2015 County and City Extra

Annual Metro, City, and County Data Book

23rd Edition

2015 County and City Extra

Annual Metro, City, and County Data Book

23rd Edition

Edited by Deirdre A. Gaquin
and Mary Meghan Ryan

Bernan Press

Lanham, MD

Published by Bernan Press
An imprint of
The Rowman & Littlefield Publishing Group, Inc.
4501 Forbes Boulevard, Lanham, Maryland 20706

www.rowman.com
800-462-6420
info@bernan.com

ISBN: 978-159888-789-1

E-ISBN: 978-159888-790-7

ISSN: 1059-9096

∞ ™ The paper used in this publication meets the minimum requirements of American National Standard for Information Sciences—Permanence of Paper for Printed Library Materials, ANSI/NISO Z39.48-1992.
Manufactured in the United States of America.

Contents

Contents

INTRODUCTION

County and City Extra is an annual publication that provides the most up-to-date statistical information available for every state, county, metropolitan area, and congressional district, as well as all cities in the United States with a 2010 census population of 25,000 or more. Data for places, including towns and cities with populations of fewer than 25,000 people are published by Bernan Press in a separate companion volume, *Places, Towns and Townships*. These two volumes are designed to meet the needs of libraries, businesses, and other organizations or individuals who desire convenient and timely sources of the most frequently sought information about geographic entities within the United States. The annual updating of *County and City Extra* for more than 20 years ensures its stature as a reliable and authoritative source for statistical information.

Bernan Press has recently published a new companion volume, the *State and Metropolitan Area Data Book,* previously published by the Census Bureau. That edition provides an expanded collection of data about states and metropolitan areas, including micropolitan areas and their component counties. Another recent addition is the *County and City Extra: Special Historical Edition, 1790–2010* with data from the earliest days of the nation, and states, counties, and cities from their beginnings.

County and City Extra, Places, Towns and Townships, and *State and Metropolitan Area Data Book* are large volumes, but are not big enough to accommodate the wealth of information from the decennial census and the American Community Survey. Two additional volumes in the *County and City Extra* series include this information. *County and City Extra—Special Decennial Census Edition* provides detailed population and housing data from the 2010 census and was published by Bernan Press in December 2011. *The Who, What, and Where of America—Understanding the American Community Survey* includes social and economic details from the ongoing American Community Survey, and the *County and City Extra* series includes additional books on special topics, such as the recently published *Aging in America*.

The American Community Survey (ACS) is a national survey that has replaced the census long form as the key source of detailed social and economic data. *County and City Extra* includes data from both the 2010 census and the ACS.

New and Updated Information for the 2015 Edition

County and City Extra includes updated data including 2014 population estimates for states, counties, metropolitan areas, and cities. Also included are the latest available data for education, vital statistics, income and poverty, employment and unemployment, residential construction, production by industry, health resources, crime, land use, city government finances, and many other topics.

This edition includes state finance data from the 2013 Annual Survey of State Government Finance and newly released finance data from the 2012 Census of Governments. Tables B and C include finance data for all government entities operating within each county and each metropolitan area. Table D includes municipal government finance data.

Table E (Congressional Districts) includes a wide selection of 2013 American Community Survey data, Social Security data, and data from the 2012 Census of Agriculture for the congressional districts of the 113th Congress, along with the 114th Congressional representatives.

In February 2013, the Office of Management and Budget released a completely new list of Core Based Statistical Areas (metropolitan and micropolitan areas) based on the 2010 census and some changes in the way these areas are defined. These newly delineated metropolitan areas are used in Table C. Appendixes B and C provide details about the component counties of these metropolitan and micropolitan areas and their 2010 census and 2014 estimated populations. Appendix D has a map for each state showing the metropolitan and micropolitan areas.

This edition includes data from the 2010 census, 2013 and 2014 population estimates, and the ACS. Annual ACS data are available for all states and almost all metropolitan areas (all geographic areas with populations of 65,000 or more), but three years are needed to build a sample large enough for reliable estimates for areas of 20,000 to 64,999, and smaller areas need five years of data collection.

With the now annual release of 1-year, 3-year, and 5-year estimates, *County and City Extra* uses ACS data for all geographic areas. ACS 1-year data for 2013 are included in Table A (States), Table C (metropolitan areas), and Table E (Congressional Districts)—all areas with populations of 65,000 or more. Table B (Counties), includes 5-year data (2009–2013), and Table D (Cities) includes 3-year data (2011–2013). The release of 5-year data for even the smallest geographic areas means that annual social and economic characteristics are available for all counties and cities.

Although some of the state data are also included in Table B (States and Counties), the separate state data table offers several important features:

- Additional data not available at the county level are provided. Examples include population projections, health insurance coverage, number of immigrants, personal tax payments, information about health service firms not subject to federal tax, and exports by state of origin.

- Additional data that exceeds the space limitations for counties can be found for states. Examples are age of householder, more detailed information about employment in retail trade and services, and the expanded presentation of federal grants and payments to individuals by type.

- State totals can be found more quickly and compared more readily.

Appendix F, **Source Notes and Explanations**, includes internet references for all data sources. This is especially helpful in today's environment where the data sources are updated at a faster pace. The sources referenced here can be used to track down additional information too cumbersome for this book. Some of the data can be directly found in data tables on the websites; some can be assembled through on line access tools; others can be obtained by downloading files and processing them with statistical software; and some need to be ordered from the agencies.

Rankings

The rankings present the geography types by various subjects, including population, land area, population density, population change, age, immigration, birth rate, housing characteristics, race, Hispanic origin, educational attainment, income, unemployment rate, per capita local taxes, poverty rate, defense contracts, value of agricultural products, and violent crime rate.

Subjects Covered and Volume Organization

A summary of the **subjects covered** in each of the five tables appears on **page x**. The **colored map** portfolio begins on **page xiii**.

The main body of this volume contains five basic parts. Each part includes a table that is preceded by highlights and rankings, as well as the complete column headings for the table. **Part A**, which begins on **page 1**, contains data for states. **Part B**, beginning on **page 49**, contains information for states and counties. The county geography codes include county typology codes from the Economic Research Service of the Department of Agriculture. These codes characterize counties by size of the largest place as well as by other criteria for nonmetropolitan counties. (See Appendix A for the definition of each code.) **Part C**, beginning on **page 771**, contains information for metropolitan areas. Statistics for cities with a 2010 census population of 25,000 or more can be found in **Part D**, which begins on **page 893**. **Part E**, beginning on **page 1173**, contains data for the congressional districts of the 113th Congress.

A contents page preceding tables B through E lists the page number on which the data for a given geographic area begin. Counties and cities are listed alphabetically by state. Metropolitan areas are listed alphabetically, except that metropolitan divisions are listed alphabetically within the metropolitan statistical area of which they are components. Congressional districts are listed in numeric order within states.

The appendixes include definitions of geographic concepts (**Appendix A**); sources and definitions of each data item included in this volume (**Appendix F**); an alphabetical listing of metropolitan areas with their component counties delineated as of February 2013, with 2010 census populations (**Appendix B**); a listing of metropolitan and micropolitan areas and their component counties as of February 2013, with 2010 census populations and 2014 estimated populations (**Appendix C**); a list of cities by county (**Appendix E**); and maps showing congressional districts in the United States and metropolitan areas, counties, and selected places within each state (**Appendix D**).

Symbols

D Indicates that the number has been withheld to avoid disclosure of information pertaining to a specific organization or individual, or because the number does not meet statistical standards for publication.

NA Indicates that data are not available.

X Indicates that data are not applicable or are not meaningful for this geographic unit.

In this volume, a figure that is less than half the unit of measure shown will appear as zero.

Sources

The great majority of the data in this volume have been obtained from federal government sources. A few items are obtained from private sources that are widely recognized as reliable basic sources of those particular data items. For a complete list of these sources, see **Appendix F**.

Data included in this volume meet the publication standards established by the U.S. Census Bureau and the other federal statistical agencies from which they were obtained. Every effort has been made to select data that are accurate, meaningful, and useful. All data from censuses, surveys, and administrative records are subject to errors arising from factors such as sampling variability, reporting errors, incomplete coverage, nonresponse, imputations, and processing error. Responsibility of the editors and publishers of this volume is limited to reasonable care in the reproduction and presentation of data obtained from sources believed to be reliable.

County and City Extra: Annual Metro, City, and County Data Book is part of Bernan Press's *County and City Extra* series. The editors of *County and City Extra* acknowledge the contributions of Courtenay Slater and the late George Hall, the originators of this publication. Their initial contributions continue to enrich the *County and City Extra* series. As always, we are especially grateful to the many federal agency personnel who assisted us in obtaining the data, provided excellent resources on their Web sites, and patiently answered questions.

Deirdre A. Gaquin has been a data use consultant to private organizations, government agencies, and universities for over 30 years. Prior to that, she was Director of Data Access Services at Data Use & Access Laboratories, a pioneer in private sector distribution of federal statistical data. A former President of the Association of Public Data Users, Ms. Gaquin has served on numerous boards, panels, and task forces concerned with federal statistical data and has worked on five decennial censuses. She holds a Master of Urban Planning (MUP) degree from Hunter College. Ms. Gaquin is also an editor of Bernan Press's *The Who, What, and Where of America: Understanding the American Community Survey*; *Places, Towns and Townships*; *The Congressional District Atlas*; *The Almanac of American Education; Race and Employment in America;* and *the State and Metropolitan Area Data Book.*

Mary Meghan Ryan is the senior research editor for Bernan Press. She is also the editor for the *Handbook of U.S. Labor Statistics* and *State Profiles*, and the associate editor for *Business Statistics of the United States.*

SUBJECTS COVERED, BY GEOGRAPHY TYPE

State data begin on page 1
County data begin on page 49
Metropolitan area data begin on page 771
City data begin on page 893
Congressional district data begin on page 1173

Subject	Column Number				
	Table A. States	Table B. States and Counties	Table C. Metropolitan Areas	Table D. Cities	Table E. Congressional Districts
Land area	1	1	1	1	1
Population					
Total persons, 1990	31				
Total persons, 2000	32	20	20	23	
Total persons, 2010	33	21	21	24	
Total persons, 2013					2
Total persons, 2014	2	2	2	2	
Rank, 2014	3	3	3	3	
Persons per square kilometer	4	4	4	4	
Race and Hispanic or Latino origin, 2010	45–50				
Race and Hispanic or Latino origin, 2013	5–9	5–9	5–9		4–11
Race and Hispanic or Latino origin, 2011–2013				5–10	
Percent female	21	19	19	22	12
Foreign-born population	22			11	13
Percent born in state of residence	23				14
Immigrants	24				
Age distribution, 2010	52–61				
Age distribution, 2013	10–19	10–18	10–18		15–23
Age distribution, 2011–2013				12–20	
Median age	20, 62			21	24
Percent population change, 1990–2000	34				
Percent population change, 2000–2010	35	22	22	25	
Percent population change, 2010–2014	36	23	23	26	
Components of population change	37–41	24–26	24–26		
Daytime population		33–34	33–34		
Population projections	42–44				
Households					
Total households, 2010	64	27	27		
Total households, 2013	25				28
Total households, 2009–2013		27–31			
Total households, 2011–2013				27	
Percent change in number of households	26, 65			29–30	
Household type	28–30, 67–68	29–31	29–31		30–33
Persons per household	27, 66	28	28	28	29
Persons in group quarters		32	32	31–34	34–39
Housing					
Housing units in 2010	69–78			47–49	
Housing units in 2013	79–92		89–96		40–45
Housing units in 2014		87–88	87–88		
Housing units in 2009–2013		89–96			
Housing units in 2011–2013				50–58	
Percent change in number of housing units	70, 80	88	88	48	
Housing costs	73–77, 83–90	91–95	91–95	52–57	43–45
Substandard housing units	78, 91	96	96		
Percent with no vehicle available				58	
Percent who lived in same house one year ago	92			59	
Percent who lived outside city one year ago				60	
New residential construction	93–95	169–170	169–170	69–71	
Manufactured housing	96				
Vital statistics					
Births	97–98	35–36	35–36		
Deaths	99–103	37–38	37–38		

SUBJECTS COVERED, BY GEOGRAPHY TYPE — Continued

State data begin on page 1
County data begin on page 49
Metropolitan area data begin on page 771
City data begin on page 893
Congressional district data begin on page 1173

Subject	Column Number				
	Table A. States	Table B. States and Counties	Table C. Metropolitan Areas	Table D. Cities	Table E. Congressional Districts
Health					
Persons in nursing facilities				33	37
Medicare enrollees	106	41–43	41–43		
Persons lacking health insurance	104–105	39–40	39–40		59
Crime	107–110	44–47	44–47	35–38	
Education					
School enrollment	111–112	48–49	48–49		25
Educational attainment	113–116	50–51	50–51	39–41	26–27
Expenditures for education	117–118	52–53	52–53		
Income					
Personal income	134–149	62–71	62–71		
Per capita income	122, 136, 149	54, 64	54, 64	42	46
Household income	123–126	55–58	55–58	43–45	47–48
Poverty	127–133	59–61	59–61	46	49–50
Food stamps					51
Personal income by type	138–140	66–70	66–70		
Earnings by industry	150–158	72–83	72–83		
Transfer payments	141–146	71	71		
Gross state product	159				
Personal tax payments	147				
Disposable personal income	148–149				
Social Security	160–162	84–86	84–86		60–62
Labor Force and Employment					
Labor force and unemployment	167–171	97–100	97–100	61–68	52–54
Employment in selected occupations	163–166	101–103	101–103		55–58
Employment by industry	172–183, 207–216	104–112	104–112		
Exports of goods produced	119–121				
Establishments, employment, sales, and payroll					
Manufacturing	207–216	151–154	151–154	88–91	
Construction	217–221				
Wholesale trade	222–226	135–138	135–138	72–75	
Retail trade	227–235	139–142	139–142	76–79	
Information	236–246				
Utilities	247–251				
Transportation and warehousing	252–256				
Finance and insurance	257–261				
Real estate and rental and leasing	262–266	143–146	143–146	80–83	
Professional, scientific, and technical services	267–275	147–150	147–150	84–87	
Health care and social assistance	276–289	159–162	159–162	100–103	
Arts, entertainment and recreation	290–294			96–99	
Accommodation and food services	295–300	155–158	155–158	92–95	
Other services, except public administration	301–308	163–166	163–166	104–108	
Nonemployer businesses		167–168	167–168		
Government employment	309–314	171, 194–196	171, 194–196	108	
Government payroll	315–330	172–179	172–179	109–116	
Government finances	331–350	180–193	180–193	117–139	

SUBJECTS COVERED, BY GEOGRAPHY TYPE — Continued

State data begin on page 1
County data begin on page 49
Metropolitan area data begin on page 771
City data begin on page 893
Congressional district data begin on page 1173

Subject	Column Number				
	Table A. States	Table B. States and Counties	Table C. Metropolitan Areas	Table D. Cities	Table E. Congressional Districts
Agriculture	184–202	113–132	113–132		63–72
Land and water	203–206	133–134	133–134		
Voting and elections	351–355	197–199	197–199		
Climate				140–146	

Population Change 2010–2014

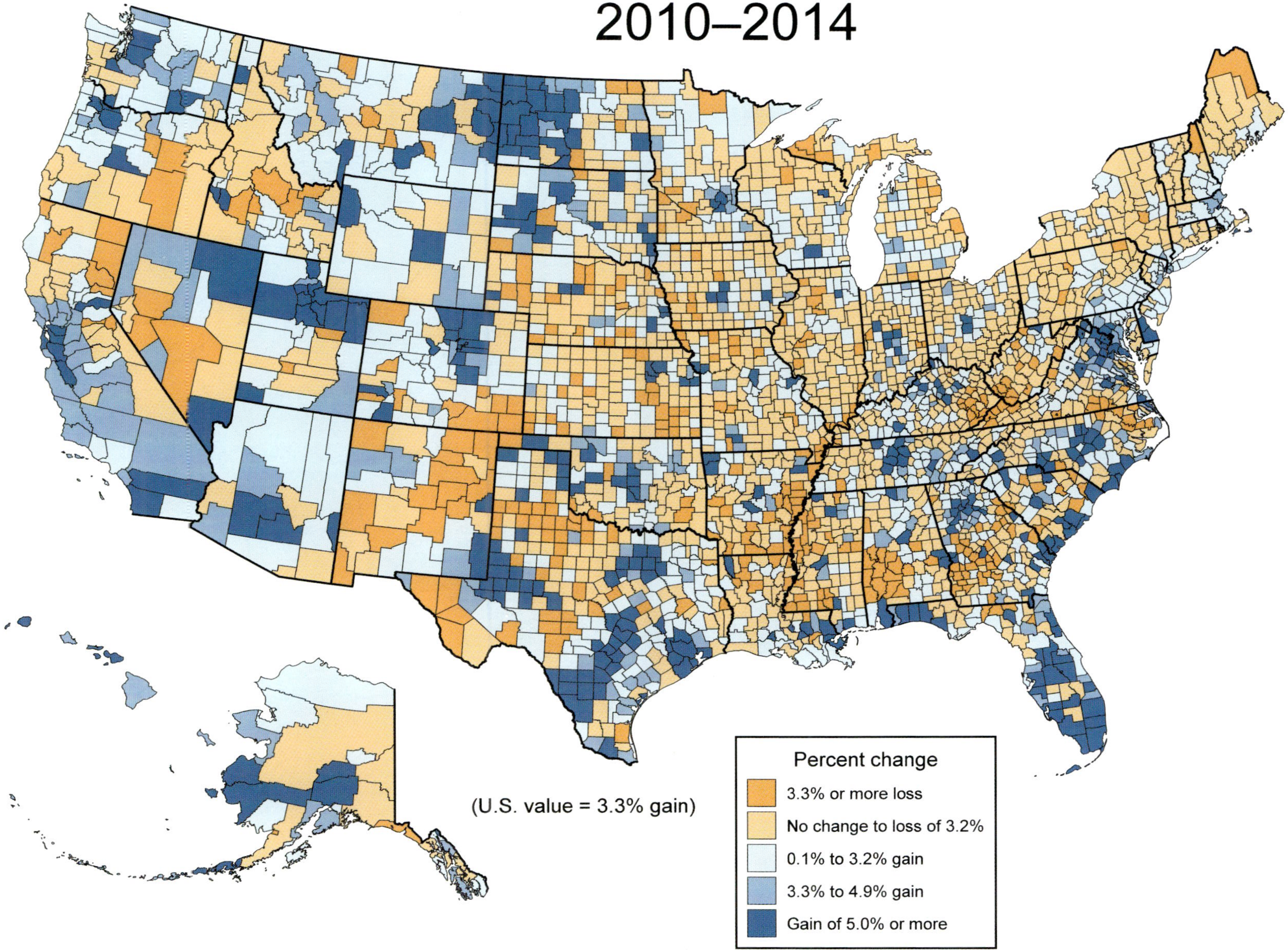

Black, Not Hispanic or Latino, Population 2013

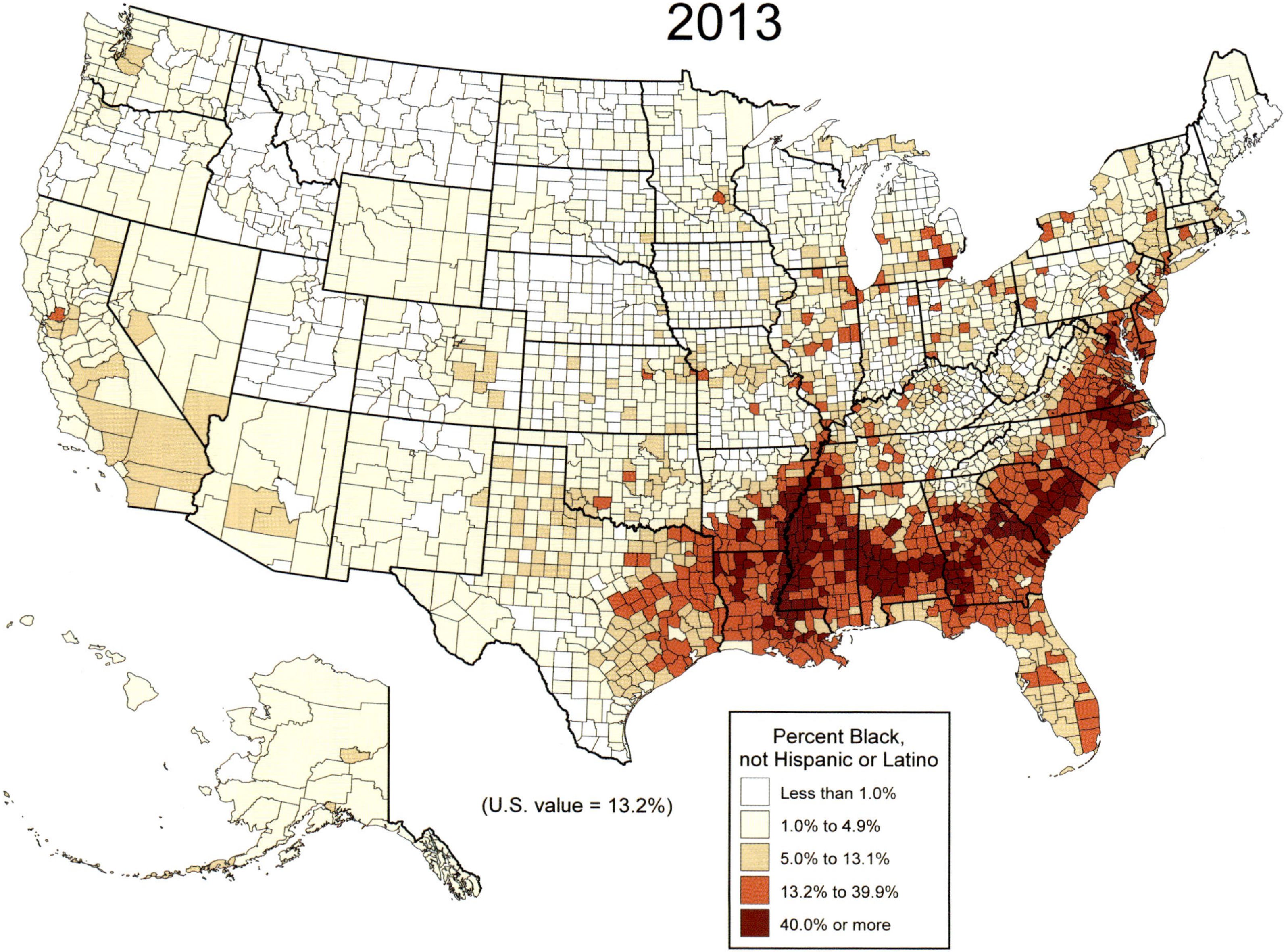

(U.S. value = 13.2%)

Hispanic or Latino Population 2013

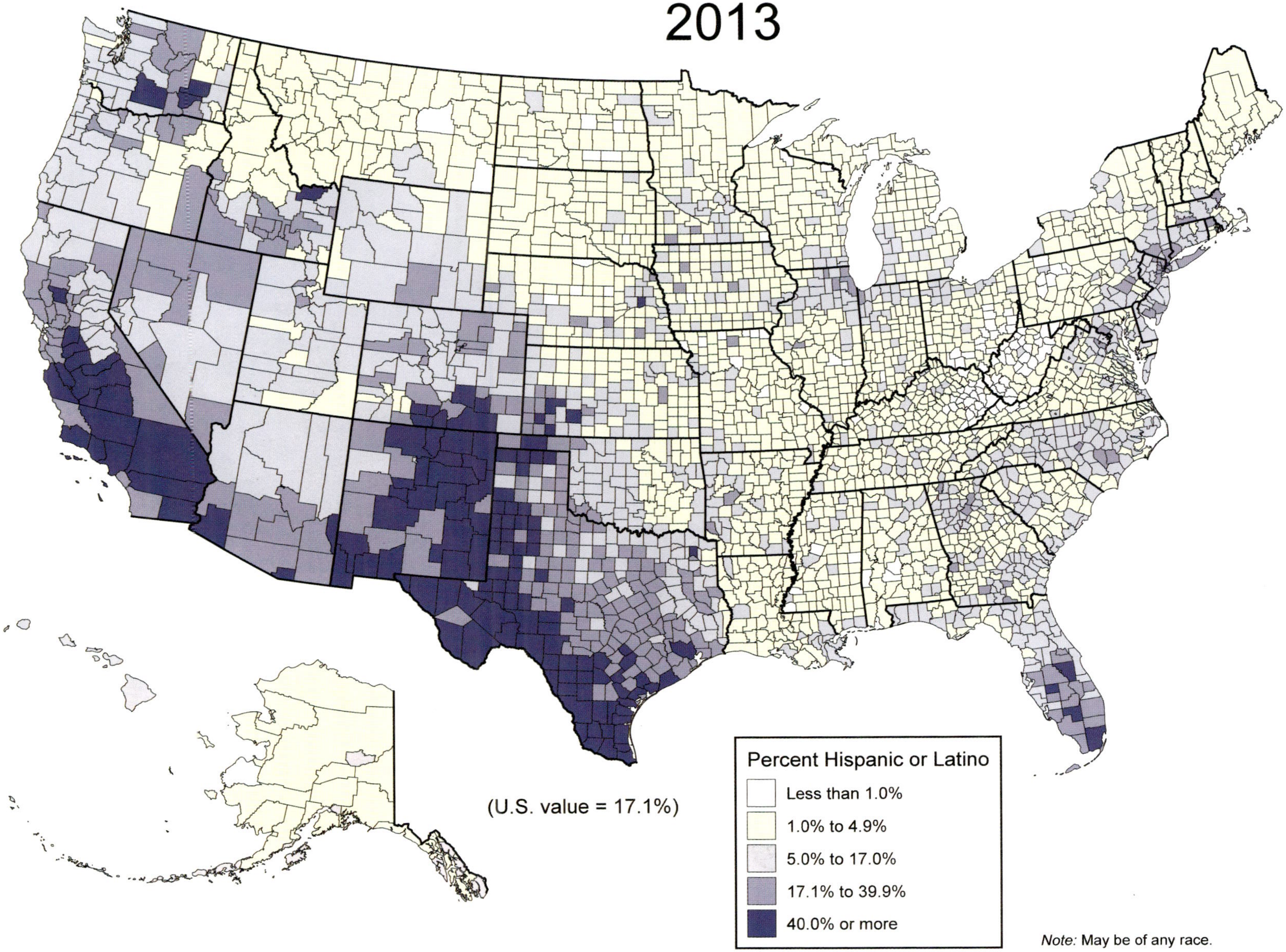

Population Under 18 Years Old
2013

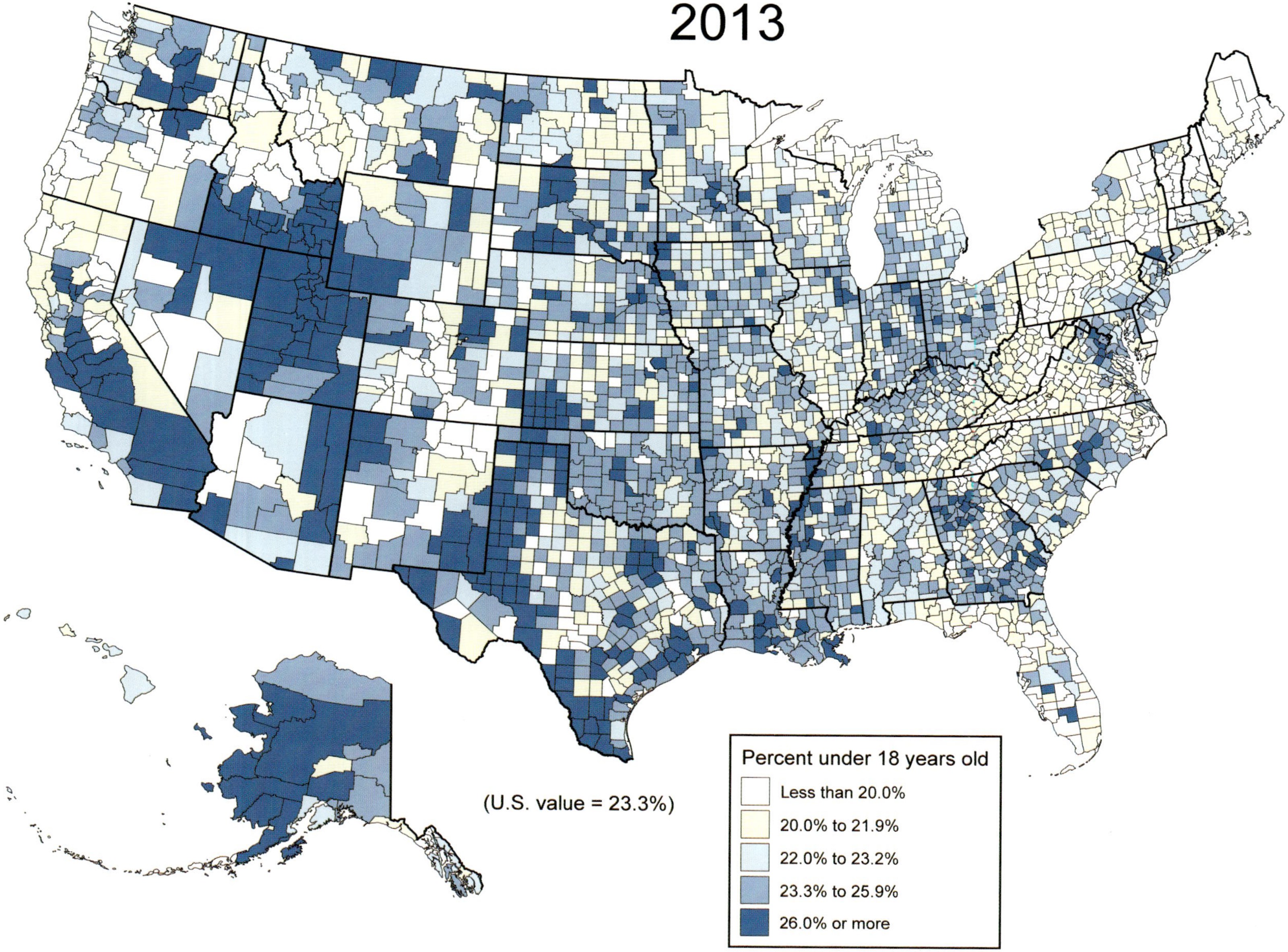

Population 65 Years Old and Over
2013

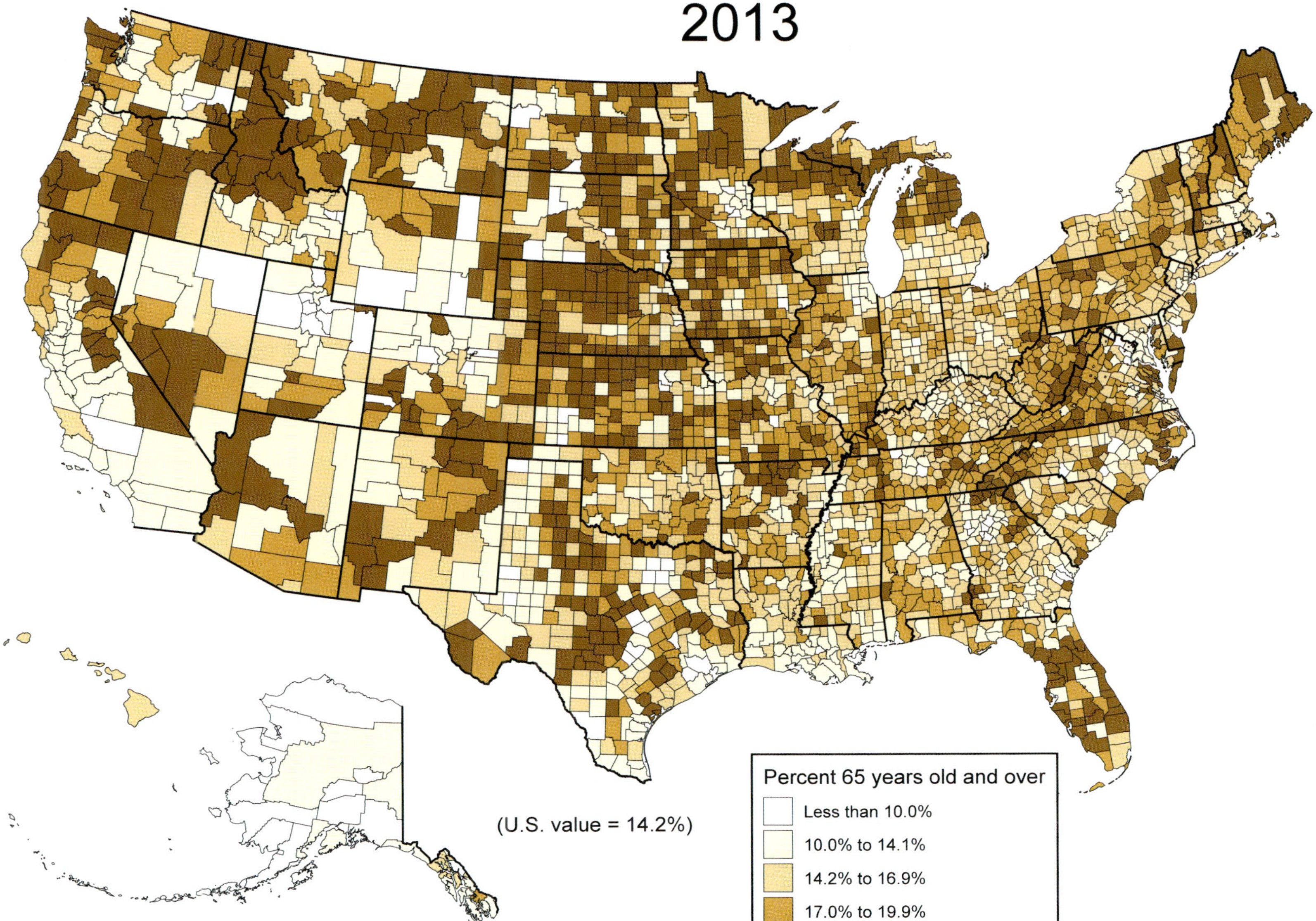

Population Density 2014

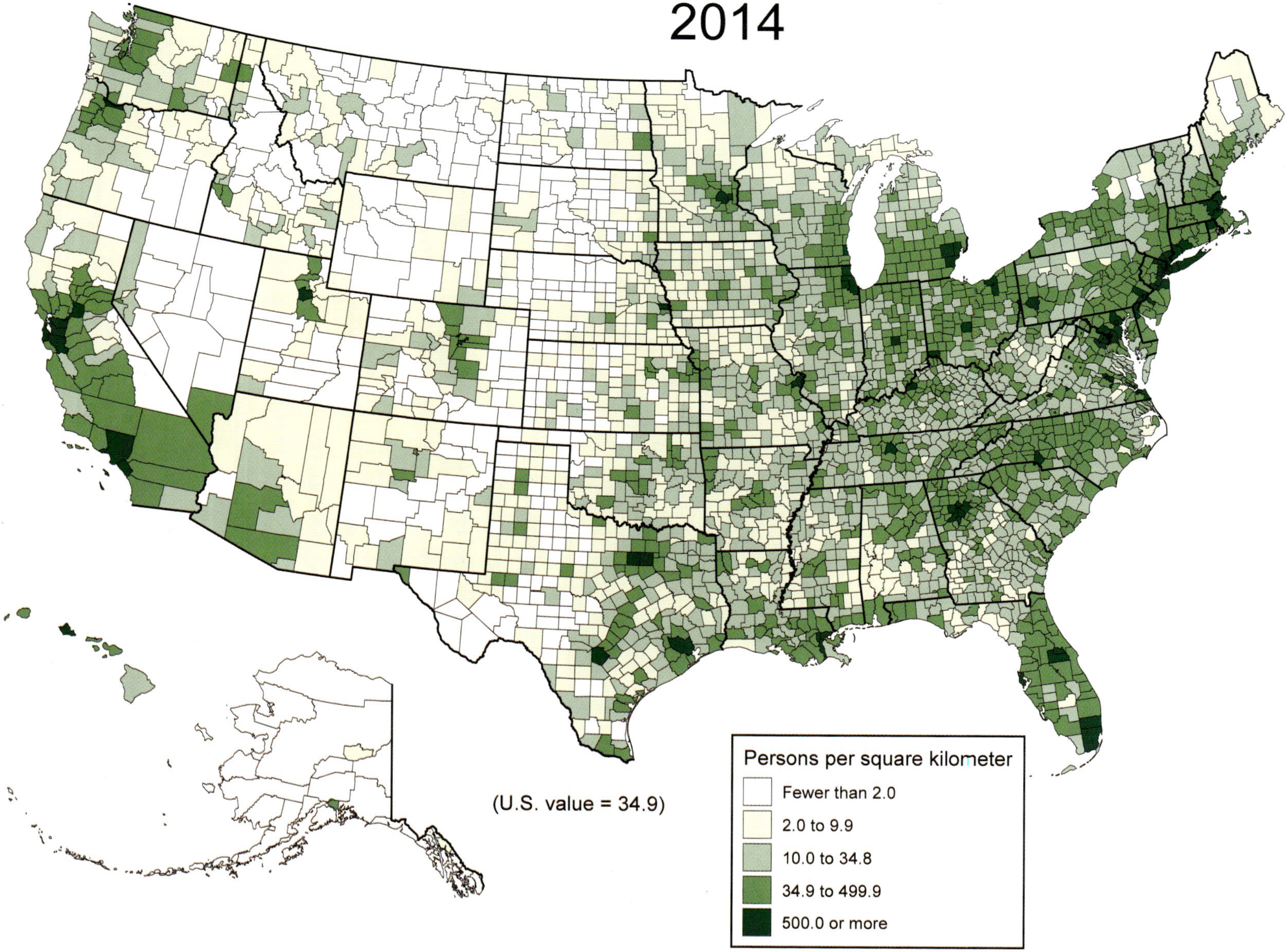

Unemployment Rate 2014

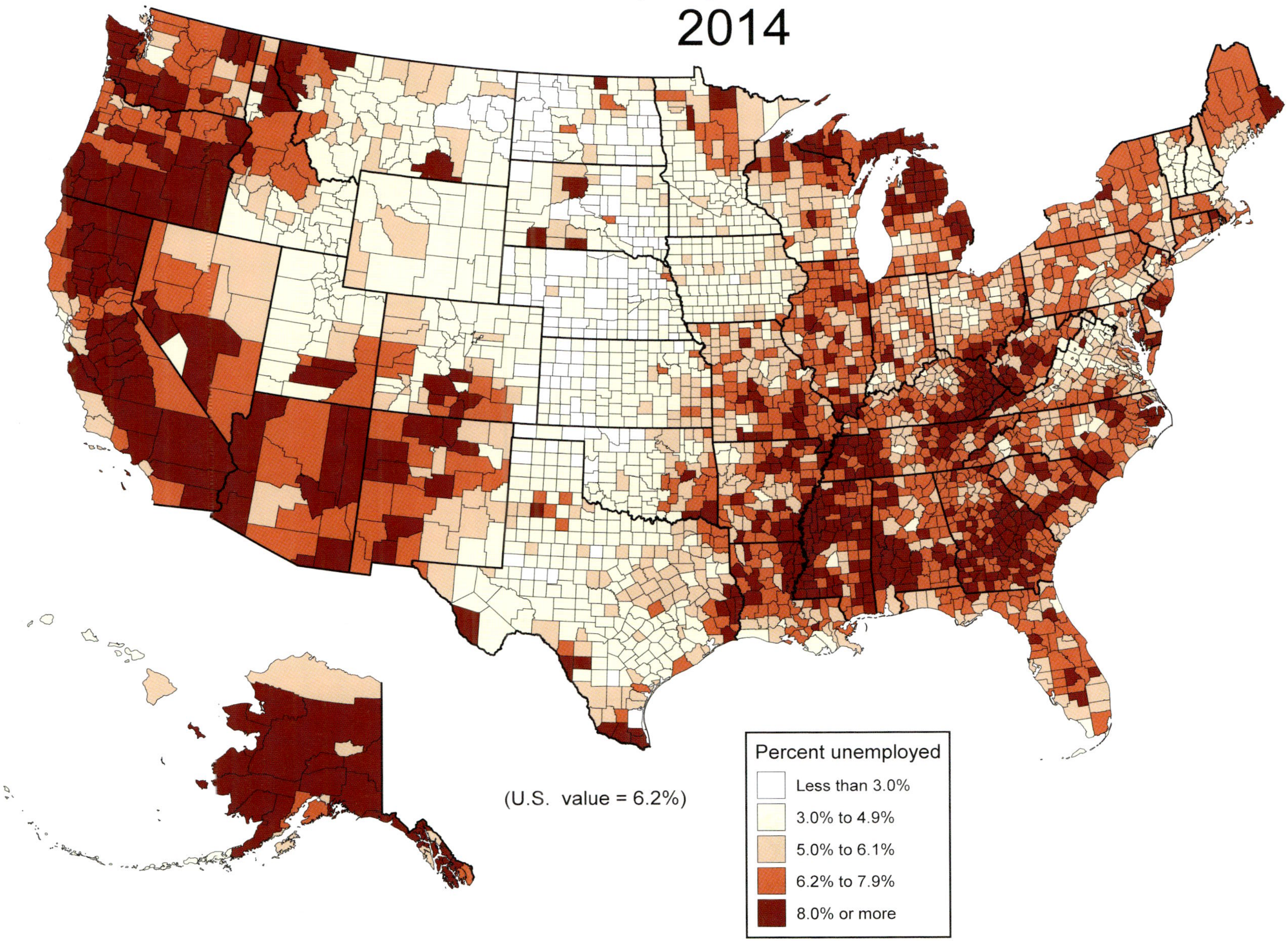

Educational Expenditures Per Student 2012–2013

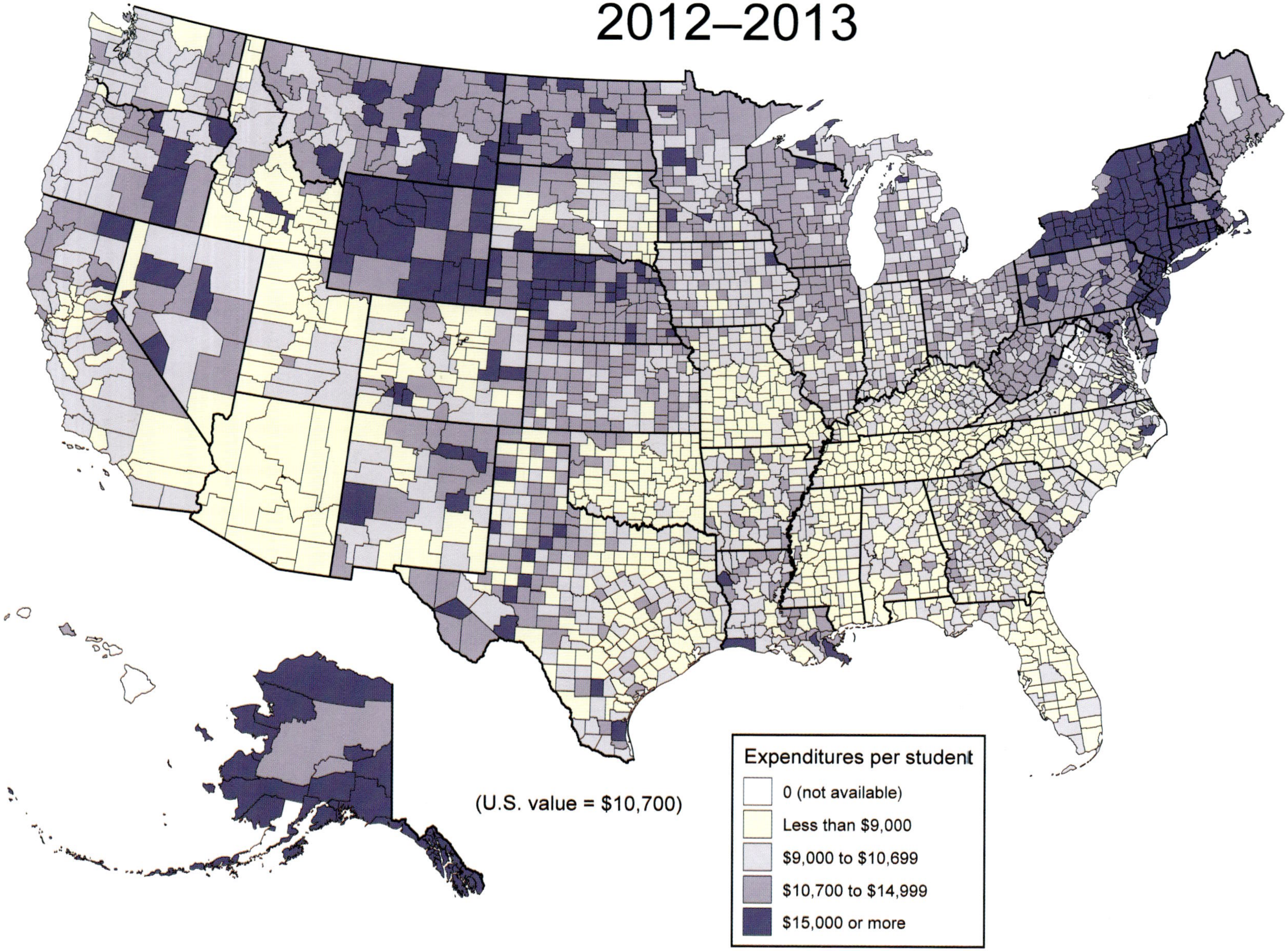

Population with High School Diploma or Less
2009–2013

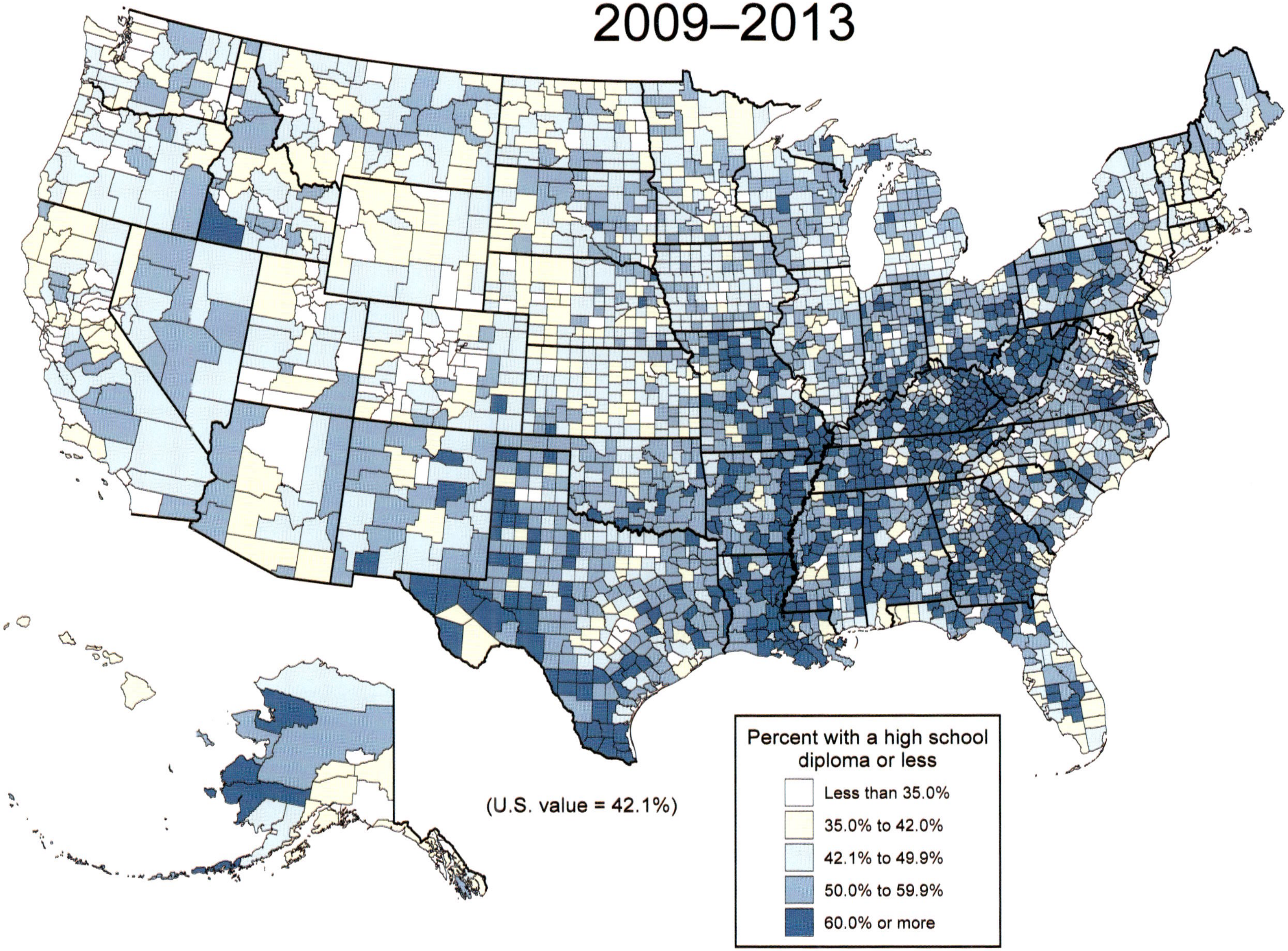

Earnings from Manufacturing 2013

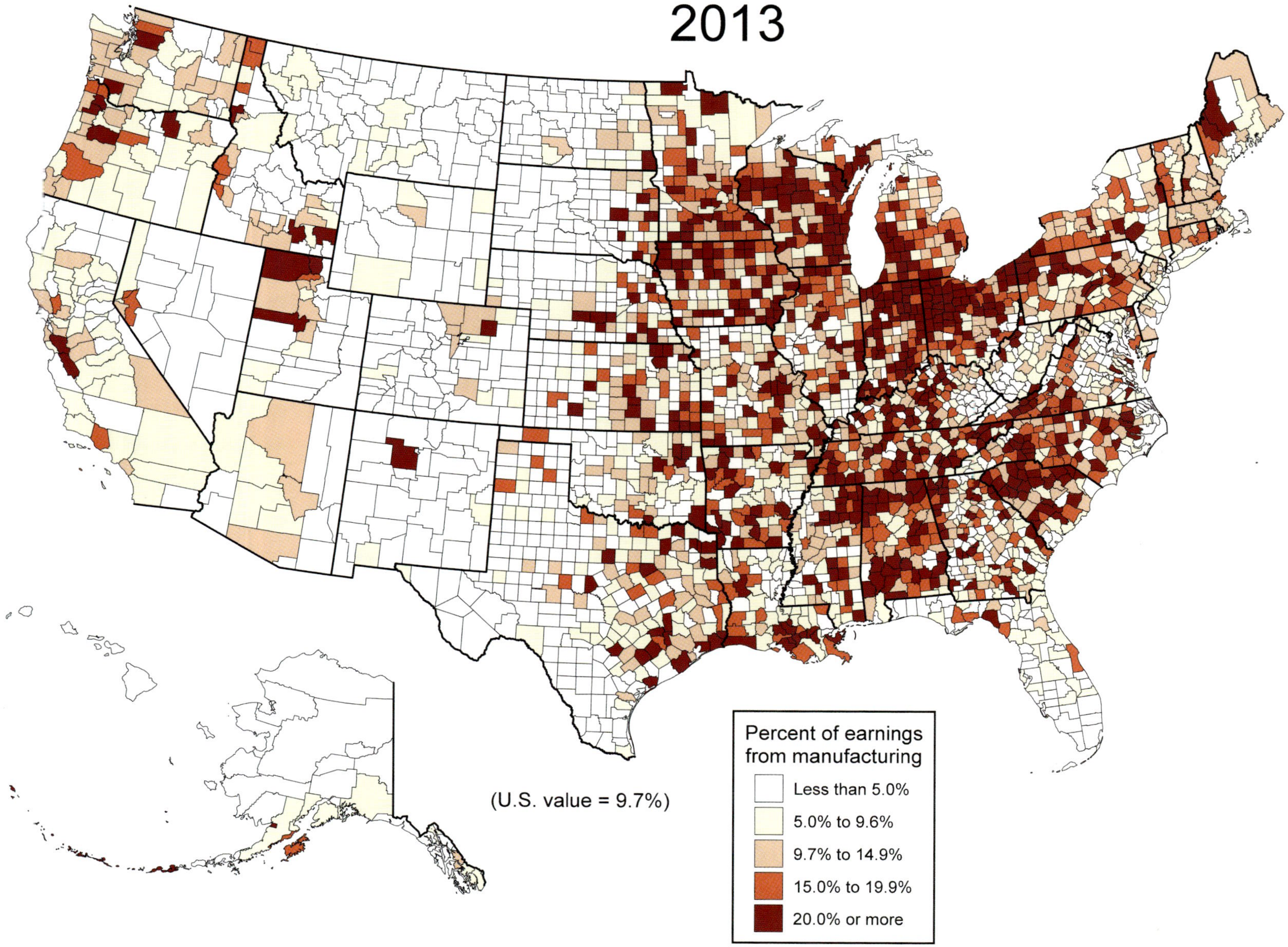

Employment in Management, Business, Science, and Arts Occupations: 2009–2013

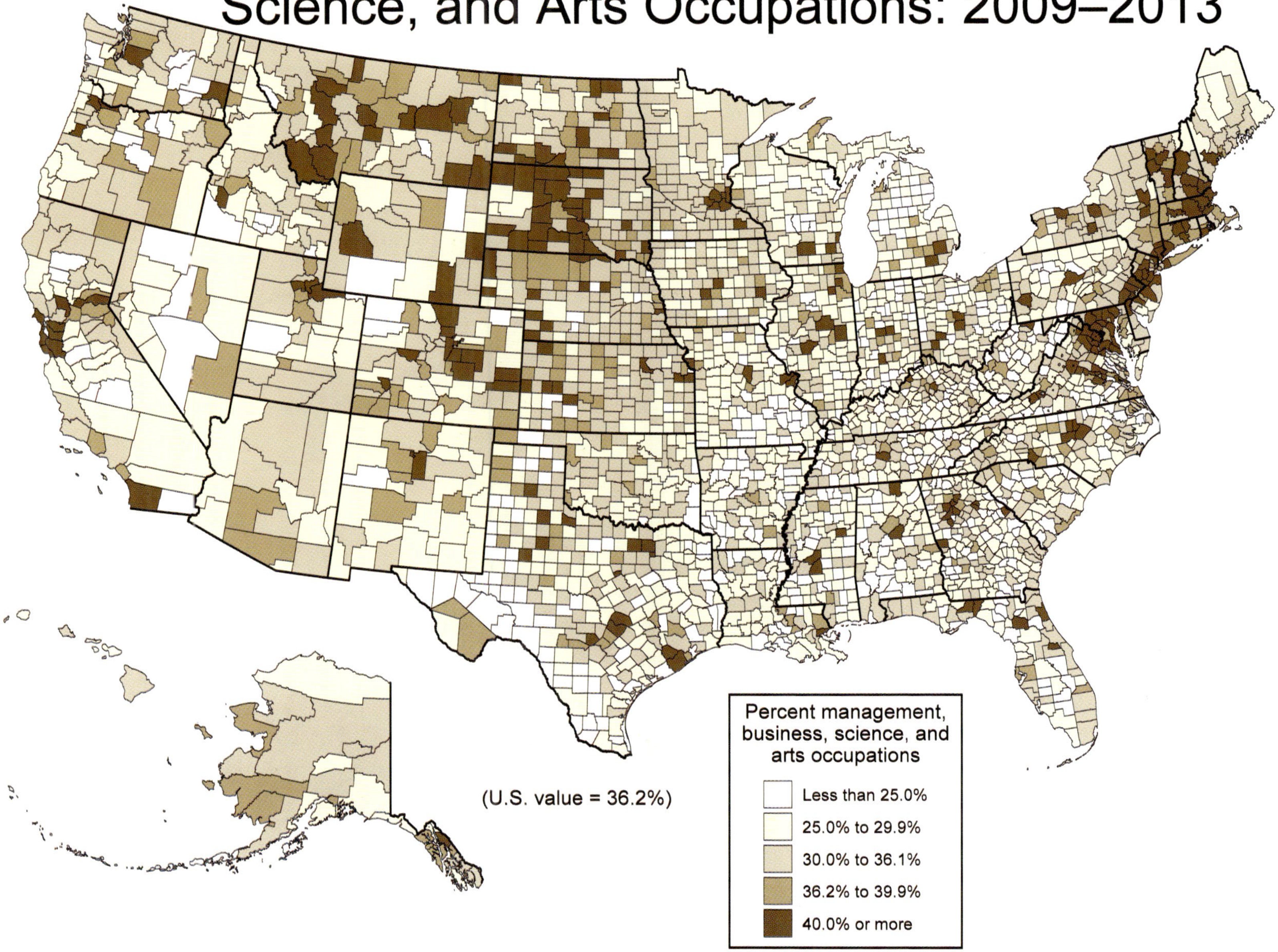

Land in Farms
2012

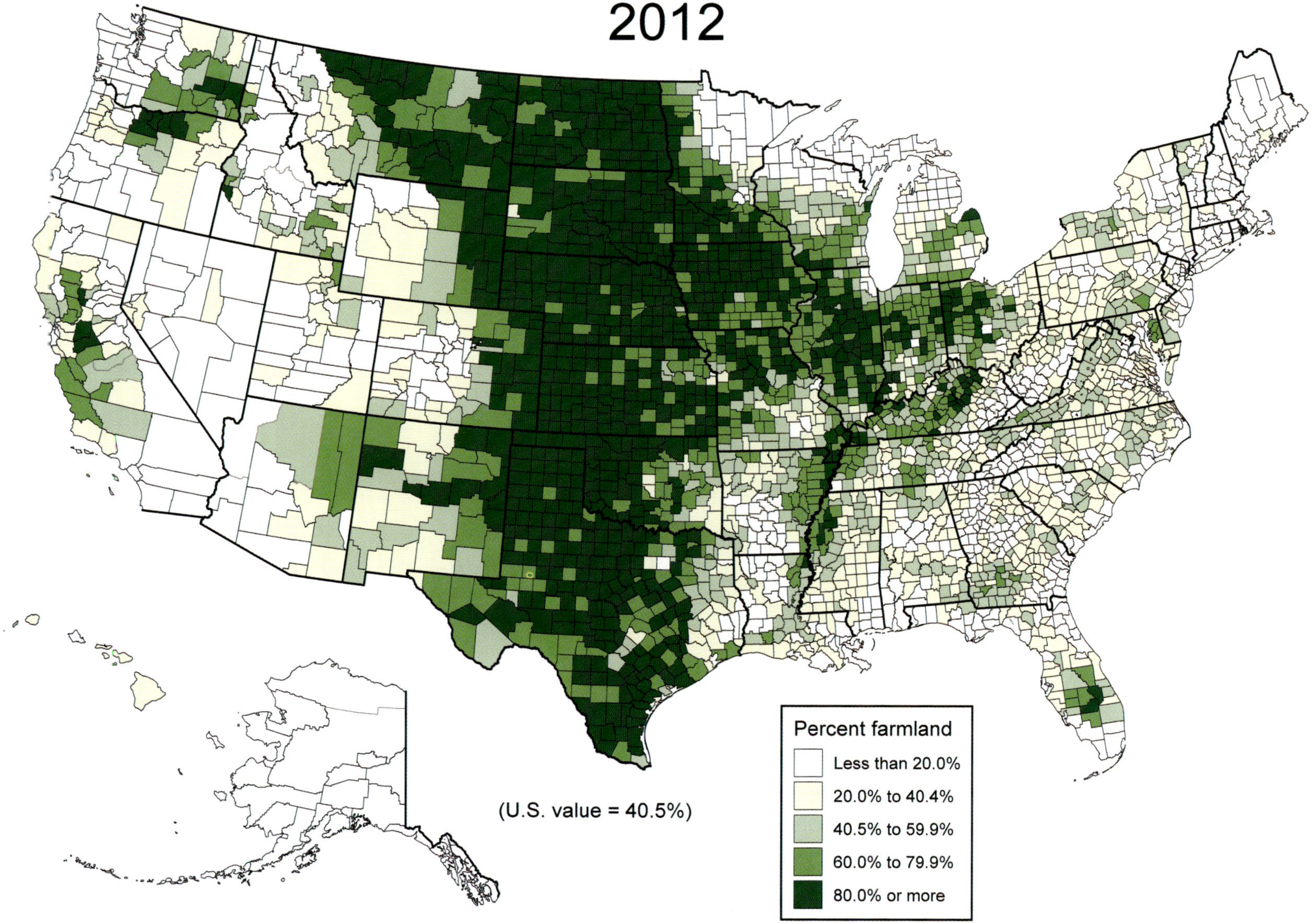

Persons Under Age 65 with No Health Insurance 2013

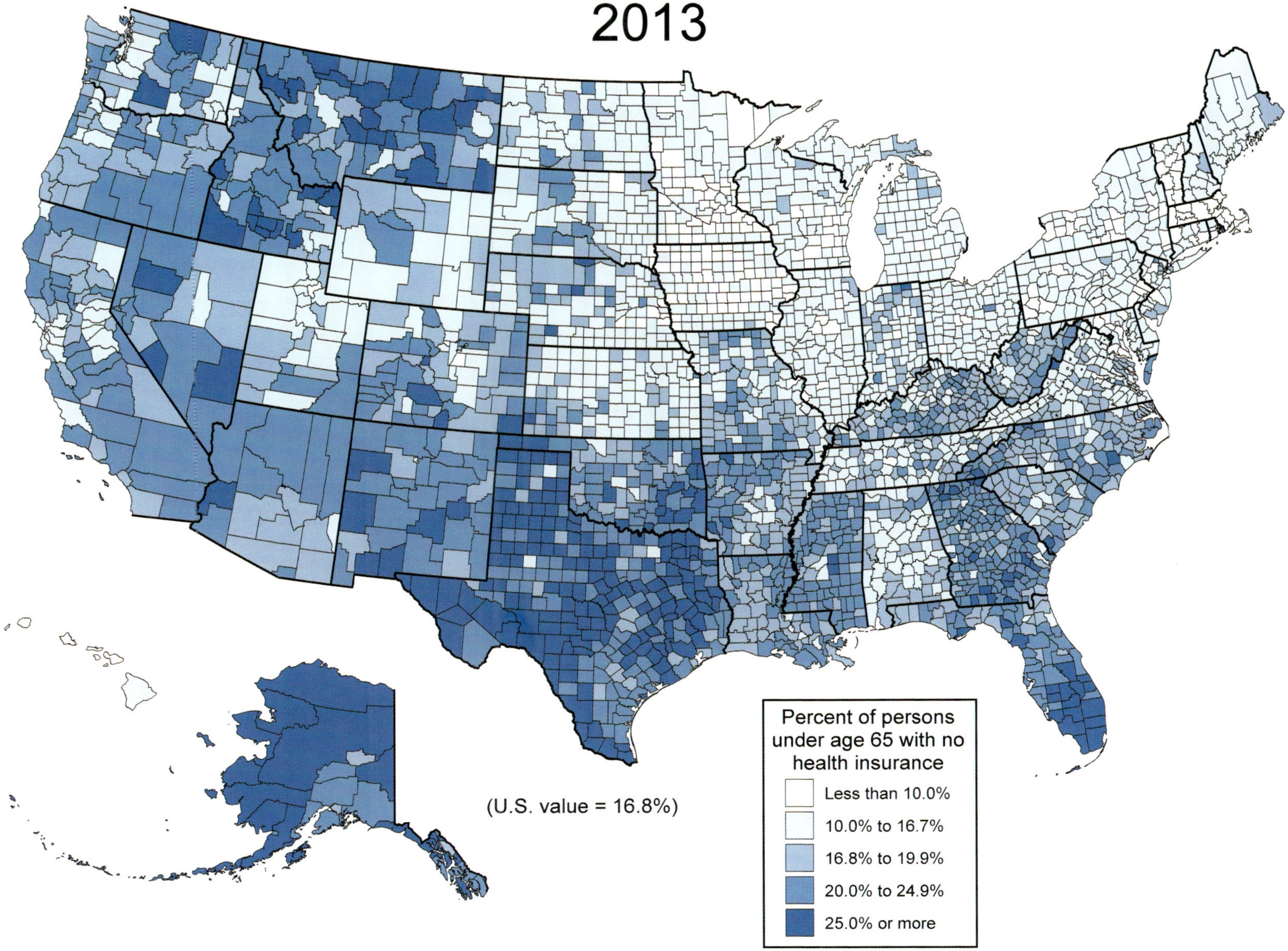

Median Household Income 2013

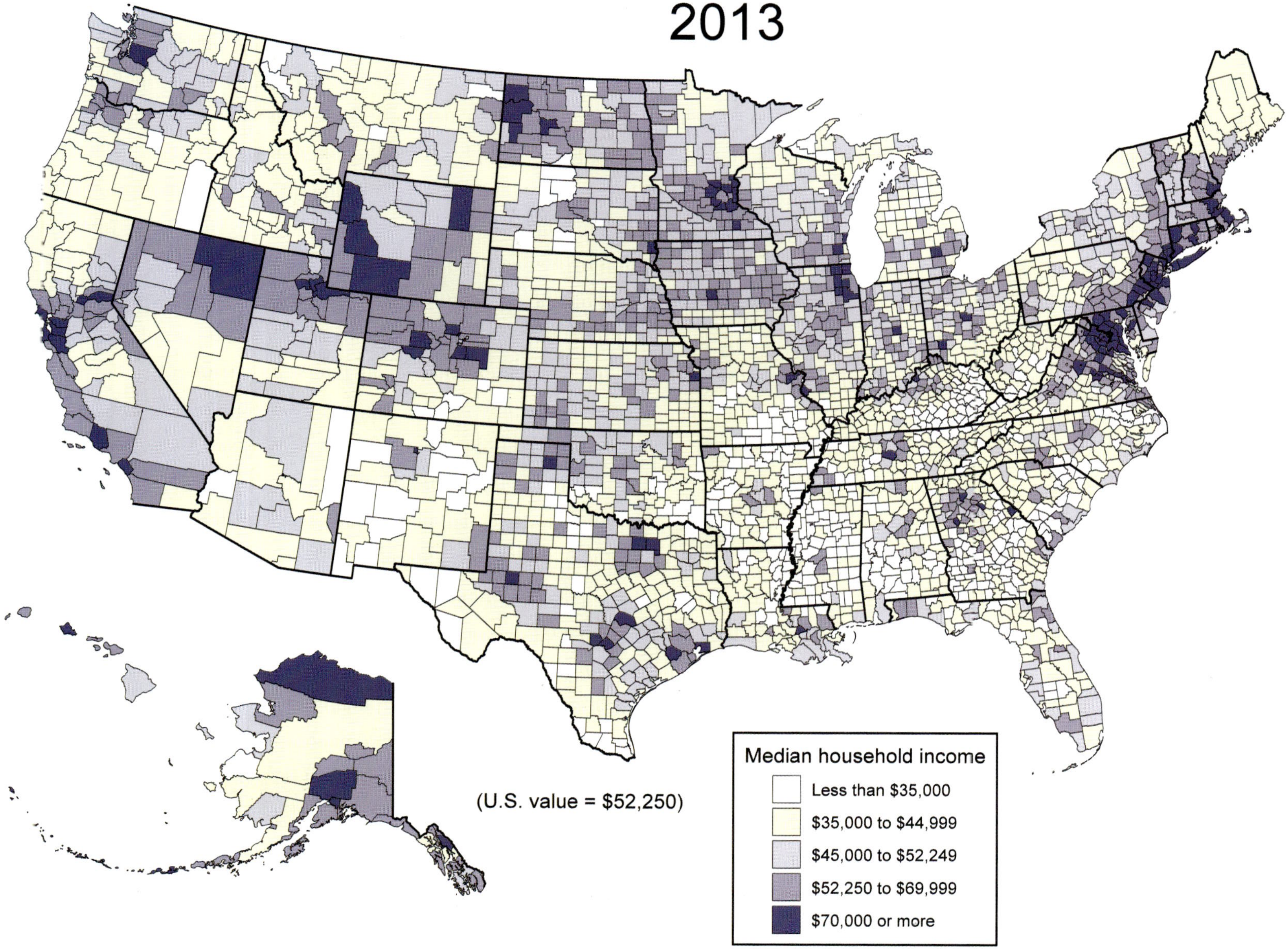

Percent in Poverty
2013

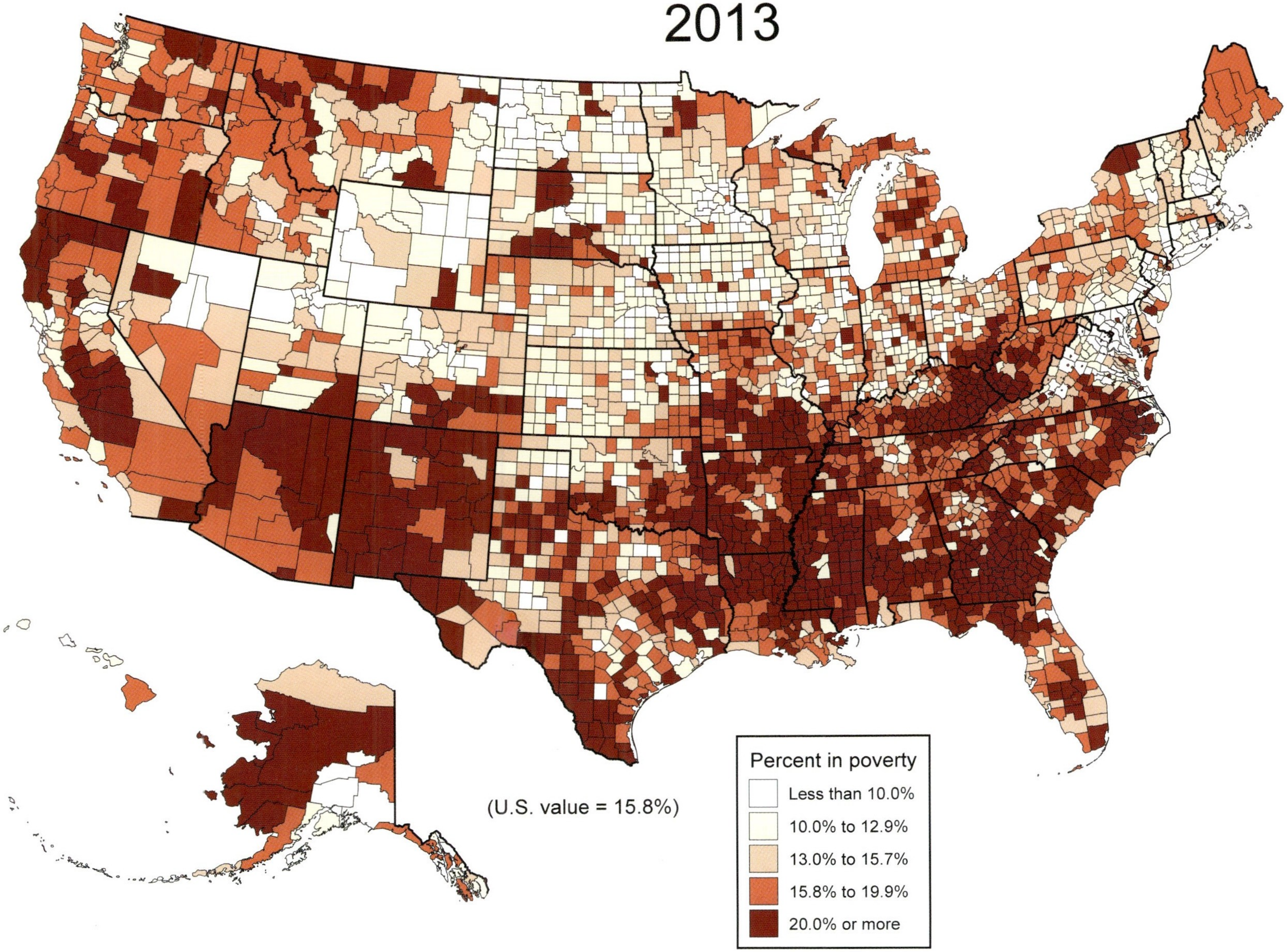

Vote for President Obama 2012

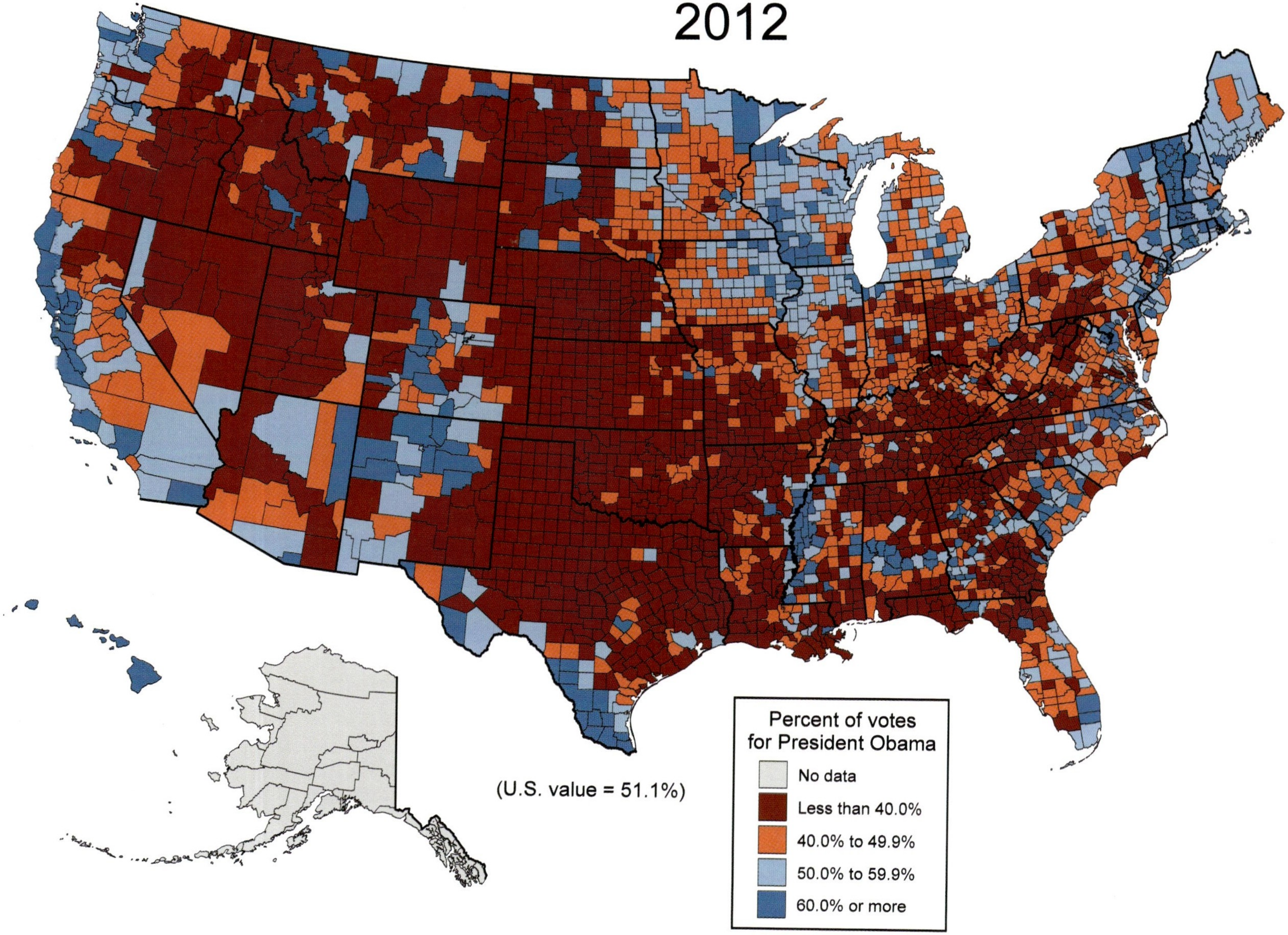

State Highlights and Rankings

Figure A-1. Top 10 Fastest Growing States, 2010–2014

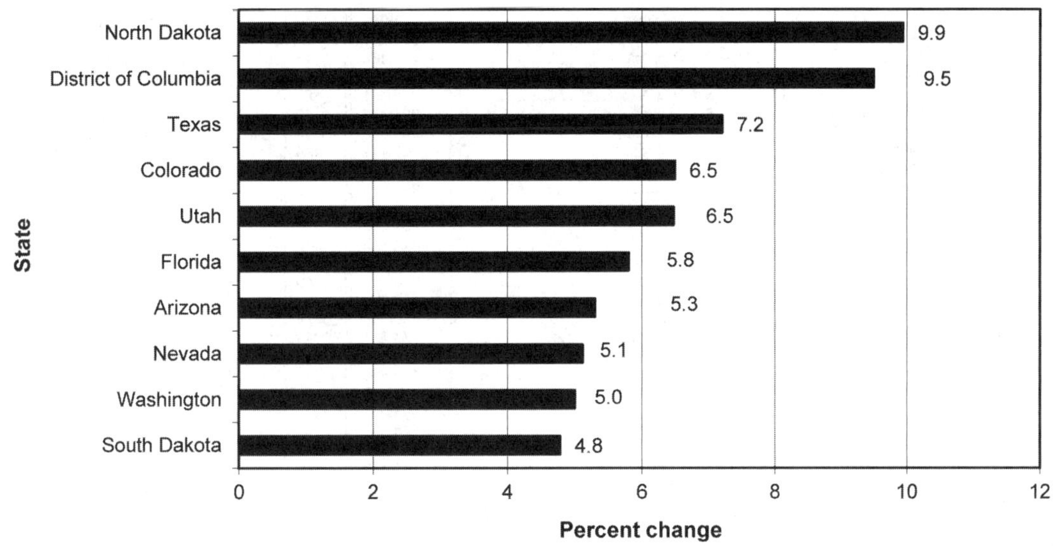

There is no simple relationship between population size and land area for most of the geographic entities included in this publication. According to the Census Bureau's 2014 estimates, state populations ranged from a high of over 38 million in California to a low of 584,153 in Wyoming. (The median population for states—with half having a larger population and half having a smaller population—was over 4.4 million people.) California was also one of the largest states in land area (ranking third). Alaska was by far the largest state in area; it was more than twice the size of Texas, the second-largest state, even though its population rank was close to the bottom (ranked 48th). Texas was also the second-largest state in terms of total population with nearly 27.0 million residents. At the other end of the geographic size spectrum were many of the New England states (with Rhode Island ranking as the smallest), plus Delaware, Hawaii, and New Jersey. As a consequence of differing area size and population rank, New Jersey was the most densely settled state, with 469.3 persons per square kilometer, while Alaska was the least densely settled, with about 0.5 persons per square kilometer. California, which had the largest population and third-largest land area, ranked 12th in terms of population density (96 persons per square kilometer). The 15 most populous states remained almost unchanged between 2010 and 2014, but there were changes within their ranks. Florida became the third most populous state, pushing ahead of New York, and Michigan and North Carolina swapped places. North Carolina moved up to 9th place while Michigan dropped to 10th.

Not surprisingly, states with higher population density also had higher proportions of developed land. According to the Department of Agriculture's most recent National Resources Inventory, 35.3 percent of New Jersey's land was developed. Connecticut had the second highest proportion with 33.7 percent, followed by Massachusetts at 32.8 percent. Among the reporting states, Nevada had the lowest proportion of developed land, at just 0.8 percent, followed by Wyoming and Montana, each with 1.1 percent of its land developed. Nearly 85 percent of Nevada's land was owned by the federal government. This was by far the highest percentage in the nation. Federal land accounted for nearly 21 percent of the United States' total land area. (Estimates are not available for Alaska and the District of Columbia. See Appendix F for definitions and additional information.)

The total population of the United States increased 3.3 percent between 2010 and 2014, with 24 states matching or exceeding this rate of growth and the remainder growing more slowly. North Dakota and the District of Columbia experienced the highest growth rates (9.9 and 9.5 percent) even though they ranked 47th and 49th respectively in population among all the states. Despite its growth, North Dakota ranked 47th for total population and 48th for density. It was among five states with population densities of fewer than five persons per square kilometer. Texas and Florida ranked among the top 10 states for total population and for population growth from 2010 to 2014. Texas, with the second-largest population, grew by 7.2 percent, increasing its population by 1.8 million people. New Hampshire, Rhode Island, and Vermont all ranked among the 10 least populous states, as well as among the 10 states with the lowest population growth between 2010 and 2014. While most states have increased their populations in the four years, West Virginia's population declined by a small amount. Ten other states experienced increases below one percent. Louisiana's population has rebounded from a loss of about 250,000 residents after Hurricane Katrina hit the state in August 2005. Its 2014 population of 4.6 million is slightly higher than its 2005 estimated population on July 1 of that year.

States and the District of Columbia, Selected Rankings

Population, 2014			Land area, 2010				Population density, 2014			
Population rank	State	Population [col 2]	Population rank	Land area rank	State	Land area (square kilometers) [col 1]	Population rank	Density rank	State	Density (per square kilometer) [col 4]
	United States	318 857 056			United States	9 147 593			United States	34.9
1	California	38 802 500	48	1	Alaska	1 477 953	49	1	District of Columbia	4 170.2
2	Texas	26 956 958	2	2	Texas	676 587	11	2	New Jersey	469.3
3	Florida	19 893 297	1	3	California	403 466	43	3	Rhode Island	394.0
4	New York	19 746 227	44	4	Montana	376 962	14	4	Massachusetts	333.9
5	Illinois	12 880 580	36	5	New Mexico	314 161	29	5	Connecticut	286.8
6	Pennsylvania	12 787 209	15	6	Arizona	294 207	19	6	Maryland	237.7
7	Ohio	11 594 163	35	7	Nevada	284 332	45	7	Delaware	185.4
8	Georgia	10 097 343	22	8	Colorado	268 431	4	8	New York	161.8
9	North Carolina	9 943 964	51	9	Wyoming	251 470	3	9	Florida	143.2
10	Michigan	9 909 877	27	10	Oregon	248 608	6	10	Pennsylvania	110.3
11	New Jersey	8 938 175	39	11	Idaho	214 045	7	11	Ohio	109.6
12	Virginia	8 326 289	33	12	Utah	212 818	1	12	California	96.2
13	Washington	7 061 530	34	13	Kansas	211 754	5	13	Illinois	89.6
14	Massachusetts	6 745 408	21	14	Minnesota	206 232	40	14	Hawaii	85.3
15	Arizona	6 731 484	37	15	Nebraska	198 974	12	15	Virginia	81.4
16	Indiana	6 596 855	46	16	South Dakota	196 350	9	16	North Carolina	79.0
17	Tennessee	6 549 352	47	17	North Dakota	178 711	16	17	Indiana	71.1
18	Missouri	6 063 589	18	18	Missouri	178 040	8	18	Georgia	67.8
19	Maryland	5 976 407	28	19	Oklahoma	177 660	10	19	Michigan	67.7
20	Wisconsin	5 757 564	13	20	Washington	172 119	24	20	South Carolina	62.1
21	Minnesota	5 457 173	8	21	Georgia	148 959	17	21	Tennessee	61.3
22	Colorado	5 355 866	10	22	Michigan	146 435	42	22	New Hampshire	57.2
23	Alabama	4 849 377	30	23	Iowa	144 669	26	23	Kentucky	43.2
24	South Carolina	4 832 482	5	24	Illinois	143 793	25	24	Louisiana	41.6
25	Louisiana	4 649 676	20	25	Wisconsin	140 268	20	25	Wisconsin	41.0
26	Kentucky	4 413 457	3	26	Florida	138 887	13	26	Washington	41.0
27	Oregon	3 970 239	32	27	Arkansas	134 771	2	27	Texas	39.8
28	Oklahoma	3 878 051	23	28	Alabama	131 171	23	28	Alabama	37.0
29	Connecticut	3 596 677	9	29	North Carolina	125 920	18	29	Missouri	34.1
30	Iowa	3 107 126	4	30	New York	122 057	38	30	West Virginia	29.7
31	Mississippi	2 994 079	31	31	Mississippi	121 531	21	31	Minnesota	26.5
32	Arkansas	2 966 369	6	32	Pennsylvania	115 883	50	32	Vermont	26.2
33	Utah	2 942 902	25	33	Louisiana	111 898	31	33	Mississippi	24.6
34	Kansas	2 904 021	17	34	Tennessee	106 798	15	34	Arizona	22.9
35	Nevada	2 839 099	7	35	Ohio	105 829	32	35	Arkansas	22.0
36	New Mexico	2 085 572	12	36	Virginia	102 279	28	36	Oklahoma	21.8
37	Nebraska	1 881 503	26	37	Kentucky	102 269	30	37	Iowa	21.5
38	West Virginia	1 850 326	16	38	Indiana	92 789	22	38	Colorado	20.0
39	Idaho	1 634 464	41	39	Maine	79 883	41	39	Maine	16.7
40	Hawaii	1 419 561	24	40	South Carolina	77 857	27	40	Oregon	16.0
41	Maine	1 330 089	38	41	West Virginia	62 259	33	41	Utah	13.8
42	New Hampshire	1 326 813	19	42	Maryland	25 142	34	42	Kansas	13.7
43	Rhode Island	1 055 173	50	43	Vermont	23 871	35	43	Nevada	10.0
44	Montana	1 023 579	42	44	New Hampshire	23 187	37	44	Nebraska	9.5
45	Delaware	935 614	14	45	Massachusetts	20 202	39	45	Idaho	7.6
46	South Dakota	853 175	11	46	New Jersey	19 047	36	46	New Mexico	6.6
47	North Dakota	739 482	40	47	Hawaii	16 635	46	47	South Dakota	4.3
48	Alaska	736 732	29	48	Connecticut	12 542	47	48	North Dakota	4.1
49	District of Columbia	658 893	45	49	Delaware	5 047	44	49	Montana	2.7
50	Vermont	626 562	43	50	Rhode Island	2 678	51	50	Wyoming	2.3
51	Wyoming	584 153	49	51	District of Columbia	158	48	51	Alaska	0.5

States and the District of Columbia, Selected Rankings

Percent population change, 2010-2014				Percent under 18 years old, 2013				Percent 65 years old and over, 2013			
Population rank	Percent change rank	State	Percent change [col 36]	Population rank	Under 18 years old rank	State	Percent under 18 years old [cols 10 + 11]	Population rank	65 years old and over rank	State	Percent 65 years old and over [cols 17 + 18 + 19]
		United States	3.3			United States	23.3			United States	14.1
47	1	North Dakota	9.9	33	1	Utah	30.9	3	1	Florida	18.7
49	2	District of Columbia	9.5	2	2	Texas	26.6	41	2	Maine	17.7
2	3	Texas	7.2	39	3	Idaho	26.5	38	3	West Virginia	17.3
22	4	Colorado	6.5	48	4	Alaska	25.6	6	4	Pennsylvania	16.4
33	4	Utah	6.5	34	5	Kansas	25.0	50	4	Vermont	16.4
3	6	Florida	5.8	8	6	Georgia	24.9	44	6	Montana	16.2
15	7	Arizona	5.3	37	6	Nebraska	24.9	45	7	Delaware	15.9
35	8	Nevada	5.1	31	8	Mississippi	24.7	30	8	Iowa	15.6
13	9	Washington	5.0	28	9	Oklahoma	24.6	40	8	Hawaii	15.6
46	10	South Dakota	4.8	46	9	South Dakota	24.6	27	10	Oregon	15.5
24	11	South Carolina	4.5	15	11	Arizona	24.4	43	10	Rhode Island	15.5
40	12	Hawaii	4.4	36	12	New Mexico	24.3	15	12	Arizona	15.4
39	13	Idaho	4.3	16	13	Indiana	24.1	32	12	Arkansas	15.4
9	13	North Carolina	4.3	25	13	Louisiana	24.1	42	12	New Hampshire	15.4
1	15	California	4.2	32	15	Arkansas	24.0	24	15	South Carolina	15.2
45	15	Delaware	4.2	1	16	California	23.9	29	15	Connecticut	15.2
8	15	Georgia	4.2	35	17	Nevada	23.7	7	17	Ohio	15.1
12	18	Virginia	4.1	21	18	Minnesota	23.6	18	18	Missouri	15.0
48	19	Alaska	3.7	51	18	Wyoming	23.6	10	18	Michigan	15.0
27	20	Oregon	3.6	22	20	Colorado	23.5	46	20	South Dakota	14.9
51	20	Wyoming	3.6	5	20	Illinois	23.5	23	20	Alabama	14.9
19	22	Maryland	3.5	30	22	Iowa	23.4	20	22	Wisconsin	14.8
44	22	Montana	3.5	9	23	North Carolina	23.2	14	22	Massachusetts	14.8
28	24	Oklahoma	3.4	26	24	Kentucky	23.1	36	24	New Mexico	14.7
17	25	Tennessee	3.2	18	24	Missouri	23.1	17	24	Tennessee	14.7
14	26	Massachusetts	3.0	23	26	Alabama	23.0	26	26	Kentucky	14.4
37	26	Nebraska	3.0	17	26	Tennessee	23.0	11	26	New Jersey	14.4
21	28	Minnesota	2.9	7	28	Ohio	22.9	4	26	New York	14.4
25	29	Louisiana	2.6	13	28	Washington	22.9	28	29	Oklahoma	14.3
30	30	Iowa	2.0	20	30	Wisconsin	22.8	9	29	North Carolina	14.3
4	31	New York	1.9	19	31	Maryland	22.7	47	31	North Dakota	14.2
34	32	Kansas	1.8	10	31	Michigan	22.7	37	32	Nebraska	14.1
32	33	Arkansas	1.7	11	31	New Jersey	22.7	34	33	Kansas	14.0
16	33	Indiana	1.7	24	34	South Carolina	22.6	31	34	Mississippi	13.9
26	33	Kentucky	1.7	12	34	Virginia	22.6	16	34	Indiana	13.9
11	33	New Jersey	1.7	47	36	North Dakota	22.5	21	34	Minnesota	13.9
23	37	Alabama	1.5	44	37	Montana	22.1	39	37	Idaho	13.8
36	38	New Mexico	1.3	45	38	Delaware	22.0	35	38	Nevada	13.7
18	39	Missouri	1.2	40	39	Hawaii	21.9	13	39	Washington	13.6
20	39	Wisconsin	1.2	29	40	Connecticut	21.8	51	40	Wyoming	13.5
31	41	Mississippi	0.9	27	40	Oregon	21.8	5	40	Illinois	13.5
42	42	New Hampshire	0.8	4	42	New York	21.6	19	42	Maryland	13.4
6	43	Pennsylvania	0.7	6	43	Pennsylvania	21.3	12	42	Virginia	13.4
29	44	Connecticut	0.6	14	44	Massachusetts	20.8	25	44	Louisiana	13.3
7	45	Ohio	0.5	3	45	Florida	20.6	1	45	California	12.5
5	46	Illinois	0.4	38	45	West Virginia	20.6	22	46	Colorado	12.3
10	47	Michigan	0.3	42	47	New Hampshire	20.5	8	47	Georgia	12.0
43	48	Rhode Island	0.2	43	48	Rhode Island	20.4	49	48	District Of Columbia	11.4
41	49	Maine	0.1	41	49	Maine	19.7	2	49	Texas	11.2
50	49	Vermont	0.1	50	50	Vermont	19.6	33	50	Utah	9.8
38	51	West Virginia	-0.1	49	51	District Of Columbia	17.2	48	51	Alaska	9.0

States and the District of Columbia, Selected Rankings

Percent born in state of residence, 2013

Population rank	Born in state of residence rank	State	Percent born in state of residence [col 23]
		United States	58.8
25	1	Louisiana	77.9
10	2	Michigan	76.9
7	3	Ohio	75.4
6	4	Pennsylvania	73.5
20	5	Wisconsin	71.8
31	6	Mississippi	71.7
30	7	Iowa	71.2
26	8	Kentucky	70.1
38	9	West Virginia	70.0
23	10	Alabama	70.0
16	11	Indiana	68.5
21	12	Minnesota	68.1
5	13	Illinois	67.2
18	14	Missouri	66.2
47	15	North Dakota	65.1
37	16	Nebraska	65.0
46	17	South Dakota	64.3
41	18	Maine	63.7
4	19	New York	63.6
33	20	Utah	62.7
32	21	Arkansas	62.2
14	22	Massachusetts	62.1
17	23	Tennessee	61.1
28	24	Oklahoma	61.1
2	25	Texas	60.2
34	26	Kansas	58.8
24	27	South Carolina	57.8
43	28	Rhode Island	57.8
9	29	North Carolina	57.4
8	30	Georgia	55.1
29	31	Connecticut	55.1
1	32	California	54.7
44	33	Montana	54.5
40	34	Hawaii	54.2
11	35	New Jersey	52.6
36	36	New Mexico	52.0
50	37	Vermont	50.5
12	38	Virginia	49.8
19	39	Maryland	47.6
13	40	Washington	47.4
39	41	Idaho	47.1
45	42	Delaware	46.8
27	43	Oregon	46.2
22	44	Colorado	43.4
48	45	Alaska	42.9
42	46	New Hampshire	42.2
51	47	Wyoming	41.9
15	48	Arizona	38.7
49	49	District of Columbia	36.7
3	50	Florida	36.2
35	51	Nevada	25.7

Number of immigrants, 2013

Population rank	Immigrant rank	State	Number of immigrants [col 24]
		United States	990 553
1	1	California	191 806
4	2	New York	133 601
3	3	Florida	102 939
2	4	Texas	92 674
11	5	New Jersey	53 082
5	6	Illinois	35 988
14	7	Massachusetts	29 482
12	8	Virginia	27 861
19	9	Maryland	25 361
6	10	Pennsylvania	24 720
8	11	Georgia	24 387
13	12	Washington	22 994
10	13	Michigan	16 952
9	14	North Carolina	16 798
15	15	Arizona	16 097
7	16	Ohio	13 819
21	17	Minnesota	12 781
22	18	Colorado	11 108
29	19	Connecticut	10 985
35	20	Nevada	9 886
17	21	Tennessee	8 380
16	22	Indiana	7 668
27	23	Oregon	7 171
18	24	Missouri	6 345
40	25	Hawaii	6 226
20	26	Wisconsin	5 918
33	27	Utah	5 503
26	28	Kentucky	5 159
34	29	Kansas	5 000
28	30	Oklahoma	4 648
25	31	Louisiana	4 355
24	32	South Carolina	4 266
37	33	Nebraska	4 141
30	34	Iowa	4 105
23	35	Alabama	3 848
36	36	New Mexico	3 664
43	37	Rhode Island	3 337
49	38	District of Columbia	2 981
32	39	Arkansas	2 900
45	40	Delaware	2 325
42	41	New Hampshire	2 227
39	42	Idaho	2 120
31	43	Mississippi	1 716
48	44	Alaska	1 460
47	45	North Dakota	1 234
46	46	South Dakota	1 231
41	47	Maine	1 208
50	48	Vermont	838
38	49	West Virginia	760
51	50	Wyoming	522
44	51	Montana	445

Birth rate, 2013

Population rank	Birth rate rank	State	Birth rate (per 1,000 population) [col 98]
		United States	12.4
33	1	Utah	17.6
48	2	Alaska	15.6
47	3	North Dakota	14.7
2	4	Texas	14.6
46	5	South Dakota	14.5
49	6	District of Columbia	14.4
37	7	Nebraska	14.0
39	8	Idaho	13.9
28	8	Oklahoma	13.9
25	10	Louisiana	13.7
40	11	Hawaii	13.5
34	12	Kansas	13.4
51	13	Wyoming	13.1
15	14	Arizona	12.9
1	14	California	12.9
8	14	Georgia	12.9
31	14	Mississippi	12.9
32	18	Arkansas	12.8
21	18	Minnesota	12.8
30	20	Iowa	12.7
26	20	Kentucky	12.7
16	22	Indiana	12.6
35	22	Nevada	12.6
36	22	New Mexico	12.6
18	25	Missouri	12.5
12	26	Virginia	12.4
13	26	Washington	12.4
22	28	Colorado	12.3
17	28	Tennessee	12.3
5	30	Illinois	12.2
44	30	Montana	12.2
19	32	Maryland	12.1
4	32	New York	12.1
9	32	North Carolina	12.1
23	35	Alabama	12.0
7	35	Ohio	12.0
24	37	South Carolina	11.9
45	38	Delaware	11.7
20	39	Wisconsin	11.6
10	40	Michigan	11.5
11	40	New Jersey	11.5
27	40	Oregon	11.5
38	43	West Virginia	11.2
3	44	Florida	11.0
6	44	Pennsylvania	11.0
14	46	Massachusetts	10.7
43	47	Rhode Island	10.3
29	48	Connecticut	10.0
41	49	Maine	9.6
50	50	Vermont	9.5
42	51	New Hampshire	9.4

Figure A-2. States with the Highest Proportion of Foreign-Born Population and States with the Highest Proportion of Population Born in State of Residence, 2013

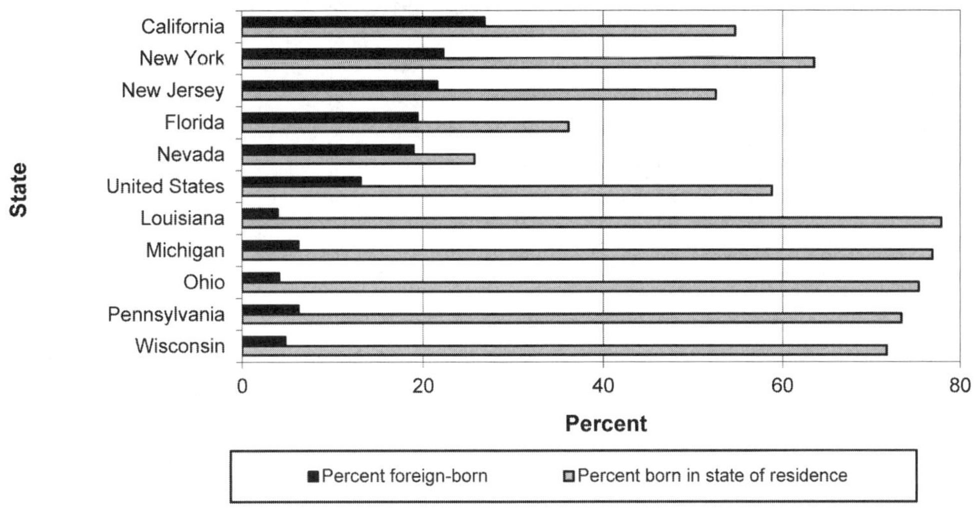

The U.S. median age increased slightly from 37.2 years in 2010 to 37.6 years in 2013, primarily caused by the aging Baby Boomer population. This increase was much less than the jump from 32.1 years to 35.3 years between 1990 and 2000. The population between 65 and 74 years showed the largest proportional increase, while the proportion between 45 and 54 showed the largest decrease. The proportion under age 18 decreased slightly, and there were small increases in the young adult age groups, ages 18 to 34, sometimes referred to as the Echo Boom. The median age by state ranged from 30.2 years in Utah to 43.9 years in Maine. Utah had the highest proportion of young residents; in 2013, 30.9 percent of the state's population was younger than 18 years old. The population age 65 years and over ranged from 9.0 percent in Alaska to 18.7 percent in Florida. Alaska, North Dakota, Wyoming, and Hawaii had the lowest proportions of female residents and were among just ten states in which men outnumbered women. Delaware had the highest proportion of female residents with 52.6 percent, followed by Rhode Island and the District of Columbia with 51.6 percent.

Natural growth is the difference between the number of births and the number of deaths. Vermont had the fewest births between 2010 and 2014. Maine and West Virginia were the only states to have more deaths than births. A net migration of more than 2,768 people prevented Maine from having a population loss from 2010 to 2014, but West Virginia did experience a population decline. California, the largest state in the nation, had over 1.1 million more births than deaths and 459,574 new residents through net migration. From 2010 to 2014, California gained 648,856 residents from foreign countries and lost 189,282 residents to other states. Texas and Florida each had a net gain of over 900,000 new residents during this period. In Texas, 62.1 percent of these new residents were from other states; in Florida, nearly half were from other states. Thirteen states had a net loss of residents due to migration including New York, which lost over 486,000 residents to other states but gained almost as many new residents from other countries.

In ten states, 70 percent or more of the residents were born in that same state. Louisiana ranked highest with 77.9 percent. The ten highest rates were mainly in the Midwest and the South. Thirteen states and the District of Columbia had proportions less than 50 percent. Nevada had the lowest proportion by far, with just 25.7 percent of its residents having been born in the state. Nationally, 58.8 percent of Americans lived in the state of their birth.

The U.S. birth rate in 2013 was 12.4, the lowest rate ever recorded and the 6th year of a decline in the rate. Utah had the highest birth rate in the nation, with 17.6 births per 1,000 population. Alaska had the second highest birth rate at 15.6, followed by the District of Columbia with a birth rate of 14.7. Maine, Vermont, and New Hampshire had the lowest birth rates in the nation, all below 10 births per 1,000 population. Alaska had the lowest crude death rate with 5.4 deaths per 1,000 population followed by Utah at 5.6 deaths. However, both states had relatively young populations. (In Utah, 42.4 percent of the population was under 25 years old while 36.8 percent of the population was under 25 in Alaska.) Once adjusted for age, Alaska's death rate increased to 7.2, and Utah's to 7.1, just under the U.S. rate of 7.3. West Virginia, Alabama, and Arkansas had the highest crude death rates in the nation. Mississippi had the highest age-adjusted death rate followed by Alabama, both with a mix of younger and older residents. Florida had, by far, the highest proportion of senior citizens. However, Florida also had a high proportion of younger people, which helped give the state a crude death rate of 9.3 per 1,000 population, ranking it 15th among the states. When Florida's death rate was age-adjusted, it dropped to 6.6, which was well below the national age-adjusted rate of 7.3 and among the lowest eight states. Hawaii had the lowest age-adjusted death rate at 5.9, one of 13 states with rates below 7.0. Mississippi, Louisiana, and Alabama had the highest infant mortality rates, while Iowa, Massachusets, and Vermont had the lowest infant death rates.

States and the District of Columbia, Selected Rankings

Percent of owners with a mortgage paying 30 percent or more of income for housing expenses, 2013

Population rank	Percent of income for housing rank	State	Percent of income for housing [col 83]
		United States	31.6
40	1	Hawaii	43.5
1	2	California	41.6
11	3	New Jersey	40.7
3	4	Florida	38.6
4	5	New York	37.6
43	6	Rhode Island	36.1
35	7	Nevada	35.7
29	8	Connecticut	35.1
27	8	Oregon	35.1
50	10	Vermont	34.8
13	11	Washington	34.1
14	12	Massachusetts	33.7
42	12	New Hampshire	33.7
5	14	Illinois	32.6
19	15	Maryland	31.6
41	16	Maine	31.5
15	17	Arizona	31.4
36	18	New Mexico	31.1
45	19	Delaware	30.6
8	20	Georgia	30.5
31	21	Mississippi	30.3
22	22	Colorado	30.0
39	23	Idaho	29.9
24	24	South Carolina	29.8
12	25	Virginia	29.4
20	26	Wisconsin	29.1
33	27	Utah	29.0
44	28	Montana	28.9
9	28	North Carolina	28.9
6	30	Pennsylvania	28.8
49	31	District of Columbia	28.4
17	31	Tennessee	28.4
10	33	Michigan	27.5
2	34	Texas	27.4
25	35	Louisiana	27.2
48	36	Alaska	26.7
18	37	Missouri	26.4
23	38	Alabama	26.3
7	39	Ohio	26.0
21	40	Minnesota	25.6
26	41	Kentucky	25.5
32	42	Arkansas	24.7
28	43	Oklahoma	24.2
51	44	Wyoming	23.7
38	45	West Virginia	23.4
16	46	Indiana	23.3
37	47	Nebraska	23.2
34	48	Kansas	22.1
46	49	South Dakota	21.9
30	50	Iowa	20.9
47	51	North Dakota	17.6

Median value of owner-occupied housing units, 2013

Population rank	Median value rank	State	Median value (dollars) [col 88]
		United States	173 900
40	1	Hawaii	500 000
49	2	District of Columbia	470 500
1	3	California	373 100
14	4	Massachusetts	327 200
11	5	New Jersey	307 700
19	6	Maryland	280 200
4	7	New York	277 600
29	8	Connecticut	267 000
48	9	Alaska	254 000
13	10	Washington	250 800
22	11	Colorado	240 500
12	12	Virginia	239 300
42	13	New Hampshire	233 300
43	14	Rhode Island	232 300
27	15	Oregon	229 700
45	16	Delaware	226 200
50	17	Vermont	218 300
33	18	Utah	211 400
51	19	Wyoming	195 500
44	20	Montana	190 100
21	21	Minnesota	180 100
41	22	Maine	172 800
5	23	Illinois	169 600
15	24	Arizona	166 000
35	25	Nevada	165 300
6	26	Pennsylvania	164 200
20	27	Wisconsin	163 000
36	28	New Mexico	159 200
39	29	Idaho	159 000
47	30	North Dakota	155 400
9	31	North Carolina	154 300
3	32	Florida	153 300
8	33	Georgia	141 600
25	34	Louisiana	140 300
17	34	Tennessee	140 300
24	36	South Carolina	139 200
46	37	South Dakota	138 400
18	38	Missouri	133 200
37	39	Nebraska	132 700
2	40	Texas	132 000
34	41	Kansas	129 700
7	42	Ohio	127 000
30	43	Iowa	126 900
23	44	Alabama	122 700
16	45	Indiana	122 200
26	46	Kentucky	120 900
10	47	Michigan	117 500
28	48	Oklahoma	116 500
32	49	Arkansas	109 500
38	50	West Virginia	103 200
31	51	Mississippi	97 500

Median gross rent of renter-occupied housing units, 2013

Population rank	Median rent rank	State	Median rent (dollars) [col 90]
		United States	905
40	1 414	Hawaii	1 414
49	1 307	District of Columbia	1 307
1	1 224	California	1 224
19	1 210	Maryland	1 210
11	1 171	New Jersey	1 171
48	1 117	Alaska	1 117
4	1 109	New York	1 109
12	1 086	Virginia	1 086
14	1 077	Massachusetts	1 077
29	1 040	Connecticut	1 040
45	999	Delaware	999
42	995	New Hampshire	995
13	989	Washington	989
3	972	Florida	972
22	971	Colorado	971
35	952	Nevada	952
43	918	Rhode Island	918
15	890	Arizona	890
27	887	Oregon	887
5	885	Illinois	885
33	881	Utah	881
50	865	Vermont	865
2	857	Texas	857
8	850	Georgia	850
21	832	Minnesota	832
6	828	Pennsylvania	828
51	780	Wyoming	780
9	778	North Carolina	778
36	772	New Mexico	772
10	768	Michigan	768
24	766	South Carolina	766
25	763	Louisiana	763
41	760	Maine	760
20	758	Wisconsin	758
17	748	Tennessee	748
34	745	Kansas	745
18	734	Missouri	734
16	730	Indiana	730
39	725	Idaho	725
37	714	Nebraska	714
7	709	Ohio	709
31	708	Mississippi	708
28	705	Oklahoma	705
23	694	Alabama	694
44	690	Montana	690
47	690	North Dakota	690
30	679	Iowa	679
26	668	Kentucky	668
32	659	Arkansas	659
46	637	South Dakota	637
38	620	West Virginia	620

Figure A-3. Top 10 Median Housing Values and Percentage of Owners Paying 30% or More of Income for Housing Expenses, 2013

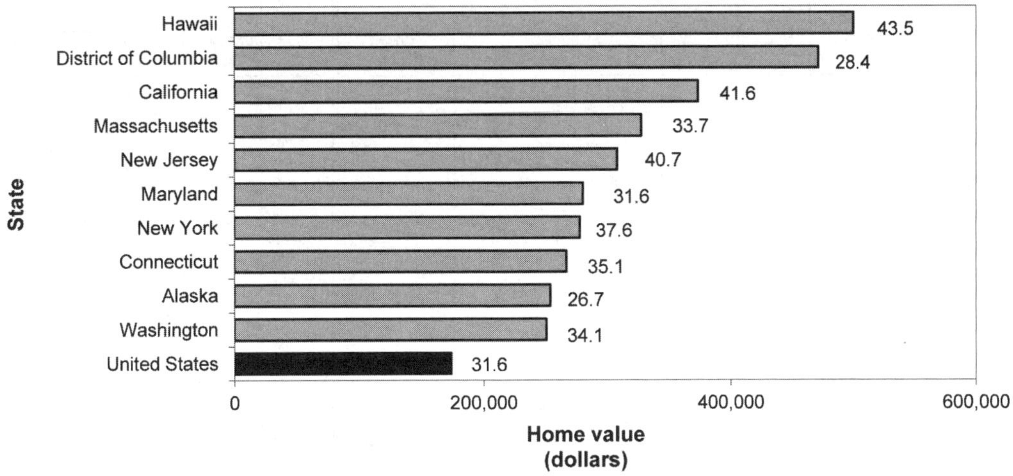

Note: Median values are of owner-occupied units, and housing expenses are a percentage of household income for owners with mortgages.

In 2013, homeowners with mortgages paid a median of 25.1 percent of their incomes for monthly owner costs (mortgage, insurance, taxes, utilities, fuel, etc.). This ranged from a high of 30.6 percent in California to 19.6 percent in North Dakota. Nationally, 31.6 percent of owners with a mortgage paid 30 percent or more of income for housing expenses in 2013. Hawaii had the highest proportion of mortgage holders paying 30 percent or more of their income with 43.5 percent, followed by California at 41.6 percent, New Jersey at 40.7 percent, and Florida at 38.6 percent. In 28 states and the District of Columbia, less than 30 percent of all mortgaged owners paid this high level of owner costs. North Dakota had the lowest proportion in the nation with 17.6 percent. Four states and the District of Columbia had median home values exceeding $300,000 in 2013, led by Hawaii with a median home value of $500,000. Nationally, the median value of owner-occupied housing units was $173,900. Hawaii also had the highest median gross rent, at $1,414. The District of Columbia, California, Maryland, New Jersey, Alaska, New York, Virginia, Massachusetts, and Connecticut all had median gross monthly rents exceeding $1,000.

Many minority groups had above average growth rates since 2000. Currently, in four states and the District of Columbia, the minority population outnumbers the non-Hispanic White population. Nationally, 64.3 percent of the U.S. population was non-Hispanic White alone or in combination, but the racial and ethnic compositions of the states varied widely. In Hawaii, the state with the highest proportion of minorities, Asian and Pacific Islander alone or in combination was the largest race group, representing over 74 percent of the state's population. Hispanic or Latino residents made up over 47 percent of New Mexico's population and over 38 percent of residents in both California and Texas. The District of Columbia had the highest proportion of Black residents at just under half the population at 49.2 percent, down from 60.5 percent in 2000. Among the states, Mississippi and Louisiana ranked first and second, with Black populations of 37.7 and 32.8 percent, respectively. Alaska had the highest proportion of American Indians and Alaska Natives, who made up 18.4 percent of the population. Oklahoma, New Mexico, and South Dakota all had high proportions of American Indian populations. As might be expected, the states with the largest number of minorities were among the states with the highest total populations. New York was home to approximately 3.6 million Black residents, and California had the largest number of Hispanics, Asian and Pacific Islanders, and American Indians and Alaska Natives. California had over 380,000 non-Hispanic American Indian and Alaska Native residents, though they made up just 1.0 percent of the state's population. Oklahoma ranked second for both the total number of Native Americans as well as for their representative proportion of the state's population. Despite having only about 83,000 Native American residents, South Dakota had the third highest proportion in the nation.

States and the District of Columbia, Selected Rankings

Percent White, not Hispanic or Latino, alone or in combination, 2013			
Population rank	Percent White rank	State	Percent White [col 5]
		United States	64.3
41	1	Maine	95.5
50	2	Vermont	95.4
38	3	West Virginia	94.1
42	4	New Hampshire	92.9
44	5	Montana	89.2
30	6	Iowa	89.0
47	7	North Dakota	88.9
26	8	Kentucky	87.1
51	9	Wyoming	85.6
46	10	South Dakota	85.1
39	11	Idaho	84.9
20	12	Wisconsin	83.9
21	13	Minnesota	83.8
37	14	Nebraska	82.5
16	15	Indiana	82.2
7	15	Ohio	82.2
18	17	Missouri	82.1
33	18	Utah	81.4
27	19	Oregon	80.3
6	20	Pennsylvania	79.7
34	21	Kansas	79.3
10	22	Michigan	77.9
43	23	Rhode Island	76.9
14	24	Massachusetts	76.6
17	25	Tennessee	76.3
32	26	Arkansas	75.2
13	27	Washington	74.4
28	28	Oklahoma	72.4
22	29	Colorado	71.3
29	30	Connecticut	71.0
48	31	Alaska	68.2
23	32	Alabama	67.6
45	33	Delaware	65.9
9	33	North Carolina	65.9
12	35	Virginia	65.7
24	36	South Carolina	65.2
5	37	Illinois	64.0
25	38	Louisiana	60.7
11	39	New Jersey	58.8
15	40	Arizona	58.4
4	40	New York	58.4
31	42	Mississippi	58.3
3	43	Florida	57.7
8	44	Georgia	56.2
19	45	Maryland	55.1
35	46	Nevada	54.8
2	47	Texas	45.2
1	48	California	41.2
36	49	New Mexico	40.6
49	50	District of Columbia	37.4
40	51	Hawaii	36.9

Percent Black, not Hispanic or Latino, alone or in combination, 2013			
Population rank	Percent Black rank	State	Percent Black [col 6]
		United States	13.2
49	1	District of Columbia	49.2
31	2	Mississippi	37.7
25	3	Louisiana	32.8
8	4	Georgia	31.5
19	5	Maryland	30.5
24	6	South Carolina	28.3
23	7	Alabama	26.9
45	8	Delaware	22.5
9	9	North Carolina	22.3
12	10	Virginia	20.2
17	11	Tennessee	17.6
3	12	Florida	16.3
32	13	Arkansas	16.0
4	14	New York	15.4
10	15	Michigan	15.0
5	16	Illinois	14.9
11	17	New Jersey	13.6
7	18	Ohio	13.4
18	19	Missouri	12.5
2	20	Texas	12.3
6	21	Pennsylvania	11.5
29	22	Connecticut	10.6
16	23	Indiana	10.1
35	24	Nevada	9.2
26	25	Kentucky	8.9
28	26	Oklahoma	8.7
14	27	Massachusetts	7.4
34	28	Kansas	7.0
20	28	Wisconsin	7.0
43	30	Rhode Island	6.6
1	31	California	6.5
21	31	Minnesota	6.5
37	33	Nebraska	5.4
48	34	Alaska	4.8
13	34	Washington	4.8
15	36	Arizona	4.7
22	36	Colorado	4.7
38	38	West Virginia	4.3
30	39	Iowa	3.9
40	40	Hawaii	3.1
27	41	Oregon	2.5
46	42	South Dakota	2.4
36	43	New Mexico	2.3
47	44	North Dakota	2.2
51	45	Wyoming	2.0
41	46	Maine	1.8
42	47	New Hampshire	1.7
50	48	Vermont	1.6
33	49	Utah	1.5
39	50	Idaho	1.0
44	51	Montana	0.9

Percent Hispanic or Latino,[1] 2013			
Population rank	Hispanic or Latino rank	State	Percent Hispanic or Latino [col 9]
		United States	17.1
36	1	New Mexico	47.3
1	2	California	38.3
2	2	Texas	38.3
15	4	Arizona	30.2
35	5	Nevada	27.5
3	6	Florida	23.6
22	7	Colorado	21.0
11	8	New Jersey	18.9
4	9	New York	18.3
5	10	Illinois	16.5
29	11	Connecticut	14.6
43	12	Rhode Island	13.6
33	13	Utah	13.4
27	14	Oregon	12.3
13	15	Washington	11.9
39	16	Idaho	11.8
34	17	Kansas	11.2
14	18	Massachusetts	10.5
49	19	District of Columbia	10.1
37	20	Nebraska	9.9
40	21	Hawaii	9.8
51	22	Wyoming	9.7
28	23	Oklahoma	9.6
8	24	Georgia	9.2
19	25	Maryland	9.0
9	26	North Carolina	8.9
45	27	Delaware	8.7
12	28	Virginia	8.6
32	29	Arkansas	6.9
48	30	Alaska	6.6
16	31	Indiana	6.4
6	32	Pennsylvania	6.3
20	32	Wisconsin	6.3
30	34	Iowa	5.5
24	35	South Carolina	5.3
21	36	Minnesota	5.0
17	37	Tennessee	4.9
25	38	Louisiana	4.7
10	38	Michigan	4.7
23	40	Alabama	4.1
18	41	Missouri	3.9
7	42	Ohio	3.4
46	42	South Dakota	3.4
26	44	Kentucky	3.3
44	44	Montana	3.3
42	46	New Hampshire	3.2
31	47	Mississippi	2.9
47	47	North Dakota	2.9
50	49	Vermont	1.7
41	50	Maine	1.4
38	50	West Virginia	1.4

1. May be of any race.

States and the District of Columbia, Selected Rankings

Percent high school graduates or more,[1] 2013

Population rank	Percent high school graduates rank	State	Percent high school graduates [col 115]
		United States	86.6
51	1	Wyoming	93.5
42	2	New Hampshire	92.8
44	3	Montana	92.7
21	4	Minnesota	92.4
41	5	Maine	91.8
48	6	Alaska	91.6
30	6	Iowa	91.6
46	6	South Dakota	91.6
47	9	North Dakota	91.5
33	9	Utah	91.5
50	9	Vermont	91.5
40	12	Hawaii	91.0
20	13	Wisconsin	90.9
22	14	Colorado	90.5
37	15	Nebraska	90.2
49	16	District of Columbia	90.1
34	16	Kansas	90.1
13	16	Washington	90.1
14	19	Massachusetts	89.9
29	20	Connecticut	89.7
27	20	Oregon	89.7
39	22	Idaho	89.4
10	22	Michigan	89.4
6	24	Pennsylvania	89.2
19	25	Maryland	89.1
7	26	Ohio	89.0
18	27	Missouri	88.7
11	28	New Jersey	88.5
12	29	Virginia	88.4
45	30	Delaware	88.3
5	31	Illinois	87.8
16	32	Indiana	87.6
3	33	Florida	86.8
28	34	Oklahoma	86.7
15	35	Arizona	85.9
43	35	Rhode Island	85.9
9	37	North Carolina	85.7
4	38	New York	85.6
24	38	South Carolina	85.6
17	38	Tennessee	85.6
8	41	Georgia	85.5
35	42	Nevada	85.2
38	43	West Virginia	84.6
23	44	Alabama	84.5
32	45	Arkansas	84.4
36	46	New Mexico	84.3
26	47	Kentucky	84.1
25	48	Louisiana	83.1
31	49	Mississippi	82.4
2	50	Texas	81.9
1	51	California	81.7

Percent college graduates (bachelor's degree or more),[1] 2013

Population rank	Percent college graduates rank	State	Percent college graduates [col 116]
		United States	29.6
49	1	District of Columbia	55.1
14	2	Massachusetts	40.3
22	3	Colorado	37.8
19	4	Maryland	37.4
29	5	Connecticut	37.2
11	6	New Jersey	36.6
12	7	Virginia	36.1
50	8	Vermont	35.7
42	9	New Hampshire	34.6
4	10	New York	34.1
21	11	Minnesota	33.5
13	12	Washington	32.7
43	13	Rhode Island	32.4
5	14	Illinois	32.1
33	15	Utah	31.3
40	16	Hawaii	31.2
34	17	Kansas	31.1
1	18	California	31.0
27	19	Oregon	30.7
45	20	Delaware	29.8
37	21	Nebraska	29.4
44	22	Montana	29.0
6	23	Pennsylvania	28.7
9	24	North Carolina	28.4
8	25	Georgia	28.3
41	26	Maine	28.2
48	27	Alaska	28.0
20	28	Wisconsin	27.7
2	29	Texas	27.5
15	30	Arizona	27.4
3	31	Florida	27.2
47	32	North Dakota	27.1
18	33	Missouri	27.0
10	34	Michigan	26.9
46	35	South Dakota	26.6
51	35	Wyoming	26.6
30	37	Iowa	26.4
36	37	New Mexico	26.4
39	39	Idaho	26.2
7	40	Ohio	26.1
24	40	South Carolina	26.1
17	42	Tennessee	24.8
16	43	Indiana	23.8
28	43	Oklahoma	23.8
23	45	Alabama	23.5
26	46	Kentucky	22.6
25	47	Louisiana	22.5
35	47	Nevada	22.5
32	49	Arkansas	20.6
31	50	Mississippi	20.4
38	51	West Virginia	18.9

Median household income, 2013

Population rank	Median income rank	State	Median income (dollars) [col 123]
		United States	52 250
19	1	Maryland	72 483
48	2	Alaska	72 237
11	3	New Jersey	70 165
40	4	Hawaii	68 020
49	5	District of Columbia	67 572
29	6	Connecticut	67 098
14	7	Massachusetts	66 768
42	8	New Hampshire	64 230
12	9	Virginia	62 666
21	10	Minnesota	60 702
1	11	California	60 190
33	12	Utah	59 770
22	13	Colorado	58 823
51	14	Wyoming	58 752
13	15	Washington	58 405
45	16	Delaware	57 846
4	17	New York	57 369
5	18	Illinois	56 210
43	19	Rhode Island	55 902
47	20	North Dakota	55 759
50	21	Vermont	52 578
30	22	Iowa	52 229
6	23	Pennsylvania	52 007
2	24	Texas	51 704
20	25	Wisconsin	51 467
37	26	Nebraska	51 440
35	27	Nevada	51 230
34	28	Kansas	50 972
27	29	Oregon	50 251
46	30	South Dakota	48 947
15	31	Arizona	48 510
10	32	Michigan	48 273
7	33	Ohio	48 081
8	34	Georgia	47 829
16	35	Indiana	47 529
41	36	Maine	46 974
44	37	Montana	46 972
18	38	Missouri	46 931
39	39	Idaho	46 783
3	40	Florida	46 036
9	41	North Carolina	45 906
28	42	Oklahoma	45 690
17	43	Tennessee	44 297
25	44	Louisiana	44 164
24	45	South Carolina	44 163
36	46	New Mexico	43 872
26	47	Kentucky	43 399
23	48	Alabama	42 849
38	49	West Virginia	41 253
32	50	Arkansas	40 511
31	51	Mississippi	37 963

1. Persons 25 years old and over

States and the District of Columbia, Selected Rankings

Unemployment rate, 2014

Population rank	Unemployment rate rank	State	Unemployment rate [col 171]
		United States	6.2
49	1	District of Columbia	7.8
31	1	Mississippi	7.8
35	1	Nevada	7.8
43	4	Rhode Island	7.7
1	5	California	7.5
10	6	Michigan	7.3
8	7	Georgia	7.2
5	8	Illinois	7.1
15	9	Arizona	6.9
27	9	Oregon	6.9
23	11	Alabama	6.8
48	11	Alaska	6.8
17	13	Tennessee	6.7
29	14	Connecticut	6.6
11	14	New Jersey	6.6
26	16	Kentucky	6.5
36	16	New Mexico	6.5
38	16	West Virginia	6.5
25	19	Louisiana	6.4
24	19	South Carolina	6.4
3	21	Florida	6.3
4	21	New York	6.3
13	23	Washington	6.2
32	24	Arkansas	6.1
18	24	Missouri	6.1
9	24	North Carolina	6.1
16	27	Indiana	6.0
19	28	Maryland	5.8
14	28	Massachusetts	5.8
6	28	Pennsylvania	5.8
45	31	Delaware	5.7
41	31	Maine	5.7
7	31	Ohio	5.7
20	34	Wisconsin	5.5
12	35	Virginia	5.2
2	36	Texas	5.1
22	37	Colorado	5.0
39	38	Idaho	4.8
44	39	Montana	4.7
34	40	Kansas	4.5
28	40	Oklahoma	4.5
40	42	Hawaii	4.4
30	42	Iowa	4.4
42	44	New Hampshire	4.3
51	44	Wyoming	4.3
21	46	Minnesota	4.1
50	46	Vermont	4.1
33	48	Utah	3.8
46	49	South Dakota	3.4
37	50	Nebraska	3.3
47	51	North Dakota	2.8

Per capita state taxes, 2013

Population rank	State taxes rank	State	State taxes per capita (dollars) [col 337]
		United States	X
47	1	North Dakota	7 325
48	2	Alaska	6 982
50	3	Vermont	4 594
29	4	Connecticut	4 502
40	5	Hawaii	4 340
21	6	Minnesota	3 880
51	7	Wyoming	3 752
4	8	New York	3 749
45	9	Delaware	3 615
14	10	Massachusetts	3 571
1	11	California	3 474
11	12	New Jersey	3 267
19	13	Maryland	3 056
5	14	Illinois	3 006
41	15	Maine	2 924
32	16	Arkansas	2 901
38	17	West Virginia	2 900
20	18	Wisconsin	2 876
43	19	Rhode Island	2 796
30	20	Iowa	2 710
13	21	Washington	2 678
6	22	Pennsylvania	2 659
34	23	Kansas	2 633
44	24	Montana	2 605
16	25	Indiana	2 577
37	26	Nebraska	2 526
10	27	Michigan	2 520
35	28	Nevada	2 518
36	29	New Mexico	2 494
31	30	Mississippi	2 475
26	31	Kentucky	2 461
9	32	North Carolina	2 414
7	33	Ohio	2 378
27	34	Oregon	2 331
12	35	Virginia	2 323
28	36	Oklahoma	2 309
39	37	Idaho	2 220
33	38	Utah	2 180
22	39	Colorado	2 135
15	40	Arizona	2 033
25	41	Louisiana	1 994
2	42	Texas	1 955
23	43	Alabama	1 917
17	44	Tennessee	1 904
18	45	Missouri	1 843
24	46	South Carolina	1 827
46	47	South Dakota	1 815
3	48	Florida	1 809
8	49	Georgia	1 781
42	50	New Hampshire	1 775
49	X	District of Columbia	X

Exports of goods by state of origin, 2014

Population rank	Exports rank	State	Exports (milions of dollars) [col 119]
		United States	1 623 273
2	1	Texas	289 023
1	2	California	174 129
13	3	Washington	90 646
47	4	North Dakota	86 007
5	5	Illinois	68 182
25	6	Louisiana	65 085
3	7	Florida	58 637
10	8	Michigan	55 751
7	9	Ohio	52 130
6	10	Pennsylvania	40 227
8	11	Georgia	39 365
36	12	New Mexico	36 836
16	13	Indiana	35 452
17	14	Tennessee	32 957
37	15	Nebraska	31 290
24	16	South Carolina	29 704
26	17	Kentucky	27 541
41	18	Maine	27 364
38	19	West Virginia	23 433
21	20	Minnesota	21 372
15	21	Arizona	21 124
27	22	Oregon	20 920
23	23	Alabama	19 518
50	24	Vermont	19 194
29	25	Connecticut	15 941
30	26	Iowa	15 101
31	27	Mississippi	14 141
33	28	Utah	12 266
19	29	Maryland	12 241
34	30	Kansas	12 004
18	31	Missouri	11 414
22	32	Colorado	8 368
42	33	New Hampshire	7 863
9	34	North Carolina	7 701
20	35	Wisconsin	7 496
32	36	Arkansas	6 857
28	37	Oklahoma	6 300
45	38	Delaware	5 293
35	39	Nevada	5 290
48	40	Alaska	5 153
39	41	Idaho	5 136
11	42	New Jersey	4 424
4	43	New York	3 789
12	44	Virginia	3 643
14	45	Massachusetts	2 752
43	46	Rhode Island	2 394
51	47	Wyoming	1 757
46	48	South Dakota	1 590
44	49	Montana	1 529
40	50	Hawaii	1 452
49	51	District of Columbia	936

Figure A-4. States with the Highest and Lowest Poverty Rates for All Persons and Children, 2013

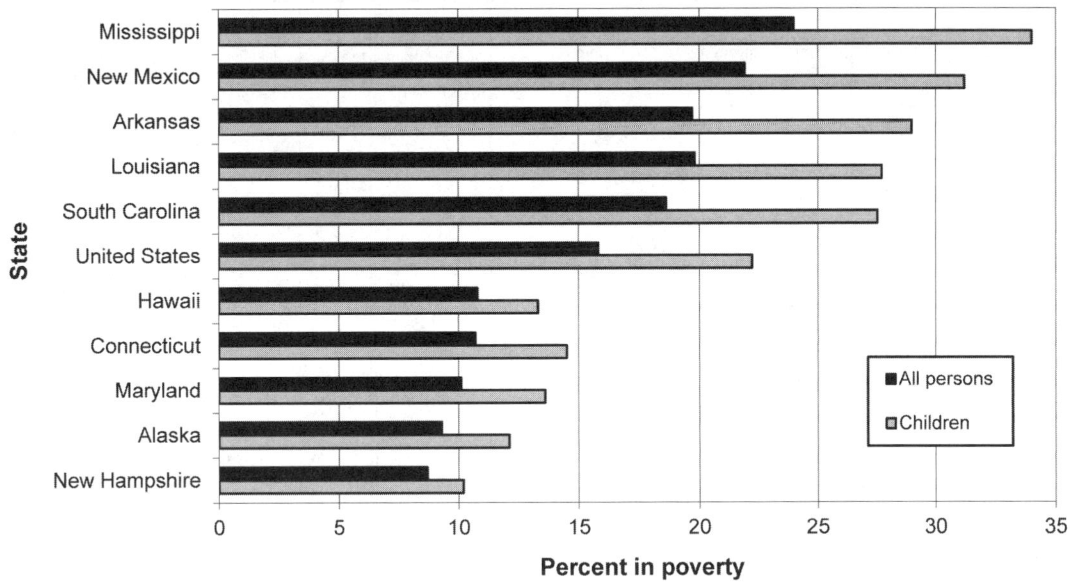

Nationally, 86.6 percent of the population 25 years old and over had graduated from high school. Eighteen states had high school attainment levels of 90 percent or more, led by Wyoming with 93.5 percent. States in the Midwest and the West tended to have above average high school attainment rates, although California had the lowest rate at 81.7 percent, followed by Texas at at 81.9 percent. States with above average high school attainment levels do not necessarily have high proportions of college graduates. Nationally, 29.6 percent of the population held bachelor's degrees. In the District of Columbia, 55.1 percent of the population had graduated from college. Even when compared with other large cities, the District of Columbia had among the 10 highest proportions of college graduates in the nation. Of the 50 states, Massachusetts, Colorado, Maryland, Connecticut, New Jersey, Virginia, and Vermont each had more than 35 percent of their populations holding bachelor's degrees or more. States in the Northeast tended to have above average college attainment levels, while states in the South had below average rates.

Median household income ranged from $37,963 in Mississippi to $72,483 in Maryland. Nationally, the median household income was $52,250. In six states—Mississippi, West Virginia, Arkansas, Louisiana, New Mexico, and Alabama, 30 percent or more of households had incomes below $25,000. The District of Columbia and Maryland had the highest proportions of households earning $100,000 or more, at 35.8 percent and 35.1 percent respectively, followed by New Jersey at 34.6 percent.

The poverty threshold for an individual was $11,888 in 2013. Mississippi had the highest poverty rate in the nation, with 24.0 percent of its population living in poverty. New Mexico, Louisiana, Arkansas, and Georgia all had poverty rates of 19 percent or higher. The poverty threshold for a four-person family was $23,834. Among children under 18 years old, 22.2 percent were living in poverty. Over 30 percent of children in Mississippi and New Mexico lived in poverty. New Hampshire had the lowest proportion of children in poverty, at 10.2 percent. The District of Columbia had the highest proportion of residents 65 years and over living in poverty, 17.5 percent, followed by Mississippi at 14.7 percent.

The United States labor force increased by 0.3 percent between 2013 and 2014. From 2000 to 2008, it grew about an average of 1 percent a year but then declined from 2009 to 2011 followed by small increases in recent years. Nineteen states experienced a decline in their labor force between 2013 and 2014. Mississippi experienced the largest decline, dropping 3.0 percent. Meanwhile, the labor force in Hawaii, Louisiana, Delaware, and North Dakota grew by more than 2 percent in the same period. In 2014, the unemployment rate was 6.2 percent, down from 7.4 percent in 2013. Eight states had an unemployment rate over 7 percent. The District of Columbia, Mississippi, and Nevada shared the highest unemployment rate in the nation at 7.8 percent, followed by Rhode Island at 7.7 percent. North Dakota, South Dakota, Nebraska, and Utah had the lowest unemployment rates in 2014, all below 4 percent.

States and the District of Columbia, Selected Rankings

Percent of persons below the poverty level, 2013

Population rank	Poverty rate rank	State	Poverty rate [col 127]
		United States	15.8
31	1	Mississippi	24.0
36	2	New Mexico	21.9
25	3	Louisiana	19.8
32	4	Arkansas	19.7
8	5	Georgia	19.0
49	6	District of Columbia	18.9
26	7	Kentucky	18.8
23	8	Alabama	18.7
15	9	Arizona	18.6
24	9	South Carolina	18.6
38	11	West Virginia	18.5
9	12	North Carolina	17.9
17	13	Tennessee	17.8
2	14	Texas	17.5
3	15	Florida	17.0
10	15	Michigan	17.0
1	17	California	16.8
28	17	Oklahoma	16.8
27	19	Oregon	16.7
44	20	Montana	16.5
4	21	New York	16.0
7	21	Ohio	16.0
16	23	Indiana	15.9
18	23	Missouri	15.9
35	25	Nevada	15.8
39	26	Idaho	15.6
5	27	Illinois	14.7
43	28	Rhode Island	14.3
46	29	South Dakota	14.2
13	30	Washington	14.1
34	31	Kansas	14.0
41	31	Maine	14.0
6	33	Pennsylvania	13.7
20	34	Wisconsin	13.5
37	35	Nebraska	13.2
22	36	Colorado	13.0
30	37	Iowa	12.7
33	37	Utah	12.7
45	39	Delaware	12.4
50	40	Vermont	12.3
14	41	Massachusetts	11.9
47	42	North Dakota	11.8
12	43	Virginia	11.7
11	44	New Jersey	11.4
21	45	Minnesota	11.2
51	46	Wyoming	10.9
40	47	Hawaii	10.8
29	48	Connecticut	10.7
19	49	Maryland	10.1
48	50	Alaska	9.3
42	51	New Hampshire	8.7

Percent of children under 18 years old below the poverty level, 2013

Population rank	Poverty rate rank	State	Poverty rate [col 128]
		United States	22.2
31	1	Mississippi	34.0
36	2	New Mexico	31.2
32	3	Arkansas	29.0
25	4	Louisiana	27.7
24	5	South Carolina	27.5
23	6	Alabama	27.2
49	6	District of Columbia	27.2
38	8	West Virginia	27.0
15	9	Arizona	26.5
8	9	Georgia	26.5
17	9	Tennessee	26.5
26	12	Kentucky	25.3
9	13	North Carolina	25.2
2	14	Texas	25.0
3	15	Florida	24.5
28	16	Oklahoma	24.0
10	17	Michigan	23.8
1	18	California	23.5
4	19	New York	22.8
35	20	Nevada	22.7
7	20	Ohio	22.7
16	22	Indiana	22.2
18	22	Missouri	22.2
27	24	Oregon	21.6
43	25	Rhode Island	21.5
44	26	Montana	21.3
5	27	Illinois	20.7
6	28	Pennsylvania	19.4
39	29	Idaho	19.1
13	30	Washington	18.8
34	31	Kansas	18.7
46	32	South Dakota	18.6
20	33	Wisconsin	18.4
45	34	Delaware	18.0
41	35	Maine	17.7
37	35	Nebraska	17.7
22	37	Colorado	16.9
11	38	New Jersey	16.7
14	39	Massachusetts	16.3
30	40	Iowa	16.2
12	41	Virginia	15.7
50	42	Vermont	15.3
33	43	Utah	14.8
29	44	Connecticut	14.5
21	45	Minnesota	14.0
19	46	Maryland	13.6
40	47	Hawaii	13.3
51	48	Wyoming	13.2
48	49	Alaska	12.1
47	50	North Dakota	12.0
42	51	New Hampshire	10.2

Percent of persons lacking health insurance, 2013

Population rank	Percent lacking health insurance rank	State	Percent lacking health insurance [col 104]
		United States	14.5
2	1	Texas	22.1
35	2	Nevada	20.7
3	3	Florida	20.0
8	4	Georgia	18.8
36	5	New Mexico	18.6
48	6	Alaska	18.5
28	7	Oklahoma	17.7
1	8	California	17.2
15	9	Arizona	17.1
31	9	Mississippi	17.1
25	11	Louisiana	16.6
44	12	Montana	16.5
39	13	Idaho	16.2
32	14	Arkansas	16.0
24	15	South Carolina	15.8
9	16	North Carolina	15.6
27	17	Oregon	14.7
26	18	Kentucky	14.3
22	19	Colorado	14.1
16	20	Indiana	14.0
33	20	Utah	14.0
13	20	Washington	14.0
38	20	West Virginia	14.0
17	24	Tennessee	13.9
23	25	Alabama	13.6
51	26	Wyoming	13.4
11	27	New Jersey	13.2
18	28	Missouri	13.0
5	29	Illinois	12.7
34	30	Kansas	12.3
12	30	Virginia	12.3
43	32	Rhode Island	11.6
37	33	Nebraska	11.3
46	33	South Dakota	11.3
41	35	Maine	11.2
10	36	Michigan	11.0
7	36	Ohio	11.0
42	38	New Hampshire	10.7
4	38	New York	10.7
47	40	North Dakota	10.4
19	41	Maryland	10.2
6	42	Pennsylvania	9.7
29	43	Connecticut	9.4
45	44	Delaware	9.1
20	44	Wisconsin	9.1
21	46	Minnesota	8.2
30	47	Iowa	8.1
50	48	Vermont	7.2
49	49	District of Columbia	6.7
40	49	Hawaii	6.7
14	51	Massachusetts	3.7

States and the District of Columbia, Selected Rankings

State government employment, 2013

Population rank	State government employment rank	State	State government employment [col 312]
		United States	4 312 054
1	1	California	395 489
2	2	Texas	310 549
4	3	New York	242 299
3	4	Florida	181 262
6	5	Pennsylvania	158 094
9	6	North Carolina	150 424
11	7	New Jersey	146 220
10	8	Michigan	146 163
7	9	Ohio	135 594
5	10	Illinois	130 206
8	11	Georgia	128 445
12	12	Virginia	126 520
13	13	Washington	111 888
14	14	Massachusetts	96 752
16	15	Indiana	89 332
19	16	Maryland	86 981
23	17	Alabama	86 976
18	18	Missouri	85 919
26	19	Kentucky	85 315
17	20	Tennessee	84 514
21	21	Minnesota	79 730
25	22	Louisiana	79 378
24	23	South Carolina	78 364
22	24	Colorado	73 458
20	25	Wisconsin	70 851
15	26	Arizona	69 392
27	27	Oregon	65 777
28	28	Oklahoma	65 209
32	29	Arkansas	63 606
29	30	Connecticut	61 578
31	31	Mississippi	58 090
40	32	Hawaii	57 293
33	33	Utah	53 255
34	34	Kansas	48 491
30	35	Iowa	47 921
36	36	New Mexico	45 216
38	37	West Virginia	40 227
37	38	Nebraska	32 094
48	39	Alaska	27 290
45	40	Delaware	26 588
35	41	Nevada	26 388
39	42	Idaho	21 548
41	43	Maine	21 022
44	44	Montana	20 251
43	45	Rhode Island	18 969
47	46	North Dakota	18 897
42	47	New Hampshire	18 589
50	48	Vermont	15 023
46	49	South Dakota	14 971
51	50	Wyoming	13 646
49	X	District of Columbia	X

Value of agricultural products sold, 2012

Population rank	Agricultural sales rank	State	Value of sales (millions of dollars) [col 197]
		United States	394 644
1	1	California	42 627
30	2	Iowa	30 822
2	3	Texas	25 376
37	4	Nebraska	23 069
21	5	Minnesota	21 280
34	6	Kansas	18 461
5	7	Illinois	17 187
9	8	North Carolina	12 588
20	9	Wisconsin	11 744
16	10	Indiana	11 211
47	11	North Dakota	10 951
46	12	South Dakota	10 170
7	13	Ohio	10 064
32	14	Arkansas	9 776
8	15	Georgia	9 255
18	16	Missouri	9 165
13	17	Washington	9 121
10	18	Michigan	8 678
39	19	Idaho	7 801
22	20	Colorado	7 781
3	21	Florida	7 702
6	22	Pennsylvania	7 401
28	23	Oklahoma	7 130
31	24	Mississippi	6 441
23	25	Alabama	5 571
4	26	New York	5 415
26	27	Kentucky	5 067
27	28	Oregon	4 884
44	29	Montana	4 230
25	30	Louisiana	3 809
12	31	Virginia	3 753
15	32	Arizona	3 732
17	33	Tennessee	3 611
24	34	South Carolina	3 040
36	35	New Mexico	2 550
19	36	Maryland	2 271
33	37	Utah	1 816
51	38	Wyoming	1 689
45	39	Delaware	1 274
11	40	New Jersey	1 007
38	41	West Virginia	807
50	42	Vermont	776
35	43	Nevada	764
41	44	Maine	763
40	45	Hawaii	661
29	46	Connecticut	551
14	47	Massachusetts	492
42	48	New Hampshire	191
43	49	Rhode Island	60
48	50	Alaska	59
49	X	District of Columbia	X

Violent crime rate, 2013

Population rank	Violent crime rate rank	State	Violent crime rate (per 100,000 population) [col 108]
		United States	376.6
49	1	District of Columbia	1 300.3
48	2	Alaska	640.4
36	3	New Mexico	613.0
35	4	Nevada	603.0
17	5	Tennessee	590.6
25	6	Louisiana	518.5
24	7	South Carolina	508.5
45	8	Delaware	491.4
19	9	Maryland	473.8
3	10	Florida	470.4
32	11	Arkansas	460.3
10	12	Michigan	449.9
28	13	Oklahoma	441.2
18	14	Missouri	433.4
23	15	Alabama	430.8
15	16	Arizona	416.5
14	17	Massachusetts	413.4
2	18	Texas	408.3
1	19	California	402.1
4	20	New York	393.7
5	21	Illinois	380.2
8	22	Georgia	365.7
16	23	Indiana	357.4
9	24	North Carolina	342.2
34	25	Kansas	339.9
6	26	Pennsylvania	335.4
46	27	South Dakota	316.5
22	28	Colorado	308.0
38	29	West Virginia	300.3
13	30	Washington	289.1
11	31	New Jersey	288.5
7	32	Ohio	286.2
20	33	Wisconsin	277.9
31	34	Mississippi	274.6
30	35	Iowa	271.4
47	36	North Dakota	270.1
29	37	Connecticut	262.5
37	38	Nebraska	262.1
43	39	Rhode Island	257.2
27	40	Oregon	254.0
44	41	Montana	252.9
40	42	Hawaii	251.6
21	43	Minnesota	234.4
33	44	Utah	224.0
39	45	Idaho	217.0
42	46	New Hampshire	215.3
26	47	Kentucky	209.8
51	48	Wyoming	205.1
12	49	Virginia	196.2
41	50	Maine	129.3
50	51	Vermont	121.1

Table A. States — Land Area and Population Characteristics

State code	STATE		Population, 2014			Population characteristics, 2013										
						Race alone or in combination, not Hispanic or Latino (percent)					Age (percent)					
		Land area,[1] 2010 (sq km)	Total persons, 2014	Rank	Per square kilometer	White	Black	American Indian, Alaska Native	Asian and Pacific Islander	Hispanic or Latino[2] (percent)	Under 5 years	5 to 17 years	18 to 24 years	25 to 34 years	35 to 44 years	45 to 54 years
		1	2	3	4	5	6	7	8	9	10	11	12	13	14	15

1. Dry land or land partially or temporarily covered by water. 2. May be of any race.

Table A. States — Population Characteristics, Immigration, and Households

STATE	Population characteristics, 2013 (cont.)									Households, 2013					
	Age (percent) (cont.)												Household type		
	55 to 64 years	65 to 74 years	75 to 84 years	85 years and over	Median age	Percent female	Percent foreign born	Percent born in state of residence	Immigrants admitted to legal status, 2013	Number	Percent change, 2012–2013	Persons per household	Married couple	Female householder[1]	Householder living alone
	16	17	18	19	20	21	22	23	24	25	26	27	28	29	30

1. No spouse present.

Table A. States — Population Change

STATE	Population, 1990–2010			Population change, 1990–2014								Population, 2020–2030		
	Census counts			Percent change			Components of change, 2010–2014					Projections		
									Migration					
	1990	2000	2010	1990–2000	2000–2010	2010–2014	Births	Deaths	Net migration	International	Net internal	2020	2025	2030
	31	32	33	34	35	36	37	38	39	40	41	42	43	44

Table A. States — Population Characteristics

STATE	Population characteristics, 2010																		
	Race (percent)							Age (percent)											
	White alone	Black alone	American Indian, Alaska Native alone	Asian and Pacific Islander alone	Some other race or two or more races	Percent Hispanic or Latino[1]	Percent foreign born	Under 5 years	5 to 17 years	18 to 24 years	25 to 34 years	35 to 44 years	45 to 54 years	55 to 64 years	65 to 74 years	75 to 84 years	85 years and over	Median age	Percent female
	45	46	47	48	49	50	51	52	53	54	55	56	57	58	59	60	61	62	63

1 May be of any race.

Table A. States — Households and Housing Units

STATE	Households, 2010					Housing units, 2010									
				Percent				Occupied units							
									Owner-occupied				Renter-occupied		
											Median owner cost				
	Number	Percent change, 2000–2010	Persons per household	Female family householder[1]	One person	Total	Percent change, 2000–2010	Total	Percent	Median value[2] (dollars)	With a mortgage	Without a mortgage[3]	Median rent[4] (dollars)	Median rent as a percent of income	Substandard units[5] (percent)
	64	65	66	67	68	69	70	71	72	73	74	75	76	77	78

1. No spouse present. 2. Specified owner-occupied units. 3. Median monthly costs is often in the minimum category—10.0 percent or less, which is indicated as 10.0 percent. 4. Specified renter-occupied units. 5. Overcrowded or lacking complete plumbing facilities.

Table A. States — Housing Units

STATE	Housing units, 2013													
			Occupied units											
					Percent who pay 30 percent or more of income for housing expenses		Median owner cost as a percent of income							
	Total	Percent change, 2012–2013	Total	Percent owner-occupied	Owners with a mortgage	Renter[1]	With a mortgage	Without a mortgage[2]	Median monthly housing costs (dollars)	Median value of units[3] (dollars)	Percent valued over $500,000	Median gross rent[4] (dollars)	Substandard units[5] (percent)	Percent living in a different house than 1 year ago
	79	80	81	82	83	84	85	86	87	88	89	90	91	92

1. Excludes units where owner costs or gross rent as a percentage of households income cannot be calculated. 2. Median monthly costs is often in the minimum category—10.0 percent or less, which is indicated as 10.0 percent. 3. Specified owner-occupied units. 4. Specified renter-occupied units. 5. Overcrowded or lacking complete plumbing facilities.

Table A. States — Residential Construction, Vital Statistics, and Health

STATE	Value of residential construction authorized by building permits, 2014				Births, 2013		Deaths, 2011					Percent lacking health insurance, 2013		
							Number		Rate					
									Total					
	New construction ($1,000)	Number of housing units	Percent single family	Manufactured housing units put in place, 2013 (1,000)	Total	Rate[1]	Total	Infant[2]	Crude[1]	Age-adjusted	Infant[3]	All persons	Children under 18 years	Medicare enrollees, 2012
	93	94	95	96	97	98	99	100	101	102	103	104	105	106

1. Per 1,000 resident population. 2. Deaths of infants under 1 year old. 3. Deaths of infants under 1 year old per 1,000 live births.

Table A. States — Crime and Education

STATE	Serious crime known to police,[1] 2013				Public elementary and secondary school enrollment, 2012–2013		Educational attainment[3] (percent)				Local government expenditures for education, 2011–2012	
	Violent Crime		Property Crime				2010		2013			
	Number	Rate[2]	Number	Rate[2]	Total	Student/teacher ratio	High school graduate or more	Bachelor's degree or more	High school graduate or more	Bachelor's degree or more	Total current expenditures (mil dol)	Current expenditures per student (dollars)
	107	108	109	110	111	112	113	114	115	116	117	118

1. Data for serious crimes have not been adjusted for underreporting; this may affect comparability between geographic areas and over time. 2. Per 100,000 population estimated by the FBI. 3. Persons 25 years old and over.

Table A. States — Exports, Income, and Poverty

STATE	Exports of goods by state of origin, 2014			Income, 2013					Percent below poverty level, 2013						
					Households								Families with children under 18		
	Total	Manu-factured	Non-manu-factured	Per capita income (dollars)	Median income (dollars)	Percent with income of $25,000 or less	Percent with income of $100,000 or more	Median income of family of four	All persons	Children under 18 years	Persons 65 years and over	All families	Married-couple families	Male house-holder[1] families	Female house-holder[1] families
	119	120	121	122	123	124	125	126	127	128	129	130	131	132	133

1. No spouse present.

Table A. States — Personal Income

STATE	Personal income, 2013												
			Per capita[1]		Sources of personal income (mil dol)								
								Transfer payments					
									Government payments to individuals				
	Total (mil dol)	Percent change, 2012–2013	Dollars	Rank	Wages and salaries[2]	Proprietors' income	Dividends, interest, and rent	Total	Total	Social Security	Medical payments	Income main-tenance	Unemploy-ment insurance
	134	135	136	137	138	139	140	141	142	143	144	145	146

1. Based on the resident population estimated as of July 1 of the year shown. 2. Includes supplements to wages and salaries.

Table A. States — Personal Income and Earnings

STATE		Disposable personal income, 2013		Earnings, 2013										
					Percent by selected industries									
						Goods-related[2]		Service-related and other[3]						
	Personal tax payments, 2013 (mil dol)	Total (mil dol)	Per capita[1] (dollars)	Total (mil dol)	Farm	Total	Manu-facturing	Total	Retail trade	Finance, insurance, real estate, rental and leasing	Health care and social assist-ance	Government	Gross state product, 2013 (mil dol)
	147	148	149	150	151	152	153	154	155	156	157	158	159

1. Based on the resident population estimated as of July 1 of the year shown. 2. Total includes mining, construction, and manufacturing. 3. Includes private sector earnings in forestry, fishing, related activities, and other; utilities; wholesale trade; transportation and warehousing; and information.

Table A. States — Social Security, Employment, and Labor Force

STATE	Social Security beneficiaries, December 2013			Civilian employment and selected occupations,[2] 2013				Civilian labor force (annual average), 2014				
					Percent						Unemployed	
	Number	Rate[1]	Supple-mental Security Income recipients, December 2013	Total	Management, business, science and art occupations	Services, sales, and office occupations	Construction and production occupations	Total (1,000)	Percent change, 2013–2014	Employed (1,000)	Total (1,000)	Rate[3]
	160	161	162	163	164	165	166	167	168	169	170	171

1. Per 1,000 resident population estimated as of July 1 of the year shown. 2. Persons 16 years old and over. 3. Percent of civilian labor force.

Table A. States — Nonfarm Employment and Earnings

STATE	Private nonfarm employment and earnings, 2014											
	Employed		Manufacturing			Employment (1,000)						
				Average earnings of production workers								
	Total (1,000)	Percent change, 2013–2014	Employment (1,000)	Hourly	Weekly	Construction	Transportation and public utilities	Wholesale trade	Retail trade	Information	Financial activities	Services[1]
	172	173	174	175	176	177	178	179	180	181	182	183

1. Includes professional and business services, educational and health services, leisure and hospitality, and other services.

Table A. States — Agriculture

STATE	Agriculture, 2012											
	Farms					Land in farms					Value of land and buildings (dollars)	
		Percent with:						Acres				
	Number	Fewer than 50 acres	500 acres or more	Farm operators whose principal occupation is farming (percent)	Government payments, average per farm (dollars)	Acreage (1,000)	Percent change, 2007–2012	Average size of farm	Total irrigated (1,000)	Total cropland (1,000)	Average per farm	Average per acre
	184	185	186	187	188	189	190	191	192	193	194	195

Table A. States — Agriculture, Land, and Water

STATE	Agriculture, 2012 (cont.)							Land, 2010			
		Value of products sold				Percent of farms with sales of:					
				Percent from:							
	Value of machinery and equipment, average per farm (dollars)	Total (mil dol)	Average per farm (dollars)	Crops	Livestock and poultry products	$10,000 or more	$100,000 or more	Cropland (percent)	Owned by the federal government (percent)	Developed (percent)	Water consumption, 2010 (mil gal per day)
	196	197	198	199	200	201	202	203	204	205	206

Table A. States — Manufactures and Construction

STATE	Manufactures, 2013										Construction, 2007				
	All employees			Production workers								Employees			
						Wages									
	Number (1,000)	Percent change, 2011–2013	Annual payroll (mil dol)	Number (1,000)	Work hours (millions)	Total (mil dol)	Average per worker (dollars)	Value added by manufacture (mil dol)	Value of shipments (mil dol)	Total cost of materials (mil dol)	Number of establishments	Number	Percent change, 2002–2007	Value (mil dol)	Annual payroll (mil dol)
	207	208	209	210	211	212	213	214	215	216	217	218	219	220	221

Table A. States — Wholesale Trade and Retail Trade

STATE	Wholesale trade, 2007					Retail trade,[1] 2007								
		Employees					Employees							
	Number of estab-lishments	Number	Percent change, 2002–2007	Sales (mil dol)	Annual payroll (mil dol)	Number of estab-lishments	Total	Percent change, 2002–2007	Motor vehicle and parts dealers	Food and beverage stores	Clothing and clothing accessory stores	General merchan-dise stores	Sales (mil dol)	Annual payroll (mil dol)
	222	223	224	225	226	227	228	229	230	231	232	233	234	235

1. Establishments with payroll.

Table A. States — Information

STATE	Information, 2007										
		Employees									
	Number of establishments	Number	Percent change, 2002–2007	Publishing, except Internet	Motion picture and sound recording	Broadcasting, except Internet	Internet publishing and broad-casting and web search portals	Telecom-munications	Data processing, hosting, and related services	Receipts (mil dol)	Annual payroll (mil dol)
	236	237	238	239	240	241	242	243	244	245	246

Table A. States — Utilities, Transportation and Warehousing, and Finance and Insurance

STATE	Utilities, 2007					Transportation and warehousing, 2007					Finance and insurance, 2007				
		Employees					Employees					Employees			
	Number of estab-lishments	Number	Percent change, 2002–2007	Receipts (mil dol)	Annual payroll (mil dol)	Number of estab-lishments	Number	Percent change, 2002–2007	Receipts (mil dol)	Annual payroll (mil dol)	Number of estab-lishments	Number	Percent change, 2002–2007	Receipts (mil dol)	Annual payroll (mil dol)
	247	248	249	250	251	252	253	254	255	256	257	258	259	260	261

Table A. States — Real Estate and Rental and Leasing and Professional, Scientific, and Technical Services

STATE	Real estate and rental and leasing, 2007					Professional, scientific, and technical services, 2007								
		Employees					Employees							
	Number of estab-lishments	Number	Percent change, 2002–2007	Receipts (mil dol)	Annual payroll (mil dol)	Number of estab-lishments	Total	Percent change, 2002–2007	Legal services	Accounting and related services	Architectural, engineering, and related services	Computer systems design and related services	Receipts (mil dol)	Annual payroll (mil dol)
	262	263	264	265	266	267	268	269	270	271	272	273	274	275

Table A. States — Health Care and Social Assistance

STATE	Health care and social assistance, 2007													
	Subject to federal tax							Tax-exempt						
		Employees							Employees					
	Number of establishments	Total	Percent change, 2002–2007	Ambulatory health care services	Hospitals	Receipts (mil dol)	Annual payroll (mil dol)	Number of establishments	Total	Percent change, 2002–2007	Ambulatory health care services	Hospitals	Receipts (mil dol)	Annual payroll (mil dol)
	276	277	278	279	280	281	282	283	284	285	286	287	288	289

Table A. States — Arts, Entertainment, and Recreation and Accommodation and Food Services

STATE	Arts, entertainment, and recreation, 2007					Accommodation and food services, 2007					
		Employees					Employees				
	Number of establishments	Number	Percent change, 2002–2007	Receipts (mil dol)	Annual payroll (mil dol)	Number of establishments	Total	Percent change, 2002–2007	Food services and drinking places	Receipts (mil dol)	Annual payroll (mil dol)
	290	291	292	293	294	295	296	297	298	299	300

Table A. States — Other Services, Except Public Administration, and Government Employment

STATE	Other services, except public administration, 2007								Government employment, 2013		
		Employees									
	Number of establishments	Total	Percent change, 2002–2007	Repair and maintenance	Personal and laundry services	Religious, civic, and similar services	Receipts (mil dol)	Annual payroll (mil dol)	Federal civilian	Federal military	State and local
	301	302	303	304	305	306	307	308	309	310	311

Table A. States — State Government Employment and Payroll

STATE	State government employment and payroll, 2012											
	State government employment, 2013			State government payroll, 2012		Full-time equivalent payroll (1,000 dollars)						
							Percent of total for:					
	Full-time equivalent employees	Full-time employees	Part-time employees	Full-time March payroll (1,000 dollars)	Part-time March payroll (1,000 dollars)	Total March payroll (1,000 dollars)[1]	Administration	Judicial and legal	Police	Corrections	Highways and transportation	Public Welfare
	312	313	314	315	316	317	318	319	320	321	322	323

1. Includes program categories not shown separately.

Table A. States — State Government Employment and Payroll and State Government Finances

STATE	State government employment and payroll, 2012 (cont.)							State government finances, 2013							
	Full-time equivalent payroll (1,000 dollars) (cont.)							General revenue (mil dol)							
	Percent of total for:								From federal government		From own sources				
												Taxes		Taxes per capita[1] (dollars)	
	Health	Hospitals	Social Insurance administration	Natural resources and parks	Utilities, sewerage, and waste management	Elementary and secondary education and libraries	Higher education	Total	Total	Per capita (dollars)	Total	Total	Sales and gross receipts	Total	Sales and gross receipts
	324	325	326	327	328	329	330	331	332	333	334	335	336	337	338

1. Based on resident population estimated as of July 1 of the year shown.

Table A. States — State Government Finances and Voting

STATE	State government finances, 2013 (cont.)												Voting and registration, November 2014		Presidential election,[2] 2012 (percent of vote cast)		
	General expenditures (mil dol)										Debt outstanding						
			Direct general expenditures		By selected function												
	Total	To local governments	Total	Per capita[1] (dollars)	Education	Health and hospitals	Highways	Public safety	Public welfare	Natural resources, parks, and recreation	Total (mil dol)	Per capita[1]	Percent registered	Percent voted	Democratic	Republican	All other
	339	340	341	342	343	344	345	346	347	348	349	350	351	352	353	354	355

1. Based on resident population estimated as of July 1 of the year shown. 2. © 2013 Election Data Services, Inc. All rights reserved.

Table A. States — **Land Area and Population Characteristics**

State code	STATE	Land area,[1] 2010 (sq km)	Population, 2014: Total persons, 2014	Population, 2014: Rank	Population, 2014: Per square kilometer	Population characteristics, 2013: Race alone or in combination, not Hispanic or Latino (percent): White	Black	American Indian, Alaska Native	Asian and Pacific Islander	Hispanic or Latino[2] (percent)	Age (percent): Under 5 years	5 to 17 years	18 to 24 years	25 to 34 years	35 to 44 years	45 to 54 years
		1	2	3	4	5	6	7	8	9	10	11	12	13	14	15
0	United States	9 147 593	318 857 056	X	34.9	64.3	13.2	1.3	6.2	17.1	6.3	17.0	10.0	13.6	12.8	13.8
1	Alabama	131 171	4 849 377	23	37.0	67.6	26.9	1.1	1.6	4.1	6.1	16.8	10.0	12.8	12.6	13.7
2	Alaska	1 477 953	736 732	48	0.5	68.2	4.8	18.4	8.9	6.6	7.5	18.1	11.2	15.6	12.3	13.7
4	Arizona	294 207	6 731 484	15	22.9	58.4	4.7	4.6	4.0	30.2	6.5	17.9	10.1	13.3	12.5	12.6
5	Arkansas	134 771	2 966 369	32	22.0	75.2	16.0	1.6	2.0	6.9	6.5	17.5	9.7	13.0	12.3	13.2
6	California	403 466	38 802 500	1	96.2	41.2	6.5	1.0	15.6	38.3	6.5	17.4	10.5	14.6	13.4	13.6
8	Colorado	268 431	5 355 866	22	20.0	71.3	4.7	1.3	4.0	21.0	6.4	17.1	9.8	14.8	13.6	13.6
9	Connecticut	12 542	3 596 677	29	286.8	71.0	10.6	0.6	4.8	14.6	5.3	16.5	9.6	12.2	12.4	15.5
10	Delaware	5 047	935 614	45	185.4	65.9	22.5	0.9	4.2	8.7	6.1	15.9	10.0	13.0	12.0	14.2
11	District of Columbia	158	658 893	49	4 170.2	37.4	49.2	0.8	4.8	10.1	6.3	10.9	12.5	22.6	13.9	11.8
12	Florida	138 887	19 893 297	3	143.2	57.7	16.3	0.6	3.3	23.6	5.5	15.1	9.1	12.6	12.3	14.0
13	Georgia	148 959	10 097 343	8	67.8	56.2	31.5	0.7	4.2	9.2	6.7	18.2	10.2	13.7	13.7	14.0
15	Hawaii	16 635	1 419 561	40	85.3	36.9	3.1	1.7	74.3	9.8	6.5	15.4	9.8	14.7	12.4	12.8
16	Idaho	214 045	1 634 464	39	7.6	84.9	1.0	1.9	2.3	11.8	7.0	19.5	9.7	13.2	12.2	12.4
17	Illinois	143 793	12 880 580	5	89.6	64.0	14.9	0.5	5.6	16.5	6.2	17.3	9.8	13.9	13.1	13.9
18	Indiana	92 789	6 596 855	16	71.1	82.2	10.1	0.7	2.3	6.4	6.4	17.7	10.1	12.8	12.6	13.8
19	Iowa	144 669	3 107 126	30	21.5	89.0	3.9	0.7	2.5	5.5	6.3	17.1	10.3	12.6	11.7	13.4
20	Kansas	211 754	2 904 021	34	13.7	79.3	7.0	1.8	3.3	11.2	6.9	18.1	10.4	13.4	11.9	13.0
21	Kentucky	102 269	4 413 457	26	43.2	87.1	8.9	0.7	1.7	3.3	6.3	16.8	9.7	12.8	12.9	14.1
22	Louisiana	111 898	4 649 676	25	41.6	60.7	32.8	1.1	2.1	4.7	6.7	17.4	10.2	14.3	12.2	13.5
23	Maine	79 883	1 330 089	41	16.7	95.5	1.8	1.4	1.6	1.4	4.9	14.8	8.6	11.3	11.9	15.5
24	Maryland	25 142	5 976 407	19	237.7	55.1	30.5	0.8	7.0	9.0	6.2	16.5	9.5	13.8	13.0	15.0
25	Massachusetts	20 202	6 745 408	14	333.9	76.6	7.4	0.6	6.7	10.5	5.5	15.4	10.3	13.6	12.6	14.9
26	Michigan	146 435	9 909 877	10	67.7	77.9	15.0	1.3	3.3	4.7	5.8	16.9	10.2	12.0	12.2	14.4
27	Minnesota	206 232	5 457 173	21	26.5	83.8	6.5	1.7	5.2	5.0	6.4	17.2	9.4	13.7	12.3	14.2
28	Mississippi	121 531	2 994 079	31	24.6	58.3	37.7	0.8	1.3	2.9	6.6	18.0	10.5	13.0	12.4	13.2
29	Missouri	178 040	6 063 589	18	34.1	82.1	12.5	1.1	2.4	3.9	6.2	16.9	9.9	13.2	12.1	13.9
30	Montana	376 962	1 023 579	44	2.7	89.2	0.9	7.6	1.3	3.3	6.0	16.0	9.9	12.5	11.3	13.3
31	Nebraska	198 974	1 881 503	37	9.5	82.5	5.4	1.3	2.6	9.9	7.0	17.9	10.1	13.5	12.0	13.0
32	Nevada	284 332	2 839 099	35	10.0	54.8	9.2	1.5	10.3	27.5	6.4	17.3	9.1	14.2	13.6	13.6
33	New Hampshire	23 187	1 326 813	42	57.2	92.9	1.7	0.7	2.9	3.2	5.0	15.5	9.6	11.5	12.3	16.2
34	New Jersey	19 047	8 938 175	11	469.3	58.8	13.6	0.5	9.8	18.9	6.0	16.7	8.9	12.8	13.3	15.2
35	New Mexico	314 161	2 085 572	36	6.6	40.6	2.3	9.3	2.0	47.3	6.7	17.7	10.1	13.3	11.7	13.0
36	New York	122 057	19 746 227	4	161.8	58.4	15.4	0.7	8.8	18.3	6.0	15.6	10.1	14.3	12.8	14.3
37	North Carolina	125 920	9 943 964	9	79.0	65.9	22.3	1.7	3.0	8.9	6.2	17.0	10.0	12.9	13.3	13.9
38	North Dakota	178 711	739 482	47	4.1	88.9	2.2	6.1	1.7	2.9	6.7	15.7	12.8	14.4	11.0	12.6
39	Ohio	105 829	11 594 163	7	109.6	82.2	13.4	0.7	2.3	3.4	6.0	16.9	9.6	12.6	12.2	14.1
40	Oklahoma	177 660	3 878 051	28	21.8	72.4	8.7	12.3	2.6	9.6	6.9	17.7	10.2	13.7	12.1	12.9
41	Oregon	248 608	3 970 239	27	16.0	80.3	2.5	2.4	5.8	12.3	5.9	16.0	9.3	13.6	13.0	13.1
42	Pennsylvania	115 883	12 787 209	6	110.3	79.7	11.5	0.5	3.5	6.3	5.6	15.7	9.7	12.6	12.0	14.4
44	Rhode Island	2 678	1 055 173	43	394.0	76.9	6.6	1.0	3.9	13.6	5.2	15.2	11.2	12.9	12.0	14.8
45	South Carolina	77 857	4 832 482	24	62.1	65.2	28.3	0.8	1.9	5.3	6.1	16.5	10.2	12.9	12.5	13.6
46	South Dakota	196 350	853 175	46	4.3	85.1	2.4	9.6	1.6	3.4	7.1	17.5	10.1	13.2	11.2	13.0
47	Tennessee	106 798	6 549 352	17	61.3	76.3	17.6	0.8	2.0	4.9	6.2	16.8	9.7	13.0	13.0	13.9
48	Texas	676 587	26 956 958	2	39.8	45.2	12.3	0.7	4.8	38.3	7.3	19.3	10.3	14.5	13.5	13.0
49	Utah	212 818	2 942 902	33	13.8	81.4	1.5	1.4	4.3	13.4	8.8	22.2	11.5	15.2	12.8	10.5
50	Vermont	23 871	626 562	50	26.2	95.4	1.6	1.1	1.9	1.7	4.9	14.7	10.7	11.5	11.6	15.1
51	Virginia	102 279	8 326 289	12	81.4	65.7	20.2	0.8	7.2	8.6	6.2	16.4	10.0	14.1	13.2	14.4
53	Washington	172 119	7 061 530	13	41.0	74.4	4.8	2.5	10.5	11.9	6.4	16.5	9.6	14.3	13.1	13.6
54	West Virginia	62 259	1 850 326	38	29.7	94.1	4.3	0.7	1.1	1.4	5.5	15.1	9.3	11.8	12.5	13.9
55	Wisconsin	140 268	5 757 564	20	41.0	83.9	7.0	1.4	2.9	6.3	6.0	16.8	9.7	12.8	12.1	14.5
56	Wyoming	251 470	584 153	51	2.3	85.6	2.0	2.9	1.5	9.7	6.6	17.0	10.1	14.0	11.9	13.1

1. Dry land or land partially or temporarily covered by water. 2. May be of any race.

Table A. States — **Population Characteristics, Immigration, and Households**

STATE	Population characteristics, 2013 (cont.)									Households, 2013					
	Age (percent) (cont.)												Household type		
	55 to 64 years	65 to 74 years	75 to 84 years	85 years and over	Median age	Percent female	Percent foreign born	Percent born in state of residence	Immigrants admitted to legal status, 2013	Number	Percent change, 2012–2013	Persons per household	Married couple	Female householder[1]	Householder living alone
	16	17	18	19	20	21	22	23	24	25	26	27	28	29	30
United States	12.4	8.0	4.3	1.9	37.6	50.8	13.1	58.8	990 553	116 291 033	0.3	2.65	48.0	13.1	27.7
Alabama	12.9	8.7	4.6	1.7	38.4	51.5	3.4	70.0	3 848	1 822 439	-1.2	2.59	47.1	15.6	29.0
Alaska	12.6	6.0	2.3	0.8	33.2	47.6	6.9	42.9	1 460	246 015	-2.2	2.88	51.4	10.1	25.5
Arizona	11.7	8.9	4.7	1.8	36.8	50.3	13.5	38.7	16 097	2 400 809	0.4	2.70	47.3	12.8	27.6
Arkansas	12.4	8.8	4.7	1.8	37.7	50.9	4.5	62.2	2 900	1 125 899	-1.6	2.56	48.7	13.3	27.9
California	11.5	7.0	3.7	1.7	35.8	50.3	26.9	54.7	191 806	12 650 592	0.8	2.97	48.7	13.7	24.3
Colorado	12.5	7.3	3.5	1.5	36.4	49.8	9.5	43.4	11 108	2 002 800	0.3	2.57	49.0	10.5	27.9
Connecticut	13.3	8.2	4.5	2.5	40.5	51.2	13.9	55.1	10 985	1 339 860	-1.3	2.60	49.1	13.1	27.7
Delaware	13.1	9.3	4.7	1.9	39.5	52.6	8.3	46.8	2 325	339 071	-0.4	2.66	48.6	14.4	26.5
District of Columbia	10.6	6.3	3.3	1.7	33.8	51.6	14.4	36.7	2 981	271 651	1.9	2.23	24.2	15.8	42.2
Florida	12.8	10.2	5.9	2.6	41.5	51.1	19.4	36.2	102 939	7 211 584	0.2	2.65	46.2	13.3	29.3
Georgia	11.6	7.3	3.4	1.3	35.9	51.1	9.7	55.1	24 387	3 546 965	0.4	2.74	47.2	15.3	27.0
Hawaii	12.8	8.6	4.5	2.5	38.0	49.5	17.6	54.2	6 226	450 120	0.5	3.02	52.3	11.8	24.1
Idaho	12.2	8.1	4.0	1.7	35.5	49.9	5.9	47.1	2 120	588 489	0.9	2.69	55.2	9.8	24.1
Illinois	12.3	7.5	4.1	2.0	37.2	50.9	14.0	67.2	35 988	4 783 421	0.3	2.63	48.1	12.7	28.9
Indiana	12.6	7.8	4.2	1.9	37.4	50.7	4.8	68.5	7 668	2 498 395	0.7	2.55	49.1	12.3	28.2
Iowa	13.0	8.1	4.9	2.5	38.1	50.4	4.8	71.2	4 105	1 236 209	0.7	2.42	50.6	9.4	29.0
Kansas	12.3	7.5	4.3	2.2	36.0	50.2	6.8	58.8	5 000	1 113 729	0.0	2.53	51.0	10.7	28.3
Kentucky	13.0	8.4	4.3	1.7	38.5	50.8	3.4	70.1	5 159	1 705 623	-0.1	2.50	48.9	12.9	27.7
Louisiana	12.5	7.7	4.0	1.6	36.1	51.1	3.9	77.9	4 355	1 728 149	0.5	2.60	43.1	17.0	29.3
Maine	15.4	10.0	5.3	2.3	43.9	51.0	3.4	63.7	1 208	547 686	-1.2	2.36	48.1	9.4	30.0
Maryland	12.7	7.7	3.9	1.8	38.2	51.5	14.2	47.6	25 361	2 161 680	0.2	2.68	47.3	14.8	27.2
Massachusetts	13.0	8.0	4.4	2.3	39.4	51.5	15.6	62.1	29 482	2 536 321	0.6	2.54	46.9	12.7	28.4
Michigan	13.6	8.4	4.5	2.1	39.5	50.9	6.2	76.9	16 952	3 832 466	0.4	2.52	47.2	12.9	29.0
Minnesota	12.8	7.6	4.2	2.1	37.7	50.3	7.4	68.1	12 781	2 119 954	0.4	2.49	50.8	9.8	28.3
Mississippi	12.3	8.0	4.2	1.6	36.5	51.4	2.1	71.7	1 716	1 091 002	0.0	2.66	44.7	18.7	27.2
Missouri	12.9	8.4	4.6	2.0	38.2	51.0	3.9	66.2	6 345	2 362 853	0.2	2.48	48.0	12.2	29.3
Montana	14.7	9.3	4.8	2.1	39.9	49.8	1.9	54.5	445	406 288	-0.6	2.43	49.0	9.3	30.3
Nebraska	12.4	7.4	4.5	2.2	36.2	50.2	6.6	65.0	4 141	730 579	-0.4	2.49	51.0	9.8	28.8
Nevada	12.1	8.5	3.9	1.3	37.2	49.6	19.0	25.7	9 886	1 002 571	-0.4	2.75	45.5	12.7	28.6
New Hampshire	14.6	8.9	4.4	2.1	42.3	50.6	5.7	42.2	2 227	519 246	0.0	2.47	52.4	10.1	25.5
New Jersey	12.7	7.9	4.4	2.2	39.4	51.2	21.6	52.6	53 082	3 176 139	-0.7	2.74	50.7	13.8	25.5
New Mexico	12.9	8.6	4.4	1.7	36.9	50.4	10.1	52.0	3 664	753 507	-1.5	2.71	44.7	14.2	29.6
New York	12.5	7.9	4.4	2.2	38.2	51.5	22.3	63.6	133 601	7 219 356	-0.3	2.64	43.7	14.7	29.9
North Carolina	12.4	8.4	4.2	1.7	38.1	51.3	7.6	57.4	16 798	3 757 480	0.7	2.55	47.5	13.8	28.1
North Dakota	12.5	7.2	4.6	2.4	35.3	48.9	2.9	65.1	1 234	298 298	2.5	2.33	48.6	7.4	30.5
Ohio	13.4	8.3	4.7	2.1	39.3	51.1	4.1	75.4	13 819	4 564 745	0.2	2.47	46.4	13.0	29.9
Oklahoma	12.2	8.1	4.4	1.7	36.2	50.5	5.7	61.1	4 648	1 447 277	0.0	2.58	48.6	12.5	28.6
Oregon	13.7	9.0	4.4	2.1	39.0	50.5	10.0	46.2	7 171	1 523 799	0.5	2.52	48.0	10.7	28.3
Pennsylvania	13.6	8.7	5.1	2.6	40.7	51.1	6.2	73.5	24 720	4 938 894	-0.4	2.50	47.7	11.9	30.1
Rhode Island	13.3	8.2	4.6	2.7	39.9	51.6	12.9	57.8	3 337	406 366	-1.6	2.49	44.5	14.2	29.8
South Carolina	13.0	9.2	4.4	1.6	38.6	51.3	4.8	57.8	4 266	1 794 989	0.4	2.58	46.8	15.2	28.0
South Dakota	13.0	7.8	4.7	2.4	36.8	49.8	2.9	64.3	1 231	331 406	2.4	2.45	50.3	9.6	29.2
Tennessee	12.8	8.7	4.3	1.7	38.5	51.2	4.7	61.1	8 380	2 490 249	0.4	2.55	48.5	13.4	28.1
Texas	10.9	6.6	3.3	1.3	34.0	50.3	16.5	60.2	92 674	9 110 853	1.6	2.84	50.0	14.4	25.0
Utah	9.3	5.6	3.0	1.2	30.2	49.7	8.2	62.7	5 503	899 475	0.4	3.17	61.4	9.6	19.1
Vermont	15.2	9.5	4.7	2.2	42.4	50.7	4.3	50.5	838	253 234	-2.0	2.37	48.6	9.1	29.9
Virginia	12.4	7.9	3.9	1.6	37.6	50.8	11.5	49.8	27 861	3 055 863	0.6	2.62	50.1	12.6	26.7
Washington	12.9	8.0	3.8	1.8	37.5	50.0	13.5	47.4	22 994	2 644 557	0.3	2.58	49.5	10.3	27.5
West Virginia	14.7	9.9	5.3	2.1	41.9	50.6	1.4	70.0	760	738 653	-0.4	2.44	48.2	11.7	30.2
Wisconsin	13.3	8.1	4.6	2.2	39.0	50.3	4.8	71.8	5 918	2 289 424	0.0	2.44	49.1	10.2	29.2
Wyoming	13.8	7.9	4.0	1.7	36.8	49.0	3.1	41.9	522	224 003	0.2	2.54	52.7	9.0	27.1

1. No spouse present.

Table A. States — **Population Change**

STATE	Population, 1990–2010			Population change, 1990–2014								Population, 2020–2030		
	Census counts			Percent change			Components of change, 2010–2014					Projections		
									Migration					
	1990	2000	2010	1990–2000	2000–2010	2010–2014	Births	Deaths	Net migration	International	Net internal	2020	2025	2030
	31	32	33	34	35	36	37	38	39	40	41	42	43	44
United States	248 709 873	281 421 906	308 745 538	13.2	9.7	3.3	16 811 002	10 775 362	4 063 311	4 063 311	(X)	335 804 546	349 439 199	363 584 435
Alabama	4 040 587	4 447 100	4 779 736	10.1	7.5	1.5	249 818	207 826	26 687	23 159	3 528	4 728 915	4 800 092	4 874 243
Alaska	550 043	626 932	710 231	14.0	13.3	3.7	47 988	17 081	-4 700	9 311	-14 011	774 421	820 881	867 674
Arizona	3 665 228	5 130 632	6 392 017	40.0	24.6	5.3	367 725	210 702	172 848	56 493	116 355	8 456 448	9 531 537	10 712 397
Arkansas	2 350 725	2 673 400	2 915 918	13.7	9.1	1.7	162 691	124 578	13 316	13 118	198	3 060 219	3 151 005	3 240 208
California	29 760 021	33 871 648	37 253 956	13.8	10.0	4.2	2 144 767	1 041 844	459 574	648 856	-189 282	42 206 743	44 305 177	46 444 861
Colorado	3 294 394	4 301 261	5 029 196	30.6	16.9	6.5	278 842	140 585	183 324	43 208	140 116	5 278 867	5 522 803	5 792 357
Connecticut	3 287 116	3 405 565	3 574 097	3.6	4.9	0.6	156 554	124 313	-5 861	69 991	-75 852	3 675 650	3 691 016	3 688 630
Delaware	666 168	783 600	897 934	17.6	14.6	4.2	47 400	33 845	23 974	9 921	14 053	963 209	990 694	1 012 658
District of Columbia	606 900	572 059	601 723	-5.7	5.2	9.5	39 983	20 670	37 229	15 126	22 103	480 540	455 108	433 414
Florida	12 937 926	15 982 378	18 801 310	23.5	17.6	5.8	908 600	760 861	917 135	467 201	449 934	23 406 525	25 912 458	28 685 769
Georgia	6 478 216	8 186 453	9 687 653	26.4	18.3	4.2	556 992	308 766	151 661	102 677	48 984	10 843 753	11 438 622	12 017 838
Hawaii	1 108 229	1 211 537	1 360 301	9.3	12.3	4.4	80 734	45 388	24 911	35 968	-11 057	1 412 373	1 438 720	1 466 046
Idaho	1 006 749	1 293 953	1 567 582	28.5	21.1	4.3	96 826	49 597	18 656	6 766	11 890	1 741 333	1 852 627	1 969 624
Illinois	11 430 602	12 419 293	12 830 632	8.6	3.3	0.4	678 650	433 772	-190 144	128 843	-318 987	13 236 720	13 340 507	13 432 892
Indiana	5 544 159	6 080 485	6 483 802	9.7	6.6	1.7	353 871	246 674	8 366	41 995	-33 629	6 627 008	6 721 322	6 810 108
Iowa	2 776 755	2 926 324	3 046 355	5.4	4.1	2.0	163 391	118 503	16 872	21 447	-4 575	3 020 496	2 993 222	2 955 172
Kansas	2 477 574	2 688 418	2 853 118	8.5	6.1	1.8	170 209	104 162	-15 299	24 874	-40 173	2 890 566	2 919 002	2 940 084
Kentucky	3 685 296	4 041 769	4 339 367	9.7	7.4	1.7	235 345	181 384	21 472	25 060	-3 588	4 424 431	4 489 662	4 554 998
Louisiana	4 219 973	4 468 976	4 533 372	5.9	1.4	2.6	264 495	176 623	28 462	31 499	-3 037	4 719 160	4 762 398	4 802 633
Maine	1 227 928	1 274 923	1 328 361	3.8	4.2	0.1	53 972	55 009	2 768	5 517	-2 749	1 408 665	1 414 402	1 411 097
Maryland	4 781 468	5 296 486	5 773 552	10.8	9.0	3.5	310 306	191 599	86 740	118 187	-31 447	6 497 626	6 762 732	7 022 251
Massachusetts	6 016 425	6 349 097	6 547 629	5.5	3.1	3.0	309 219	228 008	122 642	151 731	-29 089	6 855 546	6 938 636	7 012 009
Michigan	9 295 297	9 938 444	9 883 640	6.9	-0.6	0.3	481 063	381 059	-72 674	80 485	-153 159	10 695 993	10 713 730	10 694 172
Minnesota	4 375 099	4 919 479	5 303 925	12.4	7.8	2.9	291 521	168 050	31 088	56 239	-25 151	5 900 769	6 108 787	6 306 130
Mississippi	2 573 216	2 844 658	2 967 297	10.5	4.3	0.9	165 775	123 715	-16 999	9 779	-26 778	3 044 812	3 069 420	3 092 410
Missouri	5 117 073	5 595 211	5 988 927	9.3	7.0	1.2	321 112	236 479	-8 048	35 491	-43 539	6 199 882	6 315 366	6 430 173
Montana	799 065	902 195	989 415	12.9	9.7	3.5	51 465	38 383	20 502	3 240	17 262	1 022 735	1 037 387	1 044 898
Nebraska	1 578 385	1 711 263	1 826 341	8.4	6.7	3.0	109 785	63 958	10 030	15 473	-5 443	1 802 678	1 812 787	1 820 247
Nevada	1 201 833	1 998 257	2 700 551	66.3	35.1	5.1	149 568	88 521	74 737	33 685	41 052	3 452 283	3 863 298	4 282 102
New Hampshire	1 109 252	1 235 786	1 316 470	11.4	6.5	0.8	53 225	45 357	3 013	8 137	-5 124	1 524 751	1 586 348	1 646 471
New Jersey	7 730 188	8 414 350	8 791 894	8.9	4.5	1.7	444 933	300 194	6 968	211 165	-204 197	9 461 635	9 636 644	9 802 440
New Mexico	1 515 069	1 819 046	2 059 179	20.1	13.2	1.3	115 471	70 216	-18 886	10 869	-29 755	2 084 341	2 106 584	2 099 708
New York	17 990 455	18 976 457	19 378 102	5.5	2.1	1.9	1 023 877	638 192	-1 626	485 224	-486 850	19 576 920	19 540 179	19 477 429
North Carolina	6 628 637	8 049 313	9 535 483	21.4	18.5	4.3	511 558	345 465	233 880	90 452	143 428	10 709 289	11 449 153	12 227 739
North Dakota	638 800	642 200	672 591	0.5	4.7	9.9	42 376	25 140	48 867	5 521	43 346	630 112	620 777	606 566
Ohio	10 847 115	11 353 140	11 536 504	4.7	1.6	0.5	586 295	471 142	-50 959	71 072	-122 031	11 644 058	11 605 738	11 550 528
Oklahoma	3 145 585	3 450 654	3 751 351	9.7	8.7	3.4	224 135	157 577	58 870	23 852	35 018	3 735 690	3 820 994	3 913 251
Oregon	2 842 321	3 421 399	3 831 074	20.4	12.0	3.6	191 586	139 246	85 464	27 111	58 353	4 260 393	4 536 418	4 833 918
Pennsylvania	11 881 643	12 281 054	12 702 379	3.4	3.4	0.7	604 903	539 878	29 004	118 159	-89 155	12 787 354	12 801 945	12 768 184
Rhode Island	1 003 464	1 048 319	1 052 567	4.5	0.4	0.2	46 520	40 353	-3 441	17 656	-21 097	1 154 230	1 157 855	1 152 941
South Carolina	3 486 703	4 012 012	4 625 364	15.1	15.3	4.5	244 058	182 009	139 545	27 161	112 384	4 822 577	4 989 550	5 148 569
South Dakota	696 004	754 844	814 180	8.5	7.9	4.8	51 014	30 398	18 038	5 951	12 087	801 939	801 845	800 462
Tennessee	4 877 185	5 689 283	6 346 105	16.7	11.5	3.2	339 088	258 632	121 745	37 402	84 343	6 780 670	7 073 125	7 380 634
Texas	16 986 510	20 851 820	25 145 561	22.8	20.6	7.2	1 626 353	733 219	905 754	343 093	562 661	28 634 896	30 865 134	33 317 744
Utah	1 722 850	2 233 169	2 763 885	29.6	23.8	6.5	218 387	64 878	25 597	21 857	3 740	2 990 094	3 225 680	3 485 367
Vermont	562 758	608 827	625 741	8.2	2.8	0.1	25 598	22 735	-1 653	2 852	-4 505	690 686	703 288	711 867
Virginia	6 187 358	7 078 515	8 001 024	14.4	13.0	4.1	437 406	259 805	145 072	141 687	3 385	8 917 395	9 364 304	9 825 019
Washington	4 866 692	5 894 121	6 724 540	21.1	14.1	5.0	370 520	214 584	179 873	95 873	84 000	7 432 136	7 996 400	8 624 801
West Virginia	1 793 477	1 808 344	1 852 994	0.8	2.5	-0.1	87 357	92 030	3 010	4 756	-1 746	1 801 112	1 766 435	1 719 959
Wisconsin	4 891 769	5 363 675	5 686 986	9.6	6.0	1.2	285 690	203 329	-11 288	26 088	-37 376	6 004 954	6 088 374	6 150 764
Wyoming	453 588	493 782	563 626	8.9	14.1	3.6	31 985	19 028	7 195	2 033	5 162	530 948	529 031	522 979

Table A. States — **Population Characteristics**

STATE	Population characteristics, 2010																		
	Race (percent)							Age (percent)											
	White alone	Black alone	American Indian, Alaska Native alone	Asian and Pacific Islander alone	Some other race or two or more races	Percent Hispanic or Latino[1]	Percent foreign born	Under 5 years	5 to 17 years	18 to 24 years	25 to 34 years	35 to 44 years	45 to 54 years	55 to 64 years	65 to 74 years	75 to 84 years	85 years and over	Median age	Percent female
	45	46	47	48	49	50	51	52	53	54	55	56	57	58	59	60	61	62	63
United States	72.4	12.6	0.9	5.0	9.1	16.3	12.9	6.5	17.5	9.9	13.3	13.3	14.6	11.8	7.0	4.2	1.8	37.2	50.8
Alabama	68.5	26.2	0.6	1.2	3.5	3.9	3.5	6.4	17.3	10.0	12.6	13.0	14.5	12.3	7.8	4.4	1.6	37.9	51.5
Alaska	66.7	3.3	14.8	6.4	8.9	5.5	6.9	7.6	18.8	10.5	14.5	13.1	15.6	12.1	5.0	2.1	0.6	33.8	48.0
Arizona	73.0	4.1	4.6	3.0	15.3	29.6	13.4	7.1	18.4	9.9	13.4	12.9	13.2	11.4	7.8	4.4	1.6	35.9	50.3
Arkansas	77.0	15.4	0.8	1.4	5.4	6.4	4.5	6.8	17.6	9.7	12.6	12.6	14.0	12.0	8.0	4.6	1.8	37.4	50.9
California	57.6	6.2	1.0	13.4	21.9	37.6	27.2	6.8	18.2	10.5	14.2	13.9	14.1	10.8	6.1	3.7	1.6	35.2	50.3
Colorado	81.3	4.0	1.1	2.9	10.6	20.7	9.8	6.8	17.5	9.7	14.4	13.9	14.8	11.9	6.2	3.4	1.4	36.1	49.9
Connecticut	77.6	10.1	0.3	3.8	8.2	13.4	13.6	5.7	17.2	9.1	11.8	13.6	16.1	12.4	7.1	4.6	2.4	40.0	51.3
Delaware	68.9	21.4	0.5	3.2	6.1	8.2	8.0	6.2	16.7	10.1	12.3	12.9	14.9	12.4	8.1	4.5	1.8	38.8	51.6
District of Columbia	38.5	50.7	0.3	3.6	7.0	9.1	13.5	5.4	11.3	14.5	20.9	13.4	12.6	10.6	6.1	3.5	1.8	33.8	52.8
Florida	75.0	16.0	0.4	2.5	6.1	22.5	19.4	5.7	15.6	9.3	12.1	12.9	14.6	12.4	9.2	5.7	2.4	40.7	51.1
Georgia	59.7	30.5	0.3	3.3	6.1	8.8	9.7	7.1	18.6	10.0	13.6	14.4	14.4	11.0	6.3	3.1	1.2	35.3	51.2
Hawaii	24.7	1.6	0.3	48.6	24.8	8.9	18.2	6.4	15.9	9.6	13.3	13.0	14.2	12.9	7.4	4.7	2.3	38.6	49.9
Idaho	89.1	0.6	1.4	1.3	7.6	11.2	5.5	7.8	19.6	9.9	13.3	12.2	13.3	11.5	7.0	3.8	1.7	34.6	49.9
Illinois	71.5	14.5	0.3	4.6	9.0	15.8	13.7	6.5	17.9	9.7	13.9	13.5	14.6	11.5	6.6	4.0	1.9	36.6	51.0
Indiana	84.3	9.1	0.3	1.6	4.7	6.0	4.6	6.7	18.1	10.0	12.7	13.0	14.6	11.9	7.0	4.3	1.7	37.0	50.8
Iowa	91.3	2.9	0.4	1.8	3.6	5.0	4.6	6.6	17.3	10.0	12.6	12.0	14.4	12.2	7.4	5.0	2.5	38.1	50.5
Kansas	83.8	5.9	1.0	2.5	6.9	10.5	6.5	7.2	18.3	10.1	13.0	12.2	14.2	11.6	6.7	4.3	2.1	36.0	50.4
Kentucky	87.8	7.8	0.2	1.2	3.0	3.1	3.2	6.5	17.1	9.5	13.0	13.3	14.8	12.4	7.5	4.2	1.6	38.1	50.8
Louisiana	62.6	32.0	0.7	1.5	3.1	4.2	3.8	6.9	17.7	10.5	13.7	12.5	14.4	11.8	6.9	3.9	1.5	35.8	51.0
Maine	95.2	1.2	0.6	1.0	1.9	1.3	3.4	5.2	15.4	8.7	10.9	12.9	16.5	14.5	8.5	5.3	2.1	42.7	51.1
Maryland	58.2	29.4	0.4	5.6	6.5	8.2	13.9	6.3	17.1	9.7	13.2	13.8	15.6	12.1	6.7	3.9	1.7	38.0	51.6
Massachusetts	80.4	6.6	0.3	5.3	7.3	9.6	15.0	5.6	16.1	10.4	12.9	13.5	15.5	12.3	7.0	4.6	2.2	39.1	51.6
Michigan	78.9	14.2	0.6	2.4	3.8	4.4	6.0	6.0	17.7	9.9	11.7	12.9	15.3	12.7	7.3	4.5	1.9	38.9	50.9
Minnesota	85.3	5.2	1.1	4.0	4.3	4.7	7.1	6.7	17.5	9.5	13.5	12.8	15.2	11.9	6.7	4.2	2.0	37.4	50.4
Mississippi	59.1	37.0	0.5	0.9	2.4	2.7	2.1	7.1	18.4	10.3	12.6	12.6	14.1	11.7	7.2	4.1	1.5	36.0	51.4
Missouri	82.8	11.6	0.5	1.7	3.4	3.5	3.9	6.5	17.3	9.8	12.9	12.5	14.8	12.1	7.5	4.5	2.0	37.9	51.0
Montana	89.4	0.4	6.3	0.7	3.1	2.9	2.0	6.3	16.3	9.6	12.3	11.4	15.1	14.0	8.2	4.7	2.0	39.8	49.8
Nebraska	86.1	4.5	1.0	1.9	6.5	9.2	6.1	7.2	17.9	10.0	13.2	12.1	14.2	11.7	6.7	4.7	2.2	36.2	50.4
Nevada	66.2	8.1	1.2	7.8	16.7	26.5	18.8	6.9	17.7	9.2	14.3	14.2	13.9	11.7	7.3	3.6	1.1	36.3	49.5
New Hampshire	93.9	1.1	0.2	2.2	2.5	2.8	5.3	5.3	16.5	9.4	11.0	13.6	17.2	13.5	7.4	4.4	1.8	41.1	50.7
New Jersey	68.6	13.7	0.3	8.3	9.1	17.7	21.0	6.2	17.3	8.7	12.6	14.1	15.7	11.9	7.0	4.5	2.0	39.0	51.3
New Mexico	68.4	2.1	9.4	1.5	18.7	46.3	9.9	7.0	18.1	9.9	12.8	12.1	14.2	12.5	7.5	4.3	1.5	36.7	50.6
New York	65.7	15.9	0.6	7.3	10.4	17.6	22.2	6.0	16.4	10.2	13.7	13.5	14.9	11.9	7.0	4.5	2.0	38.0	51.6
North Carolina	68.5	21.5	1.3	2.3	6.5	8.4	7.5	6.6	17.3	9.8	13.0	13.9	14.4	11.9	7.3	4.1	1.6	37.4	51.3
North Dakota	90.0	1.2	5.4	1.0	2.3	2.0	2.5	6.6	15.7	12.0	13.1	11.2	14.4	12.2	7.0	5.1	2.5	37.0	49.5
Ohio	82.7	12.2	0.2	1.7	3.2	3.1	4.1	6.2	17.4	9.5	12.4	12.8	15.1	12.6	7.4	4.7	2.0	38.8	51.2
Oklahoma	72.2	7.4	8.6	1.8	10.0	8.9	5.5	7.0	17.7	10.2	13.5	12.3	14.0	11.7	7.5	4.4	1.6	36.2	50.5
Oregon	83.6	1.8	1.4	4.0	9.1	11.7	9.8	6.2	16.4	9.4	13.7	13.0	14.1	13.3	7.6	4.3	2.0	38.4	50.5
Pennsylvania	81.9	10.8	0.2	2.7	4.3	5.7	5.8	5.7	16.2	9.9	11.9	12.7	15.3	12.8	7.7	5.3	2.5	40.1	51.3
Rhode Island	81.4	5.7	0.6	3.0	9.3	12.4	12.8	5.5	15.8	11.4	12.0	13.0	15.4	12.4	7.0	4.9	2.5	39.4	51.7
South Carolina	66.2	27.9	0.4	1.4	4.2	5.1	4.7	6.5	16.8	10.3	12.7	13.0	14.3	12.6	8.0	4.1	1.6	37.9	51.4
South Dakota	85.9	1.3	8.8	0.9	3.0	2.7	2.7	7.3	17.6	10.0	12.8	11.4	14.4	12.0	7.1	4.8	2.4	36.9	50.0
Tennessee	77.6	16.7	0.3	1.5	3.9	4.6	4.5	6.4	17.1	9.6	12.8	13.5	14.6	12.4	7.7	4.2	1.6	38.0	51.3
Texas	70.4	11.8	0.7	3.9	13.2	37.6	16.4	7.7	19.6	10.2	14.3	13.8	13.7	10.3	5.9	3.3	1.2	33.6	50.4
Utah	86.1	1.1	1.2	2.9	8.7	13.0	8.0	9.5	22.0	11.5	16.2	12.0	11.1	8.7	5.0	2.9	1.1	29.2	49.8
Vermont	95.3	1.0	0.4	1.3	2.0	1.5	4.4	5.1	15.5	10.4	11.2	12.5	16.4	14.4	7.9	4.5	2.1	41.5	50.7
Virginia	68.6	19.4	0.4	5.6	6.1	7.9	11.4	6.4	16.8	10.0	13.6	13.9	15.2	11.9	6.9	3.8	1.5	37.5	50.9
Washington	77.3	3.6	1.5	7.8	9.9	11.2	13.1	6.5	17.0	9.7	13.9	13.5	14.7	12.4	6.8	3.7	1.8	37.3	50.2
West Virginia	93.9	3.4	0.2	0.7	1.8	1.2	1.2	5.6	15.3	9.1	11.7	12.8	14.9	14.3	8.8	5.2	2.0	41.3	50.7
Wisconsin	86.2	6.3	1.0	2.3	4.2	5.9	4.5	6.3	17.3	9.7	12.6	12.8	15.4	12.3	7.0	4.6	2.1	38.5	50.4
Wyoming	90.7	0.8	2.4	0.9	5.2	8.9	2.8	7.1	16.9	10.0	13.6	11.9	14.8	13.0	7.0	3.8	1.6	36.8	49.0

1. May be of any race.

Table A. States — **Households and Housing Units**

STATE	Households, 2010					Housing units, 2010									
				Percent				Occupied units							
									Owner-occupied				Renter-occupied		
											Median owner cost				
	Number	Percent change, 2000–2010	Persons per household	Female family householder[1]	One person	Total	Percent change, 2000–2010	Total	Percent	Median value[2] (dollars)	With a mortgage	Without a mortgage[3]	Median rent[4] (dollars)	Median rent as a percent of income	Substandard units[5] (percent)
	64	65	66	67	68	69	70	71	72	73	74	75	76	77	78
United States	116 716 292	10.7	2.58	13.1	26.7	131 791 065	13.7	114 567 419	65.4	179 900	25.1	12.8	855	31.6	3.9
Alabama	1 883 791	8.4	2.48	15.3	27.4	2 174 428	10.7	1 815 152	70.1	123 900	23.0	12.3	667	32.2	2.4
Alaska	258 058	16.5	2.65	10.7	25.6	307 065	17.7	254 610	63.9	241 400	23.3	10.8	981	29.0	10.2
Arizona	2 380 990	25.2	2.63	12.4	26.1	2 846 738	30.0	2 334 050	65.2	168 800	26.5	11.3	844	31.6	5.1
Arkansas	1 147 084	10.0	2.47	13.4	27.1	1 317 818	12.3	1 114 902	67.4	106 300	21.5	10.9	638	29.9	3.2
California	12 577 498	9.3	2.90	13.3	23.3	13 682 976	12.0	12 406 475	55.6	370 900	30.6	11.4	1 163	33.8	9.1
Colorado	1 972 868	19.0	2.49	10.1	27.9	2 214 262	22.5	1 960 585	65.9	236 600	25.2	10.7	863	31.2	3.2
Connecticut	1 371 087	5.3	2.52	12.9	27.3	1 488 215	7.4	1 358 809	68.0	288 800	26.8	17.6	992	32.1	2.4
Delaware	342 297	14.6	2.55	14.2	25.6	406 489	18.5	328 765	73.0	243 600	24.8	11.8	952	32.3	2.9
District of Columbia	266 707	7.4	2.11	16.4	44.0	296 836	8.0	252 388	42.5	426 900	24.8	11.0	1 198	30.4	3.5
Florida	7 420 802	17.1	2.48	13.5	27.2	8 994 091	23.2	7 035 068	68.1	164 200	29.5	14.4	947	35.5	3.1
Georgia	3 585 584	19.3	2.63	15.8	25.4	4 091 482	24.7	3 482 420	66.2	156 200	25.2	12.3	819	32.4	3.2
Hawaii	455 338	12.9	2.89	12.6	23.3	519 992	12.9	445 812	58.0	525 400	30.1	10.1	1 291	33.5	9.1
Idaho	579 408	23.4	2.66	9.6	23.8	668 634	26.7	576 709	69.6	165 100	24.7	10.6	683	30.5	3.6
Illinois	4 836 972	5.3	2.59	12.9	27.8	5 297 077	8.4	4 752 857	67.7	191 800	25.9	13.8	848	31.5	3.1
Indiana	2 502 154	7.1	2.52	12.4	26.9	2 797 172	10.5	2 470 905	70.3	123 300	21.6	11.0	683	30.8	2.2
Iowa	1 221 576	6.3	2.41	9.3	28.4	1 337 563	8.5	1 223 439	72.4	123 400	21.3	11.5	629	28.1	1.7
Kansas	1 112 096	7.1	2.49	10.4	27.8	1 234 037	9.1	1 101 658	68.1	127 300	21.8	11.8	682	28.1	2.2
Kentucky	1 719 965	8.1	2.45	12.7	27.5	1 928 617	10.1	1 684 348	68.6	121 600	22.2	11.3	613	29.8	2.5
Louisiana	1 728 360	4.4	2.55	17.2	26.9	1 967 947	6.5	1 689 822	67.6	137 500	21.6	10.5	736	31.7	3.7
Maine	557 219	7.5	2.32	10.0	28.6	722 217	10.8	545 417	72.7	179 100	24.1	13.9	707	29.8	2.5
Maryland	2 156 411	8.9	2.61	14.6	26.1	2 380 605	11.0	2 127 439	67.0	301 400	25.4	12.9	1 131	30.8	2.4
Massachusetts	2 547 075	4.2	2.48	12.5	28.7	2 808 727	7.1	2 520 419	62.2	334 100	26.1	15.3	1 009	30.4	2.0
Michigan	3 872 508	2.3	2.49	13.2	27.9	4 531 231	7.0	3 806 621	72.8	123 300	24.6	13.9	730	33.3	2.1
Minnesota	2 087 227	10.1	2.48	9.5	28.0	2 348 242	13.7	2 091 548	73.0	194 300	24.1	11.9	764	30.2	2.3
Mississippi	1 115 768	6.6	2.58	18.5	26.3	1 276 441	9.9	1 079 999	69.8	100 100	23.5	12.0	672	33.2	4.0
Missouri	2 375 611	8.2	2.45	12.3	28.3	2 714 017	11.1	2 350 628	69.0	139 000	22.6	11.7	682	30.1	2.2
Montana	409 607	14.2	2.35	9.0	29.7	483 006	17.1	402 747	69.7	181 200	24.1	11.3	642	28.3	2.8
Nebraska	721 130	8.2	2.46	9.8	28.7	797 677	10.4	719 304	67.4	127 600	21.4	12.6	669	27.7	2.2
Nevada	1 006 250	34.0	2.65	12.7	25.7	1 175 070	42.0	989 811	57.2	174 800	28.1	12.2	952	31.6	5.0
New Hampshire	518 973	9.3	2.46	9.7	25.6	614 996	12.4	515 431	71.7	243 000	26.5	16.5	951	30.3	1.9
New Jersey	3 214 360	4.9	2.68	13.3	25.2	3 554 909	7.4	3 172 421	66.4	339 200	28.7	18.9	1 114	32.4	4.1
New Mexico	791 395	16.7	2.55	14.0	28.0	902 242	15.6	765 183	67.9	161 200	24.3	10.0	699	29.3	4.7
New York	7 317 755	3.7	2.57	14.9	29.1	8 108 211	5.6	7 196 427	54.3	296 500	26.3	15.5	1 020	31.7	5.5
North Carolina	3 745 155	19.6	2.48	13.7	27.0	4 333 479	23.0	3 670 859	67.2	154 200	24.0	12.5	731	31.3	2.8
North Dakota	281 192	9.3	2.30	8.2	31.5	318 099	9.8	280 412	66.9	123 000	19.6	10.0	583	25.8	1.3
Ohio	4 603 435	3.5	2.44	13.1	28.9	5 128 113	7.2	4 525 066	68.4	134 400	23.4	13.1	685	31.1	1.8
Oklahoma	1 460 450	8.8	2.49	12.3	27.5	1 666 205	10.0	1 432 959	67.8	111 400	21.9	11.2	659	28.9	3.0
Oregon	1 518 938	13.9	2.47	10.5	27.4	1 676 476	15.4	1 507 137	62.5	244 500	27.3	12.9	816	32.7	3.4
Pennsylvania	5 018 904	5.1	2.45	12.2	28.6	5 568 820	6.1	4 936 030	70.1	165 500	23.8	13.7	763	30.4	1.6
Rhode Island	413 600	1.3	2.44	13.5	29.6	463 416	5.4	402 295	60.8	254 500	27.7	15.4	868	30.9	2.6
South Carolina	1 801 181	17.4	2.49	15.6	26.5	2 140 337	22.0	1 761 393	68.7	138 100	23.5	12.0	728	32.2	2.7
South Dakota	322 282	11.0	2.42	9.7	29.4	364 031	12.6	318 955	68.0	129 700	21.9	10.9	591	26.9	2.7
Tennessee	2 493 552	11.7	2.48	13.9	26.9	2 815 087	15.4	2 440 663	68.1	139 000	23.7	11.4	697	31.4	2.5
Texas	8 922 933	20.7	2.75	14.1	24.2	9 996 209	22.5	8 738 664	63.6	128 100	23.4	12.5	801	30.2	5.8
Utah	877 692	25.2	3.1	9.7	18.7	981 821	27.7	880 025	69.9	217 200	24.8	10.0	796	29.5	4.6
Vermont	256 442	6.6	2.34	9.6	28.2	322 698	9.6	256 922	70.4	216 800	26.0	16.3	823	31.8	2.2
Virginia	3 056 058	13.2	2.54	12.4	26.0	3 368 674	16.0	2 992 732	67.7	249 100	24.7	11.4	1 019	30.2	2.6
Washington	2 620 076	15.4	2.51	10.5	27.2	2 888 594	17.9	2 606 863	63.1	271 800	26.7	12.1	908	30.6	3.4
West Virginia	763 831	3.7	2.36	11.2	28.4	882 213	4.5	741 940	74.6	95 100	20.1	10.0	571	29.7	1.8
Wisconsin	2 279 768	9.4	2.43	10.3	28.2	2 625 477	13.1	2 279 532	68.7	169 400	24.5	14.0	715	29.8	2.2
Wyoming	226 879	17.2	2.42	8.9	28.0	262 286	17.2	222 803	69.7	180 100	22.0	10.0	693	25.3	2.8

1. No spouse present. 2. Specified owner-occupied units. 3. Median monthly costs is often in the minimum category—10.0 percent or less, which is indicated as 10.0 percent.
4. Specified renter-occupied units. 5. Overcrowded or lacking complete plumbing facilities.

STATE	Housing units, 2013													
			Occupied units											
					Percent who pay 30 percent or more of income for housing expenses		Median owner cost as a percent of income							
	Total	Percent change, 2012–2013	Total	Percent owner-occupied	Owners with a mortgage	Renter[1]	With a mortgage	Without a mortgage[2]	Median monthly housing costs (dollars)	Median value of units[3] (dollars)	Percent valued over $500,000	Median gross rent[4] (dollars)	Substandard units[5] (percent)	Percent living in a different house than 1 year ago
	79	80	81	82	83	84	85	86	87	88	89	90	91	92
United States	132 808 137	0.3	116 291 033	63.5	31.6	47.6	22.8	11.8	966	173 900	10.2	905	3.7	15.0
Alabama	2 190 027	0.0	1 822 439	68.0	26.3	43.6	20.7	10.6	706	122 700	2.9	694	2.0	14.9
Alaska	307 417	-0.1	246 015	63.5	26.7	39.8	22.1	10.3	1 201	254 000	7.0	1 117	9.2	19.5
Arizona	2 892 359	0.7	2 400 809	62.1	31.4	45.8	22.6	10.5	915	166 000	6.6	890	5.0	18.7
Arkansas	1 329 777	0.1	1 125 899	65.7	24.7	42.2	19.9	10.0	648	109 500	2.1	659	3.0	15.3
California	13 791 262	0.6	12 650 592	53.8	41.6	54.1	26.8	11.1	1 367	373 100	34.1	1 224	8.5	15.0
Colorado	2 247 291	0.8	2 002 800	64.5	30.0	49.0	22.4	10.0	1 107	240 500	11.9	971	2.9	19.6
Connecticut	1 488 072	0.0	1 339 860	66.3	35.1	49.3	24.3	16.3	1 337	267 000	16.2	1 040	2.3	12.2
Delaware	412 015	0.4	339 071	71.7	30.6	46.7	22.4	11.1	1 068	226 200	6.6	999	2.3	13.4
District of Columbia	302 975	0.9	271 651	40.7	28.4	46.7	22.1	11.4	1 477	470 500	46.2	1 307	3.4	19.9
Florida	9 047 973	0.2	7 211 584	64.8	38.6	53.4	25.0	12.6	956	153 300	6.9	972	3.2	16.3
Georgia	4 110 162	0.1	3 546 965	62.7	30.5	47.8	22.2	10.8	908	141 600	5.0	850	2.7	16.4
Hawaii	526 305	0.4	450 120	56.2	43.5	50.8	27.6	10.0	1 505	500 000	50.0	1 414	9.4	15.1
Idaho	676 192	0.5	588 489	69.4	29.9	43.1	22.6	10.0	813	159 000	4.7	725	3.6	17.3
Illinois	5 289 653	0.0	4 783 421	65.9	32.6	45.8	23.1	13.0	1 004	169 600	7.0	885	3.0	13.4
Indiana	2 809 640	0.0	2 498 395	68.5	23.3	45.2	19.6	10.6	777	122 200	2.2	730	2.2	15.3
Iowa	1 349 607	0.3	1 236 209	70.8	20.9	39.6	19.2	10.9	746	126 900	2.1	679	2.0	15.3
Kansas	1 239 755	0.1	1 113 729	66.1	22.1	41.3	20.1	11.5	797	129 700	2.6	745	2.5	16.4
Kentucky	1 936 634	0.0	1 705 623	67.4	25.5	40.1	20.2	10.1	691	120 900	2.6	668	2.2	15.6
Louisiana	1 990 967	0.2	1 728 149	66.0	27.2	45.5	20.3	10.0	726	140 300	3.1	763	2.7	13.7
Maine	723 140	-0.1	547 686	70.2	31.5	47.8	22.9	13.7	841	172 800	5.5	760	1.8	14.2
Maryland	2 404 177	0.4	2 161 680	66.5	31.6	48.4	23.2	11.2	1 381	280 200	16.8	1 210	2.2	13.3
Massachusetts	2 813 641	0.1	2 536 321	61.5	33.7	47.5	23.8	14.3	1 314	327 200	21.3	1 077	2.1	13.5
Michigan	4 525 266	0.0	3 832 466	70.6	27.5	48.2	21.3	12.8	824	117 500	2.6	768	2.0	15.2
Minnesota	2 368 754	0.3	2 119 954	71.6	25.6	44.8	21.5	11.1	976	180 100	5.6	832	2.3	14.4
Mississippi	1 283 192	-0.1	1 091 002	67.2	30.3	43.5	21.8	11.4	657	97 500	1.8	708	3.4	14.4
Missouri	2 719 109	0.0	2 362 853	67.0	26.4	44.7	20.8	11.5	783	133 200	3.1	734	1.9	16.0
Montana	485 767	-0.1	406 288	66.9	28.9	42.5	22.4	10.7	730	190 100	7.1	690	2.9	17.5
Nebraska	806 888	0.3	730 579	66.0	23.2	41.3	20.3	11.7	801	132 700	2.3	714	2.8	16.1
Nevada	1 186 936	0.3	1 002 571	54.3	35.7	46.7	24.0	10.0	1 001	165 300	4.8	952	4.6	21.4
New Hampshire	616 496	-0.1	519 246	70.2	33.7	45.3	24.2	16.4	1 206	233 300	6.6	995	2.1	13.9
New Jersey	3 578 260	0.1	3 176 139	64.0	40.7	51.1	26.4	17.6	1 462	307 700	19.5	1 171	3.5	9.8
New Mexico	905 134	-0.2	753 507	67.9	31.1	46.0	22.5	10.0	758	159 200	5.1	772	4.5	14.3
New York	8 126 399	0.0	7 219 356	53.7	37.6	50.8	24.6	14.5	1 199	277 600	22.5	1 109	5.3	11.0
North Carolina	4 394 515	0.4	3 757 480	64.3	28.9	45.1	21.6	11.3	829	154 300	5.1	778	2.9	15.4
North Dakota	339 293	3.1	298 298	64.8	17.6	38.6	18.5	10.0	715	155 400	2.6	690	1.7	16.9
Ohio	5 124 126	-0.1	4 564 745	66.1	26.0	44.6	21.0	11.9	800	127 000	2.4	709	1.8	14.8
Oklahoma	1 682 358	0.3	1 447 277	65.5	24.2	40.4	20.1	10.4	720	116 500	2.3	705	3.2	17.6
Oregon	1 684 107	0.1	1 523 799	60.8	35.1	50.2	24.2	12.4	991	229 700	9.2	887	3.6	18.9
Pennsylvania	5 565 354	-0.1	4 938 894	68.9	28.8	46.1	21.9	13.1	892	164 200	5.1	828	1.7	12.1
Rhode Island	461 658	-0.2	406 366	60.4	36.1	49.3	24.5	14.8	1 106	232 300	9.0	918	1.8	13.1
South Carolina	2 158 784	0.1	1 794 989	68.2	29.8	45.2	21.7	10.8	776	139 200	5.0	766	2.1	15.3
South Dakota	370 207	0.5	331 406	67.2	21.9	36.4	20.5	10.7	699	138 400	3.1	637	3.2	16.9
Tennessee	2 840 998	0.2	2 490 249	66.4	28.4	44.6	21.8	10.4	769	140 300	4.1	748	2.4	15.4
Texas	10 256 203	1.0	9 110 853	61.8	27.4	44.2	21.3	11.2	899	132 000	4.4	857	5.5	17.0
Utah	1 006 164	0.9	899 475	69.2	29.0	43.6	22.6	10.0	1 023	211 400	6.8	881	3.9	17.3
Vermont	323 936	0.0	253 234	71.0	34.8	50.3	24.3	16.9	1 004	218 300	6.9	865	2.1	12.8
Virginia	3 412 577	0.4	3 055 863	65.6	29.4	45.6	22.5	10.3	1 165	239 300	15.9	1 086	2.3	15.8
Washington	2 928 300	0.5	2 644 557	61.9	34.1	48.0	24.0	11.6	1 136	250 800	13.5	989	3.5	17.2
West Virginia	879 424	-0.4	738 653	72.3	23.4	38.4	19.5	10.0	558	103 200	1.5	620	1.7	11.8
Wisconsin	2 633 420	0.0	2 289 424	67.2	29.1	44.3	22.4	13.4	877	163 000	3.6	758	2.1	14.2
Wyoming	265 471	0.1	224 003	69.1	23.7	37.4	20.9	10.0	833	195 500	5.7	780	1.9	18.5

1. Excludes units where owner costs or gross rent as a percentage of households income cannot be calculated. 2. Median monthly costs is often in the minimum category—10.0 percent or less, which is indicated as 10.0 percent. 3. Specified owner-occupied units. 4. Specified renter-occupied units. 5. Overcrowded or lacking complete plumbing facilities.

Table A. States — Residential Construction, Vital Statistics, and Health

STATE	Value of residential construction authorized by building permits, 2014: New construction ($1,000)	Value of residential construction authorized by building permits, 2014: Number of housing units	Value of residential construction authorized by building permits, 2014: Percent single family	Manufactured housing units put in place, 2013 (1,000)	Births, 2013: Total	Births, 2013: Rate[1]	Deaths, 2011: Number: Total	Deaths, 2011: Number: Infant[2]	Deaths, 2011: Rate: Total: Crude[1]	Deaths, 2011: Rate: Total: Age-adjusted	Deaths, 2011: Rate: Infant[3]	Percent lacking health insurance, 2013: All persons	Percent lacking health insurance, 2013: Children under 18 years	Medicare enrollees, 2012
	93	94	95	96	97	98	99	100	101	102	103	104	105	106
United States	193 243 022	1 046 363	60.6	56.3	3 932 181	12.4	2 596 993	23 440	8.2	7.3	5.96	14.5	7.1	49 682 146
Alabama	2 204 675	13 369	71.1	2.4	58 167	12.0	50 189	501	10.4	9.3	8.61	13.6	4.3	896 274
Alaska	353 712	1 518	74.1	0.1	11 446	15.6	3 997	64	5.4	7.2	5.59	18.5	11.6	72 898
Arizona	5 666 004	26 997	62.4	1.0	85 600	12.9	50 534	451	7.6	6.7	5.27	17.1	11.9	1 009 292
Arkansas	1 250 185	7 666	68.6	1.5	37 832	12.8	30 437	288	10.3	8.9	7.61	16.0	5.5	558 620
California	18 742 105	83 645	46.9	2.2	494 705	12.9	248 359	2 353	6.5	6.3	4.76	17.2	7.4	5 111 208
Colorado	6 479 529	28 686	59.6	0.8	65 007	12.3	33 712	331	6.4	6.6	5.09	14.1	8.2	688 283
Connecticut	1 148 276	5 329	51.8	0.1	36 085	10.0	29 632	169	8.2	6.5	4.68	9.4	4.3	595 294
Delaware	615 472	5 194	79.8	0.3	10 831	11.7	7 967	68	8.6	7.3	6.28	9.1	4.5	161 422
District of Columbia	374 396	4 189	6.9	X	9 288	14.4	4 719	63	7.3	7.5	6.78	6.7	2.4	82 493
Florida	19 548 769	84 075	66.9	2.8	215 407	11.0	181 112	1 326	9.3	6.6	6.16	20.0	11.1	3 621 057
Georgia	6 541 383	39 423	69.8	1.5	128 748	12.9	75 088	894	7.5	8.1	6.94	18.8	9.6	1 350 944
Hawaii	1 011 786	3 066	71.7	D	18 987	13.5	10 505	124	7.5	5.9	6.53	6.7	3.0	221 514
Idaho	1 654 793	8 797	71.5	0.3	22 383	13.9	12 434	126	7.7	7.3	5.63	16.2	8.9	249 626
Illinois	4 211 740	20 578	51.3	0.9	156 931	12.2	103 401	942	8.0	7.2	6	12.7	4.2	1 934 703
Indiana	3 222 176	17 816	68.1	0.9	83 102	12.6	60 716	600	9.2	8.3	7.22	14.0	8.2	1 064 511
Iowa	1 907 579	10 256	68.1	0.3	39 094	12.7	28 948	162	9.4	7.2	4.14	8.1	4.1	537 430
Kansas	1 417 358	7 459	65.3	0.2	38 839	13.4	25 414	250	8.8	7.6	6.44	12.3	6.1	453 927
Kentucky	1 304 713	9 536	63.7	2.3	55 686	12.7	43 759	355	10.0	9.0	6.38	14.3	5.9	804 245
Louisiana	2 888 790	15 255	84.2	3.5	63 201	13.7	43 270	547	9.4	9.0	8.65	16.6	5.7	729 271
Maine	612 903	3 242	83.7	0.3	12 776	9.6	13 547	90	10.2	7.5	7.04	11.2	5.9	281 968
Maryland	2 889 171	16 331	64.5	0.3	71 953	12.1	45 689	477	7.7	7.1	6.63	10.2	4.4	844 862
Massachusetts	3 300 622	14 486	50.6	0.2	71 788	10.7	54 567	298	8.2	6.6	4.15	3.7	1.5	1 125 661
Michigan	3 314 833	15 933	77.7	1.6	113 489	11.5	92 408	799	9.3	7.8	7.04	11.0	4.0	1 754 367
Minnesota	3 680 420	16 990	62.9	0.3	69 159	12.8	40 987	349	7.6	6.5	5.05	8.2	5.6	836 205
Mississippi	1 033 059	6 871	80.7	2.3	38 634	12.9	30 703	373	10.3	9.6	9.65	17.1	7.6	523 625
Missouri	2 682 665	16 003	56.7	0.9	75 296	12.5	57 444	491	9.5	8.1	6.52	13.0	7.0	1 058 418
Montana	647 022	3 884	52.6	0.4	12 377	12.2	9 511	70	9.4	7.6	5.66	16.5	10.1	181 710
Nebraska	1 205 827	7 605	62.4	0.2	26 095	14.0	15 754	139	8.4	7.1	5.33	11.3	5.5	291 333
Nevada	1 754 597	13 016	68.3	0.2	35 030	12.6	21 468	191	7.7	7.7	5.45	20.7	14.9	394 066
New Hampshire	653 428	3 403	64.3	0.2	12 396	9.4	10 897	70	8.2	6.8	5.65	10.7	3.8	240 551
New Jersey	4 069 959	28 155	39.1	0.2	102 575	11.5	71 403	460	8.0	6.8	4.48	13.2	5.6	1 397 532
New Mexico	881 907	4 799	84.5	1.0	26 354	12.6	16 805	144	8.1	7.3	5.46	18.6	8.5	336 413
New York	5 581 783	36 286	28.6	1.5	236 980	12.1	150 919	1 167	7.7	6.5	4.92	10.7	4.0	3 138 042
North Carolina	8 619 650	49 911	70.2	2.1	119 002	12.1	83 329	832	8.5	7.8	6.99	15.6	6.3	1 604 085
North Dakota	1 636 051	12 178	37.2	0.7	10 599	14.7	6 233	65	8.6	7.1	6.13	10.4	7.9	112 330
Ohio	3 753 786	19 872	63.1	0.9	138 936	12.0	113 258	1 018	9.8	8.1	7.33	11.0	5.3	2 003 455
Oklahoma	2 457 497	14 179	72.2	2.1	53 369	13.9	38 384	364	10.0	9.1	6.82	17.7	10.0	635 525
Oregon	3 243 361	16 645	51.5	0.5	45 155	11.5	33 939	224	8.6	7.2	4.96	14.7	5.8	671 822
Pennsylvania	4 714 443	25 059	65.3	1.3	140 921	11.0	129 123	938	10.1	7.6	6.66	9.7	5.4	2 385 084
Rhode Island	195 030	952	83.6	D	10 809	10.3	9 792	70	9.3	7.1	6.48	11.6	5.4	191 420
South Carolina	5 424 387	27 537	77.9	2.2	56 795	11.9	44 582	389	9.3	8.4	6.85	15.8	6.7	839 989
South Dakota	689 248	4 722	59.3	0.4	12 248	14.5	7 099	80	8.4	6.8	6.53	11.3	6.3	143 014
Tennessee	4 550 319	27 632	64.7	1.8	79 992	12.3	63 406	544	9.8	8.8	6.8	13.9	5.7	1 132 942
Texas	26 295 841	166 982	59.7	10.0	387 340	14.6	179 183	2 264	6.8	7.5	5.84	22.1	12.6	3 256 477
Utah	3 360 911	17 510	64.4	0.2	50 957	17.6	16 366	263	5.6	7.1	5.16	14.0	9.5	307 361
Vermont	281 490	1 546	63.3	0.2	5 975	9.5	5 639	26	9.0	7.1	4.35	7.2	3.1	119 759
Virginia	4 655 664	28 682	65.7	1.2	102 147	12.4	62 716	634	7.6	7.2	6.21	12.3	5.4	1 226 577
Washington	7 016 518	33 898	52.8	0.6	86 577	12.4	51 264	388	7.4	6.8	4.48	14.0	5.9	1 055 977
West Virginia	395 354	2 677	71.3	1.2	20 825	11.2	21 843	158	11.8	9.2	7.59	14.0	5.3	396 705
Wisconsin	2 599 187	14 622	58.7	0.3	66 649	11.6	50 026	416	8.7	7.2	6.24	9.1	4.7	966 151
Wyoming	502 643	1 901	84.9	0.2	7 644	13.1	4 516	35	7.8	7.3	4.58	13.4	5.7	85 708

1. Per 1,000 resident population. 2. Deaths of infants under 1 year old. 3. Deaths of infants under 1 year old per 1,000 live births.

Table A. States — **Crime and Education**

STATE	Serious crime known to police,[1] 2013				Public elementary and secondary school enrollment, 2012–2013		Educational attainment[3] (percent)				Local government expenditures for education, 2011–2012	
	Violent Crime		Property Crime				2010		2013			
	Number	Rate[2]	Number	Rate[2]	Total	Student/ teacher ratio	High school graduate or more	Bachelor's degree or more	High school graduate or more	Bachelor's degree or more	Total current expenditures (mil dol)	Current expenditures per student (dollars)
	107	108	109	110	111	112	113	114	115	116	117	118
United States	1 191 988	376.6	8 632 512	2 730.70	49 771 118	16.0	85.6	28.2	86.6	29.6	527 096	10 667
Alabama	20 826	430.8	161 993	3 351.30	744 637	14.4	82.1	21.9	84.5	23.5	6 387	8 577
Alaska	4 708	640.4	21 210	2 885.20	131 489	17.1	91.0	27.9	91.6	28.0	2 292	17 475
Arizona	27 599	416.5	225 243	3 399.10	1 089 384	22.3	85.6	25.9	85.9	27.4	7 975	7 382
Arkansas	13 621	460.3	106 613	3 602.60	486 157	14.2	82.9	19.5	84.4	20.6	4 607	9 536
California	154 129	402.1	1 018 907	2 658.10	6 299 451	23.7	80.7	30.1	81.7	31.0	57 975	9 329
Colorado	16 226	308.0	140 057	2 658.50	863 561	17.7	89.7	36.4	90.5	37.8	7 342	8 594
Connecticut	9 440	262.5	70 990	1 974.10	550 954	12.5	88.6	35.5	89.7	37.2	9 345	16 855
Delaware	4 549	491.4	28 379	3 065.50	129 026	13.9	87.7	27.8	88.3	29.8	1 751	13 580
District of Columbia	8 406	1 300.3	31 083	4 808.30	76 140	12.9	87.4	50.1	90.1	55.1	1 467	19 847
Florida	91 986	470.4	607 172	3 105.30	2 692 162	15.3	85.5	25.8	86.8	27.2	22 733	8 520
Georgia	36 541	365.7	334 399	3 346.60	1 703 332	15.6	84.3	27.3	85.5	28.3	15 624	9 272
Hawaii	3 533	251.6	42 875	3 053.70	184 760	15.9	89.9	29.5	91.0	31.2	2 187	11 973
Idaho	3 498	217.0	30 055	1 864.30	284 834	19.6	88.3	24.4	89.4	26.2	1 855	6 626
Illinois	48 974	380.2	292 983	2 274.30	2 072 880	15.3	86.9	30.8	87.8	32.1	25 013	12 011
Indiana	23 487	357.4	187 536	2 854.00	1 041 369	17.4	87.0	22.7	87.6	23.8	9 978	9 588
Iowa	8 388	271.4	67 800	2 193.90	499 825	14.3	90.6	24.9	91.6	26.4	4 972	10 027
Kansas	9 838	339.9	85 280	2 946.80	489 043	11.9	89.2	29.8	90.1	31.1	4 871	10 021
Kentucky	9 222	209.8	103 857	2 362.90	685 167	16.0	81.9	20.5	84.1	22.6	6 361	9 327
Louisiana	23 984	518.5	165 686	3 582.00	710 903	15.3	81.9	21.4	83.1	22.5	7 545	10 726
Maine	1 718	129.3	30 447	2 292.20	185 739	12.2	90.3	26.8	91.8	28.2	2 331	12 335
Maryland	28 089	473.8	157 913	2 663.50	859 638	14.9	88.1	36.1	89.1	37.4	11 847	13 871
Massachusetts	27 667	413.4	137 285	2 051.20	954 773	13.5	89.1	39.0	89.9	40.3	14 152	14 844
Michigan	44 523	449.9	230 334	2 327.60	1 555 370	18.1	88.7	25.2	89.4	26.9	16 485	10 477
Minnesota	12 705	234.4	131 195	2 420.40	845 404	15.8	91.8	31.8	92.4	33.5	9 053	10 781
Mississippi	8 214	274.6	81 500	2 724.70	493 650	15.1	81.0	19.5	82.4	20.4	3 973	8 097
Missouri	26 197	433.4	189 606	3 137.00	917 900	13.9	86.9	25.6	88.7	27.0	8 720	9 514
Montana	2 567	252.9	25 953	2 556.50	142 908	14.0	91.7	28.8	92.7	29.0	1 505	10 569
Nebraska	4 897	262.1	49 018	2 623.40	303 505	13.7	90.4	28.6	90.2	29.4	3 357	11 640
Nevada	16 824	603.0	79 177	2 837.70	445 707	21.5	84.7	21.7	85.2	22.5	3 574	8 130
New Hampshire	2 849	215.3	29 040	2 194.30	188 974	12.7	91.5	32.8	92.8	34.6	2 643	13 774
New Jersey	25 674	288.5	167 556	1 882.80	1 372 203	12.4	88.0	35.4	88.5	36.6	24 391	17 982
New Mexico	12 782	613.0	77 256	3 704.80	338 220	15.2	83.3	25.0	84.3	26.4	3 039	9 013
New York	77 372	393.7	358 598	1 824.80	2 710 703	13.1	84.9	32.5	85.6	34.1	52 460	19 396
North Carolina	33 700	342.2	308 049	3 128.00	1 518 465	15.4	84.7	26.5	85.7	28.4	12 303	8 160
North Dakota	1 954	270.1	15 148	2 094.00	101 111	11.7	90.3	27.6	91.5	27.1	1 098	11 246
Ohio	33 121	286.2	338 731	2 927.50	1 729 916	16.3	88.1	24.6	89.0	26.1	19 702	11 323
Oklahoma	16 989	441.2	126 057	3 273.70	673 483	16.1	86.2	22.9	86.7	23.8	5 171	7 763
Oregon	9 984	254.0	124 737	3 173.90	587 564	22.3	88.8	28.8	89.7	30.7	5 389	9 485
Pennsylvania	42 849	335.4	263 240	2 060.80	1 763 677	14.3	88.4	27.1	89.2	28.7	23 190	13 091
Rhode Island	2 705	257.2	25 678	2 442.00	142 481	14.4	83.5	30.2	85.9	32.4	2 167	15 172
South Carolina	24 278	508.5	173 049	3 624.20	735 998	15.3	84.1	24.5	85.6	26.1	6 601	9 077
South Dakota	2 674	316.5	16 177	1 914.70	130 471	14.0	89.6	26.3	91.6	26.6	1 100	8 593
Tennessee	38 364	590.6	206 629	3 180.90	993 496	15.0	83.6	23.1	85.6	24.8	8 351	8 354
Texas	107 998	408.3	861 734	3 258.20	5 077 659	15.5	80.7	25.9	81.9	27.5	41 068	8 213
Utah	6 498	224.0	85 586	2 950.40	613 279	23.1	90.6	29.3	91.5	31.3	3 780	6 441
Vermont	759	121.1	13 875	2 214.20	89 624	10.7	91.0	33.6	91.5	35.7	1 497	16 651
Virginia	16 205	196.2	170 654	2 065.90	1 265 419	14.2	86.5	34.2	88.4	36.1	13 404	10 656
Washington	20 153	289.1	258 662	3 710.30	1 051 694	19.6	89.8	31.1	90.1	32.7	10 054	9 617
West Virginia	5 568	300.3	39 013	2 103.90	283 044	14.1	83.2	17.5	84.6	18.9	3 275	11 579
Wisconsin	15 961	277.9	125 688	2 188.70	872 436	15.2	90.1	26.3	90.9	27.7	9 705	11 233
Wyoming	1 195	205.1	12 809	2 198.40	91 533	12.5	92.3	24.1	93.5	26.6	1 432	15 988

1. Data for serious crimes have not been adjusted for underreporting; this may affect comparability between geographic areas and over time. 2. Per 100,000 population estimated by the FBI. 3. Persons 25 years old and over.

Table A. States — **Exports, Income, and Poverty**

STATE	Exports of goods by state of origin, 2014			Income, 2013					Percent below poverty level, 2013						
					Households								Families with children under 18		
	Total	Manu-factured	Non-manu-factured	Per capita income (dollars)	Median income (dollars)	Percent with income of $25,000 or less	Percent with income of $100,000 or more	Median income of family of four	All persons	Children under 18 years	Persons 65 years and over	All families	Married-couple families	Male house-holder[1] families	Female house-holder[1] families
	119	120	121	122	123	124	125	126	127	128	129	130	131	132	133
United States	1 623 273	1 193 380	180 853	28 184	52 250	23.7	22.6	77 953	15.8	22.2	9.6	11.6	8.5	23.1	41.0
Alabama	19 518	16 972	1 879	23 384	42 849	30.0	15.7	65 381	18.7	27.2	10.6	14.3	8.7	26.5	49.1
Alaska	5 153	389	4 560	32 474	72 237	14.3	33.1	95 010	9.3	12.1	5.2	5.9	3.9	15.5	27.8
Arizona	21 124	12 433	4 082	25 164	48 510	25.1	18.9	67 800	18.6	26.5	8.9	13.6	12.6	25.3	39.3
Arkansas	6 857	4 568	465	21 927	40 511	31.2	13.3	58 149	19.7	29.0	10.5	14.5	11.1	31.7	49.5
California	174 129	112 497	22 694	29 513	60 190	21.2	28.7	78 150	16.8	23.5	10.4	12.6	11.0	25.9	38.8
Colorado	8 368	6 817	618	31 421	58 823	19.6	25.7	84 998	13.0	16.9	7.4	8.7	7.0	15.8	33.6
Connecticut	15 941	14 459	580	37 726	67 098	18.7	33.0	107 360	10.7	14.5	7.4	7.6	3.7	13.8	32.2
Delaware	5 292	4 082	178	29 484	57 846	19.3	24.5	84 179	12.4	18.0	7.2	8.5	6.5	14.9	31.0
District of Columbia	936	821	54	45 477	67 572	22.7	35.8	72 523	18.9	27.2	17.5	15.7	4.8	27.9	41.4
Florida	58 637	43 701	3 974	25 834	46 036	26.4	17.7	66 461	17.0	24.5	10.7	12.4	10.4	25.4	38.7
Georgia	39 365	33 065	3 333	24 923	47 829	26.4	19.2	68 066	19.0	26.5	10.7	14.5	10.1	25.8	43.8
Hawaii	1 452	1 169	173	29 577	68 020	17.2	31.7	88 217	10.8	13.3	7.2	7.1	4.4	18.6	28.1
Idaho	5 136	2 891	477	22 652	46 783	24.1	14.4	61 353	15.6	19.1	8.2	10.4	8.5	25.3	39.9
Illinois	68 182	52 366	6 339	29 856	56 210	22.3	24.7	83 546	14.7	20.7	8.8	10.8	7.4	24.4	40.5
Indiana	35 452	32 038	502	24 796	47 529	25.2	16.5	73 020	15.9	22.2	7.9	11.9	8.2	25.3	44.4
Iowa	15 101	12 260	2 358	27 740	52 229	22.0	19.1	81 219	12.7	16.2	7.8	8.1	4.5	18.1	40.7
Kansas	12 004	8 979	2 363	27 175	50 972	22.9	19.6	74 804	14.0	18.7	7.9	9.6	7.2	14.2	41.5
Kentucky	27 541	22 449	567	23 668	43 399	29.7	15.2	68 680	18.8	25.3	11.2	14.5	10.4	28.9	49.4
Louisiana	65 085	45 184	19 048	24 695	44 164	30.4	18.3	72 828	19.8	27.7	12.7	15.3	7.0	21.9	49.4
Maine	27 364	1 520	1 111	26 630	46 974	26.1	16.4	75 290	14.0	17.7	9.1	9.6	6.2	19.4	40.2
Maryland	12 241	8 458	1 013	36 177	72 483	15.9	35.1	105 382	10.1	13.6	8.0	7.1	4.1	12.6	26.0
Massachusetts	2 752	21 987	1 482	35 879	66 768	20.3	32.5	106 812	11.9	16.3	8.8	8.6	4.6	21.6	35.9
Michigan	55 751	46 808	3 762	25 918	48 273	25.6	18.3	76 622	17.0	23.8	8.3	12.3	8.6	26.9	45.9
Minnesota	21 372	18 113	1 610	31 358	60 702	19.3	25.5	93 294	11.2	14.0	7.4	7.2	4.4	15.7	35.1
Mississippi	14 141	9 582	530	20 156	37 963	34.4	12.5	58 182	24.0	34.0	14.7	19.0	11.5	28.7	54.7
Missouri	11 414	12 111	1 289	25 384	46 931	26.1	17.0	71 550	15.9	22.2	9.4	11.5	8.2	25.5	41.7
Montana	1 529	938	512	26 054	46 972	26.9	16.7	67 614	16.5	21.3	9.2	11.3	7.6	27.7	46.3
Nebraska	31 291	6 146	1 364	27 093	51 440	22.2	19.1	78 363	13.2	17.7	8.4	8.8	6.7	19.2	36.7
Nevada	5 289	5 314	746	25 918	51 230	22.6	19.3	68 560	15.8	22.7	8.7	11.6	10.1	22.3	35.8
New Hampshire	7 863	3 093	459	33 269	64 230	17.4	27.8	94 432	8.7	10.2	5.6	5.1	2.4	10.1	25.1
New Jersey	4 424	26 723	3 658	35 728	70 165	18.2	34.6	105 737	11.4	16.7	8.2	8.7	5.5	21.4	34.8
New Mexico	36 836	2 148	149	23 334	43 872	30.1	16.7	61 837	21.9	31.2	11.7	16.3	14.2	28.6	45.9
New York	3 789	42 972	12 859	32 514	57 369	23.3	27.6	88 156	16.0	22.8	11.6	12.1	9.3	21.1	38.8
North Carolina	7 701	26 671	1 934	25 377	45 906	26.8	17.2	69 370	17.9	25.2	10.0	13.1	9.3	26.8	43.7
North Dakota	86 007	2 176	3 033	30 855	55 759	20.9	22.1	88 887	11.8	12.0	9.4	7.0	4.5	13.7	34.4
Ohio	52 130	44 112	3 514	26 354	48 081	25.9	18.4	77 367	16.0	22.7	8.4	11.6	7.3	25.0	44.7
Oklahoma	6 300	5 410	329	24 284	45 690	26.6	16.2	63 419	16.8	24.0	9.5	12.5	9.3	19.9	46.7
Oregon	20 920	15 590	3 061	27 048	50 251	24.4	19.4	71 508	16.7	21.6	9.0	11.3	9.1	23.5	40.5
Pennsylvania	40 227	32 069	3 481	28 647	52 007	23.6	21.6	84 396	13.7	19.4	8.5	9.3	5.6	20.2	40.6
Rhode Island	2 394	1 520	701	30 748	55 902	23.2	24.7	88 389	14.3	21.5	8.5	10.7	7.5	22.9	37.3
South Carolina	29 704	27 584	786	23 687	44 163	28.4	15.9	66 561	18.6	27.5	10.2	14.1	9.8	24.5	46.8
South Dakota	1 590	1 428	124	25 860	48 947	22.4	16.2	73 089	14.2	18.6	10.1	9.2	5.7	22.3	41.2
Tennessee	32 957	24 576	1 136	24 678	44 297	28.0	15.8	66 846	17.8	26.5	9.7	13.3	9.8	25.8	47.9
Texas	289 023	215 596	27 312	26 327	51 704	23.7	22.7	70 824	17.5	25.0	11.0	13.6	11.2	22.4	42.2
Utah	12 266	10 548	679	24 250	59 770	17.9	22.9	72 274	12.7	14.8	7.2	9.3	7.9	19.2	36.6
Vermont	19 194	2 568	81	29 136	52 578	23.3	20.2	82 047	12.3	15.3	8.0	7.8	3.1	21.4	41.8
Virginia	3 643	14 513	2 864	33 145	62 666	18.6	29.8	91 859	11.7	15.7	7.4	8.4	5.1	19.3	33.7
Washington	90 646	71 651	15 398	30 672	58 405	20.3	25.7	84 786	14.1	18.8	8.1	9.5	7.3	19.4	39.4
West Virginia	23 433	4 071	3 230	23 159	41 253	31.7	13.7	66 009	18.5	27.0	9.4	13.5	11.2	28.0	51.4
Wisconsin	7 496	20 245	1 398	27 448	51 467	22.7	19.0	82 350	13.5	18.4	9.0	9.2	5.4	20.8	42.5
Wyoming	1 757	1 216	505	28 889	58 752	19.8	23.3	80 477	10.9	13.2	7.6	8.4	3.9	12.6	38.7

1. No spouse present.

STATE	Personal income, 2013												
			Per capita[1]		Sources of personal income (mil dol)								
								Transfer payments					
									Government payments to individuals				
	Total (mil dol)	Percent change, 2012–2013	Dollars	Rank	Wages and salaries[2]	Proprietors' income	Dividends, interest, and rent	Total	Total	Social Security	Medical payments	Income main-tenance	Unemploy-ment insurance
	134	135	136	137	138	139	140	141	142	143	144	145	146
United States	14 151 427	2.0	44 765	X	8 823 703	1 341 560	2 670 719	2 414 501	2 349 356	799 044	1 040 885	267 804	62 769
Alabama	176 341	1.8	36 481	45	102 689	16 084	29 735	39 514	38 511	14 708	15 232	4 761	467
Alaska	36 867	1.2	50 150	10	26 521	3 476	6 689	5 210	5 060	1 158	1 929	827	197
Arizona	245 070	2.1	36 983	42	150 316	19 205	45 102	49 003	47 633	16 823	20 403	4 896	590
Arkansas	108 603	1.1	36 698	43	60 274	9 590	22 528	24 709	24 101	8 791	10 045	2 573	471
California	1 856 614	2.8	48 434	12	1 162 588	176 024	377 314	281 173	273 243	75 232	128 772	34 646	10 677
Colorado	247 069	2.8	46 897	18	157 171	25 677	51 310	31 601	30 512	10 832	12 654	2 868	936
Connecticut	218 132	0.8	60 658	2	128 630	21 680	47 996	29 736	29 001	10 051	13 826	2 507	1 315
Delaware	41 487	2.7	44 815	23	28 032	4 029	7 239	8 039	7 849	2 819	3 653	652	170
District of Columbia	48 697	1.2	75 329	1	78 406	6 004	8 265	5 885	5 757	1 013	3 383	874	164
Florida	811 377	2.3	41 497	29	439 687	49 333	216 149	160 614	156 554	57 693	67 907	17 366	2 071
Georgia	378 156	2.4	37 845	41	248 891	31 533	63 256	65 997	63 941	22 493	25 049	9 283	1 325
Hawaii	63 468	2.4	45 204	22	40 847	4 829	13 384	9 839	9 551	3 449	3 760	1 316	273
Idaho	58 272	3.9	36 146	47	31 983	7 110	11 934	10 745	10 411	4 059	4 087	1 074	214
Illinois	605 201	2.2	46 980	17	396 619	53 194	112 563	92 572	89 913	31 084	38 991	10 850	3 528
Indiana	253 779	1.8	38 622	40	158 708	22 589	38 795	49 234	47 885	18 584	19 735	5 196	892
Iowa	138 337	2.2	44 763	24	79 957	20 768	24 675	22 362	21 730	8 643	8 990	1 962	527
Kansas	128 541	2.7	44 417	25	77 161	15 903	24 770	19 605	19 011	7 445	7 634	2 011	449
Kentucky	159 172	1.4	36 214	46	99 281	12 708	25 301	36 655	35 753	12 586	14 916	4 264	795
Louisiana	190 590	2.0	41 204	30	112 973	21 795	32 612	36 491	35 531	11 049	17 218	4 675	307
Maine	54 359	2.6	40 924	32	31 205	4 140	9 477	12 521	12 248	4 184	5 786	1 189	241
Maryland	319 125	1.1	53 826	6	187 308	24 893	61 625	41 855	40 632	13 458	18 799	4 129	1 252
Massachusetts	383 152	1.7	57 248	3	257 648	32 024	73 193	57 085	55 723	17 188	27 656	5 995	2 406
Michigan	386 471	1.4	39 055	38	241 781	27 670	63 638	83 546	81 503	31 442	34 045	9 362	2 064
Minnesota	257 466	1.0	47 500	14	170 378	23 089	47 043	40 395	39 278	13 679	18 102	3 718	1 008
Mississippi	101 442	1.6	33 913	51	55 112	10 608	14 824	25 334	24 718	8 252	11 214	3 300	329
Missouri	245 771	2.2	40 663	33	155 277	22 657	44 625	47 746	46 505	17 087	20 918	4 378	780
Montana	39 963	1.5	39 366	36	22 327	4 139	9 406	7 344	7 136	2 797	2 745	618	171
Nebraska	88 114	3.4	47 157	15	52 090	14 812	16 805	12 277	11 893	4 517	4 900	1 121	153
Nevada	109 471	1.3	39 235	37	67 784	8 186	24 713	17 067	16 485	6 466	6 339	1 697	765
New Hampshire	67 513	2.1	51 013	9	38 745	6 052	12 939	9 520	9 249	4 052	3 638	825	141
New Jersey	492 897	1.2	55 386	4	288 956	42 438	90 189	70 447	68 606	24 216	29 655	6 686	4 061
New Mexico	74 996	0.5	35 965	48	44 799	5 657	13 859	16 143	15 712	5 125	6 688	2 078	325
New York	1 070 236	1.1	54 462	5	707 600	101 183	206 943	185 354	181 325	50 489	94 448	21 566	4 971
North Carolina	380 954	1.4	38 683	39	238 743	35 381	65 159	74 869	72 841	26 621	31 100	8 207	1 534
North Dakota	38 472	-2.6	53 182	7	26 209	4 363	7 589	4 764	4 617	1 664	1 881	412	101
Ohio	474 973	2.2	41 049	31	307 774	40 182	73 616	93 599	91 220	31 530	40 869	10 157	1 805
Oklahoma	161 188	2.0	41 861	28	90 088	24 611	28 130	29 176	28 386	10 106	11 939	3 054	338
Oregon	156 605	2.3	39 848	34	100 245	11 622	30 847	30 731	29 919	11 037	11 920	3 250	1 106
Pennsylvania	590 171	1.4	46 202	19	361 326	52 782	103 002	112 900	110 292	39 363	50 307	10 422	4 047
Rhode Island	49 410	1.7	46 989	16	29 395	3 965	9 083	9 515	9 302	3 033	4 194	1 058	331
South Carolina	171 088	2.5	35 831	49	102 040	13 105	28 705	37 988	37 009	14 202	14 284	4 412	512
South Dakota	38 897	2.1	46 039	20	20 172	7 605	8 448	5 586	5 414	2 164	2 177	543	41
Tennessee	256 969	2.1	39 558	35	154 094	34 202	36 710	53 284	51 944	18 583	22 535	6 449	660
Texas	1 160 079	2.9	43 862	26	715 202	173 546	190 441	168 168	162 701	50 975	73 862	21 145	3 633
Utah	106 289	3.7	36 640	44	72 432	9 457	19 241	14 489	13 886	5 019	5 239	1 852	282
Vermont	28 501	2.5	45 483	21	16 759	2 354	5 471	5 746	5 619	1 923	2 701	568	97
Virginia	403 425	1.2	48 838	11	259 762	27 371	82 869	53 440	51 745	19 690	20 617	5 261	756
Washington	332 655	2.5	47 717	13	212 429	25 279	69 758	50 993	49 550	17 466	18 467	5 761	1 808
West Virginia	65 889	1.0	35 533	50	37 889	5 028	9 368	17 640	17 259	6 396	7 206	1 727	354
Wisconsin	248 335	2.1	43 244	27	160 042	18 264	44 614	42 217	41 035	16 400	17 072	4 006	1 235
Wyoming	30 779	1.7	52 826	8	17 358	3 365	8 772	3 778	3 658	1 407	1 401	260	94

1. Based on the resident population estimated as of July 1 of the year shown.
2. Includes supplements to wages and salaries.

Table A. States — **Personal Income and Earnings**

STATE	Personal tax payments, 2013 (mil dol)	Disposable personal income, 2013: Total (mil dol)	Disposable personal income, 2013: Per capita[1] (dollars)	Earnings, 2013: Total (mil dol)	Earnings, 2013: Percent by selected industries: Farm	Goods-related[2]: Total	Goods-related[2]: Manu-facturing	Service-related and other[3]: Total	Service-related and other[3]: Retail trade	Service-related and other[3]: Finance, insurance, real estate, rental and leasing	Service-related and other[3]: Health care and social assist-ance	Government	Gross state product, 2013 (mil dol)
	147	148	149	150	151	152	153	154	155	156	157	158	159
United States	1 660 181	12 491 246	39 513	10 165 263	1.2	16.8	9.7	65.0	6.0	9.2	10.9	17.1	16 665 215
Alabama	16 104	160 236	33 150	118 772	1.4	20.9	13.8	56.9	6.8	6.7	10.5	20.9	194 671
Alaska	3 345	33 522	45 600	29 997	0.0	19.3	3.0	49.6	5.3	4.4	10.6	31.1	57 276
Arizona	23 746	221 325	33 399	169 521	0.5	14.6	8.1	67.3	7.4	10.3	12.3	17.6	274 734
Arkansas	10 337	98 267	33 205	69 864	3.7	19.4	12.3	59.2	7.0	5.6	11.8	17.7	118 553
California	251 801	1 604 813	41 866	1 338 612	1.3	14.6	9.5	66.7	5.7	8.8	9.5	17.4	2 212 991
Colorado	30 344	216 725	41 137	182 848	0.8	16.7	6.1	65.9	5.6	8.2	8.8	16.5	288 338
Connecticut	35 656	182 475	50 743	150 310	0.1	16.8	11.6	69.4	5.6	17.0	11.5	13.7	246 897
Delaware	4 658	36 829	39 783	32 060	0.8	11.2	6.0	71.1	5.9	16.8	12.4	16.7	60 816
District of Columbia	6 349	42 347	65 507	84 410	0.0	1.7	0.2	58.2	1.0	4.6	5.5	40.1	111 695
Florida	81 423	729 954	37 332	489 020	0.6	10.0	4.8	72.8	7.9	9.6	12.9	16.5	800 697
Georgia	40 098	338 059	33 832	280 425	1.3	14.2	9.2	67.0	6.2	8.4	9.8	17.5	456 483
Hawaii	6 282	57 187	40 730	45 676	0.8	9.1	1.8	59.3	6.1	7.2	9.5	30.9	75 095
Idaho	5 481	52 792	32 746	39 093	7.1	17.6	10.7	58.0	8.1	6.0	11.4	17.3	61 117
Illinois	77 166	528 036	40 990	449 814	2.2	16.1	11.2	67.2	5.2	9.9	10.1	14.5	724 795
Indiana	26 605	227 174	34 573	181 297	2.6	27.6	20.8	56.4	6.1	5.8	12.4	13.4	311 188
Iowa	14 486	123 852	40 076	100 726	8.9	23.4	16.9	52.5	6.0	9.5	9.4	15.1	166 787
Kansas	13 766	114 774	39 660	93 064	4.3	21.8	13.9	56.3	5.7	7.1	10.4	17.5	142 449
Kentucky	15 977	143 195	32 579	111 990	1.7	21.2	14.2	56.4	6.3	6.5	12.1	20.7	183 582
Louisiana	18 030	172 560	37 307	134 768	1.2	24.1	9.6	57.4	6.4	6.6	10.5	17.3	246 660
Maine	5 491	48 868	36 790	35 345	0.6	16.5	10.0	64.9	8.2	7.8	16.3	18.0	54 609
Maryland	41 182	277 943	46 880	212 201	0.2	11.7	4.5	63.4	5.5	7.8	11.0	24.7	339 409
Massachusetts	56 489	326 663	48 808	289 672	0.1	13.8	8.7	73.2	4.7	12.2	13.5	13.0	441 467
Michigan	43 718	342 754	34 637	269 451	0.8	21.9	16.8	62.2	6.2	6.5	12.5	15.1	434 674
Minnesota	34 066	223 400	41 215	193 467	2.3	18.4	12.8	66.1	5.4	10.5	12.3	13.2	307 270
Mississippi	8 223	93 219	31 164	65 719	3.5	21.2	12.3	53.3	7.4	5.6	10.7	22.0	104 095
Missouri	25 447	220 324	36 452	177 934	1.7	16.5	10.5	65.6	6.3	8.0	12.1	16.1	276 715
Montana	4 386	35 577	35 045	26 466	3.1	16.5	4.1	59.8	8.1	6.1	13.3	20.7	43 006
Nebraska	9 180	78 934	42 244	66 902	10.2	16.6	10.1	57.5	5.5	8.0	10.1	15.7	109 364
Nevada	11 026	98 445	35 283	75 970	0.3	12.4	3.8	69.9	7.2	6.0	8.9	17.4	127 989
New Hampshire	6 540	60 973	46 071	44 797	0.1	18.8	12.1	67.6	8.8	9.3	12.6	13.5	68 701
New Jersey	65 626	427 271	48 012	331 395	0.1	13.0	7.6	71.1	6.2	10.0	11.2	15.7	537 396
New Mexico	6 565	68 431	32 816	50 456	2.8	15.8	4.3	54.1	6.7	4.7	11.2	27.3	90 828
New York	164 328	905 908	46 100	808 784	0.2	9.0	4.6	74.0	5.0	18.1	10.8	16.8	1 341 591
North Carolina	40 328	340 626	34 588	274 124	1.2	16.9	11.7	62.0	6.2	10.7	10.1	19.9	467 075
North Dakota	4 888	33 584	46 425	30 572	5.2	24.8	5.1	54.4	6.0	7.0	10.1	15.6	51 048
Ohio	53 308	421 665	36 442	347 956	0.7	20.2	14.4	63.5	6.1	8.2	12.9	15.6	562 845
Oklahoma	15 882	145 306	37 736	114 699	1.0	28.4	9.2	52.1	6.4	6.0	9.6	18.5	176 398
Oregon	18 994	137 611	35 015	111 867	1.4	18.6	12.7	62.9	6.8	6.2	12.4	17.1	204 867
Pennsylvania	67 499	522 672	40 917	414 108	0.4	17.2	10.3	68.5	5.7	8.3	13.9	14.0	640 294
Rhode Island	5 383	44 026	41 870	33 360	0.1	14.0	8.8	68.2	5.7	10.2	14.9	17.5	53 300
South Carolina	16 117	154 972	32 456	115 145	0.6	19.5	13.9	58.9	7.3	8.3	9.3	21.1	182 400
South Dakota	3 357	35 540	42 065	27 777	13.0	15.7	9.5	55.5	6.7	10.4	12.9	15.9	44 673
Tennessee	20 104	236 864	36 463	188 296	0.4	18.3	12.0	66.7	6.9	7.8	15.3	14.6	290 125
Texas	114 634	1 045 445	39 528	888 748	0.5	25.7	9.3	59.7	5.8	7.9	8.9	14.1	1 557 193
Utah	11 353	94 936	32 727	81 888	0.4	19.2	10.3	62.7	7.6	8.6	8.7	17.7	134 974
Vermont	2 876	25 625	40 894	19 113	1.0	19.2	11.7	60.6	7.7	6.2	14.3	19.2	28 838
Virginia	49 817	353 607	42 807	287 133	0.2	11.6	5.8	64.5	5.2	7.0	8.8	23.7	454 984
Washington	33 326	299 329	42 937	237 707	1.4	17.1	11.1	62.0	6.7	6.0	10.1	19.5	407 160
West Virginia	6 224	59 664	32 176	42 917	0.0	24.2	8.7	55.2	7.1	4.8	14.8	20.6	70 595
Wisconsin	28 209	220 126	38 331	178 305	1.8	24.1	18.6	58.3	6.0	7.4	12.4	15.8	284 728
Wyoming	3 961	26 819	46 028	20 722	1.7	30.7	3.7	44.6	5.7	5.4	7.0	22.9	41 782

1. Based on the resident population estimated as of July 1 of the year shown. 2. Total includes mining, construction, and manufacturing. 3. Includes private sector earnings in forestry, fishing, related activities, and other; utilities; wholesale trade; transportation and warehousing; and information.

Table A. States — **Social Security, Employment, and Labor Force**

STATE	Social Security beneficiaries, December 2013		Supple-mental Security Income recipients, December 2013	Civilian employment and selected occupations,[2] 2013				Civilian labor force (annual average), 2014				
					Percent						Unemployed	
	Number	Rate[1]		Total	Management, business, science and art occupations	Services, sales, and office occupations	Construction and production occupations	Total (1,000)	Percent change, 2013–2014	Employed (1,000)	Total (1,000)	Rate[3]
	160	161	162	163	164	165	166	167	168	169	170	171
United States	56 480 451	178.5	8 362 414	145 128 676	36.3	42.6	21.1	155 922	0.3	146 305	9 617	6.2
Alabama	1 081 046	223.6	176 562	2 010 934	33.3	40.9	25.7	2 150	-0.9	2 004	146	6.8
Alaska	86 861	118.2	12 689	352 822	35.8	40.7	23.4	367	0.3	342	25	6.8
Arizona	1 174 944	177.3	118 216	2 791 546	35.1	46.1	18.8	3 091	1.6	2 878	213	6.9
Arkansas	666 172	225.1	112 741	1 241 828	31.9	41.0	27.1	1 301	-0.5	1 221	80	6.1
California	5 414 499	141.3	1 304 222	17 132 696	36.9	42.8	20.3	18 811	0.7	17 397	1 414	7.5
Colorado	774 056	146.9	72 154	2 593 798	40.1	41.6	18.3	2 817	1.3	2 676	141	5.0
Connecticut	648 466	180.3	62 537	1 771 141	40.4	42.5	17.1	1 885	0.9	1 760	125	6.6
Delaware	187 246	202.3	16 697	430 247	38.6	43.4	18.0	452	2.3	426	26	5.7
District of Columbia	78 416	121.3	26 806	333 111	61.7	32.4	5.8	377	1.1	348	29	7.8
Florida	4 114 745	210.4	548 178	8 459 990	33.6	48.3	18.1	9 638	1.7	9 034	603	6.3
Georgia	1 632 953	163.4	253 498	4 347 839	35.6	42.4	22.1	4 757	0.0	4 414	342	7.2
Hawaii	246 477	175.5	25 342	643 571	34.2	47.5	18.3	668	2.6	639	29	4.4
Idaho	298 269	185.0	30 317	710 293	33.0	42.3	24.7	777	0.8	740	37	4.8
Illinois	2 133 829	165.6	278 543	6 074 089	36.6	42.2	21.2	6 525	-0.5	6 064	460	7.1
Indiana	1 267 542	192.9	127 355	3 025 786	32.1	40.4	27.5	3 231	1.2	3 036	195	6.0
Iowa	609 067	197.1	50 849	1 576 091	34.3	40.4	25.3	1 705	1.9	1 629	75	4.4
Kansas	515 969	178.3	49 071	1 399 578	37.4	39.5	23.1	1 500	0.9	1 432	68	4.5
Kentucky	944 041	214.8	190 721	1 894 116	32.7	40.7	26.5	2 005	-2.5	1 875	130	6.5
Louisiana	842 160	182.1	181 598	2 011 783	32.1	43.1	24.8	2 157	2.4	2 020	138	6.4
Maine	320 482	241.3	37 428	643 378	34.6	42.5	22.9	699	-1.1	659	40	5.7
Maryland	917 497	154.8	117 605	2 983 367	44.5	40.1	15.4	3 111	-0.4	2 930	181	5.8
Massachusetts	1 206 184	180.2	188 015	3 398 003	44.0	40.4	15.6	3 557	1.4	3 353	205	5.8
Michigan	2 098 078	212.0	277 210	4 369 787	34.4	42.5	23.1	4 750	0.5	4 402	348	7.3
Minnesota	948 229	174.9	93 748	2 828 280	38.8	40.5	20.7	2 974	0.3	2 852	122	4.1
Mississippi	632 191	211.3	126 240	1 196 784	30.5	42.5	27.0	1 236	-3.0	1 140	96	7.8
Missouri	1 232 526	203.9	142 219	2 808 535	34.8	43.2	21.9	3 058	1.4	2 871	187	6.1
Montana	208 546	205.4	18 673	482 603	34.8	43.6	21.5	516	0.4	492	24	4.7
Nebraska	321 882	172.3	27 457	965 779	35.7	40.7	23.6	1 022	0.0	988	34	3.3
Nevada	459 536	164.7	48 817	1 262 730	28.0	53.0	19.0	1 395	0.8	1 286	108	7.8
New Hampshire	278 664	210.6	19 507	694 508	39.0	40.2	20.8	741	-0.1	709	32	4.3
New Jersey	1 548 525	174.0	180 354	4 252 626	40.4	42.0	17.6	4 519	-0.3	4 218	300	6.6
New Mexico	392 306	188.1	64 300	872 487	34.7	43.5	21.8	918	-0.5	858	60	6.5
New York	3 444 200	175.3	698 928	9 213 552	39.2	44.1	16.6	9 569	-0.7	8 964	605	6.3
North Carolina	1 907 394	193.7	234 362	4 355 481	35.9	41.8	22.3	4 656	-0.5	4 370	286	6.1
North Dakota	123 363	170.5	8 350	390 647	34.3	39.6	26.1	416	2.2	405	12	2.8
Ohio	2 239 797	193.6	311 195	5 347 801	34.9	41.6	23.5	5 719	-0.1	5 392	328	5.7
Oklahoma	741 822	192.7	97 616	1 716 784	32.5	42.4	25.1	1 784	-1.1	1 704	80	4.5
Oregon	777 832	197.9	83 264	1 785 619	36.7	42.3	20.9	1 942	1.6	1 807	135	6.9
Pennsylvania	2 697 111	211.1	379 194	5 987 761	36.5	42.0	21.6	6 378	-1.0	6 009	370	5.8
Rhode Island	214 095	203.6	33 133	515 340	36.8	44.2	19.0	553	-0.7	511	42	7.7
South Carolina	1 014 683	212.5	118 384	2 080 718	32.8	43.7	23.4	2 198	0.8	2 056	141	6.4
South Dakota	162 695	192.6	14 833	431 256	33.6	43.0	23.4	448	0.7	433	15	3.4
Tennessee	1 348 004	207.5	183 784	2 881 431	33.7	42.1	24.2	3 011	-2.3	2 811	201	6.7
Texas	3 756 420	142.0	666 258	12 074 980	34.9	42.2	22.9	13 112	1.6	12 448	664	5.1
Utah	356 984	123.1	31 093	1 327 452	37.0	42.0	21.0	1 431	1.5	1 377	54	3.8
Vermont	138 418	220.9	15 741	322 899	39.5	39.8	20.7	349	-0.6	335	14	4.1
Virginia	1 384 419	167.6	153 632	3 986 665	42.2	40.1	17.7	4 261	0.4	4 041	220	5.2
Washington	1 197 824	171.8	150 239	3 229 431	38.5	40.5	21.0	3 488	0.8	3 270	218	6.2
West Virginia	460 494	248.3	79 136	752 310	30.9	43.3	25.8	790	-1.3	739	52	6.5
Wisconsin	1 134 358	197.5	116 715	2 873 231	33.9	40.7	25.5	3 094	0.3	2 924	170	5.5
Wyoming	99 134	170.1	6 888	295 192	34.1	39.1	26.8	307	0.0	294	13	4.3

1. Per 1,000 resident population estimated as of July 1 of the year shown. 2. Persons 16 years old and over. 3. Percent of civilian labor force.

Table A. States — **Nonfarm Employment and Earnings**

STATE	Private nonfarm employment and earnings, 2014											
	Employed		Manufacturing			Employment (1,000)						
				Average earnings of production workers								
	Total (1,000)	Percent change, 2013–2014	Employment (1,000)	Hourly	Weekly	Construction	Transportation and public utilities	Wholesale trade	Retail trade	Information	Financial activities	Services[1]
	172	173	174	175	176	177	178	179	180	181	182	183
United States	139 042	1.9	12 188	19.56	822.24	6 138	5 193.3	5 826.0	15 364.3	2 740	7 979	60 854
Alabama	1 923	1.1	253	18.31	774.51	79.6	72.3	73.0	227.8	22.0	94.8	711.6
Alaska	337	0.4	14	20.38	703.11	17.3	21.6	6.5	36.8	6.2	12.2	122.5
Arizona	2 568	1.9	157	18.49	748.85	125.3	86.9	93.8	312.3	43.1	189.0	1 138.1
Arkansas	1 189	1.1	155	15.96	655.96	45.9	62.3	46.6	135.9	13.7	49.7	457.9
California	15 645	3.0	1 270	20.91	865.67	675.4	522.2	715.1	1 633.8	457.9	784.3	7 144.7
Colorado	2 461	3.3	137	25.05	986.97	142.3	77.8	99.7	254.3	69.9	153.3	1 085.1
Connecticut	1 666	0.8	160	22.40	913.92	55.5	52.6	63.0	185.6	31.8	128.6	750.8
Delaware	438	2.1	26	16.63	676.84	20.4	15.3	11.9	52.2	4.9	45.1	197.2
District of Columbia	754	0.7	1	NA	NA	14.3	4.3	4.9	21.6	17.2	30.3	425.4
Florida	7 825	3.2	331	20.09	837.75	397.4	254.2	327.8	1 040.6	136.2	522.7	3 734.7
Georgia	4 156	3.0	367	18.09	757.97	156.1	194.0	210.2	467.6	107.3	232.8	1 726.8
Hawaii	625	1.1	14	18.37	718.27	31.6	30.0	17.7	69.7	8.5	27.4	301.1
Idaho	655	2.7	60	21.49	878.94	36.0	22.4	29.2	80.3	9.3	33.0	262.3
Illinois	5 873	1.2	579	19.49	824.43	201.3	270.9	299.2	604.9	99.0	369.3	2 610.3
Indiana	2 980	1.5	507	18.77	782.71	122.6	138.6	117.6	319.2	35.6	128.3	1 177.6
Iowa	1 548	1.3	217	18.87	792.54	74.5	64.5	69.2	179.1	25.6	104.1	556.3
Kansas	1 393	1.5	162	18.51	790.38	59.9	56.4	61.5	145.8	27.9	79.8	531.9
Kentucky	1 858	1.5	235	19.73	864.17	72.4	97.2	74.4	205.1	26.3	89.8	717.8
Louisiana	1 981	1.4	148	22.04	994.00	139.3	88.4	73.4	227.4	26.0	91.8	803.9
Maine	604	0.4	50	20.55	861.05	25.8	17.7	19.7	81.6	7.5	30.4	269.2
Maryland	2 619	0.9	103	19.34	765.86	151.1	81.5	84.7	288.8	37.9	144.2	1 223.7
Massachusetts	3 414	1.6	250	21.40	877.40	127.7	88.8	123.7	348.9	86.2	208.0	1 727.9
Michigan	4 180	1.7	576	20.47	898.63	141.3	129.0	168.0	460.3	57.0	204.8	1 839.7
Minnesota	2 813	1.3	312	19.88	829.00	107.0	95.6	131.9	289.3	52.8	178.6	1 219.4
Mississippi	1 120	0.7	139	17.83	741.73	49.0	50.3	34.1	135.4	13.1	43.5	400.6
Missouri	2 734	0.9	256	19.02	796.94	109.8	97.5	120.9	304.3	57.2	164.2	1 187.9
Montana	454	1.0	19	17.29	651.83	24.8	18.6	17.0	57.3	6.5	24.9	187.6
Nebraska	993	1.3	97	17.19	715.10	47.0	53.3	42.7	107.9	17.1	72.5	385.2
Nevada	1 215	3.5	42	16.38	678.13	62.8	56.9	34.1	139.2	13.6	57.2	643.4
New Hampshire	648	1.2	67	18.76	767.28	23.3	15.1	27.1	94.6	12.0	35.8	282.1
New Jersey	3 962	0.7	243	19.55	793.73	141.9	168.5	213.8	455.0	75.1	247.0	1 796.5
New Mexico	820	0.8	28	16.71	663.39	42.6	24.0	21.7	92.5	12.4	33.4	345.9
New York	9 084	1.6	452	19.42	790.39	339.6	276.5	338.0	940.7	264.3	691.7	4 339.0
North Carolina	4 142	2.1	449	16.71	720.20	179.5	127.6	176.7	471.5	72.4	211.1	1 733.9
North Dakota	461	3.8	26	19.17	759.13	34.4	28.1	27.3	50.7	6.8	24.0	153.2
Ohio	5 331	1.3	673	19.80	843.48	194.1	196.4	232.4	564.4	72.6	288.3	2 336.1
Oklahoma	1 654	1.1	139	18.08	748.51	75.5	59.1	63.4	178.3	21.7	79.5	628.2
Oregon	1 717	2.8	179	19.31	776.26	79.2	56.8	72.3	195.8	32.2	92.1	710.4
Pennsylvania	5 790	0.8	567	19.02	781.72	231.0	250.6	225.8	634.4	85.2	315.2	2 731.5
Rhode Island	477	1.2	41	18.38	737.04	16.5	11.1	16.8	47.0	8.9	32.5	243.4
South Carolina	1 949	2.5	230	18.65	770.25	82.3	67.3	68.2	237.6	26.5	96.5	780.1
South Dakota	423	1.4	42	17.33	729.59	22.2	13.0	20.8	51.8	6.1	29.6	159.6
Tennessee	2 815	2.1	325	17.50	729.75	111.0	147.9	123.3	320.5	43.9	141.4	1 177.4
Texas	11 550	3.1	885	21.09	932.18	650.5	477.7	577.2	1 255.3	203.3	700.6	4 666.0
Utah	1 328	2.9	121	18.39	728.24	78.3	52.7	48.6	151.9	33.3	75.0	525.4
Vermont	310	1.1	31	18.45	706.64	14.7	8.6	9.2	37.9	4.8	12.1	134.7
Virginia	3 774	0.4	232	19.46	827.05	177.9	119.5	110.9	412.9	71.3	193.2	1 741.0
Washington	3 076	2.8	289	25.16	1 034.08	159.4	97.5	129.9	342.3	109.5	153.7	1 236.7
West Virginia	762	-0.4	48	19.29	798.61	33.4	25.3	22.6	86.9	9.6	30.9	322.3
Wisconsin	2 845	1.3	465	18.95	775.06	103.7	101.2	120.7	302.8	47.8	150.6	1 138.2
Wyoming	293	1.1	10	20.99	812.31	23.6	15.7	9.5	29.7	3.8	11.2	90.6

1. Includes professional and business services, educational and health services, leisure and hospitality, and other services.

STATE	Agriculture, 2012											
	Farms					Land in farms					Value of land and buildings (dollars)	
		Percent with:						Acres				
	Number	Fewer than 50 acres	500 acres or more	Farm operators whose principal occupation is farming (percent)	Government payments, average per farm (dollars)	Acreage (1,000)	Percent change, 2007–2012	Average size of farm	Total irrigated (1,000)	Total cropland (1,000)	Average per farm	Average per acre
	184	185	186	187	188	189	190	191	192	193	194	195
United States	2 109 303	38.6	15.0	47.8	9 925	914 528	-0.8	434	55 822	389 690	1 075 491	2 481
Alabama	43 223	37.4	8.6	44.2	6 802	8 903	-1.4	206	113	2 759	547 524	2 658
Alaska	762	56.2	11.3	54.1	12 473	834	-5.4	1 094	2	84	681 479	623
Arizona	20 005	79.9	8.1	66.1	10 245	26 249	0.5	1 312	881	1 151	844 065	643
Arkansas	45 071	30.8	13.0	47.3	20 013	13 811	-0.4	306	4 804	7 931	807 965	2 637
California	77 857	64.8	9.9	54.5	19 349	25 569	0.8	328	7 862	9 592	2 061 792	6 278
Colorado	36 180	39.4	24.3	49.6	14 897	31 887	0.9	881	2 517	10 650	1 128 277	1 280
Connecticut	5 977	69.8	1.8	46.3	9 328	437	7.6	73	9	151	809 375	11 082
Delaware	2 451	56.5	9.8	63.9	10 553	509	-0.3	208	127	439	1 694 584	8 166
District of Columbia	X	X	X	X	X	X	X	X	X	X	X	X
Florida	47 740	68.6	5.6	48.0	10 158	9 548	3.4	200	1 493	2 744	1 040 259	5 201
Georgia	42 257	39.9	10.4	47.0	9 793	9 621	-5.2	228	1 125	4 191	702 282	3 085
Hawaii	7 000	88.1	2.6	52.0	8 325	1 129	0.7	161	82	174	1 461 342	9 058
Idaho	24 816	47.9	17.1	49.8	10 673	11 497	2.3	474	3 365	5 793	1 052 941	2 222
Illinois	75 087	34.1	20.4	50.4	9 829	26 775	0.6	359	522	23 753	2 261 778	6 305
Indiana	58 695	46.6	12.8	43.7	8 331	14 773	-0.4	251	437	12 591	1 342 826	5 354
Iowa	88 637	30.9	22.4	54.1	11 262	30 748	-0.4	345	172	26 256	2 207 220	6 389
Kansas	61 773	19.0	31.6	48.3	10 426	46 346	-0.4	747	2 881	28 503	1 218 662	1 632
Kentucky	77 064	36.5	6.2	41.7	5 087	13 993	-6.7	169	74	6 336	512 033	3 024
Louisiana	28 093	43.7	11.6	43.2	14 625	8 110	-2.6	281	1 093	4 276	718 179	2 554
Maine	8 173	43.0	6.7	48.5	7 629	1 348	7.9	178	31	477	410 633	2 308
Maryland	12 256	49.2	7.6	48.9	7 784	2 052	-1.0	166	105	1 396	1 148 268	6 930
Massachusetts	7 755	67.5	1.5	50.0	10 416	518	1.1	68	23	161	704 071	10 430
Michigan	52 194	43.9	8.8	48.4	7 567	10 032	-0.8	191	592	7 669	766 148	4 020
Minnesota	74 542	25.2	18.2	52.9	8 962	26 918	-3.3	349	524	21 597	1 474 057	4 220
Mississippi	38 076	28.1	11.8	43.0	10 983	11 456	-4.6	287	1 652	5 076	652 593	2 273
Missouri	99 171	25.5	13.7	44.2	7 834	29 027	-2.6	285	1 181	15 259	795 444	2 791
Montana	28 008	28.1	42.2	55.1	16 865	61 388	-2.7	2 134	1 903	17 022	1 674 568	785
Nebraska	49 969	23.3	37.7	59.7	11 436	45 480	-0.3	907	8 297	21 597	2 159 268	2 380
Nevada	4 137	53.2	18.9	53.0	9 566	5 865	0.8	1 429	688	757	1 324 673	927
New Hampshire	4 391	55.5	3.5	48.0	7 434	472	0.5	108	3	98	449 848	4 167
New Jersey	9 071	71.2	3.1	49.5	7 332	733	-2.5	79	88	457	1 008 402	12 792
New Mexico	24 721	51.3	25.3	50.1	12 829	43 238	-0.1	1 748	680	1 977	755 185	432
New York	35 537	32.6	8.4	57.4	7 955	7 175	0.1	202	60	4 217	525 587	2 600
North Carolina	50 218	48.1	6.8	48.9	8 332	8 475	-0.7	168	175	4 745	726 944	4 338
North Dakota	30 961	11.0	48.8	56.6	15 398	39 675	-1.0	1 268	218	27 147	1 808 801	1 426
Ohio	75 462	41.1	8.3	43.9	6 603	13 957	0.0	185	47	10 749	894 933	4 837
Oklahoma	80 245	25.0	19.0	42.1	8 634	35 087	-2.1	428	480	11 279	573 858	1 340
Oregon	35 439	61.5	10.6	49.9	16 054	16 400	-0.6	460	1 630	4 690	865 613	1 882
Pennsylvania	59 309	39.3	4.1	51.7	5 395	7 809	-1.3	130	39	4 546	704 712	5 425
Rhode Island	1 243	71.1	0.9	49.8	12 344	68	2.6	56	4	23	786 093	14 041
South Carolina	25 266	44.1	8.1	41.0	6 867	4 889	1.7	197	159	1 967	586 518	2 981
South Dakota	31 989	19.6	43.6	58.9	12 451	43 666	-0.9	1 352	379	19 147	2 281 026	1 687
Tennessee	68 050	39.4	5.5	41.8	4 184	10 970	-0.9	160	146	5 330	569 416	3 565
Texas	248 809	37.7	15.8	42.1	12 293	130 399	-0.2	523	4 489	29 148	876 614	1 676
Utah	18 027	57.9	12.3	38.5	8 584	11 095	-1.1	609	1 104	1 646	888 886	1 460
Vermont	7 338	39.2	7.3	51.5	8 929	1 233	1.5	171	4	488	546 627	3 205
Virginia	46 030	38.6	7.7	45.1	7 719	8 104	2.4	180	69	2 991	776 719	4 306
Washington	37 249	63.2	11.0	47.4	22 014	14 973	-1.5	396	1 634	7 527	910 249	2 299
West Virginia	21 489	28.3	5.8	42.6	3 203	3 698	-2.5	168	2	804	413 407	2 463
Wisconsin	69 754	32.2	8.8	49.8	6 093	15 191	-4.1	209	422	9 911	819 551	3 924
Wyoming	11 736	28.8	36.3	49.8	10 027	30 170	0.6	2 587	1 436	2 419	1 759 200	680

STATE	Agriculture, 2012 (cont.)							Land, 2010			
		Value of products sold				Percent of farms with sales of:					
				Percent from:							
	Value of machinery and equipment, average per farm (dollars)	Total (mil dol)	Average per farm (dollars)	Crops	Livestock and poultry products	$10,000 or more	$100,000 or more	Cropland (percent)	Owned by the federal government (percent)	Developed (percent)	Water consumption, 2010 (mil gal per day)
	196	197	198	199	200	201	202	203	204	205	206
United States	115 706	394 644	187 097	53.8	46.2	43.4	18.4	18.6	20.7	5.8	351 417.1
Alabama	71 211	5 571	128 894	23.6	76.4	33.8	11.2	6.7	3.0	8.6	9 960.0
Alaska	87 445	59	77 329	42.2	57.8	42.3	11.4	NA	NA	NA	1 094.5
Arizona	63 624	3 732	186 559	55.6	44.4	20.3	7.3	1.2	41.7	2.9	6 088.2
Arkansas	115 438	9 776	216 897	49.5	50.5	44.0	16.7	21.2	9.1	5.4	11 327.0
California	124 720	42 627	547 510	71.2	28.8	57.0	26.4	9.0	45.9	6.1	37 962.2
Colorado	110 134	7 781	215 060	31.3	68.7	37.7	15.6	12.1	35.7	2.8	10 994.2
Connecticut	58 958	551	92 123	70.7	29.3	30.0	7.7	5.5	0.5	33.7	3 311.0
Delaware	161 559	1 274	519 794	33.7	66.3	64.6	41.7	26.9	2.0	18.8	717.5
District of Columbia	X	X	X	X	X	X	X	NA	NA	NA	0.1
Florida	60 845	7 702	161 322	77.5	22.5	34.3	11.0	7.3	10.1	14.6	14 936.0
Georgia	93 146	9 255	219 020	39.7	60.3	37.4	17.3	10.9	5.6	12.3	4 718.8
Hawaii	43 999	661	94 478	81.5	18.5	41.6	7.2	2.8	8.7	5.8	1 273.8
Idaho	143 835	7 801	314 372	44.1	55.9	44.3	20.5	9.6	62.7	1.7	17 230.5
Illinois	203 192	17 187	228 895	82.3	17.7	54.5	33.0	66.2	1.4	9.5	13 091.3
Indiana	143 252	11 211	191 001	67.2	32.8	48.3	24.4	57.4	2.0	10.8	8 643.0
Iowa	213 856	30 822	347 728	56.3	43.7	62.8	41.0	71.6	0.5	5.4	3 070.5
Kansas	156 740	18 461	298 845	37.8	62.2	56.0	25.5	49.0	1.0	4.0	4 004.8
Kentucky	70 190	5 067	65 755	45.0	55.0	36.5	8.2	20.5	5.0	8.1	4 326.5
Louisiana	104 418	3 809	135 600	73.1	26.9	33.0	11.7	15.9	4.2	6.0	8 540.3
Maine	69 780	763	93 364	62.1	37.9	34.6	9.5	1.7	1.0	4.1	449.3
Maryland	115 879	2 271	185 329	46.3	53.7	43.1	20.6	17.8	2.1	19.1	7 382.0
Massachusetts	53 948	492	63 470	77.8	22.2	32.7	9.8	4.3	1.8	32.8	2 995.9
Michigan	122 533	8 678	166 265	63.5	36.5	44.0	18.0	21.2	8.8	11.3	10 837.2
Minnesota	197 715	21 280	285 479	65.2	34.8	60.0	33.5	39.0	6.2	4.5	3 821.2
Mississippi	91 917	6 441	169 162	46.2	53.8	33.0	12.4	15.4	5.9	6.0	3 933.0
Missouri	88 960	9 165	92 415	49.8	50.2	46.8	12.5	30.3	4.3	6.7	8 568.5
Montana	137 625	4 230	151 031	53.3	46.7	50.4	26.2	14.9	28.8	1.1	7 645.2
Nebraska	230 222	23 069	461 661	49.3	50.7	68.5	43.0	39.8	1.3	2.4	8 036.3
Nevada	134 658	764	184 710	47.9	52.1	42.0	21.2	0.8	84.6	0.8	2 623.1
New Hampshire	56 439	191	43 477	52.8	47.2	26.6	6.0	2.0	12.8	12.2	1 214.6
New Jersey	81 470	1 007	111 006	88.5	11.5	36.1	12.3	9.5	2.8	35.3	5 670.7
New Mexico	60 610	2 550	103 157	24.2	75.8	24.4	7.0	1.9	34.0	1.7	3 161.0
New York	117 163	5 415	152 380	41.5	58.5	49.2	20.0	16.2	0.7	12.2	10 574.5
North Carolina	92 887	12 588	250 670	34.2	65.8	37.3	16.6	15.3	7.4	14.2	12 420.1
North Dakota	300 334	10 951	353 693	88.3	11.7	59.0	40.6	54.3	3.9	2.2	1 147.1
Ohio	116 899	10 064	133 366	65.6	34.4	47.4	20.3	42.0	1.4	15.8	9 442.8
Oklahoma	74 212	7 130	88 848	26.3	73.7	40.8	10.0	19.8	2.6	4.8	3 168.2
Oregon	90 222	4 884	137 805	66.5	33.5	35.6	13.1	5.6	50.3	2.3	6 734.5
Pennsylvania	89 735	7 401	124 783	37.6	62.4	48.1	19.9	17.1	2.5	15.1	8 134.9
Rhode Island	56 065	60	47 990	82.1	17.9	35.7	8.7	2.2	0.4	28.2	375.5
South Carolina	72 400	3 040	120 323	42.6	57.4	27.0	8.6	11.1	5.2	13.3	6 782.2
South Dakota	241 388	10 170	317 929	59.7	40.3	65.0	40.7	35.4	6.3	1.9	625.8
Tennessee	69 248	3 611	53 064	57.8	42.2	30.2	6.1	16.0	4.8	11.5	7 696.6
Texas	72 185	25 376	101 988	29.0	71.0	29.7	7.0	14.2	1.7	5.1	24 796.7
Utah	84 537	1 816	100 746	31.6	68.4	37.2	11.0	2.8	63.1	1.6	4 463.8
Vermont	86 947	776	105 765	22.9	77.1	40.6	15.1	8.9	6.9	6.4	430.5
Virginia	72 561	3 753	81 540	36.2	63.8	37.9	9.6	9.9	9.8	11.5	7 648.0
Washington	98 588	9 121	244 859	71.2	28.8	34.2	16.4	13.9	27.1	5.8	4 955.8
West Virginia	50 027	807	37 544	17.2	82.8	25.3	4.0	4.7	7.8	7.4	3 533.0
Wisconsin	129 561	11 744	168 370	39.2	60.8	52.3	24.6	28.4	5.1	7.7	6 157.6
Wyoming	114 212	1 689	143 952	26.0	74.0	48.8	23.5	3.6	45.9	1.1	4 701.5

STATE	Manufactures, 2013										Construction, 2007				
	All employees			Production workers								Employees			
						Wages									
	Number (1,000)	Percent change, 2011–2013	Annual payroll (mil dol)	Number (1,000)	Work hours (millions)	Total (mil dol)	Average per worker (dollars)	Value added by manufacture (mil dol)	Value of shipments (mil dol)	Total cost of materials (mil dol)	Number of establishments	Number	Percent change, 2002–2007	Value (mil dol)	Annual payroll (mil dol)
	207	208	209	210	211	212	213	214	215	216	217	218	219	220	221
United States	11 082	4.1	602 878	7 747	15 736	340 635	43 967	2 398 392	5 846 768	3 456 983	729 345	7 316 240	1.7	1 731 842	331 003
Alabama	233	9.4	11 426	176	362	7 420	42 210	47 357	128 280	81 507	9 239	107 166	8.7	24 714	4 188
Alaska	12	9.1	521	10	20	369	38 827	1 726	7 444	5 792	2 404	22 082	3.4	6 263	1 352
Arizona	130	2.4	8 207	74	149	3 311	44 758	27 451	52 848	25 142	15 470	221 585	26.7	56 159	9 182
Arkansas	151	3.4	6 380	122	247	4 526	37 001	25 152	62 128	36 902	5 764	50 407	8.1	10 341	1 814
California	1 138	2.2	70 111	724	1 452	32 522	44 931	245 765	524 494	279 418	72 173	873 789	0.4	217 933	43 134
Colorado	112	1.8	6 351	74	148	3 267	44 109	23 683	52 196	28 530	17 787	173 559	-1.0	42 990	7 711
Connecticut	163	5.2	10 761	98	197	4 823	49 346	34 068	58 164	24 893	9 004	71 649	-6.5	18 056	3 830
Delaware	26	-3.7	1 433	18	36	797	43 331	5 923	22 220	16 439	2 724	25 646	2.0	5 609	1 150
District of Columbia	1	0.0	56	1	1	31	41 112	151	249	99	375	7 833	30.7	2 473	422
Florida	271	6.3	14 455	180	358	7 387	40 984	51 285	101 260	50 647	51 143	473 703	11.5	117 804	19 587
Georgia	334	6.7	16 060	253	517	9 958	39 352	66 159	161 453	95 722	20 568	223 557	1.0	59 375	9 651
Hawaii	11	0.0	465	7	13	268	38 779	1 140	6 418	5 264	2 771	35 523	30.2	10 420	1 907
Idaho	53	10.4	2 608	39	78	1 618	41 188	8 815	20 840	12 071	7 919	50 382	39.6	10 052	1 730
Illinois	545	1.9	29 949	382	777	16 531	43 274	112 179	284 863	172 801	30 236	272 682	-11.9	72 778	14 623
Indiana	454	5.8	23 876	342	705	15 402	45 013	100 326	245 119	144 352	15 640	147 467	-0.5	30 164	6 456
Iowa	203	5.7	10 197	148	300	6 171	41 701	45 848	119 366	73 606	8 019	70 357	4.7	14 961	2 900
Kansas	159	5.3	8 346	114	230	5 196	45 596	28 874	89 324	59 728	7 159	67 769	-1.3	13 829	2 793
Kentucky	215	6.4	10 580	167	341	7 350	43 944	44 475	133 906	89 579	8 615	83 154	-0.9	16 493	3 131
Louisiana	131	4.8	8 407	94	196	5 173	55 273	57 752	263 037	205 182	8 564	135 781	9.7	25 569	5 806
Maine	48	0.0	2 464	36	70	1 618	45 546	7 942	16 507	8 567	4 942	29 908	-1.6	5 441	1 128
Maryland	98	-5.8	5 954	60	121	2 706	45 289	22 098	40 516	18 553	15 618	191 293	5.5	44 327	8 953
Massachusetts	232	3.6	14 770	139	277	6 496	46 848	46 539	82 533	36 151	17 194	135 485	-18.2	36 835	7 470
Michigan	525	13.9	28 908	382	795	18 045	47 235	98 438	250 874	153 269	21 790	160 110	-26.9	35 373	7 244
Minnesota	296	2.1	16 268	193	387	8 220	42 635	55 721	126 899	71 234	15 863	134 584	-9.3	37 052	6 821
Mississippi	133	3.9	5 953	103	209	3 969	38 470	22 522	66 029	43 436	4 737	55 936	13.7	11 765	2 093
Missouri	236	2.2	12 053	174	346	7 594	43 574	46 364	109 517	62 367	15 230	164 362	6.8	35 463	7 141
Montana	16	23.1	787	11	22	477	43 350	3 592	12 443	9 114	5 316	30 353	34.9	6 158	1 105
Nebraska	91	1.1	4 100	70	144	2 768	39 351	20 041	57 683	37 782	5 447	44 605	-3.0	8 490	1 667
Nevada	38	-2.6	2 100	26	52	1 145	44 668	8 720	16 178	7 480	5 280	122 900	29.0	29 314	5 743
New Hampshire	66	-5.7	3 938	40	81	1 746	43 510	10 628	19 381	8 925	4 357	30 054	-10.4	5 960	1 366
New Jersey	223	-5.1	13 730	143	290	6 606	46 067	43 341	103 300	60 091	23 142	180 251	-14.4	46 383	9 643
New Mexico	25	0.0	1 299	17	34	752	44 714	13 790	25 169	11 306	5 306	55 006	21.5	10 324	2 003
New York	414	-1.2	22 013	277	552	11 756	42 375	72 861	144 754	72 407	43 409	349 415	-5.6	90 318	18 393
North Carolina	400	3.1	18 612	298	600	11 455	38 404	106 757	212 569	106 457	25 457	242 488	7.6	55 786	9 364
North Dakota	23	4.5	1 079	18	35	687	39 180	5 729	15 552	9 939	2 082	19 378	14.9	3 674	768
Ohio	629	5.0	33 854	451	930	20 489	45 425	124 349	320 150	196 248	22 937	224 342	-12.8	48 315	10 016
Oklahoma	128	2.4	6 563	94	196	4 150	44 074	24 257	74 969	50 397	7 611	69 842	11.4	14 132	2 608
Oregon	147	14.0	7 699	103	207	4 379	42 362	37 145	63 488	26 428	13 434	102 974	17.0	23 265	4 443
Pennsylvania	534	0.8	28 358	376	760	16 621	44 255	103 791	235 470	132 292	28 505	265 925	-4.1	59 187	12 480
Rhode Island	38	5.6	2 037	25	50	1 064	42 044	6 053	11 522	5 610	3 587	21 658	-20.6	5 777	1 082
South Carolina	208	7.2	10 476	157	320	6 629	42 350	39 443	104 350	65 253	12 118	108 199	-2.4	22 820	3 910
South Dakota	42	7.7	1 799	30	63	1 137	37 392	6 483	16 967	10 458	3 128	20 601	8.2	3 944	723
Tennessee	291	5.1	14 471	212	425	8 863	41 878	61 365	143 613	82 362	10 907	124 488	0.4	27 964	5 210
Texas	760	8.4	43 747	524	1 094	24 916	47 530	239 012	731 708	493 340	37 200	596 499	7.5	146 638	26 534
Utah	107	7.0	5 798	71	144	3 163	44 355	21 891	48 418	26 968	10 055	88 880	31.5	20 012	3 375
Vermont	29	3.6	1 509	19	39	792	41 262	3 885	9 209	5 288	2 838	17 475	10.0	3 171	678
Virginia	224	0.9	11 991	158	321	6 920	43 677	57 435	99 971	42 318	22 431	235 312	11.1	51 968	10 004
Washington	249	8.3	15 012	164	328	8 328	50 791	62 637	139 165	78 586	22 382	199 064	18.6	48 104	9 568
West Virginia	46	-8.0	2 564	35	71	1 649	47 639	10 912	24 566	13 553	3 992	31 965	9.3	5 033	1 200
Wisconsin	434	1.4	22 175	311	628	12 938	41 635	83 725	179 294	95 569	14 673	126 261	-11.2	28 611	5 941
Wyoming	10	25.0	610	7	15	437	59 190	2 797	10 396	7 563	2 803	22 534	30.1	4 250	956

Table A. States — **Wholesale Trade and Retail Trade**

STATE	Wholesale trade, 2007					Retail trade,[1] 2007								
		Employees					Employees							
	Number of establishments	Number	Percent change, 2002–2007	Sales (mil dol)	Annual payroll (mil dol)	Number of establishments	Total	Percent change, 2002–2007	Motor vehicle and parts dealers	Food and beverage stores	Clothing and clothing accessory stores	General merchandise stores	Sales (mil dol)	Annual payroll (mil dol)
	222	223	224	225	226	227	228	229	230	231	232	233	234	235
United States	434 983	6 227 389	5.9	6 515 709	336 207	1 128 112	15 515 396	5.9	1 914 466	2 827 162	1 644 025	2 763 474	3 917 663	362 819
Alabama	5 663	81 076	8.2	68 625	3 600	19 722	238 922	7.4	31 887	35 110	23 832	54 410	57 345	5 112
Alaska	753	9 063	22.1	7 355	443	2 641	34 977	6.0	4 517	7 519	2 333	8 105	9 303	937
Arizona	7 045	102 200	15.4	85 607	5 224	19 384	337 529	25.7	47 174	67 301	28 497	64 405	86 759	8 011
Arkansas	3 501	47 949	11.8	63 511	2 019	11 906	140 018	4.3	D	18 949	10 948	D	32 974	2 889
California	61 451	888 079	9.5	925 328	53 724	114 438	1 683 023	10.4	212 872	323 171	212 039	262 169	455 032	44 329
Colorado	7 290	105 366	4.2	101 410	6 147	19 428	261 962	5.9	31 207	46 934	24 488	46 357	65 897	6 538
Connecticut	4 620	75 993	-3.9	143 640	4 923	13 807	196 133	2.3	23 359	41 163	24 850	23 395	52 165	5 160
Delaware	983	19 452	-8.1	28 365	1 467	3 907	55 432	6.8	7 360	8 859	5 468	8 764	14 202	1 323
District of Columbia	416	5 184	-10.3	3 247	333	1 827	19 117	3.3	D	5 287	4 003	D	3 844	486
Florida	32 361	326 878	9.2	323 340	15 150	73 794	1 016 290	12.6	132 389	199 431	118 091	174 854	262 341	24 050
Georgia	14 165	213 227	6.1	254 298	11 604	36 218	475 344	6.2	62 488	83 542	51 939	89 896	117 517	10 760
Hawaii	1 844	20 252	4.3	12 672	836	5 012	70 661	10.8	7 390	12 966	12 215	12 724	17 612	1 766
Idaho	2 103	26 519	15.6	20 210	1 136	6 300	80 447	15.5	12 293	10 928	4 892	16 553	20 527	1 834
Illinois	20 062	320 942	-3.2	405 962	18 813	43 055	639 147	6.3	72 057	111 756	68 703	117 382	165 451	14 895
Indiana	8 147	115 868	5.7	101 259	5 324	23 692	333 172	-3.0	42 332	50 449	28 083	70 472	78 746	7 123
Iowa	5 017	64 891	4.6	55 108	2 724	13 203	177 156	0.5	21 717	34 508	13 035	33 571	39 235	3 561
Kansas	4 544	57 551	-0.6	69 668	2 789	11 463	149 672	3.3	18 661	26 074	12 203	30 111	34 538	3 134
Kentucky	4 485	70 882	2.4	94 546	3 409	16 404	214 782	0.3	26 128	33 299	17 512	47 875	50 406	4 502
Louisiana	5 614	75 568	2.7	67 152	3 460	17 135	231 365	1.3	30 846	35 276	22 636	47 780	56 543	5 096
Maine	1 629	18 734	-3.6	12 458	790	6 911	83 279	3.8	10 679	17 274	6 140	11 617	20 444	1 894
Maryland	5 997	99 648	6.6	83 494	5 590	19 601	294 806	3.2	39 773	57 680	35 385	45 187	75 664	7 291
Massachusetts	8 765	152 513	-1.6	145 729	10 030	25 469	360 218	0.3	36 748	90 032	45 200	38 996	88 083	8 916
Michigan	12 047	172 356	-3.2	226 532	9 367	37 619	470 794	-9.6	48 960	76 602	45 331	105 937	109 103	10 001
Minnesota	8 623	138 822	9.5	140 335	8 537	20 777	307 034	0.2	32 763	53 089	26 289	57 166	71 384	6 686
Mississippi	2 922	37 214	5.4	27 995	1 466	12 452	141 426	4.1	17 947	18 625	12 686	34 157	33 751	2 911
Missouri	8 338	129 138	1.4	117 329	5 802	23 360	317 318	1.8	40 043	45 890	26 639	65 680	76 575	7 155
Montana	1 461	14 184	3.3	10 741	559	5 258	58 883	11.3	8 311	8 692	3 659	9 791	14 687	1 318
Nebraska	3 093	38 752	5.3	34 283	1 721	7 888	108 209	2.4	12 325	18 326	7 804	20 056	26 487	2 231
Nevada	3 046	41 664	31.1	27 115	2 031	8 492	139 829	24.5	18 723	22 123	19 203	24 415	37 434	3 692
New Hampshire	1 886	24 960	6.0	19 023	1 490	6 603	98 333	4.8	12 937	20 704	8 378	14 523	25 354	2 380
New Jersey	16 174	283 501	3.5	366 292	18 714	34 482	460 843	6.0	48 275	107 638	63 287	57 782	124 814	12 050
New Mexico	2 036	22 943	15.5	14 702	966	7 208	97 385	8.9	13 659	13 897	7 455	20 724	24 470	2 251
New York	34 672	412 962	-0.1	438 854	23 018	76 637	892 863	6.6	78 920	194 012	138 550	114 888	230 718	22 337
North Carolina	12 256	180 664	11.4	148 758	9 342	36 592	466 577	7.2	62 076	75 817	47 335	87 515	114 578	10 343
North Dakota	1 525	17 596	10.3	15 408	741	3 361	44 054	6.6	5 853	7 242	2 947	8 011	10 527	891
Ohio	15 332	243 652	3.8	241 334	12 100	40 075	591 237	-3.4	72 230	99 666	50 924	114 955	138 816	12 729
Oklahoma	4 584	61 265	12.0	66 516	2 802	13 554	170 984	1.8	D	21 975	14 278	D	43 095	3 610
Oregon	5 789	77 547	4.0	72 660	3 943	14 991	204 793	11.5	27 048	38 697	17 632	40 184	50 371	4 916
Pennsylvania	15 769	246 422	5.3	229 254	13 164	46 532	672 042	1.5	80 992	143 626	65 190	108 007	166 843	14 862
Rhode Island	1 479	21 502	21.6	12 557	1 062	4 080	50 865	0.4	5 484	11 571	5 639	5 973	12 286	1 215
South Carolina	5 034	68 229	13.0	55 125	3 111	18 886	231 685	8.8	28 786	41 184	26 215	42 730	54 298	4 878
South Dakota	1 425	15 655	4.6	14 765	623	4 172	50 842	3.4	6 713	9 025	2 880	9 028	12 266	1 045
Tennessee	7 413	123 575	1.3	126 919	6 065	24 234	320 739	5.3	42 090	48 065	31 283	65 120	77 547	7 245
Texas	31 898	495 225	12.6	663 680	27 146	78 795	1 138 440	10.9	156 304	192 056	125 866	224 986	311 335	26 395
Utah	3 659	52 935	20.1	38 764	2 503	8 984	142 266	16.9	18 008	22 968	12 114	26 087	36 574	3 241
Vermont	852	10 628	-1.5	5 893	472	3 852	40 416	0.8	5 116	9 473	3 301	2 499	9 310	939
Virginia	7 740	120 111	13.7	94 659	6 059	29 633	431 634	7.4	57 291	70 445	47 329	75 598	105 663	9 992
Washington	9 743	132 047	9.0	116 016	6 919	23 075	328 053	10.6	44 839	59 754	29 651	59 721	92 969	8 585
West Virginia	1 580	20 653	2.4	15 506	868	7 047	92 227	3.2	11 609	16 316	6 260	20 406	20 539	1 776
Wisconsin	7 326	117 706	4.4	94 009	5 707	21 205	320 140	2.7	37 848	56 874	21 749	60 781	72 283	6 778
Wyoming	826	7 646	22.2	7 699	372	2 951	32 033	11.2	4 644	5 302	1 659	5 766	8 958	758

1. Establishments with payroll.

STATE	Information, 2007										
		Employees									
	Number of establishments	Number	Percent change, 2002–2007	Publishing, except Internet	Motion picture and sound recording	Broadcasting, except Internet	Internet publishing and broad-casting and web search portals	Telecom-munications	Data processing, hosting, and related services	Receipts (mil dol)	Annual payroll (mil dol)
	236	237	238	239	240	241	242	243	244	245	246
United States	141 566	3 496 773	-6.4	1 093 047	335 807	294 876	75 506	1 250 993	393 741	1 072 342.856	228 837
Alabama	1 700	40 054	0.1	13 226	2 109	3 991	110	16 907	3 562	NA	1 875
Alaska	407	6 754	-5.4	983	590	926	D	4 121	103	NA	374
Arizona	2 275	52 573	-7.4	15 967	3 690	4 143	524	17 966	9 635	NA	3 006
Arkansas	1 034	26 074	-17.1	D	D	D	D	9 273	D	NA	1 343
California	21 068	556 535	-1.3	166 140	142 848	35 660	30 580	129 756	47 851	NA	48 147
Colorado	3 183	84 564	-17.2	24 635	4 730	5 621	D	35 283	13 369	NA	5 663
Connecticut	1 834	40 345	-16.3	12 288	D	4 073	D	13 380	4 805	NA	2 556
Delaware	383	8 565	4.9	D	D	D	D	3 537	D	NA	457
District of Columbia	749	24 499	-14.1	10 544	D	D	934	4 689	D	NA	2 129
Florida	8 296	175 382	-5.0	50 552	13 190	17 527	1 783	73 873	17 265	NA	9 663
Georgia	4 328	122 496	-15.7	29 487	6 548	12 544	2 971	54 327	14 641	NA	8 156
Hawaii	622	10 083	-13.6	2 409	1 080	1 012	52	4 672	797	NA	510
Idaho	717	15 163	37.9	3 267	866	1 352	D	7 681	1 828	NA	528
Illinois	5 696	136 589	-8.9	45 443	9 545	9 391	3 221	46 662	20 343	NA	8 630
Indiana	2 282	45 786	-7.7	14 847	3 746	4 461	112	17 838	4 375	NA	2 089
Iowa	1 590	34 397	-22.2	11 130	1 758	2 716	45	10 635	8 066	NA	1 426
Kansas	1 502	52 737	6.0	9 902	1 653	2 622	182	33 823	3 597	NA	3 064
Kentucky	1 594	33 996	15.4	7 694	1 837	3 219	572	12 130	7 836	NA	1 252
Louisiana	1 455	30 537	-2.8	5 866	2 191	3 468	68	17 171	1 609	NA	1 361
Maine	777	13 520	14.7	4 235	546	1 225	102	5 353	852	NA	523
Maryland	2 571	63 081	-13.2	15 239	D	6 334	D	26 069	9 536	NA	3 764
Massachusetts	3 772	110 038	-11.7	51 791	4 212	5 552	D	30 501	13 623	NA	8 623
Michigan	3 791	77 639	-20.0	26 606	6 017	6 296	347	28 682	9 182	NA	4 314
Minnesota	2 772	70 314	0.2	32 666	4 123	4 831	637	18 110	9 547	NA	4 232
Mississippi	1 017	15 902	-19.9	3 290	970	1 930	D	8 728	761	NA	646
Missouri	2 627	73 040	-11.1	20 630	3 802	5 463	510	28 911	13 041	NA	3 880
Montana	638	9 500	1.5	2 648	D	1 135	D	3 949	1 023	NA	343
Nebraska	957	20 217	-10.3	7 748	1 316	1 809	D	5 361	3 338	NA	984
Nevada	1 109	17 914	0.4	4 621	1 775	2 787	389	6 907	1 368	NA	973
New Hampshire	790	15 482	5.9	8 604	824	666	D	4 387	710	NA	1 149
New Jersey	4 092	134 356	5.0	46 384	D	D	D	61 510	13 802	NA	8 950
New Mexico	828	13 987	-7.6	3 017	1 186	1 503	D	7 737	412	NA	495
New York	11 326	301 340	-2.1	94 777	34 555	48 850	D	77 655	21 289	NA	22 538
North Carolina	3 481	76 413	-1.5	23 062	4 656	6 291	609	33 854	6 856	NA	4 263
North Dakota	367	7 124	-7.5	2 910	345	1 261	D	1 790	611	NA	332
Ohio	4 199	97 360	-13.8	32 911	5 711	7 982	5 160	34 879	10 095	NA	5 178
Oklahoma	1 585	32 481	-10.8	D	D	D	D	17 759	D	NA	1 463
Oregon	1 992	39 258	-1.7	13 074	3 121	3 330	325	12 853	6 211	NA	2 055
Pennsylvania	5 302	137 115	-4.7	45 951	7 704	9 256	756	54 148	13 664	NA	7 774
Rhode Island	394	8 059	-8.4	2 778	374	927	D	3 097	386	NA	416
South Carolina	1 410	33 052	11.3	8 239	1 825	3 324	152	16 878	2 213	NA	1 581
South Dakota	437	7 296	-8.8	1 968	475	1 177	D	3 170	462	NA	313
Tennessee	2 491	50 778	-6.3	13 093	5 330	6 313	D	21 126	4 465	NA	2 370
Texas	9 541	250 410	-11.4	62 632	14 855	18 854	1 548	111 021	39 565	NA	15 460
Utah	1 412	33 310	-4.8	11 345	3 278	1 726	918	9 619	6 121	NA	1 762
Vermont	514	6 048	-17.6	1 993	404	720	D	1 778	637	NA	255
Virginia	4 064	104 147	-20.5	27 600	5 140	7 133	D	48 597	13 230	NA	7 533
Washington	3 301	111 840	10.0	59 057	5 065	4 532	2 532	29 709	9 182	NA	11 277
West Virginia	679	10 285	-18.8	2 633	553	1 541	6	4 726	764	NA	387
Wisconsin	2 286	54 179	-2.0	19 751	3 497	5 327	307	16 856	8 376	NA	2 625
Wyoming	329	4 159	-1.4	1 293	499	515	D	1 549	234	NA	151

STATE	Utilities, 2007					Transportation and warehousing, 2007					Finance and insurance, 2007				
	Number of establishments	Employees: Number	Employees: Percent change, 2002–2007	Receipts (mil dol)	Annual payroll (mil dol)	Number of establishments	Employees: Number	Employees: Percent change, 2002–2007	Receipts (mil dol)	Annual payroll (mil dol)	Number of establishments	Employees: Number	Employees: Percent change, 2002–2007	Receipts (mil dol)	Annual payroll (mil dol)
	247	248	249	250	251	252	253	254	255	256	257	258	259	260	261
United States	16 578	637 247	-3.9	584 193	51 654	219 706	4 454 383	22.0	639 916	173 183	501 713	6 607 511	0.4	3 669 303	502 417
Alabama	373	14 396	-10.1	NA	1 171	3 266	61 799	19.0	8 167	2 210	7 059	72 010	-3.0	NA	3 912
Alaska	90	1 731	0.6	NA	125	1 125	20 143	30.3	5 495	1 114	810	7 778	9.5	NA	437
Arizona	227	11 957	NA	NA	952	3 405	83 777	10.1	9 626	3 271	10 496	147 894	NA	NA	7 997
Arkansas	346	7 127	-3.1	NA	514	2 613	60 118	1.9	7 420	2 199	4 579	37 798	11.3	NA	1 685
California	1 145	63 954	11.3	NA	5 437	21 616	452 017	13.8	70 603	18 055	54 395	720 191	5.7	NA	57 431
Colorado	371	8 468	-0.4	NA	614	3 463	64 731	36.9	10 471	2 450	10 905	107 119	5.2	NA	6 920
Connecticut	151	10 210	-3.5	NA	997	1 714	44 117	9.7	5 273	1 739	6 431	137 353	-5.9	NA	16 598
Delaware	49	2 615	-2.1	NA	224	725	11 638	33.7	1 050	402	2 117	42 443	-11.8	NA	3 031
District of Columbia	37	2 029	NA	NA	201	197	8 810	52.5	3 765	607	1 036	19 474	NA	NA	2 486
Florida	588	30 920	8.6	NA	2 218	13 417	218 128	23.7	40 830	8 204	34 389	371 543	8.8	NA	21 520
Georgia	561	24 495	-3.8	NA	1 821	6 430	169 568	44.7	22 064	7 499	15 707	179 053	0.1	NA	11 189
Hawaii	54	2 953	20.8	NA	214	883	32 361	100.0	4 275	1 108	1 672	20 747	13.6	NA	1 095
Idaho	186	3 330	-10.1	NA	233	1 772	16 991	31.7	2 198	544	2 997	22 586	27.0	NA	980
Illinois	455	27 635	-21.0	NA	2 551	11 753	237 877	30.8	36 208	9 947	24 106	348 163	-0.2	NA	28 584
Indiana	605	14 982	-2.2	NA	1 016	5 282	118 144	21.7	16 577	4 108	10 453	110 143	1.6	NA	5 739
Iowa	260	7 718	-5.0	NA	507	3 778	54 447	24.4	6 825	1 909	6 261	91 157	-4.1	NA	4 756
Kansas	230	9 158	38.7	NA	474	2 656	46 861	15.5	5 881	1 647	6 065	61 657	11.6	NA	3 224
Kentucky	329	8 282	-9.1	NA	578	3 176	78 936	17.5	11 791	3 517	6 594	66 825	-2.8	NA	3 076
Louisiana	532	10 857	-8.8	NA	928	3 805	72 064	11.9	12 491	3 284	7 825	64 290	-1.2	NA	3 096
Maine	84	2 513	-12.0	NA	165	1 251	15 211	14.9	1 658	523	2 031	26 977	-0.1	NA	1 380
Maryland	115	10 058	-17.8	NA	1 162	3 704	67 301	20.1	7 266	2 548	8 553	125 201	2.4	NA	8 944
Massachusetts	243	13 230	-6.9	NA	1 139	3 741	79 518	11.4	10 036	2 998	9 941	222 383	3.0	NA	22 299
Michigan	397	22 221	NA	NA	1 734	5 876	106 859	16.8	17 723	4 454	15 165	175 299	-1.2	NA	9 308
Minnesota	269	11 780	-5.6	NA	876	4 739	80 323	39.9	15 056	3 185	10 114	156 603	2.5	NA	10 928
Mississippi	586	8 677	0.7	NA	587	2 340	36 419	23.3	4 041	1 251	4 906	35 919	6.6	NA	1 514
Missouri	375	16 032	-18.0	NA	1 199	5 091	89 027	13.0	14 974	3 277	11 219	137 221	0.3	NA	7 277
Montana	194	2 761	-9.7	NA	184	1 350	11 658	28.2	1 640	375	2 110	17 011	25.1	NA	715
Nebraska	130	1 296	8.1	NA	147	2 334	47 793	63.4	6 323	1 629	4 169	64 519	12.5	NA	3 280
Nevada	108	5 327	-7.0	NA	442	1 543	48 376	68.6	5 319	1 548	4 841	42 034	16.7	NA	2 098
New Hampshire	97	3 178	-3.8	NA	240	847	12 703	-17.5	1 384	439	2 095	28 111	10.2	NA	1 763
New Jersey	337	18 334	-13.7	NA	1 728	7 440	181 595	12.4	25 333	7 536	12 886	213 509	-4.0	NA	18 545
New Mexico	220	5 012	-0.6	NA	331	1 374	17 192	27.7	2 181	577	2 973	25 485	-37.4	NA	1 216
New York	547	38 328	-17.0	NA	3 490	12 067	242 097	21.2	35 690	9 358	28 241	590 838	-24.4	NA	104 090
North Carolina	392	20 490	-0.1	NA	1 648	5 971	116 932	21.8	13 265	4 252	13 722	192 422	8.7	NA	12 575
North Dakota	114	3 331	0.5	NA	265	1 051	10 258	26.6	1 579	347	1 666	16 220	24.0	NA	662
Ohio	610	26 511	5.8	NA	2 159	7 612	177 614	10.4	22 380	6 906	19 047	266 335	2.4	NA	15 422
Oklahoma	334	9 822	1.5	NA	632	2 704	48 079	35.5	6 441	1 912	6 727	60 399	8.3	NA	2 702
Oregon	268	7 984	-4.7	NA	657	3 254	57 290	17.1	7 203	2 209	6 729	66 714	3.6	NA	3 570
Pennsylvania	611	29 183	-13.8	NA	2 790	8 158	206 663	20.0	21 206	7 109	18 954	279 472	-10.0	NA	18 603
Rhode Island	28	1 283	-17.3	NA	99	703	10 686	14.2	1 275	345	1 594	31 415	19.7	NA	1 882
South Carolina	323	12 139	21.3	NA	769	2 759	56 053	19.8	6 300	2 042	7 549	66 489	1.7	NA	3 036
South Dakota	151	2 122	2.8	NA	127	1 102	9 168	21.8	1 253	286	1 916	29 806	27.3	NA	1 187
Tennessee	150	3 249	-7.0	NA	169	4 218	132 044	11.6	15 208	4 701	10 242	116 358	1.4	NA	6 629
Texas	1 860	46 175	-11.2	NA	3 958	16 274	373 340	37.3	62 952	15 768	37 761	465 405	11.6	NA	28 764
Utah	203	4 639	9.9	NA	346	2 194	49 364	30.1	7 522	1 942	5 351	58 648	38.9	NA	2 769
Vermont	47	1 902	7.6	NA	167	539	6 243	14.0	717	202	1 039	9 422	-17.7	NA	532
Virginia	312	16 629	10.1	NA	1 395	5 358	95 040	14.1	10 993	3 316	12 396	168 511	5.8	NA	10 456
Washington	297	5 819	3.6	NA	396	5 111	87 038	33.3	14 983	3 626	11 061	119 201	7.4	NA	7 280
West Virginia	211	6 448	4.2	NA	463	1 403	16 588	8.3	2 764	613	2 174	19 975	-10.6	NA	752
Wisconsin	265	15 721	11.1	NA	1 244	5 606	104 717	19.5	12 814	3 723	9 663	144 531	7.6	NA	8 191
Wyoming	111	2 236	0.8	NA	170	916	8 667	47.8	1 425	372	981	6 854	6.0	NA	291

Real Estate and Rental and Leasing and Professional, Scientific, and Technical Services

STATE	Real estate and rental and leasing, 2007					Professional, scientific, and technical services, 2007								
		Employees					Employees							
	Number of establishments	Number	Percent change, 2002–2007	Receipts (mil dol)	Annual payroll (mil dol)	Number of establishments	Total	Percent change, 2002–2007	Legal services	Accounting and related services	Architectural, engineering, and related services	Computer systems design and related services	Receipts (mil dol)	Annual payroll (mil dol)
	262	263	264	265	266	267	268	269	270	271	272	273	274	275
United States	384 297	2 188 479	12.3	485 059	84 765	847 492	7 870 414	8.7	1 203 763	1 375 685	1 432 209	1 252 197	1 251 004	502 074
Alabama	4 554	27 100	27.2	4 073	823	9 489	94 051	15.7	D	15 126	25 354	14 691	13 863	5 072
Alaska	852	4 370	2.8	841	160	1 828	12 843	11.3	2 010	1 521	5 419	831	2 042	759
Arizona	9 441	52 627	NA	10 078	1 994	16 640	129 368	20.7	17 688	21 946	27 186	23 092	17 802	7 311
Arkansas	3 162	14 115	15.1	1 968	375	5 609	32 361	6.2	D	7 407	6 711	2 134	3 443	1 325
California	51 597	312 488	14.1	76 805	13 447	112 709	1 260 896	8.3	145 772	364 118	185 972	169 890	200 037	82 881
Colorado	10 011	47 568	1.1	8 461	1 793	22 629	160 601	3.0	17 955	17 283	39 320	37 318	29 572	10 800
Connecticut	3 609	22 455	-3.0	5 687	994	9 881	102 071	-4.7	D	11 868	16 515	13 484	15 895	8 029
Delaware	1 248	5 807	1.7	11 057	222	2 390	23 389	1.9	D	2 610	3 568	3 902	4 269	1 722
District of Columbia	1 140	9 663	NA	2 748	625	4 595	89 006	6.6	35 547	4 379	6 494	12 379	25 809	9 137
Florida	33 653	170 859	25.3	32 235	6 094	69 263	430 211	13.6	91 579	62 515	89 807	55 962	61 990	24 395
Georgia	12 620	65 875	10.1	14 022	2 903	27 752	215 705	12.0	32 613	35 950	44 517	36 072	35 259	12 809
Hawaii	2 084	16 759	13.6	3 974	654	3 291	22 460	5.9	D	3 424	5 908	2 452	3 172	1 229
Idaho	2 530	8 371	49.7	1 242	234	4 209	31 650	-0.6	4 631	3 580	9 229	1 901	3 822	1 491
Illinois	13 899	87 468	0.7	21 725	3 985	38 934	369 279	5.8	60 900	70 693	47 136	52 381	62 953	24 624
Indiana	6 389	34 272	1.2	5 448	1 062	13 017	96 189	-1.7	D	19 014	21 049	8 902	12 184	4 809
Iowa	2 969	14 667	7.4	2 556	473	6 214	42 376	12.0	7 996	9 570	5 363	4 530	5 043	1 896
Kansas	3 314	15 160	3.5	2 429	440	7 078	56 302	5.7	D	12 215	12 266	8 234	7 889	2 753
Kentucky	3 898	20 146	11.8	3 894	593	8 114	61 944	11.5	D	11 253	11 185	9 205	7 917	2 852
Louisiana	4 625	30 922	5.3	6 015	1 195	11 190	85 415	6.8	20 106	16 657	27 672	4 887	11 967	4 265
Maine	1 771	6 942	15.0	1 054	209	3 484	22 242	1.5	4 348	3 085	5 191	2 374	2 916	1 087
Maryland	6 768	49 766	9.7	12 392	2 263	19 516	251 806	26.9	D	21 041	38 889	72 913	40 162	16 882
Massachusetts	7 053	48 576	11.6	14 030	2 288	21 974	252 905	5.5	32 489	25 994	46 532	46 723	51 285	21 358
Michigan	8 862	54 874	NA	12 859	1 686	22 691	251 684	-7.5	27 771	51 164	57 694	28 751	29 800	15 402
Minnesota	6 889	39 430	6.5	9 208	1 317	16 678	141 819	13.3	21 404	20 035	20 294	22 362	20 575	8 473
Mississippi	2 517	10 169	5.2	1 735	284	4 770	30 999	6.8	D	6 352	6 128	3 251	3 986	1 357
Missouri	7 003	39 625	3.0	7 186	1 249	13 582	132 339	10.3	D	22 088	21 693	25 803	19 916	7 540
Montana	1 892	6 410	34.6	848	153	3 455	16 889	8.1	3 210	2 924	4 424	1 415	1 802	685
Nebraska	2 032	9 974	6.0	1 646	292	4 220	40 829	31.6	5 560	10 983	5 718	6 226	4 851	2 018
Nevada	4 613	31 603	62.2	6 187	1 106	7 925	58 085	25.4	9 593	8 275	17 170	5 486	8 991	3 272
New Hampshire	1 534	7 266	-3.1	1 372	248	3 993	29 453	1.7	D	6 964	4 848	5 577	3 758	1 584
New Jersey	9 618	64 021	11.0	16 348	2 939	31 141	331 838	15.5	D	45 727	43 790	76 963	52 696	23 765
New Mexico	2 525	11 678	26.1	1 955	356	4 832	44 310	43.2	5 732	5 561	8 713	3 977	6 186	2 589
New York	32 588	171 601	7.2	49 867	7 942	58 526	565 273	0.4	129 554	91 780	66 137	63 579	115 484	42 815
North Carolina	11 258	53 563	15.9	11 175	1 881	22 488	184 998	17.3	24 385	28 145	31 819	28 769	26 574	10 883
North Dakota	770	3 748	10.4	669	96	1 445	9 794	-10.7	1 678	1 666	2 069	1 250	1 122	420
Ohio	10 973	67 048	5.6	15 011	2 339	25 083	228 670	-4.7	39 115	37 230	44 190	33 677	33 028	12 619
Oklahoma	4 003	24 887	30.3	3 852	806	9 174	65 879	12.4	12 586	15 304	12 412	9 186	8 084	3 062
Oregon	6 391	30 978	16.1	5 077	950	11 465	85 253	10.0	12 504	14 448	16 090	10 583	9 964	4 967
Pennsylvania	9 904	68 954	7.2	13 603	2 612	29 726	298 754	-2.4	54 156	48 633	58 726	38 256	46 680	18 523
Rhode Island	1 233	6 493	13.4	1 463	227	3 110	22 892	16.9	D	3 561	3 543	6 163	2 796	1 182
South Carolina	5 473	30 417	23.8	5 194	990	9 518	74 923	17.2	15 302	15 902	18 083	5 925	9 484	3 658
South Dakota	888	3 844	8.2	524	90	1 750	10 197	-2.2	1 869	2 052	1 666	919	1 108	391
Tennessee	6 087	37 737	14.8	6 950	1 243	11 339	100 859	4.7	15 457	21 889	19 552	10 974	12 836	5 100
Texas	26 593	173 745	13.0	36 399	7 067	57 586	540 528	9.1	81 046	76 120	144 800	79 341	91 869	35 742
Utah	4 886	20 413	41.4	3 391	617	8 255	68 452	31.5	8 319	18 562	11 171	8 730	8 373	3 212
Vermont	797	3 395	20.2	497	96	2 122	16 534	30.1	2 203	5 776	2 152	1 989	1 637	658
Virginia	9 475	60 502	21.3	12 637	2 409	27 254	387 272	25.0	28 391	29 108	65 996	148 375	68 693	27 939
Washington	10 480	51 196	7.3	10 467	1 819	19 394	159 711	12.2	22 408	21 957	37 630	24 995	24 809	10 391
West Virginia	1 586	7 055	6.6	1 171	175	2 960	22 233	4.3	5 998	3 247	4 715	2 145	2 650	921
Wisconsin	5 119	27 226	5.4	4 043	789	11 305	98 050	9.0	D	17 712	17 133	12 681	12 871	5 028
Wyoming	1 121	4 651	49.7	992	160	1 899	8 827	21.2	1 559	1 271	2 570	592	1 093	393

Table A. States — **Health Care and Social Assistance**

STATE	Health care and social assistance, 2007													
	Subject to federal tax							Tax-exempt						
		Employees							Employees					
	Number of establishments	Total	Percent change, 2002–2007	Ambulatory health care services	Hospitals	Receipts (mil dol)	Annual payroll (mil dol)	Number of establishments	Total	Percent change, 2002–2007	Ambulatory health care services	Hospitals	Receipts (mil dol)	Annual payroll (mil dol)
	276	277	278	279	280	281	282	283	284	285	286	287	288	289
United States	647 120	8 322 326	18.5	4 984 940	601 899	818 395	330 888	137 506	8 469 748	5.5	718 501	4 926 944	849 882	331 832
Alabama	8 502	134 925	19.3	71 265	18 878	12 637	5 167	1 890	103 145	3.2	9 310	69 965	9 968	3 723
Alaska	1 603	15 416	59.8	10 193	1 740	1 821	714	528	25 202	-3.0	4 401	12 925	2 842	1 077
Arizona	13 643	154 061	35.1	91 394	D	16 656	6 572	1 803	124 772	26.1	11 535	D	13 751	5 081
Arkansas	5 718	77 215	19.8	39 750	9 239	7 151	2 895	1 498	75 649	8.1	6 435	D	6 289	2 387
California	84 335	883 552	15.2	563 016	63 134	102 703	38 944	12 953	708 878	6.2	55 838	433 199	88 903	33 587
Colorado	11 557	127 029	21.3	75 024	9 821	12 599	5 234	2 087	111 913	14.6	16 882	64 076	11 729	4 491
Connecticut	7 687	122 425	11.8	68 206	D	11 535	5 062	2 362	130 935	9.0	14 051	D	13 278	5 378
Delaware	1 877	25 319	26.8	15 335	D	2 621	1 156	502	29 421	7.1	2 200	17 353	2 810	1 215
District of Columbia	1 419	19 710	9.3	10 263	3 431	2 099	944	711	41 365	-6.7	1 484	23 722	5 151	1 998
Florida	46 687	538 050	13.8	318 090	70 644	61 637	22 586	4 992	365 954	9.4	33 165	219 986	40 393	14 648
Georgia	18 379	229 101	14.5	135 432	19 522	23 274	9 145	2 461	190 195	8.8	11 570	132 958	20 669	7 336
Hawaii	2 778	29 023	45.3	20 431	D	2 979	1 244	706	34 617	-4.4	4 955	D	3 586	1 477
Idaho	3 974	44 499	31.1	24 110	2 799	3 510	1 423	571	29 433	8.2	1 609	20 808	2 701	1 088
Illinois	25 651	325 085	15.9	205 032	11 797	32 056	13 445	5 411	381 584	0.2	20 692	228 320	37 987	14 564
Indiana	11 919	181 493	21.8	102 701	13 359	17 015	6 813	3 053	188 600	1.4	13 317	115 514	17 754	6 640
Iowa	5 399	70 263	14.1	40 123	D	5 854	2 732	2 458	128 022	6.9	6 804	D	9 518	3 872
Kansas	5 778	83 531	16.6	48 409	7 241	7 948	3 176	1 917	94 997	3.3	6 005	49 462	7 181	2 968
Kentucky	8 686	115 673	13.0	62 383	7 842	10 090	4 218	1 914	119 609	2.8	10 428	78 156	12 062	4 177
Louisiana	9 725	145 174	11.6	77 250	21 393	13 179	4 935	1 820	110 905	-3.4	3 396	71 075	10 507	3 926
Maine	3 203	39 757	10.4	21 408	D	3 016	1 397	1 672	64 394	11.2	7 955	D	5 577	2 294
Maryland	12 542	143 677	15.8	91 164	D	15 364	6 218	2 762	172 104	10.2	8 902	D	18 463	6 871
Massachusetts	12 828	202 678	8.1	113 995	11 095	21 342	9 280	5 027	308 334	6.7	30 689	162 079	30 605	12 896
Michigan	21 150	228 681	10.0	156 808	2 591	21 055	9 169	4 883	320 801	5.4	24 972	207 748	31 703	12 420
Minnesota	10 263	157 035	25.2	93 957	D	13 230	6 021	3 733	229 109	1.9	22 776	D	20 768	8 851
Mississippi	4 858	72 601	18.0	37 002	11 694	7 229	2 753	1 018	74 257	5.4	3 996	54 573	6 885	2 619
Missouri	12 881	159 529	14.2	84 426	13 808	14 102	5 912	3 103	202 811	3.3	15 615	124 941	18 785	7 007
Montana	2 438	21 763	18.1	13 791	D	1 945	802	863	36 097	8.3	2 481	D	3 026	1 182
Nebraska	3 830	49 338	19.7	27 155	2 050	4 447	1 889	1 090	65 590	2.6	2 796	39 933	5 634	2 219
Nevada	5 269	72 716	37.5	39 241	17 329	9 226	3 345	503	23 917	1.0	1 516	15 577	2 965	1 053
New Hampshire	2 655	32 711	11.4	18 356	D	3 096	1 386	837	51 006	14.5	8 546	D	4 990	1 992
New Jersey	22 056	253 078	18.0	169 075	3 984	26 416	10 530	3 721	250 292	6.5	20 063	149 193	25 498	10 784
New Mexico	3 713	57 423	42.1	28 655	7 403	4 855	1 958	1 019	48 073	14.0	5 072	25 291	3 980	1 823
New York	41 201	459 964	15.3	341 364	4 431	46 578	18 428	12 747	866 075	3.7	98 596	411 842	82 017	35 995
North Carolina	17 964	286 998	36.1	160 857	6 844	22 795	10 133	3 748	236 399	12.4	15 003	155 137	23 894	8 915
North Dakota	1 176	14 135	16.4	9 015	1 404	1 427	571	572	38 062	6.3	1 465	18 719	2 480	1 145
Ohio	22 693	346 386	13.0	204 606	6 227	28 637	12 631	5 272	394 808	4.7	30 467	247 224	37 246	14 990
Oklahoma	8 577	121 175	26.5	58 561	21 197	10 860	4 172	1 755	79 602	-2.2	6 397	D	7 503	2 653
Oregon	9 011	91 816	18.6	58 522	D	9 445	3 751	2 250	100 417	13.6	10 889	D	10 715	4 144
Pennsylvania	27 138	368 531	20.3	228 474	21 985	35 089	15 093	8 018	506 212	5.7	43 780	252 464	46 889	18 339
Rhode Island	2 502	34 762	20.5	19 520	D	3 015	1 310	772	47 185	6.2	4 505	D	4 146	1 782
South Carolina	7 883	115 669	23.3	64 005	13 933	11 213	4 523	1 408	84 547	-1.5	4 245	57 911	9 195	3 238
South Dakota	1 535	17 404	-0.1	10 080	1 187	1 697	667	706	39 076	7.2	3 632	22 299	3 070	1 372
Tennessee	11 720	185 582	23.8	104 883	23 380	19 249	7 600	2 547	152 159	4.6	11 097	97 202	14 550	5 494
Texas	48 875	780 459	26.2	450 190	105 928	71 221	27 772	6 116	386 154	2.0	28 558	257 127	42 609	15 346
Utah	5 731	67 064	19.3	38 665	D	6 411	2 365	661	45 582	10.8	3 873	D	4 449	1 791
Vermont	1 469	15 381	14.9	8 992	D	1 147	532	707	26 536	11.1	6 426	D	2 390	963
Virginia	14 942	203 981	19.5	121 014	18 113	19 705	8 418	2 598	167 086	5.9	11 227	101 016	17 817	6 544
Washington	15 513	172 010	19.4	103 216	D	16 739	6 871	2 961	173 151	10.1	21 900	D	19 148	7 479
West Virginia	3 741	51 790	5.0	25 186	6 094	4 339	1 708	1 119	62 873	-2.1	6 739	38 307	5 536	2 121
Wisconsin	11 149	165 008	14.9	96 982	D	15 006	6 808	3 268	204 281	5.9	19 528	D	18 835	7 274
Wyoming	1 297	11 680	20.6	7 368	644	1 139	470	413	17 562	13.3	718	9 886	1 437	603

Table A. States — Arts, Entertainment, and Recreation and Accommodation and Food Services

STATE	Arts, entertainment, and recreation, 2007					Accommodation and food services, 2007					
	Number of establishments	Employees: Number	Employees: Percent change, 2002–2007	Receipts (mil dol)	Annual payroll (mil dol)	Number of establishments	Employees: Total	Employees: Percent change, 2002–2007	Employees: Food services and drinking places	Receipts (mil dol)	Annual payroll (mil dol)
	290	291	292	293	294	295	296	297	298	299	300
United States	124 620	2 061 348	11.5	189 417	58 359	634 361	11 600 751	14.6	9 630 090	613 796	170 827
Alabama	1 129	17 981	24.2	1 256	300	8 093	150 791	17.5	136 439	6 426	1 751
Alaska	495	4 456	20.1	350	72	1 996	25 638	8.3	19 114	1 851	530
Arizona	1 819	46 524	18.2	4 275	1 322	11 610	250 716	21.5	199 909	13 269	3 766
Arkansas	812	9 212	15.4	484	141	5 112	89 933	15.5	79 512	3 560	994
California	20 090	302 015	5.2	36 444	11 869	75 989	1 366 926	19.3	1 128 817	80 853	22 375
Colorado	2 414	49 688	9.8	3 911	1 256	12 075	231 721	12.2	186 986	11 440	3 408
Connecticut	1 652	25 179	8.4	2 546	730	7 941	132 001	11.5	100 129	9 138	2 483
Delaware	389	6 855	-8.9	545	139	1 850	32 194	19.4	28 359	1 911	469
District of Columbia	290	7 318	3.2	876	319	2 148	52 998	22.4	37 156	4 278	1 238
Florida	7 537	166 847	13.7	15 381	4 218	35 012	746 214	20.1	598 276	41 922	11 470
Georgia	2 797	45 047	27.7	3 422	1 137	18 640	355 423	21.3	312 688	16 976	4 704
Hawaii	502	11 988	12.1	824	246	3 528	98 353	14.8	60 304	8 042	2 210
Idaho	718	9 020	30.0	397	126	3 482	56 662	24.7	45 340	2 416	663
Illinois	4 608	79 603	9.2	7 329	2 242	26 774	468 827	11.4	409 186	25 469	6 894
Indiana	2 175	35 876	14.0	3 025	953	12 932	254 293	10.0	221 408	11 670	3 175
Iowa	1 453	21 677	6.1	1 534	363	7 014	116 838	11.7	96 927	4 738	1 276
Kansas	1 114	15 643	16.6	807	232	5 866	104 795	13.8	92 897	4 192	1 174
Kentucky	1 341	18 556	15.6	1 205	368	7 309	151 551	11.1	136 285	6 301	1 787
Louisiana	1 356	24 761	-16.6	2 801	674	8 169	180 289	6.0	142 855	9 730	2 579
Maine	894	7 792	22.1	505	134	3 938	49 363	9.8	39 919	2 516	748
Maryland	2 149	37 507	17.5	2 776	976	10 802	192 619	9.1	170 707	10 758	2 916
Massachusetts	3 078	52 731	12.7	4 691	1 612	16 039	257 302	6.6	225 602	14 917	4 340
Michigan	3 654	55 118	-7.2	4 792	1 482	19 678	339 181	2.9	302 866	14 537	4 207
Minnesota	2 747	42 057	13.4	2 924	1 057	11 340	221 081	8.9	181 622	10 424	2 978
Mississippi	673	8 179	-12.0	525	146	4 817	119 626	9.3	79 146	7 045	1 812
Missouri	2 161	37 529	12.3	3 411	1 254	12 261	241 438	11.9	207 557	11 071	3 109
Montana	1 083	10 294	11.3	674	140	3 360	46 137	12.8	36 177	2 079	554
Nebraska	841	11 364	10.6	622	168	4 241	69 142	10.3	61 544	2 686	749
Nevada	1 261	30 274	13.3	3 367	783	5 570	325 544	21.0	97 104	28 816	8 595
New Hampshire	739	11 595	10.6	776	245	3 508	55 268	15.5	45 825	2 631	800
New Jersey	3 543	51 054	16.4	3 867	1 273	19 526	291 327	8.3	221 700	19 994	5 232
New Mexico	664	14 341	5.4	1 488	304	4 090	80 415	14.9	64 319	3 734	1 055
New York	11 230	158 275	15.6	21 135	6 424	43 791	591 653	12.1	504 817	39 813	10 956
North Carolina	3 422	55 306	19.0	4 462	1 458	18 268	343 235	21.8	302 669	16 127	4 395
North Dakota	407	4 581	29.4	198	56	1 840	30 307	15.8	23 926	1 214	338
Ohio	4 077	65 326	3.5	5 526	1 849	23 959	436 598	4.2	401 245	17 780	5 079
Oklahoma	1 099	26 237	77.3	2 569	487	6 900	129 159	16.2	117 572	5 107	1 401
Oregon	1 597	24 334	8.4	1 476	546	10 241	150 538	15.8	127 821	7 556	2 153
Pennsylvania	4 648	83 594	13.7	6 702	2 299	26 910	420 209	10.0	369 097	19 625	5 454
Rhode Island	524	8 829	32.9	679	192	2 926	44 426	15.2	40 319	2 149	622
South Carolina	1 547	25 300	18.8	1 426	426	9 291	182 899	19.7	156 272	8 383	2 311
South Dakota	661	6 436	17.2	469	101	2 426	36 710	13.9	27 654	1 623	436
Tennessee	2 377	32 436	18.2	3 421	1 079	11 592	239 379	18.1	210 513	10 627	3 009
Texas	6 260	109 689	12.6	8 824	2 855	43 509	866 189	21.0	768 821	42 055	11 502
Utah	842	18 487	-1.1	961	336	4 541	91 808	13.7	74 282	3 981	1 149
Vermont	474	8 009	0.8	379	112	1 942	31 176	4.4	19 700	1 368	428
Virginia	2 730	51 160	11.2	3 803	1 097	15 765	302 446	18.0	256 469	15 340	4 273
Washington	2 675	57 631	14.4	4 907	1 538	15 893	233 235	16.8	199 322	12 389	3 618
West Virginia	699	10 801	12.6	1 354	180	3 650	61 711	18.7	51 734	2 553	713
Wisconsin	2 738	42 791	22.1	3 028	969	14 439	227 475	13.3	192 650	9 247	2 535
Wyoming	435	4 045	-0.6	269	75	1 768	26 992	11.7	18 532	1 469	412

STATE	Other services, except public administration, 2007								Government employment, 2013		
		Employees									
	Number of establishments	Total	Percent change, 2002–2007	Repair and maintenance	Personal and laundry services	Religious, civic, and similar services	Receipts (mil dol)	Annual payroll (mil dol)	Federal civilian	Federal military	State and local
	301	302	303	304	305	306	307	308	309	310	311
United States	540 148	3 479 011	0.1	1 261 083	1 337 539	880 389	405 284	99 123	2 826 000	2 032 000	19 187 000
Alabama	6 718	40 488	-2.8	18 034	15 757	6 697	4 154	1 050	54 685	30 557	315 459
Alaska	1 328	7 566	-0.9	2 487	2 387	2 692	811	223	15 504	27 457	64 073
Arizona	8 906	68 368	19.6	27 251	24 794	16 323	6 220	1 726	55 613	33 307	352 837
Arkansas	4 153	23 188	-3.8	9 961	8 460	4 767	2 188	558	20 441	18 718	196 177
California	57 626	399 336	-1.4	158 848	149 940	90 548	52 326	11 914	246 734	213 744	2 128 214
Colorado	10 151	62 767	-2.1	23 065	22 293	17 409	7 789	1 823	53 639	53 966	358 177
Connecticut	7 392	47 992	3.7	14 885	21 839	11 268	5 061	1 395	17 392	14 618	227 886
Delaware	1 587	10 012	-14.9	3 300	4 593	2 119	898	265	5 551	9 141	59 570
District of Columbia	3 284	49 853	5.4	703	6 308	42 842	15 500	3 154	200 751	15 119	35 270
Florida	35 597	201 687	5.1	66 378	82 991	52 318	20 757	5 174	132 244	98 336	932 145
Georgia	14 588	98 047	15.3	42 248	38 992	16 807	10 386	2 837	100 257	98 339	567 208
Hawaii	2 916	20 119	4.3	3 805	7 864	8 450	1 918	513	33 919	57 357	91 305
Idaho	2 640	13 681	4.6	6 567	4 464	2 650	1 094	316	12 450	9 510	104 947
Illinois	23 510	167 675	-5.3	62 578	60 360	44 737	20 639	5 203	81 231	43 324	753 486
Indiana	11 458	75 292	-5.0	29 915	26 816	18 561	8 451	1 893	37 032	21 468	385 342
Iowa	6 088	31 869	-5.5	12 559	11 772	7 538	3 063	779	17 420	12 673	237 564
Kansas	5 498	31 665	-1.7	12 126	12 139	7 400	3 326	804	25 442	36 331	234 658
Kentucky	6 150	40 956	-1.2	17 582	16 359	7 015	3 751	1 009	38 508	53 700	281 672
Louisiana	6 637	42 223	-8.7	20 353	14 686	7 184	4 664	1 170	30 602	39 737	307 701
Maine	2 840	13 297	-4.3	4 697	4 439	4 161	1 280	328	14 157	7 145	85 639
Maryland	10 365	77 368	3.9	25 182	32 326	19 860	9 689	2 487	173 770	49 956	344 732
Massachusetts	13 516	90 268	-0.9	27 823	38 899	23 546	9 841	2 690	46 281	20 281	392 272
Michigan	17 040	101 568	-10.3	38 528	40 665	22 375	10 844	2 648	51 924	18 864	539 265
Minnesota	11 137	81 829	4.7	23 556	28 659	29 614	8 301	2 355	31 296	20 254	366 245
Mississippi	3 853	20 421	-7.9	8 894	7 307	4 220	1 950	490	25 524	29 259	222 452
Missouri	11 111	67 476	-6.8	27 126	26 623	13 727	6 771	1 800	57 379	37 855	380 478
Montana	2 287	10 323	0.3	4 533	2 727	3 063	995	246	13 076	8 299	73 423
Nebraska	4 073	22 543	-1.7	9 368	7 918	5 257	2 391	543	16 532	12 799	144 108
Nevada	3 571	27 234	15.0	10 557	12 199	4 478	2 584	702	18 387	18 608	129 983
New Hampshire	2 886	16 153	-3.5	5 849	6 420	3 884	1 574	458	7 403	4 668	82 405
New Jersey	19 047	105 659	-0.4	35 166	50 036	20 457	11 204	3 003	49 510	25 222	545 485
New Mexico	2 953	18 061	0.4	8 051	5 410	4 600	1 690	450	30 398	18 350	162 612
New York	42 575	249 391	-0.5	56 440	98 809	94 142	39 147	8 073	116 234	59 347	1 283 015
North Carolina	14 105	85 304	3.4	34 948	32 550	17 806	9 362	2 217	69 318	136 770	655 105
North Dakota	1 708	9 261	-5.4	2 869	3 190	3 202	746	199	9 198	11 893	65 139
Ohio	20 349	135 272	-8.6	48 306	57 766	29 200	13 048	3 464	76 666	36 168	681 086
Oklahoma	5 541	31 654	-2.5	12 605	12 458	6 591	3 318	759	47 221	35 621	286 659
Oregon	6 888	39 129	4.0	16 415	13 094	9 620	4 462	1 091	27 606	12 151	236 918
Pennsylvania	25 316	154 379	0.2	51 384	62 406	40 589	17 622	3 933	97 070	36 241	654 389
Rhode Island	2 382	14 379	-0.9	4 226	5 847	4 306	1 449	373	10 197	7 548	54 032
South Carolina	7 088	45 520	7.7	18 456	16 777	10 287	3 902	1 127	32 658	54 937	311 585
South Dakota	1 815	8 518	-2.7	3 471	2 725	2 322	750	182	11 151	8 283	64 473
Tennessee	8 811	62 425	6.7	23 758	26 667	12 000	6 339	1 681	49 929	22 273	374 444
Texas	34 462	253 503	2.5	116 002	93 700	43 801	25 779	6 994	197 794	177 742	1 598 375
Utah	4 141	26 236	9.5	12 620	9 314	4 302	2 356	653	34 606	16 432	192 194
Vermont	1 629	7 269	-1.7	2 306	2 133	2 830	799	183	6 588	4 402	47 851
Virginia	15 072	111 129	1.3	34 685	41 436	35 008	16 498	3 915	193 383	140 677	534 725
Washington	12 324	71 213	3.7	27 026	27 518	16 669	8 921	2 030	71 772	80 410	470 315
West Virginia	2 927	16 527	-4.0	6 735	5 647	4 145	1 550	388	23 397	9 419	125 347
Wisconsin	10 724	66 392	-2.8	23 560	27 506	15 326	6 360	1 679	28 730	16 491	386 484
Wyoming	1 385	6 526	4.0	3 296	1 554	1 676	766	179	7 430	6 233	62 074

STATE	State government employment and payroll, 2012											
	State government employment, 2013			State government payroll, 2012		Full-time equivalent payroll (1,000 dollars)						
							Percent of total for:					
	Full-time equivalent employees	Full-time employees	Part-time employees	Full-time March payroll (1,000 dollars)	Part-time March payroll (1,000 dollars)	Total March payroll (1,000 dollars)[1]	Administration	Judicial and legal	Police	Corrections	Highways and transportation	Public Welfare
	312	313	314	315	316	317	318	319	320	321	322	323
United States	4 312 054	3 729 798	1 556 304	18 043 224	2 129 612	20 172 836	4.8	4.5	2.9	9.2	6.0	4.4
Alabama	86 976	77 517	28 604	331 712	28 856	360 567	3.8	4.0	1.5	4.6	5.0	3.9
Alaska	27 290	24 918	5 815	135 810	7 886	143 696	7.5	6.2	2.9	7.0	12.7	5.8
Arizona	69 392	58 514	26 931	260 708	28 154	288 862	4.7	3.2	3.3	13.0	4.0	5.7
Arkansas	63 606	57 847	16 286	229 115	15 557	244 672	4.2	2.2	1.9	7.4	5.1	5.1
California	395 489	326 477	156 478	2 120 834	336 730	2 457 564	5.7	1.6	3.2	14.3	6.1	0.7
Colorado	73 458	54 751	46 029	280 779	78 844	359 622	3.3	6.3	1.9	8.4	3.9	2.5
Connecticut	61 578	52 297	25 677	300 870	41 393	342 263	6.4	6.9	3.7	10.6	4.5	8.9
Delaware	26 588	23 291	8 552	101 629	11 673	113 302	4.0	7.1	5.8	10.0	8.5	4.8
District of Columbia	X	X	X	X	X	X	X	X	X	X	X	X
Florida	181 262	164 607	45 828	663 992	55 666	719 658	4.2	10.7	2.3	11.4	4.2	3.8
Georgia	128 445	112 991	48 384	453 601	50 586	504 187	3.5	3.2	1.5	9.0	4.3	5.2
Hawaii	57 293	51 888	20 205	216 629	19 306	235 935	2.3	4.6	-	4.1	3.5	0.7
Idaho	21 548	18 373	9 769	80 469	9 413	89 882	7.4	4.2	2.4	8.5	6.0	6.3
Illinois	130 206	103 578	52 784	578 721	88 551	667 272	5.9	3.4	3.5	9.4	5.9	7.7
Indiana	89 332	75 516	41 334	318 653	35 662	354 315	3.2	2.7	2.2	5.5	3.7	4.3
Iowa	47 921	40 529	26 452	235 274	22 930	258 203	2.7	4.5	2.1	5.6	4.3	4.9
Kansas	48 491	43 464	15 942	193 147	16 776	209 923	4.1	4.2	2.1	4.8	5.2	3.5
Kentucky	85 315	74 613	27 413	300 097	26 192	326 289	4.0	6.1	2.9	3.5	4.5	5.8
Louisiana	79 378	72 132	21 890	314 181	20 764	334 944	6.3	2.2	2.8	7.3	5.8	5.7
Maine	21 022	18 437	8 778	77 329	8 897	86 226	8.1	4.5	3.1	5.4	9.3	11.2
Maryland	86 981	77 971	13 779	375 742	41 110	416 852	5.3	6.5	2.9	12.4	6.7	6.8
Massachusetts	96 752	86 528	34 485	454 156	46 893	501 048	5.9	9.7	10.5	6.2	4.9	7.1
Michigan	146 163	110 576	73 228	604 390	114 397	718 787	3.9	1.4	1.9	9.3	1.8	6.9
Minnesota	79 730	65 879	35 765	357 098	50 517	407 615	4.7	4.4	1.2	4.5	8.4	2.7
Mississippi	58 090	52 720	12 872	192 721	14 411	207 132	3.4	2.1	1.9	3.9	4.8	4.7
Missouri	85 919	76 691	24 257	273 599	24 257	297 857	4.9	4.9	3.3	10.5	6.2	6.2
Montana	20 251	16 670	9 731	70 838	10 655	81 493	6.9	3.8	2.7	5.9	11.2	7.0
Nebraska	32 094	26 690	10 484	109 648	11 947	121 595	3.5	2.9	2.7	7.9	6.3	6.2
Nevada	26 388	23 454	9 793	114 145	11 893	126 038	7.3	3.7	4.2	11.9	6.1	5.1
New Hampshire	18 589	14 911	10 273	70 081	11 769	81 850	6.0	4.4	3.2	6.1	8.0	7.4
New Jersey	146 220	132 767	31 358	791 775	50 680	842 456	4.2	9.7	3.6	6.5	10.1	5.7
New Mexico	45 216	39 561	14 735	178 747	18 211	196 957	2.8	7.0	1.3	6.2	3.7	2.9
New York	242 299	225 854	50 467	1 278 224	78 854	1 357 078	5.7	9.8	3.7	12.8	12.7	1.6
North Carolina	150 424	131 676	45 614	572 887	60 149	633 036	3.1	5.0	2.6	10.1	6.5	0.6
North Dakota	18 897	15 721	9 456	68 016	8 783	76 799	4.7	3.7	1.2	3.9	6.3	2.2
Ohio	135 594	108 649	76 720	552 665	93 378	646 043	5.8	1.9	2.0	9.1	4.5	2.2
Oklahoma	65 209	57 853	25 930	225 635	22 730	248 365	3.3	4.8	3.3	6.7	3.9	6.5
Oregon	65 777	56 703	24 711	275 865	42 823	318 689	6.6	4.4	2.1	7.0	5.5	8.4
Pennsylvania	158 094	141 130	64 863	660 252	102 880	763 133	5.9	2.9	5.2	10.6	7.3	5.8
Rhode Island	18 969	17 149	6 812	95 313	7 102	102 415	7.3	6.6	2.5	9.9	8.4	6.9
South Carolina	78 364	70 684	21 150	269 261	22 369	291 630	4.9	1.3	2.4	7.9	5.9	4.4
South Dakota	14 971	13 062	6 288	55 711	5 204	60 915	5.4	4.4	2.0	4.5	6.0	9.6
Tennessee	84 514	75 441	27 123	310 019	25 812	335 831	6.2	7.5	2.2	6.1	3.7	7.2
Texas	310 549	274 987	87 871	1 255 897	117 136	1 373 033	2.8	2.1	2.1	8.1	3.9	5.0
Utah	53 255	44 301	25 942	198 285	29 195	227 480	5.7	3.1	1.4	4.7	2.9	4.2
Vermont	15 023	13 630	4 468	61 543	7 458	69 001	7.2	4.2	4.5	6.4	7.4	7.9
Virginia	126 520	107 379	55 602	483 099	68 155	551 254	3.8	3.2	2.6	8.0	6.0	2.1
Washington	111 888	94 477	44 049	430 779	64 591	495 370	3.7	2.2	2.4	7.0	7.0	8.6
West Virginia	40 227	36 387	12 500	134 189	11 193	145 381	5.0	4.9	2.9	6.1	11.5	6.1
Wisconsin	70 851	56 094	49 328	275 072	48 008	323 080	4.6	4.2	1.2	12.5	2.2	2.6
Wyoming	13 646	12 463	3 499	54 022	3 216	57 238	6.6	5.2	2.4	8.8	12.7	5.7

1. Includes program categories not shown separately.

STATE	State government employment and payroll, 2012 (cont.)							State government finances, 2013							
	Full-time equivalent payroll (1,000 dollars) (cont.)							General revenue (mil dol)							
	Percent of total for:								From federal government		From own sources				
												Taxes		Taxes per capita[1] (dollars)	
	Health	Hospitals	Social Insurance administration	Natural resources and parks	Utilities, sewerage, and waste management	Elementary and secondary education and libraries	Higher education	Total	Total	Per capita (dollars)	Total	Total	Sales and gross receipts	Total	Sales and gross receipts
	324	325	326	327	328	329	330	331	332	333	334	335	336	337	338
United States	4.2	9.2	1.8	3.4	0.3	1.1	42.0	X	X	X	X	X	X	X	X
Alabama	5.8	13.7	0.9	2.5	-	-	48.2	22 760	8 227	1 702	14 422	9 268	4 709	1 917	974
Alaska	2.8	0.9	1.3	9.4	-	9.0	21.8	12 280	2 747	3 737	9 526	5 133	250	6 982	340
Arizona	3.2	0.9	1.7	2.4	-	-	49.7	29 176	10 166	1 534	18 596	13 472	8 207	2 033	1 238
Arkansas	6.2	10.1	2.2	3.8	-	-	45.6	17 310	5 689	1 922	11 585	8 586	4 019	2 901	1 358
California	3.2	13.1	3.1	3.8	0.1	-	39.4	219 693	54 828	1 430	161 596	133 184	48 075	3 474	1 254
Colorado	2.0	6.4	1.3	1.9	-	-	56.8	23 129	6 428	1 220	16 620	11 246	4 280	2 135	812
Connecticut	6.0	11.5	1.1	1.1	0.1	-	30.4	25 446	5 949	1 654	19 484	16 190	6 776	4 502	1 884
Delaware	7.0	4.6	1.0	2.5	0.5	-	36.5	7 794	1 929	2 084	5 798	3 346	487	3 615	526
District of Columbia								X	X	X	X	X	X	X	X
Florida	8.7	1.9	1.2	4.3	-	-	43.1	74 726	23 506	1 202	50 846	35 378	29 316	1 809	1 499
Georgia	4.4	3.4	1.1	3.5	-	-	55.6	38 392	14 323	1 433	23 773	17 794	7 408	1 781	741
Hawaii	3.7	9.5	0.5	1.6	-	42.2	21.2	10 825	2 327	1 657	8 494	6 093	3 932	4 340	2 801
Idaho	5.1	2.0	3.0	9.6	-	-	38.6	7 340	2 523	1 565	4 799	3 579	1 773	2 220	1 100
Illinois	2.3	8.2	1.9	2.4	-	-	42.7	65 562	16 974	1 318	48 249	38 729	14 720	3 006	1 143
Indiana	1.9	1.7	1.1	2.4	-	-	67.8	33 499	11 192	1 703	22 231	16 931	10 298	2 577	1 567
Iowa	0.9	16.9	1.4	3.4	-	-	45.4	18 534	5 915	1 914	12 542	8 374	3 609	2 710	1 168
Kansas	2.5	16.3	0.2	2.4	-	-	47.8	15 246	3 789	1 309	11 401	7 620	3 743	2 633	1 293
Kentucky	3.7	7.6	0.9	4.1	-	-	49.6	22 927	8 047	1 831	14 843	10 816	5 110	2 461	1 163
Louisiana	4.0	13.5	1.3	6.0	-	1.3	36.5	25 255	10 593	2 290	14 595	9 224	4 975	1 994	1 075
Maine	5.1	2.4	1.6	5.7	-	0.2	35.0	7 991	2 821	2 124	5 161	3 884	1 780	2 924	1 340
Maryland	6.4	3.8	1.1	2.8	-	-	36.1	34 779	9 953	1 679	24 454	18 118	7 347	3 056	1 239
Massachusetts	6.7	5.1	1.8	2.2	1.7	0.1	30.2	46 180	13 233	1 977	32 474	23 901	7 455	3 571	1 114
Michigan	3.3	11.1	0.8	2.1	-	-	53.7	54 343	17 830	1 802	36 336	24 936	12 298	2 520	1 243
Minnesota	4.0	5.1	1.3	4.2	0.9	-	49.3	34 651	9 142	1 687	25 336	21 032	8 290	3 880	1 529
Mississippi	4.5	20.0	1.4	5.0	0.1	-	40.4	17 511	7 510	2 511	9 861	7 403	4 571	2 475	1 528
Missouri	3.0	10.9	0.6	3.0	-	-	40.1	26 662	10 188	1 686	16 165	11 139	4 791	1 843	793
Montana	4.4	2.4	4.0	7.7	-	-	35.5	5 768	2 158	2 126	3 606	2 645	559	2 605	551
Nebraska	2.1	11.6	0.7	6.7	-	-	41.3	9 819	3 155	1 688	6 607	4 719	2 198	2 526	1 176
Nevada	4.6	4.8	1.8	2.9	0.2	-	39.6	11 402	2 845	1 020	8 322	7 027	5 468	2 518	1 960
New Hampshire	4.7	2.8	1.4	2.6	0.2	-	40.3	6 132	1 660	1 254	4 249	2 350	945	1 775	714
New Jersey	3.3	9.5	1.0	2.2	0.5	12.1	25.5	53 864	13 756	1 546	39 392	29 077	12 198	3 267	1 371
New Mexico	3.6	16.7	0.9	2.9	-	-	45.6	14 295	5 228	2 507	8 879	5 202	2 652	2 494	1 272
New York	3.7	16.7	3.1	1.9	1.0	-	20.7	165 201	46 273	2 355	93 518	73 667	23 217	3 749	1 181
North Carolina	1.6	12.2	1.8	3.8	0.3	-	47.1	47 575	15 471	1 571	31 805	23 769	9 714	2 414	986
North Dakota	6.3	3.6	1.8	4.0	-	-	52.2	8 060	1 529	2 114	6 487	5 299	1 763	7 325	2 438
Ohio	2.8	13.0	1.4	2.0	-	-	50.1	60 946	20 483	1 770	39 832	27 517	13 822	2 378	1 195
Oklahoma	7.6	2.0	1.9	3.4	1.4	-	48.2	20 800	7 029	1 825	13 640	8 893	3 848	2 309	999
Oregon	2.4	12.5	3.9	3.9	-	-	39.8	22 833	7 987	2 032	14 830	9 161	1 369	2 331	348
Pennsylvania	1.2	5.2	2.3	5.1	-	-	40.6	69 756	21 219	1 661	48 343	33 966	17 106	2 659	1 339
Rhode Island	5.2	4.1	2.2	2.5	1.7	2.7	27.3	6 933	2 331	2 217	4 564	2 940	1 516	2 796	1 442
South Carolina	6.6	7.2	1.5	2.7	3.7	-	46.2	22 161	6 699	1 403	14 958	8 721	4 477	1 827	938
South Dakota	4.4	5.3	1.5	7.5	-	-	42.2	4 036	1 575	1 864	2 430	1 534	1 228	1 815	1 454
Tennessee	9.2	4.4	1.4	5.1	-	-	41.8	27 402	10 820	1 666	16 501	12 367	9 128	1 904	1 405
Texas	8.7	8.6	1.1	3.7	-	-	50.1	112 936	36 845	1 393	75 356	51 714	39 278	1 955	1 485
Utah	3.4	12.8	1.3	2.5	-	-	52.8	14 811	4 299	1 482	10 507	6 325	2 740	2 180	945
Vermont	2.9	1.5	1.5	4.6	-	-	41.5	5 635	1 870	2 984	3 763	2 879	983	4 594	1 569
Virginia	3.9	10.5	1.1	2.8	-	-	49.3	41 140	9 412	1 139	31 181	19 187	6 193	2 323	750
Washington	4.5	7.0	3.5	4.5	0.6	-	42.7	35 670	9 737	1 397	25 639	18 667	14 647	2 678	2 101
West Virginia	1.8	3.3	1.2	5.4	-	-	42.2	12 391	4 231	2 282	8 066	5 378	2 579	2 900	1 391
Wisconsin	2.3	4.2	1.2	2.9	-	-	53.2	32 281	8 952	1 559	23 052	16 514	7 088	2 876	1 234
Wyoming	6.0	4.5	0.8	8.8	-	-	29.0	5 929	2 086	3 580	3 610	2 186	826	3 752	1 418

1. Based on resident population estimated as of July 1 of the year shown.

Table A. States — State Government Finances and Voting

STATE	State government finances, 2013 (cont.)												Voting and registration, November 2014		Presidential election,[2] 2012 (percent of vote cast)		
	General expenditures (mil dol)										Debt outstanding						
			Direct general expenditures		By selected function												
	Total	To local govern-ments	Total	Per capita[1] (dollars)	Educa-tion	Health and hospitals	High-ways	Public safety	Public welfare	Natural resources, parks, and recreation	Total (mil dol)	Per capita[1]	Percent registered	Percent voted	Demo-cratic	Repub-lican	All other
	339	340	341	342	343	344	345	346	347	348	349	350	351	352	353	354	355
United States	X	X	X	X	X	X	X	X	X	X	X	X	59.3	38.5	51.1	47.2	3.6
Alabama	24 602	6 476	18 126	3 750	10 617	2 691	1 753	694	6 387	296	9 055	1 873	64.7	40.9	38.4	60.5	1.1
Alaska	10 707	2 032	8 675	11 801	2 807	429	1 153	502	2 084	361	6 218	8 459	64.6	49.0	40.8	54.8	4.4
Arizona	27 751	8 210	19 541	2 949	9 423	2 608	1 972	1 061	8 495	341	13 723	2 071	54.8	35.7	44.6	53.7	1.8
Arkansas	17 560	4 938	12 622	4 265	7 518	1 234	1 219	513	5 140	307	3 947	1 334	59.0	36.5	36.9	60.6	2.6
California	233 454	95 069	138 385	3 610	80 196	17 893	13 193	9 446	80 014	4 626	152 186	3 970	48.6	30.8	60.2	37.1	2.6
Colorado	23 189	6 291	16 898	3 207	9 479	1 766	1 449	1 148	5 840	404	16 309	3 096	66.2	55.2	51.5	46.1	2.4
Connecticut	23 719	4 909	18 811	5 231	7 019	2 239	1 056	902	7 319	226	32 357	8 998	59.9	43.0	58.1	40.7	1.2
Delaware	7 783	1 271	6 512	7 034	2 745	497	595	408	1 971	117	5 755	6 216	62.0	42.0	58.6	40.0	1.4
District of Columbia	X	X	X	X	X	X	X	X	X	X	X	X	65.6	45.8	90.9	7.3	1.8
Florida	71 098	17 810	53 288	2 725	23 904	4 584	5 869	2 660	22 528	1 205	37 892	1 938	56.4	40.4	50.0	49.1	0.9
Georgia	38 702	10 361	28 341	2 836	17 338	2 153	2 171	1 807	11 518	651	13 293	1 330	58.9	40.0	45.5	53.3	1.2
Hawaii	10 098	221	9 877	7 035	3 404	1 295	409	235	2 099	209	8 318	5 925	47.4	38.6	70.5	27.8	1.6
Idaho	7 378	1 982	5 397	3 347	2 659	231	692	306	2 191	256	3 648	2 263	56.8	39.1	32.6	64.5	2.8
Illinois	61 222	15 549	45 673	3 545	17 272	3 586	4 969	1 795	20 425	500	63 660	4 942	58.6	38.3	57.6	40.7	1.7
Indiana	33 450	9 292	24 158	3 676	14 613	657	2 530	926	10 748	412	22 564	3 434	62.0	33.5	43.9	54.1	1.9
Iowa	17 902	4 754	13 148	4 254	6 469	1 777	1 658	431	5 265	326	6 648	2 151	67.8	51.5	52.0	46.2	1.8
Kansas	14 516	4 058	10 458	3 614	6 057	1 913	1 182	452	3 387	271	6 825	2 358	63.7	45.3	38.0	59.7	2.3
Kentucky	24 458	4 803	19 655	4 472	9 453	1 824	2 366	730	7 084	433	14 984	3 409	69.2	45.9	37.8	60.5	1.7
Louisiana	27 800	6 241	21 559	4 661	8 881	2 455	1 716	1 058	7 165	1 160	18 589	4 019	69.5	48.6	40.6	57.8	1.6
Maine	7 877	1 239	6 638	4 998	2 019	596	615	212	2 892	197	5 375	4 046	75.4	60.5	56.3	41.0	2.7
Maryland	34 171	8 641	25 530	4 306	11 398	2 667	1 949	1 947	10 045	609	26 067	4 397	65.9	44.7	62.0	35.9	2.1
Massachusetts	46 360	9 401	36 959	5 522	13 010	1 642	2 005	1 926	15 560	626	76 161	11 379	61.6	42.8	60.7	37.5	1.8
Michigan	53 550	19 250	34 300	3 466	22 972	4 410	2 419	2 259	14 986	432	30 377	3 070	68.1	45.1	54.2	44.7	1.1
Minnesota	35 059	12 976	22 083	4 074	15 026	697	2 464	898	11 324	857	13 573	2 504	68.8	49.9	52.7	45.0	2.4
Mississippi	17 387	5 053	12 334	4 123	5 456	1 535	1 377	489	5 817	381	7 113	2 378	74.6	41.6	43.8	55.3	0.9
Missouri	26 039	5 772	20 267	3 353	8 952	3 269	1 595	951	7 988	381	19 308	3 194	70.9	38.0	44.4	53.8	1.9
Montana	6 061	1 373	4 688	4 618	1 857	225	683	242	1 421	340	3 558	3 505	64.3	49.7	41.7	55.4	2.9
Nebraska	9 184	2 171	7 014	3 754	3 367	738	754	333	2 517	296	1 847	988	62.4	41.4	38.0	59.8	2.2
Nevada	10 639	4 215	6 425	2 303	4 365	541	722	386	2 400	135	3 610	1 294	51.1	32.6	52.4	45.7	2.0
New Hampshire	6 207	1 301	4 907	3 707	2 068	190	558	169	1 682	100	8 763	6 622	66.3	48.6	52.0	46.4	1.6
New Jersey	50 052	11 102	38 950	4 377	16 426	3 366	3 192	2 255	14 701	772	64 264	7 221	57.5	31.5	58.3	40.6	1.0
New Mexico	15 015	4 501	10 515	5 042	5 406	1 445	756	535	3 946	234	7 233	3 469	59.9	42.1	53.0	42.8	4.2
New York	147 156	56 237	90 920	4 627	41 152	13 966	4 239	4 434	58 010	974	136 014	6 921	52.9	30.6	63.4	35.2	1.3
North Carolina	46 103	13 173	32 930	3 344	19 251	3 389	3 688	1 913	12 977	683	19 055	1 935	64.5	42.8	48.3	50.4	1.3
North Dakota	5 786	1 632	4 154	5 743	1 931	215	1 052	132	943	369	1 834	2 536	64.1	49.2	38.7	58.3	3.0
Ohio	59 502	16 517	42 984	3 715	21 607	5 619	3 678	1 862	19 187	474	33 133	2 863	64.5	38.5	50.7	47.7	1.6
Oklahoma	19 579	4 213	15 366	3 991	7 322	1 120	1 803	803	6 258	313	9 514	2 471	57.7	32.3	33.2	66.8	0.0
Oregon	21 465	5 495	15 970	4 064	7 172	2 341	1 313	914	6 575	531	13 598	3 460	65.2	51.8	54.2	42.1	3.6
Pennsylvania	72 244	18 834	53 410	4 181	22 629	6 870	7 601	3 031	23 079	970	47 021	3 681	61.7	38.3	52.1	46.7	1.2
Rhode Island	6 563	1 170	5 392	5 128	1 987	225	319	255	2 395	88	9 568	9 100	59.4	40.4	62.7	35.3	2.1
South Carolina	22 331	5 454	16 877	3 535	8 352	2 456	924	674	6 051	283	14 724	3 084	67.0	41.3	44.1	54.6	1.4
South Dakota	4 011	740	3 271	3 872	1 266	200	653	155	972	224	3 425	4 054	64.2	43.7	39.9	57.9	2.2
Tennessee	27 831	7 075	20 757	3 195	9 811	1 078	1 752	1 123	10 960	377	6 192	953	62.1	35.4	39.1	59.5	1.4
Texas	108 025	27 590	80 435	3 041	47 479	8 012	7 536	4 502	30 781	1 208	39 625	1 498	51.4	30.2	41.4	57.2	1.4
Utah	14 956	3 069	11 887	4 098	6 875	1 572	962	454	3 018	210	7 050	2 430	54.3	34.7	24.7	72.8	2.5
Vermont	5 608	1 502	4 106	6 553	2 407	236	455	226	1 629	96	3 330	5 315	65.7	41.6	66.6	31.0	2.5
Virginia	42 530	11 256	31 274	3 786	15 214	4 942	3 913	2 266	9 855	367	28 023	3 392	63.1	39.4	51.2	47.3	1.6
Washington	37 865	9 778	28 087	4 029	15 582	4 346	3 184	1 312	8 389	986	30 474	4 371	61.5	44.8	56.2	41.3	2.5
West Virginia	11 709	2 470	9 239	4 983	4 334	472	1 103	376	3 527	277	7 356	3 967	61.8	33.4	35.5	62.3	2.2
Wisconsin	31 878	9 637	22 241	3 873	10 878	2 193	2 409	1 214	8 849	693	23 188	4 038	69.0	53.8	52.8	45.9	1.3
Wyoming	5 037	1 681	3 356	5 759	1 724	279	548	194	783	423	1 021	1 752	54.7	39.1	27.8	68.6	3.5

1. Based on resident population estimated as of July 1 of the year shown. 2.

PART B.

States and Counties

(For explanation of symbols, see page viii)

County Highlights and Rankings

Figure B-1. Fastest Growing Counties Among the 75 Largest, 2010–2014

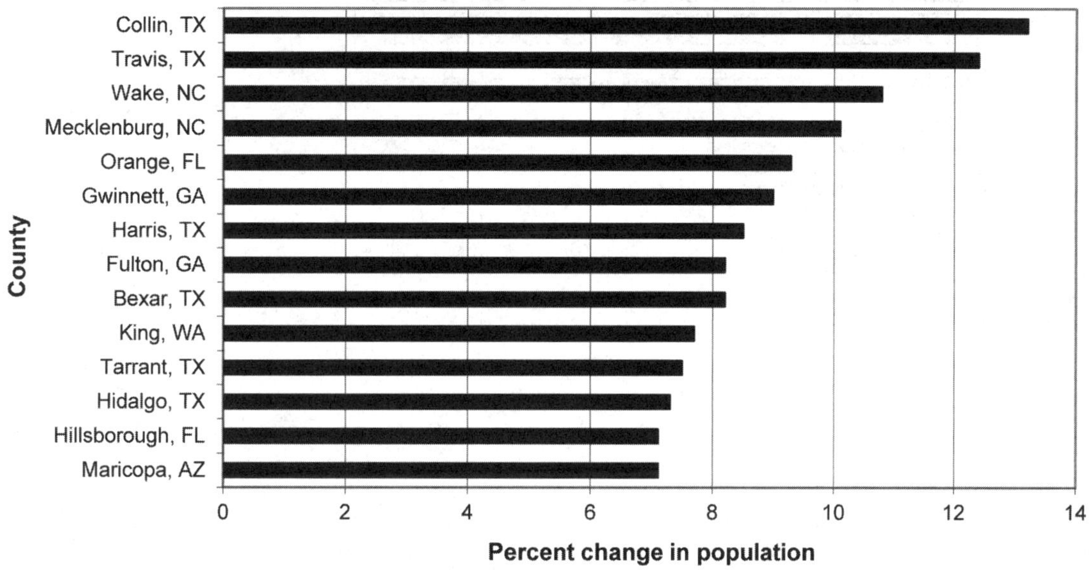

Four years after the 2010 census, the 2014 population estimates show that Los Angeles County, CA, remains, by far, the most populous county, with over 10.0 million residents. Next is Cook County, IL, which includes Chicago, with over 5.2 million people. Its population declined 3.4 percent from 2000 to 2010 but increased 1.0 percent from 2010 to 2014. New York City consists of five counties (the five boroughs), with Kings (Brooklyn) and Queens each with over 2 million residents. Queens county moved out of the top 10 in 2014, but Brooklyn's 4.7 percent growth keeps Kings the 8th most populous county in the nation. Among the 75 most populous counties, the highest growth rates from 2010 to 2014 were found in the West and the South. From 2010 to 2014, the fastest-growing of these large counties was Collin, TX, in the Dallas metropolitan area. During the past four years, Collin County's population increased by 13.2 percent followed by Travis County, TX (Austin) at 12.4 percent. In 2014, Collin County ranked 60th among the most populous counties. Two counties in North Carolina also had growth rates over 10 percent—Wake County (Raleigh) and Mecklenburg County (Charlotte). More than 1,600 counties lost population during this period. The largest proportional losses were in counties with very small populations. Among the largest counties, only New Haven County, CT, Cuyahoga County, OH (Cleveland), and Wayne County, MI (Detroit), declined in population between 2010 and 2014. Eighty-three counties had population growth rates at or above 10 percent from 2010 to 2014. Forty-nine of these fast-growing counties had more than 50,000 residents, and thirty-seven counties had more than 100,000 residents.

Within states, the number and physical size of counties varied considerably: Delaware had three counties while Texas had 254 counties. For the 3,143 counties (and county equivalents—see Appendix A) in the United States, population in 2014 ranged from 10.0 million in Los Angeles, CA, to 86 in Loving County, TX. Other particularly large counties in terms of population are Cook County, IL (over 5.2 million people), encompassing Chicago and its suburbs, Harris County, TX (containing Houston) with 4.4 million people, and Maricopa County, AZ (containing Phoenix), with over 4.0 million people. There were 43 counties with a population of 1,000,000 or more; these counties combined contain more than one-fourth of the U.S. population. Over half of the U.S. population lived in the 150 largest counties, those with a population of 450,000 or more. At the other extreme, there were 35 counties with fewer than 1,000 people in 2014. The median county population size was 25,715.

In terms of land area, counties range from the nearly 377,000 square kilometers of Yukon-Koyukuk Census Area, AK; to Kalawao County, HI, with 31 square kilometers; New York County, NY (Manhattan), with 59 square kilometers; Bristol County, RI, with 63 square kilometers; and Arlington County, VA, with 67 square kilometers.[1] Counties tend to be larger in the western United States (most of the largest 50 in

[1]Several independent cities in Virginia, which are treated as counties for tabulation purposes, were excluded here.

Figure B-2. Counties Among the 75 Largest with the Highest and Lowest Proportion of Population with a Bachelor's Degree or More, 2009–2013

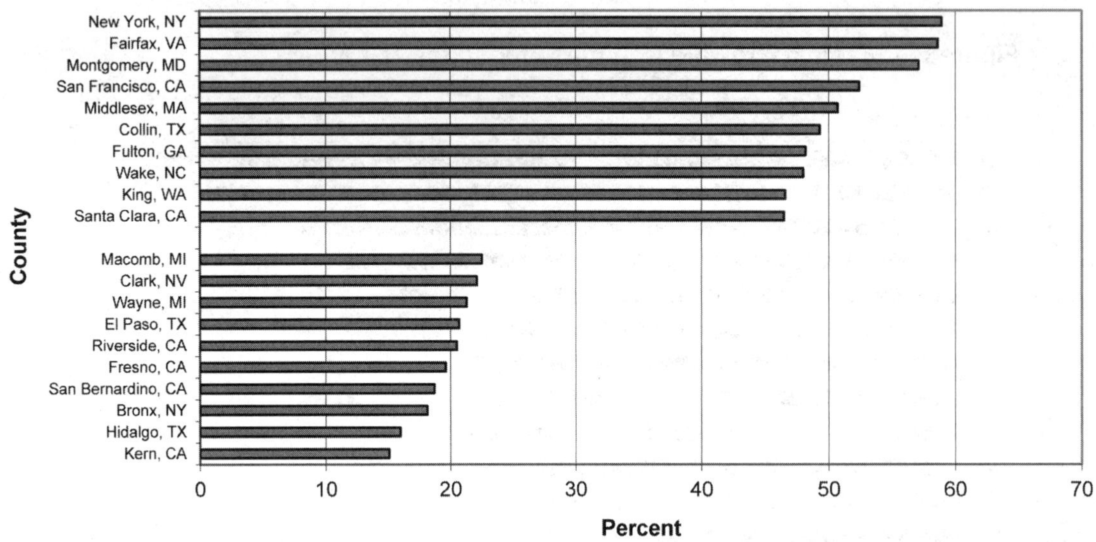

size are in that region). The median land area for all U.S. counties was about 1,600 square kilometers in 2010.

While New York County, NY, had one of the smallest land areas, it had by far the highest population density among U.S. counties in 2014, with over 27,000 persons per square kilometer. No other county approached that density (although three other New York City boroughs were among the top five counties in population density). San Francisco had the highest population density outside of New York City, with Suffolk County, MA (Boston); Philadelphia County, PA; and Washington, DC, also among the top 10 counties. The median county only had about 17 persons per square kilometer, with only 116 counties having more than 500 persons per square kilometer. The nation's largest county in terms of population (Los Angeles) had a population density of 962.6 persons per square kilometer. This density ranked 21st among the 75 most populous U.S. counties.

Proportionally large year-to-year labor force changes are not unusual for counties with small populations. The 2014 annual averages reflect a national labor force that increased by 0.3 percent. Among the 75 most populous counties, 12 counties' labor forces grew by 2.0 percent or more between 2013 and 2014. Travis County, TX and Honolulu County, HI, experienced the largest increase among the 75 most populous counties at 2.7 percent each followed by Orange County, FL and Collin County, TX at 2.6 percent each. A total of 12 counties experienced increases of between 2.0 and 3.0 percent. Nearly 1,700 counties experienced declines in their labor forces from 2013 to 2014, with 66 counties losing 5 percent or more. Among the most populous 75 counties, 16 counties had decreases in their labor forces, led by Shelby County, TN at 3.1 percent.

The national annual average unemployment rate was 6.2 percent in 2014, down from 7.4 in 2013 and 8.1 in 2012 but still higher than the unemployment rate of 5.8 percent in 2008. Over 1,400 counties had unemployment rates above the national average of 6.2 percent in 2014 and over 169 counties had unemployment rates greater than 10 percent, down from 1,100 counties in 2010 but still higher than the 125 counties in 2008. Of the 10 counties with the highest unemployment rates, only Imperial County, CA, and Yuma County, AZ, had populations over 100,000. Among the 75 most populous counties, 30 exceeded the national unemployment rate of 6.2 percent. Unemployment was 11.6 percent in Fresno County, CA. Hennepin, MN and Salt Lake, UT had the lowest unemployment rate at 3.7 percent followed by Travis, TX at 4.0 percent. In 2014, seven counties in North Dakota had unemployment rates of less than 2 percent.

Among the 75 largest counties, two of the three counties with the highest unemployment rates, Fresno and Kern counties in CA, ranked among the top counties for agricultural sales. Meanwhile, Wayne County, MI, which ranked second highest in manufacturing employment, had the third highest unemployment rate among the 75 most populous counties. Two of the ten lowest unemployment rates were in the two counties that topped the rankings for employment in professional, scientific, and technical occupations (Fairfax County, VA and Montgomery County, MD.) These two counties were also at the top of the rankings for median household income and educational attainment, with more than 57 percent of residents holding bachelor's, master's, doctoral, or professional degrees. Five large counties had college-educated proportions of less than 20 percent, and all five were among the 10 counties with the highest unemployment rates. Nationally, 29.6 percent of the population held bachelor's degrees or higher in 2013.

75 Largest Counties by 2014 Population

Selected Rankings

Population, 2014			Land area, 2010				Population density, 2014				
Population rank		Population [col 2]	Population rank	Land area rank	County	Land area (Square kilometers) [col 1]	Population rank	Density rank	County	Density (per square kilometer) [col 4]
1	Los Angeles, CA	10 116 705	12	1	San Bernardino, CA	51 947	20	1	New York, NY	27 733.4
2	Cook, IL	5 246 456	4	2	Maricopa, AZ	23 828	8	2	Kings, NY	14 326.7
3	Harris, TX	4 441 370	42	3	Pima, AZ	23 794	26	3	Bronx, NY	13 194.1
4	Maricopa, AZ	4 087 191	62	4	Kern, CA	21 062	11	4	Queens, NY	8 261.9
5	San Diego, CA	3 263 431	14	5	Clark, NV	20 439	65	5	San Francisco, CA	7 045.2
6	Orange, CA	3 145 515	10	6	Riverside, CA	18 665	23	6	Philadelphia, PA	4 496.5
7	Miami-Dade, FL	2 662 874	48	7	Fresno, CA	15 431	75	7	Essex, NJ	2 433.4
8	Kings, NY	2 621 793	5	8	San Diego, CA	10 895	2	8	Cook, IL	2 143.2
9	Dallas, TX	2 518 638	1	9	Los Angeles, CA	10 510	28	9	Nassau, NY	1 843.5
10	Riverside, CA	2 329 271	13	10	King, WA	5 479	54	10	Bergen, NJ	1 548.2
11	Queens, NY	2 321 580	27	11	Palm Beach, FL	5 102	6	11	Orange, CA	1 535.9
12	San Bernardino, CA	2 112 619	7	12	Miami-Dade, FL	4 915	49	12	Milwaukee, WI	1 530.2
13	King, WA	2 079 967	66	13	Ventura, CA	4 774	52	13	Pinellas, FL	1 323.1
14	Clark, NV	2 069 681	3	14	Harris, TX	4 412	37	14	Fairfax, VA	1 122.9
15	Tarrant, TX	1 945 360	69	15	Pierce, WA	4 324	9	15	Dallas, TX	1 115.9
16	Santa Clara, CA	1 894 605	70	16	Hidalgo, TX	4 069	19	16	Wayne, MI	1 113.4
17	Broward, FL	1 869 235	73	17	Worcester, MA	3 913	55	17	Du Page, IL	1 099.9
18	Bexar, TX	1 855 866	16	18	Santa Clara, CA	3 341	30	18	Cuyahoga, OH	1 064.0
19	Wayne, MI	1 764 804	18	19	Bexar, TX	3 211	67	19	Middlesex, NJ	1 045.4
20	New York, NY	1 636 268	17	20	Broward, FL	3 133	3	20	Harris, TX	1 006.7
21	Alameda, CA	1 610 921	56	21	Erie, NY	2 701	1	21	Los Angeles, CA	962.6
22	Middlesex, MA	1 570 315	29	22	Hillsborough, FL	2 642	53	22	Marion, IN	910.6
23	Philadelphia, PA	1 560 297	68	23	El Paso, TX	2 623	33	23	Franklin, OH	893.6
24	Suffolk, NY	1 502 968	36	24	Travis, TX	2 565	47	24	Westchester, NY	872.3
25	Sacramento, CA	1 482 026	25	25	Sacramento, CA	2 498	15	25	Tarrant, TX	869.6
26	Bronx, NY	1 438 159	2	26	Cook, IL	2 448	35	26	Hennepin, MN	845.2
27	Palm Beach, FL	1 397 710	24	27	Suffolk, NY	2 362	21	27	Alameda, CA	841.7
28	Nassau, NY	1 358 627	31	28	Orange, FL	2 340	40	28	Montgomery, MD	810.1
29	Hillsborough, FL	1 316 298	9	29	Dallas, TX	2 257	61	29	Gwinnett, GA	787.4
30	Cuyahoga, OH	1 259 828	32	30	Oakland, MI	2 247	74	30	Hamilton, OH	767.5
31	Orange, FL	1 253 001	15	31	Tarrant, TX	2 237	43	31	St. Louis, MO	761.9
32	Oakland, MI	1 237 868	60	32	Collin, TX	2 179	41	32	Mecklenburg, NC	746.2
33	Franklin, OH	1 231 393	44	33	Wake, NC	2 163	22	33	Middlesex, MA	741.4
34	Allegheny, PA	1 231 255	22	34	Middlesex, MA	2 118	45	34	Fulton, GA	730.4
35	Hennepin, MN	1 212 064	6	35	Orange, CA	2 048	57	35	Prince George's, MD	723.5
36	Travis, TX	1 151 145	51	36	Shelby, TN	1 977	64	36	Macomb, MI	693.1
37	Fairfax, VA	1 137 538	59	37	Duval, FL	1 974	72	37	Montgomery, PA	653.0
38	Contra Costa, CA	1 111 339	39	38	Salt Lake, UT	1 923	34	38	Allegheny, PA	651.1
39	Salt Lake, UT	1 091 742	21	39	Alameda, CA	1 914	46	39	Honolulu, HI	637.4
40	Montgomery, MD	1 030 447	58	40	Hartford, CT	1 904	24	40	Suffolk, NY	636.3
41	Mecklenburg, NC	1 012 539	34	41	Allegheny, PA	1 891	38	41	Contra Costa, CA	599.4
42	Pima, AZ	1 004 516	38	42	Contra Costa, CA	1 854	17	42	Broward, FL	596.6
43	St. Louis, MO	1 001 876	50	43	Fairfield, CT	1 618	25	43	Sacramento, CA	593.3
44	Wake, NC	998 691	19	44	Wayne, MI	1 585	50	44	Fairfield, CT	584.3
45	Fulton, GA	996 319	63	45	New Haven, CT	1 566	18	45	Bexar, TX	578.0
46	Honolulu, HI	991 788	46	46	Honolulu, HI	1 556	39	46	Salt Lake, UT	567.7
47	Westchester, NY	972 634	71	47	Baltimore, MD	1 550	16	47	Santa Clara, CA	567.1
48	Fresno, CA	965 974	35	48	Hennepin, MN	1 434	32	48	Oakland, MI	550.9
49	Milwaukee, WI	956 406	33	49	Franklin, OH	1 378	63	49	New Haven, CT	550.0
50	Fairfield, CT	945 438	45	50	Fulton, GA	1 364	7	50	Miami-Dade, FL	541.8
51	Shelby, TN	938 803	41	51	Mecklenburg, NC	1 357	31	51	Orange, FL	535.5
52	Pinellas, FL	938 098	43	52	St. Louis, MO	1 315	71	52	Baltimore, MD	533.5
53	Marion, IN	934 243	40	53	Montgomery, MD	1 272	29	53	Hillsborough, FL	498.2
54	Bergen, NJ	933 572	72	54	Montgomery, PA	1 251	51	54	Shelby, TN	474.9
55	Du Page, IL	932 708	57	55	Prince George's, MD	1 250	58	55	Hartford, CT	471.6
56	Erie, NY	922 835	64	56	Macomb, MI	1 241	44	56	Wake, NC	461.7
57	Prince George's, MD	904 430	30	57	Cuyahoga, OH	1 184	59	57	Duval, FL	454.8
58	Hartford, CT	897 985	47	58	Westchester, NY	1 115	36	58	Travis, TX	448.8
59	Duval, FL	897 698	61	58	Gwinnett, GA	1 115	60	59	Collin, TX	406.3
60	Collin, TX	885 241	74	60	Hamilton, OH	1 051	13	60	King, WA	379.6
61	Gwinnett, GA	877 922	53	61	Marion, IN	1 026	56	61	Erie, NY	341.7
62	Kern, CA	874 589	37	62	Fairfax, VA	1 013	68	62	El Paso, TX	317.8
63	New Haven, CT	861 277	55	63	Du Page, IL	848	5	63	San Diego, CA	299.5
64	Macomb, MI	860 112	67	64	Middlesex, NJ	800	27	64	Palm Beach, FL	274.0
65	San Francisco, CA	852 469	28	65	Nassau, NY	737	73	65	Worcester, MA	207.9
66	Ventura, CA	846 178	52	66	Pinellas, FL	709	70	66	Hidalgo, TX	204.2
67	Middlesex, NJ	836 297	49	67	Milwaukee, WI	625	69	67	Pierce, WA	192.4
68	El Paso, TX	833 487	54	68	Bergen, NJ	603	66	68	Ventura, CA	177.2
69	Pierce, WA	831 928	23	69	Philadelphia, PA	347	4	69	Maricopa, AZ	171.5
70	Hidalgo, TX	831 073	75	70	Essex, NJ	327	10	70	Riverside, CA	124.8
71	Baltimore, MD	826 925	11	71	Queens, NY	281	14	71	Clark, NV	101.3
72	Montgomery, PA	816 857	8	72	Kings, NY	183	48	72	Fresno, CA	62.6
73	Worcester, MA	813 475	65	73	San Francisco, CA	121	42	73	Pima, AZ	42.2
74	Hamilton, OH	806 631	26	74	Bronx, NY	109	62	74	Kern, CA	41.5
75	Essex, NJ	795 723	20	75	New York, NY	59	12	75	San Bernardino, CA	40.7

75 Largest Counties by 2014 Population

Selected Rankings

Percent population change, 2010-2014				Employment/residence ratio, 2009-2013				Percent White, not Hispanic or Latino, alone or in combination, 2013			
Population rank	Percent change rank	County	Percent change [col 23]	Population rank	Number of employees per resident rank	County	Number of employees per resident [col 34]	Population rank	White rank	County	Percent white [col 5]
60	1	Collin, TX	13.2	20	1	New York, NY	2.79	64	1	Macomb, MI	83.4
36	2	Travis, TX	12.4	45	2	Fulton, GA	1.81	34	2	Allegheny, PA	81.5
44	3	Wake, NC	10.8	65	3	San Francisco, CA	1.38	73	3	Worcester, MA	81.1
41	4	Mecklenburg, NC	10.1	35	4	Hennepin, MN	1.36	72	4	Montgomery, PA	79.2
31	5	Orange, FL	9.3	74	5	Hamilton, OH	1.32	56	5	Erie, NY	78.3
61	6	Gwinnett, GA	9.0	53	6	Marion, IN	1.31	52	6	Pinellas, FL	77.3
3	7	Harris, TX	8.5	9	7	Dallas, TX	1.29	22	7	Middlesex, MA	77.2
18	8	Bexar, TX	8.2	41	8	Mecklenburg, NC	1.28	32	8	Oakland, MI	75.4
45	8	Fulton, GA	8.2	31	9	Orange, FL	1.26	39	9	Salt Lake, UT	75.0
13	10	King, WA	7.7	30	10	Cuyahoga, OH	1.24	69	10	Pierce, WA	74.1
15	11	Tarrant, TX	7.5	33	11	Franklin, OH	1.20	35	11	Hennepin, MN	73.2
70	12	Hidalgo, TX	7.3	55	11	Du Page, IL	1.20	24	12	Suffolk, NY	71.1
4	13	Maricopa, AZ	7.1	23	13	Philadelphia, PA	1.19	55	13	Du Page, IL	70.2
29	13	Hillsborough, FL	7.1	36	13	Travis, TX	1.19	43	14	St. Louis, MO	69.6
17	15	Broward, FL	6.9	43	13	St. Louis, MO	1.19	33	15	Franklin, OH	68.8
7	16	Miami-Dade, FL	6.7	59	13	Duval, FL	1.19	74	15	Hamilton, OH	68.8
21	16	Alameda, CA	6.7	51	17	Shelby, TN	1.18	63	17	New Haven, CT	67.1
9	18	Dallas, TX	6.4	58	18	Hartford, CT	1.17	13	18	King, WA	66.9
10	18	Riverside, CA	6.4	13	19	King, WA	1.16	50	19	Fairfield, CT	65.7
16	20	Santa Clara, CA	6.3	34	19	Allegheny, PA	1.16	58	20	Hartford, CT	65.6
14	21	Clark, NV	6.1	3	21	Harris, TX	1.15	28	21	Nassau, NY	64.2
39	22	Salt Lake, UT	6.0	39	21	Salt Lake, UT	1.15	60	22	Collin, TX	63.1
40	22	Montgomery, MD	6.0	72	21	Montgomery, PA	1.15	44	23	Wake, NC	62.9
27	24	Palm Beach, FL	5.9	16	24	Santa Clara, CA	1.13	71	24	Baltimore, MD	62.2
38	24	Contra Costa, CA	5.9	32	24	Oakland, MI	1.13	30	25	Cuyahoga, OH	62.1
65	24	San Francisco, CA	5.9	29	26	Hillsborough, FL	1.11	54	26	Bergen, NJ	60.7
33	27	Franklin, OH	5.8	19	27	Wayne, MI	1.09	53	27	Marion, IN	60.5
5	28	San Diego, CA	5.4	22	27	Middlesex, MA	1.09	4	28	Maricopa, AZ	59.3
35	29	Hennepin, MN	5.2	49	27	Milwaukee, WI	1.09	27	29	Palm Beach, FL	59.2
37	29	Fairfax, VA	5.2	2	30	Cook, IL	1.08	59	30	Duval, FL	57.5
8	31	Kings, NY	4.7	56	31	Erie, NY	1.07	47	31	Westchester, NY	56.9
57	31	Prince George's, MD	4.7	75	31	Essex, NJ	1.07	42	32	Pima, AZ	55.5
69	33	Pierce, WA	4.6	7	33	Miami-Dade, FL	1.06	37	33	Fairfax, VA	55.4
6	34	Orange, CA	4.5	18	33	Bexar, TX	1.06	49	34	Milwaukee, WI	55.2
22	34	Middlesex, MA	4.5	6	35	Orange, CA	1.05	29	35	Hillsborough, FL	53.9
25	34	Sacramento, CA	4.5	44	35	Wake, NC	1.05	19	36	Wayne, MI	51.8
62	37	Kern, CA	4.2	50	35	Fairfield, CT	1.05	15	37	Tarrant, TX	51.6
11	38	Queens, NY	4.1	1	38	Los Angeles, CA	1.03	36	37	Travis, TX	51.6
68	38	El Paso, TX	4.1	25	38	Sacramento, CA	1.03	25	39	Sacramento, CA	50.9
46	40	Honolulu, HI	4.0	27	38	Palm Beach, FL	1.03	41	40	Mecklenburg, NC	50.8
59	41	Duval, FL	3.9	4	41	Maricopa, AZ	1.02	5	41	San Diego, CA	49.9
12	42	San Bernardino, CA	3.8	5	41	San Diego, CA	1.02	38	42	Contra Costa, CA	49.6
26	42	Bronx, NY	3.8	52	41	Pinellas, FL	1.02	66	43	Ventura, CA	49.3
48	42	Fresno, CA	3.8	14	44	Clark, NV	1.01	40	44	Montgomery, MD	49.2
53	45	Marion, IN	3.4	48	44	Fresno, CA	1.01	20	45	New York, NY	49.1
67	46	Middlesex, NJ	3.3	62	44	Kern, CA	1.01	14	46	Clark, NV	48.8
20	47	New York, NY	3.2	37	47	Fairfax, VA	1.00	67	47	Middlesex, NJ	47.5
50	48	Fairfield, CT	3.1	42	47	Pima, AZ	1.00	31	48	Orange, FL	45.5
54	48	Bergen, NJ	3.1	46	47	Honolulu, HI	1.00	6	49	Orange, CA	44.8
1	50	Los Angeles, CA	3.0	21	50	Alameda, CA	0.99	2	50	Cook, IL	44.5
32	50	Oakland, MI	3.0	68	50	El Paso, TX	0.99	65	51	San Francisco, CA	44.4
66	52	Ventura, CA	2.8	15	52	Tarrant, TX	0.98	61	52	Gwinnett, GA	43.2
71	53	Baltimore, MD	2.7	54	53	Bergen, NJ	0.97	45	53	Fulton, GA	42.0
42	54	Pima, AZ	2.5	47	54	Westchester, NY	0.96	17	54	Broward, FL	41.9
47	54	Westchester, NY	2.5	70	54	Hidalgo, TX	0.96	10	55	Riverside, CA	39.9
52	56	Pinellas, FL	2.4	67	56	Middlesex, NJ	0.95	51	56	Shelby, TN	38.6
64	57	Macomb, MI	2.3	63	57	New Haven, CT	0.94	62	56	Kern, CA	38.6
23	58	Philadelphia, PA	2.2	40	58	Montgomery, MD	0.93	23	58	Philadelphia, PA	37.7
72	59	Montgomery, PA	2.1	17	59	Broward, FL	0.92	8	59	Kings, NY	37.1
73	60	Worcester, MA	1.9	12	60	San Bernardino, CA	0.91	16	60	Santa Clara, CA	36.5
55	61	Du Page, IL	1.7	61	61	Gwinnett, GA	0.89	21	61	Alameda, CA	36.4
75	62	Essex, NJ	1.5	66	61	Ventura, CA	0.89	75	62	Essex, NJ	33.8
28	63	Nassau, NY	1.4	28	63	Nassau, NY	0.88	12	63	San Bernardino, CA	33.1
51	64	Shelby, TN	1.2	60	63	Collin, TX	0.88	48	64	Fresno, CA	33.0
2	65	Cook, IL	1.0	69	63	Pierce, WA	0.88	3	65	Harris, TX	32.9
49	66	Milwaukee, WI	0.9	24	66	Suffolk, NY	0.87	46	65	Honolulu, HI	32.9
24	67	Suffolk, NY	0.6	71	66	Baltimore, MD	0.87	9	67	Dallas, TX	32.7
34	67	Allegheny, PA	0.6	73	66	Worcester, MA	0.87	18	68	Bexar, TX	30.7
74	69	Hamilton, OH	0.5	64	69	Macomb, MI	0.83	1	69	Los Angeles, CA	28.8
56	70	Erie, NY	0.4	10	70	Riverside, CA	0.80	11	70	Queens, NY	27.8
58	70	Hartford, CT	0.4	38	71	Contra Costa, CA	0.77	57	71	Prince George's, MD	15.8
43	72	St. Louis, MO	0.3	8	72	Kings, NY	0.74	7	72	Miami-Dade, FL	15.7
63	73	New Haven, CT	-0.1	57	73	Prince George's, MD	0.73	68	73	El Paso, TX	14.2
30	74	Cuyahoga, OH	-1.6	26	74	Bronx, NY	0.70	26	74	Bronx, NY	11.2
19	75	Wayne, MI	-3.1	11	75	Queens, NY	0.67	70	75	Hidalgo, TX	7.4

75 Largest Counties by 2014 Population

Selected Rankings

Percent Black, not Hispanic or Latino, alone or in combination, 2013				Percent American Indian, Alaska Native, alone or in combination, 2013				Percent Asian or Pacific Islander, alone or in combination, 2013			
Population rank	Black rank	County	Percent black [col 6]	Population rank	American Indian Alaska native rank	County	Percent American Indian, Alaska native [col 7]	Population rank	Asian or Pacific Islander rank	County	Percent Asian or Pacific Islander [col 8]
57	1	Prince George's, MD	64.3	42	1	Pima, AZ	3.1	46	1	Honolulu, HI	77.3
51	2	Shelby, TN	53.3	69	2	Pierce, WA	2.6	65	2	San Francisco, CA	36.7
45	3	Fulton, GA	44.5	4	3	Maricopa, AZ	2.1	16	3	Santa Clara, CA	36.2
23	4	Philadelphia, PA	42.8	13	4	King, WA	1.7	21	4	Alameda, CA	31.5
19	5	Wayne, MI	40.3	25	5	Sacramento, CA	1.6	11	5	Queens, NY	26.3
75	6	Essex, NJ	39.9	35	6	Hennepin, MN	1.5	67	6	Middlesex, NJ	24.1
8	7	Kings, NY	32.1	46	6	Honolulu, HI	1.5	6	7	Orange, CA	20.9
41	8	Mecklenburg, NC	32.0	62	8	Kern, CA	1.3	37	8	Fairfax, VA	20.7
26	9	Bronx, NY	30.6	48	9	Fresno, CA	1.2	13	9	King, WA	19.2
30	9	Cuyahoga, OH	30.6	49	9	Milwaukee, WI	1.2	25	10	Sacramento, CA	18.6
59	11	Duval, FL	30.2	39	11	Salt Lake, UT	1.1	38	10	Contra Costa, CA	18.6
53	12	Marion, IN	28.6	5	12	San Diego, CA	1.0	54	12	Bergen, NJ	16.6
71	13	Baltimore, MD	28.1	10	12	Riverside, CA	1.0	40	13	Montgomery, MD	16.2
17	14	Broward, FL	28.0	12	12	San Bernardino, CA	1.0	1	14	Los Angeles, CA	15.6
49	15	Milwaukee, WI	27.6	14	12	Clark, NV	1.0	5	15	San Diego, CA	13.9
74	16	Hamilton, OH	27.1	19	12	Wayne, MI	1.0	60	16	Collin, TX	13.4
61	17	Gwinnett, GA	25.9	38	12	Contra Costa, CA	1.0	20	17	New York, NY	12.9
43	18	St. Louis, MO	24.5	57	12	Prince George's, MD	1.0	8	18	Kings, NY	12.4
2	19	Cook, IL	24.4	15	19	Tarrant, TX	0.9	14	19	Clark, NV	12.1
33	20	Franklin, OH	23.2	21	19	Alameda, CA	0.9	61	20	Gwinnett, GA	11.9
9	21	Dallas, TX	22.8	33	19	Franklin, OH	0.9	55	21	Du Page, IL	11.7
44	22	Wake, NC	21.6	41	19	Mecklenburg, NC	0.9	22	22	Middlesex, MA	11.5
31	23	Orange, FL	20.9	56	19	Erie, NY	0.9	48	23	Fresno, CA	10.8
3	24	Harris, TX	19.1	60	19	Collin, TX	0.9	69	23	Pierce, WA	10.8
11	24	Queens, NY	19.1	64	19	Macomb, MI	0.9	28	25	Nassau, NY	9.3
40	26	Montgomery, MD	18.4	11	26	Queens, NY	0.8	66	26	Ventura, CA	8.6
27	27	Palm Beach, FL	18.3	23	26	Philadelphia, PA	0.8	12	27	San Bernardino, CA	7.9
7	28	Miami-Dade, FL	17.2	32	26	Oakland, MI	0.8	35	28	Hennepin, MN	7.8
29	29	Hillsborough, FL	16.8	44	26	Wake, NC	0.8	10	29	Riverside, CA	7.7
15	30	Tarrant, TX	16.0	53	26	Marion, IN	0.8	72	29	Montgomery, PA	7.7
32	31	Oakland, MI	15.1	59	26	Duval, FL	0.8	2	31	Cook, IL	7.4
34	32	Allegheny, PA	14.3	65	26	San Francisco, CA	0.8	23	31	Philadelphia, PA	7.4
47	32	Westchester, NY	14.3	66	26	Ventura, CA	0.8	3	33	Harris, TX	7.2
56	34	Erie, NY	14.0	71	26	Baltimore, MD	0.8	32	34	Oakland, MI	7.0
20	35	New York, NY	13.7	9	35	Dallas, TX	0.7	36	34	Travis, TX	7.0
58	35	Hartford, CT	13.7	16	35	Santa Clara, CA	0.7	45	34	Fulton, GA	7.0
35	37	Hennepin, MN	13.6	36	35	Travis, TX	0.7	44	37	Wake, NC	6.8
63	38	New Haven, CT	13.1	45	35	Fulton, GA	0.7	47	38	Westchester, NY	6.6
21	39	Alameda, CA	12.8	52	35	Pinellas, FL	0.7	39	39	Salt Lake, UT	6.4
14	40	Clark, NV	11.7	61	35	Gwinnett, GA	0.7	71	39	Baltimore, MD	6.4
28	40	Nassau, NY	11.7	1	41	Los Angeles, CA	0.6	31	41	Orange, FL	6.2
25	42	Sacramento, CA	11.6	6	41	Orange, CA	0.6	9	42	Dallas, TX	6.1
64	43	Macomb, MI	11.3	8	41	Kings, NY	0.6	50	43	Fairfield, CT	5.9
50	44	Fairfield, CT	11.2	18	41	Bexar, TX	0.6	15	44	Tarrant, TX	5.8
52	44	Pinellas, FL	11.2	26	41	Bronx, NY	0.6	41	45	Mecklenburg, NC	5.7
37	46	Fairfax, VA	10.2	29	41	Hillsborough, FL	0.6	59	46	Duval, FL	5.6
38	47	Contra Costa, CA	10.0	30	41	Cuyahoga, OH	0.6	75	46	Essex, NJ	5.6
67	48	Middlesex, NJ	9.9	31	41	Orange, FL	0.6	58	48	Hartford, CT	5.3
72	49	Montgomery, PA	9.8	37	41	Fairfax, VA	0.6	62	48	Kern, CA	5.3
60	50	Collin, TX	9.7	40	41	Montgomery, MD	0.6	33	50	Franklin, OH	5.0
12	51	San Bernardino, CA	9.2	43	41	St. Louis, MO	0.6	57	50	Prince George's, MD	5.0
69	52	Pierce, WA	9.1	51	41	Shelby, TN	0.6	73	50	Worcester, MA	5.0
1	53	Los Angeles, CA	8.9	58	41	Hartford, CT	0.6	4	53	Maricopa, AZ	4.9
36	54	Travis, TX	8.7	63	41	New Haven, CT	0.6	29	54	Hillsborough, FL	4.6
18	55	Bexar, TX	7.7	73	41	Worcester, MA	0.6	43	55	St. Louis, MO	4.5
24	55	Suffolk, NY	7.7	74	41	Hamilton, OH	0.6	17	56	Broward, FL	4.4
13	57	King, WA	7.6	75	41	Essex, NJ	0.6	63	56	New Haven, CT	4.4
10	58	Riverside, CA	6.9	2	58	Cook, IL	0.5	24	58	Suffolk, NY	4.3
65	59	San Francisco, CA	6.3	3	58	Harris, TX	0.5	49	59	Milwaukee, WI	4.2
62	60	Kern, CA	5.9	17	58	Broward, FL	0.5	26	60	Bronx, NY	4.1
4	61	Maricopa, AZ	5.8	20	58	New York, NY	0.5	64	60	Macomb, MI	4.1
54	61	Bergen, NJ	5.8	24	58	Suffolk, NY	0.5	52	62	Pinellas, FL	4.0
5	63	San Diego, CA	5.7	34	58	Allegheny, PA	0.5	34	63	Allegheny, PA	3.7
22	64	Middlesex, MA	5.4	67	58	Middlesex, NJ	0.5	42	63	Pima, AZ	3.7
55	64	Du Page, IL	5.4	68	58	El Paso, TX	0.5	19	65	Wayne, MI	3.6
48	66	Fresno, CA	5.3	22	66	Middlesex, MA	0.4	56	66	Erie, NY	3.5
73	67	Worcester, MA	4.8	27	66	Palm Beach, FL	0.4	30	67	Cuyahoga, OH	3.4
42	68	Pima, AZ	4.0	28	66	Nassau, NY	0.4	18	68	Bexar, TX	3.3
46	69	Honolulu, HI	3.8	47	66	Westchester, NY	0.4	27	69	Palm Beach, FL	3.2
68	70	El Paso, TX	3.4	50	66	Fairfield, CT	0.4	53	70	Marion, IN	3.0
16	71	Santa Clara, CA	3.0	55	66	Du Page, IL	0.4	51	71	Shelby, TN	2.9
66	72	Ventura, CA	2.2	72	66	Montgomery, PA	0.4	74	72	Hamilton, OH	2.8
39	73	Salt Lake, UT	2.1	54	73	Bergen, NJ	0.3	7	73	Miami-Dade, FL	2.0
6	74	Orange, CA	2.0	7	74	Miami-Dade, FL	0.2	68	74	El Paso, TX	1.6
70	75	Hidalgo, TX	0.5	70	75	Hidalgo, TX	0.1	70	75	Hidalgo, TX	1.1

75 Largest Counties by 2014 Population

Selected Rankings

Percent Hispanic or Latino,[1] 2013				Percent under 18 years old, 2013				Percent 65 years old and over, 2013			
Population rank	Hispanic or Latino rank	County	Percent Hispanic or Latino [col 9]	Population rank	Under 18 years old rank	County	Percent under 18 years old [cols 10 and 11]	Population rank	65 years old and over rank	County	Percent 65 years old and over [cols 17 and 18]
70	1	Hidalgo, TX	90.7	70	1	Hidalgo, TX	34.0	52	1	Pinellas, FL	22.6
68	2	El Paso, TX	80.8	62	2	Kern, CA	29.6	27	2	Palm Beach, FL	22.5
7	3	Miami-Dade, FL	65.0	48	3	Fresno, CA	29.2	42	3	Pima, AZ	17.2
18	4	Bexar, TX	59.0	68	4	El Paso, TX	28.9	34	4	Allegheny, PA	17.1
26	5	Bronx, NY	54.3	39	5	Salt Lake, UT	28.5	56	5	Erie, NY	16.4
48	6	Fresno, CA	51.5	61	6	Gwinnett, GA	28.1	30	6	Cuyahoga, OH	16.2
12	7	San Bernardino, CA	50.9	12	7	San Bernardino, CA	27.7	28	7	Nassau, NY	16.1
62	8	Kern, CA	50.8	60	8	Collin, TX	27.6	43	7	St. Louis, MO	16.1
1	9	Los Angeles, CA	48.1	3	9	Harris, TX	27.4	72	7	Montgomery, PA	16.1
10	10	Riverside, CA	46.8	15	10	Tarrant, TX	27.3	54	10	Bergen, NJ	15.8
66	11	Ventura, CA	41.5	9	11	Dallas, TX	27.1	46	11	Honolulu, HI	15.5
3	12	Harris, TX	41.4	10	12	Riverside, CA	26.8	47	11	Westchester, NY	15.5
9	13	Dallas, TX	38.9	18	13	Bexar, TX	26.4	71	11	Baltimore, MD	15.5
42	14	Pima, AZ	35.6	26	14	Bronx, NY	25.7	58	14	Hartford, CT	15.4
6	15	Orange, CA	34.1	51	15	Shelby, TN	25.6	63	15	New Haven, CT	15.3
36	16	Travis, TX	33.8	4	16	Maricopa, AZ	25.4	64	15	Macomb, MI	15.3
5	17	San Diego, CA	32.8	44	17	Wake, NC	25.3	17	17	Broward, FL	15.0
14	18	Clark, NV	30.0	53	18	Marion, IN	24.9	7	18	Miami-Dade, FL	14.9
4	18	Maricopa, AZ	30.0	41	19	Mecklenburg, NC	24.8	24	18	Suffolk, NY	14.9
31	20	Orange, FL	28.7	25	20	Sacramento, CA	24.7	32	20	Oakland, MI	14.6
11	21	Queens, NY	27.9	49	21	Milwaukee, WI	24.5	20	21	New York, NY	14.2
15	22	Tarrant, TX	27.5	66	21	Ventura, CA	24.5	50	21	Fairfield, CT	14.2
17	23	Broward, FL	26.8	14	23	Clark, NV	24.2	65	21	San Francisco, CA	14.2
16	24	Santa Clara, CA	26.6	19	23	Wayne, MI	24.2	74	24	Hamilton, OH	14.0
29	25	Hillsborough, FL	26.0	69	23	Pierce, WA	24.2	73	25	Worcester, MA	13.9
20	26	New York, NY	25.7	75	23	Essex, NJ	24.2	22	26	Middlesex, MA	13.8
38	27	Contra Costa, CA	24.9	37	27	Fairfax, VA	24.0	38	26	Contra Costa, CA	13.8
2	28	Cook, IL	24.7	50	28	Fairfield, CT	23.9	19	28	Wayne, MI	13.5
47	29	Westchester, NY	23.3	38	29	Contra Costa, CA	23.8	4	29	Maricopa, AZ	13.4
21	30	Alameda, CA	22.6	55	29	Du Page, IL	23.8	11	29	Queens, NY	13.4
25	31	Sacramento, CA	22.2	33	31	Franklin, OH	23.7	40	29	Montgomery, MD	13.4
75	32	Essex, NJ	21.6	40	32	Montgomery, MD	23.6	66	32	Ventura, CA	13.2
61	33	Gwinnett, GA	20.5	16	33	Santa Clara, CA	23.4	67	32	Middlesex, NJ	13.2
27	34	Palm Beach, FL	20.2	29	33	Hillsborough, FL	23.4	55	34	Du Page, IL	13.0
67	35	Middlesex, NJ	19.5	45	33	Fulton, GA	23.4	6	35	Orange, CA	12.8
8	35	Kings, NY	19.5	6	36	Orange, CA	23.3	10	35	Riverside, CA	12.8
50	37	Fairfield, CT	18.2	8	36	Kings, NY	23.3	14	35	Clark, NV	12.8
40	37	Montgomery, MD	18.2	36	36	Travis, TX	23.3	2	38	Cook, IL	12.7
54	39	Bergen, NJ	17.8	74	36	Hamilton, OH	23.3	29	38	Hillsborough, FL	12.7
24	40	Suffolk, NY	17.7	1	40	Los Angeles, CA	23.2	5	40	San Diego, CA	12.4
39	41	Salt Lake, UT	17.6	47	41	Westchester, NY	23.1	23	40	Philadelphia, PA	12.4
58	42	Hartford, CT	16.6	59	42	Duval, FL	23.0	25	40	Sacramento, CA	12.4
63	43	New Haven, CT	16.4	2	43	Cook, IL	22.9	59	43	Duval, FL	12.3
37	44	Fairfax, VA	16.2	31	43	Orange, FL	22.9	69	43	Pierce, WA	12.3
57	45	Prince George's, MD	16.1	57	45	Prince George's, MD	22.7	35	45	Hennepin, MN	12.2
28	46	Nassau, NY	15.6	5	46	San Diego, CA	22.6	75	45	Essex, NJ	12.2
65	47	San Francisco, CA	15.3	24	46	Suffolk, NY	22.6	21	47	Alameda, CA	12.1
60	48	Collin, TX	14.9	43	48	St. Louis, MO	22.5	8	48	Kings, NY	12.0
49	49	Milwaukee, WI	14.0	32	49	Oakland, MI	22.4	49	48	Milwaukee, WI	12.0
55	50	Du Page, IL	13.9	35	49	Hennepin, MN	22.4	1	50	Los Angeles, CA	11.9
23	51	Philadelphia, PA	13.2	28	51	Nassau, NY	22.3	13	50	King, WA	11.9
41	52	Mecklenburg, NC	12.6	23	52	Philadelphia, PA	22.2	16	50	Santa Clara, CA	11.9
73	53	Worcester, MA	10.1	67	52	Middlesex, NJ	22.2	51	53	Shelby, TN	11.2
69	54	Pierce, WA	9.9	72	52	Montgomery, PA	22.2	26	54	Bronx, NY	11.1
44	54	Wake, NC	9.9	73	52	Worcester, MA	22.2	37	54	Fairfax, VA	11.1
53	56	Marion, IN	9.7	42	56	Pima, AZ	22.1	18	56	Bexar, TX	11.0
13	57	King, WA	9.3	64	56	Macomb, MI	22.1	53	56	Marion, IN	11.0
46	58	Honolulu, HI	9.2	58	58	Hartford, CT	22.0	48	50	Fresno, CA	10.9
52	59	Pinellas, FL	8.6	54	59	Bergen, NJ	21.9	68	58	El Paso, TX	10.9
59	60	Duval, FL	8.3	17	60	Broward, FL	21.8	57	60	Prince George's, MD	10.8
45	61	Fulton, GA	7.7	30	60	Cuyahoga, OH	21.8	33	61	Franklin, OH	10.6
22	62	Middlesex, MA	7.3	21	62	Alameda, CA	21.7	31	62	Orange, FL	10.5
35	63	Hennepin, MN	6.8	46	62	Honolulu, HI	21.7	45	63	Fulton, GA	10.1
51	64	Shelby, TN	5.9	71	64	Baltimore, MD	21.6	70	63	Hidalgo, TX	10.1
19	65	Wayne, MI	5.6	63	65	New Haven, CT	21.3	12	65	San Bernardino, CA	10.0
30	66	Cuyahoga, OH	5.2	13	66	King, WA	21.1	15	66	Tarrant, TX	9.9
33	67	Franklin, OH	5.0	7	67	Miami-Dade, FL	20.8	41	67	Mecklenburg, NC	9.8
56	68	Erie, NY	4.9	56	67	Erie, NY	20.8	44	68	Wake, NC	9.7
71	69	Baltimore, MD	4.8	22	69	Middlesex, MA	20.7	62	69	Kern, CA	9.6
72	70	Montgomery, PA	4.6	11	70	Queens, NY	20.4	9	70	Dallas, TX	9.4
32	71	Oakland, MI	0.7	27	71	Palm Beach, FL	19.8	39	70	Salt Lake, UT	9.4
74	72	Hamilton, OH	2.8	34	72	Allegheny, PA	19.1	60	72	Collin, TX	9.3
43	73	St. Louis, MO	2.7	52	73	Pinellas, FL	17.2	3	73	Harris, TX	9.0
64	74	Macomb, MI	2.4	20	74	New York, NY	14.7	61	74	Gwinnett, GA	8.2
34	75	Allegheny, PA	1.8	65	75	San Francisco, CA	13.4	36	75	Travis, TX	8.1

75 Largest Counties by 2014 Population

Selected Rankings

Percent female-headed family households, 2009-2013				Birth rate, 2014				Percent under 65 who have no health insurance, 2013			
Population rank	Female households rank	County	Percent female households [col 30]	Population rank	Live birth rate rank	County	Birth rate [col 36]	Population rank	No health insurance rank	County	Percent with no health insurance [col 40]
26	1	Bronx, NY	31.4	70	1	Hidalgo, TX	19.4	70	1	Hidalgo, TX	38.2
51	2	Shelby, TN	20.8	62	2	Kern, CA	16.9	7	2	Miami-Dade, FL	33.1
57	3	Prince George's, MD	20.6	39	3	Salt Lake, UT	16.6	68	3	El Paso, TX	30.7
75	4	Essex, NJ	20.5	48	4	Fresno, CA	16.5	9	4	Dallas, TX	29.4
23	5	Philadelphia, PA	20.4	8	5	Kings, NY	16.4	3	5	Harris, TX	27.5
8	6	Kings, NY	20.2	68	6	El Paso, TX	16.2	17	6	Broward, FL	25.8
68	7	El Paso, TX	20.1	53	7	Marion, IN	15.7	27	7	Palm Beach, FL	25.4
70	8	Hidalgo, TX	19.9	3	8	Harris, TX	15.4	31	8	Orange, FL	24.1
19	9	Wayne, MI	19.6	9	8	Dallas, TX	15.4	14	9	Clark, NV	23.8
7	10	Miami-Dade, FL	18.1	33	10	Franklin, OH	15.1	1	10	Los Angeles, CA	23.7
48	11	Fresno, CA	17.1	26	11	Bronx, NY	14.9	61	11	Gwinnett, GA	23.6
53	12	Marion, IN	17.0	23	12	Philadelphia, PA	14.8	15	12	Tarrant, TX	23.2
49	13	Milwaukee, WI	16.8	49	13	Milwaukee, WI	14.6	18	13	Bexar, TX	22.3
12	14	San Bernardino, CA	16.4	51	13	Shelby, TN	14.6	10	14	Riverside, CA	21.9
18	14	Bexar, TX	16.4	12	15	San Bernardino, CA	14.5	52	14	Pinellas, FL	21.9
62	14	Kern, CA	16.4	18	15	Bexar, TX	14.5	36	16	Travis, TX	21.0
30	17	Cuyahoga, OH	16.2	15	17	Tarrant, TX	14.4	45	16	Fulton, GA	21.0
11	18	Queens, NY	16.1	36	18	Travis, TX	13.9	29	18	Hillsborough, FL	20.5
9	19	Dallas, TX	16.0	41	18	Mecklenburg, NC	13.9	12	19	San Bernardino, CA	20.4
59	20	Duval, FL	15.7	46	18	Honolulu, HI	13.9	62	19	Kern, CA	20.4
1	21	Los Angeles, CA	15.6	59	18	Duval, FL	13.9	48	21	Fresno, CA	20.3
3	22	Harris, TX	15.5	5	22	San Diego, CA	13.7	4	22	Maricopa, AZ	19.8
17	22	Broward, FL	15.5	35	22	Hennepin, MN	13.7	59	23	Duval, FL	19.4
2	24	Cook, IL	15.2	69	24	Pierce, WA	13.6	53	24	Marion, IN	19.3
45	24	Fulton, GA	15.2	74	24	Hamilton, OH	13.6	11	25	Queens, NY	19.2
74	24	Hamilton, OH	15.2	4	26	Maricopa, AZ	13.5	6	26	Orange, CA	18.8
25	27	Sacramento, CA	15.0	2	27	Cook, IL	13.3	42	26	Pima, AZ	18.8
31	28	Orange, FL	14.9	25	27	Sacramento, CA	13.3	41	28	Mecklenburg, NC	18.5
58	28	Hartford, CT	14.9	10	29	Riverside, CA	13.2	75	28	Essex, NJ	18.5
63	28	New Haven, CT	14.9	57	29	Prince George's, MD	13.2	2	30	Cook, IL	18.4
41	31	Mecklenburg, NC	14.4	11	31	Queens, NY	13.1	66	31	Ventura, CA	18.1
43	31	St. Louis, MO	14.4	37	31	Fairfax, VA	13.1	5	32	San Diego, CA	17.9
15	33	Tarrant, TX	14.3	75	31	Essex, NJ	13.1	51	33	Shelby, TN	17.4
29	34	Hillsborough, FL	14.2	1	34	Los Angeles, CA	13.0	25	34	Sacramento, CA	16.9
33	35	Franklin, OH	14.1	19	34	Wayne, MI	13.0	39	35	Salt Lake, UT	16.7
71	35	Baltimore, MD	14.1	16	36	Santa Clara, CA	12.9	23	36	Philadelphia, PA	16.5
56	37	Erie, NY	13.9	45	36	Fulton, GA	12.9	57	36	Prince George's, MD	16.5
61	37	Gwinnett, GA	13.9	31	38	Orange, FL	12.8	60	38	Collin, TX	16.2
14	39	Clark, NV	13.8	40	38	Montgomery, MD	12.8	19	39	Wayne, MI	15.8
10	40	Riverside, CA	13.5	61	40	Gwinnett, GA	12.7	26	40	Bronx, NY	15.6
47	41	Westchester, NY	13.2	14	41	Clark, NV	12.6	8	41	Kings, NY	14.8
4	42	Maricopa, AZ	12.7	44	41	Wake, NC	12.6	69	41	Pierce, WA	14.8
42	42	Pima, AZ	12.7	29	43	Hillsborough, FL	12.5	33	43	Franklin, OH	14.7
64	42	Macomb, MI	12.7	66	43	Ventura, CA	12.5	21	44	Alameda, CA	14.4
21	45	Alameda, CA	12.5	21	45	Alameda, CA	12.4	44	44	Wake, NC	14.4
66	46	Ventura, CA	12.4	13	46	King, WA	12.3	67	44	Middlesex, NJ	14.4
46	47	Honolulu, HI	12.3	6	47	Orange, CA	12.2	54	47	Bergen, NJ	14.3
73	47	Worcester, MA	12.3	20	48	New York, NY	11.9	38	48	Contra Costa, CA	14.0
5	49	San Diego, CA	12.1	42	48	Pima, AZ	11.9	49	49	Milwaukee, WI	13.8
24	49	Suffolk, NY	12.1	60	50	Collin, TX	11.8	13	50	King, WA	13.7
27	51	Palm Beach, FL	12.0	30	51	Cuyahoga, OH	11.7	30	51	Cuyahoga, OH	13.3
28	51	Nassau, NY	12.0	67	51	Middlesex, NJ	11.7	50	51	Fairfield, CT	13.3
38	51	Contra Costa, CA	12.0	71	51	Baltimore, MD	11.7	74	53	Hamilton, OH	13.2
69	51	Pierce, WA	12.0	43	54	St. Louis, MO	11.5	16	54	Santa Clara, CA	12.6
6	55	Orange, CA	11.9	7	55	Miami-Dade, FL	11.4	40	55	Montgomery, MD	12.5
50	55	Fairfield, CT	11.9	17	55	Broward, FL	11.4	64	55	Macomb, MI	12.5
34	57	Allegheny, PA	11.8	22	55	Middlesex, MA	11.4	65	57	San Francisco, CA	12.4
67	57	Middlesex, NJ	11.8	55	58	Du Page, IL	11.2	37	58	Fairfax, VA	12.3
20	59	New York, NY	11.6	38	59	Contra Costa, CA	11.0	43	59	St. Louis, MO	12.0
36	60	Travis, TX	11.5	32	60	Oakland, MI	10.9	47	60	Westchester, NY	11.9
44	60	Wake, NC	11.5	56	60	Erie, NY	10.9	71	61	Baltimore, MD	11.5
40	62	Montgomery, MD	11.2	72	60	Montgomery, PA	10.9	20	62	New York, NY	10.9
52	62	Pinellas, FL	11.2	47	63	Westchester, NY	10.8	55	63	Du Page, IL	10.8
54	62	Bergen, NJ	11.2	65	63	San Francisco, CA	10.8	24	64	Suffolk, NY	10.7
32	65	Oakland, MI	10.8	73	63	Worcester, MA	10.8	32	64	Oakland, MI	10.7
39	65	Salt Lake, UT	10.8	34	66	Allegheny, PA	10.7	63	64	New Haven, CT	10.7
16	67	Santa Clara, CA	10.5	50	66	Fairfield, CT	10.7	28	67	Nassau, NY	10.3
35	68	Hennepin, MN	10.3	64	66	Macomb, MI	10.7	58	67	Hartford, CT	10.3
60	69	Collin, TX	10.0	58	69	Hartford, CT	10.6	35	69	Hennepin, MN	10.2
22	70	Middlesex, MA	9.8	24	70	Suffolk, NY	10.4	34	70	Allegheny, PA	9.8
55	71	Du Page, IL	9.4	63	70	New Haven, CT	10.4	56	71	Erie, NY	8.4
72	72	Montgomery, PA	9.2	28	72	Nassau, NY	10.3	72	72	Montgomery, PA	8.3
37	73	Fairfax, VA	9.1	27	73	Palm Beach, FL	10.1	46	73	Honolulu, HI	6.7
13	74	King, WA	8.8	54	74	Bergen, NJ	9.8	73	74	Worcester, MA	4.2
65	75	San Francisco, CA	8.6	52	75	Pinellas, FL	9.1	22	75	Middlesex, MA	4.0

75 Largest Counties by 2014 Population

Selected Rankings

Percent college graduates (bachelor's degree or more), 2009–2013

Population rank	College graduates rank	County	Percent college graduates [col 51]
20	1	New York, NY	58.9
37	2	Fairfax, VA	58.6
40	3	Montgomery, MD	57.1
65	4	San Francisco, CA	52.4
22	5	Middlesex, MA	50.7
60	6	Collin, TX	49.3
45	7	Fulton, GA	48.2
44	8	Wake, NC	48.0
13	9	King, WA	46.6
16	10	Santa Clara, CA	46.5
55	11	Du Page, IL	46.3
54	12	Bergen, NJ	45.9
35	13	Hennepin, MN	45.8
72	14	Montgomery, PA	45.5
47	15	Westchester, NY	45.4
36	16	Travis, TX	44.9
50	17	Fairfield, CT	44.8
32	18	Oakland, MI	43.1
21	19	Alameda, CA	41.8
28	20	Nassau, NY	41.5
41	21	Mecklenburg, NC	40.7
43	22	St. Louis, MO	40.6
67	23	Middlesex, NJ	40.1
38	24	Contra Costa, CA	39.0
6	25	Orange, CA	36.8
33	26	Franklin, OH	36.4
34	27	Allegheny, PA	35.9
71	28	Baltimore, MD	35.7
58	29	Hartford, CT	34.9
2	30	Cook, IL	34.7
5	31	San Diego, CA	34.6
61	32	Gwinnett, GA	33.9
73	33	Worcester, MA	33.8
74	34	Hamilton, OH	33.7
24	35	Suffolk, NY	32.9
63	35	New Haven, CT	32.9
27	37	Palm Beach, FL	32.4
46	38	Honolulu, HI	32.1
75	39	Essex, NJ	32.0
66	40	Ventura, CA	31.4
39	41	Salt Lake, UT	31.0
56	42	Erie, NY	30.9
8	43	Kings, NY	30.6
31	44	Orange, FL	30.1
11	45	Queens, NY	30.0
17	46	Broward, FL	29.9
4	47	Maricopa, AZ	29.8
42	47	Pima, AZ	29.8
57	47	Prince George's, MD	29.8
1	50	Los Angeles, CA	29.7
30	50	Cuyahoga, OH	29.7
15	52	Tarrant, TX	29.5
29	52	Hillsborough, FL	29.5
51	54	Shelby, TN	29.0
9	55	Dallas, TX	28.6
3	56	Harris, TX	28.4
49	57	Milwaukee, WI	28.1
25	58	Sacramento, CA	28.0
52	59	Pinellas, FL	27.5
53	60	Marion, IN	27.4
59	61	Duval, FL	26.4
7	62	Miami-Dade, FL	26.3
18	62	Bexar, TX	26.3
69	64	Pierce, WA	24.0
23	65	Philadelphia, PA	23.9
64	66	Macomb, MI	22.5
14	67	Clark, NV	22.1
19	68	Wayne, MI	21.3
68	69	El Paso, TX	20.7
10	70	Riverside, CA	20.5
48	71	Fresno, CA	19.6
12	72	San Bernardino, CA	18.7
26	73	Bronx, NY	18.1
70	74	Hidalgo, TX	15.9
62	75	Kern, CA	15.0

Expenditures per student, 2012–2013

Population rank	Expenditures rank	County	Expenditures per student (dollars) [col 53]
28	1	Nassau, NY	$24 744
47	2	Westchester, NY	$23 561
75	3	Essex, NJ	$23 340
20	4	New York, NY	$22 518
8	4	Kings, NY	$22 518
11	4	Queens, NY	$22 518
26	4	Bronx, NY	$22 518
24	8	Suffolk, NY	$21 944
23	9	Philadelphia, PA	$20 194
54	10	Bergen, NJ	$18 298
56	11	Erie, NY	$17 775
50	12	Fairfield, CT	$17 442
58	13	Hartford, CT	$17 118
67	14	Middlesex, NJ	$16 984
72	15	Montgomery, PA	$16 934
63	16	New Haven, CT	$16 895
22	17	Middlesex, MA	$16 245
34	18	Allegheny, PA	$15 859
40	19	Montgomery, MD	$15 097
30	20	Cuyahoga, OH	$14 915
57	21	Prince George's, MD	$14 120
55	22	Du Page, IL	$14 074
73	23	Worcester, MA	$14 064
37	24	Fairfax, VA	$13 756
2	25	Cook, IL	$13 671
33	26	Franklin, OH	$13 463
43	27	St. Louis, MO	$13 436
74	28	Hamilton, OH	$13 313
71	29	Baltimore, MD	$13 209
35	30	Hennepin, MN	$13 139
49	31	Milwaukee, WI	$12 389
65	32	San Francisco, CA	$12 109
46	33	Honolulu, HI	$11 903
32	34	Oakland, MI	$11 726
19	35	Wayne, MI	$11 693
45	36	Fulton, GA	$11 224
53	37	Marion, IN	$10 927
64	38	Macomb, MI	$10 692
1	39	Los Angeles, CA	$10 053
13	40	King, WA	$10 005
69	41	Pierce, WA	$9 826
62	42	Kern, CA	$9 682
16	43	Santa Clara, CA	$9 510
51	44	Shelby, TN	$9 480
27	45	Palm Beach, FL	$9 429
48	46	Fresno, CA	$9 403
36	47	Travis, TX	$9 261
21	48	Alameda, CA	$9 173
70	49	Hidalgo, TX	$9 112
5	50	San Diego, CA	$9 033
7	51	Miami-Dade, FL	$8 986
25	52	Sacramento, CA	$8 976
38	53	Contra Costa, CA	$8 969
61	54	Gwinnett, GA	$8 891
66	55	Ventura, CA	$8 813
29	56	Hillsborough, FL	$8 766
52	56	Pinellas, FL	$8 766
6	58	Orange, CA	$8 692
10	59	Riverside, CA	$8 583
68	60	El Paso, TX	$8 554
12	61	San Bernardino, CA	$8 544
59	62	Duval, FL	$8 414
17	63	Broward, FL	$8 390
31	64	Orange, FL	$8 338
18	65	Bexar, TX	$8 334
41	66	Mecklenburg, NC	$8 224
9	67	Dallas, TX	$8 157
42	68	Pima, AZ	$8 133
3	69	Harris, TX	$8 132
14	70	Clark, NV	$8 066
60	71	Collin, TX	$7 958
15	72	Tarrant, TX	$7 941
44	73	Wake, NC	$7 788
4	74	Maricopa, AZ	$7 248
39	75	Salt Lake, UT	$6 906

Per capita personal income, 2013

Population rank	Per capita income rank	County	Per capita income (dollars) [col 64]
20	1	New York, NY	$121 632
65	2	San Francisco, CA	$84 356
50	3	Fairfield, CT	$82 009
47	4	Westchester, NY	$80 363
40	5	Montgomery, MD	$72 746
28	6	Nassau, NY	$72 549
37	7	Fairfax, VA	$71 752
16	8	Santa Clara, CA	$70 151
72	9	Montgomery, PA	$70 050
54	10	Bergen, NJ	$69 495
22	11	Middlesex, MA	$66 498
38	12	Contra Costa, CA	$63 403
13	13	King, WA	$62 770
35	14	Hennepin, MN	$60 601
45	15	Fulton, GA	$58 123
55	16	Du Page, IL	$58 064
27	17	Palm Beach, FL	$57 985
43	18	St. Louis, MO	$57 183
32	19	Oakland, MI	$57 035
24	20	Suffolk, NY	$56 940
58	21	Hartford, CT	$55 845
60	22	Collin, TX	$55 520
21	23	Alameda, CA	$55 338
75	24	Essex, NJ	$54 606
6	25	Orange, CA	$54 519
71	26	Baltimore, MD	$54 009
34	27	Allegheny, PA	$53 208
3	28	Harris, TX	$53 141
67	29	Middlesex, NJ	$52 291
63	30	New Haven, CT	$51 685
5	31	San Diego, CA	$51 384
66	32	Ventura, CA	$50 507
74	33	Hamilton, OH	$50 235
2	34	Cook, IL	$49 661
41	35	Mecklenburg, NC	$49 109
46	36	Honolulu, HI	$48 798
9	37	Dallas, TX	$48 638
36	38	Travis, TX	$48 562
73	39	Worcester, MA	$48 415
30	40	Cuyahoga, OH	$47 294
1	41	Los Angeles, CA	$46 530
44	42	Wake, NC	$46 097
52	43	Pinellas, FL	$45 574
56	44	Erie, NY	$45 496
11	45	Queens, NY	$44 966
15	46	Tarrant, TX	$44 417
69	47	Pierce, WA	$43 982
17	48	Broward, FL	$43 792
33	49	Franklin, OH	$43 506
25	50	Sacramento, CA	$43 438
57	51	Prince George's, MD	$43 362
51	52	Shelby, TN	$43 210
59	53	Duval, FL	$42 423
8	54	Kings, NY	$42 306
39	55	Salt Lake, UT	$42 189
23	56	Philadelphia, PA	$42 155
49	57	Milwaukee, WI	$41 017
29	58	Hillsborough, FL	$40 680
4	59	Maricopa, AZ	$40 030
53	60	Marion, IN	$39 963
7	61	Miami-Dade, FL	$39 880
18	62	Bexar, TX	$39 005
64	63	Macomb, MI	$38 456
31	64	Orange, FL	$37 844
14	65	Clark, NV	$37 457
42	66	Pima, AZ	$37 063
19	67	Wayne, MI	$36 021
62	68	Kern, CA	$35 847
48	69	Fresno, CA	$35 635
61	70	Gwinnett, GA	$34 061
10	71	Riverside, CA	$33 278
26	72	Bronx, NY	$32 852
12	73	San Bernardino, CA	$32 747
68	74	El Paso, TX	$31 156
70	75	Hidalgo, TX	$23 073

75 Largest Counties by 2014 Population

Selected Rankings

Median household income, 2013

Population rank	Median income rank	County	Median income (dollars) [col 58]
37	1	Fairfax, VA	$110 658
40	2	Montgomery, MD	$97 873
28	3	Nassau, NY	$95 395
16	4	Santa Clara, CA	$91 843
24	5	Suffolk, NY	$84 940
47	6	Westchester, NY	$83 094
22	7	Middlesex, MA	$82 118
50	8	Fairfield, CT	$81 816
54	9	Bergen, NJ	$81 615
60	10	Collin, TX	$81 315
38	11	Contra Costa, CA	$78 909
72	12	Montgomery, PA	$77 021
65	13	San Francisco, CA	$76 933
67	14	Middlesex, NJ	$76 515
66	15	Ventura, CA	$76 513
55	16	Du Page, IL	$76 269
6	17	Orange, CA	$73 827
46	18	Honolulu, HI	$72 649
21	19	Alameda, CA	$72 128
13	20	King, WA	$71 779
57	21	Prince George's, MD	$71 682
20	22	New York, NY	$71 443
32	23	Oakland, MI	$67 281
44	24	Wake, NC	$65 433
71	25	Baltimore, MD	$64 624
35	26	Hennepin, MN	$64 331
58	27	Hartford, CT	$63 491
73	28	Worcester, MA	$62 268
39	29	Salt Lake, UT	$61 716
5	30	San Diego, CA	$61 365
36	31	Travis, TX	$60 372
43	32	St. Louis, MO	$59 284
61	33	Gwinnett, GA	$59 081
63	34	New Haven, CT	$58 672
69	35	Pierce, WA	$57 619
15	36	Tarrant, TX	$56 906
11	37	Queens, NY	$56 307
45	38	Fulton, GA	$55 474
41	39	Mecklenburg, NC	$54 657
1	40	Los Angeles, CA	$54 443
10	41	Riverside, CA	$53 909
2	42	Cook, IL	$53 795
75	43	Essex, NJ	$53 358
25	44	Sacramento, CA	$52 980
64	45	Macomb, MI	$52 954
3	46	Harris, TX	$52 533
12	47	San Bernardino, CA	$52 112
4	48	Maricopa, AZ	$52 066
27	49	Palm Beach, FL	$51 768
33	50	Franklin, OH	$51 456
34	51	Allegheny, PA	$51 400
56	52	Erie, NY	$51 123
14	53	Clark, NV	$51 071
17	54	Broward, FL	$50 343
18	55	Bexar, TX	$49 655
29	56	Hillsborough, FL	$49 510
9	57	Dallas, TX	$47 902
59	58	Duval, FL	$47 876
74	59	Hamilton, OH	$47 123
8	60	Kings, NY	$47 067
62	61	Kern, CA	$46 688
31	62	Orange, FL	$46 675
51	63	Shelby, TN	$45 067
42	64	Pima, AZ	$43 926
52	65	Pinellas, FL	$43 773
48	66	Fresno, CA	$43 741
30	67	Cuyahoga, OH	$43 653
49	68	Milwaukee, WI	$42 058
7	69	Miami-Dade, FL	$41 840
53	70	Marion, IN	$41 478
19	71	Wayne, MI	$40 485
68	72	El Paso, TX	$39 748
23	73	Philadelphia, PA	$36 918
70	74	Hidalgo, TX	$34 607
26	75	Bronx, NY	$33 079

Median value of owner-occupied housing units, 2009–2013

Population rank	Median value rank	County	Median value (dollars) [col 91]
20	1	New York, NY	$828 100
65	2	San Francisco, CA	$744 600
16	3	Santa Clara, CA	$645 600
8	4	Kings, NY	$557 100
46	5	Honolulu, HI	$556 300
6	6	Orange, CA	$519 600
47	7	Westchester, NY	$518 400
21	8	Alameda, CA	$493 800
37	9	Fairfax, VA	$476 600
28	10	Nassau, NY	$454 500
54	11	Bergen, NJ	$451 400
11	12	Queens, NY	$450 900
40	13	Montgomery, MD	$446 300
66	14	Ventura, CA	$442 200
50	15	Fairfield, CT	$432 100
1	16	Los Angeles, CA	$420 200
38	17	Contra Costa, CA	$404 000
5	18	San Diego, CA	$402 100
22	19	Middlesex, MA	$398 200
24	20	Suffolk, NY	$383 400
13	21	King, WA	$377 300
26	22	Bronx, NY	$374 500
75	23	Essex, NJ	$364 800
67	24	Middlesex, NJ	$330 000
72	25	Montgomery, PA	$292 600
55	26	Du Page, IL	$286 500
57	27	Prince George's, MD	$269 800
73	28	Worcester, MA	$259 200
63	29	New Haven, CT	$256 900
71	30	Baltimore, MD	$253 300
58	31	Hartford, CT	$241 500
69	32	Pierce, WA	$240 400
45	33	Fulton, GA	$238 200
25	34	Sacramento, CA	$234 200
39	35	Salt Lake, UT	$232 100
2	36	Cook, IL	$231 200
10	37	Riverside, CA	$231 000
35	38	Hennepin, MN	$230 900
44	39	Wake, NC	$229 000
12	40	San Bernardino, CA	$222 300
36	41	Travis, TX	$219 200
60	42	Collin, TX	$206 100
7	43	Miami-Dade, FL	$201 000
27	44	Palm Beach, FL	$199 700
48	45	Fresno, CA	$195 400
41	46	Mecklenburg, NC	$181 900
17	47	Broward, FL	$181 500
4	48	Maricopa, AZ	$176 500
43	49	St. Louis, MO	$174 500
61	50	Gwinnett, GA	$171 300
32	51	Oakland, MI	$170 500
31	52	Orange, FL	$167 800
42	53	Pima, AZ	$167 500
14	54	Clark, NV	$165 000
62	55	Kern, CA	$161 700
29	56	Hillsborough, FL	$160 000
49	57	Milwaukee, WI	$158 400
52	58	Pinellas, FL	$151 500
59	59	Duval, FL	$151 400
33	60	Franklin, OH	$150 800
74	61	Hamilton, OH	$144 400
23	62	Philadelphia, PA	$142 500
15	63	Tarrant, TX	$136 400
51	64	Shelby, TN	$132 700
3	65	Harris, TX	$131 400
9	66	Dallas, TX	$128 300
30	67	Cuyahoga, OH	$125 700
56	68	Erie, NY	$124 300
18	69	Bexar, TX	$123 700
64	70	Macomb, MI	$123 100
34	71	Allegheny, PA	$122 400
53	72	Marion, IN	$118 000
68	73	El Paso, TX	$111 800
19	74	Wayne, MI	$86 800
70	75	Hidalgo, TX	$78 100

Median gross rent of renter-occupied housing units, 2009–2013

Population rank	Median rent rank	County	Median rent (dollars) [col 94]
37	1	Fairfax, VA	$1 687
40	2	Montgomery, MD	$1 568
16	3	Santa Clara, CA	$1 566
28	4	Nassau, NY	$1 504
6	5	Orange, CA	$1 498
24	6	Suffolk, NY	$1 495
65	7	San Francisco, CA	$1 488
66	8	Ventura, CA	$1 470
46	9	Honolulu, HI	$1 467
20	10	New York, NY	$1 442
38	11	Contra Costa, CA	$1 365
54	12	Bergen, NJ	$1 334
47	13	Westchester, NY	$1 325
11	14	Queens, NY	$1 315
50	15	Fairfield, CT	$1 302
5	16	San Diego, CA	$1 300
21	17	Alameda, CA	$1 289
22	18	Middlesex, MA	$1 286
67	19	Middlesex, NJ	$1 265
57	20	Prince George's, MD	$1 241
1	21	Los Angeles, CA	$1 204
17	22	Broward, FL	$1 171
10	23	Riverside, CA	$1 168
8	24	Kings, NY	$1 149
27	24	Palm Beach, FL	$1 149
71	26	Baltimore, MD	$1 139
13	27	King, WA	$1 131
72	28	Montgomery, PA	$1 128
55	29	Du Page, IL	$1 104
12	30	San Bernardino, CA	$1 102
7	31	Miami-Dade, FL	$1 085
60	32	Collin, TX	$1 063
63	33	New Haven, CT	$1 060
75	34	Essex, NJ	$1 055
26	35	Bronx, NY	$1 032
25	36	Sacramento, CA	$1 024
31	37	Orange, FL	$1 022
14	38	Clark, NV	$1 019
61	39	Gwinnett, GA	$1 002
69	40	Pierce, WA	$997
36	41	Travis, TX	$988
58	42	Hartford, CT	$974
45	43	Fulton, GA	$971
2	44	Cook, IL	$963
29	45	Hillsborough, FL	$952
52	46	Pinellas, FL	$947
4	47	Maricopa, AZ	$943
59	48	Duval, FL	$935
32	49	Oakland, MI	$919
35	50	Hennepin, MN	$917
44	51	Wake, NC	$913
73	52	Worcester, MA	$911
39	53	Salt Lake, UT	$895
23	54	Philadelphia, PA	$893
41	55	Mecklenburg, NC	$889
62	56	Kern, CA	$885
9	57	Dallas, TX	$883
15	58	Tarrant, TX	$881
3	59	Harris, TX	$880
48	60	Fresno, CA	$875
43	61	St. Louis, MO	$861
51	62	Shelby, TN	$842
18	63	Bexar, TX	$839
64	64	Macomb, MI	$824
33	65	Franklin, OH	$819
42	66	Pima, AZ	$798
19	67	Wayne, MI	$792
49	67	Milwaukee, WI	$792
53	69	Marion, IN	$768
34	70	Allegheny, PA	$751
30	71	Cuyahoga, OH	$732
56	72	Erie, NY	$724
68	73	El Paso, TX	$720
74	74	Hamilton, OH	$698
70	75	Hidalgo, TX	$641

75 Largest Counties by 2014 Population

Selected Rankings

Percent of population below the poverty level, 2013				Percent under 18 years old below the poverty level, 2013				Unemployment rate, 2014			
Population rank	Poverty rate rank	County	Poverty rate [col 59]	Population rank	Poverty rate for children rank	County	Poverty rate for children under 18 years [col 60]	Population rank	Unemployment rate rank	County	Unemployment rate [col 100]
70	1	Hidalgo, TX	34.0	70	1	Hidalgo, TX	44.5	48	1	Fresno, CA	11.6
26	2	Bronx, NY	30.7	48	2	Fresno, CA	42.0	62	2	Kern, CA	10.4
48	3	Fresno, CA	28.6	26	3	Bronx, NY	41.6	19	3	Wayne, MI	10.0
23	4	Philadelphia, PA	26.0	19	4	Wayne, MI	36.9	26	4	Bronx, NY	9.8
19	5	Wayne, MI	25.1	23	5	Philadelphia, PA	36.3	70	5	Hidalgo, TX	8.7
8	6	Kings, NY	23.3	51	6	Shelby, TN	34.7	1	6	Los Angeles, CA	8.3
62	7	Kern, CA	22.7	8	7	Kings, NY	33.3	10	7	Riverside, CA	8.2
68	7	El Paso, TX	22.7	49	8	Milwaukee, WI	33.2	64	7	Macomb, MI	8.2
49	9	Milwaukee, WI	22.4	68	9	El Paso, TX	31.2	12	9	San Bernardino, CA	8.1
51	10	Shelby, TN	21.6	62	10	Kern, CA	30.5	23	10	Philadelphia, PA	8.0
53	11	Marion, IN	21.3	53	11	Marion, IN	30.1	51	11	Shelby, TN	7.9
7	12	Miami-Dade, FL	21.0	9	12	Dallas, TX	29.5	75	11	Essex, NJ	7.9
9	13	Dallas, TX	19.5	30	13	Cuyahoga, OH	28.1	14	13	Clark, NV	7.8
42	14	Pima, AZ	19.3	7	14	Miami-Dade, FL	27.8	8	14	Kings, NY	7.7
12	15	San Bernardino, CA	19.2	1	15	Los Angeles, CA	27.4	2	15	Cook, IL	7.4
30	15	Cuyahoga, OH	19.2	3	16	Harris, TX	26.7	25	16	Sacramento, CA	7.3
1	17	Los Angeles, CA	19.0	12	16	San Bernardino, CA	26.7	45	17	Fulton, GA	7.2
20	17	New York, NY	19.0	20	18	New York, NY	26.6	63	17	New Haven, CT	7.2
25	19	Sacramento, CA	18.9	42	19	Pima, AZ	26.5	69	17	Pierce, WA	7.2
74	20	Hamilton, OH	18.7	2	20	Cook, IL	26.0	49	20	Milwaukee, WI	7.0
3	21	Harris, TX	18.4	31	20	Orange, FL	26.0	58	21	Hartford, CT	6.9
31	22	Orange, FL	18.2	25	22	Sacramento, CA	25.9	7	22	Miami-Dade, FL	6.8
45	22	Fulton, GA	18.2	74	23	Hamilton, OH	25.8	32	22	Oakland, MI	6.8
2	24	Cook, IL	17.8	45	24	Fulton, GA	25.6	59	24	Duval, FL	6.7
33	25	Franklin, OH	17.7	59	24	Duval, FL	25.6	66	24	Ventura, CA	6.7
75	25	Essex, NJ	17.7	33	26	Franklin, OH	25.4	53	26	Marion, IN	6.5
4	27	Maricopa, AZ	17.6	4	27	Maricopa, AZ	25.1	68	26	El Paso, TX	6.5
10	28	Riverside, CA	17.4	75	28	Essex, NJ	24.9	5	28	San Diego, CA	6.4
18	28	Bexar, TX	17.4	10	29	Riverside, CA	24.2	11	28	Queens, NY	6.4
59	30	Duval, FL	17.1	29	30	Hillsborough, FL	24.0	30	28	Cuyahoga, OH	6.4
29	31	Hillsborough, FL	16.8	18	31	Bexar, TX	23.9	38	31	Contra Costa, CA	6.2
14	32	Clark, NV	16.3	14	32	Clark, NV	23.7	42	31	Pima, AZ	6.2
36	33	Travis, TX	15.9	52	33	Pinellas, FL	23.6	50	31	Fairfield, CT	6.2
41	34	Mecklenburg, NC	15.5	56	34	Erie, NY	23.1	71	31	Baltimore, MD	6.2
11	35	Queens, NY	15.4	27	35	Palm Beach, FL	22.7	73	31	Worcester, MA	6.2
5	36	San Diego, CA	15.3	11	36	Queens, NY	21.6	20	36	New York, NY	6.1
15	37	Tarrant, TX	15.2	15	37	Tarrant, TX	21.5	56	36	Erie, NY	6.1
17	37	Broward, FL	15.2	36	38	Travis, TX	21.0	61	36	Gwinnett, GA	6.1
52	39	Pinellas, FL	15.1	41	39	Mecklenburg, NC	20.5	67	39	Middlesex, NJ	6.0
56	39	Erie, NY	15.1	61	40	Gwinnett, GA	20.0	4	40	Maricopa, AZ	5.9
27	41	Palm Beach, FL	15.0	64	41	Macomb, MI	19.7	21	40	Alameda, CA	5.9
69	42	Pierce, WA	14.1	17	42	Broward, FL	19.5	27	40	Palm Beach, FL	5.9
65	43	San Francisco, CA	13.8	5	43	San Diego, CA	19.4	41	40	Mecklenburg, NC	5.9
61	44	Gwinnett, GA	13.7	69	44	Pierce, WA	19.3	57	40	Prince George's, MD	5.9
6	45	Orange, CA	13.5	6	45	Orange, CA	18.8	17	45	Broward, FL	5.8
34	45	Allegheny, PA	13.5	34	46	Allegheny, PA	18.5	29	45	Hillsborough, FL	5.8
64	47	Macomb, MI	13.4	66	47	Ventura, CA	18.0	31	45	Orange, FL	5.8
21	48	Alameda, CA	13.0	73	47	Worcester, MA	18.0	43	45	St. Louis, MO	5.8
73	48	Worcester, MA	13.0	63	49	New Haven, CT	17.7	52	45	Pinellas, FL	5.8
63	50	New Haven, CT	12.8	58	50	Hartford, CT	17.4	55	50	Du Page, IL	5.6
39	51	Salt Lake, UT	12.7	43	51	St. Louis, MO	16.2	6	51	Orange, CA	5.5
13	52	King, WA	12.4	39	52	Salt Lake, UT	15.9	9	52	Dallas, TX	5.4
35	53	Hennepin, MN	12.2	13	53	King, WA	15.7	54	52	Bergen, NJ	5.4
58	54	Hartford, CT	12.1	21	54	Alameda, CA	15.4	24	54	Suffolk, NY	5.3
66	55	Ventura, CA	12.0	35	55	Hennepin, MN	15.3	34	54	Allegheny, PA	5.3
43	56	St. Louis, MO	10.9	44	56	Wake, NC	14.5	74	54	Hamilton, OH	5.3
44	56	Wake, NC	10.9	65	57	San Francisco, CA	14.4	16	57	Santa Clara, CA	5.2
38	58	Contra Costa, CA	10.8	57	58	Prince George's, MD	14.1	47	58	Westchester, NY	5.1
16	59	Santa Clara, CA	10.5	38	59	Contra Costa, CA	13.4	15	59	Tarrant, TX	5.0
32	60	Oakland, MI	10.2	47	59	Westchester, NY	13.4	3	60	Harris, TX	4.9
47	61	Westchester, NY	9.9	32	61	Oakland, MI	13.1	28	61	Nassau, NY	4.8
57	61	Prince George's, MD	9.9	16	62	Santa Clara, CA	12.9	33	61	Franklin, OH	4.8
46	63	Honolulu, HI	9.6	71	62	Baltimore, MD	12.9	44	61	Wake, NC	4.8
50	63	Fairfield, CT	9.6	67	64	Middlesex, NJ	12.6	13	64	King, WA	4.6
71	65	Baltimore, MD	9.5	46	65	Honolulu, HI	12.2	18	64	Bexar, TX	4.6
67	66	Middlesex, NJ	9.4	50	66	Fairfield, CT	11.9	22	64	Middlesex, MA	4.6
22	67	Middlesex, MA	8.7	22	67	Middlesex, MA	10.6	72	64	Montgomery, PA	4.6
54	68	Bergen, NJ	8.1	54	67	Bergen, NJ	10.6	60	68	Collin, TX	4.5
60	69	Collin, TX	7.9	24	69	Suffolk, NY	10.1	40	69	Montgomery, MD	4.4
24	70	Suffolk, NY	7.5	60	70	Collin, TX	9.9	65	69	San Francisco, CA	4.4
40	71	Montgomery, MD	7.0	55	71	Du Page, IL	9.8	37	71	Fairfax, VA	4.1
55	71	Du Page, IL	7.0	40	72	Montgomery, MD	9.7	46	71	Honolulu, HI	4.1
72	73	Montgomery, PA	6.8	28	73	Nassau, NY	9.1	36	73	Travis, TX	4.0
28	74	Nassau, NY	6.5	72	74	Montgomery, PA	8.2	35	74	Hennepin, MN	3.7
37	75	Fairfax, VA	6.0	37	75	Fairfax, VA	7.7	39	74	Salt Lake, UT	3.7

75 Largest Counties by 2014 Population

Selected Rankings

Manufacturing employment as a percent of total nonfarm employment, 2013

Population rank	Manufacturing rank	County	Percent employed in manufacturing [col 107/ col 105]
64	1	Macomb, MI	22.0
19	2	Wayne, MI	13.0
73	3	Worcester, MA	11.7
49	4	Milwaukee, WI	10.9
58	4	Hartford, CT	10.9
6	6	Orange, CA	10.8
56	7	Erie, NY	10.7
15	8	Tarrant, TX	10.6
30	9	Cuyahoga, OH	10.4
21	10	Alameda, CA	10.1
48	11	Fresno, CA	9.7
16	12	Santa Clara, CA	9.6
63	12	New Haven, CT	9.6
24	14	Suffolk, NY	9.5
1	15	Los Angeles, CA	9.4
66	16	Ventura, CA	9.3
12	17	San Bernardino, CA	9.1
55	18	Du Page, IL	9.0
39	19	Salt Lake, UT	8.9
3	20	Harris, TX	8.7
10	21	Riverside, CA	8.6
74	21	Hamilton, OH	8.6
5	23	San Diego, CA	8.5
53	24	Marion, IN	8.4
50	25	Fairfield, CT	8.3
35	26	Hennepin, MN	8.2
72	27	Montgomery, PA	8.1
42	28	Pima, AZ	8.0
2	29	Cook, IL	7.8
52	30	Pinellas, FL	7.7
54	31	Bergen, NJ	7.6
13	32	King, WA	7.4
32	32	Oakland, MI	7.4
69	32	Pierce, WA	7.4
67	35	Middlesex, NJ	7.3
9	36	Dallas, TX	7.1
22	37	Middlesex, MA	6.9
61	38	Gwinnett, GA	6.7
62	39	Kern, CA	6.6
68	40	El Paso, TX	6.4
4	41	Maricopa, AZ	6.3
43	41	St. Louis, MO	6.3
75	43	Essex, NJ	6.1
51	44	Shelby, TN	5.9
71	45	Baltimore, MD	5.6
36	46	Travis, TX	5.5
34	47	Allegheny, PA	5.3
60	48	Collin, TX	5.2
33	49	Franklin, OH	4.9
18	50	Bexar, TX	4.7
38	50	Contra Costa, CA	4.7
59	52	Duval, FL	4.6
25	53	Sacramento, CA	4.5
41	53	Mecklenburg, NC	4.5
11	55	Queens, NY	4.0
8	56	Kings, NY	3.9
70	56	Hidalgo, TX	3.9
31	58	Orange, FL	3.8
29	59	Hillsborough, FL	3.7
23	60	Philadelphia, PA	3.6
7	61	Miami-Dade, FL	3.5
17	62	Broward, FL	3.4
28	63	Nassau, NY	3.1
44	63	Wake, NC	3.1
47	65	Westchester, NY	3.0
27	66	Palm Beach, FL	2.9
57	66	Prince George's, MD	2.9
46	68	Honolulu, HI	2.7
26	69	Bronx, NY	2.5
45	69	Fulton, GA	2.5
14	71	Clark, NV	2.4
40	72	Montgomery, MD	1.9
65	73	San Francisco, CA	1.3
37	74	Fairfax, VA	1.1
20	75	New York, NY	0.9

Professional, scientific, and technical employment as a percent of total nonfarm employment, 2013

Population rank	Professional services rank	County	Percent employed in professional services [col 110/ col 105]
37	1	Fairfax, VA	33.6
40	2	Montgomery, MD	18.8
65	3	San Francisco, CA	16.2
16	4	Santa Clara, CA	14.3
20	5	New York, NY	13.7
22	5	Middlesex, MA	13.7
32	7	Oakland, MI	13.4
67	8	Middlesex, NJ	13.2
45	9	Fulton, GA	12.9
36	10	Travis, TX	11.6
57	11	Prince George's, MD	11.5
44	11	Wake, NC	11.5
5	13	San Diego, CA	11.2
60	14	Collin, TX	10.6
64	15	Macomb, MI	10.5
21	16	Alameda, CA	10.2
29	17	Hillsborough, FL	10.0
9	18	Dallas, TX	9.7
13	19	King, WA	9.4
2	19	Cook, IL	9.4
43	19	St. Louis, MO	9.4
72	22	Montgomery, PA	9.2
3	22	Harris, TX	9.2
38	24	Contra Costa, CA	9.0
66	24	Ventura, CA	9.0
35	26	Hennepin, MN	8.9
50	27	Fairfield, CT	8.8
6	28	Orange, CA	8.5
1	28	Los Angeles, CA	8.5
75	28	Essex, NJ	8.5
74	31	Hamilton, OH	8.4
24	31	Suffolk, NY	8.4
41	33	Mecklenburg, NC	8.3
52	34	Pinellas, FL	8.2
34	34	Allegheny, PA	8.2
54	36	Bergen, NJ	8.1
27	36	Palm Beach, FL	8.1
71	36	Baltimore, MD	8.1
28	39	Nassau, NY	7.9
39	39	Salt Lake, UT	7.9
23	41	Philadelphia, PA	7.8
61	41	Gwinnett, GA	7.8
55	43	Du Page, IL	7.7
58	43	Hartford, CT	7.7
25	43	Sacramento, CA	7.7
17	46	Broward, FL	7.6
53	47	Marion, IN	7.3
56	48	Erie, NY	7.1
7	49	Miami-Dade, FL	6.8
47	49	Westchester, NY	6.8
19	51	Wayne, MI	6.7
31	51	Orange, FL	6.7
62	53	Kern, CA	6.6
33	54	Franklin, OH	6.5
4	55	Maricopa, AZ	6.3
30	56	Cuyahoga, OH	6.1
18	56	Bexar, TX	6.1
59	56	Duval, FL	6.1
73	59	Worcester, MA	5.9
42	60	Pima, AZ	5.5
15	61	Tarrant, TX	5.4
46	62	Honolulu, HI	5.3
14	63	Clark, NV	5.2
49	64	Milwaukee, WI	5.1
48	65	Fresno, CA	4.6
63	66	New Haven, CT	4.5
68	67	El Paso, TX	4.3
69	68	Pierce, WA	4.0
51	69	Shelby, TN	3.6
8	70	Kings, NY	3.4
12	71	San Bernardino, CA	3.3
10	71	Riverside, CA	3.3
70	73	Hidalgo, TX	2.9
11	74	Queens, NY	2.7
26	75	Bronx, NY	1.5

Per capita local government taxes, 2012

Population rank	Local taxes rank	County	Per capita local taxes (dollars) [col 183]
28	1	Nassau, NY	$5 254
47	2	Westchester, NY	$5 135
20	3	New York, NY	$5 096
8	3	Kings, NY	$5 096
11	3	Queens, NY	$5 096
26	3	Bronx, NY	$5 096
24	7	Suffolk, NY	$4 295
65	8	San Francisco, CA	$4 001
54	9	Bergen, NJ	$3 788
50	10	Fairfield, CT	$3 419
40	11	Montgomery, MD	$3 168
55	12	Du Page, IL	$3 002
75	13	Essex, NJ	$2 846
37	14	Fairfax, VA	$2 810
45	15	Fulton, GA	$2 802
2	16	Cook, IL	$2 765
30	16	Cuyahoga, OH	$2 765
67	18	Middlesex, NJ	$2 730
33	19	Franklin, OH	$2 717
23	20	Philadelphia, PA	$2 636
16	21	Santa Clara, CA	$2 621
58	22	Hartford, CT	$2 571
13	23	King, WA	$2 543
27	24	Palm Beach, FL	$2 542
72	25	Montgomery, PA	$2 541
22	26	Middlesex, MA	$2 471
36	27	Travis, TX	$2 455
74	28	Hamilton, OH	$2 403
60	29	Collin, TX	$2 390
56	30	Erie, NY	$2 368
21	31	Alameda, CA	$2 358
63	31	New Haven, CT	$2 358
9	33	Dallas, TX	$2 338
34	34	Allegheny, PA	$2 228
3	35	Harris, TX	$2 171
43	36	St. Louis, MO	$2 133
7	37	Miami-Dade, FL	$2 132
15	38	Tarrant, TX	$2 029
41	39	Mecklenburg, NC	$1 923
71	40	Baltimore, MD	$1 917
35	41	Hennepin, MN	$1 910
1	42	Los Angeles, CA	$1 891
49	43	Milwaukee, WI	$1 888
38	44	Contra Costa, CA	$1 861
51	45	Shelby, TN	$1 828
31	46	Orange, FL	$1 815
6	47	Orange, CA	$1 806
5	48	San Diego, CA	$1 791
57	49	Prince George's, MD	$1 761
17	50	Broward, FL	$1 742
18	51	Bexar, TX	$1 675
66	52	Ventura, CA	$1 650
73	53	Worcester, MA	$1 630
52	54	Pinellas, FL	$1 597
59	55	Duval, FL	$1 536
61	56	Gwinnett, GA	$1 529
69	57	Pierce, WA	$1 521
32	58	Oakland, MI	$1 515
4	59	Maricopa, AZ	$1 506
19	60	Wayne, MI	$1 499
53	61	Marion, IN	$1 447
42	62	Pima, AZ	$1 438
44	63	Wake, NC	$1 436
39	64	Salt Lake, UT	$1 428
14	65	Clark, NV	$1 367
62	66	Kern, CA	$1 365
10	67	Riverside, CA	$1 362
29	68	Hillsborough, FL	$1 359
25	69	Sacramento, CA	$1 357
46	70	Honolulu, HI	$1 348
68	71	El Paso, TX	$1 318
12	72	San Bernardino, CA	$1 287
48	73	Fresno, CA	$1 131
64	74	Macomb, MI	$1 112
70	75	Hidalgo, TX	$1 071

75 Largest Counties by 2014 Population

Selected Rankings

Violent crime rate, 2013				Military as a percent of all federal employment, 2013				Percent of votes for Barack Obama, 2012			
Population rank	Violent crime rate rank	County	Violent crime rate per 100,000 population [col 46]	Population rank	Military employment rank	County	Percent military federal employment [col 195/ col 194 + 195]	Population rank	Vote for Obama rank	County	Percent of votes for Obama [col 197]
51	1	Shelby, TN	1 240	69	1	Pierce, WA	75.6	57	1	Prince George's, MD	88.9
53	2	Marion, IN	1 204	68	2	El Paso, TX	69.3	26	2	Bronx, NY	88.7
23	3	Philadelphia, PA	1 100	5	3	San Diego, CA	68.5	20	3	New York, NY	85.7
19	4	Wayne, MI	1 052	46	4	Honolulu, HI	63.6	65	4	San Francisco, CA	84.2
49	5	Milwaukee, WI	919	12	5	San Bernardino, CA	59.7	23	5	Philadelphia, PA	83.1
65	6	San Francisco, CA	859	60	6	Collin, TX	57.3	8	6	Kings, NY	79.4
45	7	Fulton, GA	785	14	7	Clark, NV	55.8	21	7	Alameda, CA	78.8
21	8	Alameda, CA	747	61	8	Gwinnett, GA	51.0	2	8	Cook, IL	76.2
75	9	Essex, NJ	733	18	9	Bexar, TX	50.1	75	9	Essex, NJ	76.0
3	10	Harris, TX	712	59	10	Duval, FL	47.9	11	10	Queens, NY	75.1
14	11	Clark, NV	678	72	11	Montgomery, PA	45.8	19	11	Wayne, MI	74.1
31	11	Orange, FL	678	67	12	Middlesex, NJ	43.1	40	12	Montgomery, MD	71.6
7	13	Miami-Dade, FL	655	54	13	Bergen, NJ	42.6	13	13	King, WA	70.3
20	14	New York, NY	625	66	14	Ventura, CA	41.9	46	14	Honolulu, HI	69.8
8	14	Kings, NY	625	42	15	Pima, AZ	40.4	16	15	Santa Clara, CA	69.4
11	14	Queens, NY	625	50	16	Fairfield, CT	40.3	1	16	Los Angeles, CA	69.2
26	14	Bronx, NY	625	8	17	Kings, NY	40.2	70	17	Hidalgo, TX	69.0
59	18	Duval, FL	623	73	18	Worcester, MA	39.7	30	18	Cuyahoga, OH	68.9
30	19	Cuyahoga, OH	613	4	19	Maricopa, AZ	39.2	38	19	Contra Costa, CA	68.0
2	20	Cook, IL	594	43	20	St. Louis, MO	37.8	49	20	Milwaukee, WI	67.3
62	21	Kern, CA	576	29	21	Hillsborough, FL	37.1	45	21	Fulton, GA	67.2
52	22	Pinellas, FL	552	44	22	Wake, NC	36.5	17	22	Broward, FL	67.1
41	23	Mecklenburg, NC	539	10	23	Riverside, CA	36.3	68	23	El Paso, TX	65.9
18	24	Bexar, TX	532	17	24	Broward, FL	35.5	58	24	Hartford, CT	65.2
25	25	Sacramento, CA	514	6	25	Orange, CA	33.3	22	25	Middlesex, MA	64.2
48	26	Fresno, CA	510	28	26	Nassau, NY	32.6	36	26	Travis, TX	63.9
57	27	Prince George's, MD	506	70	27	Hidalgo, TX	32.4	53	27	Marion, IN	63.8
71	28	Baltimore, MD	469	39	28	Salt Lake, UT	32.3	35	28	Hennepin, MN	63.4
74	29	Hamilton, OH	461	32	29	Oakland, MI	32.3	47	28	Westchester, NY	63.4
27	30	Palm Beach, FL	450	41	30	Mecklenburg, NC	31.5	51	28	Shelby, TN	63.4
69	31	Pierce, WA	445	21	31	Alameda, CA	30.6	41	31	Mecklenburg, NC	61.8
56	32	Erie, NY	444	22	32	Middlesex, MA	29.8	27	32	Palm Beach, FL	61.2
9	33	Dallas, TX	439	27	33	Palm Beach, FL	29.7	63	33	New Haven, CT	61.0
73	34	Worcester, MA	436	52	34	Pinellas, FL	29.4	67	34	Middlesex, NJ	60.4
17	35	Broward, FL	435	3	35	Harris, TX	29.0	37	35	Fairfax, VA	60.1
42	36	Pima, AZ	431	38	36	Contra Costa, CA	28.6	72	36	Montgomery, PA	60.0
35	37	Hennepin, MN	427	62	37	Kern, CA	28.3	33	37	Franklin, OH	59.7
15	38	Tarrant, TX	409	1	38	Los Angeles, CA	27.6	43	38	St. Louis, MO	59.5
33	39	Franklin, OH	407	55	39	Du Page, IL	27.3	31	39	Orange, FL	59.0
4	40	Maricopa, AZ	405	7	40	Miami-Dade, FL	27.1	50	40	Fairfield, CT	58.6
1	41	Los Angeles, CA	403	35	41	Hennepin, MN	27.0	14	41	Clark, NV	58.5
12	42	San Bernardino, CA	402	63	42	New Haven, CT	26.5	25	41	Sacramento, CA	58.5
34	43	Allegheny, PA	392	26	43	Bronx, NY	26.4	56	43	Erie, NY	58.0
63	43	New Haven, CT	392	47	44	Westchester, NY	25.9	7	44	Miami-Dade, FL	57.9
39	45	Salt Lake, UT	368	25	45	Sacramento, CA	25.8	9	45	Dallas, TX	57.3
38	46	Contra Costa, CA	363	15	46	Tarrant, TX	25.5	34	45	Allegheny, PA	57.3
5	47	San Diego, CA	348	13	47	King, WA	25.3	44	47	Wake, NC	56.7
68	48	El Paso, TX	341	58	48	Hartford, CT	25.3	32	48	Oakland, MI	56.5
29	49	Hillsborough, FL	336	16	49	Santa Clara, CA	24.8	71	49	Baltimore, MD	56.2
36	50	Travis, TX	324	49	50	Milwaukee, WI	24.0	73	50	Worcester, MA	55.8
13	51	King, WA	315	57	51	Prince George's, MD	22.9	66	51	Ventura, CA	55.2
64	52	Macomb, MI	298	34	52	Allegheny, PA	22.5	69	51	Pierce, WA	55.2
58	53	Hartford, CT	289	2	53	Cook, IL	22.1	55	53	Du Page, IL	54.7
70	54	Hidalgo, TX	286	51	54	Shelby, TN	21.6	54	54	Bergen, NJ	54.3
43	55	St. Louis, MO	281	33	55	Franklin, OH	21.5	5	55	San Diego, CA	54.1
10	56	Riverside, CA	270	11	56	Queens, NY	20.8	28	56	Nassau, NY	53.8
50	57	Fairfield, CT	245	31	57	Orange, FL	20.2	52	57	Pinellas, FL	53.6
16	58	Santa Clara, CA	244	19	58	Wayne, MI	19.8	64	58	Macomb, MI	53.4
44	59	Wake, NC	232	74	59	Hamilton, OH	19.6	29	59	Hillsborough, FL	53.2
47	60	Westchester, NY	229	36	60	Travis, TX	19.2	74	60	Hamilton, OH	53.0
61	61	Gwinnett, GA	210	9	61	Dallas, TX	19.2	24	61	Suffolk, NY	52.6
22	62	Middlesex, MA	208	24	62	Suffolk, NY	18.8	18	62	Bexar, TX	52.4
32	63	Oakland, MI	203	30	63	Cuyahoga, OH	18.6	42	62	Pima, AZ	52.4
6	64	Orange, CA	194	53	64	Marion, IN	17.9	12	64	San Bernardino, CA	52.1
66	64	Ventura, CA	194	64	65	Macomb, MI	17.8	3	65	Harris, TX	50.4
40	66	Montgomery, MD	174	37	66	Fairfax, VA	17.4	10	66	Riverside, CA	50.2
72	67	Montgomery, PA	168	56	67	Erie, NY	17.2	48	66	Fresno, CA	50.2
28	68	Nassau, NY	154	75	68	Essex, NJ	15.4	39	68	Salt Lake, UT	48.7
67	69	Middlesex, NJ	151	40	69	Montgomery, MD	14.7	59	68	Duval, FL	48.7
60	70	Collin, TX	148	23	70	Philadelphia, PA	14.5	6	70	Orange, CA	47.6
24	71	Suffolk, NY	127	71	71	Baltimore, MD	14.0	61	71	Gwinnett, GA	44.5
46	72	Honolulu, HI	115	48	72	Fresno, CA	13.6	4	72	Maricopa, AZ	44.1
37	73	Fairfax, VA	96	20	73	New York, NY	11.6	15	73	Tarrant, TX	43.7
54	74	Bergen, NJ	90	65	74	San Francisco, CA	10.4	62	74	Kern, CA	40.1
55	75	Du Page, IL	81	45	75	Fulton, GA	10.2	60	75	Collin, TX	36.8

75 Largest Counties by 2014 Population

Selected Rankings

Nonemployer businesses, 2013				Value of residential construction authorized by building permits, 2014				Full-time equivalent government employees, 2012			
Population rank	Nonemployer Businesses rank	County	Nonemployer businesses [col 167]	Population rank	Value ($1,000) rank	County	Value ($1,000) [col 169]	Population rank	Government Employment rank	County	Government employees [col 172]
1	1	Los Angeles, CA	945 941	3	1	Harris, TX	5 358 419	20	1	New York, NY	411 393
2	2	Cook, IL	447 401	1	2	Los Angeles, CA	4 059 026	1	2	Los Angeles, CA	386 456
7	3	Miami-Dade, FL	407 551	4	3	Maricopa, AZ	3 991 073	2	3	Cook, IL	198 590
3	4	Harris, TX	367 449	13	4	King, WA	2 880 007	3	4	Harris, TX	166 045
6	5	Orange, CA	278 270	60	5	Collin, TX	2 389 272	4	5	Maricopa, AZ	129 919
4	6	Maricopa, AZ	275 014	9	6	Dallas, TX	2 030 691	9	6	Dallas, TX	105 099
8	7	Kings, NY	249 647	31	7	Orange, FL	2 015 453	7	7	Miami-Dade, FL	102 308
5	8	San Diego, CA	246 649	29	8	Hillsborough, FL	1 971 955	5	8	San Diego, CA	97 178
11	9	Queens, NY	229 249	6	9	Orange, CA	1 923 311	6	9	Orange, CA	85 251
17	10	Broward, FL	225 162	16	10	Santa Clara, CA	1 867 633	18	10	Bexar, TX	76 821
20	11	New York, NY	219 326	36	11	Travis, TX	1 850 112	15	11	Tarrant, TX	76 274
9	12	Dallas, TX	210 881	7	12	Miami-Dade, FL	1 812 541	17	12	Broward, FL	73 864
10	13	Riverside, CA	152 801	44	13	Wake, NC	1 691 319	10	13	Riverside, CA	68 997
13	14	King, WA	151 561	15	14	Tarrant, TX	1 536 130	12	14	San Bernardino, CA	68 989
27	15	Palm Beach, FL	151 331	2	15	Cook, IL	1 524 679	13	15	King, WA	65 821
15	16	Tarrant, TX	151 025	5	16	San Diego, CA	1 504 007	24	16	Suffolk, NY	63 444
14	17	Clark, NV	141 658	10	17	Riverside, CA	1 471 177	30	17	Cuyahoga, OH	62 490
12	18	San Bernardino, CA	135 455	27	18	Palm Beach, FL	1 265 400	23	18	Philadelphia, PA	60 937
28	19	Nassau, NY	132 134	41	19	Mecklenburg, NC	1 265 076	41	19	Mecklenburg, NC	60 489
16	20	Santa Clara, CA	128 730	45	20	Fulton, GA	1 177 766	28	20	Nassau, NY	60 368
19	21	Wayne, MI	126 314	14	21	Clark, NV	1 132 984	16	21	Santa Clara, CA	59 919
22	22	Middlesex, MA	125 980	35	22	Hennepin, MN	1 125 448	21	22	Alameda, CA	56 184
21	23	Alameda, CA	124 216	18	23	Bexar, TX	1 020 999	19	23	Wayne, MI	52 078
24	24	Suffolk, NY	123 386	21	24	Alameda, CA	889 512	14	24	Clark, NV	51 796
18	25	Bexar, TX	120 595	23	25	Philadelphia, PA	879 066	22	25	Middlesex, MA	51 015
26	26	Bronx, NY	112 552	39	26	Salt Lake, UT	864 159	25	26	Sacramento, CA	50 509
31	27	Orange, FL	110 458	69	27	Pierce, WA	827 177	27	27	Palm Beach, FL	46 198
32	28	Oakland, MI	108 991	33	28	Franklin, OH	811 638	29	28	Hillsborough, FL	45 811
29	29	Hillsborough, FL	106 573	65	29	San Francisco, CA	768 892	31	29	Orange, FL	45 111
40	30	Montgomery, MD	103 731	24	30	Suffolk, NY	750 599	36	30	Travis, TX	45 034
36	31	Travis, TX	101 952	8	31	Kings, NY	734 465	34	31	Allegheny, PA	43 945
45	32	Fulton, GA	99 463	42	32	Pima, AZ	697 362	33	32	Franklin, OH	43 936
35	33	Hennepin, MN	99 234	22	33	Middlesex, MA	695 156	45	33	Fulton, GA	43 801
37	34	Fairfax, VA	97 330	32	34	Oakland, MI	630 334	37	34	Fairfax, VA	43 275
25	35	Sacramento, CA	95 166	12	35	San Bernardino, CA	627 861	47	35	Westchester, NY	42 725
47	36	Westchester, NY	92 896	40	36	Montgomery, MD	625 089	51	36	Shelby, TN	39 378
61	37	Gwinnett, GA	90 033	50	37	Fairfield, CT	614 243	70	37	Hidalgo, TX	39 042
65	38	San Francisco, CA	89 078	59	38	Duval, FL	591 516	65	38	San Francisco, CA	38 712
30	39	Cuyahoga, OH	88 494	61	39	Gwinnett, GA	591 439	40	39	Montgomery, MD	38 590
50	40	Fairfield, CT	88 363	20	40	New York, NY	524 215	68	40	El Paso, TX	38 262
33	41	Franklin, OH	87 914	54	41	Bergen, NJ	514 764	35	41	Hennepin, MN	35 312
54	42	Bergen, NJ	86 102	38	42	Contra Costa, CA	493 802	56	42	Erie, NY	35 259
41	43	Mecklenburg, NC	83 428	55	43	Du Page, IL	485 653	43	43	St. Louis, MO	35 141
38	44	Contra Costa, CA	82 405	34	44	Allegheny, PA	461 426	48	44	Fresno, CA	34 954
23	45	Philadelphia, PA	80 370	11	45	Queens, NY	458 159	55	45	Du Page, IL	34 627
51	46	Shelby, TN	77 761	48	46	Fresno, CA	445 222	39	46	Salt Lake, UT	34 230
55	47	Du Page, IL	77 413	68	47	El Paso, TX	439 382	53	47	Marion, IN	34 223
39	48	Salt Lake, UT	76 464	25	48	Sacramento, CA	439 041	49	48	Milwaukee, WI	34 086
52	49	Pinellas, FL	76 324	62	49	Kern, CA	409 139	54	49	Bergen, NJ	32 531
44	50	Wake, NC	76 044	17	50	Broward, FL	404 301	62	50	Kern, CA	32 191
60	51	Collin, TX	75 827	46	51	Honolulu, HI	376 973	52	51	Pinellas, FL	32 162
34	52	Allegheny, PA	74 402	70	52	Hidalgo, TX	372 000	32	52	Oakland, MI	32 137
43	53	St. Louis, MO	72 436	64	53	Macomb, MI	354 503	50	53	Fairfield, CT	32 029
57	54	Prince George's, MD	71 062	43	54	St. Louis, MO	348 478	58	54	Hartford, CT	31 675
72	55	Montgomery, PA	66 225	28	55	Nassau, NY	333 009	42	55	Pima, AZ	31 634
70	56	Hidalgo, TX	66 167	52	56	Pinellas, FL	315 192	44	56	Wake, NC	31 235
66	57	Ventura, CA	64 224	56	57	Erie, NY	307 875	38	57	Contra Costa, CA	31 030
71	58	Baltimore, MD	62 218	37	58	Fairfax, VA	302 407	74	58	Hamilton, OH	30 330
59	59	Duval, FL	62 201	67	59	Middlesex, NJ	298 858	63	59	New Haven, CT	28 448
42	60	Pima, AZ	60 686	66	60	Ventura, CA	279 531	60	60	Collin, TX	28 433
75	61	Essex, NJ	60 582	57	61	Prince George's, MD	275 090	73	61	Worcester, MA	28 380
46	62	Honolulu, HI	60 220	51	62	Shelby, TN	259 660	75	62	Essex, NJ	27 818
64	63	Macomb, MI	59 636	72	63	Montgomery, PA	256 177	61	63	Gwinnett, GA	27 778
53	64	Marion, IN	58 749	73	64	Worcester, MA	250 082	66	64	Ventura, CA	27 714
63	65	New Haven, CT	57 091	75	65	Essex, NJ	243 184	57	65	Prince George's, MD	27 062
58	66	Hartford, CT	56 271	47	66	Westchester, NY	238 056	59	66	Duval, FL	26 681
74	67	Hamilton, OH	54 764	74	67	Hamilton, OH	237 253	67	67	Middlesex, NJ	26 592
68	68	El Paso, TX	53 783	19	68	Wayne, MI	196 344	71	68	Baltimore, MD	26 532
67	69	Middlesex, NJ	51 540	26	69	Bronx, NY	185 203	69	69	Pierce, WA	23 934
73	70	Worcester, MA	49 892	30	70	Cuyahoga, OH	184 863	72	70	Montgomery, PA	23 690
48	71	Fresno, CA	49 304	71	71	Baltimore, MD	177 875	64	71	Macomb, MI	20 477
49	72	Milwaukee, WI	47 132	53	72	Marion, IN	177 765	46	72	Honolulu, HI	9 304
56	73	Erie, NY	45 745	63	73	New Haven, CT	150 265	8		Kings, NY (included in New York, NY)	NA
62	74	Kern, CA	43 515	58	74	Hartford, CT	134 850	11		Queens, NY (included in New York, NY)	NA
69	75	Pierce, WA	38 934	49	75	Milwaukee, WI	90 206	26		Bronx, NY (included in New York, NY)	NA

75 Counties with Highest Agricultural Sales

Selected Rankings

Value of agricultural sales, 2013			Average agricultural sales per farm, 2013				Number of farms, 2013			
Value of sales rank	County	Value of sales (millions of dollars) [col 125]	Value of sales rank	Average sales rank	County	Average sales per farm (dollars) [col 126]	Value of sales rank	Number of farms rank	County	Number of farms [col 113]
1	Fresno, CA	4 973	28	1	Haskell, KS	5 400 412	50	1	San Diego, CA	5 732
2	Tulare, CA	4 017	22	2	Hartley, TX	4 630 969	1	2	Fresno, CA	5 683
3	Kern, CA	3 999	8	3	Imperial, CA	4 486 078	15	3	Lancaster, PA	5 657
4	Monterey, CA	2 980	32	4	Scott, KS	3 642 543	2	4	Tulare, CA	4 931
5	Merced, CA	2 968	46	5	Hansford, TX	2 977 973	7	5	Stanislaus, CA	4 143
6	San Joaquin, CA	2 250	40	6	Grant, KS	2 790 860	6	6	San Joaquin, CA	3 580
7	Stanislaus, CA	2 228	4	7	Monterey, CA	2 527 341	33	7	Sonoma, CA	3 579
8	Imperial, CA	1 889	19	8	Castro, TX	2 466 429	9	8	Weld, CO	3 525
9	Weld, CO	1 861	62	9	Wichita, KS	2 357 736	45	9	Stearns, MN	3 501
10	Kings, CA	1 829	18	10	Parmer, TX	2 332 523	12	10	Yakima, WA	3 143
11	Grant, WA	1 762	66	11	Moore, TX	2 318 107	67	11	Miami-Dade, FL	2 954
12	Yakima, WA	1 646	36	12	Gray, KS	2 247 407	26	12	Riverside, CA	2 949
13	Sioux, IA	1 613	17	13	Deaf Smith, TX	2 220 734	53	13	San Luis Obispo, CA	2 666
14	Madera, CA	1 603	3	14	Kern, CA	2 063 462	71	14	Marion, OR	2 567
15	Lancaster, PA	1 475	72	15	Sherman, TX	1 886 121	5	15	Merced, CA	2 486
16	Ventura, CA	1 440	49	16	Phelps, NE	1 824 185	29	16	Maricopa, AZ	2 479
17	Deaf Smith, TX	1 379	41	17	Finney, KS	1 822 062	16	17	Ventura, CA	2 150
18	Parmer, TX	1 330	58	18	Dallam, TX	1 756 642	3	18	Kern, CA	1 938
19	Castro, TX	1 312	31	19	Yuma, AZ	1 752 685	55	19	Rockingham, VA	1 902
20	Duplin, NC	1 276	10	20	Kings, CA	1 732 231	54	20	Chester, PA	1 730
21	Sampson, NC	1 259	35	21	Gooding, ID	1 581 904	13	21	Sioux, IA	1 618
22	Hartley, TX	1 181	34	22	Cassia, ID	1 427 737	23	22	Santa Barbara, CA	1 597
23	Santa Barbara, CA	1 178	24	23	Yuma, CO	1 379 309	11	23	Grant, WA	1 552
24	Yuma, CO	1 150	20	24	Duplin, NC	1 357 895	38	24	Benton, WA	1 509
25	Cuming, NE	1 081	5	25	Merced, CA	1 193 694	14	25	Madera, CA	1 507
26	Riverside, CA	1 039	21	26	Sampson, NC	1 179 750	30	26	Palm Beach, FL	1 409
27	Texas, OK	1 014	25	27	Cuming, NE	1 177 889	75	27	Allegan, MI	1 396
28	Haskell, KS	1 010	11	28	Grant, WA	1 135 499	42	28	Custer, NE	1 352
29	Maricopa, AZ	1 004	64	29	Jerome, ID	1 101 943	51	29	Kossuth, IA	1 349
30	Palm Beach, FLIf	999	14	30	Madera, CA	1 063 547	59	30	Plymouth, IA	1 331
31	Yuma, AZ	985	73	31	Swisher, TX	1 038 602	70	31	Polk, MN	1 322
32	Scott, KS	980	44	32	Dawson, NE	1 025 163	60	32	Glenn, CA	1 311
33	Sonoma, CA	974	13	33	Sioux, IA	996 964	68	33	Twin Falls, ID	1 294
34	Cassia, ID	954	27	34	Texas, OK	990 157	61	34	Holt, NE	1 279
35	Gooding, ID	943	37	35	Pinal, AZ	989 059	74	35	San Bernardino, CA	1 249
36	Gray, KS	939	1	36	Fresno, CA	875 073	39	36	Sussex, DE	1 214
37	Pinal, AZ	928	48	37	Franklin, WA	838 068	69	37	Mercer, OH	1 208
38	Benton, WA	923	65	38	Morgan, CO	816 073	56	38	Huron, MI	1 205
39	Sussex, DE	921	2	39	Tulare, CA	814 657	4	39	Monterey, CA	1 179
40	Grant, KS	918	39	40	Sussex, DE	758 755	47	40	Lincoln, NE	1 168
41	Finney, KS	909	23	41	Santa Barbara, CA	737 581	43	41	Lyon, IA	1 139
42	Custer, NE	845	43	42	Lyon, IA	734 068	21	42	Sampson, NC	1 067
43	Lyon, IA	836	30	43	Palm Beach, FL	709 041	52	43	Renville, MN	1 061
44	Dawson, NE	826	57	44	Platte, NE	692 256	10	44	Kings, CA	1 056
45	Stearns, MN	808	63	45	Martin, MN	690 708	27	45	Texas, OK	1 024
46	Hansford, TX	783	47	46	Lincoln, NE	670 087	57	46	Platte, NE	942
47	Lincoln, NE	783	16	47	Ventura, CA	669 829	20	47	Duplin, NC	940
48	Franklin, WA	740	52	48	Renville, MN	669 506	37	48	Pinal, AZ	938
49	Phelps, NE	739	6	49	San Joaquin, CA	628 536	25	49	Cuming, NE	918
50	San Diego, CA	726	42	50	Custer, NE	625 226	63	50	Martin, MN	897
51	Kossuth, IA	722	38	51	Benton, WA	611 771	48	51	Franklin, WA	883
52	Renville, MN	710	56	52	Huron, MI	543 207	24	52	Yuma, CO	834
53	San Luis Obispo, CA	665	7	53	Stanislaus, CA	537 807	44	53	Dawson, NE	806
54	Chester, PA	661	51	54	Kossuth, IA	535 440	65	54	Morgan, CO	754
55	Rockingham, VA	659	9	55	Weld, CO	527 863	34	55	Cassia, ID	668
56	Huron, MI	655	12	56	Yakima, WA	523 548	17	56	Deaf Smith, TX	621
57	Platte, NE	652	61	57	Holt, NE	497 540	35	57	Gooding, ID	596
58	Dallam, TX	652	69	58	Mercer, OH	493 681	18	58	Parmer, TX	570
59	Plymouth, IA	643	60	59	Glenn, CA	486 166	73	59	Swisher, TX	565
60	Glenn, CA	637	59	60	Plymouth, IA	483 173	31	60	Yuma, AZ	562
61	Holt, NE	636	74	61	San Bernardino, CA	466 156	64	61	Jerome, ID	560
62	Wichita, KS	625	68	62	Twin Falls, ID	463 355	19	62	Castro, TX	532
63	Martin, MN	620	70	63	Polk, MN	449 722	41	63	Finney, KS	499
64	Jerome, ID	617	75	64	Allegan, MI	416 071	8	64	Imperial, CA	421
65	Morgan, CO	615	29	65	Maricopa, AZ	404 790	36	65	Gray, KS	418
66	Moore, TX	605	54	66	Chester, PA	381 933	49	66	Phelps, NE	405
67	Miami-Dade, FL	604	26	67	Riverside, CA	352 306	58	67	Dallam, TX	371
68	Twin Falls, ID	600	55	68	Rockingham, VA	346 475	40	68	Grant, KS	329
69	Mercer, OH	596	33	69	Sonoma, CA	272 253	72	69	Sherman, TX	313
70	Polk, MN	594	15	70	Lancaster, PA	260 731	32	70	Scott, KS	269
71	Marion, OR	590	50	71	San Luis Obispo, CA	249 431	62	71	Wichita, KS	265
72	Sherman, TX	590	71	72	Marion, OR	230 953	46	72	Hansford, TX	263
73	Swisher, TX	587	45	73	Stearns, MN	230 933	66	73	Moore, TX	261
74	San Bernardino, CA	582	67	74	Miami-Dade, FL	204 549	22	74	Hartley, TX	255
75	Allegan, MI	581	50	75	San Diego, CA	126 657	28	75	Haskell, KS	187

75 Counties with Highest Agricultural Sales

Selected Rankings

Average size of farm, 2012

Value of sales rank	Size of farm rank	County	Average size of farm (acres) [col 119]
22	1	Hartley, TX	3 541
58	2	Dallam, TX	2 296
46	3	Hansford, TX	2 155
66	4	Moore, TX	2 006
28	5	Haskell, KS	1 944
72	6	Sherman, TX	1 863
62	7	Wichita, KS	1 750
32	8	Scott, KS	1 686
41	9	Finney, KS	1 635
24	10	Yuma, CO	1 623
17	11	Deaf Smith, TX	1 487
36	12	Gray, KS	1 309
27	13	Texas, OK	1 257
37	14	Pinal, AZ	1 252
8	15	Imperial, CA	1 225
47	16	Lincoln, NE	1 219
3	17	Kern, CA	1 202
42	18	Custer, NE	1 112
61	19	Holt, NE	1 106
40	20	Grant, KS	1 105
4	21	Monterey, CA	1 076
19	22	Castro, TX	1 030
18	23	Parmer, TX	971
73	24	Swisher, TX	966
34	25	Cassia, ID	915
65	26	Morgan, CO	858
70	27	Polk, MN	828
49	28	Phelps, NE	818
44	29	Dawson, NE	782
48	30	Franklin, WA	708
10	31	Kings, CA	638
11	32	Grant, WA	621
52	33	Renville, MN	586
12	34	Yakima, WA	566
9	35	Weld, CO	555
60	36	Glenn, CA	510
53	37	San Luis Obispo, CA	502
63	38	Martin, MN	478
38	39	Benton, WA	466
57	40	Platte, NE	453
51	41	Kossuth, IA	444
23	42	Santa Barbara, CA	439
14	43	Madera, CA	434
59	44	Plymouth, IA	407
35	45	Gooding, ID	402
25	46	Cuming, NE	395
5	47	Merced, CA	394
31	48	Yuma, AZ	382
56	49	Huron, MI	375
68	50	Twin Falls, ID	374
30	51	Palm Beach, FL	365
64	52	Jerome, ID	336
43	53	Lyon, IA	325
1	54	Fresno, CA	303
13	55	Sioux, IA	299
21	56	Sampson, NC	273
2	57	Tulare, CA	251
20	58	Duplin, NC	246
69	59	Mercer, OH	226
39	60	Sussex, DE	224
6	61	San Joaquin, CA	220
45	62	Stearns, MN	216
75	63	Allegan, MI	194
29	64	Maricopa, AZ	192
7	65	Stanislaus, CA	185
33	66	Sonoma, CA	165
16	67	Ventura, CA	131
26	68	Riverside, CA	117
55	68	Rockingham, VA	117
71	70	Marion, OR	111
54	71	Chester, PA	95
15	72	Lancaster, PA	78
74	73	San Bernardino, CA	62
50	74	San Diego, CA	39
67	75	Miami-Dade, FL	28

Average value of land and buildings per farm, 2012

Value of sales rank	Value of land and buildings per farm rank	County	Average value per farm (dollars) [col 122]
8	1	Imperial, CA	8 577 865
3	2	Kern, CA	5 332 548
4	3	Monterey, CA	5 263 068
10	4	Kings, CA	3 847 243
49	5	Phelps, NE	3 684 978
22	6	Hartley, TX	3 557 855
52	7	Renville, MN	3 547 517
51	8	Kossuth, IA	3 380 844
14	9	Madera, CA	3 302 033
23	10	Santa Barbara, CA	3 233 061
5	11	Merced, CA	3 045 778
59	12	Plymouth, IA	2 992 740
37	13	Pinal, AZ	2 979 541
63	14	Martin, MN	2 931 235
31	15	Yuma, AZ	2 758 098
13	16	Sioux, IA	2 726 452
43	17	Lyon, IA	2 677 244
28	18	Haskell, KS	2 676 770
30	19	Palm Beach, FL	2 586 187
32	20	Scott, KS	2 556 929
1	21	Fresno, CA	2 509 484
44	22	Dawson, NE	2 429 274
33	23	Sonoma, CA	2 409 158
70	24	Polk, MN	2 403 190
62	25	Wichita, KS	2 375 008
41	26	Finney, KS	2 353 291
60	27	Glenn, CA	2 342 959
61	28	Holt, NE	2 314 973
57	29	Platte, NE	2 302 510
24	30	Yuma, CO	2 223 818
6	31	San Joaquin, CA	2 218 140
58	32	Dallam, TX	2 164 833
34	33	Cassia, ID	2 143 115
11	34	Grant, WA	2 128 600
25	35	Cuming, NE	2 120 511
53	36	San Luis Obispo, CA	2 115 410
42	37	Custer, NE	2 110 533
48	38	Franklin, WA	2 071 813
16	39	Ventura, CA	2 041 990
72	40	Sherman, TX	2 006 652
46	41	Hansford, TX	1 994 289
56	42	Huron, MI	1 952 800
2	43	Tulare, CA	1 893 271
66	44	Moore, TX	1 884 521
7	45	Stanislaus, CA	1 786 289
69	46	Mercer, OH	1 775 939
39	47	Sussex, DE	1 761 092
47	48	Lincoln, NE	1 749 910
36	49	Gray, KS	1 747 136
35	50	Gooding, ID	1 539 908
40	51	Grant, KS	1 471 553
17	52	Deaf Smith, TX	1 470 176
64	53	Jerome, ID	1 289 525
38	54	Benton, WA	1 276 306
54	55	Chester, PA	1 242 743
65	56	Morgan, CO	1 224 219
26	57	Riverside, CA	1 191 416
68	58	Twin Falls, ID	1 155 801
19	59	Castro, TX	1 131 530
9	60	Weld, CO	1 098 289
29	61	Maricopa, AZ	1 087 145
21	62	Sampson, NC	1 086 479
12	63	Yakima, WA	1 021 212
18	64	Parmer, TX	1 010 667
27	65	Texas, OK	1 005 370
20	66	Duplin, NC	1 001 313
15	67	Lancaster, PA	973 388
75	68	Allegan, MI	927 485
73	69	Swisher, TX	888 986
71	70	Marion, OR	885 406
45	71	Stearns, MN	844 095
74	72	San Bernardino, CA	831 612
55	73	Rockingham, VA	823 606
67	74	Miami-Dade, FL	699 727
50	75	San Diego, CA	694 313

Average value of land and buildings per acre, 2012

Value of sales rank	Value of land and buildings per acre rank	County	Average value per acre (dollars) [col 123]
67	1	Miami-Dade, FL	25 423
50	2	San Diego, CA	17 964
16	3	Ventura, CA	15 621
33	4	Sonoma, CA	14 620
74	5	San Bernardino, CA	13 455
54	6	Chester, PA	13 070
15	7	Lancaster, PA	12 529
26	8	Riverside, CA	10 212
6	9	San Joaquin, CA	10 090
7	10	Stanislaus, CA	9 636
13	11	Sioux, IA	9 105
1	12	Fresno, CA	8 286
43	13	Lyon, IA	8 245
71	14	Marion, OR	7 942
69	15	Mercer, OH	7 854
39	16	Sussex, DE	7 853
5	17	Merced, CA	7 737
14	18	Madera, CA	7 614
51	19	Kossuth, IA	7 608
2	20	Tulare, CA	7 535
23	21	Santa Barbara, CA	7 365
59	22	Plymouth, IA	7 352
31	23	Yuma, AZ	7 220
30	24	Palm Beach, FL	7 090
55	25	Rockingham, VA	7 055
8	26	Imperial, CA	7 002
63	27	Martin, MN	6 134
52	28	Renville, MN	6 055
10	29	Kings, CA	6 031
29	30	Maricopa, AZ	5 663
25	31	Cuming, NE	5 364
56	32	Huron, MI	5 202
57	33	Platte, NE	5 088
4	34	Monterey, CA	4 893
75	35	Allegan, MI	4 790
60	36	Glenn, CA	4 593
49	37	Phelps, NE	4 504
3	38	Kern, CA	4 435
53	39	San Luis Obispo, CA	4 212
20	40	Duplin, NC	4 076
21	41	Sampson, NC	3 975
45	42	Stearns, MN	3 901
64	43	Jerome, ID	3 840
35	44	Gooding, ID	3 830
11	45	Grant, WA	3 428
44	46	Dawson, NE	3 106
68	47	Twin Falls, ID	3 090
48	48	Franklin, WA	2 927
70	49	Polk, MN	2 902
38	50	Benton, WA	2 738
37	51	Pinal, AZ	2 379
34	52	Cassia, ID	2 343
61	53	Holt, NE	2 093
9	54	Weld, CO	1 979
42	55	Custer, NE	1 898
12	56	Yakima, WA	1 803
32	57	Scott, KS	1 517
41	58	Finney, KS	1 439
47	59	Lincoln, NE	1 436
65	60	Morgan, CO	1 426
28	61	Haskell, KS	1 377
24	62	Yuma, CO	1 370
62	63	Wichita, KS	1 357
36	64	Gray, KS	1 335
40	65	Grant, KS	1 332
19	66	Castro, TX	1 098
72	67	Sherman, TX	1 077
18	68	Parmer, TX	1 040
22	69	Hartley, TX	1 005
17	70	Deaf Smith, TX	989
58	71	Dallam, TX	943
66	72	Moore, TX	939
46	73	Hansford, TX	925
73	74	Swisher, TX	921
27	75	Texas, OK	800

Table B. States and Counties — **Land Area and Population**

STATE/ County code	CBSA code[1]	County type[2]	STATE County		Population, 2014			Population and population characteristics, 2013										
								Race alone or in combination, not Hispanic or Latino (percent)					Age (percent)					
				Land area,[3] (sq km) 2010	Total persons 2014	Rank	Per square kilometer	White	Black	American Indian, Alaska Native	Asian and Pacific Islander	Percent Hispanic or Latino[4]	Under 5 years	5 to 17 years	18 to 24 years	25 to 34 years	35 to 44 years	45 to 54 years
				1	2	3	4	5	6	7	8	9	10	11	12	13	14	15

1. CBSA = Core Based Statistical Area. See Appendix A for explanation. See Appendix B for list of metropolitan areas with component counties. 2. County type code from the Economic Research Service of USDA Rural-Urban Continuum Codes. See Appendix A for definition. 3. Dry land or land partially or temporarily covered by water. 4. May be of any race.

Table B. States and Counties — **Population and Households**

STATE County	Population, 2013 (cont.)				Population change and components of change, 2000–2014							Households, 2009–2013				
	Age (percent) (cont.)				Total persons		Percent change		Components of change, 2010–2014					Percent		
	55 to 64 years	65 to 74 years	75 years and over	Percent female	2000	2010	2000–2010	2010–2014	Births	Deaths	Net migration	Number	Persons per house-hold	Family house-holds	Female family house-holder[1]	One per-son
	16	17	18	19	20	21	22	23	24	25	26	27	28	29	30	31

1. No spouse present.

Table B. States and Counties — **Population, Vital Statistics, Medicare, and Crime**

STATE County		Daytime population, 2009–2013		Births, 2014		Deaths, 2014		Persons under 65 with no health insurance, 2013		Medicare, 2014			Serious crimes known to police,[2] 2013	
													Total	
	Persons in group quarters, 2014	Number	Employ-ment/ resi-dence ratio	Total	Rate[1]	Number	Rate[1]	Number	Percent	Eligible for Medicare	Enrolled in Medicare Advantage	Enrolled in a Medicare prescription drug plan	Number	Rate[3]
	32	33	34	35	36	37	38	39	40	41	42	43	44	45

1. Per 1,000 estimated resident population. 2. Data for serious crimes have not been adjusted for underreporting; this may affect comparability between geographic areas and over time. 3. Per 100,000 population estimated by the FBI.

Table B. States and Counties — **Crime, Education, Money Income, and Poverty**

STATE County	Serious crimes known to police, 2013 (cont.)[1]		Education						Money income, 2009–2013				Income and poverty, 2013			
	Rate[2]		School enrollment and attainment, 2009–2013				Local government expenditures,[5] 2012–2013			Households				Percent below poverty level		
			Enrollment[3]		Attainment[4] (percent)											
	Violent	Property	Total	Per-cent private	High school grad-uate or less	Bach-elor's degree or more	Total current spending (mil dol)	Current spend-ing per student (dollars)	Per capita income[6] (dollars)	Median income (dollars)	Mean income (dollars)	Percent with income of $200,000 or more	Median house-hold income (dollars)	All per-sons	Children under 18 years	Children 5 to 17 years in families
	46	47	48	49	50	51	52	53	54	55	56	57	58	59	60	61

1. Data for serious crimes have not been adjusted for underreporting; this may affect comparability between geographic areas and over time. 2. Per 100,000 population estimated by the FBI. 3. All persons 3 years old and over enrolled in nursery school through college. 4. Persons 25 years old and over. 5. Elementary and secondary education expenditures. 6. Based on population estimated by the American Community Survey, 2009–2013.

Table B. States and Counties — **Personal Income**

STATE County	Personal income, 2013										Earnings, 2013		
			Per capita[1]			Supplements to wages and salaries; employer contributions (mil dol)						Contributions for government social insurance (mil dol)	
	Total (mil dol)	Percent change, 2012–2013	Dollars	Rank	Wages and salaries (mil dol)	Pension and insurance	Government social insurance	Proprietors' income (mil dol)	Dividends, interest, and rent (mil dol)	Personal transfer receipts (mil dol)	Total (mil dol)	From employee and self-employed	From employer
	62	63	64	65	66	67	68	69	70	71	72	73	74

1. Based on the resident population estimated as of July 1 of the year shown.

Table B. States and Counties — **Earnings, Social Security, and Housing**

STATE County	Earnings, 2013 (cont.)									Social Security beneficiaries, December 2013			Housing units, 2014	
	Percent by selected industries													
	Farm	Mining	Construction	Manu-facturing	Infor-mation: professional, scientific, technical services	Retail trade	Finance, insur-ance, real estate and leasing	Health care and social assistance	Govern-ment	Number	Rate[1]	Supple-mental Security Income recipients, December 2013	Total	Percent change, 2010–2014
	75	76	77	78	79	80	81	82	83	84	85	86	87	88

1. Per 1,000 resident population estimated as of July 1 of the year shown.

Table B. States and Counties — **Housing, Labor Force, and Employment**

STATE County	Housing units, 2009–2013								Civilian labor force, 2014				Civilian employment,[6] 2009–2013		
	Occupied units										Unemployment			Percent	
		Owner-occupied				Renter-occupied									
				Median owner cost as a percent of income											
	Total	Percent	Median value[1]	With a mort-gage	Without a mort-gage[2]	Median rent[3]	Median rent as a per-cent of income[2]	Sub-stand-ard units[4] (percent)	Total	Percent change, 2013–2014	Total	Rate[5]	Total	Manage-ment, business, science and arts	Con-struction, produc-tion, and mainte-nance occu-pations
	89	90	91	92	93	94	95	96	97	98	99	100	101	102	103

1. Specified owner-occupied units. 2. A value of 10.0 represents 10 percent or less; a value of 50.0 represents 50 percent or more. 3. Specified renter-occupied units.
4. Overcrowded or lacking complete plumbing facilities. 5. Percent of civilian labor force. 6. Persons 16 years old and over.

Table B. States and Counties — **Nonfarm Employment and Agriculture**

STATE County	Private nonfarm establishments, employment and payroll, 2013									Agriculture, 2012			
		Employment						Annual payroll		Farms			
											Percent with:		
	Number of establish-ments	Total	Health care and social assistance	Manufac-turing	Retail trade	Finance and insurance	Professional, scientific, and technical services	Total (mil dol)	Average per employee (dollars)	Number	Fewer than 50 acres	500 acres or more	Farm operators whose principal occu-pation is farming (percent)
	104	105	106	107	108	109	110	111	112	113	114	115	116

Table B. States and Counties — Agriculture

STATE County	Agriculture, 2012 (cont.)															
	Land in farms					Value of land and buildings (dollars)			Value of products sold				Percent of farms with sales of:		Government payments	
			Acres								Percent from:					
	Acreage (1,000)	Percent change, 2007–2012	Average size of farm	Total irrigated (1,000)	Total cropland (1,000)	Average per farm	Average per acre	Value of machinery and equipment, average per farm (dollars)	Total (mil dol)	Average per farm (dollars)	Crops	Livestock and poultry products	$10,000 or more	$100,000 or more	Total ($1,000)	Percent of farms
	117	118	119	120	121	122	123	124	125	126	127	128	129	130	131	132

Table B. States and Counties — Water Use, Wholesale Trade, Retail Trade, and Real Estate

STATE County	Water use, 2010		Wholesale trade,[1] 2007				Retail trade,[2] 2007				Real estate and rental and leasing,[2] 2007			
	Total water withdrawn (mil gal/day)	Gallons withdrawn per person per day	Number of establishments	Number of employees	Sales (mil dol)	Annual payroll (mil dol)	Number of establishments	Number of employees	Sales (mil dol)	Annual payroll (mil dol)	Number of establishments	Number of employees	Receipts (mil dol)	Annual payroll (mil dol)
	133	134	135	136	137	138	139	140	141	142	143	144	145	146

1. Merchant wholesalers, except manufacturers' sales branches and offices. 2. Employer establishments.

Table B. States and Counties — Professional Services, Manufacturing, and Accommodation and Food Services

STATE County	Professional, scientific, and technical services,[1] 2007				Manufacturing, 2007				Accommodation and food services, 2007			
	Number of establishments	Number of employees	Receipts (mil dol)	Annual payroll (mil dol)	Number of establishments	Number of employees	Receipts (mil dol)	Annual payroll (mil dol)	Number of establishments	Number of employees	Sales (mil dol)	Annual payroll (mil dol)
	147	148	149	150	151	152	153	154	155	156	157	158

1. Establishment subject to federal tax.

Table B. States and Counties — Health Care and Social Assistance, Other Services, Nonemployer Businesses, and Residential Construction

STATE County	Health care and social assistance, 2007				Other services, 2007				Nonemployer businesses, 2013		Value of residential construction authorized by building permits, 2014	
	Number of establishments	Number of employees	Receipts (mil dol)	Annual payroll (mil dol)	Number of establishments	Number of employees	Receipts (mil dol)	Annual payroll (mil dol)	Number	Receipts (mil dol)	New Construction ($1,000)	Number of housing units
	159	160	161	162	163	164	165	166	167	168	169	170

Table B. States and Counties — Government Employment and Payroll, and Local Government Finances

STATE County	Government employment and payroll, 2012									Local government finances, 2012				
			March payroll (percent of total)							General revenue				
												Taxes		
													Per capita[1] (dollars)	
	Full-time equivalent employees	March payroll (dollars)	Adminis-tration, judicial, and legal	Police and Corrections	Fire Protection	Highways and transpor-tation	Health and Welfare	Natural resources and utilities	Education and libraries	Total (mil dol)	Inter-govern-mental (mil dol)	Total (mil dol)	Total	Property
	171	172	173	174	175	176	177	178	179	180	181	182	183	184

1. Based on the resident population estimated as of July 1 of the year shown.

Table B. States and Counties — Local Government Finances, Government Employment, and Voting

STATE County	Local government finances, 2012 (cont.)									Government employment, 2013			Presidential election,[2] 2012		
	Direct general expenditure							Debt outstanding					Percent of vote cast:		
			Percent of total for:												
	Total (mil dol)	Per capita[1] (dollars)	Educa-tion	Health and hospitals	Police protec-tion	Public welfare	High-ways	Total (mil dol)	Per capita[1] (dollars)	Federal civilian	Federal military	State and local	Demo-cratic	Republi-can	All other
	185	186	187	188	189	190	191	192	193	194	195	196	197	198	199

1. Based on the resident population estimated as of July 1 of the year shown. 2.

STATE/ County code	CBSA code[1]	County type[2]	STATE County	Land area,[3] (sq km) 2010	Population, 2014: Total persons 2014	Population, 2014: Rank	Population, 2014: Per square kilometer	Population and population characteristics, 2013: Race alone or in combination, not Hispanic or Latino (percent): White	Black	American Indian, Alaska Native	Asian and Pacific Islander	Percent Hispanic or Latino[4]	Age (percent): Under 5 years	5 to 17 years	18 to 24 years	25 to 34 years	35 to 44 years	45 to 54 years
				1	2	3	4	5	6	7	8	9	10	11	12	13	14	15
00 000	...	X	UNITED STATES	9 147 593	318 857 056	X	34.9	64.3	13.2	1.3	6.2	17.1	6.3	17.0	10.0	13.6	12.8	13.8
01 000	...	X	ALABAMA	131 171	4 849 377	X	37.0	67.6	26.9	1.1	1.6	4.1	6.1	16.8	10.0	12.8	12.6	13.7
01 001	33860	2	Autauga	1 540	55 395	912	36.0	77.3	19.0	0.9	1.6	2.7	6.1	19.3	9.0	12.0	14.0	14.8
01 003	19300	4	Baldwin	4 118	200 111	325	48.6	84.4	9.9	1.3	1.3	4.6	5.7	16.7	7.8	11.5	12.5	13.9
01 005	...	6	Barbour	2 292	26 887	1 540	11.7	47.0	47.7	0.6	0.7	4.9	5.8	15.3	9.1	14.2	12.8	14.0
01 007	13820	1	Bibb	1 612	22 506	1 710	14.0	75.3	22.4	0.8	0.3	2.1	5.3	15.9	8.8	14.1	14.4	14.8
01 009	13820	1	Blount	1 670	57 719	885	34.6	88.8	2.0	1.1	0.5	8.7	6.1	17.7	8.2	11.8	13.1	13.9
01 011	...	6	Bullock	1 613	10 764	2 375	6.7	22.8	69.2	0.5	0.4	7.8	6.3	14.7	9.3	14.4	12.9	14.3
01 013	...	6	Butler	2 012	20 296	1 820	10.1	54.1	43.6	0.7	1.1	1.2	6.1	17.2	8.3	12.0	11.6	12.7
01 015	11500	3	Calhoun	1 569	115 916	528	73.9	74.5	21.4	1.0	1.3	3.5	5.8	16.4	10.4	12.6	12.1	13.6
01 017	46740	6	Chambers	1 545	34 076	1 326	22.1	58.3	39.4	0.6	0.8	2.0	5.9	15.6	8.8	11.5	12.2	14.2
01 019	...	8	Cherokee	1 434	26 037	1 558	18.2	93.2	5.1	1.3	0.4	1.5	4.8	15.9	7.6	9.7	11.9	14.7
01 021	13820	1	Chilton	1 794	43 931	1 090	24.5	81.6	10.5	0.7	0.6	7.7	6.5	17.7	8.7	12.3	13.3	13.6
01 023	...	9	Choctaw	2 366	13 323	2 218	5.6	56.3	42.8	0.5	0.3	0.7	5.0	16.1	7.8	10.0	11.4	14.8
01 025	...	7	Clarke	3 208	24 945	1 611	7.8	53.8	44.3	0.7	0.7	1.3	5.5	17.5	9.0	10.5	12.2	14.6
01 027	...	9	Clay	1 564	13 552	2 200	8.7	81.7	15.2	1.3	0.4	3.3	5.4	16.3	7.9	10.8	12.1	14.8
01 029	...	8	Cleburne	1 451	15 080	2 095	10.4	93.6	4.2	0.7	0.3	2.2	5.5	17.1	8.2	10.8	12.9	14.1
01 031	21460	6	Coffee	1 759	50 909	974	28.9	73.4	17.9	2.0	2.3	6.6	6.3	17.4	8.5	13.2	13.2	13.6
01 033	22520	3	Colbert	1 535	54 543	918	35.5	80.2	16.9	1.2	0.7	2.5	5.7	16.0	8.5	11.4	12.3	13.9
01 035	...	9	Conecuh	2 202	12 670	2 252	5.8	52.2	46.0	0.9	0.4	1.7	5.5	16.5	8.7	9.9	11.2	13.8
01 037	45180	8	Coosa	1 686	10 886	2 367	6.5	66.2	31.4	1.0	0.3	2.1	4.6	14.3	7.8	10.0	12.6	15.8
01 039	...	7	Covington	2 669	37 914	1 225	14.2	84.7	13.3	1.2	0.6	1.6	5.9	16.2	7.8	11.3	11.5	13.7
01 041	...	8	Crenshaw	1 577	13 977	2 171	8.9	72.0	25.0	1.1	1.8	1.8	6.2	16.8	8.7	10.8	11.9	14.1
01 043	18980	6	Cullman	1 903	81 289	686	42.7	93.2	1.6	1.2	0.7	4.4	5.9	16.6	8.6	11.9	12.6	13.9
01 045	37120	4	Dale	1 453	49 484	990	34.1	72.9	20.4	1.5	2.1	5.7	6.5	17.2	9.1	14.7	12.2	13.1
01 047	42820	4	Dallas	2 535	41 711	1 132	16.5	29.1	69.7	0.4	0.6	0.9	6.8	18.8	9.4	11.6	10.9	13.6
01 049	...	6	DeKalb	2 013	71 065	756	35.3	82.5	2.1	2.6	0.5	14.2	6.3	18.5	8.7	11.9	13.3	13.5
01 051	33860	2	Elmore	1 602	80 977	688	50.5	75.1	21.5	0.9	1.1	2.8	6.0	17.2	9.8	13.2	13.8	14.4
01 053	...	6	Escambia	2 448	37 733	1 233	15.4	62.1	32.7	4.1	0.5	2.1	6.3	15.8	8.9	13.1	13.2	13.7
01 055	23460	3	Etowah	1 386	103 531	572	74.7	79.8	16.0	1.0	1.0	3.6	5.8	16.5	8.9	11.6	12.9	13.7
01 057	...	6	Fayette	1 626	16 874	1 987	10.4	86.1	12.3	0.7	0.4	1.5	5.5	16.2	8.5	10.4	11.9	14.0
01 059	...	6	Franklin	1 642	31 601	1 395	19.2	79.8	4.6	1.0	0.4	15.4	6.7	17.7	8.8	12.5	13.0	13.2
01 061	20020	3	Geneva	1 488	26 712	1 543	18.0	85.7	10.4	1.5	0.7	3.4	5.7	16.5	7.8	11.1	12.0	14.1
01 063	...	3	Greene	1 676	8 553	2 555	5.1	18.6	80.2	0.4	0.4	1.0	6.0	17.2	9.4	10.7	9.4	13.7
01 065	46220	3	Hale	1 668	15 184	2 086	9.1	40.7	57.9	0.4	0.4	1.1	6.2	17.1	9.4	11.2	10.8	14.5
01 067	20020	3	Henry	1 455	17 190	1 972	11.8	69.2	27.8	0.7	1.0	2.5	5.4	15.9	7.3	10.7	12.3	13.2
01 069	20020	3	Houston	1 502	104 193	568	69.4	69.1	27.0	1.0	1.3	3.3	6.4	17.6	8.3	12.9	12.8	13.6
01 071	42460	6	Jackson	2 792	52 665	949	18.9	92.1	3.9	3.1	0.7	2.8	5.4	16.5	8.1	10.6	12.8	14.1
01 073	13820	1	Jefferson	2 878	660 793	99	229.6	51.8	43.0	0.6	1.8	3.8	6.6	16.6	9.4	14.3	12.7	13.4
01 075	...	9	Lamar	1 567	14 086	2 161	9.0	87.0	11.9	0.7	0.3	1.4	5.2	17.0	7.3	9.9	12.3	14.1
01 077	22520	3	Lauderdale	1 729	93 096	627	53.8	86.2	10.7	0.9	1.0	2.4	5.3	15.4	11.9	11.1	11.5	13.3
01 079	19460	3	Lawrence	1 789	33 477	1 339	18.7	80.6	12.0	9.2	0.5	2.1	5.5	16.4	8.6	11.1	12.7	15.7
01 081	12220	3	Lee	1 574	154 255	416	98.0	69.5	23.8	0.7	3.6	3.8	5.7	16.1	19.8	14.6	12.2	11.7
01 083	26620	2	Limestone	1 450	90 787	636	62.6	79.2	13.6	1.3	1.7	5.8	6.1	17.4	8.0	13.3	14.0	15.4
01 085	33860	2	Lowndes	1 854	10 580	2 392	5.7	25.7	73.0	0.5	0.3	1.1	6.7	16.8	10.1	11.1	10.7	14.6
01 087	...	6	Macon	1 577	19 425	1 857	12.3	16.9	81.5	0.6	0.6	1.5	5.0	14.0	18.6	10.0	9.6	12.5
01 089	26620	2	Madison	2 076	350 299	194	168.7	67.7	25.1	1.5	3.3	4.7	5.9	16.8	9.9	13.7	12.5	15.6
01 091	...	7	Marengo	2 530	20 110	1 831	7.9	46.4	51.2	0.5	0.5	2.2	6.0	17.0	9.1	10.6	11.7	13.5
01 093	...	8	Marion	1 923	30 271	1 424	15.7	92.7	4.6	0.8	0.4	2.5	5.2	15.9	7.6	10.8	12.4	14.6
01 095	10700	4	Marshall	1 466	94 636	618	64.6	83.8	2.5	1.3	0.9	12.9	6.8	17.9	8.7	12.4	12.5	13.5
01 097	33660	2	Mobile	3 184	415 123	165	130.4	59.3	35.7	1.5	2.3	2.6	6.7	17.5	9.9	13.4	12.1	13.5
01 099	...	7	Monroe	2 656	21 947	1 736	8.3	56.0	41.8	1.9	0.6	1.1	5.7	18.2	8.8	10.1	11.7	14.1
01 101	33860	2	Montgomery	2 031	226 189	285	111.4	37.8	56.6	0.6	2.8	3.4	6.8	17.4	10.9	14.5	12.5	12.8
01 103	19460	3	Morgan	1 500	119 607	515	79.7	78.5	12.9	1.6	1.0	7.8	6.1	17.1	8.5	12.2	12.8	14.6
01 105	...	8	Perry	1 864	9 826	2 453	5.3	30.8	67.5	0.4	0.5	1.4	6.0	17.1	14.6	10.2	10.3	11.5
01 107	46220	8	Pickens	2 283	20 365	1 814	8.9	50.7	41.2	0.5	0.4	2.2	5.5	16.4	8.8	11.1	10.8	15.0
01 109	45980	6	Pike	1 741	33 389	1 342	19.2	58.3	37.1	1.2	2.4	2.3	5.8	14.1	22.4	11.6	10.3	10.9
01 111	...	6	Randolph	1 504	22 539	1 707	15.0	76.0	20.7	0.9	0.5	3.2	5.6	16.5	8.9	10.3	11.7	14.1
01 113	17980	2	Russell	1 661	59 608	874	35.9	52.1	42.6	1.1	1.6	4.9	7.8	17.5	9.7	15.5	12.6	13.1
01 115	13820	1	St. Clair	1 637	86 697	662	53.0	87.3	9.7	0.9	1.0	2.3	6.2	17.0	7.9	13.1	13.9	14.3
01 117	13820	1	Shelby	2 033	206 655	311	101.7	79.9	12.2	0.7	2.5	6.0	6.1	18.6	8.1	13.1	14.8	14.5
01 119	...	8	Sumter	2 341	13 166	2 227	5.6	25.2	73.5	0.3	0.4	1.0	4.7	15.1	18.0	9.6	9.9	12.6
01 121	45180	4	Talladega	1 908	81 322	685	42.6	64.9	32.7	0.9	0.7	2.2	5.6	16.8	8.9	12.1	13.0	14.1
01 123	...	6	Tallapoosa	1 856	41 165	1 147	22.2	69.8	27.3	0.7	0.6	2.5	5.8	15.6	8.5	10.5	11.6	14.1
01 125	46220	3	Tuscaloosa	3 423	202 212	318	59.1	64.6	30.9	0.6	1.8	3.2	6.0	15.1	19.5	13.7	11.6	11.4
01 127	13820	1	Walker	2 049	65 471	804	32.0	90.7	6.7	0.9	0.5	2.3	5.9	16.3	8.2	11.4	12.4	14.1

1. CBSA = Core Based Statistical Area. See Appendix A for explanation. See Appendix B for list of metropolitan areas with component counties. 2. County type code from the Economic Research Service of USDA Rural-Urban Continuum Codes. See Appendix A for definition. 3. Dry land or land partially or temporarily covered by water. 4. May be of any race.

STATE County	Population, 2013 (cont.) Age (percent) (cont.) 55 to 64 years	65 to 74 years	75 years and over	Percent female	Population change and components of change, 2000–2014 Total persons 2000	2010	Percent change 2000–2010	2010–2014	Components of change, 2010–2014 Births	Deaths	Net migration	Households, 2009–2013 Number	Persons per household	Percent Family households	Female family householder[1]	One person
	16	17	18	19	20	21	22	23	24	25	26	27	28	29	30	31
UNITED STATES	12.4	8.0	6.2	50.8	281 421 906	308 745 538	9.7	3.3	16 811 002	10 775 362	4 063 311	115 610 216	2.63	66.4	13.0	27.5
ALABAMA	12.9	8.7	6.3	51.5	4 447 100	4 779 736	7.5	1.4	249 818	207 826	26 687	1 838 683	2.55	67.5	15.3	28.4
Autauga	11.3	8.1	5.4	51.5	43 671	54 571	25.0	1.5	2 633	2 247	347	20 071	2.71	70.4	12.9	25.7
Baldwin	13.7	10.8	7.3	51.2	140 415	182 265	29.8	9.8	9 159	8 099	16 080	73 283	2.52	70.8	11.0	25.1
Barbour	12.9	9.5	6.4	46.5	29 038	27 457	-5.4	-2.1	1 251	1 334	-504	9 200	2.66	65.9	19.0	31.2
Bibb	12.4	8.6	5.6	46.0	20 826	22 915	10.0	-1.8	1 061	1 000	-461	7 091	3.03	75.3	16.0	22.7
Blount	12.8	9.9	6.5	50.6	51 024	57 322	12.3	0.7	2 928	2 417	-130	21 108	2.70	74.2	9.3	23.2
Bullock	13.5	8.4	6.2	45.2	11 714	10 914	-6.8	-1.4	591	506	-233	3 741	2.73	63.9	24.5	29.5
Butler	14.2	9.4	8.4	53.4	21 399	20 947	-2.1	-3.1	1 082	1 102	-621	8 235	2.47	64.9	19.3	32.6
Calhoun	13.5	8.9	6.6	51.7	112 249	118 572	5.6	-2.3	5 682	5 818	-2 391	45 196	2.54	66.4	15.5	29.0
Chambers	14.1	10.2	7.6	52.0	36 583	34 215	-6.5	-0.3	1 688	1 921	118	13 722	2.46	65.6	17.7	32.1
Cherokee	15.3	12.5	7.6	50.4	23 988	25 989	8.3	0.2	1 000	1 388	418	11 656	2.20	71.9	12.6	26.1
Chilton	13.0	8.8	6.1	50.8	39 593	43 643	10.2	0.7	2 387	2 053	-37	16 232	2.67	74.6	13.5	22.7
Choctaw	14.6	12.0	8.4	52.5	15 922	13 859	-13.0	-3.9	518	698	-363	5 518	2.45	64.4	16.0	32.8
Clarke	13.2	10.0	7.5	52.7	27 867	25 833	-7.3	-3.5	1 173	1 216	-866	9 631	2.63	64.6	17.1	33.1
Clay	13.8	10.6	8.5	50.8	14 254	13 932	-2.3	-2.7	607	773	-217	5 649	2.38	69.4	13.7	28.1
Cleburne	13.3	10.8	7.2	50.4	14 123	14 972	6.0	0.7	773	709	5	5 601	2.64	72.1	11.5	25.6
Coffee	12.3	9.0	6.6	50.3	43 615	49 948	14.5	1.9	2 676	2 052	336	18 820	2.65	69.1	14.2	27.5
Colbert	14.0	10.2	7.9	51.9	54 984	54 428	-1.0	0.2	2 594	2 846	433	22 260	2.42	67.9	13.6	29.1
Conecuh	14.8	11.5	8.2	51.7	14 089	13 228	-6.1	-4.2	629	706	-472	4 994	2.61	68.8	16.9	29.4
Coosa	16.9	10.9	7.2	50.2	12 202	11 539	-5.4	-7.4	404	520	-756	4 506	2.42	64.2	11.6	29.0
Covington	14.1	10.7	8.9	51.6	37 631	37 765	0.4	0.4	1 867	2 048	301	15 041	2.48	68.4	15.6	28.3
Crenshaw	13.8	10.1	7.4	51.5	13 665	13 906	1.8	0.5	640	685	118	5 601	2.46	66.1	14.5	30.9
Cullman	13.2	10.2	7.0	50.4	77 483	80 406	3.8	1.1	4 089	4 015	757	31 342	2.53	71.5	12.7	25.4
Dale	12.3	8.8	6.1	50.5	49 129	50 251	2.3	-1.5	2 857	1 975	-1 607	19 345	2.52	66.1	14.1	29.5
Dallas	13.6	9.0	6.2	53.5	46 365	43 820	-5.5	-4.8	2 402	2 199	-2 308	16 173	2.63	60.4	23.6	36.9
DeKalb	12.7	9.0	6.2	50.7	64 452	71 109	10.3	-0.1	3 607	3 122	-514	24 923	2.82	72.9	10.4	24.8
Elmore	12.1	8.4	5.1	51.4	65 874	79 303	20.4	2.1	4 070	3 047	582	28 324	2.62	73.7	13.9	23.7
Escambia	12.8	9.4	6.8	48.5	38 440	38 319	-0.3	-1.5	1 901	1 869	-603	13 681	2.59	68.1	17.1	30.1
Etowah	13.8	9.9	7.0	51.5	103 459	104 430	0.9	-0.9	5 020	5 834	12	40 217	2.55	69.3	14.7	28.0
Fayette	14.5	11.0	7.9	50.4	18 495	17 241	-6.8	-2.1	782	973	-171	6 956	2.41	69.2	13.3	29.3
Franklin	12.1	9.2	6.7	50.1	31 223	31 704	1.5	-0.3	1 814	1 621	-303	12 437	2.52	70.7	12.0	26.8
Geneva	14.2	10.7	7.9	51.0	25 764	26 790	4.0	-0.3	1 310	1 469	104	10 945	2.43	70.2	15.2	26.7
Greene	16.3	9.3	7.8	52.3	9 974	9 045	-9.3	-5.4	446	450	-483	3 264	2.72	61.0	20.5	37.1
Hale	14.0	9.5	7.4	52.5	17 185	15 760	-8.3	-3.7	825	745	-667	5 969	2.56	65.7	23.1	31.3
Henry	15.0	11.9	8.1	51.8	16 310	17 302	6.1	-0.6	747	905	36	7 001	2.44	69.1	13.1	28.8
Houston	12.8	8.9	6.7	52.0	88 787	101 547	14.4	2.6	5 499	4 363	1 492	39 250	2.58	67.7	15.9	28.5
Jackson	14.4	10.9	7.1	50.7	53 926	53 227	-1.3	-1.1	2 442	2 768	-206	20 765	2.53	70.5	10.8	26.7
Jefferson	13.1	7.6	6.3	52.7	662 047	658 466	-0.5	0.4	37 726	29 127	-5 254	259 634	2.48	64.0	18.0	31.3
Lamar	14.3	11.0	8.9	51.2	15 904	14 564	-8.4	-3.3	607	826	-244	6 084	2.32	72.9	11.9	25.4
Lauderdale	13.6	10.1	7.8	52.1	87 966	92 709	5.4	0.4	3 915	4 541	1 059	38 458	2.36	65.7	11.2	29.6
Lawrence	13.6	10.1	6.2	51.4	34 803	34 339	-1.3	-2.5	1 524	1 618	-744	13 382	2.52	71.6	14.2	25.7
Lee	9.9	6.1	3.9	50.5	115 092	140 247	21.9	9.9	7 368	3 969	10 314	55 864	2.49	59.9	12.5	29.1
Limestone	12.2	8.3	5.2	49.6	65 676	82 782	26.0	9.7	4 238	2 918	6 491	31 794	2.56	72.5	12.4	24.9
Lowndes	13.5	10.1	6.5	52.4	13 473	11 299	-16.1	-6.4	615	538	-828	4 212	2.61	62.2	24.3	36.2
Macon	13.9	9.4	7.1	53.9	24 105	21 452	-11.0	-9.4	835	988	-1 905	8 107	2.29	62.6	26.7	33.5
Madison	12.3	7.5	5.7	51.1	276 700	334 811	21.0	4.6	17 386	11 460	9 254	132 975	2.50	65.7	12.5	30.1
Marengo	13.7	10.0	8.3	52.9	22 539	21 027	-6.7	-4.4	1 024	1 094	-885	8 464	2.42	67.7	18.3	30.1
Marion	13.7	11.6	8.3	50.4	31 214	30 776	-1.4	-1.6	1 309	1 683	-131	12 700	2.34	70.2	12.5	26.5
Marshall	12.4	9.4	6.5	50.9	82 231	93 019	13.1	1.7	5 386	4 530	750	34 250	2.70	70.7	12.9	26.3
Mobile	12.8	8.3	5.8	52.1	399 843	412 992	3.3	0.5	23 716	17 784	-3 698	155 178	2.60	67.5	18.6	28.2
Monroe	14.1	9.7	7.5	52.3	24 324	23 068	-5.2	-4.9	1 033	1 079	-1 050	8 333	2.71	67.8	19.2	31.0
Montgomery	12.1	7.2	5.7	52.5	223 510	229 363	2.6	-1.4	13 174	8 547	-7 795	88 844	2.49	64.2	20.9	30.8
Morgan	13.1	9.1	6.4	50.8	111 064	119 490	7.6	0.1	6 001	5 182	-609	46 192	2.55	69.2	12.9	27.4
Perry	13.1	9.3	7.8	53.2	11 861	10 591	-10.7	-7.1	503	579	-681	3 400	2.84	67.9	28.9	30.6
Pickens	14.3	10.2	7.9	52.0	20 949	19 746	-5.7	3.1	916	1 012	658	7 926	2.42	65.9	19.8	32.4
Pike	11.1	8.0	5.8	51.9	29 605	32 899	11.1	1.5	1 617	1 403	258	12 959	2.40	61.0	16.4	30.2
Randolph	14.1	10.9	7.9	51.5	22 380	22 913	2.4	-1.6	1 042	1 134	-333	9 013	2.48	68.0	12.9	28.8
Russell	11.6	7.2	5.0	51.0	49 756	52 947	6.4	12.6	3 657	2 382	5 279	21 142	2.60	63.9	19.5	31.6
St. Clair	12.9	9.2	5.5	50.1	64 742	83 593	29.1	3.7	4 506	3 539	1 988	31 353	2.63	73.9	11.6	21.8
Shelby	12.4	7.7	4.7	51.2	143 293	195 085	36.1	5.9	10 279	5 538	6 499	74 144	2.64	72.0	9.9	24.2
Sumter	14.2	8.3	7.6	54.7	14 798	13 763	-7.0	4.3	500	684	-494	5 060	2.57	62.8	27.6	30.7
Talladega	13.9	9.5	6.2	51.3	80 321	82 291	2.5	-1.2	3 698	4 149	-401	31 486	2.50	71.0	17.9	26.2
Tallapoosa	14.9	11.3	7.8	51.5	41 475	41 616	0.3	-1.1	1 990	2 244	-225	16 373	2.49	71.1	16.7	25.8
Tuscaloosa	11.3	6.6	4.9	51.6	164 875	194 656	18.1	3.9	10 366	6 951	4 227	67 882	2.76	65.5	15.1	28.2
Walker	14.1	10.5	7.2	51.4	70 713	67 023	-5.2	-2.3	3 368	4 128	-798	25 751	2.55	70.2	15.6	26.8

1. No spouse present.

STATE County	Persons in group quarters, 2014	Daytime population, 2009–2013: Number	Daytime population, 2009–2013: Employment/residence ratio	Births, 2014: Total	Births, 2014: Rate[1]	Deaths, 2014: Number	Deaths, 2014: Rate[1]	Persons under 65 with no health insurance, 2013: Number	Persons under 65 with no health insurance, 2013: Percent	Medicare, 2014: Eligible for Medicare	Medicare, 2014: Enrolled in Medicare Advantage	Medicare, 2014: Enrolled in a Medicare prescription drug plan	Serious crimes known to police,[2] 2013: Total: Number	Serious crimes known to police,[2] 2013: Total: Rate[3]
	32	33	34	35	36	37	38	39	40	41	42	43	44	45
UNITED STATES	8 064 161	311 536 594	1.00	3 957 577	12.4	2 593 996	8.1	44 477 968	16.8	53 234 408	14 553 102	22 437 083	9 824 500	3 108
ALABAMA	118 470	4 758 150	0.98	58 059	12.0	49 793	10.3	636 216	15.9	953 663	230 100	450 531	182 819	3 782
Autauga	455	44 081	0.55	618	11.2	492	8.9	6 351	13.4	9 688	3 080	3 342	1 820	3 314
Baldwin	2 296	172 239	0.82	2 169	10.8	1 947	9.7	27 538	17.5	43 284	13 751	16 521	5 249	2 715
Barbour	3 402	27 034	0.97	285	10.6	307	11.4	3 402	17.4	6 170	912	3 465	767	2 855
Bibb	2 224	19 581	0.60	243	10.8	227	10.1	2 576	15.0	4 685	1 711	1 871	309	1 373
Blount	489	44 839	0.43	676	11.7	564	9.8	8 470	17.6	11 486	4 703	4 380	1 419	2 448
Bullock	1 726	10 054	0.83	132	12.3	111	10.3	1 386	18.5	1 848	470	1 004	108	1 044
Butler	333	19 692	0.88	252	12.4	238	11.7	2 578	15.5	4 627	463	3 053	526	2 617
Calhoun	2 809	120 936	1.07	1 292	11.1	1 401	12.1	15 348	16.0	25 849	3 733	12 278	4 987	4 266
Chambers	458	29 467	0.63	404	11.9	452	13.3	4 678	16.8	8 540	1 373	4 848	1 462	4 296
Cherokee	290	22 253	0.62	243	9.3	307	11.8	3 415	16.4	6 642	1 570	3 520	1 069	4 107
Chilton	393	37 090	0.62	558	12.7	466	10.6	7 109	19.2	8 506	3 846	2 876	1 536	3 503
Choctaw	129	13 079	0.87	127	9.5	177	13.3	1 692	15.9	3 747	310	2 632	95	736
Clarke	280	25 575	1.00	288	11.5	303	12.1	3 233	15.7	6 051	1 291	3 449	456	1 852
Clay	255	12 701	0.80	141	10.4	187	13.8	2 081	19.2	3 476	452	1 964	156	1 174
Cleburne	178	12 029	0.48	198	13.1	179	11.9	2 032	16.7	3 385	408	1 935	206	1 393
Coffee	600	47 756	0.87	589	11.6	501	9.8	7 128	16.8	9 803	859	4 806	1 318	2 553
Colbert	474	55 886	1.07	613	11.2	660	12.1	6 419	14.5	13 229	1 520	7 724	2 029	3 729
Conecuh	45	12 611	0.87	140	11.0	170	13.4	1 863	18.1	3 460	375	2 190	386	2 990
Coosa	338	9 009	0.43	93	8.5	106	9.7	1 527	17.3	2 475	340	1 432	225	2 513
Covington	575	36 681	0.92	434	11.4	500	13.2	5 119	16.9	9 342	791	5 811	1 200	3 202
Crenshaw	132	12 418	0.73	137	9.8	176	12.6	1 902	16.5	3 364	706	1 844	291	2 136
Cullman	1 044	75 839	0.86	968	11.9	952	11.7	12 445	18.8	18 326	4 008	10 109	1 764	2 194
Dale	917	52 055	1.09	644	13.0	511	10.3	6 207	14.9	9 667	947	4 465	1 578	3 175
Dallas	856	42 855	0.98	539	12.9	530	12.7	5 039	14.3	9 661	2 017	5 523	2 444	5 744
DeKalb	782	66 889	0.84	826	11.6	739	10.4	13 780	23.0	14 692	2 808	8 062	1 603	2 256
Elmore	5 432	64 190	0.53	954	11.8	745	9.2	7 932	12.3	15 136	4 134	5 674	2 498	3 085
Escambia	3 213	39 030	1.07	419	11.1	450	11.9	5 377	18.7	8 362	933	5 056	853	2 251
Etowah	2 083	99 599	0.88	1 144	11.0	1 431	13.8	13 664	16.1	24 273	5 887	12 884	4 725	4 859
Fayette	291	15 566	0.74	176	10.4	215	12.7	2 083	15.4	4 828	569	2 787	206	1 219
Franklin	272	30 139	0.88	412	13.0	363	11.5	5 376	20.4	6 528	507	4 290	780	2 455
Geneva	229	22 310	0.57	305	11.4	337	12.6	4 180	19.3	6 564	654	3 614	763	2 830
Greene	45	8 428	0.81	98	11.5	90	10.5	1 230	17.0	2 143	154	1 449	250	3 047
Hale	272	13 506	0.61	194	12.8	182	12.0	2 032	16.1	3 852	249	2 554	224	1 742
Henry	199	14 719	0.60	168	9.8	192	11.2	2 323	16.9	4 378	849	2 213	345	2 059
Houston	1 418	109 094	1.15	1 254	12.0	1 086	10.4	13 714	15.9	21 537	2 894	11 698	3 611	3 475
Jackson	597	50 092	0.85	574	10.9	642	12.2	7 740	17.9	12 334	1 747	7 436	1 386	2 694
Jefferson	16 030	726 226	1.24	8 766	13.3	6 999	10.6	81 122	14.7	122 823	50 540	44 863	34 260	5 366
Lamar	217	13 209	0.79	144	10.2	191	13.6	1 794	15.8	3 779	314	2 483	93	656
Lauderdale	2 042	87 594	0.87	914	9.8	1 079	11.6	11 158	15.0	20 419	2 415	11 965	2 468	2 669
Lawrence	229	28 347	0.56	359	10.7	381	11.4	5 086	18.2	7 517	869	4 851	657	1 988
Lee	4 552	134 287	0.84	1 837	11.9	1 006	6.5	21 142	16.1	19 919	2 706	10 190	NA	NA
Limestone	2 907	73 674	0.67	1 002	11.0	696	7.7	11 888	16.1	15 447	2 670	8 251	1 891	2 121
Lowndes	96	10 375	0.79	138	13.0	133	12.6	1 360	15.3	2 624	1 006	1 156	262	2 937
Macon	1 811	19 146	0.78	174	9.0	256	13.2	2 367	15.9	4 356	959	1 815	1 135	5 747
Madison	7 660	373 950	1.22	4 031	11.5	2 799	8.0	39 932	13.7	56 903	8 263	24 380	14 787	4 282
Marengo	254	20 145	0.93	238	11.8	255	12.7	2 522	15.4	5 218	487	3 477	639	3 220
Marion	868	30 146	0.96	307	10.1	381	12.6	3 838	16.1	6 875	764	4 376	608	2 015
Marshall	1 059	94 971	1.03	1 211	12.8	1 082	11.4	17 315	21.9	19 479	2 195	11 409	2 606	3 006
Mobile	7 274	422 654	1.06	5 501	13.3	4 290	10.3	58 018	16.6	76 799	31 601	26 499	20 988	5 069
Monroe	230	22 714	0.99	223	10.2	250	11.4	3 353	18.3	5 097	668	3 201	705	3 179
Montgomery	9 027	265 269	1.37	2 995	13.2	2 085	9.2	28 932	15.3	39 263	10 707	15 660	9 270	4 026
Morgan	2 120	118 919	0.99	1 370	11.5	1 200	10.0	17 209	17.3	23 960	2 816	14 702	3 434	2 847
Perry	764	9 522	0.68	105	10.7	148	15.1	1 182	15.4	2 383	155	1 671	NA	NA
Pickens	1 661	16 845	0.59	222	10.9	232	11.4	2 608	16.8	4 852	324	3 041	195	1 042
Pike	2 126	34 973	1.14	363	10.9	348	10.4	4 715	17.4	5 919	1 240	3 201	1 263	3 799
Randolph	407	19 941	0.65	246	10.9	269	11.9	3 405	10.7	5 022	701	3 051	419	1 854
Russell	574	46 733	0.61	898	15.1	578	9.7	8 884	17.1	10 552	2 255	4 627	2 717	4 618
St. Clair	1 895	67 980	0.52	1 061	12.2	871	10.0	10 299	14.4	16 088	6 679	5 417	1 470	1 726
Shelby	2 652	178 839	0.80	2 400	11.6	1 345	6.5	21 163	12.1	31 211	11 173	11 479	3 189	1 593
Sumter	853	12 951	0.87	137	10.4	159	12.1	1 813	17.2	2 949	199	2 117	320	2 499
Talladega	3 288	80 655	0.96	876	10.8	1 029	12.7	9 573	14.6	18 569	4 564	9 145	3 791	4 643
Tallapoosa	576	39 732	0.89	463	11.2	526	12.8	5 298	16.0	10 608	1 266	6 368	1 351	3 309
Tuscaloosa	10 360	203 559	1.08	2 469	12.2	1 681	8.3	25 589	15.2	32 897	3 945	18 019	8 123	4 066
Walker	851	63 361	0.86	767	11.7	950	14.5	8 591	16.0	17 074	6 079	6 155	2 499	3 846

1. Per 1,000 estimated resident population. 2. Data for serious crimes have not been adjusted for underreporting; this may affect comparability between geographic areas and over time.
3. Per 100,000 population estimated by the FBI.

STATE County	Serious crimes known to police, 2013 (cont.)[1] Rate[2] Violent	Property	Education: School enrollment and attainment, 2009–2013 Enrollment[3] Total	Per-cent private	Attainment[4] (percent) High school grad-uate or less	Bach-elor's degree or more	Local government expenditures,[5] 2012–2013 Total current spending (mil dol)	Current spend-ing per student (dollars)	Money income, 2009–2013 Per capita income[6] (dollars)	Households Median income (dollars)	Mean income (dollars)	Percent with income of $200,000 or more	Income and poverty, 2013 Median house-hold income (dollars)	Percent below poverty level All per-sons	Children under 18 years	Children 5 to 17 years in families
	46	47	48	49	50	51	52	53	54	55	56	57	58	59	60	61
UNITED STATES	377	2 731	82 624 806	16.5	42.1	28.8	530 552.8	10 700	28 155	53 046	73 487	4.8	52 250	15.8	22.2	20.8
ALABAMA	431	3 351	1 222 995	14.3	47.9	22.6	6 642.0	8 755	23 680	43 253	59 631	2.6	42 882	18.9	27.4	25.6
Autauga	279	3 036	15 314	21.3	48.6	20.9	71.0	7 303	24 571	53 682	64 699	1.9	51 868	13.5	19.6	17.6
Baldwin	219	2 496	41 925	15.6	40.1	27.7	243.6	8 279	26 766	50 221	66 835	3.6	47 539	14.2	20.8	19.2
Barbour	402	2 453	6 014	12.8	59.2	13.4	33.8	8 742	16 829	32 911	43 926	0.6	30 981	28.2	42.4	41.2
Bibb	116	1 258	4 988	6.6	63.3	12.1	28.7	8 260	17 427	36 447	48 885	0.6	39 781	23.1	35.6	31.4
Blount	209	2 239	13 162	8.2	57.7	12.1	75.6	7 711	20 730	44 145	54 820	0.9	44 392	17.2	26.6	24.2
Bullock	203	841	2 178	11.1	66.2	12.5	16.8	11 000	18 628	32 033	49 022	2.3	25 937	35.2	44.2	44.4
Butler	438	2 179	4 779	10.2	60.7	14.0	28.9	8 904	17 403	29 918	41 089	0.4	31 041	28.8	39.8	41.6
Calhoun	531	3 735	29 894	10.1	54.3	16.1	164.3	9 010	20 828	39 962	52 130	1.7	37 898	21.4	28.7	27.0
Chambers	520	3 776	7 367	8.3	60.7	11.8	39.7	8 386	19 291	32 402	44 998	1.4	33 883	22.5	34.7	34.7
Cherokee	442	3 665	4 978	9.5	56.3	12.8	36.4	8 819	22 030	34 907	49 817	1.3	37 478	20.1	31.6	28.8
Chilton	356	3 147	10 055	11.7	64.2	12.9	59.7	7 792	20 701	41 250	54 226	1.5	41 348	20.3	33.7	32.7
Choctaw	101	636	3 192	25.3	62.1	11.8	15.9	9 250	20 323	33 941	47 640	1.7	33 581	22.4	31.0	28.8
Clarke	386	1 466	6 122	9.6	63.8	11.2	41.1	8 712	18 979	29 357	46 106	0.9	34 593	25.4	35.3	32.4
Clay	309	866	2 820	5.5	61.1	9.2	17.3	8 414	18 694	34 002	44 118	0.4	33 344	19.6	28.9	27.9
Cleburne	149	1 245	3 389	8.4	63.3	9.0	22.6	8 466	19 108	38 019	48 783	1.3	40 407	18.9	27.6	25.9
Coffee	331	2 222	12 269	9.0	47.2	22.5	81.4	8 795	23 380	43 768	59 150	1.7	44 666	18.5	27.9	25.8
Colbert	413	3 315	12 308	6.3	51.1	17.7	79.9	9 728	21 572	39 077	50 990	1.2	40 032	16.3	25.8	24.3
Conecuh	527	2 464	2 752	11.7	66.3	8.8	18.0	10 922	15 605	24 658	38 807	0.8	27 196	30.5	43.4	40.2
Coosa	145	2 368	2 167	4.7	67.6	9.8	12.1	10 513	18 493	37 277	44 275	0.0	35 175	19.9	30.9	28.7
Covington	299	2 903	8 438	7.5	55.9	14.2	52.9	8 493	20 391	35 869	49 532	1.3	35 187	19.2	29.2	27.1
Crenshaw	484	1 651	3 003	9.3	61.2	12.7	19.4	8 660	21 343	36 275	51 287	2.4	34 105	22.2	31.3	29.9
Cullman	124	2 069	19 023	10.8	51.9	14.8	108.6	8 542	20 760	38 847	51 556	1.5	40 142	16.4	22.6	20.1
Dale	358	2 816	12 502	12.6	46.6	17.0	56.6	8 697	22 685	44 889	55 648	1.5	41 805	20.1	28.2	25.0
Dallas	717	5 027	11 430	12.0	58.2	14.2	71.0	9 144	17 245	26 519	42 696	1.7	27 524	31.3	49.6	50.6
DeKalb	293	1 963	16 789	6.2	64.4	10.7	98.1	8 315	18 149	37 851	48 351	1.2	36 713	20.0	30.3	28.6
Elmore	312	2 773	20 067	18.2	47.6	21.0	101.9	7 724	23 856	54 766	65 915	2.1	51 650	13.4	20.2	19.1
Escambia	401	1 850	8 380	13.5	60.3	11.7	54.1	9 386	16 540	30 687	42 834	0.9	33 455	27.8	37.1	34.9
Etowah	591	4 268	23 813	9.0	50.9	14.8	132.2	8 058	20 204	38 013	50 389	1.3	38 587	19.6	28.1	25.5
Fayette	130	1 089	3 729	12.7	64.2	13.2	22.0	9 046	18 494	33 838	44 371	1.5	35 661	20.7	29.6	27.3
Franklin	315	2 141	6 889	6.5	60.6	11.0	52.4	9 163	18 888	36 415	48 488	1.6	33 332	23.1	36.3	33.7
Geneva	315	2 514	5 405	4.8	61.0	10.4	31.9	7 946	20 199	35 625	48 200	0.7	35 378	23.6	38.2	35.9
Greene	987	2 060	2 127	4.1	63.2	12.8	13.3	10 626	14 930	24 226	37 375	0.8	25 864	35.0	50.5	46.7
Hale	319	1 423	3 970	9.8	63.8	12.8	24.8	8 679	18 812	30 051	45 816	1.0	33 597	25.7	38.8	37.5
Henry	269	1 790	3 926	17.0	55.0	16.6	21.5	8 061	21 924	41 650	52 310	0.3	41 590	18.2	28.7	27.3
Houston	427	3 048	24 374	16.1	50.1	19.7	133.1	8 492	23 316	40 948	57 876	2.5	39 636	18.1	30.1	28.6
Jackson	350	2 344	12 303	9.8	62.6	13.0	76.8	9 160	20 486	37 634	49 609	1.4	37 204	16.9	28.1	28.3
Jefferson	738	4 627	169 964	17.0	39.1	30.0	1 025.5	9 862	26 906	45 429	66 269	3.8	45 024	18.9	26.8	24.7
Lamar	42	614	2 961	8.1	62.1	9.5	19.4	8 144	19 026	36 028	44 828	1.3	36 475	23.0	30.8	27.9
Lauderdale	276	2 393	23 607	12.2	50.5	21.1	119.5	9 100	23 510	42 844	55 172	1.8	43 586	17.1	24.5	23.0
Lawrence	236	1 752	7 778	10.3	61.8	11.9	45.6	8 956	20 181	38 551	49 679	0.9	40 713	17.4	26.2	25.6
Lee	NA	NA	53 127	9.6	39.7	32.5	193.4	8 989	23 506	43 542	59 102	2.3	44 647	19.8	21.8	18.8
Limestone	144	1 977	19 940	13.4	49.4	22.7	108.5	8 926	25 020	48 619	65 254	2.6	50 148	15.9	21.2	18.9
Lowndes	426	2 511	2 664	18.9	62.9	14.4	25.4	14 501	18 368	26 230	45 950	2.7	29 734	37.0	53.1	50.6
Macon	638	5 109	6 668	41.8	50.2	19.6	24.5	10 375	16 826	30 724	41 814	0.5	29 228	33.8	46.4	42.6
Madison	571	3 711	92 940	16.8	31.3	38.5	486.2	9 248	31 933	58 434	79 504	5.5	58 258	13.9	19.6	17.5
Marengo	504	2 716	4 964	11.8	56.2	17.4	39.0	9 580	22 072	35 079	52 993	1.8	33 749	31.5	50.0	58.7
Marion	278	1 737	6 415	10.9	61.0	9.5	40.2	8 473	19 576	32 888	46 574	2.1	34 162	20.8	30.5	28.2
Marshall	165	2 841	20 878	7.2	56.4	15.2	148.3	8 802	20 382	39 526	53 362	1.9	38 399	18.1	29.5	28.3
Mobile	582	4 486	108 714	20.0	49.0	20.7	563.8	8 881	22 501	43 028	57 634	2.3	42 278	20.3	31.3	28.8
Monroe	446	2 732	5 253	11.6	62.9	10.6	33.0	8 855	15 749	29 203	40 216	0.4	32 696	29.7	39.1	35.6
Montgomery	367	3 659	65 878	22.5	40.7	31.5	266.5	8 499	24 975	44 790	62 418	3.1	44 013	22.1	33.0	30.4
Morgan	169	2 677	28 607	11.6	50.1	19.9	183.0	9 487	23 764	44 800	59 811	1.9	44 079	17.4	25.1	22.9
Perry	NA	NA	2 641	18.8	68.3	10.4	16.7	9 580	13 716	28 209	37 475	1.2	25 461	36.4	52.6	49.4
Pickens	192	850	4 548	11.7	62.2	11.0	25.1	9 201	17 153	28 741	40 214	0.6	32 314	23.8	36.3	35.2
Pike	472	3 327	11 887	6.8	54.3	23.0	41.3	9 354	19 715	33 090	48 614	1.3	35 944	25.3	34.8	33.1
Randolph	164	1 690	5 067	10.5	64.1	11.1	32.4	8 559	19 830	35 213	49 335	1.3	35 121	23.4	34.1	32.1
Russell	406	4 212	15 246	10.9	51.7	16.0	85.0	8 189	19 678	36 143	48 813	0.7	35 762	23.9	34.0	35.1
St. Clair	180	1 546	19 075	14.1	53.2	15.5	102.7	7 909	23 872	50 786	62 411	2.5	52 437	14.0	20.7	20.7
Shelby	109	1 484	53 615	22.5	30.1	40.3	242.8	8 473	33 313	68 770	86 995	6.1	68 718	8.3	11.2	10.6
Sumter	469	2 030	4 486	4.8	62.6	14.9	18.6	9 875	14 156	22 186	35 053	0.2	24 504	38.0	48.8	44.4
Talladega	377	4 266	18 766	9.2	58.4	13.0	111.6	9 088	19 410	35 409	48 737	1.2	38 505	19.8	28.9	27.3
Tallapoosa	534	2 775	8 910	8.6	56.5	16.3	52.5	8 538	21 434	39 130	52 395	1.6	37 747	22.2	36.3	38.1
Tuscaloosa	399	3 667	60 735	8.9	44.3	27.0	249.3	8 935	22 637	45 408	60 978	2.5	45 959	17.2	23.4	22.7
Walker	397	3 449	13 871	8.3	58.9	10.5	99.1	9 109	20 698	37 566	51 040	1.3	37 193	22.0	32.2	29.2

1. Data for serious crimes have not been adjusted for underreporting; this may affect comparability between geographic areas and over time. 2. Per 100,000 population estimated by the FBI.
3. All persons 3 years old and over enrolled in nursery school through college. 4. Persons 25 years old and over. 5. Elementary and secondary education expenditures.
6. Based on population estimated by the American Community Survey, 2009–2013.

STATE County	Personal income, 2013										Earnings, 2013		
			Per capita[1]			Supplements to wages and salaries; employer contributions (mil dol)						Contributions for government social insurance (mil dol)	
	Total (mil dol)	Percent change, 2012–2013	Dollars	Rank	Wages and salaries (mil dol)	Pension and insurance	Government social insurance	Proprietors' income (mil dol)	Dividends, interest, and rent (mil dol)	Personal transfer receipts (mil dol)	Total (mil dol)	From employee and self-employed	From employer
	62	63	64	65	66	67	68	69	70	71	72	73	74
UNITED STATES	14 151 427	2.0	44 765	X	7 110 424	1 188 031	525 248	1 341 560	2 670 719	2 414 501	10 165 263	577 486	525 248
ALABAMA	176 341	1.8	36 481	X	82 476	13 948	6 265	16 084	29 735	39 514	118 772	7 435	6 265
Autauga	1 925	1.6	34 843	1 924	396	68	29	140	283	395	634	43	29
Baldwin	7 646	3.2	39 100	1 280	2 242	348	173	542	1 557	1 540	3 306	227	173
Barbour	773	4.8	28 559	2 846	296	60	24	88	129	246	468	30	24
Bibb	571	1.4	25 352	3 043	170	32	13	45	67	185	260	19	13
Blount	1 691	2.3	29 222	2 779	291	56	23	144	240	438	513	40	23
Bullock	256	2.5	24 043	3 080	93	20	7	12	42	89	133	9	7
Butler	630	3.7	31 082	2 537	224	41	18	58	85	203	341	23	18
Calhoun	3 786	-1.1	32 432	2 347	1 721	357	134	219	694	1 067	2 431	157	134
Chambers	1 028	2.6	30 082	2 677	286	52	22	58	140	334	418	33	22
Cherokee	754	2.8	28 761	2 825	172	34	14	58	120	250	278	22	14
Chilton	1 321	1.4	30 060	2 680	325	60	26	70	178	352	482	36	26
Choctaw	437	2.4	32 528	2 325	183	28	13	46	55	149	270	19	13
Clarke	794	3.4	31 497	2 481	321	58	23	85	108	241	488	33	23
Clay	392	3.3	29 056	2 801	116	23	9	42	57	130	190	13	9
Cleburne	483	3.4	32 226	2 380	98	19	7	45	54	131	169	12	7
Coffee	1 936	1.2	38 002	1 431	502	92	40	194	372	414	828	52	40
Colbert	1 824	2.1	33 459	2 180	988	177	78	135	295	528	1 378	89	78
Conecuh	394	4.1	30 602	2 611	121	25	10	43	56	144	198	14	10
Coosa	271	0.4	24 838	3 061	49	10	4	11	41	94	74	7	4
Covington	1 187	1.9	31 341	2 501	440	86	34	96	186	370	656	45	34
Crenshaw	477	6.2	34 122	2 057	133	24	11	80	60	132	249	15	11
Cullman	2 697	4.1	33 370	2 196	982	165	76	263	406	710	1 485	100	76
Dale	1 602	0.8	32 116	2 402	1 195	294	101	107	317	415	1 697	90	101
Dallas	1 262	1.1	30 042	2 685	481	88	39	108	184	474	717	49	39
DeKalb	2 034	4.1	28 649	2 831	704	130	57	235	318	588	1 126	74	57
Elmore	2 934	1.8	36 261	1 699	663	123	51	148	432	622	985	69	51
Escambia	1 203	2.6	31 684	2 450	486	95	36	133	210	345	750	48	36
Etowah	3 447	1.2	33 162	2 233	1 254	211	99	279	531	1 022	1 843	129	99
Fayette	503	1.4	29 737	2 722	126	29	10	34	78	179	198	16	10
Franklin	883	1.9	27 997	2 899	330	66	27	67	123	270	490	33	27
Geneva	846	1.8	31 637	2 457	159	34	12	81	124	254	286	21	12
Greene	289	7.0	33 060	2 242	60	14	5	36	48	96	116	7	5
Hale	478	4.5	31 007	2 547	101	20	8	55	72	157	184	13	8
Henry	588	1.9	33 977	2 087	130	23	10	62	99	172	225	15	10
Houston	3 871	1.4	37 338	1 532	1 862	319	141	317	684	870	2 640	165	141
Jackson	1 732	2.3	32 719	2 301	569	110	45	196	254	466	920	60	45
Jefferson	30 311	1.4	45 961	618	18 283	2 700	1 346	4 975	5 466	5 392	27 303	1 627	1 346
Lamar	422	2.1	29 629	2 738	125	23	10	36	59	150	195	15	10
Lauderdale	3 147	1.8	33 907	2 097	1 006	179	79	283	579	765	1 547	103	79
Lawrence	1 073	3.2	31 947	2 417	268	46	19	111	117	295	444	30	19
Lee	4 603	2.7	30 499	2 629	1 927	390	145	347	858	830	2 810	168	145
Limestone	3 234	2.4	36 398	1 675	974	191	76	382	445	624	1 624	98	76
Lowndes	387	3.7	36 127	1 725	113	24	9	65	42	113	211	12	9
Macon	636	3.4	32 323	2 364	217	58	17	23	100	194	315	20	17
Madison	15 023	2.0	43 308	816	10 575	1 724	810	759	2 996	2 264	13 868	814	810
Marengo	741	3.9	36 787	1 626	271	52	20	94	113	217	437	29	20
Marion	869	2.5	28 656	2 829	320	59	26	99	142	272	503	34	26
Marshall	3 055	2.0	32 243	2 376	1 175	219	93	174	487	779	1 660	111	93
Mobile	13 599	0.8	32 843	2 275	7 689	1 222	583	1 201	2 111	3 411	10 694	675	583
Monroe	661	1.2	29 744	2 721	260	46	20	73	106	215	399	27	20
Montgomery	9 105	1.0	40 168	1 152	6 041	1 117	465	919	1 751	1 862	8 542	493	465
Morgan	4 099	1.0	34 219	2 049	1 971	341	151	265	664	954	2 729	176	151
Perry	315	4.1	31 432	2 491	71	16	6	45	41	112	138	9	6
Pickens	598	4.5	30 822	2 574	121	24	9	58	81	198	212	15	9
Pike	1 182	2.1	35 448	1 830	505	97	38	138	189	300	779	47	38
Randolph	645	3.7	28 360	2 859	149	30	12	57	105	215	248	19	12
Russell	1 821	2.1	30 558	2 617	499	90	38	71	240	476	698	49	38
St. Clair	2 920	2.1	33 837	2 112	661	112	51	109	334	625	934	70	51
Shelby	9 452	1.0	46 201	602	4 018	550	289	336	1 611	1 164	5 192	328	289
Sumter	380	6.4	28 464	2 852	120	27	9	42	51	135	199	13	9
Talladega	2 732	3.5	33 686	2 145	1 288	214	100	136	352	753	1 739	117	100
Tallapoosa	1 377	2.3	33 417	2 190	441	77	35	67	235	431	621	46	35
Tuscaloosa	7 249	1.6	36 095	1 732	3 885	693	289	553	1 257	1 451	5 420	327	289
Walker	2 276	1.2	34 493	1 988	685	126	52	206	280	727	1 068	78	52

1. Based on the resident population estimated as of July 1 of the year shown.

Table B. States and Counties — **Earnings, Social Security, and Housing**

STATE County	Earnings, 2013 (cont.) Percent by selected industries: Farm	Mining	Construction	Manufacturing	Information: professional, scientific, technical services	Retail trade	Finance, insurance, real estate and leasing	Health care and social assistance	Government	Social Security beneficiaries, December 2013: Number	Rate[1]	Supplemental Security Income recipients, December 2013	Housing units, 2014: Total	Percent change, 2010–2014
	75	76	77	78	79	80	81	82	83	84	85	86	87	88
UNITED STATES	1.2	1.6	5.5	9.7	13.1	6.0	9.2	10.9	17.1	56 480 451	178	8 362 414	133 957 180	1.7
ALABAMA	1.4	0.7	6.3	13.8	9.3	6.8	6.7	10.5	20.9	1 081 046	224	176 562	2 207 912	1.7
Autauga	4.6	D	6.9	13.6	3.3	10.1	7.3	8.8	18.4	10 995	199	1 495	22 751	2.8
Baldwin	0.9	0.2	8.4	6.6	5.2	13.5	8.4	11.9	15.1	47 355	242	3 494	107 374	3.2
Barbour	9.0	2.3	2.8	24.1	D	6.6	3.0	D	18.9	6 950	258	1 589	11 799	-0.3
Bibb	4.8	D	25.0	6.9	D	6.0	2.4	D	25.3	5 550	247	1 072	8 978	-0.1
Blount	4.2	D	8.2	11.0	4.3	8.6	3.4	D	20.5	13 250	230	1 529	23 826	-0.3
Bullock	5.7	0.0	D	D	3.3	4.7	2.4	13.5	27.7	2 065	195	686	4 461	-0.7
Butler	6.6	0.0	5.1	18.2	D	8.8	2.7	D	14.3	5 375	265	1 234	9 916	-0.5
Calhoun	0.4	D	2.9	14.4	5.3	8.1	3.2	10.2	32.2	29 475	253	4 731	53 289	0.0
Chambers	0.7	D	4.2	17.4	3.1	10.1	2.5	D	16.8	9 815	287	1 663	16 894	-0.6
Cherokee	4.6	0.0	4.5	17.3	D	12.3	4.5	7.0	22.5	7 730	296	1 026	16 241	-0.2
Chilton	3.7	D	9.7	19.9	D	10.6	3.2	6.7	19.4	9 945	227	1 579	19 221	-0.3
Choctaw	1.7	0.8	D	D	D	9.1	2.2	D	9.2	4 325	323	881	7 231	-0.5
Clarke	3.0	0.9	2.5	26.8	D	10.6	5.0	D	20.0	7 040	280	1 501	12 583	-0.4
Clay	6.5	D	4.1	32.2	2.7	5.5	3.3	D	22.4	3 925	291	593	6 736	-0.6
Cleburne	11.8	0.0	23.2	10.8	1.2	8.6	2.4	1.9	23.7	3 970	264	566	6 690	-0.4
Coffee	5.4	0.0	5.0	15.5	D	10.0	4.7	11.2	16.6	11 020	217	1 445	22 852	2.3
Colbert	2.6	0.5	8.4	23.7	1.9	7.8	3.5	8.2	23.9	15 035	276	2 226	26 192	1.7
Conecuh	7.7	D	2.7	13.5	1.7	5.2	1.3	D	20.6	3 985	309	826	7 055	-0.5
Coosa	6.5	0.0	3.0	37.2	D	3.1	D	3.8	24.1	2 875	260	480	6 458	-0.5
Covington	4.4	0.1	5.5	16.6	2.8	9.7	4.0	D	16.5	10 590	280	1 569	18 778	-0.3
Crenshaw	15.0	0.0	4.3	21.3	1.5	4.5	2.7	D	12.1	3 855	276	706	6 708	-0.4
Cullman	3.2	D	6.4	18.5	5.1	9.5	4.1	12.6	14.5	20 875	258	2 736	37 131	0.2
Dale	1.7	D	2.8	23.9	3.2	2.2	1.5	1.9	48.4	10 950	220	1 912	22 832	0.7
Dallas	4.3	D	3.4	25.8	2.2	8.2	3.1	12.7	19.4	11 010	262	4 317	20 240	0.2
DeKalb	5.9	D	5.5	27.2	3.1	7.7	3.1	9.0	14.9	16 850	238	2 366	31 035	-0.2
Elmore	0.6	0.2	8.1	16.2	5.2	12.3	4.6	9.2	22.3	17 135	212	2 293	33 326	2.1
Escambia	4.0	2.6	4.7	22.5	1.8	7.4	3.9	6.6	27.7	9 815	259	1 536	16 402	-0.5
Etowah	0.3	0.2	4.9	15.4	3.7	8.4	5.0	21.5	15.8	28 310	272	4 789	47 505	0.1
Fayette	0.9	1.5	5.6	17.7	2.7	10.6	3.3	D	29.7	5 465	323	910	8 404	-0.4
Franklin	5.2	0.7	3.3	34.6	2.3	6.0	3.9	D	19.7	7 700	244	1 149	14 048	0.2
Geneva	14.1	D	5.2	9.5	D	8.5	3.6	4.4	23.7	7 350	275	1 277	12 646	-0.3
Greene	24.3	0.0	2.9	17.7	D	4.6	1.8	D	25.4	2 535	291	890	4 988	-0.4
Hale	18.5	0.0	7.3	14.9	1.8	6.4	2.8	D	24.0	4 585	299	1 162	7 639	-0.2
Henry	15.5	0.0	6.4	13.2	D	4.8	2.6	D	15.6	4 965	288	675	8 961	0.8
Houston	1.6	D	6.8	7.2	4.6	10.4	4.7	17.3	18.3	24 160	233	4 110	46 442	2.5
Jackson	8.2	0.3	3.8	26.7	4.0	8.1	2.8	5.4	21.8	14 230	269	1 744	24 755	-0.1
Jefferson	0.0	0.9	8.8	7.3	11.0	5.4	10.7	14.1	14.8	138 320	210	25 463	305 040	1.5
Lamar	4.7	D	4.2	28.4	D	6.8	4.2	6.9	15.7	4 425	312	653	7 326	-0.4
Lauderdale	5.0	D	6.4	11.8	4.8	11.9	5.7	14.9	18.4	23 260	251	2 746	44 353	1.3
Lawrence	14.1	D	5.2	28.7	D	7.0	2.3	D	16.8	8 795	262	1 433	15 171	-0.4
Lee	0.2	0.1	5.6	11.9	5.1	7.3	4.9	6.6	35.8	22 660	149	3 440	65 566	5.1
Limestone	4.7	D	13.2	10.6	5.4	10.2	3.4	4.7	30.7	17 550	197	2 119	35 445	1.3
Lowndes	21.0	D	7.9	33.8	D	3.0	D	2.0	14.6	3 125	291	975	5 089	-1.0
Macon	3.0	D	D	D	D	3.2	1.1	D	63.6	4 780	241	1 248	10 217	-0.4
Madison	0.4	0.0	2.9	11.7	25.7	4.9	3.2	6.9	29.7	59 835	172	6 846	154 452	5.5
Marengo	4.3	0.0	5.0	20.8	D	6.6	3.7	D	18.7	6 030	298	1 647	10 207	-0.3
Marion	4.5	D	3.3	29.4	D	7.7	4.6	D	15.7	8 095	267	1 145	14 704	-0.2
Marshall	0.5	D	4.0	28.9	5.0	9.5	5.1	6.6	19.1	22 065	233	2 970	40 328	0.0
Mobile	0.2	0.8	6.6	14.1	9.0	6.8	7.1	11.4	16.0	87 650	211	15 409	181 611	1.9
Monroe	4.2	D	2.2	23.6	D	6.8	3.3	D	17.8	5 975	269	1 093	11 274	-0.5
Montgomery	0.4	0.0	6.1	10.5	9.2	5.5	6.7	10.8	30.1	43 855	193	10 211	103 434	1.8
Morgan	0.9	0.1	8.0	31.0	4.5	6.9	4.3	7.1	15.1	27 410	229	3 485	51 496	0.6
Perry	16.8	0.0	2.9	13.8	D	4.4	2.2	6.8	21.3	2 800	281	1 189	4 691	-0.9
Pickens	14.9	D	3.2	17.8	1.8	6.5	D	D	20.4	5 635	291	1 246	9 441	-0.4
Pike	3.5	0.0	4.0	22.1	2.3	6.2	4.2	D	20.7	6 655	198	1 653	15 807	3.5
Randolph	6.5	D	4.5	16.7	2.3	10.4	3.8	D	23.1	6 115	270	913	11 928	-0.5
Russell	1.8	0.1	7.7	25.2	D	9.1	5.4	10.0	20.9	12 195	205	2 166	26 787	8.9
St. Clair	0.4	D	7.9	16.8	5.5	9.3	3.9	8.4	17.3	18 485	214	2 193	35 844	0.9
Shelby	0.1	0.7	6.8	6.6	10.5	7.1	18.8	7.1	9.2	34 120	167	2 555	83 498	3.1
Sumter	13.1	0.0	4.5	10.5	D	5.1	2.4	D	34.2	3 330	250	1 227	6 748	-0.6
Talladega	1.2	1.7	3.5	40.5	2.1	4.9	1.9	8.0	17.0	21 340	262	4 360	37 177	0.2
Tallapoosa	0.7	D	5.3	18.2	3.8	8.4	3.9	D	17.7	12 215	296	1 889	22 029	-0.4
Tuscaloosa	0.3	5.4	5.1	17.5	5.8	6.2	4.5	9.3	27.5	37 725	188	6 864	87 795	3.4
Walker	0.4	4.0	5.2	9.5	4.8	11.3	4.6	16.5	15.8	20 330	309	3 345	30 669	-0.5

1. Per 1,000 resident population estimated as of July 1 of the year shown.

STATE County	Housing units, 2009–2013								Civilian labor force, 2014				Civilian employment,[6] 2009–2013		
	Occupied units										Unemployment			Percent	
		Owner-occupied				Renter-occupied									
				Median owner cost as a percent of income											
	Total	Percent	Median value[1]	With a mortgage	Without a mortgage[2]	Median rent[3]	Median rent as a percent of income[2]	Substandard units[4] (percent)	Total	Percent change, 2013–2014	Total	Rate[5]	Total	Management, business, science and arts	Construction, production, and maintenance occupations
	89	90	91	92	93	94	95	96	97	98	99	100	101	102	103
UNITED STATES	115 610 216	64.9	176 700	24.2	12.5	904	31.3	3.7	155 922 000	0.3	9 617 000	6.2	141 864 697	36.2	21.1
ALABAMA	1 838 683	69.7	122 500	21.9	11.6	705	31.1	2.3	2 150 118	-0.9	146 208	6.8	2 002 163	32.6	26.0
Autauga	20 071	76.8	136 200	21.0	10.0	851	30.4	2.4	25 429	-1.3	1 496	5.9	23 937	31.7	24.3
Baldwin	73 283	72.6	168 600	23.4	11.2	876	31.6	2.3	85 815	0.8	5 195	6.1	81 969	32.9	22.7
Barbour	9 200	67.7	89 200	21.2	13.5	587	31.2	0.6	8 798	-3.2	951	10.8	9 344	26.3	31.6
Bibb	7 091	79.0	90 500	24.5	11.9	568	33.4	1.7	8 560	-1.3	611	7.1	8 022	21.3	42.0
Blount	21 108	81.0	117 100	22.5	11.4	600	25.1	3.6	24 614	-0.9	1 513	6.1	23 015	26.8	34.8
Bullock	3 741	74.3	70 600	23.8	13.4	492	30.4	2.2	4 679	-2.1	425	9.1	4 076	19.0	47.8
Butler	8 235	70.3	74 700	24.2	14.4	560	36.4	1.4	9 253	1.3	793	8.6	7 606	28.1	32.7
Calhoun	45 196	68.7	100 600	21.1	11.2	615	30.1	4.0	46 924	-2.6	3 716	7.9	45 644	26.7	30.3
Chambers	13 722	67.9	81 200	23.3	13.7	635	34.8	2.2	15 190	-0.3	1 025	6.7	12 802	25.5	34.7
Cherokee	11 656	76.1	99 400	23.7	14.3	609	30.9	4.3	11 299	-0.6	661	5.9	10 217	28.2	36.5
Chilton	16 232	74.5	102 600	22.2	11.8	626	30.0	2.8	19 121	-1.0	1 201	6.3	17 824	26.1	33.1
Choctaw	5 518	83.7	58 200	22.4	12.7	593	27.8	3.1	4 479	-4.5	406	9.1	4 713	30.9	36.2
Clarke	9 631	72.9	85 600	20.8	15.8	479	32.3	4.7	8 101	-2.2	1 010	12.5	8 505	23.9	34.3
Clay	5 649	75.0	79 900	23.6	10.9	424	25.1	5.4	5 446	1.2	393	7.2	5 132	26.5	41.1
Cleburne	5 601	77.6	100 800	21.0	12.5	574	24.1	1.8	5 764	-0.9	387	6.7	5 799	26.2	37.4
Coffee	18 820	69.9	131 000	21.4	10.1	647	28.5	1.9	20 213	-1.3	1 351	6.7	19 596	31.5	26.8
Colbert	22 260	72.1	99 300	21.6	12.2	617	29.3	5.6	24 016	0.9	1 971	8.2	21 470	27.9	32.3
Conecuh	4 994	79.1	69 600	26.6	13.9	525	37.9	3.7	4 629	-1.3	497	10.7	3 802	20.7	33.9
Coosa	4 506	83.0	75 100	24.4	13.7	574	27.8	2.5	4 400	-0.7	389	8.8	4 005	20.9	39.0
Covington	15 041	75.1	88 800	21.8	12.5	579	29.9	1.7	15 771	-1.5	1 224	7.8	14 928	24.5	35.6
Crenshaw	5 601	69.9	70 800	19.5	12.1	505	25.3	2.2	6 244	-0.7	434	7.0	5 678	29.1	34.3
Cullman	31 342	75.0	106 100	22.6	12.0	605	30.8	1.9	35 477	-0.6	2 163	6.1	33 043	28.2	32.0
Dale	19 345	61.1	99 400	19.2	10.0	616	27.9	8.3	20 397	-1.6	1 459	7.2	19 406	26.4	31.7
Dallas	16 173	60.9	75 700	23.7	15.0	537	36.4	4.0	15 747	-3.3	1 821	11.6	13 931	25.1	35.2
DeKalb	24 923	76.3	93 400	23.2	12.1	518	25.9	2.5	28 655	-1.0	1 989	6.9	27 390	23.7	39.4
Elmore	28 324	75.5	144 600	21.4	10.8	774	28.2	2.3	36 381	-1.3	2 100	5.8	34 061	33.6	25.1
Escambia	13 681	72.5	84 100	20.5	14.2	582	35.1	2.2	14 194	-0.4	1 167	8.2	12 346	24.7	28.4
Etowah	40 217	72.4	100 000	22.7	12.8	615	30.4	1.7	43 578	-0.3	3 063	7.0	39 289	27.2	32.1
Fayette	6 956	74.9	71 400	21.4	11.6	451	32.0	4.8	6 281	-1.7	496	7.9	6 141	23.7	38.5
Franklin	12 437	69.5	82 300	20.1	13.8	527	26.1	3.4	13 641	-0.1	1 063	7.8	12 648	20.3	47.2
Geneva	10 945	72.1	78 100	20.3	10.3	573	28.6	4.3	10 783	-2.2	727	6.7	10 795	23.5	35.6
Greene	3 264	73.2	72 700	32.0	13.5	428	31.1	4.1	3 000	0.1	379	12.6	2 652	18.5	36.7
Hale	5 969	78.0	79 900	25.6	15.0	426	28.4	1.2	6 142	-0.9	602	9.8	5 462	25.1	35.1
Henry	7 001	77.7	97 000	22.6	11.9	545	23.2	1.6	6 799	-2.0	506	7.4	6 749	32.4	29.5
Houston	39 250	64.6	122 300	20.8	10.0	663	29.2	1.9	44 834	-1.7	3 053	6.8	44 194	29.7	25.0
Jackson	20 765	75.2	93 400	21.2	11.2	516	26.7	1.6	23 306	-1.2	1 680	7.2	21 246	25.5	38.3
Jefferson	259 634	64.7	140 800	23.2	12.1	809	32.8	2.9	311 833	-0.9	19 672	6.3	291 158	37.7	18.8
Lamar	6 084	71.5	66 800	19.5	10.4	447	27.8	1.0	5 547	-4.2	396	7.1	5 583	27.0	39.5
Lauderdale	38 458	69.9	114 300	21.2	10.0	588	30.2	1.3	43 367	0.7	3 114	7.2	39 261	29.1	27.4
Lawrence	13 382	80.1	94 200	22.2	13.0	531	25.8	2.0	13 988	-1.7	1 153	8.2	12 984	23.4	39.0
Lee	55 864	61.7	146 900	22.0	11.5	767	35.2	2.6	70 960	0.8	3 969	5.6	65 065	37.6	22.6
Limestone	31 794	76.6	134 500	20.6	10.0	615	29.1	6.0	39 016	-0.9	2 381	6.1	36 166	33.4	28.3
Lowndes	4 212	74.9	71 400	27.8	20.7	534	28.2	2.4	3 906	-2.5	504	12.9	3 543	23.8	39.0
Macon	8 107	65.7	75 700	27.4	12.8	584	33.0	1.6	8 211	-2.2	750	9.1	7 587	25.0	26.7
Madison	132 975	69.3	164 500	19.0	10.0	744	27.6	2.8	169 656	-0.8	10 453	6.2	160 131	44.5	17.0
Marengo	8 464	71.3	89 600	22.1	11.8	527	30.1	2.4	7 597	-0.2	611	8.0	7 495	27.2	34.4
Marion	12 700	75.9	78 700	22.2	12.2	477	29.5	3.8	12 160	-2.4	979	8.1	11 559	25.7	36.1
Marshall	34 250	71.9	114 000	21.9	11.7	594	27.8	2.7	39 588	-2.3	2 652	6.7	37 950	27.3	36.1
Mobile	155 178	66.6	124 300	22.9	12.3	756	34.0	2.2	184 133	-1.2	14 186	7.7	169 678	31.0	24.4
Monroe	8 333	74.0	76 900	24.2	12.3	536	33.1	2.2	7 530	-3.0	851	11.3	7 247	23.6	38.3
Montgomery	88 844	61.4	122 900	22.1	10.4	812	33.7	2.2	104 838	-1.1	7 246	6.9	99 071	35.7	19.6
Morgan	46 192	71.5	120 500	20.3	10.0	603	26.7	9.0	55 799	-1.8	3 694	6.6	51 905	29.1	30.8
Perry	3 400	67.0	58 000	23.2	16.6	461	33.3	2.7	3 454	-3.1	430	12.4	2 793	22.7	34.5
Pickens	7 026	72.0	81 900	21.9	12.4	412	30.9	2.2	7 429	0.5	611	8.2	6 661	21.5	37.5
Pike	12 959	57.8	101 000	20.8	10.0	587	34.4	5.6	14 839	-0.3	1 082	7.0	14 431	27.6	29.7
Randolph	9 013	72.3	88 600	23.1	12.2	588	33.9	2.1	9 166	-0.3	629	6.9	8 440	25.3	41.5
Russell	21 142	61.3	104 400	24.4	13.3	712	30.5	2.2	24 634	-1.4	1 633	6.6	22 048	26.3	26.7
St. Clair	31 353	81.5	134 600	21.9	11.8	757	27.8	1.4	38 380	-1.0	2 227	5.8	35 366	30.1	29.0
Shelby	74 144	79.0	193 000	21.1	10.0	917	28.0	4.5	106 051	-0.7	4 797	4.5	98 202	42.6	15.1
Sumter	5 060	64.7	74 100	23.6	15.0	550	43.7	2.8	5 321	-2.5	471	8.9	4 897	26.8	27.5
Talladega	31 486	71.2	92 600	22.6	12.9	589	31.4	5.2	34 916	-2.0	2 682	7.7	30 760	26.3	33.0
Tallapoosa	16 373	72.2	94 900	22.1	11.5	585	30.1	2.1	18 136	-1.2	1 388	7.7	16 422	30.3	33.8
Tuscaloosa	67 882	64.4	153 300	22.3	10.5	762	33.4	1.7	96 911	1.5	5 771	6.0	86 458	34.3	25.0
Walker	25 751	75.0	82 100	20.6	11.8	614	28.7	3.0	25 912	-1.2	1 988	7.7	24 153	25.3	32.0

1. Specified owner-occupied units. 2. A value of 10.0 represents 10 percent or less; a value of 50.0 represents 50 percent or more. 3. Specified renter-occupied units.
4. Overcrowded or lacking complete plumbing facilities. 5. Percent of civilian labor force. 6. Persons 16 years old and over.

STATE County	Private nonfarm establishments, employment and payroll, 2013									Agriculture, 2012			
		Employment						Annual payroll		Farms			
											Percent with:		
	Number of establish-ments	Total	Health care and social assistance	Manufac-turing	Retail trade	Finance and insurance	Professional, scientific, and technical services	Total (mil dol)	Average per employee (dollars)	Number	Fewer than 50 acres	500 acres or more	Farm operators whose principal occu-pation is farming (percent)
	104	105	106	107	108	109	110	111	112	113	114	115	116
UNITED STATES	7 488 353	118 266 253	18 598 711	11 276 438	15 023 362	6 063 761	8 275 350	5 621 697	47 534	2 109 303	38.6	15.0	47.8
ALABAMA	97 578	1 603 100	240 549	242 093	222 277	69 332	92 520	62 408	38 930	43 223	37.4	8.6	44.2
Autauga	817	10 120	1 535	907	2 488	425	290	292	28 821	389	31.6	14.4	51.2
Baldwin	4 871	54 988	6 843	3 939	12 940	1 611	1 979	1 669	30 351	989	52.6	8.1	45.8
Barbour	464	6 611	724	2 647	887	185	110	213	32 182	571	13.8	17.3	46.1
Bibb	275	3 145	657	292	475	76	D	115	36 484	189	29.6	13.8	38.6
Blount	660	6 798	933	1 182	1 202	206	217	197	28 988	1 241	40.6	3.1	48.8
Bullock	112	D	D	D	235	D	22	D	D	273	17.2	30.4	40.7
Butler	393	5 711	D	1 332	933	151	52	167	29 262	407	25.1	8.6	45.2
Calhoun	2 311	34 871	6 102	5 643	6 032	890	1 024	1 105	31 681	592	45.4	3.5	46.1
Chambers	515	6 431	1 268	1 441	1 107	D	152	199	30 984	301	22.6	15.6	38.9
Cherokee	379	3 864	D	1 157	879	122	55	114	29 449	561	32.1	11.6	45.6
Chilton	703	7 396	739	1 795	1 427	235	97	209	28 273	543	37.9	7.0	41.1
Choctaw	255	2 900	D	D	348	68	D	141	48 528	248	37.1	14.5	40.3
Clarke	586	6 648	916	1 756	1 448	347	82	229	34 502	263	38.8	9.9	35.4
Clay	190	2 993	468	1 437	285	85	56	84	27 994	401	24.7	7.7	39.7
Cleburne	152	1 548	D	D	261	59	D	61	39 267	341	36.7	5.3	47.8
Coffee	954	12 762	1 955	3 221	2 289	533	411	378	29 616	899	27.9	9.1	50.5
Colbert	1 226	19 820	2 552	5 350	2 839	D	302	714	36 042	687	39.6	9.0	36.7
Conecuh	194	2 197	321	328	284	41	34	68	31 169	346	19.1	8.4	44.8
Coosa	93	992	D	393	142	D	20	30	29 789	152	23.7	11.8	52.6
Covington	834	10 824	1 775	2 287	1 816	345	285	322	29 784	1 051	31.4	6.8	40.3
Crenshaw	211	3 139	453	1 187	282	D	32	104	33 279	575	21.6	12.3	40.2
Cullman	1 714	22 185	3 430	4 721	3 351	784	429	747	33 679	2 007	47.6	2.1	48.6
Dale	766	11 924	1 292	480	1 189	388	975	524	43 955	487	27.9	12.7	30.8
Dallas	757	10 420	2 016	2 948	1 700	D	204	323	30 988	506	22.9	25.7	45.7
DeKalb	1 082	16 841	2 280	6 727	2 273	452	336	527	31 284	2 035	44.9	3.4	50.7
Elmore	1 135	14 056	2 082	2 662	2 824	410	388	437	31 061	552	46.4	7.8	40.9
Escambia	723	9 977	1 208	1 841	1 680	460	168	327	32 795	454	44.1	13.9	39.6
Etowah	2 008	29 796	7 277	5 068	4 355	1 015	1 185	923	30 980	853	51.1	2.9	40.3
Fayette	306	3 323	729	756	569	D	27	116	34 914	414	24.6	8.0	38.9
Franklin	510	9 369	1 152	D	932	376	154	293	31 260	825	25.7	7.8	47.5
Geneva	400	3 791	608	D	739	147	197	108	28 478	1 017	31.6	9.8	43.1
Greene	99	1 379	D	536	174	27	D	40	29 311	304	26.0	24.0	50.3
Hale	195	1 966	429	D	279	72	D	69	35 006	456	27.0	16.0	49.8
Henry	293	2 754	D	295	360	92	114	91	33 004	498	19.5	17.1	43.0
Houston	2 702	43 139	9 320	4 025	7 725	1 189	1 089	1 587	36 787	816	38.8	12.3	44.5
Jackson	856	12 440	1 865	5 047	1 909	D	249	386	31 009	1 376	40.1	6.0	37.4
Jefferson	16 232	319 199	55 306	23 743	39 475	22 933	15 159	14 721	46 120	394	59.9	3.0	46.7
Lamar	241	2 943	312	D	407	121	53	102	34 719	353	31.7	8.5	33.4
Lauderdale	1 967	25 839	4 478	3 592	5 404	1 036	770	723	27 983	1 466	45.9	5.2	44.8
Lawrence	407	4 232	657	D	769	104	D	191	45 243	1 551	41.5	4.3	43.2
Lee	2 500	38 782	5 625	6 177	6 458	1 021	1 410	1 172	30 226	315	32.7	7.6	37.1
Limestone	1 308	15 305	2 087	2 944	2 801	D	740	501	32 708	1 230	40.6	6.9	46.6
Lowndes	98	1 835	D	1 088	166	D	D	110	59 901	441	24.5	21.8	48.5
Macon	217	5 381	D	D	384	58	43	212	39 410	352	26.4	15.9	48.3
Madison	8 095	153 304	23 122	16 460	19 067	3 551	32 607	7 213	47 051	1 033	48.4	8.0	49.5
Marengo	478	5 876	949	1 419	883	D	78	202	34 365	499	27.3	16.8	33.9
Marion	547	8 006	1 278	2 841	1 015	369	74	233	29 149	715	32.3	3.8	37.5
Marshall	1 795	30 306	3 587	10 284	4 590	759	586	902	29 771	1 505	53.2	3.1	41.9
Mobile	8 567	147 574	20 148	17 209	19 298	5 836	9 030	5 784	39 195	698	60.9	4.4	48.6
Monroe	393	5 029	665	D	860	203	43	203	40 326	480	37.1	12.1	44.6
Montgomery	5 533	101 517	16 028	12 956	12 282	3 911	5 985	4 046	39 853	603	28.0	19.2	50.4
Morgan	2 589	42 569	6 008	11 149	5 615	1 410	1 348	1 654	38 864	1 237	44.2	3.7	42.1
Perry	125	1 570	D	553	202	D	D	47	29 686	389	26.2	19.0	39.8
Pickens	266	2 707	642	562	412	D	D	79	29 197	433	28.4	9.9	46.9
Pike	628	11 009	1 102	1 467	1 402	344	D	357	32 384	600	21.5	14.7	39.5
Randolph	340	3 481	570	978	731	154	43	92	26 403	611	27.8	8.3	52.2
Russell	783	10 489	1 440	D	1 839	343	184	343	32 656	280	28.9	21.8	35.4
St. Clair	1 266	15 265	1 948	3 021	2 626	468	568	473	31 016	540	44.3	3.3	51.1
Shelby	4 845	76 137	6 713	5 512	7 993	9 125	1 866	3 561	40 777	401	45.4	6.7	44.6
Sumter	202	2 966	398	D	294	61	D	108	36 297	428	22.7	22.9	46.0
Talladega	1 230	23 763	2 887	8 588	2 598	484	419	992	41 736	519	38.2	8.5	50.3
Tallapoosa	721	10 771	2 241	2 373	1 454	D	206	320	29 748	345	35.1	5.5	42.0
Tuscaloosa	4 009	72 917	11 839	13 009	10 074	1 685	2 255	2 790	38 257	497	43.7	9.5	37.0
Walker	1 250	15 669	3 226	2 197	3 304	498	608	512	32 645	482	46.9	3.7	33.8

STATE County	Agriculture, 2012 (cont.)															
	Land in farms					Value of land and buildings (dollars)		Value of machinery and equipment, average per farm (dollars)	Value of products sold				Percent of farms with sales of:		Government payments	
	Acreage (1,000)	Percent change, 2007–2012	Acres						Total (mil dol)	Average per farm (dollars)	Percent from:					
			Average size of farm	Total irrigated (1,000)	Total cropland (1,000)	Average per farm	Average per acre				Crops	Livestock and poultry products	$10,000 or more	$100,000 or more	Total ($1,000)	Percent of farms
	117	118	119	120	121	122	123	124	125	126	127	128	129	130	131	132
UNITED STATES	914 528	-0.8	434	55 822.2	389 690.4	1 075 491	2 481	115 662	394 644.5	187 097	53.8	46.2	43.4	18.4	8 053 346	38.5
ALABAMA	8 903	-1.4	206	113.0	2 758.5	547 524	2 658	71 210	5 571.2	128 894	23.6	76.4	33.8	11.2	88 145	30.0
Autauga	112	0.9	287	1.6	41.3	655 057	2 285	73 658	19.8	50 928	D	D	33.7	6.9	1 245	31.9
Baldwin	192	1.3	194	7.7	100.9	773 980	3 980	107 905	135.6	137 070	85.3	14.7	35.2	11.7	2 649	26.7
Barbour	204	2.6	358	2.3	41.3	808 758	2 261	80 371	104.4	182 760	14.1	85.9	32.7	9.6	1 806	62.5
Bibb	56	47.7	298	0.1	12.6	624 810	2 098	66 159	D	D	D	D	23.8	1.6	138	14.3
Blount	146	-3.4	118	0.5	37.1	427 880	3 632	58 512	178.2	143 587	7.0	93.0	37.4	12.7	897	19.1
Bullock	165	22.9	603	1.4	26.1	1 312 890	2 178	107 813	54.5	199 813	62.0	38.0	38.8	13.6	721	31.5
Butler	88	-4.5	217	0.0	21.3	527 472	2 429	65 489	110.1	270 634	D	D	28.7	10.8	355	26.3
Calhoun	81	6.6	137	0.9	21.4	418 128	3 046	61 630	92.4	156 052	11.8	88.2	30.1	7.3	406	17.4
Chambers	96	-8.2	320	0.1	15.3	832 784	2 602	61 761	8.3	27 708	24.3	75.7	35.2	5.3	397	15.6
Cherokee	124	-6.5	221	1.3	58.8	757 134	3 419	84 629	120.0	213 913	30.0	70.0	36.4	17.3	1 985	38.1
Chilton	91	-8.8	168	0.5	23.7	493 578	2 933	55 048	16.0	29 538	63.8	36.2	36.8	5.3	296	10.3
Choctaw	68	24.5	276	0.0	8.0	517 085	1 872	53 851	D	D	D	D	18.5	2.0	194	11.3
Clarke	47	-35.6	181	0.0	7.7	369 251	2 045	38 399	2.6	9 863	49.1	50.9	24.3	0.8	153	17.5
Clay	78	4.6	194	0.0	13.0	480 421	2 474	54 217	58.1	144 850	1.8	98.2	38.4	8.7	585	19.5
Cleburne	50	1.4	147	0.3	7.7	404 111	2 745	60 522	84.3	247 170	3.9	96.1	45.2	18.5	106	12.6
Coffee	202	-4.2	225	3.3	85.5	593 148	2 636	90 236	258.2	287 171	14.3	85.7	37.9	19.7	3 459	57.7
Colbert	153	18.5	222	3.7	65.7	626 991	2 820	80 017	67.0	97 531	54.3	45.7	32.3	8.7	1 996	31.4
Conecuh	94	8.6	271	0.1	20.1	539 208	1 991	72 494	16.4	47 436	44.6	55.4	35.0	6.4	770	41.0
Coosa	36	-20.8	236	D	4.3	489 967	2 072	52 934	2.1	13 763	D	D	30.3	2.0	39	5.9
Covington	209	4.2	198	1.4	65.5	447 436	2 255	67 858	119.8	114 025	26.0	74.0	30.9	12.9	2 582	43.8
Crenshaw	130	-1.9	226	0.9	29.0	458 381	2 029	80 572	143.8	250 132	3.5	96.5	36.2	17.0	919	51.0
Cullman	194	-15.5	97	0.5	58.4	403 876	4 176	64 375	417.1	207 820	3.8	96.2	43.3	21.1	567	12.0
Dale	130	-6.1	267	2.6	49.6	668 934	2 510	86 197	118.0	242 400	21.6	78.4	32.6	15.8	1 495	55.6
Dallas	255	-0.7	504	2.0	76.8	925 310	1 835	106 532	70.2	138 800	39.5	60.5	32.6	12.3	2 616	45.8
DeKalb	229	-2.5	113	0.3	72.3	427 088	3 790	70 291	461.7	226 882	5.3	94.7	37.4	17.5	2 652	24.1
Elmore	90	-12.1	164	3.1	30.2	519 685	3 175	64 795	26.5	47 986	65.6	34.4	29.3	4.3	959	15.9
Escambia	107	-4.8	236	0.8	47.7	537 068	2 271	93 018	40.9	89 991	88.5	11.5	28.4	11.5	2 602	48.9
Etowah	86	-8.6	101	0.1	19.5	359 368	3 559	51 635	83.7	98 161	6.5	93.5	27.8	8.2	450	11.8
Fayette	81	2.9	196	D	27.6	415 915	2 124	83 215	36.3	87 751	D	D	30.2	7.0	903	37.4
Franklin	150	6.8	182	0.8	35.0	383 861	2 104	57 796	132.7	160 807	5.6	94.4	39.3	13.8	782	21.8
Geneva	219	-0.8	215	2.7	93.1	465 026	2 161	89 514	178.5	175 499	26.4	73.6	36.0	15.6	4 741	59.2
Greene	120	-11.3	396	0.3	21.8	803 934	2 030	58 648	22.4	73 658	7.7	92.3	28.0	9.2	790	35.5
Hale	161	-5.2	352	D	29.9	735 855	2 091	81 908	65.2	142 934	D	D	39.9	11.4	797	32.0
Henry	170	2.5	341	8.1	72.9	762 197	2 235	108 992	75.0	150 647	53.5	46.5	38.4	15.5	3 315	64.3
Houston	198	-3.3	243	9.1	97.4	631 875	2 604	89 566	89.2	109 336	71.7	28.3	31.1	14.8	5 065	59.3
Jackson	232	-4.5	168	0.4	89.4	440 304	2 613	65 429	117.2	85 181	30.5	69.5	35.0	8.6	1 849	34.4
Jefferson	39	-3.6	99	0.2	9.1	446 142	4 507	49 924	10.4	26 277	10.5	89.5	20.6	1.3	98	8.1
Lamar	82	-2.8	233	D	13.9	344 326	1 477	42 527	7.5	21 337	20.7	79.3	21.5	2.0	203	27.5
Lauderdale	212	-7.1	144	0.4	100.0	428 690	2 970	56 675	72.4	49 385	55.6	44.4	30.7	6.8	2 973	34.7
Lawrence	244	9.6	157	4.7	114.7	480 849	3 059	81 876	192.1	123 829	29.4	70.6	32.0	13.9	4 764	40.4
Lee	59	-6.6	187	0.9	12.2	707 330	3 775	71 403	D	D	D	D	32.4	4.8	692	19.0
Limestone	247	4.0	201	13.1	146.1	815 963	4 068	103 711	132.7	107 913	64.2	35.8	36.3	10.7	3 605	34.6
Lowndes	218	16.6	494	3.8	40.0	852 254	1 726	73 297	76.3	173 052	D	D	41.0	10.0	880	34.7
Macon	103	-11.5	294	1.9	20.1	721 324	2 458	81 386	15.2	43 230	80.5	19.5	31.5	4.0	622	33.2
Madison	209	5.0	203	5.1	125.4	752 873	3 715	88 137	74.2	71 833	86.2	13.8	31.0	8.3	3 156	34.1
Marengo	165	-7.1	332	0.4	32.8	591 148	1 783	59 990	19.4	38 964	27.5	72.5	34.7	5.6	912	28.9
Marion	114	-2.9	159	0.0	21.8	353 441	2 221	47 490	100.1	139 948	3.2	96.8	27.6	11.2	599	29.0
Marshall	163	5.5	108	0.2	46.7	410 550	3 791	61 688	256.5	170 433	2.9	97.1	34.2	12.3	2 102	23.7
Mobile	89	-21.9	127	2.8	36.6	516 701	4 062	78 354	84.7	121 289	90.7	9.3	33.2	8.5	796	12.2
Monroe	141	18.3	293	0.2	53.9	576 181	1 967	103 242	44.5	92 663	72.1	27.9	34.6	10.0	2 925	59.2
Montgomery	220	-1.4	365	1.7	61.2	957 657	2 624	76 778	77.4	128 421	21.5	78.5	40.6	11.8	927	23.7
Morgan	153	-5.5	123	0.3	52.6	460 337	3 732	52 647	109.3	88 335	12.7	87.3	32.7	9.1	1 462	19.6
Perry	157	-5.1	404	0.3	39.5	709 424	1 755	68 270	29.6	76 177	32.6	67.4	31.1	11.8	1 428	53.5
Pickens	103	-21.5	237	D	24.6	490 279	2 068	68 935	110.6	255 370	6.0	94.0	39.5	20.6	511	20.1
Pike	167	-6.6	279	3.2	35.2	635 038	2 278	66 467	130.4	217 322	8.9	91.1	42.5	16.0	1 573	54.2
Randolph	114	-0.7	186	0.1	14.4	523 882	2 810	66 257	111.5	182 509	1.9	98.1	40.4	13.9	831	21.1
Russell	117	24.6	419	3.4	29.4	947 768	2 261	83 646	28.9	103 057	56.0	44.0	29.6	8.6	738	34.6
St. Clair	67	-5.8	125	0.3	13.6	479 537	3 839	55 039	64.8	120 028	15.2	84.8	30.4	9.1	119	6.1
Shelby	58	6.6	146	1.1	18.7	612 140	4 199	68 581	12.2	30 347	80.4	19.6	25.9	6.2	659	10.5
Sumter	240	32.5	560	1.5	33.3	797 215	1 423	58 586	30.5	71 199	D	D	33.2	10.0	1 057	36.4
Talladega	100	-16.1	192	4.8	39.7	559 618	2 909	63 229	40.7	78 428	41.8	58.2	28.3	5.8	717	17.1
Tallapoosa	61	-4.9	177	1.1	8.4	426 409	2 414	53 971	10.6	30 635	32.2	67.8	24.6	3.2	266	10.4
Tuscaloosa	86	-22.2	173	1.1	25.3	512 952	2 965	60 022	27.7	55 682	33.8	66.2	27.0	6.0	493	17.1
Walker	55	-22.5	113	0.0	13.1	291 614	2 578	51 429	33.1	68 683	11.4	88.6	24.3	5.6	105	4.8

STATE County	Water use, 2010		Wholesale trade,[1] 2007				Retail trade,[2] 2007				Real estate and rental and leasing,[2] 2007			
	Total water withdrawn (mil gal/day)	Gallons withdrawn per person per day	Number of establish-ments	Number of employees	Sales (mil dol)	Annual payroll (mil dol)	Number of establish-ments	Number of employees	Sales (mil dol)	Annual payroll (mil dol)	Number of establish-ments	Number of employees	Receipts (mil dol)	Annual payroll (mil dol)
	133	134	135	136	137	138	139	140	141	142	143	144	145	146
UNITED STATES	351 417.1	1 138	369 387	5 098 545	4 174 286.5	260 532.1	1 128 112	15 515 396	3 917 663.5	362 818.7	384 297	2 188 479	485 058.6	84 764.9
ALABAMA	9 960.0	2 084	4 824	70 469	52 252.8	3 032.2	19 722	238 922	57 344.9	5 112.0	4 554	27 100	4 073.2	823.4
Autauga	55.6	1 018	26	D	D	D	182	2 373	598.2	56.4	31	D	D	D
Baldwin	64.4	353	183	D	D	D	1 019	12 920	2 966.5	282.6	358	1 987	266.7	59.5
Barbour	11.1	402	19	D	D	D	104	994	188.3	17.4	20	D	D	D
Bibb	7.6	332	13	D	D	D	64	515	124.7	10.6	11	27	3.5	0.9
Blount	57.1	996	32	D	D	D	155	1 263	319.7	25.4	16	49	3.6	0.7
Bullock	3.2	292	6	D	D	D	22	251	43.8	4.8	4	10	0.7	0.1
Butler	4.5	216	10	74	56.7	2.9	106	1 084	229.3	19.6	21	88	3.8	0.7
Calhoun	29.3	247	104	D	D	D	552	6 854	1 543.0	139.1	93	459	66.3	10.2
Chambers	5.4	158	16	D	D	D	130	1 205	264.7	23.9	17	79	7.5	1.3
Cherokee	5.5	213	17	74	62.3	2.5	86	884	186.3	17.5	18	58	8.3	1.1
Chilton	7.3	168	23	292	155.1	10.5	170	1 503	359.9	31.1	27	87	6.4	1.2
Choctaw	42.9	3 095	13	57	52.9	2.1	66	360	84.6	6.1	4	9	0.5	0.1
Clarke	24.3	941	14	206	85.8	6.1	153	1 477	344.3	28.7	22	74	6.2	1.5
Clay	2.5	180	5	D	D	D	50	358	70.6	5.3	7	17	1.3	0.5
Cleburne	1.8	120	4	10	5.9	0.3	49	362	133.4	10.3	3	D	D	D
Coffee	14.7	294	25	275	131.6	9.7	224	2 514	639.6	54.9	62	261	29.7	6.7
Colbert	1 344.3	24 699	84	848	351.4	30.2	238	2 912	821.3	66.4	38	211	23.1	4.0
Conecuh	2.4	181	7	174	76.7	4.9	45	303	71.2	4.5	8	12	1.0	0.2
Coosa	0.9	81	7	37	31.6	1.8	18	89	20.5	1.4	7	10	1.1	0.1
Covington	10.3	273	39	610	338.7	17.7	191	1 902	424.9	39.2	33	128	12.1	2.4
Crenshaw	3.2	227	13	346	131.9	14.4	50	343	75.5	6.5	7	17	0.9	0.3
Cullman	37.9	471	91	D	D	D	341	3 346	867.1	69.6	56	231	26.1	5.9
Dale	10.3	204	22	257	69.3	7.5	149	1 431	332.5	27.0	31	169	21.1	3.6
Dallas	49.1	1 121	31	D	D	D	200	2 085	437.4	41.8	39	119	14.0	2.5
DeKalb	11.9	168	43	D	D	D	269	2 532	635.2	55.3	36	153	11.8	3.4
Elmore	16.0	202	32	291	104.9	8.8	225	2 479	618.3	50.6	48	125	17.4	3.1
Escambia	45.2	1 180	27	221	93.1	6.5	190	1 639	379.6	33.5	25	119	10.3	2.1
Etowah	146.3	1 401	96	1 064	518.4	36.1	453	4 786	1 114.8	92.7	79	428	68.7	12.1
Fayette	4.7	270	7	34	22.5	1.1	62	633	130.4	11.5	6	15	0.9	0.2
Franklin	6.4	203	20	111	67.4	3.5	119	1 060	269.1	19.3	15	45	4.6	0.6
Geneva	7.5	278	21	423	231.7	23.0	102	872	170.0	15.0	8	27	1.7	0.4
Greene	366.4	40 504	3	D	D	D	28	185	33.6	3.0	1	D	D	D
Hale	20.3	1 285	6	D	D	D	49	361	86.7	7.0	5	D	D	D
Henry	6.5	375	14	D	D	D	60	425	92.6	8.2	13	21	1.9	0.3
Houston	118.0	1 162	159	D	D	D	618	7 934	1 909.6	179.1	122	553	81.5	17.2
Jackson	1 067.5	20 055	38	D	D	D	187	1 923	411.0	37.0	28	106	11.4	2.6
Jefferson	81.3	124	1 052	18 937	13 756.8	930.6	3 026	42 765	11 066.3	971.5	810	7 976	1 193.0	289.1
Lamar	2.1	143	6	D	D	D	51	349	70.8	6.0	5	22	1.1	0.3
Lauderdale	17.5	189	78	1 286	514.6	34.0	445	5 190	1 131.6	100.7	86	345	45.1	8.5
Lawrence	72.8	2 120	11	34	23.8	1.0	86	825	167.0	15.6	7	30	2.8	1.0
Lee	18.2	130	68	D	D	D	472	6 391	1 451.6	125.3	122	636	79.4	15.0
Limestone	2 744.2	33 150	51	407	248.3	17.8	246	2 611	723.2	58.8	55	156	24.0	3.9
Lowndes	4.5	394	2	D	D	D	32	395	103.6	7.1	7	D	D	D
Macon	7.1	333	9	D	D	D	50	455	87.5	7.1	11	D	D	D
Madison	79.1	236	342	4 519	2 970.4	212.4	1 348	18 840	4 438.7	421.1	432	2 091	345.3	65.4
Marengo	25.1	1 191	25	133	64.6	4.2	109	1 039	197.2	18.8	17	85	24.8	3.5
Marion	7.0	227	23	195	162.5	6.2	110	976	209.9	18.1	14	33	3.9	0.6
Marshall	30.5	327	86	1 486	1 138.7	55.3	465	4 990	1 357.7	102.8	80	603	39.4	8.6
Mobile	1 096.7	2 656	546	6 904	3 268.7	296.1	1 644	22 271	5 225.5	483.4	448	2 460	417.2	77.8
Monroe	50.6	2 194	15	148	92.8	7.2	93	872	212.6	16.1	13	50	5.5	1.1
Montgomery	37.6	164	290	5 684	3 275.6	235.8	1 009	14 325	3 238.2	314.6	303	2 358	292.8	72.5
Morgan	123.6	1 035	163	2 046	1 213.9	86.5	545	5 851	1 637.6	128.4	102	418	60.2	10.4
Perry	10.8	1 023	4	69	10.4	1.8	37	178	34.1	3.4	3	D	D	D
Pickens	6.2	312	12	72	36.6	1.8	66	524	113.2	9.2	6	31	1.0	0.6
Pike	7.8	237	22	D	D	D	147	1 578	367.9	31.5	28	89	21.5	1.7
Randolph	2.9	125	8	61	26.8	0.9	95	714	161.4	15.1	20	49	5.8	1.0
Russell	40.7	768	16	D	D	D	165	2 010	428.2	38.5	46	157	23.2	3.5
St. Clair	18.1	216	68	726	317.5	30.1	232	2 502	581.3	51.6	45	157	28.4	3.8
Shelby	688.6	3 530	328	4 622	4 385.6	255.1	707	10 135	2 520.5	237.8	217	1 474	454.8	57.9
Sumter	8.6	628	13	173	76.5	4.8	47	334	59.6	4.4	9	25	3.1	0.9
Talladega	46.0	559	59	D	D	D	310	3 233	730.7	63.6	52	400	28.6	4.9
Tallapoosa	12.1	290	22	D	D	D	155	1 534	362.3	33.3	38	139	26.6	4.2
Tuscaloosa	39.2	202	142	1 655	760.6	72.6	781	10 551	2 445.9	223.5	198	1 170	173.8	32.0
Walker	955.0	14 248	52	300	256.4	13.2	322	3 789	903.6	74.7	41	159	24.7	4.2

1. Merchant wholesalers, except manufacturers' sales branches and offices. 2. Employer establishments.

STATE County	Professional, scientific, and technical services,[1] 2007				Manufacturing, 2007				Accommodation and food services, 2007			
	Number of establish-ments	Number of employees	Receipts (mil dol)	Annual payroll (mil dol)	Number of establish-ments	Number of employees	Receipts (mil dol)	Annual payroll (mil dol)	Number of establish-ments	Number of employees	Sales (mil dol)	Annual payroll (mil dol)
	147	148	149	150	151	152	153	154	155	156	157	158
UNITED STATES	842 607	7 678 304	1 220 434.1	489 965.4	332 536	13 395 670	5 319 456.3	613 768.6	634 361	11 600 751	613 795.7	170 826.8
ALABAMA	9 437	92 759	13 623.2	4 996.4	4 928	271 986	112 858.8	11 351.6	8 093	150 791	6 426.3	1 751.4
Autauga	61	386	42.3	15.5	33	1 506	D	D	92	2 182	88.2	25.5
Baldwin	458	D	D	D	162	4 795	1 410.3	169.3	414	8 368	437.0	122.4
Barbour	48	D	D	D	38	D	D	D	45	D	D	D
Bibb	14	D	D	D	NA	NA	NA	NA	19	255	10.8	2.6
Blount	47	229	16.7	8.2	53	1 517	341.5	44.3	46	490	20.9	5.1
Bullock	7	20	2.6	0.9	3	D	D	D	8	110	3.7	1.1
Butler	25	85	6.9	2.2	23	1 170	399.1	38.5	40	673	28.4	7.5
Calhoun	171	D	D	D	141	6 961	2 680.0	279.3	224	5 129	186.5	51.5
Chambers	29	D	D	D	27	D	667.3	73.6	47	611	23.2	5.9
Cherokee	17	60	6.3	1.5	24	1 171	307.4	34.7	39	354	13.9	3.7
Chilton	39	D	D	D	52	1 444	D	41.8	60	868	34.1	8.5
Choctaw	18	51	3.3	1.1	7	D	D	D	21	170	11.3	1.5
Clarke	30	94	13.2	2.1	31	1 592	571.5	70.2	53	611	23.6	5.4
Clay	10	56	5.2	0.8	12	2 526	330.9	72.9	12	139	4.4	1.1
Cleburne	8	36	1.7	0.6	NA	NA	NA	NA	13	164	4.1	1.0
Coffee	71	373	45.2	11.2	36	3 128	613.8	80.6	89	1 474	50.1	13.2
Colbert	94	D	D	D	112	4 162	2 083.2	185.2	99	1 560	61.9	16.2
Conecuh	11	19	2.2	0.4	12	672	183.5	21.5	16	202	8.7	1.9
Coosa	6	15	1.7	0.7	9	782	89.6	D	3	5	0.6	0.1
Covington	63	301	28.4	9.7	34	2 476	561.2	76.7	67	745	30.3	7.2
Crenshaw	11	31	2.8	0.8	10	986	270.8	29.1	11	173	5.6	1.4
Cullman	118	566	38.5	14.0	124	5 306	1 393.4	188.9	126	2 457	102.3	25.6
Dale	81	974	129.4	45.3	35	652	115.0	19.8	85	1 219	37.2	10.1
Dallas	45	D	D	D	46	3 594	1 174.8	137.7	63	855	33.7	7.9
DeKalb	79	399	30.1	13.1	134	9 028	1 831.6	304.3	108	1 426	67.9	18.3
Elmore	86	449	79.2	17.0	73	3 312	766.3	130.3	82	1 209	47.9	11.8
Escambia	41	176	16.2	5.4	39	1 660	665.3	80.5	54	728	31.9	7.6
Etowah	156	876	76.6	26.8	118	5 430	1 253.0	203.7	177	3 381	138.0	38.1
Fayette	15	47	3.4	1.1	25	974	186.2	28.5	22	258	10.9	2.6
Franklin	28	123	9.7	2.8	49	4 071	672.0	135.0	51	691	25.4	6.1
Geneva	34	D	D	D	27	960	153.3	27.2	31	313	10.4	2.7
Greene	6	D	D	D	NA	NA	NA	NA	6	58	1.2	0.4
Hale	8	D	D	D	11	820	D	D	12	148	3.1	0.8
Henry	22	D	D	D	17	826	425.8	25.3	25	252	7.4	1.8
Houston	236	D	D	D	126	5 562	1 310.7	201.1	226	4 442	177.2	48.6
Jackson	55	D	D	D	70	5 707	1 525.4	206.5	77	1 068	39.3	10.6
Jefferson	1 946	D	D	D	674	28 833	10 261.0	1 331.4	1 271	26 530	1 268.2	354.2
Lamar	18	51	4.3	1.5	17	1 113	234.9	49.9	19	153	6.0	1.4
Lauderdale	176	D	D	D	91	3 150	1 083.7	116.1	150	3 568	136.6	40.1
Lawrence	35	112	7.7	2.4	24	1 411	D	D	42	543	22.7	6.0
Lee	189	D	D	D	123	D	D	D	271	5 515	201.2	55.8
Limestone	98	666	92.9	34.5	72	4 272	947.3	173.9	96	1 548	68.1	17.2
Lowndes	8	58	9.4	3.3	13	1 103	1 156.9	63.8	6	14	0.6	0.1
Macon	15	D	D	D	NA	NA	NA	NA	22	436	19.4	5.5
Madison	1 276	31 697	5 668.6	2 209.6	319	23 499	8 650.7	1 129.7	643	13 989	596.3	167.6
Marengo	25	88	11.0	2.2	25	1 886	542.1	74.7	41	422	16.7	3.9
Marion	23	75	5.0	1.5	48	3 474	794.5	114.3	46	491	19.1	5.3
Marshall	133	623	54.6	17.9	125	10 842	3 029.5	334.0	169	2 473	103.5	27.5
Mobile	901	D	D	D	385	16 776	12 407.2	840.9	652	13 252	562.4	155.0
Monroe	25	62	4.4	1.3	28	2 329	1 251.9	119.7	32	349	14.8	3.3
Montgomery	662	6 385	890.0	341.8	199	12 828	7 956.6	567.2	473	9 754	402.9	112.8
Morgan	227	1 451	116.6	48.1	199	12 152	D	D	207	3 756	154.7	41.4
Perry	6	D	D	D	NA	NA	NA	NA	11	58	2.6	0.5
Pickens	18	42	2.5	0.7	22	630	107.6	18.7	16	138	6.3	1.7
Pike	34	173	14.6	4.0	32	D	D	D	63	1 197	45.7	11.8
Randolph	20	78	4.2	1.6	21	1 537	401.7	49.3	30	219	9.2	2.4
Russell	48	D	D	D	37	D	D	D	84	1 428	56.4	14.7
St. Clair	93	475	40.8	16.1	76	2 830	985.4	102.2	109	1 641	70.3	18.8
Shelby	570	D	D	D	191	6 672	1 723.0	272.3	334	6 596	301.9	83.6
Sumter	12	32	2.0	0.5	NA	NA	NA	NA	20	262	8.2	2.1
Talladega	72	310	21.8	8.1	88	9 749	9 054.2	514.4	111	1 775	67.1	17.7
Tallapoosa	57	209	24.5	9.2	39	1 473	D	39.7	65	843	28.2	7.9
Tuscaloosa	356	2 555	223.1	83.7	154	13 216	10 852.5	715.5	377	8 183	327.4	87.4
Walker	98	558	46.1	21.7	59	1 679	314.8	52.3	102	1 565	73.9	17.9

1. Establishment subject to federal tax.

Table B. States and Counties — **Health Care and Social Assistance, Other Services, Nonemployer Businesses, and Residential Construction**

STATE County	Health care and social assistance, 2007				Other services, 2007				Nonemployer businesses, 2013		Value of residential construction authorized by building permits, 2014	
	Number of establish-ments	Number of employees	Receipts (mil dol)	Annual payroll (mil dol)	Number of establish-ments	Number of employees	Receipts (mil dol)	Annual payroll (mil dol)	Number	Receipts (mil dol)	New Construction ($1,000)	Number of housing units
	159	160	161	162	163	164	165	166	167	168	169	170
UNITED STATES	784 626	16 792 074	1 668 276.8	662 719.9	540 148	3 479 011	405 284.0	99 123.3	23 005 620	1 052 025.3	193 243 022	1 046 363
ALABAMA	10 392	238 070	22 604.9	8 890.1	6 718	40 488	4 154.1	1 050.0	311 578	12 468.3	2 204 675	13 369
Autauga	82	1 059	82.1	29.5	65	D	D	D	2 947	108.5	34 660	131
Baldwin	388	6 647	624.0	230.6	274	1 202	169.0	32.1	16 508	774.3	264 926	1 384
Barbour	59	D	D	D	32	D	D	D	1 546	49.5	1 608	8
Bibb	30	602	33.2	14.3	22	D	D	D	1 126	38.5	3 358	19
Blount	47	805	57.0	24.2	59	241	17.5	4.6	3 563	134.7	421	3
Bullock	17	365	25.3	8.9	9	19	1.4	0.3	470	14.8	94	1
Butler	42	798	63.4	25.1	25	152	6.0	3.6	1 095	38.6	320	2
Calhoun	283	6 307	545.7	206.7	186	944	81.3	22.1	6 352	223.1	14 522	114
Chambers	66	1 070	95.8	34.1	41	D	D	D	2 354	50.8	943	8
Cherokee	30	389	28.4	12.3	19	70	5.4	1.3	1 560	76.5	186	2
Chilton	65	808	53.3	23.4	35	D	D	D	2 719	99.7	6 491	78
Choctaw	27	283	18.8	8.4	20	51	5.8	1.2	809	22.9	0	0
Clarke	58	1 007	72.7	29.6	40	190	17.0	3.5	1 640	57.7	1 556	11
Clay	23	665	34.4	15.6	13	D	D	D	792	31.2	0	0
Cleburne	13	D	D	D	10	60	6.3	1.6	930	33.5	170	1
Coffee	104	D	D	D	62	D	D	D	2 602	96.8	9 956	58
Colbert	140	2 680	261.2	103.9	83	572	69.8	16.2	3 630	131.8	17 330	143
Conecuh	23	371	30.4	11.2	15	30	4.0	0.8	756	23.1	598	3
Coosa	8	D	D	D	6	14	1.6	0.3	367	11.7	0	0
Covington	98	1 692	136.6	49.2	49	224	20.1	5.4	2 201	74.9	1 455	8
Crenshaw	15	D	D	D	15	D	D	D	811	27.0	620	2
Cullman	184	3 542	317.2	123.9	110	515	45.3	12.2	5 549	234.3	10 107	77
Dale	72	D	D	D	57	D	D	D	2 444	82.3	879	17
Dallas	119	2 172	185.6	73.4	64	419	35.7	8.0	2 179	74.1	2 210	17
DeKalb	109	2 260	160.7	62.4	59	206	16.1	4.0	4 679	182.4	5 324	31
Elmore	122	1 880	122.5	48.8	77	D	D	D	4 850	175.8	17 998	259
Escambia	79	1 323	98.7	38.8	59	225	17.1	4.0	2 111	64.9	1 829	26
Etowah	302	6 515	626.7	229.8	121	691	54.0	15.8	6 988	303.1	10 935	79
Fayette	58	896	48.2	21.4	23	D	D	D	1 073	41.2	0	0
Franklin	78	1 317	97.3	37.1	37	135	11.5	3.0	1 863	63.7	1 072	13
Geneva	42	D	D	D	22	D	D	D	1 584	62.5	1 382	8
Greene	9	D	D	D	8	30	1.7	0.5	506	14.7	417	4
Hale	17	D	D	D	7	17	1.2	0.3	762	23.1	1 263	8
Henry	28	D	D	D	18	D	D	D	1 034	35.2	2 306	17
Houston	320	9 099	920.9	365.4	198	1 104	104.3	24.4	6 819	293.6	59 995	311
Jackson	112	D	D	D	43	161	14.7	3.7	3 098	115.4	6 857	39
Jefferson	1 730	54 356	6 502.2	2 422.6	1 192	9 162	1 145.4	295.9	44 987	1 975.0	423 892	2 280
Lamar	21	346	17.8	8.1	15	46	3.6	0.9	932	36.3	0	0
Lauderdale	265	4 604	399.7	147.1	136	821	51.1	15.7	6 576	276.5	7 398	54
Lawrence	40	732	46.9	19.7	32	101	8.3	2.1	1 990	63.9	0	0
Lee	221	6 157	469.5	191.8	152	748	49.7	14.2	9 361	387.5	237 589	943
Limestone	130	1 927	136.8	58.8	75	358	26.2	6.9	5 417	194.0	20 815	140
Lowndes	9	288	25.9	4.6	4	D	D	D	685	22.7	595	5
Macon	27	1 920	130.1	93.4	17	D	D	D	1 166	23.0	255	1
Madison	871	18 475	1 883.4	769.3	494	3 661	593.3	96.2	22 681	883.1	328 681	2 677
Marengo	61	973	71.1	28.3	37	137	9.1	2.0	1 019	30.8	0	0
Marion	72	1 139	95.0	36.9	32	96	7.9	2.2	1 828	70.6	0	0
Marshall	201	3 356	290.8	108.0	107	378	27.1	6.8	6 781	309.0	4 973	28
Mobile	741	23 845	2 160.0	894.7	666	4 681	412.6	116.5	29 500	1 070.8	124 217	746
Monroe	31	725	49.6	21.0	22	76	6.9	1.4	1 265	42.7	0	0
Montgomery	704	16 381	1 747.0	658.7	508	3 504	329.9	96.2	15 129	653.7	107 643	734
Morgan	344	6 131	501.0	200.4	180	1 058	91.4	26.4	7 506	286.4	22 527	136
Perry	18	306	15.5	7.6	4	D	D	D	488	17.6	0	0
Pickens	26	646	40.6	17.4	17	D	D	D	1 073	34.3	474	3
Pike	65	1 086	92.5	34.2	38	D	D	D	1 970	64.9	5 501	44
Randolph	41	720	44.4	19.9	24	70	5.1	1.5	1 388	50.7	0	0
Russell	75	1 653	105.4	40.5	68	342	22.5	7.6	3 523	97.6	45 596	244
St. Clair	94	1 669	120.3	45.2	91	398	35.5	8.3	5 172	191.9	11 773	00
Shelby	392	5 700	522.0	203.0	324	2 137	191.2	61.4	15 634	774.3	167 461	896
Sumter	24	447	27.5	10.7	7	24	1.5	0.4	823	26.8	920	3
Talladega	170	3 016	230.4	90.0	79	365	29.2	8.5	3 988	137.6	5 339	65
Tallapoosa	97	D	D	D	46	204	16.7	4.3	2 478	106.9	3 582	16
Tuscaloosa	396	D	D	D	242	1 742	134.7	38.3	11 107	491.2	201 037	1 375
Walker	174	3 208	273.4	108.2	85	441	37.0	10.5	3 509	140.4	1 602	8

STATE County	Government employment and payroll, 2012: Full-time equivalent employees	Government employment and payroll, 2012: March payroll (dollars)	March payroll (percent of total): Administration, judicial, and legal	March payroll (percent of total): Police and Corrections	March payroll (percent of total): Fire Protection	March payroll (percent of total): Highways and transportation	March payroll (percent of total): Health and Welfare	March payroll (percent of total): Natural resources and utilities	March payroll (percent of total): Education and libraries	Local government finances, 2012: General revenue: Total (mil dol)	General revenue: Intergovernmental (mil dol)	Taxes: Total (mil dol)	Taxes: Per capita[1] (dollars): Total	Taxes: Per capita[1] (dollars): Property
	171	172	173	174	175	176	177	178	179	180	181	182	183	184
UNITED STATES	X	X	X	X	X	X	X	X	X	X	X	X	X	X
ALABAMA	X	X	X	X	X	X	X	X	X	X	X	X	X	X
Autauga	1 582	5 202 816	4.0	9.6	6.8	2.7	1.7	5.0	67.1	125.4	65.8	41.7	751	262
Baldwin	7 374	22 581 577	7.4	8.0	2.9	4.3	20.7	5.6	47.7	640.7	189.9	231.1	1 211	537
Barbour	1 162	3 226 895	2.8	6.5	3.7	2.8	22.4	6.2	54.3	79.4	44.6	19.5	719	241
Bibb	837	2 413 468	3.7	5.9	0.0	3.6	26.0	2.1	58.0	59.5	31.7	7.9	351	147
Blount	1 539	4 659 233	4.8	7.3	1.6	3.1	0.9	5.3	75.6	107.3	70.3	23.0	398	220
Bullock	552	1 468 315	4.4	5.2	0.0	4.7	37.7	0.1	46.6	28.4	20.9	4.8	454	337
Butler	934	2 423 650	4.8	7.9	2.9	6.4	14.6	5.7	55.8	65.7	35.4	23.2	1 142	306
Calhoun	5 708	17 129 463	3.6	6.8	2.8	2.8	32.2	7.0	43.2	507.7	169.3	112.4	958	366
Chambers	1 193	3 265 131	6.9	10.3	3.6	6.5	3.3	9.0	58.5	79.2	43.1	21.6	634	304
Cherokee	997	3 526 515	5.0	5.1	0.1	2.9	16.9	6.0	63.4	50.9	29.6	16.6	640	293
Chilton	1 218	3 862 506	5.9	8.9	0.5	4.3	1.4	6.0	72.4	95.1	55.9	25.1	572	321
Choctaw	383	970 992	9.1	5.8	0.0	6.4	0.0	1.9	74.4	27.8	15.9	7.3	536	470
Clarke	1 107	3 358 366	4.7	9.6	0.0	3.2	12.7	8.4	59.5	70.9	38.1	25.5	1 015	336
Clay	699	1 916 771	2.1	5.9	0.1	5.2	39.3	5.7	40.5	52.0	20.5	9.5	704	493
Cleburne	633	2 123 561	3.8	6.3	0.1	3.4	9.9	5.1	70.2	36.9	24.6	7.3	490	274
Coffee	2 026	5 912 313	3.1	6.9	2.2	3.8	13.7	5.8	63.9	136.4	72.2	40.1	782	349
Colbert	3 178	10 303 212	2.2	5.5	2.5	2.4	36.7	11.6	37.7	258.1	88.3	46.3	850	424
Conecuh	486	1 319 565	6.8	10.8	0.0	6.5	1.3	10.9	62.6	33.3	20.8	7.6	588	279
Coosa	265	695 770	2.4	13.6	0.0	6.3	0.6	1.2	75.2	21.9	15.4	4.4	397	290
Covington	1 587	4 552 054	7.2	6.3	1.6	5.3	1.1	22.2	53.7	120.6	57.2	30.6	805	249
Crenshaw	472	1 600 404	4.4	5.5	0.0	6.3	0.9	7.4	75.5	27.8	16.6	6.6	471	206
Cullman	3 911	11 764 023	3.0	6.7	1.9	3.3	31.4	8.4	43.9	194.4	96.2	54.4	676	276
Dale	1 600	4 956 908	3.8	7.4	2.7	2.6	26.4	5.1	50.9	131.8	55.8	34.7	688	250
Dallas	1 746	4 733 521	4.8	9.2	3.2	2.5	1.5	6.4	67.0	113.7	68.6	33.9	791	371
DeKalb	2 193	6 908 865	4.2	8.4	2.2	3.5	4.3	10.3	66.0	169.1	97.9	42.8	602	293
Elmore	2 265	6 703 799	3.5	10.3	1.2	3.1	0.8	4.6	75.0	153.6	86.5	43.7	541	251
Escambia	1 604	4 378 782	4.5	9.0	2.3	4.4	15.2	2.8	58.4	116.3	47.9	27.6	726	330
Etowah	3 980	11 900 349	4.3	10.5	6.2	3.7	6.9	8.4	56.6	284.1	137.1	99.7	955	293
Fayette	541	1 471 267	6.2	6.8	1.8	7.2	2.2	10.0	65.4	50.8	33.7	12.6	742	260
Franklin	1 331	3 838 038	4.8	7.1	2.1	3.7	3.3	12.5	65.2	84.8	50.1	15.5	488	176
Geneva	1 102	3 351 087	3.2	5.0	0.1	3.9	27.3	3.4	56.6	106.8	34.4	20.2	751	302
Greene	456	1 298 955	3.6	6.0	0.0	5.0	31.6	4.7	48.5	30.5	13.4	5.5	620	359
Hale	605	1 537 609	4.7	7.4	0.0	3.8	23.7	1.0	59.3	51.7	27.1	9.4	613	301
Henry	549	1 493 829	6.9	8.0	2.0	5.6	2.8	4.3	68.4	33.3	19.9	9.4	546	269
Houston	5 714	19 682 365	3.7	6.6	3.6	2.3	45.1	5.9	30.9	590.6	124.8	126.4	1 222	429
Jackson	2 490	8 016 220	3.3	6.6	1.8	3.9	29.0	8.0	46.4	205.9	91.7	40.1	756	359
Jefferson	27 700	103 543 070	5.4	12.8	7.2	3.5	7.3	9.3	49.8	2 895.7	935.7	1 334.8	2 022	856
Lamar	454	1 337 464	7.1	9.0	0.8	4.9	2.6	9.6	64.8	31.4	20.5	6.5	457	274
Lauderdale	2 704	9 293 198	4.1	8.4	4.2	4.1	2.8	16.3	57.5	230.1	103.9	91.1	984	414
Lawrence	1 156	3 399 543	4.4	7.8	0.4	3.4	14.2	4.4	64.8	74.9	46.2	11.0	324	217
Lee	6 506	23 295 526	2.9	5.8	2.5	1.6	40.7	4.1	41.4	640.1	158.1	164.2	1 115	594
Limestone	2 694	10 450 795	2.4	6.2	1.4	1.9	21.8	7.7	57.3	213.7	86.7	39.0	445	236
Lowndes	502	1 360 565	8.1	8.4	0.0	4.3	0.5	2.4	75.6	38.0	25.6	9.0	830	443
Macon	731	2 048 937	7.8	7.7	2.4	4.5	1.6	16.0	58.1	49.6	28.9	15.3	746	268
Madison	17 330	64 421 407	3.9	6.3	3.3	2.9	40.3	7.4	32.3	1 978.9	813.4	389.2	1 134	579
Marengo	1 007	2 884 299	5.2	7.8	3.8	5.1	8.0	6.1	61.8	87.7	38.7	15.2	746	331
Marion	992	2 975 248	4.1	7.5	1.3	5.2	1.2	15.9	64.8	75.9	39.2	22.6	745	282
Marshall	4 582	15 491 666	2.4	5.3	2.4	1.7	30.3	11.3	46.0	395.1	144.9	75.8	799	378
Mobile	15 334	47 151 677	5.5	11.5	5.1	4.9	9.2	7.3	53.7	1 405.0	626.1	561.4	1 356	491
Monroe	1 069	3 209 902	3.2	6.5	1.2	3.7	34.3	2.7	48.2	82.1	40.2	13.0	573	337
Montgomery	8 484	27 145 960	5.0	15.4	8.4	3.3	4.4	0.6	49.6	1 098.6	290.3	265.5	1 154	360
Morgan	4 927	17 209 848	3.0	7.3	3.3	2.5	22.7	9.2	50.8	514.7	208.9	123.2	1 023	501
Perry	634	1 533 195	4.2	5.7	0.1	9.3	22.6	2.7	54.6	35.7	28.0	5.6	546	240
Pickens	699	1 770 074	5.4	8.5	0.0	6.6	2.9	6.6	68.1	65.0	32.5	7.6	389	243
Pike	1 061	3 438 644	6.1	11.4	3.5	4.1	4.1	13.7	55.5	103.3	44.5	21.4	644	263
Randolph	771	2 493 832	3.6	8.3	0.1	4.4	13.3	1.8	67.8	67.1	30.1	11.3	500	257
Russell	2 491	7 257 682	19.9	8.4	3.1	2.7	1.7	7.6	53.3	148.3	81.2	49.2	851	413
St. Clair	2 191	7 157 617	7.3	9.7	4.9	3.2	0.1	3.1	71.1	184.8	107.5	55.3	649	287
Shelby	5 778	16 879 679	6.7	14.3	5.9	3.1	2.9	4.8	60.5	441.4	172.8	191.6	954	567
Sumter	560	1 553 057	5.4	7.7	1.9	5.9	1.9	7.7	67.6	34.6	20.5	8.9	664	293
Talladega	3 476	9 539 423	3.6	6.8	2.5	2.7	19.3	8.7	54.0	201.6	106.6	60.5	740	379
Tallapoosa	1 698	5 118 158	4.4	8.1	3.8	2.6	22.1	9.3	47.3	118.2	65.1	34.0	826	434
Tuscaloosa	10 215	37 068 838	3.6	7.2	3.6	3.5	48.2	3.7	29.3	991.4	234.1	212.4	1 070	420
Walker	2 414	6 546 224	3.1	8.7	1.3	3.2	3.4	7.9	70.5	157.6	87.1	48.0	726	246

1. Based on the resident population estimated as of July 1 of the year shown

STATE County	Local government finances, 2012 (cont.)									Government employment, 2013			Presidential election,[2] 2012		
	Direct general expenditure							Debt outstanding					Percent of vote cast:		
			Percent of total for:												
	Total (mil dol)	Per capita[1] (dollars)	Educa-tion	Health and hospitals	Police protec-tion	Public welfare	High-ways	Total (mil dol)	Per capita[1] (dollars)	Federal civilian	Federal military	State and local	Demo-cratic	Republi-can	All other
	185	186	187	188	189	190	191	192	193	194	195	196	197	198	199
UNITED STATES	X	X	X	X	X	X	X	X	X	2 826 000	2 032 000	19 187 000	51.1	47.2	1.7
ALABAMA	X	X	X	X	X	X	X	X	X	54 685	30 557	315 459	38.7	60.3	0.9
Autauga	119.9	2 161	60.8	0.1	7.0	0.5	2.9	149.8	2 699	78	256	2 137	25.8	73.6	0.6
Baldwin	700.0	3 669	34.5	19.2	6.1	0.1	7.7	911.0	4 775	330	898	8 598	23.8	75.3	0.9
Barbour	74.3	2 732	47.4	18.7	6.4	0.0	3.9	37.2	1 369	55	122	1 657	49.0	50.4	0.6
Bibb	57.9	2 564	51.4	26.2	4.4	0.0	4.1	55.2	2 445	83	94	1 211	26.6	72.4	1.0
Blount	108.1	1 870	72.0	0.8	5.8	0.3	6.1	48.6	841	93	266	1 908	14.5	84.0	1.5
Bullock	30.6	2 921	53.3	22.5	3.6	0.7	8.6	14.8	1 416	34	41	682	74.1	25.7	0.2
Butler	60.7	2 987	47.3	9.6	5.4	0.5	9.3	65.0	3 202	38	92	893	43.1	56.5	0.4
Calhoun	517.7	4 414	32.7	36.2	5.9	0.0	3.9	358.0	3 052	3 968	587	8 252	33.2	65.7	1.1
Chambers	78.6	2 308	50.4	1.2	8.3	0.3	7.0	72.0	2 112	49	156	1 334	45.5	53.9	0.6
Cherokee	48.3	1 856	75.1	0.1	4.8	0.0	4.5	60.1	2 309	44	120	1 223	23.7	74.9	1.4
Chilton	96.3	2 198	62.9	0.6	7.0	0.4	5.7	23.3	533	66	202	1 761	20.7	78.5	0.8
Choctaw	28.4	2 080	53.7	0.0	6.0	0.1	13.4	22.9	1 681	27	62	499	46.1	53.5	0.4
Clarke	67.0	2 664	60.9	0.3	7.8	0.2	6.2	111.3	4 422	78	116	1 788	44.0	55.6	0.4
Clay	70.4	5 240	51.0	26.2	4.1	0.1	4.4	26.5	1 971	51	61	870	25.8	73.1	1.1
Cleburne	41.7	2 813	52.6	0.1	4.4	17.0	6.0	35.4	2 387	43	69	763	18.0	80.3	1.7
Coffee	144.1	2 812	62.6	0.4	4.8	0.2	4.8	136.0	2 654	200	234	2 372	25.2	74.1	0.6
Colbert	259.3	4 762	32.1	37.0	3.6	0.2	3.5	178.7	3 282	892	251	4 244	39.1	59.3	1.6
Conecuh	37.1	2 859	59.4	0.0	8.0	0.6	6.4	64.7	4 982	27	60	754	49.4	50.0	0.6
Coosa	22.3	2 029	59.1	0.1	7.7	0.2	19.6	8.9	810	22	50	359	40.9	58.4	0.8
Covington	141.5	3 727	42.0	0.3	6.6	0.1	12.6	930.5	24 517	118	173	1 992	20.5	78.8	0.7
Crenshaw	29.8	2 119	65.1	6.8	9.7	0.0	3.3	16.9	1 199	35	64	563	30.8	68.7	0.5
Cullman	206.4	2 566	52.3	2.1	7.2	1.1	7.3	191.6	2 381	208	370	4 179	16.6	81.8	1.5
Dale	146.4	2 902	56.7	19.7	4.5	0.2	2.5	62.7	1 242	3 139	3 830	2 181	27.3	71.9	0.8
Dallas	143.5	3 347	61.4	0.1	8.3	0.4	3.2	105.2	2 455	172	191	2 646	67.1	32.6	0.3
DeKalb	174.9	2 461	64.2	3.0	8.3	0.4	7.1	113.8	1 602	159	326	3 141	23.6	74.8	1.7
Elmore	159.9	1 983	65.0	0.8	7.4	0.0	7.2	169.3	2 100	145	350	3 968	24.2	75.1	0.7
Escambia	124.2	3 269	45.2	24.5	6.3	0.4	4.3	40.7	1 071	58	161	4 022	35.4	63.9	0.8
Etowah	278.9	2 672	46.7	1.9	11.2	0.2	4.8	218.9	2 097	327	472	5 211	30.2	68.4	1.4
Fayette	33.4	1 968	66.1	1.2	2.5	0.0	10.0	12.4	731	37	77	1 245	25.1	73.9	1.0
Franklin	94.1	2 961	58.5	0.1	4.4	0.0	6.5	55.6	1 752	86	145	1 807	29.7	68.8	1.5
Geneva	79.5	2 953	44.2	28.4	5.0	0.2	5.9	34.0	1 262	57	123	1 435	18.3	80.8	0.9
Greene	31.5	3 551	49.2	28.3	3.2	0.5	3.8	17.4	1 960	23	40	607	83.1	16.5	0.4
Hale	48.8	3 170	51.5	17.8	6.3	0.0	12.3	13.5	876	47	70	845	60.7	39.0	0.4
Henry	34.2	1 979	64.6	0.0	6.7	0.7	13.2	44.3	2 565	43	79	641	34.9	64.6	0.5
Houston	591.0	5 716	25.3	46.6	3.9	0.1	3.3	407.2	3 938	313	507	8 059	29.3	70.1	0.6
Jackson	209.8	3 957	51.6	23.7	4.0	0.3	4.2	118.1	2 227	402	243	3 096	30.5	67.5	2.0
Jefferson	2 885.7	4 372	40.1	5.3	6.6	0.0	4.0	7 596.1	11 509	7 790	3 387	50 445	52.2	47.1	0.8
Lamar	32.3	2 262	61.7	0.0	6.4	0.4	4.7	29.7	2 081	36	65	596	22.8	76.6	0.6
Lauderdale	225.0	2 431	58.9	0.1	6.2	0.1	6.7	265.7	2 871	283	424	4 759	35.0	63.2	1.9
Lawrence	78.1	2 309	60.0	13.5	6.3	0.5	6.4	41.6	1 229	89	155	1 335	35.2	63.2	1.6
Lee	638.8	4 338	33.9	39.7	4.1	0.0	2.6	782.4	5 313	296	720	17 037	39.6	59.3	1.1
Limestone	276.5	3 155	51.2	23.1	4.8	0.2	3.7	282.8	3 227	1 632	399	5 216	28.4	70.3	1.2
Lowndes	39.8	3 667	69.6	0.0	5.6	0.0	9.7	34.2	3 148	34	49	560	74.9	24.9	0.3
Macon	52.1	2 539	58.2	0.3	5.4	0.0	2.5	68.8	3 349	894	95	2 165	86.9	12.8	0.3
Madison	1 830.4	5 335	30.6	39.1	3.7	0.0	2.5	1 931.7	5 631	18 944	2 375	24 320	41.9	56.9	1.2
Marengo	94.5	4 633	40.6	31.0	3.2	0.0	2.7	33.7	1 651	55	109	1 560	51.7	48.1	0.3
Marion	72.1	2 379	61.7	0.0	6.4	0.0	5.4	62.6	2 065	73	137	1 506	21.0	77.2	1.8
Marshall	395.8	4 177	40.0	33.4	5.5	0.2	1.9	306.5	3 234	250	435	5 817	21.2	77.6	1.2
Mobile	1 433.8	3 464	41.2	6.0	6.8	0.5	8.3	1 386.2	3 349	2 634	2 829	23 568	45.3	54.0	0.7
Monroe	83.9	3 713	40.0	33.9	5.1	0.1	8.3	7.6	334	53	102	1 400	44.7	54.9	0.5
Montgomery	1 084.1	4 711	25.4	43.2	5.2	0.3	2.1	1 050.3	4 564	6 283	3 699	26 313	59.4	40.1	0.5
Morgan	592.0	4 917	54.2	17.4	4.2	0.3	2.9	883.2	7 336	318	549	6 976	27.5	71.3	1.3
Perry	37.4	3 675	46.2	24.5	3.6	0.4	7.2	37.3	3 663	25	81	539	72.4	27.3	0.4
Pickens	72.8	3 752	37.4	29.1	3.2	0.1	5.3	52.7	2 716	50	88	814	45.6	54.0	0.4
Pike	119.3	3 594	39.5	22.5	7.4	0.0	3.2	140.0	4 218	88	149	2 997	42.1	57.4	0.5
Randolph	70.0	3 087	46.0	32.1	4.6	0.0	1.9	57.2	2 521	51	104	1 085	29.5	69.1	1.4
Russell	149.9	2 593	59.3	0.1	5.7	0.1	3.0	302.5	5 233	94	274	2 786	53.3	46.0	0.7
St. Clair	188.6	2 213	57.2	6.9	10.0	0.1	4.2	290.2	3 404	106	391	2 831	17.9	81.1	1.0
Shelby	463.8	2 308	61.2	1.7	10.9	0.2	3.8	773.4	3 840	300	905	8 059	22.8	76.2	1.1
Sumter	37.0	2 754	54.6	0.8	7.3	0.1	13.6	25.2	1 879	41	58	1 342	75.0	24.7	0.4
Talladega	213.4	2 610	55.2	4.8	7.5	0.4	5.6	225.8	2 762	699	362	4 704	40.3	58.8	0.9
Tallapoosa	123.8	3 008	45.4	17.8	6.1	0.0	4.1	118.8	2 886	89	188	1 985	31.4	67.9	0.7
Tuscaloosa	994.6	5 008	29.0	43.5	4.8	0.0	4.7	615.9	3 101	1 565	896	21 861	41.6	57.5	0.9
Walker	158.5	2 394	61.5	0.1	5.4	0.0	8.0	116.9	1 765	187	303	3 169	25.9	72.3	1.8

1. Based on the resident population estimated as of July 1 of the year shown. 2.

STATE/ County code	CBSA code[1]	County type[2]	STATE County	Land area,[3] (sq km) 2010	Population, 2014 Total persons 2014	Population, 2014 Rank	Population, 2014 Per square kilometer	Race alone or in combination, not Hispanic or Latino (percent) White	Black	American Indian, Alaska Native	Asian and Pacific Islander	Percent Hispanic or Latino[4]	Age (percent) Under 5 years	5 to 17 years	18 to 24 years	25 to 34 years	35 to 44 years	45 to 54 years
				1	2	3	4	5	6	7	8	9	10	11	12	13	14	15
			ALABAMA—Cont'd															
01 129	...	8	Washington	2 798	16 834	1 993	6.0	66.5	24.9	8.2	0.4	1.3	5.1	17.8	8.8	11.0	12.0	14.6
01 131	...	8	Wilcox	2 301	11 098	2 349	4.8	28.0	71.1	0.4	0.2	0.9	5.8	19.4	9.1	10.4	11.2	12.7
01 133	...	6	Winston	1 588	24 150	1 640	15.2	95.5	1.2	1.3	0.5	2.7	4.9	16.1	7.6	10.4	12.3	15.0
02 000	...	X	ALASKA	1 477 953	736 732	X	0.5	68.2	4.8	18.4	8.9	6.6	7.5	18.1	11.2	15.6	12.3	13.7
02 013	...	9	Aleutians East	18 083	3 360	2 949	0.2	15.7	8.0	23.3	42.9	12.5	3.0	7.7	9.0	15.5	19.0	24.5
02 016	...	7	Aleutians West	11 371	5 750	2 783	0.5	32.6	7.7	15.1	34.5	14.1	3.3	9.4	9.1	17.1	19.0	21.8
02 020	11260	2	Anchorage	4 415	301 010	223	68.2	66.5	7.6	11.4	13.6	8.6	7.4	17.7	11.9	16.9	12.6	13.3
02 050	...	7	Bethel	105 076	17 868	1 921	0.2	15.0	1.1	84.5	1.9	1.6	10.9	25.0	11.3	14.7	10.2	12.1
02 060	...	9	Bristol Bay	1 305	957	3 109	0.7	60.4	1.8	45.7	4.7	3.9	5.7	15.7	8.9	12.2	12.4	19.1
02 068	...	8	Denali	33 026	1 921	3 059	0.1	90.4	2.1	6.8	2.0	2.9	5.2	15.5	5.6	13.0	16.4	17.9
02 070	...	9	Dillingham	48 093	4 988	2 837	0.1	25.9	1.2	77.1	2.3	2.4	10.9	21.5	11.5	13.3	9.6	12.8
02 090	21820	3	Fairbanks North Star	19 006	99 357	593	5.2	77.0	6.3	10.2	5.1	7.7	7.9	16.8	14.8	18.1	12.0	11.7
02 100	...	9	Haines	6 005	2 566	3 004	0.4	86.2	1.3	14.9	1.9	2.7	5.1	14.6	6.2	9.7	11.7	16.5
02 105	...		Hoonah-Angoon	19 489	2 082	3 042	0.1	57.3	1.5	44.3	2.2	4.5	6.0	13.7	7.5	10.7	10.2	16.1
02 110	27940	5	Juneau	6 998	32 406	1 377	4.6	73.2	2.2	17.7	10.3	6.2	6.2	16.4	9.5	15.0	13.1	15.4
02 122	...	7	Kenai Peninsula	41 635	57 477	888	1.4	86.4	1.2	11.2	2.8	3.8	6.4	16.6	8.9	12.2	11.5	14.4
02 130	28540	7	Ketchikan Gateway	12 583	13 787	2 187	1.1	72.6	1.4	20.2	9.7	5.0	6.6	16.2	9.2	13.4	11.9	15.4
02 150	...	7	Kodiak Island	16 963	13 986	2 170	0.8	56.7	1.7	16.9	22.8	8.4	7.9	18.9	10.7	16.3	12.3	14.2
02 164	...	9	Lake and Peninsula	61 258	1 631	3 076	0.0	31.7	2.0	69.8	2.9	3.2	8.9	20.6	11.0	15.1	9.7	14.1
02 170	11260	2	Matanuska-Susitna	63 734	97 882	602	1.5	86.8	2.1	10.1	3.3	4.4	7.4	20.3	9.5	13.5	12.9	14.3
02 180	...	7	Nome	59 471	9 817	2 455	0.2	22.7	1.1	78.5	2.2	1.8	11.4	23.5	10.9	14.4	10.7	11.9
02 185	...	7	North Slope	229 720	9 703	2 460	0.0	36.8	2.0	55.5	8.2	3.4	8.3	17.0	9.7	15.9	12.3	18.0
02 188	...	7	Northwest Arctic	92 133	7 717	2 619	0.1	17.8	1.4	83.6	1.8	1.5	11.8	24.0	12.1	15.0	9.7	11.9
02 195	...		Petersburg	8 500	3 160	2 961	0.4	74.5	1.9	21.9	5.0	5.5	6.1	16.5	7.8	11.9	12.0	15.4
02 198	...		Prince of Wales-Hyder	10 160	6 396	2 725	0.6	55.7	1.1	45.9	3.2	2.8	7.1	17.9	7.8	12.3	11.7	16.0
02 220	...	7	Sitka	7 434	8 900	2 523	1.2	71.1	1.8	22.0	8.3	5.8	6.6	16.3	8.2	14.3	13.2	13.8
02 230	...		Skagway	1 172	1 036	3 107	0.9	90.1	0.9	6.7	1.8	4.2	5.2	7.5	7.3	18.9	16.8	14.6
02 240	...	8	Southeast Fairbanks	64 151	6 931	2 683	0.1	80.7	2.0	14.8	2.5	4.9	7.9	17.6	9.2	13.4	12.1	13.7
02 261	...	9	Valdez-Cordova	88 681	9 488	2 470	0.1	76.8	1.3	18.4	6.1	4.4	6.9	18.0	8.3	13.6	11.6	16.2
02 270	...	9	Wade Hampton	44 241	8 010	2 597	0.2	6.8	0.6	93.6	0.8	0.7	14.0	28.1	12.5	13.9	8.8	10.4
02 275	...		Wrangell	6 582	2 364	3 015	0.4	79.7	1.7	23.0	3.5	1.8	4.7	16.6	7.9	9.8	8.8	16.1
02 282	...	9	Yakutat	19 812	635	3 132	0.0	50.6	3.9	47.4	11.2	3.2	5.8	14.2	8.9	11.8	14.3	17.1
02 290	...	8	Yukon-Koyukuk	376 856	5 547	2 798	0.0	26.8	1.1	74.5	1.3	1.7	8.8	19.0	9.1	12.8	9.5	13.2
04 000	...	X	ARIZONA	294 207	6 731 484	X	22.9	58.4	4.7	4.6	4.0	30.2	6.5	17.9	10.1	13.3	12.5	12.6
04 001	...	6	Apache	29 001	71 828	753	2.5	20.4	1.3	72.9	0.8	6.3	7.8	21.8	10.6	11.5	10.9	12.8
04 003	43420	4	Cochise	15 969	127 448	485	8.0	58.9	4.8	1.6	3.5	33.8	6.4	16.1	9.5	12.7	10.7	12.2
04 005	22380	3	Coconino	48 223	137 682	459	2.9	56.9	1.9	27.0	2.7	13.8	6.2	16.1	19.6	13.3	10.9	11.8
04 007	37740	4	Gila	12 323	53 119	939	4.3	64.8	0.8	16.0	1.0	18.4	5.7	14.7	7.3	9.1	8.7	12.5
04 009	40940	6	Graham	11 972	37 957	1 222	3.2	53.2	2.1	13.3	1.1	31.6	8.0	20.4	11.3	14.5	12.2	11.2
04 011	...	7	Greenlee	4 774	9 346	2 482	2.0	48.7	1.4	2.9	1.0	47.8	7.0	21.2	8.5	14.8	12.4	12.3
04 012	...	6	La Paz	11 654	20 231	1 823	1.7	62.1	1.2	12.7	1.1	24.9	4.4	13.0	6.3	8.3	7.4	10.8
04 013	38060	1	Maricopa	23 828	4 087 191	4	171.5	59.3	5.8	2.1	4.9	30.0	6.8	18.6	9.7	14.2	13.4	13.0
04 015	29420	4	Mohave	34 476	203 361	315	5.9	79.9	1.5	2.9	1.9	15.5	4.8	14.3	6.9	9.7	9.6	12.9
04 017	43320	4	Navajo	25 771	108 101	556	4.2	43.8	1.6	44.2	1.0	11.0	7.4	20.9	9.6	11.4	10.7	12.4
04 019	46060	2	Pima	23 794	1 004 516	42	42.2	55.5	4.0	3.1	3.7	35.6	6.0	16.1	12.1	12.3	11.4	12.2
04 021	38060	1	Pinal	13 897	401 918	170	28.9	59.8	5.0	5.5	2.7	28.9	6.4	18.6	8.0	13.6	13.3	11.5
04 023	35700	4	Santa Cruz	3 204	46 695	1 031	14.6	16.2	0.5	0.5	0.6	81.9	7.4	21.5	9.7	10.3	11.1	12.4
04 025	39140	3	Yavapai	21 040	218 844	291	10.4	82.8	1.1	2.3	1.6	13.9	4.2	13.5	6.8	8.9	9.0	12.6
04 027	49740	3	Yuma	14 281	203 247	316	14.2	34.5	2.3	1.5	1.8	60.9	7.5	19.2	11.9	13.0	10.9	11.1
05 000	...	X	ARKANSAS	134 771	2 966 369	X	22.0	75.2	16.0	1.6	2.0	6.9	6.5	17.5	9.7	13.0	12.3	13.2
05 001	...	6	Arkansas	2 561	18 594	1 887	7.3	71.5	25.2	0.8	1.1	2.8	6.6	16.5	8.3	11.5	12.1	13.5
05 003	...	7	Ashley	2 397	20 948	1 778	8.7	68.8	25.9	0.8	0.4	5.2	6.5	17.1	8.4	10.5	12.4	13.9
05 005	34260	7	Baxter	1 436	40 857	1 157	28.5	96.5	0.5	1.6	0.8	2.0	4.5	13.6	5.9	8.9	9.6	12.5
05 007	22220	2	Benton	2 195	242 321	275	110.4	77.2	2.1	2.7	4.2	16.0	7.4	19.9	8.0	14.0	14.1	12.0
05 009	25460	7	Boone	1 529	37 196	1 245	24.3	96.1	0.6	2.0	0.7	2.3	5.9	16.8	8.1	11.1	11.9	13.7
05 011	...	6	Bradley	1 682	11 148	2 343	6.6	58.0	27.5	1.0	0.4	14.4	6.7	16.7	7.8	11.9	11.9	13.4
05 013	15780	9	Calhoun	1 628	5 202	2 824	3.2	74.2	22.0	0.9	0.6	3.7	4.7	13.1	9.6	10.2	11.6	16.2
05 015	...	6	Carroll	1 632	27 744	1 506	17.0	82.9	0.8	2.2	1.2	14.5	5.6	16.9	7.0	10.7	10.8	13.2
05 017	...	7	Chicot	1 669	11 180	2 341	6.7	40.1	54.2	0.6	0.6	5.3	6.9	16.3	8.1	11.1	10.9	13.4
05 019	11660	7	Clark	2 243	22 576	1 705	10.1	70.8	24.2	1.0	0.9	4.4	5.1	14.4	21.8	10.4	10.1	11.5
05 021	...	7	Clay	1 656	15 118	2 091	9.1	97.1	0.9	1.1	0.3	1.7	4.8	16.4	8.2	10.1	11.7	14.3
05 023	...	6	Cleburne	1 434	25 634	1 578	17.9	96.3	0.7	1.5	0.4	2.3	5.0	14.7	6.6	9.9	10.4	14.0

1. CBSA = Core Based Statistical Area. See Appendix A for explanation. See Appendix B for list of metropolitan areas with component counties. 2. County type code from the Economic Research Service of USDA Rural-Urban Continuum Codes. See Appendix A for definition. 3. Dry land or land partially or temporarily covered by water. 4. May be of any race.

STATE County	Population, 2013 (cont.): Age (percent) (cont.): 55 to 64 years	65 to 74 years	75 years and over	Percent female	Population change and components of change, 2000–2014: Total persons: 2000	2010	Percent change: 2000–2010	2010–2014	Components of change, 2010–2014: Births	Deaths	Net migration	Households, 2009–2013: Number	Persons per house-hold	Percent: Family house-holds	Female family house-holder[1]	One per-son
	16	17	18	19	20	21	22	23	24	25	26	27	28	29	30	31
ALABAMA—Cont'd																
Washington	14.3	9.8	6.7	51.2	18 097	17 581	-2.9	-4.3	674	798	-615	6 620	2.59	73.0	13.1	24.1
Wilcox	14.3	9.7	7.3	52.3	13 183	11 670	-11.5	-4.9	587	627	-549	3 866	2.90	66.5	27.5	32.5
Winston	14.2	11.9	7.7	51.0	24 843	24 484	-1.4	-1.4	1 038	1 281	-77	9 489	2.52	69.1	11.2	28.8
ALASKA	12.6	6.0	3.0	47.6	626 932	710 231	13.3	3.7	47 988	17 081	-4 700	251 899	2.75	67.2	11.4	25.4
Aleutians East	14.4	4.6	2.4	32.6	2 697	3 141	16.5	7.0	72	20	163	435	2.46	64.1	15.9	28.0
Aleutians West	15.3	4.1	0.9	32.3	5 465	5 561	1.8	3.4	142	36	77	1 033	3.52	60.3	7.5	30.2
Anchorage	11.7	5.5	2.9	48.6	260 283	291 826	12.1	3.1	19 855	6 717	-3 898	105 208	2.73	66.5	12.3	25.3
Bethel	9.4	4.2	2.2	48.3	16 006	17 013	6.3	5.0	1 851	513	-482	4 358	3.90	74.0	14.4	17.9
Bristol Bay	16.5	6.1	3.4	44.6	1 258	997	-20.7	-4.0	51	32	-62	384	2.42	68.0	8.1	25.8
Denali	17.7	6.4	2.2	45.3	1 893	1 826	-3.5	5.2	79	30	31	716	2.26	57.8	2.4	36.2
Dillingham	12.4	5.2	2.8	48.1	4 922	4 847	-1.5	2.9	445	185	-127	1 339	3.59	65.3	15.0	29.6
Fairbanks North Star	11.2	5.1	2.4	46.2	82 840	97 581	17.8	1.8	6 996	1 907	-3 422	35 588	2.67	64.3	9.9	27.3
Haines	20.4	10.6	5.3	49.8	2 392	2 508	4.8	2.3	91	72	34	1 245	2.01	54.1	9.6	41.8
Hoonah-Angoon	20.3	10.8	4.7	46.9	0	2 150	NA	-3.1	92	48	-121	930	2.23	62.2	9.5	31.7
Juneau	14.5	6.6	3.3	48.9	30 711	31 275	1.8	3.6	1 671	719	195	12 099	2.58	66.2	11.7	25.1
Kenai Peninsula	16.5	9.1	4.4	47.6	49 691	55 400	11.5	3.7	3 046	1 658	707	21 720	2.50	66.7	8.9	27.8
Ketchikan Gateway	15.4	7.6	4.3	47.9	14 070	13 477	-4.2	2.3	768	351	-98	5 295	2.50	63.1	11.0	29.6
Kodiak Island	12.0	5.5	2.3	46.1	13 913	13 592	-2.3	2.8	937	235	-333	4 501	2.97	75.6	10.3	20.6
Lake and Peninsula	11.7	6.3	2.5	46.8	1 823	1 631	-10.5	-0.2	127	49	-86	508	2.83	75.0	21.1	20.3
Matanuska-Susitna	13.0	6.2	2.9	48.0	59 322	88 995	50.0	10.0	5 683	2 170	5 290	31 123	2.89	72.1	9.4	22.0
Nome	10.0	4.6	2.5	47.3	9 196	9 492	3.2	3.4	993	372	-341	2 797	3.37	74.3	19.3	21.0
North Slope	14.2	3.3	1.4	37.9	7 385	9 430	27.7	2.9	752	187	-282	1 990	3.48	72.0	24.3	24.1
Northwest Arctic	8.9	4.1	2.5	46.0	7 208	7 523	4.4	2.6	799	210	-384	1 828	4.00	80.1	21.6	15.0
Petersburg	17.4	8.9	4.1	48.2	0	3 815	NA	-1.5	174	79	-140	1 643	2.20	58.1	6.6	32.1
Prince of Wales-Hyder	16.4	7.6	3.2	45.2	0	5 559	NA	3.6	336	164	45	2 240	2.49	64.1	12.1	29.9
Sitka	14.8	7.2	5.7	49.3	8 835	8 881	0.5	0.2	449	252	-185	3 554	2.42	64.9	9.3	28.1
Skagway	19.1	7.6	2.9	47.2	0	968	NA	7.0	40	19	47	412	2.23	55.3	6.1	28.9
Southeast Fairbanks	14.6	7.8	3.6	44.3	6 174	7 029	13.8	-1.4	470	167	-412	2 326	2.84	67.2	7.1	29.1
Valdez-Cordova	15.8	6.8	2.7	46.9	10 195	9 636	-5.5	-1.5	548	209	-514	3 424	2.73	75.1	9.2	19.6
Wade Hampton	7.2	3.2	1.9	47.3	7 028	7 459	6.1	7.4	1 012	327	-128	1 744	4.39	83.2	26.3	13.7
Wrangell	18.8	10.5	6.8	48.5	0	2 369	NA	0.0	103	79	-12	1 149	2.01	56.2	11.5	36.6
Yakutat	16.0	7.3	4.5	43.8	808	662	-18.1	-4.1	31	10	-51	254	2.15	63.4	11.8	34.3
Yukon-Koyukuk	14.8	7.7	5.1	46.0	6 551	5 588	-14.7	-0.7	375	264	-211	2 056	2.72	59.4	16.5	33.3
ARIZONA	11.7	8.9	6.5	50.3	5 130 632	6 392 017	24.6	5.3	367 725	210 702	172 848	2 370 289	2.67	65.9	12.6	27.1
Apache	11.6	7.8	5.1	50.5	69 423	71 518	3.0	0.4	4 371	2 397	-1 608	19 055	3.70	68.2	21.3	28.4
Cochise	13.3	11.2	7.9	48.9	117 755	131 346	11.5	-3.0	7 194	5 154	-5 955	49 174	2.47	66.3	12.0	28.6
Coconino	11.8	6.6	3.7	50.6	116 320	134 421	15.6	2.4	7 353	3 135	-1 134	46 198	2.74	64.6	13.6	24.3
Gila	16.2	15.4	10.4	50.4	51 335	53 597	4.4	-0.9	2 650	3 035	-120	20 601	2.54	65.8	11.0	29.5
Graham	10.2	7.0	5.3	46.8	33 489	37 220	11.1	2.0	2 413	1 144	-543	11 031	3.01	73.0	14.1	23.7
Greenlee	11.9	6.5	5.3	47.5	8 547	8 437	-1.3	10.8	501	238	644	3 386	2.54	71.8	14.3	20.5
La Paz	14.3	20.0	15.5	48.9	19 715	20 489	3.9	-1.3	841	907	-166	10 221	1.97	62.1	10.8	32.6
Maricopa	10.9	7.7	5.7	50.5	3 072 149	3 817 117	24.2	7.1	232 032	113 638	146 372	1 411 727	2.72	65.9	12.7	26.8
Mohave	15.8	15.4	10.5	49.7	155 032	200 186	29.1	1.6	8 005	10 954	5 464	80 230	2.43	64.4	9.8	28.0
Navajo	12.7	9.3	5.8	49.9	97 470	107 449	10.2	0.6	7 011	3 941	-2 465	34 343	3.05	72.1	19.0	24.9
Pima	12.6	9.6	7.6	50.8	843 746	980 263	16.2	2.5	51 183	37 412	9 905	384 041	2.50	62.0	12.7	30.8
Pinal	11.6	10.9	6.2	47.8	179 727	375 770	109.1	7.0	20 023	10 588	14 917	123 733	2.87	72.6	11.6	22.3
Santa Cruz	12.3	9.1	6.2	51.9	38 381	47 420	23.6	-1.5	2 876	1 183	-2 485	15 078	3.11	75.4	17.5	21.1
Yavapai	17.6	16.1	11.3	51.2	167 517	211 033	26.0	3.7	7 763	11 180	10 862	91 349	2.28	62.3	8.8	31.1
Yuma	9.6	9.1	7.7	48.9	160 026	195 751	22.3	3.8	13 509	5 796	-840	70 122	2.73	77.6	14.0	18.2
ARKANSAS	12.4	8.8	6.5	50.9	2 673 400	2 915 918	9.1	1.7	162 691	124 578	13 316	1 129 723	2.53	67.5	13.4	27.7
Arkansas	14.5	9.3	7.7	51.6	20 749	19 019	-8.3	-2.2	1 092	979	-499	7 883	2.36	66.0	13.2	30.5
Ashley	13.4	10.5	7.2	51.6	24 209	21 853	-9.7	-4.1	1 144	1 018	-996	8 656	2.47	70.2	14.4	28.4
Baxter	15.4	16.4	13.2	51.9	38 386	41 513	8.1	-1.6	1 442	2 795	734	18 155	2.24	66.8	8.1	28.8
Benton	10.3	7.3	5.5	50.5	153 406	221 339	44.3	9.5	13 911	6 674	13 442	82 150	2.74	74.3	10.0	20.8
Boone	13.3	10.8	8.5	50.7	33 948	36 903	8.7	0.8	1 886	1 777	188	15 086	2.43	71.1	10.7	25.6
Bradley	13.4	9.9	8.2	51.2	12 600	11 508	-8.7	-3.1	596	662	-294	4 789	2.32	67.5	14.6	29.4
Calhoun	15.2	10.8	8.7	48.9	5 744	5 368	-6.5	-3.1	197	214	-169	2 046	2.55	66.3	12.8	31.9
Carroll	15.6	12.2	8.1	50.8	25 357	27 446	8.2	1.1	1 294	1 199	280	11 019	2.47	68.1	9.2	25.9
Chicot	14.5	9.7	9.1	50.8	14 117	11 800	-16.4	-5.3	656	654	-611	4 510	2.41	65.2	18.7	32.7
Clark	11.2	8.5	7.1	52.3	23 546	22 995	-2.3	-1.8	1 021	1 101	-365	8 341	2.41	64.2	13.7	30.2
Clay	13.5	11.8	9.2	50.9	17 609	16 083	-8.7	-6.0	428	1 016	-359	6 814	2.30	64.5	10.8	32.4
Cleburne	14.6	14.0	10.9	50.7	24 046	25 970	8.0	-1.3	1 037	1 534	177	10 286	2.47	69.7	10.1	27.8

1. No spouse present.

STATE County	Persons in group quarters, 2014	Daytime population, 2009–2013: Number	Daytime population, 2009–2013: Employment/residence ratio	Births, 2014: Total	Births, 2014: Rate[1]	Deaths, 2014: Number	Deaths, 2014: Rate[1]	Persons under 65 with no health insurance, 2013: Number	Persons under 65 with no health insurance, 2013: Percent	Medicare, 2014: Eligible for Medicare	Medicare, 2014: Enrolled in Medicare Advantage	Medicare, 2014: Enrolled in a Medicare prescription drug plan	Serious crimes known to police,[2] 2013: Total: Number	Serious crimes known to police,[2] 2013: Total: Rate[3]
	32	33	34	35	36	37	38	39	40	41	42	43	44	45
ALABAMA—Cont'd														
Washington	147	16 810	0.92	159	9.4	200	11.9	2 271	16.2	3 872	489	2 349	247	1 458
Wilcox	108	11 691	1.06	129	11.6	136	12.3	1 579	16.9	3 073	284	2 153	139	1 221
Winston	301	23 610	0.92	247	10.2	302	12.5	3 245	16.8	5 878	743	3 701	299	1 245
ALASKA	28 311	728 417	1.02	11 221	15.2	4 245	5.8	137 170	20.8	78 788	NA	30 990	25 918	3 526
Aleutians East	1 726	3 346	1.08	12	3.6	5	1.5	1 177	40.5	159	NA	41	NA	NA
Aleutians West	2 531	6 310	1.20	38	6.6	5	0.9	1 422	28.0	220	NA	52	NA	NA
Anchorage	8 906	304 878	1.06	4 686	15.6	1 698	5.6	49 274	18.2	31 851	134	12 545	NA	NA
Bethel	361	17 520	1.03	431	24.1	135	7.6	4 645	27.9	1 263	NA	664	NA	NA
Bristol Bay	16	1 211	1.57	11	11.5	7	7.3	194	22.6	118	NA	32	NA	NA
Denali	50	2 460	1.38	18	9.4	4	2.1	371	22.2	199	NA	56	NA	NA
Dillingham	52	4 999	1.04	100	20.0	48	9.6	1 287	27.5	428	NA	209	NA	NA
Fairbanks North Star	5 084	97 890	0.98	1 611	16.2	445	4.5	16 771	18.8	9 216	40	3 176	NA	NA
Haines	0	2 451	0.93	18	7.0	9	3.5	654	29.9	507	NA	203	NA	NA
Hoonah-Angoon	0	2 131	0.99	18	8.6	9	4.3	595	32.5	NA	NA	NA	NA	NA
Juneau	923	32 264	1.02	380	11.7	152	4.7	4 993	17.3	4 147	NA	1 266	NA	NA
Kenai Peninsula	1 576	54 943	0.95	730	12.7	437	7.6	11 194	23.2	9 468	41	4 125	NA	NA
Ketchikan Gateway	277	14 060	1.07	172	12.5	68	4.9	2 742	22.9	2 076	NA	846	NA	NA
Kodiak Island	362	14 088	1.03	227	16.2	55	3.9	3 489	27.0	1 389	NA	527	NA	NA
Lake and Peninsula	37	1 573	1.20	30	18.4	13	8.0	477	31.3	171	NA	77	NA	NA
Matanuska-Susitna	2 153	79 099	0.67	1 354	13.8	509	5.2	17 901	20.9	10 987	66	4 473	NA	NA
Nome	192	9 772	1.02	220	22.4	105	10.7	2 662	29.2	775	NA	322	NA	NA
North Slope	2 653	17 152	2.50	178	18.3	57	5.9	2 389	25.8	474	NA	114	NA	NA
Northwest Arctic	382	7 941	1.13	182	23.6	75	9.7	2 200	30.5	533	NA	297	NA	NA
Petersburg	43	4 041	1.12	46	14.6	27	8.5	789	23.9	NA	NA	NA	NA	NA
Prince of Wales-Hyder	50	5 671	1.00	69	10.8	37	5.8	1 591	30.6	NA	NA	NA	NA	NA
Sitka	252	8 953	1.00	99	11.1	45	5.1	1 915	24.5	1 211	NA	387	NA	NA
Skagway	32	981	0.85	6	5.8	15	14.5	206	23.2	NA	NA	NA	NA	NA
Southeast Fairbanks	370	7 713	1.22	102	14.7	30	4.3	1 675	27.2	1 026	NA	402	NA	NA
Valdez-Cordova	201	10 439	1.17	129	13.6	39	4.1	2 000	22.8	1 236	NA	474	NA	NA
Wade Hampton	18	7 736	1.03	237	29.6	111	13.9	2 210	28.6	507	NA	330	NA	NA
Wrangell	15	2 368	1.00	28	11.8	30	12.7	461	23.1	NA	NA	NA	NA	NA
Yakutat	18	648	1.12	7	11.0	0	0.0	200	34.9	95	NA	38	NA	NA
Yukon-Koyukuk	31	5 779	1.06	82	14.8	75	13.5	1 686	33.5	732	NA	334	NA	NA
ARIZONA	151 403	6 457 238	0.99	86 868	12.9	51 748	7.7	1 093 575	20.0	1 094 469	415 162	369 524	252 842	3 816
Apache	942	71 257	0.96	1 041	14.5	636	8.9	14 874	23.6	10 939	642	5 918	595	804
Cochise	5 017	132 338	1.03	1 622	12.7	1 205	9.5	17 527	17.7	27 654	8 289	7 897	NA	NA
Coconino	10 628	135 072	1.00	1 697	12.3	772	5.6	24 148	21.1	16 970	1 939	8 394	4 620	3 372
Gila	897	54 196	1.05	610	11.5	760	14.3	7 661	19.6	14 802	1 753	7 630	1 676	3 210
Graham	3 321	35 416	0.85	556	14.6	267	7.0	5 239	17.6	5 173	1 665	1 923	473	1 673
Greenlee	37	10 441	1.58	121	12.9	38	4.1	912	11.5	1 183	129	499	236	2 624
La Paz	400	21 063	1.10	215	10.6	245	12.1	3 531	27.4	4 986	739	2 118	548	3 170
Maricopa	58 775	3 928 925	1.02	55 318	13.5	28 067	6.9	675 795	19.8	581 187	245 313	187 879	146 884	3 674
Mohave	4 809	191 276	0.84	1 857	9.1	2 799	13.8	32 388	22.2	56 259	14 887	23 070	7 152	3 571
Navajo	2 248	108 278	1.03	1 635	15.1	960	8.9	19 437	21.5	19 697	3 851	9 620	2 509	2 338
Pima	25 764	986 728	1.00	11 980	11.9	9 087	9.0	151 382	18.8	186 122	85 371	52 860	52 482	5 250
Pinal	25 971	328 910	0.62	4 596	11.4	2 550	6.3	59 008	19.8	65 039	23 093	20 537	9 546	2 470
Santa Cruz	376	47 253	1.01	662	14.2	300	6.4	9 553	24.4	8 020	3 767	2 284	766	1 645
Yavapai	3 750	208 313	0.95	1 821	8.3	2 647	12.1	33 933	22.0	66 641	17 547	26 768	4 700	2 194
Yuma	8 468	197 772	0.98	3 137	15.4	1 415	7.0	38 185	24.0	29 797	6 177	12 127	6 172	3 102
ARKANSAS	82 184	2 933 538	1.00	38 049	12.8	29 231	9.9	458 560	18.8	589 148	114 626	292 191	120 234	4 063
Arkansas	247	20 214	1.15	259	13.9	226	12.2	2 769	18.0	4 111	449	2 565	812	4 304
Ashley	191	21 546	0.99	266	12.7	250	11.9	2 988	17.3	5 056	657	3 358	653	3 047
Baxter	595	42 292	1.07	329	8.1	661	16.2	5 394	18.9	14 406	3 796	6 355	1 228	3 003
Bonton	2 109	232 911	1.05	3 311	13.7	1 566	6.5	36 938	18.0	36 874	11 196	15 093	4 641	1 970
Boone	465	38 630	1.10	463	12.4	436	11.7	5 491	10.0	9 523	2 086	4 377	1 158	3 090
Bradley	221	11 459	1.01	136	12.2	148	13.3	2 167	23.8	2 538	275	1 605	184	1 618
Calhoun	175	4 979	0.85	51	9.8	47	9.0	772	19.1	1 189	153	664	60	1 131
Carroll	230	27 381	0.99	302	10.9	277	10.0	5 618	25.6	6 707	1 836	2 802	734	2 655
Chicot	728	11 522	0.97	145	13.0	165	14.8	1 750	20.5	2 706	340	1 728	382	3 374
Clark	2 627	22 949	1.00	226	10.0	248	11.0	2 928	17.6	4 406	831	2 047	643	2 803
Clay	125	14 318	0.76	127	8.4	209	13.8	2 432	20.2	4 168	474	2 486	289	1 857
Cleburne	339	24 981	0.91	229	8.9	361	14.1	3 893	20.4	7 551	906	4 000	951	3 693

1. Per 1,000 estimated resident population. 2. Data for serious crimes have not been adjusted for underreporting; this may affect comparability between geographic areas and over time.
3. Per 100,000 population estimated by the FBI.

Table B. States and Counties — **Crime, Education, Money Income, and Poverty**

STATE County	Serious crimes known to police, 2013 (cont.)[1] Rate[2] Violent	Serious crimes known to police, 2013 (cont.)[1] Rate[2] Property	Education: School enrollment and attainment, 2009–2013 Enrollment[3] Total	Education: Enrollment[3] Percent private	Education: Attainment[4] (percent) High school graduate or less	Education: Attainment[4] (percent) Bachelor's degree or more	Education: Local government expenditures,[5] 2012–2013 Total current spending (mil dol)	Education: Local government expenditures,[5] 2012–2013 Current spending per student (dollars)	Money income, 2009–2013 Per capita income[6] (dollars)	Money income, 2009–2013 Households Median income (dollars)	Money income, 2009–2013 Households Mean income (dollars)	Money income, 2009–2013 Households Percent with income of $200,000 or more	Income and poverty, 2013 Median household income (dollars)	Income and poverty, 2013 Percent below poverty level All persons	Income and poverty, 2013 Percent below poverty level Children under 18 years	Income and poverty, 2013 Percent below poverty level Children 5 to 17 years in families
	46	47	48	49	50	51	52	53	54	55	56	57	58	59	60	61
ALABAMA—Cont'd																
Washington	277	1 180	3 987	5.8	67.9	9.5	27.8	8 681	20 395	42 156	52 809	1.0	41 115	19.7	29.2	25.9
Wilcox	308	914	2 699	14.5	66.2	11.1	18.6	9 760	13 379	23 642	35 565	0.3	23 184	32.4	50.1	45.9
Winston	158	1 087	5 263	4.9	59.6	10.4	39.5	9 109	18 995	32 900	46 093	1.6	33 578	21.9	33.9	30.2
ALASKA	640	2 885	195 215	11.8	35.7	27.5	2 394.3	18 175	32 651	70 760	87 235	5.6	70 058	10.1	13.6	12.5
Aleutians East	NA	NA	309	12.9	63.1	12.0	9.4	36 588	26 535	61 250	75 766	3.4	56 856	15.2	13.3	11.6
Aleutians West	NA	NA	854	5.3	53.8	13.3	14.1	26 956	31 790	81 853	91 901	6.2	74 088	8.1	7.6	6.9
Anchorage	NA	NA	82 233	13.1	30.7	32.8	764.2	15 555	36 214	77 454	96 935	7.6	76 362	7.7	10.2	9.7
Bethel	NA	NA	5 422	1.7	61.4	11.7	153.8	30 987	18 497	51 689	69 262	4.3	42 876	25.1	30.8	29.1
Bristol Bay	NA	NA	278	9.0	34.3	19.4	20.9	38 998	37 024	79 531	92 359	4.7	65 283	9.5	10.4	9.7
Denali	NA	NA	361	15.8	37.3	28.1	9.7	11 282	35 295	72 500	86 625	5.2	68 103	5.4	3.9	3.5
Dillingham	NA	NA	1 511	3.8	47.7	17.8	33.3	29 748	21 498	54 150	71 258	4.8	47 930	20.9	28.6	28.0
Fairbanks North Star	NA	NA	28 434	11.7	32.3	29.0	275.6	17 384	32 143	69 223	83 145	4.0	67 204	8.8	11.2	10.5
Haines	NA	NA	485	4.3	34.2	30.1	6.8	23 873	31 096	52 866	62 807	0.8	55 295	11.4	17.8	16.3
Hoonah-Angoon	NA	NA	394	5.8	40.9	26.9	9.8	35 466	28 806	49 545	63 204	2.6	42 276	19.2	29.1	26.8
Juneau	NA	NA	8 216	11.7	26.9	36.7	88.5	17 468	37 558	81 490	96 025	6.6	83 642	7.5	9.7	8.1
Kenai Peninsula	NA	NA	12 970	12.5	38.9	23.7	160.9	17 855	31 256	61 793	77 022	3.7	61 629	10.1	13.9	12.8
Ketchikan Gateway	NA	NA	3 049	10.4	39.7	25.4	39.5	17 574	31 589	62 519	78 081	4.2	62 619	10.3	14.3	12.9
Kodiak Island	NA	NA	3 828	11.7	36.6	20.0	51.0	20 007	28 562	68 718	80 343	4.7	64 782	8.5	9.8	9.0
Lake and Peninsula	NA	NA	472	2.5	48.7	15.4	NA	NA	21 616	51 786	64 040	3.0	43 936	17.3	24.4	22.9
Matanuska-Susitna	NA	NA	25 679	15.9	39.1	21.3	267.1	15 274	29 534	71 037	83 413	4.7	72 371	9.4	12.0	10.3
Nome	NA	NA	2 943	1.2	55.9	17.1	79.7	31 129	20 271	49 974	67 207	2.7	46 471	26.3	28.4	26.9
North Slope	NA	NA	2 128	3.2	47.5	14.5	72.7	37 481	46 457	80 761	89 995	5.2	74 174	13.3	16.7	15.4
Northwest Arctic	NA	NA	2 161	2.8	63.5	11.0	61.2	30 582	21 461	61 607	74 256	3.2	54 600	23.3	28.6	27.2
Petersburg	NA	NA	803	5.1	35.1	25.7	12.8	22 590	34 183	63 934	77 905	3.5	58 176	10.7	13.0	11.4
Prince of Wales-Hyder	NA	NA	1 197	7.6	52.1	15.7	30.9	23 553	24 581	46 071	60 647	2.2	48 175	17.4	24.1	22.0
Sitka	NA	NA	2 158	5.2	30.3	34.1	26.6	20 141	32 521	69 405	80 018	3.6	66 038	9.8	12.6	10.9
Skagway	NA	NA	156	7.1	35.1	24.3	2.4	25 880	37 139	71 667	87 987	9.5	63 930	4.2	5.6	6.8
Southeast Fairbanks	NA	NA	1 877	15.8	37.4	23.1	27.0	22 153	29 437	56 801	72 533	3.7	54 922	16.1	21.3	20.7
Valdez-Cordova	NA	NA	2 491	11.4	33.3	23.9	34.0	23 316	32 579	74 878	84 959	4.5	63 541	9.2	10.9	9.6
Wade Hampton	NA	NA	2 670	1.0	69.4	5.4	70.7	28 443	11 210	40 176	48 906	0.6	31 274	34.7	42.4	39.6
Wrangell	NA	NA	467	1.9	48.8	16.7	8.0	20 420	28 474	45 841	58 422	1.4	49 039	13.9	20.7	17.6
Yakutat	NA	NA	157	0.6	37.6	22.7	3.2	34 699	34 317	72 500	76 460	3.5	56 365	16.7	26.8	25.8
Yukon-Koyukuk	NA	NA	1 512	6.5	56.8	9.3	60.6	11 024	19 729	34 710	48 862	0.7	35 114	24.4	30.1	27.5
ARIZONA	416	3 399	1 738 721	10.8	38.8	26.9	6 836.6	7 208	25 358	49 774	66 971	3.5	48 504	18.6	26.6	25.0
Apache	130	674	21 399	5.2	57.6	10.4	84.5	7 250	12 709	31 476	41 303	0.8	30 252	38.7	49.3	46.5
Cochise	NA	NA	32 938	9.3	38.3	22.5	125.5	7 181	23 608	45 755	59 695	2.2	45 294	18.8	29.1	28.1
Coconino	329	3 043	45 319	6.3	34.8	31.1	134.3	7 962	23 382	49 555	65 130	2.8	48 732	23.2	28.1	25.8
Gila	414	2 796	10 407	10.8	46.7	16.1	51.8	7 122	20 792	39 954	49 941	0.7	39 868	22.6	36.5	35.8
Graham	357	1 315	10 531	5.3	49.9	12.3	41.3	6 402	17 168	44 943	54 155	1.0	43 497	21.6	26.8	25.7
Greenlee	556	2 068	2 593	9.8	53.9	11.1	11.9	6 958	20 516	47 992	53 415	0.6	54 673	11.6	13.8	12.3
La Paz	399	2 771	3 106	1.3	58.3	9.3	19.7	8 013	22 200	35 776	44 728	0.7	33 994	23.2	36.9	34.0
Maricopa	405	3 269	1 071 338	11.6	36.8	29.8	4 361.4	7 248	27 256	53 596	72 691	4.4	52 066	17.6	25.1	24.0
Mohave	211	3 360	40 516	12.5	50.9	11.9	131.8	6 291	20 833	39 200	50 929	1.4	38 560	21.3	34.0	30.1
Navajo	352	1 986	30 101	6.3	47.6	14.9	132.0	7 305	16 626	36 927	49 240	1.4	37 182	31.8	43.1	42.4
Pima	431	4 819	267 463	10.9	35.6	29.8	1 033.5	8 133	25 269	45 841	62 852	2.9	43 926	19.3	26.5	23.7
Pinal	190	2 280	92 353	9.7	44.9	18.0	299.1	6 692	20 910	50 027	60 265	1.6	49 887	16.7	24.3	22.5
Santa Cruz	88	1 557	13 482	4.8	55.5	19.8	63.3	6 530	17 664	37 745	52 793	2.1	35 753	22.7	34.7	32.4
Yavapai	240	1 953	43 125	12.7	35.8	24.2	139.2	6 708	25 186	42 987	57 111	1.9	40 486	16.4	24.4	21.6
Yuma	409	2 694	54 050	6.9	53.4	14.3	207.3	5 941	18 840	41 595	53 339	1.6	40 498	19.2	29.4	28.8
ARKANSAS	460	3 603	750 822	10.9	51.3	20.1	4 521.6	9 394	22 170	40 768	55 749	2.1	40 605	19.4	28.3	26.4
Arkansas	424	3 880	4 140	7.0	61.0	12.4	27.4	8 799	23 045	39 633	54 360	1.4	38 497	19.8	29.6	26.8
Ashley	294	2 753	5 025	4.2	60.6	12.2	36.6	9 245	19 761	35 683	48 294	0.8	36 479	21.9	35.4	32.9
Baxter	112	2 890	7 758	8.8	49.2	16.5	44.8	8 710	21 334	35 343	47 411	1.3	36 082	15.6	27.0	24.0
Benton	220	1 750	58 507	13.5	45.3	28.7	353.7	8 996	26 715	54 515	72 645	4.1	56 518	11.7	17.1	16.1
Boone	342	2 749	8 354	8.2	52.8	15.4	53.7	8 462	22 160	38 506	53 140	2.0	38 410	17.2	26.5	24.0
Bradley	273	1 346	2 668	9.1	66.5	10.8	21.7	10 555	19 386	30 409	46 192	2.5	31 733	27.0	39.8	39.4
Calhoun	170	962	995	3.0	68.5	7.4	5.6	10 290	17 763	30 980	41 618	0.3	37 497	18.9	25.9	24.2
Carroll	166	2 489	5 221	11.7	53.5	17.3	35.3	8 946	20 637	36 584	49 539	1.0	34 109	22.2	36.7	35.0
Chicot	415	2 959	2 683	8.1	60.1	12.0	18.9	11 842	16 538	26 201	42 338	1.3	28 006	32.4	46.6	44.7
Clark	275	2 529	7 795	19.0	49.7	21.4	41.5	14 627	17 960	32 721	47 105	1.5	36 517	22.7	31.1	29.4
Clay	263	1 594	3 148	3.0	67.4	9.5	22.4	8 686	18 509	31 502	41 690	0.6	33 488	20.0	29.5	25.9
Cleburne	229	3 464	4 980	6.1	53.4	16.8	30.7	8 955	23 044	40 246	53 648	1.7	41 612	16.3	26.4	24.1

1. Data for serious crimes have not been adjusted for underreporting; this may affect comparability between geographic areas and over time. 2. Per 100,000 population estimated by the FBI.
3. All persons 3 years old and over enrolled in nursery school through college. 4. Persons 25 years old and over. 5. Elementary and secondary education expenditures.
6. Based on population estimated by the American Community Survey, 2009–2013.

STATE County	Personal income, 2013										Earnings, 2013		
			Per capita[1]			Supplements to wages and salaries; employer contributions (mil dol)						Contributions for government social insurance (mil dol)	
	Total (mil dol)	Percent change, 2012–2013	Dollars	Rank	Wages and salaries (mil dol)	Pension and insurance	Government social insurance	Proprietors' income (mil dol)	Dividends, interest, and rent (mil dol)	Personal transfer receipts (mil dol)	Total (mil dol)	From employee and self-employed	From employer
	62	63	64	65	66	67	68	69	70	71	72	73	74
ALABAMA—Cont'd													
Washington	493	1.0	29 208	2 780	199	43	14	39	59	154	294	20	14
Wilcox	327	10.2	28 932	2 815	109	21	8	53	47	133	190	12	8
Winston	666	3.6	27 597	2 926	237	45	20	33	117	233	334	25	20
ALASKA	36 867	1.2	50 150	X	19 957	4 927	1 636	3 476	6 689	5 210	29 997	1 542	1 636
Aleutians East	103	8.1	33 430	2 186	79	23	9	3	12	9	114	6	9
Aleutians West	202	2.7	36 673	1 642	194	48	19	16	29	18	277	14	19
Anchorage	16 482	1.4	54 766	211	9 835	2 190	828	1 973	3 087	2 126	14 825	774	828
Bethel	643	-1.4	36 195	1 715	300	113	23	18	65	165	453	20	23
Bristol Bay	58	4.3	60 210	101	65	18	7	6	11	7	96	5	7
Denali	124	-2.1	66 674	60	97	20	9	1	20	27	128	7	9
Dillingham	233	2.3	46 563	579	115	36	10	17	40	41	177	9	10
Fairbanks North Star	4 551	-1.3	45 313	668	2 499	699	213	285	983	651	3 696	177	213
Haines	221	5.2	85 326	13	40	11	4	111	27	23	167	9	4
Hoonah-Angoon	96	0.9	44 619	720	28	11	2	7	19	22	49	3	2
Juneau	1 863	0.8	57 033	157	987	316	70	46	407	200	1 420	64	70
Kenai Peninsula	2 771	3.4	48 485	453	1 062	281	84	241	547	455	1 669	92	84
Ketchikan Gateway	777	0.9	56 591	173	365	107	30	90	131	118	592	29	30
Kodiak Island	690	0.6	48 804	429	361	102	34	77	148	86	574	28	34
Lake and Peninsula	78	-0.8	47 492	512	33	13	3	1	20	15	50	2	3
Matanuska-Susitna	4 393	1.9	46 149	611	939	261	78	325	565	551	1 603	89	78
Nome	409	0.0	41 310	1 016	192	67	14	16	46	102	289	13	14
North Slope	491	1.2	50 719	338	1 491	212	103	5	64	48	1 810	101	103
Northwest Arctic	309	0.3	40 241	1 146	193	50	14	11	28	84	268	14	14
Petersburg	195	-2.8	51 541	316	64	22	5	39	42	34	130	7	5
Prince of Wales-Hyder	210	6.7	36 354	1 682	93	33	7	15	33	46	148	7	7
Sitka	475	3.4	52 608	283	222	63	19	69	106	64	372	19	19
Skagway	70	7.9	70 065	48	35	9	3	10	13	6	57	3	3
Southeast Fairbanks	330	-0.2	47 270	531	167	40	12	20	54	59	239	13	12
Valdez-Cordova	504	1.2	51 646	311	270	78	21	45	99	64	414	21	21
Wade Hampton	200	-1.9	25 066	3 052	68	42	4	2	19	80	116	4	4
Wrangell	98	1.3	40 890	1 066	36	13	3	9	22	22	61	3	3
Yakutat	32	2.6	49 269	404	13	5	1	1	5	6	20	1	1
Yukon-Koyukuk	259	-1.9	45 494	656	111	45	7	19	46	79	182	8	7
ARIZONA	245 070	2.1	36 983	X	122 564	18 744	9 008	19 205	45 102	49 003	169 521	10 328	9 008
Apache	1 894	0.3	26 331	3 015	762	195	59	56	271	793	1 072	66	59
Cochise	4 740	-1.3	36 612	1 650	1 886	443	156	195	983	1 361	2 679	157	156
Coconino	4 906	3.4	35 933	1 759	2 462	525	184	314	896	929	3 485	198	184
Gila	1 791	1.4	33 762	2 131	593	117	45	71	375	682	826	60	45
Graham	1 033	6.1	27 548	2 933	363	74	27	29	139	333	493	31	27
Greenlee	338	17.7	37 355	1 530	352	47	26	8	29	74	432	25	26
La Paz	634	0.5	31 204	2 518	195	41	15	74	117	209	325	19	15
Maricopa	160 498	2.4	40 030	1 169	89 074	12 312	6 454	14 755	27 951	26 651	122 595	7 329	6 454
Mohave	5 679	2.4	27 971	2 902	1 697	298	131	316	1 016	1 910	2 442	194	131
Navajo	2 870	1.5	26 739	2 990	1 090	224	89	116	455	1 112	1 519	103	89
Pima	36 935	1.4	37 063	1 572	16 428	2 962	1 225	2 044	8 313	8 359	22 659	1 411	1 225
Pinal	9 933	1.4	25 511	3 038	2 395	483	179	422	1 398	2 731	3 479	243	179
Santa Cruz	1 297	2.9	27 734	2 913	597	125	47	104	298	340	873	54	47
Yavapai	6 993	2.8	32 503	2 330	2 126	373	160	295	1 971	2 141	2 955	233	160
Yuma	5 530	1.9	27 483	2 938	2 544	524	211	406	890	1 379	3 685	204	211
ARKANSAS	108 603	1.1	36 698	X	48 820	7 610	3 845	9 590	22 528	24 709	69 864	4 437	3 845
Arkansas	868	0.8	46 240	606	398	62	33	173	156	170	666	36	33
Ashley	780	2.5	36 634	1 647	317	48	26	134	109	223	525	31	26
Baxter	1 458	0.8	35 604	1 813	509	85	41	77	414	485	713	58	41
Benton	9 766	5.5	41 157	1 034	5 759	716	404	613	1 936	1 389	7 492	468	404
Boone	1 225	0.9	32 763	2 289	522	88	41	109	263	350	761	52	41
Bradley	362	1.5	32 144	2 395	115	20	10	42	58	129	187	13	10
Calhoun	160	0.7	30 473	2 634	121	17	10	6	24	43	155	10	10
Carroll	837	3.4	30 101	2 674	299	54	25	73	217	229	451	31	25
Chicot	419	-1.4	36 933	1 596	114	18	9	95	65	131	237	12	9
Clark	759	0.1	33 387	2 194	328	58	27	43	182	205	456	30	27
Clay	542	-1.5	35 175	1 874	120	21	10	112	89	162	263	15	10
Cleburne	971	-0.1	37 809	1 459	235	41	20	94	252	260	390	30	20

1. Based on the resident population estimated as of July 1 of the year shown.

STATE County	Earnings, 2013 (cont.) — Percent by selected industries: Farm	Mining	Construction	Manu-facturing	Infor-mation: professional, scientific, technical services	Retail trade	Finance, insur-ance, real estate and leasing	Health care and social assistance	Govern-ment	Social Security beneficiaries, December 2013: Number	Rate[1]	Supple-mental Security Income recipients, December 2013	Housing units, 2014: Total	Percent change, 2010–2014
	75	76	77	78	79	80	81	82	83	84	85	86	87	88
ALABAMA—Cont'd														
Washington	4.3	D	5.3	40.2	D	3.8	D	D	15.3	4 665	277	778	8 377	-0.4
Wilcox	19.4	0.0	3.2	24.0	D	4.6	D	D	19.9	3 710	329	1 529	5 615	-0.6
Winston	1.2	D	4.4	35.4	D	7.0	3.3	9.1	17.6	6 835	283	1 015	13 406	-0.5
ALASKA	0.0	8.9	7.4	3.0	8.4	5.3	4.4	10.6	31.1	86 861	118	12 689	308 583	0.5
Aleutians East	0.0	0.0	D	D	D	1.5	D	D	17.9	180	54	8	747	0.0
Aleutians West	-0.5	D	3.7	47.4	D	4.0	D	2.7	16.8	230	40	24	1 932	0.2
Anchorage	0.0	5.1	7.7	1.1	12.9	5.3	5.8	12.0	27.2	33 040	110	5 832	114 332	1.2
Bethel	0.0	D	D	1.2	D	5.4	D	D	46.8	1 575	88	411	5 920	0.0
Bristol Bay	0.0	0.0	D	41.8	D	D	D	D	22.9	125	131	0	965	-0.4
Denali	0.0	D	D	0.0	D	1.2	D	D	26.1	220	114	9	1 760	-0.6
Dillingham	0.0	D	1.5	D	D	3.9	D	24.3	29.8	540	108	112	2 422	-0.2
Fairbanks North Star	0.2	4.6	8.2	1.4	4.6	5.7	3.5	9.3	46.4	9 760	97	1 143	41 684	-0.2
Haines	0.0	D	11.7	6.5	9.1	9.6	14.2	11.0	9.6	535	208	53	1 639	0.5
Hoonah-Angoon	0.0	0.0	3.3	D	D	4.9	D	D	53.1	430	201	56	1 755	-0.3
Juneau	-0.2	D	5.0	1.3	4.5	5.6	2.6	7.0	51.9	4 205	129	664	13 207	1.2
Kenai Peninsula	0.0	11.6	8.3	5.1	4.5	6.4	4.3	11.7	27.0	10 275	180	1 030	30 698	0.4
Ketchikan Gateway	0.0	0.0	7.8	6.1	D	8.2	5.1	10.5	35.2	2 225	162	267	6 239	1.2
Kodiak Island	0.0	0.0	4.9	19.3	1.7	3.5	2.7	D	36.3	1 500	106	154	5 327	0.5
Lake and Peninsula	0.0	D	D	7.0	D	D	D	0.0	51.5	185	111	16	1 501	-0.3
Matanuska-Susitna	0.4	0.5	15.3	0.8	7.7	9.9	4.9	15.5	26.7	11 970	125	1 527	41 313	0.0
Nome	0.0	D	3.1	D	D	5.1	2.7	17.5	46.4	1 020	103	229	4 045	0.9
North Slope	0.0	69.3	D	D	1.4	0.7	D	D	10.6	625	64	26	2 586	3.4
Northwest Arctic	0.0	D	D	0.0	D	D	D	D	30.5	710	92	120	2 704	-0.1
Petersburg	0.0	D	3.2	14.3	2.5	5.3	D	D	35.1	675	210	47	1 646	0.1
Prince of Wales-Hyder	0.0	0.0	8.2	4.9	D	7.1	3.0	4.2	47.6	905	141	132	3 319	-1.2
Sitka	0.0	0.0	9.5	D	3.6	5.0	2.3	12.6	32.8	1 240	138	98	4 122	0.5
Skagway	0.0	0.0	17.5	2.6	0.7	17.6	D	D	25.6	95	94	5	662	4.1
Southeast Fairbanks	0.0	D	4.7	D	5.8	4.9	1.0	D	33.2	1 100	158	153	3 890	-0.6
Valdez-Cordova	0.0	0.5	4.8	7.6	4.1	4.6	D	5.2	30.5	1 335	137	117	6 089	-0.2
Wade Hampton	0.0	0.0	0.0	D	D	6.8	0.1	D	70.8	775	97	203	2 183	0.0
Wrangell	0.0	0.0	5.3	8.3	D	6.3	1.3	D	45.0	455	189	37	1 422	0.1
Yakutat	0.0	0.0	D	D	D	D	D	D	56.1	110	174	0	450	0.0
Yukon-Koyukuk	0.0	5.3	12.3	D	D	4.3	D	10.4	53.1	820	145	203	4 024	-0.3
ARIZONA	0.5	0.9	5.7	8.1	10.0	7.4	10.3	12.3	17.6	1 174 944	177	118 216	2 909 218	2.3
Apache	-1.2	0.8	2.3	0.6	1.7	4.1	2.3	12.6	61.6	11 895	166	4 512	32 651	0.4
Cochise	2.2	0.2	2.9	1.0	9.4	6.2	2.8	7.3	52.1	29 815	230	2 990	60 504	2.5
Coconino	0.0	D	3.7	10.6	3.4	6.9	3.7	16.1	33.5	18 115	133	2 746	64 217	1.4
Gila	-0.2	D	4.7	13.1	D	7.4	2.6	12.0	32.7	16 160	305	1 463	33 099	1.2
Graham	3.2	D	4.7	2.0	15.1	9.3	2.3	11.4	35.4	5 995	160	774	13 238	2.0
Greenlee	0.4	D	D	0.0	D	1.4	0.2	D	6.7	1 395	156	112	4 416	1.0
La Paz	17.8	D	D	1.9	1.9	10.5	2.1	D	38.4	5 455	268	503	16 209	1.0
Maricopa	0.2	0.3	6.2	8.2	11.1	7.5	12.5	11.8	12.6	623 135	155	60 234	1 680 068	2.5
Mohave	0.4	1.6	5.0	6.1	4.6	12.7	5.6	20.8	19.6	61 605	304	4 529	112 313	1.3
Navajo	0.7	3.9	4.8	0.7	7.3	8.0	2.8	12.5	36.5	21 350	199	4 916	57 408	0.8
Pima	0.1	1.4	4.5	10.4	9.8	6.8	5.9	14.7	25.8	197 965	198	20 132	448 843	1.8
Pinal	5.7	4.8	3.3	6.0	3.1	7.1	3.2	7.3	37.1	69 830	179	6 033	165 710	4.1
Santa Cruz	0.3	0.1	1.6	2.3	D	10.1	3.1	4.2	40.3	8 600	183	1 355	18 101	0.5
Yavapai	0.3	3.2	6.2	6.4	4.7	10.2	5.0	16.1	22.3	70 725	328	3 687	112 523	1.9
Yuma	7.0	0.1	4.0	3.0	5.5	7.3	3.5	11.4	34.6	32 905	163	4 230	89 918	2.4
ARKANSAS	3.7	1.5	5.6	12.3	6.4	7.0	5.6	11.8	17.7	666 172	225	112 741	1 341 033	1.9
Arkansas	15.5	0.0	3.1	28.1	1.8	6.6	3.2	6.4	8.6	4 620	245	780	9 441	0.1
Ashley	17.4	0.0	7.8	30.3	D	5.2	2.4	D	10.0	5 820	274	1 044	10 106	-0.3
Baxter	0.7	D	5.2	16.7	5.2	9.6	8.9	25.7	11.7	16 020	391	1 085	22 633	0.2
Benton	1.0	0.3	4.1	7.2	7.7	5.3	3.8	6.2	7.1	40 955	173	3 603	97 542	4.8
Boone	2.8	D	D	11.6	3.9	8.6	4.5	8.6	21.2	10 730	287	1 142	16 904	0.5
Bradley	6.6	D	7.1	15.7	D	5.7	3.8	12.7	20.1	2 915	260	540	5 820	-0.7
Calhoun	0.5	D	3.9	72.6	D	D	D	1.6	7.3	1 385	265	184	2 886	-0.4
Carroll	8.2	D	5.5	28.3	2.8	7.6	5.0	9.7	12.3	7 585	273	638	13 568	0.1
Chicot	33.3	0.0	5.0	3.9	1.6	5.4	4.7	D	18.9	3 075	271	974	5 403	-0.3
Clark	2.0	0.0	1.5	19.7	3.7	10.1	4.2	D	23.9	4 965	219	735	10 435	0.5
Clay	35.1	0.0	3.9	6.4	1.7	5.7	2.5	6.7	14.9	4 705	308	602	8 037	0.1
Cleburne	2.2	5.6	10.4	14.7	2.8	10.0	4.3	D	11.7	8 350	325	714	15 849	0.2

1. Per 1,000 resident population estimated as of July 1 of the year shown.

STATE County	Housing units, 2009–2013: Occupied units: Total	Owner-occupied: Percent	Owner-occupied: Median value[1]	Median owner cost as a percent of income: With a mortgage	Median owner cost as a percent of income: Without a mortgage[2]	Renter-occupied: Median rent[3]	Renter-occupied: Median rent as a percent of income[2]	Substandard units[4] (percent)	Civilian labor force, 2014: Total	Percent change, 2013–2014	Unemployment: Total	Unemployment: Rate[5]	Civilian employment,[6] 2009–2013: Total	Percent: Management, business, science and arts	Percent: Construction, production, and maintenance occupations
	89	90	91	92	93	94	95	96	97	98	99	100	101	102	103
ALABAMA—Cont'd															
Washington	6 620	86.5	83 900	19.3	12.4	614	29.4	4.1	6 556	-2.3	648	9.9	5 997	21.4	49.6
Wilcox	3 866	74.5	67 000	26.5	18.2	395	33.5	1.7	2 849	2.4	495	17.4	2 579	24.0	38.4
Winston	9 489	74.9	82 500	23.8	13.2	520	30.6	5.5	9 485	-1.5	832	8.8	9 136	23.8	36.6
ALASKA	251 899	63.8	241 800	23.2	10.9	1 098	27.8	9.7	367 166	0.4	24 956	6.8	343 366	35.8	23.4
Aleutians East	435	54.7	118 500	20.0	10.0	888	19.5	11.0	2 246	1.3	103	4.6	2 612	9.2	77.6
Aleutians West	1 033	36.4	218 400	19.0	15.1	1 246	20.3	4.7	4 419	3.7	218	4.9	3 842	16.2	57.6
Anchorage	105 208	60.6	282 800	23.3	11.0	1 142	28.4	54.2	159 955	0.8	8 224	5.1	148 695	39.2	18.0
Bethel	4 358	64.2	189 600	19.9	12.7	1 177	24.3	7.3	7 325	-0.9	1 171	16.0	6 049	36.2	21.5
Bristol Bay	384	57.3	175 000	17.7	10.0	1 117	21.9	16.5	499	2.7	40	8.0	500	37.4	25.2
Denali	716	68.9	192 500	17.7	10.0	837	14.5	28.0	1 070	-0.6	108	10.1	1 147	25.4	30.8
Dillingham	1 339	57.8	194 000	16.7	13.0	979	22.8	10.0	2 144	1.0	213	9.9	1 777	39.6	19.0
Fairbanks North Star	35 588	59.2	212 500	24.6	11.2	1 179	30.7	13.1	47 119	-0.5	2 708	5.7	45 920	35.3	24.0
Haines	1 245	64.2	171 900	22.8	10.0	828	29.2	13.8	1 109	-2.8	116	10.5	1 350	28.6	26.9
Hoonah-Angoon	930	63.4	200 500	26.9	10.0	733	24.6	5.8	1 141	1.4	172	15.1	1 018	39.0	26.4
Juneau	12 099	64.5	309 900	24.2	11.1	1 178	26.8	9.8	17 457	-0.9	883	5.1	17 248	46.3	15.7
Kenai Peninsula	21 720	72.7	204 900	22.9	10.0	917	25.3	4.4	27 969	0.4	2 180	7.8	25 455	29.7	29.1
Ketchikan Gateway	5 295	58.5	265 600	23.1	12.8	1 022	27.8	8.6	7 108	-0.6	540	7.6	6 708	31.5	28.7
Kodiak Island	4 501	56.9	224 500	23.3	12.7	973	26.1	26.4	6 617	0.2	374	5.7	6 725	23.3	36.8
Lake and Peninsula	508	64.4	136 400	23.6	10.0	768	15.8	9.2	637	1.8	98	15.4	630	35.1	30.3
Matanuska-Susitna	31 123	76.7	218 900	23.2	11.1	1 026	29.4	37.5	44 183	0.6	3 538	8.0	39 190	32.6	27.2
Nome	2 797	55.1	142 800	18.1	14.4	1 127	25.8	33.2	4 190	1.2	508	12.1	3 580	36.6	22.3
North Slope	1 990	48.3	154 600	14.4	10.0	1 025	15.8	50.2	4 326	6.3	251	5.8	5 217	28.1	38.5
Northwest Arctic	1 828	56.0	131 000	20.5	14.2	1 121	19.0	5.8	3 061	-0.3	510	16.7	2 489	32.4	28.2
Petersburg	1 643	69.2	215 100	19.8	15.3	847	24.1	12.7	1 636	-2.2	161	9.8	2 143	33.6	33.0
Prince of Wales-Hyder	2 240	70.7	162 500	21.6	10.6	761	22.7	4.8	2 799	-0.3	372	13.3	2 480	28.3	34.1
Sitka	3 554	56.2	323 200	24.1	10.7	1 139	29.8	4.9	4 701	1.5	240	5.1	4 704	39.5	22.5
Skagway	412	59.2	305 600	29.9	11.3	1 057	19.1	18.5	805	1.5	95	11.8	695	21.6	42.3
Southeast Fairbanks	2 326	66.5	175 000	23.6	10.8	1 175	23.2	11.5	2 946	-2.2	384	13.0	2 989	35.9	30.0
Valdez-Cordova	3 424	74.5	177 700	19.0	10.0	871	23.5	67.4	4 907	-0.6	468	9.5	4 703	29.7	26.3
Wade Hampton	1 744	71.1	109 300	14.5	11.8	666	18.1	4.7	2 835	2.5	671	23.7	2 032	30.4	27.4
Wrangell	1 149	71.4	157 400	25.2	10.0	772	31.5	13.4	1 063	0.3	92	8.7	1 089	30.7	29.5
Yakutat	254	49.6	147 500	17.1	10.0	972	21.7	47.0	277	-3.1	27	9.7	363	29.2	36.1
Yukon-Koyukuk	2 056	70.4	106 500	21.8	13.3	669	22.4	27.4	2 620	-4.2	490	18.7	2 016	32.5	29.9
ARIZONA	2 370 289	64.4	165 100	24.8	11.1	896	30.8	5.0	3 090 628	1.6	212 985	6.9	2 721 866	35.1	18.6
Apache	19 055	76.5	83 100	23.8	10.0	536	19.6	3.9	21 185	-3.4	3 383	16.0	18 594	29.1	26.2
Cochise	49 174	68.8	146 200	22.4	10.2	778	28.2	9.9	50 978	-0.6	4 301	8.4	46 250	35.6	17.3
Coconino	46 198	59.5	220 400	24.6	10.0	996	32.8	5.1	71 901	1.2	5 146	7.2	64 440	32.5	20.3
Gila	20 601	75.8	134 000	26.8	11.5	743	30.9	7.7	21 363	2.0	1 797	8.4	18 378	29.4	23.0
Graham	11 031	74.3	122 200	22.8	10.3	711	26.3	9.2	14 418	0.4	1 102	7.6	12 143	29.3	30.3
Greenlee	3 386	46.1	81 000	20.2	10.0	381	10.0	9.3	4 699	2.6	306	6.5	3 229	27.4	46.5
La Paz	10 221	74.0	88 800	25.4	10.0	553	25.4	4.5	8 011	-0.8	637	8.0	6 635	25.9	29.6
Maricopa	1 411 727	62.5	176 500	24.6	11.1	943	30.7	3.7	1 956 284	2.2	114 919	5.9	1 734 641	36.6	17.6
Mohave	80 230	69.4	133 900	26.5	11.9	803	30.7	15.0	78 247	1.3	6 905	8.8	68 228	25.1	21.9
Navajo	34 343	72.0	112 200	24.1	10.0	668	27.8	4.1	41 593	-1.2	4 685	11.3	32 413	30.2	23.1
Pima	384 041	62.7	167 500	24.7	11.6	798	32.3	4.6	461 806	0.7	28 485	6.2	414 967	36.2	17.1
Pinal	123 733	74.4	120 200	25.5	11.4	966	30.0	5.5	151 645	1.7	10 966	7.2	133 164	31.0	23.3
Santa Cruz	15 078	66.3	140 000	25.0	11.4	630	30.2	3.5	20 258	0.3	2 665	13.2	17 334	27.1	22.0
Yavapai	91 349	70.0	184 100	28.4	12.1	847	32.0	7.5	95 402	2.9	6 049	6.3	82 623	30.7	20.1
Yuma	70 122	69.6	118 000	25.5	10.9	827	31.1	1.7	92 838	-2.5	21 640	23.3	68 827	25.3	27.1
ARKANSAS	1 129 723	66.7	107 300	20.7	10.7	661	29.7	3.0	1 300 608	-0.5	79 733	6.1	1 245 432	31.2	27.5
Arkansas	7 883	67.5	75 500	20.7	10.0	631	26.3	2.8	9 291	-1.8	504	5.4	8 681	28.5	35.1
Ashley	8 656	75.6	62 500	19.1	11.5	572	28.8	1.7	8 470	-4.1	795	9.4	8 515	25.2	37.9
Baxter	18 155	76.5	120 000	24.2	11.8	592	30.3	3.1	15 740	-0.8	1 069	6.8	14 826	30.2	25.2
Benton	82 150	68.6	147 500	20.3	10.0	774	25.0	0.5	113 328	2.6	5 260	4.6	103 176	34.5	25.0
Boone	15 086	72.6	106 400	21.1	10.8	587	28.7	5.9	15 417	-2.8	948	6.1	14 971	27.7	26.8
Bradley	4 789	68.8	62 900	23.3	10.8	606	38.2	0.0	4 123	1.1	350	8.5	4 374	21.4	35.3
Calhoun	2 046	80.0	58 300	21.2	15.4	593	29.1	3.2	2 353	-1.8	159	6.8	2 321	21.2	47.7
Carroll	11 019	73.2	120 000	24.8	10.0	600	26.9	3.2	12 379	2.0	651	5.3	11 843	25.2	38.2
Chicot	4 510	66.3	54 700	24.2	15.0	513	32.3	1.6	3 837	0.9	407	10.6	3 705	31.8	27.0
Clark	8 341	63.5	86 600	20.6	11.4	588	32.9	2.5	9 443	-3.7	664	7.0	9 563	33.9	22.0
Clay	6 814	72.6	62 400	19.1	11.8	463	31.7	3.3	6 334	-2.0	510	8.1	6 322	23.7	38.8
Cleburne	10 286	76.9	117 900	21.2	11.3	662	28.4	2.1	9 607	-2.9	800	8.3	9 686	23.9	35.7

1. Specified owner-occupied units. 2. A value of 10.0 represents 10 percent or less; a value of 50.0 represents 50 percent or more. 3. Specified renter-occupied units.
4. Overcrowded or lacking complete plumbing facilities. 5. Percent of civilian labor force. 6. Persons 16 years old and over.

Table B. States and Counties — **Nonfarm Employment and Agriculture**

STATE County	Private nonfarm establishments, employment and payroll, 2013: Number of establish-ments	Employment: Total	Employment: Health care and social assistance	Employment: Manufac-turing	Employment: Retail trade	Employment: Finance and insurance	Employment: Professional, scientific, and technical services	Annual payroll: Total (mil dol)	Annual payroll: Average per employee (dollars)	Agriculture, 2012: Farms: Number	Farms: Percent with: Fewer than 50 acres	Farms: Percent with: 500 acres or more	Farm operators whose principal occu-pation is farming (percent)
	104	105	106	107	108	109	110	111	112	113	114	115	116
ALABAMA—Cont'd													
Washington	217	5 756	297	4 210	249	D	D	372	64 620	371	31.3	6.2	43.4
Wilcox	189	1 738	262	D	245	97	D	73	41 750	316	30.7	24.1	44.9
Winston	439	6 321	685	3 143	720	D	97	178	28 161	520	32.3	3.3	51.0
ALASKA	20 519	266 627	48 057	12 406	33 175	7 512	18 996	14 601	54 762	762	56.2	11.3	54.1
Aleutians East	59	D	D	D	NA	D	D	D	D	NA	NA	NA	NA
Aleutians West	117	4 668	D	3 418	D	D	D	145	31 121	NA	NA	NA	NA
Anchorage	8 609	152 377	24 940	1 790	15 152	4 895	14 376	9 029	59 257	291	56.7	5.8	56.4
Bethel	232	3 174	D	D	852	D	D	136	42 989	NA	NA	NA	NA
Bristol Bay	66	299	D	51	39	D	D	38	126 171	NA	NA	NA	NA
Denali	103	408	D	NA	D	D	D	46	113 944	NA	NA	NA	NA
Dillingham	92	1 264	621	D	221	D	D	60	47 645	NA	NA	NA	NA
Fairbanks North Star	2 471	27 466	5 945	622	4 891	765	1 632	1 376	50 111	217	39.2	20.7	47.9
Haines	134	635	120	D	115	D	D	29	46 139	NA	NA	NA	NA
Hoonah-Angoon	71	216	D	D	NA	NA	D	9	43 690	NA	NA	NA	NA
Juneau	1 135	10 932	2 346	245	1 687	370	506	522	47 757	52	92.3	0.0	63.5
Kenai Peninsula	2 058	14 734	3 707	686	2 533	298	554	683	46 366	162	67.9	4.9	57.4
Ketchikan Gateway	583	4 722	844	439	773	214	D	226	47 881	NA	NA	NA	NA
Kodiak Island	478	4 787	D	1 792	466	80	66	181	37 843	NA	NA	NA	NA
Lake and Peninsula	51	135	NA	D	NA	D	D	14	103 089	NA	NA	NA	NA
Matanuska-Susitna	2 070	16 807	3 781	253	3 387	489	887	773	46 004	NA	NA	NA	NA
Nome	167	1 910	866	D	322	D	D	93	48 615	NA	NA	NA	NA
North Slope	155	3 414	D	D	267	D	D	233	68 377	NA	NA	NA	NA
Northwest Arctic	72	1 591	D	NA	141	D	D	133	83 833	NA	NA	NA	NA
Petersburg	167	1 079	D	D	212	24	D	49	45 305	NA	NA	NA	NA
Prince of Wales-Hyder	134	894	188	D	NA	D	NA	32	35 721	NA	NA	NA	NA
Sitka	382	2 867	889	262	428	64	70	129	44 977	NA	NA	NA	NA
Skagway	109	337	D	D	80	D	D	23	68 596	NA	NA	NA	NA
Southeast Fairbanks	172	1 265	108	22	190	D	68	81	63 839	NA	NA	NA	NA
Valdez-Cordova	461	2 786	454	D	351	D	99	164	58 851	NA	NA	NA	NA
Wade Hampton	71	575	D	D	NA	D	D	15	25 605	NA	NA	NA	NA
Wrangell	86	524	D	D	125	D	D	19	36 345	NA	NA	NA	NA
Yakutat	30	147	D	D	NA	NA	NA	6	41 068	NA	NA	NA	NA
Yukon-Koyukuk	99	434	D	D	NA	NA	D	19	44 924	NA	NA	NA	NA
ARIZONA	132 762	2 173 205	326 256	136 644	296 132	132 038	128 691	92 770	42 688	20 005	79.9	8.1	66.1
Apache	463	6 796	2 768	D	1 264	74	128	253	37 262	5 591	85.6	4.2	73.3
Cochise	2 245	26 387	4 895	328	5 270	646	3 654	905	34 297	1 093	43.8	22.4	56.1
Coconino	3 518	44 834	7 671	D	7 486	827	1 522	1 657	36 962	2 239	92.0	3.8	72.5
Gila	1 013	10 780	2 106	128	2 067	226	D	451	41 880	195	65.6	13.3	58.5
Graham	487	6 499	1 406	206	1 521	117	D	215	33 099	412	61.4	15.8	45.4
Greenlee	90	4 834	117	NA	156	D	D	243	50 247	159	52.8	15.1	57.9
La Paz	345	3 739	557	164	962	D	D	109	29 126	125	35.2	28.8	73.6
Maricopa	86 045	1 491 582	210 570	93 374	191 196	108 563	94 008	67 741	45 415	2 479	84.6	5.7	50.9
Mohave	3 603	39 476	8 263	2 809	8 946	1 219	909	1 275	32 297	335	59.1	23.9	51.3
Navajo	1 692	16 802	3 998	167	3 934	375	346	555	33 020	3 846	91.3	3.4	75.5
Pima	19 962	305 393	56 519	24 549	45 124	11 666	16 943	11 618	38 043	855	79.4	9.4	49.0
Pinal	3 311	46 431	7 875	3 443	8 054	982	825	1 516	32 654	938	56.5	22.8	62.8
Santa Cruz	1 145	10 954	1 162	339	2 390	237	175	328	29 981	236	53.0	19.5	58.9
Yavapai	5 548	53 338	11 973	2 984	9 940	1 311	1 653	1 774	33 261	940	69.9	13.1	64.1
Yuma	2 851	39 710	6 064	3 025	7 822	1 230	1 304	1 221	30 739	562	64.4	14.4	54.8
ARKANSAS	64 772	978 094	165 607	153 711	138 007	36 295	33 686	36 808	37 632	45 071	30.8	13.0	47.3
Arkansas	527	8 181	1 023	3 312	1 082	249	64	296	36 191	492	17.9	41.7	53.7
Ashley	414	6 845	900	D	837	173	81	273	39 829	376	47.9	12.2	40.4
Baxter	1 039	12 604	3 592	2 276	2 116	521	400	416	32 988	561	38.5	6.4	44.9
Benton	5 454	98 642	8 047	9 418	11 179	2 859	6 596	5 513	55 888	2 157	43.2	5.1	47.8
Boone	864	11 897	2 319	1 654	1 892	414	241	400	33 596	1 282	32.2	9.2	52.7
Bradley	250	2 621	495	487	329	117	D	75	28 681	185	39.5	2.7	36.8
Calhoun	66	435	D	D	74	19	D	15	35 545	92	20.7	5.4	28.3
Carroll	698	8 142	D	3 275	1 142	232	D	211	26 285	1 126	27.5	10.7	49.4
Chicot	225	2 207	833	81	344	97	31	63	28 504	313	17.6	41.5	57.5
Clark	498	6 584	1 085	D	1 114	232	159	201	30 571	381	26.0	10.0	44.1
Clay	307	2 683	714	328	460	88	47	73	27 231	610	24.6	26.6	52.5
Cleburne	577	5 882	841	1 333	1 017	178	153	172	29 313	797	32.4	7.0	40.0

STATE County	Agriculture, 2012 (cont.)															
	Land in farms					Value of land and buildings (dollars)			Value of products sold				Percent of farms with sales of:		Government payments	
			Acres								Percent from:					
	Acreage (1,000)	Percent change, 2007–2012	Average size of farm	Total irrigated (1,000)	Total cropland (1,000)	Average per farm	Average per acre	Value of machinery and equipment, average per farm (dollars)	Total (mil dol)	Average per farm (dollars)	Crops	Live-stock and poultry products	$10,000 or more	$100,000 or more	Total ($1,000)	Percent of farms
	117	118	119	120	121	122	123	124	125	126	127	128	129	130	131	132
ALABAMA—Cont'd																
Washington	96	14.3	258	0.0	12.6	435 148	1 689	62 544	31.7	85 329	15.3	84.7	26.7	7.0	373	17.5
Wilcox	120	-29.2	379	D	22.3	636 839	1 682	51 880	D	D	D	D	25.9	3.2	1 142	44.9
Winston	58	-10.2	111	D	13.5	289 904	2 601	51 921	57.6	110 785	1.4	98.6	36.7	13.8	135	7.3
ALASKA	834	-5.4	1 094	2.5	84.1	681 479	623	87 445	58.9	77 329	42.2	57.8	42.3	11.4	2 432	25.6
Aleutians East	NA	NA	NA	NA	NA	NA	NA	NA	NA	NA	NA	NA	NA	NA	NA	NA
Aleutians West	NA	NA	NA	NA	NA	NA	NA	NA	NA	NA	NA	NA	NA	NA	NA	NA
Anchorage	36	-5.2	125	1.3	17.1	879 979	7 039	92 491	30.0	103 158	47.3	52.7	46.0	14.8	354	17.5
Bethel	NA	NA	NA	NA	NA	NA	NA	NA	NA	NA	NA	NA	NA	NA	NA	NA
Bristol Bay	NA	NA	NA	NA	NA	NA	NA	NA	NA	NA	NA	NA	NA	NA	NA	NA
Denali	NA	NA	NA	NA	NA	NA	NA	NA	NA	NA	NA	NA	NA	NA	NA	NA
Dillingham	NA	NA	NA	NA	NA	NA	NA	NA	NA	NA	NA	NA	NA	NA	NA	NA
Fairbanks North Star	100	-10.1	459	1.0	61.4	580 382	1 264	94 359	9.1	42 120	84.8	15.2	42.4	10.6	1 354	30.9
Haines	NA	NA	NA	NA	NA	NA	NA	NA	NA	NA	NA	NA	NA	NA	NA	NA
Hoonah-Angoon	NA	NA	NA	NA	NA	NA	NA	NA	NA	NA	NA	NA	NA	NA	NA	NA
Juneau	1	37.5	14	0.0	0.1	740 712	54 479	152 173	12.4	238 692	7.4	92.6	51.9	23.1	25	13.5
Kenai Peninsula	29	-23.9	180	0.1	4.5	435 877	2 423	46 315	D	D	D	D	30.9	3.7	353	33.3
Ketchikan Gateway	NA	NA	NA	NA	NA	NA	NA	NA	NA	NA	NA	NA	NA	NA	NA	NA
Kodiak Island	NA	NA	NA	NA	NA	NA	NA	NA	NA	NA	NA	NA	NA	NA	NA	NA
Lake and Peninsula	NA	NA	NA	NA	NA	NA	NA	NA	NA	NA	NA	NA	NA	NA	NA	NA
Matanuska-Susitna	NA	NA	NA	NA	NA	NA	NA	NA	NA	NA	NA	NA	NA	NA	NA	NA
Nome	NA	NA	NA	NA	NA	NA	NA	NA	NA	NA	NA	NA	NA	NA	NA	NA
North Slope	NA	NA	NA	NA	NA	NA	NA	NA	NA	NA	NA	NA	NA	NA	NA	NA
Northwest Arctic	NA	NA	NA	NA	NA	NA	NA	NA	NA	NA	NA	NA	NA	NA	NA	NA
Petersburg	NA	NA	NA	NA	NA	NA	NA	NA	NA	NA	NA	NA	NA	NA	NA	NA
Prince of Wales-Hyder	NA	NA	NA	NA	NA	NA	NA	NA	NA	NA	NA	NA	NA	NA	NA	NA
Sitka	NA	NA	NA	NA	NA	NA	NA	NA	NA	NA	NA	NA	NA	NA	NA	NA
Skagway	NA	NA	NA	NA	NA	NA	NA	NA	NA	NA	NA	NA	NA	NA	NA	NA
Southeast Fairbanks	NA	NA	NA	NA	NA	NA	NA	NA	NA	NA	NA	NA	NA	NA	NA	NA
Valdez-Cordova	NA	NA	NA	NA	NA	NA	NA	NA	NA	NA	NA	NA	NA	NA	NA	NA
Wade Hampton	NA	NA	NA	NA	NA	NA	NA	NA	NA	NA	NA	NA	NA	NA	NA	NA
Wrangell	NA	NA	NA	NA	NA	NA	NA	NA	NA	NA	NA	NA	NA	NA	NA	NA
Yakutat	NA	NA	NA	NA	NA	NA	NA	NA	NA	NA	NA	NA	NA	NA	NA	NA
Yukon-Koyukuk	NA	NA	NA	NA	NA	NA	NA	NA	NA	NA	NA	NA	NA	NA	NA	NA
ARIZONA	26 249	0.5	1 312	880.6	1 150.8	844 064	643	62 708	3 732.1	186 559	55.6	44.4	20.3	7.3	31 329	15.3
Apache	5 598	D	1 001	9.8	26.5	192 667	192	18 893	24.2	4 327	54.5	45.5	7.5	0.6	973	14.9
Cochise	917	11.2	839	65.5	123.3	1 175 308	1 401	81 234	150.0	137 235	D	D	37.6	13.3	2 594	16.9
Coconino	5 816	-4.7	2 597	1.9	8.3	543 406	209	23 731	25.8	11 528	9.1	90.9	9.6	1.4	987	23.0
Gila	1 189	1.9	6 098	0.8	2.8	1 993 174	327	55 646	3.8	19 241	9.1	90.9	33.8	4.6	323	10.8
Graham	1 251	-7.0	3 037	36.9	41.7	1 752 109	577	143 189	170.9	414 769	97.1	2.9	33.5	15.8	3 056	38.3
Greenlee	52	48.5	329	5.4	5.2	514 126	1 561	70 818	9.7	61 239	24.8	75.2	32.7	15.1	337	32.7
La Paz	D	D	D	93.2	120.0	2 513 648	D	345 968	183.2	1 465 944	D	D	64.8	45.6	2 011	34.4
Maricopa	476	-2.0	192	192.9	222.5	1 087 145	5 663	113 576	1 003.5	404 790	44.5	55.5	32.2	14.1	5 379	9.7
Mohave	1 244	45.0	3 714	20.8	29.1	1 792 487	483	75 743	30.2	90 102	68.9	31.1	33.7	11.9	1 242	11.3
Navajo	4 323	-4.0	1 124	6.5	20.1	291 214	259	20 164	64.5	16 775	9.0	91.0	7.6	0.6	832	13.1
Pima	D	D	D	32.4	36.7	1 651 870	D	64 622	97.3	113 786	76.8	23.2	31.2	10.3	1 085	5.3
Pinal	1 175	12.2	1 252	223.6	302.6	2 979 541	2 379	188 860	927.7	989 059	34.0	66.0	49.7	30.0	9 558	27.8
Santa Cruz	215	65.9	911	1.8	1.2	1 390 784	1 527	35 631	14.7	62 110	4.7	95.3	43.6	12.7	996	15.7
Yavapai	825	29.0	877	7.6	10.7	1 382 518	1 576	51 250	41.6	44 285	25.5	74.5	32.2	12.0	141	3.2
Yuma	215	2.0	382	181.4	200.1	2 758 098	7 220	372 064	985.0	1 752 685	D	D	61.7	28.5	1 815	17.1
ARKANSAS	13 811	-0.4	306	4 803.9	7 931.1	807 965	2 637	115 436	9 775.8	216 897	49.5	50.5	44.0	16.7	262 967	29.2
Arkansas	402	-0.7	817	314.6	360.2	2 168 250	2 653	320 372	298.2	606 043	99.7	0.3	55.5	46.5	17 373	83.9
Ashley	112	-27.7	297	70.8	83.7	861 694	2 905	127 370	72.8	193 734	91.6	8.4	31.4	15.2	3 123	31.1
Baxter	92	-5.4	164	0.1	12.8	436 902	2 668	46 217	20.4	36 305	3.0	97.0	29.8	4.1	948	16.8
Benton	305	19.7	141	0.6	88.0	626 853	4 435	68 418	529.1	245 307	1.0	99.0	46.5	17.8	1 832	13.7
Boone	257	6.2	201	0.4	38.7	515 837	2 572	54 509	124.1	96 775	1.1	98.9	45.1	10.8	3 730	34.8
Bradley	20	-21.7	107	D	5.5	372 924	3 492	57 232	43.6	235 854	D	D	41.1	16.2	133	13.0
Calhoun	14	-15.4	151	0.1	3.4	370 859	2 459	57 957	6.0	64 761	6.5	93.5	28.3	7.6	32	21.7
Carroll	256	5.7	228	0.1	48.2	579 130	2 543	70 987	307.0	272 652	0.6	99.4	56.6	20.4	2 464	25.3
Chicot	290	1.4	925	197.1	254.9	2 465 096	2 665	340 051	204.7	654 054	96.4	3.6	60.4	44.7	7 640	83.7
Clark	90	10.3	237	D	26.5	437 554	1 848	53 113	15.1	39 588	13.9	86.1	34.6	5.0	342	22.8
Clay	331	0.3	543	235.6	298.0	1 737 748	3 198	263 780	246.2	403 561	98.6	1.4	48.9	32.0	9 792	77.2
Cleburne	157	21.3	198	0.8	37.0	540 846	2 738	62 587	47.9	60 064	2.5	97.5	33.9	6.9	1 013	23.5

STATE County	Water use, 2010		Wholesale trade,[1] 2007				Retail trade,[2] 2007				Real estate and rental and leasing,[2] 2007			
	Total water withdrawn (mil gal/day)	Gallons withdrawn per person per day	Number of establish- ments	Number of employees	Sales (mil dol)	Annual payroll (mil dol)	Number of establish- ments	Number of employees	Sales (mil dol)	Annual payroll (mil dol)	Number of establish- ments	Number of employees	Receipts (mil dol)	Annual payroll (mil dol)
	133	134	135	136	137	138	139	140	141	142	143	144	145	146
ALABAMA—Cont'd														
Washington	89.6	5 098	5	78	32.9	2.8	47	325	76.3	5.9	2	D	D	D
Wilcox	22.2	1 905	7	43	21.3	1.4	46	298	75.7	5.5	7	14	0.5	0.1
Winston	2.2	89	29	310	165.6	10.5	108	915	166.7	16.6	11	32	2.4	0.4
ALASKA	1 094.5	1 541	658	8 262	4 563.6	391.6	2 641	34 977	9 303.4	936.8	852	4 370	840.6	160.2
Aleutians East	3.7	1 172	1	D	D	D	9	52	9.3	1.2	2	D	D	D
Aleutians West	5.0	892	10	82	62.1	4.0	14	155	46.8	5.1	6	39	10.0	2.0
Anchorage	46.2	158	339	5 498	2 914.0	261.0	923	15 842	4 482.7	441.8	378	2 416	453.5	94.0
Bethel	0.5	28	4	26	3.5	0.3	54	831	96.8	13.5	6	45	7.9	1.0
Bristol Bay	0.2	191	3	D	D	D	9	50	12.8	1.5	2	D	D	D
Denali	24.2	13 237	NA	NA	NA	NA	10	33	11.0	0.9	NA	NA	NA	NA
Dillingham	0.4	80	2	D	D	D	19	209	42.7	4.8	6	25	3.6	0.6
Fairbanks North Star	53.6	549	72	D	D	D	339	5 236	1 574.3	146.7	136	745	152.5	29.9
Haines	44.4	17 699	2	D	D	D	18	115	16.2	2.9	4	8	0.7	0.1
Hoonah-Angoon	141.1	65 623	NA	NA	NA	NA	NA	NA	NA	NA	NA	NA	NA	NA
Juneau	58.8	1 880	33	D	D	D	172	1 933	465.3	52.0	58	241	41.1	5.9
Kenai Peninsula	28.0	506	46	353	193.7	16.1	265	2 537	666.9	62.5	66	169	38.2	5.3
Ketchikan Gateway	29.9	2 220	10	D	D	D	109	961	268.9	31.2	22	82	16.1	2.5
Kodiak Island	6.1	449	37	D	D	D	45	481	108.2	11.6	15	75	7.8	2.2
Lake and Peninsula	0.5	294	1	D	D	D	4	D	D	D	3	9	0.5	0.1
Matanuska-Susitna	33.8	379	36	368	137.0	14.9	233	3 200	853.9	86.9	72	272	37.4	6.8
Nome	0.7	78	4	D	D	D	33	399	63.2	7.8	7	24	5.2	0.5
North Slope	221.2	23 453	8	202	135.2	14.6	18	233	70.1	6.7	5	D	D	D
Northwest Arctic	9.8	1 307	1	D	D	D	15	201	41.6	4.9	3	2	0.4	0.0
Petersburg	62.3	16 338	NA	NA	NA	NA	NA	NA	NA	NA	NA	NA	NA	NA
Prince of Wales-Hyder	73.7	13 254	NA	NA	NA	NA	NA	NA	NA	NA	NA	NA	NA	NA
Sitka	55.3	6 221	15	D	D	D	62	465	94.9	12.6	15	49	7.8	1.9
Skagway	8.7	8 988	NA	NA	NA	NA	NA	NA	NA	NA	NA	NA	NA	NA
Southeast Fairbanks	1.0	135	2	D	D	D	38	208	47.3	4.0	8	10	1.0	0.1
Valdez-Cordova	42.7	4 431	14	86	81.2	4.7	56	370	79.7	7.7	17	45	17.1	2.4
Wade Hampton	0.5	68	1	D	D	D	25	283	39.5	4.0	2	D	D	D
Wrangell	48.1	20 283	NA	NA	NA	NA	NA	NA	NA	NA	NA	NA	NA	NA
Yakutat	92.6	139 849	3	20	10.0	1.8	6	D	D	D	1	D	D	D
Yukon-Koyukuk	1.8	317	2	D	D	D	34	299	41.6	6.5	3	5	0.3	0.1
ARIZONA	6 088.2	952	5 874	84 029	57 573.5	4 116.4	19 384	337 529	86 758.8	8 010.8	9 441	52 627	10 077.6	1 994.3
Apache	49.0	685	12	32	18.1	0.8	104	1 189	276.9	24.1	20	56	5.9	0.9
Cochise	238.4	1 815	54	359	102.3	10.4	455	6 305	1 313.7	129.1	139	504	65.1	12.4
Coconino	52.2	388	98	1 149	475.6	40.2	674	7 861	1 691.7	169.3	237	754	187.5	24.2
Gila	34.7	647	29	D	D	D	186	2 450	550.8	55.6	82	269	35.9	7.5
Graham	176.2	4 734	19	193	68.0	7.5	97	1 602	389.4	36.2	29	D	D	D
Greenlee	25.9	3 069	2	D	D	D	19	159	35.6	2.8	2	D	D	D
La Paz	668.8	32 644	10	107	65.9	3.7	88	1 006	394.4	19.1	17	57	6.0	1.3
Maricopa	1 953.6	512	4 176	66 783	49 760.3	3 457.2	11 468	217 746	58 688.3	5 332.6	6 123	37 987	7 796.5	1 564.0
Mohave	121.2	605	117	976	423.8	33.0	730	10 672	2 837.7	248.0	280	876	133.3	22.7
Navajo	61.7	574	38	289	209.5	12.0	340	4 399	1 237.5	102.4	142	350	56.9	10.1
Pima	305.4	312	744	8 132	3 056.8	324.6	2 982	51 830	11 928.5	1 208.9	1 449	8 133	1 211.7	251.8
Pinal	1 130.1	3 007	110	930	450.4	35.9	524	8 552	2 033.1	175.2	202	689	107.5	18.1
Santa Cruz	17.4	368	157	D	D	D	257	3 058	681.3	60.7	61	265	42.6	5.5
Yavapai	92.3	437	175	1 652	831.4	61.1	920	11 795	2 695.4	266.6	469	1 776	293.9	55.4
Yuma	1 161.4	5 933	133	D	D	D	540	8 905	2 004.6	180.2	190	734	119.2	17.5
ARKANSAS	11 327.0	3 885	2 977	38 988	29 659.8	1 536.3	11 906	140 018	32 974.3	2 889.2	3 162	14 115	1 968.1	374.9
Arkansas	939.7	49 410	30	303	134.6	12.2	111	1 231	286.3	25.4	19	58	6.1	1.3
Ashley	205.2	9 388	18	114	107.3	4.7	95	881	170.8	16.6	13	46	4.8	0.8
Baxter	4.8	117	19	D	D	D	242	2 460	486.8	48.7	50	202	22.7	4.5
Benton	402.5	1 818	216	D	D	D	751	9 896	2 390.6	223.0	308	1 204	165.9	34.3
Boone	2.8	76	32	D	D	D	166	2 038	466.9	42.2	38	104	13.6	2.4
Bradley	2.1	180	10	137	42.8	4.2	50	346	71.5	6.0	9	20	1.6	0.4
Calhoun	0.7	121	2	D	D	D	20	65	17.9	1.0	2	D	D	D
Carroll	10.7	300	14	78	24.1	2.9	107	1 339	265.4	25.8	36	70	6.4	1.3
Chicot	273.1	23 140	13	113	120.6	4.0	50	426	67.0	7.0	11	30	3.5	0.6
Clark	11.6	505	13	D	D	D	102	1 184	247.8	25.8	36	112	11.1	2.2
Clay	407.5	25 337	12	265	116.9	7.9	67	531	132.6	9.8	10	22	1.5	0.4
Cleburne	26.0	999	18	123	54.4	3.0	123	1 131	282.4	23.2	34	83	8.3	2.0

1. Merchant wholesalers, except manufacturers' sales branches and offices. 2. Employer establishments.

Table B. States and Counties — **Professional Services, Manufacturing, and Accommodation and Food Services**

STATE County	Professional, scientific, and technical services,[1] 2007				Manufacturing, 2007				Accommodation and food services, 2007			
	Number of establish-ments	Number of employees	Receipts (mil dol)	Annual payroll (mil dol)	Number of establish-ments	Number of employees	Receipts (mil dol)	Annual payroll (mil dol)	Number of establish-ments	Number of employees	Sales (mil dol)	Annual payroll (mil dol)
	147	148	149	150	151	152	153	154	155	156	157	158
ALABAMA—Cont'd												
Washington	14	178	25.9	9.1	15	1 397	1 153.4	85.3	9	D	D	D
Wilcox	11	D	D	D	13	876	D	D	19	112	12.9	1.2
Winston	23	70	5.7	1.9	68	4 439	797.8	112.0	40	511	16.6	4.4
ALASKA	1 799	12 509	2 006.8	745.4	544	13 298	8 204.0	489.5	1 996	25 638	1 851.3	529.8
Aleutians East	NA	NA	NA	NA	5	D	D	D	12	D	D	D
Aleutians West	2	D	D	D	14	2 314	634.8	77.1	12	103	14.7	2.9
Anchorage	1 092	D	D	D	194	2 305	D	D	720	14 031	933.3	283.9
Bethel	5	D	D	D	NA	NA	NA	NA	18	39	4.1	0.8
Bristol Bay	1	D	D	D	NA	NA	NA	NA	19	74	13.3	3.9
Denali	2	D	D	D	NA	NA	NA	NA	30	110	37.1	10.5
Dillingham	4	D	D	D	NA	NA	NA	NA	18	51	7.2	1.9
Fairbanks North Star	228	1 329	174.9	64.7	78	745	D	37.3	220	3 430	221.6	60.9
Haines	4	6	0.3	0.1	NA	NA	NA	NA	19	64	6.4	1.5
Hoonah-Angoon	NA	NA	NA	NA	NA	NA	NA	NA	NA	NA	NA	NA
Juneau	95	D	D	D	NA	NA	NA	NA	97	1 228	86.9	21.6
Kenai Peninsula	111	D	D	D	64	982	D	57.4	260	1 677	131.2	33.5
Ketchikan Gateway	26	D	D	D	14	500	D	16.7	57	546	45.6	12.1
Kodiak Island	25	65	12.4	2.5	22	1 644	D	51.5	42	404	26.3	6.9
Lake and Peninsula	3	9	1.0	0.5	NA	NA	NA	NA	14	D	D	D
Matanuska-Susitna	132	D	D	D	NA	NA	NA	NA	185	1 774	113.7	30.2
Nome	5	D	D	D	NA	NA	NA	NA	15	166	10.2	2.9
North Slope	4	14	2.8	1.3	NA	NA	NA	NA	20	414	56.3	20.0
Northwest Arctic	1	D	D	D	NA	NA	NA	NA	4	D	D	D
Petersburg	NA	NA	NA	NA	NA	NA	NA	NA	NA	NA	NA	NA
Prince of Wales-Hyder	NA	NA	NA	NA	NA	NA	NA	NA	NA	NA	NA	NA
Sitka	15	48	4.0	1.1	NA	NA	NA	NA	41	500	27.1	8.2
Skagway	NA	NA	NA	NA	NA	NA	NA	NA	NA	NA	NA	NA
Southeast Fairbanks	11	23	5.5	1.2	NA	NA	NA	NA	30	165	22.2	4.1
Valdez-Cordova	21	D	D	D	14	569	543.4	19.2	56	264	23.1	6.2
Wade Hampton	1	D	D	D	NA	NA	NA	NA	NA	NA	NA	NA
Wrangell	NA	NA	NA	NA	NA	NA	NA	NA	NA	NA	NA	NA
Yakutat	NA	NA	NA	NA	NA	NA	NA	NA	7	21	3.8	1.1
Yukon-Koyukuk	1	D	D	D	NA	NA	NA	NA	12	77	5.4	1.6
ARIZONA	16 563	128 188	17 617.1	7 239.5	5 074	172 438	57 977.8	8 774.3	11 610	250 716	13 268.5	3 766.3
Apache	27	D	D	D	NA	NA	NA	NA	68	1 033	47.8	13.3
Cochise	208	D	D	D	56	576	181.3	20.6	277	4 100	171.4	47.8
Coconino	322	D	D	D	109	4 219	1 526.8	240.5	531	11 181	717.7	181.9
Gila	91	370	34.4	12.2	NA	NA	NA	NA	137	2 021	106.7	29.5
Graham	27	373	10.5	11.2	NA	NA	NA	NA	53	955	34.7	8.3
Greenlee	4	28	0.9	0.4	NA	NA	NA	NA	16	116	4.9	1.2
La Paz	15	D	D	D	NA	NA	NA	NA	73	719	38.0	9.3
Maricopa	11 727	D	D	D	3 398	121 062	40 182.1	6 043.4	6 750	156 678	8 408.9	2 446.3
Mohave	251	D	D	D	164	3 814	1 350.0	139.6	381	6 380	274.3	77.3
Navajo	117	D	D	D	57	D	D	D	244	3 308	191.5	45.7
Pima	2 692	16 250	1 886.4	777.8	760	30 567	10 365.2	1 877.0	1 758	42 002	2 135.2	601.8
Pinal	227	D	D	D	122	3 896	2 149.9	151.8	328	6 063	341.9	88.3
Santa Cruz	63	D	D	D	NA	NA	NA	NA	100	1 481	67.2	19.8
Yavapai	584	D	D	D	233	3 618	764.0	143.6	578	8 737	456.5	126.2
Yuma	208	D	D	D	82	2 856	891.6	88.0	316	5 942	271.9	69.6
ARKANSAS	5 588	D	D	D	3 088	184 568	60 735.6	6 518.4	5 112	89 933	3 559.8	994.1
Arkansas	28	85	7.0	2.7	33	3 061	1 702.2	127.5	43	448	15.5	4.2
Ashley	27	95	9.1	3.0	26	2 733	D	125.4	25	442	15.3	4.1
Baxter	75	413	29.1	11.0	57	2 496	550.1	90.6	108	1 555	60.3	16.1
Benton	535	4 702	472.6	240.4	199	12 403	D	432.3	362	7 511	295.7	85.8
Boone	66	D	D	D	69	D	D	D	63	1 023	41.9	11.7
Bradley	14	36	2.4	0.8	5	916	177.0	27.3	15	176	6.2	1.5
Calhoun	NA	NA	NA	NA	NA	NA	NA	NA	4	30	0.8	0.2
Carroll	51	139	10.0	3.4	41	2 866	D	74.2	143	1 424	54.0	15.8
Chicot	16	53	2.6	1.2	8	503	D	8.5	18	169	6.1	1.6
Clark	28	198	14.7	6.8	28	2 196	433.9	53.9	50	908	32.7	9.5
Clay	16	36	2.7	0.7	17	651	111.8	18.7	16	205	6.3	1.7
Cleburne	31	104	7.0	2.1	40	1 360	205.6	43.3	58	784	29.2	9.0

1. Establishment subject to federal tax.

Table B. States and Counties — **Health Care and Social Assistance, Other Services, Nonemployer Businesses, and Residential Construction**

STATE County	Health care and social assistance, 2007				Other services, 2007				Nonemployer businesses, 2013		Value of residential construction authorized by building permits, 2014	
	Number of establish-ments	Number of employees	Receipts (mil dol)	Annual payroll (mil dol)	Number of establish-ments	Number of employees	Receipts (mil dol)	Annual payroll (mil dol)	Number	Receipts (mil dol)	New Construction ($1,000)	Number of housing units
	159	160	161	162	163	164	165	166	167	168	169	170
ALABAMA—Cont'd												
Washington	21	295	16.4	8.4	8	16	1.3	0.2	1 031	29.8	232	2
Wilcox	20	247	12.7	6.2	10	D	D	D	613	18.1	0	0
Winston	42	915	59.1	23.9	23	D	D	D	1 641	74.7	785	7
ALASKA	2 131	40 618	4 662.6	1 791.5	1 328	7 566	811.3	222.9	52 991	2 574.1	353 712	1 518
Aleutians East	9	D	D	D	2	D	D	D	241	24.3	0	0
Aleutians West	17	146	9.7	4.9	6	29	13.9	1.4	254	10.5	196	2
Anchorage	1 033	20 722	2 678.4	964.1	580	4 060	441.0	125.5	19 252	1 019.5	211 518	770
Bethel	11	D	D	D	13	78	8.7	1.9	1 079	21.1	2 450	11
Bristol Bay	3	5	1.0	0.4	1	D	D	D	220	10.4	402	2
Denali	2	D	D	D	1	D	D	D	155	4.8	NA	NA
Dillingham	5	D	D	D	6	15	0.8	0.3	790	21.8	961	4
Fairbanks North Star	267	4 867	570.5	223.9	195	1 081	106.8	31.3	5 249	223.1	9 925	54
Haines	8	113	6.8	3.0	7	18	1.2	0.3	395	15.7	1 552	6
Hoonah-Angoon	NA	NA	NA	NA	NA	NA	NA	NA	287	11.3	1 676	8
Juneau	138	2 215	200.8	85.5	85	433	40.0	12.0	2 572	127.3	29 697	204
Kenai Peninsula	191	2 671	226.4	97.5	135	602	67.2	18.4	6 160	280.9	24 357	125
Ketchikan Gateway	31	D	D	D	35	133	12.7	3.3	1 317	79.0	8 060	37
Kodiak Island	42	534	56.7	22.0	26	130	13.7	3.0	1 551	96.5	2 284	12
Lake and Peninsula	NA	NA	NA	NA	1	D	D	D	298	18.0	NA	NA
Matanuska-Susitna	232	2 692	253.8	102.7	113	498	57.1	13.6	6 351	273.6	17 936	117
Nome	23	D	D	D	14	74	6.4	1.2	572	19.8	844	10
North Slope	3	D	D	D	8	67	8.3	3.3	255	7.3	3 862	15
Northwest Arctic	4	D	D	D	6	D	D	D	219	8.0	10 224	20
Petersburg	NA	NA	NA	NA	NA	NA	NA	NA	755	63.8	1 025	9
Prince of Wales-Hyder	NA	NA	NA	NA	NA	NA	NA	NA	540	26.6	854	4
Sitka	28	855	86.1	38.9	21	93	8.2	1.8	1 275	76.1	4 544	17
Skagway	NA	NA	NA	NA	NA	NA	NA	NA	127	7.1	719	2
Southeast Fairbanks	9	115	7.1	2.8	9	17	1.3	0.4	542	18.1	NA	NA
Valdez-Cordova	24	470	35.3	13.2	25	96	9.5	2.5	1 258	71.3	518	3
Wade Hampton	3	D	D	D	1	D	D	D	474	3.9	0	0
Wrangell	NA	NA	NA	NA	NA	NA	NA	NA	356	17.2	680	6
Yakutat	2	D	D	D	NA	NA	NA	NA	110	6.0	570	3
Yukon-Koyukuk	4	D	D	D	5	D	D	D	337	11.2	0	0
ARIZONA	15 446	278 833	30 406.8	11 653.5	8 906	68 368	6 219.6	1 725.6	420 233	19 002.7	5 666 004	26 997
Apache	57	2 616	184.3	96.8	35	D	D	D	2 644	54.3	8 649	38
Cochise	273	4 773	380.3	152.0	162	718	44.2	12.3	6 369	185.9	35 149	261
Coconino	389	6 628	878.6	305.9	247	1 493	100.8	32.2	8 342	335.1	105 407	560
Gila	141	2 366	197.5	78.0	64	262	22.1	5.3	3 387	115.9	26 286	101
Graham	70	1 242	104.3	41.1	43	287	30.5	10.0	1 314	47.6	12 852	87
Greenlee	8	121	6.8	4.2	NA	NA	NA	NA	220	6.4	90	1
La Paz	20	516	59.3	23.4	25	D	D	D	793	31.2	3 921	26
Maricopa	9 683	175 051	19 740.9	7 610.8	5 509	45 671	4 392.2	1 195.4	275 014	13 460.3	3 991 073	18 597
Mohave	456	7 612	911.1	284.4	315	1 895	129.4	38.0	10 217	431.6	105 884	535
Navajo	216	3 152	333.4	133.9	125	1 120	135.7	39.9	5 261	156.9	33 104	191
Pima	2 672	51 151	5 459.8	2 073.5	1 494	12 045	1 020.6	289.4	60 686	2 442.0	697 362	3 250
Pinal	325	5 819	476.3	211.5	241	1 445	89.3	28.5	15 902	565.7	318 721	1 744
Santa Cruz	70	1 055	89.8	31.8	52	155	11.8	3.5	4 032	155.4	10 076	44
Yavapai	737	10 268	930.0	370.7	386	1 822	141.9	41.0	17 762	697.2	226 053	968
Yuma	329	6 463	654.6	235.7	208	1 217	85.2	26.0	8 290	317.1	91 377	594
ARKANSAS	7 216	152 864	13 439.6	5 282.0	4 153	23 188	2 187.8	558.0	191 530	7 928.7	1 250 185	7 666
Arkansas	49	1 087	64.4	26.9	35	137	8.9	2.7	1 285	63.2	1 590	18
Ashley	46	567	44.8	19.0	25	131	10.8	2.8	1 078	31.8	0	0
Baxter	158	3 168	311.6	116.2	99	409	25.9	7.6	3 042	121.1	1 265	8
Benton	409	6 176	563.0	220.0	274	D	D	D	15 567	670.8	394 423	2 218
Boone	109	2 109	151.5	59.9	63	D	D	D	2 722	102.4	1 997	12
Bradley	31	574	40.8	16.0	22	71	6.8	1.5	525	20.4	175	1
Calhoun	5	D	D	D	2	D	D	D	191	5.9	0	0
Carroll	54	743	59.7	26.3	40	132	8.8	2.4	2 444	80.8	1 042	10
Chicot	42	773	49.1	21.0	17	57	4.3	1.0	551	20.5	755	6
Clark	57	D	D	D	38	115	12.9	2.9	1 246	44.6	216	3
Clay	27	643	31.4	16.3	24	60	5.1	1.3	814	31.7	984	3
Cleburne	43	718	54.9	20.7	42	153	12.2	2.8	2 143	92.4	2 577	26

STATE County	Government employment and payroll, 2012									Local government finances, 2012				
			March payroll (percent of total)							General revenue				
												Taxes		
													Per capita[1] (dollars)	
	Full-time equivalent employees	March payroll (dollars)	Adminis-tration, judicial, and legal	Police and Corrections	Fire Protection	Highways and transpor-tation	Health and Welfare	Natural resources and utilities	Education and libraries	Total (mil dol)	Inter-govern-mental (mil dol)	Total (mil dol)	Total	Property
	171	172	173	174	175	176	177	178	179	180	181	182	183	184
ALABAMA—Cont'd														
Washington	673	2 075 254	4.0	4.1	0.0	2.0	21.7	3.3	64.7	40.9	25.0	11.8	691	514
Wilcox	583	1 459 476	6.1	7.4	0.0	6.3	11.1	6.3	60.3	29.0	18.4	7.7	674	358
Winston	1 387	3 355 200	3.1	5.2	0.8	2.7	29.1	3.2	54.4	62.5	36.3	16.1	667	283
ALASKA	X	X	X	X	X	X	X	X	X	X	X	X	X	X
Aleutians East	184	728 454	19.1	7.1	0.2	11.9	2.3	7.0	41.2	34.8	17.1	10.2	3 215	0
Aleutians West	278	1 422 298	17.8	11.2	3.2	9.9	3.0	15.4	24.7	56.1	18.9	21.5	3 872	853
Anchorage	10 003	52 917 485	4.5	7.7	6.5	5.4	2.3	9.8	62.6	1 313.0	582.8	546.6	1 831	1 623
Bethel	302	1 160 315	19.0	13.8	3.3	7.0	2.2	43.9	0.1	65.9	43.9	9.6	543	0
Bristol Bay	78	333 504	12.5	13.6	0.7	18.6	2.8	5.7	46.1	16.8	7.9	5.5	5 590	3 083
Denali	82	322 133	9.4	0.0	0.0	0.0	4.0	0.0	85.9	11.0	7.8	2.8	1 472	0
Dillingham	293	1 115 865	13.8	10.5	0.7	3.7	2.6	29.8	35.5	40.8	28.5	5.7	1 140	460
Fairbanks North Star	2 949	14 833 210	7.9	3.4	2.6	2.4	1.8	5.3	75.9	380.0	201.2	148.5	1 481	1 335
Haines	105	554 027	8.6	6.3	0.8	5.6	0.6	5.8	68.5	20.5	12.5	5.3	2 089	1 020
Hoonah-Angoon	90	310 388	14.5	8.3	2.0	8.6	2.0	9.8	54.0	12.4	8.3	1.7	814	39
Juneau	2 061	10 714 562	5.3	5.1	2.9	7.0	24.9	13.7	41.0	338.0	110.1	83.0	2 549	1 125
Kenai Peninsula	2 080	9 477 210	10.6	5.1	7.7	3.9	1.5	4.4	61.5	445.9	125.4	111.8	1 965	1 014
Ketchikan Gateway	699	3 359 138	10.3	7.2	4.6	11.2	1.5	15.2	47.8	123.4	42.9	28.8	2 087	994
Kodiak Island	637	2 986 849	7.4	6.7	2.5	6.1	0.9	9.3	64.9	102.4	55.1	27.0	1 893	1 004
Lake and Peninsula	163	640 681	11.6	0.0	0.1	1.6	1.2	2.7	78.9	24.1	18.4	2.8	1 706	0
Matanuska-Susitna	2 847	12 057 275	8.3	3.7	1.6	2.4	3.8	2.2	76.5	386.7	229.3	136.9	1 458	1 165
Nome	378	1 484 923	12.5	9.6	0.1	4.9	2.6	23.5	37.5	50.2	28.5	9.5	963	231
North Slope	1 749	8 359 644	27.7	5.0	3.3	11.1	11.6	11.4	26.8	503.2	75.9	366.0	37 957	37 888
Northwest Arctic	630	2 686 215	7.5	8.0	1.7	3.7	1.1	9.5	61.6	100.8	72.5	4.2	541	0
Petersburg	512	2 386 453	4.4	6.0	0.8	10.0	32.9	10.6	32.3	82.3	42.5	9.6	2 490	1 229
Prince of Wales-Hyder	289	1 128 652	6.7	2.6	1.0	2.1	2.2	19.6	61.2	30.3	21.8	3.3	576	89
Sitka	525	2 686 315	6.2	5.6	2.0	2.6	30.9	12.2	35.9	89.4	30.2	15.4	1 705	671
Skagway	66	277 303	9.2	10.8	6.1	7.0	16.4	6.9	36.1	19.8	9.1	8.4	8 710	2 132
Southeast Fairbanks	12	40 359	51.1	0.0	0.0	7.5	18.3	0.0	17.1	1.8	1.3	0.0	0	0
Valdez-Cordova	506	2 285 718	8.9	9.3	3.5	9.2	14.4	12.9	38.6	103.7	27.4	50.7	5 213	4 747
Wade Hampton	286	832 391	24.5	17.3	0.7	6.1	0.8	19.3	17.7	58.3	48.1	1.6	208	0
Wrangell	NA	NA	NA	NA	NA	NA	NA	NA	NA	NA	NA	NA	NA	NA
Yakutat	56	174 101	20.5	10.7	0.0	9.9	2.5	2.0	50.3	6.3	4.3	1.3	1 936	647
Yukon-Koyukuk	365	1 481 198	10.8	1.7	0.6	2.6	1.1	7.6	73.3	41.9	35.8	0.9	148	52
ARIZONA	X	X	X	X	X	X	X	X	X	X	X	X	X	X
Apache	2 657	8 600 597	5.6	5.3	1.9	2.9	2.7	1.1	79.6	168.2	116.4	31.5	431	379
Cochise	4 879	16 984 358	11.7	10.2	5.2	2.9	3.0	3.3	61.1	397.9	175.5	144.2	1 092	821
Coconino	4 575	17 536 070	11.8	13.5	9.2	3.5	4.5	6.4	48.1	469.7	159.1	223.4	1 643	979
Gila	2 222	7 331 024	14.5	15.3	7.8	3.9	2.3	5.8	48.1	194.4	80.9	87.8	1 652	1 207
Graham	2 165	7 913 958	6.9	8.1	0.2	2.5	26.5	4.9	50.0	137.7	81.5	29.0	774	382
Greenlee	376	1 216 974	14.2	15.2	0.0	7.6	5.4	1.1	53.9	32.1	12.7	13.6	1 545	1 283
La Paz	799	2 443 896	12.2	19.6	6.3	4.6	4.4	6.2	44.6	60.9	26.7	21.8	1 075	779
Maricopa	129 919	553 767 788	8.2	13.2	5.3	2.8	6.3	12.4	50.5	14 121.0	4 763.7	5 936.1	1 506	958
Mohave	5 613	20 393 845	13.0	13.4	11.7	4.5	2.0	5.6	47.4	538.5	183.2	229.9	1 131	849
Navajo	4 056	13 281 721	8.7	9.6	5.1	2.8	1.5	3.5	67.5	523.9	174.9	109.2	1 020	745
Pima	31 634	115 785 276	10.5	14.5	6.6	3.5	2.2	7.1	52.9	3 257.1	1 214.5	1 427.3	1 438	1 057
Pinal	9 793	33 904 548	13.3	15.5	5.5	3.5	3.8	5.1	52.2	961.4	426.5	329.1	850	624
Santa Cruz	2 004	6 229 659	10.5	13.1	10.4	3.9	2.5	1.8	56.6	161.7	83.6	52.4	1 108	737
Yavapai	6 155	23 081 009	10.4	13.4	9.4	4.0	2.1	5.5	45.2	648.3	201.2	335.8	1 579	1 029
Yuma	7 924	25 609 990	12.0	12.1	3.1	2.2	2.4	7.3	59.9	638.9	314.0	221.6	1 108	716
ARKANSAS	X	X	X	X	X	X	X	X	X	X	X	X	X	X
Arkansas	988	2 636 492	5.7	8.3	2.3	3.4	19.7	5.4	51.8	59.0	32.8	17.1	906	316
Ashley	866	2 414 339	4.8	9.8	2.9	4.1	2.0	4.2	71.6	63.9	38.0	15.5	719	291
Baxter	1 228	3 503 816	4.6	8.5	3.2	6.2	1.3	7.6	68.0	81.3	46.3	22.7	553	251
Benton	7 214	24 863 912	5.8	8.5	5.2	2.0	0.5	6.6	70.3	624.9	346.9	196.3	845	405
Boone	1 391	3 599 052	4.9	7.8	2.9	3.4	0.3	7.1	72.7	96.8	61.2	19.7	527	210
Bradley	467	1 184 067	4.0	5.4	0.9	4.3	3.1	2.7	79.4	35.7	24.9	6.9	603	215
Calhoun	169	422 712	9.1	11.0	0.0	8.6	4.4	3.4	61.8	17.3	7.1	2.7	511	302
Carroll	1 012	2 598 555	4.9	8.8	2.4	5.9	2.4	9.3	64.4	71.0	38.3	16.2	585	295
Chicot	716	2 139 884	6.2	8.0	0.0	2.0	31.0	4.0	48.8	35.1	21.3	8.7	762	307
Clark	763	2 247 437	7.0	17.2	2.0	3.9	2.5	9.0	58.1	67.1	41.9	13.1	572	219
Clay	859	3 044 204	5.9	15.6	0.0	4.6	23.1	14.3	35.5	49.8	25.0	7.5	478	259
Cleburne	801	2 107 158	6.7	9.2	0.5	4.7	1.5	7.6	69.0	57.0	31.3	15.0	583	313

1. Based on the resident population estimated as of July 1 of the year shown.

STATE County	Local government finances, 2012 (cont.)									Government employment, 2013			Presidential election,[2] 2012		
	Direct general expenditure							Debt outstanding					Percent of vote cast:		
			Percent of total for:												
	Total (mil dol)	Per capita[1] (dollars)	Educa-tion	Health and hospitals	Police protec-tion	Public welfare	High-ways	Total (mil dol)	Per capita[1] (dollars)	Federal civilian	Federal military	State and local	Demo-cratic	Republi-can	All other
	185	186	187	188	189	190	191	192	193	194	195	196	197	198	199
ALABAMA—Cont'd															
Washington	42.8	2 504	67.0	3.3	3.6	0.1	11.2	186.5	10 900	34	78	944	35.0	64.4	0.6
Wilcox	31.8	2 786	61.3	2.7	5.4	0.0	7.4	45.1	3 945	59	52	727	71.0	28.8	0.2
Winston	67.7	2 809	62.8	0.9	3.3	0.0	6.0	53.1	2 204	77	111	1 100	17.5	80.8	1.7
ALASKA	X	X	X	X	X	X	X	X	X	15 504	27 457	64 073	37.9	59.4	2.7
Aleutians East	35.1	11 095	24.9	0.3	3.1	0.0	6.3	40.2	12 717	20	10	261	NA	NA	NA
Aleutians West	55.3	9 975	16.7	0.1	7.8	0.0	12.5	41.9	7 550	15	28	482	NA	NA	NA
Anchorage	1 268.0	4 246	52.5	2.1	9.8	0.0	5.8	1 857.9	6 222	8 750	14 545	20 336	NA	NA	NA
Bethel	70.7	3 986	0.0	0.1	6.7	0.0	3.2	8.4	476	74	124	2 911	NA	NA	NA
Bristol Bay	15.8	15 960	28.3	4.7	6.6	0.0	2.4	1.0	993	51	0	193	NA	NA	NA
Denali	10.7	5 696	75.8	0.1	0.0	0.0	0.0	0.0	0	215	22	154	NA	NA	NA
Dillingham	39.6	7 872	29.2	2.5	8.2	2.1	5.2	15.1	2 990	50	35	685	NA	NA	NA
Fairbanks North Star	342.4	3 415	63.0	1.6	2.3	0.0	6.2	170.2	1 698	3 037	8 775	8 202	NA	NA	NA
Haines	15.3	5 980	38.0	1.6	3.3	0.0	6.3	16.4	6 424	10	18	202	NA	NA	NA
Hoonah-Angoon	11.8	5 536	49.2	1.1	4.3	0.0	4.8	3.0	1 396	104	15	264			
Juneau	318.0	9 768	26.7	30.7	5.4	0.0	4.2	225.5	6 927	764	473	6 155	NA	NA	NA
Kenai Peninsula	437.7	7 692	32.5	38.4	2.0	0.0	2.4	171.8	3 019	359	486	4 413	NA	NA	NA
Ketchikan Gateway	133.0	9 654	26.9	0.8	3.6	0.0	4.1	145.8	10 581	247	256	1 795	NA	NA	NA
Kodiak Island	95.8	6 729	46.7	0.6	5.3	0.0	3.3	62.8	4 413	321	1 069	1 119	NA	NA	NA
Lake and Peninsula	20.2	12 184	72.3	0.1	0.5	0.0	0.8	3.8	2 267	42	11	366	NA	NA	NA
Matanuska-Susitna	393.6	4 190	61.3	2.3	2.6	0.0	6.9	404.7	4 309	198	667	4 640	NA	NA	NA
Nome	44.7	4 511	29.0	1.0	4.3	0.0	6.8	12.3	1 244	57	69	1 619	NA	NA	NA
North Slope	459.1	47 609	17.7	2.7	3.1	1.5	3.7	510.2	52 913	21	50	1 863	NA	NA	NA
Northwest Arctic	89.1	11 410	62.5	0.1	1.7	0.0	2.2	72.5	9 289	50	52	1 042	NA	NA	NA
Petersburg	85.2	22 155	24.0	26.0	3.2	1.2	7.1	28.2	7 342	100	54	398			
Prince of Wales-Hyder	28.0	4 867	53.2	1.1	4.5	0.0	2.7	4.0	704	88	41	875			
Sitka	79.2	8 752	28.6	27.3	5.4	0.0	1.8	117.1	12 949	131	253	1 044	NA	NA	NA
Skagway	17.6	18 327	12.7	9.9	7.3	0.1	9.4	6.5	6 776	53	0	118			
Southeast Fairbanks	1.9	262	0.2	0.1	0.0	0.0	8.6	0.9	119	420	47	433	NA	NA	NA
Valdez-Cordova	84.7	8 716	25.8	23.7	2.1	0.0	3.8	37.8	3 895	138	225	1 172	NA	NA	NA
Wade Hampton	70.2	8 985	80.8	0.2	1.6	0.0	1.3	3.8	489	21	57	1 532	NA	NA	NA
Wrangell	NA	NA	NA	NA	NA	NA	NA	NA	NA	50	17	276			
Yakutat	6.6	9 847	45.8	2.9	9.1	0.0	7.6	1.0	1 548	25	0	121	NA	NA	NA
Yukon-Koyukuk	46.4	8 035	79.2	0.3	1.0	0.0	1.2	6.9	1 200	93	40	1 402	NA	NA	NA
ARIZONA	X	X	X	X	X	X	X	X	X	55 613	33 307	352 837	45.1	53.6	1.2
Apache	161.6	2 208	65.6	3.6	3.3	0.0	6.5	280.9	3 837	2 713	156	8 111	63.4	35.2	1.3
Cochise	407.1	3 082	44.0	3.5	12.3	4.9	7.3	161.6	1 223	5 560	4 984	6 484	38.8	59.5	1.7
Coconino	457.2	3 361	35.9	3.4	6.5	1.6	7.6	377.9	2 779	2 810	289	15 449	57.8	40.8	1.3
Gila	163.2	3 071	37.4	1.4	11.8	2.5	6.1	46.8	881	462	115	4 718	35.3	63.1	1.6
Graham	132.6	3 543	64.5	0.4	8.6	1.6	4.9	28.1	752	419	75	2 287	29.0	69.8	1.2
Greenlee	31.0	3 517	44.5	5.9	11.6	0.0	6.8	16.8	1 911	31	20	511	40.0	58.8	1.2
La Paz	82.5	4 069	27.8	3.1	9.7	0.6	7.2	44.7	2 204	319	44	2 029	34.7	63.2	2.1
Maricopa	13 916.1	3 530	41.6	5.1	8.2	1.5	4.1	27 988.0	7 100	19 884	12 837	189 999	44.1	54.7	1.2
Mohave	555.1	2 730	33.9	2.7	6.9	0.1	8.7	627.7	3 087	488	437	7 431	32.7	65.6	1.7
Navajo	397.5	3 712	44.4	24.0	5.0	0.8	4.3	156.9	1 465	1 699	231	8 037	43.5	55.2	1.3
Pima	3 531.8	3 559	37.0	3.1	9.1	2.7	5.3	5 788.9	5 833	12 621	8 564	67 100	52.4	46.4	1.2
Pinal	1 130.4	2 918	46.7	4.4	9.1	1.6	3.8	1 030.3	2 660	1 742	800	18 400	42.2	56.7	1.2
Santa Cruz	148.9	3 149	48.5	3.1	10.0	0.0	3.8	161.3	3 410	1 788	102	2 109	65.3	34.0	0.8
Yavapai	653.7	3 074	36.5	2.1	7.2	1.8	9.0	725.7	3 413	1 372	475	9 106	37.0	61.4	1.6
Yuma	616.3	3 081	47.8	2.1	6.0	2.5	4.6	668.5	3 342	3 705	4 178	11 066	42.6	56.3	1.1
ARKANSAS	X	X	X	X	X	X	X	X	X	20 441	18 718	196 177	38.9	58.7	2.4
Arkansas	54.5	2 887	54.8	0.8	6.7	0.0	6.5	53.2	2 814	185	84	1 009	37.5	60.0	2.5
Ashley	63.4	2 945	60.9	0.2	5.8	0.0	6.5	95.2	4 425	67	96	1 095	34.4	62.6	3.0
Baxter	82.1	2 001	58.9	0.0	7.5	0.1	8.6	143.9	3 507	140	184	1 540	32.7	64.3	3.0
Benton	620.5	2 672	61.2	0.2	5.6	0.0	5.6	1 204.1	5 184	442	1 071	9 173	30.7	67.2	2.1
Boone	94.8	2 540	65.0	0.1	4.7	0.0	4.2	59.7	1 600	158	168	3 212	28.7	68.3	3.0
Bradley	34.0	2 985	65.5	0.0	5.4	0.1	7.3	14.7	1 294	29	50	864	41.6	56.0	2.4
Calhoun	20.8	3 913	57.2	1.1	3.3	0.5	6.0	106.6	20 089	11	23	267	31.2	65.9	2.9
Carroll	75.8	2 746	55.7	0.1	5.3	0.0	7.5	70.0	2 781	82	125	1 116	39.4	57.5	3.1
Chicot	34.4	3 008	57.3	2.8	6.4	0.1	7.0	15.4	1 344	41	48	953	58.4	40.7	0.9
Clark	65.6	2 861	64.3	0.1	4.3	0.0	5.6	101.8	4 437	85	91	2 632	46.9	50.7	2.4
Clay	49.7	3 171	48.6	25.1	4.0	0.0	5.7	31.5	2 010	53	70	858	40.7	55.0	4.3
Cleburne	54.0	2 093	60.3	0.2	4.9	0.1	9.9	57.4	2 225	83	115	885	26.0	70.2	3.7

1. Based on the resident population estimated as of July 1 of the year shown. 2.

STATE/ County code	CBSA code[1]	County type[2]	STATE County	Land area,[3] (sq km) 2010	Population, 2014: Total persons 2014	Population, 2014: Rank	Population, 2014: Per square kilometer	Population and population characteristics, 2013: Race alone or in combination, not Hispanic or Latino (percent): White	Black	American Indian, Alaska Native	Asian and Pacific Islander	Percent Hispanic or Latino[4]	Age (percent): Under 5 years	5 to 17 years	18 to 24 years	25 to 34 years	35 to 44 years	45 to 54 years
				1	2	3	4	5	6	7	8	9	10	11	12	13	14	15
			ARKANSAS—Cont'd															
05 025	38220	3	Cleveland	1 548	8 449	2 561	5.5	85.7	12.3	0.7	0.3	2.0	5.4	18.3	7.6	10.5	12.3	14.0
05 027	31620	7	Columbia	1 984	23 933	1 645	12.1	60.5	36.3	0.8	0.9	2.6	6.0	15.9	16.0	11.1	10.5	12.3
05 029	...	6	Conway	1 430	21 083	1 769	14.7	83.5	12.1	1.7	0.8	3.9	6.1	17.2	8.1	11.4	11.4	14.1
05 031	27860	3	Craighead	1 832	102 518	576	56.0	80.0	14.7	0.8	1.4	4.6	6.9	17.9	11.8	15.1	12.6	12.0
05 033	22900	2	Crawford	1 536	61 697	847	40.2	88.1	1.9	3.7	2.0	6.7	6.0	19.2	8.4	12.0	12.6	14.3
05 035	32820	1	Crittenden	1 579	49 548	986	31.4	45.6	51.8	0.7	0.9	2.2	7.8	20.3	9.3	12.9	12.3	13.6
05 037	...	6	Cross	1 596	17 227	1 969	10.8	74.7	23.2	0.8	0.8	1.8	6.7	17.8	8.5	11.1	12.3	14.1
05 039	...	6	Dallas	1 729	7 755	2 616	4.5	54.7	42.7	0.9	0.3	2.7	5.7	17.1	7.6	10.9	10.7	13.4
05 041	...	6	Desha	1 990	12 264	2 280	6.2	47.5	47.5	0.7	0.5	4.6	6.9	19.0	8.2	11.5	10.7	13.0
05 043	...	7	Drew	2 145	18 622	1 884	8.7	68.1	28.6	0.6	0.9	2.9	6.1	16.8	14.2	11.4	10.8	12.8
05 045	30780	2	Faulkner	1 678	120 768	511	72.0	83.0	11.8	1.2	1.8	4.0	6.6	17.6	15.5	14.5	12.5	12.3
05 047	...	2	Franklin	1 577	17 805	1 927	11.3	94.1	1.3	2.1	1.2	2.8	5.9	18.0	8.9	10.9	12.0	13.3
05 049	...	9	Fulton	1 601	12 125	2 289	7.6	97.5	0.9	1.6	0.5	1.1	4.9	15.6	6.7	8.8	10.4	13.5
05 051	26300	3	Garland	1 755	97 322	604	55.5	85.0	9.2	1.5	1.2	5.2	5.6	15.1	7.9	11.2	11.1	13.2
05 053	30780	2	Grant	1 636	18 144	1 913	11.1	94.0	3.0	1.2	0.6	2.3	5.8	18.0	7.8	12.1	13.2	14.7
05 055	37500	6	Greene	1 496	43 694	1 098	29.2	95.8	1.2	1.1	0.5	2.6	6.8	18.2	8.8	12.3	13.4	13.7
05 057	...	6	Hempstead	1 884	22 327	1 717	11.9	57.2	30.1	1.0	0.8	12.5	7.3	18.9	8.3	11.4	11.5	13.8
05 059	31680	6	Hot Spring	1 593	33 368	1 343	20.9	84.4	12.0	1.3	0.7	3.2	5.4	16.5	8.6	12.4	12.3	14.1
05 061	...	7	Howard	1 524	13 500	2 207	8.9	67.0	21.3	1.3	1.0	10.6	7.1	19.2	8.1	11.7	11.3	14.0
05 063	12900	7	Independence	1 979	36 959	1 250	18.7	90.3	2.6	1.1	1.3	6.1	6.5	17.4	8.9	12.0	12.5	13.3
05 065	...	9	Izard	1 504	13 486	2 208	9.0	95.6	1.9	1.7	0.5	1.7	4.4	14.0	6.8	9.9	10.8	14.1
05 067	...	6	Jackson	1 642	17 534	1 945	10.7	79.0	17.9	1.2	0.6	2.6	5.5	14.9	8.1	14.1	13.3	14.3
05 069	38220	3	Jefferson	2 255	72 297	749	32.1	41.5	56.0	0.8	1.2	1.8	6.2	17.3	10.6	12.7	11.4	13.6
05 071	...	6	Johnson	1 709	26 005	1 559	15.2	83.0	2.1	1.9	1.4	13.2	7.0	17.7	9.8	12.7	11.8	13.6
05 073	...	8	Lafayette	1 368	7 111	2 670	5.2	60.5	37.2	0.5	0.6	2.0	4.8	16.1	8.4	9.8	10.5	15.0
05 075	...	6	Lawrence	1 522	16 931	1 982	11.1	97.2	1.2	1.1	0.4	1.2	5.4	17.1	9.8	10.7	11.4	13.4
05 077	...	6	Lee	1 561	9 860	2 449	6.3	42.3	54.7	1.0	0.8	2.5	5.3	14.9	9.0	14.5	13.2	13.4
05 079	38220	3	Lincoln	1 454	13 970	2 172	9.6	65.9	30.4	0.8	0.4	3.6	4.5	13.6	10.9	16.4	14.6	15.4
05 081	45500	6	Little River	1 379	12 532	2 262	9.1	75.2	20.4	2.5	0.7	3.1	5.2	17.6	7.8	10.8	12.4	13.4
05 083	...	6	Logan	1 834	21 958	1 734	12.0	92.9	2.0	1.9	2.1	2.6	5.6	17.4	8.2	10.4	11.6	14.6
05 085	30780	2	Lonoke	1 996	71 557	755	35.9	88.6	6.5	1.1	1.4	3.9	6.8	20.0	8.4	13.9	14.0	13.6
05 087	22220	2	Madison	2 161	15 740	2 058	7.3	92.2	0.7	2.2	1.0	5.3	6.1	17.5	7.9	10.4	12.1	14.6
05 089	...	9	Marion	1 546	16 367	2 022	10.6	96.4	0.7	1.7	0.5	2.2	4.4	12.6	6.4	8.6	9.1	14.6
05 091	45500	3	Miller	1 620	43 428	1 104	26.8	71.4	25.1	1.3	0.8	3.0	7.1	17.1	8.8	13.5	12.6	13.6
05 093	14180	4	Mississippi	2 332	44 235	1 086	19.0	60.9	35.0	0.7	0.8	3.9	7.2	19.9	9.5	12.7	11.8	13.6
05 095	...	7	Monroe	1 572	7 582	2 635	4.8	56.9	40.4	1.2	0.8	2.0	5.7	15.9	8.5	9.2	10.6	14.1
05 097	...	8	Montgomery	2 020	9 082	2 509	4.5	94.2	0.8	2.4	0.9	3.7	4.4	15.3	6.5	8.1	10.6	14.9
05 099	...	7	Nevada	1 600	8 723	2 538	5.5	65.5	31.4	0.8	0.5	3.2	6.4	16.5	8.0	10.8	11.4	13.9
05 101	25460	9	Newton	2 126	7 904	2 602	3.7	96.7	0.7	2.9	0.5	1.5	4.7	15.3	6.9	10.1	10.1	13.6
05 103	15780	7	Ouachita	1 898	24 828	1 616	13.1	57.4	40.8	0.9	0.7	1.9	6.3	16.6	7.9	11.1	10.8	13.9
05 105	30780	2	Perry	1 428	10 245	2 418	7.2	93.9	2.8	1.7	0.5	2.9	5.3	16.6	8.1	10.4	12.4	14.9
05 107	25760	7	Phillips	1 802	19 930	1 839	11.1	36.2	62.1	0.6	0.6	1.6	7.8	19.3	9.3	11.1	10.2	13.0
05 109	...	9	Pike	1 556	11 024	2 358	7.1	89.1	3.6	1.5	0.7	6.6	6.0	17.6	8.2	10.7	12.6	13.8
05 111	27860	3	Poinsett	1 964	24 246	1 635	12.3	89.0	8.4	0.7	0.5	2.7	6.5	17.4	8.7	11.5	12.4	13.9
05 113	...	7	Polk	2 221	20 225	1 825	9.1	91.0	0.8	3.4	0.8	6.2	6.0	17.4	7.7	9.7	10.8	13.2
05 115	40780	5	Pope	2 104	63 201	828	30.0	87.1	3.6	1.7	1.5	8.0	6.3	16.5	14.1	12.8	11.5	13.1
05 117	...	8	Prairie	1 678	8 304	2 576	4.9	86.3	12.5	1.0	0.2	1.0	4.9	15.9	7.2	9.7	11.2	14.6
05 119	30780	2	Pulaski	1 968	392 702	175	199.5	55.9	36.4	1.0	2.7	5.9	7.0	16.9	9.1	15.2	12.8	13.1
05 121	...	7	Randolph	1 689	17 571	1 944	10.4	96.4	1.3	1.2	0.5	1.8	5.8	16.7	8.2	11.4	11.4	13.6
05 123	22620	6	St. Francis	1 644	26 899	1 539	16.4	42.3	52.8	0.9	0.9	4.4	6.5	16.3	8.5	14.7	14.1	13.5
05 125	30780	2	Saline	1 874	115 719	529	61.7	88.3	6.5	1.1	1.3	4.2	6.1	17.9	7.4	12.9	13.4	13.5
05 127	...	6	Scott	2 311	10 693	2 381	4.6	86.3	1.4	3.4	3.9	7.4	6.0	18.5	8.3	10.7	11.1	14.6
05 129	...	9	Searcy	1 725	7 929	2 601	4.6	96.1	0.7	3.1	0.5	2.0	4.9	15.3	6.5	9.5	10.6	14.2
05 131	22900	2	Sebastian	1 378	126 776	487	92.0	74.1	7.5	3.3	5.0	13.2	6.9	17.8	9.6	13.2	12.5	13.6
05 133	...	7	Sevier	1 464	17 426	1 953	11.9	60.7	4.7	3.1	0.8	32.6	8.0	21.1	9.5	12.4	12.7	12.3
05 135	...	7	Sharp	1 565	16 906	1 985	10.8	95.8	1.2	2.2	0.6	2.0	5.3	15.7	6.9	9.0	10.3	13.0
05 137	...	9	Stone	1 571	12 494	2 266	8.0	96.9	0.6	1.8	0.7	1.6	5.2	15.3	6.5	9.1	9.7	13.5
05 139	20980	5	Union	2 692	40 227	1 167	14.9	62.7	33.0	1.0	1.0	3.6	6.4	17.3	8.2	11.7	12.1	13.8
05 141	...	8	Van Buren	1 834	16 851	1 992	9.2	95.3	1.1	2.0	0.6	2.8	5.0	14.9	6.8	9.6	10.8	13.7
05 143	22220	2	Washington	2 440	220 792	290	90.5	74.8	3.9	2.2	5.4	16.1	7.4	18.0	14.9	15.4	12.7	11.4
05 145	42620	4	White	2 681	78 592	702	29.3	90.3	5.2	1.3	0.9	4.1	6.5	17.3	12.2	12.6	12.0	13.1
05 147	...	9	Woodruff	1 520	6 910	2 688	4.5	71.0	27.7	0.8	0.5	1.6	5.8	16.3	7.7	9.6	11.5	13.8
05 149	40780	6	Yell	2 409	21 951	1 735	9.1	77.0	2.0	1.3	1.7	19.4	6.7	18.7	8.3	11.6	12.5	13.7

1. CBSA = Core Based Statistical Area. See Appendix A for explanation. See Appendix B for list of metropolitan areas with component counties. 2. County type code from the Economic Research Service of USDA Rural-Urban Continuum Codes. See Appendix A for definition. 3. Dry land or land partially or temporarily covered by water. 4. May be of any race.

STATE County	Population, 2013 (cont.): Age (percent) (cont.): 55 to 64 years	65 to 74 years	75 years and over	Percent female	Population change and components of change, 2000–2014: Total persons: 2000	2010	Percent change: 2000–2010	2010–2014	Components of change, 2010–2014: Births	Deaths	Net migration	Households, 2009–2013: Number	Persons per house-hold	Percent: Family house-holds	Female family house-holder[1]	One per-son
	16	17	18	19	20	21	22	23	24	25	26	27	28	29	30	31
ARKANSAS—Cont'd																
Cleveland	13.5	10.5	7.9	51.2	8 571	8 689	1.4	-2.8	383	388	-225	3 346	2.56	74.6	13.0	22.9
Columbia	11.9	8.6	7.8	52.2	25 603	24 552	-4.1	-2.5	1 210	1 329	-469	9 449	2.43	68.8	17.5	26.2
Conway	13.7	10.0	8.0	51.0	20 336	21 273	4.6	-0.9	1 135	1 028	-264	8 154	2.57	70.5	16.0	26.4
Craighead	10.8	7.4	5.4	51.2	82 148	96 443	17.4	6.3	6 012	3 655	3 657	37 834	2.51	68.3	15.2	24.3
Crawford	12.7	9.0	5.9	50.8	53 247	61 948	16.3	-0.4	3 228	2 495	-922	23 368	2.62	75.2	13.0	22.1
Crittenden	11.8	7.1	4.7	52.7	50 866	50 902	0.1	-2.7	3 379	1 982	-2 707	18 309	2.72	69.6	23.8	27.0
Cross	12.6	10.0	6.9	51.6	19 526	17 870	-8.5	-3.6	991	871	-744	6 818	2.57	69.5	13.8	26.6
Dallas	14.8	10.6	9.1	51.5	9 210	8 116	-11.9	-4.4	354	442	-282	3 269	2.32	63.4	11.8	34.3
Desha	14.2	9.7	6.8	53.2	15 341	13 008	-15.2	-5.7	749	630	-882	5 305	2.39	63.7	20.6	32.3
Drew	12.1	8.3	7.4	51.3	18 723	18 509	-1.1	0.6	1 003	784	-87	7 496	2.37	66.5	16.9	25.0
Faulkner	10.1	6.6	4.4	51.0	86 014	113 237	31.6	6.7	6 624	3 565	4 323	42 413	2.62	67.0	11.6	25.3
Franklin	13.3	9.8	7.8	50.7	17 771	18 125	2.0	-1.8	833	900	-262	6 769	2.61	70.4	11.4	26.4
Fulton	15.6	14.4	10.2	50.7	11 642	12 245	5.2	-1.0	449	722	149	5 140	2.35	67.5	8.2	27.8
Garland	14.5	11.9	9.4	51.7	88 068	96 024	9.0	1.4	4 814	5 675	2 421	39 881	2.37	64.3	12.1	29.7
Grant	12.7	9.7	6.1	50.4	16 464	17 853	8.4	1.6	853	739	174	6 855	2.59	73.4	9.2	24.4
Greene	12.0	8.7	6.1	50.8	37 331	42 090	12.7	3.8	2 331	1 943	1 231	16 603	2.53	69.6	12.0	25.9
Hempstead	12.9	9.1	6.7	51.6	23 587	22 609	-4.1	-1.2	1 376	984	-649	8 296	2.67	66.6	17.0	31.0
Hot Spring	13.9	9.9	6.8	48.0	30 353	32 923	8.5	1.4	1 511	1 524	464	12 231	2.58	69.4	12.0	25.7
Howard	12.3	9.1	7.2	51.1	14 300	13 789	-3.6	-2.1	822	635	-448	5 208	2.60	71.1	18.1	24.9
Independence	12.8	9.2	7.4	51.2	34 233	36 647	7.1	0.9	1 995	1 709	70	14 544	2.46	68.9	13.2	25.3
Izard	15.1	13.9	11.0	48.4	13 249	13 696	3.4	-1.5	508	763	77	5 682	2.26	68.1	9.9	30.3
Jackson	13.3	9.6	6.8	50.4	18 418	17 997	-2.3	-2.6	846	927	-386	6 541	2.28	64.9	14.9	31.2
Jefferson	13.5	8.4	6.3	51.0	84 278	77 435	-8.1	-6.6	4 031	3 567	-5 585	28 367	2.47	63.8	18.9	32.8
Johnson	12.1	8.8	6.6	50.4	22 781	25 540	12.1	1.8	1 516	1 079	77	10 046	2.49	70.4	11.4	25.9
Lafayette	14.4	12.2	8.7	51.5	8 559	7 645	-10.7	-7.0	269	385	-378	2 722	2.70	62.7	16.6	33.2
Lawrence	12.9	10.6	8.7	50.9	17 774	17 415	-2.0	-2.8	795	982	-294	6 580	2.52	66.5	10.5	29.4
Lee	13.4	8.9	7.5	44.3	12 580	10 424	-17.1	-5.4	451	497	-515	3 491	2.54	62.1	19.3	34.0
Lincoln	11.5	7.2	6.0	39.0	14 492	14 134	-2.5	-1.2	509	507	-155	4 188	2.53	71.4	16.5	23.7
Little River	14.2	11.3	7.3	51.0	13 628	13 171	-3.4	-4.8	586	647	-567	5 315	2.41	72.3	17.1	25.0
Logan	13.4	10.7	8.0	50.4	22 486	22 353	-0.6	-1.8	1 083	1 166	-329	8 233	2.63	68.6	10.9	27.5
Lonoke	11.1	7.4	4.7	50.7	52 828	68 356	29.4	4.7	4 106	2 531	1 603	25 052	2.74	75.0	13.0	20.8
Madison	14.5	10.1	6.8	49.9	14 243	15 717	10.3	0.1	818	697	-90	6 048	2.58	71.2	9.9	26.3
Marion	17.9	16.5	10.0	50.1	16 140	16 653	3.2	-1.7	620	994	128	7 036	2.34	67.1	6.3	27.5
Miller	12.7	8.6	6.1	50.8	40 443	43 462	7.5	-0.1	2 570	1 897	-635	16 950	2.49	66.9	16.4	30.1
Mississippi	12.3	7.5	5.6	51.3	51 979	46 480	-10.6	-4.8	2 684	2 124	-2 785	17 058	2.64	68.5	18.9	26.6
Monroe	16.1	10.4	9.5	52.5	10 254	8 149	-20.5	-7.0	392	449	-475	3 393	2.33	63.9	14.9	32.7
Montgomery	15.4	13.8	11.0	50.0	9 245	9 487	2.6	-4.3	346	511	-226	3 873	2.39	68.0	8.0	27.2
Nevada	14.2	10.5	8.4	50.8	9 955	8 997	-9.6	-3.0	466	464	-269	3 622	2.41	65.8	12.6	32.3
Newton	16.1	14.1	9.0	49.6	8 608	8 330	-3.2	-5.1	305	399	-312	3 507	2.32	68.8	7.7	28.8
Ouachita	15.5	9.6	8.2	52.8	28 790	26 120	-9.3	-5.0	1 327	1 529	-1 079	10 733	2.36	64.5	16.7	33.1
Perry	13.9	10.6	7.8	50.2	10 209	10 445	2.3	-1.9	443	523	-150	3 903	2.61	72.0	7.7	25.2
Phillips	13.4	9.0	6.8	53.0	26 445	21 757	-17.7	-8.4	1 335	1 139	-2 026	8 339	2.52	65.5	26.6	31.1
Pike	13.2	10.2	7.6	50.1	11 303	11 291	-0.1	-2.4	507	590	-173	4 325	2.55	73.5	13.5	25.2
Poinsett	13.0	9.8	6.9	51.7	25 614	24 583	-4.0	-1.4	1 313	1 392	-239	9 369	2.56	67.8	15.4	28.7
Polk	14.3	12.4	8.6	50.9	20 229	20 662	2.1	-2.1	985	1 093	-292	8 069	2.53	69.9	11.0	27.3
Pope	11.6	8.1	5.9	50.2	54 469	61 754	13.4	2.3	3 309	2 400	607	22 603	2.63	70.2	12.1	25.6
Prairie	14.7	12.3	9.4	50.8	9 539	8 715	-8.6	-4.7	359	417	-367	3 737	2.26	66.5	11.6	28.1
Pulaski	12.8	7.5	5.5	52.0	361 474	382 748	5.9	2.6	24 113	14 768	951	153 720	2.47	61.4	16.5	33.1
Randolph	13.4	10.9	8.7	50.8	18 195	17 969	-1.2	-2.2	801	974	-177	7 244	2.42	72.0	9.6	26.0
St. Francis	13.0	8.1	5.3	45.2	29 329	28 258	-3.7	-4.8	1 487	1 172	-1 658	9 358	2.57	66.9	22.2	29.8
Saline	12.1	10.2	6.6	50.9	83 529	107 118	28.2	8.0	5 688	4 083	7 004	41 287	2.62	71.7	10.9	24.3
Scott	12.6	10.9	7.2	49.4	10 996	11 233	2.2	-4.8	529	522	-543	4 324	2.55	74.2	11.7	21.9
Searcy	15.9	13.4	9.7	49.9	8 261	8 195	-0.8	-3.2	330	465	-117	3 296	2.43	64.1	6.7	33.5
Sebastian	12.3	8.1	6.0	51.0	115 071	125 744	9.3	0.8	7 282	5 135	-1 059	49 294	2.53	65.1	12.2	30.3
Sevier	10.9	7.3	5.8	50.1	15 757	17 058	8.3	2.2	1 158	640	-113	5 745	2.95	72.1	15.3	25.3
Sharp	14.7	14.3	10.9	50.8	17 119	17 264	0.8	-2.1	727	1 036	-30	7 023	2.42	65.3	7.7	30.3
Stone	16.0	14.7	10.1	50.5	11 499	12 394	7.8	0.8	548	719	248	5 135	2.41	63.5	4.9	32.4
Union	14.0	8.9	7.4	51.3	45 629	41 639	-8.7	-3.4	2 182	2 189	-1 409	16 596	2.45	70.4	17.5	27.1
Van Buren	15.0	13.4	10.8	50.0	16 192	17 295	6.8	-2.6	724	955	-166	7 063	2.40	68.3	11.3	27.4
Washington	9.7	6.1	4.4	49.9	157 715	203 065	28.8	8.7	14 012	5 826	9 383	79 214	2.53	63.3	11.1	28.2
White	11.4	8.6	6.2	51.0	67 165	77 076	14.8	2.0	4 252	3 336	568	29 632	2.50	70.7	10.6	24.8
Woodruff	16.3	11.4	8.7	52.4	8 741	7 260	-16.9	-4.9	344	419	-295	3 070	2.29	65.2	16.5	32.0
Yell	12.4	9.1	7.1	50.2	21 139	22 185	4.9	-1.1	1 279	1 047	-512	7 917	2.74	67.5	9.9	27.3

1. No spouse present.

STATE County	Persons in group quarters, 2014	Daytime population, 2009–2013: Number	Daytime population, 2009–2013: Employment/residence ratio	Births, 2014: Total	Births, 2014: Rate[1]	Deaths, 2014: Number	Deaths, 2014: Rate[1]	Persons under 65 with no health insurance, 2013: Number	Persons under 65 with no health insurance, 2013: Percent	Medicare, 2014: Eligible for Medicare	Medicare, 2014: Enrolled in Medicare Advantage	Medicare, 2014: Enrolled in a Medicare prescription drug plan	Serious crimes known to police,[2] 2013: Total: Number	Serious crimes known to police,[2] 2013: Total: Rate[3]
	32	33	34	35	36	37	38	39	40	41	42	43	44	45
ARKANSAS—Cont'd														
Cleveland	52	6 840	0.44	82	9.7	80	9.5	1 279	18.3	1 955	228	1 122	144	1 673
Columbia	1 650	24 427	0.99	284	11.9	289	12.1	3 534	18.8	5 113	635	3 252	762	3 125
Conway	286	20 483	0.91	263	12.5	218	10.3	3 249	18.8	4 919	952	2 522	770	3 614
Craighead	3 788	102 884	1.11	1 445	14.1	903	8.8	16 136	18.9	16 960	2 517	9 576	3 894	3 863
Crawford	540	55 361	0.74	774	12.5	576	9.3	10 774	20.7	12 522	4 670	4 580	1 852	2 990
Crittenden	701	46 854	0.82	769	15.5	491	9.9	7 049	16.3	8 425	1 334	4 781	3 249	6 533
Cross	225	16 449	0.81	235	13.6	196	11.4	2 478	17.2	3 837	669	2 101	719	4 077
Dallas	403	8 667	1.22	74	9.5	89	11.5	1 115	18.5	1 904	382	988	273	3 429
Desha	56	13 064	1.06	165	13.5	159	13.0	1 912	18.5	2 789	281	1 760	NA	NA
Drew	905	17 823	0.88	243	13.0	199	10.7	2 644	17.7	3 567	386	2 148	768	4 090
Faulkner	4 366	106 719	0.83	1 544	12.8	836	6.9	16 196	15.9	17 268	1 655	9 499	4 442	3 692
Franklin	448	16 916	0.83	201	11.3	194	10.9	2 809	19.0	3 957	1 126	1 770	458	2 541
Fulton	165	10 802	0.66	108	8.9	180	14.8	2 041	22.1	3 397	726	1 753	161	1 304
Garland	2 172	96 611	1.00	1 141	11.7	1 288	13.2	16 109	21.4	26 223	5 363	12 577	5 637	5 802
Grant	143	14 440	0.55	209	11.5	154	8.5	2 478	16.5	3 602	512	1 783	442	2 452
Greene	602	42 413	0.99	535	12.2	455	10.4	6 427	17.7	9 002	1 726	4 781	2 137	4 912
Hempstead	301	22 856	1.04	322	14.4	213	9.5	4 170	22.3	4 429	799	2 438	967	4 335
Hot Spring	2 137	29 383	0.71	345	10.3	355	10.6	4 583	17.7	7 281	1 176	3 462	NA	NA
Howard	181	15 738	1.35	180	13.3	134	9.9	2 694	23.9	3 001	490	1 715	445	3 245
Independence	919	38 346	1.10	472	12.8	403	10.9	6 342	21.0	8 075	826	4 852	1 595	4 299
Izard	944	13 018	0.88	119	8.8	181	13.4	2 003	21.3	3 751	646	2 128	281	2 095
Jackson	2 129	18 046	1.04	200	11.4	203	11.6	2 448	19.2	3 908	374	2 474	851	4 874
Jefferson	4 781	78 696	1.10	916	12.7	844	11.7	8 916	15.4	14 817	3 269	7 017	4 171	5 645
Johnson	555	25 772	1.01	366	14.1	233	9.0	4 784	22.4	5 386	1 256	2 639	656	2 521
Lafayette	113	6 785	0.70	61	8.6	84	11.8	1 281	22.8	1 750	211	1 055	NA	NA
Lawrence	630	16 181	0.83	189	11.2	245	14.5	2 513	18.9	4 266	645	2 429	184	1 091
Lee	1 741	9 880	0.87	104	10.5	121	12.3	1 257	18.8	1 991	489	1 080	265	2 607
Lincoln	3 748	13 501	0.83	111	7.9	141	10.1	1 650	19.2	2 363	345	1 319	101	715
Little River	123	12 316	0.87	146	11.7	149	11.9	1 919	18.6	3 063	393	1 714	300	2 335
Logan	581	20 236	0.77	253	11.5	282	12.8	3 319	18.7	5 407	1 381	2 471	746	3 410
Lonoke	572	53 611	0.51	961	13.4	604	8.4	9 735	15.8	11 631	1 801	5 450	2 013	2 865
Madison	79	13 234	0.62	196	12.5	141	9.0	3 190	24.6	3 550	1 029	1 462	146	1 102
Marion	141	14 996	0.73	146	8.9	257	15.7	2 460	20.4	5 107	1 307	2 235	362	2 188
Miller	1 470	39 180	0.76	579	13.3	442	10.2	6 257	17.5	8 179	1 483	4 295	2 246	5 142
Mississippi	794	48 631	1.16	610	13.8	502	11.3	6 683	17.5	8 500	1 578	4 520	2 670	5 894
Monroe	84	7 940	0.98	88	11.6	125	16.5	1 152	18.9	1 997	366	1 162	160	2 067
Montgomery	121	8 344	0.69	73	8.0	129	14.2	1 624	23.6	2 525	427	1 230	83	893
Nevada	157	8 072	0.75	102	11.7	107	12.3	1 291	18.3	2 109	468	1 078	177	1 986
Newton	51	6 820	0.57	74	9.4	100	12.7	1 391	22.5	2 344	536	1 071	114	1 424
Ouachita	352	24 213	0.85	297	12.0	344	13.9	3 319	16.3	6 083	1 530	2 850	717	2 848
Perry	152	8 018	0.41	100	9.8	124	12.1	1 621	19.3	2 492	448	1 310	298	2 892
Phillips	246	20 620	0.91	314	15.8	259	13.0	2 989	17.6	4 338	903	2 451	NA	NA
Pike	196	10 913	0.93	114	10.3	137	12.4	2 371	26.3	2 643	395	1 470	149	1 326
Poinsett	341	21 709	0.70	307	12.7	315	13.0	3 622	18.2	5 710	1 019	3 354	916	3 779
Polk	155	20 439	0.99	229	11.3	270	13.3	3 819	23.8	5 302	613	2 803	568	2 782
Pope	3 687	62 803	1.02	762	12.1	558	8.8	10 065	20.0	11 730	2 384	5 662	1 951	3 096
Prairie	131	7 425	0.66	84	10.1	103	12.4	1 357	21.0	2 043	226	1 258	74	1 062
Pulaski	8 650	454 223	1.38	5 582	14.2	3 508	8.9	57 019	17.1	69 602	12 046	32 307	29 118	7 449
Randolph	349	16 651	0.81	195	11.1	229	13.0	2 885	20.5	4 533	1 100	2 322	501	2 796
St. Francis	4 089	28 083	1.02	330	12.3	304	11.3	3 492	17.8	4 837	982	2 637	1 595	6 050
Saline	1 364	85 305	0.52	1 392	12.0	989	8.5	14 401	15.3	22 671	3 617	10 186	NA	NA
Scott	79	10 723	0.91	114	10.7	118	11.0	2 128	23.8	2 584	691	1 165	345	3 157
Searcy	71	7 414	0.76	74	9.3	102	12.9	1 526	24.9	2 379	505	1 125	48	604
Sebastian	2 402	142 252	1.29	1 660	13.1	1 182	9.3	22 805	21.2	23 901	6 893	10 124	5 811	4 546
Sevier	173	16 425	0.89	269	15.4	147	8.4	4 429	29.7	2 857	306	1 656	437	2 541
Sharp	189	16 083	0.80	174	10.3	220	13.0	2 936	23.2	5 830	1 159	3 218	NA	NA
Stone	151	12 308	0.95	122	9.8	170	13.6	2 228	23.7	3 918	556	2 083	382	2 997
Union	524	43 431	1.13	503	12.5	542	13.6	5 068	17.0	9 472	1 292	5 495	1 602	4 125
Van Buren	189	16 560	0.89	159	9.4	242	14.4	2 733	21.4	4 961	946	2 490	425	2 508
Washington	7 823	210 626	1.03	3 365	15.2	1 377	6.2	38 805	20.9	29 256	6 331	13 375	7 445	3 537
White	3 536	74 827	0.91	1 005	12.8	776	9.9	11 436	18.0	15 435	2 229	7 996	NA	NA
Woodruff	106	6 755	0.84	77	11.1	94	13.6	1 066	19.0	1 831	212	1 134	NA	NA
Yell	323	20 215	0.79	292	13.3	225	10.3	4 507	24.8	4 635	788	2 351	581	2 733

1. Per 1,000 estimated resident population. 2. Data for serious crimes have not been adjusted for underreporting; this may affect comparability between geographic areas and over time.
3. Per 100,000 population estimated by the FBI.

STATE County	Serious crimes known to police, 2013 (cont.)[1]		Education						Money income, 2009–2013				Income and poverty, 2013			
	Rate[2]		School enrollment and attainment, 2009–2013				Local government expenditures,[5] 2012–2013			Households				Percent below poverty level		
			Enrollment[3]		Attainment[4] (percent)											
	Violent	Property	Total	Percent private	High school graduate or less	Bachelor's degree or more	Total current spending (mil dol)	Current spending per student (dollars)	Per capita income[6] (dollars)	Median income (dollars)	Mean income (dollars)	Percent with income of $200,000 or more	Median household income (dollars)	All persons	Children under 18 years	Children 5 to 17 years in families
	46	47	48	49	50	51	52	53	54	55	56	57	58	59	60	61
ARKANSAS—Cont'd																
Cleveland	35	1 638	2 179	4.7	59.6	13.8	12.7	9 142	20 622	39 420	51 755	1.0	42 414	17.0	26.0	23.2
Columbia	332	2 792	7 405	4.5	51.9	20.3	31.6	9 119	19 439	35 128	49 385	0.7	36 927	23.2	32.1	31.4
Conway	216	3 398	4 903	12.0	58.9	14.7	41.8	12 743	20 040	35 225	49 700	1.4	38 145	21.1	33.1	29.1
Craighead	360	3 503	27 777	6.7	48.8	24.4	145.7	8 292	23 138	41 393	59 467	2.7	41 608	20.0	28.9	25.9
Crawford	370	2 620	15 396	7.0	55.6	14.3	99.1	8 744	19 477	39 479	50 542	1.4	39 384	19.2	27.9	27.0
Crittenden	1 269	5 264	15 049	6.5	55.9	13.9	95.6	9 057	19 665	37 751	51 938	1.9	37 726	23.6	36.1	33.2
Cross	448	3 629	4 231	3.5	68.2	11.4	31.2	8 958	18 701	38 085	47 984	0.8	35 438	20.6	31.3	30.4
Dallas	239	3 190	1 820	9.9	71.1	10.2	10.2	11 530	16 838	28 931	40 286	0.9	32 591	21.4	36.9	34.7
Desha	NA	NA	3 283	9.3	63.9	12.7	26.3	9 549	19 822	28 680	46 385	1.6	30 241	34.0	47.5	43.1
Drew	431	3 659	5 397	10.6	55.3	19.1	41.9	13 279	17 057	31 171	41 796	0.6	35 249	24.8	32.7	29.6
Faulkner	291	3 401	35 798	14.6	41.6	27.2	158.5	8 522	24 401	50 314	64 110	2.4	49 936	14.9	19.7	16.6
Franklin	316	2 225	4 607	6.5	57.1	12.4	27.3	9 696	19 135	36 766	48 526	2.0	38 874	20.7	31.2	27.9
Fulton	202	1 101	2 463	8.8	58.0	10.0	14.9	8 967	19 326	35 522	45 159	0.0	33 439	22.9	40.1	36.4
Garland	472	5 329	20 880	8.1	45.2	20.9	141.5	9 550	23 170	39 162	54 240	2.2	39 057	22.1	35.1	31.3
Grant	189	2 263	4 005	4.7	54.8	17.6	39.1	8 063	23 239	49 004	59 827	1.6	47 089	14.2	21.5	20.1
Greene	331	4 581	10 805	6.8	60.0	14.7	62.8	8 495	19 652	38 413	48 994	0.8	40 840	17.7	25.3	23.0
Hempstead	645	3 689	5 810	8.7	56.3	14.1	38.4	10 324	17 376	32 056	42 962	0.9	33 715	22.9	36.2	34.1
Hot Spring	NA	NA	7 459	7.0	57.7	12.3	47.7	8 715	19 286	41 193	50 883	0.5	39 927	18.5	29.8	27.2
Howard	95	3 150	3 428	2.9	61.4	12.0	27.5	8 705	18 707	35 879	46 824	1.3	32 740	21.5	35.3	32.7
Independence	485	3 814	8 646	8.0	57.3	14.4	58.5	9 335	20 289	35 026	50 036	1.7	37 761	18.4	27.2	24.5
Izard	157	1 939	2 598	10.9	60.2	11.7	20.6	11 371	18 040	30 661	42 020	1.2	33 308	20.8	31.4	28.5
Jackson	315	4 559	3 617	4.0	69.5	8.8	28.2	9 416	15 609	30 284	40 849	0.5	32 923	27.5	40.3	35.6
Jefferson	850	4 795	21 064	7.3	54.0	17.5	123.4	10 180	19 353	37 140	50 294	1.3	36 169	25.8	38.0	37.1
Johnson	154	2 367	5 645	13.8	63.3	14.7	38.5	8 624	19 366	31 003	48 662	2.4	33 634	23.4	32.5	29.9
Lafayette	NA	NA	1 656	11.7	67.9	10.7	11.1	10 028	17 212	29 732	42 453	1.4	30 642	26.0	40.3	35.7
Lawrence	83	1 008	4 290	14.9	65.4	10.4	33.9	10 456	15 971	32 239	39 857	0.2	34 740	20.4	33.6	30.9
Lee	108	2 499	2 153	13.8	71.4	7.1	11.6	11 326	12 529	25 034	35 214	0.4	27 068	41.1	51.7	47.0
Lincoln	127	588	2 721	7.7	70.4	7.9	16.1	9 597	15 023	32 697	48 853	2.6	36 062	27.6	30.3	27.6
Little River	265	2 070	3 035	10.0	55.6	10.6	18.4	9 241	19 880	39 673	48 003	0.1	36 310	19.3	28.3	25.0
Logan	293	3 117	5 320	7.8	60.8	11.7	36.0	8 973	19 046	34 996	48 608	1.2	34 090	18.7	30.4	27.5
Lonoke	300	2 565	18 975	10.7	48.5	18.2	115.4	8 364	23 218	52 582	62 313	0.9	55 648	12.6	17.7	16.2
Madison	257	845	3 437	10.0	66.2	10.3	21.3	9 242	18 754	35 771	47 380	1.6	36 358	20.2	30.2	29.7
Marion	332	1 855	2 956	6.4	57.9	12.9	20.9	12 576	18 188	34 494	41 692	0.6	34 217	19.0	36.0	32.6
Miller	778	4 364	9 855	10.3	55.1	13.9	64.2	9 584	20 636	41 319	50 723	0.9	40 005	21.4	32.0	29.8
Mississippi	885	5 009	12 233	5.2	58.3	13.0	79.7	9 630	18 905	36 428	49 312	1.6	34 285	25.6	39.0	36.8
Monroe	194	1 874	1 859	4.5	61.4	11.3	12.2	10 127	16 939	27 263	39 821	1.5	29 870	28.7	42.0	40.6
Montgomery	129	764	1 774	5.5	57.2	12.9	10.7	9 510	19 021	31 345	45 331	1.2	31 763	22.4	37.5	33.0
Nevada	224	1 761	2 095	9.7	59.3	12.8	13.0	8 865	18 695	33 694	44 532	1.3	33 341	21.1	32.5	30.6
Newton	275	1 149	1 653	3.3	61.1	12.7	14.5	10 812	17 884	30 038	41 541	0.6	31 824	23.5	39.6	36.2
Ouachita	342	2 507	6 162	4.6	55.9	15.5	46.3	10 238	18 975	32 015	43 370	0.6	35 006	27.5	43.6	41.1
Perry	388	2 504	2 415	5.9	60.2	11.9	13.5	8 258	22 047	42 455	57 350	0.8	42 328	17.5	27.5	25.6
Phillips	NA	NA	6 025	10.0	58.0	12.0	39.7	13 123	16 830	26 737	42 723	1.1	25 894	36.6	53.0	50.6
Pike	151	1 174	2 576	3.4	55.8	13.8	19.4	9 389	18 377	32 206	46 104	1.0	35 592	21.9	34.0	31.5
Poinsett	355	3 425	5 521	8.8	68.8	8.6	44.6	10 274	16 919	32 089	41 733	0.4	34 113	24.7	37.9	35.3
Polk	206	2 577	4 706	5.3	53.8	12.3	33.7	8 967	19 116	32 835	46 274	1.1	31 818	24.4	37.9	34.8
Pope	276	2 820	17 671	5.7	51.7	20.7	91.7	9 150	19 918	40 453	52 593	1.4	39 704	20.0	25.9	23.7
Prairie	57	1 004	1 909	5.7	67.3	9.3	11.9	9 278	18 137	34 855	41 595	0.0	38 921	19.6	30.4	28.3
Pulaski	1 011	6 438	102 168	19.4	38.4	31.2	586.2	11 235	27 414	46 013	65 729	3.7	46 526	17.3	25.7	24.4
Randolph	151	2 645	4 519	7.2	57.6	12.3	20.1	8 386	18 871	34 418	46 076	1.0	33 148	22.6	34.0	32.1
St. Francis	565	5 485	6 912	8.3	61.1	11.7	44.6	10 407	15 511	30 873	41 862	1.0	29 011	37.3	50.2	48.8
Saline	NA	NA	26 656	10.4	45.9	23.4	124.3	7 676	25 962	55 348	66 165	1.7	54 921	10.3	15.5	14.7
Scott	256	2 901	2 789	3.5	60.4	11.6	23.0	8 880	18 934	37 448	48 052	1.3	32 404	21.2	35.2	31.2
Searcy	226	377	1 646	17.9	62.3	12.0	18.1	11 406	16 731	30 779	38 883	0.8	27 299	25.9	43.0	38.0
Sebastian	548	3 998	32 379	8.9	49.2	19.2	183.5	9 191	23 222	40 471	58 215	2.9	41 685	22.1	32.5	30.1
Sevier	174	2 366	4 335	4.5	66.3	8.6	38.9	11 851	16 021	35 153	44 647	0.7	33 698	22.2	32.9	29.4
Sharp	NA	NA	3 612	7.8	61.0	11.0	25.6	8 687	16 714	30 861	39 774	0.6	31 224	22.8	38.7	35.0
Stone	298	2 699	2 614	14.9	54.7	14.2	14.7	8 400	17 403	29 832	40 188	0.5	27 522	26.2	40.7	38.7
Union	554	3 572	9 867	7.8	54.6	16.1	65.6	8 736	20 718	37 435	50 778	1.8	38 132	21.0	31.0	30.1
Van Buren	260	2 248	3 265	8.6	57.6	13.6	24.6	10 660	18 782	32 517	43 752	0.8	35 111	18.9	30.0	28.2
Washington	419	3 118	65 058	8.7	45.8	28.7	354.6	9 228	23 264	41 248	60 091	3.2	43 302	20.9	25.9	25.1
White	NA	NA	21 654	27.3	54.6	18.1	117.3	9 006	21 793	42 487	56 272	1.7	43 363	17.2	22.9	21.3
Woodruff	NA	NA	1 516	2.4	71.1	10.1	7.3	13 708	19 087	28 259	43 696	1.2	29 159	28.0	41.3	39.1
Yell	263	2 470	5 296	3.9	71.4	9.4	38.3	8 910	10 992	35 505	44 505	0.3	31 670	19.7	31.3	28.7

1. Data for serious crimes have not been adjusted for underreporting; this may affect comparability between geographic areas and over time. 2. Per 100,000 population estimated by the FBI.
3. All persons 3 years old and over enrolled in nursery school through college. 4. Persons 25 years old and over. 5. Elementary and secondary education expenditures.
6. Based on population estimated by the American Community Survey, 2009–2013.

STATE County	Personal income, 2013										Earnings, 2013		
			Per capita[1]			Supplements to wages and salaries; employer contributions (mil dol)						Contributions for government social insurance (mil dol)	
	Total (mil dol)	Percent change, 2012–2013	Dollars	Rank	Wages and salaries (mil dol)	Pension and insurance	Government social insurance	Proprietors' income (mil dol)	Dividends, interest, and rent (mil dol)	Personal transfer receipts (mil dol)	Total (mil dol)	From employee and self-employed	From employer
	62	63	64	65	66	67	68	69	70	71	72	73	74
ARKANSAS—Cont'd													
Cleveland	305	2.5	35 472	1 824	36	7	3	27	36	76	72	5	3
Columbia	855	-0.3	35 364	1 844	334	57	26	83	191	231	500	34	26
Conway	772	2.6	36 345	1 683	261	42	21	66	136	206	390	27	21
Craighead	3 586	0.9	35 338	1 850	1 756	275	142	377	681	790	2 550	157	142
Crawford	1 820	1.1	29 533	2 748	711	110	60	119	294	502	1 000	71	60
Crittenden	1 685	-0.2	33 874	2 103	590	96	50	170	234	443	906	57	50
Cross	646	3.8	36 786	1 628	179	29	14	112	122	167	334	19	14
Dallas	244	-0.9	30 698	2 599	87	14	8	13	38	92	122	9	8
Desha	463	1.4	37 024	1 580	168	27	13	88	83	130	296	16	13
Drew	644	2.5	34 267	2 039	221	40	18	74	127	178	354	22	18
Faulkner	4 097	0.4	34 260	2 042	1 754	250	137	194	657	814	2 335	150	137
Franklin	600	1.3	33 267	2 213	163	35	13	40	111	155	251	17	13
Fulton	356	1.0	28 911	2 817	62	12	5	38	66	128	117	10	5
Garland	3 744	0.3	38 526	1 369	1 294	195	105	246	1 131	999	1 840	134	105
Grant	605	0.2	33 568	2 165	142	23	11	40	94	140	217	16	11
Greene	1 389	-0.9	32 238	2 378	549	93	48	123	292	371	813	52	48
Hempstead	655	-4.2	29 159	2 785	283	50	23	57	97	201	413	26	23
Hot Spring	959	-0.3	28 619	2 835	300	53	25	38	161	294	416	31	25
Howard	411	4.2	30 276	2 647	224	42	19	62	63	120	347	21	19
Independence	1 205	1.1	32 574	2 315	538	92	45	132	212	340	806	52	45
Izard	383	0.7	28 644	2 832	103	20	8	26	73	145	158	13	8
Jackson	596	-0.8	33 823	2 120	202	34	16	100	97	171	352	21	16
Jefferson	2 497	-2.0	34 110	2 063	1 248	228	103	167	448	705	1 746	109	103
Johnson	692	2.2	26 783	2 988	276	48	23	58	106	206	404	27	23
Lafayette	231	2.6	31 834	2 430	47	8	4	38	46	72	97	6	4
Lawrence	504	-0.8	29 656	2 734	135	25	11	61	92	173	232	16	11
Lee	331	1.3	33 076	2 240	74	13	6	92	50	96	185	9	6
Lincoln	408	1.2	29 070	2 799	111	22	8	47	44	101	189	11	8
Little River	393	-0.6	30 896	2 568	182	27	14	29	64	120	252	17	14
Logan	648	2.1	29 332	2 773	187	34	15	56	106	224	292	21	15
Lonoke	2 484	0.9	35 107	1 884	477	71	38	185	446	510	771	51	38
Madison	409	5.8	26 048	3 025	107	20	9	53	81	122	189	13	9
Marion	478	1.9	29 081	2 798	115	25	10	27	102	175	177	16	10
Miller	1 475	-1.0	33 980	2 085	501	76	39	174	239	345	789	52	39
Mississippi	1 526	-1.2	34 080	2 067	833	128	67	144	213	412	1 172	71	67
Monroe	274	-2.2	35 647	1 810	74	12	6	33	52	86	125	8	6
Montgomery	247	2.8	26 798	2 986	49	9	4	27	48	90	89	7	4
Nevada	277	-0.6	31 481	2 485	88	14	8	20	45	93	131	9	8
Newton	231	0.5	28 591	2 840	31	7	2	17	49	77	58	6	2
Ouachita	818	0.4	32 724	2 300	260	49	20	49	140	256	378	28	20
Perry	351	0.2	33 889	2 100	45	8	4	27	56	94	84	7	4
Phillips	686	0.4	33 608	2 163	213	36	17	103	103	226	369	21	17
Pike	352	2.2	31 451	2 490	75	13	6	44	83	97	138	9	6
Poinsett	812	-0.1	33 649	2 154	189	30	15	148	102	252	382	23	15
Polk	566	3.4	27 737	2 912	188	36	16	63	107	199	303	22	16
Pope	2 011	2.4	32 148	2 392	1 039	175	85	101	389	486	1 400	89	85
Prairie	306	-0.9	36 546	1 655	57	9	5	59	43	82	130	7	5
Pulaski	18 725	0.1	47 854	494	12 462	1 940	980	1 734	4 906	3 207	17 116	1 015	980
Randolph	543	1.9	30 718	2 595	145	27	12	65	88	194	249	17	12
St. Francis	754	-0.6	27 656	2 919	286	55	24	73	116	245	438	27	24
Saline	4 709	1.2	41 159	1 033	786	120	64	175	736	918	1 145	89	64
Scott	297	6.4	27 118	2 962	95	18	8	32	49	97	153	11	8
Searcy	223	-0.1	27 765	2 910	46	9	4	21	44	89	80	7	4
Sebastian	5 213	-0.6	40 934	1 060	2 730	416	218	485	1 433	1 005	3 849	242	218
Sevier	433	3.0	24 930	3 056	162	30	15	41	64	126	247	16	15
Sharp	469	1.3	27 497	2 937	110	19	9	15	94	216	153	15	9
Stone	349	0.9	27 704	2 915	71	14	6	30	91	141	121	11	6
Union	1 918	0.7	47 139	544	831	136	64	298	459	397	1 329	85	64
Van Buren	546	1.5	32 218	2 383	165	27	12	24	124	180	228	19	12
Washington	7 850	3.1	36 275	1 696	4 277	656	325	709	1 630	1 225	5 967	359	325
White	2 497	-0.7	31 813	2 432	980	146	79	178	518	635	1 383	94	79
Woodruff	241	-3.3	34 057	2 071	69	12	5	35	42	80	122	7	5
Yell	667	5.1	30 483	2 632	202	39	17	57	115	187	314	21	17

1. Based on the resident population estimated as of July 1 of the year shown.

STATE County	Earnings, 2013 (cont.): Percent by selected industries									Social Security beneficiaries, December 2013		Supple-mental Security Income recipients, December 2013	Housing units, 2014	
	Farm	Mining	Construction	Manu-facturing	Infor-mation: professional, scientific, technical services	Retail trade	Finance, insur-ance, real estate and leasing	Health care and social assistance	Govern-ment	Number	Rate[1]		Total	Percent change, 2010–2014
	75	76	77	78	79	80	81	82	83	84	85	86	87	88
ARKANSAS—Cont'd														
Cleveland	26.1	0.0	2.9	5.5	D	3.6	D	5.4	22.0	2 135	249	286	4 048	-0.4
Columbia	1.6	13.7	4.5	25.5	2.9	5.9	5.0	D	18.5	5 870	242	1 306	11 562	-0.3
Conway	5.9	3.6	11.2	15.2	2.6	7.8	2.8	D	16.7	5 650	267	981	9 720	0.0
Craighead	3.4	0.0	6.4	12.8	4.5	7.9	5.2	21.4	16.0	19 470	192	3 933	43 311	6.9
Crawford	1.1	3.3	6.3	20.6	D	6.3	3.8	7.2	11.8	14 730	239	2 099	26 458	1.3
Crittenden	7.4	D	4.3	10.2	2.3	7.0	3.8	11.6	16.4	9 945	200	3 647	21 624	0.6
Cross	24.6	0.0	2.7	8.7	2.0	8.9	5.5	10.5	17.0	4 435	253	887	7 888	0.5
Dallas	1.3	0.0	4.0	21.4	D	8.8	3.6	D	12.7	2 250	284	439	4 289	-0.4
Desha	25.7	0.0	3.0	17.9	1.9	5.4	3.9	D	14.4	3 205	257	820	6 306	0.7
Drew	8.9	0.0	4.4	10.3	2.4	8.5	4.0	D	27.4	4 145	221	794	8 481	0.9
Faulkner	0.3	6.0	8.3	8.6	14.8	7.4	5.0	11.0	17.0	19 445	163	2 731	48 849	4.8
Franklin	6.9	8.4	4.8	17.1	2.0	8.1	4.6	D	21.5	4 570	255	562	8 024	0.0
Fulton	10.0	D	D	3.6	D	6.9	6.1	13.4	23.6	3 935	322	509	6 762	-0.2
Garland	0.4	0.7	6.9	7.4	5.9	11.1	7.9	22.1	14.6	29 025	299	3 873	50 542	0.0
Grant	1.7	D	8.9	25.9	4.5	6.7	3.6	D	19.0	3 990	221	433	7 837	1.0
Greene	8.2	D	3.7	35.5	D	7.3	3.4	10.0	13.1	10 500	244	1 843	18 439	3.1
Hempstead	7.1	D	4.8	20.5	1.4	6.9	3.2	D	21.1	5 145	230	1 130	10 423	0.0
Hot Spring	1.2	D	5.8	18.8	D	6.4	3.8	D	22.8	8 490	254	1 258	14 283	-0.3
Howard	10.5	D	3.5	41.6	D	6.0	2.2	D	11.7	3 425	253	520	6 236	0.0
Independence	4.9	0.9	4.1	20.1	D	8.2	4.6	18.7	13.2	9 365	254	1 314	16 260	0.5
Izard	6.0	D	5.9	8.2	D	8.6	5.2	14.7	29.8	4 290	321	561	7 214	-0.2
Jackson	18.4	D	2.7	18.2	2.0	7.0	3.4	D	19.1	4 385	248	881	7 589	-0.2
Jefferson	4.8	D	3.8	17.9	2.3	6.5	4.0	13.4	27.5	16 250	222	4 566	33 242	0.7
Johnson	6.3	D	3.4	27.5	1.9	7.1	3.0	D	14.9	6 285	243	986	11 351	0.4
Lafayette	31.5	10.2	7.7	1.5	D	3.5	2.3	D	16.4	1 970	272	494	4 342	-0.3
Lawrence	14.4	0.9	5.7	8.5	D	8.1	3.4	D	23.6	4 905	287	883	7 979	-0.3
Lee	38.0	0.0	D	D	D	4.9	2.0	D	20.6	2 270	226	850	4 364	0.2
Lincoln	23.8	D	3.1	7.3	D	3.0	2.3	D	35.1	2 640	188	558	4 858	-0.1
Little River	5.6	D	5.5	48.6	D	5.1	1.9	2.6	15.6	3 430	269	437	6 446	-0.2
Logan	11.1	4.5	5.0	18.8	2.4	7.6	5.0	10.1	21.7	6 350	288	930	10 125	0.2
Lonoke	12.4	0.3	9.3	12.2	3.6	8.8	6.0	8.1	18.0	13 335	188	1 896	28 618	5.1
Madison	13.6	D	6.6	25.5	3.5	7.5	2.4	5.2	16.5	4 100	261	485	7 485	0.0
Marion	3.3	D	4.5	37.6	3.7	7.9	6.2	6.6	15.3	5 775	352	591	9 333	-0.2
Miller	4.2	0.8	9.2	20.5	D	6.8	3.8	D	14.0	9 205	212	2 041	19 415	0.7
Mississippi	7.9	0.0	5.1	39.1	5.1	4.6	2.0	D	11.3	10 105	226	3 451	20 506	0.2
Monroe	16.0	0.0	4.2	4.1	D	8.9	5.7	D	16.4	2 275	297	616	4 432	-0.5
Montgomery	10.8	D	8.9	2.6	2.5	6.9	5.3	D	27.5	2 870	311	347	5 747	-0.3
Nevada	7.5	0.2	D	D	D	6.5	2.2	11.5	14.9	2 410	274	503	4 542	-0.5
Newton	9.7	0.0	D	3.6	D	D	D	D	35.9	2 685	333	420	4 667	0.1
Ouachita	0.7	8.1	3.7	10.3	D	8.5	3.9	D	24.3	6 950	278	1 536	13 067	-0.4
Perry	15.1	D	12.3	2.1	D	5.3	D	D	21.2	2 815	272	365	4 900	-0.1
Phillips	24.1	0.0	2.0	4.8	D	6.8	3.3	12.4	18.6	5 030	246	2 084	10 163	0.4
Pike	22.1	D	2.6	5.8	1.8	8.3	7.0	D	20.4	3 005	270	402	5 569	-0.2
Poinsett	26.5	D	3.4	9.0	1.5	5.7	4.0	5.9	15.2	6 655	275	1 677	10 937	0.1
Polk	7.3	1.0	5.1	19.8	2.8	8.1	4.9	15.0	16.5	6 120	301	712	10 034	0.3
Pope	2.1	0.8	8.3	15.7	3.9	6.6	4.7	10.1	16.1	13 325	212	1 939	25 915	1.4
Prairie	42.0	0.0	D	D	D	4.7	2.7	7.2	14.2	2 310	276	358	4 493	-0.2
Pulaski	0.2	0.4	5.8	5.1	11.1	6.5	8.5	12.5	24.7	76 030	194	17 291	181 406	3.3
Randolph	17.6	D	3.4	9.7	D	7.4	2.7	18.4	19.1	5 265	299	794	8 522	0.1
St. Francis	11.0	D	2.9	6.8	D	7.8	3.3	D	31.1	5 610	205	2 072	10 929	0.2
Saline	0.2	0.2	11.3	6.9	3.9	16.0	4.9	13.3	21.3	25 060	219	2 567	46 701	4.2
Scott	12.3	0.1	D	D	0.9	5.7	2.3	D	20.4	3 030	278	430	5 183	-0.2
Searcy	2.4	D	D	8.7	D	7.8	4.4	13.9	24.9	2 785	349	460	4 895	-0.1
Sebastian	0.3	4.4	4.6	18.5	7.6	6.4	5.3	16.6	11.8	27 240	214	4 412	56 034	2.5
Sevier	10.0	D	D	D	1.5	7.9	4.4	D	20.7	3 190	184	460	6 882	-0.1
Sharp	7.5	D	D	3.1	3.8	11.1	6.8	D	22.9	6 640	389	850	9 821	0.0
Stone	4.9	1.4	6.6	5.3	2.0	15.6	4.3	16.3	22.1	4 385	350	628	6 757	0.7
Union	0.7	15.4	8.0	17.7	2.1	5.9	3.7	8.7	9.3	10 915	268	2 023	19 676	0.1
Van Buren	1.7	15.7	5.7	1.3	2.4	8.2	D	11.6	14.7	5 680	335	601	10 341	0.0
Washington	1.2	0.2	5.2	10.3	5.4	7.0	7.3	12.6	18.9	32 710	151	4 293	89 775	2.2
White	2.5	6.0	7.3	9.5	3.1	8.8	4.3	15.6	13.0	17 650	224	2 515	33 198	2.2
Woodruff	29.0	D	2.1	9.4	D	4.2	4.0	7.1	18.8	2 090	296	449	3 882	-0.3
Yell	8.9	D	5.7	27.7	D	5.0	4.1	D	21.1	5 300	243	841	9 732	-0.2

1. Per 1,000 resident population estimated as of July 1 of the year shown.

STATE County	Housing units, 2009–2013: Occupied units: Total	Owner-occupied: Percent	Owner-occupied: Median value[1]	Median owner cost as a percent of income: With a mortgage	Median owner cost as a percent of income: Without a mortgage[2]	Renter-occupied: Median rent[3]	Renter-occupied: Median rent as a percent of income[2]	Substandard units[4] (percent)	Civilian labor force, 2014: Total	Percent change, 2013–2014	Unemployment: Total	Unemployment: Rate[5]	Civilian employment,[6] 2009–2013: Total	Percent: Management, business, science and arts	Percent: Construction, production, and maintenance occupations
	89	90	91	92	93	94	95	96	97	98	99	100	101	102	103
ARKANSAS—Cont'd															
Cleveland	3 346	77.5	78 300	19.6	11.0	620	23.7	2.4	3 437	-3.5	239	7.0	3 339	31.2	33.5
Columbia	9 449	68.9	78 900	19.4	10.3	573	33.5	3.9	9 369	-2.0	684	7.3	9 697	31.3	28.4
Conway	8 154	74.0	86 100	21.4	10.0	613	41.6	2.7	8 466	-0.6	598	7.1	8 256	24.3	37.5
Craighead	37 834	58.3	120 700	18.9	10.0	648	29.5	3.8	49 142	0.8	2 701	5.5	43 572	33.7	26.4
Crawford	23 368	74.3	102 800	22.4	10.4	581	28.2	4.5	26 433	-1.2	1 610	6.1	25 540	26.8	31.2
Crittenden	18 309	56.3	99 500	21.7	11.2	693	33.1	1.3	21 184	-0.7	1 542	7.3	20 657	29.0	27.3
Cross	6 818	65.4	78 400	20.6	12.0	641	29.2	5.3	8 002	-1.5	527	6.6	7 273	23.6	34.2
Dallas	3 269	66.4	59 200	22.5	10.0	454	31.6	2.1	2 861	-1.4	271	9.5	2 883	18.3	43.5
Desha	5 305	55.9	55 100	17.3	11.6	553	34.0	2.7	5 515	-1.3	457	8.3	4 960	28.4	34.5
Drew	7 496	61.2	83 300	19.8	12.8	599	35.3	1.9	7 895	-2.3	682	8.6	7 582	36.2	26.1
Faulkner	42 413	65.2	137 800	19.8	10.0	713	28.5	2.0	58 134	-0.8	3 299	5.7	55 838	35.1	23.0
Franklin	6 769	74.0	93 000	19.8	10.0	572	28.3	4.0	7 213	-1.7	417	5.8	6 980	23.5	33.7
Fulton	5 140	78.1	88 200	20.5	10.3	469	31.4	3.0	4 710	-3.1	282	6.0	4 569	27.0	30.6
Garland	39 881	68.6	130 500	22.7	10.3	717	31.0	3.2	40 044	-0.8	2 564	6.4	38 810	31.8	23.7
Grant	6 855	77.8	100 800	18.6	10.3	715	23.6	2.0	8 116	-0.8	451	5.6	7 946	29.6	32.2
Greene	16 603	63.3	99 100	20.4	10.9	634	30.1	2.6	19 403	0.9	1 261	6.5	17 400	27.9	36.2
Hempstead	8 296	68.0	73 100	21.5	10.8	573	34.7	2.2	9 812	-1.7	600	6.1	9 211	24.4	37.9
Hot Spring	12 231	72.5	81 300	19.7	10.7	632	28.0	4.7	13 863	-0.6	814	5.9	13 488	27.8	31.8
Howard	5 208	63.3	74 500	20.9	10.0	552	27.8	3.6	6 249	1.4	366	5.9	5 936	22.2	43.5
Independence	14 544	70.6	88 900	21.8	11.3	589	33.7	3.7	15 271	-2.2	1 216	8.0	15 531	26.3	33.0
Izard	5 682	78.0	73 900	23.1	11.9	530	36.7	2.5	4 841	-2.0	369	7.6	4 449	29.3	28.7
Jackson	6 541	67.2	56 500	20.9	12.2	536	29.9	2.0	6 115	-1.4	572	9.4	5 765	23.7	35.0
Jefferson	28 367	64.5	81 100	19.8	12.2	650	32.3	3.5	29 195	-4.8	2 603	8.9	28 989	27.7	27.5
Johnson	10 046	66.2	88 700	20.3	10.0	600	34.4	1.4	10 185	-2.5	675	6.6	10 182	22.1	39.5
Lafayette	2 722	72.7	52 200	21.9	12.3	472	29.5	2.1	2 641	-2.8	211	8.0	2 492	24.0	34.8
Lawrence	6 580	70.7	59 800	19.9	11.6	516	29.1	0.7	6 994	-1.1	518	7.4	6 384	25.2	32.4
Lee	3 491	57.0	54 700	25.4	12.7	538	33.9	4.2	3 226	-1.8	254	7.9	3 026	23.0	25.8
Lincoln	4 188	69.7	59 300	19.0	11.4	567	30.2	1.8	4 144	-3.8	303	7.3	4 008	27.5	39.5
Little River	5 315	78.0	80 900	18.1	11.4	502	32.5	2.3	5 534	-1.9	368	6.6	5 490	19.5	42.3
Logan	8 233	75.4	81 100	19.0	10.2	511	31.4	3.3	9 003	-1.5	548	6.1	8 711	25.7	33.8
Lonoke	25 052	73.2	120 600	19.8	10.0	688	26.2	4.2	32 178	-0.7	1 672	5.2	31 164	33.0	25.8
Madison	6 048	76.5	92 800	21.1	10.0	584	29.3	3.5	6 954	2.6	340	4.9	6 474	25.1	41.1
Marion	7 036	79.5	92 700	22.8	11.5	558	30.6	3.2	6 436	-0.1	416	6.5	6 039	21.9	35.0
Miller	16 950	67.2	92 900	20.1	10.2	680	30.1	3.2	19 052	-1.5	1 147	6.0	18 730	25.5	31.0
Mississippi	17 058	58.8	75 300	17.2	12.3	616	30.8	2.3	18 954	0.9	1 764	9.3	17 668	25.7	37.3
Monroe	3 393	63.5	52 200	19.8	13.5	517	34.8	2.7	3 080	-0.1	210	6.8	2 743	23.6	35.9
Montgomery	3 873	79.8	76 400	22.2	11.9	569	28.2	2.5	3 321	-1.7	269	8.1	3 448	28.0	40.6
Nevada	3 622	73.1	64 600	21.2	11.2	614	32.3	6.1	3 646	-2.3	223	6.1	3 501	22.4	35.3
Newton	3 507	82.5	74 600	23.9	10.0	332	19.8	1.9	3 361	-2.7	202	6.0	3 326	21.5	39.7
Ouachita	10 733	66.3	70 000	19.5	11.9	566	32.8	5.7	9 883	-2.4	796	8.1	9 900	25.7	33.9
Perry	3 903	79.5	77 700	18.2	10.0	585	23.9	5.6	4 240	-1.6	326	7.7	4 102	24.4	39.4
Phillips	8 339	54.5	59 500	24.3	11.0	586	36.5	1.3	7 199	-4.2	691	9.6	7 110	31.2	19.8
Pike	4 325	73.1	75 200	20.3	10.9	486	27.9	4.8	4 160	0.2	311	7.5	4 553	25.1	38.7
Poinsett	9 369	62.5	71 300	21.0	12.0	498	29.3	3.9	10 073	0.5	697	6.9	9 081	23.1	35.4
Polk	8 069	77.0	82 700	23.7	10.0	526	29.5	2.7	8 362	0.0	537	6.4	8 090	27.4	35.6
Pope	22 603	69.8	110 200	21.3	10.0	633	30.1	2.4	29 204	-0.4	1 858	6.4	27 806	27.8	29.9
Prairie	3 737	72.9	72 400	20.9	12.7	477	25.8	1.9	3 767	0.2	224	5.9	3 457	26.6	32.7
Pulaski	153 720	60.4	140 500	21.2	11.3	770	30.2	3.1	182 809	-1.0	10 231	5.6	179 131	39.5	17.0
Randolph	7 244	75.3	74 100	19.8	10.1	455	31.5	3.3	6 479	-2.1	522	8.1	6 847	28.5	35.2
St. Francis	9 358	55.3	65 600	19.7	13.6	599	31.0	2.1	8 826	-2.8	787	8.9	9 384	26.5	31.2
Saline	41 287	77.7	138 600	20.6	10.0	787	27.4	5.1	53 685	-0.9	2 656	4.9	51 542	34.4	24.0
Scott	4 324	73.0	82 100	19.1	10.7	533	24.9	2.9	4 531	-0.2	235	5.2	4 386	26.6	40.5
Searcy	3 296	77.5	85 100	25.9	10.0	433	34.4	2.9	2 954	-4.3	193	6.5	2 952	24.8	31.7
Sebastian	49 294	62.8	114 500	20.3	10.2	621	29.0	5.8	56 683	-1.4	3 264	5.8	54 665	30.1	28.1
Sevier	5 745	69.6	68 800	22.5	10.0	521	27.4	4.7	5 722	-2.2	400	7.0	6 726	20.4	49.0
Sharp	7 023	80.0	73 800	22.2	11.5	581	32.1	5.7	5 874	-1.3	511	8.7	5 805	27.5	33.2
Stone	5 135	78.3	88 100	26.0	11.6	472	27.4	4.4	4 661	-2.1	371	8.0	4 738	31.8	29.1
Union	16 596	69.3	75 000	18.5	12.1	604	28.7	3.9	16 374	-0.1	1 237	7.6	16 390	29.2	30.5
Van Buren	7 063	78.1	86 700	21.3	12.2	579	28.7	5.4	6 373	-0.5	521	8.2	5 556	24.7	35.0
Washington	79 214	55.9	148 800	21.6	10.0	690	30.8	3.4	108 276	2.5	4 790	4.4	99 115	34.5	23.7
White	29 632	68.4	100 100	19.5	10.0	620	30.2	3.1	34 055	-1.9	2 457	7.2	32 776	27.2	28.8
Woodruff	3 070	62.9	58 400	19.1	12.4	427	29.0	6.0	3 150	-1.7	247	7.8	2 716	29.9	33.7
Yell	7 917	66.4	91 200	21.7	11.1	524	26.4	6.3	8 963	0.0	506	5.6	8 564	19.4	43.9

1. Specified owner-occupied units. 2. A value of 10.0 represents 10 percent or less; a value of 50.0 represents 50 percent or more. 3. Specified renter-occupied units. 4. Overcrowded or lacking complete plumbing facilities. 5. Percent of civilian labor force. 6. Persons 16 years old and over.

STATE County	Private nonfarm establishments, employment and payroll, 2013									Agriculture, 2012			
		Employment						Annual payroll		Farms			
											Percent with:		
	Number of establish-ments	Total	Health care and social assistance	Manufac-turing	Retail trade	Finance and insurance	Professional, scientific, and technical services	Total (mil dol)	Average per employee (dollars)	Number	Fewer than 50 acres	500 acres or more	Farm operators whose principal occu-pation is farming (percent)
	104	105	106	107	108	109	110	111	112	113	114	115	116
ARKANSAS—Cont'd													
Cleveland	81	584	D	78	73	D	D	16	27 570	211	39.8	2.8	58.8
Columbia	596	7 538	1 244	2 035	1 032	255	210	268	35 610	278	28.4	5.8	42.1
Conway	409	4 894	552	D	855	142	90	171	34 981	816	29.7	7.7	51.0
Craighead	2 476	38 113	8 252	5 813	6 672	1 010	950	1 294	33 960	583	38.6	29.5	52.0
Crawford	1 061	20 016	1 656	4 022	1 944	405	278	617	30 839	886	45.4	5.3	44.2
Crittenden	824	13 445	2 098	1 524	2 092	226	243	421	31 294	263	17.5	44.1	66.9
Cross	359	4 100	788	641	979	D	80	113	27 441	325	16.0	41.2	59.1
Dallas	195	2 305	732	D	334	65	D	65	28 192	90	18.9	11.1	51.1
Desha	312	3 412	593	D	576	D	48	106	31 174	244	20.5	43.4	64.8
Drew	405	4 478	D	679	982	173	189	127	28 386	308	27.3	17.2	42.9
Faulkner	2 439	35 228	4 934	3 921	5 296	1 142	861	1 363	38 698	1 288	40.7	6.2	33.8
Franklin	278	3 424	690	913	536	208	94	103	30 211	829	28.1	8.6	43.9
Fulton	162	1 460	544	161	D	61	41	36	24 484	753	20.5	13.9	47.4
Garland	2 696	32 235	7 425	2 354	5 869	972	1 596	959	29 740	361	49.3	2.5	55.4
Grant	274	2 876	D	1 045	455	73	82	88	30 600	257	37.4	5.8	44.4
Greene	767	15 717	1 625	4 900	1 866	584	434	449	28 591	711	37.6	15.3	40.6
Hempstead	386	6 036	1 161	1 973	903	173	D	182	30 124	748	25.1	15.2	54.4
Hot Spring	472	5 876	1 220	1 231	858	218	104	182	31 058	536	43.1	3.2	41.6
Howard	300	5 881	737	3 381	608	95	53	161	27 451	552	26.8	8.0	50.5
Independence	779	13 970	3 066	3 624	1 779	D	219	462	33 078	1 003	28.9	11.3	37.9
Izard	206	1 988	574	210	475	D	D	54	27 351	633	21.2	15.0	41.7
Jackson	327	3 890	869	999	720	D	100	127	32 726	437	18.5	31.8	51.0
Jefferson	1 371	21 243	4 522	5 134	3 390	D	459	725	34 130	444	35.4	26.8	52.3
Johnson	394	7 204	997	2 528	931	149	89	191	26 514	624	28.0	6.9	46.2
Lafayette	111	780	174	D	125	54	D	23	29 404	263	17.9	22.1	60.5
Lawrence	274	2 790	612	336	576	D	37	76	27 323	559	22.7	22.4	46.7
Lee	127	907	269	D	177	33	30	28	31 237	220	13.6	40.0	81.4
Lincoln	155	1 636	289	D	181	D	D	52	31 811	377	23.6	20.4	56.0
Little River	162	2 713	305	D	372	70	D	127	46 804	448	21.9	16.7	48.0
Logan	377	4 054	718	D	690	286	74	115	28 441	969	27.0	7.0	48.1
Lonoke	1 002	10 181	1 200	D	2 231	433	341	293	28 825	767	31.8	19.0	55.8
Madison	189	2 422	251	985	430	D	45	68	28 049	1 250	22.0	8.9	49.3
Marion	213	3 002	281	1 635	450	122	45	81	26 865	485	21.0	14.0	42.9
Miller	704	10 926	976	D	1 439	287	238	406	37 129	525	35.6	12.0	45.0
Mississippi	836	17 787	1 815	5 328	1 882	263	128	650	36 564	347	17.6	55.0	74.1
Monroe	197	1 723	295	108	315	68	D	46	26 798	230	20.0	51.3	64.8
Montgomery	141	920	70	D	119	46	D	27	28 807	449	24.1	5.3	50.1
Nevada	123	1 948	D	D	249	41	D	62	31 834	351	23.6	5.7	47.6
Newton	83	759	274	D	120	D	D	16	21 070	648	28.2	6.5	42.6
Ouachita	530	7 423	1 267	2 499	1 092	215	153	278	37 470	182	39.0	6.6	33.0
Perry	107	816	D	D	110	24	22	33	40 342	419	31.7	6.2	43.2
Phillips	414	4 195	989	389	953	D	83	124	29 639	282	13.5	50.7	68.8
Pike	201	1 792	270	217	334	88	38	45	24 900	346	24.0	8.7	55.8
Poinsett	365	3 546	590	658	763	131	D	110	30 913	397	22.2	53.4	66.2
Polk	453	5 036	1 007	1 231	902	150	D	132	26 295	893	38.4	4.4	42.6
Pope	1 536	23 438	3 229	5 096	3 240	1 023	453	762	32 497	977	36.6	6.3	48.2
Prairie	157	905	203	D	193	D	D	23	25 871	445	20.9	29.7	50.8
Pulaski	12 010	204 171	42 543	14 095	25 510	12 782	10 586	8 534	41 796	417	50.6	7.4	42.7
Randolph	325	3 500	913	658	663	111	77	89	25 507	667	21.0	15.4	39.7
St. Francis	462	5 148	1 148	D	1 035	192	114	145	28 240	326	21.2	37.1	65.3
Saline	1 837	19 290	4 061	1 441	3 936	499	557	560	29 038	386	52.8	4.9	46.9
Scott	154	2 178	262	D	288	47	D	54	24 990	602	25.6	5.3	49.8
Searcy	116	1 083	337	130	259	35	D	21	19 848	592	18.6	15.2	50.3
Sebastian	3 482	61 045	10 974	13 095	7 880	1 684	1 513	2 237	36 650	770	36.8	5.5	43.4
Sevier	270	4 148	536	D	701	130	50	110	26 554	543	28.4	6.4	44.8
Sharp	309	2 394	515	D	644	186	41	55	23 070	648	20.4	12.7	39.4
Stone	234	2 024	530	130	529	119	51	46	22 838	523	19.9	13.4	49.9
Union	1 140	16 689	2 238	2 809	2 167	442	246	769	46 075	280	34.3	5.7	48.6
Van Buren	338	3 484	699	D	590	109	65	126	36 145	587	21.8	7.7	47.5
Washington	4 934	79 392	13 569	12 130	11 431	2 250	3 238	2 897	36 485	2 502	43.2	4.1	42.3
White	1 519	22 276	4 324	2 271	3 532	634	480	701	31 462	1 836	35.6	7.3	35.9
Woodruff	138	1 307	D	D	252	46	D	41	31 162	217	14.7	48.8	60.8
Yell	307	4 940	959	D	602	172	67	136	27 468	794	29.7	8.3	47.9

STATE County	Agriculture, 2012 (cont.) — Land in farms — Acreage (1,000)	Land in farms — Percent change, 2007–2012	Land in farms — Acres — Average size of farm	Land in farms — Acres — Total irrigated (1,000)	Land in farms — Acres — Total cropland (1,000)	Value of land and buildings (dollars) — Average per farm	Value of land and buildings (dollars) — Average per acre	Value of machinery and equipment, average per farm (dollars)	Value of products sold — Total (mil dol)	Value of products sold — Average per farm (dollars)	Value of products sold — Percent from: — Crops	Value of products sold — Percent from: — Livestock and poultry products	Percent of farms with sales of: — $10,000 or more	Percent of farms with sales of: — $100,000 or more	Government payments — Total ($1,000)	Government payments — Percent of farms
	117	118	119	120	121	122	123	124	125	126	127	128	129	130	131	132
ARKANSAS—Cont'd																
Cleveland	27	-12.5	129	D	6.0	502 071	3 895	83 725	105.8	501 427	0.4	99.6	48.8	36.0	237	10.4
Columbia	46	-3.1	164	0.3	12.5	353 727	2 157	65 011	41.7	150 032	12.2	87.8	38.5	11.5	84	8.6
Conway	179	-4.2	220	14.8	76.4	568 464	2 587	77 902	161.6	198 098	10.3	89.7	44.6	16.9	1 554	17.4
Craighead	338	0.2	579	271.6	314.2	1 857 806	3 208	276 847	261.6	448 714	98.9	1.1	55.1	36.5	10 157	57.8
Crawford	125	5.1	141	4.5	48.6	424 447	3 001	59 635	67.4	76 081	33.4	66.6	32.6	7.8	342	8.7
Crittenden	338	7.7	1 285	173.3	306.5	3 568 985	2 778	506 837	215.0	817 551	99.8	0.2	71.9	52.5	6 850	76.4
Cross	279	-1.4	858	214.7	255.2	2 181 258	2 542	375 991	188.8	580 855	99.8	0.2	56.9	44.9	11 662	84.9
Dallas	21	6.7	236	D	3.2	377 989	1 600	49 933	1.3	14 500	59.5	40.5	31.1	1.1	54	26.7
Desha	267	-12.9	1 095	202.1	243.9	3 053 189	2 789	683 840	212.9	872 512	97.0	3.0	68.0	49.2	7 594	87.3
Drew	130	4.4	422	66.9	86.8	1 062 338	2 520	147 227	88.3	286 841	72.0	28.0	44.8	19.5	2 580	44.8
Faulkner	185	-2.7	144	6.8	54.5	470 804	3 279	52 585	26.3	20 386	38.3	61.7	30.4	2.6	1 254	13.8
Franklin	160	4.6	193	0.6	44.8	439 010	2 277	64 706	158.2	190 806	2.7	97.3	50.5	13.9	542	10.0
Fulton	204	15.3	271	0.0	25.9	434 740	1 601	44 228	27.7	36 819	4.0	96.0	42.0	5.8	1 708	21.9
Garland	36	-9.6	99	0.3	8.4	364 504	3 688	43 119	24.1	66 756	18.6	81.4	24.7	5.3	93	8.9
Grant	65	86.9	252	0.1	10.3	567 051	2 253	61 296	20.9	81 183	2.6	97.4	26.5	6.6	55	9.7
Greene	260	-2.6	366	166.0	216.6	1 251 740	3 418	167 745	177.3	249 404	94.3	5.7	37.1	18.3	8 391	53.4
Hempstead	196	-6.7	263	D	48.9	537 639	2 047	76 608	198.5	265 362	2.3	97.7	52.1	19.5	814	24.5
Hot Spring	69	-4.7	128	0.1	19.3	329 142	2 567	48 366	23.9	44 675	4.8	95.2	30.2	3.9	202	13.1
Howard	147	32.6	266	0.5	23.2	627 100	2 357	72 839	179.1	324 422	0.8	99.2	60.3	31.5	99	15.0
Independence	248	-0.7	247	32.7	87.2	517 500	2 094	76 524	131.9	131 473	25.7	74.3	44.5	8.5	1 541	17.0
Izard	173	1.3	273	0.3	28.3	481 487	1 766	56 648	49.4	78 044	D	D	41.7	6.2	2 095	30.8
Jackson	307	1.6	703	206.5	271.7	1 768 018	2 516	289 577	186.8	427 545	98.3	1.7	54.0	37.1	12 642	70.9
Jefferson	292	-3.8	657	207.5	257.5	1 905 205	2 900	305 345	215.3	484 831	91.2	8.8	45.0	30.9	10 681	71.2
Johnson	118	11.9	190	1.0	38.7	456 329	2 405	59 563	141.0	226 029	3.1	96.9	48.7	14.6	348	12.2
Lafayette	115	18.1	438	21.7	60.8	886 065	2 022	177 734	127.9	486 259	24.7	75.3	61.2	38.0	1 817	41.4
Lawrence	253	-4.1	452	130.3	179.2	1 208 589	2 673	190 691	149.1	266 798	84.6	15.4	50.4	24.7	7 345	49.0
Lee	261	-13.8	1 185	158.0	245.9	3 313 277	2 796	452 068	171.9	781 227	99.9	0.1	76.4	47.7	6 373	82.7
Lincoln	200	7.4	530	135.0	157.5	1 481 042	2 795	274 745	219.5	582 101	53.6	46.4	54.1	35.5	7 190	55.7
Little River	172	23.2	383	10.0	59.9	643 661	1 681	86 491	76.5	170 781	23.4	76.6	45.1	16.5	833	28.8
Logan	198	23.2	204	0.9	66.8	458 086	2 246	64 342	188.0	193 997	3.4	96.6	49.0	16.4	229	9.8
Lonoke	339	-8.8	442	199.6	274.6	1 228 919	2 781	204 691	223.4	291 236	85.6	14.4	39.5	19.0	12 927	51.4
Madison	269	3.8	216	0.5	57.5	585 871	2 718	63 058	208.2	166 530	1.5	98.5	48.3	14.0	2 670	24.7
Marion	137	4.8	282	D	19.3	567 852	2 014	58 499	39.7	81 788	1.4	98.6	39.8	7.4	1 159	26.6
Miller	164	-6.3	312	5.5	85.3	620 006	1 986	71 606	45.5	86 739	53.8	46.2	39.2	8.4	1 229	18.3
Mississippi	476	3.1	1 371	286.9	462.6	3 905 478	2 849	614 256	314.6	906 764	99.9	0.1	80.7	62.8	9 887	83.3
Monroe	268	10.8	1 167	199.5	248.9	2 804 648	2 404	458 365	194.4	845 100	D	D	64.8	54.3	8 137	84.3
Montgomery	74	1.0	166	0.3	20.8	415 392	2 506	56 347	42.1	93 871	2.1	97.9	40.5	12.0	464	16.7
Nevada	67	2.2	190	0.1	16.1	360 188	1 897	66 954	47.9	136 519	2.4	97.6	47.0	13.7	178	21.7
Newton	114	1.1	176	0.1	17.2	388 836	2 206	44 318	28.7	44 221	3.5	96.5	35.2	2.2	784	29.6
Ouachita	26	-20.0	143	0.0	6.9	318 632	2 228	55 341	16.5	90 467	2.5	97.5	26.4	4.4	113	19.8
Perry	70	-3.2	168	4.7	25.4	409 379	2 438	65 847	33.1	78 955	14.8	85.2	43.7	9.1	602	17.4
Phillips	352	-19.4	1 250	231.9	345.6	3 260 908	2 610	512 504	248.0	879 426	99.9	0.1	77.7	61.3	10 328	87.2
Pike	70	-16.2	202	1.0	14.9	431 405	2 132	65 754	82.3	237 962	0.7	99.3	52.0	22.0	201	21.1
Poinsett	385	13.1	970	310.0	369.8	2 978 222	3 069	481 224	287.4	723 980	99.8	0.2	67.3	57.2	15 715	83.1
Polk	119	-10.9	133	0.4	31.9	352 879	2 651	54 186	117.8	131 885	1.4	98.6	37.0	11.3	185	14.4
Pope	154	0.1	157	6.2	51.3	432 140	2 745	67 052	150.1	153 636	6.9	93.1	39.4	11.3	828	9.7
Prairie	275	-17.1	618	179.1	214.1	1 546 649	2 501	236 348	165.1	370 933	96.7	3.3	43.6	30.6	10 031	76.4
Pulaski	84	-11.4	202	21.5	47.9	692 978	3 438	77 942	40.0	95 851	75.4	24.6	30.5	8.4	1 439	18.9
Randolph	211	-16.6	316	56.9	89.9	636 148	2 015	92 799	79.6	119 318	72.1	27.9	41.1	10.3	3 472	29.4
St. Francis	300	17.5	919	209.3	273.3	2 175 083	2 366	355 064	189.9	582 448	99.5	0.5	60.1	42.0	7 971	72.1
Saline	45	0.1	116	0.4	12.1	408 819	3 519	61 010	4.5	11 645	40.6	59.4	26.7	1.6	55	8.0
Scott	100	4.0	167	0.0	30.1	365 899	2 197	57 341	132.0	219 276	1.0	99.0	54.7	16.3	283	11.0
Searcy	169	-13.4	285	D	25.0	475 546	1 668	49 813	13.0	22 024	7.8	92.2	42.1	3.9	2 000	27.7
Sebastian	119	13.8	154	0.0	35.0	411 097	2 663	53 995	97.4	126 507	2.5	97.5	37.7	11.2	374	6.1
Sevier	129	10.9	238	D	27.4	555 635	2 335	70 293	137.4	253 066	0.6	99.4	46.8	20.1	224	24.9
Sharp	158	-14.0	244	0.1	28.8	444 068	1 818	58 008	75.6	116 607	1.4	98.6	40.7	8.5	1 522	24.1
Stone	135	-5.1	259	0.2	22.1	504 455	1 951	69 801	63.7	102 608	1.6	90.4	44.0	10.7	1 122	32.5
Union	43	12.1	152	0.0	7.8	384 639	2 534	58 164	28.0	99 829	2.0	98.0	26.4	6.4	91	15.0
Van Buren	123	7.5	209	0.3	29.5	519 421	2 481	59 424	19.9	33 981	5.3	94.7	43.3	3.4	648	17.9
Washington	312	-4.7	125	0.6	83.5	512 264	4 111	57 567	443.0	177 068	1.6	98.4	41.4	11.6	1 611	14.1
White	356	-13.5	194	39.4	138.3	498 108	2 571	61 275	100.4	54 669	39.0	61.0	27.0	5.3	4 909	26.6
Woodruff	274	-0.1	1 263	197.0	246.0	3 152 682	2 495	489 051	167.6	772 295	D	D	60.4	48.4	6 684	88.9
Yell	160	-8.5	202	3.1	56.5	458 194	2 271	73 649	196.4	247 331	3.2	96.8	49.5	18.8	1 339	22.9

STATE County	Water use, 2010		Wholesale trade,[1] 2007				Retail trade,[2] 2007				Real estate and rental and leasing,[2] 2007			
	Total water withdrawn (mil gal/day)	Gallons withdrawn per person per day	Number of establish-ments	Number of employees	Sales (mil dol)	Annual payroll (mil dol)	Number of establish-ments	Number of employees	Sales (mil dol)	Annual payroll (mil dol)	Number of establish-ments	Number of employees	Receipts (mil dol)	Annual payroll (mil dol)
	133	134	135	136	137	138	139	140	141	142	143	144	145	146
ARKANSAS—Cont'd														
Cleveland	1.4	165	3	12	1.2	0.2	11	81	12.3	0.8	1	D	D	D
Columbia	11.3	458	22	D	D	D	116	1 100	197.9	19.3	27	139	16.9	4.2
Conway	29.2	1 371	20	236	124.9	5.9	90	960	270.4	20.1	9	38	11.3	1.1
Craighead	422.7	4 383	129	1 418	605.9	56.8	499	6 536	1 440.9	125.1	103	473	73.6	11.8
Crawford	34.7	561	49	D	D	D	158	1 937	452.5	39.4	60	169	24.3	5.6
Crittenden	219.7	4 317	53	663	795.8	28.3	175	2 313	750.5	44.9	37	153	20.4	4.7
Cross	561.7	31 433	17	265	174.7	9.2	73	693	185.7	15.2	22	149	13.0	3.0
Dallas	0.8	99	6	22	10.9	0.5	52	399	79.7	7.7	7	17	2.1	0.4
Desha	484.0	37 207	22	195	230.9	8.2	85	598	119.2	10.9	18	56	3.9	0.8
Drew	37.3	2 013	12	106	87.6	3.7	96	932	199.0	17.6	21	66	6.5	1.4
Faulkner	8.8	78	71	601	266.1	23.0	381	5 250	1 227.7	102.7	120	384	52.8	9.7
Franklin	11.1	615	7	25	3.1	0.4	55	483	140.2	9.1	7	19	1.1	0.3
Fulton	84.4	6 894	7	25	8.2	1.1	46	236	42.4	3.4	3	5	0.3	0.1
Garland	17.6	183	91	D	D	D	523	5 898	1 443.4	126.9	158	614	88.0	14.6
Grant	5.3	298	13	130	48.5	4.1	49	460	107.6	9.0	7	41	2.7	0.8
Greene	367.0	8 719	47	D	D	D	180	1 655	373.1	33.6	29	85	12.1	1.7
Hempstead	4.7	206	15	157	32.8	3.8	87	973	204.4	19.2	20	77	9.7	1.7
Hot Spring	125.0	3 797	17	154	77.0	5.7	101	941	207.4	19.2	19	122	8.2	2.9
Howard	4.4	321	12	73	45.1	3.0	63	591	160.8	12.2	12	32	3.3	0.5
Independence	156.7	4 276	29	464	175.0	14.1	167	1 664	384.2	34.4	28	98	10.9	2.3
Izard	4.6	339	4	D	D	D	51	417	104.7	7.7	8	53	3.3	0.8
Jackson	442.0	24 559	27	217	95.4	6.2	72	669	190.9	13.4	18	48	4.6	0.8
Jefferson	350.6	4 528	66	D	D	D	321	4 024	867.4	79.8	76	D	D	D
Johnson	5.6	218	9	83	44.2	2.8	81	938	196.8	16.5	19	57	8.8	1.6
Lafayette	25.1	3 286	3	D	D	D	24	194	32.9	3.1	7	11	0.8	0.1
Lawrence	198.5	11 401	15	114	58.0	3.3	75	644	163.7	14.7	10	30	2.2	0.4
Lee	307.0	29 451	11	136	84.7	4.0	20	205	35.8	3.0	8	18	2.2	0.5
Lincoln	224.2	15 862	8	D	D	D	31	248	57.5	4.1	6	D	D	D
Little River	105.2	7 986	8	32	13.5	1.0	45	335	88.2	7.1	5	12	0.8	0.1
Logan	4.2	187	6	D	D	D	78	700	178.1	13.4	13	31	2.6	0.5
Lonoke	489.5	7 161	42	320	161.6	10.8	185	2 041	497.2	40.9	49	144	13.4	2.8
Madison	1.8	113	3	D	D	D	40	446	114.7	8.2	5	6	0.3	0.1
Marion	2.0	122	4	D	D	D	41	501	87.9	9.5	14	19	2.3	0.3
Miller	15.5	357	42	D	D	D	142	1 474	407.7	30.7	21	66	10.5	1.5
Mississippi	381.2	8 201	51	D	D	D	191	1 911	421.9	37.1	45	180	24.3	4.1
Monroe	297.5	36 509	13	100	64.7	3.7	44	364	82.2	6.2	4	9	1.1	0.1
Montgomery	1.0	105	3	D	D	D	25	152	32.4	2.8	10	41	1.4	0.4
Nevada	1.4	150	5	D	D	D	28	295	136.8	5.1	6	14	0.9	0.2
Newton	1.4	163	2	D	D	D	16	67	13.3	1.2	3	9	0.7	0.1
Ouachita	43.4	1 663	22	D	D	D	113	1 086	185.7	18.9	22	D	D	D
Perry	2.0	193	3	12	1.5	0.2	22	194	32.8	3.5	6	9	0.9	0.4
Phillips	266.7	12 256	33	D	D	D	99	1 120	229.4	22.1	22	53	5.1	1.2
Pike	1.8	163	17	163	92.1	3.6	35	276	52.8	5.0	8	26	1.5	0.3
Poinsett	937.3	38 126	21	D	D	D	88	883	193.1	14.7	12	72	6.1	1.4
Polk	4.0	191	22	126	47.8	2.5	98	861	176.9	16.8	18	128	10.4	2.6
Pope	987.2	15 985	71	426	234.5	16.1	303	3 633	919.3	73.8	78	241	45.3	6.0
Prairie	334.2	38 344	8	59	28.4	2.0	38	201	39.5	3.0	5	9	0.9	0.4
Pulaski	82.1	215	704	13 507	13 419.0	594.4	1 771	25 621	6 163.1	566.9	644	3 614	671.4	113.1
Randolph	156.2	8 692	10	89	39.3	2.1	67	708	137.4	12.4	15	41	3.6	0.6
St. Francis	363.1	12 848	20	D	D	D	136	1 248	353.8	26.3	17	54	4.8	0.8
Saline	31.9	298	68	751	265.2	31.5	301	3 996	1 157.7	90.7	78	225	27.2	4.7
Scott	1.9	170	8	39	9.2	1.2	28	299	48.7	5.3	5	11	0.8	0.2
Searcy	1.8	221	3	D	D	D	33	299	59.1	5.1	6	31	0.9	0.2
Sebastian	3.7	30	198	2 474	1 313.8	95.9	604	8 058	1 825.5	167.8	170	919	158.6	26.8
Sevier	4.6	268	4	D	D	D	73	657	160.6	12.6	8	32	3.0	0.6
Sharp	3.5	203	7	D	D	D	73	648	156.0	12.1	17	35	4.4	0.7
Stone	2.8	225	8	75	32.6	1.6	62	583	108.4	13.4	10	13	1.8	0.2
Union	20.4	490	55	D	D	D	237	2 457	526.4	47.3	37	184	35.1	5.2
Van Buren	4.4	252	14	81	50.7	2.2	66	603	152.1	12.4	6	34	4.9	0.7
Washington	3.1	15	236	2 578	1 328.1	110.5	798	11 512	2 723.3	247.4	289	2 262	196.0	59.1
White	88.0	1 142	63	D	D	D	311	3 384	803.5	69.1	70	267	34.4	6.8
Woodruff	246.3	33 928	12	183	90.9	7.2	32	200	64.7	3.0	7	11	1.0	0.1
Yell	4.1	186	9	24	5.8	0.6	57	575	109.3	9.4	11	20	1.8	0.3

1. Merchant wholesalers, except manufacturers' sales branches and offices. 2. Employer establishments.

STATE County	Professional, scientific, and technical services,[1] 2007				Manufacturing, 2007				Accommodation and food services, 2007			
	Number of establish-ments	Number of employees	Receipts (mil dol)	Annual payroll (mil dol)	Number of establish-ments	Number of employees	Receipts (mil dol)	Annual payroll (mil dol)	Number of establish-ments	Number of employees	Sales (mil dol)	Annual payroll (mil dol)
	147	148	149	150	151	152	153	154	155	156	157	158
ARKANSAS—Cont'd												
Cleveland	1	D	D	D	NA	NA	NA	NA	2	D	D	D
Columbia	33	149	10.4	3.9	35	2 688	1 164.3	93.4	38	590	21.8	5.5
Conway	31	94	7.4	2.5	27	1 137	432.6	43.4	36	424	16.2	3.9
Craighead	173	D	D	D	120	6 455	1 830.3	229.9	178	3 963	146.7	41.4
Crawford	90	D	D	D	62	3 576	848.0	97.1	84	1 364	53.2	15.2
Crittenden	53	D	D	D	44	1 396	701.3	55.1	82	1 626	65.1	17.6
Cross	28	74	5.2	1.8	11	664	D	17.9	24	369	12.5	3.3
Dallas	10	23	1.6	0.4	13	749	184.5	27.2	13	115	4.6	1.3
Desha	23	59	4.5	1.4	14	982	400.8	43.4	28	279	9.8	2.5
Drew	28	105	7.6	2.7	24	891	156.1	30.2	31	657	19.7	5.1
Faulkner	214	759	76.5	22.7	100	5 342	1 587.6	216.5	165	3 781	137.9	37.1
Franklin	15	D	D	D	19	954	327.7	28.9	21	262	10.4	2.7
Fulton	15	57	3.6	1.5	NA	NA	NA	NA	16	163	5.3	1.6
Garland	218	D	D	D	119	2 786	661.7	99.9	265	5 080	203.3	62.2
Grant	14	D	D	D	18	1 294	489.9	D	18	249	10.2	2.4
Greene	55	360	20.1	8.0	53	4 942	1 434.1	160.7	61	984	37.6	10.4
Hempstead	15	45	4.1	1.5	30	D	D	D	38	586	21.2	6.0
Hot Spring	22	105	7.0	2.4	33	1 749	858.5	62.4	32	456	16.8	4.4
Howard	18	62	4.1	1.2	23	3 645	1 081.1	100.3	16	307	9.2	2.5
Independence	57	343	17.6	5.6	44	4 491	920.0	147.5	59	990	34.7	9.7
Izard	5	D	D	D	NA	NA	NA	NA	13	111	3.3	1.0
Jackson	24	D	D	D	17	982	D	33.4	26	237	9.7	2.7
Jefferson	89	D	D	D	60	4 684	D	D	140	2 147	87.1	22.4
Johnson	26	99	7.6	2.5	37	2 798	546.8	71.9	35	480	20.5	5.0
Lafayette	7	32	1.4	0.3	NA	NA	NA	NA	5	50	1.5	0.4
Lawrence	13	42	2.4	0.8	NA	NA	NA	NA	19	292	9.3	2.4
Lee	11	47	4.4	1.2	NA	NA	NA	NA	7	84	2.8	0.7
Lincoln	9	D	D	D	5	D	D	D	14	D	D	D
Little River	13	70	5.4	1.6	16	1 339	D	83.8	14	166	6.1	1.5
Logan	28	66	7.5	1.9	23	1 824	692.1	51.9	27	312	10.0	2.9
Lonoke	92	D	D	D	38	1 502	D	56.4	75	1 222	46.4	12.7
Madison	13	D	D	D	21	1 082	D	31.4	13	126	3.2	1.0
Marion	13	40	2.3	0.9	20	1 756	350.1	49.7	32	237	8.6	2.1
Miller	39	187	25.6	6.7	29	2 246	712.9	129.1	66	1 188	43.7	12.7
Mississippi	49	195	17.2	5.6	51	5 962	5 010.2	319.6	81	1 091	45.8	11.8
Monroe	11	33	1.8	0.6	NA	NA	NA	NA	16	212	8.2	2.2
Montgomery	9	22	1.2	0.5	NA	NA	NA	NA	17	232	18.2	5.1
Nevada	4	19	1.6	0.5	8	D	D	D	9	95	3.2	0.9
Newton	6	D	D	D	NA	NA	NA	NA	12	46	3.3	0.7
Ouachita	27	154	17.1	5.0	32	D	D	D	26	421	14.6	3.7
Perry	8	D	D	D	NA	NA	NA	NA	5	58	1.7	0.5
Phillips	39	D	D	D	NA	NA	NA	NA	29	382	13.5	3.7
Pike	3	D	D	D	NA	NA	NA	NA	14	162	6.8	1.7
Poinsett	21	D	D	D	19	834	172.0	29.1	37	361	11.6	2.8
Polk	34	107	8.8	2.6	38	1 218	303.5	34.5	35	418	14.4	3.8
Pope	138	D	D	D	75	4 620	1 436.7	159.3	113	2 349	79.4	21.3
Prairie	7	21	2.2	0.5	NA	NA	NA	NA	14	90	4.3	0.8
Pulaski	1 549	D	D	D	382	15 031	5 969.5	665.4	858	17 807	810.0	231.0
Randolph	21	81	6.0	2.0	35	822	148.1	28.1	22	413	13.9	3.6
St. Francis	35	D	D	D	12	1 011	D	30.7	45	739	28.5	7.5
Saline	136	438	40.4	14.1	74	1 579	366.9	63.9	117	1 919	81.2	23.3
Scott	9	14	1.4	0.3	19	1 070	203.0	27.2	16	100	3.1	0.8
Searcy	8	31	1.5	0.4	NA	NA	NA	NA	11	73	2.9	0.9
Sebastian	297	D	D	D	198	19 654	5 676.5	648.5	262	5 124	207.8	56.8
Sevier	12	17	2.1	0.7	0	D	D	D	14	191	6.9	1.6
Sharp	19	41	2.5	0.7	NA	NA	NA	NA	41	387	13.0	3.3
Stone	8	D	D	D	NA	NA	NA	NA	29	316	12.1	2.9
Union	66	D	D	D	60	4 711	3 901.9	198.3	70	975	40.0	9.8
Van Buren	18	60	4.4	1.5	NA	NA	NA	NA	22	319	12.5	3.1
Washington	570	D	D	D	213	14 703	3 497.6	482.9	454	9 536	355.7	102.3
White	77	343	30.6	11.0	79	3 831	1 168.2	128.4	116	2 005	79.8	20.4
Woodruff	6	D	D	D	NA	NA	NA	NA	7	45	1.3	0.3
Yell	19	D	D	D	17	2 683	449.6	65.3	22	318	9.2	2.5

1. Establishment subject to federal tax.

STATE County	Health care and social assistance, 2007				Other services, 2007				Nonemployer businesses, 2013		Value of residential construction authorized by building permits, 2014	
	Number of establish-ments	Number of employees	Receipts (mil dol)	Annual payroll (mil dol)	Number of establish-ments	Number of employees	Receipts (mil dol)	Annual payroll (mil dol)	Number	Receipts (mil dol)	New Construction ($1,000)	Number of housing units
	159	160	161	162	163	164	165	166	167	168	169	170
ARKANSAS—Cont'd												
Cleveland	8	D	D	D	7	D	D	D	404	16.4	0	0
Columbia	63	1 190	69.7	27.3	39	169	11.7	3.3	1 215	51.0	6 677	49
Conway	45	556	32.1	12.5	16	98	22.6	5.1	1 337	50.4	869	10
Craighead	307	7 706	769.0	283.2	141	835	67.6	16.9	7 113	317.2	66 814	671
Crawford	92	1 542	100.4	46.9	67	420	33.1	9.9	3 573	145.1	5 900	43
Crittenden	117	1 897	166.2	65.5	71	476	34.7	9.7	3 542	124.4	15 537	95
Cross	47	657	43.2	16.2	22	49	4.1	1.0	1 381	51.4	3 830	18
Dallas	22	877	45.3	17.9	14	42	2.9	0.8	364	12.5	10	1
Desha	34	600	42.0	15.6	17	40	2.2	0.6	732	28.1	812	7
Drew	41	1 011	46.4	21.7	21	143	9.9	3.7	1 006	44.1	640	4
Faulkner	273	4 581	366.0	136.1	121	571	44.6	12.3	7 738	308.2	52 386	341
Franklin	28	574	26.5	12.1	15	59	5.7	1.1	1 025	38.3	0	0
Fulton	27	418	17.8	9.1	10	27	1.4	0.4	790	26.5	25	1
Garland	276	6 590	613.4	244.4	179	1 309	80.6	26.6	7 724	304.3	12 298	43
Grant	20	237	13.0	5.7	18	D	D	D	1 155	48.7	1 043	9
Greene	86	1 572	117.8	42.4	45	145	12.1	3.4	2 718	127.7	17 745	193
Hempstead	54	1 160	72.6	26.7	36	D	D	D	1 060	37.9	631	3
Hot Spring	44	1 070	62.1	27.3	28	135	9.1	2.4	1 793	64.1	0	0
Howard	30	589	32.7	12.6	21	88	6.8	2.0	740	32.5	246	3
Independence	106	2 730	243.6	90.6	54	249	16.7	5.0	2 431	105.1	5 143	48
Izard	22	589	41.6	12.9	16	78	3.0	1.0	847	35.1	473	3
Jackson	56	1 002	67.9	26.0	22	161	7.9	2.3	842	32.9	575	5
Jefferson	267	4 422	387.1	142.7	94	665	44.7	17.2	3 802	124.6	5 064	55
Johnson	44	977	63.5	26.3	27	161	6.2	2.9	1 376	52.7	240	3
Lafayette	9	217	7.5	4.0	5	D	D	D	321	10.4	0	0
Lawrence	29	608	34.6	16.2	19	58	4.6	1.0	1 154	45.1	160	3
Lee	20	243	17.6	6.9	11	18	1.5	0.4	643	25.8	0	0
Lincoln	14	D	D	D	15	D	D	D	575	21.8	0	0
Little River	17	362	19.4	9.9	13	D	D	D	598	22.1	140	1
Logan	44	695	40.6	15.7	27	88	7.0	1.9	1 218	40.1	705	8
Lonoke	96	1 085	74.7	29.8	59	215	16.1	4.9	4 220	175.6	27 898	263
Madison	16	D	D	D	11	D	D	D	1 237	44.4	0	0
Marion	18	379	12.1	5.8	14	36	2.8	0.6	1 165	36.6	167	2
Miller	69	1 367	81.7	29.5	40	274	20.9	5.8	2 423	103.6	5 654	37
Mississippi	124	1 699	115.5	45.6	44	208	13.8	3.9	2 083	74.7	3 881	30
Monroe	21	337	12.4	6.4	13	58	5.0	0.9	534	25.1	180	1
Montgomery	11	D	D	D	7	D	D	D	740	27.0	NA	NA
Nevada	14	441	17.8	8.4	13	D	D	D	471	17.6	0	0
Newton	9	218	7.0	3.1	4	D	D	D	697	23.0	213	1
Ouachita	61	D	D	D	34	D	D	D	1 292	46.5	263	3
Perry	16	162	9.4	3.8	6	D	D	D	700	27.1	286	1
Phillips	80	1 168	78.4	28.1	30	D	D	D	1 419	47.7	2 778	34
Pike	13	300	10.9	5.0	8	D	D	D	866	34.5	NA	NA
Poinsett	39	506	23.6	11.3	20	52	4.0	1.1	1 424	52.0	811	9
Polk	52	947	53.0	22.8	26	84	5.4	1.4	1 461	53.6	115	2
Pope	146	2 593	180.7	78.6	99	515	33.5	10.3	3 684	129.5	5 482	53
Prairie	18	180	10.2	4.5	11	34	1.9	0.5	496	19.8	1 198	11
Pulaski	1 462	39 444	4 389.9	1 688.5	856	5 641	690.3	155.4	26 975	1 239.2	197 509	1 142
Randolph	37	769	53.7	21.7	18	43	3.7	0.9	1 252	53.4	895	11
St. Francis	59	1 290	76.2	31.5	26	D	D	D	1 882	58.8	0	0
Saline	174	3 387	248.2	100.2	128	668	53.1	16.7	7 532	326.6	54 375	326
Scott	16	269	15.5	6.5	8	38	1.7	1.5	613	21.2	4 484	42
Searcy	13	292	11.4	5.0	2	D	D	D	754	27.6	0	0
Sebastian	403	11 362	1 021.0	423.8	201	981	81.7	22.2	8 225	437.1	55 403	414
Sevier	33	593	28.4	12.8	23	90	4.9	1.4	779	31.9	302	8
Sharp	40	501	19.8	8.7	26	112	7.8	1.9	1 276	44.5	797	8
Stone	20	458	25.7	11.5	13	41	3.8	1.3	1 183	44.1	963	8
Union	135	2 440	192.8	79.3	81	446	42.6	10.8	2 733	118.6	5 767	87
Van Buren	34	682	39.2	17.1	24	159	13.5	2.6	1 259	41.9	360	3
Washington	494	11 569	1 179.7	472.0	314	D	D	D	14 580	653.2	263 928	1 131
White	154	3 259	282.5	110.2	100	573	46.7	16.1	5 198	203.3	13 426	116
Woodruff	22	161	10.0	3.8	9	10	1.1	0.3	393	17.4	0	0
Yell	45	791	46.1	18.4	13	55	4.1	1.0	1 159	41.5	66	1

STATE County	Government employment and payroll, 2012: Full-time equivalent employees	March payroll (dollars)	March payroll (percent of total): Adminis-tration, judicial, and legal	Police and Corrections	Fire Protection	Highways and transpor-tation	Health and Welfare	Natural resources and utilities	Education and libraries	Local government finances, 2012: General revenue: Total (mil dol)	Inter-govern-mental (mil dol)	Taxes: Total (mil dol)	Taxes: Per capita[1] (dollars): Total	Property
	171	172	173	174	175	176	177	178	179	180	181	182	183	184
ARKANSAS—Cont'd														
Cleveland	330	806 062	9.0	5.0	0.0	5.3	0.7	2.9	76.0	20.0	15.3	2.4	280	186
Columbia	810	2 122 431	5.9	8.7	1.9	4.1	0.6	7.5	70.9	84.2	34.7	16.8	686	216
Conway	751	2 035 580	5.2	11.1	0.6	3.9	0.8	8.1	70.0	72.1	44.8	15.9	748	377
Craighead	3 565	10 924 637	4.8	9.2	2.9	3.7	1.2	10.0	67.7	285.0	164.7	77.8	780	344
Crawford	2 079	8 936 720	9.1	2.8	0.0	1.4	5.5	24.0	57.1	156.8	108.4	28.6	461	213
Crittenden	2 243	7 239 687	5.6	10.1	4.1	1.8	1.6	6.1	67.6	182.3	109.3	39.6	792	258
Cross	603	1 548 890	10.4	9.4	1.4	3.4	1.1	2.8	71.5	51.1	33.6	9.9	562	280
Dallas	261	612 066	9.1	13.5	0.3	5.1	2.7	7.1	61.9	19.8	11.6	4.3	544	186
Desha	795	2 143 489	5.0	5.6	0.5	2.7	22.4	3.6	59.5	57.2	28.7	12.9	1 031	405
Drew	969	2 684 507	3.1	4.7	1.1	2.3	30.7	2.1	55.8	79.4	41.6	12.6	671	211
Faulkner	3 393	11 696 206	5.6	8.1	3.7	2.3	1.7	2.7	75.5	324.2	171.2	77.9	656	297
Franklin	616	1 780 777	6.6	4.8	0.5	3.5	2.3	1.9	77.8	48.5	35.0	9.5	525	268
Fulton	446	1 158 320	4.4	3.4	0.7	4.9	23.0	2.8	60.2	31.9	18.9	3.9	319	163
Garland	2 929	9 379 603	4.7	8.8	4.0	3.5	3.4	5.5	68.3	270.5	155.0	62.1	640	262
Grant	736	2 167 090	4.0	5.7	0.2	2.7	0.5	2.6	83.3	54.6	40.7	8.6	480	234
Greene	1 593	4 613 388	4.1	5.9	2.2	3.0	2.1	8.3	68.5	112.0	67.4	19.6	455	189
Hempstead	991	2 866 901	6.3	9.8	1.5	3.8	2.3	7.5	64.3	63.0	40.8	14.1	629	190
Hot Spring	1 020	3 135 235	4.3	4.3	1.6	3.0	1.9	5.9	78.5	75.0	50.6	15.7	471	242
Howard	721	2 467 138	7.2	17.5	1.7	5.0	3.5	21.0	42.7	46.1	28.6	9.7	704	226
Independence	1 442	3 864 054	4.6	7.4	0.9	3.5	2.2	8.2	72.6	113.1	69.9	22.7	614	314
Izard	479	1 132 741	7.6	7.8	0.2	5.9	1.2	5.3	71.6	32.9	23.1	5.4	399	259
Jackson	623	1 641 667	7.2	8.7	4.1	4.3	2.8	5.1	65.5	43.2	27.4	9.3	528	229
Jefferson	2 803	8 103 678	6.2	13.3	4.7	3.4	1.8	1.9	66.2	217.6	136.9	51.2	686	285
Johnson	832	2 711 188	3.4	5.5	0.7	2.3	0.4	12.2	75.6	63.8	42.9	12.1	466	209
Lafayette	324	1 024 900	6.7	6.5	0.5	5.3	1.6	2.4	77.1	19.1	12.6	3.8	516	258
Lawrence	1 057	2 598 077	3.2	3.6	0.8	2.1	33.0	2.4	54.7	79.8	45.0	7.8	459	210
Lee	422	1 112 758	5.2	7.2	1.9	5.4	2.5	8.4	68.7	24.4	17.7	4.1	401	201
Lincoln	362	919 481	6.2	5.9	0.1	3.6	0.2	2.7	80.4	24.4	16.8	4.2	297	152
Little River	689	1 796 446	3.9	4.0	0.1	2.7	34.8	3.7	50.8	44.7	19.0	7.9	615	273
Logan	771	2 027 835	5.6	7.0	0.2	4.0	2.6	4.4	76.0	49.8	33.4	9.6	437	237
Lonoke	2 693	7 148 935	4.2	6.7	2.0	2.1	0.5	4.6	79.3	189.2	129.4	38.9	558	260
Madison	571	1 449 917	5.1	4.6	0.0	6.7	5.3	2.7	75.2	31.5	20.9	6.6	420	180
Marion	420	1 177 227	8.0	10.7	0.3	8.0	1.6	5.5	65.4	26.6	17.6	6.1	370	207
Miller	1 370	3 792 335	7.1	17.4	7.1	4.8	0.8	2.2	58.3	120.6	70.4	29.4	674	250
Mississippi	2 048	5 872 177	5.4	9.7	2.9	3.6	2.1	9.0	65.1	191.6	104.8	32.2	707	241
Monroe	360	1 055 919	8.0	11.9	0.8	5.2	0.9	10.4	61.7	25.7	17.8	4.5	571	283
Montgomery	294	752 749	7.1	6.2	0.0	6.4	2.9	4.0	72.7	19.1	14.5	3.0	317	201
Nevada	405	978 364	8.6	11.3	0.0	8.2	3.9	6.8	59.4	20.3	14.7	3.3	374	180
Newton	434	1 232 173	2.8	2.8	0.0	2.9	1.0	1.0	89.0	59.7	55.7	2.4	298	215
Ouachita	1 097	3 081 016	5.9	8.9	2.9	5.3	2.7	5.6	68.4	75.4	51.1	15.8	623	202
Perry	344	973 732	8.1	7.6	0.0	4.4	0.3	3.1	72.6	20.7	15.2	3.5	334	164
Phillips	872	2 319 840	6.4	8.7	2.9	4.6	0.0	7.6	68.3	70.5	48.6	14.3	689	239
Pike	507	1 198 447	2.9	2.6	0.0	2.3	0.6	3.0	88.0	32.5	23.2	6.0	533	207
Poinsett	959	2 599 342	5.4	11.1	1.0	3.7	0.5	5.4	72.6	69.5	51.1	10.0	411	173
Polk	1 139	3 233 326	3.5	4.4	0.5	3.3	0.1	3.1	84.0	84.7	45.1	10.6	516	173
Pope	2 245	7 108 185	4.8	9.2	3.2	2.4	3.2	4.5	71.3	165.6	100.1	42.3	674	270
Prairie	351	1 159 649	15.7	11.7	0.5	12.8	1.1	5.2	52.5	20.8	12.8	4.0	470	235
Pulaski	15 078	52 069 152	6.0	12.7	6.6	4.5	3.5	11.7	52.8	1 476.7	724.3	418.1	1 075	551
Randolph	552	1 387 909	7.5	7.1	2.0	4.5	1.7	6.7	68.7	37.2	24.0	9.9	551	358
St. Francis	1 036	3 954 323	5.7	6.9	1.6	2.0	2.7	7.1	73.4	75.8	52.5	14.7	527	164
Saline	2 671	8 478 497	6.2	7.9	4.2	2.4	0.6	6.1	71.0	238.1	147.9	54.6	489	267
Scott	364	909 428	4.1	3.6	0.0	5.1	1.8	4.7	79.2	25.0	18.3	4.3	391	127
Searcy	296	714 402	4.4	5.2	0.0	5.9	1.5	2.7	80.0	16.3	12.2	2.5	308	178
Sebastian	4 285	15 121 933	5.9	9.8	4.3	4.0	2.6	7.8	65.5	399.0	208.5	123.0	966	364
Sevier	764	2 036 880	4.0	5.6	0.4	2.6	1.5	12.6	72.8	59.3	43.9	8.4	490	157
Sharp	745	1 804 388	5.9	6.5	3.5	5.1	0.2	6.1	71.2	44.2	31.2	7.0	408	175
Stone	424	1 109 650	6.3	5.7	0.0	5.5	1.2	9.6	70.0	26.1	18.0	5.4	423	148
Union	1 719	4 970 357	4.4	7.3	3.6	3.5	2.6	4.4	72.2	125.7	71.2	35.1	859	292
Van Buren	757	1 902 959	7.4	21.6	1.0	6.7	1.1	2.5	58.5	49.1	26.5	14.0	822	502
Washington	7 560	23 284 035	5.1	10.7	3.9	4.1	1.3	4.1	69.5	691.8	396.1	183.9	870	333
White	2 609	7 296 125	4.8	6.2	2.5	2.4	2.0	5.5	75.7	192.0	122.5	42.8	545	227
Woodruff	367	874 741	9.7	5.0	0.3	4.3	1.5	8.7	68.2	25.9	19.0	3.7	521	309
Yell	877	2 241 720	3.8	7.4	0.3	4.0	0.5	4.0	79.4	58.7	42.0	10.7	489	268

1. Based on the resident population estimated as of July 1 of the year shown.

STATE County	Local government finances, 2012 (cont.) — Direct general expenditure: Total (mil dol)	Per capita[1] (dollars)	Percent of total for: Education	Health and hospitals	Police protection	Public welfare	Highways	Debt outstanding: Total (mil dol)	Per capita[1] (dollars)	Government employment, 2013: Federal civilian	Federal military	State and local	Presidential election,[2] 2012 — Percent of vote cast: Democratic	Republican	All other
	185	186	187	188	189	190	191	192	193	194	195	196	197	198	199
ARKANSAS—Cont'd															
Cleveland	19.8	2 299	72.2	0.7	3.3	0.2	9.2	7.9	916	13	39	355	26.0	69.9	4.1
Columbia	85.3	3 484	43.3	28.4	3.6	0.1	3.9	107.4	4 388	41	103	1 959	37.2	61.3	1.5
Conway	70.4	3 308	65.7	1.5	5.0	0.2	8.3	39.8	1 868	60	95	1 497	38.7	57.6	3.7
Craighead	279.3	2 800	56.9	0.3	5.7	0.1	5.4	482.8	4 841	321	451	7 768	36.5	61.0	2.6
Crawford	160.3	2 588	67.2	0.0	5.0	0.0	7.4	203.0	3 277	90	278	2 192	25.5	71.5	3.0
Crittenden	177.1	3 540	57.7	0.2	7.9	0.0	4.9	305.8	6 114	95	223	2 836	56.6	41.9	1.5
Cross	50.3	2 847	65.6	4.4	4.9	0.2	5.5	15.3	867	58	79	1 087	36.2	61.6	2.2
Dallas	18.2	2 276	53.5	0.2	7.1	0.0	9.3	15.1	1 887	18	34	380	44.3	53.0	2.7
Desha	54.8	4 365	49.1	21.1	6.0	0.1	3.4	43.6	3 478	58	57	900	54.9	42.7	2.4
Drew	81.1	4 329	53.9	22.7	3.7	0.2	6.4	39.5	2 108	58	81	2 030	39.3	58.4	2.3
Faulkner	340.2	2 866	58.3	0.1	4.3	0.0	5.9	686.1	5 780	203	534	7 629	36.3	61.6	2.1
Franklin	46.2	2 558	73.0	3.3	3.8	0.3	6.5	43.4	2 406	158	80	888	28.9	68.1	3.0
Fulton	30.6	2 485	53.3	24.1	3.1	0.1	8.4	14.3	1 159	26	55	618	38.9	57.8	3.3
Garland	268.9	2 775	57.5	0.3	5.6	0.0	3.6	344.1	3 551	505	433	4 251	36.4	61.4	2.3
Grant	54.3	3 022	74.8	0.6	4.5	0.1	4.4	31.4	1 747	28	81	820	23.0	73.9	3.1
Greene	119.5	2 769	59.8	0.2	3.6	0.1	4.4	136.1	3 152	82	193	2 030	33.4	63.0	3.6
Hempstead	64.4	2 877	60.7	0.2	4.3	0.1	5.2	53.7	2 402	92	101	1 721	39.0	58.1	2.8
Hot Spring	76.2	2 283	72.0	1.7	3.4	0.1	4.0	94.3	2 823	67	143	1 996	35.9	60.3	3.8
Howard	46.0	3 350	63.9	0.8	4.9	0.1	4.2	74.9	5 451	58	61	840	36.0	61.0	3.0
Independence	118.5	3 202	52.8	0.2	3.5	0.1	6.2	274.1	7 403	124	164	2 239	30.0	67.1	2.9
Izard	33.6	2 497	65.3	1.3	4.8	0.2	6.9	26.2	1 942	28	57	1 085	34.3	61.2	4.5
Jackson	41.6	2 363	54.0	1.4	7.4	0.1	6.9	23.9	1 357	44	71	1 487	39.5	55.9	4.6
Jefferson	217.7	2 914	59.7	0.1	7.5	0.1	4.0	226.1	3 025	1 644	339	7 064	62.2	35.9	1.9
Johnson	65.1	2 514	63.3	0.2	4.4	0.0	7.2	48.8	1 883	91	115	1 073	37.1	60.2	2.7
Lafayette	20.9	2 805	68.4	0.2	6.4	0.1	6.3	10.0	1 344	23	32	332	39.0	58.1	2.9
Lawrence	75.1	4 412	56.5	22.2	3.3	4.3	3.1	40.2	2 361	57	75	1 244	36.7	57.6	5.7
Lee	21.6	2 110	53.3	0.4	9.2	0.2	10.8	5.6	551	38	38	808	60.1	38.6	1.2
Lincoln	25.2	1 788	68.0	0.1	4.2	0.0	7.9	12.9	913	22	47	1 353	38.8	57.0	4.2
Little River	45.4	3 511	41.4	20.9	4.1	6.7	4.1	77.9	6 027	46	57	836	34.0	63.0	3.0
Logan	50.5	2 295	64.1	5.2	5.3	0.1	5.4	41.6	1 893	104	98	1 355	28.9	67.7	3.4
Lonoke	184.1	2 636	69.9	0.2	4.3	0.0	2.8	172.0	2 463	104	319	2 805	25.1	72.6	2.2
Madison	31.6	2 021	66.4	3.3	5.6	0.0	11.6	24.7	1 576	42	71	600	33.9	62.8	3.4
Marion	28.0	1 688	60.5	0.2	8.4	0.2	11.9	19.4	1 172	33	74	559	33.3	63.2	3.5
Miller	112.1	2 568	56.8	0.3	9.6	0.0	4.3	109.3	2 504	59	191	2 158	32.3	65.8	1.9
Mississippi	189.3	4 154	49.4	0.5	5.1	0.1	2.9	796.0	17 471	97	200	2 924	47.6	49.8	2.6
Monroe	25.5	3 252	52.9	1.3	5.1	0.2	10.3	10.9	1 390	26	35	448	46.8	50.9	2.3
Montgomery	18.0	1 926	60.2	0.1	3.4	0.0	10.6	13.6	1 457	55	41	506	30.1	65.3	4.6
Nevada	20.5	2 300	61.8	0.3	6.5	0.2	8.5	12.4	1 394	25	39	472	40.6	56.7	2.7
Newton	30.3	3 746	81.8	0.1	1.5	0.1	7.3	72.1	8 919	55	36	453	29.8	65.4	4.8
Ouachita	71.1	2 801	66.5	0.1	4.9	0.0	5.4	60.6	2 386	92	112	2 004	43.6	54.5	1.9
Perry	19.2	1 861	72.5	0.1	5.9	0.3	7.5	14.0	1 359	22	46	405	31.6	64.1	4.3
Phillips	71.5	3 442	65.5	0.1	5.3	0.1	3.5	34.7	1 670	64	92	1 502	63.5	34.5	2.0
Pike	30.8	2 738	73.7	0.4	3.3	0.2	7.6	17.3	1 541	61	50	574	27.5	68.8	3.8
Poinsett	65.0	2 676	70.6	0.2	6.9	0.1	4.4	35.9	1 479	64	108	1 185	34.6	61.8	3.6
Polk	82.4	4 025	54.6	28.8	2.5	0.0	3.6	60.1	2 937	87	92	1 083	25.5	71.3	3.3
Pope	163.1	2 599	67.0	1.6	6.5	0.1	6.0	190.1	3 029	270	270	4 380	27.2	70.5	2.3
Prairie	19.8	2 343	62.2	2.0	6.4	0.0	9.5	17.3	2 050	42	38	358	31.0	65.7	3.3
Pulaski	1 448.1	3 723	46.0	4.2	6.9	0.0	3.8	1 780.8	4 578	9 120	7 263	45 670	55.1	43.5	1.4
Randolph	35.5	1 979	57.5	0.0	7.8	0.0	9.3	8.9	498	32	79	1 151	39.1	57.2	3.7
St. Francis	73.2	2 628	65.4	0.5	5.9	0.1	4.9	21.2	759	666	105	1 562	57.7	41.2	1.1
Saline	246.7	2 206	68.6	0.3	4.4	0.0	5.3	376.7	3 368	80	515	4 541	28.4	69.4	2.2
Scott	25.5	2 315	68.6	0.5	4.5	0.0	7.8	31.9	2 901	74	49	622	26.4	69.9	3.8
Searcy	16.1	2 010	62.9	0.2	4.8	0.2	10.4	2.8	353	38	36	457	25.0	70.9	4.2
Sebastian	398.6	3 131	51.6	0.2	5.7	0.1	6.2	717.8	5 639	1 014	608	6 733	31.6	66.3	2.1
Sevier	59.7	3 477	77.9	0.0	3.5	0.1	3.6	19.8	1 151	66	78	1 126	28.2	68.2	3.6
Sharp	43.7	2 563	62.6	0.1	5.0	0.0	10.0	23.8	1 398	44	77	806	33.6	62.5	3.9
Stone	24.5	1 931	63.3	0.1	5.7	0.2	9.7	8.6	681	65	57	551	30.0	66.4	3.6
Union	124.9	3 056	60.5	0.1	5.9	0.0	7.4	143.9	3 521	147	184	2 547	36.0	62.2	1.8
Van Buren	45.8	2 692	53.0	4.9	8.6	0.2	14.4	61.6	3 616	33	76	733	32.1	63.8	4.1
Washington	690.9	3 268	59.8	0.3	5.5	0.0	3.8	886.2	4 192	1 922	966	17 559	42.4	55.5	2.0
White	187.6	2 389	67.8	0.2	5.9	0.1	5.3	228.1	2 907	161	342	3 653	25.0	72.2	2.8
Woodruff	27.6	3 888	46.7	0.3	3.9	20.3	8.1	12.6	1 776	40	32	512	51.1	43.7	5.2
Yell	56.6	2 581	70.7	0.1	6.1	0.0	5.0	53.5	2 439	113	98	1 261	33.2	63.1	3.7

1. Based on the resident population estimated as of July 1 of the year shown.
2.

STATE/ County code	CBSA code[1]	County type[2]	STATE County	Land area,[3] (sq km) 2010	Population, 2014: Total persons 2014	Population, 2014: Rank	Population, 2014: Per square kilometer	Population and population characteristics, 2013: Race alone or in combination, not Hispanic or Latino (percent): White	Black	American Indian, Alaska Native	Asian and Pacific Islander	Percent Hispanic or Latino[4]	Age (percent): Under 5 years	5 to 17 years	18 to 24 years	25 to 34 years	35 to 44 years	45 to 54 years
				1	2	3	4	5	6	7	8	9	10	11	12	13	14	15
06 000	...	X	CALIFORNIA	403 466	38 802 500	X	96.2	41.2	6.5	1.0	15.6	38.3	6.5	17.4	10.5	14.6	13.4	13.6
06 001	41860	1	Alameda	1 914	1 610 921	21	841.7	36.4	12.8	0.9	31.5	22.6	6.1	15.6	9.5	15.6	14.9	14.2
06 003	...	8	Alpine	1 912	1 116	3 105	0.6	68.5	1.2	21.2	1.5	9.9	3.3	17.6	6.9	7.9	10.0	15.4
06 005	...	6	Amador	1 540	36 742	1 257	23.9	82.4	2.5	2.8	2.2	12.7	3.6	11.9	6.5	9.8	10.9	15.1
06 007	17020	3	Butte	4 238	224 241	287	52.9	77.1	2.4	3.0	5.9	15.1	5.4	14.9	15.9	11.8	10.3	11.8
06 009	...	6	Calaveras	2 612	44 624	1 079	16.9	85.1	1.4	2.7	2.0	11.1	3.8	14.2	6.6	8.4	9.2	14.5
06 011	...	6	Colusa	2 980	21 419	1 755	7.2	38.5	1.3	1.8	2.2	57.3	7.5	20.7	10.0	12.9	12.0	12.6
06 013	41860	1	Contra Costa	1 854	1 111 339	38	599.4	49.6	10.0	1.0	18.6	24.9	5.9	17.9	8.6	12.4	13.5	15.0
06 015	18860	7	Del Norte	2 606	27 212	1 524	10.4	66.5	4.1	9.1	4.8	19.2	5.9	15.3	8.5	14.6	12.7	14.1
06 017	40900	1	El Dorado	4 423	183 087	349	41.4	81.8	1.3	1.9	5.6	12.5	4.6	16.7	7.9	9.7	11.2	15.9
06 019	23420	2	Fresno	15 431	965 974	48	62.6	33.0	5.3	1.2	10.8	51.5	8.4	20.8	11.3	14.7	12.1	11.9
06 021	...	6	Glenn	3 403	27 955	1 494	8.2	55.4	1.2	2.5	3.1	39.6	7.3	19.8	9.2	12.5	11.4	12.7
06 023	21700	5	Humboldt	9 241	134 809	470	14.6	80.3	2.1	7.4	4.4	10.5	5.3	14.1	13.2	13.9	11.8	12.1
06 025	20940	3	Imperial	10 817	179 091	358	16.6	13.3	2.7	1.0	1.7	81.4	8.3	20.5	11.2	14.0	12.2	12.1
06 027	...	7	Inyo	26 368	18 410	1 901	0.7	66.6	1.2	11.6	2.1	20.8	6.0	15.0	7.1	10.8	10.5	13.7
06 029	12540	2	Kern	21 062	874 589	62	41.5	38.6	5.9	1.3	5.3	50.8	8.4	21.2	11.2	14.9	12.5	12.2
06 031	25260	3	Kings	3 599	150 269	428	41.8	36.0	7.0	1.4	5.1	52.7	8.2	19.5	11.5	16.6	13.8	12.6
06 033	17340	4	Lake	3 254	64 184	818	19.7	75.6	2.6	4.2	2.6	18.4	5.6	14.7	7.7	10.5	10.4	14.0
06 035	45000	6	Lassen	11 762	31 749	1 391	2.7	68.8	8.9	4.2	2.6	18.2	4.6	12.9	10.5	18.0	15.0	14.7
06 037	31080	1	Los Angeles	10 510	10 116 705	1	962.6	28.8	8.9	0.6	15.6	48.1	6.4	16.8	10.7	15.4	14.1	13.7
06 039	31460	3	Madera	5 535	154 548	414	27.9	37.8	3.5	1.9	2.7	55.8	7.8	20.4	10.3	13.6	12.3	12.2
06 041	41860	1	Marin	1 348	260 750	257	193.4	75.4	3.2	0.8	8.0	15.7	5.0	15.6	6.3	9.1	13.3	16.1
06 043	...	8	Mariposa	3 752	17 682	1 934	4.7	84.6	1.6	4.5	2.4	10.0	4.2	12.7	7.0	9.6	9.3	14.9
06 045	46380	4	Mendocino	9 081	87 869	649	9.7	69.6	1.3	5.5	3.0	23.5	5.9	15.7	7.9	11.9	11.7	12.7
06 047	32900	3	Merced	5 012	266 353	254	53.1	31.7	3.8	1.0	8.7	56.7	8.2	22.2	11.9	14.0	12.2	11.8
06 049	...	6	Modoc	10 147	9 023	2 517	0.9	79.7	1.8	4.3	1.9	14.8	5.1	15.4	6.8	9.6	10.7	13.3
06 051	...	7	Mono	7 897	13 997	2 169	1.8	67.9	1.1	2.3	2.8	27.8	5.4	14.6	9.4	16.2	13.0	15.2
06 053	41500	2	Monterey	8 497	431 344	161	50.8	33.5	3.3	0.9	8.0	56.8	7.8	18.7	10.9	15.0	13.0	12.2
06 055	34900	3	Napa	1 938	141 667	448	73.1	56.5	2.4	1.1	9.0	33.3	5.7	16.6	9.1	12.3	12.6	13.8
06 057	46020	4	Nevada	2 481	98 893	596	39.9	88.1	0.9	2.0	2.5	9.0	4.2	13.7	6.9	9.9	10.4	13.9
06 059	31080	1	Orange	2 048	3 145 515	6	1 535.9	44.8	2.0	0.6	20.9	34.1	6.1	17.2	10.2	14.0	13.8	14.6
06 061	40900	1	Placer	3 644	371 694	182	102.0	77.7	2.1	1.4	8.9	13.4	5.6	17.7	7.9	11.2	12.9	14.5
06 063	...	7	Plumas	6 612	18 606	1 885	2.8	87.1	1.7	4.1	1.9	8.3	4.5	12.8	7.3	8.7	9.0	13.7
06 065	40140	1	Riverside	18 665	2 329 271	10	124.8	39.9	6.9	1.0	7.7	46.8	6.9	19.9	10.6	13.3	12.8	13.1
06 067	40900	1	Sacramento	2 498	1 482 026	25	593.3	50.9	11.6	1.6	18.6	22.2	6.8	17.9	9.8	14.9	13.0	13.5
06 069	41940	1	San Benito	3 597	58 267	883	16.2	38.0	1.2	1.0	3.6	57.9	7.0	20.4	9.8	12.9	12.9	14.3
06 071	40140	1	San Bernardino	51 947	2 112 619	12	40.7	33.1	9.2	1.0	7.9	50.9	7.4	20.3	11.5	14.3	12.9	13.1
06 073	41740	1	San Diego	10 895	3 263 431	5	299.5	49.9	5.7	1.0	13.9	32.8	6.5	16.1	11.4	15.9	13.2	13.2
06 075	41860	1	San Francisco	121	852 469	65	7 045.2	44.4	6.3	0.8	36.7	15.3	4.6	8.8	8.0	22.3	16.3	13.6
06 077	44700	2	San Joaquin	3 604	715 597	87	198.6	37.3	7.9	1.2	17.0	40.1	7.5	20.7	10.5	13.4	12.8	13.0
06 079	42020	3	San Luis Obispo	8 543	279 083	240	32.7	72.2	2.4	1.3	5.0	21.7	4.9	13.5	15.6	11.5	10.7	12.7
06 081	41860	1	San Mateo	1 161	758 581	82	653.4	44.0	3.2	0.6	30.5	25.3	6.1	15.5	7.6	14.0	14.7	14.8
06 083	42200	2	Santa Barbara	7 084	440 668	157	62.2	48.4	2.3	1.0	6.5	44.1	6.5	16.1	16.1	13.2	11.4	12.0
06 085	41940	1	Santa Clara	3 341	1 894 605	16	567.1	36.5	3.0	0.7	36.2	26.6	6.5	16.9	8.8	15.1	15.1	14.5
06 087	42100	2	Santa Cruz	1 153	271 804	247	235.7	61.2	1.6	1.2	6.1	32.9	5.7	14.8	15.4	12.0	12.0	13.4
06 089	39820	3	Shasta	9 778	179 804	357	18.4	84.7	1.7	4.1	4.1	9.1	5.7	16.0	8.7	12.1	10.6	13.5
06 091	...	8	Sierra	2 469	3 003	2 977	1.2	88.3	1.2	2.4	0.9	9.2	4.0	12.4	5.3	7.7	9.4	14.9
06 093	...	7	Siskiyou	16 260	43 628	1 100	2.7	81.6	2.2	6.2	2.6	11.6	5.3	15.0	7.3	9.9	9.7	12.8
06 095	46700	2	Solano	2 128	431 131	162	202.6	44.1	15.9	1.4	19.0	25.2	6.2	17.1	10.0	13.9	12.4	14.3
06 097	42220	2	Sonoma	4 081	500 292	136	122.6	67.6	2.2	1.6	5.7	25.8	5.4	15.5	9.2	12.9	12.1	14.1
06 099	33700	2	Stanislaus	3 872	531 997	125	137.4	47.3	3.2	1.3	7.5	43.4	7.4	20.2	10.4	13.9	12.6	12.9
06 101	49700	3	Sutter	1 560	95 847	613	61.4	51.4	2.7	2.0	17.7	29.6	6.9	19.7	9.8	13.3	12.2	13.1
06 103	39780	4	Tehama	7 640	63 067	831	8.3	72.6	1.2	3.4	2.0	23.4	6.2	17.8	8.6	11.4	11.1	13.8
06 105	...	8	Trinity	8 234	13 170	2 226	1.6	87.1	1.3	7.1	1.9	7.1	4.6	12.7	6.2	9.0	9.9	14.4
06 107	47300	2	Tulare	12 495	458 198	148	36.7	32.2	1.7	1.2	4.1	62.2	9.0	22.9	10.9	14.1	12.2	11.5
06 109	43760	4	Tuolumne	5 752	53 831	931	9.4	83.9	2.4	2.9	2.1	11.2	4.1	12.8	7.8	11.4	10.3	13.4
06 111	37100	2	Ventura	4 774	846 178	66	177.2	49.3	2.2	0.8	8.6	41.5	6.4	18.1	10.1	12.9	12.8	14.3
06 113	40900	1	Yolo	2 628	207 590	309	79.0	52.0	3.2	1.3	16.0	31.0	5.0	10.0	10.5	10.0	11.0	11.0
06 115	49700	3	Yuba	1 636	73 966	739	45.2	61.1	4.5	3.5	8.9	26.9	8.4	19.9	10.4	15.2	11.8	12.1
08 000	...	X	COLORADO	268 431	5 355 866	X	20.0	71.3	4.7	1.3	4.0	21.0	6.4	17.1	9.8	14.8	13.6	13.6
08 001	19740	1	Adams	3 024	480 718	143	159.0	54.0	3.6	1.1	4.7	38.4	7.8	20.1	9.1	16.0	14.6	12.8
08 003	...	7	Alamosa	1 872	16 177	2 033	8.6	51.2	1.7	1.9	1.6	45.4	7.6	16.1	18.2	13.2	9.9	11.2
08 005	19740	1	Arapahoe	2 067	618 821	108	299.4	65.3	11.4	1.1	6.7	18.5	6.6	18.1	8.6	14.9	14.2	13.9
08 007	...	7	Archuleta	3 497	12 244	2 283	3.5	79.1	0.8	2.4	1.3	18.2	4.8	14.0	6.2	9.7	9.7	14.0
08 009	...	9	Baca	6 617	3 645	2 931	0.6	87.8	1.2	1.9	0.7	9.9	6.1	14.8	6.9	10.2	9.0	12.5
08 011	...	7	Bent	3 918	5 630	2 793	1.4	59.8	6.9	1.8	1.2	30.8	4.0	12.7	8.9	16.0	14.4	14.6

1. CBSA = Core Based Statistical Area. See Appendix A for explanation. See Appendix B for list of metropolitan areas with component counties. 2. County type code from the Economic Research Service of USDA Rural-Urban Continuum Codes. See Appendix A for definition. 3. Dry land or land partially or temporarily covered by water. 4. May be of any race.

STATE County	Population, 2013 (cont.): Age (percent) (cont.): 55 to 64 years	65 to 74 years	75 years and over	Percent female	Population change and components of change, 2000–2014: Total persons: 2000	2010	Percent change: 2000–2010	2010–2014	Components of change, 2010–2014: Births	Deaths	Net migration	Households, 2009–2013: Number	Persons per household	Percent: Family households	Female family householder[1]	One person
	16	17	18	19	20	21	22	23	24	25	26	27	28	29	30	31
CALIFORNIA	11.5	7.0	5.5	50.3	33 871 648	37 253 956	10.0	4.2	2 144 767	1 041 844	459 574	12 542 460	2.94	68.6	13.5	24.2
Alameda	12.0	6.9	5.2	51.0	1 443 741	1 510 271	4.6	6.7	82 793	40 237	59 746	545 071	2.76	65.0	12.5	26.9
Alpine	19.8	12.1	7.0	47.4	1 208	1 175	-2.7	-5.0	33	29	-71	394	2.90	66.8	6.6	30.2
Amador	17.9	14.4	9.8	46.9	35 100	38 091	8.5	-3.5	1 184	1 754	-757	14 262	2.32	66.8	9.0	26.9
Butte	13.3	9.1	7.6	50.4	203 171	220 000	8.3	1.9	10 200	9 512	3 513	84 816	2.53	60.2	11.3	29.3
Calaveras	19.0	15.0	9.2	50.0	40 554	45 578	12.4	-2.1	1 467	2 000	-323	18 702	2.38	69.5	8.1	25.1
Colusa	11.7	7.4	5.4	48.3	18 804	21 419	13.9	0.0	1 350	554	-781	6 853	3.07	72.9	10.2	23.1
Contra Costa	12.8	7.9	5.9	51.2	948 816	1 049 025	10.6	5.9	51 614	31 232	41 374	375 855	2.81	70.6	12.0	23.5
Del Norte	14.0	8.6	6.2	44.6	27 507	28 610	4.0	-4.9	1 360	1 151	-1 576	9 593	2.58	62.1	13.7	33.0
El Dorado	16.8	10.4	6.7	50.0	156 299	181 058	15.8	1.1	6 652	5 964	1 284	67 885	2.64	72.2	8.7	22.0
Fresno	10.0	6.1	4.8	50.0	799 407	930 450	16.4	3.8	68 262	27 223	-5 425	289 811	3.18	72.9	17.1	21.4
Glenn	12.5	8.0	6.5	49.5	26 453	28 122	6.3	-0.6	1 621	912	-897	9 628	2.87	70.7	11.4	24.2
Humboldt	14.7	8.8	6.0	50.0	126 518	134 623	6.4	0.1	6 328	5 334	-636	53 296	2.44	57.3	11.7	31.8
Imperial	10.2	6.2	5.3	48.8	142 361	174 528	22.6	2.6	12 966	3 967	-4 593	48 099	3.42	78.9	19.6	17.9
Inyo	16.4	11.0	9.4	49.8	17 945	18 546	3.3	-0.7	916	818	-254	7 873	2.30	56.7	10.9	38.4
Kern	9.8	5.7	3.9	48.7	661 645	839 631	26.9	4.2	61 710	23 511	-2 517	255 271	3.19	75.1	16.4	19.9
Kings	9.0	5.1	3.7	44.3	129 461	152 982	18.2	-1.8	10 344	3 385	-9 845	40 785	3.28	77.4	15.6	17.9
Lake	17.2	11.9	7.9	50.0	58 309	64 665	10.9	-0.7	3 092	3 342	-138	26 505	2.38	62.4	12.9	29.4
Lassen	12.3	7.1	4.8	36.6	33 828	34 895	3.2	-9.0	1 270	969	-3 471	9 945	2.36	64.8	10.0	28.4
Los Angeles	11.1	6.6	5.3	50.7	9 519 338	9 818 605	3.1	3.0	558 921	254 353	3 777	3 230 383	3.01	67.2	15.6	25.6
Madera	10.9	7.4	5.2	51.3	123 109	150 865	22.5	2.4	9 823	4 266	-1 705	42 516	3.37	77.3	14.9	18.5
Marin	15.6	11.0	7.9	51.1	247 289	252 409	2.1	3.3	9 831	7 858	6 698	102 912	2.39	62.5	8.8	30.3
Mariposa	18.6	14.1	9.6	49.2	17 130	18 251	6.5	-3.1	641	674	-488	7 238	2.36	66.4	9.3	26.6
Mendocino	16.1	11.1	7.1	50.1	86 265	87 841	1.8	0.0	4 676	3 435	-1 063	33 878	2.52	60.8	11.4	31.9
Merced	9.5	5.8	4.4	49.4	210 554	255 793	21.5	4.1	18 116	6 717	-679	75 409	3.36	77.3	17.6	18.2
Modoc	16.8	13.7	8.7	49.6	9 449	9 686	2.5	-6.8	374	453	-585	3 983	2.23	60.2	8.3	35.3
Mono	15.0	7.1	4.1	46.5	12 853	14 202	10.5	-1.4	585	185	-623	5 268	2.65	60.1	6.2	30.5
Monterey	10.8	6.4	5.2	48.6	401 762	415 057	3.3	3.9	28 447	10 023	-1 696	125 428	3.20	72.2	13.1	21.6
Napa	13.4	9.1	7.4	50.2	124 279	136 484	9.8	3.8	6 314	5 106	3 924	49 431	2.69	68.6	10.6	24.6
Nevada	18.6	13.3	9.2	50.7	92 033	98 764	7.3	0.1	3 369	3 827	830	40 991	2.38	63.9	8.6	28.7
Orange	11.5	7.1	5.7	50.5	2 846 289	3 010 232	5.8	4.5	162 288	77 737	52 028	995 512	3.02	71.6	11.9	21.6
Placer	13.0	9.7	7.5	51.2	248 399	348 432	40.3	6.7	15 877	12 110	18 912	132 709	2.66	70.9	9.8	23.1
Plumas	20.0	15.2	8.8	49.9	20 824	20 007	-3.9	-7.0	657	948	-1 066	8 997	2.13	59.8	10.4	33.8
Riverside	10.5	7.2	5.6	50.2	1 545 387	2 189 641	41.7	6.4	129 896	63 586	71 401	683 144	3.21	73.9	13.5	20.4
Sacramento	11.7	6.9	5.5	51.1	1 223 499	1 418 788	16.0	4.5	84 065	44 841	23 552	517 243	2.72	65.3	15.0	27.1
San Benito	11.7	6.4	4.5	49.9	53 234	55 269	3.8	5.4	3 090	1 181	1 112	16 995	3.28	79.2	13.8	17.0
San Bernardino	10.5	5.9	4.1	50.2	1 709 434	2 035 210	19.1	3.8	130 705	54 093	559	603 879	3.33	76.1	16.4	19.2
San Diego	11.3	6.8	5.6	49.7	2 813 833	3 095 313	10.0	5.4	188 675	86 169	65 485	1 076 483	2.83	66.4	12.1	25.0
San Francisco	12.2	7.4	6.8	49.1	776 733	805 235	3.7	5.9	38 182	24 511	33 886	345 344	2.31	45.4	8.6	38.7
San Joaquin	10.7	6.5	4.9	50.2	563 598	685 306	21.6	4.4	43 512	20 912	7 325	215 563	3.14	74.4	15.4	20.2
San Luis Obispo	14.2	9.4	7.4	49.0	246 681	269 637	9.3	3.5	11 123	9 431	7 564	102 154	2.50	63.4	9.1	26.4
San Mateo	12.9	7.9	6.5	50.7	707 161	718 451	1.6	5.6	38 945	20 089	22 252	257 941	2.79	67.7	10.2	25.4
Santa Barbara	11.1	7.1	6.6	49.7	399 347	423 895	6.1	3.9	24 146	12 491	5 121	141 720	2.89	65.4	11.6	24.9
Santa Clara	11.1	6.6	5.3	49.7	1 682 585	1 781 642	5.9	6.3	102 357	40 746	53 447	609 377	2.92	71.5	10.5	21.7
Santa Cruz	14.0	7.7	5.1	50.3	255 602	262 382	2.7	3.6	13 337	7 379	3 463	93 504	2.72	62.5	10.7	26.2
Shasta	14.7	10.9	7.9	50.9	163 256	177 223	8.6	1.5	8 866	8 700	2 201	68 980	2.54	65.6	12.0	28.0
Sierra	21.2	15.5	9.6	49.7	3 555	3 240	-8.9	-7.3	81	159	-171	1 253	2.45	61.4	7.9	32.0
Siskiyou	18.0	13.2	8.8	50.3	44 301	44 900	1.4	-2.8	2 036	2 241	-970	19 417	2.26	62.8	9.6	30.7
Solano	13.1	7.7	5.3	50.1	394 542	413 344	4.8	4.3	21 742	12 699	8 558	141 464	2.85	71.3	15.1	22.6
Sonoma	14.7	9.3	6.7	50.9	458 614	483 878	5.5	3.4	22 052	16 792	10 856	185 660	2.57	63.1	10.4	27.8
Stanislaus	10.8	6.6	5.1	50.5	446 997	514 453	15.1	3.4	32 444	15 917	938	166 883	3.07	74.4	15.5	20.3
Sutter	11.1	7.7	6.2	50.2	78 930	94 737	20.0	1.2	5 490	3 167	-1 292	31 725	2.95	73.4	13.3	21.6
Tehama	13.5	10.1	7.3	50.2	56 039	63 463	13.2	-0.6	3 248	2 506	-1 130	23 374	2.66	68.8	12.7	25.2
Trinity	20.2	14.4	8.6	48.7	13 022	13 786	5.9	-4.5	509	678	-415	5 668	2.35	59.8	7.4	31.7
Tulare	9.5	5.8	4.3	49.8	368 021	442 179	20.2	3.6	34 179	11 918	-5 743	131 642	3.35	78.3	16.3	17.6
Tuolumne	17.5	13.1	9.7	47.9	54 501	55 365	1.6	-2.8	1 935	2 474	-954	22 025	2.31	67.4	10.8	27.8
Ventura	12.2	7.4	5.8	50.4	753 197	823 318	9.3	2.8	45 529	22 396	-544	267 076	3.06	73.7	12.4	20.5
Yolo	10.5	6.3	4.8	51.3	168 660	200 849	19.1	3.4	10 299	5 028	1 345	70 347	2.76	62.3	10.4	24.8
Yuba	11.1	6.6	4.4	49.4	60 219	72 155	19.8	2.5	5 243	2 154	-1 169	24 300	2.93	73.0	14.5	20.8
COLORADO	12.5	7.3	5.0	49.8	4 301 261	5 029 196	16.9	6.5	278 842	140 585	183 324	1 977 591	2.53	64.2	10.2	28.1
Adams	10.2	5.6	3.7	49.7	348 618	441 603	NA	8.8	30 126	11 433	19 636	152 803	2.93	70.9	13.3	23.0
Alamosa	11.7	7.2	4.9	50.0	14 966	15 445	3.2	4.7	953	500	205	5 801	2.61	62.4	13.0	32.7
Arapahoe	12.2	6.8	4.7	50.8	487 967	572 003	17.2	8.2	33 210	15 000	27 688	225 552	2.58	65.7	12.4	28.2
Archuleta	20.4	14.1	7.2	49.9	9 898	12 084	22.1	1.3	501	345	36	4 881	2.45	69.6	9.3	28.0
Baca	15.2	11.8	13.5	50.3	4 517	3 788	-16.1	-3.8	197	234	-101	1 651	2.20	66.7	6.5	31.3
Bent	13.4	8.8	7.3	36.2	5 998	6 499	8.4	-13.4	191	223	-843	1 873	2.17	64.8	16.4	31.8

1. No spouse present.

Table B. States and Counties — **Population, Vital Statistics, Medicare, and Crime**

STATE County	Persons in group quarters, 2014	Daytime population, 2009–2013: Number	Daytime population, 2009–2013: Employment/residence ratio	Births, 2014: Total	Births, 2014: Rate[1]	Deaths, 2014: Number	Deaths, 2014: Rate[1]	Persons under 65 with no health insurance, 2013: Number	Persons under 65 with no health insurance, 2013: Percent	Medicare, 2014: Eligible for Medicare	Medicare, 2014: Enrolled in Medicare Advantage	Medicare, 2014: Enrolled in a Medicare prescription drug plan	Serious crimes known to police,[2] 2013: Total: Number	Serious crimes known to police,[2] 2013: Total: Rate[3]
	32	33	34	35	36	37	38	39	40	41	42	43	44	45
CALIFORNIA	817 130	37 654 586	1.00	505 903	13.0	255 787	6.6	6 382 717	19.4	5 521 829	2 216 451	2 025 558	1 173 036	3 060
Alameda	37 119	1 530 075	0.99	19 989	12.4	10 027	6.2	197 119	14.4	217 221	94 488	75 519	71 872	4 575
Alpine	24	1 549	1.85	10	9.0	4	3.6	166	17.6	229	16	155	39	3 479
Amador	3 287	37 529	1.01	290	7.9	396	10.8	3 966	16.1	10 103	1 953	5 249	898	2 439
Butte	5 327	219 845	0.99	2 409	10.7	2 287	10.2	31 203	17.1	46 647	650	31 480	6 857	3 084
Calaveras	494	39 382	0.66	357	8.0	490	11.0	5 405	16.2	12 026	1 574	6 463	1 210	2 716
Colusa	260	21 745	1.04	314	14.7	114	5.3	4 467	24.2	3 318	211	2 168	578	2 697
Contra Costa	10 555	955 597	0.77	12 221	11.0	7 744	7.0	130 734	14.0	173 910	79 415	55 161	35 312	3 239
Del Norte	3 140	29 081	1.08	294	10.8	246	9.0	3 434	16.7	5 503	422	3 486	764	2 706
El Dorado	1 690	158 057	0.71	1 526	8.3	1 486	8.1	19 825	13.3	36 909	11 434	15 180	3 662	2 028
Fresno	17 319	941 687	1.01	15 977	16.5	6 721	7.0	170 295	20.3	124 126	35 776	59 029	41 566	4 356
Glenn	338	26 835	0.88	361	12.9	215	7.7	5 307	22.5	5 241	46	3 563	865	3 090
Humboldt	5 453	135 098	1.01	1 476	10.9	1 292	9.6	23 337	20.8	25 884	830	16 742	5 458	4 045
Imperial	8 800	174 922	1.00	3 028	16.9	935	5.2	31 736	21.5	27 061	2 946	17 110	6 215	3 658
Inyo	440	19 264	1.09	220	12.0	184	10.0	2 637	18.2	4 257	55	2 892	383	2 069
Kern	31 798	850 166	1.01	14 763	16.9	5 763	6.6	153 624	20.4	103 910	36 598	42 487	38 350	4 448
Kings	17 030	151 133	0.99	2 345	15.6	818	5.4	22 593	18.8	15 486	1 821	8 836	4 448	2 941
Lake	1 164	60 523	0.83	731	11.4	769	12.0	10 307	20.3	16 357	658	10 035	2 189	3 430
Lassen	8 705	34 846	1.09	286	9.0	211	6.6	2 553	12.8	4 636	72	2 817	703	2 110
Los Angeles	177 864	10 046 216	1.03	131 668	13.0	63 063	6.2	2 064 660	23.7	1 336 467	625 754	447 994	268 803	2 682
Madera	8 151	150 914	0.99	2 224	14.4	960	6.2	29 028	22.8	21 951	6 942	9 608	4 951	3 241
Marin	8 333	257 924	1.03	2 256	8.7	1 833	7.0	24 063	11.9	52 809	18 940	20 935	5 503	2 137
Mariposa	726	17 015	0.85	160	9.0	155	8.8	2 092	15.6	4 572	185	2 630	390	2 189
Mendocino	1 985	88 643	1.03	1 138	13.0	817	9.3	15 604	22.0	20 371	1 413	12 418	2 323	2 657
Merced	6 452	246 767	0.87	4 267	16.0	1 625	6.1	48 769	21.0	32 325	2 505	19 951	9 651	3 649
Modoc	357	9 195	0.92	75	8.3	109	12.1	1 598	23.0	2 457	179	1 417	237	2 572
Mono	336	14 843	1.08	124	8.9	40	2.9	2 885	23.5	1 426	30	881	250	1 737
Monterey	17 598	419 488	0.99	6 613	15.3	2 450	5.7	88 415	24.4	57 067	988	34 202	12 734	2 955
Napa	5 028	143 575	1.09	1 446	10.2	1 241	8.8	20 081	17.6	26 532	9 908	9 789	2 991	2 137
Nevada	1 155	93 591	0.88	815	8.2	877	8.9	13 143	17.4	25 663	3 860	13 395	2 221	2 260
Orange	42 968	3 129 596	1.05	38 295	12.2	19 073	6.1	506 359	18.8	439 930	205 160	147 499	67 692	2 170
Placer	3 856	349 673	0.96	3 708	10.0	2 924	7.9	38 368	12.7	71 355	31 672	22 762	7 869	2 149
Plumas	277	19 430	0.98	144	7.7	208	11.2	2 586	18.3	5 610	397	3 277	482	2 504
Riverside	33 627	2 058 938	0.80	30 694	13.2	15 706	6.7	431 410	21.9	318 513	176 506	77 649	71 337	3 109
Sacramento	23 222	1 450 489	1.03	19 720	13.3	10 985	7.4	214 090	16.9	224 838	100 274	76 189	51 841	3 547
San Benito	397	48 840	0.70	721	12.4	295	5.1	9 805	19.3	7 421	313	4 411	1 037	1 807
San Bernardino	40 532	1 987 367	0.91	30 733	14.5	13 486	6.4	377 512	20.4	255 492	144 921	60 057	66 032	3 148
San Diego	104 750	3 168 586	1.02	44 860	13.7	21 128	6.5	490 023	17.9	460 117	209 452	122 473	81 449	2 540
San Francisco	24 003	987 028	1.38	9 168	10.8	6 026	7.1	88 387	12.4	136 413	52 113	58 413	56 602	6 788
San Joaquin	14 176	664 819	0.89	10 078	14.1	5 074	7.1	118 403	19.2	98 033	33 935	41 704	33 583	4 739
San Luis Obispo	16 619	268 461	0.97	2 610	9.4	2 199	7.9	33 835	15.8	54 090	5 973	31 782	7 277	2 629
San Mateo	8 852	732 246	1.01	9 267	12.2	4 898	6.5	76 798	12.1	115 900	50 617	35 739	16 527	2 213
Santa Barbara	19 070	440 990	1.07	5 636	12.8	3 013	6.8	75 743	21.1	69 035	9 576	38 386	11 240	2 589
Santa Clara	30 962	1 921 118	1.13	24 362	12.9	10 248	5.4	204 201	12.6	244 093	91 150	98 042	49 013	2 639
Santa Cruz	12 910	253 497	0.91	3 105	11.4	1 804	6.6	41 619	18.5	41 915	3 503	25 734	9 142	3 408
Shasta	2 745	179 187	1.02	2 107	11.7	2 058	11.4	25 986	18.0	44 177	2 299	27 741	7 044	3 930
Sierra	33	2 902	0.80	18	6.0	36	12.0	465	20.4	837	19	507	84	2 759
Siskiyou	578	45 197	1.04	480	11.0	537	12.3	6 877	20.3	12 082	928	7 110	889	2 023
Solano	11 255	376 831	0.78	5 151	11.9	3 175	7.4	52 961	14.7	67 117	30 163	15 069	15 534	3 667
Sonoma	10 750	466 614	0.91	5 196	10.4	4 115	8.2	70 240	17.2	92 253	36 517	33 484	10 000	2 021
Stanislaus	6 310	502 376	0.92	7 550	14.2	3 747	7.0	95 255	20.7	77 509	32 428	30 493	23 254	4 433
Sutter	794	87 114	0.79	1 260	13.1	729	7.6	17 150	20.9	15 719	349	10 134	3 182	3 343
Tehama	846	60 021	0.85	773	12.3	592	9.4	9 911	19.2	14 088	173	9 077	2 027	3 197
Trinity	390	13 959	1.07	126	9.6	162	12.3	2 043	19.9	3 569	189	2 214	169	1 255
Tulare	5 066	438 174	0.95	8 019	17.5	2 862	6.2	85 820	21.2	56 263	6 787	35 745	16 387	3 597
Tuolumne	3 856	54 995	1.01	465	8.6	555	10.3	6 115	16.0	14 373	514	9 022	1 330	2 477
Ventura	10 452	785 988	0.89	10 602	12.5	5 597	6.6	129 926	18.1	128 467	38 105	53 515	18 029	2 145
Yolo	5 721	214 421	1.14	2 455	11.8	1 201	5.8	29 856	16.9	26 931	12 121	9 142	7 076	3 445
Yuba	1 185	70 224	0.90	1 217	16.5	482	6.5	11 924	18.5	11 225	628	6 606	2 415	3 299
COLORADO	117 480	5 105 364	0.99	66 284	12.4	34 337	6.4	722 071	16.0	762 461	55 902	268 724	156 283	2 966
Adams	4 038	403 888	0.77	6 915	14.4	2 739	5.7	88 148	20.9	53 267	27 547	13 041	14 850	3 173
Alamosa	1 155	17 961	1.32	228	14.1	113	7.0	2 528	19.1	2 518	626	1 365	NA	NA
Arapahoe	4 726	573 122	0.96	7 896	12.8	3 717	6.0	87 632	16.4	79 616	34 498	22 590	17 930	2 957
Archuleta	129	11 834	0.95	114	9.3	91	7.4	2 227	23.4	2 994	399	1 539	250	2 058
Baca	82	3 741	0.99	49	13.4	44	12.1	732	26.8	978	NA	682	31	823
Bent	1 725	6 110	0.98	47	8.3	40	7.1	555	17.2	1 009	46	532	98	1 754

1. Per 1,000 estimated resident population. 2. Data for serious crimes have not been adjusted for underreporting; this may affect comparability between geographic areas and over time.
3. Per 100,000 population estimated by the FBI.

STATE County	Serious crimes known to police, 2013 (cont.)[1]		Education						Money income, 2009–2013				Income and poverty, 2013		
	Rate[2]		School enrollment and attainment, 2009–2013				Local government expenditures,[5] 2012–2013			Households				Percent below poverty level	
			Enrollment[3]		Attainment[4] (percent)										
	Violent	Property	Total	Percent private	High school graduate or less	Bachelor's degree or more	Total current spending (mil dol)	Current spending per student (dollars)	Per capita income[6] (dollars)	Median income (dollars)	Mean income (dollars)	Percent with income of $200,000 or more	Median household income (dollars)	All persons	Children under 18 years	Children 5 to 17 years in families
	46	47	48	49	50	51	52	53	54	55	56	57	58	59	60	61
CALIFORNIA	402	2 658	10 600 340	14.0	39.5	30.7	58 252.1	9 220	29 527	61 094	85 408	7.2	60 185	16.8	23.5	22.5
Alameda	747	3 828	414 999	15.4	32.7	41.8	2 002.1	9 173	35 763	72 112	96 982	10.3	72 128	13.0	15.4	15.3
Alpine	535	2 944	306	18.0	42.0	31.2	3.7	35 067	25 527	58 636	69 097	2.0	49 392	19.7	31.9	23.8
Amador	272	2 167	7 222	11.8	40.1	19.3	37.2	8 886	27 347	53 684	69 891	2.5	52 357	14.3	22.1	19.8
Butte	285	2 799	64 723	8.2	35.3	24.4	306.8	9 812	23 787	43 752	59 081	2.2	42 395	21.4	25.0	22.4
Calaveras	292	2 424	8 849	11.3	35.3	21.2	63.0	10 578	29 329	55 295	70 161	3.9	52 598	15.0	21.8	19.8
Colusa	201	2 497	5 861	6.4	56.1	13.8	49.0	10 463	21 579	52 158	63 743	2.2	48 897	13.0	20.0	19.3
Contra Costa	363	2 876	289 437	16.5	30.4	39.0	1 536.7	8 969	38 219	78 756	106 018	11.7	78 909	10.8	13.4	12.7
Del Norte	620	2 086	6 596	15.4	52.2	14.0	43.0	10 243	19 072	37 909	53 185	1.8	38 663	23.7	32.6	30.1
El Dorado	216	1 812	46 132	11.8	28.7	32.0	252.9	9 301	34 884	69 297	90 247	7.9	63 002	11.4	13.8	11.9
Fresno	510	3 846	290 833	7.7	49.5	19.6	1 841.6	9 403	20 208	45 563	63 079	3.0	43 741	28.6	42.0	39.6
Glenn	539	2 550	7 993	11.1	54.0	14.6	61.1	11 492	22 148	43 023	62 856	3.6	42 129	19.1	28.5	27.4
Humboldt	351	3 694	35 804	7.6	35.3	27.5	184.6	11 006	23 540	41 426	56 127	2.0	40 882	21.5	25.6	22.3
Imperial	304	3 354	54 684	5.2	57.2	13.3	354.7	9 692	16 763	41 807	57 847	2.2	40 106	22.7	30.9	31.5
Inyo	405	1 664	3 926	10.4	43.6	21.4	52.0	11 672	27 441	44 796	61 137	2.4	45 784	15.7	23.1	21.6
Kern	576	3 872	249 780	8.6	54.1	15.0	1 708.5	9 682	20 295	48 552	64 677	3.0	46 688	22.7	30.5	29.4
Kings	479	2 461	42 647	9.9	54.5	12.9	255.8	8 888	18 429	48 133	63 130	2.4	45 794	21.8	28.0	27.9
Lake	558	2 872	13 989	10.2	42.1	16.2	89.2	9 752	21 537	36 548	51 573	1.7	36 973	23.3	33.7	30.0
Lassen	381	1 728	6 864	18.5	46.3	13.1	40.7	9 551	19 931	53 107	63 149	1.8	50 487	19.1	19.9	18.2
Los Angeles	403	2 279	2 794 386	15.5	43.9	29.7	15 689.0	10 053	27 749	55 909	81 416	6.6	54 443	19.0	27.4	26.6
Madera	666	2 575	41 742	6.5	54.6	13.6	269.6	8 845	17 847	45 625	60 240	2.2	41 223	23.4	32.2	29.8
Marin	191	1 947	59 926	25.1	20.0	54.6	377.6	11 849	56 791	90 839	137 795	18.6	94 347	8.7	10.3	9.2
Mariposa	472	1 718	3 397	8.0	40.8	21.3	21.3	11 108	26 988	49 820	62 748	1.7	45 251	16.4	25.5	24.0
Mendocino	540	2 117	20 132	10.9	40.6	22.0	146.7	11 197	23 306	43 469	57 774	2.1	42 001	20.9	28.9	28.2
Merced	588	3 061	83 431	5.7	57.7	12.6	540.7	9 596	18 177	42 591	59 420	2.6	41 003	24.8	34.1	33.4
Modoc	749	1 823	1 986	12.6	42.2	18.7	16.2	16 665	21 200	36 212	48 765	0.7	37 055	20.0	33.4	30.2
Mono	201	1 535	3 211	3.5	36.1	29.8	27.0	13 247	28 046	61 757	68 616	1.7	55 107	11.8	18.7	17.8
Monterey	416	2 539	118 659	9.4	49.4	23.0	734.8	9 999	24 775	59 168	79 378	5.5	55 411	17.5	24.4	23.8
Napa	298	1 839	34 787	16.1	36.4	31.3	216.5	10 447	34 795	70 443	94 451	8.3	68 619	9.7	13.7	12.6
Nevada	441	1 820	21 156	12.2	26.9	32.3	168.1	10 232	32 346	57 353	75 824	4.7	55 246	12.8	17.8	16.3
Orange	194	1 977	868 966	14.6	34.2	36.8	4 361.7	8 692	34 057	75 422	101 134	10.2	73 827	13.5	18.8	18.6
Placer	180	1 969	96 013	13.9	26.6	35.1	511.4	7 823	34 886	72 725	91 628	7.2	73 643	8.3	9.5	8.1
Plumas	478	2 026	3 808	10.5	33.2	22.6	25.6	11 854	29 806	45 794	62 345	3.7	47 645	15.7	24.9	23.2
Riverside	270	2 839	653 024	11.6	45.8	20.5	3 649.3	8 583	23 591	56 529	73 752	4.0	53 909	17.4	24.2	22.2
Sacramento	514	3 033	415 521	12.9	36.1	28.0	2 112.8	8 976	26 739	55 064	72 200	3.9	52 980	18.9	25.9	24.3
San Benito	427	1 380	16 255	11.0	46.3	18.2	97.0	8 661	25 914	66 237	80 980	5.3	66 780	12.7	18.6	17.4
San Bernardino	402	2 746	631 175	11.1	47.9	18.7	3 521.5	8 544	21 332	54 090	69 091	3.2	52 112	19.2	26.7	24.9
San Diego	348	2 192	866 784	14.2	33.6	34.6	4 493.3	9 033	30 668	62 962	84 889	6.7	61 365	15.3	19.4	19.5
San Francisco	859	5 929	173 305	30.6	27.0	52.4	697.6	12 109	48 486	75 604	110 208	14.1	76 933	13.8	14.4	14.7
San Joaquin	703	4 036	206 976	12.6	48.5	18.1	1 189.0	8 545	22 589	53 380	70 435	3.4	51 219	19.8	26.4	25.1
San Luis Obispo	386	2 243	75 735	9.2	31.3	31.5	324.7	9 366	29 954	58 697	77 043	4.9	57 743	15.0	16.1	15.3
San Mateo	238	1 975	185 894	22.5	28.7	44.4	980.8	10 484	45 732	88 202	126 129	16.3	91 061	8.0	10.0	9.4
Santa Barbara	326	2 263	132 532	10.4	38.4	31.3	640.6	9 585	30 352	62 779	88 230	7.1	60 803	16.2	20.9	20.2
Santa Clara	244	2 395	499 609	20.3	29.0	46.5	2 598.2	9 510	41 513	91 702	120 718	16.1	91 843	10.5	12.9	12.0
Santa Cruz	374	3 034	79 297	11.4	30.7	37.0	399.3	9 881	32 295	66 519	88 776	8.2	65 282	14.9	18.9	18.5
Shasta	642	3 288	44 427	15.8	37.9	18.8	276.2	10 161	23 670	44 651	59 066	2.5	41 236	19.7	28.3	26.8
Sierra	230	2 529	479	10.4	45.2	18.5	6.5	17 126	24 996	39 009	55 972	4.7	46 449	14.5	20.4	19.1
Siskiyou	264	1 759	9 838	12.8	37.3	23.9	76.2	11 968	22 293	37 709	50 428	1.6	37 108	20.4	28.0	26.5
Solano	472	3 195	111 642	13.5	37.1	24.3	544.6	8 255	28 929	67 177	82 971	5.5	63 398	12.9	17.8	16.6
Sonoma	360	1 661	122 859	12.1	33.3	32.2	674.3	9 575	32 835	63 356	83 823	6.2	61 020	12.4	16.0	15.0
Stanislaus	518	3 915	149 678	9.5	51.9	16.4	996.5	9 467	21 663	49 297	65 123	2.8	47 808	21.8	30.5	29.6
Sutter	256	3 086	26 923	9.2	45.6	18.7	166.5	7 876	23 602	50 408	68 744	2.8	47 903	17.2	25.4	23.9
Tehama	554	2 643	15 474	8.6	48.0	13.5	109.0	10 382	20 439	41 924	54 024	1.7	43 459	17.9	28.7	26.3
Trinity	223	1 033	2 528	10.2	37.2	21.3	23.2	14 298	22 905	36 890	51 299	1.4	35 708	22.1	34.6	34.0
Tulare	460	3 137	138 307	6.7	56.0	13.3	974.8	9 752	17 894	42 708	58 700	2.4	39 657	29.6	39.8	37.3
Tuolumne	192	2 285	11 365	15.2	39.9	19.5	64.4	10 312	25 943	48 426	62 918	3.4	50 774	14.6	21.6	20.1
Ventura	194	1 951	232 395	14.7	36.1	31.4	1 248.7	8 813	32 930	76 544	98 869	9.4	76 513	12.0	18.0	15.9
Yolo	313	3 132	74 953	8.3	34.2	37.9	261.6	8 942	27 730	55 918	77 162	5.3	55 011	17.8	17.9	16.5
Yuba	372	2 927	21 120	8.2	46.3	13.7	137.0	9 926	19 244	44 902	55 847	1.2	41 824	20.6	28.0	27.0
COLORADO	308	2 658	1 370 879	13.5	32.0	37.0	7 431.8	8 647	31 109	58 433	78 383	5.2	58 942	12.9	16.8	15.7
Adams	309	2 864	121 425	11.4	48.3	20.9	712.4	8 178	24 195	56 270	69 009	2.7	54 876	13.2	17.5	16.7
Alamosa	NA	NA	5 513	6.3	42.6	24.2	24.7	10 361	19 487	34 520	50 549	2.8	37 484	25.6	35.3	35.9
Arapahoe	206	2 661	157 516	11.7	20.6	38.8	1 023.3	8 951	32 595	60 651	82 593	6.0	61 092	12.3	16.6	15.5
Archuleta	198	1 860	2 261	17.2	37.4	32.9	13.7	9 993	29 793	48 933	70 257	5.8	44 417	15.1	26.1	24.6
Baca	239	584	753	5.3	45.0	17.2	8.7	11 183	22 318	38 829	50 022	2.2	35 787	19.1	29.3	28.7
Bent	179	1 575	965	5.2	63.1	8.8	7.1	8 872	15 081	37 340	48 573	1.3	34 440	33.0	37.0	35.0

1. Data for serious crimes have not been adjusted for underreporting; this may affect comparability between geographic areas and over time. 2. Per 100,000 population estimated by the FBI.
3. All persons 3 years old and over enrolled in nursery school through college. 4. Persons 25 years old and over. 5. Elementary and secondary education expenditures.
6. Based on population estimated by the American Community Survey, 2009–2013.

STATE County	Personal income, 2013: Total (mil dol)	Percent change, 2012–2013	Per capita[1]: Dollars	Per capita[1]: Rank	Wages and salaries (mil dol)	Supplements to wages and salaries; employer contributions (mil dol): Pension and insurance	Supplements: Government social insurance	Proprietors' income (mil dol)	Dividends, interest, and rent (mil dol)	Personal transfer receipts (mil dol)	Earnings, 2013: Total (mil dol)	Contributions for government social insurance (mil dol): From employee and self-employed	From employer
	62	63	64	65	66	67	68	69	70	71	72	73	74
CALIFORNIA	1 856 614	2.8	48 434	X	934 699	164 218	63 671	176 024	377 314	281 173	1 338 612	76 446	63 671
Alameda	87 373	3.4	55 338	198	46 745	7 956	3 256	5 868	16 431	11 505	63 824	3 611	3 256
Alpine	67	4.1	57 981	134	40	8	2	6	20	13	58	3	2
Amador	1 496	2.3	40 961	1 059	485	144	31	102	365	346	762	49	31
Butte	8 251	3.4	37 150	1 557	2 984	704	219	710	1 793	2 159	4 616	289	219
Calaveras	1 833	3.6	41 166	1 032	307	91	21	159	468	455	578	46	21
Colusa	1 049	4.0	49 101	410	346	80	25	355	169	152	806	27	25
Contra Costa	69 376	2.4	63 403	73	22 394	3 913	1 543	5 147	14 279	7 757	32 997	1 990	1 543
Del Norte	859	1.8	30 818	2 575	301	107	19	47	164	288	473	29	19
El Dorado	10 454	1.9	57 520	147	2 311	478	167	1 031	2 034	1 393	3 987	258	167
Fresno	34 041	4.0	35 635	1 811	14 589	3 336	1 087	3 858	5 753	7 928	22 871	1 235	1 087
Glenn	1 107	1.7	39 605	1 216	318	80	23	264	215	239	685	29	23
Humboldt	5 063	2.9	37 646	1 482	1 788	483	126	498	1 251	1 253	2 895	175	126
Imperial	5 690	3.6	32 225	2 381	2 312	690	165	699	761	1 436	3 866	188	165
Inyo	829	2.1	44 886	696	308	102	19	87	194	183	516	28	19
Kern	30 976	3.0	35 847	1 773	14 653	3 218	1 053	4 566	4 424	5 724	23 490	1 204	1 053
Kings	4 927	1.9	32 635	2 307	2 009	570	152	753	792	961	3 484	150	152
Lake	2 392	4.3	37 460	1 514	551	151	39	152	447	729	893	67	39
Lassen	1 093	-0.2	33 995	2 082	449	173	29	82	196	245	733	37	29
Los Angeles	466 099	2.3	46 530	582	244 407	42 559	17 125	52 789	93 241	80 733	356 879	20 645	17 125
Madera	4 920	3.1	32 287	2 366	1 888	457	135	838	779	1 071	3 318	161	135
Marin	25 093	1.7	97 124	5	7 085	1 129	485	2 608	7 647	1 864	11 306	668	485
Mariposa	688	1.7	38 731	1 331	185	55	14	56	160	183	310	22	14
Mendocino	3 551	3.6	40 727	1 087	1 156	292	84	317	975	907	1 849	120	84
Merced	8 406	4.6	31 935	2 419	2 847	748	204	1 155	1 293	2 126	4 954	244	204
Modoc	369	1.5	40 293	1 139	95	33	7	46	86	111	181	10	7
Mono	639	3.2	45 410	660	261	66	19	66	190	60	412	21	19
Monterey	19 233	4.0	44 851	702	8 299	1 796	632	2 101	4 635	2 782	12 828	656	632
Napa	7 947	3.8	56 634	171	3 589	748	265	720	1 829	1 050	5 322	295	265
Nevada	4 925	2.3	50 148	363	1 255	280	92	536	1 424	898	2 163	146	92
Orange	169 793	1.9	54 519	219	87 037	13 783	6 247	18 511	34 435	18 870	125 578	7 291	6 247
Placer	20 174	3.8	54 924	205	7 359	1 242	549	1 424	4 242	2 614	10 574	648	549
Plumas	863	2.1	45 776	634	254	79	19	75	241	226	427	28	19
Riverside	76 289	3.5	33 278	2 211	26 048	5 936	1 897	5 651	14 184	14 812	39 532	2 417	1 897
Sacramento	63 513	3.5	43 438	808	35 401	8 787	2 286	5 168	11 213	12 347	51 642	2 666	2 286
San Benito	2 224	3.3	38 619	1 350	649	153	48	192	404	339	1 042	60	48
San Bernardino	68 387	2.7	32 747	2 292	29 755	6 580	2 246	4 101	10 205	14 445	42 682	2 529	2 246
San Diego	165 008	2.5	51 384	318	83 427	15 768	6 089	13 362	36 859	22 163	118 647	6 631	6 089
San Francisco	70 643	4.8	84 356	14	56 434	7 943	3 411	9 796	13 739	6 376	77 583	4 241	3 411
San Joaquin	24 481	3.4	34 755	1 941	9 503	2 074	713	2 326	4 033	5 924	14 616	839	713
San Luis Obispo	12 547	3.1	45 388	666	4 761	1 127	339	1 233	3 555	1 898	7 461	436	339
San Mateo	59 710	1.8	79 893	23	38 970	4 145	1 973	4 879	15 389	4 282	49 967	2 942	1 973
Santa Barbara	21 726	2.0	49 864	372	9 656	1 940	690	2 054	6 652	2 743	14 341	797	690
Santa Clara	130 624	4.7	70 151	47	98 478	10 576	5 604	7 886	26 832	11 191	122 543	7 114	5 604
Santa Cruz	14 810	3.9	54 970	202	4 716	964	325	1 320	3 479	1 795	7 325	417	325
Shasta	6 941	2.6	38 780	1 321	2 470	581	184	531	1 482	2 050	3 766	251	184
Sierra	123	1.5	40 443	1 118	25	9	2	7	31	29	43	3	2
Siskiyou	1 685	1.7	38 467	1 377	478	136	37	171	424	525	821	55	37
Solano	18 057	4.5	42 509	888	7 271	1 577	520	809	3 186	3 114	10 177	600	520
Sonoma	24 906	3.8	50 312	354	9 158	1 778	676	2 241	6 348	3 588	13 852	843	676
Stanislaus	18 528	3.2	35 259	1 865	7 462	1 595	557	1 811	2 963	4 112	11 424	652	557
Sutter	3 541	3.4	37 141	1 559	1 082	235	81	537	649	755	1 935	109	81
Tehama	2 006	3.2	31 810	2 434	630	151	47	182	439	619	1 010	65	47
Trinity	471	2.6	34 991	1 898	96	36	7	30	122	159	169	13	7
Tulare	14 782	3.1	32 550	2 319	5 511	1 416	403	2 094	2 290	3 635	9 423	469	403
Tuolumne	2 269	1.3	42 116	928	661	183	46	130	649	565	1 019	70	46
Ventura	42 406	1.7	50 507	347	17 253	3 183	1 227	3 056	8 867	5 384	24 720	1 420	1 227
Yolo	8 890	1.7	43 452	806	5 166	1 463	329	697	1 978	1 305	7 654	356	329
Yuba	2 470	4.5	33 679	2 149	1 032	331	81	136	412	759	1 580	80	81
COLORADO	247 069	2.8	46 897	X	129 597	18 267	9 307	25 677	51 310	31 601	182 848	9 892	9 307
Adams	16 578	3.0	35 334	1 851	8 950	1 332	637	1 000	2 371	2 570	12 009	[illegible]	637
Alamosa	582	2.7	35 784	1 784	293	54	20	74	105	128	441	21	20
Arapahoe	31 833	2.6	52 437	289	18 647	2 261	1 322	5 689	7 265	3 422	27 918	1 515	1 322
Archuleta	430	3.2	35 263	1 864	119	20	9	62	138	93	209	13	9
Baca	181	4.9	49 171	407	40	9	2	59	39	38	110	3	2
Bent	161	3.4	28 342	2 862	41	8	3	25	39	45	76	3	3

1. Based on the resident population estimated as of July 1 of the year shown.

STATE County	Earnings, 2013 (cont.) Percent by selected industries: Farm	Mining	Construction	Manu-facturing	Infor-mation: professional, scientific, technical services	Retail trade	Finance, insur-ance, real estate and leasing	Health care and social assistance	Govern-ment	Social Security beneficiaries, December 2013: Number	Rate[1]	Supple-mental Security Income recipients, December 2013	Housing units, 2014: Total	Percent change, 2010–2014
	75	76	77	78	79	80	81	82	83	84	85	86	87	88
CALIFORNIA	1.3	0.5	4.6	9.5	17.9	5.7	8.8	9.5	17.4	5 414 499	141	1 304 222	13 900 766	1.6
Alameda	0.0	0.1	6.1	10.4	17.5	5.6	4.9	11.4	17.3	202 205	128	53 547	592 355	1.7
Alpine	0.0	0.0	D	0.0	D	0.7	D	1.7	32.7	235	204	39	1 765	0.3
Amador	0.2	1.4	5.7	6.6	6.3	7.6	3.7	D	41.5	10 505	287	738	18 249	1.2
Butte	4.6	0.1	5.6	5.1	7.0	8.9	5.1	19.7	22.4	49 185	221	11 679	97 486	1.7
Calaveras	0.7	D	12.8	2.6	6.1	8.5	4.7	6.8	31.5	12 865	288	1 135	28 053	0.5
Colusa	41.6	D	1.8	8.4	0.8	3.0	2.2	D	17.3	3 505	164	573	7 938	0.7
Contra Costa	0.1	2.0	7.2	8.1	14.6	5.9	11.8	13.3	12.9	170 450	156	26 486	406 772	1.6
Del Norte	1.1	D	3.0	1.4	3.0	7.7	2.2	14.4	52.5	5 895	212	1 965	11 336	1.3
El Dorado	-0.1	0.2	9.0	2.9	12.1	6.5	16.9	11.2	18.8	38 610	213	3 183	88 866	0.8
Fresno	8.1	0.2	4.7	6.2	6.0	6.5	6.6	13.2	22.0	127 580	133	43 157	324 126	2.7
Glenn	36.3	D	3.2	5.3	D	4.4	2.1	D	20.6	5 670	203	1 211	10 917	1.3
Humboldt	2.3	D	5.9	4.2	5.8	9.9	6.2	13.2	30.3	27 195	202	6 726	62 348	1.3
Imperial	14.5	D	3.0	3.4	2.4	6.9	2.6	5.4	38.8	29 090	164	10 735	56 972	1.6
Inyo	1.5	1.9	3.4	9.9	2.9	7.4	1.7	D	46.3	4 320	234	463	9 513	0.4
Kern	10.7	8.8	6.3	4.6	5.4	5.6	3.9	7.6	21.8	113 340	131	34 210	291 454	2.5
Kings	19.8	0.0	2.1	8.3	2.2	4.6	2.0	8.5	39.5	16 800	111	4 698	44 864	2.3
Lake	1.3	D	5.0	1.8	4.2	9.6	3.6	18.6	27.8	17 760	278	3 867	35 657	0.5
Lassen	6.3	D	2.4	0.2	2.3	4.7	1.9	7.0	65.6	4 960	154	972	12 741	0.2
Los Angeles	0.0	0.6	3.3	8.4	20.1	5.6	9.3	10.0	15.0	1 245 490	124	423 076	3 482 516	1.1
Madera	20.8	D	3.4	9.0	2.8	5.1	2.0	14.0	22.2	23 915	157	4 751	49 891	1.5
Marin	0.2	0.7	5.6	1.7	20.8	7.0	14.9	10.9	13.5	49 380	191	3 739	112 295	1.0
Mariposa	1.1	0.2	6.1	2.0	4.1	6.2	D	3.6	41.6	4 935	278	499	10 329	1.4
Mendocino	0.9	D	6.6	9.0	5.3	10.8	4.1	13.5	24.8	20 555	235	3 718	40 718	1.0
Merced	17.3	D	3.7	10.8	2.5	6.2	2.8	9.2	25.5	35 005	133	11 291	84 167	0.6
Modoc	18.4	0.0	D	D	D	6.4	1.9	D	42.0	2 620	288	468	5 238	0.9
Mono	2.1	D	6.6	0.7	4.1	6.0	5.7	1.8	36.8	1 390	99	110	14 002	0.6
Monterey	9.6	0.3	3.5	2.9	5.8	5.7	4.7	7.7	26.3	58 140	135	9 293	140 144	0.8
Napa	2.9	D	6.0	18.7	6.3	5.4	6.1	10.5	16.4	26 200	186	2 738	55 317	1.0
Nevada	-0.1	D	12.7	4.9	9.4	8.0	9.5	13.5	20.7	26 235	267	2 049	53 080	0.9
Orange	0.0	0.2	6.2	11.5	14.3	5.9	14.5	8.6	10.8	413 340	132	74 566	1 072 011	2.2
Placer	0.1	0.1	9.3	5.7	9.2	10.2	13.1	16.1	13.4	71 370	194	5 584	157 446	3.1
Plumas	1.5	D	7.9	7.9	D	5.8	2.9	7.0	37.0	5 745	304	694	15 692	0.8
Riverside	0.7	0.3	8.7	7.0	5.5	9.3	6.3	11.0	25.0	337 145	147	61 401	819 936	2.4
Sacramento	0.3	0.0	4.6	4.1	12.6	5.1	7.4	10.8	36.8	223 715	153	66 892	561 842	1.1
San Benito	6.1	D	6.2	20.2	D	11.8	3.8	4.6	21.7	7 840	136	938	18 113	1.4
San Bernardino	0.1	0.2	5.8	7.5	5.4	8.0	4.9	12.5	25.2	269 515	129	73 392	708 297	1.2
San Diego	0.3	0.1	4.8	8.1	17.5	5.3	8.9	8.4	24.3	452 445	140	84 827	1 187 625	2.0
San Francisco	0.0	0.1	2.6	1.3	30.6	3.8	16.8	5.2	15.5	117 715	140	44 989	386 564	2.6
San Joaquin	6.3	0.1	5.4	8.3	4.0	7.3	6.0	12.3	20.6	101 855	144	29 545	237 542	1.6
San Luis Obispo	2.2	0.2	8.4	6.2	8.0	8.2	6.8	10.9	22.8	54 445	197	5 142	119 143	1.6
San Mateo	0.1	D	4.3	10.6	39.3	3.8	10.2	5.9	6.1	109 450	146	12 545	273 539	0.9
Santa Barbara	3.5	1.9	4.7	7.7	13.6	6.2	6.7	10.3	21.8	69 435	159	9 438	154 401	1.0
Santa Clara	0.1	0.0	3.1	22.8	32.3	4.3	5.3	6.8	7.2	222 270	119	48 376	651 156	3.0
Santa Cruz	4.7	D	8.2	7.8	7.7	6.8	5.1	12.9	20.3	41 770	155	5 792	105 275	0.8
Shasta	0.3	D	6.6	3.7	6.4	10.1	5.5	19.4	24.5	47 510	265	10 006	77 915	0.8
Sierra	3.6	D	8.6	D	D	1.7	D	13.7	50.5	865	285	98	2 341	0.6
Siskiyou	8.9	D	4.8	4.3	4.6	7.2	2.9	12.8	31.2	12 765	292	2 620	24 106	0.8
Solano	1.1	0.3	8.2	14.1	3.9	6.9	5.4	15.7	26.0	68 670	161	12 621	154 981	1.5
Sonoma	1.4	0.2	7.8	12.6	9.5	7.7	7.2	13.9	15.3	91 640	185	9 551	207 232	1.3
Stanislaus	8.2	0.0	4.8	13.2	4.0	7.7	5.0	16.0	18.1	82 435	157	22 290	180 278	0.4
Sutter	12.9	0.6	4.8	5.3	4.2	9.5	5.1	13.8	17.3	16 330	171	3 999	34 096	0.7
Tehama	11.7	0.0	5.9	9.8	2.4	7.6	2.7	11.5	23.4	15 385	244	3 489	27 239	0.9
Trinity	2.5	D	4.4	6.7	3.6	10.0	2.2	D	50.3	3 890	289	714	8 784	1.2
Tulare	15.4	0.1	3.8	8.1	3.3	7.1	3.5	6.7	24.6	60 930	134	19 316	145 503	2.7
Tuolumne	-0.4	0.6	5.6	5.2	5.7	8.1	4.2	16.7	35.8	15 360	285	1 763	31 361	0.4
Ventura	3.7	1.9	4.4	15.5	9.6	6.8	9.3	9.0	17.1	127 775	152	16 662	284 504	1.0
Yolo	3.8	0.2	3.7	6.1	6.7	4.5	3.3	6.4	44.2	26 480	129	5 737	76 720	2.2
Yuba	3.9	0.5	3.4	2.7	3.4	3.4	1.4	9.7	58.4	12 380	169	4 119	28 015	1.4
COLORADO	0.8	4.3	6.3	6.1	18.0	5.6	8.2	8.8	16.5	774 056	147	72 154	2 276 184	2.9
Adams	0.3	0.6	10.9	7.9	6.9	6.6	3.2	8.9	22.8	56 525	120	6 882	166 243	1.9
Alamosa	10.6	D	4.9	1.4	6.2	8.7	5.2	D	25.1	2 695	166	561	6 684	2.0
Arapahoe	0.0	2.9	6.4	2.3	26.9	5.7	13.2	9.5	8.8	79 805	131	7 399	243 745	2.3
Archuleta	-0.6	1.3	11.1	1.5	9.3	11.8	8.4	D	19.3	3 110	255	140	8 943	2.1
Baca	47.2	0.8	D	D	D	6.1	D	D	23.5	1 030	280	79	2 232	-0.7
Bent	34.8	0.0	D	D	D	4.5	D	2.3	26.6	1 010	176	193	2 217	-1.1

1. Per 1,000 resident population estimated as of July 1 of the year shown.

STATE County	Housing units, 2009–2013: Occupied units: Total	Owner-occupied: Percent	Owner-occupied: Median value[1]	Median owner cost as a percent of income: With a mortgage	Median owner cost as a percent of income: Without a mortgage[2]	Renter-occupied: Median rent[3]	Renter-occupied: Median rent as a percent of income[2]	Substandard units[4] (percent)	Civilian labor force, 2014: Total	Civilian labor force, 2014: Percent change, 2013–2014	Unemployment: Total	Unemployment: Rate[5]	Civilian employment,[6] 2009–2013: Total	Percent: Management, business, science and arts	Percent: Construction, production, and maintenance occupations
	89	90	91	92	93	94	95	96	97	98	99	100	101	102	103
CALIFORNIA	12 542 460	55.3	366 400	29.2	11.3	1 224	33.7	8.6	18 811 395	0.7	1 414 276	7.5	16 635 854	36.9	20.1
Alameda	545 071	53.2	493 800	27.9	10.2	1 289	31.1	1.0	811 346	0.6	47 683	5.9	732 923	45.6	16.0
Alpine	394	81.5	333 600	30.8	14.4	1 018	36.5	1.5	491	-5.8	43	8.8	467	39.0	21.6
Amador	14 262	76.1	270 500	30.0	13.4	1 006	34.8	3.6	14 459	0.3	1 207	8.3	12 609	30.3	22.1
Butte	84 816	60.1	225 900	27.7	12.7	890	35.5	2.3	101 924	0.0	8 820	8.7	87 159	33.8	18.7
Calaveras	18 702	78.4	254 800	30.1	14.0	1 061	30.5	7.5	20 307	0.4	1 641	8.1	17 598	34.3	24.7
Colusa	6 853	63.3	181 600	27.8	10.1	923	28.9	4.6	11 152	-1.0	1 947	17.5	8 653	25.1	38.9
Contra Costa	375 855	65.9	404 000	28.5	11.5	1 365	32.7	4.1	544 022	0.7	33 509	6.2	491 161	42.3	15.7
Del Norte	9 593	60.2	198 400	27.9	13.7	914	34.9	2.7	10 041	-3.1	1 022	10.2	9 006	32.8	15.3
El Dorado	67 885	74.8	359 500	29.1	13.2	1 090	32.6	10.7	88 797	0.2	6 212	7.0	81 175	39.4	16.0
Fresno	289 811	53.8	195 400	27.1	11.2	875	34.6	6.0	441 022	0.3	51 217	11.6	363 912	28.5	28.7
Glenn	9 628	63.1	217 700	28.8	11.7	720	29.0	4.2	12 908	-0.5	1 375	10.7	10 813	23.2	36.7
Humboldt	53 296	55.9	288 300	28.4	11.7	889	37.4	10.1	62 751	-0.6	4 256	6.8	59 294	33.0	20.2
Imperial	48 099	56.4	147 300	27.1	12.1	744	33.0	4.9	80 266	1.9	18 957	23.6	58 169	23.9	27.5
Inyo	7 873	64.1	236 100	24.8	13.3	829	32.5	9.2	9 213	-1.7	643	7.0	8 692	29.3	19.7
Kern	255 271	58.0	161 700	25.9	11.1	885	33.3	9.4	394 849	0.2	41 204	10.4	317 047	26.0	33.2
Kings	40 785	51.8	176 900	26.5	10.0	871	30.3	4.5	57 393	-1.2	6 920	12.1	51 566	24.9	33.2
Lake	26 505	62.7	183 600	31.9	14.9	900	40.1	3.5	29 928	1.0	2 653	8.9	22 718	27.7	22.8
Lassen	9 945	62.9	185 500	24.9	10.4	867	29.7	12.5	10 808	-1.7	1 002	9.3	9 583	32.9	18.8
Los Angeles	3 230 383	46.9	420 200	31.3	11.3	1 204	35.1	10.9	5 025 883	0.9	415 088	8.3	4 489 974	35.3	20.7
Madera	42 516	60.8	182 000	30.8	11.9	914	32.0	3.5	63 184	0.8	6 981	11.0	52 029	25.2	36.0
Marin	102 912	62.8	781 900	28.5	12.0	1 628	32.9	3.0	140 051	0.8	5 980	4.3	124 625	51.6	10.0
Mariposa	7 238	71.6	235 000	28.1	10.6	866	29.7	6.2	8 128	-0.8	715	8.8	7 365	29.3	21.8
Mendocino	33 878	58.2	323 600	32.3	13.4	953	35.8	9.2	41 067	-0.2	2 838	6.9	37 335	28.7	24.4
Merced	75 409	53.6	146 400	26.9	10.9	860	33.6	2.0	115 386	0.4	14 771	12.8	93 207	21.9	37.4
Modoc	3 983	68.8	164 100	22.0	12.1	633	35.0	5.2	3 365	-3.3	353	10.5	3 635	38.2	22.0
Mono	5 268	55.6	344 500	34.4	14.0	1 118	28.3	12.4	8 161	-2.4	589	7.2	7 852	34.8	14.0
Monterey	125 428	49.7	362 400	30.0	10.7	1 209	33.3	6.6	219 814	1.4	19 920	9.1	174 453	27.6	30.2
Napa	49 431	60.6	428 600	28.7	11.7	1 350	32.0	2.8	74 041	1.6	4 129	5.6	66 087	35.2	22.7
Nevada	40 991	72.6	357 300	31.5	14.4	1 217	37.6	9.5	47 906	-0.3	3 153	6.6	42 077	39.5	16.1
Orange	995 512	58.7	519 600	29.1	10.2	1 498	33.6	2.5	1 575 606	0.6	86 442	5.5	1 453 951	39.7	16.8
Placer	132 709	70.6	342 000	28.5	12.9	1 242	32.3	4.0	176 474	0.3	11 053	6.3	157 675	41.5	14.4
Plumas	8 997	69.7	243 700	30.9	14.2	799	28.9	7.7	8 140	-1.2	952	11.7	7 461	36.0	22.5
Riverside	683 144	66.5	231 000	30.3	13.7	1 168	35.7	5.2	1 010 706	1.2	83 372	8.2	877 030	29.2	24.0
Sacramento	517 243	56.7	234 200	27.8	10.5	1 024	34.0	8.0	682 174	0.2	49 979	7.3	610 662	37.5	16.4
San Benito	16 995	61.6	343 000	31.7	12.1	1 233	32.9	9.3	29 242	1.4	2 731	9.3	24 793	27.5	27.3
San Bernardino	603 879	61.9	222 300	29.1	11.9	1 102	35.7	6.3	909 188	1.2	73 197	8.1	801 850	28.4	26.6
San Diego	1 076 483	53.8	402 100	29.6	10.9	1 300	34.1	8.0	1 546 363	0.0	99 216	6.4	1 390 197	40.1	16.0
San Francisco	345 344	36.6	744 600	29.2	10.2	1 488	28.4	7.7	532 645	2.5	23 307	4.4	456 845	51.7	9.3
San Joaquin	215 563	58.3	208 000	28.7	11.3	1 026	34.8	3.8	311 061	-0.1	33 094	10.6	270 795	28.3	28.9
San Luis Obispo	102 154	58.4	426 600	29.9	11.8	1 211	35.4	7.4	139 865	1.4	7 838	5.6	122 909	35.6	18.3
San Mateo	257 941	59.4	722 200	28.9	10.6	1 602	30.3	9.5	430 778	2.5	18 117	4.2	371 212	44.4	13.9
Santa Barbara	141 720	52.6	453 000	28.8	11.2	1 340	34.1	8.1	218 721	0.7	13 300	6.1	196 190	35.2	22.0
Santa Clara	609 377	57.5	645 600	27.8	10.0	1 566	28.9	6.8	995 256	2.1	51 736	5.2	865 327	49.8	14.8
Santa Cruz	93 504	58.8	557 500	30.8	11.8	1 385	35.0	3.3	142 626	0.3	12 469	8.7	127 850	40.6	19.2
Shasta	68 980	64.2	220 000	28.8	13.1	919	36.0	0.3	75 458	0.0	7 293	9.7	67 746	32.4	19.4
Sierra	1 253	77.8	231 400	26.9	15.0	1 040	32.7	4.5	1 448	0.5	145	10.0	1 140	29.7	30.3
Siskiyou	19 417	62.7	200 800	29.7	13.7	802	37.1	4.6	18 001	-1.1	2 028	11.3	16 329	34.0	19.6
Solano	141 464	61.7	262 400	28.1	10.0	1 264	34.1	5.5	203 706	-0.3	15 186	7.5	182 801	33.4	21.4
Sonoma	185 660	60.1	407 400	29.5	12.4	1 265	33.5	7.6	257 295	1.8	14 351	5.6	232 206	35.7	19.9
Stanislaus	166 883	58.1	172 900	28.5	12.2	992	35.2	7.6	241 446	-0.1	27 085	11.2	203 232	26.5	30.9
Sutter	31 725	59.6	188 500	26.5	11.0	889	32.2	5.1	44 455	-0.9	5 653	12.7	37 230	28.3	27.8
Tehama	23 374	67.5	177 100	28.6	11.9	821	31.0	6.3	25 250	1.1	2 443	9.7	22 495	24.8	29.4
Trinity	5 668	71.2	257 400	27.5	12.9	758	32.1	11.1	5 045	-1.9	501	9.9	4 552	31.8	18.2
Tulare	131 642	57.5	163 100	27.6	11.4	821	33.3	3.4	198 631	-1.1	26 272	13.2	168 845	23.7	36.1
Tuolumne	22 025	69.9	269 400	29.0	13.9	919	36.0	7.0	21 638	-0.2	1 888	8.7	18 988	32.3	19.9
Ventura	267 076	64.9	442 200	28.7	10.7	1 470	34.3	5.4	431 547	-0.6	28 827	6.7	389 297	37.4	20.5
Yolo	70 347	52.9	314 300	26.3	10.0	1 082	34.8	8.5	101 799	0.4	7 814	7.7	90 984	45.1	17.8
Yuba	24 000	59.1	171 000	20.0	11.0	803	34.4	4.8	28 165	-0.8	3 158	11.2	24 078	27.3	25.6
COLORADO	1 977 591	65.4	236 200	24.0	10.2	939	30.9	2.9	2 817 334	1.4	141 387	5.0	2 509 777	39.9	18.4
Adams	152 803	65.6	186 600	25.3	11.4	967	31.1	3.0	245 361	1.1	14 004	5.7	215 131	29.0	27.3
Alamosa	5 891	61.5	137 300	23.8	10.0	586	34.8	3.2	7 558	-0.2	536	7.1	6 450	31.0	21.8
Arapahoe	225 552	62.7	230 700	23.9	10.0	981	32.0	4.3	333 429	1.8	16 343	4.9	295 023	39.7	16.6
Archuleta	4 881	73.7	279 700	30.3	10.2	913	29.8	2.1	5 751	0.6	344	6.0	5 503	34.6	22.1
Baca	1 651	74.4	73 500	21.5	11.4	508	24.1	2.0	1 962	3.0	55	2.8	1 837	36.6	26.2
Bent	1 873	63.5	75 500	23.3	11.2	635	29.1	2.4	1 673	1.3	88	5.3	1 553	34.6	25.6

1. Specified owner-occupied units. 2. A value of 10.0 represents 10 percent or less; a value of 50.0 represents 50 percent or more. 3. Specified renter-occupied units. 4. Overcrowded or lacking complete plumbing facilities. 5. Percent of civilian labor force. 6. Persons 16 years old and over.

STATE County	Private nonfarm establishments, employment and payroll, 2013: Number of establishments	Employment: Total	Employment: Health care and social assistance	Employment: Manufacturing	Employment: Retail trade	Employment: Finance and insurance	Employment: Professional, scientific, and technical services	Annual payroll: Total (mil dol)	Annual payroll: Average per employee (dollars)	Agriculture, 2012: Farms: Number	Farms: Percent with: Fewer than 50 acres	Farms: Percent with: 500 acres or more	Farm operators whose principal occupation is farming (percent)
	104	105	106	107	108	109	110	111	112	113	114	115	116
CALIFORNIA	874 243	13 401 863	1 786 656	1 146 841	1 595 788	590 753	1 148 692	742 524	55 405	77 857	64.8	9.9	54.5
Alameda	37 108	598 309	84 622	60 432	64 151	19 435	61 290	36 923	61 713	452	60.2	12.2	48.7
Alpine	36	176	D	NA	D	D	D	4	23 028	3	0.0	33.3	0.0
Amador	786	7 768	1 335	736	1 533	D	317	266	34 223	461	47.7	11.3	49.2
Butte	4 637	56 166	13 454	4 102	10 494	2 126	2 507	1 962	34 940	2 056	66.8	7.0	59.4
Calaveras	881	5 729	961	365	1 130	129	D	177	30 843	663	60.0	10.0	46.6
Colusa	376	3 956	431	615	473	101	40	147	37 179	782	27.5	23.0	61.6
Contra Costa	22 338	306 661	50 357	14 326	42 982	22 737	27 602	18 063	58 903	602	73.3	8.0	52.0
Del Norte	417	3 966	1 187	D	962	90	113	115	28 918	121	59.5	6.6	57.9
El Dorado	4 236	40 712	6 193	2 298	5 835	2 930	2 071	1 633	40 111	1 358	78.4	3.0	52.1
Fresno	15 973	239 776	41 485	23 176	35 099	9 301	10 967	9 121	38 041	5 683	59.7	11.2	59.6
Glenn	453	4 574	602	581	707	130	D	215	46 973	1 311	51.3	15.3	62.9
Humboldt	3 169	32 396	6 845	2 108	6 553	989	1 614	1 050	32 399	930	54.0	15.5	56.1
Imperial	2 419	31 319	4 634	3 670	7 589	D	775	979	31 268	421	29.7	40.6	69.4
Inyo	525	5 085	1 133	D	926	95	D	183	36 034	125	50.4	31.2	63.2
Kern	12 344	195 927	29 499	12 864	28 943	6 076	12 859	8 449	43 122	1 938	40.6	26.6	63.2
Kings	1 575	23 441	4 955	3 932	4 143	495	456	820	34 973	1 056	51.2	18.6	66.0
Lake	1 032	9 233	2 299	280	2 111	D	233	318	34 480	838	68.7	5.1	43.9
Lassen	409	3 947	814	D	856	D	D	122	30 793	448	40.6	25.2	51.8
Los Angeles	253 227	3 799 831	504 700	358 922	400 418	156 838	323 290	194 175	51 101	1 294	88.9	2.9	60.6
Madera	1 883	25 438	5 879	3 483	3 437	475	512	954	37 507	1 507	44.8	14.3	57.9
Marin	9 654	98 110	15 375	1 835	14 967	5 863	8 558	5 552	56 584	323	39.9	34.1	58.5
Mariposa	349	3 246	436	86	387	D	D	90	27 602	364	37.9	23.6	51.9
Mendocino	2 466	22 157	4 344	2 523	4 606	558	667	735	33 152	1 220	48.8	14.3	49.8
Merced	2 852	41 183	6 643	8 757	7 899	946	821	1 447	35 131	2 486	56.7	12.8	64.5
Modoc	158	1 228	440	D	201	35	37	42	34 407	437	22.4	37.8	60.4
Mono	562	6 264	D	D	625	30	D	161	25 694	72	31.9	27.8	58.3
Monterey	8 408	101 020	15 086	5 614	16 469	3 260	7 823	4 218	41 755	1 179	42.0	26.4	61.7
Napa	4 043	58 272	10 351	10 409	6 843	1 402	1 760	2 801	48 063	1 685	71.9	5.3	34.9
Nevada	2 966	26 259	4 576	2 249	4 005	732	1 390	995	37 875	742	79.0	2.0	46.6
Orange	89 496	1 381 148	151 017	149 604	148 811	87 572	117 334	73 286	53 062	312	85.3	4.8	58.7
Placer	9 707	129 592	18 248	3 799	21 868	7 734	11 828	6 261	48 316	1 355	82.2	2.4	45.5
Plumas	593	3 656	934	D	587	131	120	144	39 512	141	37.6	34.0	44.0
Riverside	34 773	493 307	68 777	42 275	85 173	10 757	16 443	17 833	36 149	2 949	86.0	3.5	49.1
Sacramento	27 571	428 475	76 436	19 394	58 656	27 350	33 130	20 878	48 725	1 352	72.3	7.6	48.2
San Benito	927	10 161	1 388	2 145	1 288	227	211	399	39 221	628	51.6	23.2	58.3
San Bernardino	32 426	538 336	82 865	48 764	81 444	14 037	17 712	20 861	38 751	1 249	85.9	2.1	57.0
San Diego	78 379	1 181 133	152 207	100 475	145 051	51 448	132 252	59 966	50 770	5 732	91.6	0.9	47.6
San Francisco	32 360	542 366	60 840	7 095	44 258	47 382	87 818	46 667	86 044	6	100.0	0.0	83.3
San Joaquin	10 668	166 252	27 516	18 531	25 203	6 167	4 460	6 522	39 229	3 580	63.5	8.3	59.0
San Luis Obispo	7 873	86 125	15 276	5 943	14 346	2 431	4 792	3 288	38 176	2 666	55.8	12.2	47.0
San Mateo	20 342	347 658	32 046	D	34 628	19 797	34 278	36 799	105 849	334	61.7	6.3	56.0
Santa Barbara	11 211	137 623	20 275	13 333	19 242	4 385	9 753	6 353	46 162	1 597	63.9	11.3	51.7
Santa Clara	46 212	926 766	98 895	88 694	81 908	24 185	132 910	88 740	95 752	1 003	76.4	5.6	56.0
Santa Cruz	6 779	70 493	12 437	4 516	11 769	2 030	3 977	2 955	41 914	667	73.8	4.6	62.1
Shasta	4 126	47 159	10 049	2 031	9 284	1 970	2 033	1 690	35 842	1 544	72.9	6.1	44.9
Sierra	67	198	D	D	34	D	D	6	31 540	48	14.6	27.1	56.3
Siskiyou	1 075	8 222	1 681	670	1 544	247	325	254	30 932	929	35.5	22.5	58.2
Solano	6 677	103 470	22 106	9 571	18 725	4 338	3 634	4 697	45 398	860	62.9	11.7	53.7
Sonoma	13 370	152 105	23 442	18 224	23 924	5 782	9 228	6 984	45 916	3 579	71.3	6.0	51.3
Stanislaus	8 516	128 728	23 373	18 837	22 227	3 337	5 057	5 390	41 874	4 143	68.8	5.9	59.1
Sutter	1 696	19 962	3 569	1 498	4 369	639	875	725	36 324	1 358	51.8	14.1	64.4
Tehama	956	11 381	2 010	D	1 802	232	186	417	36 607	1 743	61.6	10.7	52.3
Trinity	253	1 477	321	D	396	43	D	45	30 800	247	55.5	8.1	48.6
Tulare	6 142	88 795	15 293	12 212	15 419	3 095	2 576	3 131	35 263	4 931	61.2	8.4	58.3
Tuolumne	1 289	12 223	2 726	830	2 202	322	441	431	35 229	391	53.5	9.7	40.7
Ventura	20 089	247 116	33 429	23 031	38 595	13 531	22 247	12 013	48 614	2 150	78.0	5.2	48.7
Yolo	3 878	60 719	6 650	6 519	7 220	1 636	3 434	2 602	42 859	1 011	47.5	14.7	59.1
Yuba	820	9 130	2 094	567	1 450	216	434	323	35 324	795	61.4	10.4	44.2
COLORADO	154 875	2 090 975	265 893	118 701	254 679	101 049	182 594	102 237	48 894	36 180	39.4	24.3	49.6
Adams	8 559	137 849	19 741	10 606	17 524	2 843	4 651	6 205	45 011	841	50.4	20.0	43.0
Alamosa	475	5 383	1 626	D	1 066	359	140	171	31 840	322	22.4	24.5	51.2
Arapahoe	17 284	259 423	29 825	7 408	31 996	21 784	24 340	14 275	55 026	755	65.4	10.9	39.3
Archuleta	490	2 965	266	D	600	92	123	90	30 202	372	34.9	22.3	54.0
Baca	90	525	D	NA	119	36	D	15	27 688	737	3.4	62.0	48.4
Bent	57	551	45	D	73	D	D	16	29 864	277	15.9	46.6	53.4

STATE County	Agriculture, 2012 (cont.): Land in farms: Acreage (1,000)	Land in farms: Percent change, 2007–2012	Land in farms: Acres: Average size of farm	Land in farms: Acres: Total irrigated (1,000)	Land in farms: Acres: Total cropland (1,000)	Value of land and buildings (dollars): Average per farm	Value of land and buildings (dollars): Average per acre	Value of machinery and equipment, average per farm (dollars)	Value of products sold: Total (mil dol)	Value of products sold: Average per farm (dollars)	Value of products sold: Percent from: Crops	Value of products sold: Percent from: Livestock and poultry products	Percent of farms with sales of: $10,000 or more	Percent of farms with sales of: $100,000 or more	Government payments: Total ($1,000)	Government payments: Percent of farms
	117	118	119	120	121	122	123	124	125	126	127	128	129	130	131	132
CALIFORNIA	25 569	0.8	328	7 862.0	9 591.8	2 061 792	6 278	124 710	42 627.5	547 510	71.2	28.8	57.0	26.4	146 919	9.8
Alameda	178	-13.1	393	8.9	20.3	2 170 265	5 517	47 292	57.5	127 261	82.7	17.3	42.7	9.7	49	3.5
Alpine	D	D	D	0.2	0.6	1 800 000	D	20 333	0.3	88 333	D	D	100.0	33.3	0	0.0
Amador	155	-5.1	337	11.3	16.0	1 324 401	3 934	51 321	32.0	69 345	68.1	31.9	49.7	15.4	37	2.8
Butte	381	1.9	185	199.7	227.3	1 408 199	7 599	135 591	541.3	263 266	97.3	2.7	59.7	26.2	9 386	13.7
Calaveras	212	5.5	320	4.5	6.1	1 043 833	3 262	40 736	26.0	39 222	45.5	54.5	36.2	7.7	8	0.6
Colusa	453	-4.4	579	260.9	285.7	3 146 341	5 431	300 276	577.3	738 252	98.7	1.3	80.7	59.1	13 629	48.5
Contra Costa	128	-13.1	212	27.3	46.5	1 786 847	8 425	80 620	89.4	148 435	84.7	15.3	43.2	13.1	232	5.6
Del Norte	D	D	D	9.2	8.6	1 481 355	D	115 661	35.7	294 636	46.5	53.5	34.7	11.6	96	12.4
El Dorado	128	19.9	95	6.8	11.1	777 782	8 228	30 537	30.5	22 465	79.8	20.2	32.3	5.7	237	3.0
Fresno	1 721	5.2	303	968.7	1 153.4	2 509 484	8 286	161 509	4 973.0	875 073	74.4	25.6	71.9	41.9	10 149	9.0
Glenn	669	36.7	510	242.9	274.3	2 342 959	4 593	192 225	637.4	486 166	79.9	20.1	68.6	38.0	13 136	35.5
Humboldt	594	-0.6	638	17.1	20.9	1 649 520	2 584	57 685	203.3	218 559	D	D	45.4	16.8	1 242	8.8
Imperial	516	20.7	1 225	455.0	487.9	8 577 865	7 002	745 304	1 888.6	4 486 078	69.4	30.6	84.3	66.7	2 788	29.5
Inyo	331	13.1	2 647	23.8	18.7	2 062 976	779	86 688	19.6	156 904	34.6	65.4	40.8	16.0	D	1.6
Kern	2 330	-1.3	1 202	730.0	899.4	5 332 548	4 435	332 960	3 999.0	2 063 462	80.8	19.2	62.0	43.8	5 306	15.5
Kings	674	-1.0	638	407.4	501.5	3 847 243	6 031	340 454	1 829.2	1 732 231	46.7	53.3	68.3	45.1	7 901	36.4
Lake	151	21.4	180	13.5	29.1	1 095 199	6 089	55 516	99.5	118 691	98.0	2.0	52.6	13.6	100	4.8
Lassen	483	5.1	1 077	66.0	70.9	2 075 935	1 927	113 085	72.7	162 212	D	D	42.0	16.3	186	9.6
Los Angeles	92	-15.5	71	39.7	59.6	882 832	12 459	45 905	193.1	149 225	90.1	9.9	34.2	11.6	247	3.1
Madera	654	-3.8	434	292.3	304.2	3 302 033	7 614	182 022	1 602.8	1 063 547	77.4	22.6	70.2	46.8	2 400	11.4
Marin	171	28.2	529	3.7	14.4	3 295 415	6 229	69 226	91.8	284 238	9.3	90.7	64.1	34.1	1 283	16.4
Mariposa	284	33.4	779	1.8	12.6	1 638 973	2 104	44 742	22.3	61 321	11.7	88.3	37.1	8.8	515	7.4
Mendocino	770	26.5	631	25.7	49.3	2 533 399	4 013	51 877	148.9	122 047	92.1	7.9	50.2	16.9	426	2.3
Merced	979	-6.0	394	468.2	522.6	3 045 778	7 737	236 454	2 967.5	1 193 694	42.9	57.1	76.0	45.7	9 528	20.2
Modoc	524	-12.4	1 198	128.4	154.7	2 061 595	1 721	125 055	106.6	243 950	66.0	34.0	60.4	37.1	701	24.7
Mono	56	26.4	783	21.5	11.4	2 205 819	2 817	144 722	18.0	249 667	49.0	51.0	48.6	40.3	D	1.4
Monterey	1 268	-4.5	1 076	263.8	358.3	5 263 068	4 893	396 806	2 979.7	2 527 341	98.5	1.5	59.6	35.4	635	7.0
Napa	253	13.5	150	54.6	63.0	3 278 130	21 801	85 134	536.1	318 188	97.8	2.2	74.5	34.1	85	1.1
Nevada	42	-40.0	57	5.3	3.3	614 920	10 834	31 177	9.1	12 256	63.9	36.1	27.9	2.4	126	2.2
Orange	60	-30.8	194	8.1	15.2	4 237 538	21 854	70 968	158.5	508 055	99.0	1.0	41.3	18.3	43	4.8
Placer	91	-30.9	67	20.7	33.6	719 330	10 664	35 897	43.4	32 057	D	D	27.2	5.0	1 305	2.8
Plumas	174	44.9	1 236	19.1	26.0	2 194 518	1 776	95 652	22.6	160 404	19.7	80.3	51.8	22.0	0	0.0
Riverside	344	-3.0	117	146.0	227.2	1 191 416	10 212	76 009	1 038.9	352 306	71.7	28.3	50.2	13.9	2 189	4.7
Sacramento	247	-24.9	183	86.0	105.7	1 302 636	7 135	85 653	326.6	241 559	63.9	36.1	43.2	18.6	2 474	10.3
San Benito	604	4.2	962	19.2	38.5	2 737 111	2 844	93 435	164.0	261 198	76.9	23.1	50.2	18.9	174	7.5
San Bernardino	77	-85.0	62	21.8	29.8	831 612	13 455	83 151	582.2	466 156	11.5	88.5	42.4	16.7	849	4.1
San Diego	222	-27.1	39	45.2	68.2	694 313	17 964	34 672	726.0	126 657	89.3	10.7	42.9	9.1	451	1.7
San Francisco	0	71.4	2	0.0	0.0	252 167	126 083	52 000	D	D	D	D	0.0	0.0	0	0.0
San Joaquin	787	6.7	220	485.4	517.9	2 218 140	10 090	145 302	2 250.2	628 536	73.7	26.3	73.5	39.3	5 508	9.4
San Luis Obispo	1 339	-2.2	502	81.6	255.4	2 115 410	4 212	92 222	665.0	249 431	92.9	7.1	52.2	19.1	3 488	9.0
San Mateo	48	-15.6	144	2.8	8.5	1 629 243	11 299	69 497	75.9	227 213	96.4	3.6	49.1	14.7	182	4.2
Santa Barbara	701	-3.6	439	96.7	132.3	3 233 061	7 365	125 663	1 177.9	737 581	95.8	4.2	58.8	29.4	554	1.5
Santa Clara	230	-23.3	229	17.8	38.4	1 538 866	6 713	69 246	243.8	243 100	95.7	4.3	45.3	12.8	20	1.2
Santa Cruz	100	110.5	150	28.9	41.1	1 857 240	12 390	113 943	565.8	848 328	96.9	3.1	59.2	28.0	D	0.1
Shasta	376	-3.7	244	38.2	36.9	682 565	2 801	36 550	65.6	42 501	36.6	63.4	26.2	4.8	420	4.6
Sierra	39	36.0	815	9.7	4.0	1 226 333	1 504	92 896	D	D	D	D	62.5	22.9	D	2.1
Siskiyou	723	21.0	778	160.0	194.8	1 586 712	2 039	121 981	223.1	240 146	85.4	14.6	42.2	18.0	2 029	19.7
Solano	407	13.6	473	130.9	169.6	2 631 010	5 558	146 770	307.4	357 463	79.0	21.0	53.1	22.7	1 911	15.7
Sonoma	590	11.1	165	75.0	130.6	2 409 158	14 620	78 965	974.4	272 253	62.2	37.8	60.3	24.3	2 615	4.1
Stanislaus	768	-2.7	185	320.8	340.9	1 786 289	9 636	117 810	2 228.1	537 807	47.7	52.3	66.5	33.9	7 049	10.7
Sutter	375	4.3	276	244.3	275.8	1 828 515	6 619	179 143	508.2	374 208	98.8	1.2	77.1	40.8	11 326	27.1
Tehama	617	15.8	354	84.9	89.3	1 053 199	2 978	71 962	240.8	138 163	70.6	29.4	46.2	13.8	1 627	9.0
Trinity	176	40.8	712	1.6	2.1	811 870	1 140	29 838	5.2	20 895	D	D	23.1	2.0	247	12.1
Tulare	1 239	6.0	251	557.4	677.5	1 893 271	7 535	144 666	4 017.1	814 657	41.6	58.4	70.2	36.6	12 174	13.5
Tuolumne	88	-25.0	225	2.3	2.8	1 039 974	4 631	59 552	27.7	70 721	9.4	90.6	25.6	3.1	D	0.5
Ventura	281	8.5	131	87.1	101.1	2 041 990	15 621	94 136	1 440.1	669 829	99.3	0.7	65.1	24.7	154	2.0
Yolo	461	-4.0	456	229.9	306.9	2 571 454	5 642	218 361	561.2	555 135	93.6	6.4	61.7	34.2	6 240	28.1
Yuba	188	16.6	236	82.5	89.8	1 367 039	5 792	149 175	193.4	243 332	79.8	20.2	47.0	25.4	3 341	15.3
COLORADO	31 887	0.9	881	2 516.8	10 649.7	1 128 277	1 280	109 260	7 780.9	215 060	31.3	68.7	37.7	15.6	165 576	30.7
Adams	691	-1.6	821	17.6	550.3	1 179 177	1 436	121 985	116.5	138 483	88.0	12.0	31.6	15.2	5 479	40.7
Alamosa	182	3.3	567	68.6	71.5	825 866	1 458	154 025	92.5	287 354	87.5	12.5	46.0	23.0	821	29.8
Arapahoe	283	12.5	375	2.5	137.2	632 109	1 685	62 514	31.7	41 933	D	D	20.9	4.6	1 635	23.2
Archuleta	210	40.5	565	24.2	13.2	1 213 137	2 147	55 333	15.5	41 653	8.3	91.7	31.7	7.3	329	4.6
Baca	1 503	15.6	2 040	62.6	872.6	1 133 718	556	153 448	125.3	170 012	63.0	37.0	48.3	28.9	15 510	87.9
Bent	726	-17.3	2 620	31.5	107.1	1 219 368	465	156 993	70.8	255 574	17.9	82.1	55.6	27.8	2 945	58.8

STATE County	Water use, 2010		Wholesale trade,[1] 2007				Retail trade,[2] 2007				Real estate and rental and leasing,[2] 2007			
	Total water withdrawn (mil gal/day)	Gallons withdrawn per person per day	Number of establish-ments	Number of employees	Sales (mil dol)	Annual payroll (mil dol)	Number of establish-ments	Number of employees	Sales (mil dol)	Annual payroll (mil dol)	Number of establish-ments	Number of employees	Receipts (mil dol)	Annual payroll (mil dol)
	133	134	135	136	137	138	139	140	141	142	143	144	145	146
CALIFORNIA	37 962.2	1 019	53 963	745 785	598 456.5	42 334.5	114 438	1 683 023	455 032.3	44 328.9	51 597	312 488	76 805.0	13 446.7
Alameda	254.9	169	2 553	45 364	35 674.0	2 786.6	4 503	67 335	17 909.1	1 882.1	2 032	12 754	3 081.7	508.7
Alpine	4.5	3 804	NA	NA	NA	NA	4	D	D	D	1	D	D	D
Amador	32.4	850	24	D	D	D	163	1 960	1 800.8	49.7	44	98	16.4	2.6
Butte	715.3	3 252	165	1 824	796.4	71.6	798	11 316	2 400.7	256.8	264	1 462	158.8	32.6
Calaveras	23.4	513	20	77	24.2	3.3	151	1 388	292.8	32.6	61	173	29.5	3.9
Colusa	835.0	38 985	18	224	183.2	11.6	60	506	208.5	12.1	17	42	5.8	1.2
Contra Costa	302.7	289	779	7 116	6 644.0	409.6	2 822	46 065	11 763.8	1 242.9	1 452	7 236	1 607.0	311.8
Del Norte	13.7	478	9	D	D	D	74	1 029	206.3	22.6	35	122	16.6	3.0
El Dorado	55.7	308	118	718	363.6	32.8	591	6 384	1 619.7	175.6	265	1 545	190.8	40.7
Fresno	2 813.2	3 024	814	12 843	7 846.8	582.0	2 579	38 046	9 808.3	905.0	755	4 478	695.2	132.1
Glenn	606.6	21 571	29	415	148.4	14.4	85	766	204.0	18.0	25	97	9.0	2.3
Humboldt	114.0	847	99	D	D	D	659	7 782	1 726.4	172.4	186	622	102.8	15.7
Imperial	1 169.2	6 699	212	D	D	D	534	8 052	1 727.3	170.2	134	555	73.4	12.5
Inyo	111.6	6 016	15	D	D	D	116	975	242.0	21.8	28	94	10.6	2.5
Kern	2 159.9	2 572	559	7 850	5 730.5	377.0	1 993	30 123	7 876.0	725.6	627	3 414	565.5	112.8
Kings	1 298.9	8 490	60	D	D	D	326	4 267	1 035.9	93.9	95	343	55.4	7.2
Lake	50.9	786	21	D	D	D	196	2 267	557.9	50.6	67	223	28.2	5.0
Lassen	202.6	5 806	7	D	D	D	95	993	260.4	24.5	25	65	6.1	1.3
Los Angeles	3 064.0	312	21 677	259 831	198 435.8	12 262.9	30 179	418 153	119 111.8	10 849.2	14 085	90 847	26 790.4	4 129.2
Madera	748.7	4 963	79	678	353.1	28.8	368	3 883	1 010.2	89.3	100	409	36.7	9.4
Marin	42.9	170	381	3 631	2 373.1	218.5	1 161	15 432	4 589.3	472.8	633	3 122	1 148.2	137.8
Mariposa	5.3	291	7	D	D	D	72	427	84.5	8.6	21	85	9.3	2.4
Mendocino	81.5	928	84	D	D	D	492	5 097	1 259.1	120.7	141	597	91.3	12.6
Merced	1 494.7	5 843	97	D	D	D	578	8 005	2 001.3	179.9	153	641	85.6	15.1
Modoc	261.5	27 001	8	D	D	D	33	271	53.0	5.4	11	D	D	D
Mono	229.7	16 174	9	D	D	D	90	812	154.3	16.9	65	346	39.5	9.9
Monterey	545.5	1 314	392	D	D	D	1 497	18 392	4 541.1	487.8	487	2 423	500.6	86.6
Napa	96.9	710	143	D	D	D	537	6 463	1 665.0	180.7	206	893	153.0	31.1
Nevada	48.7	493	88	D	D	D	443	4 713	1 077.2	124.6	185	820	142.5	26.1
Orange	765.4	254	6 559	94 938	97 963.6	5 642.5	9 991	159 810	45 022.5	4 304.3	5 566	43 366	10 688.2	2 161.6
Placer	191.2	549	334	5 272	3 898.6	275.6	1 254	22 112	6 180.1	604.9	602	4 113	674.9	146.7
Plumas	118.7	5 934	5	D	D	D	118	769	175.3	17.6	42	77	13.7	2.8
Riverside	1 099.3	502	1 601	22 180	16 912.3	979.6	5 320	89 543	24 146.4	2 257.3	2 189	11 787	2 056.8	376.9
Sacramento	681.1	480	1 144	16 959	15 728.1	773.4	3 821	63 609	15 600.0	1 613.6	1 673	9 979	1 677.6	360.4
San Benito	85.4	1 546	36	1 645	319.6	60.7	124	1 522	352.9	40.7	56	115	16.5	3.4
San Bernardino	659.4	324	2 284	33 335	27 579.9	1 434.7	5 018	84 312	21 717.4	2 018.8	1 771	9 935	2 310.1	354.5
San Diego	2 818.2	910	4 002	55 934	33 704.9	4 120.7	9 948	151 425	38 710.6	3 889.2	5 810	33 067	7 190.2	1 345.2
San Francisco	93.5	116	1 195	11 786	10 562.2	668.1	3 710	45 079	12 400.0	1 395.9	1 843	14 332	4 309.7	984.3
San Joaquin	1 753.4	2 559	558	9 517	9 001.3	437.3	1 756	27 329	7 109.7	653.0	634	3 363	577.5	104.4
San Luis Obispo	2 579.1	9 565	277	2 329	955.0	104.1	1 262	14 652	3 548.4	353.6	475	2 050	293.4	56.7
San Mateo	93.1	130	1 076	15 170	12 607.8	1 094.9	2 216	36 139	10 198.8	1 084.2	1 246	8 041	2 077.1	365.1
Santa Barbara	264.3	623	438	5 713	4 023.6	350.4	1 605	20 281	4 983.4	524.4	681	3 452	620.7	119.5
Santa Clara	298.2	167	2 487	61 835	60 644.1	6 157.9	5 297	86 410	26 491.5	2 906.4	2 608	14 831	5 172.6	748.6
Santa Cruz	66.4	253	273	D	D	D	981	12 454	3 725.4	316.0	380	1 793	311.1	58.6
Shasta	239.0	1 349	179	1 748	829.0	69.4	722	10 287	2 526.4	260.1	225	1 201	128.2	26.1
Sierra	39.0	12 046	2	D	D	D	14	D	D	D	NA	NA	NA	NA
Siskiyou	411.1	9 155	37	358	169.1	11.2	209	1 859	403.3	37.2	67	203	22.1	4.1
Solano	452.8	1 095	249	D	D	D	1 167	19 117	4 828.0	482.7	404	1 913	347.9	58.5
Sonoma	259.5	536	585	7 631	3 953.6	454.3	1 925	26 177	6 427.2	718.5	718	3 237	604.1	114.2
Stanislaus	1 642.7	3 193	397	5 460	3 759.1	248.8	1 500	23 394	5 661.9	561.1	500	2 988	472.6	90.3
Sutter	722.0	7 621	66	1 421	879.0	71.7	304	4 614	1 065.4	112.0	99	602	60.4	12.9
Tehama	825.6	13 009	32	D	D	D	180	2 244	735.4	54.7	60	216	23.8	4.7
Trinity	22.5	1 634	4	D	D	D	52	383	69.2	6.7	8	D	D	D
Tulare	2 600.3	5 881	337	D	D	D	1 140	16 005	3 900.9	367.4	294	1 260	189.1	32.3
Tuolumne	35.8	646	37	D	D	D	213	2 419	582.4	56.1	90	271	39.9	6.6
Ventura	719.5	874	1 024	D	D	D	2 766	40 773	11 083.6	1 074.8	1 051	5 064	1 006.1	196.0
Yolo	780.2	3 885	251	6 048	6 483.6	271.2	500	7 812	1 765.7	189.2	268	1 560	247.0	53.4
Yuba	261.7	3 627	27	D	D	D	126	1 522	423.6	35.0	37	121	20.5	2.6
COLORADO	10 994.2	2 186	5 850	81 144	53 599.0	4 191.0	19 428	261 962	65 896.8	6 537.5	10 011	47 568	8 460.9	1 793.0
Adams	230.9	523	654	15 465	11 193.4	747.6	907	17 102	4 848.0	400.9	455	3 029	458.8	98.1
Alamosa	152.4	9 868	17	136	85.3	4.7	90	1 115	263.0	27.6	26	122	14.2	2.8
Arapahoe	187.0	327	684	9 551	5 774.1	550.7	1 890	32 052	9 932.0	848.7	1 109	6 048	1 207.1	241.7
Archuleta	59.3	4 905	8	29	8.8	0.8	104	647	142.7	14.9	51	178	37.2	4.7
Baca	98.5	26 006	16	43	52.7	1.2	17	124	32.9	2.5	3	3	0.1	0.0
Bent	152.4	23 454	1	D	D	D	16	85	16.4	1.4	2	D	D	D

1. Merchant wholesalers, except manufacturers' sales branches and offices. 2. Employer establishments.

Table B. States and Counties — **Professional Services, Manufacturing, and Accommodation and Food Services**

STATE County	Professional, scientific, and technical services,[1] 2007				Manufacturing, 2007				Accommodation and food services, 2007			
	Number of establish-ments	Number of employees	Receipts (mil dol)	Annual payroll (mil dol)	Number of establish-ments	Number of employees	Receipts (mil dol)	Annual payroll (mil dol)	Number of establish-ments	Number of employees	Sales (mil dol)	Annual payroll (mil dol)
	147	148	149	150	151	152	153	154	155	156	157	158
CALIFORNIA	111 954	1 231 372	194 406.3	80 738.1	44 296	1 448 485	491 372.1	71 247.3	75 989	1 366 926	80 852.8	22 374.8
Alameda	5 143	D	D	D	2 081	81 002	25 236.9	4 645.4	3 385	47 408	2 807.8	770.0
Alpine	5	D	D	D	NA	NA	NA	NA	12	D	D	D
Amador	77	279	26.1	8.9	51	760	143.0	29.4	109	1 249	61.2	17.1
Butte	426	D	D	D	224	4 404	987.4	150.6	429	7 708	355.8	96.7
Calaveras	80	347	36.7	12.9	NA	NA	NA	NA	114	976	42.4	11.1
Colusa	22	50	3.9	1.1	24	745	288.4	27.5	39	1 124	91.6	21.0
Contra Costa	3 273	D	D	D	622	18 551	32 021.4	1 146.1	1 777	28 524	1 562.3	433.1
Del Norte	38	135	13.1	4.2	NA	NA	NA	NA	74	748	32.2	7.9
El Dorado	538	2 808	515.1	151.4	204	3 534	662.2	142.5	447	5 885	301.7	83.5
Fresno	1 564	D	D	D	646	26 898	7 827.3	1 018.0	1 460	25 553	1 147.2	320.9
Glenn	36	149	11.0	3.4	31	721	278.3	27.7	58	608	31.0	8.3
Humboldt	259	D	D	D	158	3 105	877.0	117.7	352	4 649	209.0	58.4
Imperial	153	D	D	D	58	2 846	1 207.9	96.9	261	3 719	167.8	46.2
Inyo	34	D	D	D	NA	NA	NA	NA	98	1 570	91.7	25.3
Kern	1 123	D	D	D	390	12 789	9 456.2	583.7	1 203	19 344	940.3	252.2
Kings	101	535	52.9	16.9	73	4 291	2 107.7	148.7	171	4 209	360.1	77.5
Lake	79	D	D	D	NA	NA	NA	NA	133	1 325	68.1	17.3
Lassen	33	120	11.9	4.0	NA	NA	NA	NA	61	651	29.7	7.6
Los Angeles	30 754	D	D	D	15 158	451 656	153 343.7	20 520.1	19 476	339 815	20 238.1	5 570.1
Madera	124	D	D	D	116	4 143	1 452.9	170.3	192	2 265	125.1	33.1
Marin	1 797	D	D	D	229	2 205	397.2	88.0	694	10 913	626.6	185.9
Mariposa	21	76	5.8	1.9	NA	NA	NA	NA	51	1 430	133.0	27.5
Mendocino	206	D	D	D	146	3 057	773.4	113.6	347	3 796	194.2	53.6
Merced	170	D	D	D	122	9 208	3 954.2	348.6	302	5 130	219.4	55.2
Modoc	11	35	3.7	0.8	NA	NA	NA	NA	26	156	8.8	2.0
Mono	36	217	24.3	9.6	NA	NA	NA	NA	138	3 848	217.4	68.9
Monterey	818	D	D	D	301	7 333	2 227.6	268.4	983	18 026	1 197.1	345.4
Napa	419	D	D	D	436	13 165	4 529.3	632.4	363	8 904	620.4	195.4
Nevada	389	D	D	D	164	2 488	664.6	156.1	235	5 604	199.4	64.4
Orange	14 013	D	D	D	5 351	177 115	49 131.9	8 641.4	6 854	141 702	8 247.8	2 366.7
Placer	1 188	D	D	D	292	9 197	3 023.4	354.3	824	16 575	773.6	228.8
Plumas	57	D	D	D	21	593	130.6	26.5	112	560	30.1	8.5
Riverside	3 174	D	D	D	1 611	56 388	13 623.5	2 314.9	3 292	73 824	4 835.3	1 275.0
Sacramento	3 735	D	D	D	925	26 030	7 282.8	1 126.9	2 634	45 903	2 252.9	628.3
San Benito	70	206	25.8	7.8	63	2 867	630.3	102.0	93	1 109	50.2	14.6
San Bernardino	2 488	D	D	D	2 057	65 702	18 907.3	2 540.2	3 112	54 839	2 754.7	746.0
San Diego	11 972	117 497	18 834.7	7 694.0	3 182	102 168	27 541.1	5 244.6	6 599	144 287	9 551.5	2 567.2
San Francisco	5 600	D	D	D	788	11 339	2 077.5	422.5	3 525	66 365	5 039.2	1 496.8
San Joaquin	801	D	D	D	585	23 442	8 272.5	938.6	1 079	15 195	745.8	199.3
San Luis Obispo	930	5 709	593.8	222.6	377	6 517	2 548.2	260.4	850	14 903	767.9	219.7
San Mateo	2 916	D	D	D	742	30 221	17 918.2	1 975.0	1 785	30 836	2 107.2	613.5
Santa Barbara	1 359	D	D	D	505	13 149	3 174.1	676.8	1 029	21 380	1 361.5	360.1
Santa Clara	7 815	123 627	21 567.5	13 553.6	2 620	142 713	45 088.8	10 295.9	4 097	68 514	4 147.6	1 159.3
Santa Cruz	914	D	D	D	329	6 689	1 502.4	301.6	657	9 774	513.8	148.8
Shasta	400	D	D	D	167	2 794	662.9	117.1	403	5 862	281.0	74.9
Sierra	4	D	D	D	NA	NA	NA	NA	16	D	D	D
Siskiyou	98	D	D	D	38	911	257.8	36.0	149	1 684	78.5	22.0
Solano	598	D	D	D	296	10 357	8 377.3	578.9	731	12 523	573.3	153.4
Sonoma	1 538	D	D	D	885	24 077	5 841.9	1 201.2	1 173	17 739	1 005.4	283.8
Stanislaus	701	D	D	D	443	24 127	9 476.0	1 032.9	842	13 881	615.1	171.7
Sutter	129	D	D	D	71	1 549	494.9	61.3	153	2 498	100.7	28.1
Tehama	75	280	29.1	10.2	47	2 356	556.7	97.0	124	1 215	56.1	14.8
Trinity	22	82	8.1	2.6	NA	NA	NA	NA	53	291	14.6	3.7
Tulare	446	D	D	D	278	12 443	5 016.0	458.3	558	8 282	379.4	102.8
Tuolumne	120	D	D	D	66	1 030	222.5	40.4	169	1 817	86.5	23.6
Ventura	2 597	16 457	6 370.8	1 032.7	954	33 602	8 769.0	1 643.4	1 602	29 832	1 478.2	422.9
Yolo	395	D	D	D	177	5 743	1 853.3	235.7	399	8 693	840.3	159.7
Yuba	70	D	D	D	45	921	170.0	33.3	85	1 055	52.4	14.0
COLORADO	22 522	156 859	28 932.6	10 515.7	5 288	137 880	46 332.0	6 789.7	12 075	231 721	11 440.4	3 408.2
Adams	658	D	D	D	417	11 757	6 161.5	515.1	635	11 997	578.0	164.1
Alamosa	51	D	D	D	NA	NA	NA	NA	48	766	30.3	9.2
Arapahoe	2 727	D	D	D	436	8 358	2 043.0	395.2	1 136	20 947	1 008.5	301.4
Archuleta	43	119	10.1	3.5	NA	NA	NA	NA	64	649	33.2	9.0
Baca	3	5	0.5	0.1	NA	NA	NA	NA	8	D	D	D
Bent	2	D	D	D	NA	NA	NA	NA	10	98	3.0	0.8

1. Establishment subject to federal tax.

Table B. States and Counties — **Health Care and Social Assistance, Other Services, Nonemployer Businesses, and Residential Construction**

STATE County	Health care and social assistance, 2007				Other services, 2007				Nonemployer businesses, 2013		Value of residential construction authorized by building permits, 2014	
	Number of establish-ments	Number of employees	Receipts (mil dol)	Annual payroll (mil dol)	Number of establish-ments	Number of employees	Receipts (mil dol)	Annual payroll (mil dol)	Number	Receipts (mil dol)	New Construction ($1,000)	Number of housing units
	159	160	161	162	163	164	165	166	167	168	169	170
CALIFORNIA	97 288	1 592 430	191 605.7	72 531.1	57 626	399 336	52 326.5	11 913.7	2 983 996	152 884.8	18 742 105	83 645
Alameda	4 238	74 258	9 681.4	3 987.0	2 742	19 921	2 359.3	670.7	124 216	6 028.7	889 512	3 438
Alpine	4	D	D	D	1	D	D	D	101	3.8	1 486	3
Amador	89	1 281	127.6	48.1	50	158	17.4	4.4	2 678	110.5	4 926	22
Butte	737	12 120	1 179.3	427.5	321	2 168	173.6	49.9	13 031	603.4	92 522	550
Calaveras	99	1 134	106.8	40.4	63	226	18.2	4.9	3 521	150.9	20 733	70
Colusa	25	D	D	D	22	94	10.4	2.6	974	53.8	12 753	58
Contra Costa	2 737	44 257	5 652.4	2 302.8	1 528	8 902	1 054.4	276.2	82 405	4 647.3	493 802	2 001
Del Norte	75	1 352	117.0	51.3	26	98	10.5	2.1	1 210	50.1	2 081	9
El Dorado	452	5 802	624.8	240.9	285	1 513	137.8	38.8	15 627	744.3	87 274	190
Fresno	2 099	36 707	4 150.8	1 713.0	1 069	7 309	704.7	191.7	49 304	2 326.6	445 222	1 892
Glenn	37	479	33.7	14.5	21	51	6.9	1.1	1 353	65.5	5 316	30
Humboldt	462	6 762	589.0	217.0	259	1 304	157.0	32.8	11 071	425.4	30 521	234
Imperial	265	4 257	394.1	142.6	163	1 046	83.2	25.1	9 691	317.4	43 915	246
Inyo	63	1 047	92.8	38.2	44	164	16.2	4.2	1 298	49.7	1 995	7
Kern	1 456	25 119	2 746.4	1 042.9	857	5 637	569.1	145.0	43 515	2 079.8	409 139	2 297
Kings	204	4 106	433.8	153.1	105	582	47.0	13.4	4 180	170.1	56 757	434
Lake	154	2 242	237.7	86.7	79	258	24.4	7.0	3 929	145.1	7 901	45
Lassen	61	722	75.5	23.7	29	92	7.4	1.9	1 031	36.1	1 131	6
Los Angeles	27 728	444 806	53 200.9	19 568.8	16 089	117 748	15 230.4	3 369.6	945 941	48 573.4	4 059 026	17 659
Madera	221	5 836	554.7	255.8	119	609	48.9	12.9	6 970	312.2	56 882	214
Marin	1 066	13 958	1 595.2	649.1	617	4 249	630.4	167.2	36 468	2 583.1	112 423	390
Mariposa	31	456	29.9	13.3	18	62	5.6	1.4	1 232	46.2	6 921	24
Mendocino	294	4 185	369.1	147.2	165	674	74.3	16.3	8 223	315.2	14 189	109
Merced	443	6 048	592.2	235.3	209	899	73.9	19.3	10 521	492.7	42 954	169
Modoc	18	D	D	D	7	54	4.5	1.2	555	20.4	1 441	8
Mono	28	D	D	D	53	199	20.1	5.0	1 346	78.5	13 690	29
Monterey	970	13 789	1 876.6	723.7	556	3 651	425.9	104.6	23 865	1 293.0	72 040	361
Napa	425	10 004	1 150.0	502.2	219	1 172	142.5	38.4	11 274	677.7	44 721	147
Nevada	365	4 469	451.4	171.9	176	878	94.0	25.8	11 651	544.0	58 676	290
Orange	9 967	133 174	16 300.4	5 915.0	5 111	34 627	3 636.0	967.4	278 270	16 104.5	1 923 311	9 291
Placer	979	13 655	1 934.7	676.1	547	7 590	1 955.4	444.6	29 974	1 632.9	576 047	1 990
Plumas	53	912	75.2	30.3	41	128	10.6	3.0	1 529	64.9	6 165	32
Riverside	3 779	57 969	6 621.0	2 365.0	2 474	15 480	1 335.4	383.7	152 801	6 536.6	1 471 177	6 761
Sacramento	3 232	70 675	9 072.3	3 587.6	2 200	17 591	1 974.9	573.8	95 166	4 302.6	439 041	1 761
San Benito	100	D	D	D	69	251	22.4	5.7	3 307	160.1	26 779	105
San Bernardino	3 446	71 731	8 350.6	3 149.6	2 336	16 862	1 592.3	467.0	135 455	5 464.0	627 861	3 405
San Diego	7 924	133 893	15 954.7	5 872.9	5 176	37 084	3 732.5	1 015.3	246 649	12 284.5	1 504 007	6 875
San Francisco	2 967	57 946	7 752.0	3 039.4	2 239	17 261	5 992.0	626.7	89 078	5 373.5	768 892	2 711
San Joaquin	1 351	26 658	3 045.8	1 141.3	879	5 576	462.8	144.6	34 735	1 719.2	329 445	1 265
San Luis Obispo	864	14 341	1 341.2	546.4	464	2 808	222.0	60.3	23 558	1 179.3	271 870	983
San Mateo	2 095	30 901	4 046.3	1 591.8	1 411	9 356	2 520.3	331.9	63 460	4 041.2	528 575	1 461
Santa Barbara	1 322	19 124	2 076.4	784.0	767	5 005	816.9	141.4	32 058	1 820.0	172 342	755
Santa Clara	5 061	D	D	D	2 901	19 386	2 816.0	658.4	128 730	7 450.0	1 867 633	9 932
Santa Cruz	863	11 416	1 441.4	505.0	452	2 702	258.2	72.1	23 649	1 176.8	52 652	291
Shasta	661	10 015	1 124.5	420.3	320	1 697	168.2	43.3	11 542	521.8	50 129	242
Sierra	11	D	D	D	NA	NA	NA	NA	235	6.3	1 365	4
Siskiyou	117	1 721	151.9	59.3	71	212	20.9	5.1	3 249	127.2	3 783	19
Solano	861	18 135	2 136.5	895.9	541	3 240	324.0	92.5	21 658	868.0	167 513	646
Sonoma	1 516	23 219	2 623.9	1 065.9	873	4 877	508.1	138.8	43 454	2 224.5	130 619	663
Stanislaus	1 108	21 628	2 662.6	967.7	650	4 205	380.9	119.5	25 939	1 252.0	97 036	454
Sutter	251	3 085	409.2	116.9	132	741	61.9	16.6	5 193	318.9	20 900	79
Tehama	129	1 917	171.5	62.1	71	614	31.8	23.9	3 232	134.5	16 097	78
Trinity	29	198	12.9	4.7	17	D	D	D	970	33.5	5 445	30
Tulare	806	13 734	1 295.3	493.8	384	2 298	208.1	62.9	19 668	900.7	200 613	1 092
Tuolumne	173	2 662	307.7	112.2	76	435	41.0	11.2	4 033	162.7	12 440	55
Ventura	2 317	29 522	3 140.0	1 200.9	1 196	7 303	839.6	195.9	64 224	3 413.3	279 531	1 314
Yolo	364	5 936	660.5	234.6	282	2 000	208.0	63.8	11 858	558.5	69 863	218
Yuba	96	2 708	313.1	111.6	54	250	33.9	9.9	3 141	108.0	31 026	201
COLORADO	13 644	238 942	24 328.4	9 724.8	10 151	62 767	7 789.2	1 823.2	447 586	20 808.6	6 479 529	28 686
Adams	582	18 364	2 227.9	770.6	620	4 315	458.5	122.1	28 516	1 182.4	250 104	1 115
Alamosa	69	1 507	114.3	50.8	44	222	11.6	3.6	1 096	40.2	4 469	52
Arapahoe	1 714	28 246	3 010.4	1 196.9	1 110	7 321	943.9	242.5	50 623	2 548.5	390 710	1 897
Archuleta	37	186	13.3	4.7	29	139	10.0	3.2	1 892	86.0	21 997	75
Baca	7	D	D	D	6	D	D	D	363	13.5	0	0
Bent	7	D	D	D	3	D	D	D	219	10.5	0	0

STATE County	Government employment and payroll, 2012: Full-time equivalent employees	Government employment and payroll, 2012: March payroll (dollars)	March payroll (percent of total): Adminis-tration, judicial, and legal	March payroll (percent of total): Police and Corrections	March payroll (percent of total): Fire Protection	March payroll (percent of total): Highways and transpor-tation	March payroll (percent of total): Health and Welfare	March payroll (percent of total): Natural resources and utilities	March payroll (percent of total): Education and libraries	Local government finances, 2012, General revenue: Total (mil dol)	General revenue: Inter-govern-mental (mil dol)	Taxes: Total (mil dol)	Taxes: Per capita[1] (dollars): Total	Taxes: Per capita[1] (dollars): Property
	171	172	173	174	175	176	177	178	179	180	181	182	183	184
CALIFORNIA	X	X	X	X	X	X	X	X	X	X	X	X	X	X
Alameda	56 184	365 163 607	5.7	11.5	5.1	11.1	17.4	11.1	35.4	11 581.0	4 300.9	3 665.4	2 358	1 599
Alpine	214	872 045	11.7	13.5	1.0	7.4	8.2	7.0	43.1	24.5	12.2	8.3	7 356	6 651
Amador	1 266	6 168 436	11.2	19.0	1.9	5.8	6.8	6.0	39.5	128.1	55.8	50.2	1 356	1 204
Butte	8 734	37 694 370	6.4	9.6	2.6	2.0	12.6	5.9	58.9	1 079.1	643.7	243.0	1 097	878
Calaveras	1 448	6 209 937	7.6	9.6	4.4	4.6	11.0	10.4	49.5	186.0	75.8	74.1	1 657	1 522
Colusa	1 069	4 506 211	9.2	12.0	1.8	3.7	9.6	7.3	55.3	146.1	73.1	36.5	1 707	1 430
Contra Costa	31 030	175 288 765	5.0	11.0	4.7	3.1	16.5	6.7	49.7	5 884.2	1 770.2	2 008.9	1 861	1 450
Del Norte	840	3 504 433	11.7	12.1	0.5	4.3	15.7	4.5	48.9	153.3	93.2	23.2	819	669
El Dorado	6 061	31 562 790	7.6	11.3	7.2	4.8	7.4	6.9	49.3	878.4	352.8	300.6	1 665	1 450
Fresno	34 954	165 436 346	4.1	10.3	2.1	3.3	9.7	4.5	65.0	5 127.4	3 047.2	1 071.6	1 131	789
Glenn	1 427	5 989 936	3.6	9.7	0.6	3.0	13.1	9.7	56.4	178.6	102.2	29.6	1 057	878
Humboldt	5 913	25 492 898	6.6	10.3	1.9	3.5	17.6	6.2	50.4	699.2	403.7	159.8	1 185	901
Imperial	10 122	49 143 599	4.2	6.0	1.7	1.1	19.5	16.2	45.5	1 293.3	740.8	180.2	1 019	733
Inyo	1 429	7 084 588	6.7	10.0	0.3	4.1	40.9	3.3	30.9	203.7	66.4	52.2	2 825	2 089
Kern	32 191	158 787 344	5.1	10.1	4.5	2.2	16.0	4.2	56.8	6 098.2	2 797.6	1 169.0	1 365	1 151
Kings	4 882	22 137 016	6.6	11.1	2.5	1.2	11.7	3.6	60.7	623.0	383.4	130.2	860	727
Lake	2 729	12 022 755	11.2	10.5	3.8	2.4	16.8	9.3	43.1	271.7	144.5	78.7	1 231	1 043
Lassen	1 280	5 212 652	7.9	9.0	1.2	3.2	10.4	8.7	58.1	128.4	89.5	24.8	738	648
Los Angeles	386 456	2 230 095 495	9.6	12.3	4.7	5.7	13.7	9.3	42.7	62 878.6	29 034.6	18 834.7	1 891	1 234
Madera	4 578	20 019 402	8.1	8.1	0.2	2.2	10.1	5.2	64.4	627.3	366.3	154.2	1 013	706
Marin	8 544	51 753 682	10.8	11.2	8.5	4.2	8.9	10.4	44.3	1 521.9	327.6	825.0	3 222	2 533
Mariposa	919	3 214 468	8.2	10.8	0.6	5.1	32.1	3.0	35.0	106.5	45.5	33.4	1 867	1 123
Mendocino	3 596	16 441 501	8.4	10.8	1.7	3.8	21.2	5.0	47.9	1 037.3	251.8	144.5	1 653	1 355
Merced	10 959	49 202 192	6.5	7.6	1.6	1.1	10.0	6.7	63.4	1 305.5	840.8	219.3	836	680
Modoc	586	2 160 529	8.3	8.7	1.4	11.9	22.7	4.7	40.8	67.3	46.4	10.6	1 140	1 021
Mono	1 012	5 526 104	7.8	11.4	5.1	6.0	35.5	9.2	22.9	195.2	38.3	79.1	5 511	4 023
Monterey	16 674	95 953 296	5.6	9.2	2.7	3.8	28.8	5.1	41.4	3 062.0	1 376.2	682.3	1 599	1 199
Napa	5 012	27 819 123	11.8	13.2	3.0	2.1	9.4	6.0	49.6	811.6	274.6	367.8	2 645	2 138
Nevada	3 125	16 593 333	8.7	9.9	4.8	4.6	26.3	10.1	30.7	498.3	165.7	159.3	1 620	1 417
Orange	85 251	527 595 855	5.4	11.0	4.8	3.1	7.4	5.7	58.4	14 543.9	5 867.6	5 580.4	1 806	1 406
Placer	12 015	67 291 627	7.1	9.6	4.2	2.3	5.5	9.5	58.5	1 867.4	613.0	730.0	2 018	1 673
Plumas	1 484	5 779 631	5.2	6.8	2.3	4.1	39.9	3.6	35.0	189.6	75.9	44.6	2 300	2 099
Riverside	68 997	380 597 495	8.6	11.0	1.9	2.3	12.6	7.6	54.4	10 975.4	5 598.2	3 090.1	1 362	1 054
Sacramento	50 509	274 337 834	5.2	13.3	5.5	4.2	8.8	13.3	46.1	7 904.0	3 980.4	1 968.0	1 357	948
San Benito	2 079	11 695 733	4.3	7.2	1.9	1.9	29.7	5.0	47.9	317.3	147.3	81.2	1 428	1 245
San Bernardino	68 989	370 218 367	5.5	10.6	4.1	2.1	13.3	5.1	56.9	11 897.3	6 945.9	2 679.6	1 287	987
San Diego	97 178	529 647 292	9.3	10.8	3.9	3.4	11.1	7.0	52.0	16 495.7	6 780.5	5 691.2	1 791	1 381
San Francisco	38 712	274 384 267	11.0	13.8	5.8	19.9	21.2	9.0	18.6	8 696.0	2 927.1	3 303.9	4 001	2 234
San Joaquin	23 911	123 453 125	6.5	12.7	3.3	2.6	14.7	5.0	53.3	3 894.7	2 276.8	855.2	1 217	851
San Luis Obispo	8 194	48 094 004	7.2	11.4	2.8	2.5	6.9	6.4	57.6	1 189.7	435.4	547.8	1 994	1 615
San Mateo	20 873	132 351 507	8.3	12.6	5.3	5.4	14.1	7.1	44.7	4 326.2	1 099.6	2 039.6	2 759	2 118
Santa Barbara	15 712	89 085 924	7.3	11.4	5.3	3.7	14.4	7.2	48.4	2 761.9	960.5	877.6	2 035	1 531
Santa Clara	59 919	402 121 133	7.6	10.2	5.0	5.0	20.4	6.5	42.7	12 701.2	3 946.9	4 816.5	2 621	1 963
Santa Cruz	9 292	50 504 116	8.1	10.1	3.9	7.3	13.5	7.9	47.1	1 432.9	632.4	483.8	1 813	1 441
Shasta	6 528	30 533 939	6.7	8.7	2.8	3.4	15.6	9.0	52.2	922.9	498.8	217.9	1 220	1 000
Sierra	204	851 638	16.3	12.9	0.1	11.6	17.0	3.1	35.4	28.6	16.9	7.5	2 443	2 207
Siskiyou	2 067	8 289 776	11.3	10.4	0.5	6.1	10.7	5.7	53.1	242.6	147.2	54.2	1 228	1 028
Solano	14 386	72 410 858	7.6	13.9	3.4	2.8	9.9	7.1	53.4	1 896.3	937.5	594.6	1 413	1 051
Sonoma	16 072	90 178 192	9.5	12.6	3.9	2.6	12.9	7.2	47.9	2 545.8	918.8	972.6	1 978	1 555
Stanislaus	19 446	94 702 481	5.9	8.3	2.5	1.6	11.8	9.4	58.2	2 696.4	1 547.9	554.1	1 062	825
Sutter	3 010	14 970 086	9.1	8.0	3.7	3.1	14.1	4.9	55.0	556.7	302.3	112.6	1 185	908
Tehama	2 320	9 999 317	7.1	9.2	1.1	3.3	13.4	2.6	61.2	246.2	160.2	57.2	902	755
Trinity	1 131	4 471 095	2.7	3.4	0.7	7.0	27.1	7.4	48.8	140.6	56.9	13.9	1 024	919
Tulare	21 502	97 324 423	4.7	7.2	1.7	1.1	30.4	3.5	50.1	3 132.9	1 499.7	450.9	998	665
Tuolumne	1 609	7 837 540	9.3	11.4	1.9	4.0	9.2	5.7	53.0	206.6	92.6	69.5	1 287	1 105
Ventura	27 714	159 457 912	10.1	10.8	4.6	3.0	13.0	7.6	49.2	4 630.9	2 005.3	1 379.1	1 650	1 378
Yolo	6 203	32 178 923	11.0	12.7	5.3	1.8	9.0	7.7	48.4	954.1	449.2	304.9	1 494	1 014
Yuba	3 659	17 894 536	5.9	8.6	0.7	1.5	7.2	2.0	71.6	385.0	230.2	77.0	1 056	932
COLORADO	X	X	X	X	X	X	X	X	X	X	X	X	X	X
Adams	14 341	67 598 280	8.2	13.6	4.3	2.6	4.0	12.3	52.8	1 856.9	785.2	806.6	1 755	1 137
Alamosa	647	1 959 302	10.3	10.3	0.7	4.6	18.5	7.3	47.7	73.8	42.5	23.1	1 428	843
Arapahoe	21 249	96 139 327	5.9	11.9	9.5	2.0	4.3	8.1	56.7	2 508.7	756.4	1 211.5	2 034	1 426
Archuleta	516	2 016 002	9.3	6.9	2.2	5.2	24.8	8.6	30.1	79.3	24.7	31.1	2 580	1 862
Baca	511	1 703 710	8.5	7.0	0.0	11.1	42.4	7.3	21.4	31.5	11.2	5.7	1 519	1 381
Bent	294	918 613	7.0	10.4	0.0	4.8	21.4	18.4	36.0	56.2	15.6	20.3	3 509	2 068

1. Based on the resident population estimated as of July 1 of the year shown.

STATE County	Local government finances, 2012 (cont.) — Direct general expenditure — Total (mil dol)	Per capita[1] (dollars)	Percent of total for: Education	Health and hospitals	Police protection	Public welfare	Highways	Debt outstanding — Total (mil dol)	Per capita[1] (dollars)	Government employment, 2013 — Federal civilian	Federal military	State and local	Presidential election,[2] 2012 — Percent of vote cast: Democratic	Republican	All other
	185	186	187	188	189	190	191	192	193	194	195	196	197	198	199
CALIFORNIA	X	X	X	X	X	X	X	X	X	246 734	213 744	2 128 214	61.0	37.0	2.0
Alameda	12 422.0	7 990	22.9	13.4	5.2	5.4	2.3	24 528.0	15 776	9 404	4 137	97 171	78.8	19.3	2.0
Alpine	26.0	23 015	19.6	7.3	10.1	5.8	8.6	23.6	20 861	11	0	253	61.0	36.4	2.6
Amador	133.4	3 602	30.1	6.7	9.8	7.2	5.6	61.9	1 670	87	53	4 094	41.5	56.1	2.3
Butte	1 098.2	4 957	46.2	6.8	4.4	11.8	3.6	480.5	2 169	561	348	14 319	49.8	47.5	2.7
Calaveras	179.1	4 002	37.4	6.3	5.0	8.1	5.2	135.0	3 017	130	70	2 123	42.1	55.1	2.8
Colusa	142.2	6 642	35.7	6.2	5.7	4.9	6.5	51.5	2 404	74	34	2 080	40.0	58.1	2.0
Contra Costa	6 294.4	5 830	33.6	19.1	6.3	5.7	4.7	7 234.2	6 701	4 498	1 802	41 204	68.0	30.2	1.8
Del Norte	142.9	5 052	31.7	5.8	3.7	12.4	2.6	70.4	2 488	145	51	3 489	45.4	52.1	2.5
El Dorado	940.2	5 207	36.4	3.7	4.8	5.2	6.4	905.2	5 013	732	288	9 086	43.6	54.1	2.2
Fresno	5 031.5	5 308	44.7	7.0	5.6	10.3	3.4	3 847.5	4 059	10 051	1 581	54 713	50.2	48.1	1.7
Glenn	186.6	6 665	40.1	6.9	4.5	11.9	5.2	33.9	1 212	239	44	1 767	37.8	59.8	2.4
Humboldt	731.8	5 428	44.2	7.8	4.7	10.6	4.7	396.3	2 939	705	392	12 132	62.3	34.1	3.6
Imperial	1 172.3	6 625	40.7	23.6	4.1	7.5	2.9	1 408.8	7 962	2 445	480	15 020	62.2	36.1	1.7
Inyo	199.3	10 776	23.8	41.6	4.6	3.3	3.2	72.4	3 915	371	29	2 707	43.9	53.0	3.1
Kern	5 683.5	6 638	55.4	8.5	3.6	6.7	3.0	3 571.0	4 171	10 091	3 983	46 676	40.1	57.9	2.0
Kings	602.9	3 983	45.9	6.6	4.9	9.6	2.9	261.9	1 730	1 146	5 069	11 566	42.0	56.1	1.9
Lake	267.3	4 177	39.4	7.1	5.3	13.9	3.9	107.2	1 675	150	100	3 719	58.2	38.9	2.9
Lassen	133.2	3 956	45.5	7.1	5.0	10.9	6.5	58.3	1 734	1 935	40	4 363	31.5	65.7	2.8
Los Angeles	60 312.8	6 054	35.0	11.1	7.8	8.7	3.1	84 320.3	8 464	47 626	18 171	502 818	69.2	28.8	2.0
Madera	649.2	4 265	45.6	3.7	3.9	8.8	6.2	475.5	3 124	311	233	9 482	42.4	55.7	1.9
Marin	1 569.1	6 127	34.5	6.9	6.2	4.1	3.1	2 304.2	8 998	756	623	14 416	78.0	20.2	1.8
Mariposa	101.6	5 675	21.1	24.5	6.6	10.1	6.4	22.6	1 262	734	27	1 069	42.5	54.9	2.6
Mendocino	1 025.1	11 725	70.9	7.3	2.3	5.1	2.4	577.0	6 600	340	164	6 279	69.6	26.8	3.6
Merced	1 403.1	5 349	48.6	3.6	4.1	10.0	2.7	901.0	3 435	746	412	16 241	53.3	45.0	1.7
Modoc	67.1	7 198	38.4	16.9	4.0	6.8	8.8	4.6	497	242	14	928	29.7	67.4	2.9
Mono	192.0	13 383	15.1	34.5	6.6	4.9	8.7	76.3	5 321	234	247	1 250	55.5	42.3	2.2
Monterey	2 904.3	6 806	36.5	22.7	4.6	5.4	2.6	1 444.4	3 385	5 553	6 527	24 805	68.2	29.9	2.0
Napa	821.7	5 909	37.5	5.9	7.5	4.2	4.0	746.0	5 365	223	216	9 638	65.1	32.7	2.2
Nevada	537.0	5 464	23.8	31.3	4.9	5.6	4.7	392.6	3 994	361	155	5 087	51.4	46.1	2.5
Orange	13 915.7	4 503	41.4	2.9	7.7	7.3	4.5	22 316.3	7 222	11 036	5 519	134 370	47.6	50.2	2.2
Placer	1 896.3	5 243	41.7	2.8	5.8	5.9	6.0	2 500.4	6 913	677	601	16 247	43.4	54.7	1.9
Plumas	177.2	9 133	26.8	34.8	4.1	4.9	5.8	57.6	2 967	412	30	1 821	42.8	54.7	2.5
Riverside	11 682.2	5 149	39.3	8.1	6.7	7.1	4.3	13 164.6	5 802	6 894	3 932	113 036	50.2	47.9	1.9
Sacramento	7 966.3	5 494	34.4	6.0	4.9	8.6	5.8	16 350.5	11 275	8 807	3 062	171 578	58.5	39.5	2.0
San Benito	327.5	5 757	32.1	32.0	3.9	5.6	3.2	125.8	2 211	137	91	2 426	60.5	37.7	1.8
San Bernardino	11 798.5	5 669	38.7	15.6	6.0	7.5	5.5	11 574.3	5 561	13 600	20 166	97 939	52.1	45.8	2.2
San Diego	16 846.0	5 302	37.0	9.8	5.3	6.9	2.9	27 732.0	8 729	46 943	101 931	180 024	54.1	43.9	1.9
San Francisco	7 412.4	8 975	16.3	24.7	5.1	6.5	3.4	17 985.0	21 777	14 094	1 639	87 075	84.2	13.7	2.2
San Joaquin	3 717.2	5 291	40.5	9.2	5.9	8.8	3.5	3 309.2	4 710	3 524	1 178	31 880	54.4	43.8	1.8
San Luis Obispo	1 206.8	4 391	38.5	5.9	6.2	8.2	3.9	850.7	3 096	610	567	19 818	51.4	46.0	2.6
San Mateo	4 256.2	5 757	34.0	11.6	7.7	4.4	3.8	4 651.4	6 292	3 630	1 352	26 719	73.5	24.7	1.8
Santa Barbara	2 786.6	6 462	32.4	18.7	5.7	6.7	3.0	1 346.9	3 123	3 799	3 394	30 596	60.4	37.5	2.1
Santa Clara	11 865.9	6 458	32.5	21.8	5.2	5.2	2.2	17 898.2	9 740	9 905	3 273	75 617	69.4	28.6	2.0
Santa Cruz	1 415.2	5 305	36.6	6.6	6.3	8.5	2.3	1 074.8	4 029	525	412	17 693	77.5	19.8	2.7
Shasta	906.1	5 074	43.3	8.1	5.8	10.6	4.0	544.3	3 048	1 306	324	11 153	35.9	61.7	2.4
Sierra	29.0	9 401	28.7	10.0	10.3	10.1	12.9	6.1	1 986	51	0	307	37.3	58.2	4.5
Siskiyou	251.0	5 684	48.4	6.3	5.8	7.4	5.5	80.4	1 822	750	69	3 108	43.3	53.7	3.1
Solano	1 873.8	4 454	35.1	6.1	9.3	7.8	4.2	1 624.0	3 860	3 799	7 412	19 731	63.4	34.8	1.8
Sonoma	2 601.9	5 290	35.4	10.3	6.3	6.4	5.0	2 547.1	5 179	1 423	1 349	24 840	73.6	24.0	2.3
Stanislaus	2 792.3	5 352	50.1	6.9	4.9	10.2	3.4	4 496.8	8 619	849	834	25 239	49.9	48.1	2.0
Sutter	526.6	5 542	44.9	7.7	4.4	6.1	1.8	241.8	2 545	118	152	4 265	40.7	57.4	1.9
Tehama	244.9	3 862	49.8	6.6	5.9	14.9	4.0	28.9	456	231	99	3 360	36.6	60.7	2.7
Trinity	128.3	9 486	22.7	15.7	2.1	6.0	7.0	47.2	3 487	258	21	966	50.7	46.1	3.2
Tulare	3 186.6	7 050	39.0	24.4	3.2	8.0	4.7	1 380.8	3 055	1 123	719	29 814	41.5	56.8	1.7
Tuolumne	214.2	3 966	35.6	9.8	6.8	8.2	4.3	66.5	1 230	485	80	4 731	42.4	55.1	2.4
Ventura	4 471.8	5 349	38.6	13.1	7.5	4.6	3.5	3 011.8	3 603	7 082	5 110	35 491	55.2	42.9	1.9
Yolo	951.1	4 659	30.3	3.8	6.2	8.0	5.9	944.3	4 626	3 407	330	34 343	67.1	30.8	2.1
Yuba	436.2	5 982	54.3	2.1	4.1	10.8	4.0	399.0	5 472	1 358	4 801	5 532	41.4	56.1	2.5
COLORADO	X	X	X	X	X	X	X	X	X	53 639	53 966	358 177	53.7	44.7	1.6
Adams	1 860.3	4 048	42.2	0.3	5.7	9.9	5.6	2 579.2	5 612	1 343	1 599	36 465	58.2	39.9	1.9
Alamosa	68.0	4 210	38.8	5.3	7.5	20.9	5.9	38.4	2 379	154	40	2 214	56.0	41.9	2.1
Arapahoe	2 593.0	4 354	41.7	1.1	7.2	3.0	5.0	6 000.2	10 075	3 309	3 216	33 532	55.7	42.8	1.5
Archuleta	68.6	5 681	20.6	27.4	2.8	7.3	11.0	57.7	4 780	48	32	671	42.8	54.9	2.3
Baca	31.8	8 484	29.7	35.6	3.0	11.3	8.9	2.1	559	38	10	645	24.6	72.3	3.1
Bent	42.9	7 437	18.7	2.0	8.7	5.5	17.8	8.1	1 402	42	11	444	41.6	56.1	2.3

1. Based on the resident population estimated as of July 1 of the year shown. 2.

STATE/ County code	CBSA code[1]	County type[2]	STATE County	Land area,[3] (sq km) 2010	Population, 2014: Total persons 2014	Population, 2014: Rank	Population, 2014: Per square kilometer	Population and population characteristics, 2013: Race alone or in combination, not Hispanic or Latino (percent): White	Black	American Indian, Alaska Native	Asian and Pacific Islander	Percent Hispanic or Latino[4]	Age (percent): Under 5 years	5 to 17 years	18 to 24 years	25 to 34 years	35 to 44 years	45 to 54 years
				1	2	3	4	5	6	7	8	9	10	11	12	13	14	15
			COLORADO—Cont'd															
08 013	14500	2	Boulder	1 881	313 333	213	166.6	80.6	1.4	0.9	5.6	13.7	5.1	15.4	15.3	13.0	13.2	13.7
08 014	19740	1	Broomfield	86	62 138	841	722.5	79.6	1.7	1.0	7.1	12.5	6.4	18.6	8.5	16.8	14.8	12.9
08 015	...	7	Chaffee	2 625	18 363	1 902	7.0	86.4	1.8	1.6	1.0	10.4	4.2	11.8	7.1	12.1	11.4	13.6
08 017	...	9	Cheyenne	4 606	1 871	3 064	0.4	85.8	0.8	1.3	0.7	12.1	8.0	17.1	6.9	12.6	9.8	14.0
08 019	19740	1	Clear Creek	1 024	9 187	2 497	9.0	92.4	1.1	1.6	1.2	5.1	3.7	11.4	5.5	9.6	14.2	17.6
08 021	...	9	Conejos	3 334	8 265	2 584	2.5	44.5	0.5	1.3	0.7	54.0	6.7	20.7	8.5	10.4	10.2	12.9
08 023	...	9	Costilla	3 178	3 568	2 935	1.1	32.9	0.7	1.5	1.2	64.2	3.9	14.7	8.0	8.1	8.5	13.5
08 025	...	8	Crowley	2 039	5 360	2 811	2.6	58.4	9.5	2.3	1.5	29.6	3.6	9.6	9.8	19.1	16.4	16.5
08 027	...	8	Custer	1 913	4 361	2 877	2.3	92.6	1.4	1.5	0.7	5.2	2.7	12.2	5.3	5.8	8.8	14.5
08 029	...	6	Delta	2 958	29 870	1 431	10.1	83.4	0.8	1.4	1.1	14.7	5.2	16.1	7.1	9.8	10.2	13.1
08 031	19740	1	Denver	396	663 862	97	1 676.4	55.3	10.4	1.3	4.6	31.0	7.0	14.0	8.9	21.8	15.5	11.6
08 033	...	9	Dolores	2 764	1 978	3 051	0.7	92.0	1.3	4.4	0.7	4.1	5.1	16.4	6.1	9.2	11.4	14.2
08 035	19740	1	Douglas	2 176	314 638	211	144.6	86.3	1.8	0.7	5.3	8.1	6.5	22.4	6.7	10.6	16.6	16.4
08 037	20780	5	Eagle	4 363	52 921	943	12.1	68.1	0.8	0.6	1.5	29.8	6.4	17.1	7.6	17.4	17.0	14.9
08 039	19740	1	Elbert	4 794	24 195	1 637	5.0	91.4	1.1	1.2	1.5	6.3	4.1	19.0	7.2	7.4	11.7	19.5
08 041	17820	2	El Paso	5 508	663 519	98	120.5	74.0	7.6	1.5	4.8	15.9	7.0	18.3	11.4	15.0	12.5	13.4
08 043	15860	4	Fremont	3 971	46 502	1 035	11.7	81.1	4.2	2.4	1.0	12.8	4.1	12.6	7.2	13.9	13.0	14.9
08 045	24060	5	Garfield	7 634	57 461	889	7.5	69.9	0.8	1.2	1.2	28.3	7.4	18.9	8.3	14.3	14.3	14.0
08 047	19740	1	Gilpin	388	5 851	2 767	15.1	90.3	1.6	1.7	2.0	6.1	3.9	13.2	4.9	9.3	15.7	19.0
08 049	...	8	Grand	4 782	14 546	2 132	3.0	90.3	0.8	1.1	1.4	7.9	4.3	13.9	7.2	13.3	13.3	15.6
08 051	...	7	Gunnison	8 389	15 725	2 060	1.9	89.1	0.8	1.3	1.2	9.1	5.0	13.3	18.0	14.2	13.3	12.2
08 053	...	9	Hinsdale	2 894	786	3 119	0.3	94.3	1.0	1.5	1.1	3.9	5.0	14.0	5.9	9.7	8.5	14.6
08 055	...	6	Huerfano	4 121	6 462	2 719	1.6	62.8	0.8	2.1	1.2	34.7	3.9	11.7	6.7	7.8	8.0	13.9
08 057	...	9	Jackson	4 180	1 396	3 088	0.3	87.5	0.5	1.5	0.2	11.4	3.6	14.9	6.7	9.7	11.3	15.3
08 059	19740	1	Jefferson	1 979	558 503	115	282.2	80.7	1.5	1.1	3.5	15.0	5.3	15.9	8.4	13.0	12.9	15.5
08 061	...	9	Kiowa	4 578	1 402	3 086	0.3	92.9	0.8	0.9	0.2	6.1	6.4	14.3	8.4	9.2	9.1	13.2
08 063	...	7	Kit Carson	5 597	8 072	2 596	1.4	77.4	2.4	1.1	1.2	18.9	6.3	16.1	8.0	13.8	12.1	13.7
08 065	...	7	Lake	976	7 357	2 647	7.5	59.8	0.8	1.3	0.8	38.5	6.6	17.1	9.1	14.9	14.4	13.2
08 067	20420	6	La Plata	4 382	53 989	926	12.3	81.2	0.8	6.1	1.2	12.5	5.1	14.3	10.7	14.2	12.7	13.8
08 069	22660	2	Larimer	6 724	324 122	205	48.2	85.5	1.4	1.1	3.0	10.9	5.5	15.1	14.6	13.9	12.0	12.4
08 071	...	7	Las Animas	12 361	14 052	2 165	1.1	53.9	1.7	1.8	1.3	42.3	5.2	14.3	8.9	10.7	10.2	13.4
08 073	...	8	Lincoln	6 676	5 510	2 803	0.8	80.2	5.5	1.3	1.3	12.8	5.7	13.8	8.1	15.7	11.9	15.3
08 075	44540	7	Logan	4 762	22 524	1 709	4.7	78.3	4.4	1.4	1.0	16.0	4.9	13.9	12.1	14.7	12.4	13.4
08 077	24300	3	Mesa	8 622	148 255	434	17.2	83.9	1.2	1.4	1.5	13.8	6.4	16.3	10.1	13.3	11.2	12.7
08 079	...	9	Mineral	2 268	698	3 127	0.3	94.7	0.8	0.8	1.0	3.6	4.3	8.7	4.9	10.5	8.6	15.1
08 081	18780	7	Moffat	12 285	12 928	2 236	1.1	83.9	1.0	1.4	1.2	14.1	6.8	19.0	8.2	13.4	11.5	14.0
08 083	...	6	Montezuma	5 256	25 772	1 569	4.9	75.7	0.7	12.5	1.1	11.9	6.1	16.5	7.3	10.8	10.9	13.6
08 085	33940	7	Montrose	5 803	40 873	1 155	7.0	77.9	0.7	1.3	1.1	20.3	5.7	17.2	6.9	10.6	11.0	13.3
08 087	22820	6	Morgan	3 316	28 328	1 479	8.5	61.4	3.0	0.8	0.8	35.0	7.5	19.2	9.1	12.6	11.3	13.3
08 089	...	6	Otero	3 268	18 488	1 895	5.7	56.2	1.0	1.3	1.2	41.8	6.5	17.7	9.7	10.6	10.6	12.3
08 091	...	9	Ouray	1 403	4 629	2 857	3.3	93.7	0.7	1.1	0.9	4.9	3.5	13.4	4.7	7.0	10.4	15.5
08 093	19740	1	Park	5 682	16 345	2 023	2.9	92.2	1.0	1.7	1.4	5.7	3.9	13.0	5.7	8.3	11.9	19.5
08 095	...	9	Phillips	1 782	4 363	2 876	2.4	78.2	1.0	0.7	1.1	20.0	5.9	18.6	7.3	10.0	10.6	12.9
08 097	24060	7	Pitkin	2 514	17 626	1 941	7.0	87.7	1.0	0.7	2.0	9.8	4.0	12.6	6.4	15.2	14.2	15.9
08 099	...	7	Prowers	4 243	12 034	2 296	2.8	62.0	0.9	1.1	0.7	36.3	7.0	19.6	9.7	11.4	11.2	12.3
08 101	39380	3	Pueblo	6 180	161 875	393	26.2	54.3	2.2	1.3	1.2	42.3	6.1	17.4	9.7	12.3	11.7	12.9
08 103	...	9	Rio Blanco	8 342	6 707	2 703	0.8	85.5	1.5	2.1	1.1	12.0	7.0	17.7	11.3	13.4	10.9	13.0
08 105	...	7	Rio Grande	2 362	11 607	2 317	4.9	54.1	0.6	1.5	0.7	44.3	6.3	17.8	8.3	11.0	10.9	13.0
08 107	44460	7	Routt	6 118	23 865	1 646	3.9	91.3	0.7	0.8	1.3	7.0	4.8	14.8	8.0	14.6	14.8	15.2
08 109	...	9	Saguache	8 206	6 196	2 742	0.8	58.8	0.9	2.2	1.4	38.4	6.5	15.6	6.7	9.5	10.0	14.7
08 111	...	9	San Juan	1 004	720	3 126	0.7	82.9	0.4	1.4	1.0	15.5	2.9	12.6	6.1	12.9	13.7	15.2
08 113	...	9	San Miguel	3 332	7 840	2 606	2.4	88.7	0.7	1.1	1.5	9.4	5.1	14.3	5.6	16.7	16.4	16.2
08 115	...	9	Sedgwick	1 419	2 348	3 019	1.7	83.9	1.1	0.9	1.0	14.5	5.7	14.4	6.4	10.6	9.8	12.2
08 117	14720	7	Summit	1 576	29 404	1 443	18.7	83.5	1.1	0.6	1.4	14.3	4.9	11.8	8.2	20.0	16.2	14.5
08 119	17820	2	Teller	1 443	23 389	1 667	16.2	91.6	1.0	1.7	1.5	6.1	3.9	15.1	6.4	8.2	10.8	17.9
08 121	...	9	Washington	6 522	4 780	2 852	0.7	89.1	1.1	0.6	0.6	9.7	5.1	16.6	8.0	10.5	10.4	14.1
08 123	24540	3	Weld	10 327	277 670	243	26.9	68.6	1.3	1.1	1.9	28.3	7.3	19.7	10.3	14.1	13.5	12.9
08 125	...	7	Yuma	6 124	10 202	2 421	1.7	77.4	0.5	0.6	0.4	21.6	7.6	18.9	7.8	12.1	11.3	12.6
09 000	...	X	CONNECTICUT	12 542	3 596 677	X	286.8	71.0	10.6	0.6	4.8	14.6	5.3	16.5	9.6	12.2	12.4	15.5
09 001	14860	2	Fairfield	1 618	945 438	50	584.3	65.7	11.2	0.4	5.9	18.2	5.8	18.1	8.6	11.7	13.2	15.9
09 003	25540	1	Hartford	1 904	897 985	58	471.6	65.6	13.7	0.6	5.3	16.6	5.5	16.5	9.1	13.0	12.4	15.1
09 005	45860	4	Litchfield	2 384	184 993	348	77.6	91.5	1.9	0.6	2.2	5.2	4.3	15.7	7.3	9.7	11.7	17.2
09 007	25540	1	Middlesex	956	164 943	385	172.5	86.6	5.5	0.5	3.5	5.5	4.6	15.2	8.5	10.9	12.0	16.7
09 009	35300	2	New Haven	1 566	861 277	63	550.0	67.1	13.1	0.6	4.4	16.4	5.3	16.0	10.0	13.1	12.3	14.9
09 011	35980	2	New London	1 722	273 676	246	158.9	79.2	7.2	1.8	5.3	9.6	5.2	15.5	10.4	12.6	11.8	15.3

1. CBSA = Core Based Statistical Area. See Appendix A for explanation. See Appendix B for list of metropolitan areas with component counties. 2. County type code from the Economic Research Service of USDA Rural-Urban Continuum Codes. See Appendix A for definition. 3. Dry land or land partially or temporarily covered by water. 4. May be of any race.

STATE County	Population, 2013 (cont.): Age (percent) (cont.): 55 to 64 years	65 to 74 years	75 years and over	Percent female	Population change and components of change, 2000–2014: Total persons: 2000	2010	Percent change: 2000–2010	2010–2014	Components of change, 2010–2014: Births	Deaths	Net migration	Households, 2009–2013: Number	Persons per household	Percent: Family households	Female family householder[1]	One person
	16	17	18	19	20	21	22	23	24	25	26	27	28	29	30	31
COLORADO—Cont'd																
Boulder	12.6	7.0	4.7	49.8	269 814	294 567	NA	6.4	12 720	6 847	12 836	120 521	2.42	58.7	8.0	28.2
Broomfield	10.1	6.7	5.2	50.4	38 272	55 889	NA	11.2	2 997	1 392	4 602	22 016	2.59	66.7	8.2	26.8
Chaffee	17.8	13.2	8.8	47.0	16 242	17 809	9.6	3.1	579	660	632	7 832	2.15	65.4	7.9	29.7
Cheyenne	14.0	8.4	9.0	49.8	2 231	1 836	-17.7	1.9	126	79	-3	839	2.55	65.4	3.3	30.5
Clear Creek	21.2	11.9	5.0	48.3	9 322	9 088	-2.5	1.1	290	231	23	4 024	2.21	58.7	4.3	32.0
Conejos	13.5	9.7	7.3	50.2	8 400	8 256	-1.7	0.1	472	312	-171	3 099	2.64	71.6	13.1	27.1
Costilla	18.2	15.7	9.4	48.2	3 663	3 524	-3.8	1.2	126	134	67	1 361	2.61	60.3	9.5	37.9
Crowley	11.9	7.9	5.1	29.9	5 518	5 823	5.5	-8.0	155	139	-504	1 173	3.40	66.5	14.7	25.4
Custer	23.6	18.9	8.2	49.0	3 503	4 255	21.5	2.5	94	129	168	2 048	2.06	62.4	3.3	34.3
Delta	16.1	12.8	9.6	49.7	27 834	30 952	11.2	-3.5	1 381	1 471	-987	12 671	2.33	66.5	8.4	28.0
Denver	10.5	6.0	4.7	49.9	554 636	600 158	8.2	10.6	40 649	18 232	40 514	266 069	2.27	48.1	10.5	40.2
Dolores	16.3	12.7	8.6	48.5	1 844	2 064	11.9	-4.2	79	57	-124	780	2.19	64.0	8.8	33.2
Douglas	11.5	6.2	3.1	50.4	175 766	285 465	62.4	10.2	14 866	4 362	18 199	103 780	2.82	78.1	7.3	17.5
Eagle	12.2	5.7	1.8	46.9	41 659	52 197	25.3	1.4	2 831	411	-1 724	17 966	2.90	63.0	6.7	24.0
Elbert	18.0	9.2	3.9	49.9	19 872	23 086	16.2	4.8	703	495	844	8 240	2.81	77.3	4.2	18.9
El Paso	11.3	6.6	4.5	49.7	516 929	622 263	20.4	6.6	39 074	16 590	18 448	237 039	2.60	67.8	11.2	26.3
Fremont	14.7	11.4	8.3	42.4	46 145	46 824	1.5	-0.7	1 555	2 227	302	16 938	2.10	64.9	9.5	29.1
Garfield	12.7	6.3	3.8	48.8	43 791	56 389	28.8	1.9	3 488	1 220	-1 237	20 163	2.76	70.2	9.9	24.2
Gilpin	20.9	9.8	3.2	47.3	4 757	5 441	14.4	7.5	185	90	309	2 504	2.16	57.1	6.0	33.3
Grand	19.1	9.5	3.7	46.9	12 442	14 843	19.3	-2.0	481	214	-586	5 227	2.72	63.3	5.2	30.4
Gunnison	13.1	7.6	3.3	45.9	13 956	15 324	9.8	2.6	630	275	35	6 293	2.27	54.1	6.4	31.7
Hinsdale	19.4	15.7	7.0	49.2	790	843	6.7	-6.8	39	17	-83	388	2.06	65.5	1.5	28.9
Huerfano	19.3	17.0	11.6	49.9	7 862	6 711	-14.6	-3.7	213	394	-64	3 059	2.00	60.0	8.0	34.9
Jackson	17.6	12.4	8.5	45.9	1 577	1 394	-11.6	0.1	42	38	-8	648	2.08	60.2	5.4	36.1
Jefferson	14.8	8.4	5.8	50.3	525 507	534 543	NA	4.5	23 995	16 791	16 505	219 562	2.42	65.3	9.9	27.8
Kiowa	16.1	11.3	11.9	50.7	1 622	1 398	-13.8	0.3	58	73	3	559	2.49	69.1	7.2	29.3
Kit Carson	13.0	8.8	8.3	44.9	8 011	8 270	3.2	-2.4	386	314	-264	3 046	2.43	66.9	7.6	32.2
Lake	14.2	6.8	3.7	46.6	7 812	7 310	-6.4	0.6	361	143	-178	3 079	2.33	55.7	9.7	39.2
La Plata	15.6	8.6	5.0	49.2	43 941	51 334	16.8	5.2	2 263	1 298	1 666	20 947	2.39	62.5	9.2	27.2
Larimer	13.0	8.0	5.5	50.3	251 494	299 630	19.1	8.2	14 376	8 162	17 677	121 423	2.45	63.3	8.2	25.1
Las Animas	16.3	12.6	8.4	48.4	15 207	15 507	2.0	-9.4	623	701	-1 386	5 992	2.43	65.6	10.9	29.8
Lincoln	12.0	8.6	9.0	41.1	6 087	5 467	-10.2	0.7	243	198	-5	1 845	2.11	63.0	9.4	34.6
Logan	13.0	7.9	7.7	43.1	20 504	22 709	10.8	-0.8	981	814	-371	8 015	2.68	64.2	11.6	32.1
Mesa	13.7	9.0	7.3	50.3	116 255	146 723	26.2	1.0	7 884	5 718	-710	58 598	2.45	67.0	10.2	26.4
Mineral	23.6	15.7	8.6	49.2	831	712	-14.3	-2.0	22	16	-17	393	1.85	60.1	0.8	38.9
Moffat	14.8	7.6	4.8	48.2	13 184	13 795	4.6	-6.3	771	392	-1 278	5 062	2.61	65.6	5.7	29.3
Montezuma	16.3	10.9	7.6	50.2	23 830	25 535	7.2	0.9	1 289	1 118	108	10 688	2.36	67.6	11.3	27.2
Montrose	14.7	11.6	8.9	50.8	33 432	41 276	23.5	-1.0	1 909	1 677	-638	16 586	2.44	68.7	8.3	26.3
Morgan	11.7	7.8	7.4	50.2	27 171	28 159	3.6	0.6	1 844	1 031	-717	10 446	2.65	72.1	14.6	24.1
Otero	13.7	9.8	9.0	50.7	20 311	18 831	-7.3	-1.8	999	949	-387	7 427	2.45	65.1	11.9	30.3
Ouray	22.0	16.9	6.5	51.4	3 742	4 436	18.5	4.4	133	117	161	1 943	2.30	67.6	2.9	22.5
Park	22.8	11.4	3.6	47.4	14 523	16 206	11.6	0.9	463	315	61	7 038	2.27	67.2	5.3	26.6
Phillips	13.8	9.2	11.6	50.5	4 480	4 442	-0.8	-1.8	210	209	-74	1 668	2.59	69.7	6.1	27.6
Pitkin	16.9	10.4	4.3	47.1	14 872	17 148	15.3	2.8	570	186	122	7 507	2.27	52.4	4.2	35.5
Prowers	13.4	8.6	6.7	50.1	14 483	12 551	-13.3	-4.1	693	480	-707	4 935	2.45	66.4	11.4	30.1
Pueblo	13.4	9.1	7.5	50.8	141 472	159 063	12.4	1.8	8 081	6 902	1 664	62 439	2.49	64.1	13.7	30.6
Rio Blanco	13.4	7.7	5.7	47.6	5 986	6 666	11.4	0.6	359	196	-128	2 638	2.24	66.6	4.9	29.9
Rio Grande	14.8	10.4	7.4	50.1	12 413	11 982	-3.5	-3.1	603	485	-494	4 722	2.46	66.6	9.6	27.0
Routt	16.4	8.1	3.2	47.3	19 690	23 509	19.4	1.5	899	398	-182	9 647	2.38	63.4	7.0	26.2
Saguache	19.3	12.1	5.6	49.5	5 917	6 108	3.2	1.4	295	127	-71	2 692	2.29	59.2	9.9	35.8
San Juan	18.8	13.9	4.0	42.3	558	699	25.3	3.0	16	15	17	321	2.05	45.8	8.4	46.4
San Miguel	15.9	7.4	2.4	46.4	6 594	7 359	11.6	6.5	299	94	270	3 234	2.31	52.6	4.9	33.8
Sedgwick	16.9	11.9	12.2	49.7	2 747	2 379	-13.4	-1.3	108	135	0	943	2.47	64.9	9.0	30.1
Summit	14.2	7.9	2.3	45.5	23 548	27 994	18.9	5.0	1 187	211	438	11 138	2.48	56.6	5.4	28.0
Teller	21.3	12.1	4.4	49.0	20 555	23 350	13.6	0.2	776	587	-131	9 434	2.44	70.3	7.8	25.7
Washington	15.1	10.7	9.7	48.5	4 926	4 814	-2.3	-0.7	172	189	-27	2 019	2.27	69.7	6.7	27.1
Weld	11.3	6.6	4.3	49.7	180 926	252 825	NA	9.8	16 389	6 371	14 339	90 465	2.79	71.8	10.3	22.1
Yuma	12.4	9.1	8.2	49.9	9 841	10 043	2.1	1.6	632	414	-111	3 811	2.61	61.2	6.3	34.6
CONNECTICUT	13.3	8.2	7.0	51.2	3 405 565	3 574 097	4.9	0.6	156 554	124 313	-5 861	1 355 849	2.55	66.6	13.0	27.6
Fairfield	12.5	7.6	6.6	51.3	882 567	916 829	3.9	3.1	43 273	27 599	13 990	332 655	2.73	69.2	11.9	25.7
Hartford	13.1	8.1	7.3	51.5	857 183	894 014	4.3	0.4	40 515	33 203	2 382	347 874	2.40	65.0	14.9	20.0
Litchfield	16.2	10.1	7.7	50.7	182 193	189 927	4.2	-2.6	6 278	7 357	-3 658	75 755	2.45	67.3	9.1	27.3
Middlesex	15.0	9.6	7.6	51.2	155 071	165 676	6.8	-0.4	6 156	6 084	-545	66 141	2.41	66.3	9.1	27.6
New Haven	13.1	8.2	7.1	51.7	824 008	862 477	4.7	-0.1	38 580	32 109	-6 836	328 013	2.54	65.1	14.9	29.1
New London	13.7	8.7	6.9	50.0	259 088	274 055	5.8	-0.1	11 799	9 737	-2 139	107 066	2.44	65.7	11.5	27.7

1. No spouse present.

STATE County	Persons in group quarters, 2014	Daytime population, 2009–2013: Number	Daytime population, 2009–2013: Employment/residence ratio	Births, 2014: Total	Births, 2014: Rate[1]	Deaths, 2014: Number	Deaths, 2014: Rate[1]	Persons under 65 with no health insurance, 2013: Number	Persons under 65 with no health insurance, 2013: Percent	Medicare, 2014: Eligible for Medicare	Medicare, 2014: Enrolled in Medicare Advantage	Medicare, 2014: Enrolled in a Medicare prescription drug plan	Serious crimes known to police,[2] 2013: Total: Number	Serious crimes known to police,[2] 2013: Total: Rate[3]
	32	33	34	35	36	37	38	39	40	41	42	43	44	45
COLORADO—Cont'd														
Boulder	10 468	328 873	1.18	3 028	9.7	1 725	5.5	36 902	13.9	42 139	15 392	15 397	6 763	2 742
Broomfield	282	61 758	1.16	737	11.9	337	5.4	5 499	10.5	8 195	4 023	2 157	1 241	2 088
Chaffee	1 363	18 238	1.02	129	7.0	146	8.0	2 365	18.1	4 632	789	2 360	329	1 790
Cheyenne	42	2 410	1.19	34	18.2	16	8.6	383	24.9	324	15	193	9	474
Clear Creek	84	7 704	0.73	61	6.6	53	5.8	936	12.6	1 569	526	524	164	1 810
Conejos	36	7 161	0.65	111	13.4	62	7.5	1 371	20.1	1 713	519	924	38	456
Costilla	0	3 270	0.77	26	7.3	23	6.4	788	29.9	1 059	291	526	16	440
Crowley	2 264	5 688	1.05	37	6.9	29	5.4	455	19.1	780	102	431	7	133
Custer	151	3 945	0.80	20	4.6	33	7.6	663	22.3	1 334	222	601	54	1 265
Delta	552	29 096	0.87	316	10.6	359	12.0	5 006	21.7	7 832	1 917	3 431	579	1 900
Denver	16 157	767 669	1.46	10 051	15.1	4 630	7.0	103 341	18.2	82 916	40 317	24 349	28 089	4 328
Dolores	0	1 620	0.86	21	10.6	6	3.0	385	24.1	491	55	243	9	453
Douglas	612	249 681	0.71	3 462	11.0	1 108	3.5	21 565	7.8	33 449	13 296	10 734	3 289	1 082
Eagle	74	51 670	0.98	640	12.1	103	1.9	10 830	22.4	4 374	296	2 481	950	1 822
Elbert	73	16 539	0.42	167	6.9	118	4.9	2 746	13.4	3 479	987	1 217	23	100
El Paso	18 564	633 683	1.00	9 305	14.0	4 178	6.3	75 427	13.4	89 274	26 019	26 532	24 193	3 714
Fremont	8 390	46 512	0.98	339	7.3	530	11.4	4 960	16.9	10 819	3 101	4 433	947	2 012
Garfield	858	55 365	0.95	806	14.0	310	5.4	12 031	23.7	6 797	730	3 653	1 239	2 151
Gilpin	49	7 799	1.77	43	7.3	20	3.4	469	9.7	774	285	212	299	5 401
Grand	223	14 331	0.98	116	8.0	47	3.2	2 295	18.6	2 052	234	1 038	NA	NA
Gunnison	933	16 313	1.10	141	9.0	57	3.6	3 076	23.6	1 962	106	1 141	282	1 807
Hinsdale	56	801	0.98	15	19.1	6	7.6	116	18.4	207	16	111	6	746
Huerfano	165	6 574	0.98	47	7.3	85	13.2	961	20.7	2 115	353	1 156	146	2 205
Jackson	2	1 480	1.15	9	6.4	8	5.7	251	23.2	319	NA	189	10	744
Jefferson	8 001	492 846	0.83	5 801	10.4	4 118	7.4	60 010	12.9	91 308	48 478	20 141	16 688	3 025
Kiowa	14	1 440	1.03	12	8.6	14	10.0	217	19.9	319	NA	234	3	204
Kit Carson	822	8 417	1.06	88	10.9	74	9.2	1 411	23.8	1 437	53	1 004	160	1 977
Lake	140	6 345	0.74	84	11.4	24	3.3	1 619	25.2	857	67	456	82	1 107
La Plata	1 941	52 892	1.03	541	10.0	328	6.1	8 174	18.4	8 476	871	4 522	786	1 554
Larimer	8 637	298 569	0.95	3 447	10.6	1 965	6.1	37 675	14.1	50 304	13 470	23 275	7 452	2 359
Las Animas	795	15 239	1.02	135	9.6	156	11.1	1 987	18.4	3 599	595	1 859	141	947
Lincoln	1 030	5 843	1.23	53	9.6	40	7.3	636	18.2	950	46	605	37	675
Logan	3 898	22 254	0.97	245	10.9	204	9.1	2 909	19.2	3 839	421	2 512	623	2 741
Mesa	4 494	145 058	0.96	1 825	12.3	1 356	9.1	21 117	17.5	28 383	10 319	10 965	4 294	2 891
Mineral	0	811	1.14	6	8.6	3	4.3	89	16.4	227	25	142	1	140
Moffat	102	12 700	0.89	179	13.8	76	5.9	2 028	17.8	1 936	129	1 073	266	2 033
Montezuma	237	24 689	0.92	305	11.8	267	10.4	4 785	22.9	5 529	620	2 973	522	2 042
Montrose	542	39 591	0.92	439	10.7	388	9.5	7 246	22.5	9 406	2 087	4 441	839	2 055
Morgan	564	28 660	1.03	429	15.1	220	7.8	4 846	20.5	4 574	387	2 854	621	2 303
Otero	459	18 742	0.99	219	11.8	211	11.4	2 710	18.3	4 294	670	2 462	433	2 363
Ouray	0	4 446	0.99	31	6.7	29	6.3	722	20.7	1 084	155	604	NA	NA
Park	92	11 216	0.42	112	6.9	81	5.0	2 406	17.7	2 836	719	1 018	86	536
Phillips	60	4 411	1.01	48	11.0	53	12.1	779	22.7	889	16	656	25	573
Pitkin	72	24 097	1.70	119	6.8	33	1.9	2 682	18.2	2 487	98	1 617	412	2 367
Prowers	343	12 309	0.97	160	13.3	104	8.6	2 262	22.3	2 269	56	1 604	323	2 602
Pueblo	4 556	158 490	0.98	1 908	11.8	1 638	10.1	20 197	15.4	33 645	11 294	14 136	9 903	6 102
Rio Blanco	301	7 112	1.11	80	11.9	37	5.5	947	16.7	987	162	521	70	1 004
Rio Grande	198	11 496	0.92	140	12.1	116	10.0	2 034	21.1	2 749	713	1 549	244	2 034
Routt	286	24 488	1.08	196	8.2	102	4.3	3 249	15.8	2 997	245	1 762	352	1 502
Saguache	18	5 730	0.83	60	9.7	42	6.8	1 537	30.2	1 061	187	504	111	1 733
San Juan	0	693	1.09	4	5.6	0	0.0	130	22.8	136	15	66	14	2 035
San Miguel	9	8 463	1.22	71	9.1	23	2.9	1 581	22.9	800	74	415	151	1 960
Sedgwick	35	2 268	0.89	23	9.8	20	8.5	369	20.7	614	28	398	14	583
Summit	274	29 611	1.09	271	9.2	59	2.0	5 429	21.2	2 840	267	1 551	831	2 944
Teller	132	20 754	0.77	171	7.3	145	6.2	2 868	14.9	4 900	1 558	1 611	381	1 622
Washington	184	4 202	0.72	41	8.6	47	9.8	673	18.4	941	20	631	101	2 111
Weld	5 778	236 223	0.81	3 980	14.3	1 546	5.6	40 203	17.1	34 980	10 501	15 392	5 913	2 255
Yuma	213	10 423	1.07	151	14.8	85	8.3	1 904	23.0	1 821	34	1 389	71	695
CONNECTICUT	118 226	3 570 703	0.99	36 499	10.1	29 579	8.2	323 606	10.9	623 712	152 344	293 221	80 430	2 237
Fairfield	19 745	948 316	1.05	10 087	10.7	6 579	7.0	105 291	13.3	144 985	31 114	72 687	17 212	1 869
Hartford	27 887	968 504	1.17	9 501	10.6	7 912	8.8	76 285	10.3	160 676	45 152	73 223	22 782	2 604
Litchfield	2 685	160 278	0.71	1 436	7.8	1 771	9.6	14 926	9.8	37 966	7 439	19 369	NA	NA
Middlesex	4 924	150 998	0.83	1 423	8.6	1 419	8.6	10 985	8.2	32 130	7 599	15 060	NA	NA
New Haven	29 800	838 082	0.94	8 974	10.4	7 625	8.9	75 876	10.7	152 836	41 574	66 286	26 013	3 216
New London	12 755	276 702	1.02	2 761	10.1	2 361	8.6	20 276	9.2	50 329	8 718	24 463	NA	NA

1. Per 1,000 estimated resident population. 2. Data for serious crimes have not been adjusted for underreporting; this may affect comparability between geographic areas and over time.
3. Per 100,000 population estimated by the FBI.

STATE County	Serious crimes known to police, 2013 (cont.)[1]		Education						Money income, 2009–2013				Income and poverty, 2013			
	Rate[2]		School enrollment and attainment, 2009–2013				Local government expenditures,[5] 2012–2013			Households				Percent below poverty level		
			Enrollment[3]		Attainment[4] (percent)											
	Violent	Property	Total	Percent private	High school graduate or less	Bachelor's degree or more	Total current spending (mil dol)	Current spending per student (dollars)	Per capita income[6] (dollars)	Median income (dollars)	Mean income (dollars)	Percent with income of $200,000 or more	Median household income (dollars)	All persons	Children under 18 years	Children 5 to 17 years in families
	46	47	48	49	50	51	52	53	54	55	56	57	58	59	60	61
COLORADO—Cont'd																
Boulder	219	2 523	94 472	12.5	18.5	58.3	[7]521.1	[7]8 769	38 011	67 956	93 225	8.8	71 405	13.5	12.8	11.9
Broomfield	56	2 033	16 998	17.3	21.2	47.5	[7]	[7]	37 442	77 998	95 619	7.1	79 117	6.4	7.0	6.8
Chaffee	109	1 681	2 974	12.4	36.9	33.9	21.0	9 786	27 182	46 504	60 923	2.0	48 012	13.0	19.3	18.6
Cheyenne	53	421	482	9.8	44.3	21.3	4.9	15 665	23 647	51 641	59 073	0.7	50 379	13.1	20.3	21.1
Clear Creek	397	1 413	1 749	19.3	26.8	39.8	10.4	10 869	41 716	67 259	93 639	6.1	63 489	9.1	13.5	12.4
Conejos	84	372	2 246	3.4	52.3	19.1	15.0	9 394	17 316	34 526	44 584	0.2	34 923	22.9	30.4	28.0
Costilla	82	357	745	1.7	52.4	19.5	5.8	12 539	20 742	29 145	49 197	1.8	28 233	26.0	37.8	34.0
Crowley	95	38	1 091	13.7	58.7	12.3	4.4	9 930	17 187	31 477	42 893	2.6	31 477	43.2	38.5	36.9
Custer	141	1 125	701	14.0	32.4	32.7	3.9	9 309	25 761	32 427	52 620	2.7	47 268	14.4	29.7	26.2
Delta	108	1 792	6 262	10.7	48.8	18.3	41.7	7 796	24 771	42 078	58 899	3.1	41 730	15.1	21.5	20.1
Denver	631	3 697	150 270	20.9	33.1	42.9	881.5	10 572	33 251	50 313	74 746	5.8	51 156	18.7	28.7	29.2
Dolores	50	403	316	1.9	48.3	18.4	3.0	10 399	22 880	37 750	49 240	1.4	42 416	14.0	18.3	16.8
Douglas	76	1 006	89 294	16.8	15.9	55.8	505.8	7 824	43 634	101 591	121 999	13.2	105 192	3.6	3.8	3.4
Eagle	140	1 682	12 347	16.4	29.9	47.0	62.3	9 717	39 497	74 456	106 458	9.2	78 517	9.5	13.6	12.4
Elbert	13	87	5 999	13.4	31.6	29.6	28.5	7 917	36 077	82 118	99 457	8.0	80 972	6.7	9.1	7.6
El Paso	370	3 345	185 665	13.5	27.8	35.2	907.8	8 136	28 867	57 125	74 750	4.1	57 072	11.4	13.8	12.4
Fremont	242	1 770	8 191	16.4	52.5	15.6	43.4	8 061	18 954	39 943	51 391	1.4	41 412	19.7	31.2	30.0
Garfield	215	1 936	14 829	12.1	40.3	26.6	97.2	8 606	26 603	57 022	71 727	3.0	57 364	12.4	16.4	16.6
Gilpin	253	5 148	1 064	5.6	27.6	29.1	4.8	12 788	38 022	63 885	80 095	5.2	64 962	8.1	10.3	7.2
Grand	NA	NA	2 829	13.3	33.0	32.8	17.4	10 368	31 684	64 664	75 959	3.4	57 312	11.0	16.4	15.1
Gunnison	122	1 686	4 815	12.0	21.7	54.5	15.7	8 483	27 654	52 332	65 678	3.4	48 391	13.7	18.1	16.6
Hinsdale	124	622	82	41.5	23.8	42.2	1.5	17 963	36 365	56 667	75 014	3.6	52 188	10.6	31.2	28.2
Huerfano	498	1 707	1 091	14.6	41.8	28.0	7.6	10 143	24 058	33 298	51 126	2.4	32 418	22.8	40.2	36.9
Jackson	149	595	313	4.2	48.2	22.2	2.6	12 515	25 936	43 606	53 039	0.8	43 549	15.7	26.2	23.2
Jefferson	209	2 816	135 043	14.2	27.7	40.7	728.8	8 520	36 087	68 984	87 315	6.2	68 161	9.1	12.6	12.0
Kiowa	0	204	395	9.1	36.1	20.6	3.3	12 588	22 482	40 813	54 779	2.1	42 378	12.9	20.2	20.5
Kit Carson	272	1 705	1 752	12.1	48.9	13.5	13.6	9 442	21 850	44 157	54 491	1.1	39 633	15.1	19.5	18.6
Lake	310	796	1 853	7.2	41.1	28.1	15.0	12 853	25 029	44 610	56 657	0.9	47 547	14.7	26.8	25.2
La Plata	172	1 382	13 301	12.0	25.2	41.4	68.6	10 229	30 151	58 080	72 066	3.7	58 675	12.4	14.6	13.6
Larimer	203	2 156	91 942	9.6	24.2	43.8	379.0	8 405	30 740	58 626	75 962	4.4	59 337	13.8	12.7	12.2
Las Animas	94	853	3 505	7.8	46.0	16.3	21.6	9 062	22 180	42 261	53 022	1.0	38 547	18.0	25.3	24.3
Lincoln	146	529	912	11.1	59.0	15.6	13.0	17 489	19 703	41 910	57 565	2.2	41 510	19.1	24.5	24.9
Logan	158	2 583	5 311	5.8	45.9	15.8	27.5	9 077	22 581	40 415	55 757	2.7	43 561	16.9	19.0	18.0
Mesa	312	2 578	37 092	11.5	40.4	25.7	174.7	7 802	26 700	49 471	66 456	2.8	48 108	15.4	19.3	19.3
Mineral	140	0	50	22.0	28.3	39.3	1.6	20 885	42 255	47 083	78 223	3.1	50 286	9.9	14.0	14.8
Moffat	138	1 895	3 499	6.9	48.5	15.6	19.5	8 561	24 577	53 231	62 411	0.4	58 890	11.5	16.4	14.5
Montezuma	184	1 859	5 534	8.3	39.2	27.3	32.0	8 142	23 548	43 188	55 701	2.1	43 655	19.1	30.2	27.4
Montrose	179	1 876	9 427	15.7	45.9	24.5	51.8	8 002	22 897	45 718	56 020	1.6	43 946	15.1	23.3	21.7
Morgan	204	2 099	7 448	3.8	51.8	15.1	44.3	8 105	20 680	43 774	55 018	2.0	46 332	13.5	20.4	19.3
Otero	131	2 232	4 934	5.5	46.9	15.5	32.7	10 103	19 078	33 848	46 294	0.6	36 811	22.5	35.1	34.3
Ouray	NA	NA	766	13.7	22.2	47.5	7.6	14 531	33 015	64 601	74 762	4.0	58 137	9.8	16.6	14.7
Park	100	436	3 041	9.1	29.3	32.0	15.7	9 416	31 504	61 570	70 976	2.2	57 510	10.3	15.9	13.9
Phillips	183	390	1 026	12.5	49.2	16.8	12.0	12 473	20 720	43 011	52 131	1.4	46 805	12.4	17.3	16.4
Pitkin	80	2 286	3 290	22.0	13.7	56.8	24.3	14 046	51 814	72 745	111 601	10.3	71 012	7.3	8.9	8.1
Prowers	121	2 481	3 400	2.4	49.3	14.1	21.0	8 660	18 941	34 391	47 783	0.8	38 830	21.7	31.0	29.0
Pueblo	651	5 451	42 569	9.2	41.8	21.5	210.6	7 852	21 940	41 777	54 290	1.3	41 352	20.1	27.4	24.4
Rio Blanco	72	932	1 621	13.6	42.8	23.1	13.1	10 430	27 586	60 128	71 206	2.3	59 364	10.7	11.7	11.2
Rio Grande	150	1 884	2 953	9.0	47.1	20.3	17.2	8 351	20 557	38 993	50 543	1.7	39 834	17.9	28.9	28.1
Routt	183	1 319	4 881	13.1	22.0	48.0	36.9	11 744	34 873	62 002	81 406	4.6	63 763	8.9	12.1	10.9
Saguache	265	1 468	1 421	3.6	47.5	23.8	12.2	12 751	20 726	34 600	47 297	1.5	35 310	29.4	43.0	39.3
San Juan	436	1 599	58	0.0	35.9	24.8	1.6	25 129	24 711	39 583	46 770	0.0	41 683	15.7	27.2	23.5
San Miguel	78	1 882	1 254	16.8	22.6	53.5	12.6	11 673	40 827	63 594	94 314	8.3	53 674	11.9	18.0	17.0
Sedgwick	42	541	508	3.7	48.0	15.0	8.5	6 725	21 536	40 221	51 523	1.3	39 980	14.5	22.9	22.8
Summit	220	2 725	5 003	10.7	20.6	47.7	33.1	10 477	34 025	63 697	81 097	5.0	63 236	9.3	13.1	11.8
Teller	111	1 511	4 753	11.5	31.2	31.6	27.1	9 054	31 075	59 040	73 321	2.2	62 725	8.4	15.1	13.5
Washington	105	2 007	1 119	9.5	46.2	18.5	11.1	12 710	24 977	44 683	58 823	2.5	45 572	14.0	19.9	17.8
Weld	299	1 956	75 434	9.0	40.8	25.9	325.5	8 426	25 468	57 180	70 978	3.2	58 404	13.2	16.6	14.9
Yuma	29	666	2 496	6.7	45.9	17.7	17.6	9 658	22 498	44 308	56 592	1.5	45 487	13.0	18.9	17.9
CONNECTICUT	263	1 974	951 377	20.7	38.6	36.5	8 888.7	16 631	37 892	69 461	97 650	9.1	67 262	10.7	14.5	13.3
Fairfield	245	1 623	251 802	24.4	33.7	44.8	2 503.2	17 442	48 721	82 283	132 661	17.0	81 816	9.6	11.9	11.1
Hartford	289	2 314	237 957	17.8	39.5	34.9	2 281.9	17 118	34 698	64 967	87 148	7.1	63 491	12.1	17.4	16.6
Litchfield	NA	NA	43 669	18.5	38.2	33.4	424.0	17 647	37 667	71 338	92 137	6.6	70 519	7.2	9.2	8.0
Middlesex	NA	NA	41 279	22.6	34.6	39.1	380.6	17 229	39 992	76 994	98 414	8.6	75 335	7.3	7.6	6.9
New Haven	392	2 824	229 093	24.2	42.2	32.9	2 073.6	16 895	32 523	61 996	82 562	6.1	58 672	12.8	17.7	16.1
New London	NA	NA	67 539	18.3	40.4	31.3	618.5	17 545	33 782	66 583	84 806	5.4	62 638	9.4	13.4	11.6

1. Data for serious crimes have not been adjusted for underreporting; this may affect comparability between geographic areas and over time. 2. Per 100,000 population estimated by the FBI.
3. All persons 3 years old and over enrolled in nursery school through college. 4. Persons 25 years old and over. 5. Elementary and secondary education expenditures.
6. Based on population estimated by the American Community Survey, 2009–2013. 7. Broomfield county is included with Boulder county.

STATE County	Personal income, 2013: Total (mil dol)	Personal income, 2013: Percent change, 2012–2013	Per capita[1]: Dollars	Per capita[1]: Rank	Wages and salaries (mil dol)	Supplements to wages and salaries; employer contributions (mil dol): Pension and insurance	Supplements to wages and salaries; employer contributions (mil dol): Government social insurance	Proprietors' income (mil dol)	Dividends, interest, and rent (mil dol)	Personal transfer receipts (mil dol)	Earnings, 2013: Total (mil dol)	Contributions for government social insurance (mil dol): From employee and self-employed	Contributions for government social insurance (mil dol): From employer
	62	63	64	65	66	67	68	69	70	71	72	73	74
COLORADO—Cont'd													
Boulder	17 043	2.4	54 968	203	10 261	1 347	707	1 441	4 452	1 517	13 756	743	707
Broomfield	2 906	5.3	48 867	424	2 567	287	169	294	672	282	3 317	191	169
Chaffee	664	3.5	35 862	1 767	238	42	16	43	217	147	339	20	16
Cheyenne	108	2.2	57 131	154	32	6	2	34	29	12	74	2	2
Clear Creek	542	2.1	59 970	106	163	22	11	113	109	52	310	16	11
Conejos	221	2.6	26 753	2 989	48	10	3	20	40	71	81	5	3
Costilla	115	6.7	32 714	2 302	25	5	2	12	20	39	43	2	2
Crowley	108	1.0	20 244	3 110	42	8	2	11	20	33	63	3	2
Custer	162	2.6	37 894	1 447	27	5	2	19	56	39	53	4	2
Delta	1 057	1.8	34 681	1 956	319	57	22	122	232	251	520	32	22
Denver	36 999	3.1	56 967	158	29 011	3 781	2 018	7 874	6 686	4 033	42 685	2 264	2 018
Dolores	65	8.4	32 107	2 404	20	3	2	3	15	16	29	2	2
Douglas	23 176	3.5	75 747	28	6 215	717	430	494	3 177	1 218	7 855	453	430
Eagle	2 645	3.5	50 416	348	1 297	142	101	344	756	163	1 883	100	101
Elbert	1 154	2.1	48 645	440	140	22	11	36	186	122	208	14	11
El Paso	26 941	1.7	41 128	1 037	13 967	2 522	1 115	1 229	5 946	4 310	18 833	976	1 115
Fremont	1 388	1.5	29 884	2 705	508	108	35	66	296	393	717	43	35
Garfield	2 359	2.3	41 171	1 029	1 207	174	89	215	545	275	1 686	89	89
Gilpin	250	3.3	44 584	722	229	19	17	20	43	27	285	16	17
Grand	612	5.2	42 858	858	234	36	18	80	161	70	368	19	18
Gunnison	575	1.6	37 098	1 564	297	49	21	41	191	68	407	21	21
Hinsdale	39	3.7	48 322	463	7	2	1	2	20	6	12	1	1
Huerfano	217	2.8	33 264	2 214	55	11	4	11	58	84	82	6	4
Jackson	66	5.3	48 540	448	19	4	1	16	18	9	40	1	1
Jefferson	26 077	2.3	47 259	532	11 538	1 679	844	1 184	5 797	3 446	15 245	885	844
Kiowa	85	13.9	59 765	110	21	4	1	31	19	12	58	1	1
Kit Carson	356	2.4	44 345	736	107	18	7	120	67	53	253	9	7
Lake	248	1.1	33 995	2 082	81	15	6	10	49	38	112	6	6
La Plata	2 485	2.7	46 633	574	1 124	161	79	335	680	285	1 699	89	79
Larimer	13 545	3.9	42 866	856	6 500	1 005	454	848	3 105	1 805	8 808	475	454
Las Animas	527	1.9	36 500	1 663	217	38	16	26	104	161	298	18	16
Lincoln	173	-7.2	31 875	2 426	80	16	5	8	47	37	109	5	5
Logan	900	1.0	40 106	1 161	323	58	23	226	167	152	630	29	23
Mesa	5 492	1.0	37 222	1 544	2 551	384	193	395	1 222	1 048	3 524	209	193
Mineral	40	2.5	55 859	190	16	2	1	2	18	6	22	1	1
Moffat	589	2.2	44 956	692	239	43	17	91	85	86	390	20	17
Montezuma	937	2.6	36 524	1 659	330	61	23	54	218	202	468	27	23
Montrose	1 333	2.7	32 750	2 290	531	92	39	147	318	314	809	48	39
Morgan	1 052	3.7	37 041	1 574	483	84	36	148	167	193	751	37	36
Otero	637	4.8	34 033	2 073	230	43	18	53	114	203	344	20	18
Ouray	212	4.7	46 496	589	60	9	4	18	77	32	91	5	4
Park	607	2.6	37 635	1 483	81	15	6	36	137	95	137	9	6
Phillips	186	0.0	42 618	880	61	12	4	41	43	34	118	5	4
Pitkin	1 450	2.1	83 425	15	773	80	57	193	616	80	1 104	58	57
Prowers	463	2.2	37 668	1 477	161	30	11	84	103	105	285	13	11
Pueblo	5 427	1.7	33 616	2 160	2 366	390	179	317	987	1 492	3 253	195	179
Rio Blanco	292	2.4	42 931	851	171	29	12	36	53	40	248	12	12
Rio Grande	476	4.5	40 294	1 138	140	26	11	93	104	117	270	14	11
Routt	1 396	4.8	59 384	116	655	84	50	175	482	101	964	51	50
Saguache	188	5.4	30 281	2 645	62	11	5	30	38	40	107	4	5
San Juan	24	1.0	34 922	1 911	7	1	1	2	8	4	11	1	1
San Miguel	376	3.6	49 006	415	182	24	14	54	129	25	274	14	14
Sedgwick	129	0.7	54 615	213	30	6	2	40	22	23	78	2	2
Summit	1 414	4.4	49 369	397	697	84	52	126	524	96	960	51	52
Teller	1 040	0.7	44 680	716	257	38	18	41	216	174	354	23	18
Washington	193	-1.9	40 159	1 157	48	10	3	43	37	33	105	4	3
Weld	9 009	5.0	33 393	2 193	4 284	626	313	937	1 560	1 456	6 161	330	313
Yuma	530	1.7	52 188	296	169	27	11	190	93	73	398	12	11
CONNECTICUT	218 132	0.8	60 658	X	105 366	15 923	7 341	21 680	47 996	29 736	150 310	8 196	7 341
Fairfield	77 080	1.0	82 009	20	36 272	4 499	2 199	10 591	19 037	7 024	53 561	2 902	2 199
Hartford	50 164	1.0	55 845	191	32 744	4 938	2 354	4 525	9 938	7 957	44 561	2 412	2 354
Litchfield	10 609	0.9	56 757	166	2 729	496	219	965	2 546	1 417	4 408	256	219
Middlesex	9 503	0.4	57 400	150	3 524	620	267	750	2 085	1 220	5 160	286	267
New Haven	44 568	0.9	51 685	309	19 824	3 191	1 540	3 339	8 678	7 916	27 894	1 555	1 540
New London	13 796	0.2	50 322	353	6 763	1 370	501	781	3 402	2 260	9 415	492	501

1. Based on the resident population estimated as of July 1 of the year shown.

STATE County	Earnings, 2013 (cont.) — Percent by selected industries — Farm	Mining	Construction	Manu-facturing	Infor-mation: professional, scientific, technical services	Retail trade	Finance, insur-ance, real estate and leasing	Health care and social assistance	Govern-ment	Social Security beneficiaries, December 2013 — Number	Rate[1]	Supple-mental Security Income recipients, December 2013	Housing units, 2014 — Total	Percent change, 2010–2014
	75	76	77	78	79	80	81	82	83	84	85	86	87	88
COLORADO—Cont'd														
Boulder	0.0	0.4	3.8	12.3	31.0	4.9	5.4	9.4	14.9	40 405	130	2 526	130 938	3.0
Broomfield	0.0	D	3.9	17.1	38.0	4.9	4.7	3.4	2.5	7 855	130	374	25 900	14.4
Chaffee	0.4	1.7	12.0	2.7	D	10.7	6.9	6.8	28.3	4 725	258	227	10 319	3.0
Cheyenne	35.7	16.2	D	D	D	3.4	D	D	16.0	310	163	9	970	-0.5
Clear Creek	0.0	D	9.7	D	D	3.4	D	D	12.4	1 620	178	83	5 690	0.1
Conejos	7.1	D	10.4	1.6	D	9.3	D	11.0	31.0	1 810	219	362	4 293	0.2
Costilla	30.2	D	D	D	D	D	D	4.1	29.1	1 130	319	230	2 686	2.8
Crowley	16.8	0.0	D	0.1	0.8	4.7	D	D	45.1	855	160	142	1 547	-0.8
Custer	5.4	0.8	26.2	4.4	8.8	9.6	3.7	D	19.3	1 350	316	46	4 167	5.3
Delta	2.1	24.5	5.2	4.9	3.8	7.9	3.4	8.2	23.5	8 205	271	492	14 485	-0.6
Denver	0.0	9.9	3.6	3.5	19.2	2.9	11.5	6.8	12.4	81 835	126	14 955	298 864	4.6
Dolores	3.7	D	34.5	D	D	6.5	D	D	28.4	545	269	22	1 450	-1.2
Douglas	0.0	1.9	6.1	2.1	26.9	7.3	11.1	8.1	8.8	32 985	108	1 017	113 777	6.5
Eagle	0.6	D	11.5	1.0	7.5	8.5	11.2	10.0	9.9	4 220	80	108	31 528	0.7
Elbert	-4.7	D	26.1	3.2	D	7.2	4.5	D	20.1	3 740	158	92	9 084	1.6
El Paso	0.0	0.3	5.0	4.6	16.3	6.4	6.2	9.0	34.4	93 775	143	8 476	262 154	3.7
Fremont	-0.1	1.1	6.2	4.9	3.5	7.7	2.7	12.5	46.8	11 525	248	1 051	19 223	-0.1
Garfield	0.4	13.7	14.7	1.3	6.5	7.2	5.7	9.8	17.1	6 980	122	340	23 361	0.2
Gilpin	0.0	0.0	1.4	D	D	0.3	D	D	9.9	830	149	36	3 581	0.6
Grand	3.7	0.9	11.7	2.0	10.6	6.9	6.2	2.2	20.5	2 045	143	69	16 724	4.1
Gunnison	0.8	17.1	9.2	0.9	7.8	7.3	4.6	3.8	24.7	1 980	128	73	11 574	1.4
Hinsdale	2.8	D	13.5	0.0	D	D	D	D	30.7	205	252	0	1 413	1.8
Huerfano	-0.1	D	6.7	2.5	5.3	10.1	2.5	D	24.9	2 170	333	271	5 128	1.0
Jackson	36.0	0.0	9.3	2.0	D	5.6	D	1.1	20.7	315	231	12	1 290	0.3
Jefferson	0.0	0.8	5.9	12.6	16.8	6.7	5.8	11.6	16.9	90 410	164	5 302	233 275	1.4
Kiowa	56.3	3.6	4.4	0.0	D	1.8	1.8	D	18.1	330	232	15	811	0.7
Kit Carson	39.0	D	3.0	2.4	1.9	4.3	3.3	2.4	12.8	1 490	186	98	3 514	-0.4
Lake	0.0	D	7.9	D	2.0	5.0	1.4	D	30.4	915	126	76	4 273	0.0
La Plata	-0.2	8.6	10.7	1.9	10.6	6.9	9.2	11.5	20.4	8 580	161	400	26 475	2.4
Larimer	0.3	0.6	8.3	13.1	13.0	6.7	4.7	9.1	23.3	50 315	159	2 625	138 534	4.4
Las Animas	0.2	19.1	6.9	1.3	3.9	7.0	4.1	D	25.8	3 660	253	586	8 244	0.3
Lincoln	3.8	0.0	3.3	D	D	9.0	4.1	5.9	48.1	985	181	67	2 427	0.2
Logan	15.3	9.3	3.8	5.9	1.7	9.3	2.8	D	19.6	3 910	174	393	8 952	-0.3
Mesa	0.3	9.1	7.7	4.4	6.7	8.0	5.8	15.5	16.7	29 385	199	2 412	63 779	1.8
Mineral	-1.4	D	7.5	D	D	7.6	D	D	17.1	240	332	0	1 225	2.0
Moffat	2.9	27.5	5.2	1.1	2.2	7.8	2.5	D	16.5	2 150	164	163	6 162	-0.5
Montezuma	0.3	5.2	8.8	3.6	4.1	10.7	3.5	D	28.0	5 815	227	439	11 981	-0.9
Montrose	0.4	4.5	9.6	8.1	5.9	9.6	4.5	D	21.5	9 950	244	643	18 338	0.5
Morgan	11.0	7.9	6.3	21.1	D	4.5	3.1	D	13.6	4 740	167	438	11 474	-0.1
Otero	8.6	D	7.9	7.5	3.0	7.5	4.1	D	23.4	4 340	234	795	8 881	-1.0
Ouray	1.6	D	13.8	2.7	10.4	8.1	4.2	D	19.6	1 115	244	40	3 151	2.2
Park	2.0	D	14.9	2.5	11.4	6.9	3.4	2.0	27.5	3 000	186	123	14 171	1.6
Phillips	27.9	D	6.4	0.6	D	4.6	2.8	D	22.4	910	209	55	2 088	0.0
Pitkin	0.1	D	6.9	0.5	9.8	6.6	12.2	3.0	13.3	2 290	132	26	13 039	0.7
Prowers	21.1	2.2	7.4	5.5	4.2	8.6	4.8	5.8	23.2	2 370	193	334	5 885	-1.0
Pueblo	0.4	0.3	7.4	11.6	5.1	8.0	3.2	19.9	21.8	34 195	212	6 265	70 054	0.8
Rio Blanco	4.6	28.7	13.6	0.6	1.5	4.6	1.4	1.0	24.8	1 045	155	38	3 346	1.1
Rio Grande	18.3	D	5.0	2.0	2.4	4.4	3.0	7.2	17.4	3 030	258	429	6 617	-0.2
Routt	0.7	7.4	19.5	0.9	8.7	6.5	8.3	9.0	10.2	2 930	125	92	16 387	0.5
Saguache	36.6	D	2.8	2.0	D	4.4	0.6	2.6	21.4	1 075	173	98	3 930	2.3
San Juan	0.0	D	D	D	D	12.0	D	D	32.6	125	179	0	757	0.1
San Miguel	1.0	D	12.4	3.3	D	6.4	8.4	4.0	15.9	815	106	26	6 736	1.5
Sedgwick	53.4	0.0	D	1.4	D	3.8	D	D	18.3	640	272	40	1 408	-0.5
Summit	0.0	D	8.3	0.6	9.9	9.8	9.1	7.9	13.7	2 655	92	41	30 405	1.9
Teller	-0.5	D	4.8	D	10.5	7.8	4.0	5.6	17.9	5 300	228	224	12 742	0.8
Washington	33.2	D	2.3	1.2	D	5.3	D	0.8	19.4	960	201	51	2 414	-0.8
Weld	4.6	10.8	12.4	10.8	4.1	6.0	5.2	7.7	13.1	36 935	137	3 440	100 070	3.9
Yuma	46.4	6.1	2.6	3.7	1.6	3.9	3.2	2.7	12.6	1 860	183	100	4 429	-0.8
CONNECTICUT	0.1	0.1	5.1	11.6	11.6	5.6	17.0	11.5	13.7	648 466	180	62 537	1 493 564	0.4
Fairfield	0.0	0.2	4.3	9.4	14.1	5.3	26.3	8.4	7.6	147 460	157	12 134	364 954	1.0
Hartford	0.1	0.0	4.4	12.5	11.6	4.9	20.0	11.8	14.2	167 975	187	20 706	374 695	0.1
Litchfield	0.4	0.2	D	15.3	6.8	8.8	4.0	12.5	14.6	39 930	214	1 700	87 434	-0.1
Middlesex	0.1	D	7.4	17.1	8.4	6.9	4.6	15.0	18.2	33 110	200	1 562	75 274	0.6
New Haven	0.1	0.1	5.8	10.6	10.2	6.2	6.2	15.9	15.2	159 190	184	19 439	362 262	0.1
New London	0.5	0.1	4.8	17.7	8.2	5.8	2.8	11.5	29.7	53 050	194	3 927	121 248	0.2

1. Per 1,000 resident population estimated as of July 1 of the year shown.

Table B. States and Counties — **Housing, Labor Force, and Employment**

STATE County	Housing units, 2009–2013: Occupied units: Total	Owner-occupied: Percent	Owner-occupied: Median value[1]	Median owner cost as a percent of income: With a mortgage	Median owner cost as a percent of income: Without a mortgage[2]	Renter-occupied: Median rent[3]	Renter-occupied: Median rent as a percent of income[2]	Substandard units[4] (percent)	Civilian labor force, 2014: Total	Percent change, 2013–2014	Unemployment: Total	Unemployment: Rate[5]	Civilian employment,[6] 2009–2013: Total	Percent: Management, business, science and arts	Percent: Construction, production, and maintenance occupations
	89	90	91	92	93	94	95	96	97	98	99	100	101	102	103
COLORADO—Cont'd															
Boulder	120 521	63.1	350 900	22.8	10.0	1 113	35.0	2.3	177 744	1.2	7 276	4.1	159 754	52.7	11.7
Broomfield	22 016	68.3	275 900	22.3	10.9	1 165	27.4	1.3	33 583	2.0	1 436	4.3	29 828	49.1	12.5
Chaffee	7 832	76.2	262 300	26.6	10.2	818	30.0	3.5	8 501	1.9	376	4.4	8 154	37.2	18.3
Cheyenne	839	76.5	81 700	21.9	10.0	508	16.3	0.4	998	2.5	29	2.9	1 138	41.7	27.7
Clear Creek	4 024	81.3	268 500	23.2	10.4	803	23.1	4.9	5 564	1.8	259	4.7	5 129	33.9	23.2
Conejos	3 099	77.3	109 700	24.0	11.2	526	30.8	4.6	3 629	0.2	284	7.8	3 135	33.9	26.0
Costilla	1 361	79.6	93 800	28.0	11.1	669	42.8	3.2	1 622	1.2	148	9.1	1 227	27.5	34.5
Crowley	1 173	79.6	78 800	26.7	13.1	583	26.6	5.4	1 313	-1.3	80	6.1	1 280	27.4	25.0
Custer	2 048	80.6	216 200	34.0	10.3	685	28.6	2.7	1 994	3.4	93	4.7	1 537	27.2	31.4
Delta	12 671	75.7	191 200	24.8	13.7	797	31.2	3.7	13 743	-0.9	949	6.9	12 145	30.6	29.3
Denver	266 069	50.2	249 100	23.6	10.6	883	29.9	4.7	370 487	1.6	18 060	4.9	324 278	43.1	15.6
Dolores	780	80.8	121 800	30.6	10.8	738	25.7	0.9	1 285	26.1	52	4.0	663	35.4	34.4
Douglas	103 780	80.9	335 600	22.8	10.0	1 273	26.9	3.8	168 842	2.2	6 779	4.0	149 780	54.0	8.9
Eagle	17 966	66.0	453 300	29.1	12.0	1 196	29.2	2.3	32 739	2.2	1 382	4.2	31 461	35.3	18.0
Elbert	8 240	90.4	333 600	26.9	10.0	1 085	29.5	2.7	13 036	2.2	556	4.3	11 823	40.7	21.8
El Paso	237 039	63.7	213 500	23.8	10.0	910	30.1	1.6	308 020	-0.1	18 605	6.0	279 591	40.3	17.0
Fremont	16 938	70.7	159 500	25.6	11.8	713	31.6	5.4	14 641	-2.4	1 192	8.1	14 168	26.9	20.2
Garfield	20 163	64.8	302 700	30.6	10.2	1 129	32.3	3.2	31 505	1.5	1 634	5.2	28 736	28.0	29.3
Gilpin	2 504	75.5	281 700	27.0	10.0	1 029	33.8	3.1	3 387	1.7	148	4.4	3 056	35.2	19.2
Grand	5 227	74.9	282 000	26.8	10.0	957	22.8	3.4	8 934	1.4	363	4.1	8 330	30.9	30.7
Gunnison	6 293	59.1	329 500	27.8	10.0	844	31.9	0.5	9 721	0.4	396	4.1	8 807	35.0	23.4
Hinsdale	388	78.9	261 700	24.8	10.0	808	22.3	4.4	444	2.3	17	3.8	381	39.6	21.0
Huerfano	3 059	72.5	152 400	26.9	13.2	744	34.3	3.2	2 437	-4.4	245	10.1	2 306	38.0	23.3
Jackson	648	72.2	123 200	29.1	11.2	717	22.4	1.7	848	6.4	30	3.5	730	28.8	36.8
Jefferson	219 562	70.6	262 400	23.4	10.0	979	30.1	1.8	311 855	1.7	14 198	4.6	281 421	43.6	16.1
Kiowa	559	72.8	79 400	21.9	11.1	661	25.8	1.1	763	-0.4	26	3.4	697	41.2	20.1
Kit Carson	3 046	65.8	121 600	23.0	13.0	612	22.2	5.0	4 373	6.7	134	3.1	3 790	27.9	29.5
Lake	3 079	65.6	164 400	23.3	10.2	858	31.9	1.9	4 569	2.3	220	4.8	3 840	31.9	29.3
La Plata	20 947	66.5	339 400	26.0	10.0	1 012	29.3	1.8	30 136	1.5	1 275	4.2	27 001	39.0	18.5
Larimer	121 423	65.6	247 100	23.8	10.0	973	33.8	3.0	177 264	1.3	7 578	4.3	156 980	42.6	16.6
Las Animas	5 992	69.4	151 500	25.4	11.7	711	32.5	2.1	6 522	-3.5	498	7.6	6 483	25.7	31.8
Lincoln	1 845	68.3	115 000	22.6	11.1	647	29.1	2.6	2 144	1.4	87	4.1	1 736	33.1	18.3
Logan	8 015	69.4	119 800	22.8	12.4	617	26.4	2.7	11 088	2.2	421	3.8	10 659	22.9	29.2
Mesa	58 598	71.7	210 100	25.0	10.0	842	32.4	0.0	73 608	-0.2	4 540	6.2	67 217	32.3	24.3
Mineral	393	83.7	275 000	23.9	10.6	670	32.5	2.6	427	0.0	22	5.2	363	36.4	28.7
Moffat	5 062	75.9	176 500	22.8	11.1	724	30.5	4.9	7 353	-2.7	422	5.7	6 716	23.0	31.4
Montezuma	10 688	70.5	189 400	25.6	11.0	700	31.2	2.5	12 711	-0.4	777	6.1	10 799	36.2	21.8
Montrose	16 586	73.1	193 700	27.5	12.1	848	29.8	6.7	19 393	0.1	1 325	6.8	17 761	28.0	29.4
Morgan	10 446	63.5	137 000	23.8	13.2	695	27.3	3.7	15 010	1.9	691	4.6	13 000	26.2	37.7
Otero	7 427	64.7	91 800	22.9	12.0	630	31.7	1.1	8 097	-1.5	615	7.6	7 377	31.8	21.9
Ouray	1 943	75.4	383 900	32.6	10.6	1 102	23.2	1.6	2 135	0.3	117	5.5	2 166	46.2	17.7
Park	7 038	88.5	247 300	27.2	10.7	1 180	30.4	5.9	9 469	1.8	439	4.6	8 712	31.8	24.9
Phillips	1 668	69.2	132 700	22.9	14.2	595	26.4	2.7	2 260	5.9	75	3.3	1 962	34.5	30.7
Pitkin	7 507	68.7	611 200	28.5	12.3	1 377	25.8	2.7	11 030	1.9	539	4.9	10 074	40.9	10.0
Prowers	4 935	65.8	86 100	20.2	13.9	541	27.7	2.2	5 783	-1.7	276	4.8	5 330	31.4	26.3
Pueblo	62 439	65.7	138 700	24.5	12.3	736	33.6	3.2	73 037	-0.8	5 358	7.3	64 628	29.4	21.6
Rio Blanco	2 638	68.8	200 400	21.4	10.0	755	19.9	3.3	2 954	-4.1	172	5.8	3 263	24.8	38.6
Rio Grande	4 722	67.4	129 500	25.4	11.7	604	24.1	1.3	4 862	-0.4	439	9.0	5 080	30.5	28.6
Routt	9 647	70.6	390 100	28.3	10.0	1 160	29.5	5.1	14 458	-0.7	606	4.2	14 012	36.7	19.6
Saguache	2 692	66.9	135 400	27.6	10.0	626	31.2	7.5	3 022	2.1	261	8.6	2 819	29.4	36.9
San Juan	321	59.8	242 300	32.9	11.2	875	37.9	4.5	473	-1.0	25	5.3	377	31.3	29.4
San Miguel	3 234	64.4	448 000	31.6	10.9	1 127	29.2	1.3	4 922	2.6	233	4.7	4 581	38.8	17.9
Sedgwick	943	68.6	81 400	20.7	11.4	514	23.0	4.5	1 091	-0.3	50	4.6	1 034	28.4	27.8
Summit	11 138	65.9	460 000	29.2	10.0	1 142	29.1	1.9	20 263	4.2	683	3.4	17 593	32.0	17.8
Teller	9 434	81.4	226 900	24.6	10.0	868	33.6	1.1	11 724	-0.3	686	5.9	10 990	38.3	16.9
Washington	2 019	73.3	110 500	20.0	11.1	575	22.5	4.8	2 679	4.6	86	3.2	2 227	39.8	27.5
Weld	90 465	70.1	191 500	23.9	10.3	835	32.2	1.2	146 103	4.5	6 584	4.5	121 383	33.2	25.7
Yuma	3 811	67.4	136 600	23.4	10.0	562	23.1	2.9	5 007	5.2	167	3.3	4 772	25.2	34.9
CONNECTICUT	1 355 849	67.8	278 900	25.9	16.9	1 056	31.8	2.3	1 885 126	0.9	124 705	6.6	1 759 412	40.8	17.2
Fairfield	332 655	69.0	432 100	27.6	18.3	1 302	32.4	2.2	475 888	1.1	29 360	6.2	449 106	43.0	15.0
Hartford	347 874	65.5	241 500	24.6	16.1	974	30.8	1.3	471 431	0.8	32 377	6.9	435 942	41.4	16.5
Litchfield	75 755	78.1	263 600	26.2	16.8	926	30.1	1.0	105 945	1.2	6 295	5.9	99 302	39.6	20.1
Middlesex	66 141	76.2	292 000	25.2	16.2	1 007	29.1	2.5	92 018	1.2	5 179	5.6	86 214	45.1	16.1
New Haven	328 013	63.7	256 900	26.6	18.1	1 060	34.2	1.6	455 537	0.7	32 912	7.2	418 622	39.6	18.3
New London	107 066	67.5	252 900	25.0	15.2	1 012	29.5	1.2	137 254	-0.3	9 254	6.7	132 657	37.5	17.5

1. Specified owner-occupied units. 2. A value of 10.0 represents 10 percent or less; a value of 50.0 represents 50 percent or more. 3. Specified renter-occupied units.
4. Overcrowded or lacking complete plumbing facilities. 5. Percent of civilian labor force. 6. Persons 16 years old and over.

STATE County	Private nonfarm establishments, employment and payroll, 2013									Agriculture, 2012			
		Employment						Annual payroll		Farms			
											Percent with:		
	Number of establish-ments	Total	Health care and social assistance	Manufac-turing	Retail trade	Finance and insurance	Professional, scientific, and technical services	Total (mil dol)	Average per employee (dollars)	Number	Fewer than 50 acres	500 acres or more	Farm operators whose principal occu-pation is farming (percent)
	104	105	106	107	108	109	110	111	112	113	114	115	116
COLORADO—Cont'd													
Boulder	11 696	139 136	19 197	14 133	16 688	3 395	23 750	7 965	57 247	855	72.0	4.3	44.9
Broomfield	1 810	33 426	1 945	2 822	4 539	D	5 851	2 093	62 627	25	60.0	20.0	44.0
Chaffee	860	5 367	775	178	1 010	244	224	162	30 168	223	33.2	17.0	52.9
Cheyenne	58	745	D	NA	63	D	4	42	56 352	345	5.5	70.4	67.5
Clear Creek	327	2 574	69	26	236	D	66	104	40 497	25	60.0	12.0	24.0
Conejos	106	697	206	D	195	D	D	21	29 597	605	26.1	19.8	47.4
Costilla	42	255	41	D	NA	D	D	6	21 773	251	34.3	15.1	65.3
Crowley	33	478	D	NA	86	D	D	15	31 084	228	11.8	50.4	58.3
Custer	143	543	D	40	141	D	53	16	29 459	198	20.7	27.8	47.0
Delta	818	6 620	1 449	534	1 192	228	185	225	33 982	1 250	58.9	5.9	56.4
Denver	22 834	399 744	48 148	16 142	28 333	23 739	40 445	22 534	56 370	10	100.0	0.0	40.0
Dolores	53	D	D	D	D	D	4	6	D	283	21.9	27.2	48.8
Douglas	8 040	91 934	9 536	2 131	16 572	7 165	8 971	4 796	52 166	1 116	64.3	6.3	51.1
Eagle	3 217	29 062	1 934	D	3 896	813	1 229	1 010	34 764	165	38.2	21.2	41.2
Elbert	564	2 271	147	117	414	66	173	78	34 561	1 330	32.6	21.3	42.3
El Paso	16 008	221 972	32 432	10 568	29 946	9 664	20 571	9 444	42 544	1 206	45.4	17.2	49.5
Fremont	821	7 420	1 717	527	1 567	248	169	214	28 800	809	68.0	12.0	40.8
Garfield	2 410	18 983	2 554	223	2 914	711	1 011	863	45 472	625	52.2	13.8	48.3
Gilpin	111	4 970	D	D	D	D	D	174	34 999	24	33.3	4.2	45.8
Grand	797	7 582	365	124	619	107	796	217	28 677	205	29.3	30.7	52.2
Gunnison	1 053	6 056	479	80	883	D	334	186	30 757	244	32.4	20.9	47.5
Hinsdale	75	183	D	NA	D	D	D	5	27 694	26	3.8	30.8	38.5
Huerfano	156	1 188	446	52	217	D	D	33	27 484	407	22.9	34.6	54.8
Jackson	71	279	D	44	66	D	D	7	25 566	105	14.3	63.8	63.8
Jefferson	16 222	188 932	25 582	17 708	28 897	8 657	23 797	8 776	46 450	521	72.6	5.6	41.8
Kiowa	36	D	D	NA	D	D	D	8	D	395	2.5	64.8	58.0
Kit Carson	263	1 952	282	131	325	101	D	60	30 508	704	8.9	57.4	55.5
Lake	205	1 226	225	D	177	D	D	31	25 143	23	17.4	30.4	52.2
La Plata	2 296	20 661	3 035	592	3 255	1 031	1 145	891	43 124	1 124	44.3	11.3	45.7
Larimer	9 723	112 150	18 490	9 922	17 565	3 624	8 790	4 556	40 626	1 625	60.7	8.5	46.5
Las Animas	371	3 228	727	48	686	139	89	102	31 454	602	17.6	49.5	47.3
Lincoln	123	1 114	254	D	305	67	24	37	33 257	464	8.2	69.8	57.3
Logan	577	5 312	969	360	1 140	206	94	164	30 940	891	12.3	47.3	53.6
Mesa	4 431	49 355	9 740	2 389	8 259	1 749	2 477	1 980	40 116	2 264	75.4	5.4	48.6
Mineral	66	220	D	D	D	D	D	8	35 436	14	21.4	14.3	57.1
Moffat	415	3 527	484	54	734	D	100	147	41 677	492	29.1	31.9	37.2
Montezuma	758	6 746	1 466	278	1 202	176	292	225	33 282	1 138	49.4	9.6	45.3
Montrose	1 270	11 253	2 444	1 171	2 116	347	520	383	34 021	1 128	52.7	10.6	48.4
Morgan	667	8 794	1 235	2 696	988	266	145	316	35 985	754	20.2	34.9	56.5
Otero	442	4 256	D	509	767	165	121	121	28 395	541	29.6	25.0	48.6
Ouray	263	963	D	56	129	D	67	31	32 397	108	38.0	15.7	73.1
Park	434	1 196	78	D	165	D	D	34	28 824	209	23.4	26.3	41.6
Phillips	135	909	D	29	126	49	D	33	35 754	319	11.0	60.5	69.0
Pitkin	1 559	16 314	726	D	1 555	225	646	564	34 574	82	36.6	18.3	46.3
Prowers	340	2 901	605	181	733	191	100	81	28 023	553	19.5	46.5	52.8
Pueblo	3 036	46 754	12 228	4 248	8 013	1 150	1 715	1 684	36 026	894	38.9	21.3	52.3
Rio Blanco	229	2 131	D	D	235	144	36	122	57 345	313	31.0	36.7	53.7
Rio Grande	348	2 646	431	D	424	112	D	75	28 339	377	27.1	24.9	54.1
Routt	1 592	16 630	1 252	122	1 553	249	519	668	40 194	799	43.7	20.9	41.3
Saguache	117	799	71	D	114	D	D	24	30 220	277	14.1	44.4	59.6
San Juan	68	203	D	D	NA	NA	9	4	20 882	0	0.0	0.0	0.0
San Miguel	614	4 430	134	79	482	D	D	122	27 601	135	40.0	23.7	48.9
Sedgwick	71	510	D	D	108	D	D	14	27 025	226	13.7	51.3	72.1
Summit	2 140	18 614	925	160	3 075	245	583	501	26 930	38	26.3	21.1	26.3
Teller	673	5 377	407	57	813	145	D	187	34 861	123	45.5	21.1	39.0
Washington	105	524	27	D	D	D	D	17	33 195	824	11.5	47.7	48.4
Weld	5 376	71 783	8 029	11 023	8 979	3 718	2 195	3 131	43 619	3 525	35.5	19.6	49.8
Yuma	370	2 535	587	90	461	147	61	94	36 937	834	12.8	56.7	61.4
CONNECTICUT	88 498	1 473 605	271 611	153 370	183 805	118 693	105 226	85 897	58 290	5 977	69.8	1.8	46.3
Fairfield	26 972	403 375	64 409	33 541	49 718	38 384	35 648	30 707	76 125	439	82.2	1.6	57.0
Hartford	22 613	446 375	80 508	48 580	49 753	55 935	34 393	25 577	57 299	899	71.2	1.3	49.6
Litchfield	4 782	51 115	9 534	8 809	8 795	1 451	1 689	2 044	39 989	1 207	67.9	2.5	41.5
Middlesex	4 147	60 406	14 077	9 253	8 639	1 925	2 822	2 765	45 773	518	78.2	1.2	48.6
New Haven	19 431	331 081	72 961	31 847	42 507	12 359	15 043	16 252	49 088	695	77.3	1.2	43.0
New London	5 698	103 244	17 133	D	14 424	2 095	7 714	5 107	49 467	949	64.0	1.3	48.6

STATE County	Agriculture, 2012 (cont.) — Land in farms: Acreage (1,000)	Land in farms: Percent change, 2007–2012	Land in farms — Acres: Average size of farm	Acres: Total irrigated (1,000)	Acres: Total cropland (1,000)	Value of land and buildings (dollars): Average per farm	Value of land and buildings (dollars): Average per acre	Value of machinery and equipment, average per farm (dollars)	Value of products sold: Total (mil dol)	Value of products sold: Average per farm (dollars)	Percent from: Crops	Percent from: Livestock and poultry products	Percent of farms with sales of: $10,000 or more	Percent of farms with sales of: $100,000 or more	Government payments: Total ($1,000)	Government payments: Percent of farms
	117	118	119	120	121	122	123	124	125	126	127	128	129	130	131	132
COLORADO—Cont'd																
Boulder	133	-3.4	155	30.1	39.2	888 591	5 715	49 384	33.9	39 629	D	D	22.8	5.8	474	12.0
Broomfield	11	78.5	446	1.1	11.1	874 920	1 960	90 840	1.5	61 480	90.9	9.1	28.0	20.0	37	24.0
Chaffee	78	-2.2	348	13.5	15.9	1 053 157	3 024	75 278	9.6	43 130	30.5	69.5	30.9	9.9	74	7.6
Cheyenne	977	8.6	2 832	26.6	536.6	2 203 649	778	216 333	87.1	252 417	68.1	31.9	64.3	40.6	6 203	78.3
Clear Creek	8	-33.4	332	D	0.3	910 680	2 744	41 080	0.3	13 720	D	D	32.0	0.0	0	0.0
Conejos	258	12.7	426	100.1	112.6	646 739	1 518	97 661	42.7	70 650	61.8	38.2	47.8	16.0	1 240	28.9
Costilla	376	-6.2	1 499	34.3	49.9	1 646 637	1 099	126 490	29.0	115 398	84.7	15.3	39.8	11.2	475	28.3
Crowley	500	10.8	2 193	5.9	45.3	750 031	342	73 939	161.5	708 268	1.0	99.0	47.4	23.2	2 044	61.4
Custer	189	37.0	953	12.3	20.3	1 451 495	1 523	76 455	8.2	41 379	27.2	72.8	38.9	13.1	301	23.7
Delta	251	-0.7	201	59.2	60.7	665 865	3 319	63 422	55.6	44 511	42.4	57.6	36.3	8.2	728	9.5
Denver	0	-76.5	14	0.0	0.0	775 500	54 231	93 200	D	D	D	D	60.0	20.0	0	0.0
Dolores	160	-8.0	565	7.4	73.1	815 583	1 443	71 901	10.1	35 629	62.9	37.1	28.6	9.9	1 153	63.3
Douglas	200	5.7	179	1.7	23.3	900 148	5 022	53 598	13.7	12 234	33.5	66.5	19.5	1.3	502	4.4
Eagle	129	4.4	785	12.7	14.9	3 090 273	3 939	91 448	7.9	48 109	42.2	57.8	30.9	8.5	68	4.8
Elbert	1 043	-8.0	784	8.4	180.5	879 390	1 121	60 820	45.0	33 805	19.9	80.1	28.9	8.1	2 328	17.4
El Paso	649	5.3	538	7.9	53.7	650 029	1 208	45 053	43.9	36 403	47.1	52.9	24.5	5.1	1 232	10.3
Fremont	290	-1.8	359	8.4	17.7	839 582	2 339	42 611	21.2	26 214	20.2	79.8	19.0	2.8	313	7.0
Garfield	311	-7.3	497	32.3	46.2	1 380 994	2 777	72 635	22.7	36 272	24.9	75.1	30.2	8.8	604	12.6
Gilpin	6	-56.7	240	D	0.4	679 792	2 832	30 250	0.2	6 875	D	D	25.0	0.0	D	20.8
Grand	227	8.8	1 107	27.5	34.9	2 530 395	2 286	94 561	13.5	65 883	15.6	84.4	40.5	13.2	91	6.8
Gunnison	190	9.5	780	42.2	41.6	2 197 246	2 818	95 365	13.0	53 221	13.8	86.2	37.7	13.5	52	4.9
Hinsdale	10	73.5	394	2.4	1.1	2 083 538	5 293	91 308	0.7	27 385	15.4	84.6	38.5	3.8	0	0.0
Huerfano	581	12.0	1 427	11.7	25.1	1 233 226	864	48 887	11.3	27 656	13.1	86.9	26.8	4.7	675	13.0
Jackson	342	-11.5	3 261	59.6	65.5	3 397 571	1 042	187 457	23.6	224 771	19.8	80.1	61.9	35.2	34	11.4
Jefferson	68	-26.8	131	2.3	10.1	719 981	5 493	39 426	9.1	17 465	81.0	19.0	15.7	3.5	41	4.0
Kiowa	1 113	16.2	2 818	3.1	713.3	1 924 033	683	177 504	96.1	243 205	38.5	61.5	54.4	28.6	7 743	86.8
Kit Carson	1 377	1.8	1 956	110.2	872.3	2 214 455	1 132	320 912	499.8	709 908	28.1	71.9	58.8	37.5	12 129	75.6
Lake	12	-17.9	530	3.6	0.8	1 544 261	2 916	26 957	0.9	37 478	8.9	91.0	43.5	13.0	0	0.0
La Plata	590	3.6	525	61.7	85.9	975 981	1 858	66 034	25.0	22 234	33.4	66.6	29.5	4.3	752	9.8
Larimer	450	-8.0	277	52.5	106.4	854 599	3 083	72 401	128.6	79 167	44.6	55.4	28.8	7.6	1 061	11.2
Las Animas	2 141	-1.8	3 556	11.3	71.1	1 441 724	405	60 860	28.4	47 228	11.1	88.9	39.4	14.1	3 371	28.1
Lincoln	1 473	5.2	3 175	4.8	581.6	1 514 664	477	163 039	75.6	162 860	53.5	46.5	61.6	33.4	7 741	70.0
Logan	1 099	-2.9	1 234	94.0	516.0	1 071 964	869	167 899	566.9	636 255	20.8	79.2	63.0	34.9	9 526	76.1
Mesa	387	3.9	171	75.3	71.4	575 360	3 367	51 431	84.6	37 360	48.1	51.9	25.7	6.1	821	7.1
Mineral	7	-25.2	473	D	0.5	2 055 643	4 342	34 286	0.1	6 357	16.9	83.1	14.3	0.0	0	0.0
Moffat	930	11.2	1 890	23.5	119.6	1 380 283	730	77 575	27.0	54 866	13.0	87.0	28.9	10.6	1 866	33.9
Montezuma	691	-1.9	607	62.6	97.4	672 749	1 108	67 594	46.4	40 748	64.7	35.3	30.8	6.6	1 387	15.6
Montrose	330	2.7	292	70.4	70.0	838 902	2 871	74 786	103.2	91 508	32.6	67.4	39.5	12.9	930	17.7
Morgan	647	-11.1	858	100.9	303.6	1 224 219	1 426	198 156	615.3	816 073	17.3	82.7	59.7	32.9	6 315	66.7
Otero	707	13.2	1 306	43.6	74.3	852 516	653	124 166	144.2	266 608	20.8	79.2	53.6	22.7	2 473	54.5
Ouray	81	-13.3	753	9.8	10.1	2 138 602	2 840	88 769	4.3	39 574	16.5	83.5	40.7	13.0	24	6.5
Park	180	-44.4	861	3.8	10.2	1 146 282	1 331	64 617	7.7	37 057	9.2	90.8	22.5	2.9	140	7.7
Phillips	436	1.2	1 368	72.9	370.8	2 477 361	1 810	329 323	208.0	652 056	56.5	43.5	70.5	51.7	6 831	82.8
Pitkin	32	12.5	391	7.5	4.8	2 190 561	5 597	95 427	3.0	36 122	13.3	86.7	28.0	7.3	149	12.2
Prowers	1 022	-1.5	1 848	79.9	480.5	1 270 078	687	180 617	318.2	575 496	20.4	79.6	53.2	27.8	6 892	62.6
Pueblo	895	-1.7	1 001	18.6	88.5	735 098	734	62 169	51.1	57 149	35.4	64.6	27.2	8.1	2 223	20.6
Rio Blanco	507	31.2	1 621	25.6	42.7	2 154 358	1 329	101 540	24.4	77 994	16.2	83.8	39.3	18.8	786	15.0
Rio Grande	185	3.7	492	93.6	105.4	1 163 151	2 364	237 934	106.5	282 470	88.9	11.1	57.8	37.7	1 003	29.2
Routt	613	14.9	767	46.6	117.3	1 700 572	2 218	75 899	46.5	58 148	16.8	83.2	29.8	10.1	847	14.1
Saguache	311	8.4	1 124	90.5	115.3	1 670 177	1 486	284 354	110.0	397 069	84.2	15.8	54.5	32.9	1 298	31.0
San Juan	0	0.0	0	0.0	0.0	0	0	0	0.0	0	0.0	0.0	0.0	0.0	0	0.0
San Miguel	127	-16.2	937	12.7	14.6	1 366 578	1 458	66 570	4.7	35 089	11.3	88.7	30.4	9.6	209	14.8
Sedgwick	336	13.2	1 487	38.1	207.2	1 889 363	1 271	249 558	101.3	448 066	56.8	43.2	70.8	46.0	3 427	80.5
Summit	25	-47.0	668	4.2	5.8	2 218 579	3 324	63 553	D	D	D	D	23.7	10.5	D	2.6
Teller	71	-3.2	577	0.4	3.4	1 156 211	2 006	33 358	1.3	10 195	12.6	87.4	17.9	2.4	102	8.9
Washington	1 216	-11.6	1 476	47.0	699.7	1 441 458	977	177 691	220.7	267 856	44.6	55.4	54.0	29.2	11 607	76.5
Weld	1 956	-6.3	555	299.9	850.2	1 098 289	1 979	146 652	1 860.7	527 863	20.1	79.9	42.8	20.2	15 649	39.7
Yuma	1 353	1.4	1 623	233.0	607.2	2 223 818	1 370	298 933	1 150.3	1 379 309	27.1	72.9	60.0	43.5	12 866	73.5
CONNECTICUT	437	7.6	73	9.3	151.1	809 375	11 082	58 958	550.6	92 123	70.7	29.3	30.0	7.7	4 841	8.7
Fairfield	54	36.4	123	0.3	5.0	1 492 513	12 145	68 132	34.8	79 317	60.1	39.9	35.3	7.5	160	5.5
Hartford	54	1.0	60	4.9	25.7	760 429	12 645	63 402	113.9	126 692	94.1	5.9	36.9	12.0	583	8.8
Litchfield	91	4.1	75	0.4	37.2	859 063	11 399	52 797	46.3	38 344	60.5	39.5	26.3	5.3	1 209	10.8
Middlesex	24	44.8	46	0.6	7.7	654 002	14 074	59 284	53.5	103 257	94.5	5.5	27.0	4.6	167	5.4
New Haven	42	-7.4	61	1.3	14.1	764 679	12 561	56 881	84.6	121 755	91.7	8.3	31.9	10.1	383	7.3
New London	65	2.8	69	0.8	22.8	709 299	10 330	47 891	118.3	124 690	43.2	56.8	26.9	6.7	537	9.2

STATE County	Water use, 2010		Wholesale trade,[1] 2007				Retail trade,[2] 2007				Real estate and rental and leasing,[2] 2007			
	Total water withdrawn (mil gal/day)	Gallons withdrawn per person per day	Number of establish-ments	Number of employees	Sales (mil dol)	Annual payroll (mil dol)	Number of establish-ments	Number of employees	Sales (mil dol)	Annual payroll (mil dol)	Number of establish-ments	Number of employees	Receipts (mil dol)	Annual payroll (mil dol)
	133	134	135	136	137	138	139	140	141	142	143	144	145	146
COLORADO—Cont'd														
Boulder	231.6	786	397	5 129	2 782.1	427.1	1 244	17 620	4 039.3	444.5	669	2 365	441.7	83.2
Broomfield	6.4	115	68	D	D	D	279	5 355	1 139.8	111.3	91	525	105.3	15.3
Chaffee	101.9	5 719	16	71	23.6	1.7	135	989	252.6	24.4	74	210	25.9	4.7
Cheyenne	37.9	20 632	5	46	51.2	1.9	11	67	13.0	1.1	1	D	D	D
Clear Creek	1.8	200	13	33	7.0	0.8	48	238	73.1	6.2	23	180	6.5	1.5
Conejos	382.5	46 330	5	8	3.6	0.2	20	179	33.1	3.6	2	D	D	D
Costilla	139.9	39 702	2	D	D	D	8	24	5.7	0.4	NA	NA	NA	NA
Crowley	13.7	2 358	NA	NA	NA	NA	9	84	15.7	1.8	1	D	D	D
Custer	27.2	6 402	3	D	D	D	21	145	58.7	3.0	15	38	3.0	0.6
Delta	359.5	11 615	25	231	60.9	8.4	141	1 319	312.9	29.1	42	90	14.1	2.6
Denver	150.5	251	1 174	21 245	14 920.9	1 064.5	2 271	27 979	6 835.4	752.6	1 451	11 600	2 536.4	623.7
Dolores	5.6	2 708	5	33	19.2	0.9	8	58	15.0	0.9	NA	NA	NA	NA
Douglas	51.6	181	236	D	D	D	845	15 346	3 765.5	361.9	498	1 368	239.1	45.7
Eagle	137.9	2 642	70	D	D	D	449	4 343	928.8	120.2	414	1 728	268.8	66.5
Elbert	13.8	598	17	51	13.8	1.5	38	251	80.7	6.4	18	22	5.5	0.5
El Paso	116.1	187	457	5 400	2 810.6	264.3	2 079	31 302	7 950.2	773.3	1 132	3 870	588.1	114.0
Fremont	146.2	3 123	21	D	D	D	143	1 531	352.4	34.1	46	217	26.5	3.8
Garfield	261.5	4 637	63	625	442.2	32.2	325	3 798	1 184.7	116.0	182	676	114.7	22.6
Gilpin	3.4	618	NA	NA	NA	NA	7	13	3.2	0.1	7	10	0.8	0.2
Grand	186.5	12 567	6	17	5.1	0.5	124	918	193.1	21.3	99	720	75.7	17.4
Gunnison	562.7	36 723	10	D	D	D	142	1 024	211.6	21.9	92	233	27.6	6.0
Hinsdale	30.4	36 074	NA	NA	NA	NA	15	33	7.8	0.8	11	D	D	D
Huerfano	38.3	5 701	1	D	D	D	32	222	55.3	4.4	12	19	3.5	0.4
Jackson	347.9	249 541	1	D	D	D	13	88	19.4	1.9	2	D	D	D
Jefferson	78.3	146	529	4 492	2 514.1	238.5	2 054	31 020	7 282.2	750.6	925	3 134	538.0	104.9
Kiowa	5.6	3 977	8	18	27.0	0.5	6	50	8.0	0.7	NA	NA	NA	NA
Kit Carson	130.5	15 780	17	184	166.3	6.1	46	348	84.4	6.5	7	19	2.4	0.7
Lake	14.7	2 005	1	D	D	D	30	235	51.4	4.6	17	71	6.8	1.4
La Plata	336.6	6 558	59	D	D	D	345	3 345	790.4	83.2	169	552	109.5	17.3
Larimer	412.9	1 378	290	3 156	1 265.2	146.8	1 306	17 510	3 922.9	402.7	562	2 181	327.1	63.6
Las Animas	73.7	4 755	14	119	51.6	3.4	62	733	164.4	16.0	23	84	10.2	1.8
Lincoln	4.5	821	2	D	D	D	36	336	134.7	7.3	3	6	0.3	0.0
Logan	164.4	7 239	25	D	D	D	106	1 135	281.3	24.9	22	67	7.2	1.4
Mesa	754.7	5 144	219	2 463	1 179.3	103.2	693	8 856	2 389.5	223.8	323	1 101	246.9	40.1
Mineral	18.5	25 955	1	D	D	D	11	45	6.0	0.7	3	4	0.8	0.0
Moffat	170.1	12 332	27	159	73.2	6.9	77	707	213.0	18.7	20	41	6.5	0.8
Montezuma	255.1	9 989	24	160	52.1	5.6	117	1 335	301.4	31.2	34	111	18.7	2.8
Montrose	702.9	17 028	48	D	D	D	208	2 195	610.9	58.3	67	200	33.8	6.8
Morgan	186.0	6 606	30	D	D	D	105	1 071	232.8	22.1	35	84	7.9	1.6
Otero	436.8	23 195	24	188	59.8	4.9	87	837	171.5	17.4	21	119	14.7	2.4
Ouray	111.0	25 020	3	11	1.0	0.3	46	207	27.0	4.1	9	12	3.1	0.3
Park	24.4	1 506	8	17	3.4	0.5	47	209	55.4	5.1	31	39	4.9	1.0
Phillips	58.9	13 267	11	121	150.9	4.4	23	165	45.6	3.4	4	6	0.4	0.4
Pitkin	123.4	7 194	18	85	64.7	7.1	250	1 864	399.5	57.1	204	1 213	210.3	49.3
Prowers	152.3	12 131	21	174	82.0	4.3	69	709	147.0	14.6	17	49	4.6	0.9
Pueblo	288.9	1 816	85	850	431.0	37.8	548	8 064	1 864.6	192.4	165	667	94.9	18.3
Rio Blanco	267.2	40 078	2	D	D	D	43	247	54.7	5.0	8	11	1.8	0.4
Rio Grande	579.2	48 339	29	435	218.2	13.2	62	465	110.2	10.6	15	55	5.2	0.8
Routt	204.0	8 678	40	246	187.8	12.1	223	1 982	421.5	45.9	148	1 082	165.7	30.9
Saguache	270.9	44 355	12	156	57.1	5.4	18	86	20.9	1.6	1	D	D	D
San Juan	1.6	2 232	1	D	D	D	14	44	6.6	0.7	1	D	D	D
San Miguel	37.9	5 156	1	D	D	D	75	572	97.8	12.8	89	362	61.5	9.4
Sedgwick	61.4	25 818	5	D	D	D	12	106	33.3	1.9	1	D	D	D
Summit	68.7	2 454	26	D	D	D	371	3 391	641.0	73.9	271	1 980	236.7	51.6
Teller	7.6	325	14	78	26.3	2.0	79	668	169.0	14.4	51	158	15.2	3.2
Washington	73.4	15 247	7	44	42.6	1.9	20	87	23.1	1.3	2	D	D	D
Weld	462.1	1 828	248	D	D	D	650	8 735	2 246.1	212.9	227	838	115.6	23.7
Yuma	220.8	21 986	26	178	193.6	6.2	68	462	106.1	7.8	8	31	5.8	0.9
CONNECTICUT	3 311.0	926	3 848	58 291	107 917.0	3 587.9	13 807	196 133	52 165.5	5 160.4	3 609	22 455	5 686.6	994.0
Fairfield	494.3	539	1 220	17 035	78 881.6	1 391.9	3 770	53 738	15 702.2	1 648.8	1 174	7 466	2 283.1	450.7
Hartford	200.7	225	1 014	19 472	15 631.4	1 021.7	3 423	53 241	13 820.7	1 310.7	932	6 289	1 204.5	248.3
Litchfield	68.4	360	176	D	D	D	788	9 059	2 458.2	239.8	162	680	89.9	18.1
Middlesex	133.6	807	171	2 189	953.9	111.5	749	8 300	2 129.2	209.8	146	915	233.2	38.1
New Haven	113.5	132	980	14 619	9 890.7	814.1	3 172	46 058	11 785.3	1 112.5	780	5 470	1 611.1	192.9
New London	2 249.8	8 209	147	D	D	D	1 123	15 660	3 883.0	390.4	232	D	D	D

1. Merchant wholesalers, except manufacturers' sales branches and offices. 2. Employer establishments.

Table B. States and Counties — **Professional Services, Manufacturing, and Accommodation and Food Services**

STATE County	Professional, scientific, and technical services,[1] 2007				Manufacturing, 2007				Accommodation and food services, 2007			
	Number of establish-ments	Number of employees	Receipts (mil dol)	Annual payroll (mil dol)	Number of establish-ments	Number of employees	Receipts (mil dol)	Annual payroll (mil dol)	Number of establish-ments	Number of employees	Sales (mil dol)	Annual payroll (mil dol)
	147	148	149	150	151	152	153	154	155	156	157	158
COLORADO—Cont'd												
Boulder	2 447	23 459	5 054.5	1 781.8	534	16 791	3 855.9	896.9	815	14 563	668.9	208.4
Broomfield	271	D	D	D	85	3 939	2 255.5	192.9	137	3 370	163.4	53.3
Chaffee	87	D	D	D	NA	NA	NA	NA	107	1 197	49.2	14.6
Cheyenne	5	5	0.4	0.1	NA	NA	NA	NA	3	10	0.4	0.1
Clear Creek	59	77	9.4	3.9	NA	NA	NA	NA	49	481	25.0	7.6
Conejos	4	5	0.3	0.1	NA	NA	NA	NA	12	49	4.5	0.9
Costilla	1	D	D	D	NA	NA	NA	NA	5	D	D	D
Crowley	1	D	D	D	NA	NA	NA	NA	3	D	D	D
Custer	16	28	1.9	0.8	NA	NA	NA	NA	19	125	5.5	1.5
Delta	80	D	D	D	48	570	141.4	19.1	80	708	26.9	7.6
Denver	3 856	D	D	D	840	19 480	5 189.9	826.0	1 778	38 701	2 279.0	656.3
Dolores	4	4	0.4	0.1	NA	NA	NA	NA	5	22	1.7	0.7
Douglas	1 360	D	D	D	130	6 965	1 950.8	442.7	467	9 878	435.1	136.6
Eagle	422	D	D	D	NA	NA	NA	NA	254	7 882	469.7	152.7
Elbert	80	198	20.3	7.8	NA	NA	NA	NA	16	177	6.9	1.8
El Paso	2 328	D	D	D	499	D	D	D	1 240	24 124	1 153.8	350.5
Fremont	63	184	13.7	4.2	51	663	168.8	29.6	97	1 120	40.8	12.0
Garfield	317	1 270	163.3	63.5	NA	NA	NA	NA	187	2 900	161.2	46.3
Gilpin	16	D	D	D	NA	NA	NA	NA	9	1 610	291.5	49.5
Grand	97	D	D	D	NA	NA	NA	NA	133	1 581	73.9	24.8
Gunnison	121	D	D	D	NA	NA	NA	NA	123	2 501	89.7	29.8
Hinsdale	5	D	D	D	NA	NA	NA	NA	18	58	3.6	0.9
Huerfano	11	26	1.8	0.6	NA	NA	NA	NA	31	221	9.7	2.8
Jackson	3	6	0.8	0.1	NA	NA	NA	NA	11	49	2.4	0.7
Jefferson	2 934	D	D	D	489	16 816	6 566.6	1 063.6	1 109	21 096	960.5	293.0
Kiowa	2	D	D	D	NA	NA	NA	NA	2	D	D	D
Kit Carson	15	41	2.4	1.0	NA	NA	NA	NA	22	194	10.3	2.2
Lake	13	D	D	D	NA	NA	NA	NA	36	412	12.6	4.3
La Plata	342	D	D	D	65	748	D	22.5	204	4 188	206.2	63.3
Larimer	1 327	7 876	867.5	387.3	420	11 764	3 226.8	664.5	807	14 244	604.4	181.9
Las Animas	28	112	15.3	5.6	NA	NA	NA	NA	43	547	22.4	6.0
Lincoln	13	66	6.3	1.8	NA	NA	NA	NA	17	194	8.4	2.4
Logan	39	175	11.5	5.9	NA	NA	NA	NA	43	553	23.3	6.3
Mesa	547	D	D	D	177	2 691	539.6	104.9	301	6 307	268.8	77.6
Mineral	4	4	0.4	0.1	NA	NA	NA	NA	18	62	9.5	2.8
Moffat	41	152	12.2	5.3	NA	NA	NA	NA	37	556	35.3	6.8
Montezuma	79	D	D	D	NA	NA	NA	NA	86	1 424	84.9	22.0
Montrose	138	D	D	D	66	1 436	218.2	38.8	85	1 363	51.1	16.9
Morgan	37	D	D	D	31	2 463	D	85.3	55	741	27.7	8.1
Otero	33	D	D	D	NA	NA	NA	NA	57	558	20.3	5.3
Ouray	36	65	8.5	3.3	NA	NA	NA	NA	56	397	21.2	6.4
Park	58	102	10.3	4.1	NA	NA	NA	NA	44	224	11.1	3.6
Phillips	6	15	1.6	0.4	NA	NA	NA	NA	9	63	1.9	0.5
Pitkin	274	D	D	D	NA	NA	NA	NA	146	4 550	270.8	91.9
Prowers	31	87	12.0	2.7	NA	NA	NA	NA	37	393	16.3	3.9
Pueblo	251	D	D	D	106	3 838	1 705.8	180.3	344	5 602	220.9	61.8
Rio Blanco	20	46	4.0	1.2	NA	NA	NA	NA	31	278	11.3	3.2
Rio Grande	20	58	5.1	2.2	NA	NA	NA	NA	40	328	14.2	3.9
Routt	186	D	D	D	NA	NA	NA	NA	130	4 813	184.4	61.6
Saguache	11	16	1.3	0.6	NA	NA	NA	NA	10	D	D	D
San Juan	4	D	D	D	NA	NA	NA	NA	22	67	5.1	1.6
San Miguel	83	214	27.7	9.1	NA	NA	NA	NA	74	1 422	77.1	22.8
Sedgwick	5	10	0.8	0.2	NA	NA	NA	NA	8	59	1.7	0.5
Summit	220	D	D	D	NA	NA	NA	NA	208	6 952	281.6	97.8
Teller	95	D	D	D	NA	NA	NA	NA	76	1 790	128.0	38.1
Washington	7	17	1.2	0.4	NA	NA	NA	NA	8	46	1.5	0.4
Weld	462	D	D	D	284	10 186	4 193.7	451.8	379	6 099	217.2	63.8
Yuma	23	D	D	D	NA	NA	NA	NA	31	284	8.8	2.3
CONNECTICUT	9 828	101 384	15 771.7	7 988.8	4 924	190 790	58 404.9	10 345.1	7 941	132 001	9 138.4	2 483.1
Fairfield	3 778	38 942	7 103.5	3 058.3	1 029	42 123	20 028.4	2 455.4	2 094	27 883	1 861.9	523.1
Hartford	2 304	29 103	5 011.1	2 180.3	1 392	63 880	15 016.2	3 584.0	1 956	32 809	1 638.0	483.8
Litchfield	457	D	D	D	405	D	D	509.9	424	4 558	245.2	70.5
Middlesex	396	D	D	D	280	10 104	3 336.0	530.4	410	5 266	293.4	89.8
New Haven	2 015	D	D	D	1 289	40 188	10 493.0	1 976.9	1 920	24 768	1 345.9	371.7
New London	555	D	D	D	201	D	D	848.8	690	30 404	3 444.7	856.8

1. Establishment subject to federal tax.

Table B. States and Counties — **Health Care and Social Assistance, Other Services, Nonemployer Businesses, and Residential Construction**

STATE County	Health care and social assistance, 2007: Number of establish-ments	Health care and social assistance, 2007: Number of employees	Health care and social assistance, 2007: Receipts (mil dol)	Health care and social assistance, 2007: Annual payroll (mil dol)	Other services, 2007: Number of establish-ments	Other services, 2007: Number of employees	Other services, 2007: Receipts (mil dol)	Other services, 2007: Annual payroll (mil dol)	Nonemployer businesses, 2013: Number	Nonemployer businesses, 2013: Receipts (mil dol)	Value of residential construction authorized by building permits, 2014: New Construction ($1,000)	Value of residential construction authorized by building permits, 2014: Number of housing units
	159	160	161	162	163	164	165	166	167	168	169	170
COLORADO—Cont'd												
Boulder	1 158	17 109	1 712.5	716.4	711	4 509	794.5	161.0	35 710	1 846.2	288 246	1 371
Broomfield	110	1 007	89.0	35.0	92	760	127.7	45.5	5 010	213.1	190 713	820
Chaffee	60	661	58.9	22.2	43	153	10.4	3.2	2 113	80.7	26 778	105
Cheyenne	1	D	D	D	6	11	0.8	0.2	197	7.6	170	1
Clear Creek	15	D	D	D	15	33	3.5	1.0	978	44.8	3 713	11
Conejos	10	D	D	D	4	D	D	D	623	26.0	1 504	13
Costilla	7	27	0.9	0.4	2	D	D	D	241	9.4	6 807	30
Crowley	4	80	3.2	1.5	1	D	D	D	163	6.5	500	7
Custer	3	D	D	D	6	D	D	D	655	25.1	10 823	43
Delta	82	1 316	91.7	38.5	56	204	20.6	5.1	2 656	93.3	4 159	47
Denver	1 981	45 826	5 232.8	2 172.8	1 627	12 532	1 821.5	381.8	59 296	3 136.4	811 547	5 958
Dolores	5	D	D	D	NA	NA	NA	NA	149	5.3	255	1
Douglas	598	7 186	765.6	283.9	468	2 646	224.2	66.6	28 689	1 448.1	745 614	3 230
Eagle	144	D	D	D	174	1 998	140.3	36.4	6 887	397.0	117 992	256
Elbert	19	138	8.9	3.3	34	83	7.9	2.3	2 629	119.0	33 254	116
El Paso	1 733	27 411	2 913.8	1 102.7	1 078	8 039	1 315.5	256.3	45 032	1 761.1	1 187 576	3 533
Fremont	104	2 028	126.5	52.7	48	169	12.8	3.6	2 692	95.3	11 985	55
Garfield	143	2 266	286.8	106.0	147	719	64.6	20.0	5 918	303.2	22 647	83
Gilpin	5	D	D	D	7	D	D	D	493	16.4	3 448	13
Grand	32	230	19.0	8.1	42	99	15.3	3.1	1 803	77.8	37 921	137
Gunnison	54	513	37.8	14.4	63	183	25.9	4.2	2 243	89.1	20 262	58
Hinsdale	1	D	D	D	5	D	D	D	167	5.5	1 032	6
Huerfano	17	417	18.1	8.9	9	28	3.2	0.5	580	20.1	3 160	13
Jackson	3	D	D	D	2	D	D	D	175	5.4	0	0
Jefferson	1 441	21 470	1 946.8	821.0	1 124	5 971	579.9	150.6	51 004	2 227.1	492 031	2 519
Kiowa	2	D	D	D	3	D	D	D	145	6.1	0	0
Kit Carson	22	328	18.6	8.3	15	46	4.9	0.9	657	30.0	510	2
Lake	13	D	D	D	12	31	2.1	0.5	608	21.9	0	0
La Plata	223	2 766	275.7	106.7	126	582	47.7	15.2	5 970	281.5	61 007	278
Larimer	908	15 177	1 400.5	610.6	612	3 123	286.8	77.2	28 499	1 234.1	524 427	2 498
Las Animas	41	543	43.0	15.1	43	580	34.6	11.5	911	34.8	817	5
Lincoln	6	212	15.7	7.9	14	D	D	D	392	14.4	160	2
Logan	72	1 203	81.0	32.7	55	261	26.9	7.3	1 219	56.9	2 456	19
Mesa	425	8 480	847.4	336.2	317	1 599	160.1	42.3	11 002	495.1	114 228	504
Mineral	2	D	D	D	4	D	D	D	151	7.9	1 277	6
Moffat	43	485	44.5	15.3	29	217	17.2	4.7	951	40.6	1 103	9
Montezuma	94	1 118	83.6	31.4	55	183	15.4	3.5	2 219	86.8	2 584	15
Montrose	157	2 065	164.6	68.3	85	397	33.0	9.2	3 557	138.3	15 422	89
Morgan	69	1 093	94.8	36.5	45	146	12.1	3.3	1 701	76.5	4 608	20
Otero	62	1 398	79.2	35.4	37	108	8.9	1.9	1 008	32.4	387	2
Ouray	18	60	4.6	1.7	9	16	2.0	0.3	873	42.0	16 357	33
Park	16	64	3.5	1.2	29	D	D	D	1 720	62.9	13 271	88
Phillips	9	261	15.8	7.3	13	43	5.2	1.1	413	19.9	1 689	9
Pitkin	80	709	110.5	37.2	105	777	101.4	24.2	3 528	249.2	207 877	98
Prowers	32	637	46.1	18.0	24	100	8.1	1.9	833	38.3	150	1
Pueblo	410	11 085	872.7	388.5	237	1 160	92.3	25.4	7 860	297.9	28 074	157
Rio Blanco	11	258	22.3	9.2	12	50	3.8	0.9	576	27.1	2 406	10
Rio Grande	34	417	24.3	9.5	31	93	11.1	2.4	1 017	33.6	2 653	12
Routt	100	1 147	124.5	50.9	76	362	30.4	8.3	3 543	164.3	54 449	132
Saguache	7	49	2.7	1.2	9	D	D	D	576	18.4	3 011	32
San Juan	2	D	D	D	2	D	D	D	106	5.0	0	0
San Miguel	26	128	8.7	3.4	38	245	37.5	5.7	1 660	79.1	54 327	36
Sedgwick	4	D	D	D	4	D	D	D	188	6.5	205	1
Summit	84	942	87.7	34.3	112	478	47.6	12.2	4 139	228.0	109 562	207
Teller	63	313	20.6	8.0	49	183	12.7	3.0	2 388	106.9	25 321	140
Washington	7	31	1.5	0.5	9	D	D	D	371	16.0	850	5
Weld	429	8 538	763.1	292.3	340	1 513	161.2	40.0	19 020	875.3	540 224	2 708
Yuma	27	574	43.7	17.8	24	53	5.5	1.0	943	40.5	670	3
CONNECTICUT	10 049	253 360	24 813.2	10 440.0	7 392	47 992	5 061.3	1 395.4	263 511	15 242.6	1 148 276	5 329
Fairfield	2 730	60 407	6 023.6	2 601.2	2 066	13 367	1 722.7	431.1	88 363	6 108.6	611 213	1 880
Hartford	2 686	72 837	7 022.9	3 107.3	1 989	15 781	1 599.2	458.6	56 271	3 052.9	134 850	962
Litchfield	503	9 629	820.4	349.7	391	1 900	158.3	57.7	16 961	923.8	44 875	145
Middlesex	476	12 803	1 175.5	543.0	325	1 527	158.7	43.3	13 156	724.4	46 886	228
New Haven	2 371	68 663	6 467.8	2 792.6	1 772	10 629	948.2	288.9	57 091	2 961.1	150 265	1 140
New London	703	16 048	1 467.8	617.5	479	2 549	234.3	59.3	15 978	754.8	99 302	646

STATE County	Government employment and payroll, 2012									Local government finances, 2012				
			March payroll (percent of total)							General revenue				
												Taxes		
													Per capita[1] (dollars)	
	Full-time equivalent employees	March payroll (dollars)	Adminis-tration, judicial, and legal	Police and Corrections	Fire Protection	Highways and transpor-tation	Health and Welfare	Natural resources and utilities	Education and libraries	Total (mil dol)	Inter-govern-mental (mil dol)	Total (mil dol)	Total	Property
	171	172	173	174	175	176	177	178	179	180	181	182	183	184
COLORADO—Cont'd														
Boulder	11 666	48 102 144	8.2	10.8	5.0	2.7	5.3	10.3	53.3	1 374.3	334.5	816.3	2 674	1 840
Broomfield	687	3 465 698	16.4	35.0	0.0	2.4	10.3	27.3	3.9	167.6	16.5	123.6	2 120	775
Chaffee	981	3 205 729	12.3	6.1	0.6	3.3	43.6	2.3	30.5	122.6	43.2	31.0	1 707	1 041
Cheyenne	186	506 783	7.0	5.9	0.0	7.9	25.6	3.5	46.1	11.6	3.9	4.8	2 562	2 163
Clear Creek	426	1 607 157	17.1	24.4	1.0	10.4	10.2	4.5	29.9	55.5	7.7	41.0	4 539	4 152
Conejos	417	1 165 848	8.0	8.9	0.0	4.9	9.9	3.0	62.1	35.4	24.9	8.0	965	500
Costilla	216	594 990	12.8	7.1	0.6	14.3	13.6	6.0	39.9	21.5	11.8	7.4	2 049	1 959
Crowley	149	372 979	13.1	7.4	0.2	7.6	12.0	7.9	49.2	13.0	9.3	3.0	554	412
Custer	188	561 207	16.3	10.1	0.7	9.8	17.6	3.0	41.1	14.0	3.5	7.4	1 741	1 402
Delta	1 667	6 363 576	6.3	7.6	0.1	3.4	39.9	9.2	32.0	159.9	41.2	32.5	1 067	738
Denver	31 444	153 513 001	5.5	11.6	4.4	12.7	23.1	10.5	30.8	5 569.5	1 334.4	2 071.4	3 266	1 406
Dolores	125	332 266	21.5	7.7	0.0	17.4	6.7	1.6	42.7	5.7	2.5	2.8	1 418	1 324
Douglas	8 978	36 551 403	6.0	11.8	1.8	3.0	0.7	5.6	68.6	1 187.6	326.8	623.8	2 092	1 621
Eagle	1 753	9 241 964	10.1	13.6	8.4	9.4	9.0	14.1	30.0	388.1	36.2	240.3	4 632	3 109
Elbert	793	2 420 569	5.3	13.3	4.8	6.6	3.6	3.3	61.8	68.8	28.9	26.5	1 132	853
El Paso	24 223	94 407 600	4.8	9.4	3.9	2.0	15.6	15.5	46.2	2 544.0	807.4	804.8	1 248	728
Fremont	1 361	4 257 494	6.5	12.3	3.9	5.6	7.8	6.9	53.3	113.3	43.1	39.2	837	567
Garfield	2 715	10 773 217	7.9	10.4	4.9	3.5	18.8	8.7	43.3	377.7	79.3	217.3	3 815	3 060
Gilpin	323	1 493 439	17.4	31.0	11.0	10.9	2.8	6.6	15.7	64.3	18.7	33.2	6 047	1 928
Grand	899	3 399 937	11.0	8.9	1.9	8.6	29.9	12.4	25.0	112.4	11.3	66.9	4 715	3 643
Gunnison	938	4 262 174	12.1	9.1	1.5	9.8	23.1	10.8	16.9	118.1	21.2	51.6	3 335	2 295
Hinsdale	78	213 518	22.4	6.9	0.0	16.9	17.4	4.9	28.8	6.8	1.9	3.5	4 346	3 385
Huerfano	683	2 657 574	9.1	15.2	0.3	8.0	42.0	6.2	18.4	59.2	16.3	13.5	2 049	1 649
Jackson	109	283 034	16.2	7.4	0.3	12.1	6.1	7.8	43.4	7.5	4.3	2.3	1 700	1 447
Jefferson	16 292	67 925 819	8.0	14.5	6.3	2.7	4.7	8.0	53.4	1 796.8	529.1	959.0	1 758	1 296
Kiowa	195	518 331	6.2	3.4	0.1	6.2	53.7	0.0	26.7	13.7	4.6	3.5	2 400	2 321
Kit Carson	599	1 765 320	8.1	7.1	2.1	6.4	30.3	7.6	36.2	45.5	15.1	12.7	1 565	1 397
Lake	1 036	3 786 124	2.2	2.4	4.0	1.7	9.4	2.1	76.3	123.9	28.5	61.1	8 331	7 915
La Plata	2 067	7 718 347	12.2	16.8	4.4	5.9	9.2	7.1	41.1	215.9	60.0	121.8	2 324	1 552
Larimer	10 782	47 317 101	8.8	11.5	1.1	2.8	7.5	18.4	46.2	1 178.8	292.6	577.8	1 861	1 211
Las Animas	790	3 154 143	13.1	10.3	5.0	7.2	4.0	23.0	36.5	67.9	34.0	24.1	1 610	1 155
Lincoln	433	1 393 504	11.8	4.7	0.0	8.0	44.9	2.8	25.9	42.3	17.3	9.6	1 763	1 199
Logan	1 057	3 288 524	7.3	7.7	3.0	24.9	6.5	4.7	43.0	98.6	25.5	33.4	1 475	969
Mesa	5 197	18 735 519	8.2	13.3	5.0	4.1	7.0	9.6	48.8	498.4	180.8	228.0	1 542	966
Mineral	54	178 882	27.1	10.8	0.0	16.4	3.6	2.1	40.0	2.9	0.6	1.5	2 123	1 523
Moffat	596	2 538 838	9.9	13.4	0.2	10.3	6.2	10.3	44.2	92.8	17.6	36.4	2 760	2 173
Montezuma	1 215	5 805 045	11.6	22.2	1.0	7.2	7.7	14.6	27.4	95.8	39.0	40.1	1 577	1 113
Montrose	2 104	7 665 788	7.4	9.0	2.9	5.0	34.2	6.0	34.1	212.1	63.1	64.1	1 574	943
Morgan	1 340	3 811 946	7.6	9.5	0.4	4.0	9.8	9.7	57.0	108.9	39.6	44.8	1 573	1 252
Otero	1 005	2 762 692	7.5	7.2	2.0	3.8	7.9	18.7	51.8	77.3	47.6	18.6	995	589
Ouray	217	778 899	20.7	8.6	4.2	8.7	4.3	7.5	43.5	24.2	6.0	13.1	2 889	2 250
Park	565	1 709 266	7.9	11.7	9.4	8.8	7.9	2.6	45.3	79.9	43.2	27.9	1 739	1 620
Phillips	387	1 231 524	5.8	2.8	0.0	4.9	50.9	5.0	28.5	41.2	11.7	7.9	1 819	1 329
Pitkin	1 617	8 457 732	10.5	7.7	1.5	20.9	24.6	13.9	14.7	334.3	32.9	154.4	8 946	4 437
Prowers	976	3 070 921	6.7	5.7	0.9	3.5	37.0	8.6	32.8	89.1	35.2	16.6	1 340	781
Pueblo	5 698	21 434 409	5.8	12.3	11.0	3.0	6.6	9.0	49.7	552.8	247.0	223.3	1 388	895
Rio Blanco	743	2 764 159	6.3	7.4	0.2	5.5	52.7	8.3	15.4	118.7	16.4	59.8	8 716	7 064
Rio Grande	594	2 555 313	11.1	23.0	0.0	5.2	6.7	1.8	52.0	64.6	42.5	16.8	1 408	981
Routt	1 184	5 565 786	14.7	11.9	5.9	17.1	2.2	12.5	30.0	144.8	31.4	79.2	3 394	2 136
Saguache	347	1 034 643	14.8	8.6	0.3	8.8	6.1	10.3	48.3	55.6	45.0	6.6	1 042	909
San Juan	40	161 715	24.7	12.1	0.0	15.7	7.6	8.1	30.7	9.6	6.5	2.6	3 820	2 945
San Miguel	502	2 269 390	18.4	15.3	2.9	13.4	5.4	10.0	33.5	93.6	14.2	55.2	7 283	5 078
Sedgwick	255	812 165	5.4	2.7	1.9	4.4	48.8	7.8	27.6	22.9	7.9	4.8	2 001	1 581
Summit	1 631	6 095 822	12.4	10.1	11.6	10.3	3.7	14.3	28.7	206.4	13.5	141.5	5 044	2 991
Teller	955	3 818 256	16.1	19.9	2.6	7.0	8.6	7.5	33.5	87.9	28.6	45.4	1 942	1 236
Washington	385	1 126 606	13.3	11.8	0.0	8.2	7.0	2.5	56.0	43.4	28.9	10.2	2 145	1 945
Weld	8 663	35 763 495	8.2	17.4	4.0	5.2	6.6	11.0	45.5	919.9	308.8	411.9	1 562	1 194
Yuma	749	2 253 233	4.4	5.3	0.0	6.1	43.0	5.1	34.4	88.3	21.8	23.8	2 349	2 036
CONNECTICUT	X	X	X	X	X	X	X	X	X	X	X	X	X	X
Fairfield	32 029	179 963 079	3.5	9.1	5.1	3.1	3.2	3.7	70.6	4 597.7	963.2	3 193.1	3 419	3 370
Hartford	31 675	164 755 032	3.0	8.6	3.8	2.4	3.4	4.9	72.4	4 279.2	1 571.4	2 306.6	2 571	2 541
Litchfield	5 578	26 405 841	4.3	6.4	1.8	5.2	1.9	2.5	76.6	698.9	167.1	476.8	2 542	2 521
Middlesex	5 503	26 698 181	4.2	7.4	4.5	3.5	3.5	3.2	71.4	656.2	154.4	441.0	2 663	2 643
New Haven	28 448	140 929 161	3.5	10.1	6.3	2.6	2.7	5.4	68.7	3 790.8	1 443.5	2 034.2	2 358	2 333
New London	8 967	42 369 410	4.4	7.7	3.8	3.8	2.3	8.0	68.3	1 101.6	386.5	598.5	2 183	2 159

1. Based on the resident population estimated as of July 1 of the year shown.

STATE County	Local government finances, 2012 (cont.) — Direct general expenditure: Total (mil dol)	Per capita[1] (dollars)	Percent of total for: Education	Health and hospitals	Police protection	Public welfare	Highways	Debt outstanding: Total (mil dol)	Per capita[1] (dollars)	Government employment, 2013: Federal civilian	Federal military	State and local	Presidential election,[2] 2012 — Percent of vote cast: Democratic	Republican	All other
	185	186	187	188	189	190	191	192	193	194	195	196	197	198	199
COLORADO—Cont'd															
Boulder	1 414.6	4 633	43.6	2.5	8.2	2.3	4.6	1 940.0	6 354	1 990	887	30 192	72.3	26.1	1.6
Broomfield	144.5	2 479	0.0	1.3	11.0	7.9	6.3	650.9	11 165	137	158	1 151	54.9	43.3	1.8
Chaffee	126.2	6 953	33.9	30.5	2.8	4.5	3.0	96.2	5 298	84	45	1 700	49.0	49.1	1.9
Cheyenne	10.0	5 359	50.3	1.1	4.3	21.9	4.7	4.3	2 284	12	0	273	17.8	80.1	2.1
Clear Creek	50.3	5 569	22.6	4.4	10.8	5.5	14.8	19.7	2 186	37	24	650	57.8	39.9	2.3
Conejos	32.7	3 950	48.7	4.8	3.1	18.2	5.7	7.1	857	47	22	539	55.6	42.7	1.7
Costilla	19.3	5 383	36.1	8.6	3.1	5.2	18.0	10.6	2 962	11	0	339	73.4	24.5	2.2
Crowley	12.3	2 296	34.8	0.9	4.5	16.8	7.5	5.3	989	13	0	507	35.4	62.6	1.9
Custer	14.0	3 302	29.4	21.6	5.5	3.1	12.9	5.3	1 249	16	11	224	34.7	63.6	1.7
Delta	164.5	5 405	28.7	38.1	3.5	2.1	6.4	79.3	2 607	171	79	2 158	32.9	65.2	1.8
Denver	4 720.3	7 442	20.3	15.1	4.8	3.6	3.3	12 146.9	19 151	14 014	2 398	51 221	75.5	23.0	1.5
Dolores	8.4	4 230	38.7	1.5	9.3	1.7	28.9	3.1	1 535	10	0	198	30.3	67.2	2.5
Douglas	1 073.0	3 598	46.7	0.7	5.5	1.9	8.1	1 832.6	6 145	378	815	11 140	40.8	58.0	1.2
Eagle	360.2	6 944	19.9	3.1	5.6	0.9	7.0	691.4	13 329	136	141	2 957	60.9	37.8	1.3
Elbert	66.6	2 849	52.4	1.1	2.8	6.7	8.4	163.8	7 006	30	63	906	28.9	69.0	2.1
El Paso	2 502.2	3 880	37.1	21.9	6.0	2.0	8.1	4 398.1	6 819	13 059	39 056	35 517	39.9	58.7	1.4
Fremont	111.0	2 373	42.2	0.5	8.6	5.0	5.7	106.8	2 282	1 117	101	3 991	34.4	63.6	2.0
Garfield	343.8	6 036	29.4	12.6	5.3	5.4	6.2	453.7	7 965	270	150	5 008	49.2	49.2	1.6
Gilpin	50.9	9 270	11.0	2.3	12.0	3.9	11.8	57.5	10 467	10	15	429	59.2	38.0	2.8
Grand	101.5	7 151	19.1	14.0	6.2	1.0	9.3	159.5	11 235	135	37	1 217	48.6	49.7	1.7
Gunnison	122.5	7 917	13.3	24.8	4.1	3.0	11.9	140.6	9 086	168	39	1 813	62.6	35.3	2.1
Hinsdale	7.9	9 716	19.4	25.6	3.8	0.3	8.5	0.7	895	0	0	84	40.1	57.4	2.5
Huerfano	56.4	8 549	15.8	41.7	1.6	2.4	10.2	12.0	1 821	13	17	479	54.6	43.4	2.0
Jackson	7.0	5 173	38.5	4.4	6.1	2.3	23.7	0.7	487	39	0	142	30.3	68.3	1.3
Jefferson	1 793.4	3 289	42.8	1.2	9.3	2.3	4.8	1 397.5	2 563	8 760	1 498	27 197	53.6	44.6	1.8
Kiowa	14.6	10 098	23.1	43.2	3.7	4.8	11.6	4.6	3 195	21	0	234	20.9	76.3	2.8
Kit Carson	45.0	5 561	31.8	27.5	3.7	5.2	8.8	19.9	2 455	40	19	727	26.5	71.3	2.2
Lake	135.4	18 454	79.4	5.5	1.1	1.4	2.2	36.4	4 957	56	19	698	61.9	35.9	2.2
La Plata	202.8	3 869	35.0	1.1	7.0	2.7	5.9	291.6	5 566	366	137	5 229	57.4	41.1	1.5
Larimer	1 080.2	3 479	37.9	4.5	6.4	3.0	9.0	1 388.6	4 472	2 460	845	31 720	54.0	44.3	1.7
Las Animas	67.0	4 482	36.8	3.7	4.8	14.4	8.4	26.1	1 744	63	36	1 625	52.7	45.6	1.7
Lincoln	47.4	8 698	36.7	27.0	2.8	5.8	9.1	9.7	1 786	24	12	964	23.7	74.5	1.8
Logan	73.2	3 236	40.5	1.4	5.0	4.8	10.0	99.6	4 400	68	49	2 381	31.7	66.9	1.4
Mesa	517.8	3 502	35.4	1.7	13.1	5.6	9.4	476.5	3 223	1 474	395	8 127	34.5	64.0	1.5
Mineral	2.9	4 056	57.4	0.8	5.3	0.0	15.9	1.2	1 746	0	0	83	43.3	53.6	3.0
Moffat	93.2	7 060	24.3	30.6	5.6	6.2	10.7	40.3	3 050	153	35	1 011	26.9	70.4	2.6
Montezuma	95.7	3 762	36.0	3.0	10.1	11.6	6.2	60.5	2 379	347	68	2 420	39.4	58.9	1.7
Montrose	215.1	5 283	25.1	29.4	6.1	3.0	9.2	127.2	3 123	312	107	2 598	33.9	63.7	2.4
Morgan	102.1	3 585	44.8	1.5	4.7	4.6	7.3	72.8	2 556	120	74	2 173	37.3	61.3	1.5
Otero	73.8	3 949	48.8	9.4	2.9	2.4	5.4	37.0	1 981	109	48	1 731	44.0	54.5	1.6
Ouray	18.2	4 027	38.4	1.5	6.2	7.7	14.2	11.3	2 485	12	12	363	53.5	44.7	1.9
Park	79.6	4 968	50.7	2.8	3.8	4.7	6.8	28.9	1 800	54	43	750	45.3	52.2	2.5
Phillips	43.4	9 946	35.1	40.0	2.6	1.2	5.0	19.5	4 468	23	11	545	27.5	71.3	1.2
Pitkin	271.6	15 734	9.3	32.7	4.0	1.8	4.6	380.2	22 024	98	46	2 015	73.7	24.9	1.3
Prowers	85.2	6 880	36.9	27.3	5.4	4.4	4.5	184.4	14 887	37	32	1 377	32.2	65.9	1.8
Pueblo	566.4	3 521	40.3	1.5	6.6	5.3	3.7	456.3	2 837	1 014	436	11 541	56.7	41.8	1.5
Rio Blanco	94.0	13 703	15.7	31.1	5.7	2.8	9.7	113.7	16 584	73	17	1 125	20.8	77.4	1.7
Rio Grande	62.5	5 236	64.5	2.5	4.3	3.9	5.0	22.1	1 851	106	31	816	45.0	53.8	1.2
Routt	151.7	6 501	26.1	0.5	3.9	3.9	7.2	168.4	7 217	112	62	1 770	62.7	35.8	1.5
Saguache	54.4	8 636	66.9	1.8	1.8	8.1	6.5	14.0	2 225	47	17	481	63.0	34.7	2.3
San Juan	9.9	14 307	73.7	1.8	5.2	0.9	5.5	1.8	2 645	0	0	73	53.2	44.0	2.8
San Miguel	78.7	10 376	17.1	8.1	5.4	1.7	11.2	104.6	13 797	45	20	729	77.0	21.4	1.6
Sedgwick	21.9	9 187	35.7	36.4	2.6	2.8	4.4	1.7	700	18	0	335	34.6	63.4	1.9
Summit	193.3	6 894	18.6	1.3	5.5	1.0	7.9	128.1	4 569	49	76	2 466	65.8	32.8	1.4
Teller	84.7	3 621	35.6	6.2	7.8	2.8	8.5	55.5	2 371	58	62	1 282	35.0	63.1	1.9
Washington	40.7	8 539	68.2	2.8	2.6	6.4	6.5	14.9	3 135	49	12	448	21.1	77.6	1.4
Weld	839.9	3 185	42.6	1.2	7.3	4.0	6.6	868.6	3 294	579	707	15 375	44.7	53.4	1.9
Yuma	77.9	7 698	25.5	39.3	3.2	4.7	6.7	65.7	6 497	49	27	962	24.9	73.3	1.8
CONNECTICUT	X	X	X	X	X	X	X	X	X	17 392	14 618	227 886	60.7	38.1	1.1
Fairfield	4 616.0	4 044	50.0	1.2	6.6	1.0	3.1	4 013.1	4 207	2 820	1 000	43 880	58.6	40.6	0.7
Hartford	4 219.6	4 703	56.1	0.9	6.3	0.8	4.1	2 673.7	2 980	5 363	1 813	67 163	65.2	33.7	1.1
Litchfield	765.4	4 081	66.1	1.3	3.5	0.2	6.7	390.3	2 081	410	376	8 163	51.6	46.7	1.7
Middlesex	673.0	4 064	63.2	0.8	4.2	0.4	4.0	355.1	2 144	358	327	10 711	60.8	37.8	1.5
New Haven	4 427.8	5 132	58.4	0.6	4.3	0.3	2.5	3 649.0	4 229	5 377	1 935	44 161	61.0	37.8	1.2
New London	1 142.0	4 165	60.1	0.7	5.5	0.6	6.1	911.5	3 324	2 545	7 723	30 905	59.9	38.8	1.3

1. Based on the resident population estimated as of July 1 of the year shown. 2.

STATE/ County code	CBSA code[1]	County type[2]	STATE County	Land area,[3] (sq km) 2010	Population, 2014: Total persons 2014	Population, 2014: Rank	Population, 2014: Per square kilometer	Population and population characteristics, 2013 — Race alone or in combination, not Hispanic or Latino (percent): White	Black	American Indian, Alaska Native	Asian and Pacific Islander	Percent Hispanic or Latino[4]	Age (percent): Under 5 years	5 to 17 years	18 to 24 years	25 to 34 years	35 to 44 years	45 to 54 years
				1	2	3	4	5	6	7	8	9	10	11	12	13	14	15
			CONNECTICUT—Cont'd															
09 013	25540	1	Tolland	1 062	151 367	424	142.5	88.0	3.7	0.5	4.5	4.8	4.1	14.9	17.7	10.4	11.1	15.1
09 015	49340	4	Windham	1 328	116 998	524	88.1	85.9	2.6	1.1	1.7	10.5	5.2	15.8	10.4	12.3	12.6	15.8
10 000	...	X	DELAWARE	5 047	935 614	X	185.4	65.9	22.5	0.9	4.2	8.7	6.1	15.9	10.0	13.0	12.0	14.2
10 001	20100	3	Kent	1 518	171 987	370	113.3	66.2	26.0	1.4	3.1	6.6	6.6	17.2	11.0	13.0	11.7	13.6
10 003	37980	1	New Castle	1 104	552 778	119	500.7	61.8	24.9	0.7	5.5	9.2	6.2	16.2	10.7	13.9	12.7	14.6
10 005	41540	4	Sussex	2 424	210 849	304	87.0	76.6	13.5	1.0	1.5	9.2	5.5	14.1	7.2	10.5	10.3	13.4
11 000	...	X	DISTRICT OF COLUMBIA	158	658 893	X	4 170.2	37.4	49.2	0.8	4.8	10.1	6.3	10.9	12.5	22.6	13.9	11.8
11 001	47900	1	District of Columbia	158	658 893	100	4 170.2	37.4	49.2	0.8	4.8	10.1	6.3	10.9	12.5	22.6	13.9	11.8
12 000	...	X	FLORIDA	138 887	19 893 297	X	143.2	57.7	16.3	0.6	3.3	23.6	5.5	15.1	9.1	12.6	12.3	14.0
12 001	23540	3	Alachua	2 266	256 380	260	113.1	65.2	20.9	0.7	6.7	8.9	5.6	12.4	22.7	15.0	10.2	10.7
12 003	27260	1	Baker	1 516	27 093	1 532	17.9	83.5	13.8	1.0	1.0	2.3	6.4	18.6	8.9	13.7	13.4	14.4
12 005	37460	3	Bay	1 964	178 985	359	91.1	80.6	12.0	1.5	3.4	5.4	6.2	15.4	9.2	13.7	12.1	14.6
12 007	...	6	Bradford	761	26 702	1 544	35.1	76.3	19.9	0.8	0.9	3.6	5.9	14.4	8.3	14.4	12.2	14.4
12 009	37340	2	Brevard	2 631	556 885	116	211.7	78.2	11.0	0.9	3.2	9.0	4.7	14.2	7.9	10.5	10.5	15.2
12 011	33100	1	Broward	3 133	1 869 235	17	596.6	41.9	28.0	0.5	4.4	26.8	5.9	15.9	8.6	13.3	13.5	15.2
12 013	...	6	Calhoun	1 469	14 532	2 134	9.9	79.3	14.0	2.1	1.0	5.7	5.6	15.5	7.8	14.0	13.4	14.2
12 015	39460	3	Charlotte	1 762	168 474	377	95.6	86.1	6.2	0.7	1.8	6.5	3.2	10.2	5.6	7.2	8.0	12.2
12 017	26140	4	Citrus	1 507	139 377	453	92.5	90.2	3.4	0.9	2.0	4.9	3.8	11.4	5.7	7.4	8.3	12.6
12 019	27260	1	Clay	1 565	199 798	326	127.7	77.7	11.0	1.0	4.3	8.7	5.6	19.0	8.8	11.7	13.2	15.3
12 021	34940	2	Collier	5 176	348 777	195	67.4	65.5	7.0	0.4	1.7	26.2	4.9	13.6	6.9	10.0	10.3	12.4
12 023	29380	6	Columbia	2 066	67 857	784	32.8	74.8	18.9	1.0	1.5	5.4	5.9	15.7	9.5	12.7	11.7	13.7
12 027	11580	6	DeSoto	1 650	35 012	1 301	21.2	56.2	13.1	0.5	0.8	30.1	5.8	15.6	9.7	13.7	11.9	12.3
12 029	...	6	Dixie	1 826	15 907	2 047	8.7	87.0	9.2	1.1	0.6	3.5	5.6	13.4	7.1	11.3	11.0	14.8
12 031	27260	1	Duval	1 974	897 698	59	454.8	57.5	30.2	0.8	5.6	8.3	6.8	16.2	9.9	15.6	12.9	13.9
12 033	37860	2	Escambia	1 700	310 659	215	182.7	68.2	23.6	1.7	4.3	5.2	6.1	14.9	12.9	13.6	10.9	13.2
12 035	19660	4	Flagler	1 257	102 408	577	81.5	77.1	11.5	0.7	2.9	9.4	4.3	14.2	6.7	8.9	10.5	12.7
12 037	...	6	Franklin	1 385	11 815	2 308	8.5	79.9	15.0	1.0	0.8	4.9	4.4	12.1	7.6	15.7	12.3	13.7
12 039	45220	2	Gadsden	1 337	46 281	1 045	34.6	33.9	55.2	0.6	0.9	10.3	6.3	16.3	8.6	12.3	12.8	14.2
12 041	23540	3	Gilchrist	906	16 997	1 979	18.8	88.3	5.9	1.0	0.8	5.2	5.1	15.1	12.4	10.0	10.7	13.5
12 043	...	6	Glades	2 088	13 635	2 196	6.5	61.2	12.3	4.5	0.9	22.1	4.3	13.0	7.1	13.2	12.0	12.3
12 045	37460	6	Gulf	1 461	15 944	2 044	10.9	75.4	19.6	1.2	0.7	4.8	4.3	11.3	7.9	15.2	14.3	15.8
12 047	...	6	Hamilton	1 331	14 048	2 167	10.6	56.1	34.0	1.1	1.1	9.3	5.4	13.6	12.4	13.3	12.5	13.7
12 049	48100	6	Hardee	1 652	27 469	1 514	16.6	48.4	7.3	0.7	1.6	43.1	7.3	19.5	10.7	13.7	11.9	12.1
12 051	17500	4	Hendry	2 986	38 505	1 208	12.9	35.0	12.4	1.7	1.2	49.9	7.9	20.4	9.8	13.9	12.4	12.6
12 053	45300	1	Hernando	1 224	175 855	362	143.7	82.1	5.6	0.8	1.8	11.2	4.5	14.5	7.0	9.2	10.3	13.0
12 055	42700	4	Highlands	2 633	98 236	599	37.3	70.3	10.1	0.9	1.8	18.1	4.7	13.2	6.5	8.9	8.7	11.0
12 057	45300	1	Hillsborough	2 642	1 316 298	29	498.2	53.9	16.8	0.6	4.6	26.0	6.4	17.0	9.9	14.6	13.7	14.0
12 059	...	6	Holmes	1 240	19 650	1 849	15.8	89.1	7.1	1.9	1.1	2.7	5.2	15.1	9.3	12.1	12.2	14.1
12 061	42680	3	Indian River	1 302	144 755	444	111.2	77.7	9.5	0.6	1.8	11.7	4.5	13.5	6.8	9.0	9.4	12.8
12 063	...	6	Jackson	2 377	48 801	1 006	20.5	67.5	27.4	1.2	1.0	4.5	4.9	13.8	9.1	12.9	13.9	14.1
12 065	45220	2	Jefferson	1 549	14 050	2 166	9.1	59.9	35.8	0.8	0.7	4.1	4.8	12.7	7.3	11.5	12.5	15.4
12 067	...	8	Lafayette	1 407	8 835	2 527	6.3	71.8	15.5	0.7	0.5	12.6	5.4	15.3	11.2	14.8	15.2	13.5
12 069	36740	1	Lake	2 430	315 690	210	129.9	74.3	10.5	0.8	2.6	13.3	5.1	15.0	7.0	10.0	11.1	13.0
12 071	15980	2	Lee	2 032	679 513	93	334.4	70.9	8.7	0.5	2.0	19.1	4.9	14.0	7.4	10.6	10.8	12.6
12 073	45220	2	Leon	1 727	283 988	238	164.4	59.6	31.8	0.8	3.9	6.0	5.4	13.9	23.3	14.0	10.6	11.1
12 075	...	8	Levy	2 896	39 613	1 182	13.7	81.7	10.0	1.1	0.9	7.8	5.1	14.9	7.3	10.2	10.5	14.2
12 077	...	8	Liberty	2 164	8 360	2 570	3.9	73.5	19.6	1.3	0.5	6.5	4.8	15.2	8.9	16.6	15.9	15.4
12 079	...	6	Madison	1 802	18 518	1 894	10.3	55.5	39.2	0.9	0.6	5.0	5.5	14.8	9.2	12.7	12.1	13.8
12 081	35840	2	Manatee	1 924	351 746	192	182.8	73.8	9.4	0.6	2.3	15.3	5.2	14.7	7.1	10.2	10.7	13.1
12 083	36100	2	Marion	4 104	339 167	197	82.6	73.9	13.1	0.8	2.0	11.7	5.0	13.9	7.3	10.0	10.0	12.6
12 085	38940	2	Martin	1 408	153 392	420	108.9	80.0	6.0	0.5	1.6	13.0	4.1	13.0	6.8	8.9	9.6	14.0
12 086	33100	1	Miami-Dade	4 915	2 662 874	7	541.8	15.7	17.2	0.2	2.0	65.0	5.9	14.9	9.6	14.0	14.3	14.9
12 087	28580	4	Monroe	2 547	77 136	715	30.3	70.3	6.8	0.9	1.8	21.0	4.0	10.4	7.1	12.5	12.4	10.2
12 089	27260	1	Nassau	1 680	76 619	717	45.6	88.5	6.9	0.8	1.5	3.8	5.1	15.7	7.6	10.7	12.0	14.7
12 091	18880	3	Okaloosa	2 409	196 512	332	81.6	78.2	10.7	1.3	5.0	8.3	6.7	15.6	10.4	15.5	11.3	13.8
12 093	36380	4	Okeechobee	1 991	39 149	1 192	19.7	64.9	9.0	1.1	1.3	24.8	6.4	16.7	8.9	12.7	12.2	13.5
12 095	36740	1	Orange	2 340	1 253 001	31	535.5	45.5	20.9	0.6	6.2	28.7	6.3	16.6	11.8	16.2	14.0	13.8
12 097	36740	1	Osceola	3 438	310 211	216	90.2	38.5	10.4	0.6	3.4	48.5	6.5	18.9	9.9	13.8	14.1	13.7
12 099	33100	1	Palm Beach	5 102	1 397 710	27	274.0	59.2	18.3	0.4	3.2	20.2	5.2	14.6	8.1	11.4	11.8	13.9
12 101	45300	1	Pasco	1 934	485 331	140	250.9	79.6	5.4	0.7	2.9	13.0	5.1	15.5	7.3	10.6	12.3	14.0
12 103	45300	1	Pinellas	709	938 098	52	1 323.1	77.3	11.2	0.7	4.0	8.6	4.5	12.7	7.4	11.2	11.3	15.1
12 105	29460	2	Polk	4 656	634 638	101	136.3	64.2	15.4	0.7	2.2	19.0	6.0	17.0	8.8	12.1	11.8	12.8

1. CBSA = Core Based Statistical Area. See Appendix A for explanation. See Appendix B for list of metropolitan areas with component counties. 2. County type code from the Economic Research Service of USDA Rural-Urban Continuum Codes. See Appendix A for definition. 3. Dry land or land partially or temporarily covered by water. 4. May be of any race.

STATE County	Population, 2013 (cont.) Age (percent) (cont.) 55 to 64 years	65 to 74 years	75 years and over	Percent female	Population change and components of change, 2000–2014 Total persons 2000	2010	Percent change 2000–2010	2010–2014	Components of change, 2010–2014 Births	Deaths	Net migration	Households, 2009–2013 Number	Persons per house-hold	Percent Family house-holds	Female family house-holder[1]	One per-son
	16	17	18	19	20	21	22	23	24	25	26	27	28	29	30	31
CONNECTICUT—Cont'd																
Tolland	13.2	7.9	5.6	49.9	136 364	152 691	12.0	-0.9	4 897	4 149	-1 937	54 327	2.52	68.8	9.5	24.5
Windham	13.7	8.1	6.2	50.3	109 091	118 428	8.6	-1.2	5 056	4 075	-2 354	44 018	2.57	67.7	12.5	25.7
DELAWARE	13.1	9.3	6.6	51.6	783 600	897 934	14.6	4.2	47 400	33 845	23 974	335 707	2.63	67.6	13.9	26.2
Kent	11.8	8.9	6.2	51.8	126 697	162 310	28.1	5.9	9 320	6 172	6 319	58 524	2.74	69.8	15.4	24.6
New Castle	12.5	7.5	5.8	51.6	500 265	538 479	7.6	2.7	28 460	18 399	4 737	200 739	2.62	66.8	14.3	26.8
Sussex	15.5	14.3	9.1	51.4	156 638	197 145	25.9	7.0	9 620	9 274	12 918	76 444	2.58	67.8	11.8	25.8
DISTRICT OF COLUMBIA	10.6	6.3	5.0	52.6	572 059	601 723	5.2	9.5	39 983	20 670	37 229	263 649	2.20	42.6	15.9	45.4
District of Columbia	10.6	6.3	5.0	52.6	572 059	601 723	5.2	9.5	39 983	20 670	37 229	263 649	2.20	42.6	15.9	45.4
FLORIDA	12.8	10.2	8.5	51.1	15 982 378	18 801 310	17.6	5.8	908 600	760 861	917 135	7 158 980	2.61	64.7	13.2	28.8
Alachua	11.4	6.9	5.1	51.7	217 955	247 336	13.5	3.7	12 254	7 454	4 123	96 043	2.43	53.5	12.0	32.3
Baker	12.1	7.7	4.7	47.8	22 259	27 115	21.8	-0.1	1 449	969	-490	8 216	3.01	76.7	12.1	19.0
Bay	12.9	9.0	6.8	50.4	148 217	168 852	13.9	6.0	9 520	7 173	7 510	67 561	2.48	64.7	11.8	28.6
Bradford	13.3	9.6	7.4	45.4	26 088	28 520	9.3	-6.4	1 350	1 220	-2 033	8 857	2.72	69.6	14.8	25.1
Brevard	14.9	11.7	10.3	51.2	476 230	543 376	14.1	2.5	21 451	26 811	17 928	220 277	2.44	64.5	11.5	29.5
Broward	12.5	8.0	7.0	51.4	1 623 018	1 748 066	7.7	6.9	90 351	62 161	92 844	663 458	2.67	63.1	15.5	30.1
Calhoun	12.6	9.6	7.3	45.6	13 017	14 625	12.4	-0.6	622	598	-139	4 696	2.70	67.5	13.6	27.1
Charlotte	16.7	19.9	17.2	51.4	141 627	159 978	13.0	5.3	4 312	9 854	13 557	70 545	2.24	65.4	7.7	28.9
Citrus	16.3	18.9	15.6	51.6	118 085	141 236	19.6	-1.3	4 421	10 004	3 553	60 319	2.29	63.9	8.4	30.3
Clay	12.6	8.5	5.2	50.9	140 814	190 865	35.5	4.7	8 882	6 449	6 395	67 805	2.82	75.2	13.2	19.6
Collier	13.0	15.2	13.6	50.7	251 377	321 520	27.9	8.5	13 602	12 684	25 365	122 972	2.64	67.1	9.1	28.1
Columbia	13.8	10.0	6.9	48.3	56 513	67 531	19.5	0.5	3 346	3 239	294	23 604	2.69	64.9	15.1	31.3
DeSoto	11.6	11.0	8.4	43.7	32 209	34 862	8.2	0.4	1 611	1 197	-221	10 622	2.89	69.7	15.0	25.3
Dixie	15.2	13.4	8.0	46.4	13 827	16 422	18.8	-3.1	661	843	-288	6 130	2.49	62.8	8.8	33.0
Duval	12.3	7.2	5.1	51.5	778 879	864 263	11.0	3.9	52 992	31 874	12 280	330 897	2.58	62.8	15.7	30.7
Escambia	12.9	8.8	6.7	50.3	294 410	297 619	1.1	4.4	16 423	13 317	9 784	111 689	2.51	61.9	14.4	31.5
Flagler	15.3	16.0	11.4	52.0	49 832	95 696	92.0	7.0	3 415	4 684	7 551	35 647	2.71	70.7	9.4	24.3
Franklin	14.4	12.7	7.1	42.7	11 057	11 549	4.4	2.3	461	512	307	4 294	2.23	68.1	13.4	26.9
Gadsden	14.4	8.7	6.2	49.9	45 087	46 389	2.9	-3.1	2 440	1 953	-1 961	16 662	2.62	65.1	19.5	31.4
Gilchrist	14.2	10.8	8.0	47.5	14 437	16 939	17.3	0.3	818	730	-35	6 240	2.51	71.0	9.4	23.4
Glades	12.9	14.6	10.7	43.4	10 576	12 884	21.8	5.8	308	424	672	3 843	3.05	66.3	13.6	27.6
Gulf	13.8	10.2	7.1	40.0	13 332	15 863	19.0	0.5	534	662	174	5 414	2.49	68.7	12.6	25.7
Hamilton	13.8	9.5	5.9	42.1	13 327	14 799	11.0	-5.1	658	516	-924	4 657	2.45	65.8	18.6	31.3
Hardee	10.3	8.2	6.3	46.5	26 938	27 731	2.9	-0.9	1 697	812	-1 179	7 463	3.38	76.4	15.9	19.2
Hendry	10.2	7.4	5.4	47.8	36 210	39 140	8.1	-1.6	2 544	1 154	-2 096	11 223	3.15	69.9	17.5	22.7
Hernando	14.2	14.7	12.5	52.1	130 802	172 778	32.1	1.8	6 199	10 694	7 180	70 210	2.44	68.2	11.7	27.5
Highlands	13.2	16.9	16.7	51.3	87 366	98 786	13.1	-0.6	3 848	6 168	1 709	39 931	2.42	64.0	9.1	30.7
Hillsborough	11.6	7.2	5.5	51.3	998 948	1 229 226	23.1	7.1	70 010	41 002	56 858	471 340	2.63	63.8	14.2	29.0
Holmes	13.4	10.6	7.9	46.7	18 564	19 927	7.3	-1.4	803	1 062	-12	6 808	2.65	69.3	10.9	26.7
Indian River	14.7	14.6	14.6	52.0	112 947	138 028	22.2	4.9	5 362	7 600	8 312	58 038	2.37	64.1	9.8	30.6
Jackson	13.5	9.8	7.8	45.0	46 755	49 746	6.4	-1.9	2 066	2 332	-538	16 244	2.55	65.6	13.7	30.9
Jefferson	16.4	11.8	7.7	47.7	12 902	14 761	14.4	-4.8	559	609	-661	5 347	2.36	68.0	14.9	28.2
Lafayette	10.9	7.7	6.0	40.2	7 022	8 870	26.3	-0.4	335	307	-63	2 710	2.75	64.1	11.4	30.7
Lake	13.1	14.1	11.6	51.6	210 528	297 052	41.1	6.3	12 984	14 816	19 849	117 250	2.53	69.3	9.7	25.1
Lee	14.0	14.6	11.1	50.9	440 888	618 754	40.3	9.8	27 063	26 381	57 918	241 531	2.59	66.2	10.1	27.7
Leon	10.9	6.5	4.4	52.5	239 452	275 487	15.0	3.1	12 801	7 313	2 864	110 377	2.40	55.9	13.4	29.7
Levy	15.6	13.6	8.6	50.8	34 450	40 801	18.4	-2.9	1 643	2 155	-673	15 582	2.54	67.3	14.0	27.1
Liberty	11.6	7.0	4.5	38.3	7 021	8 365	19.1	-0.1	328	246	-94	2 305	2.91	64.8	12.3	28.1
Madison	14.4	10.0	7.5	47.3	18 733	19 224	2.6	-3.7	915	888	-761	6 739	2.52	69.9	16.0	27.0
Manatee	14.0	13.5	11.6	51.6	264 002	322 833	22.3	9.0	14 504	14 866	28 022	131 197	2.48	64.4	10.2	29.4
Marion	13.9	15.3	12.0	52.0	258 916	331 298	28.0	2.4	14 131	19 089	12 313	134 002	2.43	67.1	11.7	27.1
Martin	14.7	14.3	14.6	50.4	126 731	146 318	15.5	4.5	4 965	7 524	8 903	59 891	2.41	62.2	7.7	33.1
Miami-Dade	11.4	7.9	7.0	51.4	2 253 362	2 496 435	10.8	6.6	131 349	80 077	112 470	828 031	3.02	68.6	18.1	25.9
Monroe	17.2	12.2	7.5	47.3	79 589	73 090	-8.2	5.5	3 077	2 777	3 753	28 503	2.54	58.2	7.2	31.3
Nassau	15.3	12.0	7.0	50.8	57 663	73 314	27.1	4.5	3 218	2 997	2 837	28 044	2.62	73.5	11.2	21.8
Okaloosa	12.1	8.2	6.5	49.2	170 498	180 822	6.1	8.7	11 245	6 631	10 850	73 253	2.47	67.3	12.7	26.7
Okeechobee	12.2	10.0	7.4	46.2	35 910	39 996	11.4	-2.1	2 249	1 654	-1 619	12 999	2.86	69.2	13.8	26.0
Orange	10.7	6.1	4.4	50.7	896 344	1 145 956	27.8	9.3	66 309	30 210	70 490	415 790	2.76	64.2	14.9	27.1
Osceola	10.8	7.5	4.8	50.8	172 493	268 685	55.8	15.5	18 341	7 709	02 203	90 413	3.07	74.8	17.4	20.0
Palm Beach	12.5	10.7	11.8	51.6	1 131 184	1 320 134	16.7	5.9	59 251	57 431	73 904	526 007	2.51	61.8	12.0	31.6
Pasco	13.1	12.2	10.0	51.4	344 765	464 697	34.8	4.4	20 181	23 605	22 959	182 707	2.53	66.3	10.6	27.8
Pinellas	15.2	11.7	10.9	52.0	921 482	916 542	-0.5	2.3	36 037	48 733	33 481	401 708	2.24	55.6	11.2	37.0
Polk	12.3	10.9	8.3	51.0	483 924	602 095	24.4	5.4	30 903	25 499	26 568	219 540	2.71	69.1	13.8	25.5

1. No spouse present.

STATE County	Persons in group quarters, 2014	Daytime population, 2009–2013: Number	Daytime population, 2009–2013: Employment/residence ratio	Births, 2014: Total	Births, 2014: Rate[1]	Deaths, 2014: Number	Deaths, 2014: Rate[1]	Persons under 65 with no health insurance, 2013: Number	Persons under 65 with no health insurance, 2013: Percent	Medicare, 2014: Eligible for Medicare	Medicare, 2014: Enrolled in Medicare Advantage	Medicare, 2014: Enrolled in a Medicare prescription drug plan	Serious crimes known to police,[2] 2013: Total: Number	Serious crimes known to police,[2] 2013: Total: Rate[3]
	32	33	34	35	36	37	38	39	40	41	42	43	44	45
CONNECTICUT—Cont'd														
Tolland	15 515	124 485	0.64	1 135	7.5	958	6.3	8 969	7.7	23 861	6 186	11 044	NA	NA
Windham	4 915	103 338	0.74	1 182	10.1	954	8.2	10 998	11.3	20 929	4 562	11 089	NA	NA
DELAWARE	25 510	908 798	1.00	11 134	11.9	8 278	8.8	82 412	10.9	175 549	13 357	112 437	32 928	3 557
Kent	4 578	156 883	0.89	2 219	12.9	1 542	9.0	14 497	10.4	31 124	2 107	18 980	5 826	3 433
New Castle	18 117	558 811	1.06	6 609	12.0	4 402	8.0	45 752	10.0	88 618	8 417	57 525	20 325	3 695
Sussex	2 815	193 104	0.91	2 306	10.9	2 334	11.1	22 163	14.1	55 807	2 833	35 932	7 469	3 628
DISTRICT OF COLUMBIA	40 293	1 103 540	2.55	9 647	14.6	5 228	7.9	40 951	7.6	87 008	10 557	38 264	39 489	6 109
District of Columbia	40 293	1 103 540	2.55	9 647	14.6	5 228	7.9	40 951	7.6	87 008	10 557	38 264	39 512	6 112
FLORIDA	431 463	19 046 722	0.99	214 567	10.8	187 102	9.4	3 775 449	24.3	3 895 288	1 514 669	1 380 667	699 158	3 576
Alachua	13 311	265 198	1.14	2 856	11.1	1 847	7.2	40 292	19.1	37 434	6 045	15 719	9 274	3 655
Baker	2 349	23 872	0.67	336	12.4	217	8.0	3 641	17.0	4 282	999	1 833	464	1 706
Bay	3 937	172 461	1.02	2 300	12.9	1 800	10.1	27 807	19.3	34 191	5 829	13 914	7 839	4 520
Bradford	3 209	25 615	0.75	305	11.4	316	11.8	3 601	18.7	5 151	1 018	2 210	516	1 971
Brevard	6 726	538 632	0.97	5 043	9.1	6 512	11.7	84 893	20.0	135 515	47 077	42 429	18 282	3 321
Broward	16 161	1 718 849	0.92	21 354	11.4	15 069	8.1	398 540	25.8	282 197	149 012	77 864	71 058	3 855
Calhoun	1 959	13 518	0.72	143	9.8	138	9.5	2 146	20.5	2 647	689	1 172	84	567
Charlotte	3 221	156 785	0.91	1 037	6.2	2 420	14.4	23 743	23.4	57 516	17 229	25 473	3 799	2 317
Citrus	2 249	134 442	0.87	1 009	7.2	2 410	17.3	19 393	21.5	51 527	15 547	21 384	3 177	2 333
Clay	1 251	155 487	0.56	2 093	10.5	1 591	8.0	28 359	16.9	34 150	7 330	11 500	4 672	2 383
Collier	4 548	335 346	1.05	3 187	9.1	3 156	9.0	71 254	29.9	82 582	16 186	44 026	6 021	1 787
Columbia	4 948	68 070	1.02	769	11.3	768	11.3	10 471	20.2	13 813	2 493	6 043	2 757	4 035
DeSoto	3 827	34 608	1.00	360	10.3	279	8.0	9 092	36.8	6 387	1 419	3 057	972	2 794
Dixie	1 440	15 330	0.82	154	9.7	194	12.2	2 268	20.3	3 868	802	1 743	524	3 256
Duval	20 568	950 175	1.19	12 472	13.9	7 921	8.8	146 935	19.4	138 506	40 093	52 567	40 731	4 589
Escambia	20 874	314 295	1.10	3 885	12.5	3 272	10.5	44 621	18.5	61 972	16 152	19 929	15 914	5 211
Flagler	684	87 059	0.70	798	7.8	1 114	10.9	15 952	22.1	30 461	11 365	11 206	2 189	2 200
Franklin	1 926	11 448	0.97	111	9.4	99	8.4	1 950	25.8	2 548	617	1 122	230	1 952
Gadsden	3 418	42 416	0.74	523	11.3	491	10.6	8 339	22.6	9 189	4 237	2 530	1 034	2 264
Gilchrist	1 094	14 651	0.60	204	12.0	174	10.2	3 087	24.1	3 520	721	1 521	201	1 195
Glades	1 483	12 035	0.72	77	5.6	107	7.8	2 911	34.3	2 213	590	932	201	1 521
Gulf	3 596	14 952	0.85	124	7.8	151	9.5	2 280	23.5	3 287	538	1 641	444	2 819
Hamilton	2 480	13 913	0.82	149	10.6	114	8.1	1 913	20.2	2 650	479	1 330	413	2 794
Hardee	2 004	26 981	0.96	386	14.1	168	6.1	6 685	30.7	4 012	845	2 123	761	2 746
Hendry	698	38 235	0.99	596	15.5	284	7.4	10 718	33.2	5 087	1 142	2 529	1 466	3 954
Hernando	1 835	158 947	0.74	1 435	8.2	2 561	14.6	27 997	22.3	52 557	26 410	15 068	4 519	2 594
Highlands	1 733	97 186	0.96	881	9.0	1 442	14.7	17 847	27.8	29 986	8 058	13 789	3 309	3 696
Hillsborough	22 028	1 318 553	1.11	16 500	12.5	10 392	7.9	226 659	20.5	200 222	90 331	59 560	32 820	2 529
Holmes	1 860	17 603	0.64	182	9.3	236	12.0	3 029	21.1	4 685	731	2 187	350	1 763
Indian River	1 320	139 410	1.00	1 256	8.7	1 887	13.0	26 288	26.5	42 657	9 149	20 639	3 402	2 398
Jackson	8 439	48 963	0.98	493	10.1	577	11.8	5 869	18.0	10 684	1 711	4 732	993	2 146
Jefferson	1 307	12 449	0.60	133	9.5	140	10.0	2 030	19.9	3 177	1 293	964	229	1 618
Lafayette	1 804	7 827	0.73	74	8.4	72	8.1	1 633	27.8	998	138	520	54	611
Lake	3 913	274 286	0.77	3 111	9.9	3 728	11.8	47 972	21.2	85 907	25 557	35 817	7 754	2 612
Lee	8 482	622 252	0.95	6 516	9.6	6 568	9.7	131 059	27.1	159 250	48 298	70 988	16 584	2 527
Leon	15 136	296 716	1.13	2 936	10.3	1 762	6.2	40 863	17.3	36 652	15 646	8 615	13 140	4 571
Levy	336	35 688	0.66	377	9.5	498	12.6	7 996	26.1	10 483	2 421	4 654	NA	NA
Liberty	2 140	7 968	0.87	76	9.1	58	6.9	1 203	22.3	1 267	427	447	65	784
Madison	2 015	17 643	0.77	212	11.4	218	11.8	2 728	20.0	3 906	925	1 850	593	3 143
Manatee	4 816	310 197	0.85	3 493	9.9	3 620	10.3	62 214	24.6	82 891	26 886	34 105	12 523	3 697
Marion	9 223	325 445	0.93	3 268	9.6	4 566	13.5	57 134	24.1	100 422	37 689	36 988	8 413	2 492
Martin	4 177	150 108	1.04	1 161	7.6	1 878	12.2	23 960	23.0	40 641	9 599	18 881	3 539	2 357
Miami-Dade	41 775	2 614 256	1.06	30 445	11.4	19 975	7.5	725 898	33.1	418 177	255 829	113 430	126 865	4 823
Monroe	2 014	76 645	1.07	750	9.7	695	9.0	16 534	27.4	15 316	1 373	7 822	3 374	4 461
Nassau	543	63 172	0.65	751	9.8	795	10.4	10 576	17.4	16 952	4 066	7 364	1 284	1 705
Okaloosa	4 852	194 030	1.09	2 707	13.8	1 658	8.4	30 669	19.1	34 858	4 320	10 385	5 238	2 699
Okeechobee	2 647	39 086	0.96	514	13.1	385	9.8	8 647	28.8	7 597	2 487	3 006	1 682	4 265
Orange	34 696	1 319 173	1.26	15 980	12.8	7 533	6.0	258 379	24.1	157 008	66 828	46 600	58 773	4 797
Osceola	3 282	248 508	0.74	4 025	13.0	1 960	6.3	69 454	26.8	46 367	25 143	11 329	10 173	3 452
Palm Beach	20 684	1 355 593	1.03	14 144	10.1	14 180	10.1	265 486	25.4	286 114	104 560	117 399	48 469	3 531
Pasco	5 821	409 743	0.67	4 757	9.8	5 680	11.7	76 844	21.0	112 707	58 282	31 555	13 950	2 944
Pinellas	19 858	929 660	1.02	8 568	9.1	11 960	12.7	155 304	21.9	218 130	98 230	67 792	38 570	4 163
Polk	12 575	584 399	0.89	7 268	11.5	6 215	9.8	117 135	23.8	132 554	59 478	42 013	20 402	3 276

1. Per 1,000 estimated resident population. 2. Data for serious crimes have not been adjusted for underreporting; this may affect comparability between geographic areas and over time.
3. Per 100,000 population estimated by the FBI.

Table B. States and Counties — **Crime, Education, Money Income, and Poverty**

STATE County	Serious crimes known to police, 2013 (cont.)[1] — Rate[2]		Education — School enrollment and attainment, 2009–2013				Education — Local government expenditures,[5] 2012–2013		Money income, 2009–2013				Income and poverty, 2013			
			Enrollment[3]		Attainment[4] (percent)					Households				Percent below poverty level		
	Violent	Property	Total	Percent private	High school graduate or less	Bachelor's degree or more	Total current spending (mil dol)	Current spending per student (dollars)	Per capita income[6] (dollars)	Median income (dollars)	Mean income (dollars)	Percent with income of $200,000 or more	Median household income (dollars)	All persons	Children under 18 years	Children 5 to 17 years in families
	46	47	48	49	50	51	52	53	54	55	56	57	58	59	60	61
CONNECTICUT—Cont'd																
Tolland	NA	NA	49 754	10.8	34.2	36.9	340.0	15 804	34 392	80 529	94 146	6.8	73 660	6.4	7.0	6.2
Windham	NA	NA	30 284	10.1	50.0	22.3	266.9	17 361	27 893	59 333	72 403	2.8	55 948	13.0	18.0	16.4
DELAWARE	491	3 066	234 336	20.5	43.9	28.9	1 689.5	13 833	29 819	59 878	77 915	4.8	58 244	12.9	19.1	17.5
Kent	456	2 977	45 701	17.2	48.3	21.4	306.6	13 046	24 851	55 149	66 276	2.3	53 811	13.5	20.2	17.5
New Castle	534	3 160	149 223	23.3	39.8	33.8	984.7	14 721	32 406	64 537	85 404	6.1	63 033	11.9	16.9	15.6
Sussex	446	3 182	39 412	13.8	51.0	22.2	398.2	14 075	26 908	52 710	67 161	3.2	50 207	14.8	24.6	23.0
DISTRICT OF COLUMBIA	1 300	4 808	157 837	43.8	30.4	52.4	883.2	17 953	45 290	65 830	101 076	11.9	66 326	18.8	29.3	29.9
District of Columbia	1 302	4 810	157 837	43.8	30.4	52.4	883.2	19 990	45 290	65 830	101 076	11.9	66 326	18.8	29.3	29.9
FLORIDA	470	3 105	4 625 006	17.5	43.7	26.4	23 144.9	8 433	26 236	46 956	66 368	3.7	46 021	17.1	24.8	23.5
Alachua	564	3 092	93 312	9.1	30.1	40.5	243.3	8 744	24 857	42 149	62 061	4.0	39 614	25.7	25.7	24.8
Baker	346	1 360	6 747	13.0	67.0	10.0	40.0	8 036	19 852	49 236	61 205	2.4	46 505	18.8	25.6	24.0
Bay	510	4 010	40 039	11.4	44.0	21.1	209.8	7 876	24 498	47 461	59 743	2.2	45 249	18.0	28.4	25.1
Bradford	489	1 482	5 203	12.9	61.4	9.2	30.7	9 378	17 749	40 259	52 033	2.0	40 668	21.8	29.1	28.0
Brevard	525	2 796	121 195	18.5	39.4	26.3	568.2	7 977	27 009	48 039	64 115	2.9	46 677	15.0	21.9	20.2
Broward	435	3 420	466 525	21.8	40.0	29.9	2 183.4	8 390	28 205	51 251	71 963	4.5	50 343	15.2	19.5	18.0
Calhoun	122	446	3 111	4.3	65.9	7.8	19.8	8 730	14 675	32 780	43 352	1.1	33 977	23.8	32.7	28.9
Charlotte	238	2 079	25 438	17.6	45.7	21.2	146.4	8 952	26 286	44 378	57 495	1.6	43 611	14.4	25.3	22.1
Citrus	388	1 945	22 913	14.3	52.0	16.6	136.2	8 895	23 148	39 100	51 597	1.5	39 285	17.3	29.1	27.2
Clay	336	2 047	54 840	14.0	38.8	24.0	278.4	7 900	26 577	59 482	73 178	3.2	57 991	9.9	14.1	13.2
Collier	233	1 554	63 240	15.9	41.8	31.7	445.8	10 182	36 439	55 843	91 387	8.3	55 584	13.4	24.1	22.9
Columbia	685	3 350	15 895	13.8	52.2	13.3	80.5	8 212	19 306	38 070	50 730	1.6	41 722	18.8	29.5	26.6
DeSoto	532	2 263	7 228	7.9	68.4	10.6	44.2	9 298	15 088	34 963	43 594	0.5	33 198	33.9	46.5	44.4
Dixie	416	2 840	2 935	7.1	60.2	8.4	17.8	8 696	16 851	33 981	41 341	0.7	31 649	27.1	39.5	40.0
Duval	623	3 966	228 850	20.8	40.7	26.4	1 057.5	8 414	26 143	48 323	65 569	3.2	47 876	17.1	25.6	22.6
Escambia	714	4 497	75 544	20.9	40.6	23.7	338.9	8 334	23 441	43 918	58 570	2.1	42 742	17.6	29.6	27.8
Flagler	289	1 910	19 932	14.2	43.1	23.3	109.4	8 468	24 497	47 233	62 177	2.5	47 872	14.5	24.4	23.2
Franklin	289	1 664	1 812	6.3	57.7	14.4	13.1	10 655	19 843	38 328	52 360	1.9	33 471	25.9	38.9	37.0
Gadsden	416	1 848	11 059	15.1	58.2	14.9	61.8	10 174	17 615	35 380	46 489	0.8	34 348	25.3	39.6	41.3
Gilchrist	214	981	3 577	11.8	58.2	11.1	24.3	9 445	20 180	38 406	53 081	1.1	39 854	21.9	32.2	31.1
Glades	318	1 203	2 104	11.1	63.9	12.2	13.6	8 987	16 011	34 694	43 249	0.6	39 003	24.1	36.0	31.3
Gulf	591	2 229	2 833	9.6	57.6	13.6	18.0	9 344	18 546	40 455	50 251	1.3	38 880	22.4	29.7	28.8
Hamilton	453	2 341	2 736	12.5	64.9	9.4	17.9	10 769	16 295	37 716	49 578	0.8	33 836	29.2	40.5	39.7
Hardee	267	2 479	6 378	4.2	71.5	8.8	45.2	8 927	15 366	37 125	51 321	1.6	34 884	28.8	38.7	36.4
Hendry	728	3 225	10 174	7.2	68.0	9.9	58.8	8 603	16 133	35 425	50 399	1.1	37 085	25.1	38.4	37.1
Hernando	309	2 285	36 694	12.8	51.9	15.5	176.6	7 950	21 411	41 024	50 957	1.3	39 280	15.6	25.6	24.0
Highlands	390	3 307	17 083	11.6	55.7	14.9	103.3	8 558	20 072	35 560	46 645	1.1	34 054	20.1	33.4	31.8
Hillsborough	336	2 193	339 917	16.5	41.2	29.5	1 757.4	8 766	27 149	49 596	69 525	4.4	49 510	16.8	24.0	22.9
Holmes	358	1 406	4 185	7.6	60.8	12.0	27.7	8 331	16 845	35 511	45 505	0.7	33 220	27.5	38.3	35.9
Indian River	295	2 102	27 481	14.6	41.7	26.6	144.9	8 047	30 532	44 772	70 719	5.1	44 326	14.1	24.1	22.8
Jackson	417	1 729	11 024	18.0	56.7	14.2	61.9	8 938	17 525	36 809	47 623	1.5	36 332	26.3	38.1	35.9
Jefferson	728	890	2 688	23.4	52.7	16.9	11.7	11 210	21 184	44 170	56 670	2.2	39 494	19.6	30.9	29.8
Lafayette	328	283	1 859	13.3	60.3	9.3	10.1	8 448	18 660	39 722	56 160	1.5	37 120	25.2	32.5	29.6
Lake	317	2 296	62 446	16.8	47.8	20.5	320.6	7 727	24 183	45 035	59 808	1.8	44 244	14.5	23.7	22.4
Lee	333	2 194	132 085	13.3	45.5	24.7	756.4	8 819	27 348	47 439	67 429	4.0	46 605	16.3	27.2	26.7
Leon	638	3 933	107 403	10.5	27.8	44.2	290.1	8 677	26 196	46 369	64 947	3.5	46 975	21.7	22.6	21.8
Levy	NA	NA	8 938	11.3	58.5	11.1	48.0	8 486	18 304	34 348	45 171	1.0	33 193	23.6	39.3	38.5
Liberty	145	639	1 767	2.7	65.7	12.8	14.7	9 966	16 266	39 681	53 639	1.7	36 561	27.7	33.3	31.6
Madison	832	2 311	3 999	8.6	60.2	9.7	25.0	9 443	15 538	33 833	43 551	0.9	30 391	28.9	42.1	42.4
Manatee	576	3 121	66 966	15.2	43.9	26.6	396.2	8 583	27 322	47 876	65 293	3.5	48 066	16.0	28.3	26.8
Marion	430	2 061	66 229	16.0	51.4	17.4	350.4	8 344	21 992	39 453	52 739	1.8	38 783	19.6	30.1	28.4
Martin	185	2 171	28 734	16.8	37.6	29.9	164.2	8 789	34 057	49 846	80 143	6.7	51 159	13.5	20.6	18.5
Miami-Dade	655	4 168	646 306	21.0	49.5	26.3	3 183.4	8 986	23 174	43 100	65 616	4.3	41 840	21.0	27.8	26.6
Monroe	517	3 944	12 445	13.9	40.1	28.0	87.1	10 425	33 974	53 607	80 531	6.5	50 380	16.8	23.6	25.6
Nassau	116	1 590	16 854	13.9	45.7	22.8	89.7	8 099	28 926	55 315	74 307	3.9	56 987	13.4	20.4	19.7
Okaloosa	430	2 269	45 112	12.2	36.3	27.4	249.9	8 388	28 600	54 684	70 388	3.7	54 265	13.4	20.8	21.7
Okeechobee	385	3 880	9 104	9.1	65.6	10.2	55.9	8 598	17 787	34 570	49 995	1.6	35 954	25.7	37.0	36.0
Orange	678	4 119	343 444	18.6	39.8	30.1	1 526.4	8 338	24 877	47 581	66 709	3.8	46 675	18.2	26.0	25.0
Osceola	478	2 974	75 769	13.9	51.0	17.6	455.4	8 073	19 007	43 891	54 987	1.7	41 592	20.7	32.0	32.4
Palm Beach	450	3 080	305 449	19.2	38.7	32.1	1 692.7	9 129	32 858	52 432	70 066	6.2	61 768	15.0	22.7	21.6
Pasco	289	2 656	102 924	15.9	47.4	20.4	535.8	7 978	23 736	43 888	58 132	2.0	45 454	13.5	19.2	18.2
Pinellas	552	3 611	186 012	17.9	41.4	27.5	908.1	8 766	29 262	45 535	64 120	3.5	43 773	15.1	23.6	22.6
Polk	367	2 908	146 414	16.1	53.3	18.1	888.4	9 165	21 285	43 113	56 379	1.9	42 447	19.3	29.4	28.3

1. Data for serious crimes have not been adjusted for underreporting; this may affect comparability between geographic areas and over time. 2. Per 100,000 population estimated by the FBI. 3. All persons 3 years old and over enrolled in nursery school through college. 4. Persons 25 years old and over. 5. Elementary and secondary education expenditures. 6. Based on population estimated by the American Community Survey, 2009–2013.

STATE County	Personal income, 2013: Total (mil dol)	Personal income, 2013: Percent change, 2012–2013	Personal income, 2013: Per capita[1]: Dollars	Personal income, 2013: Per capita[1]: Rank	Personal income, 2013: Wages and salaries (mil dol)	Personal income, 2013: Supplements to wages and salaries; employer contributions (mil dol): Pension and insurance	Personal income, 2013: Supplements to wages and salaries; employer contributions (mil dol): Government social insurance	Personal income, 2013: Proprietors' income (mil dol)	Personal income, 2013: Dividends, interest, and rent (mil dol)	Personal income, 2013: Personal transfer receipts (mil dol)	Earnings, 2013: Total (mil dol)	Earnings, 2013: Contributions for government social insurance (mil dol): From employee and self-employed	Earnings, 2013: Contributions for government social insurance (mil dol): From employer
	62	63	64	65	66	67	68	69	70	71	72	73	74
CONNECTICUT—Cont'd													
Tolland	7 601	0.0	50 213	358	1 864	465	131	485	1 456	950	2 945	156	131
Windham	4 811	0.3	40 905	1 064	1 647	345	130	243	856	992	2 366	136	130
DELAWARE	41 487	2.7	44 815	X	22 620	3 760	1 651	4 029	7 239	8 039	32 060	1 794	1 651
Kent	6 252	2.4	36 905	1 601	2 825	705	223	580	1 027	1 472	4 333	230	223
New Castle	27 266	2.6	49 604	382	17 149	2 558	1 219	2 809	4 448	4 317	23 737	1 313	1 219
Sussex	7 968	3.4	38 560	1 366	2 646	497	209	639	1 765	2 250	3 991	250	209
DISTRICT OF COLUMBIA	48 697	1.2	75 329	X	62 074	11 797	4 536	6 004	8 265	5 885	84 410	4 245	4 536
District of Columbia	48 697	1.2	75 329	31	62 074	11 797	4 536	6 004	8 265	5 885	84 410	4 245	4 536
FLORIDA	811 377	2.3	41 497	X	358 174	55 446	26 067	49 333	216 149	160 614	489 020	30 481	26 067
Alachua	9 688	2.3	38 225	1 406	5 472	1 190	394	393	2 142	1 690	7 449	414	394
Baker	720	0.6	26 670	2 996	232	57	17	18	97	199	325	21	17
Bay	6 635	1.9	37 915	1 445	3 060	574	241	332	1 529	1 493	4 207	251	241
Bradford	863	0.3	32 151	2 391	241	53	18	27	119	231	338	23	18
Brevard	21 714	1.2	39 420	1 240	9 398	1 493	694	868	5 201	5 136	12 453	813	694
Broward	80 526	2.8	43 792	775	37 092	5 304	2 674	5 162	18 058	12 598	50 231	3 046	2 674
Calhoun	345	1.6	23 484	3 084	94	24	7	20	53	115	145	10	7
Charlotte	6 192	3.2	37 588	1 492	1 637	269	123	269	2 055	1 934	2 298	189	123
Citrus	4 788	1.3	34 380	2 015	1 253	227	93	168	1 332	1 741	1 740	153	93
Clay	7 068	1.7	35 987	1 749	1 741	306	130	184	1 379	1 434	2 361	159	130
Collier	22 033	1.9	64 872	67	5 979	781	416	1 245	11 993	2 823	8 421	544	416
Columbia	1 980	1.8	29 315	2 774	822	180	63	54	373	602	1 119	72	63
DeSoto	851	5.0	24 664	3 066	318	61	24	47	174	258	449	28	24
Dixie	372	3.0	23 333	3 087	86	22	6	19	66	154	132	11	6
Duval	37 581	1.4	42 423	895	25 179	3 796	1 888	2 576	8 163	6 640	33 439	1 931	1 888
Escambia	11 740	1.8	38 389	1 390	6 027	1 189	479	452	2 799	2 689	8 147	468	479
Flagler	3 674	2.3	36 753	1 631	712	137	53	27	1 093	1 015	929	83	53
Franklin	351	2.6	30 301	2 642	114	25	8	24	106	99	171	12	8
Gadsden	1 307	0.9	28 290	2 866	451	107	32	43	226	384	634	41	32
Gilchrist	567	1.8	33 491	2 177	103	24	7	54	76	138	188	12	7
Glades	326	4.1	24 421	3 070	76	16	6	51	55	80	150	8	6
Gulf	428	2.4	27 053	2 967	134	31	10	18	101	128	192	14	10
Hamilton	299	0.6	20 807	3 106	143	37	10	8	49	114	198	13	10
Hardee	709	1.8	25 752	3 030	256	55	19	73	110	187	403	21	19
Hendry	1 161	5.6	30 973	2 553	493	80	36	146	154	257	755	34	36
Hernando	5 481	2.2	31 422	2 494	1 355	248	104	216	1 184	1 975	1 922	167	104
Highlands	3 022	1.6	30 962	2 556	925	170	70	118	781	1 106	1 283	100	70
Hillsborough	52 541	2.1	40 680	1 090	32 824	4 858	2 378	4 207	11 125	9 237	44 266	2 583	2 378
Holmes	539	0.6	27 347	2 953	106	30	8	39	82	192	183	14	8
Indian River	7 731	0.9	54 448	221	1 960	295	146	320	3 878	1 455	2 721	192	146
Jackson	1 469	1.8	30 037	2 686	508	126	38	114	249	472	787	47	38
Jefferson	443	1.5	31 183	2 520	85	20	6	14	87	127	126	10	6
Lafayette	180	1.9	20 294	3 109	52	14	4	15	35	45	85	5	4
Lake	10 714	2.6	34 782	1 936	3 120	549	234	386	2 415	3 067	4 290	323	234
Lee	28 292	3.5	42 795	860	9 342	1 530	682	1 747	10 492	5 801	13 301	892	682
Leon	10 807	1.2	38 345	1 395	6 186	1 338	439	589	2 367	1 640	8 552	472	439
Levy	1 150	2.3	29 002	2 806	270	58	21	68	209	396	417	31	21
Liberty	209	1.9	25 062	3 053	74	19	6	6	28	53	104	7	6
Madison	497	2.2	26 557	3 004	143	37	10	32	85	169	223	15	10
Manatee	14 404	3.1	42 104	930	4 513	698	332	997	4 207	3 013	6 540	434	332
Marion	11 618	1.9	34 437	2 001	3 572	647	267	389	2 785	3 658	4 875	378	267
Martin	8 199	1.6	54 205	227	2 436	369	178	437	3 788	1 396	3 420	229	178
Miami-Dade	104 373	2.0	39 880	1 184	54 535	8 072	3 893	10 440	22 057	21 177	76 941	4 667	3 893
Monroe	4 415	1.0	57 829	140	1 620	260	121	251	1 834	551	2 252	134	121
Nassau	3 469	1.6	45 817	630	819	136	60	98	995	610	1 114	78	60
Okaloosa	8 775	2.7	45 277	670	4 562	985	385	387	2 523	1 489	6 319	333	385
Okeechobee	1 079	3.2	27 423	2 942	404	74	30	80	176	346	588	37	30
Orange	46 369	3.0	37 844	1 455	34 389	4 648	2 458	3 160	8 862	7 644	44 654	2 581	2 458
Osceola	8 065	4.3	27 019	2 968	2 954	472	222	217	1 101	2 016	3 865	257	222
Palm Beach	79 565	2.5	57 985	133	28 495	3 846	1 985	5 266	31 314	11 492	39 591	2 474	1 985
Pasco	15 680	3.1	32 975	2 256	3 912	687	293	278	2 927	4 343	5 169	412	293
Pinellas	42 340	2.0	45 574	650	19 172	2 889	1 388	2 183	11 152	8 890	25 632	1 634	1 388
Polk	21 427	3.4	34 393	2 012	8 323	1 406	611	1 080	4 513	5 303	11 420	757	611

1. Based on the resident population estimated as of July 1 of the year shown.

STATE County	Earnings, 2013 (cont.) Percent by selected industries: Farm	Mining	Construction	Manu-facturing	Infor-mation: professional, scientific, technical services	Retail trade	Finance, insur-ance, real estate and leasing	Health care and social assistance	Govern-ment	Social Security beneficiaries, December 2013: Number	Rate[1]	Supple-mental Security Income recipients, December 2013	Housing units, 2014: Total	Percent change, 2010–2014
	75	76	77	78	79	80	81	82	83	84	85	86	87	88
CONNECTICUT—Cont'd														
Tolland	0.6	D	8.5	6.9	6.2	6.9	3.1	12.1	37.6	24 950	164	1 044	58 529	1.0
Windham	0.4	D	D	18.2	4.9	8.1	2.4	15.8	21.4	22 800	194	2 025	49 168	0.2
DELAWARE	0.8	D	5.3	6.0	14.8	5.9	16.8	12.4	16.7	187 246	202	16 697	417 437	2.8
Kent	1.8	D	4.8	D	4.8	7.3	7.1	12.0	38.9	34 155	201	3 732	67 874	3.9
New Castle	0.0	D	4.9	D	18.2	4.9	20.0	12.0	13.0	94 590	172	9 938	220 118	1.2
Sussex	4.0	0.0	8.3	11.8	5.1	10.5	8.2	15.2	14.7	58 500	283	3 027	129 445	5.2
DISTRICT OF COLUMBIA	0.0	0.0	1.5	0.2	26.3	1.0	4.6	5.5	40.1	78 416	121	26 806	306 174	3.2
District of Columbia	0.0	0.0	1.5	0.2	26.3	1.0	4.6	5.5	40.1	78 416	121	26 806	306 174	3.2
FLORIDA	0.6	0.1	5.1	4.8	12.1	7.9	9.6	12.9	16.5	4 114 745	210	548 178	9 144 250	1.7
Alachua	0.3	D	3.4	4.7	D	5.8	5.7	17.4	39.7	40 030	158	6 000	114 060	1.1
Baker	0.3	0.0	3.6	1.6	3.0	8.1	1.8	D	44.2	4 960	184	635	9 620	-0.7
Bay	0.0	0.1	5.5	5.7	8.3	9.0	6.0	13.7	26.9	37 535	215	4 840	100 322	0.7
Bradford	0.4	D	3.9	3.8	2.9	9.1	2.3	12.3	32.6	5 875	218	882	10 909	-0.9
Brevard	0.1	0.0	4.4	15.5	11.2	7.2	4.3	14.3	17.9	146 240	265	11 302	272 297	0.9
Broward	0.0	0.1	5.4	3.8	13.9	8.6	9.9	10.2	15.0	296 985	161	43 214	817 277	0.9
Calhoun	6.1	D	5.2	1.1	D	7.8	2.4	18.7	36.1	2 965	202	548	5 928	-1.2
Charlotte	1.1	0.2	6.2	1.5	7.2	12.8	5.7	24.6	16.7	60 510	367	2 615	101 365	0.7
Citrus	0.1	0.3	7.3	1.0	6.2	11.4	4.0	23.6	14.9	55 645	400	3 122	77 717	-0.4
Clay	-0.1	0.1	7.5	3.2	11.1	11.0	5.0	17.7	19.7	37 035	188	2 776	77 439	2.6
Collier	2.3	0.4	9.1	2.4	8.8	9.2	10.1	14.5	11.0	83 055	244	3 793	203 070	2.9
Columbia	0.2	D	3.3	8.9	D	10.2	4.5	13.7	32.3	15 460	229	2 580	28 309	-1.1
DeSoto	11.7	D	3.8	4.0	1.7	6.3	2.9	D	22.9	6 950	201	975	14 729	1.0
Dixie	2.0	0.0	3.7	15.9	D	7.2	2.0	3.9	37.8	4 445	279	786	9 155	-1.8
Duval	0.1	0.1	4.6	5.5	12.0	6.2	14.6	12.7	15.4	148 825	168	24 209	395 841	1.9
Escambia	0.5	0.1	4.6	4.8	8.1	6.9	6.9	15.4	31.7	67 870	220	10 227	138 636	1.4
Flagler	1.2	D	4.5	4.7	9.0	11.3	4.9	15.6	23.0	32 455	325	1 699	49 562	2.0
Franklin	0.0	0.0	5.5	D	7.1	8.9	7.5	7.5	32.0	2 750	236	356	8 569	-1.0
Gadsden	4.6	2.0	7.7	8.5	D	6.2	2.0	3.8	38.4	10 265	222	2 728	19 432	-0.4
Gilchrist	12.4	0.0	9.6	1.3	D	4.2	2.0	D	30.7	3 950	234	455	7 229	-1.1
Glades	25.8	0.0	3.2	5.0	D	D	1.2	D	19.7	2 365	179	224	6 825	-2.2
Gulf	0.0	0.0	9.5	1.6	5.9	7.9	7.7	D	36.0	3 570	226	374	9 181	0.9
Hamilton	1.0	0.0	D	D	D	4.1	D	D	31.6	2 980	208	636	5 704	-1.3
Hardee	18.9	D	1.8	2.5	1.7	5.8	3.8	D	23.7	4 575	167	850	9 618	-1.1
Hendry	29.3	D	3.6	3.3	6.1	4.7	2.2	4.6	17.0	5 695	151	1 437	14 376	-1.3
Hernando	0.2	0.2	5.9	4.4	5.2	11.7	3.9	23.0	19.5	58 395	335	4 026	84 623	0.1
Highlands	6.2	0.0	3.2	2.4	4.0	10.8	3.8	23.4	18.4	32 190	329	2 662	54 894	-0.9
Hillsborough	0.5	0.1	4.6	4.0	16.8	6.9	12.6	11.3	14.5	215 180	166	39 240	554 070	3.4
Holmes	2.6	D	6.2	4.8	D	8.4	3.3	D	40.3	5 330	271	872	8 559	-0.9
Indian River	1.6	0.2	6.0	4.3	9.4	10.6	8.1	18.4	12.4	44 485	313	2 255	77 340	1.3
Jackson	10.0	0.4	5.3	4.2	D	7.6	2.8	D	39.1	12 105	247	1 962	20 821	-0.9
Jefferson	3.1	0.0	6.4	0.3	D	6.6	3.2	D	33.2	3 475	245	617	6 589	-0.6
Lafayette	16.6	D	3.0	2.4	D	5.1	D	D	41.2	1 185	134	145	3 300	-0.8
Lake	1.1	0.3	7.9	4.1	6.4	11.9	5.3	19.8	18.2	91 335	296	6 457	146 687	1.2
Lee	0.2	0.3	7.7	2.7	10.2	10.0	6.5	12.2	20.3	166 040	251	12 198	375 682	1.2
Leon	0.0	D	3.4	1.2	14.0	6.1	6.1	12.6	40.0	38 785	137	5 856	126 724	2.1
Levy	10.7	0.3	9.2	6.9	2.9	9.7	4.2	7.5	22.9	11 825	298	1 530	19 856	-1.3
Liberty	-0.3	0.0	1.2	16.6	D	2.2	D	18.5	40.3	1 430	172	294	3 324	-1.0
Madison	7.5	D	1.8	10.4	2.5	6.7	2.5	10.0	33.0	4 450	238	1 003	8 422	-0.7
Manatee	3.5	0.1	7.2	8.3	9.6	9.4	6.7	14.2	12.6	86 890	254	5 848	179 035	3.7
Marion	-0.3	0.1	5.9	8.8	6.0	11.0	5.4	16.4	21.1	108 585	323	9 121	163 542	-0.3
Martin	1.0	D	6.8	6.3	10.5	10.6	7.7	17.6	11.2	42 660	282	1 612	78 948	0.8
Miami-Dade	0.3	0.1	4.1	3.0	13.2	7.5	10.7	11.8	14.8	400 300	152	155 746	1 004 371	1.5
Monroe	0.0	0.2	5.7	0.5	6.7	10.1	6.0	7.1	24.3	16 045	210	1 296	52 935	0.3
Nassau	0.0	0.1	3.6	9.5	9.5	8.0	4.6	8.8	22.9	17 860	236	1 118	35 972	2.8
Okaloosa	0.1	0.1	3.8	4.2	11.4	6.0	5.5	7.3	44.9	37 450	193	3 110	95 055	2.9
Okeechobee	9.5	0.2	5.5	7.1	D	8.7	3.3	D	21.6	8 405	215	1 000	18 223	-1.5
Orange	0.2	0.0	4.5	5.1	14.0	6.4	9.7	10.7	11.3	171 080	139	32 957	508 051	4.1
Osceola	0.4	0.0	5.6	1.8	4.5	10.4	6.8	15.5	20.2	52 320	175	10 183	133 981	4.5
Palm Beach	1.1	0.2	4.9	3.5	13.5	7.4	12.3	13.4	12.1	298 055	217	22 828	674 844	1.5
Pasco	0.2	0.1	6.6	3.8	6.4	12.4	4.7	21.8	19.2	124 735	262	11 030	232 348	1.5
Pinellas	0.0	0.1	4.1	9.0	13.5	8.0	10.3	15.8	12.3	232 515	250	21 124	504 674	0.2
Polk	1.0	0.7	5.2	8.9	5.6	8.6	7.8	14.1	14.8	144 565	232	19 954	282 730	0.5

1. Per 1,000 resident population estimated as of July 1 of the year shown.

STATE County	Housing units, 2009–2013								Civilian labor force, 2014				Civilian employment,[6] 2009–2013		
	Occupied units										Unemployment			Percent	
		Owner-occupied				Renter-occupied									
				Median owner cost as a percent of income											
	Total	Percent	Median value[1]	With a mortgage	Without a mortgage[2]	Median rent[3]	Median rent as a percent of income[2]	Substandard units[4] (percent)	Total	Percent change, 2013–2014	Total	Rate[5]	Total	Management, business, science and arts	Construction, production, and maintenance occupations
	89	90	91	92	93	94	95	96	97	98	99	100	101	102	103
CONNECTICUT—Cont'd															
Tolland	54 327	74.4	254 800	23.8	14.2	1 017	29.5	2.0	84 100	1.2	4 735	5.6	79 479	42.3	18.8
Windham	44 018	70.1	211 100	26.0	16.7	863	29.7	2.1	62 958	1.2	4 597	7.3	58 090	30.6	24.9
DELAWARE	335 707	72.5	235 800	24.0	11.4	999	31.2	2.4	451 767	2.1	25 854	5.7	422 009	37.8	19.3
Kent	58 524	72.3	199 500	24.5	11.6	945	32.4	2.2	75 239	2.0	4 780	6.4	71 671	32.8	24.2
New Castle	200 739	70.0	246 300	23.3	10.6	1 025	31.1	3.0	282 787	2.2	15 693	5.5	263 522	41.8	16.4
Sussex	76 444	79.0	236 600	25.8	12.2	954	30.2	3.5	93 742	1.7	5 382	5.7	86 816	30.0	24.1
DISTRICT OF COLUMBIA	263 649	42.1	445 200	23.8	10.7	1 242	29.9	3.5	377 448	1.1	29 399	7.8	315 177	60.2	6.9
District of Columbia	263 649	42.1	445 200	23.8	10.7	1 242	29.9	2.1	377 448	1.1	29 399	7.8	315 177	60.2	6.9
FLORIDA	7 158 980	67.1	160 200	28.0	13.6	990	34.9	3.0	9 637 536	1.7	603 296	6.3	8 202 636	33.7	18.1
Alachua	96 043	54.1	167 900	23.9	11.4	886	37.1	4.5	130 895	1.0	6 785	5.2	114 147	45.5	11.3
Baker	8 216	79.7	124 300	23.6	11.1	705	32.3	2.2	11 385	0.9	712	6.3	10 023	29.8	25.2
Bay	67 561	62.5	157 600	25.7	11.5	932	31.8	2.9	87 777	1.4	5 495	6.3	76 287	31.3	20.9
Bradford	8 857	77.8	108 000	23.6	12.0	635	31.9	1.6	10 884	-1.0	605	5.6	9 434	26.8	24.9
Brevard	220 277	73.5	144 900	25.6	12.5	899	33.0	3.7	260 004	0.2	17 991	6.9	226 768	36.0	18.5
Broward	663 458	65.9	181 500	30.8	17.1	1 171	36.6	4.6	994 081	2.0	58 071	5.8	850 199	35.3	15.8
Calhoun	4 696	79.0	70 000	25.9	10.5	573	38.2	1.3	4 943	-0.3	340	6.9	4 387	24.1	22.2
Charlotte	70 545	79.0	143 700	30.7	13.3	912	33.1	2.1	67 003	1.2	4 510	6.7	53 974	30.3	17.0
Citrus	60 319	82.6	117 400	25.2	12.4	790	34.8	1.5	48 578	-1.7	4 108	8.5	43 751	27.9	19.5
Clay	67 805	76.6	158 600	24.2	10.0	1 013	28.5	3.7	98 450	1.4	5 627	5.7	84 902	35.2	20.0
Collier	122 972	74.1	261 300	30.5	14.1	1 020	33.6	3.4	161 233	3.4	9 506	5.9	132 180	29.3	18.8
Columbia	23 604	70.8	108 700	25.4	11.3	765	28.8	7.9	28 619	1.7	1 855	6.5	24 435	30.2	25.2
DeSoto	10 622	71.8	89 900	26.8	11.1	693	30.2	3.1	13 011	-1.7	924	7.1	11 969	16.8	38.9
Dixie	6 130	78.5	85 300	30.1	11.6	618	26.9	2.3	5 621	-2.6	419	7.5	5 207	26.9	32.8
Duval	330 897	61.6	151 400	25.6	12.5	935	33.2	2.2	463 985	1.2	31 069	6.7	397 396	34.7	18.4
Escambia	111 689	64.1	130 100	24.7	11.8	869	33.2	1.6	141 015	0.9	8 948	6.3	123 875	32.2	18.2
Flagler	35 647	80.2	169 300	29.3	13.5	1 039	33.3	3.8	43 115	-2.3	3 228	7.5	34 404	31.5	16.8
Franklin	4 294	69.7	143 900	27.6	12.9	694	27.4	6.4	5 038	0.7	277	5.5	4 175	23.3	28.1
Gadsden	16 662	71.2	111 200	24.8	12.1	690	39.2	4.9	19 039	1.0	1 522	8.0	17 094	27.4	23.0
Gilchrist	6 240	79.7	102 300	23.5	13.4	793	31.5	2.5	6 707	1.3	439	6.5	5 750	25.9	29.9
Glades	3 843	72.1	87 700	27.5	11.8	720	29.6	3.7	5 303	-4.2	381	7.2	3 835	23.7	27.9
Gulf	5 414	71.3	120 200	28.1	11.0	813	35.6	2.3	6 309	2.1	379	6.0	5 564	25.0	26.0
Hamilton	4 657	75.1	73 500	23.9	10.0	606	30.7	10.9	4 612	-1.3	362	7.8	4 390	24.6	29.1
Hardee	7 463	70.5	85 800	25.0	12.1	677	31.5	8.3	10 377	-7.0	800	7.7	9 643	20.6	46.0
Hendry	11 223	69.6	81 400	23.8	11.6	753	32.0	2.2	16 851	0.8	1 782	10.6	14 351	20.9	41.7
Hernando	70 210	79.3	117 400	27.6	12.8	885	37.3	2.7	67 159	1.1	5 279	7.9	56 716	29.2	20.8
Highlands	39 931	77.9	93 600	26.9	12.6	719	34.4	3.1	36 531	1.1	2 984	8.2	30 935	25.5	24.0
Hillsborough	471 340	60.0	160 000	25.8	12.5	952	33.1	1.8	684 400	1.3	39 964	5.8	580 852	36.6	17.1
Holmes	6 808	79.3	83 400	23.5	11.4	602	30.0	2.0	6 960	-0.6	475	6.8	6 363	30.6	23.8
Indian River	58 038	74.9	157 400	26.9	13.7	854	35.9	2.3	62 028	0.7	4 852	7.8	52 296	30.2	19.8
Jackson	16 244	74.3	88 100	23.1	13.5	619	33.1	0.8	17 948	-1.2	1 147	6.4	16 149	28.4	21.0
Jefferson	5 347	75.5	121 100	23.1	12.7	696	33.6	2.3	5 535	1.4	358	6.5	5 194	41.2	19.3
Lafayette	2 710	79.9	116 600	29.7	10.9	655	28.0	2.5	3 396	-3.5	177	5.2	3 383	22.2	27.8
Lake	117 250	75.3	142 700	26.5	13.6	946	35.6	3.1	139 296	2.6	8 857	6.4	117 409	30.7	20.2
Lee	241 531	70.8	149 400	28.2	13.9	943	33.1	3.4	311 695	4.0	18 617	6.0	247 502	29.8	18.8
Leon	110 377	53.8	183 300	23.8	11.1	923	38.1	2.2	150 980	1.7	8 339	5.5	136 171	44.9	11.3
Levy	15 582	77.5	92 200	25.9	12.3	685	32.5	6.9	16 410	-0.2	1 131	6.9	13 931	24.4	28.5
Liberty	2 305	78.7	78 800	20.7	11.0	576	23.0	4.7	2 802	-1.2	181	6.5	2 660	34.6	29.4
Madison	6 739	75.8	81 000	24.7	13.5	651	41.1	2.7	7 768	0.1	575	7.4	6 456	26.6	30.5
Manatee	131 197	71.4	165 400	28.1	13.7	933	33.4	2.4	160 590	3.1	9 213	5.7	133 379	32.6	19.4
Marion	134 002	76.7	119 400	27.3	12.8	822	35.2	1.7	132 815	1.2	9 669	7.3	117 005	27.7	20.8
Martin	59 891	76.2	197 900	28.1	13.5	939	34.9	5.9	69 303	2.4	4 242	6.1	58 300	36.3	17.5
Miami-Dade	828 031	55.7	201 000	33.2	16.1	1 085	39.1	5.2	1 320 447	2.2	89 806	6.8	1 139 865	31.1	19.7
Monroe	28 503	61.7	381 200	34.8	15.0	1 367	37.3	2.2	45 263	1.4	1 877	4.1	00 707	29.9	18.7
Nassau	28 044	78.4	181 100	26.0	11.0	958	30.5	2.2	36 634	1.2	2 135	5.8	31 577	32.5	25.2
Okaloosa	73 253	66.1	182 100	25.2	10.8	1 001	31.2	6.5	93 119	0.9	4 773	5.1	82 413	34.0	17.7
Okeechobee	12 999	73.9	105 300	29.8	13.0	687	31.3	2.8	18 062	-1.2	1 312	7.3	13 492	20.0	33.0
Orange	415 790	57.4	167 800	28.2	12.8	1 022	35.8	3.1	681 733	2.6	39 504	5.8	569 109	34.8	16.0
Osceola	90 413	63.1	129 900	31.2	13.9	1 030	37.0	3.1	151 665	2.4	10 133	6.7	122 341	24.0	20.2
Palm Beach	526 007	71.2	199 700	30.0	15.9	1 149	36.5	2.1	688 244	2.1	40 598	5.9	586 528	35.4	16.2
Pasco	182 707	76.5	120 000	27.2	13.0	911	33.3	1.8	213 279	1.1	14 304	6.7	181 254	34.4	17.4
Pinellas	401 708	67.0	151 500	27.6	15.2	947	33.3	3.5	477 751	1.3	27 767	5.8	412 104	37.3	16.1
Polk	219 540	70.5	111 400	25.7	12.8	862	32.7	2.6	281 330	0.7	19 982	7.1	240 565	28.9	24.1

1. Specified owner-occupied units. 2. A value of 10.0 represents 10 percent or less; a value of 50.0 represents 50 percent or more. 3. Specified renter-occupied units. 4. Overcrowded or lacking complete plumbing facilities. 5. Percent of civilian labor force. 6. Persons 16 years old and over.

Table B. States and Counties — **Nonfarm Employment and Agriculture**

STATE County	Private nonfarm establishments, employment and payroll, 2013									Agriculture, 2012			
		Employment						Annual payroll		Farms			
											Percent with:		
	Number of establish-ments	Total	Health care and social assistance	Manufac-turing	Retail trade	Finance and insurance	Professional, scientific, and technical services	Total (mil dol)	Average per employee (dollars)	Number	Fewer than 50 acres	500 acres or more	Farm operators whose principal occu-pation is farming (percent)
	104	105	106	107	108	109	110	111	112	113	114	115	116
CONNECTICUT—Cont'd													
Tolland	2 398	30 798	5 907	3 513	4 963	657	1 139	1 070	34 754	578	64.5	2.4	34.3
Windham	2 092	29 397	6 898	5 312	4 983	721	584	1 129	38 415	692	62.0	3.0	51.3
DELAWARE	24 151	382 128	61 496	26 239	52 945	39 196	31 437	19 541	51 138	2 451	56.5	9.8	63.9
Kent	3 166	48 071	9 638	4 450	9 019	1 242	2 111	1 712	35 624	863	54.5	9.0	56.8
New Castle	15 452	270 062	41 202	12 612	31 318	35 326	26 205	15 474	57 298	374	64.7	9.4	57.8
Sussex	5 343	61 111	10 535	9 177	12 607	1 867	1 702	2 149	35 163	1 214	55.4	10.5	70.8
DISTRICT OF COLUMBIA	21 919	491 130	65 595	1 047	20 263	16 596	97 936	35 131	71 532	NA	NA	NA	NA
District of Columbia	21 919	491 130	65 595	1 047	20 263	16 596	97 936	35 131	71 532	NA	NA	NA	NA
FLORIDA	510 389	7 134 644	1 010 544	281 852	985 663	338 792	444 688	294 142	41 227	47 740	68.6	5.6	48.0
Alachua	5 850	84 425	22 147	3 170	13 375	4 116	4 822	3 124	37 001	1 662	69.7	4.9	42.3
Baker	388	5 150	1 787	D	773	128	111	157	30 562	381	74.8	3.4	35.7
Bay	4 380	56 839	9 669	4 518	10 579	1 882	3 349	1 920	33 782	115	71.3	2.6	42.6
Bradford	421	4 067	784	161	910	D	D	121	29 710	470	68.3	1.9	46.0
Brevard	13 084	161 218	29 730	18 801	25 978	4 479	12 336	6 604	40 962	513	80.3	5.1	38.8
Broward	57 607	626 529	85 936	21 387	101 429	32 353	47 848	27 283	43 547	615	93.7	1.3	50.1
Calhoun	191	1 729	661	D	305	66	D	46	26 704	218	51.8	8.3	31.2
Charlotte	3 692	35 239	9 018	396	8 520	1 103	1 361	1 094	31 055	284	61.3	12.0	51.1
Citrus	2 665	26 477	8 268	221	5 352	694	811	854	32 241	559	73.9	3.4	49.7
Clay	3 596	36 060	7 469	1 032	8 160	970	2 790	1 110	30 788	403	75.9	2.0	44.7
Collier	10 622	108 607	16 923	2 705	19 578	3 722	4 885	4 313	39 711	319	74.0	10.3	43.9
Columbia	1 320	17 648	4 402	695	2 973	537	407	624	35 355	945	65.4	4.6	46.5
DeSoto	427	4 876	1 048	D	1 053	162	D	154	31 638	836	63.0	9.4	48.4
Dixie	184	1 411	132	450	250	D	25	41	29 309	204	60.3	6.4	30.9
Duval	23 807	403 647	59 569	18 505	47 901	45 796	24 776	18 914	46 859	352	76.4	3.1	59.9
Escambia	6 581	98 366	20 868	3 994	15 281	5 630	6 093	3 596	36 558	729	68.2	4.5	43.2
Flagler	1 863	15 920	2 659	728	3 193	520	515	461	28 962	118	46.6	14.4	54.2
Franklin	304	2 226	291	D	417	D	48	58	25 844	20	65.0	0.0	40.0
Gadsden	640	9 016	2 504	1 147	1 146	155	135	302	33 505	402	56.5	5.2	39.6
Gilchrist	214	1 424	465	D	167	54	60	42	29 537	581	66.3	5.3	44.8
Glades	106	881	D	D	41	D	D	26	29 402	331	53.5	15.7	39.3
Gulf	275	2 023	532	D	351	D	82	59	29 000	34	41.2	5.9	52.9
Hamilton	166	1 890	216	D	D	D	43	90	47 874	292	36.0	9.6	64.4
Hardee	380	4 172	1 263	302	725	251	D	130	31 059	982	57.3	9.4	50.2
Hendry	546	5 579	1 085	D	1 060	210	248	184	32 920	406	49.8	22.7	51.2
Hernando	2 984	29 704	7 501	1 475	6 982	760	1 110	870	29 281	799	76.0	3.3	51.2
Highlands	1 862	18 901	5 286	626	4 309	544	639	564	29 815	969	64.3	11.0	49.3
Hillsborough	33 302	538 119	73 341	20 176	65 064	45 677	53 709	24 618	45 748	2 466	80.3	2.1	51.7
Holmes	267	1 804	593	116	367	51	68	44	24 217	801	41.7	4.2	52.6
Indian River	3 976	39 372	8 099	1 668	7 980	1 316	1 630	1 373	34 882	461	73.1	7.2	49.0
Jackson	767	8 740	1 728	548	1 832	297	217	256	29 290	1 160	39.0	8.7	42.1
Jefferson	239	1 490	199	56	279	D	47	44	29 425	617	56.1	6.6	37.0
Lafayette	94	762	125	D	136	56	20	17	22 806	221	29.9	13.6	59.7
Lake	6 526	70 757	15 666	2 846	14 064	1 854	2 478	2 222	31 400	1 784	76.7	3.3	43.9
Lee	16 403	184 629	31 751	4 527	36 112	5 342	9 980	6 545	35 450	844	79.5	4.5	48.1
Leon	7 396	94 117	16 783	1 507	15 561	4 162	12 381	3 607	38 327	284	63.4	4.6	38.4
Levy	703	5 121	553	D	1 369	202	160	138	26 997	1 053	64.7	4.4	49.9
Liberty	79	1 334	D	D	127	D	D	40	29 718	80	30.0	5.0	30.0
Madison	298	2 775	639	418	474	78	69	76	27 284	669	36.2	10.3	38.6
Manatee	7 925	85 188	14 992	7 848	16 638	2 732	3 531	3 030	35 568	689	62.6	9.6	43.4
Marion	6 787	74 910	15 911	5 482	14 864	2 338	3 741	2 516	33 591	3 870	76.7	2.2	49.5
Martin	5 141	49 754	9 096	2 822	9 329	1 811	2 990	1 829	36 771	587	74.3	9.7	54.7
Miami-Dade	78 629	886 497	134 519	31 382	130 369	45 212	60 257	38 829	43 801	2 954	92.8	1.2	56.5
Monroe	3 615	29 697	2 500	191	5 488	696	1 086	936	31 533	28	92.9	0.0	25.0
Nassau	1 648	15 434	2 293	1 289	2 832	391	502	531	34 375	444	74.1	2.9	45.0
Okaloosa	5 031	58 285	9 115	2 503	11 750	2 389	6 167	2 044	35 064	477	52.0	4.8	37.9
Okeechobee	738	6 486	1 286	D	1 591	199	164	202	31 185	678	47.9	25.1	56.6
Orange	33 317	640 229	69 010	24 260	79 042	22 122	42 775	26 273	41 036	662	80.5	4.1	51.8
Osceola	5 090	65 594	9 897	1 168	13 305	1 231	1 759	1 924	29 339	365	58.1	15.9	58.9
Palm Beach	44 234	466 399	75 043	13 685	71 438	22 622	37 745	21 087	45 213	1 409	90.0	3.5	56.7
Pasco	8 784	84 928	18 166	3 070	19 743	2 489	4 364	2 747	32 343	1 065	75.1	5.3	52.1
Pinellas	26 751	365 099	67 819	28 108	49 631	24 357	29 991	14 852	40 680	118	91.5	0.0	45.8
Polk	10 922	166 924	27 427	13 997	23 914	10 647	6 305	6 176	36 996	2 415	64.4	7.2	45.3

STATE County	Agriculture, 2012 (cont.) — Land in farms — Acreage (1,000)	Land in farms — Percent change, 2007–2012	Land in farms — Acres — Average size of farm	Land in farms — Acres — Total irrigated (1,000)	Land in farms — Acres — Total cropland (1,000)	Value of land and buildings (dollars) — Average per farm	Value of land and buildings (dollars) — Average per acre	Value of machinery and equipment, average per farm (dollars)	Value of products sold — Total (mil dol)	Value of products sold — Average per farm (dollars)	Value of products sold — Percent from: Crops	Value of products sold — Percent from: Livestock and poultry products	Percent of farms with sales of: $10,000 or more	Percent of farms with sales of: $100,000 or more	Government payments — Total ($1,000)	Government payments — Percent of farms
	117	118	119	120	121	122	123	124	125	126	127	128	129	130	131	132
CONNECTICUT—Cont'd																
Tolland	48	21.4	83	0.5	18.5	820 254	9 926	78 550	55.0	95 107	64.9	35.1	26.8	8.0	544	7.8
Windham	58	-3.1	84	0.5	20.1	642 272	7 628	58 766	44.2	63 890	40.8	59.2	31.8	7.1	1 259	10.8
DELAWARE	509	-0.3	208	127.3	439.2	1 694 584	8 166	161 559	1 274.0	519 794	33.7	66.3	64.6	41.7	9 677	37.4
Kent	172	-0.9	200	31.8	147.4	1 596 656	7 999	121 074	277.7	321 816	D	D	53.3	29.8	2 550	37.2
New Castle	64	-4.2	172	4.6	56.1	1 704 668	9 935	138 596	75.2	200 957	D	D	51.6	18.7	1 802	31.0
Sussex	272	1.0	224	90.8	235.7	1 761 092	7 853	197 414	921.1	758 755	27.1	72.9	76.7	57.2	5 325	39.5
DISTRICT OF COLUMBIA	NA	NA	NA	NA	NA	NA	NA	NA	NA	NA	NA	NA	NA	NA	NA	NA
District of Columbia	NA	NA	NA	NA	NA	NA	NA	NA	NA	NA	NA	NA	NA	NA	NA	NA
FLORIDA	9 548	3.4	200	1 493.3	2 744.1	1 040 259	5 201	60 838	7 701.5	161 322	77.5	22.5	34.3	10.9	40 164	8.3
Alachua	188	8.8	113	10.7	58.7	608 861	5 383	50 010	101.2	60 865	68.5	31.5	31.5	6.3	654	6.2
Baker	33	23.2	86	0.3	4.4	560 165	6 483	29 995	15.8	41 491	14.9	85.1	20.7	2.1	103	4.2
Bay	10	-15.9	91	D	2.7	473 730	5 193	36 009	2.7	23 635	83.6	16.4	20.0	0.9	65	7.0
Bradford	35	18.4	75	0.7	9.2	312 011	4 181	34 200	13.1	27 962	18.7	81.3	19.1	2.6	52	4.5
Brevard	146	-12.3	286	13.4	19.3	1 545 698	5 414	45 433	46.0	89 651	77.2	22.8	36.8	6.6	142	2.1
Broward	14	65.9	24	1.8	4.3	540 185	22 916	31 886	47.4	77 099	91.2	8.8	41.0	8.6	246	2.9
Calhoun	43	9.6	197	1.6	18.9	417 583	2 124	60 647	19.9	91 096	83.4	16.6	27.5	7.8	332	22.9
Charlotte	217	30.8	765	13.7	18.4	3 875 556	5 067	65 965	103.4	364 088	91.8	8.2	38.0	13.0	92	1.8
Citrus	41	1.3	73	0.7	7.3	480 195	6 621	29 451	14.1	25 190	54.9	45.1	17.7	3.4	146	3.6
Clay	52	24.2	128	0.6	5.2	450 531	3 520	28 380	9.3	22 970	62.8	37.2	17.1	2.2	24	3.2
Collier	124	12.4	387	26.4	66.9	1 736 727	4 482	151 806	202.8	635 583	98.1	1.9	36.4	14.7	207	2.8
Columbia	101	18.0	107	6.1	33.4	486 956	4 536	73 098	108.6	114 893	17.4	82.6	18.0	5.0	709	10.4
DeSoto	303	16.4	362	47.7	62.4	1 701 201	4 696	60 083	198.3	237 166	82.2	17.8	39.4	14.4	196	1.3
Dixie	45	7.6	222	3.4	10.6	873 338	3 943	72 917	19.1	93 686	D	D	20.6	2.9	124	5.4
Duval	28	5.6	80	1.1	5.5	557 054	6 935	32 875	16.2	45 903	75.9	24.1	21.3	2.6	141	5.1
Escambia	75	-9.0	102	4.6	40.1	499 244	4 880	59 298	42.6	58 375	89.4	10.6	18.7	6.0	1 426	24.1
Flagler	44	-25.3	369	3.9	5.5	1 566 102	4 239	60 636	16.9	143 602	91.9	8.1	33.1	11.0	D	2.5
Franklin	2	251.6	90	0.0	0.8	174 150	1 943	48 400	0.6	28 500	44.7	55.4	40.0	10.0	63	30.0
Gadsden	51	7.9	126	2.7	13.1	559 923	4 430	38 505	54.4	135 388	97.7	2.3	23.1	4.5	255	18.2
Gilchrist	84	18.0	144	12.6	43.7	481 217	3 332	62 892	88.7	152 732	31.6	68.4	27.4	7.4	746	12.0
Glades	443	10.0	1 338	88.5	56.5	4 087 441	3 056	84 066	106.5	321 807	73.2	26.8	32.3	14.8	383	7.9
Gulf	5	-3.1	135	D	0.5	565 500	4 184	39 588	0.9	27 147	4.8	95.2	14.7	5.9	D	8.8
Hamilton	72	11.0	246	9.5	28.4	710 452	2 886	87 274	45.5	155 771	80.2	19.8	31.8	9.2	234	31.8
Hardee	274	-2.1	279	36.0	51.8	1 150 569	4 125	52 140	218.4	222 378	66.4	33.6	48.1	20.0	345	2.4
Hendry	496	6.6	1 221	193.1	262.4	4 953 187	4 057	206 352	499.9	1 231 345	95.8	4.2	53.4	31.8	527	5.9
Hernando	62	10.1	78	2.7	15.5	650 753	8 394	38 645	28.4	35 492	56.1	43.9	24.8	6.1	441	1.8
Highlands	490	2.9	506	61.8	84.0	1 484 852	2 937	82 911	273.4	282 121	72.6	27.4	41.4	21.4	609	2.2
Hillsborough	215	-2.2	87	26.1	75.8	788 988	9 052	54 052	378.1	153 316	84.2	15.8	32.5	10.5	865	2.5
Holmes	106	-30.5	132	1.1	34.4	371 996	2 823	42 097	28.9	36 105	46.0	54.0	25.1	7.7	754	26.7
Indian River	162	3.3	352	57.6	54.8	1 359 020	3 856	54 672	144.9	314 419	92.2	7.8	49.7	18.4	809	4.1
Jackson	262	-15.8	226	21.5	117.6	761 272	3 367	65 673	92.7	79 907	81.4	18.6	34.0	11.0	3 805	41.3
Jefferson	130	-12.1	210	2.4	24.6	884 258	4 212	53 783	48.3	78 292	43.6	56.4	25.6	4.7	425	19.0
Lafayette	91	12.3	413	10.7	22.3	1 703 208	4 124	114 973	87.6	396 217	13.0	87.0	39.8	24.0	914	32.6
Lake	152	25.3	85	15.2	36.0	642 919	7 539	34 263	142.1	79 631	94.0	6.0	32.7	9.9	255	1.2
Lee	87	1.6	103	13.6	22.8	979 161	9 485	53 895	105.9	125 478	95.8	4.2	32.8	7.3	61	1.7
Leon	81	-10.4	286	2.0	6.6	1 574 884	5 501	37 673	3.8	13 493	72.7	27.3	22.5	3.5	42	5.6
Levy	167	-3.9	159	13.7	59.8	949 232	5 972	62 627	80.4	76 335	52.4	47.6	32.5	10.8	1 244	8.0
Liberty	14	-40.0	177	D	1.2	479 600	2 705	34 450	1.5	18 750	2.9	97.1	22.5	5.0	39	8.8
Madison	143	-4.0	214	8.1	38.5	719 737	3 367	49 706	51.8	77 463	30.4	69.6	28.4	8.4	520	26.3
Manatee	186	-17.2	271	50.1	70.4	1 512 093	5 590	115 546	298.4	433 160	91.4	8.6	42.4	13.2	11	0.9
Marion	321	20.6	83	13.2	69.8	776 909	9 353	37 481	188.2	48 624	23.3	76.7	27.8	8.2	483	2.1
Martin	139	7.7	237	34.8	43.8	1 561 876	6 581	64 925	165.5	281 862	68.1	31.9	39.0	11.6	398	4.8
Miami-Dade	81	21.3	28	45.2	64.9	699 727	25 423	47 644	604.2	204 549	98.0	2.0	58.5	16.0	6 944	8.5
Monroe	0	154.5	17	0.0	0.1	322 607	18 077	00 030	10.8	386 964	6.0	94.0	50.0	21.4	0	0.0
Nassau	39	25.8	89	0.1	4.9	424 045	4 786	37 444	6.5	14 739	18.7	81.3	14.6	1.1	D	0.9
Okaloosa	61	-6.7	129	0.2	18.6	467 688	3 628	51 556	10.3	21 562	81.1	18.9	21.0	4.4	983	30.8
Okeechobee	442	30.6	652	19.4	52.1	2 992 147	4 592	82 420	256.9	378 876	19.7	80.3	45.0	21.4	2 120	18.1
Orange	132	-2.7	200	9.5	13.8	1 673 992	8 365	56 754	261.6	395 193	96.2	3.8	51.5	26.1	11	0.6
Osceola	547	-15.4	1 499	29.2	29.7	5 917 241	3 948	89 249	108.6	297 660	63.4	36.6	38.9	16.4	326	4.4
Palm Beach	514	-2.2	365	362.7	440.7	2 586 187	7 090	182 476	999.0	709 041	98.3	1.7	43.2	16.2	1 536	6.0
Pasco	171	14.1	161	6.6	24.7	1 086 574	6 763	41 420	73.9	69 351	40.4	59.6	31.2	7.1	355	2.4
Pinellas	1	1.6	13	0.1	0.6	377 805	30 143	43 763	2.6	22 415	72.9	27.1	39.0	4.2	9	5.1
Polk	521	-5.1	216	79.9	125.1	1 182 091	5 480	64 954	350.3	145 042	90.2	9.8	48.1	18.3	419	1.4

STATE County	Water use, 2010		Wholesale trade,[1] 2007				Retail trade,[2] 2007				Real estate and rental and leasing,[2] 2007			
	Total water withdrawn (mil gal/day)	Gallons withdrawn per person per day	Number of establish-ments	Number of employees	Sales (mil dol)	Annual payroll (mil dol)	Number of establish-ments	Number of employees	Sales (mil dol)	Annual payroll (mil dol)	Number of establish-ments	Number of employees	Receipts (mil dol)	Annual payroll (mil dol)
	133	134	135	136	137	138	139	140	141	142	143	144	145	146
CONNECTICUT—Cont'd														
Tolland	15.9	104	69	571	214.3	25.7	406	5 207	1 206.3	126.3	110	457	62.7	12.2
Windham	34.6	292	71	1 132	546.7	60.0	376	4 870	1 180.6	122.0	73	D	D	D
DELAWARE	717.5	799	819	9 065	5 727.4	416.9	3 907	55 432	14 202.1	1 322.8	1 248	5 807	11 057.2	222.4
Kent	43.3	267	100	D	D	D	632	9 614	2 589.2	224.6	127	604	91.0	22.0
New Castle	404.7	752	559	D	D	D	2 093	33 010	8 633.4	795.0	823	3 786	10 740.6	155.1
Sussex	269.5	1 367	160	D	D	D	1 182	12 808	2 979.4	303.1	298	1 417	225.5	45.3
DISTRICT OF COLUMBIA	0.1	0	316	3 680	2 118.0	216.4	1 827	19 117	3 843.7	485.9	1 140	9 663	2 747.8	624.8
District of Columbia	0.1	0	316	3 680	2 118.0	216.4	1 827	19 117	3 843.7	485.9	1 140	9 663	2 747.8	624.8
FLORIDA	14 936.0	794	27 442	279 300	221 641.5	12 566.1	73 794	1 016 290	262 341.1	24 049.7	33 653	170 859	32 235.4	6 094.2
Alachua	53.8	218	188	D	D	D	969	14 610	3 152.2	300.1	397	2 048	311.6	59.0
Baker	5.2	191	8	D	D	D	74	888	180.6	16.3	11	D	D	D
Bay	301.4	1 785	174	1 481	645.0	62.9	816	10 186	2 472.0	227.1	314	1 172	167.7	33.6
Bradford	4.3	151	14	D	D	D	87	961	215.6	20.7	22	47	6.2	1.0
Brevard	251.4	463	493	3 683	1 852.7	155.1	2 073	28 911	6 594.0	630.4	777	2 795	401.1	74.8
Broward	1 279.1	732	3 946	37 891	31 411.6	1 819.5	7 382	104 336	30 886.3	2 710.6	3 624	18 044	3 555.6	648.1
Calhoun	4.1	281	12	D	D	D	42	295	64.8	6.2	5	13	1.1	0.2
Charlotte	58.8	367	94	592	211.7	22.0	582	8 761	1 898.1	187.9	289	877	120.7	22.1
Citrus	1 201.2	8 505	84	D	D	D	516	5 836	1 405.6	131.1	202	605	59.4	12.3
Clay	23.3	122	115	803	394.3	34.8	609	9 363	2 005.7	195.5	230	797	143.2	21.4
Collier	256.9	799	331	2 678	1 649.0	137.9	1 500	20 122	5 186.5	535.5	958	2 874	552.3	118.0
Columbia	13.7	203	75	871	478.6	35.6	265	3 113	862.2	74.2	66	206	31.5	5.4
DeSoto	97.4	2 793	20	D	D	D	75	1 023	280.8	23.1	38	106	13.0	2.2
Dixie	4.6	280	4	D	D	D	34	237	49.1	4.2	7	11	1.1	0.1
Duval	758.1	877	1 154	19 865	17 205.8	969.5	3 464	51 916	13 316.7	1 228.5	1 427	8 481	2 040.1	368.9
Escambia	311.7	1 047	278	3 171	1 838.9	126.6	1 233	16 777	4 055.7	374.3	413	1 539	278.0	45.0
Flagler	23.4	245	53	D	D	D	208	2 899	684.1	66.3	195	508	66.9	13.8
Franklin	2.3	198	8	D	D	D	71	438	92.3	9.3	33	194	20.5	6.1
Gadsden	17.8	383	34	707	384.0	23.9	137	1 462	440.3	29.4	29	88	13.3	2.2
Gilchrist	9.1	538	3	10	2.3	0.2	41	239	52.5	4.7	8	38	4.6	1.0
Glades	162.3	12 599	5	D	D	D	15	83	13.1	1.4	5	14	1.1	0.2
Gulf	2.3	142	3	D	D	D	48	371	76.3	7.3	22	68	8.6	1.6
Hamilton	37.5	2 533	4	D	D	D	54	343	103.2	5.6	4	22	1.8	0.3
Hardee	52.4	1 891	21	D	D	D	75	740	400.1	16.0	25	65	8.3	1.3
Hendry	424.1	10 834	32	273	212.1	8.3	131	1 373	345.7	28.2	29	94	10.3	1.9
Hernando	38.8	225	114	592	177.9	20.8	469	7 191	1 654.1	156.1	192	467	63.0	9.8
Highlands	107.8	1 091	83	D	D	D	364	4 513	1 089.6	99.0	112	337	52.6	8.1
Hillsborough	1 960.7	1 595	1 764	28 080	17 752.9	1 233.9	4 369	70 015	19 110.3	1 745.9	1 983	12 821	2 504.2	500.3
Holmes	4.5	226	14	D	D	D	49	332	73.1	5.5	8	18	1.4	0.3
Indian River	154.5	1 119	132	D	D	D	699	9 096	1 851.7	203.3	260	945	146.5	24.1
Jackson	62.8	1 263	26	185	70.6	5.2	188	2 056	541.9	43.0	47	131	13.1	2.5
Jefferson	7.3	495	9	39	43.7	1.5	55	390	88.7	6.6	10	24	1.9	0.4
Lafayette	6.4	722	4	D	D	D	20	139	66.5	3.1	2	D	D	D
Lake	104.9	353	224	1 745	726.3	62.3	1 003	14 137	3 441.9	310.3	477	2 116	266.9	69.5
Lee	746.6	1 207	589	5 590	2 271.6	225.7	2 624	38 417	9 193.1	923.2	1 307	5 643	1 000.1	171.3
Leon	37.6	136	228	2 254	791.2	88.4	1 043	16 881	3 533.8	343.1	451	2 412	361.5	68.3
Levy	32.5	797	32	170	62.8	4.2	145	1 546	346.4	32.8	44	129	10.2	2.0
Liberty	1.5	181	4	D	D	D	16	76	24.4	1.4	1	D	D	D
Madison	14.0	730	9	D	D	D	71	585	124.8	9.4	13	25	2.4	0.4
Manatee	126.5	392	303	3 314	1 725.5	148.1	1 163	16 937	3 874.8	382.0	550	2 227	390.6	66.0
Marion	65.4	197	318	3 812	1 639.5	149.7	1 208	16 639	4 218.8	379.2	466	1 598	217.9	39.9
Martin	101.1	691	195	1 393	741.6	65.3	809	10 666	2 470.4	243.3	326	1 595	203.0	40.7
Miami-Dade	461.0	185	7 819	65 657	60 760.1	2 818.0	10 293	123 559	34 530.5	3 055.6	4 935	25 546	5 367.9	985.2
Monroe	1.2	16	86	D	D	D	657	6 267	1 387.6	146.7	308	808	150.5	26.5
Nassau	50.3	686	37	D	D	D	280	2 998	630.9	63.0	97	D	D	D
Okaloosa	26.3	145	110	563	236.9	23.0	903	12 427	3 031.0	272.4	398	1 772	260.5	57.0
Okeechobee	61.9	1 548	29	179	85.3	6.0	156	1 680	430.6	37.5	49	115	16.5	3.3
Orange	238.3	208	1 643	23 425	17 080.7	1 148.0	4 670	71 848	19 195.0	1 050.3	2 000	26 517	6 177.0	1 063.1
Osceola	97.6	363	128	1 819	3 044.2	69.6	822	12 171	2 868.7	264.6	504	4 643	732.0	155.4
Palm Beach	706.5	535	2 007	17 634	12 017.5	900.5	5 564	76 129	19 321.7	1 916.5	2 691	12 359	2 083.2	503.8
Pasco	1 658.8	3 570	311	1 847	807.4	70.4	1 336	18 995	4 746.2	426.6	529	1 602	197.5	35.1
Pinellas	493.0	538	1 247	14 111	12 378.4	625.8	3 850	52 539	14 826.9	1 232.7	1 687	7 648	1 222.6	268.2
Polk	298.7	496	580	8 024	13 241.7	337.4	1 876	25 321	6 420.1	586.4	741	3 423	517.8	95.9

1. Merchant wholesalers, except manufacturers' sales branches and offices. 2. Employer establishments.

STATE County	Professional, scientific, and technical services,[1] 2007				Manufacturing, 2007				Accommodation and food services, 2007			
	Number of establish-ments	Number of employees	Receipts (mil dol)	Annual payroll (mil dol)	Number of establish-ments	Number of employees	Receipts (mil dol)	Annual payroll (mil dol)	Number of establish-ments	Number of employees	Sales (mil dol)	Annual payroll (mil dol)
	147	148	149	150	151	152	153	154	155	156	157	158
CONNECTICUT—Cont'd												
Tolland	200	D	D	D	141	3 962	1 021.8	185.1	211	3 472	173.1	48.7
Windham	123	D	D	D	187	6 135	1 776.5	254.7	236	2 841	136.3	38.7
DELAWARE	2 383	D	D	D	673	34 866	25 679.9	1 759.7	1 850	32 194	1 910.8	468.8
Kent	248	D	D	D	87	5 253	2 361.8	213.8	236	5 352	447.9	76.2
New Castle	1 804	D	D	D	421	18 556	20 268.8	1 167.8	1 051	19 118	999.2	267.2
Sussex	331	D	D	D	165	11 057	3 049.3	378.0	563	7 724	463.7	125.4
DISTRICT OF COLUMBIA	4 373	82 107	24 177.7	8 660.6	137	2 015	332.8	80.8	2 148	52 998	4 278.2	1 238.4
District of Columbia	4 373	82 107	24 177.7	8 660.6	137	2 015	332.8	80.8	2 148	52 998	4 278.2	1 238.4
FLORIDA	69 083	427 536	61 599.8	24 264.5	14 324	355 386	104 832.9	15 227.2	35 012	746 214	41 922.1	11 470.0
Alachua	792	5 262	625.4	263.6	147	3 803	D	D	524	11 170	494.0	133.7
Baker	16	90	7.2	2.9	NA	NA	NA	NA	34	446	19.8	4.8
Bay	406	D	D	D	116	3 702	1 254.3	153.4	442	9 154	480.4	135.8
Bradford	44	163	11.9	4.2	NA	NA	NA	NA	42	752	37.1	9.1
Brevard	1 683	19 711	3 364.7	1 589.6	473	22 772	6 767.6	1 172.5	1 019	19 057	855.5	240.1
Broward	9 509	46 243	6 635.1	2 550.4	1 734	29 333	7 160.8	1 185.5	3 693	70 373	4 209.1	1 140.1
Calhoun	9	19	1.1	0.5	NA	NA	NA	NA	20	285	9.3	2.8
Charlotte	366	D	D	D	NA	NA	NA	NA	240	4 322	178.0	53.2
Citrus	274	D	D	D	NA	NA	NA	NA	188	2 931	109.7	32.4
Clay	423	D	D	D	81	1 464	D	D	274	5 413	213.8	61.9
Collier	1 271	D	D	D	228	3 035	606.7	109.5	704	17 421	1 037.2	308.3
Columbia	115	D	D	D	38	988	351.5	37.5	120	2 220	103.3	25.9
DeSoto	32	189	14.9	6.1	NA	NA	NA	NA	38	579	24.3	6.5
Dixie	13	63	3.5	2.0	11	529	D	D	23	192	7.4	1.6
Duval	3 126	D	D	D	647	26 119	11 222.1	1 242.1	1 811	34 979	1 719.4	488.1
Escambia	778	D	D	D	191	5 152	2 117.0	253.4	534	11 014	493.9	137.2
Flagler	197	674	105.6	46.6	52	1 031	235.7	29.9	131	2 401	114.8	31.6
Franklin	21	41	7.2	2.0	NA	NA	NA	NA	43	623	37.6	10.4
Gadsden	48	D	D	D	33	1 462	262.9	50.8	38	466	18.9	4.7
Gilchrist	18	64	4.4	1.6	NA	NA	NA	NA	19	163	8.1	2.0
Glades	6	D	D	D	NA	NA	NA	NA	11	110	4.9	1.3
Gulf	31	143	14.6	5.4	NA	NA	NA	NA	25	298	18.8	3.4
Hamilton	11	19	1.8	0.3	1	D	D	D	18	151	7.9	1.6
Hardee	23	105	7.0	2.5	NA	NA	NA	NA	25	413	17.9	3.4
Hendry	41	193	17.3	7.0	22	1 014	D	D	71	754	37.3	9.3
Hernando	281	D	D	D	80	1 111	312.5	44.1	237	4 101	166.2	44.3
Highlands	152	D	D	D	56	927	306.1	33.1	133	2 408	100.8	28.0
Hillsborough	4 983	40 574	6 205.8	2 518.5	911	28 213	9 444.9	1 112.6	2 117	47 384	2 619.8	706.8
Holmes	24	160	6.1	3.4	NA	NA	NA	NA	18	206	8.3	2.3
Indian River	473	2 076	235.3	97.2	99	2 179	413.0	87.7	232	4 557	190.5	56.2
Jackson	46	253	23.5	9.1	22	636	180.6	21.1	72	1 014	43.2	11.1
Jefferson	20	98	8.7	3.2	NA	NA	NA	NA	18	79	7.0	1.2
Lafayette	8	28	1.4	0.5	NA	NA	NA	NA	9	47	2.7	0.6
Lake	644	D	D	D	163	3 531	825.5	132.4	428	8 283	436.0	110.6
Lee	1 848	10 115	1 305.2	511.3	403	5 988	1 181.8	222.6	1 095	23 070	1 192.0	344.2
Leon	1 373	D	D	D	100	2 155	593.4	90.3	594	13 745	551.6	150.8
Levy	47	205	15.6	6.1	27	681	131.0	22.3	75	862	32.4	8.2
Liberty	2	D	D	D	NA	NA	NA	NA	4	60	3.4	0.8
Madison	21	111	5.6	2.5	NA	NA	NA	NA	21	356	12.3	3.1
Manatee	919	D	D	D	297	10 012	2 985.1	434.2	529	9 788	443.8	129.5
Marion	698	3 459	361.6	132.0	221	8 904	1 841.5	320.9	443	7 784	353.1	100.0
Martin	675	D	D	D	154	3 242	856.1	118.6	329	6 648	279.0	85.3
Miami-Dade	11 294	60 310	9 603.2	3 755.1	2 312	40 446	9 347.1	1 556.0	4 358	91 230	6 005.9	1 659.8
Monroe	325	D	D	D	NA	NA	NA	NA	484	9 814	748.1	202.4
Nassau	164	495	62.3	23.3	33	D	696.2	68.0	152	3 971	287.0	78.0
Okaloosa	637	D	D	D	98	3 858	656.7	166.4	431	10 619	491.9	148.9
Okeechobee	51	202	14.3	5.1	NA	NA	NA	NA	59	914	46.9	11.5
Orange	4 656	D	D	D	822	30 097	10 921.8	1 555.9	2 426	87 369	6 645.1	1 567.8
Osceola	423	D	D	D	88	1 907	644.9	75.7	532	14 153	890.5	239.0
Palm Beach	6 944	35 002	6 092.8	2 284.2	995	13 919	4 240.7	628.6	2 618	56 542	3 088.6	919.0
Pasco	875	D	D	D	211	3 057	745.2	122.8	581	10 306	432.4	126.7
Pinellas	4 036	D	D	D	1 121	33 564	8 062.0	1 483.6	2 060	37 374	1 925.1	545.3
Polk	1 093	6 654	781.8	310.5	438	16 160	7 178.0	697.4	765	16 084	699.6	199.4

1. Establishment subject to federal tax.

Table B. States and Counties — **Health Care and Social Assistance, Other Services, Nonemployer Businesses, and Residential Construction**

STATE County	Health care and social assistance, 2007				Other services, 2007				Nonemployer businesses, 2013		Value of residential construction authorized by building permits, 2014	
	Number of establish- ments	Number of employees	Receipts (mil dol)	Annual payroll (mil dol)	Number of establish- ments	Number of employees	Receipts (mil dol)	Annual payroll (mil dol)	Number	Receipts (mil dol)	New Construction ($1,000)	Number of housing units
	159	160	161	162	163	164	165	166	167	168	169	170
CONNECTICUT—Cont'd												
Tolland	297	5 867	434.0	197.6	201	1 517	177.9	39.1	9 190	433.2	39 862	203
Windham	274	7 016	501.3	228.1	179	732	62.2	17.4	6 501	283.9	17 994	116
DELAWARE	2 379	54 740	5 430.9	2 370.5	1 587	10 012	898.4	264.6	56 861	3 303.7	615 472	5 194
Kent	354	7 773	672.8	269.3	249	1 460	100.8	32.3	9 126	499.0	134 398	998
New Castle	1 517	37 843	3 886.5	1 750.7	982	6 854	671.1	195.4	32 974	2 068.6	158 116	1 908
Sussex	508	9 124	871.6	350.6	356	1 698	126.5	36.8	14 761	736.1	322 958	2 288
DISTRICT OF COLUMBIA	2 130	61 075	7 250.2	2 942.1	3 284	49 853	15 499.7	3 154.3	52 262	2 506.8	374 396	4 189
District of Columbia	2 130	61 075	7 250.2	2 942.1	3 284	49 853	15 499.7	3 154.3	52 262	2 506.8	374 397	4 189
FLORIDA	51 679	904 004	102 029.3	37 234.1	35 597	201 687	20 757.0	5 173.7	1 838 864	77 785.6	19 548 769	84 075
Alachua	708	D	D	D	379	2 781	655.1	87.6	16 536	619.8	106 852	762
Baker	39	1 844	109.1	65.5	30	D	D	D	1 181	36.8	7 071	47
Bay	493	9 501	985.3	354.0	315	1 767	122.2	38.1	12 463	609.1	125 069	601
Bradford	38	913	59.5	26.4	28	139	11.0	3.1	1 161	41.6	493	2
Brevard	1 417	26 415	2 796.8	1 085.6	1 039	4 868	395.3	121.0	39 045	1 549.9	424 956	1 286
Broward	5 732	88 155	10 883.5	3 647.7	4 174	22 705	2 171.8	586.7	225 162	9 331.7	404 301	2 462
Calhoun	28	525	29.7	12.6	7	D	D	D	767	25.9	869	8
Charlotte	474	7 731	897.1	308.2	275	1 186	90.0	24.7	11 764	523.6	140 869	610
Citrus	340	6 762	661.8	239.8	221	857	52.8	16.3	8 790	337.9	6 838	233
Clay	376	6 167	611.2	227.6	288	1 423	89.0	29.3	11 616	441.2	170 489	915
Collier	914	14 861	1 796.1	703.8	828	4 364	393.3	113.0	34 947	1 935.6	1 111 396	3 610
Columbia	155	3 542	372.3	149.5	82	340	29.7	6.6	3 691	156.5	10 958	80
DeSoto	53	1 134	96.7	39.1	23	82	4.2	1.3	1 572	55.4	16 895	112
Dixie	12	D	D	D	8	25	1.8	0.5	775	26.5	3 159	24
Duval	2 292	52 877	5 928.8	2 230.4	1 745	11 890	1 242.6	358.0	62 201	2 407.8	591 516	3 446
Escambia	751	19 847	2 101.2	785.1	477	2 727	229.0	69.1	19 187	775.9	117 915	698
Flagler	149	1 807	175.1	70.7	126	484	35.2	9.4	8 112	410.2	168 986	548
Franklin	24	D	D	D	22	99	5.9	1.9	1 270	49.0	2 207	8
Gadsden	60	D	D	D	42	147	11.2	3.2	2 780	79.3	5 335	23
Gilchrist	21	D	D	D	11	25	3.0	0.7	913	31.1	4 780	37
Glades	9	D	D	D	6	25	1.5	0.4	517	15.5	2 822	14
Gulf	25	387	18.1	8.5	18	93	4.4	1.1	1 063	51.7	26 285	92
Hamilton	18	275	14.3	5.8	12	41	2.6	0.7	556	19.6	767	9
Hardee	59	1 242	82.1	35.1	25	71	4.9	1.3	1 272	58.2	2 709	17
Hendry	63	843	55.0	23.6	49	170	12.3	3.2	2 707	92.1	3 075	24
Hernando	411	6 711	741.9	248.6	230	1 115	65.9	21.1	10 326	387.2	59 706	378
Highlands	300	4 876	483.4	180.7	142	540	40.7	10.4	5 719	221.6	21 357	92
Hillsborough	3 248	63 269	7 585.5	2 791.8	2 065	16 278	1 576.0	415.9	106 573	4 554.6	1 971 955	7 490
Holmes	33	623	31.4	14.7	16	55	4.4	1.3	1 091	35.3	6 728	31
Indian River	446	7 230	836.4	300.9	264	1 169	97.0	26.7	12 372	651.4	271 374	707
Jackson	91	1 819	135.0	54.3	56	297	27.7	6.9	2 687	85.6	5 010	29
Jefferson	27	D	D	D	15	62	2.4	0.8	1 015	33.0	2 795	17
Lafayette	10	D	D	D	5	D	D	D	325	12.9	2 323	11
Lake	704	13 216	1 382.3	533.6	450	1 864	145.2	43.3	22 148	855.2	553 492	2 488
Lee	1 389	25 867	3 068.2	1 115.8	1 206	6 552	589.9	162.5	57 794	2 755.3	934 206	4 095
Leon	676	15 657	1 691.6	614.8	629	4 537	704.3	161.8	19 062	751.8	158 053	1 114
Levy	59	583	34.1	13.8	61	156	13.3	2.8	2 599	106.8	7 938	49
Liberty	11	D	D	D	3	D	D	D	371	11.0	1 233	9
Madison	39	754	42.5	17.9	21	63	4.5	1.4	938	40.7	4 115	33
Manatee	793	12 166	1 279.6	448.6	524	2 524	167.0	48.4	26 634	1 216.2	624 199	3 565
Marion	817	14 493	1 590.4	566.1	467	2 408	201.6	51.4	22 900	927.4	154 202	754
Martin	506	8 500	859.2	340.2	379	2 024	155.2	49.0	14 370	760.3	203 873	432
Miami-Dade	8 311	120 152	15 042.3	5 194.3	5 065	27 878	3 185.8	659.3	407 551	16 224.0	1 812 541	7 731
Monroe	210	2 293	264.8	91.3	257	1 118	110.4	28.1	11 729	666.5	64 953	188
Nassau	131	1 974	161.7	63.9	106	D	D	D	5 403	238.5	152 755	587
Okaloosa	499	8 357	845.8	312.4	393	2 053	166.4	46.1	14 078	701.2	171 556	590
Okeechobee	103	1 591	153.7	50.6	55	235	16.9	4.8	2 078	72.8	5 537	17
Orange	2 011	57 144	5 005.1	2 466.0	2 012	15 428	1 610.4	450.9	110 458	4 328.9	2 015 453	9 246
Osceola	407	7 041	965.6	297.2	329	1 411	156.7	33.0	25 694	846.3	744 229	3 414
Palm Beach	4 815	67 881	8 382.6	2 978.3	3 180	17 714	1 812.2	460.1	151 331	7 503.0	1 265 400	5 066
Pasco	1 016	15 549	1 718.4	624.2	638	2 901	211.0	61.0	31 285	1 200.5	498 465	2 785
Pinellas	3 194	61 564	6 733.7	2 496.3	2 104	10 928	963.9	283.2	76 324	3 408.4	315 192	1 733
Polk	971	24 347	2 613.7	926.8	727	3 850	323.5	94.6	38 465	1 453.7	502 521	2 559

STATE County	Government employment and payroll, 2012: Full-time equivalent employees	March payroll (dollars)	March payroll (percent of total): Adminis-tration, judicial, and legal	Police and Corrections	Fire Protection	Highways and transpor-tation	Health and Welfare	Natural resources and utilities	Education and libraries	Local government finances, 2012 — General revenue: Total (mil dol)	Inter-govern-mental (mil dol)	Taxes: Total (mil dol)	Per capita[1] (dollars): Total	Property
	171	172	173	174	175	176	177	178	179	180	181	182	183	184
CONNECTICUT—Cont'd														
Tolland	4 711	21 137 708	4.8	2.7	1.1	3.4	2.1	2.9	81.0	531.4	189.3	302.4	1 996	1 971
Windham	3 899	15 623 446	4.2	2.5	1.2	4.0	0.5	3.9	82.0	430.6	207.6	189.4	1 611	1 586
DELAWARE	X	X	X	X	X	X	X	X	X	X	X	X	X	X
Kent	4 210	17 226 252	4.7	6.0	0.1	0.6	1.6	5.6	79.4	494.8	323.1	88.0	525	459
New Castle	13 350	61 131 759	5.7	9.5	1.4	3.2	2.2	5.4	70.9	1 685.7	768.1	591.4	1 083	883
Sussex	5 143	20 898 662	5.1	4.6	0.0	1.2	3.3	4.3	80.0	633.4	356.0	169.5	833	671
DISTRICT OF COLUMBIA	X	X	X	X	X	X	X	X	X	X	X	X	X	X
District of Columbia	44 423	263 772 974	11.1	14.2	4.3	27.8	12.5	5.9	19.0	11 142.1	3 474.2	5 933.8	9 384	2 970
FLORIDA	X	X	X	X	X	X	X	X	X	X	X	X	X	X
Alachua	9 411	34 346 743	10.1	15.9	4.6	4.8	3.1	12.0	45.8	854.0	266.5	363.0	1 444	1 113
Baker	867	2 564 944	5.5	3.7	1.2	2.9	5.4	3.6	77.0	73.2	44.3	18.9	699	507
Bay	8 014	30 150 146	3.2	6.0	2.6	3.8	35.9	4.9	42.5	823.2	190.5	261.0	1 518	1 060
Bradford	881	2 067 161	5.4	1.3	0.4	2.7	7.1	1.3	75.8	71.8	37.9	23.1	853	598
Brevard	19 755	66 076 682	7.5	12.3	7.0	4.4	7.8	7.9	52.0	1 764.4	557.0	634.8	1 160	923
Broward	73 864	331 154 408	5.1	13.2	6.2	3.7	29.6	6.0	33.6	9 918.0	2 186.8	3 161.3	1 742	1 392
Calhoun	510	1 309 655	4.9	3.6	0.2	5.5	0.9	3.7	80.8	46.1	34.0	8.6	581	443
Charlotte	4 654	16 650 878	13.2	15.5	8.9	5.6	2.0	7.8	45.5	559.2	101.1	264.1	1 626	1 290
Citrus	3 890	11 674 757	8.6	11.3	0.1	3.6	5.4	3.4	65.1	322.4	98.7	162.1	1 163	1 064
Clay	6 995	21 858 185	5.6	10.0	3.5	1.9	1.2	5.5	71.3	556.6	210.2	185.3	953	696
Collier	9 918	41 162 175	6.9	15.7	6.7	3.5	4.2	9.1	52.0	1 300.6	231.7	737.4	2 218	2 006
Columbia	2 446	7 323 140	6.4	8.1	2.5	3.8	3.8	3.8	69.3	195.9	99.6	58.8	865	641
DeSoto	1 506	4 657 631	3.9	13.7	4.7	2.2	25.3	4.7	44.3	123.0	39.7	31.6	911	665
Dixie	584	1 731 414	9.6	25.5	0.3	3.8	8.6	2.7	49.0	42.4	22.0	12.7	789	669
Duval	26 681	104 173 723	5.7	15.6	6.2	2.1	1.2	7.3	52.4	3 353.2	1 044.0	1 351.0	1 536	1 039
Escambia	10 348	32 971 310	5.4	14.5	2.6	2.7	4.7	8.0	59.2	937.6	348.0	338.3	1 118	772
Flagler	2 869	10 004 315	13.0	9.5	8.0	1.8	3.2	8.7	53.9	286.1	72.0	141.3	1 437	1 235
Franklin	399	1 124 749	9.6	10.0	1.7	7.1	5.5	9.5	54.3	60.6	21.8	24.9	2 130	1 812
Gadsden	1 850	4 901 351	12.9	12.9	1.7	6.4	3.2	4.9	56.6	109.5	61.3	33.5	721	528
Gilchrist	624	1 705 173	8.0	8.7	0.9	3.7	4.8	1.4	69.5	43.8	24.4	13.1	781	660
Glades	401	1 250 845	13.0	0.2	0.5	3.3	5.2	7.6	67.4	65.1	17.5	12.8	974	884
Gulf	661	1 888 717	10.9	17.7	0.2	5.5	8.9	6.1	46.3	58.3	19.3	27.3	1 735	1 504
Hamilton	602	1 883 338	4.3	14.6	0.6	4.0	4.1	19.8	50.0	60.4	31.4	21.4	1 452	1 298
Hardee	1 238	3 660 532	9.3	12.4	2.4	3.4	4.4	4.8	59.9	83.9	40.3	30.3	1 103	950
Hendry	1 671	5 341 045	10.9	8.7	1.0	3.6	17.8	12.2	43.4	156.7	60.3	45.0	1 201	842
Hernando	5 261	17 523 253	4.9	11.1	6.5	1.8	0.9	20.4	52.8	557.9	169.7	301.2	1 737	1 597
Highlands	3 358	10 445 615	8.2	12.8	2.4	5.5	3.7	6.4	56.9	264.2	111.3	100.2	1 021	799
Hillsborough	45 811	168 419 971	6.8	14.7	5.5	5.2	2.8	7.1	56.0	4 882.0	2 046.8	1 736.7	1 359	996
Holmes	889	2 422 344	5.2	5.1	0.0	3.5	20.9	5.0	58.1	71.8	52.9	10.8	548	332
Indian River	4 188	14 858 891	4.7	16.3	4.8	5.0	5.1	12.6	48.7	445.1	88.8	266.5	1 896	1 553
Jackson	2 760	8 398 373	4.9	6.0	2.2	2.8	34.8	2.6	46.1	203.4	76.8	40.3	823	456
Jefferson	365	927 774	7.8	2.9	2.0	7.8	9.8	3.9	63.2	30.2	13.1	12.4	871	675
Lafayette	373	1 167 432	11.8	22.1	0.0	1.9	8.3	6.2	48.5	18.5	10.9	4.9	555	451
Lake	10 347	30 892 756	6.4	14.3	6.8	2.9	1.5	7.4	57.3	851.0	286.9	352.0	1 161	905
Lee	29 739	118 190 826	4.0	7.9	5.4	3.4	39.4	4.7	33.6	3 672.5	586.2	1 065.4	1 651	1 448
Leon	11 335	40 616 545	8.8	12.0	3.5	5.4	3.6	15.1	47.5	1 138.8	359.2	388.1	1 368	952
Levy	1 489	4 220 044	6.6	13.3	0.6	4.8	6.8	4.6	61.2	107.5	52.0	38.2	954	772
Liberty	390	1 120 616	1.3	0.1	28.3	3.3	4.3	2.5	59.6	26.9	19.5	5.1	613	482
Madison	949	2 696 175	4.6	8.3	1.1	3.0	18.6	2.7	50.5	73.1	37.0	16.5	874	617
Manatee	11 893	40 190 709	10.2	12.9	5.6	2.7	2.6	5.6	58.7	1 162.4	346.0	503.0	1 507	1 276
Marion	10 760	33 096 942	6.2	11.8	9.0	0.5	2.5	5.9	63.0	875.9	312.2	296.0	883	746
Martin	4 603	17 106 522	8.9	17.9	12.8	2.6	1.6	5.7	48.8	500.0	104.9	304.6	2 047	1 811
Miami-Dade	102 308	498 941 928	4.9	14.9	6.0	5.9	20.8	6.6	32.3	14 058.6	3 695.7	5 524.1	2 132	1 564
Monroe	3 585	14 624 150	5.7	22.6	8.9	2.9	3.9	19.5	34.7	567.8	118.5	263.2	3 519	2 437
Nassau	1 980	6 570 847	4.2	2.9	11.2	4.6	1.0	4.9	66.5	222.9	55.5	123.9	1 660	1 424
Okaloosa	6 391	22 546 268	5.1	9.5	4.5	3.0	2.3	7.4	65.4	596.0	213.5	239.6	1 260	1 023
Okeechobee	1 527	4 441 541	4.9	15.8	5.3	1.7	1.2	7.3	62.2	123.6	58.3	42.0	1 065	682
Orange	45 111	168 174 502	6.0	14.3	7.4	5.4	6.3	9.8	48.0	5 410.1	1 451.5	2 181.6	1 815	1 273
Osceola	10 876	36 955 599	7.4	13.0	6.2	2.3	1.1	9.5	58.0	1 052.2	358.1	406.0	1 412	1 006
Palm Beach	46 198	195 497 482	7.6	16.4	10.2	2.6	5.1	13.1	41.6	6 353.4	1 180.9	3 449.0	2 542	2 211
Pasco	14 918	46 238 730	6.6	11.6	5.0	1.2	1.2	4.8	67.1	1 276.0	533.4	417.6	888	715
Pinellas	32 162	118 407 394	7.7	19.5	5.8	3.8	3.8	10.1	45.5	3 227.6	836.8	1 470.9	1 597	1 224
Polk	22 910	75 047 946	7.9	12.5	4.2	2.1	2.6	10.6	56.6	1 844.2	710.5	644.8	1 047	726

1. Based on the resident population estimated as of July 1 of the year shown.

STATE County	Local government finances, 2012 (cont.)									Government employment, 2013			Presidential election,[2] 2012		
	Direct general expenditure							Debt outstanding					Percent of vote cast:		
			Percent of total for:												
	Total (mil dol)	Per capita[1] (dollars)	Educa-tion	Health and hospitals	Police protec-tion	Public welfare	High-ways	Total (mil dol)	Per capita[1] (dollars)	Federal civilian	Federal military	State and local	Demo-cratic	Republi-can	All other
	185	186	187	188	189	190	191	192	193	194	195	196	197	198	199
CONNECTICUT—Cont'd															
Tolland	554.3	3 658	66.0	0.7	2.3	0.3	5.5	321.3	2 121	256	314	15 170	59.6	38.8	1.6
Windham	416.8	3 544	69.2	0.6	2.8	0.4	4.7	176.2	1 498	263	230	7 724	60.7	37.7	1.6
DELAWARE	X	X	X	X	X	X	X	X	X	5 551	9 141	59 570	61.9	36.9	1.1
Kent	527.3	3 145	73.4	1.1	4.4	0.0	1.5	478.7	2 856	1 801	4 542	17 489	54.4	44.6	1.1
New Castle	1 812.2	3 319	59.7	0.8	7.5	0.0	2.5	1 735.3	3 178	3 237	3 307	34 135	69.7	29.1	1.2
Sussex	613.0	3 014	69.2	2.1	4.3	0.1	1.7	515.0	2 532	513	1 292	7 946	45.2	53.8	0.9
DISTRICT OF COLUMBIA	X	X	X	X	X	X	X	X	X	200 751	15 119	35 270	92.5	6.5	1.0
District of Columbia	10 765.0	17 025	22.0	6.3	5.2	26.6	4.9	13 246.6	20 949	200 751	15 119	35 270	92.5	6.5	1.0
FLORIDA	X	X	X	X	X	X	X	X	X	132 244	98 336	932 145	51.0	48.2	0.8
Alachua	900.5	3 582	38.5	3.8	8.3	1.7	4.6	1 948.7	7 751	4 414	554	37 327	60.2	38.6	1.1
Baker	88.4	3 262	47.4	4.9	5.7	1.3	10.3	18.5	682	66	47	2 520	21.0	78.4	0.5
Bay	927.6	5 396	32.4	24.5	6.6	0.0	4.4	885.7	5 152	3 671	3 761	8 491	29.2	69.9	1.0
Bradford	72.8	2 691	44.9	6.1	6.5	0.0	6.2	13.5	501	32	45	2 033	29.4	69.7	0.9
Brevard	1 830.9	3 345	36.4	11.6	7.9	0.4	4.3	1 872.2	3 421	6 251	2 879	22 525	44.3	54.7	0.9
Broward	10 214.0	5 627	24.6	26.3	10.2	1.2	1.4	8 639.5	4 760	7 192	3 954	92 921	67.1	32.4	0.5
Calhoun	49.3	3 348	43.9	2.4	5.2	0.1	28.4	3.8	256	23	25	964	29.2	69.6	1.2
Charlotte	563.6	3 470	33.1	3.8	11.0	1.5	11.1	628.4	3 868	312	313	5 335	45.8	53.1	1.1
Citrus	362.7	2 602	47.4	5.5	9.1	2.5	6.6	493.5	3 541	216	288	4 259	41.3	57.4	1.3
Clay	560.4	2 884	52.3	0.7	8.2	0.5	6.0	488.9	2 515	337	402	7 033	28.2	71.1	0.7
Collier	1 313.8	3 952	37.5	3.0	12.1	0.6	6.0	2 257.5	6 791	637	645	12 042	38.3	60.8	0.8
Columbia	210.8	3 101	53.8	3.7	6.1	0.1	6.0	94.4	1 389	1 299	122	4 299	32.6	66.4	1.0
DeSoto	129.0	3 717	35.1	28.2	5.2	0.4	2.7	71.9	2 070	46	59	1 701	43.3	55.6	1.1
Dixie	42.5	2 637	45.4	10.3	7.8	0.0	6.5	11.2	694	11	28	941	26.5	71.5	2.0
Duval	3 336.4	3 793	39.0	1.9	9.4	1.4	4.4	11 704.3	13 306	15 537	14 307	36 921	48.7	50.6	0.6
Escambia	1 097.8	3 627	40.4	3.3	6.7	0.2	4.3	1 910.8	6 312	5 890	13 779	15 325	39.9	59.2	0.9
Flagler	307.1	3 122	38.2	1.4	7.1	0.2	6.7	437.4	4 447	138	191	3 493	50.4	48.8	0.7
Franklin	62.9	5 386	27.2	14.8	10.5	0.2	5.5	56.4	4 826	14	19	1 005	35.4	63.3	1.3
Gadsden	120.4	2 588	50.5	4.7	7.8	0.8	7.5	55.7	1 197	105	83	4 427	69.2	30.3	0.5
Gilchrist	44.2	2 629	55.7	5.0	6.8	0.4	8.4	4.7	282	29	30	1 072	25.5	72.3	2.1
Glades	69.5	5 305	21.6	4.0	6.8	0.1	6.4	202.1	15 417	20	23	493	41.1	57.7	1.2
Gulf	59.6	3 791	32.4	9.7	5.8	0.4	7.6	52.0	3 310	14	24	1 250	29.8	69.1	1.1
Hamilton	59.7	4 061	31.9	3.6	5.9	0.1	5.3	3.7	253	23	22	1 141	42.3	56.9	0.8
Hardee	86.6	3 149	54.2	4.1	11.3	0.2	5.3	9.9	360	43	49	1 639	34.6	64.3	1.1
Hendry	180.1	4 810	32.7	25.6	7.7	0.4	3.5	74.6	1 991	73	71	2 024	45.9	53.1	0.9
Hernando	566.7	3 268	33.0	2.6	5.9	0.1	3.9	365.6	2 108	289	333	5 749	47.7	51.2	1.1
Highlands	276.6	2 818	46.6	3.7	7.8	0.6	6.0	143.0	1 457	238	186	3 784	40.5	58.6	1.0
Hillsborough	5 230.4	4 093	38.8	3.2	7.5	2.6	3.9	6 006.8	4 701	14 157	8 365	66 012	53.2	46.0	0.8
Holmes	71.5	3 610	38.8	22.5	3.3	0.1	8.7	33.4	1 686	58	35	1 353	16.8	81.9	1.3
Indian River	470.0	3 343	38.2	4.8	9.4	0.8	8.2	436.2	3 103	349	271	4 708	42.1	56.9	1.0
Jackson	226.5	4 626	38.1	33.8	3.4	0.0	8.3	82.2	1 680	472	78	4 876	35.6	63.6	0.8
Jefferson	31.4	2 204	37.8	7.2	14.4	0.5	9.5	3.9	274	35	26	760	51.4	47.7	0.9
Lafayette	19.1	2 172	55.0	7.9	4.8	0.6	8.7	1.7	189	13	14	629	19.1	79.8	1.1
Lake	925.8	3 054	40.3	3.7	8.1	0.5	5.1	1 090.4	3 596	553	586	12 547	42.8	56.4	0.8
Lee	3 730.8	5 782	25.4	32.3	4.8	0.5	3.9	5 119.6	7 934	2 407	1 324	35 542	44.5	54.8	0.7
Leon	1 138.4	4 012	38.2	0.6	7.6	0.0	7.4	4 257.0	15 002	1 738	606	51 651	61.7	37.5	0.8
Levy	112.3	2 806	46.8	5.0	8.6	0.8	9.0	30.9	772	67	107	1 755	35.8	62.8	1.4
Liberty	27.8	3 361	51.9	8.1	3.7	0.3	10.1	4.7	568	40	12	769	27.3	71.4	1.3
Madison	78.8	4 166	46.8	15.6	5.2	0.4	9.1	16.3	861	39	32	1 381	47.9	51.0	1.0
Manatee	1 227.1	3 675	40.6	2.5	8.5	0.7	4.4	1 359.0	4 070	759	682	11 153	46.1	53.1	0.8
Marion	879.1	2 623	48.9	2.0	7.6	0.7	6.3	732.6	2 186	689	634	16 034	43.7	55.3	1.0
Martin	526.0	3 534	36.8	8.1	9.7	2.3	3.4	296.9	1 995	276	284	5 452	42.8	56.4	0.8
Miami-Dade	14 468.1	5 584	25.8	12.2	7.5	3.5	2.2	23 549.3	9 089	20 053	7 437	119 756	57.9	41.8	0.4
Monroe	536.4	7 170	22.9	4.6	11.0	0.5	2.3	1 453.0	19 423	1 194	1 426	4 418	51.9	47.0	1.1
Nassau	230.5	3 089	41.0	5.2	7.0	0.2	6.7	231.3	3 100	587	145	2 720	27.7	71.5	0.7
Okaloosa	687.4	3 616	51.5	2.4	6.6	0.3	2.9	368.2	1 937	8 227	17 244	7 956	27.1	72.0	0.9
Okeechobee	121.9	3 087	49.3	2.5	8.0	0.7	4.0	78.4	1 987	65	71	2 106	39.9	59.1	0.9
Orange	5 320.5	4 426	36.8	4.6	7.1	0.7	4.0	9 996.1	8 315	10 411	2 632	61 344	59.0	40.4	0.6
Osceola	1 153.9	4 015	42.2	1.2	7.2	1.7	8.7	2 678.5	9 319	369	569	11 507	59.6	39.8	0.6
Palm Beach	6 575.2	4 847	27.6	4.7	9.3	2.5	2.5	7 440.3	5 485	6 511	2 752	54 500	61.2	38.3	0.5
Pasco	1 277.5	2 716	49.4	2.0	7.9	0.8	5.8	1 324.5	2 816	740	905	15 485	47.7	51.2	1.1
Pinellas	3 402.6	3 693	34.6	4.2	11.2	3.0	4.2	3 555.7	3 859	6 991	2 910	36 745	53.6	45.3	1.1
Polk	1 992.7	3 234	48.6	3.2	8.2	1.6	5.5	2 776.3	4 506	1 068	1 238	26 981	46.5	52.6	0.9

1. Based on the resident population estimated as of July 1 of the year shown. 2.

STATE/ County code	CBSA code[1]	County type[2]	STATE County	Land area,[3] (sq km) 2010	Population, 2014: Total persons 2014	Population, 2014: Rank	Population, 2014: Per square kilometer	Race alone or in combination, not Hispanic or Latino (percent): White	Race: Black	Race: American Indian, Alaska Native	Race: Asian and Pacific Islander	Percent Hispanic or Latino[4]	Age (percent): Under 5 years	Age: 5 to 17 years	Age: 18 to 24 years	Age: 25 to 34 years	Age: 35 to 44 years	Age: 45 to 54 years
				1	2	3	4	5	6	7	8	9	10	11	12	13	14	15
			FLORIDA—Cont'd															
12 107	37260	4	Putnam	1 885	72 143	750	38.3	73.4	16.7	1.0	1.0	9.4	5.8	16.0	8.1	10.5	10.3	13.6
12 109	27260	1	St. Johns	1 556	217 919	294	140.1	85.9	6.0	0.6	3.2	5.8	4.9	17.3	7.8	10.1	12.7	15.3
12 111	38940	2	St. Lucie	1 481	291 028	231	196.5	61.4	20.1	0.7	2.4	17.2	5.3	15.9	7.8	10.8	11.5	13.5
12 113	37860	2	Santa Rosa	2 620	163 422	390	62.4	85.6	7.1	1.7	3.5	5.1	5.8	17.0	8.7	13.4	13.0	15.4
12 115	35840	2	Sarasota	1 440	396 962	172	275.7	85.1	5.2	0.5	1.9	8.6	3.8	11.4	6.1	8.2	9.2	12.8
12 117	36740	1	Seminole	801	442 516	155	552.5	66.1	11.8	0.7	4.8	18.6	5.2	16.5	9.5	13.7	13.3	15.1
12 119	45540	4	Sumter	1 417	114 350	533	80.7	84.8	8.6	0.6	1.0	5.6	2.1	5.7	3.5	6.1	6.9	7.8
12 121	...	6	Suwannee	1 783	44 022	1 088	24.7	76.7	13.7	1.0	0.9	9.1	5.9	15.5	8.4	12.9	11.4	13.2
12 123	...	6	Taylor	2 702	22 582	1 704	8.4	73.8	21.3	1.6	1.1	3.9	5.4	13.5	8.6	14.3	12.9	14.3
12 125	...	6	Union	631	15 190	2 085	24.1	71.9	22.8	0.7	0.5	5.4	5.1	14.1	9.1	15.4	13.8	15.6
12 127	19660	2	Volusia	2 852	507 531	134	178.0	75.7	11.0	0.8	2.2	12.0	4.7	13.5	8.7	10.8	10.7	13.9
12 129	45220	2	Wakulla	1 571	31 432	1 401	20.0	80.3	15.6	1.3	0.9	3.6	5.3	15.7	7.9	14.4	15.1	15.9
12 131	18880	6	Walton	2 687	61 530	852	22.9	86.0	6.3	1.9	1.7	6.3	5.5	14.9	7.2	12.6	12.4	14.8
12 133	...	6	Washington	1 509	24 451	1 628	16.2	79.1	16.3	2.1	1.0	3.4	5.0	15.4	8.7	12.9	13.5	14.8
13 000	...	X	GEORGIA	148 959	10 097 343	X	67.8	56.2	31.5	0.7	4.2	9.2	6.7	18.2	10.2	13.7	13.7	14.0
13 001	...	7	Appling	1 313	18 540	1 892	14.1	70.6	19.6	0.5	0.9	9.4	6.9	18.5	8.2	12.0	12.3	13.6
13 003	...	9	Atkinson	879	8 223	2 588	9.4	57.5	17.6	0.8	0.6	24.6	8.2	20.0	9.5	12.6	13.2	13.2
13 005	...	7	Bacon	670	11 281	2 339	16.8	75.9	16.8	0.3	0.6	7.5	6.9	18.8	8.6	12.3	13.7	12.6
13 007	10500	3	Baker	886	3 255	2 953	3.7	49.4	45.6	0.4	1.2	4.5	5.7	16.0	7.9	10.3	12.2	14.2
13 009	33300	4	Baldwin	668	45 909	1 050	68.7	54.4	42.0	0.5	2.0	2.1	5.3	14.2	19.3	12.0	10.4	13.1
13 011	...	8	Banks	601	18 295	1 905	30.4	89.6	3.1	0.8	1.4	6.2	5.4	18.2	8.3	11.3	13.7	14.9
13 013	12060	1	Barrow	415	73 240	743	176.5	75.7	12.1	0.7	4.1	9.2	7.5	19.9	8.3	14.8	14.5	13.5
13 015	12060	1	Bartow	1 190	101 736	585	85.5	80.5	11.2	0.8	1.2	7.8	6.4	19.1	8.9	12.7	13.9	14.8
13 017	22340	7	Ben Hill	648	17 464	1 949	27.0	57.8	35.3	0.7	0.9	6.4	7.9	18.0	8.6	12.1	12.0	13.2
13 019	...	6	Berrien	1 170	18 700	1 881	16.0	83.3	11.4	0.6	0.8	5.0	6.1	18.0	8.3	11.9	12.8	14.6
13 021	31420	3	Bibb	647	153 905	417	237.9	41.8	53.6	0.5	2.2	3.2	7.4	18.0	10.7	13.2	11.9	13.0
13 023	...	6	Bleckley	559	12 795	2 246	22.9	69.9	27.1	0.3	1.1	2.6	5.4	16.3	14.6	11.0	11.2	14.0
13 025	15260	3	Brantley	1 146	18 417	1 899	16.1	94.1	3.8	1.1	0.4	2.0	6.0	19.1	8.2	11.4	13.1	14.8
13 027	46660	3	Brooks	1 277	15 418	2 075	12.1	59.0	35.0	0.8	0.6	5.6	6.6	15.4	8.3	11.5	11.4	14.6
13 029	42340	2	Bryan	1 129	33 906	1 328	30.0	76.5	15.9	0.9	2.7	6.3	7.3	21.7	8.5	13.6	15.1	13.5
13 031	44340	4	Bulloch	1 743	72 087	751	41.4	65.8	29.3	0.6	2.1	3.6	5.7	14.8	26.4	13.1	10.2	10.3
13 033	12260	2	Burke	2 142	22 709	1 701	10.6	48.2	48.8	0.7	0.7	3.0	6.9	19.6	9.5	11.9	11.4	13.8
13 035	12060	1	Butts	478	23 368	1 668	48.9	68.5	28.2	0.6	0.7	3.0	5.9	15.7	9.6	14.0	13.6	14.7
13 037	...	8	Calhoun	726	6 463	2 718	8.9	34.0	61.3	0.6	0.6	4.4	4.8	14.3	9.4	15.8	15.7	15.1
13 039	41220	4	Camden	1 588	52 027	959	32.8	72.7	20.2	1.1	2.7	5.9	7.7	18.0	13.2	15.5	11.6	13.0
13 043	...	7	Candler	629	10 888	2 366	17.3	64.2	24.9	0.5	0.8	10.7	6.6	19.6	8.4	11.6	12.0	12.5
13 045	12060	1	Carroll	1 293	114 093	535	88.2	73.9	19.6	0.7	1.2	6.5	6.6	18.0	13.9	12.8	12.6	12.9
13 047	16860	2	Catoosa	420	65 621	803	156.2	93.0	3.2	0.9	1.8	2.7	5.7	18.3	8.3	11.8	13.9	14.2
13 049	...	6	Charlton	2 004	12 897	2 239	6.4	63.4	32.9	0.9	0.9	3.5	5.4	13.1	10.4	16.4	15.3	15.4
13 051	42340	2	Chatham	1 104	283 379	239	256.7	51.5	40.4	0.7	3.4	5.9	7.0	15.3	12.2	16.4	11.9	12.2
13 053	17980	2	Chattahoochee	644	11 837	2 305	18.4	63.6	18.7	1.6	4.2	15.7	10.0	15.9	28.4	24.0	9.7	4.9
13 055	44900	6	Chattooga	812	24 939	1 612	30.7	84.2	11.0	0.7	0.7	4.8	5.7	16.9	8.6	12.6	12.9	13.9
13 057	12060	1	Cherokee	1 092	230 985	282	211.5	81.8	6.6	0.7	2.5	10.1	6.5	20.0	8.1	12.0	15.4	15.3
13 059	12020	3	Clarke	309	120 938	509	391.4	58.0	27.5	0.5	5.1	10.7	5.8	11.6	28.7	16.7	10.7	8.7
13 061	...	9	Clay	506	3 102	2 967	6.1	38.5	60.0	0.6	0.7	1.2	6.8	14.6	7.4	10.5	8.4	12.3
13 063	12060	1	Clayton	367	267 542	251	729.0	15.2	67.2	0.7	5.6	13.1	8.0	20.4	10.6	14.9	14.3	13.6
13 065	...	6	Clinch	2 073	6 831	2 696	3.3	67.7	28.0	1.0	0.4	4.2	7.4	18.1	9.4	12.1	12.5	12.7
13 067	12060	1	Cobb	879	730 981	85	831.6	56.4	26.8	0.7	5.6	12.6	6.7	18.2	9.3	14.2	15.1	14.9
13 069	20060	7	Coffee	1 489	42 811	1 115	28.8	60.7	28.3	0.5	1.0	10.6	6.8	18.4	10.8	13.8	13.4	13.6
13 071	34220	6	Colquitt	1 409	46 102	1 047	32.7	58.3	23.4	0.6	1.0	17.6	7.9	19.1	9.4	13.3	12.6	12.8
13 073	12260	2	Columbia	751	139 257	454	185.4	73.4	17.1	0.8	5.4	5.9	6.5	19.9	8.7	13.1	13.9	14.5
13 075	...	6	Cook	588	17 214	1 970	29.3	65.6	27.9	0.7	0.9	5.9	6.8	19.6	8.3	12.7	12.5	13.6
13 077	12060	1	Coweta	1 142	135 571	467	118.7	73.5	18.3	0.7	2.4	6.8	6.4	19.8	8.2	12.3	14.5	15.2
13 079	31420	3	Crawford	841	12 387	2 273	14.7	74.9	21.9	1.0	0.5	3.0	5.0	16.2	8.6	10.7	12.2	16.8
13 081	18380	6	Crisp	706	22 934	1 689	32.5	52.1	43.9	0.5	1.3	3.3	6.9	18.1	9.3	12.0	11.4	13.1
13 083	16860	2	Dade	451	16 389	2 019	36.3	95.1	1.7	1.1	1.2	2.1	5.1	14.9	13.6	10.9	11.6	13.7
13 085	12060	1	Dawson	546	22 957	1 687	42.0	94.1	1.1	0.9	1.0	4.1	5.4	17.0	7.4	11.3	12.7	15.0
13 087	12460	6	Decatur	1 547	27 220	1 522	17.6	52.7	41.3	0.6	0.8	5.6	6.8	18.2	9.6	11.9	12.4	13.9
13 089	12060	1	DeKalb	693	722 161	86	1 042.1	31.2	54.5	0.7	6.2	9.1	7.4	16.3	9.4	16.7	15.1	13.8
13 091	...	7	Dodge	1 284	20 976	1 775	16.3	66.4	29.9	0.5	0.6	3.6	6.3	15.3	10.1	12.7	13.3	14.8
13 093	...	6	Dooly	1 015	14 188	2 155	14.0	43.5	49.2	0.4	0.9	6.8	5.0	15.0	8.5	13.3	13.6	14.9
13 095	10500	3	Dougherty	851	92 407	630	108.6	28.6	68.2	0.6	1.3	2.5	7.5	17.6	12.4	13.5	11.4	12.1
13 097	12060	1	Douglas	518	138 776	456	267.9	47.8	42.4	0.8	2.2	8.9	6.7	20.5	9.1	12.3	15.5	15.0
13 099	...	6	Early	1 328	10 491	2 396	7.9	47.8	49.6	0.7	0.6	2.0	6.7	18.3	9.0	10.0	11.8	13.4
13 101	46660	3	Echols	1 075	4 003	2 902	3.7	64.8	4.9	2.3	0.6	29.4	8.6	18.5	9.5	15.1	13.4	12.9

1. CBSA = Core Based Statistical Area. See Appendix A for explanation. See Appendix B for list of metropolitan areas with component counties. 2. County type code from the Economic Research Service of USDA Rural-Urban Continuum Codes. See Appendix A for definition. 3. Dry land or land partially or temporarily covered by water. 4. May be of any race.

STATE County	Population, 2013 (cont.): Age (percent) (cont.): 55 to 64 years	65 to 74 years	75 years and over	Percent female	Population change and components of change, 2000–2014: Total persons: 2000	2010	Percent change: 2000–2010	2010–2014	Components of change, 2010–2014: Births	Deaths	Net migration	Households, 2009–2013: Number	Persons per house-hold	Percent: Family house-holds	Female family house-holder[1]	One per-son
	16	17	18	19	20	21	22	23	24	25	26	27	28	29	30	31
FLORIDA—Cont'd																
Putnam	15.0	11.8	8.8	50.6	70 423	74 364	5.6	-3.0	3 562	3 987	-1 649	28 047	2.57	65.3	14.2	29.5
St. Johns	14.3	10.4	7.1	51.4	123 135	190 039	54.3	14.7	8 066	6 642	25 543	75 558	2.57	69.4	9.4	24.5
St. Lucie	13.1	11.9	10.1	51.2	192 695	277 789	44.2	5.0	12 690	12 048	12 189	106 060	2.62	68.6	13.3	25.8
Santa Rosa	12.6	8.7	5.4	49.0	117 743	151 372	28.6	8.0	7 724	5 372	9 359	57 368	2.64	73.4	10.8	20.9
Sarasota	15.2	16.8	16.4	52.2	325 957	379 448	16.4	4.6	12 215	21 609	25 856	170 555	2.21	60.6	8.7	32.9
Seminole	12.7	7.9	5.9	51.6	365 196	422 718	15.8	4.7	18 753	12 884	13 348	147 529	2.87	67.2	12.9	26.6
Sumter	16.4	33.0	18.6	48.9	53 345	93 420	75.1	22.4	1 939	5 575	23 294	43 507	2.04	70.0	5.2	26.0
Suwannee	13.4	10.9	8.4	47.6	34 844	41 551	19.2	5.9	2 015	2 152	2 562	15 712	2.64	69.4	14.6	26.4
Taylor	13.6	10.3	7.1	43.6	19 256	22 570	17.2	0.1	1 018	937	-54	7 672	2.55	68.5	16.0	26.7
Union	15.0	7.8	4.0	35.3	13 442	15 535	15.6	-2.2	742	785	-322	3 807	2.79	74.2	18.6	22.6
Volusia	14.9	12.2	10.6	51.3	443 343	494 593	11.6	2.6	19 842	26 706	19 298	195 907	2.47	62.5	10.9	31.3
Wakulla	13.1	8.3	4.4	44.9	22 863	30 776	34.6	2.1	1 360	996	274	10 455	2.61	72.8	15.0	23.7
Walton	14.6	11.1	7.0	49.2	40 601	55 043	35.6	11.8	2 877	2 302	5 700	22 639	2.41	64.6	10.7	30.2
Washington	13.1	10.2	6.7	45.4	20 973	24 896	18.7	-1.8	999	1 137	-316	8 533	2.63	66.7	10.4	28.9
GEORGIA	11.6	7.3	4.7	51.1	8 186 453	9 687 653	18.3	4.2	556 992	308 766	151 661	3 518 097	2.71	68.2	15.3	26.5
Appling	13.3	9.2	5.9	49.7	17 419	18 236	4.7	1.7	1 140	756	-78	6 934	2.59	67.3	13.4	28.2
Atkinson	11.8	7.3	4.1	49.7	7 609	8 375	10.1	-1.9	544	258	-453	2 758	3.00	68.2	15.3	29.2
Bacon	13.2	8.5	5.4	50.8	10 103	11 096	9.8	1.7	640	510	59	4 036	2.66	68.5	12.3	27.3
Baker	16.9	9.6	7.3	51.9	4 074	3 451	-15.3	-5.7	139	83	-240	1 374	2.47	62.3	18.3	33.9
Baldwin	12.2	8.2	5.3	49.9	44 700	45 720	2.3	0.2	2 022	1 690	-271	16 338	2.55	60.2	17.6	30.5
Banks	13.1	10.0	5.2	49.4	14 422	18 395	27.5	-0.5	756	570	-323	6 772	2.71	73.9	8.9	20.8
Barrow	10.7	6.9	3.9	50.7	46 144	69 367	50.3	5.6	4 524	2 170	1 425	23 413	2.97	76.1	13.3	19.5
Bartow	11.9	7.8	4.5	50.7	76 019	100 157	31.8	1.6	5 413	3 534	-373	34 567	2.88	74.6	12.5	20.8
Ben Hill	13.1	8.9	6.2	52.1	17 484	17 634	0.9	-1.0	1 014	869	-309	6 110	2.83	66.1	19.7	30.6
Berrien	12.6	9.5	6.3	50.5	16 235	19 286	18.8	-3.0	943	775	-758	7 040	2.69	71.0	12.2	26.1
Bibb	12.4	7.6	5.9	52.9	153 887	155 547	1.1	-1.0	9 666	6 885	-4 330	56 585	2.63	64.0	20.3	30.9
Bleckley	11.0	9.0	7.6	52.3	11 666	13 063	12.0	-2.1	580	563	-296	3 955	2.90	67.6	16.1	27.1
Brantley	13.2	9.0	5.2	50.5	14 629	18 411	25.9	0.0	853	743	-90	6 550	2.79	76.0	13.1	22.1
Brooks	14.2	11.0	7.1	51.7	16 450	16 243	-1.3	-5.6	890	780	-1 020	6 573	2.39	64.1	14.1	31.7
Bryan	10.7	6.1	3.6	50.4	23 417	30 233	29.1	12.1	2 106	914	2 435	11 230	2.79	77.3	11.4	17.8
Bulloch	9.4	6.1	4.0	50.5	55 983	70 217	25.4	2.7	3 460	2 065	310	25 254	2.61	59.7	15.5	24.0
Burke	13.4	8.5	5.1	52.1	22 243	23 316	4.8	-2.6	1 360	1 030	-985	7 881	2.91	69.0	20.5	26.7
Butts	12.5	8.6	5.5	46.8	19 522	23 655	21.2	-1.2	1 212	1 031	-428	7 776	2.74	70.6	10.9	24.8
Calhoun	12.8	6.4	5.7	40.4	6 320	6 694	5.9	-3.5	280	236	-315	1 804	2.19	60.8	16.7	36.1
Camden	10.4	7.3	3.5	48.8	43 664	50 513	15.7	3.0	3 485	1 237	-774	18 386	2.69	75.2	13.2	19.3
Candler	13.2	10.2	5.9	50.9	9 577	10 998	14.8	-1.0	628	481	-279	3 861	2.78	69.8	14.6	23.5
Carroll	11.0	7.5	4.7	51.2	87 268	110 527	26.7	3.2	6 286	4 028	1 277	39 494	2.72	70.4	15.1	23.8
Catoosa	12.3	9.1	6.2	51.4	53 282	63 942	20.0	2.6	3 196	2 252	579	23 941	2.68	73.4	12.0	23.8
Charlton	11.2	7.8	5.0	39.4	10 282	12 171	18.4	6.0	565	389	448	3 727	3.12	69.5	15.9	26.3
Chatham	11.6	7.7	5.6	51.7	232 048	265 128	14.3	6.9	16 739	9 525	10 750	102 484	2.55	61.7	16.5	31.3
Chattahoochee	3.1	2.4	1.4	34.8	14 882	11 267	-24.3	5.1	1 056	116	-425	2 613	3.54	80.4	13.9	13.7
Chattooga	13.3	9.3	6.8	48.9	25 470	26 015	2.1	-4.1	1 199	1 279	-989	9 457	2.52	68.8	14.1	26.3
Cherokee	11.5	7.5	3.8	50.7	141 903	214 346	51.1	7.8	11 759	5 175	9 782	76 144	2.85	75.7	11.3	20.0
Clarke	8.4	5.3	4.0	52.2	101 489	116 714	15.0	3.6	6 166	2 912	876	41 358	2.61	49.9	13.5	33.8
Clay	16.7	13.9	9.3	53.9	3 357	3 183	-5.2	-2.5	150	152	-83	1 235	2.49	57.7	18.8	38.1
Clayton	10.4	5.1	2.7	52.4	236 517	259 424	9.7	3.1	17 584	6 338	-3 270	86 274	2.99	65.2	23.3	29.7
Clinch	13.3	9.6	5.0	50.3	6 878	6 798	-1.2	0.5	440	284	-119	2 586	2.53	64.8	17.3	31.9
Cobb	11.5	6.4	3.8	51.6	607 751	688 078	13.2	6.2	40 063	16 346	19 096	261 242	2.64	67.6	12.9	26.0
Coffee	11.3	7.4	4.6	48.8	37 413	42 356	13.2	1.1	2 516	1 544	-554	14 497	2.73	70.6	16.9	26.0
Colquitt	11.2	8.0	5.7	50.4	42 053	45 498	8.2	1.3	3 040	1 929	-462	15 918	2.81	73.7	17.9	23.8
Columbia	12.1	7.0	4.3	51.1	89 288	124 053	38.9	12.3	6 862	3 354	11 430	43 975	2.90	78.7	12.7	18.5
Cook	11.9	8.8	5.8	51.4	15 771	17 212	9.1	0.0	959	781	-168	6 308	2.67	74.6	16.2	22.0
Coweta	11.6	7.6	4.3	51.1	89 215	127 317	42.7	6.5	6 964	3 718	4 830	46 912	2.74	74.6	11.4	21.4
Crawford	14.6	10.5	5.4	49.3	12 495	12 630	1.1	-1.9	525	488	-295	4 620	2.70	73.2	17.5	23.7
Crisp	14.0	8.6	6.7	52.3	21 996	23 439	6.6	-2.2	1 290	1 037	-723	8 832	2.61	71.8	23.9	25.5
Dade	14.1	9.5	6.6	50.7	15 154	16 633	9.8	-1.5	755	695	-301	6 325	2.44	75.4	9.8	21.3
Dawson	14.1	11.7	5.3	50.1	15 999	22 330	39.6	2.8	1 031	693	227	8 506	2.61	76.4	9.3	19.3
Decatur	12.2	8.5	6.6	51.3	28 240	27 842	-1.4	-2.2	1 574	1 296	-912	10 525	2.51	67.5	19.5	28.9
DeKalb	11.4	6.0	3.9	52.2	665 865	691 893	3.9	4.4	46 517	18 057	1 624	264 496	2.59	59.1	17.4	33.4
Dodge	12.7	8.6	6.1	47.5	19 171	21 796	13.7	-3.8	1 064	946	-976	8 186	2.36	66.6	16.4	30.8
Dooly	14.5	9.5	5.7	45.9	11 525	14 918	29.4	-4.9	499	511	-730	5 133	2.37	63.5	14.7	33.1
Dougherty	12.3	7.3	5.7	53.6	96 065	94 565	-1.6	-2.3	6 013	3 774	-4 423	35 661	2.53	63.8	25.1	31.5
Douglas	11.0	6.5	3.4	51.9	92 174	132 403	43.6	4.9	7 425	3 615	2 512	46 295	2.86	74.3	17.8	22.0
Early	12.9	10.3	7.7	53.2	12 354	11 008	-10.9	-4.7	637	566	-613	4 030	2.61	64.9	20.2	32.2
Echols	10.9	6.0	5.1	50.6	3 754	4 034	7.5	-0.8	270	104	-216	1 382	2.93	78.9	16.1	16.9

1. No spouse present.

STATE County	Persons in group quarters, 2014	Daytime population, 2009–2013 Number	Daytime population, 2009–2013 Employ-ment/ resi-dence ratio	Births, 2014 Total	Births, 2014 Rate[1]	Deaths, 2014 Number	Deaths, 2014 Rate[1]	Persons under 65 with no health insurance, 2013 Number	Persons under 65 with no health insurance, 2013 Percent	Medicare, 2014 Eligible for Medicare	Medicare, 2014 Enrolled in Medicare Advantage	Medicare, 2014 Enrolled in a Medicare prescription drug plan	Serious crimes known to police,[2] 2013 Total Number	Serious crimes known to police,[2] 2013 Total Rate[3]
	32	33	34	35	36	37	38	39	40	41	42	43	44	45
FLORIDA—Cont'd														
Putnam	1 428	68 393	0.78	812	11.3	917	12.7	13 875	24.6	17 548	4 457	7 873	2 941	4 056
St. Johns	2 833	175 804	0.76	2 012	9.2	1 668	7.7	26 432	15.6	42 258	9 017	18 435	4 727	2 286
St. Lucie	3 051	257 201	0.77	2 949	10.1	3 021	10.4	56 783	25.7	65 756	22 934	25 953	7 666	2 674
Santa Rosa	6 154	128 943	0.60	1 865	11.4	1 333	8.2	24 381	18.4	28 512	7 393	9 161	2 301	1 429
Sarasota	5 627	396 607	1.09	2 871	7.2	5 308	13.4	59 411	23.1	121 623	29 176	59 558	11 167	2 866
Seminole	3 517	397 968	0.86	4 458	10.1	3 218	7.3	72 404	19.4	68 586	25 300	22 546	12 479	2 868
Sumter	8 302	102 034	1.18	479	4.2	1 439	12.6	7 898	18.2	58 076	17 543	25 788	1 157	1 125
Suwannee	3 465	41 293	0.90	466	10.6	515	11.7	7 746	24.0	10 300	1 855	5 018	976	2 204
Taylor	3 367	22 914	1.03	231	10.2	225	10.0	3 002	19.5	4 528	829	2 083	544	2 376
Union	4 785	15 799	1.11	175	11.5	196	12.9	1 440	16.2	1 956	341	797	161	1 061
Volusia	13 174	474 104	0.89	4 682	9.2	6 379	12.6	90 489	24.0	127 042	56 215	40 209	18 716	3 760
Wakulla	3 681	24 430	0.50	316	10.1	222	7.1	4 222	18.0	4 969	2 340	1 196	637	2 060
Walton	2 047	57 920	1.06	740	12.0	550	8.9	11 507	24.4	11 987	2 154	5 225	1 735	2 961
Washington	2 760	23 433	0.85	227	9.3	260	10.6	3 561	19.9	5 277	796	2 529	448	1 790
GEORGIA	261 656	9 808 847	1.00	129 389	12.8	75 557	7.5	1 806 594	21.1	1 485 186	437 376	613 917	370 940	3 712
Appling	393	18 888	1.07	268	14.5	189	10.2	3 682	24.1	3 502	854	1 739	414	2 252
Atkinson	25	7 283	0.67	131	15.9	47	5.7	2 328	31.9	1 314	341	669	NA	NA
Bacon	307	10 987	0.96	144	12.8	101	9.0	2 386	25.4	2 024	552	976	NA	NA
Baker	0	3 060	0.66	28	8.6	25	7.7	639	23.0	693	176	327	NA	NA
Baldwin	5 910	46 756	1.05	467	10.2	416	9.1	6 651	19.1	8 007	3 285	2 735	1 911	4 098
Banks	0	15 586	0.65	169	9.2	113	6.2	3 655	23.4	3 245	848	1 671	561	3 068
Barrow	338	55 946	0.54	1 069	14.6	534	7.3	14 210	22.3	10 305	3 045	4 534	2 649	3 767
Bartow	945	94 182	0.85	1 277	12.6	846	8.3	19 035	21.6	16 154	4 329	7 201	3 719	3 736
Ben Hill	312	17 767	1.04	222	12.7	200	11.5	3 108	21.1	3 530	1 030	1 726	716	4 091
Berrien	180	16 329	0.58	230	12.3	196	10.5	3 806	23.8	3 536	954	1 593	477	2 518
Bibb	6 074	178 298	1.38	2 240	14.6	1 648	10.7	26 693	20.8	28 729	8 890	11 625	10 291	6 575
Bleckley	1 268	11 508	0.66	138	10.8	115	9.0	1 644	17.3	2 446	461	997	496	3 855
Brantley	61	14 582	0.41	196	10.6	182	9.9	3 800	24.2	3 158	728	1 514	472	2 534
Brooks	90	13 931	0.67	199	12.9	192	12.5	3 199	25.2	3 370	895	1 561	498	3 404
Bryan	99	23 575	0.46	546	16.1	213	6.3	4 718	15.8	4 429	1 276	1 604	506	1 541
Bulloch	5 511	68 813	0.92	775	10.8	488	6.8	12 943	21.9	9 042	2 092	4 391	2 213	3 015
Burke	283	22 641	0.93	305	13.4	230	10.1	3 949	20.0	4 172	1 452	1 659	805	3 541
Butts	2 327	21 756	0.80	294	12.6	258	11.0	3 680	20.8	4 227	1 455	1 690	530	2 260
Calhoun	1 687	6 299	0.88	67	10.4	46	7.1	970	23.7	1 072	342	527	361	6 172
Camden	1 875	48 417	0.90	824	15.8	291	5.6	7 497	17.0	7 028	1 402	2 762	1 511	3 002
Candler	288	10 065	0.77	142	13.0	110	10.1	2 178	24.2	2 141	566	1 077	NA	NA
Carroll	4 658	104 850	0.86	1 474	12.9	983	8.6	19 310	20.2	18 554	5 547	8 344	3 769	3 369
Catoosa	472	51 654	0.55	747	11.4	558	8.5	9 849	17.9	12 038	3 267	5 657	1 991	3 044
Charlton	2 941	11 486	0.61	133	10.3	84	6.5	1 710	19.9	1 930	401	956	170	1 263
Chatham	14 096	298 020	1.23	3 958	14.0	2 329	8.2	49 919	21.8	43 560	13 797	16 152	11 277	4 027
Chattahoochee	3 268	19 092	2.12	228	19.3	26	2.2	1 354	14.8	543	149	155	27	196
Chattooga	1 485	23 636	0.77	278	11.1	287	11.5	4 346	21.9	5 439	1 583	2 673	593	2 362
Cherokee	1 626	176 061	0.59	2 707	11.7	1 232	5.3	37 821	19.2	31 205	9 681	12 266	3 146	1 408
Clarke	10 306	137 782	1.37	1 465	12.1	721	6.0	23 315	23.6	14 665	3 677	7 359	4 869	4 015
Clay	58	2 812	0.64	34	11.0	33	10.6	506	21.8	729	249	338	NA	NA
Clayton	4 448	250 989	0.89	3 806	14.2	1 561	5.8	62 789	26.2	29 459	10 946	10 311	13 048	4 869
Clinch	132	6 900	1.06	104	15.2	55	8.1	1 397	24.1	1 386	375	717	286	4 273
Cobb	9 269	681 521	0.95	9 471	13.0	4 086	5.6	133 700	21.2	87 368	26 097	33 494	19 819	2 777
Coffee	3 111	43 682	1.05	583	13.6	364	8.5	8 914	25.5	6 664	1 781	3 309	1 887	4 479
Colquitt	1 001	44 580	0.93	680	14.7	449	9.7	11 153	28.3	8 251	2 198	3 837	NA	NA
Columbia	743	100 955	0.54	1 607	11.5	820	5.9	17 876	15.0	18 474	4 655	5 832	2 370	1 769
Cook	145	15 046	0.71	219	12.7	188	10.9	3 481	23.9	3 214	838	1 529	421	2 636
Coweta	553	107 494	0.63	1 632	12.0	923	6.8	19 596	16.9	19 119	5 825	7 576	3 009	2 280
Crawford	135	9 447	0.37	98	7.9	118	9.5	2 233	21.3	2 367	791	925	416	3 301
Crisp	406	24 170	1.08	284	12.4	266	11.6	4 088	21.0	4 169	1 379	1 869	1 298	5 480
Dade	974	13 694	0.61	185	11.3	179	10.9	2 570	20.0	3 278	948	1 521	200	1 216
Dawson	142	20 438	0.80	251	10.9	163	7.1	4 086	22.0	3 984	956	1 942	476	2 119
Decatur	1 011	27 158	0.95	366	13.4	307	11.3	5 010	22.3	5 283	1 391	2 626	985	3 594
DeKalb	11 905	678 024	0.93	10 784	14.9	4 351	6.0	139 408	22.2	89 091	32 269	31 988	42 844	6 016
Dodge	1 826	19 384	0.73	225	10.7	225	10.7	3 364	20.5	3 848	1 043	1 675	943	4 977
Dooly	1 870	13 757	0.83	111	7.8	107	7.5	2 497	24.3	2 208	677	887	NA	NA
Dougherty	4 327	108 018	1.40	1 337	14.5	897	9.7	15 836	20.4	16 296	4 351	6 981	5 934	6 284
Douglas	1 372	117 016	0.72	1 726	12.4	926	6.7	25 723	21.2	17 377	5 405	6 735	4 411	3 281
Early	134	10 794	1.00	152	14.5	138	13.2	1 706	19.9	2 290	716	1 102	476	4 650
Echols	0	2 725	0.20	53	13.2	19	4.7	1 202	33.5	473	91	238	11	277

1. Per 1,000 estimated resident population. 2. Data for serious crimes have not been adjusted for underreporting; this may affect comparability between geographic areas and over time.
3. Per 100,000 population estimated by the FBI.

STATE County	Serious crimes known to police, 2013 (cont.)[1] Rate[2] Violent	Property	Education: School enrollment and attainment, 2009–2013 Enrollment[3] Total	Per-cent private	Attainment[4] (percent) High school grad-uate or less	Bach-elor's degree or more	Local government expenditures,[5] 2012–2013 Total current spending (mil dol)	Current spend-ing per student (dollars)	Money income, 2009–2013 Per capita income[6] (dollars)	Households Median income (dollars)	Mean income (dollars)	Percent with income of $200,000 or more	Income and poverty, 2013 Median house-hold income (dollars)	Percent below poverty level All per-sons	Children under 18 years	Children 5 to 17 years in families
	46	47	48	49	50	51	52	53	54	55	56	57	58	59	60	61
FLORIDA—Cont'd																
Putnam	603	3 453	15 029	11.0	62.7	11.4	98.0	8 853	18 377	32 497	45 391	0.9	32 852	26.9	42.8	44.7
St. Johns	259	2 027	51 685	22.2	28.1	41.4	259.0	7 982	36 836	64 876	93 325	8.4	66 312	9.6	11.7	10.7
St. Lucie	416	2 258	66 578	13.0	48.9	19.5	330.8	8 344	23 285	43 413	58 639	2.1	42 825	19.0	28.6	26.3
Santa Rosa	124	1 305	40 541	12.3	38.1	25.9	204.5	7 903	26 861	57 703	71 126	3.3	54 876	13.8	17.7	16.5
Sarasota	289	2 577	66 963	15.9	38.8	30.8	423.7	10 310	32 313	49 052	70 251	4.4	48 717	13.0	20.4	17.7
Seminole	350	2 519	121 245	16.8	32.5	35.0	492.4	7 639	28 675	58 175	77 098	4.6	55 195	12.9	17.3	16.1
Sumter	170	955	9 628	13.5	44.3	25.2	68.5	8 569	27 504	48 493	59 959	1.9	52 670	12.0	33.5	33.0
Suwannee	400	1 804	8 733	12.5	64.4	9.8	51.0	8 512	18 431	35 698	46 650	1.6	35 666	24.6	37.5	34.1
Taylor	882	1 494	4 436	20.5	60.6	11.6	26.7	9 585	17 045	36 356	47 769	0.7	38 370	23.9	32.9	32.8
Union	349	712	2 888	8.2	63.1	10.0	19.4	8 474	13 590	42 660	49 840	0.6	40 841	23.8	27.0	26.3
Volusia	413	3 346	109 907	18.6	45.2	20.8	484.6	7 935	23 973	42 457	56 975	2.3	40 908	16.6	25.3	24.4
Wakulla	249	1 811	6 895	9.6	50.3	17.2	39.8	7 928	21 797	52 691	61 632	0.9	47 430	15.9	22.2	20.1
Walton	357	2 605	11 881	10.5	45.9	24.1	75.1	9 611	25 845	43 640	62 249	3.9	45 357	19.3	29.9	29.6
Washington	232	1 558	5 646	11.8	60.1	11.4	36.6	10 646	17 385	38 501	46 476	0.4	35 671	23.4	34.5	31.9
GEORGIA	366	3 347	2 754 113	15.1	44.0	28.0	15 444.1	9 099	25 182	49 179	67 572	3.9	47 765	19.0	26.7	24.9
Appling	103	2 148	4 344	4.4	66.1	12.8	33.4	9 364	19 643	36 786	49 647	0.7	36 915	28.6	40.3	36.3
Atkinson	NA	NA	2 340	3.2	72.5	7.7	15.7	8 941	15 958	30 049	43 350	1.5	30 883	26.0	38.4	36.6
Bacon	NA	NA	2 432	7.2	67.2	12.1	18.1	8 932	18 558	33 757	48 806	1.2	33 781	22.8	36.5	32.8
Baker	NA	NA	864	4.4	65.4	10.9	3.8	11 418	17 019	27 353	41 751	1.3	37 135	27.7	43.2	40.8
Baldwin	613	3 484	13 829	14.1	55.0	19.0	49.5	8 856	18 622	32 751	49 753	1.1	35 815	31.8	40.2	36.3
Banks	93	2 975	4 224	8.9	66.5	11.6	25.1	8 854	20 231	41 141	53 488	1.7	42 495	17.4	27.4	25.0
Barrow	509	3 258	18 736	11.7	52.1	17.1	105.4	8 091	21 379	53 274	61 465	1.1	54 668	14.4	20.5	19.6
Bartow	376	3 361	25 277	8.7	58.3	15.9	170.0	9 241	21 022	47 197	58 409	1.5	46 330	19.1	25.4	25.0
Ben Hill	383	3 709	4 708	5.6	62.0	9.8	30.2	9 176	14 204	28 547	37 574	0.6	30 090	31.9	44.0	42.0
Berrien	222	2 296	5 278	5.9	55.4	12.8	27.1	8 386	16 784	32 258	43 702	0.2	37 903	24.0	35.4	32.4
Bibb	510	6 065	43 804	19.8	50.3	22.5	239.7	9 782	20 982	37 550	55 272	2.6	36 816	29.2	44.6	40.2
Bleckley	311	3 545	4 236	10.2	60.3	14.9	22.5	9 219	20 156	36 073	58 881	2.4	40 369	22.0	28.7	26.8
Brantley	129	2 405	4 566	7.2	68.8	6.4	30.5	8 583	16 938	36 070	44 033	0.2	36 758	22.5	34.5	30.9
Brooks	417	2 987	3 790	6.8	59.4	11.4	23.6	10 366	19 409	34 419	46 464	1.4	34 367	25.4	37.9	38.5
Bryan	88	1 452	9 079	14.3	38.8	30.6	58.7	7 341	27 556	64 707	76 441	2.8	66 066	10.1	14.5	13.9
Bulloch	162	2 852	29 952	7.3	44.2	27.7	92.1	9 311	18 587	35 840	51 299	1.9	36 484	30.6	29.8	28.4
Burke	682	2 859	6 557	11.4	62.9	9.9	55.2	12 364	16 171	31 494	43 580	0.3	32 675	32.0	46.0	43.3
Butts	222	2 038	4 924	13.8	68.0	8.4	29.8	8 829	20 363	49 754	57 516	0.7	43 330	22.0	29.6	28.7
Calhoun	1 846	4 326	1 561	17.1	66.2	11.5	8.1	12 287	14 868	26 986	45 981	1.8	30 727	39.1	42.6	39.1
Camden	417	2 585	13 898	13.0	41.8	19.5	80.4	8 688	22 701	51 990	60 187	1.6	49 098	15.6	22.7	22.3
Candler	NA	NA	2 928	7.3	62.1	14.6	19.2	8 880	17 974	35 070	48 396	1.2	31 427	29.1	43.2	40.2
Carroll	266	3 102	33 601	8.7	56.0	18.3	168.4	8 761	21 227	46 147	58 875	1.9	45 493	17.9	25.2	24.2
Catoosa	180	2 864	16 152	14.9	49.5	17.5	103.1	9 423	21 690	47 087	56 365	0.7	50 847	16.0	22.9	19.8
Charlton	82	1 181	2 680	6.3	65.3	9.4	15.0	8 922	17 102	40 111	50 044	1.6	35 165	31.2	36.3	32.7
Chatham	387	3 639	76 048	25.3	38.9	31.3	344.1	9 400	25 093	45 794	62 966	3.5	45 254	20.3	30.2	29.3
Chattahoochee	0	196	3 934	11.6	33.9	27.5	10.1	10 902	20 042	48 758	57 142	1.0	46 893	20.5	24.4	27.3
Chattooga	219	2 143	5 413	7.5	69.3	7.7	34.3	8 101	16 045	33 228	43 096	1.4	34 440	28.3	41.2	37.5
Cherokee	68	1 340	59 699	16.9	35.2	34.2	323.2	8 230	29 615	67 261	83 210	4.9	67 686	11.0	13.9	12.2
Clarke	346	3 670	50 652	7.0	37.0	39.5	150.8	11 892	19 295	33 060	51 128	2.7	32 864	37.2	38.4	41.0
Clay	NA	NA	620	9.0	61.8	7.9	3.7	10 802	12 982	21 192	31 766	0.0	27 102	35.5	55.7	55.7
Clayton	562	4 307	79 797	13.9	50.1	18.0	410.5	7 931	17 950	40 606	49 971	0.8	40 606	25.4	36.6	34.8
Clinch	388	3 885	1 518	3.6	69.4	12.5	13.3	9 416	17 815	30 345	44 426	1.3	30 094	33.5	39.8	37.6
Cobb	277	2 501	198 312	18.4	28.9	43.7	1 075.2	9 196	33 069	63 920	86 949	7.3	62 866	13.8	18.0	17.2
Coffee	415	4 064	11 030	4.6	63.2	12.9	70.9	9 032	17 031	35 693	48 651	1.5	33 615	28.2	38.1	35.6
Colquitt	NA	NA	12 139	5.0	65.1	13.1	84.2	8 817	17 025	32 484	46 599	1.0	33 095	25.9	37.1	35.2
Columbia	49	1 721	36 652	14.1	33.1	34.1	193.7	7 928	30 949	69 306	87 167	6.2	72 531	8.3	10.5	9.9
Cook	232	2 404	4 653	2.7	63.8	12.4	29.6	8 892	18 592	34 985	49 941	1.5	32 327	25.3	35.7	31.8
Coweta	169	2 111	34 978	14.3	44.9	26.9	197.2	8 692	26 757	60 813	73 184	2.5	61 469	13.7	19.4	17.6
Crawford	230	3 071	3 064	9.5	58.3	13.0	16.5	8 920	20 556	41 586	51 341	0.9	43 392	21.5	32.6	28.9
Crisp	401	5 079	6 625	6.7	56.1	15.5	38.8	9 035	18 185	35 240	46 889	1.5	30 481	30.7	48.9	45.7
Dade	365	851	4 455	29.5	54.2	17.0	20.4	8 957	21 690	43 205	56 931	1.6	43 446	16.7	21.8	20.1
Dawson	80	2 039	5 203	10.0	44.9	24.4	35.4	10 139	27 330	53 525	72 492	4.6	52 804	15.2	20.6	18.7
Decatur	478	3 116	7 360	6.9	53.8	14.7	47.9	8 590	18 059	30 619	46 861	1.6	34 102	26.6	40.7	38.4
DeKalb	590	5 427	192 970	24.7	33.1	39.7	909.6	8 868	28 810	50 856	73 002	5.3	49 894	19.9	30.1	28.7
Dodge	433	4 544	4 521	7.2	62.6	15.2	33.9	10 156	18 114	37 292	46 931	0.2	33 893	25.9	37.1	36.3
Dooly	NA	NA	3 095	9.4	68.4	10.1	15.0	10 214	14 510	29 012	40 802	0.8	31 620	30.9	41.1	37.0
Dougherty	825	5 459	30 714	8.5	48.6	17.8	149.3	9 437	18 619	31 671	47 137	1.9	31 575	31.3	44.5	43.5
Douglas	337	2 944	40 145	15.5	44.1	24.4	230.8	9 168	23 626	52 691	66 072	2.6	51 941	17.9	25.9	23.4
Early	938	3 712	3 165	6.3	61.1	12.9	21.2	9 495	17 579	28 853	44 492	1.5	32 357	27.4	43.3	40.2
Echols	101	176	1 298	4.9	68.1	5.7	7.6	9 621	15 861	31 375	45 160	2.0	34 809	28.3	45.0	42.4

1. Data for serious crimes have not been adjusted for underreporting; this may affect comparability between geographic areas and over time. 2. Per 100,000 population estimated by the FBI.
3. All persons 3 years old and over enrolled in nursery school through college. 4. Persons 25 years old and over. 5. Elementary and secondary education expenditures.
6. Based on population estimated by the American Community Survey, 2009–2013.

STATE County	Personal income, 2013: Total (mil dol)	Percent change, 2012–2013	Per capita[1]: Dollars	Per capita[1]: Rank	Wages and salaries (mil dol)	Supplements to wages and salaries; employer contributions (mil dol): Pension and insurance	Supplements: Government social insurance	Proprietors' income (mil dol)	Dividends, interest, and rent (mil dol)	Personal transfer receipts (mil dol)	Earnings, 2013: Total (mil dol)	Contributions for government social insurance (mil dol): From employee and self-employed	From employer
	62	63	64	65	66	67	68	69	70	71	72	73	74
FLORIDA—Cont'd													
Putnam	2 075	1.0	28 594	2 838	623	134	46	36	368	754	840	63	46
St. Johns	11 338	3.5	54 082	231	2 550	398	186	276	3 303	1 465	3 410	225	186
St. Lucie	8 944	1.8	31 182	2 521	2 726	501	204	314	2 360	2 586	3 746	272	204
Santa Rosa	6 080	2.1	37 739	1 470	1 340	263	105	148	1 263	1 137	1 856	124	105
Sarasota	22 122	1.9	56 661	168	6 586	944	479	1 221	9 277	4 025	9 230	641	479
Seminole	18 744	2.4	42 986	842	7 575	1 092	557	969	3 359	2 780	10 193	623	557
Sumter	3 983	6.0	37 206	1 547	1 026	188	75	86	1 313	1 709	1 375	138	75
Suwannee	1 246	2.8	28 501	2 849	367	84	27	98	218	415	576	38	27
Taylor	626	2.9	27 395	2 944	289	56	21	23	112	185	388	25	21
Union	308	0.8	20 321	3 108	139	42	10	12	47	86	203	12	10
Volusia	17 293	1.8	34 530	1 980	6 006	1 005	451	552	4 707	4 801	8 015	575	451
Wakulla	952	2.1	30 699	2 598	183	46	13	29	145	198	271	19	13
Walton	2 271	3.6	37 976	1 434	793	126	59	142	824	442	1 119	72	59
Washington	622	1.3	25 248	3 047	203	48	15	20	96	228	286	20	15
GEORGIA	378 156	2.4	37 845	X	200 896	33 727	14 269	31 533	63 256	65 997	280 425	15 895	14 269
Appling	555	3.2	30 106	2 672	281	74	19	62	69	152	436	23	19
Atkinson	210	5.3	25 375	3 041	58	13	4	46	27	62	121	6	4
Bacon	315	4.5	28 042	2 895	118	28	8	45	36	95	200	11	8
Baker	142	-3.3	42 479	891	19	4	1	49	16	30	73	2	1
Baldwin	1 325	5.0	28 781	2 822	541	126	38	65	223	411	770	46	38
Banks	590	4.1	32 016	2 411	99	22	7	74	83	132	201	12	7
Barrow	2 348	2.8	32 865	2 270	637	125	45	135	253	429	941	58	45
Bartow	3 022	2.1	29 844	2 712	1 364	259	100	319	388	699	2 041	120	100
Ben Hill	495	2.7	28 256	2 872	192	41	15	51	91	169	300	18	15
Berrien	592	0.6	31 060	2 541	125	32	9	98	95	160	264	13	9
Bibb	5 684	2.0	36 738	1 634	3 525	611	254	432	1 129	1 432	4 822	283	254
Bleckley	404	0.0	31 625	2 459	82	24	6	35	84	109	146	8	6
Brantley	449	0.7	24 552	3 067	66	19	5	23	48	140	112	9	5
Brooks	585	7.1	37 728	1 473	96	21	7	93	89	147	217	11	7
Bryan	1 374	3.7	41 448	1 001	240	51	17	79	211	197	387	23	17
Bulloch	1 963	3.1	27 560	2 928	832	194	58	138	326	441	1 222	66	58
Burke	694	0.4	30 289	2 644	361	92	24	94	96	214	572	30	24
Butts	618	1.2	26 436	3 010	209	48	15	33	90	182	304	19	15
Calhoun	170	-3.5	26 056	3 024	35	10	2	41	31	47	88	4	2
Camden	1 736	1.1	33 719	2 141	883	224	74	38	343	324	1 218	62	74
Candler	315	0.5	28 775	2 824	91	22	6	45	44	103	165	9	6
Carroll	3 462	3.0	30 814	2 577	1 617	309	114	181	511	805	2 221	132	114
Catoosa	2 046	1.5	31 329	2 505	499	99	37	150	221	460	784	53	37
Charlton	259	1.6	19 527	3 111	80	16	6	10	35	89	113	8	6
Chatham	11 655	2.0	41 859	952	6 614	1 193	493	719	2 470	2 100	9 020	504	493
Chattahoochee	485	0.7	37 783	1 466	1 088	331	113	3	222	38	1 535	53	113
Chattooga	649	4.0	25 801	3 029	197	48	15	37	88	222	297	21	15
Cherokee	8 989	4.7	39 930	1 179	1 990	340	141	387	1 215	1 172	2 858	179	141
Clarke	3 237	2.4	26 694	2 993	2 842	666	190	247	808	680	3 945	204	190
Clay	105	2.7	34 575	1 973	19	5	2	16	17	34	42	2	2
Clayton	7 093	3.4	26 846	2 980	5 666	1 105	402	399	888	1 682	7 571	417	402
Clinch	179	2.0	26 305	3 018	76	17	6	12	21	68	110	7	6
Cobb	34 420	2.3	47 993	482	18 620	2 530	1 290	3 840	5 502	3 675	26 280	1 484	1 290
Coffee	1 185	5.3	27 428	2 941	529	111	40	130	181	332	809	44	40
Colquitt	1 396	2.4	30 170	2 662	472	108	33	171	239	387	785	42	33
Columbia	5 923	1.5	43 739	781	1 164	213	84	241	945	781	1 703	104	84
Cook	471	5.5	27 601	2 925	121	30	9	74	68	146	234	12	9
Coweta	4 799	2.3	36 037	1 740	1 352	253	98	188	689	768	1 891	116	98
Crawford	418	0.9	33 456	2 182	46	11	3	48	45	102	109	7	3
Crisp	679	3.6	29 091	2 795	275	54	20	64	119	204	413	24	20
Dade	482	0.9	29 173	2 784	114	23	8	27	72	121	172	12	8
Dawson	797	2.6	35 128	1 880	223	43	17	75	151	146	357	22	17
Decatur	910	3.9	33 264	2 214	280	68	19	168	163	248	535	26	19
DeKalb	29 652	1.8	41 568	986	15 382	2 338	1 107	3 216	5 078	4 223	22 043	1 250	1 107
Dodge	532	-0.3	25 092	3 050	165	47	11	38	88	172	262	16	11
Dooly	344	-1.8	24 026	3 081	93	24	6	72	53	99	195	9	6
Dougherty	2 783	1.0	29 931	2 696	2 004	408	145	157	606	864	2 714	153	145
Douglas	4 200	2.7	30 798	2 580	1 456	262	106	168	490	802	1 992	120	106
Early	432	1.7	40 964	1 058	190	38	13	80	56	108	321	15	13
Echols	114	10.0	28 050	2 894	21	5	1	23	11	24	50	2	1

1. Based on the resident population estimated as of July 1 of the year shown.

STATE County	Earnings, 2013 (cont.) Percent by selected industries: Farm	Mining	Construction	Manu-facturing	Infor-mation: professional, scientific, technical services	Retail trade	Finance, insur-ance, real estate and leasing	Health care and social assistance	Govern-ment	Social Security beneficiaries, December 2013: Number	Rate[1]	Supple-mental Security Income recipients, December 2013	Housing units, 2014: Total	Percent change, 2010–2014
	75	76	77	78	79	80	81	82	83	84	85	86	87	88
FLORIDA—Cont'd														
Putnam	1.7	0.4	3.7	14.2	D	9.2	2.7	13.2	30.0	19 865	274	3 031	36 662	-1.8
St. Johns	1.1	D	5.9	5.8	7.5	9.3	8.4	12.6	16.6	43 970	210	2 360	96 900	7.9
St. Lucie	0.7	0.1	4.9	3.9	6.3	9.7	4.2	16.1	22.5	71 115	248	6 615	137 339	0.4
Santa Rosa	0.9	0.7	6.9	2.2	10.4	9.0	3.7	12.6	29.1	31 355	195	2 476	67 604	4.4
Sarasota	0.1	0.2	7.5	4.7	11.8	9.7	10.3	18.0	11.0	124 840	320	4 577	230 987	1.1
Seminole	0.0	0.0	8.0	3.9	15.2	9.6	11.9	10.1	10.6	73 725	169	7 323	185 882	2.5
Sumter	0.9	0.7	12.1	5.8	D	8.5	4.6	14.1	23.4	57 715	532	1 537	64 510	21.7
Suwannee	10.4	D	D	D	2.8	9.1	1.8	9.1	26.0	11 670	267	1 477	18 848	-1.6
Taylor	0.1	D	9.7	31.1	D	8.1	2.2	D	21.6	5 140	225	786	10 872	-1.2
Union	1.3	D	4.0	D	D	D	D	D	61.5	2 270	150	386	4 458	-1.1
Volusia	0.5	0.0	5.5	7.8	7.0	10.1	5.7	18.8	16.4	137 985	275	11 633	256 093	0.7
Wakulla	-0.1	0.0	6.4	15.9	6.4	8.7	2.7	D	36.2	5 645	182	600	12 838	0.3
Walton	1.2	0.1	9.1	1.6	6.5	11.7	7.3	10.2	16.8	12 775	215	1 069	47 807	5.9
Washington	1.0	D	7.3	3.6	4.6	7.1	2.5	D	40.4	6 010	244	1 001	10 680	-1.1
GEORGIA	1.3	0.2	4.8	9.2	13.6	6.2	8.4	9.8	17.5	1 632 953	163	253 498	4 151 190	1.5
Appling	9.7	0.0	4.4	8.2	1.6	6.3	1.8	2.4	16.1	3 975	216	714	8 414	-1.2
Atkinson	31.1	D	D	26.8	D	4.3	2.2	D	16.0	1 525	184	367	3 461	-1.8
Bacon	15.7	0.0	1.9	15.0	D	4.9	D	D	14.8	2 280	203	430	4 739	-1.3
Baker	68.7	0.0	D	D	D	1.1	D	2.0	7.5	790	238	218	1 628	-1.5
Baldwin	0.3	D	D	15.0	D	8.9	3.9	14.5	30.3	8 930	194	1 504	20 226	0.2
Banks	14.6	0.0	7.9	7.0	4.1	9.3	1.6	D	20.2	3 765	205	441	7 540	-0.7
Barrow	2.0	D	9.2	11.9	4.3	9.9	4.0	7.2	17.9	11 820	165	1 648	26 833	1.6
Bartow	1.3	0.4	7.6	27.1	D	6.3	3.8	7.0	14.1	18 405	182	2 324	39 827	0.0
Ben Hill	7.8	0.0	2.1	22.1	D	7.2	3.4	D	18.1	3 890	222	862	7 893	-0.6
Berrien	28.3	D	3.9	19.6	1.5	7.1	3.4	D	17.7	3 960	208	772	8 640	-0.8
Bibb	0.0	D	3.4	7.2	7.7	8.2	13.3	21.4	12.8	31 425	203	7 303	70 297	0.9
Bleckley	13.4	0.0	5.7	1.4	D	8.5	5.1	5.0	38.7	2 675	210	408	5 276	-0.5
Brantley	5.6	D	9.9	8.5	D	5.2	1.8	4.5	36.5	3 550	194	536	7 923	-2.0
Brooks	39.0	0.0	2.3	4.7	D	4.2	2.5	7.5	16.4	3 755	240	772	7 659	-0.6
Bryan	1.8	0.0	9.2	5.5	D	9.5	6.5	6.7	26.4	4 965	150	554	12 908	9.0
Bulloch	4.4	0.0	5.9	6.8	4.0	7.6	4.4	11.9	32.9	9 950	140	1 716	29 771	3.4
Burke	10.8	0.0	1.7	6.2	D	4.3	1.6	D	14.7	4 920	215	1 198	9 829	-0.4
Butts	1.7	0.0	4.0	12.4	D	8.9	3.3	D	28.3	4 855	209	633	9 281	-0.8
Calhoun	40.1	0.0	D	D	D	3.4	D	D	27.6	1 175	180	300	2 383	-1.1
Camden	0.0	0.0	2.5	5.4	10.8	4.7	4.9	4.4	55.1	7 890	153	859	21 389	1.3
Candler	17.5	0.0	5.4	6.9	6.1	8.2	D	D	23.4	2 415	221	509	4 697	-1.3
Carroll	1.6	D	6.9	16.0	D	8.2	3.1	15.2	18.6	21 610	192	3 188	44 757	0.3
Catoosa	0.3	0.0	7.6	9.6	2.7	12.6	4.7	14.7	18.6	13 505	207	1 321	26 803	0.7
Charlton	2.7	0.0	2.7	10.5	D	5.6	D	4.3	25.5	2 175	167	365	4 414	-1.4
Chatham	0.0	0.0	3.9	16.2	5.3	6.6	5.0	13.3	19.3	46 710	168	6 633	122 600	2.7
Chattahoochee	0.0	0.0	0.8	D	D	0.3	D	D	90.8	715	58	148	3 343	-1.0
Chattooga	2.6	0.0	4.1	36.9	D	8.3	2.6	D	22.9	6 260	249	966	10 883	-0.9
Cherokee	0.1	0.1	10.1	8.2	9.3	9.9	6.6	10.4	17.2	33 195	148	1 842	85 507	3.8
Clarke	0.1	D	3.0	11.3	3.9	6.3	6.4	17.0	35.8	15 935	131	3 089	51 781	1.4
Clay	37.7	0.0	D	0.0	0.0	3.8	D	6.2	27.6	820	270	192	2 083	-0.9
Clayton	0.0	D	2.6	4.6	2.1	5.5	2.4	6.2	12.6	34 205	129	8 439	104 535	-0.2
Clinch	3.9	0.0	2.6	35.4	2.9	3.7	D	3.7	21.5	1 590	234	415	2 967	-1.3
Cobb	0.0	0.1	9.2	6.8	16.4	6.5	9.2	8.9	8.5	91 790	128	9 165	292 870	2.2
Coffee	10.6	0.0	3.6	14.8	2.7	9.2	2.9	D	17.0	7 720	179	1 627	16 925	-0.8
Colquitt	16.4	0.0	3.3	14.2	D	8.4	4.4	D	23.5	9 270	200	1 996	18 291	-0.1
Columbia	0.1	D	8.2	11.3	7.9	11.3	6.9	10.9	18.4	20 075	147	1 460	53 375	9.8
Cook	29.4	D	5.9	10.0	D	5.5	2.6	D	24.5	3 630	213	696	7 241	-0.6
Coweta	0.5	D	4.9	14.0	5.6	9.7	3.9	14.6	17.1	21 305	160	2 105	52 000	3.6
Crawford	11.4	D	11.4	1.5	D	7.9	3.1	D	19.9	2 700	216	469	5 250	-0.8
Crisp	8.5	0.0	2.8	10.0	D	8.0	4.8	D	17.1	4 705	203	1 101	10 712	-0.2
Dade	1.0	0.0	D	18.2	D	7.8	D	7.0	16.6	3 715	225	409	7 260	-0.6
Dawson	4.7	0.1	6.9	8.5	3.7	22.9	4.7	4.5	15.8	4 405	194	357	10 595	1.6
Decatur	22.4	D	3.8	5.7	3.0	10.0	4.1	4.5	25.0	5 935	217	1 360	12 120	0.0
DeKalb	0.0	D	5.2	4.4	15.6	5.7	7.7	12.3	13.5	94 690	132	18 279	306 954	0.7
Dodge	6.9	D	2.4	9.9	2.0	7.5	3.4	D	38.1	4 295	202	918	9 744	-1.2
Dooly	32.3	D	0.9	15.9	0.7	5.2	D	D	21.5	2 460	172	532	6 225	-1.6
Dougherty	0.8	0.0	3.9	9.7	7.4	6.6	4.0	18.7	27.0	18 195	195	5 123	40 701	-0.2
Douglas	0.0	D	7.1	9.8	3.9	11.2	4.7	11.7	17.7	19 975	146	2 732	51 861	0.4
Early	22.7	0.0	3.8	20.6	1.3	4.7	D	D	17.7	2 580	245	655	4 918	-1.1
Echols	32.1	0.0	7.3	0.0	0.8	D	D	D	18.0	560	140	91	1 537	-1.3

1. Per 1,000 resident population estimated as of July 1 of the year shown.

STATE County	Housing units, 2009–2013: Occupied units: Total	Owner-occupied: Percent	Owner-occupied: Median value[1]	Median owner cost as a percent of income: With a mortgage	Median owner cost as a percent of income: Without a mortgage[2]	Renter-occupied: Median rent[3]	Renter-occupied: Median rent as a percent of income[2]	Substandard units[4] (percent)	Civilian labor force, 2014: Total	Percent change, 2013–2014	Unemployment: Total	Unemployment: Rate[5]	Civilian employment,[6] 2009–2013: Total	Percent: Management, business, science and arts	Percent: Construction, production, and maintenance occupations
	89	90	91	92	93	94	95	96	97	98	99	100	101	102	103
FLORIDA—Cont'd															
Putnam	28 047	76.3	89 600	28.0	11.1	634	36.0	1.3	28 321	-0.6	2 464	8.7	24 821	23.3	31.8
St. Johns	75 558	77.0	242 900	26.6	11.9	1 073	32.6	2.2	109 004	1.3	5 138	4.7	90 997	43.8	12.6
St. Lucie	106 060	73.0	122 900	29.8	14.3	1 006	38.5	2.1	131 012	1.2	10 457	8.0	109 216	28.1	20.5
Santa Rosa	57 368	73.6	162 300	24.3	11.2	1 003	30.0	1.4	74 167	1.0	4 033	5.4	64 373	35.5	19.6
Sarasota	170 555	74.5	175 000	28.8	13.8	1 003	33.3	1.4	176 427	3.1	10 277	5.8	149 482	34.0	15.7
Seminole	147 529	70.5	184 300	26.5	12.1	1 046	32.0	1.4	239 413	2.6	13 447	5.6	204 633	42.2	13.2
Sumter	43 507	90.2	194 100	25.5	11.9	827	27.3	3.7	28 306	2.9	2 186	7.7	20 740	27.3	21.8
Suwannee	15 712	72.2	98 400	24.9	11.1	669	32.3	2.5	18 251	-0.1	1 126	6.2	15 801	24.4	32.5
Taylor	7 672	78.1	87 400	24.2	11.6	569	26.5	3.6	9 394	-2.2	662	7.0	7 972	26.1	25.3
Union	3 807	66.5	89 200	24.1	10.0	588	25.2	2.1	4 730	-5.5	286	6.0	4 522	24.0	18.7
Volusia	195 907	72.0	142 800	27.8	13.9	898	35.4	2.6	239 225	1.5	15 997	6.7	196 102	30.7	20.0
Wakulla	10 455	78.7	138 300	23.9	10.2	858	33.0	4.1	14 266	1.2	744	5.2	13 078	30.6	22.2
Walton	22 639	73.3	159 500	29.0	11.5	970	34.9	2.7	27 226	0.9	1 431	5.3	23 751	30.0	21.2
Washington	8 533	78.6	85 900	24.6	12.2	597	30.0	3.3	9 824	-0.9	663	6.7	8 292	27.4	21.7
GEORGIA	3 518 097	65.1	151 300	23.9	11.7	860	31.9	2.9	4 756 708	0.0	342 365	7.2	4 254 879	35.7	22.3
Appling	6 934	69.6	75 600	23.4	10.0	524	23.4	5.1	8 679	0.0	776	8.9	7 689	24.3	42.5
Atkinson	2 758	69.9	75 000	23.2	11.9	436	27.9	1.9	3 628	4.0	281	7.7	3 223	18.2	47.3
Bacon	4 036	67.5	77 000	17.9	10.7	572	30.1	8.4	4 854	4.9	338	7.0	4 347	28.2	39.9
Baker	1 374	72.0	72 700	40.7	13.1	471	38.6	1.9	1 139	1.2	101	8.9	1 041	29.7	36.3
Baldwin	16 338	57.2	103 900	24.9	11.6	686	40.8	5.0	18 366	-1.0	1 636	8.9	16 724	35.1	22.0
Banks	6 772	77.3	140 200	25.9	11.2	681	32.9	2.6	8 100	1.5	538	6.6	7 926	26.0	39.4
Barrow	23 413	78.2	127 000	24.2	11.7	894	30.9	3.1	34 873	0.5	2 206	6.3	31 292	28.7	26.6
Bartow	34 567	67.7	128 500	23.9	10.6	786	31.9	3.1	47 108	0.2	3 372	7.2	42 434	29.7	29.7
Ben Hill	6 110	64.4	79 700	28.6	13.0	591	34.6	1.8	5 624	-2.7	579	10.3	5 426	26.3	31.9
Berrien	7 040	76.8	80 100	26.0	11.6	484	33.1	2.4	7 160	-3.4	645	9.0	6 791	28.7	32.2
Bibb	56 585	54.4	123 000	23.9	12.2	736	36.3	0.7	69 480	-0.6	5 599	8.1	60 953	32.6	18.9
Bleckley	3 955	71.3	79 900	21.4	15.3	635	28.9	1.6	4 599	-4.0	526	11.4	4 374	29.7	22.6
Brantley	6 550	80.4	68 500	23.6	13.2	498	24.1	5.7	6 938	-1.4	641	9.2	6 602	25.7	33.3
Brooks	6 573	67.6	101 400	26.6	14.0	584	38.7	1.7	6 754	1.1	499	7.4	6 228	25.7	35.8
Bryan	11 230	70.2	182 400	22.8	10.0	1 076	28.8	2.4	15 480	0.4	1 005	6.5	13 622	35.6	24.1
Bulloch	25 254	50.9	134 900	22.7	10.1	717	37.2	3.7	34 379	0.5	2 559	7.4	30 073	33.7	22.9
Burke	7 881	70.2	80 000	22.9	13.7	567	31.6	3.1	9 363	-1.4	949	10.1	8 473	24.5	31.0
Butts	7 776	75.2	125 400	25.6	11.6	807	28.9	0.6	10 187	-0.2	773	7.6	9 294	20.2	33.6
Calhoun	1 804	70.6	53 000	24.9	16.9	496	34.0	2.6	2 142	1.1	159	7.4	2 473	20.0	35.1
Camden	18 386	63.1	154 500	25.9	10.9	886	28.9	2.5	21 740	0.6	1 485	6.8	19 861	31.5	21.1
Candler	3 861	64.0	86 700	24.2	11.3	538	25.6	3.0	5 049	-1.3	364	7.2	4 429	23.0	34.9
Carroll	39 494	66.7	118 500	23.1	11.0	793	34.9	2.2	51 954	0.1	4 256	8.2	46 226	28.5	31.3
Catoosa	23 941	72.6	130 200	22.5	10.6	705	28.2	1.8	31 056	-1.9	1 932	6.2	29 438	30.8	26.3
Charlton	3 727	77.9	76 100	22.0	10.4	706	33.4	1.8	4 841	-1.8	376	7.8	4 322	22.0	36.9
Chatham	102 484	57.5	174 500	24.9	12.7	926	33.6	3.2	131 738	0.4	9 594	7.3	118 110	35.2	20.7
Chattahoochee	2 613	28.8	97 100	16.6	14.1	1 212	29.6	7.9	2 417	-2.1	238	9.8	2 133	26.4	31.0
Chattooga	9 457	69.7	72 400	23.7	13.1	566	27.4	2.2	10 482	-0.6	824	7.9	9 084	23.1	44.4
Cherokee	76 144	79.1	190 400	23.4	10.5	998	30.3	2.7	116 873	1.0	6 503	5.6	104 824	38.9	17.1
Clarke	41 358	43.9	156 600	23.2	11.4	774	37.3	4.0	57 688	-0.2	3 985	6.9	51 379	40.0	16.7
Clay	1 235	66.6	72 300	26.5	17.2	553	32.0	4.8	916	-3.8	101	11.0	903	23.4	38.4
Clayton	86 274	55.3	97 500	26.4	11.7	881	35.5	2.7	125 119	0.0	11 697	9.3	110 243	23.3	28.6
Clinch	2 586	68.7	62 900	21.4	13.6	466	25.5	2.7	2 791	-1.6	244	8.7	2 375	24.8	38.8
Cobb	261 242	66.4	196 700	22.6	10.0	974	30.3	3.4	392 464	0.8	23 691	6.0	352 080	44.4	15.2
Coffee	14 497	69.4	80 700	23.7	10.9	545	30.2	5.3	17 503	-0.1	1 485	8.5	15 647	26.5	32.6
Colquitt	15 918	66.2	83 500	24.2	12.2	574	32.9	1.0	20 384	0.1	1 680	8.2	18 616	25.8	39.2
Columbia	43 975	78.9	170 400	21.5	10.0	1 044	27.4	2.9	65 341	-0.4	3 860	5.9	57 914	42.2	17.6
Cook	6 308	73.4	83 100	27.0	11.2	664	31.7	2.3	7 404	-0.6	624	8.4	6 910	26.8	33.1
Coweta	46 912	74.5	176 400	23.5	11.5	928	29.6	1.5	66 404	0.8	4 146	6.2	59 209	33.4	25.9
Crawford	4 620	79.0	90 800	26.3	13.5	690	34.5	3.4	5 673	-0.2	425	7.5	5 029	28.6	31.4
Crisp	8 832	59.8	95 600	21.2	13.7	582	34.0	2.1	9 450	-2.4	870	9.2	8 610	30.7	24.5
Dade	6 325	77.8	112 800	23.0	10.3	667	29.7	2.1	7 998	-1.6	520	6.5	7 677	25.2	29.9
Dawson	8 506	73.7	186 000	28.3	10.0	960	33.1	7.1	10 002	0.0	001	0.1	9 045	31.2	20.8
Decatur	10 525	64.3	102 900	23.5	13.4	598	32.8	3.3	11 415	-1.5	951	8.3	10 418	28.5	30.2
DeKalb	264 496	56.7	168 900	24.9	12.4	970	32.7	2.0	370 122	0.4	27 014	7.3	329 740	42.3	16.3
Dodge	8 186	65.7	70 000	20.9	10.1	559	29.8	3.5	7 537	-3.3	755	10.0	8 039	31.3	31.3
Dooly	5 133	66.7	67 600	23.0	13.5	531	34.4	3.8	4 655	3.0	454	9.8	4 702	22.9	35.4
Dougherty	35 661	47.3	101 700	23.7	13.5	689	35.6	2.4	38 774	-2.4	3 630	9.4	34 939	29.1	25.8
Douglas	46 295	69.8	135 700	24.7	10.3	918	31.6	3.8	67 568	0.3	5 033	7.4	59 925	32.1	24.3
Early	4 030	64.7	82 400	25.5	13.3	551	37.2	7.5	4 271	-2.0	385	9.0	3 722	27.6	28.5
Echols	1 382	62.7	71 600	19.8	11.8	679	24.0	3.2	1 826	2.5	107	5.9	1 667	15.5	45.2

1. Specified owner-occupied units. 2. A value of 10.0 represents 10 percent or less; a value of 50.0 represents 50 percent or more. 3. Specified renter-occupied units.
4. Overcrowded or lacking complete plumbing facilities. 5. Percent of civilian labor force. 6. Persons 16 years old and over.

STATE County	Private nonfarm establishments, employment and payroll, 2013									Agriculture, 2012			
		Employment						Annual payroll		Farms			
											Percent with:		
	Number of establish-ments	Total	Health care and social assistance	Manufac-turing	Retail trade	Finance and insurance	Professional, scientific, and technical services	Total (mil dol)	Average per employee (dollars)	Number	Fewer than 50 acres	500 acres or more	Farm operators whose principal occu-pation is farming (percent)
	104	105	106	107	108	109	110	111	112	113	114	115	116
FLORIDA—Cont'd													
Putnam	1 232	11 917	2 453	1 822	2 565	332	279	392	32 863	430	64.0	7.9	44.7
St. Johns	5 305	49 016	7 273	1 540	9 052	1 628	3 288	1 691	34 498	188	67.0	12.2	47.3
St. Lucie	5 062	53 629	10 212	2 111	12 391	1 245	2 483	1 783	33 256	406	50.7	18.0	53.0
Santa Rosa	2 469	22 056	3 615	466	4 667	592	1 893	735	33 346	666	59.6	6.9	41.3
Sarasota	12 905	127 514	26 606	5 995	21 808	5 211	9 021	4 741	37 177	283	72.1	7.1	44.5
Seminole	12 639	152 363	17 707	5 655	25 541	13 237	10 698	6 057	39 754	312	84.6	2.2	49.4
Sumter	1 319	17 523	3 438	1 006	2 917	591	583	645	36 781	1 367	70.1	4.0	34.7
Suwannee	671	7 738	1 454	1 790	1 429	124	198	211	27 276	1 266	50.6	5.5	54.2
Taylor	401	4 447	648	D	949	77	100	166	37 260	181	44.8	7.2	57.5
Union	135	1 822	D	D	158	22	D	59	32 141	291	58.4	4.1	41.2
Volusia	11 972	131 926	26 075	7 923	24 368	4 560	6 349	4 306	32 641	1 363	81.6	2.5	55.1
Wakulla	413	3 101	172	D	799	83	132	89	28 567	171	70.2	5.3	49.7
Walton	1 873	17 445	2 135	D	3 842	274	452	533	30 582	670	43.0	6.4	44.8
Washington	378	3 751	774	D	706	D	233	113	30 173	406	41.9	5.7	36.0
GEORGIA	217 559	3 458 050	457 707	340 638	440 474	163 566	230 143	154 628	44 715	42 257	39.9	10.4	47.0
Appling	364	5 222	960	558	691	148	49	227	43 482	475	38.5	13.9	43.2
Atkinson	89	1 115	D	557	135	D	D	36	32 576	194	28.4	20.6	70.1
Bacon	214	2 553	D	548	273	147	53	77	30 280	268	35.1	12.7	48.1
Baker	23	218	D	NA	D	D	D	8	35 468	150	17.3	32.7	72.7
Baldwin	815	12 245	3 671	1 530	2 138	379	D	397	32 389	124	38.7	7.3	42.7
Banks	264	2 947	149	D	D	47	D	72	24 350	519	40.7	1.9	59.5
Barrow	1 072	13 953	1 379	D	2 392	D	868	437	31 334	304	52.3	3.3	35.9
Bartow	1 853	28 229	2 814	7 420	3 708	650	492	1 072	37 959	458	53.1	5.0	50.7
Ben Hill	318	4 597	656	1 521	715	154	66	137	29 741	209	38.8	13.9	44.0
Berrien	254	2 815	343	1 086	463	159	D	80	28 565	380	28.4	25.3	64.2
Bibb	4 060	71 200	15 435	4 555	9 910	8 723	2 573	2 592	36 407	113	38.1	1.8	50.4
Bleckley	163	1 469	269	24	352	78	D	37	25 322	219	31.5	15.5	39.3
Brantley	187	1 232	D	D	287	D	22	35	28 549	215	49.3	2.8	49.8
Brooks	199	1 986	510	D	325	64	D	57	28 725	364	39.3	19.5	51.9
Bryan	597	5 686	1 035	310	1 102	122	232	151	26 552	60	65.0	11.7	58.3
Bulloch	1 373	17 227	2 965	1 727	3 330	534	549	461	26 757	544	28.9	18.6	42.1
Burke	300	4 993	463	813	737	152	D	273	54 664	393	29.3	20.4	43.3
Butts	347	4 048	538	634	721	D	88	121	29 894	140	44.3	5.0	58.6
Calhoun	74	725	160	NA	101	36	D	19	26 514	151	25.2	37.1	48.3
Camden	792	8 460	933	134	2 378	342	D	213	25 197	69	60.9	10.1	44.9
Candler	200	2 182	532	163	363	119	63	60	27 715	238	29.4	11.3	47.5
Carroll	1 988	31 002	4 775	6 856	4 704	738	644	1 212	39 089	909	45.5	1.8	50.8
Catoosa	892	11 569	2 014	1 694	2 492	D	D	364	31 469	269	50.2	1.1	43.9
Charlton	146	1 804	254	D	219	41	53	58	32 365	84	48.8	8.3	51.2
Chatham	7 229	120 438	18 700	13 978	16 276	2 956	4 186	4 836	40 157	35	37.1	5.7	57.1
Chattahoochee	97	1 690	40	D	126	D	299	65	38 225	13	15.4	15.4	30.8
Chattooga	295	4 390	362	D	638	137	85	120	27 248	292	31.8	7.5	39.0
Cherokee	4 830	42 481	5 414	3 761	8 360	1 357	2 800	1 388	32 680	430	69.5	1.9	49.1
Clarke	2 912	44 643	9 528	5 302	7 026	1 047	1 793	1 558	34 895	90	64.4	3.3	23.3
Clay	37	D	43	NA	60	D	D	D	D	70	17.1	21.4	45.7
Clayton	3 767	70 120	6 979	3 613	10 846	1 862	895	2 504	35 712	23	87.0	0.0	69.6
Clinch	127	1 806	D	D	174	D	31	53	29 552	80	35.0	16.3	55.0
Cobb	19 159	302 767	30 518	D	36 576	16 865	26 199	15 453	51 039	110	81.8	0.0	55.5
Coffee	830	11 855	2 016	2 522	1 852	329	212	361	30 469	587	29.1	15.2	43.8
Colquitt	872	11 360	2 279	3 020	1 794	319	166	327	28 822	484	30.2	19.2	60.5
Columbia	2 092	26 336	3 147	2 995	5 281	D	1 220	892	33 882	145	57.2	2.8	45.5
Cook	299	2 782	D	551	529	117	47	71	25 639	234	41.0	18.4	41.0
Coweta	2 109	28 918	4 044	4 157	5 212	640	847	1 001	34 622	357	52.1	4.5	44.5
Crawford	101	548	D	39	D	19	D	18	31 982	155	38.7	8.4	53.5
Crisp	514	6 614	1 174	965	1 418	217	143	199	30 131	244	30.3	23.4	51.2
Dade	214	2 718	204	492	490	97	D	80	29 447	192	38.5	3.1	38.5
Dawson	588	6 340	325	D	2 769	90	D	140	22 022	182	64.3	1.6	41.2
Decatur	578	6 459	962	1 348	1 389	247	159	204	31 603	358	27.7	25.7	55.0
DeKalb	16 052	260 194	38 691	10 725	30 861	8 984	18 941	12 917	49 646	25	84.0	4.0	36.0
Dodge	338	3 507	873	D	701	126	103	96	27 356	401	26.4	8.7	53.4
Dooly	160	1 935	163	745	281	D	D	51	26 249	290	27.2	21.0	58.6
Dougherty	2 336	38 273	8 343	3 078	6 475	1 149	1 840	1 335	34 878	121	45.5	18.2	51.2
Douglas	2 392	33 246	4 522	2 459	7 379	700	889	1 051	31 603	117	67.5	2.6	43.6
Early	211	2 843	D	806	368	132	60	132	46 559	334	25.1	27.8	47.3
Echols	23	114	D	D	NA	D	NA	3	27 789	40	17.5	17.5	40.0

STATE County	Agriculture, 2012 (cont.) — Land in farms: Acreage (1,000)	Land in farms: Percent change, 2007–2012	Land in farms: Acres: Average size of farm	Land in farms: Acres: Total irrigated (1,000)	Land in farms: Acres: Total cropland (1,000)	Value of land and buildings (dollars): Average per farm	Value of land and buildings (dollars): Average per acre	Value of machinery and equipment, average per farm (dollars)	Value of products sold: Total (mil dol)	Value of products sold: Average per farm (dollars)	Value of products sold: Percent from: Crops	Value of products sold: Percent from: Livestock and poultry products	Percent of farms with sales of: $10,000 or more	Percent of farms with sales of: $100,000 or more	Government payments: Total ($1,000)	Government payments: Percent of farms
	117	118	119	120	121	122	123	124	125	126	127	128	129	130	131	132
FLORIDA—Cont'd																
Putnam	70	-5.5	164	5.5	10.3	904 658	5 529	50 742	44.2	102 761	85.0	15.0	31.9	9.5	153	5.3
St. Johns	34	0.3	179	11.7	18.5	1 172 793	6 556	259 819	69.7	370 527	98.7	1.3	38.8	16.5	162	5.9
St. Lucie	195	27.1	481	59.2	66.6	2 287 172	4 758	82 488	168.1	413 975	87.5	12.5	48.3	25.1	872	6.7
Santa Rosa	98	39.1	147	2.4	69.6	518 886	3 539	87 569	62.8	94 249	94.9	5.1	31.7	13.2	2 545	31.5
Sarasota	80	31.3	283	2.0	4.7	1 363 223	4 814	44 753	25.0	88 456	60.0	40.0	28.6	10.6	384	2.5
Seminole	22	-39.0	70	1.2	2.4	547 465	7 872	35 391	27.5	88 042	95.1	4.9	34.0	9.3	40	2.2
Sumter	183	14.7	134	3.1	20.7	717 143	5 350	45 931	42.1	30 773	58.9	41.1	19.3	5.3	164	2.9
Suwannee	193	15.5	153	27.8	84.1	613 355	4 014	92 742	296.3	234 060	29.2	70.8	35.8	13.3	1 332	12.1
Taylor	37	11.7	207	D	2.3	787 271	3 805	39 011	5.8	32 160	58.7	41.3	26.0	4.4	19	5.5
Union	46	-0.7	159	1.0	7.3	567 890	3 574	39 282	7.4	25 495	75.8	24.2	25.4	3.4	111	4.8
Volusia	106	27.3	78	9.0	23.4	477 479	6 137	44 275	111.5	81 802	89.7	10.3	35.2	9.5	1 427	8.0
Wakulla	31	9.1	181	0.2	2.0	632 977	3 502	31 655	2.3	13 322	D	D	31.0	2.3	39	7.6
Walton	148	16.6	221	1.3	30.7	634 997	2 876	47 294	28.6	42 633	37.5	62.5	22.8	6.0	819	25.2
Washington	58	-21.1	144	1.1	18.4	412 480	2 874	59 667	13.5	33 370	69.3	30.7	25.9	4.4	450	30.0
GEORGIA	9 621	-5.2	228	1 125.4	4 190.9	702 282	3 085	93 143	9 255.1	219 020	39.7	60.3	37.4	17.3	142 322	34.4
Appling	123	21.0	259	7.5	73.8	605 707	2 341	143 872	139.6	293 888	45.8	54.2	48.8	28.8	2 049	44.8
Atkinson	87	12.5	448	6.6	35.1	1 195 005	2 669	136 820	70.0	360 840	43.0	57.0	60.3	36.6	961	49.5
Bacon	58	-8.7	215	4.4	30.3	624 134	2 896	108 507	65.2	243 127	48.6	51.4	56.0	23.5	624	34.3
Baker	146	8.4	977	30.5	60.6	2 680 720	2 745	266 427	84.4	562 620	74.0	26.0	56.7	38.7	3 011	74.7
Baldwin	19	-37.7	151	0.0	4.5	368 589	2 448	60 427	1.2	9 936	42.4	57.6	26.6	0.8	10	7.3
Banks	60	27.8	115	0.1	14.3	631 780	5 494	70 378	179.5	345 890	1.0	99.0	56.1	40.1	247	16.8
Barrow	30	-12.0	98	0.1	6.5	538 576	5 493	46 885	39.9	131 306	1.4	98.6	29.9	10.9	123	10.5
Bartow	64	-1.9	140	2.2	25.6	618 074	4 430	68 517	95.4	208 210	15.5	84.5	35.2	17.0	1 141	21.2
Ben Hill	57	-23.3	274	6.9	26.5	695 507	2 536	93 340	27.0	129 029	86.7	13.3	32.5	13.4	762	58.9
Berrien	143	20.7	377	21.6	76.4	1 001 384	2 653	184 247	101.6	267 384	80.0	20.0	55.3	29.7	2 653	56.6
Bibb	15	2.2	130	0.3	6.2	425 690	3 267	48 389	11.4	100 770	11.3	88.7	28.3	10.6	86	17.7
Bleckley	66	-25.1	301	13.0	33.3	701 356	2 328	91 685	24.6	112 502	93.9	6.1	32.0	16.9	1 049	66.7
Brantley	23	-7.6	109	0.8	7.5	315 219	2 893	50 674	7.7	35 967	52.0	48.0	37.2	5.1	143	22.3
Brooks	148	-21.6	407	19.7	77.0	1 344 739	3 303	144 365	112.1	308 014	66.7	33.3	38.7	17.9	3 095	53.8
Bryan	15	-25.0	254	D	4.4	743 867	2 932	105 567	D	D	D	D	20.0	6.7	D	25.0
Bulloch	180	-8.5	331	7.8	108.9	802 399	2 421	124 037	105.3	193 612	84.7	15.3	40.1	20.0	3 610	68.4
Burke	161	-15.9	411	27.5	88.7	924 547	2 252	159 715	106.4	270 817	67.0	33.0	39.2	19.3	3 146	52.2
Butts	21	-16.9	151	0.0	4.9	526 171	3 484	47 029	2.4	17 143	51.2	48.9	35.0	3.6	21	14.3
Calhoun	108	-12.3	712	21.1	61.4	1 560 185	2 191	279 291	93.2	617 053	72.4	27.6	53.6	32.5	2 817	78.8
Camden	16	17.4	228	0.1	1.0	497 348	2 180	32 899	0.5	6 594	71.0	29.0	14.5	1.4	102	15.9
Candler	54	-27.6	225	3.0	23.4	536 151	2 383	64 819	22.4	94 277	60.6	39.4	34.0	14.3	832	49.2
Carroll	86	-10.7	95	D	19.4	419 188	4 435	51 799	192.1	211 382	4.7	95.3	29.9	13.0	513	9.9
Catoosa	21	0.3	77	0.3	7.3	434 822	5 669	62 424	43.4	161 260	10.1	89.9	31.6	14.5	77	9.7
Charlton	13	-34.5	159	0.1	1.5	324 679	2 040	56 214	8.8	105 214	6.2	93.8	23.8	4.8	25	10.7
Chatham	4	-10.8	110	0.0	1.5	565 600	5 162	52 943	4.1	118 029	93.1	6.9	31.4	11.4	4	11.4
Chattahoochee	4	-4.3	314	0.0	0.3	652 846	2 080	42 462	0.0	3 154	D	D	7.7	0.0	13	46.2
Chattooga	50	-5.6	172	0.2	13.0	528 260	3 079	54 678	23.8	81 565	7.7	92.3	34.2	6.5	152	23.3
Cherokee	25	7.5	59	0.1	5.0	555 347	9 486	39 460	44.0	102 426	14.6	85.4	27.7	9.8	16	3.0
Clarke	9	-15.0	99	0.1	2.1	557 689	5 648	38 556	41.1	457 111	D	D	34.4	6.7	68	25.6
Clay	40	-10.2	571	6.8	18.7	945 343	1 654	150 500	17.8	254 800	96.3	3.7	27.1	22.9	718	81.4
Clayton	1	-50.9	36	D	0.2	202 348	5 574	23 609	0.1	4 130	34.7	65.3	13.0	0.0	0	0.0
Clinch	27	41.0	333	2.9	5.4	903 375	2 710	152 763	23.5	293 513	91.7	8.3	67.5	41.3	68	25.0
Cobb	5	-39.5	47	0.0	1.4	572 027	12 235	30 482	3.4	31 227	88.6	11.4	20.0	3.6	20	14.5
Coffee	168	-9.2	286	22.8	87.0	753 704	2 633	133 838	200.2	341 043	44.3	55.7	47.2	29.8	3 049	56.0
Colquitt	189	-4.1	390	47.5	106.6	1 144 308	2 938	154 525	251.6	519 804	65.2	34.8	50.8	28.3	4 920	60.5
Columbia	13	-30.5	90	0.1	2.0	443 579	4 910	51 034	3.0	20 538	65.0	35.0	23.4	3.4	10	2.8
Cook	68	5.1	293	14.8	44.2	804 987	2 751	158 726	87.0	371 714	64.5	35.5	50.4	23.9	1 661	55.6
Coweta	55	-25.8	155	0.4	11.4	766 835	4 942	50 751	11.5	32 140	51.9	48.1	19.6	3.1	161	7.6
Crawford	34	-9.9	219	4.7	14.0	675 006	3 084	92 968	52.2	336 626	50.9	49.1	38.7	20.0	125	24.5
Crisp	117	40.8	481	22.3	81.9	1 004 480	2 090	216 049	77.1	315 783	90.0	10.0	42.2	27.0	2 312	62.7
Dade	32	-7.9	169	0.0	7.2	535 115	3 163	50 755	29.4	153 193	1.8	98.2	27.1	8.9	195	9.9
Dawson	13	-24.8	70	0.0	2.3	543 434	7 782	82 945	54.3	298 418	1.2	98.8	32.4	20.9	21	6.6
Decatur	199	10.6	556	54.7	123.6	1 545 198	2 780	229 341	209.4	584 919	90.7	9.3	40.2	29.1	4 158	72.9
DeKalb	3	205.2	118	0.0	0.3	335 920	2 857	32 920	0.6	25 800	84.5	15.5	44.0	12.0	22	20.0
Dodge	90	-29.3	225	7.9	27.7	494 833	2 202	61 095	35.6	88 838	52.9	47.1	26.2	6.7	1 142	61.3
Dooly	127	-18.5	437	28.0	86.6	1 025 624	2 345	215 472	80.9	279 052	86.4	13.6	41.0	24.1	3 688	77.9
Dougherty	65	-25.5	541	13.0	19.7	1 771 504	3 277	134 256	33.6	277 562	94.2	5.8	24.8	12.4	408	42.1
Douglas	8	17.3	71	D	2.2	469 940	6 591	30 325	1.2	9 974	69.8	30.2	17.1	2.6	55	9.4
Early	169	-4.6	507	32.7	93.8	1 089 147	2 148	143 674	86.5	258 934	91.2	8.8	43.1	26.3	4 347	72.8
Echols	13	-7.1	333	2.3	4.8	878 025	2 638	152 050	8.3	208 125	88.8	11.2	42.5	20.0	80	47.5

STATE County	Water use, 2010		Wholesale trade,[1] 2007				Retail trade,[2] 2007				Real estate and rental and leasing,[2] 2007			
	Total water withdrawn (mil gal/day)	Gallons withdrawn per person per day	Number of establish-ments	Number of employees	Sales (mil dol)	Annual payroll (mil dol)	Number of establish-ments	Number of employees	Sales (mil dol)	Annual payroll (mil dol)	Number of establish-ments	Number of employees	Receipts (mil dol)	Annual payroll (mil dol)
	133	134	135	136	137	138	139	140	141	142	143	144	145	146
FLORIDA—Cont'd														
Putnam	74.7	1 004	24	D	D	D	261	2 918	671.6	60.2	72	182	22.0	3.9
St. Johns	43.9	231	165	1 817	871.1	83.5	763	8 967	2 039.7	189.1	376	1 383	207.0	41.8
St. Lucie	1 201.3	4 325	244	1 899	693.6	72.5	705	13 381	3 697.7	335.1	327	1 014	174.2	31.8
Santa Rosa	26.2	173	72	266	148.9	8.9	363	4 472	1 108.0	96.6	178	469	55.3	10.7
Sarasota	31.3	82	477	3 442	1 560.3	147.8	1 764	22 887	5 599.5	561.1	929	3 175	539.4	103.3
Seminole	69.1	164	661	6 783	2 852.7	314.2	1 800	28 169	6 872.1	642.2	877	3 376	682.0	120.3
Sumter	32.0	342	42	D	D	D	178	2 696	672.1	52.1	90	153	19.7	3.7
Suwannee	138.2	3 325	31	271	108.7	6.3	152	1 606	353.8	33.3	29	66	7.7	1.1
Taylor	42.9	1 901	14	D	D	D	93	980	207.1	18.6	21	76	6.8	1.2
Union	2.7	172	2	D	D	D	28	146	42.0	3.6	2	D	D	D
Volusia	228.3	462	443	4 426	2 002.9	168.8	1 970	26 205	6 099.9	575.9	842	3 978	531.8	101.5
Wakulla	5.3	173	13	63	7.0	1.5	63	908	167.7	17.2	15	41	4.6	0.7
Walton	13.9	252	47	722	205.1	21.7	381	3 317	705.0	72.2	176	950	145.3	33.0
Washington	3.7	148	9	D	D	D	70	805	177.3	16.0	18	42	3.0	0.9
GEORGIA	4 718.8	487	11 545	166 619	141 962.4	8 246.5	36 218	475 344	117 516.9	10 760.2	12 620	65 875	14 021.9	2 903.2
Appling	60.9	3 341	20	112	58.1	3.1	83	705	179.4	14.1	8	38	4.3	0.6
Atkinson	2.6	313	6	D	D	D	26	162	35.7	2.6	1	D	D	D
Bacon	2.3	203	15	171	120.7	5.0	45	313	68.6	5.3	3	9	0.4	0.1
Baker	36.5	10 568	2	D	D	D	5	43	5.3	0.4	2	D	D	D
Baldwin	6.9	151	25	D	D	D	199	2 326	524.2	46.9	34	D	D	D
Banks	3.7	200	12	108	23.3	3.0	68	994	233.9	19.9	4	D	D	D
Barrow	6.5	94	64	1 476	466.3	50.4	159	2 308	660.9	59.8	59	165	22.7	3.4
Bartow	109.2	1 090	120	1 378	649.0	51.3	342	4 069	1 177.4	96.3	137	466	51.6	11.9
Ben Hill	6.0	339	9	D	D	D	96	987	225.0	17.5	11	44	4.5	0.9
Berrien	4.9	256	20	132	68.4	3.3	77	478	129.2	10.4	7	16	1.5	0.2
Bibb	41.9	270	209	2 975	1 613.7	132.6	860	11 834	2 536.2	250.1	223	1 223	221.8	34.9
Bleckley	8.3	634	6	42	16.9	2.2	50	385	76.3	6.5	6	36	1.1	1.0
Brantley	1.7	95	3	D	D	D	37	249	62.4	3.9	3	10	0.7	0.1
Brooks	8.7	536	12	66	65.9	2.6	43	302	88.2	6.5	8	D	D	D
Bryan	3.3	107	20	249	154.4	13.0	96	705	225.0	15.6	39	105	21.5	3.2
Bulloch	9.0	128	48	D	D	D	292	3 603	733.4	71.6	88	319	45.9	6.6
Burke	74.6	3 201	22	D	D	D	64	686	177.5	15.4	12	31	3.4	0.6
Butts	3.0	127	17	364	465.4	12.1	69	760	295.5	15.2	28	60	7.6	1.2
Calhoun	27.8	4 154	7	42	16.5	1.4	21	133	19.6	2.0	NA	NA	NA	NA
Camden	6.4	127	10	D	D	D	188	2 512	648.3	55.9	59	201	26.4	3.6
Candler	2.2	200	6	43	24.3	0.9	63	463	114.5	8.9	6	20	1.6	0.3
Carroll	15.0	136	78	1 560	985.9	58.9	390	4 606	1 252.5	98.0	98	364	49.7	9.0
Catoosa	6.9	109	40	444	151.2	15.6	203	3 053	795.1	70.5	44	144	24.3	4.1
Charlton	1.3	104	5	34	46.0	1.7	46	258	68.4	4.8	5	33	1.3	0.4
Chatham	278.2	1 049	327	4 287	3 780.1	216.0	1 287	17 094	4 004.2	381.0	409	2 007	351.2	63.6
Chattahoochee	0.9	78	1	D	D	D	11	69	13.0	1.0	1	D	D	D
Chattooga	10.8	416	13	47	66.4	1.8	77	798	147.2	13.8	5	D	D	D
Cherokee	24.4	114	233	1 702	849.0	71.4	545	8 242	2 114.9	193.8	255	721	125.4	20.3
Clarke	15.1	130	106	1 994	1 782.5	84.1	553	7 752	1 669.1	161.5	224	839	128.3	24.3
Clay	4.8	1 508	5	12	1.5	0.3	9	64	11.0	0.9	2	D	D	D
Clayton	7.7	30	276	6 131	3 582.3	253.8	808	12 447	3 207.0	297.7	231	1 247	302.1	44.0
Clinch	3.4	496	2	D	D	D	26	135	39.8	2.7	4	19	0.6	0.1
Cobb	55.0	80	1 189	20 206	15 524.8	1 094.7	2 413	39 613	10 480.7	961.7	1 235	7 548	2 171.2	383.1
Coffee	9.4	223	47	433	323.9	17.3	208	1 981	458.7	39.9	35	D	D	D
Colquitt	24.2	531	44	370	184.9	10.9	195	1 997	432.4	43.1	42	142	18.6	3.1
Columbia	19.1	154	71	791	357.5	32.5	308	5 023	1 406.3	126.7	93	380	71.4	10.9
Cook	8.6	501	16	125	51.5	5.2	78	530	118.1	9.7	11	34	4.1	0.8
Coweta	53.1	417	68	815	524.6	33.6	343	4 895	1 291.0	111.5	141	390	65.7	12.3
Crawford	3.5	276	5	D	D	D	20	98	18.2	1.5	NA	NA	NA	NA
Crisp	21.0	897	34	D	D	D	131	1 538	326.5	28.8	30	220	16.8	4.3
Dade	2.3	137	4	D	D	D	65	516	189.3	8.3	5	D	D	D
Dawson	2.5	110	16	144	103.9	6.0	185	2 524	466.6	44.2	27	84	27.0	2.3
Decatur	73.5	2 641	28	D	D	D	158	1 945	395.4	33.4	20	55	10.8	1.0
DeKalb	2.7	4	905	11 028	9 361.1	559.4	2 456	35 506	7 973.4	810.1	1 086	5 761	1 542.4	311.4
Dodge	13.6	620	13	82	9.8	1.3	91	851	167.1	16.2	15	86	7.5	1.9
Dooly	29.3	1 962	13	115	61.9	3.8	42	303	151.4	7.3	2	D	D	D
Dougherty	82.3	871	148	2 086	1 175.7	81.2	538	6 934	1 543.7	136.4	146	654	87.9	17.3
Douglas	23.0	174	114	1 552	929.2	69.7	447	8 396	2 055.8	192.2	135	553	78.5	16.0
Early	146.4	13 299	16	68	131.9	2.1	59	401	75.8	6.3	8	22	1.8	0.4
Echols	1.5	374	1	D	D	D	2	D	D	D	1	D	D	D

1. Merchant wholesalers, except manufacturers' sales branches and offices. 2. Employer establishments.

STATE County	Professional, scientific, and technical services,[1] 2007				Manufacturing, 2007				Accommodation and food services, 2007			
	Number of establishments	Number of employees	Receipts (mil dol)	Annual payroll (mil dol)	Number of establishments	Number of employees	Receipts (mil dol)	Annual payroll (mil dol)	Number of establishments	Number of employees	Sales (mil dol)	Annual payroll (mil dol)
	147	148	149	150	151	152	153	154	155	156	157	158
FLORIDA—Cont'd												
Putnam	100	D	D	D	40	2 163	982.6	91.3	96	1 103	48.9	11.5
St. Johns	724	D	D	D	104	2 074	533.3	81.9	442	9 172	507.6	153.6
St. Lucie	503	D	D	D	141	2 864	916.5	113.2	336	6 503	268.3	76.3
Santa Rosa	264	D	D	D	55	558	74.9	17.6	184	3 385	135.1	36.4
Sarasota	1 768	D	D	D	333	7 786	1 366.7	328.9	806	16 412	844.4	251.9
Seminole	1 944	D	D	D	400	7 482	1 634.7	296.1	804	16 975	764.1	226.1
Sumter	99	D	D	D	29	889	367.9	33.5	95	2 367	79.9	22.5
Suwannee	53	241	18.6	5.8	23	D	D	D	40	633	31.9	7.5
Taylor	32	138	9.7	3.6	23	1 428	595.5	69.1	41	306	20.0	4.0
Union	10	30	2.0	0.8	NA	NA	NA	NA	20	148	10.5	1.9
Volusia	1 353	D	D	D	369	9 491	1 948.6	366.2	1 006	19 359	899.2	245.8
Wakulla	47	D	D	D	8	D	D	D	34	489	20.1	5.1
Walton	191	D	D	D	NA	NA	NA	NA	165	4 382	312.7	93.2
Washington	30	200	16.3	6.5	13	676	D	16.0	36	525	18.1	4.4
GEORGIA	27 668	213 419	34 966.0	12 689.5	8 699	411 158	144 280.8	16 128.1	18 640	355 423	16 976.2	4 704.4
Appling	20	63	4.8	1.4	23	948	347.1	39.1	31	444	15.8	4.2
Atkinson	5	8	0.4	0.1	12	663	D	D	6	40	0.9	0.2
Bacon	12	57	3.4	1.4	15	817	165.4	20.7	15	141	5.9	1.5
Baker	2	D	D	D	NA	NA	NA	NA	2	D	D	D
Baldwin	57	D	D	D	30	D	D	D	85	1 781	57.9	15.8
Banks	12	37	3.7	1.4	NA	NA	NA	NA	46	950	44.3	12.4
Barrow	89	687	60.2	28.3	65	2 159	768.4	77.4	73	1 711	125.1	25.0
Bartow	142	858	84.3	31.1	143	8 447	3 723.6	359.4	184	3 306	140.7	41.9
Ben Hill	15	178	14.6	6.9	34	2 445	D	D	38	632	20.0	4.9
Berrien	13	29	2.0	0.7	12	1 872	415.9	57.5	21	285	9.3	2.6
Bibb	405	D	D	D	147	5 429	1 693.9	236.8	395	7 493	306.3	81.2
Bleckley	10	45	2.9	1.4	6	D	D	D	10	221	6.6	1.4
Brantley	4	D	D	D	NA	NA	NA	NA	10	94	4.3	1.1
Brooks	13	D	D	D	NA	NA	NA	NA	10	D	D	D
Bryan	66	D	D	D	NA	NA	NA	NA	65	841	34.8	8.3
Bulloch	115	641	64.0	20.8	48	1 904	523.8	63.9	133	2 611	95.3	25.9
Burke	15	D	D	D	15	788	D	29.4	22	306	11.1	2.8
Butts	28	124	10.3	3.1	17	726	287.0	19.9	28	393	18.0	4.2
Calhoun	3	5	0.5	0.1	NA	NA	NA	NA	5	18	0.9	0.2
Camden	76	367	32.8	11.7	NA	NA	NA	NA	101	1 825	71.8	19.8
Candler	16	63	4.9	1.5	NA	NA	NA	NA	20	394	14.7	3.2
Carroll	149	846	63.8	23.3	134	8 222	3 175.6	317.4	201	3 552	142.4	38.6
Catoosa	60	274	25.3	10.1	56	2 563	562.1	90.2	93	1 862	76.5	20.7
Charlton	6	20	1.4	0.5	NA	NA	NA	NA	19	222	9.8	2.6
Chatham	694	D	D	D	185	13 508	D	786.4	807	16 946	872.9	237.9
Chattahoochee	19	D	D	D	NA	NA	NA	NA	4	24	0.8	0.2
Chattooga	18	D	D	D	22	3 502	629.6	84.8	34	D	D	D
Cherokee	711	2 756	381.9	120.5	188	4 008	823.7	146.0	308	6 116	246.9	71.8
Clarke	283	D	D	D	91	6 632	1 971.2	255.2	331	7 062	293.4	80.3
Clay	1	D	D	D	NA	NA	NA	NA	1	D	D	D
Clayton	256	4 947	1 113.8	358.3	127	4 254	1 604.6	179.7	414	8 175	398.9	121.1
Clinch	9	28	3.2	1.1	9	851	D	33.4	11	89	3.3	0.7
Cobb	3 360	23 747	4 225.6	1 464.5	540	20 106	5 651.6	1 033.3	1 460	28 640	1 393.5	395.8
Coffee	58	269	22.7	8.3	48	3 503	D	D	67	1 313	47.1	12.7
Colquitt	63	203	19.6	5.4	59	3 472	599.5	90.0	59	904	35.0	9.5
Columbia	208	D	D	D	52	3 637	2 411.2	183.2	164	3 198	119.1	31.8
Cook	25	102	10.3	3.4	33	976	360.7	32.8	38	410	18.1	4.5
Coweta	202	742	83.0	29.5	87	5 466	2 270.1	227.6	159	3 633	146.6	42.7
Crawford	3	D	D	D	NA	NA	NA	NA	6	60	1.1	0.3
Crisp	25	D	D	D	29	1 405	410.8	54.4	51	1 062	39.0	11.2
Dade	12	D	D	D	15	889	187.8	31.7	22	412	15.8	4.2
Dawson	55	221	24.4	7.8	NA	NA	NA	NA	51	1 049	49.9	14.0
Decatur	38	165	11.5	4.5	34	2 301	1 021.4	74.8	50	600	24.1	5.7
DeKalb	2 872	D	D	D	511	19 626	7 489.0	821.2	1 425	22 495	1 207.7	320.2
Dodge	24	98	8.1	2.9	15	762	199.1	24.5	28	366	12.5	3.5
Dooly	5	11	1.0	0.3	12	1 118	303.8	34.4	16	180	6.6	1.8
Dougherty	214	D	D	D	78	5 380	D	260.0	216	4 151	171.0	42.7
Douglas	251	1 122	115.6	38.2	116	3 656	989.9	149.6	214	5 146	212.3	59.0
Early	14	D	D	D	16	912	832.3	72.6	21	164	6.3	1.5
Echols	NA	NA	NA	NA	NA	NA	NA	NA	NA	NA	NA	NA

1. Establishment subject to federal tax.

Table B. States and Counties — **Health Care and Social Assistance, Other Services, Nonemployer Businesses, and Residential Construction**

STATE County	Health care and social assistance, 2007				Other services, 2007				Nonemployer businesses, 2013		Value of residential construction authorized by building permits, 2014	
	Number of establish-ments	Number of employees	Receipts (mil dol)	Annual payroll (mil dol)	Number of establish-ments	Number of employees	Receipts (mil dol)	Annual payroll (mil dol)	Number	Receipts (mil dol)	New Construction ($1,000)	Number of housing units
	159	160	161	162	163	164	165	166	167	168	169	170
FLORIDA—Cont'd												
Putnam	146	2 213	203.5	70.2	99	444	34.2	9.1	3 853	119.8	4 286	29
St. Johns	432	6 152	554.8	213.0	316	D	D	D	18 006	871.5	752 216	2 786
St. Lucie	581	8 754	998.2	331.1	355	1 685	132.8	36.8	21 562	771.6	147 599	962
Santa Rosa	232	3 352	311.7	109.1	172	741	54.3	17.1	10 394	418.9	144 619	1 127
Sarasota	1 451	23 670	2 493.2	935.9	907	4 837	410.7	111.7	38 127	1 929.8	672 444	2 093
Seminole	1 141	15 588	1 600.4	612.0	820	5 329	433.5	137.6	38 346	1 538.2	253 491	967
Sumter	83	1 335	136.0	51.0	59	245	17.9	4.5	5 521	218.7	733 957	2 570
Suwannee	64	1 372	106.0	37.5	43	178	15.2	4.1	2 307	89.4	8 002	41
Taylor	45	757	60.6	27.8	29	106	8.8	2.4	930	33.3	2 212	24
Union	18	D	D	D	6	22	1.3	0.4	518	20.9	2 033	22
Volusia	1 246	24 171	2 513.9	949.0	1 028	5 409	499.6	119.4	37 963	1 518.5	387 951	1 373
Wakulla	20	D	D	D	35	79	9.4	2.2	1 981	68.5	14 544	106
Walton	100	1 534	133.4	51.6	77	401	42.0	10.4	6 588	410.2	434 305	1 076
Washington	42	1 042	53.0	22.9	22	70	5.6	1.2	1 400	44.4	3 335	21
GEORGIA	20 840	419 296	43 943.0	16 481.2	14 588	98 047	10 386.0	2 836.9	816 360	31 306.4	6 541 383	39 423
Appling	29	811	43.7	19.7	29	118	9.8	2.5	1 170	38.4	333	3
Atkinson	5	D	D	D	1	D	D	D	514	18.8	0	0
Bacon	17	436	35.8	11.1	18	D	D	D	652	22.5	0	0
Baker	5	D	D	D	2	D	D	D	193	5.0	0	0
Baldwin	107	D	D	D	58	353	21.3	6.6	2 976	88.1	6 537	39
Banks	15	130	8.9	2.7	11	47	5.1	1.0	1 236	49.2	1 281	17
Barrow	67	1 176	98.4	51.1	77	294	23.0	6.6	5 317	202.8	54 106	444
Bartow	158	2 538	286.3	94.7	115	547	53.6	15.1	7 663	304.5	44 530	221
Ben Hill	31	601	40.9	17.8	29	D	D	D	1 154	34.3	1 162	11
Berrien	25	D	D	D	14	45	3.2	0.7	1 061	43.5	2 340	15
Bibb	557	15 350	1 686.3	611.8	302	1 835	190.0	51.3	12 382	401.0	15 107	92
Bleckley	21	330	20.1	7.4	15	40	4.7	0.9	758	20.4	2 373	16
Brantley	10	D	D	D	14	39	3.9	0.6	973	32.3	1 847	11
Brooks	20	D	D	D	23	D	D	D	819	30.6	5 161	15
Bryan	39	D	D	D	35	163	9.3	2.6	2 258	93.6	67 220	412
Bulloch	163	2 345	259.9	79.3	99	479	37.6	9.8	4 308	164.5	51 406	521
Burke	33	484	32.0	13.1	20	57	3.3	0.8	1 381	48.6	7 095	43
Butts	27	700	37.8	16.3	27	178	30.7	3.4	1 461	53.7	2 315	12
Calhoun	8	262	13.4	6.9	5	D	D	D	295	9.9	0	0
Camden	99	889	90.2	32.3	53	261	17.7	5.5	2 319	68.2	34 143	126
Candler	15	409	25.1	12.2	4	22	1.9	0.4	776	29.5	0	0
Carroll	188	4 028	431.0	169.3	124	596	51.5	12.5	8 017	277.3	12 416	111
Catoosa	96	2 366	207.9	82.0	61	359	20.9	6.5	4 002	164.9	24 877	144
Charlton	10	218	15.5	5.9	8	15	1.5	0.3	507	15.0	1 509	7
Chatham	682	18 344	1 941.2	793.5	460	3 091	275.9	83.1	19 018	817.1	251 726	1 317
Chattahoochee	5	D	D	D	7	105	8.2	2.7	251	4.8	300	3
Chattooga	24	D	D	D	18	D	D	D	1 348	63.3	0	0
Cherokee	362	3 977	378.5	141.6	327	1 341	106.2	33.0	20 922	882.0	418 226	2 123
Clarke	394	8 593	871.8	372.4	209	1 635	186.6	31.3	7 804	286.8	50 528	538
Clay	7	99	3.6	1.6	2	D	D	D	200	4.1	800	5
Clayton	405	7 206	763.0	298.9	293	1 549	133.4	38.7	25 549	569.9	57 869	340
Clinch	11	158	13.2	4.3	7	20	1.4	0.4	428	13.5	580	4
Cobb	1 567	29 429	3 293.2	1 282.3	1 259	13 391	902.7	459.0	71 103	3 038.1	585 896	3 103
Coffee	95	D	D	D	57	D	D	D	2 837	104.6	5 230	35
Colquitt	97	2 018	153.0	59.9	60	326	23.7	7.7	2 854	102.3	11 332	88
Columbia	187	2 303	172.5	75.1	148	920	62.3	19.0	8 724	364.8	219 999	1 289
Cook	31	437	30.1	10.8	13	50	3.1	0.9	1 002	47.7	4 900	33
Coweta	160	2 909	277.0	113.6	143	553	51.2	14.5	10 042	346.8	250 815	745
Crawford	9	D	D	D	11	28	1.8	0.6	851	26.0	4 312	20
Crisp	58	1 212	96.1	34.8	29	D	D	D	1 610	51.8	1 560	12
Dade	14	D	D	D	13	D	D	D	1 069	38.5	85	1
Dawson	32	252	21.6	9.4	40	159	15.8	3.9	2 055	100.0	38 161	177
Decatur	60	1 010	71.2	31.8	41	227	11.1	3.5	1 854	66.6	4 413	32
DeKalb	1 747	38 838	4 338.3	1 602.9	1 072	7 368	837.2	238.7	71 233	2 335.9	199 239	1 231
Dodge	55	1 150	69.9	28.1	20	109	6.9	1.9	1 378	41.5	1 541	8
Dooly	12	144	7.5	3.1	9	30	3.2	0.6	747	34.3	0	0
Dougherty	307	8 298	838.5	311.6	188	1 106	85.5	25.7	6 777	193.1	7 154	80
Douglas	235	4 268	392.5	151.3	212	1 027	121.2	32.5	11 313	343.6	29 869	224
Early	23	254	26.1	10.4	14	34	3.2	0.8	647	24.7	1 475	9
Echols	3	D	D	D	1	D	D	D	183	5.9	230	1

STATE County	Government employment and payroll, 2012									Local government finances, 2012				
			March payroll (percent of total)							General revenue				
												Taxes		
													Per capita[1] (dollars)	
	Full-time equivalent employees	March payroll (dollars)	Adminis-tration, judicial, and legal	Police and Corrections	Fire Protection	Highways and transpor-tation	Health and Welfare	Natural resources and utilities	Education and libraries	Total (mil dol)	Inter-govern-mental (mil dol)	Total (mil dol)	Total	Property
	171	172	173	174	175	176	177	178	179	180	181	182	183	184
FLORIDA—Cont'd														
Putnam	3 846	14 358 652	7.4	13.9	0.8	1.5	2.5	26.1	46.6	395.8	157.9	190.3	2 597	2 417
St. Johns	6 382	21 674 061	7.3	12.2	6.8	2.0	1.9	5.0	59.5	671.6	162.3	311.6	1 541	1 380
St. Lucie	10 618	40 360 120	6.2	13.8	7.0	2.1	1.9	6.5	59.0	1 062.2	343.2	409.9	1 444	1 184
Santa Rosa	4 424	14 124 230	11.2	10.2	1.2	2.6	1.4	3.0	69.2	350.7	153.5	129.3	816	709
Sarasota	15 008	61 458 391	6.0	10.2	6.3	3.8	31.5	5.2	34.0	2 009.8	280.1	709.8	1 838	1 447
Seminole	13 257	48 666 111	6.8	14.5	7.5	2.5	1.1	6.0	60.1	1 274.8	440.7	579.9	1 346	977
Sumter	1 509	4 669 736	4.3	3.1	1.1	6.4	1.4	4.3	72.3	251.5	43.7	105.9	1 042	834
Suwannee	1 250	3 665 519	1.8	2.1	4.9	6.0	1.5	1.5	76.2	111.4	59.1	33.8	773	579
Taylor	786	2 148 026	10.9	14.9	3.3	3.6	2.4	3.5	59.2	67.3	33.3	26.1	1 148	904
Union	487	1 232 008	5.4	0.2	0.0	3.3	7.6	4.3	78.2	32.6	21.2	6.6	433	280
Volusia	20 784	73 359 257	5.4	11.5	4.2	2.1	24.3	6.2	44.1	2 117.9	503.9	753.8	1 517	1 158
Wakulla	827	2 245 238	3.1	0.4	1.1	0.0	4.2	3.1	87.4	79.8	43.2	24.2	784	664
Walton	2 328	7 662 784	10.7	15.8	12.5	4.9	2.3	2.2	47.4	217.6	48.3	141.1	2 450	1 824
Washington	925	2 765 292	6.8	13.6	0.1	3.5	2.8	2.9	69.5	77.2	44.1	22.4	901	681
GEORGIA	X	X	X	X	X	X	X	X	X	X	X	X	X	X
Appling	1 166	3 357 745	5.4	4.9	0.2	3.4	40.2	2.3	42.9	101.3	23.2	31.5	1 717	1 055
Atkinson	477	2 010 541	3.8	3.1	0.0	1.5	3.3	1.4	85.2	27.4	15.3	7.7	927	571
Bacon	457	1 275 084	6.8	7.3	3.9	3.1	3.3	3.9	70.6	31.3	15.9	11.6	1 032	637
Baker	109	265 135	10.3	11.8	0.0	4.2	6.9	0.3	66.0	7.6	2.8	4.1	1 214	935
Baldwin	2 074	6 857 034	4.5	7.7	2.8	1.2	39.8	4.6	38.7	195.7	44.2	53.0	1 143	638
Banks	669	1 937 141	7.1	10.1	4.9	1.5	0.8	3.5	69.3	49.3	16.9	23.2	1 267	661
Barrow	2 271	8 023 913	5.3	11.2	6.0	1.9	0.4	3.2	70.8	183.6	75.3	79.2	1 129	694
Bartow	3 986	13 981 683	6.0	7.9	4.2	1.8	11.2	5.6	61.8	329.5	108.9	176.5	1 753	972
Ben Hill	1 147	3 286 219	4.4	6.3	2.0	2.8	28.8	5.8	44.8	73.5	21.8	20.5	1 168	664
Berrien	719	2 060 957	6.9	9.8	0.2	4.4	3.1	4.2	71.1	50.3	26.7	17.3	911	561
Bibb	6 298	22 932 839	6.6	10.3	5.2	2.3	5.6	6.2	62.4	582.3	249.1	239.3	1 530	1 004
Bleckley	611	1 809 213	5.2	7.5	1.5	2.9	15.6	2.6	64.0	43.0	19.1	12.4	960	647
Brantley	674	1 858 203	5.0	7.6	1.1	3.5	4.4	0.6	76.4	47.4	24.7	17.9	963	714
Brooks	547	1 728 938	6.4	10.4	2.7	2.7	0.2	3.5	70.4	39.5	17.4	16.6	1 079	809
Bryan	1 408	4 117 520	6.2	9.0	3.9	3.1	0.9	1.8	72.5	105.5	39.0	54.1	1 679	990
Bulloch	2 932	8 670 844	4.4	9.3	1.3	2.3	13.2	5.4	62.9	203.4	80.5	82.0	1 128	580
Burke	1 329	4 107 904	4.5	7.8	10.8	4.1	1.0	2.7	66.7	98.4	35.0	53.8	2 324	1 816
Butts	841	2 814 107	8.3	12.6	6.9	3.6	1.8	7.2	58.7	67.2	18.6	39.3	1 671	1 021
Calhoun	366	979 335	10.2	7.4	0.7	2.9	40.9	1.9	35.5	30.9	10.8	7.0	1 076	732
Camden	2 030	7 548 391	6.8	8.0	6.1	2.8	1.4	3.1	70.2	151.8	54.9	73.4	1 428	963
Candler	567	1 831 024	5.7	4.7	0.3	2.6	32.8	2.7	50.3	45.3	16.5	11.4	1 029	561
Carroll	4 120	14 298 798	4.5	9.2	3.6	1.3	0.9	5.5	74.6	321.7	126.8	135.2	1 212	693
Catoosa	521	1 425 530	21.0	30.9	13.0	7.3	4.0	13.5	1.6	366.0	65.6	70.0	1 077	575
Charlton	616	1 655 066	4.2	6.4	0.0	3.2	24.8	3.3	57.2	42.4	11.9	18.8	1 412	1 079
Chatham	10 068	34 099 398	11.9	16.1	3.9	3.9	4.3	8.5	48.0	1 650.2	303.7	617.1	2 233	1 331
Chattahoochee	245	688 357	6.1	3.3	0.0	3.3	1.1	3.7	81.0	12.5	8.2	2.8	217	112
Chattooga	892	2 643 680	6.6	8.6	0.4	3.0	1.5	9.6	68.8	64.8	29.2	23.2	901	517
Cherokee	7 029	24 643 064	5.0	7.9	5.8	1.4	0.4	4.0	73.8	584.3	192.5	290.4	1 312	942
Clarke	4 598	14 811 444	7.4	13.2	5.1	3.9	6.5	8.9	52.4	786.3	118.3	156.8	1 304	951
Clay	153	338 738	12.0	11.6	0.0	5.9	10.5	4.9	53.7	11.6	5.8	4.5	1 443	1 081
Clayton	10 173	35 407 764	8.8	11.0	2.0	2.2	3.2	6.1	63.2	920.8	359.2	426.5	1 604	962
Clinch	408	1 264 709	7.4	6.1	2.4	2.4	26.1	1.7	53.7	37.6	11.7	10.4	1 552	1 170
Cobb	21 811	86 644 451	7.5	8.4	4.5	1.1	2.0	6.1	69.0	2 213.0	659.3	1 157.2	1 636	1 103
Coffee	1 488	4 411 069	6.7	9.4	3.0	2.6	0.9	5.5	70.9	107.8	47.8	44.0	1 020	537
Colquitt	2 449	7 687 804	4.2	6.3	1.7	2.0	30.8	3.3	49.7	222.7	74.9	47.4	1 028	553
Columbia	3 933	13 876 194	6.0	9.6	0.3	1.7	1.1	3.8	75.8	345.5	122.6	173.7	1 319	749
Cook	873	2 387 884	12.7	9.3	2.3	3.3	2.5	4.1	61.5	46.6	20.7	17.3	1 025	578
Coweta	4 492	16 492 046	4.9	10.2	4.8	1.9	0.7	3.7	71.5	348.5	120.9	183.0	1 397	887
Crawford	409	1 190 596	12.1	7.9	0.3	4.3	0.0	2.2	71.6	30.1	16.0	10.8	855	645
Crisp	1 725	5 432 319	3.5	6.3	2.7	2.0	36.6	9.1	38.4	77.9	34.1	32.8	1 391	767
Dade	530	1 479 400	6.8	9.6	0.2	3.2	0.6	3.0	72.4	34.2	13.9	16.9	1 027	529
Dawson	883	2 870 993	9.9	10.6	5.7	1.7	1.3	5.5	64.0	77.9	18.2	53.2	2 374	1 408
Decatur	1 769	5 577 746	4.6	10.6	0.9	2.4	30.0	3.0	47.3	136.5	40.7	37.7	1 372	723
DeKalb	26 888	103 868 526	7.1	8.8	3.1	0.8	23.2	3.6	52.3	2 945.3	639.0	1 074.5	1 520	1 096
Dodge	906	3 199 644	3.3	4.7	0.8	1.5	30.4	2.0	56.5	119.4	31.6	18.8	881	486
Dooly	464	1 464 602	8.7	18.6	0.6	3.5	5.3	4.9	57.6	43.0	17.6	16.5	1 150	731
Dougherty	4 532	14 341 822	8.6	11.0	5.2	3.2	6.8	9.3	52.1	390.9	181.4	135.1	1 429	878
Douglas	4 786	16 883 097	6.3	9.7	3.9	1.7	1.1	5.1	70.7	416.9	160.6	203.6	1 520	907
Early	569	1 743 416	4.9	3.4	2.7	3.8	5.9	5.5	72.8	41.8	16.7	18.3	1 726	1 066
Echols	193	553 759	4.6	9.7	0.0	4.1	4.2	1.7	75.0	10.7	5.7	4.4	1 110	953

1. Based on the resident population estimated as of July 1 of the year shown.

STATE County	Local government finances, 2012 (cont.)									Government employment, 2013			Presidential election,[2] 2012		
	Direct general expenditure							Debt outstanding					Percent of vote cast:		
			Percent of total for:												
	Total (mil dol)	Per capita[1] (dollars)	Educa-tion	Health and hospitals	Police protec-tion	Public welfare	High-ways	Total (mil dol)	Per capita[1] (dollars)	Federal civilian	Federal military	State and local	Demo-cratic	Republi-can	All other
	185	186	187	188	189	190	191	192	193	194	195	196	197	198	199
FLORIDA—Cont'd															
Putnam	399.5	5 452	34.5	1.8	5.6	0.6	3.0	210.9	2 879	112	137	4 026	39.9	59.2	0.9
St. Johns	735.8	3 639	40.2	2.2	9.5	1.0	5.3	1 504.0	7 439	598	402	8 215	33.8	65.4	0.8
St. Lucie	1 134.8	3 998	41.4	1.0	7.9	0.9	6.3	2 450.5	8 632	756	620	12 016	55.7	43.5	0.8
Santa Rosa	415.0	2 618	54.4	1.5	8.3	0.0	4.4	1 574.0	9 930	786	1 372	5 548	25.6	73.5	1.0
Sarasota	2 019.2	5 229	26.3	30.5	5.5	0.1	4.4	1 927.4	4 991	1 005	792	13 171	49.5	49.6	0.9
Seminole	1 294.2	3 004	46.2	1.0	8.8	0.8	9.2	890.7	2 067	1 063	834	15 803	48.2	51.0	0.7
Sumter	263.4	2 592	27.3	1.6	6.0	0.5	7.8	594.1	5 846	1 598	189	2 982	36.1	63.2	0.7
Suwannee	116.7	2 674	46.6	3.1	7.6	0.8	7.6	34.0	778	101	78	2 540	27.8	71.0	1.2
Taylor	68.5	3 013	44.4	2.4	9.4	0.2	11.3	16.9	741	34	37	1 575	29.9	68.9	1.1
Union	34.6	2 273	56.6	4.9	7.0	1.2	3.9	2.9	192	15	20	2 251	24.6	74.4	1.0
Volusia	2 177.8	4 382	29.7	25.3	7.3	0.4	3.5	2 589.6	5 211	1 128	998	18 529	52.4	46.7	0.9
Wakulla	81.9	2 657	52.0	3.7	9.6	0.2	3.4	16.7	542	85	53	1 713	36.9	61.7	1.3
Walton	219.9	3 819	35.9	5.8	9.3	0.1	9.2	133.4	2 316	142	138	2 950	26.5	72.3	1.1
Washington	78.4	3 150	61.0	1.7	5.4	0.1	8.3	30.5	1 226	33	42	1 972	25.7	73.5	0.8
GEORGIA	X	X	X	X	X	X	X	X	X	100 257	98 339	567 208	47.0	52.2	0.8
Appling	103.6	5 642	37.2	40.4	3.0	1.1	5.8	23.1	1 257	44	52	1 370	26.4	72.7	0.9
Atkinson	26.9	3 242	60.6	0.2	3.6	0.4	3.5	11.0	1 324	17	24	391	32.3	66.8	0.9
Bacon	33.2	2 969	55.2	3.2	4.9	1.2	7.9	46.1	4 115	22	32	587	20.7	78.4	0.8
Baker	7.5	2 220	56.9	5.0	7.4	0.6	8.6	0.8	252	0	10	127	50.1	49.1	0.8
Baldwin	184.3	3 974	29.8	43.5	4.6	0.1	2.8	85.5	1 843	68	135	4 432	51.9	47.3	0.8
Banks	40.1	2 192	68.6	0.3	5.3	0.4	2.2	21.8	1 192	15	54	834	16.5	82.1	1.5
Barrow	186.4	2 657	60.5	0.7	6.9	0.3	2.8	222.6	3 172	166	207	2 701	27.1	71.7	1.2
Bartow	347.5	3 452	58.9	1.4	8.8	0.2	4.1	306.7	3 047	187	292	4 581	26.8	72.0	1.3
Ben Hill	81.8	4 663	37.3	32.7	4.5	0.4	3.3	18.0	1 027	26	50	1 090	42.9	56.6	0.5
Berrien	45.9	2 409	60.4	2.4	5.6	0.4	7.6	17.9	939	30	55	961	22.8	76.0	1.2
Bibb	601.4	3 844	44.1	7.1	6.5	0.3	1.9	510.5	3 262	1 085	522	9 241	58.7	40.7	0.5
Bleckley	45.7	3 536	52.6	19.3	4.9	1.0	4.6	14.9	1 152	25	34	1 199	27.2	72.1	0.7
Brantley	50.2	2 701	61.4	2.5	3.2	0.6	11.1	13.3	715	26	81	808	17.8	80.9	1.2
Brooks	42.2	2 737	55.7	1.6	6.5	0.4	4.6	12.1	786	25	45	676	43.0	56.6	0.4
Bryan	99.9	3 100	63.6	2.1	7.7	0.9	3.7	45.2	1 404	201	96	1 520	28.3	70.9	0.8
Bulloch	216.1	2 973	48.2	11.2	5.7	0.0	4.0	302.9	4 167	135	199	7 393	40.1	59.3	0.7
Burke	98.6	4 264	55.4	3.2	4.7	0.4	6.1	14.9	643	42	66	1 483	54.4	45.1	0.5
Butts	62.8	2 668	49.4	2.9	7.3	0.3	5.2	43.9	1 866	44	61	1 581	33.7	65.4	0.9
Calhoun	30.5	4 684	35.5	34.1	3.8	0.3	3.0	4.2	644	19	14	539	60.7	39.0	0.3
Camden	144.7	2 816	55.4	4.1	7.1	0.2	4.1	84.7	1 648	2 241	4 155	2 315	37.9	61.5	0.6
Candler	48.2	4 334	45.1	28.6	3.5	0.0	4.0	21.3	1 913	19	31	737	34.4	65.0	0.7
Carroll	329.8	2 956	58.0	0.6	6.4	0.2	2.6	335.3	3 005	196	318	7 332	33.0	65.9	1.2
Catoosa	277.3	4 263	51.2	31.2	2.8	0.4	2.1	143.9	2 212	87	189	2 561	24.6	74.4	1.0
Charlton	40.5	3 046	38.8	25.3	5.1	0.3	7.6	12.6	947	43	29	532	32.5	66.9	0.6
Chatham	1 559.0	5 640	26.6	30.7	10.1	0.3	2.2	741.4	2 682	2 710	5 917	15 826	56.9	42.5	0.6
Chattahoochee	16.1	1 234	73.5	1.4	3.7	4.7	3.0	4.9	376	84	17 086	279	50.2	49.1	0.7
Chattooga	68.3	2 655	56.6	0.3	5.8	0.3	4.1	31.8	1 237	33	69	1 298	31.3	67.1	1.7
Cherokee	581.9	2 629	63.6	3.8	4.8	0.4	2.5	701.9	3 172	279	651	7 410	23.8	74.9	1.2
Clarke	854.7	7 107	20.1	50.3	3.2	0.1	1.3	564.4	4 693	1 122	395	23 338	65.0	33.7	1.3
Clay	11.5	3 685	36.6	23.2	6.0	0.7	6.5	1.6	517	44	0	189	61.0	38.8	0.2
Clayton	908.8	3 418	54.3	3.7	8.1	0.7	2.7	457.9	1 722	1 500	805	13 765	83.0	16.6	0.4
Clinch	33.2	4 943	44.6	27.7	3.7	0.3	5.5	16.1	2 403	17	19	487	36.7	62.2	1.1
Cobb	2 261.5	3 197	56.3	1.0	7.2	0.7	7.3	3 722.8	5 262	2 375	2 497	33 069	44.8	54.2	1.0
Coffee	114.8	2 659	57.4	0.3	6.5	0.2	5.8	18.7	434	106	116	2 621	35.0	64.5	0.5
Colquitt	216.3	4 688	39.4	34.4	3.5	0.1	4.0	54.2	1 175	116	132	3 389	30.8	68.4	0.8
Columbia	330.5	2 511	64.3	0.9	6.4	0.3	6.0	242.1	1 840	257	392	4 788	28.4	71.0	0.6
Cook	49.1	2 900	54.5	1.3	8.1	0.5	6.5	18.8	1 112	27	49	1 212	35.2	64.1	0.8
Coweta	343.0	2 620	61.2	1.1	6.1	0.1	4.2	213.3	1 629	223	386	4 960	29.0	70.2	0.9
Crawford	30.2	2 394	59.2	1.1	4.7	0.3	5.5	12.0	952	0	36	447	35.0	64.1	1.0
Crisp	83.6	3 542	57.8	1.1	7.1	0.3	5.0	31.7	1 343	53	67	1 267	40.9	58.6	0.5
Dade	36.5	2 215	63.4	1.1	8.9	0.2	6.0	9.7	586	20	45	562	25.2	73.4	1.5
Dawson	84.8	3 783	48.5	2.7	4.7	0.9	3.3	124.1	5 535	51	66	1 056	16.4	82.6	1.0
Decatur	143.5	5 218	34.0	27.4	5.0	0.1	3.7	45.5	1 655	49	77	2 730	42.6	56.8	0.6
DeKalb	2 937.7	4 155	37.1	33.5	4.6	0.5	1.6	2 476.3	3 502	10 004	2 184	30 066	79.0	20.3	0.7
Dodge	77.8	3 646	46.0	31.2	3.4	1.0	3.8	21.4	1 005	41	56	1 993	31.6	67.5	0.9
Dooly	37.4	2 615	43.0	10.8	9.8	0.5	6.6	10.1	704	50	36	785	51.4	47.9	0.7
Dougherty	400.6	4 239	40.5	13.1	5.7	0.1	2.1	219.4	2 322	2 936	605	7 369	67.3	32.3	0.4
Douglas	492.1	3 674	53.7	0.9	4.5	0.4	2.1	632.2	4 719	159	394	5 570	50.5	48.7	0.8
Early	43.1	4 068	53.5	7.9	10.2	0.0	3.3	13.2	1 250	37	30	1 105	48.8	50.8	0.4
Echols	10.8	2 706	74.2	0.3	4.4	0.4	3.7	19.9	4 981	0	12	215	16.9	82.6	0.4

1. Based on the resident population estimated as of July 1 of the year shown. 2.

STATE/ County code	CBSA code[1]	County type[2]	STATE County	Land area,[3] (sq km) 2010	Population, 2014: Total persons 2014	Population, 2014: Rank	Population, 2014: Per square kilometer	Population and population characteristics, 2013: Race alone or in combination, not Hispanic or Latino (percent): White	Black	American Indian, Alaska Native	Asian and Pacific Islander	Percent Hispanic or Latino[4]	Age (percent): Under 5 years	5 to 17 years	18 to 24 years	25 to 34 years	35 to 44 years	45 to 54 years
				1	2	3	4	5	6	7	8	9	10	11	12	13	14	15
			GEORGIA—Cont'd															
13 103	42340	2	Effingham	1 237	55 423	911	44.8	81.6	14.5	0.9	1.4	3.3	6.6	20.6	8.9	12.9	14.4	14.8
13 105	...	6	Elbert	909	19 438	1 856	21.4	64.5	29.5	0.5	1.0	5.3	6.3	16.0	8.7	11.3	11.2	14.3
13 107	...	7	Emanuel	1 763	22 755	1 699	12.9	60.7	34.2	0.5	0.8	4.7	6.8	18.2	9.4	13.2	11.8	13.1
13 109	...	6	Evans	474	10 898	2 365	23.0	57.6	30.0	0.5	1.0	11.9	7.3	18.8	8.9	13.5	12.0	13.2
13 111	...	8	Fannin	1 002	23 753	1 650	23.7	96.6	1.0	1.1	0.6	1.9	4.4	13.6	6.4	9.0	10.1	13.8
13 113	12060	1	Fayette	503	109 664	549	218.0	67.3	21.9	0.7	5.0	6.9	4.2	20.1	8.8	7.9	11.7	17.0
13 115	40660	3	Floyd	1 321	96 063	611	72.7	73.8	15.3	0.6	1.7	10.1	6.3	17.5	10.5	12.2	12.5	13.3
13 117	12060	1	Forsyth	580	204 302	314	352.2	78.8	3.5	0.6	8.8	9.6	6.5	22.8	6.6	9.9	17.0	16.3
13 119	...	8	Franklin	677	22 264	1 719	32.9	85.7	9.7	0.7	1.0	4.4	5.6	16.1	10.0	11.1	11.6	13.9
13 121	12060	1	Fulton	1 364	996 319	45	730.4	42.0	44.5	0.7	7.0	7.7	6.6	16.8	10.7	16.4	15.0	13.8
13 123	...	6	Gilmer	1 105	28 829	1 462	26.1	88.0	0.9	1.0	0.5	10.6	5.3	15.5	7.2	10.2	11.7	13.8
13 125	...	9	Glascock	372	3 053	2 971	8.2	88.4	9.9	1.0	0.5	1.6	5.0	19.7	7.8	10.5	13.5	13.9
13 127	15260	3	Glynn	1 087	82 175	679	75.6	65.6	27.0	0.7	2.0	6.5	6.5	16.9	8.5	12.1	11.8	13.8
13 129	15660	6	Gordon	922	56 047	904	60.8	79.9	4.7	0.6	1.3	14.6	6.7	19.1	9.0	12.6	13.8	14.3
13 131	...	6	Grady	1 177	25 359	1 596	21.5	59.7	28.7	1.0	0.7	10.9	7.0	18.5	8.4	12.3	11.7	13.5
13 133	...	6	Greene	1 003	16 490	2 010	16.4	56.8	36.6	0.7	0.7	6.4	5.5	14.0	6.9	10.1	9.6	12.1
13 135	12060	1	Gwinnett	1 115	877 922	61	787.4	43.2	25.9	0.7	11.9	20.5	7.1	21.0	9.1	13.5	15.6	15.0
13 137	18460	6	Habersham	717	43 752	1 093	61.0	79.9	4.3	0.7	2.8	13.6	6.1	17.3	9.2	12.2	12.6	13.0
13 139	23580	3	Hall	1 017	190 761	338	187.6	63.3	7.9	0.6	2.2	27.2	7.1	19.9	9.3	12.9	13.5	13.3
13 141	33300	7	Hancock	1 222	8 509	2 557	7.0	24.9	72.7	0.5	0.9	1.8	4.6	11.9	9.5	13.5	11.6	14.7
13 143	12060	1	Haralson	731	28 641	1 468	39.2	92.9	5.5	0.9	0.9	1.3	6.1	18.7	8.2	11.8	12.8	14.4
13 145	17980	2	Harris	1 201	32 876	1 358	27.4	78.8	17.4	0.8	1.4	3.0	4.8	17.5	8.1	9.2	13.3	16.0
13 147	...	6	Hart	602	25 377	1 594	42.2	76.9	19.4	0.4	1.2	3.5	5.5	16.1	8.1	10.6	11.4	14.0
13 149	12060	1	Heard	767	11 603	2 318	15.1	86.3	11.4	0.8	1.0	2.2	5.7	17.8	9.0	10.3	12.9	15.4
13 151	12060	1	Henry	834	213 869	299	256.4	51.3	39.8	0.8	3.9	6.3	6.1	21.5	9.4	11.5	15.3	15.6
13 153	47580	3	Houston	973	149 111	431	153.2	60.9	30.6	0.9	3.8	6.5	7.0	18.9	9.8	14.7	12.9	14.3
13 155	...	7	Irwin	918	9 104	2 506	9.9	69.1	27.2	0.3	0.9	3.3	5.5	17.2	9.0	13.0	12.8	13.7
13 157	27600	6	Jackson	880	61 870	844	70.3	84.3	7.7	0.7	2.2	6.7	6.8	19.1	8.1	12.0	14.4	14.6
13 159	12060	1	Jasper	954	13 432	2 213	14.1	73.2	22.7	0.8	0.6	4.2	6.1	18.3	7.9	11.7	12.6	14.6
13 161	...	7	Jeff Davis	857	14 859	2 110	17.3	73.1	15.6	0.5	0.8	10.9	7.4	19.7	8.5	12.3	12.8	13.2
13 163	...	6	Jefferson	1 364	16 272	2 026	11.9	42.3	54.2	0.4	0.6	3.2	6.5	17.6	8.8	11.6	11.7	13.6
13 165	...	6	Jenkins	899	9 125	2 504	10.2	51.9	42.7	0.5	0.7	5.1	5.8	16.7	10.3	13.3	12.8	13.9
13 167	20140	9	Johnson	785	9 701	2 461	12.4	62.8	34.7	0.5	0.5	2.4	4.5	15.4	8.3	13.6	14.2	15.7
13 169	31420	3	Jones	1 020	28 787	1 466	28.2	73.2	25.0	0.6	1.0	1.3	5.5	19.2	8.3	11.2	13.1	14.6
13 171	12060	1	Lamar	475	18 207	1 909	38.3	66.1	31.9	0.7	0.9	2.1	5.8	15.3	14.6	11.0	11.4	13.1
13 173	46660	3	Lanier	480	10 373	2 407	21.6	70.0	23.8	1.2	2.1	5.2	7.7	17.3	9.2	16.6	13.1	13.5
13 175	20140	6	Laurens	2 091	47 851	1 019	22.9	60.3	36.7	0.5	1.2	2.4	6.8	18.0	9.0	11.8	12.3	13.6
13 177	10500	3	Lee	921	29 191	1 447	31.7	74.6	20.9	0.7	2.8	2.4	6.5	20.4	8.6	12.8	15.2	14.2
13 179	25980	3	Liberty	1 269	65 198	809	51.4	45.7	41.5	1.2	3.9	11.6	11.1	17.9	14.9	19.1	10.9	10.4
13 181	12260	8	Lincoln	545	7 622	2 631	14.0	66.3	31.7	0.7	0.7	1.5	4.6	14.7	7.9	9.8	10.7	15.5
13 183	25980	3	Long	1 037	17 113	1 976	16.5	61.5	26.2	1.2	2.5	11.8	8.5	20.6	9.6	16.7	14.3	12.8
13 185	46660	3	Lowndes	1 285	113 523	537	88.3	56.4	37.1	0.7	2.3	5.4	7.5	17.4	18.6	14.2	11.2	11.1
13 187	...	6	Lumpkin	733	31 176	1 409	42.5	92.4	2.1	1.4	1.2	4.6	5.2	14.1	18.1	11.3	10.7	12.6
13 189	12260	2	McDuffie	667	21 370	1 758	32.0	56.4	40.9	0.6	0.8	2.7	6.9	18.9	8.7	11.4	11.6	13.9
13 191	15260	3	McIntosh	1 099	14 214	2 153	12.9	62.4	35.5	0.8	0.7	1.8	4.6	14.1	8.1	9.3	11.2	14.8
13 193	...	6	Macon	1 038	13 792	2 186	13.3	34.7	60.0	0.4	1.9	4.0	5.2	14.9	10.5	14.2	12.0	14.4
13 195	12020	3	Madison	731	28 312	1 480	38.7	85.5	9.5	0.6	1.3	4.3	5.5	17.9	8.4	11.5	12.9	15.0
13 197	17980	2	Marion	948	8 797	2 531	9.3	60.4	32.0	1.1	1.4	6.5	6.1	16.5	8.0	10.5	11.5	15.9
13 199	12060	1	Meriwether	1 298	21 198	1 762	16.3	58.1	39.6	0.6	0.8	2.0	5.6	16.8	8.4	11.3	11.0	14.3
13 201	...	8	Miller	731	5 958	2 760	8.2	69.9	27.8	0.7	0.8	1.9	6.3	16.7	8.2	10.6	11.6	13.7
13 205	...	6	Mitchell	1 326	22 771	1 698	17.2	47.1	47.9	0.5	0.9	4.4	6.3	17.8	9.1	13.1	13.2	13.7
13 207	31420	3	Monroe	1 025	27 051	1 534	26.4	73.3	23.5	0.6	1.2	2.4	5.3	16.1	8.8	11.2	12.2	15.3
13 209	47080	9	Montgomery	620	8 991	2 520	14.5	67.5	26.1	0.4	0.6	6.6	5.5	16.6	11.7	11.9	12.7	13.8
13 211	12060	6	Morgan	900	17 956	1 917	20.0	73.1	23.7	0.6	0.9	2.9	5.4	18.2	7.8	9.5	12.4	14.7
13 213	19140	3	Murray	892	39 410	1 186	44.2	84.6	1.5	0.6	0.5	13.7	6.4	19.3	9.2	12.2	13.9	14.8
13 215	17980	2	Muscogee	560	200 887	323	358.7	44.7	46.3	0.9	3.3	7.3	7.4	17.2	11.5	16.3	12.4	12.6
13 217	12060	1	Newton	705	103 675	570	147.1	52.1	42.8	0.7	1.5	4.8	6.8	20.6	9.5	12.1	14.3	14.2
13 219	12020	3	Oconee	477	35 093	1 298	73.6	86.5	5.7	0.4	4.1	4.6	5.4	21.4	8.3	9.1	14.1	15.4
13 221	12020	3	Oglethorpe	1 137	14 673	2 125	12.9	77.6	18.5	0.7	0.9	4.0	5.3	16.5	8.2	11.0	12.6	15.5
13 223	12060	1	Paulding	809	148 987	432	184.2	76.0	18.3	0.8	1.6	5.3	6.7	21.7	8.6	12.7	16.4	15.0
13 225	47580	6	Peach	389	26 922	1 538	69.2	46.6	45.5	0.9	1.4	7.4	6.2	16.4	16.3	11.9	10.7	13.5
13 227	12060	1	Pickens	601	29 997	1 429	49.9	94.7	1.7	0.9	0.8	3.0	5.1	16.1	7.4	10.2	12.2	14.3
13 229	48180	6	Pierce	820	18 991	1 875	23.2	84.8	9.7	0.8	0.9	5.0	6.5	19.0	8.0	11.9	13.4	13.7
13 231	12060	1	Pike	560	17 784	1 928	31.8	87.3	11.3	0.8	0.7	1.3	5.3	20.4	8.0	10.3	14.0	15.3
13 233	16340	6	Polk	804	41 133	1 150	51.2	73.6	13.5	0.5	1.0	12.8	7.0	19.3	8.7	13.0	12.2	13.3
13 235	47580	6	Pulaski	645	11 483	2 329	17.8	63.7	31.9	0.5	1.3	3.5	4.8	15.2	7.8	12.2	12.8	14.7

1. CBSA = Core Based Statistical Area. See Appendix A for explanation. See Appendix B for list of metropolitan areas with component counties. 2. County type code from the Economic Research Service of USDA Rural-Urban Continuum Codes. See Appendix A for definition. 3. Dry land or land partially or temporarily covered by water. 4. May be of any race.

STATE County	Population, 2013 (cont.) Age (percent) (cont.) 55 to 64 years	65 to 74 years	75 years and over	Percent female	Population change and components of change, 2000–2014 Total persons 2000	2010	Percent change 2000–2010	2010–2014	Components of change, 2010–2014 Births	Deaths	Net migration	Households, 2009–2013 Number	Persons per house-hold	Percent Family house-holds	Female family house-holder[1]	One per-son
	16	17	18	19	20	21	22	23	24	25	26	27	28	29	30	31
GEORGIA—Cont'd																
Effingham	11.4	6.8	3.6	50.3	37 535	52 250	39.2	6.1	2 989	1 463	1 592	17 830	2.96	78.1	11.3	17.7
Elbert	13.7	10.3	8.3	52.3	20 511	20 166	-1.7	-3.6	1 002	1 065	-660	7 635	2.57	70.5	18.2	26.1
Emanuel	12.3	9.1	6.2	50.8	21 837	22 598	3.5	0.7	1 389	1 159	-124	8 026	2.71	68.8	18.8	27.1
Evans	11.6	8.2	6.4	51.0	10 495	11 000	4.8	-0.9	731	426	-432	4 067	2.55	62.8	16.1	30.8
Fannin	18.1	14.7	9.9	51.2	19 798	23 682	19.6	0.3	848	1 252	471	9 940	2.36	69.5	11.7	27.4
Fayette	14.9	9.5	5.9	51.5	91 263	106 567	16.8	2.9	3 414	3 223	2 793	37 930	2.81	78.4	10.4	19.6
Floyd	12.3	8.6	6.7	51.5	90 565	96 317	6.4	-0.3	5 024	4 277	-971	34 646	2.66	68.0	12.4	26.6
Forsyth	10.0	6.9	3.8	50.3	98 407	175 511	78.4	16.4	9 320	3 920	22 743	58 080	3.14	80.3	8.7	16.7
Franklin	13.3	10.6	7.8	51.0	20 285	22 084	8.9	0.8	1 148	1 141	150	8 618	2.47	68.5	11.6	27.1
Fulton	10.6	6.0	4.1	51.3	816 006	920 581	12.8	8.2	54 502	25 398	45 345	368 184	2.49	56.1	15.2	36.8
Gilmer	15.5	13.1	7.6	49.7	23 456	28 292	20.6	1.9	1 292	1 028	186	11 513	2.44	70.9	8.8	23.1
Glascock	13.0	9.5	7.2	51.4	2 556	3 082	20.6	-0.9	123	157	-9	1 189	2.53	71.9	13.0	23.7
Glynn	13.5	10.2	6.7	52.8	67 568	79 626	17.8	3.2	4 269	3 398	1 586	31 547	2.51	69.0	16.3	27.3
Gordon	11.6	8.1	4.9	50.2	44 104	55 186	25.1	1.6	3 014	1 972	-150	19 066	2.88	70.5	12.9	24.2
Grady	12.9	9.2	6.5	51.3	23 659	25 011	5.7	1.4	1 538	1 031	-139	9 290	2.69	70.2	14.3	26.4
Greene	16.3	17.0	8.4	51.4	14 406	15 994	11.0	3.1	698	796	540	6 353	2.50	71.4	14.3	24.9
Gwinnett	10.4	5.3	2.9	50.9	588 448	805 321	36.9	9.0	48 706	15 591	39 048	266 952	3.07	76.3	13.9	19.2
Habersham	12.4	9.9	7.1	52.6	35 902	43 041	19.9	1.7	2 157	1 715	226	14 805	2.74	71.9	10.3	24.8
Hall	10.7	7.8	5.3	50.0	139 277	179 684	29.0	6.2	10 789	5 343	5 294	61 220	2.93	74.4	12.5	21.0
Hancock	15.9	11.0	7.3	44.9	10 076	9 429	-6.4	-9.5	341	344	-893	2 742	2.78	57.4	20.7	39.9
Haralson	12.2	9.6	6.1	51.7	25 690	28 780	12.0	-0.5	1 485	1 423	-213	10 806	2.60	72.9	13.4	24.4
Harris	15.2	10.4	5.5	50.1	23 695	32 024	35.2	2.7	1 261	990	542	11 426	2.79	78.5	9.0	18.9
Hart	14.1	11.8	8.3	50.8	22 997	25 213	9.6	0.7	1 109	1 152	171	10 009	2.45	66.9	12.7	29.1
Heard	13.7	9.7	5.5	50.5	11 012	11 834	7.5	-2.0	547	488	-283	4 321	2.68	67.3	10.4	25.7
Henry	10.7	6.5	3.4	52.0	119 341	203 922	70.9	4.9	10 420	5 345	4 744	69 238	2.97	76.4	16.2	20.2
Houston	11.0	6.5	4.8	51.2	110 765	139 900	26.3	6.6	8 738	4 420	4 655	52 330	2.70	69.4	14.0	26.6
Irwin	11.6	9.9	7.4	48.6	9 931	9 538	-4.0	-4.6	435	381	-517	3 277	2.69	74.9	15.0	21.1
Jackson	11.9	8.4	4.7	50.4	41 589	60 485	45.4	2.3	3 331	2 185	13	21 293	2.81	77.2	11.5	17.8
Jasper	14.3	8.9	5.6	51.0	11 426	13 900	21.7	-3.4	746	538	-701	5 132	2.66	70.8	12.6	24.4
Jeff Davis	12.1	8.5	5.3	50.4	12 684	15 068	18.8	-1.4	889	610	-471	5 509	2.71	71.7	11.0	23.5
Jefferson	13.8	9.6	6.9	51.6	17 266	16 930	-1.9	-3.9	931	941	-678	6 220	2.58	67.3	21.1	30.1
Jenkins	12.2	8.8	6.0	46.9	8 575	8 340	-2.7	9.4	441	445	734	3 354	2.54	66.6	23.1	30.5
Johnson	13.2	9.0	6.2	43.5	8 560	9 980	16.6	-2.8	372	384	-280	3 250	2.71	71.3	16.8	27.0
Jones	13.1	9.2	5.8	51.6	23 639	28 669	21.3	0.4	1 319	1 101	-191	10 384	2.73	74.1	16.0	20.8
Lamar	13.1	9.6	6.2	52.3	15 912	18 317	15.1	-0.6	817	818	-128	6 393	2.65	69.3	13.8	27.5
Lanier	11.0	7.2	4.4	49.0	7 241	10 078	39.2	3.0	533	334	100	3 725	2.66	68.8	11.5	29.1
Laurens	12.6	9.1	6.9	52.3	44 874	48 434	7.9	-1.2	2 824	2 322	-1 156	17 632	2.67	69.4	18.5	27.6
Lee	12.1	6.5	3.6	49.9	24 757	28 298	14.3	3.2	1 552	795	108	9 773	2.79	75.7	11.1	21.1
Liberty	8.5	4.9	2.4	49.2	61 610	63 453	3.0	2.7	6 169	1 323	-3 358	23 046	2.73	74.2	17.3	21.0
Lincoln	17.2	12.3	7.4	50.7	8 348	7 996	-4.2	-4.7	299	345	-303	3 394	2.30	67.1	17.7	31.3
Long	9.8	4.7	3.0	50.0	10 304	14 464	40.4	18.4	901	340	2 023	4 841	3.11	73.7	17.9	22.0
Lowndes	9.5	6.2	4.4	50.9	92 115	109 233	18.6	3.9	7 120	3 532	443	39 722	2.70	63.6	16.6	26.4
Lumpkin	13.1	9.8	5.2	50.0	21 016	29 966	42.6	4.0	1 359	965	732	10 999	2.62	65.5	8.8	26.7
McDuffie	13.2	9.5	6.0	53.1	21 231	21 875	3.0	-2.3	1 124	1 013	-606	8 143	2.62	72.7	19.3	24.1
McIntosh	16.7	13.5	7.6	50.9	10 847	14 333	32.1	-0.8	701	438	-404	4 993	2.81	67.1	14.8	28.7
Macon	14.3	9.4	5.1	45.5	14 074	14 740	4.7	-6.4	565	642	-903	4 887	2.64	65.8	22.3	29.6
Madison	13.8	9.4	5.8	50.8	25 730	28 120	9.3	0.7	1 365	1 153	4	9 732	2.86	71.6	11.3	23.5
Marion	14.7	11.0	5.7	50.7	7 144	8 742	22.4	0.6	432	314	-49	3 000	2.87	62.6	15.7	33.8
Meriwether	14.5	11.3	6.8	52.1	22 534	21 992	-2.4	-3.6	1 037	1 061	-762	8 135	2.62	70.9	19.8	26.0
Miller	13.5	9.8	9.6	51.0	6 383	6 125	-4.0	-2.8	319	332	-156	2 458	2.39	69.4	17.7	29.0
Mitchell	12.4	8.5	5.9	47.8	23 932	23 498	-1.8	-3.1	1 207	977	-972	8 131	2.61	64.5	20.7	31.6
Monroe	15.0	9.8	6.3	49.7	21 757	26 424	21.5	2.2	1 147	1 090	460	9 550	2.66	75.3	14.8	22.7
Montgomery	13.1	9.3	5.5	48.7	8 270	9 123	10.3	-1.4	455	335	-264	3 185	2.60	66.9	15.7	29.3
Morgan	14.4	10.4	7.2	51.5	15 457	17 868	15.6	0.5	765	701	-5	6 513	2.71	74.9	13.6	22.0
Murray	11.7	8.2	4.5	50.6	36 506	39 628	8.6	-0.6	2 102	1 525	-848	14 092	2.79	75.6	13.2	20.6
Muscogee	11.0	6.4	5.2	50.9	186 291	189 885	1.9	5.4	13 622	7 570	4 123	72 243	2.53	64.7	21.5	30.7
Newton	10.8	7.2	4.3	52.4	62 001	99 958	61.2	3.7	5 645	3 319	1 407	33 840	2.93	73.8	19.7	22.7
Oconee	13.5	8.0	4.8	51.3	26 225	32 808	25.1	6.9	1 355	879	1 752	11 485	2.88	80.2	10.4	16.8
Oglethorpe	13.6	10.6	6.6	50.3	12 635	14 899	17.9	-1.5	641	541	-386	5 201	2.80	71.8	10.1	23.9
Paulding	9.8	6.0	3.0	51.1	81 678	142 324	74.3	4.7	7 892	3 306	1 857	47 881	2.99	80.5	14.2	15.9
Peach	12.3	7.8	5.0	51.6	23 668	27 695	17.0	-2.8	1 382	950	-1 247	9 525	2.62	71.9	18.4	24.0
Pickens	15.1	12.7	6.9	51.0	22 983	29 431	28.1	2.0	1 249	1 249	512	11 083	2.63	75.8	6.9	20.8
Pierce	12.3	9.5	5.7	50.6	15 636	18 758	20.0	1.2	1 009	794	46	6 970	2.67	72.1	14.5	23.7
Pike	12.5	8.9	5.2	50.5	13 688	17 869	30.5	-0.5	702	638	-148	6 140	2.86	80.2	13.4	17.6
Polk	11.9	8.8	5.7	50.7	38 127	41 475	8.8	-0.8	2 455	1 919	-894	14 645	2.78	73.2	14.3	23.9
Pulaski	14.1	11.0	7.4	57.0	9 588	12 010	25.3	-4.3	384	432	-465	4 034	2.54	72.8	20.8	23.8

1. No spouse present.

STATE County	Persons in group quarters, 2014	Daytime population, 2009–2013: Number	Daytime population, 2009–2013: Employment/residence ratio	Births, 2014: Total	Births, 2014: Rate[1]	Deaths, 2014: Number	Deaths, 2014: Rate[1]	Persons under 65 with no health insurance, 2013: Number	Persons under 65 with no health insurance, 2013: Percent	Medicare, 2014: Eligible for Medicare	Medicare, 2014: Enrolled in Medicare Advantage	Medicare, 2014: Enrolled in a Medicare prescription drug plan	Serious crimes known to police,[2] 2013: Total: Number	Serious crimes known to police,[2] 2013: Total: Rate[3]
	32	33	34	35	36	37	38	39	40	41	42	43	44	45
GEORGIA—Cont'd														
Effingham	488	40 010	0.45	742	13.4	382	6.9	8 064	16.7	7 386	1 945	2 868	551	1 028
Elbert	264	18 915	0.87	230	11.8	267	13.7	3 318	20.9	4 804	1 387	2 079	814	4 166
Emanuel	934	22 144	0.94	325	14.3	262	11.5	4 196	22.7	4 583	1 377	2 211	622	2 794
Evans	391	11 511	1.15	183	16.8	113	10.4	2 136	24.2	1 996	602	879	196	1 850
Fannin	157	22 812	0.90	207	8.7	293	12.3	4 440	24.8	6 859	1 466	3 167	395	1 686
Fayette	507	102 119	0.90	827	7.5	775	7.1	12 710	14.1	19 301	5 028	7 943	1 761	1 635
Floyd	3 922	101 014	1.13	1 125	11.7	1 032	10.7	17 517	22.5	18 861	4 230	9 567	4 208	4 378
Forsyth	600	167 214	0.81	2 161	10.6	1 004	4.9	24 616	14.3	22 124	6 864	8 922	1 958	1 021
Franklin	801	22 717	1.09	273	12.3	265	11.9	3 951	22.6	5 015	1 231	2 564	540	2 562
Fulton	33 606	1 305 616	1.81	12 844	12.9	6 766	6.8	178 722	21.0	117 602	39 516	46 659	57 133	5 737
Gilmer	178	26 405	0.82	291	10.1	290	10.1	6 312	28.1	6 972	1 521	3 368	497	1 765
Glascock	85	2 387	0.40	30	9.8	30	9.8	473	18.3	570	150	271	10	402
Glynn	1 189	86 408	1.18	996	12.1	818	10.0	14 175	21.2	16 333	3 804	7 063	4 095	5 029
Gordon	661	55 291	0.99	703	12.5	477	8.5	12 136	25.3	9 307	1 804	4 931	1 777	3 220
Grady	165	21 660	0.59	340	13.4	255	10.1	5 910	27.9	4 791	1 402	2 079	561	2 194
Greene	167	16 523	1.07	162	9.8	195	11.8	2 699	22.4	4 851	1 264	2 441	468	2 902
Gwinnett	5 267	784 778	0.89	11 185	12.7	3 929	4.5	184 164	23.6	84 738	27 167	32 871	21 351	2 501
Habersham	2 445	41 867	0.92	508	11.6	415	9.5	7 857	23.2	8 774	2 301	4 121	1 193	2 732
Hall	2 812	183 987	1.01	2 494	13.1	1 367	7.2	39 337	24.5	30 016	7 909	14 082	4 499	2 402
Hancock	1 182	8 478	0.67	73	8.6	95	11.2	1 203	20.2	2 123	909	772	108	1 219
Haralson	332	27 420	0.89	337	11.8	316	11.0	4 566	19.0	5 781	1 713	2 800	1 222	4 322
Harris	437	22 932	0.37	286	8.7	281	8.5	4 049	15.0	5 796	1 485	2 091	381	1 203
Hart	682	23 025	0.75	249	9.8	273	10.8	4 134	20.8	5 899	1 335	2 942	1 004	3 924
Heard	132	9 591	0.53	122	10.5	105	9.0	1 942	19.9	2 139	687	950	202	1 747
Henry	889	172 102	0.62	2 537	11.9	1 344	6.3	33 551	17.8	27 263	9 139	9 854	6 210	2 952
Houston	1 664	145 435	1.03	2 025	13.6	1 122	7.5	23 282	18.0	21 478	3 509	5 981	6 354	4 294
Irwin	667	8 534	0.68	97	10.7	93	10.2	1 510	21.2	1 943	533	994	298	3 105
Jackson	698	54 747	0.78	775	12.5	509	8.2	10 676	20.3	10 841	2 957	4 826	1 217	2 073
Jasper	82	10 498	0.45	155	11.5	123	9.2	2 576	22.3	2 654	851	1 139	153	1 130
Jeff Davis	113	13 986	0.81	203	13.7	156	10.5	2 927	22.8	2 685	580	1 405	460	3 031
Jefferson	587	16 470	0.96	207	12.7	221	13.6	2 826	21.2	3 599	1 035	1 763	438	3 245
Jenkins	1 199	7 509	0.63	103	11.3	106	11.6	1 692	25.0	1 632	534	786	NA	NA
Johnson	1 738	8 424	0.58	87	9.0	97	10.0	1 411	21.1	1 810	474	902	29	294
Jones	310	20 942	0.35	268	9.3	264	9.2	4 310	17.9	5 167	1 852	1 978	531	1 859
Lamar	1 286	15 663	0.65	183	10.1	202	11.1	2 989	21.1	3 582	1 307	1 392	627	3 604
Lanier	214	8 502	0.50	117	11.3	82	7.9	1 973	21.9	1 442	334	701	289	2 751
Laurens	1 001	49 459	1.07	657	13.7	538	11.2	7 705	19.3	9 868	2 801	4 058	1 918	4 002
Lee	927	20 868	0.39	366	12.5	198	6.8	4 087	16.2	3 888	857	1 545	976	3 854
Liberty	2 505	71 241	1.23	1 457	22.3	303	4.6	9 848	17.3	5 781	1 354	1 592	2 210	3 327
Lincoln	67	6 399	0.52	70	9.2	84	11.0	1 295	21.0	1 866	542	742	243	3 171
Long	298	10 726	0.22	215	12.6	88	5.1	3 830	25.4	1 340	284	502	195	1 179
Lowndes	6 399	119 229	1.17	1 613	14.2	872	7.7	19 134	20.2	15 739	3 323	7 160	3 471	2 987
Lumpkin	2 569	26 130	0.68	297	9.5	242	7.8	5 461	22.8	5 447	1 254	2 610	379	1 234
McDuffie	267	21 012	0.91	282	13.2	245	11.5	3 529	19.5	4 302	1 631	1 479	NA	NA
McIntosh	71	12 017	0.59	129	9.1	102	7.2	2 444	22.3	2 743	836	1 106	311	2 624
Macon	1 884	13 919	0.88	133	9.6	155	11.2	2 616	25.8	2 193	809	939	828	6 065
Madison	249	21 375	0.42	321	11.3	257	9.1	5 295	22.3	5 605	1 544	2 608	729	2 728
Marion	74	7 564	0.65	87	9.9	77	8.8	1 707	23.8	1 464	450	556	101	1 161
Meriwether	249	19 185	0.68	222	10.5	243	11.5	3 536	20.4	4 772	1 863	1 962	732	3 613
Miller	150	5 570	0.79	66	11.1	78	13.1	993	21.1	1 207	330	615	118	1 996
Mitchell	2 180	23 822	1.06	256	11.2	223	9.8	3 720	21.0	4 281	1 309	1 823	583	2 573
Monroe	1 217	23 666	0.73	254	9.4	288	10.6	3 919	18.1	5 188	1 364	2 209	669	2 504
Montgomery	670	7 777	0.61	102	11.3	72	8.0	1 673	23.9	1 573	443	758	NA	NA
Morgan	147	19 056	1.15	169	9.4	156	8.7	2 961	20.4	3 911	1 230	1 628	424	2 481
Murray	226	34 368	0.66	482	12.2	384	9.7	8 271	24.1	6 870	1 042	4 042	1 039	2 641
Muscogee	7 898	221 726	1.32	3 284	16.3	1 836	9.1	34 682	20.0	31 440	8 917	10 368	13 575	6 748
Newton	1 707	87 019	0.67	1 313	12.7	802	7.7	18 385	20.6	15 466	5 076	6 209	3 115	3 054
Oconee	114	29 584	0.76	309	8.8	184	5.2	4 541	15.5	5 388	1 239	2 550	567	1 677
Oglethorpe	177	10 831	0.37	147	10.0	129	8.8	2 841	23.7	2 877	720	1 370	398	2 740
Paulding	498	104 164	0.40	1 778	11.9	837	5.6	24 100	18.1	16 480	4 911	6 531	3 138	2 157
Peach	1 302	25 986	0.87	353	13.1	233	8.7	5 005	22.4	4 842	1 256	1 715	1 068	3 873
Pickens	348	27 022	0.80	284	9.5	307	10.2	4 917	20.8	7 835	1 943	3 647	520	2 035
Pierce	182	16 025	0.60	246	13.0	196	10.3	3 649	22.9	3 850	858	2 001	286	1 517
Pike	218	13 271	0.39	167	9.4	155	8.7	2 889	19.2	3 150	934	1 348	281	1 615
Polk	373	37 550	0.76	577	14.0	463	11.3	8 221	23.5	8 162	2 086	3 841	2 243	5 460
Pulaski	1 217	11 253	0.87	89	7.8	120	10.5	1 863	22.6	2 012	439	843	NA	NA

1. Per 1,000 estimated resident population. 2. Data for serious crimes have not been adjusted for underreporting; this may affect comparability between geographic areas and over time.
3. Per 100,000 population estimated by the FBI.

Table B. States and Counties — **Crime, Education, Money Income, and Poverty**

STATE County	Serious crimes known to police, 2013 (cont.)[1] — Rate[2] — Violent	Property	Education — School enrollment and attainment, 2009–2013 — Enrollment[3] — Total	Percent private	Attainment[4] (percent) — High school graduate or less	Bachelor's degree or more	Local government expenditures,[5] 2012–2013 — Total current spending (mil dol)	Current spending per student (dollars)	Money income, 2009–2013 — Per capita income[6] (dollars)	Households — Median income (dollars)	Mean income (dollars)	Percent with income of $200,000 or more	Income and poverty, 2013 — Median household income (dollars)	Percent below poverty level — All persons	Children under 18 years	Children 5 to 17 years in families
	46	47	48	49	50	51	52	53	54	55	56	57	58	59	60	61
GEORGIA—Cont'd																
Effingham	76	952	15 228	12.1	52.0	16.8	95.0	8 242	24 824	63 030	71 732	2.1	61 062	11.8	15.8	14.2
Elbert	409	3 756	4 646	11.9	67.7	11.3	32.3	10 249	18 835	35 817	46 475	1.1	34 487	23.4	34.0	32.3
Emanuel	341	2 453	5 598	6.0	62.8	11.6	37.4	8 572	17 064	32 046	46 041	1.6	30 348	34.1	49.6	47.6
Evans	113	1 737	2 818	12.8	62.7	14.1	16.8	9 003	18 998	36 788	48 892	1.0	32 838	27.9	44.2	43.0
Fannin	188	1 498	4 704	9.3	61.9	14.4	32.1	10 561	19 164	34 239	45 059	0.5	35 673	22.5	34.8	32.3
Fayette	86	1 549	31 522	16.6	27.0	42.6	183.0	9 014	35 344	79 977	97 636	8.5	81 368	7.2	9.9	8.6
Floyd	375	4 003	25 398	19.7	53.3	18.1	163.8	10 091	20 500	40 821	54 791	1.8	39 381	22.2	30.3	28.1
Forsyth	62	959	54 848	17.1	29.2	43.8	306.6	7 891	34 582	86 569	104 524	9.8	87 565	7.7	8.9	7.9
Franklin	128	2 433	5 101	15.3	64.0	13.0	29.7	8 096	18 234	34 830	45 318	0.2	40 114	20.9	31.4	30.0
Fulton	785	4 952	274 495	22.5	27.9	48.2	1 610.2	11 224	36 757	56 857	90 989	9.9	55 474	18.2	25.6	24.2
Gilmer	195	1 570	5 853	8.7	55.9	16.4	41.5	9 625	21 317	39 140	52 527	2.5	39 323	25.1	39.9	34.7
Glascock	0	402	759	5.7	65.1	9.6	6.2	9 630	17 984	37 760	48 108	0.0	37 955	19.2	24.2	20.4
Glynn	591	4 438	19 064	10.1	42.4	26.1	118.4	9 266	26 724	46 407	66 720	4.3	43 533	20.3	31.0	29.0
Gordon	313	2 906	13 829	8.7	61.3	14.2	92.0	8 701	19 177	40 926	52 683	1.8	42 291	18.4	25.7	24.1
Grady	278	1 916	6 671	5.4	66.5	11.3	37.8	8 100	15 734	30 571	41 623	0.4	35 212	25.7	39.5	39.0
Greene	248	2 654	3 223	13.8	58.4	21.4	29.8	13 463	27 828	42 565	68 720	5.0	42 842	23.1	41.2	39.4
Gwinnett	210	2 291	250 443	13.9	36.5	33.9	1 500.4	8 891	25 932	60 445	77 273	4.3	59 081	13.7	20.0	18.6
Habersham	149	2 583	10 674	10.8	56.2	17.1	66.3	9 594	18 910	39 306	52 611	1.3	40 530	21.2	30.4	27.7
Hall	156	2 246	48 219	11.1	51.4	22.8	290.9	8 521	23 645	50 853	68 004	3.5	46 986	20.8	30.1	28.4
Hancock	147	1 072	1 778	4.8	67.8	9.9	15.8	14 483	12 381	25 000	35 388	0.5	26 281	38.5	48.8	47.8
Haralson	746	3 575	7 063	6.6	63.0	14.1	51.6	9 042	19 789	39 993	52 025	0.7	39 548	22.2	30.8	28.3
Harris	79	1 124	8 223	9.2	39.5	27.3	45.6	8 775	31 482	69 223	85 920	6.6	60 977	10.6	15.0	13.6
Hart	356	3 568	5 614	13.8	58.0	15.5	32.0	9 138	20 371	35 615	49 770	1.1	40 225	20.8	31.5	29.5
Heard	130	1 618	2 928	7.4	66.2	8.2	19.6	9 599	18 964	39 909	49 727	0.5	40 123	20.3	30.9	27.7
Henry	177	2 775	65 927	18.3	41.4	26.1	346.6	8 626	25 299	60 781	72 845	2.3	60 087	11.6	16.7	15.0
Houston	348	3 946	42 765	10.1	40.2	24.0	258.1	9 349	25 195	54 893	66 641	2.5	52 297	15.4	21.9	19.9
Irwin	344	2 761	2 032	2.7	59.0	10.3	16.1	9 271	18 207	40 771	51 145	1.9	35 854	26.5	35.0	32.5
Jackson	145	1 928	15 841	10.1	54.3	19.5	106.3	9 133	23 247	53 179	65 241	2.1	52 385	14.0	18.6	17.1
Jasper	170	960	3 351	17.3	57.9	13.3	18.9	8 297	21 297	42 192	54 981	1.5	42 343	19.7	31.3	29.7
Jeff Davis	468	2 563	3 979	3.6	63.4	9.6	24.2	7 796	17 684	36 296	46 158	0.8	34 481	22.7	36.9	34.6
Jefferson	363	2 882	4 145	8.7	69.5	8.8	27.0	9 363	14 757	26 968	38 028	0.5	29 152	27.5	39.5	38.0
Jenkins	NA	NA	2 474	9.4	65.4	13.1	14.2	10 141	17 565	26 104	43 809	2.5	28 445	38.3	48.9	44.3
Johnson	61	233	2 225	3.9	62.8	11.5	11.4	9 520	16 807	36 722	46 453	1.4	29 565	31.3	39.1	34.9
Jones	60	1 800	7 410	12.5	52.5	17.8	47.9	8 669	24 485	51 497	64 655	3.2	51 650	16.3	23.0	21.2
Lamar	109	3 495	5 261	10.3	56.8	14.2	24.5	9 396	18 800	41 016	51 416	0.3	40 915	19.7	29.4	27.4
Lanier	419	2 332	2 629	5.2	53.5	12.0	15.3	8 624	17 264	39 452	45 289	1.1	35 101	27.2	37.5	36.3
Laurens	232	3 771	11 705	7.5	63.3	15.0	81.6	8 392	18 625	34 793	48 492	1.4	33 974	29.1	38.3	35.1
Lee	363	3 491	8 716	11.5	45.9	20.5	48.6	7 703	26 357	60 104	75 666	3.7	63 272	11.6	16.1	14.7
Liberty	328	2 999	19 065	10.3	41.4	20.2	97.6	9 576	20 791	43 832	55 827	1.7	40 175	20.0	28.1	30.1
Lincoln	365	2 806	1 563	1.2	63.3	11.4	12.0	10 218	20 641	35 625	47 155	0.5	35 683	22.3	32.0	30.2
Long	60	1 118	4 231	9.6	54.8	14.0	22.8	7 897	17 158	42 651	50 240	0.0	41 147	21.8	30.6	27.9
Lowndes	187	2 800	35 753	8.3	46.5	23.1	154.5	8 430	18 897	37 365	51 068	1.5	37 138	26.3	30.5	28.8
Lumpkin	65	1 169	9 353	9.5	45.7	25.4	35.1	9 241	20 908	43 775	54 431	1.9	42 919	21.5	27.0	27.3
McDuffie	NA	NA	5 572	6.3	62.1	13.7	40.1	9 406	17 922	37 487	46 708	0.7	37 328	23.7	37.4	34.6
McIntosh	194	2 430	3 396	11.2	55.7	15.8	15.8	9 477	21 484	39 068	54 887	1.0	36 346	23.1	36.5	33.6
Macon	740	5 325	3 500	9.7	67.5	10.1	18.6	10 633	13 865	30 240	37 843	0.3	28 844	33.5	43.7	40.2
Madison	142	2 586	6 745	12.5	60.2	14.9	47.5	10 009	19 939	42 549	54 314	1.4	43 611	18.7	27.0	24.7
Marion	103	1 057	2 047	6.9	65.7	10.6	12.8	9 706	17 479	33 301	45 687	0.8	34 680	24.7	38.8	35.3
Meriwether	355	3 257	4 870	13.1	67.0	8.9	31.5	9 842	18 821	37 333	48 388	0.9	34 962	27.2	42.6	44.2
Miller	203	1 793	1 446	5.9	59.3	11.9	9.8	8 753	19 674	32 260	45 795	1.1	32 535	26.0	39.5	36.9
Mitchell	190	2 383	5 667	12.0	67.1	9.6	41.1	10 247	15 694	32 054	41 885	0.9	32 280	32.8	42.2	38.7
Monroe	191	2 313	6 589	18.6	55.8	18.7	40.3	9 863	22 888	48 630	62 034	1.4	54 793	13.9	21.3	19.8
Montgomery	NA	NA	2 283	22.0	63.2	15.5	9.3	9 393	16 460	32 702	44 561	1.0	37 128	25.5	35.8	33.4
Morgan	135	2 346	4 555	13.2	53.4	22.7	31.1	9 330	25 933	47 729	68 867	4.7	48 337	17.1	24.9	22.6
Murray	203	2 438	9 904	7.1	66.9	9.6	59.7	7 876	16 449	34 888	44 840	0.5	40 343	21.9	29.8	26.0
Muscogee	510	6 239	57 106	11.3	42.6	22.6	322.7	10 031	22 856	41 339	58 556	2.5	40 414	22.9	34.0	32.6
Newton	410	2 645	30 269	13.1	48.2	19.4	167.2	8 715	21 484	50 580	61 273	1.4	50 862	15.0	24.1	21.3
Oconee	98	1 579	10 123	17.8	28.6	43.1	58.5	8 756	33 801	75 004	95 213	8.0	72 478	8.6	10.9	9.3
Oglethorpe	303	2 437	3 663	11.1	57.0	18.0	21.5	9 523	20 493	45 729	54 750	1.0	44 026	17.6	25.3	22.8
Paulding	132	2 025	44 599	12.5	46.7	23.4	222.1	7 817	24 168	61 837	70 599	2.2	60 008	11.6	14.9	13.7
Peach	479	3 394	9 296	10.8	49.5	19.2	37.4	9 923	19 431	39 844	54 488	1.0	42 602	21.1	32.2	29.4
Pickens	180	1 855	6 368	10.6	52.3	22.5	46.0	10 509	26 686	51 383	69 605	3.9	53 332	15.1	25.6	23.2
Pierce	176	1 342	4 310	5.6	61.2	11.8	28.0	7 703	20 001	30 067	52 880	1.0	36 214	21.8	31.3	20.1
Pike	63	1 551	5 172	12.7	50.5	17.0	26.3	7 630	22 191	53 865	63 422	1.4	52 393	13.8	19.4	16.8
Polk	304	5 155	10 208	13.4	63.6	13.1	64.7	8 476	18 336	39 208	50 356	1.4	38 730	22.5	33.0	29.9
Pulaski	NA	NA	2 413	9.0	66.9	9.6	14.2	9 992	17 781	41 550	49 946	0.4	37 012	23.5	33.7	30.3

1. Data for serious crimes have not been adjusted for underreporting; this may affect comparability between geographic areas and over time. 2. Per 100,000 population estimated by the FBI.
3. All persons 3 years old and over enrolled in nursery school through college. 4. Persons 25 years old and over. 5. Elementary and secondary education expenditures.
6. Based on population estimated by the American Community Survey, 2009–2013.

STATE County	Personal income, 2013										Earnings, 2013		
	Total (mil dol)	Percent change, 2012–2013	Per capita[1]		Wages and salaries (mil dol)	Supplements to wages and salaries; employer contributions (mil dol)		Proprietors' income (mil dol)	Dividends, interest, and rent (mil dol)	Personal transfer receipts (mil dol)	Total (mil dol)	Contributions for government social insurance (mil dol)	
			Dollars	Rank		Pension and insurance	Government social insurance					From employee and self-employed	From employer
	62	63	64	65	66	67	68	69	70	71	72	73	74
GEORGIA—Cont'd													
Effingham	1 957	3.1	35 932	1 760	397	87	27	55	190	313	565	35	27
Elbert	600	1.7	30 596	2 614	199	47	14	52	112	186	313	21	14
Emanuel	639	1.6	27 929	2 905	213	54	15	54	89	226	336	21	15
Evans	325	2.5	29 989	2 690	139	31	9	27	54	86	206	12	9
Fannin	745	3.1	31 339	2 503	170	36	13	63	142	242	282	22	13
Fayette	5 246	2.0	48 413	456	1 711	278	122	349	1 052	682	2 459	148	122
Floyd	3 319	1.4	34 641	1 967	1 567	289	114	205	534	854	2 176	133	114
Forsyth	8 975	7.7	45 930	621	3 313	465	232	35	1 227	791	4 045	239	232
Franklin	717	5.5	32 566	2 317	233	46	17	123	123	197	419	23	17
Fulton	57 210	2.5	58 123	130	55 155	7 115	3 736	8 714	10 752	5 606	74 719	4 134	3 736
Gilmer	861	4.6	30 132	2 669	228	50	17	101	157	250	396	25	17
Glascock	75	0.0	24 121	3 077	11	4	1	4	12	24	19	1	1
Glynn	3 157	1.8	38 735	1 330	1 500	298	108	142	826	645	2 048	120	108
Gordon	1 620	3.3	29 050	2 803	813	147	60	149	199	392	1 170	69	60
Grady	755	0.8	29 883	2 706	204	43	14	92	119	190	353	21	14
Greene	755	2.4	46 242	605	189	34	13	58	270	177	294	20	13
Gwinnett	29 269	2.8	34 061	2 070	17 056	2 396	1 189	1 481	3 913	3 734	22 121	1 265	1 189
Habersham	1 267	4.1	29 258	2 776	497	120	35	72	226	326	725	45	35
Hall	6 373	4.0	33 945	2 091	3 318	570	223	509	1 139	1 216	4 620	271	223
Hancock	204	3.5	22 954	3 093	57	17	4	15	37	87	92	7	4
Haralson	882	1.8	30 954	2 560	250	52	18	48	135	253	368	25	18
Harris	1 676	0.0	51 313	321	137	34	10	178	262	223	358	23	10
Hart	741	3.4	29 109	2 792	225	46	17	67	148	222	356	23	17
Heard	344	1.1	29 732	2 723	96	25	7	16	36	92	143	9	7
Henry	6 596	2.4	31 242	2 516	1 973	385	144	315	818	1 167	2 816	171	144
Houston	5 490	1.5	37 183	1 550	2 876	749	224	246	1 097	993	4 094	214	224
Irwin	314	1.2	33 259	2 216	65	19	5	75	50	85	163	7	5
Jackson	2 017	3.0	33 046	2 244	781	144	56	134	271	417	1 115	66	56
Jasper	428	1.3	31 454	2 489	64	16	5	26	64	108	111	8	5
Jeff Davis	428	3.2	28 513	2 848	150	33	11	73	56	123	267	15	11
Jefferson	466	-0.4	28 539	2 847	157	37	11	50	77	163	255	15	11
Jenkins	227	-1.2	24 459	3 069	45	12	3	29	32	79	90	5	3
Johnson	212	1.0	21 688	3 101	54	15	4	11	30	82	83	6	4
Jones	1 031	0.1	36 097	1 731	153	34	11	36	117	217	234	17	11
Lamar	519	1.1	28 920	2 816	124	31	9	37	70	160	201	13	9
Lanier	286	3.9	27 473	2 940	47	12	3	26	31	71	88	5	3
Laurens	1 521	2.3	31 678	2 453	663	144	50	109	251	431	966	58	50
Lee	1 315	1.0	45 222	674	217	42	15	55	165	172	329	19	15
Liberty	1 973	1.2	30 756	2 586	1 825	554	173	43	586	367	2 594	105	173
Lincoln	244	1.3	31 512	2 476	41	10	3	16	51	71	70	5	3
Long	346	3.8	20 792	3 107	32	11	2	7	60	85	52	3	2
Lowndes	3 660	1.4	32 410	2 350	1 935	453	148	233	748	791	2 769	145	148
Lumpkin	899	3.8	29 062	2 800	248	61	18	50	166	214	376	23	18
McDuffie	701	1.0	32 494	2 335	230	48	17	45	108	187	341	20	17
McIntosh	348	2.4	24 861	3 060	60	16	4	17	65	107	97	8	4
Macon	369	4.0	26 321	3 016	109	25	8	64	65	108	206	10	8
Madison	904	2.8	32 215	2 384	108	29	7	62	131	227	206	15	7
Marion	250	0.9	28 970	2 807	46	12	3	25	36	63	85	5	3
Meriwether	641	2.3	30 192	2 658	157	42	11	33	99	201	243	17	11
Miller	229	0.3	38 611	1 353	54	15	4	52	37	54	124	5	4
Mitchell	750	1.3	32 527	2 326	246	59	17	136	131	192	457	21	17
Monroe	1 155	1.4	42 808	859	271	69	18	31	151	206	389	24	18
Montgomery	253	3.1	28 071	2 889	50	12	4	21	37	68	86	5	4
Morgan	713	1.6	40 085	1 165	219	41	16	76	155	149	351	21	16
Murray	1 044	1.4	26 577	3 002	336	68	26	31	110	280	460	31	26
Muscogee	8 117	1.7	40 021	1 170	4 531	921	335	345	1 782	1 665	6 132	336	335
Newton	2 704	2.2	26 398	3 013	861	182	62	65	360	676	1 169	76	62
Oconee	2 035	2.3	59 802	109	366	69	25	63	359	186	523	31	25
Oglethorpe	505	1.3	34 746	1 942	57	15	4	59	68	107	134	7	4
Paulding	5 667	2.1	38 561	1 365	733	149	52	193	458	720	1 127	73	52
Peach	884	-0.1	32 714	2 302	320	67	24	59	143	225	471	26	24
Pickens	1 150	3.3	38 858	1 311	276	53	20	54	251	276	402	29	20
Pierce	581	1.8	30 689	2 601	136	30	10	49	84	169	224	15	10
Pike	593	1.3	33 335	2 198	90	22	6	33	80	126	151	11	6
Polk	1 192	2.3	28 937	2 811	412	86	30	62	169	358	591	39	30
Pulaski	329	0.2	28 485	2 850	98	22	7	12	69	83	139	9	7

1. Based on the resident population estimated as of July 1 of the year shown.

STATE County	Earnings, 2013 (cont.) — Percent by selected industries: Farm	Mining	Construction	Manu-facturing	Infor-mation: professional, scientific, technical services	Retail trade	Finance, insur-ance, real estate and leasing	Health care and social assistance	Govern-ment	Social Security beneficiaries, December 2013: Number	Rate[1]	Supple-mental Security Income recipients, December 2013	Housing units, 2014: Total	Percent change, 2010–2014
	75	76	77	78	79	80	81	82	83	84	85	86	87	88
GEORGIA—Cont'd														
Effingham	0.9	D	4.6	24.2	4.9	7.1	2.9	D	28.0	8 300	152	922	20 549	3.3
Elbert	3.8	5.1	2.9	29.2	D	5.9	4.2	D	22.8	5 420	278	863	9 513	-0.7
Emanuel	6.5	D	3.1	19.7	2.8	7.3	3.6	D	28.8	5 370	235	1 322	9 879	-0.9
Evans	7.5	0.0	6.2	35.3	D	6.7	D	D	16.3	2 250	208	452	4 636	-0.6
Fannin	0.9	0.0	D	3.3	5.0	10.4	6.9	D	17.9	7 630	321	723	16 589	2.3
Fayette	0.1	D	8.3	9.4	7.8	8.5	5.5	14.7	13.6	20 050	185	970	41 344	1.4
Floyd	0.4	D	2.4	16.8	D	6.8	4.2	24.8	15.1	21 405	223	3 336	40 428	-0.3
Forsyth	0.3	0.1	7.9	13.9	15.7	5.9	3.7	10.0	10.5	22 870	117	1 018	71 045	10.9
Franklin	18.0	0.0	D	16.6	D	7.2	2.8	D	13.1	5 830	264	842	10 460	-0.9
Fulton	0.0	0.2	2.5	4.4	26.3	3.6	14.2	8.1	11.3	121 315	123	25 878	448 897	2.7
Gilmer	11.7	D	5.5	16.5	D	8.9	5.1	7.4	16.5	7 645	267	653	16 653	0.6
Glascock	5.3	D	D	0.0	D	D	D	D	43.1	670	217	80	1 501	-1.2
Glynn	0.0	D	6.7	7.2	4.9	7.7	4.6	8.7	32.2	17 750	218	1 928	41 726	2.5
Gordon	3.2	0.0	3.7	41.0	2.5	6.1	2.6	8.3	13.7	10 685	191	1 401	22 254	-0.1
Grady	11.5	0.0	5.6	10.1	2.6	7.8	D	D	19.0	5 285	209	1 099	10 684	-0.7
Greene	7.2	0.4	13.4	8.3	4.7	7.8	7.0	9.8	14.6	5 160	317	628	9 006	3.7
Gwinnett	0.0	D	6.1	9.6	15.1	8.9	9.8	7.0	9.9	90 755	106	11 497	298 611	2.4
Habersham	2.0	D	3.6	29.6	5.4	8.1	3.2	4.5	22.0	9 685	224	887	18 111	-0.2
Hall	0.7	D	5.2	20.4	4.1	6.8	5.8	15.2	12.5	32 980	176	3 083	69 492	1.0
Hancock	3.0	D	D	D	D	5.1	D	D	39.3	2 350	264	481	5 279	-1.1
Haralson	0.9	0.0	7.0	25.0	3.5	7.5	2.9	8.9	23.3	6 710	236	1 069	12 241	-0.4
Harris	0.3	0.0	13.3	10.9	D	3.3	12.1	D	16.9	6 350	194	466	13 690	2.2
Hart	12.5	0.0	4.6	24.2	5.0	6.6	2.6	5.7	17.1	6 580	258	723	12 943	-0.5
Heard	2.8	D	6.1	23.7	D	1.8	D	2.1	22.3	2 485	215	401	5 103	-0.9
Henry	0.1	0.3	5.3	7.0	4.3	11.2	6.0	12.4	21.6	30 870	146	3 415	77 530	1.3
Houston	0.2	D	2.4	6.8	8.4	5.8	2.4	5.7	56.2	22 785	154	3 533	60 555	3.8
Irwin	40.5	0.0	2.7	5.8	2.0	4.8	1.6	6.3	23.9	2 180	232	406	4 022	-0.3
Jackson	5.2	D	4.7	26.3	5.0	7.3	3.1	4.1	14.0	12 080	198	1 453	23 752	0.0
Jasper	4.8	0.0	6.1	15.7	2.4	7.2	3.6	D	26.1	2 960	219	365	6 230	1.3
Jeff Davis	10.8	0.0	1.1	19.0	1.1	9.2	1.9	3.3	15.7	3 100	207	513	6 412	-1.2
Jefferson	11.6	D	4.7	11.7	1.9	7.5	3.2	D	20.7	4 105	251	956	7 246	-0.7
Jenkins	23.6	0.0	2.2	0.6	D	4.5	2.0	4.8	29.8	1 840	199	464	4 175	-1.1
Johnson	3.4	0.0	4.8	6.4	1.0	5.2	D	13.3	35.1	1 975	202	473	4 066	-1.3
Jones	1.5	D	13.0	1.5	D	5.5	4.1	D	26.2	5 860	204	733	11 576	-1.0
Lamar	7.5	D	3.5	16.4	D	6.9	3.3	4.6	31.1	4 080	227	498	7 504	0.4
Lanier	22.1	0.0	5.2	6.5	D	5.0	D	9.1	25.6	1 685	162	398	4 295	1.1
Laurens	2.1	0.0	5.0	12.9	D	8.6	3.7	14.1	28.0	11 165	233	2 191	21 283	-0.4
Lee	7.6	D	11.9	3.2	D	6.8	3.0	D	23.0	4 535	156	488	10 698	4.1
Liberty	0.1	0.0	1.3	5.6	D	2.3	1.3	1.5	78.8	6 605	103	1 124	27 198	1.7
Lincoln	1.3	0.0	20.4	D	1.4	7.5	5.0	2.3	27.7	2 055	266	255	4 779	-0.1
Long	5.3	D	4.4	D	D	2.7	D	1.9	60.8	1 555	93	298	6 205	2.9
Lowndes	0.6	D	6.0	7.6	5.7	9.0	4.7	10.0	37.2	17 815	158	3 512	45 665	4.0
Lumpkin	2.2	D	6.2	8.9	D	7.4	3.0	9.2	37.5	6 060	196	552	13 073	1.1
McDuffie	7.8	0.3	5.9	21.9	4.0	9.0	3.1	D	20.5	4 850	226	974	9 248	-0.8
McIntosh	0.8	D	4.6	1.1	D	7.7	2.1	1.8	36.2	3 035	214	440	9 299	0.9
Macon	25.5	D	3.0	21.4	D	3.6	1.6	D	20.6	2 495	179	682	6 052	-1.4
Madison	13.9	1.4	9.3	5.1	D	6.0	4.2	D	30.7	6 520	232	980	11 732	-0.4
Marion	11.5	D	4.9	24.5	D	5.2	D	4.1	21.7	1 645	189	332	4 109	-1.1
Meriwether	3.5	0.0	7.1	14.9	1.6	6.3	3.2	D	34.3	5 245	247	975	9 911	-0.5
Miller	37.6	0.0	2.9	0.7	D	6.2	5.5	3.0	28.3	1 375	232	254	2 752	-1.4
Mitchell	27.6	0.0	1.0	24.2	D	5.1	2.6	D	17.0	4 745	206	1 129	8 938	-0.6
Monroe	1.7	D	5.9	2.6	D	5.3	1.9	5.0	35.1	5 670	210	624	10 954	2.2
Montgomery	17.0	0.0	3.6	7.6	0.5	5.2	6.9	D	21.0	1 830	204	315	3 886	-0.9
Morgan	6.1	0.0	6.3	16.4	D	7.4	6.3	3.6	15.9	4 350	245	438	7 497	0.3
Murray	0.5	D	2.2	43.7	D	7.1	2.9	D	16.9	7 925	202	1 211	15 777	-1.3
Muscogee	0.0	D	3.7	6.8	7.4	6.0	15.8	12.8	29.1	35 460	174	7 284	83 846	1.4
Newton	0.3	D	6.1	26.7	D	7.5	2.9	9.3	22.2	17 800	174	2 777	38 351	0.0
Oconee	3.5	D	5.9	4.6	8.0	7.6	10.7	10.4	16.6	5 740	169	342	13 147	6.1
Oglethorpe	40.5	3.3	7.6	4.4	D	3.1	2.1	D	20.5	3 185	219	448	6 487	0.0
Paulding	0.3	D	12.4	4.2	5.4	11.3	4.3	8.9	26.0	18 915	129	1 885	53 105	1.9
Peach	10.2	0.1	4.8	27.4	1.6	7.0	2.4	5.5	24.6	5 155	192	985	11 273	2.0
Pickens	0.7	3.6	7.2	10.0	5.1	9.1	8.3	16.8	18.4	8 425	286	654	13 688	0.0
Pierce	11.1	0.0	8.5	8.0	2.8	6.7	2.6	7.2	19.6	4 110	217	716	7 961	-0.3
Pike	1.7	D	13.7	11.2	D	6.4	3.1	6.4	23.2	3 615	203	337	6 819	0.0
Polk	2.0	D	4.5	33.1	D	8.8	2.0	5.6	16.6	9 360	227	1 461	16 940	0.2
Pulaski	8.0	0.0	D	D	5.7	6.8	D	D	24.9	2 190	190	359	5 136	-0.2

1. Per 1,000 resident population estimated as of July 1 of the year shown.

STATE County	Housing units, 2009–2013: Occupied units: Total	Owner-occupied: Percent	Owner-occupied: Median value[1]	Median owner cost as a percent of income: With a mortgage	Median owner cost as a percent of income: Without a mortgage[2]	Renter-occupied: Median rent[3]	Renter-occupied: Median rent as a percent of income[2]	Substandard units[4] (percent)	Civilian labor force, 2014: Total	Civilian labor force, 2014: Percent change, 2013–2014	Unemployment: Total	Unemployment: Rate[5]	Civilian employment,[6] 2009–2013: Total	Percent: Management, business, science and arts	Percent: Construction, production, and maintenance occupations
	89	90	91	92	93	94	95	96	97	98	99	100	101	102	103
GEORGIA—Cont'd															
Effingham	17 830	76.6	155 400	22.2	10.5	924	28.1	3.9	26 275	0.4	1 632	6.2	23 793	30.3	29.8
Elbert	7 635	68.4	84 500	22.8	12.8	620	29.7	4.1	8 140	-2.8	711	8.7	7 522	23.1	38.6
Emanuel	8 026	65.6	69 900	25.1	13.4	576	29.6	4.0	8 557	-3.3	917	10.7	8 447	25.0	34.3
Evans	4 067	63.7	89 700	22.2	14.2	571	26.7	1.5	4 715	-0.3	309	6.6	4 191	31.8	36.1
Fannin	9 940	78.2	161 300	29.1	12.7	634	32.4	1.3	9 760	0.0	757	7.8	8 344	27.1	27.5
Fayette	37 930	82.9	231 500	23.3	10.9	1 090	30.4	3.4	53 998	1.0	3 346	6.2	48 997	43.1	18.7
Floyd	34 646	64.2	114 800	23.5	12.6	697	31.3	1.5	43 404	-0.9	3 441	7.9	38 841	30.9	27.2
Forsyth	58 080	85.6	258 200	22.4	10.0	1 141	30.6	2.1	97 533	1.0	5 171	5.3	84 654	46.4	14.0
Franklin	8 618	73.1	114 800	26.8	12.2	597	29.5	2.8	9 223	-1.3	764	8.3	8 515	26.9	32.7
Fulton	368 184	53.9	238 200	24.0	12.3	971	30.8	4.7	511 786	0.6	36 791	7.2	448 135	48.1	11.8
Gilmer	11 513	73.4	142 200	27.0	11.7	699	31.2	2.4	11 909	0.0	880	7.4	11 043	24.9	30.7
Glascock	1 189	70.8	70 000	24.8	10.7	474	26.8	4.1	1 274	-1.5	107	8.4	1 200	25.6	41.7
Glynn	31 547	61.9	162 900	24.3	10.6	823	31.6	3.2	37 373	-1.9	2 828	7.6	35 568	31.0	18.9
Gordon	19 066	66.8	116 100	23.6	11.2	664	31.5	2.8	26 047	-0.7	1 937	7.4	22 898	26.5	36.7
Grady	9 290	58.5	110 800	24.1	14.5	713	37.3	2.1	10 420	-0.5	772	7.4	8 616	30.0	31.4
Greene	6 353	75.6	145 200	26.4	13.2	660	35.6	3.4	6 367	0.3	528	8.3	5 946	23.2	31.9
Gwinnett	266 952	68.4	171 300	24.7	10.5	1 002	32.1	4.0	442 046	0.8	27 155	6.1	390 589	37.6	19.8
Habersham	14 805	76.3	137 900	24.0	12.8	659	31.5	5.4	18 876	-2.2	1 318	7.0	16 625	25.9	30.5
Hall	61 220	67.8	165 300	24.8	10.9	844	30.8	2.0	90 087	0.6	5 338	5.9	80 685	29.4	31.6
Hancock	2 742	77.7	67 800	37.5	18.7	666	39.6	5.5	2 613	-1.2	312	11.9	2 390	25.5	28.9
Haralson	10 806	70.3	106 800	22.9	13.1	721	32.8	1.6	11 977	0.1	934	7.8	10 858	29.0	32.4
Harris	11 426	86.7	203 800	22.7	13.1	893	29.9	1.4	15 615	-1.3	954	6.1	14 945	41.7	21.3
Hart	10 009	73.7	118 400	26.8	12.2	546	29.4	3.1	10 314	-1.9	801	7.8	9 552	28.7	35.0
Heard	4 321	76.0	93 200	23.2	12.9	641	31.9	2.0	5 023	0.2	398	7.9	4 589	21.8	38.4
Henry	69 238	75.0	147 500	24.5	10.4	1 061	30.7	2.6	103 815	0.4	7 550	7.3	92 015	33.1	23.0
Houston	52 330	67.1	132 900	20.1	10.0	818	29.6	3.7	66 049	-2.1	4 547	6.9	62 716	37.4	23.0
Irwin	3 277	72.4	83 400	21.6	11.4	616	31.2	2.0	3 162	-6.3	318	10.1	3 375	30.9	29.8
Jackson	21 293	77.1	161 300	24.8	11.8	775	30.2	2.8	29 658	0.0	1 783	6.0	26 235	32.6	26.7
Jasper	5 132	76.1	120 200	24.3	14.5	758	42.1	3.5	6 527	0.1	433	6.6	6 037	22.6	34.1
Jeff Davis	5 509	71.3	79 900	20.5	11.1	459	24.3	4.9	6 409	0.3	538	8.4	5 780	23.9	36.5
Jefferson	6 220	65.5	67 200	24.9	17.3	555	33.3	6.1	6 630	-3.2	766	11.6	5 296	26.2	31.4
Jenkins	3 354	69.6	63 400	27.6	14.1	505	38.3	3.2	3 289	-1.1	338	10.3	3 138	19.9	34.5
Johnson	3 250	78.9	65 000	20.6	13.8	465	29.5	1.6	3 930	-1.8	346	8.8	3 614	21.3	38.9
Jones	10 384	79.1	138 900	23.6	12.2	812	28.9	1.3	13 620	0.1	875	6.4	12 147	29.9	26.7
Lamar	6 393	70.1	122 600	24.6	13.4	645	27.7	5.2	7 799	-0.4	743	9.5	6 984	27.3	29.8
Lanier	3 725	60.9	111 800	24.2	12.0	646	30.0	2.3	3 838	0.1	302	7.9	3 375	28.0	26.5
Laurens	17 632	65.7	85 200	22.8	11.6	605	31.0	1.0	18 950	-2.5	1 803	9.5	17 127	29.7	28.0
Lee	9 773	76.2	159 000	22.0	12.8	939	29.0	1.5	14 042	-1.8	893	6.4	12 706	37.9	21.1
Liberty	23 046	51.1	126 900	24.2	11.4	914	30.3	1.6	25 798	-1.7	2 026	7.9	22 474	31.3	26.2
Lincoln	3 394	78.7	103 700	24.4	19.1	508	26.1	4.0	3 428	-0.7	286	8.3	3 183	20.6	32.8
Long	4 841	62.2	111 900	23.9	10.0	710	28.8	2.9	6 631	-0.8	485	7.3	5 304	25.1	30.5
Lowndes	39 722	53.9	133 700	24.1	11.0	776	33.6	1.7	50 839	-0.5	3 697	7.3	44 955	28.7	20.4
Lumpkin	10 999	68.2	165 900	27.4	12.4	840	35.7	2.1	15 184	0.1	997	6.6	13 338	31.8	21.2
McDuffie	8 143	66.0	106 100	25.9	12.0	607	35.9	2.5	8 963	-1.3	886	9.9	8 080	24.8	36.1
McIntosh	4 993	81.5	103 700	25.4	13.2	578	29.2	4.2	5 884	-1.0	481	8.2	5 688	28.0	34.2
Macon	4 887	66.5	65 500	26.4	14.9	540	31.5	3.3	4 618	-7.0	570	12.3	4 851	22.3	39.7
Madison	9 732	73.3	127 800	22.9	10.2	646	32.2	3.6	12 853	-0.2	831	6.5	11 746	27.2	31.1
Marion	3 000	71.8	87 000	26.3	14.1	495	31.3	4.0	3 390	-1.5	260	7.7	3 240	23.9	39.7
Meriwether	8 135	69.9	91 200	25.1	14.9	713	35.6	4.6	8 894	0.8	871	9.8	8 037	18.3	43.4
Miller	2 458	74.5	83 200	21.2	14.3	587	30.1	3.8	2 667	0.5	169	6.3	2 355	28.2	31.3
Mitchell	8 131	65.3	77 900	25.8	13.2	565	33.2	2.7	8 795	-2.5	700	8.0	8 121	25.3	34.1
Monroe	9 550	76.3	148 300	23.2	10.4	703	36.5	4.4	12 716	-0.2	853	6.7	11 134	33.8	25.0
Montgomery	3 185	69.4	74 300	30.0	11.5	529	29.3	1.2	3 920	-3.1	401	10.2	3 302	28.8	35.6
Morgan	6 513	77.1	175 700	27.5	12.8	901	30.4	7.1	8 400	0.8	551	6.6	7 742	34.6	24.6
Murray	14 092	68.9	94 100	23.8	12.4	652	31.5	2.1	15 963	0.3	1 516	9.5	15 369	22.6	41.9
Muscogee	72 243	52.6	133 300	23.6	11.4	807	30.9	2.5	81 544	-1.9	6 965	8.5	74 010	33.7	18.8
Newton	33 840	73.5	125 600	26.4	11.0	962	36.8	1.3	48 115	0.0	3 958	8.2	42 533	30.8	27.2
Oconee	11 485	78.9	238 200	21.4	11.0	862	29.0	1.4	17 130	0.2	871	5.1	15 521	48.5	14.0
Oglethorpe	5 201	77.0	120 800	23.1	13.8	715	28.2	1.8	6 738	0.2	432	6.4	6 237	29.9	36.1
Paulding	47 881	82.1	135 500	23.5	10.5	997	31.3	2.3	75 002	0.5	4 660	6.2	67 383	33.8	23.4
Peach	9 525	66.6	120 000	22.5	10.0	647	35.0	1.8	11 662	-2.0	1 119	9.6	11 250	26.9	31.9
Pickens	11 083	78.9	166 300	24.4	12.0	781	29.8	3.5	13 842	0.3	921	6.7	12 607	28.2	26.2
Pierce	6 970	73.3	79 600	23.4	12.9	531	24.9	2.0	8 038	-1.5	610	7.6	7 110	28.2	32.6
Pike	6 140	84.2	152 800	24.1	13.5	850	36.6	4.2	8 322	0.2	582	7.0	7 590	31.4	29.5
Polk	14 645	70.8	107 900	25.2	12.9	660	30.0	4.5	18 328	-0.9	1 436	7.8	15 879	22.9	39.9
Pulaski	4 034	68.0	87 300	22.1	10.2	523	28.0	1.8	4 134	-1.7	330	8.0	4 068	28.9	32.9

1. Specified owner-occupied units. 2. A value of 10.0 represents 10 percent or less; a value of 50.0 represents 50 percent or more. 3. Specified renter-occupied units.
4. Overcrowded or lacking complete plumbing facilities. 5. Percent of civilian labor force. 6. Persons 16 years old and over.

STATE County	Private nonfarm establishments, employment and payroll, 2013									Agriculture, 2012			
		Employment						Annual payroll		Farms			
											Percent with:		
	Number of establish-ments	Total	Health care and social assistance	Manufac-turing	Retail trade	Finance and insurance	Professional, scientific, and technical services	Total (mil dol)	Average per employee (dollars)	Number	Fewer than 50 acres	500 acres or more	Farm operators whose principal occu-pation is farming (percent)
	104	105	106	107	108	109	110	111	112	113	114	115	116
GEORGIA—Cont'd													
Effingham	673	7 394	880	D	1 318	158	254	275	37 168	186	48.9	9.1	35.5
Elbert	423	4 505	535	1 956	601	D	54	131	29 174	411	35.3	4.6	55.2
Emanuel	385	4 899	830	1 753	772	166	D	133	27 172	438	24.9	19.6	39.3
Evans	212	3 744	466	D	476	86	48	109	29 202	202	32.2	8.4	45.5
Fannin	553	4 496	1 049	366	977	165	203	122	27 195	198	62.6	1.0	41.4
Fayette	3 182	38 001	5 835	2 423	6 599	1 054	2 292	1 447	38 075	126	50.8	3.2	52.4
Floyd	1 950	32 861	7 668	5 800	4 282	D	768	1 166	35 476	559	44.4	3.6	36.5
Forsyth	5 513	64 358	6 793	7 124	8 763	1 851	4 705	2 811	43 680	311	68.8	0.0	53.7
Franklin	414	5 869	744	1 390	754	151	115	183	31 104	775	44.6	1.8	52.3
Fulton	33 874	723 886	74 484	17 883	49 743	54 164	93 349	46 351	64 031	187	66.3	2.1	56.7
Gilmer	522	5 524	611	D	1 093	126	163	153	27 657	296	43.9	0.7	66.2
Glascock	22	D	D	D	20	D	D	D	D	96	30.2	17.7	47.9
Glynn	2 427	29 435	4 905	2 265	4 688	700	831	968	32 869	53	77.4	1.9	45.3
Gordon	986	18 965	1 505	7 430	2 355	D	221	657	34 640	671	47.5	4.2	53.1
Grady	402	3 841	403	D	750	150	100	122	31 706	471	34.2	13.2	35.2
Greene	420	4 549	637	415	691	182	109	138	30 399	193	34.7	11.9	58.5
Gwinnett	21 547	305 293	25 584	20 416	42 410	13 853	23 880	14 034	45 968	179	67.6	1.1	37.4
Habersham	802	11 576	1 291	D	1 840	387	243	346	29 881	422	58.5	2.4	53.8
Hall	3 953	64 743	10 804	17 461	7 754	2 010	1 624	2 612	40 339	622	59.0	2.3	51.3
Hancock	73	601	D	D	102	38	D	18	30 025	133	30.8	11.3	40.6
Haralson	441	5 221	810	1 494	890	98	D	190	36 398	299	48.5	1.7	38.5
Harris	377	3 921	D	1 414	273	70	70	97	24 724	252	42.5	4.0	50.0
Hart	393	5 319	431	2 106	874	122	117	193	36 215	584	42.8	4.1	58.9
Heard	118	1 181	D	601	D	25	D	45	37 934	168	38.1	6.0	39.9
Henry	3 354	46 159	6 918	2 876	9 298	1 337	1 351	1 433	31 043	254	56.7	2.8	47.6
Houston	2 318	36 198	6 375	3 868	6 820	1 035	4 080	1 177	32 513	226	52.7	13.3	38.9
Irwin	125	1 727	611	D	144	D	29	54	31 017	373	23.6	22.3	50.7
Jackson	1 162	16 656	1 202	4 909	2 997	D	630	595	35 746	774	53.0	3.2	47.5
Jasper	147	1 383	D	369	D	56	D	35	25 637	239	39.3	7.1	51.0
Jeff Davis	239	3 344	321	1 125	695	90	36	99	29 628	192	32.8	24.0	46.4
Jefferson	300	3 935	546	977	624	160	D	128	32 410	358	23.7	20.7	40.5
Jenkins	97	946	281	D	139	36	D	28	29 795	224	24.6	23.2	41.5
Johnson	120	994	239	130	164	D	D	28	27 870	255	22.0	10.2	31.8
Jones	315	2 523	453	D	435	69	59	74	29 423	175	37.1	2.9	41.1
Lamar	234	2 811	310	506	519	D	46	85	30 128	252	44.4	4.4	33.3
Lanier	92	757	D	108	117	D	D	19	25 723	86	38.4	26.7	41.9
Laurens	1 037	14 748	3 053	2 455	2 573	494	274	507	34 361	694	26.2	12.1	32.1
Lee	369	3 810	298	209	578	202	492	135	35 486	192	28.1	19.3	46.4
Liberty	812	12 380	2 039	1 934	1 928	378	878	448	36 215	46	47.8	10.9	34.8
Lincoln	135	935	D	D	D	41	27	24	25 174	150	44.0	6.7	37.3
Long	71	252	29	D	65	D	D	5	20 960	67	34.3	4.5	46.3
Lowndes	2 640	38 679	7 320	3 124	6 316	1 017	1 185	1 149	29 710	411	50.6	5.4	46.0
Lumpkin	506	4 388	746	650	871	D	126	122	27 778	220	63.6	0.9	53.6
McDuffie	433	5 938	878	1 633	1 023	143	97	178	30 011	208	44.2	11.1	35.1
McIntosh	184	1 199	41	26	401	D	29	29	24 078	56	62.5	8.9	42.9
Macon	179	2 194	478	671	233	45	D	81	36 716	279	26.5	17.2	60.2
Madison	355	2 078	349	267	447	D	75	53	25 407	745	46.3	0.9	46.4
Marion	81	1 357	D	D	98	D	D	36	26 198	203	24.1	12.3	42.4
Meriwether	302	3 248	932	722	532	127	43	102	31 362	295	32.9	8.1	44.7
Miller	132	1 066	D	D	226	47	D	32	29 917	183	20.8	30.1	56.3
Mitchell	365	5 868	504	D	764	154	D	156	26 630	443	30.5	25.5	47.9
Monroe	507	6 593	961	D	D	127	211	205	31 041	183	41.0	8.7	38.8
Montgomery	111	924	22	107	168	26	D	25	26 819	229	30.6	13.1	36.2
Morgan	445	5 451	500	1 269	896	173	338	190	34 777	572	35.1	6.1	45.5
Murray	395	6 831	428	3 650	763	D	47	217	31 753	320	48.4	3.8	39.1
Muscogee	4 256	75 855	14 608	5 231	11 241	D	2 322	2 866	37 781	22	40.9	13.6	45.5
Newton	1 306	17 729	2 153	3 808	2 755	484	427	622	35 064	285	50.2	6.0	53.3
Oconee	1 000	9 398	1 607	563	1 750	429	715	321	34 207	375	44.8	5.1	43.2
Oglethorpe	168	1 046	106	64	D	D	D	24	23 351	406	34.7	8.1	50.2
Paulding	1 716	15 576	2 156	786	4 200	333	582	435	27 908	142	66.2	0.7	35.2
Peach	456	5 767	692	D	814	139	101	196	34 037	190	58.9	8.9	36.8
Pickens	643	5 800	1 240	643	1 176	260	151	106	33 103	262	63.0	1.1	48.6
Pierce	322	2 930	230	351	388	85	67	86	29 285	356	46.3	11.8	52.8
Pike	240	1 463	248	D	D	D	65	43	29 088	296	44.6	5.7	35.1
Polk	584	9 161	806	3 224	1 433	D	110	309	33 724	353	45.0	2.8	41.4
Pulaski	173	1 895	717	D	357	74	48	65	34 096	176	37.5	18.2	52.8

STATE County	Agriculture, 2012 (cont.)															
	Land in farms					Value of land and buildings (dollars)		Value of machinery and equipment, average per farm (dollars)	Value of products sold				Percent of farms with sales of:		Government payments	
			Acres								Percent from:					
	Acreage (1,000)	Percent change, 2007–2012	Average size of farm	Total irrigated (1,000)	Total cropland (1,000)	Average per farm	Average per acre		Total (mil dol)	Average per farm (dollars)	Crops	Livestock and poultry products	$10,000 or more	$100,000 or more	Total ($1,000)	Percent of farms
	117	118	119	120	121	122	123	124	125	126	127	128	129	130	131	132
GEORGIA—Cont'd																
Effingham	40	0.0	217	1.1	17.4	604 253	2 779	106 022	13.8	74 038	90.5	9.5	36.0	10.2	255	28.5
Elbert	57	-9.4	139	0.1	13.6	490 494	3 537	53 966	79.2	192 749	3.7	96.3	37.2	17.3	362	32.6
Emanuel	152	9.5	346	3.7	65.1	738 584	2 132	92 105	57.3	130 845	92.8	7.2	37.4	17.1	2 136	58.2
Evans	36	-31.7	178	3.0	14.7	461 465	2 587	75 366	39.8	197 055	40.8	59.2	39.1	17.8	429	33.7
Fannin	14	-26.3	70	0.2	3.7	455 722	6 505	47 121	16.1	81 293	8.0	92.0	23.7	7.1	16	5.6
Fayette	11	-6.8	91	0.1	2.7	557 341	6 110	48 786	4.0	31 635	90.4	9.6	21.4	4.0	9	6.3
Floyd	70	-17.1	126	0.8	19.6	489 283	3 898	54 420	77.0	137 828	6.9	93.1	29.3	8.6	616	19.7
Forsyth	16	-18.8	52	0.1	3.3	568 206	10 995	41 273	31.7	101 897	8.2	91.8	24.8	10.9	30	4.5
Franklin	77	-5.0	100	0.3	19.7	539 779	5 412	76 230	367.1	473 618	1.2	98.8	52.8	36.4	328	14.3
Fulton	14	-9.3	75	0.8	3.0	511 385	6 780	35 460	4.6	24 460	71.8	28.2	29.4	3.2	44	9.6
Gilmer	26	-30.1	86	0.1	5.3	530 159	6 141	88 270	213.9	722 466	1.0	99.0	56.1	44.3	140	8.4
Glascock	24	13.1	250	0.3	6.4	461 958	1 847	50 208	3.4	35 135	77.8	22.2	33.3	5.2	160	25.0
Glynn	4	-38.3	68	0.0	0.3	266 472	3 923	116 453	0.4	6 943	60.3	39.7	22.6	0.0	16	15.1
Gordon	85	7.3	127	1.8	32.8	607 225	4 797	66 523	261.2	389 270	4.9	95.1	45.5	23.1	1 200	16.5
Grady	130	9.5	277	9.2	54.4	850 864	3 077	104 682	99.2	210 690	64.1	35.9	43.1	17.4	2 083	52.4
Greene	49	-12.2	252	0.2	8.3	811 705	3 225	67 798	47.8	247 829	4.5	95.5	43.0	16.1	215	13.5
Gwinnett	10	25.4	58	0.1	2.1	604 374	10 335	53 011	12.1	67 425	92.5	7.5	27.4	4.5	33	10.1
Habersham	38	29.5	90	0.0	9.6	516 374	5 746	66 038	125.8	298 085	1.3	98.7	48.1	31.3	142	9.2
Hall	52	-9.3	84	0.1	12.3	686 416	8 212	68 188	166.3	267 434	2.1	97.9	34.9	19.8	115	8.2
Hancock	32	-15.9	240	0.2	4.8	822 805	3 424	61 669	4.5	34 008	35.8	64.2	33.1	6.8	165	18.0
Haralson	27	-22.0	90	0.0	5.4	377 763	4 212	46 033	42.6	142 539	0.8	99.2	23.4	7.7	172	9.7
Harris	32	-46.7	129	0.2	6.9	618 067	4 802	39 357	2.3	9 183	62.8	37.2	18.7	0.8	42	5.2
Hart	68	-3.0	117	1.6	21.7	605 507	5 181	79 663	208.1	356 355	3.7	96.3	46.9	26.2	793	22.8
Heard	27	14.7	161	D	3.4	559 560	3 473	58 190	36.1	215 137	2.4	97.6	38.7	17.3	70	6.5
Henry	22	-7.9	85	0.1	5.6	489 512	5 735	26 445	3.3	12 917	58.6	41.4	24.0	2.0	70	9.8
Houston	47	1.7	210	9.0	23.1	650 288	3 097	94 969	22.5	99 668	69.3	30.7	31.0	10.2	756	25.7
Irwin	148	2.1	398	31.6	95.7	1 012 070	2 542	182 375	117.5	314 944	86.3	13.7	52.5	33.0	4 677	71.0
Jackson	77	-8.8	100	0.3	17.7	553 712	5 539	69 008	189.4	244 758	2.9	97.1	39.7	20.8	502	14.7
Jasper	44	-22.3	183	0.4	8.1	634 649	3 462	64 134	25.2	105 586	13.7	86.3	28.0	4.2	114	9.2
Jeff Davis	79	35.7	411	9.8	44.5	1 364 479	3 321	119 953	51.9	270 260	78.6	21.4	43.8	26.0	1 115	49.0
Jefferson	146	33.7	407	22.3	74.7	812 567	1 998	116 911	72.9	203 567	72.7	27.3	43.0	22.6	2 695	65.4
Jenkins	91	7.9	408	14.2	44.1	766 795	1 879	141 826	37.5	167 295	90.5	9.5	37.5	20.5	1 808	68.3
Johnson	57	-14.2	224	1.7	15.1	401 690	1 796	53 239	6.7	26 443	78.9	21.2	28.2	3.9	405	45.9
Jones	23	-28.9	132	0.0	6.3	417 766	3 176	68 857	10.4	59 269	5.3	94.7	23.4	5.1	156	9.1
Lamar	35	-0.6	141	1.7	12.0	540 194	3 837	77 290	54.4	215 821	19.7	80.3	34.9	14.3	268	21.4
Lanier	42	-21.7	484	6.9	19.7	1 649 140	3 408	207 430	21.2	246 209	98.1	1.9	39.5	25.6	824	58.1
Laurens	184	11.7	265	10.3	60.7	544 447	2 051	74 219	35.9	51 713	84.5	15.5	31.0	7.8	2 023	61.1
Lee	105	-16.5	549	16.9	52.7	1 579 948	2 877	164 563	72.5	377 734	D	D	39.6	19.3	1 529	59.9
Liberty	6	-33.7	135	0.0	0.6	285 370	2 111	33 000	0.3	6 761	47.9	52.1	28.3	0.0	23	17.4
Lincoln	24	-14.5	157	0.0	3.6	436 273	2 772	62 560	4.1	27 020	12.9	87.1	22.7	3.3	127	20.7
Long	10	-21.9	153	D	2.8	377 328	2 463	58 806	11.5	172 179	6.1	93.9	35.8	11.9	120	40.3
Lowndes	65	-4.4	158	8.0	25.4	559 107	3 538	72 920	31.1	75 786	79.1	20.9	30.4	7.8	464	40.1
Lumpkin	17	-21.1	79	0.1	3.0	710 636	8 994	47 768	52.5	238 436	3.8	96.2	37.7	18.6	71	6.8
McDuffie	38	5.2	183	0.3	8.2	523 361	2 866	40 394	27.8	133 582	D	D	26.0	4.3	251	14.4
McIntosh	17	87.3	305	0.3	1.0	786 375	2 581	88 643	3.5	62 732	63.5	36.5	37.5	12.5	5	5.4
Macon	101	-17.4	362	29.3	53.9	928 871	2 563	145 670	172.5	618 305	21.0	79.0	51.3	33.7	2 301	58.4
Madison	71	-6.9	96	0.2	19.5	536 699	5 616	54 460	213.3	286 311	1.4	98.6	43.4	21.9	611	16.8
Marion	47	1.6	233	2.1	13.2	524 025	2 246	69 227	27.4	134 818	20.9	79.1	33.5	9.9	367	41.9
Meriwether	62	-23.8	210	0.9	16.0	666 929	3 171	63 573	12.4	42 003	46.0	54.0	28.1	5.8	287	16.6
Miller	96	-5.9	523	31.7	61.0	1 289 738	2 465	233 066	69.8	381 339	91.7	8.3	63.4	36.6	2 746	67.2
Mitchell	191	-6.5	431	67.2	117.4	1 233 991	2 860	189 664	277.8	627 196	51.4	48.6	54.2	34.5	4 902	57.8
Monroe	34	-12.2	189	0.0	5.3	642 836	3 410	79 377	37.3	203 885	2.2	97.8	27.9	9.8	354	18.0
Montgomery	58	11.9	252	5.0	18.1	435 651	1 728	75 183	14.3	62 358	85.3	14.7	25.8	8.7	795	61.6
Morgan	95	2.3	165	1.4	30.0	722 206	4 371	118 593	103.0	180 004	6.9	93.1	37.6	16.1	858	32.9
Murray	47	17.6	147	0.6	18.8	629 225	4 288	81 572	78.7	246 072	14.2	85.8	40.0	17.5	273	16.6
Muscogee	4	-44.5	194	0.0	2.0	997 818	5 137	43 500	0.1	2 273	34.0	66.0	0.0	0.0	6	22.7
Newton	41	5.7	143	0.1	8.8	603 568	4 224	46 418	D	D	D	D	27.1	2.6	81	12.3
Oconee	45	-7.2	121	2.1	12.7	872 227	7 223	56 709	73.7	196 496	32.0	68.0	34.7	13.9	336	30.4
Oglethorpe	81	-6.7	199	0.7	17.2	644 724	3 239	78 283	180.7	445 118	4.6	95.4	43.3	27.3	697	24.4
Paulding	8	-26.7	59	0.0	2.4	385 641	6 544	37 458	13.9	97 789	3.6	96.4	23.9	4.9	8	8.5
Peach	35	-11.7	186	4.7	22.2	743 532	3 999	102 589	31.0	163 116	94.4	5.6	26.3	8.9	307	19.5
Pickens	17	-29.1	64	0.0	4.0	431 542	6 715	42 969	72.6	277 233	1.4	98.6	29.4	15.6	22	2.3
Pierce	78	9.0	220	10.8	44.9	523 298	2 381	125 357	64.4	180 787	61.1	38.9	42.7	16.9	2 363	46.3
Pike	38	-17.4	129	0.6	9.0	469 351	3 650	40 432	11.1	37 419	22.3	77.7	22.0	2.7	248	22.0
Polk	45	2.5	127	0.0	13.7	459 448	3 606	51 759	35.1	99 442	8.6	91.4	27.8	6.8	437	18.7
Pulaski	63	9.8	355	19.5	43.7	929 739	2 617	236 636	76.2	433 119	64.8	35.2	35.2	27.3	1 512	60.8

STATE County	Water use, 2010		Wholesale trade,[1] 2007				Retail trade,[2] 2007				Real estate and rental and leasing,[2] 2007			
	Total water withdrawn (mil gal/day)	Gallons withdrawn per person per day	Number of establish- ments	Number of employees	Sales (mil dol)	Annual payroll (mil dol)	Number of establish- ments	Number of employees	Sales (mil dol)	Annual payroll (mil dol)	Number of establish- ments	Number of employees	Receipts (mil dol)	Annual payroll (mil dol)
	133	134	135	136	137	138	139	140	141	142	143	144	145	146
GEORGIA—Cont'd														
Effingham	122.8	2 350	12	95	63.0	4.8	108	1 190	322.6	26.1	39	111	14.9	1.9
Elbert	3.5	172	44	377	106.3	11.2	88	650	137.0	13.0	10	23	1.7	0.4
Emanuel	6.6	292	27	172	93.4	4.3	104	896	184.0	17.8	19	54	6.2	1.0
Evans	5.0	455	5	D	D	D	54	451	153.9	11.5	5	21	2.4	0.3
Fannin	9.3	391	22	139	41.8	4.1	122	1 173	293.1	24.1	51	97	18.4	1.9
Fayette	12.9	121	190	1 798	877.2	81.8	464	7 315	1 390.0	147.0	216	535	80.7	15.7
Floyd	474.7	4 928	94	1 274	636.2	46.9	431	4 718	1 039.8	94.0	82	353	58.0	10.1
Forsyth	27.4	156	386	4 565	2 503.5	249.0	541	7 952	1 960.9	194.3	314	829	147.9	30.9
Franklin	4.7	214	20	334	107.8	7.5	115	985	315.1	22.2	17	31	2.1	0.5
Fulton	208.5	227	1 596	28 186	40 824.1	1 744.0	3 625	54 054	13 239.7	1 361.0	2 312	20 719	4 881.9	1 234.2
Gilmer	6.8	240	20	160	45.8	5.2	117	1 298	370.5	32.8	32	84	13.0	1.9
Glascock	0.4	130	NA	NA	NA	NA	3	14	4.8	0.2	NA	NA	NA	NA
Glynn	64.6	811	93	598	270.9	20.8	507	4 954	1 351.8	117.0	195	721	93.4	20.4
Gordon	13.5	245	70	D	D	D	249	2 641	659.4	53.3	55	170	32.2	4.4
Grady	9.8	392	23	356	201.3	10.3	87	762	168.1	15.8	21	75	6.5	1.4
Greene	4.5	280	18	90	31.9	4.1	77	638	137.1	12.9	30	54	8.0	1.7
Gwinnett	10.6	13	1 774	33 042	28 829.1	1 851.4	2 959	47 523	13 857.0	1 178.7	1 212	5 730	1 396.1	258.1
Habersham	12.2	283	35	D	D	D	175	1 983	492.1	40.0	33	240	23.3	5.0
Hall	100.2	558	252	3 732	4 914.5	170.8	630	8 134	2 220.7	206.5	229	558	125.5	18.4
Hancock	2.3	246	NA	NA	NA	NA	18	98	21.0	2.4	2	D	D	D
Haralson	3.9	136	19	174	53.2	6.6	96	969	313.1	21.1	14	40	3.5	0.6
Harris	7.1	222	10	D	D	D	51	335	66.1	5.6	15	D	D	D
Hart	4.2	168	19	227	59.0	7.3	94	879	170.7	15.6	19	72	8.9	2.3
Heard	50.5	4 267	2	D	D	D	21	113	24.8	2.1	1	D	D	D
Henry	43.0	211	101	1 508	3 076.6	71.4	556	8 291	1 907.4	183.5	210	636	116.4	19.8
Houston	34.2	245	49	D	D	D	452	6 600	1 524.3	143.9	133	510	72.6	12.5
Irwin	8.8	924	14	160	94.1	4.4	34	137	27.3	2.6	4	8	1.1	0.4
Jackson	13.5	224	63	1 050	568.8	32.8	232	2 175	559.4	47.1	62	144	19.4	2.7
Jasper	2.9	208	3	D	D	D	30	228	33.4	3.6	6	D	D	D
Jeff Davis	4.7	309	12	138	35.9	4.2	74	751	204.4	15.4	8	32	4.5	0.7
Jefferson	17.1	1 007	14	141	127.2	3.6	74	694	129.4	12.6	13	D	D	D
Jenkins	2.7	320	2	D	D	D	33	212	53.9	3.8	2	D	D	D
Johnson	2.0	196	11	D	D	D	21	145	25.2	2.2	2	D	D	D
Jones	10.3	358	12	86	42.4	4.2	42	364	70.6	6.8	18	D	D	D
Lamar	3.8	209	4	D	D	D	48	480	114.0	10.9	5	D	D	D
Lanier	2.0	199	2	D	D	D	18	D	D	D	4	D	D	D
Laurens	27.7	571	47	663	252.1	18.7	262	2 779	613.1	51.4	46	D	D	D
Lee	43.1	1 523	10	216	118.3	8.8	48	584	124.0	15.5	25	75	11.3	1.9
Liberty	16.6	262	7	D	D	D	191	1 946	539.3	41.0	51	233	28.9	5.8
Lincoln	1.8	229	6	27	9.4	0.8	31	218	39.6	3.7	4	9	0.7	0.2
Long	2.2	149	2	D	D	D	13	58	17.4	1.0	4	5	0.5	0.1
Lowndes	29.1	266	130	1 731	756.5	55.9	569	7 019	1 804.8	142.9	131	764	80.8	18.7
Lumpkin	3.3	110	12	171	37.4	5.1	86	806	206.6	18.7	28	116	15.5	2.8
McDuffie	7.0	318	10	D	D	D	109	1 196	350.4	26.9	21	90	11.3	2.2
McIntosh	1.6	110	3	D	D	D	69	574	114.0	10.2	12	15	4.1	0.3
Macon	30.8	2 088	12	80	39.5	3.1	38	282	47.9	5.1	7	28	2.6	0.6
Madison	3.3	116	16	186	57.8	5.5	60	501	119.2	8.5	13	D	D	D
Marion	3.0	347	4	D	D	D	25	337	71.7	7.2	NA	NA	NA	NA
Meriwether	1.7	79	8	D	D	D	88	682	100.8	12.0	9	28	1.8	0.5
Miller	46.8	7 639	3	37	15.0	1.2	42	257	53.5	4.3	6	8	0.6	0.1
Mitchell	67.4	2 870	27	302	169.2	8.2	102	816	151.0	14.6	15	70	5.4	1.4
Monroe	68.9	2 607	19	D	D	D	71	526	114.4	10.7	17	D	D	D
Montgomery	2.5	270	8	D	D	D	22	100	24.7	2.1	4	6	0.6	0.0
Morgan	5.4	299	16	200	54.9	5.7	91	1 014	276.4	21.1	27	63	7.8	1.5
Murray	3.9	97	29	338	89.4	12.4	101	818	218.9	18.1	11	40	4.8	1.0
Muscogee	44.1	232	173	1 906	1 173.6	81.2	845	12 642	2 889.2	260.7	259	1 549	292.8	54.0
Newton	14.3	143	52	512	226.6	19.6	223	2 699	679.4	57.2	70	256	33.2	5.8
Oconee	7.3	222	28	254	72.9	10.7	101	1 557	326.4	33.3	60	114	14.4	3.5
Oglethorpe	2.2	148	8	27	8.5	0.9	36	256	69.6	4.7	2	D	D	D
Paulding	2.1	15	62	366	176.5	15.2	233	3 920	973.0	83.7	78	243	44.9	9.5
Peach	10.4	376	19	D	D	D	118	945	317.4	22.1	25	61	11.7	2.1
Pickens	4.1	138	21	100	112.0	4.4	110	1 335	320.5	27.0	49	105	15.3	3.0
Pierce	4.1	219	18	D	D	D	67	460	99.7	8.7	6	22	1.6	0.3
Pike	8.1	453	9	97	16.7	2.9	35	183	33.9	3.1	9	33	2.8	0.4
Polk	7.8	187	17	D	D	D	145	1 500	314.7	29.7	23	68	6.9	1.4
Pulaski	18.0	1 495	8	80	21.4	1.8	47	391	84.5	7.5	12	22	2.2	0.3

1. Merchant wholesalers, except manufacturers' sales branches and offices. 2. Employer establishments.

STATE County	Professional, scientific, and technical services,[1] 2007				Manufacturing, 2007				Accommodation and food services, 2007			
	Number of establishments	Number of employees	Receipts (mil dol)	Annual payroll (mil dol)	Number of establishments	Number of employees	Receipts (mil dol)	Annual payroll (mil dol)	Number of establishments	Number of employees	Sales (mil dol)	Annual payroll (mil dol)
	147	148	149	150	151	152	153	154	155	156	157	158
GEORGIA—Cont'd												
Effingham	56	D	D	D	25	D	D	D	49	637	26.1	6.6
Elbert	26	84	5.8	1.5	108	2 522	515.2	82.4	29	437	14.6	4.3
Emanuel	27	189	26.3	9.6	30	1 936	448.4	51.9	33	406	14.8	3.5
Evans	12	60	5.1	1.6	14	1 895	354.8	47.9	17	161	6.4	1.7
Fannin	41	183	12.8	5.2	NA	NA	NA	NA	59	651	29.7	8.4
Fayette	431	D	D	D	113	3 690	1 744.7	170.2	204	4 586	171.2	49.2
Floyd	174	703	80.1	24.8	109	7 726	3 346.1	312.7	198	3 423	144.3	38.1
Forsyth	855	4 197	650.9	207.2	223	8 127	2 318.6	329.8	240	3 904	183.1	48.4
Franklin	31	D	D	D	41	2 180	430.4	69.3	45	664	22.8	6.3
Fulton	6 560	77 813	16 269.2	5 882.0	677	24 993	10 428.5	1 051.8	2 782	66 711	4 133.8	1 154.9
Gilmer	52	207	14.8	5.4	34	2 099	354.6	64.1	57	872	36.6	10.8
Glascock	1	D	D	D	NA	NA	NA	NA	2	D	D	D
Glynn	268	D	D	D	73	2 554	D	123.6	251	7 394	398.3	162.5
Gordon	73	232	23.8	8.3	104	6 291	2 528.1	214.2	89	1 358	62.5	16.2
Grady	14	58	5.6	1.5	22	771	183.2	28.0	26	364	13.1	2.7
Greene	39	120	15.6	5.5	14	533	673.2	20.7	27	897	60.6	15.9
Gwinnett	3 256	D	D	D	772	22 797	6 480.3	1 030.7	1 629	27 397	1 264.7	353.6
Habersham	59	250	23.8	7.1	58	4 357	968.5	140.7	81	995	41.8	10.5
Hall	419	D	D	D	265	17 296	6 069.0	602.5	272	4 930	224.1	62.5
Hancock	3	D	D	D	NA	NA	NA	NA	9	28	1.0	0.3
Haralson	36	141	13.6	4.2	37	2 239	952.1	87.8	34	409	14.6	3.7
Harris	32	D	D	D	20	693	D	D	38	731	43.5	14.2
Hart	34	118	10.9	3.5	31	1 246	244.8	48.7	36	480	16.8	4.4
Heard	7	D	D	D	NA	NA	NA	NA	6	50	1.9	0.5
Henry	305	D	D	D	82	3 092	1 695.8	122.6	348	6 217	243.2	63.1
Houston	281	D	D	D	64	2 511	1 422.9	97.2	248	5 246	206.1	54.8
Irwin	5	30	2.9	0.9	NA	NA	NA	NA	6	97	2.6	0.7
Jackson	98	417	50.4	17.0	77	5 675	1 801.5	202.3	58	811	33.3	9.3
Jasper	8	D	D	D	19	839	187.5	27.7	11	104	3.4	0.9
Jeff Davis	17	87	3.9	1.8	24	1 229	242.9	34.3	21	364	9.9	2.6
Jefferson	13	44	3.0	0.9	30	1 343	303.6	47.6	26	327	11.2	2.6
Jenkins	4	13	0.9	0.4	10	665	116.9	20.6	13	140	3.8	1.0
Johnson	3	8	0.4	0.2	NA	NA	NA	NA	6	39	1.4	0.4
Jones	32	95	7.3	2.9	NA	NA	NA	NA	20	369	13.4	3.5
Lamar	20	83	4.2	1.2	NA	NA	NA	NA	28	379	12.0	3.3
Lanier	6	D	D	D	NA	NA	NA	NA	10	D	D	D
Laurens	73	322	29.7	11.1	47	3 870	D	D	97	1 608	66.8	17.8
Lee	23	79	9.0	2.3	NA	NA	NA	NA	16	205	6.9	2.0
Liberty	54	D	D	D	17	D	D	D	95	1 665	62.9	15.9
Lincoln	9	30	2.5	1.0	NA	NA	NA	NA	11	106	5.2	1.0
Long	3	D	D	D	NA	NA	NA	NA	6	102	1.8	0.6
Lowndes	211	D	D	D	106	4 324	2 237.8	162.9	252	5 498	209.5	55.3
Lumpkin	37	121	9.3	4.5	28	1 063	207.8	30.8	53	757	33.4	9.1
McDuffie	28	D	D	D	36	1 983	D	67.7	41	637	23.6	5.6
McIntosh	16	D	D	D	NA	NA	NA	NA	40	531	19.8	5.4
Macon	9	16	1.5	0.6	17	733	397.4	32.9	19	191	5.6	1.5
Madison	30	D	D	D	30	505	D	17.2	23	182	7.2	1.7
Marion	6	D	D	D	NA	NA	NA	NA	7	18	1.0	0.2
Meriwether	13	41	3.7	1.2	15	812	233.4	33.8	31	434	14.8	4.5
Miller	9	37	1.4	0.5	NA	NA	NA	NA	10	96	2.9	0.9
Mitchell	26	183	8.8	4.1	19	D	D	69.8	29	333	15.4	4.4
Monroe	42	99	9.0	2.8	19	855	118.1	25.9	42	668	23.8	7.2
Montgomery	7	12	0.8	0.2	NA	NA	NA	NA	7	61	2.9	0.7
Morgan	46	222	23.2	8.9	27	1 105	239.5	40.0	56	1 004	40.3	10.8
Murray	20	D	D	D	82	5 446	1 605.7	153.3	43	573	24.6	6.6
Muscogee	348	D	D	D	141	7 055	2 111.4	266.7	418	9 898	428.2	120.7
Newton	127	565	48.1	16.7	90	4 175	2 205.1	187.4	103	1 714	93.5	20.3
Oconee	145	709	58.9	25.7	31	747	D	25.4	58	946	38.9	9.6
Oglethorpe	18	D	D	D	NA	NA	NA	NA	9	45	1.8	0.5
Paulding	141	582	59.3	24.0	61	1 114	255.4	38.9	123	2 863	109.0	31.0
Peach	32	117	8.2	2.7	30	4 378	1 057.8	124.1	49	761	28.7	6.8
Pickens	83	177	18.3	6.4	44	694	104.8	23.0	49	719	27.8	7.8
Pierce	23	D	D	D	NA	NA	NA	NA	19	343	8.7	2.4
Pike	24	59	6.1	1.7	NA	NA	NA	NA	12	53	2.4	0.6
Polk	34	D	D	D	35	3 271	698.6	117.8	63	843	35.2	8.7
Pulaski	12	80	5.0	2.2	NA	NA	NA	NA	21	432	13.7	3.5

1. Establishment subject to federal tax.

STATE County	Health care and social assistance, 2007				Other services, 2007				Nonemployer businesses, 2013		Value of residential construction authorized by building permits, 2014	
	Number of establish-ments	Number of employees	Receipts (mil dol)	Annual payroll (mil dol)	Number of establish-ments	Number of employees	Receipts (mil dol)	Annual payroll (mil dol)	Number	Receipts (mil dol)	New Construction ($1,000)	Number of housing units
	159	160	161	162	163	164	165	166	167	168	169	170
GEORGIA—Cont'd												
Effingham	46	D	D	D	43	213	21.2	5.4	3 311	119.7	82 776	482
Elbert	39	615	41.6	16.2	27	84	7.5	2.1	1 369	47.3	1 219	12
Emanuel	52	897	54.7	24.8	30	127	12.0	2.5	1 849	67.4	478	7
Evans	20	448	32.8	14.4	16	114	8.4	2.2	692	22.9	2 270	20
Fannin	67	865	78.7	33.2	26	161	11.2	2.9	2 648	110.3	35 006	168
Fayette	301	4 309	437.3	158.9	211	1 273	101.7	31.7	9 875	438.1	76 357	314
Floyd	259	7 910	785.1	310.9	108	D	D	D	6 748	237.1	14 421	75
Forsyth	368	4 193	403.4	152.7	274	1 618	308.6	83.9	17 610	848.9	378 883	3 194
Franklin	38	768	56.6	21.8	28	171	15.6	3.5	1 591	61.1	300	2
Fulton	3 204	67 143	8 483.0	3 072.6	2 139	20 887	3 560.9	707.4	99 463	4 918.0	1 177 766	8 098
Gilmer	45	625	43.7	16.5	49	424	21.9	6.0	2 567	97.3	13 255	102
Glascock	5	D	D	D	3	D	D	D	172	6.2	NA	NA
Glynn	265	4 708	897.7	183.8	151	912	72.1	21.1	6 218	264.6	112 632	427
Gordon	74	1 314	133.1	51.2	50	355	32.4	10.3	3 429	148.3	10 387	63
Grady	36	452	41.7	13.6	29	153	14.2	3.7	1 483	50.2	4 347	31
Greene	35	393	33.9	13.4	24	98	11.7	3.9	1 439	58.5	62 642	203
Gwinnett	1 583	21 698	2 302.0	879.7	1 431	8 527	813.1	257.3	90 033	3 569.9	591 439	3 379
Habersham	87	1 406	93.6	41.9	46	170	15.2	4.7	2 865	103.2	7 785	35
Hall	398	8 599	1 046.7	384.6	272	1 384	136.1	36.5	13 987	599.8	120 068	722
Hancock	8	D	D	D	7	20	1.5	0.3	500	12.3	1 996	15
Haralson	41	608	53.4	22.9	39	171	11.0	3.1	2 025	73.3	4 073	23
Harris	23	212	11.1	4.6	19	D	D	D	2 338	97.4	29 572	113
Hart	36	697	50.1	20.7	23	80	5.8	1.3	1 798	62.1	6 194	35
Heard	6	D	D	D	7	D	D	D	705	28.3	1 826	15
Henry	351	5 004	459.2	183.6	242	1 172	91.9	27.6	17 787	586.9	207 535	1 047
Houston	256	4 784	461.8	176.5	166	932	67.1	17.0	8 976	263.9	118 054	602
Irwin	18	529	39.7	13.8	9	D	D	D	561	17.8	1 785	10
Jackson	63	975	58.9	30.1	67	230	23.7	7.1	4 692	172.7	95 975	455
Jasper	13	169	12.5	5.4	13	D	D	D	1 055	37.2	7 101	53
Jeff Davis	18	264	19.8	7.6	13	39	1.8	0.6	852	30.4	220	1
Jefferson	25	501	41.1	13.6	19	57	3.3	0.9	1 139	34.4	671	5
Jenkins	8	258	12.8	6.3	10	23	3.1	0.6	545	18.2	1 000	10
Johnson	11	D	D	D	9	29	2.3	0.7	599	19.8	0	0
Jones	24	D	D	D	22	57	3.6	1.0	1 890	66.3	5 744	28
Lamar	21	204	18.2	5.5	13	147	10.7	4.0	1 145	33.9	2 337	18
Lanier	15	D	D	D	4	D	D	D	516	18.8	2 052	15
Laurens	133	D	D	D	66	335	24.6	6.6	3 871	136.4	719	9
Lee	25	322	19.4	7.1	27	141	11.6	3.5	1 950	68.3	20 823	175
Liberty	66	D	D	D	68	D	D	D	2 805	81.1	50 602	242
Lincoln	6	33	2.1	1.1	13	71	5.1	1.1	502	18.0	3 727	17
Long	4	D	D	D	4	D	D	D	532	13.8	NA	NA
Lowndes	321	7 074	593.7	243.1	162	794	64.4	21.3	6 635	341.4	52 880	379
Lumpkin	53	609	52.9	19.8	33	108	9.5	2.3	2 309	88.9	20 686	91
McDuffie	48	1 011	55.9	26.0	35	120	39.1	3.3	1 412	45.5	3 330	19
McIntosh	13	D	D	D	15	33	3.4	0.8	884	39.6	4 690	24
Macon	21	460	37.2	13.5	9	D	D	D	793	19.0	574	3
Madison	17	D	D	D	21	D	D	D	2 080	67.7	14 229	66
Marion	7	D	D	D	5	D	D	D	436	12.8	896	10
Meriwether	36	717	52.9	25.7	18	48	4.0	1.0	1 494	42.1	4 842	24
Miller	14	388	24.0	11.9	10	36	2.7	0.7	380	12.0	0	0
Mitchell	25	500	35.8	14.2	33	191	13.8	3.8	1 312	43.3	2 025	10
Monroe	39	D	D	D	30	130	16.3	4.0	1 875	78.2	18 075	77
Montgomery	5	15	1.0	0.4	4	10	0.8	0.3	544	15.3	1 515	11
Morgan	28	500	29.7	15.4	35	135	11.8	2.8	1 820	74.2	11 856	52
Murray	33	505	39.2	14.5	28	113	9.1	2.8	1 756	69.4	4 733	22
Muscogee	555	13 088	1 332.5	521.1	353	2 323	178.4	54.7	13 691	411.8	53 634	585
Newton	133	2 037	203.9	75.8	90	414	33.3	9.6	8 657	249.1	29 715	181
Oconee	81	D	D	D	47	474	42.8	13.1	3 547	161.2	80 203	299
Oglethorpe	10	D	D	D	11	D	D	D	980	29.8	405	27
Paulding	109	1 492	105.5	40.6	108	455	30.3	9.8	10 643	354.0	100 140	930
Peach	40	D	D	D	31	D	D	D	1 823	62.7	15 431	161
Pickens	50	1 003	72.6	28.5	42	188	15.7	5.0	2 864	117.4	14 075	53
Pierce	27	298	11.5	6.2	26	68	4.5	1.0	1 152	39.4	3 986	38
Pike	15	D	D	D	15	57	3.4	1.0	1 352	59.3	4 501	26
Polk	42	891	53.3	23.2	45	495	46.0	11.2	2 581	78.2	1 645	10
Pulaski	24	786	61.5	28.0	10	14	1.0	0.3	671	18.4	1 331	17

STATE County	Government employment and payroll, 2012									Local government finances, 2012				
			March payroll (percent of total)							General revenue				
												Taxes		
													Per capita[1] (dollars)	
	Full-time equivalent employees	March payroll (dollars)	Adminis-tration, judicial, and legal	Police and Corrections	Fire Protection	Highways and transpor-tation	Health and Welfare	Natural resources and utilities	Education and libraries	Total (mil dol)	Inter-govern-mental (mil dol)	Total (mil dol)	Total	Property
	171	172	173	174	175	176	177	178	179	180	181	182	183	184
GEORGIA—Cont'd														
Effingham	2 486	7 934 109	4.0	6.9	1.7	0.8	16.1	2.9	65.1	191.3	66.5	72.8	1 366	843
Elbert	1 023	2 910 130	6.0	7.4	1.7	2.3	20.0	5.2	54.4	74.4	24.4	21.3	1 084	728
Emanuel	1 380	4 099 290	4.7	6.6	1.2	3.3	32.4	1.6	49.5	134.4	38.4	25.2	1 102	650
Evans	411	1 161 088	7.5	7.5	1.2	2.3	0.9	7.4	72.6	32.8	16.8	10.9	1 022	548
Fannin	760	2 415 781	6.9	7.2	1.6	5.7	4.3	5.2	68.0	63.1	21.3	34.9	1 484	927
Fayette	4 677	16 227 469	6.0	9.6	6.9	2.0	0.0	3.4	70.7	331.0	78.7	204.0	1 897	1 391
Floyd	3 631	12 476 709	5.7	9.3	4.2	4.2	1.7	5.5	67.7	620.3	284.0	151.4	1 574	957
Forsyth	5 440	15 768 647	8.4	9.3	5.1	2.1	0.8	5.4	66.7	548.8	158.2	323.5	1 721	1 160
Franklin	907	2 573 274	6.9	12.5	0.0	2.6	4.2	5.9	64.4	64.2	24.6	29.2	1 334	759
Fulton	43 801	165 333 873	9.4	12.0	4.7	15.4	3.4	6.1	47.6	5 335.6	1 131.9	2 739.7	2 802	1 941
Gilmer	920	2 851 278	9.0	12.0	2.0	3.3	4.8	1.4	67.0	76.9	24.5	43.0	1 524	1 036
Glascock	129	342 830	4.9	4.2	0.0	3.5	1.7	4.2	80.7	8.3	4.5	3.0	970	705
Glynn	4 919	18 972 711	4.6	6.1	2.8	0.9	46.3	3.8	35.3	515.4	78.5	158.8	1 960	1 234
Gordon	2 032	7 129 189	6.2	7.7	4.0	2.9	0.3	5.2	71.1	172.1	62.6	78.3	1 404	810
Grady	1 132	2 874 976	6.5	7.8	2.0	1.9	2.7	6.1	69.6	66.6	29.6	25.7	1 009	623
Greene	269	680 713	19.0	33.4	1.8	17.6	6.5	14.2	0.0	58.7	12.0	38.3	2 379	1 693
Gwinnett	27 778	103 170 776	5.7	8.0	3.3	0.8	1.5	3.8	75.9	2 774.6	950.1	1 287.6	1 529	1 100
Habersham	3 305	10 231 305	4.4	3.6	1.2	1.1	19.8	2.2	67.1	181.0	64.5	53.3	1 225	714
Hall	6 523	22 620 107	6.4	9.1	7.3	1.6	4.4	4.9	65.4	563.5	217.3	266.2	1 436	890
Hancock	382	962 206	6.0	11.2	0.0	2.9	5.0	4.4	68.0	28.6	10.2	16.3	1 811	1 568
Haralson	1 277	3 955 709	6.4	9.3	4.8	2.9	2.1	6.3	67.7	88.2	38.2	39.1	1 375	852
Harris	1 034	3 285 198	4.4	8.8	0.1	2.2	4.9	3.4	74.7	80.5	24.1	43.3	1 331	974
Hart	900	2 651 269	5.4	6.4	1.0	2.6	1.4	3.1	73.5	59.3	20.8	30.8	1 208	771
Heard	504	1 507 476	3.9	8.3	9.3	3.8	1.5	6.9	62.5	42.2	12.2	27.6	2 376	938
Henry	7 960	25 579 364	7.4	7.5	4.5	1.4	1.0	5.6	71.5	718.9	328.0	305.3	1 460	969
Houston	5 500	18 181 428	5.3	9.1	2.9	2.2	2.3	3.3	73.1	461.3	189.3	203.0	1 389	803
Irwin	623	2 698 793	4.3	21.9	4.3	7.8	23.1	6.2	32.3	40.3	14.0	9.7	1 013	702
Jackson	2 530	7 918 962	6.3	11.0	0.4	1.4	3.5	4.7	71.2	198.5	64.2	107.0	1 767	1 201
Jasper	596	1 714 273	5.5	6.8	0.6	0.7	23.1	3.8	56.7	44.3	14.2	16.0	1 176	880
Jeff Davis	671	2 209 748	5.1	5.1	1.9	1.6	22.2	2.5	60.6	64.7	22.7	14.5	959	451
Jefferson	926	2 709 948	7.4	10.5	1.1	0.9	22.0	2.9	53.3	61.2	24.1	20.9	1 273	787
Jenkins	429	1 431 503	7.7	9.7	1.7	6.7	21.4	3.0	48.9	28.0	15.0	8.5	923	581
Johnson	327	789 670	7.1	8.8	1.3	2.1	5.8	3.8	70.5	20.2	10.3	7.8	788	516
Jones	1 142	2 976 385	4.8	7.6	0.3	3.1	1.4	2.8	79.5	77.2	38.1	33.3	1 165	839
Lamar	637	1 432 522	7.9	19.7	2.3	3.0	3.1	7.3	55.8	44.4	15.3	19.3	1 069	698
Lanier	309	907 306	5.1	6.3	0.4	4.9	0.6	0.8	81.4	22.8	12.3	8.7	840	599
Laurens	2 333	6 680 665	4.4	7.5	2.2	2.2	14.7	4.0	62.8	168.6	86.7	55.3	1 151	626
Lee	1 281	3 572 458	6.0	9.8	3.1	2.1	3.3	1.7	73.1	83.1	33.8	38.4	1 337	897
Liberty	2 620	8 517 567	5.5	9.7	1.7	0.8	17.6	1.9	58.9	231.2	86.6	70.0	1 070	640
Lincoln	343	943 673	7.0	8.3	0.1	4.6	4.7	4.1	70.2	24.9	9.7	11.6	1 495	1 126
Long	484	1 237 309	6.2	6.7	0.0	3.9	0.5	1.1	81.0	41.0	26.8	10.9	678	497
Lowndes	6 045	19 639 563	3.1	7.2	1.9	1.4	42.6	2.7	39.9	581.5	129.5	139.2	1 215	637
Lumpkin	914	2 710 822	6.9	9.8	4.9	4.4	1.3	4.6	66.2	65.6	21.0	35.6	1 164	771
McDuffie	1 115	3 376 988	4.5	5.8	1.9	1.8	17.5	5.3	60.7	89.6	43.8	29.4	1 357	750
McIntosh	543	1 451 916	10.8	16.2	0.3	3.5	4.5	2.5	58.6	37.8	12.8	19.7	1 422	1 061
Macon	468	1 330 912	6.2	9.8	1.1	3.9	3.2	8.0	66.6	35.4	15.4	15.7	1 103	778
Madison	1 012	3 107 942	5.4	7.1	0.0	1.8	4.3	1.4	78.7	69.1	34.5	27.9	998	714
Marion	276	887 260	6.5	7.1	0.0	4.2	3.2	3.5	74.6	27.1	16.3	8.1	933	664
Meriwether	1 203	3 245 971	5.5	9.3	0.8	1.8	22.0	3.1	55.0	84.2	30.1	25.7	1 210	867
Miller	558	1 697 352	5.4	6.0	0.2	1.6	45.2	3.2	35.5	39.7	21.9	7.8	1 308	873
Mitchell	1 021	2 901 088	6.0	10.9	2.5	2.8	3.0	6.3	61.9	77.9	28.7	31.6	1 366	899
Monroe	1 172	3 579 175	4.2	11.4	1.2	4.4	12.1	3.3	61.1	93.8	21.4	53.1	1 992	1 362
Montgomery	230	587 331	8.4	7.4	0.5	6.6	3.1	1.4	72.5	17.7	8.0	7.4	835	546
Morgan	953	3 020 860	6.6	5.9	0.9	3.0	17.7	3.8	59.5	58.7	20.9	31.5	1 763	1 132
Murray	1 247	3 919 836	4.1	6.6	2.6	2.5	1.1	1.8	77.8	92.6	46.9	36.7	932	519
Muscogee	9 038	29 241 738	4.1	12.0	4.8	2.6	7.5	7.2	60.0	741.6	293.1	273.0	1 376	1 010
Newton	4 446	13 949 576	4.8	7.6	3.4	1.7	14.6	4.6	61.7	372.2	178.8	121.8	1 200	823
Oconee	1 252	3 915 501	7.1	6.7	0.4	2.2	1.3	3.9	74.9	100.2	32.7	57.1	1 698	1 106
Oglethorpe	532	1 614 557	5.6	5.6	0.8	1.8	3.5	1.4	81.2	31.8	13.7	15.1	1 034	808
Paulding	5 393	14 332 833	3.2	7.3	2.8	1.5	0.5	2.6	80.1	356.7	171.7	150.3	1 038	665
Peach	1 087	3 443 843	6.7	12.0	3.0	1.1	15.5	2.4	56.5	102.9	28.0	38.7	1 399	851
Pickens	1 155	3 419 594	7.3	9.4	3.0	2.8	3.9	5.3	64.6	83.1	24.1	47.4	1 618	1 120
Pierce	624	2 237 998	1.9	4.1	0.0	2.0	2.7	2.2	84.6	46.0	24.2	18.2	963	622
Pike	638	1 686 429	6.9	9.0	0.0	3.2	0.0	2.0	78.9	39.8	18.6	17.9	1 005	826
Polk	1 548	4 904 910	5.6	10.2	2.6	2.4	1.4	4.0	66.8	116.2	53.1	48.3	1 172	717
Pulaski	358	909 842	9.2	11.0	3.6	4.3	1.3	4.5	64.6	27.3	12.1	11.6	990	649

1. Based on the resident population estimated as of July 1 of the year shown.

STATE County	Local government finances, 2012 (cont.)									Government employment, 2013			Presidential election,[2] 2012		
	Direct general expenditure							Debt outstanding					Percent of vote cast:		
			Percent of total for:												
	Total (mil dol)	Per capita[1] (dollars)	Educa-tion	Health and hospitals	Police protec-tion	Public welfare	High-ways	Total (mil dol)	Per capita[1] (dollars)	Federal civilian	Federal military	State and local	Demo-cratic	Republi-can	All other
	185	186	187	188	189	190	191	192	193	194	195	196	197	198	199
GEORGIA—Cont'd															
Effingham	215.1	4 037	47.5	28.2	3.7	0.3	2.7	102.6	1 925	61	157	2 786	24.3	75.0	0.7
Elbert	78.1	3 967	39.3	26.1	4.2	0.7	4.5	17.7	901	128	56	1 175	40.5	58.5	1.0
Emanuel	128.4	5 609	29.9	50.2	2.4	0.2	2.9	34.5	1 507	64	63	1 930	37.2	62.0	0.8
Evans	39.2	3 664	67.4	1.1	4.4	0.0	3.4	8.1	760	38	30	658	35.6	63.9	0.5
Fannin	65.9	2 803	54.6	3.5	4.0	0.5	11.3	12.3	524	44	69	906	24.7	73.8	1.6
Fayette	360.7	3 354	57.2	1.1	6.8	0.2	4.4	279.1	2 596	483	349	4 456	34.2	64.9	0.9
Floyd	658.4	6 846	27.4	47.2	2.2	0.1	2.6	238.0	2 474	211	270	5 773	31.2	67.6	1.1
Forsyth	529.3	2 816	59.8	0.4	6.1	0.5	4.9	349.8	1 861	174	567	6 348	20.4	78.5	1.1
Franklin	58.5	2 670	56.1	3.0	9.3	0.4	6.3	16.0	730	48	62	1 043	23.7	75.2	1.1
Fulton	4 905.9	5 017	36.2	1.9	6.5	2.3	2.4	20 181.5	20 640	25 064	2 860	77 969	67.2	32.1	0.7
Gilmer	71.0	2 520	60.5	0.4	6.0	0.2	2.7	75.3	2 672	80	82	1 144	23.4	75.4	1.1
Glascock	8.8	2 789	73.4	1.9	3.4	1.5	6.9	0.4	113	0	0	199	14.7	84.2	1.1
Glynn	522.7	6 452	28.7	45.8	4.4	0.1	1.6	353.6	4 364	1 660	274	6 908	38.0	61.4	0.6
Gordon	172.7	3 096	59.5	1.2	6.0	0.4	3.7	114.7	2 057	86	160	2 695	24.2	74.5	1.3
Grady	73.3	2 881	53.7	1.8	4.8	0.0	6.5	41.6	1 635	76	73	1 126	37.8	61.7	0.5
Greene	66.3	4 122	48.1	0.3	8.8	1.2	6.7	33.3	2 068	44	47	771	42.2	57.2	0.6
Gwinnett	2 810.6	3 338	58.1	1.5	5.7	0.1	4.5	3 709.8	4 406	2 392	2 486	32 013	44.5	54.7	0.8
Habersham	168.2	3 865	41.0	30.6	3.5	0.3	3.1	147.2	3 382	105	119	2 861	19.6	79.5	1.0
Hall	566.0	3 053	55.8	6.1	4.5	0.8	2.5	1 522.9	8 213	449	539	9 688	24.1	75.0	0.8
Hancock	25.7	2 852	59.1	3.1	5.4	1.7	5.0	11.1	1 235	16	22	773	81.4	18.3	0.3
Haralson	90.4	3 182	64.8	1.4	5.5	0.3	2.9	42.6	1 502	44	82	1 568	20.3	78.0	1.7
Harris	77.2	2 371	65.4	3.4	5.0	0.0	4.2	45.3	1 392	54	94	1 155	28.1	71.4	0.5
Hart	58.4	2 289	53.1	3.2	5.6	0.4	4.4	16.0	628	85	72	1 073	33.6	65.4	1.0
Heard	36.5	3 133	56.5	4.4	5.1	2.9	4.3	21.9	1 878	12	33	652	24.7	74.2	1.2
Henry	565.4	2 705	60.8	0.4	5.5	0.9	6.1	704.9	3 372	960	613	7 878	45.9	53.4	0.7
Houston	446.8	3 057	57.5	4.7	6.4	0.0	5.5	209.8	1 435	15 572	4 094	9 257	39.5	59.7	0.8
Irwin	42.7	4 450	40.9	35.7	4.1	0.2	7.1	10.1	1 048	22	25	794	31.3	68.1	0.7
Jackson	211.8	3 497	53.3	2.4	5.8	0.3	7.5	505.9	8 352	136	175	2 853	21.6	77.4	1.0
Jasper	43.8	3 215	45.0	24.5	4.1	0.6	6.1	15.0	1 099	20	39	616	32.8	66.3	0.9
Jeff Davis	60.0	3 960	38.1	36.0	3.5	0.2	7.6	20.3	1 337	26	43	823	25.7	73.3	1.0
Jefferson	64.9	3 950	43.6	21.7	4.9	1.0	3.6	24.3	1 480	40	46	1 050	57.4	42.3	0.3
Jenkins	26.9	2 917	51.4	4.2	4.4	0.8	9.3	4.9	533	19	24	537	43.1	56.3	0.6
Johnson	19.4	1 960	61.3	3.0	5.3	0.3	6.1	0.9	88	17	23	629	32.8	66.5	0.6
Jones	72.0	2 520	65.4	0.6	5.4	0.6	6.1	11.5	403	33	82	1 131	36.8	62.6	0.7
Lamar	47.0	2 605	52.2	0.8	7.4	0.7	3.3	56.0	3 100	39	49	1 075	35.8	63.4	0.8
Lanier	22.1	2 125	69.1	0.5	7.1	0.4	6.2	11.4	1 096	15	30	469	37.0	62.2	0.8
Laurens	182.6	3 801	47.1	15.1	4.8	0.3	4.0	54.7	1 138	1 317	137	2 828	39.0	60.5	0.6
Lee	84.5	2 939	66.3	3.3	5.2	0.0	3.2	70.7	2 459	37	82	1 493	23.7	75.8	0.5
Liberty	250.0	3 818	53.4	19.3	4.8	0.0	2.3	82.6	1 262	4 129	17 890	3 409	64.0	35.6	0.5
Lincoln	23.8	3 082	54.0	3.7	3.6	2.7	6.6	35.4	4 577	13	22	418	37.4	61.8	0.8
Long	36.7	2 284	68.5	0.5	5.4	1.5	8.2	6.7	417	10	47	690	37.3	61.4	1.2
Lowndes	649.1	5 667	24.9	53.1	3.9	0.7	2.3	369.8	3 228	1 137	4 913	10 585	45.0	54.3	0.7
Lumpkin	67.2	2 197	60.3	1.9	7.6	0.1	3.6	75.2	2 455	69	235	2 233	23.3	75.2	1.5
McDuffie	90.0	4 153	49.0	21.0	4.1	1.3	2.2	31.7	1 464	28	135	1 246	42.3	57.2	0.5
McIntosh	35.7	2 581	47.5	2.9	9.5	0.0	4.1	3.4	246	24	41	669	46.6	52.7	0.7
Macon	36.4	2 549	51.7	1.7	6.1	0.5	5.1	4.5	314	22	35	884	65.3	34.4	0.4
Madison	72.1	2 583	67.3	2.6	3.1	0.5	4.4	51.6	1 850	44	81	1 219	26.2	72.6	1.3
Marion	31.7	3 643	77.5	1.8	2.4	2.2	1.7	21.1	2 425	34	25	343	43.4	55.7	0.9
Meriwether	85.0	3 997	44.3	21.9	5.5	0.2	2.8	60.8	2 859	45	61	1 617	47.0	52.4	0.6
Miller	38.7	6 487	24.8	50.2	3.2	0.1	3.5	25.7	4 303	19	17	705	29.9	69.4	0.8
Mitchell	87.6	3 783	42.9	4.0	5.8	0.0	7.0	58.1	2 509	78	61	1 458	47.7	51.7	0.6
Monroe	92.6	3 477	43.8	14.7	6.5	0.1	5.1	33.5	1 257	34	75	2 467	33.8	65.4	0.8
Montgomery	17.6	1 979	59.5	3.0	4.8	1.0	4.3	1.9	217	17	24	351	29.1	70.2	0.7
Morgan	72.8	4 070	44.7	20.5	4.7	0.9	5.4	29.9	1 674	37	51	1 083	33.8	65.4	0.8
Murray	90.2	2 289	67.5	2.4	4.0	0.9	5.5	39.4	1 001	102	114	1 351	26.6	71.9	1.5
Muscogee	832.5	4 196	45.9	7.7	5.9	2.3	4.4	677.3	3 413	6 696	6 619	13 409	59.6	39.9	0.5
Newton	383.8	3 782	52.5	20.5	4.2	0.0	2.1	387.3	3 816	210	293	4 223	50.3	49.1	0.7
Oconee	98.9	2 943	63.3	1.2	4.1	0.6	5.9	108.6	3 230	130	99	1 401	28.2	70.7	1.1
Oglethorpe	32.9	2 254	68.3	2.8	3.0	1.0	3.7	24.2	1 653	16	42	566	34.6	64.3	1.1
Paulding	341.1	2 355	68.6	0.9	5.0	0.1	7.3	260.6	1 800	120	426	4 737	30.2	68.8	1.0
Peach	89.7	3 247	45.2	13.6	6.8	0.2	2.5	47.6	1 722	103	81	1 990	53.1	46.3	0.6
Pickens	82.3	2 812	55.3	3.3	6.4	0.2	4.6	22.2	758	53	85	1 282	20.3	78.2	1.5
Pierce	44.8	2 375	64.8	2.3	3.1	0.8	6.5	18.5	982	44	55	790	18.5	81.0	0.6
Pike	37.6	2 114	69.3	2.4	7.0	0.2	3.7	11.8	662	28	51	713	19.2	79.8	1.0
Polk	111.7	2 712	59.9	1.2	7.3	0.3	4.7	44.4	1 079	65	119	1 591	28.7	69.8	1.5
Pulaski	35.2	3 007	42.6	2.6	5.9	0.2	5.4	5.9	508	18	30	709	34.8	64.6	0.6

1. Based on the resident population estimated as of July 1 of the year shown. 2.

STATE/ County code	CBSA code[1]	County type[2]	STATE County	Land area,[3] (sq km) 2010	Population, 2014: Total persons 2014	Population, 2014: Rank	Population, 2014: Per square kilometer	Race alone or in combination, not Hispanic or Latino (percent): White	Black	American Indian, Alaska Native	Asian and Pacific Islander	Percent Hispanic or Latino[4]	Age (percent): Under 5 years	5 to 17 years	18 to 24 years	25 to 34 years	35 to 44 years	45 to 54 years
				1	2	3	4	5	6	7	8	9	10	11	12	13	14	15
			GEORGIA—Cont'd															
13 237	...	6	Putnam	893	21 192	1 763	23.7	65.9	27.1	0.4	0.9	6.7	6.1	15.3	7.4	11.2	10.8	13.3
13 239	...	9	Quitman	392	2 315	3 024	5.9	51.0	47.5	0.5	0.5	1.5	4.2	13.5	6.8	8.6	9.8	13.4
13 241	...	9	Rabun	958	16 243	2 027	17.0	89.2	1.9	1.1	1.1	8.1	4.2	14.6	7.4	9.2	11.3	13.3
13 243	...	6	Randolph	1 109	7 313	2 651	6.6	37.3	60.7	0.3	0.7	1.7	5.8	15.1	9.7	10.6	9.3	13.3
13 245	12260	2	Richmond	840	201 368	321	239.7	38.6	55.7	0.9	2.8	4.6	7.2	16.6	12.1	15.8	11.3	12.7
13 247	12060	1	Rockdale	336	87 754	653	261.2	39.1	49.4	0.7	2.5	10.1	6.2	19.7	9.5	11.5	13.1	15.0
13 249	11140	8	Schley	432	5 163	2 827	12.0	73.0	22.0	0.4	1.2	4.2	5.2	22.6	8.1	10.1	13.6	15.0
13 251	...	6	Screven	1 671	14 085	2 162	8.4	55.6	42.5	0.7	0.7	1.6	6.6	16.4	9.6	11.1	11.0	14.2
13 253	...	6	Seminole	609	8 686	2 543	14.3	63.4	33.5	0.5	0.9	2.8	5.5	16.8	8.1	9.8	10.9	13.7
13 255	12060	1	Spalding	509	63 988	820	125.7	61.4	33.9	0.7	1.3	4.2	6.8	17.6	9.0	12.7	12.5	13.3
13 257	45740	7	Stephens	464	25 480	1 588	54.9	84.8	12.2	0.7	1.1	2.9	5.7	16.7	10.0	11.0	11.4	13.5
13 259	...	8	Stewart	1 188	5 744	2 784	4.8	28.6	45.4	0.6	1.3	26.8	4.6	10.2	11.5	20.1	14.0	12.7
13 261	11140	6	Sumter	1 250	31 232	1 405	25.0	41.2	52.4	0.6	1.6	5.0	6.7	17.3	13.8	12.5	10.8	12.9
13 263	...	8	Talbot	1 014	6 390	2 728	6.3	40.7	57.4	0.8	0.4	1.8	4.6	14.1	8.3	8.7	10.5	16.7
13 265	...	8	Taliaferro	504	1 693	3 074	3.4	37.6	59.3	0.6	0.7	3.3	6.3	12.4	8.1	9.6	10.4	14.0
13 267	...	6	Tattnall	1 242	25 224	1 600	20.3	59.2	29.6	0.5	0.7	10.9	6.1	15.1	10.3	16.1	14.9	14.4
13 269	...	8	Taylor	976	8 442	2 563	8.6	59.1	38.1	0.4	0.9	2.3	5.4	16.9	9.1	10.2	12.2	14.6
13 271	...	7	Telfair	1 133	16 518	2 005	14.6	50.7	34.7	0.3	0.9	14.0	4.4	13.4	8.4	15.6	15.8	14.6
13 273	10500	3	Terrell	869	9 132	2 502	10.5	36.9	60.4	0.6	0.7	2.3	6.8	16.7	9.5	11.7	9.9	14.0
13 275	45620	4	Thomas	1 410	44 959	1 070	31.9	58.8	37.0	0.8	1.0	3.4	6.5	17.7	8.2	12.0	11.9	14.2
13 277	45700	4	Tift	671	40 704	1 160	60.7	57.6	30.4	0.5	1.7	10.9	6.9	18.6	11.7	13.1	12.0	12.7
13 279	47080	7	Toombs	943	27 282	1 520	28.9	62.3	26.1	0.5	1.1	11.3	7.9	19.7	8.5	12.6	11.9	12.6
13 281	...	9	Towns	431	11 098	2 349	25.7	95.7	1.2	0.5	0.8	2.5	3.5	10.7	12.3	7.2	8.9	11.4
13 283	...	7	Treutlen	517	6 778	2 701	13.1	64.5	33.0	0.5	0.5	2.5	6.3	18.2	9.1	13.7	12.1	12.6
13 285	29300	4	Troup	1 072	69 469	769	64.8	59.7	35.5	0.5	2.1	3.6	6.8	18.9	10.5	12.7	12.3	13.4
13 287	...	6	Turner	739	8 153	2 592	11.0	55.7	39.3	0.5	1.0	4.2	5.9	19.8	8.7	11.5	10.9	12.7
13 289	31420	3	Twiggs	928	8 320	2 574	9.0	56.4	41.8	0.8	0.3	1.8	5.5	14.0	8.5	10.5	10.0	16.2
13 291	...	9	Union	834	21 984	1 732	26.4	95.7	1.1	1.0	0.6	2.7	3.5	13.3	6.1	7.8	9.2	13.0
13 293	45580	6	Upson	838	26 256	1 552	31.3	69.1	28.1	0.6	0.9	2.5	6.2	16.3	9.0	11.0	12.2	14.4
13 295	16860	2	Walker	1 156	68 218	782	59.0	93.0	5.1	0.8	0.7	1.8	5.6	17.2	8.1	11.8	13.2	14.1
13 297	12060	1	Walton	844	87 615	656	103.8	78.1	17.0	0.6	1.8	3.8	6.3	19.6	8.5	11.5	13.7	14.8
13 299	48180	4	Ware	2 311	35 515	1 286	15.4	65.7	30.0	0.7	1.3	3.6	6.9	16.5	9.5	13.4	12.0	13.3
13 301	...	8	Warren	736	5 520	2 800	7.5	38.5	60.6	0.5	0.5	0.9	6.1	15.5	8.2	9.8	10.2	14.6
13 303	...	7	Washington	1 757	20 635	1 795	11.7	44.9	52.8	0.3	0.7	2.2	6.3	16.3	9.3	12.5	11.6	15.4
13 305	27700	6	Wayne	1 662	29 949	1 430	18.0	72.7	21.0	0.8	0.9	6.3	7.0	17.7	8.5	13.2	13.6	13.7
13 307	...	8	Webster	542	2 649	2 999	4.9	54.2	42.1	0.3	0.5	4.0	3.8	18.3	8.0	9.0	11.8	14.7
13 309	...	9	Wheeler	765	7 995	2 600	10.5	57.2	38.0	0.3	0.4	5.0	4.4	12.6	10.0	17.9	15.5	15.3
13 311	...	8	White	623	27 970	1 493	44.9	93.8	2.9	1.1	0.8	2.9	4.9	16.6	9.1	9.7	11.4	14.1
13 313	19140	3	Whitfield	752	103 542	571	137.7	61.6	4.3	0.6	1.7	32.9	7.3	20.0	9.7	13.3	13.3	13.4
13 315	...	9	Wilcox	978	8 847	2 525	9.0	59.6	35.9	0.8	0.7	4.0	5.0	13.7	9.2	15.2	14.2	14.6
13 317	...	6	Wilkes	1 216	9 940	2 443	8.2	53.4	43.1	0.4	0.8	3.7	5.9	15.9	7.7	9.8	10.6	14.4
13 319	...	8	Wilkinson	1 159	9 326	2 485	8.0	58.8	38.8	0.5	0.7	2.5	6.6	17.0	8.0	11.5	10.5	14.7
13 321	10500	3	Worth	1 478	20 940	1 779	14.2	68.4	29.3	0.5	0.7	2.0	6.1	17.1	8.9	11.8	11.7	14.3
15 000	...	X	HAWAII	16 635	1 419 561	X	85.3	36.9	3.1	1.7	74.3	9.8	6.5	15.4	9.8	14.7	12.4	12.8
15 001	25900	5	Hawaii	10 434	194 190	335	18.6	48.0	1.7	2.5	67.9	12.2	6.3	15.8	8.4	12.4	11.4	12.8
15 003	46520	2	Honolulu	1 556	991 788	46	637.4	32.9	3.8	1.5	77.3	9.2	6.5	15.2	10.5	15.4	12.6	12.5
15 005	27980	9	Kalawao	31	89	3 141	2.9	40.0	8.9	3.3	62.2	1.1	0.0	0.0	0.0	12.2	10.0	18.9
15 007	28180	5	Kauai	1 606	70 475	762	43.9	45.0	1.4	1.9	67.8	10.5	6.5	15.8	7.5	12.7	12.0	13.4
15 009	27980	5	Maui	3 008	163 019	391	54.2	45.0	1.5	1.8	66.8	10.6	6.2	16.3	7.6	13.4	13.2	14.4
16 000	...	X	IDAHO	214 045	1 634 464	X	7.6	84.9	1.0	1.9	2.3	11.8	7.0	19.5	9.7	13.2	12.2	12.4
16 001	14260	2	Ada	2 726	426 236	163	156.4	88.0	1.7	1.2	4.1	7.5	6.4	19.1	8.8	14.6	14.0	13.4
16 003	...	8	Adams	3 530	3 861	2 915	1.1	95.1	0.5	1.8	0.9	3.3	4.2	13.3	5.6	8.1	9.0	13.7
16 005	38540	3	Bannock	2 880	83 347	673	28.9	87.4	1.1	3.5	2.3	7.6	7.5	19.4	10.9	15.5	11.6	11.1
16 007	...	7	Bear Lake	2 525	5 957	2 761	2.4	94.5	0.4	1.2	0.7	4.2	6.8	20.6	7.0	10.3	10.5	11.6
16 009	...	6	Benewah	2 011	9 118	2 505	4.5	88.2	0.7	10.7	1.0	3.1	5.7	16.5	6.9	9.1	10.1	14.3
16 011	13940	6	Bingham	5 423	45 269	1 065	8.3	75.8	0.4	6.2	1.2	17.5	8.6	23.1	8.6	12.4	11.6	11.6
16 013	25200	7	Blaine	6 847	21 482	1 754	3.1	78.4	0.4	0.6	1.4	20.1	5.5	18.0	6.5	11.2	13.2	15.1
16 015	14260	2	Boise	4 919	6 824	2 698	1.4	94.4	0.8	2.2	1.2	3.6	3.5	16.0	5.0	6.5	10.3	16.6
16 017	41760	6	Bonner	4 493	41 585	1 136	9.3	95.7	0.5	2.0	1.3	2.6	4.8	15.6	6.3	9.3	10.8	14.1
16 019	26820	3	Bonneville	4 833	108 623	550	22.5	85.4	1.0	1.2	1.6	12.4	8.9	22.4	8.5	14.3	11.9	11.5
16 021	...	7	Boundary	3 286	10 979	2 361	3.3	93.1	0.7	2.9	1.1	4.2	5.3	18.3	6.4	9.4	11.2	13.0
16 023	26820	8	Butte	5 780	2 622	3 000	0.5	93.3	0.6	1.8	1.3	5.4	5.6	19.8	7.0	8.9	10.1	12.5
16 025	25200	9	Camas	2 783	1 039	3 106	0.4	90.9	1.3	3.1	0.6	7.2	4.6	18.3	4.1	9.8	13.1	13.7
16 027	14260	2	Canyon	1 521	203 143	317	133.6	73.4	0.9	1.5	1.8	24.4	8.1	22.3	9.5	13.2	12.9	11.6

1. CBSA = Core Based Statistical Area. See Appendix A for explanation. See Appendix B for list of metropolitan areas with component counties. 2. County type code from the Economic Research Service of USDA Rural-Urban Continuum Codes. See Appendix A for definition. 3. Dry land or land partially or temporarily covered by water. 4. May be of any race.

STATE County	Population, 2013 (cont.) — Age (percent) (cont.) — 55 to 64 years	65 to 74 years	75 years and over	Percent female	Population change and components of change, 2000–2014 — Total persons — 2000	2010	Percent change — 2000–2010	2010–2014	Components of change, 2010–2014 — Births	Deaths	Net migration	Households, 2009–2013 — Number	Persons per household	Percent — Family households	Female family householder[1]	One person
	16	17	18	19	20	21	22	23	24	25	26	27	28	29	30	31
GEORGIA—Cont'd																
Putnam	15.6	13.1	7.3	51.6	18 812	21 218	12.8	-0.1	1 059	970	-99	8 457	2.49	76.3	15.7	18.3
Quitman	18.0	16.1	9.5	52.6	2 598	2 513	-3.3	-7.9	109	118	-186	932	2.57	71.5	13.9	26.4
Rabun	15.5	15.0	9.6	50.7	15 050	16 276	8.1	-0.2	603	785	149	6 997	2.28	64.1	7.6	29.2
Randolph	15.6	11.5	9.2	53.6	7 791	7 719	-0.9	-5.3	377	369	-421	3 020	2.38	64.8	21.1	29.5
Richmond	12.1	7.1	5.1	51.5	199 775	200 549	0.4	0.4	12 891	8 062	-3 954	72 281	2.66	61.3	21.5	33.6
Rockdale	12.8	7.7	4.6	52.6	70 111	85 215	21.5	3.0	4 284	2 568	784	29 317	2.89	73.1	18.6	22.5
Schley	11.0	9.8	4.8	52.0	3 766	5 010	33.0	3.1	224	121	57	1 829	2.73	69.1	10.3	27.3
Screven	14.7	9.9	6.5	51.0	15 374	14 593	-5.1	-3.5	839	722	-628	5 165	2.72	65.4	16.8	30.4
Seminole	14.3	12.3	8.6	52.0	9 369	8 729	-6.8	-0.5	451	439	-48	3 317	2.63	71.0	17.5	25.7
Spalding	12.7	9.5	6.0	51.5	58 417	64 073	9.7	-0.1	3 586	2 942	-792	22 997	2.74	70.6	19.8	25.3
Stephens	13.9	10.9	6.9	52.0	25 435	26 175	2.9	-2.7	1 316	1 417	-607	9 227	2.70	71.0	12.1	26.7
Stewart	12.0	8.1	6.9	39.1	5 252	6 058	15.3	-5.2	220	287	-284	1 851	2.74	57.1	23.8	38.4
Sumter	11.8	8.4	5.8	52.5	33 200	32 819	-1.1	-4.8	1 760	1 409	-1 961	11 493	2.63	65.1	21.2	30.7
Talbot	18.3	11.8	6.9	52.0	6 498	6 865	5.6	-6.9	258	292	-450	2 682	2.49	70.2	21.7	27.7
Taliaferro	17.1	12.2	9.8	50.4	2 077	1 717	-17.3	-1.4	77	90	-6	704	2.49	61.1	14.2	35.8
Tattnall	11.3	7.3	4.7	41.7	22 305	25 520	14.4	-1.2	1 377	964	-756	7 885	2.62	68.8	15.3	27.7
Taylor	14.1	10.6	6.8	52.3	8 815	8 906	1.0	-5.2	389	397	-503	3 681	2.24	71.9	23.6	26.6
Telfair	12.9	8.2	6.8	41.1	11 794	16 500	39.9	0.1	584	591	-12	5 567	2.27	68.0	18.9	28.7
Terrell	14.1	10.1	7.1	52.2	10 970	9 315	-15.1	-3.9	557	395	-545	3 351	2.66	69.4	22.6	28.2
Thomas	13.2	9.3	7.1	52.6	42 737	44 720	4.6	0.5	2 515	2 093	-231	17 377	2.51	64.0	16.7	31.8
Tift	11.3	8.0	5.9	51.9	38 407	40 118	4.5	1.5	2 382	1 597	-261	13 691	2.84	68.1	17.3	27.7
Toombs	11.9	8.6	6.2	52.5	26 067	27 223	4.4	0.2	1 707	1 218	-420	10 310	2.60	66.5	14.2	30.6
Towns	14.3	17.3	14.3	52.0	9 319	10 471	12.4	6.0	342	658	904	4 261	2.29	63.8	5.4	32.5
Treutlen	13.5	8.3	6.2	49.6	6 854	6 885	0.5	-1.6	335	261	-154	2 515	2.52	65.7	19.1	32.3
Troup	12.1	7.7	5.7	51.8	58 779	67 044	14.1	3.6	3 879	2 851	1 415	24 441	2.70	70.1	20.7	25.9
Turner	12.2	10.4	7.8	50.7	9 504	8 930	-6.0	-8.7	471	418	-867	3 166	2.61	69.0	21.4	28.8
Twiggs	16.7	12.0	6.7	51.3	10 590	9 023	-14.8	-7.8	403	483	-638	3 056	2.85	70.2	15.7	28.4
Union	16.5	18.2	12.5	51.5	17 289	21 356	23.5	2.9	673	1 200	1 049	9 141	2.30	71.9	8.3	25.3
Upson	13.5	10.3	7.0	52.4	27 597	27 153	-1.6	-3.3	1 363	1 533	-722	10 341	2.55	69.3	16.1	27.5
Walker	13.7	9.5	6.7	50.8	61 053	68 756	12.6	-0.8	3 123	2 949	-676	26 191	2.57	70.1	12.0	26.0
Walton	11.9	8.5	5.2	51.4	60 687	83 768	38.0	4.6	4 613	3 114	2 315	29 520	2.84	77.9	12.9	19.2
Ware	12.7	8.6	7.2	50.3	35 483	36 312	2.3	-2.2	2 103	1 859	-1 100	13 460	2.48	66.2	14.6	30.2
Warren	15.7	11.3	8.5	53.0	6 336	5 834	-7.9	-5.4	259	294	-278	2 208	2.55	61.1	21.2	36.0
Washington	13.2	9.0	6.4	49.5	21 176	21 187	0.1	-2.6	1 017	903	-697	7 119	2.70	70.2	19.3	28.1
Wayne	12.1	8.6	5.6	48.0	26 565	30 099	13.3	-0.5	1 729	1 323	-556	10 171	2.76	72.0	14.0	23.9
Webster	15.4	10.8	8.1	49.6	2 390	2 799	17.1	-5.4	73	62	-185	1 129	2.45	65.1	16.6	33.6
Wheeler	11.7	7.5	5.1	34.8	6 179	7 421	20.1	7.7	259	233	505	2 096	2.03	71.3	18.3	27.5
White	14.1	12.5	7.6	51.0	19 944	27 144	36.1	3.0	1 115	1 049	730	11 788	2.29	69.4	8.1	26.0
Whitfield	10.6	7.3	5.1	50.1	83 525	102 599	22.8	0.9	6 010	3 215	-1 805	34 450	2.95	74.7	13.6	20.1
Wilcox	12.7	8.4	6.9	40.8	8 577	9 255	7.9	-4.4	397	442	-378	2 705	2.60	70.1	15.7	27.8
Wilkes	14.7	12.5	8.5	52.1	10 687	10 593	-0.9	-6.2	495	575	-586	4 083	2.47	60.9	17.5	37.2
Wilkinson	14.2	10.4	7.1	51.8	10 220	9 563	-6.4	-2.5	469	459	-258	3 348	2.81	68.9	18.0	28.8
Worth	13.8	9.9	6.3	52.1	21 967	21 679	-1.3	-3.4	1 053	901	-896	7 851	2.74	72.7	15.8	24.9
HAWAII	12.8	8.6	7.1	49.5	1 211 537	1 360 301	12.3	4.4	80 734	45 388	24 911	449 771	2.96	69.4	12.4	23.9
Hawaii	16.1	10.0	6.7	49.9	148 677	185 079	24.5	4.9	10 341	6 618	5 250	64 909	2.83	66.3	13.1	26.6
Honolulu	11.7	8.2	7.3	49.3	876 156	953 207	8.8	4.0	58 047	31 518	13 102	309 803	3.00	70.2	12.3	23.4
Kalawao	28.9	6.7	23.3	53.3	147	90	-38.8	-1.1	0	1	0	46	1.39	26.1	0.0	60.9
Kauai	15.2	9.7	7.1	49.8	58 463	67 091	14.8	5.0	3 727	2 448	2 125	22 390	2.99	69.7	11.0	22.4
Maui	14.2	8.9	5.8	49.6	128 094	154 834	20.9	5.3	8 619	4 803	4 434	52 623	2.93	68.5	12.3	24.0
IDAHO	12.2	8.1	5.7	49.9	1 293 953	1 567 582	21.1	4.3	96 826	49 597	18 656	579 797	2.68	69.8	9.6	23.9
Ada	11.7	7.2	4.9	50.0	300 904	392 365	30.4	8.6	21 692	10 583	22 344	151 600	2.60	67.9	9.2	24.6
Adams	22.0	15.3	8.7	48.9	3 476	3 976	14.4	-2.9	122	115	-95	1 707	2.27	69.5	7.6	26.0
Bannock	11.8	7.1	5.3	50.2	75 565	82 839	9.6	0.6	5 606	2 720	-2 323	30 271	2.68	66.1	10.5	27.3
Bear Lake	13.7	11.1	8.3	50.3	6 411	5 986	-6.6	-0.5	343	263	-96	2 442	2.42	73.8	8.5	23.3
Benewah	16.8	13.1	7.6	49.1	9 171	9 285	1.2	-1.8	483	437	-207	3 888	2.34	68.2	8.8	25.3
Bingham	11.5	7.1	5.4	49.7	41 735	45 607	9.3	-0.7	3 215	1 326	-2 211	14 650	3.08	77.1	10.1	19.8
Blaine	15.7	10.1	4.8	49.1	18 991	21 376	12.6	0.5	963	392	-477	9 207	2.28	65.9	7.8	26.0
Boise	21.8	15.0	5.4	48.7	6 670	7 028	5.4	-2.9	171	216	-148	2 994	2.29	62.1	4.9	32.2
Bonner	18.5	13.0	7.5	50.0	36 835	40 877	11.0	1.7	1 677	1 636	532	17 388	2.32	66.0	8.4	26.9
Bonneville	10.8	6.7	5.1	50.3	82 522	104 234	26.3	4.1	8 276	3 185	806	36 066	2.00	74.1	11.0	21.0
Boundary	16.4	12.6	7.4	49.2	9 871	10 972	11.2	0.1	514	460	-46	4 144	2.59	70.0	8.0	24.2
Butte	16.6	11.7	7.9	48.4	2 899	2 891	-0.3	-9.4	120	90	-319	1 022	2.68	66.5	8.7	29.5
Camas	17.9	12.1	6.3	47.4	991	1 117	12.7	-7.0	45	18	-125	464	2.73	69.2	6.7	26.3
Canyon	10.3	7.3	4.8	50.5	131 441	188 923	43.7	7.5	13 237	5 461	6 202	63 442	2.98	74.1	12.4	21.4

1. No spouse present.

STATE County	Persons in group quarters, 2014	Daytime population, 2009–2013: Number	Daytime population, 2009–2013: Employment/residence ratio	Births, 2014: Total	Births, 2014: Rate[1]	Deaths, 2014: Number	Deaths, 2014: Rate[1]	Persons under 65 with no health insurance, 2013: Number	Persons under 65 with no health insurance, 2013: Percent	Medicare, 2014: Eligible for Medicare	Medicare, 2014: Enrolled in Medicare Advantage	Medicare, 2014: Enrolled in a Medicare prescription drug plan	Serious crimes known to police,[2] 2013: Total: Number	Serious crimes known to police,[2] 2013: Total: Rate[3]
	32	33	34	35	36	37	38	39	40	41	42	43	44	45
GEORGIA—Cont'd														
Putnam	161	18 990	0.74	239	11.3	244	11.5	3 978	23.6	5 040	1 339	2 139	704	3 321
Quitman	0	2 011	0.43	26	11.2	13	5.6	435	24.6	683	199	275	5	211
Rabun	391	16 808	1.09	140	8.6	202	12.4	3 593	29.7	4 520	863	2 348	403	2 471
Randolph	432	7 470	0.99	91	12.4	74	10.1	1 097	19.9	1 573	522	695	167	2 315
Richmond	10 793	238 462	1.46	3 046	15.1	1 916	9.5	31 506	18.7	33 183	11 306	10 331	11 657	5 855
Rockdale	771	84 646	0.97	1 019	11.6	638	7.3	16 723	22.2	13 334	4 598	5 032	3 616	4 206
Schley	0	4 090	0.51	49	9.5	28	5.4	923	21.2	748	241	322	58	1 164
Screven	358	13 393	0.80	188	13.3	173	12.3	2 405	20.6	2 968	878	1 346	469	3 463
Seminole	100	8 374	0.84	104	12.0	96	11.1	1 549	22.0	2 222	570	1 085	187	2 073
Spalding	1 166	62 457	0.94	793	12.4	716	11.2	10 579	19.9	13 055	4 319	5 585	3 756	5 888
Stephens	574	25 796	0.99	328	12.9	305	12.0	3 885	18.8	6 090	1 351	2 948	1 078	4 179
Stewart	1 511	5 692	0.82	47	8.2	74	12.9	732	21.5	989	366	398	4	86
Sumter	1 721	32 829	1.06	406	13.0	300	9.6	5 401	21.2	5 822	1 868	2 626	1 826	5 999
Talbot	17	5 128	0.33	59	9.2	69	10.8	1 171	22.3	1 486	539	567	88	1 456
Taliaferro	7	1 467	0.49	16	9.5	24	14.2	332	24.9	454	171	190	NA	NA
Tattnall	4 516	24 085	0.83	312	12.4	227	9.0	4 684	26.3	3 766	1 186	1 496	373	1 686
Taylor	144	7 705	0.70	88	10.4	80	9.5	1 469	21.2	1 744	623	742	140	1 686
Telfair	3 828	17 224	1.20	133	8.1	160	9.7	2 216	20.9	2 334	637	1 120	NA	NA
Terrell	270	8 446	0.75	129	14.1	93	10.2	1 542	21.2	2 089	725	838	216	2 412
Thomas	828	46 846	1.13	619	13.8	473	10.5	7 505	20.2	9 679	2 846	4 266	2 012	4 501
Tift	1 619	45 021	1.29	554	13.6	387	9.5	8 148	24.4	7 068	2 106	3 185	2 270	5 488
Toombs	407	28 800	1.15	390	14.3	295	10.8	5 346	23.2	5 421	1 252	2 809	991	4 321
Towns	1 035	10 587	1.01	90	8.1	153	13.8	1 663	25.2	4 092	1 040	1 835	215	2 052
Treutlen	388	5 737	0.52	80	11.8	59	8.7	1 165	21.2	1 328	427	589	NA	NA
Troup	2 288	76 073	1.31	912	13.1	711	10.2	10 731	18.5	11 742	3 186	5 602	2 399	3 481
Turner	381	7 751	0.69	110	13.5	95	11.7	1 500	23.5	1 929	679	830	341	4 141
Twiggs	89	7 728	0.58	86	10.3	147	17.7	1 452	21.1	2 198	770	906	143	1 726
Union	289	20 739	0.91	151	6.9	265	12.1	3 645	24.7	7 152	1 705	3 176	326	1 516
Upson	401	25 248	0.83	312	11.9	377	14.4	4 085	18.7	6 120	2 239	2 592	850	3 208
Walker	1 282	56 386	0.56	742	10.9	737	10.8	11 431	20.3	13 936	3 997	6 654	2 996	4 417
Walton	701	69 063	0.58	1 137	13.0	762	8.7	14 846	20.3	14 239	4 295	6 128	2 710	3 198
Ware	2 172	39 614	1.28	484	13.6	410	11.5	5 893	20.9	7 733	1 855	4 083	1 669	4 685
Warren	89	5 202	0.73	55	10.0	65	11.8	918	20.6	1 325	441	538	156	2 832
Washington	1 634	21 042	1.01	231	11.2	217	10.5	3 147	19.6	4 163	1 652	1 672	NA	NA
Wayne	2 313	29 003	0.89	369	12.3	311	10.4	4 800	20.1	5 518	1 455	2 534	1 697	5 586
Webster	0	2 208	0.49	16	6.0	9	3.4	492	22.3	507	164	208	19	679
Wheeler	2 574	7 574	0.88	63	7.9	61	7.6	1 005	22.8	1 113	321	483	100	1 261
White	623	25 288	0.81	264	9.4	250	8.9	4 709	21.6	6 142	1 627	2 812	538	1 944
Whitfield	997	114 849	1.29	1 373	13.3	757	7.3	24 408	27.3	15 809	2 323	9 192	3 185	3 150
Wilcox	1 953	8 724	0.84	94	10.6	101	11.4	1 255	21.9	1 667	478	675	198	2 331
Wilkes	133	9 912	0.90	107	10.8	135	13.6	1 734	22.1	2 531	705	1 214	180	1 810
Wilkinson	114	9 580	1.02	100	10.7	114	12.2	1 556	20.1	2 199	666	931	132	1 644
Worth	164	17 495	0.49	233	11.1	208	9.9	3 944	22.2	3 832	943	1 629	705	3 236
HAWAII	44 216	1 377 140	1.00	19 125	13.5	11 482	8.1	89 341	7.6	239 170	17 196	10 454	46 408	3 305
Hawaii	3 730	186 762	1.00	2 447	12.6	1 721	8.9	17 294	10.7	36 527	15 361	11 459	5 833	3 058
Honolulu	36 546	965 761	1.00	13 743	13.9	7 869	7.9	54 264	6.7	164 800	78 921	38 197	16 890	1 715
Kalawao	3	125	1.93	0	0.0	0	0.0	0	0.0	18	NA	NA	NA	NA
Kauai	1 184	67 952	1.00	889	12.6	639	9.1	5 064	8.6	12 865	5 085	4 199	1 730	2 509
Maui	2 753	156 540	1.00	2 046	12.6	1 253	7.7	12 719	9.2	24 960	12 111	6 255	6 154	3 855
IDAHO	29 601	1 563 097	0.97	22 945	14.0	11 628	7.1	255 932	18.8	273 054	43 912	100 536	33 553	2 081
Ada	10 088	420 244	1.10	5 124	12.0	2 563	6.0	51 854	14.5	62 157	28 283	15 534	7 997	1 920
Adams	21	3 659	0.83	29	7.5	20	5.2	691	24.1	1 083	196	435	11	281
Bannock	1 980	81 361	0.95	1 261	15.1	629	7.5	11 377	16.0	13 016	4 297	5 633	2 752	3 257
Bear Lake	31	5 513	0.81	92	15.4	59	9.9	909	19.1	1 328	42	825	117	1 978
Benewah	70	9 648	1.13	117	12.8	104	11.4	1 543	21.6	2 349	442	1 096	107	1 175
Bingham	324	42 588	0.84	760	16.8	308	6.8	8 712	22.2	7 023	1 522	3 191	846	1 855
Blaine	258	22 423	1.10	223	10.4	87	4.0	4 429	24.5	3 071	070	1 501	202	063
Boise	34	6 551	0.86	39	5.7	52	7.6	1 121	20.9	1 617	682	409	117	1 843
Bonner	353	39 827	0.94	403	9.7	368	8.8	6 658	20.8	9 984	2 804	3 630	936	2 310
Bonneville	1 242	111 051	1.12	1 950	18.0	764	7.0	16 955	18.1	15 652	3 404	7 108	2 508	2 325
Boundary	73	10 552	0.92	120	10.9	118	10.7	2 072	24.1	2 659	736	894	166	1 538
Butte	18	4 566	2.75	26	9.9	12	4.6	388	18.4	563	NA	320	7	259
Camas	0	1 121	0.74	10	9.6	3	2.9	242	28.6	194	35	73	6	560
Canyon	3 365	174 826	0.77	3 202	15.8	1 321	6.5	36 086	21.1	30 505	15 149	8 339	4 050	2 062

1. Per 1,000 estimated resident population. 2. Data for serious crimes have not been adjusted for underreporting; this may affect comparability between geographic areas and over time.
3. Per 100,000 population estimated by the FBI.

STATE County	Serious crimes known to police, 2013 (cont.)[1] Rate[2] Violent	Rate[2] Property	Education: School enrollment and attainment, 2009–2013: Enrollment[3] Total	Enrollment[3] Percent private	Attainment[4] (percent) High school graduate or less	Attainment[4] (percent) Bachelor's degree or more	Local government expenditures,[5] 2012–2013 Total current spending (mil dol)	Current spending per student (dollars)	Money income, 2009–2013 Per capita income[6] (dollars)	Households Median income (dollars)	Households Mean income (dollars)	Households Percent with income of $200,000 or more	Income and poverty, 2013 Median household income (dollars)	Percent below poverty level All persons	Children under 18 years	Children 5 to 17 years in families
	46	47	48	49	50	51	52	53	54	55	56	57	58	59	60	61
GEORGIA—Cont'd																
Putnam	509	2 811	4 663	21.3	54.1	18.7	31.2	11 126	26 321	44 764	66 115	3.6	42 934	19.0	35.3	33.4
Quitman	0	211	539	3.0	67.9	3.2	3.8	11 119	14 201	31 068	36 153	0.3	29 111	26.9	46.6	43.2
Rabun	141	2 330	3 147	15.1	47.6	26.6	27.4	11 962	22 260	35 423	50 786	2.1	38 114	19.4	32.2	29.5
Randolph	610	1 705	1 629	25.1	61.4	17.4	11.9	10 861	18 094	30 023	42 552	1.2	28 105	31.7	45.1	44.5
Richmond	394	5 461	55 300	14.4	47.4	20.5	296.7	9 257	20 526	37 749	51 380	1.8	36 069	27.7	43.6	44.4
Rockdale	362	3 844	24 703	16.7	42.7	26.0	152.7	9 624	23 461	52 579	65 431	2.4	50 646	16.8	24.2	21.8
Schley	261	903	1 541	4.1	60.7	14.2	13.2	9 521	19 037	38 425	50 889	1.2	38 944	20.1	28.6	24.0
Screven	532	2 931	3 714	8.1	62.4	13.0	22.4	9 316	18 640	34 848	47 856	1.4	35 087	27.9	40.5	41.2
Seminole	266	1 807	2 065	6.7	59.6	12.2	15.2	9 136	17 641	30 521	45 083	0.6	34 814	27.3	43.4	38.5
Spalding	472	5 416	15 413	10.2	59.3	14.8	97.6	9 220	19 783	41 534	52 685	1.9	39 068	21.1	34.9	35.4
Stephens	333	3 846	6 361	17.2	60.3	14.2	36.1	8 897	18 557	37 898	49 639	1.3	36 318	20.4	31.1	28.6
Stewart	0	86	1 042	14.3	75.9	10.0	6.9	12 286	13 238	23 451	34 876	0.5	28 304	38.7	44.0	44.6
Sumter	818	5 181	9 722	8.4	57.9	18.5	47.9	9 751	17 879	33 796	46 546	1.1	32 474	36.1	54.0	47.5
Talbot	33	1 423	1 490	19.8	64.2	12.3	6.3	12 194	16 993	32 424	41 425	0.9	33 168	24.5	40.7	38.6
Taliaferro	NA	NA	313	5.8	73.9	9.3	2.9	14 640	14 381	25 465	34 733	1.0	28 917	31.0	45.4	47.6
Tattnall	108	1 577	5 591	11.1	67.0	11.6	32.4	8 796	15 280	37 587	47 373	1.8	35 983	28.3	37.6	36.7
Taylor	265	1 421	2 027	13.0	63.5	10.1	15.3	9 886	17 078	27 455	40 803	1.4	30 538	29.1	41.0	39.7
Telfair	NA	NA	2 776	1.5	73.9	10.9	15.5	8 825	12 489	26 634	35 672	0.3	28 334	32.8	40.6	36.1
Terrell	547	1 865	2 203	14.7	68.0	8.7	14.8	9 980	16 836	32 628	44 237	0.3	31 826	30.4	44.6	42.7
Thomas	353	4 148	11 509	13.1	53.5	18.1	77.8	9 143	19 983	34 035	49 397	2.2	38 914	20.4	29.2	27.5
Tift	600	4 888	11 739	9.8	55.8	16.0	73.4	9 280	18 933	34 591	51 410	2.4	33 902	31.3	40.7	36.3
Toombs	493	3 829	7 570	9.0	59.8	15.2	47.1	8 283	18 716	31 189	47 652	1.6	32 311	28.3	40.8	36.4
Towns	172	1 880	2 338	22.8	51.8	22.7	12.7	11 252	20 419	36 570	47 843	1.4	39 854	18.1	29.3	27.8
Treutlen	NA	NA	1 693	5.7	69.6	12.3	10.1	8 274	19 410	37 894	52 298	1.9	31 917	30.9	43.9	39.6
Troup	200	3 281	18 059	12.9	53.9	18.6	113.8	8 955	21 443	41 161	57 446	2.7	42 044	23.8	33.5	31.3
Turner	583	3 558	2 390	9.2	62.1	9.8	15.7	10 035	17 609	28 326	45 256	0.7	31 817	30.5	45.8	41.4
Twiggs	97	1 630	1 721	9.7	71.3	10.8	9.7	10 613	17 952	31 234	47 723	0.6	36 107	22.9	33.8	33.6
Union	214	1 302	3 817	22.5	49.5	19.6	27.4	10 497	22 156	40 009	52 283	1.2	39 677	16.9	29.2	25.5
Upson	264	2 944	6 518	7.0	59.5	11.4	38.9	8 878	17 978	35 329	45 344	0.6	34 709	22.3	34.6	32.8
Walker	476	3 941	15 350	13.1	57.6	14.0	94.6	9 075	20 865	39 963	53 394	1.7	40 512	17.3	25.7	23.8
Walton	237	2 961	22 502	16.4	49.5	18.4	127.9	8 487	22 824	52 369	63 895	2.4	54 294	14.2	20.3	17.6
Ware	359	4 326	8 333	6.3	60.4	13.9	60.1	9 988	18 842	34 572	48 880	1.3	32 211	27.6	40.7	41.1
Warren	454	2 378	1 262	21.3	71.7	7.3	7.4	10 452	17 884	27 796	42 859	2.0	30 967	27.5	42.8	40.6
Washington	NA	NA	4 888	8.6	66.0	11.1	31.3	10 081	17 515	33 652	48 065	1.5	36 807	26.5	36.8	34.2
Wayne	520	5 066	7 371	10.4	60.4	11.4	44.5	8 152	17 270	35 830	47 575	0.7	38 081	25.3	33.8	32.7
Webster	36	644	694	13.1	65.4	11.2	4.5	10 092	19 082	35 718	45 208	0.3	34 374	23.0	33.7	27.2
Wheeler	113	1 147	803	1.1	80.0	8.5	9.8	9 796	8 948	24 382	35 356	0.0	30 779	45.0	45.6	41.5
White	152	1 792	6 341	16.6	48.9	19.3	46.6	11 959	22 059	40 670	51 891	1.7	41 337	19.0	30.1	27.2
Whitfield	251	2 898	28 269	6.6	60.3	14.0	186.2	8 923	19 497	40 471	55 969	2.4	39 946	19.9	27.5	25.8
Wilcox	271	2 060	1 735	7.8	69.1	8.6	13.1	10 336	13 228	32 928	40 890	0.7	33 308	33.2	39.5	37.4
Wilkes	332	1 478	2 391	9.1	64.2	14.5	17.2	10 393	17 120	28 983	40 042	0.9	33 662	24.0	37.5	37.2
Wilkinson	87	1 557	2 140	6.5	67.8	8.2	17.7	11 032	17 228	36 173	45 387	0.2	35 745	23.6	34.8	34.1
Worth	482	2 754	5 387	9.7	66.6	8.1	30.3	8 873	18 551	35 792	48 701	1.3	36 616	23.1	34.4	33.3
HAWAII	252	3 054	337 054	23.6	37.7	30.1	2 199.3	11 823	29 305	67 402	84 933	5.9	67 798	11.2	14.4	13.9
Hawaii	287	2 771	43 387	18.2	41.5	25.6	(7)	(7)	24 635	51 250	65 809	2.8	47 377	19.5	25.8	24.5
Honolulu	115	1 600	242 764	25.7	36.4	32.1	(7)2 199.3	(7)11 903	30 361	72 764	89 741	6.6	72 649	9.6	12.2	11.9
Kalawao	NA	NA	6	0.0	40.0	41.5	(7)	(7)	45 515	59 375	66 591	0.0	0	0.0	0.0	0.0
Kauai	149	2 360	14 736	15.7	38.9	25.1	(7)	(7)	26 658	62 052	76 516	4.2	55 844	11.8	15.6	15.1
Maui	282	3 573	36 161	19.3	40.6	25.7	(7)	(7)	29 517	63 512	83 816	6.1	62 277	10.7	13.8	12.7
IDAHO	217	1 864	440 280	13.7	39.0	25.1	1 852.2	6 791	22 568	46 767	60 192	2.2	46 621	15.6	19.2	18.3
Ada	224	1 697	115 090	11.7	28.0	36.0	453.2	6 700	27 452	55 210	71 473	3.7	53 420	13.6	14.7	13.9
Adams	26	255	788	14.0	44.4	21.9	4.1	10 554	21 555	35 434	49 558	1.6	37 630	17.3	26.8	25.5
Bannock	283	2 975	25 689	8.4	36.3	26.8	89.6	6 374	21 327	43 534	56 564	1.3	42 665	17.7	20.5	18.9
Bear Lake	101	1 877	1 414	10.6	48.7	16.1	7.6	6 913	21 853	44 964	54 892	1.3	45 589	13.0	17.3	16.2
Benewah	329	846	1 845	6.3	56.0	13.4	13.1	9 610	20 198	39 049	47 772	0.5	39 530	16.5	24.3	22.7
Bingham	140	1 715	13 281	7.1	46.6	17.3	61.2	6 317	18 872	47 941	57 131	1.7	47 721	14.1	18.7	17.6
Blaine	132	821	4 358	19.1	25.3	44.7	53.7	16 157	35 524	64 042	83 687	5.5	67 936	9.9	14.0	12.6
Boise	157	1 685	1 389	10.6	41.8	24.1	8.0	9 373	24 324	41 056	54 602	0.7	48 974	14.9	22.9	19.7
Bonner	148	2 162	8 079	17.4	40.1	21.1	41.7	8 090	23 221	41 414	53 502	2.1	41 797	17.0	25.9	23.8
Bonneville	177	2 148	30 120	12.3	36.9	26.0	126.4	5 986	22 657	50 872	65 066	2.7	50 559	12.0	16.1	15.8
Boundary	176	1 362	2 214	12.6	52.4	15.4	10.6	7 199	19 877	37 003	40 450	2.0	30 681	17.0	24.9	23.4
Butte	222	37	682	8.8	46.9	17.9	3.5	8 280	20 995	41 131	55 367	2.7	41 739	17.1	20.6	18.0
Camas	0	560	311	5.5	44.3	22.3	1.9	13 397	21 830	41 154	56 289	5.8	47 911	13.1	20.8	16.7
Canyon	221	1 841	55 885	15.2	48.8	16.8	213.0	5 949	17 755	42 105	51 692	1.0	42 237	20.1	24.6	24.5

1. Data for serious crimes have not been adjusted for underreporting; this may affect comparability between geographic areas and over time. 2. Per 100,000 population estimated by the FBI.
3. All persons 3 years old and over enrolled in nursery school through college. 4. Persons 25 years old and over. 5. Elementary and secondary education expenditures.
6. Based on population estimated by the American Community Survey, 2009–2013. 7. Hawaii, Kalawao, Kauai, and Maui counties are included with Honolulu county.

STATE County	Personal income, 2013										Earnings, 2013		
			Per capita[1]			Supplements to wages and salaries; employer contributions (mil dol)						Contributions for government social insurance (mil dol)	
	Total (mil dol)	Percent change, 2012–2013	Dollars	Rank	Wages and salaries (mil dol)	Pension and insurance	Government social insurance	Proprietors' income (mil dol)	Dividends, interest, and rent (mil dol)	Personal transfer receipts (mil dol)	Total (mil dol)	From employee and self-employed	From employer
	62	63	64	65	66	67	68	69	70	71	72	73	74
GEORGIA—Cont'd													
Putnam	731	2.3	34 191	2 050	191	48	13	52	171	193	304	20	13
Quitman	63	0.7	26 624	2 999	12	4	1	3	8	24	20	2	1
Rabun	548	3.1	33 747	2 139	151	31	11	35	158	161	229	16	11
Randolph	249	2.9	34 532	1 979	63	16	5	76	32	68	160	8	5
Richmond	6 400	1.7	31 683	2 451	5 234	1 178	401	291	1 362	1 775	7 103	372	401
Rockdale	2 828	2.3	32 534	2 322	1 452	248	105	126	403	586	1 931	114	105
Schley	114	2.3	22 483	3 096	39	10	3	13	18	30	65	4	3
Screven	453	-0.9	31 811	2 433	117	27	8	45	81	130	197	11	8
Seminole	334	0.8	37 385	1 524	81	17	6	79	43	91	183	9	6
Spalding	1 871	1.8	29 308	2 775	749	162	55	100	316	572	1 065	68	55
Stephens	861	2.8	33 542	2 167	350	72	25	76	136	242	523	33	25
Stewart	137	-1.2	23 417	3 086	46	10	3	9	24	47	68	4	3
Sumter	964	0.1	30 727	2 592	357	87	26	93	189	287	562	31	26
Talbot	194	1.1	30 051	2 681	28	7	2	6	33	63	43	4	2
Taliaferro	51	1.7	29 660	2 733	5	2	0	4	9	17	12	1	0
Tattnall	703	5.4	27 554	2 930	194	52	13	115	101	174	374	17	13
Taylor	246	3.6	29 041	2 804	61	15	4	32	37	78	112	6	4
Telfair	291	0.2	17 536	3 113	105	27	9	22	43	114	164	10	9
Terrell	313	1.1	34 702	1 950	80	19	5	48	62	91	153	8	5
Thomas	1 725	1.2	38 443	1 384	866	155	61	129	358	415	1 211	71	61
Tift	1 344	2.0	33 358	2 197	681	154	46	155	219	329	1 036	54	46
Toombs	938	3.9	34 378	2 016	433	84	32	89	126	247	638	36	32
Towns	405	2.4	37 603	1 490	99	24	7	26	107	132	156	12	7
Treutlen	170	1.0	25 372	3 042	32	8	2	13	25	57	56	4	2
Troup	2 449	4.2	35 461	1 827	1 597	268	120	107	422	529	2 092	123	120
Turner	291	3.3	35 782	1 785	71	16	5	54	40	87	147	7	5
Twiggs	293	0.2	34 577	1 972	43	10	3	3	30	93	59	6	3
Union	721	2.5	33 434	2 185	210	50	15	37	165	235	312	23	15
Upson	804	2.1	30 252	2 648	253	51	18	32	142	255	355	25	18
Walker	1 925	1.3	28 224	2 874	448	110	34	85	268	562	676	49	34
Walton	3 099	2.1	36 133	1 724	754	145	55	73	418	576	1 028	67	55
Ware	1 022	1.8	28 613	2 836	560	114	46	73	169	375	793	50	46
Warren	153	1.2	27 506	2 936	53	11	4	7	24	56	75	5	4
Washington	705	2.0	34 083	2 066	252	62	17	49	186	183	380	22	17
Wayne	924	0.3	30 720	2 594	346	78	25	58	138	257	507	30	25
Webster	83	1.7	30 616	2 610	20	5	1	9	17	20	35	2	1
Wheeler	154	0.7	19 418	3 112	49	11	4	9	21	46	72	4	4
White	778	4.5	28 005	2 898	218	43	16	51	143	221	328	23	16
Whitfield	3 142	2.4	30 520	2 626	2 243	382	168	339	506	675	3 131	179	168
Wilcox	261	-2.3	29 082	2 796	39	12	3	64	36	73	118	5	3
Wilkes	302	1.0	30 135	2 666	96	24	7	26	61	102	152	10	7
Wilkinson	280	0.3	29 723	2 724	149	26	11	11	38	92	197	13	11
Worth	765	0.0	35 940	1 757	126	28	9	112	102	166	275	13	9
HAWAII	63 468	2.4	45 204	X	31 487	6 548	2 812	4 829	13 384	9 839	45 676	2 618	2 812
Hawaii	6 545	4.0	34 297	2 033	2 635	529	234	545	1 428	1 618	3 943	248	234
Honolulu	47 990	2.0	48 798	432	24 625	5 291	2 205	3 420	10 031	6 645	35 541	1 998	2 205
Kalawao	(3)6 206	(3)3.3	(3)38 714	(3)1 333	(3)2 983	(3)507	(3)263	(3)617	(3)1 344	(3)1 040	(3)4 370	(3)261	(3)263
Kauai	2 728	4.0	39 251	1 259	1 243	221	111	247	580	536	1 822	111	111
Maui	(3)	(3)	(3)	(3)	(3)	(3)	(3)	(3)	(3)	(3)	(3)	(3)	(3)
IDAHO	58 272	3.9	36 146	X	25 360	4 306	2 317	7 110	11 934	10 745	39 093	2 296	2 317
Ada	17 656	4.7	42 395	897	9 572	1 465	840	2 192	3 488	2 458	14 069	846	840
Adams	126	2.3	33 017	2 249	36	8	4	7	41	33	55	4	4
Bannock	2 575	1.7	30 926	2 564	1 158	231	111	160	438	628	1 660	105	111
Bear Lake	206	3.2	34 618	1 969	57	13	6	19	38	48	95	6	6
Benewah	320	0.9	35 341	1 849	128	26	12	31	62	85	197	13	12
Bingham	1 488	4.9	32 855	2 273	523	97	48	299	246	292	966	49	48
Blaine	1 440	1.2	67 513	58	488	66	46	133	692	117	734	44	46
Boise	270	1.5	39 730	1 198	43	10	4	7	56	54	64	5	4
Bonner	1 420	3.0	34 890	1 915	459	85	45	100	437	326	689	48	45
Bonneville	4 152	3.0	38 616	1 352	1 592	264	150	726	763	683	2 732	157	150
Boundary	322	3.2	29 668	2 731	125	24	12	32	76	86	193	12	12
Butte	97	1.4	36 664	1 643	636	52	49	14	18	22	751	46	49
Camas	51	9.3	49 054	413	21	3	2	4	11	6	31	2	2
Canyon	5 092	5.0	25 606	3 036	1 903	337	184	416	875	1 313	2 839	181	184

1. Based on the resident population estimated as of July 1 of the year shown. 3. Kalawao county is included with Maui county.

STATE County	Earnings, 2013 (cont.) Percent by selected industries: Farm	Mining	Construction	Manu-facturing	Infor-mation: professional, scientific, technical services	Retail trade	Finance, insur-ance, real estate and leasing	Health care and social assistance	Govern-ment	Social Security beneficiaries, December 2013: Number	Rate[1]	Supple-mental Security Income recipients, December 2013	Housing units, 2014: Total	Percent change, 2010–2014
	75	76	77	78	79	80	81	82	83	84	85	86	87	88
GEORGIA—Cont'd														
Putnam	2.5	0.0	11.9	7.3	3.3	9.7	4.5	D	26.3	5 495	258	498	12 735	-0.5
Quitman	13.7	0.0	D	D	D	D	D	D	33.9	755	319	146	2 008	-2.0
Rabun	2.4	D	8.9	7.6	3.3	14.6	5.5	D	20.8	4 955	305	445	12 460	1.2
Randolph	21.3	0.0	D	D	D	8.8	3.5	D	18.4	1 750	244	435	4 100	-1.3
Richmond	0.0	0.1	4.2	8.0	7.3	4.9	3.5	13.5	41.3	37 900	188	8 281	87 076	0.9
Rockdale	0.1	D	10.7	20.9	10.0	8.2	5.0	11.0	12.9	14 760	170	1 891	33 286	0.0
Schley	10.4	0.0	D	29.3	D	D	D	D	25.6	865	171	143	2 159	-2.2
Screven	17.6	0.0	3.3	22.3	D	6.0	3.0	D	24.5	3 400	239	736	6 650	-1.3
Seminole	33.2	0.0	1.3	7.7	D	5.0	2.6	11.7	12.8	2 470	277	500	4 785	-0.3
Spalding	0.1	D	3.0	18.8	D	7.7	3.9	15.6	23.0	14 695	231	2 645	26 983	0.8
Stephens	0.4	D	D	19.6	3.1	7.6	3.0	D	19.3	6 865	268	1 085	12 506	-1.2
Stewart	4.2	0.0	D	0.0	D	1.9	D	18.0	31.0	1 085	198	273	2 336	-2.0
Sumter	9.8	D	2.7	8.9	D	7.6	2.7	13.3	25.6	6 510	208	1 404	13 849	-0.4
Talbot	5.6	11.4	20.0	0.0	D	2.3	D	D	27.3	1 630	253	315	3 363	-1.0
Taliaferro	29.7	0.0	D	D	0.0	D	D	D	44.1	490	289	100	1 005	-1.0
Tattnall	29.3	0.0	3.9	1.9	1.4	4.7	2.8	D	27.4	4 260	167	903	9 860	-1.1
Taylor	21.9	D	2.8	2.2	D	5.7	2.1	12.7	20.0	2 000	237	448	4 502	-1.3
Telfair	8.4	0.0	2.0	D	1.7	5.5	3.4	D	23.4	2 710	162	599	7 208	-1.2
Terrell	23.4	0.0	1.9	12.0	2.5	5.7	4.8	D	20.0	2 295	249	580	4 157	-0.1
Thomas	4.3	D	4.1	15.5	3.2	6.2	5.6	D	16.4	10 755	240	2 328	20 352	0.9
Tift	7.9	0.0	3.3	6.5	4.6	9.0	3.5	6.8	31.4	8 045	200	1 622	16 402	-0.2
Toombs	8.5	0.0	4.6	9.6	D	8.2	2.5	D	12.9	5 990	219	1 366	12 089	-0.5
Towns	3.4	D	6.5	3.0	D	8.5	6.6	D	16.5	4 385	408	242	7 887	2.0
Treutlen	12.8	0.0	D	D	D	9.6	D	D	30.0	1 515	227	367	2 982	-0.3
Troup	0.1	D	4.6	34.5	4.8	8.3	4.0	8.9	10.5	13 545	196	2 304	28 250	0.7
Turner	33.2	0.0	1.1	8.4	D	5.1	D	3.1	20.4	2 200	270	484	3 807	-0.9
Twiggs	-1.3	D	D	D	D	2.9	D	D	25.7	2 450	290	482	4 190	-1.1
Union	0.9	D	5.6	4.0	3.2	10.6	6.1	D	25.7	7 740	358	488	14 255	1.4
Upson	1.1	0.0	6.1	20.2	D	7.8	5.0	18.9	19.9	7 055	266	1 211	12 103	-0.5
Walker	2.7	D	4.1	31.8	2.7	6.1	5.0	5.7	24.1	15 860	232	1 944	30 098	0.0
Walton	1.9	0.1	11.6	14.8	4.1	12.1	3.0	7.9	21.0	15 820	184	2 033	32 544	0.3
Ware	2.3	0.0	3.9	8.9	D	10.0	3.5	19.1	20.3	7 895	221	1 754	16 408	0.5
Warren	4.0	D	D	20.7	D	4.5	D	D	16.6	1 505	271	305	2 946	-1.3
Washington	5.0	3.6	4.8	6.7	4.3	6.1	4.7	D	29.4	4 735	229	976	9 055	0.1
Wayne	4.5	0.0	8.8	20.8	D	7.2	2.8	D	30.4	6 330	211	1 083	12 118	-0.7
Webster	23.0	D	0.3	D	0.0	5.0	0.8	0.0	18.6	540	199	90	1 504	-1.3
Wheeler	12.4	0.0	1.5	0.0	D	2.3	D	11.5	20.5	1 225	154	248	2 594	-1.2
White	3.4	D	12.9	15.3	D	11.2	4.0	D	18.7	6 915	249	611	15 994	-0.4
Whitfield	0.3	0.2	2.3	35.8	9.1	7.0	2.1	8.9	10.2	17 885	173	2 431	39 642	-0.6
Wilcox	49.8	0.0	D	D	D	2.8	D	D	24.2	1 780	198	381	3 480	-0.9
Wilkes	8.6	0.0	3.1	16.7	D	7.9	4.8	6.2	27.9	2 875	289	472	5 155	-0.1
Wilkinson	-0.3	45.5	6.9	12.4	1.2	2.0	D	2.8	12.4	2 515	267	371	4 439	-1.1
Worth	35.4	0.0	4.2	6.2	2.0	5.0	2.3	D	17.9	4 385	208	786	9 196	-0.6
HAWAII	0.8	0.1	7.2	1.8	7.3	6.1	7.2	9.5	30.9	246 477	175	25 342	530 106	2.0
Hawaii	2.0	D	D	D	D	D	6.9	D	24.2	39 695	207	5 400	85 163	3.4
Honolulu	0.3	0.1	6.9	1.9	8.1	5.5	7.3	9.8	33.8	165 805	168	16 925	343 017	1.8
Kalawao	(3)2.9	(3)D	(3)8.1	(3)1.4	(3)4.3	(3)8.4	(3)6.5	(3)7.1	(3)17.3	0	0	0	113	0.0
Kauai	2.3	D	D	D	D	D	8.1	D	20.2	13 925	200	990	30 346	1.9
Maui	(3)	(3)	(3)	(3)	(3)	(3)	(3)	(3)	(3)	27 050	168	2 027	71 467	1.5
IDAHO	7.1	0.8	6.1	10.7	8.6	8.1	6.0	11.4	17.3	298 269	185	30 317	685 099	2.6
Ada	0.5	0.4	6.9	11.9	9.7	8.1	8.9	13.7	14.8	66 850	160	6 509	167 215	4.9
Adams	-1.0	D	6.0	12.3	5.2	7.5	4.0	D	30.7	1 135	296	52	2 636	0.0
Bannock	1.3	D	5.0	7.4	D	8.2	6.6	15.9	25.5	13 690	164	1 850	33 380	0.6
Bear Lake	10.1	D	3.0	2.7	D	8.0	2.7	3.1	33.6	1 440	243	104	3 987	1.9
Benewah	2.3	D	2.8	16.5	2.6	11.9	1.6	D	33.6	2 605	288	238	4 614	-0.3
Bingham	21.1	D	6.4	12.8	D	4.3	2.7	8.3	18.4	7 845	173	904	16 225	0.5
Blaine	2.1	D	11.9	4.4	13.6	9.0	9.7	10.1	12.5	3 695	173	116	15 121	0.5
Boise	0.4	D	6.2	2.2	D	5.3	D	3.0	38.4	1 800	267	126	5 339	0.9
Bonner	0.1	1.4	6.9	15.5	6.7	15.3	4.9	7.7	18.3	10 995	270	843	24 580	-0.4
Bonneville	4.9	D	6.5	5.4	9.0	9.9	5.4	16.2	12.2	17 480	163	2 139	40 718	2.5
Boundary	10.3	D	5.4	15.8	3.6	7.4	2.6	7.0	28.3	2 915	268	256	5 247	1.4
Butte	1.6	0.0	0.3	0.3	93.0	0.3	D	0.5	2.1	635	242	53	1 351	-0.3
Camas	19.7	0.0	D	D	D	D	D	D	18.7	200	192	15	836	0.6
Canyon	7.3	0.1	8.1	15.4	4.6	9.2	4.0	9.6	15.9	33 540	169	4 635	71 326	2.8

1. Per 1,000 resident population estimated as of July 1 of the year shown. 3. Kalawao county is included with Maui county.

STATE County	Housing units, 2009–2013								Civilian labor force, 2014				Civilian employment,[6] 2009–2013		
	Occupied units										Unemployment			Percent	
		Owner-occupied				Renter-occupied									
				Median owner cost as a percent of income											
	Total	Percent	Median value[1]	With a mortgage	Without a mortgage[2]	Median rent[3]	Median rent as a percent of income[2]	Substandard units[4] (percent)	Total	Percent change, 2013–2014	Total	Rate[5]	Total	Management, business, science and arts	Construction, production, and maintenance occupations
	89	90	91	92	93	94	95	96	97	98	99	100	101	102	103
GEORGIA—Cont'd															
Putnam	8 457	77.1	140 600	24.0	11.6	695	32.1	3.1	8 094	-0.7	745	9.2	8 953	29.2	28.3
Quitman	932	77.3	62 300	24.4	13.5	624	33.4	1.8	891	-1.5	77	8.6	685	15.0	31.2
Rabun	6 997	73.2	168 300	29.2	13.1	718	39.1	5.1	6 568	-3.8	548	8.3	6 439	28.6	24.6
Randolph	3 020	71.2	70 300	30.6	13.1	622	31.9	2.8	2 702	-3.3	261	9.7	2 639	23.9	33.2
Richmond	72 281	54.5	100 900	23.9	12.1	763	33.4	3.2	85 777	-1.1	7 436	8.7	77 529	30.1	21.5
Rockdale	29 317	69.0	149 900	24.6	10.2	943	31.7	4.5	42 296	0.2	3 339	7.9	37 583	33.2	25.0
Schley	1 829	64.4	93 000	20.2	14.6	570	23.8	1.6	2 148	0.8	166	7.7	1 950	26.9	39.7
Screven	5 165	70.8	77 000	24.6	12.1	541	32.3	5.0	5 482	-1.6	550	10.0	5 378	27.6	32.7
Seminole	3 317	77.0	71 200	27.4	13.2	613	30.0	2.8	3 134	0.0	299	9.5	2 968	25.6	24.0
Spalding	22 997	63.1	113 900	24.3	13.0	773	34.1	3.9	27 639	-0.6	2 625	9.5	24 560	25.0	30.8
Stephens	9 227	74.7	106 600	23.5	13.2	593	30.5	3.2	11 258	-2.0	856	7.6	10 316	26.7	26.8
Stewart	1 851	63.3	50 600	24.4	14.3	476	38.6	3.2	2 194	-4.3	174	7.9	1 735	21.2	35.1
Sumter	11 493	58.2	90 300	24.0	13.3	608	29.3	2.6	13 517	0.7	1 296	9.6	12 475	31.0	26.3
Talbot	2 682	75.9	76 500	27.9	17.2	557	28.0	3.3	2 834	-0.8	224	7.9	2 356	25.4	33.3
Taliaferro	704	73.2	68 300	23.9	18.6	488	30.6	3.2	598	1.2	66	11.0	569	14.1	42.5
Tattnall	7 885	71.3	86 100	25.0	12.9	535	24.2	3.6	9 584	-0.1	705	7.4	7 836	29.8	30.2
Taylor	3 681	69.3	60 800	24.0	17.2	543	22.2	3.4	2 879	-9.4	301	10.5	3 196	27.2	32.5
Telfair	5 567	64.8	58 300	26.5	14.5	514	29.9	3.3	5 158	-2.7	524	10.2	4 382	29.7	26.1
Terrell	3 351	63.4	78 800	24.6	15.0	548	31.4	2.0	3 567	-2.6	292	8.2	3 294	21.3	35.7
Thomas	17 377	56.5	127 000	25.6	13.7	690	36.5	4.5	17 312	-2.5	1 483	8.6	16 253	34.0	22.7
Tift	13 691	61.1	117 300	23.7	11.6	612	29.4	3.0	18 119	-3.1	1 336	7.4	15 489	30.3	29.0
Toombs	10 310	62.4	88 100	21.6	11.7	552	33.2	1.9	12 403	-3.1	1 229	9.9	10 453	25.4	31.1
Towns	4 261	84.8	164 000	32.6	12.6	664	32.7	1.0	4 067	-1.9	363	8.9	3 649	28.2	27.2
Treutlen	2 515	68.0	64 300	25.9	10.1	521	27.0	3.5	2 779	-1.8	299	10.8	2 280	19.8	29.4
Troup	24 441	60.9	121 300	23.7	12.1	733	33.8	4.5	36 187	0.0	2 699	7.5	27 654	28.7	30.8
Turner	3 166	64.7	83 800	21.0	17.9	603	38.0	1.3	3 215	-3.5	255	7.9	2 919	33.5	28.8
Twiggs	3 056	80.0	54 700	21.8	12.5	587	37.4	1.1	3 066	-1.9	349	11.4	2 671	26.7	35.2
Union	9 141	78.3	198 300	25.2	12.6	607	33.6	2.9	9 413	1.1	613	6.5	7 393	28.6	21.3
Upson	10 341	67.0	86 600	23.6	12.9	661	33.9	4.5	11 276	-5.5	1 036	9.2	10 306	23.8	32.4
Walker	26 191	72.6	104 700	22.1	11.4	637	29.8	1.7	29 506	-1.9	2 114	7.2	28 100	27.4	34.6
Walton	29 520	75.1	157 100	24.4	11.9	839	34.0	3.9	41 172	0.3	2 665	6.5	37 092	30.6	25.1
Ware	13 460	65.3	79 600	22.0	12.5	646	31.2	2.1	14 800	-2.1	1 205	8.1	13 222	30.2	25.9
Warren	2 208	65.9	66 700	26.0	15.5	543	34.3	2.6	2 723	-0.2	270	9.9	1 904	19.6	42.1
Washington	7 119	72.5	82 300	23.1	12.3	554	35.3	2.1	7 520	-2.3	633	8.4	7 405	27.1	29.1
Wayne	10 171	69.1	80 400	22.5	12.1	637	29.6	2.3	11 828	-3.9	1 063	9.0	10 702	25.6	35.0
Webster	1 129	79.7	48 800	25.9	10.4	584	15.0	0.7	1 017	-1.4	86	8.5	1 128	36.6	31.6
Wheeler	2 096	66.6	54 200	22.6	11.8	476	27.1	2.9	1 899	0.3	230	12.1	1 504	25.2	37.9
White	11 788	74.3	169 600	27.8	12.4	759	39.4	6.4	13 846	0.3	874	6.3	11 175	27.3	25.5
Whitfield	34 450	65.7	122 800	23.9	10.3	677	29.2	5.4	44 869	0.4	3 558	7.9	43 553	22.8	40.0
Wilcox	2 705	75.6	71 200	25.7	12.2	470	31.2	1.7	2 865	1.6	270	9.4	2 451	31.0	28.4
Wilkes	4 083	72.1	95 200	32.2	16.7	569	34.8	3.3	3 766	0.7	354	9.4	3 608	26.7	34.8
Wilkinson	3 348	78.2	71 600	22.0	11.9	572	37.5	1.8	3 722	0.1	326	8.8	3 197	20.3	36.6
Worth	7 851	74.1	75 400	23.4	12.1	616	30.7	9.8	9 050	-1.9	709	7.8	8 332	25.3	32.9
HAWAII	449 771	57.6	503 100	29.3	10.0	1 380	33.3	9.5	668 177	2.6	29 153	4.4	640 072	33.7	18.2
Hawaii	64 909	65.7	309 800	30.4	10.0	1 049	34.3	9.0	87 346	1.5	4 846	5.5	81 463	31.4	19.5
Honolulu	309 803	55.5	556 300	28.5	10.0	1 467	33.6	0.0	463 568	2.7	18 890	4.1	446 822	35.5	17.8
Kalawao	46	0.0	0	0.0	0.0	850	16.3	9.8	NA	NA	NA	NA	51	45.1	21.6
Kauai	22 390	62.6	484 500	32.0	11.9	1 239	29.4	12.0	34 623	2.0	1 684	4.9	32 247	29.4	19.2
Maui	52 623	58.1	523 700	32.0	10.0	1 291	31.8	2.2	82 639	3.5	3 732	4.5	79 489	28.1	18.8
IDAHO	579 797	69.8	162 100	24.1	10.2	728	29.8	3.4	777 238	0.8	37 404	4.8	696 190	33.3	24.2
Ada	151 600	68.1	183 600	23.2	10.0	833	30.1	3.6	210 284	1.8	8 620	4.1	190 542	41.6	15.2
Adams	1 707	81.6	150 500	27.4	12.6	565	27.1	2.7	1 662	-2.6	166	10.0	1 642	26.1	29.0
Bannock	30 271	68.8	142 600	22.7	10.5	614	31.1	1.6	41 703	0.7	1 911	4.6	37 606	34.1	22.1
Bear Lake	2 442	81.3	129 700	18.8	11.1	559	24.9	4.2	2 859	-0.8	127	4.4	2 428	25.7	33.5
Benewah	3 888	75.2	136 000	24.1	12.3	605	24.5	5.8	3 943	-1.2	321	8.1	3 744	29.0	37.4
Bingham	14 650	74.8	135 400	21.7	10.0	605	24.6	3.6	22 042	-1.1	1 002	4.5	10 954	20.4	32.6
Blaine	9 207	70.1	375 000	28.6	11.7	932	23.3	4.1	11 429	-1.3	510	4.5	11 725	34.4	19.2
Boise	2 994	78.3	195 600	25.4	10.8	600	29.9	5.3	2 935	0.7	176	6.0	2 845	37.7	23.6
Bonner	17 388	73.1	222 200	30.3	10.7	716	30.0	2.7	18 138	-0.7	1 280	7.1	16 311	28.7	27.5
Bonneville	36 066	73.0	154 700	22.3	10.0	703	29.7	4.3	49 556	1.2	2 088	4.2	46 735	34.6	21.7
Boundary	4 144	74.4	174 300	26.7	11.8	660	34.1	2.6	4 880	-0.7	293	6.0	3 792	31.2	27.6
Butte	1 022	79.5	110 300	24.5	11.7	535	35.6	1.7	1 309	1.2	68	5.2	1 028	34.6	28.3
Camas	464	67.7	163 000	29.3	10.0	676	30.9	4.5	628	-0.9	30	4.8	575	28.5	35.1
Canyon	63 442	69.3	122 800	25.9	11.3	738	31.5	1.4	88 595	1.1	5 191	5.9	77 089	26.7	29.0

1. Specified owner-occupied units. 2. A value of 10.0 represents 10 percent or less; a value of 50.0 represents 50 percent or more. 3. Specified renter-occupied units.
4. Overcrowded or lacking complete plumbing facilities. 5. Percent of civilian labor force. 6. Persons 16 years old and over.

STATE County	Private nonfarm establishments, employment and payroll, 2013									Agriculture, 2012			
		Employment						Annual payroll		Farms			
											Percent with:		
	Number of establish-ments	Total	Health care and social assistance	Manufac-turing	Retail trade	Finance and insurance	Professional, scientific, and technical services	Total (mil dol)	Average per employee (dollars)	Number	Fewer than 50 acres	500 acres or more	Farm operators whose principal occu-pation is farming (percent)
	104	105	106	107	108	109	110	111	112	113	114	115	116
GEORGIA—Cont'd													
Putnam	396	4 444	486	562	670	161	61	134	30 048	165	37.0	6.7	41.2
Quitman	38	231	D	D	D	D	D	5	23 719	21	19.0	23.8	23.8
Rabun	454	3 987	578	309	D	141	116	114	28 617	114	57.0	0.9	62.3
Randolph	132	1 384	D	D	168	D	D	43	31 341	197	11.2	27.4	45.7
Richmond	4 313	85 077	23 934	7 507	10 727	2 305	4 280	3 313	38 946	123	59.3	5.7	40.7
Rockdale	1 927	28 615	3 784	4 568	4 448	738	863	1 138	39 778	103	77.7	1.0	58.3
Schley	58	763	D	D	71	D	D	30	38 819	92	17.4	19.6	41.3
Screven	213	2 384	278	D	370	100	D	75	31 362	344	14.8	26.2	48.5
Seminole	187	1 559	418	D	329	D	31	45	28 897	149	28.2	27.5	67.1
Spalding	1 117	16 590	4 197	2 918	2 605	491	357	524	31 582	258	63.6	1.9	49.2
Stephens	544	7 966	1 349	2 036	1 154	176	D	271	34 002	218	45.0	0.9	53.7
Stewart	62	787	172	NA	64	D	D	21	26 882	108	7.4	36.1	36.1
Sumter	629	8 951	2 536	1 147	1 380	216	233	253	28 239	369	19.2	19.0	38.2
Talbot	57	538	D	D	43	D	D	18	34 236	90	22.2	23.3	43.3
Taliaferro	17	45	NA	D	NA	D	NA	1	28 044	55	16.4	10.9	43.6
Tattnall	289	3 016	757	65	423	118	73	97	32 195	565	35.6	8.3	59.1
Taylor	120	855	187	55	124	47	D	28	32 873	224	21.0	15.2	46.9
Telfair	190	3 171	396	D	294	96	25	68	21 514	300	29.3	9.0	36.7
Terrell	164	1 705	152	D	254	D	D	50	29 100	248	21.4	24.2	42.3
Thomas	1 051	14 947	D	2 747	2 056	620	294	580	38 775	407	35.4	21.1	54.3
Tift	1 017	15 454	3 015	1 444	2 468	402	520	530	34 304	285	39.6	15.4	43.2
Toombs	673	9 231	2 217	1 264	1 619	271	523	283	30 705	268	36.9	12.7	29.9
Towns	285	2 731	466	45	383	78	58	69	25 124	109	58.7	0.0	49.5
Treutlen	82	571	125	D	150	D	D	14	24 287	149	31.5	11.4	27.5
Troup	1 410	33 030	3 098	11 183	3 125	1 008	787	1 301	39 393	212	48.1	7.1	50.5
Turner	153	1 392	159	353	168	69	32	39	27 874	262	34.7	20.2	40.8
Twiggs	75	1 484	223	NA	D	D	21	51	34 259	108	36.1	12.0	37.0
Union	531	4 895	1 162	271	1 048	D	186	152	30 975	249	51.8	2.8	42.6
Upson	446	5 903	1 425	1 320	1 029	D	150	187	31 657	296	43.6	5.1	39.9
Walker	707	9 999	921	D	1 415	315	146	300	29 956	528	40.3	6.3	53.4
Walton	1 520	15 244	1 708	1 761	2 373	425	536	519	34 049	477	50.3	3.4	54.3
Ware	849	11 477	2 923	1 276	2 472	328	234	359	31 238	280	44.3	8.9	43.9
Warren	65	599	D	D	73	D	D	21	35 780	134	26.1	13.4	38.1
Washington	336	5 366	1 051	477	742	157	179	206	38 396	408	22.5	13.0	36.8
Wayne	538	5 671	D	D	1 213	177	D	212	37 393	287	37.3	13.9	41.5
Webster	29	346	D	D	NA	D	NA	13	37 913	102	19.6	22.5	39.2
Wheeler	67	1 011	D	NA	65	D	D	31	30 862	136	15.4	17.6	25.7
White	584	5 191	438	650	1 133	141	D	149	28 709	299	64.2	2.7	53.8
Whitfield	2 175	46 606	4 402	15 685	4 824	745	1 624	1 737	37 271	378	45.2	2.6	49.2
Wilcox	92	470	152	D	D	50	D	14	28 745	365	21.6	23.6	47.9
Wilkes	197	2 235	532	D	332	D	29	62	27 724	317	24.0	13.2	47.0
Wilkinson	149	2 049	188	D	148	36	D	96	46 721	114	29.8	4.4	39.5
Worth	282	2 578	488	260	440	76	66	70	27 114	487	27.3	28.5	51.1
HAWAII	31 622	502 530	67 974	12 172	70 051	20 125	22 384	19 881	39 562	7 000	88.1	2.6	52.0
Hawaii	3 923	50 266	8 299	1 259	9 128	1 210	1 500	1 728	34 367	4 282	87.6	2.3	48.2
Honolulu	21 173	347 954	50 413	9 555	47 539	16 589	18 269	14 466	41 573	999	90.6	2.1	66.3
Kalawao	1	D	NA	NA	NA	NA	NA	D	D	NA	NA	NA	NA
Kauai	1 986	25 186	3 038	301	3 992	381	747	881	34 967	591	85.3	4.2	52.3
Maui	4 409	60 720	6 209	1 057	9 389	1 002	1 475	2 162	35 609	1 128	89.0	3.5	54.0
IDAHO	43 124	509 986	84 446	56 982	74 858	21 335	32 485	18 559	36 391	24 816	47.9	17.1	49.8
Ada	12 216	174 796	29 696	16 447	21 130	9 215	12 633	7 455	42 650	1 233	80.0	3.1	43.6
Adams	115	455	D	D	86	D	D	12	26 927	234	35.5	20.1	53.4
Bannock	1 953	23 611	4 795	1 752	4 446	1 892	1 223	714	30 228	819	46.6	16.1	42.6
Bear Lake	117	938	D	D	237	D	D	26	27 239	493	25.2	24.7	46.9
Benewah	228	2 190	409	D	285	D	D	77	35 179	274	35.0	16.8	45.6
Bingham	819	9 700	1 791	2 293	1 141	305	174	332	34 212	1 265	56.4	17.1	58.5
Blaine	1 339	10 413	684	316	1 346	270	D	378	36 305	186	39.2	30.1	58.6
Boise	151	491	D	D	100	D	7	12	23 953	105	43.8	12.4	57.1
Bonner	1 398	10 977	1 572	1 739	1 879	200	510	392	35 725	686	51.0	3.4	42.9
Bonneville	3 244	44 031	7 772	2 566	7 077	1 203	D	1 718	39 010	893	53.1	18.6	39.0
Boundary	355	2 340	547	366	385	D	74	68	28 959	370	44.3	12.2	41.4
Butte	59	D	D	D	D	D	D	D	D	214	21.5	31.3	71.0
Camas	27	D	D	D	NA	D	NA	D	D	114	24.6	36.8	56.1
Canyon	3 627	45 609	7 002	8 045	7 406	1 017	1 349	1 390	30 471	2 331	71.3	6.0	45.6

STATE County	Agriculture, 2012 (cont.)															
	Land in farms					Value of land and buildings (dollars)		Value of machinery and equipment, average per farm (dollars)	Value of products sold				Percent of farms with sales of:		Government payments	
	Acreage (1,000)	Percent change, 2007–2012	Acres: Average size of farm	Acres: Total irrigated (1,000)	Acres: Total cropland (1,000)	Average per farm	Average per acre		Total (mil dol)	Average per farm (dollars)	Percent from: Crops	Percent from: Livestock and poultry products	$10,000 or more	$100,000 or more	Total ($1,000)	Percent of farms
	117	118	119	120	121	122	123	124	125	126	127	128	129	130	131	132
GEORGIA—Cont'd																
Putnam	28	-24.5	173	0.8	9.6	656 891	3 803	91 436	38.0	230 521	3.8	96.2	35.8	13.3	567	20.0
Quitman	9	-20.0	433	0.0	2.4	924 667	2 133	66 762	D	D	D	D	14.3	9.5	D	57.1
Rabun	8	1.7	71	D	3.6	500 658	7 078	73 737	21.3	186 719	20.8	79.2	50.9	21.9	138	11.4
Randolph	119	32.4	605	22.0	64.7	1 171 264	1 935	185 523	50.3	255 442	95.8	4.2	40.1	22.3	2 025	79.7
Richmond	14	11.1	113	0.1	3.9	299 699	2 650	58 967	2.0	16 276	45.6	54.4	28.5	6.5	42	12.2
Rockdale	5	-13.6	53	0.0	0.9	370 515	6 982	38 777	0.5	4 660	56.5	43.5	11.7	1.0	4	6.8
Schley	35	-2.3	385	0.8	7.1	875 543	2 273	56 413	18.1	196 239	11.2	88.8	34.8	15.2	284	58.7
Screven	180	1.0	525	17.9	103.0	1 119 872	2 134	170 779	66.6	193 669	92.3	7.7	37.5	18.3	2 076	75.0
Seminole	88	-14.8	592	38.9	62.0	1 600 074	2 703	268 034	74.7	501 631	90.7	9.3	63.1	35.6	1 883	65.1
Spalding	19	-28.8	73	0.0	5.1	381 438	5 229	37 888	5.2	20 298	19.2	80.8	17.4	3.9	60	12.8
Stephens	18	19.7	84	0.0	4.8	445 170	5 272	96 917	79.7	365 583	0.6	99.4	50.5	25.7	189	12.4
Stewart	59	28.6	549	4.4	19.7	1 076 824	1 963	127 593	14.6	135 417	80.6	19.4	30.6	17.6	917	68.5
Sumter	160	4.8	435	44.3	90.4	983 650	2 264	167 710	123.3	334 236	68.4	31.6	36.3	18.4	3 044	68.6
Talbot	34	-18.7	377	D	4.9	784 578	2 084	42 133	0.7	8 200	37.0	63.1	18.9	2.2	266	21.1
Taliaferro	14	-2.1	251	0.1	3.6	552 345	2 202	66 745	8.5	153 709	5.0	95.0	40.0	18.2	75	23.6
Tattnall	108	-20.7	190	13.8	49.2	528 524	2 778	97 715	236.2	418 099	36.7	63.3	49.4	27.1	1 594	36.5
Taylor	62	-29.0	275	6.0	21.7	556 027	2 025	65 634	22.7	101 505	55.5	44.5	29.0	6.7	510	51.3
Telfair	67	7.9	222	4.0	13.8	422 643	1 903	46 887	6.1	20 390	78.8	21.2	25.7	4.7	581	57.3
Terrell	121	-11.6	487	25.8	73.2	1 150 536	2 364	163 758	68.2	274 843	96.7	3.3	33.9	26.2	3 795	81.5
Thomas	173	-15.2	426	11.5	81.6	1 423 002	3 344	159 329	83.5	205 061	77.8	22.2	43.7	22.6	2 676	56.3
Tift	84	-36.4	296	20.6	50.0	941 074	3 176	135 681	70.6	247 653	94.0	6.0	43.5	23.5	1 695	50.5
Toombs	73	-18.5	273	9.9	30.6	647 821	2 371	84 123	58.9	219 746	78.3	21.7	31.3	11.2	745	48.5
Towns	8	12.3	77	0.0	2.1	456 587	5 913	50 862	3.2	29 367	36.6	63.4	30.3	8.3	35	4.6
Treutlen	35	16.7	236	D	9.7	423 060	1 794	64 107	8.3	55 376	95.0	5.0	20.1	3.4	259	60.4
Troup	32	-14.4	153	0.2	5.2	608 769	3 981	52 245	4.2	19 660	23.6	76.3	25.9	2.4	94	8.0
Turner	87	-25.0	332	19.1	47.5	791 313	2 384	141 511	58.4	223 050	86.8	13.2	39.7	19.8	2 000	72.1
Twiggs	39	-13.9	358	5.1	14.3	895 907	2 501	93 389	9.3	85 685	93.5	6.5	23.1	7.4	738	30.6
Union	21	-1.2	83	0.0	6.1	500 076	6 015	65 426	19.4	77 751	23.5	76.5	39.8	5.6	221	15.7
Upson	45	-6.1	151	D	8.2	478 044	3 160	51 111	23.0	77 770	8.5	91.5	20.9	5.7	193	14.5
Walker	80	12.0	151	0.3	28.5	589 797	3 907	71 972	108.2	204 932	8.1	91.9	42.8	13.6	1 049	16.3
Walton	52	-2.3	110	0.9	14.3	590 239	5 367	39 698	29.4	61 660	21.2	78.8	32.1	7.5	371	21.0
Ware	57	12.8	203	4.9	18.5	499 896	2 468	72 825	30.6	109 114	65.6	34.4	40.4	10.4	339	32.9
Warren	34	-7.5	257	0.1	9.2	518 627	2 019	54 731	5.6	41 694	58.0	42.0	27.6	8.2	225	23.1
Washington	100	-9.3	245	7.8	42.8	506 213	2 067	88 184	27.5	67 507	73.8	26.2	32.8	9.8	1 104	52.0
Wayne	62	9.6	217	6.6	35.6	595 854	2 746	115 289	44.3	154 456	59.8	40.2	42.5	19.5	748	42.5
Webster	48	-12.1	471	4.8	22.2	834 667	1 772	59 471	17.2	168 471	88.7	11.3	32.4	16.7	619	74.5
Wheeler	51	-11.4	372	2.5	11.6	556 206	1 493	60 529	8.1	59 706	95.5	4.5	28.7	6.6	473	66.9
White	23	11.8	79	0.1	5.9	539 097	6 866	50 181	77.4	258 957	2.9	97.1	45.2	27.1	129	9.7
Whitfield	39	-8.5	103	0.0	10.6	501 405	4 846	66 577	144.2	381 362	1.2	98.8	36.0	17.2	85	7.4
Wilcox	115	14.5	316	28.4	75.2	771 348	2 439	146 175	104.9	287 512	64.5	35.5	41.9	26.3	2 491	80.3
Wilkes	94	4.4	296	0.1	19.7	820 962	2 777	62 407	58.7	185 306	5.6	94.4	45.1	16.7	662	33.1
Wilkinson	16	-46.8	140	0.5	4.8	297 851	2 134	40 939	4.5	39 614	29.3	70.7	24.6	8.8	42	23.7
Worth	229	19.1	471	47.2	137.4	1 216 889	2 584	177 600	153.5	315 187	90.6	9.4	42.5	28.7	5 342	67.8
HAWAII	1 129	0.7	161	81.8	174.0	1 461 342	9 058	43 999	661.3	94 478	81.5	18.5	41.6	7.2	5 228	9.0
Hawaii	687	0.4	160	7.0	72.0	1 280 898	7 985	36 698	247.2	57 741	63.3	36.7	40.6	6.1	4 153	8.2
Honolulu	69	14.5	69	10.8	22.2	1 396 597	20 171	56 908	161.5	161 650	90.0	10.0	54.6	12.7	283	6.1
Kalawao	NA	NA	NA	NA	NA	NA	NA	NA	NA	NA	NA	NA	NA	NA	NA	NA
Kauai	144	-4.9	244	22.5	30.2	1 853 486	7 600	57 464	64.5	109 161	86.3	13.7	35.2	6.6	234	16.2
Maui	229	1.6	203	41.5	49.6	1 998 207	9 836	53 229	188.1	166 755	96.5	3.5	37.1	7.1	558	10.5
IDAHO	11 760	2.3	474	3 365.3	5 793.3	1 052 941	2 222	143 835	7 801.4	314 372	44.1	55.9	44.3	20.5	99 789	37.7
Ada	144	-24.8	117	55.3	53.4	616 596	5 278	70 942	221.0	179 229	20.2	79.8	26.8	7.9	704	10.2
Adams	136	-8.6	582	19.0	19.8	885 517	1 521	67 226	13.5	57 902	25.1	74.9	41.9	11.5	104	16.7
Bannock	295	-8.3	360	52.6	164.1	651 077	1 807	83 179	54.3	66 267	66.6	33.4	29.4	9.2	3 067	37.0
Bear Lake	258	10.6	523	54.5	112.5	743 225	1 421	101 310	29.5	59 850	35.4	64.6	52.7	15.8	1 316	47.1
Benewah	147	-4.5	505	0.0	81.7	849 000	1 587	106 938	23.9	87 058	96.9	3.1	29.6	10.9	1 516	45.6
Bingham	870	-4.7	687	333.4	369.5	1 536 482	2 235	194 538	453.3	358 314	82.7	17.3	46.5	23.7	5 568	33.9
Blaine	179	-6.7	963	41.9	47.6	2 752 371	2 858	165 301	38.6	207 376	72.2	27.8	62.9	32.8	415	40.3
Boise	D	D	D	2.4	3.0	667 895	D	34 914	3.1	29 133	39.8	60.3	29.5	6.7	D	6.7
Bonner	81	-14.6	118	1.2	26.1	513 108	4 366	43 496	10.2	14 940	60.1	39.9	24.2	1.9	96	4.7
Bonneville	409	-9.7	458	133.6	278.8	1 061 908	2 317	134 569	204.2	228 641	71.8	28.2	39.9	17.9	5 044	43.2
Boundary	75	2.3	203	2.1	46.7	694 997	3 420	72 922	27.8	75 203	84.1	15.8	41.1	15.7	785	23.5
Butte	125	3.3	585	58.7	68.6	901 136	1 540	148 860	39.3	183 640	82.4	17.6	71.0	38.8	1 539	67.3
Camas	168	21.1	1 471	20.4	82.7	2 182 649	1 484	176 982	21.6	189 500	83.5	16.5	51.8	26.3	406	55.3
Canyon	304	16.7	130	225.3	217.8	694 984	5 332	109 214	513.7	220 387	53.0	47.0	38.9	15.6	2 241	20.6

Table B. States and Counties — **Water Use, Wholesale Trade, Retail Trade, and Real Estate**

STATE County	Water use, 2010		Wholesale trade,[1] 2007				Retail trade,[2] 2007				Real estate and rental and leasing,[2] 2007			
	Total water withdrawn (mil gal/day)	Gallons withdrawn per person per day	Number of establish-ments	Number of employees	Sales (mil dol)	Annual payroll (mil dol)	Number of establish-ments	Number of employees	Sales (mil dol)	Annual payroll (mil dol)	Number of establish-ments	Number of employees	Receipts (mil dol)	Annual payroll (mil dol)
	133	134	135	136	137	138	139	140	141	142	143	144	145	146
GEORGIA—Cont'd														
Putnam	957.6	45 130	16	96	75.5	3.6	95	899	204.1	21.4	34	203	16.3	3.0
Quitman	0.5	183	3	D	D	D	5	26	2.8	0.3	1	D	D	D
Rabun	3.2	194	5	D	D	D	92	949	234.4	23.4	27	54	10.4	1.3
Randolph	25.2	3 263	9	53	41.7	1.5	31	211	44.3	3.6	4	12	0.8	0.2
Richmond	114.4	571	196	2 249	916.4	94.3	895	11 084	2 505.1	233.6	233	1 449	220.1	38.5
Rockdale	13.6	160	101	726	515.6	33.7	329	5 488	1 450.1	138.0	98	389	85.3	14.0
Schley	1.0	202	3	D	D	D	13	110	18.6	1.9	NA	NA	NA	NA
Screven	7.1	488	7	31	17.5	0.6	51	427	93.6	7.7	12	36	1.9	0.5
Seminole	45.6	5 224	11	58	48.8	2.1	53	382	76.5	6.6	5	14	0.8	0.2
Spalding	6.3	98	54	565	604.3	20.9	252	2 948	661.6	63.1	62	243	28.1	5.8
Stephens	5.9	225	30	D	D	D	101	1 164	274.7	24.5	12	30	3.2	0.8
Stewart	1.6	262	3	16	2.6	0.4	22	89	23.9	1.6	1	D	D	D
Sumter	42.1	1 282	31	462	239.0	12.6	150	1 575	326.1	29.3	24	86	11.3	1.7
Talbot	2.9	415	3	D	D	D	7	23	4.7	0.3	NA	NA	NA	NA
Taliaferro	0.1	76	NA	NA	NA	NA	4	14	1.7	0.2	2	D	D	D
Tattnall	9.0	351	21	446	152.0	11.9	70	518	102.4	9.9	11	31	2.3	0.4
Taylor	6.0	671	5	93	21.4	3.0	28	190	46.4	3.6	4	10	0.7	0.1
Telfair	6.2	378	12	66	30.5	1.7	51	396	77.3	6.5	3	D	D	D
Terrell	26.1	2 798	10	D	D	D	52	343	68.3	5.7	5	D	D	D
Thomas	11.1	249	63	752	575.3	35.4	239	2 567	627.5	55.4	44	167	23.7	4.0
Tift	17.3	432	70	1 205	612.2	41.2	242	2 515	721.6	52.1	51	217	32.4	5.0
Toombs	10.8	396	35	611	665.0	20.7	158	1 702	386.3	33.9	25	86	12.0	1.7
Towns	4.5	429	11	28	6.2	0.7	72	446	102.3	8.6	28	71	16.6	1.8
Treutlen	2.2	312	5	D	D	D	25	199	30.4	3.0	1	D	D	D
Troup	12.0	179	57	D	D	D	295	3 357	798.8	71.3	66	445	41.7	9.0
Turner	9.4	1 053	15	148	103.2	4.8	34	193	64.5	3.4	4	D	D	D
Twiggs	6.6	729	2	D	D	D	18	99	30.3	2.1	1	D	D	D
Union	8.0	375	12	99	38.1	3.3	117	981	246.7	20.1	60	153	17.5	3.3
Upson	6.3	231	3	D	D	D	97	1 152	208.7	21.5	18	37	5.5	0.9
Walker	8.6	125	33	D	D	D	170	1 472	344.2	28.5	20	D	D	D
Walton	6.8	81	63	598	260.4	25.3	207	2 660	797.2	64.4	91	193	27.1	4.6
Ware	5.8	159	45	450	762.7	13.5	244	2 811	621.1	55.7	34	139	12.4	2.3
Warren	1.8	300	4	D	D	D	22	154	23.2	3.1	2	D	D	D
Washington	24.4	1 151	17	122	70.0	4.2	94	920	213.7	18.7	17	84	9.9	1.3
Wayne	62.0	2 059	14	D	D	D	134	1 367	310.3	29.3	20	102	7.6	1.5
Webster	9.3	3 323	4	22	3.5	0.3	4	29	4.7	0.5	NA	NA	NA	NA
Wheeler	2.9	385	3	47	8.2	0.8	19	92	18.1	1.2	1	D	D	D
White	2.9	106	18	154	40.4	4.5	137	960	280.7	23.8	28	48	8.1	1.5
Whitfield	22.6	220	235	3 548	1 351.9	136.0	504	5 707	1 440.2	128.8	89	372	56.7	11.0
Wilcox	8.9	966	3	D	D	D	24	128	27.4	2.1	NA	NA	NA	NA
Wilkes	1.9	180	6	38	19.0	1.1	60	401	73.4	7.0	7	22	2.5	0.5
Wilkinson	15.1	1 578	7	28	13.3	1.2	26	153	24.3	2.6	NA	NA	NA	NA
Worth	19.0	876	27	188	116.4	5.8	70	497	132.2	11.0	13	34	2.1	0.4
HAWAII	1 273.8	936	1 629	17 707	8 894.7	699.1	5 012	70 661	17 611.9	1 766.4	2 084	16 759	3 974.0	653.8
Hawaii	134.7	728	185	1 847	732.2	62.1	722	9 730	2 566.0	250.0	303	2 729	474.1	106.3
Honolulu	799.2	838	1 244	14 049	7 377.1	565.1	3 058	46 613	11 518.3	1 144.1	1 294	9 867	2 660.2	399.9
Kalawao	0.0	111	NA	NA	NA	NA	NA	NA	NA	NA	NA	NA	NA	NA
Kauai	61.8	921	61	525	209.4	16.4	379	4 457	1 052.7	110.3	168	1 387	245.6	50.7
Maui	278.1	1 796	139	1 286	575.9	55.5	853	9 861	2 474.8	262.0	319	2 776	594.1	96.8
IDAHO	17 230.5	10 992	1 846	21 844	14 286.7	900.0	6 300	80 447	20 526.6	1 833.6	2 530	8 371	1 241.7	233.5
Ada	832.2	2 121	561	7 490	6 006.9	371.8	1 483	23 080	5 855.1	545.1	916	3 614	551.8	121.0
Adams	78.2	19 663	1	D	D	D	17	120	20.0	1.8	12	17	1.7	0.2
Bannock	168.1	2 029	78	636	386.6	24.1	350	4 972	1 099.2	97.7	96	323	52.2	6.9
Bear Lake	177.0	29 571	4	63	23.4	1.7	32	288	58.7	4.0	7	16	1.2	0.3
Benewah	2.5	265	5	37	6.1	1.0	39	366	93.9	7.5	5	9	0.6	0.2
Bingham	956.8	20 979	50	D	D	D	124	1 357	339.9	27.6	24	75	8.4	1.7
Blaine	109.2	5 107	35	678	285.9	29.8	201	1 579	356.0	44.6	111	363	59.4	10.5
Boise	6.8	966	NA	NA	NA	NA	21	100	18.7	1.5	8	13	2.0	0.2
Bonner	20.1	491	37	276	140.7	10.0	200	2 128	485.3	48.0	95	257	34.8	7.1
Bonneville	716.8	6 877	158	2 081	1 881.6	89.0	512	7 375	1 871.5	159.4	142	501	86.8	11.5
Boundary	100.8	9 191	10	39	19.7	1.7	45	369	86.3	8.3	9	9	0.9	0.2
Butte	160.7	55 597	4	31	5.2	0.5	15	98	18.1	1.5	7	26	0.8	0.2
Camas	164.7	147 449	NA	NA	NA	NA	2	D	D	D	NA	NA	NA	NA
Canyon	746.5	3 951	182	1 766	992.9	79.2	510	7 916	2 176.0	196.0	212	643	67.7	12.5

1. Merchant wholesalers, except manufacturers' sales branches and offices. 2. Employer establishments.

STATE County	Professional, scientific, and technical services,[1] 2007				Manufacturing, 2007				Accommodation and food services, 2007			
	Number of establish-ments	Number of employees	Receipts (mil dol)	Annual payroll (mil dol)	Number of establish-ments	Number of employees	Receipts (mil dol)	Annual payroll (mil dol)	Number of establish-ments	Number of employees	Sales (mil dol)	Annual payroll (mil dol)
	147	148	149	150	151	152	153	154	155	156	157	158
GEORGIA—Cont'd												
Putnam	37	81	9.5	2.2	27	1 352	316.1	42.7	39	545	19.8	5.2
Quitman	1	D	D	D	NA	NA	NA	NA	3	D	D	D
Rabun	31	119	10.3	4.0	25	591	138.7	19.4	66	676	41.1	10.4
Randolph	9	42	2.4	1.5	NA	NA	NA	NA	14	81	3.9	0.9
Richmond	437	3 181	397.2	144.3	129	9 055	5 256.3	452.0	431	9 726	395.4	108.6
Rockdale	229	1 139	131.5	50.5	87	4 437	1 778.8	192.6	193	4 190	196.6	49.7
Schley	2	D	D	D	12	919	215.9	32.0	6	29	0.9	0.2
Screven	13	39	2.4	0.8	17	1 063	183.8	32.9	20	206	8.3	1.9
Seminole	11	40	3.7	0.9	NA	NA	NA	NA	19	140	5.4	1.3
Spalding	81	481	51.1	19.6	57	4 266	2 285.2	170.1	111	2 023	77.4	20.8
Stephens	42	160	17.9	6.2	52	1 981	535.7	69.0	50	771	26.2	6.8
Stewart	2	D	D	D	NA	NA	NA	NA	7	69	2.7	0.6
Sumter	34	D	D	D	35	1 940	412.0	64.7	56	1 069	33.7	9.8
Talbot	3	5	0.3	0.2	NA	NA	NA	NA	NA	NA	NA	NA
Taliaferro	NA	NA	NA	NA	NA	NA	NA	NA	1	D	D	D
Tattnall	17	78	7.3	2.0	NA	NA	NA	NA	21	269	9.5	2.2
Taylor	9	11	0.8	0.1	NA	NA	NA	NA	8	57	1.6	0.5
Telfair	11	48	3.2	1.2	13	D	D	D	19	216	11.1	2.6
Terrell	8	36	3.3	1.1	14	535	D	17.8	10	D	D	D
Thomas	78	426	44.9	16.2	51	3 166	657.6	112.5	82	1 313	49.9	13.5
Tift	79	559	47.4	20.4	54	2 370	547.5	75.6	102	2 195	92.0	26.1
Toombs	46	225	20.1	6.6	36	D	D	D	65	1 042	42.3	11.2
Towns	21	88	6.7	2.7	NA	NA	NA	NA	42	539	31.0	9.2
Treutlen	3	D	D	D	NA	NA	NA	NA	4	50	1.8	0.5
Troup	88	429	42.3	18.6	92	6 857	2 470.8	288.4	131	2 359	88.7	23.8
Turner	13	33	2.9	0.8	NA	NA	NA	NA	17	172	6.5	1.7
Twiggs	4	D	D	D	NA	NA	NA	NA	7	29	1.3	0.4
Union	49	197	13.8	5.6	NA	NA	NA	NA	43	452	21.6	5.7
Upson	36	D	D	D	24	D	526.5	56.5	50	569	22.9	5.3
Walker	53	197	21.3	9.4	65	5 417	2 060.6	181.2	56	745	25.4	6.4
Walton	151	574	53.1	20.3	55	1 698	591.8	69.5	90	1 397	58.4	15.0
Ware	61	D	D	D	33	1 552	D	43.2	75	1 645	55.5	14.7
Warren	3	D	D	D	NA	NA	NA	NA	7	17	0.7	0.2
Washington	22	193	12.6	8.9	NA	NA	NA	NA	32	516	16.5	4.4
Wayne	28	106	6.9	5.5	28	1 505	663.4	74.0	57	875	32.9	8.7
Webster	1	D	D	D	NA	NA	NA	NA	1	D	D	D
Wheeler	3	8	0.3	0.1	NA	NA	NA	NA	3	D	D	D
White	50	122	10.1	3.1	34	584	103.9	20.3	88	831	51.1	11.6
Whitfield	167	D	D	D	317	22 283	7 524.9	710.4	189	3 428	144.8	38.8
Wilcox	2	D	D	D	NA	NA	NA	NA	3	17	0.6	0.1
Wilkes	16	87	7.3	3.6	17	622	174.3	18.3	18	176	7.1	1.7
Wilkinson	7	69	5.6	1.9	15	973	521.5	52.4	7	39	1.4	0.4
Worth	10	D	D	D	NA	NA	NA	NA	17	178	6.5	1.7
HAWAII	3 254	21 772	3 068.3	1 193.5	984	14 127	8 799.3	511.5	3 528	98 353	8 042.2	2 209.8
Hawaii	321	D	D	D	138	1 516	290.1	53.6	421	12 280	874.7	284.5
Honolulu	2 433	18 508	2 686.9	1 056.8	684	10 996	8 201.9	398.9	2 347	57 064	4 123.8	1 126.5
Kalawao	NA	NA	NA	NA	NA	NA	NA	NA	NA	NA	NA	NA
Kauai	132	D	D	D	NA	NA	NA	NA	234	7 082	591.5	168.8
Maui	368	D	D	D	114	1 319	262.7	50.7	526	21 927	2 452.2	630.1
IDAHO	4 189	D	D	D	1 942	64 778	18 011.0	2 829.4	3 482	56 662	2 416.0	662.7
Ada	1 602	D	D	D	419	21 075	4 942.4	1 248.3	900	17 928	796.0	219.9
Adams	8	D	D	D	NA	NA	NA	NA	16	D	D	D
Bannock	104	D	D	D	58	D	D	D	180	3 056	117.8	31.9
Bear Lake	3	D	D	D	NA	NA	NA	NA	15	D	D	D
Benewah	12	D	D	D	10	576	D	25.0	21	D	D	D
Bingham	49	209	23.0	7.9	45	2 334	624.5	79.9	55	1 046	24.3	6.2
Blaine	163	727	114.2	47.3	NA	NA	NA	NA	114	3 186	153.3	52.2
Boise	12	D	D	D	NA	NA	NA	NA	23	165	5.7	1.7
Bonner	145	576	43.8	26.7	87	2 091	498.6	79.6	124	2 018	63.3	20.8
Bonneville	382	D	D	D	144	2 580	D	92.8	200	3 824	153.5	41.3
Boundary	27	108	6.0	2.6	NA	NA	NA	NA	23	D	D	D
Butte	2	D	D	D	NA	NA	NA	NA	8	D	D	D
Camas	NA	NA	NA	NA	NA	NA	NA	NA	6	89	1.5	0.4
Canyon	252	D	D	D	233	9 848	D	335.1	242	3 905	140.9	38.1

1. Establishment subject to federal tax.

STATE County	Health care and social assistance, 2007				Other services, 2007				Nonemployer businesses, 2013		Value of residential construction authorized by building permits, 2014	
	Number of establish-ments	Number of employees	Receipts (mil dol)	Annual payroll (mil dol)	Number of establish-ments	Number of employees	Receipts (mil dol)	Annual payroll (mil dol)	Number	Receipts (mil dol)	New Construction ($1,000)	Number of housing units
	159	160	161	162	163	164	165	166	167	168	169	170
GEORGIA—Cont'd												
Putnam	25	380	27.0	11.2	31	73	5.4	1.2	1 733	77.4	7 932	35
Quitman	2	D	D	D	1	D	D	D	136	3.2	400	5
Rabun	32	455	36.0	13.7	34	96	10.0	2.3	1 707	61.3	18 170	47
Randolph	8	246	16.2	6.3	8	22	2.2	0.4	423	10.2	0	0
Richmond	617	20 772	2 482.3	911.5	290	1 956	193.4	49.9	12 458	380.5	79 400	730
Rockdale	228	3 606	335.9	127.4	175	838	65.4	19.0	7 816	242.9	35 936	133
Schley	5	D	D	D	5	D	D	D	296	10.6	0	0
Screven	20	468	24.6	11.8	20	65	6.7	1.5	906	33.6	1 519	10
Seminole	22	464	41.2	14.3	14	48	2.9	0.9	623	24.4	645	4
Spalding	128	3 753	277.7	96.8	88	502	38.6	11.8	4 635	146.9	13 216	141
Stephens	49	1 335	108.0	45.9	36	190	20.0	4.3	1 620	54.6	5 320	25
Stewart	12	196	12.8	4.3	7	18	1.8	0.4	316	5.8	0	0
Sumter	88	D	D	D	49	D	D	D	1 824	55.3	1 478	11
Talbot	2	D	D	D	6	5	0.4	0.1	506	14.3	1 500	10
Taliaferro	2	D	D	D	3	D	D	D	104	3.5	260	2
Tattnall	26	615	30.8	13.7	14	42	2.9	0.6	1 224	43.1	2 124	17
Taylor	19	267	13.4	4.6	8	D	D	D	561	18.2	1 547	11
Telfair	18	647	32.7	15.6	17	69	7.8	1.6	686	24.6	0	0
Terrell	17	D	D	D	16	D	D	D	660	19.9	380	3
Thomas	134	3 303	369.8	130.7	74	470	41.2	10.2	3 142	134.4	15 316	71
Tift	110	2 811	267.4	121.2	65	543	65.3	17.1	2 986	121.9	6 062	59
Toombs	117	1 787	151.4	58.2	43	241	19.6	5.4	2 010	74.2	1 898	23
Towns	25	416	32.1	12.8	15	35	2.2	0.6	1 108	42.7	17 339	103
Treutlen	9	150	5.9	2.8	7	29	1.7	0.5	425	12.3	0	0
Troup	132	3 341	281.4	114.9	96	456	40.6	9.8	5 252	156.0	28 109	133
Turner	9	D	D	D	9	31	1.4	0.4	576	18.6	7 195	65
Twiggs	8	D	D	D	6	16	1.9	0.4	541	13.3	205	1
Union	56	941	74.6	28.9	32	202	19.8	4.4	2 055	75.2	18 611	87
Upson	61	1 360	121.7	45.9	38	D	D	D	1 667	48.0	2 667	22
Walker	52	D	D	D	48	D	D	D	4 151	157.2	12 739	84
Walton	107	1 661	223.7	51.1	113	349	29.1	8.1	7 448	264.4	36 617	271
Ware	114	2 824	260.2	94.7	70	349	22.5	6.3	1 868	62.8	11 634	94
Warren	5	110	6.4	3.0	7	D	D	D	344	9.7	0	0
Washington	36	949	48.6	23.3	34	88	7.1	1.6	1 231	34.7	5 782	53
Wayne	56	1 634	94.1	36.4	29	D	D	D	1 769	58.5	631	4
Webster	1	D	D	D	2	D	D	D	148	6.8	NA	NA
Wheeler	9	98	11.5	5.1	5	12	1.3	0.3	352	11.2	0	0
White	33	427	20.9	9.8	46	204	15.6	4.2	2 482	88.3	7 819	38
Whitfield	195	3 776	441.3	168.8	138	726	68.5	21.2	5 738	271.0	14 617	99
Wilcox	14	213	9.2	3.9	6	17	0.9	0.2	491	17.5	NA	NA
Wilkes	30	514	28.6	13.1	14	46	4.0	0.8	612	22.7	180	3
Wilkinson	14	141	10.9	3.9	11	40	2.3	0.7	651	14.6	88	1
Worth	27	D	D	D	28	75	7.0	1.4	1 265	45.0	2 614	13
HAWAII	3 484	63 640	6 565.0	2 721.4	2 916	20 119	1 917.8	512.6	98 490	4 567.5	1 011 786	3 066
Hawaii	452	7 285	623.3	271.8	310	1 673	162.5	42.6	16 499	688.9	444 829	958
Honolulu	2 473	47 727	5 055.4	2 047.9	2 083	15 228	1 462.7	388.7	60 220	2 873.7	376 973	1 578
Kalawao	NA	NA	NA	NA	NA	NA	NA	NA	NA	NA	NA	NA
Kauai	172	2 729	266.5	119.7	134	866	65.6	20.6	6 621	269.0	104 787	192
Maui	387	5 899	619.8	282.0	389	2 352	227.1	60.6	15 150	735.9	85 196	338
IDAHO	4 545	73 932	6 211.0	2 510.8	2 640	13 681	1 094.0	315.6	115 043	4 803.8	1 654 793	8 797
Ada	1 298	25 055	2 433.7	1 020.4	790	4 663	395.2	122.6	33 207	1 476.9	771 405	3 968
Adams	9	44	2.1	1.0	3	D	D	D	360	12.2	3 566	4
Bannock	291	D	D	D	132	669	59.4	14.2	5 073	186.7	19 128	162
Bear Lake	14	295	18.1	7.6	8	23	2.2	0.4	420	14.4	8 410	35
Benewah	19	362	23.0	9.7	16	79	6.4	2.0	540	20.7	2 533	14
Bingham	84	1 417	105.3	51.0	56	310	27.0	8.5	2 685	126.5	10 387	88
Blaine	79	595	69.3	27.7	82	331	45.8	10.9	3 337	190.2	75 462	89
Boise	5	22	1.3	0.5	8	D	D	D	564	19.3	7 655	32
Bonner	132	1 448	112.6	44.2	84	376	22.5	7.1	3 687	140.9	8 730	55
Bonneville	404	D	D	D	166	954	83.6	22.4	7 757	333.4	54 818	398
Boundary	34	507	25.7	13.6	23	36	3.3	0.8	871	35.2	11 894	51
Butte	8	191	8.5	5.4	3	18	1.2	0.2	189	6.2	705	5
Camas	3	D	D	D	NA	NA	NA	NA	87	3.3	408	3
Canyon	340	5 703	422.5	175.9	207	1 172	83.0	24.4	11 596	440.7	173 113	1 130

STATE County	Government employment and payroll, 2012									Local government finances, 2012				
			March payroll (percent of total)							General revenue				
												Taxes		
													Per capita[1] (dollars)	
	Full-time equivalent employees	March payroll (dollars)	Adminis-tration, judicial, and legal	Police and Corrections	Fire Protection	Highways and transpor-tation	Health and Welfare	Natural resources and utilities	Education and libraries	Total (mil dol)	Inter-govern-mental (mil dol)	Total (mil dol)	Total	Property
	171	172	173	174	175	176	177	178	179	180	181	182	183	184
GEORGIA—Cont'd														
Putnam	984	3 113 107	7.0	8.5	2.1	1.9	21.4	3.9	53.4	77.1	16.7	40.8	1 927	1 196
Quitman	121	315 487	9.9	7.4	0.2	4.3	8.7	2.9	65.7	8.3	4.1	3.2	1 332	1 155
Rabun	712	2 242 761	6.8	10.9	2.2	4.4	7.2	5.6	61.5	63.4	12.6	43.0	2 638	1 882
Randolph	534	1 324 386	4.1	6.0	1.2	2.8	42.1	4.5	38.3	42.9	11.1	14.3	1 951	1 486
Richmond	7 950	24 545 151	7.9	10.6	4.4	2.7	3.5	7.3	62.0	723.6	324.4	222.4	1 098	673
Rockdale	3 955	12 355 812	6.2	9.9	4.2	1.3	0.7	4.5	71.2	266.8	93.9	129.0	1 503	1 071
Schley	221	708 164	2.4	6.6	0.0	3.3	4.8	4.1	78.8	16.0	8.4	5.0	1 011	733
Screven	656	1 803 310	6.3	10.5	2.8	3.9	4.8	5.5	64.2	45.6	23.1	16.0	1 128	780
Seminole	372	1 424 704	4.2	9.3	2.0	3.8	4.4	1.3	74.5	27.2	10.7	13.1	1 463	928
Spalding	2 703	8 758 007	4.7	13.1	5.5	2.0	7.8	7.1	56.8	223.0	90.1	90.6	1 418	906
Stephens	894	2 549 588	7.6	10.7	2.8	2.5	1.9	9.9	61.7	120.9	28.0	31.7	1 223	823
Stewart	231	632 898	9.4	19.7	2.8	4.9	5.1	4.7	52.5	14.0	5.9	5.5	915	668
Sumter	1 492	4 667 090	4.8	12.0	4.4	1.8	14.0	4.3	55.3	123.8	56.0	47.3	1 498	959
Talbot	263	648 950	15.0	7.1	0.0	6.9	4.5	5.3	60.1	16.0	5.2	8.8	1 350	1 039
Taliaferro	95	252 316	11.8	15.2	0.0	6.8	1.6	0.9	60.8	6.4	2.1	3.2	1 880	1 613
Tattnall	764	2 267 688	6.8	7.3	0.0	4.7	3.0	3.2	73.4	51.7	24.6	20.6	810	496
Taylor	402	1 087 805	6.6	7.8	0.7	2.6	1.3	2.5	76.3	24.2	12.5	8.6	1 017	618
Telfair	434	1 158 142	7.7	9.9	4.9	3.3	2.8	4.0	66.4	30.4	12.8	13.3	813	533
Terrell	443	1 230 523	6.4	14.1	3.6	2.3	4.9	4.0	64.2	29.7	13.0	12.4	1 376	912
Thomas	2 420	7 648 981	5.7	7.9	3.2	3.4	8.3	6.5	59.1	194.9	58.8	64.1	1 432	870
Tift	3 242	12 909 421	2.9	4.3	0.8	1.6	59.8	2.1	26.8	404.4	50.3	64.4	1 568	788
Toombs	1 085	3 290 743	4.9	9.0	1.7	1.4	3.9	3.2	74.9	191.8	42.5	32.2	1 177	561
Towns	518	1 438 233	4.8	7.4	0.8	3.1	0.3	24.8	49.8	26.3	6.4	15.9	1 518	962
Treutlen	241	645 937	7.5	7.8	0.4	3.2	1.3	4.5	74.0	28.8	21.1	5.0	740	446
Troup	3 339	10 586 640	4.7	11.9	4.4	1.8	9.1	6.2	59.3	240.0	99.8	101.3	1 480	879
Turner	509	1 317 091	10.3	7.4	1.7	4.5	3.8	5.8	62.7	31.0	13.3	10.2	1 209	826
Twiggs	296	826 420	11.0	20.1	0.5	4.9	0.4	1.5	60.0	20.2	6.9	10.5	1 247	910
Union	1 493	4 119 774	3.0	5.1	1.6	1.3	48.9	4.1	35.5	56.7	15.8	34.2	1 593	1 016
Upson	965	2 830 552	6.4	11.2	2.1	2.0	0.7	3.7	72.7	154.8	37.1	28.6	1 073	730
Walker	2 622	7 660 154	5.8	5.5	2.5	2.1	10.7	4.8	66.0	172.5	90.6	54.3	798	474
Walton	3 007	10 183 150	6.0	8.9	3.5	2.6	2.5	5.6	68.5	253.5	88.7	125.8	1 487	1 043
Ware	1 747	5 214 214	5.1	10.2	4.2	3.4	17.2	1.0	56.2	150.2	74.1	48.2	1 345	705
Warren	197	551 517	8.8	6.8	0.0	4.0	6.1	5.3	64.2	16.7	6.7	7.4	1 320	928
Washington	1 131	3 414 908	4.5	6.7	0.9	3.9	35.1	4.5	42.2	125.1	24.7	31.9	1 530	951
Wayne	1 486	4 440 469	3.8	6.1	0.9	3.2	35.1	2.4	45.9	139.5	38.9	37.7	1 243	759
Webster	104	294 610	7.7	5.3	0.0	3.0	2.2	1.0	80.8	9.5	3.7	4.2	1 493	1 310
Wheeler	259	643 558	10.3	8.6	0.0	6.2	1.6	4.0	68.1	17.9	10.2	6.1	772	542
White	868	2 678 650	6.8	11.0	0.9	2.2	1.2	3.4	72.6	77.2	27.9	40.3	1 464	942
Whitfield	4 096	14 180 499	3.9	6.7	4.0	3.4	7.2	11.9	61.8	347.4	152.6	112.5	1 088	733
Wilcox	281	825 846	7.4	8.9	0.0	5.0	0.3	1.5	76.4	20.6	10.9	7.4	819	578
Wilkes	700	2 101 724	4.1	4.7	2.3	3.1	36.0	3.8	45.3	48.7	11.7	15.5	1 540	1 102
Wilkinson	479	1 156 738	10.2	14.5	0.0	4.8	0.4	1.9	66.2	39.7	18.0	19.1	1 997	1 336
Worth	797	2 247 660	7.4	8.5	3.1	4.5	0.1	4.6	69.5	50.7	23.4	19.6	900	588
HAWAII	X	X	X	X	X	X	X	X	X	X	X	X	X	X
Hawaii	2 415	11 250 002	15.2	26.6	22.6	11.1	5.5	17.0	0.0	375.6	91.7	253.3	1 339	1 101
Honolulu	9 304	47 881 176	14.1	35.4	14.0	2.6	6.8	20.8	0.0	2 232.4	331.8	1 316.4	1 348	833
Kalawao	NA	NA	NA	NA	NA	NA	NA	NA	NA	NA	NA	NA	NA	NA
Kauai	1 232	5 830 608	20.2	19.2	15.5	10.5	6.2	20.4	0.0	188.8	66.9	100.2	1 465	1 179
Maui	2 328	11 762 934	19.0	23.7	16.4	6.9	6.2	25.4	0.0	252.6	23.1	224.7	1 420	1 317
IDAHO	X	X	X	X	X	X	X	X	X	X	X	X	X	X
Ada	12 112	39 983 613	9.7	14.3	6.3	4.1	3.0	5.8	55.5	1 138.5	454.6	413.3	1 010	956
Adams	147	443 031	15.8	17.4	0.0	11.4	1.6	4.6	45.7	11.9	6.2	4.4	1 132	952
Bannock	2 618	8 746 568	9.9	14.1	5.7	4.5	6.0	6.6	51.4	238.0	114.9	73.0	871	828
Bear Lake	229	654 192	13.1	9.9	0.2	7.8	3.3	5.5	57.6	22.6	13.4	2.6	441	419
Benewah	501	1 444 872	5.0	6.6	1.0	3.3	36.5	3.9	43.4	44.1	19.2	5.9	652	616
Bingham	1 565	4 338 272	6.4	11.2	2.5	4.1	0.9	3.8	70.0	101.5	63.5	23.4	514	501
Blaine	959	4 228 217	10.2	10.1	5.2	3.3	0.5	6.4	61.6	114.6	26.2	66.7	3 152	3 047
Boise	251	737 278	24.2	12.1	0.6	8.0	2.0	2.2	50.8	23.1	11.0	7.0	1 022	1 015
Bonner	1 368	4 223 862	11.1	13.5	5.6	4.8	4.5	6.4	51.1	107.8	42.8	46.9	1 158	1 112
Bonneville	3 464	10 839 917	6.9	10.9	5.5	3.6	4.1	8.8	57.9	271.5	135.2	82.8	776	747
Boundary	529	1 491 650	6.9	7.2	0.6	4.2	37.3	5.6	37.2	38.9	14.5	7.6	707	698
Butte	218	969 719	3.5	4.5	0.0	4.1	61.6	0.6	25.3	15.1	4.0	3.5	1 273	1 204
Camas	63	187 878	16.7	9.7	0.0	19.8	0.0	1.9	52.0	4.7	2.8	1.5	1 353	1 312
Canyon	5 895	18 424 410	6.4	13.6	4.1	2.0	2.4	5.1	63.5	487.9	253.1	149.0	768	705

1. Based on the resident population estimated as of July 1 of the year shown.

STATE County	Local government finances, 2012 (cont.)									Government employment, 2013			Presidential election,[2] 2012		
	Direct general expenditure							Debt outstanding					Percent of vote cast:		
			Percent of total for:												
	Total (mil dol)	Per capita[1] (dollars)	Education	Health and hospitals	Police protection	Public welfare	Highways	Total (mil dol)	Per capita[1] (dollars)	Federal civilian	Federal military	State and local	Democratic	Republican	All other
	185	186	187	188	189	190	191	192	193	194	195	196	197	198	199
GEORGIA—Cont'd															
Putnam	72.9	3 441	44.6	23.5	6.0	0.8	3.3	32.9	1 552	64	62	1 474	34.0	65.3	0.7
Quitman	8.2	3 406	52.3	7.2	6.2	1.8	4.5	6.3	2 614	0	0	142	53.6	45.7	0.7
Rabun	76.9	4 718	60.5	4.4	4.4	0.2	5.2	64.1	3 932	49	46	778	26.3	72.2	1.5
Randolph	40.0	5 457	32.6	34.8	3.1	0.0	2.6	8.5	1 166	19	20	624	57.0	42.6	0.4
Richmond	773.0	3 816	44.0	5.8	5.2	0.1	2.9	1 078.9	5 326	7 446	10 725	21 445	65.7	33.8	0.5
Rockdale	265.4	3 093	63.2	1.2	6.2	0.4	1.5	131.0	1 526	103	252	4 137	54.4	44.9	0.7
Schley	15.2	3 050	68.7	0.6	3.4	0.2	3.0	10.5	2 102	0	15	300	27.6	72.0	0.4
Screven	51.6	3 634	47.5	4.3	4.4	0.5	7.2	16.6	1 168	34	40	962	46.7	52.8	0.5
Seminole	28.0	3 127	58.5	3.1	7.8	0.0	6.4	2.0	222	19	26	467	41.5	57.9	0.5
Spalding	220.8	3 457	49.2	9.1	6.7	0.1	2.5	97.8	1 531	125	182	4 599	40.2	58.9	0.9
Stephens	131.2	5 068	39.4	38.7	2.9	0.3	1.2	65.0	2 510	65	73	1 829	25.7	73.1	1.2
Stewart	14.4	2 389	48.8	0.7	7.9	0.1	8.9	2.2	358	83	12	264	62.0	37.2	0.8
Sumter	189.6	6 009	27.5	40.2	3.7	0.1	1.5	43.4	1 374	131	86	2 666	52.8	46.7	0.5
Talbot	16.6	2 545	46.5	5.7	6.5	0.7	8.6	6.3	967	14	19	258	64.0	35.2	0.8
Taliaferro	6.4	3 816	48.9	2.7	14.8	2.5	5.5	0.7	438	0	0	127	64.9	34.2	0.8
Tattnall	52.9	2 082	60.1	2.7	5.1	0.1	7.0	17.8	701	36	60	2 151	28.8	70.4	0.8
Taylor	23.7	2 820	66.0	2.8	6.0	0.4	4.5	3.3	389	20	24	465	42.9	56.4	0.7
Telfair	30.5	1 866	55.4	3.3	8.2	0.4	6.3	11.0	675	30	37	797	42.6	56.8	0.6
Terrell	29.3	3 236	51.1	4.8	7.0	0.1	4.1	9.0	992	65	25	548	56.6	42.8	0.6
Thomas	190.8	4 266	41.2	9.8	5.5	0.1	5.3	245.9	5 499	193	129	3 454	41.8	57.7	0.5
Tift	381.3	9 285	20.1	64.4	1.5	0.1	1.9	195.8	4 767	201	114	5 257	33.3	66.1	0.5
Toombs	186.3	6 822	31.2	50.6	2.8	0.0	1.5	76.6	2 805	62	78	1 612	30.6	68.7	0.7
Towns	27.3	2 598	47.1	4.4	6.0	2.9	4.7	28.4	2 702	26	29	512	24.2	74.8	1.0
Treutlen	32.8	4 842	80.8	1.3	2.9	0.7	1.9	13.3	1 965	13	18	356	37.6	61.8	0.5
Troup	264.2	3 858	45.4	7.1	6.4	0.4	8.6	84.1	1 228	139	194	3 838	40.2	59.1	0.7
Turner	30.7	3 654	53.3	4.1	8.0	0.8	7.1	13.4	1 596	27	23	603	40.2	59.0	0.8
Twiggs	20.6	2 444	54.2	2.1	10.0	1.2	8.4	10.3	1 223	0	24	325	53.2	46.2	0.7
Union	54.6	2 546	54.2	3.2	5.7	0.9	3.8	28.4	1 326	49	62	1 552	23.4	75.4	1.3
Upson	143.4	5 384	30.0	51.3	2.2	0.0	1.4	37.4	1 403	36	76	1 318	35.6	63.8	0.6
Walker	177.3	2 604	57.4	15.8	4.9	0.8	3.6	84.0	1 233	104	195	3 282	25.9	72.7	1.4
Walton	248.4	2 937	56.6	1.1	6.4	1.4	4.9	295.1	3 490	138	247	3 510	23.5	75.6	0.8
Ware	150.8	4 210	40.9	26.4	5.2	0.2	4.1	43.3	1 209	107	98	2 955	32.5	66.9	0.6
Warren	15.9	2 855	53.9	0.2	11.9	1.1	8.2	9.0	1 620	17	16	276	58.4	40.9	0.7
Washington	93.4	4 474	37.1	33.1	4.7	0.1	6.2	65.8	3 153	48	55	2 361	52.0	47.6	0.5
Wayne	133.6	4 408	40.5	35.6	3.7	0.5	4.6	47.0	1 550	388	81	2 270	27.1	72.0	1.0
Webster	9.9	3 552	48.2	4.4	3.0	0.6	5.2	2.9	1 037	0	0	135	46.4	52.9	0.7
Wheeler	20.1	2 548	57.2	2.6	5.1	0.0	4.0	7.1	901	11	16	314	35.9	63.7	0.4
White	82.8	3 003	62.2	1.4	5.2	0.4	3.1	24.2	879	46	79	1 087	20.2	78.7	1.1
Whitfield	397.4	3 845	52.0	10.1	3.9	0.2	4.6	103.9	1 005	138	297	5 323	29.5	69.5	1.0
Wilcox	20.2	2 223	65.8	2.8	6.4	1.0	7.1	1.1	120	21	20	611	30.9	68.3	0.8
Wilkes	56.9	5 644	29.5	36.5	4.0	0.5	3.2	51.2	5 077	35	29	817	45.8	53.5	0.6
Wilkinson	52.8	5 509	73.3	2.0	4.8	0.6	3.6	25.9	2 707	21	27	510	49.2	50.3	0.6
Worth	55.0	2 532	54.0	1.3	8.3	0.1	10.1	14.9	684	37	62	868	30.4	69.1	0.6
HAWAII	X	X	X	X	X	X	X	X	X	33 919	57 357	91 305	71.8	26.6	1.6
Hawaii	354.9	1 876	0.0	0.0	13.4	1.9	13.5	415.5	2 196	1 414	1 349	11 220	75.9	22.2	1.8
Honolulu	1 596.7	1 635	0.0	1.5	15.2	0.0	7.8	5 300.0	5 428	31 103	54 254	67 083	69.8	28.7	1.4
Kalawao	NA	NA	NA	NA	NA	NA	NA	NA	NA	(3)855	(3)1 151	(3)8 919	0.0	0.0	0.0
Kauai	196.1	2 865	0.0	0.0	13.7	5.8	8.0	246.2	3 598	547	603	4 083	75.0	22.9	2.1
Maui	264.1	1 669	0.0	0.0	15.8	6.0	2.7	281.6	1 780	(3)	(3)	(3)	76.7	21.5	1.8
IDAHO	X	X	X	X	X	X	X	X	X	12 450	9 510	104 947	36.1	61.5	2.4
Ada	1 060.4	2 592	40.6	0.3	10.7	0.9	7.6	516.6	1 263	5 398	1 599	27 223	45.8	52.0	2.1
Adams	10.4	2 645	37.6	0.0	12.3	0.0	13.2	4.7	1 205	103	14	204	31.4	65.4	3.2
Bannock	221.0	2 637	41.2	2.7	8.1	1.0	5.5	54.8	654	537	306	7 576	42.1	55.1	2.7
Bear Lake	24.3	4 106	33.5	22.5	2.2	0.4	1.3	2.5	424	51	22	614	17.1	80.8	2.2
Benewah	38.9	4 264	35.2	40.0	2.3	0.7	4.2	11.6	1 277	51	34	1 281	33.8	63.5	2.7
Bingham	100.2	2 204	61.5	0.3	7.5	0.7	6.2	46.6	1 024	227	169	3 639	25.8	71.3	2.9
Blaine	113.0	5 346	53.5	2.2	8.7	3.0	3.7	69.4	3 281	96	79	1 383	65.7	32.5	1.8
Boise	17.6	2 582	45.9	0.8	0.9	0.9	9.6	15.5	2 261	140	25	314	32.9	64.5	2.7
Bonner	109.1	2 696	37.9	3.6	6.5	0.6	9.0	31.1	769	182	151	2 117	40.1	57.0	2.9
Bonneville	269.0	2 527	48.0	1.3	7.4	0.3	4.9	252.9	2 370	755	402	5 074	27.4	70.3	2.3
Boundary	40.5	3 751	26.8	27.6	9.8	1.0	7.6	14.5	1 345	159	40	905	31.4	65.0	3.6
Butte	12.7	4 635	28.6	45.0	2.1	0.8	3.4	2.7	1 003	73	27	158	22.6	74.9	2.6
Camas	4.6	4 281	41.0	0.3	12.3	0.2	19.9	3.6	3 301	23	0	88	30.3	68.3	1.5
Canyon	467.4	2 411	45.9	1.7	8.3	1.0	4.9	465.5	2 401	344	735	8 551	31.4	66.5	2.1

1. Based on the resident population estimated as of July 1 of the year shown. 2. 3. Kalawao county is included with Maui county.

STATE/ County code	CBSA code[1]	County type[2]	STATE County	Land area,[3] (sq km) 2010	Population, 2014 Total persons 2014	Rank	Per square kilometer	Population and population characteristics, 2013 — Race alone or in combination, not Hispanic or Latino (percent): White	Black	American Indian, Alaska Native	Asian and Pacific Islander	Percent Hispanic or Latino[4]	Age (percent): Under 5 years	5 to 17 years	18 to 24 years	25 to 34 years	35 to 44 years	45 to 54 years
				1	2	3	4	5	6	7	8	9	10	11	12	13	14	15
			IDAHO—Cont'd															
16 029	...	6	Caribou	4 569	6 837	2 693	1.5	93.3	0.5	1.0	0.9	5.4	7.2	21.2	7.5	11.1	11.3	11.7
16 031	15420	7	Cassia	6 644	23 540	1 657	3.5	72.3	0.4	1.1	1.1	26.3	8.4	24.1	9.2	11.8	11.3	11.1
16 033	...	8	Clark	4 569	867	3 114	0.2	56.1	0.9	1.5	1.0	42.5	6.9	20.2	8.9	12.7	12.2	12.5
16 035	...	6	Clearwater	6 364	8 562	2 554	1.3	93.4	0.7	3.4	1.3	3.3	3.8	12.4	6.2	9.5	10.7	15.2
16 037	...	9	Custer	12 745	4 140	2 893	0.3	94.4	0.6	1.5	0.8	4.3	4.4	13.9	5.9	9.4	10.7	14.5
16 039	34300	4	Elmore	7 964	26 094	1 556	3.3	77.1	3.4	1.9	4.6	16.1	8.2	18.3	13.5	15.7	11.3	11.6
16 041	30860	3	Franklin	1 719	13 021	2 230	7.6	92.4	0.5	1.0	0.6	6.8	8.1	26.0	7.8	10.9	12.2	10.8
16 043	39940	6	Fremont	4 827	12 867	2 242	2.7	86.1	0.5	1.3	0.7	12.5	7.1	21.8	8.1	11.6	11.6	12.2
16 045	14260	2	Gem	1 453	16 866	1 988	11.6	89.9	0.5	1.8	1.7	8.2	5.6	17.7	7.5	9.4	10.2	14.2
16 047	...	7	Gooding	1 888	15 064	2 096	8.0	69.7	0.3	1.3	1.1	28.8	6.9	21.9	8.4	11.4	11.6	12.3
16 049	...	6	Idaho	21 956	16 215	2 028	0.7	93.5	0.5	3.8	0.9	3.0	5.3	14.7	6.6	9.1	9.3	13.4
16 051	26820	3	Jefferson	2 832	27 021	1 535	9.5	88.1	0.5	1.1	1.0	10.5	9.1	25.6	8.2	13.0	11.9	11.6
16 053	46300	7	Jerome	1 547	22 818	1 696	14.7	65.0	0.5	1.3	0.9	33.4	9.1	21.7	9.0	13.9	11.3	11.9
16 055	17660	3	Kootenai	3 222	147 326	438	45.7	93.3	0.7	2.2	1.7	4.2	6.1	17.7	8.5	12.2	12.1	13.4
16 057	34140	4	Latah	2 787	38 411	1 212	13.8	92.6	1.2	1.7	3.0	3.9	5.8	12.6	25.8	13.8	9.7	10.1
16 059	...	7	Lemhi	11 819	7 726	2 618	0.7	95.4	0.8	1.8	0.9	2.9	4.2	13.7	5.7	9.2	8.4	13.5
16 061	...	8	Lewis	1 240	3 838	2 918	3.1	89.1	0.9	7.6	1.2	4.1	5.3	17.4	6.2	10.1	8.6	13.4
16 063	25200	9	Lincoln	3 112	5 316	2 813	1.7	69.8	0.9	1.4	0.8	28.4	7.0	23.7	8.6	13.1	11.9	11.5
16 065	39940	6	Madison	1 215	38 038	1 219	31.3	91.2	0.8	0.8	2.3	6.5	9.6	17.1	31.5	15.9	7.4	6.5
16 067	15420	7	Minidoka	1 962	20 323	1 818	10.4	65.4	0.4	1.5	0.8	33.0	8.1	20.4	9.1	11.8	10.8	12.1
16 069	30300	3	Nez Perce	2 197	40 007	1 171	18.2	90.0	0.8	6.7	1.6	3.3	5.8	15.6	9.5	12.3	11.2	13.1
16 071	...	8	Oneida	3 108	4 184	2 888	1.3	95.6	0.6	0.9	0.9	3.2	6.9	21.5	6.5	9.9	10.3	11.6
16 073	14260	2	Owyhee	19 854	11 353	2 333	0.6	70.2	0.5	3.8	1.0	26.1	6.5	21.0	8.7	10.6	12.1	12.8
16 075	36620	6	Payette	1 054	22 836	1 695	21.7	81.4	0.5	2.1	1.6	16.4	7.1	20.0	8.3	11.0	11.6	13.3
16 077	...	3	Power	3 637	7 617	2 632	2.1	66.1	0.6	2.9	0.9	31.2	9.7	20.8	9.0	11.6	10.6	12.1
16 079	...	6	Shoshone	6 811	12 390	2 272	1.8	94.1	0.5	2.9	1.0	3.3	4.8	15.0	7.4	9.8	10.9	14.4
16 081	27220	9	Teton	1 164	10 341	2 410	8.9	81.6	0.4	0.7	0.8	17.3	8.1	20.5	6.1	14.4	18.1	13.7
16 083	46300	5	Twin Falls	4 976	80 914	689	16.3	82.7	0.8	1.2	1.9	14.7	7.7	19.8	9.2	13.6	11.8	11.7
16 085	...	8	Valley	9 491	9 826	2 453	1.0	94.7	0.5	1.2	0.9	4.0	4.4	13.7	5.6	9.1	12.2	13.4
16 087	...	6	Washington	3 763	10 021	2 436	2.7	80.8	0.5	1.8	1.2	17.2	4.9	18.3	7.5	8.8	10.7	12.6
17 000	...	X	ILLINOIS	143 793	12 880 580	X	89.6	64.0	14.9	0.5	5.6	16.5	6.2	17.3	9.8	13.9	13.1	13.9
17 001	39500	5	Adams	2 215	66 988	793	30.2	94.1	4.7	0.4	1.0	1.4	6.3	16.3	8.8	12.1	11.1	13.8
17 003	16020	7	Alexander	610	7 492	2 640	12.3	61.1	37.1	0.9	0.8	2.3	6.3	16.4	8.6	11.7	10.9	13.9
17 005	41180	1	Bond	985	17 269	1 965	17.5	89.2	7.1	0.8	0.9	3.3	4.7	14.9	10.0	13.0	13.2	14.6
17 007	40420	2	Boone	727	53 869	929	74.1	76.0	2.7	0.6	1.7	20.4	5.9	20.9	9.0	10.4	13.8	14.8
17 009	...	7	Brown	792	6 832	2 695	8.6	74.6	19.0	0.3	0.4	6.1	3.7	11.3	12.2	18.4	15.8	14.9
17 011	36860	6	Bureau	2 251	33 840	1 331	15.0	89.8	1.1	0.5	1.0	8.5	5.2	16.9	7.6	10.7	11.5	14.1
17 013	41180	1	Calhoun	657	4 956	2 839	7.5	98.2	0.5	0.3	0.4	1.0	5.6	15.6	7.1	9.4	10.9	14.9
17 015	...	7	Carroll	1 152	14 715	2 122	12.8	94.8	1.5	0.6	0.8	3.3	4.5	15.1	7.3	9.9	10.8	13.7
17 017	...	6	Cass	973	13 156	2 229	13.5	77.4	3.9	0.4	0.6	18.4	6.3	18.5	8.0	12.0	12.4	13.9
17 019	16580	3	Champaign	2 580	207 133	310	80.3	72.1	13.6	0.5	10.7	5.6	5.6	13.6	23.4	14.9	10.7	10.5
17 021	45380	6	Christian	1 837	33 892	1 329	18.4	96.1	2.1	0.4	0.8	1.5	5.6	15.9	8.4	11.8	12.0	14.5
17 023	...	6	Clark	1 299	16 180	2 032	12.5	97.6	0.8	0.5	0.5	1.4	5.8	17.0	7.6	11.4	11.7	14.4
17 025	...	7	Clay	1 213	13 520	2 204	11.1	97.1	0.8	0.6	0.9	1.4	6.0	16.5	8.0	10.9	11.5	14.4
17 027	41180	1	Clinton	1 228	37 857	1 227	30.8	92.6	4.1	0.5	0.8	3.0	5.5	16.0	8.6	13.4	12.6	15.4
17 029	16660	5	Coles	1 316	53 320	936	40.5	92.6	4.6	0.5	1.4	2.3	4.9	13.1	21.2	12.9	10.0	11.4
17 031	16980	1	Cook	2 448	5 246 456	2	2 143.2	44.5	24.4	0.5	7.4	24.7	6.5	16.4	9.6	16.3	13.6	13.3
17 033	...	6	Crawford	1 149	19 393	1 863	16.9	92.4	5.1	0.6	0.7	2.1	5.4	14.6	8.4	12.7	12.6	14.6
17 035	16660	9	Cumberland	896	10 833	2 371	12.1	97.9	0.8	0.6	0.7	0.9	6.0	17.0	7.5	11.5	11.6	14.2
17 037	16980	1	DeKalb	1 635	105 462	563	64.5	79.7	7.5	0.5	3.2	10.6	5.9	16.0	20.9	13.5	11.0	11.8
17 039	14010	6	De Witt	1 030	16 284	2 025	15.8	96.2	1.2	0.5	0.9	2.3	5.6	16.4	7.5	11.2	12.3	14.8
17 041	...	6	Douglas	1 079	19 889	1 841	18.4	91.8	0.8	0.6	0.7	7.1	6.8	18.9	7.9	12.0	11.8	13.4
17 043	16980	1	DuPage	848	932 708	55	1 099.9	70.2	5.4	0.4	11.7	13.9	6.0	17.8	8.7	12.8	13.1	15.3
17 045	...	6	Edgar	1 615	17 841	1 925	11.0	98.1	0.8	0.5	0.4	1.0	5.0	16.1	7.5	11.0	11.8	14.0
17 047	...	9	Edwards	576	6 617	2 712	11.5	97.6	1.1	0.5	0.5	1.2	5.6	17.6	7.5	10.2	12.0	14.0
17 049	20020	7	Effingham	1 240	34 320	1 321	27.7	97.2	0.7	0.3	0.7	1.8	6.6	17.4	8.8	12.3	11.0	14.6
17 051	...	6	Fayette	1 856	21 870	1 741	11.8	93.3	4.9	0.5	0.6	1.7	5.4	16.1	8.2	12.7	12.7	14.1
17 053	16580	3	Ford	1 258	13 688	2 194	10.9	95.6	1.1	0.6	0.6	2.9	5.5	17.5	7.3	10.5	11.5	14.4
17 055	...	5	Franklin	1 059	39 411	1 185	37.2	97.2	0.9	0.7	0.7	1.5	6.0	16.3	7.8	11.2	12.1	13.7
17 057	15900	6	Fulton	2 242	36 007	1 271	16.1	93.0	4.0	0.6	0.5	2.7	5.0	15.3	8.1	12.3	12.6	14.0
17 059	...	8	Gallatin	837	5 291	2 815	6.3	97.1	1.2	1.0	0.4	1.8	4.5	15.4	7.7	10.6	12.2	13.4
17 061	...	6	Greene	1 406	13 434	2 212	9.6	97.6	1.4	0.4	0.2	1.0	5.6	16.5	8.1	11.2	12.2	14.6
17 063	16980	1	Grundy	1 083	50 425	980	46.6	88.8	1.8	0.4	1.2	8.9	6.6	19.7	8.2	12.9	13.8	14.6
17 065	...	7	Hamilton	1 126	8 296	2 578	7.4	97.5	0.9	0.5	0.5	1.5	6.0	16.7	7.4	10.7	11.3	13.3
17 067	22800	7	Hancock	2 056	18 564	1 890	9.0	97.7	0.8	0.5	0.5	1.4	5.3	15.7	7.3	10.1	10.7	14.2

1. CBSA = Core Based Statistical Area. See Appendix A for explanation. See Appendix B for list of metropolitan areas with component counties. 2. County type code from the Economic Research Service of USDA Rural-Urban Continuum Codes. See Appendix A for definition. 3. Dry land or land partially or temporarily covered by water. 4. May be of any race.

STATE County	Population, 2013 (cont.): Age (percent) (cont.): 55 to 64 years	Population, 2013 (cont.): Age (percent) (cont.): 65 to 74 years	Population, 2013 (cont.): Age (percent) (cont.): 75 years and over	Population, 2013 (cont.): Percent female	Population change and components of change, 2000–2014: Total persons: 2000	Population change and components of change, 2000–2014: Total persons: 2010	Population change and components of change, 2000–2014: Percent change: 2000–2010	Population change and components of change, 2000–2014: Percent change: 2010–2014	Components of change, 2010–2014: Births	Components of change, 2010–2014: Deaths	Components of change, 2010–2014: Net migration	Households, 2009–2013: Number	Households, 2009–2013: Persons per household	Households, 2009–2013: Percent: Family households	Households, 2009–2013: Percent: Female family householder[1]	Households, 2009–2013: Percent: One person
	16	17	18	19	20	21	22	23	24	25	26	27	28	29	30	31
IDAHO—Cont'd																
Caribou	13.4	9.4	7.2	50.1	7 304	6 963	-4.7	-1.8	398	270	-233	2 644	2.56	73.8	3.0	24.0
Cassia	10.8	7.2	6.1	49.3	21 416	22 952	7.2	2.5	1 662	784	-275	7 653	2.96	72.1	7.5	24.7
Clark	11.6	8.3	6.7	46.7	1 022	982	-3.9	-11.7	41	27	-131	304	2.41	74.7	12.2	22.0
Clearwater	17.4	14.8	10.0	45.4	8 930	8 761	-1.9	-2.3	286	464	-22	3 545	2.19	66.2	6.0	27.0
Custer	19.1	14.0	8.1	48.5	4 342	4 368	0.6	-5.2	151	148	-227	1 870	2.26	61.3	4.1	33.9
Elmore	10.0	6.8	4.6	47.9	29 130	27 038	-7.2	-3.5	1 980	701	-2 266	9 555	2.70	70.0	8.9	24.4
Franklin	10.6	7.4	6.1	49.4	11 329	12 786	12.9	1.8	859	394	-229	4 150	3.07	76.2	6.1	22.7
Fremont	12.2	8.9	6.5	47.6	11 819	13 242	12.0	-2.8	845	433	-786	4 549	2.76	75.6	4.5	22.3
Gem	14.5	12.2	8.8	50.5	15 181	16 719	10.1	0.9	841	766	56	6 323	2.62	71.8	11.4	23.9
Gooding	11.3	8.8	7.3	48.7	14 155	15 464	9.2	-2.6	867	594	-655	5 552	2.73	71.1	7.3	23.0
Idaho	18.1	14.1	9.5	47.9	15 511	16 267	4.9	-0.3	669	699	1	6 534	2.40	69.0	8.8	24.7
Jefferson	10.1	6.4	4.3	49.7	19 155	26 140	36.5	3.4	2 131	589	-661	8 058	3.26	83.0	7.3	14.0
Jerome	11.1	7.0	4.9	48.8	18 342	22 374	22.0	2.0	1 719	612	-660	7 676	2.90	74.1	10.6	21.7
Kootenai	13.7	9.8	6.6	50.7	108 685	138 494	27.4	6.4	7 300	5 151	6 431	55 679	2.50	69.5	11.1	22.9
Latah	10.8	6.6	4.8	48.7	34 935	37 244	6.6	3.1	1 914	956	241	14 941	2.31	56.7	6.2	25.7
Lemhi	18.9	15.9	10.5	49.0	7 806	7 936	1.7	-2.6	276	358	-134	3 832	2.00	60.5	6.0	36.3
Lewis	15.6	13.0	10.4	49.1	3 747	3 821	2.0	0.4	173	139	0	1 660	2.28	63.3	8.5	31.9
Lincoln	11.9	6.8	5.4	48.7	4 044	5 208	28.8	2.1	332	164	-64	1 617	3.21	77.6	6.5	17.1
Madison	6.0	3.4	2.6	49.9	27 467	37 536	36.7	1.3	4 510	525	-3 530	10 323	3.53	78.3	6.4	11.8
Minidoka	12.2	8.4	7.0	49.6	20 174	20 069	-0.5	1.3	1 438	731	-448	6 994	2.86	74.8	7.6	22.9
Nez Perce	13.8	9.8	9.0	50.5	37 410	39 265	5.0	1.9	2 032	2 044	800	16 019	2.41	64.3	10.4	29.4
Oneida	14.9	9.4	9.1	49.9	4 125	4 286	3.9	-2.4	220	144	-184	1 579	2.67	71.2	9.6	27.9
Owyhee	12.8	9.2	6.3	49.2	10 644	11 526	8.3	-1.5	601	374	-408	3 911	2.90	71.2	9.8	25.0
Payette	12.0	9.6	7.0	50.6	20 578	22 623	9.9	0.9	1 336	788	-311	8 056	2.79	71.6	11.0	24.6
Power	12.7	7.9	5.5	49.0	7 538	7 817	3.7	-2.6	569	223	-546	2 568	2.99	79.1	11.6	16.2
Shoshone	16.9	12.0	8.9	49.8	13 771	12 765	-7.3	-2.9	525	758	-126	5 714	2.17	62.6	6.6	32.9
Teton	11.4	5.0	2.8	48.0	5 999	10 170	69.5	1.7	681	139	-356	3 583	2.82	65.8	6.6	27.8
Twin Falls	11.5	8.0	6.6	50.6	64 284	77 230	20.1	4.8	5 193	2 987	1 463	28 166	2.72	70.8	10.7	23.2
Valley	20.8	14.0	6.7	48.3	7 651	9 862	28.9	-0.4	370	240	-186	3 519	2.70	68.0	5.1	27.9
Washington	15.1	12.7	9.6	50.0	9 977	10 198	2.2	-1.7	443	493	-123	3 938	2.52	65.7	11.0	28.3
ILLINOIS	12.3	7.5	6.0	50.9	12 419 293	12 830 632	3.3	0.4	678 650	433 772	-190 144	4 772 723	2.63	65.7	12.7	28.6
Adams	13.2	9.2	9.1	51.3	68 277	67 103	-1.7	-0.2	3 377	3 287	-282	26 912	2.43	65.0	10.3	29.8
Alexander	14.3	9.9	8.0	49.5	9 590	8 238	-14.1	-9.1	435	401	-756	2 860	2.62	67.7	22.3	30.3
Bond	13.4	8.6	7.6	47.5	17 633	17 768	0.8	-2.8	680	688	-504	6 373	2.65	66.9	6.6	30.5
Boone	11.8	8.1	5.4	50.2	41 786	54 165	29.6	-0.6	2 484	1 525	-1 239	17 938	3.00	78.3	11.5	17.8
Brown	10.8	6.9	5.9	35.5	6 950	6 937	-0.2	-1.5	209	223	-78	2 105	2.47	64.9	7.6	30.5
Bureau	14.5	10.0	9.5	51.0	35 503	34 978	-1.5	-3.3	1 398	1 519	-969	13 998	2.44	65.8	9.6	28.4
Calhoun	14.4	12.0	10.1	49.7	5 084	5 089	0.1	-2.6	200	224	-121	2 061	2.41	70.2	5.4	26.9
Carroll	15.8	12.7	10.2	50.1	16 674	15 387	-7.7	-4.4	547	782	-396	6 671	2.24	65.5	10.4	29.3
Cass	12.8	8.3	7.7	49.1	13 695	13 642	-0.4	-3.5	794	601	-678	5 134	2.59	68.6	11.3	26.5
Champaign	10.5	5.9	5.0	50.0	179 669	201 081	11.9	3.0	10 080	5 166	1 213	79 137	2.35	53.9	10.1	32.9
Christian	13.6	9.4	8.8	49.1	35 372	34 800	-1.6	-2.6	1 510	1 706	-697	14 138	2.32	64.2	10.8	29.9
Clark	13.7	9.9	8.4	50.9	17 008	16 335	-4.0	-0.9	857	836	-160	6 568	2.44	70.0	9.3	26.7
Clay	14.1	9.9	8.7	50.8	14 560	13 815	-5.1	-2.1	735	722	-277	5 486	2.45	65.9	10.2	30.9
Clinton	12.9	8.2	7.4	48.4	35 535	37 762	6.3	0.3	1 770	1 398	-336	14 051	2.55	69.7	9.8	25.4
Coles	11.9	7.6	7.0	51.7	53 196	53 873	1.3	-1.0	2 171	2 090	-557	21 046	2.33	56.4	11.0	33.4
Cook	11.7	7.0	5.7	51.5	5 376 741	5 194 675	-3.4	1.0	300 639	168 890	-75 659	1 933 335	2.65	61.4	15.2	32.1
Crawford	13.6	9.4	8.6	48.3	20 452	19 817	-3.1	-2.1	869	979	-318	7 731	2.41	67.0	8.1	29.4
Cumberland	14.7	9.4	8.1	50.0	11 253	11 048	-1.8	-1.9	451	466	-190	4 184	2.59	68.8	9.0	28.6
DeKalb	10.1	6.0	4.9	50.5	88 969	105 160	18.2	0.3	5 117	2 938	-1 952	37 844	2.59	60.7	9.5	28.7
De Witt	14.5	9.9	7.8	50.1	16 798	16 561	-1.4	-1.7	771	762	-300	6 802	2.38	66.7	8.5	29.7
Douglas	13.1	8.2	8.0	50.4	19 922	19 980	0.3	-0.5	1 090	763	-398	7 509	2.62	70.7	9.9	24.2
DuPage	13.3	7.5	5.5	50.9	904 161	916 924	1.4	1.7	44 983	25 217	-3 232	336 028	2.71	71.1	9.4	24.7
Edgar	14.6	10.8	9.2	51.5	19 704	18 576	-5.7	-4.0	786	981	-524	7 893	2.28	68.2	10.7	28.9
Edwards	14.4	9.8	8.8	51.2	6 971	6 721	-3.6	-1.5	322	283	-109	2 728	2.43	63.6	7.2	33.1
Effingham	13.1	8.5	7.7	50.2	34 264	34 242	-0.1	0.2	1 875	1 454	-414	13 544	2.50	68.0	8.4	27.8
Fayette	12.7	8.8	8.0	47.3	21 802	22 140	1.6	-1.2	1 002	916	-352	8 124	2.57	69.0	8.2	27.3
Ford	13.7	9.4	10.2	50.5	14 241	14 081	-1.1	-2.8	566	812	-177	5 651	2.40	62.7	7.9	33.2
Franklin	13.7	10.8	8.4	50.9	39 018	39 561	1.4	-1.4	1 910	2 186	-241	16 110	2.42	64.0	11.9	31.6
Fulton	13.7	10.0	9.0	47.8	38 250	37 069	-3.1	-2.9	1 519	1 901	-685	14 610	2.37	65.9	9.3	28.1
Gallatin	14.1	13.1	9.0	51.4	6 445	5 589	-13.3	-5.3	220	341	-100	2 369	2.32	65.6	11.1	28.4
Greene	14.0	9.4	8.4	49.6	14 761	13 886	-5.9	-3.3	636	630	-464	5 790	2.33	67.4	8.6	27.5
Grundy	11.8	7.4	4.9	50.2	37 535	50 063	33.4	0.7	2 649	1 610	-746	18 082	2.75	70.7	11.2	24.4
Hamilton	14.5	10.6	9.4	50.8	8 621	8 457	-1.9	-1.9	353	473	-10	3 512	2.36	67.5	6.6	27.4
Hancock	15.2	11.4	10.0	50.7	20 121	19 104	-5.1	-2.8	718	832	-484	8 101	2.30	67.5	9.3	28.1

1. No spouse present.

STATE County	Persons in group quarters, 2014	Daytime population, 2009–2013		Births, 2014		Deaths, 2014		Persons under 65 with no health insurance, 2013		Medicare, 2014			Serious crimes known to police,[2] 2013	
													Total	
		Number	Employment/residence ratio	Total	Rate[1]	Number	Rate[1]	Number	Percent	Eligible for Medicare	Enrolled in Medicare Advantage	Enrolled in a Medicare prescription drug plan	Number	Rate[3]
	32	33	34	35	36	37	38	39	40	41	42	43	44	45
IDAHO—Cont'd														
Caribou	79	7 424	1.19	93	13.6	63	9.2	930	16.6	1 270	198	642	148	2 189
Cassia	286	23 991	1.10	391	16.6	168	7.1	4 636	23.3	3 681	754	1 692	478	2 041
Clark	2	762	1.03	8	9.2	1	1.2	282	38.8	121	25	53	6	715
Clearwater	649	8 905	1.09	74	8.6	96	11.2	1 176	20.0	2 604	20	1 443	196	2 274
Custer	21	4 295	0.98	33	8.0	26	6.3	740	22.5	1 058	16	553	19	438
Elmore	693	25 949	0.95	441	16.9	174	6.7	4 922	22.0	3 683	617	1 195	321	1 231
Franklin	102	10 985	0.65	205	15.7	80	6.1	1 984	18.0	1 968	18	1 267	85	662
Fremont	460	11 182	0.65	192	14.9	94	7.3	2 616	25.1	2 281	428	1 015	117	905
Gem	151	14 075	0.58	209	12.4	182	10.8	2 936	22.5	4 053	1 763	1 245	136	812
Gooding	52	14 830	0.93	197	13.1	112	7.4	3 447	27.6	2 714	600	1 179	159	1 039
Idaho	524	15 689	0.91	157	9.7	168	10.4	2 634	22.3	3 693	40	2 261	202	1 232
Jefferson	111	22 443	0.64	491	18.2	139	5.1	4 718	19.8	3 488	751	1 495	233	864
Jerome	106	21 576	0.91	407	17.8	148	6.5	5 368	27.4	3 195	1 011	1 271	387	1 710
Kootenai	1 488	134 150	0.89	1 745	11.8	1 242	8.4	22 209	18.6	30 308	8 921	11 256	4 479	3 106
Latah	3 139	34 577	0.83	455	11.8	209	5.4	4 957	16.1	5 313	829	2 620	960	2 482
Lemhi	80	7 795	0.98	59	7.6	72	9.3	1 122	20.0	2 326	27	1 173	78	1 009
Lewis	74	3 954	1.07	39	10.2	32	8.3	670	22.6	1 794	16	1 039	71	1 806
Lincoln	37	4 566	0.70	79	14.9	38	7.1	1 324	28.7	796	183	451	28	526
Madison	943	38 417	1.06	1 059	27.8	111	2.9	5 598	16.3	2 568	569	902	306	814
Minidoka	82	19 273	0.91	361	17.8	168	8.3	4 257	25.0	3 453	865	1 425	396	1 968
Nez Perce	961	42 079	1.14	506	12.6	463	11.6	4 954	15.5	8 978	2 104	4 275	1 356	3 407
Oneida	50	3 886	0.79	49	11.7	33	7.9	669	19.4	911	152	446	46	1 093
Owyhee	160	10 414	0.75	147	12.9	80	7.0	2 953	31.1	2 038	740	647	181	1 576
Payette	94	20 052	0.71	310	13.6	187	8.2	4 154	22.3	4 701	1 753	1 630	474	2 083
Power	47	8 104	1.10	136	17.9	55	7.2	1 658	25.1	1 210	270	592	119	1 527
Shoshone	160	12 796	1.01	131	10.6	165	13.3	1 735	17.5	3 327	608	1 520	355	2 783
Teton	7	8 569	0.68	162	15.7	28	2.7	2 590	27.5	1 045	82	623	74	735
Twin Falls	1 001	79 112	1.03	1 253	15.5	732	9.0	14 276	21.2	13 938	4 000	5 823	1 775	2 237
Valley	66	9 985	1.07	89	9.1	57	5.8	1 456	19.3	2 183	540	811	214	2 249
Washington	119	9 332	0.80	111	11.1	97	9.7	1 924	25.2	2 555	828	944	73	722
ILLINOIS	300 410	12 842 258	1.00	157 330	12.2	103 766	8.1	1 587 714	14.6	2 043 638	396 742	1 032 576	341 957	2 655
Adams	2 283	70 532	1.11	771	11.5	792	11.8	5 685	10.6	14 259	1 620	8 739	1 764	2 625
Alexander	543	7 697	0.88	100	13.3	102	13.6	798	13.7	1 685	143	1 046	447	5 885
Bond	2 060	16 000	0.78	148	8.6	160	9.3	1 436	11.3	3 341	420	2 107	219	1 280
Boone	310	46 256	0.67	565	10.5	332	6.2	6 620	14.3	8 768	2 098	4 409	736	1 367
Brown	2 110	8 167	1.48	50	7.3	57	8.3	406	10.4	1 018	148	554	54	781
Bureau	456	31 697	0.82	328	9.7	368	10.9	3 535	13.0	7 336	979	4 392	465	1 425
Calhoun	90	3 963	0.49	43	8.7	60	12.1	513	13.1	1 211	135	790	NA	NA
Carroll	223	13 719	0.79	145	9.9	187	12.7	1 521	13.3	4 034	796	2 047	230	1 974
Cass	184	13 409	0.98	184	14.0	132	10.0	1 739	15.6	2 447	342	1 341	63	476
Champaign	16 104	211 702	1.09	2 372	11.5	1 257	6.1	21 179	12.6	25 803	11 439	6 853	6 537	3 226
Christian	1 609	30 808	0.75	346	10.2	377	11.1	3 034	11.4	7 429	1 497	3 837	456	1 367
Clark	221	14 425	0.74	205	12.7	206	12.7	1 531	11.6	3 550	627	2 118	130	1 060
Clay	305	13 514	0.96	183	13.5	175	12.9	1 343	12.3	3 100	184	2 067	226	1 644
Clinton	2 072	31 499	0.66	418	11.0	359	9.5	2 872	9.5	6 856	650	4 134	467	1 495
Coles	4 498	55 607	1.08	505	9.5	470	8.8	5 559	13.2	9 058	1 892	4 756	737	1 376
Cook	90 625	5 396 994	1.08	69 752	13.3	40 954	7.8	830 462	18.4	767 814	150 117	383 721	180 666	3 497
Crawford	1 495	19 815	1.01	193	10.0	239	12.3	1 692	11.5	4 126	331	2 699	NA	NA
Cumberland	117	8 562	0.50	92	8.5	103	9.5	1 038	11.5	2 187	353	1 237	110	1 005
DeKalb	6 681	95 705	0.82	1 178	11.2	683	6.5	11 311	13.0	13 718	2 401	7 205	2 373	2 380
De Witt	249	14 556	0.75	180	11.1	211	13.0	1 393	10.4	3 366	808	1 598	226	1 574
Douglas	168	18 538	0.85	248	12.5	168	8.4	2 687	16.2	3 777	1 254	1 550	194	1 180
DuPage	12 149	1 015 558	1.20	10 447	11.2	6 120	6.6	85 937	10.8	137 880	19 666	73 779	13 301	1 429
Edgar	283	17 594	0.90	187	10.5	225	12.6	1 699	11.9	4 087	576	2 454	278	1 658
Edwards	52	6 499	0.93	78	11.8	69	10.4	622	11.5	1 494	97	987	89	1 540
Effingham	440	38 563	1.25	441	12.8	324	9.4	2 870	10.1	6 669	601	4 024	672	1 954
Fayette	1 784	20 382	0.81	231	10.6	206	9.4	2 338	14.0	4 488	490	2 704	274	1 247
Ford	410	12 869	0.82	126	9.2	191	14.0	1 193	10.8	2 846	650	1 371	253	1 922
Franklin	517	34 734	0.69	429	10.9	508	12.9	4 180	13.3	9 353	1 662	5 300	719	2 051
Fulton	2 682	31 542	0.65	348	9.7	457	12.7	3 459	12.7	7 782	1 977	4 032	673	2 131
Gallatin	25	5 210	0.86	48	9.1	77	14.6	563	13.4	1 404	128	855	NA	NA
Greene	284	11 100	0.56	148	11.0	162	12.1	1 408	12.8	2 996	270	1 971	131	972
Grundy	254	44 637	0.76	602	11.9	372	7.4	4 275	9.8	7 662	569	4 213	829	1 681
Hamilton	117	7 258	0.66	75	9.0	111	13.4	873	13.1	1 912	214	1 181	NA	NA
Hancock	223	15 439	0.60	186	10.0	195	10.5	1 941	13.3	4 534	488	2 593	NA	NA

1. Per 1,000 estimated resident population. 2. Data for serious crimes have not been adjusted for underreporting; this may affect comparability between geographic areas and over time.
3. Per 100,000 population estimated by the FBI.

STATE County	Serious crimes known to police, 2013 (cont.)[1] Rate[2] Violent	Rate[2] Property	Education: School enrollment and attainment, 2009–2013: Enrollment[3] Total	Enrollment[3] Percent private	Attainment[4] (percent) High school graduate or less	Attainment[4] (percent) Bachelor's degree or more	Local government expenditures,[5] 2012–2013: Total current spending (mil dol)	Current spending per student (dollars)	Money income, 2009–2013: Per capita income[6] (dollars)	Households: Median income (dollars)	Households: Mean income (dollars)	Households: Percent with income of $200,000 or more	Income and poverty, 2013: Median household income (dollars)	Percent below poverty level: All persons	Children under 18 years	Children 5 to 17 years in families
	46	47	48	49	50	51	52	53	54	55	56	57	58	59	60	61
IDAHO—Cont'd																
Caribou	207	1 982	1 767	9.8	47.1	17.5	11.5	7 748	23 586	53 586	61 042	1.9	54 579	11.1	14.8	13.6
Cassia	252	1 789	6 564	6.0	48.2	15.6	31.9	6 202	17 801	42 039	52 316	1.4	44 160	15.3	20.4	18.8
Clark	0	715	148	0.0	59.5	11.4	2.2	13 393	20 032	33 200	46 237	0.0	42 940	17.5	24.7	23.3
Clearwater	209	2 065	1 465	14.1	51.8	15.5	9.6	9 637	20 256	40 134	49 889	1.0	40 068	17.8	26.4	24.4
Custer	23	415	841	9.6	48.7	26.3	5.6	8 691	23 965	39 541	52 723	0.3	41 522	14.3	20.0	18.4
Elmore	196	1 036	7 027	8.8	45.8	16.9	28.9	6 797	20 646	42 842	54 028	1.3	42 680	16.6	22.9	22.3
Franklin	62	599	3 829	6.6	45.6	17.4	16.7	5 374	17 620	44 962	53 117	0.2	44 790	12.3	16.7	14.6
Fremont	70	836	3 450	12.4	43.5	19.7	15.0	6 540	19 475	44 520	55 739	0.6	44 130	16.7	23.8	22.7
Gem	125	686	3 898	11.3	51.0	15.8	18.1	7 159	20 250	44 432	51 976	0.6	44 173	18.4	26.2	24.3
Gooding	157	882	3 704	10.9	56.7	12.1	19.8	6 903	18 373	37 050	50 377	1.9	41 310	16.3	22.9	21.8
Idaho	134	1 098	3 165	19.3	52.2	14.8	17.5	10 416	19 168	37 349	45 155	0.3	39 434	15.8	23.3	22.8
Jefferson	78	786	8 195	13.9	39.3	22.0	34.7	5 528	19 598	52 023	62 564	1.6	52 950	13.1	16.8	16.8
Jerome	208	1 503	6 071	7.5	56.9	13.4	24.4	5 875	17 182	40 126	49 120	0.7	41 595	15.3	22.4	22.2
Kootenai	321	2 785	34 510	13.2	37.3	23.3	136.4	6 501	24 685	49 002	61 930	2.6	51 681	13.3	17.9	16.6
Latah	111	2 371	14 808	9.5	25.3	44.1	42.6	8 996	22 322	41 735	55 557	1.6	43 699	18.1	15.2	14.6
Lemhi	194	815	1 291	11.4	39.5	23.8	8.2	8 557	23 998	34 122	49 824	1.7	38 367	18.0	25.0	23.0
Lewis	178	1 628	779	12.7	47.1	16.2	9.0	10 168	19 910	36 000	44 428	0.1	41 190	17.0	25.3	23.5
Lincoln	413	113	1 425	6.5	59.6	11.8	8.5	8 843	16 530	42 433	50 423	0.2	42 625	15.6	23.8	21.1
Madison	56	758	19 799	58.4	20.8	33.7	39.1	5 895	15 133	32 059	51 535	1.8	37 142	29.1	19.1	19.5
Minidoka	134	1 834	5 143	7.6	57.4	9.9	25.8	6 335	19 597	43 266	54 597	2.5	41 968	14.4	20.5	20.1
Nez Perce	153	3 254	9 109	9.4	41.8	21.1	48.3	8 785	24 257	46 503	57 608	1.4	46 753	13.4	18.0	16.5
Oneida	214	879	1 148	6.8	44.8	13.2	5.9	6 660	18 920	40 842	47 532	0.6	45 040	13.8	19.8	17.9
Owyhee	148	1 428	2 901	8.4	63.0	8.2	16.5	6 827	15 945	32 175	44 333	0.7	35 017	18.4	26.4	24.9
Payette	176	1 907	5 825	8.9	50.5	16.4	25.0	5 908	19 165	43 649	51 952	1.0	43 642	17.6	22.9	21.4
Power	51	1 476	2 151	7.9	54.9	15.9	14.1	8 705	17 684	44 212	52 091	0.4	44 450	17.6	25.7	27.7
Shoshone	447	2 336	2 458	8.3	48.6	13.5	19.5	10 196	20 487	38 440	46 317	0.3	37 431	19.4	28.3	25.6
Teton	149	586	2 419	12.2	34.5	34.4	12.4	7 416	22 436	53 931	58 443	1.0	52 650	12.8	20.1	19.5
Twin Falls	221	2 017	20 654	9.0	45.4	16.3	89.3	6 630	20 588	43 886	55 320	1.7	44 602	16.0	21.1	20.1
Valley	284	1 965	2 205	24.4	35.6	34.3	14.5	11 953	25 785	50 473	60 737	1.7	48 879	11.7	18.2	17.1
Washington	89	633	2 386	10.4	48.5	16.7	13.6	7 552	20 380	37 453	50 385	2.8	37 539	17.9	25.1	21.9
ILLINOIS	380	2 274	3 494 514	18.7	39.9	31.4	25 785.0	12 288	29 666	56 797	77 660	5.3	56 212	14.6	20.6	19.6
Adams	323	2 302	15 818	19.4	46.6	21.3	92.5	9 504	24 217	45 073	58 447	2.1	43 604	15.9	19.9	18.0
Alexander	1 843	4 042	1 903	5.8	61.5	8.4	13.2	12 087	13 619	26 972	35 154	0.3	30 141	33.0	53.2	51.9
Bond	29	1 251	4 819	18.2	50.4	19.1	22.2	9 062	23 195	48 163	60 502	2.5	48 464	16.0	20.5	18.1
Boone	113	1 253	15 052	18.3	50.2	19.3	103.2	10 101	25 888	60 893	75 809	4.4	59 537	10.2	14.6	13.0
Brown	174	608	1 437	5.6	55.2	12.2	7.5	9 866	20 555	42 194	61 648	1.9	46 522	16.0	14.8	14.2
Bureau	107	1 318	8 130	10.3	49.8	17.4	62.5	11 448	26 705	48 977	64 773	2.4	49 062	12.0	17.7	16.4
Calhoun	NA	NA	1 114	23.8	55.0	14.4	6.6	11 522	26 924	50 436	64 626	3.5	48 504	12.0	16.9	15.6
Carroll	146	1 828	3 103	8.2	52.7	15.1	27.2	10 946	27 118	47 985	62 035	2.4	43 643	14.0	21.4	19.3
Cass	113	363	3 374	9.2	60.4	13.0	22.6	9 269	22 257	45 734	56 363	1.2	45 257	12.9	19.9	18.6
Champaign	526	2 700	80 858	7.5	29.4	42.4	292.7	12 063	25 713	45 808	64 105	3.7	46 917	21.6	20.8	21.3
Christian	135	1 232	7 711	11.2	55.6	13.5	53.1	11 344	23 915	45 145	59 109	2.2	49 391	13.1	20.7	19.0
Clark	228	831	3 971	5.7	49.2	17.6	24.5	8 841	24 296	47 405	59 554	2.2	46 287	13.7	22.1	20.0
Clay	36	1 608	3 037	5.5	54.8	14.0	21.6	8 815	22 279	40 640	52 009	1.4	42 369	14.2	21.5	20.6
Clinton	186	1 309	8 998	15.7	42.9	20.3	49.6	9 318	27 802	61 720	72 516	3.2	61 843	9.5	12.1	11.3
Coles	191	1 186	18 840	5.6	42.4	24.2	79.7	12 255	21 970	37 040	54 058	2.1	39 353	19.8	22.3	20.0
Cook	594	2 903	1 396 496	23.2	39.7	34.7	10 615.4	13 671	30 183	54 548	78 472	6.0	53 795	17.8	26.0	25.9
Crawford	NA	NA	4 463	5.1	46.2	17.1	30.7	10 293	25 214	46 216	62 111	2.7	47 517	14.0	19.5	18.9
Cumberland	219	786	2 474	7.1	50.5	13.8	16.2	8 892	22 952	43 958	57 780	2.2	47 382	12.1	17.6	16.3
DeKalb	279	2 101	39 292	8.9	35.7	29.8	218.9	12 809	23 696	53 375	63 525	1.9	54 204	18.7	17.9	15.6
De Witt	167	1 407	3 710	7.2	51.0	16.8	28.3	10 090	26 704	51 051	64 361	2.1	53 303	13.8	20.6	19.2
Douglas	261	918	4 562	13.1	54.2	16.2	32.1	9 714	23 732	52 741	61 851	1.7	49 179	10.7	17.4	15.4
DuPage	81	1 348	254 541	22.4	27.3	46.3	2 227.0	14 074	38 570	78 487	104 013	10.1	76 269	7.0	9.8	9.2
Edgar	262	1 395	3 933	6.2	51.9	18.2	30.2	8 247	23 368	42 133	53 981	1.3	44 433	18.5	24.9	22.2
Edwards	294	1 246	1 498	9.4	49.0	10.5	8.9	9 148	20 898	39 075	49 147	0.6	45 675	12.7	19.7	18.1
Effingham	128	1 826	8 176	12.9	45.7	20.0	51.6	9 526	27 051	52 108	67 796	3.5	50 900	11.1	15.9	15.0
Fayette	146	1 102	5 020	9.2	57.8	13.1	29.8	10 117	21 523	44 722	55 917	1.3	43 014	16.9	25.5	23.1
Ford	137	1 785	3 255	7.8	51.3	16.3	33.2	11 146	25 448	48 866	60 720	2.8	52 375	11.4	18.1	16.5
Franklin	268	1 783	9 061	7.7	47.6	13.1	72.7	11 154	20 394	36 273	48 075	0.7	35 681	20.0	30.1	28.0
Fulton	215	1 916	8 058	6.3	51.0	14.5	53.1	9 935	22 318	45 130	54 790	1.2	46 342	14.8	20.4	18.4
Gallatin	NA	NA	1 093	2.0	54.3	12.0	7.9	9 852	23 862	40 330	55 570	1.5	40 349	17.1	27.9	25.4
Greene	119	853	3 170	12.7	54.5	12.9	20.5	10 101	22 307	43 502	53 174	0.9	41 588	18.3	21.0	20.0
Grundy	81	1 600	10 129	11.7	45.6	20.2	142.2	11 032	28 725	64 541	77 086	3.2	68 474	8.0	10.7	9.9
Hamilton	NA	NA	1 633	5.4	51.4	15.7	12.6	9 839	21 960	38 417	53 550	0.7	42 330	14.9	23.8	22.5
Hancock	NA	NA	3 952	7.0	47.7	18.4	32.5	10 326	23 714	43 925	54 668	1.2	47 965	12.2	19.7	17.9

1. Data for serious crimes have not been adjusted for underreporting; this may affect comparability between geographic areas and over time. 2. Per 100,000 population estimated by the FBI.
3. All persons 3 years old and over enrolled in nursery school through college. 4. Persons 25 years old and over. 5. Elementary and secondary education expenditures.
6. Based on population estimated by the American Community Survey, 2009–2013.

STATE County	Personal income, 2013										Earnings, 2013		
	Total (mil dol)	Percent change, 2012–2013	Per capita[1]		Wages and salaries (mil dol)	Supplements to wages and salaries; employer contributions (mil dol)		Proprietors' income (mil dol)	Dividends, interest, and rent (mil dol)	Personal transfer receipts (mil dol)	Total (mil dol)	Contributions for government social insurance (mil dol)	
			Dollars	Rank		Pension and insurance	Government social insurance					From employee and self-employed	From employer
	62	63	64	65	66	67	68	69	70	71	72	73	74
IDAHO—Cont'd													
Caribou	274	0.8	40 316	1 135	173	33	15	43	50	46	263	14	15
Cassia	884	5.3	37 885	1 449	363	61	34	248	143	143	706	29	34
Clark	46	2.3	53 416	256	19	3	2	17	5	4	41	1	2
Clearwater	279	2.3	32 502	2 331	102	23	10	21	60	86	156	11	10
Custer	151	2.8	35 466	1 826	69	13	6	18	42	32	106	6	6
Elmore	1 008	5.2	38 503	1 372	419	113	42	68	233	165	642	28	42
Franklin	405	4.5	31 497	2 481	94	21	9	46	66	68	171	9	9
Fremont	412	8.4	31 887	2 424	101	23	9	60	85	83	193	10	9
Gem	511	4.9	30 597	2 613	100	21	10	27	115	141	158	13	10
Gooding	697	5.7	46 244	604	227	35	20	218	100	105	500	15	20
Idaho	508	2.0	31 502	2 478	156	33	15	60	135	122	264	17	15
Jefferson	844	4.4	31 353	2 500	193	37	18	185	113	136	434	19	18
Jerome	785	5.5	34 880	1 920	320	49	29	197	106	132	595	25	29
Kootenai	5 263	3.0	36 478	1 666	1 960	350	188	338	1 172	1 069	2 836	188	188
Latah	1 343	0.5	35 274	1 863	479	125	42	98	321	214	743	42	42
Lemhi	273	1.1	35 391	1 837	75	18	7	22	89	76	122	8	7
Lewis	169	0.0	43 378	813	51	11	5	24	31	59	91	6	5
Lincoln	192	5.0	36 168	1 718	60	12	5	64	24	37	141	5	5
Madison	861	3.8	22 987	3 090	431	79	40	126	142	177	676	36	40
Minidoka	762	8.0	37 546	1 499	252	44	23	157	156	122	476	21	23
Nez Perce	1 525	3.1	38 209	1 410	818	141	72	127	311	342	1 158	74	72
Oneida	136	5.7	31 703	2 448	32	8	3	28	23	31	70	4	3
Owyhee	388	5.1	33 843	2 109	89	16	8	96	66	77	209	7	8
Payette	745	4.3	32 967	2 258	217	38	22	70	150	170	346	22	22
Power	316	5.2	40 979	1 054	133	25	12	89	44	50	259	10	12
Shoshone	468	1.5	36 899	1 603	199	32	18	17	96	131	267	19	18
Teton	318	5.5	30 910	2 566	93	16	9	44	79	42	163	9	9
Twin Falls	2 780	4.3	34 763	1 939	1 164	199	111	410	529	579	1 884	105	111
Valley	401	1.5	41 727	969	134	26	13	34	142	70	207	13	13
Washington	314	5.0	31 621	2 461	94	20	10	19	64	88	142	10	10
ILLINOIS	605 201	2.2	46 980	X	319 855	53 879	22 886	53 194	112 563	92 572	449 814	24 240	22 886
Adams	2 888	3.2	43 023	838	1 359	262	103	253	670	551	1 977	109	103
Alexander	230	2.7	30 144	2 664	77	22	5	9	32	90	113	6	5
Bond	658	3.7	37 658	1 479	184	47	14	78	116	133	323	17	14
Boone	2 053	2.8	38 040	1 427	776	145	68	121	379	333	1 109	62	68
Brown	234	12.1	34 111	2 060	156	30	11	37	47	38	234	11	11
Bureau	1 528	10.5	44 854	700	476	97	37	270	297	268	880	41	37
Calhoun	187	8.5	36 977	1 590	24	7	2	20	36	43	54	3	2
Carroll	632	11.7	42 394	898	156	36	12	92	142	141	295	16	12
Cass	506	9.4	38 007	1 430	215	49	16	78	77	102	359	17	16
Champaign	8 122	3.9	39 637	1 212	4 420	1 100	283	545	1 889	1 032	6 348	280	283
Christian	1 432	8.6	41 740	967	415	91	32	247	264	302	785	38	32
Clark	663	10.9	40 988	1 053	165	40	13	123	116	135	340	17	13
Clay	527	7.3	38 812	1 319	186	45	15	94	91	137	339	17	15
Clinton	1 616	3.1	42 639	877	392	90	29	166	313	266	677	35	29
Coles	2 007	5.5	37 385	1 524	947	233	67	168	466	391	1 415	67	67
Cook	260 257	1.7	49 661	380	156 561	24 200	11 066	26 638	46 187	41 136	218 464	11 914	11 066
Crawford	815	4.3	41 773	962	350	104	25	126	155	153	606	30	25
Cumberland	473	11.6	43 276	820	86	20	7	96	70	83	209	9	7
DeKalb	3 662	4.5	34 959	1 902	1 567	400	107	299	767	588	2 373	109	107
De Witt	734	11.4	44 673	718	274	61	19	136	114	130	489	22	19
Douglas	865	10.1	43 489	802	317	66	25	186	156	139	594	28	25
DuPage	54 123	1.4	58 064	132	37 692	5 307	2 744	4 169	10 913	5 250	49 911	2 734	2 744
Edgar	759	12.1	42 255	913	242	54	20	163	120	167	479	21	20
Edwards	245	7.1	36 731	1 635	90	19	7	50	52	49	166	8	7
Effingham	1 468	2.3	42 790	862	757	142	59	165	376	244	1 123	60	59
Fayette	688	7.5	31 188	2 519	193	46	14	116	133	175	369	19	14
Ford	734	11.4	53 098	266	187	41	14	205	119	113	448	18	14
Franklin	1 286	0.7	32 795	2 283	311	75	24	78	236	398	488	33	24
Fulton	1 348	4.6	37 080	1 568	286	76	20	157	229	312	539	29	20
Gallatin	246	20.8	45 390	665	45	10	3	00	43	66	125	5	3
Greene	506	11.9	37 158	1 555	90	22	6	116	78	117	235	10	6
Grundy	1 957	5.1	38 963	1 307	952	197	67	208	335	296	1 424	73	67
Hamilton	347	9.9	41 509	993	69	17	5	68	67	80	158	7	5
Hancock	772	14.4	41 459	998	142	36	10	165	142	158	353	16	10

1. Based on the resident population estimated as of July 1 of the year shown.

Table B. States and Counties — **Earnings, Social Security, and Housing**

STATE County	Earnings, 2013 (cont.) Percent by selected industries									Social Security beneficiaries, December 2013		Supple-mental Security Income recipients, December 2013	Housing units, 2014	
	Farm	Mining	Construction	Manu-facturing	Infor-mation: professional, scientific, technical services	Retail trade	Finance, insur-ance, real estate and leasing	Health care and social assistance	Govern-ment	Number	Rate[1]		Total	Percent change, 2010–2014
	75	76	77	78	79	80	81	82	83	84	85	86	87	88
IDAHO—Cont'd														
Caribou	14.4	D	9.3	31.8	2.8	3.4	2.5	1.3	12.0	1 370	201	70	3 217	-0.3
Cassia	33.8	1.0	3.7	10.8	D	7.0	2.1	8.0	10.3	4 085	175	421	8 434	0.7
Clark	51.0	0.0	D	2.0	D	D	1.6	D	16.1	125	145	7	533	0.4
Clearwater	1.9	D	5.9	4.1	3.0	6.2	2.4	D	33.7	2 865	333	243	4 479	0.6
Custer	10.3	D	3.6	0.5	D	5.1	1.5	D	21.3	1 160	274	69	3 090	-0.4
Elmore	10.3	D	1.9	3.0	1.8	4.8	1.8	4.6	60.8	4 020	154	494	12 193	0.3
Franklin	21.8	D	7.4	4.8	D	9.1	2.8	D	22.0	2 215	172	163	4 650	2.7
Fremont	24.7	D	10.2	0.9	D	5.2	2.3	3.1	27.7	2 485	192	186	8 651	1.4
Gem	8.0	D	7.1	2.9	2.9	9.1	3.3	15.8	26.1	4 565	273	478	7 100	0.0
Gooding	55.9	D	1.9	10.1	D	2.3	D	1.9	9.9	2 995	198	297	6 059	-0.6
Idaho	8.7	1.7	7.8	8.0	2.9	9.0	5.1	8.6	25.8	4 085	252	379	8 648	-1.1
Jefferson	33.6	0.1	7.9	11.8	D	6.0	2.3	3.2	12.0	3 950	147	292	8 878	1.8
Jerome	34.5	0.0	2.7	12.6	D	6.2	1.9	4.1	7.8	3 610	160	392	8 238	1.7
Kootenai	0.1	0.9	7.6	9.2	6.9	11.0	6.8	12.4	21.6	32 900	228	2 625	66 130	4.7
Latah	4.5	D	3.5	3.0	5.6	7.5	2.8	9.8	45.8	5 640	148	490	16 330	2.1
Lemhi	5.6	D	8.8	2.8	D	9.3	2.9	D	38.9	2 535	328	188	4 746	0.4
Lewis	23.5	D	2.5	14.9	D	5.7	3.2	D	21.5	2 040	533	257	1 868	-0.6
Lincoln	52.7	0.0	D	D	D	2.1	D	4.4	16.9	1 155	218	81	1 958	-0.9
Madison	7.9	D	4.3	5.0	6.6	7.6	3.6	D	14.7	2 840	76	243	12 708	12.7
Minidoka	34.1	0.0	4.4	14.9	2.6	3.6	1.4	D	13.3	3 545	175	357	7 787	1.6
Nez Perce	2.1	D	4.2	20.5	4.4	7.6	7.7	17.0	18.7	10 010	251	1 053	17 417	-0.1
Oneida	29.4	D	1.4	1.1	2.1	12.8	5.3	2.5	23.7	1 015	238	63	1 935	1.5
Owyhee	54.0	2.1	3.0	3.9	D	2.9	D	D	13.5	2 285	200	250	4 769	-0.3
Payette	12.2	D	4.8	15.9	D	4.4	D	11.6	13.5	5 300	235	576	9 070	1.4
Power	36.6	0.0	1.2	27.8	D	2.3	D	D	11.1	1 385	180	120	2 936	-0.3
Shoshone	-0.1	30.6	5.0	3.0	4.8	17.2	2.1	4.9	18.0	3 765	297	456	6 976	-1.2
Teton	12.2	0.0	13.5	2.3	D	7.0	5.8	5.1	17.4	1 155	112	59	5 503	0.5
Twin Falls	13.8	0.0	3.9	11.9	5.7	9.0	4.3	14.7	12.4	15 215	191	1 791	31 772	2.3
Valley	0.9	D	9.1	0.6	D	10.4	9.3	D	28.1	2 350	245	114	11 906	1.0
Washington	10.0	0.0	4.7	16.9	6.5	6.7	4.7	D	23.4	2 780	279	263	4 543	0.3
ILLINOIS	2.2	0.3	4.6	11.2	13.3	5.2	9.9	10.1	14.5	2 133 829	166	278 543	5 307 222	0.2
Adams	6.3	0.9	4.3	17.9	4.3	7.7	7.4	16.5	11.9	15 245	227	1 386	29 967	0.4
Alexander	3.5	D	1.2	6.4	D	2.8	D	D	46.0	1 910	250	498	3 953	-1.3
Bond	15.0	1.1	3.9	15.8	2.7	3.1	2.9	D	22.3	3 620	207	347	7 094	0.1
Boone	5.4	D	5.9	47.8	2.5	4.4	2.5	3.7	12.2	9 595	178	510	19 973	0.0
Brown	13.2	0.1	6.2	0.2	D	D	1.5	D	12.9	1 095	160	98	2 442	-0.8
Bureau	23.8	0.3	4.5	11.9	D	4.0	2.9	D	14.8	7 850	230	389	15 651	-0.4
Calhoun	27.5	D	4.7	1.1	D	7.1	D	D	26.5	1 305	259	83	2 835	0.0
Carroll	24.8	D	5.0	15.7	D	5.0	4.1	3.7	16.2	4 180	281	248	8 412	-0.3
Cass	17.6	0.0	2.9	D	D	4.1	3.7	D	14.1	2 640	198	253	5 781	-0.9
Champaign	4.0	D	4.0	7.0	8.3	4.7	4.2	12.5	39.3	26 015	126	3 030	89 194	1.9
Christian	24.3	0.4	4.7	12.9	3.9	6.0	3.2	10.6	13.6	8 235	241	712	15 533	-0.2
Clark	24.7	2.9	7.1	20.9	D	5.0	2.7	4.4	13.5	3 875	239	281	7 739	-0.4
Clay	16.6	4.7	2.2	28.8	D	4.4	3.2	D	15.9	3 295	243	327	6 353	-0.8
Clinton	13.8	D	11.2	6.1	3.2	8.3	4.4	10.3	21.4	7 075	187	419	15 541	1.5
Coles	8.2	0.4	4.3	11.1	D	5.6	3.4	15.0	29.2	9 675	180	1 051	23 434	0.0
Cook	0.0	0.1	4.1	7.4	18.3	4.2	13.6	9.7	13.1	779 575	149	158 840	2 175 146	-0.2
Crawford	9.5	3.8	5.8	38.1	D	4.2	2.7	D	16.3	4 490	230	311	8 637	-0.3
Cumberland	34.5	D	3.5	11.8	D	7.5	D	6.3	13.8	2 465	227	201	4 838	-0.7
DeKalb	6.3	D	6.3	10.6	3.4	6.8	3.5	11.8	33.2	14 400	137	850	41 003	-0.2
De Witt	21.8	D	7.5	8.0	D	4.8	1.8	D	12.0	3 545	216	253	7 502	-0.3
Douglas	20.3	D	5.5	34.3	2.2	5.0	2.4	3.0	9.9	3 960	200	221	8 374	-0.2
DuPage	0.0	0.1	4.7	10.1	15.9	5.5	9.0	8.7	8.0	137 770	148	8 196	357 407	0.3
Edgar	28.5	D	3.0	22.6	2.1	3.9	6.1	D	13.0	4 495	250	449	8 741	-0.7
Edwards	20.9	D	3.0	D	D	3.0	D	2.0	8.9	1 605	240	99	3 158	-0.9
Effingham	6.3	0.4	6.2	17.5	D	9.1	3.7	17.2	10.2	7 205	210	490	14 714	1.0
Fayette	21.4	2.0	4.3	10.3	2.8	6.8	3.5	D	18.6	4 750	216	481	9 216	-0.9
Ford	32.3	D	2.9	7.9	1.8	7.6	2.0	D	10.2	3 075	223	201	6 334	0.8
Franklin	4.3	1.9	7.1	8.3	D	9.7	3.5	9.5	27.0	10 495	265	1 406	18 546	-0.9
Fulton	20.3	D	4.9	2.9	2.5	7.0	3.7	D	26.1	8 460	233	733	16 180	-0.1
Gallatin	44.1	D	4.9	0.7	D	4.1	D	D	11.2	1 550	287	225	2 725	-0.8
Greene	43.4	D	3.5	2.6	1.8	4.9	D	D	16.0	3 245	238	390	6 341	-0.8
Grundy	7.3	0.1	10.1	10.5	3.1	5.6	2.6	8.8	11.9	8 565	171	387	20 337	1.7
Hamilton	31.4	14.9	3.7	3.0	D	3.7	2.7	4.4	19.9	2 070	249	203	4 062	-1.0
Hancock	36.1	D	4.0	0.0	5.2	3.9	3.4	D	15.8	4 820	260	319	9 221	-0.6

1. Per 1,000 resident population estimated as of July 1 of the year shown.

Table B. States and Counties — **Housing, Labor Force, and Employment**

STATE County	Housing units, 2009–2013: Occupied units: Total	Owner-occupied: Percent	Owner-occupied: Median value[1]	Median owner cost as a percent of income: With a mortgage	Median owner cost as a percent of income: Without a mortgage[2]	Renter-occupied: Median rent[3]	Renter-occupied: Median rent as a percent of income[2]	Substandard units[4] (percent)	Civilian labor force, 2014: Total	Percent change, 2013–2014	Unemployment: Total	Unemployment: Rate[5]	Civilian employment,[6] 2009–2013: Total	Percent: Management, business, science and arts	Percent: Construction, production, and maintenance occupations
	89	90	91	92	93	94	95	96	97	98	99	100	101	102	103
IDAHO—Cont'd															
Caribou	2 644	84.1	116 300	19.3	10.0	524	15.7	4.5	3 852	-1.2	163	4.2	3 013	32.0	33.8
Cassia	7 653	69.0	125 900	23.1	10.0	548	27.6	10.2	11 117	0.0	477	4.3	9 360	27.7	37.4
Clark	304	59.5	111 700	36.2	10.0	510	15.3	1.8	441	4.0	20	4.5	397	25.9	49.9
Clearwater	3 545	80.1	138 300	24.6	11.6	613	24.3	1.3	3 110	-2.4	293	9.4	2 954	29.5	30.9
Custer	1 870	83.5	150 600	22.8	10.0	439	27.3	4.4	2 120	-3.9	142	6.7	1 958	27.1	38.3
Elmore	9 555	62.4	136 800	25.4	10.4	714	25.5	2.5	11 011	2.1	585	5.3	10 200	27.7	33.3
Franklin	4 150	80.9	156 800	25.9	12.2	638	26.9	5.3	6 386	2.0	220	3.4	5 327	24.9	39.6
Fremont	4 549	82.5	147 600	23.2	11.1	651	31.1	1.6	7 013	1.4	280	4.0	5 519	26.4	34.8
Gem	6 323	74.6	150 400	23.3	11.2	757	31.9	7.6	7 529	0.4	441	5.9	6 370	30.4	22.7
Gooding	5 552	70.5	123 800	26.7	10.1	643	31.6	2.6	7 953	-1.2	319	4.0	6 445	26.6	43.5
Idaho	6 534	78.2	150 900	26.1	10.9	619	25.4	3.4	6 455	-1.7	486	7.5	6 453	25.7	33.4
Jefferson	8 058	83.8	157 500	24.6	10.0	690	26.4	8.2	12 275	1.1	493	4.0	11 108	33.6	30.2
Jerome	7 676	63.5	135 200	25.6	11.6	689	28.5	3.2	11 077	1.1	449	4.1	9 457	22.9	42.1
Kootenai	55 679	70.6	188 800	24.9	10.6	825	31.2	2.7	70 488	1.8	3 982	5.6	62 668	30.8	23.1
Latah	14 941	56.7	189 100	22.4	10.0	661	34.0	3.2	19 091	-1.7	788	4.1	18 372	39.9	18.2
Lemhi	3 832	71.3	186 900	24.0	10.0	524	37.3	2.4	3 358	-2.3	258	7.7	3 313	31.8	28.6
Lewis	1 660	74.1	116 600	21.6	11.1	556	29.6	6.9	1 606	-0.4	68	4.2	1 509	30.8	25.7
Lincoln	1 617	71.7	120 300	23.0	11.3	724	27.3	8.4	2 606	-1.5	149	5.7	2 217	21.0	40.4
Madison	10 323	49.1	169 600	23.8	10.0	635	41.0	5.0	18 851	2.2	622	3.3	15 627	37.4	18.1
Minidoka	6 994	72.8	108 500	20.7	10.0	542	24.5	1.8	10 385	0.0	476	4.6	9 037	22.0	41.8
Nez Perce	16 019	69.3	165 900	23.1	11.7	645	27.1	1.8	20 412	1.0	829	4.1	18 719	29.3	26.9
Oneida	1 579	81.2	126 100	27.1	13.7	504	30.1	7.1	2 132	1.8	84	3.9	1 792	31.2	32.2
Owyhee	3 911	64.2	121 200	26.7	10.0	530	24.0	3.1	5 086	-0.6	166	3.3	4 286	24.4	44.1
Payette	8 056	74.6	132 700	27.2	12.2	678	30.4	6.4	10 910	0.9	608	5.6	8 887	30.6	28.1
Power	2 568	70.8	125 600	25.1	10.0	622	19.4	3.0	3 991	0.3	193	4.8	3 414	26.3	46.9
Shoshone	5 714	68.4	123 200	22.3	11.7	586	28.1	2.8	5 215	-5.0	524	10.0	4 796	26.4	30.7
Teton	3 583	72.1	222 700	28.5	10.8	852	27.4	4.2	5 589	2.5	220	3.9	5 138	34.5	24.2
Twin Falls	28 166	66.8	148 900	24.5	10.0	710	27.5	3.9	38 168	-1.0	1 655	4.3	34 609	28.1	29.5
Valley	3 519	77.8	221 200	24.6	11.4	676	27.1	4.1	4 506	-0.9	337	7.5	4 418	33.5	26.4
Washington	3 938	76.3	122 700	27.0	10.0	631	37.3	1.6	4 544	-4.6	293	6.4	3 811	28.8	32.4
ILLINOIS	4 772 723	67.5	182 300	24.7	13.6	890	30.8	3.0	6 524 579	-0.5	460 363	7.1	5 998 320	36.4	21.2
Adams	26 912	72.0	104 200	20.7	10.6	576	28.9	4.4	32 629	-0.9	1 757	5.4	32 358	29.3	26.3
Alexander	2 860	65.8	54 400	22.5	14.0	338	25.7	1.4	2 617	-2.6	276	10.5	2 459	20.2	26.2
Bond	6 373	74.7	103 300	21.9	12.3	659	25.5	2.5	7 962	-0.6	518	6.5	7 528	29.8	26.9
Boone	17 938	82.5	158 800	25.1	13.0	721	29.9	2.5	26 253	-0.6	2 076	7.9	23 891	28.6	32.6
Brown	2 105	78.2	83 600	20.0	11.7	545	24.1	1.4	2 747	5.2	116	4.2	2 703	29.8	32.7
Bureau	13 998	75.7	101 200	20.8	12.6	636	26.4	1.7	17 539	-1.0	1 291	7.4	16 100	24.9	32.2
Calhoun	2 061	81.5	112 300	24.8	12.2	593	23.2	1.5	2 411	0.0	200	8.3	2 212	29.0	31.7
Carroll	6 671	76.5	100 100	21.6	12.1	541	28.5	2.1	7 888	0.1	513	6.5	7 049	28.4	33.8
Cass	5 134	72.2	76 100	20.1	11.1	613	24.1	1.3	6 398	-0.6	443	6.9	5 972	23.4	38.9
Champaign	79 137	54.9	149 500	20.9	11.5	804	36.1	2.1	103 145	0.1	6 243	6.1	100 244	43.8	14.9
Christian	14 138	74.7	82 400	19.4	11.9	600	27.5	1.3	15 830	-1.3	1 206	7.6	15 535	26.4	29.4
Clark	6 568	75.6	87 800	19.8	13.2	622	24.7	1.9	7 962	0.3	578	7.3	7 447	31.0	30.8
Clay	5 486	79.6	75 300	20.2	11.7	524	21.9	1.8	6 441	1.9	522	8.1	6 041	23.7	37.9
Clinton	14 051	82.4	127 300	19.8	12.3	692	22.9	1.2	19 958	0.2	1 105	5.5	18 885	30.8	27.7
Coles	21 046	62.0	90 200	21.4	12.3	607	34.8	4.3	24 362	-0.1	1 658	6.8	24 643	29.1	24.4
Cook	1 933 335	58.3	231 200	27.9	15.4	963	31.8	2.0	2 666 625	-0.4	196 439	7.4	2 414 798	37.8	19.2
Crawford	7 731	79.9	76 600	18.2	10.0	563	26.8	2.8	9 857	-1.2	654	6.6	8 508	27.2	33.9
Cumberland	4 184	80.8	83 800	19.6	10.8	515	22.0	3.0	5 883	0.9	358	6.1	4 998	29.4	33.0
DeKalb	37 844	60.2	173 000	25.8	14.9	830	34.9	0.7	54 706	0.1	3 592	6.6	51 992	32.9	21.8
De Witt	6 802	77.0	107 100	19.3	11.8	600	25.7	3.0	7 977	-2.1	523	6.6	7 846	25.9	29.7
Douglas	7 509	78.3	99 300	20.8	11.0	686	25.3	2.4	9 853	0.8	583	5.9	9 425	26.8	33.0
DuPage	336 028	74.4	286 500	25.7	14.2	1 104	29.2	0.9	512 869	0.2	28 970	5.6	470 864	44.3	15.6
Edgar	7 893	73.4	72 900	18.8	12.8	586	32.0	1.1	9 160	1.6	658	7.2	7 993	27.2	32.5
Edwards	2 728	79.9	65 800	21.1	10.8	477	26.0	0.9	2 863	-0.1	195	6.8	2 887	22.4	41.6
Effingham	13 544	78.3	115 200	21.0	10.6	553	22.8	1.7	18 367	1.7	1 022	5.6	17 528	27.9	29.8
Fayette	0 124	80.5	82 000	20.3	10.6	540	27.2	1.4	9 745	-3.9	746	7.7	9 424	27.0	30.6
Ford	5 651	76.6	89 600	19.7	12.9	598	24.6	1.9	6 566	0.1	401	6.1	6 434	30.0	29.5
Franklin	16 110	75.6	64 300	20.7	12.0	572	29.5	1.8	16 504	-2.1	1 544	9.4	15 631	25.6	30.6
Fulton	14 610	75.5	80 600	19.8	12.4	608	28.8	2.6	15 762	-2.6	1 361	8.6	15 156	30.4	29.0
Gallatin	2 369	78.3	61 100	19.5	11.3	432	23.9	2.6	2 410	-1.7	180	7.5	2 209	30.0	30.7
Greene	5 790	75.8	75 200	19.9	11.7	586	24.5	2.7	6 223	-1.5	431	6.9	6 250	27.7	34.1
Grundy	18 082	76.2	182 200	24.8	12.6	956	30.3	2.3	25 608	-1.2	2 180	8.5	22 931	28.6	28.6
Hamilton	3 512	76.7	72 800	19.1	12.5	558	29.4	1.5	4 342	6.5	257	5.9	3 515	26.1	32.1
Hancock	8 101	78.3	81 600	19.7	11.6	539	22.3	1.9	8 831	-0.8	592	6.7	8 835	26.6	30.9

1. Specified owner-occupied units. 2. A value of 10.0 represents 10 percent or less; a value of 50.0 represents 50 percent or more. 3. Specified renter-occupied units.
4. Overcrowded or lacking complete plumbing facilities. 5. Percent of civilian labor force. 6. Persons 16 years old and over.

Table B. States and Counties — **Nonfarm Employment and Agriculture**

STATE County	Private nonfarm establishments, employment and payroll, 2013: Number of establishments	Employment: Total	Employment: Health care and social assistance	Employment: Manufacturing	Employment: Retail trade	Employment: Finance and insurance	Employment: Professional, scientific, and technical services	Annual payroll: Total (mil dol)	Annual payroll: Average per employee (dollars)	Agriculture, 2012: Farms: Number	Farms: Percent with: Fewer than 50 acres	Farms: Percent with: 500 acres or more	Farm operators whose principal occupation is farming (percent)
	104	105	106	107	108	109	110	111	112	113	114	115	116
IDAHO—Cont'd													
Caribou	193	2 639	237	736	279	49	D	153	57 887	436	19.3	40.4	55.3
Cassia	644	7 301	1 212	1 282	1 373	227	186	224	30 659	668	42.7	27.1	56.1
Clark	18	75	D	D	33	D	D	2	26 653	72	12.5	41.7	61.1
Clearwater	229	1 867	503	269	D	43	41	62	33 294	256	35.5	11.7	34.8
Custer	167	681	43	24	166	40	D	20	28 950	272	36.4	23.9	52.9
Elmore	431	3 936	735	D	999	185	D	104	26 302	349	53.9	21.2	47.6
Franklin	281	1 928	D	266	523	74	48	53	27 387	834	40.0	19.2	43.5
Fremont	272	1 377	D	D	237	44	D	40	29 070	601	33.8	22.1	52.2
Gem	337	2 154	721	81	376	63	67	57	26 306	830	68.1	7.3	48.3
Gooding	348	2 498	517	433	363	81	66	82	32 671	596	53.4	14.1	52.0
Idaho	478	3 292	684	596	449	144	147	113	34 254	731	24.5	33.0	51.8
Jefferson	430	3 769	309	D	461	75	D	108	28 738	776	53.5	16.8	43.9
Jerome	524	5 770	D	1 358	848	116	113	192	33 302	560	46.3	15.4	63.2
Kootenai	4 345	44 971	8 639	4 268	8 164	2 035	2 881	1 564	34 779	824	58.4	6.7	48.1
Latah	885	8 299	1 363	298	1 860	227	469	221	26 649	1 053	30.6	15.9	43.3
Lemhi	289	1 651	484	D	367	39	54	43	26 166	350	46.6	20.0	48.6
Lewis	121	763	D	D	159	25	D	21	27 701	216	13.9	44.9	54.6
Lincoln	87	635	79	D	88	D	D	21	32 710	310	27.1	23.5	57.7
Madison	757	14 065	1 386	1 026	1 726	D	362	318	22 636	472	48.3	19.7	46.2
Minidoka	403	4 355	484	925	468	76	104	156	35 788	622	51.1	14.0	56.6
Nez Perce	1 110	16 434	3 028	3 346	2 305	1 232	459	600	36 491	430	41.4	30.0	52.1
Oneida	88	692	D	D	161	D	2	18	26 632	503	28.2	27.8	45.5
Owyhee	181	1 612	192	156	158	D	31	43	26 895	578	41.0	26.6	67.6
Payette	483	4 326	588	1 110	427	180	132	134	30 970	655	65.8	6.6	52.1
Power	150	2 027	170	D	D	D	D	70	34 350	308	24.4	50.3	63.3
Shoshone	355	4 166	494	D	D	D	189	176	42 302	36	61.1	0.0	33.3
Teton	418	1 882	D	D	284	52	93	69	36 530	291	30.2	21.3	42.3
Twin Falls	2 455	27 449	5 576	3 295	4 863	961	1 473	851	30 997	1 294	42.9	13.4	55.3
Valley	567	2 927	433	D	462	72	79	86	29 348	117	35.9	22.2	47.0
Washington	218	1 664	220	452	276	49	62	48	28 556	559	42.4	20.9	54.4
ILLINOIS	315 364	5 209 070	786 018	547 259	592 779	301 696	392 549	262 263	50 347	75 087	34.1	20.4	50.4
Adams	1 833	31 182	5 449	5 616	4 848	1 790	777	1 225	39 301	1 298	28.2	18.3	44.5
Alexander	107	1 037	157	D	126	22	D	38	36 227	144	25.0	19.4	56.9
Bond	303	3 825	600	832	380	130	81	120	31 316	661	39.2	16.5	46.1
Boone	847	15 398	1 001	8 671	1 334	232	729	644	41 796	479	49.9	15.7	53.0
Brown	116	2 988	D	D	150	D	D	123	41 299	413	23.2	16.7	41.2
Bureau	768	9 484	2 177	1 503	1 071	379	331	358	37 704	1 056	26.1	26.1	55.8
Calhoun	93	605	92	D	118	69	D	12	20 582	478	30.5	10.0	39.3
Carroll	399	3 198	461	718	455	182	63	104	32 631	643	26.7	22.4	56.9
Cass	254	4 471	382	D	472	D	D	155	34 582	446	29.6	24.2	48.2
Champaign	4 133	67 335	D	6 979	10 337	2 941	2 861	2 481	36 849	1 312	29.3	30.6	57.7
Christian	718	8 699	1 722	1 002	1 362	360	528	283	32 518	816	34.1	27.2	51.6
Clark	334	3 763	356	D	450	160	D	120	31 865	677	34.0	21.4	47.6
Clay	364	4 555	645	1 935	436	156	109	154	33 731	774	35.4	18.7	49.6
Clinton	880	8 679	1 715	696	1 521	299	194	256	29 545	915	29.0	16.3	47.9
Coles	1 186	17 476	4 180	2 619	2 635	560	392	598	34 205	704	37.2	23.2	56.7
Cook	129 972	2 286 711	370 907	178 683	224 197	152 449	214 618	128 494	56 192	127	81.1	3.9	44.1
Crawford	427	6 607	859	1 841	760	228	D	267	40 409	599	32.4	18.9	51.3
Cumberland	178	1 657	230	D	178	D	D	46	27 910	733	40.5	13.5	38.5
DeKalb	1 959	26 056	4 949	3 797	4 389	801	655	912	35 013	880	32.7	26.9	61.1
De Witt	397	4 445	550	493	679	D	100	218	49 016	511	42.3	24.7	55.4
Douglas	586	6 396	314	2 220	1 275	198	79	231	36 094	735	40.7	21.1	54.8
DuPage	33 329	583 086	65 203	52 726	59 269	32 764	44 673	32 135	55 111	74	82.4	2.7	35.1
Edgar	347	5 966	855	1 935	618	273	94	212	35 548	673	27.3	31.1	54.4
Edwards	145	1 983	129	D	203	68	D	72	36 150	365	41.4	16.4	39.7
Effingham	1 185	21 580	2 803	3 012	2 881	463	330	743	34 434	1 302	37.6	12.5	47.2
Fayette	479	4 800	941	404	853	232	135	135	28 039	1 240	39.2	12.6	42.7
Ford	374	3 971	1 107	674	538	D	101	137	34 486	546	26.4	35.7	53.5
Franklin	763	6 837	1 272	576	1 479	272	204	204	29 795	711	42.9	10.4	38.8
Fulton	662	6 412	1 952	209	1 363	327	197	181	28 288	970	29.7	20.2	53.1
Gallatin	102	911	D	D	D	17	23	42	45 951	203	24.1	36.0	56.2
Greene	254	1 740	354	150	395	100	74	51	29 265	689	30.2	22.9	52.8
Grundy	1 075	14 102	1 953	1 344	1 750	421	503	767	54 406	431	23.2	29.5	63.8
Hamilton	194	1 370	459	84	178	45	D	50	36 780	695	37.6	12.5	25.6
Hancock	378	2 737	519	D	440	190	150	92	33 442	1 090	28.4	21.5	50.0

STATE County	Agriculture, 2012 (cont.) Land in farms: Acreage (1,000)	Land in farms: Percent change, 2007–2012	Land in farms, Acres: Average size of farm	Acres: Total irrigated (1,000)	Acres: Total cropland (1,000)	Value of land and buildings (dollars): Average per farm	Value of land and buildings (dollars): Average per acre	Value of machinery and equipment, average per farm (dollars)	Value of products sold: Total (mil dol)	Value of products sold: Average per farm (dollars)	Value of products sold, Percent from: Crops	Percent from: Livestock and poultry products	Percent of farms with sales of: $10,000 or more	Percent of farms with sales of: $100,000 or more	Government payments: Total ($1,000)	Government payments: Percent of farms
	117	118	119	120	121	122	123	124	125	126	127	128	129	130	131	132
IDAHO—Cont'd																
Caribou	395	-6.4	905	66.0	215.4	1 267 638	1 401	196 009	88.0	201 934	76.8	23.2	51.6	27.3	4 068	62.8
Cassia	611	-5.2	915	237.8	333.8	2 143 115	2 343	350 045	953.7	1 427 737	27.0	73.0	58.5	37.3	5 934	43.9
Clark	151	-4.2	2 101	29.2	52.5	3 059 583	1 456	304 333	35.2	488 792	75.1	24.9	66.7	38.9	572	56.9
Clearwater	73	4.4	284	0.2	28.9	534 063	1 883	59 699	9.7	38 078	74.6	25.4	25.8	6.3	797	43.0
Custer	143	15.0	525	51.6	44.4	1 208 224	2 302	107 033	26.2	96 471	33.6	66.4	50.4	22.8	588	23.2
Elmore	345	-0.5	988	89.9	117.9	2 021 562	2 046	204 605	350.6	1 004 536	26.9	73.1	41.0	21.5	838	20.9
Franklin	263	16.8	315	61.2	140.8	632 061	2 007	117 307	106.1	127 228	23.1	76.9	45.1	18.5	3 420	48.7
Fremont	316	9.8	526	124.8	207.8	1 175 121	2 233	216 087	158.6	263 942	89.5	10.5	47.4	24.0	3 473	52.1
Gem	179	-6.2	216	34.2	31.7	595 434	2 761	57 441	42.4	51 031	39.1	60.9	34.5	9.3	517	19.9
Gooding	240	7.4	402	142.0	150.7	1 539 908	3 830	272 973	942.8	1 581 904	10.7	89.3	59.9	33.7	1 873	29.0
Idaho	639	8.2	874	5.0	209.8	1 219 897	1 395	99 766	80.8	110 564	77.4	22.6	47.2	23.1	5 658	50.5
Jefferson	323	-0.8	416	175.3	191.1	1 089 749	2 620	162 642	257.2	331 387	57.8	42.2	51.3	25.4	2 332	41.0
Jerome	188	-0.4	336	149.0	148.9	1 289 525	3 840	304 766	617.1	1 101 943	23.5	76.5	65.9	36.4	1 880	47.3
Kootenai	124	-5.1	151	13.8	64.3	624 138	4 139	57 726	23.7	28 750	83.8	16.2	19.5	4.1	1 075	20.1
Latah	416	20.9	396	0.5	254.2	713 039	1 803	102 611	87.9	83 435	94.5	5.5	26.7	12.6	8 001	69.0
Lemhi	187	-1.2	535	56.7	49.7	1 189 800	2 222	89 217	32.2	91 863	15.1	84.9	44.6	20.0	533	12.6
Lewis	221	-10.0	1 024	D	158.7	1 437 389	1 403	201 764	62.5	289 292	95.4	4.6	57.4	40.7	3 763	80.6
Lincoln	130	10.5	418	71.4	72.6	1 098 352	2 625	208 332	175.6	566 510	21.8	78.2	64.2	33.2	1 703	44.2
Madison	201	-4.4	427	122.3	167.4	1 413 886	3 314	232 362	131.1	277 674	94.2	5.8	54.0	26.9	2 678	49.4
Minidoka	244	7.9	392	204.5	217.4	1 360 826	3 468	253 349	368.9	593 125	72.6	27.4	57.2	33.9	2 782	52.6
Nez Perce	322	-8.8	749	0.8	181.4	1 261 165	1 683	150 307	81.2	188 777	89.0	11.0	46.0	26.3	5 030	56.0
Oneida	329	4.7	653	34.1	175.7	775 891	1 187	106 209	32.5	64 545	58.1	41.9	42.5	12.1	3 972	66.4
Owyhee	749	31.5	1 295	133.5	140.7	1 590 689	1 228	183 332	291.6	504 424	32.2	67.8	66.8	36.7	2 041	40.1
Payette	157	-5.5	240	56.9	51.6	724 612	3 021	117 252	236.2	360 676	21.3	78.7	43.4	16.9	652	22.1
Power	467	3.5	1 517	120.9	361.7	2 293 497	1 512	378 549	238.3	773 747	85.4	14.6	48.7	31.5	6 836	67.9
Shoshone	D	D	D	D	0.8	387 167	D	43 778	0.1	3 944	32.4	66.9	11.1	0.0	D	2.8
Teton	133	8.8	458	56.4	87.6	1 506 742	3 292	137 058	35.8	123 086	83.9	16.1	44.0	18.6	1 206	44.0
Twin Falls	484	10.1	374	257.0	275.1	1 155 801	3 090	159 620	599.6	463 355	36.0	64.0	63.3	36.9	3 657	48.1
Valley	61	-1.3	524	26.2	8.8	1 294 667	2 473	72 564	6.6	56 675	18.2	81.8	36.8	11.1	62	12.8
Washington	426	2.3	763	42.7	79.5	762 163	999	96 005	75.3	134 664	49.1	50.9	48.3	20.4	1 036	39.9
ILLINOIS	26 938	0.6	359	522.5	23 752.8	2 261 778	6 305	203 184	17 187.1	228 895	82.3	17.7	54.5	33.0	553 300	75.0
Adams	389	3.9	299	2.3	294.2	1 479 562	4 940	147 340	174.0	134 044	74.9	25.1	55.5	27.4	7 898	73.2
Alexander	62	31.1	434	5.0	51.8	1 433 333	3 306	145 569	25.7	178 771	97.9	2.1	39.6	20.8	778	66.0
Bond	198	-11.8	300	0.0	176.7	1 941 345	6 470	174 467	66.0	99 800	82.0	18.0	46.3	24.5	3 940	74.7
Boone	135	-1.8	281	0.9	126.9	1 926 883	6 849	204 127	99.0	206 676	89.1	10.9	56.8	35.5	3 391	51.4
Brown	138	-9.0	333	0.4	85.5	1 327 644	3 987	105 603	42.0	101 717	79.4	20.6	40.2	20.1	3 102	87.9
Bureau	450	-5.9	426	10.6	410.8	3 125 461	7 332	246 925	420.2	397 908	89.9	10.1	68.7	49.0	8 943	80.8
Calhoun	88	-0.2	184	0.0	48.5	697 808	3 801	80 816	23.7	49 513	83.1	16.9	35.8	11.1	2 053	76.4
Carroll	256	-3.4	398	11.3	218.8	2 723 677	6 838	250 918	270.7	421 009	69.6	30.4	57.5	43.7	6 884	81.3
Cass	183	5.3	410	21.3	151.1	2 290 363	5 592	209 209	123.7	277 296	77.8	22.2	53.1	29.8	3 866	80.5
Champaign	616	12.0	470	17.9	591.1	3 740 816	7 961	294 914	424.2	323 295	94.5	5.5	73.5	50.7	11 068	84.7
Christian	374	-16.9	458	D	352.7	3 469 135	7 576	240 299	288.7	353 750	90.6	9.4	60.2	44.2	5 962	79.0
Clark	267	11.8	394	6.6	230.3	1 935 795	4 912	234 895	130.8	193 163	69.9	30.1	47.1	25.1	6 033	79.8
Clay	270	28.8	349	0.1	235.2	1 663 978	4 764	148 499	66.7	86 142	81.2	18.8	38.6	19.3	6 246	85.5
Clinton	285	6.4	312	1.9	259.6	1 824 631	5 848	228 694	206.0	225 184	42.9	57.1	62.4	33.1	5 669	81.5
Coles	267	4.7	379	0.0	245.9	2 671 436	7 050	235 723	136.0	193 229	96.3	3.7	54.5	34.8	4 927	77.6
Cook	8	3.7	67	0.4	7.5	700 701	10 471	76 598	10.7	84 150	79.4	20.6	51.2	18.1	104	15.0
Crawford	215	4.7	359	8.3	186.7	1 793 496	4 997	228 519	65.9	110 018	86.3	13.7	43.4	22.7	6 248	85.1
Cumberland	170	17.4	232	0.1	143.5	1 262 847	5 440	150 681	89.1	121 583	68.5	31.5	41.9	21.4	4 423	84.2
DeKalb	398	7.3	452	3.3	383.5	3 549 751	7 853	289 255	474.9	539 677	70.8	29.2	70.2	55.3	11 835	76.1
De Witt	196	-1.6	383	0.1	182.6	2 749 990	7 188	228 883	154.9	303 139	89.0	11.0	53.8	36.6	3 265	73.6
Douglas	263	0.5	358	0.3	247.8	2 721 101	7 609	214 850	166.7	226 789	85.4	14.6	61.6	40.5	4 948	63.8
DuPage	7	-8.8	98	0.1	5.9	680 851	6 947	82 162	10.0	135 514	95.3	4.7	37.8	14.9	80	14.9
Edgar	352	-0.2	523	D	326.3	3 432 028	6 568	287 382	205.1	304 807	D	D	62.3	42.9	6 450	83.2
Edwards	107	-8.5	292	D	88.1	1 176 600	4 024	173 096	33.7	92 282	85.7	14.3	39.7	18.4	2 276	80.8
Effingham	287	18.6	220	1.7	241.9	1 277 618	5 796	157 144	165.8	127 337	50.5	49.5	49.9	27.3	6 722	80.2
Fayette	303	0.0	244	0.3	248.2	1 089 291	4 456	131 927	97.4	78 521	80.1	10.9	40.0	18.8	5 615	73.7
Ford	308	13.8	564	0.8	298.0	4 278 846	7 581	312 397	191.7	351 125	82.5	17.5	74.4	50.0	5 740	85.3
Franklin	181	-12.8	255	0.1	152.7	946 098	3 709	113 533	55.8	78 457	73.0	27.0	27.3	12.8	3 330	66.5
Fulton	355	-7.9	366	2.1	266.4	1 921 065	5 249	166 037	212.1	218 637	71.7	28.3	53.8	28.9	6 943	67.1
Gallatin	186	0.3	917	25.9	170.3	4 030 990	4 394	455 074	90.1	443 606	98.8	1.2	69.5	40.9	2 545	83.3
Greene	290	6.2	421	8.8	233.4	2 373 734	5 637	220 164	186.2	270 305	77.0	23.0	55.7	32.4	6 005	74.0
Grundy	217	0.7	504	0.0	206.0	3 835 093	7 617	315 223	128.9	298 993	96.7	3.3	74.9	54.1	3 667	80.0
Hamilton	223	1.6	321	0.0	195.3	1 163 304	3 620	146 839	55.7	80 098	98.0	2.0	26.9	14.5	4 621	84.7
Hancock	386	-1.7	354	2.6	315.7	2 029 171	5 726	194 508	317.2	290 977	66.7	33.3	57.7	35.0	8 365	78.3

STATE County	Water use, 2010: Total water withdrawn (mil gal/day)	Water use, 2010: Gallons withdrawn per person per day	Wholesale trade,[1] 2007: Number of establish-ments	Wholesale trade,[1] 2007: Number of employees	Wholesale trade,[1] 2007: Sales (mil dol)	Wholesale trade,[1] 2007: Annual payroll (mil dol)	Retail trade,[2] 2007: Number of establish-ments	Retail trade,[2] 2007: Number of employees	Retail trade,[2] 2007: Sales (mil dol)	Retail trade,[2] 2007: Annual payroll (mil dol)	Real estate and rental and leasing,[2] 2007: Number of establish-ments	Real estate and rental and leasing,[2] 2007: Number of employees	Real estate and rental and leasing,[2] 2007: Receipts (mil dol)	Real estate and rental and leasing,[2] 2007: Annual payroll (mil dol)
	133	134	135	136	137	138	139	140	141	142	143	144	145	146
IDAHO—Cont'd														
Caribou	307.9	44 221	14	63	94.6	2.3	34	340	68.4	6.0	5	6	0.6	0.1
Cassia	812.7	35 410	30	267	335.9	8.5	128	1 436	318.9	30.2	26	D	D	D
Clark	96.9	98 625	1	D	D	D	3	D	D	D	NA	NA	NA	NA
Clearwater	68.9	7 859	5	32	13.7	1.1	42	265	69.8	5.8	5	D	D	D
Custer	678.7	155 389	NA	NA	NA	NA	30	150	35.1	2.7	7	20	0.6	0.1
Elmore	362.8	13 418	14	101	53.4	4.0	75	970	241.2	20.1	16	50	5.6	1.0
Franklin	224.1	17 523	19	146	49.5	4.5	42	508	113.5	9.3	11	D	D	D
Fremont	358.7	27 087	14	184	76.7	4.9	41	250	68.2	4.9	6	11	2.5	0.3
Gem	468.3	28 011	11	75	13.6	2.7	47	392	113.9	8.8	20	37	3.8	0.5
Gooding	1 284.6	83 072	19	174	118.9	5.0	44	419	88.2	6.5	9	D	D	D
Idaho	24.4	1 500	17	115	64.8	3.7	68	519	97.6	11.2	14	28	2.8	0.5
Jefferson	1 405.3	53 760	23	D	D	D	56	474	92.4	8.0	13	47	5.0	0.8
Jerome	1 437.6	64 252	36	226	103.7	8.4	73	982	300.4	21.5	26	51	8.2	0.9
Kootenai	56.5	408	142	1 550	843.3	64.0	609	7 398	2 175.2	187.5	249	876	155.3	27.4
Latah	10.5	282	24	D	D	D	156	1 960	361.7	37.1	49	120	17.6	2.9
Lemhi	268.8	33 875	5	D	D	D	53	444	123.0	8.9	19	33	2.7	0.6
Lewis	1.5	390	9	D	D	D	20	138	29.7	2.3	5	15	1.3	0.2
Lincoln	281.4	54 038	NA	NA	NA	NA	13	77	16.9	1.1	4	D	D	D
Madison	481.2	12 820	38	475	162.0	11.6	124	1 718	407.7	37.6	59	174	23.4	3.1
Minidoka	629.2	31 352	40	745	347.0	24.9	66	543	162.9	10.4	10	D	D	D
Nez Perce	128.3	3 268	45	D	D	D	216	2 822	703.0	70.0	40	160	23.0	4.7
Oneida	177.0	41 295	1	D	D	D	15	145	24.1	2.0	4	D	D	D
Owyhee	811.3	70 386	10	71	34.6	2.8	25	219	50.9	4.4	10	23	0.7	0.1
Payette	242.0	10 697	26	187	133.1	6.3	70	596	145.6	14.2	29	46	6.4	0.8
Power	452.0	57 827	11	D	D	D	23	213	50.4	3.9	7	27	1.8	0.3
Shoshone	3.0	231	9	71	25.0	2.8	80	1 019	623.1	32.1	11	44	3.1	0.7
Teton	180.3	17 731	12	D	D	D	46	329	84.1	6.9	46	56	22.5	2.4
Twin Falls	1 462.0	18 930	123	1 301	497.6	44.6	423	5 363	1 259.1	117.5	113	359	49.1	8.4
Valley	71.3	7 228	11	62	20.5	2.4	83	643	135.6	13.5	60	111	16.5	2.6
Washington	203.2	19 924	12	439	63.4	7.2	38	335	76.3	6.1	13	43	3.3	0.5
ILLINOIS	13 091.3	1 020	16 704	259 758	231 082.8	14 319.6	43 055	639 147	165 450.5	14 895.5	13 899	87 468	21 725.0	3 985.2
Adams	19.4	289	114	D	D	D	330	4 813	928.3	89.9	65	294	34.9	7.0
Alexander	2.2	271	7	D	D	D	24	165	22.9	2.5	2	D	D	D
Bond	2.0	113	18	414	217.6	17.0	60	490	104.5	8.7	13	D	D	D
Boone	6.0	110	35	223	146.2	11.0	103	1 555	454.9	36.6	25	68	7.9	1.3
Brown	0.5	75	7	D	D	D	25	166	30.0	2.7	2	D	D	D
Bureau	6.0	173	42	823	977.6	30.0	120	1 269	332.0	27.2	17	D	D	D
Calhoun	0.5	104	2	D	D	D	15	104	22.3	2.1	2	D	D	D
Carroll	6.5	422	23	250	301.8	10.5	59	428	88.7	7.6	10	34	2.8	0.4
Cass	5.6	411	17	355	331.3	13.2	50	478	115.4	9.1	6	D	D	D
Champaign	32.3	161	170	3 166	2 576.0	118.7	667	10 960	2 347.1	213.1	233	1 655	349.4	51.0
Christian	838.9	24 107	46	D	D	D	122	1 385	369.9	30.7	20	83	10.4	1.8
Clark	5.6	345	17	154	176.1	4.8	60	390	109.6	8.2	5	18	2.4	0.5
Clay	1.3	94	28	315	168.8	9.7	55	531	114.8	10.2	11	30	3.6	0.7
Clinton	11.9	315	48	544	282.0	19.7	151	1 538	383.2	35.5	22	161	16.5	4.0
Coles	5.0	94	59	496	382.9	19.9	193	2 894	635.1	60.6	47	162	21.8	4.1
Cook	1 672.7	322	6 657	98 030	83 964.6	5 379.0	16 288	241 745	60 585.6	5 793.8	6 626	47 857	13 137.3	2 511.3
Crawford	69.2	3 493	15	157	90.9	4.3	63	709	164.2	14.0	17	39	4.2	0.5
Cumberland	1.4	125	18	D	D	D	27	160	22.9	2.1	NA	NA	NA	NA
DeKalb	10.4	99	72	579	249.7	21.7	320	4 713	1 090.2	94.6	66	524	57.2	11.2
De Witt	767.1	46 317	25	262	248.9	12.4	64	740	188.2	14.5	9	45	6.4	0.6
Douglas	3.0	150	30	318	290.1	13.1	136	1 081	218.4	18.9	11	38	5.2	1.0
DuPage	16.6	18	2 423	46 343	49 574.9	2 924.4	3 512	65 944	18 043.4	1 646.3	1 485	11 690	3 917.2	614.7
Edgar	4.3	232	23	197	126.7	8.0	66	743	197.1	16.3	9	39	3.4	1.1
Edwards	0.7	103	17	213	147.1	7.5	27	191	40.6	3.3	3	D	D	D
Effingham	4.5	130	60	D	D	D	205	3 141	857.8	68.7	44	222	36.8	6.7
Fayette	3.9	176	25	396	322.6	13.3	88	970	227.3	19.1	12	34	3.4	0.7
Ford	3.9	280	30	312	323.1	10.8	62	599	112.3	9.1	6	12	1.1	0.2
Franklin	15.3	388	31	191	72.7	6.6	152	1 545	362.2	33.5	21	75	8.2	1.3
Fulton	283.6	7 650	23	D	D	D	128	1 343	288.9	25.5	18	D	D	D
Gallatin	28.2	5 000	8	44	23.2	1.2	18	108	21.9	2.2	NA	NA	NA	NA
Greene	1.9	136	22	148	151.3	5.1	56	389	95.9	7.6	3	11	0.3	0.1
Grundy	501.9	10 026	46	393	438.5	16.4	161	1 928	522.6	42.5	41	149	23.5	3.4
Hamilton	0.7	84	10	D	D	D	33	158	41.9	2.9	6	41	0.5	0.2
Hancock	2.9	152	28	160	200.5	5.2	82	569	106.5	9.8	3	8	3.4	0.1

1. Merchant wholesalers, except manufacturers' sales branches and offices. 2. Employer establishments.

STATE County	Professional, scientific, and technical services,[1] 2007				Manufacturing, 2007				Accommodation and food services, 2007			
	Number of establish-ments	Number of employees	Receipts (mil dol)	Annual payroll (mil dol)	Number of establish-ments	Number of employees	Receipts (mil dol)	Annual payroll (mil dol)	Number of establish-ments	Number of employees	Sales (mil dol)	Annual payroll (mil dol)
	147	148	149	150	151	152	153	154	155	156	157	158
IDAHO—Cont'd												
Caribou	9	D	D	D	11	D	443.2	D	11	D	D	D
Cassia	45	173	14.6	4.3	28	1 032	371.3	41.2	47	656	33.5	6.5
Clark	2	D	D	D	NA	NA	NA	NA	1	D	D	D
Clearwater	12	D	D	D	NA	NA	NA	NA	34	D	D	D
Custer	8	D	D	D	NA	NA	NA	NA	33	205	11.3	2.7
Elmore	27	D	D	D	NA	NA	NA	NA	55	702	27.0	7.9
Franklin	12	D	D	D	NA	NA	NA	NA	20	194	5.8	1.7
Fremont	12	27	6.0	0.6	NA	NA	NA	NA	33	170	10.1	2.7
Gem	20	61	4.5	1.3	NA	NA	NA	NA	28	342	9.2	2.6
Gooding	20	80	8.5	2.8	25	510	D	20.4	30	D	D	D
Idaho	22	88	16.0	3.6	NA	NA	NA	NA	66	353	14.7	3.5
Jefferson	44	D	D	D	33	1 069	D	26.3	24	238	7.4	1.8
Jerome	30	D	D	D	24	1 246	764.2	36.6	33	329	14.0	3.5
Kootenai	438	D	D	D	246	4 401	992.2	163.3	363	6 773	303.7	96.0
Latah	84	D	D	D	NA	NA	NA	NA	104	1 756	55.2	15.9
Lemhi	24	68	4.0	1.4	NA	NA	NA	NA	34	232	7.7	2.4
Lewis	1	D	D	D	NA	NA	NA	NA	13	D	D	D
Lincoln	4	D	D	D	NA	NA	NA	NA	10	68	2.4	0.7
Madison	64	910	38.1	11.4	35	D	D	D	50	1 090	32.0	9.0
Minidoka	23	98	7.0	2.8	27	864	381.1	32.2	28	336	18.9	3.4
Nez Perce	78	D	D	D	37	2 874	D	D	95	1 687	64.5	20.2
Oneida	1	D	D	D	NA	NA	NA	NA	9	85	2.1	0.5
Owyhee	10	35	2.9	1.1	NA	NA	NA	NA	21	144	4.2	1.2
Payette	28	D	D	D	31	1 228	D	39.9	33	329	12.8	2.4
Power	6	D	D	D	8	D	D	D	17	70	2.6	0.6
Shoshone	27	254	24.2	8.1	NA	NA	NA	NA	50	310	11.1	3.4
Teton	32	D	D	D	NA	NA	NA	NA	29	201	10.7	2.9
Twin Falls	221	D	D	D	101	3 175	970.3	104.3	177	2 825	112.0	29.5
Valley	47	165	31.8	6.2	NA	NA	NA	NA	82	803	43.2	13.0
Washington	17	70	4.2	1.3	NA	NA	NA	NA	25	D	D	D
ILLINOIS	38 797	363 231	61 896.1	24 197.9	15 704	663 586	257 760.7	31 715.9	26 774	468 827	25 469.0	6 894.3
Adams	136	D	D	D	96	D	D	D	142	D	D	D
Alexander	9	D	D	D	NA	NA	NA	NA	19	D	D	D
Bond	23	D	D	D	16	821	D	30.0	31	333	13.1	3.4
Boone	73	D	D	D	71	6 534	5 553.7	387.3	71	883	40.2	10.4
Brown	8	D	D	D	NA	NA	NA	NA	15	D	D	D
Bureau	41	D	D	D	43	2 062	D	D	78	765	27.4	7.5
Calhoun	2	D	D	D	NA	NA	NA	NA	20	138	5.4	1.4
Carroll	19	66	5.4	1.6	28	926	320.8	34.1	40	297	13.0	2.8
Cass	16	59	4.6	1.5	13	D	D	D	33	235	8.1	2.0
Champaign	453	2 913	299.3	127.9	143	8 995	3 248.9	337.2	502	9 836	374.5	104.4
Christian	46	5 377	69.6	32.6	25	1 339	392.4	46.6	76	762	29.3	7.5
Clark	20	132	8.2	3.8	18	1 622	664.4	59.5	38	543	17.0	5.0
Clay	16	57	4.1	1.1	17	1 980	737.1	71.3	30	D	D	D
Clinton	50	244	20.6	8.0	35	1 005	D	30.6	76	808	32.4	8.6
Coles	83	494	43.4	15.2	54	3 537	D	D	127	2 465	75.6	21.7
Cook	18 818	D	D	D	6 018	236 509	77 932.9	11 039.2	10 887	201 766	13 094.4	3 525.6
Crawford	30	124	12.3	4.0	19	2 007	D	120.1	37	423	15.3	3.9
Cumberland	7	30	2.0	0.8	NA	NA	NA	NA	11	140	3.1	0.9
DeKalb	158	D	D	D	140	4 608	1 435.9	191.2	214	3 247	128.2	32.7
De Witt	29	91	7.0	2.3	NA	NA	NA	NA	38	483	13.9	4.1
Douglas	30	108	6.4	2.3	92	2 731	699.9	102.2	54	674	24.5	7.2
DuPage	5 172	D	D	D	1 881	62 578	16 862.5	2 977.7	2 071	41 256	2 226.2	638.5
Edgar	28	105	8.4	2.5	23	2 061	521.8	75.8	28	384	12.0	3.4
Edwards	11	37	2.0	0.7	7	D	D	D	8	83	2.5	0.8
Effingham	57	315	31.9	9.0	63	3 440	890.3	119.2	107	2 265	85.2	24.3
Fayette	26	132	7.8	3.6	21	833	174.6	24.8	46	511	18.3	5.2
Ford	26	93	9.0	2.7	20	D	D	D	36	302	11.4	3.2
Franklin	56	345	23.3	7.6	38	782	223.2	25.7	82	956	34.2	10.1
Fulton	43	D	D	D	NA	NA	NA	NA	84	844	29.4	8.4
Gallatin	7	21	1.6	0.7	NA	NA	NA	NA	10	D	D	D
Greene	16	79	6.7	2.7	NA	NA	NA	NA	24	D	D	D
Grundy	93	D	D	D	49	1 755	2 082.4	D	101	1 406	56.3	14.7
Hamilton	11	25	2.2	0.5	NA	NA	NA	NA	8	95	2.8	0.8
Hancock	25	127	21.2	4.9	24	726	193.2	35.2	34	254	10.9	3.0

1. Establishment subject to federal tax.

STATE County	Health care and social assistance, 2007				Other services, 2007				Nonemployer businesses, 2013		Value of residential construction authorized by building permits, 2014	
	Number of establish- ments	Number of employees	Receipts (mil dol)	Annual payroll (mil dol)	Number of establish- ments	Number of employees	Receipts (mil dol)	Annual payroll (mil dol)	Number	Receipts (mil dol)	New Construction ($1,000)	Number of housing units
	159	160	161	162	163	164	165	166	167	168	169	170
IDAHO—Cont'd												
Caribou	20	224	14.8	5.7	18	39	4.0	0.8	451	17.1	1 976	9
Cassia	83	1 165	74.8	27.8	45	135	11.9	2.5	1 486	77.0	10 152	46
Clark	2	D	D	D	NA	NA	NA	NA	53	1.3	422	3
Clearwater	25	551	34.5	17.8	10	98	4.1	1.9	478	17.2	1 665	19
Custer	9	49	2.1	0.8	3	7	0.3	0.1	440	14.0	0	0
Elmore	52	711	46.7	17.4	40	167	8.6	2.4	1 198	41.1	9 829	57
Franklin	27	D	D	D	20	D	D	D	958	37.7	7 325	35
Fremont	18	209	10.2	4.4	19	62	5.8	1.4	1 081	43.9	9 328	65
Gem	41	574	33.9	13.1	29	D	D	D	1 238	40.6	4 850	37
Gooding	32	482	28.8	12.2	24	D	D	D	848	34.5	2 142	13
Idaho	35	535	38.2	17.6	19	51	3.1	0.6	1 209	42.3	111	1
Jefferson	33	D	D	D	17	24	3.4	0.7	2 037	87.7	15 453	79
Jerome	36	471	26.3	13.8	45	214	19.0	4.9	1 101	50.0	9 489	57
Kootenai	458	7 004	573.4	238.0	240	1 242	82.8	24.6	10 934	468.0	208 068	1 047
Latah	71	1 210	92.7	36.9	59	407	25.4	8.0	2 444	87.2	23 774	136
Lemhi	32	431	24.3	10.4	27	69	5.3	1.2	685	19.5	1 802	11
Lewis	15	59	3.7	1.3	1	D	D	D	310	10.2	1 157	10
Lincoln	7	D	D	D	2	D	D	D	284	8.4	508	4
Madison	84	1 183	99.2	35.9	31	163	9.6	2.5	2 421	96.6	59 439	386
Minidoka	39	588	34.0	13.9	26	186	17.1	4.5	1 151	43.6	6 525	29
Nez Perce	140	2 949	271.7	95.2	89	484	31.7	9.5	2 152	81.4	9 573	55
Oneida	8	174	7.8	3.5	4	D	D	D	319	10.3	2 191	18
Owyhee	13	128	6.2	3.0	8	D	D	D	635	26.6	2 675	16
Payette	39	512	29.6	11.9	21	D	D	D	1 366	57.0	13 208	110
Power	12	D	D	D	13	43	4.0	0.9	372	14.1	1 360	8
Shoshone	32	458	31.1	11.8	23	84	5.9	1.6	768	20.5	1 406	7
Teton	29	D	D	D	20	75	6.2	1.9	1 293	46.0	7 846	28
Twin Falls	311	4 734	373.6	134.8	167	976	70.1	20.6	5 099	228.2	59 807	361
Valley	40	399	32.5	12.4	31	109	8.9	2.7	1 224	54.8	31 936	99
Washington	22	413	24.3	9.6	11	40	5.5	1.0	635	20.4	2 555	17
ILLINOIS	31 062	706 669	70 042.9	28 009.4	23 510	167 675	20 639.2	5 203.0	928 461	38 826.0	4 211 740	20 578
Adams	156	5 096	509.4	185.2	158	D	D	D	3 874	142.2	11 695	83
Alexander	8	D	D	D	6	D	D	D	416	8.5	0	0
Bond	30	D	D	D	26	88	7.0	2.0	1 069	29.7	2 473	12
Boone	65	745	39.7	15.8	66	345	27.5	7.9	3 056	120.3	2 254	11
Brown	7	152	8.7	4.0	10	D	D	D	334	8.8	0	0
Bureau	77	2 024	157.6	64.9	76	304	22.3	6.9	1 982	70.8	4 412	15
Calhoun	6	D	D	D	6	6	1.0	0.2	339	10.8	2 365	12
Carroll	28	550	18.9	8.6	32	164	12.0	3.4	1 051	35.1	4 522	17
Cass	23	366	14.8	7.3	23	100	7.2	1.9	690	20.0	1 350	8
Champaign	363	10 977	1 251.3	490.5	290	2 154	428.6	56.4	11 532	418.6	235 631	1 458
Christian	71	1 664	107.0	42.0	68	319	19.1	4.8	1 960	64.3	4 312	29
Clark	20	393	18.9	9.1	23	71	4.6	1.0	1 089	35.3	425	7
Clay	37	711	44.4	17.5	31	116	9.0	1.8	1 026	36.6	485	4
Clinton	76	D	D	D	62	257	17.0	4.6	2 248	79.0	16 568	85
Coles	156	3 631	290.3	105.3	100	498	35.4	10.7	2 671	91.5	3 158	16
Cook	13 580	325 243	34 227.7	13 682.6	9 784	79 024	11 900.2	2 789.2	447 401	18 954.7	1 524 679	7 753
Crawford	44	894	54.7	21.0	44	183	14.2	3.4	1 196	43.0	1 375	5
Cumberland	18	229	15.1	6.9	14	84	5.1	1.9	742	22.4	0	0
DeKalb	202	4 374	368.3	143.8	148	838	59.9	16.2	5 934	213.8	9 563	45
De Witt	26	473	30.1	12.3	24	128	7.8	2.2	866	27.2	5 413	25
Douglas	33	331	19.6	8.6	30	140	13.4	2.9	1 504	60.0	3 465	25
DuPage	2 894	56 847	6 379.9	2 541.4	2 038	17 829	2 120.8	647.6	77 413	4 102.5	485 653	1 341
Edgar	32	744	53.7	21.5	29	108	7.4	1.8	992	30.1	6 657	45
Edwards	15	145	5.9	2.9	15	54	3.0	0.9	481	15.6	NA	NA
Effingham	120	2 550	231.6	88.4	95	783	48.6	19.2	2 732	124.0	4 973	24
Fayette	47	814	50.9	20.6	37	121	12.0	2.4	1 363	49.9	595	4
Ford	33	D	D	D	25	79	4.8	1.1	974	36.5	3 316	11
Franklin	70	1 329	77.8	32.8	62	227	20.0	6.1	2 278	75.0	493	7
Fulton	67	1 528	129.4	47.1	70	375	15.7	4.9	1 774	52.3	6 177	44
Gallatin	6	D	D	D	10	23	1.9	0.4	293	12.3	NA	NA
Greene	26	481	29.3	13.5	19	D	D	D	791	29.1	2 890	27
Grundy	97	1 780	171.5	67.5	78	400	33.7	9.1	2 796	109.6	20 913	194
Hamilton	17	422	21.2	9.4	19	40	3.2	0.6	556	18.2	0	0
Hancock	39	554	32.8	13.5	32	81	5.9	1.5	1 326	42.0	1 213	5

Table B. States and Counties — **Government Employment and Payroll, and Local Government Finances**

STATE County	Government employment and payroll, 2012: Full-time equivalent employees	Government employment and payroll, 2012: March payroll (dollars)	March payroll (percent of total): Adminis-tration, judicial, and legal	March payroll (percent of total): Police and Corrections	March payroll (percent of total): Fire Protection	March payroll (percent of total): Highways and transpor-tation	March payroll (percent of total): Health and Welfare	March payroll (percent of total): Natural resources and utilities	March payroll (percent of total): Education and libraries	Local government finances, 2012 — General revenue: Total (mil dol)	General revenue: Inter-govern-mental (mil dol)	Taxes: Total (mil dol)	Taxes: Per capita[1] (dollars): Total	Taxes: Per capita[1] (dollars): Property
	171	172	173	174	175	176	177	178	179	180	181	182	183	184
IDAHO—Cont'd														
Caribou	536	1 743 847	5.7	7.1	0.0	5.1	23.6	2.6	54.8	30.0	15.1	9.8	1 451	1 424
Cassia	841	2 609 053	6.9	10.2	1.3	4.4	1.0	7.7	66.0	72.2	36.8	15.3	658	460
Clark	64	182 907	15.4	10.5	0.0	12.5	0.0	3.3	58.1	5.0	3.3	1.2	1 353	1 265
Clearwater	338	951 830	12.2	14.7	0.3	8.5	5.3	6.8	50.6	26.1	13.8	8.4	974	934
Custer	193	546 688	12.5	6.7	0.1	16.9	1.2	5.5	56.7	15.9	9.6	3.8	876	845
Elmore	1 019	3 030 975	6.9	10.0	0.6	5.4	25.3	5.0	45.8	85.0	33.0	18.8	717	631
Franklin	560	1 720 585	5.4	4.8	0.0	3.4	34.4	1.8	50.0	29.4	21.3	5.3	417	394
Fremont	515	1 419 098	11.6	16.1	2.7	6.1	2.9	5.3	54.6	35.8	16.2	14.1	1 086	1 034
Gem	557	1 566 566	7.1	9.6	1.2	2.9	21.3	5.1	50.7	48.1	18.9	14.1	844	831
Gooding	579	1 442 650	8.1	9.0	1.3	5.5	3.6	3.7	66.2	56.3	24.7	15.8	1 036	1 004
Idaho	626	1 781 949	5.1	6.7	0.0	7.5	28.5	2.9	44.8	45.1	21.7	8.0	491	490
Jefferson	872	2 231 238	5.7	8.4	1.8	4.0	1.4	0.9	76.4	54.6	35.5	14.4	541	538
Jerome	672	1 876 675	11.2	10.1	3.4	5.6	0.5	5.4	62.3	54.6	29.4	15.7	697	673
Kootenai	6 580	25 436 541	6.0	8.3	3.6	2.4	37.6	3.3	38.1	678.7	158.8	148.1	1 040	972
Latah	1 001	3 595 367	11.4	10.5	0.8	5.9	0.5	6.2	63.7	82.9	35.0	31.3	819	745
Lemhi	403	1 235 515	7.2	7.5	0.2	3.9	46.4	3.5	30.0	38.3	15.0	4.0	511	478
Lewis	228	620 176	8.8	8.6	0.0	7.6	0.3	4.4	69.1	19.4	10.6	6.1	1 560	1 538
Lincoln	225	639 708	10.8	7.0	0.8	6.1	0.7	4.7	69.2	12.7	7.9	3.6	675	614
Madison	1 018	2 964 631	10.1	13.1	1.9	4.4	1.9	2.7	63.6	142.6	48.3	21.2	565	517
Minidoka	971	2 994 496	5.6	6.8	1.4	1.2	25.7	9.8	49.0	70.9	29.8	11.3	562	530
Nez Perce	1 348	5 048 001	7.1	13.3	6.7	5.6	4.0	8.5	50.0	119.0	49.4	44.7	1 132	1 075
Oneida	180	488 815	12.4	9.4	0.2	6.7	2.2	3.2	65.1	13.7	7.2	3.0	709	690
Owyhee	420	1 130 203	5.4	8.3	0.9	4.7	0.4	2.7	73.7	36.6	20.4	12.9	1 130	780
Payette	742	2 179 486	8.8	11.0	1.4	4.1	2.9	4.4	66.6	54.2	28.9	16.9	747	643
Power	430	1 383 820	5.4	5.9	0.3	7.0	26.0	3.4	51.1	39.7	13.4	10.9	1 398	1 360
Shoshone	609	1 865 396	6.7	7.4	2.8	7.1	21.4	5.7	48.1	52.0	20.0	14.5	1 140	1 102
Teton	450	1 567 917	7.7	3.7	5.3	2.4	33.2	1.8	43.6	55.4	16.6	14.5	1 445	1 299
Twin Falls	3 114	9 543 688	6.8	11.2	2.7	2.8	5.5	3.6	66.3	357.5	212.6	68.8	876	846
Valley	517	1 760 075	11.5	14.1	6.6	9.0	7.9	8.9	39.9	49.2	15.8	24.3	2 542	2 475
Washington	545	1 653 304	6.7	8.4	0.8	4.2	28.1	6.1	43.6	48.8	16.8	12.1	1 202	1 131
ILLINOIS	X	X	X	X	X	X	X	X	X	X	X	X	X	X
Adams	2 703	8 715 868	5.5	10.4	4.2	4.1	5.0	6.1	62.7	223.4	108.4	76.6	1 140	966
Alexander	313	970 447	7.7	9.2	0.0	10.6	2.3	10.0	57.2	30.3	20.7	4.6	595	522
Bond	553	1 740 375	8.4	8.6	0.2	5.4	9.2	6.9	61.0	47.8	21.7	14.3	811	782
Boone	1 665	6 568 081	5.5	11.2	2.8	2.0	1.2	4.1	72.4	168.6	64.4	88.0	1 632	1 512
Brown	202	635 285	9.5	7.4	0.4	13.0	4.1	3.1	62.1	17.3	8.3	5.3	772	738
Bureau	1 639	5 498 491	7.7	6.6	1.2	2.6	22.0	6.1	53.1	152.9	48.9	47.1	1 371	1 315
Calhoun	170	503 707	8.6	7.8	0.2	10.3	6.6	2.8	63.7	12.8	6.7	4.6	917	910
Carroll	571	1 922 747	6.7	10.1	1.2	4.6	1.4	4.6	70.2	50.2	17.9	26.2	1 744	1 700
Cass	549	1 630 366	5.5	5.1	0.7	5.7	1.6	4.6	73.9	47.1	27.4	13.9	1 039	967
Champaign	7 295	27 910 700	5.6	8.8	3.9	7.8	5.7	5.8	60.6	779.8	297.9	355.6	1 749	1 502
Christian	1 070	3 699 842	8.2	9.1	2.1	5.7	2.0	6.3	66.0	97.0	49.7	35.0	1 009	963
Clark	656	1 941 162	6.3	7.0	1.4	5.2	2.5	7.5	65.2	49.9	25.6	16.5	1 017	965
Clay	731	2 318 318	7.1	5.7	0.1	3.7	25.1	6.3	51.0	65.8	22.2	11.1	807	758
Clinton	1 065	3 651 290	8.0	9.9	0.0	4.7	3.6	5.9	67.0	83.0	32.3	37.3	980	957
Coles	2 055	7 515 260	6.6	9.1	4.4	3.1	2.6	3.4	70.1	193.9	95.6	62.8	1 170	1 079
Cook	198 590	1 055 085 174	5.5	19.7	3.8	8.4	5.0	6.1	49.9	30 214.0	10 506.2	14 465.1	2 765	2 126
Crawford	1 004	3 546 258	3.9	4.8	1.2	4.9	40.2	1.7	42.6	92.3	22.6	23.8	1 214	1 192
Cumberland	489	1 701 831	5.1	5.3	0.6	4.4	1.3	6.8	75.7	24.9	13.2	8.4	765	749
DeKalb	3 677	13 579 842	6.4	11.5	5.3	3.7	5.7	4.9	61.7	427.7	136.1	235.3	2 247	1 839
De Witt	856	2 898 838	6.6	7.9	0.9	3.4	26.5	4.6	49.0	74.5	16.6	32.1	1 956	1 907
Douglas	604	1 931 336	13.2	8.9	0.8	4.9	0.1	2.9	68.4	57.7	23.4	26.8	1 352	1 325
DuPage	34 627	161 978 004	4.8	10.0	5.2	2.3	1.4	8.6	66.1	4 380.5	931.7	2 785.7	3 002	2 700
Edgar	762	2 449 135	5.9	7.4	2.5	12.8	1.9	5.1	63.4	53.8	26.7	21.4	1 175	1 081
Edwards	230	593 869	6.7	6.9	0.5	3.2	1.4	6.8	74.3	13.3	7.7	3.8	573	568
Effingham	1 139	4 092 064	7.6	10.0	2.5	4.1	2.3	4.6	67.2	103.7	48.7	39.5	1 151	1 088
Fayette	798	2 298 002	8.1	12.9	0.0	4.6	5.0	3.9	65.2	56.1	29.6	16.6	754	737
Ford	495	1 697 539	6.4	9.3	0.0	5.1	0.0	3.3	75.1	45.2	18.3	21.4	1 530	1 465
Franklin	1 582	5 056 096	5.7	8.6	1.7	3.6	12.7	9.1	58.0	140.8	72.3	25.5	646	571
Fulton	1 688	5 342 718	6.0	7.3	2.2	3.1	5.4	5.4	70.1	131.1	60.0	46.1	1 259	1 214
Gallatin	190	667 273	12.7	6.1	0.2	4.8	0.2	7.6	67.8	16.8	10.0	3.8	699	636
Greene	546	1 577 821	8.0	6.8	0.3	8.5	4.3	8.2	63.4	36.4	17.9	12.3	908	861
Grundy	1 993	7 671 944	5.9	9.9	3.1	2.7	1.3	1.8	74.1	223.4	53.5	147.8	2 939	2 877
Hamilton	413	1 340 057	6.2	3.3	0.0	3.7	34.5	5.5	46.3	33.7	13.2	5.1	604	603
Hancock	809	2 296 207	7.2	7.6	0.4	6.0	1.8	4.7	71.8	55.0	25.2	21.7	1 147	1 101

1. Based on the resident population estimated as of July 1 of the year shown.

STATE County	Local government finances, 2012 (cont.) — Direct general expenditure: Total (mil dol)	Per capita[1] (dollars)	Percent of total for: Education	Health and hospitals	Police protection	Public welfare	Highways	Debt outstanding: Total (mil dol)	Per capita[1] (dollars)	Government employment, 2013: Federal civilian	Federal military	State and local	Presidential election,[2] 2012 — Percent of vote cast: Democratic	Republican	All other
	185	186	187	188	189	190	191	192	193	194	195	196	197	198	199
IDAHO—Cont'd															
Caribou	29.0	4 268	41.5	0.2	10.7	0.5	13.5	1.0	151	46	25	612	16.7	80.4	2.8
Cassia	58.1	2 497	57.1	0.4	5.3	0.8	5.6	30.3	1 303	146	86	1 465	17.0	80.5	2.6
Clark	5.2	6 037	40.8	0.2	6.5	0.5	26.7	4.2	4 807	35	0	105	17.1	81.3	1.6
Clearwater	26.0	3 028	39.9	2.2	7.1	1.3	13.0	2.0	229	174	30	789	31.0	65.8	3.2
Custer	16.4	3 790	37.4	7.3	4.7	0.5	14.1	0.2	42	150	16	294	26.0	72.0	2.0
Elmore	76.8	2 930	37.5	27.0	6.8	0.0	7.2	27.5	1 049	830	3 546	1 204	30.7	67.2	2.1
Franklin	28.7	2 243	61.1	1.8	7.2	0.4	7.4	5.0	394	34	48	930	11.8	83.7	4.5
Fremont	39.0	3 014	39.0	1.3	7.0	0.8	11.9	29.5	2 277	72	47	954	18.1	79.9	2.0
Gem	41.4	2 481	43.1	21.4	5.8	0.6	5.5	23.5	1 409	78	62	799	27.3	70.3	2.5
Gooding	85.0	5 557	26.2	51.3	2.6	0.7	3.7	49.5	3 236	59	56	1 106	27.6	69.8	2.5
Idaho	41.4	2 537	44.3	2.9	4.7	1.4	20.3	6.4	391	330	58	859	24.6	71.8	3.6
Jefferson	64.3	2 411	54.0	0.0	6.7	0.2	4.6	89.0	3 335	48	101	1 240	15.7	81.8	2.5
Jerome	53.8	2 393	44.7	0.3	5.9	1.1	9.0	39.2	1 743	41	84	968	26.2	71.5	2.3
Kootenai	637.0	4 475	29.8	40.2	5.8	0.4	3.9	121.1	851	551	536	9 629	35.7	62.0	2.3
Latah	87.4	2 290	48.2	0.3	11.6	1.1	4.1	40.7	1 065	170	155	6 471	51.9	45.1	3.0
Lemhi	34.8	4 485	25.3	39.2	3.9	0.7	4.9	15.4	1 987	217	29	608	25.8	71.6	2.6
Lewis	21.4	5 498	42.3	0.7	5.0	0.7	11.4	4.3	1 109	45	14	406	26.6	70.7	2.8
Lincoln	12.3	2 332	69.2	0.0	4.6	0.1	9.2	6.3	1 194	84	20	381	29.1	65.9	5.0
Madison	144.7	3 862	27.9	37.4	3.3	0.2	4.1	137.2	3 662	56	137	1 971	12.5	85.2	2.3
Minidoka	75.3	3 760	38.1	24.8	4.2	0.5	5.7	46.9	2 341	68	76	1 325	23.7	73.8	2.5
Nez Perce	119.5	3 023	41.4	0.7	8.3	0.2	7.5	25.2	637	202	147	3 852	40.0	58.1	1.9
Oneida	14.2	3 368	42.9	22.5	6.2	0.3	7.9	2.7	633	17	16	426	17.6	79.7	2.6
Owyhee	32.2	2 814	58.3	0.0	6.5	0.9	6.7	21.0	1 836	49	42	644	23.3	74.5	2.2
Payette	52.4	2 315	48.3	3.5	7.4	1.5	7.7	25.3	1 117	32	84	1 022	28.0	69.5	2.4
Power	34.2	4 401	40.1	20.7	3.4	0.6	11.8	11.5	1 480	22	29	634	36.1	61.7	2.1
Shoshone	52.1	4 102	38.6	21.3	5.0	0.8	10.7	38.7	3 043	69	47	913	44.5	52.1	3.4
Teton	51.0	5 069	26.2	24.7	2.1	0.1	4.7	22.8	2 269	43	39	477	49.4	48.6	2.0
Twin Falls	356.9	4 541	65.8	1.8	3.6	0.9	4.2	190.1	2 418	366	297	4 322	30.4	67.1	2.4
Valley	50.0	5 243	33.1	0.0	8.0	0.2	14.2	52.4	5 495	230	36	737	45.4	52.3	2.2
Washington	43.6	4 322	34.4	33.0	5.6	1.2	5.7	9.6	952	47	37	677	27.5	70.3	2.2
ILLINOIS	X	X	X	X	X	X	X	X	X	81 231	43 324	753 486	61.9	36.8	1.3
Adams	201.0	2 991	56.5	3.5	5.7	0.2	5.8	99.6	1 482	269	132	3 994	38.3	60.7	1.0
Alexander	30.3	3 916	49.2	1.4	5.2	0.5	5.8	3.3	426	27	14	648	55.6	43.0	1.4
Bond	45.6	2 583	46.2	7.7	7.5	0.1	9.0	52.0	2 948	330	31	761	48.5	49.8	1.7
Boone	156.0	2 893	62.0	1.2	6.0	0.1	5.4	126.3	2 341	67	108	2 039	51.1	47.0	1.9
Brown	16.0	2 312	46.9	4.0	5.1	0.0	14.3	5.3	774	43	10	378	38.4	60.1	1.5
Bureau	156.2	4 551	37.8	25.0	3.8	0.0	9.0	77.1	2 245	126	68	2 191	51.9	46.2	1.8
Calhoun	11.5	2 294	52.1	0.5	3.8	0.1	22.6	8.5	1 693	25	10	244	52.7	45.2	2.0
Carroll	49.2	3 280	55.2	1.4	4.9	0.0	10.6	31.3	2 088	69	30	791	51.7	46.9	1.5
Cass	48.5	3 633	48.0	10.6	5.0	0.1	5.9	32.3	2 418	54	27	913	49.7	48.4	1.9
Champaign	826.4	4 066	48.3	2.5	5.1	1.9	5.6	670.9	3 301	1 230	418	35 056	57.8	40.3	2.0
Christian	110.2	3 182	62.3	1.4	5.2	0.2	6.9	48.6	1 404	73	66	1 791	45.8	52.1	2.1
Clark	50.6	3 123	49.6	1.9	5.8	0.2	12.5	27.6	1 705	49	32	870	45.1	53.2	1.7
Clay	65.1	4 732	32.8	32.8	3.4	0.1	5.2	24.2	1 756	47	27	890	37.6	60.8	1.6
Clinton	81.6	2 145	54.7	2.6	8.5	0.0	9.4	57.5	1 510	102	72	2 265	44.2	54.0	1.7
Coles	224.0	4 175	60.6	1.0	4.9	0.1	7.5	97.1	1 809	134	102	6 396	50.8	47.6	1.7
Cook	29 791.5	5 695	39.4	4.1	7.7	1.3	4.1	59 701.4	11 412	38 179	10 833	283 993	76.2	22.8	1.0
Crawford	103.4	5 277	28.7	46.8	2.5	0.1	5.6	46.4	2 366	52	36	1 780	42.5	55.5	1.9
Cumberland	25.4	2 316	59.2	2.1	4.8	0.2	11.9	9.6	878	29	22	489	38.6	59.3	2.1
DeKalb	465.9	4 450	45.9	1.7	5.4	3.0	4.9	394.6	3 769	179	201	13 231	57.5	40.8	1.7
De Witt	72.0	4 384	38.0	25.7	5.5	0.1	7.2	34.3	2 088	49	33	1 004	42.4	55.7	1.9
Douglas	56.1	2 825	47.8	1.8	6.3	0.3	11.0	34.9	1 760	60	40	1 085	38.6	59.9	1.5
DuPage	4 276.8	4 609	55.0	0.8	6.9	1.6	4.5	4 424.5	4 768	5 106	1 913	46 227	54.7	43.9	1.4
Edgar	59.4	3 263	54.0	3.0	5.0	0.0	11.2	50.5	2 777	55	36	984	45.3	53.3	1.4
Edwards	13.2	1 968	61.7	1.1	4.8	0.1	7.8	6.7	1 005	24	13	292	34.0	63.8	2.2
Effingham	107.8	3 137	47.2	2.6	6.9	0.7	10.6	58.0	1 688	152	69	1 663	31.3	67.3	1.5
Fayette	56.3	2 557	53.8	6.6	7.2	0.0	7.1	24.9	1 130	59	41	1 084	41.0	56.8	2.2
Ford	49.5	3 535	64.3	0.7	5.7	0.0	8.3	21.0	1 501	51	27	821	34.9	63.9	1.3
Franklin	143.4	3 639	47.5	12.4	7.3	0.3	5.1	32.0	811	216	78	1 860	47.6	50.4	1.9
Fulton	132.3	3 611	54.8	3.6	4.8	2.2	7.8	85.5	2 332	91	68	2 286	50.6	[illegible]	2.1
Gallatin	16.0	2 938	50.0	0.8	2.9	0.3	11.8	8.2	1 509	25	11	244	55.5	42.4	2.1
Greene	37.1	2 735	54.1	5.0	5.5	0.4	12.8	12.2	901	43	27	694	45.1	52.6	2.3
Grundy	239.2	4 757	60.5	1.0	4.2	0.0	7.5	311.7	6 199	110	101	2 582	49.9	48.2	1.9
Hamilton	35.0	4 183	33.6	40.5	2.7	0.1	8.6	25.1	3 002	33	17	539	42.1	55.2	2.7
Hancock	59.2	3 132	56.6	5.9	3.8	1.1	11.6	21.0	1 109	82	37	1 117	43.7	54.5	1.8

1. Based on the resident population estimated as of July 1 of the year shown. 2.

STATE/ County code	CBSA code[1]	County type[2]	STATE County	Land area,[3] (sq km) 2010	Population, 2014: Total persons 2014	Population, 2014: Rank	Population, 2014: Per square kilometer	Population and population characteristics, 2013: Race alone or in combination, not Hispanic or Latino (percent): White	Black	American Indian, Alaska Native	Asian and Pacific Islander	Percent Hispanic or Latino[4]	Age (percent): Under 5 years	5 to 17 years	18 to 24 years	25 to 34 years	35 to 44 years	45 to 54 years
				1	2	3	4	5	6	7	8	9	10	11	12	13	14	15
			ILLINOIS—Cont'd															
17 069	...	9	Hardin	460	4 129	2 894	9.0	96.3	0.8	1.0	0.9	1.8	5.3	15.0	6.3	8.7	11.0	14.5
17 071	15460	9	Henderson	981	6 916	2 686	7.0	97.7	0.9	0.7	0.5	1.2	4.6	14.7	6.6	9.1	9.7	15.5
17 073	19340	2	Henry	2 132	49 635	985	23.3	92.2	2.4	0.5	0.8	5.4	5.5	17.4	7.8	10.5	11.9	14.1
17 075	...	6	Iroquois	2 894	28 879	1 459	10.0	92.0	1.5	0.5	0.7	6.2	5.4	17.2	7.6	10.3	11.1	14.2
17 077	16060	5	Jackson	1 513	59 677	871	39.4	77.2	15.6	1.0	4.5	4.2	5.1	12.8	24.3	14.2	9.7	10.5
17 079	...	7	Jasper	1 281	9 623	2 464	7.5	98.0	0.5	0.4	0.5	1.3	6.1	16.7	7.3	11.3	11.1	15.3
17 081	34500	7	Jefferson	1 479	38 534	1 206	26.1	88.1	9.5	0.6	1.1	2.3	6.2	15.6	8.6	12.6	12.3	13.7
17 083	41180	1	Jersey	956	22 571	1 706	23.6	97.4	1.0	0.7	0.8	1.2	5.0	16.8	9.7	11.0	11.5	15.2
17 085	...	6	Jo Daviess	1 557	22 254	1 720	14.3	95.7	0.9	0.4	0.7	3.2	4.9	15.1	6.4	9.2	10.5	13.9
17 087	...	7	Johnson	891	12 601	2 258	14.1	88.2	8.4	0.6	0.4	3.2	4.8	13.7	9.2	12.6	12.5	14.6
17 089	16980	1	Kane	1 347	527 306	126	391.5	59.5	5.9	0.4	4.2	31.2	6.9	20.8	8.8	12.4	14.2	14.3
17 091	28100	3	Kankakee	1 752	111 375	542	63.6	74.2	16.0	0.5	1.4	9.5	6.1	18.3	10.5	12.1	12.2	13.7
17 093	16980	1	Kendall	830	121 350	507	146.2	74.3	6.5	0.3	4.0	16.4	7.5	22.6	7.6	13.7	17.0	13.6
17 095	23660	4	Knox	1 855	52 069	957	28.1	86.1	9.0	0.5	1.1	5.2	4.9	15.1	10.0	11.6	11.5	13.3
17 097	16980	1	Lake	1 149	705 186	88	613.7	65.4	7.5	0.5	7.7	20.6	6.0	19.8	9.9	11.1	13.2	15.6
17 099	36860	4	LaSalle	2 940	111 241	543	37.8	88.2	2.6	0.5	1.1	8.7	5.6	16.8	8.4	11.8	11.5	14.7
17 101	...	7	Lawrence	964	16 519	2 004	17.1	86.2	10.2	0.4	0.5	3.5	5.0	14.1	9.7	14.6	14.2	13.8
17 103	19940	4	Lee	1 877	34 735	1 309	18.5	88.2	5.6	0.5	1.1	5.7	5.2	15.4	8.3	12.1	12.1	15.5
17 105	38700	4	Livingston	2 705	37 903	1 226	14.0	89.5	6.0	0.4	0.8	4.4	5.4	16.3	8.8	12.4	12.1	14.8
17 107	30660	6	Logan	1 601	29 746	1 435	18.6	88.0	8.4	0.5	1.0	3.3	4.9	14.4	11.1	13.7	12.5	13.9
17 109	31380	5	McDonough	1 527	31 880	1 387	20.9	89.8	6.1	0.6	2.6	2.6	4.7	11.7	26.0	12.3	9.0	10.1
17 111	16980	1	McHenry	1 562	307 283	219	196.7	83.8	1.6	0.4	3.3	12.1	5.7	19.7	8.5	10.8	13.7	17.0
17 113	14010	3	McLean	3 065	174 061	365	56.8	82.4	8.7	0.5	5.8	4.7	6.0	16.1	18.1	13.3	12.2	12.5
17 115	19500	3	Macon	1 504	108 350	552	72.0	79.6	18.6	0.6	1.6	2.1	6.0	16.2	9.6	11.7	11.5	13.3
17 117	41180	1	Macoupin	2 235	46 453	1 037	20.8	97.2	1.4	0.7	0.6	1.1	5.1	16.6	8.3	11.2	11.8	14.2
17 119	41180	1	Madison	1 853	266 560	253	143.9	87.7	9.0	0.6	1.4	3.0	5.9	16.3	9.3	13.2	12.3	14.3
17 121	16460	4	Marion	1 482	38 571	1 205	26.0	93.4	5.1	0.5	0.9	1.7	6.3	16.7	8.3	11.4	11.4	13.9
17 123	37900	2	Marshall	1 002	12 014	2 297	12.0	95.6	0.8	0.5	0.9	3.1	5.1	15.8	7.8	9.7	11.1	14.2
17 125	...	6	Mason	1 397	13 898	2 179	9.9	97.8	1.0	0.7	0.7	1.0	5.1	16.0	7.7	10.1	11.4	14.5
17 127	37140	7	Massac	614	14 905	2 107	24.3	91.1	7.0	0.8	0.7	2.5	6.1	16.1	7.5	10.4	12.1	14.1
17 129	44100	3	Menard	814	12 570	2 259	15.4	97.1	1.6	0.7	0.6	1.2	5.3	17.0	7.6	10.4	11.8	15.4
17 131	19340	2	Mercer	1 454	15 945	2 043	11.0	96.9	0.8	0.4	0.5	2.2	5.3	17.0	7.1	9.7	11.5	14.8
17 133	41180	1	Monroe	997	33 722	1 336	33.8	97.4	0.6	0.5	0.8	1.5	5.2	18.2	7.4	10.9	12.6	16.2
17 135	...	6	Montgomery	1 823	29 359	1 444	16.1	94.4	3.7	0.4	0.6	1.7	5.2	15.6	8.3	12.4	12.1	14.7
17 137	27300	4	Morgan	1 473	34 929	1 302	23.7	90.8	7.2	0.4	0.7	2.3	5.3	14.9	10.3	12.6	11.2	14.2
17 139	...	6	Moultrie	870	14 837	2 115	17.1	98.0	0.8	0.4	0.4	1.1	6.1	18.7	7.7	11.7	11.1	13.4
17 141	40300	4	Ogle	1 965	52 085	955	26.5	89.1	1.5	0.5	0.7	9.2	5.3	18.2	8.2	10.4	12.1	15.5
17 143	37900	2	Peoria	1 604	187 319	343	116.8	73.9	19.6	0.6	4.2	4.4	6.8	17.0	10.0	13.9	12.1	12.7
17 145	...	7	Perry	1 144	21 672	1 746	18.9	87.6	9.6	0.5	0.7	3.0	4.9	15.0	10.2	12.9	13.4	13.8
17 147	16580	3	Piatt	1 138	16 431	2 013	14.4	97.7	0.9	0.5	0.8	1.1	5.1	17.6	7.4	10.4	11.7	15.6
17 149	...	7	Pike	2 153	16 022	2 039	7.4	96.4	2.2	0.5	0.4	1.3	5.6	16.5	7.7	11.4	11.6	13.4
17 151	...	9	Pope	955	4 276	2 882	4.5	90.8	7.0	0.9	0.6	1.6	3.5	12.9	11.2	9.3	10.0	14.8
17 153	...	9	Pulaski	516	5 815	2 770	11.3	65.2	33.4	0.9	0.8	1.7	5.4	16.8	8.0	10.4	10.7	13.7
17 155	36860	8	Putnam	415	5 814	2 771	14.0	93.7	1.2	0.5	0.5	5.1	4.2	15.5	7.5	10.7	10.6	15.2
17 157	...	6	Randolph	1 491	32 869	1 359	22.0	86.7	10.3	0.4	0.6	2.8	5.0	14.3	8.1	14.1	13.1	14.8
17 159	...	7	Richland	932	16 061	2 037	17.2	96.7	0.9	0.5	1.3	1.4	6.0	15.9	8.0	11.4	11.3	13.7
17 161	19340	2	Rock Island	1 108	146 063	441	131.8	76.2	10.5	0.6	2.7	12.3	6.3	16.0	9.1	12.7	11.6	13.2
17 163	41180	1	St. Clair	1 704	265 729	256	155.9	64.4	31.3	0.6	2.2	3.7	6.5	17.8	9.3	13.0	12.6	14.4
17 165	...	7	Saline	984	24 612	1 624	25.0	93.5	5.0	0.9	0.8	1.6	6.1	16.1	8.6	11.5	11.4	13.6
17 167	44100	3	Sangamon	2 249	198 997	328	88.5	83.7	13.5	0.6	2.4	2.1	6.1	17.0	8.5	13.0	12.2	14.3
17 169	...	7	Schuyler	1 133	7 330	2 650	6.5	94.5	3.4	0.3	0.4	1.9	5.1	15.8	7.1	10.4	13.4	14.7
17 171	27300	9	Scott	650	5 204	2 823	8.0	98.1	0.8	0.5	0.4	1.1	4.8	17.4	7.6	10.2	11.8	15.6
17 173	...	6	Shelby	1 965	22 048	1 727	11.2	98.3	0.6	0.4	0.4	0.8	5.3	16.4	7.6	10.4	11.3	14.1
17 175	37900	2	Stark	746	5 813	2 772	7.8	97.5	1.1	0.7	0.8	1.1	4.8	16.5	7.1	9.1	11.3	13.3
17 177	23300	4	Stephenson	1 462	46 435	1 038	31.8	86.4	11.0	0.4	1.1	3.3	5.6	16.3	8.1	10.3	10.8	14.4
17 179	37900	2	Tazewell	1 681	135 707	466	80.7	95.5	1.8	0.6	1.2	2.2	6.0	17.1	7.7	12.6	12.9	13.8
17 101	...	7	Union	1 071	17 447	1 952	16.3	92.9	1.7	0.8	0.9	5.1	5.2	15.6	8.0	11.0	12.0	14.3
17 183	19180	3	Vermilion	2 327	79 728	695	34.3	81.3	14.3	0.6	1.1	4.7	6.5	17.4	8.6	11.7	11.7	10.5
17 185	...	6	Wabash	578	11 549	2 324	20.0	96.9	1.3	0.6	1.0	1.4	5.9	16.2	8.3	11.2	11.1	13.7
17 187	...	7	Warren	1 405	17 874	1 920	12.7	87.3	2.7	0.5	1.8	9.0	6.0	16.0	12.5	10.6	10.9	12.7
17 189	...	6	Washington	1 457	14 337	2 143	9.8	97.1	1.2	0.4	0.6	1.6	4.8	16.3	7.7	11.6	11.9	15.1
17 191	...	7	Wayne	1 849	16 543	2 003	8.9	97.4	0.8	0.5	0.8	1.3	6.0	16.7	7.5	11.2	11.4	13.6
17 193	...	6	White	1 281	14 374	2 140	11.2	97.7	0.7	0.5	0.5	1.2	6.5	15.3	6.9	11.4	10.4	14.0
17 195	44580	4	Whiteside	1 772	56 876	894	32.1	86.3	2.1	0.4	0.7	11.7	5.8	17.1	8.1	10.5	11.6	14.0
17 197	16980	1	Will	2 168	685 419	90	316.2	67.2	11.9	0.4	5.6	16.3	6.3	21.0	9.0	11.6	14.8	15.5
17 199	16060	5	Williamson	1 088	67 008	792	61.6	92.3	5.0	0.7	1.3	2.2	5.7	16.1	8.1	13.1	12.8	13.8

1. CBSA = Core Based Statistical Area. See Appendix A for explanation. See Appendix B for list of metropolitan areas with component counties. 2. County type code from the Economic Research Service of USDA Rural-Urban Continuum Codes. See Appendix A for definition. 3. Dry land or land partially or temporarily covered by water. 4. May be of any race.

STATE County	Population, 2013 (cont.): Age (percent) (cont.): 55 to 64 years	65 to 74 years	75 years and over	Percent female	Population change and components of change, 2000–2014: Total persons: 2000	2010	Percent change: 2000–2010	2010–2014	Components of change, 2010–2014: Births	Deaths	Net migration	Households, 2009–2013: Number	Persons per house-hold	Percent: Family house-holds	Female family house-holder[1]	One per-son
	16	17	18	19	20	21	22	23	24	25	26	27	28	29	30	31
ILLINOIS—Cont'd																
Hardin	16.5	13.7	9.0	49.7	4 800	4 320	-10.0	-4.4	145	232	-96	1 800	2.33	62.4	9.2	33.7
Henderson	16.9	12.5	10.3	51.1	8 213	7 331	-10.7	-5.6	188	342	-248	3 202	2.22	67.5	9.1	27.9
Henry	14.4	10.0	8.3	50.2	51 020	50 486	-1.0	-1.7	2 223	2 218	-836	20 393	2.43	68.6	9.6	26.7
Iroquois	14.3	10.4	9.6	51.2	31 334	29 718	-5.2	-2.8	1 310	1 505	-609	11 892	2.42	68.2	9.4	27.4
Jackson	10.9	6.8	5.7	49.5	59 612	60 218	1.0	-0.9	2 773	1 897	-1 392	23 567	2.33	50.7	10.1	37.0
Jasper	14.4	9.4	8.6	49.9	10 117	9 698	-4.1	-0.8	494	398	-147	3 904	2.46	71.0	9.6	25.3
Jefferson	13.8	9.6	7.6	48.6	40 045	38 827	-3.0	-0.7	1 988	1 860	-361	15 288	2.40	65.6	10.6	30.2
Jersey	13.7	9.2	7.9	51.1	21 668	22 985	6.1	-1.8	934	942	-402	8 752	2.50	74.2	11.5	23.0
Jo Daviess	16.5	13.4	10.1	49.8	22 289	22 678	1.7	-1.9	688	1 013	-63	9 616	2.33	68.8	8.1	25.9
Johnson	13.8	11.5	7.2	44.2	12 878	12 582	-2.3	0.2	498	507	79	4 362	2.45	68.9	9.2	28.9
Kane	11.4	6.7	4.6	50.1	404 119	515 269	27.5	2.3	29 293	12 663	-5 435	170 358	3.01	74.8	10.9	20.7
Kankakee	12.6	7.9	6.6	50.9	103 833	113 449	9.3	-1.8	5 744	4 514	-3 292	41 245	2.62	68.5	15.1	26.3
Kendall	9.1	5.5	3.2	50.5	54 544	114 736	110.4	5.8	7 240	2 127	1 462	38 075	3.05	77.4	9.1	18.7
Knox	14.3	10.1	9.2	49.7	55 836	52 919	-5.2	-1.6	2 280	2 752	-271	21 481	2.25	59.6	11.3	34.6
Lake	12.6	6.8	5.0	50.1	644 356	703 462	9.2	0.3	34 272	17 996	-14 804	241 072	2.84	74.3	10.6	21.9
LaSalle	13.9	8.9	8.4	49.9	111 509	113 924	2.2	-2.4	4 943	5 374	-2 257	44 257	2.50	67.2	10.8	28.1
Lawrence	12.3	8.5	7.8	43.9	15 452	16 833	8.9	-2.3	705	869	-222	4 872	2.26	68.2	13.1	29.5
Lee	14.4	9.2	7.9	47.3	36 062	36 031	-0.1	-3.6	1 547	1 470	-1 296	13 504	2.45	66.8	9.2	27.8
Livingston	13.6	8.4	8.1	49.8	39 678	38 950	-1.8	-2.7	1 905	1 730	-1 203	14 446	2.37	67.6	8.5	28.2
Logan	12.8	8.5	8.2	49.4	31 183	30 305	-2.8	-1.8	1 231	1 295	-512	10 963	2.13	65.6	12.2	29.4
McDonough	11.3	7.8	7.1	50.5	32 913	32 612	-0.9	-2.2	1 286	1 198	-853	12 620	2.18	54.3	10.4	32.9
McHenry	12.8	7.2	4.5	50.2	260 077	308 760	18.7	-0.5	13 952	8 081	-7 645	108 852	2.82	75.8	9.6	19.9
McLean	10.9	6.0	4.9	51.2	150 433	169 572	12.7	2.6	9 126	4 744	149	64 016	2.54	61.9	9.3	28.2
Macon	14.3	9.2	8.2	52.0	114 706	110 768	-3.4	-2.2	5 767	4 936	-3 174	45 142	2.36	62.1	12.0	32.7
Macoupin	14.4	9.7	8.6	50.6	49 019	47 765	-2.6	-2.7	1 940	2 347	-911	19 254	2.41	68.9	10.2	26.0
Madison	13.3	8.3	7.0	51.1	258 941	269 282	4.0	-1.0	13 327	11 193	-4 622	107 238	2.45	66.9	12.3	26.3
Marion	14.0	9.7	8.4	51.1	41 691	39 437	-5.4	-2.2	2 109	2 031	-956	15 893	2.41	65.8	13.1	29.9
Marshall	15.4	10.9	10.0	50.5	13 180	12 640	-4.1	-5.0	460	628	-433	5 021	2.42	64.5	6.8	29.7
Mason	14.6	10.8	9.8	50.7	16 038	14 666	-8.6	-5.2	575	789	-649	6 310	2.27	66.0	9.7	28.6
Massac	13.8	10.2	9.5	52.4	15 161	15 429	1.8	-3.4	685	870	-356	6 053	2.48	64.5	10.1	31.5
Menard	15.0	9.9	7.5	51.4	12 486	12 705	1.8	-1.1	523	548	-108	5 071	2.47	67.7	7.1	27.7
Mercer	14.7	11.1	8.8	50.6	16 957	16 434	-3.1	-3.0	609	754	-370	6 716	2.40	72.5	9.9	24.1
Monroe	14.3	7.8	7.5	50.5	27 619	32 957	19.3	2.3	1 377	1 101	419	12 506	2.63	75.3	7.6	21.0
Montgomery	13.8	9.0	9.0	47.7	30 652	30 104	-1.8	-2.5	1 280	1 482	-527	11 192	2.19	67.2	12.7	27.0
Morgan	13.8	9.4	8.3	49.6	36 616	35 547	-2.9	-1.7	1 590	1 607	-566	13 926	2.32	64.9	12.7	30.2
Moultrie	12.8	9.3	9.3	51.3	14 287	14 846	3.9	-0.1	713	769	16	5 676	2.54	70.8	9.7	24.3
Ogle	13.4	9.4	7.4	50.4	51 032	53 497	4.8	-2.6	2 246	2 013	-1 647	20 745	2.53	67.0	8.2	27.1
Peoria	12.7	8.0	6.7	51.5	183 433	186 494	1.7	0.4	11 334	7 467	-2 820	75 892	2.39	61.8	13.7	31.9
Perry	13.0	9.3	7.5	45.5	23 094	22 350	-3.2	-3.0	869	986	-535	7 982	2.51	63.3	10.0	33.4
Piatt	14.5	9.6	8.1	50.2	16 365	16 729	2.2	-1.8	688	704	-269	6 546	2.52	72.1	7.5	24.0
Pike	14.0	10.2	9.5	50.0	17 384	16 430	-5.5	-2.5	750	826	-334	6 708	2.35	66.8	8.9	28.1
Pope	17.4	11.9	9.0	47.6	4 413	4 470	1.3	-4.3	136	174	-142	1 736	2.33	66.4	10.7	31.9
Pulaski	15.6	10.4	9.1	52.0	7 348	6 161	-16.2	-5.6	252	326	-265	2 419	2.45	62.1	14.0	35.9
Putnam	16.7	11.4	8.1	48.9	6 086	6 006	-1.3	-3.2	228	224	-171	2 471	2.39	67.4	5.6	25.1
Randolph	13.6	9.0	7.9	45.0	33 893	33 476	-1.2	-1.8	1 470	1 512	-575	11 889	2.50	67.6	11.7	28.7
Richland	13.7	9.7	10.2	50.8	16 149	16 233	0.5	-1.1	797	808	-161	6 620	2.41	63.4	7.8	32.2
Rock Island	13.9	9.2	8.0	50.8	149 374	147 546	-1.2	-1.0	7 409	6 326	-2 362	60 456	2.37	62.4	12.4	33.2
St. Clair	12.9	7.3	6.2	51.7	256 082	270 056	5.5	-1.6	14 544	10 404	-8 365	102 885	2.57	67.3	17.6	28.6
Saline	13.6	10.2	8.7	50.8	26 733	24 913	-6.8	-1.2	1 315	1 441	-141	10 174	2.38	65.3	11.9	31.0
Sangamon	13.9	8.3	6.7	52.1	188 951	197 465	4.5	0.8	10 055	8 134	-340	82 807	2.35	62.8	12.6	31.4
Schuyler	14.9	10.1	8.5	47.0	7 189	7 544	4.9	-2.8	288	352	-153	3 056	2.31	70.9	6.9	25.4
Scott	14.1	9.5	8.9	51.3	5 537	5 355	-3.3	-2.8	226	241	-129	2 113	2.48	68.3	9.2	26.9
Shelby	14.5	10.9	9.3	50.4	22 893	22 363	-2.3	-1.4	987	992	-288	8 991	2.45	70.2	7.9	26.8
Stark	14.5	12.5	10.9	50.3	6 332	5 994	-5.3	-3.0	237	351	-49	2 416	2.41	68.5	6.8	28.8
Stephenson	14.5	10.1	9.9	51.7	48 979	47 711	-2.6	-2.7	2 137	2 260	-1 136	19 408	2.40	64.1	12.5	31.0
Tazewell	13.4	8.7	7.8	50.6	128 485	135 394	5.4	0.2	6 914	5 791	-763	54 428	2.45	68.6	10.3	27.2
Union	14.7	10.8	8.4	50.0	18 293	17 808	-2.7	-2.0	777	929	-192	6 852	2.47	68.2	10.4	29.5
Vermilion	13.6	9.3	7.8	50.3	83 919	81 625	-2.7	-2.3	4 567	3 951	-2 417	31 575	2.51	63.9	13.7	31.3
Wabash	15.2	9.4	9.0	50.9	12 937	11 947	-7.7	-3.3	633	553	-436	4 785	2.45	69.6	8.4	27.2
Warren	13.8	9.2	8.2	51.3	18 735	17 707	-5.5	0.9	878	764	31	6 972	2.37	65.0	10.8	30.2
Washington	14.4	9.4	8.8	49.8	15 148	14 716	-2.9	-2.6	578	594	-363	5 882	2.44	69.4	7.6	27.2
Wayne	13.9	10.5	9.3	50.8	17 151	16 760	-2.3	-1.3	836	877	-169	7 063	2.34	70.1	10.9	28.1
White	14.0	10.9	10.7	51.5	15 371	14 665	-4.6	-2.0	707	904	-73	6 240	2.28	68.2	9.4	28.4
Whiteside	14.5	9.7	8.7	50.7	60 653	58 498	-3.6	-2.8	2 516	2 688	-1 363	23 370	2.44	67.2	10.4	28.3
Will	11.2	6.5	4.3	50.3	502 266	677 560	34.9	1.2	34 243	16 858	-9 641	222 652	3.02	76.9	10.6	19.4
Williamson	13.1	10.0	7.4	50.4	61 296	66 357	8.3	1.0	3 339	3 131	531	26 819	2.41	66.2	12.0	29.2

1. No spouse present.

STATE County	Persons in group quarters, 2014	Daytime population, 2009–2013: Number	Daytime population, 2009–2013: Employment/residence ratio	Births, 2014: Total	Births, 2014: Rate[1]	Deaths, 2014: Number	Deaths, 2014: Rate[1]	Persons under 65 with no health insurance, 2013: Number	Persons under 65 with no health insurance, 2013: Percent	Medicare, 2014: Eligible for Medicare	Medicare, 2014: Enrolled in Medicare Advantage	Medicare, 2014: Enrolled in a Medicare prescription drug plan	Serious crimes known to police,[2] 2013: Total: Number	Serious crimes known to police,[2] 2013: Total: Rate[3]
	32	33	34	35	36	37	38	39	40	41	42	43	44	45
ILLINOIS—Cont'd														
Hardin	17	3 956	0.78	28	6.8	59	14.3	428	13.2	1 185	143	706	31	731
Henderson	51	5 385	0.48	45	6.5	81	11.7	697	12.9	1 701	221	927	10	148
Henry	726	42 478	0.67	531	10.7	529	10.7	4 344	10.8	10 591	1 645	5 951	701	1 535
Iroquois	468	26 612	0.79	308	10.7	327	11.3	2 969	12.9	6 735	824	4 186	486	1 670
Jackson	4 094	64 504	1.17	631	10.6	431	7.2	6 899	14.1	9 092	1 813	4 562	2 294	3 865
Jasper	54	8 379	0.72	112	11.6	86	8.9	976	12.5	2 073	211	1 355	86	898
Jefferson	2 203	42 933	1.26	464	12.0	428	11.1	3 784	12.6	7 869	940	4 765	1 475	3 813
Jersey	848	18 737	0.59	223	9.9	193	8.6	1 876	10.3	4 766	631	2 881	437	1 928
Jo Daviess	167	20 364	0.80	217	9.8	246	11.1	2 279	13.4	5 840	2 156	3 414	237	1 144
Johnson	1 553	11 302	0.66	117	9.3	124	9.8	1 147	13.1	2 866	600	1 475	128	1 092
Kane	6 793	485 159	0.86	6 700	12.7	3 115	5.9	72 557	15.8	66 239	12 317	32 540	7 993	1 524
Kankakee	5 113	108 966	0.92	1 305	11.7	1 091	9.8	11 349	12.3	20 325	3 202	11 289	3 193	2 850
Kendall	208	89 322	0.52	1 660	13.7	493	4.1	9 915	9.2	12 989	2 317	6 240	1 607	1 350
Knox	3 956	51 942	0.97	545	10.5	583	11.2	4 875	12.6	11 780	3 633	5 362	1 586	3 394
Lake	18 654	718 072	1.05	7 950	11.3	4 339	6.2	76 887	12.8	96 538	10 241	52 972	12 995	1 862
LaSalle	2 942	107 923	0.89	1 093	9.8	1 210	10.9	11 404	12.5	22 464	2 623	12 222	1 955	1 782
Lawrence	2 542	16 822	1.03	169	10.2	209	12.7	1 400	12.2	3 193	228	2 032	148	1 058
Lee	2 872	34 283	0.92	354	10.2	376	10.8	3 001	11.3	7 375	1 051	4 225	605	1 742
Livingston	3 389	38 124	0.96	457	12.1	358	9.4	2 914	10.1	7 220	1 378	3 829	795	2 062
Logan	4 361	28 996	0.89	277	9.3	309	10.4	2 109	10.1	5 671	1 442	2 444	656	2 323
McDonough	4 042	33 487	1.06	308	9.7	283	8.9	3 348	14.0	5 551	1 356	2 847	729	2 242
McHenry	1 648	262 454	0.70	3 167	10.3	1 868	6.1	29 452	10.9	44 387	3 984	25 015	3 394	1 157
McLean	10 688	176 745	1.06	2 176	12.5	1 123	6.5	13 625	9.4	22 954	6 445	10 790	4 266	2 466
Macon	4 062	116 230	1.13	1 351	12.5	1 138	10.5	9 296	10.6	23 008	4 284	12 517	3 186	2 900
Macoupin	876	38 376	0.57	438	9.4	563	12.1	4 502	11.9	10 219	1 148	6 205	615	1 392
Madison	3 809	251 782	0.86	3 038	11.4	2 696	10.1	22 837	10.2	50 393	14 356	24 838	6 358	2 457
Marion	758	38 348	0.96	491	12.7	403	10.4	3 866	12.3	9 053	883	5 693	1 388	3 706
Marshall	255	10 810	0.70	100	8.3	138	11.5	1 039	10.9	2 843	477	1 328	92	852
Mason	206	12 957	0.74	123	8.9	180	13.0	1 339	11.9	3 404	513	1 793	NA	NA
Massac	292	14 106	0.80	154	10.3	169	11.3	1 369	11.3	3 621	490	1 991	319	2 103
Menard	154	9 015	0.41	125	9.9	131	10.4	1 028	10.0	2 514	687	992	61	583
Mercer	185	12 454	0.50	143	9.0	173	10.8	1 352	10.5	3 834	815	1 956	152	961
Monroe	343	25 550	0.53	332	9.8	292	8.7	2 174	7.7	5 866	1 826	2 546	168	502
Montgomery	2 415	29 954	1.01	295	10.0	373	12.7	2 617	11.7	6 349	742	3 872	568	1 952
Morgan	3 071	36 167	1.05	371	10.6	359	10.3	2 851	10.8	7 536	1 290	4 048	608	1 758
Moultrie	395	14 020	0.87	156	10.5	153	10.3	1 504	12.5	2 954	410	1 700	NA	NA
Ogle	525	46 412	0.73	504	9.7	464	8.9	5 020	11.6	10 056	2 220	5 214	346	803
Peoria	4 984	210 499	1.28	2 707	14.5	1 739	9.3	17 601	11.2	33 383	10 468	12 425	6 586	3 512
Perry	2 500	19 809	0.72	199	9.2	220	10.2	1 864	11.7	4 346	734	2 583	192	874
Piatt	72	13 076	0.57	164	10.0	162	9.9	1 238	9.2	3 337	1 212	1 119	130	863
Pike	627	14 813	0.78	174	10.9	175	10.9	1 850	14.8	3 533	379	2 163	59	363
Pope	389	3 798	0.64	31	7.2	20	4.7	478	14.8	942	130	405	NA	NA
Pulaski	21	6 180	1.07	54	9.3	65	11.2	668	14.1	1 457	177	821	70	1 419
Putnam	2	5 241	0.74	57	9.8	64	11.0	589	12.7	1 309	190	607	39	667
Randolph	4 298	33 918	1.05	341	10.4	368	11.2	2 549	10.9	6 416	1 077	3 592	409	1 321
Richland	364	15 974	0.97	176	11.0	186	11.6	1 518	11.8	3 665	330	2 461	NA	NA
Rock Island	4 319	159 697	1.18	1 859	12.7	1 438	9.8	15 870	13.4	29 015	6 202	14 270	4 105	2 799
St. Clair	4 607	256 347	0.89	3 307	12.4	2 572	9.7	26 969	11.9	44 404	12 884	18 221	9 424	3 727
Saline	882	25 648	1.08	303	12.3	324	13.2	2 489	12.6	5 888	693	3 498	510	2 190
Sangamon	3 967	212 761	1.15	2 295	11.5	2 026	10.2	16 736	10.0	36 708	12 817	12 804	9 490	4 960
Schuyler	463	6 406	0.67	63	8.6	69	9.4	890	14.8	1 614	236	880	48	646
Scott	43	4 302	0.58	56	10.8	48	9.2	543	12.8	972	153	532	NA	NA
Shelby	205	18 709	0.64	239	10.8	249	11.3	2 111	12.0	4 892	394	2 900	99	589
Stark	92	5 060	0.66	52	8.9	81	13.9	525	11.7	1 292	273	521	NA	NA
Stephenson	835	46 460	0.96	503	10.8	537	11.6	4 241	11.4	10 748	3 592	5 173	584	1 270
Tazewell	2 844	128 014	0.88	1 622	12.0	1 381	10.2	10 655	9.5	26 044	6 691	9 648	2 532	2 060
Union	566	15 943	0.74	184	10.5	217	12.4	2 071	14.6	4 398	851	2 349	304	1 727
Vermilion	2 903	80 081	0.97	1 080	13.5	919	11.5	7 843	12.2	17 102	6 321	6 355	3 628	4 586
Wabash	88	10 395	0.73	150	13.0	113	9.8	1 133	11.9	2 555	197	1 705	275	2 358
Warren	1 116	16 746	0.87	211	11.8	177	9.9	1 927	14.2	3 389	625	1 858	501	2 906
Washington	246	14 985	1.05	127	8.9	132	9.2	1 209	10.3	2 962	348	1 768	238	1 634
Wayne	76	15 510	0.85	192	11.6	203	12.3	1 747	13.1	3 726	276	2 544	262	1 691
White	391	13 494	0.82	154	10.7	207	14.4	1 299	11.5	3 595	383	2 289	NA	NA
Whiteside	1 010	54 239	0.85	605	10.6	605	10.6	5 597	12.1	12 914	1 900	7 901	1 152	2 050
Will	8 564	600 243	0.75	7 854	11.5	4 160	6.1	67 282	11.2	88 897	14 198	44 926	11 058	1 634
Williamson	1 870	65 874	0.97	801	12.0	747	11.1	6 771	12.6	13 931	2 178	7 462	1 118	1 839

1. Per 1,000 estimated resident population. 2. Data for serious crimes have not been adjusted for underreporting; this may affect comparability between geographic areas and over time.
3. Per 100,000 population estimated by the FBI.

STATE County	Serious crimes known to police, 2013 (cont.)[1] Rate[2] Violent	Property	Education: School enrollment and attainment, 2009–2013 Enrollment[3] Total	Per-cent private	Attainment[4] (percent) High school grad-uate or less	Bach-elor's degree or more	Local government expenditures,[5] 2012–2013 Total current spending (mil dol)	Current spend-ing per student (dollars)	Money income, 2009–2013 Per capita income[6] (dollars)	Households Median income (dollars)	Mean income (dollars)	Percent with income of $200,000 or more	Income and poverty, 2013 Median house-hold income (dollars)	Percent below poverty level All per-sons	Children under 18 years	Children 5 to 17 years in families
	46	47	48	49	50	51	52	53	54	55	56	57	58	59	60	61
ILLINOIS—Cont'd																
Hardin	165	566	902	4.5	55.1	12.2	5.5	8 671	22 366	37 071	50 418	2.3	36 567	20.3	32.7	29.8
Henderson	30	118	1 422	10.3	52.6	15.7	9.4	10 084	25 902	49 389	58 602	0.7	45 022	12.8	20.7	19.1
Henry	109	1 426	11 729	8.5	46.3	19.8	86.6	9 943	27 117	52 940	66 361	2.6	52 117	11.2	16.0	14.6
Iroquois	165	1 505	6 793	12.3	53.4	14.6	55.4	11 742	25 098	47 079	61 213	2.7	46 977	14.0	20.5	19.1
Jackson	556	3 309	24 356	7.3	34.8	35.1	90.3	12 079	20 527	33 479	49 930	1.7	34 243	29.5	34.0	32.3
Jasper	42	856	2 220	17.6	46.6	16.2	19.6	13 880	24 174	52 233	59 235	1.1	52 187	10.5	18.0	17.4
Jefferson	651	3 162	8 903	8.8	47.7	15.9	63.0	10 260	22 620	42 981	56 414	2.0	40 663	18.4	26.7	24.6
Jersey	124	1 805	5 993	24.1	45.4	16.2	26.7	9 808	25 467	53 954	64 902	1.8	54 331	10.5	15.3	13.8
Jo Daviess	111	1 033	4 600	13.2	46.5	23.7	39.6	11 720	29 675	50 817	69 287	3.0	49 573	10.2	15.5	14.5
Johnson	265	828	2 658	6.1	49.4	15.1	19.4	9 850	18 763	40 760	52 790	1.3	39 965	17.9	21.1	18.4
Kane	153	1 371	149 394	15.7	41.0	31.7	1 350.7	11 026	30 082	69 530	89 378	6.9	71 444	10.9	16.2	15.4
Kankakee	302	2 548	31 047	19.7	48.2	17.1	204.9	10 598	23 779	50 102	62 913	1.7	49 584	16.7	23.0	21.6
Kendall	91	1 259	35 674	14.1	33.0	34.2	284.0	10 312	31 276	81 765	93 784	5.0	79 648	5.8	7.8	7.6
Knox	321	3 073	12 386	17.6	51.4	17.0	87.4	11 680	22 093	40 667	52 500	1.1	39 494	19.6	28.2	25.4
Lake	158	1 704	201 326	17.1	32.2	41.9	1 963.5	14 339	38 018	77 469	108 570	11.8	75 106	9.5	13.7	12.0
LaSalle	121	1 661	27 258	11.2	49.6	15.9	210.5	12 311	25 709	52 640	63 810	1.8	49 487	13.8	19.8	18.7
Lawrence	136	922	3 673	16.0	57.9	8.4	21.4	9 061	14 147	40 145	50 663	1.7	39 670	18.2	25.4	24.4
Lee	72	1 670	8 090	14.4	49.5	16.0	48.9	10 937	25 409	50 060	64 375	3.2	53 126	12.4	17.0	15.9
Livingston	213	1 849	8 995	9.0	54.1	14.5	76.5	11 956	24 952	54 614	66 263	2.2	52 819	12.5	17.4	15.4
Logan	223	2 100	7 597	17.2	50.6	16.2	38.4	11 397	21 445	47 133	59 347	1.7	50 991	13.6	19.1	17.5
McDonough	234	2 009	12 959	7.3	37.3	33.3	47.5	13 364	20 042	36 031	49 451	1.6	41 661	21.1	22.9	22.5
McHenry	80	1 077	88 365	16.1	34.9	32.4	597.9	11 522	32 341	76 145	90 181	6.0	75 713	7.1	9.2	8.1
McLean	329	2 137	57 741	13.1	31.1	42.8	276.7	10 992	30 460	62 089	79 136	4.7	62 261	13.8	12.7	11.5
Macon	354	2 546	26 920	20.1	46.5	22.3	211.2	12 747	26 232	46 559	62 668	2.8	46 179	18.1	26.5	23.6
Macoupin	177	1 216	11 191	11.0	49.6	15.9	77.9	8 710	24 658	49 590	59 895	1.5	50 089	13.9	20.9	18.8
Madison	222	2 236	71 125	15.6	42.4	24.4	424.2	10 110	27 407	53 633	67 568	3.0	53 864	13.7	18.9	16.7
Marion	246	3 460	9 150	10.6	50.1	13.9	80.9	11 485	21 887	41 010	52 548	1.0	40 969	19.2	32.4	29.7
Marshall	130	723	2 703	10.8	51.5	17.0	15.3	11 136	25 975	51 504	62 809	2.0	50 899	10.2	16.6	14.9
Mason	NA	NA	3 177	5.7	54.1	14.2	29.8	10 150	23 199	42 260	53 684	0.7	45 563	14.0	22.7	20.2
Massac	290	1 813	3 517	6.7	48.3	16.7	23.4	9 432	22 047	43 615	53 372	1.2	41 373	17.5	28.6	27.5
Menard	19	563	3 032	12.7	46.6	22.1	22.6	8 981	28 330	58 190	69 327	2.3	60 151	10.8	16.9	15.8
Mercer	152	809	3 767	8.9	50.8	14.7	26.7	9 189	26 620	53 136	64 189	2.3	53 626	9.7	13.6	12.6
Monroe	42	460	8 456	19.7	41.7	25.9	49.2	9 239	31 758	68 482	83 526	4.9	71 604	4.9	5.8	4.7
Montgomery	344	1 608	6 372	9.1	56.8	12.1	41.3	8 963	19 917	41 952	55 155	1.1	42 614	16.1	21.7	19.6
Morgan	147	1 610	8 866	27.7	52.8	20.7	57.4	11 568	24 337	46 809	60 318	2.0	48 223	16.0	24.7	23.0
Moultrie	NA	NA	3 355	13.8	54.6	14.1	15.9	9 344	23 786	46 622	59 987	1.7	47 645	12.4	18.3	16.2
Ogle	60	742	13 979	11.2	46.2	19.9	115.8	12 191	26 635	54 541	66 757	1.9	51 334	13.0	16.6	14.8
Peoria	497	3 015	49 098	25.5	39.6	28.9	327.2	11 127	28 438	50 712	68 651	3.6	49 827	17.0	25.7	23.7
Perry	132	742	4 975	6.5	50.7	14.3	27.0	9 639	19 716	42 078	51 418	0.5	41 931	17.6	24.8	23.1
Piatt	173	690	4 032	9.6	41.8	26.5	31.0	9 546	31 190	63 027	78 783	4.3	66 279	7.2	10.1	8.9
Pike	25	338	3 789	9.0	58.7	13.5	26.2	9 637	21 344	39 845	51 186	1.2	39 430	17.3	27.3	24.4
Pope	NA	NA	838	6.8	48.9	13.5	5.2	9 014	20 448	38 371	47 949	1.2	38 676	19.9	31.6	30.0
Pulaski	567	851	1 474	7.1	55.4	12.0	14.1	13 790	19 867	33 717	46 783	1.5	34 828	21.5	36.8	33.1
Putnam	17	650	1 345	7.3	50.0	14.1	9.9	10 935	27 074	54 196	65 815	2.3	58 438	9.0	15.0	13.4
Randolph	129	1 192	7 015	11.4	59.1	11.8	47.6	11 339	21 976	47 427	57 840	1.3	44 991	14.1	21.2	19.8
Richland	NA	NA	3 721	11.0	43.5	20.4	23.2	9 245	23 621	44 070	55 949	2.1	41 985	16.4	24.4	22.5
Rock Island	328	2 471	36 080	20.4	44.5	21.8	243.3	11 043	26 455	48 702	62 867	2.8	48 160	15.8	25.1	23.2
St. Clair	811	2 916	76 120	13.7	38.7	25.3	483.6	11 350	26 234	50 578	66 066	3.0	48 343	18.3	26.6	25.1
Saline	292	1 898	5 603	5.7	46.9	14.6	41.0	9 628	21 596	37 800	51 976	1.5	39 281	18.6	29.4	28.4
Sangamon	840	4 120	51 301	17.3	36.2	32.5	356.0	11 926	29 974	55 449	70 931	3.5	55 255	15.2	21.9	18.6
Schuyler	54	592	1 630	4.2	49.4	18.6	12.9	10 538	23 656	48 138	57 476	0.9	49 808	13.2	19.4	18.1
Scott	NA	NA	1 263	9.7	57.2	13.7	9.1	9 608	24 471	49 669	59 303	1.9	46 004	13.3	19.0	17.2
Shelby	54	535	4 903	6.0	52.8	14.4	22.8	9 374	23 069	47 188	55 709	0.8	50 569	12.6	20.4	20.1
Stark	NA	NA	1 339	8.8	51.9	16.7	10.4	10 169	26 843	54 203	65 787	5.2	52 428	11.0	17.3	15.9
Stephenson	63	1 207	11 478	12.1	47.6	17.9	81.0	11 837	23 350	43 472	54 923	1.1	42 897	18.6	26.7	26.1
Tazewell	228	1 832	33 617	15.7	41.8	23.6	206.6	10 159	28 037	56 067	69 037	2.5	57 544	8.9	12.0	10.9
Union	239	1 488	4 050	5.8	48.4	20.1	27.3	9 346	21 719	41 848	53 527	1.9	42 799	16.7	24.5	22.9
Vermilion	662	3 924	18 262	9.1	54.2	13.9	146.8	10 877	21 225	41 400	52 248	1.1	44 085	19.6	30.5	26.3
Wabash	189	2 170	3 053	12.8	43.6	16.8	15.6	8 680	24 096	47 365	59 199	2.1	47 351	14.6	20.0	18.8
Warren	360	2 546	5 032	27.8	47.7	20.9	23.9	8 633	21 832	43 536	54 826	1.1	45 770	15.1	21.7	21.2
Washington	426	1 209	3 195	15.4	42.4	20.5	18.3	9 520	26 325	52 832	63 448	1.3	53 967	9.9	14.4	12.6
Wayne	155	1 536	3 813	10.4	49.2	11.8	25.0	9 743	22 526	43 605	52 738	1.3	42 896	17.4	27.4	24.1
White	NA	NA	3 096	3.5	46.8	14.3	35.0	13 985	25 375	42 914	59 089	2.2	42 621	15.6	23.0	20.0
Whiteside	125	1 925	13 730	13.9	49.7	16.2	104.5	10 918	24 525	47 667	59 290	1.3	50 489	12.1	19.2	17.5
Will	173	1 461	204 367	17.3	36.7	32.3	1 321.6	11 250	30 377	76 147	90 649	6.1	74 669	8.5	11.5	10.9
Williamson	36	1 803	15 456	8.1	40.2	22.5	103.8	10 093	23 605	43 125	56 600	1.7	44 041	16.2	25.1	22.2

1. Data for serious crimes have not been adjusted for underreporting; this may affect comparability between geographic areas and over time. 2. Per 100,000 population estimated by the FBI.
3. All persons 3 years old and over enrolled in nursery school through college. 4. Persons 25 years old and over. 5. Elementary and secondary education expenditures.
6. Based on population estimated by the American Community Survey, 2009–2013.

Table B. States and Counties — **Personal Income**

STATE County	Personal income, 2013										Earnings, 2013		
	Total (mil dol)	Percent change, 2012–2013	Per capita[1]		Wages and salaries (mil dol)	Supplements to wages and salaries; employer contributions (mil dol)		Proprietors' income (mil dol)	Dividends, interest, and rent (mil dol)	Personal transfer receipts (mil dol)	Total (mil dol)	Contributions for government social insurance (mil dol)	
			Dollars	Rank		Pension and insurance	Government social insurance					From employee and self-employed	From employer
	62	63	64	65	66	67	68	69	70	71	72	73	74
ILLINOIS—Cont'd													
Hardin	141	3.5	33 757	2 137	35	9	3	13	25	50	60	4	3
Henderson	326	24.8	46 615	576	37	11	3	90	57	58	140	5	3
Henry	2 177	7.2	43 671	785	518	122	37	371	441	366	1 049	51	37
Iroquois	1 351	12.8	46 629	575	284	64	21	323	259	255	693	28	21
Jackson	2 181	2.3	36 467	1 670	1 126	320	69	145	420	422	1 660	74	69
Jasper	423	10.5	44 052	751	88	23	6	107	92	75	225	9	6
Jefferson	1 407	0.8	36 402	1 673	815	158	63	109	250	339	1 146	63	63
Jersey	937	4.9	41 379	1 007	176	42	12	69	151	184	299	18	12
Jo Daviess	1 069	6.8	47 697	500	283	63	22	140	297	180	508	28	22
Johnson	370	1.8	29 202	2 781	83	25	5	30	63	101	142	9	5
Kane	21 021	1.7	40 145	1 159	9 664	1 793	722	1 105	3 611	2 765	13 284	711	722
Kankakee	4 136	4.0	36 892	1 607	1 746	363	132	259	633	935	2 500	136	132
Kendall	4 836	2.7	40 518	1 112	1 078	226	78	164	554	485	1 546	82	78
Knox	1 994	5.3	38 289	1 401	793	168	69	214	377	515	1 243	69	69
Lake	42 781	1.0	60 853	97	24 025	3 808	1 592	2 266	10 395	3 910	31 691	1 707	1 592
LaSalle	4 564	5.2	40 682	1 089	1 822	376	137	483	837	886	2 818	148	137
Lawrence	560	8.4	33 818	2 122	160	40	12	86	99	144	298	15	12
Lee	1 452	10.9	41 660	978	499	102	37	255	271	280	893	43	37
Livingston	1 901	10.3	49 789	376	590	126	43	410	299	279	1 169	48	43
Logan	1 189	13.5	39 666	1 210	345	74	25	251	192	227	695	29	25
McDonough	1 191	7.6	36 698	1 639	498	147	31	156	241	217	832	33	31
McHenry	13 366	0.8	43 479	803	4 294	815	326	361	2 291	1 631	5 797	324	326
McLean	7 930	3.7	45 405	661	4 888	855	325	735	1 331	893	6 803	345	325
Macon	4 730	1.8	43 280	819	2 458	450	188	428	907	976	3 524	198	188
Macoupin	1 889	7.1	40 303	1 137	379	87	27	214	347	390	707	38	27
Madison	10 896	1.7	40 776	1 080	4 239	869	322	480	2 139	2 110	5 910	342	322
Marion	1 444	2.8	37 385	1 524	534	116	44	96	271	428	790	47	44
Marshall	604	9.9	49 739	378	121	26	9	125	109	106	281	12	9
Mason	625	11.5	43 891	768	123	33	8	128	100	132	292	12	8
Massac	510	1.9	33 825	2 119	168	39	12	29	95	152	248	15	12
Menard	548	8.7	43 506	800	67	19	4	99	95	89	190	7	4
Mercer	779	15.0	48 180	468	111	28	8	145	140	130	291	13	8
Monroe	1 629	2.6	48 642	441	306	63	22	118	329	207	510	30	22
Montgomery	1 082	9.0	36 474	1 667	355	79	26	169	218	252	629	31	26
Morgan	1 358	8.2	38 738	1 328	570	120	42	195	277	296	928	46	42
Moultrie	621	10.5	41 730	968	147	30	11	155	99	113	343	16	11
Ogle	2 184	7.8	41 695	973	726	163	52	284	405	379	1 224	62	52
Peoria	9 042	-1.5	47 988	483	5 248	865	396	516	1 820	1 429	7 026	389	396
Perry	663	4.2	30 306	2 641	183	49	12	61	131	180	305	17	12
Piatt	941	10.0	57 279	152	125	31	8	153	156	114	316	12	8
Pike	652	15.3	40 347	1 129	145	34	11	142	125	136	332	14	11
Pope	136	2.3	31 556	2 471	23	7	2	9	23	37	41	3	2
Pulaski	222	4.9	37 658	1 479	73	21	5	28	29	77	126	6	5
Putnam	260	3.9	44 820	706	70	14	5	22	58	45	111	6	5
Randolph	1 065	4.1	32 369	2 356	445	110	32	62	239	258	649	35	32
Richland	579	5.4	35 798	1 781	229	51	18	71	129	151	368	20	18
Rock Island	6 063	0.9	41 171	1 029	4 320	792	302	362	1 222	1 126	5 776	321	302
St. Clair	10 430	1.7	39 069	1 286	4 475	1 003	359	443	2 156	2 171	6 280	344	359
Saline	926	2.4	37 132	1 561	395	86	29	77	164	269	587	34	29
Sangamon	8 622	2.6	43 294	818	4 562	942	317	790	1 855	1 436	6 612	330	317
Schuyler	318	10.0	42 747	867	107	23	7	53	49	55	190	8	7
Scott	217	14.4	41 606	983	38	10	3	53	31	37	104	4	3
Shelby	879	11.6	39 760	1 194	165	39	12	210	151	179	427	17	12
Stark	287	25.7	48 539	449	50	12	4	83	46	48	149	5	4
Stephenson	1 907	4.7	40 790	1 077	762	149	58	208	394	401	1 177	65	58
Tazewell	5 704	-4.4	41 829	954	3 557	549	255	374	1 123	989	4 736	265	255
Union	612	3.0	34 791	1 934	159	42	11	30	118	188	242	15	11
Vermilion	2 883	4.5	35 892	1 764	1 184	268	90	311	498	729	1 853	101	90
Wabash	475	5.2	40 748	1 086	125	33	9	60	110	100	226	12	9
Warren	755	16.3	42 597	881	221	47	16	168	134	132	452	19	16
Washington	679	0.5	47 006	554	251	57	19	106	139	112	433	22	19
Wayne	657	3.5	39 572	1 220	162	40	12	141	117	146	355	17	12
White	661	8.8	45 404	662	185	38	14	148	135	143	386	20	14
Whiteside	2 422	6.4	42 076	932	833	199	60	293	494	515	1 385	71	60
Will	31 112	1.2	45 564	651	10 176	1 931	771	920	4 168	3 678	13 797	758	771
Williamson	2 496	1.4	37 289	1 537	1 097	252	83	140	483	571	1 572	89	83

1. Based on the resident population estimated as of July 1 of the year shown.

Table B. States and Counties — **Earnings, Social Security, and Housing**

STATE County	Earnings, 2013 (cont.) Percent by selected industries: Farm	Mining	Construction	Manu-facturing	Infor-mation: professional, scientific, technical services	Retail trade	Finance, insur-ance, real estate and leasing	Health care and social assistance	Govern-ment	Social Security beneficiaries, December 2013: Number	Rate[1]	Supple-mental Security Income recipients, December 2013	Housing units, 2014: Total	Percent change, 2010–2014
	75	76	77	78	79	80	81	82	83	84	85	86	87	88
ILLINOIS—Cont'd														
Hardin	9.0	13.0	D	D	D	4.0	D	20.6	21.3	1 345	323	191	2 459	-1.2
Henderson	54.8	D	3.2	D	D	2.4	D	3.5	13.2	1 805	261	102	3 821	-0.1
Henry	21.4	D	6.2	15.2	3.1	6.4	4.3	6.1	18.6	11 110	223	622	22 107	-0.2
Iroquois	40.3	0.1	5.4	5.1	D	5.3	2.9	D	11.8	7 150	246	496	13 438	-0.1
Jackson	1.8	D	4.7	2.3	4.4	6.2	3.3	15.7	45.2	9 195	153	1 485	28 615	0.1
Jasper	37.8	3.4	2.6	4.4	3.2	5.3	D	D	14.5	2 245	234	162	4 329	-0.4
Jefferson	3.3	D	2.5	22.9	4.6	6.4	4.8	D	14.4	8 565	221	1 012	16 818	-0.8
Jersey	13.3	0.0	7.8	1.5	D	9.0	2.7	D	24.5	5 240	231	381	10 034	1.9
Jo Daviess	19.1	D	6.4	13.9	4.1	6.3	3.7	D	15.4	6 110	275	178	13 596	0.2
Johnson	4.3	D	6.5	0.9	4.0	4.7	D	D	47.0	3 105	245	253	5 552	-0.8
Kane	0.6	0.2	7.0	17.2	9.0	6.2	5.3	11.3	17.6	68 760	131	4 990	184 014	1.1
Kankakee	6.3	D	3.9	17.6	D	7.2	4.8	17.1	16.3	21 910	195	2 765	45 154	-0.2
Kendall	4.8	0.1	6.6	16.5	5.1	8.7	3.3	6.0	23.8	14 060	118	651	41 183	2.1
Knox	12.7	D	2.8	5.5	D	8.3	3.3	D	17.2	12 075	231	1 283	23 894	-0.8
Lake	0.0	D	3.3	21.8	10.1	7.5	7.4	6.9	13.8	98 945	141	7 725	261 366	0.4
LaSalle	10.3	2.6	4.4	17.1	3.8	8.0	3.8	9.3	14.5	24 780	221	1 584	49 869	-0.2
Lawrence	18.9	12.6	4.0	12.6	1.7	4.2	6.2	8.2	18.1	3 545	212	312	6 944	0.1
Lee	20.4	0.7	2.3	19.7	D	5.2	3.5	13.9	14.6	7 925	227	529	15 038	-0.1
Livingston	28.6	D	4.2	15.1	D	5.2	2.6	7.0	14.6	7 915	207	538	15 829	-0.4
Logan	31.4	D	2.0	12.3	2.4	6.0	3.4	8.3	13.9	6 145	205	381	12 033	-0.6
McDonough	15.3	D	2.9	10.6	2.4	5.4	3.0	D	44.6	5 720	176	568	14 390	-0.2
McHenry	1.5	0.1	8.9	18.7	6.0	7.7	3.6	10.9	17.4	46 845	152	1 811	117 051	0.8
McLean	4.9	D	3.2	4.4	D	4.6	22.6	8.6	14.5	24 400	140	1 749	71 417	2.5
Macon	4.2	0.1	6.6	27.5	5.0	5.3	3.5	12.5	11.1	24 670	225	3 253	50 353	-0.2
Macoupin	22.6	D	5.1	7.7	2.5	5.9	3.6	D	18.1	11 150	238	969	21 539	-0.2
Madison	1.1	0.2	7.5	18.4	6.7	7.2	4.4	11.5	17.9	54 525	204	5 860	118 186	0.9
Marion	6.4	2.6	5.2	17.0	D	5.9	3.5	15.6	17.2	9 320	241	1 096	18 118	-1.0
Marshall	37.2	0.3	5.3	19.7	1.7	2.5	2.6	5.7	10.2	3 135	258	125	5 896	-0.3
Mason	38.2	D	2.8	1.2	1.6	4.0	2.8	3.9	23.3	3 720	262	273	7 028	-0.7
Massac	3.9	0.0	D	13.1	D	5.2	2.5	6.1	24.4	4 025	269	493	7 076	-0.5
Menard	45.6	D	4.8	0.6	D	4.2	4.0	D	18.5	2 765	219	154	5 658	0.1
Mercer	42.6	0.0	4.6	10.2	1.4	4.2	3.4	5.9	15.3	4 040	251	181	7 367	0.1
Monroe	5.0	0.2	8.0	3.9	16.8	9.1	7.8	6.2	16.6	6 150	183	160	13 764	2.8
Montgomery	20.9	7.5	3.7	5.4	3.0	6.9	4.3	D	16.3	6 990	236	667	13 054	-0.2
Morgan	14.0	0.0	3.3	15.5	3.7	6.8	6.9	11.2	17.7	8 040	229	943	15 411	-0.7
Moultrie	25.9	D	6.4	26.8	3.5	3.8	3.0	D	8.9	3 140	211	164	6 349	1.4
Ogle	15.0	D	6.1	19.5	D	4.7	3.3	5.0	15.2	10 920	208	560	22 545	-0.1
Peoria	1.6	D	5.0	11.5	16.5	5.0	5.5	21.8	11.3	36 150	192	4 865	83 555	0.6
Perry	9.6	D	4.4	10.8	D	5.8	3.7	10.0	31.4	4 805	220	446	9 465	0.4
Piatt	40.7	D	3.1	3.5	D	3.9	3.9	8.3	17.0	3 425	208	108	7 344	1.0
Pike	35.1	D	4.7	1.3	2.1	7.2	4.8	D	14.9	3 790	235	339	7 936	-0.2
Pope	11.8	D	5.4	D	D	D	D	D	43.4	1 060	245	106	2 468	-0.9
Pulaski	16.2	0.0	3.2	2.8	D	3.2	D	1.0	43.4	1 575	267	285	3 129	-0.8
Putnam	18.0	0.0	D	20.4	D	2.9	D	1.9	13.7	1 470	252	45	3 114	1.3
Randolph	6.1	0.3	4.9	22.4	D	7.2	3.1	7.9	26.5	7 005	213	507	13 814	0.8
Richland	11.5	6.1	2.0	7.4	2.5	6.0	5.1	14.0	16.4	4 000	249	428	7 478	-0.5
Rock Island	1.2	0.1	3.6	13.7	6.3	4.8	5.4	9.3	19.8	30 825	210	2 854	65 775	0.0
St. Clair	0.9	D	4.7	6.0	9.2	6.8	4.2	12.4	32.5	47 740	179	8 499	118 323	1.8
Saline	4.1	21.4	6.7	3.8	4.2	7.1	3.9	D	20.5	6 470	260	1 150	11 608	-0.8
Sangamon	4.4	D	4.4	3.0	7.5	5.8	8.9	21.3	25.2	40 210	202	4 739	90 538	0.7
Schuyler	24.2	D	4.5	1.5	0.9	3.6	1.9	3.2	22.1	1 675	226	100	3 435	-0.7
Scott	46.5	0.0	D	D	D	2.8	D	D	15.2	1 040	199	67	2 441	-0.7
Shelby	43.6	D	2.5	10.5	D	4.0	4.8	6.1	10.7	5 395	243	385	10 467	0.7
Stark	48.6	0.0	3.5	9.0	D	4.7	D	2.8	12.3	1 405	239	88	2 663	-0.4
Stephenson	11.0	0.0	8.1	22.4	3.5	4.9	8.6	12.8	13.7	11 685	250	1 113	21 926	-0.7
Tazewell	3.1	0.0	5.5	44.7	2.7	4.5	3.6	4.8	9.7	28 565	209	1 824	58 058	0.9
Union	4.4	D	4.5	6.2	3.0	9.8	3.4	D	32.2	4 620	263	673	7 914	-0.1
Vermilion	9.8	D	2.5	18.8	2.1	6.1	5.5	8.7	21.0	18 815	234	2 825	36 008	-0.9
Wabash	12.0	14.7	7.8	6.7	3.9	5.4	3.3	D	26.8	2 735	235	216	5 529	-1.0
Warren	32.7	D	1.6	21.2	D	3.8	D	D	9.1	3 555	201	297	7 673	-0.1
Washington	13.7	D	4.3	17.0	1.9	8.7	2.6	D	11.0	3 085	214	163	6 570	0.6
Wayne	26.5	9.4	2.8	9.0	2.0	5.4	2.4	D	14.9	4 095	246	294	7 886	-1.1
White	20.1	25.3	3.0	4.4	1.7	6.6	2.9	D	12.1	3 925	270	390	7 125	-0.8
Whiteside	12.4	D	3.0	24.2	3.1	5.5	3.0	5.2	23.0	14 185	248	1 139	25 773	0.0
Will	0.7	0.2	8.4	12.3	6.4	7.0	4.0	10.8	17.2	94 860	139	6 000	200 024	1.0
Williamson	1.0	D	5.0	8.8	4.1	7.4	7.5	17.1	27.2	14 935	223	1 699	30 801	1.5

1. Per 1,000 resident population estimated as of July 1 of the year shown.

STATE County	Housing units, 2009–2013: Occupied units: Total	Owner-occupied: Percent	Owner-occupied: Median value[1]	Median owner cost as a percent of income: With a mortgage	Median owner cost as a percent of income: Without a mortgage[2]	Renter-occupied: Median rent[3]	Renter-occupied: Median rent as a percent of income[2]	Substandard units[4] (percent)	Civilian labor force, 2014: Total	Civilian labor force, 2014: Percent change, 2013–2014	Unemployment: Total	Unemployment: Rate[5]	Civilian employment,[6] 2009–2013: Total	Percent: Management, business, science and arts	Percent: Construction, production, and maintenance occupations
	89	90	91	92	93	94	95	96	97	98	99	100	101	102	103
ILLINOIS—Cont'd															
Hardin	1 800	79.5	72 600	18.3	12.8	297	31.1	1.0	1 628	-3.0	143	8.8	1 481	27.6	30.7
Henderson	3 202	79.6	83 700	19.1	10.0	545	24.2	1.3	3 750	2.3	237	6.3	3 480	29.0	33.3
Henry	20 393	78.1	109 800	19.5	12.4	632	24.8	2.7	25 336	-0.3	1 702	6.7	23 893	30.6	27.5
Iroquois	11 892	75.3	96 500	22.3	11.8	621	29.0	1.6	14 801	-1.1	965	6.5	13 562	28.5	30.6
Jackson	23 567	53.4	100 600	20.3	12.0	650	42.1	0.8	27 791	-1.1	1 822	6.6	26 408	37.1	17.3
Jasper	3 904	84.0	88 100	19.0	10.5	520	23.3	2.3	4 736	0.1	305	6.4	4 839	27.9	32.2
Jefferson	15 288	72.7	86 300	20.2	12.4	585	27.7	1.0	17 591	-1.1	1 313	7.5	16 619	26.1	29.4
Jersey	8 752	79.9	117 900	21.0	11.4	642	27.9	0.9	11 086	-0.4	794	7.2	10 423	29.9	26.4
Jo Daviess	9 616	78.3	138 000	22.7	13.4	625	23.6	0.9	11 589	0.1	719	6.2	11 180	29.0	28.6
Johnson	4 362	81.3	89 800	20.6	13.2	614	26.8	4.4	4 133	-3.1	404	9.8	4 123	25.9	24.8
Kane	170 358	75.4	223 100	26.7	14.5	984	32.7	1.8	263 989	-0.1	18 372	7.0	247 519	33.5	23.9
Kankakee	41 245	68.9	145 900	24.1	13.8	795	29.3	1.3	55 367	-0.6	4 484	8.1	49 441	29.0	27.7
Kendall	38 075	83.6	210 800	26.7	14.7	1 205	28.7	1.5	64 498	-0.1	4 091	6.3	57 882	40.2	19.9
Knox	21 481	68.4	81 100	19.8	12.4	606	29.9	2.9	23 483	-0.7	1 640	7.0	21 663	29.2	27.3
Lake	241 072	75.9	254 800	26.2	15.0	1 022	30.2	1.5	366 147	0.2	23 858	6.5	332 723	41.8	17.5
LaSalle	44 257	75.8	125 200	22.4	12.6	680	28.1	1.6	57 094	-1.7	4 717	8.3	52 238	26.1	30.2
Lawrence	4 872	78.1	65 900	18.2	11.1	526	26.8	1.1	6 352	0.9	481	7.6	4 211	28.8	28.2
Lee	13 504	73.9	112 100	21.6	12.2	620	25.1	0.8	18 153	0.1	1 178	6.5	16 042	30.2	28.2
Livingston	14 446	73.9	110 200	21.5	12.2	632	25.7	0.7	17 576	-0.6	1 132	6.4	16 259	27.5	32.7
Logan	10 963	69.0	97 200	18.5	11.9	585	27.5	1.4	13 097	0.0	849	6.5	11 210	31.5	23.0
McDonough	12 620	61.0	86 400	19.7	11.2	683	41.2	1.7	14 295	-2.3	991	6.9	14 798	33.1	20.5
McHenry	108 852	82.3	220 500	26.6	15.1	1 068	31.5	1.6	166 668	-0.3	10 635	6.4	153 608	37.3	20.6
McLean	64 016	67.3	157 200	20.1	11.7	742	28.3	1.8	90 929	-1.7	5 036	5.5	88 807	42.0	14.7
Macon	45 142	69.2	93 300	19.3	11.8	659	29.3	2.2	50 806	-3.2	4 406	8.7	48 357	31.3	25.4
Macoupin	19 254	76.7	93 900	19.8	11.5	626	27.2	1.5	23 283	-0.6	1 733	7.4	21 862	27.8	29.5
Madison	107 238	72.5	124 600	21.6	12.1	780	31.4	2.2	132 323	-0.5	9 339	7.1	124 212	33.6	23.7
Marion	15 893	75.0	70 300	21.1	13.0	635	33.0	1.1	17 872	-1.3	1 394	7.8	16 938	25.7	30.5
Marshall	5 021	82.0	100 600	20.8	12.2	589	26.0	1.1	5 787	-1.8	403	7.0	5 576	24.4	35.2
Mason	6 310	77.4	82 100	20.5	11.8	594	30.4	2.0	6 632	-1.5	578	8.7	6 037	27.6	33.2
Massac	6 053	75.6	80 200	20.6	12.2	625	29.4	1.9	6 350	-0.8	509	8.0	6 143	29.5	28.1
Menard	5 071	80.8	119 100	19.8	10.6	625	24.7	1.0	6 733	0.1	386	5.7	6 357	33.6	23.1
Mercer	6 716	78.7	98 100	19.4	11.6	590	23.9	1.0	8 394	0.0	589	7.0	7 879	29.8	34.3
Monroe	12 506	81.1	193 900	22.1	12.9	832	26.8	1.1	17 727	0.1	963	5.4	16 691	35.0	22.2
Montgomery	11 192	75.3	79 500	19.4	12.3	656	29.6	0.7	12 283	-2.5	1 080	8.8	10 361	30.5	23.7
Morgan	13 926	69.9	91 000	19.6	10.0	607	29.1	2.4	17 199	-1.2	1 060	6.2	16 484	30.3	25.0
Moultrie	5 676	78.7	95 400	20.0	11.4	590	24.8	1.5	7 062	-0.4	386	5.5	6 746	27.5	34.5
Ogle	20 745	76.1	149 500	22.5	14.4	690	25.2	1.9	25 530	-1.0	1 951	7.6	25 332	29.0	31.9
Peoria	75 892	65.5	123 200	19.9	12.0	704	29.2	2.1	91 630	-2.0	7 105	7.8	85 513	38.3	19.0
Perry	7 982	76.7	78 000	20.6	12.0	515	28.4	1.4	8 857	-1.6	765	8.6	8 787	24.8	33.7
Piatt	6 546	82.4	120 800	18.8	11.3	727	22.8	1.6	8 394	0.2	485	5.8	8 316	36.6	25.9
Pike	6 708	77.9	74 700	20.0	12.4	526	26.1	2.3	7 798	1.5	451	5.8	7 125	22.7	32.8
Pope	1 736	81.1	98 900	21.3	15.0	473	22.9	2.4	1 800	-1.6	147	8.2	1 650	22.7	34.7
Pulaski	2 419	78.1	55 300	22.0	12.8	465	31.6	2.8	2 164	-2.2	224	10.4	2 192	24.5	30.5
Putnam	2 471	79.6	126 500	21.6	11.9	636	23.9	1.3	3 047	-0.3	239	7.8	2 666	24.2	33.3
Randolph	11 889	76.0	92 100	19.1	11.1	653	25.9	2.8	14 130	-1.7	953	6.7	13 986	25.1	35.4
Richland	6 620	74.9	78 100	19.5	10.2	541	26.8	2.0	7 141	-3.3	483	6.8	7 284	27.4	33.1
Rock Island	60 456	70.2	113 800	21.0	11.9	650	28.3	1.7	73 101	-0.6	5 159	7.1	68 496	30.3	26.8
St. Clair	102 885	67.2	123 700	22.3	13.0	795	31.9	1.7	126 821	-0.7	10 044	7.9	118 336	33.5	20.3
Saline	10 174	72.2	70 500	20.4	12.8	567	28.7	1.7	10 909	-3.0	889	8.1	9 143	27.8	28.3
Sangamon	82 807	70.0	126 200	19.9	11.1	735	29.8	3.9	103 918	0.0	6 242	6.0	97 035	40.1	14.8
Schuyler	3 056	81.0	76 600	19.3	11.1	540	27.5	1.5	3 541	1.4	231	6.5	3 331	27.3	30.9
Scott	2 113	75.9	82 900	18.9	10.0	508	23.1	1.3	2 571	-1.3	176	6.8	2 489	30.3	29.2
Shelby	8 991	81.2	86 100	19.8	11.2	646	23.6	1.2	10 109	-1.9	702	6.9	9 981	29.0	33.7
Stark	2 416	82.0	88 300	18.9	11.3	562	20.5	0.6	2 833	-1.7	213	7.5	2 654	32.4	28.3
Stephenson	19 408	71.8	101 800	22.1	13.5	601	32.0	1.3	22 265	-2.1	1 671	7.5	21 188	29.1	30.1
Tazewell	54 428	76.0	132 000	20.4	11.4	667	26.0	1.5	67 781	-1.8	4 626	6.8	63 979	34.2	24.2
Union	6 852	75.7	87 500	19.6	13.5	513	28.7	1.3	7 223	-2.1	650	9.0	6 982	32.1	26.8
Vermilion	31 575	70.6	75 300	20.1	11.9	618	29.8	2.0	35 643	-1.1	3 059	8.6	32 883	26.3	31.1
Wabash	4 785	78.7	80 900	19.4	12.3	575	24.6	2.8	5 558	-1.5	339	6.1	5 536	26.2	35.9
Warren	6 972	73.4	81 500	21.2	12.3	610	27.0	1.5	8 714	-1.2	516	5.9	8 036	28.2	27.3
Washington	5 882	80.6	107 900	21.8	12.0	629	24.1	1.6	9 069	1.8	442	4.9	7 463	32.3	32.3
Wayne	7 063	79.1	75 700	19.4	10.7	531	28.2	1.5	7 685	-2.5	514	6.7	7 713	26.3	37.5
White	6 240	78.6	72 200	18.9	10.1	502	22.1	1.7	7 042	0.2	426	6.0	6 480	25.0	33.1
Whiteside	23 370	75.6	99 400	20.9	13.0	633	29.7	2.2	28 598	-2.7	2 028	7.1	26 515	27.2	30.7
Will	222 652	82.9	219 400	26.2	14.2	983	30.8	1.2	357 282	-0.5	26 531	7.4	323 606	36.2	22.0
Williamson	26 819	72.0	93 700	19.8	12.5	624	29.1	2.1	30 556	-1.4	2 247	7.4	28 566	31.8	20.7

1. Specified owner-occupied units. 2. A value of 10.0 represents 10 percent or less; a value of 50.0 represents 50 percent or more. 3. Specified renter-occupied units. 4. Overcrowded or lacking complete plumbing facilities. 5. Percent of civilian labor force. 6. Persons 16 years old and over.

STATE County	Private nonfarm establishments, employment and payroll, 2013									Agriculture, 2012			
		Employment						Annual payroll		Farms			
											Percent with:		
	Number of establish-ments	Total	Health care and social assistance	Manufac-turing	Retail trade	Finance and insurance	Professional, scientific, and technical services	Total (mil dol)	Average per employee (dollars)	Number	Fewer than 50 acres	500 acres or more	Farm operators whose principal occu-pation is farming (percent)
	104	105	106	107	108	109	110	111	112	113	114	115	116
ILLINOIS—Cont'd													
Hardin	65	785	348	D	70	D	D	23	29 161	150	22.0	6.7	34.0
Henderson	119	680	D	D	109	D	36	17	24 744	396	24.2	28.8	68.7
Henry	1 077	13 024	1 576	4 064	1 812	551	306	445	34 194	1 373	30.6	21.5	56.6
Iroquois	702	6 237	1 708	637	987	327	89	197	31 626	1 470	25.4	29.2	55.0
Jackson	1 310	17 040	3 925	886	3 766	602	689	527	30 949	783	34.7	10.9	42.1
Jasper	203	1 620	106	287	282	97	16	60	37 226	910	34.5	19.6	41.2
Jefferson	956	17 619	3 468	3 697	2 326	433	621	646	36 650	1 063	38.4	8.8	33.1
Jersey	424	4 645	1 146	82	886	183	159	125	26 811	509	37.9	17.5	47.0
Jo Daviess	719	6 736	639	1 078	905	241	184	216	32 004	935	26.4	13.6	50.6
Johnson	165	1 289	267	69	211	60	D	27	20 581	558	33.0	5.7	30.1
Kane	12 318	180 958	21 514	29 435	22 923	8 733	8 966	7 234	39 975	590	51.4	16.1	66.3
Kankakee	2 369	37 103	7 539	5 345	5 639	2 019	736	1 309	35 268	818	33.7	24.4	56.8
Kendall	2 008	21 251	1 709	2 141	4 829	574	733	672	31 627	364	35.2	21.2	61.5
Knox	1 079	15 413	3 500	1 022	3 568	454	304	447	28 979	856	29.7	22.1	56.9
Lake	19 636	324 805	33 404	41 839	35 738	14 884	32 669	21 823	67 188	349	79.7	4.3	56.2
LaSalle	2 715	37 250	5 864	4 545	6 173	1 365	998	1 380	37 035	1 583	29.1	24.1	58.8
Lawrence	278	3 416	611	627	366	296	49	121	35 536	379	36.4	26.4	58.8
Lee	712	10 140	2 171	2 969	1 257	327	273	386	38 078	835	28.0	26.7	55.2
Livingston	879	11 604	2 087	3 158	1 620	404	228	414	35 707	1 349	25.2	31.9	62.9
Logan	601	7 477	1 551	1 002	1 062	302	168	234	31 236	779	32.6	31.2	54.8
McDonough	680	9 442	1 868	1 545	1 567	356	250	272	28 832	740	26.9	23.9	58.4
McHenry	7 693	84 168	10 310	15 842	14 825	2 497	3 191	3 444	40 915	911	52.3	13.0	62.5
McLean	3 730	77 572	8 513	3 993	9 395	22 541	2 938	3 872	49 915	1 489	30.2	29.0	55.6
Macon	2 456	46 406	7 968	7 758	5 775	1 415	1 239	1 876	40 430	674	35.9	29.5	59.1
Macoupin	913	8 536	1 527	589	1 357	491	139	271	31 765	1 190	29.9	19.6	48.7
Madison	5 856	83 255	13 883	12 552	12 237	3 063	3 493	3 329	39 986	1 110	45.2	15.1	41.9
Marion	924	10 863	2 905	2 500	1 321	373	261	379	34 909	1 152	36.4	11.8	44.1
Marshall	280	2 752	477	731	322	124	D	92	33 512	440	20.9	29.3	58.0
Mason	295	2 377	D	D	428	140	D	79	33 174	490	25.5	33.9	58.4
Massac	229	3 279	761	D	312	99	35	129	39 277	412	39.8	11.7	40.5
Menard	216	1 248	77	35	305	D	78	37	29 745	369	37.4	26.8	56.9
Mercer	280	2 441	455	621	360	129	28	74	30 488	715	32.2	21.1	59.3
Monroe	788	8 083	879	329	1 429	349	624	261	32 298	563	39.6	20.2	43.9
Montgomery	707	7 262	1 387	826	1 489	402	185	234	32 245	1 021	31.5	22.8	48.1
Morgan	843	12 331	2 470	1 612	1 804	987	627	403	32 647	757	31.0	26.0	62.1
Moultrie	320	4 928	786	D	347	129	66	169	34 386	553	45.8	20.3	55.3
Ogle	1 056	12 693	1 541	3 448	1 361	509	D	524	41 258	1 148	36.8	19.5	52.3
Peoria	4 567	108 908	21 444	8 015	10 860	3 809	5 870	5 982	54 924	917	35.2	16.5	49.9
Perry	424	4 380	920	D	738	167	58	134	30 684	560	30.7	19.5	43.0
Piatt	335	2 133	191	D	433	171	99	66	31 012	426	28.6	35.2	58.2
Pike	375	2 995	568	164	598	230	D	89	29 599	970	24.8	23.1	55.6
Pope	53	245	104	D	50	D	7	5	18 469	349	20.9	9.7	35.5
Pulaski	98	652	D	NA	111	41	D	17	26 078	230	30.4	20.0	34.8
Putnam	131	1 089	D	370	118	45	D	55	50 721	183	25.7	16.4	46.4
Randolph	677	10 556	2 166	2 803	1 360	301	229	361	34 178	793	27.9	17.7	47.7
Richland	461	5 183	1 009	483	659	177	99	172	33 096	554	41.5	19.3	37.9
Rock Island	3 263	63 252	9 381	9 122	7 887	2 791	3 065	3 162	49 989	666	41.3	11.9	50.3
St. Clair	5 325	77 072	15 148	4 712	13 184	2 403	5 281	2 774	35 995	732	38.4	21.2	47.4
Saline	583	7 199	1 665	344	1 244	350	170	284	39 502	483	40.4	14.9	37.5
Sangamon	5 074	81 996	20 979	2 717	12 257	7 095	4 327	3 242	39 538	1 092	41.4	20.0	50.5
Schuyler	155	1 201	D	D	D	D	27	38	31 483	542	24.0	16.6	35.2
Scott	84	577	D	150	76	52	8	21	35 735	356	29.5	23.0	43.8
Shelby	444	4 035	600	1 055	596	200	227	130	32 181	1 282	32.9	19.9	51.6
Stark	117	998	D	233	156	81	D	35	34 573	348	29.0	33.0	62.4
Stephenson	1 087	15 212	2 387	3 070	1 980	1 299	454	586	38 494	1 087	36.0	17.7	56.9
Tazewell	2 799	44 972	5 259	8 544	6 893	D	1 180	1 654	36 790	942	36.5	22.7	49.8
Union	342	3 382	1 268	D	682	141	73	88	26 143	623	35.8	6.9	37.4
Vermilion	1 460	23 526	5 001	5 043	3 518	1 417	407	887	37 693	956	36.6	29.5	54.5
Wabash	267	2 824	831	210	315	101	137	101	35 884	213	29.6	25.4	52.1
Warren	353	5 693	D	1 976	594	199	83	159	27 859	605	25.8	32.2	59.2
Washington	385	4 671	D	D	543	165	109	174	37 194	777	27.0	26.9	50.7
Wayne	378	3 472	913	D	634	126	71	100	30 599	1 187	34.5	13.6	34.5
White	381	3 410	660	D	506	D	78	123	36 007	582	35.6	19.6	38.3
Whiteside	1 244	17 674	3 212	4 027	2 742	556	335	609	34 454	1 110	33.4	20.4	50.5
Will	14 384	204 956	24 132	19 707	28 121	4 781	9 473	8 308	40 535	882	55.8	15.4	54.8
Williamson	1 595	22 792	6 019	2 203	3 675	1 456	623	797	34 961	702	44.7	6.1	39.6

STATE County	Agriculture, 2012 (cont.)															
	Land in farms					Value of land and buildings (dollars)			Value of products sold				Percent of farms with sales of:		Government payments	
			Acres								Percent from:					
	Acreage (1,000)	Percent change, 2007–2012	Average size of farm	Total irrigated (1,000)	Total cropland (1,000)	Average per farm	Average per acre	Value of machinery and equipment, average per farm (dollars)	Total (mil dol)	Average per farm (dollars)	Crops	Live-stock and poultry products	$10,000 or more	$100,000 or more	Total ($1,000)	Percent of farms
	117	118	119	120	121	122	123	124	125	126	127	128	129	130	131	132
ILLINOIS—Cont'd																
Hardin	33	-4.4	221	0.0	16.8	782 720	3 536	68 840	4.0	26 513	D	D	27.3	5.3	288	48.7
Henderson	172	0.7	433	10.9	141.7	2 681 811	6 190	237 106	138.4	349 467	84.8	15.2	70.2	51.5	3 974	81.8
Henry	479	-2.2	349	8.7	436.8	2 384 519	6 831	226 993	397.9	289 824	79.6	20.4	62.6	42.4	11 930	78.6
Iroquois	669	-1.3	455	3.1	638.2	3 096 555	6 801	256 896	493.5	335 710	86.4	13.6	72.0	50.5	15 428	87.8
Jackson	214	-4.6	274	1.5	172.9	1 077 216	3 938	144 249	67.4	86 087	87.9	12.1	34.6	13.9	2 883	59.9
Jasper	251	3.0	276	D	218.2	1 396 085	5 066	154 589	159.3	175 074	46.9	53.1	51.3	27.3	11 040	87.4
Jefferson	214	-8.0	201	0.3	172.5	725 120	3 604	102 292	60.2	56 591	81.3	18.7	34.2	11.9	3 775	69.3
Jersey	155	-17.9	305	0.0	126.1	1 800 929	5 896	165 061	69.2	135 959	94.7	5.3	50.5	27.7	2 589	73.5
Jo Daviess	272	-3.4	291	0.1	190.2	1 411 296	4 855	151 134	154.1	164 857	54.0	46.0	50.8	27.4	8 935	79.9
Johnson	90	-10.7	161	0.1	48.2	485 810	3 022	71 670	12.1	21 685	70.6	29.4	23.8	4.3	1 747	52.7
Kane	169	-12.4	286	1.8	154.3	2 535 083	8 874	199 881	196.2	332 464	84.1	15.9	60.7	37.1	4 322	45.3
Kankakee	343	-11.2	419	14.6	327.9	2 769 373	6 612	264 800	287.5	351 460	90.2	9.8	71.8	48.5	5 827	76.5
Kendall	130	-22.3	356	D	123.6	3 094 407	8 682	229 712	103.0	283 091	83.8	16.2	70.6	42.0	1 986	69.2
Knox	348	-4.2	406	0.0	288.7	2 788 956	6 868	193 379	293.1	342 459	80.2	19.8	56.2	34.7	8 091	74.6
Lake	30	-13.0	86	0.5	22.0	894 759	10 396	88 287	35.4	101 544	72.6	27.4	43.0	14.6	272	9.2
LaSalle	602	-6.4	380	5.0	569.0	3 001 877	7 890	247 122	459.3	290 132	94.7	5.3	71.4	48.3	10 769	78.8
Lawrence	184	-5.1	486	13.6	169.3	2 378 997	4 897	257 005	101.5	267 902	71.6	28.4	53.3	34.3	4 542	76.5
Lee	369	-6.7	442	25.4	348.9	3 344 959	7 568	293 399	361.0	432 352	86.7	13.3	67.9	51.7	8 885	81.8
Livingston	656	4.4	486	0.4	632.1	3 496 319	7 187	280 713	409.6	303 664	81.4	18.6	76.6	52.2	11 676	85.5
Logan	363	13.4	466	1.1	343.0	3 349 367	7 182	250 374	240.0	308 109	91.0	9.0	62.3	43.9	8 215	85.5
McDonough	292	-5.1	395	0.1	253.5	2 773 084	7 027	210 159	209.2	282 639	88.7	11.3	60.7	38.9	6 739	76.5
McHenry	234	8.6	257	11.2	212.6	2 074 731	8 070	177 105	182.4	200 256	83.6	16.4	51.0	27.6	4 732	38.1
McLean	692	2.4	465	1.6	653.9	3 803 046	8 180	297 883	501.0	336 465	88.6	11.4	69.4	47.8	13 140	81.7
Macon	337	15.8	499	0.0	321.7	3 911 432	7 833	294 921	211.3	313 540	95.7	4.3	66.0	42.7	5 762	80.1
Macoupin	439	11.3	369	0.0	371.0	2 291 757	6 218	186 864	221.8	186 369	81.3	18.7	53.4	31.9	8 416	79.0
Madison	307	-1.9	277	2.4	276.5	1 765 512	6 381	184 861	141.7	127 692	87.3	12.7	54.8	23.8	4 518	60.8
Marion	267	2.4	232	0.2	216.9	972 948	4 201	103 237	68.8	59 693	75.6	24.4	28.0	12.7	5 884	82.6
Marshall	209	2.2	475	2.2	183.7	3 290 455	6 924	274 420	136.1	309 418	96.2	3.8	71.8	51.4	4 416	85.7
Mason	290	6.0	592	102.3	265.5	3 458 004	5 846	344 157	201.2	410 545	88.7	11.3	63.9	43.9	5 881	84.1
Massac	102	14.0	248	6.1	83.3	887 687	3 577	115 689	39.5	95 782	81.8	18.2	37.6	15.3	2 256	66.7
Menard	158	-6.4	428	4.3	139.9	2 703 653	6 324	240 477	84.6	229 138	94.3	5.7	52.0	35.2	2 978	77.8
Mercer	252	-17.7	352	7.9	212.3	2 139 906	6 072	196 516	216.9	303 290	82.2	17.8	55.5	38.0	6 391	78.2
Monroe	193	8.5	343	3.8	167.7	1 777 323	5 179	209 716	111.7	198 455	81.0	19.0	50.1	31.3	2 792	68.0
Montgomery	382	10.0	375	D	346.7	2 230 784	5 956	197 314	227.3	222 582	78.6	21.4	54.9	34.3	7 252	80.6
Morgan	309	-3.5	408	3.8	272.3	2 729 232	6 683	232 711	201.9	266 663	86.0	14.0	60.2	38.8	5 870	78.1
Moultrie	205	22.2	371	0.0	194.2	2 849 613	7 687	206 665	130.7	236 318	94.8	5.2	58.8	34.7	3 550	59.1
Ogle	376	2.7	328	1.1	335.9	2 273 063	6 932	209 389	323.7	281 925	76.4	23.6	58.5	37.7	9 746	69.3
Peoria	250	-3.4	273	3.2	211.1	1 888 508	6 920	163 937	187.4	204 315	87.3	12.7	60.5	32.5	4 738	64.6
Perry	181	-9.8	323	0.2	143.9	1 313 157	4 071	168 170	45.4	81 054	88.6	11.4	43.6	22.5	2 310	78.9
Piatt	259	-3.1	608	1.0	251.4	5 262 390	8 654	359 110	187.0	438 925	98.2	1.8	70.9	50.9	4 294	81.9
Pike	411	5.6	424	1.7	310.2	2 085 246	4 916	160 991	232.2	239 381	65.5	34.5	51.5	26.9	9 067	79.0
Pope	78	28.3	223	0.3	43.6	582 077	2 605	67 040	12.7	36 364	81.0	19.0	25.5	8.0	1 251	66.2
Pulaski	82	-18.8	357	1.2	64.7	1 436 774	4 022	155 809	28.3	123 191	95.4	4.6	30.9	17.0	1 604	72.2
Putnam	60	-4.1	329	1.0	52.3	2 068 290	6 294	239 754	81.7	446 224	97.1	2.9	61.2	41.5	1 727	84.7
Randolph	279	10.1	351	1.1	228.0	1 566 426	4 459	174 168	104.4	131 629	89.1	10.9	53.0	26.6	4 034	73.4
Richland	189	-6.9	341	D	167.3	1 498 597	4 395	160 653	81.4	146 910	53.9	46.1	42.8	20.0	5 909	82.1
Rock Island	149	-16.5	224	4.0	119.6	1 396 574	6 235	141 845	101.4	152 303	88.7	11.3	50.6	28.4	3 369	66.8
St. Clair	252	-17.8	344	0.5	227.4	2 173 104	6 314	225 559	119.2	162 816	89.3	10.7	56.8	33.1	4 174	69.4
Saline	140	19.3	290	0.0	117.7	1 221 402	4 218	137 004	58.7	121 449	65.7	34.3	35.0	17.8	1 878	68.1
Sangamon	514	-0.8	471	1.0	475.8	3 468 062	7 367	270 515	358.4	328 162	93.9	6.1	50.6	34.0	9 359	72.4
Schuyler	182	-12.2	336	1.7	124.6	1 470 393	4 377	119 697	78.4	144 705	67.2	32.8	43.4	19.2	3 899	85.2
Scott	148	8.7	414	7.0	122.8	2 412 295	5 821	232 750	89.2	250 511	85.6	14.4	57.0	30.9	2 904	79.5
Shelby	406	4.8	317	0.0	362.7	1 910 895	6 037	175 446	214.3	167 165	82.0	18.0	54.7	29.4	8 301	76.5
Stark	168	-1.0	483	D	159.5	3 592 802	7 437	309 853	133.0	382 089	94.4	5.6	68.1	53.2	3 634	85.1
Stephenson	352	4.3	324	0.0	315.8	2 205 409	6 801	208 247	313.2	288 094	57.7	42.3	58.5	36.4	9 449	73.2
Tazewell	337	2.5	358	38.5	304.0	2 664 259	7 439	207 022	263.7	279 942	88.7	11.3	59.3	41.7	6 853	77.5
Union	121	-1.0	194	0.8	79.3	689 525	3 545	81 409	33.9	54 413	91.2	8.8	30.2	6.3	2 516	58.4
Vermilion	434	-5.0	454	0.2	409.5	3 200 276	7 043	259 283	283.6	296 653	95.7	4.3	60.4	41.8	7 122	76.2
Wabash	106	-6.9	500	1.1	94.4	2 653 826	5 311	244 742	43.5	204 188	95.3	4.7	49.3	33.3	1 690	77.9
Warren	338	14.8	559	8.0	306.0	3 871 392	6 921	290 898	274.6	453 820	87.1	12.9	74.9	51.7	6 194	77.4
Washington	355	0.3	457	0.6	325.7	2 366 162	5 180	263 172	144.8	186 342	65.5	34.5	62.9	35.8	6 187	85.5
Wayne	369	10.6	310	2.9	318.7	1 387 644	4 470	115 500	150.3	126 600	70.1	29.9	32.3	17.0	7 260	85.2
White	311	4.7	534	15.2	275.1	2 394 223	4 482	260 127	130.9	224 912	94.5	5.5	41.4	23.9	4 491	79.7
Whiteside	403	-0.5	363	57.4	370.0	2 485 254	6 841	238 705	435.7	392 487	77.4	22.6	62.8	42.4	11 400	78.3
Will	234	6.1	266	1.5	221.2	2 080 146	7 832	185 451	169.1	191 723	94.2	5.8	54.6	29.3	3 639	53.4
Williamson	103	9.9	147	0.0	72.1	649 405	4 408	74 148	22.5	32 031	74.2	25.8	24.6	6.1	1 392	46.7

STATE County	Water use, 2010		Wholesale trade,[1] 2007				Retail trade,[2] 2007				Real estate and rental and leasing,[2] 2007			
	Total water withdrawn (mil gal/day)	Gallons withdrawn per person per day	Number of establish-ments	Number of employees	Sales (mil dol)	Annual payroll (mil dol)	Number of establish-ments	Number of employees	Sales (mil dol)	Annual payroll (mil dol)	Number of establish-ments	Number of employees	Receipts (mil dol)	Annual payroll (mil dol)
	133	134	135	136	137	138	139	140	141	142	143	144	145	146
ILLINOIS—Cont'd														
Hardin	1.3	306	NA	NA	NA	NA	11	70	14.4	1.1	2	D	D	D
Henderson	9.1	1 240	10	D	D	D	18	103	26.1	1.7	2	D	D	D
Henry	7.8	155	60	D	D	D	200	2 173	477.6	45.0	32	74	5.8	1.1
Iroquois	5.7	191	50	463	614.9	16.1	99	964	265.4	20.4	18	46	6.8	1.2
Jackson	70.3	1 167	26	D	D	D	244	3 759	684.1	66.9	76	381	38.6	6.6
Jasper	660.1	68 062	16	142	257.2	4.9	34	282	82.6	5.2	4	D	D	D
Jefferson	1.3	34	49	D	D	D	190	2 262	567.6	50.1	28	101	13.5	3.1
Jersey	4.0	174	24	D	D	D	76	978	250.3	21.2	13	24	2.9	0.4
Jo Daviess	7.7	341	21	107	120.5	4.7	145	1 060	310.7	21.6	29	63	11.5	1.6
Johnson	1.6	130	7	40	16.7	1.0	36	272	65.5	5.3	4	D	D	D
Kane	65.8	128	775	10 899	9 589.6	620.8	1 624	25 240	5 688.3	543.7	502	2 803	430.3	89.0
Kankakee	26.8	236	116	D	D	D	389	5 737	1 258.5	118.1	105	342	63.5	9.5
Kendall	12.5	109	63	1 164	1 299.8	44.8	243	4 360	1 064.0	106.6	67	195	25.4	4.3
Knox	1.9	36	50	D	D	D	206	3 653	681.4	67.7	36	148	19.4	2.8
Lake	657.3	934	1 121	26 870	26 053.3	2 054.7	2 530	44 334	20 336.3	1 407.1	846	3 956	1 082.2	213.0
LaSalle	110.6	971	131	1 577	1 208.2	59.7	478	6 904	1 739.9	149.9	103	692	76.2	22.4
Lawrence	16.9	1 003	12	220	82.7	8.3	46	432	81.7	8.7	8	16	1.4	0.2
Lee	15.8	439	31	D	D	D	118	1 421	366.5	31.4	32	162	13.2	2.9
Livingston	7.6	196	51	D	D	D	152	1 841	396.5	34.8	21	61	5.4	1.3
Logan	13.5	446	43	D	D	D	109	1 234	275.5	24.4	29	105	12.2	2.3
McDonough	3.9	120	22	D	D	D	142	1 657	338.1	32.0	26	85	14.5	2.3
McHenry	35.2	114	438	4 815	2 391.2	251.9	979	15 034	3 578.6	331.8	295	1 358	178.3	39.0
McLean	14.5	85	174	2 701	5 309.3	149.1	608	9 660	2 231.4	197.0	153	934	139.2	24.9
Macon	39.4	356	113	D	D	D	432	6 231	1 450.6	132.5	91	454	64.6	12.6
Macoupin	6.2	129	49	610	350.4	24.5	160	1 464	326.0	31.8	24	96	6.1	1.8
Madison	404.8	1 503	231	2 470	1 643.6	113.7	906	12 733	3 104.2	285.8	241	1 284	158.5	32.3
Marion	4.1	104	39	D	D	D	168	1 434	345.7	30.7	29	D	D	D
Marshall	3.3	259	17	D	D	D	42	329	78.5	6.1	6	D	D	D
Mason	98.6	6 722	19	206	192.3	8.1	48	453	98.8	7.3	3	5	1.1	0.1
Massac	665.5	43 134	9	D	D	D	44	287	75.9	6.5	5	D	D	D
Menard	2.0	158	14	113	128.7	4.3	33	352	68.9	5.6	8	58	9.5	0.5
Mercer	3.2	195	16	D	D	D	45	405	85.3	7.8	4	6	0.5	0.1
Monroe	3.3	100	22	D	D	D	105	1 395	405.7	35.1	37	123	13.0	2.9
Montgomery	478.7	15 901	41	312	254.3	13.0	138	1 647	401.5	34.2	19	58	5.2	1.1
Morgan	109.6	3 084	45	697	425.5	23.5	162	1 984	403.1	37.0	24	D	D	D
Moultrie	1.8	119	15	86	95.2	3.5	48	480	118.7	9.3	4	D	D	D
Ogle	66.2	1 237	44	D	D	D	151	1 587	454.3	30.1	45	120	13.0	2.4
Peoria	535.9	2 873	226	3 127	1 609.8	147.5	786	11 618	2 425.9	241.0	230	1 167	194.6	31.7
Perry	2.1	93	8	53	42.9	1.7	58	650	168.3	13.9	7	26	1.6	0.3
Piatt	5.8	344	27	237	263.9	10.1	44	496	118.8	10.7	7	40	1.7	0.5
Pike	14.6	890	21	171	265.3	6.1	56	551	136.5	10.5	8	24	2.5	0.4
Pope	0.1	16	NA	NA	NA	NA	11	60	9.2	0.9	1	D	D	D
Pulaski	0.7	117	5	D	D	D	18	96	31.8	1.9	1	D	D	D
Putnam	200.4	33 370	8	D	D	D	14	112	21.7	1.8	1	D	D	D
Randolph	37.1	1 109	32	422	166.4	17.3	116	1 472	332.3	31.0	14	34	3.0	0.7
Richland	3.0	184	22	382	250.3	11.6	70	756	161.5	15.2	8	D	D	D
Rock Island	1 140.0	7 726	163	3 145	1 437.5	131.4	545	8 158	1 711.4	174.9	136	615	96.1	14.1
St. Clair	20.7	77	182	1 800	1 661.6	72.9	976	13 864	3 087.2	299.7	245	1 167	153.2	33.2
Saline	2.6	103	16	D	D	D	120	1 214	271.2	26.0	13	70	6.0	1.4
Sangamon	323.6	1 639	192	2 763	1 841.3	109.2	809	12 446	2 862.6	250.1	227	1 011	153.5	24.6
Schuyler	1.5	192	3	D	D	D	37	285	53.1	6.1	4	D	D	D
Scott	7.9	1 466	2	D	D	D	12	119	34.9	2.3	1	D	D	D
Shelby	4.0	177	27	184	157.3	6.0	72	549	140.9	9.6	11	27	1.7	0.4
Stark	0.8	140	10	D	D	D	19	174	57.3	5.5	1	D	D	D
Stephenson	8.3	174	46	D	D	D	167	2 045	480.6	42.4	37	105	11.6	2.5
Tazewell	98.9	731	134	1 946	1 225.1	86.6	455	6 798	1 758.1	156.7	85	321	55.1	8.9
Union	4.0	224	8	64	20.5	2.0	70	678	145.1	14.2	14	42	4.4	0.9
Vermilion	14.0	171	77	D	D	D	281	3 443	757.9	68.5	59	254	34.3	6.6
Wabash	4.5	379	12	143	89.5	4.5	43	496	109.2	8.4	5	20	1.8	0.4
Warren	3.4	189	20	281	219.8	10.1	66	634	133.7	11.5	8	19	1.7	0.3
Washington	4.0	273	31	482	270.5	18.8	65	610	197.3	15.4	14	30	1.4	0.2
Wayne	7.0	415	16	128	126.6	6.2	68	645	140.0	12.4	8	22	1.9	0.5
White	23.4	1 594	26	280	400.3	8.9	59	491	123.1	10.0	10	49	4.9	1.4
Whiteside	24.3	415	64	431	926.8	16.7	222	2 823	570.6	57.2	47	179	16.4	3.2
Will	2 363.1	3 488	699	12 694	11 061.8	636.9	1 654	28 627	6 841.5	624.0	530	2 767	424.1	80.9
Williamson	216.9	3 269	58	D	D	D	308	3 900	987.5	84.7	61	242	43.7	9.5

1. Merchant wholesalers, except manufacturers' sales branches and offices. 2. Employer establishments.

STATE County	Professional, scientific, and technical services,[1] 2007				Manufacturing, 2007				Accommodation and food services, 2007			
	Number of establish-ments	Number of employees	Receipts (mil dol)	Annual payroll (mil dol)	Number of establish-ments	Number of employees	Receipts (mil dol)	Annual payroll (mil dol)	Number of establish-ments	Number of employees	Sales (mil dol)	Annual payroll (mil dol)
	147	148	149	150	151	152	153	154	155	156	157	158
ILLINOIS—Cont'd												
Hardin	4	D	D	D	NA	NA	NA	NA	7	32	1.0	0.3
Henderson	6	24	1.5	0.4	NA	NA	NA	NA	20	57	1.9	0.5
Henry	67	D	D	D	57	4 272	D	D	97	1 119	42.0	10.4
Iroquois	29	111	8.9	3.6	30	880	338.7	24.3	64	539	20.8	5.6
Jackson	119	D	D	D	31	716	177.4	D	155	3 138	108.3	31.2
Jasper	9	22	1.7	0.6	NA	NA	NA	NA	13	110	3.2	0.8
Jefferson	71	471	39.8	17.1	36	D	D	D	82	1 650	67.8	19.3
Jersey	27	163	13.2	6.0	NA	NA	NA	NA	59	749	26.7	7.4
Jo Daviess	54	184	26.7	8.1	36	1 106	419.5	42.8	101	1 730	81.3	22.7
Johnson	16	361	9.9	3.6	NA	NA	NA	NA	16	163	6.8	1.8
Kane	1 522	D	D	D	885	34 075	9 879.5	1 552.1	904	15 459	680.9	201.2
Kankakee	169	D	D	D	115	5 633	3 418.9	280.8	229	D	D	D
Kendall	169	D	D	D	84	2 766	685.7	D	152	2 153	99.9	25.7
Knox	65	D	D	D	40	D	D	D	132	1 800	68.3	19.1
Lake	3 021	D	D	D	922	49 414	16 381.5	3 717.8	1 492	24 968	1 299.3	365.8
LaSalle	181	D	D	D	155	5 964	2 244.0	274.7	322	4 263	158.6	44.1
Lawrence	19	77	7.8	2.6	12	D	D	D	22	D	D	D
Lee	46	271	26.3	10.7	43	4 115	1 098.2	145.9	89	884	35.0	8.8
Livingston	59	302	24.5	10.9	55	4 021	1 261.5	188.0	79	898	38.3	9.5
Logan	42	177	13.7	5.2	20	1 329	631.6	51.7	73	844	30.4	9.4
McDonough	42	D	D	D	22	1 369	248.8	49.9	107	1 598	52.8	13.5
McHenry	973	3 730	488.0	167.7	576	21 462	5 291.2	958.4	539	8 438	365.6	104.5
McLean	338	D	D	D	115	5 497	2 578.8	270.5	375	8 558	336.1	97.4
Macon	181	1 185	125.8	51.1	112	8 762	9 590.8	409.4	219	4 733	170.9	52.0
Macoupin	55	471	40.2	18.2	40	704	180.4	25.2	84	786	26.1	6.5
Madison	528	D	D	D	213	13 490	18 978.2	769.9	596	10 249	382.7	111.6
Marion	63	232	15.0	6.6	56	2 930	689.7	113.5	88	1 016	36.8	9.9
Marshall	13	D	D	D	21	1 045	D	D	30	345	9.2	2.7
Mason	12	34	3.0	0.8	NA	NA	NA	NA	36	279	10.4	2.5
Massac	12	D	D	D	6	514	D	D	27	D	D	D
Menard	14	77	4.9	1.5	NA	NA	NA	NA	22	185	6.9	1.5
Mercer	13	D	D	D	NA	NA	NA	NA	20	222	5.6	1.8
Monroe	75	766	82.7	43.1	NA	NA	NA	NA	66	971	35.9	10.7
Montgomery	37	217	16.7	5.1	28	1 081	305.6	40.1	74	992	36.4	10.8
Morgan	50	D	D	D	34	2 349	D	D	88	1 248	44.4	13.0
Moultrie	19	100	8.6	3.6	31	1 777	541.2	70.0	19	D	D	D
Ogle	81	729	46.1	21.1	68	4 590	1 137.6	192.5	108	1 140	43.4	11.8
Peoria	426	D	D	D	165	11 683	4 951.3	502.0	486	8 169	343.1	99.3
Perry	21	93	6.2	2.6	19	831	369.0	30.9	34	526	15.4	4.5
Piatt	34	119	8.9	3.9	NA	NA	NA	NA	31	299	10.0	2.7
Pike	18	67	8.1	2.0	NA	NA	NA	NA	40	434	13.7	3.7
Pope	3	D	D	D	NA	NA	NA	NA	10	26	1.2	0.2
Pulaski	NA	NA	NA	NA	NA	NA	NA	NA	9	D	D	D
Putnam	6	D	D	D	10	613	D	D	13	59	2.3	0.5
Randolph	39	201	22.8	5.5	34	3 104	532.2	80.7	74	800	26.8	7.0
Richland	27	84	9.2	3.1	32	543	94.6	17.4	31	357	14.2	3.7
Rock Island	297	D	D	D	166	7 961	3 714.3	395.9	364	5 853	224.2	64.9
St. Clair	514	D	D	D	181	5 788	2 324.5	245.6	564	11 181	615.4	149.4
Saline	48	223	27.0	7.3	27	501	92.4	D	45	833	28.3	7.5
Sangamon	580	4 649	562.7	228.8	117	D	D	D	521	9 265	366.8	110.7
Schuyler	9	19	1.2	0.4	NA	NA	NA	NA	14	D	D	D
Scott	3	D	D	D	NA	NA	NA	NA	9	33	1.7	0.4
Shelby	24	164	15.4	6.3	18	1 163	D	44.9	38	364	14.1	4.1
Stark	14	D	D	D	NA	NA	NA	NA	8	40	1.4	0.3
Stephenson	76	460	48.5	17.0	57	3 631	905.1	168.4	95	1 192	44.8	13.6
Tazewell	183	1 197	106.3	47.0	121	9 985	5 145.7	395.7	334	6 334	353.9	83.9
Union	24	91	9.8	4.7	11	584	176.1	21.0	29	314	10.0	4.0
Vermilion	93	396	44.7	12.9	100	5 458	2 576.4	239.7	156	2 370	85.0	24.6
Wabash	21	108	11.0	3.7	NA	NA	NA	NA	21	301	10.2	2.9
Warren	20	D	D	D	21	D	D	D	29	414	14.3	4.0
Washington	21	97	16.2	6.1	17	1 983	409.2	73.5	37	313	12.3	2.9
Wayne	23	54	4.6	1.1	17	D	D	D	26	D	D	D
White	20	80	5.3	1.4	NA	NA	NA	NA	26	338	11.4	3.2
Whiteside	73	583	128.8	24.9	103	3 985	1 022.5	178.9	119	1 647	60.6	16.4
Will	1 516	D	D	D	642	22 470	13 628.2	1 098.3	1 029	20 905	1 404.9	308.1
Williamson	128	D	D	D	50	1 863	681.4	72.1	145	2 588	118.6	31.0

1. Establishment subject to federal tax.

Table B. States and Counties — **Health Care and Social Assistance, Other Services, Nonemployer Businesses, and Residential Construction**

STATE County	Health care and social assistance, 2007				Other services, 2007				Nonemployer businesses, 2013		Value of residential construction authorized by building permits, 2014	
	Number of establish-ments	Number of employees	Receipts (mil dol)	Annual payroll (mil dol)	Number of establish-ments	Number of employees	Receipts (mil dol)	Annual payroll (mil dol)	Number	Receipts (mil dol)	New Construction ($1,000)	Number of housing units
	159	160	161	162	163	164	165	166	167	168	169	170
ILLINOIS—Cont'd												
Hardin	11	311	17.9	8.9	3	D	D	D	242	6.0	0	0
Henderson	8	D	D	D	5	D	D	D	394	15.7	564	6
Henry	87	1 421	116.2	43.3	96	640	48.8	11.7	2 815	91.7	8 247	43
Iroquois	78	1 648	93.3	42.0	52	148	15.0	3.8	2 161	71.3	4 491	28
Jackson	161	3 872	370.4	127.7	96	436	42.6	7.3	3 149	105.9	16 260	130
Jasper	15	130	5.9	2.3	23	89	5.7	1.2	838	29.7	0	0
Jefferson	139	3 158	316.6	118.3	88	391	26.6	8.1	2 331	94.0	896	7
Jersey	37	D	D	D	33	126	5.6	1.5	1 307	39.8	3 832	25
Jo Daviess	41	615	32.0	15.4	58	277	19.9	5.5	1 991	76.1	7 057	28
Johnson	20	192	9.4	3.9	10	D	D	D	729	20.9	0	0
Kane	1 068	20 650	2 107.5	861.5	849	5 753	583.3	165.6	31 570	1 358.7	223 886	1 283
Kankakee	290	6 260	618.8	228.6	193	1 080	105.7	26.6	6 232	207.4	23 395	127
Kendall	128	1 021	95.7	35.6	148	767	55.4	16.9	7 348	272.4	51 749	283
Knox	143	4 266	356.7	134.4	83	621	204.5	15.2	2 337	67.6	6 709	27
Lake	1 818	30 953	3 380.3	1 372.6	1 246	8 449	787.7	218.6	52 367	2 777.9	286 680	1 341
LaSalle	277	5 599	404.0	164.3	249	1 337	87.7	25.5	5 827	199.5	22 745	147
Lawrence	27	713	33.8	13.4	28	153	16.5	3.7	809	30.3	7 245	42
Lee	87	2 082	161.8	71.7	64	338	25.1	7.8	1 935	66.3	13 477	21
Livingston	67	1 622	123.6	50.2	77	321	29.4	7.2	1 969	59.0	4 722	22
Logan	59	1 296	91.4	33.5	55	222	16.6	3.3	1 436	44.8	3 660	13
McDonough	83	1 816	120.0	52.5	72	265	17.8	4.6	1 570	52.0	1 488	8
McHenry	667	10 348	1 013.9	409.5	561	3 226	240.5	75.1	21 914	912.7	91 487	558
McLean	333	8 693	875.8	354.5	260	2 362	187.8	59.7	9 321	371.7	43 042	246
Macon	282	7 449	750.1	281.3	197	1 526	222.4	33.5	5 900	180.0	9 541	53
Macoupin	96	1 761	96.0	39.1	80	276	23.7	5.6	2 553	79.9	9 802	47
Madison	655	12 765	1 066.8	412.7	479	3 210	273.5	80.8	14 059	503.2	104 868	525
Marion	113	2 852	210.8	80.0	77	279	20.3	5.3	2 139	75.1	0	0
Marshall	22	D	D	D	21	D	D	D	628	22.1	235	1
Mason	27	460	28.2	12.8	27	88	7.3	1.4	727	26.8	195	1
Massac	31	628	40.7	16.7	28	150	8.3	3.0	809	24.3	140	2
Menard	15	D	D	D	19	61	4.8	1.2	806	23.5	4 714	24
Mercer	27	369	21.7	9.4	23	65	7.3	1.5	930	33.8	1 180	6
Monroe	70	793	45.2	19.2	68	292	23.6	6.6	2 116	79.4	31 205	118
Montgomery	75	1 538	111.7	41.8	57	220	17.2	4.6	1 558	45.7	4 674	24
Morgan	125	D	D	D	66	273	17.1	5.0	1 971	67.5	468	2
Moultrie	30	721	33.9	15.5	23	66	6.6	1.7	1 018	38.5	3 577	40
Ogle	92	1 424	86.4	34.5	80	346	28.1	7.8	3 326	110.2	6 204	38
Peoria	536	20 744	2 106.8	883.9	338	3 786	332.4	141.5	9 452	349.8	43 854	174
Perry	44	1 018	61.6	24.8	50	162	13.3	2.6	1 053	34.1	9 737	50
Piatt	29	D	D	D	19	70	4.2	0.9	1 090	36.5	5 256	20
Pike	31	585	41.0	15.6	29	103	7.8	1.7	1 075	39.1	2 854	20
Pope	13	143	4.9	2.5	4	D	D	D	206	6.6	0	0
Pulaski	14	184	6.6	2.8	14	37	5.0	0.7	323	9.1	450	3
Putnam	4	20	1.0	0.3	6	17	1.2	0.3	365	13.3	1 740	13
Randolph	73	2 120	147.9	69.0	66	248	17.0	5.7	1 471	51.3	5 237	21
Richland	48	945	60.5	26.1	44	187	13.3	3.7	1 149	44.3	1 230	4
Rock Island	397	9 031	742.0	324.9	263	1 765	152.2	44.1	6 652	238.7	43 906	241
St. Clair	620	14 718	1 246.8	517.7	439	2 502	196.7	60.3	14 000	434.9	125 354	762
Saline	62	2 059	116.0	53.1	53	D	D	D	1 528	58.1	0	0
Sangamon	462	D	D	D	482	3 494	382.6	108.4	12 256	455.1	83 436	431
Schuyler	15	345	20.3	8.4	13	39	6.0	0.7	486	16.0	NA	NA
Scott	5	D	D	D	5	14	2.2	0.3	309	9.9	NA	NA
Shelby	37	683	43.3	16.3	27	96	7.8	1.8	1 299	42.1	4 849	32
Stark	7	D	D	D	3	D	D	D	357	13.8	718	3
Stephenson	104	2 586	208.5	88.9	98	594	30.6	9.9	2 958	96.5	3 231	8
Tazewell	238	5 102	335.4	135.1	252	1 270	109.9	32.3	6 333	222.9	152 361	637
Union	53	1 156	47.5	22.0	20	71	5.3	1.5	1 076	38.1	1 986	13
Vermilion	149	4 729	437.7	203.4	138	780	54.8	14.5	4 382	137.8	922	6
Wabash	28	733	42.2	16.6	23	D	D	D	837	31.6	400	1
Warren	44	732	33.5	13.4	34	112	11.3	1.9	874	32.0	1 422	6
Washington	26	489	26.2	12.1	28	101	5.8	1.4	1 009	35.9	4 011	20
Wayne	32	727	41.8	18.5	28	112	0.1	2.0	1 259	42.2	270	1
White	38	536	25.7	10.2	34	141	16.1	3.9	1 187	50.9	131	1
Whiteside	112	3 834	248.3	104.9	135	695	71.1	14.2	2 802	94.2	4 041	19
Will	1 127	18 527	1 782.4	714.9	1 013	6 548	638.9	169.8	43 952	1 865.4	299 452	1 185
Williamson	210	5 288	539.0	197.2	102	472	44.1	10.8	4 286	148.3	16 995	115

STATE County	Government employment and payroll, 2012									Local government finances, 2012				
			March payroll (percent of total)							General revenue				
												Taxes		
													Per capita[1] (dollars)	
	Full-time equivalent employees	March payroll (dollars)	Adminis-tration, judicial, and legal	Police and Corrections	Fire Protection	Highways and transpor-tation	Health and Welfare	Natural resources and utilities	Education and libraries	Total (mil dol)	Inter-govern-mental (mil dol)	Total (mil dol)	Total	Property
	171	172	173	174	175	176	177	178	179	180	181	182	183	184
ILLINOIS—Cont'd														
Hardin	285	791 768	2.8	3.0	0.0	56.6	0.9	4.7	31.7	16.6	13.4	1.6	384	331
Henderson	266	806 748	8.3	7.3	0.3	7.4	10.9	2.4	62.8	21.4	9.7	7.4	1 047	1 030
Henry	1 997	6 801 070	4.9	8.8	1.9	3.9	16.2	5.8	57.8	199.6	66.8	68.8	1 372	1 289
Iroquois	1 017	3 877 441	5.9	6.3	0.5	4.2	0.4	1.9	79.8	90.3	38.3	39.1	1 337	1 242
Jackson	2 101	6 263 626	8.2	10.9	3.5	4.0	8.7	8.4	55.9	187.5	83.7	70.9	1 181	879
Jasper	379	1 198 050	10.1	7.5	0.4	7.8	10.7	3.7	59.8	34.3	16.7	13.8	1 437	1 424
Jefferson	1 638	5 345 187	5.0	7.6	2.9	4.0	1.2	3.6	74.9	147.2	83.4	43.3	1 119	882
Jersey	837	3 076 248	4.5	7.9	0.3	2.8	30.8	3.6	48.9	78.3	24.9	21.1	926	828
Jo Daviess	997	3 300 597	8.1	8.4	0.4	5.4	17.9	2.0	56.6	94.9	21.9	52.5	2 329	2 191
Johnson	372	1 081 737	6.4	5.0	0.0	5.0	0.2	4.9	77.4	26.5	15.8	7.0	547	545
Kane	21 805	101 252 430	5.2	10.1	5.2	2.0	0.9	6.8	68.3	2 745.0	798.1	1 591.7	3 046	2 837
Kankakee	4 413	16 356 166	7.8	13.5	3.6	3.7	1.5	3.4	65.4	441.9	208.0	169.2	1 496	1 433
Kendall	3 451	14 665 867	5.1	10.4	5.3	1.3	0.8	4.9	71.6	446.4	125.8	268.8	2 276	2 192
Knox	2 362	8 240 583	5.2	9.0	3.0	3.3	7.4	6.1	64.9	191.6	87.1	68.2	1 306	1 155
Lake	27 930	134 406 176	5.8	8.4	4.0	2.3	3.7	6.6	68.5	3 687.1	912.8	2 300.4	3 276	3 089
LaSalle	4 146	16 025 437	6.1	10.7	2.6	3.3	2.5	3.9	69.6	433.1	147.6	217.8	1 928	1 756
Lawrence	525	1 443 702	5.9	7.2	0.3	7.5	2.8	3.7	71.9	44.1	29.2	8.7	523	515
Lee	1 249	4 093 940	7.1	9.2	4.8	4.5	2.0	3.9	68.0	116.7	37.8	58.8	1 677	1 531
Livingston	1 564	5 591 107	6.4	8.8	1.4	4.2	3.1	3.6	72.0	146.1	52.6	67.2	1 738	1 641
Logan	897	2 996 965	7.7	10.0	3.8	5.0	4.3	2.9	65.3	74.1	29.9	31.4	1 045	1 003
McDonough	1 625	5 796 187	4.2	7.7	1.7	2.8	51.0	3.4	28.6	163.5	47.6	32.0	983	944
McHenry	11 260	47 454 823	5.9	10.6	5.0	2.9	2.6	5.6	65.8	1 313.1	295.8	821.5	2 666	2 473
McLean	6 296	24 583 518	6.5	10.3	4.7	4.3	5.2	5.3	61.6	657.7	182.2	354.7	2 059	1 702
Macon	4 204	17 133 160	5.9	11.8	4.5	3.0	2.0	8.2	63.3	407.1	180.7	163.9	1 488	1 260
Macoupin	1 579	5 464 855	7.7	8.5	0.5	3.9	2.1	5.6	71.2	159.2	103.8	40.1	850	818
Madison	8 550	34 777 691	7.6	11.4	3.9	3.8	1.5	6.9	63.4	966.9	418.8	400.7	1 496	1 338
Marion	1 941	6 738 024	6.0	6.5	2.0	6.9	1.1	4.0	73.0	188.6	94.3	42.9	1 104	1 038
Marshall	389	1 147 988	11.1	7.9	0.1	5.9	0.0	3.3	70.7	32.3	9.0	19.1	1 547	1 484
Mason	923	2 905 218	5.6	6.6	1.1	4.1	31.2	2.1	49.0	70.8	24.6	21.1	1 473	1 402
Massac	642	2 312 058	4.9	5.8	3.7	5.1	27.2	5.6	47.5	66.0	26.3	12.5	822	786
Menard	629	1 816 714	5.1	6.6	0.0	3.4	18.6	6.4	58.9	48.9	20.5	18.4	1 447	1 400
Mercer	808	2 500 408	4.4	7.5	0.1	4.2	27.9	2.7	52.0	60.4	20.7	22.0	1 356	1 324
Monroe	1 183	4 219 452	6.0	6.8	0.1	3.0	9.8	5.0	68.2	102.0	27.3	50.1	1 503	1 423
Montgomery	1 039	3 506 922	6.9	10.8	2.5	5.7	5.0	6.3	61.4	82.3	39.4	28.5	963	919
Morgan	1 212	4 876 454	5.8	9.2	2.8	3.7	1.9	5.1	70.1	101.9	48.0	40.0	1 135	1 038
Moultrie	521	1 796 777	7.8	7.6	2.7	4.3	1.3	9.1	66.3	36.7	14.6	17.0	1 135	1 079
Ogle	2 397	8 623 161	5.6	8.6	3.0	3.7	0.9	6.5	71.3	242.2	66.1	126.2	2 388	2 325
Peoria	6 795	26 829 973	7.0	12.3	5.0	5.9	4.2	8.9	54.4	819.7	356.0	319.4	1 706	1 383
Perry	777	2 700 659	4.7	8.5	1.5	3.8	27.6	5.4	47.3	84.4	42.3	13.8	627	594
Piatt	763	2 418 221	6.8	10.0	0.5	5.3	14.9	3.4	57.7	66.5	26.6	26.9	1 631	1 599
Pike	558	1 854 503	4.9	7.2	0.0	8.0	4.7	8.8	66.1	46.6	23.4	15.2	932	910
Pope	138	448 003	20.0	12.1	0.0	2.4	0.2	11.1	54.2	9.3	5.8	2.3	545	536
Pulaski	327	899 884	7.1	8.9	0.0	20.1	0.0	3.3	59.6	25.7	17.3	2.4	395	366
Putnam	225	602 290	16.8	7.7	4.2	6.1	0.0	5.9	58.5	21.9	11.9	8.0	1 357	1 315
Randolph	1 307	4 546 917	4.9	6.9	0.2	2.7	38.8	4.6	41.3	133.8	44.5	27.5	833	774
Richland	975	3 144 076	4.3	4.3	0.6	2.4	0.2	3.1	84.3	57.1	27.3	13.0	807	742
Rock Island	5 596	23 551 782	5.9	9.4	3.6	6.1	4.6	7.6	61.4	620.9	245.3	250.9	1 701	1 489
St. Clair	9 810	39 541 919	4.8	9.2	1.9	2.6	2.2	3.8	73.7	1 194.0	627.0	382.0	1 421	1 216
Saline	1 108	4 428 993	4.7	6.7	0.9	2.6	0.3	6.0	77.8	90.8	50.3	23.2	930	837
Sangamon	8 380	36 468 884	5.0	9.4	3.8	4.6	1.2	19.7	56.0	774.9	316.2	329.5	1 654	1 429
Schuyler	476	1 475 450	5.3	4.7	0.2	4.4	42.6	3.1	38.9	44.3	11.9	8.0	1 069	1 046
Scott	279	678 856	8.7	3.5	0.5	4.1	18.9	5.6	57.3	16.8	8.0	4.6	873	829
Shelby	598	1 947 657	9.5	8.9	1.8	7.6	2.8	6.4	62.1	47.8	23.5	17.9	808	790
Stark	247	745 997	7.9	3.6	5.2	4.9	5.8	1.4	71.0	24.8	11.5	10.9	1 837	1 825
Stephenson	2 084	7 077 197	4.5	9.2	3.6	2.9	5.4	4.5	68.9	190.9	85.0	73.4	1 563	1 449
Tazewell	4 864	18 067 473	5.1	9.0	3.1	2.4	2.6	4.8	70.8	521.3	190.4	225.1	1 655	1 450
Union	758	2 771 148	9.5	6.1	0.8	5.1	0.0	5.2	72.8	60.0	30.9	17.9	1 015	992
Vermilion	3 642	12 242 579	7.0	7.8	2.7	3.5	3.6	4.2	67.9	289.5	151.8	91.4	1 132	940
Wabash	629	2 227 140	2.9	4.6	1.3	1.8	48.4	3.1	37.5	63.3	16.1	9.7	830	795
Warren	522	1 914 920	7.4	10.5	4.1	3.6	0.2	4.0	69.9	49.1	22.4	18.5	1 044	1 001
Washington	568	1 952 729	6.8	5.6	0.6	5.3	31.1	4.1	46.3	61.8	13.6	15.4	1 056	1 044
Wayne	680	1 956 742	7.1	7.6	1.1	3.6	2.2	8.9	66.5	46.0	28.5	12.0	724	652
White	705	2 274 585	7.3	7.6	0.6	4.7	1.6	8.1	69.3	49.9	30.9	10.9	747	707
Whiteside	3 387	13 850 341	3.2	4.6	1.2	1.9	52.6	3.0	32.7	404.5	88.0	74.4	1 287	1 222
Will	22 376	101 738 743	4.7	11.4	5.8	2.2	2.7	5.6	66.5	2 654.5	767.6	1 489.2	2 182	2 004
Williamson	2 123	8 108 041	5.1	8.0	3.0	3.7	0.5	5.2	72.9	224.1	117.2	75.8	1 137	974

1. Based on the resident population estimated as of July 1 of the year shown.

STATE County	Local government finances, 2012 (cont.) — Direct general expenditure: Total (mil dol)	Per capita[1] (dollars)	Percent of total for: Education	Health and hospitals	Police protection	Public welfare	Highways	Debt outstanding: Total (mil dol)	Per capita[1] (dollars)	Government employment, 2013: Federal civilian	Federal military	State and local	Presidential election,[2] 2012 — Percent of vote cast: Democratic	Republican	All other
	185	186	187	188	189	190	191	192	193	194	195	196	197	198	199
ILLINOIS—Cont'd															
Hardin	9.4	2 219	53.6	4.3	2.9	0.3	6.9	3.9	917	0	0	229	39.6	59.0	1.5
Henderson	23.7	3 370	36.9	8.9	3.5	0.0	12.3	3.3	465	39	14	371	58.1	40.4	1.5
Henry	218.5	4 357	39.3	20.6	5.2	2.4	5.6	98.2	1 957	114	99	3 546	53.2	45.4	1.4
Iroquois	91.6	3 132	53.4	3.1	3.5	0.1	7.9	32.1	1 098	99	58	1 645	34.1	64.0	1.9
Jackson	186.2	3 100	49.6	4.1	7.0	4.9	4.5	96.1	1 600	187	121	12 208	59.7	37.9	2.3
Jasper	35.9	3 739	55.0	4.2	2.9	0.1	13.9	9.9	1 031	41	19	575	40.2	57.8	2.0
Jefferson	141.2	3 647	60.3	0.7	5.4	0.0	6.2	65.0	1 679	143	75	2 522	43.5	54.3	2.2
Jersey	88.3	3 885	32.7	37.7	3.8	0.1	7.5	73.1	3 212	39	44	1 120	47.6	50.4	2.0
Jo Daviess	84.9	3 767	44.0	15.8	6.1	0.0	11.0	34.5	1 528	65	45	1 321	54.5	44.0	1.5
Johnson	27.3	2 141	60.1	1.3	4.1	0.1	8.6	19.6	1 535	72	22	815	31.7	66.3	2.0
Kane	2 646.1	5 064	55.1	0.4	6.5	0.1	5.6	4 427.4	8 474	1 611	1 047	29 126	55.2	43.4	1.3
Kankakee	442.3	3 912	52.1	0.7	6.1	0.1	5.9	327.2	2 894	229	217	6 182	51.5	46.9	1.5
Kendall	434.1	3 676	60.8	0.5	5.2	0.9	3.7	902.1	7 638	113	241	5 554	53.1	45.8	1.1
Knox	198.6	3 801	51.6	1.5	5.0	4.2	8.6	156.9	3 002	165	97	3 406	59.2	39.3	1.6
Lake	3 519.2	5 012	56.6	2.1	5.9	0.6	4.2	3 079.5	4 386	5 603	13 427	36 959	59.3	39.6	1.1
LaSalle	473.9	4 195	57.8	1.3	5.1	1.1	6.6	284.6	2 520	339	222	6 154	54.7	43.6	1.7
Lawrence	51.2	3 083	63.6	1.4	3.9	0.1	9.0	34.7	2 091	44	28	847	46.1	52.1	1.8
Lee	113.4	3 238	58.0	1.7	5.2	0.1	7.1	71.5	2 040	75	66	1 943	47.6	50.6	1.8
Livingston	169.3	4 381	47.9	3.0	3.8	0.2	5.0	65.3	1 689	102	70	2 346	39.6	58.8	1.6
Logan	71.3	2 376	51.1	5.0	5.4	0.1	7.6	26.9	895	100	52	1 422	40.7	57.6	1.7
McDonough	169.8	5 218	27.4	39.5	3.7	3.4	9.6	21.4	657	95	60	5 753	52.0	46.4	1.6
McHenry	1 256.5	4 078	49.3	2.2	6.5	1.2	7.2	1 209.9	3 926	478	618	15 014	51.9	46.6	1.5
McLean	663.9	3 853	46.3	1.2	4.8	1.3	5.4	781.5	4 536	525	336	14 887	49.8	48.5	1.7
Macon	452.8	4 112	52.8	2.0	7.8	0.1	8.1	462.5	4 200	324	224	5 565	49.8	48.7	1.5
Macoupin	129.5	2 741	63.8	2.0	7.1	0.2	7.8	66.0	1 397	118	93	2 246	54.0	44.2	1.8
Madison	939.6	3 507	50.9	0.8	6.8	1.6	6.8	839.9	3 135	543	538	15 930	53.7	44.6	1.7
Marion	186.5	4 794	59.6	11.4	3.2	0.2	3.5	110.6	2 844	126	77	2 132	48.1	50.1	1.9
Marshall	33.3	2 698	45.3	2.0	5.5	0.1	16.2	9.4	759	34	24	499	48.6	49.7	1.7
Mason	72.0	5 027	41.2	33.1	3.0	0.0	4.5	27.4	1 914	53	28	1 099	52.0	46.1	1.8
Massac	63.9	4 197	33.1	34.0	4.6	0.0	6.8	35.3	2 315	47	30	932	37.5	60.8	1.7
Menard	46.5	3 652	52.7	4.5	4.3	13.7	7.4	27.0	2 121	28	25	669	41.9	56.8	1.3
Mercer	59.7	3 679	42.8	21.8	3.5	0.1	6.2	15.9	978	58	32	809	55.2	43.3	1.4
Monroe	99.7	2 990	44.6	3.1	5.8	10.1	10.9	136.3	4 085	70	67	1 421	44.0	54.6	1.4
Montgomery	84.4	2 851	51.5	3.4	7.1	0.1	10.4	52.7	1 779	99	55	1 538	50.4	47.8	1.8
Morgan	103.7	2 940	52.8	1.6	5.8	3.3	9.0	36.7	1 040	83	65	2 306	48.6	49.4	1.9
Moultrie	39.7	2 658	46.1	1.8	4.8	0.0	9.9	11.4	763	30	29	510	42.6	55.4	1.9
Ogle	280.5	5 307	64.6	0.8	3.1	0.0	5.5	269.6	5 101	117	105	2 966	45.3	52.9	1.8
Peoria	776.9	4 149	41.7	1.1	6.6	3.2	6.5	850.1	4 540	1 617	444	9 500	56.2	42.3	1.5
Perry	91.6	4 151	51.3	22.3	3.7	0.2	4.4	32.0	1 453	46	39	1 263	47.0	50.9	2.1
Piatt	65.0	3 940	47.2	2.6	3.6	12.4	9.9	36.4	2 205	38	33	992	42.9	55.5	1.7
Pike	48.7	2 986	53.6	6.0	6.0	0.3	9.7	27.7	1 701	61	31	924	39.7	58.5	1.8
Pope	9.6	2 241	48.1	0.0	2.7	0.0	16.4	0.3	64	74	0	202	37.9	60.2	1.9
Pulaski	23.9	3 981	59.8	1.8	6.4	0.3	6.2	12.7	2 118	66	12	795	50.1	48.7	1.2
Putnam	21.7	3 688	43.8	2.5	4.8	0.3	13.3	3.0	508	22	12	314	56.9	41.3	1.8
Randolph	140.7	4 269	35.0	36.0	4.5	2.8	6.9	54.6	1 657	92	58	2 451	48.6	49.6	1.8
Richland	75.7	4 677	78.3	0.4	3.6	0.1	5.2	28.2	1 746	49	32	992	41.6	56.6	1.8
Rock Island	636.7	4 318	45.3	1.1	6.6	3.0	5.2	418.1	2 835	5 339	713	7 880	61.7	37.1	1.2
St. Clair	1 159.8	4 314	54.3	1.3	5.1	0.1	4.2	908.3	3 378	6 327	5 244	13 233	60.6	38.1	1.3
Saline	95.1	3 814	54.7	1.0	5.6	0.6	5.5	54.8	2 197	100	49	1 892	44.5	53.4	2.2
Sangamon	823.4	4 132	52.9	1.4	7.6	0.2	4.4	2 513.3	12 612	1 837	440	18 851	51.4	47.0	1.6
Schuyler	47.2	6 325	29.5	48.7	2.2	0.1	10.2	10.5	1 403	25	14	661	49.7	47.9	2.4
Scott	17.4	3 281	46.2	2.2	3.3	13.9	8.8	6.2	1 174	16	10	306	41.9	56.0	2.1
Shelby	50.5	2 273	53.6	3.0	5.5	0.1	12.8	14.9	670	97	44	847	39.1	58.9	2.1
Stark	18.9	3 183	55.8	0.5	5.0	0.5	11.8	11.4	1 922	23	12	325	46.7	52.0	1.3
Stephenson	184.9	3 937	57.2	2.4	4.7	3.3	6.3	98.3	2 092	131	93	2 890	52.5	45.9	1.6
Tazewell	547.5	4 028	52.3	1.6	5.5	0.1	6.4	349.0	2 567	510	270	7 303	46.0	52.1	1.9
Union	60.8	3 445	72.9	2.7	4.1	0.0	5.3	53.7	3 042	57	34	1 171	43.0	54.9	2.1
Vermilion	308.3	3 819	56.4	0.7	6.4	3.5	6.3	102.1	1 265	1 535	156	4 360	49.4	48.8	1.7
Wabash	60.5	5 156	29.5	47.7	4.0	0.5	5.0	14.7	1 254	28	23	1 080	42.6	56.3	1.1
Warren	53.0	2 987	53.6	0.4	5.3	0.0	6.7	45.8	2 584	64	34	827	53.4	45.3	1.3
Washington	72.8	4 985	42.5	34.2	2.5	0.1	6.1	55.0	3 766	47	29	853	42.1	56.4	1.5
Wayne	47.3	2 854	59.1	1.9	4.8	0.1	9.4	21.3	1 285	55	33	900	31.0	66.8	1.7
White	56.9	3 908	63.4	1.7	4.0	0.1	9.2	23.5	1 610	49	29	800	44.5	53.5	2.0
Whiteside	392.0	6 777	27.5	52.5	2.6	0.2	2.3	129.8	2 244	147	114	4 729	58.0	40.4	1.5
Will	2 568.4	3 763	52.2	1.6	6.9	0.8	5.1	3 781.8	5 541	931	1 375	33 641	56.0	42.8	1.2
Williamson	279.8	4 196	65.4	0.0	3.9	0.1	4.9	229.8	3 447	1 667	132	4 141	41.9	56.4	1.7

1. Based on the resident population estimated as of July 1 of the year shown. 2.

STATE/ County code	CBSA code[1]	County type[2]	STATE County	Land area,[3] (sq km) 2010	Population, 2014: Total persons 2014	Population, 2014: Rank	Population, 2014: Per square kilometer	Race alone or in combination, not Hispanic or Latino (percent): White	Black	American Indian, Alaska Native	Asian and Pacific Islander	Percent Hispanic or Latino[4]	Age (percent): Under 5 years	5 to 17 years	18 to 24 years	25 to 34 years	35 to 44 years	45 to 54 years
				1	2	3	4	5	6	7	8	9	10	11	12	13	14	15
			ILLINOIS—Cont'd															
17 201	40420	2	Winnebago	1 330	288 542	234	216.9	73.2	13.5	0.6	3.0	11.7	6.3	17.8	8.7	12.2	12.4	14.1
17 203	37900	2	Woodford	1 367	39 187	1 190	28.7	96.9	1.1	0.5	0.9	1.7	6.3	18.6	8.8	10.6	11.8	14.2
18 000	...	X	INDIANA	92 789	6 596 855	X	71.1	82.2	10.1	0.7	2.3	6.4	6.4	17.7	10.1	12.8	12.6	13.8
18 001	19540	6	Adams	878	34 791	1 307	39.6	94.8	0.7	0.4	0.4	4.4	9.1	22.0	8.8	11.2	11.0	12.1
18 003	23060	2	Allen	1 702	365 918	184	215.0	77.8	13.4	0.8	3.7	6.9	7.2	19.1	9.4	13.3	12.7	13.2
18 005	18020	3	Bartholomew	1 054	80 217	691	76.1	86.2	2.8	0.6	5.4	6.4	6.5	17.8	8.4	13.4	13.3	13.5
18 007	29200	3	Benton	1 053	8 700	2 541	8.3	93.4	1.1	0.5	0.4	5.5	6.4	18.4	7.9	11.3	11.9	15.0
18 009	...	6	Blackford	428	12 401	2 270	29.0	97.4	1.2	0.8	0.6	1.5	6.1	16.3	7.9	10.2	11.7	14.2
18 011	26900	1	Boone	1 095	61 915	843	56.5	93.7	1.8	0.5	2.7	2.5	6.5	20.7	7.5	11.1	13.8	15.7
18 013	26900	1	Brown	808	14 962	2 104	18.5	97.2	0.9	1.0	0.7	1.4	4.2	15.3	6.7	8.6	11.0	15.1
18 015	29200	3	Carroll	964	19 923	1 840	20.7	95.2	0.8	0.5	0.3	4.0	5.1	18.5	8.0	10.1	12.4	14.4
18 017	30900	4	Cass	1 067	38 438	1 209	36.0	83.3	2.0	0.6	1.5	13.6	6.5	18.0	8.4	11.5	12.6	14.0
18 019	31140	1	Clark	966	114 262	534	118.3	86.5	8.4	0.7	1.5	5.1	6.3	16.8	8.1	13.9	13.7	14.2
18 021	45460	3	Clay	926	26 562	1 545	28.7	97.5	1.0	0.6	0.5	1.2	6.0	17.3	8.2	11.8	12.5	14.1
18 023	23140	6	Clinton	1 049	32 776	1 363	31.2	84.6	0.8	0.5	0.3	14.5	6.5	19.5	8.2	11.9	12.2	13.7
18 025	...	8	Crawford	792	10 655	2 384	13.5	97.3	0.8	0.8	0.5	1.6	5.2	17.6	7.6	10.2	12.1	15.4
18 027	47780	7	Daviess	1 112	32 729	1 365	29.4	93.8	1.2	0.5	0.8	4.6	8.4	20.9	8.9	11.9	11.2	12.5
18 029	17140	1	Dearborn	790	49 506	988	62.7	97.3	1.1	0.5	0.7	1.2	5.6	18.4	7.9	10.7	12.8	15.7
18 031	24700	6	Decatur	965	26 524	1 547	27.5	96.4	0.7	0.5	1.4	1.8	6.2	18.8	8.4	11.8	12.4	14.4
18 033	12140	4	DeKalb	940	42 383	1 121	45.1	96.1	0.9	0.5	0.7	2.7	6.2	19.1	8.4	11.5	12.6	14.6
18 035	34620	3	Delaware	1 016	117 074	522	115.2	89.5	8.1	0.7	1.7	2.0	5.2	14.0	20.1	10.9	10.5	12.0
18 037	27540	7	Dubois	1 107	42 345	1 122	38.3	92.5	0.6	0.3	0.6	6.5	6.2	18.3	7.8	11.5	11.9	15.3
18 039	21140	3	Elkhart	1 200	201 971	319	168.3	78.1	6.9	0.7	1.4	14.9	7.5	20.5	8.9	12.7	12.7	13.0
18 041	18220	7	Fayette	557	23 468	1 663	42.1	96.9	2.0	0.5	0.5	1.1	5.5	17.6	7.7	10.5	13.0	13.5
18 043	31140	1	Floyd	383	76 179	722	198.9	90.6	6.3	0.7	1.5	2.9	5.8	17.4	8.9	12.3	12.8	15.0
18 045	...	6	Fountain	1 025	16 658	1 999	16.3	96.6	0.7	0.8	0.5	2.5	5.9	17.2	8.1	10.3	12.1	14.6
18 047	...	1	Franklin	996	22 934	1 689	23.0	98.2	0.5	0.5	0.4	1.1	5.6	19.3	7.9	10.2	12.7	15.1
18 049	...	7	Fulton	954	20 500	1 801	21.5	93.4	1.3	0.7	0.8	4.8	5.9	18.0	7.9	10.9	12.0	13.9
18 051	...	2	Gibson	1 263	33 759	1 334	26.7	95.9	3.0	0.6	0.7	1.5	6.3	17.2	8.6	11.6	12.1	14.3
18 053	31980	4	Grant	1 072	68 569	778	64.0	87.9	8.3	0.8	1.1	4.0	5.7	15.4	13.6	10.3	11.0	13.3
18 055	...	3	Greene	1 405	32 726	1 366	23.3	97.8	0.5	0.8	0.6	1.2	5.6	17.4	7.7	10.9	12.0	14.9
18 057	26900	1	Hamilton	1 021	302 623	221	296.4	86.8	4.5	0.4	6.2	3.7	7.1	21.9	6.8	12.5	15.8	15.2
18 059	26900	1	Hancock	793	71 978	752	90.8	94.7	2.6	0.6	1.3	2.0	5.7	19.2	7.6	11.2	13.4	15.5
18 061	31140	1	Harrison	1 255	39 299	1 188	31.3	97.0	0.9	0.7	0.7	1.7	5.5	17.2	7.7	11.8	12.6	15.4
18 063	26900	1	Hendricks	1 054	156 056	407	148.1	88.3	6.4	0.5	2.9	3.4	6.4	20.0	7.8	12.7	14.8	14.8
18 065	35220	4	Henry	1 015	48 995	998	48.3	95.2	3.1	0.6	0.7	1.6	4.9	16.2	8.3	11.2	13.0	15.0
18 067	29020	3	Howard	759	82 982	675	109.3	88.6	8.5	0.9	1.5	2.9	6.0	17.0	8.2	11.3	12.0	14.2
18 069	26540	6	Huntington	991	36 706	1 259	37.0	96.6	0.8	0.7	0.8	2.0	5.6	16.9	10.1	11.7	11.9	14.5
18 071	42980	4	Jackson	1 319	43 705	1 096	33.1	91.3	1.3	0.7	1.6	6.2	6.5	17.6	8.1	12.7	13.1	14.1
18 073	16980	1	Jasper	1 449	33 475	1 340	23.1	92.8	1.2	0.5	0.6	5.7	6.0	18.9	9.5	10.8	12.4	14.3
18 075	...	6	Jay	994	21 179	1 764	21.3	96.1	0.6	0.5	0.7	2.9	7.1	19.0	8.4	10.9	11.9	13.7
18 077	31500	6	Jefferson	934	32 494	1 375	34.8	94.7	2.5	0.6	1.0	2.4	5.3	15.9	10.5	11.6	12.5	14.8
18 079	35860	6	Jennings	975	28 000	1 492	28.7	96.4	1.3	0.6	0.5	2.3	6.2	18.7	8.8	10.8	13.3	15.3
18 081	26900	1	Johnson	830	147 538	437	177.8	92.4	2.2	0.6	2.7	3.4	6.6	19.2	8.5	12.8	13.7	14.1
18 083	47180	4	Knox	1 337	37 938	1 223	28.4	94.4	3.5	0.6	1.0	1.8	5.8	15.2	13.9	11.8	10.5	13.3
18 085	47700	4	Kosciusko	1 376	78 564	703	57.1	89.9	1.3	0.6	1.4	7.8	6.5	18.4	9.2	12.3	12.1	13.8
18 087	...	6	LaGrange	983	38 436	1 210	39.1	95.2	0.6	0.4	0.6	3.8	9.5	24.3	9.0	11.6	11.2	11.3
18 089	16980	1	Lake	1 292	490 228	138	379.4	56.0	25.3	0.6	1.7	17.8	6.4	18.4	9.1	12.4	12.5	13.9
18 091	33140	3	LaPorte	1 550	111 444	540	71.9	82.3	12.1	0.7	0.9	5.9	6.0	16.2	8.6	13.1	12.6	14.3
18 093	13260	4	Lawrence	1 163	45 704	1 055	39.3	97.0	0.8	0.9	0.8	1.5	5.5	17.0	7.6	10.9	12.4	14.6
18 095	26900	3	Madison	1 170	130 069	478	111.2	87.3	9.3	0.6	0.8	3.6	5.8	16.5	9.0	12.4	12.8	13.9
18 097	26900	1	Marion	1 026	934 243	53	910.6	60.5	28.6	0.8	3.0	9.7	7.5	17.4	9.9	16.4	12.9	13.2
18 099	38500	6	Marshall	1 149	47 107	1 028	41.0	89.3	1.0	0.6	0.8	9.3	6.5	19.4	8.4	10.9	12.0	13.9
18 101	...	6	Martin	870	10 203	2 420	11.7	98.2	0.6	0.5	0.5	0.9	5.8	17.3	7.2	11.0	11.8	15.0
18 103	37940	6	Miami	968	35 954	1 275	37.1	91.6	5.3	1.5	0.7	2.6	5.2	16.7	8.5	12.5	13.7	14.8
18 105	14020	3	Monroe	1 022	143 339	445	140.3	87.2	4.2	0.7	7.0	3.2	4.5	11.5	28.2	14.6	10.0	10.1
18 107	18820	6	Montgomery	1 307	38 146	1 216	29.2	93.5	1.5	0.6	0.9	4.7	6.2	17.0	10.0	11.1	12.1	14.3
18 109	26900	1	Morgan	1 046	69 693	767	66.6	97.2	0.9	0.7	0.8	1.4	6.0	18.2	8.1	10.9	12.7	15.7
18 111	16980	1	Newton	1 041	14 156	2 157	13.6	93.0	0.9	0.7	0.4	5.8	5.1	17.2	7.4	11.0	11.5	15.3
18 113	28340	6	Noble	1 064	47 618	1 022	44.8	88.8	0.9	0.6	0.8	9.9	6.5	19.4	8.4	11.5	12.8	14.0
18 115	17140	1	Ohio	223	6 035	2 755	27.1	97.6	0.8	0.4	0.5	1.4	4.1	15.6	6.9	10.7	12.0	16.7
18 117	...	6	Orange	1 032	19 626	1 850	19.0	97.0	1.7	0.8	0.6	1.2	5.6	18.5	7.9	10.6	12.0	14.5
18 119	14020	3	Owen	998	20 969	1 776	21.0	97.6	0.9	0.8	0.7	1.2	5.0	17.1	7.7	10.1	11.8	16.2
18 121	...	6	Parke	1 152	17 233	1 967	15.0	95.5	2.9	0.6	0.3	1.3	5.8	15.6	8.3	12.5	12.1	15.0
18 123	...	6	Perry	989	19 454	1 854	19.7	95.1	3.3	0.5	0.6	1.3	5.7	15.3	8.3	13.3	12.7	14.5

1. CBSA = Core Based Statistical Area. See Appendix A for explanation. See Appendix B for list of metropolitan areas with component counties. 2. County type code from the Economic Research Service of USDA Rural-Urban Continuum Codes. See Appendix A for definition. 3. Dry land or land partially or temporarily covered by water. 4. May be of any race.

STATE County	Population, 2013 (cont.): Age (percent) (cont.): 55 to 64 years	65 to 74 years	75 years and over	Percent female	Population change and components of change, 2000–2014: Total persons: 2000	2010	Percent change: 2000–2010	2010–2014	Components of change, 2010–2014: Births	Deaths	Net migration	Households, 2009–2013: Number	Persons per household	Percent: Family households	Female family householder[1]	One person
	16	17	18	19	20	21	22	23	24	25	26	27	28	29	30	31
ILLINOIS—Cont'd																
Winnebago	13.1	8.4	6.8	51.2	278 418	295 266	6.1	-2.3	15 386	11 261	-10 842	113 449	2.55	65.8	14.3	29.0
Woodford	13.6	8.3	7.7	50.4	35 469	38 664	9.0	1.4	1 865	1 546	184	14 362	2.63	76.4	8.0	21.6
INDIANA	12.6	7.8	6.1	50.7	6 080 485	6 483 802	6.6	1.7	353 871	246 674	8 366	2 481 793	2.55	66.7	12.3	27.7
Adams	11.4	7.3	7.1	50.5	33 625	34 387	2.3	1.2	2 874	1 222	-1 238	12 127	2.80	71.5	8.3	25.5
Allen	12.2	7.1	5.7	51.2	331 849	355 329	7.1	3.0	22 362	12 211	798	138 212	2.55	65.5	13.0	28.7
Bartholomew	12.4	8.4	6.3	50.2	71 435	76 794	7.5	4.5	4 469	2 963	1 973	30 041	2.56	68.8	10.6	26.5
Benton	13.2	9.0	6.9	50.4	9 421	8 854	-6.0	-1.7	422	344	-202	3 444	2.53	67.8	10.1	27.8
Blackford	14.2	10.8	8.7	50.3	14 048	12 766	-9.1	-2.9	607	618	-362	5 190	2.41	69.8	12.1	26.4
Boone	12.3	6.9	5.5	50.5	46 107	56 640	22.8	9.3	3 069	1 918	3 996	21 908	2.62	73.8	9.1	21.9
Brown	18.8	13.1	7.3	50.2	14 957	15 242	1.9	-1.8	515	636	-165	5 889	2.54	70.3	10.4	25.8
Carroll	14.3	9.8	7.4	50.0	20 165	20 155	0.0	-1.2	942	740	-391	7 995	2.50	69.4	8.8	26.7
Cass	13.1	8.6	7.4	50.0	40 930	38 966	-4.8	-1.4	2 176	1 628	-1 065	14 827	2.54	68.0	11.3	27.4
Clark	13.1	8.3	5.7	50.9	96 472	110 232	14.3	3.7	6 109	4 533	2 423	42 502	2.58	66.6	12.5	27.6
Clay	13.9	9.1	7.2	50.8	26 556	26 890	1.3	-1.2	1 351	1 207	-495	10 230	2.59	71.9	9.8	23.5
Clinton	12.6	7.9	7.5	50.8	33 866	33 224	-1.9	-1.3	1 921	1 439	-952	11 745	2.76	71.6	11.1	23.7
Crawford	15.2	10.4	6.1	49.3	10 743	10 713	-0.3	-0.5	479	472	-51	4 237	2.49	68.2	11.0	28.0
Daviess	11.9	7.9	6.4	50.1	29 820	31 648	6.1	3.4	2 253	1 387	265	11 160	2.81	71.1	9.6	25.7
Dearborn	14.3	8.7	5.9	50.2	46 109	50 047	8.5	-1.1	2 259	1 838	-896	18 556	2.66	71.5	8.6	23.7
Decatur	12.9	8.2	6.8	50.7	24 555	25 740	4.8	3.0	1 355	1 048	499	9 792	2.61	69.8	11.6	26.8
DeKalb	13.2	8.2	6.2	50.4	40 285	42 223	4.8	0.4	2 102	1 581	-345	16 032	2.61	71.6	10.9	24.7
Delaware	11.6	8.6	7.1	51.8	118 769	117 671	-0.9	-0.5	5 271	4 978	-726	46 325	2.36	60.2	12.6	29.1
Dubois	13.6	8.2	7.3	50.6	39 674	41 889	5.6	1.1	2 165	1 630	-113	15 890	2.59	71.7	8.5	25.0
Elkhart	11.6	7.1	5.9	50.5	182 791	197 559	8.1	2.2	12 815	6 556	-1 749	70 130	2.78	72.5	12.4	23.5
Fayette	14.5	9.9	7.8	50.7	25 588	24 277	-5.1	-3.4	999	1 265	-539	9 536	2.48	67.8	12.4	28.4
Floyd	13.8	8.1	5.8	51.4	70 823	74 578	5.3	2.1	3 748	2 977	881	29 087	2.54	69.3	14.7	25.8
Fountain	13.2	10.0	8.7	50.1	17 954	17 240	-4.0	-3.4	752	807	-509	6 925	2.44	68.1	11.0	26.5
Franklin	14.1	8.5	6.8	49.9	22 151	23 087	4.2	-0.7	1 067	879	-314	8 551	2.67	75.5	7.5	20.3
Fulton	14.1	9.8	7.7	49.8	20 511	20 836	1.6	-1.6	1 040	1 006	-344	8 221	2.49	70.5	8.9	26.9
Gibson	13.7	8.7	7.4	50.2	32 500	33 503	3.1	0.8	1 717	1 484	32	13 094	2.50	70.0	8.5	25.4
Grant	13.4	9.5	7.9	52.2	73 403	70 061	-4.6	-2.1	3 252	3 361	-1 290	26 981	2.39	64.9	13.6	30.6
Greene	13.9	10.1	7.5	50.0	33 157	33 165	0.0	-1.3	1 511	1 612	-344	12 894	2.53	69.6	9.6	27.7
Hamilton	10.8	6.0	3.9	51.2	182 740	274 569	50.3	10.2	15 955	5 886	17 503	103 234	2.73	74.3	8.6	21.8
Hancock	13.0	8.8	5.7	50.8	55 391	70 002	26.4	2.8	3 247	2 447	1 071	26 071	2.68	74.8	11.2	21.2
Harrison	14.1	9.3	6.3	50.1	34 325	39 364	14.7	-0.2	1 699	1 530	-204	14 499	2.67	70.5	8.7	25.0
Hendricks	11.7	7.0	4.8	50.1	104 093	145 448	39.7	7.3	7 286	4 097	7 181	52 946	2.75	75.7	9.9	20.7
Henry	13.8	9.8	7.8	48.5	48 508	49 462	2.0	-0.9	1 956	2 332	-132	18 367	2.50	67.5	11.4	29.0
Howard	13.7	10.0	7.7	51.8	84 964	82 752	-2.6	0.3	4 309	3 746	-316	34 544	2.36	65.1	11.0	30.2
Huntington	13.5	8.4	7.2	50.9	38 075	37 124	-2.5	-1.1	1 785	1 654	-537	14 138	2.52	69.1	9.1	25.5
Jackson	12.7	8.6	6.7	50.2	41 335	42 376	2.5	3.1	2 414	1 837	723	16 713	2.52	68.8	11.1	26.7
Jasper	12.8	8.9	6.5	50.1	30 043	33 478	11.4	0.0	1 664	1 344	-316	11 924	2.71	76.7	8.3	21.0
Jay	12.7	9.2	7.1	50.8	21 806	21 253	-2.5	-0.3	1 277	941	-382	8 179	2.57	67.3	9.6	27.4
Jefferson	13.7	9.3	6.5	51.9	31 705	32 428	2.3	0.2	1 538	1 483	53	12 668	2.38	66.9	12.1	28.1
Jennings	12.7	9.0	5.2	49.8	27 554	28 525	3.5	-1.8	1 454	1 178	-785	10 632	2.63	68.8	12.9	26.1
Johnson	11.7	7.7	5.7	50.7	115 209	139 654	21.2	5.5	7 879	5 046	4 668	52 239	2.66	71.9	10.3	23.4
Knox	13.1	9.0	7.5	49.4	39 256	38 440	-2.1	-1.3	2 043	1 811	-694	14 738	2.40	64.7	9.9	30.8
Kosciusko	13.1	8.5	6.2	50.2	74 057	77 358	4.5	1.6	4 332	2 821	-190	29 705	2.56	71.3	9.0	24.9
LaGrange	10.7	7.5	5.0	49.6	34 909	37 128	6.4	3.5	3 184	1 088	-776	11 833	3.13	78.2	7.9	19.4
Lake	13.3	7.8	6.4	51.7	484 564	496 005	2.4	-1.2	25 807	19 694	-11 412	182 080	2.68	67.2	16.7	28.7
LaPorte	13.9	8.9	6.4	48.2	110 106	111 467	1.2	0.0	5 505	4 829	-633	42 690	2.41	65.6	12.8	29.1
Lawrence	14.2	10.2	7.5	50.5	45 922	46 134	0.5	-0.9	2 079	2 277	-188	18 592	2.44	70.8	9.9	25.3
Madison	13.0	9.3	7.3	50.1	133 358	131 636	-1.3	-1.2	6 427	6 138	-1 660	50 637	2.46	64.6	12.7	30.4
Marion	11.5	6.1	4.9	51.8	860 454	903 393	5.0	3.4	61 939	32 236	2 079	360 072	2.49	59.2	17.0	33.7
Marshall	13.2	8.4	7.3	50.4	45 128	47 051	4.3	0.1	2 491	1 858	-561	17 581	2.63	69.7	9.7	26.4
Martin	15.1	9.7	7.0	49.4	10 369	10 334	-0.3	-1.7	552	430	-264	4 146	2.45	65.3	9.6	30.8
Miami	13.2	8.9	6.4	46.4	36 082	36 903	2.3	-2.6	1 549	1 487	-1 027	13 210	2.64	68.9	10.2	26.7
Monroe	10.0	6.1	4.9	50.3	120 563	137 974	14.4	3.9	5 506	3 662	3 542	53 914	2.32	50.9	9.0	34.3
Montgomery	13.1	9.0	7.3	49.7	37 629	38 124	1.3	0.1	2 021	1 590	-334	14 590	2.53	70.3	9.0	24.8
Morgan	14.0	8.8	5.7	50.5	66 689	68 894	3.3	1.1	3 234	2 588	167	25 621	2.67	75.5	11.0	19.9
Newton	15.2	10.1	7.2	49.3	14 566	14 244	-2.2	-0.6	642	641	-64	5 374	2.60	71.8	9.4	24.6
Noble	13.2	8.1	6.0	50.1	46 275	47 536	2.7	0.2	2 480	1 885	-562	17 722	2.64	71.7	11.4	24.7
Ohio	15.0	11.7	7.3	50.3	5 623	6 128	9.0	-1.5	248	254	-105	2 422	2.40	69.3	7.8	24.9
Orange	14.1	9.8	7.0	50.6	19 306	19 840	2.8	-1.1	924	875	-236	7 688	2.54	67.8	9.7	27.4
Owen	15.5	10.5	6.2	49.8	21 786	21 575	-1.0	-2.8	911	934	-578	8 552	2.47	71.1	9.9	24.0
Parke	13.8	10.1	6.7	53.2	17 241	17 339	0.6	-0.7	844	697	-243	5 893	2.66	70.3	7.7	23.9
Perry	14.1	8.7	7.5	46.5	18 899	19 338	2.3	0.6	885	808	43	7 411	2.40	66.8	8.3	28.7

1. No spouse present.

STATE County	Persons in group quarters, 2014	Daytime population, 2009–2013		Births, 2014		Deaths, 2014		Persons under 65 with no health insurance, 2013		Medicare, 2014			Serious crimes known to police,[2] 2013	
													Total	
		Number	Employ-ment/ resi-dence ratio	Total	Rate[1]	Number	Rate[1]	Number	Percent	Eligible for Medicare	Enrolled in Medicare Advantage	Enrolled in a Medicare prescription drug plan	Number	Rate[3]
	32	33	34	35	36	37	38	39	40	41	42	43	44	45
ILLINOIS—Cont'd														
Winnebago	4 687	298 887	1.04	3 519	12.2	2 669	9.2	32 163	13.2	54 286	14 400	26 196	12 478	4 342
Woodford	1 021	31 473	0.60	441	11.3	391	10.0	2 544	7.9	6 874	1 269	3 214	357	1 041
INDIANA	189 082	6 459 613	0.98	83 206	12.6	58 212	8.8	885 240	16.1	1 133 461	254 854	594 371	211 023	3 211
Adams	421	33 737	0.95	695	20.0	252	7.2	5 541	18.8	5 496	1 987	2 808	NA	NA
Allen	6 101	372 121	1.09	5 283	14.4	2 961	8.1	53 558	17.2	58 591	24 665	25 128	12 446	3 429
Bartholomew	1 147	86 895	1.24	1 089	13.6	674	8.4	9 971	14.9	14 258	2 445	8 821	2 822	3 523
Benton	92	7 589	0.70	96	11.0	82	9.4	1 307	17.9	1 715	245	973	NA	NA
Blackford	163	11 618	0.79	136	11.0	163	13.1	1 657	16.7	3 089	554	1 831	309	2 509
Boone	574	51 397	0.77	767	12.4	453	7.3	5 688	10.9	8 835	1 954	4 612	NA	NA
Brown	163	11 730	0.50	127	8.5	136	9.1	2 079	17.5	3 670	890	1 865	97	643
Carroll	106	16 439	0.60	231	11.6	184	9.2	2 666	16.2	4 041	748	2 208	NA	NA
Cass	1 055	37 896	0.95	508	13.2	404	10.5	6 204	19.5	7 523	1 347	4 283	940	2 438
Clark	1 464	103 795	0.86	1 452	12.7	1 085	9.5	15 378	16.0	21 146	4 324	10 981	NA	NA
Clay	341	22 850	0.66	314	11.8	280	10.5	3 441	15.4	5 359	677	3 113	NA	NA
Clinton	830	30 616	0.83	481	14.7	313	9.5	5 224	19.0	6 028	936	3 403	1 216	3 679
Crawford	62	8 834	0.57	115	10.8	108	10.1	1 575	17.8	2 316	375	1 278	108	1 012
Daviess	581	30 739	0.91	536	16.4	316	9.7	5 648	20.6	5 283	422	2 908	912	2 827
Dearborn	530	41 736	0.65	525	10.6	421	8.5	5 548	13.2	9 591	2 115	4 650	NA	NA
Decatur	377	26 785	1.07	327	12.3	254	9.6	3 472	15.7	5 011	1 094	2 814	NA	NA
DeKalb	615	43 424	1.06	488	11.5	384	9.1	5 507	15.3	7 833	3 406	3 071	NA	NA
Delaware	9 139	119 008	1.03	1 226	10.5	1 159	9.9	14 921	16.4	22 784	3 564	13 713	4 023	3 422
Dubois	893	47 101	1.23	519	12.3	388	9.2	4 923	14.0	7 775	642	4 905	NA	NA
Elkhart	3 760	218 340	1.23	3 042	15.1	1 542	7.6	37 492	21.8	31 389	8 351	15 093	4 811	2 395
Fayette	392	22 558	0.82	224	9.5	271	11.5	3 293	16.9	5 821	811	3 719	NA	NA
Floyd	1 329	69 921	0.85	888	11.7	701	9.2	8 837	13.7	13 813	2 476	7 492	2 642	3 638
Fountain	172	15 187	0.74	170	10.2	182	10.9	2 053	15.0	3 786	531	2 065	NA	NA
Franklin	187	17 806	0.50	258	11.2	191	8.3	2 790	14.4	5 074	1 351	2 458	191	831
Fulton	224	18 912	0.79	248	12.1	204	10.0	3 038	18.1	4 329	1 607	1 803	NA	NA
Gibson	738	36 949	1.22	395	11.7	375	11.1	3 470	12.6	6 421	1 515	3 242	NA	NA
Grant	5 020	71 454	1.06	733	10.7	792	11.6	7 954	15.1	15 335	2 933	8 814	1 747	2 521
Greene	281	26 726	0.56	342	10.5	405	12.4	4 393	16.4	6 858	616	3 506	384	1 249
Hamilton	1 630	260 487	0.84	3 739	12.4	1 466	4.8	25 248	9.6	35 150	8 699	17 160	2 242	873
Hancock	649	57 321	0.61	771	10.7	560	7.8	7 169	11.9	12 815	3 491	6 367	804	1 127
Harrison	461	33 095	0.65	388	9.9	333	8.5	4 827	14.8	7 580	1 314	4 179	601	1 535
Hendricks	4 182	128 834	0.73	1 697	10.9	963	6.2	14 253	10.9	21 410	5 643	10 260	2 391	1 722
Henry	3 599	43 487	0.70	457	9.3	550	11.2	5 805	15.6	10 663	2 062	6 806	896	1 812
Howard	1 280	87 006	1.12	1 031	12.4	903	10.9	9 708	14.4	18 386	2 234	13 737	2 686	3 232
Huntington	1 330	34 835	0.87	429	11.7	379	10.3	4 538	15.1	7 493	3 316	3 057	426	1 150
Jackson	595	43 648	1.05	587	13.4	418	9.6	6 436	17.6	8 388	2 280	5 025	1 884	4 344
Jasper	926	30 832	0.82	388	11.6	314	9.4	3 956	14.5	6 340	760	3 805	NA	NA
Jay	243	20 320	0.89	298	14.1	223	10.5	2 934	16.5	4 367	1 107	2 163	361	1 875
Jefferson	1 963	31 818	0.95	372	11.4	335	10.3	4 298	16.8	6 774	800	4 076	NA	NA
Jennings	298	24 329	0.66	348	12.4	281	10.0	3 850	16.0	5 525	1 136	3 184	824	2 929
Johnson	2 530	121 896	0.71	1 891	12.8	1 194	8.1	15 576	12.6	23 751	5 880	11 567	4 269	2 978
Knox	2 531	39 546	1.08	498	13.1	394	10.4	4 922	16.7	7 645	580	4 589	240	681
Kosciusko	1 594	77 758	1.01	1 044	13.3	656	8.3	11 525	17.7	13 824	5 327	5 572	1 531	1 965
LaGrange	325	36 294	0.92	751	19.5	239	6.2	8 730	26.4	5 242	1 679	2 226	240	636
Lake	6 422	481 769	0.94	5 848	11.9	4 753	9.7	68 112	16.4	85 102	11 776	47 616	19 320	3 926
LaPorte	6 819	107 229	0.91	1 280	11.5	1 172	10.5	13 541	15.4	21 183	2 348	12 157	3 138	2 905
Lawrence	653	41 203	0.75	492	10.8	528	11.6	6 173	16.5	9 851	1 538	5 436	900	2 150
Madison	6 136	120 770	0.81	1 464	11.3	1 398	10.7	16 553	16.0	27 478	6 236	17 992	3 913	3 004
Marion	16 979	1 042 615	1.31	14 640	15.7	7 692	8.2	156 117	19.3	133 572	33 892	65 620	57 258	6 512
Marshall	670	45 930	0.95	583	12.4	448	9.5	7 450	18.9	8 577	2 945	3 628	564	1 196
Martin	134	13 877	1.76	136	13.3	90	8.8	1 234	14.8	2 185	182	1 095	NA	NA
Miami	3 370	31 779	0.67	353	9.8	343	9.5	4 356	15.9	6 516	1 052	3 874	376	1 031
Monroe	15 145	148 711	1.14	1 306	9.1	844	5.9	17 642	15.8	18 813	3 109	10 163	4 527	3 183
Montgomery	1 173	37 407	0.95	489	12.0	373	9.8	5 271	17.0	7 419	1 601	3 957	939	2 444
Morgan	592	54 341	0.53	738	10.6	607	8.7	8 365	14.2	13 236	2 887	7 103	NA	NA
Newton	168	11 671	0.60	153	10.8	137	9.7	1 995	17.3	2 688	330	1 532	168	1 199
Noble	813	45 178	0.89	586	12.3	432	9.1	7 619	18.9	8 220	3 433	3 215	320	670
Ohio	52	4 858	0.59	66	10.9	72	11.9	711	14.7	1 183	238	592	NA	NA
Orange	258	19 070	0.90	211	10.8	208	10.6	2 573	15.8	4 397	792	2 323	NA	NA
Owen	197	17 533	0.57	194	9.3	226	10.8	3 219	18.3	4 503	847	2 411	NA	NA
Parke	1 665	14 862	0.64	205	11.9	162	9.4	2 263	17.8	3 311	479	1 749	59	346
Perry	1 661	18 594	0.90	202	10.4	174	8.9	2 254	15.2	3 785	324	2 246	154	856

1. Per 1,000 estimated resident population. 2. Data for serious crimes have not been adjusted for underreporting; this may affect comparability between geographic areas and over time.
3. Per 100,000 population estimated by the FBI.

Table B. States and Counties — **Crime, Education, Money Income, and Poverty**

STATE County	Serious crimes known to police, 2013 (cont.)[1]: Rate[2]: Violent	Rate[2]: Property	Education: School enrollment and attainment, 2009–2013: Enrollment[3]: Total	Enrollment[3]: Percent private	Attainment[4] (percent): High school graduate or less	Attainment[4] (percent): Bachelor's degree or more	Local government expenditures,[5] 2012–2013: Total current spending (mil dol)	Current spending per student (dollars)	Money income, 2009–2013: Per capita income[6] (dollars)	Households: Median income (dollars)	Households: Mean income (dollars)	Households: Percent with income of $200,000 or more	Income and poverty, 2013: Median household income (dollars)	Percent below poverty level: All persons	Children under 18 years	Children 5 to 17 years in families
	46	47	48	49	50	51	52	53	54	55	56	57	58	59	60	61
ILLINOIS—Cont'd																
Winnebago	845	3 497	74 744	20.8	47.7	21.2	541.9	11 618	24 495	47 072	61 506	2.7	47 214	16.3	26.0	23.6
Woodford	50	991	10 723	18.0	39.1	27.6	85.3	10 690	30 926	66 639	81 828	4.5	67 036	7.0	9.3	9.0
INDIANA	357	2 854	1 748 724	16.4	48.0	23.2	9 658.7	9 566	24 635	48 248	62 988	2.6	47 508	15.8	21.9	20.0
Adams	NA	NA	8 953	29.1	59.1	14.7	45.9	10 451	20 160	46 695	56 982	1.7	48 001	15.5	28.6	27.9
Allen	303	3 126	102 162	21.3	41.2	26.3	495.5	9 289	25 279	49 370	64 359	2.6	45 587	17.0	24.8	22.8
Bartholomew	185	3 338	19 941	14.3	45.9	26.5	112.6	9 142	27 359	54 165	69 369	3.3	54 341	11.6	16.5	15.4
Benton	NA	NA	2 102	13.4	57.9	16.0	18.6	10 064	23 049	48 711	58 250	0.9	49 318	11.9	18.4	16.8
Blackford	57	2 452	2 730	5.5	64.8	9.8	16.8	9 299	20 322	39 225	49 741	0.9	39 373	15.4	25.1	23.6
Boone	NA	NA	15 959	13.5	34.8	41.0	105.1	9 347	37 482	67 255	98 989	10.2	68 047	7.3	8.7	7.8
Brown	13	630	3 239	7.5	51.4	21.1	23.6	11 569	25 833	51 568	63 457	1.7	51 074	13.4	19.9	18.0
Carroll	NA	NA	4 825	13.8	54.0	16.0	21.9	8 032	24 531	50 542	60 718	1.7	52 587	10.9	15.9	14.1
Cass	70	2 368	9 677	8.3	59.8	13.7	69.8	10 648	21 700	41 940	55 509	1.8	41 611	13.8	21.2	19.7
Clark	NA	NA	26 222	14.5	49.2	18.9	151.9	9 217	24 312	50 496	60 836	1.7	50 296	11.7	18.4	16.1
Clay	NA	NA	6 179	10.6	58.0	14.0	38.9	8 824	21 474	46 430	55 760	1.0	47 030	15.0	22.7	20.5
Clinton	157	3 521	7 953	9.4	62.4	13.0	58.3	9 435	21 554	48 953	58 130	1.3	47 279	14.4	20.6	18.1
Crawford	122	890	2 290	11.4	66.7	12.1	17.2	11 164	20 504	39 700	49 750	0.8	38 014	19.3	30.4	26.1
Daviess	170	2 656	7 363	22.5	63.6	12.4	42.4	9 825	21 416	47 165	59 051	1.6	45 578	13.9	23.5	22.0
Dearborn	NA	NA	12 543	17.3	51.7	17.6	78.3	8 806	27 058	56 946	71 112	2.7	55 077	10.8	15.9	14.0
Decatur	NA	NA	6 484	9.7	60.6	13.7	40.1	9 102	22 046	48 047	56 518	0.8	47 666	12.9	18.0	16.7
DeKalb	NA	NA	11 350	17.4	53.6	16.3	88.9	12 062	22 827	47 247	58 744	1.6	50 279	12.9	18.7	16.5
Delaware	275	3 147	38 504	5.3	49.1	22.5	148.2	9 741	20 854	37 474	51 500	1.5	37 116	23.0	27.8	26.5
Dubois	NA	NA	10 426	9.1	54.1	18.9	67.8	9 147	25 589	54 780	65 584	2.0	55 606	8.9	10.4	9.0
Elkhart	287	2 108	52 342	15.0	56.0	18.2	347.2	9 626	21 109	45 693	58 065	1.7	46 123	15.5	20.3	19.6
Fayette	NA	NA	5 702	5.7	65.4	8.9	41.9	10 710	18 757	37 391	46 082	0.8	40 212	17.3	25.9	23.6
Floyd	134	3 504	19 400	15.8	46.5	22.6	107.3	9 502	27 185	53 961	68 257	3.2	55 844	13.1	17.7	16.7
Fountain	NA	NA	3 833	7.8	60.2	11.9	26.3	8 660	23 063	45 884	56 429	0.6	42 732	13.8	19.2	17.2
Franklin	52	778	5 686	19.2	58.7	18.1	41.4	8 259	24 085	49 516	63 547	2.3	53 538	11.4	15.9	14.2
Fulton	NA	NA	4 958	11.4	60.1	12.7	23.5	8 939	21 226	40 168	52 804	1.2	44 337	16.3	25.2	21.4
Gibson	NA	NA	8 033	14.3	49.7	16.1	47.8	9 648	24 258	49 329	61 416	1.6	48 579	12.0	15.9	14.7
Grant	179	2 342	19 278	30.4	56.2	16.8	107.5	9 774	20 516	39 747	51 236	1.3	39 325	21.7	33.3	29.9
Greene	29	1 220	7 399	9.2	56.0	12.1	51.7	9 771	22 235	43 980	55 501	1.1	43 786	13.7	20.8	18.8
Hamilton	26	847	83 892	18.6	20.1	55.1	483.9	8 733	39 521	82 468	107 384	10.0	84 022	5.5	6.1	5.7
Hancock	50	1 076	18 867	13.8	42.7	26.3	92.0	7 356	28 111	62 981	73 897	3.3	67 738	6.5	9.1	7.9
Harrison	117	1 417	9 120	12.9	56.2	14.9	55.8	9 363	23 244	50 510	59 761	0.9	50 321	13.0	17.3	16.3
Hendricks	123	1 599	39 785	14.7	37.0	32.2	223.5	8 128	29 830	68 297	82 006	4.0	68 575	6.4	7.7	6.8
Henry	22	1 790	11 828	9.1	59.1	14.9	75.5	9 920	20 309	40 679	51 655	1.1	42 133	17.2	23.8	19.9
Howard	265	2 967	20 925	10.0	48.9	20.0	128.0	9 608	24 071	43 590	57 187	1.5	45 211	15.8	24.2	21.7
Huntington	78	1 072	9 523	23.8	53.1	16.9	49.3	8 734	22 601	46 148	57 099	1.3	44 828	13.0	18.5	16.9
Jackson	281	4 062	10 114	20.9	60.5	14.5	59.5	8 831	22 568	46 501	56 180	1.1	49 614	12.9	17.8	16.5
Jasper	NA	NA	8 698	17.9	55.7	14.9	41.9	8 025	24 297	57 500	65 320	1.6	53 757	10.7	14.7	13.6
Jay	73	1 803	5 253	7.5	64.7	10.0	36.5	10 409	19 236	40 235	49 157	0.8	41 847	16.0	27.2	24.4
Jefferson	NA	NA	7 893	22.5	54.1	17.8	45.3	10 471	21 524	43 795	54 077	0.7	44 569	15.3	22.3	20.1
Jennings	348	2 581	7 269	12.9	61.7	9.6	53.2	11 134	20 109	44 128	52 493	0.9	44 554	16.9	24.0	22.6
Johnson	262	2 717	37 530	18.0	43.7	26.8	226.5	8 954	28 575	61 231	76 423	4.0	58 936	11.8	14.7	12.5
Knox	14	667	10 473	8.3	51.0	14.1	49.5	9 397	21 047	42 119	52 344	1.6	44 091	15.9	23.8	22.8
Kosciusko	374	1 592	19 089	14.9	52.8	20.3	129.3	9 362	24 881	50 859	64 212	2.7	51 603	12.7	17.8	16.4
LaGrange	58	578	8 829	30.8	69.2	10.3	55.7	9 335	19 356	47 617	60 164	2.0	51 810	12.7	19.3	18.3
Lake	433	3 493	132 803	15.8	49.1	19.8	788.0	10 095	23 918	49 035	62 295	2.2	48 341	17.8	27.7	25.7
LaPorte	163	2 742	27 171	14.0	53.2	17.3	178.6	10 209	22 852	47 538	59 211	1.8	46 610	17.0	26.9	23.4
Lawrence	363	1 787	10 686	11.0	57.5	13.7	68.1	9 778	22 169	42 627	54 165	2.0	44 435	12.9	20.4	18.0
Madison	187	2 817	30 347	17.3	53.2	16.7	162.2	9 467	21 527	43 120	53 392	1.1	41 117	19.6	29.6	28.4
Marion	1 204	5 309	242 246	19.7	44.6	27.4	1 403.5	10 927	24 124	42 334	58 836	2.4	41 478	21.3	30.1	28.2
Marshall	72	1 124	12 217	16.8	56.1	16.6	72.2	9 438	21 933	45 709	57 529	1.5	45 855	13.8	18.2	16.0
Martin	NA	NA	2 389	15.0	57.0	10.8	14.2	9 212	22 817	44 740	55 067	0.9	46 839	14.9	21.4	19.8
Miami	101	929	9 483	4.8	59.1	10.6	48.8	9 047	20 475	42 023	53 283	1.1	43 694	17.7	25.8	22.1
Monroe	285	2 898	60 236	7.9	31.5	43.4	130.9	9 712	23 032	40 052	57 267	2.9	42 404	24.0	17.8	16.0
Montgomery	276	2 168	9 295	14.9	56.9	17.8	59.1	9 766	22 679	46 797	57 199	1.2	50 889	12.5	19.4	18.2
Morgan	NA	NA	16 849	13.1	54.0	16.1	99.9	8 649	25 781	55 354	68 595	2.3	56 491	12.7	18.7	16.7
Newton	79	1 121	3 313	11.8	63.3	8.5	23.3	9 929	25 594	50 262	63 557	2.4	53 715	11.4	17.2	15.9
Noble	52	618	12 186	15.2	58.2	13.2	67.5	8 956	21 889	47 117	57 759	1.2	48 789	13.6	19.3	15.7
Ohio	NA	NA	1 290	10.5	62.1	13.1	8.5	9 998	25 443	50 377	61 382	1.2	50 518	10.5	17.2	14.7
Orange	NA	NA	4 417	8.8	63.9	12.6	41.1	12 062	18 576	38 826	46 360	0.5	39 411	10.8	27.8	25.7
Owen	NA	NA	4 516	12.9	62.6	11.0	26.2	9 586	21 318	43 950	53 213	1.3	42 994	15.0	25.2	22.7
Parke	35	311	3 779	8.9	57.8	13.7	16.1	7 075	20 534	43 870	56 460	1.7	41 964	17.2	28.5	27.5
Perry	39	818	3 737	9.3	62.6	10.9	27.6	9 383	20 934	47 596	54 398	0.7	45 722	14.2	19.4	17.6

1. Data for serious crimes have not been adjusted for underreporting; this may affect comparability between geographic areas and over time. 2. Per 100,000 population estimated by the FBI.
3. All persons 3 years old and over enrolled in nursery school through college. 4. Persons 25 years old and over. 5. Elementary and secondary education expenditures.
6. Based on population estimated by the American Community Survey, 2009–2013.

STATE County	Personal income, 2013: Total (mil dol)	Percent change, 2012–2013	Per capita[1]: Dollars	Per capita[1]: Rank	Wages and salaries (mil dol)	Supplements to wages and salaries; employer contributions (mil dol): Pension and insurance	Supplements: Government social insurance	Proprietors' income (mil dol)	Dividends, interest, and rent (mil dol)	Personal transfer receipts (mil dol)	Earnings, 2013: Total (mil dol)	Contributions for government social insurance (mil dol): From employee and self-employed	From employer
	62	63	64	65	66	67	68	69	70	71	72	73	74
ILLINOIS—Cont'd													
Winnebago	10 873	1.5	37 406	1 519	5 759	1 059	444	654	1 931	2 311	7 917	454	444
Woodford	1 892	3.2	48 183	467	420	86	31	190	389	243	728	36	31
INDIANA	253 779	1.8	38 622	X	127 681	21 317	9 709	22 589	38 795	49 234	181 297	10 961	9 709
Adams	1 124	2.6	32 459	2 343	465	88	37	174	168	218	763	45	37
Allen	13 635	0.6	37 560	1 496	7 831	1 246	606	1 203	2 314	2 606	10 886	667	606
Bartholomew	3 496	0.6	43 923	763	2 423	365	179	270	581	568	3 237	194	179
Benton	408	7.4	46 556	580	86	17	6	129	58	64	239	10	6
Blackford	417	1.2	33 405	2 191	118	24	9	45	61	125	196	13	9
Boone	3 484	4.4	57 604	146	1 023	159	80	526	564	337	1 788	101	80
Brown	595	0.0	39 593	1 217	83	18	7	49	101	132	158	12	7
Carroll	758	4.6	37 731	1 471	188	36	14	125	119	147	362	20	14
Cass	1 334	2.8	34 692	1 952	518	103	40	113	204	345	774	47	40
Clark	4 174	2.0	36 956	1 594	1 924	354	150	278	587	893	2 707	169	150
Clay	919	3.5	34 277	2 038	249	52	20	96	125	227	417	26	20
Clinton	1 129	0.5	34 305	2 030	426	78	32	109	172	246	646	37	32
Crawford	317	0.5	29 818	2 715	59	14	4	22	39	97	100	8	4
Daviess	1 208	5.4	37 261	1 541	399	72	30	189	201	237	690	38	30
Dearborn	1 917	1.3	38 411	1 389	558	105	43	145	292	369	851	56	43
Decatur	1 023	2.7	38 939	1 309	543	93	42	125	150	201	802	46	42
DeKalb	1 466	0.9	34 646	1 964	914	147	73	114	215	311	1 248	77	73
Delaware	3 789	0.9	32 255	2 371	1 772	344	137	280	625	1 028	2 534	160	137
Dubois	2 049	3.7	48 359	461	1 100	169	85	387	451	287	1 741	98	85
Elkhart	7 266	3.3	36 229	1 705	5 028	827	408	623	1 120	1 333	6 885	409	408
Fayette	747	2.5	31 286	2 511	231	44	18	59	115	262	351	25	18
Floyd	3 241	0.7	42 503	889	1 148	206	88	215	488	599	1 657	104	88
Fountain	627	3.6	37 157	1 556	178	37	14	85	89	146	314	18	14
Franklin	906	2.1	39 470	1 235	134	29	10	64	141	183	237	17	10
Fulton	731	1.7	35 753	1 790	241	45	18	86	133	169	390	24	18
Gibson	1 371	8.2	40 776	1 080	956	148	72	224	198	256	1 400	81	72
Grant	2 405	0.7	34 793	1 932	1 095	194	87	215	334	707	1 591	102	87
Greene	1 153	1.3	35 166	1 877	214	46	16	82	178	283	359	24	16
Hamilton	16 767	2.3	56 515	175	6 446	869	470	1 667	2 667	1 288	9 451	558	470
Hancock	3 389	6.2	47 342	523	928	146	69	328	425	481	1 470	92	69
Harrison	1 348	1.2	34 410	2 008	357	65	28	85	199	295	535	36	28
Hendricks	5 993	3.9	38 948	1 308	2 113	357	164	605	750	806	3 239	193	164
Henry	1 572	3.0	32 051	2 408	436	84	33	124	242	448	677	47	33
Howard	2 854	1.9	34 488	1 990	1 805	280	141	163	444	784	2 388	154	141
Huntington	1 302	0.8	35 400	1 835	519	96	40	103	229	292	759	47	40
Jackson	1 573	1.8	36 200	1 714	807	151	62	152	231	327	1 173	69	62
Jasper	1 353	2.1	40 513	1 113	486	86	38	220	169	245	829	44	38
Jay	736	1.8	34 499	1 986	266	54	21	133	90	170	474	26	21
Jefferson	1 054	1.7	32 484	2 338	490	98	37	76	181	295	701	45	37
Jennings	979	0.5	34 656	1 963	280	51	22	50	98	276	403	27	22
Johnson	5 732	2.2	39 385	1 243	1 808	296	142	456	832	913	2 702	170	142
Knox	1 555	4.5	40 966	1 057	687	141	51	182	253	368	1 061	60	51
Kosciusko	3 216	4.8	41 249	1 021	1 787	354	133	205	522	527	2 478	145	133
LaGrange	1 050	4.0	27 627	2 923	503	90	41	129	164	192	762	44	41
Lake	18 576	0.5	37 797	1 464	9 294	1 498	698	1 109	2 458	4 166	12 599	790	698
LaPorte	3 716	0.4	33 397	2 192	1 672	289	131	252	560	883	2 344	148	131
Lawrence	1 523	0.6	33 219	2 223	475	85	38	83	237	408	681	48	38
Madison	4 196	1.1	32 158	2 390	1 445	248	112	241	544	1 208	2 045	144	112
Marion	37 097	1.0	39 963	1 174	31 834	4 860	2 355	3 499	5 477	7 170	42 547	2 501	2 355
Marshall	1 640	3.9	34 804	1 930	675	120	54	150	260	339	999	61	54
Martin	379	3.7	37 350	1 531	461	126	38	39	66	81	664	34	38
Miami	1 072	1.4	29 675	2 728	355	79	29	79	175	281	543	34	29
Monroe	4 667	0.7	32 892	2 265	2 568	583	191	238	943	783	3 580	206	191
Montgomery	1 348	3.7	35 320	1 852	619	107	48	163	194	289	938	54	48
Morgan	2 792	2.1	40 013	1 172	547	100	43	107	325	517	797	56	43
Newton	524	4.7	37 208	1 546	131	24	10	82	70	104	247	12	10
Noble	1 545	1.0	32 472	2 340	671	122	54	96	200	321	944	60	54
Ohio	220	0.6	36 656	1 645	45	8	3	0	26	44	65	5	3
Orange	656	2.2	33 183	2 231	250	41	21	53	91	185	365	24	21
Owen	705	1.3	33 239	2 220	177	44	13	44	97	184	279	19	13
Parke	556	8.9	32 344	2 361	100	24	8	79	87	143	210	12	8
Perry	637	1.4	32 577	2 313	246	49	18	40	97	153	353	23	18

1. Based on the resident population estimated as of July 1 of the year shown.

STATE County	Earnings, 2013 (cont.) Percent by selected industries: Farm	Mining	Construction	Manu- facturing	Infor- mation: professional, scientific, technical services	Retail trade	Finance, insur- ance, real estate and leasing	Health care and social assistance	Govern- ment	Social Security beneficiaries, December 2013: Number	Rate[1]	Supple- mental Security Income recipients, December 2013	Housing units, 2014: Total	Percent change, 2010–2014
	75	76	77	78	79	80	81	82	83	84	85	86	87	88
ILLINOIS—Cont'd														
Winnebago	0.8	D	4.5	23.6	4.8	7.1	5.4	17.2	12.7	59 680	205	7 148	125 536	-0.3
Woodford	19.6	D	7.0	20.3	3.2	5.6	2.5	7.5	14.8	7 420	190	298	15 367	1.5
INDIANA	2.6	0.6	6.2	20.8	7.0	6.1	5.8	12.4	13.4	1 267 542	193	127 355	2 829 532	1.2
Adams	6.9	D	9.4	33.8	D	6.5	3.0	4.9	13.5	6 145	177	370	13 098	0.6
Allen	0.5	0.1	5.8	18.5	7.4	6.2	8.1	17.2	10.1	65 415	180	7 700	154 477	1.5
Bartholomew	1.5	D	3.5	46.4	4.5	5.3	3.6	6.7	9.9	16 025	201	1 250	33 548	1.4
Benton	34.7	D	2.6	8.3	D	4.1	D	D	11.8	1 925	220	137	3 921	-0.4
Blackford	12.2	D	1.8	28.1	D	11.1	2.6	D	13.0	3 555	285	290	5 996	-0.9
Boone	5.0	D	8.3	9.8	D	13.9	5.1	5.9	11.4	9 585	158	470	25 212	10.8
Brown	1.1	0.0	12.2	3.2	D	7.7	4.2	10.6	23.4	4 135	275	205	8 506	2.7
Carroll	20.9	D	7.1	D	2.5	4.9	3.0	D	10.7	4 535	226	203	9 434	-0.4
Cass	9.4	D	5.1	26.2	2.2	6.4	3.1	D	22.4	8 375	217	780	16 337	-0.8
Clark	0.8	D	6.8	16.9	3.7	9.8	6.3	8.9	17.0	23 755	211	2 373	48 986	2.5
Clay	9.2	1.1	5.0	33.1	2.1	7.0	2.5	7.2	14.2	6 130	229	632	11 694	-0.1
Clinton	14.0	0.0	4.8	33.9	D	4.4	2.6	8.8	12.6	6 740	205	504	13 248	-0.5
Crawford	1.4	D	5.6	D	D	5.7	4.4	5.4	24.1	2 680	253	326	5 455	-1.2
Daviess	12.8	3.8	15.8	13.1	3.8	7.8	2.9	D	13.9	5 770	179	557	12 481	0.1
Dearborn	0.5	D	8.7	13.7	3.6	8.5	3.5	8.0	20.5	10 685	215	639	20 238	0.3
Decatur	9.0	D	2.8	40.2	D	4.4	2.7	3.1	11.2	5 610	214	461	11 231	0.2
DeKalb	2.3	0.1	3.5	44.3	3.6	4.0	2.1	6.4	8.6	9 035	214	675	17 624	0.4
Delaware	1.9	D	3.9	10.3	7.3	7.9	5.8	19.4	22.8	25 740	219	2 998	52 512	0.3
Dubois	5.9	D	3.5	33.2	2.5	6.6	2.3	D	6.3	8 510	201	424	17 595	1.2
Elkhart	1.2	0.0	3.3	47.9	2.8	4.6	2.7	8.5	6.7	34 540	172	3 247	77 933	0.2
Fayette	8.3	D	2.7	21.2	3.8	8.3	3.3	18.6	16.1	6 680	280	882	10 816	-0.8
Floyd	0.1	D	7.9	21.6	6.5	5.9	5.1	11.2	20.9	15 120	199	1 529	32 300	1.0
Fountain	17.1	0.0	3.6	35.3	1.9	7.1	3.0	D	12.7	4 280	254	298	7 801	-0.8
Franklin	12.8	0.3	7.9	15.4	D	9.1	D	D	19.6	5 665	247	370	9 563	0.3
Fulton	10.4	D	8.4	25.9	2.9	7.5	4.1	4.8	18.1	4 840	237	373	9 653	-0.6
Gibson	5.8	8.4	2.6	45.3	2.7	3.7	1.0	D	5.1	7 095	211	483	14 729	0.6
Grant	3.8	D	3.0	23.5	2.8	6.1	3.2	17.6	14.3	17 425	252	2 063	30 288	-0.5
Greene	12.5	2.2	6.8	6.1	4.7	8.7	3.7	D	26.0	7 725	235	757	15 051	-1.0
Hamilton	0.5	0.2	7.2	4.5	D	6.7	18.3	10.1	8.1	36 760	124	1 443	116 286	8.9
Hancock	3.4	0.1	9.3	14.9	18.7	5.7	3.3	8.4	13.8	14 115	199	611	28 881	2.6
Harrison	6.6	1.0	4.6	14.9	2.2	7.8	4.0	D	19.7	8 560	219	605	16 665	0.8
Hendricks	3.5	0.2	6.8	8.6	D	10.3	3.3	8.3	14.8	23 350	152	907	58 326	5.2
Henry	8.6	D	6.9	17.3	2.7	8.1	4.1	D	21.9	12 245	250	1 050	21 139	-0.7
Howard	2.0	D	2.9	44.5	3.3	6.2	3.4	12.1	10.6	21 140	255	2 201	38 688	0.0
Huntington	8.5	D	4.2	29.3	D	5.5	4.6	8.3	10.4	8 325	226	544	15 879	0.5
Jackson	6.8	D	3.7	35.7	1.7	6.6	2.6	4.6	14.3	9 655	222	845	18 524	1.8
Jasper	17.1	D	12.7	12.5	2.3	6.9	2.4	4.5	11.3	7 265	218	378	13 349	1.4
Jay	18.9	D	3.6	38.2	1.8	3.9	2.3	3.9	14.2	4 935	232	408	9 194	-0.3
Jefferson	0.9	0.0	D	26.8	D	8.1	2.6	14.7	16.6	7 625	235	795	14 320	0.1
Jennings	8.8	D	12.1	23.6	1.5	5.6	2.0	D	17.0	6 490	230	728	12 063	0.0
Johnson	1.7	D	7.4	13.2	4.8	9.9	5.0	12.3	15.1	26 125	179	1 397	58 738	3.7
Knox	8.4	9.3	3.1	9.0	3.4	5.7	3.9	11.1	24.5	8 550	225	987	16 974	-0.4
Kosciusko	3.7	D	2.6	49.8	2.2	5.1	2.5	6.6	6.4	15 420	198	877	37 557	1.4
LaGrange	7.2	D	4.0	51.0	1.6	4.8	2.3	D	9.1	5 845	154	326	14 378	2.0
Lake	0.2	0.1	11.4	21.6	4.5	7.4	3.4	15.3	11.3	95 760	195	13 070	210 362	0.8
LaPorte	2.9	D	8.1	20.8	2.9	6.9	3.5	14.2	15.8	23 820	214	2 250	48 769	0.7
Lawrence	1.9	1.0	5.8	21.5	6.8	8.9	4.4	15.8	15.3	11 155	243	965	20 923	-0.7
Madison	3.0	D	4.9	14.7	4.2	7.2	4.5	16.1	16.4	31 535	242	3 379	58 789	-0.5
Marion	0.0	D	6.2	14.3	12.0	4.8	8.3	14.4	13.0	149 940	162	25 758	419 350	0.4
Marshall	6.8	D	4.0	36.4	2.7	6.6	4.8	7.3	10.8	9 750	207	666	19 961	0.6
Martin	5.1	0.0	0.6	3.6	11.9	1.4	0.5	0.6	73.0	2 395	234	221	4 742	-0.9
Miami	9.7	0.5	5.4	18.1	1.6	4.8	3.7	D	28.4	7 165	198	738	15 314	-1.1
Monroe	0.2	0.5	4.6	12.7	6.4	5.7	4.0	15.6	32.8	20 035	141	1 793	60 112	1.7
Montgomery	11.9	D	3.2	37.1	D	5.2	2.3	D	10.8	8 360	219	621	16 540	0.0
Morgan	6.1	0.4	8.6	17.0	3.9	9.1	4.2	11.7	16.7	14 970	216	981	27 951	0.6
Newton	33.1	D	3.5	12.9	D	2.9	2.9	4.1	13.7	3 015	214	212	6 028	0.0
Noble	2.7	0.1	4.0	50.8	D	5.0	2.1	5.7	10.4	9 515	200	679	20 190	0.4
Ohio	1.8	0.0	4.0	D	D	2.5	D	5.9	24.5	1 325	220	84	2 793	0.3
Orange	6.4	D	14.5	15.4	1.5	5.3	1.5	D	13.0	4 945	251	534	9 095	-0.9
Owen	6.0	0.0	5.0	42.4	D	4.9	2.8	D	13.2	5 170	244	440	9 982	-1.1
Parke	23.4	D	6.5	11.1	D	6.0	3.6	D	24.2	3 805	221	258	0 003	-0.3
Perry	3.6	D	4.4	39.6	2.5	5.4	3.2	D	21.8	4 340	223	343	8 522	0.3

1. Per 1,000 resident population estimated as of July 1 of the year shown.

STATE County	Housing units, 2009–2013: Occupied units: Total	Owner-occupied: Percent	Owner-occupied: Median value[1]	Median owner cost as a percent of income: With a mortgage	Median owner cost as a percent of income: Without a mortgage[2]	Renter-occupied: Median rent[3]	Renter-occupied: Median rent as a percent of income[2]	Substandard units[4] (percent)	Civilian labor force, 2014: Total	Percent change, 2013–2014	Unemployment: Total	Unemployment: Rate[5]	Civilian employment,[6] 2009–2013: Total	Percent: Management, business, science and arts	Percent: Construction, production, and maintenance occupations
	89	90	91	92	93	94	95	96	97	98	99	100	101	102	103
ILLINOIS—Cont'd															
Winnebago	113 449	66.9	123 400	23.2	13.4	735	30.4	1.5	142 408	-0.5	11 876	8.3	130 062	30.0	27.0
Woodford	14 362	81.6	158 600	20.7	11.0	680	26.8	8.6	19 635	-1.4	1 100	5.6	18 652	37.9	23.7
INDIANA	2 481 793	70.0	122 800	20.8	11.1	730	30.1	2.1	3 230 540	1.2	194 959	6.0	2 963 879	32.1	26.8
Adams	12 127	78.9	116 100	20.8	10.0	570	29.2	2.1	16 386	2.9	774	4.7	14 788	24.5	37.1
Allen	138 212	69.8	112 700	19.5	10.0	668	27.7	2.2	175 530	0.7	10 160	5.8	164 621	34.4	23.7
Bartholomew	30 041	70.9	134 900	19.8	11.2	786	25.9	1.3	42 798	2.8	1 906	4.5	37 480	38.3	25.2
Benton	3 444	74.4	84 300	19.5	10.9	721	25.6	1.1	4 561	1.9	250	5.5	4 164	27.6	35.6
Blackford	5 190	75.0	70 400	20.0	10.7	595	29.0	1.2	5 297	-2.8	395	7.5	5 152	21.2	36.2
Boone	21 908	76.8	179 000	20.0	12.5	790	27.6	2.5	31 774	2.1	1 428	4.5	28 633	44.3	20.0
Brown	5 889	83.0	157 400	22.7	14.6	887	34.9	3.0	7 461	1.9	450	6.0	7 001	32.9	27.8
Carroll	7 995	78.8	103 900	20.1	10.8	644	26.9	3.4	10 082	1.6	532	5.3	9 320	27.5	35.0
Cass	14 827	75.9	81 900	21.2	10.6	599	28.3	2.1	17 831	0.8	1 036	5.8	17 407	24.6	38.3
Clark	42 502	71.6	127 400	21.3	11.5	739	28.3	1.3	57 432	2.0	3 144	5.5	52 793	29.1	25.8
Clay	10 230	76.2	91 300	19.6	11.7	650	30.8	2.6	12 482	-1.0	856	6.9	11 893	27.8	30.7
Clinton	11 745	72.1	97 300	20.1	11.3	682	27.5	2.9	16 665	1.3	876	5.3	14 956	21.7	44.0
Crawford	4 237	82.0	83 300	21.4	12.9	555	26.2	2.0	4 908	1.3	379	7.7	4 331	20.1	42.5
Daviess	11 160	75.8	105 500	19.2	10.0	584	22.3	1.5	15 149	1.8	689	4.5	14 104	23.4	41.7
Dearborn	18 556	77.0	160 400	21.5	12.2	713	29.6	2.3	25 449	1.2	1 648	6.5	23 654	27.4	31.1
Decatur	9 792	70.6	112 000	21.8	10.9	711	24.6	1.0	14 254	2.6	714	5.0	11 527	25.7	38.3
DeKalb	16 032	78.7	107 800	22.1	10.0	630	25.7	1.2	21 229	1.2	1 130	5.3	18 744	28.3	36.2
Delaware	46 325	63.8	89 600	19.8	12.0	675	37.7	1.9	53 717	-1.0	3 821	7.1	50 114	31.9	21.2
Dubois	15 890	78.2	133 200	20.2	10.0	626	24.5	3.4	22 027	1.7	915	4.2	21 799	27.9	35.4
Elkhart	70 130	71.6	121 700	21.7	10.8	708	29.2	1.8	102 117	3.0	5 305	5.2	88 591	24.9	37.4
Fayette	9 536	72.0	81 700	22.3	14.3	638	36.3	2.2	9 124	0.9	729	8.0	8 926	25.2	31.2
Floyd	29 087	71.8	150 400	21.2	10.7	718	29.8	1.4	39 447	2.3	2 040	5.2	36 359	33.5	23.3
Fountain	6 925	76.5	88 800	18.8	11.7	617	24.9	2.9	8 224	-1.7	581	7.1	7 563	25.5	42.4
Franklin	8 551	79.4	150 100	21.6	10.6	626	27.2	1.1	10 846	0.9	706	6.5	10 724	30.9	32.9
Fulton	8 221	76.5	95 600	22.5	12.8	608	30.9	1.8	9 838	-1.2	622	6.3	8 825	26.2	41.1
Gibson	13 094	77.8	104 400	18.6	10.5	615	27.0	1.5	18 502	2.5	848	4.6	15 621	26.8	38.7
Grant	26 981	69.7	80 100	19.9	10.8	610	27.9	4.2	32 723	0.6	2 284	7.0	28 810	28.9	25.4
Greene	12 894	78.4	88 800	18.5	12.4	577	27.5	0.8	13 788	0.4	1 100	8.0	14 302	28.0	33.2
Hamilton	103 234	79.2	215 600	20.5	10.0	963	25.1	0.6	159 577	2.3	6 577	4.1	143 762	51.3	10.7
Hancock	26 071	80.2	155 400	21.3	10.1	820	29.3	1.3	36 754	1.8	1 902	5.2	33 751	37.4	22.5
Harrison	14 499	81.2	122 100	20.8	10.6	690	29.3	1.4	19 135	2.2	1 083	5.7	17 832	28.5	31.7
Hendricks	52 946	82.4	159 800	20.4	10.9	906	25.9	1.4	80 397	2.1	3 753	4.7	72 882	39.6	21.3
Henry	18 367	73.3	94 200	20.8	11.7	621	28.6	1.3	21 527	0.9	1 480	6.9	19 155	28.4	30.2
Howard	34 544	70.5	98 500	19.4	10.0	637	33.9	1.9	37 099	1.7	2 360	6.4	34 523	30.0	27.2
Huntington	14 138	77.4	97 100	20.8	11.9	663	27.2	2.4	18 590	0.4	1 084	5.8	17 490	26.8	35.8
Jackson	16 713	73.0	117 100	20.1	11.1	686	28.9	1.7	21 289	2.0	1 077	5.1	19 331	26.4	37.4
Jasper	11 924	79.6	146 200	20.6	10.0	688	25.5	2.8	16 112	0.9	1 099	6.8	14 620	27.1	36.2
Jay	8 179	76.0	79 300	19.9	12.4	551	26.7	3.1	10 194	1.6	592	5.8	9 476	23.1	43.6
Jefferson	12 668	72.6	111 500	21.8	10.8	652	28.2	2.7	15 196	-0.6	917	6.0	14 276	26.2	33.4
Jennings	10 632	75.9	89 700	22.1	12.9	693	27.7	2.1	13 072	0.2	892	6.8	11 836	25.5	35.5
Johnson	52 239	72.6	144 300	20.5	10.5	830	29.6	1.5	75 262	2.0	3 790	5.0	68 489	35.1	22.8
Knox	14 738	67.4	84 100	19.0	11.5	609	27.1	1.9	18 845	1.1	1 000	5.3	17 220	27.0	31.8
Kosciusko	29 705	77.7	132 200	20.5	10.6	682	25.5	4.7	40 312	1.3	1 989	4.9	36 713	27.5	38.4
LaGrange	11 833	78.9	160 200	25.1	11.0	680	26.6	2.5	18 154	3.3	826	4.5	14 946	20.8	49.1
Lake	182 080	69.6	136 600	22.6	12.3	799	32.7	2.4	231 350	0.4	18 636	8.1	211 287	29.5	27.1
LaPorte	42 690	72.7	122 800	21.1	10.7	694	30.9	2.0	48 934	-0.2	3 779	7.7	47 049	27.2	30.1
Lawrence	18 592	78.3	98 200	21.6	13.0	606	29.4	1.9	20 463	-1.1	1 677	8.2	19 359	27.8	31.6
Madison	50 637	69.9	92 800	20.5	11.9	688	31.6	2.5	58 691	1.0	4 193	7.1	53 796	28.3	25.4
Marion	360 072	55.8	118 000	21.7	11.9	768	32.1	3.0	468 845	1.2	30 362	6.5	425 049	34.0	21.4
Marshall	17 581	77.9	124 600	21.6	12.7	655	28.1	2.1	23 669	2.2	1 323	5.6	21 083	26.8	36.0
Martin	4 146	80.5	88 500	19.5	10.0	542	26.9	2.3	4 968	0.2	266	5.4	4 743	30.5	34.8
Miami	13 210	75.3	84 100	19.9	12.4	632	26.5	1.3	15 760	0.8	1 068	6.8	14 740	23.6	37.8
Monroe	53 914	54.0	156 300	21.1	10.1	799	41.7	1.1	67 249	0.7	3 907	5.8	66 347	42.8	16.3
Montgomery	14 590	72.2	108 300	20.4	10.0	667	30.4	1.4	18 633	1.1	1 032	5.5	17 402	26.2	35.3
Morgan	25 621	76.5	141 200	20.8	10.0	760	28.1	1.1	35 384	1.5	2 065	5.8	32 573	28.2	30.7
Newton	5 374	76.6	112 000	20.4	10.0	717	24.3	3.7	6 915	0.1	486	7.0	6 297	20.6	40.2
Noble	17 722	76.1	112 700	21.7	10.0	613	26.6	1.9	23 104	2.0	1 225	5.3	21 080	23.4	44.1
Ohio	2 422	74.4	137 900	21.6	12.8	698	25.7	2.8	3 218	1.7	222	6.9	3 023	22.1	35.2
Orange	7 688	74.6	88 100	21.8	12.6	592	29.7	3.4	8 534	-2.0	660	7.7	7 951	24.2	35.1
Owen	8 552	78.7	101 900	22.4	11.7	679	28.1	3.9	9 635	0.0	776	8.1	9 481	24.3	39.8
Parke	5 893	83.8	87 600	21.0	10.1	590	27.5	1.8	6 951	0.3	486	7.0	6 838	23.2	38.0
Perry	7 411	79.9	97 300	19.9	11.1	568	24.7	1.7	9 157	3.3	543	5.9	8 339	20.1	43.7

1. Specified owner-occupied units. 2. A value of 10.0 represents 10 percent or less; a value of 50.0 represents 50 percent or more. 3. Specified renter-occupied units.
4. Overcrowded or lacking complete plumbing facilities. 5. Percent of civilian labor force. 6. Persons 16 years old and over.

STATE County	Private nonfarm establishments, employment and payroll, 2013									Agriculture, 2012			
		Employment						Annual payroll		Farms			
											Percent with:		
	Number of establish-ments	Total	Health care and social assistance	Manufac-turing	Retail trade	Finance and insurance	Professional, scientific, and technical services	Total (mil dol)	Average per employee (dollars)	Number	Fewer than 50 acres	500 acres or more	Farm operators whose principal occu-pation is farming (percent)
	104	105	106	107	108	109	110	111	112	113	114	115	116
ILLINOIS—Cont'd													
Winnebago	6 481	116 977	20 339	25 335	14 657	3 603	4 374	4 678	39 987	807	46.0	12.4	44.2
Woodford	759	8 969	1 368	2 148	965	227	195	327	36 465	958	32.7	20.5	52.8
INDIANA	143 515	2 555 979	402 148	463 363	309 333	97 071	106 114	103 134	40 350	58 695	46.6	12.8	43.7
Adams	713	11 483	1 427	4 426	1 464	281	210	365	31 829	1 476	61.9	6.8	32.4
Allen	9 044	161 708	30 258	25 255	20 183	9 084	5 548	6 472	40 022	1 725	57.7	7.8	43.4
Bartholomew	1 827	43 638	4 750	11 686	4 655	926	3 362	1 954	44 780	623	44.1	14.4	44.8
Benton	188	1 443	59	349	198	92	48	48	33 482	381	26.0	36.7	63.5
Blackford	232	2 718	387	1 019	337	D	D	89	32 928	263	43.7	16.3	46.8
Boone	1 414	20 400	2 328	1 789	2 743	382	778	724	35 485	607	49.6	21.4	47.3
Brown	349	1 982	298	139	335	43	D	46	23 280	173	54.9	2.3	24.9
Carroll	380	4 464	267	D	371	99	98	142	31 800	491	35.6	23.2	50.7
Cass	742	12 379	2 359	3 779	1 522	312	220	397	32 091	688	42.7	16.9	42.9
Clark	2 405	44 691	6 125	7 380	7 010	1 866	1 021	1 536	34 376	515	49.3	7.4	41.6
Clay	469	5 735	641	2 146	951	123	86	168	29 318	579	44.9	16.1	39.4
Clinton	577	9 225	1 226	3 594	994	D	135	313	33 966	597	43.4	22.8	50.9
Crawford	125	1 346	D	D	193	D	11	36	26 518	338	27.8	3.6	29.9
Daviess	865	10 143	1 367	1 929	1 456	265	606	334	32 969	1 325	60.1	7.0	28.6
Dearborn	908	13 630	2 589	1 801	1 963	444	263	415	30 455	561	39.9	1.6	39.8
Decatur	624	11 818	1 171	4 204	1 327	D	107	444	37 540	610	31.1	19.0	49.0
DeKalb	985	18 643	1 668	8 087	1 471	354	457	757	40 593	924	49.9	8.5	28.2
Delaware	2 321	37 892	9 184	4 288	6 152	2 617	1 463	1 281	33 814	610	49.5	13.3	54.8
Dubois	1 295	25 617	3 142	9 957	3 018	515	D	995	38 854	720	34.2	12.4	40.3
Elkhart	4 853	112 276	10 183	57 400	8 753	1 962	1 865	4 523	40 288	1 724	62.8	3.9	38.3
Fayette	435	5 696	1 645	1 164	1 074	152	194	190	33 311	347	40.9	12.4	44.4
Floyd	1 777	26 086	5 487	5 546	3 115	790	1 096	925	35 454	277	67.9	2.9	48.0
Fountain	322	4 348	D	2 213	595	160	76	131	30 028	460	34.6	22.8	48.0
Franklin	409	5 187	660	607	645	D	D	166	32 018	727	32.2	7.7	47.9
Fulton	473	5 391	818	1 922	899	D	128	180	33 347	653	40.9	13.9	49.0
Gibson	705	17 450	1 766	6 900	1 572	176	324	765	43 848	589	36.8	23.6	52.3
Grant	1 327	29 170	5 791	4 557	3 142	635	375	927	31 796	500	37.6	22.2	53.6
Greene	579	4 991	942	D	1 055	192	277	138	27 716	810	41.0	8.5	42.0
Hamilton	8 081	114 197	16 823	5 606	15 516	12 772	8 841	5 620	49 212	598	62.2	11.5	40.1
Hancock	1 333	19 756	2 503	3 273	2 117	333	4 015	727	36 816	604	60.1	15.1	41.6
Harrison	651	8 805	1 393	1 497	1 290	259	163	258	29 336	967	48.5	4.7	43.3
Hendricks	2 954	51 362	7 205	2 936	8 958	843	1 223	1 737	33 811	694	55.9	15.6	54.3
Henry	831	10 567	2 894	1 853	1 543	348	203	330	31 214	702	50.4	13.0	42.3
Howard	1 753	30 882	5 488	9 015	4 845	684	685	1 346	43 585	476	40.8	15.5	57.4
Huntington	872	12 923	1 795	3 867	1 332	403	170	394	30 477	695	47.5	16.3	44.9
Jackson	1 000	17 926	2 193	5 965	2 292	407	261	668	37 275	744	37.0	13.2	39.5
Jasper	744	8 589	1 309	1 365	1 370	270	183	295	34 354	615	38.7	24.7	47.2
Jay	401	6 162	799	2 855	596	161	88	197	32 014	836	50.6	11.2	38.9
Jefferson	678	11 028	2 037	3 036	1 600	208	229	393	35 627	615	42.4	5.9	38.2
Jennings	404	6 280	888	1 828	752	110	108	213	33 903	528	47.2	11.0	39.2
Johnson	3 046	43 122	7 295	5 160	8 556	1 256	1 363	1 444	33 488	562	57.8	14.9	45.0
Knox	917	13 149	D	D	1 982	347	217	442	33 610	496	30.2	31.5	61.3
Kosciusko	1 914	34 469	3 899	13 466	3 910	791	508	1 726	50 063	1 247	54.2	10.2	39.9
LaGrange	802	11 359	918	5 887	1 107	D	178	433	38 083	2 419	58.7	2.3	43.3
Lake	9 843	167 680	33 942	23 472	24 108	4 205	5 804	7 141	42 587	430	57.2	15.1	47.0
LaPorte	2 299	35 042	5 660	7 682	5 713	832	966	1 224	34 928	731	43.8	17.1	51.4
Lawrence	838	11 748	2 545	2 049	1 942	365	720	385	32 764	800	42.0	6.5	39.5
Madison	2 233	35 209	6 629	2 808	4 808	900	721	1 109	31 511	737	52.6	16.1	54.5
Marion	22 741	508 703	83 408	42 539	46 854	24 455	37 025	25 211	49 558	231	79.7	4.8	36.4
Marshall	1 038	16 068	1 865	5 699	2 037	357	311	560	34 846	878	46.8	12.3	40.7
Martin	182	2 206	135	350	329	D	657	82	37 198	283	44.9	9.5	35.3
Miami	561	6 767	1 082	1 702	898	332	101	208	30 719	666	45.0	14.6	44.4
Monroe	2 901	49 288	8 550	D	7 159	1 291	1 889	1 733	35 161	462	48.3	3.7	37.7
Montgomery	857	12 985	1 190	4 823	1 643	288	178	497	38 276	732	44.3	20.8	48.9
Morgan	1 163	12 330	2 034	1 876	2 179	D	318	394	31 930	583	55.6	11.1	42.5
Newton	257	2 497	284	574	271	107	63	77	30 667	348	29.6	32.2	54.9
Noble	867	15 213	1 485	7 989	1 475	251	183	522	34 312	1 163	52.0	0.0	38.5
Ohio	89	1 194	91	D	77	D	D	29	24 567	171	38.0	2.9	33.9
Orange	390	7 570	809	1 408	691	91	D	221	29 252	478	33.7	9.4	36.8
Owen	290	2 904	416	984	399	113	78	85	29 123	549	39.5	7.1	40.3
Parke	255	2 053	1 211	526	307	68	D	61	29 706	574	38.0	13.4	43.4
Perry	367	4 954	840	1 799	715	101	86	178	35 932	413	26.6	5.1	39.2

STATE County	Agriculture, 2012 (cont.) — Land in farms: Acreage (1,000)	Land in farms: Percent change, 2007–2012	Land in farms — Acres: Average size of farm	Acres: Total irrigated (1,000)	Acres: Total cropland (1,000)	Value of land and buildings (dollars): Average per farm	Value of land and buildings (dollars): Average per acre	Value of machinery and equipment, average per farm (dollars)	Value of products sold: Total (mil dol)	Value of products sold: Average per farm (dollars)	Value of products sold — Percent from: Crops	Percent from: Livestock and poultry products	Percent of farms with sales of: $10,000 or more	Percent of farms with sales of: $100,000 or more	Government payments: Total ($1,000)	Government payments: Percent of farms
	117	118	119	120	121	122	123	124	125	126	127	128	129	130	131	132
ILLINOIS—Cont'd																
Winnebago	183	-0.4	227	0.5	159.6	1 434 529	6 329	127 939	106.4	131 822	79.1	20.9	43.2	23.4	5 109	61.6
Woodford	323	12.0	337	0.5	291.6	2 612 922	7 750	210 760	240.6	251 196	78.5	21.5	62.3	40.6	6 107	79.2
INDIANA	14 720	-0.4	251	437.4	12 590.6	1 342 826	5 354	143 235	11 210.8	191 001	67.2	32.8	48.3	24.4	267 287	54.7
Adams	210	15.2	142	0.1	186.0	825 272	5 794	92 331	250.3	169 571	48.1	51.9	55.8	25.1	3 765	37.6
Allen	271	6.6	157	0.4	241.5	969 217	6 174	87 928	187.6	108 776	79.6	20.4	48.8	20.6	6 302	52.5
Bartholomew	172	3.2	275	13.5	153.4	1 619 191	5 878	151 406	95.6	153 387	89.5	10.5	54.9	27.1	4 647	63.7
Benton	254	-6.1	667	D	247.4	4 308 843	6 457	328 864	210.9	553 499	80.8	19.2	73.5	59.8	4 782	85.0
Blackford	88	4.0	335	D	81.2	1 414 730	4 228	176 620	71.5	271 764	D	D	56.3	28.9	1 380	66.2
Boone	222	-0.5	365	0.9	210.3	2 253 794	6 171	194 476	146.0	240 486	88.5	11.5	52.9	32.6	3 428	54.7
Brown	15	-14.0	84	0.1	6.6	337 468	4 002	37 514	4.2	24 486	D	D	16.8	2.9	156	28.3
Carroll	204	6.1	416	0.4	189.5	2 837 483	6 826	234 244	221.4	450 982	61.5	38.5	65.4	46.4	3 497	63.7
Cass	200	-12.2	291	1.9	181.6	1 575 185	5 412	185 317	158.4	230 281	78.2	21.8	55.8	30.5	4 080	73.3
Clark	79	-9.4	153	0.4	54.2	644 767	4 228	83 882	32.1	62 418	82.4	17.6	37.9	11.5	1 034	48.2
Clay	163	3.4	281	0.2	137.4	1 226 095	4 358	143 682	60.3	104 079	92.2	7.8	42.8	22.3	2 433	76.0
Clinton	223	-12.5	374	D	211.6	2 497 002	6 672	245 072	251.5	421 293	71.0	29.0	61.1	40.7	4 216	69.5
Crawford	46	2.2	137	0.0	16.2	351 639	2 561	40 038	7.2	21 323	D	D	17.2	2.4	288	29.6
Daviess	225	12.9	170	5.8	189.4	1 100 902	6 479	108 929	190.1	143 498	41.9	58.1	44.5	17.1	3 949	24.0
Dearborn	57	-14.1	101	0.1	26.8	410 578	4 071	46 287	12.4	22 191	74.9	25.1	27.3	6.1	650	33.9
Decatur	187	-8.9	306	0.0	162.6	1 627 090	5 321	166 746	159.4	261 293	58.0	42.0	62.8	37.0	3 721	74.1
DeKalb	161	0.1	174	0.8	136.8	771 247	4 429	92 135	106.9	115 738	65.5	34.5	35.8	16.6	4 689	73.6
Delaware	175	13.5	287	0.0	160.4	1 522 762	5 300	152 951	125.6	205 836	93.2	6.8	52.1	26.9	3 980	67.4
Dubois	175	-4.0	243	0.2	130.0	1 086 538	4 473	142 382	241.0	334 742	21.8	78.2	55.7	25.1	3 256	63.5
Elkhart	173	5.8	100	25.5	140.2	808 782	8 067	83 012	296.8	172 178	28.0	72.0	51.8	27.4	2 785	20.1
Fayette	78	-15.4	225	D	63.8	1 047 712	4 647	117 945	40.1	115 651	82.7	17.3	49.3	25.1	1 421	61.1
Floyd	21	-10.6	77	0.0	12.2	413 040	5 331	53 170	4.6	16 621	78.7	21.4	17.3	3.2	299	23.8
Fountain	214	13.6	466	D	190.5	2 236 072	4 797	218 709	116.7	253 644	D	D	52.4	30.9	3 690	68.9
Franklin	125	-1.1	172	0.1	85.1	786 644	4 577	92 254	54.0	74 304	78.8	21.2	47.3	17.6	2 101	61.9
Fulton	188	1.9	289	22.9	169.4	1 449 573	5 024	178 933	140.7	215 464	84.9	15.1	57.7	31.1	3 180	61.1
Gibson	268	16.0	455	4.8	250.3	2 426 261	5 329	255 418	146.4	248 542	87.7	12.3	63.2	35.5	4 803	70.6
Grant	183	-9.3	367	D	171.5	2 046 020	5 579	209 740	138.0	275 964	90.4	9.6	60.0	36.8	3 298	68.4
Greene	181	6.7	224	2.2	132.9	881 351	3 942	108 274	97.4	120 212	55.7	44.3	37.9	12.3	2 470	40.7
Hamilton	131	5.9	219	3.7	120.9	1 406 630	6 428	132 154	116.2	194 256	97.1	2.9	45.8	21.7	1 833	44.1
Hancock	166	-3.4	275	0.2	156.6	1 570 192	5 718	148 467	110.4	182 821	83.7	16.3	47.2	24.8	3 001	50.8
Harrison	135	-12.9	140	0.0	85.0	513 898	3 681	71 044	58.0	59 968	47.1	52.9	29.2	8.0	1 556	38.8
Hendricks	218	27.2	315	0.1	200.9	1 835 824	5 834	163 981	89.4	128 772	92.0	8.0	42.9	20.7	3 783	48.4
Henry	176	1.2	251	0.0	158.4	1 244 617	4 952	157 963	115.5	164 479	74.6	25.4	49.1	23.8	3 282	58.4
Howard	144	-11.1	303	D	134.5	1 924 391	6 353	182 880	140.4	294 874	81.1	18.9	68.1	37.2	2 993	67.0
Huntington	189	-5.1	272	0.7	172.6	1 481 458	5 452	216 573	174.8	251 550	65.7	34.3	50.5	28.2	4 185	71.7
Jackson	184	-12.1	247	2.9	139.9	1 132 552	4 582	174 212	184.4	247 907	42.2	57.8	50.8	24.5	3 876	66.7
Jasper	283	-16.9	460	21.1	256.7	2 819 873	6 132	250 876	357.4	581 142	58.3	41.7	61.3	40.0	4 736	72.8
Jay	176	-10.9	210	D	156.3	1 380 341	6 565	137 579	282.0	337 292	35.2	64.8	53.7	29.3	3 621	64.6
Jefferson	95	-6.9	155	0.0	61.7	549 182	3 540	72 820	40.4	65 737	76.7	23.3	32.4	8.8	1 907	53.3
Jennings	123	-10.8	234	0.1	87.7	910 475	3 896	126 716	79.7	150 917	57.8	42.2	37.5	16.9	3 214	57.4
Johnson	145	1.7	257	3.1	131.6	1 567 699	6 091	140 655	70.6	125 575	87.1	12.9	42.7	23.5	2 779	50.5
Knox	329	0.6	664	34.9	304.0	3 748 448	5 646	405 986	218.1	439 627	83.4	16.6	70.8	45.8	5 837	72.6
Kosciusko	255	1.4	204	18.0	219.6	1 198 890	5 866	110 144	282.1	226 226	47.0	53.0	42.4	20.8	4 140	51.7
LaGrange	204	26.2	84	25.6	147.4	628 366	7 448	56 611	262.6	108 542	26.1	73.9	55.2	23.1	2 276	12.5
Lake	133	3.6	309	8.1	124.2	1 755 500	5 673	178 735	100.8	234 374	98.1	1.9	44.4	30.0	2 419	49.1
LaPorte	228	-11.0	312	54.4	209.3	1 896 432	6 084	188 253	223.1	305 215	80.5	19.5	55.7	33.8	4 036	58.4
Lawrence	135	0.0	168	D	70.8	534 073	3 172	64 313	33.2	41 486	68.1	31.9	31.5	5.3	2 091	48.1
Madison	205	-5.6	278	0.9	191.5	1 677 897	6 028	169 689	164.4	223 026	91.7	8.3	53.5	29.0	3 565	58.8
Marion	20	16.5	87	0.2	16.0	558 134	6 422	60 861	27.3	117 991	D	D	29.4	10.8	220	16.5
Marshall	206	15.2	235	13.4	181.8	1 222 325	5 202	140 648	147.6	168 141	73.5	26.5	49.7	26.9	3 430	49.2
Martin	63	2.0	221	0.4	39.0	892 177	4 037	105 095	54.3	191 735	24.9	75.1	36.7	13.4	701	33.2
Miami	175	-1.5	263	3.1	158.1	1 333 943	5 069	145 643	156.9	235 605	67.1	32.9	55.0	32.6	3 696	68.8
Monroe	53	-1.4	114	0.1	27.6	551 762	4 831	55 294	13.0	28 134	66.7	33.3	28.4	5.6	754	29.0
Montgomery	287	-4.8	392	1.0	264.6	2 189 187	5 585	199 959	175.4	239 638	83.9	16.1	53.4	30.6	6 178	68.6
Morgan	137	20.2	235	0.0	114.2	1 158 144	4 922	130 446	51.8	88 768	87.9	12.1	36.4	14.8	2 146	46.0
Newton	192	0.8	552	6.3	174.3	3 131 055	5 674	315 417	242.6	697 187	53.1	46.9	66.1	46.3	3 086	79.6
Noble	181	13.5	156	13.7	150.1	754 298	4 834	95 800	143.7	123 588	57.4	42.6	44.3	18.4	4 236	52.5
Ohio	21	-0.2	126	0.2	10.5	446 731	3 560	57 649	4.2	24 462	74.7	25.3	28.7	4.1	368	34.5
Orange	98	0.9	206	0.0	56.9	717 036	3 488	102 278	64.0	133 902	22.4	77.6	30.3	8.6	1 599	47.9
Owen	96	8.8	174	0.1	62.5	590 885	3 396	76 073	23.5	42 805	82.7	17.3	29.0	8.0	1 537	49.7
Parke	177	-0.4	308	2.7	120.9	1 282 422	4 169	131 817	64.2	111 779	81.9	18.1	43.7	22.1	2 785	50.7
Perry	66	-5.9	160	0.0	30.7	481 276	2 999	62 182	20.3	49 208	47.4	52.6	35.1	7.5	605	42.4

STATE County	Water use, 2010		Wholesale trade,[1] 2007				Retail trade,[2] 2007				Real estate and rental and leasing,[2] 2007			
	Total water withdrawn (mil gal/day)	Gallons withdrawn per person per day	Number of establish-ments	Number of employees	Sales (mil dol)	Annual payroll (mil dol)	Number of establish-ments	Number of employees	Sales (mil dol)	Annual payroll (mil dol)	Number of establish-ments	Number of employees	Receipts (mil dol)	Annual payroll (mil dol)
	133	134	135	136	137	138	139	140	141	142	143	144	145	146
ILLINOIS—Cont'd														
Winnebago	35.6	120	363	4 931	2 624.7	209.7	1 051	16 095	3 852.0	346.4	245	1 585	211.3	46.2
Woodford	9.6	248	48	D	D	D	102	1 089	278.3	21.6	30	D	D	D
INDIANA	8 643.0	1 333	6 756	97 219	67 634.9	4 295.6	23 692	333 172	78 745.6	7 123.1	6 389	34 272	5 448.1	1 061.6
Adams	7.8	226	36	D	D	D	150	1 672	369.9	32.3	30	99	8.0	2.3
Allen	48.6	137	548	D	D	D	1 345	21 214	4 774.2	440.3	410	1 913	323.3	54.3
Bartholomew	18.2	237	80	1 012	747.3	50.5	375	5 133	1 075.2	106.7	74	319	50.1	8.9
Benton	0.9	101	16	D	D	D	43	241	50.9	4.0	3	6	0.3	0.2
Blackford	2.0	155	11	112	158.9	3.0	51	435	97.9	9.3	12	38	2.9	0.6
Boone	4.4	78	58	532	386.4	22.8	176	1 769	484.5	37.7	47	110	20.7	3.1
Brown	0.3	21	8	64	4.3	1.0	93	467	61.5	7.1	17	47	6.0	1.6
Carroll	5.1	255	21	D	D	D	58	529	102.1	8.4	14	20	4.6	1.0
Cass	28.8	738	42	458	439.0	14.8	134	1 561	340.9	34.6	21	72	7.5	1.3
Clark	25.7	233	101	1 375	1 062.0	67.1	446	7 214	1 729.5	157.4	100	593	91.4	15.1
Clay	1.2	43	15	D	D	D	96	1 040	312.4	20.8	13	41	4.7	0.5
Clinton	6.2	185	29	D	D	D	115	1 009	223.6	22.1	19	90	5.9	1.5
Crawford	2.8	262	2	D	D	D	32	189	40.7	3.5	6	D	D	D
Daviess	8.6	271	28	282	153.7	10.3	121	1 563	381.5	33.9	16	57	6.2	1.0
Dearborn	601.2	12 013	32	D	D	D	151	1 866	509.7	43.3	39	212	29.7	5.6
Decatur	5.3	204	32	D	D	D	119	1 403	315.0	29.7	21	60	8.7	1.6
DeKalb	8.8	208	45	D	D	D	147	1 744	408.9	36.8	33	184	18.3	5.8
Delaware	15.6	132	97	984	424.1	31.6	484	6 563	1 516.8	130.8	113	575	89.0	17.2
Dubois	7.6	182	64	846	530.6	33.3	242	3 215	763.4	74.3	38	D	D	D
Elkhart	33.0	167	371	6 096	3 231.4	255.2	727	9 710	2 416.9	219.0	180	813	109.4	20.4
Fayette	2.9	117	14	126	85.9	5.7	84	1 018	208.9	19.7	21	61	7.2	1.2
Floyd	254.6	3 414	78	873	1 420.5	33.3	221	3 457	787.4	71.9	81	351	43.9	7.4
Fountain	2.2	129	14	105	124.8	3.6	72	672	142.5	10.8	8	29	0.9	0.3
Franklin	3.9	169	8	61	18.6	2.1	79	614	171.3	11.2	8	36	2.5	0.5
Fulton	7.7	368	15	125	62.1	4.1	82	925	200.8	17.6	19	66	3.5	0.9
Gibson	59.8	1 785	20	D	D	D	133	1 597	442.6	30.4	17	58	10.3	1.4
Grant	11.8	169	44	D	D	D	282	3 380	765.8	69.7	60	217	23.2	5.1
Greene	5.5	166	15	D	D	D	118	1 087	226.1	18.9	14	54	2.4	0.5
Hamilton	72.7	265	346	4 043	2 779.5	231.5	821	14 029	3 295.4	323.6	367	2 871	558.5	129.1
Hancock	7.0	100	51	826	519.9	32.6	165	2 012	568.5	47.9	43	137	22.1	3.1
Harrison	3.7	95	27	296	98.6	8.7	134	1 421	400.9	32.3	19	61	7.4	1.0
Hendricks	8.6	59	103	2 465	2 520.7	103.1	437	8 440	2 088.7	176.6	110	350	54.5	8.4
Henry	5.1	103	23	280	180.2	13.3	167	1 861	455.0	41.3	34	83	8.2	1.5
Howard	17.5	212	62	510	319.5	24.1	374	5 240	1 194.7	105.6	83	320	47.7	7.5
Huntington	4.7	125	38	D	D	D	136	1 539	328.0	29.2	32	109	8.4	1.6
Jackson	9.9	233	42	D	D	D	199	2 193	529.5	49.2	43	171	20.0	3.1
Jasper	55.6	1 662	37	234	163.4	9.8	127	1 425	405.5	28.1	26	112	36.5	3.3
Jay	4.2	195	21	270	413.7	8.3	68	690	139.5	14.7	8	20	1.8	0.4
Jefferson	1 249.1	38 519	14	D	D	D	162	1 754	382.7	37.2	38	126	15.8	2.8
Jennings	3.1	107	15	D	D	D	80	776	223.8	18.0	13	26	3.6	0.8
Johnson	13.6	97	108	1 181	682.3	52.8	513	9 056	2 072.9	189.7	153	532	90.4	13.0
Knox	47.1	1 224	59	618	321.5	21.7	192	2 194	471.8	44.8	39	163	17.1	3.1
Kosciusko	24.4	315	87	D	D	D	314	3 780	794.9	80.9	80	196	49.4	6.3
LaGrange	19.9	536	33	318	104.6	7.3	166	1 212	276.9	25.1	24	65	9.0	1.1
Lake	1 696.0	3 419	396	5 198	3 348.8	254.9	1 715	26 506	7 102.4	559.8	441	2 376	328.0	64.1
LaPorte	44.0	395	123	1 446	856.2	54.1	495	6 054	1 363.6	114.9	102	438	60.4	11.1
Lawrence	8.2	177	22	D	D	D	169	2 041	481.6	44.7	29	85	12.5	1.9
Madison	19.1	145	75	1 113	574.2	44.1	431	5 542	1 234.9	108.0	103	434	61.5	10.2
Marion	283.5	314	1 358	25 490	15 780.3	1 254.1	3 291	53 214	12 951.3	1 278.7	1 297	10 411	1 935.6	390.8
Marshall	7.3	154	65	D	D	D	191	2 164	551.0	41.0	34	98	11.0	1.9
Martin	1.5	149	5	39	51.1	1.0	34	361	81.2	6.2	6	14	1.7	0.2
Miami	21.2	575	30	D	D	D	109	936	235.4	19.8	30	103	6.8	1.8
Monroe	18.3	133	83	1 331	683.2	47.0	508	7 479	1 530.8	146.7	187	1 133	144.0	29.5
Montgomery	6.1	160	43	338	368.6	15.1	147	1 759	429.2	34.9	28	113	11.8	2.0
Morgan	183.8	2 668	44	310	185.0	13.6	212	2 578	586.9	54.2	62	179	21.7	3.7
Newton	6.0	422	17	128	121.6	5.7	55	391	96.7	7.5	10	25	2.5	0.4
Noble	11.2	235	36	D	D	D	140	1 572	357.0	31.0	41	121	13.2	2.3
Ohio	1.0	162	2	D	D	D	11	107	23.7	1.7	4	10	0.6	0.1
Orange	1.5	77	12	83	52.8	2.2	75	729	153.2	13.9	15	60	5.4	1.2
Owen	2.5	115	11	D	D	D	44	427	106.3	8.8	11	19	2.6	0.2
Parke	2.8	163	6	44	24.5	1.5	50	404	84.5	6.7	16	50	5.5	2.1
Perry	2.5	131	10	65	12.9	1.8	72	796	153.4	13.9	16	46	6.2	0.8

1. Merchant wholesalers, except manufacturers' sales branches and offices. 2. Employer establishments.

Table B. States and Counties — **Professional Services, Manufacturing, and Accommodation and Food Services**

STATE County	Professional, scientific, and technical services,[1] 2007				Manufacturing, 2007				Accommodation and food services, 2007			
	Number of establish-ments	Number of employees	Receipts (mil dol)	Annual payroll (mil dol)	Number of establish-ments	Number of employees	Receipts (mil dol)	Annual payroll (mil dol)	Number of establish-ments	Number of employees	Sales (mil dol)	Annual payroll (mil dol)
	147	148	149	150	151	152	153	154	155	156	157	158
ILLINOIS—Cont'd												
Winnebago	654	D	D	D	685	27 367	7 913.4	1 354.8	591	10 526	452.2	125.1
Woodford	43	137	12.0	4.6	47	1 869	963.3	78.4	62	746	26.0	7.2
INDIANA	12 959	95 701	12 128.9	4 785.9	9 015	536 907	221 877.8	24 474.7	12 932	254 293	11 669.8	3 175.2
Adams	48	198	16.1	6.3	65	5 564	2 127.7	215.6	53	948	27.1	7.8
Allen	889	6 829	716.2	333.7	568	30 612	19 741.9	1 526.0	703	15 470	550.5	169.0
Bartholomew	157	D	D	D	143	11 711	4 843.9	502.9	160	3 416	139.7	39.9
Benton	10	D	D	D	NA	NA	NA	NA	10	81	2.6	0.5
Blackford	14	92	8.6	2.7	30	1 437	397.1	62.4	20	213	8.0	2.0
Boone	154	618	133.3	28.8	74	2 131	D	D	102	1 473	54.5	15.5
Brown	40	D	D	D	NA	NA	NA	NA	47	559	19.8	6.8
Carroll	28	D	D	D	29	2 536	D	D	33	556	18.4	5.3
Cass	48	257	18.3	7.0	49	4 628	1 302.0	151.9	80	1 032	33.8	9.3
Clark	177	848	122.2	30.7	165	8 119	2 114.9	332.5	204	4 834	197.5	60.4
Clay	29	D	D	D	36	1 705	D	D	46	571	18.4	4.7
Clinton	43	149	13.7	3.7	50	3 910	2 283.5	139.2	56	759	25.1	6.9
Crawford	6	D	D	D	NA	NA	NA	NA	19	D	D	D
Daviess	36	346	36.4	14.2	71	2 036	643.4	54.6	62	772	25.9	6.9
Dearborn	76	316	28.4	10.8	48	D	786.1	D	79	D	D	D
Decatur	38	138	13.9	5.5	55	4 294	1 869.7	174.5	56	836	29.9	8.4
DeKalb	72	521	36.7	14.1	120	8 220	3 818.9	381.7	85	1 353	47.5	13.6
Delaware	169	D	D	D	150	5 268	1 280.6	232.7	216	4 981	160.8	48.3
Dubois	86	757	42.4	42.8	125	D	D	D	104	1 649	58.8	17.7
Elkhart	338	D	D	D	852	64 309	15 779.8	2 508.4	385	7 395	272.4	76.0
Fayette	29	D	D	D	30	2 265	486.5	107.8	47	594	21.6	5.6
Floyd	185	D	D	D	119	6 166	1 558.4	250.7	119	D	D	D
Fountain	20	90	4.2	1.4	23	2 228	498.4	90.0	36	387	12.0	3.6
Franklin	34	D	D	D	17	D	D	D	41	676	28.5	7.5
Fulton	30	190	14.9	5.2	51	2 248	524.3	83.6	47	D	D	D
Gibson	46	D	D	D	40	6 362	D	D	71	1 134	38.5	11.0
Grant	87	D	D	D	69	4 653	1 670.1	272.3	148	2 496	88.1	24.3
Greene	41	D	D	D	NA	NA	NA	NA	49	665	19.5	5.2
Hamilton	1 054	D	D	D	200	6 001	1 569.9	241.0	499	10 012	437.2	127.2
Hancock	123	683	59.1	50.5	67	3 118	1 256.0	129.8	97	1 823	66.3	19.0
Harrison	44	D	D	D	46	1 522	410.7	56.4	55	D	D	D
Hendricks	248	1 491	144.9	57.3	109	3 566	2 819.4	139.0	250	5 771	227.6	66.7
Henry	55	D	D	D	49	2 300	1 026.6	118.6	76	1 019	36.2	10.3
Howard	131	D	D	D	76	11 980	2 923.2	877.5	186	3 921	150.5	44.5
Huntington	42	186	16.3	5.2	71	4 357	1 478.6	195.1	100	1 333	44.3	13.4
Jackson	64	372	29.7	11.0	74	7 015	2 585.5	279.3	83	1 557	58.4	17.4
Jasper	54	D	D	D	38	1 549	601.1	62.1	65	1 051	33.9	9.3
Jay	23	90	5.6	1.8	33	2 523	835.1	100.5	36	D	D	D
Jefferson	57	280	18.6	6.5	60	3 881	1 477.0	165.4	77	1 152	43.2	11.3
Jennings	20	D	D	D	43	1 995	377.2	70.5	29	433	16.1	4.4
Johnson	253	1 235	107.4	37.6	133	5 904	1 609.9	233.2	265	5 447	208.4	62.7
Knox	57	227	20.2	5.8	38	1 917	774.3	68.2	83	1 502	56.8	14.9
Kosciusko	129	545	48.8	15.2	198	14 469	5 705.3	706.3	151	2 342	92.3	25.8
LaGrange	35	137	8.8	3.2	147	6 694	1 602.3	280.9	65	761	33.9	9.4
Lake	933	D	D	D	411	26 654	21 914.5	1 489.0	993	19 402	1 069.2	265.5
LaPorte	169	D	D	D	184	8 808	2 364.0	363.9	259	5 254	389.7	80.1
Lawrence	63	406	42.5	16.5	71	3 016	716.5	160.7	74	1 227	43.0	12.5
Madison	202	D	D	D	118	4 652	1 046.9	191.8	246	4 343	155.1	43.6
Marion	2 816	D	D	D	1 016	57 069	24 333.9	3 137.1	2 111	45 923	2 248.4	663.8
Marshall	69	386	28.9	9.9	125	6 310	1 239.4	230.3	98	1 408	50.5	13.8
Martin	10	D	D	D	NA	NA	NA	NA	25	D	D	D
Miami	34	140	9.4	3.9	50	2 576	711.3	88.0	59	805	25.8	0.9
Monroe	282	D	D	D	108	6 389	1 799.3	279.5	335	7 271	287.8	79.1
Montgomery	55	242	17.9	6.3	57	6 258	2 768.4	298.5	86	1 152	48.5	12.6
Morgan	103	342	32.3	10.8	66	D	D	92.5	80	1 530	59.1	17.4
Newton	15	D	D	D	27	1 108	197.5	32.0	32	256	8.0	2.0
Noble	56	259	30.3	8.5	138	9 525	2 454.5	345.8	82	1 028	35.9	9.9
Ohio	2	D	D	D	NA	NA	NA	NA	15	D	D	D
Orange	22	71	4.5	1.6	24	1 414	201.7	45.1	28	D	D	D
Owen	22	D	D	D	33	2 040	D	D	23	316	10.4	3.0
Parke	12	D	D	D	13	660	137.6	21.5	36	D	D	D
Perry	25	76	8.1	2.1	29	2 003	600.2	92.4	41	D	D	D

1. Establishment subject to federal tax.

STATE County	Health care and social assistance, 2007				Other services, 2007				Nonemployer businesses, 2013		Value of residential construction authorized by building permits, 2014	
	Number of establish-ments	Number of employees	Receipts (mil dol)	Annual payroll (mil dol)	Number of establish-ments	Number of employees	Receipts (mil dol)	Annual payroll (mil dol)	Number	Receipts (mil dol)	New Construction ($1,000)	Number of housing units
	159	160	161	162	163	164	165	166	167	168	169	170
ILLINOIS—Cont'd												
Winnebago	669	19 367	1 909.7	798.6	551	3 698	305.0	89.8	18 184	626.0	16 123	139
Woodford	42	1 252	56.4	27.8	55	D	D	D	2 370	80.4	17 318	75
INDIANA	14 972	370 093	34 768.4	13 453.8	11 458	75 292	8 451.2	1 892.9	390 233	15 418.6	3 222 176	17 816
Adams	53	1 727	103.5	38.9	73	307	24.5	6.4	3 001	144.6	10 253	79
Allen	1 011	28 617	2 769.4	1 073.6	692	5 000	403.4	127.8	22 540	906.7	201 106	1 115
Bartholomew	228	5 095	439.1	178.5	120	857	82.8	19.5	4 130	161.4	62 387	254
Benton	13	114	6.5	2.9	14	32	3.9	0.8	625	22.9	1 184	2
Blackford	25	D	D	D	23	65	6.5	1.3	621	20.9	357	3
Boone	116	2 134	175.6	71.9	97	563	40.9	11.6	4 861	225.7	122 884	526
Brown	26	228	12.6	5.7	20	65	6.6	1.7	1 423	53.2	9 058	48
Carroll	29	299	15.3	7.5	33	87	6.4	1.8	1 234	46.6	4 039	24
Cass	75	2 973	173.8	80.2	75	492	26.6	9.2	1 760	62.1	1 817	12
Clark	233	5 037	453.1	182.3	182	1 226	105.3	30.9	6 448	259.0	92 349	531
Clay	56	D	D	D	46	255	12.1	3.2	1 461	48.4	1 732	14
Clinton	50	1 235	77.3	29.7	55	314	26.9	7.3	1 634	55.8	4 495	24
Crawford	14	166	8.3	3.6	9	D	D	D	683	22.9	0	0
Daviess	79	1 468	96.7	40.4	64	365	65.4	8.7	2 132	93.8	400	4
Dearborn	107	D	D	D	71	326	24.3	6.6	2 967	112.2	14 207	65
Decatur	58	1 026	78.0	33.1	47	251	19.2	4.2	1 591	62.7	8 318	50
DeKalb	89	1 615	121.4	47.6	79	303	20.8	6.3	2 496	92.3	18 867	94
Delaware	316	10 078	836.1	335.6	203	1 206	119.8	26.7	5 564	205.1	15 776	98
Dubois	125	2 965	239.4	103.7	86	478	56.8	10.9	2 740	107.1	23 441	124
Elkhart	347	9 746	1 024.6	358.1	374	2 298	195.7	60.1	12 323	511.3	57 187	270
Fayette	65	1 217	114.0	48.1	44	190	17.8	3.9	1 158	39.3	1 431	11
Floyd	233	5 234	437.2	172.7	140	846	71.3	16.9	5 001	204.8	32 723	142
Fountain	25	493	27.6	10.8	29	90	8.9	1.8	941	37.5	289	2
Franklin	58	D	D	D	37	D	D	D	1 608	65.4	8 433	35
Fulton	45	838	68.0	29.8	36	112	11.8	2.6	1 392	47.7	3 204	15
Gibson	83	D	D	D	58	267	18.1	5.1	1 698	58.8	18 995	121
Grant	176	5 003	435.1	182.6	124	549	38.1	10.4	3 248	111.9	7 913	68
Greene	71	1 104	65.8	26.4	50	D	D	D	1 830	61.1	NA	NA
Hamilton	729	12 555	1 354.4	494.5	461	3 217	218.4	68.8	24 778	1 281.1	729 080	3 684
Hancock	131	2 265	187.3	70.9	105	472	39.4	9.4	4 837	192.0	73 451	395
Harrison	69	1 327	88.4	36.0	46	150	17.0	3.6	2 575	90.3	14 513	84
Hendricks	260	4 706	427.5	170.6	208	1 051	84.9	24.2	10 069	418.0	186 405	1 145
Henry	92	2 418	155.5	68.2	71	316	32.0	5.6	2 424	84.4	4 757	18
Howard	223	5 618	513.4	195.6	131	711	53.2	14.1	4 233	137.9	19 488	140
Huntington	73	1 823	122.2	47.3	77	341	18.8	5.6	1 912	64.0	10 328	53
Jackson	108	2 174	158.1	69.7	80	431	35.9	9.2	2 167	73.1	19 468	178
Jasper	56	1 432	92.1	38.3	52	157	14.4	3.4	1 789	76.3	10 632	51
Jay	35	707	59.8	22.4	40	123	8.6	2.0	1 330	53.0	2 969	21
Jefferson	86	2 209	178.0	82.7	57	254	19.4	4.8	1 755	68.1	3 518	29
Jennings	60	886	69.7	29.3	27	D	D	D	1 454	50.8	4 996	47
Johnson	276	5 814	446.4	176.6	216	1 434	113.7	35.6	9 184	404.4	136 000	668
Knox	129	3 581	296.3	116.5	71	491	32.2	8.8	1 875	70.6	5 190	34
Kosciusko	144	3 432	225.9	101.9	160	877	81.6	20.2	4 896	181.7	38 626	261
LaGrange	45	770	57.0	21.6	49	217	17.7	4.8	3 429	142.7	18 433	121
Lake	1 220	31 776	3 101.1	1 205.3	902	6 829	548.1	167.1	27 379	1 011.6	211 716	908
LaPorte	236	4 900	521.2	188.2	207	1 172	74.6	22.2	5 747	202.7	24 548	125
Lawrence	101	2 407	184.2	75.6	85	417	26.1	7.6	2 470	80.9	6 336	42
Madison	266	6 713	556.4	223.6	201	1 239	83.4	24.0	6 466	210.3	18 789	92
Marion	2 402	74 201	8 186.4	3 168.6	1 780	16 477	2 991.1	535.3	58 749	2 281.9	177 765	1 195
Marshall	80	1 947	152.3	56.3	87	509	45.3	14.4	2 921	109.8	18 071	83
Martin	12	D	D	D	14	D	D	D	619	20.6	1 075	8
Miami	43	1 226	77.8	29.9	56	295	18.8	5.7	1 675	55.6	2 397	10
Monroe	304	7 565	690.6	298.4	211	2 080	609.7	56.0	8 760	332.8	80 041	521
Montgomery	87	1 367	103.3	47.0	83	525	50.5	13.0	2 103	74.5	7 556	45
Morgan	111	1 668	145.8	55.5	110	480	37.5	10.0	4 485	176.6	24 221	129
Newton	15	165	7.7	4.0	16	58	7.9	1.4	767	34.1	4 852	22
Noble	76	1 354	97.2	40.6	82	000	54.2	6.8	2 504	91.2	14 224	87
Ohio	8	D	D	D	6	D	D	D	348	10.3	3 524	20
Orange	43	951	49.1	20.3	30	132	9.2	1.9	1 167	39.8	100	1
Owen	23	390	18.9	8.6	31	D	D	D	1 415	51.8	3 051	18
Parke	27	484	24.6	10.0	27	84	9.7	1.8	1 046	50.5	3 046	26
Perry	42	832	69.7	22.2	30	81	7.2	1.7	876	35.6	4 277	48

STATE / County	Government employment and payroll, 2012: Full-time equivalent employees	March payroll (dollars)	March payroll (percent of total): Adminis-tration, judicial, and legal	Police and Corrections	Fire Protection	Highways and transpor-tation	Health and Welfare	Natural resources and utilities	Education and libraries	Local government finances, 2012: General revenue: Total (mil dol)	Inter-govern-mental (mil dol)	Taxes: Total (mil dol)	Taxes: Per capita[1] (dollars): Total	Per capita[1] (dollars): Property
	171	172	173	174	175	176	177	178	179	180	181	182	183	184
ILLINOIS—Cont'd														
Winnebago	10 237	41 731 581	5.0	11.9	6.0	3.7	3.9	7.5	61.2	1 183.6	493.6	527.0	1 804	1 627
Woodford	1 508	5 339 422	4.9	6.4	1.3	4.5	0.9	2.8	78.6	119.7	45.6	61.2	1 570	1 555
INDIANA	X	X	X	X	X	X	X	X	X	X	X	X	X	X
Adams	1 561	4 888 145	4.7	5.9	0.8	2.1	44.7	3.1	37.8	145.4	46.1	31.4	914	779
Allen	10 511	40 339 187	6.4	12.9	4.3	4.7	1.4	5.9	62.8	1 115.0	515.1	426.4	1 183	960
Bartholomew	4 371	15 688 309	3.2	6.6	2.9	1.3	44.5	3.1	37.7	469.7	111.3	106.7	1 348	1 076
Benton	555	1 313 464	8.3	7.4	0.0	6.3	5.5	2.3	69.0	40.6	19.2	16.2	1 838	1 489
Blackford	419	1 328 279	7.1	13.0	1.8	3.7	2.2	4.2	65.8	39.7	21.9	11.2	898	707
Boone	2 618	9 699 681	4.3	6.4	4.6	1.8	30.1	1.6	50.8	311.1	88.4	80.6	1 367	1 089
Brown	487	1 429 248	8.6	9.6	0.0	3.1	3.6	3.8	70.3	49.6	24.3	20.7	1 373	893
Carroll	613	1 723 537	7.5	7.8	0.0	5.1	6.1	5.3	66.8	54.7	26.6	20.7	1 030	776
Cass	2 403	7 224 020	3.1	5.7	1.4	1.6	31.7	7.4	48.9	182.8	62.7	46.0	1 192	797
Clark	4 732	18 084 071	3.7	7.9	2.7	2.4	38.3	3.7	41.0	466.1	142.4	134.5	1 201	884
Clay	1 049	2 619 145	6.8	6.9	1.9	3.0	1.0	5.5	72.4	75.7	42.8	22.3	831	529
Clinton	1 323	4 321 114	6.4	5.1	2.9	2.8	0.7	8.5	67.5	112.5	54.4	40.9	1 238	878
Crawford	416	1 229 568	6.6	5.4	0.0	4.7	3.2	1.7	77.0	32.3	18.4	8.3	783	640
Daviess	1 354	4 234 993	5.9	7.5	1.3	3.1	36.1	7.1	38.5	148.6	57.8	30.0	937	730
Dearborn	2 410	9 132 488	4.4	7.5	0.7	1.6	40.1	3.6	41.5	318.7	143.7	50.2	1 007	864
Decatur	1 237	4 252 343	4.4	5.2	2.3	2.0	40.2	2.9	42.7	119.2	37.5	26.3	1 009	794
DeKalb	1 614	5 058 353	9.1	8.5	2.6	3.0	1.3	8.0	66.9	153.8	68.7	51.5	1 216	955
Delaware	3 335	10 832 587	6.2	9.0	3.6	4.7	3.7	4.2	64.9	345.4	171.1	109.1	930	778
Dubois	1 643	4 804 962	7.3	8.1	0.8	5.6	2.5	16.6	59.1	155.2	64.9	49.7	1 180	905
Elkhart	6 985	24 411 992	5.4	8.4	4.1	2.5	1.6	3.6	73.6	630.5	315.1	218.4	1 094	907
Fayette	815	2 807 530	4.2	10.7	4.2	2.9	3.8	5.1	67.2	77.2	42.2	24.8	1 032	701
Floyd	4 128	15 144 305	3.0	3.9	2.2	0.8	54.1	2.1	33.3	467.4	119.9	81.4	1 081	846
Fountain	702	1 835 852	6.6	8.5	1.6	5.5	6.2	3.5	67.3	53.7	31.0	15.9	930	767
Franklin	568	1 607 664	8.0	8.8	0.0	4.5	1.5	2.6	73.5	47.8	26.1	16.2	704	477
Fulton	976	3 541 251	3.8	5.5	1.3	2.2	47.4	1.8	37.3	96.4	27.9	20.7	1 000	751
Gibson	1 093	3 390 759	8.4	7.1	3.0	3.7	4.8	4.6	68.3	107.6	54.3	38.1	1 140	1 012
Grant	2 226	7 247 230	7.6	13.8	3.6	3.3	0.8	2.9	67.7	198.6	103.6	70.9	1 023	759
Greene	1 299	4 191 866	4.9	6.2	1.0	2.4	23.5	4.2	56.9	123.7	53.8	24.9	756	573
Hamilton	9 749	38 707 131	4.7	8.4	7.3	2.0	14.0	2.7	59.9	1 219.3	387.4	488.6	1 688	1 330
Hancock	2 896	9 851 360	4.6	8.2	3.9	1.7	31.8	2.5	45.9	327.9	103.5	93.6	1 319	977
Harrison	1 349	4 713 395	5.2	4.9	0.0	2.6	36.7	2.0	47.0	155.4	72.7	26.9	689	469
Hendricks	6 025	22 075 204	3.7	5.6	5.8	1.4	30.4	2.6	50.1	681.2	209.2	213.8	1 421	1 074
Henry	2 369	7 555 604	4.3	5.2	1.2	2.3	32.1	3.4	50.6	241.5	75.8	42.1	853	643
Howard	4 091	15 459 399	5.0	6.2	3.5	2.0	35.8	3.0	42.2	435.8	136.7	118.7	1 433	1 170
Huntington	1 237	3 734 687	5.5	8.0	4.3	3.5	1.1	5.4	69.0	101.2	49.3	39.0	1 055	770
Jackson	2 118	8 012 413	3.8	6.5	2.3	1.6	47.5	1.4	36.3	212.1	54.8	30.5	707	506
Jasper	1 433	4 507 418	5.5	8.1	0.3	2.6	29.7	5.3	47.8	131.9	42.0	40.9	1 224	719
Jay	1 099	3 415 778	5.2	6.1	1.4	1.7	36.1	3.1	45.2	123.7	55.6	25.5	1 196	860
Jefferson	902	3 038 763	7.5	7.5	0.7	2.5	2.6	4.5	74.2	89.4	47.0	26.9	826	757
Jennings	908	2 922 410	4.4	7.4	0.6	3.0	2.6	5.4	75.0	78.7	47.6	22.3	793	611
Johnson	4 964	16 948 881	4.8	8.7	2.9	1.9	18.6	2.7	59.4	506.1	198.1	162.0	1 131	885
Knox	2 489	8 335 443	2.7	4.6	1.9	1.6	60.2	2.8	25.4	286.7	52.9	33.9	890	737
Kosciusko	2 569	8 158 465	6.1	8.0	0.4	2.3	0.9	3.7	77.8	243.0	119.1	85.5	1 101	909
LaGrange	1 149	3 367 799	4.8	6.5	0.3	3.1	0.6	2.5	80.6	95.5	51.4	32.4	865	663
Lake	18 892	64 877 066	9.2	9.9	4.1	4.4	2.1	8.2	60.1	2 367.0	1 042.1	989.0	2 003	1 956
LaPorte	4 264	12 639 630	5.9	11.9	4.3	3.5	3.5	6.6	63.1	369.8	180.5	137.0	1 231	1 055
Lawrence	1 833	6 258 969	4.2	7.1	2.2	2.7	24.3	3.4	55.6	143.8	73.1	50.7	1 100	799
Madison	3 695	12 894 572	8.1	13.7	4.5	3.9	1.5	11.3	55.4	411.1	191.4	142.7	1 095	811
Marion	34 223	145 207 021	3.0	7.6	6.1	1.6	14.0	18.4	48.0	4 321.3	1 815.1	1 329.5	1 447	1 014
Marshall	1 390	4 686 571	6.2	10.5	1.5	4.0	1.4	5.1	69.8	140.9	76.1	48.0	1 020	856
Martin	313	962 585	8.0	8.2	0.0	3.8	2.8	1.5	67.8	29.8	16.1	7.1	689	541
Miami	1 311	4 091 188	4.5	6.1	2.6	3.8	0.7	6.7	70.0	119.6	65.2	34.0	931	637
Monroe	3 589	12 483 781	10.4	10.4	5.5	5.0	2.7	8.7	56.9	339.2	139.6	147.6	1 046	827
Montgomery	1 366	4 441 185	3.7	7.5	4.2	3.9	1.0	10.2	68.9	131.4	58.1	56.2	1 468	1 078
Morgan	2 356	7 692 514	4.7	7.9	3.4	3.0	18.5	1.3	60.5	238.5	98.7	72.4	1 044	538
Newton	607	1 789 217	10.0	9.0	0.0	3.9	4.7	2.6	67.9	61.2	25.8	18.1	1 291	1 109
Noble	1 526	4 688 687	7.9	9.1	1.0	3.1	0.3	4.9	73.3	132.6	63.7	46.2	972	770
Ohio	248	804 741	9.9	6.7	0.0	5.5	3.4	20.4	52.3	29.4	20.3	4.8	786	579
Orange	656	2 087 602	7.2	6.3	0.2	4.7	1.4	5.5	73.3	74.2	49.7	16.5	838	620
Owen	478	1 467 231	7.6	11.8	0.0	5.3	4.5	1.2	68.4	51.9	27.2	15.9	742	538
Parke	550	1 469 526	6.3	9.1	0.8	4.5	3.5	4.2	69.9	47.3	28.5	14.7	862	531
Perry	892	2 938 269	4.0	4.8	0.4	4.2	35.8	7.7	42.5	92.9	30.5	18.1	929	744

1. Based on the resident population estimated as of July 1 of the year shown.

STATE County	Local government finances, 2012 (cont.)									Government employment, 2013			Presidential election,[2] 2012		
	Direct general expenditure							Debt outstanding					Percent of vote cast:		
			Percent of total for:												
	Total (mil dol)	Per capita[1] (dollars)	Educa-tion	Health and hospitals	Police protec-tion	Public welfare	High-ways	Total (mil dol)	Per capita[1] (dollars)	Federal civilian	Federal military	State and local	Demo-cratic	Republi-can	All other
	185	186	187	188	189	190	191	192	193	194	195	196	197	198	199
ILLINOIS—Cont'd															
Winnebago	1 135.0	3 886	50.2	1.7	8.1	3.0	5.4	750.7	2 570	856	602	13 663	55.6	42.8	1.7
Woodford	116.2	2 982	68.7	1.1	3.9	0.0	7.1	40.0	1 026	68	77	1 872	35.9	62.6	1.5
INDIANA	X	X	X	X	X	X	X	X	X	37 032	21 468	385 342	49.9	48.9	1.1
Adams	133.8	3 893	35.3	41.5	1.9	0.6	3.0	120.4	3 505	56	111	2 064	36.5	62.2	1.3
Allen	969.6	2 690	50.6	0.7	6.5	0.4	3.3	1 061.3	2 945	1 869	1 184	16 940	47.4	51.8	0.8
Bartholomew	465.6	5 883	32.7	40.9	1.8	0.5	0.9	364.3	4 603	158	255	6 081	43.7	55.0	1.3
Benton	35.9	4 079	50.7	2.9	2.6	0.5	7.6	27.8	3 163	27	28	617	41.0	57.2	1.8
Blackford	31.6	2 526	55.3	0.6	5.0	0.9	4.4	22.9	1 830	23	40	528	49.2	49.4	1.4
Boone	254.2	4 312	38.4	34.0	3.4	0.2	3.0	422.2	7 162	91	194	3 268	36.6	62.4	1.0
Brown	46.1	3 056	59.2	0.2	2.0	0.2	4.2	23.3	1 545	16	48	819	47.8	50.4	1.8
Carroll	44.9	2 233	56.6	1.7	3.2	1.1	6.3	15.9	791	60	65	783	42.8	55.6	1.6
Cass	169.3	4 387	43.5	32.2	4.5	0.2	2.9	80.8	2 094	88	121	3 128	44.8	53.3	1.9
Clark	456.8	4 081	34.1	34.1	3.8	0.2	1.1	411.3	3 674	1 845	363	6 104	46.0	53.1	0.9
Clay	70.5	2 627	57.4	1.1	2.7	0.5	3.4	38.3	1 426	81	86	1 210	43.5	55.0	1.5
Clinton	106.0	3 210	57.5	0.5	2.8	0.7	3.5	96.4	2 919	57	104	1 558	42.8	55.8	1.3
Crawford	28.5	2 676	60.9	2.8	2.1	0.1	4.3	20.9	1 955	24	34	561	48.2	50.4	1.4
Daviess	136.7	4 263	34.6	34.7	1.9	0.2	4.2	136.4	4 253	71	103	1 717	31.8	67.1	1.1
Dearborn	292.4	5 869	28.3	29.1	2.1	0.0	1.6	199.3	3 999	104	160	2 903	32.1	67.0	0.9
Decatur	123.9	4 759	32.1	32.1	1.8	0.1	1.8	144.4	5 545	73	84	1 531	37.1	61.5	1.4
DeKalb	141.5	3 344	61.2	0.3	3.3	0.3	3.6	92.5	2 185	84	135	1 930	41.8	57.0	1.1
Delaware	323.3	2 755	48.4	0.8	3.9	0.5	2.7	191.9	1 635	290	355	10 569	56.9	41.9	1.1
Dubois	122.5	2 913	62.4	0.6	3.1	0.1	4.8	195.3	4 641	103	134	2 067	47.1	51.3	1.6
Elkhart	609.8	3 055	58.2	1.0	3.9	0.2	3.5	758.8	3 801	253	638	8 359	43.9	55.1	0.9
Fayette	72.1	3 001	59.5	1.8	4.9	0.2	5.4	37.9	1 577	45	76	1 063	46.4	52.0	1.6
Floyd	441.6	5 865	25.8	49.3	1.8	0.0	1.1	309.6	4 113	212	242	5 957	44.5	54.6	0.9
Fountain	45.0	2 632	61.9	2.3	2.9	0.3	7.1	40.9	2 387	58	54	796	41.8	56.1	2.1
Franklin	38.8	1 688	69.0	0.1	2.0	0.3	4.9	26.8	1 166	40	75	966	32.1	66.1	1.8
Fulton	83.1	4 008	31.5	45.7	2.8	0.1	2.5	22.8	1 097	45	65	1 307	41.1	57.2	1.7
Gibson	99.3	2 969	54.6	1.5	3.1	0.1	6.2	186.7	5 581	85	106	1 300	42.8	56.0	1.3
Grant	175.3	2 529	54.4	0.3	7.8	0.2	3.4	108.6	1 566	996	208	2 921	42.9	56.0	1.0
Greene	110.5	3 356	48.9	22.9	1.7	0.1	3.4	52.3	1 587	71	105	1 747	41.9	56.4	1.7
Hamilton	1 098.2	3 794	43.5	16.9	3.8	0.1	2.9	2 131.8	7 364	351	954	12 318	38.5	60.7	0.7
Hancock	259.1	3 652	38.3	36.3	2.5	0.1	3.7	430.2	6 065	103	229	3 428	34.7	64.3	1.1
Harrison	142.1	3 631	38.8	32.2	0.5	0.1	1.6	105.0	2 682	98	125	1 982	40.3	58.3	1.4
Hendricks	586.7	3 900	37.8	29.3	2.6	0.1	1.7	985.7	6 552	270	484	7 991	37.8	61.2	1.0
Henry	226.4	4 588	34.1	40.7	1.5	0.1	1.6	118.3	2 397	91	147	2 821	47.2	51.1	1.7
Howard	406.5	4 907	32.7	36.7	3.9	0.3	1.8	200.3	2 417	234	265	5 031	46.3	52.4	1.3
Huntington	90.3	2 442	58.2	0.3	3.7	0.1	4.3	59.5	1 608	86	115	1 425	35.8	63.0	1.2
Jackson	185.0	4 294	31.0	55.4	1.0	0.1	1.1	103.4	2 400	84	139	2 814	42.3	56.0	1.7
Jasper	124.9	3 732	37.4	35.2	2.1	0.1	2.1	207.7	6 207	86	105	1 885	39.2	59.6	1.3
Jay	94.3	4 414	38.3	35.4	2.3	0.6	3.7	67.3	3 148	45	68	1 369	45.1	52.9	2.0
Jefferson	77.9	2 394	64.1	1.2	3.5	0.2	4.5	52.1	1 600	76	99	2 420	46.4	52.3	1.3
Jennings	82.7	2 935	66.8	0.7	2.7	0.2	2.8	49.5	1 758	70	90	1 199	44.9	52.9	2.2
Johnson	466.1	3 255	49.3	17.5	3.5	0.1	2.7	489.4	3 417	390	704	6 406	36.8	62.2	1.0
Knox	274.0	7 186	18.6	63.3	1.2	0.1	2.8	128.9	3 381	195	115	4 872	46.1	52.6	1.3
Kosciusko	216.4	2 788	61.0	1.0	3.8	0.1	4.8	226.2	2 915	165	247	2 919	30.6	68.0	1.4
LaGrange	85.5	2 278	67.1	0.1	1.4	0.1	3.8	71.2	1 896	58	122	1 299	38.6	60.1	1.3
Lake	1 850.2	3 748	45.8	0.6	5.4	1.1	1.8	1 929.7	3 909	1 360	1 569	25 260	66.7	32.5	0.8
LaPorte	330.9	2 974	53.0	1.0	4.1	0.3	2.3	311.4	2 799	172	360	6 755	60.2	38.2	1.6
Lawrence	114.9	2 494	59.2	0.4	4.2	0.2	6.0	97.1	2 107	123	146	2 018	38.9	59.4	1.7
Madison	322.0	2 470	48.2	0.7	5.0	0.2	3.7	497.2	3 814	252	402	5 834	52.6	46.0	1.4
Marion	4 896.8	5 329	31.1	23.0	4.5	0.2	0.9	11 765.5	12 803	14 767	3 218	65 855	63.8	35.4	0.8
Marshall	129.3	2 749	63.4	1.7	4.8	0.2	5.4	98.6	2 098	93	150	2 031	42.5	56.1	1.4
Martin	26.7	2 598	58.5	0.8	2.4	0.3	8.0	14.6	1 421	4 187	76	459	34.8	63.7	1.5
Miami	111.4	3 054	57.5	0.2	2.1	0.2	4.7	101.3	2 777	653	119	1 969	39.4	58.9	1.7
Monroe	289.9	2 055	45.2	1.2	4.9	0.4	4.3	383.5	2 719	282	449	21 436	65.6	33.4	1.0
Montgomery	110.0	2 875	52.3	0.3	3.9	0.5	5.8	103.4	2 703	84	120	1 947	39.3	59.3	1.4
Morgan	210.4	3 033	48.5	21.5	2.5	0.1	2.6	96.0	1 385	93	224	2 529	35.9	62.9	1.2
Newton	55.2	3 932	46.4	2.3	2.3	0.2	6.4	34.2	2 435	27	45	739	43.4	54.6	2.0
Noble	113.5	2 385	60.5	0.3	5.9	0.1	4.5	94.3	1 982	74	151	1 040	41.0	57.0	1.4
Ohio	23.6	3 888	36.5	0.1	3.4	0.1	3.1	15.6	2 573	13	19	336	39.7	58.7	1.6
Orange	63.7	3 235	54.0	0.2	0.9	0.1	3.8	72.0	3 654	41	63	946	41.9	56.1	2.0
Owen	40.1	1 878	63.7	0.0	2.5	0.2	4.4	41.4	1 939	36	68	741	43.7	54.0	2.3
Parke	44.2	2 588	55.1	0.9	2.6	0.1	6.9	39.4	2 308	46	50	1 089	42.0	56.1	1.9
Perry	80.3	4 126	33.1	41.5	1.7	0.0	3.6	65.0	3 340	69	58	1 420	60.6	37.7	1.7

1. Based on the resident population estimated as of July 1 of the year shown. 2.

STATE/ County code	CBSA code[1]	County type[2]	STATE County	Land area,[3] (sq km) 2010	Population, 2014: Total persons 2014	Population, 2014: Rank	Population, 2014: Per square kilometer	Population and population characteristics, 2013: Race alone or in combination, not Hispanic or Latino (percent): White	Black	American Indian, Alaska Native	Asian and Pacific Islander	Percent Hispanic or Latino[4]	Age (percent): Under 5 years	5 to 17 years	18 to 24 years	25 to 34 years	35 to 44 years	45 to 54 years
				1	2	3	4	5	6	7	8	9	10	11	12	13	14	15
			INDIANA—Cont'd															
18 125	27540	6	Pike	866	12 624	2 255	14.6	97.8	0.9	0.6	0.4	1.1	5.7	16.2	7.3	10.3	11.9	14.8
18 127	16980	1	Porter	1 083	167 076	380	154.3	85.9	3.9	0.6	1.8	9.2	5.5	17.6	9.3	12.3	13.1	14.3
18 129	21780	2	Posey	1 061	25 540	1 582	24.1	97.5	1.5	0.4	0.5	1.0	5.7	17.0	8.3	10.6	11.8	15.4
18 131	...	6	Pulaski	1 123	12 967	2 234	11.5	95.7	1.2	0.7	0.6	2.7	5.4	17.7	7.9	10.7	11.8	14.7
18 133	26900	1	Putnam	1 245	37 618	1 236	30.2	93.2	4.5	0.6	1.1	1.7	4.9	15.3	13.8	11.9	12.1	14.5
18 135	...	6	Randolph	1 172	25 384	1 593	21.7	95.6	1.1	0.7	0.5	3.2	5.7	17.9	7.9	10.3	12.3	14.1
18 137	...	6	Ripley	1 156	28 497	1 470	24.7	97.1	0.7	0.6	0.9	1.6	6.1	18.5	7.9	10.8	12.3	14.7
18 139	...	6	Rush	1 057	16 892	1 986	16.0	97.2	1.3	0.5	0.6	1.2	5.3	18.2	8.1	10.5	12.2	15.0
18 141	43780	2	St. Joseph	1 186	267 618	250	225.6	76.9	14.1	0.9	2.8	7.9	6.5	17.6	11.2	12.9	12.0	13.0
18 143	31140	6	Scott	493	23 712	1 653	48.1	97.1	0.7	0.5	0.8	1.7	6.0	17.4	8.2	11.5	13.2	15.2
18 145	26900	1	Shelby	1 065	44 579	1 081	41.9	93.9	1.5	0.5	1.1	4.0	6.2	17.6	8.2	11.4	12.6	15.3
18 147	...	8	Spencer	1 028	20 801	1 785	20.2	96.0	1.1	0.4	0.5	2.8	5.9	17.0	7.5	10.5	11.8	15.4
18 149	...	6	Starke	801	23 074	1 681	28.8	95.5	0.8	0.8	0.5	3.4	5.6	17.7	8.4	10.8	12.1	14.3
18 151	11420	7	Steuben	800	34 308	1 322	42.9	95.2	1.1	0.6	0.8	3.3	5.1	16.4	10.8	10.3	11.6	14.3
18 153	45460	3	Sullivan	1 158	21 050	1 770	18.2	93.2	5.0	0.8	0.4	1.8	5.2	15.3	8.9	13.4	13.6	14.4
18 155	...	8	Switzerland	571	10 452	2 399	18.3	97.6	0.8	0.5	0.4	1.6	6.4	18.4	8.0	11.1	12.0	15.1
18 157	29200	3	Tippecanoe	1 294	183 074	350	141.5	80.5	5.3	0.6	7.5	7.9	6.1	14.4	24.1	14.4	10.7	10.4
18 159	...	3	Tipton	675	15 415	2 076	22.8	96.4	0.8	0.4	0.6	2.5	4.7	17.4	7.9	10.0	12.3	14.9
18 161	17140	8	Union	418	7 246	2 656	17.3	97.4	1.2	0.7	0.6	1.3	5.0	18.4	8.1	9.9	12.3	15.7
18 163	21780	2	Vanderburgh	605	182 006	353	300.8	86.8	10.7	0.6	1.8	2.4	6.3	15.6	10.8	14.2	11.4	13.4
18 165	45460	3	Vermillion	665	15 693	2 062	23.6	98.1	0.7	0.5	0.5	1.1	5.3	17.5	7.4	10.6	12.7	13.7
18 167	45460	3	Vigo	1 045	108 175	555	103.5	88.1	8.4	0.8	2.4	2.5	5.9	15.0	15.2	12.9	11.8	12.7
18 169	47340	6	Wabash	1 068	32 252	1 379	30.2	95.9	1.1	1.1	0.7	2.2	5.4	16.5	10.1	10.3	11.3	13.6
18 171	...	8	Warren	945	8 352	2 571	8.8	97.7	0.5	0.5	0.6	1.2	5.9	16.2	7.9	9.8	11.9	15.7
18 173	21780	2	Warrick	997	61 149	857	61.3	94.9	2.0	0.5	2.3	1.7	5.9	19.1	7.3	10.8	13.2	14.6
18 175	31140	1	Washington	1 331	27 878	1 498	20.9	97.9	0.6	0.5	0.4	1.3	5.6	18.3	8.0	11.2	12.8	15.4
18 177	39980	5	Wayne	1 041	67 671	789	65.0	91.1	6.5	0.7	1.5	2.7	6.2	16.4	9.1	11.4	12.0	13.9
18 179	23060	2	Wells	953	27 862	1 500	29.2	96.4	0.9	0.6	0.6	2.4	6.6	17.5	8.1	11.5	11.1	14.4
18 181	...	6	White	1 308	24 453	1 627	18.7	91.2	0.8	0.7	0.7	7.7	6.3	17.4	7.8	9.9	11.9	13.7
18 183	23060	2	Whitley	869	33 403	1 341	38.4	97.1	0.8	0.8	0.7	1.8	5.9	17.8	7.9	11.2	12.6	14.6
19 000	...	X	IOWA	144 669	3 107 126	X	21.5	89.0	3.9	0.7	2.5	5.5	6.3	17.1	10.3	12.6	11.7	13.4
19 001	...	8	Adair	1 474	7 454	2 644	5.1	97.7	0.5	0.4	0.5	1.5	5.0	16.9	6.5	10.7	9.8	14.8
19 003	...	9	Adams	1 097	3 875	2 914	3.5	97.6	0.5	0.8	0.7	1.1	5.7	14.7	7.2	11.1	9.9	14.9
19 005	...	6	Allamakee	1 655	14 038	2 168	8.5	92.1	1.6	0.5	0.6	5.8	6.1	16.2	7.4	10.3	10.0	14.1
19 007	...	7	Appanoose	1 288	12 661	2 253	9.8	97.2	1.0	0.7	0.6	1.6	6.1	15.9	7.4	10.5	10.2	13.7
19 009	...	8	Audubon	1 147	5 794	2 776	5.1	98.1	0.6	0.4	0.7	0.9	4.7	15.6	6.9	8.8	9.9	15.2
19 011	16300	3	Benton	1 855	25 680	1 574	13.8	97.8	0.9	0.4	0.5	1.3	5.7	18.3	7.5	10.2	12.2	16.2
19 013	47940	3	Black Hawk	1 465	132 897	474	90.7	85.1	10.0	0.5	2.5	4.0	6.1	15.3	16.0	13.1	10.7	11.6
19 015	14340	6	Boone	1 480	26 433	1 548	17.9	95.9	1.5	0.6	0.8	2.3	5.6	17.4	7.7	12.1	11.7	14.3
19 017	47940	3	Bremer	1 128	24 721	1 620	21.9	96.9	1.4	0.3	1.2	1.2	5.3	16.6	12.4	11.1	11.1	12.8
19 019	...	6	Buchanan	1 479	21 038	1 772	14.2	97.6	0.8	0.5	0.7	1.4	6.9	19.7	7.4	11.7	11.2	14.0
19 021	44740	7	Buena Vista	1 489	20 578	1 796	13.8	64.7	2.6	0.4	8.5	24.8	7.0	18.2	12.3	11.9	10.4	12.9
19 023	...	8	Butler	1 503	15 006	2 102	10.0	98.0	0.8	0.4	0.6	1.1	6.2	17.4	6.6	10.5	11.0	13.1
19 025	...	9	Calhoun	1 476	9 866	2 448	6.7	95.6	2.2	0.6	0.5	1.9	5.5	15.0	7.3	10.7	10.5	13.3
19 027	...	7	Carroll	1 475	20 562	1 798	13.9	96.5	1.1	0.4	0.7	2.2	6.6	17.5	7.4	10.3	11.0	14.1
19 029	...	6	Cass	1 461	13 448	2 211	9.2	96.2	0.7	0.4	0.9	2.5	5.8	16.8	7.0	10.2	10.4	13.9
19 031	...	6	Cedar	1 501	18 411	1 900	12.3	97.0	0.8	0.6	0.8	1.9	5.5	17.7	6.8	10.4	11.8	15.3
19 033	32380	5	Cerro Gordo	1 472	43 254	1 106	29.4	93.4	2.0	0.5	1.5	4.1	5.6	15.3	8.4	11.2	10.7	14.3
19 035	...	6	Cherokee	1 494	11 836	2 306	7.9	95.0	1.2	0.6	0.8	3.3	5.9	15.0	7.1	10.1	9.9	13.9
19 037	...	6	Chickasaw	1 306	12 264	2 280	9.4	96.9	0.8	0.3	0.5	2.2	6.1	17.6	7.5	9.8	10.0	14.7
19 039	...	6	Clarke	1 117	9 217	2 494	8.3	87.1	0.9	0.6	0.9	11.6	6.7	18.1	7.9	11.2	11.2	13.9
19 041	43980	7	Clay	1 469	16 515	2 006	11.2	95.6	1.0	0.5	0.9	3.0	5.8	16.8	7.5	11.5	11.0	13.5
19 043	...	8	Clayton	2 016	17 692	1 933	8.8	97.0	0.9	0.4	0.6	1.9	5.6	16.6	7.1	9.7	10.2	14.5
19 045	17540	4	Clinton	1 800	48 051	1 012	26.7	93.2	4.0	0.7	0.9	2.9	6.1	16.9	8.4	10.9	11.3	14.6
19 047	...	6	Crawford	1 850	17 228	1 968	9.3	69.3	1.9	0.4	1.6	27.6	7.4	18.7	9.2	11.2	11.5	13.0
19 049	19780	2	Dallas	1 521	77 400	711	50.8	88.4	2.1	0.5	3.9	6.3	8.2	20.5	6.3	15.7	15.3	13.1
19 051	36900	9	Davis	1 301	8 781	2 534	6.7	98.0	0.5	0.6	0.6	1.3	8.0	20.8	7.9	10.0	10.7	12.5
19 053	...	9	Decatur	1 378	8 263	2 585	6.0	94.4	2.2	0.8	1.2	2.5	5.1	16.2	16.5	9.5	9.7	11.4
19 055	...	6	Delaware	1 496	17 398	1 954	11.6	98.1	0.8	0.3	0.4	1.1	5.6	18.3	7.4	10.0	11.0	15.5
19 057	15460	5	Des Moines	1 078	40 255	1 166	37.3	90.4	6.9	0.7	1.2	2.9	6.1	16.9	7.9	11.8	11.2	13.5
19 059	44020	7	Dickinson	986	16 935	1 981	17.2	97.4	0.6	0.4	0.8	1.6	5.0	14.3	6.3	10.0	10.7	13.3
19 061	20220	3	Dubuque	1 576	96 370	610	61.1	93.4	3.4	0.5	1.9	2.1	6.1	16.9	10.2	12.8	11.0	13.9
19 063	...	7	Emmet	1 025	9 990	2 440	9.7	88.5	1.0	0.7	1.0	9.6	5.6	16.0	10.0	11.7	10.2	12.6
19 065	...	6	Fayette	1 893	20 343	1 817	10.7	95.7	1.8	0.4	1.0	2.2	6.1	15.6	10.0	10.1	10.0	14.1
19 067	...	7	Floyd	1 297	16 077	2 036	12.4	94.5	1.9	0.3	1.7	2.2	5.9	17.2	8.0	10.1	10.7	13.6

1. CBSA = Core Based Statistical Area. See Appendix A for explanation. See Appendix B for list of metropolitan areas with component counties. 2. County type code from the Economic Research Service of USDA Rural-Urban Continuum Codes. See Appendix A for definition. 3. Dry land or land partially or temporarily covered by water. 4. May be of any race.

STATE County	Population, 2013 (cont.) — Age (percent) (cont.) — 55 to 64 years	65 to 74 years	75 years and over	Percent female	Population change and components of change, 2000–2014 — Total persons — 2000	2010	Percent change — 2000–2010	2010–2014	Components of change, 2010–2014 — Births	Deaths	Net migration	Households, 2009–2013 — Number	Persons per household	Percent — Family households	Female family householder[1]	One person
	16	17	18	19	20	21	22	23	24	25	26	27	28	29	30	31
INDIANA—Cont'd																
Pike	15.2	10.3	8.2	49.9	12 837	12 845	0.1	-1.7	578	577	-210	5 149	2.44	71.8	8.4	25.5
Porter	14.1	8.2	5.7	50.9	146 798	164 343	12.0	1.7	7 433	5 849	1 236	61 502	2.63	70.6	11.6	24.5
Posey	15.4	9.0	6.9	50.3	27 061	25 910	-4.3	-1.4	1 201	995	-551	10 050	2.53	74.0	9.3	23.5
Pulaski	14.3	9.9	7.8	49.2	13 755	13 402	-2.6	-3.2	562	630	-352	5 058	2.58	71.3	7.0	26.2
Putnam	12.6	8.3	6.5	47.1	36 019	37 963	5.4	-0.9	1 437	1 376	-365	12 414	2.60	73.1	9.8	22.1
Randolph	13.6	9.8	8.4	50.7	27 401	26 171	-4.5	-3.0	1 306	1 155	-941	10 429	2.46	67.7	9.8	27.7
Ripley	13.2	9.3	7.4	50.6	26 523	28 818	8.7	-1.1	1 391	1 233	-531	10 761	2.62	72.2	10.4	23.9
Rush	13.7	9.2	7.8	50.6	18 261	17 392	-4.8	-2.9	788	795	-473	6 874	2.47	71.8	10.9	23.7
St. Joseph	12.9	7.4	6.7	51.5	265 559	266 931	0.5	0.3	14 880	10 441	-3 415	101 947	2.49	64.2	13.6	29.7
Scott	13.3	9.4	5.8	50.8	22 960	24 181	5.3	-1.9	1 217	1 259	-452	8 914	2.66	71.3	12.0	24.3
Shelby	13.8	8.5	6.5	50.4	43 445	44 436	2.3	0.4	2 139	1 839	-108	17 171	2.55	69.3	12.6	25.8
Spencer	14.7	10.2	7.1	49.5	20 391	20 952	2.8	-0.7	908	851	-271	7 984	2.58	72.6	7.0	23.3
Starke	14.5	9.8	6.7	50.5	23 556	23 363	-0.8	-1.2	1 161	1 146	-305	8 964	2.58	70.8	10.9	25.3
Steuben	14.7	10.1	6.7	49.2	33 214	34 185	2.9	0.4	1 498	1 242	-110	13 514	2.44	70.9	10.1	23.5
Sullivan	13.3	9.1	6.8	45.8	21 751	21 475	-1.3	-2.0	982	970	-442	7 764	2.46	70.4	11.0	24.0
Switzerland	13.0	9.5	6.4	49.0	9 065	10 613	17.1	-1.5	496	434	-227	4 099	2.54	72.9	11.7	23.7
Tippecanoe	9.7	5.7	4.5	48.9	148 955	172 780	16.0	6.0	9 627	4 621	5 359	66 667	2.43	57.3	9.8	29.2
Tipton	14.1	10.8	8.0	50.0	16 577	15 936	-3.9	-3.3	592	715	-340	6 622	2.36	73.2	9.8	22.8
Union	14.1	10.0	6.6	50.7	7 349	7 516	2.3	-3.6	312	260	-335	2 943	2.49	68.6	8.6	28.7
Vanderburgh	13.4	7.8	7.2	51.6	171 922	179 703	4.5	1.3	9 859	7 844	543	73 963	2.34	60.8	12.8	32.7
Vermillion	14.7	10.3	7.8	50.8	16 788	16 212	-3.4	-3.2	679	889	-299	6 466	2.45	65.8	9.9	30.2
Vigo	12.3	7.9	6.3	49.3	105 848	107 848	1.9	0.3	5 448	4 792	-305	39 597	2.49	61.8	12.2	31.2
Wabash	13.6	9.5	9.5	51.3	34 960	32 888	-5.9	-1.9	1 455	1 720	-393	12 703	2.41	71.1	8.5	25.9
Warren	14.3	10.2	8.1	50.2	8 419	8 508	1.1	-1.8	412	294	-281	3 283	2.55	74.0	6.1	23.4
Warrick	13.7	9.2	6.1	50.6	52 383	59 689	13.9	2.4	2 720	2 219	912	22 454	2.65	75.7	8.6	20.4
Washington	13.6	9.1	6.0	50.0	27 223	28 262	3.8	-1.4	1 289	1 206	-445	10 631	2.61	70.0	12.1	26.2
Wayne	13.6	9.4	8.1	51.5	71 097	68 917	-3.1	-1.9	3 523	3 459	-1 379	28 185	2.34	66.8	14.9	28.1
Wells	13.9	8.8	7.9	50.6	27 600	27 636	0.1	0.8	1 478	1 058	-205	10 904	2.49	71.8	10.9	26.1
White	14.7	10.0	8.3	50.4	25 267	24 643	-2.5	-0.8	1 233	1 095	-342	9 541	2.54	71.8	7.3	25.3
Whitley	14.6	8.7	6.8	50.2	30 707	33 292	8.4	0.3	1 599	1 246	-215	13 094	2.51	70.4	9.4	25.3
IOWA	13.0	8.1	7.5	50.4	2 926 324	3 046 355	4.1	2.0	163 391	118 503	16 872	1 226 547	2.42	64.8	9.4	28.8
Adair	14.3	9.9	12.2	50.5	8 243	7 682	-6.8	-3.0	319	436	-121	3 295	2.26	62.9	5.5	30.8
Adams	14.6	10.8	11.0	50.0	4 482	4 029	-10.1	-3.8	205	198	-128	1 745	2.20	67.7	5.4	28.8
Allamakee	15.2	10.9	9.7	48.9	14 675	14 330	-2.4	-2.0	734	671	-338	5 862	2.36	66.5	5.7	27.2
Appanoose	14.9	11.0	10.2	50.7	13 721	12 887	-6.1	-1.8	657	726	-150	5 534	2.28	62.8	8.5	33.4
Audubon	14.7	11.2	13.0	52.1	6 830	6 119	-10.4	-5.3	243	337	-236	2 684	2.18	63.0	7.0	33.4
Benton	13.4	8.7	7.9	50.0	25 308	26 076	3.0	-1.5	1 151	960	-580	10 079	2.55	73.5	9.6	23.0
Black Hawk	12.6	7.6	7.0	51.1	128 012	131 090	2.4	1.4	7 136	5 006	-210	52 276	2.40	59.7	10.7	31.3
Boone	14.6	8.5	8.2	49.8	26 224	26 306	0.3	0.5	1 320	1 243	57	10 574	2.41	64.7	8.7	30.1
Bremer	12.6	9.5	8.6	50.8	23 325	24 276	4.1	1.8	1 048	867	292	9 258	2.46	70.7	6.0	25.8
Buchanan	13.2	8.6	7.4	50.3	21 093	20 958	-0.6	0.4	1 180	828	-225	8 187	2.52	71.7	7.6	24.0
Buena Vista	12.6	6.5	8.0	49.4	20 411	20 260	-0.7	1.6	1 390	760	-294	7 615	2.53	64.5	7.8	30.5
Butler	14.6	10.3	10.4	50.7	15 305	14 867	-2.9	0.9	684	732	210	6 189	2.37	70.6	7.1	25.8
Calhoun	15.2	10.3	12.3	48.4	11 115	9 670	-13.0	-3.1	450	594	-144	4 356	2.15	66.6	7.1	30.7
Carroll	14.2	8.4	10.6	51.2	21 421	20 816	-2.8	-1.2	1 096	1 003	-353	8 626	2.35	65.6	9.4	32.2
Cass	14.5	10.6	10.7	50.9	14 684	13 956	-5.0	-3.6	635	798	-329	6 081	2.21	64.6	8.0	32.3
Cedar	14.5	9.2	8.8	50.4	18 187	18 499	1.7	-0.5	782	702	-140	7 665	2.37	69.8	8.2	26.1
Cerro Gordo	15.4	9.4	9.7	50.9	46 447	44 151	-4.9	-2.0	1 973	2 042	-820	19 967	2.14	58.8	7.2	35.1
Cherokee	16.0	9.9	12.1	50.5	13 035	12 072	-7.4	-2.0	561	649	-141	5 354	2.17	62.6	8.5	32.9
Chickasaw	15.1	9.7	9.4	49.9	13 095	12 439	-5.0	-1.4	608	574	-162	5 364	2.27	68.3	7.3	27.6
Clarke	13.9	9.0	8.1	50.1	9 133	9 286	1.7	-0.7	520	434	-141	3 672	2.49	61.6	8.9	33.9
Clay	14.6	9.2	10.2	50.9	17 372	16 667	-4.1	-0.9	827	807	-167	7 148	2.28	63.1	7.8	30.4
Clayton	15.9	10.2	10.3	49.9	18 678	18 129	-2.9	-2.4	832	806	-429	7 707	2.29	67.4	8.2	27.1
Clinton	14.0	9.3	8.5	50.9	50 149	49 116	-2.1	-2.2	2 439	2 248	-1 252	20 008	2.40	65.2	10.1	29.3
Crawford	12.3	8.6	8.0	49.1	16 942	17 096	0.9	0.8	1 002	669	-185	6 300	2.65	69.7	9.3	26.8
Dallas	10.1	6.0	4.8	50.9	40 750	66 135	62.3	17.0	4 805	1 538	7 664	26 262	2.63	71.9	8.8	22.6
Davis	12.7	9.0	8.4	50.6	8 541	8 753	2.5	0.3	579	344	-202	3 115	2.76	69.4	6.8	27.8
Decatur	12.8	9.3	9.5	49.9	8 689	8 457	-2.7	-2.3	373	407	-178	3 106	2.43	65.9	7.5	29.4
Delaware	14.6	8.7	8.9	49.9	18 404	17 764	-3.5	-2.1	830	711	-485	7 129	2.44	70.4	7.4	26.1
Des Moines	14.2	9.8	8.6	51.0	42 351	40 325	-4.8	-0.2	1 979	1 946	-71	16 993	2.33	64.0	13.1	30.8
Dickinson	17.1	11.8	11.5	50.3	16 424	16 667	1.5	1.6	683	834	404	7 981	2.07	66.0	5.4	29.2
Dubuque	13.3	8.1	7.7	50.6	89 143	93 653	5.1	2.9	4 992	3 649	1 411	37 366	2.41	65.0	8.9	28.7
Emmet	14.8	8.9	10.2	49.9	11 027	10 302	-6.6	-3.0	473	528	-263	4 119	2.31	64.6	8.6	30.9
Fayette	14.2	10.0	10.0	50.1	22 008	20 880	-5.1	-2.6	922	1 028	-408	8 328	2.40	63.1	7.6	31.5
Floyd	13.9	10.3	10.3	51.0	16 900	16 303	-3.5	-1.4	815	829	-195	7 007	2.26	65.5	10.1	30.1

1. No spouse present.

STATE County	Persons in group quarters, 2014	Daytime population, 2009–2013: Number	Daytime population, 2009–2013: Employment/residence ratio	Births, 2014: Total	Births, 2014: Rate[1]	Deaths, 2014: Number	Deaths, 2014: Rate[1]	Persons under 65 with no health insurance, 2013: Number	Persons under 65 with no health insurance, 2013: Percent	Medicare, 2014: Eligible for Medicare	Medicare, 2014: Enrolled in Medicare Advantage	Medicare, 2014: Enrolled in a Medicare prescription drug plan	Serious crimes known to police,[2] 2013: Total: Number	Serious crimes known to police,[2] 2013: Total: Rate[3]
	32	33	34	35	36	37	38	39	40	41	42	43	44	45
INDIANA—Cont'd														
Pike	213	11 159	0.70	127	10.1	140	11.1	1 513	14.8	2 881	550	1 476	271	2 605
Porter	3 410	148 082	0.77	1 767	10.6	1 484	8.9	18 289	13.1	28 421	4 275	16 510	2 791	1 696
Posey	242	22 936	0.77	291	11.4	240	9.4	2 340	11.0	4 917	1 111	2 561	NA	NA
Pulaski	193	12 554	0.87	134	10.3	133	10.3	1 756	16.6	2 823	433	1 605	NA	NA
Putnam	5 264	35 920	0.87	321	8.5	317	8.4	4 145	15.4	6 669	1 685	3 495	NA	NA
Randolph	329	22 621	0.70	313	12.3	257	10.1	3 522	16.9	5 594	804	3 123	266	1 256
Ripley	449	27 538	0.91	321	11.3	281	9.9	3 330	14.2	4 992	1 000	2 699	407	1 424
Rush	178	14 946	0.71	196	11.6	183	10.8	2 156	15.4	3 471	566	2 073	NA	NA
St. Joseph	11 217	272 494	1.05	3 495	13.1	2 420	9.0	36 763	16.7	45 103	13 288	19 675	9 959	3 740
Scott	312	21 247	0.70	280	11.8	289	12.2	3 139	15.6	5 151	905	3 073	718	3 672
Shelby	683	41 689	0.86	475	10.7	414	9.3	6 001	16.0	8 202	1 754	4 600	937	2 100
Spencer	368	18 850	0.78	193	9.3	220	10.6	2 508	14.7	4 072	593	2 149	NA	NA
Starke	16	19 054	0.54	274	11.9	274	11.9	3 304	17.1	5 269	795	2 955	145	624
Steuben	1 302	32 887	0.92	349	10.2	300	8.7	4 315	15.8	6 928	2 763	2 929	882	2 578
Sullivan	2 238	20 121	0.85	228	10.8	200	9.5	2 596	16.5	4 093	417	2 277	225	1 325
Switzerland	107	8 720	0.59	109	10.4	107	10.2	1 590	18.1	1 663	218	925	NA	NA
Tippecanoe	14 492	186 601	1.13	2 340	12.8	1 077	5.9	25 630	17.3	21 974	3 707	11 554	5 588	3 150
Tipton	205	13 726	0.70	127	8.2	155	10.1	1 775	14.1	3 257	498	2 365	226	1 442
Union	67	5 524	0.44	65	9.0	61	8.4	968	16.1	1 370	247	819	NA	NA
Vanderburgh	7 420	202 197	1.26	2 357	13.0	1 822	10.0	22 155	14.9	34 376	8 923	16 759	7 289	4 012
Vermillion	209	14 459	0.75	156	9.9	195	12.4	1 970	15.2	3 507	367	1 927	107	667
Vigo	9 562	117 483	1.20	1 261	11.7	1 124	10.4	13 346	15.8	19 932	2 308	11 600	4 659	4 369
Wabash	1 837	31 960	0.95	333	10.3	395	12.2	3 996	16.0	7 622	2 911	3 391	NA	NA
Warren	84	6 845	0.58	93	11.1	80	9.6	971	14.3	1 760	169	1 010	NA	NA
Warrick	726	48 598	0.60	625	10.2	561	9.2	6 031	11.8	11 118	2 585	4 892	935	1 537
Washington	261	22 471	0.54	305	10.9	276	9.9	4 349	18.6	5 521	1 385	2 801	NA	NA
Wayne	2 683	70 263	1.06	807	11.9	859	12.7	9 286	17.1	15 186	1 692	9 339	NA	NA
Wells	472	25 494	0.83	344	12.3	239	8.6	3 237	14.1	5 426	2 064	2 549	634	2 287
White	307	22 909	0.85	294	12.0	277	11.3	3 386	17.1	5 288	807	2 917	152	623
Whitley	436	29 199	0.74	376	11.3	285	8.5	4 026	14.5	6 333	3 136	2 284	NA	NA
IOWA	99 927	3 065 497	1.00	38 673	12.4	27 706	8.9	243 546	9.6	565 475	8 250	352 289	76 188	2 465
Adair	163	6 750	0.79	68	9.1	91	12.2	547	9.5	1 601	141	1 143	48	645
Adams	101	3 499	0.76	55	14.2	43	11.1	378	12.5	981	27	709	25	644
Allamakee	259	12 805	0.79	180	12.8	169	12.0	1 620	14.6	3 303	332	2 189	52	365
Appanoose	125	12 656	0.97	151	11.9	172	13.6	1 168	11.8	3 171	414	2 102	345	2 722
Audubon	138	5 333	0.78	57	9.8	63	10.9	508	11.5	1 522	48	1 156	18	307
Benton	312	19 547	0.50	260	10.1	224	8.7	1 720	8.1	4 860	866	2 860	NA	NA
Black Hawk	5 555	141 931	1.16	1 691	12.7	1 193	9.0	10 690	9.9	23 633	3 140	15 896	3 496	2 641
Boone	753	23 571	0.79	314	11.9	288	10.9	1 944	9.0	5 342	634	3 490	391	1 490
Bremer	1 731	23 232	0.91	257	10.4	208	8.4	1 223	6.6	4 911	390	3 620	220	894
Buchanan	300	18 344	0.74	276	13.1	188	8.9	1 656	9.5	3 918	545	2 676	NA	NA
Buena Vista	989	21 444	1.11	345	16.8	161	7.8	2 649	15.8	3 313	158	2 336	397	1 915
Butler	230	12 076	0.60	164	10.9	162	10.8	1 099	9.3	3 451	326	2 430	16	106
Calhoun	738	8 746	0.73	116	11.8	142	14.4	694	9.7	2 413	95	1 745	62	630
Carroll	466	22 063	1.12	245	11.9	244	11.9	1 307	7.9	4 444	312	3 277	NA	NA
Cass	300	13 702	0.99	150	11.2	167	12.4	1 052	10.0	3 393	267	2 392	152	1 110
Cedar	318	14 483	0.59	174	9.5	166	9.0	1 191	8.0	3 608	626	2 009	160	987
Cerro Gordo	1 130	46 610	1.12	453	10.5	482	11.1	3 173	9.2	10 134	221	6 901	1 513	3 455
Cherokee	368	11 737	0.95	135	11.4	159	13.4	854	9.4	2 698	343	1 831	128	1 074
Chickasaw	168	11 399	0.84	145	11.8	123	10.0	1 049	10.6	2 632	60	1 953	63	514
Clarke	139	9 233	0.98	124	13.5	94	10.2	901	11.8	1 883	128	1 241	196	2 081
Clay	253	17 576	1.11	194	11.7	173	10.5	1 221	9.3	3 678	NA	2 695	307	1 846
Clayton	270	16 588	0.84	199	11.2	179	10.1	1 617	11.5	4 263	695	2 997	71	399
Clinton	886	49 433	1.02	552	11.5	494	10.3	3 015	7.7	10 195	1 421	6 320	1 475	3 028
Crawford	570	16 635	0.93	229	13.3	153	8.9	2 372	16.4	3 279	258	2 221	89	511
Dallas	481	60 425	0.75	1 210	15.6	391	5.1	4 575	6.9	9 392	1 411	5 434	1 178	1 591
Davis	106	7 895	0.76	136	15.5	77	8.8	1 235	17.2	1 638	122	1 096	39	449
Decatur	788	7 882	0.88	90	10.9	89	10.8	796	13.4	1 623	159	1 089	33	402
Delaware	222	15 878	0.81	198	11.4	170	9.8	1 500	10.5	3 324	591	2 330	159	906
Des Moines	702	43 642	1.19	461	11.5	438	10.9	3 137	9.7	8 891	632	5 718	1 400	3 459
Dickinson	210	16 917	1.01	161	9.5	190	11.2	1 143	8.8	4 543	197	3 298	252	1 472
Dubuque	4 256	102 203	1.16	1 194	12.4	872	9.0	6 092	7.9	18 105	7 477	13 943	2 043	2 134
Emmet	433	9 793	0.93	118	11.8	108	10.8	1 068	13.7	2 163	56	1 611	141	1 397
Fayette	920	19 966	0.91	207	10.2	228	11.2	1 648	10.5	4 699	465	3 348	235	1 128
Floyd	304	14 716	0.81	186	11.6	207	12.9	1 203	9.5	3 727	84	2 648	190	1 186

1. Per 1,000 estimated resident population. 2. Data for serious crimes have not been adjusted for underreporting; this may affect comparability between geographic areas and over time.
3. Per 100,000 population estimated by the FBI.

STATE County	Serious crimes known to police, 2013 (cont.)[1] Rate[2] Violent	Property	Education: School enrollment and attainment, 2009–2013 Enrollment[3] Total	Percent private	Attainment[4] (percent) High school graduate or less	Bachelor's degree or more	Local government expenditures,[5] 2012–2013 Total current spending (mil dol)	Current spending per student (dollars)	Money income, 2009–2013 Per capita income[6] (dollars)	Households Median income (dollars)	Mean income (dollars)	Percent with income of $200,000 or more	Income and poverty, 2013 Median household income (dollars)	Percent below poverty level All persons	Children under 18 years	Children 5 to 17 years in families
	46	47	48	49	50	51	52	53	54	55	56	57	58	59	60	61
INDIANA—Cont'd																
Pike	279	2 326	2 733	4.9	62.2	11.2	23.2	11 719	22 245	40 680	54 064	1.6	45 679	12.3	18.6	16.7
Porter	98	1 597	44 027	19.5	43.8	25.4	230.9	8 502	28 669	62 794	75 404	3.2	64 530	11.7	15.0	13.1
Posey	NA	NA	6 409	15.9	47.5	20.5	37.4	10 243	29 187	58 750	73 218	2.8	58 477	9.6	13.4	11.8
Pulaski	NA	NA	3 160	11.5	60.1	13.1	23.1	11 098	21 641	44 764	54 813	1.2	44 821	14.3	19.9	18.5
Putnam	NA	NA	10 108	29.9	55.4	16.2	60.2	9 835	21 520	50 821	62 845	1.3	51 052	13.2	18.2	15.9
Randolph	9	1 247	6 386	4.5	59.3	12.4	42.6	9 776	21 592	40 904	53 152	1.1	41 057	18.1	26.2	24.0
Ripley	105	1 319	7 308	14.1	59.7	15.9	36.6	11 410	22 059	47 537	58 138	1.3	47 495	10.2	15.1	13.6
Rush	NA	NA	4 080	7.4	61.8	15.1	23.4	9 388	23 396	47 401	58 363	1.8	46 910	12.8	19.1	17.2
St. Joseph	343	3 398	78 225	31.5	44.4	26.5	385.8	10 137	23 509	44 582	60 014	2.6	40 978	20.1	29.1	26.7
Scott	205	3 467	5 897	8.8	62.0	11.5	36.8	8 918	20 481	42 898	52 814	0.9	43 650	17.0	24.5	23.6
Shelby	450	1 650	10 294	10.8	57.0	14.8	65.9	9 077	24 459	51 440	61 580	2.1	49 657	12.6	18.1	16.4
Spencer	NA	NA	4 711	8.5	57.5	15.5	33.0	9 841	23 641	52 991	60 498	1.3	50 533	10.5	13.8	12.9
Starke	86	538	5 431	10.3	60.9	12.3	38.3	10 098	19 773	40 126	50 681	0.7	39 552	19.4	28.4	24.9
Steuben	73	2 505	8 794	20.8	51.0	19.4	38.1	9 279	23 975	48 080	60 411	1.9	46 275	12.3	19.0	17.1
Sullivan	124	1 202	4 199	7.9	56.2	13.2	29.1	9 513	19 821	43 510	53 678	1.3	41 978	18.3	23.8	21.0
Switzerland	NA	NA	2 168	12.1	64.5	9.9	15.1	10 265	20 019	44 143	50 404	0.8	43 243	19.9	32.6	29.2
Tippecanoe	266	2 885	69 011	8.8	37.5	35.7	202.8	9 426	23 691	44 246	60 870	2.9	47 808	19.6	18.5	16.7
Tipton	147	1 295	3 586	9.5	52.5	16.4	21.6	8 228	25 093	52 686	61 392	2.2	53 185	10.3	14.5	12.7
Union	NA	NA	1 854	5.9	53.8	18.4	16.9	11 313	20 883	44 161	51 464	0.0	45 411	13.1	21.2	18.5
Vanderburgh	343	3 669	44 190	17.7	45.7	22.6	234.9	10 202	24 378	43 540	58 048	2.1	42 014	18.7	26.9	25.2
Vermillion	112	555	3 774	8.2	57.8	13.0	24.8	9 576	22 875	42 524	54 591	1.6	40 813	13.9	20.3	17.4
Vigo	203	4 166	31 638	12.3	47.9	21.2	147.4	9 569	21 192	40 692	54 562	2.1	39 014	23.9	29.7	28.3
Wabash	NA	NA	8 205	20.4	56.6	17.0	53.6	10 147	21 201	45 286	53 170	1.1	45 833	14.2	21.3	19.5
Warren	NA	NA	1 863	12.1	57.1	16.0	11.2	9 671	27 390	52 317	68 952	5.1	53 623	9.9	16.0	14.7
Warrick	156	1 381	15 284	18.4	40.4	27.2	85.3	8 559	29 927	62 351	79 483	4.2	61 820	7.9	11.1	9.9
Washington	NA	NA	6 608	13.2	63.8	11.9	40.6	9 382	21 370	41 986	54 575	1.5	43 981	15.5	24.7	22.1
Wayne	NA	NA	17 025	15.8	55.6	17.4	95.9	9 302	21 114	38 350	50 745	1.2	36 623	23.0	30.6	26.3
Wells	50	2 236	6 548	15.1	50.9	15.7	40.4	8 536	24 269	48 136	60 243	1.4	49 452	11.8	17.3	16.3
White	57	565	5 554	9.1	53.6	15.4	44.2	9 068	23 666	51 444	60 695	1.3	48 581	12.4	19.3	18.4
Whitley	NA	NA	8 073	17.1	52.5	16.7	41.8	8 738	24 613	51 914	61 532	1.7	52 673	8.9	13.2	12.3
IOWA	271	2 194	811 848	16.3	41.9	25.7	5 177.7	10 313	27 027	51 843	66 136	2.8	52 286	12.6	16.0	15.0
Adair	13	632	1 630	4.4	52.4	16.3	9.5	10 642	25 564	47 892	57 482	1.3	47 905	10.1	15.6	13.7
Adams	154	489	825	10.8	48.9	13.7	5.9	10 846	23 707	45 871	53 374	0.9	44 004	13.2	20.4	20.1
Allamakee	56	309	3 077	14.2	54.7	14.9	21.2	9 326	24 926	48 831	59 712	1.8	44 673	13.9	21.2	20.8
Appanoose	347	2 375	2 684	6.7	49.8	18.3	18.9	9 148	21 599	39 208	49 057	1.1	37 683	17.2	25.3	23.8
Audubon	17	290	1 298	6.4	51.0	16.6	7.8	9 635	30 919	48 313	68 572	4.3	47 227	11.2	16.0	14.2
Benton	NA	NA	6 716	14.8	46.1	18.8	35.1	8 949	26 624	56 669	66 970	1.5	59 179	8.8	11.6	10.6
Black Hawk	514	2 127	38 424	10.7	44.7	25.3	233.5	12 526	24 273	45 747	59 277	1.9	46 281	16.7	20.3	19.6
Boone	320	1 170	6 558	13.6	44.4	20.3	36.8	9 325	27 149	51 826	65 563	2.4	52 578	11.3	15.5	14.2
Bremer	240	654	7 142	27.3	40.4	28.3	47.0	9 314	28 727	61 216	72 510	2.4	61 665	6.5	6.2	5.8
Buchanan	NA	NA	5 136	17.5	52.7	17.1	28.6	9 540	27 038	55 553	70 484	3.3	54 383	9.2	14.4	12.9
Buena Vista	333	1 582	5 432	21.9	51.9	20.0	40.8	10 034	22 899	46 951	59 444	2.2	47 514	12.5	17.5	16.2
Butler	20	86	3 299	5.4	52.1	15.0	18.2	9 223	25 269	52 026	60 765	1.3	53 920	9.3	12.8	12.5
Calhoun	61	569	2 032	4.2	45.9	19.1	17.6	10 119	25 766	44 484	58 407	2.7	47 351	14.0	16.1	15.4
Carroll	NA	NA	4 846	30.0	50.7	18.8	25.0	9 737	25 430	48 361	59 108	1.6	51 328	9.5	11.4	10.8
Cass	139	972	2 924	6.7	51.4	19.0	28.7	10 912	25 448	43 481	56 876	2.8	45 191	14.8	21.3	20.2
Cedar	49	938	4 428	4.0	47.5	19.5	33.2	9 607	26 567	58 088	63 829	1.2	58 530	7.4	9.0	8.3
Cerro Gordo	89	3 366	9 949	13.5	39.7	21.0	55.1	9 835	27 291	44 795	60 060	2.4	46 063	11.9	15.8	15.0
Cherokee	143	931	2 529	5.9	45.7	19.6	16.5	9 336	26 330	48 977	57 887	2.1	51 655	11.1	15.5	14.4
Chickasaw	65	449	2 950	13.5	56.7	13.8	20.0	9 729	24 139	43 971	55 635	2.0	50 342	10.6	14.6	13.9
Clarke	170	1 911	2 153	7.9	58.8	14.3	16.1	8 742	23 472	43 216	56 399	1.2	42 776	13.3	20.5	19.9
Clay	156	1 690	4 061	12.7	45.0	18.4	23.1	9 478	29 060	49 035	68 107	2.0	51 399	10.7	16.6	14.8
Clayton	73	326	3 748	7.3	54.2	15.5	46.1	18 843	25 074	47 494	58 464	1.9	48 626	12.0	17.9	16.6
Clinton	423	2 605	11 916	11.7	46.8	17.7	81.1	10 105	25 966	49 559	61 912	2.1	49 702	13.9	19.6	18.3
Crawford	29	482	4 269	7.0	58.6	14.7	37.3	9 625	22 748	46 548	59 637	2.0	48 555	13.0	18.6	18.4
Dallas	140	1 451	18 735	20.9	27.9	43.6	133.8	8 938	35 844	73 847	93 577	7.4	79 309	6.0	6.7	6.3
Davis	115	334	2 073	24.5	49.7	16.4	11.6	9 265	22 210	45 040	58 663	2.7	44 477	16.5	28.8	28.1
Decatur	61	341	2 423	35.8	53.1	18.4	11.5	10 672	18 845	36 326	48 768	1.8	37 534	21.6	29.7	27.5
Delaware	125	780	4 397	18.0	52.6	15.5	21.9	9 390	26 261	54 076	63 990	1.4	54 587	10.1	13.5	12.5
Des Moines	418	3 042	9 179	10.1	45.0	18.9	62.6	9 420	24 408	42 451	56 854	1.9	42 882	12.3	22.2	21.2
Dickinson	111	1 361	3 156	7.6	37.4	25.4	25.4	9 826	31 790	56 136	68 515	3.2	58 610	8.7	11.7	10.5
Dubuque	160	1 974	25 290	34.0	44.9	27.1	144.7	9 945	26 254	51 475	64 995	2.6	61 007	12.8	14.5	10.4
Emmet	307	1 090	2 657	6.4	44.0	15.3	17.3	9 830	27 908	48 601	67 422	3.1	46 892	14.7	20.7	20.4
Fayette	202	927	5 272	20.8	50.8	18.4	36.1	9 740	23 391	45 542	56 255	1.2	44 739	13.9	18.7	17.7
Floyd	144	1 043	3 498	14.4	49.3	15.9	21.0	10 033	24 590	43 826	56 013	1.5	48 964	12.1	17.6	15.8

1. Data for serious crimes have not been adjusted for underreporting; this may affect comparability between geographic areas and over time. 2. Per 100,000 population estimated by the FBI.
3. All persons 3 years old and over enrolled in nursery school through college. 4. Persons 25 years old and over. 5. Elementary and secondary education expenditures.
6. Based on population estimated by the American Community Survey, 2009–2013.

STATE County	Personal income, 2013										Earnings, 2013		
			Per capita[1]			Supplements to wages and salaries; employer contributions (mil dol)						Contributions for government social insurance (mil dol)	
	Total (mil dol)	Percent change, 2012–2013	Dollars	Rank	Wages and salaries (mil dol)	Pension and insurance	Government social insurance	Proprietors' income (mil dol)	Dividends, interest, and rent (mil dol)	Personal transfer receipts (mil dol)	Total (mil dol)	From employee and self-employed	From employer
	62	63	64	65	66	67	68	69	70	71	72	73	74
INDIANA—Cont'd													
Pike	439	3.1	34 643	1 965	171	34	12	44	57	112	261	16	12
Porter	7 995	1.0	48 002	481	2 615	405	199	492	991	1 149	3 712	235	199
Posey	1 154	4.0	45 296	669	464	101	33	158	185	195	755	42	33
Pulaski	502	2.2	38 620	1 349	168	32	12	78	94	110	291	15	12
Putnam	1 305	4.9	34 783	1 935	449	82	37	114	169	256	682	41	37
Randolph	952	3.7	37 161	1 553	270	52	21	177	129	228	521	30	21
Ripley	907	1.5	31 921	2 420	544	101	40	46	156	200	731	44	40
Rush	734	10.5	43 167	832	175	35	13	144	97	142	368	17	13
St. Joseph	10 132	0.5	37 989	1 432	5 116	827	397	1 094	1 699	2 002	7 434	455	397
Scott	720	0.2	30 051	2 681	243	46	20	29	85	219	338	24	20
Shelby	1 776	4.4	39 699	1 204	708	120	55	159	234	351	1 043	61	55
Spencer	758	3.8	36 212	1 708	264	50	20	77	106	149	411	24	20
Starke	700	2.7	30 176	2 659	142	30	11	63	88	218	246	17	11
Steuben	1 164	2.7	33 887	2 101	515	94	42	74	217	257	724	47	42
Sullivan	698	4.7	32 883	2 268	257	54	18	91	95	178	420	24	18
Switzerland	343	2.4	32 575	2 314	79	12	6	13	33	70	110	8	6
Tippecanoe	5 939	1.3	32 961	2 259	3 631	712	272	405	1 060	951	5 020	287	272
Tipton	658	0.6	42 068	933	157	28	12	65	111	130	263	16	12
Union	288	6.4	39 553	1 226	45	10	3	46	33	56	104	6	3
Vanderburgh	7 584	0.5	41 808	957	4 561	733	351	888	1 490	1 495	6 532	397	351
Vermillion	593	4.6	37 333	1 534	208	39	15	69	80	145	331	19	15
Vigo	3 652	0.5	33 725	2 140	1 989	369	157	270	643	925	2 784	171	157
Wabash	1 244	2.1	38 453	1 380	430	81	33	156	210	313	701	44	33
Warren	343	6.8	40 789	1 078	75	13	6	79	45	68	173	8	6
Warrick	2 747	1.1	45 003	687	685	115	51	160	459	424	1 011	67	51
Washington	914	2.7	32 897	2 264	207	40	16	74	114	233	338	22	16
Wayne	2 299	1.8	33 869	2 104	1 115	199	87	169	370	668	1 570	101	87
Wells	1 053	0.6	37 854	1 453	420	75	31	98	179	209	625	38	31
White	943	4.4	38 563	1 364	324	59	25	117	157	205	526	28	25
Whitley	1 233	2.2	37 023	1 581	460	85	35	64	183	234	644	40	35
IOWA	138 337	2.2	44 763	X	64 169	10 689	5 099	20 768	24 675	22 362	100 726	5 661	5 099
Adair	332	9.4	44 451	731	93	17	8	77	56	57	195	9	8
Adams	242	7.0	62 055	86	43	9	3	108	34	39	163	7	3
Allamakee	549	3.5	38 745	1 326	167	35	13	111	111	113	326	18	13
Appanoose	421	4.1	33 132	2 237	141	29	11	49	78	119	231	16	11
Audubon	343	14.7	58 335	129	61	12	5	137	61	52	214	7	5
Benton	1 217	3.2	47 344	522	206	41	16	235	202	176	498	25	16
Black Hawk	5 281	1.3	39 840	1 186	3 289	525	257	398	910	1 007	4 469	272	257
Boone	1 182	1.3	44 842	703	388	73	32	100	205	246	593	36	32
Bremer	1 123	2.7	45 602	648	395	70	31	123	210	174	618	36	31
Buchanan	857	3.6	40 837	1 075	222	43	18	138	178	150	421	22	18
Buena Vista	957	2.8	46 522	584	372	70	29	277	163	138	748	36	29
Butler	752	10.3	50 065	364	138	27	11	216	120	122	392	16	11
Calhoun	473	0.6	47 688	501	99	20	8	139	91	86	265	11	8
Carroll	1 048	5.4	50 876	336	423	71	32	272	196	161	797	40	32
Cass	672	7.5	49 441	393	204	41	16	163	131	128	424	20	16
Cedar	845	1.1	45 953	619	193	35	16	139	157	120	383	20	16
Cerro Gordo	2 053	0.1	47 104	547	937	148	76	345	394	383	1 506	89	76
Cherokee	732	1.8	61 273	92	195	37	15	316	107	95	564	25	15
Chickasaw	676	4.4	54 857	207	178	31	15	236	119	95	461	23	15
Clarke	335	4.6	35 967	1 752	137	26	11	58	49	77	232	13	11
Clay	785	-1.5	47 594	505	336	58	27	180	155	125	601	31	27
Clayton	759	2.4	42 699	870	228	44	20	125	191	147	417	24	20
Clinton	1 980	1.9	40 882	1 067	847	147	71	234	323	452	1 299	77	71
Crawford	835	5.4	47 899	489	281	52	21	276	132	121	631	28	21
Dallas	3 643	3.8	48 813	428	1 891	239	141	231	664	334	2 501	146	141
Davis	279	3.5	31 741	2 442	65	14	5	56	45	61	140	9	5
Decatur	246	4.4	30 176	2 659	67	15	6	33	42	65	121	7	6
Delaware	822	6.7	46 900	558	249	49	21	191	162	116	510	26	21
Des Moines	1 954	1.7	48 263	465	863	142	77	462	344	367	1 543	91	77
Dickinson	851	0.1	50 211	359	298	57	26	130	233	142	511	30	26
Dubuque	3 945	0.9	41 229	1 023	2 341	351	192	344	782	682	3 228	201	192
Emmet	420	-1.2	42 039	934	146	28	12	88	65	88	274	14	12
Fayette	815	2.0	39 775	1 193	239	44	19	148	158	191	450	24	19
Floyd	662	4.6	41 122	1 038	212	42	17	110	136	145	381	21	17

1. Based on the resident population estimated as of July 1 of the year shown.

STATE County	Earnings, 2013 (cont.) — Percent by selected industries: Farm	Mining	Construction	Manu-facturing	Infor-mation: professional, scientific, technical services	Retail trade	Finance, insur-ance, real estate and leasing	Health care and social assistance	Govern-ment	Social Security beneficiaries, December 2013: Number	Rate[1]	Supple-mental Security Income recipients, December 2013	Housing units, 2014: Total	Percent change, 2010–2014
	75	76	77	78	79	80	81	82	83	84	85	86	87	88
INDIANA—Cont'd														
Pike	7.5	24.7	6.3	4.2	D	3.1	D	3.7	11.9	3 220	254	270	5 752	0.3
Porter	0.9	D	10.5	26.5	5.2	6.3	3.6	12.1	9.8	31 665	190	1 928	67 059	1.3
Posey	9.8	1.1	5.1	39.9	3.7	7.4	2.0	3.1	7.9	5 535	217	369	11 331	1.1
Pulaski	22.5	D	3.5	25.0	2.2	4.9	3.2	D	17.3	3 190	245	242	6 043	-0.3
Putnam	10.9	0.6	3.4	21.0	D	5.0	2.8	D	17.5	7 465	199	431	14 828	0.8
Randolph	15.7	D	5.1	30.6	D	4.4	1.5	D	11.0	6 345	248	484	11 651	-0.8
Ripley	3.4	0.2	4.3	17.6	4.2	4.1	5.7	D	9.1	5 685	200	374	12 108	1.3
Rush	33.2	D	4.8	16.3	D	5.2	2.4	3.5	15.1	3 955	232	311	7 469	-0.5
St. Joseph	0.6	0.0	4.6	15.6	9.3	6.2	5.5	15.4	10.1	50 125	188	5 730	115 587	0.6
Scott	3.6	0.3	2.7	32.1	2.6	8.7	3.3	D	17.4	6 110	256	871	10 443	0.0
Shelby	9.6	0.4	6.0	29.7	2.4	4.7	2.0	D	13.4	9 250	208	719	19 091	0.1
Spencer	11.2	0.2	4.6	18.1	D	4.0	1.7	4.1	11.5	4 495	216	275	8 931	0.7
Starke	15.7	0.0	3.0	22.2	2.1	7.7	1.8	D	20.1	6 120	264	613	10 999	0.3
Steuben	3.4	0.1	4.5	35.2	3.9	7.9	2.6	D	10.2	7 800	227	437	19 529	0.8
Sullivan	14.9	D	4.6	8.7	3.2	5.5	1.8	3.4	21.9	4 750	224	397	8 860	-0.9
Switzerland	5.3	D	D	D	D	4.0	D	5.4	21.0	1 935	184	195	5 083	2.3
Tippecanoe	1.5	D	3.7	21.3	5.5	5.5	4.7	13.7	28.4	24 250	134	2 088	73 901	3.9
Tipton	16.6	D	8.4	18.7	4.6	9.0	2.7	D	14.0	3 675	236	178	6 969	-0.4
Union	28.7	0.0	5.5	11.5	1.1	5.6	D	D	20.1	1 560	213	111	3 225	-0.4
Vanderburgh	0.3	4.1	9.6	16.0	6.9	6.4	3.6	16.8	8.9	38 085	210	4 592	83 400	0.5
Vermillion	15.7	D	13.9	22.7	2.1	6.0	D	8.5	9.9	3 955	249	306	7 480	-0.1
Vigo	1.0	0.9	5.6	18.9	3.7	6.9	4.6	18.5	17.9	22 085	204	3 209	46 443	0.9
Wabash	7.9	D	6.2	30.6	3.0	6.8	3.6	D	13.9	8 500	263	615	14 098	-0.5
Warren	39.8	D	3.5	15.0	D	3.5	D	7.4	10.2	1 975	235	104	3 680	0.0
Warrick	1.5	2.4	8.0	21.6	5.8	5.6	4.9	20.9	11.4	12 185	200	660	24 936	3.0
Washington	14.1	D	5.7	24.8	3.5	8.0	3.5	8.5	17.5	6 475	233	707	12 192	-0.2
Wayne	3.6	0.1	3.1	21.0	D	8.6	4.1	19.2	14.7	17 105	252	2 105	31 144	-0.3
Wells	7.0	D	3.9	25.8	D	4.8	3.8	11.4	9.9	6 030	217	324	11 707	0.4
White	21.8	0.3	3.6	24.8	D	8.1	2.4	D	11.8	5 865	241	302	12 966	0.0
Whitley	8.2	0.1	4.7	42.6	D	5.3	2.2	6.6	11.5	7 025	211	318	14 453	1.2
IOWA	8.9	0.2	6.4	16.9	6.0	6.0	9.5	9.4	15.1	609 067	197	50 849	1 362 124	1.9
Adair	28.5	D	8.1	12.7	D	4.6	3.6	D	12.1	1 735	232	89	3 674	-0.6
Adams	24.4	D	D	39.4	D	2.6	D	8.9	7.3	1 050	270	63	2 010	0.0
Allamakee	15.4	0.2	8.3	18.7	2.1	6.8	3.9	7.0	15.6	3 535	252	185	7 650	0.4
Appanoose	5.9	D	5.3	19.7	3.0	8.7	3.3	D	15.5	3 390	268	447	6 578	-0.8
Audubon	53.5	0.0	4.6	4.5	D	3.5	D	D	9.8	1 640	279	70	2 997	0.8
Benton	25.1	D	8.0	14.2	D	6.6	3.5	D	16.2	5 315	207	289	11 079	-0.1
Black Hawk	1.8	D	4.8	27.0	4.6	6.3	6.5	12.0	15.2	25 780	194	3 204	56 890	1.8
Boone	10.8	D	7.2	5.1	4.8	6.1	3.1	D	24.8	5 640	214	356	11 793	0.3
Bremer	11.3	D	5.2	19.3	D	5.7	12.3	D	16.9	5 205	212	182	10 136	2.2
Buchanan	24.3	D	8.0	15.5	2.1	6.3	4.5	D	18.4	4 290	205	306	8 990	0.2
Buena Vista	19.5	0.0	3.3	21.3	D	4.9	3.2	D	12.5	3 605	175	262	8 299	0.8
Butler	45.1	D	5.5	14.0	2.0	3.4	2.4	4.1	9.7	3 700	247	173	6 731	0.7
Calhoun	43.8	0.0	5.1	1.6	1.4	4.3	2.7	D	13.4	2 625	265	135	5 088	-0.4
Carroll	20.0	D	5.2	14.7	2.7	6.1	7.4	D	7.9	4 730	230	273	9 419	0.5
Cass	27.6	D	6.9	8.4	3.2	6.1	3.7	6.7	18.7	3 690	271	333	6 564	-0.4
Cedar	21.0	0.0	7.8	9.4	5.3	5.4	2.4	D	14.1	3 870	211	151	8 116	0.7
Cerro Gordo	5.5	D	5.3	19.8	5.5	7.3	5.4	21.0	10.9	10 855	250	815	22 238	0.3
Cherokee	24.6	D	5.0	35.7	1.4	3.7	1.8	D	9.8	2 890	242	135	5 791	0.2
Chickasaw	18.3	D	6.9	37.9	1.3	4.1	2.3	D	7.3	2 880	234	145	5 664	-0.3
Clarke	14.5	D	D	26.6	1.7	6.7	2.8	6.1	17.8	2 080	225	146	4 132	1.1
Clay	19.3	D	4.9	10.1	D	11.6	3.6	9.5	15.3	3 995	243	231	8 112	0.6
Clayton	19.4	D	12.4	11.5	D	6.2	4.2	D	17.0	4 605	259	247	9 032	0.4
Clinton	9.6	D	4.9	26.1	2.4	6.8	4.3	12.8	10.6	11 050	229	1 175	21 792	0.3
Crawford	28.2	0.0	4.4	29.6	D	4.1	2.2	4.0	12.2	3 560	204	191	6 985	0.6
Dallas	4.5	D	4.4	4.2	4.1	6.6	44.6	6.9	8.1	9 865	132	511	29 884	9.6
Davis	4.0	D	10.7	10.8	12.2	6.7	3.3	D	21.9	1 820	208	141	3 578	-0.6
Decatur	15.6	D	D	D	D	4.9	D	D	23.5	1 805	219	200	3 847	0.3
Delaware	18.3	D	7.2	28.1	2.0	4.4	3.7	D	14.0	3 605	206	222	8 026	0.0
Des Moines	2.4	D	5.2	40.8	2.9	6.1	3.0	12.6	9.4	9 675	239	1 082	18 463	-0.4
Dickinson	10.7	D	8.4	21.9	3.5	9.1	5.4	6.4	12.8	4 835	285	195	13 191	2.7
Dubuque	3.0	D	5.7	19.4	9.0	6.8	8.6	13.9	8.2	19 835	207	1 523	40 369	3.6
Emmet	21.4	D	5.7	17.6	3.6	5.5	2.8	D	14.3	2 340	234	126	4 752	-0.1
Fayette	26.7	D	5.2	6.1	2.1	5.8	3.2	D	13.1	5 030	215	400	9 522	-0.4
Floyd	18.8	0.0	7.9	22.6	2.5	5.6	4.8	D	13.7	4 120	256	340	7 516	-0.1

1. Per 1,000 resident population estimated as of July 1 of the year shown.

STATE County	Housing units, 2009–2013								Civilian labor force, 2014				Civilian employment,[6] 2009–2013		
	Occupied units										Unemployment			Percent	
		Owner-occupied				Renter-occupied									
	Total	Percent	Median value[1]	Median owner cost as a percent of income: With a mortgage	Median owner cost as a percent of income: Without a mortgage[2]	Median rent[3]	Median rent as a percent of income[2]	Substandard units[4] (percent)	Total	Percent change, 2013–2014	Total	Rate[5]	Total	Management, business, science and arts	Construction, production, and maintenance occupations
	89	90	91	92	93	94	95	96	97	98	99	100	101	102	103
INDIANA—Cont'd															
Pike	5 149	83.1	85 800	20.1	12.6	596	27.4	2.0	6 447	2.8	329	5.1	5 617	23.1	45.1
Porter	61 502	77.4	165 700	20.4	11.1	857	27.9	2.6	83 829	0.7	5 318	6.3	76 896	33.3	26.3
Posey	10 050	85.0	127 900	19.0	10.2	605	27.5	1.2	13 172	1.6	643	4.9	12 510	29.0	33.8
Pulaski	5 058	80.0	94 900	20.7	10.5	607	28.8	1.7	6 189	0.6	338	5.5	5 694	27.6	38.0
Putnam	12 414	79.1	125 800	22.3	11.3	653	25.6	2.1	16 357	1.3	1 070	6.5	15 119	30.1	31.1
Randolph	10 429	73.4	76 200	20.0	11.0	606	27.7	1.6	12 542	0.1	825	6.6	11 306	26.9	37.4
Ripley	10 761	76.2	132 000	21.1	12.1	653	24.0	0.7	13 641	-0.2	915	6.7	12 853	26.4	32.6
Rush	6 874	71.9	104 700	20.2	11.3	607	27.1	1.4	8 524	2.7	477	5.6	7 939	30.0	35.3
St. Joseph	101 947	69.5	115 100	20.5	10.2	711	30.2	1.4	128 906	1.2	8 647	6.7	120 386	34.2	22.4
Scott	8 914	73.2	101 400	23.5	11.8	716	30.2	2.1	10 369	1.3	695	6.7	9 558	22.3	38.5
Shelby	17 171	71.1	125 000	21.0	11.5	697	26.5	2.0	22 714	1.7	1 279	5.6	20 963	26.7	35.4
Spencer	7 984	82.1	113 300	19.4	10.7	566	25.4	2.0	10 753	0.5	568	5.3	9 912	27.2	36.7
Starke	8 964	81.1	96 900	24.6	11.1	666	28.3	1.4	10 246	0.3	761	7.4	9 223	23.7	37.4
Steuben	13 514	77.3	123 000	22.0	11.0	656	26.5	4.2	19 930	2.7	1 006	5.0	16 185	26.3	32.3
Sullivan	7 764	72.2	77 600	17.9	11.7	611	32.5	4.7	8 687	-0.6	642	7.4	8 176	26.7	33.2
Switzerland	4 099	76.3	110 800	25.8	13.1	740	30.5	2.1	4 824	-1.3	283	5.9	4 551	16.5	36.1
Tippecanoe	66 667	54.2	130 900	19.9	10.0	788	34.7	1.0	91 071	1.4	4 650	5.1	83 361	38.9	21.1
Tipton	6 622	77.2	108 300	19.5	10.8	661	25.6	1.1	8 144	1.9	445	5.5	7 062	27.6	35.3
Union	2 943	76.1	103 200	22.5	13.0	605	33.6	2.4	3 581	1.5	202	5.6	3 387	30.2	24.3
Vanderburgh	73 963	63.6	112 900	20.5	11.8	709	30.9	2.1	92 094	1.2	5 051	5.5	86 186	29.7	24.8
Vermillion	6 466	78.2	75 100	19.2	11.7	570	24.8	2.2	7 277	-0.8	635	8.7	6 837	22.7	34.3
Vigo	39 597	63.9	91 600	19.4	11.4	673	32.4	1.9	49 306	-0.6	3 845	7.8	46 551	31.7	24.7
Wabash	12 703	76.2	95 000	20.1	10.0	599	28.3	2.1	15 441	-0.1	871	5.6	14 301	28.5	31.7
Warren	3 283	76.6	99 500	19.3	10.0	709	25.0	1.9	4 121	-1.0	250	6.1	3 929	24.9	38.2
Warrick	22 454	83.3	146 300	21.1	10.6	766	31.1	1.9	31 233	1.6	1 553	5.0	29 194	34.3	22.8
Washington	10 631	80.3	101 500	22.7	11.1	631	27.3	2.0	13 369	1.9	889	6.6	12 289	23.8	39.2
Wayne	28 185	66.8	94 100	21.8	12.1	636	31.9	1.6	31 047	1.5	2 067	6.7	28 520	30.3	27.6
Wells	10 904	78.3	112 500	18.9	10.0	577	28.7	2.0	13 836	1.2	676	4.9	13 083	26.8	33.9
White	9 541	76.6	109 800	19.2	11.6	687	29.1	1.7	13 371	3.5	700	5.2	11 289	26.2	33.0
Whitley	13 094	81.7	126 300	22.0	10.0	631	28.2	1.8	16 910	0.8	886	5.2	16 061	24.3	37.4
IOWA	1 226 547	72.2	124 300	20.4	11.5	670	27.8	1.9	1 704 575	1.9	75 249	4.4	1 553 030	34.0	25.4
Adair	3 295	77.1	90 900	21.5	12.0	526	22.0	1.1	4 175	2.6	175	4.2	3 968	28.3	34.2
Adams	1 745	78.5	85 200	20.0	13.1	475	21.6	2.0	2 218	3.2	78	3.5	1 989	32.2	33.2
Allamakee	5 862	79.5	114 400	21.3	12.3	529	22.3	2.5	7 777	1.6	457	5.9	7 107	30.4	35.2
Appanoose	5 534	72.5	77 600	19.8	12.9	528	28.3	0.6	6 173	4.1	368	6.0	5 790	30.8	34.3
Audubon	2 684	80.4	71 100	18.8	10.0	545	18.1	1.2	3 306	2.2	148	4.5	3 090	32.7	26.6
Benton	10 079	80.4	131 500	20.9	11.6	603	23.5	2.1	13 900	1.3	666	4.8	13 085	31.2	29.0
Black Hawk	52 276	67.8	123 600	19.6	10.7	671	32.3	1.7	72 478	1.0	3 698	5.1	65 028	30.7	26.0
Boone	10 574	75.6	117 300	21.9	12.2	616	26.7	1.0	15 248	2.5	537	3.5	13 245	31.5	29.1
Bremer	9 258	81.3	145 300	19.7	10.0	588	23.4	3.7	14 215	1.6	544	3.8	12 814	36.7	24.5
Buchanan	8 187	78.1	122 200	19.8	10.3	646	25.3	5.6	11 528	3.3	556	4.8	10 366	30.1	33.4
Buena Vista	7 615	68.0	97 700	20.3	10.0	565	23.7	1.6	11 532	2.0	476	4.1	10 582	25.5	38.0
Butler	6 189	79.6	100 400	18.3	11.0	562	21.2	0.4	8 410	1.8	372	4.4	7 299	27.5	32.4
Calhoun	4 356	79.0	72 200	18.2	10.1	493	26.3	0.6	4 433	1.7	225	5.1	4 566	30.6	26.0
Carroll	8 626	75.4	105 700	19.7	10.0	540	28.8	1.0	11 293	0.2	372	3.3	11 024	27.2	27.8
Cass	6 081	71.8	88 100	20.6	12.0	531	23.9	1.2	7 430	1.9	336	4.5	6 893	28.8	29.1
Cedar	7 665	78.8	132 800	20.6	11.8	686	22.3	1.1	10 938	1.2	440	4.0	9 915	30.0	30.5
Cerro Gordo	19 967	71.6	110 800	20.1	12.1	584	26.8	0.7	23 373	0.2	1 131	4.8	22 844	29.9	27.1
Cherokee	5 354	74.9	80 200	18.0	10.0	506	23.8	1.7	6 680	-2.3	356	5.3	6 160	29.7	32.0
Chickasaw	5 364	80.1	95 900	19.0	11.3	511	25.6	1.0	6 541	2.8	322	4.9	6 008	28.0	37.1
Clarke	3 672	71.0	84 900	19.9	17.7	631	28.2	1.8	4 729	3.1	221	4.7	4 381	25.1	35.6
Clay	7 148	74.2	105 400	18.7	11.4	524	26.5	2.0	8 989	2.0	388	4.3	8 500	26.7	31.2
Clayton	7 707	78.2	102 400	22.1	12.5	552	25.3	1.0	10 254	1.8	531	5.2	9 090	27.1	33.9
Clinton	20 008	74.4	110 300	19.8	12.6	594	28.1	3.3	24 855	-0.2	1 363	5.5	23 647	27.4	30.7
Crawford	6 300	75.9	83 100	19.4	10.4	485	25.0	1.3	8 772	0.1	373	4.3	8 223	26.5	38.6
Dallas	26 262	77.4	184 100	20.2	11.2	842	24.4	4.8	42 082	2.9	1 436	3.4	36 809	47.6	14.5
Davis	3 115	80.2	99 700	23.0	12.4	550	25.0	0.5	4 142	0.6	220	5.3	3 675	30.6	37.6
Decatur	3 106	70.1	77 700	23.7	13.6	467	26.8	0.7	4 461	3.8	174	3.9	3 591	32.8	27.8
Delaware	7 129	78.8	125 300	22.0	10.5	559	23.3	1.9	10 585	1.9	418	3.9	9 446	26.9	37.9
Des Moines	16 993	73.1	93 900	20.9	13.0	614	28.3	1.0	20 968	2.3	1 089	5.2	18 250	27.9	31.5
Dickinson	7 981	75.6	159 700	22.2	10.4	612	24.1	1.2	9 770	4.7	474	4.9	8 871	33.1	28.5
Dubuque	37 366	73.0	145 900	20.8	12.2	670	28.8	1.4	55 858	1.5	2 387	4.3	49 672	33.7	23.4
Emmet	4 119	79.8	82 200	19.0	10.9	589	31.5	1.5	5 736	0.9	238	4.1	5 207	24.5	35.2
Fayette	8 328	77.6	85 400	19.4	12.0	523	25.1	1.6	10 860	1.8	566	5.2	10 103	31.3	31.9
Floyd	7 007	72.9	90 200	18.7	11.4	530	27.7	1.4	8 391	1.5	398	4.7	8 054	31.1	34.1

1. Specified owner-occupied units. 2. A value of 10.0 represents 10 percent or less; a value of 50.0 represents 50 percent or more. 3. Specified renter-occupied units.
4. Overcrowded or lacking complete plumbing facilities. 5. Percent of civilian labor force. 6. Persons 16 years old and over.

Table B. States and Counties — **Nonfarm Employment and Agriculture**

STATE County	Private nonfarm establishments, employment and payroll, 2013									Agriculture, 2012			
		Employment						Annual payroll		Farms			
											Percent with:		
	Number of establish-ments	Total	Health care and social assistance	Manufac-turing	Retail trade	Finance and insurance	Professional, scientific, and technical services	Total (mil dol)	Average per employee (dollars)	Number	Fewer than 50 acres	500 acres or more	Farm operators whose principal occu-pation is farming (percent)
	104	105	106	107	108	109	110	111	112	113	114	115	116
INDIANA—Cont'd													
Pike	196	2 411	351	D	255	D	D	116	48 279	321	34.0	11.2	32.1
Porter	3 448	51 077	7 849	9 551	6 867	1 147	1 974	2 170	42 489	481	53.4	15.2	48.0
Posey	488	8 892	424	2 766	709	115	307	483	54 361	408	31.6	31.6	60.5
Pulaski	323	3 519	587	1 176	495	D	65	126	35 789	536	38.6	20.7	46.6
Putnam	683	10 907	1 750	2 280	1 187	254	192	318	29 189	847	49.6	11.9	41.0
Randolph	491	6 033	705	D	578	D	102	206	34 101	772	40.7	18.3	52.7
Ripley	642	10 321	1 306	2 371	930	261	D	432	41 843	876	41.3	10.0	43.8
Rush	357	3 635	505	D	442	92	124	128	35 144	601	32.6	20.6	54.2
St. Joseph	5 782	112 678	18 207	13 761	14 700	3 892	3 879	4 227	37 513	691	54.7	11.7	45.0
Scott	399	5 761	960	1 769	852	108	D	175	30 290	321	51.4	5.9	35.5
Shelby	907	14 624	D	4 920	1 350	196	224	568	38 832	569	39.4	24.4	56.8
Spencer	395	5 190	296	1 326	724	143	D	192	36 964	597	32.8	15.1	38.5
Starke	304	2 836	309	896	651	79	60	79	27 819	511	50.7	13.3	33.9
Steuben	971	13 140	1 351	4 291	2 109	214	165	402	30 597	562	39.0	8.5	38.3
Sullivan	338	4 619	D	695	543	D	D	196	42 362	433	32.3	23.8	55.2
Switzerland	131	1 814	170	D	86	30	D	47	26 008	383	41.0	3.1	39.9
Tippecanoe	3 369	64 443	10 882	14 311	8 874	2 726	2 483	2 440	37 863	702	56.7	15.2	39.3
Tipton	305	3 162	D	697	476	D	D	114	36 169	377	35.3	23.3	53.8
Union	111	884	D	45	196	27	30	25	27 958	242	31.0	19.8	49.6
Vanderburgh	4 981	109 426	19 193	10 807	12 622	3 662	4 034	3 953	36 126	275	46.5	16.4	42.5
Vermillion	262	3 360	543	D	583	D	25	157	46 677	270	37.8	23.7	48.1
Vigo	2 491	45 346	8 978	8 693	6 687	1 274	1 154	1 612	35 544	450	56.2	14.2	44.7
Wabash	756	10 901	2 113	2 667	1 321	292	349	342	31 358	745	44.8	13.4	44.4
Warren	119	1 349	D	501	123	32	D	46	34 405	413	43.1	22.0	46.2
Warrick	1 109	13 443	3 056	D	1 610	563	418	550	40 903	379	47.8	16.1	44.9
Washington	435	4 305	736	1 431	693	128	111	125	28 959	831	40.7	9.7	49.8
Wayne	1 527	25 456	5 032	5 320	3 756	828	444	874	34 317	805	41.5	8.9	44.7
Wells	619	9 553	1 643	2 537	933	187	239	327	34 218	636	40.1	17.5	49.2
White	601	6 867	832	2 437	1 054	191	112	231	33 684	631	39.9	25.0	53.2
Whitley	672	10 185	1 102	4 275	1 340	234	188	374	36 755	710	51.7	8.5	34.4
IOWA	80 581	1 305 216	215 820	208 190	178 668	91 984	49 897	50 343	38 571	88 637	30.9	22.4	54.1
Adair	187	1 663	324	D	D	D	71	51	30 915	726	25.5	28.5	55.2
Adams	118	884	D	D	114	38	D	28	31 612	467	24.4	27.4	53.3
Allamakee	396	4 517	1 069	1 207	607	179	76	128	28 278	1 011	25.4	17.5	41.5
Appanoose	312	3 437	720	862	666	107	64	97	28 256	744	30.1	13.4	46.1
Audubon	181	1 176	303	203	186	55	D	35	29 535	622	33.1	28.1	61.1
Benton	566	4 366	786	643	765	176	79	143	32 741	1 215	30.1	24.1	54.3
Black Hawk	3 203	68 753	14 278	14 072	9 093	2 859	3 848	2 518	36 628	924	33.0	21.4	55.6
Boone	553	6 824	D	D	1 048	193	148	225	33 023	938	42.6	19.9	49.7
Bremer	607	9 369	1 740	2 080	1 208	875	183	362	38 680	982	34.7	16.6	49.1
Buchanan	490	5 218	1 266	1 020	883	212	90	171	32 826	1 075	30.6	19.7	57.6
Buena Vista	556	9 218	1 406	3 328	1 178	449	190	304	33 009	858	27.9	32.5	65.3
Butler	333	2 594	486	785	400	D	60	95	36 547	1 096	37.2	19.9	51.3
Calhoun	284	2 197	636	106	355	116	D	65	29 524	826	29.5	31.1	52.7
Carroll	879	10 604	2 174	1 343	1 497	800	206	352	33 242	1 065	29.1	21.6	57.0
Cass	478	4 709	1 196	D	853	226	108	146	30 916	703	25.3	29.2	50.2
Cedar	465	4 282	657	632	604	D	89	129	30 145	955	37.6	21.3	51.8
Cerro Gordo	1 399	20 910	4 790	2 855	3 633	1 084	608	743	35 539	780	35.1	27.4	59.0
Cherokee	354	4 379	929	927	647	174	D	143	32 687	805	22.0	28.6	64.0
Chickasaw	418	3 942	624	1 355	430	149	61	135	34 210	1 036	34.0	18.8	55.5
Clarke	189	3 154	587	D	545	87	34	90	28 621	627	27.1	15.3	35.9
Clay	608	7 313	1 505	835	1 443	278	168	257	35 121	720	26.1	32.1	57.6
Clayton	537	4 851	1 120	887	624	178	96	158	32 498	1 577	29.2	13.9	50.3
Clinton	1 181	27 036	3 647	4 316	2 707	687	292	888	32 829	1 244	30.9	23.4	63.1
Crawford	460	6 534	1 009	2 587	832	206	94	208	31 763	900	26.6	30.6	61.7
Dallas	1 718	34 419	3 414	1 902	5 405	12 234	1 359	1 649	47 914	1 001	43.6	17.5	43.7
Davis	170	1 451	424	140	265	60	55	44	30 356	917	28.9	10.9	44.1
Decatur	130	1 697	311	D	210	38	D	33	19 669	711	27.3	18.3	44.6
Delaware	496	5 725	1 062	1 746	717	262	118	195	34 117	1 382	29.7	16.2	60.2
Des Moines	1 107	19 430	3 692	4 671	3 008	500	304	893	35 654	663	37.4	17.3	46.5
Dickinson	770	6 877	932	1 712	1 100	235	155	236	34 343	441	29.5	32.0	58.0
Dubuque	2 772	53 122	7 764	9 030	7 207	3 283	2 700	1 982	37 306	1 462	28.3	10.3	52.5
Emmet	317	3 639	986	893	461	135	81	118	32 501	475	25.9	37.3	64.0
Fayette	553	6 298	1 297	597	852	190	D	173	27 471	1 286	30.4	18.2	56.2
Floyd	414	4 552	974	D	767	175	98	169	37 030	944	35.1	22.9	51.8

STATE County	Agriculture, 2012 (cont.) Land in farms Acreage (1,000)	Percent change, 2007–2012	Acres: Average size of farm	Acres: Total irrigated (1,000)	Acres: Total cropland (1,000)	Value of land and buildings (dollars): Average per farm	Value of land and buildings (dollars): Average per acre	Value of machinery and equipment, average per farm (dollars)	Value of products sold: Total (mil dol)	Value of products sold: Average per farm (dollars)	Percent from: Crops	Percent from: Livestock and poultry products	Percent of farms with sales of: $10,000 or more	Percent of farms with sales of: $100,000 or more	Government payments: Total ($1,000)	Government payments: Percent of farms
	117	118	119	120	121	122	123	124	125	126	127	128	129	130	131	132
INDIANA—Cont'd																
Pike	80	8.7	249	D	65.0	1 064 710	4 271	115 533	50.8	158 343	57.1	42.9	39.6	20.9	1 395	71.3
Porter	121	4.8	251	10.0	109.4	1 502 112	5 993	176 526	106.8	222 133	93.2	6.8	48.6	31.0	2 268	55.5
Posey	229	12.1	561	16.4	215.7	2 689 417	4 797	375 517	139.7	342 500	87.5	12.5	69.4	44.4	3 332	75.2
Pulaski	217	-6.8	404	18.5	197.1	2 080 849	5 152	192 328	185.3	345 784	67.9	32.1	53.9	34.9	4 080	79.7
Putnam	198	17.3	233	0.1	156.0	979 574	4 198	116 544	76.1	89 791	80.9	19.1	33.6	14.0	3 467	50.6
Randolph	241	4.0	312	0.2	216.6	1 588 816	5 088	181 580	227.0	294 035	56.6	43.4	60.4	34.7	4 656	66.8
Ripley	167	4.8	190	0.1	124.1	776 272	4 079	98 368	94.0	107 283	80.6	19.4	47.7	20.2	2 604	66.4
Rush	208	-4.3	345	0.5	188.7	2 103 171	6 089	216 255	162.5	270 401	60.6	39.4	68.1	42.1	4 158	67.1
St. Joseph	152	-14.9	220	27.6	136.3	1 350 298	6 140	142 120	123.5	178 734	86.6	13.4	48.3	24.6	2 468	54.7
Scott	51	-17.0	160	D	38.4	575 841	3 591	96 140	24.0	74 903	97.3	2.7	25.5	9.0	877	45.5
Shelby	233	13.4	410	4.3	220.6	2 508 759	6 125	238 496	128.9	226 522	86.5	13.5	65.7	38.7	4 519	63.4
Spencer	170	13.4	285	0.2	132.5	1 104 744	3 870	158 107	91.9	153 982	65.6	34.4	52.8	22.9	2 593	66.3
Starke	133	-13.1	261	25.6	115.4	1 144 699	4 383	156 188	69.8	136 528	95.0	5.0	32.9	19.0	3 463	82.0
Steuben	105	-1.7	186	2.1	84.6	834 635	4 486	109 486	61.8	109 888	65.9	34.1	36.7	14.6	1 868	72.6
Sullivan	170	-4.0	393	6.0	150.0	1 642 543	4 178	216 111	91.5	211 358	79.0	21.0	56.4	31.2	2 788	71.6
Switzerland	51	6.4	132	0.1	25.9	465 300	3 528	56 084	12.3	32 180	D	D	28.2	5.2	940	50.7
Tippecanoe	220	0.9	314	4.3	201.7	2 111 205	6 731	195 491	150.6	214 583	88.0	12.0	43.2	24.2	4 159	53.1
Tipton	145	-12.5	385	1.2	138.7	2 812 836	7 304	249 233	159.9	424 141	82.5	17.5	74.5	46.9	2 774	80.9
Union	74	1.7	308	D	63.9	1 525 157	4 955	172 099	41.7	172 190	88.3	11.7	61.6	33.1	1 200	69.4
Vanderburgh	77	6.4	278	D	70.6	1 177 945	4 231	157 189	36.1	131 247	90.2	9.8	52.4	28.4	1 078	64.0
Vermillion	118	-10.5	438	D	100.3	2 083 200	4 751	218 111	62.2	230 389	74.1	25.9	45.6	28.9	2 502	67.8
Vigo	118	-3.2	261	1.1	101.3	1 012 440	3 876	123 420	47.4	105 222	97.7	2.3	40.2	17.8	1 437	55.1
Wabash	198	-1.5	265	2.1	172.9	1 370 395	5 167	177 270	227.2	305 032	51.3	48.7	52.5	29.9	4 325	67.8
Warren	176	-10.2	426	2.1	156.5	2 509 559	5 890	222 634	111.7	270 574	94.8	5.2	43.3	29.3	3 349	66.3
Warrick	100	-9.4	263	D	88.6	1 276 810	4 856	164 979	39.7	104 873	93.1	6.9	37.7	22.4	2 192	63.6
Washington	200	-0.2	240	0.1	142.8	797 445	3 321	105 395	129.2	155 489	43.2	56.8	40.7	17.1	3 448	42.5
Wayne	156	-5.0	194	0.7	124.6	1 002 708	5 177	111 768	91.9	114 170	73.6	26.4	49.6	23.7	3 828	59.6
Wells	200	2.9	315	0.0	189.0	1 993 800	6 330	195 305	210.2	330 434	67.1	32.9	64.6	39.5	3 322	73.6
White	288	-9.4	457	4.2	267.7	3 122 778	6 837	265 100	297.4	471 342	57.0	43.0	59.1	40.1	4 960	71.2
Whitley	140	2.2	197	2.2	120.3	1 013 832	5 138	132 938	100.2	141 182	75.9	24.1	48.6	21.3	2 465	60.7
IOWA	30 623	-0.4	345	171.7	26 256.3	2 207 220	6 389	213 849	30 821.5	347 728	56.3	43.7	62.8	41.0	782 290	78.4
Adair	324	3.8	446	0.0	251.5	2 085 152	4 679	214 081	188.2	259 185	65.6	34.4	64.0	38.0	5 695	76.0
Adams	229	1.9	491	D	165.9	2 107 058	4 292	208 206	120.3	257 557	64.8	35.2	61.2	36.2	4 107	79.4
Allamakee	289	5.2	286	0.0	185.8	1 217 119	4 255	144 265	220.6	218 199	41.4	58.6	51.8	29.8	7 526	82.7
Appanoose	188	-5.1	252	D	111.8	749 059	2 969	84 641	38.4	51 620	55.5	44.5	43.5	10.2	3 704	69.1
Audubon	280	0.5	451	0.0	251.9	3 003 379	6 663	236 170	287.9	462 814	48.9	51.1	62.7	43.4	7 006	82.0
Benton	422	5.3	347	0.1	381.8	2 508 267	7 219	235 523	381.4	313 927	72.2	27.8	67.1	47.0	10 826	78.0
Black Hawk	297	5.2	321	0.1	273.8	2 559 448	7 969	245 895	287.2	310 850	65.4	34.6	68.2	44.2	7 606	81.4
Boone	313	-5.6	334	0.1	283.3	2 520 885	7 546	180 946	301.8	321 707	74.9	25.1	54.6	34.2	6 378	75.8
Bremer	272	11.7	276	0.7	242.5	2 132 518	7 713	222 672	271.7	276 729	63.2	36.8	62.9	41.1	7 929	81.6
Buchanan	342	-5.1	318	0.0	318.5	2 331 990	7 332	246 866	390.7	363 461	63.2	36.8	71.5	47.6	10 788	71.9
Buena Vista	361	-0.5	421	0.7	334.0	3 070 632	7 301	290 162	577.1	672 564	44.5	55.5	73.5	60.1	8 715	83.4
Butler	363	-3.5	331	0.4	330.9	2 260 181	6 829	206 931	358.2	326 838	55.1	44.9	59.7	38.0	9 333	81.2
Calhoun	358	-0.3	434	0.3	337.4	3 332 812	7 685	276 166	366.3	443 500	57.8	42.2	68.3	51.9	7 928	88.7
Carroll	359	0.2	337	D	328.1	2 535 277	7 524	243 800	540.6	507 578	35.6	64.4	75.6	53.0	8 377	81.3
Cass	290	-8.8	412	0.3	240.7	2 253 533	5 464	220 265	228.3	324 761	57.7	42.3	63.4	41.8	5 974	78.1
Cedar	312	-7.3	327	0.4	275.6	2 346 182	7 171	250 577	315.9	330 800	69.4	30.6	58.2	42.2	8 363	75.2
Cerro Gordo	327	-2.9	419	D	306.3	2 778 794	6 631	282 482	245.0	314 089	80.4	19.6	60.1	42.3	8 384	82.3
Cherokee	337	7.1	419	0.0	290.4	3 110 383	7 422	272 880	407.5	506 183	56.5	43.5	84.8	65.0	6 226	82.7
Chickasaw	299	3.5	289	0.3	271.3	2 067 023	7 158	208 558	336.2	324 558	52.2	47.8	64.0	41.3	11 550	82.2
Clarke	169	-11.4	269	0.0	98.9	910 281	3 378	87 847	93.4	148 973	29.5	70.5	43.7	15.3	4 294	67.3
Clay	319	-2.9	443	0.3	292.5	3 269 768	7 385	292 085	403.5	560 428	58.5	41.5	71.5	54.6	7 683	83.6
Clayton	398	-2.7	252	0.2	291.7	1 207 906	4 786	149 960	402.6	255 286	47.8	52.2	54.4	32.4	15 965	80.9
Clinton	417	5.5	335	0.0	372.1	2 381 902	7 103	228 046	381.3	306 518	70.4	29.6	68.2	46.8	10 432	78.9
Crawford	451	4.3	501	1.0	404.7	3 465 877	6 918	324 907	417.6	463 991	63.3	36.7	74.3	49.4	7 985	77.0
Dallas	[illegible]	0.1	[illegible]	0.1	270.7	2 059 497	6 728	168 490	237.2	236 924	73.6	26.4	51.0	29.8	6 868	65.7
Davis	214	-2.1	233	0.1	135.2	686 799	2 943	94 828	90.8	99 061	32.3	67.7	49.8	15.2	4 670	59.2
Decatur	232	1.3	326	D	127.0	972 918	2 988	121 181	92.4	130 018	34.7	65.3	47.5	19.3	5 905	66.4
Delaware	366	9.5	265	0.1	321.2	1 906 151	7 206	228 110	495.1	358 221	41.9	58.1	70.2	49.6	14 190	85.2
Des Moines	173	-6.6	260	3.1	137.6	1 451 878	5 574	166 958	118.7	179 054	82.3	17.7	54.1	30.6	4 631	82.8
Dickinson	187	-17.2	425	0.9	173.6	2 999 796	7 061	278 673	192.3	435 941	67.6	32.4	67.1	52.6	3 868	80.7
Dubuque	291	-6.2	199	0.0	224.3	1 214 544	6 093	172 274	387.8	265 260	31.0	69.0	67.5	39.7	11 080	81.2
Emmet	219	-12.3	461	0.4	201.9	3 356 078	7 280	322 318	292.2	615 097	53.7	46.3	71.8	57.3	4 456	82.3
Fayette	388	-6.9	302	0.3	333.3	2 077 995	6 879	214 755	432.2	336 045	54.0	46.0	61.5	44.3	13 738	87.1
Floyd	318	6.4	337	2.1	291.1	2 154 441	6 401	225 738	280.4	297 050	65.8	34.2	58.3	41.2	8 273	80.8

STATE County	Water use, 2010		Wholesale trade,[1] 2007				Retail trade,[2] 2007				Real estate and rental and leasing,[2] 2007			
	Total water withdrawn (mil gal/day)	Gallons withdrawn per person per day	Number of establish-ments	Number of employees	Sales (mil dol)	Annual payroll (mil dol)	Number of establish-ments	Number of employees	Sales (mil dol)	Annual payroll (mil dol)	Number of establish-ments	Number of employees	Receipts (mil dol)	Annual payroll (mil dol)
	133	134	135	136	137	138	139	140	141	142	143	144	145	146
INDIANA—Cont'd														
Pike	595.1	46 329	8	41	64.7	3.2	35	265	55.9	4.6	3	D	D	D
Porter	599.5	3 648	143	2 004	1 463.1	99.8	500	7 393	1 956.3	162.9	168	779	89.8	18.3
Posey	18.9	731	23	381	346.7	12.1	74	711	268.4	17.1	10	30	4.5	0.6
Pulaski	9.2	687	28	396	262.9	14.1	67	456	112.8	8.5	11	15	0.9	0.2
Putnam	8.7	228	19	134	43.0	4.8	111	1 134	310.8	25.9	23	69	6.3	1.3
Randolph	5.1	193	16	184	113.3	6.8	84	735	273.3	14.6	11	27	2.0	0.3
Ripley	3.3	116	18	112	44.5	3.3	106	1 027	255.4	21.6	22	D	D	D
Rush	2.8	163	17	119	162.3	4.8	56	535	113.4	10.9	10	25	3.1	0.4
St. Joseph	45.6	171	345	D	D	D	951	16 607	3 683.4	349.9	242	1 442	215.2	43.4
Scott	3.6	147	14	D	D	D	95	1 025	241.2	19.9	19	73	6.4	1.0
Shelby	9.3	210	40	739	291.0	18.4	136	1 707	487.6	41.5	44	127	16.6	2.7
Spencer	33.5	1 600	13	223	181.1	8.3	72	908	166.0	22.2	13	37	3.0	0.6
Starke	6.1	262	11	63	61.5	2.4	76	893	156.7	14.8	16	36	3.1	0.6
Steuben	4.9	144	33	246	97.2	8.2	198	2 293	575.1	40.8	46	114	16.4	2.9
Sullivan	423.9	19 741	22	159	201.5	4.8	65	630	146.9	11.3	8	24	1.5	0.3
Switzerland	2.2	209	4	10	3.9	0.3	13	96	19.9	1.6	3	D	D	D
Tippecanoe	33.9	196	99	1 033	413.3	44.0	567	9 881	2 079.6	193.0	196	1 073	185.3	34.5
Tipton	1.9	116	10	132	141.6	4.4	52	425	136.0	11.8	15	35	2.0	0.5
Union	0.7	96	4	D	D	D	27	179	31.0	3.0	4	11	0.7	0.2
Vanderburgh	31.3	174	271	5 495	2 907.8	282.2	855	13 949	3 025.8	297.7	214	1 431	217.0	38.9
Vermillion	623.2	38 441	12	D	D	D	57	687	184.6	12.8	6	27	1.3	0.2
Vigo	334.3	3 100	101	1 212	584.1	46.5	487	7 679	1 668.2	154.6	102	628	80.5	18.4
Wabash	7.0	212	30	420	168.9	12.4	148	1 475	325.6	31.9	29	103	11.2	2.6
Warren	1.5	181	13	154	118.3	5.8	16	106	24.0	1.5	3	D	D	D
Warrick	761.3	12 754	41	342	412.3	17.9	134	1 436	331.2	29.7	39	172	27.5	3.4
Washington	4.7	166	12	67	16.3	1.9	87	750	190.7	15.0	16	45	3.9	0.7
Wayne	11.1	160	58	517	325.2	20.8	302	4 153	1 004.3	85.8	60	274	30.5	6.9
Wells	7.2	259	40	D	D	D	103	1 219	221.3	22.8	26	86	7.6	1.7
White	5.9	239	40	424	235.1	11.6	108	1 205	283.4	25.4	22	90	7.4	1.4
Whitley	4.4	132	23	D	D	D	121	1 644	343.5	30.8	30	103	12.4	2.9
IOWA	3 070.5	1 008	4 361	55 874	41 068.3	2 276.7	13 203	177 156	39 234.6	3 561.1	2 969	14 667	2 556.0	473.0
Adair	2.3	301	6	60	29.4	2.3	31	245	49.6	3.5	5	D	D	D
Adams	1.8	454	4	27	14.2	0.8	25	155	32.6	2.4	3	5	0.7	0.1
Allamakee	123.3	8 602	35	383	154.5	12.3	62	586	128.7	11.0	9	15	2.1	0.4
Appanoose	11.1	864	11	60	23.1	1.7	65	681	133.5	12.5	13	24	1.8	0.3
Audubon	2.1	346	14	81	47.8	2.8	19	200	37.3	3.3	5	4	0.5	0.1
Benton	3.3	126	30	253	213.2	8.5	96	844	176.4	15.9	15	54	5.1	1.4
Black Hawk	37.0	282	149	2 492	1 278.5	95.1	532	8 624	1 929.4	175.3	148	707	114.7	19.2
Boone	3.6	136	30	D	D	D	75	960	210.6	21.5	16	D	D	D
Bremer	3.9	162	23	149	105.6	6.2	94	1 112	268.4	24.6	21	D	D	D
Buchanan	4.3	207	30	357	624.5	12.5	90	861	214.8	18.0	13	D	D	D
Buena Vista	8.2	402	29	D	D	D	104	1 100	260.8	22.2	22	77	9.3	2.6
Butler	5.9	397	29	228	288.4	7.7	66	332	79.1	5.9	7	D	D	D
Calhoun	2.9	295	21	253	200.7	11.1	53	316	103.5	5.9	4	18	1.2	0.3
Carroll	6.8	326	58	1 519	1 350.5	59.9	156	1 572	298.1	32.2	23	125	24.7	4.2
Cass	3.0	212	26	207	151.5	6.7	79	927	178.2	18.1	14	68	11.8	2.2
Cedar	4.8	261	29	290	221.8	10.6	66	585	131.3	10.9	16	23	1.9	0.3
Cerro Gordo	9.9	224	88	800	650.5	32.7	246	3 917	887.1	77.2	63	D	D	D
Cherokee	6.6	544	13	101	114.7	3.7	71	660	139.4	11.8	7	18	1.2	0.2
Chickasaw	4.0	318	31	266	210.1	10.1	52	453	103.9	8.0	5	D	D	D
Clarke	2.2	235	3	16	6.3	0.5	38	436	95.4	8.3	7	D	D	D
Clay	4.2	254	46	542	425.1	19.4	124	1 650	298.7	31.9	27	102	16.9	2.4
Clayton	6.5	360	33	349	564.6	13.7	87	682	163.6	11.6	8	10	1.0	0.2
Clinton	106.9	2 176	49	319	190.1	11.2	219	2 789	635.7	57.5	46	136	27.6	3.9
Crawford	7.0	408	14	126	122.0	5.3	85	854	162.4	14.4	10	21	1.3	0.2
Dallas	5.3	80	49	420	218.3	17.3	263	5 073	905.7	90.7	47	298	68.3	15.0
Davis	1.6	184	7	47	17.9	1.3	32	330	71.6	6.8	7	13	1.4	0.2
Decatur	1.6	184	9	121	76.7	2.6	27	223	39.6	3.3	3	D	D	D
Delaware	8.4	472	34	369	302.4	14.9	82	700	171.4	14.4	11	27	2.0	0.4
Des Moines	77.3	1 916	47	D	D	D	221	3 193	616.0	60.0	41	D	D	D
Dickinson	7.3	440	20	D	D	D	116	1 044	255.2	22.8	49	88	16.4	2.6
Dubuque	40.5	432	154	2 388	1 847.7	91.6	467	7 056	1 433.5	135.0	103	446	73.6	16.6
Emmet	3.3	320	18	105	103.9	3.1	60	510	92.7	9.7	5	D	D	D
Fayette	4.5	217	39	476	304.2	18.4	100	830	157.2	15.4	15	48	9.4	1.1
Floyd	4.1	252	24	143	121.9	7.4	74	762	149.1	12.7	10	30	4.3	0.7

1. Merchant wholesalers, except manufacturers' sales branches and offices. 2. Employer establishments.

STATE County	Professional, scientific, and technical services,[1] 2007				Manufacturing, 2007				Accommodation and food services, 2007			
	Number of establish-ments	Number of employees	Receipts (mil dol)	Annual payroll (mil dol)	Number of establish-ments	Number of employees	Receipts (mil dol)	Annual payroll (mil dol)	Number of establish-ments	Number of employees	Sales (mil dol)	Annual payroll (mil dol)
	147	148	149	150	151	152	153	154	155	156	157	158
INDIANA—Cont'd												
Pike	7	26	2.0	0.6	NA	NA	NA	NA	11	164	5.6	1.6
Porter	333	2 132	224.9	83.1	152	9 716	7 318.8	615.5	301	5 474	211.3	58.6
Posey	45	D	D	D	24	2 564	D	182.9	41	477	17.1	5.5
Pulaski	22	64	3.9	1.0	20	1 268	D	59.4	28	D	D	D
Putnam	47	172	10.6	3.9	30	3 004	676.0	99.9	79	1 224	45.9	11.6
Randolph	34	90	6.6	2.0	46	2 134	577.4	84.8	42	D	D	D
Ripley	44	142	10.9	3.6	44	2 574	757.4	92.2	40	495	18.7	5.3
Rush	31	122	11.1	3.2	36	1 160	523.3	47.0	27	D	D	D
St. Joseph	561	D	D	D	427	17 667	8 011.0	862.2	555	11 175	439.7	126.6
Scott	31	133	11.1	3.5	32	2 096	978.7	78.0	44	804	30.7	8.6
Shelby	69	379	23.6	11.8	87	5 730	2 354.9	247.4	68	1 322	46.4	13.3
Spencer	23	112	9.8	3.0	26	1 346	D	58.4	29	390	16.3	4.1
Starke	16	54	4.5	1.4	24	996	243.7	32.1	32	D	D	D
Steuben	57	185	12.7	3.8	97	4 542	1 148.0	163.1	100	1 391	57.0	15.8
Sullivan	25	D	D	D	NA	NA	NA	NA	35	396	14.3	3.9
Switzerland	8	D	D	D	NA	NA	NA	NA	20	D	D	D
Tippecanoe	296	D	D	D	125	13 836	D	693.0	389	8 352	316.0	92.3
Tipton	23	D	D	D	24	1 094	362.1	37.4	27	299	9.8	2.8
Union	6	D	D	D	NA	NA	NA	NA	7	88	3.0	0.8
Vanderburgh	455	D	D	D	276	14 248	6 447.6	607.9	457	11 318	516.8	146.4
Vermillion	18	D	D	D	12	816	D	56.3	39	376	16.3	3.5
Vigo	207	1 181	110.8	37.7	126	8 821	3 565.9	393.7	252	4 838	195.5	54.9
Wabash	53	352	24.3	7.9	62	3 950	1 045.4	153.9	62	900	30.3	8.3
Warren	7	D	D	D	15	572	93.1	D	9	173	8.4	2.2
Warrick	94	D	D	D	46	2 973	D	D	72	1 073	36.9	11.1
Washington	32	D	D	D	41	1 763	248.3	60.7	31	D	D	D
Wayne	86	377	30.9	11.5	128	6 830	2 483.1	265.6	147	3 153	107.2	31.8
Wells	42	231	23.1	7.7	54	2 855	699.1	107.5	42	667	19.3	5.5
White	31	112	7.1	2.4	44	2 058	715.2	76.3	70	682	24.5	6.5
Whitley	47	193	14.0	5.2	72	4 783	2 107.5	203.9	58	860	28.3	7.7
IOWA	6 181	42 118	5 015.6	1 883.8	3 802	223 049	97 592.1	9 525.7	7 014	116 838	4 737.7	1 276.0
Adair	12	44	2.7	0.8	NA	NA	NA	NA	14	129	4.1	1.2
Adams	5	D	D	D	NA	NA	NA	NA	7	D	D	D
Allamakee	21	151	9.8	2.7	33	1 557	D	50.6	37	313	8.5	2.1
Appanoose	26	68	4.3	1.4	14	755	151.6	28.8	30	297	8.0	2.2
Audubon	11	D	D	D	NA	NA	NA	NA	8	D	D	D
Benton	32	82	6.3	2.2	30	819	176.8	27.8	42	348	9.6	2.6
Black Hawk	234	D	D	D	163	12 539	5 880.3	531.7	288	6 172	194.6	59.7
Boone	40	170	17.7	5.3	33	782	161.3	30.1	45	592	16.2	4.6
Bremer	44	D	D	D	39	1 950	699.7	99.5	46	546	16.7	4.5
Buchanan	28	115	9.8	2.6	41	1 216	640.8	42.8	39	388	11.5	3.2
Buena Vista	40	178	15.6	6.5	32	2 906	1 578.0	92.9	47	796	25.5	6.9
Butler	19	62	5.2	1.1	26	696	D	22.9	22	D	D	D
Calhoun	16	39	3.7	0.9	NA	NA	NA	NA	19	D	D	D
Carroll	51	224	21.2	6.7	44	1 551	794.0	67.1	56	637	20.8	5.7
Cass	29	121	10.0	3.8	23	560	D	21.6	33	374	11.6	3.1
Cedar	32	96	7.5	2.4	34	530	178.8	19.8	36	326	9.5	2.6
Cerro Gordo	96	D	D	D	54	3 761	1 357.5	152.3	148	2 429	83.9	24.2
Cherokee	17	71	10.8	1.8	21	813	279.3	26.3	30	259	8.7	2.7
Chickasaw	20	58	5.0	1.2	35	1 170	278.3	40.8	30	263	7.4	1.7
Clarke	12	39	3.0	0.8	15	1 054	416.6	33.8	22	791	84.9	12.9
Clay	36	181	16.9	6.4	30	D	D	D	49	618	23.4	6.2
Clayton	27	84	6.6	1.8	31	1 010	206.4	31.6	57	768	53.7	10.1
Clinton	04	066	30.8	13.0	61	4 678	3 914.9	218.3	117	1 440	54.1	14.4
Crawford	20	101	7.0	2.6	26	2 477	1 266.8	91.4	35	412	12.9	3.5
Dallas	133	1 072	167.9	47.8	41	2 384	574.2	79.9	132	2 621	110.4	31.3
Davis	11	41	4.2	0.9	NA	NA	NA	NA	13	128	3.1	0.9
Decatur	7	D	D	D	NA	NA	NA	NA	13	180	4.3	1.2
Delaware	30	131	9.3	3.8	37	1 573	326.4	59.9	34	377	9.0	2.7
Des Moines	55	336	30.0	15.1	67	D	D	D	98	2 012	68.8	20.6
Dickinson	48	D	D	D	37	1 878	647.5	66.3	104	1 284	54.6	16.2
Dubuque	168	D	D	D	150	9 378	4 711.2	380.3	253	4 502	145.7	42.5
Emmet	17	66	7.0	2.5	16	1 138	331.4	40.9	23	252	7.9	2.2
Fayette	39	147	10.0	3.3	32	735	157.7	23.9	50	479	14.6	3.6
Floyd	28	92	6.9	1.8	19	708	461.4	40.5	43	378	13.7	3.1

1. Establishment subject to federal tax.

Table B. States and Counties — **Health Care and Social Assistance, Other Services, Nonemployer Businesses, and Residential Construction**

STATE County	Health care and social assistance, 2007				Other services, 2007				Nonemployer businesses, 2013		Value of residential construction authorized by building permits, 2014	
	Number of establish-ments	Number of employees	Receipts (mil dol)	Annual payroll (mil dol)	Number of establish-ments	Number of employees	Receipts (mil dol)	Annual payroll (mil dol)	Number	Receipts (mil dol)	New Construction ($1,000)	Number of housing units
	159	160	161	162	163	164	165	166	167	168	169	170
INDIANA—Cont'd												
Pike	14	359	17.2	6.5	22	78	5.8	1.6	581	18.7	2 816	20
Porter	363	7 157	632.1	248.0	290	1 827	155.6	44.4	9 095	375.6	109 639	448
Posey	44	D	D	D	38	130	12.1	2.7	1 402	49.0	10 468	55
Pulaski	33	619	40.4	17.7	27	105	9.2	1.8	800	30.6	1 835	13
Putnam	74	1 612	93.6	38.7	63	273	19.9	5.3	1 961	74.7	11 669	65
Randolph	34	591	44.0	17.0	46	177	13.9	3.2	1 431	53.1	2 204	6
Ripley	67	903	43.9	20.9	55	191	17.1	3.6	1 748	67.7	12 281	86
Rush	31	528	35.5	14.3	40	138	12.7	2.6	1 095	42.6	1 390	10
St. Joseph	668	D	D	D	519	3 816	403.4	96.4	15 389	584.4	67 951	428
Scott	66	955	68.4	25.0	23	106	8.4	2.0	1 156	38.7	3 427	26
Shelby	86	1 604	148.4	56.2	75	525	40.4	11.3	2 774	121.5	9 189	59
Spencer	33	404	17.4	7.7	35	110	6.8	2.3	1 203	41.0	6 650	36
Starke	31	663	45.7	17.4	39	141	10.6	2.1	1 159	43.5	6 861	36
Steuben	77	1 278	86.3	32.0	81	580	56.3	11.5	2 162	95.9	26 941	98
Sullivan	40	D	D	D	25	100	6.9	1.6	913	28.4	240	2
Switzerland	16	125	8.9	3.4	13	D	D	D	555	21.4	3 146	54
Tippecanoe	322	9 181	913.3	342.8	252	1 861	239.1	46.9	8 694	354.1	158 393	1 055
Tipton	30	575	58.0	21.3	29	127	13.2	3.1	1 019	41.1	1 284	7
Union	12	D	D	D	10	D	D	D	542	21.0	675	3
Vanderburgh	563	17 053	1 720.0	649.2	367	3 041	274.3	82.1	9 388	387.7	45 522	322
Vermillion	24	D	D	D	22	48	3.7	0.6	771	22.2	70	1
Vigo	357	8 792	917.0	305.2	191	1 408	110.4	30.8	4 768	181.4	32 872	321
Wabash	73	2 139	134.8	51.1	61	242	21.2	4.8	1 702	57.0	4 970	24
Warren	11	D	D	D	8	D	D	D	518	21.3	2 102	19
Warrick	117	2 329	225.4	75.4	91	440	37.1	11.0	3 646	154.0	49 312	304
Washington	45	738	55.2	27.9	31	157	12.8	3.9	1 718	58.2	4 422	32
Wayne	184	5 306	530.7	195.2	136	612	52.8	13.4	3 583	141.9	9 853	85
Wells	51	1 419	105.3	42.5	67	273	22.0	4.9	1 585	55.2	7 974	36
White	36	742	58.2	24.3	46	173	13.0	2.8	1 420	59.8	4 755	31
Whitley	52	1 115	69.5	26.1	66	413	31.7	8.1	2 141	76.5	16 980	94
IOWA	7 857	198 285	15 371.6	6 603.6	6 088	31 869	3 063.2	779.2	203 763	8 608.0	1 907 579	10 256
Adair	16	297	15.3	6.2	15	D	D	D	626	21.2	1 399	8
Adams	17	301	18.4	8.9	8	21	1.9	0.4	321	13.7	180	1
Allamakee	41	937	41.7	19.9	34	101	11.2	2.1	1 179	52.2	4 895	41
Appanoose	39	723	42.3	17.6	27	103	6.6	1.8	919	41.7	408	6
Audubon	14	297	17.4	7.1	20	61	5.4	1.4	494	21.9	1 592	5
Benton	52	755	39.1	18.1	52	138	12.3	3.1	1 828	60.9	5 506	28
Black Hawk	340	10 326	850.4	362.6	212	1 670	127.4	36.5	7 189	331.6	64 981	314
Boone	57	1 538	87.6	39.8	46	155	15.5	4.1	1 747	64.1	7 178	44
Bremer	54	1 604	91.5	43.0	59	D	D	D	1 591	70.2	16 486	74
Buchanan	39	1 104	61.6	33.7	31	84	6.2	1.3	1 508	68.0	4 376	27
Buena Vista	51	1 322	76.4	33.0	35	D	D	D	1 260	53.6	1 992	8
Butler	26	460	19.3	9.3	24	61	5.9	1.1	1 115	39.2	3 885	21
Calhoun	31	684	39.3	17.0	16	35	4.9	0.6	732	28.4	2 935	12
Carroll	108	2 280	146.4	55.0	51	211	17.4	3.8	1 856	85.0	7 382	26
Cass	41	1 180	63.3	29.2	42	205	15.2	3.0	1 179	44.8	2 954	12
Cedar	57	585	23.9	11.9	37	96	7.5	1.9	1 258	47.0	6 530	29
Cerro Gordo	134	D	D	D	115	526	36.3	11.0	3 031	117.5	15 711	86
Cherokee	36	911	53.8	27.1	29	61	6.2	1.5	812	32.5	1 580	6
Chickasaw	30	490	28.8	10.9	40	123	14.2	2.3	954	33.3	814	5
Clarke	30	625	37.6	17.3	21	67	6.1	1.0	598	23.7	171	1
Clay	52	1 341	113.3	48.7	51	239	17.0	4.4	1 305	60.3	3 155	14
Clayton	54	897	42.0	18.8	36	72	6.1	1.3	1 382	49.5	5 921	28
Clinton	142	3 835	240.7	101.4	114	563	28.6	13.5	2 677	94.4	16 345	102
Crawford	37	943	51.8	23.3	31	133	8.3	2.5	924	41.5	2 512	11
Dallas	147	2 453	183.0	92.3	82	888	105.8	45.0	5 486	267.9	132 705	661
Davis	23	413	25.9	10.6	13	30	2.1	0.5	748	49.5	352	4
Decatur	23	408	21.9	9.9	7	D	D	D	655	24.7	156	2
Delaware	44	843	48.4	21.9	31	110	7.1	1.5	1 312	54.6	993	5
Des Moines	140	D	D	D	92	D	D	D	2 359	81.2	6 139	41
Dickinson	57	D	D	D	43	191	13.1	3.4	1 818	78.8	28 790	134
Dubuque	242	7 056	592.0	264.0	208	1 505	102.2	27.4	6 130	268.6	48 756	276
Emmet	31	666	37.9	16.0	27	85	6.5	1.6	720	28.4	5 703	48
Fayette	62	1 251	69.1	30.2	54	200	21.0	5.7	1 412	50.2	3 865	24
Floyd	58	966	55.6	23.6	35	111	8.3	2.0	1 202	39.3	3 650	21

STATE County	Government employment and payroll, 2012									Local government finances, 2012				
			March payroll (percent of total)							General revenue				
												Taxes		
													Per capita[1] (dollars)	
	Full-time equivalent employees	March payroll (dollars)	Adminis-tration, judicial, and legal	Police and Corrections	Fire Protection	Highways and transpor-tation	Health and Welfare	Natural resources and utilities	Education and libraries	Total (mil dol)	Inter-govern-mental (mil dol)	Total (mil dol)	Total	Property
	171	172	173	174	175	176	177	178	179	180	181	182	183	184
INDIANA—Cont'd														
Pike	517	1 538 013	6.0	5.7	0.0	2.8	2.9	3.1	78.9	37.9	19.2	13.1	1 029	1 017
Porter	4 682	15 472 739	6.2	11.3	4.3	3.7	2.1	4.6	66.6	488.1	210.9	195.5	1 180	1 059
Posey	911	2 762 902	6.5	6.5	1.9	5.2	4.2	4.8	69.9	91.5	46.7	35.1	1 370	1 173
Pulaski	708	2 273 852	6.2	7.1	0.1	2.4	37.6	1.9	44.1	67.8	28.8	13.4	1 019	724
Putnam	1 642	4 711 936	4.0	5.6	1.1	2.5	24.9	2.7	57.3	152.8	52.1	46.2	1 223	1 010
Randolph	1 040	2 903 572	6.2	8.7	2.2	3.1	2.3	2.6	74.3	87.0	51.7	23.2	898	698
Ripley	1 010	3 272 378	6.6	6.7	0.8	3.3	2.0	5.4	74.4	92.3	48.8	27.6	967	752
Rush	863	2 783 719	5.3	5.5	1.8	3.6	34.1	2.2	47.2	62.7	23.4	13.5	788	596
St. Joseph	9 537	31 853 965	4.7	12.0	7.2	4.2	1.2	7.1	62.0	1 039.1	434.1	391.0	1 468	1 064
Scott	984	3 352 561	6.3	6.5	0.1	1.7	23.7	3.5	56.0	87.7	37.4	20.6	865	696
Shelby	1 997	6 919 558	3.0	7.4	2.7	1.5	36.5	2.1	46.2	272.2	100.9	54.8	1 233	968
Spencer	769	2 237 381	7.1	8.1	0.1	3.7	2.1	4.2	74.1	70.8	38.9	21.7	1 042	882
Starke	708	2 237 301	6.6	4.8	2.5	3.1	0.7	1.7	75.9	73.3	44.3	20.2	868	715
Steuben	1 096	3 394 672	9.6	9.3	2.3	3.8	4.4	6.2	63.6	108.5	47.5	40.3	1 182	873
Sullivan	911	2 516 743	6.1	5.1	1.0	4.1	30.7	3.5	49.0	93.6	35.3	20.1	951	859
Switzerland	398	1 091 343	11.4	6.6	0.0	5.1	2.6	5.1	68.7	40.0	28.0	6.9	658	486
Tippecanoe	4 468	15 188 885	7.3	12.7	5.8	5.8	2.2	5.7	59.5	457.5	213.5	170.7	962	767
Tipton	903	3 143 238	4.0	4.5	1.9	2.0	42.8	4.2	38.9	44.9	22.7	15.5	989	726
Union	448	1 183 280	9.6	3.8	1.0	2.9	1.2	2.3	78.6	26.8	13.9	8.2	1 116	890
Vanderburgh	5 583	20 513 638	6.9	13.0	6.2	3.9	1.5	8.7	57.8	578.5	275.8	204.6	1 131	901
Vermillion	614	1 596 357	7.0	7.2	0.5	4.5	1.0	2.1	76.9	49.4	28.3	15.4	963	931
Vigo	3 145	11 398 778	8.5	10.1	5.8	4.8	0.9	6.3	62.4	343.5	178.1	110.8	1 022	808
Wabash	1 443	4 610 578	4.1	7.2	4.2	2.4	29.9	2.5	49.7	143.9	51.1	32.9	1 017	612
Warren	295	823 372	8.8	8.6	0.0	7.3	2.3	2.0	70.9	26.8	11.8	11.6	1 393	1 027
Warrick	1 757	5 629 245	7.9	6.7	0.8	2.6	1.7	3.6	76.2	168.5	76.5	59.4	982	827
Washington	845	2 699 186	6.9	6.0	1.0	3.5	1.8	2.8	76.4	72.6	43.4	21.5	769	601
Wayne	2 355	8 196 624	6.3	10.4	3.9	3.3	3.6	11.9	58.9	225.2	109.7	75.5	1 104	906
Wells	917	2 758 659	6.4	11.3	1.0	3.1	1.4	4.9	70.3	82.1	43.3	25.6	927	656
White	1 059	3 072 979	5.9	7.0	4.5	4.1	1.4	4.8	71.6	119.7	51.9	36.9	1 509	1 286
Whitley	1 054	3 089 365	6.7	13.1	0.0	4.8	0.9	1.6	71.8	89.8	43.2	27.3	820	609
IOWA	X	X	X	X	X	X	X	X	X	X	X	X	X	X
Adair	361	1 122 671	8.0	6.1	0.0	8.8	28.8	3.4	44.3	37.5	13.2	12.9	1 725	1 407
Adams	179	522 990	8.9	6.5	0.0	10.7	6.7	3.3	62.4	16.9	7.2	7.4	1 901	1 634
Allamakee	647	2 079 591	5.0	5.7	0.1	6.8	25.3	3.2	53.2	65.4	22.8	22.7	1 596	1 243
Appanoose	443	1 437 537	5.8	7.1	0.8	6.8	1.1	3.0	74.6	41.7	21.0	16.6	1 308	1 005
Audubon	328	1 089 236	5.8	5.2	0.0	7.5	33.7	1.3	45.9	32.8	8.6	11.6	1 971	1 623
Benton	846	2 776 401	7.0	6.1	0.1	7.7	1.3	7.5	70.0	87.3	37.6	37.9	1 468	1 188
Black Hawk	4 471	16 944 268	4.8	10.2	4.6	4.7	6.0	11.4	55.6	566.6	249.4	219.9	1 668	1 325
Boone	1 271	4 353 230	3.6	5.2	1.3	4.7	29.4	4.3	50.3	126.6	35.0	39.6	1 510	1 205
Bremer	952	3 191 387	7.1	7.5	0.0	5.7	7.0	3.2	66.5	149.1	41.3	41.6	1 698	1 343
Buchanan	834	2 711 732	5.2	6.6	0.5	5.4	22.7	8.0	51.3	79.4	27.4	29.1	1 389	1 115
Buena Vista	1 236	4 037 429	5.3	5.7	0.3	4.3	36.7	2.1	45.6	128.8	34.8	37.1	1 802	1 417
Butler	352	1 075 176	10.9	10.2	0.1	14.2	6.9	7.8	48.7	80.8	53.4	20.5	1 365	1 136
Calhoun	506	1 374 475	7.1	6.8	0.0	9.4	7.0	3.4	64.2	42.3	15.6	21.9	2 208	1 889
Carroll	828	2 504 489	5.6	6.3	0.2	7.0	5.5	7.6	66.7	87.4	32.6	36.2	1 753	1 373
Cass	903	2 917 219	3.3	2.3	0.2	3.9	43.1	0.9	45.0	91.1	26.3	27.8	2 024	1 557
Cedar	668	1 997 014	6.7	9.8	0.1	8.4	4.5	4.8	63.2	67.2	27.0	32.7	1 774	1 427
Cerro Gordo	1 766	6 541 728	4.4	8.2	2.8	8.5	5.2	5.1	64.4	203.2	74.2	86.1	1 967	1 505
Cherokee	418	1 242 156	8.2	6.7	0.6	9.2	1.4	5.2	66.5	40.1	14.5	20.3	1 703	1 336
Chickasaw	502	1 552 970	6.1	5.4	0.0	7.3	4.9	6.3	69.5	40.9	17.3	18.5	1 511	1 176
Clarke	529	1 675 579	5.4	5.8	0.0	5.3	31.8	3.4	47.7	54.9	15.5	16.8	1 795	1 452
Clay	1 187	4 281 441	3.5	4.2	0.5	6.0	45.8	8.0	29.0	143.1	24.9	30.2	1 822	1 405
Clayton	718	2 326 866	6.3	6.5	0.1	7.1	14.8	3.5	61.2	88.3	36.5	28.8	1 614	1 312
Clinton	1 731	6 177 764	5.4	9.5	3.6	5.4	2.6	5.5	66.4	199.4	80.5	85.7	1 760	1 345
Crawford	917	3 208 303	4.3	4.0	0.1	5.6	29.6	4.8	49.8	89.7	30.6	26.4	1 524	1 243
Dallas	2 341	8 457 626	5.2	4.5	0.6	2.8	6.9	2.8	76.8	257.1	92.3	126.9	1 764	1 534
Davis	419	1 521 730	4.6	4.0	0.1	5.6	40.7	2.5	42.4	45.3	13.6	10.3	1 184	967
Decatur	476	1 395 435	5.0	5.3	0.0	7.8	24.8	1.6	54.5	38.0	14.7	12.4	1 498	1 205
Delaware	974	3 412 646	4.0	3.6	0.0	4.3	41.3	2.0	44.6	99.6	31.6	29.8	1 695	1 409
Des Moines	1 756	6 340 038	4.4	7.5	3.3	4.2	1.8	4.4	73.0	171.7	72.6	68.2	1 691	1 253
Dickinson	844	3 005 898	7.0	6.0	0.0	4.6	29.5	6.9	45.5	102.7	15.7	50.1	2 950	2 520
Dubuque	3 261	12 486 456	6.7	9.6	3.9	7.2	5.0	6.0	60.6	400.9	169.8	165.8	1 743	1 320
Emmet	840	2 701 635	4.3	4.2	0.0	4.0	1.6	3.9	81.5	71.8	26.5	22.1	2 185	1 847
Fayette	775	2 536 072	6.6	8.5	0.5	8.6	2.3	3.9	69.1	78.2	37.2	31.6	1 519	1 194
Floyd	655	2 381 344	4.8	5.4	1.3	6.9	31.5	3.8	44.8	76.5	22.6	24.9	1 552	1 207

1. Based on the resident population estimated as of July 1 of the year shown.

STATE County	Local government finances, 2012 (cont.)									Government employment, 2013			Presidential election,[2] 2012		
	Direct general expenditure							Debt outstanding					Percent of vote cast:		
			Percent of total for:												
	Total (mil dol)	Per capita[1] (dollars)	Educa-tion	Health and hospitals	Police protec-tion	Public welfare	High-ways	Total (mil dol)	Per capita[1] (dollars)	Federal civilian	Federal military	State and local	Demo-cratic	Republi-can	All other
	185	186	187	188	189	190	191	192	193	194	195	196	197	198	199
INDIANA—Cont'd															
Pike	34.3	2 684	63.8	1.9	2.6	0.2	4.1	28.8	2 253	30	40	629	44.8	53.4	1.8
Porter	434.6	2 623	59.0	1.1	3.4	0.2	3.6	510.5	3 081	424	529	6 441	53.0	45.8	1.2
Posey	70.6	2 759	61.6	1.8	2.5	0.3	4.9	54.0	2 108	65	82	1 121	45.6	53.3	1.1
Pulaski	61.0	4 646	39.3	31.3	2.5	0.3	4.3	30.0	2 286	39	41	973	41.3	56.8	1.8
Putnam	123.0	3 258	52.6	25.9	2.2	0.1	3.9	99.5	2 636	74	104	2 394	43.2	55.2	1.5
Randolph	72.4	2 803	61.3	1.1	3.3	0.3	5.5	45.1	1 749	63	82	1 199	44.8	53.6	1.7
Ripley	77.1	2 698	69.6	0.9	2.4	0.1	3.5	73.8	2 582	74	90	1 264	34.4	63.9	1.7
Rush	60.9	3 561	39.7	33.6	2.8	0.2	6.5	41.7	2 438	41	54	1 076	42.3	56.0	1.7
St. Joseph	848.7	3 186	49.9	0.6	4.9	0.4	3.0	856.7	3 216	935	901	12 762	58.0	41.0	1.0
Scott	82.2	3 453	49.0	26.1	3.2	0.1	2.3	53.4	2 245	66	77	1 064	48.1	50.1	1.8
Shelby	217.7	4 896	31.6	43.4	3.2	0.1	2.2	156.3	3 515	122	142	2 377	39.8	58.8	1.4
Spencer	60.9	2 923	50.0	0.5	2.5	0.2	3.3	52.3	2 510	65	67	951	49.5	49.1	1.4
Starke	57.6	2 481	62.7	1.4	2.4	0.1	5.1	49.3	2 124	44	75	1 004	50.5	47.3	2.3
Steuben	88.6	2 597	53.3	1.0	3.4	0.2	3.8	103.6	3 037	61	107	1 517	44.4	54.2	1.3
Sullivan	83.4	3 936	37.2	35.1	0.9	0.2	3.7	81.5	3 848	47	61	1 823	48.8	49.5	1.8
Switzerland	38.7	3 712	40.1	0.3	1.1	0.2	3.1	17.5	1 683	22	34	434	45.0	53.3	1.7
Tippecanoe	406.1	2 288	50.8	0.2	6.3	0.6	5.9	369.7	2 083	486	584	23 348	55.2	43.6	1.2
Tipton	40.8	2 597	56.2	0.2	3.5	0.2	6.7	38.3	2 442	34	50	763	41.5	56.9	1.6
Union	23.2	3 150	73.7	0.1	2.6	0.0	4.3	25.2	3 429	14	23	449	36.6	61.6	1.9
Vanderburgh	605.3	3 347	39.0	0.7	7.5	0.3	2.7	673.3	3 723	877	571	9 304	50.8	48.3	0.9
Vermillion	47.0	2 933	53.2	0.4	2.5	0.4	5.1	23.9	1 493	32	51	668	56.1	42.2	1.7
Vigo	303.7	2 801	52.3	0.6	4.1	0.6	2.7	415.8	3 835	1 129	341	7 522	57.3	41.5	1.2
Wabash	128.9	3 983	46.9	29.1	2.8	0.1	3.3	49.4	1 525	75	99	1 861	39.3	59.4	1.3
Warren	25.3	3 032	48.5	1.2	1.6	1.1	6.3	5.8	698	14	28	353	43.9	54.2	1.9
Warrick	150.3	2 485	55.3	0.5	3.2	0.1	2.8	121.4	2 008	103	195	2 161	43.0	55.9	1.1
Washington	72.9	2 611	64.1	0.6	1.7	0.2	4.2	47.7	1 710	55	89	1 114	40.4	57.7	2.0
Wayne	192.9	2 822	52.8	1.7	4.5	0.3	3.0	101.7	1 489	157	211	4 659	47.1	51.0	1.9
Wells	73.2	2 646	66.0	0.6	4.1	0.1	4.5	54.7	1 977	53	88	1 197	33.7	65.1	1.3
White	92.9	3 804	53.9	0.2	2.1	0.1	3.9	122.7	5 024	58	78	1 328	44.9	53.2	1.8
Whitley	83.9	2 515	50.7	0.4	3.1	0.1	5.2	89.8	2 693	74	106	1 401	38.6	60.1	1.3
IOWA	X	X	X	X	X	X	X	X	X	17 420	12 673	237 564	53.9	44.4	1.7
Adair	35.9	4 797	29.3	28.1	3.8	0.1	14.9	30.8	4 112	25	30	459	47.5	50.8	1.7
Adams	18.9	4 842	43.4	5.1	6.6	0.8	17.5	25.1	6 408	26	16	220	50.7	47.4	1.9
Allamakee	60.7	4 262	38.8	26.8	3.5	0.2	12.3	42.3	2 969	62	57	1 050	56.2	42.0	1.8
Appanoose	38.5	3 030	55.1	4.8	8.0	0.2	13.4	8.5	670	50	52	608	48.1	49.9	2.0
Audubon	32.4	5 481	33.4	34.9	4.0	0.2	13.4	10.0	1 694	27	24	401	50.6	47.6	1.8
Benton	81.0	3 135	52.4	3.2	3.8	0.1	11.3	122.8	4 756	67	105	1 459	51.5	47.0	1.5
Black Hawk	637.5	4 836	53.7	3.2	4.6	0.3	7.4	430.8	3 268	504	547	11 569	60.5	38.1	1.5
Boone	124.1	4 739	36.1	35.5	3.3	0.4	7.7	248.4	9 484	106	106	2 403	52.8	45.2	2.0
Bremer	157.5	6 436	38.3	35.9	2.7	0.2	6.4	95.8	3 915	63	95	1 888	53.9	44.6	1.5
Buchanan	82.2	3 927	41.5	24.9	4.2	0.1	11.1	83.7	3 995	45	86	1 438	58.5	40.0	1.5
Buena Vista	124.9	6 065	34.7	32.6	3.3	0.1	7.7	93.1	4 522	114	81	1 617	48.4	50.2	1.4
Butler	80.9	5 400	24.9	40.1	2.8	0.3	13.2	30.8	2 054	41	61	771	46.9	51.6	1.4
Calhoun	44.1	4 453	58.6	8.7	3.3	0.5	11.4	14.8	1 490	38	38	662	45.1	52.8	2.2
Carroll	82.7	4 011	45.1	5.7	3.3	4.3	11.5	57.3	2 780	84	83	1 198	51.0	47.3	1.6
Cass	117.4	8 552	29.2	40.3	2.1	0.2	6.2	80.0	5 832	76	55	1 309	43.7	54.5	1.8
Cedar	69.5	3 774	57.4	5.4	4.1	0.0	10.6	54.8	2 977	89	75	1 003	54.0	44.4	1.6
Cerro Gordo	204.6	4 672	54.1	4.7	5.2	0.6	6.3	164.2	3 750	162	177	2 656	59.7	38.8	1.5
Cherokee	39.0	3 267	46.5	3.5	4.6	0.1	19.0	23.5	1 969	47	48	977	45.4	53.0	1.7
Chickasaw	44.7	3 641	56.0	3.0	4.0	0.2	13.2	29.3	2 390	52	50	607	59.6	38.8	1.6
Clarke	51.9	5 544	32.9	36.7	3.5	0.4	8.8	35.1	3 750	33	38	748	49.9	47.6	2.5
Clay	129.8	7 817	21.1	46.9	2.7	0.2	5.4	102.7	6 185	59	67	1 562	46.7	51.8	1.5
Clayton	98.8	5 538	51.9	15.0	3.1	0.4	9.5	56.2	3 150	84	72	1 248	57.8	40.6	1.6
Clinton	230.7	4 735	45.9	4.9	4.2	0.3	8.2	231.1	4 743	118	197	2 486	60.7	37.7	1.5
Crawford	93.1	5 378	36.5	33.2	2.6	0.1	10.1	85.1	4 916	82	70	1 274	51.7	46.5	1.8
Dallas	257.2	3 574	65.5	8.1	2.9	0.2	6.0	404.2	5 617	97	307	3 523	46.4	51.9	1.7
Davis	44.2	5 085	27.2	43.8	2.8	0.2	9.8	35.8	4 115	37	36	525	44.0	53.1	2.9
Decatur	44.9	5 439	33.8	43.0	3.1	1.0	8.7	35.6	4 310	35	31	585	48.4	49.2	2.4
Delaware	94.8	5 392	30.9	40.4	2.9	0.2	10.4	55.0	3 130	43	72	1 225	52.2	46.2	1.6
Des Moines	184.0	4 560	60.7	3.6	4.8	0.2	4.9	138.1	3 424	109	107	2 498	60.6	37.5	1.9
Dickinson	103.1	6 073	27.9	30.2	3.5	0.3	13.2	137.6	8 106	63	69	1 138	46.7	52.1	1.2
Dubuque	405.9	4 268	37.6	4.5	4.7	2.0	7.0	372.4	3 916	247	397	4 424	59.7	38.9	1.5
Emmet	70.6	6 975	75.4	3.2	3.2	0.1	6.0	24.8	2 448	39	40	758	51.2	47.3	1.4
Fayette	72.6	3 494	51.6	4.0	5.1	0.2	16.4	32.0	1 541	77	81	1 140	57.6	41.0	1.5
Floyd	71.8	4 475	33.5	31.9	2.8	0.9	9.2	26.4	1 647	46	65	951	59.6	37.7	2.7

1. Based on the resident population estimated as of July 1 of the year shown. 2.

STATE/ County code	CBSA code[1]	County type[2]	STATE County	Land area,[3] (sq km) 2010	Population, 2014: Total persons 2014	Population, 2014: Rank	Population, 2014: Per square kilometer	Population and population characteristics, 2013: Race alone or in combination, not Hispanic or Latino (percent): White	Black	American Indian, Alaska Native	Asian and Pacific Islander	Percent Hispanic or Latino[4]	Age (percent): Under 5 years	5 to 17 years	18 to 24 years	25 to 34 years	35 to 44 years	45 to 54 years
				1	2	3	4	5	6	7	8	9	10	11	12	13	14	15
			IOWA—Cont'd															
19 069	...	7	Franklin	1 507	10 436	2 400	6.9	87.4	0.7	0.5	0.6	11.5	5.8	17.0	7.4	10.8	10.6	13.5
19 071	...	8	Fremont	1 324	7 022	2 676	5.3	96.3	0.7	0.7	0.5	2.7	5.5	16.3	6.7	9.6	10.7	13.8
19 073	...	6	Greene	1 475	9 200	2 495	6.2	96.2	0.8	0.7	0.8	2.5	5.2	17.2	7.1	9.7	10.2	14.1
19 075	47940	3	Grundy	1 300	12 375	2 274	9.5	98.1	0.8	0.3	0.5	1.1	6.1	17.1	7.3	10.5	11.2	14.1
19 077	19780	2	Guthrie	1 530	10 722	2 378	7.0	96.9	0.6	0.5	0.7	2.1	5.3	16.9	6.5	9.5	10.8	14.4
19 079	...	6	Hamilton	1 494	15 117	2 092	10.1	91.7	0.9	0.6	2.5	5.4	5.6	17.7	6.8	10.9	11.4	14.7
19 081	...	7	Hancock	1 479	11 027	2 357	7.5	95.2	1.0	0.5	0.8	3.5	5.2	17.4	6.6	10.1	11.0	14.4
19 083	...	6	Hardin	1 474	17 311	1 962	11.7	94.1	1.8	0.6	0.7	3.9	5.3	16.7	8.7	10.4	10.1	13.4
19 085	36540	2	Harrison	1 805	14 324	2 146	7.9	97.6	0.6	0.7	0.5	1.5	5.4	17.3	7.4	9.9	11.6	15.1
19 087	...	7	Henry	1 125	20 217	1 828	18.0	90.0	3.2	0.6	3.1	4.6	5.9	16.7	9.5	11.8	11.8	13.8
19 089	...	7	Howard	1 226	9 449	2 474	7.7	97.5	0.8	0.4	0.6	1.5	6.8	18.1	6.9	10.9	10.4	13.9
19 091	...	7	Humboldt	1 125	9 640	2 463	8.6	95.1	0.9	0.5	0.6	3.8	5.7	17.5	7.3	10.8	10.0	13.9
19 093	...	8	Ida	1 118	7 042	2 672	6.3	97.2	0.7	0.6	0.6	1.7	6.9	17.1	6.7	10.3	9.9	13.0
19 095	...	8	Iowa	1 519	16 375	2 021	10.8	96.6	0.9	0.3	0.6	2.3	5.8	17.7	7.3	10.5	11.5	15.1
19 097	...	6	Jackson	1 647	19 482	1 853	11.8	96.9	1.0	0.5	1.2	1.3	5.5	17.1	7.4	9.8	10.9	15.4
19 099	35500	6	Jasper	1 892	36 872	1 253	19.5	95.8	2.0	0.6	0.8	1.7	5.6	16.9	7.3	11.9	12.1	14.9
19 101	21840	7	Jefferson	1 128	17 325	1 960	15.4	86.6	2.0	0.7	9.2	2.8	4.3	13.1	11.2	12.4	10.0	11.7
19 103	26980	3	Johnson	1 590	142 287	447	89.5	83.6	6.2	0.6	6.4	5.4	6.1	14.1	21.0	16.8	11.5	10.6
19 105	16300	3	Jones	1 491	20 454	1 807	13.7	95.3	2.6	0.3	0.7	1.6	5.1	16.4	7.4	11.5	12.1	15.1
19 107	...	8	Keokuk	1 500	10 231	2 419	6.8	97.5	0.9	0.4	0.4	1.6	6.3	16.7	7.3	10.4	10.6	14.4
19 109	...	7	Kossuth	2 519	15 222	2 084	6.0	96.9	0.9	0.3	0.7	2.0	5.6	16.6	7.0	9.7	9.4	14.1
19 111	22800	5	Lee	1 340	35 286	1 292	26.3	92.6	4.2	0.7	1.0	3.4	5.9	15.6	8.0	11.7	11.3	14.4
19 113	16300	3	Linn	1 857	217 751	296	117.3	90.6	5.5	0.6	2.7	2.9	6.4	17.5	9.6	13.6	12.8	13.8
19 115	...	8	Louisa	1 041	11 161	2 342	10.7	80.8	1.1	0.5	2.2	16.1	5.3	18.6	8.1	11.2	11.9	15.5
19 117	...	6	Lucas	1 115	8 701	2 540	7.8	98.0	0.4	0.4	0.5	1.3	5.6	17.6	7.4	9.2	10.4	14.1
19 119	...	8	Lyon	1 522	11 683	2 312	7.7	96.8	0.4	0.4	0.4	2.5	7.5	20.4	7.2	11.2	11.6	12.5
19 121	19780	2	Madison	1 453	15 609	2 066	10.7	97.5	0.7	0.5	0.7	1.4	5.9	20.0	6.5	9.9	13.4	14.8
19 123	36820	7	Mahaska	1 479	22 370	1 714	15.1	95.5	1.8	0.5	1.5	1.8	6.3	17.6	9.7	11.7	11.4	13.3
19 125	...	6	Marion	1 436	33 365	1 344	23.2	95.8	1.3	0.5	1.6	1.8	6.0	18.2	10.7	10.8	11.3	13.6
19 127	32260	4	Marshall	1 483	40 866	1 156	27.6	76.0	2.3	0.7	2.9	19.4	7.0	18.1	8.7	11.7	10.8	13.0
19 129	36540	2	Mills	1 133	14 831	2 116	13.1	95.8	1.0	0.8	0.9	2.7	5.8	18.9	7.1	9.9	12.4	15.3
19 131	...	7	Mitchell	1 215	10 779	2 374	8.9	97.8	0.7	0.3	0.4	1.2	5.6	18.6	7.5	9.3	10.0	14.4
19 133	...	6	Monona	1 798	8 996	2 519	5.0	96.5	1.0	1.3	0.5	1.7	5.1	16.5	6.5	9.1	9.8	13.9
19 135	...	7	Monroe	1 123	8 001	2 599	7.1	96.2	0.9	0.4	1.0	2.5	5.6	17.8	7.4	10.7	11.7	13.7
19 137	...	6	Montgomery	1 098	10 421	2 401	9.5	95.6	0.6	0.7	0.6	3.3	5.5	17.4	6.9	9.2	11.1	13.9
19 139	34700	4	Muscatine	1 133	42 903	1 113	37.9	80.2	2.2	0.6	1.3	16.8	6.7	18.8	8.5	12.0	12.2	13.9
19 141	...	7	O'Brien	1 484	14 056	2 164	9.5	94.4	0.9	0.4	1.0	4.0	5.9	17.2	7.3	10.6	10.2	13.6
19 143	...	7	Osceola	1 033	6 218	2 741	6.0	92.5	0.5	0.5	0.6	6.5	5.6	17.1	7.0	10.3	10.9	14.1
19 145	...	7	Page	1 385	15 496	2 073	11.2	93.0	3.0	1.0	1.2	3.2	5.6	15.3	7.7	11.2	12.1	13.2
19 147	...	7	Palo Alto	1 460	9 099	2 507	6.2	96.6	1.0	0.6	0.9	1.9	5.8	16.0	9.0	10.6	10.0	13.0
19 149	43580	6	Plymouth	2 235	24 874	1 614	11.1	95.2	0.8	0.5	0.9	3.5	6.0	19.1	7.3	10.4	11.5	14.2
19 151	...	9	Pocahontas	1 495	7 138	2 666	4.8	95.4	1.3	0.5	0.6	3.1	5.6	16.6	6.9	9.2	9.2	14.9
19 153	19780	2	Polk	1 486	459 862	147	309.5	81.5	7.4	0.6	4.6	8.0	7.2	18.1	9.0	15.8	13.6	13.5
19 155	36540	2	Pottawattamie	2 461	93 128	626	37.8	90.5	2.1	0.9	1.0	7.0	6.6	17.1	9.0	12.4	11.8	14.1
19 157	...	7	Poweshiek	1 515	18 668	1 882	12.3	94.1	1.7	0.6	2.3	2.8	5.3	15.3	13.8	9.7	10.0	13.1
19 159	...	9	Ringgold	1 387	5 051	2 835	3.6	96.6	0.6	0.5	0.9	2.1	6.1	18.0	5.9	9.5	9.5	12.1
19 161	...	9	Sac	1 489	10 035	2 434	6.7	96.7	0.7	0.4	0.4	2.6	5.4	16.9	6.6	9.3	10.1	13.8
19 163	19340	2	Scott	1 186	171 387	371	144.5	84.1	8.7	0.8	2.8	6.1	6.6	17.6	8.7	13.7	12.5	13.8
19 165	...	6	Shelby	1 530	11 948	2 300	7.8	96.6	0.8	0.6	0.6	2.2	5.5	17.1	7.0	8.3	10.4	14.9
19 167	...	6	Sioux	1 990	34 681	1 311	17.4	88.9	0.8	0.3	0.9	9.7	7.5	19.4	13.4	12.3	10.3	11.6
19 169	11180	3	Story	1 484	94 073	621	63.4	87.5	3.1	0.5	7.1	3.2	5.0	12.5	30.3	13.3	9.2	9.4
19 171	...	6	Tama	1 867	17 451	1 951	9.3	85.0	0.9	7.2	0.8	7.9	5.9	18.4	7.6	9.9	11.0	14.1
19 173	...	9	Taylor	1 378	6 143	2 746	4.5	92.0	0.5	0.6	0.5	7.2	5.6	17.1	7.0	11.4	10.0	13.7
19 175	...	6	Union	1 097	12 516	2 264	11.4	95.8	1.3	0.5	0.8	2.4	6.2	17.2	8.7	11.4	10.8	13.3
19 177	...	9	Van Buren	1 256	7 468	2 643	5.9	97.9	0.5	0.5	0.7	1.1	6.5	16.5	7.0	9.8	10.8	13.7
19 179	36900	5	Wapello	1 118	35 212	1 293	31.5	86.9	2.4	0.7	1.3	9.9	6.2	16.4	9.3	12.3	11.7	13.4
19 181	19780	2	Warren	1 470	47 056	1 016	32.5	96.1	1.1	0.5	1.0	2.4	5.9	19.4	9.4	10.9	12.6	14.6
19 183	26980	3	Washington	1 473	22 070	1 726	15.0	93.1	1.3	0.5	0.9	5.2	6.4	18.3	7.4	10.6	11.3	14.3
19 185	...	9	Wayne	1 361	6 395	2 726	4.7	97.5	0.8	0.6	0.5	1.5	6.6	17.3	7.1	10.2	9.0	13.4
19 187	22700	5	Webster	1 853	36 955	1 251	19.9	90.7	5.1	0.6	1.1	4.2	5.7	15.9	11.6	12.0	10.3	13.3
19 189	...	7	Winnebago	1 037	10 559	2 393	10.2	93.9	1.6	0.5	1.1	3.9	5.1	15.8	9.2	10.5	10.6	13.1
19 191	...	7	Winneshiek	1 787	20 768	1 789	11.6	95.8	1.1	0.3	1.3	2.2	4.5	14.7	16.6	9.6	9.5	13.4
19 193	43580	3	Woodbury	2 261	102 271	579	45.2	78.5	3.7	2.3	3.1	14.7	7.4	18.8	10.2	12.9	12.0	12.9
19 195	32380	9	Worth	1 036	7 624	2 630	7.4	96.2	0.9	0.5	0.6	2.6	5.1	16.6	7.7	10.0	11.2	14.8
19 197	...	7	Wright	1 503	12 840	2 245	8.5	89.1	0.8	0.6	0.5	9.9	5.8	17.3	7.2	9.9	10.6	13.2

1. CBSA = Core Based Statistical Area. See Appendix A for explanation. See Appendix B for list of metropolitan areas with component counties. 2. County type code from the Economic Research Service of USDA Rural-Urban Continuum Codes. See Appendix A for definition. 3. Dry land or land partially or temporarily covered by water. 4. May be of any race.

STATE County	Population, 2013 (cont.): Age (percent) (cont.): 55 to 64 years	65 to 74 years	75 years and over	Percent female	Population change and components of change, 2000–2014: Total persons: 2000	2010	Percent change: 2000–2010	2010–2014	Components of change, 2010–2014: Births	Deaths	Net migration	Households, 2009–2013: Number	Persons per household	Percent: Family households	Female family householder[1]	One person
	16	17	18	19	20	21	22	23	24	25	26	27	28	29	30	31
IOWA—Cont'd																
Franklin	15.2	9.5	10.1	49.9	10 704	10 680	-0.2	-2.3	484	494	-213	4 358	2.40	69.4	8.4	25.1
Fremont	16.5	10.6	10.3	50.8	8 010	7 441	-7.1	-5.6	305	367	-332	2 965	2.40	68.5	9.7	27.5
Greene	15.2	9.8	11.3	51.3	10 366	9 336	-9.9	-1.5	417	490	-54	3 969	2.29	65.7	8.7	29.3
Grundy	14.0	9.8	9.8	50.8	12 369	12 453	0.7	-0.6	559	513	-94	5 073	2.42	69.8	6.0	26.4
Guthrie	15.3	10.8	10.4	50.0	11 353	10 954	-3.5	-2.1	434	496	-141	4 641	2.29	71.0	9.0	27.1
Hamilton	13.7	8.9	10.1	50.7	16 438	15 673	-4.7	-3.5	678	724	-529	6 395	2.39	64.7	8.6	32.0
Hancock	15.4	9.7	10.1	49.7	12 100	11 341	-6.3	-2.8	453	546	-211	4 648	2.37	67.6	5.9	28.3
Hardin	14.2	9.8	11.4	50.2	18 812	17 534	-6.8	-1.3	764	916	-32	7 061	2.35	65.3	5.9	30.2
Harrison	14.6	9.8	8.9	50.4	15 666	14 928	-4.7	-4.1	641	775	-470	5 996	2.41	69.0	8.3	28.0
Henry	13.2	9.2	8.1	48.7	20 336	20 145	-0.9	0.4	970	901	8	7 493	2.53	67.9	10.9	28.1
Howard	13.3	9.4	10.2	50.1	9 932	9 566	-3.7	-1.2	499	461	-148	3 884	2.39	62.8	6.9	31.0
Humboldt	14.4	9.4	11.1	51.2	10 381	9 815	-5.5	-1.8	455	485	-131	4 222	2.28	67.1	7.1	27.4
Ida	14.8	9.5	11.7	50.0	7 837	7 089	-9.5	-0.7	355	416	0	3 182	2.19	63.2	9.1	30.7
Iowa	14.2	8.4	9.5	50.4	15 671	16 355	4.4	0.1	790	745	-37	6 745	2.37	70.5	6.2	25.2
Jackson	14.5	10.2	9.2	50.2	20 296	19 848	-2.2	-1.8	855	956	-253	8 479	2.30	68.7	7.8	26.4
Jasper	13.6	9.3	8.5	49.2	37 213	36 842	-1.0	0.1	1 766	1 544	-159	14 826	2.34	67.3	10.1	26.9
Jefferson	19.1	10.6	7.4	47.0	16 181	16 843	4.1	2.9	599	669	555	6 919	2.21	59.1	5.5	34.7
Johnson	10.3	5.5	4.1	50.1	111 006	130 882	17.9	8.7	7 601	2 713	6 422	54 005	2.33	53.8	8.2	31.3
Jones	14.2	9.2	9.0	47.9	20 221	20 638	2.1	-0.9	895	842	-195	8 063	2.38	68.9	7.5	25.6
Keokuk	14.3	9.6	10.4	50.0	11 400	10 511	-7.8	-2.7	541	452	-365	4 354	2.36	62.3	6.2	32.8
Kossuth	15.5	9.9	12.1	49.8	17 163	15 543	-9.4	-2.1	679	759	-216	6 728	2.25	64.9	6.6	31.2
Lee	15.0	10.0	8.2	49.5	38 052	35 862	-5.8	-1.6	1 781	1 788	-534	14 241	2.44	65.3	10.3	29.5
Linn	12.2	7.6	6.4	50.7	191 701	211 226	10.2	3.1	11 502	6 843	2 017	86 052	2.42	62.4	10.0	30.3
Louisa	13.4	8.7	7.3	48.9	12 183	11 387	-6.5	-2.0	551	422	-351	4 381	2.56	70.1	9.8	25.0
Lucas	14.9	10.4	10.3	49.8	9 422	8 898	-5.6	-2.2	402	423	-187	3 734	2.32	66.3	9.3	29.9
Lyon	12.9	7.5	9.3	49.8	11 763	11 581	-1.5	0.9	704	488	-79	4 425	2.60	71.1	5.6	26.3
Madison	13.6	8.7	7.2	50.2	14 019	15 679	11.8	-0.4	701	621	-164	6 092	2.52	69.3	5.9	24.1
Mahaska	13.4	8.3	8.3	49.7	22 335	22 381	0.2	0.0	1 167	929	-233	9 073	2.40	64.2	7.0	29.9
Marion	12.9	8.5	8.0	50.2	32 052	33 309	3.9	0.2	1 582	1 387	-104	12 691	2.48	70.9	6.4	26.0
Marshall	13.6	8.8	8.4	49.7	39 311	40 648	3.4	0.5	2 366	2 001	-145	15 350	2.58	68.5	9.9	26.5
Mills	15.6	8.9	6.2	49.8	14 547	15 059	3.5	-1.5	669	583	-298	5 375	2.67	75.1	6.9	21.8
Mitchell	13.2	9.4	12.1	50.5	10 874	10 776	-0.9	0.1	512	549	46	4 389	2.39	66.7	5.6	30.3
Monona	14.8	11.5	12.7	50.6	10 020	9 243	-7.8	-2.7	362	615	-10	3 981	2.26	63.1	7.8	34.8
Monroe	14.1	9.6	9.3	50.0	8 016	7 970	-0.6	0.4	366	394	71	3 361	2.34	66.9	8.3	27.4
Montgomery	15.2	10.0	10.7	51.2	11 771	10 740	-8.8	-3.0	457	616	-157	4 553	2.28	67.6	11.5	27.4
Muscatine	13.1	8.2	6.6	50.3	41 722	42 745	2.5	0.4	2 361	1 571	-597	16 410	2.58	69.7	11.1	25.1
O'Brien	14.6	8.8	11.9	50.2	15 102	14 398	-4.7	-2.4	682	757	-271	6 098	2.27	63.2	5.6	33.4
Osceola	14.6	9.7	10.8	49.4	7 003	6 462	-7.7	-3.8	301	283	-261	2 676	2.33	68.5	4.5	27.5
Page	14.8	9.9	10.2	47.7	16 976	15 932	-6.1	-2.8	748	894	-303	6 415	2.27	64.9	7.9	31.3
Palo Alto	14.2	9.4	12.1	50.2	10 147	9 421	-7.2	-3.4	413	524	-195	3 948	2.28	60.8	7.3	34.8
Plymouth	14.2	8.8	8.7	50.5	24 849	24 986	0.6	-0.4	1 198	1 005	-261	9 867	2.49	70.7	7.6	25.2
Pocahontas	15.4	10.4	11.9	50.2	8 662	7 310	-15.6	-2.4	330	377	-109	3 227	2.19	59.5	6.3	36.0
Polk	11.5	6.5	4.9	50.8	374 601	430 640	15.0	6.8	28 241	13 353	14 270	173 164	2.48	65.1	11.4	28.0
Pottawattamie	13.6	8.3	7.0	50.9	87 704	93 158	6.2	0.0	5 134	3 730	-1 349	36 460	2.49	67.8	12.9	26.1
Poweshiek	13.6	9.6	9.6	50.9	18 815	18 914	0.5	-1.3	769	938	-30	7 488	2.28	63.9	7.9	30.1
Ringgold	14.2	11.6	13.0	50.7	5 469	5 131	-6.2	-1.6	228	317	-2	2 074	2.39	67.3	5.8	29.8
Sac	15.3	9.8	12.8	51.0	11 529	10 350	-10.2	-3.0	440	576	-140	4 435	2.25	64.1	6.3	31.2
Scott	13.1	7.8	6.2	51.0	158 668	165 224	4.1	3.7	9 426	5 967	2 869	67 049	2.44	63.4	11.2	30.1
Shelby	14.4	10.1	12.1	51.0	13 173	12 167	-7.6	-1.8	536	563	-191	5 083	2.33	66.2	7.1	30.2
Sioux	11.2	6.8	7.5	49.9	31 589	33 704	6.7	2.9	2 157	1 059	-92	11 623	2.72	75.9	6.6	20.9
Story	9.7	5.6	5.0	48.2	79 981	89 542	12.0	5.1	4 018	1 960	2 552	35 196	2.34	53.6	5.4	28.5
Tama	14.0	9.3	9.8	51.2	18 103	17 767	-1.9	-1.8	915	855	-361	6 794	2.53	72.2	10.6	24.2
Taylor	14.2	9.9	10.9	49.6	6 958	6 317	-9.2	-2.8	316	307	-188	2 764	2.22	66.6	7.9	28.6
Union	13.6	9.6	9.3	51.8	12 309	12 534	1.8	-0.1	574	604	25	5 339	2.29	64.6	9.2	29.7
Van Buren	15.3	10.9	9.6	49.2	7 809	7 570	-3.1	-1.3	398	364	-131	3 023	2.45	69.3	6.9	26.5
Wapello	13.9	8.8	8.1	50.8	36 051	35 625	-1.2	-1.2	1 837	1 654	-557	14 534	2.38	65.0	11.8	30.0
Warren	12.6	8.1	6.5	51.1	40 671	46 225	13.7	3.7	2 242	1 594	1 089	17 378	2.58	74.1	10.3	21.9
Washington	13.5	9.1	9.1	50.9	20 670	21 704	5.0	1.7	1 192	985	175	8 948	2.40	67.6	7.7	27.4
Wayne	13.7	10.9	11.5	51.4	6 730	6 403	-4.9	-0.1	380	362	-40	2 589	2.42	65.1	7.3	31.2
Webster	14.0	8.6	8.5	48.5	40 235	38 013	-5.5	-2.8	1 858	1 927	-922	15 458	2.28	58.6	11.6	35.2
Winnebago	15.5	9.1	11.1	51.3	11 723	10 866	-7.3	-2.8	470	538	-254	4 591	2.23	65.9	5.3	32.0
Winneshiek	14.0	8.5	9.2	50.6	21 310	21 056	-1.2	-1.4	723	738	-227	8 042	2.32	67.0	6.0	27.7
Woodbury	12.3	7.3	6.2	50.5	103 877	102 172	-1.6	0.1	6 487	3 855	-2 401	38 654	2.57	66.0	13.5	28.9
Worth	15.1	10.0	9.5	50.2	7 909	7 598	-3.9	0.3	322	343	55	3 197	2.33	69.9	8.1	26.0
Wright	14.9	9.6	11.7	49.7	14 334	13 229	-7.7	-2.9	590	676	-279	5 367	2.40	62.5	6.6	32.6

1. No spouse present.

STATE County	Persons in group quarters, 2014	Daytime population, 2009–2013: Number	Daytime population, 2009–2013: Employment/residence ratio	Births, 2014: Total	Births, 2014: Rate[1]	Deaths, 2014: Number	Deaths, 2014: Rate[1]	Persons under 65 with no health insurance, 2013: Number	Persons under 65 with no health insurance, 2013: Percent	Medicare, 2014: Eligible for Medicare	Medicare, 2014: Enrolled in Medicare Advantage	Medicare, 2014: Enrolled in a Medicare prescription drug plan	Serious crimes known to police,[2] 2013: Total: Number	Serious crimes known to police,[2] 2013: Total: Rate[3]
	32	33	34	35	36	37	38	39	40	41	42	43	44	45
IOWA—Cont'd														
Franklin	193	9 905	0.86	110	10.5	110	10.5	1 133	13.5	2 279	40	1 719	20	190
Fremont	132	6 576	0.79	70	10.0	81	11.5	529	9.5	1 711	153	1 130	NA	NA
Greene	131	8 859	0.91	106	11.5	118	12.8	714	10.0	2 243	240	1 502	65	713
Grundy	153	10 544	0.69	124	10.0	109	8.8	810	8.2	2 679	288	1 884	76	609
Guthrie	166	9 196	0.68	106	9.9	113	10.5	841	10.1	2 715	364	1 737	43	400
Hamilton	192	14 891	0.92	159	10.5	171	11.3	1 380	11.2	3 319	275	2 199	288	1 884
Hancock	183	10 841	0.93	112	10.2	128	11.6	835	9.5	2 358	36	1 699	29	261
Hardin	846	17 149	0.96	179	10.3	228	13.2	1 268	9.7	3 958	211	2 850	317	1 835
Harrison	272	12 045	0.63	150	10.5	171	11.9	1 095	9.4	3 137	268	2 086	57	486
Henry	1 488	20 553	1.04	223	11.0	190	9.4	1 474	9.6	4 070	343	2 720	308	1 670
Howard	201	9 208	0.93	121	12.8	121	12.8	861	11.4	2 078	33	1 511	93	970
Humboldt	127	9 153	0.87	110	11.4	111	11.5	708	9.2	2 147	85	1 508	132	1 357
Ida	118	7 556	1.13	91	12.9	100	14.2	539	9.6	1 624	131	1 122	54	756
Iowa	288	16 270	0.99	199	12.2	195	11.9	976	7.3	3 267	482	2 089	132	816
Jackson	204	16 447	0.66	194	10.0	216	11.1	1 718	11.0	4 382	940	3 085	NA	NA
Jasper	1 812	31 801	0.71	420	11.4	357	9.7	2 455	8.6	7 609	931	5 226	800	2 184
Jefferson	1 726	17 388	1.07	147	8.5	159	9.2	1 563	12.7	3 595	428	2 210	401	2 368
Johnson	7 989	143 412	1.13	1 834	12.9	680	4.8	11 355	9.6	16 204	2 055	7 921	3 486	2 521
Jones	1 189	17 824	0.71	210	10.3	207	10.1	1 427	9.1	4 136	766	2 554	143	691
Keokuk	142	8 669	0.63	127	12.4	107	10.5	893	10.9	2 325	320	1 384	53	511
Kossuth	244	15 057	0.95	156	10.2	165	10.8	1 069	9.0	3 882	53	2 682	121	789
Lee	1 351	37 889	1.13	431	12.2	415	11.8	2 770	9.9	7 860	760	5 222	1 033	2 899
Linn	5 175	225 583	1.11	2 684	12.3	1 633	7.5	13 790	7.6	36 124	9 471	18 765	6 256	2 882
Louisa	123	9 808	0.71	128	11.5	110	9.9	1 174	12.5	2 082	292	1 242	63	558
Lucas	75	8 676	0.96	88	10.1	94	10.8	858	12.5	1 988	217	1 238	282	3 226
Lyon	155	10 607	0.82	163	14.0	109	9.3	943	9.8	2 090	147	1 513	63	682
Madison	190	11 921	0.52	160	10.3	151	9.7	1 129	8.7	2 817	445	1 673	174	1 110
Mahaska	688	20 622	0.83	265	11.8	223	10.0	1 669	9.2	4 275	478	2 864	285	1 265
Marion	1 445	34 253	1.06	373	11.2	318	9.5	1 959	7.4	6 424	536	4 117	NA	NA
Marshall	1 391	40 935	1.01	566	13.9	469	11.5	4 033	12.2	8 122	1 021	5 508	1 017	2 479
Mills	607	12 216	0.60	155	10.5	121	8.2	1 000	8.2	2 976	350	1 865	310	2 094
Mitchell	239	10 358	0.93	119	11.0	120	11.1	883	10.6	2 399	NA	1 719	85	885
Monona	201	8 546	0.84	83	9.2	153	17.0	751	11.0	2 305	354	1 507	112	1 229
Monroe	122	7 512	0.87	84	10.5	90	11.2	883	13.7	1 695	178	1 166	129	1 590
Montgomery	201	10 748	1.03	111	10.7	131	12.6	874	10.7	2 505	167	1 737	NA	NA
Muscatine	524	43 756	1.05	555	12.9	339	7.9	3 719	10.3	7 621	1 633	4 238	857	1 991
O'Brien	369	13 844	0.94	159	11.3	177	12.6	1 062	9.6	3 205	131	2 364	174	1 231
Osceola	99	5 578	0.77	79	12.7	63	10.1	585	12.0	1 357	41	960	5	82
Page	1 374	16 115	1.04	182	11.7	198	12.8	1 145	10.2	3 704	245	2 570	355	2 264
Palo Alto	318	9 056	0.93	94	10.3	115	12.6	640	9.1	2 054	32	1 495	98	1 058
Plymouth	311	23 433	0.89	285	11.5	234	9.4	1 693	8.3	4 743	690	2 901	313	1 254
Pocahontas	136	6 837	0.88	76	10.6	83	11.6	524	9.5	1 759	76	1 270	51	715
Polk	9 688	480 594	1.19	6 795	14.8	3 232	7.0	36 591	9.3	65 058	11 751	35 655	15 900	3 543
Pottawattamie	2 215	86 449	0.86	1 166	12.5	909	9.8	8 060	10.5	17 726	3 971	9 390	5 887	6 331
Poweshiek	1 612	20 079	1.14	174	9.3	211	11.3	1 132	8.3	3 808	347	2 474	273	1 457
Ringgold	182	4 825	0.87	53	10.5	57	11.3	508	13.4	1 283	94	943	41	804
Sac	208	9 163	0.79	104	10.4	130	13.0	809	10.5	2 418	91	1 737	92	1 157
Scott	3 497	170 965	1.05	2 231	13.0	1 400	8.2	13 128	9.1	29 228	6 114	13 225	5 828	3 448
Shelby	214	12 313	1.04	129	10.8	132	11.0	797	8.6	3 012	215	2 049	NA	NA
Sioux	2 396	35 931	1.10	504	14.5	249	7.2	3 242	11.8	5 431	324	3 942	NA	NA
Story	10 372	92 480	1.04	938	10.0	492	5.2	6 421	8.7	11 515	1 221	7 298	1 968	2 311
Tama	339	15 442	0.73	222	12.7	187	10.7	1 849	13.1	3 765	461	2 486	225	1 532
Taylor	70	5 422	0.72	84	13.7	68	11.1	672	13.9	1 508	NA	1 107	22	355
Union	355	13 493	1.15	131	10.5	140	11.2	1 028	10.3	2 754	213	1 870	137	1 083
Van Buren	93	6 858	0.81	94	12.6	93	12.5	804	13.7	1 756	204	1 149	77	1 036
Wapello	828	36 843	1.09	426	12.1	381	10.8	3 530	12.3	7 453	684	5 061	1 499	4 238
Warren	1 606	33 818	0.47	543	11.3	399	8.3	2 702	6.9	7 949	1 303	4 384	818	1 733
Washington	308	19 916	0.83	287	13.0	216	9.8	1 887	10.6	4 609	498	2 911	244	1 107
Wayne	93	5 930	0.83	96	15.0	88	13.4	007	14.0	1 561	101	003	20	315
Webster	2 761	39 358	1.10	440	11.9	423	11.4	2 795	9.9	7 696	562	5 161	1 500	4 035
Winnebago	381	11 551	1.15	114	10.8	122	11.6	732	9.1	2 414	72	1 730	28	265
Winneshiek	2 222	21 719	1.06	164	7.9	185	8.9	1 363	9.0	4 144	613	2 674	78	369
Woodbury	2 630	102 358	1.00	1 481	14.5	887	8.7	11 281	13.1	17 200	3 729	9 343	4 244	4 138
Worth	90	6 340	0.68	81	10.6	63	8.3	568	9.4	1 643	83	1 085	92	1 223
Wright	193	13 303	1.03	133	10.4	153	11.9	1 187	11.7	2 990	98	2 166	82	772

1. Per 1,000 estimated resident population. 2. Data for serious crimes have not been adjusted for underreporting; this may affect comparability between geographic areas and over time.
3. Per 100,000 population estimated by the FBI.

STATE County	Serious crimes known to police, 2013 (cont.)[1] Rate[2] Violent	Serious crimes known to police, 2013 (cont.)[1] Rate[2] Property	Education: School enrollment and attainment, 2009–2013 Enrollment[3] Total	Enrollment[3] Percent private	Attainment[4] (percent) High school graduate or less	Attainment[4] (percent) Bachelor's degree or more	Local government expenditures,[5] 2012–2013 Total current spending (mil dol)	Local government expenditures,[5] 2012–2013 Current spending per student (dollars)	Money income, 2009–2013 Per capita income[6] (dollars)	Households Median income (dollars)	Households Mean income (dollars)	Households Percent with income of $200,000 or more	Income and poverty, 2013 Median household income (dollars)	Percent below poverty level All persons	Percent below poverty level Children under 18 years	Percent below poverty level Children 5 to 17 years in families
	46	47	48	49	50	51	52	53	54	55	56	57	58	59	60	61
IOWA—Cont'd																
Franklin	28	161	2 308	4.4	51.0	15.1	22.4	9 649	26 102	48 355	62 123	2.7	47 879	13.6	20.6	20.3
Fremont	NA	NA	1 587	3.9	49.7	20.5	10.2	11 603	26 930	50 520	64 866	3.9	50 934	13.1	19.6	18.0
Greene	11	702	2 184	5.5	47.5	17.4	17.5	10 761	26 205	45 865	60 896	2.5	47 936	12.8	19.5	17.4
Grundy	80	529	2 978	8.1	42.1	20.7	26.1	9 397	31 164	56 827	75 004	4.1	61 381	6.9	8.5	8.2
Guthrie	37	363	2 465	5.5	48.5	17.1	23.7	8 927	28 030	50 609	65 992	3.0	53 708	10.3	13.7	12.8
Hamilton	294	1 590	3 892	7.2	44.7	18.0	27.5	9 939	24 510	43 589	58 016	1.6	50 867	10.1	15.9	15.1
Hancock	27	234	2 434	7.5	47.4	16.6	17.2	9 871	25 814	50 105	61 140	2.0	54 835	10.1	13.9	12.1
Hardin	185	1 650	4 275	13.0	42.9	19.7	32.7	10 253	25 153	49 342	60 440	1.8	51 907	11.0	18.5	17.1
Harrison	34	451	3 493	7.0	49.5	17.7	28.8	9 924	26 184	54 583	63 207	1.9	53 764	10.6	14.6	13.4
Henry	239	1 431	4 665	15.4	46.2	20.0	33.8	9 854	22 687	46 376	58 340	2.2	50 084	14.2	18.7	17.5
Howard	125	845	2 078	15.9	59.2	11.6	16.1	9 461	24 286	46 429	57 890	3.0	45 975	11.9	16.7	16.4
Humboldt	103	1 254	2 252	18.7	47.5	18.2	15.4	9 801	26 746	47 897	61 492	1.6	52 286	11.2	16.4	15.2
Ida	56	700	1 544	5.7	49.7	19.6	12.0	10 176	25 869	43 449	57 572	2.2	51 948	11.5	15.9	15.6
Iowa	86	729	3 871	14.9	44.6	21.0	25.7	9 524	28 068	58 008	68 595	1.8	58 028	10.1	10.5	9.7
Jackson	NA	NA	4 477	13.7	57.1	14.5	29.5	9 551	24 493	46 467	57 451	1.8	46 180	11.8	17.1	15.8
Jasper	167	2 018	8 648	10.4	48.6	17.8	55.4	9 385	24 905	50 513	61 050	1.2	55 492	9.8	13.5	12.4
Jefferson	77	2 292	4 363	35.8	37.1	31.2	24.1	10 143	27 593	48 814	64 943	3.0	41 942	16.1	22.0	19.5
Johnson	294	2 226	50 332	8.3	22.2	51.1	165.7	10 036	29 592	53 424	72 180	4.5	53 204	16.0	12.7	12.4
Jones	53	638	4 630	16.0	49.6	17.2	29.6	9 179	26 762	55 041	67 608	2.2	54 749	10.2	13.3	12.0
Keokuk	97	415	2 482	6.4	55.3	13.4	11.5	9 390	22 243	42 167	51 876	0.9	47 626	13.3	17.5	16.9
Kossuth	144	646	3 369	19.6	46.2	18.3	22.6	11 211	29 127	51 812	66 841	3.4	55 972	9.8	14.0	12.4
Lee	494	2 405	8 099	14.3	51.5	15.8	50.0	9 645	22 649	42 469	53 891	1.1	45 307	16.2	23.2	21.9
Linn	221	2 661	58 574	20.2	33.2	31.2	416.4	11 500	29 943	57 260	72 497	3.2	56 503	9.7	12.1	11.4
Louisa	53	505	2 664	2.9	56.7	13.5	27.0	10 107	24 272	50 583	61 414	1.0	51 387	11.3	15.7	14.1
Lucas	240	2 986	1 862	6.2	56.9	11.3	13.0	9 122	21 126	43 288	50 381	0.8	41 011	15.1	23.6	22.4
Lyon	97	584	2 785	20.1	50.8	17.6	18.7	8 805	23 683	52 152	61 246	2.4	60 548	7.6	10.2	10.0
Madison	128	983	3 942	7.8	46.9	21.5	29.6	8 592	27 685	57 581	70 727	3.5	59 074	8.4	10.1	9.1
Mahaska	231	1 035	6 306	28.9	49.2	21.5	28.7	9 337	23 788	47 967	57 616	1.5	48 978	14.0	17.9	16.9
Marion	NA	NA	9 058	33.3	42.5	25.0	52.0	9 248	25 477	54 723	65 299	2.2	56 883	9.3	11.0	10.5
Marshall	436	2 043	10 055	7.0	47.9	19.3	68.8	9 727	24 117	51 555	62 277	1.6	51 382	13.4	19.6	18.7
Mills	412	1 682	3 939	10.4	42.7	24.0	29.6	9 264	27 101	63 076	73 117	2.3	56 504	10.0	13.6	12.3
Mitchell	83	801	2 454	16.1	51.9	15.7	14.6	8 840	24 518	51 078	59 179	1.0	53 049	10.2	15.7	14.3
Monona	154	1 076	2 087	7.1	53.8	14.3	18.1	10 983	24 557	42 025	55 844	1.9	41 461	12.5	19.1	17.4
Monroe	148	1 442	1 786	7.9	54.7	19.3	11.3	9 128	24 508	45 997	57 528	0.6	49 012	12.6	18.3	16.7
Montgomery	NA	NA	2 405	5.3	47.9	15.1	18.6	10 313	22 868	44 281	53 726	1.5	44 669	15.0	22.3	20.5
Muscatine	411	1 580	10 830	5.4	49.3	16.2	72.1	9 370	25 038	51 425	63 684	2.4	54 025	12.7	18.5	17.3
O'Brien	163	1 068	3 451	17.8	48.9	18.9	23.2	9 745	28 086	48 185	65 053	3.2	57 287	9.4	12.2	11.3
Osceola	0	82	1 394	9.6	52.1	15.6	7.8	9 764	24 653	48 659	58 268	1.5	51 017	9.1	14.2	13.6
Page	236	2 028	3 461	13.4	48.6	17.4	25.2	10 548	23 496	43 010	56 409	2.2	47 438	17.3	24.8	22.2
Palo Alto	162	896	2 162	13.4	43.3	16.5	17.4	10 296	25 055	44 663	57 801	2.3	49 536	10.8	14.5	13.6
Plymouth	104	1 150	6 393	20.2	45.0	20.9	38.9	9 511	27 942	58 888	69 639	2.0	58 113	8.3	10.3	9.4
Pocahontas	42	673	1 532	14.7	47.7	17.8	33.0	30 206	25 556	44 073	56 145	2.0	50 401	11.5	16.8	16.1
Polk	295	3 249	115 559	20.6	34.1	34.9	800.4	10 808	30 442	59 018	75 743	4.1	59 388	12.4	16.0	14.5
Pottawattamie	725	5 606	22 730	11.7	46.6	19.1	182.7	11 613	25 847	51 304	64 127	2.1	50 570	13.6	18.9	17.8
Poweshiek	214	1 244	5 388	36.2	45.6	24.1	27.4	9 496	25 318	50 349	61 676	2.2	50 799	12.0	14.2	13.3
Ringgold	0	804	1 113	13.9	49.4	17.6	8.6	11 034	23 324	44 551	56 788	2.4	47 319	16.4	28.5	25.9
Sac	138	1 019	2 126	5.9	49.7	19.1	18.6	10 570	26 350	48 093	59 783	2.4	51 399	10.6	14.3	13.2
Scott	484	2 964	43 693	17.7	35.3	31.6	299.8	10 525	28 948	52 735	70 690	3.9	54 444	14.2	19.9	18.5
Shelby	NA	NA	2 718	12.8	49.3	18.2	17.8	10 417	26 387	48 783	61 932	2.1	54 740	9.4	12.0	11.1
Sioux	NA	NA	10 287	48.2	46.2	23.4	44.0	9 463	24 324	57 227	69 278	3.0	61 817	8.2	9.7	9.5
Story	156	2 155	39 419	4.4	23.4	47.7	105.8	9 640	25 986	50 516	64 853	2.9	53 782	21.1	10.5	10.0
Tama	565	967	4 414	9.4	49.3	16.1	23.3	9 629	25 311	51 670	63 876	2.5	53 844	11.5	17.0	15.6
Taylor	0	355	1 379	2.8	52.8	13.8	10.8	10 340	23 793	43 804	54 477	1.7	45 009	14.1	18.0	17.0
Union	71	1 012	3 181	9.2	46.6	16.5	19.7	9 400	23 007	44 838	54 639	1.6	43 357	13.5	20.1	18.7
Van Buren	175	861	1 571	19.2	55.2	14.4	10.0	9 849	21 368	43 181	52 111	0.9	43 019	16.2	26.3	26.3
Wapello	235	4 003	8 460	11.2	52.9	16.2	78.3	12 444	22 699	41 425	54 062	1.5	40 629	19.9	24.5	23.1
Warren	318	1 415	13 029	20.2	38.2	26.7	81.0	8 867	29 088	62 535	75 993	2.7	66 328	7.0	9.1	8.0
Washington	372	735	5 302	14.0	46.1	20.8	36.7	9 566	26 459	54 554	65 360	1.5	54 480	9.3	14.8	14.2
Wayne	32	284	1 478	13.4	55.7	14.1	10.7	9 814	22 127	40 024	52 783	1.2	38 981	14.2	26.5	25.5
Webster	487	3 548	9 873	16.4	44.3	19.2	50.0	9 687	24 203	41 624	56 241	1.7	45 202	15.9	22.1	22.1
Winnebago	28	237	2 712	23.3	44.6	18.6	23.9	11 050	24 547	45 603	55 970	0.8	50 383	11.1	15.6	15.0
Winneshiek	5	365	6 629	46.4	44.0	26.5	30.1	10 541	25 062	53 122	64 052	1.9	53 194	10.9	11.6	10.8
Woodbury	359	3 779	27 861	18.0	48.3	20.3	207.2	11 321	23 269	45 856	59 500	1.0	45 670	10.5	22.7	22.5
Worth	106	1 117	1 670	13.6	42.0	16.3	13.7	9 457	26 187	50 476	61 944	2.1	49 605	10.9	16.1	14.5
Wright	160	612	2 984	5.8	49.1	16.0	26.6	9 805	25 827	45 205	61 244	1.9	49 369	10.6	16.8	16.2

1. Data for serious crimes have not been adjusted for underreporting; this may affect comparability between geographic areas and over time. 2. Per 100,000 population estimated by the FBI.
3. All persons 3 years old and over enrolled in nursery school through college. 4. Persons 25 years old and over. 5. Elementary and secondary education expenditures.
6. Based on population estimated by the American Community Survey, 2009–2013.

STATE County	Personal income, 2013										Earnings, 2013		
			Per capita[1]			Supplements to wages and salaries; employer contributions (mil dol)						Contributions for government social insurance (mil dol)	
	Total (mil dol)	Percent change, 2012–2013	Dollars	Rank	Wages and salaries (mil dol)	Pension and insurance	Government social insurance	Proprietors' income (mil dol)	Dividends, interest, and rent (mil dol)	Personal transfer receipts (mil dol)	Total (mil dol)	From employee and self-employed	From employer
	62	63	64	65	66	67	68	69	70	71	72	73	74
IOWA—Cont'd													
Franklin	580	4.4	54 963	204	163	30	12	188	116	82	393	15	12
Fremont	373	4.9	52 741	277	114	19	10	104	54	68	248	11	10
Greene	453	4.0	49 552	384	122	25	10	107	92	80	263	12	10
Grundy	676	0.0	54 868	206	165	28	14	136	153	92	342	16	14
Guthrie	487	4.2	45 611	646	118	23	9	99	95	93	249	12	9
Hamilton	778	-0.1	50 796	337	205	39	16	257	133	124	517	24	16
Hancock	573	5.2	51 631	313	266	46	28	156	109	84	497	23	28
Hardin	867	0.4	49 699	379	265	52	21	228	183	148	566	26	21
Harrison	686	7.8	47 504	510	153	28	12	149	103	125	342	16	12
Henry	751	1.5	37 129	1 562	347	63	29	102	155	153	540	32	29
Howard	402	-2.2	42 167	921	140	27	13	87	92	71	267	14	13
Humboldt	507	1.1	52 290	295	146	28	12	166	82	78	352	18	12
Ida	432	3.5	60 438	100	136	24	11	153	87	58	323	13	11
Iowa	797	3.3	48 802	431	352	73	32	154	174	111	611	32	32
Jackson	750	4.1	38 302	1 398	188	36	15	98	152	158	338	21	15
Jasper	1 352	0.8	36 895	1 606	401	77	32	197	240	273	707	41	32
Jefferson	623	4.9	37 032	1 576	264	51	21	76	148	122	411	25	21
Johnson	6 338	2.7	45 549	652	3 751	877	287	464	1 297	640	5 380	286	287
Jones	741	5.4	35 962	1 753	231	43	19	111	163	150	405	23	19
Keokuk	452	3.1	43 799	773	84	17	7	100	84	83	208	11	7
Kossuth	884	-0.6	57 672	143	265	44	21	294	160	128	624	28	21
Lee	1 235	0.6	34 614	1 970	642	112	57	89	234	310	900	58	57
Linn	9 893	1.3	45 776	634	6 198	915	484	724	1 792	1 443	8 321	502	484
Louisa	448	0.9	39 709	1 202	130	26	10	60	77	79	226	12	10
Lucas	294	5.0	33 599	2 164	119	21	9	31	56	75	181	12	9
Lyon	704	3.6	60 140	102	156	28	11	277	114	69	473	17	11
Madison	628	2.9	40 647	1 093	124	24	10	89	105	103	247	13	10
Mahaska	876	2.4	39 096	1 281	289	56	24	125	150	165	494	27	24
Marion	1 297	2.3	39 012	1 298	692	112	62	93	293	237	960	58	62
Marshall	1 587	0.3	38 709	1 336	735	129	60	140	286	353	1 064	64	60
Mills	755	5.1	50 716	339	161	35	12	124	96	195	331	17	12
Mitchell	609	0.0	56 861	162	143	26	12	253	100	81	433	21	12
Monona	446	15.6	48 941	420	92	17	7	143	83	83	259	10	7
Monroe	303	4.7	37 805	1 462	151	26	12	27	46	62	216	13	12
Montgomery	458	5.0	43 904	766	157	30	12	97	85	102	296	15	12
Muscatine	1 872	0.9	43 691	783	1 013	157	87	305	319	307	1 562	92	87
O'Brien	748	5.1	53 253	259	204	39	16	203	153	122	462	20	16
Osceola	337	3.6	54 204	228	79	14	6	123	60	44	223	7	6
Page	610	4.4	38 838	1 314	212	42	17	105	123	141	376	21	17
Palo Alto	519	-2.6	56 458	177	124	25	9	214	79	75	372	14	9
Plymouth	1 369	7.3	54 841	208	452	77	35	390	230	166	954	44	35
Pocahontas	385	-2.3	53 750	243	104	19	9	120	71	61	252	10	9
Polk	21 734	2.1	48 118	471	14 353	1 995	1 104	2 847	3 396	2 800	20 297	1 194	1 104
Pottawattamie	3 787	2.6	40 841	1 074	1 467	239	123	421	553	753	2 250	136	123
Poweshiek	819	1.3	44 003	757	388	61	33	127	164	131	609	33	33
Ringgold	191	9.2	37 752	1 468	48	11	4	39	40	47	102	6	4
Sac	563	2.5	55 891	189	120	22	9	184	113	84	336	14	9
Scott	8 023	-0.7	47 090	550	3 725	556	304	727	1 330	1 411	5 312	322	304
Shelby	683	9.7	57 080	155	217	41	17	174	125	108	448	20	17
Sioux	1 679	3.9	48 603	444	703	123	55	460	334	189	1 341	61	55
Story	3 821	0.5	41 349	1 011	1 939	448	145	449	793	444	2 981	162	145
Tama	729	-2.4	41 483	995	171	35	13	153	137	134	372	17	13
Taylor	296	8.8	48 088	475	67	13	5	100	40	54	185	7	5
Union	473	4.5	37 610	1 488	234	46	19	61	77	104	360	21	19
Van Buren	251	1.0	33 719	2 141	67	15	5	40	52	60	127	7	5
Wapello	1 233	1.9	34 839	1 925	616	109	50	95	184	325	870	56	50
Warren	2 065	1.9	43 623	788	365	67	30	92	299	290	555	38	30
Washington	1 023	0.9	46 455	594	280	53	23	173	194	164	528	29	23
Wayne	223	12.8	34 815	1 927	66	16	5	30	45	57	118	7	5
Webster	1 584	1.3	42 756	865	762	132	63	279	279	307	1 235	69	63
Winnebago	428	-0.8	40 550	1 107	150	28	12	64	96	84	254	14	12
Winneshiek	892	3.7	42 486	890	371	68	30	153	195	140	622	34	30
Woodbury	3 896	3.4	38 148	1 417	1 954	328	160	453	619	734	2 895	170	160
Worth	302	-2.5	40 097	1 162	76	15	6	57	60	55	155	8	6
Wright	686	4.7	52 880	272	231	43	19	187	122	117	480	20	19

1. Based on the resident population estimated as of July 1 of the year shown.

STATE County	Earnings, 2013 (cont.) — Percent by selected industries: Farm	Mining	Construction	Manu-facturing	Infor-mation: professional, scientific, technical services	Retail trade	Finance, insur-ance, real estate and leasing	Health care and social assistance	Govern-ment	Social Security beneficiaries, December 2013: Number	Rate[1]	Supple-mental Security Income recipients, December 2013	Housing units, 2014: Total	Percent change, 2010–2014
	75	76	77	78	79	80	81	82	83	84	85	86	87	88
IOWA—Cont'd														
Franklin	41.5	D	6.6	13.4	1.7	3.1	2.5	3.3	10.0	2 430	231	119	4 860	-0.7
Fremont	31.4	0.0	2.0	22.9	D	11.5	2.4	D	9.0	1 925	273	166	3 445	0.4
Greene	32.1	D	3.8	16.1	3.5	4.1	4.6	D	16.2	2 400	262	159	4 533	-0.3
Grundy	33.8	0.0	11.8	5.6	D	4.5	4.8	D	10.0	2 880	234	86	5 549	0.3
Guthrie	35.9	0.0	8.4	5.4	2.9	3.2	8.1	5.4	17.9	2 915	273	146	5 749	-0.1
Hamilton	24.9	D	4.3	27.8	3.0	3.9	3.4	4.0	11.9	3 605	235	213	7 184	-0.5
Hancock	23.3	D	2.7	39.9	1.1	2.3	1.9	D	6.9	2 560	231	118	5 308	-0.4
Hardin	29.9	D	4.9	12.2	2.7	4.6	3.3	D	15.5	4 275	245	235	8 175	-0.6
Harrison	34.5	D	4.2	5.1	2.8	5.5	3.3	D	13.0	3 310	229	232	6 747	0.2
Henry	7.1	D	4.0	25.7	D	5.4	3.0	D	19.1	4 520	224	340	8 274	-0.1
Howard	22.0	0.0	7.3	25.3	D	6.5	4.1	D	13.7	2 210	232	96	4 365	0.0
Humboldt	17.1	D	5.1	35.9	2.1	4.0	2.2	D	9.5	2 360	244	148	4 684	0.0
Ida	34.4	0.0	4.0	28.9	0.9	2.8	3.8	6.3	5.8	1 740	244	62	3 430	0.1
Iowa	10.9	D	5.7	47.6	D	5.5	1.6	D	8.5	3 545	217	147	7 267	0.1
Jackson	18.7	0.0	5.9	12.6	3.7	9.0	4.8	7.6	16.1	4 770	244	370	9 458	0.5
Jasper	17.5	D	5.8	17.0	6.1	5.8	3.7	6.1	20.1	8 490	231	535	16 160	-0.1
Jefferson	6.3	D	3.8	13.6	10.4	7.8	13.3	6.0	14.7	3 715	215	328	7 542	-0.7
Johnson	1.9	D	4.4	6.9	6.8	5.3	3.9	7.0	45.1	16 640	119	1 611	58 783	5.0
Jones	20.3	D	8.6	12.5	D	8.3	3.2	7.9	18.4	4 590	224	251	8 907	0.0
Keokuk	29.3	D	5.7	4.5	D	8.3	3.0	4.7	13.5	2 490	241	203	4 886	-0.9
Kossuth	29.9	0.2	4.7	23.2	3.1	4.2	6.0	D	9.1	4 155	272	197	7 481	-0.1
Lee	2.0	0.2	6.5	32.9	D	7.0	3.3	12.0	14.6	8 590	243	993	16 173	-0.2
Linn	1.0	0.1	6.2	22.2	9.1	7.0	10.8	10.6	10.4	39 005	181	3 525	94 663	2.6
Louisa	19.3	D	3.8	28.6	D	2.9	2.5	D	17.3	2 290	203	192	5 006	0.1
Lucas	5.1	0.0	6.6	4.7	2.6	6.4	3.7	D	20.6	2 145	246	215	4 204	-0.8
Lyon	39.6	D	4.4	21.0	D	2.4	2.3	3.3	6.6	2 220	190	56	4 965	2.4
Madison	22.7	1.1	10.4	7.8	4.0	6.3	5.4	5.6	20.5	3 155	204	133	6 684	2.0
Mahaska	16.5	D	5.6	20.0	3.5	6.1	2.9	5.7	17.2	4 765	213	468	9 726	-0.4
Marion	4.7	D	4.5	46.2	D	4.8	2.8	10.6	9.4	6 965	210	406	13 984	0.5
Marshall	7.3	D	4.7	29.8	D	5.5	2.8	10.3	18.7	8 865	216	719	16 718	-0.7
Mills	22.2	D	5.6	4.5	D	7.9	4.2	D	29.2	3 240	217	268	6 088	-0.3
Mitchell	18.5	D	7.3	42.8	1.1	3.6	2.3	D	8.2	2 595	242	113	4 916	1.4
Monona	48.3	0.0	3.6	1.9	D	4.5	D	11.4	10.6	2 540	279	128	4 715	0.4
Monroe	5.1	D	6.4	41.5	D	4.4	3.0	4.3	14.0	1 875	235	121	3 892	0.2
Montgomery	26.8	D	5.2	12.9	5.6	4.9	3.2	D	17.8	2 755	264	260	5 200	-0.7
Muscatine	2.1	0.1	3.8	44.3	5.8	5.2	2.3	5.7	10.1	8 435	197	752	17 996	0.5
O'Brien	34.1	0.0	4.3	10.4	D	4.5	4.0	9.6	10.9	3 470	247	208	6 635	-0.2
Osceola	55.5	D	3.9	7.5	D	2.0	D	4.7	7.3	1 475	237	72	2 968	-0.7
Page	19.4	D	4.0	14.5	D	7.0	3.2	D	21.4	4 065	261	360	7 186	0.1
Palo Alto	38.8	0.0	2.1	23.2	1.3	3.3	2.4	D	12.5	2 195	239	120	4 617	-0.2
Plymouth	26.4	D	3.6	22.3	D	3.6	3.5	3.6	8.5	5 125	206	225	10 668	1.1
Pocahontas	44.3	D	4.6	11.0	1.9	3.5	D	D	11.8	1 850	259	92	3 771	-0.6
Polk	0.2	D	8.2	5.9	10.3	5.2	22.2	10.4	12.6	69 320	153	7 687	192 980	5.9
Pottawattamie	7.0	0.2	7.8	16.3	3.8	7.7	4.0	12.7	15.0	18 600	200	2 150	39 589	0.7
Poweshiek	14.1	D	8.0	15.0	D	4.1	9.5	D	7.7	4 085	219	212	8 953	0.0
Ringgold	26.3	D	12.1	D	D	5.1	D	7.8	24.7	1 360	270	114	2 605	-0.3
Sac	39.0	D	2.9	15.9	D	2.9	D	D	8.9	2 575	256	91	5 407	-0.4
Scott	0.9	0.0	7.4	17.0	8.9	8.8	5.9	12.9	10.1	31 440	184	3 898	73 040	1.7
Shelby	30.8	0.8	3.9	10.2	5.4	3.7	3.7	D	12.3	3 185	267	186	5 561	0.3
Sioux	24.3	0.2	5.9	26.4	3.3	3.8	3.8	5.2	8.3	5 610	162	184	12 582	2.5
Story	2.3	D	5.2	17.5	6.5	4.7	3.0	6.9	39.1	11 925	128	678	38 103	3.6
Tama	35.4	0.0	5.2	4.7	D	3.7	2.4	D	25.9	4 100	234	198	7 753	-0.2
Taylor	51.3	D	2.7	12.5	D	1.9	D	D	10.5	1 620	262	92	3 091	-0.5
Union	9.7	D	5.6	23.7	D	6.5	3.7	5.8	21.4	2 970	236	277	5 907	-0.5
Van Buren	24.2	D	D	23.2	D	4.8	2.9	2.8	21.5	1 905	256	118	3 623	-1.3
Wapello	1.5	D	6.3	30.6	2.5	7.7	3.3	13.6	16.3	8 220	232	1 112	16 019	-0.5
Warren	3.6	0.0	11.4	6.2	6.2	9.1	5.3	10.9	22.8	8 535	180	390	19 162	4.3
Washington	16.3	D	11.3	16.2	2.4	7.1	3.6	6.5	14.5	4 925	224	346	9 540	0.3
Wayne	15.4	0.0	D	22.8	D	4.7	D	4.1	28.4	1 710	267	131	3 181	-1.0
Webster	9.9	0.4	9.4	21.1	4.0	6.1	2.7	11.9	13.7	8 490	228	797	17 035	0.0
Winnebago	20.3	D	8.1	15.9	4.0	6.6	4.4	D	14.6	2 605	248	120	5 183	-0.2
Winneshiek	12.7	D	7.2	16.0	D	7.1	3.2	D	16.5	4 390	210	192	8 813	1.0
Woodbury	5.7	D	9.9	11.0	4.5	8.3	4.6	15.5	14.7	18 735	183	1 978	41 510	0.1
Worth	28.0	0.8	5.6	12.2	1.1	3.2	D	3.4	14.7	1 720	228	86	3 523	-0.7
Wright	37.5	D	3.1	18.2	3.9	3.0	2.3	2.8	16.4	3 255	251	101	6 404	-0.5

1. Per 1,000 resident population estimated as of July 1 of the year shown.

STATE County	Housing units, 2009–2013: Occupied units: Total	Owner-occupied: Percent	Owner-occupied: Median value[1]	Median owner cost as a percent of income: With a mortgage	Median owner cost as a percent of income: Without a mortgage[2]	Renter-occupied: Median rent[3]	Renter-occupied: Median rent as a percent of income[2]	Substandard units[4] (percent)	Civilian labor force, 2014: Total	Percent change, 2013–2014	Unemployment: Total	Unemployment: Rate[5]	Civilian employment,[6] 2009–2013: Total	Percent: Management, business, science and arts	Percent: Construction, production, and maintenance occupations
	89	90	91	92	93	94	95	96	97	98	99	100	101	102	103
IOWA—Cont'd															
Franklin	4 358	73.7	87 500	19.3	10.2	525	20.2	0.8	6 034	2.1	250	4.1	5 235	25.9	36.9
Fremont	2 965	77.5	94 100	19.2	11.3	575	25.1	1.5	4 184	1.4	170	4.1	3 463	35.8	27.0
Greene	3 969	76.0	78 200	21.9	11.3	610	24.0	0.8	5 340	4.3	221	4.1	4 356	32.0	28.6
Grundy	5 073	81.9	123 700	19.2	11.1	549	25.2	1.5	6 736	2.1	294	4.4	6 093	31.2	30.7
Guthrie	4 641	80.4	97 100	19.9	11.8	545	26.7	1.8	5 701	3.1	256	4.5	5 280	31.9	27.8
Hamilton	6 395	71.0	91 400	20.8	12.1	607	26.2	1.2	7 146	1.5	339	4.7	7 198	30.6	33.5
Hancock	4 648	80.1	85 300	19.6	10.8	530	24.9	0.7	6 329	1.9	217	3.4	5 552	29.9	35.4
Hardin	7 061	74.4	89 900	18.2	12.0	564	22.2	1.2	8 782	1.0	393	4.5	8 088	32.2	31.0
Harrison	5 996	77.2	108 200	20.3	11.6	607	27.3	2.5	7 691	2.5	318	4.1	7 304	32.3	28.8
Henry	7 493	74.0	103 700	20.9	12.2	587	29.9	1.9	9 596	0.5	438	4.6	9 096	29.4	29.7
Howard	3 884	79.8	91 800	21.9	11.7	553	33.0	0.6	5 363	2.6	227	4.2	4 858	28.0	36.4
Humboldt	4 222	76.7	84 900	18.6	10.5	574	24.2	1.2	5 284	1.3	209	4.0	4 726	32.1	31.8
Ida	3 182	73.3	76 400	17.1	10.0	410	21.4	2.4	3 915	2.7	147	3.8	3 559	32.3	33.1
Iowa	6 745	79.7	138 000	21.1	11.0	527	20.9	0.9	10 266	3.4	446	4.3	8 846	32.7	29.4
Jackson	8 479	76.2	110 000	21.2	12.3	564	28.6	1.7	11 042	1.8	582	5.3	9 953	26.5	35.6
Jasper	14 826	71.3	113 100	22.8	11.1	629	26.6	1.7	19 463	2.1	896	4.6	17 255	29.5	30.4
Jefferson	6 919	71.9	92 400	19.7	10.5	602	25.6	2.3	9 104	2.0	409	4.5	8 181	38.5	22.4
Johnson	54 005	59.7	186 000	21.3	10.7	819	34.8	0.5	84 241	1.9	2 669	3.2	75 636	44.9	15.3
Jones	8 063	80.2	122 100	20.8	11.8	598	23.4	2.2	10 903	1.6	560	5.1	10 086	29.2	32.2
Keokuk	4 354	80.6	75 700	19.6	12.8	517	27.8	1.7	5 598	2.2	256	4.6	4 883	27.9	32.5
Kossuth	6 728	80.5	91 100	18.8	10.0	552	23.3	1.9	8 690	2.6	292	3.4	7 853	32.9	29.2
Lee	14 241	73.9	83 100	19.6	11.8	572	26.1	1.5	17 693	3.2	1 108	6.3	16 336	24.4	35.1
Linn	86 052	73.0	144 300	20.0	12.3	672	27.0	6.5	120 339	0.6	5 521	4.6	112 075	37.6	20.8
Louisa	4 381	78.6	95 400	22.1	11.8	618	22.1	3.5	5 965	2.0	280	4.7	5 418	26.1	41.5
Lucas	3 734	77.5	82 700	21.1	13.6	449	26.6	1.8	4 323	1.9	176	4.1	3 865	23.1	29.6
Lyon	4 425	82.3	105 700	19.7	10.0	542	21.4	1.7	7 074	3.3	187	2.6	5 880	33.7	28.4
Madison	6 092	76.8	160 700	21.8	13.2	755	25.4	1.2	8 320	2.9	389	4.7	7 752	36.7	25.1
Mahaska	9 073	70.5	100 900	20.8	11.3	560	26.6	1.4	11 938	2.5	544	4.6	10 917	29.4	30.9
Marion	12 691	75.8	132 000	20.8	11.1	652	25.2	2.8	17 534	1.3	694	4.0	16 913	34.4	25.5
Marshall	15 350	73.4	105 400	20.6	12.1	622	24.9	1.9	20 008	1.1	1 120	5.6	19 117	29.9	33.2
Mills	5 375	83.7	149 400	21.8	10.6	766	24.0	1.9	7 528	2.8	338	4.5	7 053	33.8	26.5
Mitchell	4 389	81.4	108 100	19.3	11.0	501	23.5	0.8	5 522	0.3	202	3.7	5 252	30.4	37.0
Monona	3 981	70.7	77 800	17.4	10.9	517	25.0	3.7	4 790	3.6	249	5.2	4 170	28.9	29.1
Monroe	3 361	75.5	95 200	18.4	12.9	541	22.6	1.5	4 109	2.1	215	5.2	3 791	34.6	32.0
Montgomery	4 553	71.8	79 600	19.1	11.7	565	26.4	2.1	5 187	1.3	223	4.3	4 803	31.2	27.8
Muscatine	16 410	74.9	124 400	20.9	12.5	716	30.6	1.3	22 164	2.2	1 046	4.7	20 854	26.8	34.8
O'Brien	6 098	74.9	93 000	18.4	10.0	538	22.1	2.2	8 230	2.4	282	3.4	7 327	29.0	31.4
Osceola	2 676	74.9	75 600	17.8	10.0	547	22.8	2.7	3 461	1.6	120	3.5	3 379	30.6	36.0
Page	6 415	73.2	77 700	18.5	11.4	553	24.3	0.8	6 639	1.3	308	4.6	7 194	33.2	29.1
Palo Alto	3 948	77.2	83 400	19.3	10.5	469	24.9	0.5	4 859	1.8	184	3.8	4 599	29.7	29.5
Plymouth	9 867	79.3	129 800	18.3	10.0	589	22.5	1.1	14 827	2.4	526	3.5	13 418	31.4	29.4
Pocahontas	3 227	79.4	60 600	17.3	10.9	504	21.8	2.8	4 383	4.6	158	3.6	3 524	33.3	31.2
Polk	173 164	69.2	154 400	21.2	11.5	779	28.2	2.4	256 666	2.5	11 207	4.4	232 170	39.3	17.4
Pottawattamie	36 460	70.2	126 300	21.4	11.8	738	28.7	0.6	49 647	2.1	2 197	4.4	46 744	29.2	25.1
Poweshiek	7 488	72.9	117 600	21.3	11.0	606	27.8	2.9	10 379	0.4	462	4.5	9 500	35.3	24.0
Ringgold	2 074	76.5	78 500	19.8	13.0	458	18.6	1.8	2 548	1.4	102	4.0	2 220	37.2	32.1
Sac	4 435	81.4	79 700	18.2	10.5	537	22.4	1.0	5 585	1.3	228	4.1	5 147	29.3	29.2
Scott	67 049	69.0	143 600	20.2	11.3	685	28.7	0.5	88 327	0.6	4 808	5.4	80 912	36.1	22.8
Shelby	5 083	77.7	104 700	20.9	11.4	612	26.5	2.3	7 068	1.9	230	3.3	6 097	31.7	27.8
Sioux	11 623	80.0	131 200	19.8	10.0	587	21.8	1.8	20 260	3.6	616	3.0	18 618	31.9	29.0
Story	35 196	55.0	162 200	20.5	10.0	738	34.6	1.8	56 826	3.8	1 669	2.9	48 954	44.4	17.7
Tama	6 794	74.7	101 300	19.6	10.9	651	25.4	2.6	9 217	1.2	512	5.6	8 274	29.2	31.0
Taylor	2 764	76.2	66 400	19.4	11.0	582	25.4	1.6	3 266	3.2	125	3.8	3 071	30.9	36.1
Union	5 339	73.2	91 600	20.0	14.2	600	32.0	4.3	6 858	-0.5	336	4.9	6 264	25.8	35.3
Van Buren	3 023	85.8	69 700	20.9	12.7	506	24.1	2.2	3 926	2.4	185	4.7	3 461	25.3	36.7
Wapello	14 534	72.8	78 800	19.8	13.0	604	30.7	1.4	18 264	0.7	1 046	5.7	16 212	25.0	37.0
Warren	17 378	78.7	154 100	20.5	11.8	730	25.5	1.6	26 998	2.5	1 100	4.1	24 848	35.9	19.7
Washington	8 948	75.7	121 800	22.2	11.9	070	26.7	3.3	12 676	2.5	463	3.7	11 445	33.4	26.0
Wayne	2 589	82.7	62 300	19.8	13.1	487	25.2	0.9	2 896	1.6	151	5.2	2 762	33.0	36.1
Webster	15 458	68.5	84 300	18.6	10.5	546	26.6	0.8	19 887	0.7	1 003	5.0	17 436	28.7	27.2
Winnebago	4 591	76.1	91 900	18.9	11.7	497	22.7	0.5	5 256	1.8	230	4.4	5 395	28.9	31.3
Winneshiek	8 042	77.3	151 500	22.1	11.8	577	25.4	2.7	12 149	2.2	537	4.4	11 842	35.5	25.4
Woodbury	38 654	67.7	97 900	19.9	11.4	643	29.8	2.0	56 358	2.1	2 563	4.5	51 034	27.1	29.5
Worth	3 197	81.1	96 900	19.4	11.6	553	25.2	1.8	4 224	1.0	198	4.7	3 956	27.5	33.7
Wright	5 367	77.4	71 700	18.2	10.8	506	22.2	0.9	7 006	2.4	299	4.3	6 238	30.6	30.8

1. Specified owner-occupied units. 2. A value of 10.0 represents 10 percent or less; a value of 50.0 represents 50 percent or more. 3. Specified renter-occupied units.
4. Overcrowded or lacking complete plumbing facilities. 5. Percent of civilian labor force. 6. Persons 16 years old and over.

Table B. States and Counties — **Nonfarm Employment and Agriculture**

STATE County	Private nonfarm establishments, employment and payroll, 2013									Agriculture, 2012			
		Employment						Annual payroll		Farms			
											Percent with:		
	Number of establish- ments	Total	Health care and social assistance	Manufac- turing	Retail trade	Finance and insurance	Professional, scientific, and technical services	Total (mil dol)	Average per employee (dollars)	Number	Fewer than 50 acres	500 acres or more	Farm operators whose principal occu- pation is farming (percent)
	104	105	106	107	108	109	110	111	112	113	114	115	116
IOWA—Cont'd													
Franklin	334	3 131	570	804	320	99	72	122	38 822	853	29.9	29.3	54.3
Fremont	187	2 210	377	575	641	67	38	76	34 541	533	27.0	32.8	62.3
Greene	261	2 697	D	370	353	118	73	92	33 992	780	31.0	30.5	60.8
Grundy	308	3 285	699	536	418	D	34	133	40 413	737	33.0	27.0	56.3
Guthrie	323	2 650	D	372	362	258	70	87	32 743	829	29.2	24.2	53.3
Hamilton	383	4 304	665	670	698	171	111	146	33 853	761	36.4	27.1	56.6
Hancock	309	3 197	534	1 008	411	78	154	107	33 570	889	32.2	28.0	65.8
Hardin	565	5 394	1 044	563	859	263	172	199	36 844	819	31.3	28.0	54.1
Harrison	357	3 060	862	D	507	132	83	93	30 233	819	28.2	32.5	57.4
Henry	514	7 980	1 143	2 437	870	172	141	264	33 066	903	31.3	16.4	47.5
Howard	256	2 808	534	910	390	D	45	85	30 392	883	30.2	19.3	51.4
Humboldt	324	3 394	443	1 019	514	124	62	119	35 021	574	28.6	30.1	52.4
Ida	248	2 865	475	1 022	296	D	D	111	38 912	547	30.2	30.5	55.4
Iowa	487	7 775	834	D	1 382	121	D	291	37 392	1 019	32.0	17.0	48.4
Jackson	545	4 892	865	868	876	255	82	138	28 278	1 255	29.6	12.7	47.4
Jasper	746	8 706	1 582	D	1 392	332	440	268	30 819	1 098	34.9	21.8	52.8
Jefferson	670	6 855	667	1 112	929	767	694	228	33 324	685	29.6	15.6	46.3
Johnson	3 186	59 466	16 001	5 138	9 029	1 974	2 087	2 355	39 595	1 342	34.7	14.7	50.2
Jones	503	4 877	845	893	1 005	202	114	150	30 754	1 061	28.8	20.8	53.3
Keokuk	250	1 685	390	224	199	113	D	58	34 396	982	27.2	20.0	47.5
Kossuth	571	5 699	D	1 304	908	486	174	203	35 657	1 349	25.0	33.5	67.4
Lee	912	13 010	2 234	3 937	2 083	D	196	453	34 850	917	32.4	16.4	42.6
Linn	5 415	115 744	15 898	16 927	14 609	9 187	5 728	5 176	44 723	1 402	37.4	15.5	58.6
Louisa	217	2 887	377	D	210	80	D	98	34 118	612	34.3	18.1	43.0
Lucas	179	2 772	544	D	436	84	34	99	35 628	648	25.0	14.8	37.7
Lyon	389	3 344	422	D	409	156	118	109	32 663	1 139	25.2	21.3	62.6
Madison	354	2 450	582	153	488	124	89	78	31 652	961	37.3	15.7	40.9
Mahaska	576	6 881	1 039	1 329	1 154	194	125	233	33 850	1 012	30.4	22.6	48.7
Marion	810	15 685	2 313	D	1 500	310	320	614	39 132	1 024	38.3	16.0	39.9
Marshall	792	14 459	2 101	D	2 086	D	300	549	38 000	882	34.4	25.3	60.1
Mills	294	2 089	614	35	346	106	D	66	31 413	500	32.0	30.8	61.4
Mitchell	326	3 097	565	979	373	121	D	99	32 126	903	29.1	24.9	65.7
Monona	233	2 086	640	D	402	117	D	61	29 408	538	19.5	39.2	65.8
Monroe	173	1 895	459	455	295	74	39	53	27 778	592	24.2	17.1	34.8
Montgomery	308	3 056	738	451	542	124	D	100	32 684	499	21.2	34.1	62.3
Muscatine	940	19 720	2 078	6 749	2 176	415	D	899	45 564	786	34.4	18.1	51.4
O'Brien	506	5 345	1 392	563	932	216	186	145	27 172	884	24.8	25.1	61.3
Osceola	183	1 526	277	D	168	82	28	49	32 092	555	22.2	33.0	71.4
Page	416	5 313	1 426	D	656	178	120	172	32 343	739	20.7	29.1	58.9
Palo Alto	278	2 802	729	484	392	D	46	84	30 127	874	31.5	27.0	54.6
Plymouth	703	9 761	1 413	2 360	1 007	308	D	390	39 973	1 331	24.0	28.8	67.8
Pocahontas	222	2 021	244	365	234	98	50	60	29 886	742	25.6	34.9	72.0
Polk	11 914	243 983	33 958	16 644	29 276	35 392	14 256	11 376	46 625	773	51.2	16.0	51.5
Pottawattamie	1 986	30 845	4 920	5 125	6 131	777	718	1 000	32 411	1 188	29.5	30.3	66.2
Poweshiek	549	9 458	1 056	1 596	1 136	D	113	325	34 396	852	27.6	24.8	55.4
Ringgold	144	1 022	373	D	211	48	D	28	27 669	651	20.4	24.9	46.2
Sac	353	2 624	569	404	360	135	51	81	31 010	914	32.5	28.9	53.9
Scott	4 408	82 196	12 884	11 147	11 718	2 665	2 841	3 070	37 346	759	35.4	18.7	55.3
Shelby	398	5 209	955	539	577	250	190	175	33 670	869	21.7	33.1	65.0
Sioux	1 233	17 949	2 583	5 267	1 623	D	897	611	34 049	1 618	31.4	19.2	61.0
Story	2 006	30 774	5 106	4 967	5 012	733	1 220	1 106	35 952	966	42.8	20.9	49.1
Tama	341	3 564	471	364	522	122	66	120	33 678	1 132	29.7	24.1	62.4
Taylor	134	1 594	252	567	130	40	33	57	35 756	639	25.2	22.1	44.4
Union	334	5 025	859	1 434	763	200	71	158	31 360	648	33.0	16.7	44.3
Van Buren	155	1 859	309	D	190	D	22	59	31 917	753	27.2	14.1	48.2
Wapello	758	14 912	2 842	4 324	2 351	388	270	511	34 271	742	31.4	15.0	45.0
Warren	773	7 742	1 199	339	1 504	253	315	220	28 447	1 334	43.4	10.0	37.3
Washington	705	6 828	1 228	1 020	1 060	218	D	204	29 817	1 139	31.3	17.3	53.8
Wayne	146	1 381	D	423	195	31	39	45	32 403	691	27.4	21.3	43.0
Webster	1 032	15 629	2 925	1 521	2 617	403	D	569	36 386	968	29.8	29.3	64.2
Winnebago	329	6 152	618	D	511	176	213	227	36 969	642	34.0	26.2	52.5
Winneshiek	619	9 585	1 389	1 390	1 220	259	174	201	30 300	1 505	33.4	15.2	49.1
Woodbury	2 692	45 624	8 818	5 160	7 457	1 411	945	1 517	33 253	973	28.5	28.6	58.6
Worth	172	1 790	177	449	163	59	D	52	28 955	640	33.4	28.0	54.5
Wright	390	3 908	940	987	538	130	123	133	33 999	775	34.2	32.8	61.3

STATE County	Agriculture, 2012 (cont.) — Land in farms — Acreage (1,000)	Land in farms — Percent change, 2007–2012	Land in farms — Acres — Average size of farm	Land in farms — Acres — Total irrigated (1,000)	Land in farms — Acres — Total cropland (1,000)	Value of land and buildings (dollars) — Average per farm	Value of land and buildings (dollars) — Average per acre	Value of machinery and equipment, average per farm (dollars)	Value of products sold — Total (mil dol)	Value of products sold — Average per farm (dollars)	Value of products sold — Percent from: Crops	Value of products sold — Percent from: Livestock and poultry products	Percent of farms with sales of: $10,000 or more	Percent of farms with sales of: $100,000 or more	Government payments — Total ($1,000)	Government payments — Percent of farms
	117	118	119	120	121	122	123	124	125	126	127	128	129	130	131	132
IOWA—Cont'd																
Franklin	355	-3.1	417	D	336.7	2 769 033	6 646	259 810	454.4	532 687	55.9	44.1	69.3	51.9	9 424	83.0
Fremont	287	17.2	539	8.5	253.9	3 311 917	6 141	274 623	180.4	338 409	89.6	10.4	62.7	46.5	5 009	83.1
Greene	357	0.9	458	D	325.6	3 185 444	6 962	289 094	308.1	395 058	67.7	32.3	65.3	47.9	7 356	82.3
Grundy	318	0.7	432	0.0	301.1	3 465 753	8 031	330 237	362.7	492 126	76.6	23.4	69.2	56.9	7 556	82.8
Guthrie	328	-7.7	395	D	262.2	2 291 450	5 798	193 695	257.5	310 555	52.5	47.5	55.9	31.8	8 272	81.3
Hamilton	327	-5.6	430	D	305.1	3 489 958	8 121	268 636	540.4	710 103	44.2	55.8	64.9	50.2	9 809	80.0
Hancock	353	-2.1	397	1.2	338.4	2 765 206	6 957	268 795	475.1	534 388	49.3	50.7	69.0	51.6	8 438	86.6
Hardin	332	-2.0	406	0.0	306.2	2 996 061	7 385	272 880	534.5	652 620	48.8	51.2	66.3	50.5	9 829	80.0
Harrison	394	7.8	481	29.1	343.3	2 799 425	5 824	257 150	249.2	304 277	85.9	14.1	64.2	44.1	7 528	83.9
Henry	270	12.5	299	0.0	220.7	1 471 299	4 929	145 765	171.8	190 219	70.4	29.6	45.4	27.5	8 270	82.5
Howard	300	7.6	340	0.2	273.3	2 239 316	6 593	243 708	322.3	365 058	57.3	42.7	62.7	41.0	9 932	81.9
Humboldt	235	-13.1	409	0.0	220.1	3 120 220	7 627	258 958	242.1	421 793	70.1	29.9	72.5	57.1	6 158	81.9
Ida	261	-4.3	477	D	234.1	3 237 473	6 786	276 272	272.2	497 678	60.1	39.9	72.8	53.9	7 024	83.7
Iowa	336	-2.6	330	D	275.5	1 996 335	6 053	170 894	276.9	271 734	64.8	35.2	58.5	36.3	8 803	80.0
Jackson	309	4.2	246	0.2	214.2	1 312 333	5 331	150 764	236.1	188 110	45.6	54.4	58.1	26.8	8 990	76.2
Jasper	374	-12.7	340	0.8	324.8	2 115 648	6 217	209 787	327.0	297 853	76.7	23.3	63.2	42.5	7 997	74.4
Jefferson	198	0.4	289	0.1	153.4	1 328 096	4 591	134 391	104.1	151 991	70.2	29.8	43.8	22.6	6 713	78.4
Johnson	329	2.3	245	0.2	285.1	1 682 142	6 868	154 571	258.3	192 443	67.9	32.1	58.7	34.1	8 623	67.7
Jones	314	-3.1	296	0.1	255.7	1 982 445	6 699	205 726	276.2	260 306	59.6	40.4	65.7	39.2	9 960	80.5
Keokuk	295	-7.1	301	0.0	240.6	1 499 580	4 984	164 024	230.8	234 996	57.0	43.0	54.9	33.2	12 904	85.0
Kossuth	599	-0.3	444	0.3	568.6	3 380 844	7 608	295 763	722.3	535 440	64.2	35.8	74.9	62.1	13 183	87.5
Lee	236	-0.9	257	1.1	172.3	1 098 520	4 268	114 699	130.1	141 845	70.7	29.3	49.5	23.8	5 417	72.5
Linn	339	1.2	242	0.2	292.6	1 626 668	6 722	173 044	260.8	185 998	76.1	23.9	58.3	30.0	8 202	72.7
Louisa	169	-9.4	275	9.9	139.5	1 581 547	5 743	187 708	172.5	281 889	60.8	39.2	53.8	33.5	5 560	77.8
Lucas	177	3.6	274	D	101.5	786 495	2 874	99 623	51.1	78 872	47.7	52.3	42.1	15.3	4 571	73.6
Lyon	370	14.5	325	1.5	334.0	2 677 244	8 245	275 852	836.1	734 068	30.7	69.3	87.4	65.6	7 064	79.0
Madison	276	-2.6	287	0.1	184.1	1 408 613	4 903	122 793	132.9	138 322	65.2	34.8	47.9	19.9	5 013	65.9
Mahaska	323	9.4	319	0.1	273.9	1 794 609	5 623	204 132	311.1	307 382	54.9	45.1	60.8	36.9	11 369	79.8
Marion	265	7.6	259	0.1	200.0	1 154 279	4 462	117 525	137.9	134 660	80.5	19.5	46.4	22.4	6 603	72.3
Marshall	312	-3.7	354	0.2	280.6	2 345 805	6 623	227 533	313.1	354 966	75.1	24.9	63.7	45.7	7 063	76.1
Mills	206	4.8	413	D	182.3	2 606 084	6 316	242 756	120.6	241 170	95.4	4.6	59.8	44.2	4 403	77.6
Mitchell	296	0.7	328	1.0	272.8	2 418 524	7 372	214 307	363.4	402 482	47.0	53.0	73.6	51.9	6 663	75.0
Monona	338	-14.1	629	61.1	300.6	3 451 381	5 491	370 487	221.3	411 253	86.6	13.4	73.6	51.9	5 639	82.0
Monroe	195	-3.0	330	D	111.8	1 045 139	3 171	95 228	59.0	99 581	55.3	44.7	49.3	17.2	3 873	70.9
Montgomery	245	11.1	491	0.4	207.4	2 753 371	5 610	272 595	189.4	379 615	71.3	28.7	71.1	47.9	4 831	82.8
Muscatine	215	-3.1	274	7.4	183.2	1 720 141	6 289	166 092	187.3	238 233	72.5	27.5	56.4	35.1	6 401	76.0
O'Brien	304	-11.9	344	0.9	276.5	2 940 939	8 538	244 251	533.4	603 437	43.4	56.6	84.8	66.9	5 935	81.9
Osceola	238	-5.2	429	1.3	223.3	3 021 315	7 039	277 225	410.6	739 865	42.8	57.2	81.8	66.5	5 504	86.8
Page	317	16.9	429	0.2	263.0	2 158 371	5 031	221 513	198.3	268 369	81.6	18.4	70.5	44.8	6 816	83.8
Palo Alto	359	1.5	410	4.8	340.8	3 088 190	7 523	288 436	498.6	570 531	55.0	45.0	65.7	50.2	8 245	86.3
Plymouth	542	4.7	407	2.0	479.8	2 992 740	7 352	280 373	643.1	483 173	40.8	59.2	77.9	51.8	11 860	80.5
Pocahontas	332	-8.4	448	0.6	317.5	3 416 818	7 635	309 951	406.7	548 144	64.8	35.2	76.7	61.7	9 485	90.3
Polk	198	-20.8	256	0.5	178.6	1 802 039	7 052	169 371	153.9	199 128	92.3	7.7	54.5	27.0	4 768	62.0
Pottawattamie	533	9.6	449	3.9	481.8	3 154 295	7 033	280 880	464.5	391 035	70.1	29.9	67.3	47.6	9 377	72.9
Poweshiek	334	6.9	393	0.0	286.8	2 386 670	6 080	231 304	350.4	411 247	60.1	39.9	64.9	42.3	7 393	79.3
Ringgold	270	1.8	414	D	178.8	1 417 304	3 420	149 154	116.6	179 161	41.8	58.2	58.7	26.0	6 034	76.8
Sac	357	-1.7	391	0.5	333.0	2 898 569	7 420	255 801	474.7	519 315	45.6	54.4	71.6	50.1	9 715	82.5
Scott	221	-11.3	291	0.6	201.4	2 359 184	8 118	234 090	248.2	326 949	66.5	33.5	65.9	43.1	7 134	71.5
Shelby	372	3.9	428	0.0	344.3	2 901 694	6 772	255 117	351.3	404 253	70.4	29.6	80.9	58.1	8 494	85.7
Sioux	484	1.2	299	8.5	442.4	2 726 452	9 105	277 347	1 613.1	996 964	19.7	80.3	83.9	66.1	11 514	74.1
Story	306	-13.1	317	0.4	279.4	2 482 983	7 838	205 934	292.8	303 082	79.6	20.4	60.0	37.3	6 566	73.5
Tama	403	-6.5	356	0.0	351.7	2 313 300	6 503	214 804	355.2	313 764	78.5	21.5	65.4	43.1	9 820	81.4
Taylor	279	-1.4	436	0.0	212.0	1 668 700	3 827	195 518	144.2	225 667	58.6	41.4	56.3	28.5	6 371	78.7
Union	214	-0.1	331	0.0	147.6	1 138 708	3 441	138 670	118.2	182 338	46.2	53.8	50.5	24.7	4 243	70.7
Van Buren	213	-3.7	283	0.0	140.8	984 527	3 475	101 955	110.1	146 246	52.6	47.4	43.8	17.9	5 497	68.7
Wapello	189	13.6	255	0.1	138.7	1 049 902	4 125	126 195	86.2	116 235	72.4	27.6	42.0	19.5	5 473	67.7
Warren	264	9.1	198	0.0	184.0	1 010 263	5 114	93 412	110.1	82 542	81.6	18.4	42.1	12.1	7 169	57.6
Washington	314	-3.5	276	0.2	264.6	1 685 741	6 107	175 919	526.8	462 551	31.7	68.3	59.3	39.4	12 460	75.9
Wayne	274	0.2	396	0.1	199.0	1 280 719	3 233	143 864	74.3	107 534	64.5	35.5	47.9	19.0	7 885	72.4
Webster	409	-9.9	422	D	383.6	3 106 004	7 352	252 019	353.6	365 319	82.4	17.6	65.4	48.7	11 421	85.4
Winnebago	235	-6.4	367	0.0	222.0	2 474 578	6 748	266 843	281.5	438 438	59.4	40.6	61.4	44.7	6 474	87.1
Winneshiek	376	19.9	245	0.0	305.3	1 460 745	5 959	173 344	345.9	225 362	50.0	50.0	56.7	35.2	14 181	83.2
Woodbury	446	0.0	458	5.3	384.6	2 736 038	5 974	230 038	416.5	428 025	56.6	43.4	66.9	46.5	9 174	77.6
Worth	235	1.4	367	1.1	218.4	2 255 917	6 145	240 556	188.1	293 936	86.8	13.2	60.2	43.9	6 708	86.1
Wright	360	9.8	464	0.0	344.6	3 345 938	7 209	316 590	484.9	625 738	53.0	47.0	65.5	51.7	11 670	84.3

STATE County	Water use, 2010		Wholesale trade,[1] 2007				Retail trade,[2] 2007				Real estate and rental and leasing,[2] 2007			
	Total water withdrawn (mil gal/day)	Gallons withdrawn per person per day	Number of establish-ments	Number of employees	Sales (mil dol)	Annual payroll (mil dol)	Number of establish-ments	Number of employees	Sales (mil dol)	Annual payroll (mil dol)	Number of establish-ments	Number of employees	Receipts (mil dol)	Annual payroll (mil dol)
	133	134	135	136	137	138	139	140	141	142	143	144	145	146
IOWA—Cont'd														
Franklin	4.1	386	29	176	154.6	6.3	42	353	65.9	5.6	14	36	3.6	0.4
Fremont	2.6	345	13	93	105.5	3.4	35	478	102.9	8.5	2	D	D	D
Greene	5.8	624	18	380	144.9	14.9	44	374	87.9	6.5	6	19	2.3	0.3
Grundy	2.2	178	17	225	269.9	9.8	57	490	109.4	9.0	8	D	D	D
Guthrie	3.2	294	18	D	D	D	41	350	91.3	5.6	7	22	2.1	0.5
Hamilton	4.1	264	31	772	558.3	31.8	65	683	149.3	11.0	10	19	2.0	0.2
Hancock	4.6	406	27	214	171.7	7.2	52	437	119.3	7.5	13	37	2.4	0.6
Hardin	9.2	526	42	892	1 191.0	40.6	90	815	161.8	14.6	17	31	3.4	0.6
Harrison	10.6	712	29	255	130.2	7.8	55	466	100.9	7.5	10	29	1.7	0.4
Henry	3.3	164	32	207	90.6	6.0	64	900	214.7	17.7	20	50	5.9	0.8
Howard	4.3	448	15	135	143.6	5.1	53	375	83.2	6.8	7	11	3.3	0.4
Humboldt	3.1	311	38	275	183.1	10.7	51	467	82.0	9.3	9	27	1.8	0.5
Ida	3.3	464	13	185	147.1	7.1	41	357	61.1	5.0	8	D	D	D
Iowa	3.2	196	19	115	80.2	4.0	145	1 204	213.4	18.3	4	D	D	D
Jackson	3.2	161	28	200	109.1	6.1	87	935	210.0	15.7	16	35	2.7	0.6
Jasper	7.9	213	41	D	D	D	122	1 424	274.0	25.8	31	81	8.4	1.6
Jefferson	2.2	132	48	319	114.6	9.7	84	1 205	333.5	33.9	20	43	6.2	0.8
Johnson	37.3	285	81	1 183	567.6	48.4	537	8 424	1 653.1	168.8	146	D	D	D
Jones	4.1	200	33	236	144.7	7.7	81	1 060	257.7	23.6	11	15	1.4	0.2
Keokuk	3.1	299	26	215	122.3	7.3	38	265	66.9	3.9	2	D	D	D
Kossuth	6.5	417	43	525	318.4	17.2	107	959	195.8	16.4	16	51	3.6	0.7
Lee	28.3	790	36	400	396.3	15.3	164	2 011	420.8	38.0	28	80	7.7	1.5
Linn	146.0	691	300	4 412	2 506.1	207.7	794	14 096	3 592.8	307.0	238	1 696	356.8	91.5
Louisa	15.7	1 378	12	D	D	D	27	237	56.5	3.7	6	7	0.4	0.1
Lucas	1.3	148	6	30	1.5	0.2	33	372	84.3	6.9	4	7	1.9	0.3
Lyon	7.4	642	23	226	215.3	7.7	54	419	91.1	6.5	7	7	1.0	0.1
Madison	2.1	135	13	D	D	D	52	422	80.6	7.7	7	16	2.1	0.2
Mahaska	4.2	189	36	D	D	D	109	1 229	242.9	22.7	12	56	5.9	1.0
Marion	4.0	121	41	D	D	D	153	1 726	333.1	30.8	40	92	9.9	1.5
Marshall	11.3	279	43	379	298.1	16.4	166	2 126	407.7	41.6	40	400	46.1	10.9
Mills	2.1	136	10	56	23.0	1.8	42	339	78.6	5.8	11	40	10.4	0.9
Mitchell	5.8	539	26	208	228.7	7.7	65	394	93.1	8.0	7	16	1.0	0.2
Monona	16.5	1 780	15	102	77.6	3.7	43	386	99.2	7.0	5	9	0.5	0.1
Monroe	2.6	324	13	162	46.2	4.9	33	290	62.5	5.2	2	D	D	D
Montgomery	2.1	198	13	109	150.7	4.5	56	510	88.3	8.6	9	49	4.9	1.1
Muscatine	235.3	5 505	52	481	377.5	17.2	158	2 086	448.6	42.3	49	160	19.9	4.2
O'Brien	6.5	451	33	407	322.7	13.9	104	844	169.7	14.0	7	33	4.8	0.7
Osceola	7.0	1 077	9	D	D	D	28	162	40.5	2.8	2	D	D	D
Page	3.3	208	16	155	116.4	5.6	92	738	163.0	12.8	11	20	1.7	0.3
Palo Alto	4.8	511	15	118	132.5	4.1	47	378	65.8	6.1	8	D	D	D
Plymouth	10.5	419	42	345	243.0	12.8	111	1 184	299.7	22.2	22	112	6.9	1.4
Pocahontas	2.2	298	14	229	86.9	6.4	38	306	79.9	3.6	1	D	D	D
Polk	58.3	135	668	11 440	6 697.2	536.1	1 658	28 621	6 714.4	655.9	567	3 399	673.2	120.0
Pottawattamie	568.5	6 102	91	1 618	2 256.7	64.7	326	6 025	1 503.4	117.5	95	425	66.3	10.5
Poweshiek	3.0	161	24	220	118.1	7.6	95	1 109	241.3	22.0	15	36	3.2	0.6
Ringgold	1.5	298	7	49	26.0	1.7	29	213	63.6	4.1	2	D	D	D
Sac	8.8	848	33	223	165.0	9.5	63	391	92.5	6.6	6	6	0.2	0.0
Scott	120.6	730	265	D	D	D	702	11 831	2 853.0	252.6	185	1 826	276.5	47.1
Shelby	3.5	284	25	423	158.6	11.7	66	588	135.1	10.5	7	D	D	D
Sioux	20.8	618	78	1 345	753.1	44.9	173	1 674	394.4	32.6	26	76	13.1	3.2
Story	12.5	140	80	599	432.0	24.7	320	4 611	968.3	91.7	96	371	38.1	10.1
Tama	5.8	325	27	163	154.9	5.4	78	548	112.5	9.3	7	17	0.9	0.2
Taylor	1.0	158	8	72	41.0	2.4	23	154	25.1	1.8	4	D	D	D
Union	6.1	483	16	236	384.7	8.1	60	779	153.8	15.1	18	46	4.8	0.9
Van Buren	1.2	152	6	D	D	D	30	243	36.9	3.0	3	4	0.6	0.1
Wapello	14.6	410	28	D	D	D	160	2 461	500.7	46.1	30	81	13.1	2.0
Warren	2.6	56	43	527	628.1	21.6	104	1 438	328.4	30.4	27	75	8.8	1.6
Washington	5.3	244	40	315	185.7	10.6	102	993	195.0	16.9	11	D	D	D
Wayne	0.8	120	5	36	27.0	1.4	36	247	49.2	3.7	1	D	D	D
Webster	16.5	433	68	D	D	D	194	2 723	577.5	52.3	42	120	18.9	2.9
Winnebago	2.8	256	19	130	170.0	4.6	60	538	115.0	8.2	8	D	D	D
Winneshiek	6.3	298	30	260	167.0	9.0	129	1 221	289.6	24.7	13	41	4.8	0.9
Woodbury	1 021.4	9 997	155	2 452	1 740.0	104.2	471	7 502	1 512.0	142.8	98	592	92.1	15.5
Worth	10.2	1 344	12	D	D	D	22	154	28.7	2.9	2	D	D	D
Wright	6.2	470	22	274	291.1	12.0	65	554	100.2	8.7	15	33	2.3	0.5

1. Merchant wholesalers, except manufacturers' sales branches and offices. 2. Employer establishments.

Table B. States and Counties — **Professional Services, Manufacturing, and Accommodation and Food Services**

STATE County	Professional, scientific, and technical services,[1] 2007				Manufacturing, 2007				Accommodation and food services, 2007			
	Number of establish-ments	Number of employees	Receipts (mil dol)	Annual payroll (mil dol)	Number of establish-ments	Number of employees	Receipts (mil dol)	Annual payroll (mil dol)	Number of establish-ments	Number of employees	Sales (mil dol)	Annual payroll (mil dol)
	147	148	149	150	151	152	153	154	155	156	157	158
IOWA—Cont'd												
Franklin	19	89	5.0	2.1	24	798	260.0	28.8	13	169	4.4	1.4
Fremont	8	34	2.4	0.8	7	D	D	D	26	241	14.8	2.0
Greene	24	80	6.6	3.1	NA	NA	NA	NA	14	145	3.9	1.1
Grundy	17	D	D	D	13	648	143.8	21.2	21	167	4.3	1.0
Guthrie	23	68	7.3	1.9	NA	NA	NA	NA	25	259	8.3	2.2
Hamilton	31	122	9.7	3.3	27	2 916	1 162.4	95.9	33	308	12.2	3.1
Hancock	19	109	7.3	2.4	27	1 126	266.8	49.0	17	159	4.1	1.0
Hardin	35	158	12.2	3.6	27	661	743.1	23.5	33	336	11.4	3.0
Harrison	21	D	D	D	NA	NA	NA	NA	31	304	10.4	2.8
Henry	39	D	D	D	32	2 520	889.9	79.3	54	693	22.2	6.1
Howard	15	38	2.9	1.2	26	1 562	273.0	D	21	187	4.8	1.1
Humboldt	20	67	5.6	1.9	27	1 214	289.8	41.4	24	244	7.5	2.0
Ida	12	44	3.8	1.1	15	1 241	373.0	53.3	14	D	D	D
Iowa	22	70	9.2	1.3	37	3 819	1 478.9	152.4	41	684	25.0	8.0
Jackson	32	85	4.9	1.7	34	1 047	248.0	27.0	45	485	14.5	3.3
Jasper	56	566	134.1	18.9	34	733	170.8	24.3	68	960	30.1	8.4
Jefferson	122	D	D	D	37	1 252	246.6	46.9	39	468	16.6	4.3
Johnson	241	D	D	D	83	5 598	D	230.1	329	6 906	258.8	75.7
Jones	33	130	10.6	4.3	30	859	180.8	31.6	34	359	9.8	2.8
Keokuk	6	29	3.7	1.0	NA	NA	NA	NA	11	D	D	D
Kossuth	41	193	22.8	5.5	25	946	474.8	38.2	40	393	11.5	2.8
Lee	50	255	18.9	6.7	66	D	D	D	96	1 154	37.0	9.5
Linn	503	4 587	574.9	244.7	237	17 801	8 229.2	1 123.9	488	9 343	353.6	103.2
Louisa	12	D	D	D	11	1 389	D	41.8	20	139	4.5	1.0
Lucas	12	D	D	D	NA	NA	NA	NA	13	D	D	D
Lyon	20	108	12.2	6.8	23	645	100.9	26.6	17	D	D	D
Madison	32	112	10.1	3.9	NA	NA	NA	NA	26	224	7.6	2.0
Mahaska	33	149	19.8	8.3	34	1 763	1 618.5	75.9	36	495	16.8	4.6
Marion	52	245	22.0	9.7	40	7 392	1 856.9	376.7	68	936	29.0	8.2
Marshall	52	340	50.4	12.0	45	5 546	1 848.0	232.3	86	1 180	40.4	11.1
Mills	25	D	D	D	NA	NA	NA	NA	16	109	5.4	0.8
Mitchell	13	66	5.9	1.5	20	941	252.0	34.8	20	186	5.1	1.1
Monona	15	96	5.1	1.6	NA	NA	NA	NA	28	193	7.2	1.6
Monroe	13	39	3.7	1.1	NA	NA	NA	NA	20	D	D	D
Montgomery	18	81	10.4	2.1	12	813	180.8	36.3	26	256	7.6	2.1
Muscatine	63	D	D	D	68	7 982	D	366.4	88	1 266	44.2	12.1
O'Brien	25	103	11.8	2.9	25	511	305.0	18.7	34	406	9.8	2.6
Osceola	7	25	3.0	0.6	NA	NA	NA	NA	14	D	D	D
Page	20	158	5.8	2.5	24	2 019	348.2	80.9	34	439	12.6	3.6
Palo Alto	12	35	3.3	1.1	21	577	401.4	23.6	23	566	34.6	7.3
Plymouth	40	203	13.7	7.0	30	2 228	D	D	60	982	22.0	6.5
Pocahontas	19	51	3.8	1.1	NA	NA	NA	NA	13	D	D	D
Polk	1 366	11 826	1 761.6	645.1	378	17 620	7 519.9	797.2	1 064	19 898	825.2	243.1
Pottawattamie	143	D	D	D	68	5 371	D	D	193	5 771	451.5	97.0
Poweshiek	40	181	18.9	5.1	34	1 997	462.2	71.6	48	632	17.0	4.9
Ringgold	9	25	3.7	0.7	NA	NA	NA	NA	15	D	D	D
Sac	16	54	6.4	1.1	NA	NA	NA	NA	27	D	D	D
Scott	389	D	D	D	189	12 506	5 745.1	590.4	421	9 171	423.9	112.7
Shelby	26	150	11.4	3.7	NA	NA	NA	NA	27	292	8.7	2.3
Sioux	81	769	67.0	18.4	95	5 479	1 152.4	179.0	78	1 187	31.7	9.2
Story	193	D	D	D	75	4 668	1 970.8	213.4	224	4 388	151.0	43.4
Tama	21	90	14.7	7.7	NA	NA	NA	NA	33	D	D	D
Taylor	9	D	D	D	NA	NA	NA	NA	10	D	D	D
Union	17	60	5.0	1.9	12	1 450	214.3	47.7	27	344	11.2	2.8
Van Buren	11	23	2.0	0.7	12	734	D	22.1	12	D	D	D
Wapello	48	D	D	D	28	4 309	1 840.4	178.0	76	1 116	41.5	11.3
Warren	62	218	18.4	6.3	27	545	D	D	60	792	25.1	6.5
Washington	52	D	D	D	39	1 114	D	33.7	41	1 224	114.7	21.3
Wayne	7	28	2.6	0.6	NA	NA	NA	NA	10	D	D	D
Webster	75	419	31.4	15.1	50	2 483	1 909.4	122.4	81	1 399	61.9	15.7
Winnebago	21	76	7.6	2.0	21	4 215	1 094.3	170.7	18	231	6.4	1.4
Winneshiek	31	145	15.2	5.8	31	1 721	288.7	58.0	58	732	21.5	6.2
Woodbury	190	D	D	D	98	5 073	2 827.5	210.2	262	4 699	158.4	47.3
Worth	10	D	D	D	13	593	248.9	20.7	13	110	4.7	1.0
Wright	24	158	11.2	3.3	26	1 096	863.3	49.5	37	242	7.6	2.0

1. Establishment subject to federal tax.

Table B. States and Counties — **Health Care and Social Assistance, Other Services, Nonemployer Businesses, and Residential Construction**

STATE County	Health care and social assistance, 2007				Other services, 2007				Nonemployer businesses, 2013		Value of residential construction authorized by building permits, 2014	
	Number of establish-ments	Number of employees	Receipts (mil dol)	Annual payroll (mil dol)	Number of establish-ments	Number of employees	Receipts (mil dol)	Annual payroll (mil dol)	Number	Receipts (mil dol)	New Construction ($1,000)	Number of housing units
	159	160	161	162	163	164	165	166	167	168	169	170
IOWA—Cont'd												
Franklin	31	524	28.1	13.3	27	64	5.5	1.5	795	34.8	775	3
Fremont	16	324	18.3	8.0	14	D	D	D	517	19.0	2 310	10
Greene	27	652	29.8	15.1	23	92	5.6	1.3	716	32.4	1 530	6
Grundy	29	387	21.1	9.2	23	D	D	D	836	28.9	4 297	19
Guthrie	33	505	27.2	12.6	25	D	D	D	1 015	42.8	2 618	10
Hamilton	36	633	47.0	18.1	36	118	13.1	3.5	1 059	36.5	1 101	5
Hancock	17	453	27.1	10.7	30	214	25.9	8.1	839	33.7	4 239	20
Hardin	41	995	48.9	23.7	49	140	12.5	3.2	1 290	51.0	1 634	7
Harrison	36	657	43.3	18.1	23	D	D	D	1 037	44.5	5 076	29
Henry	60	1 081	80.3	38.6	41	158	8.7	3.3	1 336	43.5	3 473	20
Howard	24	431	24.2	12.3	19	47	3.4	0.8	829	37.2	320	1
Humboldt	22	444	25.6	11.2	18	38	4.0	0.7	724	30.2	4 240	24
Ida	19	420	23.8	10.8	16	59	4.1	1.3	560	28.3	2 815	11
Iowa	38	727	36.5	17.8	22	52	5.5	1.1	1 241	48.7	2 563	23
Jackson	40	896	45.3	22.1	44	114	13.4	2.3	1 515	55.2	5 580	35
Jasper	83	1 565	97.5	46.1	60	249	16.5	4.2	2 261	90.3	8 561	33
Jefferson	50	697	48.1	18.8	44	152	21.6	2.9	1 927	66.4	1 428	14
Johnson	357	15 466	1 501.0	577.8	213	1 376	173.4	35.3	8 843	425.3	190 615	1 080
Jones	44	794	40.3	18.4	40	86	10.2	2.1	1 346	54.0	2 602	15
Keokuk	21	373	15.5	7.6	18	49	4.0	0.9	705	33.6	0	0
Kossuth	41	864	57.4	23.1	57	129	17.4	2.5	1 401	62.8	4 575	19
Lee	114	D	D	D	73	285	22.5	5.0	1 914	62.1	2 659	22
Linn	540	13 371	1 173.9	491.2	402	2 594	243.7	63.2	12 912	554.8	94 172	838
Louisa	24	322	11.2	5.3	14	D	D	D	621	24.0	1 753	9
Lucas	29	550	31.0	13.3	9	23	2.3	0.5	622	25.7	659	3
Lyon	23	403	18.2	7.6	31	88	7.2	1.4	983	44.1	9 750	55
Madison	27	598	30.4	13.6	27	D	D	D	1 271	54.6	12 855	55
Mahaska	59	934	61.5	28.0	41	156	12.4	2.9	1 442	51.6	9 382	64
Marion	93	2 430	170.3	73.0	65	242	22.1	5.2	2 134	73.7	26 007	125
Marshall	84	2 143	139.6	66.8	69	465	33.2	10.0	1 875	62.7	1 507	10
Mills	29	733	27.6	14.3	25	D	D	D	926	33.2	644	3
Mitchell	30	561	33.9	13.4	31	70	6.1	1.5	864	40.9	4 409	25
Monona	23	690	40.7	19.5	16	40	3.2	0.9	646	24.3	835	7
Monroe	22	485	24.8	11.1	7	19	2.2	0.4	553	19.7	4 026	82
Montgomery	38	849	49.6	22.4	34	93	8.6	1.7	731	28.6	2 038	13
Muscatine	92	1 866	111.1	50.1	77	D	D	D	2 085	81.9	7 917	51
O'Brien	49	1 391	66.5	29.4	43	170	16.9	3.9	984	48.2	4 556	22
Osceola	14	307	16.1	6.6	15	26	2.5	0.4	468	22.8	300	1
Page	51	1 587	91.4	43.4	33	102	6.6	1.5	919	30.2	2 119	11
Palo Alto	37	688	40.3	16.8	20	22	2.0	0.4	733	32.8	350	2
Plymouth	54	986	65.3	25.4	55	164	14.4	3.0	1 700	74.9	9 812	37
Pocahontas	21	318	17.9	8.0	14	38	2.4	0.5	539	26.3	690	4
Polk	1 021	32 180	3 108.7	1 332.6	965	6 980	751.7	206.0	30 761	1 427.3	682 044	3 350
Pottawattamie	194	4 453	364.2	159.4	148	678	52.0	15.7	4 975	213.8	24 643	122
Poweshiek	59	1 281	89.6	42.0	35	113	9.3	2.5	1 275	50.7	20 562	123
Ringgold	15	337	19.9	8.8	12	32	4.0	0.9	470	21.6	220	2
Sac	24	558	28.5	14.0	24	57	6.1	1.1	845	38.1	1 830	5
Scott	456	10 963	944.3	414.0	342	2 063	168.0	47.5	10 040	423.1	78 835	365
Shelby	38	1 065	52.4	24.4	24	85	7.4	1.6	972	45.6	2 851	16
Sioux	74	2 078	119.2	49.1	87	292	26.9	6.5	2 577	113.5	21 689	112
Story	172	5 026	415.3	172.4	148	1 096	212.9	28.7	5 377	216.0	88 153	539
Tama	30	314	15.3	7.6	21	64	5.3	1.1	1 130	42.3	3 214	17
Taylor	15	206	7.8	3.8	12	53	4.2	1.0	556	24.5	814	4
Union	38	904	55.5	24.8	30	139	13.1	2.6	800	26.1	964	7
Van Buren	14	353	17.0	8.5	11	D	D	D	660	29.2	0	0
Wapello	103	2 848	199.1	88.0	58	234	15.9	4.5	1 763	63.2	1 994	22
Warren	74	1 230	67.1	31.9	58	218	14.2	4.5	3 431	153.0	67 301	360
Washington	66	1 248	61.5	29.4	50	153	19.8	3.4	1 780	65.7	3 411	24
Wayne	19	309	18.5	8.2	12	31	2.7	0.5	523	32.4	0	0
Webster	117	2 977	239.7	108.3	77	404	43.4	11.0	2 082	78.0	4 489	20
Winnebago	41	628	27.5	12.0	15	37	15.7	0.7	794	32.6	1 539	6
Winneshiek	58	1 455	[illegible]	40.4	42	177	16.2	3.1	1 859	65.0	11 716	47
Woodbury	333	8 054	718.5	273.3	193	1 279	90.6	28.8	5 654	239.7	31 155	151
Worth	13	D	D	D	13	34	4.3	0.7	530	17.8	570	4
Wright	40	915	68.4	26.0	30	73	5.7	1.1	868	32.9	2 798	12

STATE County	Government employment and payroll, 2012: Full-time equivalent employees	March payroll (dollars)	March payroll (percent of total): Adminis-tration, judicial, and legal	Police and Corrections	Fire Protection	Highways and transpor-tation	Health and Welfare	Natural resources and utilities	Education and libraries	Local government finances, 2012 — General revenue: Total (mil dol)	Inter-govern-mental (mil dol)	Taxes: Total (mil dol)	Per capita[1] (dollars): Total	Property
	171	172	173	174	175	176	177	178	179	180	181	182	183	184
IOWA—Cont'd														
Franklin	668	2 088 400	4.9	4.3	0.0	6.1	28.3	1.6	54.1	66.9	22.7	23.0	2 183	1 785
Fremont	347	973 340	7.5	7.8	0.0	11.0	2.0	3.1	66.2	34.7	15.8	16.0	2 243	1 866
Greene	666	2 223 582	5.3	3.9	0.1	5.8	41.2	3.9	39.3	57.4	14.6	19.1	2 082	1 727
Grundy	563	1 970 199	5.6	4.4	0.0	5.6	33.3	4.7	45.8	64.2	18.4	21.5	1 731	1 370
Guthrie	748	2 384 845	4.1	2.8	0.0	5.3	24.8	3.4	59.0	68.4	20.6	29.3	2 716	2 276
Hamilton	889	2 941 083	5.3	6.3	0.7	5.4	28.8	4.7	47.5	85.2	24.2	29.7	1 934	1 608
Hancock	533	1 678 758	4.9	4.9	1.1	7.4	29.0	1.1	50.1	52.6	15.5	18.7	1 678	1 364
Hardin	771	2 439 397	10.0	8.8	0.3	7.6	3.2	3.8	65.7	93.9	30.1	33.2	1 921	1 546
Harrison	661	2 116 699	6.1	6.5	0.0	7.4	2.6	6.5	68.9	60.2	26.0	28.5	1 960	1 608
Henry	1 101	3 801 450	6.1	5.0	0.3	3.4	27.7	5.1	50.9	103.1	34.1	30.0	1 484	1 188
Howard	610	1 837 491	3.8	4.1	0.0	6.3	32.8	4.1	48.6	53.0	15.0	18.0	1 887	1 526
Humboldt	551	1 979 695	10.2	4.3	0.1	15.7	23.2	4.8	41.3	51.5	15.8	17.9	1 843	1 479
Ida	324	944 758	6.5	5.6	0.0	8.7	0.4	3.6	73.9	24.5	9.5	11.8	1 661	1 328
Iowa	946	2 546 590	3.6	5.9	0.1	6.6	25.6	2.5	55.1	74.3	23.2	29.8	1 838	1 381
Jackson	760	2 545 154	6.2	8.0	0.2	6.2	18.9	3.4	56.7	78.0	28.3	27.5	1 395	1 119
Jasper	1 510	5 999 123	4.8	6.2	2.0	4.5	25.8	3.5	51.2	155.2	47.6	58.5	1 597	1 284
Jefferson	662	2 186 709	5.0	7.9	0.9	5.5	30.3	6.8	43.2	74.0	18.6	24.1	1 426	1 178
Johnson	2 791	12 750 946	7.7	8.1	1.5	4.7	5.9	5.3	62.3	508.5	160.5	263.7	1 934	1 579
Jones	764	2 287 665	6.5	6.6	0.0	6.9	3.4	2.6	72.1	73.5	35.1	28.3	1 369	1 067
Keokuk	574	1 571 936	7.3	3.7	0.0	8.5	14.2	3.5	62.2	51.8	19.5	19.7	1 897	1 573
Kossuth	791	2 418 144	8.4	5.5	0.2	7.0	33.0	4.1	41.0	91.7	21.6	29.7	1 937	1 582
Lee	1 300	4 660 014	5.4	7.2	3.1	4.7	4.4	9.0	64.9	121.2	55.2	48.2	1 353	989
Linn	9 095	37 187 147	3.6	5.9	2.8	6.2	2.3	4.9	72.4	1 182.6	511.6	437.3	2 031	1 562
Louisa	609	1 866 882	4.6	6.3	0.0	4.4	2.1	2.8	79.3	56.0	27.3	22.6	2 003	1 495
Lucas	520	1 767 462	3.7	2.9	0.0	5.3	32.1	16.9	38.6	45.7	14.5	12.3	1 406	1 112
Lyon	499	1 482 179	6.0	6.8	0.0	8.4	4.9	6.3	65.1	46.7	19.3	20.2	1 715	1 324
Madison	798	2 825 675	6.6	2.7	0.0	7.8	22.7	7.6	52.2	80.3	28.9	28.9	1 848	1 518
Mahaska	1 014	3 634 697	4.3	4.7	0.9	4.1	46.1	1.9	35.8	108.1	29.6	33.7	1 503	1 164
Marion	1 252	3 936 638	5.4	7.6	0.0	6.5	4.1	9.6	65.6	122.5	47.7	49.1	1 469	1 141
Marshall	1 954	7 209 585	3.6	6.6	1.9	3.7	0.6	4.3	78.3	184.2	83.4	70.1	1 715	1 332
Mills	661	1 998 540	5.5	6.9	1.4	7.4	5.2	1.1	71.4	51.3	23.3	23.3	1 569	1 336
Mitchell	526	1 692 873	5.0	4.8	0.0	5.4	33.0	2.6	47.2	57.0	14.0	18.3	1 705	1 409
Monona	396	1 218 905	10.0	7.1	0.0	11.2	2.6	8.7	59.5	37.4	15.9	15.8	1 736	1 419
Monroe	387	1 402 370	4.4	6.0	0.1	5.9	41.4	2.3	39.4	25.8	12.4	11.4	1 418	1 109
Montgomery	722	2 440 051	4.3	3.9	1.5	5.4	42.7	3.0	37.5	72.5	19.7	21.2	2 004	1 573
Muscatine	1 797	6 903 785	4.4	8.5	3.1	3.4	2.3	23.5	51.0	179.8	71.9	69.9	1 630	1 298
O'Brien	688	2 291 194	4.3	7.0	0.0	6.3	0.5	5.0	75.2	67.6	25.7	28.4	2 007	1 628
Osceola	225	737 061	10.1	8.0	0.0	13.2	1.6	6.2	60.4	21.0	8.0	9.8	1 588	1 342
Page	735	2 422 895	5.4	5.6	0.4	5.2	28.7	4.2	50.0	75.7	24.0	22.9	1 458	1 116
Palo Alto	595	1 986 443	5.8	3.7	0.8	6.9	35.4	3.3	43.7	67.2	16.0	23.3	2 512	2 103
Plymouth	1 172	4 151 413	4.7	5.6	0.3	5.4	25.2	3.7	54.8	126.6	33.5	46.1	1 850	1 539
Pocahontas	388	1 255 236	7.6	7.3	0.0	7.9	24.8	7.4	43.9	40.0	11.0	14.7	2 054	1 718
Polk	17 358	73 983 487	5.6	9.0	3.6	4.4	8.6	5.6	61.7	2 215.8	755.8	962.0	2 168	1 882
Pottawattamie	3 555	14 074 472	5.1	12.0	3.8	3.4	3.5	4.9	66.5	469.3	187.7	200.8	2 162	1 672
Poweshiek	616	2 161 055	7.6	7.8	1.1	6.4	2.2	6.6	67.8	70.4	26.8	32.7	1 745	1 368
Ringgold	380	1 133 677	4.5	3.2	0.0	9.7	40.0	2.0	40.3	38.0	10.1	11.1	2 172	1 874
Sac	370	1 168 894	8.0	8.4	0.0	9.1	4.9	9.7	53.3	38.8	16.2	16.8	1 655	1 346
Scott	6 132	26 019 745	5.1	9.3	3.9	3.8	2.4	4.0	69.8	729.6	283.5	333.3	1 974	1 565
Shelby	746	2 472 519	5.4	3.6	0.2	6.1	48.6	4.6	28.4	74.6	17.8	20.6	1 705	1 402
Sioux	1 410	5 040 852	7.0	4.6	0.0	3.5	32.1	5.9	45.0	155.5	40.9	50.2	1 466	1 159
Story	2 892	10 932 541	7.4	7.6	2.9	7.7	10.1	9.9	52.8	476.0	102.3	138.3	1 518	1 219
Tama	838	2 616 822	5.8	6.4	0.0	7.4	4.6	3.7	70.0	73.1	34.0	30.1	1 717	1 370
Taylor	283	832 177	7.3	5.5	0.0	10.1	5.8	4.1	65.8	26.1	12.6	9.8	1 572	1 285
Union	985	3 478 275	2.6	3.0	0.6	3.4	37.5	2.3	50.1	116.7	47.2	22.5	1 788	1 421
Van Buren	420	1 439 759	4.4	3.0	0.0	5.3	38.1	2.3	46.6	36.7	12.5	10.5	1 409	1 133
Wapello	1 563	6 980 218	2.5	3.5	1.9	4.5	2.0	4.5	80.0	186.1	86.6	52.4	1 482	1 084
Warren	1 608	6 242 328	5.6	5.6	1.1	3.5	2.5	5.3	75.5	156.4	71.0	65.1	1 387	1 216
Washington	1 128	3 614 174	5.4	6.2	0.4	4.7	26.2	4.4	52.3	111.8	34.7	38.8	1 771	1 403
Wayne	428	1 412 234	4.6	3.7	0.0	5.5	52.3	1.9	31.5	45.4	11.7	10.9	1 714	1 444
Webster	1 646	5 911 455	5.2	5.8	2.4	3.6	3.2	3.1	76.3	189.7	73.6	61.4	1 648	1 262
Winnebago	563	1 699 897	5.9	5.4	0.0	5.7	4.8	5.5	71.6	53.4	20.2	24.6	2 324	1 932
Winneshiek	1 453	4 847 620	2.3	3.4	0.2	3.7	28.1	2.1	59.9	162.1	45.6	40.6	1 928	1 635
Woodbury	3 937	16 380 806	4.5	9.7	4.1	5.4	2.2	5.6	67.1	475.0	216.3	177.2	1 732	1 265
Worth	353	1 078 114	9.5	7.7	0.0	8.8	3.7	3.5	65.9	35.3	14.3	16.5	2 191	1 830
Wright	944	3 639 368	3.1	3.8	0.0	4.6	48.9	2.0	37.6	120.8	27.5	28.8	2 216	1 856

1. Based on the resident population estimated as of July 1 of the year shown.

STATE County	Local government finances, 2012 (cont.) — Direct general expenditure: Total (mil dol)	Per capita[1] (dollars)	Percent of total for: Education	Health and hospitals	Police protection	Public welfare	Highways	Debt outstanding: Total (mil dol)	Per capita[1] (dollars)	Government employment, 2013: Federal civilian	Federal military	State and local	Presidential election,[2] 2012 — Percent of vote cast: Democratic	Republican	All other
	185	186	187	188	189	190	191	192	193	194	195	196	197	198	199
IOWA—Cont'd															
Franklin	74.7	7 078	38.7	27.4	2.8	0.1	7.5	53.7	5 092	36	43	788	50.0	48.6	1.4
Fremont	36.0	5 034	46.9	4.3	4.1	0.1	19.2	10.1	1 415	29	29	470	47.4	51.1	1.5
Greene	58.6	6 398	31.8	39.4	3.0	0.2	8.2	19.5	2 133	36	37	793	49.4	48.9	1.7
Grundy	60.9	4 889	35.4	29.1	3.1	0.1	12.1	34.5	2 773	45	50	671	40.9	57.8	1.4
Guthrie	64.7	6 005	45.4	24.0	2.4	0.1	9.0	71.3	6 614	56	44	855	44.9	52.6	2.6
Hamilton	89.3	5 820	41.9	27.7	3.4	0.2	7.1	95.4	6 215	35	63	1 191	49.7	48.4	1.9
Hancock	59.9	5 378	31.9	38.4	3.3	0.1	11.3	36.3	3 260	48	45	642	47.3	50.9	1.8
Hardin	98.1	5 668	39.4	22.8	3.6	0.1	10.4	60.0	3 470	65	69	1 768	49.6	48.7	1.7
Harrison	56.0	3 853	56.3	5.5	3.7	0.3	12.4	33.4	2 299	67	59	840	46.9	51.5	1.6
Henry	99.5	4 919	39.9	36.4	3.0	0.3	4.6	76.0	3 758	64	78	1 739	46.4	51.4	2.2
Howard	49.9	5 214	37.9	32.9	2.9	0.4	8.5	14.5	1 518	33	39	773	62.2	36.4	1.4
Humboldt	60.5	6 223	36.7	23.4	2.9	0.2	10.8	37.9	3 894	52	40	630	42.2	56.5	1.3
Ida	25.1	3 531	55.4	4.9	4.2	0.2	13.6	14.0	1 973	30	29	372	41.0	57.4	1.6
Iowa	74.5	4 600	48.3	23.2	3.7	0.4	9.2	69.2	4 275	49	66	971	49.2	49.0	1.8
Jackson	75.2	3 817	46.3	20.7	4.1	0.1	9.2	36.7	1 860	75	80	1 000	61.3	36.9	1.8
Jasper	146.8	4 011	39.1	28.3	4.3	0.3	6.0	102.6	2 802	92	145	2 294	52.8	45.3	1.9
Jefferson	72.9	4 323	28.0	30.9	3.6	0.2	10.0	71.8	4 254	61	63	1 010	58.7	38.5	2.8
Johnson	524.4	3 847	35.0	4.1	4.1	0.9	6.0	708.3	5 196	1 805	585	33 297	69.9	28.4	1.7
Jones	81.7	3 958	56.2	5.0	3.3	0.1	12.9	52.6	2 548	56	80	1 335	54.4	44.0	1.6
Keokuk	46.7	4 504	42.3	19.6	2.4	0.1	11.3	24.3	2 344	52	42	541	47.0	50.6	2.5
Kossuth	92.1	6 004	26.6	34.3	2.6	0.2	10.8	73.1	4 765	63	62	1 061	50.8	47.6	1.6
Lee	137.2	3 851	55.0	7.3	5.0	0.5	5.8	121.6	3 414	94	158	2 052	57.0	41.0	2.0
Linn	1 336.0	6 206	46.5	3.0	3.7	1.2	4.7	1 559.7	7 244	1 054	876	12 875	60.0	38.5	1.5
Louisa	54.0	4 790	58.9	3.9	3.7	0.1	10.4	92.9	8 237	53	46	700	51.3	47.0	1.7
Lucas	45.7	5 216	36.3	40.7	2.3	0.2	8.8	77.6	8 862	36	36	651	45.3	52.1	2.6
Lyon	43.5	3 701	45.1	4.4	4.6	0.1	20.2	26.6	2 260	35	48	647	26.9	71.9	1.2
Madison	80.3	5 130	45.0	29.6	2.4	0.1	8.2	120.8	7 718	35	63	924	44.0	54.0	2.0
Mahaska	103.0	4 588	32.3	43.1	3.7	0.2	7.0	35.6	1 584	55	90	1 395	40.8	57.4	1.8
Marion	110.4	3 302	53.4	5.1	4.5	0.3	11.9	105.0	3 142	133	131	1 664	43.6	54.3	2.1
Marshall	192.9	4 722	64.1	3.0	4.2	0.3	6.4	177.1	4 335	118	164	3 482	53.7	44.4	1.9
Mills	49.6	3 346	58.3	5.0	5.7	1.1	10.6	46.3	3 118	37	59	1 621	40.9	57.4	1.7
Mitchell	58.6	5 460	27.5	34.6	2.8	0.1	12.4	39.9	3 723	39	43	681	55.1	42.8	2.0
Monona	39.6	4 341	49.5	4.3	4.7	0.4	17.8	19.2	2 100	40	37	550	47.8	50.3	1.9
Monroe	25.6	3 175	52.7	6.3	5.3	0.3	19.1	18.5	2 294	38	33	534	46.4	51.6	2.0
Montgomery	75.5	7 150	27.3	38.4	8.7	0.2	5.5	34.3	3 246	40	42	950	44.0	54.6	1.4
Muscatine	169.3	3 949	47.2	3.6	5.1	0.4	6.8	78.4	1 828	89	175	2 680	57.1	41.5	1.4
O'Brien	67.2	4 738	61.1	4.1	3.9	0.2	8.1	45.7	3 226	45	57	1 105	31.9	66.7	1.4
Osceola	20.4	3 288	41.6	8.9	9.7	0.1	18.2	8.6	1 389	27	25	299	33.1	64.8	2.1
Page	86.1	5 483	33.4	39.4	2.8	0.1	7.4	65.9	4 192	71	59	1 345	39.4	59.1	1.5
Palo Alto	64.4	6 948	31.7	32.8	2.9	0.1	15.3	37.1	4 003	35	37	1 026	50.5	47.7	1.8
Plymouth	123.5	4 958	40.4	28.0	3.4	2.2	7.8	86.7	3 483	73	102	1 421	37.0	62.0	1.0
Pocahontas	41.8	5 851	31.5	27.7	4.1	0.5	11.0	23.7	3 313	36	29	550	44.9	53.3	1.8
Polk	2 428.8	5 474	46.0	7.6	4.5	1.5	5.2	2 789.0	6 286	5 834	1 980	29 217	56.4	41.8	1.8
Pottawattamie	475.8	5 121	56.9	3.4	5.2	0.3	4.5	433.2	4 662	211	376	5 135	48.3	50.2	1.5
Poweshiek	66.2	3 533	47.3	5.0	4.5	0.2	10.8	65.3	3 483	56	70	875	55.0	43.3	1.7
Ringgold	38.2	7 503	25.9	44.8	2.8	0.2	9.0	42.2	8 280	44	20	428	46.0	52.1	1.9
Sac	42.6	4 196	49.4	6.2	4.3	0.1	13.4	17.5	1 720	47	41	571	44.6	53.5	1.8
Scott	760.2	4 504	54.4	2.6	4.9	0.1	3.6	683.1	4 047	575	695	8 180	56.6	42.1	1.3
Shelby	87.3	7 233	22.6	50.5	1.7	0.1	7.8	52.5	4 348	48	49	1 053	44.4	54.0	1.6
Sioux	160.8	4 691	31.1	29.5	3.1	0.1	6.7	182.6	5 329	99	133	2 063	18.2	80.9	0.9
Story	440.2	4 830	30.3	42.8	3.2	0.5	3.7	391.5	4 295	1 023	367	18 601	57.0	40.8	2.2
Tama	71.1	4 056	60.3	5.1	3.5	0.1	12.6	36.6	2 088	53	71	2 070	55.3	43.2	1.5
Taylor	30.7	4 937	39.9	4.5	3.6	0.1	25.2	25.0	4 034	39	25	407	44.5	53.1	2.4
Union	122.3	9 707	35.7	41.6	1.4	0.1	4.0	91.1	7 230	57	51	1 312	50.7	47.0	2.2
Van Buren	35.9	4 821	31.7	41.5	2.3	0.1	11.2	9.2	1 230	39	30	567	42.8	55.0	2.2
Wapello	204.9	5 795	64.7	3.0	2.8	0.3	9.3	88.9	2 514	114	143	2 388	55.3	41.8	2.9
Warren	173.5	3 701	60.2	4.1	4.2	0.3	5.2	262.4	5 595	79	189	2 192	49.4	48.8	1.8
Washington	127.8	5 831	38.9	20.4	2.8	0.3	9.4	155.3	7 085	64	90	1 445	48.6	49.4	2.0
Wayne	43.2	6 809	20.6	52.3	2.4	0.2	7.7	24.6	3 877	35	26	580	45.5	52.5	2.0
Webster	231.6	6 213	65.0	3.5	2.6	0.2	5.7	235.4	6 314	207	145	2 881	53.4	44.9	1.6
Winnebago	54.8	5 168	50.8	4.8	4.2	0.1	18.2	51.9	4 900	44	42	721	53.5	44.9	1.7
Winneshiek	175.5	8 333	54.9	26.3	1.7	0.1	5.5	125.1	6 054	69	70	2 145	60.5	37.9	1.6
Woodbury	498.8	4 875	56.0	4.2	4.6	0.6	3.9	465.5	4 550	686	415	6 397	49.1	49.6	1.4
Worth	37.0	4 920	43.7	3.8	4.3	0.1	12.6	25.7	3 424	26	31	460	60.3	37.8	1.9
Wright	134.7	10 370	22.1	58.1	1.8	0.2	4.2	130.1	10 011	62	53	1 305	48.5	50.0	1.5

1. Based on the resident population estimated as of July 1 of the year shown. 2.

STATE/ County code	CBSA code[1]	County type[2]	STATE County	Land area,[3] (sq km) 2010	Population, 2014: Total persons 2014	Population, 2014: Rank	Population, 2014: Per square kilometer	Race alone or in combination, not Hispanic or Latino (percent): White	Black	American Indian, Alaska Native	Asian and Pacific Islander	Percent Hispanic or Latino[4]	Age (percent): Under 5 years	5 to 17 years	18 to 24 years	25 to 34 years	35 to 44 years	45 to 54 years
				1	2	3	4	5	6	7	8	9	10	11	12	13	14	15
20 000	...	X	KANSAS	211 754	2 904 021	X	13.7	79.3	7.0	1.8	3.3	11.2	6.9	18.1	10.4	13.4	11.9	13.0
20 001	...	7	Allen	1 296	12 909	2 238	10.0	93.3	3.1	1.8	1.0	3.2	6.1	17.0	9.5	11.2	10.9	13.0
20 003	...	6	Anderson	1 501	7 883	2 604	5.3	96.2	1.2	1.6	0.8	1.8	6.7	18.7	7.5	9.9	10.4	13.4
20 005	11860	6	Atchison	1 117	16 513	2 007	14.8	90.9	6.4	1.5	0.9	2.8	6.5	17.3	14.1	10.9	10.5	12.6
20 007	...	9	Barber	2 937	4 897	2 842	1.7	95.1	1.2	1.3	0.7	3.2	6.8	15.7	7.6	11.3	9.7	13.2
20 009	24460	7	Barton	2 319	27 385	1 517	11.8	83.6	1.9	1.1	0.5	14.1	6.8	17.7	9.2	12.1	10.0	13.4
20 011	...	6	Bourbon	1 646	14 772	2 117	9.0	93.3	4.0	1.9	0.9	2.3	7.0	18.0	9.9	11.4	10.4	12.0
20 013	...	6	Brown	1 479	9 815	2 456	6.6	86.2	2.3	9.7	0.7	3.6	7.3	17.9	7.3	11.0	10.2	13.0
20 015	48620	2	Butler	3 703	66 227	798	17.9	92.0	2.4	1.9	1.4	4.4	5.8	20.2	9.2	11.5	12.3	14.2
20 017	...	8	Chase	2 002	2 692	2 997	1.3	93.9	1.7	1.4	0.6	3.9	4.4	16.6	7.6	9.2	10.6	14.0
20 019	...	9	Chautauqua	1 655	3 481	2 941	2.1	91.4	1.7	7.8	0.7	2.9	5.3	14.8	7.2	9.8	8.8	13.4
20 021	...	6	Cherokee	1 522	20 787	1 786	13.7	92.5	1.4	6.8	0.9	2.1	6.0	18.5	7.5	10.9	11.7	14.5
20 023	...	9	Cheyenne	2 641	2 693	2 996	1.0	91.9	0.4	0.7	0.7	6.9	5.5	15.6	6.2	9.1	9.4	12.0
20 025	...	9	Clark	2 524	2 144	3 038	0.8	88.6	1.6	1.9	1.8	8.6	6.3	19.0	7.6	10.2	9.8	13.5
20 027	...	7	Clay	1 671	8 317	2 575	5.0	96.1	0.9	1.1	0.6	2.5	6.5	16.7	7.0	11.0	11.4	12.3
20 029	...	7	Cloud	1 853	9 385	2 480	5.1	95.1	1.4	1.0	0.7	3.2	6.0	15.9	10.8	11.1	9.6	12.6
20 031	...	6	Coffey	1 624	8 433	2 564	5.2	95.4	1.2	1.6	0.7	2.4	4.8	17.8	7.3	10.1	11.0	14.9
20 033	...	9	Comanche	2 042	1 954	3 055	1.0	94.4	1.0	1.1	0.6	4.5	8.2	18.2	5.2	9.0	10.7	11.9
20 035	11680	4	Cowley	2 916	35 963	1 274	12.3	83.6	3.8	3.3	2.2	10.0	6.6	17.6	10.4	12.0	11.1	13.1
20 037	38260	4	Crawford	1 527	39 290	1 189	25.7	90.3	3.0	2.0	2.1	5.0	6.2	15.9	18.0	12.6	10.3	11.3
20 039	...	9	Decatur	2 314	2 908	2 982	1.3	96.6	1.3	1.0	0.6	1.8	5.8	13.6	5.7	9.5	8.0	13.4
20 041	...	7	Dickinson	2 194	19 394	1 862	8.8	93.4	1.8	1.3	0.8	4.5	6.7	17.8	7.5	11.2	11.6	13.6
20 043	41140	3	Doniphan	1 019	7 874	2 605	7.7	92.2	4.3	2.4	0.6	2.6	5.6	16.2	12.4	11.3	11.0	12.8
20 045	29940	3	Douglas	1 181	116 585	526	98.7	83.5	5.6	3.6	5.3	5.5	5.2	13.8	24.1	15.4	11.1	10.3
20 047	...	9	Edwards	1 611	3 030	2 975	1.9	78.7	0.6	0.9	0.7	19.9	5.5	17.4	6.9	9.4	10.5	14.5
20 049	...	8	Elk	1 669	2 694	2 995	1.6	94.8	1.2	2.5	1.0	3.4	3.7	15.9	6.2	7.8	9.1	14.0
20 051	25700	5	Ellis	2 331	29 013	1 455	12.4	92.0	1.6	0.7	1.7	5.4	6.9	14.9	17.6	14.1	9.9	11.0
20 053	...	7	Ellsworth	1 854	6 392	2 727	3.4	87.8	5.6	1.2	1.0	5.8	5.1	13.1	8.6	13.9	11.1	14.3
20 055	23780	5	Finney	3 372	37 184	1 246	11.0	45.3	2.9	0.9	4.1	47.8	9.6	21.8	11.0	13.8	11.7	12.7
20 057	19980	5	Ford	2 845	34 795	1 306	12.2	43.3	3.0	0.9	2.0	51.8	9.8	20.9	10.6	14.6	12.5	11.9
20 059	36840	1	Franklin	1 481	25 611	1 579	17.3	93.6	2.1	1.8	0.8	3.9	6.2	18.6	9.3	11.7	11.6	14.4
20 061	27920	5	Geary	996	36 713	1 258	36.9	62.9	19.8	1.9	6.1	14.8	11.4	19.5	16.1	20.4	11.0	7.8
20 063	...	9	Gove	2 776	2 727	2 991	1.0	96.9	0.7	0.4	0.6	2.3	7.2	17.5	6.7	10.4	9.0	11.7
20 065	...	9	Graham	2 327	2 566	3 004	1.1	91.7	5.2	1.8	1.0	3.0	6.0	14.0	6.0	9.6	8.8	14.1
20 067	...	7	Grant	1 489	7 816	2 612	5.2	52.2	0.6	0.9	0.6	47.1	9.0	23.4	8.5	12.4	12.7	11.9
20 069	...	9	Gray	2 250	6 082	2 751	2.7	84.1	0.9	0.7	0.3	14.7	7.8	21.6	8.1	11.4	12.0	13.4
20 071	...	9	Greeley	2 016	1 301	3 096	0.6	83.6	0.5	0.7	0.4	15.7	7.5	15.0	6.0	11.5	8.6	15.0
20 073	...	6	Greenwood	2 961	6 328	2 732	2.1	94.1	1.0	2.4	0.5	3.9	5.2	16.3	6.6	8.9	9.9	14.3
20 075	...	9	Hamilton	2 581	2 603	3 001	1.0	65.9	0.8	1.5	0.7	32.4	9.1	19.7	7.9	14.1	11.8	13.3
20 077	...	8	Harper	2 075	5 818	2 769	2.8	91.8	0.8	1.9	0.3	6.4	6.9	16.9	7.3	10.5	10.4	11.8
20 079	48620	2	Harvey	1 398	34 820	1 305	24.9	85.7	2.5	1.4	1.2	11.1	6.7	18.4	9.2	11.4	10.9	12.8
20 081	...	9	Haskell	1 496	4 106	2 896	2.7	69.9	0.6	0.9	1.7	27.9	7.7	21.4	9.6	11.3	12.1	12.5
20 083	...	9	Hodgeman	2 227	1 916	3 060	0.9	91.3	1.8	0.7	0.6	6.9	5.9	16.4	7.1	10.1	9.2	14.2
20 085	45820	3	Jackson	1 700	13 539	2 203	8.0	87.3	1.2	9.3	0.7	4.2	6.2	19.6	7.1	10.3	12.0	14.2
20 087	45820	3	Jefferson	1 379	18 855	1 877	13.7	95.6	1.0	2.0	0.5	2.4	5.1	18.3	6.9	10.0	11.5	16.3
20 089	...	9	Jewell	2 356	3 043	2 973	1.3	96.3	0.7	0.9	0.5	2.5	4.1	14.5	6.0	8.1	8.5	12.8
20 091	28140	1	Johnson	1 226	574 272	110	468.4	83.0	5.6	0.9	5.4	7.4	6.8	18.9	7.6	14.2	13.9	14.1
20 093	23780	9	Kearny	2 255	3 915	2 911	1.7	68.6	1.1	1.8	0.6	29.5	8.1	21.3	9.4	11.6	10.8	13.3
20 095	48620	6	Kingman	2 236	7 698	2 620	3.4	95.5	0.7	1.5	0.9	2.8	5.2	17.6	7.3	10.2	10.0	14.4
20 097	...	9	Kiowa	1 872	2 513	3 007	1.3	92.1	1.0	1.6	1.1	5.4	6.2	14.1	12.9	10.4	9.6	12.6
20 099	37660	7	Labette	1 671	20 960	1 777	12.5	88.7	5.9	4.0	1.1	4.3	6.1	17.1	8.8	11.3	10.9	14.2
20 101	...	9	Lane	1 858	1 687	3 075	0.9	92.6	1.5	1.5	0.7	5.6	4.7	17.6	6.5	8.4	10.9	12.9
20 103	28140	1	Leavenworth	1 199	78 797	700	65.7	81.7	10.5	1.6	2.3	6.7	6.6	17.7	8.5	13.5	14.8	14.3
20 105	...	9	Lincoln	1 863	3 167	2 959	1.7	96.3	0.9	0.9	0.6	2.5	6.5	17.6	5.9	9.2	9.9	13.1
20 107	28140	1	Linn	1 539	9 502	2 468	6.2	95.8	1.1	1.7	0.7	2.3	5.1	18.7	6.3	9.7	11.4	14.4
20 109	...	9	Logan	2 779	2 794	2 989	1.0	92.6	1.4	1.2	1.5	4.8	6.2	16.3	7.6	11.8	10.1	13.4
20 111	21380	5	Lyon	2 195	33 212	1 349	15.1	74.0	3.1	1.3	2.9	20.5	6.2	16.6	17.4	12.6	10.2	11.7
20 113	32700	6	McPherson	2 327	29 241	1 446	12.6	93.7	1.9	1.0	1.2	3.9	6.1	17.3	8.9	11.6	10.6	13.2
20 115	...	6	Marion	2 446	12 208	2 286	5.0	95.2	1.4	1.5	0.6	2.9	5.0	16.1	10.0	9.0	9.3	13.9
20 117	...	7	Marshall	2 331	10 006	2 439	4.3	96.6	0.9	1.0	0.7	2.2	6.0	17.0	6.7	10.9	9.8	13.9
20 119	...	9	Meade	2 533	4 357	2 878	1.7	82.0	1.3	1.6	0.8	16.1	6.8	20.8	8.4	9.4	10.7	13.1
20 121	28140	1	Miami	1 491	32 822	1 361	22.0	94.7	1.9	1.4	0.7	2.9	6.2	19.9	7.2	10.3	12.4	16.0
20 123	...	7	Mitchell	1 818	6 284	2 737	3.5	96.8	0.6	0.8	0.7	2.1	6.5	15.6	9.7	10.2	9.5	12.6
20 125	17700	5	Montgomery	1 667	34 065	1 327	20.4	84.3	6.9	5.9	1.3	6.1	6.5	17.0	9.9	11.6	10.5	13.2
20 127	...	9	Morris	1 801	5 698	2 786	3.2	94.4	1.2	1.3	0.6	4.1	5.3	15.5	6.4	10.2	9.2	14.6
20 129	...	9	Morton	1 890	3 110	2 964	1.6	75.1	1.4	1.6	2.3	21.5	6.5	19.6	7.5	10.5	12.0	13.1
20 131	...	8	Nemaha	1 858	10 148	2 428	5.5	96.9	1.1	1.0	0.7	1.6	6.7	18.8	7.7	10.0	10.2	13.9

1. CBSA = Core Based Statistical Area. See Appendix A for explanation. See Appendix B for list of metropolitan areas with component counties. 2. County type code from the Economic Research Service of USDA Rural-Urban Continuum Codes. See Appendix A for definition. 3. Dry land or land partially or temporarily covered by water. 4. May be of any race.

Table B. States and Counties — **Population and Households**

STATE County	Population, 2013 (cont.): Age (percent) (cont.): 55 to 64 years	65 to 74 years	75 years and over	Percent female	Population change and components of change, 2000–2014: Total persons: 2000	2010	Percent change: 2000–2010	2010–2014	Components of change, 2010–2014: Births	Deaths	Net migration	Households, 2009–2013: Number	Persons per house-hold	Percent: Family house-holds	Female family house-holder[1]	One per-son
	16	17	18	19	20	21	22	23	24	25	26	27	28	29	30	31
KANSAS	12.3	7.5	6.5	50.2	2 688 418	2 853 118	6.1	1.8	170 209	104 162	-15 299	1 110 440	2.51	65.7	10.4	28.4
Allen	13.7	9.4	9.2	51.2	14 385	13 371	-7.0	-3.5	637	744	-344	5 505	2.35	65.2	9.8	30.6
Anderson	13.0	10.5	10.0	50.5	8 110	8 102	-0.1	-2.7	400	405	-213	3 308	2.38	69.2	10.1	27.4
Atchison	12.2	8.3	7.6	51.2	16 774	16 924	0.9	-2.4	887	758	-524	6 216	2.50	65.4	10.7	30.2
Barber	15.5	11.1	9.1	49.0	5 307	4 861	-8.4	0.7	293	225	-23	2 187	2.22	65.7	7.5	31.9
Barton	13.7	8.4	8.7	50.5	28 205	27 674	-1.9	-1.0	1 642	1 311	-628	11 491	2.36	64.3	9.6	31.2
Bourbon	13.3	9.3	8.8	50.5	15 379	15 173	-1.3	-2.6	887	735	-555	5 636	2.60	68.3	10.9	27.2
Brown	14.3	10.1	8.8	50.9	10 724	9 984	-6.9	-1.7	601	543	-239	4 104	2.39	64.1	10.9	33.4
Butler	13.0	7.4	6.4	49.8	59 482	65 880	10.8	0.5	3 347	2 564	-499	24 270	2.63	71.2	8.5	25.2
Chase	15.1	12.6	9.9	49.4	3 030	2 790	-7.9	-3.5	102	118	-68	1 149	2.28	63.4	6.4	32.7
Chautauqua	14.8	13.7	12.2	48.1	4 359	3 669	-15.8	-5.1	150	219	-138	1 565	2.24	69.7	9.1	28.9
Cherokee	13.6	10.0	7.2	50.5	22 605	21 603	-4.4	-3.8	999	1 163	-627	7 936	2.65	69.5	9.6	28.1
Cheyenne	16.0	11.8	14.2	49.6	3 165	2 726	-13.9	-1.2	118	175	31	1 343	1.98	61.1	5.9	37.0
Clark	11.9	9.8	11.9	51.2	2 390	2 215	-7.3	-3.2	122	121	-87	932	2.29	65.8	7.1	31.3
Clay	13.7	10.7	10.8	50.5	8 822	8 535	-3.3	-2.6	427	440	-199	3 407	2.45	65.7	7.4	29.1
Cloud	13.2	9.9	11.0	51.1	10 268	9 533	-7.2	-1.6	555	576	-132	4 022	2.18	60.8	9.8	33.9
Coffey	15.3	10.6	8.2	50.3	8 865	8 601	-3.0	-2.0	355	410	-102	3 501	2.39	69.3	8.9	27.6
Comanche	13.7	12.4	10.7	51.4	1 967	1 891	-3.9	3.3	102	111	85	791	2.33	63.7	5.4	33.8
Cowley	12.6	8.9	7.8	50.1	36 291	36 311	0.1	-1.0	1 983	1 742	-613	13 867	2.47	64.6	9.6	29.4
Crawford	11.2	7.6	6.9	50.0	38 242	39 134	2.3	0.4	2 092	1 673	-244	15 370	2.42	60.1	10.0	30.7
Decatur	17.1	11.6	15.4	50.0	3 472	2 961	-14.7	-1.8	149	204	3	1 482	1.91	60.4	4.6	37.0
Dickinson	13.4	8.9	9.3	50.2	19 344	19 754	2.1	-1.8	965	953	-349	7 845	2.47	69.4	8.5	26.4
Doniphan	13.7	9.0	8.0	49.2	8 249	7 945	-3.7	-0.9	373	298	-135	3 161	2.30	67.6	10.6	27.7
Douglas	10.0	5.7	4.3	50.0	99 962	110 826	10.9	5.2	5 352	2 576	2 995	43 398	2.38	54.4	8.5	28.2
Edwards	16.3	9.6	9.9	49.9	3 449	3 037	-11.9	-0.2	159	136	-25	1 269	2.29	65.5	5.4	30.5
Elk	16.3	14.2	12.8	50.7	3 261	2 882	-11.6	-6.5	106	166	-121	1 271	2.14	65.1	8.9	32.4
Ellis	11.9	6.4	7.2	49.7	27 507	28 452	3.4	2.0	1 699	1 046	-74	11 824	2.32	54.4	6.6	34.0
Ellsworth	14.4	10.1	9.5	43.2	6 525	6 497	-0.4	-1.6	269	320	-60	2 528	2.15	63.9	6.1	32.2
Finney	10.2	5.3	3.9	49.3	40 523	36 776	-9.2	1.1	3 031	842	-1 763	12 515	2.91	71.8	11.4	23.6
Ford	9.6	5.2	4.9	48.4	32 458	33 848	4.3	2.8	2 898	989	-1 000	11 103	3.02	72.4	10.1	22.3
Franklin	13.0	8.6	6.6	50.4	24 784	25 992	4.9	-1.5	1 364	1 061	-672	9 909	2.56	69.0	9.1	26.1
Geary	6.4	4.0	3.3	47.3	27 947	34 362	23.0	6.8	4 261	885	-1 189	12 532	2.78	70.2	12.1	23.9
Gove	14.6	10.1	12.7	49.6	3 068	2 695	-12.2	1.2	139	148	50	1 201	2.31	70.1	5.0	26.2
Graham	15.9	12.2	13.3	50.6	2 946	2 597	-11.8	-1.2	119	129	-22	1 192	2.14	61.9	6.8	34.6
Grant	11.3	6.1	4.7	49.0	7 909	7 829	-1.0	-0.2	507	197	-343	2 793	2.79	78.7	14.5	14.5
Gray	11.6	7.7	6.4	50.3	5 904	6 006	1.7	1.3	364	176	-126	2 066	2.86	75.8	8.4	21.4
Greeley	14.7	8.8	12.8	50.8	1 534	1 247	-18.7	4.3	77	67	43	493	2.39	70.4	2.2	26.6
Greenwood	15.9	11.8	11.1	50.0	7 673	6 689	-12.8	-5.4	258	359	-238	2 855	2.27	65.1	8.6	31.8
Hamilton	11.8	6.6	5.8	48.9	2 670	2 690	0.7	-3.2	184	109	-168	1 076	2.44	69.1	9.2	26.6
Harper	14.7	11.0	10.6	49.3	6 536	6 034	-7.7	-3.6	290	400	-97	2 595	2.22	64.0	8.5	31.2
Harvey	12.9	8.2	9.5	50.9	32 869	34 684	5.5	0.4	1 953	1 519	-298	13 287	2.51	68.9	7.9	26.5
Haskell	13.6	6.0	5.7	50.9	4 307	4 256	-1.2	-3.5	244	90	-326	1 411	2.96	74.6	7.4	22.7
Hodgeman	14.6	10.2	12.2	50.1	2 085	1 916	-8.1	0.0	110	82	-52	821	2.34	72.6	6.1	25.7
Jackson	13.4	9.7	7.4	49.6	12 657	13 462	6.4	0.6	732	572	-96	5 273	2.51	73.4	11.7	23.1
Jefferson	14.9	9.8	7.2	49.1	18 426	19 126	3.8	-1.4	807	713	-339	7 421	2.52	71.9	7.4	23.0
Jewell	18.1	13.4	14.5	48.7	3 791	3 077	-18.8	-1.1	114	166	12	1 454	2.08	66.2	3.3	31.1
Johnson	12.2	6.9	5.3	51.0	451 086	544 179	20.6	5.5	31 458	14 851	13 140	216 304	2.53	67.9	9.0	26.4
Kearny	11.3	7.3	6.8	49.2	4 531	3 977	-12.2	-1.6	243	149	-157	1 301	2.97	73.6	8.8	24.4
Kingman	14.4	10.2	10.7	49.8	8 673	7 858	-9.4	-2.0	331	400	-104	3 223	2.37	66.7	8.1	28.6
Kiowa	14.9	8.6	10.7	50.4	3 278	2 553	-22.1	-1.6	138	102	-83	1 065	2.21	63.8	7.7	30.6
Labette	13.7	9.8	8.1	50.3	22 835	21 607	-5.4	-3.0	1 171	1 091	-704	8 703	2.38	65.9	8.5	29.2
Lane	15.8	10.7	12.4	50.3	2 155	1 750	-18.8	-3.6	93	99	-68	808	1.96	55.3	3.7	40.2
Leavenworth	12.4	7.2	5.0	46.6	68 691	76 227	11.0	3.4	4 101	2 326	865	26 358	2.69	70.6	10.4	24.9
Lincoln	17.1	9.3	11.4	50.2	3 578	3 241	-9.4	-2.3	146	161	-55	1 414	2.22	63.5	9.9	33.5
Linn	14.2	12.2	8.1	50.4	9 570	9 656	0.9	-1.6	414	493	-40	4 234	2.24	71.9	7.7	25.5
Logan	14.8	8.5	11.3	48.5	3 046	2 756	-9.5	1.4	136	120	20	1 282	2.12	59.3	8.9	34.2
Lyon	11.9	7.1	6.2	51.1	35 935	33 690	-6.2	-1.4	1 776	1 145	-1 154	13 170	2.46	59.2	9.2	31.0
McPherson	13.6	8.9	9.9	50.8	29 554	29 180	-1.3	0.2	1 501	1 542	109	11 540	2.42	70.1	6.2	26.0
Marion	14.3	11.0	11.3	49.9	13 361	12 660	-5.2	-3.6	479	640	-316	4 861	2.41	68.6	6.5	28.1
Marshall	14.6	9.6	11.6	50.2	10 965	10 117	-7.7	-1.1	501	515	-72	4 345	2.27	64.1	5.7	32.2
Meade	13.3	7.6	9.9	49.2	4 631	4 575	-1.2	-4.8	233	182	-259	1 714	2.55	75.1	7.6	20.4
Miami	13.4	8.2	6.5	50.5	28 351	32 787	15.6	0.1	1 564	1 082	-468	12 334	2.60	72.9	9.5	23.8
Mitchell	14.4	10.3	11.3	49.2	6 932	6 373	-8.1	-1.4	322	406	-21	2 804	2.14	63.1	6.4	34.5
Montgomery	13.4	9.5	8.3	51.0	36 252	35 471	-2.2	-4.0	2 016	1 793	-1 660	14 000	2.41	65.0	11.4	30.9
Morris	15.7	11.4	11.7	50.5	6 104	5 923	-3.0	-3.8	278	308	-169	2 503	2.32	65.0	5.3	32.5
Morton	12.6	8.4	9.7	49.2	3 496	3 233	-7.5	-3.8	179	131	-179	1 186	2.61	75.1	15.0	18.6
Nemaha	12.5	8.3	11.8	49.7	10 717	10 178	-5.0	-0.3	537	499	-76	4 117	2.36	68.8	7.1	27.6

1. No spouse present.

STATE County	Persons in group quarters, 2014	Daytime population, 2009–2013: Number	Daytime population, 2009–2013: Employment/residence ratio	Births, 2014: Total	Births, 2014: Rate[1]	Deaths, 2014: Number	Deaths, 2014: Rate[1]	Persons under 65 with no health insurance, 2013: Number	Persons under 65 with no health insurance, 2013: Percent	Medicare, 2014: Eligible for Medicare	Medicare, 2014: Enrolled in Medicare Advantage	Medicare, 2014: Enrolled in a Medicare prescription drug plan	Serious crimes known to police,[2] 2013: Total: Number	Serious crimes known to police,[2] 2013: Total: Rate[3]
	32	33	34	35	36	37	38	39	40	41	42	43	44	45
KANSAS	79 124	2 879 325	1.01	40 001	13.8	24 023	8.3	340 965	14.1	481 099	6 866	272 974	95 118	3 287
Allen	382	13 848	1.09	145	11.2	169	13.1	1 483	14.3	2 895	215	1 873	420	3 300
Anderson	103	6 894	0.70	87	11.0	96	12.2	947	15.2	1 809	83	1 201	201	2 598
Atchison	1 377	16 482	0.95	203	12.3	168	10.2	1 639	12.6	3 001	167	1 979	451	2 687
Barber	40	4 786	0.96	64	13.1	50	10.2	578	14.7	1 146	19	779	133	2 733
Barton	672	27 557	1.00	397	14.5	301	11.0	3 868	17.3	5 337	69	3 916	977	3 553
Bourbon	409	14 908	0.99	198	13.4	153	10.4	1 787	15.0	3 242	299	1 915	500	3 377
Brown	116	10 402	1.09	137	14.0	119	12.1	1 296	16.0	2 163	49	1 494	244	2 479
Butler	2 309	55 286	0.65	809	12.2	586	8.8	5 701	10.4	10 618	1 470	5 870	1 964	2 987
Chase	145	2 393	0.68	25	9.3	11	4.1	350	17.7	586	18	388	12	437
Chautauqua	79	3 150	0.69	36	10.3	42	12.1	538	20.4	975	32	649	33	932
Cherokee	202	18 930	0.74	222	10.7	256	12.3	2 499	14.5	4 446	386	2 591	638	3 150
Cheyenne	49	2 655	0.96	27	10.0	42	15.6	348	17.5	749	30	478	45	1 690
Clark	57	2 095	0.91	33	15.4	18	8.4	266	15.6	468	NA	331	28	1 289
Clay	140	8 038	0.89	95	11.4	109	13.1	769	11.8	1 902	96	1 291	133	1 561
Cloud	498	9 264	0.96	143	15.2	137	14.6	1 042	14.8	2 251	58	1 670	304	3 251
Coffey	130	9 003	1.12	81	9.6	77	9.1	825	12.1	1 972	61	1 253	80	945
Comanche	65	1 838	0.93	23	11.8	18	9.2	269	18.2	480	NA	330	NA	NA
Cowley	2 004	35 081	0.93	460	12.8	396	11.0	4 437	15.5	7 126	681	4 514	1 186	3 270
Crawford	1 771	39 618	1.02	474	12.1	355	9.0	5 262	16.3	6 944	353	4 595	1 695	4 336
Decatur	81	2 804	0.90	42	14.4	37	12.7	319	15.0	835	41	563	NA	NA
Dickinson	307	17 840	0.80	200	10.3	197	10.2	2 069	13.0	4 083	305	2 353	417	2 112
Doniphan	427	6 642	0.68	86	10.9	68	8.6	886	14.4	1 551	28	972	132	1 685
Douglas	8 794	106 407	0.90	1 269	10.9	605	5.2	13 787	14.6	14 378	1 677	8 264	4 560	4 022
Edwards	35	2 705	0.80	43	14.2	24	7.9	466	19.8	677	23	450	NA	NA
Elk	40	2 508	0.75	27	10.0	32	11.9	395	20.5	839	30	543	22	824
Ellis	1 033	29 709	1.06	396	13.6	248	8.5	2 970	12.2	4 595	76	3 201	794	2 715
Ellsworth	983	6 358	0.97	65	10.2	72	11.3	497	11.7	1 392	34	966	124	1 912
Finney	548	37 480	1.03	700	18.8	194	5.2	6 334	19.1	4 143	112	2 708	1 154	3 097
Ford	708	35 192	1.06	674	19.4	219	6.3	6 486	21.1	3 942	86	2 594	1 054	3 014
Franklin	478	23 879	0.84	319	12.5	248	9.7	2 609	12.2	4 947	327	3 142	699	2 703
Geary	847	41 990	1.38	976	26.6	206	5.6	4 893	14.5	3 574	311	1 217	897	2 302
Gove	56	3 008	1.13	34	12.5	36	13.2	361	17.0	664	19	456	18	656
Graham	40	2 528	0.94	29	11.3	28	10.9	284	14.8	714	31	469	42	1 636
Grant	79	8 267	1.11	108	13.8	23	2.9	1 259	17.9	1 015	NA	710	100	1 258
Gray	78	5 650	0.88	79	13.0	35	5.8	912	17.8	935	19	676	82	1 360
Greeley	26	1 271	1.11	20	15.4	12	9.2	163	16.1	295	NA	226	3	229
Greenwood	90	5 869	0.76	57	9.0	76	12.0	789	16.1	1 684	40	1 139	98	1 536
Hamilton	0	2 665	1.01	42	16.1	20	7.7	556	24.4	377	NA	270	33	1 261
Harper	129	5 900	0.98	64	11.0	97	16.7	765	16.7	1 380	18	1 000	119	2 682
Harvey	1 311	33 548	0.93	462	13.3	329	9.4	3 746	13.5	7 055	1 166	4 244	1 077	3 088
Haskell	33	4 185	0.98	54	13.2	21	5.1	803	22.0	565	13	392	64	1 507
Hodgeman	14	1 778	0.83	33	17.2	27	14.1	263	17.4	428	NA	284	22	1 112
Jackson	133	11 196	0.66	175	12.9	132	9.7	1 579	14.3	2 828	204	1 787	168	1 372
Jefferson	235	13 784	0.44	198	10.5	132	7.0	1 918	12.4	3 680	386	2 168	340	1 801
Jewell	27	2 729	0.77	31	10.2	34	11.2	386	17.7	879	39	608	NA	NA
Johnson	5 165	572 205	1.07	7 455	13.0	3 624	6.3	48 019	9.7	80 058	21 892	34 702	10 790	1 912
Kearny	81	3 441	0.71	53	13.5	26	6.6	682	20.3	601	NA	417	83	2 095
Kingman	190	7 341	0.85	83	10.8	101	13.1	811	13.2	1 742	37	1 167	136	1 843
Kiowa	149	2 682	1.13	32	12.7	23	9.2	294	15.5	543	NA	381	35	1 414
Labette	480	21 951	1.06	284	13.5	225	10.7	2 476	14.5	4 845	331	3 205	790	3 729
Lane	3	1 564	0.94	25	14.8	17	10.1	197	14.9	433	NA	326	35	2 069
Leavenworth	6 546	70 085	0.79	970	12.3	547	6.9	6 402	10.3	11 711	1 442	4 664	1 971	2 523
Lincoln	50	2 913	0.81	35	11.1	35	11.1	424	17.0	738	NA	511	25	793
Linn	63	8 364	0.69	97	10.2	116	12.2	1 221	16.2	2 256	504	1 082	126	1 495
Logan	41	2 867	1.07	32	11.5	18	6.4	345	15.4	613	28	427	37	1 328
Lyon	1 444	33 017	0.96	411	12.4	258	7.8	5 132	18.4	5 564	285	3 666	686	2 087
McPherson	925	29 948	1.04	378	12.9	365	12.5	2 470	10.5	5 994	448	3 956	838	3 018
Marion	723	11 304	0.80	110	9.0	137	11.2	1 311	14.6	2 915	121	2 049	183	1 495
Marshall	164	10 441	1.08	123	12.3	111	11.1	978	12.5	2 430	132	1 692	121	1 211
Meade	119	4 198	0.86	46	10.6	39	9.0	606	17.2	813	20	534	13	300
Miami	645	25 636	0.55	366	11.2	270	8.2	3 001	10.9	5 577	1 169	2 876	693	2 131
Mitchell	246	6 930	1.17	74	11.8	100	15.9	538	11.1	1 467	61	1 081	51	866
Montgomery	1 114	36 621	1.12	494	14.5	363	10.7	4 455	16.3	7 392	448	4 980	967	3 035
Morris	66	5 205	0.77	69	12.1	72	12.6	748	17.0	1 406	78	772	99	1 697
Morton	83	3 368	1.13	43	13.8	25	8.0	461	18.1	575	NA	360	40	1 473
Nemaha	259	10 499	1.07	131	12.9	82	8.1	910	11.3	2 156	34	1 517	115	1 137

1. Per 1,000 estimated resident population. 2. Data for serious crimes have not been adjusted for underreporting; this may affect comparability between geographic areas and over time.
3. Per 100,000 population estimated by the FBI.

STATE County	Serious crimes known to police, 2013 (cont.)[1] Rate[2] Violent	Serious crimes known to police, 2013 (cont.)[1] Rate[2] Property	Education: School enrollment and attainment, 2009–2013 Enrollment[3] Total	Education: Enrollment[3] Percent private	Education: Attainment[4] (percent) High school graduate or less	Education: Attainment[4] (percent) Bachelor's degree or more	Education: Local government expenditures,[5] 2012–2013 Total current spending (mil dol)	Education: Local government expenditures,[5] 2012–2013 Current spending per student (dollars)	Money income, 2009–2013: Per capita income[6] (dollars)	Money income, 2009–2013: Households Median income (dollars)	Money income, 2009–2013: Households Mean income (dollars)	Money income, 2009–2013: Households Percent with income of $200,000 or more	Income and poverty, 2013: Median household income (dollars)	Income and poverty, 2013: Percent below poverty level All persons	Income and poverty, 2013: Percent below poverty level Children under 18 years	Income and poverty, 2013: Percent below poverty level Children 5 to 17 years in families
	46	47	48	49	50	51	52	53	54	55	56	57	58	59	60	61
KANSAS	340	2 947	794 865	13.6	37.7	30.3	4 808.2	9 828	26 929	51 332	68 051	3.4	50 892	13.9	18.4	16.5
Allen	212	3 088	3 253	8.9	44.1	16.1	26.0	10 870	20 552	40 554	48 994	0.2	40 073	17.5	26.4	23.4
Anderson	207	2 391	1 732	13.4	50.8	19.0	13.6	10 413	22 139	41 713	53 830	0.6	42 386	15.4	21.0	18.9
Atchison	232	2 455	4 763	28.6	51.5	21.6	24.6	10 524	21 909	45 212	56 511	1.1	44 180	17.9	22.2	20.7
Barber	329	2 404	1 028	6.6	42.9	19.8	8.2	10 934	26 229	45 920	57 715	2.2	50 097	12.7	18.3	17.7
Barton	371	3 182	6 641	4.5	46.1	18.3	41.1	9 298	25 800	44 981	61 832	2.2	42 464	15.0	20.3	17.9
Bourbon	567	2 810	3 781	10.6	42.6	22.0	22.2	9 367	19 340	39 591	48 607	0.8	35 990	19.4	30.1	26.9
Brown	152	2 326	2 238	7.5	50.5	18.2	17.2	11 587	21 046	39 968	49 522	1.7	41 426	14.7	22.7	22.0
Butler	231	2 755	19 382	11.2	34.9	26.7	134.8	8 672	27 329	56 454	72 712	2.9	56 456	11.3	14.2	12.1
Chase	0	437	652	4.8	46.7	23.6	4.3	11 803	21 775	36 815	50 035	0.3	44 300	11.6	18.0	15.4
Chautauqua	85	847	645	7.3	49.7	16.3	6.3	11 877	21 245	39 529	48 698	1.7	38 973	15.8	25.8	24.1
Cherokee	301	2 849	5 211	4.7	48.4	14.9	39.8	10 579	19 580	39 746	50 530	1.1	40 310	18.9	27.7	24.9
Cheyenne	300	1 389	488	4.1	41.7	21.7	5.5	13 070	23 677	37 875	47 598	0.5	39 317	12.5	18.3	16.3
Clark	92	1 197	547	7.5	35.6	26.2	5.9	12 565	25 385	41 129	59 532	2.3	42 866	12.3	15.6	14.0
Clay	282	1 279	1 835	7.7	39.9	20.7	13.4	9 583	24 503	45 233	59 161	2.5	48 178	11.9	17.4	16.9
Cloud	449	2 802	2 386	9.0	44.6	16.6	19.1	11 559	20 467	38 534	46 078	0.5	40 663	14.3	17.2	15.0
Coffey	83	862	1 991	6.3	46.2	19.9	18.0	11 269	27 627	51 793	66 724	2.9	53 487	10.8	13.5	11.2
Comanche	NA	NA	448	4.2	37.7	23.9	4.1	11 284	21 041	39 375	48 231	0.5	44 076	11.3	15.9	14.2
Cowley	369	2 900	9 672	13.7	40.5	20.0	59.6	9 622	21 519	41 878	54 659	1.7	42 341	18.3	23.7	20.9
Crawford	327	4 008	12 589	8.8	39.5	27.2	63.4	10 314	20 974	37 378	51 530	1.8	36 958	22.2	24.4	23.1
Decatur	NA	NA	452	7.3	47.2	19.9	4.4	11 910	27 154	39 333	53 785	3.6	37 789	13.8	20.8	19.5
Dickinson	157	1 955	4 678	10.5	48.1	18.5	35.6	10 053	23 895	48 890	59 510	1.9	49 033	10.9	16.2	14.6
Doniphan	191	1 493	2 211	9.8	49.5	17.5	16.9	11 659	22 713	46 512	56 675	1.2	46 338	14.3	18.9	17.2
Douglas	337	3 685	45 163	8.8	24.6	49.6	137.2	9 243	26 342	49 508	66 983	3.4	51 221	16.6	15.2	13.3
Edwards	NA	NA	724	2.8	45.9	22.3	5.9	13 315	24 714	46 551	58 055	2.0	45 687	11.8	17.5	15.6
Elk	75	749	516	4.8	48.9	18.0	6.9	13 705	20 322	34 089	43 515	0.2	37 537	18.2	32.4	28.2
Ellis	332	2 383	9 184	8.1	35.5	32.3	38.6	10 084	24 291	43 085	57 012	1.9	47 454	14.4	13.7	12.7
Ellsworth	108	1 804	1 135	8.9	46.3	20.8	13.8	11 688	22 789	45 865	57 185	1.9	48 030	11.4	13.8	12.8
Finney	405	2 692	10 393	4.9	54.3	17.9	87.6	10 049	21 629	47 945	63 137	2.9	46 984	16.8	22.7	21.1
Ford	260	2 754	9 629	3.2	53.6	16.7	73.8	9 828	19 994	51 178	59 272	2.0	46 444	14.0	18.6	18.3
Franklin	263	2 440	6 763	16.9	45.8	20.2	47.1	10 293	22 979	49 543	58 959	1.2	48 297	14.1	19.5	16.4
Geary	423	1 879	10 514	11.2	37.9	20.8	79.8	9 463	21 408	46 908	58 710	1.5	41 048	15.8	24.2	24.1
Gove	36	620	560	7.7	46.1	20.3	6.8	14 079	26 233	44 866	61 388	2.5	48 042	10.5	15.0	14.4
Graham	117	1 519	497	7.6	40.2	22.9	4.3	10 135	28 146	47 500	61 376	3.9	44 422	13.3	18.6	17.3
Grant	252	1 007	1 973	6.6	53.3	17.8	15.6	8 894	26 370	53 213	74 013	3.5	54 952	11.7	17.2	15.8
Gray	199	1 161	1 587	13.5	52.1	20.2	15.2	11 342	25 537	57 808	70 019	2.8	56 615	9.4	13.6	11.9
Greeley	0	229	246	4.5	40.4	21.9	2.8	13 308	32 650	52 847	77 977	2.6	50 637	10.0	13.4	13.4
Greenwood	282	1 254	1 425	1.5	51.5	16.5	12.0	11 792	22 280	38 346	49 829	0.7	35 803	15.7	23.0	20.1
Hamilton	306	955	554	3.1	51.9	12.6	5.8	11 720	24 510	43 357	60 610	1.4	42 263	13.8	20.5	20.3
Harper	451	2 231	1 290	8.2	46.6	16.9	12.1	11 130	22 820	38 313	52 164	2.1	43 066	14.9	21.4	19.9
Harvey	413	2 675	9 764	17.4	40.3	26.3	56.6	9 174	23 775	50 287	60 533	1.7	54 135	11.3	15.1	13.2
Haskell	141	1 365	1 172	9.7	53.6	17.7	10.2	12 720	25 114	52 415	70 907	4.5	53 076	11.5	17.2	15.8
Hodgeman	101	1 011	413	4.1	38.6	22.6	3.7	11 367	30 440	52 375	71 046	3.2	49 119	9.7	13.8	13.4
Jackson	171	1 200	3 609	8.3	46.6	17.7	25.3	10 407	24 117	54 546	61 375	1.4	50 661	10.4	15.1	13.0
Jefferson	223	1 579	4 548	9.3	48.0	21.3	40.4	10 836	26 280	56 875	65 982	1.2	54 890	10.1	14.3	12.3
Jewell	NA	NA	567	4.9	44.3	14.7	3.4	10 224	23 134	39 884	48 909	1.0	41 924	13.7	20.2	18.2
Johnson	133	1 778	153 484	19.8	20.2	51.7	872.2	9 310	38 827	74 717	98 017	8.2	74 135	6.1	7.0	6.1
Kearny	303	1 792	1 092	2.7	46.2	17.2	11.0	11 763	22 292	52 264	63 199	1.3	54 399	12.2	19.2	17.7
Kingman	163	1 681	1 765	13.1	43.0	19.3	13.2	10 610	24 026	47 466	57 892	1.5	51 281	12.2	17.6	15.7
Kiowa	81	1 333	637	30.0	35.8	20.0	7.0	10 512	23 232	44 650	54 350	1.7	45 417	11.5	14.6	14.0
Labette	368	3 361	5 628	9.8	40.9	20.4	40.1	9 951	22 394	40 916	54 295	1.1	38 542	16.4	26.6	23.9
Lane	355	1 714	332	2.1	41.8	22.7	4.4	12 755	31 694	53 021	63 356	3.3	52 915	9.6	14.4	12.3
Leavenworth	399	2 124	20 907	17.5	39.8	28.7	117.1	8 857	27 017	63 435	74 904	3.4	65 424	11.2	13.7	12.8
Lincoln	63	729	697	10.0	39.4	19.7	7.3	11 571	23 686	40 811	52 272	1.2	42 521	13.2	19.9	17.7
Linn	154	1 341	2 043	5.4	50.1	14.2	20.6	10 835	26 224	45 519	60 498	2.0	44 036	15.1	21.5	17.8
Logan	179	1 148	650	17.1	45.7	15.6	6.1	10 777	25 328	41 765	54 180	2.3	46 375	10.1	13.7	12.4
Lyon	73	2 014	10 916	7.9	46.6	24.1	55.3	9 789	19 789	38 981	49 477	1.1	39 483	21.2	23.1	20.4
McPherson	205	2 813	7 176	17.5	40.7	25.7	48.1	9 930	27 462	54 167	68 973	2.4	52 734	9.4	11.7	10.1
Marion	90	1 405	3 159	19.2	47.1	20.8	23.3	11 215	22 269	45 830	54 392	0.8	45 319	12.8	16.2	13.5
Marshall	130	1 081	2 124	12.3	52.0	15.0	19.2	10 595	25 262	44 032	57 281	2.2	50 087	10.5	14.7	13.5
Meade	46	254	1 103	9.6	46.6	23.8	7.4	11 524	21 990	51 000	57 389	0.7	53 942	10.3	14.3	12.3
Miami	194	1 937	8 889	12.7	37.9	23.9	46.6	9 153	28 412	58 936	73 892	3.0	59 706	9.4	12.6	11.0
Mitchell	357	509	1 528	19.2	37.7	23.8	13.0	11 243	26 911	46 667	59 996	3.0	46 181	12.2	14.8	14.2
Montgomery	373	2 661	8 917	9.1	44.8	17.9	55.3	9 355	21 332	39 669	51 949	1.6	30 045	16.6	25.0	22.1
Morris	189	1 509	1 222	5.0	50.6	17.4	12.5	11 328	24 680	47 445	56 900	1.6	46 404	13.0	19.6	18.1
Morton	147	1 325	797	8.4	48.1	17.5	11.9	9 399	22 378	46 607	59 300	1.5	51 157	11.9	18.2	16.0
Nemaha	138	998	2 379	10.3	57.6	19.5	20.0	10 670	24 550	47 122	59 974	1.8	50 006	9.8	11.0	10.2

1. Data for serious crimes have not been adjusted for underreporting; this may affect comparability between geographic areas and over time. 2. Per 100,000 population estimated by the FBI.
3. All persons 3 years old and over enrolled in nursery school through college. 4. Persons 25 years old and over. 5. Elementary and secondary education expenditures.
6. Based on population estimated by the American Community Survey, 2009–2013.

STATE County	Personal income, 2013: Total (mil dol)	Personal income, 2013: Percent change, 2012–2013	Personal income, 2013: Per capita[1]: Dollars	Personal income, 2013: Per capita[1]: Rank	Personal income, 2013: Wages and salaries (mil dol)	Personal income, 2013: Supplements to wages and salaries; employer contributions (mil dol): Pension and insurance	Personal income, 2013: Supplements to wages and salaries; employer contributions (mil dol): Government social insurance	Personal income, 2013: Proprietors' income (mil dol)	Personal income, 2013: Dividends, interest, and rent (mil dol)	Personal income, 2013: Personal transfer receipts (mil dol)	Earnings, 2013: Total (mil dol)	Earnings, 2013: Contributions for government social insurance (mil dol): From employee and self-employed	Earnings, 2013: Contributions for government social insurance (mil dol): From employer
	62	63	64	65	66	67	68	69	70	71	72	73	74
KANSAS	128 541	2.7	44 417	X	61 897	10 400	4 863	15 903	24 770	19 605	93 064	5 329	4 863
Allen	526	5.4	40 093	1 163	204	42	17	98	86	124	361	21	17
Anderson	324	6.7	41 069	1 044	68	14	5	75	55	69	163	9	5
Atchison	557	5.9	33 256	2 218	218	40	18	85	99	125	362	21	18
Barber	269	5.5	54 359	224	66	13	5	85	71	39	169	8	5
Barton	1 376	2.1	50 022	367	517	88	40	297	313	221	942	54	40
Bourbon	502	4.6	33 829	2 117	222	40	18	43	95	131	324	21	18
Brown	468	10.0	46 826	563	182	34	14	100	86	87	330	16	14
Butler	2 806	1.9	42 644	875	695	149	54	411	437	429	1 309	77	54
Chase	167	1.3	61 931	87	21	5	2	73	31	20	101	5	2
Chautauqua	154	4.3	43 237	822	25	6	2	39	29	38	72	5	2
Cherokee	808	3.3	38 500	1 373	217	43	18	180	108	185	457	26	18
Cheyenne	107	-2.2	39 624	1 214	28	5	2	24	24	26	59	3	2
Clark	90	3.5	41 191	1 025	26	6	2	15	22	19	48	3	2
Clay	409	5.0	48 650	439	99	21	8	78	90	70	206	11	8
Cloud	367	7.6	39 472	1 234	111	22	9	87	64	84	229	12	9
Coffey	473	14.3	56 233	183	281	57	20	80	73	75	438	24	20
Comanche	90	6.7	45 874	626	21	5	2	26	20	17	54	2	2
Cowley	1 455	3.5	40 178	1 150	514	99	42	302	230	302	958	56	42
Crawford	1 287	0.5	32 770	2 288	598	121	48	23	285	318	791	51	48
Decatur	137	2.6	46 835	562	27	6	2	39	37	27	74	3	2
Dickinson	791	3.0	40 322	1 134	234	50	19	93	168	147	396	22	19
Doniphan	316	9.4	40 254	1 144	80	18	6	68	50	62	173	8	6
Douglas	4 220	2.6	36 911	1 600	1 814	360	141	226	914	596	2 542	150	141
Edwards	176	8.2	59 926	107	38	7	3	70	33	25	117	4	3
Elk	103	5.2	38 971	1 306	18	5	1	16	23	29	40	3	1
Ellis	1 455	2.5	50 055	365	615	112	47	261	347	187	1 034	59	47
Ellsworth	256	1.2	40 090	1 164	109	20	8	37	50	51	175	10	8
Finney	1 436	3.3	38 699	1 338	689	122	51	270	252	199	1 132	61	51
Ford	1 244	1.6	35 732	1 794	671	121	50	136	230	175	977	54	50
Franklin	931	1.9	36 156	1 720	361	58	29	72	148	199	520	33	29
Geary	1 545	-2.1	41 329	1 014	1 610	478	161	54	404	201	2 303	92	161
Gove	149	5.7	53 809	242	38	8	3	42	38	23	90	4	3
Graham	154	-0.6	59 579	112	38	7	3	53	29	27	100	5	3
Grant	347	6.1	43 657	786	152	27	11	109	46	38	300	13	11
Gray	341	12.5	56 721	167	105	19	8	125	60	30	256	9	8
Greeley	95	32.3	73 877	36	22	4	2	46	16	11	74	2	2
Greenwood	242	4.5	37 610	1 488	58	12	5	34	48	66	108	7	5
Hamilton	116	24.1	44 560	724	37	6	3	42	17	16	88	3	3
Harper	327	-0.6	55 740	193	100	20	8	98	59	50	226	11	8
Harvey	1 469	2.8	42 276	911	544	91	46	394	220	263	1 074	62	46
Haskell	274	11.6	66 198	63	69	12	5	126	41	22	212	5	5
Hodgeman	86	9.8	44 230	740	22	4	2	21	23	13	48	2	2
Jackson	531	5.0	39 712	1 201	135	25	10	83	87	103	253	15	10
Jefferson	692	3.4	36 809	1 621	130	25	10	35	116	133	201	14	10
Jewell	154	6.7	50 698	340	25	7	2	59	29	27	92	3	2
Johnson	34 054	2.5	60 068	103	17 978	2 274	1 358	3 643	7 012	2 956	25 253	1 489	1 358
Kearny	179	13.1	45 724	642	49	11	3	44	42	25	107	4	3
Kingman	387	3.0	49 322	400	99	19	8	101	72	64	227	11	8
Kiowa	146	6.7	57 921	137	38	8	3	43	34	21	92	4	3
Labette	835	1.5	39 904	1 181	346	70	29	88	146	216	533	33	29
Lane	99	8.1	57 725	142	27	5	2	24	29	16	59	2	2
Leavenworth	2 931	2.1	37 484	1 509	1 373	348	124	150	691	477	1 995	104	124
Lincoln	150	14.9	47 508	509	29	7	2	49	24	28	88	3	2
Linn	321	1.1	33 770	2 130	94	22	7	18	57	80	142	10	7
Logan	141	7.4	50 357	350	43	10	3	38	33	23	95	4	3
Lyon	1 058	1.3	31 576	2 470	488	100	38	57	204	241	683	42	38
McPherson	1 366	3.9	46 213	609	607	124	47	263	227	220	1 040	57	47
Marion	502	5.9	41 081	1 042	115	24	9	129	75	103	276	14	9
Marshall	527	13.2	52 649	281	203	35	18	133	104	82	389	20	18
Meade	237	8.7	54 526	218	64	13	4	69	54	28	151	6	4
Miami	1 471	2.0	44 796	711	294	53	24	38	224	217	409	29	24
Mitchell	301	5.5	47 214	536	123	24	9	70	57	55	227	11	9
Montgomery	1 310	2.5	38 200	1 411	634	120	53	131	207	311	939	59	53
Morris	229	3.3	39 835	1 187	50	10	4	22	53	49	86	5	4
Morton	174	3.0	55 408	196	49	10	3	71	26	22	133	4	3
Nemaha	560	14.1	55 089	200	187	34	15	145	141	73	381	18	15

1. Based on the resident population estimated as of July 1 of the year shown.

STATE County	Earnings, 2013 (cont.) — Percent by selected industries: Farm	Mining	Construction	Manufacturing	Information: professional, scientific, technical services	Retail trade	Finance, insurance, real estate and leasing	Health care and social assistance	Government	Social Security beneficiaries, December 2013: Number	Rate[1]	Supplemental Security Income recipients, December 2013	Housing units, 2014: Total	Percent change, 2010–2014
	75	76	77	78	79	80	81	82	83	84	85	86	87	88
KANSAS	4.3	2.5	5.3	13.9	9.0	5.7	7.1	10.4	17.5	515 969	178	49 071	1 248 813	1.3
Allen	8.4	D	4.4	29.1	1.9	5.6	2.7	6.1	19.1	3 255	249	363	6 262	0.6
Anderson	15.8	7.7	5.7	15.9	1.4	9.6	D	D	14.3	1 965	250	102	3 713	-0.2
Atchison	10.3	D	6.9	24.3	3.1	5.5	3.9	D	11.8	3 315	198	340	6 947	-0.6
Barber	21.2	23.7	8.4	6.1	D	5.6	D	D	15.5	1 215	246	70	2 744	-0.8
Barton	4.2	24.8	6.7	6.9	2.8	6.7	7.2	10.3	11.4	5 745	209	506	12 617	-0.6
Bourbon	1.2	D	4.6	15.8	4.0	6.1	7.8	18.0	15.3	3 550	239	395	7 101	-0.9
Brown	22.2	0.0	2.9	14.2	3.3	5.7	7.5	10.7	21.0	2 335	235	208	4 749	-0.6
Butler	4.1	6.8	7.6	14.0	D	8.1	4.3	14.8	20.5	11 925	181	835	26 400	1.3
Chase	9.1	17.2	8.0	2.6	4.3	4.9	9.1	D	8.9	605	223	39	1 498	-0.3
Chautauqua	7.5	D	5.7	4.1	D	5.8	D	8.9	14.4	1 120	315	115	2 137	-0.6
Cherokee	10.6	D	9.4	24.9	3.2	5.4	2.8	10.3	12.9	5 130	245	655	9 807	-0.8
Cheyenne	34.4	D	3.7	1.4	D	3.3	D	13.2	15.7	785	293	23	1 502	-1.1
Clark	21.8	2.5	D	D	D	5.4	4.2	D	41.0	510	232	28	1 131	-0.4
Clay	18.6	D	7.9	9.6	2.8	8.4	D	D	19.2	2 060	246	110	4 048	0.1
Cloud	26.9	D	3.3	11.5	4.3	6.8	3.4	D	15.5	2 405	257	177	4 624	-0.8
Coffey	5.3	3.9	12.0	2.0	3.8	3.0	2.0	1.7	12.4	2 140	254	183	4 003	1.0
Comanche	42.0	3.7	5.6	3.8	D	3.7	D	D	18.7	505	262	29	1 036	-0.8
Cowley	4.3	3.0	3.5	41.5	2.4	5.5	3.1	6.1	17.2	7 790	215	795	15 984	-0.3
Crawford	1.4	0.4	2.5	15.0	4.2	7.3	3.5	13.3	28.4	7 660	195	1 063	17 886	0.5
Decatur	37.1	2.1	D	D	D	5.7	D	10.5	12.2	875	300	40	1 806	-0.7
Dickinson	19.6	D	3.7	18.6	2.7	5.6	2.8	D	19.6	4 365	224	285	9 120	1.6
Doniphan	32.1	D	4.1	12.7	D	2.5	3.0	4.3	22.2	1 640	209	113	3 556	-0.6
Douglas	0.4	0.5	5.5	9.8	9.6	6.9	4.5	7.1	34.8	15 235	133	1 366	48 278	3.3
Edwards	56.4	0.7	2.3	5.7	0.5	2.2	1.3	5.7	8.7	710	240	52	1 625	-0.7
Elk	25.2	7.3	D	D	D	2.9	2.3	D	32.0	935	353	59	1 750	-0.6
Ellis	2.1	17.6	6.0	5.1	6.1	7.2	5.4	16.7	15.9	4 910	169	289	13 060	1.5
Ellsworth	9.0	D	2.9	13.3	5.2	3.5	D	20.3	24.3	1 480	232	76	3 210	-0.9
Finney	5.5	3.6	5.7	18.5	2.8	7.4	3.7	D	15.0	4 505	121	665	13 328	0.4
Ford	4.8	D	4.0	31.1	3.8	6.2	2.9	D	14.8	4 250	122	452	12 129	1.0
Franklin	4.1	1.7	5.0	9.9	3.0	6.2	2.4	D	19.5	5 550	215	524	11 104	-0.4
Geary	0.4	0.0	2.0	1.9	D	1.8	1.5	1.1	83.2	4 180	113	599	15 114	4.1
Gove	29.9	4.4	4.0	6.1	D	7.9	4.0	2.8	19.3	700	253	14	1 396	1.7
Graham	15.0	D	D	D	D	4.8	4.2	4.3	15.1	800	308	35	1 481	-0.2
Grant	21.9	14.8	9.2	3.6	D	3.7	3.6	4.5	10.7	1 120	142	93	2 920	-0.8
Gray	40.5	D	10.2	1.4	5.2	3.3	D	1.9	13.7	945	157	34	2 403	2.7
Greeley	63.9	D	1.8	0.0	D	4.1	2.3	D	8.4	305	237	11	631	0.3
Greenwood	19.8	19.1	2.6	7.5	2.6	3.8	2.1	D	17.4	1 890	295	163	4 036	-0.8
Hamilton	53.9	D	D	D	D	2.7	6.1	D	16.5	415	159	26	1 225	-0.9
Harper	19.2	16.6	4.7	13.3	D	6.1	3.7	D	16.2	1 485	253	88	3 167	1.6
Harvey	5.3	4.5	6.0	21.9	3.4	5.8	5.7	D	8.9	7 235	208	499	14 610	0.6
Haskell	58.2	D	D	D	D	1.9	D	D	12.9	575	139	31	1 660	-0.4
Hodgeman	40.6	D	2.6	0.0	D	4.2	D	D	24.4	460	236	16	970	-0.3
Jackson	8.0	D	D	4.5	2.9	7.2	5.1	D	35.6	3 210	240	188	5 783	0.1
Jefferson	7.3	D	20.1	5.2	D	5.2	D	D	24.2	4 010	213	245	8 218	0.7
Jewell	51.4	0.1	D	D	D	4.1	1.9	D	14.6	945	308	43	2 022	-0.5
Johnson	0.0	0.4	4.9	8.2	20.6	5.7	14.1	10.2	7.3	81 095	143	3 865	233 182	2.9
Kearny	41.6	D	D	D	D	2.7	D	0.8	29.0	640	164	54	1 547	-0.6
Kingman	21.0	12.3	9.0	11.3	D	4.0	5.6	6.9	10.2	1 855	237	98	3 814	-0.1
Kiowa	34.0	5.2	D	D	D	D	2.1	D	15.5	580	230	55	1 226	0.5
Labette	3.2	D	3.1	22.0	2.9	5.9	3.4	13.4	25.0	5 210	248	744	10 046	-0.5
Lane	40.9	D	1.2	0.0	D	3.0	3.6	D	18.0	475	276	21	981	-0.9
Leavenworth	0.1	0.1	4.5	3.5	6.6	3.6	4.3	4.8	62.5	12 450	159	952	29 088	1.4
Lincoln	46.2	D	6.6	D	D	2.7	D	2.8	19.8	765	244	40	1 856	-0.4
Linn	2.1	4.3	11.0	4.7	D	4.6	D	D	21.9	2 555	268	187	5 446	0.0
Logan	31.0	D	2.3	0.3	D	5.4	3.7	D	33.3	645	231	35	1 446	0.3
Lyon	4.1	0.7	3.7	19.2	D	7.3	3.1	8.7	31.0	5 855	175	663	15 184	-0.3
McPherson	8.2	5.6	8.8	32.3	2.7	4.0	2.8	8.4	8.7	6 400	216	309	12 846	1.0
Marion	29.5	0.8	2.1	14.3	2.8	3.3	2.8	D	14.0	3 085	252	144	5 928	-0.3
Marshall	21.3	D	3.1	22.3	4.1	5.0	3.6	5.7	8.1	2 460	245	150	4 881	0.3
Meade	42.1	1.8	4.2	0.8	D	2.3	2.6	D	17.4	845	196	34	1 991	-0.4
Miami	0.5	1.7	9.2	8.7	4.2	11.9	6.0	12.7	25.3	6 010	183	405	13 322	1.0
Mitchell	20.6	D	4.4	14.4	2.5	7.1	D	D	20.4	1 520	240	90	3 294	-0.1
Montgomery	1.7	1.8	8.3	30.5	D	5.4	2.5	D	12.7	8 340	242	1 110	16 455	-0.7
Morris	21.5	0.3	5.3	7.6	D	4.8	4.1	5.4	24.0	1 490	261	81	3 192	-0.4
Morton	50.9	4.5	D	D	D	3.5	4.0	D	21.0	640	203	47	1 454	-0.9
Nemaha	25.4	D	4.1	24.2	2.0	3.7	3.9	D	8.7	2 290	226	104	4 570	0.2

1. Per 1,000 resident population estimated as of July 1 of the year shown.

STATE County	Housing units, 2009–2013								Civilian labor force, 2014				Civilian employment,[6] 2009–2013		
	Occupied units										Unemployment			Percent	
		Owner-occupied				Renter-occupied									
				Median owner cost as a percent of income											
	Total	Percent	Median value[1]	With a mortgage	Without a mortgage[2]	Median rent[3]	Median rent as a percent of income[2]	Substandard units[4] (percent)	Total	Percent change, 2013–2014	Total	Rate[5]	Total	Management, business, science and arts	Construction, production, and maintenance occupations
	89	90	91	92	93	94	95	96	97	98	99	100	101	102	103
KANSAS	1 110 440	67.5	128 400	21.2	11.8	732	28.1	2.5	1 500 353	0.9	67 994	4.5	1 387 071	36.3	23.1
Allen	5 505	74.9	63 300	18.7	12.0	551	29.7	0.4	6 964	1.1	347	5.0	6 170	29.2	32.5
Anderson	3 308	76.4	96 300	22.0	11.6	646	31.3	1.7	4 250	0.2	216	5.1	3 756	30.1	28.7
Atchison	6 216	72.7	87 000	21.9	12.2	576	23.7	0.5	7 714	-0.7	498	6.5	7 499	34.6	29.0
Barber	2 187	72.7	61 900	17.7	10.4	560	22.5	1.9	2 717	-1.7	85	3.1	2 588	34.2	31.1
Barton	11 491	71.4	75 300	19.1	11.7	564	25.8	2.0	15 618	3.4	553	3.5	13 717	32.0	25.8
Bourbon	5 636	72.6	78 400	19.7	13.4	596	27.5	1.5	7 110	3.5	371	5.2	6 482	30.2	27.8
Brown	4 104	66.9	77 100	22.5	11.4	526	27.1	1.0	5 451	-0.1	224	4.1	4 729	31.9	26.8
Butler	24 270	76.1	127 800	21.0	11.9	699	27.5	1.0	32 034	0.6	1 564	4.9	30 798	35.9	25.6
Chase	1 149	73.5	81 100	21.4	11.1	433	23.7	1.3	1 253	0.1	50	4.0	1 212	31.1	32.8
Chautauqua	1 565	76.5	46 500	21.1	14.4	614	25.9	2.2	1 605	-0.9	88	5.5	1 544	25.5	37.0
Cherokee	7 936	75.9	71 600	21.1	12.6	580	28.3	0.8	10 385	-1.1	523	5.0	9 348	29.3	30.5
Cheyenne	1 343	74.0	76 700	20.2	13.7	526	27.9	1.6	1 312	0.2	41	3.1	1 361	34.1	23.4
Clark	932	72.4	59 800	19.0	10.9	563	24.2	0.4	1 154	-2.9	31	2.7	1 000	38.7	20.7
Clay	3 407	76.6	85 700	18.9	12.6	676	23.9	1.3	4 250	1.3	186	4.4	4 000	35.1	26.5
Cloud	4 022	76.2	66 100	18.6	12.6	554	25.6	1.3	4 439	-0.4	186	4.2	4 445	27.4	26.9
Coffey	3 501	76.5	98 200	19.4	11.4	540	24.3	0.0	5 010	1.4	279	5.6	4 151	35.0	25.1
Comanche	791	75.5	54 100	22.5	11.7	444	22.2	2.6	971	-6.1	30	3.1	902	38.5	25.8
Cowley	13 867	68.8	80 600	19.9	12.3	615	28.0	2.9	17 382	1.2	805	4.6	15 800	27.3	30.7
Crawford	15 370	60.9	83 800	19.4	13.3	670	33.6	0.7	19 312	0.1	1 026	5.3	18 068	31.6	24.2
Decatur	1 482	82.0	53 500	20.9	12.0	513	34.3	0.8	1 333	-2.1	48	3.6	1 390	39.1	23.0
Dickinson	7 845	73.4	106 700	20.9	12.0	600	26.1	2.9	9 933	0.7	496	5.0	9 236	32.2	30.6
Doniphan	3 161	74.1	83 300	19.6	11.8	548	21.8	2.0	4 321	-0.4	195	4.5	3 920	30.8	32.2
Douglas	43 398	52.0	180 300	22.6	11.6	860	34.0	1.5	64 754	1.9	2 626	4.1	60 939	43.7	14.8
Edwards	1 269	75.3	56 500	17.0	10.0	514	23.1	4.3	1 606	-0.1	52	3.2	1 481	36.1	32.9
Elk	1 271	80.2	52 100	21.4	12.8	442	25.5	0.9	1 310	-1.0	66	5.0	1 146	34.7	31.2
Ellis	11 824	62.9	138 400	22.4	12.4	603	30.8	0.8	18 201	0.8	498	2.7	16 316	30.7	20.1
Ellsworth	2 528	77.0	73 300	20.1	10.7	526	23.5	7.3	3 437	-0.3	103	3.0	2 857	32.5	29.4
Finney	12 515	64.7	109 700	23.0	11.9	670	23.7	5.7	20 340	1.7	696	3.4	18 693	24.5	36.5
Ford	11 103	61.9	88 800	21.3	11.2	589	21.6	2.4	18 486	-0.8	696	3.8	16 466	22.0	43.7
Franklin	9 909	70.9	119 700	23.2	13.3	721	28.1	4.0	14 173	1.4	729	5.1	12 605	29.2	29.5
Geary	12 532	46.6	136 500	22.8	12.2	975	27.4	1.6	12 407	-1.8	875	7.1	12 834	30.4	25.9
Gove	1 201	79.5	71 500	19.4	10.0	496	22.4	0.4	1 501	0.8	40	2.7	1 387	38.1	26.8
Graham	1 192	82.5	63 800	19.6	11.2	508	22.8	3.0	1 327	-1.8	45	3.4	1 326	35.3	26.5
Grant	2 793	73.8	90 900	17.8	10.0	534	25.8	4.8	3 969	-0.6	135	3.4	3 752	31.1	33.6
Gray	2 066	75.8	105 900	19.2	10.2	577	19.1	1.2	3 503	0.4	94	2.7	3 001	34.2	30.5
Greeley	493	80.3	78 500	14.5	13.8	440	13.7	3.1	896	-1.4	19	2.1	624	40.2	19.6
Greenwood	2 855	76.3	56 800	18.1	13.0	503	29.1	4.7	3 337	-0.7	151	4.5	3 064	29.2	33.6
Hamilton	1 076	75.2	75 100	24.7	12.1	497	19.2	1.2	1 687	-1.6	39	2.3	1 393	28.1	35.2
Harper	2 595	73.1	66 100	23.0	12.0	597	24.7	1.5	3 019	-2.8	111	3.7	2 709	32.7	28.4
Harvey	13 287	72.3	111 600	19.4	11.3	657	28.8	1.8	17 225	0.6	731	4.2	16 643	35.2	26.4
Haskell	1 411	74.3	103 300	18.3	10.0	700	18.7	2.7	2 396	0.3	62	2.6	2 067	31.0	32.9
Hodgeman	821	79.5	76 500	16.3	10.0	526	21.0	2.1	1 050	-5.9	36	3.4	970	45.6	26.5
Jackson	5 273	76.3	118 200	21.5	12.7	711	23.6	2.0	7 350	0.8	308	4.2	6 721	27.9	29.6
Jefferson	7 421	84.9	125 800	21.9	13.0	737	26.6	1.9	10 271	0.7	500	4.9	9 357	36.0	25.9
Jewell	1 454	79.4	56 500	19.4	11.6	512	18.8	1.5	1 386	-2.5	55	4.0	1 488	35.8	26.3
Johnson	216 304	70.1	210 900	21.3	10.8	918	26.8	2.8	321 092	2.2	12 097	3.8	295 268	49.3	11.9
Kearny	1 301	73.0	91 700	17.4	10.0	558	14.1	3.0	2 139	1.9	65	3.0	1 854	26.2	43.0
Kingman	3 223	71.4	86 700	21.2	11.2	619	21.9	0.7	3 700	-0.5	146	3.9	3 545	31.3	35.8
Kiowa	1 065	65.2	102 800	19.6	10.0	486	26.7	2.2	1 364	-4.1	46	3.4	1 251	34.0	24.9
Labette	8 703	71.1	66 100	20.5	12.9	551	26.7	0.0	10 834	0.9	635	5.9	9 850	30.1	28.5
Lane	808	77.8	58 200	14.6	10.8	618	19.0	1.9	868	-1.7	28	3.2	826	41.9	29.2
Leavenworth	26 358	67.4	165 800	22.0	11.4	884	26.5	1.1	35 210	1.7	1 756	5.0	32 266	36.3	20.2
Lincoln	1 414	78.9	63 500	24.3	12.1	449	24.8	5.8	1 774	-0.2	73	4.1	1 543	37.4	29.2
Linn	4 234	81.0	98 000	23.0	13.7	661	27.7	3.0	4 372	1.1	316	7.2	3 980	34.0	30.2
Logan	1 282	70.8	72 700	23.3	10.2	561	26.3	3.2	1 750	0.4	39	2.2	1 435	32.3	32.8
Lyon	13 170	58.9	93 100	21.2	12.1	590	29.2	1.5	16 396	-0.3	853	5.2	17 158	25.6	30.0
McPherson	11 540	78.3	124 600	20.0	10.0	628	23.1	2.6	16 954	2.2	554	3.3	15 130	34.3	28.9
Marion	4 861	80.8	83 000	19.7	12.2	557	25.7	4.0	6 178	0.6	262	4.1	5 914	32.3	28.9
Marshall	4 345	76.1	81 700	19.9	11.6	498	21.8	2.3	5 975	-1.2	192	3.2	5 114	31.3	32.9
Meade	1 714	71.7	85 500	19.2	10.5	599	20.6	1.6	2 427	3.2	63	2.6	2 184	36.8	28.2
Miami	12 334	79.3	162 500	23.0	13.2	758	31.1	0.9	17 093	1.8	803	4.7	15 876	33.6	26.6
Mitchell	2 804	70.4	74 600	18.6	10.3	501	21.1	2.2	3 873	-0.1	127	3.3	3 316	36.4	29.4
Montgomery	14 000	70.1	71 200	18.9	12.2	577	30.0	1.5	17 453	-2.2	1 012	5.8	15 072	26.9	31.6
Morris	2 503	78.4	81 900	20.2	10.5	549	24.1	1.2	3 134	1.0	139	4.4	2 948	30.4	34.3
Morton	1 186	70.4	82 100	19.1	11.7	549	21.9	1.4	1 514	-5.0	60	4.0	1 470	29.5	30.0
Nemaha	4 117	79.2	95 200	19.6	10.4	499	23.9	2.2	5 857	0.5	168	2.9	5 177	33.5	31.0

1. Specified owner-occupied units. 2. A value of 10.0 represents 10 percent or less; a value of 50.0 represents 50 percent or more. 3. Specified renter-occupied units.
4. Overcrowded or lacking complete plumbing facilities. 5. Percent of civilian labor force. 6. Persons 16 years old and over.

STATE County	Private nonfarm establishments, employment and payroll, 2013									Agriculture, 2012			
		Employment						Annual payroll		Farms			
											Percent with:		
	Number of establish-ments	Total	Health care and social assistance	Manufac-turing	Retail trade	Finance and insurance	Professional, scientific, and technical services	Total (mil dol)	Average per employee (dollars)	Number	Fewer than 50 acres	500 acres or more	Farm operators whose principal occu-pation is farming (percent)
	104	105	106	107	108	109	110	111	112	113	114	115	116
KANSAS	73 816	1 150 401	191 966	160 314	147 038	62 203	60 445	47 716	41 477	61 773	19.0	31.6	48.3
Allen	386	4 451	581	1 989	560	107	97	134	30 070	650	20.5	19.5	46.2
Anderson	211	1 495	334	180	D	90	D	43	28 504	707	20.8	25.5	47.5
Atchison	361	5 750	810	1 242	656	D	76	176	30 643	611	19.8	17.7	50.2
Barber	220	1 500	258	D	225	53	D	54	36 006	378	10.1	50.3	54.2
Barton	976	11 464	2 170	1 221	1 541	851	319	409	35 706	694	14.4	39.2	45.7
Bourbon	354	4 837	1 009	1 218	639	322	126	144	29 753	903	18.9	18.4	45.0
Brown	266	3 406	767	598	396	198	D	105	30 682	510	19.8	29.2	60.6
Butler	1 303	13 342	3 715	D	1 994	478	453	419	31 389	1 353	34.3	20.8	39.8
Chase	73	497	D	D	60	D	D	15	29 266	252	15.9	45.6	54.8
Chautauqua	69	450	D	D	90	D	5	12	27 244	312	8.0	38.1	53.2
Cherokee	350	5 269	968	1 459	527	117	119	200	37 983	729	27.8	24.8	50.2
Cheyenne	106	505	151	D	80	D	D	16	31 055	393	9.4	51.7	47.8
Clark	59	D	D	D	51	40	D	D	D	283	4.9	51.9	53.0
Clay	264	2 411	593	D	373	90	67	70	28 829	541	15.0	37.5	53.2
Cloud	309	2 872	707	D	558	133	80	89	30 878	461	14.8	35.1	46.4
Coffey	242	D	425	D	382	109	223	D	D	667	19.2	26.7	38.5
Comanche	83	458	164	D	86	33	D	9	20 365	234	6.8	61.1	52.1
Cowley	764	11 038	2 198	3 564	1 464	D	214	357	32 371	990	19.3	24.5	48.6
Crawford	903	13 979	3 076	2 580	1 873	322	327	404	28 931	846	25.5	19.1	36.9
Decatur	102	598	D	D	80	31	D	15	24 614	293	10.6	55.6	61.1
Dickinson	474	5 013	884	986	814	168	153	146	29 199	1 011	19.8	31.2	41.5
Doniphan	145	1 411	D	D	D	60	D	47	33 083	422	20.4	24.9	55.2
Douglas	2 635	36 252	5 965	3 240	6 061	1 011	1 698	1 103	30 413	945	38.5	9.7	35.8
Edwards	96	647	D	128	D	D	D	20	31 629	292	7.9	45.2	61.3
Elk	72	337	D	D	33	26	D	7	21 659	315	14.9	42.5	53.0
Ellis	1 140	12 848	3 244	1 113	2 169	423	321	429	33 367	645	13.2	35.0	40.2
Ellsworth	163	1 701	446	252	224	D	73	58	33 989	435	11.0	34.9	48.7
Finney	977	14 375	1 952	D	2 486	397	264	481	33 448	499	11.0	60.1	65.1
Ford	774	15 597	1 432	6 595	1 731	312	488	533	34 155	655	12.4	43.1	51.0
Franklin	575	9 031	1 121	664	1 089	160	D	308	34 129	1 024	31.1	16.3	42.5
Geary	576	8 061	1 571	D	1 263	268	389	237	29 342	238	28.2	27.3	45.4
Gove	133	927	239	127	178	47	D	27	29 379	395	8.6	55.4	57.7
Graham	108	741	D	D	125	D	D	24	32 348	431	7.4	43.2	49.2
Grant	228	2 457	D	187	D	105	49	104	42 530	329	10.6	40.7	45.9
Gray	221	1 726	D	92	192	64	44	52	29 958	418	9.6	46.2	53.1
Greeley	45	316	D	NA	D	22	D	11	34 915	262	5.0	53.8	55.7
Greenwood	189	1 201	D	D	216	62	D	37	30 659	551	13.2	37.4	52.5
Hamilton	60	564	137	NA	73	D	D	18	32 663	397	4.5	54.4	53.9
Harper	218	1 874	316	505	D	97	D	64	34 260	482	13.5	39.6	49.8
Harvey	794	13 314	3 028	3 186	1 460	322	273	472	35 473	744	30.5	25.1	48.9
Haskell	119	768	D	53	57	D	28	28	37 064	187	10.7	61.5	74.9
Hodgeman	52	301	D	NA	35	D	D	9	30 352	399	3.0	56.6	57.9
Jackson	252	2 861	D	213	381	D	75	79	27 504	1 054	26.7	15.3	36.8
Jefferson	307	2 156	418	241	305	81	58	76	35 271	996	27.9	10.9	38.2
Jewell	85	500	D	D	62	31	D	13	26 750	453	9.1	50.1	66.2
Johnson	17 242	314 916	37 071	20 845	36 227	27 827	27 677	16 136	51 241	571	52.0	8.4	35.4
Kearny	84	610	D	D	D	D	D	23	37 900	343	4.7	50.7	53.6
Kingman	210	1 940	402	452	209	124	D	61	31 399	808	14.2	31.7	43.8
Kiowa	96	757	199	NA	96	33	D	26	33 908	403	6.5	43.7	43.4
Labette	472	8 916	4 028	1 970	937	253	95	256	28 678	977	20.2	17.3	46.6
Lane	66	368	D	D	D	D	D	13	34 060	315	8.6	52.4	48.3
Leavenworth	1 208	13 833	2 904	1 023	2 330	889	1 231	496	35 851	1 133	41.0	6.6	35.4
Lincoln	86	483	134	NA	D	D	D	12	25 219	431	13.7	41.5	62.9
Linn	180	1 187	D	86	267	66	36	53	44 381	913	18.8	16.2	38.4
Logan	109	662	D	D	91	D	23	22	33 180	325	5.2	55.7	48.6
Lyon	825	11 075	1 948	2 889	1 781	315	247	337	30 468	946	21.7	26.5	47.5
McPherson	904	13 564	2 151	4 582	1 173	664	187	545	40 164	1 147	20.2	29.9	54.7
Marion	291	2 661	603	265	306	D	103	66	24 869	981	19.1	32.7	50.8
Marshall	373	4 300	604	1 504	685	216	91	157	36 517	796	14.8	34.3	55.8
Meade	130	932	D	D	160	48	22	31	33 508	439	7.7	51.9	52.4
Miami	706	6 446	1 992	495	954	246	299	226	35 081	1 305	38.4	9.7	41.5
Mitchell	245	2 690	D	D	382	130	43	86	31 824	416	11.1	13.1	60.5
Montgomery	820	12 923	2 523	3 580	1 613	391	181	447	34 565	1 012	23.9	14.4	41.3
Morris	140	1 218	288	215	176	58	57	35	28 352	454	13.4	35.0	53.1
Morton	111	914	D	D	96	D	16	34	37 358	323	3.7	49.8	50.5
Nemaha	359	4 585	871	1 309	515	181	D	163	35 505	903	15.2	26.7	49.3

STATE County	Agriculture, 2012 (cont.) Land in farms: Acreage (1,000)	Land in farms: Percent change, 2007–2012	Land in farms: Acres: Average size of farm	Land in farms: Acres: Total irrigated (1,000)	Land in farms: Acres: Total cropland (1,000)	Value of land and buildings (dollars): Average per farm	Value of land and buildings (dollars): Average per acre	Value of machinery and equipment, average per farm (dollars)	Value of products sold: Total (mil dol)	Value of products sold: Average per farm (dollars)	Value of products sold: Percent from: Crops	Value of products sold: Percent from: Livestock and poultry products	Percent of farms with sales of: $10,000 or more	Percent of farms with sales of: $100,000 or more	Government payments: Total ($1,000)	Government payments: Percent of farms
	117	118	119	120	121	122	123	124	125	126	127	128	129	130	131	132
KANSAS	46 137	-0.4	747	2 881.3	28 503.3	1 218 662	1 632	156 737	18 460.6	298 845	37.8	62.2	56.0	25.5	442 090	68.6
Allen	245	-8.3	377	D	129.5	526 683	1 396	93 555	38.2	58 702	58.5	41.5	46.9	13.1	2 652	62.9
Anderson	366	-0.3	518	1.4	224.0	806 658	1 557	132 429	73.4	103 812	55.7	44.3	57.9	21.8	4 436	66.3
Atchison	220	-13.3	361	0.5	144.4	777 051	2 154	134 581	56.5	92 530	76.6	23.4	64.2	21.8	2 999	60.9
Barber	591	-3.4	1 563	8.9	193.1	1 898 704	1 215	171 399	88.5	234 053	51.3	48.7	68.3	37.3	2 849	75.7
Barton	566	1.3	816	39.2	421.3	1 278 262	1 567	210 909	279.0	401 964	34.5	65.5	64.4	31.8	5 572	80.8
Bourbon	334	2.1	370	0.3	126.4	536 239	1 448	68 483	53.7	59 508	29.6	70.4	46.3	9.6	2 601	56.6
Brown	295	-15.0	578	5.0	232.3	1 891 461	3 271	223 178	140.5	275 506	85.4	14.6	67.5	36.1	3 416	72.9
Butler	768	-2.4	568	5.1	295.9	999 409	1 760	108 387	282.3	208 676	27.9	72.1	44.6	17.7	3 069	37.5
Chase	393	22.7	1 558	D	56.0	2 113 111	1 356	118 929	84.7	336 111	12.8	87.2	72.2	34.5	714	52.0
Chautauqua	310	0.7	995	D	39.7	1 148 269	1 155	73 324	35.2	112 805	D	D	61.5	18.3	626	34.9
Cherokee	308	-5.0	423	0.8	226.4	787 462	1 862	118 760	86.9	119 213	81.1	18.9	55.3	21.3	3 158	50.6
Cheyenne	547	-5.2	1 391	39.5	336.7	2 203 377	1 584	192 557	143.9	366 117	52.4	47.6	61.8	39.9	4 717	84.7
Clark	503	3.6	1 778	6.6	191.4	1 617 572	910	143 989	126.2	445 763	13.0	87.0	49.8	29.0	3 389	89.0
Clay	363	3.3	670	29.2	230.8	1 414 349	2 111	204 776	115.9	214 174	69.5	30.5	68.6	38.1	3 830	81.9
Cloud	322	-16.2	698	15.2	208.8	1 390 777	1 991	175 219	80.0	173 627	84.4	15.6	70.1	31.0	3 226	73.1
Coffey	329	1.4	494	1.2	183.4	753 148	1 526	94 421	61.7	92 496	53.0	47.0	46.6	18.3	3 527	76.6
Comanche	485	12.2	2 073	7.5	144.9	1 910 051	921	146 675	48.7	208 034	44.7	55.3	66.7	41.0	2 448	79.5
Cowley	575	-0.2	580	6.2	266.1	831 902	1 433	134 058	109.0	110 077	54.0	46.0	54.3	18.7	3 203	61.0
Crawford	323	-5.6	382	1.1	192.1	640 069	1 675	105 483	75.6	89 355	68.3	31.7	49.2	15.6	2 040	61.5
Decatur	462	-4.3	1 578	11.1	269.1	2 407 051	1 525	246 949	136.8	466 915	37.6	62.4	75.1	42.3	3 139	85.7
Dickinson	510	-5.0	505	4.3	335.4	1 017 926	2 017	139 688	157.1	155 342	52.5	47.5	55.2	26.0	5 935	79.7
Doniphan	180	-27.5	425	1.2	133.8	1 531 073	3 599	178 036	80.8	191 472	93.4	6.6	58.3	33.2	2 819	70.4
Douglas	211	-4.5	223	3.3	127.3	636 186	2 854	82 519	43.9	46 436	66.2	33.8	37.7	8.4	2 332	46.9
Edwards	394	-10.2	1 351	92.3	284.9	2 882 414	2 134	298 442	151.7	519 538	83.7	16.3	64.0	43.2	3 850	92.1
Elk	316	-0.1	1 004	D	51.4	1 274 378	1 269	84 156	42.1	133 556	16.0	84.0	56.5	23.5	694	41.3
Ellis	497	-5.6	770	1.9	253.4	1 025 119	1 332	130 081	99.6	154 462	32.7	67.3	59.8	19.1	3 503	78.9
Ellsworth	381	4.4	876	0.6	182.7	1 161 667	1 326	144 347	51.6	118 699	66.8	33.2	54.3	25.5	2 787	84.8
Finney	816	7.3	1 635	186.6	670.4	2 353 291	1 439	399 313	909.2	1 822 062	20.3	79.7	64.1	46.5	9 784	80.0
Ford	700	10.3	1 068	82.0	541.7	1 301 528	1 218	232 826	441.8	674 560	25.9	74.1	60.6	31.3	7 279	79.4
Franklin	362	15.4	353	2.2	200.8	820 041	2 321	103 643	101.3	98 951	54.6	45.4	43.5	10.8	3 448	52.6
Geary	146	-1.9	612	3.6	57.9	1 187 118	1 939	121 773	30.4	127 550	51.0	49.0	45.4	22.7	971	67.6
Gove	579	-2.5	1 465	21.1	368.9	1 883 304	1 286	227 359	196.1	496 537	34.9	65.1	68.1	42.3	6 300	83.5
Graham	483	-6.2	1 120	13.3	292.0	1 478 046	1 319	183 213	57.9	134 267	76.3	23.7	54.3	25.3	5 847	81.9
Grant	364	7.8	1 105	88.7	298.2	1 471 553	1 332	253 924	918.2	2 790 860	9.4	90.6	50.8	36.2	5 153	84.5
Gray	547	0.2	1 309	124.2	420.9	1 747 136	1 335	320 818	939.4	2 247 407	14.9	85.1	59.8	44.3	7 391	82.8
Greeley	497	0.9	1 898	23.2	458.2	2 823 103	1 487	306 420	123.1	470 031	47.9	52.1	64.5	42.7	5 269	90.8
Greenwood	701	15.1	1 272	0.2	104.0	1 792 824	1 409	96 279	89.6	162 530	19.8	80.2	59.9	21.4	1 382	45.6
Hamilton	635	4.0	1 600	30.9	486.4	1 617 219	1 011	198 665	367.2	925 033	15.1	84.9	47.4	29.0	6 441	88.9
Harper	506	5.1	1 050	3.8	329.0	1 592 678	1 517	176 824	109.6	227 477	58.8	41.2	60.4	35.1	5 601	85.5
Harvey	340	0.3	456	47.2	297.2	1 173 019	2 570	154 589	161.7	217 360	69.4	30.6	59.4	31.6	4 135	68.5
Haskell	364	-8.8	1 944	116.7	259.0	2 676 770	1 377	550 995	1 009.9	5 400 412	10.6	89.4	71.7	59.9	4 074	82.9
Hodgeman	543	3.2	1 360	30.7	328.1	1 461 356	1 075	227 945	182.1	456 386	29.2	70.8	65.4	36.6	6 590	87.7
Jackson	329	-3.0	312	0.8	136.1	549 724	1 760	78 991	57.9	54 893	40.3	59.7	45.7	11.4	2 322	50.4
Jefferson	244	-14.8	245	3.6	133.4	547 394	2 238	86 031	53.1	53 344	62.7	37.3	41.6	8.9	2 013	45.5
Jewell	464	-1.6	1 024	15.0	294.8	1 975 925	1 930	223 843	136.5	301 278	77.1	22.9	73.7	47.0	5 236	83.9
Johnson	99	-13.0	174	1.1	59.2	755 205	4 340	76 618	24.4	42 680	66.0	34.0	34.2	9.3	911	30.3
Kearny	547	5.3	1 594	70.9	423.6	2 067 618	1 297	238 297	337.4	983 639	23.9	76.1	56.9	38.2	6 069	86.6
Kingman	542	-0.8	671	33.7	329.3	958 710	1 429	139 131	103.2	127 708	74.0	26.0	56.7	25.0	5 868	84.2
Kiowa	455	3.4	1 130	49.9	233.2	1 391 826	1 232	141 444	80.6	199 943	79.4	20.6	56.3	26.6	3 852	88.6
Labette	371	-0.2	379	0.6	196.7	563 481	1 486	94 384	122.8	125 668	41.5	58.5	53.7	14.7	2 247	51.4
Lane	452	12.7	1 436	18.7	337.0	1 846 321	1 286	204 457	216.8	688 343	14.4	85.6	54.0	30.8	5 512	91.4
Leavenworth	184	-5.3	163	0.3	102.5	526 699	3 235	63 351	36.4	32 098	69.3	30.7	35.7	5.9	1 452	29.0
Lincoln	397	-8.2	922	1.4	204.7	1 377 181	1 494	166 234	63.5	147 355	68.1	31.9	65.7	31.8	3 280	87.9
Linn	355	33.7	388	0.0	167.8	683 687	1 760	75 490	39.5	43 245	62.7	37.3	41.9	8.1	2 608	54.3
Logan	566	0.0	1 743	11.1	329.4	2 057 326	1 180	197 542	78.8	242 551	74.3	25.7	70.8	41.2	4 297	83.4
Lyon	535	12.9	565	0.4	228.4	881 912	1 560	107 999	111.4	117 727	31.6	68.4	49.3	17.1	3 429	67.4
McPherson	572	0.9	498	42.3	409.1	1 124 564	2 257	171 576	208.5	181 763	61.5	38.5	66.4	32.3	8 021	77.6
Marion	596	-0.5	608	4.4	341.4	1 282 189	2 109	140 915	151.5	154 412	51.1	48.9	63.7	31.4	4 559	76.8
Marshall	438	-14.8	551	2.9	301.7	1 483 474	2 693	194 613	127.9	160 700	81.4	18.6	71.4	36.4	4 946	80.9
Meade	618	2.6	1 408	129.5	372.2	1 717 237	1 220	295 836	296.8	676 175	49.6	50.4	58.1	37.4	6 661	86.1
Miami	296	-3.7	227	1.3	166.5	709 454	3 131	71 108	51.0	39 090	66.4	33.6	36.9	7.4	1 946	36.2
Mitchell	439	-1.2	1 058	8.4	303.5	2 369 728	2 240	254 643	153.5	369 872	57.3	42.7	71.8	44.6	4 609	84.8
Montgomery	336	6.9	332	3.7	163.1	513 052	1 547	98 773	79.4	78 478	61.2	38.8	45.9	9.4	1 771	37.7
Morris	389	-5.9	857	0.5	153.9	1 259 154	1 469	134 231	116.8	257 302	28.1	71.9	68.3	27.1	2 296	72.9
Morton	457	3.4	1 414	59.5	389.3	1 197 084	846	156 164	169.7	525 477	34.4	65.6	47.4	30.0	6 208	86.4
Nemaha	383	-15.1	424	0.9	259.0	1 195 878	2 822	170 190	224.6	248 729	34.9	65.1	73.8	32.3	6 391	79.8

STATE County	Water use, 2010		Wholesale trade,[1] 2007				Retail trade,[2] 2007				Real estate and rental and leasing,[2] 2007			
	Total water withdrawn (mil gal/day)	Gallons withdrawn per person per day	Number of establish-ments	Number of employees	Sales (mil dol)	Annual payroll (mil dol)	Number of establish-ments	Number of employees	Sales (mil dol)	Annual payroll (mil dol)	Number of establish-ments	Number of employees	Receipts (mil dol)	Annual payroll (mil dol)
	133	134	135	136	137	138	139	140	141	142	143	144	145	146
KANSAS	4 004.8	1 404	3 747	47 285	45 863.9	2 150.4	11 463	149 672	34 538.3	3 133.7	3 314	15 160	2 428.8	439.7
Allen	3.8	284	21	164	37.2	4.6	63	541	121.7	11.2	13	44	2.0	0.5
Anderson	1.9	239	8	56	53.5	1.7	42	309	87.2	6.5	6	15	0.3	0.1
Atchison	5.4	321	17	D	D	D	58	730	130.1	12.4	13	D	D	D
Barber	5.9	1 220	8	39	35.6	1.9	35	250	70.3	4.4	3	D	D	D
Barton	36.8	1 328	62	D	D	D	138	1 543	339.4	33.1	29	113	12.5	3.3
Bourbon	3.1	203	17	541	554.9	21.9	47	567	120.6	11.6	14	53	10.1	1.3
Brown	2.5	246	16	120	87.5	4.2	34	369	67.9	6.6	5	14	0.8	0.1
Butler	15.6	237	44	243	130.1	8.7	194	2 050	567.5	43.5	61	125	18.3	2.6
Chase	1.4	516	2	D	D	D	10	60	10.9	0.7	2	D	D	D
Chautauqua	1.0	262	2	D	D	D	14	81	15.8	1.1	NA	NA	NA	NA
Cherokee	94.1	4 354	18	162	205.5	5.5	67	503	121.7	9.8	4	D	D	D
Cheyenne	42.9	15 719	10	102	54.6	2.6	22	85	12.2	1.1	2	D	D	D
Clark	5.2	2 348	2	D	D	D	14	70	9.9	0.9	1	D	D	D
Clay	9.1	1 060	15	136	99.3	5.7	44	419	76.0	6.3	3	10	1.7	0.2
Cloud	10.7	1 117	18	241	91.8	8.3	61	493	109.7	10.7	7	D	D	D
Coffey	21.1	2 451	10	90	52.3	2.6	50	442	103.0	7.1	4	5	0.5	0.1
Comanche	8.3	4 363	2	D	D	D	19	73	10.3	1.0	1	D	D	D
Cowley	8.4	230	28	D	D	D	135	1 596	317.2	31.1	19	78	6.3	1.2
Crawford	7.2	185	37	D	D	D	174	1 974	395.4	36.3	38	118	15.2	2.3
Decatur	9.4	3 168	13	80	60.5	2.6	19	119	17.2	1.4	4	D	D	D
Dickinson	5.8	292	23	255	232.6	8.5	77	787	191.4	17.4	14	21	2.4	0.3
Doniphan	0.6	70	9	D	D	D	21	132	25.2	2.2	2	D	D	D
Douglas	19.1	172	81	D	D	D	407	6 121	1 202.2	110.5	170	711	93.4	17.5
Edwards	99.3	32 697	5	81	74.7	2.9	12	73	12.4	1.1	1	D	D	D
Elk	0.9	316	2	D	D	D	7	40	8.0	0.5	1	D	D	D
Ellis	5.5	192	43	322	144.9	11.1	183	2 174	497.5	42.6	40	109	14.5	2.5
Ellsworth	2.6	405	9	47	23.0	1.4	30	185	31.9	2.3	2	D	D	D
Finney	281.3	7 650	68	D	D	D	182	2 396	504.2	47.1	34	136	23.7	4.0
Ford	96.5	2 850	57	D	D	D	139	1 632	395.7	34.2	27	115	18.8	2.7
Franklin	3.6	140	14	172	168.7	7.7	96	1 153	234.3	22.6	23	D	D	D
Geary	14.7	428	8	154	70.8	2.7	96	1 292	295.1	26.0	34	138	17.5	2.7
Gove	17.9	6 642	13	79	104.8	2.3	23	96	17.1	1.4	NA	NA	NA	NA
Graham	14.2	5 483	9	23	23.1	0.8	24	114	30.2	2.2	3	D	D	D
Grant	129.1	16 493	17	187	253.1	6.9	39	284	67.0	6.2	5	18	3.3	0.5
Gray	190.1	31 648	20	164	112.7	5.1	28	175	34.8	2.6	1	D	D	D
Greeley	17.7	14 226	1	D	D	D	8	46	9.6	0.9	1	D	D	D
Greenwood	1.8	271	10	70	14.1	1.4	37	220	53.3	3.9	2	D	D	D
Hamilton	43.5	16 186	9	60	34.4	2.4	10	85	25.4	1.4	NA	NA	NA	NA
Harper	3.7	617	15	155	91.0	3.9	38	228	50.2	4.6	NA	NA	NA	NA
Harvey	44.1	1 273	30	173	90.8	6.6	131	1 445	274.7	26.1	30	87	10.4	1.4
Haskell	198.6	46 668	14	133	147.1	4.4	15	70	13.7	0.7	2	D	D	D
Hodgeman	23.2	12 098	4	D	D	D	5	36	5.9	0.5	NA	NA	NA	NA
Jackson	2.2	162	13	89	34.5	2.6	44	413	91.1	8.3	7	18	2.5	0.5
Jefferson	3.7	196	11	35	9.6	0.8	58	392	71.3	5.1	9	D	D	D
Jewell	55.3	17 979	6	38	16.8	1.2	19	77	14.3	0.9	1	D	D	D
Johnson	18.1	33	919	13 922	16 252.0	785.5	2 001	38 008	9 255.3	870.3	1 032	5 454	1 067.3	196.3
Kearny	175.7	44 182	8	20	19.8	0.5	10	43	7.6	0.6	2	D	D	D
Kingman	22.2	2 824	19	124	57.0	4.2	32	237	43.2	3.9	4	6	0.2	0.1
Kiowa	58.5	22 902	8	91	71.5	3.3	14	77	14.6	1.1	NA	NA	NA	NA
Labette	4.5	209	21	D	D	D	109	1 004	204.3	18.3	14	65	6.4	1.3
Lane	15.4	8 811	5	31	12.2	0.7	11	57	13.6	1.0	NA	NA	NA	NA
Leavenworth	27.0	354	17	56	13.2	1.7	188	2 130	493.0	45.7	61	240	27.8	5.7
Lincoln	1.5	463	8	55	24.1	1.5	18	78	11.1	0.9	1	D	D	D
Linn	11.6	1 201	5	18	4.3	0.5	38	269	47.8	3.7	2	D	D	D
Logan	6.7	2 442	13	73	53.6	2.3	19	197	78.6	4.5	NA	NA	NA	NA
Lyon	7.7	227	30	D	D	D	169	2 028	470.7	38.0	40	D	D	D
McPherson	31.5	1 080	32	D	D	D	168	1 495	382.2	31.8	32	70	5.8	1.1
Marion	3.6	284	16	182	106.7	7.3	62	349	70.0	5.7	8	D	D	D
Marshall	3.5	348	26	182	128.9	5.5	75	707	186.0	12.5	4	3	0.3	0.1
Meade	153.3	33 510	14	106	108.3	3.4	20	125	20.3	2.1	NA	NA	NA	NA
Miami	4.9	149	21	48	72.7	2.3	103	1 068	251.7	21.4	40	D	D	D
Mitchell	13.0	2 045	25	212	73.3	7.4	53	419	98.8	7.7	4	45	2.3	0.5
Montgomery	11.7	330	36	D	D	D	167	1 772	364.6	35.4	38	140	20.4	3.0
Morris	1.7	285	5	20	9.2	0.7	34	259	45.0	4.2	3	D	D	D
Morton	47.7	14 748	10	101	54.8	2.5	17	103	28.6	2.4	NA	NA	NA	NA
Nemaha	3.3	327	20	147	79.6	5.1	83	575	106.8	9.3	NA	NA	NA	NA

1. Merchant wholesalers, except manufacturers' sales branches and offices. 2. Employer establishments.

STATE County	Professional, scientific, and technical services,[1] 2007				Manufacturing, 2007				Accommodation and food services, 2007			
	Number of establish-ments	Number of employees	Receipts (mil dol)	Annual payroll (mil dol)	Number of establish-ments	Number of employees	Receipts (mil dol)	Annual payroll (mil dol)	Number of establish-ments	Number of employees	Sales (mil dol)	Annual payroll (mil dol)
	147	148	149	150	151	152	153	154	155	156	157	158
KANSAS	7 042	55 922	7 781.4	2 736.5	3 170	177 659	76 751.8	7 983.4	5 866	104 795	4 192.3	1 173.7
Allen	25	123	8.6	3.6	24	1 971	434.7	65.6	29	384	12.4	3.1
Anderson	14	40	2.6	0.9	NA	NA	NA	NA	17	193	5.6	1.3
Atchison	20	D	D	D	23	1 994	D	D	35	540	14.9	4.2
Barber	15	55	7.8	1.5	NA	NA	NA	NA	14	93	2.7	0.6
Barton	61	324	29.9	11.5	46	1 685	561.4	58.0	61	921	35.4	9.3
Bourbon	28	129	9.2	3.4	31	1 114	179.0	35.6	34	431	16.3	4.1
Brown	15	74	9.3	2.7	17	544	91.4	19.9	24	279	7.6	2.1
Butler	100	D	D	D	44	1 535	D	78.5	100	1 479	57.4	15.0
Chase	4	D	D	D	NA	NA	NA	NA	7	67	2.3	0.8
Chautauqua	4	7	0.5	0.2	NA	NA	NA	NA	10	D	D	D
Cherokee	28	84	4.3	1.2	34	2 041	512.1	68.8	25	315	8.6	2.3
Cheyenne	7	17	1.4	0.5	NA	NA	NA	NA	5	40	0.9	0.2
Clark	6	22	4.2	0.6	NA	NA	NA	NA	7	D	D	D
Clay	15	61	3.9	1.9	NA	NA	NA	NA	19	196	5.5	1.3
Cloud	17	75	5.3	2.3	NA	NA	NA	NA	24	388	13.7	3.2
Coffey	15	57	2.2	0.7	NA	NA	NA	NA	19	152	4.9	1.3
Comanche	5	D	D	D	NA	NA	NA	NA	7	38	1.5	0.4
Cowley	54	D	D	D	44	3 726	2 025.4	132.0	71	980	34.2	9.0
Crawford	68	D	D	D	64	2 736	757.2	91.5	89	1 611	51.9	14.5
Decatur	6	25	1.8	0.5	NA	NA	NA	NA	9	69	1.5	0.4
Dickinson	32	D	D	D	20	1 236	317.3	38.4	37	454	15.3	3.8
Doniphan	8	D	D	D	13	D	D	33.8	8	74	1.5	0.4
Douglas	285	D	D	D	88	3 848	976.5	143.0	299	5 937	213.7	60.1
Edwards	4	11	0.3	0.2	NA	NA	NA	NA	6	D	D	D
Elk	6	14	1.0	0.4	NA	NA	NA	NA	6	D	D	D
Ellis	65	D	D	D	38	1 003	D	D	101	1 950	72.2	19.6
Ellsworth	7	81	5.9	2.5	NA	NA	NA	NA	12	136	4.6	1.1
Finney	61	D	D	D	27	3 510	D	110.0	74	1 190	54.9	13.3
Ford	46	D	D	D	27	5 951	D	197.1	72	960	40.3	10.0
Franklin	41	D	D	D	30	1 045	384.1	48.0	56	807	27.9	7.5
Geary	37	D	D	D	7	619	D	20.0	73	1 291	52.0	16.4
Gove	7	14	0.7	0.2	NA	NA	NA	NA	9	48	2.0	0.5
Graham	7	15	0.8	0.2	NA	NA	NA	NA	9	52	1.3	0.3
Grant	13	30	3.2	0.7	NA	NA	NA	NA	18	223	7.1	1.8
Gray	14	33	3.2	1.0	NA	NA	NA	NA	10	63	1.3	0.3
Greeley	3	6	0.6	0.2	NA	NA	NA	NA	2	D	D	D
Greenwood	13	42	2.5	0.9	NA	NA	NA	NA	14	106	3.0	0.7
Hamilton	3	14	0.5	0.1	NA	NA	NA	NA	6	35	0.6	0.2
Harper	15	26	1.8	0.5	NA	NA	NA	NA	18	184	4.4	1.3
Harvey	44	D	D	D	68	3 774	D	151.0	61	997	29.4	8.7
Haskell	7	31	3.9	1.3	NA	NA	NA	NA	6	D	D	D
Hodgeman	3	D	D	D	NA	NA	NA	NA	3	9	0.2	0.1
Jackson	19	80	4.2	1.2	NA	NA	NA	NA	19	D	D	D
Jefferson	22	57	4.9	1.6	NA	NA	NA	NA	22	158	4.4	1.2
Jewell	4	7	0.6	0.1	NA	NA	NA	NA	9	55	1.2	0.3
Johnson	2 644	D	D	D	527	20 896	7 847.7	1 004.5	1 099	24 556	1 083.0	328.1
Kearny	8	33	1.3	0.4	NA	NA	NA	NA	6	51	1.2	0.3
Kingman	12	37	2.9	0.8	NA	NA	NA	NA	13	169	4.5	1.2
Kiowa	2	D	D	D	NA	NA	NA	NA	9	71	0.9	0.2
Labette	26	2 328	9.6	17.5	39	2 446	410.2	84.4	39	496	14.2	3.8
Lane	4	17	1.3	0.5	NA	NA	NA	NA	1	D	D	D
Leavenworth	123	D	D	D	37	1 036	107.7	28.3	86	1 384	48.3	13.2
Lincoln	8	10	1.1	0.5	NA	NA	NA	NA	5	49	0.8	0.3
Linn	8	D	D	D	NA	NA	NA	NA	7	50	1.3	0.3
Logan	5	D	D	D	NA	NA	NA	NA	18	124	3.5	0.9
Lyon	45	D	D	D	37	D	D	D	104	1 528	51.0	14.3
McPherson	52	180	14.1	4.5	64	4 288	4 222.6	188.8	64	972	29.8	8.6
Marion	16	139	24.5	4.5	NA	NA	NA	NA	23	239	5.6	1.5
Marshall	17	90	9.5	2.0	19	1 091	257.7	46.6	27	270	8.8	2.3
Meade	7	42	1.5	0.6	NA	NA	NA	NA	7	44	1.5	0.3
Miami	66	D	D	D	31	527	D	D	59	695	24.0	6.7
Mitchell	15	56	3.6	1.0	NA	NA	NA	NA	17	164	5.1	1.4
Montgomery	49	206	17.3	5.7	56	5 438	3 979.7	233.2	78	1 276	43.5	10.2
Morris	12	63	4.1	1.7	NA	NA	NA	NA	16	167	4.6	1.5
Morton	7	18	1.4	0.3	NA	NA	NA	NA	6	72	2.3	0.6
Nemaha	27	D	D	D	28	1 163	243.1	44.7	18	168	4.2	1.0

1. Establishment subject to federal tax.

Table B. States and Counties — **Health Care and Social Assistance, Other Services, Nonemployer Businesses, and Residential Construction**

STATE County	Health care and social assistance, 2007				Other services, 2007				Nonemployer businesses, 2013		Value of residential construction authorized by building permits, 2014	
	Number of establish-ments	Number of employees	Receipts (mil dol)	Annual payroll (mil dol)	Number of establish-ments	Number of employees	Receipts (mil dol)	Annual payroll (mil dol)	Number	Receipts (mil dol)	New Construction ($1,000)	Number of housing units
	159	160	161	162	163	164	165	166	167	168	169	170
KANSAS	7 695	178 528	15 128.7	6 143.8	5 498	31 665	3 326.1	803.6	190 838	8 307.8	1 417 358	7 459
Allen	41	629	43.6	18.0	29	85	7.9	1.8	917	30.4	1 955	13
Anderson	25	372	21.8	8.6	14	26	1.8	0.5	611	20.1	419	11
Atchison	52	D	D	D	24	D	D	D	852	25.0	160	2
Barber	14	202	14.7	7.2	21	51	3.7	0.9	474	22.0	0	0
Barton	108	2 143	130.5	55.6	82	300	30.7	6.9	2 275	99.0	5 556	58
Bourbon	44	1 105	69.5	30.9	31	67	6.5	1.4	1 022	34.8	285	2
Brown	30	759	45.8	18.9	20	D	D	D	693	26.6	843	2
Butler	152	D	D	D	84	243	21.5	5.0	4 026	147.7	35 141	143
Chase	2	D	D	D	12	24	1.8	0.3	228	8.6	0	0
Chautauqua	10	155	7.4	3.4	5	D	D	D	316	11.4	0	0
Cherokee	39	619	27.2	12.3	28	72	5.4	1.1	1 074	41.8	983	9
Cheyenne	12	161	9.2	4.6	6	D	D	D	242	9.0	0	0
Clark	9	665	26.8	13.5	6	D	D	D	209	6.8	0	0
Clay	31	641	31.9	15.0	29	77	5.7	1.3	616	21.0	3 390	22
Cloud	38	775	36.1	16.8	24	85	6.6	1.4	665	21.6	65	1
Coffey	29	477	30.6	18.7	14	36	3.5	0.7	642	26.7	4 219	21
Comanche	7	D	D	D	8	D	D	D	158	4.9	0	0
Cowley	120	2 091	135.5	53.2	56	218	15.2	4.5	2 028	70.0	4 149	35
Crawford	141	3 013	182.6	70.4	69	D	D	D	2 158	70.1	19 486	135
Decatur	7	233	10.4	5.0	6	14	1.0	0.3	286	10.6	0	0
Dickinson	47	876	44.1	19.1	45	152	13.4	2.5	1 217	39.6	2 387	26
Doniphan	9	D	D	D	8	D	D	D	471	18.8	490	3
Douglas	283	5 331	375.5	163.3	190	1 429	277.4	33.7	7 712	298.3	56 590	347
Edwards	7	162	8.5	3.7	8	18	1.2	0.3	212	6.7	147	1
Elk	5	D	D	D	6	D	D	D	295	12.7	NA	NA
Ellis	115	3 027	252.3	98.6	81	372	37.4	7.3	2 814	119.1	14 233	69
Ellsworth	22	508	29.8	13.2	15	46	3.1	0.8	458	14.4	795	3
Finney	96	2 155	159.9	60.1	81	377	36.9	8.2	2 168	120.6	2 253	14
Ford	89	1 362	145.7	46.7	59	437	29.9	8.9	1 739	91.5	7 447	43
Franklin	66	1 159	80.3	34.4	46	298	24.9	8.4	1 544	57.6	7 556	31
Geary	53	1 554	130.2	57.3	51	261	13.9	4.1	1 168	39.1	20 658	141
Gove	11	201	12.9	5.0	14	38	4.2	0.6	311	17.7	1 297	15
Graham	14	272	12.5	6.5	9	20	3.1	0.5	287	11.4	0	0
Grant	14	191	15.9	6.8	13	55	6.0	1.1	496	27.0	138	4
Gray	13	154	6.2	3.5	13	25	2.4	0.5	630	29.6	3 074	18
Greeley	2	D	D	D	6	D	D	D	131	4.8	504	3
Greenwood	13	318	18.5	7.8	16	25	2.2	0.4	551	20.9	0	0
Hamilton	9	D	D	D	9	18	1.6	0.3	191	9.2	0	0
Harper	16	348	19.5	9.0	24	40	4.4	0.6	516	23.9	960	6
Harvey	97	2 877	208.7	86.1	67	277	19.3	5.2	2 361	73.4	12 170	73
Haskell	13	175	10.0	4.5	9	D	D	D	353	18.5	250	1
Hodgeman	5	D	D	D	5	D	D	D	184	9.2	NA	NA
Jackson	28	521	21.4	10.5	26	94	7.4	1.5	757	25.1	1 307	7
Jefferson	27	345	14.9	7.5	27	91	6.4	1.9	1 195	44.8	6 022	34
Jewell	4	D	D	D	7	D	D	D	269	10.1	112	2
Johnson	1 561	32 801	3 409.3	1 365.4	999	8 126	820.0	230.6	46 526	2 438.9	640 031	2 689
Kearny	7	D	D	D	8	D	D	D	318	12.0	0	0
Kingman	24	410	20.3	8.7	14	21	1.4	0.4	648	28.9	1 801	11
Kiowa	9	271	12.9	4.9	9	19	1.3	0.4	229	10.4	389	2
Labette	85	2 003	132.0	58.6	38	164	14.8	3.6	1 190	40.2	460	5
Lane	5	D	D	D	7	D	D	D	207	7.3	0	0
Leavenworth	122	2 682	247.8	105.6	96	510	40.6	11.4	3 682	132.9	35 733	220
Lincoln	6	138	6.8	3.5	8	28	1.5	0.4	258	8.4	60	1
Linn	11	84	3.5	1.4	13	62	4.3	1.0	697	21.9	3 718	42
Logan	8	184	11.4	5.4	14	31	2.0	0.5	260	10.7	183	1
Lyon	103	D	D	D	75	305	25.0	5.9	1 733	59.3	1 839	17
McPherson	86	2 275	111.7	51.9	83	389	31.6	8.8	2 449	99.8	13 836	124
Marion	30	669	34.6	15.6	27	108	9.3	1.8	926	25.9	3 226	17
Marshall	40	542	30.2	15.6	36	94	6.1	1.4	777	30.5	6 291	45
Meade	9	D	D	D	10	20	1.8	0.3	379	19.2	85	1
Miami	51	1 813	98.6	48.6	57	155	11.4	2.9	2 442	106.8	11 569	50
Mitchell	25	506	38.6	16.0	18	60	4.8	1.1	602	24.8	000	4
Montgomery	108	2 513	157.1	67.6	65	295	15.2	6.6	1 935	60.3	50	1
Morris	10	232	12.8	5.2	7	D	D	D	463	15.4	454	2
Morton	8	D	D	D	10	D	D	D	233	6.7	0	0
Nemaha	38	881	39.2	18.8	32	92	6.5	1.6	758	27.1	4 536	19

Table B. States and Counties — **Government Employment and Payroll, and Local Government Finances**

STATE County	Government employment and payroll, 2012: Full-time equivalent employees	March payroll (dollars)	March payroll (percent of total): Adminis-tration, judicial, and legal	Police and Corrections	Fire Protection	Highways and transpor-tation	Health and Welfare	Natural resources and utilities	Education and libraries	Local government finances, 2012 — General revenue: Total (mil dol)	Inter-govern-mental (mil dol)	Taxes: Total (mil dol)	Per capita[1] (dollars): Total	Property
	171	172	173	174	175	176	177	178	179	180	181	182	183	184
KANSAS	X	X	X	X	X	X	X	X	X	X	X	X	X	X
Allen	895	2 577 982	5.0	6.1	3.4	3.7	4.1	8.9	67.1	63.9	30.0	21.1	1 583	1 268
Anderson	497	1 619 637	6.2	5.4	1.6	4.7	1.1	6.1	73.7	23.0	11.7	7.8	980	756
Atchison	692	1 978 776	6.6	8.4	3.3	4.3	7.8	7.0	60.5	55.0	21.3	23.4	1 390	1 002
Barber	411	1 245 913	6.3	3.3	0.1	7.0	45.0	3.3	32.0	35.8	4.2	16.4	3 382	2 951
Barton	1 660	5 166 241	4.8	6.8	2.0	3.6	6.0	4.3	70.0	122.6	44.4	49.3	1 788	1 396
Bourbon	839	2 300 103	4.1	6.3	2.0	3.3	0.0	5.1	77.6	59.7	27.2	20.2	1 354	1 059
Brown	402	1 209 798	8.3	11.3	0.2	5.2	0.6	6.9	64.8	36.4	13.4	17.7	1 790	1 406
Butler	4 199	12 617 495	2.9	6.0	1.7	2.3	2.5	2.9	79.0	296.1	116.0	108.1	1 642	1 429
Chase	138	378 267	8.3	25.9	0.5	9.7	5.3	1.8	44.0	11.2	3.5	6.0	2 181	1 999
Chautauqua	172	502 746	9.7	7.9	0.0	8.5	6.3	5.4	60.4	13.8	5.5	6.9	1 943	1 619
Cherokee	874	3 187 294	11.0	10.0	0.6	9.2	3.4	2.6	61.3	64.1	33.3	21.8	1 027	758
Cheyenne	165	389 236	10.5	5.0	0.1	7.4	2.7	8.2	64.4	12.1	4.1	6.6	2 450	2 088
Clark	347	1 038 878	4.4	3.1	0.0	2.2	61.9	2.5	24.8	28.0	3.9	8.5	3 919	3 852
Clay	803	2 480 508	2.7	3.1	1.1	3.9	30.1	7.3	50.0	45.5	12.6	13.2	1 545	1 227
Cloud	581	1 796 777	3.3	5.8	1.8	7.0	2.6	3.3	72.8	44.9	18.4	15.2	1 616	1 216
Coffey	673	2 404 634	6.2	5.9	0.0	6.6	43.0	4.7	31.1	69.1	9.0	35.4	4 162	4 031
Comanche	187	510 886	10.4	5.9	0.0	8.5	34.5	11.2	28.4	18.5	6.5	6.4	3 350	3 116
Cowley	2 458	8 016 863	4.3	5.7	2.3	2.2	22.2	5.9	56.0	203.4	66.1	46.6	1 284	1 024
Crawford	1 777	5 700 396	5.1	9.6	2.5	3.3	21.7	6.6	49.1	136.9	53.7	45.9	1 166	827
Decatur	132	423 037	12.8	5.9	0.4	9.6	3.7	7.1	54.7	9.9	2.9	5.6	1 953	1 752
Dickinson	1 141	3 857 618	5.1	5.3	1.0	3.4	29.1	5.5	49.6	105.0	33.0	29.3	1 484	1 175
Doniphan	654	1 750 518	4.8	4.1	0.0	3.2	3.0	4.0	80.3	45.4	18.2	12.9	1 635	1 413
Douglas	4 535	18 551 008	5.6	11.2	5.0	2.9	33.2	7.9	33.4	537.2	114.0	188.6	1 671	1 239
Edwards	153	450 266	16.0	7.2	0.2	14.9	6.8	4.1	50.1	13.9	5.5	7.3	2 459	2 226
Elk	292	687 044	6.7	3.5	0.3	5.8	15.5	4.5	62.3	14.4	5.9	5.3	1 934	1 803
Ellis	1 003	3 461 008	7.9	9.4	2.7	5.0	5.7	5.6	61.1	88.4	23.1	51.1	1 759	1 232
Ellsworth	296	866 464	7.5	7.6	0.0	7.7	5.7	8.2	60.7	28.4	9.8	14.2	2 194	1 862
Finney	2 267	7 504 277	5.0	10.7	1.8	2.9	2.9	4.3	70.6	186.5	73.2	74.7	2 008	1 584
Ford	1 844	5 930 863	5.1	8.2	3.9	2.6	3.3	4.3	71.6	177.3	76.6	65.8	1 894	1 286
Franklin	1 501	5 023 604	6.2	8.2	1.6	2.3	29.7	5.6	44.5	115.7	36.0	39.3	1 518	1 176
Geary	2 097	7 346 708	3.8	7.7	1.7	1.2	23.2	1.3	60.2	186.7	68.2	47.0	1 236	779
Gove	329	918 512	4.3	1.7	0.0	4.8	54.5	0.9	32.9	24.5	5.7	7.8	2 849	2 457
Graham	232	804 031	8.2	3.8	0.6	8.9	44.4	4.5	28.5	22.4	4.0	9.8	3 805	3 282
Grant	403	1 281 935	6.8	7.4	0.2	7.9	5.9	5.1	65.0	41.0	11.0	26.3	3 319	3 166
Gray	309	995 915	8.2	7.4	0.0	6.0	2.2	5.2	67.3	26.3	10.8	12.0	1 998	1 829
Greeley	53	153 774	8.6	0.0	0.0	6.4	1.7	4.3	78.3	4.0	1.5	2.0	1 555	1 519
Greenwood	339	898 356	8.5	7.0	0.4	6.6	4.3	4.5	67.1	22.5	10.0	10.4	1 605	1 400
Hamilton	163	402 085	10.0	8.0	0.1	7.1	6.4	7.9	57.3	13.4	3.7	8.9	3 358	3 144
Harper	602	1 701 546	6.8	3.5	0.1	6.1	45.7	4.3	29.4	45.9	10.6	12.9	2 179	2 024
Harvey	1 517	4 865 931	8.6	8.1	5.6	3.6	3.0	5.5	65.1	120.5	49.4	44.5	1 277	900
Haskell	378	1 272 364	6.3	6.7	0.0	7.9	37.3	0.8	40.4	39.0	3.8	22.7	5 336	5 085
Hodgeman	127	312 316	11.2	6.4	0.0	12.3	7.7	10.6	49.0	11.5	3.2	6.7	3 390	3 354
Jackson	744	2 123 015	4.8	7.4	0.0	4.1	0.8	6.6	74.7	41.1	21.8	14.9	1 107	922
Jefferson	801	2 548 797	6.5	6.7	0.0	4.8	6.2	3.9	68.5	65.4	32.7	24.4	1 288	1 179
Jewell	228	595 682	6.9	3.1	0.0	12.6	38.5	5.3	30.9	15.8	4.4	6.1	2 003	1 819
Johnson	22 393	88 446 886	6.5	10.0	4.1	3.0	4.2	7.6	63.3	2 399.0	615.6	1 250.4	2 233	1 568
Kearny	501	1 624 976	4.9	5.2	1.0	3.4	47.9	3.2	32.3	40.1	5.1	19.2	4 834	4 739
Kingman	303	939 992	10.2	7.8	0.3	9.1	3.5	5.9	62.1	29.0	9.1	16.4	2 088	1 871
Kiowa	190	513 068	15.3	8.3	1.6	10.8	2.8	6.8	50.3	18.3	5.8	10.3	4 132	3 569
Labette	1 476	4 983 554	3.5	5.4	1.3	2.4	37.6	2.9	46.0	131.2	39.2	25.9	1 215	896
Lane	185	518 931	8.0	5.3	2.8	7.3	34.7	3.4	37.1	15.3	2.4	7.9	4 633	4 497
Leavenworth	2 924	9 219 623	4.7	9.0	2.4	3.1	3.7	5.2	70.5	234.3	105.0	92.8	1 194	954
Lincoln	278	791 585	5.0	2.8	0.1	6.6	36.5	5.0	42.1	16.1	5.5	7.6	2 408	2 131
Linn	469	1 414 132	7.1	7.1	0.7	5.0	2.4	6.1	70.4	38.3	14.7	20.4	2 163	2 067
Logan	328	920 118	5.1	3.8	0.2	3.2	54.6	2.9	29.9	24.5	3.1	9.2	3 298	2 915
Lyon	2 245	7 549 055	4.5	8.4	2.7	3.3	26.6	2.6	50.3	180.6	54.8	53.5	1 586	1 073
McPherson	1 486	4 467 777	5.3	7.9	1.7	5.1	4.7	13.1	58.6	102.2	34.2	49.8	1 697	1 261
Marion	702	1 972 669	7.2	6.2	0.1	6.0	17.8	6.6	54.8	54.7	18.7	20.1	1 630	1 376
Marshall	507	1 385 386	5.8	6.0	0.0	7.1	3.5	3.5	71.8	35.7	13.7	17.7	1 764	1 524
Meade	403	1 284 083	4.9	3.3	1.1	4.4	54.9	3.4	27.0	33.8	5.5	11.9	2 711	2 487
Miami	1 386	4 167 179	7.7	8.9	1.2	4.9	3.1	3.9	68.5	96.7	33.9	47.7	1 463	1 199
Mitchell	539	1 523 148	6.6	5.9	0.1	6.8	5.3	10.9	62.8	39.3	15.8	13.9	2 189	1 626
Montgomery	1 708	5 095 652	3.7	7.7	2.9	3.7	1.3	9.3	68.3	148.4	54.4	62.4	1 812	1 449
Morris	233	667 311	10.9	7.8	0.3	7.9	1.6	3.9	64.1	17.4	6.0	9.0	1 545	1 277
Morton	433	1 384 778	4.2	3.1	0.1	4.3	50.6	2.3	32.2	39.0	7.6	14.7	4 633	4 454
Nemaha	548	1 548 782	6.0	6.7	0.0	5.8	2.1	9.9	67.8	39.4	16.0	18.2	1 794	1 515

1. Based on the resident population estimated as of July 1 of the year shown.

STATE County	Local government finances, 2012 (cont.) — Direct general expenditure: Total (mil dol)	Per capita[1] (dollars)	Percent of total for: Education	Health and hospitals	Police protection	Public welfare	Highways	Debt outstanding: Total (mil dol)	Per capita[1] (dollars)	Government employment, 2013: Federal civilian	Federal military	State and local	Presidential election,[2] 2012 — Percent of vote cast: Democratic	Republican	All other
	185	186	187	188	189	190	191	192	193	194	195	196	197	198	199
KANSAS	X	X	X	X	X	X	X	X	X	25 442	36 331	234 658	41.7	56.6	1.7
Allen	63.1	4 735	58.0	4.0	3.4	0.0	6.4	50.6	3 796	61	54	1 705	37.4	60.7	1.9
Anderson	40.1	5 062	61.6	2.1	2.8	0.0	8.0	28.9	3 654	38	33	514	32.4	65.1	2.5
Atchison	59.4	3 536	45.7	1.0	4.9	4.7	7.9	33.0	1 961	44	65	886	45.1	52.7	2.2
Barber	36.3	7 477	24.0	41.7	2.6	0.0	10.3	11.4	2 336	25	21	641	24.3	74.5	1.3
Barton	120.9	4 389	60.4	2.7	3.3	0.0	7.9	58.1	2 108	75	114	2 346	27.4	70.6	2.1
Bourbon	65.3	4 385	57.0	0.9	3.2	0.0	6.3	43.5	2 920	79	61	1 116	35.3	62.5	2.2
Brown	35.1	3 553	49.9	0.9	4.2	0.0	11.2	44.1	4 465	109	42	1 650	30.1	68.2	1.7
Butler	329.4	5 004	68.1	1.1	2.9	0.0	5.2	551.1	8 372	127	269	6 016	32.9	65.1	2.0
Chase	11.4	4 131	37.7	3.0	3.4	0.0	10.4	5.1	1 857	19	11	238	27.7	70.5	1.8
Chautauqua	13.5	3 787	47.9	5.7	3.6	0.0	9.6	9.2	2 578	18	15	249	21.7	76.6	1.8
Cherokee	63.8	3 007	60.9	2.7	4.3	0.0	8.9	20.0	944	48	88	1 355	37.2	60.9	1.9
Cheyenne	11.4	4 256	50.1	5.6	3.7	0.0	9.9	0.8	296	15	11	244	21.6	76.6	1.8
Clark	28.0	12 839	20.3	57.2	4.3	0.0	4.7	5.4	2 461	10	0	437	21.1	77.4	1.5
Clay	46.8	5 482	29.6	33.0	3.0	0.0	7.6	34.9	4 095	35	35	903	24.9	74.0	1.2
Cloud	46.3	4 930	66.5	3.2	3.3	0.0	6.9	13.5	1 434	41	37	856	27.7	70.1	2.2
Coffey	70.3	8 270	29.8	34.4	3.0	0.0	10.8	13.0	1 531	42	35	1 121	26.5	72.2	1.3
Comanche	19.2	10 056	20.4	23.8	2.0	0.0	6.2	6.1	3 165	0	0	265	19.9	78.5	1.5
Cowley	191.8	5 286	45.5	21.1	3.6	0.0	3.2	166.3	4 583	98	145	3 463	36.4	61.6	2.1
Crawford	135.7	3 448	45.0	17.8	5.0	0.0	3.9	114.8	2 916	99	161	4 816	49.5	48.1	2.4
Decatur	10.3	3 573	44.7	3.6	4.6	0.0	12.8	7.9	2 755	20	12	246	22.2	76.8	1.0
Dickinson	107.2	5 425	50.6	21.7	3.1	0.0	5.6	91.6	4 637	94	82	1 699	27.9	70.2	1.9
Doniphan	45.9	5 834	72.7	2.2	2.9	0.0	6.0	12.8	1 623	36	31	974	31.3	66.6	2.2
Douglas	474.7	4 206	28.6	35.1	4.9	0.0	3.3	544.9	4 828	460	488	14 827	64.4	33.6	2.0
Edwards	14.5	4 871	42.0	3.4	4.5	0.0	14.5	1.2	396	18	12	227	24.5	73.3	2.1
Elk	14.6	5 351	44.7	2.8	2.7	13.2	10.2	3.0	1 097	18	11	344	25.3	72.7	2.0
Ellis	86.9	2 990	45.4	3.2	5.5	0.0	7.4	38.7	1 332	140	119	3 249	32.2	65.9	1.8
Ellsworth	28.5	4 390	50.2	3.3	4.0	0.0	18.7	22.2	3 424	25	23	900	29.0	68.8	2.2
Finney	182.2	4 899	60.1	1.9	6.7	0.0	4.4	162.9	4 378	125	155	3 268	31.6	66.9	1.5
Ford	201.8	5 806	49.4	1.2	3.5	1.0	2.6	336.1	9 671	228	144	2 667	33.7	64.6	1.6
Franklin	118.9	4 591	39.4	30.1	1.6	0.0	5.7	81.1	3 129	66	107	1 957	37.8	60.3	1.9
Geary	176.2	4 635	47.3	25.0	6.0	0.0	2.9	273.5	7 194	3 411	17 586	2 799	43.1	55.5	1.4
Gove	24.9	9 123	26.3	51.1	1.8	0.0	8.5	1.5	532	13	11	433	18.4	80.1	1.5
Graham	21.4	8 308	22.0	38.9	2.6	0.0	9.1	0.4	152	27	11	332	22.8	74.5	2.7
Grant	35.6	4 496	41.9	5.9	4.7	0.0	7.6	27.3	3 445	16	33	730	23.9	75.0	1.2
Gray	25.6	4 246	56.7	2.7	4.4	0.0	11.9	24.2	4 013	23	25	902	20.6	77.5	1.9
Greeley	4.0	3 089	72.8	0.0	1.1	0.0	4.3	5.0	3 847	0	0	185	20.3	79.3	0.4
Greenwood	21.3	3 303	53.1	3.8	5.8	0.0	13.3	21.4	3 323	44	27	454	27.3	71.0	1.7
Hamilton	11.6	4 401	48.9	2.0	5.9	0.0	10.1	4.6	1 740	0	11	356	21.3	77.0	1.7
Harper	45.6	7 720	25.8	36.2	2.0	6.9	9.7	21.2	3 581	32	24	833	26.3	71.5	2.2
Harvey	109.6	3 145	50.9	2.7	5.6	0.1	5.4	180.9	5 190	66	142	2 017	40.5	57.7	1.9
Haskell	39.1	9 192	29.1	42.9	3.2	0.0	10.1	10.5	2 463	14	17	595	17.7	81.3	1.0
Hodgeman	10.7	5 451	37.8	5.5	4.6	0.0	12.0	11.5	5 870	14	0	289	19.3	78.9	1.8
Jackson	41.1	3 058	62.3	0.8	5.4	0.0	10.4	21.9	1 625	47	56	1 933	36.9	60.9	2.1
Jefferson	63.2	3 338	64.8	5.4	5.1	0.0	7.4	46.3	2 446	67	79	1 041	39.6	58.3	2.1
Jewell	13.7	4 485	29.6	21.3	2.8	0.0	17.3	0.8	250	29	13	332	19.8	77.7	2.5
Johnson	2 304.6	4 116	47.4	2.5	7.7	0.9	5.7	5 877.0	10 496	2 361	2 389	28 192	44.8	53.8	1.3
Kearny	42.8	10 778	27.2	45.6	2.8	0.0	6.2	5.6	1 409	13	16	704	20.9	78.2	0.9
Kingman	29.4	3 741	43.5	3.2	4.6	0.0	13.3	19.1	2 432	35	32	579	26.3	71.0	2.7
Kiowa	16.8	6 718	43.0	3.4	4.6	0.0	10.9	3.4	1 371	14	10	383	17.6	80.4	2.0
Labette	134.7	6 331	39.7	39.0	2.6	0.0	4.0	95.8	4 500	73	87	2 793	42.5	55.4	2.1
Lane	15.6	9 127	29.8	31.7	3.9	0.0	8.7	0.5	288	13	0	260	18.8	79.3	1.9
Leavenworth	188.5	2 425	61.8	0.0	5.1	0.0	3.5	316.9	4 076	4 509	4 006	4 128	43.3	54.9	1.8
Lincoln	16.5	5 197	44.3	7.0	2.8	0.0	13.6	1.8	569	30	13	410	21.9	75.9	2.2
Linn	38.3	4 053	55.6	3.0	4.7	0.0	10.2	11.7	1 244	45	40	735	30.9	66.8	2.3
Logan	27.7	9 951	22.7	51.3	2.8	0.0	4.7	6.2	2 220	19	12	745	15.6	82.4	1.9
Lyon	166.1	4 920	39.3	28.9	4.3	0.0	4.3	94.4	2 798	104	136	4 341	45.9	51.9	2.2
McPherson	101.4	3 454	45.5	2.3	4.3	0.0	12.0	90.9	3 097	81	121	1 926	31.5	66.8	1.7
Marion	54.2	4 388	42.4	18.1	3.1	0.0	9.1	43.6	3 528	62	49	986	29.7	68.6	1.6
Marshall	34.8	3 472	53.8	2.9	4.3	0.0	13.1	19.2	1 915	55	42	853	35.4	62.7	1.9
Meade	34.5	7 851	21.7	41.1	2.2	3.8	7.6	13.7	3 120	13	18	605	18.5	79.8	1.8
Miami	87.9	2 695	49.6	2.9	5.9	0.0	9.2	104.9	3 215	61	137	2 031	37.3	61.0	1.6
Mitchell	42.4	6 669	50.7	7.8	3.9	0.0	12.6	15.4	2 417	30	26	1 037	21.9	76.2	1.9
Montgomery	142.0	4 121	61.6	2.3	3.8	0.0	5.5	137.7	3 996	104	141	2 664	31.2	66.9	1.9
Morris	25.5	4 361	59.2	5.3	2.7	0.0	10.7	21.0	3 594	35	24	459	31.9	66.0	2.1
Morton	37.0	11 666	31.7	47.6	0.9	0.0	2.7	4.6	1 453	20	13	583	16.3	82.2	1.4
Nemaha	36.9	3 640	57.0	1.5	3.6	0.0	11.8	35.6	3 511	52	42	785	26.7	71.2	2.1

1. Based on the resident population estimated as of July 1 of the year shown. 2. © 2013 Election Data Services, Inc. All rights reserved.

STATE/ County code	CBSA code[1]	County type[2]	STATE County	Land area,[3] (sq km) 2010	Population, 2014: Total persons 2014	Population, 2014: Rank	Population, 2014: Per square kilometer	Population and population characteristics, 2013: Race alone or in combination, not Hispanic or Latino (percent): White	Black	American Indian, Alaska Native	Asian and Pacific Islander	Percent Hispanic or Latino[4]	Age (percent): Under 5 years	5 to 17 years	18 to 24 years	25 to 34 years	35 to 44 years	45 to 54 years
				1	2	3	4	5	6	7	8	9	10	11	12	13	14	15
			KANSAS—Cont'd															
20 133	...	7	Neosho	1 480	16 416	2 014	11.1	92.2	1.8	1.8	1.0	4.9	6.7	17.9	8.8	11.0	10.8	13.1
20 135	...	9	Ness	2 784	3 105	2 966	1.1	89.9	0.9	0.7	0.5	8.9	4.8	17.0	5.7	10.1	9.3	14.1
20 137	...	7	Norton	2 274	5 560	2 797	2.4	90.9	3.6	0.8	1.0	5.0	5.1	14.1	8.4	13.3	11.8	15.2
20 139	45820	3	Osage	1 827	15 936	2 045	8.7	95.8	1.2	1.6	0.6	2.6	6.0	18.5	7.2	9.7	11.2	14.8
20 141	...	9	Osborne	2 312	3 756	2 924	1.6	97.1	0.7	0.7	0.6	1.7	5.5	15.7	6.8	9.9	8.6	13.8
20 143	41460	9	Ottawa	1 867	6 065	2 753	3.2	95.6	1.5	1.0	0.5	2.7	5.4	18.6	6.7	10.4	11.5	14.7
20 145	...	7	Pawnee	1 954	6 916	2 686	3.5	86.8	5.7	1.2	0.7	7.2	5.2	14.8	8.3	12.6	11.3	14.3
20 147	...	7	Phillips	2 294	5 533	2 799	2.4	95.6	0.9	0.8	1.0	2.8	5.5	17.9	6.7	10.3	9.6	13.3
20 149	31740	6	Pottawatomie	2 178	22 897	1 692	10.5	91.9	2.0	1.5	1.5	5.2	8.2	21.5	7.9	13.2	11.6	12.8
20 151	...	7	Pratt	1 904	9 850	2 450	5.2	90.9	2.0	1.3	0.9	6.8	7.3	17.1	10.2	11.3	9.8	11.8
20 153	...	9	Rawlins	2 770	2 584	3 003	0.9	94.6	0.7	0.7	0.3	4.6	4.7	14.0	6.3	10.1	7.5	13.3
20 155	26740	4	Reno	3 251	63 794	822	19.6	87.1	4.0	1.3	0.9	8.7	6.1	17.1	9.1	12.4	10.9	13.0
20 157	...	9	Republic	1 858	4 803	2 851	2.6	97.2	0.8	0.5	0.6	1.5	5.6	14.1	6.1	8.9	8.2	13.4
20 159	...	7	Rice	1 881	10 015	2 437	5.3	86.4	2.2	1.6	0.9	11.0	6.6	17.0	12.1	11.1	9.7	12.2
20 161	31740	5	Riley	1 579	75 194	732	47.6	80.4	7.7	1.3	5.7	7.8	6.9	10.8	32.9	19.2	8.6	6.9
20 163	...	9	Rooks	2 306	5 155	2 828	2.2	96.5	0.9	0.6	0.7	2.4	6.2	17.1	7.2	10.6	10.2	13.7
20 165	...	9	Rush	1 859	3 197	2 958	1.7	95.3	0.7	1.2	0.3	3.5	4.1	15.3	6.5	9.1	9.5	14.0
20 167	...	7	Russell	2 295	6 956	2 682	3.0	95.4	1.7	1.2	1.1	2.2	6.2	15.0	6.9	10.7	9.8	13.6
20 169	41460	5	Saline	1 865	55 755	907	29.9	83.4	4.7	1.2	2.9	10.6	6.9	17.6	9.4	12.7	11.6	13.5
20 171	...	7	Scott	1 858	5 080	2 833	2.7	81.2	0.5	0.7	0.7	17.4	6.9	19.2	7.5	10.9	11.2	13.5
20 173	48620	2	Sedgwick	2 584	508 803	133	196.9	72.0	10.5	2.0	5.0	13.7	7.6	19.0	9.6	14.3	12.1	12.9
20 175	30580	7	Seward	1 656	23 465	1 664	14.2	34.9	3.9	1.0	3.1	58.2	9.9	21.6	12.3	14.5	12.4	11.7
20 177	45820	3	Shawnee	1 409	178 406	360	126.6	77.8	10.0	2.2	1.9	11.5	6.7	17.8	8.6	13.0	11.5	13.3
20 179	...	9	Sheridan	2 321	2 539	3 006	1.1	95.3	0.7	0.6	0.3	4.1	5.6	17.9	6.5	8.7	9.6	13.7
20 181	...	7	Sherman	2 735	6 110	2 748	2.2	85.9	1.4	1.0	1.3	11.8	6.7	16.9	9.0	12.3	10.1	13.0
20 183	...	9	Smith	2 319	3 769	2 922	1.6	97.3	0.9	1.2	0.6	1.5	4.6	14.4	6.6	8.0	9.0	14.2
20 185	...	9	Stafford	2 051	4 297	2 880	2.1	85.0	0.9	1.5	0.6	13.4	5.6	18.8	6.5	10.3	9.3	14.8
20 187	...	9	Stanton	1 762	2 111	3 039	1.2	60.6	1.0	1.4	0.3	38.0	8.2	19.9	7.7	11.8	12.3	12.1
20 189	...	7	Stevens	1 884	5 801	2 775	3.1	65.2	0.9	1.2	0.5	33.4	7.8	22.7	8.0	11.9	12.5	12.8
20 191	48620	2	Sumner	3 061	23 528	1 659	7.7	92.3	1.7	2.3	0.6	5.1	6.4	18.7	8.0	10.8	10.8	13.9
20 193	...	7	Thomas	2 783	7 891	2 603	2.8	92.7	1.2	0.9	1.2	5.1	6.7	16.2	13.7	12.5	10.4	12.2
20 195	...	9	Trego	2 304	2 902	2 983	1.3	96.5	0.8	0.6	0.8	2.0	4.9	14.1	6.2	9.5	9.7	14.4
20 197	45820	3	Wabaunsee	2 057	7 022	2 676	3.4	94.9	1.3	1.7	0.5	3.4	6.8	18.1	6.8	10.3	11.0	14.7
20 199	...	9	Wallace	2 366	1 506	3 080	0.6	91.9	0.9	0.7	0.1	7.3	5.7	19.9	7.6	9.8	8.6	13.4
20 201	...	9	Washington	2 317	5 598	2 795	2.4	95.9	1.1	0.6	0.5	2.9	5.5	16.7	6.8	9.8	9.9	13.9
20 203	...	9	Wichita	1 861	2 176	3 036	1.2	71.4	1.0	0.5	0.5	27.2	7.0	18.8	6.8	10.5	11.7	12.4
20 205	...	7	Wilson	1 477	9 028	2 515	6.1	94.8	1.0	2.6	0.9	2.8	5.7	18.3	7.2	10.6	11.0	12.7
20 207	...	9	Woodson	1 289	3 157	2 962	2.4	95.7	1.0	2.2	0.3	2.8	5.1	17.0	5.5	11.1	8.8	13.8
20 209	28140	1	Wyandotte	393	161 636	394	411.3	44.8	25.5	1.4	3.8	27.0	8.5	19.9	9.2	15.1	12.4	12.6
21 000	...	X	KENTUCKY	102 269	4 413 457	X	43.2	87.1	8.9	0.7	1.7	3.3	6.3	16.8	9.7	12.8	12.9	14.1
21 001	...	7	Adair	1 050	19 204	1 865	18.3	94.8	3.5	0.6	0.4	1.8	5.3	15.9	12.1	11.3	11.3	14.4
21 003	14540	6	Allen	892	20 384	1 812	22.9	96.4	1.6	0.8	0.4	1.9	6.4	17.5	8.7	11.4	12.9	14.3
21 005	23180	6	Anderson	523	21 888	1 740	41.9	95.6	2.7	0.6	0.8	1.5	5.9	18.3	7.7	11.3	14.5	15.6
21 007	37140	9	Ballard	639	8 240	2 587	12.9	95.1	4.0	0.9	0.5	1.3	5.4	16.9	7.5	10.5	12.7	13.8
21 009	23980	6	Barren	1 263	43 148	1 108	34.2	92.3	4.8	0.6	0.7	2.9	6.0	17.6	8.0	11.8	12.5	14.5
21 011	34460	8	Bath	722	12 206	2 287	16.9	96.8	2.0	0.6	0.3	1.4	6.1	18.7	7.9	10.8	12.8	14.2
21 013	33180	7	Bell	930	27 778	1 503	29.9	96.1	3.0	1.1	0.5	0.9	6.0	15.3	8.7	11.8	12.7	14.6
21 015	17140	1	Boone	638	126 413	490	198.1	90.4	3.6	0.5	3.2	3.9	7.1	20.5	7.9	12.7	14.6	14.8
21 017	30460	2	Bourbon	750	19 972	1 837	26.6	86.5	7.1	0.5	0.5	7.0	6.1	17.3	8.1	10.6	12.9	14.8
21 019	26580	2	Boyd	414	48 832	1 003	118.0	94.7	3.6	0.7	0.8	1.6	5.6	15.5	7.4	12.1	13.0	14.4
21 021	19220	7	Boyle	467	29 706	1 436	63.6	88.4	8.6	0.7	1.1	3.0	5.2	15.5	11.5	10.7	12.5	13.8
21 023	17140	1	Bracken	533	8 406	2 567	15.8	97.6	1.0	0.7	0.3	1.6	6.0	18.2	8.1	11.1	12.6	15.5
21 025	...	7	Breathitt	1 275	13 409	2 216	10.5	98.0	0.6	0.4	0.8	0.7	5.5	15.8	8.8	11.6	13.3	15.3
21 027	...	8	Breckinridge	1 469	19 888	1 842	13.5	95.9	2.8	0.9	0.4	1.3	5.9	17.8	7.6	10.5	11.6	14.9
21 029	31140	1	Bullitt	769	77 955	709	101.4	96.4	1.4	0.9	0.9	1.7	5.4	18.2	8.5	12.2	14.0	15.6
21 031	14540	8	Butler	1 104	12 875	2 241	11.7	95.7	0.9	0.6	0.4	3.3	6.0	17.1	7.0	12.5	12.4	13.8
21 033	...	6	Caldwell	893	12 725	2 249	14.2	92.6	6.1	0.6	0.5	1.4	6.0	16.3	7.8	10.2	12.8	13.7
21 035	34660	7	Calloway	997	38 282	1 215	38.4	91.4	4.6	0.7	2.3	2.5	5.0	13.1	20.6	12.0	10.2	11.6
21 037	17140	1	Campbell	392	91 833	632	234.3	94.4	3.7	0.5	1.1	1.8	6.2	16.1	10.3	14.2	12.2	14.3
21 039	...	9	Carlisle	491	4 978	2 838	10.1	96.0	1.8	1.1	0.3	2.0	6.0	16.4	7.6	10.5	12.1	13.6
21 041	...	6	Carroll	333	10 815	2 372	32.5	90.4	2.9	1.0	0.7	6.9	8.3	17.3	8.6	12.7	12.1	14.2
21 043	...	6	Carter	1 061	27 223	1 521	25.7	97.6	0.9	0.7	0.4	1.2	6.1	16.5	10.1	11.3	12.6	14.1
21 045	...	9	Casey	1 151	15 891	2 050	13.8	96.0	1.0	0.6	0.4	2.9	6.2	16.8	7.7	11.4	12.6	13.5
21 047	17300	3	Christian	1 858	74 250	736	40.0	69.6	22.4	1.1	2.5	7.2	9.4	18.4	15.1	16.9	10.7	9.7
21 049	30460	2	Clark	654	35 758	1 280	54.7	91.6	5.6	0.6	0.7	2.8	5.8	17.0	7.9	11.3	13.8	14.7

1. CBSA = Core Based Statistical Area. See Appendix A for explanation. See Appendix B for list of metropolitan areas with component counties. 2. County type code from the Economic Research Service of USDA Rural-Urban Continuum Codes. See Appendix A for definition. 3. Dry land or land partially or temporarily covered by water. 4. May be of any race.

STATE County	Population, 2013 (cont.): Age (percent) (cont.): 55 to 64 years	65 to 74 years	75 years and over	Percent female	Population change and components of change, 2000–2014: Total persons: 2000	2010	Percent change: 2000–2010	2010–2014	Components of change, 2010–2014: Births	Deaths	Net migration	Households, 2009–2013: Number	Persons per household	Percent: Family households	Female family householder[1]	One person
	16	17	18	19	20	21	22	23	24	25	26	27	28	29	30	31
KANSAS—Cont'd																
Neosho	13.5	9.4	8.8	50.5	16 997	16 512	-2.9	-0.6	939	808	-225	6 508	2.45	68.0	9.8	27.3
Ness	15.4	10.5	13.3	50.0	3 454	3 107	-10.0	-0.1	158	178	17	1 340	2.26	67.1	8.3	31.7
Norton	12.7	9.5	9.9	44.5	5 953	5 671	-4.7	-2.0	226	240	-84	2 248	2.13	61.2	11.1	34.7
Osage	14.6	10.3	7.8	50.0	16 712	16 295	-2.5	-2.2	706	786	-277	6 558	2.45	70.7	9.5	26.8
Osborne	15.1	10.7	14.0	49.4	4 452	3 858	-13.3	-2.6	164	205	-63	1 727	2.16	62.4	6.7	35.7
Ottawa	14.7	9.3	8.7	48.0	6 163	6 091	-1.2	-0.4	265	258	-15	2 408	2.47	73.1	7.0	23.6
Pawnee	14.8	9.3	9.4	44.7	7 233	6 973	-3.6	-0.8	309	288	-85	2 545	2.36	62.9	8.1	32.4
Phillips	15.7	10.7	10.4	50.6	6 001	5 642	-6.0	-1.9	294	296	-101	2 388	2.29	66.5	8.1	32.4
Pottawatomie	11.9	7.0	5.9	50.0	18 209	21 604	18.6	6.0	1 571	647	383	7 974	2.72	70.6	7.6	24.7
Pratt	14.3	8.3	9.9	50.1	9 647	9 656	0.1	2.0	608	450	33	4 074	2.29	64.5	10.6	32.8
Rawlins	17.4	12.2	14.4	49.9	2 966	2 519	-15.1	2.6	112	129	72	1 224	2.04	64.1	8.1	32.1
Reno	13.6	8.8	9.0	49.7	64 790	64 511	-0.4	-1.1	3 164	3 067	-779	25 693	2.39	66.2	11.5	29.9
Republic	16.3	11.6	15.7	51.0	5 835	4 980	-14.7	-3.6	203	361	-12	2 274	2.12	60.5	6.5	37.6
Rice	13.4	9.0	8.8	49.7	10 761	10 083	-6.3	-0.7	511	490	-91	3 914	2.44	68.7	7.1	27.6
Riley	7.2	4.0	3.6	46.7	62 843	71 115	13.2	5.7	4 872	1 396	467	25 895	2.47	53.2	7.7	29.1
Rooks	14.8	9.7	10.7	51.2	5 685	5 181	-8.9	-0.5	260	266	-8	2 349	2.15	62.7	8.9	33.8
Rush	17.3	10.9	13.4	49.9	3 551	3 307	-6.9	-3.3	121	191	-47	1 529	2.07	60.7	6.0	33.2
Russell	14.9	11.1	11.7	50.5	7 370	6 970	-5.4	-0.2	360	389	41	3 317	2.06	61.9	10.7	31.7
Saline	12.9	8.2	7.2	50.4	53 597	55 606	3.7	0.3	3 260	2 103	-938	22 173	2.44	65.8	13.3	27.9
Scott	13.8	8.3	8.7	49.1	5 120	4 936	-3.6	2.9	268	251	116	2 121	2.28	68.5	4.1	28.3
Sedgwick	12.1	6.8	5.6	50.4	452 869	498 365	10.0	2.1	33 443	17 428	-5 511	192 651	2.57	64.8	12.6	29.9
Seward	8.8	4.8	4.0	48.4	22 510	22 952	2.0	2.2	1 949	548	-895	7 429	3.05	73.5	12.6	19.6
Shawnee	13.6	8.4	7.1	51.5	169 871	177 934	4.7	0.3	10 267	7 201	-2 520	72 584	2.40	63.3	12.0	30.6
Sheridan	15.6	9.6	12.8	49.3	2 813	2 556	-9.1	-0.7	111	121	-9	1 099	2.29	62.7	9.6	34.4
Sherman	13.6	9.1	9.4	49.6	6 760	6 010	-11.1	1.7	338	297	67	2 727	2.17	59.9	9.9	36.2
Smith	16.4	11.8	15.0	50.4	4 536	3 853	-15.1	-2.2	147	222	1	1 726	2.15	68.5	8.9	29.5
Stafford	14.4	9.5	10.7	49.7	4 789	4 437	-7.4	-3.2	177	224	-69	1 884	2.28	65.0	6.2	32.0
Stanton	12.1	7.1	8.8	48.5	2 406	2 235	-7.1	-5.5	126	71	-172	775	2.79	73.5	9.7	21.4
Stevens	11.2	6.4	6.8	50.0	5 463	5 724	4.8	1.3	373	156	-122	1 936	2.91	74.7	6.0	22.8
Sumner	14.6	8.7	8.0	50.0	25 946	24 132	-7.0	-2.5	1 202	1 114	-730	9 110	2.58	67.1	8.1	29.8
Thomas	12.9	7.3	8.0	50.8	8 180	7 900	-3.4	-0.1	484	292	-208	3 120	2.42	54.1	5.5	41.3
Trego	17.1	11.2	12.8	50.8	3 319	3 001	-9.6	-3.3	106	193	-31	1 232	2.35	66.0	4.0	31.5
Wabaunsee	15.6	9.3	7.5	49.1	6 885	7 053	2.4	-0.4	419	251	-168	2 693	2.58	74.2	6.5	24.0
Wallace	14.6	8.5	11.9	50.5	1 749	1 485	-15.1	1.4	75	70	12	611	2.54	70.0	2.6	29.0
Washington	13.7	11.3	12.4	49.5	6 483	5 799	-10.6	-3.5	266	302	-154	2 487	2.26	65.1	4.3	32.3
Wichita	14.6	8.9	9.3	48.2	2 531	2 234	-11.7	-2.6	122	94	-83	877	2.52	70.8	12.5	28.3
Wilson	14.7	10.8	9.0	50.9	10 332	9 409	-8.9	-4.0	506	531	-329	3 791	2.40	68.2	8.3	28.3
Woodson	16.5	10.8	11.4	50.0	3 788	3 309	-12.6	-4.6	125	202	-66	1 517	2.12	61.0	9.3	34.3
Wyandotte	11.2	6.3	4.8	50.6	157 882	157 505	-0.2	2.6	11 762	5 775	-1 756	57 291	2.74	64.5	19.3	29.7
KENTUCKY	13.0	8.4	6.0	50.8	4 041 769	4 339 367	7.4	1.7	235 345	181 384	21 472	1 694 996	2.50	67.1	12.9	27.9
Adair	13.3	9.5	6.8	50.7	17 244	18 656	8.2	2.9	876	815	497	7 241	2.44	68.3	9.6	29.6
Allen	13.1	9.5	6.2	50.7	17 800	19 956	12.1	2.1	1 055	886	297	8 061	2.46	69.8	11.1	26.8
Anderson	12.9	8.4	5.4	51.0	19 111	21 421	12.1	2.2	1 015	787	254	8 323	2.58	72.5	12.2	22.7
Ballard	14.5	10.6	8.0	50.4	8 286	8 249	-0.4	-0.1	363	427	41	3 327	2.46	68.1	6.9	28.8
Barren	13.1	9.4	7.2	51.4	38 033	42 173	10.9	2.3	2 326	1 973	585	16 584	2.51	70.7	12.4	27.0
Bath	13.7	9.4	6.4	50.8	11 085	11 591	4.6	5.3	702	580	480	4 447	2.61	69.1	11.6	26.0
Bell	13.9	10.1	6.8	51.4	30 060	28 691	-4.6	-3.2	1 553	1 575	-873	11 109	2.46	68.0	15.9	28.8
Boone	11.7	6.7	4.0	50.5	85 991	118 811	38.2	6.4	7 282	3 201	3 559	43 255	2.78	74.3	10.8	21.5
Bourbon	13.4	9.8	7.0	51.3	19 360	19 985	3.2	-0.1	943	896	-54	7 865	2.51	68.7	15.0	27.0
Boyd	14.4	9.7	7.9	50.3	49 752	49 542	-0.4	-1.4	2 519	2 435	-703	19 530	2.41	67.8	11.4	28.4
Boyle	13.3	9.7	7.8	50.7	27 697	28 432	2.7	4.5	1 254	1 266	1 260	11 100	2.38	67.3	15.1	28.7
Bracken	13.6	8.7	6.2	49.8	8 279	8 488	2.5	-1.0	452	377	-157	3 252	2.59	66.5	11.7	29.8
Breathitt	14.6	9.3	5.6	50.1	16 100	13 878	-13.8	-3.4	697	788	-381	5 290	2.52	64.9	16.1	32.0
Breckinridge	14.8	10.2	6.7	49.8	18 648	20 059	7.6	-0.8	886	933	-83	7 213	2.74	71.8	9.8	24.4
Bullitt	13.1	8.4	4.6	50.5	61 236	74 319	21.4	4.9	3 166	2 167	2 509	27 874	2.69	75.3	12.4	20.5
Butler	13.8	10.3	7.1	50.3	13 010	12 690	-2.5	1.5	577	553	136	5 124	2.45	71.9	10.6	25.1
Caldwell	14.5	10.9	7.9	51.6	13 060	12 984	-0.6	-2.0	590	688	-116	5 232	2.44	67.2	15.2	30.1
Calloway	11.6	9.3	6.6	52.0	34 177	37 191	8.8	2.9	1 664	1 661	1 106	14 937	2.28	58.7	7.2	32.2
Campbell	13.1	7.5	6.0	50.8	88 616	90 336	1.9	1.7	4 956	3 544	192	35 203	2.49	64.4	12.4	30.1
Carlisle	13.8	10.5	9.5	51.3	5 351	5 104	-4.6	-2.5	251	270	-107	2 034	2.46	75.4	12.1	22.5
Carroll	12.6	8.2	6.0	49.7	10 155	10 811	6.5	0.0	694	515	-187	4 269	2.46	67.1	12.0	27.6
Carter	13.5	9.5	6.4	50.6	26 889	27 720	3.1	-1.8	1 471	1 296	-758	10 319	2.59	69.3	9.8	25.9
Casey	13.6	11.1	7.1	51.3	15 447	15 955	3.3	-0.4	844	813	-100	6 050	2.59	69.7	9.0	27.4
Christian	9.0	6.0	4.8	47.7	72 265	73 955	2.3	0.4	6 566	2 496	-3 883	25 899	2.65	71.0	14.6	25.7
Clark	13.6	9.3	6.6	51.3	33 144	35 613	7.4	0.4	1 792	1 591	-40	14 498	2.43	70.8	12.7	24.0

1. No spouse present.

STATE County	Persons in group quarters, 2014	Daytime population, 2009–2013		Births, 2014		Deaths, 2014		Persons under 65 with no health insurance, 2013		Medicare, 2014			Serious crimes known to police,[2] 2013	
		Number	Employment/residence ratio	Total	Rate[1]	Number	Rate[1]	Number	Percent	Eligible for Medicare	Enrolled in Medicare Advantage	Enrolled in a Medicare prescription drug plan	Total Number	Total Rate[3]
	32	33	34	35	36	37	38	39	40	41	42	43	44	45
KANSAS—Cont'd														
Neosho	450	16 180	0.96	224	13.6	163	9.9	1 992	15.2	3 476	145	2 376	485	2 963
Ness	70	3 343	1.16	44	14.2	45	14.5	371	16.0	745	18	548	27	884
Norton	822	5 778	1.05	61	11.0	59	10.6	536	14.2	1 141	47	730	66	1 180
Osage	194	12 287	0.46	155	9.7	202	12.7	1 632	12.4	3 499	148	2 130	220	1 435
Osborne	100	3 676	0.91	37	9.9	40	10.6	471	16.5	970	18	645	NA	NA
Ottawa	98	4 825	0.57	65	10.7	55	9.1	674	13.8	1 270	91	796	78	1 286
Pawnee	1 026	7 615	1.19	69	10.0	70	10.1	585	12.4	1 366	20	996	173	2 504
Phillips	68	5 668	1.03	85	15.4	67	12.1	670	15.4	1 382	33	910	22	401
Pottawatomie	299	20 832	0.89	366	16.0	171	7.5	2 181	11.1	3 423	263	1 944	388	1 783
Pratt	380	9 970	1.05	144	14.6	89	9.0	1 103	14.1	1 920	17	1 414	428	4 387
Rawlins	40	2 538	0.99	33	12.8	22	8.5	316	16.7	715	20	461	41	1 590
Reno	3 124	64 014	0.99	734	11.5	689	10.8	6 661	13.3	13 225	833	8 753	2 960	4 599
Republic	103	4 794	0.95	49	10.2	72	15.0	534	15.3	1 379	37	976	128	2 652
Rice	648	9 686	0.92	118	11.8	103	10.3	1 226	16.0	1 982	59	1 401	123	1 237
Riley	9 148	72 756	0.99	1 155	15.4	328	4.4	7 240	11.8	6 786	428	3 704	1 552	2 019
Rooks	72	5 013	0.93	62	12.0	68	13.2	644	15.7	1 206	27	790	44	840
Rush	66	3 004	0.85	30	9.4	30	9.4	358	14.9	861	24	601	NA	NA
Russell	89	6 559	0.89	86	12.4	90	12.9	876	16.5	1 751	24	1 191	158	2 279
Saline	1 466	57 743	1.08	757	13.6	460	8.3	6 522	14.1	10 442	1 083	6 545	2 300	4 104
Scott	105	4 781	0.94	69	13.6	57	11.2	722	17.5	972	20	722	94	1 907
Sedgwick	7 296	519 002	1.08	7 815	15.4	4 200	8.3	67 736	15.5	77 812	13 888	41 443	26 175	5 181
Seward	476	24 496	1.13	455	19.4	116	4.9	4 994	23.9	2 328	24	1 494	628	2 647
Shawnee	4 399	191 051	1.15	2 366	13.3	1 721	9.6	20 515	13.9	35 485	3 121	21 511	8 135	4 578
Sheridan	33	2 489	0.95	26	10.2	20	7.9	292	14.8	569	NA	370	7	276
Sherman	102	5 921	0.95	84	13.7	82	13.4	840	17.1	1 276	17	931	30	488
Smith	56	3 755	0.98	39	10.3	46	12.2	428	15.9	1 095	31	701	30	803
Stafford	69	4 006	0.82	38	8.8	45	10.5	710	20.5	924	14	617	84	1 937
Stanton	47	2 250	1.04	27	12.8	13	6.2	462	25.5	356	NA	260	6	279
Stevens	72	5 176	0.80	90	15.5	30	5.2	1 001	19.9	782	12	474	23	399
Sumner	409	20 521	0.68	282	12.0	250	10.6	2 692	13.8	4 648	515	2 792	710	3 242
Thomas	353	8 152	1.06	120	15.2	64	8.1	825	12.8	1 340	40	924	169	2 129
Trego	64	2 811	0.89	22	7.6	46	15.9	298	13.3	760	NA	490	27	905
Wabaunsee	90	5 195	0.46	111	15.8	44	6.3	690	11.9	1 420	49	863	99	1 407
Wallace	19	1 477	0.88	19	12.6	14	9.3	207	16.6	329	11	231	0	0
Washington	114	5 201	0.81	63	11.3	84	15.0	754	17.6	1 509	49	1 028	25	435
Wichita	26	2 392	1.15	29	13.3	18	8.3	351	19.7	411	NA	302	21	929
Wilson	121	8 969	0.93	121	13.4	119	13.2	1 165	16.1	2 215	69	1 521	207	2 299
Woodson	39	2 867	0.71	26	8.2	46	14.6	468	18.8	760	42	496	60	1 835
Wyandotte	1 335	173 832	1.23	2 772	17.1	1 376	8.5	30 345	21.5	23 175	6 755	10 009	8 745	5 482
KENTUCKY	130 347	4 382 615	1.01	55 221	12.5	42 647	9.7	613 811	16.8	852 053	211 697	454 055	113 079	2 573
Adair	1 408	16 682	0.71	225	11.7	208	10.8	3 102	21.1	4 040	775	2 440	116	620
Allen	197	17 472	0.66	244	12.0	234	11.5	3 527	20.8	4 162	802	2 490	214	1 055
Anderson	108	16 266	0.48	233	10.6	177	8.1	2 809	15.0	4 015	1 443	1 639	191	875
Ballard	127	7 960	0.90	81	9.8	99	12.0	1 139	17.1	1 890	298	1 031	131	1 566
Barren	702	42 886	1.02	564	13.1	492	11.4	6 191	17.4	9 216	1 982	5 509	565	1 319
Bath	103	10 043	0.57	182	14.9	146	12.0	2 018	20.1	2 668	752	1 436	22	185
Bell	952	29 279	1.10	371	13.4	352	12.7	4 178	18.6	6 881	1 267	4 404	804	2 868
Boone	835	137 571	1.28	1 761	13.9	834	6.6	13 029	11.9	17 532	6 419	7 126	3 128	2 507
Bourbon	236	19 224	0.91	213	10.7	213	10.7	3 498	21.4	4 269	1 327	1 998	415	2 076
Boyd	2 316	58 077	1.49	587	12.0	572	11.7	6 130	16.0	11 678	2 460	5 971	1 276	2 602
Boyle	3 192	32 222	1.30	294	9.9	286	9.6	3 704	17.1	6 435	1 451	3 539	725	2 522
Bracken	41	6 650	0.47	110	13.1	106	12.6	1 330	18.7	1 681	463	883	92	1 172
Breathitt	322	13 221	0.86	164	12.2	187	13.9	2 046	18.0	3 424	710	2 232	NA	NA
Breckinridge	300	17 508	0.63	203	10.2	196	9.9	3 326	20.3	4 452	662	2 583	65	324
Bullitt	340	59 873	0.56	749	9.6	561	7.2	9 083	13.7	13 543	3 878	7 271	1 250	1 636
Butler	203	10 945	0.62	130	10.1	111	8.6	2 142	20.6	2 807	757	1 487	115	892
Caldwell	148	12 167	0.84	133	10.5	154	12.1	1 839	17.8	3 234	611	1 810	177	1 369
Calloway	3 310	38 126	1.04	400	10.4	389	10.2	5 494	19.1	7 251	1 786	4 140	925	2 446
Campbell	3 204	75 918	0.67	1 149	12.5	856	9.3	10 265	13.5	15 073	5 480	6 272	2 737	3 004
Carlisle	60	4 057	0.51	59	11.9	59	11.9	792	20.0	1 214	238	677	19	379
Carroll	325	13 690	1.66	153	14.1	122	11.3	1 724	18.8	2 206	453	1 231	117	1 069
Carter	653	24 454	0.70	348	12.8	320	11.8	4 193	18.8	6 373	1 470	3 549	183	672
Casey	480	14 149	0.69	203	12.8	198	12.5	2 959	23.2	3 680	620	2 323	98	607
Christian	5 384	96 215	1.74	1 533	20.6	595	8.0	10 716	17.6	10 464	2 041	5 484	2 025	2 694
Clark	458	33 192	0.84	426	11.9	346	9.7	4 482	15.2	7 489	2 086	3 593	1 268	3 535

1. Per 1,000 estimated resident population. 2. Data for serious crimes have not been adjusted for underreporting; this may affect comparability between geographic areas and over time.
3. Per 100,000 population estimated by the FBI.

STATE County	Serious crimes known to police, 2013 (cont.)[1] Rate[2] Violent	Serious crimes known to police, 2013 (cont.)[1] Rate[2] Property	Education: School enrollment and attainment, 2009–2013, Enrollment[3] Total	Education: Enrollment[3] Percent private	Education: Attainment[4] (percent) High school graduate or less	Education: Attainment[4] (percent) Bachelor's degree or more	Education: Local government expenditures,[5] 2012–2013 Total current spending (mil dol)	Education: Local government expenditures,[5] 2012–2013 Current spending per student (dollars)	Money income, 2009–2013: Per capita income[6] (dollars)	Money income, 2009–2013: Households Median income (dollars)	Money income, 2009–2013: Households Mean income (dollars)	Money income, 2009–2013: Households Percent with income of $200,000 or more	Income and poverty, 2013: Median household income (dollars)	Income and poverty, 2013: Percent below poverty level All persons	Income and poverty, 2013: Percent below poverty level Children under 18 years	Income and poverty, 2013: Percent below poverty level Children 5 to 17 years in families
	46	47	48	49	50	51	52	53	54	55	56	57	58	59	60	61
KANSAS—Cont'd																
Neosho	257	2 706	3 961	8.7	44.2	16.2	25.3	10 423	21 163	42 071	51 886	1.1	41 877	18.7	29.8	26.7
Ness	229	655	582	7.9	47.3	19.0	5.6	11 341	30 223	48 800	68 861	3.7	49 432	10.8	14.7	13.3
Norton	125	1 055	1 136	5.2	47.0	15.4	10.7	11 283	22 942	46 029	54 645	1.2	42 389	14.2	16.9	15.7
Osage	157	1 278	3 783	8.5	49.3	20.6	30.4	10 790	24 789	50 205	60 760	1.9	48 991	12.7	16.6	14.1
Osborne	NA	NA	855	15.1	48.6	18.0	6.4	13 374	26 313	37 925	56 754	3.6	38 493	15.2	23.1	21.3
Ottawa	99	1 188	1 457	9.5	40.2	21.0	13.6	10 897	26 614	58 396	67 411	2.4	52 041	9.3	12.9	11.1
Pawnee	232	2 272	1 550	4.3	41.0	22.9	12.0	10 415	23 230	44 078	58 916	2.3	45 331	14.5	18.6	16.2
Phillips	109	292	1 308	5.0	44.4	18.3	9.5	11 626	23 772	43 059	53 542	1.4	44 080	12.3	18.3	16.1
Pottawatomie	188	1 594	5 868	17.0	37.7	29.3	38.8	9 559	24 892	56 854	67 726	2.6	59 856	9.4	12.2	11.3
Pratt	420	3 967	2 207	10.9	40.9	23.4	15.9	9 358	26 209	46 035	61 679	2.3	50 970	12.4	16.3	14.9
Rawlins	155	1 435	427	5.9	38.7	23.3	3.9	12 192	26 897	43 482	57 170	1.3	45 901	12.2	16.6	15.2
Reno	485	4 114	15 616	13.2	40.5	19.8	97.7	9 589	23 382	43 798	57 119	1.7	44 099	14.9	20.2	17.9
Republic	145	2 507	965	9.1	42.8	19.8	8.1	11 230	25 531	39 572	54 197	1.9	39 819	12.8	20.5	20.0
Rice	211	1 026	2 625	19.1	44.3	20.9	21.0	11 369	23 068	45 336	57 381	0.8	45 389	13.5	18.4	16.3
Riley	200	1 819	30 207	6.5	22.7	45.0	73.8	10 053	22 948	43 962	59 788	2.6	46 267	21.8	17.4	17.4
Rooks	95	745	1 046	6.9	45.1	20.9	10.8	13 095	23 768	42 449	53 258	2.3	40 870	13.8	18.6	17.2
Rush	NA	NA	539	6.5	44.9	19.4	6.1	12 399	24 175	42 610	51 321	0.5	42 867	12.5	19.0	16.5
Russell	418	1 861	1 381	6.0	44.3	21.8	8.6	10 591	24 683	37 111	51 654	1.3	39 520	17.1	23.9	20.5
Saline	319	3 784	14 105	11.2	44.2	23.9	89.0	10 424	24 935	47 215	61 465	2.2	48 505	14.4	19.8	17.5
Scott	426	1 481	1 018	11.9	45.8	23.4	10.0	10 396	26 274	50 605	61 489	1.4	51 013	8.6	12.8	12.0
Sedgwick	643	4 538	141 778	16.6	38.4	28.7	816.9	9 782	25 603	49 865	64 938	2.9	48 671	16.0	22.1	19.3
Seward	316	2 331	6 673	5.0	61.6	12.6	55.0	9 675	19 015	50 185	58 388	1.3	45 349	18.2	25.3	25.7
Shawnee	401	4 177	46 862	15.8	41.1	28.6	283.1	9 992	26 057	48 451	63 303	2.4	50 042	16.8	22.2	19.9
Sheridan	79	197	561	2.3	39.9	22.4	6.4	10 410	26 841	48 674	59 746	3.0	50 961	11.2	16.5	14.6
Sherman	16	472	1 249	1.8	44.4	15.7	10.0	9 340	21 476	38 634	47 558	1.2	38 025	15.4	24.1	22.1
Smith	0	803	693	5.2	46.0	16.7	8.2	12 455	26 811	45 556	58 686	3.3	39 696	12.7	17.7	16.0
Stafford	415	1 522	978	5.9	43.1	19.1	11.5	13 228	23 240	43 292	54 046	1.7	42 430	14.5	20.2	17.2
Stanton	0	279	572	11.4	48.7	18.5	5.5	11 724	21 712	46 382	61 701	0.8	49 977	12.5	19.3	17.9
Stevens	69	330	1 593	5.8	52.8	17.6	14.4	10 748	24 950	54 494	69 248	3.5	57 483	10.9	15.6	13.5
Sumner	306	2 936	5 967	10.9	46.8	17.8	41.5	10 368	22 972	47 894	58 342	1.6	50 844	13.4	18.2	15.8
Thomas	302	1 827	2 278	9.9	34.0	27.9	10.4	9 519	26 903	48 187	64 724	5.3	47 654	11.1	13.1	11.5
Trego	0	905	731	14.5	44.3	21.5	4.4	11 171	23 095	45 714	55 188	0.6	43 668	10.3	13.1	12.7
Wabaunsee	185	1 222	1 681	15.1	46.4	20.6	11.5	11 838	24 199	54 694	61 045	0.8	54 414	9.4	13.2	11.7
Wallace	0	0	361	11.1	43.4	23.5	4.1	13 468	25 429	47 454	64 558	2.6	46 082	12.4	16.7	14.5
Washington	70	366	1 210	12.9	48.3	16.1	9.8	11 310	22 621	42 515	51 577	0.8	43 897	10.5	15.0	13.4
Wichita	177	752	556	2.0	49.5	16.6	5.2	12 248	23 799	53 018	61 019	1.7	51 286	11.2	17.6	16.0
Wilson	211	2 088	2 000	4.3	54.1	13.0	18.4	10 852	19 929	38 917	47 883	1.0	41 073	18.4	28.4	23.9
Woodson	92	1 744	635	7.4	50.0	18.2	5.8	12 085	21 774	33 839	47 555	1.7	40 971	17.4	30.2	25.9
Wyandotte	508	4 974	43 557	10.4	54.9	15.5	288.5	9 786	18 957	39 402	49 863	0.8	38 728	25.6	38.3	36.4
KENTUCKY	210	2 363	1 098 640	14.8	50.9	21.5	6 444.5	9 316	23 462	43 036	58 621	2.4	43 307	18.8	25.5	23.7
Adair	43	577	4 641	25.7	62.9	13.9	24.2	9 018	17 371	32 524	43 636	0.9	31 710	25.0	39.0	35.4
Allen	35	1 020	4 691	9.2	60.3	12.7	25.5	8 431	19 086	40 008	47 817	0.8	39 798	20.6	31.4	29.2
Anderson	82	792	5 634	11.5	50.3	20.4	31.7	8 092	24 161	52 646	60 700	1.4	52 852	11.4	18.5	16.8
Ballard	48	1 518	1 927	7.2	55.9	13.1	12.7	8 752	24 781	44 588	60 317	2.6	42 712	17.1	26.2	23.4
Barren	114	1 205	10 014	6.0	61.9	14.7	73.9	9 406	19 745	38 873	49 366	1.3	38 370	20.7	29.3	25.8
Bath	8	177	2 661	9.4	65.7	12.0	18.4	8 596	16 367	30 797	41 455	0.9	33 752	26.5	38.9	34.9
Bell	150	2 718	6 276	13.1	67.6	10.8	48.3	9 606	15 091	26 228	36 781	0.6	25 761	35.7	47.3	43.4
Boone	116	2 391	34 245	18.4	37.7	30.4	181.4	8 484	29 235	67 225	80 339	4.1	65 274	8.7	11.7	10.7
Bourbon	95	1 980	4 563	13.5	57.0	15.8	33.7	9 033	22 893	40 933	56 316	2.0	40 045	16.5	25.8	24.6
Boyd	114	2 488	10 662	9.6	49.1	16.3	70.1	9 289	24 530	40 379	60 903	2.8	41 443	20.3	26.6	25.6
Boyle	146	2 376	7 473	21.1	50.6	22.8	43.0	9 353	22 249	41 473	55 352	2.2	43 585	17.2	25.0	22.6
Bracken	25	1 146	1 975	5.6	61.5	14.2	13.0	8 356	20 918	39 196	52 716	1.5	43 222	16.2	24.7	22.6
Breathitt	NA	NA	3 131	5.8	68.4	9.8	27.3	10 403	14 706	24 045	35 677	0.5	26 869	33.9	43.6	42.1
Breckinridge	20	304	4 472	12.3	67.6	9.4	29.8	9 225	18 101	38 907	47 409	0.9	40 107	19.2	27.9	26.1
Bullitt	102	1 533	19 167	16.7	56.1	12.7	101.5	7 755	24 308	54 836	63 927	1.3	57 462	10.2	15.4	14.2
Butler	23	869	2 774	16.5	68.0	8.2	17.7	8 156	18 136	35 430	43 922	0.4	36 670	22.1	33.5	31.8
Caldwell	108	1 261	2 779	2.8	57.4	16.8	16.9	8 001	20 327	37 127	48 947	1.3	37 317	19.0	28.7	27.5
Calloway	164	2 282	12 566	5.5	45.9	27.7	44.3	8 988	21 490	39 677	52 122	1.8	37 977	22.8	24.5	23.0
Campbell	175	2 830	24 864	20.5	43.4	28.5	112.5	9 511	26 945	54 306	67 244	2.6	53 321	14.8	21.1	20.7
Carlisle	40	339	1 052	13.1	55.0	15.5	8.1	9 423	21 500	39 049	52 697	0.5	38 283	17.5	28.3	25.5
Carroll	64	1 005	2 363	5.2	68.1	9.5	21.7	10 794	19 429	40 160	51 038	0.8	41 792	21.0	31.6	32.3
Carter	18	653	6 691	13.3	64.6	10.4	42.0	8 701	19 201	36 406	48 215	1.2	34 767	22.5	31.4	30.2
Casey	19	589	3 508	7.7	68.1	8.4	22.2	9 542	15 603	29 934	39 613	0.4	29 303	29.7	42.8	40.9
Christian	204	2 491	20 104	12.9	49.3	15.1	85.4	9 086	19 773	38 904	51 691	1.6	41 333	18.1	26.3	26.2
Clark	176	3 359	7 912	14.3	52.0	19.4	48.5	8 411	24 524	45 853	60 235	1.8	45 516	17.1	25.7	23.6

1. Data for serious crimes have not been adjusted for underreporting; this may affect comparability between geographic areas and over time. 2. Per 100,000 population estimated by the FBI.
3. All persons 3 years old and over enrolled in nursery school through college. 4. Persons 25 years old and over. 5. Elementary and secondary education expenditures.
6. Based on population estimated by the American Community Survey, 2009–2013.

STATE County	Personal income, 2013										Earnings, 2013		
	Total (mil dol)	Percent change, 2012–2013	Per capita[1]		Wages and salaries (mil dol)	Supplements to wages and salaries; employer contributions (mil dol)		Proprietors' income (mil dol)	Dividends, interest, and rent (mil dol)	Personal transfer receipts (mil dol)	Total (mil dol)	Contributions for government social insurance (mil dol)	
			Dollars	Rank		Pension and insurance	Government social insurance					From employee and self-employed	From employer
	62	63	64	65	66	67	68	69	70	71	72	73	74
KANSAS—Cont'd													
Neosho	582	-0.8	35 429	1 832	233	45	19	77	103	150	374	22	19
Ness	209	6.7	67 907	57	54	10	4	58	57	27	126	6	4
Norton	236	7.5	42 007	937	95	19	7	56	43	39	177	8	7
Osage	577	4.4	35 744	1 791	85	20	7	36	96	132	148	11	7
Osborne	184	8.5	48 101	473	43	9	3	63	38	35	118	5	3
Ottawa	223	7.6	36 965	1 593	44	9	3	45	36	43	101	5	3
Pawnee	321	10.7	46 063	616	117	26	8	67	67	56	219	10	8
Phillips	281	2.4	50 658	343	84	21	6	70	71	48	181	10	6
Pottawatomie	886	1.6	39 027	1 295	360	65	28	101	179	129	554	32	28
Pratt	458	2.0	46 402	598	182	31	14	98	97	72	325	17	14
Rawlins	161	10.6	62 238	81	34	7	3	65	33	25	108	5	3
Reno	2 343	1.6	36 503	1 662	1 003	177	78	186	508	517	1 443	91	78
Republic	210	11.7	43 535	798	61	13	5	56	39	44	135	6	5
Rice	392	5.6	39 188	1 265	135	26	10	61	82	77	232	13	10
Riley	3 287	-1.6	43 603	790	1 122	243	85	84	737	305	1 533	86	85
Rooks	197	9.5	37 897	1 446	71	14	5	20	46	43	110	7	5
Rush	133	-2.9	41 689	975	40	9	3	20	31	31	72	4	3
Russell	268	-0.1	38 619	1 350	105	23	8	12	80	65	147	10	8
Saline	2 401	3.0	43 078	834	1 130	200	89	387	516	406	1 805	106	89
Scott	237	10.8	47 152	543	76	12	6	55	58	36	149	6	6
Sedgwick	21 127	1.7	41 801	958	11 851	1 940	935	2 557	3 744	3 359	17 283	1 015	935
Seward	806	6.1	34 459	1 997	464	85	35	140	98	113	724	39	35
Shawnee	7 439	1.2	41 598	985	4 424	747	344	381	1 422	1 525	5 897	364	344
Sheridan	159	6.4	62 215	82	39	7	3	61	36	19	109	4	3
Sherman	279	0.8	45 688	643	87	17	7	74	52	54	185	8	7
Smith	181	11.6	48 735	435	42	9	3	52	39	36	106	5	3
Stafford	209	15.3	47 961	485	42	9	3	63	50	34	118	4	3
Stanton	130	17.6	59 387	115	33	6	2	48	33	13	90	3	2
Stevens	268	13.3	46 058	617	111	18	9	74	49	30	212	9	9
Sumner	1 020	3.7	43 236	823	263	48	22	162	143	174	495	26	22
Thomas	356	8.4	44 831	705	141	25	11	74	79	52	250	12	11
Trego	134	7.5	44 876	698	45	10	3	21	29	29	79	4	3
Wabaunsee	307	3.1	43 544	796	41	9	3	16	84	50	69	5	3
Wallace	89	25.0	56 943	159	18	3	1	39	16	14	62	2	1
Washington	240	13.0	42 668	871	59	13	4	48	52	50	125	6	4
Wichita	138	10.6	63 173	76	35	6	2	53	29	18	96	3	2
Wilson	349	0.5	38 286	1 403	124	27	10	44	69	91	206	12	10
Woodson	111	-2.0	34 419	2 006	21	5	2	24	23	31	51	3	2
Wyandotte	4 811	1.3	29 996	2 688	4 237	682	347	303	589	1 224	5 569	336	347
KENTUCKY	159 172	1.4	36 214	X	78 438	14 658	6 186	12 708	25 301	36 655	111 990	6 760	6 186
Adair	503	0.4	26 878	2 976	147	33	12	29	69	176	220	16	12
Allen	644	2.1	31 710	2 447	144	30	11	145	78	166	330	21	11
Anderson	734	0.9	33 658	2 151	160	36	13	25	98	150	233	17	13
Ballard	329	6.7	39 443	1 239	124	21	9	62	40	73	216	11	9
Barren	1 355	1.1	31 485	2 483	577	110	47	140	220	370	873	55	47
Bath	332	1.3	27 777	2 909	58	14	5	10	41	112	87	8	5
Bell	745	-0.7	26 708	2 991	284	65	22	28	98	334	399	29	22
Boone	4 766	1.9	38 297	1 400	3 497	528	275	315	579	693	4 615	274	275
Bourbon	656	0.2	32 824	2 278	273	46	21	31	117	156	372	23	21
Boyd	1 654	0.4	33 829	2 117	1 221	228	93	103	227	500	1 644	102	93
Boyle	936	1.3	32 266	2 369	539	98	46	57	194	243	740	47	46
Bracken	272	1.2	32 352	2 359	51	12	4	10	32	70	77	6	4
Breathitt	399	-0.3	29 428	2 761	115	28	9	11	41	182	163	13	9
Breckinridge	643	2.6	32 071	2 407	115	27	9	51	131	175	201	14	9
Bullitt	2 520	1.4	32 791	2 284	722	127	59	158	273	533	1 066	73	59
Butler	373	5.0	29 124	2 791	96	23	8	33	46	121	160	11	8
Caldwell	433	3.8	33 760	2 132	135	27	11	54	62	124	227	14	11
Calloway	1 195	1.6	31 744	2 441	530	136	38	109	208	282	813	46	38
Campbell	3 772	1.1	41 457	1 000	1 146	222	87	190	636	636	1 645	103	87
Carlisle	195	17.0	38 990	1 305	29	7	2	55	25	47	92	4	2
Carroll	378	1.6	34 475	1 993	333	52	27	25	45	94	436	27	27
Carter	719	0.3	26 423	3 012	183	40	15	35	85	271	273	22	15
Casey	443	2.3	27 549	2 932	112	26	9	34	60	163	181	14	9
Christian	2 578	0.4	34 762	1 940	3 179	900	315	223	633	511	4 616	191	315
Clark	1 319	1.1	37 028	1 579	508	95	41	217	198	300	860	54	41

1. Based on the resident population estimated as of July 1 of the year shown.

STATE County	Earnings, 2013 (cont.) — Percent by selected industries: Farm	Mining	Construction	Manu- facturing	Infor- mation: professional, scientific, technical services	Retail trade	Finance, insur- ance, real estate and leasing	Health care and social assistance	Govern- ment	Social Security beneficiaries, December 2013: Number	Rate[1]	Supple- mental Security Income recipients, December 2013	Housing units, 2014: Total	Percent change, 2010– 2014
	75	76	77	78	79	80	81	82	83	84	85	86	87	88
KANSAS—Cont'd														
Neosho	9.5	9.0	3.5	15.4	2.4	7.2	4.1	D	25.2	3 755	228	389	7 729	2.9
Ness	22.6	27.0	4.2	1.3	D	D	D	D	14.9	800	259	19	1 732	-0.5
Norton	23.3	4.4	3.5	6.6	4.0	4.9	D	9.0	23.0	1 280	227	59	2 530	-0.5
Osage	16.5	D	5.2	3.3	2.9	7.8	5.0	8.1	33.6	3 820	238	341	7 490	-0.2
Osborne	30.7	D	2.5	4.1	D	7.4	4.3	5.9	12.6	1 080	284	50	2 188	-0.8
Ottawa	36.1	D	3.5	8.9	D	3.0	D	9.1	18.3	1 375	226	80	2 774	-0.2
Pawnee	23.0	D	6.3	0.8	D	3.4	3.1	5.0	40.5	1 475	212	79	3 163	0.3
Phillips	13.8	7.7	4.3	17.5	2.0	3.5	D	5.8	16.9	1 460	262	60	3 051	0.1
Pottawatomie	3.2	0.1	10.9	23.0	5.3	9.2	4.8	D	10.6	3 740	165	216	9 042	4.8
Pratt	15.3	15.1	6.8	1.8	3.1	7.5	4.4	D	16.3	2 070	210	145	4 481	-0.7
Rawlins	24.9	0.2	5.7	3.7	D	4.6	D	4.1	12.9	740	284	34	1 456	-0.1
Reno	4.6	2.2	6.1	13.3	5.4	7.4	4.9	14.8	17.4	14 605	228	1 400	28 323	0.2
Republic	34.5	D	4.1	7.5	2.1	5.7	5.9	D	14.3	1 475	307	71	2 873	-0.1
Rice	18.8	8.8	4.0	10.2	3.2	4.1	D	D	19.1	2 195	219	139	4 548	0.0
Riley	1.0	D	5.7	1.9	5.6	6.8	5.5	10.7	43.6	7 030	93	514	29 713	5.3
Rooks	13.8	12.2	D	D	3.2	5.8	2.8	3.6	25.2	1 340	259	71	2 760	-0.3
Rush	26.3	D	2.3	20.5	4.8	2.5	3.1	3.1	19.9	920	289	63	1 861	-0.4
Russell	4.6	19.9	3.6	17.8	D	4.6	4.2	D	17.6	1 875	271	124	3 887	-0.6
Saline	2.5	D	5.3	16.8	6.1	7.4	3.7	14.3	11.8	11 255	202	1 013	24 221	0.5
Scott	34.0	D	4.1	0.8	D	4.8	D	D	11.5	1 000	200	56	2 193	0.0
Sedgwick	0.4	3.8	5.4	25.4	6.1	5.9	4.5	11.3	12.5	85 285	169	10 878	214 408	1.3
Seward	3.6	10.7	D	D	D	6.5	2.9	D	16.4	2 570	110	347	8 101	0.5
Shawnee	0.3	0.5	5.7	7.1	7.7	5.1	10.8	15.5	23.3	37 235	209	4 897	79 466	0.4
Sheridan	41.9	D	D	D	D	3.4	D	D	12.0	590	233	18	1 261	-0.3
Sherman	32.0	D	4.0	4.1	3.2	7.2	D	D	19.8	1 385	227	131	3 123	-0.8
Smith	42.4	D	4.8	3.8	D	5.0	D	8.8	13.7	1 175	316	49	2 245	0.6
Stafford	52.4	D	D	D	D	1.5	2.6	D	19.8	1 025	236	51	2 307	-0.5
Stanton	54.5	0.5	1.0	0.3	D	2.1	3.8	D	15.8	360	166	17	980	-1.0
Stevens	29.2	3.9	23.2	3.5	D	3.3	2.2	D	16.3	870	150	38	2 287	-0.8
Sumner	27.0	1.3	1.7	14.7	3.0	5.0	3.8	D	16.6	5 000	212	420	10 834	-0.3
Thomas	25.7	D	4.9	1.8	3.1	9.9	4.3	D	14.9	1 460	182	88	3 546	0.3
Trego	24.9	D	2.2	2.5	D	4.1	D	D	26.1	815	275	32	1 676	-0.4
Wabaunsee	10.3	D	12.1	11.0	D	3.3	D	D	27.1	1 535	218	82	3 254	0.8
Wallace	61.6	0.0	D	D	D	1.9	D	D	10.1	360	230	15	778	-0.4
Washington	40.4	D	3.3	6.8	D	3.6	D	4.2	21.3	1 600	284	68	2 950	-0.2
Wichita	59.7	0.0	3.5	3.5	D	1.9	D	0.7	13.2	430	197	22	1 045	-0.9
Wilson	14.8	1.8	7.5	24.5	1.9	4.1	2.8	8.3	20.4	2 445	269	261	4 652	-0.6
Woodson	22.0	33.8	D	D	D	5.1	D	3.0	18.8	835	260	66	2 006	-0.8
Wyandotte	0.1	D	5.5	17.2	2.7	5.3	1.9	17.0	19.2	25 755	160	5 438	67 339	0.9
KENTUCKY	1.7	1.7	5.3	14.2	7.0	6.3	6.5	12.1	20.7	944 041	215	190 721	1 950 382	1.2
Adair	2.6	0.9	5.4	6.4	2.4	9.0	5.6	D	23.0	4 530	237	1 036	8 504	-0.7
Allen	4.9	0.0	D	14.4	D	31.0	2.8	D	12.8	4 750	234	897	9 320	0.1
Anderson	-1.8	D	D	28.0	2.9	8.8	4.6	D	21.0	4 555	209	439	9 254	1.4
Ballard	21.6	0.0	D	25.6	D	3.4	1.5	2.6	9.8	2 105	254	256	3 882	-0.1
Barren	4.2	0.2	5.7	21.6	D	8.8	3.0	16.1	14.4	10 555	245	1 869	19 430	1.3
Bath	1.4	0.0	D	9.0	D	6.6	4.2	9.8	31.8	3 045	254	934	5 384	-0.4
Bell	-0.1	11.5	2.1	11.5	D	10.2	4.7	16.5	23.8	7 765	278	3 056	13 097	-0.4
Boone	0.0	D	4.2	17.7	5.3	6.3	5.9	6.9	9.2	18 975	152	1 538	47 947	3.9
Bourbon	7.3	D	5.3	22.3	D	7.5	4.5	D	14.5	4 610	231	664	9 016	1.0
Boyd	-0.1	D	7.5	17.3	6.5	6.5	3.2	23.6	12.4	12 655	258	2 443	21 686	-0.5
Boyle	0.2	D	3.0	15.6	D	8.4	3.9	24.7	13.5	6 910	234	1 145	12 407	0.8
Bracken	-1.7	0.0	10.5	D	D	4.4	3.0	5.8	26.2	2 000	237	294	3 827	-0.3
Breathitt	-0.3	D	D	1.1	2.0	9.7	4.3	26.6	35.4	3 875	286	2 256	6 205	-0.4
Breckinridge	9.2	0.5	11.9	7.8	3.2	9.7	5.3	D	22.2	5 135	256	959	10 615	-0.1
Bullitt	0.1	D	11.5	15.4	4.3	5.4	3.3	4.7	14.4	15 410	201	1 697	30 461	3.9
Butler	12.3	D	6.5	27.1	1.3	4.1	3.4	D	19.3	3 250	253	603	5 861	-0.3
Caldwell	12.3	0.6	4.4	21.5	3.0	10.6	3.5	D	15.1	3 540	277	572	6 274	-0.3
Calloway	4.4	D	5.5	15.4	4.1	8.0	3.2	5.2	33.0	7 995	210	815	18 264	1.1
Campbell	-0.1	0.0	D	14.3	7.5	7.6	5.1	11.2	24.7	16 215	177	2 040	39 812	0.7
Carlisle	44.9	0.0	5.8	6.9	1.9	4.2	8.8	3.5	13.3	1 380	277	173	2 437	-0.2
Carroll	-0.3	0.0	D	46.2	7.8	4.9	1.3	D	8.9	2 540	233	516	4 685	-0.2
Carter	-0.2	1.6	8.0	12.3	3.9	12.1	4.5	D	24.4	7 070	259	1 727	12 281	-0.2
Casey	2.1	D	5.4	20.0	2.4	7.2	D	12.7	18.9	4 120	256	1 125	7 405	-1.1
Christian	2.2	0.0	1.0	0.4	3.1	2.2	1.3	3.7	71.7	11 975	161	2 519	29 746	1.0
Clark	0.7	D	8.9	19.2	7.0	7.1	4.5	9.9	10.5	8 220	231	1 090	15 713	0.2

1. Per 1,000 resident population estimated as of July 1 of the year shown.

STATE County	Housing units, 2009–2013: Occupied units: Total	Owner-occupied: Percent	Owner-occupied: Median value[1]	Median owner cost as a percent of income: With a mortgage	Median owner cost as a percent of income: Without a mortgage[2]	Renter-occupied: Median rent[3]	Renter-occupied: Median rent as a percent of income[2]	Substandard units[4] (percent)	Civilian labor force, 2014: Total	Percent change, 2013–2014	Unemployment: Total	Unemployment: Rate[5]	Civilian employment,[6] 2009–2013: Total	Percent: Management, business, science and arts	Percent: Construction, production, and maintenance occupations
	89	90	91	92	93	94	95	96	97	98	99	100	101	102	103
KANSAS—Cont'd															
Neosho	6 508	73.5	68 900	20.6	11.5	546	26.7	1.4	6 449	-3.9	467	7.2	7 511	29.8	29.8
Ness	1 340	82.5	57 200	16.1	10.0	574	21.4	3.6	1 621	1.2	44	2.7	1 539	33.0	26.8
Norton	2 248	74.6	66 000	17.0	12.8	515	19.4	2.4	3 103	0.5	74	2.4	2 820	29.1	30.5
Osage	6 558	78.2	99 000	21.0	12.8	671	26.1	1.3	8 304	0.2	453	5.5	7 512	32.4	27.8
Osborne	1 727	79.4	51 200	19.9	10.4	481	22.4	1.0	2 056	-3.2	79	3.8	1 940	37.2	26.6
Ottawa	2 408	81.0	93 400	20.3	11.8	681	22.8	0.0	3 267	0.8	135	4.1	3 019	34.3	31.8
Pawnee	2 545	72.3	73 700	23.2	10.1	463	23.5	1.3	3 440	0.7	130	3.8	3 339	36.7	23.2
Phillips	2 388	77.8	64 400	22.4	11.8	473	19.3	2.8	2 951	-0.5	103	3.5	2 849	34.3	27.1
Pottawatomie	7 974	78.0	153 700	20.5	12.0	700	23.1	0.5	11 999	0.6	470	3.9	10 725	33.2	27.4
Pratt	4 074	69.2	79 000	18.6	11.9	626	23.4	0.7	5 484	0.8	180	3.3	4 703	33.8	27.8
Rawlins	1 224	70.0	66 700	23.6	10.0	570	23.3	2.0	1 525	-1.6	38	2.5	1 328	40.2	20.8
Reno	25 693	68.2	90 600	21.2	12.2	652	26.8	1.2	31 488	-0.4	1 384	4.4	29 500	30.0	26.4
Republic	2 274	80.3	49 200	19.4	11.1	461	21.7	2.7	2 591	-2.3	79	3.0	2 395	36.1	28.1
Rice	3 914	73.1	74 200	18.3	11.0	554	24.9	9.4	5 455	0.2	194	3.6	4 673	31.3	33.8
Riley	25 895	42.5	170 400	21.4	11.1	861	32.4	1.6	36 908	0.9	1 359	3.7	33 177	42.0	16.3
Rooks	2 349	74.9	62 500	19.3	10.7	500	27.7	2.0	2 870	3.2	104	3.6	2 507	33.5	28.3
Rush	1 529	75.0	57 300	17.5	10.9	519	27.9	2.2	1 828	1.0	65	3.6	1 600	35.8	25.1
Russell	3 317	75.3	65 000	19.7	14.0	640	28.9	2.2	3 886	0.9	136	3.5	3 428	29.6	27.8
Saline	22 173	67.1	119 500	21.7	11.6	675	30.1	2.8	30 945	-0.6	1 298	4.2	28 228	29.0	30.4
Scott	2 121	73.3	104 800	24.8	10.0	771	22.9	2.6	2 858	0.6	78	2.7	2 400	40.0	31.0
Sedgwick	192 651	64.9	124 000	21.0	11.4	703	28.7	6.1	247 614	0.5	13 337	5.4	235 130	34.5	24.1
Seward	7 429	63.9	90 000	19.8	10.0	677	23.6	2.6	11 262	1.6	395	3.5	10 502	18.9	48.8
Shawnee	72 584	64.4	120 300	20.7	11.8	710	29.9	1.2	92 755	0.7	4 416	4.8	83 861	35.2	19.1
Sheridan	1 099	78.3	77 900	17.4	11.2	495	25.7	0.3	1 493	-0.3	39	2.6	1 272	37.7	27.0
Sherman	2 727	54.5	74 200	20.5	12.3	611	26.3	0.9	3 081	-1.6	99	3.2	2 900	31.3	25.5
Smith	1 726	79.7	60 800	21.9	11.1	373	25.1	2.8	2 119	-1.8	66	3.1	1 909	39.7	23.8
Stafford	1 884	81.5	60 900	17.9	12.9	530	20.9	3.6	2 207	-0.5	82	3.7	2 137	38.6	26.7
Stanton	775	77.7	81 000	23.2	10.0	531	21.6	2.6	1 039	-0.7	35	3.4	1 043	26.6	35.5
Stevens	1 936	75.2	86 200	18.3	10.4	681	38.7	2.6	3 544	6.9	102	2.9	2 759	30.4	33.5
Sumner	9 110	77.4	85 500	22.0	12.4	576	26.2	0.4	11 195	0.4	535	4.8	10 864	29.5	32.3
Thomas	3 120	68.5	97 200	18.8	10.0	432	24.6	2.4	4 487	0.4	128	2.9	4 403	34.0	25.3
Trego	1 232	74.8	74 500	17.9	10.9	593	22.6	2.0	1 505	0.9	47	3.1	1 553	27.0	29.0
Wabaunsee	2 693	84.3	112 200	21.3	12.9	717	25.6	1.0	3 801	0.8	157	4.1	3 442	35.2	28.1
Wallace	611	77.6	61 900	18.4	10.1	395	13.9	1.2	898	5.2	24	2.7	755	37.4	24.9
Washington	2 487	79.4	58 300	18.8	11.3	430	19.1	6.4	3 116	-0.4	101	3.2	3 011	30.5	35.4
Wichita	877	73.1	71 100	17.3	10.3	635	20.6	3.0	1 248	-3.2	35	2.8	1 127	34.6	33.5
Wilson	3 791	75.0	63 200	20.6	12.2	540	24.2	3.0	4 175	1.8	279	6.7	4 090	29.4	35.3
Woodson	1 517	81.0	50 900	19.3	14.3	491	27.3	4.5	1 636	0.5	86	5.3	1 488	24.9	36.7
Wyandotte	57 291	60.3	93 800	24.8	16.0	740	31.7	2.3	76 050	1.5	5 230	6.9	68 500	22.5	31.8
KENTUCKY	1 694 996	68.4	120 400	21.4	10.8	655	29.3	2.3	2 005 252	-2.5	130 106	6.5	1 857 767	32.6	26.4
Adair	7 241	74.7	78 600	21.6	11.3	454	26.8	3.3	7 206	-4.4	595	8.3	7 204	28.3	32.2
Allen	8 061	73.7	96 800	21.1	10.7	583	25.2	1.8	8 766	-2.4	521	5.9	8 005	24.0	37.2
Anderson	8 323	74.5	132 300	22.2	10.0	724	25.6	1.9	11 317	-2.1	603	5.3	10 249	31.2	28.9
Ballard	3 327	81.6	94 400	18.4	10.0	526	29.9	2.3	3 694	-3.4	293	7.9	3 467	27.9	35.0
Barren	16 584	68.2	105 400	20.1	12.2	579	32.8	4.6	18 827	-4.1	1 195	6.3	18 267	28.5	33.6
Bath	4 447	79.0	65 400	26.2	12.2	557	41.6	3.8	4 635	-4.1	419	9.0	3 992	27.2	37.2
Bell	11 109	67.7	67 300	24.4	10.7	481	30.6	2.5	9 298	-5.8	949	10.2	8 842	25.3	30.4
Boone	43 255	75.5	172 700	21.4	10.6	881	27.1	1.4	64 609	-2.2	3 366	5.2	59 917	38.4	20.6
Bourbon	7 865	59.8	139 900	21.7	10.0	642	29.1	1.1	9 720	-1.2	550	5.7	8 532	29.5	31.9
Boyd	19 530	68.8	96 900	19.2	10.5	608	31.7	0.8	18 876	-3.9	1 406	7.4	18 105	33.9	24.1
Boyle	11 100	65.0	130 700	21.8	11.1	622	28.2	3.1	12 227	-4.9	854	7.0	11 932	31.2	26.8
Bracken	3 252	78.3	90 700	22.6	11.1	527	31.6	3.7	3 822	-2.8	300	7.8	3 518	27.1	36.2
Breathitt	5 290	75.0	47 400	23.9	12.6	488	35.8	4.4	4 185	-6.6	485	11.6	4 143	25.6	25.5
Breckinridge	7 213	80.0	82 700	20.2	10.0	513	28.6	1.8	8 074	-2.0	576	7.1	7 051	25.2	38.8
Bullitt	27 874	82.2	145 500	22.4	11.9	778	25.9	2.0	38 948	-1.9	2 280	5.9	35 819	24.0	34.2
Butler	5 124	74.5	87 300	20.4	11.2	558	29.7	1.1	5 227	-2.8	385	7.4	4 867	25.4	41.3
Caldwell	5 232	72.9	86 600	19.7	10.5	520	30.7	1.8	5 472	-2.7	357	6.5	5 135	29.1	29.3
Calloway	14 937	65.6	114 800	20.9	10.7	541	33.2	1.7	18 652	2.7	1 068	5.7	17 310	33.6	24.1
Campbell	35 203	70.0	146 300	21.0	11.8	722	28.6	3.1	47 729	-2.3	2 500	5.2	45 336	36.3	20.1
Carlisle	2 034	80.8	73 800	19.9	10.9	518	21.6	6.1	2 355	-0.8	144	6.1	2 114	24.8	36.2
Carroll	4 269	62.9	99 500	21.5	10.0	646	27.8	2.6	4 858	-6.0	351	7.2	4 259	23.2	39.6
Carter	10 319	79.7	74 500	19.8	11.0	547	29.1	3.0	10 457	-5.4	1 130	10.8	10 262	25.2	35.4
Casey	6 050	80.8	70 400	24.7	13.1	459	30.3	2.8	6 573	-3.6	459	7.0	6 155	22.9	39.0
Christian	25 899	52.5	101 700	22.2	10.0	738	29.7	2.2	25 951	-2.6	1 967	7.6	23 829	28.2	29.6
Clark	14 498	64.8	141 000	20.9	11.2	671	29.3	2.0	17 020	-1.5	1 046	6.1	15 825	34.5	27.4

1. Specified owner-occupied units. 2. A value of 10.0 represents 10 percent or less; a value of 50.0 represents 50 percent or more. 3. Specified renter-occupied units.
4. Overcrowded or lacking complete plumbing facilities. 5. Percent of civilian labor force. 6. Persons 16 years old and over.

STATE County	Private nonfarm establishments, employment and payroll, 2013									Agriculture, 2012			
		Employment						Annual payroll		Farms			
											Percent with:		
	Number of establish-ments	Total	Health care and social assistance	Manufac-turing	Retail trade	Finance and insurance	Professional, scientific, and technical services	Total (mil dol)	Average per employee (dollars)	Number	Fewer than 50 acres	500 acres or more	Farm operators whose principal occu-pation is farming (percent)
	104	105	106	107	108	109	110	111	112	113	114	115	116
KANSAS—Cont'd													
Neosho	452	5 105	1 101	1 063	708	213	136	168	32 901	702	23.4	19.8	43.2
Ness	143	1 070	D	D	89	67	21	40	37 015	557	8.3	45.6	44.0
Norton	176	1 791	470	D	185	103	44	60	33 701	367	12.3	48.2	59.7
Osage	265	2 618	D	D	356	118	53	51	19 436	1 014	22.9	21.0	43.0
Osborne	154	1 139	282	D	201	77	42	33	28 570	343	10.2	50.1	65.0
Ottawa	132	893	255	D	90	67	25	25	27 774	525	12.0	35.4	49.9
Pawnee	168	2 023	1 104	D	222	79	D	72	35 348	401	13.7	45.4	53.1
Phillips	245	1 773	346	189	226	173	110	63	35 456	441	17.7	46.3	58.3
Pottawatomie	561	8 174	D	1 393	D	207	189	288	35 179	890	22.5	23.7	42.9
Pratt	387	3 515	676	73	725	147	118	127	36 108	543	7.6	37.9	45.1
Rawlins	104	630	192	D	94	D	D	21	32 881	307	6.2	67.1	63.2
Reno	1 629	22 442	4 459	3 757	3 403	827	638	763	33 977	1 633	20.6	23.6	49.0
Republic	190	1 374	319	178	208	66	D	37	26 739	575	13.0	34.6	60.7
Rice	269	2 596	390	342	286	137	D	78	30 096	532	15.0	38.9	54.5
Riley	1 568	20 159	3 404	423	4 315	843	1 016	566	28 068	493	24.3	22.7	44.6
Rooks	199	1 508	264	111	219	79	42	45	30 145	440	10.9	50.0	48.2
Rush	99	1 105	D	D	67	46	16	36	32 984	528	12.3	40.7	47.0
Russell	276	2 011	D	D	D	78	42	62	30 735	504	11.1	36.5	48.2
Saline	1 566	27 280	4 486	5 807	4 007	861	1 138	914	33 515	674	19.7	30.1	46.7
Scott	191	1 345	359	28	267	98	50	40	29 711	269	14.5	51.7	64.3
Sedgwick	11 751	221 272	32 542	45 218	28 243	9 646	9 507	9 603	43 401	1 344	36.5	19.0	46.1
Seward	556	9 890	1 109	D	1 242	223	165	353	35 730	363	8.8	39.7	44.6
Shawnee	4 259	75 553	17 664	5 887	9 555	5 255	4 343	3 151	41 701	826	39.8	11.3	39.3
Sheridan	105	685	D	D	D	D	D	24	34 931	384	6.0	60.4	67.7
Sherman	259	2 014	385	D	410	99	85	55	27 461	416	6.3	51.2	58.7
Smith	146	945	D	105	182	64	19	25	26 697	497	12.3	47.3	62.2
Stafford	129	643	D	D	D	62	D	19	29 482	536	9.0	45.0	51.3
Stanton	60	408	D	D	D	53	D	16	39 100	278	0.7	54.0	52.5
Stevens	136	1 163	D	48	163	68	33	44	38 055	315	6.0	41.0	38.4
Sumner	490	4 562	1 024	920	607	222	93	143	31 256	1 096	17.5	33.2	51.8
Thomas	333	2 834	376	D	675	137	64	87	30 556	460	10.0	51.5	58.5
Trego	119	922	D	26	147	33	D	31	33 485	384	9.9	47.9	50.3
Wabaunsee	134	866	137	144	105	44	D	23	26 076	617	18.2	27.9	43.9
Wallace	60	300	D	D	D	D	12	9	29 920	294	6.1	57.5	54.1
Washington	212	1 480	383	164	219	70	D	37	25 216	732	15.6	37.6	52.3
Wichita	86	533	D	D	71	26	D	19	36 163	265	7.9	60.0	62.6
Wilson	245	3 374	684	908	252	93	41	132	39 079	423	13.0	33.1	52.2
Woodson	87	439	132	D	63	27	8	13	28 585	315	14.0	41.9	53.0
Wyandotte	3 047	67 688	15 143	9 917	7 261	1 051	2 230	3 103	45 837	164	70.7	1.8	39.6
KENTUCKY	90 675	1 507 375	255 846	218 734	202 387	67 665	68 412	57 541	38 173	77 064	36.5	6.2	41.7
Adair	317	4 138	700	364	683	185	56	97	23 373	1 243	33.8	3.8	38.5
Allen	238	3 121	D	D	401	133	82	88	28 134	1 080	35.7	4.6	48.0
Anderson	317	3 289	331	932	711	D	95	110	33 380	676	38.2	3.4	40.4
Ballard	132	1 804	D	D	165	44	D	100	55 533	408	36.5	11.3	46.1
Barren	867	14 621	2 444	3 498	2 443	381	251	429	29 310	1 869	39.5	4.4	51.1
Bath	146	1 038	194	D	174	D	24	30	29 231	690	23.9	8.4	47.4
Bell	514	6 923	1 447	1 092	1 441	261	109	204	29 502	81	56.8	3.7	48.1
Boone	2 983	76 345	4 681	12 786	8 939	3 502	1 792	3 075	40 281	608	53.5	3.5	40.3
Bourbon	377	5 450	712	1 831	830	195	256	212	38 841	907	38.4	11.4	53.3
Boyd	1 387	23 282	D	2 440	3 878	642	765	978	41 985	214	37.9	1.4	35.5
Boyle	736	14 364	3 092	2 035	1 736	344	314	442	30 803	620	38.7	8.5	39.0
Bracken	96	843	88	D	143	D	15	25	29 075	587	28.4	3.7	42.2
Breathitt	227	3 135	1 489	D	482	110	101	89	28 520	120	34.2	10.0	26.7
Breckinridge	285	2 409	565	253	514	139	76	68	28 085	1 304	27.2	7.6	37.3
Bullitt	1 044	15 471	1 287	2 164	1 573	293	343	486	31 428	488	54.5	1.8	43.9
Butler	189	1 917	350	D	216	D	D	57	29 594	697	23.4	8.3	36.4
Caldwell	286	3 706	572	D	671	119	46	115	30 982	538	32.5	8.0	34.6
Calloway	866	13 792	2 292	2 604	1 893	398	369	379	27 499	821	40.4	9.4	38.4
Campbell	1 638	23 289	3 172	2 160	4 251	532	963	789	33 878	504	48.0	1.6	42.1
Carlisle	00	570	D	81	95	D	D	15	25 445	325	41.2	14.2	39.7
Carroll	232	5 819	D	2 548	625	72	123	300	51 598	278	20.1	5.4	37.4
Carter	409	4 918	405	768	908	D	113	125	25 388	786	30.8	3.7	31.3
Casey	230	2 957	518	D	398	D	D	77	26 095	1 118	27.4	4.1	52.6
Christian	1 315	23 451	3 557	5 068	3 097	732	709	807	34 412	1 179	27.1	10.7	45.9
Clark	744	10 685	1 507	2 385	1 561	265	315	379	35 447	883	42.7	7.1	39.2

STATE County	Agriculture, 2012 (cont.)															
	Land in farms					Value of land and buildings (dollars)			Value of products sold				Percent of farms with sales of:		Government payments	
			Acres								Percent from:					
	Acreage (1,000)	Percent change, 2007–2012	Average size of farm	Total irrigated (1,000)	Total cropland (1,000)	Average per farm	Average per acre	Value of machinery and equipment, average per farm (dollars)	Total (mil dol)	Average per farm (dollars)	Crops	Livestock and poultry products	$10,000 or more	$100,000 or more	Total ($1,000)	Percent of farms
	117	118	119	120	121	122	123	124	125	126	127	128	129	130	131	132
KANSAS—Cont'd																
Neosho	308	-4.2	439	0.1	175.4	657 053	1 497	105 855	68.0	96 806	60.8	39.2	50.1	15.1	2 284	57.0
Ness	678	9.4	1 218	4.8	412.3	1 267 795	1 041	143 088	63.5	114 077	71.7	28.3	55.1	28.4	7 435	90.7
Norton	502	-5.5	1 368	14.5	270.6	1 812 496	1 325	210 428	146.1	397 976	34.9	65.1	66.5	32.7	3 716	85.3
Osage	442	16.3	436	0.0	251.4	709 350	1 626	105 941	71.0	70 021	52.4	47.6	43.3	14.9	4 728	64.1
Osborne	440	4.7	1 283	6.7	232.5	1 758 099	1 370	162 679	69.6	202 854	67.6	32.4	70.0	42.3	3 088	85.1
Ottawa	420	-4.0	800	4.2	239.0	1 505 440	1 883	167 135	99.0	188 631	60.6	39.4	64.4	28.0	3 509	82.3
Pawnee	480	-1.4	1 198	78.5	398.5	2 184 032	1 823	247 526	362.3	903 614	25.4	74.6	61.3	35.4	5 993	90.3
Phillips	495	0.0	1 123	7.5	232.2	1 404 333	1 251	170 676	100.4	227 633	48.7	51.3	63.7	34.9	3 275	76.9
Pottawatomie	410	-4.4	460	21.9	164.9	878 335	1 908	101 524	117.0	131 421	44.8	55.2	53.9	17.9	2 860	57.2
Pratt	465	-3.3	855	86.2	356.8	1 368 877	1 600	188 613	273.4	503 547	46.0	54.0	53.6	33.0	7 049	86.6
Rawlins	609	3.1	1 984	17.7	354.9	3 461 316	1 744	266 081	91.4	297 700	75.7	24.3	85.7	54.1	4 191	87.9
Reno	790	1.1	483	58.4	591.7	868 492	1 796	138 632	267.3	163 698	56.7	43.3	50.6	22.3	9 785	73.1
Republic	361	-11.2	628	46.5	258.5	1 664 624	2 651	228 520	197.3	343 073	58.8	41.2	71.7	37.7	4 144	78.6
Rice	458	6.8	860	28.6	360.9	1 373 859	1 597	238 983	258.2	485 303	38.3	61.7	62.8	37.8	5 201	79.3
Riley	218	-5.9	443	4.1	99.4	809 619	1 829	107 047	54.4	110 404	66.7	33.3	54.6	22.7	1 265	64.9
Rooks	551	-1.8	1 253	6.9	316.9	1 644 650	1 312	187 098	85.3	193 841	66.6	33.4	58.2	35.7	3 975	85.2
Rush	453	11.6	858	13.2	321.9	1 112 680	1 297	166 716	66.8	126 566	71.4	28.6	55.7	25.9	5 200	86.7
Russell	436	-1.8	864	0.5	234.9	986 889	1 142	129 329	56.8	112 649	64.6	35.4	56.0	22.8	4 283	83.9
Saline	364	-15.5	541	4.8	236.2	1 068 445	1 976	155 677	84.4	125 258	70.5	29.5	58.6	25.4	3 461	77.0
Scott	453	0.0	1 686	36.5	363.4	2 556 929	1 517	344 584	979.8	3 642 543	6.6	93.4	71.7	46.5	4 947	76.6
Sedgwick	487	-4.6	362	45.4	396.0	860 281	2 376	133 063	148.5	110 479	87.7	12.3	52.8	20.4	4 973	58.3
Seward	402	1.5	1 107	101.0	307.7	1 274 033	1 151	214 950	465.3	1 281 838	20.6	79.4	46.3	26.4	4 481	77.4
Shawnee	194	-5.8	235	19.0	117.7	585 475	2 489	78 510	50.3	60 844	83.0	17.0	39.5	10.4	2 350	40.8
Sheridan	562	7.6	1 463	79.3	363.5	2 808 255	1 919	288 505	328.7	855 951	33.3	66.7	79.7	51.0	5 406	83.6
Sherman	595	-9.6	1 430	87.0	498.7	2 441 558	1 707	280 512	170.2	409 043	77.2	22.8	63.5	41.8	7 341	86.8
Smith	500	9.4	1 007	7.3	334.4	1 633 296	1 622	212 620	111.0	223 270	67.2	32.8	71.6	38.6	5 354	84.3
Stafford	499	-0.7	931	103.4	396.5	1 644 125	1 767	234 315	197.6	368 696	60.8	39.2	55.6	36.4	6 769	85.6
Stanton	429	3.6	1 544	76.7	390.6	1 708 899	1 107	304 309	163.7	588 986	48.6	51.4	54.7	36.3	6 864	91.4
Stevens	456	-9.5	1 446	145.2	354.3	1 982 368	1 371	373 492	328.5	1 042 711	44.0	56.0	47.3	31.4	5 414	84.4
Sumner	720	1.4	657	16.1	592.9	1 177 329	1 793	178 303	168.7	153 935	88.8	11.2	62.9	28.2	7 384	77.0
Thomas	675	2.7	1 468	90.0	576.5	3 128 313	2 132	332 954	253.4	550 976	57.6	42.4	73.3	47.0	8 819	80.7
Trego	447	4.0	1 163	6.7	258.7	1 525 997	1 312	157 602	58.9	153 425	60.8	39.2	62.8	28.4	3 651	89.6
Wabaunsee	396	-15.8	642	7.0	107.6	944 000	1 470	92 042	58.3	94 561	36.9	63.1	53.3	21.1	1 959	56.7
Wallace	488	13.6	1 660	58.0	353.3	2 093 398	1 261	233 490	97.2	330 708	66.2	33.8	64.3	40.5	6 452	85.0
Washington	490	-10.6	669	9.7	298.2	1 562 583	2 334	197 657	187.1	255 668	53.2	46.8	69.5	36.9	5 492	79.5
Wichita	464	-10.8	1 750	67.5	351.2	2 375 008	1 357	320 019	624.8	2 357 736	D	D	72.1	49.1	5 701	87.2
Wilson	255	-23.6	602	2.2	142.4	865 076	1 437	129 043	55.4	131 021	84.4	15.6	62.4	23.6	1 636	65.0
Woodson	295	12.6	935	0.0	153.9	1 286 667	1 376	140 746	54.6	173 343	49.5	50.5	60.0	28.9	1 856	69.5
Wyandotte	12	-33.7	73	D	7.3	352 140	4 809	42 561	3.3	20 067	82.2	17.8	22.6	3.0	106	9.8
KENTUCKY	13 049	-6.7	169	73.6	6 336.2	512 033	3 024	70 188	5 067.3	65 755	45.0	55.0	36.5	8.2	169 821	43.3
Adair	170	-9.5	137	0.1	66.6	350 537	2 560	49 813	53.4	42 936	25.9	74.1	37.4	7.1	2 392	54.9
Allen	146	-12.6	135	0.3	52.3	398 629	2 955	51 991	53.2	49 291	26.5	73.5	39.4	6.9	2 086	44.4
Anderson	81	-7.5	120	0.2	29.4	373 490	3 116	48 127	12.7	18 857	33.7	66.3	29.6	3.3	625	22.9
Ballard	107	-2.7	263	0.4	85.2	893 627	3 402	150 120	57.6	141 206	54.7	45.3	42.6	14.7	1 937	65.9
Barren	249	-6.1	133	0.2	130.0	391 780	2 945	68 049	113.0	60 474	33.4	66.6	45.2	8.2	4 232	40.6
Bath	142	10.2	206	0.0	47.9	402 174	1 951	58 223	19.3	27 915	46.7	53.3	42.6	5.8	1 041	41.6
Bell	8	-20.9	100	0.0	1.8	193 704	1 945	25 827	0.5	6 037	D	D	21.0	0.0	7	7.4
Boone	67	-10.1	111	0.2	28.3	682 016	6 170	64 265	12.4	20 467	66.2	33.8	26.3	4.6	450	26.2
Bourbon	184	-0.3	203	0.4	74.8	862 352	4 256	90 714	108.4	119 568	34.5	65.5	50.3	13.2	1 916	39.6
Boyd	22	-24.1	102	0.0	4.8	237 617	2 333	53 234	1.9	8 813	27.0	73.0	13.6	0.9	22	6.5
Boyle	102	7.8	164	0.2	41.9	557 629	3 405	64 198	31.0	49 953	22.9	77.1	41.5	9.8	687	33.5
Bracken	87	-13.8	148	0.2	29.0	309 826	2 095	53 532	10.9	18 547	62.5	37.5	31.9	3.4	837	39.0
Breathitt	22	-49.0	185	0.0	4.8	264 842	1 430	58 558	1.7	14 267	43.0	57.0	14.2	3.3	192	39.2
Breckinridge	260	-5.4	199	0.0	116.6	477 849	2 399	64 376	79.5	60 995	42.8	57.2	40.3	8.2	3 246	58.2
Bullitt	46	-9.8	95	D	20.2	344 717	3 645	48 629	7.7	15 873	59.6	40.4	21.5	2.7	369	23.0
Butler	153	-12.3	219	0.2	62.8	442 750	2 023	59 912	42.4	60 822	54.7	45.3	29.6	7.9	2 052	48.6
Caldwell	133	-6.5	248	D	85.5	678 645	2 735	83 006	38.5	71 561	86.7	13.3	33.1	7.4	2 270	60.4
Calloway	176	11.6	214	3.8	131.9	636 456	2 968	109 851	109.7	133 619	57.3	42.7	35.8	16.2	5 573	68.7
Campbell	42	-10.9	84	0.1	15.0	367 526	4 393	49 331	6.9	13 718	45.7	54.3	24.4	3.2	179	16.3
Carlisle	99	3.0	303	0.6	79.6	858 588	2 829	151 486	73.1	224 939	46.6	53.4	38.2	20.0	2 245	74.2
Carroll	54	-15.9	193	0.1	21.7	508 050	2 637	55 694	6.4	23 169	69.9	30.1	36.0	2.5	354	41.7
Carter	106	-15.7	135	0.1	22.6	236 774	1 758	40 621	9.5	12 080	32.7	67.3	21.5	1.7	400	23.9
Casey	179	-6.5	160	0.1	60.6	325 356	2 031	49 997	29.6	26 471	47.1	52.9	38.2	5.1	1 559	47.5
Christian	360	4.0	306	3.3	252.3	1 055 497	3 454	121 645	185.8	157 625	80.2	19.8	48.3	20.6	7 302	56.4
Clark	137	-7.9	156	0.2	50.5	510 663	3 282	63 019	34.8	39 361	31.7	68.3	40.1	8.3	790	25.3

STATE County	Water use, 2010		Wholesale trade,[1] 2007				Retail trade,[2] 2007				Real estate and rental and leasing,[2] 2007			
	Total water withdrawn (mil gal/day)	Gallons withdrawn per person per day	Number of establish-ments	Number of employees	Sales (mil dol)	Annual payroll (mil dol)	Number of establish-ments	Number of employees	Sales (mil dol)	Annual payroll (mil dol)	Number of establish-ments	Number of employees	Receipts (mil dol)	Annual payroll (mil dol)
	133	134	135	136	137	138	139	140	141	142	143	144	145	146
KANSAS—Cont'd														
Neosho	2.8	170	24	262	180.2	10.0	96	921	199.8	18.3	6	20	1.9	0.4
Ness	4.1	1 304	13	74	42.4	2.3	20	84	16.1	1.2	NA	NA	NA	NA
Norton	13.8	2 437	11	61	40.0	1.6	29	180	37.0	3.0	1	D	D	D
Osage	2.3	144	11	79	19.4	2.0	54	369	70.6	5.7	7	28	2.0	0.4
Osborne	2.0	513	13	97	86.2	3.3	31	198	38.5	2.3	1	D	D	D
Ottawa	2.8	458	9	199	48.0	5.8	17	90	19.3	1.5	1	D	D	D
Pawnee	71.5	10 260	6	92	93.8	3.8	27	215	48.5	4.2	3	12	0.8	0.3
Phillips	18.3	3 251	8	61	33.9	1.6	36	243	46.6	3.6	1	D	D	D
Pottawatomie	40.7	1 883	20	530	161.0	18.2	98	1 463	283.9	30.3	21	51	7.8	1.3
Pratt	89.1	9 225	22	131	108.3	3.7	54	690	170.2	15.4	16	40	3.7	0.7
Rawlins	14.1	5 613	6	54	83.5	2.9	23	101	16.3	1.7	2	D	D	D
Reno	70.9	1 098	65	749	573.3	27.1	316	3 722	828.6	78.4	64	166	43.2	3.9
Republic	17.7	3 544	19	272	97.4	4.8	40	250	43.7	3.9	2	D	D	D
Rice	24.3	2 409	17	111	64.0	4.1	45	279	46.9	4.2	6	D	D	D
Riley	5.3	75	35	314	93.2	10.8	270	4 028	728.6	66.5	105	489	50.3	10.1
Rooks	11.1	2 142	16	112	120.3	4.7	33	224	56.4	3.4	1	D	D	D
Rush	8.9	2 703	10	53	27.7	1.3	12	80	30.7	1.9	NA	NA	NA	NA
Russell	1.3	182	14	107	70.3	3.2	41	284	68.0	4.4	9	31	2.9	0.7
Saline	10.4	188	84	1 178	816.4	44.4	284	4 226	1 064.6	86.3	74	D	D	D
Scott	43.7	8 857	21	114	131.5	5.1	33	212	46.8	3.5	3	4	0.4	0.1
Sedgwick	94.0	189	599	8 304	12 449.4	383.6	1 771	26 921	6 574.2	590.0	605	3 411	501.8	93.7
Seward	157.4	6 857	42	392	197.5	15.5	116	1 395	314.6	29.1	27	95	12.4	2.0
Shawnee	36.0	202	166	1 966	915.3	81.2	747	10 406	2 310.1	216.4	241	D	D	D
Sheridan	72.3	28 290	11	92	88.4	4.4	20	96	18.4	1.5	NA	NA	NA	NA
Sherman	99.1	16 491	19	116	119.1	3.7	44	378	110.6	7.6	11	29	3.2	0.7
Smith	2.2	563	11	119	71.1	3.3	30	170	23.6	2.1	3	4	0.4	0.1
Stafford	88.5	19 950	6	24	18.1	0.7	19	88	15.9	1.3	NA	NA	NA	NA
Stanton	113.5	50 774	11	D	D	D	10	73	16.4	1.6	NA	NA	NA	NA
Stevens	197.6	34 521	13	84	113.7	3.0	25	187	40.3	3.4	1	D	D	D
Sumner	9.4	391	25	152	202.2	6.1	63	556	131.4	10.7	16	47	3.3	0.9
Thomas	82.4	10 433	34	242	163.1	8.6	64	633	159.4	12.2	9	23	3.7	0.4
Trego	6.1	2 029	9	34	24.1	0.9	28	127	40.4	2.5	1	D	D	D
Wabaunsee	3.7	519	6	43	13.4	1.7	23	136	26.7	2.1	5	D	D	D
Wallace	45.3	30 478	3	D	D	D	7	47	6.3	0.7	2	D	D	D
Washington	5.7	988	15	185	111.3	6.4	41	209	34.8	2.6	2	D	D	D
Wichita	53.9	24 105	10	60	68.2	2.3	15	83	18.5	1.3	1	D	D	D
Wilson	2.6	281	5	D	D	D	41	267	54.2	4.1	6	D	D	D
Woodson	1.2	369	5	43	27.4	1.2	19	79	17.2	1.6	2	D	D	D
Wyandotte	287.0	1 822	234	5 833	4 127.5	289.5	461	7 022	1 710.0	174.6	136	791	129.4	22.7
KENTUCKY	4 326.5	997	3 794	59 854	74 680.8	2 869.5	16 404	214 782	50 405.9	4 502.2	3 898	20 146	3 894.3	593.4
Adair	3.4	184	18	131	54.7	2.8	61	486	137.1	9.6	11	51	2.4	0.4
Allen	2.3	114	11	243	97.7	9.4	63	533	112.1	8.6	12	55	3.8	0.8
Anderson	4.1	190	7	D	D	D	58	709	170.7	14.2	14	52	5.3	1.1
Ballard	31.7	3 837	6	D	D	D	28	208	52.8	3.8	2	D	D	D
Barren	10.4	246	38	D	D	D	193	2 319	552.9	48.5	25	78	9.2	1.8
Bath	6.0	515	NA	NA	NA	NA	40	243	51.5	3.7	6	D	D	D
Bell	4.4	152	20	195	196.1	4.7	133	1 556	374.9	31.7	23	67	10.6	1.7
Boone	11.1	94	160	D	D	D	493	9 371	2 439.2	206.6	133	898	154.9	23.1
Bourbon	3.2	162	10	D	D	D	66	804	175.3	14.9	11	40	3.1	0.6
Boyd	44.1	890	64	D	D	D	271	4 016	934.6	75.1	53	233	41.1	6.2
Boyle	6.8	240	18	120	71.2	3.8	150	1 943	430.0	43.0	33	99	12.6	2.1
Bracken	1.7	203	3	D	D	D	19	155	25.9	2.3	2	D	D	D
Breathitt	10.3	744	5	D	D	D	51	501	103.7	9.2	7	D	D	D
Breckinridge	2.6	132	8	47	19.4	1.4	55	445	113.8	9.2	8	21	2.3	0.4
Bullitt	6.9	92	29	563	879.7	26.0	164	1 699	500.5	31.9	33	97	12.3	1.7
Butler	1.7	134	6	D	D	D	40	284	58.0	4.3	6	55	3.2	1.2
Caldwell	1.4	108	7	D	D	D	61	673	151.8	13.6	7	58	2.8	1.6
Calloway	6.4	172	39	D	D	D	158	2 030	454.8	41.2	34	129	12.1	2.2
Campbell	29.9	330	55	D	D	D	282	4 043	970.8	83.6	67	468	89.2	15.2
Carlisle	0.7	141	3	9	2.9	0.2	11	116	23.8	2.2	2	D	D	D
Carroll	42.9	3 965	7	73	13.4	1.3	55	642	182.7	14.2	5	22	5.8	0.7
Carter	5.1	184	13	406	306.2	9.7	114	1 098	268.5	18.7	17	53	3.7	0.7
Casey	1.8	115	10	95	34.9	2.6	48	316	71.8	5.1	2	D	D	D
Christian	17.4	235	65	1 028	878.4	38.6	270	3 263	936.1	70.7	66	299	29.8	5.8
Clark	94.0	2 638	34	D	D	D	147	1 861	461.8	39.2	40	135	16.6	2.5

1. Merchant wholesalers, except manufacturers' sales branches and offices. 2. Employer establishments.

STATE County	Professional, scientific, and technical services,[1] 2007				Manufacturing, 2007				Accommodation and food services, 2007			
	Number of establish-ments	Number of employees	Receipts (mil dol)	Annual payroll (mil dol)	Number of establish-ments	Number of employees	Receipts (mil dol)	Annual payroll (mil dol)	Number of establish-ments	Number of employees	Sales (mil dol)	Annual payroll (mil dol)
	147	148	149	150	151	152	153	154	155	156	157	158
KANSAS—Cont'd												
Neosho	32	133	11.5	4.6	36	1 395	291.0	48.8	35	395	13.1	3.0
Ness	6	19	1.6	0.3	NA	NA	NA	NA	11	71	1.5	0.4
Norton	11	46	2.9	0.7	NA	NA	NA	NA	13	152	5.4	1.4
Osage	16	D	D	D	NA	NA	NA	NA	21	D	D	D
Osborne	9	51	10.4	1.6	NA	NA	NA	NA	9	55	1.4	0.4
Ottawa	10	D	D	D	NA	NA	NA	NA	8	103	1.5	0.5
Pawnee	15	53	4.2	1.2	NA	NA	NA	NA	13	179	5.7	1.5
Phillips	16	84	7.6	2.6	NA	NA	NA	NA	14	146	3.7	0.8
Pottawatomie	43	D	D	D	33	1 626	329.6	64.9	32	355	11.8	3.1
Pratt	31	127	9.6	3.5	NA	NA	NA	NA	25	431	15.0	3.5
Rawlins	8	15	1.0	0.2	NA	NA	NA	NA	9	24	0.7	0.2
Reno	109	D	D	D	93	3 672	908.7	142.1	125	2 289	83.4	23.1
Republic	17	25	2.7	0.5	NA	NA	NA	NA	11	127	3.1	0.6
Rice	19	119	5.8	1.8	NA	NA	NA	NA	18	231	6.6	1.9
Riley	155	D	D	D	28	795	D	24.7	158	3 493	125.4	33.4
Rooks	13	41	3.5	1.3	NA	NA	NA	NA	11	D	D	D
Rush	6	16	1.4	0.6	NA	NA	NA	NA	4	20	0.9	0.2
Russell	14	57	4.4	1.1	NA	NA	NA	NA	20	300	10.0	2.3
Saline	124	D	D	D	77	D	D	222.7	128	2 593	96.1	26.7
Scott	19	67	6.3	1.4	NA	NA	NA	NA	13	D	D	D
Sedgwick	1 120	D	D	D	573	53 568	21 117.1	2 940.1	1 066	21 268	846.9	246.6
Seward	32	127	11.3	4.2	9	D	D	D	49	826	32.2	8.9
Shawnee	472	D	D	D	121	6 097	D	274.4	370	D	D	D
Sheridan	4	21	1.2	0.3	NA	NA	NA	NA	5	31	0.8	0.1
Sherman	18	79	6.6	2.4	NA	NA	NA	NA	23	328	11.0	3.0
Smith	9	23	2.2	0.3	NA	NA	NA	NA	8	79	1.4	0.3
Stafford	9	15	1.8	0.6	NA	NA	NA	NA	12	42	1.2	0.2
Stanton	6	16	1.1	0.4	NA	NA	NA	NA	4	22	0.8	0.1
Stevens	11	53	13.7	4.3	NA	NA	NA	NA	11	D	D	D
Sumner	24	D	D	D	39	1 253	D	43.0	39	537	16.8	4.8
Thomas	32	76	7.7	1.6	NA	NA	NA	NA	29	512	18.3	5.1
Trego	8	23	1.4	0.3	NA	NA	NA	NA	12	106	4.0	1.1
Wabaunsee	5	D	D	D	NA	NA	NA	NA	10	D	D	D
Wallace	2	D	D	D	NA	NA	NA	NA	3	D	D	D
Washington	11	34	3.5	0.9	NA	NA	NA	NA	14	123	2.5	0.7
Wichita	3	D	D	D	NA	NA	NA	NA	3	14	0.5	0.1
Wilson	14	39	4.4	0.9	22	1 428	D	D	18	191	5.8	1.4
Woodson	5	18	0.8	0.3	NA	NA	NA	NA	6	71	1.5	0.4
Wyandotte	158	D	D	D	215	11 083	7 634.5	632.0	248	4 964	241.9	66.8
KENTUCKY	8 075	61 428	7 872.2	2 831.6	4 165	247 096	119 105.4	10 773.2	7 309	151 551	6 300.9	1 787.4
Adair	16	D	D	D	NA	NA	NA	NA	20	188	9.1	1.7
Allen	11	60	5.6	1.3	12	592	164.8	22.1	14	207	8.2	2.0
Anderson	27	102	9.6	3.0	21	1 102	600.9	47.9	26	369	11.3	3.6
Ballard	5	D	D	D	11	727	D	43.3	10	70	1.8	0.5
Barren	49	292	23.2	7.3	49	4 540	1 024.9	164.9	87	1 790	64.7	17.5
Bath	11	D	D	D	NA	NA	NA	NA	10	D	D	D
Bell	37	453	31.0	17.3	21	688	D	D	47	1 044	38.1	10.5
Boone	232	3 501	381.4	146.4	183	13 239	4 691.0	647.7	269	D	D	D
Bourbon	35	D	D	D	26	1 769	D	D	25	327	13.5	3.6
Boyd	104	D	D	D	33	3 024	D	229.1	112	2 820	100.5	27.7
Boyle	72	437	43.7	15.3	28	2 839	D	D	63	1 539	57.7	16.8
Bracken	7	D	D	D	NA	NA	NA	NA	10	D	D	D
Breathitt	11	D	D	D	NA	NA	NA	NA	15	223	8.7	2.3
Breckinridge	12	66	4.6	1.9	NA	NA	NA	NA	18	273	7.9	2.5
Bullitt	76	366	26.3	10.0	47	2 823	D	104.8	84	1 818	73.0	20.1
Butler	6	126	2.4	1.4	15	573	120.5	19.5	16	170	5.4	1.4
Caldwell	18	50	4.0	1.0	16	898	213.2	27.1	24	260	9.4	2.3
Calloway	55	273	22.0	7.5	35	2 658	729.2	96.0	70	1 548	52.5	14.2
Campbell	149	D	D	D	85	2 338	798.2	105.8	192	3 734	163.3	49.0
Carlisle	3	D	D	D	NA	NA	NA	NA	4	42	1.1	0.3
Carroll	20	98	7.7	3.8	12	2 547	4 059.7	183.7	26	426	18.2	5.0
Carter	28	89	5.9	2.3	18	712	D	19.0	39	619	24.4	5.9
Casey	9	D	D	D	28	1 019	189.1	21.1	16	184	6.4	1.9
Christian	89	875	102.4	32.8	73	5 192	1 571.6	202.4	113	2 055	80.1	21.9
Clark	57	321	27.3	11.8	44	3 794	1 252.3	146.2	59	1 264	51.3	13.9

1. Establishment subject to federal tax.

Table B. States and Counties — **Health Care and Social Assistance, Other Services, Nonemployer Businesses, and Residential Construction**

STATE County	Health care and social assistance, 2007				Other services, 2007				Nonemployer businesses, 2013		Value of residential construction authorized by building permits, 2014	
	Number of establish-ments	Number of employees	Receipts (mil dol)	Annual payroll (mil dol)	Number of establish-ments	Number of employees	Receipts (mil dol)	Annual payroll (mil dol)	Number	Receipts (mil dol)	New Construction ($1,000)	Number of housing units
	159	160	161	162	163	164	165	166	167	168	169	170
KANSAS—Cont'd												
Neosho	58	1 256	85.1	31.8	41	120	11.2	2.1	1 120	38.4	705	5
Ness	11	249	13.3	6.1	10	D	D	D	303	10.5	220	1
Norton	23	448	21.5	10.7	14	40	5.0	0.7	442	17.1	535	5
Osage	30	1 533	35.5	20.5	20	D	D	D	1 070	39.6	1 812	17
Osborne	16	281	11.5	5.1	10	D	D	D	350	11.1	0	0
Ottawa	9	D	D	D	9	23	3.1	0.5	490	16.5	611	5
Pawnee	16	1 268	72.7	49.0	15	33	4.1	0.8	399	17.1	0	0
Phillips	21	294	17.1	8.0	23	64	24.8	1.2	515	18.8	3 175	18
Pottawatomie	49	1 466	56.3	28.4	46	139	10.5	2.5	1 693	70.4	49 122	220
Pratt	38	641	66.7	22.0	35	122	8.7	2.3	758	41.4	549	3
Rawlins	7	D	D	D	5	D	D	D	232	7.7	382	3
Reno	200	4 751	420.0	173.9	132	536	42.5	10.9	3 872	132.9	8 367	47
Republic	16	306	15.5	7.2	19	47	3.3	0.8	404	12.8	3 260	25
Rice	25	372	20.4	9.9	19	62	4.7	1.2	628	19.1	4 073	23
Riley	167	3 409	257.9	99.5	135	1 550	279.3	49.4	3 140	139.8	56 550	294
Rooks	13	213	11.0	4.9	15	63	6.4	1.5	581	22.0	564	3
Rush	5	128	7.2	3.3	6	D	D	D	292	9.7	160	1
Russell	18	420	21.9	11.0	14	36	3.3	0.4	805	43.3	349	1
Saline	180	D	D	D	123	582	55.4	13.1	3 472	132.3	10 421	65
Scott	12	292	15.7	7.9	19	65	6.0	1.0	434	18.4	1 696	6
Sedgwick	1 298	32 662	3 447.9	1 254.0	853	6 143	554.1	168.3	30 510	1 416.7	207 179	1 225
Seward	70	1 110	82.7	31.5	49	226	25.6	5.2	1 297	75.7	6 552	62
Shawnee	502	16 040	1 388.4	610.9	410	2 872	284.2	80.6	9 615	441.6	44 344	243
Sheridan	7	D	D	D	6	D	D	D	272	13.8	NA	NA
Sherman	35	390	23.0	9.3	23	61	5.6	1.4	435	15.8	0	0
Smith	9	260	11.2	5.4	13	30	3.0	0.5	336	9.4	636	6
Stafford	25	244	10.8	5.0	15	35	1.9	0.4	398	17.3	1 272	7
Stanton	4	D	D	D	5	D	D	D	185	9.6	0	0
Stevens	10	218	13.8	7.1	7	D	D	D	392	18.5	2 346	15
Sumner	61	D	D	D	42	112	9.3	2.1	1 459	52.5	4 700	62
Thomas	37	465	34.2	13.8	31	124	8.4	2.3	799	28.5	5 600	35
Trego	7	D	D	D	14	26	2.2	0.4	326	17.0	0	0
Wabaunsee	6	121	4.9	2.2	6	D	D	D	538	18.2	3 024	14
Wallace	5	D	D	D	6	13	0.9	0.2	145	4.4	0	0
Washington	26	378	14.8	6.9	17	55	5.3	0.8	456	16.3	1 000	2
Wichita	6	D	D	D	10	20	2.2	0.4	196	9.7	0	0
Wilson	35	588	37.1	16.1	12	26	1.6	0.5	599	21.9	266	3
Woodson	14	110	6.8	2.4	6	D	D	D	273	13.1	500	4
Wyandotte	309	10 811	1 094.6	467.5	234	1 390	232.0	34.5	7 373	248.7	57 158	493
KENTUCKY	10 600	235 282	22 151.8	8 395.1	6 150	40 956	3 751.1	1 009.3	274 987	11 196.1	1 304 713	9 536
Adair	41	883	49.2	24.4	15	37	3.0	0.7	1 525	57.5	0	0
Allen	23	D	D	D	13	42	4.0	1.2	1 390	51.1	NA	NA
Anderson	33	336	19.9	8.9	27	91	5.2	1.5	1 365	40.5	6 548	38
Ballard	8	D	D	D	9	D	D	D	458	14.9	NA	NA
Barren	106	2 498	196.0	85.7	48	D	D	D	3 208	111.9	12 726	86
Bath	13	198	9.8	4.0	12	D	D	D	769	21.8	0	0
Bell	80	1 525	116.8	46.1	37	D	D	D	1 494	40.7	1 995	20
Boone	211	3 754	311.0	123.2	184	1 641	126.9	42.9	7 102	303.7	56 168	354
Bourbon	39	D	D	D	24	127	6.3	1.7	1 310	52.0	7 098	27
Boyd	246	7 162	811.2	303.0	110	D	D	D	2 497	96.2	363	5
Boyle	110	2 486	238.4	105.7	50	219	14.2	3.9	1 952	69.4	6 266	31
Bracken	9	D	D	D	6	D	D	D	605	16.9	NA	NA
Breathitt	40	785	72.9	24.8	10	D	D	D	570	15.7	146	1
Breckinridge	30	453	30.9	11.0	23	49	4.4	1.0	1 223	52.3	280	2
Bullitt	90	906	59.6	22.8	81	1 021	27.2	23.1	4 307	164.2	47 327	231
Butler	19	250	14.4	6.4	14	51	2.8	0.8	823	30.2	0	0
Caldwell	30	515	35.2	12.9	17	62	5.4	1.3	750	26.5	365	3
Calloway	109	1 917	152.4	56.0	49	214	14.1	4.1	2 413	103.6	19 132	291
Campbell	160	3 393	288.9	114.6	124	916	111.4	26.6	5 212	193.8	41 733	212
Carlisle	7	D	D	D	3	D	D	D	401	14.8	NA	NA
Carroll	21	D	D	D	15	92	5.2	1.7	561	18.9	200	2
Carter	44	572	34.8	13.6	34	182	11.8	3.3	1 751	62.6	220	2
Casey	24	395	25.2	9.7	12	30	2.9	0.6	1 151	50.8	0	0
Christian	177	4 734	438.9	153.4	105	739	54.2	16.0	3 230	127.1	6 069	59
Clark	111	1 459	122.5	45.9	56	294	17.2	4.6	2 204	78.3	6 327	35

STATE County	Government employment and payroll, 2012									Local government finances, 2012				
			March payroll (percent of total)							General revenue				
												Taxes		
													Per capita[1] (dollars)	
	Full-time equivalent employees	March payroll (dollars)	Adminis-tration, judicial, and legal	Police and Corrections	Fire Protection	Highways and transpor-tation	Health and Welfare	Natural resources and utilities	Education and libraries	Total (mil dol)	Inter-govern-mental (mil dol)	Total (mil dol)	Total	Property
	171	172	173	174	175	176	177	178	179	180	181	182	183	184
KANSAS—Cont'd														
Neosho	1 176	4 053 546	4.7	4.8	1.4	3.1	33.7	7.7	43.8	111.1	29.1	28.8	1 755	1 392
Ness	342	928 162	3.6	3.8	0.3	7.5	55.5	2.1	25.8	27.2	3.0	10.5	3 412	3 238
Norton	415	1 296 107	5.9	8.5	0.2	5.3	36.1	4.9	38.5	21.8	9.5	8.3	1 476	1 235
Osage	664	1 848 318	7.4	9.1	0.0	4.8	2.0	8.1	66.8	51.8	25.1	19.9	1 231	1 069
Osborne	160	407 550	12.5	11.0	0.0	10.3	6.0	16.5	39.9	12.2	3.9	6.3	1 668	1 374
Ottawa	333	902 710	6.3	6.6	0.0	8.3	3.0	8.5	63.2	26.0	12.4	11.0	1 813	1 494
Pawnee	440	1 250 370	6.8	9.0	0.2	6.2	4.7	6.2	62.4	27.5	10.2	13.2	1 900	1 520
Phillips	269	733 417	9.3	5.4	0.0	11.5	9.3	7.3	56.3	24.1	8.0	10.9	1 969	1 705
Pottawatomie	900	2 555 697	7.0	7.4	0.4	6.4	5.6	4.0	68.4	81.2	25.0	45.4	2 033	1 711
Pratt	620	2 089 279	5.5	7.1	0.6	5.9	5.9	8.3	64.6	48.5	14.6	24.6	2 526	2 145
Rawlins	120	323 307	14.0	8.7	0.1	13.4	2.7	5.2	54.9	9.2	3.2	4.8	1 855	1 554
Reno	3 036	10 310 558	4.2	9.4	4.3	3.9	2.4	5.3	68.8	260.0	97.6	109.2	1 695	1 318
Republic	280	743 094	10.6	6.2	0.0	10.1	3.1	14.2	51.3	22.0	7.1	12.0	2 465	2 116
Rice	740	2 211 947	5.2	5.5	0.1	4.7	28.7	3.7	50.7	54.4	18.2	18.8	1 885	1 542
Riley	2 188	7 227 365	9.0	12.5	5.2	5.3	2.9	8.2	55.4	194.7	54.3	101.1	1 339	930
Rooks	433	1 169 894	7.0	5.2	0.1	6.4	36.2	3.6	40.2	44.1	11.5	14.8	2 837	2 597
Rush	240	677 611	5.6	5.2	0.0	9.2	28.1	6.5	42.1	19.8	4.2	7.4	2 306	2 203
Russell	400	1 117 489	12.4	9.0	1.7	7.9	3.8	13.6	49.3	31.8	7.8	19.4	2 790	2 354
Saline	2 537	8 460 384	4.0	12.5	4.8	4.8	1.1	5.4	63.9	204.8	71.4	88.3	1 578	1 104
Scott	243	604 532	5.5	5.8	0.4	5.4	1.4	5.5	73.4	23.7	6.5	15.0	3 033	2 531
Sedgwick	17 666	64 762 573	6.4	12.0	4.9	3.5	5.0	4.5	61.8	1 873.6	724.4	682.0	1 354	1 041
Seward	1 811	5 549 695	5.2	6.6	1.4	2.3	29.2	3.6	49.3	146.4	48.8	38.4	1 629	1 116
Shawnee	8 380	28 121 726	3.6	11.0	4.3	2.8	2.6	4.9	70.3	768.6	263.0	299.3	1 672	1 189
Sheridan	256	590 482	3.7	3.2	0.0	5.6	53.2	2.1	27.9	10.1	2.5	6.2	2 430	2 074
Sherman	464	1 377 731	5.7	6.0	0.9	6.3	39.8	6.9	32.6	30.8	10.9	12.2	1 999	1 467
Smith	252	661 334	7.3	6.7	0.0	9.5	8.4	7.9	57.9	20.6	8.5	9.3	2 464	2 115
Stafford	276	853 136	9.9	5.7	0.8	9.4	3.5	6.5	62.0	24.1	7.5	12.6	2 881	2 680
Stanton	212	627 118	5.8	6.3	0.0	9.1	35.1	3.1	40.4	19.3	3.0	11.2	5 142	4 980
Stevens	518	1 610 255	4.2	4.8	0.3	4.7	38.6	4.1	41.0	50.0	6.3	27.4	4 762	4 526
Sumner	1 279	3 843 881	5.5	7.0	2.2	5.1	19.6	5.9	51.4	100.9	37.4	33.6	1 421	1 151
Thomas	600	1 667 889	4.5	6.5	1.4	4.8	3.5	6.7	70.3	44.9	12.3	19.0	2 396	1 891
Trego	344	1 000 545	5.7	4.2	0.2	6.3	56.4	2.5	22.3	13.1	3.4	7.5	2 518	2 196
Wabaunsee	308	821 494	10.9	7.3	0.0	6.3	2.4	6.6	65.2	27.8	12.1	10.7	1 521	1 395
Wallace	110	277 969	12.4	3.3	0.0	9.0	2.3	2.0	66.6	8.8	2.7	5.1	3 337	3 267
Washington	376	1 063 217	7.0	4.3	0.0	6.6	18.3	6.1	55.7	29.9	10.0	12.3	2 144	1 966
Wichita	216	654 420	4.5	3.3	0.1	4.9	41.8	2.5	39.5	16.5	3.9	5.9	2 609	2 207
Wilson	601	1 662 978	4.6	6.7	0.8	4.2	19.9	9.3	49.8	43.5	17.0	11.6	1 274	1 131
Woodson	181	419 389	10.5	9.6	3.3	11.4	2.2	8.1	52.8	13.3	5.4	6.7	2 052	1 782
Wyandotte	8 144	34 012 450	5.6	11.1	6.6	2.6	2.4	14.3	54.4	766.0	289.0	302.6	1 901	1 204
KENTUCKY	X	X	X	X	X	X	X	X	X	X	X	X	X	X
Adair	919	2 441 497	2.9	3.7	0.0	1.1	35.9	4.2	51.1	55.9	21.6	8.0	427	308
Allen	767	1 841 667	2.0	8.2	0.2	1.6	4.0	4.1	78.7	41.3	23.7	11.2	555	342
Anderson	809	2 162 986	6.1	5.8	0.3	3.2	5.0	4.0	75.1	51.0	24.5	18.4	846	649
Ballard	248	590 155	9.9	12.4	0.0	2.7	9.1	4.7	61.1	23.3	12.4	8.2	986	597
Barren	1 664	5 001 627	2.5	3.2	0.0	0.8	0.2	25.7	67.1	124.1	60.3	35.4	831	508
Bath	406	1 111 046	4.3	4.3	0.9	1.2	4.3	5.5	79.0	26.0	18.6	5.0	425	253
Bell	1 171	3 090 979	2.7	6.2	2.6	2.0	1.9	1.6	81.4	75.8	50.5	15.0	534	291
Boone	3 843	13 434 279	1.9	8.5	6.9	1.7	0.4	3.4	75.6	360.0	112.7	201.9	1 637	990
Bourbon	965	3 068 260	6.3	8.4	5.9	2.9	15.6	4.1	55.9	56.7	29.4	20.5	1 028	562
Boyd	2 063	6 328 157	3.3	7.1	4.8	2.9	12.1	6.5	61.5	147.1	62.5	56.2	1 143	583
Boyle	1 287	4 095 739	3.9	9.0	16.6	1.6	5.9	2.0	59.3	83.9	32.8	34.1	1 190	651
Bracken	356	894 119	6.9	4.0	0.0	2.5	7.4	5.6	73.1	19.7	12.1	5.3	621	450
Breathitt	629	1 632 815	3.0	3.4	0.6	2.7	1.6	1.3	86.6	44.7	30.3	8.4	615	272
Breckinridge	636	1 726 384	4.2	7.6	0.0	2.7	3.3	0.7	81.4	49.9	26.8	10.3	513	381
Bullitt	2 379	7 126 688	1.5	7.4	2.5	1.5	4.1	1.8	80.6	162.7	71.4	70.4	927	693
Butler	426	1 274 899	3.6	4.6	0.0	4.2	0.0	5.4	82.2	27.2	19.3	5.9	459	211
Caldwell	534	1 550 863	4.7	6.1	2.3	3.5	12.5	10.7	58.9	23.5	15.7	6.2	481	274
Calloway	2 147	6 749 443	2.1	4.3	1.7	1.6	54.4	1.7	34.0	317.2	34.5	23.7	628	447
Campbell	2 562	8 812 479	5.0	13.2	6.5	2.9	0.4	2.0	69.5	232.7	71.5	119.3	1 312	806
Carlisle	229	547 363	15.5	2.7	0.0	3.0	7.2	0.5	71.2	13.3	8.5	2.9	573	399
Carroll	523	1 513 204	6.2	11.6	1.6	2.3	2.6	4.1	71.1	176.6	16.1	13.1	1 202	549
Carter	1 152	2 867 307	1.7	3.7	0.0	1.6	9.7	2.9	78.0	60.6	42.8	11.2	410	234
Casey	760	1 971 527	2.7	6.8	0.5	1.5	27.9	2.2	58.2	51.9	25.0	6.6	412	269
Christian	1 972	5 973 027	3.9	11.1	5.4	1.2	2.6	9.3	61.0	153.9	80.7	50.3	666	318
Clark	1 289	3 897 749	3.3	8.0	8.0	1.8	7.1	3.9	65.0	104.2	43.5	36.8	1 029	594

1. Based on the resident population estimated as of July 1 of the year shown.

STATE County	Local government finances, 2012 (cont.): Direct general expenditure: Total (mil dol)	Direct general expenditure: Per capita[1] (dollars)	Percent of total for: Education	Percent of total for: Health and hospitals	Percent of total for: Police protection	Percent of total for: Public welfare	Percent of total for: Highways	Debt outstanding: Total (mil dol)	Debt outstanding: Per capita[1] (dollars)	Government employment, 2013: Federal civilian	Government employment, 2013: Federal military	Government employment, 2013: State and local	Presidential election,[2] 2012: Percent of vote cast: Democratic	Presidential election,[2] 2012: Percent of vote cast: Republican	Presidential election,[2] 2012: Percent of vote cast: All other
	185	186	187	188	189	190	191	192	193	194	195	196	197	198	199
KANSAS—Cont'd															
Neosho	113.5	6 916	38.0	33.2	2.1	0.0	7.7	154.6	9 423	58	68	1 865	35.6	62.2	2.2
Ness	25.4	8 281	22.4	50.3	3.1	0.0	8.6	2.1	688	25	13	425	19.0	79.1	1.9
Norton	22.4	3 997	48.1	6.0	4.3	0.0	6.6	10.5	1 866	26	20	846	20.6	77.8	1.7
Osage	52.1	3 229	56.9	1.1	5.3	0.0	9.4	54.0	3 346	76	68	1 182	33.6	63.9	2.5
Osborne	12.6	3 304	32.2	8.6	8.0	0.0	13.4	3.3	875	28	16	338	20.9	77.2	1.9
Ottawa	26.4	4 347	50.1	4.7	3.2	0.0	13.3	17.8	2 933	24	25	442	22.8	75.3	1.9
Pawnee	26.1	3 762	43.8	6.6	5.2	0.0	13.5	27.5	3 968	39	25	1 834	30.6	67.6	1.8
Phillips	25.4	4 596	38.5	5.1	3.7	0.0	12.6	4.9	881	39	23	794	19.7	78.9	1.4
Pottawatomie	89.9	4 029	54.4	5.8	3.3	0.0	7.9	77.1	3 455	52	96	1 353	26.4	70.4	3.1
Pratt	49.1	5 044	57.5	3.6	5.0	0.0	9.2	35.4	3 643	30	40	1 194	30.9	67.4	1.8
Rawlins	10.8	4 225	35.7	5.3	4.3	0.0	11.1	4.4	1 700	18	11	333	17.6	80.5	1.9
Reno	245.7	3 812	58.1	2.1	5.1	0.0	4.6	208.5	3 236	168	259	5 335	37.4	60.8	1.8
Republic	23.3	4 788	35.1	4.3	3.0	0.0	14.7	7.7	1 591	32	20	507	24.0	74.1	2.0
Rice	56.5	5 654	43.4	25.1	2.5	0.0	7.7	50.8	5 088	42	40	1 068	28.9	69.1	1.9
Riley	230.8	3 057	51.3	0.7	7.0	0.0	6.1	524.1	6 941	474	318	11 006	45.6	52.7	1.7
Rooks	50.5	9 668	22.1	22.3	3.3	5.5	5.9	39.4	7 551	28	22	647	18.1	79.9	2.0
Rush	21.5	6 668	27.9	26.9	0.9	0.0	10.6	8.4	2 621	26	13	349	28.3	68.8	2.9
Russell	31.0	4 458	38.8	4.9	4.7	0.0	12.1	17.1	2 459	36	29	697	22.4	76.2	1.5
Saline	211.2	3 772	45.1	1.4	5.3	0.0	7.8	251.6	4 493	278	231	4 075	35.9	62.2	1.9
Scott	22.4	4 533	43.6	4.5	6.5	2.3	7.7	37.8	7 650	22	21	368	14.7	83.7	1.6
Sedgwick	1 940.5	3 851	46.8	4.2	5.7	0.1	5.3	5 893.5	11 696	5 004	5 023	25 588	42.7	55.4	1.8
Seward	172.9	7 343	40.9	33.7	2.9	0.0	2.5	86.1	3 658	86	97	2 286	28.0	71.0	1.0
Shawnee	739.9	4 134	52.9	2.2	6.5	0.2	2.7	1 291.7	7 217	3 439	1 009	19 071	49.0	49.3	1.7
Sheridan	9.9	3 891	38.8	11.7	2.2	0.0	16.8	0.6	238	15	11	332	18.5	80.5	1.0
Sherman	28.9	4 724	57.7	3.1	3.6	0.0	7.8	18.3	2 989	51	25	717	25.4	72.4	2.1
Smith	21.3	5 645	40.2	5.3	2.0	0.0	17.3	2.0	535	34	15	347	20.2	78.0	1.8
Stafford	24.7	5 668	48.8	4.4	4.1	0.0	14.9	2.2	513	38	18	644	26.1	72.1	1.8
Stanton	28.2	12 976	20.1	52.9	1.2	0.0	8.9	15.2	6 985	11	0	326	22.7	75.9	1.3
Stevens	55.6	9 664	30.0	27.7	3.3	0.0	8.1	24.5	4 259	24	24	738	13.3	85.3	1.4
Sumner	97.3	4 110	41.6	20.7	4.1	0.0	7.7	85.1	3 595	69	98	1 782	32.4	65.2	2.4
Thomas	47.7	6 010	55.4	1.6	2.9	0.0	9.6	33.5	4 224	30	32	1 004	21.4	77.2	1.3
Trego	13.1	4 381	37.4	4.9	2.1	0.6	14.1	16.4	5 487	16	12	459	25.1	73.3	1.6
Wabaunsee	25.0	3 546	48.3	1.1	3.9	0.0	12.8	27.4	3 889	27	29	483	29.4	68.0	2.6
Wallace	9.8	6 453	40.5	2.8	3.1	2.3	13.0	5.2	3 412	11	0	160	11.9	85.8	2.2
Washington	29.5	5 125	44.0	14.4	0.8	0.0	17.0	3.2	559	51	23	689	22.1	75.4	2.4
Wichita	16.8	7 467	32.0	38.6	3.0	0.0	8.8	7.0	3 099	12	0	280	16.0	82.4	1.6
Wilson	43.9	4 825	41.2	25.8	5.1	0.0	6.6	43.5	4 772	33	38	917	28.4	69.2	2.5
Woodson	12.5	3 824	43.4	1.9	6.1	0.0	13.6	2.8	845	13	13	269	32.0	66.0	2.0
Wyandotte	733.0	4 606	51.2	1.5	7.1	0.0	1.3	2 162.3	13 588	1 191	674	16 299	69.7	28.9	1.4
KENTUCKY	X	X	X	X	X	X	X	X	X	38 508	53 700	281 672	41.2	57.4	1.4
Adair	60.0	3 213	34.8	41.3	2.1	0.0	3.2	137.2	7 348	42	58	918	22.9	75.5	1.6
Allen	49.2	2 435	63.1	7.8	3.4	0.1	4.2	71.1	3 516	40	66	790	27.4	71.2	1.5
Anderson	51.5	2 370	63.4	5.7	3.7	0.0	3.5	69.4	3 192	36	71	963	32.8	65.2	1.9
Ballard	29.1	3 486	40.4	3.5	3.4	0.0	6.5	122.6	14 712	28	27	395	35.1	62.5	2.4
Barren	120.1	2 816	69.4	1.0	3.9	0.7	2.6	241.8	5 673	106	139	2 317	32.3	66.2	1.4
Bath	23.4	1 987	68.5	4.7	2.1	0.0	5.2	23.4	1 980	25	39	507	48.6	49.2	2.2
Bell	70.9	2 517	61.7	2.1	3.4	0.0	2.6	42.0	1 492	141	89	1 712	29.0	69.6	1.4
Boone	317.2	2 573	54.9	0.6	4.8	1.9	8.0	852.8	6 915	1 253	407	5 032	32.1	66.6	1.3
Bourbon	58.2	2 912	60.5	5.7	3.8	0.1	3.2	52.5	2 629	38	65	996	40.6	57.9	1.5
Boyd	151.0	3 072	52.9	5.0	3.7	0.0	4.0	303.6	6 176	426	153	3 299	43.0	55.3	1.7
Boyle	80.8	2 820	48.5	3.9	4.6	0.3	3.0	210.1	7 332	63	87	1 872	37.7	60.9	1.3
Bracken	19.5	2 296	59.4	6.5	3.2	0.0	7.7	14.9	1 758	20	28	420	36.5	60.8	2.7
Breathitt	41.9	3 073	57.4	8.4	3.1	0.0	7.9	24.9	1 827	55	43	1 027	43.8	53.1	3.1
Breckinridge	54.2	2 698	52.5	2.3	2.2	0.1	4.0	265.6	13 235	60	65	784	36.5	62.0	1.5
Bullitt	164.4	2 166	55.3	3.4	4.5	0.0	2.2	188.8	2 488	67	252	2 547	33.1	65.4	1.5
Butler	27.0	2 105	61.6	0.3	3.5	0.1	7.5	53.2	4 145	29	41	614	29.3	69.6	1.1
Caldwell	28.0	2 163	70.3	2.5	2.0	0.1	6.9	20.0	1 544	35	42	686	35.7	62.4	2.0
Calloway	176.1	4 676	22.2	62.3	2.8	0.0	1.6	108.2	2 874	74	114	5 376	40.0	58.4	1.6
Campbell	217.1	2 389	52.4	0.5	8.0	0.4	4.4	506.2	5 568	364	289	6 165	38.8	59.7	1.6
Carlisle	16.7	3 315	59.4	5.5	1.6	0.0	10.4	23.2	4 601	11	16	243	33.6	64.9	1.5
Carroll	170.1	15 605	12.4	0.6	0.8	0.0	1.2	3 066.5	281 328	34	35	719	44.8	53.0	2.3
Carter	66.1	2 418	70.9	4.9	3.9	0.0	3.5	99.7	3 647	58	87	1 274	44.0	53.5	2.5
Casey	49.1	3 053	40.2	33.9	1.5	0.0	4.4	63.3	3 935	25	51	701	20.5	78.5	1.0
Christian	164.3	2 178	52.4	3.1	7.2	0.2	3.3	420.2	5 571	4 719	30 693	3 815	39.0	60.1	0.9
Clark	108.6	3 033	59.0	5.7	3.5	0.1	2.7	125.2	3 499	96	116	1 575	36.8	61.8	1.4

1. Based on the resident population estimated as of July 1 of the year shown. 2.

STATE/ County code	CBSA code[1]	County type[2]	STATE County	Land area,[3] (sq km) 2010	Population, 2014: Total persons 2014	Population, 2014: Rank	Population, 2014: Per square kilometer	Population and population characteristics, 2013: Race alone or in combination, not Hispanic or Latino (percent): White	Black	American Indian, Alaska Native	Asian and Pacific Islander	Percent Hispanic or Latino[4]	Age (percent): Under 5 years	5 to 17 years	18 to 24 years	25 to 34 years	35 to 44 years	45 to 54 years
				1	2	3	4	5	6	7	8	9	10	11	12	13	14	15
			KENTUCKY—Cont'd															
21 051	...	7	Clay	1 215	21 147	1 766	17.4	93.5	4.6	0.6	0.3	2.0	6.1	15.0	8.8	14.9	15.0	14.6
21 053	...	9	Clinton	511	10 165	2 423	19.9	96.3	0.9	0.9	0.4	2.8	5.6	17.0	7.9	10.7	12.0	14.9
21 055	...	6	Crittenden	932	9 224	2 492	9.9	97.6	1.3	0.8	0.4	0.9	5.6	16.8	7.3	10.8	11.9	14.0
21 057	...	9	Cumberland	790	6 745	2 702	8.5	95.9	3.7	0.5	0.3	1.0	6.0	16.2	8.0	9.5	11.3	14.4
21 059	36980	3	Daviess	1 187	98 275	598	82.8	91.5	6.1	0.4	1.1	2.7	6.6	17.8	8.5	12.3	12.1	13.9
21 061	14540	3	Edmonson	784	12 013	2 298	15.3	96.6	2.1	0.8	0.4	1.0	4.8	15.2	9.0	11.2	12.4	14.1
21 063	...	9	Elliott	607	7 672	2 623	12.6	95.4	3.6	0.5	0.2	0.9	3.7	14.4	7.9	13.9	14.5	14.0
21 065	...	6	Estill	655	14 447	2 138	22.1	98.6	0.5	0.6	0.2	0.8	5.4	16.6	7.4	11.3	12.8	15.7
21 067	30460	2	Fayette	735	310 797	214	422.9	74.6	15.8	0.7	4.3	6.9	6.2	14.9	14.5	15.7	13.3	12.7
21 069	...	7	Fleming	903	14 545	2 133	16.1	97.0	1.9	0.5	0.3	1.2	6.4	17.5	8.1	11.0	13.1	14.4
21 071	...	7	Floyd	1 019	38 108	1 218	37.4	98.0	1.2	0.4	0.3	0.7	6.4	15.4	8.4	12.5	13.1	14.3
21 073	23180	4	Franklin	538	49 880	981	92.7	84.3	12.2	0.7	1.9	2.9	5.5	15.6	9.8	12.1	12.8	14.5
21 075	46460	7	Fulton	532	6 265	2 738	11.8	72.9	25.6	0.9	0.9	1.6	6.4	14.1	8.6	12.6	10.7	13.8
21 077	17140	1	Gallatin	262	8 589	2 552	32.8	92.8	2.4	0.6	0.5	5.2	6.5	19.5	8.5	11.4	13.1	15.9
21 079	...	6	Garrard	596	16 858	1 990	28.3	95.1	2.6	0.5	0.4	2.3	5.3	16.9	7.5	10.9	12.8	16.2
21 081	17140	1	Grant	668	24 875	1 613	37.2	96.0	1.4	0.7	0.7	2.5	7.5	20.1	8.7	12.4	13.4	14.2
21 083	32460	7	Graves	1 429	37 618	1 236	26.3	88.5	5.6	0.7	0.6	6.2	6.7	17.7	8.3	11.5	12.1	13.7
21 085	...	6	Grayson	1 286	26 194	1 554	20.4	97.2	1.5	0.7	0.5	1.2	6.0	17.5	8.3	11.7	12.7	14.0
21 087	...	8	Green	741	11 043	2 354	14.9	95.7	2.7	0.8	0.3	1.6	5.2	16.2	7.5	10.5	12.1	15.5
21 089	26580	2	Greenup	892	36 308	1 268	40.7	97.3	1.3	0.7	0.7	1.0	5.4	16.6	7.4	10.7	12.9	14.1
21 091	36980	3	Hancock	486	8 753	2 535	18.0	96.9	1.5	0.4	0.4	1.6	6.3	18.7	8.0	10.4	13.0	14.7
21 093	21060	3	Hardin	1 614	108 266	553	67.1	79.2	13.9	1.1	3.6	5.6	7.1	18.3	10.4	13.5	13.0	14.2
21 095	...	7	Harlan	1 206	28 163	1 485	23.4	96.2	2.7	0.6	0.6	0.8	6.6	15.9	8.4	12.0	12.2	14.1
21 097	...	6	Harrison	793	18 592	1 888	23.4	95.3	2.8	0.6	0.5	2.0	5.5	17.4	8.1	10.2	12.8	15.3
21 099	...	8	Hart	1 067	18 597	1 886	17.4	93.3	5.5	0.6	0.4	1.6	6.4	18.2	8.4	11.0	11.7	15.5
21 101	21780	2	Henderson	1 131	46 467	1 036	41.1	89.2	9.0	0.5	0.7	2.3	6.4	16.9	8.0	12.7	12.3	14.4
21 103	31140	1	Henry	741	15 572	2 069	21.0	93.5	3.7	1.0	0.5	3.0	6.2	17.9	7.6	10.8	12.6	14.7
21 105	...	9	Hickman	627	4 734	2 853	7.6	89.1	10.0	0.7	0.5	1.1	4.5	15.4	6.9	10.5	11.0	14.7
21 107	31580	4	Hopkins	1 404	46 376	1 043	33.0	90.7	7.9	0.6	0.8	1.8	6.0	16.8	8.0	11.8	12.4	14.0
21 109	...	9	Jackson	894	13 289	2 220	14.9	98.6	0.5	0.5	0.3	0.8	5.7	16.9	8.3	11.9	13.8	14.6
21 111	31140	1	Jefferson	985	760 026	80	771.6	71.5	22.3	0.7	3.0	4.7	6.5	16.3	8.9	14.3	12.8	13.9
21 113	30460	2	Jessamine	446	50 815	976	113.9	92.3	4.3	0.7	1.5	2.8	7.0	18.0	10.2	12.7	13.3	13.7
21 115	...	7	Johnson	678	23 262	1 674	34.3	98.4	0.7	0.5	0.6	0.6	6.1	16.3	8.3	11.7	13.4	14.5
21 117	17140	1	Kenton	415	163 929	388	395.0	91.0	5.9	0.5	1.6	2.8	7.1	17.5	8.5	14.8	13.0	14.2
21 119	...	9	Knott	910	15 892	2 049	17.5	98.2	1.0	0.5	0.3	0.8	5.4	15.2	10.0	10.9	12.6	15.8
21 121	30940	7	Knox	1 001	31 798	1 389	31.8	97.0	1.5	0.7	0.6	1.1	6.2	17.2	9.6	11.5	12.6	14.0
21 123	21060	3	Larue	677	14 180	2 156	20.9	93.2	3.9	0.8	0.6	3.1	5.3	17.2	8.0	12.0	11.9	15.1
21 125	30940	7	Laurel	1 124	60 015	867	53.4	97.0	1.2	0.8	0.7	1.4	6.2	17.4	8.2	12.6	13.6	14.3
21 127	...	6	Lawrence	1 076	15 804	2 055	14.7	98.6	0.8	0.6	0.4	0.7	6.7	16.5	8.2	11.6	13.0	14.6
21 129	...	9	Lee	541	7 594	2 634	14.0	96.8	2.1	0.7	0.4	0.9	4.4	15.2	7.9	13.1	13.0	16.5
21 131	...	9	Leslie	1 038	10 918	2 363	10.5	98.9	0.7	0.4	0.4	0.5	6.1	15.1	7.9	12.1	12.9	15.9
21 133	...	9	Letcher	875	23 359	1 669	26.7	98.4	0.7	0.4	0.3	0.7	6.3	15.4	7.3	12.0	12.8	14.7
21 135	...	8	Lewis	1 251	13 880	2 181	11.1	98.7	0.6	0.5	0.2	0.6	6.1	16.6	8.0	11.0	12.8	15.1
21 137	19220	7	Lincoln	865	24 445	1 629	28.3	95.7	2.9	0.8	0.3	1.6	6.1	17.6	7.9	11.4	13.0	14.5
21 139	37140	9	Livingston	811	9 359	2 481	11.5	97.2	0.9	0.9	0.6	1.4	5.3	14.6	7.4	10.2	11.4	15.3
21 141	...	6	Logan	1 430	26 867	1 541	18.8	90.1	7.7	0.6	0.6	2.7	5.9	18.0	8.1	11.7	11.8	14.5
21 143	...	8	Lyon	554	8 430	2 565	15.2	92.4	6.2	0.7	0.6	1.4	3.9	11.5	6.8	10.8	12.5	15.0
21 145	37140	5	McCracken	644	65 316	807	101.4	85.7	12.1	0.8	1.2	2.3	5.8	16.0	7.7	11.8	12.3	14.1
21 147	...	9	McCreary	1 105	17 863	1 922	16.2	91.1	6.1	1.4	0.4	2.4	5.9	15.8	9.2	13.7	14.7	14.6
21 149	36980	3	McLean	654	9 478	2 471	14.5	97.5	1.0	0.6	0.2	1.4	6.0	17.5	7.3	10.6	12.4	14.6
21 151	40080	4	Madison	1 133	87 340	658	77.1	91.9	5.4	0.9	1.5	2.2	5.7	15.5	17.3	12.1	12.8	12.8
21 153	...	9	Magoffin	799	12 913	2 237	16.2	98.5	0.5	0.6	0.2	0.8	5.6	17.3	8.2	11.4	13.7	15.7
21 155	...	6	Marion	888	20 007	1 836	22.5	88.1	9.6	0.5	0.9	2.5	6.2	17.6	8.3	13.4	13.1	14.8
21 157	...	7	Marshall	780	30 953	1 414	39.7	97.8	0.6	0.6	0.5	1.3	5.1	15.1	7.5	10.5	11.9	14.7
21 159	...	8	Martin	595	12 537	2 261	21.1	89.4	7.1	0.7	0.3	3.2	5.7	15.5	8.4	16.1	14.5	14.2
21 161	32500	6	Mason	622	17 166	1 974	27.6	91.1	7.6	0.6	0.9	1.5	6.3	17.5	8.0	11.1	12.4	14.5
21 163	21060	1	Meade	791	29 139	1 448	36.8	90.9	4.7	1.3	1.7	3.7	6.1	19.2	9.2	14.0	13.4	14.5
21 165	34460	9	Menifee	527	6 287	2 736	11.9	96.3	3.1	0.6	0.2	0.8	5.2	16.0	9.8	10.1	12.0	14.4
21 167	...	6	Mercer	644	21 319	1 761	33.1	93.3	4.6	0.7	0.8	2.3	6.7	16.2	7.8	10.6	11.8	14.9
21 169	23980	9	Metcalfe	750	9 990	2 440	13.3	96.4	2.1	0.5	0.4	1.5	6.8	17.0	8.2	11.0	11.4	14.6
21 171	...	9	Monroe	853	10 704	2 379	12.5	94.6	2.8	0.6	0.3	2.9	5.7	16.6	8.0	10.6	11.9	14.9
21 173	34460	6	Montgomery	511	27 474	1 513	53.8	93.9	3.3	0.5	0.5	2.7	6.6	17.6	8.2	12.4	14.3	14.0
21 175	...	7	Morgan	987	13 303	2 219	13.5	94.4	4.5	0.7	0.4	0.9	4.9	14.3	8.4	15.0	14.9	14.3
21 177	...	6	Muhlenberg	1 210	31 207	1 406	25.8	93.3	5.4	0.6	0.4	1.4	5.1	16.0	9.1	11.8	13.0	14.2
21 179	12680	1	Nelson	1 081	44 812	1 075	41.5	92.0	6.0	0.5	0.8	2.1	6.7	18.5	8.2	12.4	12.9	15.0
21 181	...	8	Nicholas	505	7 041	2 673	13.9	97.0	1.0	0.5	0.3	1.9	6.2	16.8	7.7	10.9	12.6	15.6

1. CBSA = Core Based Statistical Area. See Appendix A for explanation. See Appendix B for list of metropolitan areas with component counties. 2. County type code from the Economic Research Service of USDA Rural-Urban Continuum Codes. See Appendix A for definition. 3. Dry land or land partially or temporarily covered by water. 4. May be of any race.

STATE County	Population, 2013 (cont.) Age (percent) (cont.) 55 to 64 years	65 to 74 years	75 years and over	Percent female	Population change and components of change, 2000–2014 Total persons 2000	2010	Percent change 2000–2010	2010–2014	Components of change, 2010–2014 Births	Deaths	Net migration	Households, 2009–2013 Number	Persons per household	Percent Family households	Female family householder[1]	One person
	16	17	18	19	20	21	22	23	24	25	26	27	28	29	30	31
KENTUCKY—Cont'd																
Clay	12.3	8.2	5.0	46.9	24 556	21 730	-11.5	-2.7	1 211	1 113	-702	7 317	2.71	67.5	15.4	29.9
Clinton	14.1	10.7	7.2	50.4	9 634	10 272	6.6	-1.0	501	521	-80	3 960	2.54	65.3	11.4	33.4
Crittenden	14.6	11.2	7.8	49.6	9 384	9 315	-0.7	-1.0	439	497	-19	3 794	2.41	64.6	5.4	32.8
Cumberland	14.3	11.4	8.9	50.9	7 147	6 856	-4.1	-1.6	329	418	-9	2 604	2.59	65.6	12.0	31.4
Daviess	13.0	8.6	7.1	51.4	91 545	96 656	5.6	1.7	5 602	4 142	182	37 677	2.51	68.7	11.9	27.1
Edmonson	14.5	11.4	7.3	50.1	11 644	12 161	4.4	-1.2	427	546	-45	4 766	2.47	71.9	8.3	25.1
Elliott	13.8	10.8	7.2	43.6	6 748	7 852	16.4	-2.3	286	286	-189	2 618	2.59	67.7	13.3	26.6
Estill	14.0	10.5	6.2	50.6	15 307	14 672	-4.1	-1.5	670	724	-167	5 829	2.48	68.1	16.0	28.3
Fayette	11.4	6.5	4.9	50.9	260 512	295 803	13.5	5.1	16 952	8 808	7 021	123 142	2.34	58.3	12.8	32.3
Fleming	13.6	9.6	6.3	50.8	13 792	14 348	4.0	1.3	824	668	59	5 539	2.60	70.6	11.2	26.5
Floyd	14.7	9.3	5.9	51.3	42 441	39 451	-7.0	-3.4	2 229	2 253	-1 417	15 422	2.49	69.0	13.4	27.0
Franklin	14.1	9.2	6.4	51.8	47 687	49 285	3.4	1.2	2 328	2 072	294	21 058	2.25	60.6	13.3	33.5
Fulton	15.0	10.5	8.3	50.4	7 752	6 813	-12.1	-8.0	343	445	-452	2 744	2.30	64.9	13.3	33.6
Gallatin	12.8	8.2	4.1	49.5	7 870	8 589	9.1	0.0	481	340	-133	2 995	2.81	68.5	12.2	25.6
Garrard	14.5	9.6	6.4	50.8	14 792	16 912	14.3	-0.3	717	645	-108	6 302	2.66	76.0	11.1	22.2
Grant	11.7	7.7	4.4	49.9	22 384	24 662	10.2	0.9	1 498	884	-441	8 334	2.92	77.1	12.5	18.7
Graves	13.0	9.7	7.3	50.9	37 028	37 121	0.3	1.3	2 062	1 826	322	14 419	2.54	69.6	9.7	28.8
Grayson	13.9	9.5	6.5	49.7	24 053	25 746	7.0	1.7	1 407	1 296	360	9 897	2.57	68.7	8.4	27.6
Green	14.5	10.5	8.0	50.4	11 518	11 258	-2.3	-1.9	452	539	-124	4 495	2.47	71.7	12.4	26.5
Greenup	14.4	10.6	7.9	51.5	36 891	36 910	0.1	-1.6	1 639	1 874	-314	14 465	2.51	70.5	11.5	27.1
Hancock	13.0	10.1	5.8	48.6	8 392	8 565	2.1	2.2	461	352	82	3 361	2.53	77.7	13.7	20.5
Hardin	11.6	6.9	5.0	50.1	94 174	105 543	12.1	2.6	6 832	3 651	-561	39 401	2.60	71.8	13.6	24.4
Harlan	15.1	9.3	6.4	51.4	33 202	29 278	-11.8	-3.8	1 729	1 720	-1 122	11 343	2.51	70.9	15.1	26.2
Harrison	14.5	9.4	6.8	50.9	17 983	18 846	4.8	-1.4	829	902	-169	7 179	2.56	64.7	11.7	29.8
Hart	13.0	9.5	6.3	50.6	17 445	18 199	4.3	2.2	1 049	835	176	7 115	2.54	70.4	12.6	26.0
Henderson	14.1	8.9	6.4	51.5	44 829	46 250	3.2	0.5	2 423	2 078	-64	18 787	2.40	66.5	12.8	30.0
Henry	14.7	9.6	5.9	50.2	15 060	15 416	2.4	1.0	748	683	124	6 008	2.55	72.4	12.0	22.5
Hickman	13.9	12.2	11.0	52.4	5 262	4 902	-6.8	-3.4	183	278	-83	1 983	2.34	60.3	12.7	35.0
Hopkins	14.3	9.4	7.2	51.2	46 519	46 920	0.9	-1.2	2 305	2 403	-434	18 495	2.48	68.4	13.2	29.0
Jackson	13.9	9.4	5.6	50.3	13 495	13 494	0.0	-1.5	625	704	-124	5 712	2.33	69.8	15.0	26.8
Jefferson	13.2	7.7	6.4	51.7	693 604	741 096	6.8	2.6	42 551	30 657	8 124	305 832	2.39	61.4	15.3	32.4
Jessamine	12.1	7.4	5.5	51.3	39 041	48 586	24.4	4.6	2 770	1 581	981	18 012	2.63	74.6	12.8	19.6
Johnson	14.3	9.6	5.9	50.9	23 445	23 356	-0.4	-0.4	1 326	1 245	-134	9 154	2.50	72.5	12.0	24.8
Kenton	12.6	7.1	5.2	50.6	151 464	159 720	5.5	2.6	10 019	5 799	121	61 800	2.56	64.8	13.8	29.2
Knott	15.0	9.2	5.8	50.3	17 649	16 346	-7.4	-2.8	751	850	-337	5 892	2.63	69.0	11.9	27.0
Knox	12.4	10.2	6.3	51.5	31 795	31 883	0.3	-0.3	1 816	1 691	-317	12 350	2.53	66.7	14.0	30.2
Larue	13.9	9.1	7.7	50.4	13 373	14 193	6.1	-0.1	615	680	55	5 221	2.66	74.0	13.5	22.9
Laurel	13.2	8.8	5.6	51.1	52 715	58 849	11.6	2.0	3 055	2 452	538	22 931	2.55	73.6	13.5	22.1
Lawrence	14.3	9.4	5.7	50.1	15 569	15 860	1.9	-0.3	836	874	-44	5 823	2.70	71.0	12.2	25.9
Lee	14.6	9.1	6.1	47.2	7 916	7 887	-0.4	-3.7	318	420	-198	2 951	2.28	64.7	13.2	31.0
Leslie	14.3	9.2	6.3	50.7	12 401	11 310	-8.8	-3.5	620	699	-340	4 206	2.62	71.1	13.3	25.3
Letcher	15.5	9.7	6.2	50.6	25 277	24 519	-3.0	-4.7	1 189	1 318	-1 006	9 366	2.56	69.0	12.2	27.5
Lewis	14.1	10.0	6.3	50.3	14 092	13 870	-1.6	0.1	732	644	-68	5 003	2.74	72.6	12.6	22.6
Lincoln	13.3	9.4	6.8	50.9	23 361	24 742	5.9	-1.2	1 345	1 140	-487	9 692	2.52	71.2	12.8	25.6
Livingston	16.1	12.1	7.6	51.5	9 804	9 519	-2.9	-1.7	426	519	-79	3 569	2.62	74.7	9.2	23.6
Logan	13.1	10.0	6.8	51.0	26 573	26 835	1.0	0.1	1 535	1 203	-255	10 912	2.43	68.3	11.9	28.5
Lyon	16.5	14.3	8.8	44.4	8 080	8 314	2.9	1.3	273	454	292	3 294	2.12	57.8	8.2	37.1
McCracken	14.5	9.8	8.0	52.1	65 514	65 565	0.1	-0.4	3 276	3 365	-102	27 037	2.38	65.0	12.7	31.0
McCreary	12.3	8.7	5.0	45.6	17 080	18 306	7.2	-2.4	1 034	793	-688	6 312	2.57	71.8	10.9	26.2
McLean	13.2	10.9	7.5	50.2	9 938	9 531	-4.1	-0.6	526	495	-83	3 770	2.50	70.3	10.3	26.5
Madison	11.3	7.4	5.1	51.5	70 872	82 916	17.0	5.3	4 247	2 825	2 853	31 484	2.49	65.3	12.0	26.7
Magoffin	13.8	8.8	5.5	49.9	13 332	13 333	0.0	-3.2	641	620	-435	4 931	2.64	71.6	13.0	27.6
Marion	12.2	8.1	6.3	48.3	18 212	19 820	8.8	0.9	993	864	37	7 368	2.52	64.5	12.2	30.5
Marshall	14.7	11.9	8.6	50.9	30 125	31 448	4.4	-1.6	1 235	1 757	70	11 963	2.57	73.4	10.0	24.1
Martin	12.7	7.5	5.2	44.6	12 578	12 929	2.8	-3.0	598	608	-386	4 449	2.55	72.7	14.0	23.2
Mason	14.2	9.3	6.7	51.8	16 800	17 490	4.1	-1.9	923	776	-448	6 569	2.60	71.0	13.9	25.6
Meade	11.9	7.3	4.4	49.7	26 349	28 602	8.6	1.9	1 077	899	352	10 342	2.79	76.1	10.4	20.2
Menifee	14.6	11.0	7.0	49.5	6 556	6 306	-3.8	-0.3	305	296	-31	2 379	2.58	67.6	12.1	28.3
Mercer	14.3	10.4	7.2	51.0	20 817	21 331	2.5	-0.1	1 017	1 085	69	8 745	2.42	68.6	12.0	27.8
Metcalfe	13.6	9.7	7.7	50.7	10 037	10 099	0.6	-1.1	553	530	-142	3 919	2.53	69.3	7.4	27.1
Monroe	14.1	11.0	7.2	50.2	11 756	10 963	-6.7	-2.4	525	642	-134	4 401	2.43	65.1	12.5	29.1
Montgomery	12.8	8.5	5.7	51.4	22 554	26 499	17.5	3.7	1 701	1 111	372	10 168	2.59	66.6	12.6	27.1
Morgan	14.1	8.1	6.0	43.6	13 948	13 923	-0.2	-4.5	548	617	-560	4 697	2.54	74.6	12.1	21.1
Muhlenberg	13.5	10.3	7.2	49.3	31 839	31 499	-1.1	-0.9	1 407	1 602	-66	11 869	2.51	72.3	12.4	24.8
Nelson	13.2	7.9	5.1	50.7	37 477	43 437	15.9	3.2	2 533	1 510	374	16 571	2.62	73.4	12.6	22.6
Nicholas	13.3	9.6	7.3	50.4	6 813	7 135	4.7	-1.2	341	431	-3	2 884	2.42	68.4	13.5	26.1

1. No spouse present.

STATE County	Persons in group quarters, 2014	Daytime population, 2009–2013		Births, 2014		Deaths, 2014		Persons under 65 with no health insurance, 2013		Medicare, 2014			Serious crimes known to police,[2] 2013	
													Total	
		Number	Employment/residence ratio	Total	Rate[1]	Number	Rate[1]	Number	Percent	Eligible for Medicare	Enrolled in Medicare Advantage	Enrolled in a Medicare prescription drug plan	Number	Rate[3]
	32	33	34	35	36	37	38	39	40	41	42	43	44	45
KENTUCKY—Cont'd														
Clay	2 095	20 799	0.84	266	12.6	226	10.7	3 036	18.4	4 752	805	3 207	99	460
Clinton	136	11 072	1.25	118	11.6	109	10.7	1 677	20.3	2 536	414	1 676	0	0
Crittenden	210	8 125	0.66	111	12.0	96	10.4	1 454	19.9	2 184	385	1 211	75	808
Cumberland	86	6 498	0.86	73	10.8	111	16.5	1 131	20.9	1 677	359	1 055	62	910
Daviess	2 506	98 618	1.03	1 324	13.5	985	10.0	11 327	14.0	20 382	3 880	11 827	2 709	2 756
Edmonson	354	9 567	0.41	96	8.0	141	11.7	2 113	21.7	2 759	610	1 587	61	506
Elliott	1 061	7 174	0.68	76	9.9	62	8.1	1 045	19.8	1 597	519	792	12	155
Estill	118	12 353	0.50	151	10.5	172	11.9	2 344	19.6	3 436	741	1 997	55	381
Fayette	12 818	332 934	1.21	4 004	12.9	2 097	6.7	44 183	16.9	43 011	12 628	20 448	14 338	4 644
Fleming	22	12 541	0.67	204	14.0	162	11.1	2 664	21.9	3 359	804	1 886	91	622
Floyd	673	39 261	0.98	508	13.3	532	14.0	5 809	17.9	10 426	2 562	6 073	142	368
Franklin	1 911	59 651	1.47	553	11.1	476	9.5	6 936	17.2	12 245	4 362	6 223	1 716	3 431
Fulton	445	6 875	1.10	71	11.3	94	15.0	813	17.0	1 683	217	1 086	NA	NA
Gallatin	85	7 268	0.64	111	12.9	71	8.3	1 407	19.0	1 114	316	534	95	1 173
Garrard	109	12 759	0.40	166	9.8	164	9.7	2 792	19.8	3 621	875	1 849	141	833
Grant	457	20 930	0.63	339	13.6	214	8.6	3 489	16.4	4 826	1 525	2 032	203	831
Graves	552	34 491	0.81	469	12.5	403	10.7	6 142	20.1	8 276	1 952	4 589	533	1 439
Grayson	768	24 609	0.88	348	13.3	271	10.3	4 372	20.7	5 662	937	3 543	382	1 503
Green	113	9 051	0.49	104	9.4	123	11.1	1 985	21.9	2 771	524	1 675	36	317
Greenup	454	32 345	0.66	377	10.4	454	12.5	4 978	16.9	9 292	2 307	5 091	174	501
Hancock	90	9 590	1.27	108	12.3	81	9.3	1 010	13.9	1 806	297	915	25	287
Hardin	3 255	112 884	1.14	1 564	14.4	890	8.2	13 658	14.9	17 007	2 445	6 994	2 086	1 948
Harlan	627	29 452	1.05	409	14.5	390	13.8	4 607	19.4	7 254	1 328	4 239	185	653
Harrison	275	16 226	0.67	192	10.3	201	10.8	2 753	17.9	3 882	989	2 039	499	2 687
Hart	227	17 094	0.82	239	12.9	185	9.9	3 206	20.7	3 939	679	2 407	28	152
Henderson	1 165	45 271	0.95	556	12.0	512	11.0	5 856	15.2	9 350	2 464	4 843	1 290	2 767
Henry	80	12 065	0.50	159	10.2	153	9.8	2 311	17.8	3 206	1 003	1 624	45	327
Hickman	212	4 783	0.97	39	8.2	73	15.4	659	18.8	1 289	207	822	22	466
Hopkins	1 086	46 745	1.00	526	11.3	531	11.4	6 225	16.3	10 216	2 201	5 648	702	1 503
Jackson	110	11 534	0.56	145	10.9	145	10.9	2 354	20.8	2 935	544	1 851	89	670
Jefferson	14 939	826 053	1.23	9 986	13.1	7 169	9.4	101 551	15.9	135 865	38 412	69 696	35 901	4 765
Jessamine	1 753	44 981	0.81	640	12.6	365	7.2	7 337	17.5	8 119	2 288	3 877	1 558	3 117
Johnson	533	22 003	0.81	334	14.4	286	12.3	3 452	17.8	5 736	1 321	3 274	205	876
Kenton	2 506	147 513	0.83	2 364	14.4	1 377	8.4	19 950	14.1	25 545	8 375	10 790	4 404	2 711
Knott	791	14 781	0.71	177	11.1	183	11.5	2 402	18.4	3 789	950	2 221	34	230
Knox	652	31 617	0.97	455	14.3	417	13.1	5 178	19.8	7 525	1 243	4 955	267	842
Larue	313	11 895	0.57	145	10.2	149	10.5	2 229	19.5	3 061	623	1 708	73	516
Laurel	699	60 846	1.08	717	11.9	598	10.0	9 275	18.4	12 857	2 462	7 528	692	1 160
Lawrence	108	14 584	0.75	187	11.8	202	12.8	2 425	18.1	3 821	679	2 258	131	827
Lee	1 017	7 505	0.98	80	10.5	102	13.4	1 012	18.3	1 750	354	1 120	23	300
Leslie	227	10 456	0.74	141	12.9	162	14.8	1 716	18.8	2 829	579	1 670	17	158
Letcher	243	23 021	0.84	244	10.4	283	12.1	3 434	17.4	6 010	1 356	3 375	67	282
Lewis	139	11 512	0.51	174	12.5	141	10.2	2 390	20.9	2 840	557	1 798	43	311
Lincoln	219	20 720	0.56	316	12.9	264	10.8	4 249	21.0	5 544	1 340	2 963	88	381
Livingston	69	8 246	0.65	104	11.1	115	12.3	1 402	18.8	2 447	408	1 329	107	1 139
Logan	277	25 275	0.85	384	14.3	272	10.1	4 288	19.4	5 751	1 035	3 544	431	1 620
Lyon	1 219	7 608	0.71	65	7.7	124	14.7	967	18.0	2 240	541	1 130	65	776
McCracken	1 189	76 048	1.37	760	11.6	824	12.6	8 140	15.4	15 036	2 801	8 201	1 742	2 655
McCreary	2 023	17 176	0.79	245	13.7	164	9.2	2 890	20.8	3 833	718	2 425	81	450
McLean	82	7 834	0.56	125	13.2	111	11.7	1 362	17.7	2 217	556	1 126	39	410
Madison	6 247	81 209	0.93	1 015	11.6	658	7.5	11 157	16.1	14 410	4 233	7 309	2 580	3 021
Magoffin	127	12 370	0.74	145	11.2	145	11.2	2 228	20.2	3 009	655	1 811	22	170
Marion	1 326	20 414	1.06	229	11.4	187	9.3	2 656	16.6	3 747	726	2 364	201	1 010
Marshall	464	29 847	0.89	289	9.3	420	13.6	3 951	16.2	8 050	1 577	4 245	358	1 143
Martin	1 655	13 170	1.12	129	10.3	151	12.0	1 608	16.9	2 804	612	1 658	69	543
Mason	298	19 271	1.25	220	12.8	180	10.5	2 362	16.6	3 786	918	2 136	553	3 154
Meade	212	22 843	0.46	234	8.0	200	6.9	4 409	17.3	4 716	827	2 240	215	730
Menifee	276	5 494	0.59	72	11.5	83	13.2	1 181	23.0	1 642	571	816	50	807
Mercer	128	19 506	0.80	220	10.3	258	12.1	2 869	16.4	4 809	1 294	2 326	331	1 631
Metcalfe	121	8 682	0.65	125	12.5	133	13.3	1 729	21.1	2 347	698	1 235	72	725
Monroe	143	10 170	0.83	126	11.8	152	14.2	1 896	21.8	2 686	515	1 759	10	95
Montgomery	357	27 688	1.09	409	14.9	260	9.5	4 302	18.6	5 529	1 594	2 858	896	3 313
Morgan	1 791	13 021	0.84	121	9.1	152	11.4	1 834	18.8	2 821	805	1 534	NA	NA
Muhlenberg	2 100	30 115	0.88	330	10.6	406	13.0	4 419	18.2	7 415	1 371	4 304	178	572
Nelson	496	40 458	0.82	602	13.4	377	8.4	6 288	16.4	8 427	1 664	4 921	560	1 256
Nicholas	95	5 600	0.53	72	10.2	112	15.9	1 250	21.5	1 607	331	940	40	574

1. Per 1,000 estimated resident population. 2. Data for serious crimes have not been adjusted for underreporting; this may affect comparability between geographic areas and over time.
3. Per 100,000 population estimated by the FBI.

Table B. States and Counties — **Crime, Education, Money Income, and Poverty**

STATE County	Serious crimes known to police, 2013 (cont.)[1] Rate[2] Violent	Rate[2] Property	Education: School enrollment and attainment, 2009–2013: Enrollment[3] Total	Enrollment[3] Percent private	Attainment[4] (percent) High school graduate or less	Attainment[4] (percent) Bachelor's degree or more	Local government expenditures,[5] 2012–2013: Total current spending (mil dol)	Current spending per student (dollars)	Money income, 2009–2013: Per capita income[6] (dollars)	Households: Median income (dollars)	Households: Mean income (dollars)	Households: Percent with income of $200,000 or more	Income and poverty, 2013: Median household income (dollars)	Percent below poverty level: All persons	Children under 18 years	Children 5 to 17 years in families
	46	47	48	49	50	51	52	53	54	55	56	57	58	59	60	61
KENTUCKY—Cont'd																
Clay	46	414	4 631	4.6	74.3	9.0	34.6	10 026	13 542	21 883	34 192	0.3	24 173	42.8	52.5	50.8
Clinton	0	0	2 356	4.2	68.3	7.0	18.4	10 117	16 795	27 100	40 274	2.5	27 443	27.6	41.2	36.3
Crittenden	65	744	1 704	6.7	61.8	11.4	11.7	8 670	21 375	34 261	51 896	0.9	37 372	22.2	34.1	31.9
Cumberland	29	881	1 579	16.9	62.6	13.9	10.0	9 690	17 697	31 593	41 878	1.1	30 043	26.2	40.3	38.3
Daviess	158	2 598	24 992	18.3	51.2	18.8	150.3	9 248	22 963	46 555	57 533	1.8	46 908	15.3	21.4	18.8
Edmonson	25	481	2 702	4.2	66.7	9.8	17.7	8 761	19 481	37 646	48 484	1.0	36 324	21.2	29.3	27.7
Elliott	13	142	1 413	7.3	68.8	7.7	10.0	9 417	14 040	24 246	34 925	0.2	29 544	33.1	38.1	32.9
Estill	14	367	3 091	7.7	72.5	8.3	23.2	9 050	16 435	29 184	39 467	0.4	30 388	28.1	40.3	36.5
Fayette	313	4 331	89 799	15.2	32.1	40.1	465.6	10 755	29 251	48 398	69 728	4.5	47 959	19.0	21.8	20.7
Fleming	14	608	3 439	8.8	61.9	12.8	23.2	9 984	19 304	32 495	49 119	1.7	35 454	23.2	32.1	30.1
Floyd	36	331	8 189	7.9	60.6	12.8	61.4	9 547	17 716	30 476	43 964	1.0	31 229	30.6	37.9	37.2
Franklin	192	3 239	11 445	10.6	47.0	26.8	64.2	8 997	26 243	46 071	60 881	1.9	46 309	16.9	24.2	23.7
Fulton	NA	NA	1 385	6.9	61.6	13.1	11.6	11 532	18 602	33 582	42 749	0.0	28 550	29.2	45.6	45.1
Gallatin	25	1 148	2 063	4.5	68.2	8.8	14.9	8 857	19 020	43 793	52 185	0.9	44 142	16.3	24.5	22.2
Garrard	30	804	3 940	7.6	59.5	15.2	22.5	8 523	21 341	44 652	55 154	1.1	42 853	19.3	28.7	26.9
Grant	16	814	6 500	11.2	60.0	10.9	42.5	8 592	19 829	46 159	57 294	1.1	43 861	20.1	27.9	26.7
Graves	154	1 285	8 936	9.7	55.4	16.9	56.0	8 634	20 746	38 394	51 599	1.5	39 960	19.3	28.7	26.3
Grayson	79	1 424	6 193	9.6	65.9	9.5	36.4	8 342	19 115	32 399	47 379	1.2	32 813	25.1	34.6	31.0
Green	26	291	2 428	13.1	69.1	12.0	16.3	9 287	17 984	34 406	43 927	0.8	32 309	23.1	31.6	28.2
Greenup	43	458	8 199	7.9	52.5	15.7	53.5	8 521	22 035	44 060	54 900	1.6	44 581	19.0	25.7	23.6
Hancock	57	229	2 139	5.8	60.4	11.5	16.1	9 548	22 686	51 189	57 977	1.2	50 809	15.4	19.3	18.4
Hardin	101	1 847	28 684	13.0	45.3	20.8	149.2	8 715	24 147	48 687	62 226	2.1	48 327	14.4	20.3	19.8
Harlan	92	561	6 420	5.3	65.0	10.6	45.6	8 811	16 257	25 906	40 086	0.5	25 460	30.5	36.6	36.3
Harrison	108	2 579	4 432	8.2	58.8	14.2	26.1	8 399	21 424	36 048	52 551	1.1	42 228	17.4	25.1	23.0
Hart	16	136	4 101	11.5	70.4	8.8	22.9	9 321	17 273	33 408	44 481	0.8	33 588	27.9	37.5	35.6
Henderson	165	2 601	10 677	11.5	52.7	16.4	70.5	9 382	22 746	41 940	54 966	1.9	42 492	19.5	28.1	24.5
Henry	29	298	3 686	7.5	65.3	12.8	24.8	8 483	21 923	46 016	56 413	2.1	48 245	15.4	23.2	20.9
Hickman	0	466	1 093	7.8	57.8	10.3	8.4	10 269	19 292	34 029	44 002	0.4	38 733	19.8	30.5	26.7
Hopkins	96	1 407	10 540	7.4	56.4	14.2	69.4	8 860	22 132	40 891	53 690	1.3	40 782	17.5	26.4	24.8
Jackson	8	663	2 995	5.5	75.2	8.2	23.9	10 090	15 880	26 156	37 158	0.6	28 759	30.3	42.9	39.7
Jefferson	510	4 255	188 412	23.9	39.9	30.4	1 143.9	11 361	27 925	46 959	66 544	3.8	47 495	16.1	22.3	20.7
Jessamine	176	2 941	13 380	28.7	44.3	27.4	68.9	8 664	25 637	49 024	68 491	3.7	52 011	15.4	21.8	20.1
Johnson	47	829	5 234	5.8	66.4	10.2	44.5	9 631	19 445	34 090	49 443	1.3	34 593	25.7	32.7	30.2
Kenton	225	2 486	41 893	21.9	41.3	29.1	208.9	9 035	27 704	54 270	69 687	3.7	53 949	13.4	19.7	18.1
Knott	0	230	3 680	19.7	66.7	13.0	26.7	10 489	18 448	33 889	47 379	0.7	32 294	28.3	38.3	36.5
Knox	73	769	7 571	8.0	73.5	10.1	52.6	10 056	14 367	24 038	35 764	0.8	26 220	35.2	49.4	48.3
Larue	21	495	3 377	9.0	64.2	11.1	21.4	8 930	19 611	39 753	51 076	1.4	41 537	18.3	27.1	25.2
Laurel	80	1 079	13 590	8.2	61.9	12.6	81.9	8 170	19 923	36 570	51 061	1.6	35 372	22.2	31.4	29.1
Lawrence	50	776	3 366	8.1	65.2	10.8	22.7	8 996	17 960	33 525	45 429	0.6	33 469	25.2	32.2	30.7
Lee	26	274	1 486	5.9	71.0	5.6	10.6	9 861	13 969	22 920	34 157	0.3	25 767	35.1	50.0	44.2
Leslie	46	111	2 405	9.9	70.3	7.3	19.2	10 022	16 424	29 293	40 722	0.7	29 008	29.2	37.3	37.2
Letcher	4	278	4 965	6.3	61.8	11.5	38.0	9 846	17 886	31 200	43 987	0.5	31 799	27.1	34.4	33.0
Lewis	14	296	3 157	5.8	68.6	10.6	21.3	8 775	16 132	28 388	41 931	0.6	30 443	27.0	39.3	37.9
Lincoln	35	346	5 427	8.4	69.3	9.6	37.9	9 261	17 420	33 651	43 743	0.7	35 092	23.1	31.4	29.7
Livingston	43	1 097	1 968	16.4	62.0	11.3	12.4	9 626	19 795	40 313	49 810	0.8	41 177	15.9	22.8	21.5
Logan	109	1 511	6 004	6.5	62.7	13.3	41.8	8 889	19 143	36 590	47 006	0.8	39 513	19.7	28.1	25.9
Lyon	0	776	1 312	7.5	56.4	13.3	8.1	9 022	22 123	40 112	52 599	0.9	43 311	17.4	22.8	21.1
McCracken	172	2 483	15 089	14.9	44.7	22.5	90.0	8 982	25 957	44 898	60 932	2.4	42 069	19.8	28.7	28.5
McCreary	28	422	4 103	5.8	67.8	7.3	29.9	9 678	11 818	20 972	31 654	0.0	24 406	40.7	52.6	47.6
McLean	11	400	2 273	10.2	59.6	10.3	14.7	8 810	19 984	38 833	49 156	1.1	38 128	18.1	24.8	23.2
Madison	139	2 881	26 821	14.6	45.1	28.0	103.9	8 309	21 800	42 312	56 134	2.0	44 845	19.8	22.9	20.8
Magoffin	23	147	3 009	5.1	70.2	8.9	21.6	9 303	15 118	26 877	37 436	0.3	29 817	29.0	39.5	36.2
Marion	55	955	4 735	12.2	64.4	12.5	28.6	8 926	18 865	38 719	49 250	1.5	39 665	18.5	26.2	24.6
Marshall	48	1 095	6 576	9.7	56.5	15.3	42.2	8 761	22 381	43 907	55 183	1.2	44 157	12.7	18.9	17.3
Martin	16	527	2 625	1.6	63.6	7.5	22.2	9 936	15 525	26 261	41 078	0.6	26 931	40.5	46.0	42.6
Mason	108	3 046	3 987	7.5	57.2	14.8	26.4	9 004	23 347	41 137	60 174	2.8	42 329	20.7	31.0	27.6
Meade	41	689	7 823	6.5	53.3	12.7	41.7	8 141	20 898	46 756	57 015	0.6	45 984	15.4	21.4	19.3
Menifee	16	791	1 488	3.4	65.2	12.1	11.4	10 187	15 942	29 108	39 818	0.0	30 047	28.3	46.0	42.9
Mercer	113	1 518	5 132	15.2	53.9	18.9	30.1	8 616	24 138	45 396	56 949	1.9	43 903	16.4	23.7	22.7
Metcalfe	40	685	2 115	14.9	73.1	8.6	16.9	10 384	17 171	31 750	42 373	1.0	30 899	27.7	41.1	39.7
Monroe	28	66	2 556	5.7	69.5	12.0	19.7	10 197	16 656	29 808	40 533	0.5	29 900	23.8	35.8	32.7
Montgomery	107	3 206	6 166	4.8	60.7	14.6	42.0	8 797	20 436	37 312	51 926	1.8	41 326	20.0	26.1	25.2
Morgan	NA	NA	2 766	5.6	67.2	11.5	19.5	9 415	16 233	30 658	44 560	0.3	31 579	29.4	37.5	33.6
Muhlenberg	48	524	7 035	5.9	62.2	11.3	54.5	10 342	20 008	38 105	50 162	1.1	37 048	25.1	35.0	32.3
Nelson	56	1 200	11 055	18.9	56.0	16.6	65.5	8 711	23 545	43 833	61 104	2.4	49 444	14.7	20.0	18.5
Nicholas	57	517	1 552	17.5	58.9	13.7	9.4	8 022	20 450	43 081	49 445	0.1	37 006	20.6	31.5	30.0

1. Data for serious crimes have not been adjusted for underreporting; this may affect comparability between geographic areas and over time. 2. Per 100,000 population estimated by the FBI.
3. All persons 3 years old and over enrolled in nursery school through college. 4. Persons 25 years old and over. 5. Elementary and secondary education expenditures.
6. Based on population estimated by the American Community Survey, 2009–2013.

STATE County	Personal income, 2013										Earnings, 2013		
			Per capita[1]			Supplements to wages and salaries; employer contributions (mil dol)						Contributions for government social insurance (mil dol)	
	Total (mil dol)	Percent change, 2012–2013	Dollars	Rank	Wages and salaries (mil dol)	Pension and insurance	Government social insurance	Proprietors' income (mil dol)	Dividends, interest, and rent (mil dol)	Personal transfer receipts (mil dol)	Total (mil dol)	From employee and self-employed	From employer
	62	63	64	65	66	67	68	69	70	71	72	73	74
KENTUCKY—Cont'd													
Clay	540	-0.2	25 255	3 046	141	38	11	23	55	262	213	17	11
Clinton	285	1.9	28 094	2 886	112	27	9	19	36	116	168	12	9
Crittenden	289	3.7	31 277	2 513	63	15	5	33	37	89	116	8	5
Cumberland	191	2.8	28 132	2 882	54	12	4	10	26	83	80	6	4
Daviess	3 860	2.7	39 296	1 254	1 693	340	128	337	740	867	2 498	148	128
Edmonson	354	1.0	29 360	2 769	50	15	4	16	43	110	86	7	4
Elliott	160	0.8	20 904	3 104	27	10	2	0	17	70	39	4	2
Estill	361	0.6	24 894	3 057	78	19	7	8	43	153	112	10	7
Fayette	13 063	1.9	42 353	900	8 394	1 573	628	1 307	2 417	2 011	11 902	658	628
Fleming	401	1.9	27 628	2 922	102	27	8	28	60	131	164	12	8
Floyd	1 248	-1.4	32 230	2 379	431	88	33	144	134	490	697	50	33
Franklin	1 961	1.1	39 501	1 232	1 289	343	90	82	337	474	1 804	97	90
Fulton	224	8.2	35 079	1 886	82	18	7	49	36	73	156	8	7
Gallatin	259	2.0	30 621	2 609	103	19	8	7	24	58	138	9	8
Garrard	479	2.0	28 317	2 864	70	18	5	39	67	138	132	11	5
Grant	768	1.8	31 040	2 545	168	36	13	33	83	201	250	19	13
Graves	1 222	5.8	32 623	2 308	391	80	30	180	177	347	681	39	30
Grayson	712	2.1	27 386	2 947	241	55	20	54	103	231	369	25	20
Green	328	1.6	29 345	2 772	57	16	4	36	47	116	113	8	4
Greenup	1 396	0.2	38 214	1 409	335	63	30	43	151	392	472	38	30
Hancock	311	3.3	35 754	1 788	285	44	21	42	35	66	392	23	21
Hardin	4 299	1.0	39 735	1 197	2 454	616	215	354	858	812	3 638	184	215
Harlan	783	-4.0	27 476	2 939	283	60	21	20	100	359	384	29	21
Harrison	592	1.0	31 954	2 414	185	39	14	36	89	149	275	19	14
Hart	507	1.6	27 315	2 955	157	34	13	36	80	161	239	17	13
Henderson	1 620	4.0	34 958	1 903	738	139	59	146	243	383	1 082	63	59
Henry	512	1.2	33 146	2 235	107	25	8	25	81	128	165	12	8
Hickman	225	17.0	47 448	515	32	8	2	86	28	50	128	4	2
Hopkins	1 617	2.0	34 670	1 962	746	140	58	111	230	419	1 055	66	58
Jackson	288	0.3	21 478	3 102	65	19	5	6	35	128	95	8	5
Jefferson	33 315	0.9	44 018	755	21 877	3 285	1 689	3 301	6 246	5 984	30 151	1 807	1 689
Jessamine	1 714	1.4	34 159	2 054	578	105	47	116	271	318	845	53	47
Johnson	664	-0.4	28 304	2 865	199	44	15	29	86	264	288	22	15
Kenton	6 814	1.4	41 766	963	3 079	538	232	386	1 030	1 085	4 235	257	232
Knott	431	-3.1	26 962	2 973	93	22	7	20	42	197	142	12	7
Knox	858	0.0	26 996	2 971	244	56	20	96	91	357	417	31	20
Larue	533	1.5	37 924	1 443	79	19	6	39	75	119	143	10	6
Laurel	1 724	0.9	28 937	2 811	843	152	71	121	207	542	1 187	79	71
Lawrence	443	1.2	27 969	2 903	123	26	10	16	43	172	174	14	10
Lee	185	0.1	25 446	3 039	54	13	4	5	19	85	76	6	4
Leslie	296	-4.3	26 861	2 978	74	17	5	14	26	144	110	9	5
Letcher	646	-5.2	27 354	2 952	184	38	14	39	62	287	275	22	14
Lewis	315	2.3	22 839	3 094	63	16	5	22	35	128	105	9	5
Lincoln	665	1.5	27 307	2 956	138	32	11	36	83	221	217	17	11
Livingston	327	1.9	34 960	1 901	125	22	10	24	43	93	182	12	10
Logan	926	5.6	34 450	1 999	328	62	26	162	126	230	578	33	26
Lyon	262	2.0	30 995	2 549	65	20	5	19	45	81	108	7	5
McCracken	2 741	0.7	41 934	944	1 591	287	124	223	528	605	2 226	136	124
McCreary	392	1.3	21 806	3 099	97	29	8	14	50	199	147	12	8
McLean	358	13.7	37 658	1 479	71	14	6	84	40	87	175	8	6
Madison	2 639	1.4	30 835	2 571	1 247	273	99	144	378	613	1 763	106	99
Magoffin	328	-0.3	25 349	3 044	68	17	5	17	37	157	108	9	5
Marion	594	2.5	29 636	2 737	274	50	25	31	84	157	379	24	25
Marshall	1 118	1.8	35 946	1 756	511	94	40	75	178	297	720	47	40
Martin	330	-0.5	26 110	3 023	127	29	9	13	32	143	177	13	9
Mason	601	4.4	34 811	1 928	338	67	27	39	103	147	471	29	27
Meade	1 163	-0.2	39 811	1 188	151	36	12	46	175	204	245	17	12
Menifee	151	0.9	24 078	3 078	28	8	2	3	19	67	42	4	2
Mercer	693	1.7	32 452	2 345	282	49	22	43	109	179	397	26	22
Metcalfe	243	1.5	24 351	3 072	62	16	5	12	32	96	95	7	5
Monroe	300	0.5	28 076	2 888	91	21	7	28	39	116	148	10	7
Montgomery	804	1.7	29 501	2 751	411	77	36	44	109	217	567	37	36
Morgan	321	0.0	23 998	3 082	105	29	8	14	39	124	156	11	8
Muhlenberg	925	0.9	29 669	2 730	398	84	32	59	133	294	573	38	32
Nelson	1 568	3.0	35 201	1 872	545	103	45	102	219	323	795	50	45
Nicholas	213	0.4	30 236	2 650	29	8	2	8	24	70	47	4	2

1. Based on the resident population estimated as of July 1 of the year shown.

STATE County	Earnings, 2013 (cont.) Percent by selected industries: Farm	Mining	Construction	Manu-facturing	Infor-mation: professional, scientific, technical services	Retail trade	Finance, insur-ance, real estate and leasing	Health care and social assistance	Govern-ment	Social Security beneficiaries, December 2013: Number	Rate[1]	Supple-mental Security Income recipients, December 2013	Housing units, 2014: Total	Percent change, 2010–2014
	75	76	77	78	79	80	81	82	83	84	85	86	87	88
KENTUCKY—Cont'd														
Clay	0.4	1.3	4.0	0.7	2.7	9.9	2.2	D	45.1	5 420	255	3 495	8 860	-0.2
Clinton	3.2	D	4.4	34.3	1.1	4.7	2.3	D	18.3	2 835	280	920	5 250	-1.2
Crittenden	17.4	D	D	20.3	4.3	5.9	4.1	12.8	16.7	2 505	272	287	4 553	-0.4
Cumberland	2.2	D	D	9.2	D	6.6	4.1	30.1	21.5	1 900	279	489	3 652	-1.0
Daviess	3.7	0.6	4.7	14.9	D	7.6	8.5	9.2	22.2	22 915	233	3 676	42 541	2.6
Edmonson	3.4	0.0	11.6	D	D	5.8	D	D	45.2	3 125	259	585	6 452	-0.2
Elliott	-8.1	0.0	3.5	0.0	D	4.9	D	11.7	69.3	1 815	236	642	3 361	-0.3
Estill	-1.6	D	4.0	D	3.3	8.3	3.8	18.5	31.6	3 680	254	1 327	6 848	-0.2
Fayette	0.7	1.4	5.9	8.7	11.5	6.4	6.1	11.2	24.5	45 035	146	6 717	138 827	2.7
Fleming	2.9	D	5.8	12.2	2.3	9.8	5.0	8.2	31.8	3 845	264	751	6 608	-0.3
Floyd	0.0	D	5.8	0.8	9.9	7.0	2.9	15.9	18.9	12 425	323	4 259	18 154	-0.1
Franklin	0.1	D	3.5	8.7	5.6	4.6	4.2	7.3	52.0	13 620	274	3 209	23 201	0.2
Fulton	24.0	D	3.7	11.4	D	8.6	2.8	D	17.1	1 840	288	449	3 363	-0.3
Gallatin	0.4	D	2.4	D	D	4.3	1.2	4.7	16.9	1 325	156	233	3 832	1.2
Garrard	3.2	0.0	D	8.0	4.6	5.6	3.8	8.5	25.4	4 090	242	740	7 460	-0.1
Grant	-1.6	0.0	6.0	13.4	5.4	12.4	4.4	D	26.4	5 600	228	851	9 951	0.1
Graves	17.8	D	4.0	11.6	3.3	7.4	3.4	D	16.0	9 315	249	1 576	16 747	-0.2
Grayson	3.1	D	8.1	23.3	D	8.0	3.6	D	23.3	6 615	254	1 363	13 491	-0.5
Green	17.6	D	D	2.7	D	7.9	5.5	10.1	32.4	3 080	276	669	5 276	-0.9
Greenup	-0.3	D	3.6	9.3	D	7.5	3.1	23.8	17.3	9 045	248	1 620	16 296	-0.2
Hancock	1.9	D	13.3	65.8	D	1.2	0.9	1.6	6.4	2 120	244	252	3 720	-0.4
Hardin	0.8	0.1	2.9	11.4	7.6	5.3	3.5	5.6	50.5	19 085	177	3 008	45 726	5.7
Harlan	-0.1	25.3	3.0	0.7	4.8	7.4	3.7	D	24.6	8 355	293	2 845	13 470	-0.3
Harrison	2.1	D	D	30.2	2.5	6.6	2.4	D	16.6	4 335	234	772	8 214	0.1
Hart	1.1	D	D	39.8	1.5	6.3	2.1	D	18.1	4 530	244	1 033	8 745	2.2
Henderson	9.5	0.4	4.4	26.2	2.5	6.5	3.5	D	14.2	10 520	227	1 754	20 463	0.7
Henry	3.9	D	6.0	18.7	D	5.6	D	D	26.8	3 590	233	507	6 669	0.4
Hickman	64.2	0.0	D	D	D	2.9	2.3	D	10.1	1 430	301	247	2 338	-0.2
Hopkins	3.5	11.3	4.8	15.2	D	7.2	3.5	D	18.2	11 400	245	2 038	21 266	0.4
Jackson	-4.1	D	4.8	8.9	4.9	5.2	D	D	36.8	3 295	246	1 400	6 515	-0.1
Jefferson	0.0	0.1	4.6	12.4	10.0	5.1	11.8	15.3	11.9	145 940	193	25 260	341 449	1.1
Jessamine	0.7	D	10.0	18.3	D	13.8	3.2	4.4	15.8	8 875	177	1 338	19 910	3.0
Johnson	-0.7	D	5.6	1.2	6.8	14.7	4.0	D	27.7	6 685	285	2 129	10 531	-0.9
Kenton	0.0	D	6.5	8.5	8.4	4.6	11.0	15.2	17.8	27 415	168	3 977	69 544	0.8
Knott	-0.6	D	D	D	6.7	5.3	D	12.9	28.4	4 290	267	1 720	7 444	-0.2
Knox	-0.5	D	4.2	5.2	7.0	12.9	3.4	D	21.6	8 330	262	4 127	14 451	-0.2
Larue	12.3	0.0	11.2	12.9	D	5.3	5.4	8.0	22.8	3 415	243	535	6 277	1.7
Laurel	0.1	3.3	5.6	17.1	6.4	9.6	4.2	12.7	13.5	14 420	242	3 719	25 423	-0.1
Lawrence	-0.9	D	8.0	D	D	9.8	2.7	21.0	19.9	4 240	268	1 468	7 268	-0.2
Lee	-2.6	5.2	D	D	D	10.4	D	18.2	28.5	1 935	253	859	3 431	-0.2
Leslie	-0.2	24.4	D	D	5.4	6.3	D	D	27.1	3 310	301	1 252	5 267	-0.2
Letcher	-0.3	D	2.5	2.8	4.1	15.1	2.3	D	21.7	7 090	302	2 196	11 588	-0.1
Lewis	2.1	0.0	D	12.6	2.9	5.7	3.7	9.8	29.2	3 170	230	987	6 469	-0.2
Lincoln	4.9	0.0	7.7	15.7	5.6	7.7	3.1	12.1	24.3	6 165	253	1 531	10 851	0.3
Livingston	7.2	D	25.3	3.8	D	3.8	1.5	6.8	15.4	2 760	295	311	4 817	-0.1
Logan	16.8	0.2	5.8	32.0	2.4	5.3	2.0	D	11.2	6 385	237	969	12 318	-0.2
Lyon	8.7	0.0	6.0	D	3.6	4.7	1.7	7.3	45.1	2 445	289	178	4 807	0.3
McCracken	0.8	D	5.2	11.0	6.5	9.8	4.3	20.1	12.4	16 130	247	2 461	31 383	1.0
McCreary	-1.0	D	D	8.7	D	9.3	3.3	D	55.2	4 335	242	1 964	7 431	-1.0
McLean	43.5	0.7	14.2	4.5	D	6.0	D	2.9	14.1	2 580	271	351	4 254	-0.2
Madison	0.3	D	6.7	17.8	8.7	7.5	2.8	9.7	27.4	15 930	185	3 061	35 817	2.2
Magoffin	-0.9	D	D	D	6.6	7.5	D	12.1	29.1	3 560	276	1 722	5 930	-0.3
Marion	2.8	D	3.8	44.8	D	5.3	2.4	D	12.4	4 290	215	1 023	8 204	0.3
Marshall	1.6	D	16.5	33.9	D	6.4	3.8	D	12.7	8 995	289	839	15 976	1.4
Martin	-0.1	25.4	D	D	D	7.0	D	6.3	37.6	3 365	265	1 480	5 153	-0.2
Mason	2.1	D	8.4	18.1	D	9.3	2.8	14.4	14.8	4 230	244	764	8 137	0.4
Meade	5.2	2.6	11.8	11.8	5.8	8.8	4.8	D	24.1	5 485	188	749	12 165	3.4
Menifee	-4.8	D	D	12.0	D	5.6	2.8	D	47.1	1 825	289	594	3 748	0.1
Mercer	2.5	D	6.6	40.6	2.7	6.7	2.1	D	12.1	5 440	256	677	10 057	1.2
Metcalfe	4.3	D	D	30.5	D	7.2	D	3.7	27.5	2 680	269	627	4 671	-0.2
Monroe	9.4	0.0	5.9	15.6	D	8.9	4.0	13.6	20.5	2 995	279	740	5 201	-0.1
Montgomery	-0.4	D	7.7	37.5	D	10.0	3.6	D	12.3	6 220	228	1 355	11 753	0.5
Morgan	-1.4	D	D	10.0	5.8	7.3	D	7.8	32.9	3 180	238	1 119	5 860	0.5
Muhlenberg	4.1	D	8.1	9.0	D	6.4	2.4	D	27.4	8 400	269	1 517	13 650	-0.4
Nelson	3.6	D	9.4	20.7	D	7.4	3.2	10.2	12.9	9 550	215	1 320	18 526	2.5
Nicholas	5.7	0.0	7.5	3.5	D	6.9	D	20.0	31.5	1 820	259	344	3 243	-0.5

1. Per 1,000 resident population estimated as of July 1 of the year shown.

STATE County	Housing units, 2009–2013: Occupied units: Total	Owner-occupied: Percent	Owner-occupied: Median value[1]	Median owner cost as a percent of income: With a mortgage	Median owner cost as a percent of income: Without a mortgage[2]	Renter-occupied: Median rent[3]	Renter-occupied: Median rent as a percent of income[2]	Substandard units[4] (percent)	Civilian labor force, 2014: Total	Percent change, 2013–2014	Unemployment: Total	Unemployment: Rate[5]	Civilian employment,[6] 2009–2013: Total	Percent: Management, business, science and arts	Percent: Construction, production, and maintenance occupations
	89	90	91	92	93	94	95	96	97	98	99	100	101	102	103
KENTUCKY—Cont'd															
Clay	7 317	75.6	57 800	21.9	13.1	465	36.6	2.7	5 531	-3.9	635	11.5	5 350	25.3	32.5
Clinton	3 960	75.6	68 000	22.7	12.7	525	25.0	3.7	3 990	-2.8	363	9.1	3 504	22.8	38.9
Crittenden	3 794	78.5	72 500	20.9	10.0	473	24.8	2.3	3 913	-4.6	241	6.2	3 485	25.5	40.1
Cumberland	2 604	75.5	63 400	24.4	13.5	450	23.6	2.0	2 956	-2.8	226	7.6	2 541	30.5	37.2
Daviess	37 677	70.2	110 500	19.6	10.0	636	27.5	0.2	45 980	-3.5	2 614	5.7	42 893	29.4	28.5
Edmonson	4 766	76.5	90 600	22.5	10.7	499	29.5	2.6	4 870	-2.7	402	8.3	4 532	24.9	31.4
Elliott	2 618	79.0	71 400	27.8	15.5	433	35.7	4.4	2 147	-4.9	246	11.5	1 976	26.9	32.7
Estill	5 829	69.7	71 900	23.7	12.6	497	35.0	2.2	5 399	-2.4	404	7.5	4 711	21.5	41.8
Fayette	123 142	55.2	165 800	20.6	10.0	756	30.5	3.2	166 862	-1.0	8 059	4.8	153 591	42.5	15.7
Fleming	5 539	78.5	78 700	24.2	12.0	499	26.9	3.0	6 331	-3.0	500	7.9	5 874	31.3	34.2
Floyd	15 422	69.2	70 000	24.0	11.2	562	30.6	2.5	12 445	-5.2	1 287	10.3	12 473	29.0	25.9
Franklin	21 058	62.3	139 300	21.6	10.0	682	32.2	2.0	24 092	-2.1	1 298	5.4	21 949	37.2	21.4
Fulton	2 744	60.4	60 400	20.8	13.5	491	28.4	3.2	2 252	-5.7	189	8.4	2 311	28.2	35.3
Gallatin	2 995	68.3	98 400	24.8	13.2	657	26.7	3.0	3 825	-3.1	262	6.8	3 541	17.3	42.4
Garrard	6 302	79.0	121 400	23.0	11.1	629	34.5	3.0	7 591	-2.2	503	6.6	7 222	29.8	31.8
Grant	8 334	73.5	124 300	23.6	13.2	719	29.0	2.7	11 201	-2.6	724	6.5	10 445	21.8	36.0
Graves	14 419	76.2	85 900	21.9	11.1	561	34.4	2.5	15 940	-3.4	1 205	7.6	15 235	28.4	32.0
Grayson	9 897	72.3	87 700	23.0	11.6	515	27.8	2.1	10 822	-3.9	915	8.5	9 936	28.8	39.1
Green	4 495	76.7	70 100	19.6	10.0	510	32.1	2.3	5 111	-4.0	335	6.6	4 458	27.7	36.3
Greenup	14 465	76.4	92 000	20.7	10.7	616	31.2	1.9	14 198	-3.7	1 187	8.4	13 418	36.0	26.2
Hancock	3 361	80.3	90 800	16.0	10.0	557	22.2	1.7	3 959	-3.5	240	6.1	3 675	20.8	45.5
Hardin	39 401	62.9	140 600	20.6	10.0	732	26.1	5.1	46 567	-2.6	2 909	6.2	42 748	34.9	23.2
Harlan	11 343	69.8	52 000	20.0	11.0	469	26.9	1.7	8 536	-10.3	1 183	13.9	8 222	27.8	34.6
Harrison	7 179	66.1	109 400	21.4	12.1	588	30.4	2.1	8 404	-3.9	508	6.0	7 608	24.0	30.6
Hart	7 115	73.8	78 900	22.0	10.8	503	33.7	1.9	7 801	-3.2	496	6.4	6 889	20.9	44.0
Henderson	18 787	68.0	99 400	21.1	10.3	589	29.2	2.4	21 640	-2.3	1 326	6.1	20 299	28.6	30.1
Henry	6 008	72.0	123 300	22.4	10.8	692	30.0	3.5	7 636	-1.8	447	5.9	7 013	26.6	34.5
Hickman	1 983	79.4	62 400	19.6	10.8	548	29.9	2.5	2 129	-1.5	133	6.2	1 701	24.7	31.6
Hopkins	18 495	71.8	83 300	19.7	11.5	590	26.1	4.6	20 613	-4.2	1 324	6.4	19 762	28.8	30.1
Jackson	5 712	75.4	62 100	26.2	12.7	570	30.7	1.8	4 628	-4.3	531	11.5	4 366	23.1	42.9
Jefferson	305 832	62.7	149 100	21.6	11.3	721	29.3	3.5	378 661	-2.0	23 045	6.1	350 759	36.2	21.5
Jessamine	18 012	66.0	154 300	23.3	11.8	735	28.4	3.4	24 767	-1.3	1 311	5.3	22 846	33.4	23.6
Johnson	9 154	74.2	78 700	20.6	12.6	498	28.9	2.2	8 082	-3.3	748	9.3	7 652	24.8	29.9
Kenton	61 800	68.0	144 300	21.5	11.1	733	28.1	2.7	83 213	-2.3	4 638	5.6	77 880	35.9	21.2
Knott	5 892	80.0	59 600	19.5	10.0	481	23.6	4.2	5 149	-7.5	576	11.2	5 138	36.4	27.6
Knox	12 350	64.4	71 400	22.3	12.6	496	32.7	1.9	10 124	-3.9	1 014	10.0	9 211	25.5	31.0
Larue	5 221	76.3	101 000	22.3	10.0	561	30.3	2.6	5 714	-2.9	374	6.5	5 322	26.6	40.2
Laurel	22 931	71.3	91 300	21.2	11.6	562	27.9	2.4	23 944	-2.8	1 828	7.6	22 188	26.7	27.8
Lawrence	5 823	76.0	80 200	20.7	10.3	496	30.5	5.4	5 314	-5.0	512	9.6	5 245	24.8	37.2
Lee	2 951	73.4	62 200	25.0	14.2	424	33.9	5.7	2 257	-4.3	220	9.7	2 116	29.8	34.9
Leslie	4 206	77.8	44 700	22.3	10.0	490	22.9	3.7	3 193	-8.2	409	12.8	3 140	27.0	34.4
Letcher	9 366	75.4	54 900	20.8	10.0	535	32.2	4.2	7 337	-8.8	903	12.3	7 470	32.8	33.3
Lewis	5 003	79.3	59 900	22.4	10.4	393	27.6	3.4	5 160	-2.6	499	9.7	4 956	26.6	45.1
Lincoln	9 692	75.6	88 500	21.8	11.6	540	31.5	2.7	9 457	-4.9	827	8.7	9 207	25.8	33.8
Livingston	3 569	81.2	74 400	19.8	10.0	569	24.9	2.6	3 733	-3.7	304	8.1	3 589	21.9	34.6
Logan	10 912	71.2	89 100	22.0	12.1	562	30.8	2.0	11 887	-2.1	679	5.7	10 805	25.2	39.2
Lyon	3 294	78.3	105 500	23.9	10.0	431	19.2	1.8	2 999	-3.0	207	6.9	2 783	25.5	30.0
McCracken	27 037	68.1	117 200	19.5	10.0	588	26.4	2.3	29 359	-3.1	2 087	7.1	28 519	32.6	22.6
McCreary	6 312	67.9	65 000	24.4	12.6	470	39.6	1.8	5 063	-5.3	542	10.7	4 771	23.6	33.6
McLean	3 770	78.4	79 000	19.5	10.0	485	23.3	2.3	4 336	-3.3	282	6.5	3 967	30.3	36.0
Madison	31 484	60.5	141 100	21.5	10.7	634	30.9	1.9	44 889	-2.0	2 424	5.4	38 874	35.5	19.7
Magoffin	4 931	78.6	43 700	22.6	12.4	474	34.1	1.0	3 744	-6.5	523	14.0	3 315	32.0	35.3
Marion	7 368	76.9	100 200	23.9	12.4	535	30.4	1.4	9 062	-2.4	585	6.5	7 927	27.4	38.4
Marshall	11 963	82.3	101 800	21.7	10.0	591	28.8	4.1	15 050	-1.9	1 029	6.8	13 175	27.0	28.7
Martin	4 449	66.0	84 400	24.4	10.1	582	36.4	1.4	3 474	-4.9	317	9.1	2 868	29.0	34.3
Mason	6 569	71.2	99 000	21.1	10.0	563	28.4	2.6	7 733	-0.6	604	7.8	7 382	32.0	28.8
Meade	10 342	71.8	120 500	22.2	10.0	777	27.7	2.1	12 142	-3.2	855	7.0	11 117	29.6	34.7
Menifee	2 379	74.7	77 300	21.7	14.0	479	37.0	2.8	2 358	-5.4	233	9.9	2 110	22.3	38.6
Mercer	8 745	74.9	128 400	21.5	10.8	534	31.1	2.6	9 904	-3.0	618	6.2	9 366	30.2	30.9
Metcalfe	3 919	78.2	78 800	23.0	10.4	518	23.4	3.7	4 159	-4.2	253	6.1	4 022	23.0	44.9
Monroe	4 401	73.8	72 300	23.7	13.2	502	31.8	1.6	4 597	-3.1	257	5.6	4 189	28.7	36.4
Montgomery	10 168	65.3	109 300	22.9	11.7	613	25.7	2.8	11 659	-4.0	874	7.5	10 455	26.9	37.6
Morgan	4 697	75.3	74 500	23.2	11.5	436	29.1	1.7	4 826	-4.7	456	9.4	4 233	26.7	31.7
Muhlenberg	11 869	79.1	79 500	21.4	10.6	519	29.2	2.2	12 471	-3.8	944	7.6	11 579	27.8	36.8
Nelson	16 571	75.4	124 500	22.2	10.0	665	32.9	3.5	21 314	-2.3	1 309	6.1	19 416	28.2	35.3
Nicholas	2 884	74.1	84 900	19.7	10.9	429	24.3	3.8	3 467	-2.1	278	8.0	3 230	27.2	38.1

1. Specified owner-occupied units. 2. A value of 10.0 represents 10 percent or less; a value of 50.0 represents 50 percent or more. 3. Specified renter-occupied units.
4. Overcrowded or lacking complete plumbing facilities. 5. Percent of civilian labor force. 6. Persons 16 years old and over.

Table B. States and Counties — **Nonfarm Employment and Agriculture**

STATE County	Private nonfarm establishments, employment and payroll, 2013										Agriculture, 2012			
		Employment							Annual payroll		Farms			
												Percent with:		
	Number of establish-ments	Total	Health care and social assistance	Manufac-turing	Retail trade	Finance and insurance	Professional, scientific, and technical services	Total (mil dol)	Average per employee (dollars)	Number	Fewer than 50 acres	500 acres or more	Farm operators whose principal occu-pation is farming (percent)
	104	105	106	107	108	109	110	111	112	113	114	115	116
KENTUCKY—Cont'd													
Clay	246	2 541	878	D	533	78	57	71	28 114	243	31.7	4.5	33.3
Clinton	193	3 153	497	D	258	83	36	75	23 763	508	33.9	6.5	43.7
Crittenden	165	1 723	379	243	D	D	D	42	24 101	592	27.4	10.3	33.4
Cumberland	110	1 294	D	186	189	D	D	40	31 104	371	31.8	7.5	49.1
Daviess	2 267	41 440	8 298	5 353	5 864	3 054	1 812	1 426	34 415	837	46.5	12.7	48.7
Edmonson	127	843	215	D	166	74	D	21	25 474	638	33.1	4.2	32.0
Elliott	43	288	122	NA	NA	D	NA	7	24 767	389	26.5	4.1	38.8
Estill	182	1 552	529	D	290	D	D	41	26 580	380	27.1	4.5	39.2
Fayette	8 450	156 335	31 143	8 174	20 648	5 662	13 531	6 260	40 040	718	47.4	7.4	57.0
Fleming	249	2 092	D	378	465	105	D	61	29 329	1 087	26.9	5.7	47.7
Floyd	823	8 566	2 211	207	1 467	267	317	309	36 088	87	54.0	3.4	29.9
Franklin	1 154	14 664	1 662	2 272	2 475	960	868	498	33 992	579	35.8	5.5	37.1
Fulton	129	1 592	D	394	192	D	D	55	34 490	178	33.7	23.6	51.1
Gallatin	87	787	D	D	200	D	D	19	24 704	185	34.1	5.9	47.6
Garrard	214	1 318	D	D	166	52	D	37	28 396	805	35.5	6.7	44.5
Grant	365	3 899	470	D	889	131	D	110	28 312	812	36.5	3.1	46.1
Graves	719	9 310	D	2 376	1 303	296	494	273	29 349	1 442	41.7	8.5	45.5
Grayson	498	6 042	D	1 658	1 041	220	87	170	28 067	1 407	30.9	4.3	32.8
Green	163	1 283	555	D	246	D	D	31	24 493	1 050	32.0	3.5	41.2
Greenup	521	5 060	1 197	568	693	254	173	167	32 916	604	30.6	3.6	40.2
Hancock	127	3 531	D	2 582	133	70	D	225	63 723	350	33.4	4.0	26.6
Hardin	2 309	35 982	7 380	5 354	5 715	1 446	1 348	1 163	32 327	1 357	45.8	6.1	40.8
Harlan	457	5 817	1 265	D	1 020	147	233	211	36 194	34	58.8	11.8	29.4
Harrison	287	3 916	896	1 271	565	D	D	144	36 649	1 064	29.9	6.6	44.1
Hart	273	4 076	453	2 354	494	88	51	120	29 388	1 372	35.9	3.4	38.5
Henderson	1 018	15 968	2 418	4 830	2 098	434	483	559	34 979	465	41.9	14.8	44.7
Henry	204	2 093	255	455	372	90	D	58	27 473	869	33.9	4.1	48.3
Hickman	77	1 043	224	D	D	D	7	31	29 358	298	32.2	16.4	53.0
Hopkins	970	14 636	D	2 250	2 318	412	397	599	40 897	731	33.2	9.8	40.5
Jackson	102	1 400	234	539	167	D	D	36	25 658	588	32.1	4.1	30.8
Jefferson	19 270	401 108	66 102	40 532	41 944	27 414	22 426	17 827	44 445	382	69.6	1.0	44.0
Jessamine	1 045	14 487	997	2 565	2 622	D	577	465	32 132	668	49.6	4.0	38.6
Johnson	411	4 345	966	D	1 383	204	151	131	30 071	196	31.6	1.5	31.6
Kenton	3 014	49 837	10 467	3 328	5 439	1 318	3 358	1 959	39 306	459	51.4	1.5	34.9
Knott	174	1 519	418	D	282	46	46	46	30 302	42	31.0	9.5	19.0
Knox	466	7 535	1 020	1 073	1 227	193	D	195	25 829	243	32.5	4.9	40.3
Larue	224	1 875	337	544	250	177	D	51	27 291	720	40.1	4.9	46.5
Laurel	1 144	21 700	2 893	3 409	3 278	788	864	733	33 762	1 006	44.3	1.6	37.0
Lawrence	221	2 508	D	D	634	122	63	84	33 653	291	26.5	5.5	35.4
Lee	100	1 327	D	NA	211	D	17	31	23 181	142	38.0	3.5	30.3
Leslie	110	1 114	D	NA	225	D	68	37	32 981	15	40.0	6.7	26.7
Letcher	333	4 243	963	D	663	D	151	155	36 610	54	57.4	0.0	24.1
Lewis	119	1 297	D	405	259	84	D	42	32 145	676	25.3	6.8	39.1
Lincoln	308	2 653	472	550	563	D	73	76	28 790	1 202	40.8	7.2	45.8
Livingston	158	1 809	377	112	158	30	D	72	39 588	403	15.9	15.9	32.0
Logan	488	6 903	D	D	929	160	155	274	39 692	1 060	29.3	9.2	43.4
Lyon	140	1 098	226	D	193	D	35	28	25 753	219	27.4	4.6	32.0
McCracken	2 096	34 149	7 174	2 791	6 219	1 262	1 276	1 252	36 673	447	51.5	5.8	31.5
McCreary	160	1 470	280	D	356	100	D	35	23 979	155	45.2	3.9	36.8
McLean	163	1 047	129	D	188	D	D	32	30 768	413	38.5	16.7	56.9
Madison	1 655	21 774	3 718	3 552	4 058	664	605	732	33 600	1 219	36.8	8.2	45.9
Magoffin	172	1 526	429	D	261	55	135	42	27 563	361	31.0	2.2	34.1
Marion	358	7 285	1 238	3 719	653	138	D	238	32 641	1 016	33.4	6.7	40.1
Marshall	647	8 675	963	2 517	1 084	302	186	398	45 830	719	46.3	4.5	27.8
Martin	162	2 460	232	D	354	73	25	117	47 495	20	40.0	15.0	45.0
Mason	446	6 947	1 229	1 106	1 386	220	95	239	34 366	634	26.7	8.4	43.7
Meade	361	3 552	407	D	606	108	D	113	31 932	754	44.6	4.9	49.3
Menifee	61	473	171	92	94	D	D	13	26 641	294	31.0	5.1	38.8
Mercer	365	5 530	727	2 466	697	132	53	249	45 099	1 067	42.3	4.6	40.9
Metcalfe	120	1 224	117	624	214	43	D	34	27 945	924	32.9	4.5	48.4
Monroe	204	2 286	517	648	433	77	19	63	27 553	858	26.8	9.0	49.3
Montgomery	533	9 894	955	3 903	1 600	292	153	312	31 549	609	35.1	4.9	42.0
Morgan	154	2 068	389	322	397	114	61	62	29 910	694	23.1	7.1	35.0
Muhlenberg	560	6 266	1 275	848	1 165	204	148	204	32 528	630	33.0	7.8	39.8
Nelson	910	13 444	1 429	3 723	1 746	321	249	434	32 269	1 326	47.5	5.1	43.1
Nicholas	76	546	D	D	137	25	D	13	24 685	570	23.3	6.0	49.3

STATE County	Agriculture, 2012 (cont.)															
	Land in farms					Value of land and buildings (dollars)		Value of machinery and equipment, average per farm (dollars)	Value of products sold				Percent of farms with sales of:		Government payments	
	Acreage (1,000)	Percent change, 2007–2012	Acres: Average size of farm	Acres: Total irrigated (1,000)	Acres: Total cropland (1,000)	Average per farm	Average per acre		Total (mil dol)	Average per farm (dollars)	Percent from: Crops	Percent from: Live-stock and poultry products	$10,000 or more	$100,000 or more	Total ($1,000)	Percent of farms
	117	118	119	120	121	122	123	124	125	126	127	128	129	130	131	132
KENTUCKY—Cont'd																
Clay	35	-31.4	145	0.2	9.9	230 173	1 592	48 691	4.7	19 169	70.5	29.5	25.1	7.0	239	33.3
Clinton	74	-18.7	146	0.3	26.0	378 150	2 594	53 791	29.8	58 632	12.7	87.3	43.5	6.9	551	44.7
Crittenden	149	-7.1	251	1.1	83.0	541 215	2 153	75 215	31.6	53 311	63.0	37.0	34.0	5.9	2 672	50.7
Cumberland	65	-36.7	176	D	17.7	301 164	1 707	42 027	12.8	34 596	25.0	75.0	29.6	3.0	346	42.9
Daviess	237	-7.7	283	9.6	190.2	1 100 748	3 884	144 342	176.4	210 760	65.6	34.4	43.0	18.5	3 286	54.4
Edmonson	85	-12.1	133	0.0	34.9	316 882	2 379	44 666	20.2	31 699	33.5	66.5	28.4	4.5	1 960	44.8
Elliott	56	-15.7	145	0.1	13.5	196 622	1 358	39 936	3.2	8 321	42.9	57.1	26.7	0.0	479	30.3
Estill	52	-19.3	138	0.0	14.1	254 342	1 848	37 968	4.4	11 655	51.2	48.7	26.6	2.1	337	41.3
Fayette	115	-15.5	160	1.1	40.4	1 457 641	9 112	96 464	176.2	245 461	7.7	92.3	46.9	14.8	1 263	28.7
Fleming	183	0.9	169	0.2	73.1	353 267	2 096	62 407	52.7	48 516	34.1	65.9	50.6	9.1	1 630	63.6
Floyd	8	4.8	94	0.0	1.2	138 034	1 472	22 207	0.6	6 644	74.4	25.6	11.5	1.1	D	2.3
Franklin	79	2.9	136	0.3	30.1	499 653	3 684	55 269	19.4	33 463	41.9	58.1	35.4	4.7	546	31.3
Fulton	83	-8.8	468	2.5	74.3	1 635 017	3 490	183 713	46.6	261 562	72.4	27.6	48.3	31.5	2 716	77.0
Gallatin	28	-17.8	150	0.0	10.8	454 384	3 026	67 178	5.7	30 546	80.0	20.0	31.9	6.5	232	38.9
Garrard	127	4.6	158	0.2	43.7	390 569	2 471	61 070	38.5	47 794	27.2	72.8	43.4	9.2	805	37.6
Grant	98	-14.4	121	0.1	33.0	370 686	3 060	53 784	11.7	14 408	56.4	43.6	28.7	2.2	729	30.7
Graves	292	5.0	202	4.5	221.9	656 060	3 242	105 221	337.7	234 209	25.7	74.3	36.4	18.5	7 722	69.1
Grayson	201	-7.2	143	0.1	87.1	324 133	2 270	54 270	45.7	32 454	40.1	59.9	33.1	5.0	2 928	51.0
Green	153	4.8	145	0.1	67.4	329 032	2 265	59 282	39.2	37 304	56.1	43.9	42.5	6.4	2 908	61.1
Greenup	79	-14.4	130	0.1	17.5	230 462	1 770	45 828	5.0	8 333	56.1	43.9	20.0	0.3	311	33.3
Hancock	52	-17.2	149	0.5	23.4	419 334	2 812	81 900	14.0	40 037	72.6	27.4	30.9	3.7	515	50.3
Hardin	203	-8.7	150	0.7	114.4	524 307	3 505	74 682	57.9	42 704	70.2	29.8	35.9	6.9	2 030	40.5
Harlan	6	106.5	184	D	0.3	243 765	1 323	34 529	0.3	8 294	53.9	46.1	14.7	2.9	D	2.9
Harrison	164	1.7	155	2.0	64.2	422 032	2 730	61 867	36.0	33 848	54.0	46.0	39.4	7.3	1 123	34.7
Hart	182	-4.5	133	0.2	76.1	295 020	2 219	53 891	33.5	24 409	42.5	57.5	35.1	5.2	4 176	54.4
Henderson	176	-10.1	378	6.0	150.0	1 381 355	3 651	193 890	78.6	169 024	93.2	6.8	47.1	17.6	3 464	67.1
Henry	129	-12.2	148	0.8	58.2	494 348	3 343	59 478	30.7	35 292	60.0	40.0	42.8	6.6	1 549	47.6
Hickman	141	8.8	474	6.1	119.7	1 647 913	3 480	199 456	159.2	534 356	35.7	64.3	48.0	29.9	2 918	76.8
Hopkins	163	2.3	223	0.2	94.2	646 970	2 902	81 895	107.7	147 369	32.6	67.4	26.7	9.2	2 662	46.5
Jackson	78	-5.8	132	0.0	23.0	240 571	1 818	43 282	9.9	16 774	26.4	73.6	27.9	3.2	588	44.0
Jefferson	23	-28.5	60	0.2	11.0	521 759	8 633	43 777	7.8	20 343	79.4	20.6	22.8	3.9	288	18.1
Jessamine	84	4.4	125	0.2	33.6	685 317	5 473	49 979	25.0	37 446	21.1	78.9	35.9	7.0	863	36.4
Johnson	24	-12.5	124	D	4.9	216 969	1 750	44 179	1.3	6 561	35.8	64.3	15.8	0.5	81	20.9
Kenton	38	-10.3	83	0.1	15.1	362 353	4 360	48 092	5.3	11 475	43.2	56.8	20.5	3.3	324	29.4
Knott	7	-2.8	161	0.0	1.8	217 095	1 352	61 881	0.4	8 524	17.6	82.4	23.8	2.4	D	2.4
Knox	34	-34.4	138	0.1	9.6	241 292	1 749	50 700	2.3	9 358	60.6	39.4	19.3	0.8	206	21.4
Larue	112	-10.7	156	0.1	66.9	532 196	3 422	82 204	41.9	58 163	74.3	25.7	39.9	7.8	1 295	43.2
Laurel	96	-6.3	95	0.1	35.0	329 341	3 449	43 809	15.3	15 187	41.5	58.5	27.4	2.1	536	29.3
Lawrence	42	-30.8	143	0.0	6.5	202 818	1 416	41 120	1.6	5 375	53.4	46.6	15.8	0.0	31	12.4
Lee	22	-24.5	156	0.0	5.4	297 641	1 902	40 134	1.0	6 852	47.2	52.8	19.0	1.4	86	30.3
Leslie	D	D	D	0.0	0.2	412 867	D	33 533	0.0	267	D	D	0.0	0.0	3	20.0
Letcher	3	-20.5	53	D	0.4	123 185	2 313	43 722	0.1	2 463	64.7	34.6	3.7	0.0	0	0.0
Lewis	118	-19.6	174	0.0	32.8	256 246	1 469	49 519	12.8	18 944	70.8	29.2	27.4	4.0	968	49.6
Lincoln	181	1.4	150	0.3	72.6	374 358	2 489	59 559	57.4	47 729	30.6	69.4	42.3	9.7	1 680	43.5
Livingston	123	5.3	306	0.0	62.5	650 496	2 128	90 191	21.3	52 898	50.3	49.7	40.4	10.7	1 651	54.8
Logan	276	-4.9	260	2.7	192.4	871 373	3 349	105 848	134.9	127 283	71.8	28.2	42.8	15.2	6 034	59.8
Lyon	42	-23.1	190	D	23.6	384 995	2 025	67 187	6.8	30 968	78.0	22.0	37.0	6.4	561	52.5
McCracken	67	-10.8	150	0.3	49.7	462 497	3 077	66 349	22.2	49 738	73.3	26.7	28.6	8.1	947	53.0
McCreary	18	20.2	117	0.0	3.3	208 974	1 790	42 200	1.0	6 671	35.4	64.6	21.3	0.0	11	5.8
McLean	124	-13.7	301	1.2	96.5	1 132 448	3 760	162 719	179.7	435 218	32.1	67.9	55.9	32.0	2 451	71.7
Madison	233	6.7	191	0.2	73.0	576 284	3 018	65 868	60.5	49 656	14.2	85.8	43.3	9.5	783	43.3
Magoffin	44	-27.9	123	D	7.9	182 543	1 482	33 341	1.3	3 479	53.7	46.3	8.9	0.0	235	32.7
Marion	166	3.6	164	0.3	70.2	441 025	2 693	65 181	56.5	55 601	40.2	59.8	46.8	11.1	1 357	56.6
Marshall	95	-2.9	132	0.1	54.8	403 344	3 057	61 174	45.3	63 042	31.7	68.3	25.0	6.1	1 902	52.9
Martin	D	D	D	0.0	0.3	1 783 100	D	35 100	0.1	4 750	D	D	10.0	0.0	0	0.0
Mason	127	-9.4	200	0.0	57.9	515 345	2 578	69 967	30.9	48 784	59.5	40.5	48.3	12.1	1 693	52.8
Meade	119	-1.6	158	0.0	63.7	514 138	3 244	78 910	36.6	48 503	51.7	48.3	35.7	7.6	1 424	52.0
Menifee	41	-5.0	139	D	10.0	248 966	1 787	41 129	3.8	13 082	44.1	55.9	22.8	2.7	177	29.3
Mercer	144	2.0	135	0.0	59.4	456 854	3 379	67 196	50.7	47 495	18.6	81.4	42.4	9.3	1 472	31.8
Metcalfe	125	-16.2	136	0.1	49.7	305 962	2 256	56 923	35.0	37 899	30.1	69.9	43.5	8.4	2 185	45.0
Monroe	172	-2.0	201	0.1	62.0	473 586	2 359	68 647	77.2	90 021	23.5	76.5	51.6	11.2	1 603	48.0
Montgomery	99	-7.0	163	0.0	40.0	447 880	2 743	58 650	19.0	31 209	31.1	68.9	42.2	6.4	539	36.1
Morgan	119	-12.8	171	0.0	24.0	218 340	1 276	50 761	6.9	9 938	42.0	58.0	26.4	0.4	579	37.3
Muhlenberg	129	-8.6	204	0.2	67.1	474 975	2 324	78 500	68.9	109 373	35.6	64.4	31.0	9.5	2 162	44.6
Nelson	188	-4.3	142	0.7	97.2	476 235	3 363	65 611	64.4	48 597	53.3	46.7	34.9	8.1	2 129	35.2
Nicholas	102	-7.3	179	0.1	40.9	387 086	2 159	59 526	20.7	36 384	50.6	49.4	45.4	7.5	712	36.0

STATE County	Water use, 2010		Wholesale trade,[1] 2007				Retail trade,[2] 2007				Real estate and rental and leasing,[2] 2007			
	Total water withdrawn (mil gal/day)	Gallons withdrawn per person per day	Number of establish-ments	Number of employees	Sales (mil dol)	Annual payroll (mil dol)	Number of establish-ments	Number of employees	Sales (mil dol)	Annual payroll (mil dol)	Number of establish-ments	Number of employees	Receipts (mil dol)	Annual payroll (mil dol)
	133	134	135	136	137	138	139	140	141	142	143	144	145	146
KENTUCKY—Cont'd														
Clay	4.5	205	7	35	13.2	0.6	72	549	138.7	10.3	10	19	1.7	0.3
Clinton	4.0	393	11	79	38.7	1.6	42	232	55.3	3.7	7	28	3.3	0.8
Crittenden	1.4	151	5	108	9.4	2.5	29	286	53.4	4.9	7	27	31.7	0.9
Cumberland	1.0	144	NA	NA	NA	NA	34	225	44.2	3.6	4	D	D	D
Daviess	268.9	2 782	95	1 166	818.1	45.8	442	5 936	1 282.9	123.4	78	518	49.7	10.9
Edmonson	2.2	180	1	D	D	D	27	171	32.5	2.7	NA	NA	NA	NA
Elliott	0.6	74	NA	NA	NA	NA	14	52	12.2	0.9	NA	NA	NA	NA
Estill	1.6	111	3	D	D	D	45	321	84.2	6.0	6	27	1.7	0.4
Fayette	52.3	177	375	8 540	4 442.4	568.5	1 249	22 335	4 778.5	510.4	476	2 268	391.2	68.2
Fleming	2.3	162	19	112	29.8	2.9	70	539	128.5	10.8	7	11	1.8	0.1
Floyd	5.4	136	39	497	404.4	16.8	181	1 535	403.3	33.3	27	99	12.1	2.1
Franklin	10.2	206	23	249	223.6	10.5	198	2 719	622.1	59.4	47	146	23.8	3.6
Fulton	1.3	194	6	D	D	D	40	268	52.2	3.5	3	3	0.6	0.1
Gallatin	2.4	274	3	D	D	D	20	185	37.3	2.7	5	D	D	D
Garrard	2.4	141	5	30	7.1	0.9	38	179	39.6	3.0	5	D	D	D
Grant	2.3	95	9	D	D	D	94	1 053	285.2	22.4	19	51	4.5	1.0
Graves	10.2	273	40	D	D	D	130	1 427	342.5	31.5	25	96	6.4	1.2
Grayson	3.4	133	13	D	D	D	101	1 097	234.9	21.8	14	134	5.8	1.5
Green	2.7	239	5	14	1.9	0.2	36	242	64.4	4.0	4	8	1.8	0.2
Greenup	14.1	382	5	22	3.6	0.4	120	1 431	355.7	25.6	20	72	8.3	1.3
Hancock	306.8	35 820	4	15	3.3	0.3	17	147	28.1	2.0	5	D	D	D
Hardin	16.8	159	54	479	281.1	15.8	433	6 012	1 449.5	132.2	102	D	D	D
Harlan	5.4	185	24	227	159.3	7.5	99	1 045	211.1	19.0	16	50	5.8	0.9
Harrison	3.9	207	10	86	39.8	1.6	64	724	147.0	12.8	11	44	5.4	0.8
Hart	5.2	285	10	41	21.4	1.1	69	429	92.8	6.5	7	D	D	D
Henderson	14.8	320	44	687	545.0	26.3	183	2 508	662.0	54.6	40	218	22.0	5.1
Henry	1.3	84	11	136	46.5	4.8	38	355	153.3	6.8	3	4	0.8	0.1
Hickman	5.6	1 144	5	36	29.1	0.8	20	301	65.4	5.8	3	7	0.3	0.0
Hopkins	12.8	273	45	D	D	D	203	2 478	560.5	50.9	33	144	13.0	2.8
Jackson	2.1	156	3	D	D	D	32	221	45.2	3.0	4	14	1.2	0.3
Jefferson	687.0	927	1 026	16 413	13 000.6	763.2	2 775	43 687	10 002.4	978.5	991	6 888	1 995.1	263.3
Jessamine	7.0	144	37	D	D	D	163	2 388	731.7	60.2	46	202	28.1	6.4
Johnson	3.0	129	19	163	106.1	5.9	106	1 519	350.1	28.7	16	46	5.2	0.8
Kenton	0.5	3	140	D	D	D	426	6 589	1 262.0	124.9	132	856	180.0	26.6
Knott	2.2	136	3	D	D	D	34	203	47.6	3.8	4	11	1.0	0.2
Knox	1.0	31	12	85	63.7	2.6	106	1 260	318.6	26.8	8	75	4.4	1.8
Larue	1.1	80	9	39	19.8	0.9	31	217	49.2	4.0	4	D	D	D
Laurel	9.7	165	60	D	D	D	233	3 306	914.7	75.8	37	179	22.5	3.4
Lawrence	12.0	757	6	D	D	D	54	528	123.6	8.9	10	35	4.8	0.8
Lee	0.8	105	3	D	D	D	25	212	58.6	4.4	6	D	D	D
Leslie	1.8	156	NA	NA	NA	NA	33	306	59.4	4.8	2	D	D	D
Letcher	3.7	152	13	95	51.8	3.2	68	621	124.0	11.4	9	20	3.1	0.4
Lewis	1.6	118	2	D	D	D	38	281	56.8	3.6	5	14	0.6	0.1
Lincoln	3.3	135	15	D	D	D	61	659	127.2	10.8	11	11	2.3	0.2
Livingston	4.2	443	7	D	D	D	25	163	29.7	3.2	2	D	D	D
Logan	2.4	88	20	157	132.9	5.2	101	1 008	230.6	19.8	17	46	5.8	1.0
Lyon	3.1	368	3	D	D	D	29	235	61.0	4.4	9	16	2.1	0.4
McCracken	779.8	11 893	102	1 759	3 529.6	70.4	474	6 673	1 570.8	137.6	90	408	62.5	10.3
McCreary	2.1	114	3	9	1.3	0.2	52	406	82.5	6.8	6	29	2.2	0.7
McLean	1.9	200	7	98	38.6	2.8	29	215	48.0	4.4	2	D	D	D
Madison	11.9	144	45	405	242.1	14.3	322	4 190	976.0	82.4	75	241	36.9	5.0
Magoffin	1.3	97	4	28	11.6	0.7	33	248	52.9	4.0	3	10	0.8	0.2
Marion	5.9	298	11	66	22.9	1.3	74	625	136.2	10.5	10	36	4.6	0.9
Marshall	18.7	594	31	284	97.2	9.3	115	1 115	345.7	25.5	24	69	8.3	1.1
Martin	5.0	386	5	59	123.7	2.8	47	412	108.0	7.0	8	142	36.5	7.0
Mason	22.9	1 306	17	D	D	D	113	1 490	358.0	31.1	14	43	5.6	1.1
Meade	9.7	338	13	72	40.8	2.3	66	673	170.7	11.7	18	56	4.1	0.8
Menifee	1.3	198	NA	NA	NA	NA	17	169	24.2	1.8	4	D	D	D
Mercer	9.5	445	12	45	15.0	0.8	74	907	157.0	18.4	17	59	8.2	1.2
Metcalfe	0.8	82	1	D	D	D	32	304	58.0	5.2	5	10	0.6	0.2
Monroe	3.0	275	7	64	28.8	1.5	50	499	100.0	9.1	4	5	0.8	0.1
Montgomery	3.7	141	19	D	D	D	130	1 523	365.8	31.0	25	76	8.2	1.4
Morgan	1.7	121	1	D	D	D	56	408	88.1	7.7	5	13	1.3	0.2
Muhlenberg	1 236.8	39 263	8	D	D	D	105	1 224	265.6	24.6	22	78	6.5	1.7
Nelson	8.5	196	28	290	217.5	9.6	173	1 926	422.3	39.2	36	108	14.1	2.8
Nicholas	1.9	262	NA	NA	NA	NA	19	124	27.4	2.3	2	D	D	D

1. Merchant wholesalers, except manufacturers' sales branches and offices. 2. Employer establishments.

Table B. States and Counties — **Professional Services, Manufacturing, and Accommodation and Food Services**

STATE County	Professional, scientific, and technical services,[1] 2007				Manufacturing, 2007				Accommodation and food services, 2007			
	Number of establish-ments	Number of employees	Receipts (mil dol)	Annual payroll (mil dol)	Number of establish-ments	Number of employees	Receipts (mil dol)	Annual payroll (mil dol)	Number of establish-ments	Number of employees	Sales (mil dol)	Annual payroll (mil dol)
	147	148	149	150	151	152	153	154	155	156	157	158
KENTUCKY—Cont'd												
Clay	22	108	12.9	2.5	NA	NA	NA	NA	14	361	12.4	3.5
Clinton	14	34	2.5	0.8	14	1 731	D	44.4	16	223	7.8	1.4
Crittenden	14	42	3.6	0.7	NA	NA	NA	NA	12	152	5.1	1.1
Cumberland	9	24	1.4	0.4	NA	NA	NA	NA	11	122	4.5	1.4
Daviess	167	D	D	D	110	6 486	2 920.0	269.3	172	3 999	147.4	44.5
Edmonson	9	D	D	D	NA	NA	NA	NA	13	144	6.3	1.6
Elliott	1	D	D	D	NA	NA	NA	NA	5	37	3.2	0.5
Estill	9	23	1.0	0.3	NA	NA	NA	NA	19	223	7.9	2.0
Fayette	1 053	D	D	D	255	9 602	3 061.2	401.7	704	17 027	785.7	230.3
Fleming	13	40	3.2	1.0	NA	NA	NA	NA	12	146	6.0	1.8
Floyd	68	D	D	D	NA	NA	NA	NA	46	729	34.9	8.4
Franklin	121	705	88.9	31.4	41	3 566	1 400.8	141.7	95	2 121	80.5	25.5
Fulton	13	D	D	D	10	516	D	D	13	D	D	D
Gallatin	8	D	D	D	NA	NA	NA	NA	8	D	D	D
Garrard	17	36	2.0	0.7	NA	NA	NA	NA	12	126	4.5	1.1
Grant	23	D	D	D	17	D	D	29.1	46	864	30.0	8.7
Graves	36	D	D	D	49	2 240	D	61.8	49	D	D	D
Grayson	19	83	5.8	2.1	29	2 240	692.0	62.9	30	446	16.2	4.2
Green	14	30	2.7	0.7	NA	NA	NA	NA	10	102	4.0	1.0
Greenup	34	D	D	D	15	526	D	21.6	28	504	21.0	5.7
Hancock	7	D	D	D	14	2 709	D	D	10	71	2.2	0.5
Hardin	142	D	D	D	79	5 423	1 792.3	224.5	180	4 566	168.6	52.9
Harlan	47	D	D	D	NA	NA	NA	NA	28	528	20.3	5.1
Harrison	18	64	3.7	1.2	21	1 354	549.6	67.4	19	391	11.3	3.0
Hart	18	69	4.0	1.4	18	1 882	434.6	59.9	22	337	11.5	2.5
Henderson	81	404	34.9	11.1	77	6 420	D	D	88	1 348	54.7	15.1
Henry	21	D	D	D	10	D	D	D	13	D	D	D
Hickman	6	17	0.7	0.3	NA	NA	NA	NA	3	D	D	D
Hopkins	66	D	D	D	52	2 897	896.3	128.8	64	1 406	53.7	13.9
Jackson	6	12	1.1	0.5	NA	NA	NA	NA	5	42	2.1	0.5
Jefferson	2 266	D	D	D	797	45 142	25 695.4	2 233.8	1 561	35 897	1 629.2	480.6
Jessamine	66	224	20.6	6.4	67	2 738	1 015.6	102.8	59	1 183	46.4	13.0
Johnson	33	167	18.3	5.0	NA	NA	NA	NA	36	848	27.2	7.6
Kenton	366	D	D	D	123	4 637	1 236.4	210.3	307	7 033	323.3	94.2
Knott	12	52	5.1	1.8	NA	NA	NA	NA	4	109	3.0	0.8
Knox	40	D	D	D	18	879	210.7	34.0	37	580	27.5	5.7
Larue	14	D	D	D	20	783	90.0	20.6	14	146	5.9	1.6
Laurel	100	431	36.6	11.8	58	3 668	D	124.8	91	2 146	91.0	25.0
Lawrence	14	78	5.4	2.6	NA	NA	NA	NA	15	319	11.5	3.1
Lee	5	D	D	D	NA	NA	NA	NA	6	64	2.5	0.6
Leslie	10	D	D	D	NA	NA	NA	NA	6	81	3.9	0.9
Letcher	23	139	11.5	4.4	NA	NA	NA	NA	23	347	14.1	3.8
Lewis	4	16	0.8	0.4	NA	NA	NA	NA	13	102	3.9	0.8
Lincoln	23	128	9.8	3.3	18	737	D	D	17	259	9.4	2.6
Livingston	7	D	D	D	NA	NA	NA	NA	13	D	D	D
Logan	30	157	12.8	4.6	46	3 021	2 150.6	127.7	29	379	15.3	3.7
Lyon	9	132	2.9	1.3	NA	NA	NA	NA	23	313	12.2	3.5
McCracken	193	D	D	D	54	3 170	D	D	203	4 697	179.2	50.9
McCreary	7	33	2.3	0.5	NA	NA	NA	NA	18	247	7.1	1.9
McLean	8	D	D	D	NA	NA	NA	NA	14	101	3.1	0.8
Madison	120	D	D	D	73	5 473	D	D	143	3 368	127.3	34.7
Magoffin	13	94	13.3	6.2	NA	NA	NA	NA	11	163	7.3	2.0
Marion	23	110	7.7	2.9	30	3 349	620.2	120.1	29	417	12.3	3.6
Marshall	43	169	14.3	7.3	42	2 726	3 095.3	163.9	82	1 249	42.7	11.8
Martin	13	47	2.8	0.8	NA	NA	NA	NA	16	153	4.9	1.1
Mason	29	288	30.2	11.9	13	D	D	D	48	914	36.5	9.4
Meade	19	D	D	D	5	D	D	D	27	D	D	D
Menifee	2	D	D	D	NA	NA	NA	NA	1	D	D	D
Mercer	34	61	4.9	1.4	12	2 212	1 252.4	118.6	35	536	20.7	5.7
Metcalfe	9	16	1.2	0.3	9	979	391.3	32.4	9	101	5.1	0.7
Monroe	7	20	1.3	0.3	28	744	146.5	22.6	17	175	6.5	1.5
Montgomery	34	D	D	D	33	3 384	D	144.8	37	764	30.9	8.3
Morgan	9	42	3.0	0.8	NA	NA	NA	NA	13	226	8.1	1.9
Muhlenberg	41	166	7.1	2.1	26	547	D	22.6	55	786	27.2	7.5
Nelson	47	191	15.1	4.3	65	3 572	1 348.7	144.9	59	D	D	D
Nicholas	7	D	D	D	NA	NA	NA	NA	5	28	0.8	0.2

1. Establishment subject to federal tax.

STATE County	Health care and social assistance, 2007				Other services, 2007				Nonemployer businesses, 2013		Value of residential construction authorized by building permits, 2014	
	Number of establish-ments	Number of employees	Receipts (mil dol)	Annual payroll (mil dol)	Number of establish-ments	Number of employees	Receipts (mil dol)	Annual payroll (mil dol)	Number	Receipts (mil dol)	New Construction ($1,000)	Number of housing units
	159	160	161	162	163	164	165	166	167	168	169	170
KENTUCKY—Cont'd												
Clay	33	1 068	62.3	30.9	11	D	D	D	1 175	34.2	0	0
Clinton	24	609	35.4	14.3	8	17	1.2	0.3	812	30.2	0	0
Crittenden	17	471	28.3	12.7	14	D	D	D	619	21.7	60	1
Cumberland	14	382	22.4	9.7	7	19	1.9	0.4	582	19.2	0	0
Daviess	302	D	D	D	158	D	D	D	5 386	234.7	26 689	320
Edmonson	16	D	D	D	6	14	1.5	0.3	838	30.6	NA	NA
Elliott	9	D	D	D	4	D	D	D	314	7.6	NA	NA
Estill	22	388	26.7	9.5	11	22	2.5	0.5	883	20.5	0	0
Fayette	969	26 453	3 046.9	1 172.3	590	4 928	509.8	149.5	21 120	1 023.8	134 483	1 225
Fleming	21	614	42.1	16.0	14	33	2.9	0.5	1 303	45.6	100	1
Floyd	127	2 271	203.1	71.4	50	257	25.5	6.8	2 221	89.5	795	7
Franklin	145	2 315	256.7	76.2	142	797	90.9	26.5	3 151	115.3	13 317	87
Fulton	12	D	D	D	8	D	D	D	295	9.3	40	1
Gallatin	9	D	D	D	NA	NA	NA	NA	379	12.9	1 819	13
Garrard	21	203	13.3	5.5	14	64	3.4	1.0	1 294	42.0	0	0
Grant	33	519	43.1	17.5	34	D	D	D	1 312	50.8	7 826	55
Graves	94	1 642	113.4	39.1	31	177	25.7	6.6	2 631	106.7	0	0
Grayson	53	994	80.4	27.7	25	78	6.9	1.1	1 931	90.7	235	4
Green	27	500	31.4	13.0	15	47	3.2	0.7	984	32.7	100	1
Greenup	79	983	75.9	35.0	30	D	D	D	1 846	58.9	3 714	16
Hancock	13	136	6.2	2.1	7	D	D	D	447	12.5	638	3
Hardin	308	D	D	D	153	D	D	D	5 405	209.1	35 152	364
Harlan	54	1 362	128.9	41.6	26	125	8.9	2.6	1 415	36.3	0	0
Harrison	46	903	71.3	27.1	22	73	6.8	1.5	1 052	37.3	4 046	21
Hart	24	408	28.4	10.9	16	46	3.4	1.0	1 644	84.2	9 259	87
Henderson	141	D	D	D	70	D	D	D	2 430	90.3	9 160	46
Henry	21	D	D	D	15	55	4.6	1.4	1 064	42.0	4 016	27
Hickman	9	148	8.4	3.1	2	D	D	D	307	10.5	NA	NA
Hopkins	113	3 152	259.2	122.7	72	561	51.2	14.2	2 342	87.3	9 772	71
Jackson	17	272	15.8	6.4	4	D	D	D	887	22.0	0	0
Jefferson	2 227	58 914	6 171.5	2 309.4	1 402	12 526	1 315.0	317.2	50 359	2 293.3	292 403	2 431
Jessamine	76	726	43.7	21.6	73	281	19.6	5.9	4 020	176.6	43 971	187
Johnson	62	778	86.5	23.8	32	116	9.5	2.2	1 379	49.2	848	7
Kenton	337	9 485	1 026.0	418.4	249	1 848	150.4	43.6	9 266	408.1	51 124	278
Knott	17	380	19.3	7.4	8	D	D	D	812	29.3	NA	NA
Knox	71	1 071	76.4	29.5	21	74	6.7	1.8	2 134	69.8	0	0
Larue	15	D	D	D	16	D	D	D	1 066	34.7	7 805	43
Laurel	128	2 861	265.9	97.5	73	422	37.7	10.1	3 878	172.6	145	1
Lawrence	30	D	D	D	15	D	D	D	794	23.3	NA	NA
Lee	17	853	16.6	9.5	1	D	D	D	420	13.6	NA	NA
Leslie	15	431	33.1	12.9	3	D	D	D	520	17.6	NA	NA
Letcher	44	1 097	79.9	35.5	16	49	5.6	1.0	1 171	35.9	0	10
Lewis	13	307	25.9	10.4	3	D	D	D	910	32.9	NA	NA
Lincoln	34	543	33.4	15.4	17	45	3.9	0.8	1 643	53.0	6 740	36
Livingston	16	D	D	D	6	24	1.5	0.4	563	19.2	NA	NA
Logan	48	703	54.6	18.3	36	173	12.9	3.6	1 760	72.2	795	13
Lyon	13	238	10.4	4.7	10	12	1.1	0.3	493	15.4	425	3
McCracken	264	6 501	723.3	257.3	136	D	D	D	4 216	172.2	37 325	223
McCreary	29	360	17.3	7.3	6	21	1.6	0.3	888	31.2	0	0
McLean	9	D	D	D	13	D	D	D	517	15.5	0	0
Madison	186	3 241	238.4	91.1	89	395	31.5	7.8	5 430	195.7	14 723	225
Magoffin	14	255	21.5	5.8	8	D	D	D	667	19.0	NA	NA
Marion	43	1 019	74.2	28.1	17	76	7.4	1.9	1 176	50.5	1 304	13
Marshall	52	938	54.1	22.0	42	157	14.6	3.2	2 131	82.2	10 153	137
Martin	19	227	12.7	5.0	10	D	D	D	464	14.1	NA	NA
Mason	71	1 187	107.9	37.2	45	D	D	D	1 145	40.5	3 061	19
Meade	36	259	15.2	6.2	24	122	9.0	2.5	1 469	57.4	13 850	85
Menifee	7	142	8.7	4.0	3	D	D	D	421	13.2	NA	NA
Mercer	36	624	41.8	17.2	25	D	D	D	1 436	59.3	6 842	59
Metcalfe	16	117	6.4	2.9	6	D	D	D	855	30.7	NA	NA
Monroe	29	475	32.0	12.6	13	42	3.0	0.7	900	32.8	NA	NA
Montgomery	74	1 277	76.5	28.5	32	D	D	D	1 718	65.8	4 358	56
Morgan	18	445	30.4	11.4	17	38	3.2	0.7	758	24.4	1 275	17
Muhlenberg	58	D	D	D	43	160	12.4	3.0	1 608	52.5	426	2
Nelson	86	1 380	113.5	40.9	50	255	16.5	4.5	3 037	112.0	25 331	193
Nicholas	10	258	13.3	6.3	7	26	1.5	0.4	495	14.7	291	4

STATE County	Government employment and payroll, 2012: Full-time equivalent employees	March payroll (dollars)	March payroll (percent of total): Adminis-tration, judicial, and legal	Police and Corrections	Fire Protection	Highways and transpor-tation	Health and Welfare	Natural resources and utilities	Education and libraries	Local government finances, 2012: General revenue: Total (mil dol)	Inter-govern-mental (mil dol)	Taxes: Total (mil dol)	Per capita[1] (dollars): Total	Property
	171	172	173	174	175	176	177	178	179	180	181	182	183	184
KENTUCKY—Cont'd														
Clay	994	2 631 167	3.1	5.8	0.0	2.7	3.9	4.3	79.7	47.7	34.9	7.4	345	209
Clinton	443	1 162 284	4.8	3.5	0.0	2.1	6.0	0.7	82.6	24.4	16.8	5.6	548	258
Crittenden	318	847 790	5.5	13.8	0.0	2.2	0.0	6.6	71.2	21.9	15.1	4.5	482	288
Cumberland	454	1 348 734	2.8	4.3	0.1	1.8	42.8	3.6	43.6	42.0	9.9	4.0	592	292
Daviess	4 233	13 420 532	3.9	7.2	3.3	2.8	7.4	14.6	60.1	320.6	123.3	99.0	1 012	595
Edmonson	508	1 172 078	2.9	4.0	0.4	1.8	3.8	6.2	80.7	24.3	16.3	5.3	442	332
Elliott	264	668 556	3.5	2.6	0.0	3.1	11.5	2.5	75.8	15.4	11.7	2.1	276	169
Estill	575	2 082 079	1.7	13.1	7.0	4.2	11.0	3.5	58.3	35.1	24.2	6.6	452	275
Fayette	9 962	37 856 745	4.3	13.5	7.8	2.1	6.3	4.9	58.5	920.0	203.8	539.7	1 767	835
Fleming	697	2 194 909	3.1	2.3	0.7	1.3	36.8	2.2	53.4	87.7	20.7	8.0	553	322
Floyd	1 386	3 755 718	2.5	3.5	2.7	1.3	3.7	4.8	81.3	96.9	62.9	22.7	584	472
Franklin	1 716	6 237 758	4.5	8.7	9.2	2.6	1.1	8.1	54.8	158.6	42.6	66.3	1 332	688
Fulton	418	1 044 790	3.3	7.0	5.9	10.5	0.4	9.6	58.4	26.4	17.0	5.5	847	491
Gallatin	332	954 873	7.1	3.3	0.0	2.1	2.1	3.8	81.6	30.0	13.7	8.5	1 007	632
Garrard	526	1 692 901	3.4	1.7	0.1	1.9	5.2	1.5	86.1	39.9	19.9	12.9	761	479
Grant	998	2 854 787	5.3	7.3	1.9	1.5	0.1	5.4	77.4	59.9	37.6	15.0	611	477
Graves	1 308	3 544 113	2.9	8.2	3.0	2.3	0.0	2.8	79.5	77.1	43.4	23.1	614	366
Grayson	956	2 669 148	4.8	14.5	0.3	2.2	2.1	3.6	70.5	66.8	40.3	15.8	608	317
Green	635	2 084 431	5.8	8.4	4.2	2.1	27.5	9.5	41.8	40.4	15.6	5.1	451	288
Greenup	1 220	4 273 541	2.1	6.9	1.4	1.9	0.4	3.3	82.5	86.3	43.9	29.1	793	654
Hancock	406	1 128 193	8.8	3.1	0.0	3.6	5.5	3.0	73.5	70.5	13.2	9.1	1 052	490
Hardin	5 176	17 598 804	1.2	3.7	1.8	1.2	45.7	3.6	41.7	459.3	132.4	90.3	844	479
Harlan	1 193	3 057 085	2.8	6.7	0.2	2.7	1.0	4.6	81.1	96.7	61.1	16.0	562	404
Harrison	635	1 973 639	6.3	9.3	3.0	3.0	0.0	2.3	76.0	38.3	20.2	14.4	771	361
Hart	599	1 691 514	2.9	6.7	0.1	2.1	4.8	5.2	76.9	36.5	22.7	9.6	522	293
Henderson	2 096	5 804 471	5.3	9.5	3.7	4.2	1.2	14.4	60.1	156.8	64.1	42.2	908	550
Henry	640	1 779 003	8.8	3.5	0.0	1.4	1.9	5.1	79.3	35.5	21.0	10.1	661	488
Hickman	198	524 720	7.5	5.4	0.0	2.2	2.3	1.0	80.8	11.7	7.7	3.0	622	421
Hopkins	1 879	5 461 945	4.2	9.4	3.9	3.0	5.6	7.9	65.5	126.7	65.8	37.0	791	444
Jackson	523	1 629 435	2.4	2.5	0.0	2.9	0.5	0.3	90.4	29.9	23.5	5.0	377	231
Jefferson	25 957	96 919 915	3.8	11.0	4.8	4.5	4.7	8.9	60.3	2 308.9	694.0	1 084.7	1 445	808
Jessamine	1 836	5 035 213	4.3	7.1	3.4	1.5	7.8	4.8	68.6	116.9	46.1	57.3	1 153	712
Johnson	862	2 638 353	2.4	1.8	1.1	1.5	0.7	2.6	86.7	69.4	42.9	14.0	598	338
Kenton	5 823	21 356 962	2.4	8.9	5.6	14.3	2.9	9.7	54.0	710.4	161.7	228.8	1 415	873
Knott	613	1 519 486	4.8	3.6	0.0	2.3	3.8	6.9	78.6	39.0	27.2	8.8	546	448
Knox	1 187	3 283 773	1.7	2.6	0.1	1.9	10.4	2.7	80.2	87.2	55.9	18.9	597	369
Larue	547	1 474 160	4.8	6.4	0.0	1.7	3.2	2.6	80.9	31.5	21.6	7.0	497	357
Laurel	2 042	5 388 170	2.8	6.5	0.3	2.5	3.9	3.5	79.3	125.4	73.3	38.1	641	329
Lawrence	604	1 562 126	4.8	3.3	1.1	2.8	4.5	4.0	78.6	54.7	23.2	8.2	517	381
Lee	279	772 061	4.6	4.7	0.0	3.4	11.0	4.8	71.3	19.3	12.6	4.2	539	364
Leslie	447	1 317 537	5.5	3.0	0.0	2.8	0.0	4.1	79.4	32.5	23.5	7.5	668	472
Letcher	1 021	2 457 149	1.7	4.3	0.4	2.2	3.8	4.0	81.9	57.9	40.2	11.8	493	377
Lewis	560	1 776 699	3.4	5.5	0.0	2.3	1.5	4.2	82.9	29.1	20.7	6.3	457	316
Lincoln	879	2 396 927	2.4	4.3	0.3	1.9	3.1	3.5	84.1	50.5	35.4	11.5	471	295
Livingston	346	854 563	7.6	3.0	8.2	3.7	4.9	4.1	68.4	22.0	13.3	6.5	688	436
Logan	972	2 732 295	5.2	7.8	1.4	1.6	0.3	3.8	78.6	68.7	39.7	21.0	787	379
Lyon	237	841 257	5.7	3.3	0.2	3.5	5.4	4.3	50.3	18.0	7.4	7.1	847	615
McCracken	2 541	8 688 735	3.1	9.6	3.2	4.7	11.0	11.5	55.4	229.1	82.8	78.2	1 193	632
McCreary	751	1 960 007	1.9	4.5	0.0	1.6	6.3	4.0	80.7	47.9	30.0	16.4	907	789
McLean	404	945 835	4.5	1.7	0.0	2.1	0.7	5.7	75.6	30.6	17.9	7.4	778	382
Madison	2 628	7 891 742	2.5	5.2	3.8	2.3	9.6	4.2	68.4	199.0	81.8	79.3	935	482
Magoffin	510	1 498 254	4.1	2.3	0.8	3.5	6.7	3.0	79.4	38.5	29.7	6.1	470	216
Marion	789	2 206 926	2.6	13.7	0.3	6.2	3.0	6.0	67.3	49.3	25.1	15.3	763	452
Marshall	1 233	3 676 388	2.4	4.3	0.0	2.0	23.4	5.4	61.5	138.8	34.7	36.4	1 160	589
Martin	565	1 560 146	7.3	3.2	0.0	2.3	6.6	3.2	77.0	32.7	22.1	7.2	566	272
Mason	917	2 257 527	7.8	11.9	3.1	2.4	6.1	5.7	59.4	62.2	21.7	18.3	1 043	494
Meade	931	2 688 037	3.4	5.7	0.1	1.5	3.2	3.3	81.9	56.8	35.1	14.8	508	380
Menifee	255	589 112	3.9	0.5	0.0	2.1	3.1	2.7	87.6	17.2	10.7	4.3	691	525
Mercer	736	2 237 637	6.9	9.4	2.9	5.4	2.8	4.1	67.1	50.4	24.0	20.1	944	596
Metcalfe	377	953 969	2.6	3.0	0.0	3.1	0.6	4.9	85.9	23.2	15.8	5.4	544	294
Monroe	585	1 493 674	4.7	6.7	0.0	1.6	5.1	5.9	75.8	28.4	19.3	6.0	550	323
Montgomery	853	2 642 340	1.3	2.9	6.2	0.8	6.6	1.1	80.9	69.6	34.6	22.4	832	434
Morgan	486	1 237 685	4.6	5.7	0.0	1.9	4.7	5.7	76.6	34.6	23.0	6.2	453	241
Muhlenberg	1 235	3 174 925	4.8	7.6	1.4	3.6	3.9	4.0	74.3	72.9	47.9	14.7	471	350
Nelson	1 501	4 602 823	4.7	5.8	0.7	1.6	4.5	4.2	76.6	108.2	44.4	36.8	829	669
Nicholas	219	557 957	7.9	3.1	0.4	3.0	1.0	7.7	75.2	15.4	10.3	3.1	437	281

1. Based on the resident population estimated as of July 1 of the year shown.

STATE County	Local government finances, 2012 (cont.)									Government employment, 2013			Presidential election,[2] 2012		
	Direct general expenditure							Debt outstanding					Percent of vote cast:		
			Percent of total for:												
	Total (mil dol)	Per capita[1] (dollars)	Educa- tion	Health and hospitals	Police protec- tion	Public welfare	High- ways	Total (mil dol)	Per capita[1] (dollars)	Federal civilian	Federal military	State and local	Demo- cratic	Republi- can	All other
	185	186	187	188	189	190	191	192	193	194	195	196	197	198	199
KENTUCKY—Cont'd															
Clay	48.2	2 236	66.0	2.1	3.1	0.0	7.1	33.2	1 542	369	63	1 187	21.1	77.5	1.4
Clinton	23.1	2 250	70.0	3.9	2.9	0.0	4.7	18.9	1 842	45	33	605	18.2	80.7	1.1
Crittenden	20.2	2 174	49.6	0.3	3.2	0.0	6.6	34.3	3 698	20	30	397	31.9	66.3	1.8
Cumberland	47.8	7 014	21.3	57.7	1.5	0.0	3.3	40.3	5 903	0	22	328	24.9	73.5	1.6
Daviess	344.4	3 519	39.4	6.6	4.3	0.1	2.9	1 124.1	11 488	243	335	8 767	44.2	54.3	1.5
Edmonson	23.8	1 975	69.3	5.0	2.8	0.0	5.3	36.6	3 036	240	38	530	31.3	67.6	1.1
Elliott	14.7	1 891	60.4	9.7	1.5	1.2	7.3	16.4	2 107	0	22	558	61.0	35.9	3.1
Estill	39.4	2 719	67.4	7.2	1.3	0.0	3.6	33.1	2 286	21	47	710	29.3	69.3	1.4
Fayette	871.4	2 852	47.8	1.8	5.5	1.0	1.3	1 402.6	4 591	4 153	1 021	37 297	51.7	46.9	1.3
Fleming	60.2	4 132	42.2	39.1	1.6	0.0	3.5	101.3	6 957	47	48	950	39.1	58.8	2.1
Floyd	95.8	2 460	58.7	3.2	3.0	0.0	4.7	77.1	1 979	123	124	2 465	48.1	49.4	2.5
Franklin	148.7	2 986	38.2	6.9	4.7	0.1	3.3	147.3	2 957	516	173	13 854	48.9	49.5	1.7
Fulton	26.8	4 114	37.8	0.2	5.2	0.0	5.6	13.8	2 107	26	38	524	43.8	54.2	2.0
Gallatin	31.5	3 721	44.7	3.1	3.1	0.0	2.2	306.7	36 176	31	28	427	40.0	57.6	2.3
Garrard	36.7	2 171	53.0	18.0	3.1	0.0	3.4	63.2	3 736	21	55	706	27.9	71.0	1.1
Grant	60.7	2 479	63.9	0.5	3.4	0.1	3.7	87.4	3 568	42	80	1 196	35.5	62.9	1.5
Graves	76.9	2 049	62.2	0.3	2.9	0.2	4.8	208.0	5 539	199	121	1 731	36.2	62.2	1.6
Grayson	62.1	2 391	54.7	1.0	2.5	0.6	4.1	106.8	4 113	84	83	1 630	31.8	66.7	1.5
Green	39.0	3 443	35.6	43.0	2.1	0.0	3.4	34.9	3 088	20	36	749	23.7	74.5	1.8
Greenup	85.0	2 315	62.5	3.4	4.2	0.0	4.8	61.8	1 684	59	119	1 490	41.9	56.0	2.1
Hancock	79.0	9 101	19.3	0.8	0.8	0.1	2.2	714.6	82 360	20	28	429	51.5	46.5	2.0
Hardin	430.7	4 025	34.9	44.6	2.8	0.0	2.0	304.8	2 848	6 377	9 113	7 200	39.1	59.8	1.1
Harlan	95.7	3 353	47.6	20.0	2.5	1.4	4.6	87.7	3 072	87	92	1 835	26.1	72.3	1.6
Harrison	37.7	2 026	62.3	1.1	5.4	0.2	9.1	17.8	956	41	60	828	38.4	59.6	2.0
Hart	35.3	1 923	58.3	4.8	2.9	0.1	5.4	51.6	2 807	33	60	818	33.6	64.5	1.9
Henderson	158.7	3 411	41.1	0.2	3.9	0.4	4.8	595.8	12 809	114	149	2 770	50.6	47.9	1.5
Henry	38.5	2 513	68.2	3.6	3.2	0.0	4.4	41.2	2 690	98	51	724	39.4	59.0	1.6
Hickman	12.5	2 633	61.6	0.0	3.3	0.0	8.4	15.6	3 280	22	15	244	36.1	62.5	1.4
Hopkins	127.9	2 738	50.6	2.9	4.8	0.7	5.6	336.3	7 198	156	150	3 487	36.7	61.6	1.7
Jackson	37.2	2 791	73.7	0.3	0.9	0.0	5.1	39.0	2 924	33	44	689	14.2	84.4	1.4
Jefferson	2 460.2	3 277	46.7	1.4	4.8	0.5	3.0	4 784.1	6 372	6 487	2 685	42 354	55.5	43.5	1.0
Jessamine	118.6	2 390	54.7	4.5	6.5	0.1	5.6	197.1	3 971	77	159	2 520	30.8	67.8	1.3
Johnson	63.4	2 713	62.6	7.2	2.4	0.0	4.6	48.3	2 065	41	75	1 482	28.3	69.8	1.9
Kenton	844.4	5 222	24.0	2.1	3.6	0.0	2.7	2 312.8	14 302	4 178	561	7 359	38.8	59.7	1.5
Knott	35.4	2 196	66.3	0.1	2.3	0.2	6.1	25.7	1 594	46	50	711	44.9	52.7	2.4
Knox	85.5	2 695	53.4	8.3	1.8	0.0	3.5	96.3	3 036	157	102	1 458	27.0	71.6	1.4
Larue	29.1	2 055	63.2	2.5	2.5	0.0	4.3	46.0	3 247	42	45	561	31.0	67.2	1.8
Laurel	122.8	2 066	64.1	2.4	3.8	0.9	3.4	206.4	3 470	258	195	2 637	20.5	78.5	1.0
Lawrence	56.4	3 560	42.6	2.7	1.4	0.0	5.0	323.0	20 378	31	52	663	36.0	62.0	1.9
Lee	18.2	2 364	53.5	6.3	4.4	0.1	10.1	9.1	1 180	12	22	463	27.1	71.3	1.6
Leslie	38.3	3 427	60.6	0.3	1.6	0.0	6.1	45.7	4 093	18	35	579	17.4	81.3	1.3
Letcher	57.7	2 407	65.1	0.2	2.3	0.0	4.0	48.6	2 030	54	77	1 140	31.9	65.2	3.0
Lewis	32.1	2 322	56.5	3.9	2.6	0.0	6.9	85.2	6 155	19	45	630	31.5	67.1	1.4
Lincoln	57.7	2 358	64.0	2.6	1.3	0.1	4.4	51.0	2 086	55	79	983	30.1	68.5	1.4
Livingston	21.9	2 329	53.2	2.8	2.6	0.0	6.2	29.9	3 170	87	31	473	35.3	62.9	1.8
Logan	70.1	2 633	53.7	15.9	4.9	0.0	4.2	64.5	2 421	57	87	1 225	35.0	63.6	1.4
Lyon	19.0	2 270	40.7	6.1	4.4	0.8	10.5	27.6	3 304	30	24	988	40.9	57.6	1.5
McCracken	222.0	3 387	53.7	0.1	3.1	0.1	3.3	760.9	11 608	634	239	3 932	36.7	61.9	1.4
McCreary	46.4	2 568	59.4	1.1	0.7	0.0	4.6	41.3	2 284	469	52	774	23.3	75.4	1.3
McLean	31.1	3 277	41.5	3.3	0.7	0.6	9.6	42.6	4 483	28	31	520	44.4	54.0	1.7
Madison	191.9	2 263	56.3	9.2	4.2	0.1	3.1	375.9	4 434	1 054	273	7 436	38.1	60.5	1.4
Magoffin	33.9	2 601	61.0	4.8	2.9	0.0	5.3	40.5	3 109	13	42	623	45.3	52.3	2.4
Marion	48.7	2 426	52.2	2.0	3.7	0.0	4.4	59.9	2 983	45	62	872	47.2	50.5	2.3
Marshall	146.0	4 657	26.1	18.0	3.9	0.3	2.3	483.2	15 417	87	101	1 638	36.7	61.4	1.9
Martin	33.5	2 633	63.8	9.1	1.1	0.0	5.6	13.4	1 048	390	36	628	21.9	76.5	1.6
Mason	67.9	3 879	34.1	4.5	4.5	0.0	7.5	293.2	16 743	48	56	1 619	40.6	57.6	1.8
Meade	55.3	1 892	66.3	2.2	2.1	0.0	3.0	96.2	3 291	34	95	1 141	38.8	59.7	1.5
Menifee	19.5	3 133	66.1	3.5	3.4	0.2	4.2	20.7	3 323	51	20	345	51.3	46.4	2.3
Mercer	48.2	2 267	58.2	3.7	3.9	0.0	4.4	86.2	4 054	39	70	895	31.4	67.4	1.2
Metcalfe	34.7	3 479	78.8	1.8	2.2	0.0	4.0	60.2	6 042	24	32	514	32.2	65.1	2.7
Monroe	27.3	2 526	64.8	9.0	3.4	0.0	4.9	27.3	2 518	24	35	604	22.9	75.8	1.3
Montgomery	73.1	2 716	63.0	9.0	4.0	0.0	2.4	73.0	2 713	66	88	1 196	41.0	57.6	1.5
Morgan	36.5	2 671	54.2	4.4	1.9	6.8	7.3	55.1	4 035	34	38	1 016	42.9	54.7	2.4
Muhlenberg	94.2	3 022	66.4	2.4	2.2	0.1	4.0	83.6	2 681	549	96	1 833	48.3	50.0	1.7
Nelson	117.2	2 645	59.2	2.1	3.0	0.2	2.8	245.4	5 537	78	145	1 724	42.2	55.9	1.9
Nicholas	15.9	2 269	62.2	1.2	3.9	0.5	10.0	17.4	2 481	13	23	293	42.8	55.0	2.2

1. Based on the resident population estimated as of July 1 of the year shown. 2.

STATE/ County code	CBSA code[1]	County type[2]	STATE County	Land area,[3] (sq km) 2010	Population, 2014: Total persons 2014	Population, 2014: Rank	Population, 2014: Per square kilometer	Population and population characteristics, 2013: Race alone or in combination, not Hispanic or Latino (percent): White	Black	American Indian, Alaska Native	Asian and Pacific Islander	Percent Hispanic or Latino[4]	Age (percent): Under 5 years	5 to 17 years	18 to 24 years	25 to 34 years	35 to 44 years	45 to 54 years
				1	2	3	4	5	6	7	8	9	10	11	12	13	14	15
			KENTUCKY—Cont'd															
21 183	...	6	Ohio	1 521	23 977	1 643	15.8	95.2	1.3	0.5	0.4	3.4	6.2	18.0	7.8	12.0	12.4	13.8
21 185	31140	1	Oldham	485	63 490	824	130.9	90.2	4.9	0.7	2.0	3.6	4.7	21.7	7.7	9.9	15.0	17.3
21 187	...	8	Owen	909	10 645	2 385	11.7	96.0	1.4	0.6	0.4	2.6	5.3	18.0	7.7	10.6	13.0	14.6
21 189	...	9	Owsley	511	4 508	2 864	8.8	98.0	0.8	0.5	0.1	1.1	6.1	15.4	7.8	11.9	11.9	14.5
21 191	17140	1	Pendleton	718	14 493	2 135	20.2	98.0	0.8	0.6	0.5	1.1	5.5	17.4	9.1	11.1	12.9	16.1
21 193	...	7	Perry	880	27 597	1 508	31.4	96.9	2.2	0.5	0.7	0.8	6.6	15.1	8.1	12.6	13.4	14.9
21 195	...	7	Pike	2 038	63 034	833	30.9	97.9	0.9	0.4	0.7	0.8	5.6	15.6	8.3	11.7	13.6	14.9
21 197	...	6	Powell	464	12 434	2 269	26.8	97.6	1.1	0.6	0.3	1.3	6.5	17.4	8.2	12.4	13.5	14.3
21 199	43700	5	Pulaski	1 705	63 825	821	37.4	95.7	1.6	0.7	0.7	2.3	5.9	17.0	7.7	11.3	12.7	14.4
21 201	...	8	Robertson	259	2 197	3 035	8.5	98.4	0.6	0.8	0.1	1.1	4.3	16.1	8.5	8.9	11.2	16.2
21 203	40080	7	Rockcastle	820	16 826	1 994	20.5	98.5	0.6	0.8	0.3	0.8	5.4	16.6	8.0	10.8	13.1	15.5
21 205	...	7	Rowan	725	23 655	1 655	32.6	95.7	2.3	0.5	1.1	1.4	5.6	13.7	21.7	11.7	11.0	12.0
21 207	...	9	Russell	657	17 774	1 930	27.1	95.2	1.0	0.7	0.5	3.7	6.5	15.8	7.6	10.7	12.2	14.5
21 209	30460	2	Scott	730	51 284	969	70.3	89.0	6.5	0.6	1.4	4.1	6.7	19.2	9.7	12.7	15.3	14.5
21 211	31140	1	Shelby	983	44 875	1 072	45.7	82.5	8.4	0.7	1.2	9.0	6.9	17.5	8.5	12.3	13.6	14.9
21 213	...	6	Simpson	607	17 826	1 926	29.4	87.1	10.9	0.8	1.1	2.1	6.9	17.8	8.2	11.7	12.6	14.7
21 215	31140	1	Spencer	483	17 668	1 936	36.6	95.6	2.2	0.6	0.7	2.0	5.7	18.7	7.5	10.6	15.1	17.0
21 217	15820	7	Taylor	690	25 257	1 599	36.6	92.2	6.0	0.5	0.9	1.9	6.2	16.1	11.0	12.1	10.8	13.6
21 219	...	8	Todd	970	12 520	2 263	12.9	87.1	8.9	0.6	0.5	4.2	7.1	19.7	8.5	11.9	12.3	13.6
21 221	17300	3	Trigg	1 143	14 142	2 158	12.4	89.8	8.7	0.8	0.7	1.7	5.2	16.7	6.9	9.1	11.9	14.7
21 223	31140	1	Trimble	393	8 786	2 533	22.4	95.3	1.0	0.7	0.7	3.3	5.8	18.0	8.2	11.0	13.5	15.0
21 225	...	6	Union	888	15 165	2 089	17.1	84.4	14.2	0.6	0.6	1.7	5.2	15.7	16.5	11.0	11.1	12.6
21 227	14540	3	Warren	1 403	120 460	512	85.9	82.6	10.1	0.6	3.6	5.0	6.2	16.2	16.6	13.6	12.1	12.5
21 229	...	8	Washington	770	11 959	2 299	15.5	89.5	7.1	0.4	0.5	3.7	5.9	17.3	9.4	10.2	11.9	15.0
21 231	...	7	Wayne	1 187	20 486	1 803	17.3	94.9	2.1	0.6	0.6	2.9	5.6	16.3	8.0	11.3	12.5	14.1
21 233	...	2	Webster	860	13 236	2 223	15.4	90.4	5.0	0.7	0.6	4.6	6.5	16.4	8.1	11.9	13.0	13.9
21 235	30940	7	Whitley	1 134	35 503	1 287	31.3	97.4	1.2	0.9	0.7	1.0	7.0	17.0	11.3	11.7	11.9	13.6
21 237	...	9	Wolfe	575	7 214	2 658	12.5	98.7	0.5	0.6	0.2	0.7	6.1	17.8	6.8	11.2	11.7	15.2
21 239	30460	2	Woodford	489	25 563	1 581	52.3	87.2	6.0	0.5	0.9	6.7	5.2	17.6	8.0	10.6	12.8	15.7
22 000	...	X	LOUISIANA	111 898	4 649 676	X	41.6	60.7	32.8	1.1	2.1	4.7	6.7	17.4	10.2	14.3	12.2	13.5
22 001	29180	4	Acadia	1 697	62 486	837	36.8	79.1	19.0	0.5	0.5	2.0	7.2	19.7	9.4	12.9	11.5	13.9
22 003	...	6	Allen	1 973	25 713	1 572	13.0	72.1	23.9	3.0	1.1	1.6	6.2	16.4	8.7	15.3	14.3	14.3
22 005	12940	2	Ascension	751	117 029	523	155.8	70.9	23.1	0.6	1.5	5.0	7.3	20.6	8.5	13.9	14.6	14.3
22 007	...	6	Assumption	877	23 034	1 684	26.3	67.2	30.0	0.8	0.5	2.3	5.6	17.3	9.5	12.2	12.0	14.8
22 009	...	6	Avoyelles	2 156	41 145	1 149	19.1	67.1	30.2	1.9	0.7	1.7	6.7	17.1	8.9	13.4	12.1	14.0
22 011	19760	6	Beauregard	2 998	36 198	1 270	12.1	81.5	14.1	1.9	1.2	3.5	6.6	18.6	8.7	13.3	12.9	13.5
22 013	...	6	Bienville	2 101	13 885	2 180	6.6	55.8	42.5	0.8	0.5	1.7	6.2	17.2	8.4	11.4	10.6	14.3
22 015	43340	2	Bossier	2 176	125 064	497	57.5	70.0	22.1	1.0	2.7	6.3	7.4	17.9	10.0	15.5	13.0	12.5
22 017	43340	2	Caddo	2 275	252 603	262	111.0	47.8	48.4	0.9	1.6	2.7	7.2	17.2	9.5	14.2	11.7	12.7
22 019	29340	3	Calcasieu	2 755	197 204	331	71.6	70.2	25.9	1.1	1.6	2.9	6.8	18.1	10.0	13.9	11.8	13.3
22 021	...	8	Caldwell	1 371	9 894	2 446	7.2	79.8	17.3	0.8	0.4	2.7	6.3	16.7	8.7	12.5	12.9	13.7
22 023	29340	3	Cameron	3 328	6 679	2 705	2.0	94.0	2.6	1.0	0.3	3.2	5.5	18.4	8.3	11.6	11.7	16.9
22 025	...	9	Catahoula	1 834	10 151	2 426	5.5	66.6	32.2	0.7	0.2	1.1	5.6	16.4	9.4	14.2	11.4	13.4
22 027	...	7	Claiborne	1 955	16 412	2 016	8.4	47.2	51.0	0.8	0.7	1.4	5.2	13.4	9.2	15.1	12.7	14.0
22 029	35020	7	Concordia	1 805	20 466	1 804	11.3	57.7	40.7	0.7	0.5	1.2	6.4	17.9	9.2	13.4	11.4	13.2
22 031	43340	2	De Soto	2 268	27 142	1 527	12.0	58.4	38.3	1.4	0.4	2.6	6.5	18.1	8.4	12.0	11.9	14.0
22 033	12940	2	East Baton Rouge	1 179	446 042	154	378.3	46.9	46.3	0.6	3.6	3.9	6.5	16.4	14.7	15.0	11.4	12.1
22 035	...	7	East Carroll	1 090	7 487	2 641	6.9	29.7	67.9	0.6	0.7	2.0	7.1	17.5	10.9	14.5	11.8	13.5
22 037	12940	2	East Feliciana	1 174	19 813	1 845	16.9	53.6	44.8	0.8	0.7	1.3	5.4	14.0	9.2	13.0	12.5	15.5
22 039	...	6	Evangeline	1 716	33 700	1 337	19.6	68.7	28.8	0.6	0.6	2.3	6.9	19.4	9.9	12.7	11.8	13.5
22 041	...	7	Franklin	1 618	20 441	1 810	12.6	66.7	31.7	0.5	0.5	1.3	7.4	18.7	8.5	11.7	10.9	13.2
22 043	10780	3	Grant	1 665	22 384	1 712	13.4	78.5	16.3	1.7	0.6	4.4	5.8	16.0	8.3	16.5	14.4	13.7
22 045	29180	4	Iberia	1 487	73 913	740	49.7	61.2	32.7	0.7	3.2	3.6	7.1	19.5	9.4	12.9	11.6	14.0
22 047	12940	2	Iberville	1 602	33 327	1 345	20.8	48.6	48.6	0.5	0.6	2.4	5.8	15.5	9.8	14.6	12.7	15.2
22 049	...	6	Jackson	1 474	15 994	2 041	10.9	68.6	29.9	0.8	0.5	1.5	6.0	16.5	8.2	13.1	11.7	13.7
22 051	35380	1	Jefferson	766	435 716	159	568.8	55.8	26.8	0.8	4.6	13.4	6.3	15.7	8.6	14.7	12.3	14.1
22 053	...	6	Jefferson Davis	1 687	31 477	1 399	18.7	80.0	18.2	1.0	0.6	2.0	7.0	18.7	8.6	12.3	11.7	13.9
22 055	29180	3	Lafayette	696	235 644	277	338.6	67.9	26.5	0.7	2.0	4.3	6.8	17.2	11.1	16.4	12.5	13.3
22 057	26380	3	Lafourche	2 767	98 020	601	35.4	78.6	14.2	3.5	1.1	4.2	6.4	17.3	10.0	13.9	12.0	14.8
22 059	...	6	La Salle	1 618	14 839	2 114	9.2	84.0	12.5	1.5	0.3	2.5	5.7	17.0	9.0	14.3	12.8	12.8
22 061	40820	4	Lincoln	1 222	47 617	1 023	39.0	53.8	41.6	0.7	2.3	2.7	5.9	14.5	26.4	12.7	8.9	9.8
22 063	12940	2	Livingston	1 679	135 751	465	80.9	89.7	6.3	0.8	0.8	3.3	6.9	19.7	8.7	14.4	14.2	13.5
22 065	...	7	Madison	1 617	11 843	2 303	7.3	35.9	62.4	0.5	0.5	1.7	7.6	17.2	10.0	16.2	11.9	12.7
22 067	12820	6	Morehouse	2 059	26 760	1 542	13.0	50.5	48.0	0.5	0.7	1.3	6.9	17.3	8.8	12.1	11.3	13.1
22 069	35060	6	Natchitoches	3 243	39 166	1 191	12.1	54.9	42.0	1.8	1.1	2.1	6.5	17.5	16.6	11.4	10.2	11.5

1. CBSA = Core Based Statistical Area. See Appendix A for explanation. See Appendix B for list of metropolitan areas with component counties. 2. County type code from the Economic Research Service of USDA Rural-Urban Continuum Codes. See Appendix A for definition. 3. Dry land or land partially or temporarily covered by water. 4. May be of any race.

STATE County	Population, 2013 (cont.)				Population change and components of change, 2000–2014							Households, 2009–2013				
	Age (percent) (cont.)				Total persons		Percent change		Components of change, 2010–2014					Percent		
	55 to 64 years	65 to 74 years	75 years and over	Percent female	2000	2010	2000–2010	2010–2014	Births	Deaths	Net migration	Number	Persons per house-hold	Family house-holds	Female family house-holder[1]	One per-son
	16	17	18	19	20	21	22	23	24	25	26	27	28	29	30	31
KENTUCKY—Cont'd																
Ohio	13.2	9.8	6.7	50.1	22 916	23 842	4.0	0.6	1 286	1 117	-9	8 715	2.71	73.1	12.8	23.9
Oldham	12.4	7.6	3.7	47.5	46 178	60 316	30.6	5.3	2 145	1 498	2 536	19 532	2.89	81.5	9.0	15.2
Owen	14.8	9.9	6.1	50.2	10 547	10 841	2.8	-1.8	449	419	-190	4 601	2.34	67.8	9.5	30.2
Owsley	15.6	9.5	7.3	50.7	4 858	4 755	-2.1	-5.2	186	316	-104	1 721	2.70	65.6	13.8	34.2
Pendleton	14.2	8.4	5.4	49.7	14 390	14 877	3.4	-2.6	714	611	-482	5 357	2.71	66.5	9.8	27.1
Perry	14.6	9.0	5.8	50.5	29 390	28 712	-2.3	-3.9	1 639	1 803	-975	10 801	2.58	70.2	15.5	25.2
Pike	14.8	9.4	6.1	51.0	68 736	65 024	-5.4	-3.1	3 082	3 443	-1 631	26 362	2.41	68.1	12.4	28.6
Powell	13.6	8.6	5.4	50.5	13 237	12 613	-4.7	-1.4	709	616	-257	4 730	2.63	63.2	14.9	31.6
Pulaski	13.7	10.2	7.1	51.1	56 217	63 063	12.2	1.2	3 135	3 176	805	26 108	2.39	68.2	11.9	27.7
Robertson	13.7	11.9	9.2	47.6	2 266	2 282	0.7	-3.7	98	128	-56	884	2.50	62.4	10.7	34.3
Rockcastle	14.0	10.2	6.3	50.9	16 582	17 056	2.9	-1.3	763	866	-125	6 605	2.52	72.8	14.8	25.2
Rowan	11.1	7.7	5.5	51.5	22 094	23 333	5.6	1.4	1 142	896	115	8 305	2.49	64.4	12.2	28.5
Russell	14.1	10.8	7.9	51.2	16 315	17 565	7.7	1.2	939	919	206	7 270	2.40	65.7	11.6	30.5
Scott	11.6	6.4	3.9	50.8	33 061	47 173	42.7	8.7	2 716	1 309	2 626	17 989	2.60	72.6	13.2	23.0
Shelby	12.7	8.6	5.0	51.6	33 337	42 074	26.2	6.7	2 676	1 305	1 441	15 469	2.66	76.0	11.4	20.5
Simpson	12.8	9.1	6.2	51.1	16 405	17 327	5.6	2.9	935	768	348	6 737	2.54	67.5	10.1	27.8
Spencer	13.6	7.9	3.8	49.5	11 766	17 061	45.0	3.6	761	537	378	6 230	2.76	82.2	9.1	14.8
Taylor	13.1	9.8	7.4	51.9	22 927	24 512	6.9	3.0	1 351	1 248	600	9 708	2.43	67.8	13.3	28.0
Todd	11.7	8.8	6.4	50.8	11 971	12 460	4.1	0.5	761	554	-163	4 574	2.70	72.3	12.6	24.1
Trigg	15.0	12.7	7.7	50.8	12 597	14 339	13.8	-1.3	607	708	-93	5 935	2.38	70.7	12.1	25.9
Trimble	13.2	9.4	5.7	49.4	8 125	8 809	8.4	-0.3	440	346	-103	3 512	2.50	72.8	7.6	24.7
Union	13.3	8.4	6.2	48.2	15 637	15 007	-4.0	1.1	738	684	72	5 586	2.44	71.8	16.1	25.2
Warren	11.0	6.9	4.9	51.0	92 522	113 792	23.0	5.9	6 349	3 741	4 134	44 240	2.47	62.9	12.3	28.9
Washington	13.5	9.2	7.6	51.3	10 916	11 717	7.3	2.1	605	575	194	4 480	2.54	74.2	11.4	23.7
Wayne	14.6	10.9	6.7	50.6	19 923	20 813	4.5	-1.6	991	835	-420	8 083	2.54	71.4	12.9	25.4
Webster	14.4	9.0	6.8	50.3	14 120	13 621	-3.5	-2.8	682	714	-342	5 150	2.58	71.2	8.5	25.4
Whitley	12.7	8.9	5.8	51.0	35 865	35 637	-0.6	-0.4	2 151	1 839	-515	13 172	2.60	71.2	13.8	24.9
Wolfe	14.0	10.2	6.8	50.8	7 065	7 355	4.1	-1.9	382	421	-98	2 779	2.58	62.5	13.7	32.7
Woodford	15.1	9.1	5.9	52.2	23 208	24 939	7.5	2.5	1 181	904	348	9 698	2.55	68.1	10.2	27.3
LOUISIANA	12.5	7.7	5.6	51.1	4 468 976	4 533 372	1.4	2.6	264 495	176 623	28 462	1 707 852	2.60	66.3	16.9	28.5
Acadia	12.2	7.5	5.8	51.3	58 861	61 773	4.9	1.2	3 721	2 717	-205	22 527	2.70	70.3	16.3	25.0
Allen	11.6	7.6	5.7	43.6	25 440	25 764	1.3	-0.2	1 366	1 013	-367	8 099	2.66	67.1	15.3	30.6
Ascension	11.0	6.4	3.5	50.6	76 627	107 215	39.9	9.2	6 794	2 900	5 767	38 287	2.85	77.1	14.3	19.1
Assumption	13.7	8.8	6.1	51.0	23 388	23 421	0.1	-1.7	1 135	933	-589	8 571	2.68	71.9	13.2	22.8
Avoyelles	12.6	8.6	6.7	50.0	41 481	42 073	1.4	-2.2	2 359	2 027	-1 237	15 332	2.49	71.0	18.1	25.4
Beauregard	12.3	8.6	5.5	48.9	32 986	35 654	8.1	1.5	2 083	1 462	-76	12 948	2.67	73.4	12.6	23.1
Bienville	13.0	10.0	8.9	52.2	15 752	14 353	-8.9	-3.3	849	871	-472	5 668	2.45	65.1	18.6	31.6
Bossier	11.1	7.1	5.4	50.5	98 310	116 979	19.0	6.9	7 731	3 976	4 268	45 776	2.57	66.0	14.2	30.4
Caddo	13.0	7.8	6.5	52.5	252 161	254 969	1.1	-0.9	16 105	11 330	-6 958	98 554	2.53	62.4	19.9	33.6
Calcasieu	12.6	7.7	5.7	51.2	183 577	192 768	5.0	2.3	11 565	7 966	1 093	73 726	2.57	68.7	16.4	26.6
Caldwell	13.4	9.2	6.7	48.9	10 560	10 132	-4.1	-2.3	482	520	-187	3 935	2.46	67.2	11.8	28.3
Cameron	13.3	8.5	5.7	50.5	9 991	6 839	-31.5	-2.6	248	200	-250	2 529	2.67	75.1	6.3	22.3
Catahoula	13.9	9.0	6.6	47.0	10 920	10 407	-4.7	-2.5	532	521	-280	3 767	2.52	69.9	13.4	26.1
Claiborne	13.2	9.3	8.0	43.7	16 851	17 195	2.0	-4.6	720	766	-725	5 726	2.67	64.5	20.1	32.4
Concordia	13.2	8.5	6.8	49.5	20 247	20 822	2.8	-1.7	1 167	963	-543	7 642	2.51	69.0	23.1	28.8
De Soto	13.6	9.2	6.4	51.6	25 494	26 656	4.6	1.8	1 614	1 222	153	10 270	2.58	69.9	19.2	26.7
East Baton Rouge	11.8	6.9	5.1	52.0	412 852	440 171	6.6	1.3	25 734	15 384	-4 124	167 422	2.57	61.6	17.7	30.7
East Carroll	11.7	6.9	6.0	46.0	9 421	7 759	-17.6	-3.5	545	298	-510	2 488	2.62	65.1	25.9	31.1
East Feliciana	15.5	9.6	5.5	46.3	21 360	20 267	-5.1	-2.2	900	958	-409	6 991	2.54	72.1	17.5	25.8
Evangeline	11.9	8.2	5.7	49.4	35 434	33 984	-4.1	-0.8	2 103	1 572	-804	11 967	2.64	71.2	19.6	26.7
Franklin	12.9	9.1	7.6	51.1	21 263	20 767	-2.3	-1.6	1 224	1 122	-404	7 704	2.49	67.7	19.7	29.4
Grant	11.5	8.3	5.3	43.8	18 698	22 309	19.3	0.3	1 050	864	-112	7 340	2.60	66.8	13.6	28.7
Iberia	12.3	7.6	5.5	51.1	73 266	73 240	0.0	0.9	4 358	2 950	-717	26 496	2.71	71.3	18.7	24.3
Iberville	13.0	7.9	5.4	48.8	33 320	33 387	0.2	-0.2	1 928	1 221	-765	11 192	2.64	70.0	19.3	26.2
Jackson	12.7	10.2	7.8	48.8	15 397	16 274	5.7	-1.7	751	772	-261	6 090	2.54	73.0	15.2	24.0
Jefferson	13.5	8.4	6.4	51.4	455 466	432 552	-5.0	0.7	24 118	17 165	-3 380	167 251	2.57	64.4	16.3	30.3
Jefferson Davis	12.6	8.3	6.9	51.3	31 435	31 594	0.5	-0.4	1 824	1 505	-404	11 634	2.67	71.6	14.9	25.3
Lafayette	11.7	6.2	4.7	51.1	190 503	221 578	16.3	6.3	13 732	7 085	7 382	86 504	2.54	62.5	14.5	30.6
Lafourche	12.0	7.8	5.8	50.7	89 974	96 318	7.1	1.5	5 140	3 455	-144	35 072	2.70	72.1	14.6	22.1
La Salle	12.7	9.0	6.7	48.5	14 282	14 890	4.3	-0.3	707	702	-27	5 619	2.45	72.9	12.7	23.5
Lincoln	9.7	6.6	5.4	51.4	42 509	46 735	9.9	1.9	2 444	1 633	-4	16 877	2.56	61.0	17.8	28.7
Livingston	11.4	7.2	4.1	50.4	91 814	128 026	39.4	6.0	7 623	4 128	4 128	46 246	2.80	74.3	12.9	21.1
Madison	11.8	7.4	5.2	50.6	13 728	12 093	-11.9	-2.1	790	569	-495	4 068	2.58	60.2	21.8	37.5
Morehouse	13.9	9.0	7.6	52.0	31 021	27 979	-9.8	-4.4	1 526	1 586	-1 154	10 482	2.55	67.1	20.0	30.5
Natchitoches	11.5	8.4	6.4	52.3	39 080	39 566	1.2	-1.0	2 220	1 661	-984	14 903	2.57	64.3	17.5	28.7

1. No spouse present.

Table B. States and Counties — **Population, Vital Statistics, Medicare, and Crime**

STATE County	Persons in group quarters, 2014	Daytime population, 2009–2013: Number	Daytime population, 2009–2013: Employment/residence ratio	Births, 2014: Total	Births, 2014: Rate[1]	Deaths, 2014: Number	Deaths, 2014: Rate[1]	Persons under 65 with no health insurance, 2013: Number	Persons under 65 with no health insurance, 2013: Percent	Medicare, 2014: Eligible for Medicare	Medicare, 2014: Enrolled in Medicare Advantage	Medicare, 2014: Enrolled in a Medicare prescription drug plan	Serious crimes known to police,[2] 2013: Total: Number	Serious crimes known to police,[2] 2013: Total: Rate[3]
	32	33	34	35	36	37	38	39	40	41	42	43	44	45
KENTUCKY—Cont'd														
Ohio	307	23 184	0.91	304	12.7	255	10.6	3 481	17.6	5 315	1 183	2 786	208	861
Oldham	4 547	48 686	0.55	509	8.0	348	5.5	5 063	10.0	8 395	2 379	4 278	604	977
Owen	0	9 017	0.61	98	9.2	98	9.2	1 624	18.2	2 356	602	1 125	54	502
Owsley	90	4 433	0.71	35	7.8	61	13.5	772	20.0	1 101	191	779	19	410
Pendleton	215	11 309	0.46	170	11.7	148	10.2	2 056	16.5	2 943	925	1 315	184	1 322
Perry	611	31 889	1.36	365	13.2	420	15.2	4 106	17.4	6 691	1 278	3 982	323	1 149
Pike	1 610	67 392	1.14	707	11.2	794	12.6	9 220	17.5	16 162	3 738	9 207	564	895
Powell	188	11 294	0.67	171	13.8	133	10.7	2 046	19.3	2 888	778	1 541	187	1 503
Pulaski	962	64 834	1.06	730	11.4	751	11.8	9 618	18.4	15 764	4 014	8 553	1 237	1 948
Robertson	57	1 985	0.65	22	10.0	29	13.2	352	20.1	490	120	269	1	53
Rockcastle	341	14 956	0.65	178	10.6	234	13.9	2 568	18.7	3 793	742	2 138	83	525
Rowan	2 440	25 047	1.18	272	11.5	189	8.0	3 345	18.5	4 303	1 447	2 322	275	1 170
Russell	177	18 262	1.10	213	12.0	212	11.9	3 079	21.4	4 228	883	2 495	126	720
Scott	1 318	50 393	1.10	672	13.1	344	6.7	6 024	13.9	6 794	2 266	2 935	1 428	2 876
Shelby	1 806	38 512	0.78	656	14.6	291	6.5	6 728	18.3	7 434	2 122	3 950	891	2 024
Simpson	327	18 465	1.14	206	11.6	151	8.5	2 358	16.0	3 603	665	2 092	411	2 333
Spencer	113	10 878	0.23	162	9.2	136	7.7	2 264	14.7	2 857	745	1 487	118	673
Taylor	1 433	25 864	1.13	324	12.8	309	12.2	3 719	19.1	5 858	1 124	3 550	573	2 315
Todd	195	10 445	0.57	181	14.5	124	9.9	2 538	24.4	2 373	367	1 431	119	934
Trigg	78	12 997	0.76	143	10.1	158	11.2	2 381	21.1	3 592	890	1 769	204	1 408
Trimble	41	7 249	0.55	101	11.5	98	11.2	1 301	17.5	1 793	425	959	7	80
Union	1 663	15 350	1.04	179	11.8	166	10.9	2 138	16.8	2 966	641	1 669	149	1 007
Warren	6 312	123 002	1.14	1 534	12.7	881	7.3	18 335	18.6	18 150	3 942	10 690	3 667	3 102
Washington	425	10 221	0.70	145	12.1	125	10.5	1 789	18.6	2 529	550	1 576	53	447
Wayne	331	19 628	0.84	233	11.4	186	9.1	3 348	20.0	4 906	1 180	2 933	226	1 084
Webster	393	12 527	0.80	154	11.6	153	11.6	2 023	18.4	2 866	741	1 514	59	492
Whitley	1 590	35 923	1.02	477	13.4	428	12.1	5 128	17.6	8 330	1 530	5 204	491	1 384
Wolfe	132	6 605	0.65	86	11.9	101	14.0	1 074	18.0	1 905	453	1 248	30	449
Woodford	307	22 324	0.78	292	11.4	205	8.0	3 497	16.7	4 878	1 677	1 933	583	2 321
LOUISIANA	128 560	4 581 569	1.01	62 349	13.4	42 896	9.2	745 580	19.1	778 729	223 410	338 173	189 670	4 101
Acadia	1 050	53 573	0.66	873	14.0	636	10.2	10 368	19.4	10 371	1 012	6 270	1 488	2 459
Allen	4 183	25 666	1.00	307	11.9	231	9.0	3 526	19.4	4 277	427	2 586	NA	NA
Ascension	790	95 927	0.73	1 617	13.8	767	6.6	14 794	14.5	14 654	7 702	3 916	4 108	3 607
Assumption	199	18 214	0.41	269	11.7	220	9.6	3 784	19.4	4 298	1 073	2 396	463	2 019
Avoyelles	3 343	38 453	0.78	540	13.1	452	11.0	6 963	21.7	8 412	996	5 401	1 113	2 826
Beauregard	1 299	31 110	0.67	500	13.8	367	10.1	5 649	18.9	6 400	596	3 361	NA	NA
Bienville	319	14 116	0.98	205	14.8	199	14.3	2 202	19.6	3 199	453	1 781	268	1 914
Bossier	2 643	113 726	0.89	1 854	14.8	983	7.9	18 288	17.2	18 294	2 745	6 756	4 439	3 583
Caddo	6 252	271 306	1.14	3 696	14.6	2 669	10.6	39 735	18.6	46 086	8 369	21 320	11 914	4 689
Calcasieu	3 796	198 530	1.06	2 770	14.0	1 897	9.6	31 101	18.8	34 234	4 868	17 710	10 790	5 532
Caldwell	584	8 519	0.61	102	10.3	118	11.9	1 627	20.7	2 010	357	1 121	274	2 747
Cameron	20	7 574	1.24	51	7.6	54	8.1	1 100	19.1	1 045	139	548	152	2 277
Catahoula	865	9 227	0.68	129	12.7	113	11.1	1 822	23.4	2 180	265	1 327	252	2 583
Claiborne	2 918	15 849	0.82	170	10.4	189	11.5	2 214	20.2	3 306	451	1 945	NA	NA
Concordia	1 485	19 915	0.89	280	13.7	243	11.9	3 583	22.5	4 085	588	2 405	726	3 588
De Soto	215	25 119	0.84	388	14.3	277	10.2	4 458	19.7	5 553	639	2 836	993	3 669
East Baton Rouge	11 126	496 649	1.26	6 064	13.6	3 711	8.3	67 037	17.6	66 502	27 873	21 664	22 566	5 058
East Carroll	1 067	7 458	0.89	132	17.6	73	9.8	1 132	20.7	1 408	120	909	133	1 780
East Feliciana	2 399	17 588	0.66	202	10.2	220	11.1	2 695	18.6	4 042	1 291	1 674	222	1 374
Evangeline	1 379	31 102	0.75	516	15.3	363	10.8	5 009	18.1	6 598	496	4 546	743	2 208
Franklin	732	19 241	0.79	266	13.0	275	13.5	3 864	23.2	4 317	665	2 561	215	1 100
Grant	2 951	17 644	0.40	249	11.1	172	7.7	3 139	19.4	4 038	621	2 055	241	1 096
Iberia	944	75 554	1.07	995	13.5	745	10.1	12 722	20.1	13 085	1 035	7 772	1 927	2 593
Iberville	4 000	36 697	1.26	467	14.0	289	8.7	4 342	17.2	5 742	2 606	1 913	1 445	4 606
Jackson	1 038	14 410	0.69	162	10.1	204	12.8	2 293	18.6	3 360	583	1 861	131	808
Jefferson	3 313	426 084	0.96	5 629	12.9	4 137	9.5	78 298	21.3	78 699	43 014	19 908	17 906	4 122
Jefferson Davis	567	28 395	0.73	433	13.8	384	12.2	5 205	19.8	5 566	392	3 562	671	2 480
Lafayette	5 156	251 417	1.24	3 381	14.3	1 731	7.3	37 060	18.5	32 356	3 673	17 437	11 803	5 373
Lafourche	1 626	92 411	0.90	1 212	12.4	821	8.4	16 522	20.0	16 282	3 834	7 960	2 743	2 821
La Salle	1 243	14 287	0.90	173	11.7	169	11.4	2 020	17.9	2 777	362	1 643	115	849
Lincoln	4 908	47 058	1.01	581	12.2	395	8.3	8 565	23.1	6 552	1 023	3 305	1 569	3 336
Livingston	1 192	97 032	0.43	1 813	13.4	1 039	7.7	20 533	17.4	19 024	9 583	5 535	4 950	3 730
Madison	1 597	11 642	0.89	185	15.6	157	13.3	2 032	22.7	1 945	151	1 188	494	4 053
Morehouse	768	24 633	0.69	346	12.9	350	13.1	4 455	20.3	6 069	1 292	3 318	1 552	5 650
Natchitoches	2 197	38 456	0.94	514	13.1	380	9.7	6 155	19.7	7 081	824	4 112	2 335	5 921

1. Per 1,000 estimated resident population. 2. Data for serious crimes have not been adjusted for underreporting; this may affect comparability between geographic areas and over time.
3. Per 100,000 population estimated by the FBI.

STATE County	Serious crimes known to police, 2013 (cont.)[1] Rate[2] Violent	Serious crimes Rate[2] Property	Education: School enrollment and attainment, 2009–2013 Enrollment[3] Total	Enrollment[3] Percent private	Attainment[4] (percent) High school graduate or less	Attainment[4] (percent) Bachelor's degree or more	Local government expenditures,[5] 2012–2013 Total current spending (mil dol)	Local government expenditures,[5] Current spending per student (dollars)	Money income, 2009–2013 Per capita income[6] (dollars)	Households Median income (dollars)	Households Mean income (dollars)	Households Percent with income of $200,000 or more	Income and poverty, 2013 Median household income (dollars)	Percent below poverty level All persons	Percent below poverty level Children under 18 years	Percent below poverty level Children 5 to 17 years in families
	46	47	48	49	50	51	52	53	54	55	56	57	58	59	60	61
KENTUCKY—Cont'd																
Ohio	70	790	5 462	10.0	67.0	8.0	34.9	8 175	19 005	40 830	50 569	1.2	40 622	19.1	26.7	24.3
Oldham	49	929	18 127	16.5	31.2	40.1	101.4	8 404	33 591	83 391	103 459	10.4	86 580	6.1	7.1	5.6
Owen	9	493	2 318	8.5	58.7	15.9	16.5	8 669	23 991	41 009	56 563	0.8	42 134	19.1	27.6	24.4
Owsley	22	389	1 045	7.0	70.9	12.4	10.7	12 732	13 611	19 986	33 284	0.0	22 715	42.0	55.0	53.5
Pendleton	29	1 293	3 646	10.0	63.0	12.4	21.6	8 492	23 122	45 480	58 545	1.6	45 570	16.1	23.9	21.6
Perry	117	1 032	6 236	5.1	63.4	13.5	49.9	9 545	18 224	33 528	46 049	0.9	32 300	26.9	35.2	36.2
Pike	10	886	14 246	10.2	64.4	12.5	102.8	9 489	19 351	32 961	46 104	1.3	35 071	23.0	29.0	25.8
Powell	48	1 455	2 828	13.3	69.6	11.9	22.0	8 723	15 174	26 839	37 672	0.7	31 923	29.6	40.8	39.2
Pulaski	99	1 849	14 352	7.1	59.0	15.1	87.6	8 391	20 667	34 092	49 736	2.5	34 355	25.2	33.3	31.1
Robertson	0	53	454	5.3	64.5	12.5	4.0	11 056	17 641	31 786	42 295	0.0	38 101	23.4	35.8	31.0
Rockcastle	63	462	3 909	6.7	65.1	10.9	27.8	9 452	16 513	30 674	42 002	1.1	33 131	25.6	36.3	32.2
Rowan	68	1 102	8 066	6.0	54.4	23.8	29.3	8 776	17 094	35 236	46 839	0.8	37 690	24.7	31.3	28.8
Russell	23	697	3 606	10.3	65.4	11.9	26.9	8 794	17 107	29 721	39 772	0.8	30 985	25.5	37.9	36.0
Scott	187	2 689	13 386	23.4	43.8	27.9	70.0	8 034	27 802	61 893	72 797	2.9	61 906	10.5	14.4	13.1
Shelby	120	1 904	10 846	18.0	46.0	23.8	64.5	8 932	27 039	57 298	73 177	4.2	56 808	12.6	18.3	16.9
Simpson	125	2 208	3 930	7.2	59.1	14.8	26.2	8 756	19 441	39 546	49 464	0.6	39 117	18.5	28.5	25.2
Spencer	17	656	4 488	19.0	49.7	16.6	22.9	7 877	26 666	65 209	74 007	1.7	66 711	9.3	12.2	11.0
Taylor	255	2 060	5 983	24.5	59.7	15.1	34.4	8 999	18 790	36 384	46 262	0.8	36 599	20.7	32.2	32.4
Todd	55	879	3 015	11.8	63.7	9.4	19.1	8 886	17 846	41 541	47 545	0.4	38 533	20.5	30.3	28.4
Trigg	97	1 311	3 316	7.8	51.9	18.4	19.1	8 798	25 527	45 629	61 078	1.7	43 416	18.3	28.7	26.3
Trimble	0	80	2 149	13.6	58.6	16.1	13.5	9 176	22 070	49 718	54 832	0.0	45 394	16.1	23.8	21.8
Union	61	946	3 748	15.6	55.4	11.4	23.9	9 707	19 464	39 125	51 168	1.6	44 595	18.7	24.8	21.6
Warren	193	2 909	36 152	5.7	44.5	28.4	151.0	8 221	23 853	44 135	60 536	2.4	48 137	18.4	22.6	20.4
Washington	51	396	3 052	20.1	62.4	15.6	16.9	9 898	19 837	40 845	50 882	1.1	42 500	16.8	24.4	22.6
Wayne	24	1 060	4 472	3.5	67.8	9.8	32.1	9 249	16 396	29 497	40 146	0.4	29 878	27.5	39.3	35.3
Webster	58	434	2 890	10.1	65.8	8.4	19.1	8 328	20 337	41 415	51 359	0.6	40 881	17.0	24.1	22.8
Whitley	68	1 317	9 105	17.8	64.0	13.4	76.5	9 158	15 960	29 769	41 855	1.1	30 878	26.3	37.2	36.3
Wolfe	0	449	1 651	4.4	70.5	11.8	13.5	10 473	14 157	22 574	34 424	1.0	25 657	36.4	51.2	41.8
Woodford	131	2 189	6 133	15.2	41.5	31.6	NA	NA	29 277	57 580	73 172	4.0	59 233	11.0	16.2	14.6
LOUISIANA	519	3 582	1 186 922	19.2	51.5	21.8	7 057.3	10 490	24 442	44 874	62 773	3.2	44 234	20.0	28.4	27.0
Acadia	256	2 203	15 546	20.6	65.9	10.2	91.7	9 255	19 910	37 587	52 507	1.3	38 788	19.0	26.3	25.4
Allen	NA	NA	5 604	7.8	65.5	11.1	44.9	10 356	18 857	38 429	51 941	0.7	38 122	19.8	26.5	25.4
Ascension	371	3 235	30 877	19.3	47.1	24.9	213.4	10 161	28 178	69 070	78 478	3.5	70 303	11.1	15.7	14.6
Assumption	414	1 605	5 401	15.1	69.6	9.7	43.4	11 406	21 743	46 116	57 770	2.1	44 749	18.2	25.6	23.0
Avoyelles	556	2 270	9 464	17.0	68.2	9.7	51.7	8 639	18 006	33 942	48 388	1.0	33 240	23.8	33.9	29.8
Beauregard	NA	NA	8 271	10.0	59.6	15.0	61.0	10 026	22 509	46 385	60 076	2.0	46 225	16.6	22.7	20.9
Bienville	429	1 486	3 303	7.2	63.4	11.1	31.7	13 569	18 958	31 543	45 470	1.6	33 790	23.9	34.0	31.8
Bossier	383	3 200	30 845	10.3	43.4	25.2	205.4	9 571	27 429	53 248	69 013	3.6	51 899	14.6	19.8	19.3
Caddo	583	4 106	65 409	14.5	48.1	22.7	441.0	10 672	24 308	41 053	60 007	3.2	39 776	22.0	32.5	31.2
Calcasieu	616	4 915	49 646	13.9	50.8	19.9	324.6	10 060	24 355	43 499	61 697	2.9	43 779	16.6	23.3	21.9
Caldwell	251	2 496	2 239	9.2	69.4	8.2	17.5	10 605	22 782	39 385	55 372	2.1	35 987	23.4	32.7	30.9
Cameron	210	2 067	1 563	5.1	59.2	15.4	24.8	19 414	29 559	64 574	78 557	6.4	51 709	13.3	19.4	18.1
Catahoula	451	2 132	2 037	8.4	70.9	11.2	18.4	12 180	19 970	36 165	52 130	2.0	33 557	24.3	32.1	29.6
Claiborne	NA	NA	3 381	13.1	64.4	12.5	20.2	10 458	17 512	32 996	47 506	1.5	34 390	30.7	42.4	40.9
Concordia	430	3 158	5 056	10.0	64.2	11.3	38.5	10 081	16 431	29 022	43 043	0.5	30 432	30.6	41.8	41.3
De Soto	916	2 753	6 436	11.2	61.4	11.3	83.3	16 060	21 547	39 162	53 754	1.4	39 403	23.5	33.9	30.9
East Baton Rouge	586	4 472	133 282	20.4	37.5	34.2	609.0	11 190	27 505	48 506	69 538	4.4	47 770	20.8	28.1	27.0
East Carroll	602	1 178	1 725	9.4	72.7	9.2	13.9	12 071	12 055	25 321	35 859	1.0	26 781	44.8	57.7	57.4
East Feliciana	254	1 120	4 214	20.8	62.8	13.0	23.2	11 593	22 099	47 225	60 312	1.9	41 578	20.6	28.8	28.1
Evangeline	175	2 033	8 550	19.2	68.6	11.4	56.2	9 214	18 023	31 832	47 889	1.4	32 130	27.6	35.7	33.6
Franklin	220	880	4 902	16.7	65.8	11.6	30.1	9 316	17 752	31 214	46 199	0.8	31 243	29.1	45.1	43.2
Grant	105	991	4 857	11.3	64.4	10.2	28.7	8 715	19 018	39 654	52 751	1.5	41 208	21.2	27.9	26.6
Iberia	264	2 329	18 690	16.6	64.0	13.6	128.8	9 281	22 997	44 262	62 741	2.9	41 185	20.2	31.3	30.1
Iberville	1 157	3 449	7 858	17.1	62.2	12.8	62.8	13 595	21 177	45 368	59 897	2.3	40 449	25.7	34.9	33.9
Jackson	234	574	3 546	13.1	58.1	13.8	22.8	10 003	19 188	37 388	49 009	0.4	35 730	21.2	31.0	28.6
Jefferson	456	3 667	104 081	33.6	47.9	23.6	530.0	11 496	26 908	48 261	66 868	4.0	46 547	18.9	31.1	28.2
Jefferson Davis	222	2 258	8 100	11.5	62.4	13.0	62.4	10 630	21 132	41 622	55 134	2.0	40 760	18.0	24.3	22.3
Lafayette	605	4 769	62 532	21.7	43.9	28.3	307.1	9 997	28 901	51 462	71 992	5.1	54 978	15.6	21.1	20.4
Lafourche	166	2 655	23 818	18.0	66.4	14.8	142.9	9 768	24 798	50 572	66 074	2.4	52 115	16.5	21.9	20.7
La Salle	303	546	3 172	10.3	63.8	12.9	26.1	9 880	22 481	42 528	58 772	1.0	42 104	20.9	26.9	22.1
Lincoln	342	2 993	18 517	10.6	41.0	34.4	65.6	11 250	20 633	35 769	54 640	2.6	34 667	32.2	32.1	31.2
Livingston	324	3 406	33 913	10.6	56.3	17.5	214.1	8 466	25 076	56 811	68 673	2.4	53 118	14.3	18.1	17.2
Madison	705	3 347	2 944	15.9	63.2	11.2	19.2	10 170	13 585	25 498	36 564	0.7	26 745	40.8	55.2	54.4
Morehouse	568	5 082	5 888	11.7	65.2	12.9	46.7	10 717	16 683	28 585	41 753	0.9	28 951	27.6	41.1	39.4
Natchitoches	512	5 409	12 111	10.8	54.7	21.6	68.6	10 165	20 802	33 953	53 188	1.9	35 165	27.7	36.7	33.6

1. Data for serious crimes have not been adjusted for underreporting; this may affect comparability between geographic areas and over time. 2. Per 100,000 population estimated by the FBI.
3. All persons 3 years old and over enrolled in nursery school through college. 4. Persons 25 years old and over. 5. Elementary and secondary education expenditures.
6. Based on population estimated by the American Community Survey, 2009–2013.

STATE County	Personal income, 2013: Total (mil dol)	Personal income, 2013: Percent change, 2012–2013	Per capita[1]: Dollars	Per capita[1]: Rank	Wages and salaries (mil dol)	Supplements to wages and salaries; employer contributions (mil dol): Pension and insurance	Supplements to wages and salaries; employer contributions (mil dol): Government social insurance	Proprietors' income (mil dol)	Dividends, interest, and rent (mil dol)	Personal transfer receipts (mil dol)	Earnings, 2013: Total (mil dol)	Contributions for government social insurance (mil dol): From employee and self-employed	Contributions for government social insurance (mil dol): From employer
	62	63	64	65	66	67	68	69	70	71	72	73	74
KENTUCKY—Cont'd													
Ohio	752	4.0	31 359	2 499	236	56	19	62	93	217	372	24	19
Oldham	3 083	0.9	49 428	394	581	110	43	96	589	324	830	52	43
Owen	322	2.1	30 194	2 655	64	16	5	11	40	100	96	7	5
Owsley	121	0.0	26 022	3 026	19	6	1	1	13	65	28	3	1
Pendleton	452	1.3	31 045	2 544	97	21	7	7	59	112	133	11	7
Perry	890	-2.7	31 766	2 438	488	94	36	54	108	359	672	44	36
Pike	2 074	-2.5	32 727	2 299	969	166	75	207	238	721	1 417	97	75
Powell	362	1.4	28 934	2 813	75	19	6	31	34	130	131	10	6
Pulaski	1 965	1.0	30 750	2 588	851	173	71	109	267	699	1 205	82	71
Robertson	63	1.4	28 351	2 861	8	3	1	2	8	21	14	1	1
Rockcastle	437	1.9	26 171	3 021	110	26	9	10	48	165	156	13	9
Rowan	661	0.2	28 090	2 887	329	86	25	24	90	204	464	28	25
Russell	531	-0.7	29 917	2 700	184	42	16	63	75	181	305	20	16
Scott	1 867	1.8	37 386	1 523	1 233	171	100	84	201	269	1 588	95	100
Shelby	1 645	1.6	37 206	1 547	567	106	46	87	255	285	805	51	46
Simpson	618	4.0	34 719	1 948	314	56	27	92	80	144	488	27	27
Spencer	650	0.8	36 854	1 618	64	15	5	9	57	110	93	8	5
Taylor	766	2.0	31 066	2 540	345	69	29	42	111	241	485	32	29
Todd	397	6.6	31 760	2 439	78	18	6	84	58	96	186	9	6
Trigg	537	1.3	37 552	1 497	109	24	9	48	83	131	190	13	9
Trimble	234	1.8	26 577	3 002	45	12	3	4	30	74	65	5	3
Union	614	12.5	40 878	1 068	259	43	19	149	74	131	471	23	19
Warren	4 005	1.8	33 837	2 112	2 292	438	178	292	644	821	3 199	187	178
Washington	347	1.5	29 245	2 778	114	23	9	24	55	100	170	12	9
Wayne	522	1.5	25 239	3 048	160	37	14	28	77	204	239	17	14
Webster	497	6.7	36 945	1 595	173	34	13	89	59	116	309	16	13
Whitley	1 080	0.2	30 201	2 654	449	90	38	22	140	415	600	43	38
Wolfe	182	1.1	25 070	3 051	35	10	3	4	19	96	51	5	3
Woodford	1 150	1.1	45 482	657	409	71	31	68	194	175	580	33	31
LOUISIANA	190 590	2.0	41 204	X	91 548	15 532	5 893	21 795	32 612	36 491	134 768	7 072	5 893
Acadia	2 354	2.8	37 841	1 456	581	108	37	473	314	487	1 199	61	37
Allen	654	1.0	25 612	3 035	302	75	17	75	96	190	469	22	17
Ascension	5 414	4.8	47 325	526	2 064	348	134	1 082	540	640	3 628	182	134
Assumption	940	4.2	40 551	1 106	211	37	13	99	123	187	360	20	13
Avoyelles	1 397	-0.6	33 836	2 114	366	81	21	178	209	418	646	34	21
Beauregard	1 156	2.0	31 951	2 415	357	66	23	83	188	283	528	31	23
Bienville	473	0.7	33 815	2 123	183	37	11	54	77	152	286	16	11
Bossier	4 715	-0.6	38 075	1 423	2 057	426	151	465	866	883	3 100	153	151
Caddo	11 337	-0.1	44 478	730	5 189	923	341	1 602	2 452	2 218	8 055	413	341
Calcasieu	7 552	2.0	38 668	1 343	3 996	746	258	626	1 261	1 525	5 626	303	258
Caldwell	300	0.5	29 990	2 689	82	18	5	17	40	101	122	8	5
Cameron	263	1.8	39 069	1 286	160	29	8	9	63	36	207	11	8
Catahoula	359	1.5	35 111	1 882	78	19	5	75	44	102	177	8	5
Claiborne	553	-2.4	33 195	2 229	159	35	9	65	114	153	268	14	9
Concordia	660	0.6	32 282	2 368	210	45	13	92	116	194	360	18	13
De Soto	985	0.5	36 361	1 680	383	68	23	71	232	236	545	31	23
East Baton Rouge	19 518	2.5	43 839	771	13 467	2 198	845	1 094	3 670	3 189	17 604	904	845
East Carroll	323	5.0	42 946	847	69	16	4	96	54	88	185	5	4
East Feliciana	711	2.0	36 020	1 742	200	54	9	43	110	196	306	15	9
Evangeline	1 053	1.3	31 373	2 497	296	62	19	93	165	333	471	27	19
Franklin	713	3.5	34 674	1 959	168	39	10	166	91	218	383	16	10
Grant	609	0.6	27 667	2 918	144	39	10	42	88	175	236	15	10
Iberia	3 088	1.9	41 796	960	1 686	239	108	337	510	610	2 370	129	108
Iberville	1 157	3.1	34 672	1 960	847	160	52	124	173	283	1 182	61	52
Jackson	497	3.7	30 857	2 570	145	31	8	60	60	155	244	14	8
Jefferson	19 970	1.1	45 932	620	9 570	1 353	629	2 511	3 700	3 367	14 062	777	629
Jefferson Davis	1 120	2.6	35 794	1 782	344	69	21	124	172	257	558	29	21
Lafayette	11 925	3.2	51 656	310	7 266	966	470	2 162	2 069	1 467	10 864	562	470
Lafourche	5 038	5.4	51 863	303	2 297	380	140	1 118	603	688	3 934	196	140
La Salle	501	3.7	33 936	2 094	197	39	12	38	71	129	286	16	12
Lincoln	1 580	3.5	33 330	2 199	698	138	43	236	295	334	1 114	53	43
Livingston	4 648	3.9	34 672	1 960	970	178	63	321	502	838	1 532	91	63
Madison	362	0.7	30 359	2 638	111	29	7	68	48	110	216	8	7
Morehouse	886	-1.4	32 749	2 291	235	49	16	115	118	319	415	22	16
Natchitoches	1 354	2.1	34 608	1 971	480	107	28	206	209	349	822	40	28

1. Based on the resident population estimated as of July 1 of the year shown.

STATE County	Earnings, 2013 (cont.) Percent by selected industries: Farm	Mining	Construction	Manu-facturing	Infor-mation: professional, scientific, technical services	Retail trade	Finance, insur-ance, real estate and leasing	Health care and social assistance	Govern-ment	Social Security beneficiaries, December 2013: Number	Rate[1]	Supple-mental Security Income recipients, December 2013	Housing units, 2014: Total	Percent change, 2010–2014
	75	76	77	78	79	80	81	82	83	84	85	86	87	88
KENTUCKY—Cont'd														
Ohio	6.9	D	4.0	33.3	D	6.8	1.6	D	21.6	6 145	256	1 153	10 215	0.0
Oldham	0.2	D	9.2	6.7	10.0	6.0	11.3	12.3	23.0	8 915	143	528	21 203	2.5
Owen	1.6	0.0	3.8	D	1.4	6.2	D	11.5	27.1	2 710	255	498	5 638	0.1
Owsley	-4.0	D	D	D	D	D	4.1	20.3	50.0	1 240	269	842	2 324	-0.2
Pendleton	-3.8	D	D	21.0	D	4.1	D	D	25.4	3 230	222	519	6 312	-0.4
Perry	0.0	D	2.8	0.3	D	8.9	3.2	D	19.5	7 685	275	2 858	12 791	0.0
Pike	0.0	D	3.8	2.6	5.6	8.4	4.2	19.0	13.1	19 020	298	5 083	30 311	0.0
Powell	-0.2	D	D	6.2	1.3	10.8	3.7	8.0	27.5	3 460	276	1 142	5 590	-0.1
Pulaski	0.7	D	4.7	14.5	4.5	9.4	4.3	22.0	16.9	17 690	278	3 737	31 200	-0.8
Robertson	5.0	0.0	10.7	0.0	D	D	1.9	16.4	45.8	540	243	121	1 091	-0.4
Rockcastle	-2.3	D	D	4.7	5.7	5.8	D	28.5	25.8	4 305	257	1 277	7 690	-0.2
Rowan	0.0	D	D	9.5	2.0	8.6	3.4	D	36.5	4 860	207	1 197	10 126	0.2
Russell	3.2	0.0	D	30.3	D	9.3	3.7	D	17.9	4 770	270	1 280	9 919	-0.8
Scott	1.1	D	2.4	50.3	D	3.3	2.0	D	7.4	7 615	152	1 036	20 489	6.1
Shelby	2.0	D	5.0	29.6	4.3	7.0	4.3	7.8	15.0	8 160	184	827	16 989	2.3
Simpson	11.4	0.0	3.2	39.3	D	8.9	2.4	D	9.2	4 060	229	530	7 577	1.9
Spencer	-1.3	0.1	9.4	0.8	D	7.6	6.8	D	36.1	3 215	183	372	6 928	3.3
Taylor	2.7	0.0	D	10.8	2.8	8.3	4.4	D	21.2	6 590	262	1 292	10 961	0.9
Todd	33.1	0.0	6.6	7.3	2.2	5.0	2.8	D	15.5	2 655	213	409	5 293	0.1
Trigg	14.6	D	6.6	13.5	D	7.4	3.8	7.6	21.9	3 940	275	428	7 836	0.3
Trimble	-0.6	0.0	D	3.8	D	2.7	6.2	D	29.0	2 075	235	285	3 924	-0.2
Union	25.2	29.1	1.9	7.5	1.4	4.0	3.2	D	8.3	3 470	230	448	6 208	1.1
Warren	1.3	0.5	6.7	17.7	4.7	7.1	4.9	13.5	17.2	19 785	167	3 370	49 779	5.4
Washington	4.0	D	9.2	34.1	D	5.4	D	D	15.9	2 835	238	463	5 093	1.0
Wayne	6.6	D	3.2	26.0	D	9.3	D	D	21.9	5 460	264	1 913	10 833	-1.0
Webster	22.6	D	9.0	4.7	0.7	3.1	D	3.4	11.2	3 290	246	490	5 916	-0.3
Whitley	-0.2	1.7	2.7	9.7	7.7	7.6	2.2	D	19.4	9 170	258	3 070	15 169	0.0
Wolfe	-4.8	D	4.8	D	D	14.4	D	D	39.6	2 205	304	1 194	3 652	-0.2
Woodford	10.2	0.0	4.5	23.0	8.4	5.2	3.4	4.7	15.3	5 195	206	419	10 929	2.0
LOUISIANA	1.2	5.8	8.8	9.6	8.3	6.4	6.6	10.5	17.3	842 160	182	181 598	2 010 868	2.3
Acadia	6.6	6.5	12.2	11.4	6.5	6.6	6.9	8.8	12.8	11 575	186	2 675	25 851	1.8
Allen	0.7	D	3.5	8.4	D	5.4	4.1	D	50.3	4 830	188	862	9 787	0.6
Ascension	0.4	1.0	13.6	19.6	5.1	7.7	14.3	7.3	8.6	16 415	143	2 313	44 102	8.2
Assumption	7.8	1.9	5.6	31.6	D	5.2	3.4	5.6	16.1	4 875	210	1 125	10 496	1.4
Avoyelles	10.3	4.7	8.6	2.1	4.2	8.7	4.9	D	26.9	9 315	225	2 756	18 186	0.8
Beauregard	0.2	0.5	10.2	16.4	D	7.3	8.9	11.7	17.2	7 125	197	991	15 227	1.2
Bienville	2.3	5.8	4.3	19.5	D	4.4	6.7	7.2	16.4	3 500	250	865	7 724	0.1
Bossier	0.1	7.2	6.3	4.3	3.8	9.3	4.8	7.3	34.1	19 705	159	3 173	54 045	9.5
Caddo	0.1	9.2	5.5	6.6	6.2	6.6	6.3	17.0	19.1	49 085	192	13 223	112 696	0.6
Calcasieu	0.0	1.3	14.4	17.7	7.4	6.3	4.0	12.0	14.5	37 720	193	6 287	85 721	4.5
Caldwell	0.9	2.1	5.1	D	4.5	9.9	6.3	20.8	25.6	2 150	216	459	5 022	0.6
Cameron	0.2	9.7	10.7	22.0	D	D	D	2.3	20.5	1 170	175	110	3 836	6.8
Catahoula	29.8	4.1	D	D	D	7.7	3.2	8.4	19.3	2 340	228	640	4 904	0.6
Claiborne	12.1	14.4	6.8	5.1	2.1	4.8	2.1	D	26.2	3 515	210	921	7 759	0.0
Concordia	13.1	8.2	2.0	2.2	D	9.3	3.5	D	23.5	4 520	221	1 342	9 427	0.5
De Soto	0.7	17.0	14.0	14.8	1.6	7.3	2.6	D	20.7	6 035	223	1 355	12 402	0.9
East Baton Rouge	0.0	0.4	14.2	7.4	12.0	5.6	6.5	12.3	19.0	70 190	158	15 369	191 203	2.1
East Carroll	50.1	D	0.6	3.5	D	4.0	3.1	D	19.3	1 400	186	652	2 899	-0.2
East Feliciana	0.9	1.7	4.2	7.7	D	4.2	3.8	D	51.1	3 960	201	875	8 166	1.9
Evangeline	7.9	0.6	5.2	16.2	2.7	7.2	4.8	D	18.6	7 255	215	2 375	14 859	1.3
Franklin	29.3	D	7.3	2.3	D	9.3	3.6	D	19.3	4 565	222	1 356	9 100	0.7
Grant	1.0	D	10.7	6.5	D	3.8	D	D	47.8	4 270	191	856	9 031	1.6
Iberia	2.2	17.4	9.0	15.0	5.2	6.3	8.2	6.4	10.4	14 680	198	3 222	30 087	1.3
Iberville	3.2	0.6	10.6	41.3	2.1	3.3	3.0	D	15.2	6 245	187	1 506	13 004	2.3
Jackson	4.1	2.3	D	D	D	7.8	3.2	D	23.2	3 580	222	663	7 748	0.9
Jefferson	0.0	3.1	9.6	6.3	10.4	8.1	8.9	12.3	10.8	83 620	192	13 645	189 066	0.0
Jefferson Davis	7.6	5.4	7.0	5.3	2.6	7.4	6.5	13.5	20.4	6 270	200	1 102	13 564	1.9
Lafayette	0.2	19.0	6.7	6.8	9.5	6.0	7.9	13.0	8.4	34 110	147	5 864	97 492	4.1
Lafourche	0.9	7.4	6.6	7.3	3.5	4.0	4.7	4.8	11.1	18 110	186	3 321	39 635	2.5
La Salle	1.7	13.3	2.7	2.9	4.4	7.4	2.8	6.4	27.0	3 070	207	510	6 593	0.5
Lincoln	2.8	2.4	7.5	7.7	7.6	9.0	5.8	16.0	22.3	6 740	142	1 495	19 732	1.3
Livingston	0.0	1.1	17.6	9.4	D	10.1	7.2	6.4	20.1	21 395	159	2 932	53 715	7.1
Madison	28.1	0.0	1.4	6.5	1.0	6.4	2.6	D	26.8	2 085	175	759	4 925	2.5
Morehouse	18.6	D	4.7	5.3	D	7.9	3.6	D	18.6	6 730	249	1 830	12 535	0.9
Natchitoches	3.1	0.2	5.0	22.8	D	6.9	4.4	6.8	26.7	7 495	191	2 251	18 770	1.0

1. Per 1,000 resident population estimated as of July 1 of the year shown.

STATE County	Housing units, 2009–2013: Occupied units: Total	Owner-occupied: Percent	Owner-occupied: Median value[1]	Median owner cost as a percent of income: With a mortgage	Median owner cost as a percent of income: Without a mortgage[2]	Renter-occupied: Median rent[3]	Renter-occupied: Median rent as a percent of income[2]	Substandard units[4] (percent)	Civilian labor force, 2014: Total	Percent change, 2013–2014	Unemployment: Total	Unemployment: Rate[5]	Civilian employment,[6] 2009–2013: Total	Percent: Management, business, science and arts	Percent: Construction, production, and maintenance occupations
	89	90	91	92	93	94	95	96	97	98	99	100	101	102	103
KENTUCKY—Cont'd															
Ohio	8 715	80.8	78 800	20.7	10.7	535	26.4	1.4	9 485	-4.0	722	7.6	8 859	24.8	40.2
Oldham	19 532	84.8	245 700	21.7	10.0	822	28.2	4.8	29 948	-1.3	1 433	4.8	27 726	46.8	18.0
Owen	4 601	74.7	96 800	20.5	12.5	518	26.4	4.2	5 558	-2.2	281	5.1	4 796	26.3	38.8
Owsley	1 721	74.4	56 200	27.9	15.8	289	22.8	1.4	1 237	-3.7	127	10.3	1 092	28.0	31.5
Pendleton	5 357	76.1	105 000	25.1	10.3	584	24.3	3.7	6 836	-2.6	457	6.7	6 442	28.7	36.4
Perry	10 801	71.8	65 600	22.0	10.0	503	26.5	2.3	9 650	-6.8	997	10.3	9 821	30.6	25.6
Pike	26 362	73.1	66 400	21.0	10.7	590	30.5	5.3	22 098	-5.2	2 311	10.5	20 594	27.6	31.3
Powell	4 730	66.8	77 800	23.6	13.3	521	38.9	2.9	4 948	-2.1	424	8.6	4 008	22.9	42.8
Pulaski	26 108	71.7	106 700	21.3	12.0	582	33.5	2.9	26 325	-3.4	1 945	7.4	25 605	28.4	24.3
Robertson	884	74.2	81 900	19.5	10.8	568	32.0	3.8	808	-4.6	62	7.7	769	31.1	43.8
Rockcastle	6 605	78.3	74 800	23.5	12.6	508	28.9	2.2	6 900	-2.6	513	7.4	6 060	21.7	31.6
Rowan	8 305	65.2	96 700	19.7	10.0	610	28.8	1.9	10 512	-3.7	731	7.0	9 391	30.6	24.9
Russell	7 270	74.4	86 600	24.7	12.7	494	30.1	2.6	6 743	-3.9	674	10.0	6 219	28.0	36.6
Scott	17 989	72.0	161 300	19.7	10.0	726	26.9	3.6	25 987	-1.1	1 292	5.0	23 558	35.1	28.3
Shelby	15 469	70.8	165 000	21.7	10.0	771	25.3	3.3	22 332	-1.4	1 119	5.0	20 250	30.1	26.2
Simpson	6 737	66.2	115 200	21.7	11.4	642	29.2	2.4	8 540	-3.6	497	5.8	7 532	24.1	31.2
Spencer	6 230	84.8	170 300	20.8	10.0	626	22.4	1.8	9 209	-1.6	492	5.3	8 524	26.8	32.0
Taylor	9 708	69.8	96 800	21.2	10.0	553	30.2	2.0	11 134	-2.0	824	7.4	10 312	25.9	32.5
Todd	4 574	72.6	85 000	22.1	10.6	560	27.2	3.6	5 465	-3.0	299	5.5	4 787	19.1	43.1
Trigg	5 935	81.2	115 000	23.2	10.7	548	31.6	2.0	5 890	-2.5	408	6.9	5 346	32.9	29.9
Trimble	3 512	77.1	107 300	21.0	11.0	677	26.0	4.9	3 911	-1.3	281	7.2	3 568	25.8	39.9
Union	5 586	73.7	74 900	18.2	12.5	538	31.1	2.1	6 715	-2.1	432	6.4	5 772	26.7	35.6
Warren	44 240	60.2	140 700	21.4	10.0	663	31.4	2.3	59 281	-2.2	3 293	5.6	55 271	33.5	24.0
Washington	4 480	82.9	107 300	21.8	11.1	538	31.6	3.8	6 097	-1.0	338	5.5	5 277	28.0	36.6
Wayne	8 083	72.5	80 500	21.1	11.1	472	29.4	3.1	7 159	-4.1	710	9.9	7 223	21.5	40.5
Webster	5 150	71.9	70 500	18.6	10.8	579	27.2	2.1	6 316	2.1	351	5.6	5 234	25.1	43.3
Whitley	13 172	67.4	71 500	23.6	11.9	573	31.2	2.1	13 497	-2.5	1 176	8.7	12 420	26.2	25.5
Wolfe	2 779	71.9	52 800	24.2	11.1	461	50.0	0.6	2 047	-3.0	232	11.3	2 033	25.9	27.3
Woodford	9 698	72.5	185 900	20.9	10.0	732	25.7	4.5	14 166	-0.6	638	4.5	12 593	36.6	27.8
LOUISIANA	1 707 852	67.0	138 900	21.1	10.0	773	31.8	3.1	2 157 232	2.4	137 577	6.4	1 995 378	31.7	24.8
Acadia	22 527	70.3	88 600	19.4	10.0	524	27.0	2.4	26 895	1.8	1 538	5.7	25 197	27.6	30.1
Allen	8 099	72.3	79 600	18.5	10.0	553	26.0	3.3	9 038	2.3	650	7.2	8 356	26.0	30.4
Ascension	38 287	81.6	167 400	18.9	10.0	851	31.7	3.7	58 954	3.5	3 158	5.4	52 500	36.5	24.6
Assumption	8 571	82.0	98 100	17.1	10.0	592	31.2	3.3	10 124	2.0	770	7.6	9 055	25.1	40.3
Avoyelles	15 332	70.1	86 600	19.7	10.8	577	30.7	3.5	16 266	0.7	1 181	7.3	15 181	26.1	28.9
Beauregard	12 948	76.8	93 900	18.0	10.0	611	27.9	2.9	14 822	2.6	1 013	6.8	14 198	26.4	32.8
Bienville	5 668	71.6	58 100	19.0	10.9	501	30.2	3.7	5 965	-0.1	463	7.8	5 043	30.2	34.4
Bossier	45 776	67.0	146 300	20.6	10.0	843	28.9	2.4	57 661	1.0	3 354	5.8	56 042	34.1	24.7
Caddo	98 554	62.2	121 700	21.0	10.2	725	31.3	2.1	112 139	0.8	8 306	7.4	110 887	30.9	22.1
Calcasieu	73 726	70.6	118 300	19.5	10.0	739	30.5	2.3	94 601	5.5	5 597	5.9	85 068	29.1	26.6
Caldwell	3 935	74.2	66 200	18.8	10.0	539	28.8	2.3	4 095	3.3	313	7.6	4 105	21.8	33.6
Cameron	2 529	90.0	112 900	16.0	10.0	723	17.8	3.4	3 510	5.6	170	4.8	3 243	28.1	36.9
Catahoula	3 767	77.1	68 500	21.5	10.0	468	18.0	4.3	3 856	-1.5	312	8.1	3 589	26.2	32.7
Claiborne	5 726	70.0	70 500	19.6	11.2	616	32.5	2.7	6 408	-2.4	484	7.6	6 217	22.2	35.0
Concordia	7 642	62.1	75 000	21.8	12.3	479	28.0	4.6	7 874	0.2	685	8.7	6 851	27.1	28.0
De Soto	10 270	75.4	87 900	19.3	10.1	559	34.3	2.7	11 109	0.6	904	8.1	10 764	24.5	29.7
East Baton Rouge	167 422	61.2	166 000	21.2	10.0	817	33.3	4.7	234 099	3.3	13 516	5.8	214 379	37.5	18.3
East Carroll	2 488	56.2	48 500	18.6	11.5	460	43.2	2.3	2 238	-2.3	332	14.8	1 955	23.7	29.9
East Feliciana	6 991	79.9	116 600	19.8	10.0	629	29.7	3.7	8 242	3.2	535	6.5	7 698	24.0	26.1
Evangeline	11 967	67.4	80 000	17.8	11.0	518	33.6	3.8	13 233	2.6	893	6.7	11 160	27.3	32.4
Franklin	7 704	69.8	75 200	19.0	10.0	522	30.5	1.9	7 613	-1.6	722	9.5	7 126	29.0	30.3
Grant	7 340	78.0	78 300	19.8	10.5	711	26.4	4.3	8 352	2.2	595	7.1	7 658	26.4	32.7
Iberia	26 496	71.4	101 200	19.2	10.0	654	29.4	4.1	32 992	1.9	2 069	6.3	30 757	26.3	31.8
Iberville	11 192	77.1	93 300	19.3	10.0	607	27.6	1.8	14 536	3.1	1 138	7.8	13 124	20.7	33.2
Jackson	6 090	66.7	77 800	18.3	10.0	528	27.5	3.0	7 253	4.3	432	6.0	6 004	26.9	32.3
Jefferson	167 251	62.5	172 500	23.7	10.6	905	32.1	4.2	219 986	2.6	13 161	6.0	209 519	31.2	24.2
Jefferson Davis	11 634	74.0	86 600	18.7	10.0	576	28.2	2.3	13 603	3.0	802	5.9	11 690	28.9	33.0
Lafayette	86 504	65.5	162 500	19.9	10.0	754	28.9	3.8	121 654	2.0	5 998	4.9	112 440	34.6	21.0
Lafourche	35 072	77.7	126 500	18.9	10.0	681	28.2	2.5	48 594	3.4	2 338	4.8	43 445	27.3	33.6
La Salle	5 619	83.2	73 900	16.5	10.0	457	25.3	2.8	6 780	-3.2	348	5.1	5 959	34.0	28.3
Lincoln	16 877	54.7	116 900	20.7	10.0	645	38.1	4.3	19 865	1.3	1 557	7.8	20 136	36.0	20.9
Livingston	46 246	79.7	152 500	20.1	10.0	773	29.6	5.1	66 433	3.4	3 657	5.5	59 719	30.3	29.6
Madison	4 068	53.9	69 500	20.0	11.3	526	30.2	3.5	3 907	-1.9	441	11.3	3 892	27.9	24.9
Morehouse	10 482	66.7	74 600	22.6	11.1	545	31.3	5.3	11 270	0.8	1 270	11.3	9 941	23.3	30.2
Natchitoches	14 903	62.1	97 200	19.7	10.0	624	38.6	3.4	16 325	0.5	1 307	8.0	15 934	26.5	26.0

1. Specified owner-occupied units. 2. A value of 10.0 represents 10 percent or less; a value of 50.0 represents 50 percent or more. 3. Specified renter-occupied units.
4. Overcrowded or lacking complete plumbing facilities. 5. Percent of civilian labor force. 6. Persons 16 years old and over.

STATE County	Private nonfarm establishments, employment and payroll, 2013									Agriculture, 2012			
		Employment						Annual payroll		Farms			
											Percent with:		
	Number of establish-ments	Total	Health care and social assistance	Manufac-turing	Retail trade	Finance and insurance	Professional, scientific, and technical services	Total (mil dol)	Average per employee (dollars)	Number	Fewer than 50 acres	500 acres or more	Farm operators whose principal occu-pation is farming (percent)
	104	105	106	107	108	109	110	111	112	113	114	115	116
KENTUCKY—Cont'd													
Ohio	357	7 908	D	D	729	120	99	254	32 160	944	32.1	5.1	31.0
Oldham	1 224	11 331	2 452	834	1 148	D	537	387	34 193	419	53.9	7.2	40.1
Owen	117	1 308	D	D	181	53	8	44	33 938	701	23.3	7.4	40.8
Owsley	47	352	190	D	D	D	D	8	23 585	163	22.7	6.7	47.2
Pendleton	182	1 776	D	495	235	67	48	57	31 940	810	32.1	3.3	33.2
Perry	656	9 465	2 654	D	1 844	311	230	344	36 344	49	51.0	14.3	44.9
Pike	1 354	19 720	4 286	D	3 874	D	670	759	38 492	56	26.8	14.3	42.9
Powell	170	1 533	287	108	394	D	D	40	25 924	229	41.5	3.1	39.7
Pulaski	1 452	20 057	5 104	3 672	3 160	669	425	639	31 846	1 713	38.3	3.7	50.0
Robertson	18	125	D	NA	D	D	D	3	21 824	251	21.1	5.2	48.6
Rockcastle	218	2 572	845	103	330	92	48	71	27 660	677	36.8	4.1	36.2
Rowan	489	7 148	D	914	1 297	198	86	213	29 761	356	35.7	3.1	29.5
Russell	373	4 954	1 035	1 427	699	129	60	138	27 955	726	45.5	4.7	39.4
Scott	872	20 690	1 651	8 971	1 660	279	318	1 045	50 517	838	44.4	7.4	50.5
Shelby	878	11 978	1 392	3 666	1 632	301	297	425	35 443	1 518	50.4	4.0	40.5
Simpson	361	7 393	513	3 197	953	136	D	239	32 368	467	50.7	8.6	50.3
Spencer	198	1 100	240	D	223	D	53	26	23 673	529	44.2	4.0	41.0
Taylor	622	9 283	D	1 213	1 421	246	79	264	28 463	874	42.9	4.3	37.8
Todd	198	1 456	229	365	D	81	35	39	27 036	603	22.4	13.8	55.9
Trigg	226	2 312	D	532	394	67	D	62	26 832	397	30.2	10.1	41.3
Trimble	79	618	105	D	72	60	D	31	50 676	439	37.1	4.3	40.1
Union	272	4 666	901	D	728	123	D	206	44 203	310	35.5	25.2	46.1
Warren	2 902	49 016	7 982	8 179	7 220	1 521	1 840	1 790	36 527	1 648	45.9	4.7	32.9
Washington	241	2 779	427	867	281	D	58	88	31 526	1 011	28.7	4.3	37.1
Wayne	268	3 826	572	1 531	627	157	D	101	26 450	778	35.5	5.7	49.9
Webster	210	2 473	319	239	346	85	D	108	43 509	500	26.0	13.2	40.0
Whitley	633	10 141	2 718	996	1 435	233	839	304	29 988	496	38.7	2.6	29.8
Wolfe	84	666	288	D	195	D	D	15	22 884	297	28.6	4.7	37.7
Woodford	529	6 620	575	1 789	773	176	575	260	39 231	713	44.6	7.3	38.7
LOUISIANA	104 375	1 687 956	287 471	126 336	226 557	65 224	95 612	72 070	42 696	28 093	43.7	11.6	43.2
Acadia	1 130	13 159	2 446	1 333	2 549	432	391	434	32 982	841	50.9	14.3	47.1
Allen	325	3 515	894	D	661	131	D	108	30 683	429	48.0	9.3	35.7
Ascension	2 094	35 665	3 400	4 460	5 876	993	1 147	1 701	47 686	250	60.8	9.6	32.8
Assumption	258	2 835	723	330	461	94	87	111	39 023	81	37.0	42.0	66.7
Avoyelles	728	8 671	2 141	212	1 529	433	222	232	26 811	937	43.1	15.0	43.0
Beauregard	602	6 768	1 129	813	1 284	D	189	243	35 917	860	36.9	5.9	37.0
Bienville	233	3 409	488	D	306	156	46	119	34 993	233	33.0	6.4	54.1
Bossier	2 419	36 027	4 101	1 660	6 921	1 080	1 047	1 162	32 261	472	50.8	8.3	53.0
Caddo	6 313	107 774	27 157	5 742	13 954	3 239	4 761	4 004	37 154	614	54.4	9.6	48.2
Calcasieu	4 342	70 446	12 613	8 585	10 605	2 072	4 388	2 835	40 251	902	51.3	9.3	35.9
Caldwell	180	1 654	642	32	285	97	D	46	28 053	295	39.7	10.5	40.3
Cameron	155	1 495	D	D	D	D	58	85	56 664	342	25.7	20.5	33.9
Catahoula	188	1 580	466	D	354	D	68	40	25 448	567	25.2	18.3	34.0
Claiborne	254	2 821	853	199	359	89	D	95	33 842	295	32.5	7.8	42.0
Concordia	363	4 267	1 028	D	886	D	207	130	30 529	461	26.2	23.4	33.8
De Soto	418	5 247	621	D	829	193	113	254	48 325	669	38.1	8.5	49.6
East Baton Rouge	12 087	249 626	36 511	10 891	28 324	12 206	18 448	11 534	46 206	432	54.4	4.9	39.8
East Carroll	126	1 122	303	108	D	33	21	40	35 731	227	18.9	46.3	61.2
East Feliciana	247	3 305	1 819	270	266	D	41	121	36 588	399	36.8	12.8	32.3
Evangeline	516	6 517	2 648	953	918	287	129	189	29 049	663	45.2	10.3	36.3
Franklin	384	3 979	1 131	172	958	207	265	103	25 975	915	33.7	12.8	38.6
Grant	171	1 926	244	D	246	67	D	50	26 090	238	35.3	10.1	29.4
Iberia	1 711	29 877	3 814	4 993	3 464	828	804	1 451	48 561	279	57.7	16.8	57.3
Iberville	527	9 784	705	3 403	1 055	276	D	587	60 020	165	38.8	24.2	61.8
Jackson	244	2 699	565	D	555	112	41	106	39 372	196	48.0	1.0	49.5
Jefferson	11 630	178 459	29 521	6 756	28 601	8 887	10 783	7 747	43 410	57	70.2	3.5	14.0
Jefferson Davis	658	7 149	1 504	D	1 461	325	346	235	32 877	656	35.5	19.1	48.6
Lafayette	8 326	129 636	24 416	7 269	16 735	3 478	8 773	5 907	45 563	632	70.1	3.0	31.0
Lafourche	1 842	28 398	3 872	2 047	4 026	911	851	1 372	48 311	407	43.0	10.8	36.6
La Salle	350	3 430	776	D	573	149	D	116	33 651	186	35.5	2.7	31.2
Lincoln	1 018	14 521	2 946	1 187	2 291	662	722	471	32 434	346	33.2	4.6	41.9
Livingston	1 654	19 448	2 020	1 901	4 629	607	623	626	32 213	405	69.6	0.7	42.2
Madison	212	2 421	1 118	D	427	52	30	63	26 088	295	13.9	42.0	54.9
Morehouse	452	5 182	1 980	137	1 022	207	92	135	25 965	434	23.5	31.3	48.2
Natchitoches	819	10 944	1 790	2 434	1 718	D	244	333	30 450	630	31.9	15.7	39.5

STATE County	Agriculture, 2012 (cont.) Land in farms Acreage (1,000)	Land in farms Percent change, 2007–2012	Land in farms Acres Average size of farm	Land in farms Acres Total irrigated (1,000)	Land in farms Acres Total cropland (1,000)	Value of land and buildings (dollars) Average per farm	Value of land and buildings (dollars) Average per acre	Value of machinery and equipment, average per farm (dollars)	Value of products sold Total (mil dol)	Value of products sold Average per farm (dollars)	Value of products sold Percent from: Crops	Value of products sold Percent from: Livestock and poultry products	Percent of farms with sales of: $10,000 or more	Percent of farms with sales of: $100,000 or more	Government payments Total ($1,000)	Government payments Percent of farms
	117	118	119	120	121	122	123	124	125	126	127	128	129	130	131	132
KENTUCKY—Cont'd																
Ohio	158	-6.1	168	0.6	78.8	410 305	2 448	84 484	98.8	104 698	36.8	63.2	29.0	7.1	1 434	48.8
Oldham	60	0.5	144	0.2	24.3	899 907	6 247	68 687	14.8	35 439	61.4	38.6	41.5	5.3	296	18.4
Owen	132	-16.4	188	0.3	45.8	434 031	2 306	56 652	21.2	30 298	49.3	50.7	37.2	5.7	1 113	42.2
Owsley	28	-23.1	169	0.0	6.9	228 049	1 349	41 859	1.6	9 939	71.1	28.9	25.8	0.6	234	42.3
Pendleton	101	-19.8	125	0.9	31.7	296 179	2 368	50 151	11.5	14 167	73.6	26.4	23.6	2.5	622	26.3
Perry	11	2.7	224	D	0.9	269 490	1 206	68 408	2.1	42 082	7.3	92.7	24.5	10.2	D	2.0
Pike	13	-5.9	239	0.0	2.1	318 875	1 334	49 732	0.6	10 018	40.8	59.0	32.1	0.0	D	1.8
Powell	30	-8.3	131	0.0	7.5	208 742	1 590	42 210	2.5	10 773	63.4	36.6	22.7	1.7	133	34.9
Pulaski	228	-1.6	133	0.4	90.1	385 814	2 896	58 635	63.5	37 072	36.5	63.5	39.9	6.9	1 599	38.4
Robertson	39	-24.6	155	0.1	12.7	279 578	1 808	58 873	4.1	16 163	43.6	56.4	30.3	3.6	396	37.8
Rockcastle	91	0.5	134	0.0	30.3	272 708	2 032	49 790	12.4	18 251	53.5	46.5	29.4	3.1	557	32.6
Rowan	42	-15.4	119	0.0	15.0	253 205	2 133	47 567	5.2	14 705	48.1	51.9	18.5	2.8	262	31.2
Russell	89	-4.0	123	0.0	34.9	379 095	3 080	62 912	44.5	61 331	16.1	83.9	40.5	9.2	1 892	46.6
Scott	127	-8.3	152	0.8	48.1	695 570	4 572	63 774	38.8	46 254	34.6	65.4	36.2	10.4	1 180	31.5
Shelby	199	-2.9	131	1.3	111.3	640 994	4 881	68 175	76.8	50 596	71.4	28.6	34.1	7.6	2 489	34.3
Simpson	102	-14.8	217	0.2	78.5	905 017	4 163	107 238	73.9	158 208	60.0	40.0	43.9	12.8	2 406	57.8
Spencer	69	-5.7	131	0.4	31.2	409 495	3 134	54 915	15.6	29 516	66.0	34.0	35.9	5.3	487	42.7
Taylor	115	-3.5	131	0.1	59.5	364 644	2 782	60 556	37.9	43 362	44.5	55.5	37.4	8.1	1 458	58.7
Todd	181	-8.6	300	1.5	126.6	1 107 604	3 690	133 570	180.2	298 915	48.2	51.8	64.2	31.5	3 015	51.2
Trigg	129	-4.9	325	1.5	71.8	961 912	2 960	103 461	47.2	118 862	82.6	17.4	43.3	14.9	1 514	46.3
Trimble	56	-14.5	127	0.1	19.0	399 913	3 156	57 303	9.1	20 738	73.6	26.4	33.0	3.9	519	42.6
Union	195	-3.0	629	2.6	167.9	2 579 713	4 104	324 342	96.5	311 268	92.3	7.7	49.0	27.1	2 969	61.3
Warren	247	-6.9	150	0.4	146.2	539 892	3 606	71 369	114.7	69 603	47.9	52.1	31.9	8.1	6 190	39.2
Washington	141	-13.5	139	0.3	55.9	356 909	2 560	55 341	33.8	33 403	47.7	52.3	43.1	6.0	2 275	38.9
Wayne	129	-9.9	165	0.1	40.8	376 098	2 274	65 197	68.1	87 496	17.2	82.8	41.5	11.2	544	39.3
Webster	152	-1.7	305	0.4	107.9	973 724	3 194	135 228	102.4	204 744	43.3	56.7	33.2	16.4	4 331	73.4
Whitley	58	-20.4	118	0.0	16.9	255 401	2 168	39 494	5.4	10 851	31.4	68.6	20.6	1.6	86	14.9
Wolfe	42	-26.4	143	0.0	8.0	212 566	1 487	43 566	1.7	5 721	57.9	42.1	15.2	0.0	377	45.5
Woodford	112	-6.0	157	0.3	34.7	1 280 116	8 155	103 851	76.6	107 421	12.5	87.5	46.1	12.3	997	26.8
LOUISIANA	7 901	-2.6	281	1 092.9	4 275.6	718 179	2 554	104 418	3 809.4	135 600	73.1	26.9	33.0	11.7	138 164	33.6
Acadia	238	2.3	283	82.9	187.1	628 439	2 219	117 468	124.3	147 830	86.7	13.3	34.2	16.3	6 775	51.6
Allen	88	5.8	205	18.4	47.2	431 168	2 101	76 105	23.7	55 187	85.2	14.8	28.2	7.7	2 111	35.4
Ascension	50	11.0	202	0.0	20.3	710 252	3 519	90 016	20.5	81 968	86.4	13.6	26.4	5.6	56	3.2
Assumption	62	-2.4	768	D	56.0	2 339 247	3 048	556 259	64.8	800 235	98.6	1.4	65.4	48.1	65	8.6
Avoyelles	299	7.4	319	21.7	203.5	724 316	2 269	113 847	137.8	147 048	91.2	8.8	37.9	14.5	5 632	45.4
Beauregard	146	-18.3	170	3.1	42.6	424 519	2 497	56 241	15.7	18 269	59.7	40.3	25.1	2.7	1 523	18.3
Bienville	56	37.3	240	0.1	16.2	570 425	2 379	88 854	34.5	148 039	5.5	94.5	30.9	8.2	136	10.3
Bossier	81	-21.4	172	1.5	28.4	579 184	3 363	91 169	17.7	37 517	60.8	39.2	27.1	6.8	717	11.0
Caddo	140	-7.5	228	13.5	58.6	620 078	2 722	81 067	50.6	82 437	83.6	16.4	28.3	7.7	2 364	14.8
Calcasieu	338	-8.1	375	15.8	85.9	961 407	2 566	70 263	33.2	36 756	60.0	40.0	23.9	5.1	2 653	22.2
Caldwell	62	-7.7	211	4.1	28.8	522 678	2 476	70 064	11.5	38 929	84.1	15.9	28.5	9.2	1 762	44.4
Cameron	235	8.8	688	11.5	55.3	1 210 319	1 759	97 509	19.1	55 857	61.7	38.3	36.3	9.1	896	24.0
Catahoula	224	-3.1	395	33.7	166.2	958 256	2 427	129 684	91.9	162 157	96.0	4.0	37.0	15.7	7 435	71.4
Claiborne	57	17.8	194	D	12.5	488 681	2 518	90 197	71.2	241 434	2.7	97.3	34.2	17.6	177	15.3
Concordia	240	14.2	522	28.5	171.3	1 203 475	2 308	172 974	118.3	256 534	97.9	2.1	37.1	21.0	6 348	85.2
De Soto	164	-1.8	246	0.3	30.2	665 374	2 709	74 991	17.7	26 417	25.2	74.8	28.3	3.7	841	11.7
East Baton Rouge	58	-20.3	133	0.7	13.3	765 382	5 746	48 398	11.5	26 523	24.0	76.0	26.2	3.9	209	8.1
East Carroll	251	-3.7	1 106	125.6	214.3	3 029 084	2 739	409 366	192.3	846 934	99.6	0.4	68.3	51.1	7 976	85.5
East Feliciana	113	-12.2	282	0.2	26.0	840 722	2 981	74 306	13.5	33 802	49.6	50.4	35.8	6.3	527	15.0
Evangeline	192	11.4	289	40.1	103.9	613 686	2 121	77 027	62.6	94 450	83.6	16.4	32.0	10.6	4 088	47.7
Franklin	246	-29.1	269	88.8	162.4	613 407	2 280	106 741	143.2	156 467	96.7	3.3	35.8	17.3	7 665	80.2
Grant	48	-7.3	202	0.5	17.0	430 168	2 134	65 084	7.9	33 050	74.8	25.2	28.2	8.4	723	22.3
Iberia	107	-7.5	384	0.4	85.5	1 205 219	3 135	231 706	92.2	330 351	97.2	2.8	39.8	18.6	311	16.8
Iberville	163	90.5	990	1.0	63.0	1 785 261	1 803	395 085	67.6	409 436	96.6	3.4	52.7	20.6	223	23.6
Jackson	19	-7.3	95	0.1	3.5	268 638	2 830	49 990	30.6	155 934	1.1	98.9	27.0	9.7	48	2.6
Jefferson	8	-48.7	136	D	0.8	517 123	3 804	58 070	1.6	28 228	24.1	75.8	42.1	7.0	41	21.1
Jefferson Davis	265	-8.0	404	67.7	186.5	917 733	2 272	122 320	85.1	129 771	87.3	12.7	38.4	17.2	5 149	59.3
Lafayette	56	-17.4	88	3.2	34.8	420 315	4 770	67 704	30.5	48 180	89.2	10.8	19.0	4.0	316	11.4
Lafourche	158	49.0	389	0.4	52.4	834 602	2 148	117 747	58.0	142 462	73.7	26.3	41.0	6.6	51	2.5
La Salle	20	-3.8	105	D	4.0	269 210	2 565	56 677	1.0	5 538	34.4	65.7	13.4	0.0	186	10.8
Lincoln	56	6.4	161	0.4	9.4	536 971	3 328	65 902	101.7	293 928	1.4	98.6	37.9	18.2	387	13.6
Livingston	28	-8.1	68	0.3	5.3	391 205	5 747	46 447	4.8	11 924	25.6	74.4	20.5	1.2	103	5.7
Madison	225	-4.2	761	63.1	180.7	1 877 692	2 467	335 441	155.1	525 681	99.4	0.6	58.3	45.4	6 131	87.1
Morehouse	279	2.0	643	141.5	206.7	1 521 809	2 367	204 793	176.1	405 781	96.9	3.1	47.2	31.1	11 646	68.7
Natchitoches	201	-9.4	319	10.5	70.3	774 152	2 427	91 722	129.0	204 767	23.4	76.6	40.2	13.8	3 061	33.0

STATE County	Water use, 2010		Wholesale trade,[1] 2007				Retail trade,[2] 2007				Real estate and rental and leasing,[2] 2007			
	Total water withdrawn (mil gal/day)	Gallons withdrawn per person per day	Number of establish-ments	Number of employees	Sales (mil dol)	Annual payroll (mil dol)	Number of establish-ments	Number of employees	Sales (mil dol)	Annual payroll (mil dol)	Number of establish-ments	Number of employees	Receipts (mil dol)	Annual payroll (mil dol)
	133	134	135	136	137	138	139	140	141	142	143	144	145	146
KENTUCKY—Cont'd														
Ohio	11.3	474	12	363	149.5	6.6	60	627	142.5	12.7	7	31	1.6	0.3
Oldham	6.4	106	47	287	95.5	11.8	135	1 483	374.8	35.3	50	134	24.5	3.2
Owen	1.8	167	5	43	10.4	0.6	26	230	43.2	4.0	4	D	D	D
Owsley	0.4	90	1	D	D	D	11	87	16.7	1.5	2	D	D	D
Pendleton	2.9	198	8	D	D	D	29	233	47.2	4.0	8	21	1.6	0.3
Perry	6.7	235	32	438	267.9	21.7	158	1 952	463.1	39.5	21	64	11.1	1.7
Pike	10.9	167	59	451	589.0	21.3	290	3 876	894.9	80.4	42	122	35.2	3.0
Powell	2.2	171	5	22	3.9	0.5	43	382	95.0	6.1	4	D	D	D
Pulaski	165.0	2 616	60	1 124	989.6	29.4	316	3 495	884.4	73.3	51	181	23.8	5.0
Robertson	0.2	79	NA	NA	NA	NA	5	16	1.6	0.1	NA	NA	NA	NA
Rockcastle	2.9	168	11	D	D	D	53	316	71.6	5.1	6	37	2.5	0.7
Rowan	5.7	244	20	177	54.1	4.2	115	1 359	272.1	24.2	22	69	8.4	1.4
Russell	18.7	1 065	5	D	D	D	89	783	180.3	13.4	9	57	9.9	1.2
Scott	4.4	93	23	D	D	D	132	1 779	528.6	35.8	53	217	39.3	6.7
Shelby	4.4	104	36	618	320.8	26.8	146	1 755	498.7	37.4	45	169	21.5	3.8
Simpson	2.1	123	11	88	260.0	2.7	69	1 039	415.2	22.6	19	108	8.1	3.3
Spencer	0.5	30	4	11	1.5	0.1	23	236	68.1	4.0	9	28	2.7	0.4
Taylor	5.2	213	24	D	D	D	148	1 770	371.9	35.2	30	157	11.9	2.7
Todd	1.9	155	9	47	23.2	1.3	36	246	58.6	3.6	3	9	0.6	0.1
Trigg	3.2	222	7	D	D	D	40	364	70.9	5.9	15	40	5.0	1.0
Trimble	10.2	1 158	NA	NA	NA	NA	15	116	32.0	1.5	3	4	0.3	0.0
Union	4.9	327	12	103	94.0	3.7	65	678	144.2	12.4	7	24	3.0	0.3
Warren	19.8	174	134	D	D	D	535	7 535	1 691.2	151.0	133	1 113	114.4	28.7
Washington	2.8	237	10	94	67.7	2.5	41	262	63.3	4.6	4	5	0.4	0.1
Wayne	3.1	147	10	76	23.6	1.6	66	697	152.5	13.8	10	52	2.4	0.6
Webster	10.8	793	10	D	D	D	42	349	67.5	5.8	6	14	1.1	0.2
Whitley	6.1	170	22	D	D	D	153	1 531	373.3	30.5	26	78	10.5	1.9
Wolfe	0.5	64	3	D	D	D	26	187	45.3	3.3	2	D	D	D
Woodford	23.0	921	15	D	D	D	74	770	225.2	18.8	21	45	6.3	0.9
LOUISIANA	8 540.3	1 884	4 839	63 911	51 415.6	2 808.3	17 135	231 365	56 543.2	5 096.1	4 625	30 922	6 014.9	1 194.9
Acadia	230.9	3 738	40	D	D	D	193	2 427	526.0	49.2	39	122	11.2	2.3
Allen	24.5	951	8	D	D	D	72	741	142.9	11.7	9	32	2.2	0.5
Ascension	162.1	1 512	103	1 297	665.0	65.5	369	5 189	1 318.0	111.9	87	488	139.5	21.7
Assumption	21.2	906	12	D	D	D	53	553	100.0	8.9	7	13	2.5	0.2
Avoyelles	56.4	1 340	22	210	171.3	6.4	162	1 440	310.9	25.0	18	63	6.3	1.0
Beauregard	27.8	781	13	D	D	D	100	1 412	317.4	28.6	20	71	7.6	1.1
Bienville	13.2	918	6	D	D	D	45	338	58.7	5.3	5	D	D	D
Bossier	15.3	131	90	1 542	1 028.2	70.1	476	6 359	1 741.9	142.0	116	554	100.6	15.0
Caddo	147.0	576	312	4 511	5 467.4	198.9	1 008	14 460	3 706.8	326.5	299	1 857	260.4	49.8
Calcasieu	223.6	1 160	185	2 145	1 342.9	91.5	830	11 704	2 776.0	246.5	210	948	195.1	30.7
Caldwell	3.8	378	5	D	D	D	36	459	112.9	8.0	6	17	2.3	0.3
Cameron	26.6	3 892	13	82	62.8	3.7	23	238	36.8	3.0	5	105	36.4	4.9
Catahoula	30.0	2 883	15	156	193.1	4.5	34	244	52.7	4.2	4	18	5.6	0.6
Claiborne	2.6	152	9	69	125.9	2.3	56	444	74.2	7.3	6	18	1.7	0.3
Concordia	42.8	2 053	14	D	D	D	79	871	194.9	16.6	8	155	6.7	3.9
De Soto	36.6	1 375	11	155	22.0	5.1	73	819	184.5	15.3	7	21	1.5	0.3
East Baton Rouge	179.4	408	610	8 786	7 860.1	401.7	1 930	29 228	7 043.0	664.6	583	3 137	559.9	96.5
East Carroll	26.6	3 426	12	D	D	D	26	225	34.0	3.3	7	19	3.1	0.7
East Feliciana	3.7	183	9	D	D	D	53	394	72.8	6.1	5	D	D	D
Evangeline	203.7	5 993	17	D	D	D	130	1 078	228.6	18.6	22	65	6.0	1.3
Franklin	40.3	1 942	19	191	182.7	4.8	89	988	215.5	18.5	21	61	6.4	1.0
Grant	5.3	238	4	D	D	D	29	273	74.7	6.6	2	D	D	D
Iberia	31.0	423	84	D	D	D	290	3 631	910.2	81.0	101	2 302	553.0	164.9
Iberville	481.4	14 418	28	247	149.9	8.8	95	1 103	274.4	22.6	27	154	26.5	3.8
Jackson	4.0	245	7	D	D	D	47	569	114.5	9.8	11	33	3.8	0.5
Jefferson	816.7	1 888	802	10 311	6 049.8	489.5	1 855	30 948	8 106.2	771.5	538	5 527	960.2	183.5
Jefferson Davis	175.1	5 541	21	D	D	D	116	1 496	338.8	28.1	19	303	60.8	13.8
Lafayette	41.2	186	445	6 314	2 651.4	281.7	1 041	15 424	3 814.3	340.3	438	3 387	879.4	175.7
Lafourche	43.6	453	71	1 096	888.4	44.2	304	4 103	917.5	79.0	80	544	116.0	23.5
La Salle	2.4	164	8	D	D	D	58	517	116.1	9.0	10	42	4.5	0.9
Lincoln	8.2	176	27	388	171.3	14.6	184	2 482	527.8	48.1	46	242	51.6	6.5
Livingston	15.2	119	38	308	483.0	14.5	288	3 645	923.7	73.1	55	177	30.5	4.3
Madison	42.1	3 480	12	101	153.2	3.4	39	455	142.5	8.2	9	30	3.7	0.5
Morehouse	83.3	2 977	18	170	255.3	5.4	102	1 181	241.4	24.0	24	52	7.0	1.1
Natchitoches	34.3	868	25	D	D	D	156	1 838	414.0	35.5	46	175	15.3	2.4

1. Merchant wholesalers, except manufacturers' sales branches and offices. 2. Employer establishments.

STATE County	Professional, scientific, and technical services,[1] 2007				Manufacturing, 2007				Accommodation and food services, 2007			
	Number of establishments	Number of employees	Receipts (mil dol)	Annual payroll (mil dol)	Number of establishments	Number of employees	Receipts (mil dol)	Annual payroll (mil dol)	Number of establishments	Number of employees	Sales (mil dol)	Annual payroll (mil dol)
	147	148	149	150	151	152	153	154	155	156	157	158
KENTUCKY—Cont'd												
Ohio	25	69	5.4	1.6	27	2 377	485.5	70.5	27	416	15.3	4.2
Oldham	174	555	60.3	24.9	46	925	275.1	36.6	60	1 127	47.1	12.6
Owen	8	13	1.0	0.2	NA	NA	NA	NA	13	178	6.6	2.0
Owsley	2	D	D	D	NA	NA	NA	NA	2	D	D	D
Pendleton	9	D	D	D	17	596	D	24.3	11	182	4.5	1.2
Perry	57	D	D	D	12	690	122.2	21.4	50	1 186	43.8	11.8
Pike	104	D	D	D	28	652	D	22.2	91	1 710	75.5	19.3
Powell	7	8	0.6	0.1	NA	NA	NA	NA	14	228	9.3	2.5
Pulaski	96	D	D	D	85	4 129	1 088.0	139.4	92	1 862	73.5	19.3
Robertson	1	D	D	D	NA	NA	NA	NA	1	D	D	D
Rockcastle	14	D	D	D	NA	NA	NA	NA	25	351	11.3	3.3
Rowan	23	D	D	D	20	954	259.8	28.6	43	971	36.1	8.4
Russell	22	68	5.5	1.6	25	1 182	D	36.8	31	372	14.5	2.9
Scott	68	414	34.7	14.1	37	9 905	D	D	79	1 815	73.1	20.8
Shelby	76	317	32.0	10.6	52	4 535	1 373.1	178.2	52	D	D	D
Simpson	17	99	4.9	1.9	33	3 531	1 406.3	141.4	41	654	29.7	8.2
Spencer	13	D	D	D	NA	NA	NA	NA	13	D	D	D
Taylor	50	115	9.3	3.3	35	1 871	315.2	56.2	42	831	25.4	6.4
Todd	10	66	3.3	1.6	NA	NA	NA	NA	12	74	2.3	0.7
Trigg	11	46	3.8	0.9	17	1 134	235.1	39.3	21	344	11.3	3.4
Trimble	4	D	D	D	NA	NA	NA	NA	6	40	1.8	0.5
Union	8	28	3.2	1.1	16	901	250.4	40.7	22	261	9.8	2.4
Warren	205	D	D	D	118	D	D	D	217	5 454	231.2	63.7
Washington	15	46	3.3	1.0	12	986	259.0	35.9	12	201	6.3	1.7
Wayne	23	62	4.2	1.5	36	2 053	378.9	52.8	26	431	18.8	4.3
Webster	10	23	1.8	0.3	NA	NA	NA	NA	17	107	4.7	1.2
Whitley	55	450	53.6	15.6	27	1 233	D	40.5	58	974	39.3	9.6
Wolfe	5	11	0.7	0.2	NA	NA	NA	NA	5	42	0.6	0.1
Woodford	68	D	D	D	30	2 584	D	122.8	34	397	15.7	4.5
LOUISIANA	11 128	84 666	11 856.6	4 234.6	3 442	148 080	205 054.7	7 564.5	8 169	180 289	9 729.9	2 579.0
Acadia	89	307	35.1	13.3	51	1 148	D	38.5	67	1 145	40.8	10.5
Allen	19	59	6.0	1.7	13	655	167.5	27.2	28	422	17.4	3.7
Ascension	150	D	D	D	88	4 348	D	329.2	148	2 747	116.3	30.9
Assumption	26	70	6.0	2.4	NA	NA	NA	NA	13	135	4.1	1.0
Avoyelles	60	173	18.9	5.0	NA	NA	NA	NA	52	2 423	174.7	47.0
Beauregard	40	170	11.4	4.6	19	935	D	D	33	550	19.5	5.2
Bienville	12	31	2.7	1.3	13	1 098	D	29.3	16	164	6.6	1.6
Bossier	162	934	96.1	31.6	73	2 200	D	D	232	9 784	711.7	174.9
Caddo	604	4 224	492.8	173.4	215	9 553	D	486.2	439	12 288	675.3	175.3
Calcasieu	440	D	D	D	128	D	D	D	328	10 346	878.6	181.6
Caldwell	22	66	5.3	1.1	NA	NA	NA	NA	10	138	5.8	1.5
Cameron	15	D	D	D	NA	NA	NA	NA	4	20	1.4	0.2
Catahoula	22	56	5.6	2.4	NA	NA	NA	NA	11	127	5.0	1.3
Claiborne	14	41	4.6	1.1	NA	NA	NA	NA	8	52	2.3	0.6
Concordia	23	108	8.1	2.2	NA	NA	NA	NA	27	410	17.8	4.2
De Soto	22	54	5.1	1.3	15	766	D	D	21	300	10.4	2.6
East Baton Rouge	1 684	D	D	D	334	11 054	D	669.1	896	22 590	998.3	277.2
East Carroll	8	D	D	D	NA	NA	NA	NA	9	59	2.1	0.5
East Feliciana	24	51	4.3	1.5	NA	NA	NA	NA	17	199	6.0	1.5
Evangeline	50	198	18.2	4.8	20	698	D	33.4	22	269	9.3	2.1
Franklin	30	586	12.1	6.1	NA	NA	NA	NA	23	354	14.3	3.1
Grant	8	21	0.8	0.2	NA	NA	NA	NA	4	D	D	D
Iberia	161	754	89.1	25.4	130	6 273	1 586.2	261.8	92	1 941	73.5	18.4
Iberville	34	292	30.7	19.9	31	3 461	7 694.7	283.5	35	491	17.9	5.0
Jackson	20	122	11.4	4.1	9	D	D	D	18	223	7.9	1.9
Jefferson	1 401	D	D	D	348	14 278	2 837.2	563.6	1 032	19 590	982.9	287.8
Jefferson Davis	59	245	20.4	7.7	13	530	189.2	21.2	41	734	26.7	6.7
Lafayette	1 135	D	D	D	286	8 790	2 037.2	352.1	513	12 494	584.6	156.1
Lafourche	161	D	D	D	59	3 265	614.3	120.5	159	2 446	106.6	26.3
La Salle	31	68	6.8	2.0	NA	NA	NA	NA	14	175	7.6	1.9
Lincoln	80	419	44.1	18.4	33	D	D	D	80	1 674	72.5	17.6
Livingston	122	D	D	D	68	1 884	459.9	80.3	121	2 388	89.2	24.4
Madison	11	D	D	D	NA	NA	NA	NA	19	276	9.4	2.0
Morehouse	26	D	D	D	15	741	D	D	26	490	19.8	4.7
Natchitoches	66	D	D	D	19	2 818	1 006.3	99.6	72	1 264	52.4	13.4

1. Establishment subject to federal tax.

Table B. States and Counties — **Health Care and Social Assistance, Other Services, Nonemployer Businesses, and Residential Construction**

STATE County	Health care and social assistance, 2007				Other services, 2007				Nonemployer businesses, 2013		Value of residential construction authorized by building permits, 2014	
	Number of establish-ments	Number of employees	Receipts (mil dol)	Annual payroll (mil dol)	Number of establish-ments	Number of employees	Receipts (mil dol)	Annual payroll (mil dol)	Number	Receipts (mil dol)	New Construction ($1,000)	Number of housing units
	159	160	161	162	163	164	165	166	167	168	169	170
KENTUCKY—Cont'd												
Ohio	37	842	53.3	21.7	33	86	8.3	2.1	1 184	35.1	5 005	44
Oldham	110	1 881	139.5	61.0	82	431	30.3	8.8	4 772	228.3	57 867	215
Owen	8	201	15.8	6.8	12	40	2.8	0.6	758	26.5	0	0
Owsley	10	208	9.3	4.4	3	D	D	D	278	9.5	NA	NA
Pendleton	18	219	16.2	5.2	8	D	D	D	796	28.2	0	0
Perry	125	2 613	285.4	96.7	29	116	10.5	2.2	1 373	44.6	533	5
Pike	183	3 638	381.5	139.7	78	314	27.7	8.1	2 844	124.0	6 942	25
Powell	20	246	14.4	5.9	6	D	D	D	870	25.6	NA	NA
Pulaski	234	4 948	462.8	164.2	73	378	37.0	8.0	4 387	168.6	879	15
Robertson	4	D	D	D	1	D	D	D	134	3.8	NA	NA
Rockcastle	36	742	56.1	23.8	13	97	14.5	2.4	953	27.3	NA	NA
Rowan	74	1 718	153.8	60.1	26	166	6.9	2.1	1 405	42.6	1 190	14
Russell	47	802	47.2	19.4	19	54	4.3	0.9	1 351	54.7	780	12
Scott	80	D	D	D	62	277	21.1	5.8	3 163	115.3	41 473	313
Shelby	79	1 333	114.9	44.2	59	405	39.4	11.8	3 031	124.4	40 924	213
Simpson	37	378	34.9	10.3	26	126	12.3	3.2	1 173	55.8	2 945	15
Spencer	20	259	14.9	6.0	13	D	D	D	1 164	44.5	14 742	79
Taylor	79	1 249	100.7	39.8	47	159	10.2	2.6	1 764	62.0	2 325	27
Todd	13	193	12.3	3.6	13	50	2.8	1.0	894	39.4	196	2
Trigg	19	308	18.0	7.3	14	88	6.0	1.9	872	32.5	356	2
Trimble	8	D	D	D	5	D	D	D	476	15.7	NA	NA
Union	29	1 279	66.6	26.9	16	D	D	D	700	26.8	3 825	21
Warren	314	D	D	D	164	1 181	83.6	24.7	8 455	465.7	102 506	603
Washington	16	286	12.8	5.6	20	69	5.4	1.4	739	24.5	1 475	21
Wayne	38	D	D	D	25	66	4.8	1.1	1 208	44.1	0	0
Webster	23	D	D	D	22	D	D	D	653	18.4	851	4
Whitley	107	2 726	235.8	85.6	34	145	10.3	3.3	2 264	80.7	1 526	14
Wolfe	10	229	17.8	5.1	4	D	D	D	420	15.5	NA	NA
Woodford	48	D	D	D	39	197	12.4	3.6	2 044	88.4	20 994	101
LOUISIANA	11 545	256 079	23 685.4	8 860.6	6 637	42 223	4 664.2	1 170.0	348 367	15 268.5	2 888 790	15 255
Acadia	125	2 041	148.6	55.7	68	363	29.2	7.8	4 137	198.8	23 009	123
Allen	45	801	50.0	20.5	21	100	6.2	1.8	1 083	32.2	457	5
Ascension	152	2 232	140.7	57.8	138	940	109.6	32.1	7 976	340.1	139 993	926
Assumption	21	612	23.4	10.5	20	59	8.0	1.6	1 523	61.2	6 951	33
Avoyelles	91	2 066	104.9	41.9	44	128	10.6	2.8	2 296	87.6	8 718	66
Beauregard	60	1 182	78.5	31.5	39	140	12.7	3.6	1 894	69.6	6 588	27
Bienville	15	D	D	D	12	D	D	D	824	28.1	0	0
Bossier	207	3 397	281.4	119.5	146	990	66.9	20.5	7 956	360.8	165 844	1 347
Caddo	801	D	D	D	443	3 136	245.6	68.1	19 540	842.1	74 677	289
Calcasieu	515	10 926	1 025.2	348.4	280	D	D	D	12 556	555.6	165 628	1 263
Caldwell	23	534	32.7	14.4	15	D	D	D	576	19.8	3 574	15
Cameron	5	132	12.3	4.2	4	D	D	D	648	33.2	5 710	39
Catahoula	14	544	20.8	10.4	11	D	D	D	659	28.6	1 424	8
Claiborne	26	780	46.7	17.8	11	66	3.7	0.8	746	25.6	0	0
Concordia	46	743	48.1	20.1	25	99	6.2	1.8	1 112	45.4	1 189	19
De Soto	25	D	D	D	17	46	3.6	0.9	1 781	65.2	11 390	54
East Baton Rouge	1 386	36 001	3 477.8	1 247.2	909	6 732	776.3	206.2	36 253	1 533.9	336 813	1 464
East Carroll	12	300	15.7	7.4	7	D	D	D	438	17.7	0	0
East Feliciana	31	1 972	120.1	64.2	21	81	7.8	1.8	1 261	45.9	9 788	48
Evangeline	102	2 453	159.7	61.5	24	45	3.5	0.6	1 594	62.3	11 198	62
Franklin	53	1 068	65.6	26.2	20	69	6.0	1.2	1 399	51.6	6 564	26
Grant	17	D	D	D	6	25	1.4	0.4	1 010	40.9	8 725	41
Iberia	214	4 177	297.5	104.4	137	1 147	175.4	40.3	6 110	244.4	23 870	95
Iberville	47	D	D	D	41	285	25.4	8.6	2 154	69.0	16 899	95
Jackson	21	632	35.2	13.5	17	D	D	D	806	24.7	11 573	23
Jefferson	1 291	29 229	3 294.0	1 196.7	789	5 000	525.7	145.2	40 210	1 914.3	63 732	346
Jefferson Davis	76	1 485	106.9	42.0	39	133	9.0	2.1	1 806	76.1	12 389	89
Lafayette	951	19 023	1 871.8	681.0	448	3 481	311.8	87.5	21 781	1 207.8	384 800	1 812
Lafourche	185	3 167	335.1	120.8	115	586	57.7	15.3	6 714	329.7	82 679	398
La Salle	24	647	44.7	17.8	8	D	D	D	832	41.0	465	2
Lincoln	123	2 598	270.8	79.8	47	D	D	D	2 755	130.6	16 329	74
Livingston	131	1 632	88.1	35.0	108	620	55.0	14.4	8 757	347.0	146 386	703
Madison	35	795	37.6	17.6	17	33	2.6	0.4	712	19.7	7 977	49
Morehouse	85	1 709	102.7	39.4	29	140	9.1	2.4	1 745	47.7	3 609	16
Natchitoches	101	1 602	120.0	48.0	47	207	18.0	4.2	2 251	93.8	9 232	38

STATE County	Government employment and payroll, 2012									Local government finances, 2012				
			March payroll (percent of total)							General revenue				
												Taxes		
													Per capita[1] (dollars)	
	Full-time equivalent employees	March payroll (dollars)	Adminis-tration, judicial, and legal	Police and Corrections	Fire Protection	Highways and transpor-tation	Health and Welfare	Natural resources and utilities	Education and libraries	Total (mil dol)	Inter-govern-mental (mil dol)	Total (mil dol)	Total	Property
	171	172	173	174	175	176	177	178	179	180	181	182	183	184
KENTUCKY—Cont'd														
Ohio	1 248	3 369 261	2.7	2.9	0.0	1.3	36.2	2.8	52.4	62.2	36.1	14.2	590	347
Oldham	2 024	6 660 606	0.3	5.8	2.0	0.6	3.6	1.6	84.6	158.6	58.3	71.9	1 171	957
Owen	363	1 105 970	4.6	2.3	3.8	2.1	0.7	0.2	83.4	23.3	14.0	7.1	661	495
Owsley	278	620 892	6.0	3.8	0.0	3.9	0.3	2.8	81.2	13.2	10.6	1.4	301	184
Pendleton	588	1 671 881	4.1	2.6	1.6	2.8	15.0	6.1	67.8	38.5	22.7	9.2	631	467
Perry	1 406	4 111 977	3.0	3.4	1.5	2.6	18.7	2.8	66.7	100.4	52.4	23.0	814	540
Pike	2 126	6 896 536	3.5	4.4	1.3	2.8	7.1	1.3	78.6	183.6	110.6	49.7	775	500
Powell	571	1 479 612	5.5	7.2	0.0	1.0	5.3	5.1	75.7	31.1	21.3	6.1	493	235
Pulaski	2 626	7 286 813	4.1	5.1	1.6	1.7	17.0	5.8	64.1	151.6	74.3	49.2	773	465
Robertson	124	297 631	8.0	3.4	0.0	4.9	0.2	0.6	83.0	5.9	4.4	1.2	557	414
Rockcastle	758	1 967 231	6.5	9.5	0.0	2.3	2.6	2.4	74.7	38.4	26.7	7.6	448	184
Rowan	813	2 389 386	2.9	7.6	0.4	3.5	14.9	2.7	67.0	61.6	29.3	19.7	841	374
Russell	920	2 454 498	2.9	5.5	0.4	0.9	28.6	4.1	57.3	61.4	21.4	14.1	807	422
Scott	1 616	5 156 528	2.9	7.7	7.0	2.1	6.1	0.1	73.2	151.0	48.9	60.2	1 227	530
Shelby	1 282	4 061 414	3.4	9.9	2.6	1.9	6.5	0.8	73.8	102.9	42.5	43.5	997	724
Simpson	616	2 092 237	8.9	11.0	1.5	2.3	5.8	3.3	66.5	48.7	23.2	18.0	1 026	501
Spencer	523	1 426 278	5.8	4.0	0.7	1.4	3.1	2.3	81.4	34.5	19.5	12.1	693	525
Taylor	1 374	4 732 730	2.1	2.7	0.9	1.1	51.8	2.5	38.2	123.7	56.5	19.0	769	374
Todd	505	1 331 511	3.1	7.5	0.2	1.9	3.5	7.4	76.3	31.2	20.1	6.9	544	268
Trigg	587	1 746 830	2.8	3.6	0.1	2.4	28.3	5.6	56.1	27.8	15.3	10.2	708	456
Trimble	305	972 373	7.5	3.6	0.0	1.9	2.3	5.1	78.5	32.6	10.9	5.6	634	445
Union	599	1 762 787	11.1	6.4	2.1	5.7	0.5	5.2	67.9	38.7	23.0	11.5	777	532
Warren	4 084	12 459 019	3.2	8.5	4.4	1.8	4.7	10.4	63.3	304.6	116.1	128.4	1 096	529
Washington	407	1 176 342	5.5	5.0	0.0	4.1	9.6	4.1	69.1	26.8	14.5	8.5	718	377
Wayne	760	2 029 072	4.1	6.1	0.2	1.7	4.0	0.3	83.0	44.7	31.3	10.0	478	288
Webster	605	1 592 385	5.5	8.5	4.2	2.0	2.8	7.4	66.8	37.5	24.0	7.8	574	425
Whitley	1 867	5 263 187	2.4	4.6	3.4	1.6	6.6	7.3	73.7	112.5	68.5	23.7	669	308
Wolfe	313	774 203	3.3	1.9	0.0	1.4	0.4	3.3	85.8	23.7	18.4	2.4	336	190
Woodford	911	3 023 818	4.5	9.8	2.1	1.8	8.6	2.9	68.0	69.9	26.8	32.2	1 286	739
LOUISIANA	X	X	X	X	X	X	X	X	X	X	X	X	X	X
Acadia	1 914	5 479 946	5.7	5.4	2.7	4.1	2.9	4.6	73.3	180.8	90.9	63.9	1 033	388
Allen	973	2 882 412	11.1	8.9	0.4	3.1	19.2	2.8	54.4	94.4	48.2	28.5	1 114	473
Ascension	4 531	13 738 983	6.7	8.8	2.0	2.3	2.8	3.8	71.9	408.3	139.8	213.9	1 905	870
Assumption	1 463	4 579 903	6.7	5.0	0.6	13.3	13.8	10.4	49.4	74.9	42.1	25.4	1 102	571
Avoyelles	1 542	3 784 025	3.9	22.1	1.3	2.7	13.2	4.5	52.2	121.6	72.1	26.8	644	144
Beauregard	1 561	4 516 320	4.2	3.0	1.7	3.0	29.5	1.5	56.6	146.5	59.0	50.2	1 382	629
Bienville	604	1 849 545	7.1	11.8	0.0	5.8	0.4	1.9	72.9	72.4	15.3	51.7	3 673	2 477
Bossier	4 814	15 229 557	8.2	15.0	5.4	2.1	0.4	3.1	64.8	444.2	156.3	238.0	1 948	757
Caddo	11 080	37 545 778	5.6	16.6	7.2	2.8	2.9	5.7	57.7	1 117.9	399.7	540.3	2 102	1 067
Calcasieu	9 145	28 598 210	5.0	14.5	3.5	5.7	7.9	5.4	56.0	961.3	315.0	432.3	2 223	866
Caldwell	302	782 732	5.3	3.7	0.3	0.5	0.0	1.0	89.3	33.5	19.0	10.2	1 019	536
Cameron	525	1 990 275	6.0	0.0	0.3	7.0	7.7	4.9	74.1	94.4	45.2	42.7	6 367	6 281
Catahoula	616	1 309 075	8.8	22.3	0.4	5.1	2.5	3.4	57.4	54.6	21.6	8.9	869	412
Claiborne	847	2 308 077	5.0	2.0	2.4	2.3	47.8	2.4	38.2	69.3	34.1	15.8	939	530
Concordia	1 328	3 662 764	3.6	24.2	2.0	3.1	16.5	5.2	44.7	109.8	52.5	25.5	1 253	622
De Soto	1 141	3 608 492	7.4	7.4	0.8	6.3	2.6	3.1	71.2	213.8	37.7	149.7	5 553	2 010
East Baton Rouge	16 122	60 516 124	9.3	10.2	6.8	4.4	7.2	8.9	49.7	1 776.4	573.7	866.4	1 949	820
East Carroll	291	819 177	9.3	8.7	1.7	2.4	46.3	8.0	23.1	47.3	28.8	7.1	947	459
East Feliciana	631	1 666 825	14.0	19.9	0.0	2.6	1.1	4.2	58.2	44.3	27.0	13.4	671	245
Evangeline	1 334	3 509 396	4.9	9.7	2.3	4.2	2.0	5.9	70.6	136.3	68.0	37.5	1 111	500
Franklin	1 046	2 791 309	5.1	15.1	1.2	2.0	28.2	2.9	45.4	84.3	40.9	21.5	1 046	283
Grant	604	1 502 745	8.0	3.6	0.0	2.3	3.2	5.7	76.5	50.6	32.7	12.2	551	301
Iberia	3 450	9 630 156	4.1	12.3	3.2	2.7	20.2	5.1	51.6	320.8	141.9	101.3	1 368	514
Iberville	1 742	4 067 035	7.6	14.8	2.5	5.7	1.5	5.6	57.3	154.3	45.0	93.6	2 817	1 287
Jackson	824	2 175 796	2.6	14.3	1.3	2.9	30.0	2.2	46.2	80.9	29.0	33.0	2 033	1 323
Jefferson	16 179	70 416 195	8.0	11.6	2.9	2.3	31.2	6.3	36.3	2 140.2	681.5	696.5	1 606	721
Jefferson Davis	1 386	3 583 234	4.3	9.8	2.0	2.1	0.3	3.8	76.9	101.8	54.3	35.4	1 127	532
Lafayette	8 193	26 367 258	8.2	13.8	4.3	3.8	0.8	11.2	56.6	791.5	255.4	391.9	1 726	692
Lafourche	4 602	16 739 494	5.8	10.8	0.0	3.9	32.6	3.4	42.1	526.8	177.3	149.9	1 545	846
La Salle	890	2 469 446	4.0	15.2	0.4	1.6	31.7	2.8	44.0	119.2	60.2	20.7	1 388	759
Lincoln	1 655	6 428 631	8.8	13.7	9.5	6.9	3.8	12.8	43.0	139.1	54.9	66.4	1 414	645
Livingston	4 067	13 075 838	6.4	8.4	0.8	1.6	0.8	3.2	78.1	359.5	202.1	123.4	935	334
Madison	681	1 378 550	9.2	30.1	0.1	5.0	0.3	1.6	53.3	76.9	38.0	17.4	1 428	929
Morehouse	1 347	4 002 380	5.9	10.2	2.9	1.8	23.0	0.9	54.6	125.8	64.1	30.3	1 099	513
Natchitoches	2 176	6 441 570	5.4	11.8	1.9	2.7	29.9	5.7	41.6	198.4	86.0	59.1	1 498	518

1. Based on the resident population estimated as of July 1 of the year shown.

STATE County	Local government finances, 2012 (cont.) — Direct general expenditure: Total (mil dol)	Per capita[1] (dollars)	Percent of total for: Education	Health and hospitals	Police protection	Public welfare	Highways	Debt outstanding: Total (mil dol)	Per capita[1] (dollars)	Government employment, 2013: Federal civilian	Federal military	State and local	Presidential election,[2] 2012 — Percent of vote cast: Democratic	Republican	All other
	185	186	187	188	189	190	191	192	193	194	195	196	197	198	199
KENTUCKY—Cont'd															
Ohio	54.6	2 269	56.5	1.1	4.2	0.1	4.9	203.8	8 463	84	78	1 414	40.8	57.2	1.9
Oldham	156.7	2 552	60.0	4.3	4.0	0.4	2.1	428.5	6 978	65	191	3 328	34.1	64.8	1.1
Owen	24.6	2 286	63.4	3.3	2.4	0.5	6.5	37.0	3 440	21	35	459	35.7	62.5	1.9
Owsley	13.9	2 954	73.5	0.4	2.7	0.0	7.0	5.8	1 224	0	15	292	22.6	75.9	1.5
Pendleton	38.4	2 629	51.2	14.8	3.0	0.0	6.3	59.7	4 086	29	47	639	34.9	63.4	1.7
Perry	108.4	3 839	51.5	14.3	2.9	0.0	4.1	267.3	9 465	128	90	2 688	33.2	65.2	1.6
Pike	184.3	2 872	57.9	3.3	2.1	0.2	4.9	348.9	5 437	265	205	3 052	42.1	55.9	2.0
Powell	29.2	2 335	66.0	6.6	2.1	0.0	3.4	14.4	1 150	35	40	755	41.5	57.1	1.4
Pulaski	161.3	2 537	51.9	11.8	5.1	0.1	3.7	170.4	2 679	170	208	3 950	21.7	77.1	1.2
Robertson	15.0	6 849	83.7	0.5	0.9	0.0	3.9	36.7	16 787	0	0	147	44.4	52.5	3.1
Rockcastle	38.2	2 248	63.7	4.5	2.8	0.0	4.0	25.4	1 494	31	54	748	22.5	75.8	1.7
Rowan	57.8	2 467	44.0	13.0	4.0	0.6	5.0	89.2	3 802	85	72	3 348	50.0	47.9	2.1
Russell	56.8	3 247	41.5	34.9	2.6	0.4	3.2	42.4	2 424	74	58	1 005	21.0	77.3	1.7
Scott	139.0	2 834	46.7	7.0	4.0	0.2	2.7	633.9	12 922	55	160	2 082	39.1	59.7	1.2
Shelby	102.9	2 359	54.2	6.2	3.7	0.0	2.4	238.0	5 456	66	139	2 336	37.1	61.8	1.2
Simpson	44.9	2 560	53.3	3.9	5.1	1.0	3.9	71.7	4 088	35	57	777	38.0	60.7	1.3
Spencer	29.0	1 665	65.8	2.9	4.3	0.1	5.6	48.6	2 788	23	58	577	31.3	66.8	1.9
Taylor	135.0	5 469	23.2	57.5	1.9	0.0	2.1	111.7	4 523	81	78	1 716	29.1	69.7	1.2
Todd	33.7	2 664	60.0	5.0	3.2	0.0	4.5	102.5	8 103	32	40	600	31.2	67.5	1.3
Trigg	28.2	1 952	58.5	2.4	4.6	0.1	8.2	21.2	1 469	109	47	634	34.4	64.2	1.4
Trimble	33.1	3 770	40.0	1.5	0.6	0.0	3.9	423.4	48 190	16	29	357	38.9	58.7	2.3
Union	38.1	2 567	54.2	0.6	4.9	0.4	7.4	15.5	1 046	47	44	753	46.5	51.7	1.8
Warren	300.9	2 570	45.9	4.4	6.6	0.1	3.4	970.8	8 290	366	374	9 924	40.0	58.9	1.1
Washington	29.1	2 457	61.1	3.2	3.0	0.1	7.7	78.0	6 592	29	38	530	35.8	62.7	1.5
Wayne	46.9	2 252	65.2	3.1	3.1	0.0	3.8	44.3	2 129	37	67	953	30.6	67.6	1.8
Webster	36.1	2 657	46.4	1.2	2.4	0.0	5.6	63.7	4 692	40	43	680	43.1	54.8	2.0
Whitley	116.0	3 267	65.4	7.7	3.4	0.0	3.2	141.1	3 974	85	112	2 304	25.4	73.1	1.5
Wolfe	19.1	2 667	68.4	0.1	0.9	0.0	6.6	20.2	2 819	19	23	406	50.3	47.4	2.3
Woodford	67.4	2 689	51.3	5.2	8.7	0.0	4.7	133.5	5 323	36	82	1 517	40.9	58.0	1.1
LOUISIANA	X	X	X	X	X	X	X	X	X	30 602	39 737	307 701	39.9	58.6	1.5
Acadia	174.4	2 817	55.1	8.1	6.4	0.3	4.6	40.6	656	98	293	2 553	26.3	72.0	1.7
Allen	95.8	3 750	51.3	17.0	5.7	0.0	5.7	24.4	955	643	102	3 768	30.5	66.9	2.6
Ascension	402.3	3 583	57.6	3.1	6.1	0.0	4.1	796.9	7 097	131	546	4 833	31.4	67.1	1.5
Assumption	72.6	3 151	65.4	0.1	5.9	0.8	2.8	12.4	536	27	110	977	43.4	54.6	2.0
Avoyelles	119.8	2 877	51.1	10.8	10.3	0.0	2.9	26.7	640	80	182	3 738	37.4	60.4	2.2
Beauregard	151.0	4 161	49.3	23.5	4.9	0.0	5.2	90.4	2 493	68	168	1 649	21.8	76.2	2.0
Bienville	72.3	5 139	63.9	2.2	6.1	0.2	6.3	29.9	2 123	49	66	760	48.3	50.8	0.9
Bossier	464.2	3 799	47.3	1.0	9.1	0.1	5.0	486.1	3 978	2 024	6 094	6 756	27.7	71.4	0.9
Caddo	1 081.2	4 206	48.6	1.7	7.4	0.0	2.2	1 079.9	4 201	2 815	1 227	19 308	51.1	48.1	0.8
Calcasieu	908.6	4 671	38.0	7.0	6.7	0.4	7.0	2 311.6	11 885	533	1 021	13 418	36.8	61.4	1.8
Caldwell	34.6	3 461	63.2	7.2	3.0	0.2	3.0	14.9	1 485	28	45	618	22.8	75.5	1.6
Cameron	87.3	13 024	42.4	9.7	4.1	0.4	4.8	20.4	3 043	18	32	733	16.2	81.4	2.4
Catahoula	65.8	6 390	33.4	42.7	3.0	0.0	2.4	37.4	3 632	47	45	649	31.8	66.7	1.5
Claiborne	68.0	4 039	33.4	28.7	3.9	0.7	3.0	18.0	1 071	44	66	1 243	44.2	54.8	1.0
Concordia	116.6	5 726	35.0	12.7	6.4	0.0	2.6	38.7	1 899	61	91	1 566	39.5	59.5	1.0
De Soto	190.9	7 081	58.1	1.3	4.0	1.7	8.4	134.5	4 987	45	129	1 696	42.8	56.2	1.1
East Baton Rouge	2 083.6	4 687	38.7	5.0	6.4	0.1	5.2	2 247.5	5 056	2 309	2 288	47 213	50.5	48.3	1.2
East Carroll	50.8	6 748	38.0	18.4	3.5	0.0	2.7	36.4	4 836	19	31	712	63.7	35.2	1.1
East Feliciana	43.2	2 161	59.7	0.7	8.1	0.0	4.6	5.3	264	29	83	2 469	44.1	54.6	1.3
Evangeline	132.8	3 939	46.5	23.7	4.1	0.0	6.4	25.6	760	49	154	1 648	36.6	61.3	2.1
Franklin	83.8	4 076	38.5	25.0	7.6	0.3	4.2	14.2	691	54	95	1 332	31.6	67.1	1.3
Grant	55.3	2 505	70.8	0.2	6.0	0.0	2.2	23.9	1 085	729	103	848	17.2	80.7	2.1
Iberia	346.8	4 686	45.5	17.9	5.9	0.2	5.6	224.6	3 035	101	350	4 077	37.7	60.7	1.7
Iberville	172.3	5 186	44.7	0.6	7.8	1.5	10.8	142.1	4 275	92	141	2 853	54.9	43.8	1.3
Jackson	80.7	4 976	35.7	20.0	10.5	0.0	5.3	72.6	4 475	29	72	1 064	31.7	67.1	1.2
Jefferson	2 141.8	4 939	30.3	30.9	4.8	2.5	3.5	1 621.8	3 740	1 424	2 552	19 521	35.9	62.5	1.6
Jefferson Davis	102.5	3 259	62.2	1.3	8.7	0.1	3.0	56.9	1 811	98	147	1 973	29.1	68.7	2.2
Lafayette	816.4	3 596	40.1	0.7	7.8	0.1	5.7	1 609.2	7 087	961	1 119	13 041	33.6	64.9	1.5
Lafourche	483.7	4 985	32.9	32.8	5.3	0.5	2.6	200.2	2 064	131	482	6 585	25.5	71.5	3.0
La Salle	118.0	7 903	25.1	37.6	3.9	0.0	1.0	23.0	1 604	56	65	1 387	13.1	85.5	1.4
Lincoln	137.7	2 933	55.0	0.5	7.2	0.6	5.1	82.8	1 764	115	212	4 385	43.2	55.7	1.1
Livingston	373.0	2 827	65.1	0.6	5.1	0.0	2.6	445.0	3 373	136	637	5 358	13.1	85.0	1.9
Madison	79.7	6 557	26.6	19.8	12.1	0.1	3.5	74.6	6 141	37	50	1 070	58.5	40.6	0.9
Morehouse	124.7	4 525	44.2	20.5	4.1	0.1	2.7	101.1	3 668	62	126	1 344	43.9	55.0	1.1
Natchitoches	210.4	5 335	45.1	20.9	4.9	0.5	3.0	50.5	1 281	166	181	3 718	45.7	53.0	1.2

1. Based on the resident population estimated as of July 1 of the year shown. 2.

STATE/ County code	CBSA code[1]	County type[2]	STATE County	Land area,[3] (sq km) 2010	Population, 2014: Total persons 2014	Population, 2014: Rank	Population, 2014: Per square kilometer	Population and population characteristics, 2013: Race alone or in combination, not Hispanic or Latino (percent): White	Black	American Indian, Alaska Native	Asian and Pacific Islander	Percent Hispanic or Latino[4]	Age (percent): Under 5 years	5 to 17 years	18 to 24 years	25 to 34 years	35 to 44 years	45 to 54 years
				1	2	3	4	5	6	7	8	9	10	11	12	13	14	15
			LOUISIANA—Cont'd															
22 071	35380	1	Orleans	439	384 320	176	875.4	31.9	59.8	0.7	3.4	5.5	6.2	14.4	10.7	18.4	12.5	13.2
22 073	33740	3	Ouachita	1 581	156 325	406	98.9	59.6	37.5	0.6	1.3	2.1	7.2	18.6	10.8	13.9	12.2	12.6
22 075	35380	1	Plaquemines	2 020	23 447	1 666	11.6	68.6	21.0	2.3	4.2	6.2	6.9	19.9	9.1	12.9	13.5	14.5
22 077	12940	2	Pointe Coupee	1 444	22 406	1 711	15.5	61.7	36.0	0.4	0.5	2.4	6.3	17.1	8.0	11.3	10.7	14.4
22 079	10780	3	Rapides	3 414	132 488	475	38.8	63.1	32.6	1.4	1.8	2.8	6.9	18.6	9.1	13.2	11.8	13.6
22 081	...	6	Red River	1 008	8 669	2 544	8.6	58.7	39.7	0.6	0.3	1.4	7.0	17.9	8.5	12.2	11.0	14.4
22 083	...	6	Richland	1 448	20 740	1 790	14.3	61.6	36.0	0.6	0.5	2.1	6.6	18.4	9.1	12.8	11.8	13.2
22 085	...	6	Sabine	2 245	24 199	1 636	10.8	71.4	17.6	9.9	0.6	3.6	6.5	17.5	8.1	11.5	10.9	13.5
22 087	35380	1	St. Bernard	978	44 409	1 084	45.4	66.3	21.9	1.2	2.7	9.8	8.1	18.5	9.8	17.4	12.3	13.3
22 089	35380	1	St. Charles	723	52 745	947	73.0	66.9	26.5	0.8	1.3	5.7	6.1	19.5	9.0	12.7	12.9	15.8
22 091	12940	2	St. Helena	1 058	10 619	2 387	10.0	45.3	53.1	0.8	0.3	1.4	6.0	16.8	9.5	12.7	10.9	13.7
22 093	35380	6	St. James	626	21 638	1 750	34.6	48.6	49.5	0.5	0.4	1.7	6.4	17.8	9.5	12.6	10.5	15.2
22 095	35380	1	St. John the Baptist	552	43 745	1 094	79.2	39.3	54.9	0.6	1.1	5.2	7.0	18.5	9.4	13.0	12.3	14.8
22 097	36660	4	St. Landry	2 393	83 709	669	35.0	56.3	41.7	0.6	0.7	1.8	7.8	19.2	8.9	12.3	11.1	13.5
22 099	29180	3	St. Martin	1 910	53 315	937	27.9	65.8	31.2	0.8	1.1	2.4	6.7	18.6	9.2	13.2	12.2	14.5
22 101	34020	4	St. Mary	1 438	53 162	938	37.0	58.2	33.1	2.2	2.0	6.2	6.8	17.9	9.4	12.8	11.8	14.7
22 103	35380	1	St. Tammany	2 190	245 829	268	112.3	81.1	12.5	1.0	1.8	5.2	5.8	18.9	7.8	11.5	12.9	14.8
22 105	25220	4	Tangipahoa	2 049	127 049	486	62.0	65.1	30.6	0.8	1.0	3.8	7.1	17.8	11.7	14.3	11.8	12.6
22 107	...	9	Tensas	1 561	4 830	2 847	3.1	43.2	55.2	0.6	0.4	1.8	6.2	18.6	7.0	10.0	9.6	13.2
22 109	26380	3	Terrebonne	3 190	113 328	538	35.5	69.8	19.8	6.6	1.5	4.5	7.1	18.5	9.6	14.5	11.9	14.3
22 111	33740	3	Union	2 271	22 539	1 707	9.9	69.0	26.3	0.5	0.4	4.3	6.1	16.4	8.2	11.8	10.8	13.8
22 113	29180	4	Vermilion	3 039	59 616	873	19.6	79.7	15.4	0.7	2.4	3.0	6.8	19.5	8.5	13.1	12.1	14.1
22 115	22860	4	Vernon	3 439	52 132	954	15.2	73.1	15.5	2.2	3.3	9.1	9.1	17.7	13.6	17.8	12.6	10.1
22 117	14220	6	Washington	1 734	46 286	1 044	26.7	67.1	30.7	0.8	0.5	2.1	6.4	18.0	8.4	12.2	11.7	13.6
22 119	43340	6	Webster	1 536	40 333	1 164	26.3	63.7	34.2	0.9	0.6	1.8	6.3	16.9	8.5	12.2	11.4	13.7
22 121	12940	2	West Baton Rouge	498	25 085	1 603	50.4	58.7	38.3	0.5	0.8	2.7	6.7	17.4	9.6	15.7	11.6	14.4
22 123	...	9	West Carroll	931	11 525	2 327	12.4	80.7	16.3	0.8	0.4	2.7	6.0	18.1	8.6	11.5	12.0	13.6
22 125	12940	2	West Feliciana	1 044	15 406	2 077	14.8	52.3	46.2	0.4	0.3	1.4	4.1	12.6	6.1	14.1	18.2	18.4
22 127	...	6	Winn	2 461	14 743	2 120	6.0	66.8	30.9	1.2	0.6	1.7	5.9	16.2	8.2	13.3	12.9	14.3
23 000	...	X	MAINE	79 883	1 330 089	X	16.7	95.5	1.8	1.4	1.6	1.4	4.9	14.8	8.6	11.3	11.9	15.5
23 001	30340	3	Androscoggin	1 212	107 440	558	88.6	93.4	4.6	1.1	1.3	1.7	6.2	16.0	8.9	12.3	12.3	15.1
23 003	...	7	Aroostook	17 279	69 447	771	4.0	95.9	1.0	2.6	0.7	1.1	4.7	14.3	8.0	9.8	11.1	15.2
23 005	38860	2	Cumberland	2 163	287 797	235	133.1	92.9	3.2	0.9	2.9	1.9	4.9	14.9	9.0	12.6	12.7	15.6
23 007	...	6	Franklin	4 394	30 296	1 423	6.9	97.4	0.6	1.2	0.9	1.2	4.6	14.1	10.8	10.1	10.4	15.2
23 009	...	6	Hancock	4 110	54 696	917	13.3	96.6	0.8	1.1	1.3	1.4	4.4	13.2	7.8	10.2	11.2	15.2
23 011	12300	4	Kennebec	2 247	121 112	508	53.9	96.7	1.0	1.3	1.2	1.4	5.0	14.9	8.6	11.2	11.9	15.8
23 013	...	7	Knox	946	39 676	1 181	41.9	97.4	1.0	1.2	0.8	1.1	4.5	14.1	6.5	10.1	11.5	14.8
23 015	...	8	Lincoln	1 181	34 170	1 324	28.9	97.7	0.7	1.0	0.9	0.9	4.1	13.6	6.3	9.1	10.6	14.6
23 017	...	6	Oxford	5 379	57 238	890	10.6	97.3	0.7	1.3	1.0	1.2	4.7	15.1	7.2	10.0	11.5	16.2
23 019	12620	3	Penobscot	8 799	153 414	419	17.4	95.8	1.2	2.0	1.4	1.2	4.8	14.0	11.8	12.6	11.5	14.9
23 021	...	8	Piscataquis	10 259	17 026	1 978	1.7	96.9	0.9	1.2	1.1	1.1	4.0	13.8	6.3	8.5	10.8	15.7
23 023	38860	2	Sagadahoc	657	35 045	1 299	53.3	96.5	1.3	1.0	1.3	1.5	4.8	15.1	6.7	10.7	12.1	15.9
23 025	...	6	Somerset	10 164	51 163	971	5.0	97.4	0.8	1.2	0.9	1.0	4.8	15.4	7.0	10.4	12.3	15.9
23 027	...	6	Waldo	1 890	39 051	1 197	20.7	97.5	0.7	1.3	0.8	1.1	5.1	14.9	7.6	10.3	11.8	14.7
23 029	...	7	Washington	6 637	31 808	1 388	4.8	92.2	0.9	6.2	0.7	1.7	4.8	14.1	7.7	9.8	10.9	14.5
23 031	38860	2	York	2 566	200 710	324	78.2	96.3	1.0	0.9	1.5	1.5	4.9	15.2	7.8	11.1	12.1	16.0
24 000	...	X	MARYLAND	25 142	5 976 407	X	237.7	55.1	30.5	0.8	7.0	9.0	6.2	16.5	9.5	13.8	13.0	15.0
24 001	19060	3	Allegany	1 099	72 952	745	66.4	89.2	9.1	0.5	1.2	1.6	4.6	12.9	12.7	12.5	11.8	13.5
24 003	12580	1	Anne Arundel	1 075	560 133	114	521.1	73.1	17.1	0.8	4.8	6.9	6.3	16.5	9.1	14.0	13.2	15.3
24 005	12580	1	Baltimore	1 550	826 925	71	533.5	62.2	28.1	0.8	6.4	4.8	6.0	15.6	9.7	13.7	12.3	14.1
24 009	47900	1	Calvert	552	90 613	638	164.2	81.5	14.2	0.9	2.7	3.3	5.5	19.1	8.6	10.9	12.1	18.1
24 011	...	6	Caroline	827	32 538	1 373	39.3	78.8	15.2	0.6	1.1	6.0	6.1	17.9	8.5	11.9	12.2	15.1
24 013	12580	1	Carroll	1 159	167 830	379	144.8	91.8	4.0	0.5	2.3	2.9	4.9	18.0	9.0	10.1	12.1	17.5
24 015	37980	1	Cecil	897	102 383	578	114.1	88.2	7.3	0.7	1.8	3.9	5.9	17.8	8.7	11.8	12.8	16.1
24 017	47900	1	Charles	1 186	154 747	413	130.5	48.2	44.4	1.6	4.4	5.0	6.0	19.1	9.4	12.3	14.0	16.9
24 019	15700	6	Dorchester	1 401	32 578	1 372	23.3	66.7	28.5	0.8	1.6	4.2	6.1	15.0	8.0	11.2	10.8	14.6
24 021	47900	1	Frederick	1 710	243 675	273	142.5	78.6	9.9	0.7	5.3	8.0	6.0	18.1	8.8	12.2	13.6	16.3
24 023	...	6	Garrett	1 676	29 679	1 437	17.7	97.5	1.4	0.4	0.6	0.8	4.8	15.5	8.8	10.2	11.7	14.7
24 025	12580	1	Harford	1 132	250 105	265	220.9	79.9	14.0	0.7	3.8	4.0	5.6	17.7	8.5	12.1	12.6	16.1
24 027	12580	1	Howard	649	309 284	217	476.6	59.2	19.3	0.8	17.7	6.3	5.9	18.9	8.0	12.6	14.0	16.4
24 029	...	6	Kent	718	19 820	1 844	27.6	79.8	15.7	0.4	1.4	4.3	4.6	12.2	12.5	9.9	8.7	13.2
24 031	47900	1	Montgomery	1 272	1 030 447	40	810.1	49.2	18.4	0.6	16.2	18.2	6.5	17.1	7.7	13.7	14.0	14.9
24 033	47900	1	Prince George's	1 250	904 430	57	723.5	15.8	64.3	1.0	5.0	16.1	6.7	16.0	11.0	15.1	13.8	14.6
24 035	12580	1	Queen Anne's	963	48 804	1 005	50.7	88.4	7.6	0.6	1.6	3.4	5.5	17.2	7.8	9.6	11.8	17.2

1. CBSA = Core Based Statistical Area. See Appendix A for explanation. See Appendix B for list of metropolitan areas with component counties. 2. County type code from the Economic Research Service of USDA Rural-Urban Continuum Codes. See Appendix A for definition. 3. Dry land or land partially or temporarily covered by water. 4. May be of any race.

STATE County	Population, 2013 (cont.) Age (percent) (cont.) 55 to 64 years	65 to 74 years	75 years and over	Percent female	Population change and components of change, 2000–2014 Total persons 2000	2010	Percent change 2000–2010	2010–2014	Components of change, 2010–2014 Births	Deaths	Net migration	Households, 2009–2013 Number	Persons per house-hold	Percent Family house-holds	Female family house-holder[1]	One per-son
	16	17	18	19	20	21	22	23	24	25	26	27	28	29	30	31
LOUISIANA—Cont'd																
Orleans	12.9	6.8	4.9	52.0	484 674	343 829	-29.1	11.8	20 030	12 859	32 355	148 398	2.32	52.8	20.1	38.6
Ouachita	11.7	7.2	5.8	52.1	147 250	153 720	4.4	1.7	9 563	6 302	-646	57 551	2.57	65.8	19.4	30.2
Plaquemines	11.5	7.0	4.8	49.9	26 757	23 042	-13.9	1.8	1 296	718	-130	8 615	2.68	74.3	15.7	20.4
Pointe Coupee	14.6	10.1	7.5	51.9	22 763	22 802	0.2	-1.7	1 218	970	-633	8 818	2.55	65.2	13.6	30.6
Rapides	12.5	8.2	6.3	51.7	126 337	131 613	4.2	0.7	7 560	5 782	-770	47 606	2.68	65.3	16.9	31.0
Red River	12.9	9.4	6.6	51.6	9 622	9 091	-5.5	-4.6	553	417	-524	3 320	2.66	71.1	17.8	25.0
Richland	13.3	8.2	6.5	52.0	20 981	20 725	-1.2	0.1	1 242	998	-186	7 619	2.59	73.3	18.8	24.9
Sabine	13.8	10.9	7.2	50.2	23 459	24 233	3.3	-0.1	1 337	1 062	-229	9 175	2.60	67.2	14.0	29.5
St. Bernard	11.3	5.6	3.7	50.4	67 229	35 897	-46.6	23.7	2 664	1 321	6 892	13 714	2.81	72.2	18.9	21.5
St. Charles	12.9	6.6	4.5	50.5	48 072	52 780	9.8	-0.3	2 740	1 705	-1 195	18 547	2.81	75.9	19.6	19.3
St. Helena	13.8	9.7	7.0	50.8	10 525	11 203	6.4	-5.2	490	435	-667	4 130	2.65	72.4	22.2	26.6
St. James	13.6	8.3	6.1	51.4	21 216	22 102	4.2	-2.1	1 190	793	-903	7 786	2.78	77.7	22.4	21.0
St. John the Baptist	12.9	7.5	4.5	50.9	43 044	45 924	6.7	-4.5	2 489	1 702	-2 922	15 440	2.87	73.8	19.9	22.5
St. Landry	12.7	8.2	6.3	52.1	87 700	83 384	-4.9	0.4	5 403	3 949	-1 129	30 935	2.66	69.4	19.6	27.1
St. Martin	12.8	7.9	5.0	50.7	48 583	52 160	7.4	2.2	3 040	1 830	-29	18 756	2.76	69.6	15.9	27.0
St. Mary	12.7	8.2	5.9	50.5	53 500	54 650	2.1	-2.7	3 191	2 301	-2 332	20 092	2.65	69.9	19.1	24.8
St. Tammany	13.8	8.7	5.7	51.4	191 268	233 740	22.2	5.2	11 393	8 553	9 100	87 518	2.68	72.6	12.9	22.6
Tangipahoa	12.3	7.6	4.8	51.5	100 588	121 097	20.4	4.9	8 079	4 810	2 639	44 418	2.69	67.4	16.3	26.6
Tensas	16.1	11.3	7.9	51.2	6 618	5 252	-20.6	-8.0	288	215	-489	2 049	2.33	66.8	21.2	30.8
Terrebonne	11.8	7.4	4.9	50.6	104 503	111 860	7.0	1.6	6 729	4 231	-734	39 279	2.81	70.8	14.8	23.5
Union	14.8	10.5	7.6	50.7	22 803	22 721	-0.4	-1.1	1 219	975	-471	8 532	2.60	70.5	14.6	27.0
Vermilion	12.3	7.6	6.1	51.4	53 807	57 999	7.8	2.8	3 355	2 285	527	21 765	2.66	71.5	14.9	23.9
Vernon	8.8	6.2	4.1	47.4	52 531	52 334	-0.4	-0.4	4 514	1 512	-3 296	18 148	2.76	74.1	12.8	22.5
Washington	13.8	9.5	6.4	50.3	43 926	47 168	7.4	-1.9	2 349	2 368	-835	17 599	2.57	66.9	18.5	30.7
Webster	13.1	9.8	8.1	51.3	41 831	41 207	-1.5	-2.1	2 142	2 132	-847	15 980	2.50	67.3	17.2	29.2
West Baton Rouge	12.7	6.9	4.9	50.7	21 601	23 788	10.1	5.5	1 400	743	645	8 820	2.65	73.1	17.8	22.1
West Carroll	12.5	9.9	7.6	49.8	12 314	11 604	-5.8	-0.7	566	582	-44	4 130	2.61	69.8	14.4	27.7
West Feliciana	14.4	7.8	4.3	34.3	15 111	15 625	3.4	-1.4	553	452	-320	4 007	2.84	74.4	13.3	22.2
Winn	13.4	9.3	6.4	46.8	16 894	15 313	-9.4	-3.7	714	704	-569	5 402	2.43	71.7	17.4	26.5
MAINE	15.4	10.0	7.7	51.0	1 274 923	1 328 361	4.2	0.1	53 972	55 009	2 768	553 823	2.33	63.2	9.7	28.9
Androscoggin	13.7	8.6	6.8	50.9	103 793	107 702	3.8	-0.2	5 572	4 322	-1 526	44 006	2.37	62.6	12.0	29.4
Aroostook	16.3	11.3	9.3	50.7	73 938	71 870	-2.8	-3.4	2 784	3 502	-1 546	30 597	2.26	62.8	8.6	31.9
Cumberland	14.4	8.8	7.1	51.5	265 612	281 674	6.0	2.2	11 669	10 429	4 700	117 359	2.34	61.5	9.6	29.6
Franklin	16.0	11.0	7.7	51.0	29 467	30 768	4.4	-1.5	1 111	1 299	-248	12 098	2.44	65.6	9.8	25.8
Hancock	17.3	12.2	8.5	51.1	51 791	54 418	5.1	0.5	1 899	2 383	764	24 355	2.17	62.4	8.3	29.8
Kennebec	15.5	9.7	7.5	51.3	117 114	122 151	4.3	-0.9	5 053	5 358	-614	51 719	2.29	62.9	10.2	29.1
Knox	16.9	12.1	9.6	50.6	39 618	39 736	0.3	-0.2	1 477	1 738	229	16 941	2.28	63.3	10.0	31.0
Lincoln	17.0	14.3	10.2	51.1	33 616	34 457	2.5	-0.8	1 175	1 694	224	14 817	2.28	65.3	9.6	27.4
Oxford	16.5	10.8	8.0	50.3	54 755	57 833	5.6	-1.0	2 197	2 587	-184	22 890	2.47	63.9	9.3	29.5
Penobscot	14.4	8.8	7.2	50.6	144 919	153 923	6.2	-0.3	6 205	6 326	-427	62 608	2.34	62.5	9.3	27.3
Piscataquis	17.9	13.8	9.1	50.2	17 235	17 535	1.7	-2.9	620	917	-180	7 769	2.20	65.8	9.3	27.7
Sagadahoc	15.9	11.1	7.7	51.5	35 214	35 293	0.2	-0.7	1 389	1 402	-279	15 022	2.32	64.7	8.9	28.6
Somerset	15.8	10.9	7.3	50.4	50 888	52 228	2.6	-2.0	2 003	2 290	-745	21 692	2.36	65.5	10.7	28.2
Waldo	17.0	11.4	7.1	51.1	36 280	38 786	6.9	0.7	1 632	1 605	206	16 448	2.32	64.0	10.0	30.2
Washington	16.9	12.4	9.0	50.8	33 941	32 856	-3.2	-3.2	1 274	1 727	-552	14 209	2.20	62.7	9.7	31.4
York	15.5	9.8	7.5	51.3	186 742	197 131	5.6	1.8	7 912	7 430	2 946	81 293	2.41	65.2	9.0	27.3
MARYLAND	12.7	7.7	5.7	51.5	5 296 486	5 773 552	9.0	3.5	310 306	191 599	86 740	2 146 240	2.65	67.0	14.4	27.1
Allegany	13.0	10.1	8.8	47.9	74 930	75 087	0.2	-2.8	2 903	3 801	-1 154	28 433	2.34	61.0	11.2	32.4
Anne Arundel	12.6	7.9	5.2	50.5	489 656	537 656	9.8	4.2	29 310	16 772	10 659	199 904	2.65	69.3	11.3	24.6
Baltimore	13.1	8.1	7.4	52.6	754 292	805 029	6.7	2.7	41 372	33 146	13 995	313 912	2.52	65.1	14.1	29.0
Calvert	13.2	7.6	4.9	50.7	74 563	88 737	19.0	2.1	3 948	2 647	551	30 923	2.87	76.2	11.3	20.0
Caroline	13.3	8.6	6.3	51.5	29 772	33 066	11.1	-1.6	1 695	1 354	-884	11 806	2.73	71.6	13.5	22.9
Carroll	13.5	8.6	6.2	50.6	150 897	167 134	10.8	0.4	6 788	6 066	-209	59 909	2.73	74.3	8.9	21.5
Cecil	13.6	8.2	5.2	50.4	85 951	101 108	17.6	1.3	4 891	3 690	172	36 394	2.74	73.0	11.2	22.5
Charles	11.6	6.7	4.0	51.7	120 546	146 551	21.6	5.6	7 952	4 001	4 254	51 247	2.88	73.7	15.3	21.5
Dorchester	15.0	11.0	8.3	52.0	30 674	32 618	6.3	-0.1	1 656	1 516	-171	13 386	2.39	68.7	17.1	26.3
Frederick	12.5	7.3	5.2	50.7	195 277	233 385	19.5	4.4	11 787	6 785	5 216	86 337	2.69	72.9	10.0	22.0
Garrett	15.0	11.3	8.0	50.3	29 846	30 097	0.8	-1.4	1 217	1 284	-350	11 974	2.45	69.4	8.7	27.6
Harford	13.3	8.4	5.7	51.0	218 590	244 826	12.0	2.2	11 398	8 144	2 031	90 708	2.70	73.3	11.7	22.0
Howard	12.4	7.3	4.5	50.9	247 842	287 085	15.8	7.7	14 500	6 176	14 285	106 142	2.74	74.3	10.9	21.2
Kent	14.7	13.4	10.8	52.4	19 197	20 197	5.2	-1.9	761	1 028	-115	7 498	2.46	63.4	11.3	31.7
Montgomery	12.7	7.4	6.0	51.8	873 341	971 777	11.3	6.0	55 773	24 689	28 063	360 563	2.72	68.9	11.2	25.4
Prince George's	12.0	6.8	4.0	51.9	801 515	863 420	7.7	4.7	51 110	22 889	13 693	303 441	2.81	66.1	20.6	27.8
Queen Anne's	14.2	10.3	6.4	50.4	40 563	47 798	17.8	2.1	1 989	1 671	702	17 292	2.75	75.8	9.2	19.3

1. No spouse present.

STATE County	Persons in group quarters, 2014	Daytime population, 2009–2013		Births, 2014		Deaths, 2014		Persons under 65 with no health insurance, 2013		Medicare, 2014			Serious crimes known to police,[2] 2013	
													Total	
		Number	Employ-ment/ resi-dence ratio	Total	Rate[1]	Number	Rate[1]	Number	Percent	Eligible for Medicare	Enrolled in Medicare Advantage	Enrolled in a Medicare prescription drug plan	Number	Rate[3]
	32	33	34	35	36	37	38	39	40	41	42	43	44	45
LOUISIANA—Cont'd														
Orleans	13 400	408 560	1.33	4 830	12.6	3 213	8.4	65 010	20.2	55 434	24 515	18 443	17 824	4 728
Ouachita	5 546	160 322	1.09	2 240	14.3	1 570	10.0	24 493	18.7	26 216	4 994	13 966	9 166	6 075
Plaquemines	272	32 866	1.95	321	13.7	174	7.4	3 980	19.4	3 229	1 679	824	431	1 780
Pointe Coupee	116	19 762	0.68	277	12.4	240	10.7	3 595	19.5	4 417	1 773	1 731	444	2 475
Rapides	4 501	137 595	1.11	1 765	13.3	1 385	10.5	19 877	18.0	26 070	3 488	13 881	7 994	6 437
Red River	164	8 765	0.92	120	13.8	111	12.8	1 550	21.1	1 572	250	817	182	2 028
Richland	1 039	20 202	0.92	308	14.9	242	11.7	3 673	21.7	4 097	664	2 313	594	3 297
Sabine	439	22 783	0.82	325	13.4	224	9.3	4 466	22.8	5 146	662	2 866	425	1 743
St. Bernard	293	35 864	0.81	671	15.1	336	7.6	8 267	21.2	5 383	2 759	1 684	554	1 275
St. Charles	592	54 327	1.07	673	12.8	403	7.6	7 231	15.7	7 664	4 027	1 855	1 541	2 926
St. Helena	121	8 710	0.42	110	10.4	95	8.9	2 137	23.8	2 761	731	1 423	261	2 363
St. James	204	22 084	1.02	274	12.7	201	9.3	3 107	16.9	3 969	1 532	1 383	694	3 206
St. John the Baptist	471	42 503	0.86	533	12.2	396	9.1	6 867	18.1	7 287	3 529	2 080	1 275	2 866
St. Landry	1 105	77 959	0.82	1 250	14.9	989	11.8	12 750	18.1	17 586	1 953	11 149	3 564	4 652
St. Martin	701	43 643	0.61	722	13.5	468	8.8	9 077	20.0	9 136	1 156	5 025	1 031	1 948
St. Mary	868	58 846	1.22	750	14.1	521	9.8	10 236	22.6	9 997	1 553	5 415	2 313	4 529
St. Tammany	1 275	217 276	0.81	2 708	11.0	2 108	8.6	35 784	17.4	42 888	20 664	11 310	4 710	1 952
Tangipahoa	3 645	115 568	0.86	1 937	15.2	1 211	9.5	22 179	20.8	20 144	5 704	9 506	8 026	6 462
Tensas	16	5 217	1.06	63	13.0	49	10.1	857	21.8	1 123	112	681	NA	NA
Terrebonne	1 479	120 714	1.18	1 543	13.6	1 041	9.2	20 426	20.9	18 785	2 489	10 482	4 623	4 124
Union	476	20 020	0.70	281	12.5	221	9.8	3 793	21.2	4 746	859	2 538	406	1 818
Vermilion	536	50 600	0.68	805	13.5	558	9.4	10 503	20.6	10 186	748	6 020	1 821	3 087
Vernon	2 257	54 850	1.10	1 004	19.3	363	7.0	7 748	17.2	6 918	457	2 939	1 088	2 178
Washington	1 582	44 948	0.87	540	11.7	591	12.8	8 001	21.3	9 982	2 439	5 305	1 640	3 521
Webster	1 231	38 900	0.86	488	12.1	521	12.9	6 791	21.0	9 035	1 468	4 731	808	1 989
West Baton Rouge	556	23 210	0.93	329	13.1	190	7.6	3 330	15.8	3 825	1 881	1 166	589	2 436
West Carroll	434	10 495	0.75	125	10.8	144	12.5	2 058	22.8	2 527	236	1 611	449	3 905
West Feliciana	5 317	15 792	1.05	133	8.6	111	7.2	1 345	15.8	1 849	572	720	228	1 485
Winn	1 760	14 606	0.89	153	10.4	190	12.9	2 157	19.8	2 910	398	1 707	488	3 270
MAINE	35 630	1 314 395	0.98	12 662	9.5	13 137	9.9	143 376	13.5	302 203	62 930	150 129	32 165	2 422
Androscoggin	2 765	106 052	0.97	1 273	11.8	992	9.2	11 034	12.5	22 914	5 658	11 389	3 087	2 872
Aroostook	2 008	70 712	0.98	653	9.4	796	11.5	8 561	15.7	18 904	2 169	11 909	980	1 390
Cumberland	9 194	308 414	1.17	2 788	9.7	2 502	8.7	27 290	11.7	56 357	14 294	24 930	7 190	2 528
Franklin	1 111	29 882	0.94	260	8.6	307	10.1	3 494	14.7	6 989	1 551	3 513	644	2 107
Hancock	1 176	54 118	0.98	439	8.0	599	11.0	6 838	16.1	13 452	2 154	6 934	957	1 754
Kennebec	3 643	125 251	1.06	1 191	9.8	1 270	10.5	12 823	13.1	29 281	7 691	13 609	3 506	2 882
Knox	1 359	41 253	1.08	349	8.8	421	10.6	4 637	15.6	10 415	1 920	5 182	702	1 772
Lincoln	498	30 917	0.79	274	8.0	407	11.9	4 252	16.7	9 717	2 209	4 454	531	1 558
Oxford	850	51 648	0.76	511	8.9	633	11.1	6 773	14.7	13 917	2 498	7 670	1 518	2 648
Penobscot	7 330	156 537	1.04	1 455	9.5	1 497	9.8	17 547	14.3	33 398	6 927	16 913	4 479	2 917
Piscataquis	220	17 106	0.97	157	9.2	219	12.9	2 133	16.3	4 946	670	2 764	437	2 542
Sagadahoc	265	34 318	0.95	316	9.0	366	10.4	3 182	11.3	8 155	2 115	3 237	662	1 884
Somerset	715	49 419	0.88	443	8.7	512	10.0	6 080	14.6	11 420	1 603	7 018	1 507	2 912
Waldo	501	34 244	0.74	378	9.7	390	10.0	4 480	14.4	9 413	2 002	4 838	575	1 483
Washington	836	32 431	0.99	296	9.3	401	12.6	4 572	18.5	8 847	869	5 238	569	1 761
York	3 159	172 093	0.74	1 879	9.4	1 825	9.1	19 680	12.1	44 078	8 600	20 531	4 687	2 351
MARYLAND	139 814	5 560 766	0.91	73 047	12.2	47 373	7.9	584 983	11.7	913 471	78 719	445 929	186 002	3 137
Allegany	7 687	78 105	1.13	685	9.4	916	12.6	5 863	11.0	16 459	714	11 583	2 637	3 572
Anne Arundel	14 018	535 815	0.97	6 960	12.4	4 171	7.4	40 286	8.6	83 455	5 162	35 990	15 945	2 871
Baltimore	21 182	761 502	0.87	9 667	11.7	8 172	9.9	77 815	11.5	146 291	13 953	85 399	25 564	3 107
Calvert	639	67 415	0.52	943	10.4	671	7.4	6 188	7.9	13 302	602	5 358	1 742	1 935
Caroline	439	27 148	0.62	379	11.6	325	10.0	3 914	14.1	6 055	61	3 848	1 012	3 098
Carroll	3 398	136 660	0.65	1 630	9.7	1 478	8.8	11 488	8.3	28 974	1 537	16 678	2 683	1 602
Cecil	1 431	85 844	0.67	1 143	11.2	914	8.9	8 959	10.2	16 844	944	9 903	3 314	3 247
Charles	1 378	114 280	0.54	1 930	12.5	983	6.4	11 446	8.5	19 496	1 140	7 017	4 114	2 705
Dorchester	508	30 988	0.89	406	12.5	373	11.4	3 488	13.3	7 457	95	4 998	1 120	3 438
Frederick	4 178	218 999	0.86	2 766	11.4	1 623	6.7	19 349	9.4	35 365	2 025	16 224	4 740	1 960
Garrett	543	29 536	0.97	286	9.6	319	10.7	3 069	12.8	6 559	451	4 617	698	2 339
Harford	2 745	216 179	0.76	2 662	10.6	1 997	8.0	17 008	8.0	41 593	3 188	20 571	4 726	1 889
Howard	2 211	291 805	0.99	3 502	11.3	1 609	5.2	20 296	7.7	39 082	2 857	17 522	6 751	2 223
Kent	1 477	20 739	1.07	176	8.9	279	14.1	1 875	13.5	5 287	105	3 897	396	1 957
Montgomery	9 158	955 029	0.93	13 170	12.8	5 876	5.7	108 864	12.5	141 283	13 871	54 030	18 039	1 775
Prince George's	20 327	753 678	0.73	11 956	13.2	5 978	6.6	127 917	16.5	112 459	15 365	35 350	33 062	3 723
Queen Anne's	456	39 815	0.65	452	9.3	373	7.6	4 062	10.2	9 129	186	4 982	963	1 968

1. Per 1,000 estimated resident population. 2. Data for serious crimes have not been adjusted for underreporting; this may affect comparability between geographic areas and over time.
3. Per 100,000 population estimated by the FBI.

STATE County	Serious crimes known to police, 2013 (cont.)[1]: Rate[2]: Violent	Serious crimes known to police, 2013 (cont.)[1]: Rate[2]: Property	Education: School enrollment and attainment, 2009–2013: Enrollment[3]: Total	Education: Enrollment[3]: Percent private	Education: Attainment[4] (percent): High school graduate or less	Education: Attainment[4] (percent): Bachelor's degree or more	Education: Local government expenditures,[5] 2012–2013: Total current spending (mil dol)	Education: Local government expenditures,[5] 2012–2013: Current spending per student (dollars)	Money income, 2009–2013: Per capita income[6] (dollars)	Money income, 2009–2013: Households: Median income (dollars)	Money income, 2009–2013: Households: Mean income (dollars)	Money income, 2009–2013: Households: Percent with income of $200,000 or more	Income and poverty, 2013: Median household income (dollars)	Income and poverty, 2013: Percent below poverty level: All persons	Income and poverty, 2013: Percent below poverty level: Children under 18 years	Income and poverty, 2013: Percent below poverty level: Children 5 to 17 years in families
	46	47	48	49	50	51	52	53	54	55	56	57	58	59	60	61
LOUISIANA—Cont'd																
Orleans	787	3 940	95 009	33.3	39.7	33.7	275.4	13 627	26 500	37 146	61 211	4.3	36 240	26.6	39.0	38.9
Ouachita	624	5 450	41 414	8.6	49.0	22.9	284.0	9 903	21 917	38 955	56 872	2.9	39 976	23.8	35.1	33.1
Plaquemines	173	1 606	6 398	19.8	56.7	15.3	62.4	16 026	25 748	55 138	69 564	2.9	51 306	15.4	18.7	17.7
Pointe Coupee	513	1 962	5 374	28.4	60.7	14.3	30.1	10 306	23 742	45 363	58 614	2.6	42 129	20.2	30.7	29.2
Rapides	939	5 498	33 705	13.7	52.5	18.3	220.5	9 163	22 126	40 930	57 093	2.0	39 411	19.7	28.4	28.0
Red River	446	1 583	2 176	17.2	67.5	11.9	20.2	13 599	21 443	39 346	56 554	3.1	35 762	23.5	36.8	35.6
Richland	350	2 948	5 103	10.6	63.8	13.2	34.3	9 927	18 669	36 835	49 593	1.5	32 477	27.5	40.3	38.0
Sabine	345	1 399	5 691	7.9	60.5	13.0	47.4	10 906	22 229	35 159	53 402	2.7	37 864	21.8	30.8	27.8
St. Bernard	152	1 123	9 860	14.5	60.3	12.0	80.8	12 021	20 316	41 353	54 443	1.4	40 705	21.9	38.4	37.0
St. Charles	458	2 469	14 656	17.1	50.3	19.7	148.4	15 279	26 756	58 758	73 382	2.8	56 163	13.8	18.5	16.8
St. Helena	498	1 865	2 734	13.2	63.1	10.3	9.2	11 593	19 457	33 143	51 366	1.0	34 229	25.8	38.8	39.0
St. James	573	2 633	5 647	15.6	61.1	13.0	56.4	14 980	24 930	55 443	69 118	3.1	48 358	16.2	23.4	22.8
St. John the Baptist	157	2 708	12 624	29.7	57.6	14.5	83.2	13 296	21 335	50 635	60 671	1.2	47 389	18.5	28.4	27.9
St. Landry	929	3 722	20 011	16.9	67.2	13.2	127.5	8 586	19 387	35 503	50 167	1.8	33 781	27.1	40.5	39.3
St. Martin	240	1 708	13 582	23.1	65.9	13.3	75.1	8 973	22 164	42 186	58 681	2.5	42 110	19.4	29.0	27.7
St. Mary	627	3 903	12 063	14.4	67.0	10.8	97.7	10 377	21 313	41 571	54 786	2.2	39 608	22.3	29.5	27.2
St. Tammany	159	1 793	62 945	25.0	39.1	30.1	414.3	11 044	30 363	60 799	80 394	5.9	61 655	11.0	15.0	14.1
Tangipahoa	873	5 589	33 798	14.4	54.0	19.4	176.4	8 892	21 273	40 654	56 317	1.9	40 228	22.2	30.9	31.8
Tensas	NA	NA	1 199	17.7	66.9	10.3	9.0	13 306	17 175	27 543	43 632	1.6	28 021	33.3	50.2	46.5
Terrebonne	415	3 710	27 579	17.3	64.7	13.4	163.5	8 773	24 114	49 960	65 422	3.1	51 716	15.2	23.2	22.2
Union	278	1 541	4 433	13.4	58.9	13.1	26.0	10 998	19 412	35 828	48 293	1.2	35 825	24.6	34.0	34.9
Vermilion	451	2 636	13 895	14.3	68.1	12.6	87.7	9 258	22 589	44 665	59 730	2.0	43 434	18.6	26.6	24.0
Vernon	242	1 936	13 594	9.0	50.6	18.8	96.2	9 785	21 396	46 572	57 368	1.4	42 772	17.3	22.3	22.2
Washington	563	2 959	11 569	15.2	64.0	11.2	80.8	10 707	17 735	31 778	45 638	1.5	31 630	25.4	36.2	34.2
Webster	384	1 605	9 235	9.8	62.5	13.6	61.3	9 200	19 871	35 071	48 824	0.9	35 762	23.7	37.0	34.7
West Baton Rouge	306	2 130	6 061	21.6	55.4	18.0	45.7	11 704	24 838	50 926	65 772	2.2	48 848	16.4	24.0	22.7
West Carroll	478	3 427	2 594	3.2	71.7	9.5	21.1	9 603	17 980	33 848	48 445	1.0	34 611	23.4	34.8	32.6
West Feliciana	176	1 309	3 054	14.6	60.6	18.8	28.2	13 181	21 720	61 616	75 190	5.1	52 626	24.4	21.1	19.6
Winn	623	2 647	3 141	6.5	65.6	11.3	24.9	9 915	16 789	34 322	46 461	0.8	35 674	27.3	35.0	33.2
MAINE	129	2 292	305 865	17.0	42.8	27.9	2 335.6	12 147	26 824	48 453	63 143	2.7	47 095	14.0	18.2	16.4
Androscoggin	148	2 725	26 511	18.3	50.4	18.8	196.7	11 599	24 442	44 921	58 382	1.8	44 097	16.5	22.3	20.4
Aroostook	69	1 320	15 454	9.1	53.2	16.7	125.6	13 095	21 566	37 855	49 053	1.3	37 092	16.4	22.1	20.1
Cumberland	138	2 390	69 255	20.6	31.1	41.0	500.5	13 382	32 880	57 461	77 975	5.1	55 020	12.1	13.7	12.3
Franklin	131	1 976	7 298	10.6	46.7	23.7	40.8	12 888	22 083	41 626	53 461	1.7	41 154	15.5	21.0	19.5
Hancock	57	1 697	10 926	17.9	40.0	33.0	96.1	14 592	27 797	47 460	61 474	2.4	44 463	14.3	20.1	18.1
Kennebec	153	2 729	27 912	18.6	44.6	24.6	194.9	11 827	25 770	46 808	60 108	2.0	45 151	14.8	19.1	16.9
Knox	63	1 709	7 420	13.2	43.4	30.4	87.6	14 740	27 865	49 755	63 225	2.7	48 352	14.1	20.4	17.6
Lincoln	123	1 435	6 203	19.0	38.5	33.1	51.3	11 852	28 070	50 181	64 155	2.9	48 908	13.3	21.2	18.3
Oxford	99	2 549	12 577	14.3	55.3	18.9	120.2	12 939	21 441	40 674	51 008	1.2	38 932	15.0	20.8	18.9
Penobscot	91	2 826	41 056	14.1	45.1	23.8	262.5	11 775	23 895	43 734	57 355	2.0	43 615	15.9	19.3	17.8
Piscataquis	209	2 333	3 197	19.5	54.2	16.4	18.5	9 864	21 818	36 646	48 293	1.5	36 553	17.6	27.7	25.3
Sagadahoc	60	1 824	7 288	11.6	38.4	32.3	63.0	13 233	28 829	56 733	66 427	1.9	52 279	12.1	18.1	16.1
Somerset	108	2 804	11 112	10.5	54.7	15.4	103.2	12 703	21 513	38 642	50 542	1.2	38 279	17.8	25.1	23.0
Waldo	59	1 423	8 225	20.4	45.2	28.2	55.5	13 777	22 853	42 221	52 724	1.0	43 203	16.8	24.4	23.2
Washington	173	1 587	6 635	12.4	51.2	20.0	64.5	14 363	20 807	37 236	47 124	0.9	35 754	18.8	27.2	24.6
York	171	2 180	44 796	19.2	40.9	28.8	354.8	12 080	29 125	57 348	70 238	3.2	55 163	10.0	12.2	10.7
MARYLAND	474	2 663	1 570 717	20.1	37.2	36.8	11 905.0	13 829	36 354	73 538	96 072	8.7	72 482	10.2	13.9	12.5
Allegany	337	3 234	17 197	9.7	54.8	16.8	127.8	14 316	21 211	39 293	53 297	1.5	39 994	18.6	24.7	20.6
Anne Arundel	469	2 403	141 905	21.6	34.6	37.1	1 009.8	12 984	40 415	87 430	107 405	10.7	85 685	7.3	9.3	8.3
Baltimore	469	2 638	217 146	22.7	37.3	35.7	1 412.5	13 209	34 374	66 486	86 633	6.1	64 624	9.5	12.9	11.7
Calvert	119	1 816	24 946	10.0	39.3	30.0	217.9	13 347	38 260	95 477	108 304	9.2	91 993	6.9	8.6	7.7
Caroline	285	2 813	7 890	11.7	58.2	15.0	66.3	11 871	25 211	58 632	67 557	2.5	46 015	16.7	24.2	22.4
Carroll	204	1 397	44 761	19.8	39.6	32.7	350.4	13 129	36 153	84 790	99 179	7.6	82 073	6.8	7.8	6.5
Cecil	430	2 817	25 108	19.2	48.2	22.2	195.2	12 486	29 518	66 689	79 761	4.1	64 880	9.8	14.7	12.9
Charles	386	2 319	41 349	13.2	39.9	26.7	348.8	13 090	37 277	93 160	105 877	9.4	87 577	8.0	10.8	9.7
Dorchester	460	2 977	7 269	11.3	56.1	18.0	62.2	13 178	26 388	46 361	62 670	2.3	42 542	17.7	28.8	27.8
Frederick	254	1 706	65 199	19.8	33.7	38.2	509.0	12 583	36 917	84 570	99 911	8.2	83 489	6.9	8.6	7.6
Garrett	426	1 914	6 277	16.1	56.6	18.3	57.9	14 469	24 932	45 206	60 778	2.3	44 404	15.9	23.9	21.6
Harford	265	1 624	65 791	18.5	36.9	32.7	484.5	12 793	35 425	80 622	94 465	7.0	77 453	7.4	9.6	8.5
Howard	206	2 017	85 972	18.8	19.5	60.0	781.5	15 013	48 172	109 865	132 203	18.1	108 503	5.3	6.7	5.7
Kent	292	1 000	4 408	16.0	47.2	29.6	32.2	15 099	31 502	56 259	76 655	5.5	55 695	14.9	21.9	20.5
Montgomery	174	1 601	268 489	23.7	23.2	57.1	2 246.2	15 097	49 038	98 221	132 222	17.3	97 873	7.0	9.7	8.9
Prince George's	506	3 217	249 032	18.2	41.6	29.8	1 747.2	14 120	32 344	73 623	88 867	6.1	71 682	9.9	14.1	13.2
Queen Anne's	241	1 727	11 594	15.2	39.4	33.2	90.7	11 699	38 108	87 256	103 014	9.1	80 143	8.4	10.8	9.5

1. Data for serious crimes have not been adjusted for underreporting; this may affect comparability between geographic areas and over time. 2. Per 100,000 population estimated by the FBI.
3. All persons 3 years old and over enrolled in nursery school through college. 4. Persons 25 years old and over. 5. Elementary and secondary education expenditures.
6. Based on population estimated by the American Community Survey, 2009–2013.

STATE County	Personal income, 2013										Earnings, 2013		
	Total (mil dol)	Percent change, 2012–2013	Per capita[1] Dollars	Per capita[1] Rank	Wages and salaries (mil dol)	Supplements to wages and salaries; employer contributions (mil dol): Pension and insurance	Supplements to wages and salaries; employer contributions (mil dol): Government social insurance	Proprietors' income (mil dol)	Dividends, interest, and rent (mil dol)	Personal transfer receipts (mil dol)	Total (mil dol)	Contributions for government social insurance (mil dol): From employee and self-employed	Contributions for government social insurance (mil dol): From employer
	62	63	64	65	66	67	68	69	70	71	72	73	74
LOUISIANA—Cont'd													
Orleans	16 437	2.3	43 403	810	9 978	1 597	658	2 235	3 579	2 795	14 468	740	658
Ouachita	5 697	2.0	36 469	1 668	2 832	492	181	616	936	1 340	4 122	219	181
Plaquemines	978	0.5	41 518	991	992	177	63	215	163	146	1 448	72	63
Pointe Coupee	933	2.2	41 473	996	199	39	13	141	145	196	393	19	13
Rapides	5 353	1.3	40 333	1 132	2 394	453	157	490	944	1 403	3 495	187	157
Red River	298	-0.6	33 456	2 182	105	21	7	33	55	82	166	9	7
Richland	738	0.5	35 390	1 838	216	45	14	128	105	215	403	20	14
Sabine	788	2.2	32 532	2 323	200	42	12	96	140	220	350	20	12
St. Bernard	1 498	4.3	34 461	1 996	550	120	34	82	197	275	786	42	34
St. Charles	2 082	0.8	39 562	1 223	1 697	331	104	125	290	329	2 258	118	104
St. Helena	415	1.7	38 157	1 415	54	13	3	43	46	126	113	8	3
St. James	754	1.4	34 643	1 965	536	112	33	74	99	176	755	39	33
St. John the Baptist	1 614	-0.6	36 889	1 611	799	161	50	151	197	346	1 160	63	50
St. Landry	3 132	1.1	37 526	1 502	939	187	59	200	461	857	1 386	80	59
St. Martin	1 890	2.1	35 697	1 801	616	98	39	129	271	403	882	51	39
St. Mary	2 137	1.6	39 903	1 182	1 402	217	88	168	368	459	1 875	101	88
St. Tammany	12 196	1.8	50 328	351	3 775	608	236	1 496	2 174	1 771	6 115	326	236
Tangipahoa	4 118	1.2	32 836	2 276	1 612	327	96	278	535	1 147	2 312	122	96
Tensas	222	3.5	45 217	675	41	9	3	70	43	52	122	4	3
Terrebonne	4 983	5.5	44 197	742	3 159	423	204	199	785	822	3 984	226	204
Union	783	3.2	35 064	1 890	156	34	11	77	99	214	277	16	11
Vermilion	2 016	0.5	34 030	2 074	623	109	38	172	377	432	942	52	38
Vernon	2 218	-2.0	42 155	922	1 102	311	99	81	448	354	1 593	68	99
Washington	1 362	1.5	29 349	2 771	379	88	22	75	191	505	564	35	22
Webster	1 477	-0.1	36 308	1 693	486	88	32	126	219	407	733	44	32
West Baton Rouge	994	4.1	40 453	1 117	594	100	40	107	107	169	841	44	40
West Carroll	326	2.7	28 444	2 855	80	20	5	49	41	117	154	8	5
West Feliciana	473	2.7	30 643	2 606	286	71	15	38	81	81	410	18	15
Winn	511	0.3	34 509	1 983	177	33	12	80	73	143	301	17	12
MAINE	54 359	2.6	40 924	X	24 848	4 466	1 891	4 140	9 477	12 521	35 345	2 256	1 891
Androscoggin	4 054	2.2	37 680	1 475	1 938	327	152	267	528	1 071	2 684	176	152
Aroostook	2 567	3.4	36 647	1 646	1 007	218	76	221	372	848	1 522	98	76
Cumberland	14 122	2.7	49 472	390	8 562	1 315	645	1 120	2 646	2 320	11 642	717	645
Franklin	1 011	2.1	33 137	2 236	407	79	31	84	172	290	601	40	31
Hancock	2 183	2.6	39 804	1 190	842	147	67	214	524	506	1 270	84	67
Kennebec	4 815	3.3	39 743	1 195	2 414	495	173	313	726	1 221	3 395	205	173
Knox	1 649	2.4	41 703	972	634	116	49	185	430	373	984	65	49
Lincoln	1 459	2.5	42 795	860	388	71	30	116	399	339	605	43	30
Oxford	1 948	3.1	34 012	2 078	611	119	47	144	301	580	921	65	47
Penobscot	5 630	2.7	36 713	1 637	2 766	536	208	398	816	1 460	3 908	245	208
Piscataquis	589	3.4	34 388	2 014	186	44	14	40	102	201	285	20	14
Sagadahoc	1 538	1.5	43 935	760	741	145	58	77	308	302	1 021	65	58
Somerset	1 772	3.1	34 263	2 040	683	126	53	165	246	539	1 028	70	53
Waldo	1 370	3.9	35 195	1 873	411	73	32	103	254	377	620	45	32
Washington	1 155	3.2	35 887	1 765	364	81	28	105	184	427	578	39	28
York	8 495	2.0	42 595	882	2 892	574	228	588	1 468	1 666	4 282	277	228
MARYLAND	319 125	1.1	53 826	X	150 219	25 666	11 423	24 893	61 625	41 855	212 201	12 115	11 423
Allegany	2 606	2.5	35 450	1 829	1 201	252	101	124	507	801	1 678	110	101
Anne Arundel	33 380	1.4	60 064	104	18 505	3 574	1 442	2 623	6 536	3 503	26 143	1 422	1 442
Baltimore	44 450	1.0	54 009	235	19 941	3 255	1 519	3 316	8 722	6 467	28 031	1 662	1 519
Calvert	4 581	0.5	50 632	346	1 028	196	78	171	915	549	1 474	90	78
Caroline	1 228	3.4	37 547	1 498	366	72	29	108	207	302	575	35	29
Carroll	8 290	0.5	49 477	389	2 450	408	191	497	1 541	1 126	3 546	218	191
Cecil	4 338	3.3	42 562	886	1 438	282	114	165	655	770	2 000	124	114
Charles	7 176	1.1	46 945	557	1 895	384	151	304	1 283	892	2 734	159	151
Dorchester	1 248	2.7	38 216	1 408	440	94	35	94	260	353	662	42	35
Frederick	11 736	0.5	48 617	443	5 096	843	396	637	2 248	1 418	6 973	404	396
Garrett	1 264	3.3	42 282	910	422	84	35	210	251	280	750	46	35
Harford	13 112	0.6	52 615	282	4 728	965	378	557	2 197	1 717	6 627	387	378
Howard	21 588	1.5	70 876	43	10 707	1 302	782	1 387	3 736	1 517	14 177	815	782
Kent	987	0.8	49 495	388	318	56	25	89	330	209	488	30	25
Montgomery	73 959	0.7	72 746	38	33 258	5 110	2 430	9 086	15 873	5 411	49 883	2 758	2 430
Prince George's	38 596	0.9	43 362	814	17 564	3 477	1 374	1 843	7 063	5 175	24 257	1 358	1 374
Queen Anne's	2 659	0.7	54 810	209	540	99	43	189	575	354	871	53	43

1. Based on the resident population estimated as of July 1 of the year shown.

STATE County	Earnings, 2013 (cont.) — Percent by selected industries: Farm	Mining	Construction	Manu-facturing	Infor-mation: professional, scientific, technical services	Retail trade	Finance, insur-ance, real estate and leasing	Health care and social assistance	Govern-ment	Social Security beneficiaries, December 2013: Number	Rate[1]	Supple-mental Security Income recipients, December 2013	Housing units, 2014: Total	Percent change, 2010–2014
	75	76	77	78	79	80	81	82	83	84	85	86	87	88
LOUISIANA—Cont'd														
Orleans	0.0	4.2	4.3	2.3	16.4	3.7	7.0	7.1	21.3	57 605	152	20 325	192 445	1.3
Ouachita	0.2	0.4	5.3	9.3	10.3	8.4	9.2	17.0	16.8	28 005	179	6 836	66 292	2.8
Plaquemines	1.2	13.2	6.6	16.6	4.6	1.5	6.0	D	13.8	3 465	147	587	9 877	2.9
Pointe Coupee	19.9	3.5	7.0	6.7	3.4	8.2	6.9	5.3	15.4	4 720	210	1 063	11 287	1.4
Rapides	1.2	0.7	8.9	7.7	6.3	8.1	4.6	18.8	22.7	27 685	209	7 017	57 087	2.5
Red River	5.3	10.8	6.9	7.5	3.2	D	4.0	D	18.8	1 690	191	491	4 131	0.1
Richland	16.9	0.6	6.7	8.2	D	9.8	3.9	D	14.8	4 355	208	1 152	8 833	2.5
Sabine	8.5	2.6	6.9	17.0	6.5	8.0	5.3	D	19.7	5 630	232	1 036	14 415	2.0
St. Bernard	1.1	D	18.2	22.8	2.2	6.5	2.3	D	16.8	6 310	145	1 693	16 834	0.2
St. Charles	0.0	D	14.1	29.0	5.1	3.1	1.9	D	10.8	8 690	165	1 256	20 277	1.7
St. Helena	3.2	D	D	7.9	D	7.4	D	8.8	26.2	3 150	290	1 007	5 159	0.2
St. James	2.3	D	7.9	46.7	D	2.6	2.4	1.9	12.4	4 355	201	757	8 711	3.0
St. John the Baptist	0.5	3.8	9.4	30.3	3.7	5.4	4.7	5.2	12.2	8 365	192	1 821	17 621	0.9
St. Landry	4.9	3.0	8.9	6.8	4.7	10.6	4.5	12.8	22.0	19 345	232	5 550	36 140	1.3
St. Martin	2.9	14.5	7.0	20.5	D	6.9	6.2	6.4	14.8	10 235	193	1 947	22 526	2.7
St. Mary	1.5	15.5	4.4	20.6	3.6	4.3	6.3	D	14.7	11 155	208	2 421	23 201	0.8
St. Tammany	0.0	9.9	8.6	4.8	8.8	8.4	7.2	12.5	14.7	45 960	190	4 910	98 796	3.5
Tangipahoa	0.2	0.5	5.7	5.7	4.2	10.1	9.9	11.7	27.0	22 190	177	5 322	52 548	4.9
Tensas	55.2	D	2.7	1.6	D	D	D	D	14.2	1 190	243	407	3 373	0.5
Terrebonne	0.5	16.4	7.2	15.5	5.2	5.9	5.6	8.6	8.7	21 300	189	4 816	44 597	1.8
Union	14.8	D	6.6	D	3.2	8.7	2.9	10.4	17.1	5 245	234	931	11 431	0.7
Vermilion	6.0	17.9	7.4	7.3	4.2	7.6	7.1	D	18.4	11 320	191	1 967	25 897	2.6
Vernon	0.1	0.2	2.7	1.9	4.2	3.4	2.3	4.8	69.2	7 775	147	1 214	21 742	1.4
Washington	-0.6	1.7	9.2	15.1	D	8.1	3.9	D	33.9	11 210	242	2 995	21 288	1.2
Webster	0.3	10.2	8.3	13.8	2.7	10.0	4.6	D	16.0	9 745	239	2 025	19 428	0.5
West Baton Rouge	1.8	D	26.2	20.2	D	4.6	3.1	2.0	11.1	4 105	167	840	10 059	7.9
West Carroll	23.6	D	4.3	3.7	D	7.8	D	D	29.8	2 685	234	518	5 078	0.6
West Feliciana	0.3	D	D	6.9	2.1	2.8	3.2	D	36.2	1 820	118	351	5 254	3.1
Winn	1.9	4.0	3.3	17.0	D	4.7	7.0	22.8	13.1	3 210	217	663	7 232	0.0
MAINE	0.6	0.0	6.5	10.0	8.1	8.2	7.8	16.3	18.0	320 482	241	37 428	727 632	0.8
Androscoggin	0.5	D	7.7	11.2	7.0	8.1	8.1	20.9	11.3	25 085	234	4 011	49 142	0.1
Aroostook	5.1	0.0	4.3	10.9	3.4	9.3	4.4	17.5	24.5	20 485	292	2 751	39 470	-0.2
Cumberland	0.1	D	5.2	6.5	12.5	6.7	13.6	16.7	12.0	57 445	201	5 610	140 279	1.2
Franklin	0.6	0.0	6.8	20.1	D	9.8	4.3	D	17.7	7 695	252	933	21 935	1.0
Hancock	1.0	D	10.1	7.2	12.6	10.4	4.8	14.1	13.9	13 940	254	1 033	40 474	0.7
Kennebec	0.4	0.0	5.3	4.8	6.2	9.1	3.6	16.6	30.6	31 380	259	4 376	61 493	0.9
Knox	0.6	0.0	8.9	8.9	7.1	9.2	6.1	15.1	15.2	10 795	273	896	23 940	0.8
Lincoln	2.9	D	9.5	D	7.3	9.8	6.2	14.0	14.7	10 130	296	724	23 668	0.7
Oxford	1.7	0.1	7.1	19.1	4.2	8.1	4.5	12.9	17.9	15 355	268	1 982	36 280	0.6
Penobscot	0.1	D	5.3	5.9	5.4	9.9	4.3	22.5	20.4	35 670	232	5 507	74 282	0.6
Piscataquis	-0.2	D	5.3	D	D	10.0	2.7	D	27.2	5 315	309	722	15 393	0.3
Sagadahoc	0.0	0.0	7.3	D	6.7	6.3	3.4	5.5	11.6	8 455	241	708	18 414	0.7
Somerset	0.9	D	16.3	22.7	3.4	7.9	2.6	13.0	14.1	12 675	245	1 927	30 747	0.6
Waldo	0.7	D	7.7	10.6	4.1	8.4	12.7	15.3	13.7	10 070	258	1 244	21 772	1.0
Washington	5.0	D	5.2	10.3	2.9	9.8	4.2	15.4	25.2	9 510	295	1 376	23 063	0.3
York	0.1	0.1	7.3	11.6	5.7	8.8	5.0	11.9	27.7	46 475	233	3 628	107 280	1.4
MARYLAND	0.2	0.1	7.1	4.5	17.2	5.5	7.8	11.0	24.7	917 497	154	117 605	2 422 194	1.8
Allegany	0.1	D	4.4	9.0	D	7.2	3.6	20.7	28.7	17 390	236	2 253	33 222	-0.3
Anne Arundel	0.0	D	6.6	6.1	15.0	4.9	3.9	7.1	35.7	85 120	153	6 046	218 903	3.0
Baltimore	0.1	0.0	7.7	5.3	13.3	6.9	12.8	13.2	18.4	151 135	183	15 506	336 992	0.4
Calvert	0.1	D	10.6	2.6	D	7.4	4.0	14.5	21.8	13 710	152	975	34 597	2.4
Caroline	7.9	D	8.9	10.6	D	9.7	2.8	D	18.6	6 790	208	749	13 514	0.2
Carroll	1.0	0.1	12.9	8.3	10.7	8.0	4.6	13.7	16.1	30 025	179	1 530	63 150	1.2
Cecil	0.8	0.4	4.7	21.1	3.5	6.4	2.5	10.2	23.9	18 475	181	1 770	42 374	3.1
Charles	0.1	D	11.3	1.5	8.1	12.3	3.7	10.4	32.1	19 650	129	2 075	58 154	5.8
Dorchester	4.4	1.6	5.3	17.6	D	5.5	3.3	11.5	24.0	8 235	253	1 242	16 702	0.9
Frederick	0.7	0.1	10.1	5.5	17.4	6.7	9.6	9.7	20.4	35 970	149	2 281	93 572	3.8
Garrett	2.3	3.6	11.9	8.2	6.8	10.1	5.1	D	14.2	7 175	240	665	19 055	1.1
Harford	0.1	0.1	7.0	5.5	12.9	7.1	3.8	9.4	36.5	43 210	173	3 145	98 234	2.8
Howard	0.1	D	8.6	4.5	31.7	5.3	7.6	6.7	9.4	36 220	119	3 046	115 311	5.5
Kent	7.4	D	8.3	10.7	6.9	6.9	4.9	12.8	13.8	5 440	275	333	10 662	1.1
Montgomery	0.0	0.0	6.7	3.0	26.6	4.4	10.1	8.8	21.6	124 460	122	13 802	385 721	2.6
Prince George's	0.0	0.0	10.0	2.2	12.5	6.4	3.6	7.8	37.8	107 245	120	14 042	330 516	0.7
Queen Anne's	3.6	D	11.3	8.0	7.9	9.3	4.7	6.5	19.5	9 550	197	442	20 765	3.1

1. Per 1,000 resident population estimated as of July 1 of the year shown.

STATE County	Housing units, 2009–2013: Occupied units: Total	Owner-occupied: Percent	Owner-occupied: Median value[1]	Median owner cost as a percent of income: With a mortgage	Median owner cost as a percent of income: Without a mortgage[2]	Renter-occupied: Median rent[3]	Renter-occupied: Median rent as a percent of income[2]	Substandard units[4] (percent)	Civilian labor force, 2014: Total	Percent change, 2013–2014	Unemployment: Total	Unemployment: Rate[5]	Civilian employment,[6] 2009–2013: Total	Percent: Management, business, science and arts	Percent: Construction, production, and maintenance occupations
	89	90	91	92	93	94	95	96	97	98	99	100	101	102	103
LOUISIANA—Cont'd															
Orleans	148 398	47.3	183 700	27.0	13.9	926	37.5	2.8	178 535	2.5	12 516	7.0	158 984	40.2	16.1
Ouachita	57 551	60.4	118 200	19.6	10.0	668	32.4	2.8	72 457	1.8	5 043	7.0	65 586	33.0	20.8
Plaquemines	8 615	74.5	176 900	24.0	10.0	1 050	31.0	2.2	10 398	3.0	594	5.7	9 894	29.1	33.8
Pointe Coupee	8 818	78.0	113 100	19.7	10.0	586	24.1	2.6	10 246	3.1	715	7.0	9 447	26.8	32.8
Rapides	47 606	66.0	120 400	21.9	10.0	701	32.1	3.7	58 646	2.2	3 904	6.7	53 543	31.6	22.5
Red River	3 320	76.1	78 700	19.2	10.0	564	27.4	2.4	4 047	4.4	296	7.3	3 253	28.7	31.4
Richland	7 619	68.8	76 900	19.6	10.0	518	24.3	3.8	8 784	1.2	748	8.5	7 737	28.9	27.0
Sabine	9 175	76.6	75 300	18.2	10.0	470	28.9	2.6	9 271	0.2	609	6.6	8 806	26.4	39.0
St. Bernard	13 714	69.2	127 200	22.8	10.0	817	36.3	2.9	19 032	2.5	1 320	6.9	16 072	24.5	34.0
St. Charles	18 547	80.8	186 400	22.5	10.3	926	32.1	6.2	25 701	2.8	1 563	6.1	24 532	33.6	27.3
St. Helena	4 130	82.2	80 600	20.7	12.6	604	28.5	4.9	4 686	2.0	464	9.9	4 208	19.5	32.5
St. James	7 786	81.5	125 000	18.9	10.0	671	22.9	3.3	9 913	2.1	839	8.5	9 295	23.4	33.9
St. John the Baptist	15 440	77.7	149 900	24.0	10.2	893	32.2	3.3	20 566	2.3	1 598	7.8	19 884	25.1	29.8
St. Landry	30 935	70.0	83 600	19.5	10.0	569	33.1	3.9	34 223	1.6	2 584	7.6	31 577	25.4	29.2
St. Martin	18 756	80.3	97 300	19.0	10.0	612	26.6	4.6	24 835	1.9	1 420	5.7	23 229	20.9	32.7
St. Mary	20 092	69.7	88 800	20.0	10.1	648	26.7	1.7	25 555	1.8	1 617	6.3	21 742	23.5	35.7
St. Tammany	87 518	78.0	194 500	23.3	10.6	1 005	32.0	3.5	114 591	2.8	6 479	5.7	107 315	38.0	19.5
Tangipahoa	44 418	68.6	135 400	21.7	10.0	738	33.1	3.3	54 165	2.1	4 061	7.5	52 754	29.7	26.4
Tensas	2 049	63.5	58 900	20.3	12.1	502	34.2	4.8	1 802	1.3	169	9.4	1 761	22.4	27.8
Terrebonne	39 279	74.4	131 600	19.4	10.0	819	26.2	3.6	55 001	3.4	2 666	4.8	48 965	25.1	33.6
Union	8 532	80.2	79 700	20.4	10.0	505	35.5	4.5	9 355	1.9	697	7.5	8 609	25.2	35.3
Vermilion	21 765	75.2	96 400	19.1	10.0	607	25.3	2.7	26 725	2.0	1 487	5.6	24 845	23.7	32.8
Vernon	18 148	54.7	90 800	17.6	10.0	869	24.4	4.6	17 615	-1.5	1 483	8.4	17 641	30.4	24.7
Washington	17 599	73.0	81 900	22.7	10.2	552	33.0	3.9	17 077	3.2	1 349	7.9	15 668	26.0	27.8
Webster	15 980	69.2	79 300	19.9	10.0	566	30.4	2.3	15 770	0.5	1 328	8.4	15 523	24.6	32.9
West Baton Rouge	8 820	72.4	141 900	19.6	10.0	804	28.2	3.0	12 756	3.4	746	5.8	11 491	30.5	26.6
West Carroll	4 130	70.5	68 500	18.0	11.0	511	26.3	6.4	4 289	0.4	555	12.9	4 246	23.0	31.2
West Feliciana	4 007	73.7	196 300	19.4	10.0	748	25.2	3.6	5 436	3.5	316	5.8	5 043	39.2	24.3
Winn	5 402	72.9	64 300	17.6	10.1	519	33.0	2.0	5 470	0.9	405	7.4	4 896	28.6	32.7
MAINE	553 823	71.8	174 500	23.9	14.0	764	31.1	2.1	698 928	-1.2	39 876	5.7	647 099	35.1	22.4
Androscoggin	44 006	64.6	154 800	24.1	15.2	694	29.7	2.4	56 165	-0.7	3 070	5.5	51 767	30.8	23.8
Aroostook	30 597	71.3	90 800	21.3	13.1	555	29.1	1.9	33 120	-2.4	2 533	7.6	31 593	29.3	26.9
Cumberland	117 359	68.2	241 800	24.5	14.5	938	31.7	3.3	159 417	-1.2	7 060	4.4	149 273	43.2	16.0
Franklin	12 098	77.6	132 400	22.5	11.1	630	33.9	2.6	15 086	-2.6	1 002	6.6	14 516	30.2	26.4
Hancock	24 355	74.2	198 300	24.7	13.6	790	31.6	1.5	29 849	-1.1	2 089	7.0	27 336	35.5	25.4
Kennebec	51 719	70.6	152 800	22.5	13.1	683	31.7	2.0	63 515	-0.8	3 438	5.4	57 918	35.0	22.3
Knox	16 941	78.9	195 700	25.9	14.3	789	29.6	2.7	20 735	-0.5	1 074	5.2	19 495	31.7	24.8
Lincoln	14 817	83.5	208 000	25.6	13.3	821	28.1	2.2	17 267	-0.7	1 021	5.9	16 463	35.9	25.8
Oxford	22 890	78.6	137 200	24.2	14.7	610	32.8	2.2	27 512	-1.3	1 924	7.0	25 527	26.9	31.6
Penobscot	62 608	66.9	137 700	22.5	13.4	724	33.1	3.1	79 253	-1.4	4 928	6.2	73 043	34.0	20.5
Piscataquis	7 769	76.9	105 000	23.4	14.9	580	28.6	1.9	7 769	-2.0	582	7.5	7 203	29.2	31.8
Sagadahoc	15 022	76.1	189 700	23.4	12.9	796	33.9	3.2	19 163	-0.1	888	4.6	17 782	37.8	20.3
Somerset	21 692	78.7	111 100	23.5	14.3	660	32.3	2.4	24 520	-1.4	1 945	7.9	22 432	26.8	32.2
Waldo	16 448	78.5	156 000	25.3	14.8	706	32.0	3.2	20 902	-0.6	1 280	6.1	18 064	32.6	25.7
Washington	14 209	76.8	103 500	23.7	14.0	571	27.5	1.6	14 567	-1.2	1 222	8.4	13 155	28.7	30.0
York	81 293	73.0	227 800	25.1	15.1	890	30.1	1.4	110 083	-1.2	5 812	5.3	101 532	34.5	22.7
MARYLAND	2 146 240	67.6	292 700	24.6	12.3	1 196	31.0	2.3	3 111 329	-0.4	181 352	5.8	2 926 198	44.2	15.7
Allegany	28 433	69.8	121 300	21.9	13.5	610	31.2	1.8	33 125	-1.0	2 424	7.3	29 916	29.1	23.1
Anne Arundel	199 904	74.2	340 000	24.2	11.5	1 454	29.8	2.0	295 723	-0.2	15 231	5.2	275 387	44.9	15.1
Baltimore	313 912	66.5	253 300	23.8	12.4	1 139	30.5	1.6	440 393	-0.4	27 310	6.2	408 629	43.4	15.6
Calvert	30 923	81.4	357 000	24.4	11.8	1 452	32.7	2.8	47 581	-0.2	2 503	5.3	45 481	40.8	19.4
Caroline	11 806	72.3	212 800	27.6	14.1	895	30.3	1.1	17 487	-1.0	1 106	6.3	15 086	26.4	28.5
Carroll	59 909	82.2	325 900	24.5	12.5	1 024	29.3	1.7	92 613	-0.4	4 523	4.9	87 873	43.9	17.9
Cecil	36 394	74.1	254 800	24.8	13.9	986	30.5	1.3	52 078	-0.1	3 413	6.6	48 437	34.6	24.0
Charles	51 247	79.4	297 900	24.8	11.7	1 463	33.3	2.2	79 850	-0.2	4 494	5.6	74 982	41.3	16.5
Dorchester	13 386	65.9	191 100	26.0	15.0	811	32.5	1.7	15 820	-0.8	1 344	8.5	14 761	27.7	30.3
Frederick	86 337	75.3	307 000	23.9	11.8	1 243	29.6	1.8	127 636	-0.5	6 498	5.1	124 307	46.5	14.9
Garrett	11 974	75.5	168 600	23.8	11.3	663	30.4	1.1	15 458	-1.4	1 069	6.9	13 986	30.0	28.5
Harford	90 708	80.2	281 800	24.0	12.2	1 119	30.1	1.9	135 057	-0.4	7 801	5.8	126 050	42.1	17.9
Howard	106 142	73.9	428 100	23.0	10.0	1 489	29.2	1.9	171 079	0.0	7 523	4.4	158 202	60.5	8.7
Kent	7 498	71.4	258 200	24.7	14.2	905	31.0	2.9	10 190	-1.4	665	6.5	8 833	38.7	20.5
Montgomery	360 563	67.3	446 300	23.8	10.8	1 568	30.5	3.7	540 128	-0.4	23 708	4.4	528 089	56.0	9.9
Prince George's	303 441	62.5	269 800	27.9	12.1	1 241	31.0	1.2	482 279	-0.4	28 297	5.9	455 167	37.2	18.0
Queen Anne's	17 292	84.5	348 100	25.8	13.0	1 215	29.9	2.1	26 258	-0.6	1 352	5.1	24 621	38.6	18.6

1. Specified owner-occupied units. 2. A value of 10.0 represents 10 percent or less; a value of 50.0 represents 50 percent or more. 3. Specified renter-occupied units.
4. Overcrowded or lacking complete plumbing facilities. 5. Percent of civilian labor force. 6. Persons 16 years old and over.

STATE County	Private nonfarm establishments, employment and payroll, 2013									Agriculture, 2012			
		Employment						Annual payroll		Farms			
											Percent with:		
	Number of establishments	Total	Health care and social assistance	Manufacturing	Retail trade	Finance and insurance	Professional, scientific, and technical services	Total (mil dol)	Average per employee (dollars)	Number	Fewer than 50 acres	500 acres or more	Farm operators whose principal occupation is farming (percent)
	104	105	106	107	108	109	110	111	112	113	114	115	116
LOUISIANA—Cont'd													
Orleans	8 669	164 374	21 900	5 336	12 134	5 942	13 194	7 655	46 573	14	100.0	0.0	64.3
Ouachita	4 180	63 093	14 465	5 023	9 354	4 681	2 789	2 170	34 400	450	48.2	9.1	41.1
Plaquemines	692	11 040	454	2 110	518	112	439	710	64 334	140	52.1	20.7	42.9
Pointe Coupee	370	4 164	D	D	822	184	91	168	40 247	393	39.4	18.1	47.1
Rapides	3 147	47 643	13 756	3 546	7 884	1 549	2 228	1 686	35 390	853	54.6	9.5	50.1
Red River	130	2 049	434	D	D	74	29	80	39 226	252	32.9	21.0	56.0
Richland	414	5 845	1 793	D	778	188	93	175	29 907	762	31.8	19.2	47.1
Sabine	481	4 416	845	798	877	D	257	147	33 181	392	37.5	4.3	51.3
St. Bernard	674	7 660	957	1 224	1 726	158	138	303	39 550	56	46.4	23.2	60.7
St. Charles	943	21 116	1 451	4 496	1 276	263	1 873	1 348	63 818	70	45.7	2.9	64.3
St. Helena	119	1 146	396	148	291	32	D	33	29 213	373	41.3	7.2	44.0
St. James	319	5 977	540	2 046	524	189	D	378	63 167	63	46.0	25.4	61.9
St. John the Baptist	714	13 888	1 218	3 028	1 604	291	387	694	50 002	23	39.1	13.0	56.5
St. Landry	1 602	23 819	5 970	1 429	3 845	801	577	852	35 783	1 338	51.0	10.6	40.3
St. Martin	954	12 683	1 750	1 796	1 548	322	327	534	42 127	340	64.1	12.1	44.4
St. Mary	1 315	23 119	1 874	4 735	2 261	514	657	1 116	48 287	128	46.9	32.0	50.8
St. Tammany	6 153	72 584	14 983	2 266	13 145	3 326	5 445	2 839	39 120	604	74.3	1.8	42.4
Tangipahoa	2 280	34 973	8 780	2 387	6 320	2 542	1 010	1 106	31 621	1 070	52.1	3.0	44.1
Tensas	85	522	74	D	79	D	D	20	38 536	251	27.1	29.1	37.8
Terrebonne	3 008	51 560	7 074	6 860	7 024	1 208	2 449	2 504	48 566	189	47.6	14.8	58.7
Union	327	4 129	751	D	579	123	61	121	29 224	413	31.0	4.1	48.2
Vermilion	1 045	10 590	1 773	469	2 037	456	323	403	38 060	1 184	43.2	10.9	53.7
Vernon	728	9 040	1 993	163	1 588	314	1 247	300	33 140	471	53.1	2.5	49.7
Washington	644	7 707	2 462	D	1 309	340	123	254	32 978	826	52.8	3.1	44.1
Webster	807	10 854	2 195	1 424	2 149	397	217	395	36 351	447	40.5	2.7	44.7
West Baton Rouge	544	11 049	433	2 173	1 132	194	190	498	45 036	106	66.0	15.1	50.9
West Carroll	188	1 776	555	D	437	65	38	45	25 410	733	28.5	9.5	25.0
West Feliciana	191	2 666	462	D	263	D	D	144	54 116	163	28.2	28.2	40.5
Winn	295	4 502	D	728	523	132	52	167	37 200	179	37.4	3.4	43.6
MAINE	40 257	487 313	106 533	48 609	80 618	26 773	22 911	18 739	38 454	8 173	43.0	6.7	48.5
Androscoggin	2 678	43 936	9 327	5 218	6 072	3 206	2 006	1 604	36 508	463	51.6	5.0	56.4
Aroostook	2 000	21 157	5 864	2 757	4 331	749	341	677	31 988	895	18.2	19.1	43.9
Cumberland	10 902	158 929	32 019	9 371	21 752	12 838	10 145	6 995	44 016	718	60.6	4.2	46.5
Franklin	821	9 064	1 723	D	1 719	D	118	263	29 069	388	43.6	3.9	34.3
Hancock	2 191	16 236	3 109	1 366	3 393	524	1 680	628	38 656	404	50.0	5.0	52.0
Kennebec	3 219	45 311	13 613	2 372	8 374	1 341	1 676	1 626	35 879	604	47.4	4.6	45.7
Knox	1 701	13 515	2 983	1 436	2 592	757	426	469	34 688	314	53.8	1.6	54.8
Lincoln	1 394	8 512	1 975	768	1 580	341	306	285	33 433	344	53.2	1.5	51.2
Oxford	1 287	14 320	2 770	2 529	2 200	332	297	459	32 080	551	44.5	6.4	44.8
Penobscot	4 104	57 343	13 919	3 472	11 147	2 027	1 805	2 012	35 079	677	36.9	7.7	51.7
Piscataquis	439	4 304	1 039	1 093	837	72	D	133	30 962	203	21.7	9.4	51.2
Sagadahoc	903	12 658	1 300	D	1 875	291	804	579	45 702	229	53.7	3.1	48.9
Somerset	1 172	13 570	2 704	D	2 280	256	341	507	37 360	579	32.5	11.4	50.3
Waldo	956	8 423	1 535	1 114	1 450	D	185	289	34 336	633	41.5	3.5	48.7
Washington	836	7 039	1 789	834	1 705	267	117	227	32 318	392	35.5	8.7	44.9
York	5 440	50 703	10 753	6 386	9 309	1 652	1 959	1 832	36 140	779	53.8	1.5	54.0
MARYLAND	135 421	2 182 260	353 520	100 437	286 943	99 107	266 902	108 759	49 838	12 256	49.2	7.6	48.9
Allegany	1 613	24 448	5 888	2 511	3 812	850	987	769	31 435	291	30.9	2.1	43.0
Anne Arundel	13 750	220 926	26 116	11 248	33 382	5 618	29 481	11 266	50 994	381	66.9	2.9	57.5
Baltimore	19 782	310 635	57 993	17 409	49 201	19 957	25 202	14 190	45 680	640	63.0	3.1	49.5
Calvert	1 688	17 437	3 485	438	3 006	366	1 167	715	41 025	269	49.4	5.9	45.0
Caroline	585	6 977	840	D	1 265	154	223	233	33 347	658	37.4	14.7	60.0
Carroll	4 255	49 243	10 127	3 380	8 239	1 131	2 517	1 771	35 965	1 092	59.3	4.9	39.7
Cecil	1 784	25 767	4 603	D	3 800	440	488	1 136	44 077	496	54.4	7.3	51.2
Charles	2 622	32 448	4 775	D	8 480	832	2 163	1 168	35 999	382	52.1	5.0	52.6
Dorchester	717	8 789	1 785	2 128	1 108	210	162	295	33 618	423	36.2	16.1	54.1
Frederick	5 955	83 799	11 318	6 003	12 291	6 016	7 898	3 709	44 264	1 308	49.5	6.0	47.6
Garrett	906	11 070	1 715	1 157	1 664	345	D	364	32 885	667	31.8	4.2	49.0
Harford	5 019	60 217	11 010	4 287	14 097	1 936	8 592	2 724	39 359	582	58.4	4.5	42.8
Howard	8 946	165 518	14 552	4 809	16 582	6 745	39 636	9 724	58 749	293	65.9	7.2	37.9
Kent	636	7 070	1 158	1 077	771	201	215	235	33 289	367	27.0	17.7	49.3
Montgomery	26 739	419 956	62 621	7 951	45 341	18 987	79 057	25 559	60 861	540	66.9	4.8	42.0
Prince George's	14 281	243 260	28 620	7 019	36 368	5 877	27 855	10 583	43 503	347	61.4	2.3	44.4
Queen Anne's	1 348	11 508	969	1 143	2 580	341	471	368	31 999	530	36.6	17.0	48.9

Agriculture, 2012 (cont.)

STATE County	Land in farms: Acreage (1,000)	Land in farms: Percent change, 2007–2012	Land in farms: Acres: Average size of farm	Land in farms: Acres: Total irrigated (1,000)	Land in farms: Acres: Total cropland (1,000)	Value of land and buildings (dollars): Average per farm	Value of land and buildings (dollars): Average per acre	Value of machinery and equipment, average per farm (dollars)	Value of products sold: Total (mil dol)	Value of products sold: Average per farm (dollars)	Value of products sold: Percent from: Crops	Value of products sold: Percent from: Livestock and poultry products	Percent of farms with sales of: $10,000 or more	Percent of farms with sales of: $100,000 or more	Government payments: Total ($1,000)	Government payments: Percent of farms
	117	118	119	120	121	122	123	124	125	126	127	128	129	130	131	132
LOUISIANA—Cont'd																
Orleans	111	D	8	0.0	0.0	122 786	15 486	114 143	0.5	37 143	41.2	59.0	42.9	7.1	D	7.1
Ouachita	93	9.1	207	12.1	47.4	603 420	2 916	72 287	49.1	109 047	54.9	45.1	29.3	9.8	1 933	25.8
Plaquemines	89	-26.8	635	0.1	8.5	801 564	1 262	64 250	15.0	107 457	39.1	61.0	61.4	15.0	60	7.9
Pointe Coupee	182	-4.4	464	6.1	143.8	1 272 481	2 744	240 089	130.1	331 163	95.8	4.2	58.8	18.3	2 786	41.0
Rapides	211	19.0	247	21.1	132.1	628 930	2 543	99 732	132.2	154 972	88.3	11.7	42.3	16.4	3 644	22.2
Red River	135	31.0	537	3.0	34.3	1 049 234	1 954	129 516	38.6	153 024	33.5	66.5	41.3	15.5	1 506	34.9
Richland	279	-4.2	366	85.1	189.5	840 475	2 296	126 639	127.3	167 038	93.5	6.5	37.1	18.2	10 171	76.1
Sabine	52	2.5	132	0.1	12.0	420 495	3 180	71 528	142.1	362 612	0.9	99.1	37.8	14.0	441	11.5
St. Bernard	32	-0.5	569	0.0	4.3	946 804	1 663	68 750	5.8	103 482	2.7	97.3	32.1	12.5	19	14.3
St. Charles	16	D	232	0.0	1.9	501 871	2 166	57 929	1.2	16 571	12.8	87.3	44.3	0.0	D	8.6
St. Helena	53	1.4	142	1.4	17.0	476 399	3 346	62 539	25.6	68 542	8.3	91.7	28.4	7.5	298	18.2
St. James	40	-7.7	634	0.0	37.1	2 231 444	3 520	369 730	33.2	526 270	98.8	1.2	58.7	28.6	84	17.5
St. John the Baptist	11	-21.5	468	0.0	8.0	1 361 261	2 910	240 391	9.3	402 696	98.6	1.4	43.5	13.0	D	4.3
St. Landry	301	0.8	225	29.8	223.9	540 722	2 405	90 250	125.0	93 408	91.7	8.3	28.3	9.7	5 809	39.3
St. Martin	76	-3.8	223	6.7	58.2	552 229	2 473	154 956	52.8	155 250	91.0	9.0	37.1	14.1	506	17.6
St. Mary	76	4.6	594	0.0	63.0	1 490 961	2 508	392 164	65.8	513 867	98.4	1.6	43.8	27.3	173	21.1
St. Tammany	34	-25.0	56	0.4	7.9	413 126	7 315	44 215	11.3	18 685	61.1	38.9	22.2	4.0	38	2.5
Tangipahoa	107	-13.8	100	0.7	36.3	410 570	4 117	54 967	45.7	42 694	40.2	59.8	29.1	7.2	790	17.3
Tensas	197	-12.8	783	40.3	168.2	1 721 227	2 197	275 825	129.2	514 558	99.8	0.2	37.5	29.5	7 350	86.5
Terrebonne	93	-47.9	492	0.6	21.5	1 102 540	2 243	147 534	37.1	196 418	43.6	56.4	37.0	13.2	95	9.0
Union	63	-7.0	152	0.0	16.8	441 254	2 909	75 138	92.9	224 986	1.5	98.5	40.7	15.3	166	9.2
Vermilion	284	-2.3	240	59.2	171.9	622 631	2 599	100 574	141.1	119 207	69.7	30.3	36.7	10.3	6 832	57.3
Vernon	49	-3.2	104	0.0	8.9	328 764	3 160	43 987	3.2	6 794	29.0	70.9	14.0	0.6	89	4.0
Washington	81	-16.7	99	0.4	28.6	349 438	3 545	54 988	28.3	34 259	40.2	59.8	23.0	4.4	434	14.6
Webster	52	5.6	117	D	10.1	407 367	3 483	51 532	10.1	22 501	17.3	82.7	27.1	2.2	81	7.2
West Baton Rouge	30	17.4	286	0.1	25.6	1 071 953	3 750	222 868	31.4	295 934	88.7	11.3	39.6	17.9	181	33.0
West Carroll	166	-15.8	226	45.2	115.9	482 630	2 135	86 151	72.5	98 966	97.1	2.9	19.9	11.3	5 879	83.8
West Feliciana	101	51.9	621	0.0	28.9	1 639 712	2 639	99 767	18.7	114 497	76.8	23.2	41.1	8.0	273	30.7
Winn	25	16.7	139	0.0	4.1	337 184	2 418	59 615	18.0	100 575	4.0	96.0	24.6	4.5	118	14.0
MAINE	1 454	7.9	178	30.9	477.3	410 633	2 308	69 762	763.1	93 364	62.1	37.9	34.6	9.5	10 162	16.3
Androscoggin	59	16.9	128	0.8	22.0	329 181	2 564	72 955	53.8	116 266	22.1	77.9	32.8	8.0	445	15.6
Aroostook	351	-6.6	392	11.4	187.5	559 514	1 427	157 318	210.5	235 215	91.6	8.4	42.9	21.5	2 492	43.0
Cumberland	63	21.2	87	0.7	18.0	428 535	4 907	61 922	26.3	36 635	65.6	34.4	33.7	7.5	497	8.1
Franklin	49	21.3	127	0.1	9.6	276 724	2 172	47 778	D	D	D	D	22.4	5.4	595	17.8
Hancock	53	1.2	132	0.2	12.0	444 960	3 369	51 351	D	D	D	D	38.6	6.9	187	14.9
Kennebec	78	-5.3	129	0.4	32.8	370 354	2 866	69 992	49.8	82 505	28.9	71.1	36.8	8.8	711	12.3
Knox	29	-2.3	94	0.3	7.5	355 739	3 798	35 876	D	D	D	D	31.2	4.1	116	14.6
Lincoln	32	5.2	92	0.1	7.4	320 218	3 489	43 009	10.2	29 541	51.2	48.8	32.8	5.5	269	7.8
Oxford	75	9.5	137	0.4	15.7	347 443	2 543	48 483	19.2	34 880	75.4	24.6	27.0	5.3	488	12.5
Penobscot	113	-1.4	167	2.3	35.6	336 186	2 015	63 316	50.2	74 084	32.3	67.7	33.4	9.0	1 044	13.3
Piscataquis	47	37.1	230	0.2	12.4	394 502	1 715	49 310	D	D	D	D	29.1	9.4	405	22.2
Sagadahoc	20	7.9	88	0.2	5.2	331 555	3 779	39 664	D	D	D	D	30.1	5.7	139	7.4
Somerset	140	25.7	242	0.2	30.2	512 425	2 119	92 294	86.4	149 278	64.1	35.9	44.7	19.2	1 053	16.6
Waldo	131	91.5	206	0.2	24.8	384 874	1 865	39 363	D	D	D	D	29.1	6.5	837	16.6
Washington	149	-5.9	380	12.1	35.7	594 518	1 564	79 079	154.6	394 508	D	D	45.7	9.4	526	18.6
York	65	8.7	83	1.3	21.0	403 257	4 869	58 392	27.5	35 239	D	D	31.8	6.4	358	5.9
MARYLAND	2 031	-1.0	166	104.9	1 396.1	1 148 268	6 930	115 879	2 271.4	185 329	46.3	53.7	43.1	20.6	36 024	37.8
Allegany	36	-1.0	125	0.0	11.8	435 282	3 493	52 261	3.1	10 735	59.5	40.5	30.6	1.0	253	31.6
Anne Arundel	28	-3.9	74	0.3	14.7	854 354	11 579	71 680	19.7	51 627	84.0	16.0	25.7	5.8	160	10.0
Baltimore	70	-10.0	110	0.5	44.6	1 038 656	9 440	91 152	76.3	119 228	88.6	11.4	34.5	12.5	840	18.3
Calvert	33	24.4	122	0.2	21.2	921 743	7 536	72 149	11.1	41 416	95.3	4.7	37.2	9.7	523	23.8
Caroline	150	14.5	229	27.0	121.4	1 395 853	6 109	155 213	257.9	391 968	33.1	66.9	68.2	46.0	3 335	61.7
Carroll	133	-6.6	121	1.4	97.2	989 130	8 144	101 499	111.6	102 232	67.3	32.7	34.5	12.6	3 440	40.2
Cecil	77	-9.8	155	0.6	54.8	1 121 347	7 255	132 554	113.8	229 466	60.3	39.7	43.8	19.4	1 505	30.4
Charles	47	-10.5	122	0.5	25.3	788 220	6 453	70 134	11.9	31 272	89.8	10.2	26.4	6.5	508	22.8
Dorchester	126	-5.1	299	22.4	92.0	1 557 508	5 211	204 546	187.1	442 215	37.3	62.7	51.1	40.0	2 501	75.9
Frederick	182	-10.2	139	1.4	127.1	1 053 941	7 595	108 462	150.5	115 030	49.5	50.5	41.1	17.9	3 060	33.6
Garrett	95	-0.3	143	0.0	41.5	600 378	4 207	80 346	31.5	47 168	34.7	65.3	46.0	14.4	540	18.9
Harford	65	-12.9	112	0.5	40.4	929 613	8 264	89 722	46.0	79 041	68.1	31.9	33.8	12.9	894	28.5
Howard	37	27.6	128	0.2	20.9	1 401 898	10 961	84 051	31.9	108 816	86.9	13.1	32.4	11.9	309	20.8
Kent	133	3.9	363	8.3	104.6	2 472 676	6 813	197 866	112.3	305 858	69.8	30.2	61.3	33.2	2 931	77.9
Montgomery	63	-6.1	118	1.0	45.6	1 195 894	10 171	101 435	48.3	89 520	86.6	13.4	29.1	10.6	836	17.2
Prince George's	33	-11.9	94	0.8	14.4	741 326	7 889	56 916	18.0	51 873	91.3	8.7	30.0	5.2	157	11.5
Queen Anne's	157	6.8	296	15.8	129.9	2 204 232	7 444	181 240	166.9	314 821	61.9	38.1	53.2	35.1	4 242	73.6

STATE County	Water use, 2010		Wholesale trade,[1] 2007				Retail trade,[2] 2007				Real estate and rental and leasing,[2] 2007			
	Total water withdrawn (mil gal/day)	Gallons withdrawn per person per day	Number of establish-ments	Number of employees	Sales (mil dol)	Annual payroll (mil dol)	Number of establish-ments	Number of employees	Sales (mil dol)	Annual payroll (mil dol)	Number of establish-ments	Number of employees	Receipts (mil dol)	Annual payroll (mil dol)
	133	134	135	136	137	138	139	140	141	142	143	144	145	146
LOUISIANA—Cont'd														
Orleans	615.3	1 790	253	3 030	1 938.4	145.6	1 155	11 877	2 718.0	305.5	362	1 764	354.4	61.8
Ouachita	68.2	443	184	D	D	D	738	9 569	2 221.6	195.7	193	862	149.4	27.4
Plaquemines	85.1	3 694	59	711	921.0	34.0	66	444	113.6	10.9	36	410	102.8	20.3
Pointe Coupee	343.8	15 077	8	79	177.0	3.1	89	1 016	216.3	16.6	12	34	11.0	1.4
Rapides	547.9	4 163	142	D	D	D	603	7 960	1 910.2	169.3	140	D	D	D
Red River	4.4	484	6	D	D	D	27	186	36.7	2.8	2	D	D	D
Richland	30.6	1 474	24	213	172.6	7.7	63	737	228.4	14.8	23	69	9.4	1.3
Sabine	4.2	172	12	D	D	D	81	824	172.7	15.4	14	46	6.5	1.5
St. Bernard	260.7	7 263	26	224	164.2	7.5	104	1 056	291.8	22.6	18	47	7.8	1.7
St. Charles	2 475.5	46 903	78	1 896	2 137.7	95.2	120	1 510	389.2	32.0	38	160	52.1	8.0
St. Helena	1.1	96	2	D	D	D	18	187	35.5	2.6	2	D	D	D
St. James	192.4	8 703	14	D	D	D	50	627	162.9	10.8	7	18	1.0	0.4
St. John the Baptist	67.5	1 471	31	672	2 540.8	36.6	114	1 742	454.8	35.5	36	188	53.2	7.5
St. Landry	77.3	926	59	D	D	D	326	4 132	970.7	83.1	57	184	21.2	4.2
St. Martin	39.5	757	45	655	326.1	21.9	137	1 581	407.6	34.5	42	659	213.0	38.7
St. Mary	120.7	2 208	81	D	D	D	209	2 396	508.2	46.7	90	667	155.9	29.0
St. Tammany	28.6	122	236	2 118	2 363.2	106.8	897	13 585	3 481.1	318.5	240	973	169.5	35.1
Tangipahoa	20.1	166	89	1 782	953.7	77.1	452	6 607	1 742.4	140.8	90	417	44.6	9.0
Tensas	31.7	6 043	9	D	D	D	18	116	31.8	2.0	2	D	D	D
Terrebonne	5.9	52	194	2 105	899.0	91.0	492	7 621	1 915.4	180.9	176	1 746	372.0	79.4
Union	4.1	179	6	D	D	D	71	690	148.1	12.3	5	12	1.7	0.3
Vermilion	93.7	1 616	40	D	D	D	197	2 054	518.3	43.8	43	482	55.7	14.2
Vernon	8.5	162	19	98	51.6	3.4	156	1 535	315.7	27.3	30	213	17.3	8.3
Washington	34.6	733	23	D	D	D	152	1 513	326.3	29.0	13	32	3.3	0.7
Webster	7.3	177	27	D	D	D	161	2 045	484.8	39.4	24	216	20.9	6.2
West Baton Rouge	10.8	454	34	578	602.2	27.7	78	1 202	319.7	22.4	11	76	2.1	0.6
West Carroll	15.2	1 308	7	D	D	D	29	397	67.7	6.1	7	24	2.4	0.4
West Feliciana	41.6	2 664	7	D	D	D	35	301	66.0	5.4	8	27	3.1	0.7
Winn	2.3	152	9	D	D	D	56	579	122.5	11.6	14	49	5.1	0.9
MAINE	449.3	338	1 439	16 939	8 823.7	686.4	6 911	83 279	20 444.0	1 893.7	1 771	6 942	1 054.0	209.4
Androscoggin	15.3	142	104	1 277	444.6	51.3	489	6 386	1 704.3	145.2	119	509	82.0	13.4
Aroostook	23.0	320	70	438	230.8	17.8	388	4 657	1 105.9	92.5	74	268	29.0	5.4
Cumberland	64.1	228	474	6 730	3 427.9	290.0	1 541	22 703	5 277.2	533.9	618	2 964	505.3	104.9
Franklin	39.1	1 270	16	D	D	D	166	1 678	381.3	35.4	29	120	10.7	2.7
Hancock	31.2	573	70	409	256.6	13.1	397	3 282	820.0	81.8	86	231	28.0	5.8
Kennebec	12.9	105	107	2 450	1 195.6	102.9	605	8 718	2 382.3	203.6	114	476	70.4	13.8
Knox	5.0	126	62	356	178.0	11.5	291	2 753	640.2	62.7	64	156	23.5	5.3
Lincoln	2.5	74	42	154	65.8	4.9	226	1 773	433.2	40.7	57	143	14.0	3.4
Oxford	37.2	644	30	470	188.3	17.9	253	2 286	489.5	47.4	49	172	17.6	3.7
Penobscot	58.4	379	158	D	D	D	777	10 842	2 983.9	241.6	172	782	124.9	21.8
Piscataquis	2.5	141	11	D	D	D	102	941	196.5	18.7	17	39	4.6	0.8
Sagadahoc	2.6	74	29	144	113.9	4.9	142	1 747	415.5	37.4	44	99	15.0	2.6
Somerset	72.9	1 396	27	350	76.7	9.4	239	2 358	577.3	49.4	35	122	13.6	2.8
Waldo	4.0	103	28	271	522.3	10.3	169	1 476	340.3	33.9	29	85	8.7	2.4
Washington	31.4	956	51	161	79.1	3.9	172	1 820	405.2	37.5	26	76	4.6	1.3
York	47.3	240	160	1 349	704.2	55.9	954	9 859	2 291.4	232.1	238	700	102.1	19.3
MARYLAND	7 382.0	1 279	5 020	79 868	51 276.8	4 158.4	19 601	294 806	75 664.2	7 290.8	6 768	49 766	12 391.9	2 262.6
Allegany	42.2	562	42	D	D	D	304	4 042	865.2	72.7	58	D	D	D
Anne Arundel	341.2	635	522	10 051	6 922.2	537.1	2 126	33 592	9 465.0	812.4	627	5 356	985.8	199.5
Baltimore	673.3	836	829	12 110	5 609.3	624.5	2 991	50 468	12 074.9	1 264.2	955	7 075	2 788.3	310.3
Calvert	3 265.4	36 798	32	151	43.7	5.5	230	3 042	730.6	67.7	107	465	115.1	17.1
Caroline	19.7	594	26	228	129.7	8.4	100	1 109	406.9	27.3	24	D	D	D
Carroll	13.8	83	139	1 604	556.1	63.8	580	8 764	2 141.8	188.9	177	D	D	D
Cecil	8.4	83	72	D	D	D	286	3 925	1 099.7	86.4	80	D	D	D
Charles	1 282.1	8 748	59	D	D	D	540	9 936	2 369.8	239.0	122	534	74.6	19.6
Dorchester	21.0	643	31	D	D	D	119	1 218	318.6	28.4	34	D	D	D
Frederick	40.6	174	208	2 481	1 252.1	123.6	790	12 349	3 066.3	296.9	267	1 439	231.1	50.5
Garrett	7.7	257	28	D	D	D	160	1 754	431.4	36.0	40	D	D	D
Harford	19.1	78	191	2 139	1 871.3	95.6	771	12 630	3 380.3	308.6	216	1 017	173.2	31.7
Howard	4.1	14	478	11 257	7 170.8	654.1	866	16 094	4 555.0	424.8	406	3 189	1 040.7	176.3
Kent	5.2	257	26	D	D	D	106	990	197.1	20.4	39	D	D	D
Montgomery	737.9	759	735	9 168	7 426.6	576.9	2 952	48 390	13 255.8	1 357.8	1 465	15 301	4 335.6	871.7
Prince George's	745.3	863	582	12 603	10 449.8	634.4	2 265	37 623	9 209.7	944.3	740	6 315	1 118.6	246.8
Queen Anne's	14.0	294	68	509	212.9	22.6	249	2 822	618.3	61.9	68	D	D	D

1. Merchant wholesalers, except manufacturers' sales branches and offices. 2. Employer establishments.

Table B. States and Counties — Professional Services, Manufacturing, and Accommodation and Food Services

STATE County	Professional, scientific, and technical services,[1] 2007				Manufacturing, 2007				Accommodation and food services, 2007			
	Number of establish-ments	Number of employees	Receipts (mil dol)	Annual payroll (mil dol)	Number of establish-ments	Number of employees	Receipts (mil dol)	Annual payroll (mil dol)	Number of establish-ments	Number of employees	Sales (mil dol)	Annual payroll (mil dol)
	147	148	149	150	151	152	153	154	155	156	157	158
LOUISIANA—Cont'd												
Orleans	1 290	D	D	D	141	7 607	3 088.9	402.0	1 058	28 356	2 148.2	602.4
Ouachita	441	D	D	D	135	D	D	D	285	6 554	250.3	67.8
Plaquemines	49	691	123.1	41.4	39	2 253	D	151.0	43	616	43.2	14.5
Pointe Coupee	31	120	13.3	4.3	NA	NA	NA	NA	30	363	14.0	3.3
Rapides	281	1 746	207.2	69.2	77	D	D	192.7	224	D	D	D
Red River	7	26	2.3	0.7	NA	NA	NA	NA	9	86	3.5	1.0
Richland	31	111	9.2	2.5	NA	NA	NA	NA	22	359	14.6	3.4
Sabine	39	165	12.8	5.5	21	893	D	34.8	17	282	14.0	3.2
St. Bernard	39	161	13.6	3.4	34	1 371	D	105.1	61	869	36.3	9.2
St. Charles	85	621	68.9	28.7	38	4 864	27 354.7	440.7	81	951	40.1	10.5
St. Helena	8	42	2.4	0.7	NA	NA	NA	NA	9	47	1.7	0.4
St. James	16	46	4.0	1.3	28	2 396	D	184.1	23	330	12.0	3.1
St. John the Baptist	55	341	42.9	11.7	28	2 426	D	178.5	71	1 427	55.5	13.9
St. Landry	130	605	66.6	23.3	55	1 732	D	68.9	97	1 454	56.6	13.9
St. Martin	78	D	D	D	58	1 361	324.3	51.0	77	983	45.1	10.9
St. Mary	106	694	104.2	42.9	90	4 417	2 011.1	200.6	107	1 597	60.3	15.9
St. Tammany	791	D	D	D	136	2 468	436.3	98.1	484	8 601	370.7	105.3
Tangipahoa	189	D	D	D	92	2 773	D	81.3	225	4 169	164.6	41.3
Tensas	4	D	D	D	NA	NA	NA	NA	7	19	0.5	0.2
Terrebonne	280	D	D	D	126	5 107	1 115.6	240.3	238	4 780	233.1	68.9
Union	21	D	D	D	11	D	D	D	17	244	10.2	2.5
Vermilion	109	288	30.7	9.7	42	903	D	30.4	64	1 038	51.1	10.1
Vernon	45	747	64.7	26.2	NA	NA	NA	NA	62	1 150	39.8	11.5
Washington	49	195	23.0	6.5	35	1 383	D	75.3	61	676	28.1	6.8
Webster	52	274	15.8	5.2	33	2 237	712.0	75.3	64	801	28.7	6.3
West Baton Rouge	28	190	25.4	7.1	36	2 442	D	123.4	47	753	35.2	8.2
West Carroll	11	21	1.8	0.5	NA	NA	NA	NA	10	76	4.1	1.0
West Feliciana	17	39	4.2	1.6	6	D	D	D	27	358	11.8	3.3
Winn	15	D	D	D	19	852	D	34.8	19	316	11.2	2.4
MAINE	3 444	20 504	2 686.1	1 004.9	1 825	58 938	16 363.2	2 524.5	3 938	49 363	2 515.8	747.7
Androscoggin	182	D	D	D	158	6 945	2 186.2	300.2	226	3 422	149.7	44.0
Aroostook	104	D	D	D	103	2 441	621.6	82.3	151	1 833	71.8	20.9
Cumberland	1 350	D	D	D	423	11 005	D	479.2	898	14 351	734.9	222.3
Franklin	49	D	D	D	32	1 721	823.5	83.7	90	1 220	43.0	13.0
Hancock	136	D	D	D	107	1 838	599.1	93.3	304	2 245	167.5	45.8
Kennebec	276	D	D	D	113	2 557	584.1	104.6	300	4 073	198.5	59.6
Knox	138	D	D	D	97	1 676	387.0	65.0	178	1 697	90.1	28.4
Lincoln	105	D	D	D	78	762	122.6	27.6	152	987	72.0	20.9
Oxford	79	D	D	D	72	2 682	865.8	132.6	144	2 402	92.6	29.9
Penobscot	333	D	D	D	155	4 795	1 088.5	171.9	320	5 179	224.2	68.1
Piscataquis	10	D	D	D	27	856	119.4	26.6	49	321	13.6	3.6
Sagadahoc	95	D	D	D	41	D	D	D	81	1 048	51.5	16.7
Somerset	63	394	34.5	17.6	71	3 532	1 566.9	163.6	111	1 070	45.0	13.2
Waldo	62	185	18.9	6.6	54	1 487	210.3	42.8	88	794	37.6	10.3
Washington	39	D	D	D	43	980	444.1	42.4	92	616	24.7	6.6
York	423	D	D	D	251	D	2 904.3	D	754	8 105	499.1	144.3
MARYLAND	19 345	D	D	D	3 680	127 780	41 456.1	6 453.7	10 802	192 619	10 758.4	2 915.9
Allegany	108	D	D	D	60	2 679	D	108.9	174	2 848	124.7	34.4
Anne Arundel	2 032	19 275	3 344.9	1 310.5	333	14 020	3 610.1	995.5	1 052	22 159	1 288.1	344.0
Baltimore	2 770	23 340	3 127.1	1 295.0	512	21 919	9 247.2	1 174.1	1 546	27 814	1 414.1	385.4
Calvert	202	D	D	D	49	D	D	D	122	2 518	110.7	30.9
Caroline	39	D	D	D	35	1 351	329.0	43.8	36	466	18.9	4.5
Carroll	470	D	D	D	155	4 369	1 095.1	203.2	251	5 293	203.8	61.2
Cecil	181	D	D	D	55	4 006	1 301.1	229.2	171	2 648	133.4	35.7
Charles	265	D	D	D	62	910	158.0	35.3	231	4 741	231.6	63.3
Dorchester	49	170	16.0	6.3	56	3 077	991.9	99.3	62	1 274	81.8	20.4
Frederick	815	D	D	D	181	7 076	3 003.7	334.7	392	7 542	356.5	106.0
Garrett	58	305	26.8	13.6	54	909	143.2	29.1	79	1 059	47.3	13.8
Harford	614	D	D	D	161	5 578	2 016.1	256.0	367	7 942	361.9	96.7
Howard	1 700	D	D	D	233	6 736	2 368.3	334.6	535	10 804	565.7	160.0
Kent	59	D	D	D	29	1 065	290.2	36.9	63	676	36.0	10.6
Montgomery	5 584	D	D	D	459	10 798	3 264.1	648.1	1 753	30 058	1 872.8	508.1
Prince George's	1 639	D	D	D	347	9 985	2 504.7	494.2	1 186	20 563	1 205.0	312.2
Queen Anne's	174	D	D	D	50	1 224	238.8	48.0	94	1 937	103.0	30.8

1. Establishment subject to federal tax.

Table B. States and Counties — **Health Care and Social Assistance, Other Services, Nonemployer Businesses, and Residential Construction**

STATE County	Health care and social assistance, 2007				Other services, 2007				Nonemployer businesses, 2013		Value of residential construction authorized by building permits, 2014	
	Number of establish-ments	Number of employees	Receipts (mil dol)	Annual payroll (mil dol)	Number of establish-ments	Number of employees	Receipts (mil dol)	Annual payroll (mil dol)	Number	Receipts (mil dol)	New Construction ($1,000)	Number of housing units
	159	160	161	162	163	164	165	166	167	168	169	170
LOUISIANA—Cont'd												
Orleans	804	16 725	2 039.5	708.6	601	3 875	654.7	107.0	34 136	1 403.2	201 755	1 026
Ouachita	587	12 571	1 137.4	400.5	227	1 524	134.4	37.2	12 275	503.6	112 508	704
Plaquemines	25	D	D	D	45	D	D	D	2 248	144.7	16 172	75
Pointe Coupee	36	588	36.6	15.1	26	D	D	D	1 447	68.8	13 963	54
Rapides	487	D	D	D	228	1 192	101.7	27.8	7 650	337.6	48 875	282
Red River	17	465	27.7	12.0	9	D	D	D	540	14.1	0	0
Richland	65	1 633	95.4	39.5	23	71	5.9	1.3	1 405	48.5	7 843	33
Sabine	41	810	42.8	15.7	25	97	6.4	1.5	1 360	65.7	14 681	67
St. Bernard	45	374	31.6	10.5	32	D	D	D	3 167	133.2	6 313	39
St. Charles	74	1 397	85.3	36.9	56	344	63.0	16.2	3 955	172.6	24 106	108
St. Helena	15	376	18.4	8.9	4	D	D	D	787	19.2	0	0
St. James	29	441	32.4	13.6	13	42	4.1	0.9	1 431	41.9	12 385	47
St. John the Baptist	73	D	D	D	48	D	D	D	3 266	89.8	5 944	35
St. Landry	275	4 794	424.4	150.3	77	363	24.1	7.6	5 606	211.6	30 905	144
St. Martin	69	1 334	57.6	27.9	46	109	12.2	2.5	4 263	159.2	35 182	178
St. Mary	105	1 931	136.8	50.2	91	447	56.2	14.4	3 824	164.7	10 311	58
St. Tammany	715	12 287	1 256.7	485.5	364	2 053	168.1	51.9	22 693	1 188.5	304 234	1 315
Tangipahoa	269	7 321	568.5	226.1	150	919	86.4	21.7	9 305	344.5	78 352	592
Tensas	11	D	D	D	NA	NA	NA	NA	323	11.7	791	10
Terrebonne	255	6 396	619.2	253.0	173	1 575	222.5	63.2	7 805	389.9	75 448	266
Union	29	740	43.5	15.7	18	49	4.1	0.8	1 458	53.3	3 686	22
Vermilion	104	1 458	100.3	38.8	58	248	22.5	5.5	4 209	174.9	32 046	154
Vernon	70	1 620	170.7	55.0	50	324	32.7	9.3	2 026	77.3	16 720	76
Washington	89	1 933	132.1	55.3	42	189	13.5	3.4	2 944	102.3	13 166	68
Webster	92	2 374	166.5	59.4	36	227	20.3	5.5	2 668	104.6	6 638	29
West Baton Rouge	28	D	D	D	32	201	29.7	7.6	1 623	63.8	36 851	240
West Carroll	17	653	32.0	12.8	15	68	3.7	1.2	640	23.6	0	0
West Feliciana	20	321	26.0	9.4	7	D	D	D	759	30.2	11 733	38
Winn	43	820	52.6	21.9	18	111	10.5	4.1	659	33.7	0	0
MAINE	4 875	104 151	8 592.4	3 691.6	2 840	13 297	1 279.7	328.1	109 260	4 657.2	612 903	3 242
Androscoggin	421	9 495	872.4	355.7	203	945	69.8	21.2	5 969	269.9	17 348	91
Aroostook	252	6 327	419.9	188.5	134	410	37.3	8.8	4 148	159.4	7 825	66
Cumberland	1 316	29 849	2 669.0	1 155.5	764	4 199	398.0	107.0	26 119	1 296.1	187 702	906
Franklin	100	1 888	132.8	55.7	51	204	19.4	4.1	2 389	79.7	11 517	58
Hancock	160	2 936	252.3	110.6	137	749	120.8	22.8	7 451	318.5	51 116	183
Kennebec	496	11 949	996.5	435.9	292	1 289	146.4	36.0	8 198	304.8	42 850	344
Knox	177	3 111	215.9	88.8	118	545	58.5	15.1	5 681	272.5	23 056	101
Lincoln	102	1 878	131.4	52.9	97	491	38.4	12.2	4 587	179.0	13 645	56
Oxford	155	2 961	217.3	87.0	95	354	32.9	8.1	4 268	163.3	32 627	164
Penobscot	563	14 538	1 318.9	561.5	276	1 350	139.8	33.6	9 215	340.3	34 741	231
Piscataquis	44	1 420	81.8	38.9	21	69	6.0	1.4	1 179	38.9	2 414	20
Sagadahoc	117	1 372	80.3	34.0	65	326	27.0	8.3	3 109	116.3	18 177	97
Somerset	153	3 119	202.8	88.7	94	340	25.5	6.6	3 294	111.4	4 764	37
Waldo	111	1 526	116.3	52.0	75	243	23.3	5.4	3 756	127.3	14 343	76
Washington	110	2 256	147.2	70.0	59	191	18.0	5.0	3 649	155.7	4 780	41
York	598	9 526	737.7	315.7	359	1 592	118.8	32.6	16 248	723.9	135 641	693
MARYLAND	15 304	315 781	33 826.6	13 089.4	10 365	77 368	9 688.6	2 487.4	456 511	19 220.0	2 889 171	16 331
Allegany	256	5 848	558.7	209.7	159	858	63.4	17.4	3 087	119.4	2 993	25
Anne Arundel	1 184	21 198	2 092.9	851.2	1 095	7 437	691.4	232.8	39 029	1 851.9	365 193	2 441
Baltimore	2 645	57 385	5 767.6	2 276.7	1 499	10 625	1 072.8	320.0	62 218	2 740.8	177 875	1 004
Calvert	173	3 200	300.6	114.6	131	770	58.6	19.2	6 181	249.3	45 307	213
Caroline	49	667	33.3	17.6	52	226	19.0	5.4	2 508	92.3	6 161	35
Carroll	457	8 597	854.7	308.0	352	2 086	147.9	49.5	11 771	483.9	72 114	355
Cecil	155	5 507	637.1	280.1	152	838	65.9	19.1	5 613	240.8	80 106	278
Charles	311	4 069	384.7	150.7	231	1 471	114.6	38.3	9 636	337.5	189 167	790
Dorchester	85	1 626	130.9	56.6	63	280	18.0	4.6	2 384	83.8	4 668	27
Frederick	531	9 326	936.8	368.8	400	2 549	266.1	76.0	17 140	760.4	199 175	1 311
Garrett	73	1 602	95.8	42.7	77	702	44.7	18.3	2 394	102.7	31 364	85
Harford	545	8 231	782.3	297.9	436	2 714	196.2	65.0	15 018	663.1	142 856	860
Howard	804	12 295	1 131.0	458.3	524	4 238	452.0	147.4	24 634	1 252.8	291 524	1 446
Kent	72	1 333	121.6	47.2	52	191	21.4	5.3	1 808	81.8	12 512	54
Montgomery	3 376	54 741	6 553.4	2 574.9	1 939	17 446	3 379.3	756.2	103 731	5 249.1	625 089	3 839
Prince George's	1 763	27 511	2 588.3	1 026.7	1 212	9 385	968.3	278.2	71 062	1 958.7	275 090	1 292
Queen Anne's	67	873	56.0	24.7	109	596	47.2	12.5	4 621	247.7	29 618	173

STATE County	Government employment and payroll, 2012: Full-time equivalent employees	Government employment and payroll, 2012: March payroll (dollars)	March payroll (percent of total): Administration, judicial, and legal	March payroll (percent of total): Police and Corrections	March payroll (percent of total): Fire Protection	March payroll (percent of total): Highways and transportation	March payroll (percent of total): Health and Welfare	March payroll (percent of total): Natural resources and utilities	March payroll (percent of total): Education and libraries	Local government finances, 2012, General revenue: Total (mil dol)	General revenue: Intergovernmental (mil dol)	Taxes: Total (mil dol)	Taxes, Per capita[1] (dollars): Total	Taxes, Per capita[1] (dollars): Property
	171	172	173	174	175	176	177	178	179	180	181	182	183	184
LOUISIANA—Cont'd														
Orleans	7 189	28 500 562	12.7	30.3	9.1	2.5	3.8	25.1	9.9	1 968.9	669.4	766.2	2 075	1 020
Ouachita	7 210	21 316 630	7.2	10.3	3.6	2.2	3.7	5.2	67.2	636.4	302.9	268.8	1 730	618
Plaquemines	1 620	5 259 702	13.4	13.1	0.6	7.9	7.0	6.2	48.6	320.9	176.8	96.4	4 031	2 274
Pointe Coupee	1 063	2 905 856	7.3	13.8	0.0	1.6	21.6	5.3	50.2	93.0	34.1	31.6	1 391	766
Rapides	5 615	17 417 361	10.4	15.6	7.9	3.6	1.4	5.7	52.6	487.4	230.0	195.3	1 475	567
Red River	533	1 454 876	5.8	37.4	0.0	1.9	0.9	1.0	50.4	43.6	18.0	22.1	2 455	992
Richland	1 229	3 799 353	5.9	17.8	0.1	3.2	35.8	2.3	34.3	105.4	49.7	25.9	1 238	508
Sabine	818	2 028 527	9.4	18.3	0.0	4.8	3.6	7.0	55.7	96.4	47.5	40.6	1 668	405
St. Bernard	1 804	5 761 067	8.7	16.2	6.9	6.4	1.4	5.2	54.8	484.3	396.4	68.9	1 655	655
St. Charles	3 451	12 023 950	5.4	15.1	0.0	1.8	10.8	8.5	57.6	387.0	80.9	211.6	4 016	2 217
St. Helena	456	1 219 647	8.6	9.7	0.0	3.8	45.3	1.3	30.5	32.8	13.8	7.5	676	349
St. James	1 306	4 803 097	7.4	11.1	0.0	2.6	16.4	8.2	49.6	231.2	42.5	70.5	3 247	1 994
St. John the Baptist	1 701	5 496 602	10.6	10.0	0.0	8.8	0.1	9.7	60.5	229.3	53.3	82.6	1 845	913
St. Landry	4 416	14 852 877	5.9	10.1	3.0	2.4	26.6	3.1	48.4	409.3	165.3	100.0	1 196	372
St. Martin	1 824	5 579 531	5.5	14.8	0.1	2.7	7.9	2.9	65.6	147.8	80.2	54.1	1 026	489
St. Mary	3 043	9 174 661	6.1	12.3	1.5	2.5	10.9	8.1	57.1	251.5	102.3	102.4	1 907	1 061
St. Tammany	10 707	35 822 862	5.7	10.3	0.3	2.6	33.9	2.1	44.3	1 250.6	404.2	450.6	1 882	995
Tangipahoa	6 393	23 444 209	4.2	6.0	1.2	1.7	46.4	1.8	37.5	621.2	213.8	128.9	1 044	366
Tensas	264	627 291	16.3	4.0	0.0	4.9	1.7	3.9	68.6	27.3	17.2	7.3	1 474	872
Terrebonne	5 509	18 140 503	3.6	8.6	1.2	1.4	31.1	4.6	49.2	603.6	234.4	173.9	1 554	551
Union	834	2 308 579	6.3	18.6	0.2	2.1	11.0	6.9	53.9	62.9	32.1	20.7	923	359
Vermilion	2 406	8 239 940	6.2	8.3	1.8	3.2	23.4	6.7	50.2	227.6	95.5	73.9	1 258	572
Vernon	2 133	5 249 110	6.4	9.9	1.2	3.6	0.1	1.9	76.0	155.1	98.2	46.0	855	294
Washington	1 946	5 729 429	5.2	6.2	1.5	2.7	14.9	1.9	66.9	160.0	81.0	45.0	964	454
Webster	1 523	4 175 873	6.3	15.2	1.4	3.3	0.1	7.0	65.3	133.5	64.2	57.4	1 402	613
West Baton Rouge	1 000	3 133 887	7.9	4.1	2.2	2.9	2.9	12.2	62.7	112.9	36.3	55.4	2 296	1 199
West Carroll	438	1 121 168	6.5	2.8	0.0	4.1	3.9	2.4	79.0	46.7	23.8	13.0	1 133	428
West Feliciana	748	2 572 616	10.2	10.9	0.2	3.9	16.8	3.4	53.6	68.8	21.1	29.6	1 922	1 366
Winn	679	1 633 669	7.5	13.5	1.8	3.1	0.7	8.9	63.3	42.7	25.9	13.6	909	416
MAINE	X	X	X	X	X	X	X	X	X	X	X	X	X	X
Androscoggin	3 959	13 779 680	4.1	8.3	4.8	4.2	2.0	5.1	70.2	355.6	153.6	163.3	1 517	1 507
Aroostook	3 302	10 418 372	5.5	4.9	2.0	3.8	16.3	5.3	61.4	264.2	111.0	83.6	1 180	1 174
Cumberland	10 861	40 790 587	5.2	9.0	5.8	4.8	5.4	6.8	61.0	1 129.5	280.4	610.0	2 149	2 117
Franklin	1 043	3 602 511	5.4	8.2	1.3	4.4	1.5	4.1	73.6	80.5	29.1	43.4	1 418	1 414
Hancock	1 982	6 326 482	6.8	6.5	2.5	3.7	1.0	4.2	73.3	197.6	39.3	137.4	2 518	2 502
Kennebec	4 312	13 281 549	5.2	7.6	3.0	3.6	1.2	5.8	72.6	343.2	144.3	155.9	1 280	1 266
Knox	1 307	4 815 634	8.9	8.8	3.1	4.4	3.3	2.5	67.5	129.9	19.5	90.5	2 283	2 267
Lincoln	1 389	4 505 799	5.7	4.0	0.5	2.0	2.2	3.4	80.2	135.6	34.2	88.2	2 582	2 572
Oxford	2 319	7 212 500	4.7	5.3	2.5	4.9	0.8	2.5	78.4	186.7	69.4	103.9	1 807	1 800
Penobscot	5 352	18 128 721	5.6	7.8	5.2	7.6	1.3	6.1	64.9	466.9	185.2	205.7	1 338	1 324
Piscataquis	1 109	4 071 817	4.7	4.0	0.2	1.9	47.9	1.9	38.2	99.6	35.5	26.2	1 514	1 504
Sagadahoc	1 209	4 568 672	5.0	6.6	2.7	2.7	1.0	3.8	74.9	131.3	38.0	73.7	2 093	2 078
Somerset	2 667	8 560 527	3.4	6.5	1.2	2.5	0.5	1.6	82.6	185.9	90.8	84.4	1 626	1 622
Waldo	1 256	3 892 726	8.1	6.4	0.8	2.8	1.9	2.4	74.8	102.4	36.3	56.7	1 460	1 455
Washington	1 219	3 492 782	6.9	7.3	1.2	2.6	3.5	5.0	70.9	100.0	42.2	47.1	1 450	1 445
York	7 047	25 948 699	5.4	9.0	4.1	3.0	1.2	5.9	70.5	637.1	181.5	390.3	1 961	1 938
MARYLAND	X	X	X	X	X	X	X	X	X	X	X	X	X	X
Allegany	2 826	11 858 505	3.5	6.0	2.0	3.5	0.4	6.3	75.4	272.3	133.1	86.3	1 167	773
Anne Arundel	17 468	83 267 035	4.0	8.6	6.2	4.4	2.8	3.8	67.7	2 076.5	568.1	1 135.3	2 062	1 152
Baltimore	26 532	122 265 325	4.1	12.0	5.2	1.3	3.0	2.6	69.5	2 786.6	910.6	1 567.3	1 917	1 039
Calvert	3 256	15 584 064	4.8	7.8	0.1	1.9	2.8	4.8	74.3	388.6	117.7	224.0	2 500	1 684
Caroline	1 269	4 767 293	5.8	8.2	0.0	2.2	3.3	4.6	71.4	117.5	59.9	45.1	1 379	973
Carroll	5 844	23 979 765	5.5	5.5	0.7	1.6	1.0	2.9	80.6	641.8	205.1	366.2	2 190	1 331
Cecil	3 436	14 149 378	4.6	8.1	1.2	1.6	2.8	2.0	76.9	375.0	153.4	172.0	1 691	1 137
Charles	5 864	27 330 417	4.8	12.4	0.0	0.6	3.1	3.7	73.5	663.0	226.7	318.3	2 114	1 346
Dorchester	1 251	4 831 214	5.1	13.0	0.0	3.8	4.8	2.5	66.5	134.8	62.3	54.8	1 683	1 219
Frederick	10 553	47 827 090	4.3	6.4	4.0	1.9	4.9	3.7	73.1	1 033.9	315.3	529.5	2 210	1 385
Garrett	1 283	4 466 807	6.7	4.8	0.8	10.6	1.8	3.9	70.1	214.5	59.8	111.5	3 734	2 998
Harford	8 483	39 111 192	6.1	9.6	0.3	2.6	1.8	4.3	73.8	952.9	307.2	524.4	2 109	1 291
Howard	12 202	62 646 998	4.3	7.7	1.9	1.0	4.2	4.1	75.2	1 532.5	372.1	962.2	3 214	1 692
Kent	708	2 731 612	8.4	10.5	0.0	4.3	1.1	5.9	64.0	74.9	18.1	46.4	2 298	1 677
Montgomery	38 590	236 750 984	3.3	7.6	4.0	3.0	6.2	10.6	64.3	5 240.0	1 125.4	3 182.9	3 168	1 422
Prince George's	27 062	140 810 958	4.4	15.2	3.4	1.2	4.0	1.6	67.6	3 399.7	1 344.2	1 551.8	1 761	1 007
Queen Anne's	1 906	8 133 110	4.6	6.4	0.2	2.6	7.3	5.6	72.6	207.2	65.4	111.4	2 293	1 412

1. Based on the resident population estimated as of July 1 of the year shown.

STATE County	Local government finances, 2012 (cont.)									Government employment, 2013			Presidential election,[2] 2012		
	Direct general expenditure							Debt outstanding					Percent of vote cast:		
			Percent of total for:												
	Total (mil dol)	Per capita[1] (dollars)	Educa-tion	Health and hospitals	Police protec-tion	Public welfare	High-ways	Total (mil dol)	Per capita[1] (dollars)	Federal civilian	Federal military	State and local	Demo-cratic	Republi-can	All other
	185	186	187	188	189	190	191	192	193	194	195	196	197	198	199
LOUISIANA—Cont'd															
Orleans	1 848.6	5 006	12.2	0.7	7.8	0.1	6.6	2 707.7	7 333	9 137	4 051	28 706	79.4	19.1	1.5
Ouachita	687.9	4 428	53.4	2.3	5.8	0.1	2.6	489.7	3 152	435	723	10 803	36.9	62.1	1.0
Plaquemines	321.2	13 429	37.8	2.1	4.1	0.5	1.0	163.7	6 844	645	500	1 859	32.3	66.0	1.7
Pointe Coupee	90.9	4 001	37.3	22.2	6.6	0.4	2.1	45.9	2 021	55	107	1 106	44.4	53.9	1.7
Rapides	504.4	3 810	49.3	0.1	8.4	0.1	5.3	504.4	3 811	2 265	617	9 929	35.0	63.6	1.4
Red River	47.2	5 251	59.8	0.0	3.7	0.0	1.4	5.0	560	25	42	480	44.9	53.7	1.4
Richland	109.4	5 231	36.1	29.1	3.4	0.1	5.6	51.6	2 464	80	95	1 046	36.1	62.6	1.3
Sabine	85.0	3 493	69.8	0.2	4.8	0.0	5.6	27.9	1 145	39	114	1 310	23.3	74.9	1.9
St. Bernard	516.0	12 393	31.7	3.5	2.5	0.2	1.3	186.9	4 490	43	207	2 176	25.8	71.2	3.0
St. Charles	382.3	7 256	43.1	9.6	4.8	0.3	5.3	894.4	16 978	145	250	3 623	33.6	64.8	1.6
St. Helena	32.3	2 917	31.4	38.0	4.6	0.0	8.8	5.1	457	0	52	585	57.7	40.8	1.5
St. James	156.3	7 194	43.5	11.8	3.9	0.6	2.5	1 439.8	66 281	33	103	1 432	55.7	43.2	1.1
St. John the Baptist	252.0	5 630	34.8	0.5	4.6	0.5	5.1	1 281.3	28 626	108	208	2 049	57.4	41.2	1.5
St. Landry	414.8	4 958	43.1	29.0	4.8	0.0	3.0	98.9	1 182	159	396	5 392	47.7	50.9	1.4
St. Martin	141.4	2 682	59.3	0.9	8.4	0.2	5.1	123.9	2 349	60	251	2 205	38.8	59.6	1.6
St. Mary	245.0	4 562	42.6	10.2	6.7	0.2	3.8	139.7	2 602	132	373	4 784	40.8	57.6	1.6
St. Tammany	1 244.6	5 198	37.0	28.1	5.6	0.3	4.8	977.9	4 084	492	1 156	12 918	22.5	75.8	1.7
Tangipahoa	692.4	5 610	29.5	47.0	3.7	0.0	2.7	361.5	2 929	310	585	10 019	33.8	64.7	1.5
Tensas	26.2	5 284	36.9	2.0	4.8	0.0	4.9	26.6	5 361	24	23	315	54.1	45.0	0.9
Terrebonne	620.6	5 546	29.9	28.6	4.4	0.3	2.9	301.9	2 698	267	574	5 568	28.5	69.3	2.2
Union	60.2	2 685	49.1	8.9	5.4	0.2	6.0	5.9	265	89	105	780	28.6	70.1	1.3
Vermilion	223.8	3 812	42.2	20.8	4.9	2.1	5.1	37.7	643	134	294	2 811	25.2	72.8	2.0
Vernon	159.1	2 953	69.0	0.3	5.5	0.1	5.4	78.1	1 451	2 246	9 122	2 427	22.4	75.8	1.8
Washington	160.8	3 445	54.9	14.8	4.7	0.0	5.1	63.6	1 363	96	215	3 165	32.9	65.6	1.5
Webster	135.1	3 299	55.0	0.5	6.2	0.1	4.2	123.2	3 010	106	189	2 016	36.2	62.5	1.3
West Baton Rouge	118.0	4 896	36.6	0.9	8.9	0.6	4.0	182.2	7 559	61	115	1 506	42.5	56.1	1.4
West Carroll	47.4	4 114	52.9	20.0	3.8	2.1	3.9	8.1	701	32	53	752	17.6	81.1	1.3
West Feliciana	67.9	4 410	41.6	23.6	6.1	0.1	2.4	71.0	4 612	13	49	2 331	43.0	56.0	1.0
Winn	46.7	3 110	63.7	0.5	5.9	0.0	4.7	11.5	766	55	63	745	30.2	68.4	1.4
MAINE	X	X	X	X	X	X	X	X	X	14 157	7 145	85 639	57.7	40.4	1.9
Androscoggin	348.5	3 239	53.0	0.2	4.0	0.4	5.6	353.5	3 285	265	346	5 019	56.5	41.3	2.1
Aroostook	269.7	3 805	46.4	17.9	2.8	0.3	7.2	101.0	1 426	1 207	223	5 209	53.7	44.2	2.1
Cumberland	1 113.8	3 923	43.9	0.9	4.4	2.5	5.5	1 208.5	4 257	1 975	2 381	18 151	64.1	34.2	1.7
Franklin	104.7	3 419	60.2	0.7	3.7	0.2	8.5	100.7	3 287	115	96	1 904	58.9	38.6	2.5
Hancock	188.4	3 453	54.5	0.6	3.0	0.2	9.3	154.0	2 823	331	273	2 860	58.7	39.4	1.8
Kennebec	348.6	2 861	58.7	0.5	3.4	0.3	6.1	214.9	1 764	2 059	424	14 146	56.4	41.6	1.9
Knox	129.2	3 257	48.4	1.5	4.4	0.2	9.5	77.3	1 950	104	207	2 520	59.7	38.4	1.9
Lincoln	134.0	3 920	66.7	0.7	2.9	0.4	7.8	90.9	2 659	81	135	1 647	55.1	43.0	1.9
Oxford	185.2	3 222	64.2	0.5	2.9	0.4	8.6	87.1	1 516	154	185	3 153	56.7	40.6	2.7
Penobscot	527.2	3 429	48.1	1.1	3.8	0.2	4.2	409.3	2 662	1 222	491	13 096	51.7	46.6	1.7
Piscataquis	98.3	5 686	30.4	44.3	1.9	0.2	4.5	37.9	2 194	50	55	1 380	47.0	50.7	2.3
Sagadahoc	124.2	3 528	56.8	0.2	3.5	0.3	5.7	98.8	2 807	296	145	1 460	57.0	40.9	2.0
Somerset	179.7	3 461	69.3	0.2	2.5	0.2	6.3	81.7	1 574	189	167	2 474	51.8	46.1	2.2
Waldo	97.2	2 504	58.5	1.5	3.5	0.6	10.7	48.3	1 244	91	134	1 512	54.8	43.1	2.1
Washington	103.7	3 194	54.3	2.0	2.7	0.1	8.6	31.8	979	364	165	2 317	49.5	48.5	2.0
York	629.4	3 163	57.4	0.5	5.3	0.3	6.4	355.5	1 787	5 654	1 718	8 791	59.4	38.8	1.8
MARYLAND	X	X	X	X	X	X	X	X	X	173 770	49 956	344 732	61.9	36.5	1.6
Allegany	267.9	3 619	60.6	0.8	3.3	0.6	4.9	173.8	2 348	538	211	6 195	36.0	61.9	2.2
Anne Arundel	2 207.3	4 010	54.8	2.4	5.2	1.0	4.4	1 723.1	3 130	42 267	16 999	34 514	48.2	50.0	1.9
Baltimore	3 004.9	3 676	56.3	1.7	6.9	0.4	2.5	3 573.5	4 372	15 890	2 579	41 718	56.2	41.7	2.1
Calvert	401.4	4 479	58.4	0.8	3.8	1.0	3.2	210.1	2 344	131	323	4 166	46.1	52.4	1.5
Caroline	111.8	3 416	59.2	0.3	4.3	0.1	4.2	60.3	1 842	73	105	1 575	37.6	60.6	1.8
Carroll	634.2	3 793	62.1	0.8	3.5	1.2	4.4	467.0	2 793	271	531	8 078	33.1	64.3	2.6
Cecil	362.9	3 569	58.9	0.9	5.1	1.4	5.0	330.6	3 251	1 667	322	4 565	41.6	56.1	2.3
Charles	647.7	4 301	63.4	0.9	8.5	0.6	1.8	442.9	2 941	2 230	1 033	7 355	62.2	36.7	1.1
Dorchester	119.9	3 683	50.4	0.7	6.1	0.1	5.4	66.4	2 040	191	103	2 104	45.3	53.5	1.3
Frederick	1 022.3	4 267	56.6	0.7	5.2	3.4	3.4	1 148.1	4 792	3 804	1 924	11 914	48.6	49.6	1.8
Garrett	204.6	6 852	39.8	0.8	9.6	0.1	12.7	131.5	4 404	62	94	1 642	29.0	69.2	1.8
Harford	983.7	3 957	58.8	0.5	6.5	0.7	5.0	907.9	3 652	12 126	2 584	9 633	39.1	58.2	2.1
Howard	1 583.8	5 289	57.3	0.6	5.3	0.9	2.7	1 520.4	5 078	603	1 110	16 088	60.0	38.1	1.9
Kent	68.7	3 405	43.8	1.6	9.3	1.4	5.8	56.0	2 776	61	59	986	49.4	49.0	1.6
Montgomery	5 475.9	5 450	50.5	1.8	5.2	3.2	3.5	5 936.8	5 909	46 959	8 109	42 131	71.6	27.0	1.4
Prince George's	3 659.3	4 153	49.8	1.7	6.7	0.8	3.4	2 724.6	3 092	26 731	7 958	63 452	88.9	10.4	0.7
Queen Anne's	220.6	4 540	56.7	1.1	3.1	1.6	2.2	152.9	3 146	84	154	2 458	35.7	62.7	1.6

1. Based on the resident population estimated as of July 1 of the year shown. 2.

STATE/ County code	CBSA code[1]	County type[2]	STATE County	Land area,[3] (sq km) 2010	Population, 2014: Total persons 2014	Population, 2014: Rank	Population, 2014: Per square kilometer	Population and population characteristics, 2013: Race alone or in combination, not Hispanic or Latino (percent): White	Race: Black	Race: American Indian, Alaska Native	Race: Asian and Pacific Islander	Percent Hispanic or Latino[4]	Age (percent): Under 5 years	Age: 5 to 17 years	Age: 18 to 24 years	Age: 25 to 34 years	Age: 35 to 44 years	Age: 45 to 54 years
				1	2	3	4	5	6	7	8	9	10	11	12	13	14	15
			MARYLAND—Cont'd															
24 037	15680	4	St. Mary's	925	110 382	547	119.3	78.2	15.6	0.9	3.8	4.5	6.7	18.4	9.8	13.7	12.7	15.7
24 039	41540	3	Somerset	828	25 859	1 567	31.2	52.6	43.4	0.9	1.2	3.8	5.0	11.7	19.5	12.5	11.1	13.2
24 041	20660	6	Talbot	696	37 643	1 235	54.1	79.9	13.6	0.5	1.7	5.8	4.6	14.1	6.7	9.6	10.2	13.9
24 043	25180	3	Washington	1 186	149 573	430	126.1	83.8	11.9	0.6	2.1	4.0	5.8	16.5	8.5	12.9	13.2	15.1
24 045	41540	3	Wicomico	970	101 539	589	104.7	67.3	25.6	0.6	3.5	5.1	6.1	15.8	15.6	12.0	11.0	13.1
24 047	41540	4	Worcester	1 213	51 675	963	42.6	81.3	14.6	0.6	1.7	3.3	4.5	13.4	7.2	9.7	10.2	14.6
24 510	12580	1	Baltimore city	210	622 793	107	2 965.7	29.6	63.7	0.9	3.1	4.6	6.7	14.4	11.3	18.2	12.0	13.3
25 000	...	X	MASSACHUSETTS	20 202	6 745 408	X	333.9	76.6	7.4	0.6	6.7	10.5	5.5	15.4	10.3	13.6	12.6	14.9
25 001	12700	3	Barnstable	1 020	214 914	298	210.7	93.1	3.0	1.1	1.9	2.6	4.0	12.2	7.1	8.6	9.3	14.7
25 003	38340	3	Berkshire	2 400	128 715	483	53.6	91.7	3.8	0.6	2.0	3.8	4.5	13.8	9.7	10.3	10.7	15.1
25 005	39300	1	Bristol	1 433	554 194	117	386.7	87.1	4.6	0.7	2.7	6.7	5.3	16.0	9.7	12.1	12.9	15.5
25 007	47240	7	Dukes	267	17 356	1 958	65.0	91.2	4.7	2.4	1.8	2.9	5.0	13.6	6.3	11.2	12.0	15.7
25 009	14460	1	Essex	1 276	769 091	77	602.7	75.4	3.6	0.4	3.9	18.0	5.7	16.5	9.3	11.9	12.4	15.5
25 011	24640	2	Franklin	1 811	70 862	757	39.1	93.4	1.8	1.0	2.1	3.6	4.6	14.0	7.9	11.6	11.6	15.4
25 013	44140	2	Hampden	1 598	468 161	146	293.0	67.1	8.7	0.6	2.6	22.6	5.9	16.8	10.9	12.4	11.6	14.2
25 015	44140	2	Hampshire	1 366	160 939	396	117.8	87.1	3.2	0.6	6.1	5.1	3.6	12.2	23.0	10.3	10.1	13.3
25 017	14460	1	Middlesex	2 118	1 570 315	22	741.4	77.2	5.4	0.4	11.5	7.3	5.6	15.1	9.6	15.1	13.4	14.9
25 019	...	7	Nantucket	116	10 856	2 370	93.6	79.8	8.3	0.5	1.7	11.1	6.1	14.1	5.9	15.2	15.4	15.8
25 021	14460	1	Norfolk	1 026	692 254	89	674.7	80.1	6.8	0.4	10.6	3.8	5.4	16.4	8.5	12.4	12.9	15.7
25 023	14460	1	Plymouth	1 707	507 022	135	297.0	85.6	9.9	0.7	2.0	3.5	5.3	17.6	8.4	10.3	12.4	16.2
25 025	14460	1	Suffolk	151	767 254	78	5 081.2	49.0	21.6	0.7	9.4	21.2	5.7	11.6	15.1	22.3	12.8	11.7
25 027	49340	2	Worcester	3 913	813 475	73	207.9	81.1	4.8	0.6	5.0	10.1	5.6	16.6	9.9	12.1	12.9	15.9
26 000	...	X	MICHIGAN	146 435	9 909 877	X	67.7	77.9	15.0	1.3	3.3	4.7	5.8	16.9	10.2	12.0	12.2	14.4
26 001	...	9	Alcona	1 747	10 454	2 398	6.0	97.3	0.5	1.3	0.4	1.4	3.0	10.5	5.2	6.0	7.7	13.8
26 003	...	9	Alger	2 370	9 459	2 472	4.0	87.7	7.4	5.7	0.8	1.3	3.3	12.2	6.8	11.2	11.2	14.5
26 005	26090	4	Allegan	2 137	113 847	536	53.3	90.4	1.9	1.2	1.0	7.0	6.2	18.9	8.0	11.1	12.2	15.1
26 007	10980	7	Alpena	1 481	28 988	1 457	19.6	97.2	0.8	1.0	0.8	1.3	4.7	14.9	7.6	10.0	10.6	15.2
26 009	...	9	Antrim	1 232	23 267	1 673	18.9	96.5	0.6	1.8	0.5	1.9	4.5	15.0	6.5	8.5	9.6	14.4
26 011	...	8	Arenac	941	15 353	2 078	16.3	96.1	0.8	1.9	0.6	1.9	4.3	14.5	7.4	9.4	10.1	15.2
26 013	...	9	Baraga	2 326	8 654	2 546	3.7	77.7	8.1	16.6	0.8	1.3	4.4	14.7	8.0	11.9	12.6	14.6
26 015	24340	2	Barry	1 433	59 281	876	41.4	96.1	0.9	1.0	0.7	2.5	5.3	17.8	7.9	10.3	11.9	15.4
26 017	13020	3	Bay	1 146	106 179	561	92.7	92.4	2.5	1.1	0.9	4.9	5.3	16.0	8.4	11.7	11.6	14.5
26 019	45900	9	Benzie	828	17 519	1 946	21.2	95.4	1.0	2.2	0.5	2.2	4.1	15.2	6.4	9.2	10.7	14.9
26 021	35660	3	Berrien	1 470	155 233	412	105.6	77.5	16.2	1.2	2.4	5.0	6.2	16.6	8.6	11.1	11.5	14.3
26 023	17740	6	Branch	1 311	43 545	1 101	33.2	92.6	2.4	1.0	1.1	4.3	6.3	17.5	8.0	12.0	12.0	14.2
26 025	12980	3	Calhoun	1 829	134 878	469	73.7	82.0	12.6	1.4	2.4	4.7	6.0	17.3	9.5	11.8	11.8	14.0
26 027	43780	2	Cass	1 269	51 608	965	40.7	89.6	6.8	2.0	1.2	3.3	5.1	16.8	7.9	9.8	11.5	14.9
26 029	...	7	Charlevoix	1 078	26 121	1 555	24.2	96.0	0.8	2.6	0.7	1.6	4.8	15.9	7.0	9.6	10.1	15.1
26 031	...	7	Cheboygan	1 853	25 675	1 575	13.9	94.7	1.1	4.9	0.7	1.2	4.1	14.3	6.7	8.7	10.9	14.3
26 033	42300	5	Chippewa	4 036	38 321	1 214	9.5	75.4	7.3	19.1	1.4	1.6	5.0	14.4	11.7	12.9	12.9	14.2
26 035	...	7	Clare	1 462	30 652	1 418	21.0	96.6	1.0	1.6	0.5	1.8	5.6	14.4	7.4	9.8	10.5	14.4
26 037	29620	2	Clinton	1 467	77 297	712	52.7	91.9	2.5	0.9	2.0	4.3	5.3	18.0	9.4	11.4	12.2	15.1
26 039	...	7	Crawford	1 441	13 745	2 190	9.5	96.7	1.0	1.2	0.6	1.6	4.2	14.6	6.6	9.0	9.5	16.1
26 041	21540	5	Delta	3 033	36 559	1 262	12.1	95.7	0.7	3.8	0.8	1.0	5.3	15.2	7.5	9.7	10.8	14.3
26 043	27020	5	Dickinson	1 972	25 957	1 562	13.2	96.9	0.8	1.2	0.9	1.4	4.8	15.3	7.4	10.5	10.4	15.7
26 045	29620	2	Eaton	1 490	108 579	551	72.9	85.8	7.7	1.1	2.3	5.2	5.5	16.8	8.9	12.3	11.8	14.6
26 047	...	7	Emmet	1 211	33 204	1 350	27.4	93.6	1.1	5.0	1.0	1.5	5.0	16.2	7.9	10.6	11.2	14.1
26 049	22420	2	Genesee	1 650	412 895	167	250.2	74.6	21.9	1.3	1.4	3.2	6.0	17.7	9.2	11.6	12.3	14.4
26 051	...	6	Gladwin	1 300	25 411	1 592	19.5	97.4	0.7	1.1	0.4	1.3	4.6	14.8	6.8	8.7	10.3	13.9
26 053	...	7	Gogebic	2 854	15 737	2 059	5.5	91.4	4.8	3.5	0.7	1.2	4.0	12.2	8.4	11.0	11.1	14.6
26 055	45900	5	Grand Traverse	1 203	90 782	637	75.5	94.3	1.8	1.8	1.1	2.6	5.4	15.8	8.1	12.7	12.1	14.6
26 057	10940	6	Gratiot	1 472	41 665	1 133	28.3	87.7	6.0	1.0	0.7	5.5	5.3	15.3	11.5	12.7	12.7	14.3
26 059	25880	6	Hillsdale	1 549	45 830	1 052	29.6	96.5	1.0	1.1	0.6	2.1	5.5	17.0	9.8	10.4	11.3	14.1
26 061	26340	5	Houghton	2 614	36 495	1 265	14.0	94.3	1.2	1.2	3.3	1.4	5.3	15.2	20.7	10.4	9.3	11.0
26 063	...	7	Huron	2 164	32 065	1 384	14.8	96.5	0.7	0.7	0.7	2.1	4.6	15.0	7.0	9.4	10.2	14.5
26 065	29620	2	Ingham	1 440	284 582	237	197.6	74.7	13.4	1.3	6.4	7.6	5.7	14.7	20.2	13.6	10.8	11.7
26 067	26960	2	Ionia	1 480	64 294	817	43.4	89.6	5.3	0.9	0.7	4.7	5.8	17.6	9.5	13.4	13.7	14.6
26 069	...	7	Iosco	1 422	25 420	1 591	17.9	96.0	1.1	1.6	1.0	2.0	4.4	12.7	6.0	8.7	8.9	14.0
26 071	...	7	Iron	3 020	11 387	2 331	3.8	96.6	0.8	1.7	0.6	1.7	4.2	12.5	5.8	8.0	8.6	13.7
26 073	34380	5	Isabella	1 483	70 616	760	47.6	88.7	3.5	4.3	2.4	3.7	4.8	12.6	30.5	12.0	9.1	10.4
26 075	27100	3	Jackson	1 817	159 741	400	87.9	87.4	9.6	1.0	1.1	3.2	5.6	16.8	9.4	11.7	12.4	14.7
26 077	28020	2	Kalamazoo	1 455	258 818	258	177.9	81.6	12.6	1.2	3.3	4.5	5.9	16.3	16.1	13.0	11.4	12.1
26 079	45900	7	Kalkaska	1 450	17 394	1 955	12.0	96.5	1.0	1.8	0.6	1.7	5.4	16.2	7.2	10.7	11.5	14.8
26 081	24340	2	Kent	2 194	629 237	105	286.8	77.4	11.0	1.0	3.1	10.0	7.0	18.4	10.0	14.9	12.4	13.5

1. CBSA = Core Based Statistical Area. See Appendix A for explanation. See Appendix B for list of metropolitan areas with component counties. 2. County type code from the Economic Research Service of USDA Rural-Urban Continuum Codes. See Appendix A for definition. 3. Dry land or land partially or temporarily covered by water. 4. May be of any race.

Table B. States and Counties — **Population and Households**

STATE County	Population, 2013 (cont.): Age (percent) (cont.): 55 to 64 years	65 to 74 years	75 years and over	Percent female	Population change and components of change, 2000–2014: Total persons: 2000	2010	Percent change: 2000–2010	2010–2014	Components of change, 2010–2014: Births	Deaths	Net migration	Households, 2009–2013: Number	Persons per household	Percent: Family households	Female family householder[1]	One person
	16	17	18	19	20	21	22	23	24	25	26	27	28	29	30	31
MARYLAND—Cont'd																
St. Mary's	11.5	6.9	4.6	50.1	86 211	105 151	22.0	5.0	6 003	3 114	2 195	37 589	2.77	74.6	10.6	20.3
Somerset	12.3	8.4	6.4	45.8	24 747	26 470	7.0	-2.3	1 130	1 124	-615	8 419	2.29	59.1	14.6	31.7
Talbot	15.0	14.3	11.6	52.3	33 812	37 782	11.7	-0.4	1 407	1 795	311	16 013	2.33	67.9	11.3	29.0
Washington	12.7	8.4	7.0	48.9	131 923	147 430	11.8	1.5	7 411	6 217	946	55 960	2.51	67.3	12.4	26.9
Wicomico	12.3	8.1	6.0	52.1	84 644	98 733	16.6	2.8	5 216	3 830	1 384	36 405	2.63	67.7	17.0	24.6
Worcester	15.5	14.1	10.8	51.4	46 543	51 454	10.6	0.4	1 900	2 544	929	20 530	2.47	65.5	9.9	29.2
Baltimore city	12.0	6.8	5.3	52.8	651 154	620 961	-4.6	0.3	38 159	27 016	-9 148	241 455	2.47	51.8	22.7	39.7
MASSACHUSETTS	13.0	8.0	6.8	51.5	6 349 097	6 547 629	3.1	3.0	309 219	228 008	122 642	2 530 147	2.51	63.5	12.6	29.0
Barnstable	16.9	14.5	12.6	52.5	222 230	215 888	-2.9	-0.5	6 791	11 891	4 107	95 398	2.21	62.4	9.6	32.2
Berkshire	15.7	10.7	9.6	51.7	134 953	131 219	-2.8	-1.9	4 856	6 018	-1 183	55 301	2.24	59.3	12.2	35.2
Bristol	13.0	8.4	7.0	51.5	534 678	548 285	2.5	1.1	24 330	21 251	3 286	210 037	2.54	65.9	14.2	28.1
Dukes	17.4	11.5	7.4	50.4	14 987	16 535	10.3	5.0	681	559	705	5 891	2.80	65.8	11.1	27.9
Essex	13.6	8.3	7.0	51.8	723 419	743 159	2.7	3.5	35 959	26 589	17 039	286 008	2.56	66.4	13.9	28.0
Franklin	17.6	10.1	7.2	51.1	71 535	71 372	-0.2	-0.7	2 695	2 772	-307	30 534	2.29	60.1	11.1	29.8
Hampden	13.1	8.0	7.1	51.8	456 228	463 490	1.6	1.0	23 138	18 164	270	177 990	2.53	65.1	17.8	29.2
Hampshire	13.3	8.0	6.2	53.3	152 251	158 080	3.8	1.8	4 740	5 068	3 179	58 828	2.31	58.9	10.1	30.6
Middlesex	12.4	7.4	6.4	51.2	1 465 396	1 503 085	2.6	4.5	75 016	46 334	40 668	581 120	2.52	63.9	9.8	27.9
Nantucket	13.9	7.8	5.8	48.6	9 520	10 172	6.8	6.7	587	225	308	4 069	2.40	60.5	10.4	29.8
Norfolk	13.2	8.0	7.4	52.1	650 308	670 850	3.2	3.2	30 726	23 480	15 062	257 451	2.56	65.8	9.9	27.9
Plymouth	14.0	9.2	6.6	51.4	472 822	494 919	4.7	2.4	21 743	17 691	7 988	179 617	2.70	71.2	12.4	23.7
Suffolk	9.9	5.9	4.9	51.6	689 807	722 023	4.7	6.3	40 869	19 864	24 902	288 240	2.39	49.1	16.8	37.0
Worcester	13.1	7.6	6.3	50.7	750 963	798 552	6.3	1.9	37 088	28 102	6 618	299 663	2.59	67.1	12.3	26.5
MICHIGAN	13.6	8.4	6.6	50.9	9 938 444	9 883 640	-0.6	0.3	481 063	381 059	-72 674	3 823 280	2.53	65.7	12.8	28.7
Alcona	19.5	20.3	13.9	49.8	11 719	10 942	-6.6	-4.5	267	790	44	4 863	2.19	65.6	6.5	30.0
Alger	18.0	12.8	10.1	45.2	9 862	9 601	-2.6	-1.5	245	448	43	3 607	2.34	62.3	6.6	33.6
Allegan	13.8	8.7	6.0	50.1	105 665	111 408	5.4	2.2	5 700	3 808	333	41 794	2.64	73.8	9.6	21.3
Alpena	16.1	11.1	9.8	50.7	31 314	29 598	-5.5	-2.1	1 116	1 532	-144	12 899	2.24	63.6	9.0	30.9
Antrim	16.8	14.4	10.3	50.2	23 110	23 580	2.0	-1.3	838	1 093	-85	9 731	2.39	69.9	7.0	24.5
Arenac	17.2	12.7	9.2	49.5	17 269	15 899	-7.9	-3.4	529	895	-185	6 363	2.39	69.3	7.9	26.0
Baraga	15.3	11.1	7.4	45.2	8 746	8 860	1.3	-2.3	339	432	-115	3 234	2.07	63.8	11.6	33.7
Barry	14.8	9.8	6.7	49.7	56 755	59 173	4.3	0.2	2 630	2 158	-355	22 610	2.59	71.5	7.4	23.7
Bay	14.7	9.8	8.0	50.8	110 157	107 771	-2.2	-1.5	4 625	4 898	-1 262	44 127	2.40	65.1	11.9	28.6
Benzie	16.0	13.7	9.9	50.4	15 998	17 525	9.5	0.0	632	868	219	7 682	2.23	67.4	9.9	26.5
Berrien	14.3	9.5	7.9	51.2	162 453	156 813	-3.5	-1.0	7 791	6 971	-2 430	60 414	2.51	66.0	13.2	29.8
Branch	13.8	9.3	6.9	48.3	45 787	45 248	-1.2	-3.8	2 144	1 806	-2 045	15 862	2.64	69.7	11.3	25.1
Calhoun	13.7	8.6	7.3	51.2	137 985	136 146	-1.3	-0.9	7 045	6 195	-2 118	53 428	2.47	64.9	14.5	30.0
Cass	15.4	11.5	7.1	50.0	51 104	52 293	2.3	-1.3	1 902	2 078	-550	19 663	2.63	70.3	10.4	25.5
Charlevoix	16.7	12.1	8.7	50.5	26 090	25 949	-0.5	0.7	1 071	1 151	250	10 667	2.41	69.3	9.3	25.3
Cheboygan	17.1	14.0	9.9	50.1	26 448	26 152	-1.1	-1.8	820	1 317	35	11 477	2.24	66.4	9.5	27.7
Chippewa	13.0	9.1	6.7	44.8	38 543	38 520	-0.1	-0.9	1 500	1 499	-401	14 605	2.33	62.4	8.0	30.0
Clare	16.4	12.9	8.5	50.1	31 252	30 926	-1.0	-0.9	1 346	1 601	40	13 215	2.29	64.1	10.5	30.7
Clinton	13.7	8.6	6.2	50.6	64 753	75 382	16.4	2.5	3 319	2 351	778	28 534	2.63	70.2	8.9	23.4
Crawford	16.8	13.9	9.3	49.6	14 273	14 074	-1.4	-2.3	474	680	-103	5 781	2.37	67.1	9.4	28.4
Delta	16.7	10.9	9.7	50.3	38 520	37 069	-3.8	-1.4	1 537	1 847	-158	15 885	2.29	65.4	7.7	29.9
Dickinson	16.0	10.3	9.7	50.1	27 472	26 168	-4.7	-0.8	1 072	1 283	34	11 432	2.25	67.1	10.3	29.4
Eaton	14.5	9.2	6.5	51.2	103 655	107 759	4.0	0.8	4 876	4 060	-7	43 362	2.45	66.2	10.8	28.8
Emmet	16.2	10.4	8.4	50.6	31 437	32 694	4.0	1.6	1 310	1 407	608	13 545	2.39	67.8	8.6	25.4
Genesee	13.6	8.4	6.8	51.8	436 141	425 790	-2.4	-3.0	21 208	18 186	-15 968	165 669	2.51	64.6	16.2	30.1
Gladwin	16.5	14.5	10.0	49.8	26 023	25 692	-1.3	-1.1	994	1 414	198	10 895	2.33	69.0	8.8	26.6
Gogebic	16.4	11.6	10.7	46.0	17 370	16 427	-5.4	-4.2	530	898	-265	7 070	2.07	58.5	10.4	35.7
Grand Traverse	14.9	9.3	7.2	50.7	77 654	86 986	12.0	4.4	3 895	3 348	3 212	34 655	2.45	65.6	9.9	27.8
Gratiot	12.2	8.4	7.5	46.5	42 285	42 476	0.5	-1.9	1 768	1 805	-854	14 787	2.45	68.7	10.9	26.5
Hillsdale	14.7	10.0	7.2	50.4	46 527	46 688	0.3	-1.8	2 228	1 922	-1 100	17 642	2.55	70.2	9.8	25.0
Houghton	12.1	8.8	7.2	46.0	36 016	36 628	1.7	-0.4	1 630	1 474	-289	14 029	2.43	58.1	8.1	31.0
Huron	16.4	12.1	10.8	50.3	36 079	33 118	-8.2	-3.2	1 274	1 829	-458	13 907	2.31	65.3	8.0	30.8
Ingham	11.8	6.6	4.9	51.5	279 320	280 895	0.6	1.3	13 900	8 483	-1 671	108 823	2.41	56.9	12.0	32.4
Ionia	12.6	7.5	5.1	46.4	61 518	63 905	3.9	0.6	3 119	2 069	-641	22 152	2.67	71.2	11.7	24.2
Iosco	17.7	15.4	12.1	50.4	27 339	25 887	-5.3	-1.8	939	1 684	303	11 172	2.26	62.9	9.1	32.8
Iron	19.3	14.3	13.6	50.8	13 138	11 817	-10.1	-3.6	395	795	-14	5 289	2.13	59.4	7.7	36.8
Isabella	10.1	6.0	4.6	51.4	63 351	70 311	11.0	0.4	2 735	1 888	-515	24 817	2.58	55.2	10.0	26.7
Jackson	13.8	8.6	6.9	48.8	158 422	160 248	1.2	-0.3	7 604	6 699	-1 293	60 100	2.52	67.5	12.7	27.1
Kalamazoo	12.0	7.3	5.9	50.9	238 603	250 331	4.9	3.4	13 272	8 482	3 807	100 072	2.44	60.3	11.7	30.7
Kalkaska	15.6	11.7	6.9	49.5	16 571	17 153	3.5	1.4	753	776	274	7 035	2.40	63.4	7.2	29.8
Kent	11.9	6.5	5.4	50.9	574 335	602 622	4.9	4.4	37 620	18 520	7 563	229 373	2.61	67.1	12.5	26.2

1. No spouse present.

STATE County	Persons in group quarters, 2014	Daytime population, 2009–2013: Number	Daytime population, 2009–2013: Employment/residence ratio	Births, 2014: Total	Births, 2014: Rate[1]	Deaths, 2014: Number	Deaths, 2014: Rate[1]	Persons under 65 with no health insurance, 2013: Number	Persons under 65 with no health insurance, 2013: Percent	Medicare, 2014: Eligible for Medicare	Medicare, 2014: Enrolled in Medicare Advantage	Medicare, 2014: Enrolled in a Medicare prescription drug plan	Serious crimes known to police,[2] 2013: Total: Number	Serious crimes known to police,[2] 2013: Total: Rate[3]
	32	33	34	35	36	37	38	39	40	41	42	43	44	45
MARYLAND—Cont'd														
St. Mary's	2 861	103 916	0.94	1 389	12.6	774	7.0	8 163	8.7	14 178	169	5 981	2 731	2 476
Somerset	5 413	24 980	0.84	270	10.4	264	10.2	2 573	15.0	4 530	78	2 931	583	2 223
Talbot	383	40 676	1.16	334	8.9	447	11.9	3 556	12.8	10 269	265	6 349	737	1 927
Washington	8 457	148 843	1.01	1 756	11.7	1 494	10.0	13 261	11.1	27 808	2 602	16 258	3 494	2 330
Wicomico	4 846	100 699	1.02	1 198	11.8	989	9.7	12 299	14.8	17 241	263	11 108	3 871	3 816
Worcester	720	53 848	1.10	448	8.7	628	12.2	5 350	13.9	13 929	334	8 207	2 338	4 521
Baltimore city	25 359	724 267	1.39	8 939	14.4	6 720	10.8	67 892	12.8	96 426	12 752	57 128	40 449	6 496
MASSACHUSETTS	247 801	6 668 325	1.02	73 248	10.9	55 020	8.2	238 884	4.3	1 197 720	245 707	561 406	164 952	2 465
Barnstable	3 992	211 090	0.96	1 572	7.3	2 817	13.1	7 313	4.7	68 461	7 160	35 584	6 147	2 848
Berkshire	6 035	133 182	1.04	1 108	8.6	1 426	11.1	4 162	4.2	31 804	1 356	20 386	3 310	2 772
Bristol	16 293	503 353	0.82	5 667	10.2	5 099	9.2	21 853	4.8	109 969	16 265	61 262	15 003	2 712
Dukes	138	16 963	1.03	159	9.2	129	7.4	819	5.9	4 054	51	2 437	337	2 564
Essex	18 199	700 014	0.86	8 573	11.1	6 413	8.3	30 291	4.8	141 428	25 245	71 242	17 739	2 330
Franklin	1 521	63 854	0.79	619	8.7	657	9.3	2 471	4.2	15 744	3 085	7 075	1 092	1 874
Hampden	15 283	460 523	0.98	5 443	11.6	4 293	9.2	19 493	5.0	93 048	26 539	38 228	18 144	3 929
Hampshire	22 647	153 770	0.93	1 111	6.9	1 217	7.6	4 789	4.1	28 876	5 201	11 040	3 192	2 015
Middlesex	56 319	1 592 802	1.09	17 880	11.4	11 157	7.1	51 407	4.0	247 515	55 094	108 584	27 758	1 789
Nantucket	58	10 513	1.05	147	13.5	47	4.3	578	6.5	1 669	21	1 132	371	3 575
Norfolk	18 181	661 451	0.95	7 320	10.6	5 673	8.2	17 097	3.0	119 505	21 481	54 481	10 690	1 557
Plymouth	12 146	442 081	0.77	5 161	10.2	4 333	8.5	16 821	4.1	96 372	13 411	46 353	10 633	2 323
Suffolk	48 889	967 348	1.62	9 732	12.7	4 968	6.5	33 601	5.3	99 729	21 447	49 616	27 974	3 714
Worcester	28 100	751 381	0.87	8 756	10.8	6 791	8.3	28 189	4.2	139 546	49 351	53 986	19 580	2 442
MICHIGAN	226 720	9 848 919	0.99	112 748	11.4	90 366	9.1	1 058 668	12.9	1 871 152	575 914	1 075 367	274 857	2 778
Alcona	127	9 683	0.65	67	6.4	168	16.1	1 286	18.6	4 222	1 049	2 671	201	1 903
Alger	1 048	9 260	0.92	64	6.8	111	11.7	1 033	16.0	2 528	562	1 524	115	1 205
Allegan	954	103 280	0.83	1 341	11.8	894	7.9	12 540	13.2	19 905	9 248	8 193	1 849	1 646
Alpena	513	30 291	1.08	251	8.7	337	11.6	3 211	14.1	8 254	1 386	5 272	580	1 989
Antrim	226	20 931	0.72	180	7.7	255	11.0	2 776	15.8	6 778	2 033	4 139	343	1 466
Arenac	207	15 170	0.89	115	7.5	214	13.9	1 897	15.7	4 380	1 122	3 030	151	1 041
Baraga	1 028	9 348	1.22	81	9.4	103	11.9	1 014	16.2	1 810	347	1 019	NA	NA
Barry	614	46 678	0.52	607	10.2	527	8.9	5 680	11.7	11 753	4 671	5 335	806	1 427
Bay	1 438	98 563	0.81	1 043	9.8	1 140	10.7	10 945	12.5	24 392	6 502	16 271	2 578	2 414
Benzie	252	14 770	0.64	153	8.7	200	11.4	2 094	15.8	4 786	1 453	2 707	178	1 019
Berrien	3 532	156 516	1.00	1 823	11.7	1 610	10.4	18 760	14.9	33 395	7 897	18 758	4 712	3 063
Branch	1 979	42 322	0.88	487	11.2	413	9.5	4 973	14.2	8 858	1 738	5 814	718	1 651
Calhoun	4 015	141 911	1.11	1 683	12.5	1 373	10.2	14 469	13.0	28 814	5 374	16 312	5 019	3 766
Cass	474	41 954	0.52	474	9.2	510	9.9	6 070	14.5	11 444	2 826	6 146	611	1 315
Charlevoix	279	25 229	0.93	257	9.8	272	10.4	2 899	14.1	6 549	1 857	3 893	400	1 533
Cheboygan	388	23 765	0.77	192	7.5	326	12.7	3 390	17.5	7 574	1 807	4 690	457	1 773
Chippewa	4 944	38 581	0.99	344	9.0	355	9.3	4 721	16.8	7 599	1 633	4 348	741	1 895
Clare	444	28 587	0.77	305	10.0	367	12.0	3 584	15.0	8 665	1 936	5 791	776	2 527
Clinton	680	60 348	0.56	784	10.1	556	7.2	6 412	9.9	12 676	3 913	7 943	586	948
Crawford	197	13 719	0.94	105	7.6	163	11.9	1 512	14.2	3 635	907	2 293	293	2 091
Delta	623	36 486	0.97	354	9.7	429	11.7	3 849	13.3	9 885	2 428	5 801	942	2 556
Dickinson	453	27 951	1.16	258	9.9	299	11.5	2 551	12.3	6 414	1 515	3 398	NA	NA
Eaton	1 559	104 094	0.92	1 116	10.3	970	8.9	9 110	10.1	21 001	5 983	13 618	2 260	2 114
Emmet	505	36 028	1.21	299	9.0	324	9.8	3 711	13.9	7 623	2 056	4 470	478	1 447
Genesee	5 978	409 167	0.92	4 904	11.9	4 371	10.6	39 719	11.4	83 583	28 110	59 739	15 134	3 636
Gladwin	289	22 877	0.67	230	9.1	357	14.0	3 091	16.1	7 820	2 033	5 206	435	1 710
Gogebic	1 549	16 108	0.99	120	7.6	201	12.8	1 663	15.0	4 228	1 061	2 443	213	1 331
Grand Traverse	2 666	96 440	1.20	940	10.4	788	8.7	9 089	12.4	18 594	5 831	9 908	1 201	1 336
Gratiot	5 406	41 832	0.98	402	9.6	423	10.2	3 771	12.4	8 043	1 856	5 350	701	1 670
Hillsdale	1 642	43 191	0.82	510	11.1	451	9.8	5 443	14.7	9 376	2 301	5 837	682	1 478
Houghton	3 009	36 341	0.99	373	10.2	349	9.6	4 230	15.0	7 059	1 821	4 211	465	1 274
Huron	524	32 906	1.01	295	9.2	447	13.9	3 629	14.7	8 675	1 616	5 840	413	1 327
Ingham	18 471	313 769	1.25	3 300	11.6	2 109	7.4	28 100	12.1	42 872	10 297	26 892	8 773	3 199
Ionia	5 537	56 303	0.70	723	11.2	495	7.7	5 752	11.4	10 226	3 268	5 980	1 011	1 681
Iosco	400	26 148	1.06	232	9.1	407	16.0	2 797	15.2	8 613	1 972	5 542	540	2 140
Iron	359	11 267	0.90	90	7.9	188	16.5	1 141	13.8	3 623	743	2 071	254	2 203
Isabella	6 545	73 582	1.10	623	8.8	419	5.9	8 382	14.7	9 675	2 478	6 615	1 319	1 863
Jackson	9 481	155 293	0.92	1 756	11.0	1 592	10.0	15 291	12.1	31 584	7 461	18 061	4 226	2 718
Kalamazoo	8 534	260 249	1.07	3 159	12.2	2 075	8.0	27 724	12.8	43 250	13 907	20 943	8 542	3 374
Kalkaska	138	15 150	0.69	191	11.0	178	10.2	2 167	15.5	4 241	957	2 578	385	2 362
Kent	11 339	659 348	1.18	9 100	14.5	4 448	7.1	66 215	12.3	95 601	46 421	37 654	16 056	2 594

1. Per 1,000 estimated resident population. 2. Data for serious crimes have not been adjusted for underreporting; this may affect comparability between geographic areas and over time.
3. Per 100,000 population estimated by the FBI.

STATE County	Serious crimes known to police, 2013 (cont.)[1] Rate[2] Violent	Rate[2] Property	Education: School enrollment and attainment, 2009–2013: Enrollment[3] Total	Enrollment[3] Percent private	Attainment[4] (percent) High school graduate or less	Attainment[4] (percent) Bachelor's degree or more	Local government expenditures,[5] 2012–2013: Total current spending (mil dol)	Current spending per student (dollars)	Money income, 2009–2013: Per capita income[6] (dollars)	Households: Median income (dollars)	Households: Mean income (dollars)	Households: Percent with income of $200,000 or more	Income and poverty, 2013: Median household income (dollars)	Percent below poverty level: All persons	Children under 18 years	Children 5 to 17 years in families
	46	47	48	49	50	51	52	53	54	55	56	57	58	59	60	61
MARYLAND—Cont'd																
St. Mary's	219	2 257	30 320	15.9	41.0	29.5	217.6	12 469	36 017	85 672	99 529	7.7	78 274	8.2	11.7	10.4
Somerset	259	1 964	7 954	6.7	62.0	14.2	40.3	13 702	16 748	38 447	50 033	1.2	36 106	28.5	38.1	34.6
Talbot	191	1 736	7 876	22.8	39.4	33.3	54.5	11 934	38 022	61 597	88 215	7.1	57 525	10.9	16.7	15.0
Washington	260	2 070	35 373	12.1	51.9	19.5	281.8	12 576	26 532	55 609	68 821	3.0	55 643	12.0	17.2	15.0
Wicomico	494	3 322	29 781	10.4	46.8	26.3	188.1	12 980	25 378	51 092	66 109	3.3	47 536	16.5	23.2	21.9
Worcester	425	4 095	10 342	14.3	43.9	27.6	107.4	16 147	32 887	57 952	78 363	5.0	52 276	13.1	22.0	19.9
Baltimore city	1 408	5 088	164 648	24.1	49.4	26.8	1 275.4	15 050	24 750	41 385	59 484	3.0	41 988	22.7	32.6	30.5
MASSACHUSETTS	413	2 051	1 758 531	27.6	36.4	39.4	14 325.0	14 515	35 763	66 866	90 877	7.9	66 794	11.9	16.2	15.2
Barnstable	437	2 411	40 559	18.0	30.5	39.1	400.2	16 305	36 142	60 526	80 250	4.9	60 685	9.6	14.9	14.3
Berkshire	288	2 484	30 312	22.8	42.4	30.3	275.5	16 468	29 294	48 450	66 877	3.6	51 431	12.8	18.8	17.1
Bristol	498	2 214	137 835	18.1	48.3	25.3	1 086.4	13 970	28 837	55 298	72 971	4.1	53 626	14.1	19.2	18.3
Dukes	221	2 343	3 403	24.2	28.7	40.7	56.7	27 353	33 363	66 288	83 982	4.0	58 276	9.0	13.4	12.8
Essex	382	1 947	195 300	21.6	37.4	36.6	1 649.0	14 861	35 167	67 311	90 268	7.9	67 235	11.6	16.9	15.8
Franklin	309	1 565	16 014	15.9	36.1	34.0	160.7	16 818	29 259	53 663	67 397	2.8	51 828	12.6	17.7	17.2
Hampden	622	3 307	124 766	18.1	47.6	24.5	1 084.2	15 522	25 817	49 094	65 399	3.0	48 560	17.9	29.3	27.9
Hampshire	238	1 777	57 088	20.7	32.3	42.3	281.6	15 416	29 460	61 227	78 022	4.6	61 911	13.1	12.1	11.1
Middlesex	208	1 581	408 526	32.5	29.5	50.7	3 384.5	16 245	42 861	82 090	110 049	11.9	82 118	8.7	10.6	10.0
Nantucket	395	3 180	2 181	26.8	29.4	44.0	30.4	21 982	47 331	85 478	113 798	8.9	71 259	8.8	9.4	9.0
Norfolk	196	1 360	179 297	33.0	27.9	49.2	1 521.9	15 073	44 692	84 916	115 702	13.1	83 830	6.9	7.5	7.3
Plymouth	447	1 876	129 504	17.8	37.8	33.5	1 138.5	13 343	35 220	75 092	95 099	8.0	75 264	8.0	11.2	9.8
Suffolk	824	2 890	218 467	47.9	40.3	40.4	1 462.9	21 011	32 835	53 540	78 814	6.5	54 164	20.4	28.7	28.5
Worcester	436	2 007	215 279	21.2	39.2	33.8	1 792.5	14 064	31 537	65 223	82 259	5.7	62 268	13.0	18.0	16.3
MICHIGAN	450	2 328	2 683 622	13.3	41.5	25.9	15 409.4	10 948	25 681	48 411	64 753	3.1	48 200	17.0	23.7	21.6
Alcona	152	1 752	1 581	7.6	53.1	13.0	7.3	9 494	22 719	37 189	48 679	1.5	36 334	16.4	30.0	27.0
Alger	147	1 058	1 741	18.2	57.3	17.1	11.3	10 423	19 717	37 586	48 564	0.8	38 821	15.8	23.5	20.8
Allegan	239	1 406	27 683	14.2	48.5	20.2	177.5	10 008	24 140	52 061	63 833	1.8	55 274	13.3	18.2	15.6
Alpena	319	1 670	6 259	10.8	46.5	16.0	45.0	11 337	21 948	38 016	49 534	1.2	38 784	17.9	27.3	25.6
Antrim	120	1 346	4 943	8.6	44.5	23.8	33.4	9 322	24 370	45 362	57 580	2.3	46 890	14.0	25.1	22.5
Arenac	193	848	3 103	5.6	58.1	11.4	21.3	9 514	20 039	38 874	48 650	1.3	38 201	18.2	29.7	27.4
Baraga	NA	NA	1 431	17.7	61.9	12.0	12.6	10 673	17 701	41 189	48 646	1.5	40 402	16.6	23.9	21.5
Barry	163	1 264	14 426	10.6	47.5	17.7	84.2	9 003	25 059	52 186	64 787	1.9	51 040	11.2	16.3	14.3
Bay	302	2 113	25 370	12.7	46.8	18.2	155.3	11 226	23 799	45 376	56 825	1.5	42 305	16.9	22.8	20.7
Benzie	132	887	3 456	7.8	44.5	24.9	19.9	9 256	24 831	47 366	57 171	1.4	43 145	13.1	20.9	18.2
Berrien	441	2 622	39 816	20.6	43.9	24.2	262.7	11 019	24 013	43 633	59 724	2.3	44 291	16.9	25.8	22.3
Branch	202	1 448	10 367	11.1	54.4	13.4	74.7	12 092	19 947	41 856	53 518	1.7	43 947	16.9	26.7	24.4
Calhoun	554	3 212	35 329	11.6	45.5	19.5	239.7	12 695	22 978	42 110	56 836	1.8	44 343	18.7	28.6	25.2
Cass	138	1 177	12 628	9.7	51.2	16.2	70.3	10 377	22 743	44 346	58 045	1.4	42 875	17.2	24.7	21.2
Charlevoix	126	1 407	5 816	10.9	40.2	27.0	57.7	16 010	26 947	45 949	63 838	3.2	45 629	14.9	22.4	19.7
Cheboygan	190	1 583	4 966	9.6	53.0	16.3	37.2	12 346	23 412	38 410	52 189	1.9	37 949	18.7	33.4	30.4
Chippewa	197	1 698	8 976	9.1	48.0	18.5	55.3	12 400	20 589	41 637	52 648	1.2	45 416	16.6	23.4	21.2
Clare	293	2 234	6 632	8.2	56.1	11.1	53.8	11 999	18 148	32 668	41 987	0.6	33 605	24.1	40.1	36.4
Clinton	113	835	22 394	10.6	35.8	28.2	102.6	10 210	28 449	60 466	73 839	2.9	61 733	9.8	11.0	9.5
Crawford	378	1 713	2 783	10.2	52.3	15.2	15.3	9 388	21 492	40 295	49 624	0.4	37 627	17.6	32.3	28.6
Delta	187	2 368	8 120	9.6	46.5	18.2	51.9	10 770	22 471	42 676	51 672	1.0	41 287	16.1	22.9	21.5
Dickinson	NA	NA	5 660	7.7	48.7	20.0	43.5	11 485	24 611	44 136	55 951	1.3	43 290	15.3	18.1	16.5
Eaton	186	1 928	27 978	13.4	36.0	24.6	180.1	10 340	26 582	54 115	64 824	1.9	53 764	11.5	15.8	14.1
Emmet	115	1 332	7 982	11.2	34.3	31.8	49.6	10 194	29 718	50 929	71 028	4.3	48 399	11.3	15.4	14.1
Genesee	727	2 909	115 577	10.3	44.6	18.9	699.6	10 792	22 380	42 089	55 534	1.6	41 393	21.7	33.0	29.6
Gladwin	287	1 423	4 806	11.8	56.3	11.8	26.7	8 578	20 368	37 626	47 560	1.0	35 049	21.0	33.9	31.5
Gogebic	137	1 194	2 738	6.4	46.8	18.3	17.9	10 041	20 330	34 252	45 318	1.0	33 679	23.0	34.8	32.7
Grand Traverse	171	1 165	20 682	13.0	34.5	30.4	151.9	13 568	27 660	51 766	68 384	3.3	50 755	11.6	15.4	13.8
Gratiot	167	1 503	10 422	18.1	53.7	14.0	78.6	11 613	18 836	40 359	51 756	1.0	42 026	19.5	26.5	24.6
Hillsdale	204	1 274	11 667	23.0	54.0	15.3	63.7	10 674	20 379	41 759	52 346	1.1	40 363	18.2	28.3	26.7
Houghton	110	1 164	12 808	4.9	43.5	28.9	53.4	10 008	19 783	35 430	49 967	1.7	36 947	21.9	19.1	16.4
Huron	164	1 163	6 894	10.8	57.7	13.7	57.7	11 189	22 120	40 204	50 996	1.5	41 044	15.7	24.9	22.2
Ingham	569	2 630	102 346	8.9	30.8	36.5	449.5	12 010	24 754	45 321	62 161	3.3	44 979	22.4	26.1	24.1
Ionia	180	1 502	16 436	11.1	50.9	14.0	94.7	11 418	20 206	47 892	56 197	0.8	49 047	13.3	17.7	15.6
Iosco	266	1 874	4 543	8.6	53.1	14.0	40.4	10 180	22 047	36 236	48 282	1.1	36 103	19.9	34.5	32.4
Iron	156	2 047	2 065	7.7	52.6	18.4	12.3	9 097	21 499	34 685	45 656	1.4	34 698	15.2	26.6	24.7
Isabella	189	1 674	31 101	5.4	42.7	25.3	54.6	9 226	19 061	36 372	51 284	1.7	39 991	28.8	22.6	21.1
Jackson	409	2 309	40 604	18.1	44.8	18.8	257.0	11 350	22 010	40 015	50 065	1.7	45 002	18.0	28.5	26.2
Kalamazoo	487	2 887	81 994	10.7	32.2	34.0	367.5	11 053	25 757	45 775	63 610	3.3	46 445	17.7	21.0	18.2
Kalkaska	123	2 239	3 578	8.2	56.9	12.1	20.5	9 086	20 258	40 140	48 457	0.8	39 269	17.9	29.1	25.8
Kent	366	2 228	172 735	21.0	37.0	31.7	1 049.4	11 232	25 889	51 667	67 629	3.4	51 997	14.8	18.6	16.6

1. Data for serious crimes have not been adjusted for underreporting; this may affect comparability between geographic areas and over time. 2. Per 100,000 population estimated by the FBI.
3. All persons 3 years old and over enrolled in nursery school through college. 4. Persons 25 years old and over. 5. Elementary and secondary education expenditures.
6. Based on population estimated by the American Community Survey, 2009–2013.

STATE County	Personal income, 2013										Earnings, 2013		
			Per capita[1]			Supplements to wages and salaries; employer contributions (mil dol)						Contributions for government social insurance (mil dol)	
	Total (mil dol)	Percent change, 2012–2013	Dollars	Rank	Wages and salaries (mil dol)	Pension and insurance	Government social insurance	Proprietors' income (mil dol)	Dividends, interest, and rent (mil dol)	Personal transfer receipts (mil dol)	Total (mil dol)	From employee and self-employed	From employer
	62	63	64	65	66	67	68	69	70	71	72	73	74
MARYLAND—Cont'd													
St. Mary's	5 227	0.8	47 677	502	2 998	612	237	257	1 038	661	4 104	224	237
Somerset	813	3.1	30 941	2 563	288	76	21	68	138	233	454	26	21
Talbot	2 319	0.9	61 131	94	792	127	62	218	793	384	1 199	74	62
Washington	5 774	0.4	38 597	1 357	2 839	495	226	255	1 055	1 211	3 814	235	226
Wicomico	3 791	2.1	37 569	1 494	1 853	359	145	262	674	863	2 619	155	145
Worcester	2 598	3.2	50 325	352	824	148	72	267	805	540	1 311	82	72
Baltimore city	27 406	1.5	44 053	750	20 728	3 396	1 538	2 167	4 224	7 115	27 830	1 606	1 538
MASSACHUSETTS	383 152	1.7	57 248	X	209 911	33 130	14 607	32 024	73 193	57 085	289 672	15 484	14 607
Barnstable	13 370	1.9	62 187	83	4 106	806	316	1 037	4 208	2 408	6 266	362	316
Berkshire	6 310	1.4	48 695	438	2 641	518	200	452	1 462	1 441	3 810	215	200
Bristol	24 942	1.3	45 120	681	10 016	1 996	748	1 199	3 582	5 381	13 959	771	748
Dukes	1 192	4.6	69 105	53	388	71	31	148	485	137	638	33	31
Essex	43 101	1.7	56 522	174	16 947	2 988	1 244	2 919	8 170	6 593	24 097	1 314	1 244
Franklin	3 370	1.6	47 324	527	1 027	242	76	215	668	752	1 560	86	76
Hampden	20 183	1.6	43 189	830	9 468	1 932	694	955	2 987	5 621	13 050	707	694
Hampshire	7 222	1.8	45 255	672	2 720	706	182	397	1 681	1 053	4 006	188	182
Middlesex	103 259	1.7	66 498	61	64 485	8 567	4 446	8 252	21 578	10 415	85 750	4 639	4 446
Nantucket	933	7.1	89 722	10	340	50	28	129	406	60	548	28	28
Norfolk	48 460	1.7	70 456	44	20 231	3 101	1 469	3 408	10 389	4 737	28 210	1 517	1 469
Plymouth	28 075	1.9	55 935	188	8 923	1 743	651	2 360	4 916	4 258	13 677	727	651
Suffolk	43 562	1.6	57 660	144	51 717	7 205	3 311	8 415	6 645	7 645	70 648	3 648	3 311
Worcester	39 173	1.4	48 415	455	16 901	3 203	1 212	2 137	6 017	6 585	23 453	1 250	1 212
MICHIGAN	386 471	1.4	39 055	X	195 203	31 257	15 321	27 670	63 638	83 546	269 451	16 908	15 321
Alcona	342	3.0	32 361	2 357	58	12	5	22	82	141	97	10	5
Alger	259	1.9	27 243	2 958	90	21	7	14	53	88	132	10	7
Allegan	4 142	1.7	36 804	1 623	1 638	292	130	469	675	805	2 529	155	130
Alpena	1 027	-0.2	35 304	1 858	432	90	36	70	169	344	627	43	36
Antrim	838	1.7	35 859	1 769	160	36	14	62	239	252	272	22	14
Arenac	500	0.2	32 284	2 367	145	31	12	49	85	174	237	17	12
Baraga	264	4.2	30 400	2 637	119	31	10	14	53	76	174	11	10
Barry	2 132	1.7	36 074	1 735	454	97	35	188	350	441	774	54	35
Bay	3 770	0.5	35 293	1 861	1 513	259	118	184	646	1 059	2 073	140	118
Benzie	605	2.2	34 723	1 946	131	25	12	37	160	169	206	17	12
Berrien	5 991	2.6	38 589	1 360	2 764	532	213	360	1 044	1 434	3 869	243	213
Branch	1 333	2.1	30 541	2 620	512	100	42	109	219	370	763	49	42
Calhoun	4 924	2.5	36 468	1 669	2 753	472	215	190	796	1 253	3 630	227	215
Cass	1 906	0.3	36 716	1 636	336	69	27	96	337	450	527	40	27
Charlevoix	1 071	1.4	41 004	1 049	398	73	33	61	312	237	566	38	33
Cheboygan	838	1.9	32 573	2 316	203	39	19	55	205	277	316	26	19
Chippewa	1 212	3.2	31 326	2 506	541	137	44	46	220	336	768	47	44
Clare	937	1.5	30 647	2 605	257	57	21	85	142	350	420	33	21
Clinton	2 924	1.5	38 106	1 419	668	107	54	214	452	460	1 043	70	54
Crawford	419	1.2	30 171	2 661	148	30	12	35	76	138	224	16	12
Delta	1 241	0.2	33 630	2 159	537	99	45	48	222	373	729	51	45
Dickinson	1 069	-0.4	40 976	1 056	588	114	49	30	212	257	781	49	49
Eaton	3 874	1.9	35 754	1 788	1 509	262	118	158	630	796	2 047	135	118
Emmet	1 414	2.3	42 653	873	674	113	58	97	380	311	943	60	58
Genesee	13 709	1.0	33 003	2 252	5 761	984	466	816	1 921	4 237	8 028	548	466
Gladwin	720	0.9	28 229	2 873	143	29	12	17	134	289	201	20	12
Gogebic	523	0.8	32 883	2 268	185	44	15	24	112	178	268	19	15
Grand Traverse	3 654	2.4	40 609	1 098	1 909	326	154	525	781	707	2 914	180	154
Gratiot	1 397	-0.4	33 277	2 212	518	106	42	208	215	353	874	53	42
Hillsdale	1 427	3.8	30 958	2 558	526	98	43	108	220	379	775	51	43
Houghton	1 120	1.5	30 905	2 567	469	112	37	45	232	319	663	42	37
Huron	1 351	-1.4	41 923	946	413	79	33	230	312	342	755	43	33
Ingham	10 174	1.6	36 047	1 739	7 033	1 374	536	653	1 749	2 090	9 596	559	536
Ionia	1 780	1.0	27 779	2 908	646	133	54	119	252	422	952	59	54
Iosco	781	2.4	30 713	2 597	239	53	20	31	164	325	343	28	20
Iron	424	1.4	36 826	1 620	131	28	10	15	79	154	186	14	10
Isabella	2 192	0.8	31 125	2 529	1 057	250	84	145	361	527	1 537	89	84
Jackson	5 506	4.2	34 331	2 025	2 542	486	202	277	870	1 377	3 507	223	202
Kalamazoo	10 056	1.7	39 169	1 270	5 436	917	426	586	2 006	1 867	7 365	448	426
Kalkaska	526	3.5	30 564	2 616	185	32	15	44	78	163	276	20	15
Kent	24 747	2.9	39 806	1 189	16 122	2 405	1 283	2 359	3 911	4 190	22 170	1 337	1 283

1. Based on the resident population estimated as of July 1 of the year shown.

STATE County	Earnings, 2013 (cont.) — Percent by selected industries: Farm	Mining	Construction	Manu-facturing	Infor-mation: professional, scientific, technical services	Retail trade	Finance, insur-ance, real estate and leasing	Health care and social assistance	Govern-ment	Social Security beneficiaries, December 2013: Number	Rate[1]	Supple-mental Security Income recipients, December 2013	Housing units, 2014: Total	Percent change, 2010–2014
	75	76	77	78	79	80	81	82	83	84	85	86	87	88
MARYLAND—Cont'd														
St. Mary's	0.2	D	3.9	1.0	25.9	3.8	1.5	6.2	45.4	14 620	134	1 540	43 252	4.8
Somerset	6.0	0.0	4.5	5.0	3.1	3.5	2.3	10.9	45.4	5 100	195	776	11 168	0.3
Talbot	2.5	D	7.9	4.4	13.5	8.6	7.5	19.4	11.4	10 655	281	559	20 230	3.3
Washington	0.9	0.1	5.5	11.7	4.9	10.3	11.9	15.4	15.9	30 160	202	3 378	61 206	0.6
Wicomico	1.5	D	5.9	8.6	6.4	9.3	4.5	20.4	19.0	19 095	189	2 520	42 146	2.3
Worcester	2.8	D	6.1	3.0	4.8	15.5	6.5	8.9	19.6	14 855	288	854	55 764	0.0
Baltimore city	0.0	0.1	3.2	3.3	11.9	2.3	9.6	19.9	21.2	103 210	166	38 076	296 984	0.1
MASSACHUSETTS	0.1	0.1	5.1	8.7	18.3	4.7	12.2	13.5	13.0	1 206 184	180	188 015	2 828 492	0.7
Barnstable	0.1	D	10.0	2.3	9.5	9.5	6.6	17.1	20.1	68 700	320	3 261	161 718	0.9
Berkshire	0.0	0.1	6.9	9.9	8.7	7.9	7.6	19.0	15.1	33 380	258	3 940	68 354	-0.2
Bristol	0.1	0.0	6.3	14.6	6.8	8.2	3.8	16.1	16.5	116 590	211	18 805	231 286	0.3
Dukes	0.1	0.0	19.9	D	D	9.6	5.7	10.0	17.8	3 910	227	138	17 501	1.8
Essex	0.0	0.0	5.9	17.5	11.9	6.3	5.9	15.7	13.4	142 165	186	22 860	307 765	0.3
Franklin	0.7	D	7.2	14.8	5.3	7.7	3.5	12.4	19.9	16 065	226	2 095	33 668	-0.3
Hampden	0.0	0.1	5.6	10.8	6.2	6.3	9.5	19.3	20.0	98 530	211	30 064	191 788	-0.2
Hampshire	0.2	0.1	4.7	5.3	6.1	6.5	3.8	12.4	33.5	28 470	177	2 905	62 884	0.4
Middlesex	0.1	0.1	4.6	11.1	29.0	3.5	6.9	8.6	9.3	239 850	154	25 768	618 931	1.1
Nantucket	0.0	0.0	20.6	D	D	9.2	5.4	6.7	13.1	1 615	153	31	11 822	1.8
Norfolk	0.0	0.0	7.0	7.5	15.8	6.7	13.5	13.0	10.5	117 580	171	10 374	272 940	1.0
Plymouth	0.1	0.1	9.0	6.0	9.3	7.6	7.7	14.3	18.7	98 710	196	9 281	202 448	1.1
Suffolk	0.0	D	2.4	D	20.1	2.0	26.8	15.8	11.6	95 460	126	36 047	318 302	0.9
Worcester	0.0	0.1	5.7	13.2	9.9	6.1	7.0	16.3	17.6	145 160	179	22 446	329 085	0.7
MICHIGAN	0.8	0.4	4.7	16.8	11.7	6.2	6.5	12.5	15.1	2 098 078	212	277 210	4 539 871	0.2
Alcona	3.1	0.0	7.4	13.6	D	9.8	3.3	17.5	19.4	4 740	448	303	11 038	-0.3
Alger	1.3	0.0	4.4	22.5	D	6.2	4.0	8.0	32.2	2 865	301	201	6 593	0.6
Allegan	4.5	0.9	7.5	36.8	2.6	5.4	4.9	4.8	11.6	22 925	204	1 817	49 763	0.7
Alpena	0.9	2.1	5.4	16.3	3.8	9.7	4.0	10.1	30.5	9 490	326	1 190	15 952	-0.6
Antrim	3.0	D	9.4	15.4	5.2	7.9	5.3	D	23.6	7 485	321	512	17 854	0.2
Arenac	4.3	D	4.8	14.6	4.6	7.7	2.6	16.0	19.4	5 075	328	548	9 743	-0.6
Baraga	0.8	D	3.1	17.7	D	3.2	D	D	48.8	2 100	242	182	5 248	-0.4
Barry	3.9	0.1	6.1	25.0	D	5.3	7.3	10.4	17.1	13 325	225	882	27 063	0.2
Bay	2.0	0.1	3.7	12.8	13.8	8.2	4.0	17.8	18.4	28 105	263	3 299	48 016	-0.4
Benzie	1.6	D	12.4	8.7	3.0	9.2	5.3	D	21.2	5 220	300	351	12 294	0.8
Berrien	1.8	0.2	3.9	30.2	4.1	5.6	4.1	11.6	14.2	37 375	241	4 979	76 768	-0.2
Branch	5.3	D	4.3	17.2	D	7.6	5.4	4.8	24.5	10 140	233	986	20 611	-1.1
Calhoun	1.3	D	3.4	23.7	D	5.4	1.9	13.0	21.5	32 025	238	4 996	60 677	-0.6
Cass	5.2	0.0	6.1	19.2	3.5	5.5	4.1	D	23.2	12 625	244	1 146	25 893	0.0
Charlevoix	0.8	D	7.6	27.5	D	5.5	4.6	12.9	18.6	7 250	278	475	17 366	0.7
Cheboygan	1.0	D	14.1	3.1	5.0	13.2	5.6	D	20.7	8 705	340	748	18 286	-0.1
Chippewa	0.5	0.4	13.9	3.4	2.3	7.0	2.4	4.1	52.2	8 565	221	910	21 217	-0.2
Clare	1.3	0.1	7.9	14.5	3.6	8.8	2.6	D	24.9	9 950	326	1 295	23 120	-0.5
Clinton	5.3	0.5	9.4	18.1	D	8.3	5.5	7.1	13.5	14 265	185	819	30 867	0.6
Crawford	0.0	D	D	12.7	5.4	8.1	3.5	21.2	24.1	4 180	301	377	11 092	0.0
Delta	0.3	D	7.3	22.1	D	8.5	4.2	12.0	17.7	10 975	298	1 038	20 193	-0.1
Dickinson	0.2	0.0	17.6	19.0	D	7.2	2.5	6.9	26.9	7 210	277	550	13 995	0.0
Eaton	1.6	0.1	4.8	9.5	D	6.6	17.7	6.0	18.4	23 625	218	1 683	47 062	0.0
Emmet	0.4	D	7.1	8.8	D	10.0	5.3	22.2	16.3	8 225	249	531	21 346	0.2
Genesee	0.2	0.0	4.4	12.2	9.2	8.5	6.4	18.1	17.8	97 015	233	17 016	190 901	-0.7
Gladwin	2.7	D	8.5	15.5	1.6	12.9	3.6	10.5	24.1	8 930	350	887	17 628	-0.2
Gogebic	0.2	0.0	4.4	13.5	2.8	7.7	3.9	13.7	34.2	4 840	304	441	10 739	-0.5
Grand Traverse	0.2	4.7	6.5	9.8	8.1	8.5	7.5	23.2	14.0	20 345	226	1 403	42 327	1.8
Gratiot	7.2	0.1	2.7	15.9	D	4.7	3.4	D	17.7	9 095	216	1 063	16 203	-0.8
Hillsdale	5.8	D	3.8	31.7	D	6.4	3.2	D	19.0	10 765	233	1 156	21 652	-0.5
Houghton	0.5	D	6.9	4.6	5.2	7.3	3.5	D	41.7	7 975	217	664	18 621	-0.1
Huron	21.4	D	5.4	12.6	D	5.9	4.3	D	12.8	9 670	300	744	21 153	-0.2
Ingham	0.3	0.4	3.8	11.9	7.8	4.8	7.5	14.1	30.5	47 840	169	7 690	122 056	0.6
Ionia	7.1	D	5.2	24.3	1.7	6.9	4.2	4.9	24.1	11 920	186	1 374	24 592	-0.8
Iosco	1.1	0.6	5.6	11.6	4.2	9.4	4.4	D	26.5	9 685	382	820	20 392	-0.2
Iron	0.8	D	5.9	8.6	5.3	9.7	4.5	17.0	26.5	4 090	355	301	9 262	0.7
Isabella	1.7	3.7	8.4	8.8	3.3	6.3	5.0	8.4	37.0	10 965	156	1 339	28 674	1.0
Jackson	0.9	0.2	3.5	18.5	4.9	6.6	3.3	14.0	15.1	36 055	225	4 610	69 077	-0.5
Kalamazoo	0.7	0.1	4.9	21.8	6.0	6.0	8.6	15.9	14.2	48 135	187	6 342	110 316	0.3
Kalkaska	1.7	20.7	12.5	6.7	2.6	5.0	3.2	4.1	10.0	4 055	281	468	12 113	-0.5
Kent	0.3	0.3	4.9	20.1	8.6	6.8	7.7	14.9	8.3	106 135	171	15 188	248 724	0.7

1. Per 1,000 resident population estimated as of July 1 of the year shown.

STATE County	Housing units, 2009–2013								Civilian labor force, 2014				Civilian employment,[6] 2009–2013		
	Occupied units										Unemployment			Percent	
		Owner-occupied				Renter-occupied									
				Median owner cost as a percent of income											
	Total	Percent	Median value[1]	With a mortgage	Without a mortgage[2]	Median rent[3]	Median rent as a percent of income[2]	Substandard units[4] (percent)	Total	Percent change, 2013–2014	Total	Rate[5]	Total	Management, business, science and arts	Construction, production, and maintenance occupations
	89	90	91	92	93	94	95	96	97	98	99	100	101	102	103
MARYLAND—Cont'd															
St. Mary's	37 589	72.9	304 700	22.9	12.1	1 233	26.7	1.3	53 908	-0.5	2 913	5.4	52 113	43.5	17.9
Somerset	8 419	68.1	153 600	28.3	15.8	755	43.2	0.6	9 461	-1.2	898	9.5	8 679	28.4	23.1
Talbot	16 013	72.5	327 400	24.9	12.9	1 002	33.9	1.5	19 102	-0.3	1 079	5.6	17 726	38.1	17.5
Washington	55 960	64.9	206 100	24.1	12.5	849	28.7	2.8	76 251	-1.3	4 983	6.5	68 775	32.3	23.9
Wicomico	36 405	63.0	181 900	24.4	13.5	977	33.7	1.4	49 856	-0.3	3 801	7.6	46 752	34.2	21.3
Worcester	20 530	78.4	253 400	26.9	14.1	901	32.9	2.5	25 658	-0.6	2 902	11.3	23 287	34.7	17.9
Baltimore city	241 455	48.3	157 900	25.6	15.3	924	33.5	1.2	294 340	-0.8	25 516	8.7	269 059	38.4	16.6
MASSACHUSETTS	2 530 147	62.7	330 100	25.2	15.1	1 069	30.2	2.1	3 557 472	1.4	204 809	5.8	3 308 547	43.6	15.8
Barnstable	95 398	79.0	366 700	28.8	15.9	1 114	34.3	0.9	111 763	1.2	7 833	7.0	100 718	36.2	19.2
Berkshire	55 301	68.4	206 600	24.2	14.9	762	31.1	1.8	66 116	0.2	4 290	6.5	61 629	37.3	17.9
Bristol	210 037	63.1	278 100	25.8	15.5	810	30.1	1.6	288 918	0.9	21 206	7.3	262 667	33.7	21.5
Dukes	5 891	78.4	665 300	36.9	18.0	1 277	30.0	2.2	9 412	0.5	738	7.8	8 747	37.3	20.1
Essex	286 008	63.4	349 400	26.0	15.6	1 043	31.3	1.6	403 201	1.2	24 064	6.0	370 517	40.8	17.0
Franklin	30 534	68.5	219 500	24.9	14.4	847	29.4	2.9	39 558	0.8	2 081	5.3	37 295	39.0	21.7
Hampden	177 990	61.8	197 900	24.0	15.6	791	32.6	1.6	222 549	1.0	17 401	7.8	205 261	32.9	21.1
Hampshire	58 828	67.0	262 600	24.3	13.8	934	31.2	2.0	86 287	1.5	4 342	5.0	82 163	44.8	15.5
Middlesex	581 120	62.7	398 200	24.5	14.7	1 286	28.4	4.6	851 640	1.7	39 593	4.6	804 890	52.4	12.3
Nantucket	4 069	65.8	929 700	33.2	14.6	1 564	28.1	1.6	6 846	4.4	423	6.2	6 083	28.1	26.9
Norfolk	257 451	69.3	391 100	24.6	15.0	1 268	29.3	1.4	367 341	1.7	18 346	5.0	346 271	51.1	12.0
Plymouth	179 617	77.1	332 100	26.3	16.3	1 113	32.1	3.5	266 550	1.4	16 083	6.0	244 965	38.2	17.8
Suffolk	288 240	35.5	358 700	26.6	15.8	1 265	31.0	1.9	411 889	1.6	22 067	5.4	382 918	43.4	12.3
Worcester	299 663	65.7	259 200	24.5	14.7	911	29.4	2.2	425 404	1.4	26 342	6.2	394 423	40.8	18.5
MICHIGAN	3 823 280	72.1	121 700	23.4	13.6	768	32.7	2.0	4 750 279	0.5	347 972	7.3	4 242 948	34.4	22.5
Alcona	4 863	89.8	102 800	24.9	13.0	585	36.8	2.2	3 836	0.5	401	10.5	3 297	24.5	30.7
Alger	3 607	84.9	117 100	26.2	12.8	603	29.5	2.6	3 315	-2.3	340	10.3	3 011	29.1	26.1
Allegan	41 794	81.9	140 200	23.7	12.7	728	28.2	0.9	59 466	2.0	3 213	5.4	50 107	28.3	33.3
Alpena	12 899	77.6	96 400	23.4	12.7	545	31.1	2.3	13 527	0.7	1 067	7.9	12 176	30.0	24.8
Antrim	9 731	85.0	141 300	26.7	13.6	703	34.1	1.4	10 080	0.5	948	9.4	9 458	25.8	28.3
Arenac	6 363	83.8	90 200	24.5	13.3	572	30.1	1.6	6 453	-1.1	700	10.8	5 630	27.8	29.3
Baraga	3 234	79.3	84 000	22.7	13.9	509	26.5	1.3	3 494	-2.0	384	11.0	2 595	27.9	26.0
Barry	22 610	83.5	133 900	23.6	12.8	717	29.1	0.9	30 154	2.5	1 615	5.4	26 457	27.9	33.2
Bay	44 127	78.1	93 800	22.5	12.9	630	32.7	3.1	53 296	0.0	3 808	7.1	45 927	29.4	23.8
Benzie	7 682	83.9	149 700	25.6	12.7	763	27.9	1.6	8 735	1.1	738	8.4	7 700	31.2	25.0
Berrien	60 414	72.1	129 300	22.3	12.7	649	32.6	4.0	73 339	0.7	4 926	6.7	66 923	32.5	23.7
Branch	15 862	78.0	98 000	23.0	12.6	670	31.2	1.2	19 265	0.8	1 264	6.6	17 307	24.5	33.9
Calhoun	53 428	69.7	98 300	22.9	13.5	671	30.5	1.5	64 096	1.6	4 013	6.3	57 003	27.8	27.9
Cass	19 663	83.6	124 800	24.4	13.3	685	31.9	1.6	23 982	1.5	1 583	6.6	21 835	29.0	32.5
Charlevoix	10 667	81.6	151 400	26.1	13.5	635	31.8	2.5	13 115	0.4	1 054	8.0	11 386	29.5	26.8
Cheboygan	11 477	81.1	112 500	25.3	13.0	601	30.4	1.7	10 685	1.3	1 117	10.5	9 702	24.7	27.5
Chippewa	14 605	70.3	101 600	21.3	13.1	601	30.2	2.7	16 868	-1.4	1 591	9.4	14 956	29.3	18.0
Clare	13 215	80.4	80 000	26.7	13.6	581	35.0	0.8	11 891	-0.4	1 156	9.7	10 218	23.9	27.2
Clinton	28 534	80.8	156 300	22.1	12.1	764	31.6	3.2	39 655	1.1	1 980	5.0	35 508	36.6	20.2
Crawford	5 781	82.1	96 400	23.6	12.3	649	32.3	2.3	5 371	-0.6	503	9.4	5 151	26.6	26.3
Delta	15 885	79.3	100 200	23.4	12.7	554	33.5	0.5	17 530	-0.2	1 452	8.3	15 686	27.3	29.6
Dickinson	11 432	81.2	85 500	22.2	14.1	586	31.7	1.2	12 968	2.3	862	6.6	11 397	28.3	27.0
Eaton	43 362	72.6	138 300	22.8	13.1	759	29.0	1.6	56 133	0.9	3 180	5.7	50 505	34.1	21.9
Emmet	13 545	77.4	167 700	24.0	12.3	744	32.4	1.6	17 960	-1.4	1 684	9.4	15 658	33.9	18.9
Genesee	165 669	70.3	91 700	24.0	14.0	711	35.9	2.7	184 458	-0.2	14 299	7.8	158 199	30.4	24.0
Gladwin	10 895	84.5	103 300	25.8	13.8	572	34.5	0.8	10 045	-0.3	921	9.2	8 631	24.8	31.9
Gogebic	7 070	75.5	66 800	22.1	13.3	594	33.2	1.9	6 750	0.1	590	8.7	5 948	27.1	30.0
Grand Traverse	34 655	75.4	168 300	24.1	13.2	847	30.0	2.3	47 880	1.3	2 831	5.9	42 472	32.6	19.9
Gratiot	14 787	76.1	86 600	22.5	13.2	593	32.7	3.1	18 509	-0.2	1 314	7.1	16 097	27.4	27.8
Hillsdale	17 642	80.0	103 700	24.6	13.5	639	30.5	2.7	20 452	-0.9	1 441	7.0	18 682	26.9	34.6
Houghton	14 029	69.6	88 400	21.0	12.8	595	35.4	1.4	16 934	0.1	1 263	7.5	15 466	36.8	17.2
Huron	13 907	81.6	96 100	24.4	13.2	589	29.7	1.6	16 630	1.3	1 139	6.8	13 692	28.0	33.1
Ingham	108 823	59.3	120 500	22.8	13.2	775	34.8	1.7	145 366	0.4	8 750	6.0	130 427	38.9	16.5
Ionia	22 152	78.2	111 000	23.5	13.2	664	33.9	1.7	29 210	1.0	1 778	6.1	25 633	27.0	31.3
Iosco	11 172	81.3	90 300	24.4	12.6	588	29.8	0.6	10 353	1.0	992	9.6	8 627	24.4	27.1
Iron	5 289	84.5	75 100	24.0	15.4	490	31.0	2.1	5 124	0.6	448	8.7	4 470	25.7	26.7
Isabella	24 817	58.7	119 800	23.1	12.5	698	43.7	1.9	35 459	1.2	2 070	5.8	32 298	27.8	17.2
Jackson	60 100	73.1	112 800	22.9	13.0	722	33.0	1.3	72 918	0.5	4 834	6.6	65 357	29.3	25.8
Kalamazoo	100 072	64.7	136 700	22.3	13.0	717	34.6	3.0	127 445	1.5	7 083	5.6	117 581	38.0	18.6
Kalkaska	7 035	81.2	98 800	25.0	13.6	692	28.7	2.1	7 687	1.1	719	9.4	6 671	20.0	32.1
Kent	229 373	70.1	137 500	22.5	12.7	745	30.2	1.8	335 617	2.2	16 391	4.9	290 110	35.1	23.0

1. Specified owner-occupied units. 2. A value of 10.0 represents 10 percent or less; a value of 50.0 represents 50 percent or more. 3. Specified renter-occupied units.
4. Overcrowded or lacking complete plumbing facilities. 5. Percent of civilian labor force. 6. Persons 16 years old and over.

STATE County	Private nonfarm establishments, employment and payroll, 2013									Agriculture, 2012			
		Employment						Annual payroll		Farms			
											Percent with:		
	Number of establish-ments	Total	Health care and social assistance	Manufac-turing	Retail trade	Finance and insurance	Professional, scientific, and technical services	Total (mil dol)	Average per employee (dollars)	Number	Fewer than 50 acres	500 acres or more	Farm operators whose principal occu-pation is farming (percent)
	104	105	106	107	108	109	110	111	112	113	114	115	116
MARYLAND—Cont'd													
St. Mary's	1 928	28 844	4 078	219	4 595	476	8 541	1 454	50 404	632	48.3	3.3	53.6
Somerset	366	3 518	1 063	360	423	89	102	126	35 779	286	44.4	12.9	55.6
Talbot	1 467	17 139	3 364	1 365	2 662	620	974	653	38 101	328	34.8	22.9	46.0
Washington	3 426	58 628	9 923	5 785	9 875	6 739	1 714	2 100	35 821	860	46.3	5.3	49.8
Wicomico	2 530	36 976	8 665	3 160	6 745	1 221	1 298	1 323	35 778	510	52.4	8.0	60.2
Worcester	2 109	17 295	2 117	553	3 375	447	643	567	32 773	374	44.9	11.2	49.7
Baltimore city	12 280	284 084	75 928	11 472	17 278	16 305	21 039	15 940	56 109	NA	NA	NA	NA
MASSACHUSETTS	172 533	3 062 689	591 520	228 032	351 560	205 419	262 207	178 305	58 218	7 755	67.5	1.5	50.0
Barnstable	8 323	71 779	16 710	1 951	13 904	2 202	4 774	3 003	41 843	333	91.9	0.0	58.0
Berkshire	3 928	53 041	11 214	4 921	8 794	2 219	D	2 135	40 260	525	49.9	4.4	51.0
Bristol	12 730	193 082	40 755	25 340	34 146	5 076	6 039	7 914	40 989	717	74.5	0.7	49.0
Dukes	1 036	5 322	D	107	1 155	D	228	277	51 973	88	83.0	2.3	55.7
Essex	18 277	275 283	61 211	38 185	38 032	11 446	15 517	13 109	47 621	522	78.0	1.0	56.7
Franklin	1 584	19 917	3 538	3 689	2 946	590	595	765	38 400	780	49.4	3.3	56.9
Hampden	9 661	167 480	38 223	20 384	23 265	10 399	6 645	7 061	42 163	582	62.7	1.0	41.6
Hampshire	3 562	57 927	18 727	3 129	7 662	1 550	2 024	1 837	31 713	799	62.5	1.4	50.6
Middlesex	42 829	836 076	126 264	58 011	79 995	28 673	114 529	58 042	69 422	739	75.9	0.1	52.1
Nantucket	934	4 400	D	D	827	123	194	263	59 853	20	85.0	5.0	15.0
Norfolk	19 597	329 894	64 975	18 575	43 093	28 105	22 107	17 466	52 945	245	78.0	0.8	58.4
Plymouth	11 922	156 526	30 722	10 175	26 682	7 067	7 318	6 844	43 722	825	73.9	1.9	49.7
Suffolk	20 121	588 364	116 331	10 500	32 392	91 536	60 785	44 921	76 349	20	100.0	0.0	65.0
Worcester	17 635	281 520	61 211	33 021	38 662	14 200	16 668	12 843	45 620	1 560	64.4	1.0	43.4
MICHIGAN	217 494	3 535 685	590 060	525 565	448 929	150 244	242 932	156 830	44 356	52 194	43.9	8.8	48.4
Alcona	193	1 191	209	202	258	26	104	36	30 231	235	34.0	7.7	55.3
Alger	234	1 715	270	D	279	D	34	60	35 080	93	48.4	9.7	50.5
Allegan	2 228	34 216	3 555	12 736	3 402	403	1 356	1 485	43 415	1 396	51.8	7.9	48.2
Alpena	788	9 713	2 737	1 161	1 795	360	219	326	33 581	458	33.2	6.6	49.6
Antrim	547	3 346	307	625	565	125	99	103	30 913	415	41.0	5.5	56.9
Arenac	329	3 135	669	668	454	D	D	97	31 045	421	38.7	10.5	38.0
Baraga	195	1 722	283	483	277	D	D	52	30 256	57	29.8	15.8	43.9
Barry	869	9 487	1 354	2 788	1 270	724	316	335	35 329	1 031	44.5	6.7	43.5
Bay	2 245	30 719	7 112	3 376	5 442	1 031	1 385	1 148	37 368	766	36.9	14.6	54.4
Benzie	443	3 039	349	331	488	D	D	88	28 869	181	41.4	3.9	52.5
Berrien	3 610	51 314	8 909	8 387	6 792	1 273	2 006	2 200	42 871	1 063	57.9	7.0	51.0
Branch	808	11 025	1 515	2 604	1 616	472	400	386	35 000	1 054	41.0	10.8	46.0
Calhoun	2 630	50 801	9 284	12 096	6 077	988	2 018	2 257	44 424	1 023	35.1	10.8	45.7
Cass	737	6 650	D	2 074	793	202	190	214	32 202	798	43.4	10.0	49.0
Charlevoix	792	7 728	1 232	2 364	824	201	213	299	38 634	297	36.7	4.0	38.0
Cheboygan	754	4 759	1 091	298	1 120	205	142	146	30 583	313	39.0	4.8	40.6
Chippewa	808	8 921	2 015	516	1 751	D	263	250	28 007	409	25.4	11.7	39.1
Clare	512	5 581	1 069	1 003	1 023	D	147	175	31 310	460	40.7	5.0	50.2
Clinton	1 306	14 359	1 752	1 977	2 258	811	542	523	36 401	1 128	44.1	10.1	46.3
Crawford	302	3 269	D	559	544	D	79	114	34 830	49	61.2	0.0	49.0
Delta	1 064	11 848	1 887	D	2 164	685	421	404	34 130	283	23.3	16.3	58.3
Dickinson	883	12 202	D	2 170	1 938	323	337	491	40 260	162	27.2	8.0	35.2
Eaton	2 034	38 507	3 436	7 415	5 708	3 636	971	1 552	40 316	1 163	40.9	10.9	49.6
Emmet	1 469	14 583	3 591	1 160	2 701	348	413	545	37 364	287	33.1	3.5	44.9
Genesee	7 745	114 923	26 465	11 288	19 736	4 349	3 400	4 287	37 300	835	58.6	6.2	50.1
Gladwin	394	3 553	662	816	628	D	57	110	31 040	533	35.5	3.2	41.8
Gogebic	404	4 211	569	698	773	112	88	109	25 807	62	32.3	0.0	27.4
Grand Traverse	3 305	42 016	8 971	4 601	7 545	1 962	2 111	1 602	38 134	504	52.4	3.4	55.2
Gratiot	746	10 517	2 223	2 538	1 302	408	116	361	34 287	878	37.5	17.3	56.3
Hillsdale	780	10 601	1 397	3 807	1 364	266	190	361	34 062	1 530	44.2	7.8	38.4
Houghton	876	8 650	2 131	651	1 649	351	521	250	28 855	177	29.4	5.1	37.3
Huron	959	10 579	1 754	3 401	1 439	429	201	361	34 149	1 205	31.4	21.3	55.5
Ingham	6 129	103 894	22 532	7 811	13 577	7 802	5 870	4 273	41 133	944	55.3	8.5	51.5
Ionia	884	10 910	1 266	3 070	1 842	745	159	341	31 260	1 109	42.1	11.5	48.0
Iosco	612	6 319	1 039	954	1 246	241	158	189	29 963	283	40.3	5.3	45.2
Iron	356	2 541	427	370	433	121	126	76	30 023	117	30.8	6.8	49.6
Isabella	1 399	22 174	3 171	2 355	3 487	D	662	703	31 715	928	34.6	8.9	49.2
Jackson	2 954	49 019	9 570	8 770	7 213	1 303	2 933	2 060	42 016	1 073	48.7	7.7	45.4
Kalamazoo	5 507	103 221	18 684	15 549	12 969	5 937	3 868	4 561	44 190	734	56.1	8.9	48.6
Kalkaska	331	3 340	504	417	583	65	D	142	42 565	224	46.0	3.6	39.3
Kent	15 615	323 594	46 128	59 290	32 477	13 223	13 273	13 685	42 291	1 159	53.9	4.6	48.2

Agriculture, 2012 (cont.)

STATE County	Land in farms: Acreage (1,000)	Land in farms: Percent change, 2007–2012	Land in farms: Acres: Average size of farm	Land in farms: Acres: Total irrigated (1,000)	Land in farms: Acres: Total cropland (1,000)	Value of land and buildings (dollars): Average per farm	Value of land and buildings (dollars): Average per acre	Value of machinery and equipment, average per farm (dollars)	Value of products sold: Total (mil dol)	Value of products sold: Average per farm (dollars)	Value of products sold: Percent from: Crops	Value of products sold: Percent from: Livestock and poultry products	Percent of farms with sales of: $10,000 or more	Percent of farms with sales of: $100,000 or more	Government payments: Total ($1,000)	Government payments: Percent of farms
	117	118	119	120	121	122	123	124	125	126	127	128	129	130	131	132
MARYLAND—Cont'd																
St. Mary's	67	-2.3	106	0.7	41.2	700 921	6 603	80 758	21.8	34 494	87.4	12.6	42.6	6.6	783	30.1
Somerset	65	8.2	228	0.4	36.4	1 247 458	5 471	182 073	219.0	765 559	12.2	87.8	58.0	50.0	1 653	61.9
Talbot	119	9.6	364	7.6	98.2	2 408 598	6 612	177 098	89.5	272 893	71.2	28.8	58.5	34.8	2 380	69.2
Washington	130	13.6	151	0.8	85.3	901 269	5 981	117 867	107.7	125 219	42.2	57.8	47.6	24.2	1 078	26.2
Wicomico	84	-9.8	164	9.4	56.1	1 031 771	6 284	134 363	236.3	463 375	22.7	77.3	54.9	35.5	2 360	53.7
Worcester	99	-10.4	266	5.0	71.3	1 585 529	5 971	163 979	199.3	532 794	25.8	74.2	52.7	39.6	1 733	58.6
Baltimore city	NA	NA	NA	NA	NA	NA	NA	NA	NA	NA	NA	NA	NA	NA	NA	NA
MASSACHUSETTS	524	1.1	68	23.4	160.8	704 071	10 430	53 920	492.2	63 470	77.8	22.2	32.7	9.8	8 124	10.1
Barnstable	5	-10.6	14	1.2	1.5	500 691	35 657	50 009	19.1	57 438	50.8	49.2	40.5	11.4	358	7.5
Berkshire	62	-7.1	117	0.2	18.4	824 924	7 024	51 476	22.5	42 796	45.1	54.9	29.5	6.7	268	9.3
Bristol	35	-11.2	49	1.6	11.9	709 223	14 584	51 411	37.7	52 522	79.4	20.6	36.3	8.6	1 527	12.7
Dukes	13	60.6	145	0.2	D	1 416 193	9 800	84 943	3.5	39 671	71.9	28.1	34.1	6.8	D	3.4
Essex	22	-19.5	43	0.6	9.2	893 351	20 821	56 138	25.2	48 205	71.7	28.3	31.0	8.0	207	4.0
Franklin	90	13.0	115	2.1	22.5	700 144	6 083	68 964	55.1	70 585	71.0	29.0	31.9	10.3	1 987	16.4
Hampden	39	5.1	67	0.9	11.1	488 323	7 343	45 735	23.6	40 564	73.6	26.4	26.5	6.5	480	9.1
Hampshire	54	2.3	68	0.9	21.5	544 950	8 071	53 222	49.2	61 613	75.6	24.4	30.5	10.1	682	11.9
Middlesex	28	-16.7	38	1.7	10.7	730 977	19 135	50 583	76.6	103 593	89.7	10.3	35.7	10.1	482	9.3
Nantucket	1	100.3	62	D	0.6	1 642 150	26 658	20 950	1.7	82 800	84.0	15.9	55.0	15.0	0	0.0
Norfolk	9	-18.9	39	0.6	3.4	936 188	24 277	47 890	12.5	51 012	75.8	24.2	33.5	12.7	D	6.9
Plymouth	64	29.1	78	12.0	17.3	893 370	11 510	65 783	108.1	130 986	92.2	7.8	46.9	19.2	1 306	12.4
Suffolk	0	-75.8	1	D	D	246 000	205 000	7 700	0.2	8 100	96.3	4.3	40.0	0.0	0	0.0
Worcester	102	-4.3	65	1.3	32.2	609 428	9 338	47 396	57.5	36 845	68.9	31.1	25.4	7.0	690	8.1
MICHIGAN	9 949	-0.8	191	592.2	7 669.1	766 148	4 020	122 528	8 678.1	166 265	63.5	36.5	44.0	18.0	155 919	39.5
Alcona	38	-15.6	163	0.0	23.8	394 591	2 421	78 426	11.4	48 511	40.3	59.7	31.9	9.8	263	24.3
Alger	18	-3.1	191	0.0	8.7	395 710	2 070	54 075	3.0	32 527	29.4	70.6	38.7	6.5	119	29.0
Allegan	270	-1.8	194	28.1	223.3	927 485	4 790	152 066	580.8	416 071	33.4	66.6	45.1	19.7	3 286	27.1
Alpena	69	-19.4	151	0.0	44.1	367 974	2 433	82 430	23.7	51 644	40.2	59.8	37.3	11.4	694	32.8
Antrim	64	-4.7	155	3.4	33.9	554 149	3 584	77 942	21.0	50 593	73.0	27.0	29.9	8.7	1 324	31.1
Arenac	82	-13.7	194	D	63.0	539 781	2 782	114 143	51.2	121 620	70.0	30.0	33.0	17.8	1 570	72.2
Baraga	18	-4.9	311	0.0	7.9	574 842	1 848	71 667	1.5	25 825	53.2	46.9	38.6	7.0	79	26.3
Barry	165	-1.8	160	4.3	119.4	637 736	3 980	89 944	140.1	135 859	33.9	66.1	35.3	11.2	2 853	37.1
Bay	194	4.0	253	6.3	174.5	1 015 918	4 017	198 977	165.3	215 789	95.1	4.9	58.6	31.9	2 628	68.0
Benzie	21	-2.0	114	0.3	9.8	475 486	4 169	65 177	6.4	35 337	51.9	48.1	30.9	8.8	808	20.4
Berrien	156	-7.5	147	18.1	126.1	822 736	5 591	123 913	161.5	151 968	90.3	9.7	51.6	20.6	3 303	29.4
Branch	244	-2.4	232	44.5	197.7	823 531	3 554	132 288	175.3	166 362	71.5	28.5	44.0	20.3	4 329	54.2
Calhoun	225	-1.4	220	10.7	175.6	807 980	3 676	117 543	133.0	130 044	64.6	35.4	43.4	17.5	3 618	47.7
Cass	189	-0.9	236	57.6	148.0	936 370	3 960	147 259	187.2	234 535	67.1	32.9	43.1	19.9	2 666	47.9
Charlevoix	38	-9.4	126	0.2	20.8	465 684	3 684	52 899	9.9	33 391	60.3	39.7	30.6	6.4	182	14.5
Cheboygan	46	-4.2	146	0.5	21.8	361 479	2 483	51 425	9.3	29 633	60.5	39.5	25.2	3.2	221	20.1
Chippewa	93	-6.0	227	0.1	57.4	368 870	1 622	60 252	12.6	30 724	41.7	58.3	39.6	6.8	934	31.5
Clare	63	-8.6	136	D	30.7	385 265	2 835	54 583	20.4	44 263	30.3	69.7	31.1	8.3	438	24.8
Clinton	244	-10.2	216	4.2	205.7	939 125	4 345	133 106	262.6	232 828	46.7	53.3	49.6	21.5	3 797	54.2
Crawford	3	9.2	56	0.0	0.8	185 959	3 307	54 816	0.3	5 306	26.9	73.1	14.3	0.0	0	0.0
Delta	71	-8.9	250	0.6	35.0	488 406	1 951	83 208	15.0	52 883	51.0	49.0	38.5	13.1	588	35.7
Dickinson	29	15.0	177	0.3	15.5	390 512	2 211	77 451	5.6	34 759	51.6	48.4	34.0	7.4	186	30.2
Eaton	223	0.5	192	1.5	176.1	714 449	3 722	119 525	119.0	102 364	83.8	16.2	46.9	19.8	3 008	46.6
Emmet	40	0.6	139	0.3	17.9	438 456	3 161	55 383	6.7	23 429	66.1	33.9	34.1	4.9	117	12.5
Genesee	123	-4.6	148	1.5	102.6	570 910	3 867	107 984	91.3	109 389	88.7	11.3	38.4	12.9	2 131	32.2
Gladwin	67	-0.7	126	0.5	40.1	355 311	2 820	61 334	19.3	36 300	70.6	29.4	34.5	4.7	599	38.3
Gogebic	6	55.6	98	0.0	2.4	257 194	2 624	34 226	0.5	8 016	72.8	27.2	25.8	0.0	D	3.2
Grand Traverse	55	-12.8	108	3.0	36.4	577 258	5 333	79 274	18.2	36 202	76.3	23.7	40.1	9.7	1 273	28.8
Gratiot	289	0.9	330	9.5	259.5	1 486 503	4 510	209 694	345.0	392 976	57.7	42.3	56.3	31.7	4 522	68.6
Hillsdale	262	-2.8	171	9.1	207.9	590 512	3 444	101 482	161.5	105 577	71.8	28.2	35.6	14.5	6 159	57.7
Houghton	27	15.0	154	0.1	10.8	272 254	1 772	42 633	4.0	22 678	53.0	47.0	27.7	2.3	101	18.1
Huron	452	2.6	375	2.0	406.0	1 952 800	5 202	304 740	654.6	543 207	51.1	48.9	62.5	43.8	9 479	79.6
Ingham	201	7.7	212	1.7	167.4	866 715	4 079	128 773	131.3	139 131	77.4	22.6	42.2	17.2	2 925	27.2
Ionia	248	4.2	224	6.0	203.1	934 093	4 170	154 311	406.1	366 228	31.6	68.4	50.9	25.4	4 662	51.9
Iosco	38	-20.4	134	0.0	23.7	358 890	2 673	85 230	17.1	60 364	36.4	63.6	29.3	7.8	467	30.4
Iron	23	-17.3	196	0.5	9.5	390 043	1 989	50 376	3.7	31 222	87.3	12.7	25.6	6.8	25	17.9
Isabella	188	-3.9	203	3.4	148.9	772 920	3 806	104 693	119.4	128 664	65.7	34.3	46.7	19.2	2 703	52.3
Jackson	183	0.4	171	3.9	136.0	652 247	3 822	85 794	78.2	72 866	69.2	30.8	36.4	12.0	4 210	32.1
Kalamazoo	144	-0.9	196	39.1	112.9	909 857	4 653	148 903	244.0	332 383	79.7	20.3	48.5	21.5	2 473	26.7
Kalkaska	26	10.0	115	1.6	12.9	350 875	3 044	45 339	8.8	39 299	92.1	7.9	23.2	3.1	104	17.0
Kent	157	-7.4	136	10.0	120.5	795 991	5 858	111 424	231.9	200 053	77.8	22.2	42.6	16.6	2 417	22.7

Table B. States and Counties — **Water Use, Wholesale Trade, Retail Trade, and Real Estate**

STATE County	Water use, 2010		Wholesale trade,[1] 2007				Retail trade,[2] 2007				Real estate and rental and leasing,[2] 2007			
	Total water withdrawn (mil gal/day)	Gallons withdrawn per person per day	Number of establish-ments	Number of employees	Sales (mil dol)	Annual payroll (mil dol)	Number of establish-ments	Number of employees	Sales (mil dol)	Annual payroll (mil dol)	Number of establish-ments	Number of employees	Receipts (mil dol)	Annual payroll (mil dol)
	133	134	135	136	137	138	139	140	141	142	143	144	145	146
MARYLAND—Cont'd														
St. Mary's	7.9	75	30	D	D	D	314	4 531	1 193.0	97.9	92	466	66.1	15.0
Somerset	3.8	145	17	D	D	D	61	459	105.2	8.4	21	44	4.7	1.1
Talbot	7.2	191	61	557	252.7	23.6	262	2 750	711.9	68.0	85	242	45.9	9.0
Washington	58.8	399	144	1 978	1 265.3	81.8	673	10 226	2 463.3	219.5	131	632	136.9	17.9
Wicomico	19.9	202	112	D	D	D	445	7 431	1 780.8	167.2	152	701	107.8	22.3
Worcester	18.2	354	54	D	D	D	458	3 979	875.1	90.8	185	577	75.6	16.1
Baltimore city	25.3	41	534	9 046	4 843.4	468.9	1 950	16 682	4 348.8	401.5	647	4 677	837.5	214.9
MASSACHUSETTS	2 995.9	458	7 284	123 267	95 275.7	7 644.3	25 469	360 218	88 083.0	8 916.5	7 053	48 576	14 029.8	2 287.6
Barnstable	60.8	282	189	D	D	D	1 628	16 213	3 973.2	427.7	385	1 632	270.6	50.3
Berkshire	24.3	185	113	D	D	D	766	8 942	1 901.8	208.8	128	770	123.3	22.9
Bristol	882.1	1 609	548	10 224	7 719.8	514.7	2 419	37 079	8 647.7	846.5	472	2 451	382.1	70.6
Dukes	3.1	186	14	D	D	D	207	1 202	349.0	42.8	61	169	31.8	5.9
Essex	420.3	566	806	12 176	12 405.7	806.4	2 690	38 874	9 822.1	962.0	647	3 045	584.1	109.8
Franklin	47.1	659	56	579	460.1	31.6	290	3 153	691.0	71.3	50	127	18.2	2.9
Hampden	148.2	320	408	6 818	4 991.8	321.1	1 686	24 052	5 668.7	548.3	409	2 164	356.8	69.0
Hampshire	28.4	180	91	1 638	2 021.8	68.0	584	7 705	1 546.1	169.8	128	526	88.1	14.6
Middlesex	431.1	287	2 022	39 339	32 873.3	2 847.9	5 306	80 413	19 661.1	2 036.6	1 690	12 621	3 802.7	571.3
Nantucket	4.5	446	12	45	39.8	2.9	159	920	342.8	38.9	59	179	51.0	6.4
Norfolk	44.1	66	974	19 035	12 398.9	1 190.2	2 595	42 427	11 241.4	1 107.3	841	6 719	1 538.9	297.7
Plymouth	619.6	1 252	531	7 002	5 253.6	456.6	2 016	27 593	6 615.1	684.8	427	1 924	493.9	68.4
Suffolk	0.2	0	689	11 905	8 914.8	683.5	2 385	31 139	7 565.8	800.8	1 083	12 455	5 596.1	859.4
Worcester	282.3	353	831	11 876	6 913.7	603.7	2 738	40 506	10 057.2	971.0	673	3 794	692.2	138.6
MICHIGAN	10 837.2	1 096	9 892	137 315	107 109.3	7 016.1	37 619	470 794	109 102.6	10 001.5	8 862	54 874	12 858.6	1 685.7
Alcona	6.3	575	2	D	D	D	45	277	55.3	5.3	7	D	D	D
Alger	5.6	582	4	D	D	D	50	318	54.4	5.1	7	D	D	D
Allegan	23.6	212	115	1 316	506.7	56.6	362	3 715	881.3	77.4	77	258	46.2	8.5
Alpena	120.3	4 065	31	D	D	D	169	1 890	416.8	38.9	25	143	14.3	2.7
Antrim	58.7	2 490	11	D	D	D	103	636	156.7	13.6	21	77	7.0	1.7
Arenac	61.1	3 842	12	D	D	D	72	488	118.8	8.2	7	D	D	D
Baraga	15.5	1 752	4	5	4.6	0.2	36	324	67.7	5.5	5	D	D	D
Barry	8.2	139	33	210	72.3	8.4	150	1 528	276.2	24.6	31	100	8.3	2.9
Bay	608.3	5 644	95	D	D	D	430	5 580	1 301.0	115.5	77	316	39.9	6.0
Benzie	2.6	146	7	29	3.5	0.7	77	558	131.3	12.2	23	35	6.7	1.1
Berrien	2 019.0	12 875	143	1 836	689.1	65.2	609	7 360	1 622.8	153.9	189	796	105.6	19.3
Branch	13.2	292	30	D	D	D	148	1 887	396.9	38.5	33	79	10.8	2.2
Calhoun	28.1	206	103	D	D	D	531	7 074	1 571.3	136.0	95	475	62.7	11.7
Cass	22.6	432	44	D	D	D	121	899	183.4	17.4	25	56	10.0	1.0
Charlevoix	21.3	820	14	55	8.4	1.6	136	995	221.2	20.8	41	141	29.8	6.7
Cheboygan	7.6	291	14	D	D	D	183	1 282	316.9	28.7	31	117	15.2	2.9
Chippewa	8.9	232	22	D	D	D	169	1 654	369.5	33.0	29	93	12.1	2.1
Clare	3.8	122	12	D	D	D	127	1 144	246.1	22.8	16	29	4.2	0.7
Clinton	9.7	128	46	815	562.1	31.6	186	2 123	631.9	52.4	65	264	41.1	8.0
Crawford	2.3	161	4	D	D	D	74	621	216.8	12.6	15	28	4.0	0.6
Delta	67.4	1 817	45	D	D	D	213	2 268	459.8	46.2	31	78	7.9	1.2
Dickinson	25.2	963	51	D	D	D	181	1 975	417.3	38.8	28	D	D	D
Eaton	8.9	83	71	1 441	914.3	67.9	404	5 996	1 327.0	116.2	105	488	76.7	12.7
Emmet	6.3	193	34	D	D	D	310	2 583	580.6	62.8	53	195	23.9	5.5
Genesee	13.4	31	296	5 871	3 554.9	382.9	1 614	21 531	4 836.7	440.5	339	1 813	270.2	47.7
Gladwin	2.3	91	6	31	9.0	1.4	88	627	140.2	12.6	20	88	8.5	2.8
Gogebic	2.3	138	10	D	D	D	93	719	138.0	13.0	16	61	3.4	1.0
Grand Traverse	14.3	165	122	1 141	425.0	43.1	622	7 192	1 570.1	149.2	163	546	120.9	16.8
Gratiot	8.4	198	29	D	D	D	146	1 367	316.4	27.9	20	63	4.8	1.2
Hillsdale	9.4	201	37	384	260.6	16.5	150	1 430	323.3	31.2	27	81	10.0	1.4
Houghton	4.0	110	20	D	D	D	176	1 935	335.5	34.1	28	D	D	D
Huron	62.5	1 887	38	456	253.6	17.2	188	1 585	323.1	28.5	12	17	4.4	0.5
Ingham	220.5	785	241	3 168	4 423.7	139.6	1 000	15 174	3 156.2	299.6	286	2 596	282.0	68.2
Ionia	9.7	151	25	243	118.8	8.8	163	2 021	446.7	39.8	27	77	7.6	1.2
Iosco	4.3	168	6	D	D	D	137	1 294	270.6	25.0	24	50	5.3	0.9
Iron	1.4	115	12	47	18.6	1.3	73	519	101.4	8.6	19	65	3.0	1.2
Isabella	8.2	117	44	D	D	D	234	3 757	705.4	69.1	56	729	57.4	13.8
Jackson	20.3	127	146	D	D	D	582	7 462	1 690.9	153.6	118	608	64.9	12.5
Kalamazoo	51.8	207	250	3 102	1 207.2	139.2	918	14 148	2 808.8	278.0	226	2 512	219.2	69.1
Kalkaska	3.4	197	21	182	83.4	10.0	57	465	144.1	10.2	10	55	5.0	1.1
Kent	27.7	46	950	21 881	13 020.8	1 141.5	2 216	33 139	8 058.0	715.9	649	4 013	601.0	109.0

1. Merchant wholesalers, except manufacturers' sales branches and offices. 2. Employer establishments.

STATE County	Professional, scientific, and technical services,[1] 2007				Manufacturing, 2007				Accommodation and food services, 2007			
	Number of establish-ments	Number of employees	Receipts (mil dol)	Annual payroll (mil dol)	Number of establish-ments	Number of employees	Receipts (mil dol)	Annual payroll (mil dol)	Number of establish-ments	Number of employees	Sales (mil dol)	Annual payroll (mil dol)
	147	148	149	150	151	152	153	154	155	156	157	158
MARYLAND—Cont'd												
St. Mary's	274	D	D	D	35	D	D	D	162	3 011	132.3	34.1
Somerset	23	D	D	D	NA	NA	NA	NA	31	298	9.9	2.9
Talbot	162	1 177	176.0	67.8	47	2 422	D	83.8	124	1 997	104.9	31.8
Washington	235	D	D	D	149	6 969	2 448.7	337.4	290	5 036	229.7	65.1
Wicomico	228	D	D	D	79	D	D	136.1	194	4 002	184.8	50.3
Worcester	158	D	D	D	39	D	154.6	D	406	6 477	506.8	141.6
Baltimore city	1 506	D	D	D	479	16 253	5 730.9	726.5	1 481	21 456	1 434.7	372.1
MASSACHUSETTS	21 773	243 374	49 085.7	20 652.0	7 737	289 256	86 429.0	15 712.0	16 039	257 302	14 917.2	4 339.7
Barnstable	753	D	D	D	210	2 461	533.3	110.3	1 100	12 721	891.0	261.6
Berkshire	366	D	D	D	173	6 204	1 425.5	317.1	516	7 600	401.9	125.6
Bristol	1 110	D	D	D	797	35 101	8 878.1	1 659.4	1 206	20 866	885.2	261.7
Dukes	71	282	38.6	14.6	NA	NA	NA	NA	125	734	95.8	28.3
Essex	2 221	D	D	D	997	47 909	17 488.7	2 877.4	1 708	23 927	1 301.5	377.7
Franklin	120	D	D	D	111	4 537	1 164.4	197.3	157	1 944	80.3	24.4
Hampden	886	D	D	D	673	24 346	6 001.1	1 122.1	978	14 673	661.7	191.7
Hampshire	360	D	D	D	157	3 970	1 098.8	182.1	367	5 430	225.5	67.7
Middlesex	6 883	106 332	21 264.5	9 828.5	1 853	72 842	22 482.6	4 609.2	3 372	54 344	3 250.2	932.3
Nantucket	56	D	D	D	NA	NA	NA	NA	104	752	88.9	26.3
Norfolk	2 704	D	D	D	714	26 614	10 340.8	1 434.6	1 435	24 126	1 294.0	378.9
Plymouth	1 288	D	D	D	541	13 012	2 577.2	566.5	1 023	17 051	794.6	242.1
Suffolk	3 067	52 850	13 301.5	5 485.4	379	12 664	3 703.4	674.8	2 257	48 978	3 795.9	1 090.7
Worcester	1 888	14 149	2 693.0	917.8	1 099	39 334	10 706.1	1 953.9	1 691	24 156	1 150.7	330.8
MICHIGAN	22 552	249 864	29 536.8	15 304.5	13 675	581 739	234 455.8	29 910.3	19 678	339 181	14 536.6	4 207.3
Alcona	8	19	1.7	0.7	NA	NA	NA	NA	26	97	4.2	1.1
Alger	12	36	3.0	1.0	9	629	193.9	28.0	41	358	14.2	3.0
Allegan	169	1 012	61.7	42.4	214	13 077	4 240.7	573.6	216	2 742	118.8	34.3
Alpena	48	D	D	D	46	1 603	587.4	72.2	73	882	32.2	9.2
Antrim	43	135	10.5	3.9	52	1 039	193.6	42.2	68	1 176	35.2	14.3
Arenac	16	149	8.2	4.2	27	695	126.6	23.1	47	398	15.6	4.1
Baraga	2	D	D	D	NA	NA	NA	NA	14	183	5.6	1.3
Barry	68	266	19.6	8.6	68	2 781	977.4	118.6	81	929	32.3	9.8
Bay	174	D	D	D	126	3 532	1 107.2	191.2	238	3 973	134.7	41.3
Benzie	28	D	D	D	NA	NA	NA	NA	54	1 053	44.2	12.9
Berrien	287	D	D	D	332	10 831	2 298.3	474.7	413	5 519	219.5	64.1
Branch	46	157	12.8	4.2	80	2 990	1 061.1	127.2	83	990	44.7	10.7
Calhoun	209	D	D	D	179	11 532	4 954.0	537.5	284	4 558	182.0	54.1
Cass	55	D	D	D	85	3 114	711.3	113.6	63	743	27.1	7.5
Charlevoix	71	194	17.6	6.4	52	2 899	698.6	134.0	87	1 570	60.2	17.4
Cheboygan	55	152	14.3	4.9	NA	NA	NA	NA	116	773	46.0	14.6
Chippewa	46	D	D	D	32	578	D	19.5	114	2 428	189.9	45.0
Clare	28	166	12.5	6.8	31	969	192.5	36.1	68	736	28.9	8.0
Clinton	117	574	61.1	25.2	67	2 159	609.3	106.2	99	1 666	50.8	14.6
Crawford	19	79	9.9	2.0	18	563	152.6	23.3	49	600	19.6	6.4
Delta	81	D	D	D	73	2 695	712.6	124.6	110	1 342	46.4	13.3
Dickinson	54	D	D	D	48	2 214	D	100.4	78	873	28.6	8.1
Eaton	193	1 292	143.3	56.3	96	8 377	D	547.9	201	4 122	155.3	48.3
Emmet	118	485	56.9	22.4	51	1 026	254.4	39.9	142	2 220	108.4	33.4
Genesee	694	D	D	D	309	14 878	12 579.5	1 099.6	762	13 583	528.7	151.9
Gladwin	21	61	4.0	1.3	39	811	174.1	33.6	50	488	17.6	5.1
Gogebic	26	110	8.2	3.7	21	682	80.1	20.2	61	1 188	55.7	14.5
Grand Traverse	408	D	D	D	179	4 727	1 160.7	202.0	236	5 267	237.7	72.0
Gratiot	37	279	16.8	10.2	48	2 010	357.4	73.3	66	1 152	40.1	13.0
Hillsdale	50	346	20.3	8.2	92	3 917	1 330.8	145.8	80	752	31.4	8.0
Houghton	68	D	D	D	48	D	D	28.9	111	1 427	46.5	13.6
Huron	56	271	23.3	13.2	68	2 692	647.3	101.9	105	832	33.6	8.2
Ingham	777	5 944	724.3	293.6	222	9 829	D	533.1	601	11 648	446.1	131.8
Ionia	59	D	D	D	73	3 126	1 117.4	112.0	88	980	37.4	9.5
Iosco	40	169	12.5	5.6	37	973	190.4	33.8	77	663	27.3	7.4
Iron	31	199	8.6	4.0	NA	NA	NA	NA	44	334	11.6	3.1
Isabella	124	1 672	78.3	41.3	61	2 221	528.7	85.0	125	3 431	117.8	33.8
Jackson	235	D	D	D	284	9 250	2 783.0	403.6	300	4 999	185.4	53.5
Kalamazoo	557	D	D	D	334	17 261	7 145.9	904.1	507	11 678	414.6	130.6
Kalkaska	21	213	17.1	9.8	NA	NA	NA	NA	29	363	13.7	3.9
Kent	1 643	D	D	D	1 154	61 608	15 738.3	3 034.1	1 134	24 655	925.2	283.6

1. Establishment subject to federal tax.

STATE County	Health care and social assistance, 2007				Other services, 2007				Nonemployer businesses, 2013		Value of residential construction authorized by building permits, 2014	
	Number of establish-ments	Number of employees	Receipts (mil dol)	Annual payroll (mil dol)	Number of establish-ments	Number of employees	Receipts (mil dol)	Annual payroll (mil dol)	Number	Receipts (mil dol)	New Construction ($1,000)	Number of housing units
	159	160	161	162	163	164	165	166	167	168	169	170
MARYLAND—Cont'd												
St. Mary's	159	3 563	311.3	126.3	146	877	83.7	27.4	6 594	239.0	102 481	457
Somerset	40	1 267	77.2	37.7	28	85	11.4	1.8	1 447	52.6	16 628	140
Talbot	170	2 946	314.7	114.3	129	833	93.2	23.7	4 246	199.3	14 595	43
Washington	407	9 407	822.7	355.5	268	1 838	159.3	43.3	8 180	348.1	50 422	274
Wicomico	346	7 715	745.9	330.3	179	1 218	100.7	30.2	5 987	247.6	20 409	168
Worcester	130	1 896	160.3	64.7	150	925	72.2	22.6	4 878	240.9	39 590	200
Baltimore city	1 506	64 978	8 368.9	2 954.3	982	9 180	1 541.6	273.4	41 444	1 376.2	94 235	821
MASSACHUSETTS	17 855	511 012	51 946.1	22 176.0	13 516	90 268	9 841.0	2 690.3	484 147	25 590.0	3 300 622	14 486
Barnstable	807	15 247	1 466.2	620.7	601	3 279	334.9	88.2	24 948	1 269.6	185 209	640
Berkshire	450	10 869	981.1	429.8	309	1 742	142.3	38.5	10 054	437.5	53 836	177
Bristol	1 368	36 372	2 911.7	1 364.1	1 052	5 898	465.7	131.5	30 906	1 455.4	136 851	823
Dukes	61	590	78.1	33.0	55	177	26.1	6.1	3 695	205.5	71 742	120
Essex	2 030	47 584	4 272.0	1 909.5	1 470	8 644	1 096.7	254.2	56 791	2 856.7	305 622	1 357
Franklin	197	3 678	267.2	116.1	137	572	48.5	13.3	5 922	211.7	16 044	70
Hampden	1 162	37 111	3 243.2	1 423.3	834	5 453	431.5	133.2	23 446	1 135.2	63 712	313
Hampshire	419	8 219	764.1	309.8	297	1 550	147.2	38.9	12 700	534.8	42 910	193
Middlesex	4 386	99 055	10 192.8	4 326.2	3 202	23 744	2 577.2	790.2	125 980	6 911.8	695 156	3 241
Nantucket	34	369	52.3	17.6	41	173	26.3	6.2	2 322	173.6	107 620	149
Norfolk	2 084	53 650	4 430.5	1 984.8	1 535	9 656	1 036.5	297.6	52 921	3 310.2	379 944	1 594
Plymouth	1 157	26 215	2 209.8	978.5	921	6 294	518.6	185.1	35 386	1 889.1	249 370	1 218
Suffolk	1 755	116 467	15 525.9	6 462.1	1 716	15 391	2 216.9	483.0	49 184	2 827.4	742 524	3 323
Worcester	1 945	55 586	5 551.2	2 200.6	1 346	7 695	772.5	224.3	49 892	2 371.6	250 082	1 268
MICHIGAN	26 033	549 482	52 758.4	21 588.3	17 040	101 568	10 843.7	2 648.1	687 136	28 129.4	3 314 833	15 933
Alcona	10	D	D	D	14	36	3.1	0.5	729	26.4	2 311	23
Alger	21	308	18.1	7.7	14	D	D	D	569	19.0	5 195	28
Allegan	171	3 104	208.5	88.5	182	807	69.2	19.1	7 703	316.4	82 870	348
Alpena	92	2 734	222.1	91.5	78	348	29.5	7.7	1 965	76.1	3 683	23
Antrim	44	396	23.4	11.4	34	152	15.1	4.4	2 083	83.7	13 354	45
Arenac	32	630	46.8	17.6	25	D	D	D	914	34.1	1 734	12
Baraga	21	355	26.1	11.4	18	49	3.1	0.6	389	12.2	1 897	15
Barry	76	1 414	104.4	43.8	94	375	36.5	9.4	3 643	147.0	14 469	86
Bay	315	5 902	513.3	209.5	196	1 068	75.9	21.8	5 549	199.4	10 990	62
Benzie	34	355	26.4	9.7	25	D	D	D	1 650	68.6	8 699	41
Berrien	394	8 821	701.7	282.8	281	1 468	112.2	35.1	9 735	366.3	69 136	184
Branch	91	D	D	D	72	D	D	D	2 476	108.5	0	0
Calhoun	341	8 967	898.1	372.5	225	1 249	503.8	42.5	6 582	217.9	8 374	56
Cass	60	D	D	D	62	272	27.8	6.5	3 016	120.5	25 941	84
Charlevoix	75	862	81.4	32.6	63	251	23.8	5.9	2 570	102.6	20 581	67
Cheboygan	54	1 158	87.8	35.0	72	206	17.9	5.0	1 899	72.7	10 652	54
Chippewa	78	1 546	136.9	46.6	61	D	D	D	1 987	54.9	5 254	38
Clare	55	947	79.6	27.1	52	157	12.9	2.9	1 739	68.5	3 389	20
Clinton	95	1 370	107.1	37.9	105	592	44.7	12.6	5 142	201.4	80 233	345
Crawford	40	1 006	90.7	35.3	25	146	15.5	5.3	832	28.6	2 745	18
Delta	109	1 819	147.1	53.4	95	586	46.5	12.5	2 015	65.6	7 391	47
Dickinson	102	D	D	D	76	D	D	D	1 435	52.6	6 778	32
Eaton	239	2 995	231.0	88.7	164	1 040	118.8	38.5	7 000	247.0	19 565	95
Emmet	198	3 146	361.7	139.1	109	508	56.0	14.9	3 489	158.7	25 108	69
Genesee	1 261	25 790	2 505.1	1 005.4	648	3 695	418.1	103.4	28 250	923.3	65 470	343
Gladwin	35	701	55.6	18.3	32	211	15.5	4.3	1 600	75.3	8 275	41
Gogebic	40	738	62.9	24.7	43	131	10.2	2.6	841	25.7	8 107	23
Grand Traverse	382	7 736	798.1	305.0	232	1 314	121.8	32.0	8 953	410.3	76 184	384
Gratiot	110	2 439	216.3	81.7	62	255	30.3	7.2	2 285	86.8	3 301	17
Hillsdale	112	1 474	111.2	42.2	57	416	24.4	5.0	2 806	112.1	6 585	34
Houghton	86	2 026	146.7	61.5	69	D	D	D	1 863	54.4	6 499	34
Huron	98	1 804	130.2	50.7	61	212	18.2	4.0	2 267	102.7	10 474	47
Ingham	848	20 580	1 991.5	843.5	595	5 128	584.8	158.0	18 469	808.2	68 899	315
Ionia	108	1 287	94.2	35.9	82	366	24.1	5.7	3 184	102.6	11 203	53
Iosco	58	1 200	93.6	41.5	62	223	14.1	3.7	1 532	49.9	7 813	49
Iron	18	395	37.7	14.0	22	D	D	D	732	22.0	3 176	20
Isabella	224	3 265	193.7	86.9	101	544	34.1	9.0	3 530	159.3	13 352	111
Jackson	379	8 717	810.5	346.6	241	1 528	147.0	41.2	8 876	311.5	16 728	89
Kalamazoo	639	18 148	1 811.4	703.6	430	3 414	480.2	91.8	15 771	629.7	119 609	480
Kalkaska	25	466	32.7	13.6	36	D	D	D	1 210	46.2	3 626	21
Kent	1 497	40 522	3 956.9	1 564.3	1 100	7 828	721.7	198.8	43 713	2 052.9	344 898	1 711

STATE County	Government employment and payroll, 2012: Full-time equivalent employees	March payroll (dollars)	March payroll (percent of total): Adminis-tration, judicial, and legal	Police and Corrections	Fire Protection	Highways and transpor-tation	Health and Welfare	Natural resources and utilities	Education and libraries	Local government finances, 2012 — General revenue: Total (mil dol)	Inter-govern-mental (mil dol)	Taxes: Total (mil dol)	Per capita[1] (dollars): Total	Property
	171	172	173	174	175	176	177	178	179	180	181	182	183	184
MARYLAND—Cont'd														
St. Mary's	3 187	14 069 480	5.9	10.5	0.0	2.3	1.5	4.3	73.2	356.5	125.4	191.8	1 760	923
Somerset	890	3 320 415	5.7	9.8	0.0	2.6	2.1	5.5	67.9	83.1	45.3	26.3	1 002	735
Talbot	1 356	5 353 079	6.3	12.0	0.0	3.6	4.8	9.8	53.9	135.2	24.3	75.9	1 992	1 178
Washington	5 270	21 889 886	4.2	7.2	2.7	2.6	0.7	8.0	73.2	547.6	234.3	228.4	1 531	989
Wicomico	4 063	15 857 286	4.2	10.7	1.8	1.7	1.9	5.3	73.7	376.1	166.7	134.3	1 334	842
Worcester	2 609	11 789 178	8.3	14.2	2.1	3.0	6.7	9.7	51.9	340.0	56.3	227.1	4 403	3 313
Baltimore city	27 461	126 508 297	5.8	15.9	7.5	3.3	8.2	10.7	47.4	3 714.0	1 967.9	1 238.8	1 994	1 229
MASSACHUSETTS	X	X	X	X	X	X	X	X	X	X	X	X	X	X
Barnstable	7 548	35 968 725	7.2	11.5	10.0	4.2	3.5	6.4	53.6	1 003.5	207.7	645.0	2 994	2 809
Berkshire	4 790	19 230 480	4.3	8.5	3.3	5.5	1.3	4.1	71.5	506.3	218.2	246.7	1 897	1 828
Bristol	17 070	76 423 100	3.0	10.6	7.2	2.1	2.0	5.3	68.1	2 032.5	942.1	830.7	1 507	1 453
Dukes	1 048	4 632 999	7.6	11.3	1.4	6.7	6.9	4.4	59.7	141.2	27.4	88.5	5 195	4 963
Essex	25 587	123 574 109	3.4	8.7	6.1	2.3	1.3	6.5	69.6	2 861.5	1 081.5	1 475.0	1 952	1 898
Franklin	2 963	11 147 283	5.4	6.1	2.8	5.5	1.3	4.8	71.6	305.5	144.0	135.0	1 887	1 847
Hampden	18 660	82 237 236	2.8	9.5	5.8	2.3	1.5	8.2	68.6	2 010.8	1 105.6	711.6	1 527	1 484
Hampshire	5 845	24 568 656	4.7	9.8	7.3	3.2	2.8	5.3	64.6	489.0	185.2	236.2	1 478	1 434
Middlesex	51 015	257 135 128	5.3	9.1	7.3	2.5	5.9	5.3	61.9	7 258.0	1 991.8	3 798.4	2 471	2 386
Nantucket	564	3 317 115	5.0	8.7	5.6	10.9	11.3	6.7	48.7	127.3	11.0	80.2	7 784	6 281
Norfolk	21 584	108 297 457	3.8	9.0	7.0	2.5	1.4	5.7	68.8	2 684.4	649.6	1 685.1	2 471	2 399
Plymouth	17 576	78 325 658	3.7	8.5	6.3	2.3	1.5	4.3	71.8	1 886.5	696.4	1 001.7	2 004	1 943
Suffolk	22 999	131 415 091	3.4	16.9	11.5	2.0	7.1	7.2	49.6	3 908.1	1 488.3	1 972.4	2 650	2 442
Worcester	28 380	132 203 123	3.5	8.3	5.1	3.2	1.5	4.3	73.0	3 064.8	1 424.8	1 314.3	1 630	1 589
MICHIGAN	X	X	X	X	X	X	X	X	X	X	X	X	X	X
Alcona	260	869 231	18.9	12.8	2.7	13.1	5.9	0.9	43.1	26.7	8.8	13.3	1 250	1 247
Alger	293	1 015 817	13.5	7.1	0.5	18.5	0.2	4.4	52.0	30.8	13.5	10.2	1 071	1 037
Allegan	3 023	10 951 667	9.1	7.0	1.3	3.2	8.0	2.2	67.1	353.3	194.8	109.8	980	962
Alpena	2 199	8 769 942	4.0	2.3	1.9	3.0	58.9	0.8	28.5	257.0	79.4	32.4	1 109	1 087
Antrim	795	2 618 552	12.6	9.1	1.8	7.2	4.1	3.3	59.1	89.8	22.9	43.1	1 841	1 822
Arenac	446	1 462 195	13.6	6.7	0.0	5.4	0.6	3.4	66.5	44.9	24.2	14.4	928	920
Baraga	413	1 533 081	10.5	4.7	0.2	7.7	36.0	3.8	36.1	56.1	20.1	9.9	1 142	1 141
Barry	1 440	5 121 005	9.4	7.0	1.4	5.4	12.9	2.3	58.3	149.7	79.8	42.0	711	706
Bay	4 027	15 471 429	6.7	5.7	2.4	4.8	13.5	5.1	61.1	536.8	284.0	123.7	1 157	1 137
Benzie	473	1 629 367	11.3	8.6	1.6	6.8	9.1	2.1	57.3	57.9	16.6	24.9	1 423	1 407
Berrien	4 813	18 604 576	9.6	10.9	2.0	2.9	2.9	4.5	64.6	601.1	301.4	200.9	1 288	1 264
Branch	1 691	6 939 089	6.6	5.2	1.3	3.6	38.9	3.2	38.5	226.8	88.1	39.0	889	873
Calhoun	4 008	16 572 500	10.0	11.0	3.1	3.3	5.9	4.4	61.4	671.0	371.6	175.1	1 296	1 142
Cass	1 418	4 769 730	10.8	7.3	0.6	2.9	0.9	2.2	72.4	172.3	89.2	43.1	825	808
Charlevoix	1 150	4 194 441	10.6	5.9	1.3	5.8	28.6	3.6	42.0	158.1	43.7	73.2	2 813	2 799
Cheboygan	787	2 583 533	17.3	8.3	0.3	7.1	0.7	3.5	58.4	82.5	33.6	37.9	1 467	1 464
Chippewa	1 196	4 184 040	10.1	7.0	2.7	11.4	6.7	6.0	52.6	135.4	67.2	34.8	894	891
Clare	1 104	4 192 533	8.2	5.7	0.9	5.4	0.8	1.5	74.1	127.0	64.5	31.2	1 013	1 002
Clinton	1 742	6 413 165	10.6	9.9	0.7	3.5	0.4	3.2	69.3	200.2	105.1	60.4	794	775
Crawford	409	1 431 323	13.6	11.5	1.6	16.3	4.0	2.0	47.9	39.4	16.7	15.9	1 133	1 086
Delta	1 241	4 680 702	6.7	9.5	0.0	5.2	3.8	6.7	65.7	127.4	66.1	38.2	1 037	1 028
Dickinson	1 535	6 348 874	4.3	5.6	1.0	3.4	58.2	2.3	23.9	184.8	56.0	31.4	1 196	1 182
Eaton	2 554	9 735 640	10.8	10.4	3.7	4.1	3.2	4.4	60.8	310.5	152.5	99.7	923	899
Emmet	1 325	5 336 908	10.4	6.0	0.7	4.0	16.4	3.6	56.1	264.7	141.6	74.6	2 266	2 213
Genesee	15 234	64 330 939	5.5	5.9	1.4	3.5	24.1	3.5	55.1	2 005.4	1 056.8	353.2	844	786
Gladwin	706	2 311 382	11.6	6.0	5.6	5.3	0.0	6.6	61.0	64.7	29.2	22.5	882	866
Gogebic	622	2 249 336	12.5	6.4	0.2	9.6	0.9	8.4	60.0	90.5	45.8	17.4	1 082	1 078
Grand Traverse	3 921	13 601 114	7.7	6.2	1.5	4.9	19.6	4.5	54.3	484.0	209.1	154.5	1 733	1 707
Gratiot	1 175	3 955 893	11.4	7.1	0.6	5.7	0.5	4.7	67.3	148.7	93.4	35.9	853	831
Hillsdale	1 203	4 074 488	12.8	8.9	1.5	5.5	0.3	8.2	59.8	131.8	71.6	31.6	684	680
Houghton	1 000	3 212 799	11.7	7.0	0.3	9.7	5.5	5.2	58.7	146.4	70.0	29.8	815	804
Huron	1 172	3 974 661	13.7	7.4	3.0	6.1	17.1	4.5	45.7	144.4	58.3	49.0	1 508	1 483
Ingham	10 953	47 886 830	7.3	7.2	3.2	4.6	11.6	7.8	53.9	1 384.5	665.7	427.0	1 516	1 387
Ionia	1 653	5 904 984	8.9	6.9	0.5	4.2	2.6	4.1	71.7	208.2	123.1	53.2	832	780
Iosco	1 129	3 442 430	9.4	4.0	0.3	4.8	27.8	2.2	46.8	108.8	50.8	33.6	1 326	1 313
Iron	408	1 333 527	19.7	8.3	1.1	6.9	9.9	12.6	38.2	67.8	34.2	17.2	1 482	1 471
Isabella	1 686	5 798 126	10.7	6.7	1.2	7.0	29.5	4.2	39.4	236.5	148.6	46.1	653	641
Jackson	4 304	17 626 740	7.6	8.1	2.4	4.2	3.5	3.4	69.5	585.1	325.3	139.2	868	809
Kalamazoo	6 988	32 644 262	7.1	11.8	16.7	2.9	2.7	3.6	54.2	970.9	521.9	297.6	1 169	1 137
Kalkaska	695	2 106 824	12.6	6.6	0.4	8.0	43.8	2.8	23.7	84.6	15.9	18.4	1 075	1 058
Kent	16 442	72 374 352	7.5	10.6	3.2	4.8	1.8	4.9	66.1	2 471.0	1 223.4	763.8	1 243	1 084

1. Based on the resident population estimated as of July 1 of the year shown.

STATE County	Local government finances, 2012 (cont.) — Direct general expenditure: Total (mil dol)	Per capita[1] (dollars)	Percent of total for: Educa-tion	Health and hospitals	Police protec-tion	Public welfare	High-ways	Debt outstanding: Total (mil dol)	Per capita[1] (dollars)	Government employment, 2013: Federal civilian	Federal military	State and local	Presidential election,[2] 2012 — Percent of vote cast: Demo-cratic	Republi-can	All other
	185	186	187	188	189	190	191	192	193	194	195	196	197	198	199
MARYLAND—Cont'd															
St. Mary's	331.8	3 045	62.8	2.2	6.2	0.9	2.7	197.3	1 810	8 999	2 456	4 631	42.8	55.6	1.5
Somerset	126.9	4 833	34.0	0.9	3.5	0.2	3.0	52.4	1 996	45	98	2 991	48.2	50.8	1.1
Talbot	130.3	3 419	40.1	3.0	8.2	0.8	5.1	87.8	2 304	218	138	1 657	44.4	54.1	1.5
Washington	564.3	3 783	59.9	0.7	4.0	0.4	4.5	391.3	2 623	636	464	8 555	42.6	55.5	1.9
Wicomico	357.2	3 549	57.8	1.0	6.3	3.1	2.6	203.7	2 024	298	310	7 507	46.4	52.2	1.4
Worcester	300.6	5 827	35.7	2.9	10.6	0.7	4.0	284.8	5 522	188	197	3 620	41.6	57.1	1.3
Baltimore city	4 080.5	6 567	34.4	2.9	9.1	0.0	5.1	2 807.8	4 519	9 698	2 095	57 197	87.2	11.7	1.2
MASSACHUSETTS	X	X	X	X	X	X	X	X	X	46 281	20 281	392 272	62.0	36.2	1.7
Barnstable	1 041.6	4 835	45.9	1.1	5.3	0.2	3.5	892.5	4 143	1 703	1 241	13 169	56.1	42.4	1.5
Berkshire	629.4	4 841	60.3	0.5	3.2	0.3	5.9	274.5	2 111	365	323	8 343	75.2	22.6	2.2
Bristol	1 991.8	3 614	57.9	0.9	5.0	1.0	2.5	1 318.2	2 392	1 072	1 424	27 430	60.7	37.5	1.8
Dukes	159.8	9 379	47.0	2.7	4.8	0.1	3.1	92.7	5 440	46	44	1 444	75.1	23.2	1.6
Essex	2 925.1	3 871	57.7	0.4	4.6	0.2	2.8	1 876.8	2 484	3 471	2 015	36 596	59.4	39.0	1.6
Franklin	333.5	4 661	58.8	0.4	2.7	0.4	4.8	96.2	1 344	184	180	4 923	72.7	24.9	2.4
Hampden	2 073.1	4 449	58.0	0.5	4.5	0.6	2.9	1 537.4	3 300	3 937	1 377	30 544	61.5	36.4	2.1
Hampshire	545.4	3 413	56.1	0.8	5.8	0.5	3.8	283.7	1 775	1 284	365	17 068	71.8	26.0	2.3
Middlesex	7 035.9	4 577	49.7	11.6	4.1	0.2	2.6	4 420.3	2 876	12 064	5 122	76 090	64.2	34.1	1.7
Nantucket	106.8	10 369	26.6	0.4	4.0	6.2	0.6	224.6	21 811	59	54	617	67.5	31.0	1.5
Norfolk	2 651.4	3 889	55.1	0.5	5.1	0.2	3.0	2 012.1	2 951	1 595	1 746	32 906	58.5	40.0	1.6
Plymouth	1 986.2	3 974	61.8	0.6	4.6	0.3	2.6	1 305.2	2 612	3 220	1 308	27 944	53.0	45.4	1.5
Suffolk	3 805.2	5 112	33.9	7.5	8.8	1.3	1.5	2 110.9	2 836	14 194	3 047	65 438	77.5	21.1	1.4
Worcester	3 304.7	4 099	61.5	0.4	4.0	0.2	3.4	2 495.3	3 095	3 087	2 035	49 760	55.8	42.1	2.1
MICHIGAN	X	X	X	X	X	X	X	X	X	51 924	18 864	539 265	57.4	41.0	1.6
Alcona	27.1	2 545	30.2	4.5	5.3	0.9	24.2	3.8	359	25	18	311	45.1	53.0	1.9
Alger	32.4	3 395	36.3	4.6	2.9	0.0	17.5	26.3	2 754	83	15	664	52.0	46.1	1.9
Allegan	347.7	3 103	55.1	7.4	3.5	3.5	7.8	410.3	3 662	164	194	4 804	43.7	54.4	1.9
Alpena	248.9	8 516	25.0	59.1	1.5	0.3	2.8	47.7	1 630	113	52	2 912	51.1	47.2	1.7
Antrim	88.3	3 774	40.2	3.4	4.7	14.5	8.8	44.8	1 913	65	40	1 085	43.9	54.2	1.9
Arenac	43.2	2 790	50.7	2.2	3.0	0.5	12.9	32.8	2 122	44	26	686	51.1	46.8	2.0
Baraga	72.9	8 401	19.5	53.3	1.1	0.2	10.4	63.4	7 303	28	13	1 590	47.3	50.7	2.0
Barry	150.3	2 547	48.0	5.6	3.7	9.3	7.8	79.7	1 352	80	101	2 159	44.0	53.8	2.2
Bay	521.5	4 877	44.7	20.6	3.3	4.5	4.2	246.5	2 305	243	242	5 682	56.7	41.4	1.8
Benzie	56.3	3 226	36.8	7.9	2.1	12.2	8.7	30.3	1 734	32	47	685	52.9	45.5	1.7
Berrien	618.7	3 965	53.9	7.1	5.5	1.4	5.2	398.2	2 551	307	286	9 106	52.0	46.5	1.5
Branch	225.6	5 144	34.9	36.1	2.4	5.3	5.0	73.0	1 664	76	72	2 780	46.0	52.1	1.8
Calhoun	680.5	5 037	45.5	17.6	4.3	2.6	5.4	473.1	3 502	2 955	285	7 824	53.8	44.5	1.7
Cass	179.5	3 436	58.6	7.1	3.5	4.6	5.4	185.2	3 544	74	89	2 021	51.3	47.1	1.6
Charlevoix	145.4	5 587	41.5	16.3	2.3	9.8	7.0	79.2	3 043	49	66	1 663	47.4	50.9	1.7
Cheboygan	82.0	3 173	52.2	1.5	4.4	1.1	11.7	35.0	1 356	49	113	936	48.3	49.8	1.9
Chippewa	142.9	3 672	42.0	7.3	3.4	0.4	14.8	140.9	3 620	460	232	6 173	49.0	49.5	1.5
Clare	130.5	4 244	66.9	0.3	2.7	0.5	8.1	36.5	1 188	79	52	1 663	51.5	46.6	1.9
Clinton	197.5	2 598	55.6	0.4	4.2	0.6	7.3	261.6	3 442	184	137	1 884	49.5	48.8	1.6
Crawford	38.5	2 750	41.0	1.0	4.9	1.1	14.9	20.3	1 451	126	24	675	47.9	49.6	2.5
Delta	137.3	3 722	63.6	3.6	2.1	0.2	6.5	110.1	2 984	191	63	1 874	52.3	46.0	1.7
Dickinson	190.3	7 257	25.2	50.0	2.2	0.1	4.5	120.1	4 580	844	62	2 035	45.0	53.0	2.0
Eaton	316.4	2 929	51.9	3.6	5.8	6.6	6.0	453.6	4 200	199	204	5 316	53.4	45.0	1.7
Emmet	280.3	8 515	27.0	38.8	1.4	4.8	4.5	162.6	4 941	91	57	2 439	46.9	51.3	1.8
Genesee	2 064.7	4 935	41.9	28.1	3.5	1.1	3.3	995.9	2 380	1 067	711	20 538	65.5	32.9	1.6
Gladwin	61.5	2 415	46.1	2.0	3.8	0.6	13.3	37.6	1 474	49	44	815	49.8	48.3	2.0
Gogebic	91.1	5 666	31.9	7.4	3.1	10.2	9.5	75.9	4 719	160	25	1 571	57.6	40.3	2.1
Grand Traverse	471.3	5 288	46.6	17.8	2.7	5.6	3.8	445.4	4 998	490	276	5 896	47.7	50.7	1.6
Gratiot	152.9	3 635	57.9	7.3	3.1	1.2	8.1	103.0	2 449	72	63	2 301	51.3	46.9	1.8
Hillsdale	131.8	2 850	51.6	0.9	3.3	14.1	8.6	74.2	1 605	96	77	2 366	42.9	54.9	2.3
Houghton	140.9	3 858	41.4	5.6	2.0	13.7	7.0	113.0	3 095	166	92	3 636	46.8	50.7	2.5
Huron	148.9	4 587	35.1	11.1	2.9	10.7	18.5	113.5	3 496	94	70	1 583	48.8	49.2	1.9
Ingham	1 371.5	4 868	44.9	13.6	4.2	3.1	3.5	1 588.9	5 640	1 626	593	39 097	65.9	32.6	1.6
Ionia	225.2	3 523	60.0	7.0	2.6	0.5	5.8	294.7	4 610	110	101	3 321	46.0	51.8	2.2
Iosco	108.1	4 265	39.8	17.8	2.4	6.7	7.8	52.0	2 052	113	65	1 535	51.5	46.4	2.1
Iron	59.7	5 151	21.7	4.9	2.7	29.2	9.9	40.0	4 026	35	19	871	50.0	47.8	2.2
Isabella	230.9	3 270	25.5	39.2	3.2	5.6	6.2	128.0	1 812	158	114	10 355	58.8	39.6	1.6
Jackson	586.0	3 655	54.4	10.1	2.6	3.6	6.4	539.6	3 366	326	262	7 580	50.3	47.9	1.8
Kalamazoo	958.5	3 765	47.3	14.6	7.5	1.0	4.4	1 168.8	4 591	749	434	13 887	58.9	39.4	1.7
Kalkaska	63.6	3 721	23.4	42.5	3.6	0.2	7.4	40.1	2 342	25	30	846	44.5	53.3	2.3
Kent	2 442.6	3 975	51.3	6.7	4.7	1.7	3.6	3 992.0	6 497	2 757	1 119	23 128	49.4	48.9	1.6

1. Based on the resident population estimated as of July 1 of the year shown. 2.

STATE/ County code	CBSA code[1]	County type[2]	STATE County	Land area,[3] (sq km) 2010	Population, 2014: Total persons 2014	Population, 2014: Rank	Population, 2014: Per square kilometer	Population and population characteristics, 2013: Race alone or in combination, not Hispanic or Latino (percent): White	Black	American Indian, Alaska Native	Asian and Pacific Islander	Percent Hispanic or Latino[4]	Age (percent): Under 5 years	5 to 17 years	18 to 24 years	25 to 34 years	35 to 44 years	45 to 54 years
				1	2	3	4	5	6	7	8	9	10	11	12	13	14	15
			MICHIGAN—Cont'd															
26 083	26340	9	Keweenaw	1 399	2 217	3 032	1.6	98.5	0.5	0.5	0.3	1.0	4.4	13.3	4.7	7.3	9.0	12.6
26 085	...	8	Lake	1 469	11 341	2 334	7.7	87.3	10.2	1.8	0.7	2.5	3.6	13.5	5.5	8.3	9.7	14.6
26 087	19820	1	Lapeer	1 665	88 153	648	52.9	93.6	1.5	1.0	0.7	4.4	4.9	17.6	8.4	9.8	12.0	16.8
26 089	45900	9	Leelanau	899	21 915	1 738	24.4	92.1	0.8	3.8	0.9	3.9	3.9	13.5	6.7	7.8	8.5	13.4
26 091	10300	4	Lenawee	1 941	99 047	595	51.0	88.8	3.3	1.0	0.8	7.7	5.6	16.5	9.6	11.1	12.3	14.3
26 093	19820	1	Livingston	1 464	185 596	346	126.8	96.0	0.8	0.9	1.4	2.2	5.1	18.6	7.9	9.9	12.6	17.3
26 095	...	7	Luce	2 329	6 426	2 722	2.8	82.3	11.8	6.9	0.8	1.4	4.5	12.8	7.8	12.8	13.5	14.2
26 097	...	7	Mackinac	2 646	11 042	2 355	4.2	79.7	1.9	21.5	0.8	1.4	3.7	13.3	6.4	8.1	10.7	15.0
26 099	19820	1	Macomb	1 241	860 112	64	693.1	83.4	11.3	0.9	4.1	2.4	5.4	16.7	8.6	12.2	13.1	15.3
26 101	...	7	Manistee	1 404	24 420	1 630	17.4	91.3	3.9	3.1	0.6	2.8	3.6	14.3	7.6	9.8	10.4	14.5
26 103	32100	5	Marquette	4 684	67 676	788	14.4	94.5	2.2	2.9	1.0	1.4	4.9	13.3	15.7	12.0	10.6	12.8
26 105	31220	7	Mason	1 282	28 824	1 463	22.5	93.5	1.4	1.6	0.8	4.2	5.2	15.3	7.8	10.1	10.5	13.9
26 107	13660	6	Mecosta	1 438	43 186	1 107	30.0	93.5	3.9	1.5	1.2	2.0	4.7	14.4	20.2	10.5	9.2	11.8
26 109	31940	7	Menominee	2 704	23 714	1 651	8.8	94.9	0.9	3.3	0.7	1.5	4.5	15.2	6.9	9.5	10.4	15.4
26 111	33220	4	Midland	1 337	83 427	672	62.4	93.5	1.8	0.9	2.7	2.4	5.4	17.0	9.3	11.6	11.8	15.5
26 113	15620	9	Missaukee	1 463	15 037	2 099	10.3	96.2	0.9	1.3	0.6	2.4	5.9	17.4	7.7	10.7	10.4	14.3
26 115	33780	3	Monroe	1 423	149 824	429	105.3	93.5	3.0	0.9	0.9	3.3	5.5	17.4	8.4	10.9	12.3	15.6
26 117	24340	6	Montcalm	1 827	62 893	835	34.4	93.3	2.9	1.1	0.7	3.2	5.7	17.4	8.2	12.0	12.6	14.9
26 119	...	9	Montmorency	1 416	9 300	2 487	6.6	97.7	0.9	1.2	0.4	1.2	3.4	11.8	5.1	7.5	8.7	14.0
26 121	34740	3	Muskegon	1 293	172 344	368	133.3	79.3	15.4	1.6	1.0	5.1	6.3	17.8	9.2	12.3	11.9	14.1
26 123	...	2	Newaygo	2 106	47 900	1 017	22.7	91.9	1.6	1.3	0.6	5.9	5.8	17.7	8.1	10.6	11.1	14.9
26 125	19820	1	Oakland	2 247	1 237 868	32	550.9	75.4	15.1	0.8	7.0	3.7	5.5	16.9	8.1	12.2	13.2	15.5
26 127	...	8	Oceana	1 326	26 221	1 553	19.8	84.1	1.0	1.6	0.5	14.2	6.2	17.7	7.7	10.0	10.6	14.4
26 129	...	9	Ogemaw	1 459	21 039	1 771	14.4	96.7	0.6	1.6	0.6	1.8	4.6	14.4	7.2	9.0	9.9	14.0
26 131	...	9	Ontonagon	3 396	6 172	2 743	1.8	97.2	0.6	1.9	0.7	1.1	2.5	11.3	4.4	6.2	8.7	15.7
26 133	...	7	Osceola	1 467	23 169	1 676	15.8	96.8	1.5	1.4	0.6	1.5	5.8	18.0	7.7	10.4	11.0	14.0
26 135	...	9	Oscoda	1 465	8 371	2 569	5.7	97.8	0.6	1.7	0.4	1.1	4.8	14.4	6.5	8.2	8.5	13.9
26 137	...	7	Otsego	1 334	24 158	1 639	18.1	96.7	1.1	1.6	0.8	1.5	5.7	16.3	7.7	10.0	11.0	15.2
26 139	24340	3	Ottawa	1 459	276 292	244	189.4	86.2	2.1	0.7	3.2	9.3	6.4	18.7	13.6	11.6	11.8	13.4
26 141	...	7	Presque Isle	1 706	13 004	2 231	7.6	97.2	0.9	1.4	0.6	1.0	3.5	13.0	5.8	7.3	8.9	13.9
26 143	...	7	Roscommon	1 346	23 955	1 644	17.8	96.8	0.9	1.4	0.7	1.5	3.9	11.5	5.9	7.5	8.6	13.5
26 145	40980	3	Saginaw	2 072	195 012	334	94.1	71.8	19.6	0.8	1.5	8.0	5.7	16.5	10.5	11.4	11.3	13.8
26 147	19820	1	St. Clair	1 868	160 078	398	85.7	93.4	3.3	1.1	0.9	3.1	5.3	17.1	8.3	10.3	12.2	16.1
26 149	44780	4	St. Joseph	1 297	60 946	859	47.0	89.3	3.6	0.9	1.1	7.0	6.8	18.4	8.4	11.6	11.5	13.8
26 151	...	6	Sanilac	2 493	41 587	1 134	16.7	95.1	0.8	0.9	0.5	3.7	5.3	17.1	7.6	9.7	11.1	14.8
26 153	...	7	Schoolcraft	3 034	8 171	2 591	2.7	89.7	0.9	11.5	0.5	0.8	4.4	14.2	6.5	8.1	10.5	15.0
26 155	37020	4	Shiawassee	1 374	68 933	773	50.2	95.7	1.0	1.0	0.7	2.7	5.2	17.4	8.9	10.8	12.0	15.6
26 157	...	6	Tuscola	2 080	54 000	925	26.0	94.8	1.5	1.1	0.5	3.2	5.0	16.7	8.2	10.6	11.6	15.2
26 159	28020	2	Van Buren	1 573	75 199	731	47.8	83.8	5.0	1.7	1.0	10.8	6.3	18.0	8.2	10.9	11.8	14.6
26 161	11460	2	Washtenaw	1 828	356 874	190	195.2	74.2	14.1	1.0	9.6	4.4	5.3	14.7	18.1	13.9	11.9	12.8
26 163	19820	1	Wayne	1 585	1 764 804	19	1 113.4	51.8	40.3	1.0	3.6	5.6	6.5	17.7	10.0	12.4	12.7	14.1
26 165	15620	7	Wexford	1 463	32 886	1 357	22.5	96.4	1.0	1.4	1.0	1.7	6.4	17.0	7.7	11.2	11.4	14.6
27 000	...	X	MINNESOTA	206 232	5 457 173	X	26.5	83.8	6.5	1.7	5.2	5.0	6.4	17.2	9.4	13.7	12.3	14.2
27 001	...	8	Aitkin	4 718	15 771	2 057	3.3	95.8	0.9	3.1	0.6	1.1	4.0	13.3	5.3	7.7	8.5	13.8
27 003	33460	1	Anoka	1 096	341 864	196	311.9	86.3	6.0	1.4	5.0	3.9	6.3	18.4	8.2	13.3	13.6	16.2
27 005	...	6	Becker	3 406	33 259	1 347	9.8	89.8	0.9	9.8	0.9	1.7	6.2	18.3	6.9	10.9	10.4	13.2
27 007	13420	7	Beltrami	6 488	45 664	1 056	7.0	76.4	1.3	22.2	1.3	1.9	7.7	17.6	14.1	12.5	10.0	11.7
27 009	41060	3	Benton	1 057	39 506	1 184	37.4	94.3	2.9	0.9	1.6	2.0	6.8	17.7	9.0	16.1	12.3	13.8
27 011	...	9	Big Stone	1 292	5 127	2 831	4.0	97.6	0.6	0.8	0.3	1.3	5.7	14.6	6.3	9.2	8.5	14.5
27 013	31860	5	Blue Earth	1 937	65 385	806	33.8	91.2	3.8	0.6	2.9	3.0	5.7	13.9	21.9	14.3	10.0	10.8
27 015	35580	7	Brown	1 583	25 292	1 598	16.0	95.2	0.6	0.3	0.9	3.7	5.8	15.9	9.5	11.0	9.7	14.2
27 017	20260	2	Carlton	2 231	35 571	1 283	15.9	90.6	2.0	7.1	1.0	1.6	5.9	17.1	7.7	12.0	12.5	15.0
27 019	33460	1	Carver	918	97 338	603	106.0	91.4	1.9	0.5	3.6	4.1	6.4	21.9	7.7	11.3	14.5	17.1
27 021	14660	9	Cass	5 236	28 559	1 469	5.5	86.3	0.7	12.8	0.8	1.6	5.6	15.7	6.6	8.9	9.8	14.0
27 023	...	7	Chippewa	1 505	12 110	2 291	8.0	91.6	1.0	1.6	1.8	5.2	5.8	17.2	7.4	11.4	9.9	13.6
27 025	33460	1	Chisago	1 074	54 025	924	50.3	95.2	1.7	1.1	1.2	1.9	5.4	18.5	7.9	11.6	13.2	17.1
27 027	22020	3	Clay	2 707	61 286	854	22.6	91.7	2.2	2.0	2.0	4.0	6.6	16.4	17.1	13.8	11.2	11.6
27 029	...	8	Clearwater	2 587	8 791	2 532	3.4	88.7	0.9	10.9	0.9	1.7	6.5	18.3	7.3	10.0	11.3	13.3
27 031	...	9	Cook	3 761	5 233	2 821	1.4	88.7	1.3	9.8	1.0	1.8	4.7	12.0	5.8	9.3	10.2	14.3
27 033	...	7	Cottonwood	1 654	11 633	2 315	7.0	89.0	1.2	0.8	3.2	7.0	6.3	16.9	7.2	9.8	10.4	12.9
27 035	14660	5	Crow Wing	2 588	63 265	827	24.4	96.8	1.1	1.4	0.8	1.3	6.0	16.3	7.3	11.3	10.5	13.8
27 037	33460	1	Dakota	1 456	412 529	168	283.3	83.2	6.3	0.9	5.5	6.5	6.6	18.6	8.0	13.5	13.5	15.6
27 039	40340	3	Dodge	1 138	20 353	1 816	17.9	93.9	0.9	0.6	1.0	4.7	6.7	21.3	7.5	11.6	13.5	14.4
27 041	10820	7	Douglas	1 651	36 790	1 255	22.3	97.3	0.8	0.6	0.7	1.3	5.4	15.8	7.9	11.4	10.6	13.2
27 043	...	7	Faribault	1 845	14 192	2 154	7.7	92.9	0.6	0.7	0.6	6.0	5.5	15.9	6.7	10.1	10.1	13.6

1. CBSA = Core Based Statistical Area. See Appendix A for explanation. See Appendix B for list of metropolitan areas with component counties. 2. County type code from the Economic Research Service of USDA Rural-Urban Continuum Codes. See Appendix A for definition. 3. Dry land or land partially or temporarily covered by water. 4. May be of any race.

Table B. States and Counties — **Population and Households**

STATE County	Population, 2013 (cont.): Age (percent) (cont.): 55 to 64 years	65 to 74 years	75 years and over	Percent female	Population change and components of change, 2000–2014: Total persons: 2000	2010	Percent change: 2000–2010	2010–2014	Components of change, 2010–2014: Births	Deaths	Net migration	Households, 2009–2013: Number	Persons per household	Percent: Family households	Female family householder[1]	One person
	16	17	18	19	20	21	22	23	24	25	26	27	28	29	30	31
MICHIGAN—Cont'd																
Keweenaw	19.0	18.4	11.4	48.7	2 301	2 156	-6.3	2.8	73	69	35	1 014	2.08	60.2	5.6	35.0
Lake	18.8	16.0	9.9	49.3	11 333	11 539	1.8	-1.7	396	627	52	4 096	2.72	60.9	9.4	35.3
Lapeer	15.2	9.4	5.9	49.4	87 904	88 319	0.5	-0.2	3 452	3 257	-383	32 684	2.65	75.3	9.2	21.1
Leelanau	18.9	15.0	12.2	50.5	21 119	21 708	2.8	1.0	727	948	330	9 103	2.34	69.8	6.8	24.6
Lenawee	14.3	9.3	6.9	49.4	98 890	99 892	1.0	-0.8	4 435	4 062	-1 233	37 754	2.50	67.7	10.7	26.9
Livingston	14.6	8.8	5.3	50.0	156 951	180 967	15.3	2.6	7 299	5 642	2 741	67 691	2.68	75.4	8.8	20.5
Luce	14.8	11.1	8.5	41.8	7 024	6 631	-5.6	-3.1	223	292	-116	2 427	2.25	63.9	10.6	29.2
Mackinac	18.0	14.3	10.6	48.8	11 943	11 113	-6.9	-0.6	337	544	118	5 000	2.17	63.6	7.5	30.1
Macomb	13.5	8.3	7.0	51.4	788 149	840 978	6.7	2.3	38 799	34 202	14 807	332 818	2.52	66.8	12.7	28.8
Manistee	17.4	12.6	9.8	48.2	24 527	24 733	0.8	-1.3	779	1 304	226	10 571	2.20	64.9	9.3	29.0
Marquette	14.7	8.9	7.2	49.6	64 634	67 077	3.8	0.9	2 756	2 699	563	26 436	2.38	60.2	7.1	31.9
Mason	16.5	11.9	8.9	50.5	28 274	28 705	1.5	0.4	1 222	1 375	293	12 470	2.26	66.8	10.2	29.3
Mecosta	12.6	9.8	6.7	49.9	40 553	42 798	5.5	0.9	1 763	1 572	227	15 536	2.55	65.2	8.5	25.5
Menominee	17.2	11.2	9.7	49.5	25 326	24 029	-5.1	-1.3	931	1 090	-133	10 787	2.18	64.7	9.6	31.1
Midland	13.7	8.3	7.5	50.9	82 874	83 629	0.9	-0.2	3 617	2 944	-844	33 717	2.45	67.7	9.2	26.6
Missaukee	14.8	10.8	7.9	49.2	14 478	14 849	2.6	1.3	745	652	116	5 891	2.50	69.8	9.7	26.3
Monroe	14.7	8.7	6.5	50.7	145 945	152 021	4.2	-1.4	6 446	5 844	-2 849	58 702	2.55	70.1	11.0	25.4
Montcalm	13.5	9.0	6.6	48.2	61 266	63 342	3.4	-0.7	3 083	2 443	-1 067	23 400	2.59	70.9	11.2	25.0
Montmorency	20.4	16.6	12.6	49.2	10 315	9 765	-5.3	-4.8	272	660	-98	4 128	2.29	65.7	9.7	29.0
Muskegon	13.7	8.3	6.5	50.6	170 200	172 188	1.2	0.1	9 018	7 006	-1 850	65 008	2.54	68.8	15.2	26.3
Newaygo	14.5	10.0	7.2	49.7	47 874	48 460	1.2	-1.2	2 334	2 027	-886	18 156	2.61	70.8	10.3	24.0
Oakland	14.0	8.3	6.3	51.5	1 194 156	1 202 362	0.7	3.0	56 610	41 726	21 399	486 332	2.47	65.9	10.8	29.0
Oceana	14.5	11.0	7.7	49.9	26 873	26 570	-1.1	-1.3	1 338	1 052	-652	9 537	2.68	71.7	9.6	24.5
Ogemaw	17.2	13.9	9.8	50.4	21 645	21 699	0.2	-3.0	807	1 260	-130	8 998	2.36	65.0	10.3	29.8
Ontonagon	20.6	18.2	12.4	48.7	7 818	6 780	-13.3	-9.0	131	394	-335	3 269	1.98	58.9	5.1	35.5
Osceola	14.7	10.6	7.9	49.6	23 197	23 528	1.4	-1.5	1 162	995	-504	8 987	2.55	70.4	11.6	25.1
Oscoda	18.1	15.2	10.4	49.2	9 418	8 640	-8.3	-3.1	346	538	-72	3 781	2.26	65.0	7.7	29.9
Otsego	15.1	10.8	8.1	50.8	23 301	24 164	3.7	0.0	1 042	1 069	-19	9 818	2.42	67.5	7.7	26.5
Ottawa	11.6	7.1	5.7	50.8	238 314	263 801	10.7	4.7	14 218	7 203	5 463	94 666	2.73	73.9	8.6	20.0
Presque Isle	19.3	15.3	12.9	50.2	14 411	13 376	-7.2	-2.8	382	796	55	6 253	2.08	64.0	6.8	32.3
Roscommon	19.7	17.3	12.2	50.2	25 469	24 449	-4.0	-2.0	739	1 685	512	11 617	2.07	61.7	10.8	32.5
Saginaw	14.0	9.1	7.6	51.5	210 039	200 169	-4.7	-2.6	9 696	8 592	-6 132	77 412	2.50	64.4	14.6	30.7
St. Clair	14.7	9.2	6.9	50.5	164 235	163 040	-0.7	-1.8	6 756	7 024	-2 622	64 379	2.49	68.3	11.2	25.9
St. Joseph	13.5	9.0	7.1	50.4	62 422	61 295	-1.8	-0.6	3 420	2 542	-1 205	22 326	2.70	70.1	11.0	25.9
Sanilac	15.3	10.5	8.5	50.3	44 547	43 114	-3.2	-3.5	1 853	1 932	-1 367	16 329	2.58	65.8	8.1	29.9
Schoolcraft	18.0	12.6	10.6	50.6	8 903	8 485	-4.7	-3.7	297	443	-151	3 590	2.29	62.9	7.5	32.8
Shiawassee	14.2	9.2	6.8	50.6	71 687	70 648	-1.4	-2.4	3 054	2 906	-1 877	27 485	2.52	71.1	11.9	24.8
Tuscola	15.0	10.3	7.4	49.8	58 266	55 729	-4.4	-3.1	2 273	2 317	-1 696	21 211	2.55	70.5	9.6	25.1
Van Buren	14.8	9.1	6.3	50.6	76 263	76 258	0.0	-1.4	3 967	3 005	-1 973	28 374	2.60	69.7	11.7	26.1
Washtenaw	11.8	6.8	4.7	50.7	322 895	344 791	6.8	3.4	15 903	8 870	4 926	135 800	2.42	57.8	9.6	31.4
Wayne	13.1	7.4	6.1	51.9	2 061 162	1 820 584	-11.7	-3.1	99 655	74 536	-80 977	670 987	2.66	63.0	19.6	32.5
Wexford	14.3	10.1	7.3	50.2	30 484	32 735	7.4	0.5	1 715	1 475	-81	12 473	2.59	68.9	10.3	26.2
MINNESOTA	12.8	7.6	6.3	50.3	4 919 479	5 303 925	7.8	2.9	291 521	168 050	31 088	2 107 232	2.47	65.0	9.6	28.1
Aitkin	18.0	17.6	11.9	49.3	15 301	16 202	5.9	-2.7	520	861	-86	7 741	2.04	64.1	7.5	30.7
Anoka	12.6	7.0	4.3	50.0	298 084	330 844	11.0	3.3	17 346	7 499	1 348	122 625	2.70	71.7	10.1	22.5
Becker	15.2	10.6	8.3	50.0	30 000	32 504	8.3	2.3	1 816	1 479	395	13 476	2.40	68.9	9.9	25.5
Beltrami	12.4	7.7	6.3	50.0	39 650	44 442	12.1	2.7	3 087	1 632	-199	16 781	2.56	65.7	13.2	27.5
Benton	11.1	6.9	6.3	49.9	34 226	38 451	12.3	2.7	2 425	1 317	-104	15 359	2.47	65.0	10.3	26.4
Big Stone	15.5	11.3	14.4	51.2	5 820	5 269	-9.5	-2.7	248	315	-82	2 347	2.15	67.3	7.2	30.6
Blue Earth	10.9	6.4	6.2	49.7	55 941	64 013	14.4	2.1	3 188	1 938	98	24 476	2.48	58.0	6.9	28.7
Brown	14.1	9.2	10.6	50.1	26 911	25 893	-3.8	-2.3	1 111	1 200	-502	10 820	2.26	62.6	6.4	32.6
Carlton	14.0	8.6	7.4	48.0	31 671	35 386	11.7	0.5	1 598	1 485	63	13 789	2.44	66.8	8.2	27.9
Carver	11.6	5.5	4.1	50.3	70 205	91 042	29.7	6.9	4 797	1 891	3 283	33 486	2.74	76.0	7.5	20.3
Cass	16.2	14.4	9.0	49.2	27 150	28 567	5.2	0.0	1 435	1 238	-205	12 906	2.18	69.1	9.8	25.2
Chippewa	14.7	9.4	10.6	50.6	13 088	12 441	-4.9	-2.7	674	591	-400	5 093	2.36	64.1	8.8	32.9
Chisago	12.8	7.8	5.6	48.3	41 101	53 887	31.1	0.3	2 427	1 463	-863	19 569	2.65	72.8	8.4	21.2
Clay	10.8	6.3	6.2	50.8	51 229	58 999	15.2	3.9	3 372	1 858	739	22 463	2.47	65.9	10.9	27.9
Clearwater	14.3	10.4	8.6	49.2	8 423	8 695	3.2	1.1	434	373	41	3 586	2.40	69.5	7.4	27.0
Cook	20.1	14.6	9.1	50.7	5 168	5 176	0.2	1.1	196	174	46	2 614	1.96	65.6	9.6	27.6
Cottonwood	14.1	10.8	11.6	50.6	12 167	11 687	-3.9	-0.5	667	595	-141	4 802	2.36	67.1	8.1	28.2
Crow Wing	14.6	11.5	8.7	50.1	55 099	62 500	13.4	1.2	3 100	2 020	318	26 963	2.30	67.0	9.5	26.7
Dakota	12.6	6.8	4.8	50.8	355 904	398 552	12.0	3.5	22 099	9 528	1 171	154 275	2.59	69.7	10.3	24.3
Dodge	12.1	6.8	6.1	50.1	17 731	20 087	13.3	1.3	1 049	523	-265	7 326	2.73	73.8	8.6	22.6
Douglas	14.5	11.2	10.0	50.1	32 821	36 009	9.7	2.2	1 679	1 672	665	15 757	2.26	66.3	5.4	27.0
Faribault	15.6	10.8	11.6	50.3	16 181	14 553	-10.1	-2.5	620	774	-212	6 331	2.22	65.8	8.9	29.8

1. No spouse present.

STATE County	Persons in group quarters, 2014	Daytime population, 2009–2013		Births, 2014		Deaths, 2014		Persons under 65 with no health insurance, 2013		Medicare, 2014			Serious crimes known to police,[2] 2013	
													Total	
		Number	Employ-ment/ resi-dence ratio	Total	Rate[1]	Number	Rate[1]	Number	Percent	Eligible for Medicare	Enrolled in Medicare Advantage	Enrolled in a Medicare prescription drug plan	Number	Rate[3]
	32	33	34	35	36	37	38	39	40	41	42	43	44	45
MICHIGAN—Cont'd														
Keweenaw	10	1 793	0.53	18	8.1	12	5.4	224	14.7	692	162	387	42	1 873
Lake	393	10 656	0.73	95	8.4	141	12.4	1 359	16.7	3 562	795	2 217	230	1 999
Lapeer	1 712	76 222	0.66	807	9.2	801	9.1	8 827	12.0	17 064	5 145	11 632	1 232	1 396
Leelanau	284	19 364	0.75	174	7.9	232	10.6	2 468	15.7	6 260	2 122	3 276	91	421
Lenawee	5 431	88 798	0.74	1 026	10.4	981	9.9	9 996	12.7	20 737	5 463	13 318	NA	NA
Livingston	1 362	150 588	0.63	1 697	9.1	1 381	7.4	13 891	8.9	31 438	10 553	17 036	2 151	1 171
Luce	1 211	6 885	1.15	49	7.6	73	11.4	600	14.4	1 551	281	1 071	134	2 060
Mackinac	95	11 376	1.06	76	6.9	136	12.3	1 643	19.7	3 151	752	1 851	432	3 870
Macomb	7 522	783 230	0.83	9 241	10.7	8 163	9.5	89 512	12.5	159 406	48 240	91 828	19 490	2 292
Manistee	1 412	24 195	0.95	192	7.9	301	12.3	2 737	15.4	6 844	1 710	3 920	472	1 908
Marquette	4 619	67 562	1.01	651	9.6	648	9.6	6 630	12.6	13 585	3 373	6 725	1 154	1 691
Mason	442	28 528	0.99	289	10.0	308	10.7	3 223	14.3	7 404	1 808	4 666	890	3 101
Mecosta	3 334	42 506	0.97	412	9.5	362	8.4	4 551	13.8	8 701	2 949	5 121	1 170	2 688
Menominee	382	21 744	0.78	237	10.0	227	9.6	2 652	14.1	5 813	1 805	3 030	405	1 703
Midland	1 289	87 344	1.10	831	10.0	694	8.3	7 240	10.4	16 287	4 899	8 916	961	1 144
Missaukee	194	13 155	0.70	187	12.4	158	10.5	1 859	15.2	3 395	785	2 125	248	1 641
Monroe	1 462	129 785	0.67	1 453	9.7	1 361	9.1	13 291	10.5	28 478	8 438	17 853	3 788	2 577
Montcalm	2 944	57 013	0.73	734	11.7	572	9.1	6 834	13.5	12 782	4 073	6 190	1 204	2 018
Montmorency	175	9 454	0.95	63	6.8	169	18.2	1 126	17.1	3 556	817	2 398	46	490
Muskegon	6 496	165 171	0.91	2 100	12.2	1 666	9.7	17 395	12.2	35 550	13 615	15 802	6 794	4 002
Newaygo	557	44 036	0.77	549	11.5	475	9.9	5 678	14.4	10 776	4 622	4 721	997	2 137
Oakland	12 496	1 289 141	1.13	13 495	10.9	9 993	8.1	110 462	10.7	216 759	65 550	127 021	22 014	1 793
Oceana	303	24 350	0.79	302	11.5	239	9.1	3 739	17.6	6 193	2 030	3 020	539	2 282
Ogemaw	244	21 675	1.02	186	8.8	295	14.0	2 450	15.1	6 444	1 282	4 482	434	2 092
Ontonagon	83	6 343	0.90	28	4.5	93	15.1	720	16.4	2 304	478	1 314	35	554
Osceola	464	22 259	0.87	267	11.5	221	9.5	2 682	14.3	5 626	1 497	3 306	432	1 860
Oscoda	65	8 073	0.80	79	9.4	111	13.3	1 122	18.0	2 717	582	1 900	186	2 164
Otsego	346	25 628	1.15	233	9.6	272	11.3	2 596	13.4	5 715	1 474	3 711	507	2 113
Ottawa	8 262	251 959	0.88	3 376	12.2	1 727	6.3	25 189	11.0	43 374	24 274	14 067	4 651	1 716
Presque Isle	230	12 267	0.79	92	7.1	172	13.2	1 547	16.6	4 336	839	2 716	117	957
Roscommon	289	24 169	0.98	175	7.3	383	16.0	2 646	15.7	9 107	2 200	6 256	522	2 174
Saginaw	7 125	209 410	1.14	2 259	11.6	2 018	10.3	18 984	12.0	42 489	12 649	28 367	5 824	2 941
St. Clair	2 000	145 147	0.75	1 556	9.7	1 670	10.4	16 418	12.3	33 132	9 605	19 441	3 307	2 065
St. Joseph	765	59 066	0.91	791	13.0	577	9.5	6 935	13.6	12 131	2 698	7 139	886	1 480
Sanilac	564	39 386	0.80	419	10.1	492	11.8	5 148	15.3	9 686	2 090	6 176	516	1 307
Schoolcraft	140	8 357	0.98	71	8.7	102	12.5	988	15.6	2 182	429	1 294	NA	NA
Shiawassee	821	59 680	0.64	717	10.4	700	10.2	7 206	12.6	14 379	4 326	9 693	1 278	1 872
Tuscola	1 080	47 347	0.64	545	10.1	598	11.1	6 250	14.2	12 474	3 119	9 016	854	1 662
Van Buren	877	68 217	0.76	935	12.4	736	9.8	10 258	16.2	15 292	4 314	8 202	1 705	2 265
Washtenaw	17 791	384 788	1.22	3 690	10.3	2 139	6.0	30 716	10.4	50 709	13 584	26 381	8 518	2 412
Wayne	22 714	1 862 241	1.09	22 936	13.0	17 419	9.9	240 458	15.8	311 713	96 379	184 952	86 619	4 874
Wexford	389	34 575	1.15	384	11.7	334	10.2	3 723	13.8	7 355	1 732	4 524	1 064	3 400
MINNESOTA	134 875	5 362 552	1.01	68 982	12.6	39 728	7.3	433 806	9.5	895 484	470 182	388 912	143 900	2 655
Aitkin	274	14 653	0.79	125	7.9	199	12.6	1 381	12.6	4 335	2 484	1 862	490	3 084
Anoka	3 008	277 658	0.67	4 086	12.0	1 753	5.1	26 221	8.8	48 451	28 573	16 353	8 571	2 533
Becker	458	31 363	0.91	430	12.9	373	11.2	3 153	11.8	7 651	3 991	3 802	625	1 879
Beltrami	2 034	45 609	1.03	730	16.0	380	8.3	5 410	14.3	7 712	3 197	4 144	1 613	3 522
Benton	1 048	35 547	0.83	569	14.4	283	7.2	3 129	9.3	5 943	3 177	2 860	803	2 052
Big Stone	137	5 146	0.97	55	10.7	74	14.4	389	10.3	1 432	689	802	40	777
Blue Earth	4 083	67 881	1.10	739	11.3	444	6.8	5 053	9.4	9 869	4 643	5 902	2 175	3 313
Brown	1 124	27 434	1.14	248	9.8	270	10.7	1 615	8.3	5 729	2 570	3 212	211	832
Carlton	2 049	33 357	0.87	366	10.3	348	9.8	2 849	10.0	6 861	3 342	3 363	911	2 570
Carver	965	81 402	0.77	1 164	12.0	471	4.8	5 369	6.3	10 927	6 393	4 237	1 059	1 117
Cass	223	27 267	0.90	347	12.2	298	10.4	2 982	13.7	8 506	4 248	3 835	1 274	4 493
Chippewa	237	12 095	0.97	160	13.2	128	10.6	1 015	10.6	2 499	1 382	1 410	188	1 557
Chisago	1 660	43 345	0.61	576	10.7	342	6.3	3 616	8.0	8 533	5 098	3 072	811	1 517
Clay	3 561	49 686	0.69	803	13.1	423	6.9	4 320	8.7	9 002	4 061	4 472	1 162	1 915
Clearwater	115	8 216	0.85	96	10.9	80	9.1	923	13.0	1 900	994	904	125	1 431
Cook	51	5 313	1.04	43	8.2	44	8.4	552	13.9	1 451	660	646	163	3 130
Cottonwood	244	12 128	1.09	163	14.0	156	13.4	886	9.9	2 912	1 246	1 717	133	1 146
Crow Wing	742	64 113	1.05	709	11.2	621	9.8	5 071	10.1	15 497	8 437	7 439	1 787	2 828
Dakota	2 845	364 196	0.82	5 258	12.7	2 359	5.7	27 561	7.7	57 009	30 714	20 557	9 272	2 270
Dodge	149	15 602	0.56	236	11.6	116	5.7	1 334	7.6	3 013	1 426	1 361	295	1 451
Douglas	522	37 537	1.07	391	10.6	410	11.1	2 234	7.8	9 327	5 675	5 056	628	1 712
Faribault	336	13 589	0.88	143	10.1	151	10.6	1 116	10.3	3 507	1 913	2 146	155	1 089

1. Per 1,000 estimated resident population. 2. Data for serious crimes have not been adjusted for underreporting; this may affect comparability between geographic areas and over time.
3. Per 100,000 population estimated by the FBI.

STATE County	Serious crimes known to police, 2013 (cont.)[1] Rate[2] Violent	Serious crimes known to police, 2013 (cont.)[1] Rate[2] Property	Education: School enrollment and attainment, 2009–2013: Enrollment[3] Total	Enrollment[3] Percent private	Attainment[4] (percent) High school graduate or less	Attainment[4] (percent) Bachelor's degree or more	Local government expenditures,[5] 2012–2013: Total current spending (mil dol)	Current spending per student (dollars)	Money income, 2009–2013: Per capita income[6] (dollars)	Households: Median income (dollars)	Households: Mean income (dollars)	Households: Percent with income of $200,000 or more	Income and poverty, 2013: Median household income (dollars)	Percent below poverty level: All persons	Children under 18 years	Children 5 to 17 years in families
	46	47	48	49	50	51	52	53	54	55	56	57	58	59	60	61
MICHIGAN—Cont'd																
Keweenaw	134	1 740	373	8.8	40.6	23.9	0.2	46 250	24 802	39 038	51 415	2.4	37 229	14.0	22.6	20.8
Lake	183	1 816	1 954	7.7	60.8	8.4	7.5	13 897	16 202	29 379	38 197	0.3	30 656	31.0	52.2	45.1
Lapeer	178	1 218	21 858	10.9	48.2	17.0	120.2	9 560	23 907	52 939	64 003	1.5	53 506	11.1	16.7	13.3
Leelanau	42	380	4 446	19.4	30.1	39.2	26.2	12 590	31 462	55 018	74 759	5.0	56 335	10.2	16.2	14.4
Lenawee	NA	NA	25 835	17.6	47.7	19.3	169.2	10 775	22 395	47 766	57 679	1.2	46 693	16.0	21.4	19.8
Livingston	112	1 060	49 345	12.4	32.0	32.9	274.0	10 056	32 129	72 359	85 656	4.8	71 075	6.4	8.0	6.9
Luce	384	1 676	1 203	6.2	57.6	12.7	7.2	9 702	18 768	39 469	49 130	0.5	38 284	23.4	32.4	29.9
Mackinac	278	3 592	1 897	10.7	51.0	18.5	14.2	10 543	22 622	38 704	50 112	1.6	38 839	14.6	23.9	20.9
Macomb	298	1 994	216 575	12.3	43.0	22.5	1 319.4	10 692	26 748	53 451	66 735	2.3	52 954	13.4	19.7	17.6
Manistee	214	1 694	4 748	15.8	47.7	19.1	32.9	11 030	22 702	41 551	53 044	1.4	41 258	17.9	28.8	25.2
Marquette	107	1 584	18 740	6.5	39.4	29.1	86.0	10 705	23 789	45 622	58 015	1.8	45 170	15.4	18.0	16.5
Mason	310	2 791	6 317	10.1	44.7	19.8	53.6	13 129	23 183	41 136	53 338	1.2	40 438	15.7	26.8	24.5
Mecosta	579	2 109	15 121	9.1	46.6	21.6	66.3	12 430	19 336	39 470	50 905	1.0	39 764	23.6	31.6	29.1
Menominee	160	1 543	4 998	10.2	52.1	14.4	35.2	9 777	22 331	41 739	49 147	0.6	40 866	16.2	24.9	22.2
Midland	121	1 023	22 619	15.0	36.1	32.3	126.4	10 591	29 536	53 076	73 032	5.3	53 007	14.7	16.7	15.0
Missaukee	278	1 363	3 391	11.1	57.5	13.0	19.4	8 768	20 305	41 061	50 178	0.8	40 226	15.6	25.8	24.9
Monroe	263	2 314	38 301	12.2	46.8	18.0	245.8	10 550	25 939	53 972	66 063	2.3	55 745	12.5	16.4	15.6
Montcalm	255	1 763	15 497	12.4	52.4	13.4	96.4	10 367	18 969	40 451	49 363	0.8	40 790	18.8	26.8	24.2
Montmorency	85	405	1 618	10.4	56.6	9.9	7.8	10 091	19 661	35 261	43 270	0.5	33 742	20.4	36.5	33.7
Muskegon	469	3 533	43 792	10.5	47.0	17.2	294.0	10 921	20 621	40 979	52 917	1.2	41 556	20.4	28.1	25.6
Newaygo	311	1 827	11 620	12.7	55.3	12.9	88.9	10 994	20 623	42 571	53 398	1.4	43 238	17.2	26.1	24.3
Oakland	203	1 590	324 604	17.5	27.9	43.1	2 098.9	11 726	36 458	65 594	89 683	7.7	67 281	10.2	13.1	11.6
Oceana	182	2 100	5 855	12.2	52.1	15.0	32.5	10 204	18 986	40 023	50 095	1.1	43 134	18.3	30.9	28.4
Ogemaw	251	1 841	4 336	8.2	57.2	11.3	20.3	9 373	19 634	34 619	45 186	1.2	34 778	22.2	38.0	37.5
Ontonagon	79	475	1 038	4.7	53.0	15.3	10.9	17 311	21 585	34 620	42 976	0.1	33 116	16.4	31.6	27.2
Osceola	254	1 606	5 380	10.5	57.2	12.6	38.2	9 249	18 099	37 788	46 085	0.5	38 407	22.4	34.4	33.1
Oscoda	465	1 699	1 490	16.6	59.9	10.4	9.1	9 523	18 057	33 239	40 991	0.6	31 094	19.9	31.9	30.3
Otsego	167	1 946	5 483	16.9	47.1	19.8	35.0	8 744	24 312	47 584	59 609	1.9	47 016	13.6	21.2	19.8
Ottawa	200	1 516	82 001	18.6	39.2	30.0	447.8	10 816	25 371	56 453	70 918	2.8	57 994	11.3	12.3	11.0
Presque Isle	98	859	2 424	11.2	52.8	16.3	13.6	9 217	22 788	39 652	48 147	0.8	38 648	15.6	26.2	23.4
Roscommon	308	1 866	4 184	5.9	53.3	12.9	34.7	12 850	23 023	33 334	47 535	1.5	31 690	22.2	39.8	36.6
Saginaw	757	2 184	53 925	12.2	47.6	19.1	299.4	11 025	22 349	42 331	55 642	1.7	41 510	18.7	29.6	26.0
St. Clair	253	1 812	40 497	12.2	47.7	16.3	284.9	10 114	24 357	48 066	60 492	1.8	49 949	15.8	21.4	19.2
St. Joseph	206	1 275	14 719	8.2	54.3	14.5	109.3	10 144	20 570	44 051	53 866	1.3	43 891	17.4	26.0	22.9
Sanilac	230	1 076	9 784	7.9	59.2	11.4	67.7	10 036	20 713	40 478	51 159	1.2	41 502	15.8	25.2	22.7
Schoolcraft	NA	NA	1 587	15.2	60.0	12.4	8.1	9 534	20 892	35 260	47 071	1.3	38 514	18.0	27.3	24.3
Shiawassee	228	1 643	17 591	11.7	47.9	14.2	124.5	10 297	22 713	46 217	56 925	1.2	43 839	15.9	22.8	19.5
Tuscola	307	1 354	13 218	12.3	54.4	12.7	93.3	11 518	20 767	43 039	52 430	0.7	41 441	16.6	25.3	22.5
Van Buren	315	1 950	19 123	7.2	49.5	17.9	182.0	11 473	21 732	45 129	56 250	1.4	44 782	17.8	24.6	21.4
Washtenaw	309	2 102	124 994	10.2	21.9	51.3	462.8	12 094	33 231	59 055	81 487	6.5	59 965	16.3	15.2	13.7
Wayne	1 052	3 821	503 221	12.6	46.4	21.3	2 525.1	11 693	22 308	41 184	57 369	2.4	40 485	25.1	36.9	35.2
Wexford	361	3 039	7 484	13.2	50.6	16.8	63.2	12 630	20 573	40 965	51 923	1.4	39 566	19.8	29.1	28.6
MINNESOTA	234	2 420	1 414 545	17.2	34.8	32.6	9 329.7	11 089	30 913	59 836	77 204	4.6	60 664	11.2	14.0	13.1
Aitkin	245	2 839	2 696	9.8	51.1	14.7	19.8	9 992	24 939	41 617	52 391	1.3	41 784	13.3	23.3	20.8
Anoka	133	2 400	89 839	15.1	36.1	26.9	660.0	10 721	30 647	70 380	82 082	3.6	70 619	7.6	10.3	9.8
Becker	84	1 795	7 703	9.2	42.5	21.3	46.9	10 198	25 455	50 214	61 360	2.2	49 183	13.5	19.3	16.9
Beltrami	177	3 345	12 871	6.7	37.7	26.9	105.4	14 172	21 622	43 231	56 165	1.8	42 364	20.2	27.3	26.3
Benton	153	1 899	9 921	13.5	42.9	20.3	52.6	9 058	24 453	52 200	60 374	1.1	51 564	11.9	14.3	12.7
Big Stone	58	718	999	4.8	52.0	17.6	10.1	11 795	26 019	46 313	57 561	2.4	44 637	12.8	19.2	18.5
Blue Earth	193	3 119	21 873	8.5	35.4	30.5	105.2	10 202	25 380	49 935	64 267	2.3	51 283	17.0	13.5	13.1
Brown	71	761	6 317	40.4	47.9	20.9	39.5	11 794	26 576	48 256	62 290	2.5	52 061	9.6	11.6	10.7
Carlton	144	2 426	8 330	11.3	42.9	21.3	63.9	9 951	24 434	53 016	61 423	1.3	52 670	12.1	14.1	13.3
Carver	62	1 055	27 435	21.2	26.2	44.5	168.9	10 810	37 457	83 773	103 574	9.1	86 759	4.9	5.2	4.5
Cass	268	4 225	5 490	7.1	45.0	19.6	50.1	12 212	25 287	45 045	57 721	2.0	48 367	15.3	26.6	24.2
Chippewa	133	1 425	2 842	8.8	46.8	17.3	24.9	12 363	25 993	49 434	60 958	2.0	55 232	11.1	16.2	15.3
Chisago	88	1 429	13 926	8.9	42.0	21.0	74.4	9 907	27 914	67 157	75 524	2.4	71 397	6.8	8.2	6.9
Clay	86	1 829	18 448	21.0	35.3	30.3	90.7	9 730	24 550	52 410	63 377	2.0	52 567	12.4	13.3	12.1
Clearwater	286	1 145	1 932	6.0	53.8	13.3	15.6	10 703	22 157	43 269	53 736	1.2	44 123	16.4	24.6	22.6
Cook	77	3 053	728	8.8	32.9	37.4	5.3	11 267	32 868	52 215	67 218	3.1	48 124	10.1	16.5	15.1
Cottonwood	112	1 034	2 660	13.2	50.0	17.2	22.1	11 579	23 456	45 294	56 577	2.2	45 453	14.5	19.0	17.5
Crow Wing	146	2 683	14 425	10.2	38.7	22.5	98.5	10 531	26 527	47 058	61 707	2.2	48 661	11.3	16.4	14.4
Dakota	137	2 133	108 262	16.4	27.5	38.7	801.1	11 091	34 820	73 702	90 140	6.2	73 833	8.4	10.0	9.5
Dodge	138	1 314	5 667	8.5	40.7	23.6	36.5	8 893	29 107	69 301	78 241	2.3	73 799	7.3	9.6	8.4
Douglas	128	1 584	8 159	9.2	38.4	23.6	52.2	9 903	27 716	50 905	63 960	2.9	52 122	10.4	13.0	12.1
Faribault	91	998	3 059	10.0	50.6	16.9	21.4	11 199	25 065	44 264	56 341	1.8	47 191	11.5	18.2	16.1

1. Data for serious crimes have not been adjusted for underreporting; this may affect comparability between geographic areas and over time. 2. Per 100,000 population estimated by the FBI.
3. All persons 3 years old and over enrolled in nursery school through college. 4. Persons 25 years old and over. 5. Elementary and secondary education expenditures.
6. Based on population estimated by the American Community Survey, 2009–2013.

Table B. States and Counties — **Personal Income**

STATE County	Personal income, 2013: Total (mil dol)	Percent change, 2012–2013	Per capita[1]: Dollars	Per capita[1]: Rank	Wages and salaries (mil dol)	Supplements to wages and salaries; employer contributions (mil dol): Pension and insurance	Supplements: Government social insurance	Proprietors' income (mil dol)	Dividends, interest, and rent (mil dol)	Personal transfer receipts (mil dol)	Earnings, 2013: Total (mil dol)	Contributions for government social insurance (mil dol): From employee and self-employed	Contributions: From employer
	62	63	64	65	66	67	68	69	70	71	72	73	74
MICHIGAN—Cont'd													
Keweenaw	86	0.8	39 114	1 277	11	3	1	1	22	25	16	2	1
Lake	335	0.9	29 436	2 760	51	12	4	23	63	142	90	9	4
Lapeer	3 069	0.8	34 720	1 947	734	148	61	179	429	693	1 122	80	61
Leelanau	1 122	1.6	51 589	315	214	45	18	55	400	201	331	24	18
Lenawee	3 413	2.2	34 408	2 009	1 091	205	87	199	481	810	1 582	106	87
Livingston	8 263	1.0	44 800	710	2 236	361	181	391	1 184	1 182	3 168	209	181
Luce	178	3.2	27 404	2 943	65	18	5	9	33	69	96	7	5
Mackinac	428	3.7	38 673	1 341	151	29	15	20	100	121	215	15	15
Macomb	32 871	1.0	38 456	1 379	16 035	2 403	1 283	1 934	4 684	6 688	21 654	1 385	1 283
Manistee	794	1.2	32 490	2 336	265	64	20	38	168	276	388	28	20
Marquette	2 377	0.5	35 111	1 882	1 144	221	89	92	430	591	1 547	98	89
Mason	1 010	2.1	35 319	1 853	382	78	32	74	195	297	566	38	32
Mecosta	1 270	1.2	29 459	2 757	490	123	38	78	213	360	729	47	38
Menominee	816	1.3	34 290	2 034	251	57	21	56	159	216	385	26	21
Midland	3 879	0.2	46 228	607	1 983	330	146	172	789	644	2 631	160	146
Missaukee	428	3.4	28 466	2 851	106	21	9	48	77	131	184	13	9
Monroe	5 944	4.4	39 525	1 229	1 920	329	148	278	797	1 173	2 675	178	148
Montcalm	1 728	1.9	27 389	2 946	580	117	46	99	248	520	843	56	46
Montmorency	287	4.8	30 675	2 603	68	14	6	15	63	127	102	10	6
Muskegon	5 541	1.5	32 405	2 351	2 462	437	200	271	839	1 556	3 371	223	200
Newaygo	1 491	1.8	31 067	2 538	449	89	36	89	244	422	664	46	36
Oakland	70 247	1.8	57 035	156	39 860	4 957	3 110	7 502	12 280	9 118	55 428	3 383	3 110
Oceana	894	1.2	34 066	2 069	251	50	21	39	159	245	361	25	21
Ogemaw	623	1.6	29 360	2 769	179	38	15	39	118	246	272	22	15
Ontonagon	203	0.4	32 086	2 406	44	11	4	9	40	86	68	6	4
Osceola	641	-0.7	27 551	2 931	244	43	19	25	103	212	331	24	19
Oscoda	241	2.4	28 782	2 821	53	13	4	18	45	103	88	8	4
Otsego	795	1.7	32 955	2 260	350	61	29	79	164	213	520	35	29
Ottawa	10 343	1.5	37 928	1 442	4 841	819	388	479	2 014	1 597	6 527	397	388
Presque Isle	421	0.7	32 259	2 370	114	24	10	12	84	149	159	13	10
Roscommon	768	1.9	31 976	2 413	172	38	14	24	175	337	248	24	14
Saginaw	6 561	0.1	33 383	2 195	3 509	601	282	369	1 029	1 915	4 761	309	282
St. Clair	5 802	0.2	36 158	1 719	1 893	350	154	320	914	1 386	2 717	185	154
St. Joseph	1 962	1.9	32 177	2 389	848	155	70	123	301	494	1 196	75	70
Sanilac	1 428	-0.6	34 154	2 055	386	75	32	152	257	411	645	41	32
Schoolcraft	279	1.3	33 869	2 104	108	26	8	10	51	95	152	10	8
Shiawassee	2 144	0.5	31 120	2 532	591	122	48	69	314	591	829	61	48
Tuscola	1 678	0.1	30 923	2 565	453	95	36	106	261	517	690	50	36
Van Buren	2 492	1.7	33 032	2 247	839	180	66	76	394	642	1 161	75	66
Washtenaw	15 561	2.0	43 927	762	9 975	2 066	738	850	3 214	2 110	13 629	771	738
Wayne	63 947	-0.1	36 021	1 741	39 375	5 774	3 026	4 309	8 775	18 025	52 483	3 294	3 026
Wexford	990	2.7	30 323	2 640	489	98	40	41	176	300	668	44	40
MINNESOTA	257 466	1.0	47 500	X	139 720	19 738	10 920	23 089	47 043	40 395	193 467	11 468	10 920
Aitkin	546	1.8	34 677	1 957	122	24	10	54	124	176	209	17	10
Anoka	14 340	1.8	42 236	915	5 689	811	474	677	2 011	2 167	7 651	474	474
Becker	1 375	2.5	41 375	1 009	496	85	42	165	274	332	789	50	42
Beltrami	1 552	2.6	33 978	2 086	674	127	56	103	295	443	960	60	56
Benton	1 467	-0.7	37 410	1 518	623	97	56	242	214	278	1 017	60	56
Big Stone	245	-11.6	47 839	495	64	13	5	45	59	60	127	7	5
Blue Earth	2 567	-1.2	39 172	1 269	1 512	245	123	333	501	439	2 213	126	123
Brown	1 113	-0.2	43 932	761	507	91	42	153	238	230	793	45	42
Carlton	1 192	1.6	33 613	2 161	541	101	45	63	182	316	749	48	45
Carver	5 931	1.8	62 061	85	1 751	270	141	410	834	439	2 571	151	141
Cass	1 191	3.2	41 714	971	282	58	24	152	290	356	517	37	24
Chippewa	629	-4.4	52 030	300	204	38	17	182	108	109	441	21	17
Chisago	2 052	2.0	38 178	1 412	539	90	46	84	303	358	759	50	46
Clay	2 369	0.0	39 058	1 289	731	126	63	220	374	443	1 140	67	63
Clearwater	292	5.1	33 084	2 239	102	18	10	35	50	88	165	11	10
Cook	245	2.9	47 096	549	85	17	7	23	80	50	132	9	7
Cottonwood	536	-3.9	46 163	610	168	32	14	136	108	113	350	18	14
Crow Wing	2 273	2.6	35 962	1 753	1 022	171	90	95	498	628	1 378	93	90
Dakota	20 706	1.5	50 687	341	9 207	1 318	740	1 790	3 305	2 472	13 055	778	740
Dodge	798	-6.2	39 231	1 263	223	38	19	108	131	123	388	23	19
Douglas	1 551	0.9	42 448	892	696	115	57	146	348	349	1 013	65	57
Faribault	746	-5.4	52 583	285	296	38	22	135	143	147	491	27	22

1. Based on the resident population estimated as of July 1 of the year shown.

STATE County	Earnings, 2013 (cont.) – Percent by selected industries: Farm	Mining	Construction	Manu-facturing	Infor-mation: professional, scientific, technical services	Retail trade	Finance, insur-ance, real estate and leasing	Health care and social assistance	Govern-ment	Social Security beneficiaries, December 2013: Number	Rate[1]	Supple-mental Security Income recipients, December 2013	Housing units, 2014: Total	Percent change, 2010–2014
	75	76	77	78	79	80	81	82	83	84	85	86	87	88
MICHIGAN—Cont'd														
Keweenaw	0.0	D	D	D	D	5.3	D	D	34.7	770	353	34	2 474	0.3
Lake	1.8	0.5	6.3	3.4	D	6.8	4.7	20.7	30.0	4 060	357	613	14 925	-0.3
Lapeer	2.4	0.6	7.3	22.8	3.6	8.9	4.4	7.3	22.3	19 825	225	1 292	36 204	-0.3
Leelanau	3.7	1.8	10.6	3.6	8.6	4.8	5.9	8.3	29.2	6 655	306	208	15 221	1.9
Lenawee	4.9	D	4.0	25.7	3.6	8.1	5.7	8.8	18.9	23 650	239	1 991	43 454	0.0
Livingston	0.5	0.1	8.3	18.5	9.6	8.6	8.6	8.6	12.8	34 865	189	1 381	74 217	1.9
Luce	1.0	0.0	5.7	D	D	7.2	5.1	D	55.1	1 750	268	204	4 338	-0.1
Mackinac	1.2	D	6.0	1.7	D	8.0	4.2	D	26.6	3 590	324	239	11 013	0.0
Macomb	0.1	D	5.4	29.1	6.7	7.2	4.0	10.5	14.0	176 710	207	19 893	361 273	1.3
Manistee	0.7	0.6	4.4	15.9	2.4	6.9	2.5	D	43.6	7 585	310	676	15 639	-0.4
Marquette	0.2	12.6	5.9	3.7	5.7	6.6	4.8	21.0	22.2	15 315	226	1 170	34 495	0.5
Mason	2.9	D	5.6	18.3	3.4	7.9	4.1	12.4	19.7	8 180	285	767	17 287	0.0
Mecosta	2.0	0.2	2.4	13.6	3.6	10.1	2.6	4.2	43.2	9 880	229	1 158	21 101	-0.1
Menominee	3.1	0.1	4.0	30.4	D	5.7	3.1	D	24.8	6 600	277	505	14 154	-0.5
Midland	0.6	D	6.2	25.7	4.9	4.6	3.1	11.3	8.7	18 500	221	1 672	36 274	0.9
Missaukee	13.1	0.6	7.9	15.6	2.2	6.6	3.2	D	16.8	3 895	258	366	9 068	-0.5
Monroe	1.8	D	7.3	17.0	D	7.2	2.8	9.7	13.4	32 520	217	2 649	63 502	0.8
Montcalm	7.4	D	4.1	19.8	2.5	8.1	2.3	D	22.5	14 865	237	1 831	28 088	-0.5
Montmorency	0.5	D	6.2	12.1	1.9	7.6	17.8	D	21.4	4 095	437	317	9 548	-0.5
Muskegon	0.7	D	4.9	26.5	4.0	10.0	3.6	17.0	15.2	40 880	237	6 426	73 310	-0.3
Newaygo	6.8	D	3.9	20.8	3.3	9.5	8.0	9.3	22.3	12 455	260	1 544	24 910	-0.7
Oakland	0.0	0.2	4.5	10.8	22.8	5.8	10.4	11.4	6.3	231 540	188	22 568	533 047	1.1
Oceana	9.3	0.4	4.6	20.6	D	5.5	2.8	D	25.4	7 105	271	728	16 007	0.4
Ogemaw	4.4	2.3	4.9	4.7	2.6	16.2	3.5	D	22.3	7 400	349	867	16 037	-0.1
Ontonagon	1.5	0.0	7.0	D	D	14.3	4.8	13.9	29.5	2 645	419	148	5 642	-0.5
Osceola	2.8	2.1	27.5	18.0	1.6	4.2	1.6	11.6	18.1	6 445	277	851	13 569	-0.5
Oscoda	3.0	D	6.2	8.7	D	8.1	2.9	5.3	28.9	3 095	369	304	9 095	-0.3
Otsego	0.4	8.6	5.4	8.7	D	17.0	4.2	D	15.9	6 575	272	571	14 784	0.4
Ottawa	2.3	0.0	5.4	35.3	5.2	5.1	4.2	5.7	15.9	47 800	175	2 716	104 372	1.8
Presque Isle	3.1	D	4.9	4.0	D	8.3	3.6	12.9	21.0	4 955	380	372	10 407	-0.2
Roscommon	0.1	D	5.6	12.0	D	16.0	4.4	D	29.9	10 255	429	924	24 369	-0.4
Saginaw	1.2	0.3	3.8	19.6	6.5	7.6	5.6	18.5	15.2	48 655	247	8 669	86 783	-0.1
St. Clair	0.8	D	5.5	16.4	D	7.8	5.2	15.8	17.0	37 300	233	3 482	71 771	-0.1
St. Joseph	5.5	D	3.4	41.1	D	7.2	2.5	8.5	14.5	13 745	226	1 334	27 616	-0.6
Sanilac	14.8	0.6	5.0	17.0	D	9.4	3.9	D	16.9	11 000	263	950	22 557	-0.7
Schoolcraft	1.1	6.7	4.6	10.0	D	8.0	D	5.0	40.8	2 545	309	260	6 328	0.2
Shiawassee	2.8	0.2	4.1	12.8	D	9.9	3.5	D	22.9	16 420	238	1 721	30 071	-0.8
Tuscola	7.7	D	5.9	17.0	D	6.4	2.8	D	25.4	14 385	265	1 321	24 256	-0.8
Van Buren	5.5	D	3.6	11.2	8.3	5.7	2.1	5.9	28.7	17 475	232	2 209	36 639	-0.4
Washtenaw	0.2	0.0	2.2	9.1	15.5	4.4	4.7	11.0	36.2	53 530	151	5 392	148 470	0.6
Wayne	0.0	0.2	3.8	14.2	13.9	4.6	5.7	13.9	13.2	355 320	200	84 449	814 399	-0.9
Wexford	0.3	0.4	2.0	26.7	5.5	8.2	3.2	12.9	19.4	8 490	261	1 114	16 670	-0.4
MINNESOTA	2.3	0.5	5.2	12.8	10.8	5.4	10.5	12.3	13.2	948 229	175	93 748	2 385 544	1.6
Aitkin	2.1	D	9.0	7.3	D	12.5	4.1	D	20.4	4 705	298	261	16 237	1.3
Anoka	0.1	0.0	8.0	26.4	5.2	6.8	4.1	12.2	12.9	52 175	154	4 399	129 568	2.3
Becker	5.4	0.4	8.1	14.5	D	10.3	4.2	13.1	20.6	8 330	251	718	19 135	1.9
Beltrami	0.3	D	8.7	5.7	4.8	9.7	3.2	17.4	31.0	8 705	191	1 316	20 770	1.2
Benton	4.1	0.0	11.5	20.2	D	6.4	3.9	D	8.8	6 455	164	662	16 476	2.1
Big Stone	26.0	D	12.2	0.7	D	4.4	2.9	D	23.7	1 495	292	96	3 133	0.6
Blue Earth	5.2	D	6.3	12.4	7.9	7.8	5.2	19.4	15.0	10 585	163	1 030	27 129	3.5
Brown	11.3	D	6.9	22.9	6.9	6.4	3.7	11.6	11.5	6 125	242	267	11 583	0.8
Carlton	0.3	D	11.1	15.8	3.3	5.9	3.7	10.2	34.8	7 585	214	591	15 802	0.9
Carver	1.0	0.0	8.0	29.6	8.1	4.6	4.9	11.2	11.1	11 460	120	526	36 336	5.2
Cass	1.1	0.0	7.8	3.5	3.7	8.6	6.3	D	33.6	9 505	333	787	25 302	1.6
Chippewa	25.2	D	7.1	18.2	6.1	4.6	3.8	D	14.7	2 620	216	180	5 705	-0.3
Chisago	1.2	D	10.6	16.6	2.6	7.1	2.3	24.7	18.4	9 475	176	553	21 380	1.0
Clay	9.5	D	5.6	5.9	4.1	7.0	3.0	9.6	22.0	9 565	158	1 063	24 949	4.1
Clearwater	6.2	0.0	20.8	18.1	D	4.3	D	D	15.9	2 160	246	223	4 757	-0.3
Cook	0.0	0.0	10.4	D	2.9	8.9	3.9	3.8	36.2	1 515	292	52	5 965	2.2
Cottonwood	21.6	D	5.3	23.4	1.9	4.3	2.6	D	13.0	3 095	265	227	5 405	-0.1
Crow Wing	0.3	D	8.8	9.8	7.6	10.1	6.9	16.2	20.6	16 730	265	1 165	40 892	1.8
Dakota	0.2	0.2	7.1	16.8	13.7	6.3	10.5	7.4	10.9	59 530	146	4 320	162 861	2.0
Dodge	6.9	D	11.8	24.9	3.0	2.9	4.7	2.5	16.2	3 295	162	174	8 040	1.2
Douglas	2.9	D	9.4	19.0	4.9	8.7	4.7	8.5	18.9	9 945	272	484	20 482	2.9
Faribault	19.8	0.0	4.0	13.9	D	3.2	3.6	3.4	12.0	3 795	267	239	7 049	-0.6

1. Per 1,000 resident population estimated as of July 1 of the year shown.

STATE County	Housing units, 2009–2013: Occupied units: Total	Owner-occupied: Percent	Owner-occupied: Median value[1]	Median owner cost as a percent of income: With a mortgage	Median owner cost as a percent of income: Without a mortgage[2]	Renter-occupied: Median rent[3]	Renter-occupied: Median rent as a percent of income[2]	Substandard units[4] (percent)	Civilian labor force, 2014: Total	Civilian labor force, 2014: Percent change, 2013–2014	Unemployment: Total	Unemployment: Rate[5]	Civilian employment,[6] 2009–2013: Total	Percent: Management, business, science and arts	Percent: Construction, production, and maintenance occupations
	89	90	91	92	93	94	95	96	97	98	99	100	101	102	103
MICHIGAN—Cont'd															
Keweenaw	1 014	85.9	101 700	22.6	14.7	577	31.2	2.6	977	-1.1	105	10.7	847	39.4	20.4
Lake	4 096	81.3	79 700	28.2	14.0	544	36.0	1.9	3 613	-0.8	399	11.0	3 158	18.5	32.8
Lapeer	32 684	83.1	137 600	24.7	12.9	757	30.1	1.6	39 995	-0.2	3 944	9.9	36 210	30.5	30.8
Leelanau	9 103	85.1	235 600	27.3	11.8	822	30.5	1.9	10 531	2.0	698	6.6	9 393	37.9	21.0
Lenawee	37 754	77.8	116 900	24.0	13.4	710	32.4	0.8	48 161	0.5	3 086	6.4	42 347	28.9	27.0
Livingston	67 691	85.1	183 100	23.6	12.4	917	29.9	2.9	94 929	0.5	6 364	6.7	88 278	38.7	21.0
Luce	2 427	75.1	79 400	20.0	11.8	599	30.5	3.1	2 489	3.2	210	8.4	2 193	26.7	23.9
Mackinac	5 000	76.8	119 300	24.6	13.0	593	28.1	1.8	5 290	0.5	581	11.0	4 440	25.7	23.1
Macomb	332 818	75.5	123 100	23.5	14.2	824	31.2	2.1	418 288	0.1	34 201	8.2	382 723	33.0	22.0
Manistee	10 571	79.1	109 900	24.7	13.2	669	30.0	1.2	10 409	-1.3	867	8.3	9 277	26.9	25.2
Marquette	26 436	70.2	126 600	19.7	11.9	607	31.4	2.4	33 842	-0.8	2 348	6.9	30 298	31.9	22.3
Mason	12 470	74.1	117 000	24.5	13.4	654	29.1	3.2	14 794	1.8	1 085	7.3	12 346	30.1	28.9
Mecosta	15 536	72.9	112 200	23.3	11.8	643	38.2	2.8	18 952	0.9	1 484	7.8	16 952	27.9	27.1
Menominee	10 787	80.8	95 300	22.9	11.4	513	27.2	2.0	11 770	-0.3	793	6.7	10 219	26.5	34.0
Midland	33 717	75.4	128 600	20.7	11.8	713	29.9	2.8	41 494	1.2	2 501	6.0	37 189	39.3	21.1
Missaukee	5 891	80.8	99 400	24.3	12.8	696	29.2	1.6	7 123	1.9	552	7.7	6 161	24.4	35.6
Monroe	58 702	79.2	139 100	23.3	13.0	777	30.3	1.9	75 701	1.2	4 630	6.1	66 627	27.6	30.6
Montcalm	23 400	79.2	95 000	24.9	13.0	673	31.1	2.0	28 003	1.4	2 082	7.4	23 975	24.4	34.6
Montmorency	4 128	85.8	93 700	26.2	12.2	635	41.4	2.3	3 191	-0.9	406	12.7	2 853	23.5	31.3
Muskegon	65 008	74.4	100 900	23.2	13.1	663	36.0	2.7	76 809	0.5	5 686	7.4	67 639	28.1	28.1
Newaygo	18 156	84.1	104 100	24.2	13.5	656	32.5	1.5	22 505	1.6	1 608	7.1	18 468	24.1	36.9
Oakland	486 332	71.5	170 500	22.9	13.8	919	29.4	3.4	627 399	0.3	42 765	6.8	581 100	46.9	13.6
Oceana	9 537	81.7	106 100	24.5	13.5	676	32.4	1.5	12 905	0.9	1 270	9.8	10 460	24.4	38.5
Ogemaw	8 998	82.8	89 500	26.8	14.5	642	37.0	0.8	8 571	-0.9	833	9.7	7 334	25.5	26.4
Ontonagon	3 269	85.8	72 600	26.6	13.0	419	31.0	3.1	2 422	-1.6	270	11.1	2 337	25.4	29.0
Osceola	8 987	78.2	90 500	22.9	13.2	565	30.8	2.7	10 168	0.9	865	8.5	8 723	24.9	39.3
Oscoda	3 781	85.3	83 000	26.1	13.0	589	37.9	1.4	2 927	-1.8	350	12.0	2 710	21.3	27.9
Otsego	9 818	79.4	116 600	22.9	12.1	665	31.3	2.6	11 184	-0.8	896	8.0	10 390	29.2	22.8
Ottawa	94 666	78.1	153 200	22.1	11.8	767	30.5	1.9	148 812	2.3	7 038	4.7	128 356	33.5	27.2
Presque Isle	6 253	87.5	95 000	23.4	13.3	530	24.8	1.8	5 418	-1.4	689	12.7	4 632	29.8	29.7
Roscommon	11 617	81.1	92 000	28.4	12.6	655	37.8	1.5	7 990	-1.7	902	11.3	7 401	21.6	24.9
Saginaw	77 412	72.7	97 800	23.1	13.5	699	33.8	1.3	89 280	0.0	6 562	7.3	79 995	29.7	23.0
St. Clair	64 379	76.8	121 600	24.6	14.4	728	31.7	2.7	73 900	-0.4	7 302	9.9	67 685	26.8	28.8
St. Joseph	22 326	76.4	108 900	22.6	12.2	634	31.3	1.9	29 013	2.6	1 657	5.7	24 204	25.6	39.2
Sanilac	16 329	80.8	96 500	24.5	14.0	619	29.8	1.4	19 722	1.3	1 655	8.4	16 598	26.7	35.1
Schoolcraft	3 590	84.1	86 200	23.6	13.0	512	44.8	1.3	3 538	-1.2	383	10.8	2 784	28.1	28.1
Shiawassee	27 485	77.3	108 300	23.8	13.2	672	29.9	1.5	33 275	0.1	2 468	7.4	29 267	27.4	29.2
Tuscola	21 211	81.7	95 700	24.4	13.6	642	31.2	1.8	25 232	0.2	2 136	8.5	22 312	25.9	29.4
Van Buren	28 374	78.0	118 700	24.1	13.4	630	31.4	1.5	35 519	1.0	2 786	7.8	32 211	27.4	32.0
Washtenaw	135 800	60.8	198 400	23.2	13.3	910	32.9	3.1	186 775	1.1	8 970	4.8	170 875	50.4	12.4
Wayne	670 987	64.8	86 800	24.3	15.3	792	36.9	2.3	766 626	-0.7	76 863	10.0	679 057	31.5	22.4
Wexford	12 473	76.8	100 100	25.4	13.0	698	31.4	3.1	14 694	-0.1	1 241	8.4	12 970	26.0	34.8
MINNESOTA	2 107 232	72.5	187 900	23.1	11.7	819	29.7	2.3	2 974 102	0.3	121 626	4.1	2 748 174	38.8	20.8
Aitkin	7 741	81.8	168 700	27.8	12.8	625	28.8	1.8	6 787	-0.4	438	6.5	6 557	26.9	26.2
Anoka	122 625	81.4	192 300	23.5	11.6	938	30.9	2.3	189 696	0.5	7 681	4.0	176 279	36.9	22.2
Becker	13 476	79.0	171 500	23.6	13.0	647	29.8	3.5	17 969	-0.2	840	4.7	15 503	30.9	28.9
Beltrami	16 781	70.7	147 100	23.9	12.5	660	30.0	1.9	23 413	1.4	1 222	5.2	19 992	31.8	22.5
Benton	15 359	70.3	158 200	24.2	12.3	652	31.3	1.4	21 633	0.7	1 075	5.0	19 700	29.3	29.7
Big Stone	2 347	80.1	91 300	21.3	11.6	526	26.4	1.1	2 583	0.7	113	4.4	2 410	38.3	29.3
Blue Earth	24 476	66.4	158 100	21.8	10.9	683	33.4	1.5	38 765	0.1	1 319	3.4	35 960	30.5	22.9
Brown	10 820	77.5	121 900	21.5	11.0	583	27.6	2.7	14 133	-2.9	638	4.5	13 385	29.9	31.7
Carlton	13 789	78.2	159 000	23.4	12.7	696	29.3	1.5	17 487	-0.4	906	5.2	16 177	31.8	26.3
Carver	33 486	81.7	264 700	23.5	11.2	938	29.6	3.2	53 852	0.8	1 915	3.6	49 513	44.9	16.2
Cass	12 906	80.8	177 100	25.1	12.5	654	29.1	1.4	14 029	0.1	976	7.0	12 105	30.4	25.3
Chippewa	5 093	71.8	101 100	19.7	10.2	711	26.6	1.7	6 921	-0.6	306	4.4	6 300	30.0	30.3
Chisago	19 569	84.6	197 000	25.9	11.6	781	31.9	1.9	28 735	0.5	1 325	4.6	26 914	31.9	27.0
Clay	22 463	69.3	155 200	22.0	11.2	700	33.7	6.6	35 589	2.1	1 178	3.3	32 189	33.7	23.4
Clearwater	3 586	79.5	118 300	23.8	12.7	531	29.3	5.2	4 547	1.3	470	10.3	3 553	27.2	35.0
Cook	2 614	73.1	240 500	25.6	10.0	681	24.0	1.0	3 074	0.4	169	5.5	2 870	34.0	18.7
Cottonwood	4 802	79.0	86 800	20.5	10.3	520	28.0	1.4	5 610	-2.8	287	5.1	5 566	30.8	29.2
Crow Wing	26 963	74.5	180 300	24.3	12.1	717	29.7	1.7	31 410	-0.2	1 807	5.8	28 528	31.0	22.4
Dakota	154 275	75.8	223 300	22.8	10.9	944	29.0	1.3	231 677	0.6	8 557	3.7	216 323	41.8	16.8
Dodge	7 326	85.8	161 100	21.0	12.0	685	31.8	0.8	11 301	-0.5	460	4.1	10 628	36.0	26.6
Douglas	15 757	76.3	187 300	24.2	13.1	646	30.1	1.9	19 962	0.2	725	3.6	18 236	33.9	24.5
Faribault	6 331	78.7	85 800	20.7	11.8	509	25.4	2.8	7 420	-1.2	377	5.1	7 098	30.0	33.0

1. Specified owner-occupied units. 2. A value of 10.0 represents 10 percent or less; a value of 50.0 represents 50 percent or more. 3. Specified renter-occupied units.
4. Overcrowded or lacking complete plumbing facilities. 5. Percent of civilian labor force. 6. Persons 16 years old and over.

STATE County	Private nonfarm establishments, employment and payroll, 2013									Agriculture, 2012			
		Employment						Annual payroll		Farms			
											Percent with:		
	Number of establish-ments	Total	Health care and social assistance	Manufac-turing	Retail trade	Finance and insurance	Professional, scientific, and technical services	Total (mil dol)	Average per employee (dollars)	Number	Fewer than 50 acres	500 acres or more	Farm operators whose principal occu-pation is farming (percent)
	104	105	106	107	108	109	110	111	112	113	114	115	116
MICHIGAN—Cont'd													
Keweenaw	63	159	D	D	D	D	D	4	24 453	6	66.7	0.0	33.3
Lake	161	1 138	242	66	267	D	D	27	23 901	200	38.0	5.0	49.5
Lapeer	1 574	17 109	2 686	4 632	2 988	432	716	550	32 164	1 133	52.8	7.2	51.3
Leelanau	737	4 366	599	261	565	209	267	159	36 441	494	38.3	2.6	55.5
Lenawee	1 812	22 990	3 310	4 692	3 639	835	482	751	32 681	1 618	45.7	11.7	39.3
Livingston	4 159	47 463	5 767	8 036	8 627	3 591	2 492	1 719	36 222	734	58.3	4.6	54.8
Luce	162	1 431	D	D	268	61	D	47	32 776	43	44.2	16.3	44.2
Mackinac	449	1 995	336	104	334	84	33	97	48 737	103	30.1	11.7	57.3
Macomb	18 338	281 325	38 433	61 954	40 562	6 866	29 677	12 750	45 322	502	59.4	6.4	53.8
Manistee	560	5 402	902	D	909	171	119	181	33 460	324	35.2	2.5	43.8
Marquette	1 640	21 508	5 655	873	3 782	882	652	832	38 703	168	41.1	6.0	48.8
Mason	743	9 112	1 416	1 847	1 435	223	156	329	36 070	440	34.5	8.2	45.2
Mecosta	751	9 299	1 397	2 245	1 914	D	284	303	32 559	779	31.8	5.9	48.1
Menominee	458	5 318	295	1 789	602	147	79	165	31 063	398	25.6	9.8	47.5
Midland	1 747	36 377	5 847	6 339	4 123	D	844	2 110	58 002	555	47.9	7.0	46.7
Missaukee	289	2 101	D	403	352	D	25	63	29 756	433	38.6	10.6	48.3
Monroe	2 303	35 969	5 829	6 670	5 015	880	800	1 472	40 922	1 144	53.0	10.9	46.3
Montcalm	1 004	11 850	2 721	2 609	2 311	339	216	389	32 804	1 127	41.3	9.4	54.3
Montmorency	204	1 597	242	413	240	D	D	46	28 794	151	31.1	8.6	36.4
Muskegon	3 134	50 724	10 768	12 053	7 705	1 025	1 301	1 889	37 233	514	56.6	4.9	48.4
Newaygo	785	9 561	1 605	2 103	1 514	D	338	339	35 464	923	45.8	5.1	45.1
Oakland	38 381	644 865	101 996	47 523	72 128	37 820	86 617	35 276	54 703	537	70.9	2.0	51.6
Oceana	493	4 198	604	1 200	581	119	D	132	31 354	609	37.9	9.4	52.7
Ogemaw	566	5 740	1 557	290	1 523	D	112	163	28 351	280	24.6	11.4	49.3
Ontonagon	170	982	D	D	194	64	9	26	26 444	109	12.8	14.7	45.0
Osceola	431	6 078	944	2 194	606	92	D	235	38 725	750	34.0	4.9	35.9
Oscoda	190	1 279	150	253	239	D	51	37	28 739	145	43.4	2.1	52.4
Otsego	753	8 298	D	730	2 115	189	199	264	31 780	180	37.2	9.4	47.2
Ottawa	5 774	95 831	11 067	30 358	10 047	2 006	3 232	3 661	38 201	1 363	55.2	5.6	51.5
Presque Isle	336	2 212	D	217	380	98	D	69	31 021	323	22.9	9.9	55.1
Roscommon	554	4 616	553	593	1 356	172	61	115	24 835	58	44.8	3.4	34.5
Saginaw	4 358	78 238	18 000	10 708	12 977	2 728	2 301	2 815	35 983	1 318	41.0	12.1	48.9
St. Clair	3 070	40 247	7 941	8 357	6 889	1 392	966	1 485	36 908	1 049	46.1	7.9	56.0
St. Joseph	1 155	17 804	2 309	8 171	2 264	396	453	681	38 244	967	44.9	10.9	41.8
Sanilac	835	7 953	1 234	2 500	1 547	424	202	252	31 692	1 467	29.9	17.3	55.6
Schoolcraft	235	1 827	D	D	374	D	D	58	31 602	65	27.7	6.2	50.8
Shiawassee	1 135	12 398	2 411	1 785	2 549	403	325	379	30 550	1 033	42.1	10.6	51.2
Tuscola	854	8 641	2 256	1 347	1 522	310	199	288	33 315	1 322	40.0	12.3	48.6
Van Buren	1 270	15 280	2 579	2 657	2 351	372	D	583	38 134	1 113	49.5	4.4	53.2
Washtenaw	7 971	143 487	D	14 255	16 639	4 369	13 136	7 175	50 004	1 236	55.3	6.9	48.8
Wayne	31 821	590 972	101 515	76 534	65 804	26 459	39 451	29 065	49 181	287	77.7	1.4	59.9
Wexford	839	12 341	1 877	3 448	1 873	354	241	417	33 812	357	42.6	3.4	37.5
MINNESOTA	146 354	2 518 268	444 946	299 567	293 281	158 001	136 574	120 891	48 006	74 542	25.2	18.2	52.9
Aitkin	400	3 006	750	324	678	D	37	87	28 855	471	19.7	12.5	40.8
Anoka	7 341	111 212	14 991	20 432	15 413	2 349	3 121	5 832	52 438	396	58.3	4.5	44.7
Becker	954	11 404	2 057	2 154	1 924	231	D	367	32 142	1 107	17.3	15.4	54.9
Beltrami	1 146	13 815	3 297	871	3 035	419	387	411	29 778	573	15.5	17.6	44.9
Benton	913	16 310	3 194	4 038	1 886	191	209	552	33 829	958	29.7	7.8	51.8
Big Stone	194	1 484	553	D	195	76	45	48	32 447	400	14.8	34.0	63.0
Blue Earth	1 929	34 712	8 191	3 886	6 081	1 052	1 090	1 194	34 385	1 070	26.9	22.4	53.7
Brown	767	12 006	2 267	2 742	1 760	443	434	404	33 678	1 055	21.0	19.9	55.9
Carlton	694	8 100	2 055	1 339	1 322	412	205	293	36 175	501	21.6	5.8	43.7
Carver	2 443	37 157	4 974	9 866	3 721	1 254	1 872	1 793	48 252	789	38.3	9.6	51.3
Cass	793	6 121	1 023	299	934	190	162	168	27 446	546	20.1	12.6	54.0
Chippewa	414	5 210	1 138	1 285	677	186	83	176	33 713	674	23.7	30.4	67.1
Chisago	1 202	12 656	D	2 131	1 838	294	D	472	37 324	832	44.2	4.7	37.6
Clay	1 247	17 599	4 033	885	2 636	528	390	503	28 595	804	20.5	33.6	52.6
Clearwater	203	2 776	603	D	242	71	D	138	49 856	519	12.5	15.4	36.0
Cook	279	2 076	D	D	321	D	33	59	28 330	18	50.0	5.6	16.7
Cottonwood	352	4 277	731	1 587	529	98	D	132	30 795	813	23.1	31.1	66.8
Crow Wing	2 076	26 094	5 727	2 585	4 361	1 202	834	899	34 439	533	28.5	8.1	50.5
Dakota	10 099	172 509	22 497	16 432	22 743	11 356	9 574	8 095	46 925	892	42.2	13.6	56.8
Dodge	424	4 118	307	D	410	127	80	179	43 347	621	39.6	19.5	58.5
Douglas	1 343	17 306	3 612	3 380	3 077	474	477	615	35 561	1 091	24.6	11.2	39.4
Faribault	431	4 072	840	1 164	552	241	83	142	34 870	824	21.4	32.0	67.4

STATE County	Agriculture, 2012 (cont.) Land in farms Acreage (1,000)	Land in farms Percent change, 2007–2012	Land in farms Acres Average size of farm	Land in farms Acres Total irrigated (1,000)	Land in farms Acres Total cropland (1,000)	Value of land and buildings (dollars) Average per farm	Value of land and buildings (dollars) Average per acre	Value of machinery and equipment, average per farm (dollars)	Value of products sold Total (mil dol)	Value of products sold Average per farm (dollars)	Value of products sold Percent from: Crops	Value of products sold Percent from: Livestock and poultry products	Percent of farms with sales of: $10,000 or more	Percent of farms with sales of: $100,000 or more	Government payments Total ($1,000)	Government payments Percent of farms
	117	118	119	120	121	122	123	124	125	126	127	128	129	130	131	132
MICHIGAN—Cont'd																
Keweenaw	0	-80.1	53	0.0	0.0	133 333	2 516	34 167	D	D	D	D	0.0	0.0	0	0.0
Lake	26	21.7	130	0.0	11.5	338 075	2 598	55 965	4.1	20 305	56.4	43.6	22.0	4.0	88	12.0
Lapeer	176	-0.4	155	2.1	137.1	708 546	4 572	126 049	113.4	100 049	80.6	19.4	41.8	15.3	2 214	23.1
Leelanau	59	6.7	120	2.2	33.3	810 441	6 731	96 296	20.5	41 486	86.7	13.3	43.1	9.1	2 363	31.0
Lenawee	344	-1.2	213	4.4	299.3	863 720	4 058	134 226	204.6	126 435	70.4	29.6	42.0	17.4	10 028	62.1
Livingston	86	-10.7	117	1.4	61.0	569 114	4 849	88 651	52.3	71 187	74.1	25.9	36.0	10.4	1 090	16.5
Luce	12	31.5	270	D	4.3	619 116	2 295	97 233	3.6	84 070	81.7	18.3	39.5	11.6	79	20.9
Mackinac	22	3.3	218	0.0	11.5	452 359	2 078	57 767	5.4	52 039	22.1	77.9	45.6	7.8	142	21.4
Macomb	68	9.6	135	2.5	58.4	747 673	5 523	120 797	73.2	145 900	79.7	20.3	53.4	24.7	956	23.5
Manistee	44	-3.8	137	1.3	20.1	393 093	2 875	41 111	7.6	23 543	85.1	14.9	28.4	5.9	241	13.0
Marquette	31	2.0	183	0.1	9.2	372 268	2 038	68 690	2.3	13 679	35.5	64.5	26.8	1.2	209	8.9
Mason	79	3.4	180	3.0	56.7	512 948	2 855	109 655	52.9	120 184	59.9	40.1	43.0	15.0	828	27.0
Mecosta	123	7.2	158	14.4	79.7	471 610	2 987	90 709	113.3	145 388	40.6	59.4	46.5	13.0	904	36.5
Menominee	92	-11.3	231	0.0	50.3	463 201	2 006	84 543	41.4	104 025	19.1	80.9	37.7	14.6	1 131	37.4
Midland	90	-1.2	161	1.0	69.5	580 838	3 600	98 339	70.1	126 285	67.9	32.1	39.1	14.1	2 310	44.3
Missaukee	100	12.6	230	7.5	71.7	695 275	3 025	154 582	126.0	290 998	24.8	75.2	41.6	18.7	1 568	28.6
Monroe	215	3.2	188	9.8	196.2	853 688	4 553	135 682	173.9	152 008	95.5	4.5	54.6	20.3	3 653	50.8
Montcalm	237	-2.3	211	55.9	181.1	702 214	3 336	131 319	213.9	189 831	72.1	27.9	41.1	17.9	2 577	40.6
Montmorency	24	11.6	161	D	14.6	366 252	2 272	84 497	8.1	53 854	52.8	47.2	37.7	9.9	175	25.2
Muskegon	74	-6.8	144	9.5	49.0	741 080	5 130	95 333	76.0	147 860	61.6	38.4	38.9	15.6	658	21.8
Newaygo	126	-5.8	136	7.5	83.4	484 268	3 557	91 385	113.8	123 346	39.9	60.1	39.5	13.8	1 193	20.8
Oakland	32	-2.4	59	0.7	18.8	506 358	8 572	54 261	25.9	48 244	87.5	12.5	25.1	6.9	226	6.9
Oceana	128	3.6	210	10.4	89.4	675 791	3 221	124 509	101.2	166 141	63.3	36.7	48.6	18.7	2 529	31.2
Ogemaw	68	11.8	243	0.1	40.2	645 025	2 650	129 246	46.3	165 218	29.1	70.9	42.1	18.9	927	47.1
Ontonagon	29	-5.7	267	0.0	13.9	451 716	1 694	61 257	2.2	20 220	75.1	24.9	40.4	4.6	91	12.8
Osceola	111	-9.5	147	1.4	64.7	373 809	2 536	65 007	45.7	60 912	28.5	71.5	30.0	8.5	1 124	22.8
Oscoda	17	-4.7	116	0.0	7.9	303 648	2 629	48 641	6.9	47 635	17.1	82.9	45.5	13.8	44	6.2
Otsego	32	-3.9	179	1.2	14.3	453 122	2 526	72 189	7.1	39 250	85.5	14.5	39.4	6.1	88	32.2
Ottawa	186	9.2	137	18.1	138.1	881 996	6 458	142 875	534.4	392 080	56.2	43.8	56.9	26.9	2 689	25.5
Presque Isle	82	14.7	252	1.4	45.4	541 449	2 145	82 938	22.8	70 653	76.5	23.5	39.6	10.8	684	31.0
Roscommon	7	56.2	128	0.3	2.7	336 517	2 626	56 966	D	D	D	D	24.1	0.0	D	6.9
Saginaw	310	-4.5	235	2.3	274.5	896 656	3 816	144 832	243.6	184 855	91.7	8.3	55.8	27.6	6 093	71.6
St. Clair	180	12.1	172	0.4	151.6	640 936	3 736	122 904	107.9	102 895	90.7	9.3	47.5	17.8	1 714	32.6
St. Joseph	222	2.9	229	112.4	188.2	1 090 049	4 754	158 897	238.1	246 177	80.2	19.8	48.4	25.0	4 196	46.8
Sanilac	457	9.5	311	1.8	405.5	1 365 955	4 386	217 288	421.0	286 957	66.5	33.5	61.0	36.3	7 213	60.3
Schoolcraft	19	-27.2	299	D	5.3	485 169	1 624	59 031	2.2	33 354	63.0	37.1	32.3	9.2	93	10.8
Shiawassee	223	-1.4	216	0.8	195.2	773 484	3 577	136 423	145.2	140 532	78.1	21.9	52.6	22.0	3 634	55.3
Tuscola	325	-5.1	246	5.4	284.5	1 117 802	4 542	168 867	274.4	207 599	82.4	17.6	48.9	26.2	4 778	56.9
Van Buren	175	-5.5	157	34.0	125.1	699 335	4 445	132 358	194.7	174 900	82.9	17.1	46.6	16.4	2 425	21.5
Washtenaw	170	2.0	138	3.6	133.5	701 358	5 095	92 338	87.8	71 004	77.0	23.0	42.5	14.6	3 466	31.7
Wayne	16	-9.6	55	0.3	10.9	408 840	7 442	80 902	26.5	92 456	98.2	1.8	36.9	8.4	102	9.4
Wexford	40	4.8	113	0.9	23.7	321 616	2 847	47 675	9.7	27 104	49.9	50.1	26.1	5.0	122	15.1
MINNESOTA	26 036	-3.3	349	524.0	21 597.1	1 474 057	4 220	197 702	21 280.2	285 479	65.2	34.8	60.0	33.5	467 867	70.0
Aitkin	123	-7.6	260	3.1	61.8	458 718	1 762	64 280	15.7	33 395	52.4	47.6	36.9	6.8	275	22.1
Anoka	45	-2.5	113	2.6	33.0	683 038	6 032	84 725	47.5	119 922	81.5	18.5	35.6	11.6	329	23.7
Becker	435	9.9	393	10.4	309.9	1 067 005	2 716	145 055	261.5	236 218	67.8	32.2	45.9	21.0	6 592	62.9
Beltrami	181	-14.4	315	2.6	88.2	535 471	1 699	70 642	32.4	56 518	66.0	34.0	41.2	10.3	1 146	32.6
Benton	189	1.5	197	11.5	139.9	676 684	3 435	130 284	167.5	174 846	44.1	55.9	59.5	24.5	3 168	63.9
Big Stone	249	-1.4	622	2.1	215.7	2 426 078	3 901	304 623	164.6	411 560	84.0	16.0	72.0	47.5	3 512	85.8
Blue Earth	376	-9.4	352	1.7	338.8	2 256 415	6 413	234 723	505.4	472 358	51.8	48.2	65.8	46.4	7 732	80.4
Brown	326	-8.1	309	2.4	296.4	1 705 125	5 518	216 063	382.9	362 955	57.5	42.5	76.5	51.5	7 384	88.3
Carlton	93	-5.5	185	D	42.4	345 838	1 872	55 281	11.0	21 878	49.3	50.7	39.1	2.4	D	12.2
Carver	155	-8.3	197	0.2	131.6	1 139 812	5 793	194 842	134.4	170 340	65.4	34.6	59.6	28.9	3 149	62.4
Cass	157	-7.1	288	8.8	61.3	549 962	1 910	68 947	38.2	69 877	27.5	72.5	44.3	8.1	542	23.4
Chippewa	335	-8.9	497	4.3	310.6	2 569 132	5 167	332 969	333.2	494 408	79.3	20.7	66.5	48.5	6 261	87.5
Chisago	114	-1.3	137	1.6	76.2	595 308	4 354	79 403	56.5	67 945	77.7	22.3	47.8	12.6	1 081	38.6
Clay	611	-0.5	760	9.9	555.2	2 673 295	3 519	311 899	398.1	495 118	90.3	9.7	62.3	41.3	8 241	75.7
Clearwater	167	-14.0	322	4.0	76.2	539 944	1 679	79 719	31.1	59 836	48.3	51.7	48.4	9.8	886	41.0
Cook	2	-5.4	126	0.0	0.2	598 778	4 744	28 444	0.3	14 278	90.3	9.7	27.8	5.6	D	5.6
Cottonwood	373	-2.2	459	1.4	336.4	2 519 027	5 494	312 232	374.1	460 135	62.6	37.4	70.6	53.4	7 918	83.9
Crow Wing	100	-17.9	188	2.2	44.8	485 445	2 588	75 574	24.8	46 593	58.6	41.5	36.8	8.8	546	30.6
Dakota	220	-10.6	246	50.4	192.7	1 398 640	5 675	195 370	241.0	270 188	77.8	22.2	63.9	32.5	3 892	54.4
Dodge	225	-9.2	363	D	202.5	2 231 597	6 148	237 108	288.1	463 976	61.6	38.4	63.6	40.3	4 124	68.9
Douglas	268	1.8	245	3.4	197.8	754 903	3 078	113 163	120.9	110 813	73.7	26.3	52.6	23.1	4 467	77.7
Faribault	390	-14.0	473	0.3	370.2	2 662 949	5 624	317 608	414.2	502 671	77.9	22.1	78.9	61.0	7 763	82.8

STATE County	Water use, 2010		Wholesale trade,[1] 2007				Retail trade,[2] 2007				Real estate and rental and leasing,[2] 2007			
	Total water withdrawn (mil gal/day)	Gallons withdrawn per person per day	Number of establish-ments	Number of employees	Sales (mil dol)	Annual payroll (mil dol)	Number of establish-ments	Number of employees	Sales (mil dol)	Annual payroll (mil dol)	Number of establish-ments	Number of employees	Receipts (mil dol)	Annual payroll (mil dol)
	133	134	135	136	137	138	139	140	141	142	143	144	145	146
MICHIGAN—Cont'd														
Keweenaw	0.2	93	1	D	D	D	12	22	3.3	0.4	3	D	D	D
Lake	2.0	173	2	D	D	D	32	231	53.3	4.1	7	D	D	D
Lapeer	7.9	90	54	411	170.1	15.7	281	3 217	799.9	62.1	68	239	21.0	5.0
Leelanau	3.6	167	12	83	17.1	2.3	134	739	128.2	13.2	28	74	8.4	2.0
Lenawee	13.3	133	70	526	451.9	21.2	340	4 329	944.7	87.2	69	231	31.4	5.1
Livingston	20.0	111	208	1 475	1 293.3	78.1	611	8 734	2 059.8	186.5	139	673	110.5	16.7
Luce	1.3	201	7	D	D	D	34	317	74.0	5.8	4	D	D	D
Mackinac	10.1	908	6	D	D	D	113	462	155.8	11.0	14	D	D	D
Macomb	9.2	11	856	10 424	5 611.1	522.4	2 941	41 513	10 007.6	950.4	674	3 569	601.9	98.4
Manistee	42.9	1 736	14	D	D	D	117	906	225.4	19.5	23	76	6.1	1.1
Marquette	271.9	4 053	54	437	162.4	15.3	312	3 860	729.8	70.4	71	313	31.2	6.4
Mason	23.7	827	15	145	148.6	5.5	143	1 562	330.4	31.5	30	146	20.2	3.9
Mecosta	15.1	353	21	D	D	D	160	2 231	475.0	41.4	46	162	20.4	3.4
Menominee	5.8	243	18	D	D	D	80	690	166.9	12.6	16	41	4.6	0.7
Midland	10.6	127	49	D	D	D	323	4 382	869.3	79.5	82	D	D	D
Missaukee	3.9	263	17	D	D	D	36	329	91.9	7.4	6	18	0.8	0.2
Monroe	1 830.0	12 038	91	D	D	D	427	5 637	1 465.3	120.3	95	373	48.8	7.5
Montcalm	30.0	474	39	221	124.8	8.6	240	2 463	563.1	49.0	26	81	8.0	1.5
Montmorency	1.1	110	3	D	D	D	45	303	70.1	5.2	13	D	D	D
Muskegon	271.7	1 578	119	D	D	D	608	7 878	1 656.7	154.5	112	484	67.0	12.0
Newaygo	8.3	171	26	199	71.7	8.2	169	1 577	355.3	31.1	22	D	D	D
Oakland	50.2	42	2 150	28 244	29 825.7	1 655.5	5 189	75 573	18 183.7	1 798.7	1 821	16 685	2 929.4	642.0
Oceana	6.4	241	13	D	D	D	100	714	171.5	13.5	16	58	5.4	1.1
Ogemaw	3.2	149	18	D	D	D	126	1 501	364.7	31.6	27	82	11.2	1.9
Ontonagon	5.5	807	6	83	16.6	3.6	38	311	60.9	5.6	4	D	D	D
Osceola	5.5	234	8	122	57.7	4.9	80	609	151.6	12.1	13	20	4.3	0.6
Oscoda	1.2	142	2	D	D	D	43	264	57.1	4.7	8	D	D	D
Otsego	4.1	171	41	427	290.7	21.0	157	2 137	499.8	48.0	24	91	15.8	3.6
Ottawa	944.1	3 579	304	3 208	2 120.6	148.0	830	10 670	2 367.8	220.4	186	891	107.9	23.9
Presque Isle	23.7	1 770	8	37	8.3	0.9	69	494	101.4	9.5	7	D	D	D
Roscommon	2.7	112	12	40	6.8	0.9	133	1 610	338.4	33.1	25	63	6.0	1.2
Saginaw	22.3	111	184	2 319	1 070.8	92.0	973	12 584	2 534.3	243.3	149	751	101.8	17.4
St. Clair	1 495.2	9 171	86	818	872.3	47.0	602	7 629	1 601.6	141.9	107	408	63.0	9.7
St. Joseph	35.6	580	47	D	D	D	215	2 428	559.9	50.2	40	143	18.7	3.3
Sanilac	6.1	141	31	309	174.9	10.9	172	1 454	300.9	27.2	25	119	11.7	3.5
Schoolcraft	7.7	904	4	D	D	D	61	379	110.8	8.0	5	D	D	D
Shiawassee	7.4	104	42	D	D	D	219	2 556	614.7	54.3	39	112	13.1	2.9
Tuscola	8.9	160	29	387	283.1	15.4	163	1 764	432.3	34.2	21	77	7.4	1.3
Van Buren	167.0	2 189	55	D	D	D	262	2 431	556.7	49.6	45	189	20.0	3.0
Washtenaw	34.8	101	291	3 705	3 631.0	194.4	1 148	16 403	3 681.1	355.3	368	2 595	712.4	98.3
Wayne	1 797.3	987	1 649	26 806	26 102.9	1 405.1	6 361	68 272	17 275.8	1 451.0	1 276	7 929	5 528.0	241.0
Wexford	7.6	232	30	433	157.4	18.2	177	2 089	525.4	42.7	32	106	14.3	2.8
MINNESOTA	3 821.2	720	6 913	110 487	82 878.1	6 417.8	20 777	307 034	71 384.1	6 685.6	6 889	39 430	9 208.0	1 317.4
Aitkin	3.4	212	7	96	53.5	3.6	74	750	147.5	12.4	9	18	1.8	0.3
Anoka	126.1	381	335	8 542	7 335.9	1 054.6	986	16 716	3 738.9	363.0	388	1 857	307.3	43.7
Becker	8.6	264	31	245	88.4	8.6	158	1 680	373.5	32.2	45	113	20.7	2.6
Beltrami	6.4	144	41	D	D	D	228	3 236	627.4	60.8	38	132	15.1	2.9
Benton	21.9	568	43	943	513.0	41.0	118	1 989	495.2	40.3	37	270	16.4	7.6
Big Stone	1.4	270	8	85	185.8	2.9	30	244	32.9	3.2	4	12	0.5	0.1
Blue Earth	34.6	540	90	1 391	1 275.9	60.6	355	6 309	1 211.5	110.9	80	634	74.8	13.4
Brown	4.0	155	37	398	547.1	14.8	126	1 754	301.2	29.6	25	78	5.5	1.6
Carlton	10.7	302	21	D	D	D	130	1 490	357.4	30.8	15	76	9.8	1.0
Carver	11.2	122	129	2 044	1 484.3	132.0	235	3 440	807.1	72.1	112	D	D	D
Cass	6.0	211	17	163	44.3	5.4	160	1 122	276.8	23.1	41	262	22.5	5.7
Chippewa	2.1	170	18	212	201.4	9.0	62	697	168.3	14.2	15	98	4.4	1.2
Chisago	4.7	86	42	D	D	D	167	1 864	428.6	32.9	53	D	D	D
Clay	6.6	112	69	D	D	D	180	2 801	630.3	54.6	40	179	17.4	3.2
Clearwater	5.7	660	6	28	14.2	0.7	35	245	42.9	3.6	NA	NA	NA	NA
Cook	174.8	33 773	3	D	D	D	45	290	61.9	6.6	17	48	4.2	0.7
Cottonwood	5.4	464	25	224	177.2	8.5	66	568	90.3	7.9	8	22	2.9	0.6
Crow Wing	11.4	182	67	604	278.7	19.3	389	4 936	1 141.9	107.2	100	236	38.2	6.9
Dakota	339.7	852	552	9 217	4 415.5	491.7	1 178	22 061	5 164.0	498.1	544	2 317	356.9	70.6
Dodge	2.6	131	21	388	244.8	16.9	63	418	91.8	8.1	12	18	4.9	0.5
Douglas	5.7	159	45	D	D	D	237	2 982	625.5	58.0	49	167	32.2	3.9
Faribault	3.2	218	29	177	142.9	5.3	78	610	116.7	10.9	9	14	0.8	0.2

1. Merchant wholesalers, except manufacturers' sales branches and offices. 2. Employer establishments.

STATE County	Professional, scientific, and technical services,[1] 2007				Manufacturing, 2007				Accommodation and food services, 2007			
	Number of establish-ments	Number of employees	Receipts (mil dol)	Annual payroll (mil dol)	Number of establish-ments	Number of employees	Receipts (mil dol)	Annual payroll (mil dol)	Number of establish-ments	Number of employees	Sales (mil dol)	Annual payroll (mil dol)
	147	148	149	150	151	152	153	154	155	156	157	158
MICHIGAN—Cont'd												
Keweenaw	1	D	D	D	NA	NA	NA	NA	15	102	4.4	1.2
Lake	5	D	D	D	NA	NA	NA	NA	31	175	7.8	1.9
Lapeer	128	D	D	D	135	4 916	1 142.6	177.5	123	1 976	72.6	21.7
Leelanau	59	D	D	D	NA	NA	NA	NA	75	716	40.6	13.3
Lenawee	131	601	43.2	20.1	152	6 797	2 230.8	303.3	178	2 680	94.2	28.3
Livingston	483	2 706	327.3	155.2	268	8 278	2 715.8	377.9	263	4 955	181.0	51.3
Luce	9	16	0.9	0.5	NA	NA	NA	NA	22	231	7.4	2.2
Mackinac	16	45	3.1	1.2	NA	NA	NA	NA	106	718	56.5	15.2
Macomb	1 671	D	D	D	1 732	65 038	23 588.5	3 451.5	1 547	27 891	1 120.9	332.0
Manistee	36	104	9.7	3.6	24	973	391.2	54.7	68	654	26.8	7.4
Marquette	128	D	D	D	45	952	310.4	40.1	190	3 089	100.3	32.7
Mason	52	234	18.8	7.8	42	2 137	518.3	87.7	90	884	39.7	11.1
Mecosta	43	D	D	D	37	1 924	668.2	78.4	76	1 289	44.1	13.2
Menominee	23	89	7.4	3.2	49	1 821	418.5	76.2	38	495	17.2	4.8
Midland	164	D	D	D	55	5 103	2 821.3	363.1	129	2 545	108.0	30.6
Missaukee	8	19	1.3	0.6	NA	NA	NA	NA	24	229	9.4	2.8
Monroe	147	944	84.3	39.6	143	8 555	3 503.0	440.6	274	4 682	171.5	47.8
Montcalm	61	D	D	D	66	2 059	389.0	82.7	103	1 012	45.8	10.2
Montmorency	11	31	2.9	1.1	NA	NA	NA	NA	31	210	7.9	2.2
Muskegon	239	D	D	D	290	13 271	3 675.8	609.1	344	5 763	221.0	64.6
Newaygo	51	D	D	D	49	2 005	560.8	72.8	79	873	32.1	9.4
Oakland	6 414	D	D	D	1 862	58 971	25 885.2	3 228.0	2 700	48 801	2 284.8	661.6
Oceana	28	91	7.5	3.0	40	1 473	364.1	40.2	78	794	32.3	10.3
Ogemaw	39	139	10.9	4.2	39	838	151.7	27.0	60	833	31.1	8.3
Ontonagon	8	9	0.8	0.2	NA	NA	NA	NA	40	275	6.8	1.6
Osceola	23	69	5.8	2.1	44	2 038	968.0	81.2	41	435	19.2	5.8
Oscoda	9	24	1.4	0.7	NA	NA	NA	NA	25	253	9.0	2.6
Otsego	56	D	D	D	37	874	158.0	30.7	73	1 307	58.8	16.7
Ottawa	515	D	D	D	584	31 912	9 210.9	1 395.5	381	7 551	277.2	83.8
Presque Isle	16	36	2.1	0.7	NA	NA	NA	NA	42	262	9.2	2.6
Roscommon	35	D	D	D	NA	NA	NA	NA	80	1 063	37.3	11.7
Saginaw	355	3 009	429.9	121.3	219	11 437	4 604.8	659.0	383	8 620	337.3	102.2
St. Clair	244	D	D	D	261	9 326	2 855.5	394.0	287	4 679	178.3	52.0
St. Joseph	80	499	30.8	11.0	143	9 470	3 106.6	410.4	109	1 474	53.8	15.5
Sanilac	69	D	D	D	87	2 921	595.1	104.5	73	738	30.2	7.8
Schoolcraft	10	38	2.0	0.9	NA	NA	NA	NA	32	250	10.2	2.8
Shiawassee	93	475	39.2	12.5	69	1 865	409.5	69.6	109	1 584	57.5	15.7
Tuscola	58	D	D	D	55	1 953	581.5	78.8	68	719	24.7	7.2
Van Buren	90	D	D	D	100	3 838	1 312.9	160.9	168	2 089	80.5	23.1
Washtenaw	1 215	14 248	1 788.8	1 017.4	324	15 543	5 331.8	881.4	679	13 734	613.5	180.4
Wayne	2 880	D	D	D	1 729	87 991	55 896.9	5 545.3	3 215	57 836	3 112.4	857.5
Wexford	55	438	40.1	16.9	57	4 158	D	D	88	1 344	48.8	14.2
MINNESOTA	16 595	140 786	20 473.1	8 425.3	7 951	340 514	107 563.1	15 999.2	11 340	221 081	10 423.7	2 978.4
Aitkin	17	48	3.8	1.2	NA	NA	NA	NA	60	488	19.7	5.6
Anoka	769	D	D	D	675	23 959	6 460.2	1 247.7	461	9 936	374.9	112.1
Becker	56	272	24.5	10.7	47	1 806	284.8	59.3	88	1 130	43.4	11.4
Beltrami	66	D	D	D	38	1 249	279.8	41.5	100	1 643	65.6	18.3
Benton	48	D	D	D	77	4 248	839.1	162.7	63	1 074	42.1	11.6
Big Stone	12	31	2.2	0.9	NA	NA	NA	NA	17	D	D	D
Blue Earth	131	D	D	D	87	4 181	2 728.7	172.0	167	4 053	139.0	40.9
Brown	51	409	40.8	14.6	42	3 570	1 596.9	128.8	74	1 134	40.5	12.6
Carlton	44	D	D	D	33	1 635	D	D	66	856	32.6	9.6
Carver	306	D	D	D	153	12 361	3 149.5	579.3	138	2 511	91.1	26.9
Cass	45	D	D	D	NA	NA	NA	NA	139	2 255	146.4	41.0
Chippewa	24	107	9.7	3.8	29	1 069	175.8	36.4	32	368	11.6	3.0
Chisago	91	328	29.5	12.0	88	1 851	403.1	68.1	93	1 240	43.0	12.1
Clay	71	D	D	D	48	925	317.1	35.7	89	1 586	58.5	16.5
Clearwater	8	35	2.7	0.9	12	D	D	D	21	D	D	D
Cook	12	24	1.8	0.8	NA	NA	NA	NA	65	806	40.4	12.5
Cottonwood	19	72	7.2	1.8	19	1 590	636.1	48.2	23	282	9.0	2.4
Crow Wing	134	D	D	D	118	2 913	D	119.6	200	3 228	149.6	44.0
Dakota	1 387	8 521	971.0	469.7	490	18 815	12 930.1	929.6	645	14 819	614.3	184.9
Dodge	26	D	D	D	30	1 475	D	68.8	28	386	11.8	3.4
Douglas	74	D	D	D	91	2 672	688.2	109.6	114	2 007	71.0	20.7
Faribault	19	63	6.5	2.4	30	1 063	408.6	41.2	34	363	10.5	2.6

1. Establishment subject to federal tax.

Table B. States and Counties — **Health Care and Social Assistance, Other Services, Nonemployer Businesses, and Residential Construction**

STATE County	Health care and social assistance, 2007				Other services, 2007				Nonemployer businesses, 2013		Value of residential construction authorized by building permits, 2014	
	Number of establish-ments	Number of employees	Receipts (mil dol)	Annual payroll (mil dol)	Number of establish-ments	Number of employees	Receipts (mil dol)	Annual payroll (mil dol)	Number	Receipts (mil dol)	New Construction ($1,000)	Number of housing units
	159	160	161	162	163	164	165	166	167	168	169	170
MICHIGAN—Cont'd												
Keweenaw	NA	NA	NA	NA	1	D	D	D	152	3.6	1 400	8
Lake	12	236	12.2	6.4	9	D	D	D	636	22.8	1 552	54
Lapeer	195	2 424	196.2	72.9	118	488	35.1	9.7	6 300	258.2	21 731	120
Leelanau	56	541	43.9	17.4	43	86	9.6	2.0	2 749	128.4	26 788	113
Lenawee	252	3 345	271.9	104.2	159	787	52.0	12.6	5 890	208.9	15 124	92
Livingston	365	4 784	404.9	162.8	279	1 647	131.9	41.4	14 183	642.5	185 572	736
Luce	16	D	D	D	11	45	2.9	0.6	335	8.3	1 510	13
Mackinac	15	283	22.6	9.9	14	D	D	D	916	32.7	5 107	27
Macomb	2 085	35 424	3 299.3	1 390.3	1 450	8 269	669.0	213.7	59 636	2 512.4	354 503	1 850
Manistee	73	876	67.4	27.5	53	180	15.0	4.2	1 688	54.9	9 501	47
Marquette	228	5 390	500.7	232.0	125	711	56.9	13.1	3 390	95.7	23 251	142
Mason	98	1 359	121.4	47.8	65	245	16.9	5.1	2 002	67.7	12 157	46
Mecosta	79	1 424	105.1	45.7	66	296	23.3	5.9	2 215	74.1	8 412	79
Menominee	45	319	19.7	8.1	30	D	D	D	1 339	61.0	7 993	47
Midland	242	5 442	539.3	192.0	144	947	147.4	22.3	4 875	184.0	24 643	262
Missaukee	24	258	11.8	4.6	21	60	4.9	1.1	1 095	50.7	3 046	19
Monroe	284	4 733	381.3	158.7	195	1 172	93.7	30.3	8 193	340.8	44 179	239
Montcalm	105	2 392	188.0	81.3	100	345	28.0	6.2	3 612	129.2	11 497	67
Montmorency	17	236	12.5	5.8	15	D	D	D	584	19.5	0	0
Muskegon	398	9 463	864.8	374.1	283	1 440	116.0	27.8	9 498	339.5	38 511	181
Newaygo	74	1 473	118.8	50.3	78	308	50.4	5.4	2 739	112.0	5 844	46
Oakland	5 009	91 463	9 299.4	3 883.1	2 507	16 692	2 102.0	461.0	108 991	6 152.3	630 334	2 458
Oceana	45	660	40.9	19.4	37	D	D	D	1 670	58.8	500	4
Ogemaw	75	1 289	92.4	37.9	47	164	10.7	2.9	1 284	50.4	6 587	34
Ontonagon	24	376	18.3	11.4	9	D	D	D	378	12.6	640	7
Osceola	43	940	67.8	29.2	31	124	10.4	2.3	1 347	48.0	2 669	23
Oscoda	12	D	D	D	18	D	D	D	631	24.2	1 125	13
Otsego	92	1 486	130.0	52.1	65	229	19.6	5.3	1 930	80.1	1 377	17
Ottawa	500	9 536	761.6	294.0	425	2 575	240.5	67.4	18 114	917.6	217 926	1 307
Presque Isle	28	336	20.3	8.3	26	D	D	D	921	26.9	4 085	18
Roscommon	48	569	38.4	14.7	60	178	14.7	3.8	1 490	53.4	9 204	50
Saginaw	584	16 811	1 512.5	605.3	369	2 191	178.2	46.5	11 242	383.9	29 451	214
St. Clair	373	7 957	645.6	286.1	221	989	87.7	22.3	10 169	383.9	23 738	130
St. Joseph	109	1 928	163.5	62.8	114	494	38.8	10.4	3 614	133.7	10 608	44
Sanilac	97	1 354	89.9	37.9	64	270	20.6	5.1	3 061	117.8	5 006	39
Schoolcraft	15	341	27.5	13.6	21	D	D	D	409	12.4	2 354	10
Shiawassee	158	2 594	205.3	88.2	110	515	39.5	9.8	4 257	151.5	3 520	18
Tuscola	121	2 284	156.8	71.9	69	246	17.0	4.1	3 486	116.4	3 588	23
Van Buren	115	2 369	167.4	73.2	93	568	31.4	11.2	4 661	174.6	18 491	81
Washtenaw	958	34 745	3 715.8	1 627.0	557	3 917	443.2	122.6	27 876	1 190.6	117 826	570
Wayne	4 200	99 597	10 640.0	4 241.8	2 859	18 419	2 068.3	511.0	126 314	3 786.1	196 344	1 001
Wexford	97	2 040	172.2	68.8	64	258	22.1	5.8	2 271	84.7	9 779	45
MINNESOTA	13 996	386 144	33 997.4	14 872.0	11 137	81 829	8 301.3	2 355.0	388 900	17 268.2	3 680 420	16 990
Aitkin	25	653	57.3	20.1	34	D	D	D	1 112	41.2	34 080	175
Anoka	547	13 566	1 396.4	566.1	559	4 311	360.4	113.0	21 932	902.5	189 404	704
Becker	73	1 753	123.1	54.1	79	411	30.7	6.2	2 834	135.5	29 025	146
Beltrami	124	2 971	217.7	102.7	91	516	44.3	10.4	2 979	108.8	16 752	199
Benton	76	2 060	87.3	39.0	81	D	D	D	2 590	103.3	19 319	98
Big Stone	16	577	31.9	12.5	17	D	D	D	390	18.0	1 390	7
Blue Earth	205	7 412	541.9	232.6	155	953	69.9	18.8	4 060	172.1	42 708	332
Brown	70	2 341	148.1	61.9	85	D	D	D	1 780	69.9	13 036	90
Carlton	92	1 833	138.0	57.7	66	249	19.8	4.8	1 994	73.0	13 285	60
Carver	177	4 149	351.3	154.5	165	1 108	87.5	23.9	7 504	386.4	173 906	623
Cass	78	1 275	62.5	26.2	57	289	23.6	5.4	2 581	114.8	31 990	151
Chippewa	39	1 035	54.6	25.2	42	D	D	D	862	34.5	813	9
Chisago	121	3 843	332.3	163.9	91	D	D	D	3 753	146.4	27 582	174
Clay	148	2 670	115.1	54.5	113	D	D	D	3 807	145.9	74 912	559
Clearwater	15	419	19.6	9.6	15	D	D	D	649	25.0	247	3
Cook	14	D	D	D	10	D	D	D	782	27.6	10 434	39
Cottonwood	34	861	40.0	16.5	29	D	D	D	812	41.5	2 194	12
Crow Wing	201	5 075	343.3	139.0	148	764	50.8	11.7	4 977	223.1	58 490	331
Dakota	886	16 802	1 399.8	602.6	717	5 742	551.5	161.7	27 905	1 231.4	339 389	1 416
Dodge	29	D	D	D	45	274	24.5	7.0	1 344	69.2	10 812	51
Douglas	119	2 674	184.0	77.9	111	D	D	D	3 312	152.2	32 238	184
Faribault	39	903	51.9	23.1	31	D	D	D	1 130	54.0	1 538	8

STATE County	Government employment and payroll, 2012									Local government finances, 2012				
			March payroll (percent of total)							General revenue				
												Taxes		
													Per capita[1] (dollars)	
	Full-time equivalent employees	March payroll (dollars)	Adminis-tration, judicial, and legal	Police and Corrections	Fire Protection	Highways and transpor-tation	Health and Welfare	Natural resources and utilities	Education and libraries	Total (mil dol)	Inter-govern-mental (mil dol)	Total (mil dol)	Total	Property
	171	172	173	174	175	176	177	178	179	180	181	182	183	184
MICHIGAN—Cont'd														
Keweenaw	94	226 587	43.0	12.5	0.3	32.4	0.3	5.4	3.3	7.1	2.2	2.4	1 085	1 064
Lake	335	1 121 895	29.9	22.5	0.7	15.2	0.2	4.0	24.4	41.5	20.4	15.6	1 355	1 353
Lapeer	2 193	8 102 009	9.7	7.1	0.9	3.7	6.5	3.4	67.0	261.5	141.1	64.1	727	687
Leelanau	610	2 337 768	17.9	7.8	10.1	6.0	1.3	2.0	50.2	66.0	15.8	38.3	1 774	1 747
Lenawee	2 916	10 906 000	8.3	8.7	1.9	4.7	2.7	5.5	65.8	340.2	180.3	97.9	989	958
Livingston	3 683	15 206 225	8.3	7.3	2.3	3.3	1.3	2.2	69.7	518.2	264.0	170.8	934	916
Luce	511	1 851 870	3.9	1.5	0.5	3.4	68.0	1.9	19.9	52.1	10.7	6.0	924	922
Mackinac	650	2 008 291	8.8	6.7	0.6	5.6	41.9	4.0	30.0	45.0	12.9	23.1	2 077	1 972
Macomb	20 477	98 514 743	5.7	8.9	3.4	3.3	4.1	2.4	70.5	3 154.9	1 534.9	942.2	1 112	1 087
Manistee	1 223	4 900 512	8.6	4.0	2.1	5.6	46.5	1.1	31.4	89.4	31.4	32.7	1 326	1 315
Marquette	2 307	8 582 841	9.4	7.9	1.6	8.1	17.8	11.0	40.6	242.6	106.7	75.0	1 105	1 084
Mason	951	3 483 823	12.1	7.3	0.1	7.1	0.9	4.3	66.7	123.3	40.6	57.2	1 996	1 980
Mecosta	1 566	5 890 046	7.7	5.5	1.5	4.1	36.2	3.2	40.3	182.4	76.2	42.5	980	926
Menominee	588	2 056 771	19.0	9.3	2.8	9.0	0.0	3.2	55.6	62.8	33.4	19.2	806	799
Midland	2 175	9 622 686	11.4	7.8	3.3	4.0	3.3	5.7	62.5	271.7	113.5	103.5	1 235	1 220
Missaukee	422	1 353 016	12.8	7.9	0.0	5.9	3.8	2.5	64.8	51.3	27.9	11.7	775	714
Monroe	3 882	16 268 085	7.1	8.4	1.4	3.3	1.1	4.8	72.4	475.7	225.8	166.5	1 102	1 074
Montcalm	1 898	7 424 584	9.0	5.3	0.5	3.4	5.9	1.9	72.7	230.7	138.4	56.8	901	887
Montmorency	201	694 558	20.5	8.4	2.1	11.4	4.4	2.8	43.7	25.7	7.3	10.4	1 095	1 081
Muskegon	5 428	21 789 876	7.5	7.4	2.5	3.3	9.1	3.1	65.4	721.5	413.6	168.4	989	913
Newaygo	1 567	5 734 250	9.2	6.4	0.9	3.1	12.6	1.5	64.0	180.6	100.9	46.4	967	962
Oakland	32 137	148 761 141	8.1	11.5	4.0	2.5	1.6	3.0	67.0	4 845.3	2 149.8	1 849.8	1 515	1 468
Oceana	787	2 716 638	12.5	6.8	0.6	9.1	6.1	3.2	57.2	91.5	36.3	30.4	1 156	1 142
Ogemaw	842	2 976 350	8.9	6.3	0.2	5.1	44.2	1.3	31.8	88.5	51.5	18.2	849	836
Ontonagon	240	749 123	19.9	5.8	0.6	28.7	0.1	8.1	33.5	31.1	13.6	12.2	1 900	1 897
Osceola	733	2 622 547	9.4	6.1	0.6	5.1	5.4	1.4	70.9	69.7	41.4	19.9	853	849
Oscoda	244	725 038	18.2	5.2	0.5	9.3	2.2	2.3	61.4	22.2	10.6	9.0	1 046	1 036
Otsego	766	3 112 250	10.4	4.0	0.5	8.3	0.2	1.8	71.3	77.8	31.0	34.0	1 415	1 413
Ottawa	6 822	27 516 658	8.5	6.3	1.4	2.9	4.0	6.4	67.9	866.8	436.0	302.6	1 125	1 104
Presque Isle	353	1 093 950	16.9	10.3	0.0	9.1	0.4	3.7	54.2	39.4	19.9	14.6	1 112	1 107
Roscommon	871	3 202 024	11.2	10.4	2.9	8.2	2.8	1.9	61.8	97.6	32.0	44.6	1 849	1 841
Saginaw	5 686	21 466 345	8.3	8.5	2.2	2.7	9.8	4.8	61.7	786.5	475.8	154.2	777	684
St. Clair	4 714	19 193 428	9.3	10.1	2.3	4.7	2.9	4.1	64.9	638.8	345.1	182.6	1 136	1 082
St. Joseph	2 407	8 504 558	8.9	6.1	1.5	3.5	17.3	3.9	56.9	263.0	120.1	64.5	1 061	1 051
Sanilac	1 146	3 992 557	10.8	9.0	0.7	4.8	2.5	4.3	65.5	164.8	92.6	39.4	932	918
Schoolcraft	461	1 943 689	9.8	4.5	1.3	9.9	52.0	3.2	18.6	62.6	11.5	8.5	1 020	1 018
Shiawassee	2 564	9 090 340	7.2	7.6	1.3	2.6	17.5	2.4	59.3	229.5	141.1	48.8	706	694
Tuscola	1 649	6 143 983	21.0	6.5	0.2	4.3	0.6	1.4	64.0	203.6	117.9	44.3	810	798
Van Buren	2 988	10 792 044	6.7	6.5	1.0	3.0	15.9	2.4	63.8	369.9	183.5	110.9	1 470	1 455
Washtenaw	9 997	45 620 706	8.5	10.1	3.0	4.2	5.2	5.4	62.0	1 472.6	631.4	577.8	1 646	1 596
Wayne	52 078	243 918 311	7.3	16.2	6.7	6.5	2.2	6.4	52.0	9 260.6	4 384.4	2 686.6	1 499	1 195
Wexford	861	3 131 204	9.3	8.2	2.0	8.9	0.5	6.9	62.4	121.3	63.1	38.8	1 190	1 183
MINNESOTA	X	X	X	X	X	X	X	X	X	X	X	X	X	X
Aitkin	582	2 073 612	15.2	11.2	0.4	6.7	11.2	4.6	46.4	60.1	32.6	17.4	1 089	1 074
Anoka	10 501	53 828 905	6.5	8.8	1.4	2.5	5.0	3.0	71.0	1 331.2	702.4	418.5	1 244	1 193
Becker	932	4 604 178	7.8	4.6	0.0	8.2	10.4	5.5	61.2	127.6	63.7	39.1	1 185	1 161
Beltrami	1 932	6 706 796	6.4	7.1	0.7	3.3	9.3	2.1	68.3	213.6	142.5	38.4	846	783
Benton	983	5 694 288	6.7	6.0	0.2	10.1	6.5	2.2	67.4	129.9	70.8	39.7	1 023	988
Big Stone	457	1 386 890	7.6	3.9	0.1	6.3	36.5	4.2	39.3	61.1	19.6	7.4	1 429	1 407
Blue Earth	2 214	8 872 355	7.8	8.8	1.3	4.6	6.9	5.2	63.0	311.6	161.3	79.4	1 221	1 080
Brown	1 088	4 160 686	9.0	10.8	0.0	6.2	20.5	12.8	39.2	121.7	52.1	29.1	1 145	1 070
Carlton	1 862	6 624 488	5.4	5.5	3.7	4.3	24.0	2.7	53.1	175.9	81.0	37.5	1 060	1 044
Carver	2 896	13 125 660	8.3	9.1	0.5	3.7	9.7	7.6	58.3	405.9	156.2	153.3	1 636	1 556
Cass	1 234	4 242 722	11.4	8.7	0.0	4.7	8.0	7.4	56.2	139.1	77.1	36.0	1 270	1 262
Chippewa	807	3 441 530	7.9	4.1	0.2	6.5	37.5	2.9	37.6	70.5	36.6	15.5	1 281	1 255
Chisago	1 385	5 404 860	10.1	10.6	0.1	5.4	10.2	3.2	57.7	193.7	95.4	66.1	1 237	1 214
Clay	2 229	9 153 639	5.8	9.5	2.1	3.2	9.3	7.6	60.6	275.2	152.5	52.4	871	834
Clearwater	344	1 650 939	7.5	7.1	0.0	4.2	13.2	2.5	62.5	36.7	20.9	8.5	982	979
Cook	357	1 321 609	10.7	6.6	0.1	6.3	41.6	8.6	23.6	43.3	14.6	10.6	2 035	1 721
Cottonwood	572	1 944 398	8.0	7.4	0.1	6.3	7.4	9.1	58.7	74.4	30.9	14.0	1 205	1 195
Crow Wing	2 463	11 443 269	7.2	9.3	0.8	3.7	30.0	2.2	44.6	346.9	130.2	91.9	1 461	1 378
Dakota	12 238	59 978 327	5.3	8.3	1.1	2.3	5.3	4.9	70.7	1 651.5	821.5	536.9	1 325	1 284
Dodge	717	3 409 832	6.5	6.4	0.0	3.9	12.4	1.9	67.9	88.6	44.2	22.9	1 131	1 119
Douglas	1 101	6 909 728	5.8	7.2	0.1	2.6	9.8	5.5	66.7	237.1	64.8	46.8	1 286	1 248
Faribault	667	3 058 474	6.0	6.7	0.1	5.1	34.0	6.2	39.8	90.8	34.3	16.1	1 130	1 101

1. Based on the resident population estimated as of July 1 of the year shown.

STATE County	Local government finances, 2012 (cont.) — Direct general expenditure — Total (mil dol)	Per capita[1] (dollars)	Percent of total for: Educa-tion	Health and hospitals	Police protec-tion	Public welfare	High-ways	Debt outstanding — Total (mil dol)	Per capita[1] (dollars)	Government employment, 2013 — Federal civilian	Federal military	State and local	Presidential election,[2] 2012 — Percent of vote cast: Demo-cratic	Republi-can	All other
	185	186	187	188	189	190	191	192	193	194	195	196	197	198	199
MICHIGAN—Cont'd															
Keweenaw	6.9	3 101	2.6	1.3	7.4	0.3	34.9	4.3	1 951	20	0	103	43.3	53.6	3.1
Lake	31.5	2 738	24.3	2.6	4.3	1.0	15.0	21.8	1 898	63	19	407	55.2	42.9	2.0
Lapeer	274.0	3 108	46.0	7.1	3.5	8.9	6.8	238.6	2 706	137	151	4 077	47.3	50.3	2.4
Leelanau	61.1	2 829	43.8	4.2	3.6	0.7	9.8	51.6	2 388	130	37	1 788	50.9	48.0	1.2
Lenawee	351.5	3 551	55.5	5.5	3.4	4.6	6.5	276.7	2 796	189	162	4 584	51.6	46.6	1.8
Livingston	530.7	2 902	57.0	7.6	3.3	0.5	5.0	1 200.5	6 566	255	320	5 958	42.5	55.8	1.7
Luce	51.6	7 912	15.9	60.1	0.9	0.2	7.0	15.2	2 335	14	0	771	43.5	54.4	2.2
Mackinac	45.6	4 094	32.8	5.3	3.6	0.1	14.6	33.1	2 975	58	66	971	47.3	51.1	1.6
Macomb	3 200.9	3 777	51.2	8.3	6.2	1.5	3.9	3 701.0	4 368	8 193	1 777	28 306	53.4	44.8	1.9
Manistee	95.8	3 885	34.2	1.9	3.0	12.4	11.2	104.6	4 240	89	58	2 795	55.6	42.4	2.0
Marquette	235.2	3 464	37.8	1.8	6.5	6.4	9.7	135.1	1 989	281	128	5 448	59.2	38.9	1.9
Mason	115.8	4 037	56.0	0.9	2.9	9.4	8.9	57.5	2 005	97	67	1 924	51.3	46.9	1.7
Mecosta	174.1	4 018	38.9	30.3	3.2	0.8	5.0	74.8	1 726	87	70	5 099	48.8	49.5	1.7
Menominee	61.6	2 585	51.9	0.5	6.7	0.2	12.8	22.8	958	62	41	1 975	54.0	43.8	2.1
Midland	272.5	3 250	51.0	2.8	4.1	2.1	7.6	318.6	3 800	136	143	3 323	47.4	50.9	1.7
Missaukee	54.0	3 591	36.3	33.2	2.2	0.6	9.3	4.1	276	27	26	503	38.7	59.7	1.7
Monroe	515.6	3 414	53.6	6.7	3.7	0.2	9.1	557.6	3 691	221	258	5 421	51.3	46.9	1.8
Montcalm	236.5	3 748	58.8	7.6	2.3	0.4	7.4	191.1	3 029	119	104	2 860	48.8	49.1	2.0
Montmorency	24.1	2 539	34.8	1.0	4.8	1.0	13.9	10.5	1 103	18	16	395	44.8	53.0	2.2
Muskegon	746.4	4 386	51.2	13.2	3.2	3.6	4.5	688.6	4 046	333	312	7 478	63.9	34.6	1.5
Newaygo	194.0	4 046	57.6	5.7	2.5	6.5	7.1	159.0	3 316	134	82	2 226	46.7	51.3	2.0
Oakland	4 863.5	3 984	50.4	6.9	6.5	0.2	4.9	4 726.4	3 872	4 737	2 255	44 653	56.5	42.0	1.4
Oceana	89.5	3 401	42.0	4.4	3.7	17.2	11.9	48.9	1 859	155	45	1 387	51.2	46.8	2.0
Ogemaw	91.5	4 268	23.9	47.2	2.2	0.7	7.5	60.2	2 807	51	36	1 067	50.1	47.7	2.3
Ontonagon	29.7	4 631	39.8	1.3	2.4	0.1	24.2	24.8	3 875	41	11	334	50.6	46.9	2.5
Osceola	69.8	2 999	56.1	2.5	3.0	0.3	11.7	41.1	1 765	54	39	910	44.0	54.2	1.8
Oscoda	22.1	2 573	44.7	4.2	4.0	8.4	11.5	3.6	419	54	14	375	43.6	53.6	2.8
Otsego	81.5	3 391	48.3	3.2	2.7	0.6	12.1	42.7	1 777	150	42	1 040	44.7	53.5	1.8
Ottawa	885.8	3 292	57.1	5.1	3.6	0.9	6.5	1 000.3	3 717	403	525	15 230	37.3	61.2	1.5
Presque Isle	40.5	3 081	35.5	1.1	3.7	0.7	13.8	21.2	1 618	51	22	579	49.6	48.0	2.4
Roscommon	94.2	3 908	58.3	2.5	4.2	1.6	7.4	44.3	1 836	28	41	1 220	50.4	47.9	1.7
Saginaw	801.9	4 043	42.8	14.5	5.8	0.7	5.8	494.0	2 490	1 453	339	9 583	57.9	40.6	1.5
St. Clair	651.8	4 058	44.3	15.8	3.9	0.1	6.4	526.8	3 280	628	346	6 000	50.3	47.6	2.1
St. Joseph	268.7	4 420	49.4	24.1	3.0	0.3	4.3	186.9	3 074	97	104	2 850	47.9	50.1	1.9
Sanilac	165.3	3 911	47.1	12.6	4.3	6.0	11.0	127.3	3 011	103	71	1 769	44.9	52.9	2.2
Schoolcraft	58.9	7 054	15.2	41.3	2.0	13.4	8.4	36.7	4 402	41	14	1 072	50.5	47.6	1.9
Shiawassee	236.8	3 421	55.9	8.0	3.1	6.2	8.8	102.4	1 479	126	118	3 120	53.3	44.7	2.1
Tuscola	211.4	3 867	51.0	9.0	3.1	9.1	9.0	137.5	2 515	124	93	2 759	48.6	49.4	2.0
Van Buren	365.1	4 839	52.4	18.4	2.7	0.9	6.5	300.6	3 984	135	129	5 241	53.5	44.7	1.9
Washtenaw	1 495.8	4 262	46.0	12.6	6.5	0.9	4.9	2 033.3	5 794	3 870	633	69 462	69.8	28.8	1.4
Wayne	9 500.3	5 300	36.3	3.3	7.0	5.2	2.9	21 084.6	11 764	14 181	3 495	76 006	74.1	24.7	1.2
Wexford	112.1	3 437	54.4	1.5	4.1	1.5	9.9	59.5	1 825	125	57	1 903	47.0	51.2	1.8
MINNESOTA	X	X	X	X	X	X	X	X	X	31 296	20 254	366 245	54.1	43.8	2.1
Aitkin	64.5	4 049	33.1	1.4	4.3	8.2	22.4	16.8	1 053	44	57	780	48.8	48.8	2.4
Anoka	1 279.3	3 803	53.7	0.9	5.4	5.1	9.5	1 587.7	4 720	377	1 243	14 526	47.7	50.1	2.1
Becker	136.5	4 137	44.4	1.1	4.2	11.3	12.3	95.6	2 898	245	121	2 715	45.3	52.2	2.5
Beltrami	237.7	5 239	45.5	1.1	3.5	7.4	8.2	329.6	7 264	401	162	4 735	54.1	43.9	2.0
Benton	105.9	2 726	49.8	1.2	5.5	8.3	10.1	177.0	4 555	77	142	1 561	43.7	53.5	2.8
Big Stone	57.1	11 056	19.8	43.6	2.3	4.0	9.5	316.3	61 258	36	18	596	51.9	45.6	2.5
Blue Earth	298.5	4 586	38.2	0.6	4.8	5.4	14.5	311.4	4 785	269	274	5 156	55.1	42.1	2.7
Brown	114.6	4 507	33.1	12.3	4.8	7.0	11.5	109.7	4 315	77	89	1 597	42.7	54.7	2.6
Carlton	170.7	4 830	39.9	19.7	3.8	7.4	8.0	194.2	5 495	69	123	5 153	62.3	35.5	2.2
Carver	420.3	4 485	43.0	0.6	4.3	4.9	9.0	930.8	9 933	214	348	4 423	41.6	56.7	1.8
Cass	150.7	5 316	45.3	1.8	4.4	6.4	12.0	129.6	4 571	234	104	3 799	44.6	53.1	2.3
Chippewa	70.8	5 832	38.1	1.0	3.7	12.0	12.1	81.7	6 730	62	44	1 151	51.6	45.7	2.7
Chisago	182.5	3 415	43.9	1.5	4.9	4.7	15.5	291.7	5 458	97	192	2 333	43.6	53.9	2.5
Clay	286.2	4 758	32.4	1.9	4.5	6.9	10.4	437.1	7 267	122	209	4 297	57.0	40.9	2.1
Clearwater	40.3	4 626	44.8	0.2	5.1	9.0	18.1	19.0	2 179	35	32	491	44.1	53.8	2.2
Cook	44.8	8 644	13.1	30.8	6.2	4.2	13.3	40.0	7 721	131	19	791	60.3	37.0	2.7
Cottonwood	74.7	6 441	31.9	19.0	3.8	5.3	14.2	80.5	6 940	55	42	829	45.7	52.3	2.0
Crow Wing	333.5	5 303	34.0	22.0	4.7	6.2	6.0	491.9	7 822	186	277	4 480	45.1	52.8	2.1
Dakota	1 670.9	4 125	51.3	0.8	5.2	4.3	6.8	2 383.8	5 885	2 198	1 504	17 676	51.8	46.3	1.9
Dodge	88.6	4 380	46.8	2.3	6.2	13.6	9.3	114.3	5 648	40	74	1 182	43.7	53.5	2.8
Douglas	244.5	6 713	25.3	35.9	2.8	3.2	7.4	374.7	10 290	141	133	3 206	44.2	53.7	2.0
Faribault	106.3	7 456	21.6	34.8	2.4	1.7	14.0	77.3	5 420	57	51	1 130	45.8	51.5	2.7

1. Based on the resident population estimated as of July 1 of the year shown. 2.

STATE/ County code	CBSA code[1]	County type[2]	STATE County	Land area,[3] (sq km) 2010	Population, 2014: Total persons 2014	Population, 2014: Rank	Population, 2014: Per square kilometer	Population and population characteristics, 2013: Race alone or in combination, not Hispanic or Latino (percent): White	Black	American Indian, Alaska Native	Asian and Pacific Islander	Percent Hispanic or Latino[4]	Age (percent): Under 5 years	5 to 17 years	18 to 24 years	25 to 34 years	35 to 44 years	45 to 54 years
				1	2	3	4	5	6	7	8	9	10	11	12	13	14	15
			MINNESOTA—Cont'd															
27 045	40340	8	Fillmore	2 231	20 776	1 787	9.3	98.1	0.5	0.4	0.6	1.1	6.3	17.4	7.0	10.6	10.9	13.5
27 047	10660	7	Freeborn	1 831	30 840	1 417	16.8	88.4	1.2	0.6	1.6	9.3	5.8	16.1	7.2	10.9	10.6	14.2
27 049	39860	4	Goodhue	1 960	46 423	1 039	23.7	93.9	1.7	1.6	1.1	3.1	6.1	17.2	7.2	11.0	11.2	15.0
27 051	...	9	Grant	1 420	5 956	2 762	4.2	97.3	0.8	0.8	0.4	1.8	5.6	15.7	6.4	10.4	10.5	13.2
27 053	33460	1	Hennepin	1 434	1 212 064	35	845.2	73.2	13.6	1.5	7.8	6.8	6.6	15.8	9.1	17.0	13.1	13.9
27 055	29100	3	Houston	1 430	18 738	1 880	13.1	97.9	1.2	0.5	0.9	0.8	4.9	16.7	7.1	10.4	10.7	15.4
27 057	...	7	Hubbard	2 397	20 573	1 797	8.6	95.1	0.9	3.3	0.7	1.8	5.7	15.1	6.5	9.0	9.8	14.5
27 059	33460	1	Isanti	1 129	38 413	1 211	34.0	96.2	1.2	1.2	1.4	1.7	6.3	18.5	7.8	12.5	12.2	15.8
27 061	...	6	Itasca	6 909	45 589	1 059	6.6	94.3	0.9	5.0	0.7	1.2	5.5	15.9	7.1	10.1	10.7	13.7
27 063	...	7	Jackson	1 821	10 269	2 413	5.6	94.1	1.0	0.6	1.9	3.5	5.6	16.9	7.6	10.5	11.1	14.0
27 065	...	6	Kanabec	1 351	15 930	2 046	11.8	96.6	0.9	1.5	0.8	1.7	5.0	17.2	7.4	10.4	11.7	14.7
27 067	48820	4	Kandiyohi	2 064	42 285	1 123	20.5	84.6	3.4	0.6	0.8	11.4	6.5	17.1	9.1	12.1	10.6	13.3
27 069	...	9	Kittson	2 846	4 435	2 870	1.6	96.7	0.5	0.5	0.5	2.3	5.1	16.7	6.6	7.8	10.1	14.4
27 071	...	7	Koochiching	8 040	12 856	2 243	1.6	95.1	1.0	3.6	0.7	1.3	4.6	15.4	7.3	9.0	10.3	14.7
27 073	...	9	Lac qui Parle	1 981	6 891	2 691	3.5	96.8	0.8	0.4	1.0	2.0	5.4	15.7	5.9	8.6	9.1	13.9
27 075	...	6	Lake	5 463	10 680	2 383	2.0	97.4	0.9	1.3	0.7	1.2	5.1	13.5	6.2	9.9	9.9	14.2
27 077	...	9	Lake of the Woods	3 361	3 918	2 910	1.2	96.4	1.0	1.8	1.3	1.6	4.8	13.8	6.1	8.3	9.4	16.4
27 079	33460	6	Le Sueur	1 162	27 770	1 504	23.9	92.8	0.8	0.7	1.0	5.6	6.2	18.8	6.9	11.6	12.1	15.0
27 081	...	9	Lincoln	1 390	5 788	2 778	4.2	97.4	0.5	0.3	0.7	1.8	6.0	16.4	5.9	9.6	10.6	12.1
27 083	32140	7	Lyon	1 851	25 665	1 576	13.9	88.3	3.0	0.8	3.1	6.2	7.2	17.3	10.9	14.0	11.3	12.7
27 085	26780	6	McLeod	1 273	35 882	1 277	28.2	93.1	1.0	0.5	1.1	5.2	6.1	18.2	7.6	11.8	12.2	14.6
27 087	...	8	Mahnomen	1 445	5 505	2 805	3.8	57.3	1.5	47.1	1.0	2.3	10.8	19.6	7.8	10.6	9.9	11.7
27 089	...	8	Marshall	4 597	9 417	2 478	2.0	94.6	0.7	0.9	0.5	4.1	5.7	17.1	7.0	10.9	10.7	14.2
27 091	...	7	Martin	1 845	20 220	1 827	11.0	94.8	0.8	0.5	0.9	3.8	5.3	16.2	7.1	10.6	9.9	13.8
27 093	...	6	Meeker	1 575	23 107	1 677	14.7	95.6	0.7	0.4	0.6	3.4	6.4	18.3	7.1	10.7	11.1	14.1
27 095	33460	6	Mille Lacs	1 482	25 884	1 564	17.5	91.5	1.0	6.6	0.8	1.8	6.3	18.1	7.4	11.4	11.7	14.6
27 097	...	6	Morrison	2 914	32 810	1 362	11.3	97.4	0.8	0.8	0.7	1.4	6.3	17.6	7.4	11.6	11.1	14.6
27 099	12380	4	Mower	1 842	39 323	1 187	21.3	83.5	3.8	0.5	2.6	11.0	7.1	17.8	8.1	12.0	11.6	13.2
27 101	...	9	Murray	1 825	8 470	2 560	4.6	95.2	0.5	0.4	1.3	3.2	5.5	16.2	6.4	9.3	9.8	13.3
27 103	31860	5	Nicollet	1 162	33 093	1 352	28.5	91.9	2.8	0.6	1.8	4.2	6.1	16.1	13.6	14.1	11.3	12.9
27 105	49380	7	Nobles	1 852	21 590	1 751	11.7	64.4	4.1	0.7	6.6	25.2	8.1	18.2	9.0	13.0	11.3	12.6
27 107	...	8	Norman	2 261	6 639	2 709	2.9	92.4	1.0	3.3	1.0	4.7	4.8	18.3	7.0	8.9	10.7	14.1
27 109	40340	3	Olmsted	1 692	150 287	427	88.8	83.9	6.2	0.6	6.8	4.5	7.2	17.7	7.8	15.0	12.5	13.9
27 111	22260	6	Otter Tail	5 108	57 635	886	11.3	94.7	1.4	1.1	0.9	3.0	5.7	15.6	7.1	10.0	9.5	14.3
27 113	...	6	Pennington	1 597	14 058	2 163	8.8	92.8	2.0	2.4	1.1	3.4	6.9	16.6	8.9	13.5	11.8	13.1
27 115	...	6	Pine	3 655	29 095	1 454	8.0	91.5	2.7	4.0	1.0	2.6	5.2	15.6	7.0	12.1	12.1	15.5
27 117	...	6	Pipestone	1 204	9 281	2 491	7.7	92.4	1.5	1.7	1.2	4.6	6.4	17.9	7.2	10.6	10.4	13.7
27 119	24220	3	Polk	5 105	31 704	1 393	6.2	90.9	1.6	2.4	1.1	5.8	6.3	17.1	10.0	12.1	10.5	13.6
27 121	...	8	Pope	1 735	10 984	2 360	6.3	97.9	0.7	0.6	0.6	1.0	5.6	15.3	6.4	10.6	10.4	13.1
27 123	33460	1	Ramsey	394	532 655	124	1 351.9	67.6	12.8	1.5	14.0	7.3	7.0	16.3	11.1	16.2	11.7	12.8
27 125	...	8	Red Lake	1 120	4 043	2 900	3.6	94.2	1.2	2.3	0.4	3.2	6.6	17.4	6.3	11.0	11.2	13.8
27 127	...	7	Redwood	2 275	15 515	2 072	6.8	89.1	1.0	5.5	3.4	2.7	6.4	18.2	7.2	10.3	10.1	13.8
27 129	...	9	Renville	2 546	15 025	2 101	5.9	90.7	1.0	1.3	0.8	7.5	5.8	16.5	7.1	10.5	10.3	14.6
27 131	22060	4	Rice	1 284	65 151	810	50.7	86.0	4.2	0.7	2.8	7.8	5.8	16.4	15.1	11.6	11.9	13.7
27 133	...	6	Rock	1 250	9 553	2 466	7.6	95.6	1.2	0.7	1.0	2.5	6.1	18.8	6.9	9.8	11.6	12.8
27 135	...	7	Roseau	4 329	15 679	2 063	3.6	94.6	0.8	2.0	3.0	1.0	6.1	18.7	7.5	9.9	12.1	16.4
27 137	20260	2	St. Louis	16 181	200 949	322	12.4	93.8	2.3	3.3	1.5	1.4	5.2	14.1	12.7	11.8	10.6	13.4
27 139	33460	1	Scott	923	139 672	452	151.3	85.2	3.8	1.3	6.9	4.6	7.4	21.6	7.1	13.1	15.8	15.9
27 141	33460	1	Sherburne	1 121	91 126	634	81.3	94.0	2.5	0.9	1.7	2.4	6.8	20.9	8.3	13.5	14.8	15.3
27 143	33460	8	Sibley	1 525	14 918	2 105	9.8	90.7	0.8	0.5	0.9	8.0	6.2	18.7	7.3	11.0	11.7	14.7
27 145	41060	3	Stearns	3 479	152 912	421	44.0	91.0	4.2	0.6	2.6	3.0	6.2	16.6	15.7	12.7	11.0	13.1
27 147	36940	5	Steele	1 113	36 573	1 261	32.9	89.0	3.2	0.5	1.2	7.3	6.9	18.6	7.6	12.0	12.0	14.5
27 149	...	7	Stevens	1 460	9 800	2 457	6.7	92.1	1.7	1.9	2.0	4.0	5.3	15.4	20.4	11.4	9.0	10.4
27 151	...	7	Swift	1 922	9 436	2 475	4.9	94.2	1.3	0.6	0.6	4.3	6.0	15.7	7.6	10.5	10.3	14.6
27 153	...	6	Todd	2 447	24 264	1 633	9.9	93.2	0.8	0.8	0.9	5.3	6.7	17.2	7.6	10.0	10.2	14.3
27 155	...	9	Traverse	1 486	3 387	2 946	2.3	93.4	1.2	5.1	0.5	1.6	5.7	15.8	6.9	8.7	9.2	13.8
27 157	40340	3	Wabasha	1 355	21 362	1 760	15.8	95.9	0.8	0.5	0.8	2.9	6.0	16.7	7.2	10.6	11.4	15.1
27 159	...	7	Wadena	1 389	13 757	2 188	9.9	96.4	1.6	1.4	0.8	1.5	6.4	18.0	7.7	10.0	10.0	13.1
27 161	...	7	Waseca	1 096	19 025	1 873	17.4	90.4	2.8	1.1	1.0	5.8	5.8	17.2	7.4	13.5	12.8	13.9
27 163	33460	1	Washington	995	249 283	266	250.5	86.4	4.9	0.9	6.1	3.7	6.2	19.2	7.8	12.0	13.2	16.1
27 165	...	7	Watonwan	1 127	11 083	2 352	9.8	75.6	1.0	0.4	1.2	22.3	6.5	18.1	7.8	11.0	10.8	12.9
27 167	47420	6	Wilkin	1 945	6 495	2 717	3.3	95.8	0.8	1.5	0.7	2.4	6.0	17.9	7.1	10.6	11.1	15.4
27 169	49100	4	Winona	1 622	51 097	972	31.5	93.1	1.8	0.6	2.7	2.7	4.5	13.8	21.8	11.1	9.6	12.0
27 171	33460	1	Wright	1 713	129 918	479	75.8	94.6	1.7	0.7	1.7	2.7	7.6	21.4	7.1	12.7	14.7	14.9
27 173	...	9	Yellow Medicine	1 966	10 109	2 431	5.1	91.8	0.7	3.8	0.8	4.1	6.0	17.1	7.6	11.2	10.3	13.7

1. CBSA = Core Based Statistical Area. See Appendix A for explanation. See Appendix B for list of metropolitan areas with component counties. 2. County type code from the Economic Research Service of USDA Rural-Urban Continuum Codes. See Appendix A for definition. 3. Dry land or land partially or temporarily covered by water. 4. May be of any race.

STATE County	Population, 2013 (cont.)				Population change and components of change, 2000–2014							Households, 2009–2013				
	Age (percent) (cont.)				Total persons		Percent change		Components of change, 2010–2014					Percent		
	55 to 64 years	65 to 74 years	75 years and over	Percent female	2000	2010	2000–2010	2010–2014	Births	Deaths	Net migration	Number	Persons per house-hold	Family house-holds	Female family house-holder[1]	One per-son
	16	17	18	19	20	21	22	23	24	25	26	27	28	29	30	31
MINNESOTA—Cont'd																
Fillmore	14.3	9.8	10.3	49.9	21 122	20 866	-1.2	-0.4	1 019	960	-155	8 422	2.43	68.2	7.3	27.1
Freeborn	14.0	10.6	10.6	50.4	32 584	31 255	-4.1	-1.3	1 504	1 513	-400	13 230	2.31	63.4	8.9	32.3
Goodhue	14.4	9.4	8.7	50.3	44 127	46 183	4.7	0.5	2 246	1 972	-108	18 711	2.42	67.4	8.0	27.8
Grant	14.9	11.6	11.6	50.2	6 289	6 018	-4.3	-1.0	266	302	-28	2 580	2.27	67.0	7.3	27.8
Hennepin	12.4	6.7	5.5	50.8	1 116 200	1 152 425	3.2	5.2	69 099	33 581	25 149	481 263	2.38	58.1	10.3	32.7
Houston	15.6	9.7	9.4	50.3	19 718	19 027	-3.5	-1.5	776	724	-363	7 809	2.38	69.5	7.6	25.8
Hubbard	16.4	13.3	9.7	49.9	18 376	20 428	11.2	0.7	888	792	38	8 670	2.34	68.5	6.2	26.4
Isanti	12.7	8.2	5.9	49.7	31 287	37 816	20.9	1.6	1 890	1 212	-113	13 860	2.71	71.8	10.5	23.0
Itasca	16.7	11.6	8.9	49.5	43 992	45 058	2.4	1.2	2 019	2 049	630	18 862	2.34	68.9	8.0	25.6
Jackson	14.4	9.2	10.7	49.4	11 268	10 266	-8.9	0.0	469	455	13	4 469	2.25	67.8	6.5	28.6
Kanabec	15.5	10.6	7.5	49.4	14 996	16 239	8.3	-1.9	601	617	-265	6 277	2.54	67.8	8.5	25.1
Kandiyohi	14.2	8.7	8.3	49.9	41 203	42 239	2.5	0.1	2 335	1 582	-684	17 120	2.41	67.7	9.7	26.5
Kittson	16.4	11.0	11.9	49.7	5 285	4 552	-13.9	-2.6	194	264	-39	1 912	2.30	63.1	7.5	34.0
Koochiching	17.8	11.1	9.7	50.1	14 355	13 311	-7.3	-3.4	428	618	-260	6 134	2.11	59.9	7.5	34.9
Lac qui Parle	16.9	11.0	13.5	50.1	8 067	7 259	-10.0	-5.1	287	396	-261	3 074	2.29	68.5	6.9	27.7
Lake	17.1	12.0	12.0	49.1	11 058	10 866	-1.7	-1.7	447	576	-55	4 982	2.11	66.3	7.7	28.8
Lake of the Woods	19.6	12.2	9.2	48.6	4 522	4 045	-10.5	-3.1	133	195	-50	1 665	2.37	65.5	5.5	30.6
Le Sueur	13.8	8.7	6.9	49.6	25 426	27 703	9.0	0.2	1 319	861	-361	10 997	2.50	70.8	7.1	24.3
Lincoln	14.3	11.0	14.1	50.0	6 429	5 896	-8.3	-1.8	260	337	-59	2 485	2.28	65.0	4.9	31.7
Lyon	12.2	7.1	7.2	50.3	25 425	25 857	1.7	-0.7	1 509	917	-783	10 083	2.43	62.4	7.5	31.5
McLeod	12.6	8.8	8.1	50.3	34 898	36 651	5.0	-2.1	1 797	1 360	-1 277	14 716	2.43	68.6	7.5	26.9
Mahnomen	12.8	9.1	7.8	49.7	5 190	5 413	4.3	1.7	428	253	-92	2 058	2.62	68.3	15.9	26.9
Marshall	14.5	10.0	9.9	49.2	10 155	9 439	-7.1	-0.2	448	344	-110	4 080	2.29	65.3	5.9	29.6
Martin	15.7	10.0	11.5	50.7	21 802	20 840	-4.4	-3.0	917	1 004	-525	8 797	2.30	64.9	8.0	31.4
Meeker	14.6	9.2	8.5	49.0	22 644	23 300	2.9	-0.8	1 162	852	-510	9 288	2.46	70.3	6.2	25.3
Mille Lacs	13.0	9.4	8.1	49.7	22 330	26 097	16.9	-0.8	1 447	1 152	-489	10 312	2.46	67.0	10.9	27.3
Morrison	14.3	9.0	8.1	49.6	31 712	33 198	4.7	-1.2	1 599	1 351	-619	13 416	2.42	67.3	7.9	27.8
Mower	12.7	8.1	9.4	50.2	38 603	39 163	1.5	0.4	2 150	1 522	-469	15 855	2.44	63.6	9.0	31.9
Murray	15.9	11.6	12.1	50.3	9 165	8 725	-4.8	-2.9	379	436	-221	3 820	2.22	65.3	5.6	29.3
Nicollet	12.5	7.3	6.1	49.8	29 771	32 727	9.9	1.1	1 586	892	-315	12 192	2.47	67.7	8.1	24.9
Nobles	12.1	7.6	8.2	48.2	20 832	21 378	2.6	1.0	1 481	732	-497	7 964	2.65	71.0	7.6	25.7
Norman	14.4	10.3	11.4	49.7	7 442	6 852	-7.9	-3.1	294	399	-105	2 737	2.42	63.4	7.3	32.8
Olmsted	12.2	7.3	6.4	51.1	124 277	144 248	16.1	4.2	9 051	3 991	881	57 262	2.50	66.1	8.7	28.0
Otter Tail	15.9	11.6	10.4	49.7	57 159	57 303	0.3	0.6	2 624	2 879	666	24 356	2.30	67.9	6.8	27.8
Pennington	13.1	8.5	7.7	50.1	13 584	13 930	2.5	0.9	772	572	-59	5 806	2.35	60.8	8.9	34.3
Pine	14.5	10.2	7.9	46.6	26 530	29 750	12.1	-2.2	1 198	1 089	-752	11 758	2.35	65.9	8.1	27.6
Pipestone	13.4	8.8	11.6	51.2	9 895	9 596	-3.0	-3.3	484	454	-338	3 924	2.36	66.7	9.3	29.9
Polk	13.5	8.5	8.4	49.9	31 369	31 600	0.7	0.3	1 774	1 457	-188	12 663	2.38	65.9	10.0	29.1
Pope	16.0	11.5	11.1	49.3	11 236	10 995	-2.1	-0.1	549	536	-21	4 758	2.26	66.8	5.3	28.8
Ramsey	12.2	6.8	5.9	51.4	511 035	508 640	-0.5	4.7	32 538	16 477	8 588	205 395	2.43	58.3	12.3	33.4
Red Lake	15.4	9.4	8.8	49.3	4 299	4 089	-4.9	-1.1	257	160	-153	1 681	2.39	66.5	5.6	30.0
Redwood	13.6	9.9	10.5	50.3	16 815	16 059	-4.5	-3.4	779	760	-573	6 507	2.38	64.3	7.6	32.5
Renville	15.1	9.7	10.5	48.8	17 154	15 730	-8.3	-4.5	787	823	-672	6 400	2.37	66.9	8.1	29.6
Rice	11.9	7.4	6.2	48.9	56 665	64 142	13.2	1.6	3 153	1 899	-324	22 299	2.51	69.9	11.4	25.2
Rock	13.8	9.5	10.6	50.8	9 721	9 687	-0.3	-1.4	479	514	-130	3 970	2.36	68.6	9.4	29.5
Roseau	14.0	8.4	6.9	48.9	16 338	15 629	-4.3	0.3	775	550	-183	6 402	2.40	69.5	8.0	26.3
St. Louis	15.3	9.0	7.9	49.8	200 528	200 226	-0.2	0.4	8 818	8 790	948	85 238	2.24	58.8	9.5	32.8
Scott	10.1	5.4	3.5	50.2	89 498	129 928	45.2	7.5	8 303	2 361	3 784	45 630	2.89	76.3	8.2	18.2
Sherburne	10.6	5.8	3.9	48.9	64 417	88 499	37.4	3.0	4 999	1 953	-515	29 948	2.91	76.3	9.0	17.6
Sibley	13.3	8.4	8.6	50.0	15 356	15 226	-0.8	-2.0	770	578	-479	6 090	2.43	66.0	7.3	28.8
Stearns	11.6	6.9	6.2	49.5	133 166	150 642	13.1	1.5	7 950	3 942	-1 621	56 737	2.51	65.6	8.1	24.3
Steele	12.8	7.9	7.7	50.6	33 680	36 576	8.6	0.0	1 966	1 241	-758	14 354	2.50	68.5	8.4	26.9
Stevens	11.7	7.1	9.3	50.4	10 053	9 726	-3.3	0.8	473	362	-33	3 700	2.45	60.2	4.0	31.9
Swift	14.3	9.8	11.1	49.5	11 956	9 783	-18.2	-3.5	448	439	-345	4 315	2.19	63.0	5.9	33.6
Todd	15.1	10.5	8.3	48.7	24 426	24 895	1.9	-2.5	1 374	804	-1 239	9 904	2.45	69.0	7.4	26.9
Traverse	14.3	10.6	15.1	50.4	4 134	3 558	-13.9	-4.8	123	205	-83	1 510	2.26	62.6	5.2	34.1
Wabasha	14.7	10.0	8.3	50.2	21 610	21 676	0.3	-1.4	1 011	713	-604	8 890	2.39	69.2	8.4	26.8
Wadena	13.3	10.5	11.0	50.7	13 713	13 843	0.9	-0.6	742	776	-62	5 830	2.30	64.4	9.4	31.9
Waseca	13.5	8.0	7.8	52.8	19 526	19 136	-2.0	-0.6	933	628	-409	7 328	2.44	68.6	8.5	26.8
Washington	13.1	7.3	5.0	50.5	201 130	238 136	18.4	4.7	11 918	5 858	4 983	88 947	2.68	73.4	9.7	21.3
Watonwan	13.8	8.9	10.2	50.3	11 876	11 211	-5.6	-1.1	672	497	-286	4 445	2.48	68.1	9.1	28.6
Wilkin	13.8	8.6	9.5	49.3	7 138	6 576	-7.9	-1.2	293	334	-43	2 685	2.39	65.4	6.8	31.5
Winona	12.6	7.7	6.9	50.7	49 985	51 461	3.0	-0.7	1 934	1 689	-619	18 957	2.48	60.1	7.1	31.3
Wright	10.6	6.5	4.4	49.7	89 986	124 700	38.6	4.2	7 755	2 969	384	44 983	2.78	75.9	8.9	19.9
Yellow Medicine	14.3	9.4	10.4	49.1	11 080	10 438	-5.8	-3.2	554	501	-382	4 135	2.42	69.1	7.3	26.5

1. No spouse present.

STATE County	Persons in group quarters, 2014	Daytime population, 2009–2013: Number	Daytime population, 2009–2013: Employment/ residence ratio	Births, 2014: Total	Births, 2014: Rate[1]	Deaths, 2014: Number	Deaths, 2014: Rate[1]	Persons under 65 with no health insurance, 2013: Number	Persons under 65 with no health insurance, 2013: Percent	Medicare, 2014: Eligible for Medicare	Medicare, 2014: Enrolled in Medicare Advantage	Medicare, 2014: Enrolled in a Medicare prescription drug plan	Serious crimes known to police,[2] 2013: Total: Number	Serious crimes known to police,[2] 2013: Total: Rate[3]
	32	33	34	35	36	37	38	39	40	41	42	43	44	45
MINNESOTA—Cont'd														
Fillmore	359	17 641	0.68	228	11.0	231	11.1	1 884	11.4	4 547	2 178	2 350	131	627
Freeborn	637	29 490	0.89	354	11.5	351	11.4	2 620	10.9	7 435	3 921	3 729	585	1 881
Goodhue	899	46 687	1.02	511	11.0	453	9.8	3 313	8.8	9 335	5 170	3 923	1 008	2 166
Grant	110	5 407	0.80	63	10.6	59	9.9	455	9.9	1 620	799	944	71	1 194
Hennepin	25 903	1 390 398	1.36	16 631	13.7	8 082	6.7	106 414	10.2	173 456	93 238	64 895	43 836	3 657
Houston	257	15 026	0.60	191	10.2	184	9.8	1 307	8.7	4 099	1 813	1 988	107	568
Hubbard	154	18 221	0.75	203	9.9	178	8.7	1 939	12.3	5 351	2 757	2 678	472	2 315
Isanti	465	30 902	0.61	413	10.8	275	7.2	2 874	8.8	6 478	3 727	2 436	711	1 847
Itasca	1 022	44 144	0.94	478	10.5	456	10.0	4 041	11.3	11 168	4 878	5 280	996	2 192
Jackson	110	10 385	1.02	115	11.2	109	10.6	690	8.5	2 250	635	1 486	97	939
Kanabec	246	13 520	0.63	136	8.5	145	9.1	1 375	10.6	3 599	1 765	1 373	314	1 965
Kandiyohi	1 075	43 217	1.04	541	12.8	334	7.9	3 579	10.3	8 652	4 796	4 916	867	2 037
Kittson	111	4 333	0.91	47	10.6	65	14.7	304	8.8	1 072	475	595	27	601
Koochiching	241	13 284	1.01	88	6.8	134	10.4	1 240	12.0	3 346	1 635	1 938	314	2 375
Lac qui Parle	154	6 713	0.86	64	9.3	95	13.8	477	9.1	1 781	955	1 054	54	761
Lake	224	10 765	0.99	98	9.2	128	12.0	727	8.9	2 830	1 110	1 423	104	960
Lake of the Woods	53	3 709	0.85	27	6.9	41	10.5	371	12.1	1 008	463	476	18	454
Le Sueur	270	22 533	0.63	293	10.6	218	7.9	2 084	8.9	4 736	2 585	2 430	321	1 156
Lincoln	135	5 164	0.77	60	10.4	77	13.3	453	10.4	1 431	522	894	28	481
Lyon	1 055	27 575	1.14	345	13.4	226	8.8	2 039	9.6	4 461	1 667	2 948	447	1 751
McLeod	476	35 278	0.94	418	11.6	320	8.9	2 345	7.9	6 991	4 250	3 717	710	1 973
Mahnomen	79	6 104	1.28	92	16.7	69	12.5	658	14.2	888	355	441	96	1 716
Marshall	76	8 011	0.69	113	12.0	88	9.3	791	10.5	2 036	900	1 138	0	0
Martin	348	20 469	0.98	216	10.7	217	10.7	1 483	9.3	5 121	2 436	2 875	343	1 679
Meeker	353	20 357	0.74	271	11.7	185	8.0	1 826	9.7	4 623	2 950	2 280	323	1 401
Mille Lacs	523	25 222	0.94	355	13.7	250	9.7	2 394	11.4	5 714	3 202	2 156	900	3 500
Morrison	527	30 492	0.84	360	11.0	340	10.4	2 884	10.7	6 825	4 064	3 308	448	1 353
Mower	632	38 301	0.95	484	12.3	353	9.0	4 064	12.7	8 153	2 877	3 633	985	2 490
Murray	163	7 929	0.83	90	10.6	94	11.1	619	9.6	2 098	681	1 391	59	689
Nicollet	2 815	31 517	0.93	353	10.7	234	7.1	1 909	7.2	5 182	2 667	3 027	632	1 909
Nobles	385	22 231	1.07	335	15.5	175	8.1	2 873	15.9	3 777	1 124	2 496	227	1 051
Norman	149	6 142	0.80	80	12.1	90	13.6	540	10.5	1 588	681	820	2	30
Olmsted	2 760	161 314	1.20	2 112	14.1	962	6.4	10 118	7.9	23 596	8 888	9 829	3 128	2 108
Otter Tail	1 189	55 166	0.92	648	11.2	681	11.8	4 295	9.7	14 249	8 162	7 266	995	1 731
Pennington	327	16 387	1.33	179	12.7	126	9.0	918	7.9	2 693	1 387	1 401	222	1 567
Pine	1 734	27 094	0.81	261	9.0	250	8.6	2 717	12.3	5 992	3 375	2 253	1 389	4 765
Pipestone	205	9 502	1.01	117	12.6	115	12.4	833	11.4	1 964	627	1 247	89	957
Polk	1 389	29 275	0.85	430	13.6	338	10.7	2 527	10.0	6 247	2 835	3 431	601	1 911
Pope	184	10 015	0.82	130	11.8	116	10.6	780	9.3	2 592	1 401	1 509	135	1 238
Ramsey	17 981	577 115	1.24	7 866	14.8	3 928	7.4	52 789	11.8	80 877	43 600	30 117	20 536	3 908
Red Lake	34	3 403	0.67	63	15.6	27	6.7	378	11.5	830	531	486	19	463
Redwood	373	15 700	0.97	181	11.7	175	11.3	1 363	11.0	3 414	1 569	2 020	177	1 117
Renville	342	14 803	0.91	178	11.8	181	12.0	1 218	10.2	3 327	1 429	2 040	191	1 247
Rice	7 287	60 747	0.88	732	11.2	452	6.9	4 931	10.1	10 273	5 709	5 065	1 377	2 109
Rock	260	8 786	0.83	113	11.8	106	11.1	718	9.6	2 176	826	1 417	154	1 613
Roseau	191	16 257	1.08	182	11.6	120	7.7	1 208	9.3	2 840	1 684	1 234	222	1 433
St. Louis	9 231	207 860	1.08	2 085	10.4	2 032	10.1	15 263	9.5	42 328	20 231	20 006	7 070	3 517
Scott	1 295	107 804	0.64	1 990	14.2	571	4.1	9 520	7.7	14 652	8 373	5 947	2 433	1 773
Sherburne	2 178	68 185	0.53	1 162	12.8	488	5.4	5 600	7.1	11 262	6 314	4 420	1 345	1 495
Sibley	230	12 849	0.70	175	11.7	122	8.2	1 380	11.1	2 923	1 595	1 482	0	0
Stearns	7 835	159 443	1.11	1 815	11.9	902	5.9	11 407	9.1	24 038	12 639	11 636	4 186	2 747
Steele	594	38 716	1.12	450	12.3	299	8.2	2 248	7.4	6 614	3 751	3 317	834	2 293
Stevens	1 014	10 570	1.17	113	11.5	79	8.1	678	9.4	1 655	670	996	140	1 446
Swift	150	9 606	0.99	99	10.5	92	9.7	657	8.8	2 146	933	1 246	163	1 703
Todd	346	21 935	0.75	322	13.3	190	7.8	2 771	14.2	5 349	3 303	2 730	345	1 410
Traverse	100	3 402	0.94	26	7.7	25	7.4	304	12.0	931	390	540	0	0
Wabasha	246	17 891	0.67	236	11.0	170	8.0	1 481	8.5	4 391	2 347	1 803	230	1 070
Wadena	482	14 451	1.12	182	13.2	171	12.4	1 184	11.1	3 520	2 002	1 813	121	878
Waseca	1 317	17 713	0.86	218	11.5	132	6.9	1 318	8.9	3 749	2 017	2 124	314	1 624
Washington	3 588	203 016	0.69	2 813	11.3	1 456	5.8	13 533	6.3	35 887	21 328	12 874	5 436	2 204
Watonwan	150	10 042	0.80	164	14.8	106	9.6	1 365	15.3	2 186	936	1 214	135	1 204
Wilkin	152	6 033	0.83	68	10.5	85	13.1	448	8.4	1 388	641	740	84	1 271
Winona	4 445	51 439	1.00	472	9.2	427	8.4	3 920	9.8	8 573	3 576	4 224	591	1 139
Wright	1 105	101 970	0.63	1 771	13.6	720	5.5	8 379	7.4	16 747	10 011	6 939	2 058	1 602
Yellow Medicine	290	9 759	0.89	139	13.8	105	10.4	803	10.0	2 358	913	1 356	85	841

1. Per 1,000 estimated resident population. 2. Data for serious crimes have not been adjusted for underreporting; this may affect comparability between geographic areas and over time.
3. Per 100,000 population estimated by the FBI.

STATE County	Serious crimes known to police, 2013 (cont.)[1] Rate[2] Violent	Rate[2] Property	Education: School enrollment and attainment, 2009–2013: Enrollment[3] Total	Enrollment[3] Percent private	Attainment[4] (percent) High school graduate or less	Attainment[4] (percent) Bachelor's degree or more	Local government expenditures,[5] 2012–2013: Total current spending (mil dol)	Current spending per student (dollars)	Money income, 2009–2013: Per capita income[6] (dollars)	Households: Median income (dollars)	Households: Mean income (dollars)	Households: Percent with income of $200,000 or more	Income and poverty, 2013: Median household income (dollars)	Percent below poverty level: All persons	Children under 18 years	Children 5 to 17 years in families
	46	47	48	49	50	51	52	53	54	55	56	57	58	59	60	61
MINNESOTA—Cont'd																
Fillmore	67	560	4 697	10.8	47.9	18.4	26.0	10 593	25 249	50 657	61 786	1.7	51 323	10.7	16.1	14.4
Freeborn	141	1 739	6 768	8.4	49.1	14.8	47.4	11 538	25 668	44 683	58 814	2.3	47 698	10.5	16.9	15.2
Goodhue	110	2 056	10 988	13.2	41.1	22.9	73.2	10 645	29 932	56 836	72 339	2.8	61 428	9.3	11.6	10.7
Grant	84	1 110	1 137	7.5	43.9	18.3	11.8	11 039	26 665	50 030	61 342	2.0	49 618	10.7	16.4	15.5
Hennepin	427	3 229	308 507	18.8	26.1	45.8	1 897.8	13 139	37 485	64 403	89 707	7.7	64 331	12.2	15.3	15.0
Houston	106	462	4 393	16.9	43.5	22.7	46.0	9 399	26 450	52 545	63 352	1.8	51 160	10.4	11.9	10.9
Hubbard	137	2 177	3 976	8.2	41.1	23.6	24.3	10 311	24 880	45 961	56 999	1.7	46 530	13.4	21.0	19.8
Isanti	94	1 753	9 750	10.9	47.8	16.5	61.2	10 234	25 482	57 353	68 113	1.7	58 436	8.4	10.8	10.4
Itasca	165	2 027	9 877	8.7	40.5	21.4	71.8	11 064	24 079	46 912	57 546	1.4	46 834	13.1	20.5	17.8
Jackson	87	852	2 291	10.5	43.7	17.7	15.8	10 023	27 361	51 681	63 657	2.4	56 397	9.6	14.0	13.1
Kanabec	200	1 764	3 813	8.8	53.9	13.1	21.2	8 995	22 291	47 068	55 530	0.7	46 940	14.2	21.6	20.0
Kandiyohi	139	1 898	10 201	8.9	41.4	20.7	60.4	10 749	26 880	50 149	65 586	3.0	53 290	11.9	18.1	17.6
Kittson	22	579	903	7.1	45.3	20.7	9.6	13 726	26 927	48 875	60 389	1.4	48 458	10.1	13.2	11.7
Koochiching	136	2 239	2 627	17.9	48.8	17.2	21.8	11 609	26 045	41 108	56 480	1.8	44 817	16.9	22.9	20.6
Lac qui Parle	70	691	1 457	5.1	47.5	17.6	14.9	11 276	28 014	48 468	64 078	3.5	46 805	10.5	14.3	13.4
Lake	83	877	1 940	6.5	42.3	21.5	15.2	10 826	27 883	46 939	60 614	1.7	50 875	11.1	16.6	15.0
Lake of the Woods	50	403	724	2.3	50.2	13.8	6.0	12 490	21 903	44 069	51 410	0.4	42 644	12.4	19.9	18.9
Le Sueur	94	1 062	6 735	15.4	45.7	22.3	42.2	9 865	27 793	58 922	69 606	2.4	60 190	8.9	11.2	10.2
Lincoln	172	309	1 271	6.3	50.2	18.9	12.6	13 085	26 767	47 861	61 738	2.1	48 205	11.4	13.6	13.0
Lyon	102	1 649	7 233	11.6	42.8	26.9	72.8	17 263	26 028	49 594	64 484	2.5	51 011	12.8	15.2	13.9
McLeod	142	1 831	8 753	14.8	45.7	17.7	50.5	10 072	26 824	55 170	65 730	1.6	54 971	8.8	11.8	10.8
Mahnomen	340	1 377	1 365	9.0	51.5	13.3	16.2	13 032	19 517	40 282	51 264	1.3	39 706	24.3	38.3	37.9
Marshall	0	0	2 018	6.3	50.4	17.5	18.9	14 146	26 834	52 198	62 246	1.9	53 692	9.2	13.6	12.4
Martin	34	1 645	4 571	14.7	49.0	18.5	35.4	11 734	26 472	48 530	61 416	2.8	51 118	11.6	17.8	16.2
Meeker	87	1 314	5 370	9.5	48.1	17.7	26.1	10 355	25 665	53 904	63 446	1.9	55 327	9.4	12.2	11.3
Mille Lacs	218	3 283	6 413	13.4	48.6	15.0	62.2	9 818	22 891	47 862	56 949	1.1	48 978	12.1	17.9	16.1
Morrison	51	1 302	7 450	11.8	50.9	16.0	53.5	10 137	23 753	47 649	57 880	1.7	48 716	12.2	16.4	15.0
Mower	215	2 275	9 647	9.4	46.4	16.6	67.5	11 179	24 990	46 004	60 236	2.1	50 479	13.7	18.7	18.0
Murray	35	654	1 772	13.1	49.7	16.5	12.3	11 745	27 450	52 160	62 197	2.2	53 300	9.6	13.1	11.9
Nicollet	157	1 752	10 128	36.7	33.5	32.1	34.8	15 210	26 674	60 115	69 328	2.0	58 620	11.4	11.7	10.8
Nobles	153	898	4 996	7.0	54.6	14.5	41.4	11 013	22 598	48 208	59 590	2.7	50 936	14.2	19.4	18.5
Norman	0	30	1 547	5.6	51.8	14.3	12.8	11 710	23 707	45 389	55 851	1.3	45 276	13.6	19.8	17.6
Olmsted	160	1 947	38 122	17.7	27.8	40.1	230.7	10 322	34 073	66 252	85 226	5.8	65 829	8.3	10.3	9.7
Otter Tail	122	1 609	11 886	12.7	42.1	22.4	127.2	16 919	26 400	48 961	61 652	2.3	48 157	11.8	16.5	15.6
Pennington	99	1 469	3 441	12.1	44.6	16.1	78.6	36 352	24 554	45 633	57 255	1.2	47 300	10.7	14.6	14.5
Pine	281	4 484	6 317	12.9	54.9	13.5	40.0	10 264	21 413	43 928	53 113	0.8	43 026	15.7	23.2	20.9
Pipestone	22	936	2 220	15.2	49.7	16.8	16.8	11 232	24 137	46 019	56 824	2.1	47 613	12.4	17.2	15.8
Polk	137	1 774	8 081	8.9	41.0	21.9	53.9	10 684	25 790	50 695	62 932	2.2	52 706	13.3	17.4	16.0
Pope	92	1 146	2 071	10.4	42.4	20.5	14.1	12 755	29 128	52 350	66 653	2.5	55 404	11.0	13.5	13.0
Ramsey	476	3 432	144 805	26.3	33.2	39.4	1 077.3	14 314	29 484	54 247	72 559	4.2	56 293	16.2	22.5	21.5
Red Lake	49	414	857	6.7	51.0	16.0	9.9	13 116	23 257	47 569	54 287	0.7	45 019	11.2	14.2	13.4
Redwood	152	966	3 706	15.2	49.8	16.4	26.8	10 667	25 649	47 447	61 493	2.2	50 453	10.2	13.7	12.2
Renville	26	1 221	3 417	13.6	51.0	14.6	19.0	10 437	26 062	50 802	61 945	2.1	53 823	11.8	17.8	15.5
Rice	179	1 930	20 605	38.7	41.8	27.7	85.3	10 751	25 370	59 915	71 074	2.8	58 644	11.6	13.9	12.9
Rock	764	848	2 460	10.1	49.5	17.9	15.2	9 720	24 101	46 623	57 815	1.8	54 045	10.5	13.5	11.9
Roseau	13	1 420	3 773	5.8	48.7	17.9	31.4	10 671	25 650	50 759	62 349	2.4	51 576	8.7	11.9	10.7
St. Louis	245	3 272	51 474	13.2	37.1	26.1	267.2	11 601	25 946	46 517	59 760	2.1	46 022	16.5	19.0	18.4
Scott	95	1 679	38 780	18.7	29.3	38.0	215.3	9 586	35 467	86 112	101 817	8.0	85 481	5.9	6.7	6.1
Sherburne	94	1 400	25 367	12.2	33.9	25.1	183.2	9 667	28 071	73 098	81 329	2.6	74 915	6.5	7.7	7.0
Sibley	0	0	3 648	13.9	53.6	14.5	20.8	10 129	25 789	54 017	63 592	1.9	56 007	9.8	13.7	11.5
Stearns	172	2 575	47 037	20.2	39.6	24.6	253.9	10 612	26 065	54 551	67 580	2.6	56 705	12.7	12.6	11.8
Steele	121	2 172	9 385	15.6	42.6	24.9	63.7	9 776	27 259	56 480	68 394	2.5	53 932	10.7	14.4	13.4
Stevens	124	1 322	3 224	5.6	38.6	27.5	16.4	11 193	28 746	54 206	72 819	2.4	56 140	14.0	11.4	9.9
Swift	115	1 588	2 141	3.3	50.4	17.0	15.5	10 421	25 750	48 026	59 006	1.6	52 083	10.3	14.2	13.4
Todd	102	1 308	5 520	18.0	51.7	12.6	50.3	15 549	22 383	45 000	55 543	1.8	43 974	13.5	20.8	20.3
Traverse	0	0	707	4.8	49.5	15.1	6.1	12 351	28 030	45 714	63 145	2.8	50 451	11.9	18.3	17.1
Wabasha	98	973	4 996	11.3	47.1	20.0	41.8	9 453	28 282	53 057	67 659	2.5	52 617	9.4	11.7	11.4
Wadena	102	776	3 204	6.4	48.5	13.6	30.9	10 689	20 329	36 928	47 558	1.1	39 805	15.5	20.3	18.9
Waseca	41	1 582	4 317	11.3	46.2	18.8	34.0	9 946	25 723	53 657	64 921	2.1	53 448	10.3	14.0	13.2
Washington	77	2 128	68 039	19.7	27.0	40.5	385.6	10 468	36 706	81 540	98 422	8.1	81 052	5.8	6.9	5.9
Watonwan	160	1 043	2 558	10.2	55.0	15.9	20.9	11 363	25 635	49 698	62 384	2.3	48 064	11.2	17.3	15.9
Wilkin	91	1 180	1 564	9.5	42.1	16.5	11.4	10 506	25 148	50 507	59 656	1.2	52 849	11.0	13.7	12.8
Winona	98	1 041	16 633	19.0	41.3	26.8	64.8	13 203	23 421	47 400	50 820	1.9	49 636	14.4	14.0	12.6
Wright	67	1 535	34 863	12.8	37.1	26.5	256.1	9 967	29 623	71 598	82 160	3.5	71 999	7.1	8.2	7.2
Yellow Medicine	40	802	2 427	6.9	48.9	17.4	16.8	12 620	25 303	52 510	61 317	2.0	50 311	10.8	14.1	13.2

1. Data for serious crimes have not been adjusted for underreporting; this may affect comparability between geographic areas and over time. 2. Per 100,000 population estimated by the FBI.
3. All persons 3 years old and over enrolled in nursery school through college. 4. Persons 25 years old and over. 5. Elementary and secondary education expenditures.
6. Based on population estimated by the American Community Survey, 2009–2013.

STATE County	Personal income, 2013: Total (mil dol)	Personal income, 2013: Percent change, 2012–2013	Per capita[1]: Dollars	Per capita[1]: Rank	Wages and salaries (mil dol)	Supplements to wages and salaries; employer contributions (mil dol): Pension and insurance	Supplements to wages and salaries; employer contributions (mil dol): Government social insurance	Proprietors' income (mil dol)	Dividends, interest, and rent (mil dol)	Personal transfer receipts (mil dol)	Earnings, 2013: Total (mil dol)	Contributions for government social insurance (mil dol): From employee and self-employed	Contributions for government social insurance (mil dol): From employer
	62	63	64	65	66	67	68	69	70	71	72	73	74
MINNESOTA—Cont'd													
Fillmore	794	-5.1	38 104	1 421	194	37	16	115	159	170	363	23	16
Freeborn	1 225	-3.8	39 576	1 219	459	74	38	122	243	286	694	44	38
Goodhue	2 053	-0.5	44 182	743	936	159	76	215	402	352	1 386	82	76
Grant	282	-12.0	47 004	555	69	12	6	64	66	63	151	8	6
Hennepin	72 648	1.9	60 601	98	56 961	6 988	4 264	7 874	14 056	8 761	76 088	4 448	4 264
Houston	830	0.0	44 137	746	160	33	14	59	167	151	266	18	14
Hubbard	721	3.0	34 913	1 912	191	35	16	55	168	203	297	21	16
Isanti	1 479	1.0	38 723	1 332	415	73	35	143	196	287	666	43	35
Itasca	1 618	2.5	35 512	1 821	624	112	53	79	332	475	868	60	53
Jackson	553	-8.6	53 935	238	210	38	18	133	108	85	399	18	18
Kanabec	548	2.4	34 263	2 040	129	25	11	52	87	154	218	15	11
Kandiyohi	1 889	-1.1	44 542	726	818	140	68	278	393	359	1 304	77	68
Kittson	221	-1.5	49 096	411	57	11	4	52	49	43	125	6	4
Koochiching	481	1.3	36 386	1 678	207	38	17	18	80	143	281	19	17
Lac qui Parle	395	-4.6	56 217	184	80	16	6	132	81	75	235	10	6
Lake	484	1.7	44 873	699	188	31	16	34	88	115	269	18	16
Lake of the Woods	142	5.4	36 224	1 706	47	10	4	13	35	40	74	5	4
Le Sueur	1 137	-0.4	40 874	1 070	310	56	27	135	218	198	528	32	27
Lincoln	273	-3.8	46 796	565	61	11	5	64	59	55	141	7	5
Lyon	1 166	0.3	45 745	639	606	103	47	183	227	201	939	51	47
McLeod	1 445	-0.8	40 242	1 145	688	110	58	118	304	282	974	60	58
Mahnomen	189	2.6	34 121	2 058	63	14	5	29	32	61	111	6	5
Marshall	460	-1.7	48 758	434	100	18	8	99	87	85	225	11	8
Martin	967	-5.5	47 352	520	330	53	25	172	222	202	580	31	25
Meeker	875	-3.0	37 857	1 452	242	43	21	120	163	186	425	27	21
Mille Lacs	805	1.2	31 145	2 526	315	59	26	34	134	246	433	30	26
Morrison	1 148	-3.1	34 911	1 914	368	71	31	129	216	279	600	37	31
Mower	1 617	-3.5	41 129	1 036	704	112	52	138	300	351	1 005	61	52
Murray	458	-3.2	53 677	247	102	20	8	143	85	78	274	11	8
Nicollet	1 384	-1.5	41 913	947	532	99	44	85	270	220	760	43	44
Nobles	905	-4.2	41 849	953	385	65	30	189	175	157	668	34	30
Norman	330	-4.2	49 740	377	63	12	5	94	69	67	174	7	5
Olmsted	7 098	1.5	47 566	506	5 101	657	382	323	1 287	970	6 463	382	382
Otter Tail	2 328	1.0	40 431	1 119	802	149	67	236	528	548	1 253	80	67
Pennington	719	-0.3	50 918	334	438	67	35	50	162	125	589	34	35
Pine	912	1.8	31 341	2 501	247	54	21	43	158	268	365	26	21
Pipestone	444	-2.0	47 860	493	134	26	11	120	89	78	291	14	11
Polk	1 372	-0.8	43 476	804	449	79	38	161	248	289	727	40	38
Pope	530	-4.6	48 522	450	168	27	14	91	111	100	299	17	14
Ramsey	24 507	2.0	46 529	583	19 146	2 654	1 439	1 721	4 718	4 351	24 959	1 471	1 439
Red Lake	157	-3.7	38 598	1 356	36	8	3	24	26	33	71	4	3
Redwood	745	-5.9	47 322	528	216	43	17	196	163	143	472	22	17
Renville	785	-3.3	51 754	305	216	36	18	210	167	137	480	19	18
Rice	2 246	0.1	34 524	1 981	962	150	80	128	440	417	1 319	82	80
Rock	457	-3.1	48 036	478	126	23	9	107	94	80	265	12	9
Roseau	692	3.4	44 595	721	386	71	33	75	110	112	565	31	33
St. Louis	8 325	3.2	41 513	992	4 145	668	343	599	1 488	1 939	5 754	364	343
Scott	6 474	1.8	47 174	541	1 983	278	164	276	918	652	2 701	163	164
Sherburne	3 278	3.1	36 358	1 681	1 049	181	89	152	441	502	1 470	90	89
Sibley	647	-4.9	42 932	850	137	26	11	95	133	119	269	13	11
Stearns	5 848	0.7	38 449	1 381	3 475	557	291	378	1 145	1 080	4 701	276	291
Steele	1 527	-1.2	41 888	950	908	134	76	80	275	267	1 198	72	76
Stevens	527	-8.1	54 139	229	207	37	16	108	151	73	369	17	16
Swift	414	-13.1	43 350	815	133	26	10	77	82	94	247	14	10
Todd	836	-0.9	34 285	2 037	218	41	17	119	138	227	394	27	17
Traverse	169	-26.5	48 976	418	40	8	3	37	50	39	87	4	3
Wabasha	892	-2.2	41 600	984	242	44	21	45	175	168	352	23	21
Wadena	448	1.8	32 428	2 348	210	38	17	21	85	151	286	20	17
Waseca	747	-5.7	39 105	1 278	275	49	24	81	154	148	429	25	24
Washington	12 838	1.5	52 060	298	3 313	508	271	338	2 350	1 404	4 431	281	271
Watonwan	452	-6.1	40 616	1 097	135	26	11	92	90	93	265	13	11
Wilkin	307	-12.0	46 767	567	84	13	7	57	67	60	161	8	7
Winona	2 015	-1.2	39 327	1 248	946	178	79	94	515	365	1 297	77	79
Wright	5 010	2.5	39 000	1 302	1 504	253	131	342	634	714	2 229	138	131
Yellow Medicine	481	-3.3	47 443	516	144	29	12	94	110	103	279	13	12

1. Based on the resident population estimated as of July 1 of the year shown.

STATE County	Earnings, 2013 (cont.) — Percent by selected industries: Farm	Mining	Construction	Manufacturing	Information: professional, scientific, technical services	Retail trade	Finance, insurance, real estate and leasing	Health care and social assistance	Government	Social Security beneficiaries, December 2013: Number	Rate[1]	Supplemental Security Income recipients, December 2013	Housing units, 2014: Total	Percent change, 2010–2014
	75	76	77	78	79	80	81	82	83	84	85	86	87	88
MINNESOTA—Cont'd														
Fillmore	11.9	D	9.4	18.2	3.1	6.5	4.6	7.5	16.3	4 840	232	197	9 843	1.1
Freeborn	7.7	D	5.5	19.9	D	9.4	5.7	16.8	12.1	8 000	258	484	14 219	-0.1
Goodhue	5.5	0.0	5.0	17.3	3.7	5.3	2.7	11.6	15.9	9 905	213	456	20 320	-0.1
Grant	31.8	0.0	10.9	2.8	D	3.7	D	D	12.8	1 740	291	78	3 303	-0.6
Hennepin	0.0	0.2	3.3	8.9	16.9	4.3	17.5	9.3	9.2	176 205	147	26 444	522 864	2.6
Houston	7.3	D	9.7	9.9	D	5.3	3.2	10.9	21.5	4 420	235	199	8 634	0.4
Hubbard	8.1	D	5.8	21.7	D	8.1	3.7	D	21.2	5 960	288	377	14 604	-0.1
Isanti	0.7	0.0	7.6	16.6	D	9.8	4.7	D	16.3	7 205	189	428	15 412	0.6
Itasca	0.3	6.9	8.5	8.1	2.8	8.6	3.6	15.1	21.2	12 545	276	1 002	27 207	0.5
Jackson	27.2	0.0	3.6	27.9	D	2.3	2.0	D	8.3	2 415	235	109	4 996	0.1
Kanabec	3.0	0.4	16.0	11.7	2.6	8.5	4.6	D	27.6	4 105	256	294	7 808	-0.5
Kandiyohi	7.3	D	7.2	17.3	4.4	7.8	4.0	D	17.6	9 095	214	750	19 606	0.7
Kittson	35.8	D	3.5	5.5	D	4.1	D	D	16.8	1 180	263	49	2 598	-0.3
Koochiching	0.7	0.0	4.7	30.4	D	7.5	6.1	D	22.5	3 690	281	298	7 868	-0.4
Lac qui Parle	38.7	0.0	7.9	9.1	D	4.6	3.7	5.8	14.2	1 915	273	96	3 679	-0.4
Lake	0.1	D	D	12.9	2.1	5.5	2.8	D	17.1	2 945	273	160	7 816	1.8
Lake of the Woods	5.9	0.0	D	D	1.6	7.1	D	13.6	21.4	1 110	282	38	3 680	0.2
Le Sueur	6.8	D	9.2	28.9	2.9	4.5	4.9	5.1	12.3	5 065	183	243	12 489	0.6
Lincoln	31.2	D	6.2	1.1	2.6	4.4	2.6	D	9.5	1 515	262	64	3 115	0.2
Lyon	10.4	0.0	6.6	14.0	D	5.7	8.4	7.0	17.5	4 765	186	411	11 181	0.7
McLeod	3.9	D	4.5	36.0	3.3	6.0	3.9	14.1	10.3	7 520	209	362	15 713	-0.3
Mahnomen	21.6	0.0	3.9	D	D	3.3	D	D	48.5	985	180	160	2 765	-0.8
Marshall	33.6	D	7.5	7.4	1.9	3.7	D	5.0	14.4	2 205	234	110	4 799	-0.3
Martin	22.0	0.0	3.7	9.8	4.0	6.7	5.3	D	10.6	5 595	274	378	9 959	-0.5
Meeker	10.9	0.2	9.5	17.0	3.7	6.5	4.9	7.6	15.6	5 025	218	249	10 708	0.3
Mille Lacs	1.4	D	6.3	10.0	6.1	6.3	3.3	14.6	38.1	6 395	247	444	12 709	-0.3
Morrison	12.8	0.4	7.2	10.6	5.7	7.8	3.0	D	21.6	7 510	228	546	15 855	0.8
Mower	5.9	0.0	3.7	18.8	D	5.1	2.7	D	14.4	8 975	228	738	16 990	-0.2
Murray	41.5	0.4	7.5	6.3	2.3	4.4	3.4	D	12.0	2 225	260	90	4 596	0.9
Nicollet	9.1	D	1.9	26.3	D	4.0	2.4	D	22.8	5 440	165	319	13 196	2.5
Nobles	20.1	0.0	3.8	22.9	3.6	6.8	3.0	D	11.9	4 035	186	308	8 545	0.1
Norman	47.2	0.0	D	D	5.5	4.2	D	7.7	11.9	1 735	260	142	3 411	-0.3
Olmsted	0.5	0.0	4.1	10.9	4.2	5.1	2.9	52.2	8.6	24 595	165	2 205	61 766	2.1
Otter Tail	8.4	0.1	7.7	17.5	4.3	7.4	3.5	12.8	15.8	15 360	267	891	35 664	0.2
Pennington	4.0	0.0	3.1	11.1	D	4.8	2.0	D	12.9	2 835	201	197	6 377	1.3
Pine	3.3	D	7.7	3.0	D	7.8	2.9	8.2	43.8	6 770	233	510	17 215	-0.4
Pipestone	28.0	D	6.4	6.0	9.6	5.5	D	D	15.7	2 080	224	143	4 478	-0.1
Polk	17.8	0.2	4.9	14.1	3.4	5.7	2.5	D	19.3	6 685	211	613	14 698	0.6
Pope	20.1	0.0	5.6	16.5	1.6	4.5	2.9	D	14.4	2 690	246	132	6 544	1.7
Ramsey	0.0	D	4.2	11.1	9.3	4.2	8.5	12.6	17.4	82 795	157	16 819	218 169	0.4
Red Lake	30.1	D	3.7	D	4.2	4.4	D	4.2	18.7	875	215	44	1 938	-0.5
Redwood	28.9	D	4.4	17.5	1.6	4.5	3.8	4.4	18.2	3 720	237	218	7 252	-0.3
Renville	42.9	D	3.4	13.5	2.7	2.5	2.4	D	11.9	3 570	236	210	7 315	-0.5
Rice	2.6	0.2	7.5	19.7	4.2	5.9	3.2	9.3	16.9	10 950	169	750	24 567	0.5
Rock	33.3	D	3.3	7.8	3.5	4.5	11.4	9.5	12.2	2 305	241	111	4 270	0.2
Roseau	9.2	0.0	1.2	55.7	1.2	3.8	2.4	D	10.7	3 065	198	161	7 417	-0.7
St. Louis	0.1	9.2	5.3	5.2	6.5	7.1	5.1	23.6	17.4	45 625	227	5 275	103 218	0.2
Scott	0.9	0.3	10.9	14.0	10.4	5.7	3.3	8.6	20.2	15 540	113	1 129	49 184	4.4
Sherburne	2.1	D	11.3	14.0	3.5	7.1	2.9	13.3	17.5	12 505	139	701	32 872	1.5
Sibley	33.3	0.0	8.5	8.1	1.8	2.8	2.1	D	15.8	3 110	207	143	6 551	-0.5
Stearns	2.8	0.2	7.5	13.5	5.9	7.7	6.2	18.3	16.0	25 780	169	2 208	62 907	1.5
Steele	1.9	D	3.5	26.6	D	8.3	18.7	9.6	9.8	7 185	197	527	15 409	0.4
Stevens	23.8	D	4.7	19.0	3.7	4.4	2.5	8.8	18.4	1 785	183	119	4 157	-0.1
Swift	17.6	D	4.6	24.3	2.2	3.6	3.0	D	18.2	2 325	244	143	4 817	-0.4
Todd	5.8	D	5.0	36.1	D	5.4	2.8	D	17.8	5 800	238	406	12 954	0.3
Traverse	38.2	0.0	3.3	1.5	D	4.7	D	8.5	16.7	980	287	59	2 075	0.1
Wabasha	7.3	D	5.0	27.6	2.3	6.7	4.1	D	16.3	4 725	220	192	10 036	0.4
Wadena	2.3	0.0	4.4	8.3	2.5	6.6	3.1	D	22.0	3 805	276	410	6 982	1.2
Waseca	13.6	D	4.5	30.7	2.9	4.8	3.9	9.1	18.0	4 025	211	225	7 920	0.2
Washington	0.6	0.4	6.2	12.9	7.2	8.6	8.8	14.2	15.6	37 780	153	1 957	95 667	3.6
Watonwan	30.5	D	4.5	19.0	1.6	3.7	3.5	7.3	14.1	2 350	211	146	5 038	-0.2
Wilkin	27.7	D	2.7	0.4	D	3.4	D	12.9	12.7	1 480	226	89	3 073	-0.2
Winona	2.5	0.0	3.8	28.8	D	6.0	3.3	9.6	16.0	9 185	179	651	20 922	0.8
Wright	1.7	D	15.9	15.5	3.6	8.3	3.2	8.7	15.1	18 330	143	874	49 902	1.8
Yellow Medicine	32.4	D	7.1	4.0	2.0	3.9	2.2	D	23.5	2 505	246	134	4 746	-0.3

1. Per 1,000 resident population estimated as of July 1 of the year shown.

STATE County	Housing units, 2009–2013: Occupied units: Total	Owner-occupied: Percent	Owner-occupied: Median value[1]	Median owner cost as a percent of income: With a mortgage	Median owner cost as a percent of income: Without a mortgage[2]	Renter-occupied: Median rent[3]	Renter-occupied: Median rent as a percent of income[2]	Substandard units[4] (percent)	Civilian labor force, 2014: Total	Percent change, 2013–2014	Unemployment: Total	Unemployment: Rate[5]	Civilian employment,[6] 2009–2013: Total	Percent: Management, business, science and arts	Percent: Construction, production, and maintenance occupations
	89	90	91	92	93	94	95	96	97	98	99	100	101	102	103
MINNESOTA—Cont'd															
Fillmore	8 422	78.6	135 200	22.8	12.6	589	24.8	1.9	11 108	-0.2	478	4.3	10 423	34.0	28.2
Freeborn	13 230	77.3	104 000	22.2	11.9	546	26.6	1.4	16 300	-1.2	692	4.2	15 457	26.3	31.5
Goodhue	18 711	77.1	181 800	24.1	12.6	681	31.8	1.2	26 835	-0.2	1 033	3.8	23 645	34.8	27.6
Grant	2 580	80.3	98 600	19.6	12.6	542	27.1	2.8	3 294	0.1	162	4.9	2 981	33.8	25.9
Hennepin	481 263	63.7	230 900	23.2	12.4	917	29.5	1.7	672 114	0.5	24 897	3.7	622 838	46.5	13.6
Houston	7 809	80.9	156 500	22.4	12.6	585	29.1	2.7	10 458	-0.5	456	4.4	9 784	32.7	28.1
Hubbard	8 670	81.4	170 400	25.7	12.6	597	27.7	2.1	9 465	-0.9	595	6.3	9 170	30.1	26.4
Isanti	13 860	81.2	172 000	25.2	12.2	842	29.5	1.9	20 336	0.4	1 010	5.0	18 932	27.6	29.7
Itasca	18 862	80.8	152 200	24.8	11.8	635	29.8	2.1	21 995	0.2	1 417	6.4	19 383	31.1	27.3
Jackson	4 469	78.9	97 700	17.5	10.9	561	22.7	3.4	6 309	1.0	258	4.1	5 351	34.5	31.7
Kanabec	6 277	80.5	145 600	26.5	13.8	754	31.1	2.3	8 858	0.4	656	7.4	7 220	26.9	32.7
Kandiyohi	17 120	73.4	161 800	23.0	11.9	627	30.9	1.0	23 798	1.1	990	4.2	21 595	33.0	27.9
Kittson	1 912	82.6	68 700	18.8	10.0	465	22.6	2.6	2 388	-1.2	115	4.8	2 183	34.2	34.1
Koochiching	6 134	76.4	101 200	20.1	11.8	538	32.4	0.9	6 409	-4.9	541	8.4	6 071	26.4	30.1
Lac qui Parle	3 074	82.6	80 200	19.9	10.0	556	24.5	3.3	3 638	-1.0	172	4.7	3 512	34.0	29.2
Lake	4 982	82.6	153 200	23.1	11.4	680	31.4	2.2	5 673	-2.0	255	4.5	4 951	27.1	30.5
Lake of the Woods	1 665	88.2	121 500	25.3	14.1	547	25.0	1.6	2 396	0.7	112	4.7	1 984	25.4	35.6
Le Sueur	10 997	81.8	180 100	24.6	11.9	708	28.5	1.0	15 653	0.7	822	5.3	14 469	31.5	31.4
Lincoln	2 485	81.9	86 100	21.3	11.4	490	23.0	2.2	3 303	-0.5	140	4.2	2 988	34.6	29.4
Lyon	10 083	67.5	136 000	19.7	10.4	608	26.4	1.1	15 331	0.1	536	3.5	13 779	34.3	28.3
McLeod	14 716	76.0	155 400	23.3	13.1	684	27.2	4.0	19 808	-1.3	899	4.5	18 523	32.4	31.0
Mahnomen	2 058	72.5	97 800	21.9	12.5	486	29.7	0.7	2 356	-2.0	131	5.6	2 270	28.1	21.2
Marshall	4 080	80.8	88 100	18.4	11.1	514	23.5	1.3	5 621	0.7	369	6.6	4 761	33.4	31.7
Martin	8 797	75.6	102 600	20.4	10.2	580	28.4	1.8	10 273	-0.8	475	4.6	10 359	30.2	31.9
Meeker	9 288	81.0	156 000	24.8	12.5	686	28.9	2.0	12 901	1.0	579	4.5	11 307	31.3	35.2
Mille Lacs	10 312	74.0	146 600	25.2	14.3	702	29.5	1.6	12 790	0.6	850	6.6	11 761	30.3	30.2
Morrison	13 416	80.0	153 600	25.4	12.7	625	29.4	3.0	17 364	-2.0	1 069	6.2	16 284	28.8	32.8
Mower	15 855	71.7	106 000	20.3	10.7	695	32.2	1.2	20 328	-1.0	760	3.7	19 193	28.9	33.4
Murray	3 820	81.6	95 300	20.8	11.2	545	24.3	1.4	4 871	0.5	233	4.8	4 339	37.5	28.9
Nicollet	12 192	74.0	169 800	22.9	10.9	754	25.7	7.1	19 800	0.2	591	3.0	18 605	35.5	23.0
Nobles	7 964	72.0	107 800	21.6	11.6	633	26.6	2.5	11 220	1.2	379	3.4	10 539	24.3	40.2
Norman	2 737	80.9	84 000	21.1	11.5	521	28.7	2.1	3 327	0.2	163	4.9	3 131	35.6	26.5
Olmsted	57 262	74.9	171 100	21.4	10.2	796	28.8	1.7	82 905	-0.8	2 807	3.4	78 533	47.3	15.9
Otter Tail	24 356	78.9	159 700	22.8	11.4	594	29.3	1.5	30 991	0.2	1 378	4.4	27 641	34.0	27.9
Pennington	5 806	75.4	107 900	21.0	11.6	535	27.3	4.4	8 955	3.3	444	5.0	7 374	29.6	27.0
Pine	11 758	79.3	145 500	27.0	13.9	686	28.4	1.8	14 655	-1.5	886	6.0	12 641	24.0	29.5
Pipestone	3 924	72.7	90 600	19.9	10.8	564	25.6	1.6	4 795	2.0	178	3.7	4 711	28.3	30.0
Polk	12 663	70.7	128 100	20.0	11.9	634	28.5	1.4	17 194	0.4	770	4.5	15 527	33.6	25.3
Pope	4 758	79.7	148 000	23.0	11.4	657	22.2	4.1	6 121	2.4	222	3.6	5 432	32.1	28.8
Ramsey	205 395	59.8	198 200	23.4	11.7	840	31.0	1.7	277 177	0.5	10 942	3.9	256 770	42.6	16.9
Red Lake	1 681	80.9	87 800	18.9	12.4	497	26.0	2.4	2 278	0.8	129	5.7	2 089	30.3	28.3
Redwood	6 507	77.8	90 500	21.4	10.7	565	27.0	1.6	8 036	-0.4	348	4.3	7 634	34.0	28.0
Renville	6 400	78.6	97 600	21.1	11.3	560	24.0	2.5	8 239	-0.2	437	5.3	7 700	30.4	33.4
Rice	22 299	75.5	187 500	24.3	11.9	750	28.1	1.5	35 132	0.2	1 419	4.0	33 022	34.5	24.9
Rock	3 970	76.3	119 300	20.9	12.1	603	27.3	2.3	5 678	0.7	141	2.5	4 800	29.5	28.2
Roseau	6 402	78.1	103 800	22.1	11.4	555	24.7	1.8	8 818	2.1	317	3.6	8 305	26.1	43.0
St. Louis	85 238	71.3	137 500	21.9	11.5	654	32.8	1.4	101 800	-0.6	5 119	5.0	94 490	33.0	20.9
Scott	45 630	84.8	244 400	23.5	10.7	1 004	28.8	1.6	77 622	0.6	2 743	3.5	71 315	41.8	18.9
Sherburne	29 948	81.9	193 400	24.1	10.7	878	32.3	1.3	49 186	0.6	2 185	4.4	45 680	32.9	27.1
Sibley	6 090	79.2	136 900	23.5	12.5	602	24.7	2.4	8 425	1.0	376	4.5	7 753	30.4	36.2
Stearns	56 737	71.8	167 600	22.5	12.0	726	29.8	2.2	87 592	0.8	3 509	4.0	80 804	31.5	25.4
Steele	14 354	76.7	155 400	22.9	11.5	720	30.0	0.9	21 195	-1.2	791	3.7	18 591	31.8	26.4
Stevens	3 700	69.8	127 500	18.6	10.0	527	33.4	1.1	5 571	0.9	176	3.2	5 084	35.6	26.0
Swift	4 315	73.5	91 700	19.8	10.4	552	23.6	4.1	4 862	-0.9	234	4.8	4 975	33.6	29.3
Todd	9 904	83.0	130 000	25.4	13.3	575	25.7	0.6	12 912	0.2	588	4.6	11 287	25.8	37.6
Traverse	1 510	81.4	66 400	19.5	11.2	509	28.3	1.3	1 647	-1.0	77	4.7	1 711	36.8	26.7
Wabasha	8 890	82.4	154 000	23.4	11.8	648	29.6	1.7	11 826	-0.3	466	3.9	11 214	32.6	29.2
Wadena	5 830	75.2	114 600	26.0	13.1	555	32.0	1.4	6 158	-0.3	377	6.1	5 873	26.3	31.1
Waseca	7 328	77.3	142 700	20.9	12.3	566	26.5	1.3	9 668	-2.8	457	4.7	9 432	31.2	30.2
Washington	88 947	81.3	241 900	22.8	10.1	1 097	29.0	1.5	136 015	0.6	4 842	3.6	126 282	44.5	16.1
Watonwan	4 445	74.5	95 700	19.5	11.0	558	23.4	0.7	6 151	-0.7	301	4.9	5 730	28.1	41.1
Wilkin	2 685	77.3	107 300	19.8	10.0	442	25.6	1.6	3 599	-0.6	119	3.3	3 332	30.4	30.9
Winona	18 957	71.6	158 000	23.7	10.9	620	31.8	1.9	29 410	-0.8	1 072	3.6	27 946	30.7	25.5
Wright	44 983	83.9	195 000	23.9	12.0	889	29.9	1.6	71 124	0.6	2 934	4.1	65 806	35.8	25.0
Yellow Medicine	4 135	79.1	97 600	20.0	10.0	579	26.5	2.9	5 455	-1.8	224	4.1	5 116	32.9	29.2

1. Specified owner-occupied units. 2. A value of 10.0 represents 10 percent or less; a value of 50.0 represents 50 percent or more. 3. Specified renter-occupied units.
4. Overcrowded or lacking complete plumbing facilities. 5. Percent of civilian labor force. 6. Persons 16 years old and over.

STATE County	Private nonfarm establishments, employment and payroll, 2013									Agriculture, 2012			
		Employment						Annual payroll		Farms			
											Percent with:		
	Number of establish-ments	Total	Health care and social assistance	Manufac-turing	Retail trade	Finance and insurance	Professional, scientific, and technical services	Total (mil dol)	Average per employee (dollars)	Number	Fewer than 50 acres	500 acres or more	Farm operators whose principal occu-pation is farming (percent)
	104	105	106	107	108	109	110	111	112	113	114	115	116
MINNESOTA—Cont'd													
Fillmore	604	4 605	919	847	690	207	119	140	30 334	1 553	24.8	14.8	50.4
Freeborn	807	11 113	D	2 685	1 812	487	214	384	34 540	1 122	33.9	23.4	54.0
Goodhue	1 326	19 427	3 525	4 309	2 442	454	452	776	39 969	1 536	34.2	11.4	47.7
Grant	213	1 360	360	88	D	D	35	47	34 786	542	23.4	25.1	42.3
Hennepin	39 230	865 255	126 334	70 696	75 147	83 307	76 717	50 565	58 439	627	60.3	6.2	65.1
Houston	438	4 015	1 010	445	611	116	88	107	26 552	920	14.9	11.3	48.5
Hubbard	597	4 601	919	889	935	160	D	139	30 186	406	18.7	11.1	51.5
Isanti	816	8 760	2 069	1 621	1 582	323	191	306	34 911	844	43.4	7.8	44.1
Itasca	1 143	13 557	3 576	1 303	2 347	432	609	493	36 347	401	23.2	8.0	45.6
Jackson	315	5 945	1 331	1 550	361	97	56	195	32 758	826	21.3	30.0	59.9
Kanabec	293	3 094	907	590	510	210	D	110	35 680	648	23.1	8.6	50.8
Kandiyohi	1 399	18 349	5 238	2 575	2 876	499	529	614	33 480	1 310	27.0	14.8	44.7
Kittson	144	1 190	327	134	278	58	D	36	30 277	544	10.8	36.2	43.0
Koochiching	390	4 055	623	D	785	D	60	137	33 771	187	9.1	17.6	43.9
Lac qui Parle	204	1 954	D	237	311	93	D	57	29 405	852	18.7	35.2	57.4
Lake	299	3 263	D	D	363	D	D	122	37 504	44	50.0	2.3	29.5
Lake of the Woods	159	1 313	D	D	217	30	D	35	26 379	196	15.3	19.9	36.2
Le Sueur	692	6 651	837	2 183	756	213	140	230	34 636	1 051	35.8	11.4	40.6
Lincoln	210	1 541	532	19	230	56	44	43	27 714	699	17.6	24.5	54.6
Lyon	798	12 571	1 941	1 911	2 188	1 084	D	471	37 469	904	17.7	30.6	64.8
McLeod	979	15 789	2 977	5 214	2 226	416	378	608	38 500	966	32.6	16.6	62.6
Mahnomen	102	1 746	D	D	162	64	D	48	27 562	310	15.8	37.1	52.6
Marshall	257	1 645	257	269	254	102	D	68	41 144	1 148	8.1	33.0	44.9
Martin	612	7 931	1 792	1 295	1 336	358	202	291	36 696	897	20.3	33.2	67.8
Meeker	573	6 120	1 347	1 731	846	185	91	197	32 195	1 147	31.8	13.1	49.4
Mille Lacs	667	8 554	1 759	1 004	1 014	234	204	242	28 280	731	31.5	7.4	43.2
Morrison	882	8 301	1 706	1 326	1 508	261	201	245	29 553	1 957	18.3	8.7	50.3
Mower	861	14 009	2 561	3 999	1 798	340	251	546	38 973	1 053	30.7	22.5	64.1
Murray	315	2 830	444	D	297	145	471	89	31 369	895	20.7	31.1	59.1
Nicollet	632	11 975	2 228	3 427	950	201	451	447	37 292	764	23.6	20.9	62.6
Nobles	616	9 392	1 484	D	1 528	259	184	336	35 726	995	22.7	26.1	65.7
Norman	185	1 188	D	D	210	91	24	44	36 790	610	7.9	43.9	64.6
Olmsted	3 494	78 672	D	D	10 604	1 868	1 874	3 647	46 352	1 150	35.6	11.6	50.3
Otter Tail	1 690	19 039	4 318	4 129	2 984	582	402	627	32 919	3 033	17.0	13.9	46.6
Pennington	393	9 056	1 253	D	1 014	152	D	363	40 104	515	12.6	25.2	37.5
Pine	608	6 908	1 358	D	1 025	D	133	175	25 265	870	16.6	10.6	47.2
Pipestone	333	3 822	710	D	547	109	D	115	30 047	637	25.1	25.0	57.1
Polk	777	9 695	2 307	1 665	1 401	273	261	309	31 844	1 322	11.6	37.3	56.1
Pope	367	3 475	620	665	339	114	D	128	36 725	931	21.6	16.6	37.1
Ramsey	13 170	292 031	57 208	22 499	26 617	18 877	14 055	15 373	52 641	97	96.9	0.0	83.5
Red Lake	97	730	D	D	138	58	21	22	30 373	322	8.4	29.8	57.1
Redwood	509	5 748	841	1 151	794	247	59	176	30 637	1 163	19.9	31.2	68.5
Renville	457	4 400	914	988	583	181	196	157	35 575	1 061	20.2	32.9	63.4
Rice	1 481	22 709	3 126	3 815	2 610	510	479	770	33 904	1 304	40.9	7.7	45.6
Rock	264	2 581	650	268	405	292	87	74	28 780	689	26.6	23.9	62.1
Roseau	408	7 114	816	3 989	828	174	D	242	33 986	977	9.6	27.2	41.2
St. Louis	5 305	85 426	23 788	4 208	12 468	3 446	3 240	3 349	39 206	685	26.1	6.6	38.4
Scott	3 214	40 780	4 476	6 349	4 883	655	D	1 999	49 022	847	41.0	6.8	51.6
Sherburne	1 905	20 677	3 786	3 077	2 851	406	533	838	40 521	455	41.1	12.5	42.2
Sibley	360	3 510	549	998	D	136	56	111	31 735	949	25.7	20.9	63.8
Stearns	4 331	76 385	15 648	11 186	11 156	3 687	2 403	3 009	39 398	3 501	23.0	8.4	55.4
Steele	1 003	19 808	2 588	D	2 689	D	232	802	40 480	796	38.4	14.2	55.5
Stevens	334	4 258	1 357	D	587	D	105	146	34 308	560	25.2	31.1	56.3
Swift	306	3 342	645	D	380	109	87	109	32 493	801	22.2	26.0	55.2
Todd	559	5 774	D	1 621	795	185	D	191	33 143	1 931	18.4	6.8	52.9
Traverse	122	862	278	35	191	D	D	24	27 276	458	22.7	36.7	62.7
Wabasha	573	5 837	890	D	818	174	139	184	31 528	909	24.1	14.2	58.7
Wadena	394	3 846	901	295	D	158	72	120	31 136	643	15.7	6.4	42.8
Waseca	468	5 790	947	2 195	697	178	141	200	34 460	805	31.3	18.8	55.8
Washington	5 519	72 791	10 800	7 008	12 837	4 858	3 570	2 840	39 013	602	54.0	6.5	57.3
Watonwan	289	3 568	502	D	419	141	D	101	28 383	503	25.0	27.4	60.2
Wilkin	170	1 932	D	D	D	55	D	66	34 010	301	14.8	49.9	68.3
Winona	1 188	22 233	3 395	5 121	2 756	D	478	726	32 673	1 115	22.6	11.9	52.6
Wright	3 145	34 120	5 363	5 170	6 990	710	906	1 267	37 140	1 463	39.2	8.3	48.8
Yellow Medicine	315	4 352	795	D	398	110	55	164	37 773	885	22.7	32.3	60.8

Agriculture, 2012 (cont.)

STATE County	Land in farms: Acreage (1,000)	Land in farms: Percent change, 2007–2012	Land in farms: Acres: Average size of farm	Land in farms: Acres: Total irrigated (1,000)	Land in farms: Acres: Total cropland (1,000)	Value of land and buildings (dollars): Average per farm	Value of land and buildings (dollars): Average per acre	Value of machinery and equipment, average per farm (dollars)	Value of products sold: Total (mil dol)	Value of products sold: Average per farm (dollars)	Value of products sold: Percent from: Crops	Value of products sold: Percent from: Livestock and poultry products	Percent of farms with sales of: $10,000 or more	Percent of farms with sales of: $100,000 or more	Government payments: Total ($1,000)	Government payments: Percent of farms
	117	118	119	120	121	122	123	124	125	126	127	128	129	130	131	132
MINNESOTA—Cont'd																
Fillmore	422	-5.3	272	0.2	316.8	1 248 138	4 588	164 626	342.2	220 351	60.6	39.4	62.8	33.5	8 809	70.3
Freeborn	382	-1.7	340	2.4	356.7	1 857 024	5 454	222 874	416.0	370 784	68.8	31.2	64.0	42.7	8 422	76.1
Goodhue	398	0.4	259	4.5	330.0	1 404 395	5 418	191 857	435.7	283 650	60.9	39.1	64.1	36.1	7 646	66.3
Grant	303	-5.8	559	5.0	279.6	2 020 910	3 616	233 819	213.5	393 849	95.2	4.8	46.1	33.0	6 952	92.4
Hennepin	69	3.5	110	0.6	54.3	904 309	8 235	109 024	64.5	102 821	82.7	17.3	44.0	15.8	1 002	33.2
Houston	229	-6.2	249	0.1	129.4	860 452	3 453	133 811	146.3	158 974	51.1	48.9	59.1	28.3	4 864	78.9
Hubbard	117	-7.3	288	19.6	68.9	649 106	2 254	92 340	46.1	113 475	90.7	9.3	40.4	7.1	362	26.8
Isanti	142	12.9	169	3.1	98.9	628 475	3 724	101 475	61.0	72 306	78.5	21.5	40.9	12.0	1 812	45.9
Itasca	84	-9.9	210	D	40.1	395 067	1 884	63 691	11.2	27 870	58.4	41.6	42.1	4.7	286	13.5
Jackson	358	-10.7	433	0.1	330.0	2 646 869	6 110	298 615	376.4	455 643	66.9	33.1	77.2	54.8	6 712	82.9
Kanabec	129	-9.2	199	D	65.9	456 122	2 295	77 170	32.0	49 326	61.5	38.5	39.8	11.1	785	35.5
Kandiyohi	415	-0.5	317	21.0	354.1	1 522 722	4 806	206 989	495.4	378 160	57.4	42.6	48.7	28.6	9 979	82.8
Kittson	470	-13.2	865	D	391.1	1 516 086	1 754	285 081	180.6	331 914	94.5	5.5	44.1	30.9	8 938	86.4
Koochiching	53	-3.1	286	D	24.7	335 963	1 176	73 214	9.1	48 604	56.7	43.3	45.5	7.5	256	19.3
Lac qui Parle	446	8.4	524	4.2	407.9	2 298 670	4 386	298 212	311.8	365 912	81.1	18.9	67.3	50.1	8 663	89.2
Lake	4	9.0	85	0.0	1.5	279 023	3 285	45 000	0.4	8 841	83.5	16.5	20.5	0.0	D	2.3
Lake of the Woods	90	-6.9	461	D	56.2	686 286	1 490	112 276	19.1	97 541	92.4	7.6	45.4	15.3	962	57.7
Le Sueur	242	-3.5	230	0.9	207.5	1 276 799	5 548	158 177	224.3	213 423	63.3	36.7	55.5	26.9	5 726	78.9
Lincoln	291	1.6	416	0.4	256.6	1 614 046	3 878	224 119	198.6	284 117	68.1	31.9	66.1	41.6	7 282	89.0
Lyon	413	-3.7	457	0.0	379.7	2 373 903	5 197	279 675	403.0	445 815	59.9	40.1	73.9	54.8	8 729	83.5
McLeod	264	8.2	273	0.1	237.0	1 471 040	5 385	207 760	234.5	242 789	76.3	23.7	64.9	38.1	7 031	78.3
Mahnomen	216	13.1	696	D	178.5	1 417 135	2 035	281 677	96.0	309 745	93.8	6.2	61.0	40.0	3 698	85.5
Marshall	820	-9.9	714	1.0	740.4	1 506 519	2 109	258 963	322.3	280 777	97.7	2.3	48.3	30.4	15 614	89.4
Martin	429	-4.7	478	0.8	405.6	2 931 235	6 134	300 925	619.6	690 708	53.3	46.7	80.9	61.8	9 526	85.8
Meeker	304	-5.6	265	8.5	259.9	1 101 923	4 160	177 291	291.7	254 347	59.0	41.0	53.0	29.1	6 376	77.8
Mille Lacs	128	2.3	175	0.2	78.9	481 513	2 753	77 425	53.0	72 476	58.8	41.2	47.5	13.7	1 131	44.7
Morrison	437	1.2	223	20.3	256.1	618 675	2 774	154 393	429.9	219 691	26.0	74.0	66.8	27.6	5 626	64.3
Mower	450	7.1	427	3.2	422.9	2 557 820	5 988	260 886	475.8	451 853	68.6	31.4	70.8	46.6	8 929	78.3
Murray	408	-4.9	456	D	374.9	2 572 509	5 644	305 709	365.5	408 348	63.6	36.4	70.9	50.3	9 673	87.5
Nicollet	274	0.1	359	0.0	250.0	2 329 018	6 489	288 609	386.6	506 060	46.1	53.9	78.4	54.3	6 050	84.4
Nobles	381	-9.9	382	D	351.0	2 263 207	5 917	291 514	477.6	480 017	50.8	49.2	79.7	57.8	8 290	83.1
Norman	532	3.8	873	0.9	492.5	2 611 572	2 992	359 020	281.2	461 039	93.6	6.4	69.3	48.5	7 950	85.6
Olmsted	264	-10.7	230	0.2	209.4	1 258 339	5 473	166 763	250.1	217 472	65.8	34.2	58.4	29.4	5 524	70.8
Otter Tail	882	-1.8	291	59.0	623.3	728 692	2 505	127 789	504.3	166 272	64.2	35.8	50.4	20.6	13 475	76.7
Pennington	272	-16.5	528	0.0	225.5	958 184	1 816	167 614	82.4	160 095	90.2	9.8	50.5	24.7	5 827	87.0
Pine	204	-1.9	234	0.5	103.8	472 323	2 018	83 011	65.4	75 223	46.7	53.3	48.2	10.7	1 176	37.1
Pipestone	242	-1.1	380	2.9	206.0	1 994 403	5 250	245 870	307.9	483 356	38.1	61.9	77.7	49.5	4 263	78.6
Polk	1 095	-0.4	828	9.4	991.4	2 403 190	2 902	415 046	594.5	449 722	96.3	3.7	59.2	39.1	17 706	85.2
Pope	334	-7.3	359	28.9	267.5	1 314 806	3 666	183 074	237.7	255 321	72.5	27.5	47.5	29.4	6 786	84.1
Ramsey	1	-23.2	7	0.1	0.4	68 392	9 176	26 876	2.9	30 330	84.3	15.7	29.9	7.2	0	0.0
Red Lake	199	-11.1	617	D	167.7	1 079 854	1 750	181 960	74.8	232 242	87.8	12.2	59.3	32.3	3 215	84.5
Redwood	521	-5.9	448	0.0	489.6	2 835 987	6 325	301 476	518.4	445 711	70.4	29.6	78.3	60.4	10 261	86.1
Renville	622	0.3	586	0.3	589.1	3 547 517	6 055	357 959	710.3	669 506	76.8	23.2	76.5	61.9	10 308	83.4
Rice	237	-6.5	181	0.9	197.3	1 039 649	5 731	131 569	231.6	177 599	63.5	36.5	51.4	21.9	5 113	69.3
Rock	281	0.5	407	1.9	252.7	2 862 247	7 030	286 846	398.4	578 213	44.7	55.3	85.8	62.6	4 542	75.3
Roseau	556	-6.0	569	0.0	445.4	676 111	1 188	161 546	158.4	162 140	86.1	13.9	45.5	22.5	9 192	80.1
St. Louis	127	-14.4	186	D	60.4	349 235	1 880	49 045	17.1	24 904	59.9	40.1	36.9	3.5	245	5.0
Scott	141	20.1	167	0.2	111.6	1 038 302	6 227	115 534	112.2	132 462	61.8	38.2	56.0	22.0	2 679	53.6
Sherburne	112	5.9	247	29.7	88.7	1 062 160	4 301	153 305	88.5	194 532	77.9	22.1	40.7	17.4	1 589	46.6
Sibley	346	0.2	365	0.1	318.6	2 187 458	5 994	250 711	377.0	397 289	63.0	37.0	76.5	49.2	6 433	77.6
Stearns	758	7.0	216	52.0	582.8	844 095	3 901	175 663	808.5	230 933	32.3	67.7	68.1	38.2	16 012	74.0
Steele	238	-10.6	299	0.6	217.9	1 793 508	5 999	217 629	293.1	368 157	66.9	33.1	57.9	36.7	5 456	79.4
Stevens	319	-6.2	570	19.1	297.3	2 547 307	4 467	347 489	441.3	788 107	53.9	46.1	62.5	47.0	5 149	84.1
Swift	361	-7.1	451	27.1	326.6	2 305 811	5 116	259 010	339.2	423 437	71.0	29.0	59.4	40.1	7 598	87.1
Todd	394	4.0	204	14.1	248.1	482 272	2 364	92 717	241.0	124 812	39.3	60.7	60.7	19.4	4 869	62.6
Traverse	348	6.3	761	0.3	335.0	3 384 218	4 448	355 653	264.5	577 596	95.3	4.7	61.6	47.6	7 019	91.7
Wabasha	246	-6.3	270	1.4	177.8	1 269 843	4 698	210 095	231.2	254 341	49.7	50.3	69.3	41.0	5 237	74.4
Wadena	149	-1.5	232	20.0	83.5	412 974	1 784	74 162	57.5	89 401	62.3	37.7	49.6	14.2	1 954	61.7
Waseca	232	-9.0	288	D	213.6	1 692 842	5 881	207 745	303.9	377 523	59.1	40.9	69.6	45.1	5 979	83.5
Washington	81	-0.4	134	3.5	58.5	1 107 086	8 238	108 400	86.4	143 586	90.6	9.4	46.8	17.9	1 090	33.1
Watonwan	237	-11.9	471	3.2	223.3	2 880 443	6 111	300 348	281.0	558 740	64.3	35.7	69.6	52.1	5 266	86.7
Wilkin	444	4.6	1 136	1.9	428.8	4 434 734	3 903	532 286	303.9	777 363	99.0	1.0	71.6	57.5	7 125	86.7
Winona	277	-9.2	249	0.1	180.0	1 165 445	4 686	177 996	282.0	252 939	38.0	62.0	69.4	33.8	5 695	66.8
Wright	288	8.6	197	3.7	231.8	1 055 837	5 361	139 010	227.5	155 519	65.2	34.8	56.0	22.3	4 703	58.9
Yellow Medicine	395	-3.5	446	0.4	364.5	2 043 238	4 578	287 805	322.8	364 741	73.7	26.3	68.6	50.7	9 119	87.5

STATE County	Water use, 2010		Wholesale trade,[1] 2007				Retail trade,[2] 2007				Real estate and rental and leasing,[2] 2007			
	Total water withdrawn (mil gal/day)	Gallons withdrawn per person per day	Number of establish-ments	Number of employees	Sales (mil dol)	Annual payroll (mil dol)	Number of establish-ments	Number of employees	Sales (mil dol)	Annual payroll (mil dol)	Number of establish-ments	Number of employees	Receipts (mil dol)	Annual payroll (mil dol)
	133	134	135	136	137	138	139	140	141	142	143	144	145	146
MINNESOTA—Cont'd														
Fillmore	13.9	668	26	197	116.1	8.4	107	728	176.8	13.8	12	23	1.9	0.4
Freeborn	5.7	183	47	541	412.1	21.3	154	2 137	492.1	41.9	23	49	4.2	0.8
Goodhue	617.6	13 372	42	603	313.9	24.3	241	2 664	595.8	53.4	46	D	D	D
Grant	1.5	253	11	177	293.8	7.7	37	259	56.4	4.5	5	3	0.4	0.0
Hennepin	182.2	158	2 280	39 155	34 472.5	2 340.5	4 405	80 179	22 278.8	2 080.8	2 318	18 498	6 322.6	746.8
Houston	2.4	127	20	D	D	D	77	597	152.5	11.5	6	10	1.5	0.2
Hubbard	11.3	554	7	29	35.3	0.9	120	1 071	200.9	18.1	15	61	3.7	0.7
Isanti	4.1	108	18	D	D	D	108	1 560	405.2	34.2	27	D	D	D
Itasca	196.9	4 370	31	274	160.6	13.8	227	2 414	521.6	47.2	36	100	13.6	2.1
Jackson	2.7	267	13	182	151.7	6.6	51	399	80.3	6.0	3	13	0.7	0.1
Kanabec	1.5	95	4	15	4.9	0.4	54	582	150.5	10.4	6	59	2.5	0.9
Kandiyohi	11.1	263	77	D	D	D	231	2 921	597.6	56.7	51	198	27.2	5.8
Kittson	1.6	341	19	131	217.5	3.9	31	206	41.3	3.0	4	7	0.3	0.0
Koochiching	45.9	3 448	10	55	16.8	1.6	83	698	165.0	14.6	15	47	5.5	1.2
Lac qui Parle	3.5	478	12	121	96.2	4.4	47	302	61.6	4.8	7	30	2.3	0.7
Lake	124.7	11 474	4	D	D	D	46	384	119.8	8.9	10	67	3.1	1.3
Lake of the Woods	1.0	237	5	24	11.6	0.6	29	229	39.9	3.3	3	7	0.5	0.1
Le Sueur	23.8	860	23	299	132.0	11.4	108	884	206.2	16.5	24	91	3.8	3.0
Lincoln	2.3	383	9	64	77.6	2.3	40	274	53.1	3.9	7	11	0.8	0.1
Lyon	7.3	282	46	D	D	D	142	1 907	378.9	36.1	35	120	8.6	2.6
McLeod	7.2	197	31	D	D	D	170	2 263	477.1	43.1	38	D	D	D
Mahnomen	0.6	115	4	23	9.9	1.2	20	187	20.2	2.5	3	8	0.6	0.1
Marshall	1.1	114	24	214	246.7	8.4	43	271	118.6	5.8	2	D	D	D
Martin	10.2	487	46	D	D	D	109	1 343	268.2	22.9	16	42	4.4	0.9
Meeker	4.8	204	19	197	98.6	7.5	90	737	174.1	14.3	14	39	2.2	0.6
Mille Lacs	2.6	101	20	207	160.1	5.2	115	1 229	251.8	21.5	18	46	3.8	0.9
Morrison	14.5	437	26	280	249.7	11.0	130	1 501	361.2	31.2	13	34	4.5	0.5
Mower	10.1	259	28	198	229.8	9.7	171	1 946	347.7	33.9	25	138	8.3	1.9
Murray	2.1	241	15	149	283.2	5.3	44	321	46.6	4.3	9	49	1.7	0.7
Nicollet	6.6	200	31	349	194.3	14.0	86	790	164.9	15.5	25	132	10.1	2.7
Nobles	6.0	280	38	680	478.2	25.6	122	1 495	303.6	27.7	15	49	3.9	0.6
Norman	0.8	115	17	95	58.4	3.6	33	260	52.5	4.4	4	7	0.5	0.1
Olmsted	27.0	187	111	1 141	777.9	51.6	605	10 543	2 182.1	227.4	160	821	114.7	21.5
Otter Tail	104.3	1 820	67	432	322.5	13.2	287	3 177	704.5	61.9	67	137	22.2	2.9
Pennington	2.5	179	23	D	D	D	89	1 076	209.5	21.5	11	26	4.1	0.6
Pine	3.1	105	13	24	6.8	0.7	108	1 180	243.5	21.4	26	40	4.9	0.7
Pipestone	3.5	361	21	400	158.3	10.9	54	460	110.9	8.2	2	D	D	D
Polk	13.1	416	47	459	336.9	16.0	122	1 418	297.8	27.0	17	89	3.9	1.4
Pope	16.0	1 458	51	553	305.5	22.4	55	359	103.5	7.5	5	11	0.7	0.1
Ramsey	194.9	383	647	14 603	9 278.4	835.5	1 719	29 640	6 156.5	636.5	762	5 417	832.0	194.8
Red Lake	2.3	562	5	D	D	D	23	193	41.1	3.3	1	D	D	D
Redwood	3.1	192	29	371	210.7	17.7	93	774	156.8	14.8	16	37	2.8	0.6
Renville	3.5	219	29	236	277.7	9.1	82	582	117.0	8.4	6	9	0.6	0.1
Rice	8.5	133	59	D	D	D	219	2 596	599.2	55.9	51	168	51.4	3.7
Rock	3.7	385	15	161	88.5	6.6	47	416	109.1	7.9	9	32	1.9	0.4
Roseau	1.8	115	11	D	D	D	89	837	179.9	15.1	12	32	2.0	0.4
St. Louis	358.3	1 789	200	2 095	1 128.2	89.2	1 020	13 128	2 760.5	264.9	217	974	160.2	22.7
Scott	18.4	142	135	1 671	1 300.8	93.9	361	4 709	1 169.7	103.5	166	428	58.0	10.4
Sherburne	71.4	807	66	471	231.7	20.6	218	3 484	844.3	73.9	80	D	D	D
Sibley	3.7	243	14	99	69.3	4.5	61	426	75.5	6.4	9	17	1.5	0.3
Stearns	36.2	240	182	4 375	1 813.6	187.0	724	11 566	2 423.6	225.5	169	856	105.0	19.8
Steele	6.2	169	35	474	323.5	23.6	206	3 004	543.9	54.6	32	264	16.6	4.7
Stevens	6.2	632	19	90	130.8	3.4	52	594	170.1	12.1	11	43	2.5	0.6
Swift	9.2	936	18	282	665.6	12.1	50	376	80.6	6.8	6	82	2.4	1.3
Todd	8.6	346	12	89	18.0	2.8	100	758	160.0	13.4	20	31	2.0	0.4
Traverse	0.4	118	10	71	82.6	3.0	29	233	45.5	3.6	3	5	0.4	0.1
Wabasha	4.8	221	20	223	92.2	7.7	106	899	210.8	19.0	7	20	1.1	0.2
Wadena	7.0	507	16	487	243.4	22.4	98	892	177.7	17.3	7	25	0.7	0.3
Waseca	4.4	231	27	220	105.2	7.2	68	839	163.6	15.4	15	35	2.1	0.4
Washington	391.7	1 645	191	1 432	1 743.6	65.7	729	12 945	2 690.7	262.1	338	1 292	174.6	33.4
Watonwan	3.3	293	15	99	145.9	3.6	49	408	70.4	6.1	4	18	0.5	0.3
Wilkin	0.7	103	12	D	D	D	25	210	50.0	5.6	6	6	1.8	0.2
Winona	11.7	228	61	D	D	D	198	3 157	666.1	62.9	50	156	19.7	3.0
Wright	365.4	2 930	96	985	440.7	50.6	470	6 766	1 458.8	131.5	124	342	51.3	8.3
Yellow Medicine	2.8	265	17	205	302.3	8.1	50	449	112.9	7.7	4	10	0.9	0.2

1. Merchant wholesalers, except manufacturers' sales branches and offices. 2. Employer establishments.

STATE County	Professional, scientific, and technical services,[1] 2007				Manufacturing, 2007				Accommodation and food services, 2007			
	Number of establish-ments	Number of employees	Receipts (mil dol)	Annual payroll (mil dol)	Number of establish-ments	Number of employees	Receipts (mil dol)	Annual payroll (mil dol)	Number of establish-ments	Number of employees	Sales (mil dol)	Annual payroll (mil dol)
	147	148	149	150	151	152	153	154	155	156	157	158
MINNESOTA—Cont'd												
Fillmore	35	145	11.1	3.5	48	880	377.4	32.0	62	487	14.5	3.4
Freeborn	39	D	D	D	59	2 746	767.0	100.5	82	1 076	33.8	9.8
Goodhue	87	358	39.5	14.4	86	4 204	1 332.3	167.6	125	3 132	254.6	62.1
Grant	12	51	4.0	1.4	NA	NA	NA	NA	11	D	D	D
Hennepin	6 938	84 413	13 992.3	5 782.2	1 883	82 304	20 957.7	4 397.5	2 640	62 847	3 279.1	1 017.7
Houston	28	D	D	D	23	647	D	19.3	42	208	8.0	1.8
Hubbard	35	102	6.7	2.3	36	1 284	328.6	43.2	68	468	20.6	5.3
Isanti	59	D	D	D	70	1 515	317.7	62.1	68	936	30.4	9.2
Itasca	70	D	D	D	48	1 367	627.2	63.0	116	1 298	51.0	15.4
Jackson	13	50	3.8	1.1	11	1 025	409.6	36.2	22	454	7.8	2.1
Kanabec	17	83	5.4	1.6	19	647	114.5	22.3	28	315	10.0	2.5
Kandiyohi	89	D	D	D	71	2 957	818.7	104.6	96	1 481	52.0	14.7
Kittson	6	30	2.4	1.0	NA	NA	NA	NA	11	D	D	D
Koochiching	24	81	5.5	2.1	22	1 053	D	D	43	463	21.3	6.0
Lac qui Parle	13	37	1.7	0.5	NA	NA	NA	NA	15	D	D	D
Lake	15	74	3.3	1.2	17	612	156.8	24.6	55	661	33.9	8.9
Lake of the Woods	5	8	0.4	0.2	NA	NA	NA	NA	38	444	20.4	5.1
Le Sueur	46	174	15.4	6.4	53	2 356	623.9	91.2	47	531	17.0	4.7
Lincoln	8	22	2.3	0.5	NA	NA	NA	NA	11	D	D	D
Lyon	50	600	24.7	23.7	38	1 976	697.0	70.3	64	1 182	37.3	11.7
McLeod	68	293	24.1	9.1	75	7 486	1 603.4	362.1	67	1 111	39.8	11.3
Mahnomen	3	D	D	D	NA	NA	NA	NA	10	D	D	D
Marshall	11	32	6.3	1.3	NA	NA	NA	NA	20	D	D	D
Martin	43	217	21.4	6.9	45	1 398	779.4	55.9	49	761	24.4	7.4
Meeker	35	214	12.9	6.1	60	1 500	692.6	60.3	39	469	13.9	4.0
Mille Lacs	31	79	9.5	2.5	43	1 038	215.1	37.7	75	2 035	200.5	37.5
Morrison	33	129	13.2	4.9	58	1 953	504.1	72.1	92	953	32.1	8.7
Mower	43	267	29.1	8.9	37	3 701	D	155.4	86	1 132	41.8	11.5
Murray	15	76	5.7	1.5	NA	NA	NA	NA	19	D	D	D
Nicollet	38	D	D	D	53	4 722	872.3	136.9	47	787	25.6	7.7
Nobles	30	D	D	D	31	2 898	952.0	100.5	51	730	26.1	6.8
Norman	11	37	4.6	1.7	NA	NA	NA	NA	17	D	D	D
Olmsted	275	D	D	D	100	9 150	2 971.4	579.2	311	7 364	326.9	93.7
Otter Tail	93	D	D	D	84	4 005	1 054.4	119.3	157	1 456	62.7	17.5
Pennington	21	325	44.4	15.8	20	1 656	D	55.5	34	1 083	43.3	15.8
Pine	26	D	D	D	NA	NA	NA	NA	63	D	D	D
Pipestone	17	60	5.0	1.1	13	620	D	15.8	20	D	D	D
Polk	39	D	D	D	39	1 733	954.1	67.2	61	1 010	36.7	10.1
Pope	19	244	23.0	11.0	30	524	82.7	19.2	37	325	12.6	3.0
Ramsey	1 859	13 562	1 962.6	807.4	639	27 716	7 578.9	1 580.0	1 114	21 976	963.5	291.7
Red Lake	5	20	1.4	0.4	NA	NA	NA	NA	8	D	D	D
Redwood	26	83	6.5	2.3	30	685	148.1	23.6	38	1 286	81.5	21.4
Renville	27	120	13.5	5.9	28	908	D	40.3	31	D	D	D
Rice	130	572	61.6	27.1	78	4 215	1 397.9	179.4	114	1 936	80.6	21.1
Rock	17	43	6.1	1.5	NA	NA	NA	NA	14	D	D	D
Roseau	24	93	6.2	1.9	20	4 317	D	144.4	38	643	24.5	8.6
St. Louis	420	D	D	D	228	5 670	D	D	579	9 962	498.6	118.8
Scott	393	D	D	D	182	6 024	1 925.0	344.1	185	6 552	527.5	129.9
Sherburne	145	419	43.3	17.6	150	3 592	683.3	150.9	119	2 211	75.3	22.0
Sibley	25	73	6.2	2.6	24	928	548.5	30.9	25	D	D	D
Stearns	303	D	D	D	253	13 255	3 745.5	531.3	389	7 167	251.2	71.9
Steele	63	193	17.0	5.6	70	5 727	1 485.0	263.8	85	1 477	67.7	16.6
Stevens	15	109	10.7	4.4	17	687	192.9	27.9	27	352	11.7	2.9
Swift	15	58	5.1	1.9	NA	NA	NA	NA	28	D	D	D
Todd	25	94	6.7	2.2	48	1 794	648.1	65.3	46	439	15.1	3.8
Traverse	4	D	D	D	NA	NA	NA	NA	7	D	D	D
Wabasha	33	D	D	D	30	1 822	D	63.4	56	464	17.0	4.6
Wadena	18	49	4.5	2.3	NA	NA	NA	NA	35	400	10.9	3.0
Waseca	33	132	8.5	4.2	29	2 365	633.9	106.0	39	383	13.5	3.4
Washington	785	D	D	D	227	9 698	5 751.8	532.2	385	8 209	340.9	101.4
Watonwan	12	60	8.8	2.2	20	1 283	327.5	38.6	22	268	9.1	2.2
Wilkin	6	D	D	D	NA	NA	NA	NA	16	196	5.1	1.5
Winona	80	D	D	D	103	6 754	1 711.1	223.2	109	1 924	65.4	16.6
Wright	270	864	86.7	32.2	217	5 625	1 124.6	229.2	188	3 362	106.7	31.9
Yellow Medicine	12	96	13.4	5.4	NA	NA	NA	NA	27	577	38.3	8.8

1. Establishment subject to federal tax.

Table B. States and Counties — **Health Care and Social Assistance, Other Services, Nonemployer Businesses, and Residential Construction**

STATE County	Health care and social assistance, 2007				Other services, 2007				Nonemployer businesses, 2013		Value of residential construction authorized by building permits, 2014	
	Number of establishments	Number of employees	Receipts (mil dol)	Annual payroll (mil dol)	Number of establishments	Number of employees	Receipts (mil dol)	Annual payroll (mil dol)	Number	Receipts (mil dol)	New Construction ($1,000)	Number of housing units
	159	160	161	162	163	164	165	166	167	168	169	170
MINNESOTA—Cont'd												
Fillmore	50	1 005	44.6	21.0	46	155	16.0	3.1	1 700	68.0	6 548	45
Freeborn	76	2 686	192.7	84.1	74	D	D	D	1 851	77.7	4 802	26
Goodhue	134	3 093	235.5	110.5	97	D	D	D	2 996	129.4	15 325	64
Grant	20	601	32.6	13.6	17	D	D	D	551	21.5	0	0
Hennepin	3 556	110 510	11 773.3	5 161.1	2 653	21 236	2 352.2	583.1	99 234	4 955.2	1 125 448	4 665
Houston	44	D	D	D	42	D	D	D	1 410	63.8	8 300	44
Hubbard	50	942	71.8	30.9	37	D	D	D	1 698	60.3	2 415	18
Isanti	76	2 104	179.4	71.1	62	D	D	D	2 636	110.8	25 387	170
Itasca	140	2 936	209.2	90.0	85	D	D	D	3 000	111.4	19 449	117
Jackson	25	1 425	42.4	21.3	30	D	D	D	770	34.1	3 747	19
Kanabec	31	951	69.6	26.9	26	D	D	D	1 054	46.1	1 467	13
Kandiyohi	179	5 098	293.6	146.8	92	D	D	D	3 108	133.1	24 741	98
Kittson	8	297	13.9	6.7	13	D	D	D	327	13.5	1 685	7
Koochiching	46	735	41.1	18.8	30	D	D	D	844	24.5	803	9
Lac qui Parle	18	575	26.4	12.0	18	D	D	D	611	23.1	1 120	7
Lake	31	568	24.9	12.4	21	219	12.1	3.6	822	30.4	9 689	50
Lake of the Woods	10	D	D	D	9	D	D	D	351	13.8	2 320	11
Le Sueur	58	812	37.3	16.5	55	249	15.8	3.7	1 982	86.5	7 173	44
Lincoln	15	553	31.6	12.5	14	D	D	D	477	16.4	3 089	12
Lyon	80	1 941	122.4	49.4	59	D	D	D	1 711	79.3	6 451	36
McLeod	107	2 595	183.7	78.2	94	D	D	D	2 391	104.0	7 851	37
Mahnomen	11	189	10.0	4.5	8	D	D	D	303	13.1	0	0
Marshall	18	306	10.3	5.7	27	D	D	D	645	22.8	880	5
Martin	61	1 954	124.6	60.0	57	D	D	D	1 486	59.4	4 284	16
Meeker	52	984	57.8	23.7	46	D	D	D	1 751	66.6	7 909	42
Mille Lacs	60	1 500	89.6	38.5	55	224	18.6	3.0	1 781	72.7	10 156	46
Morrison	69	1 402	96.8	40.4	82	399	37.6	7.4	2 366	104.5	9 626	89
Mower	89	2 587	169.4	79.8	97	D	D	D	1 945	85.3	5 143	32
Murray	19	431	35.1	10.8	22	D	D	D	731	35.0	3 991	25
Nicollet	65	2 111	152.9	89.2	65	373	135.2	9.6	2 169	76.5	23 181	98
Nobles	63	1 361	73.3	34.7	50	D	D	D	1 284	57.4	8 083	67
Norman	17	384	19.7	10.2	14	D	D	D	487	23.7	3 600	12
Olmsted	344	18 305	1 975.0	801.4	248	D	D	D	9 421	401.0	137 107	639
Otter Tail	171	4 370	232.5	109.3	134	D	D	D	4 684	193.7	6 948	71
Pennington	43	1 255	95.8	38.7	41	247	11.8	3.1	893	33.6	3 294	16
Pine	62	1 240	58.3	23.0	50	306	18.8	4.9	1 723	68.8	8 127	57
Pipestone	29	722	42.7	15.1	29	D	D	D	757	33.2	1 863	10
Polk	90	2 367	124.2	60.5	62	D	D	D	2 183	84.7	13 442	68
Pope	25	605	33.8	15.6	28	D	D	D	971	42.6	9 670	45
Ramsey	1 730	51 661	4 816.8	2 087.2	1 150	10 015	1 313.1	301.5	35 978	1 463.4	154 798	728
Red Lake	5	D	D	D	7	D	D	D	231	11.6	0	0
Redwood	43	959	56.3	22.6	52	D	D	D	1 065	40.3	5 088	28
Renville	46	1 317	50.7	24.3	37	D	D	D	1 090	50.1	2 742	16
Rice	149	3 197	206.3	90.5	133	D	D	D	4 149	162.0	23 909	113
Rock	15	600	30.4	12.2	18	D	D	D	711	31.6	4 831	15
Roseau	32	798	50.3	20.0	41	D	D	D	1 162	41.4	5 208	40
St. Louis	681	22 334	2 078.2	971.3	427	2 581	218.6	55.2	11 401	433.7	83 807	466
Scott	214	4 023	340.3	139.1	220	1,372	94.2	26.8	10 136	479.3	172 070	894
Sherburne	147	3 811	244.8	124.5	152	D	D	D	6 363	260.8	48 810	245
Sibley	29	454	22.8	9.8	31	D	D	D	1 062	41.7	3 729	17
Stearns	411	13 006	1 270.1	598.4	369	D	D	D	10 267	504.2	83 888	479
Steele	120	2 225	170.1	74.0	83	532	45.7	10.6	2 359	89.7	11 929	49
Stevens	40	D	D	D	24	D	D	D	627	27.2	4 030	14
Swift	20	593	34.7	14.8	27	D	D	D	689	24.1	1 768	10
Todd	51	728	45.3	19.2	45	D	D	D	1 649	70.2	10 673	68
Traverse	11	218	12.8	4.5	9	D	D	D	261	11.9	1 389	7
Wabasha	48	D	D	D	52	170	13.0	2.6	1 517	67.5	12 386	97
Wadena	46	1 976	128.2	57.9	28	D	D	D	1 012	39.5	3 477	45
Waseca	54	1 241	51.4	21.0	39	D	D	D	1 190	55.4	3 217	15
Washington	511	9 218	826.0	327.4	384	2 490	171.5	52.7	17 472	787.6	232 080	752
Watonwan	24	546	36.7	15.5	27	D	D	D	720	27.0	965	6
Wilkin	23	D	D	D	10	D	D	D	474	43.9	2 342	12
Winona	129	3 066	187.2	80.8	90	D	D	D	2 841	111.1	12 213	109
Wright	219	4 309	315.0	134.5	225	1 270	89.9	22.0	9 447	407.2	134 275	550
Yellow Medicine	28	1 044	59.6	27.2	24	D	D	D	834	32.0	2 136	14

Table B. States and Counties — **Government Employment and Payroll, and Local Government Finances**

STATE County	Government employment and payroll, 2012: Full-time equivalent employees	Government employment and payroll, 2012: March payroll (dollars)	March payroll (percent of total): Adminis-tration, judicial, and legal	March payroll (percent of total): Police and Corrections	March payroll (percent of total): Fire Protection	March payroll (percent of total): Highways and transpor-tation	March payroll (percent of total): Health and Welfare	March payroll (percent of total): Natural resources and utilities	March payroll (percent of total): Education and libraries	Local government finances, 2012, General revenue: Total (mil dol)	General revenue: Inter-govern-mental (mil dol)	Taxes: Total (mil dol)	Taxes: Per capita[1] (dollars): Total	Taxes: Per capita[1] (dollars): Property
	171	172	173	174	175	176	177	178	179	180	181	182	183	184
MINNESOTA—Cont'd														
Fillmore	743	2 541 608	12.4	9.9	0.0	8.7	11.1	6.0	50.3	79.4	42.2	20.8	999	988
Freeborn	1 073	4 355 329	8.3	11.4	1.9	7.2	10.0	5.7	54.1	127.7	69.2	36.7	1 183	1 110
Goodhue	1 720	6 840 668	9.9	13.6	2.1	4.3	9.2	6.0	53.4	204.8	92.0	69.5	1 500	1 468
Grant	273	953 527	13.2	7.0	0.0	7.4	8.2	5.8	57.5	34.1	18.5	9.7	1 624	1 620
Hennepin	35 312	195 123 070	8.9	12.4	2.0	3.7	9.4	8.3	54.2	6 392.6	2 496.9	2 262.3	1 910	1 724
Houston	731	2 758 225	7.6	7.3	0.3	4.4	7.9	2.9	66.7	81.1	51.4	19.2	1 022	1 012
Hubbard	660	2 206 385	9.8	10.0	0.0	6.0	8.6	2.6	59.7	84.9	48.1	26.6	1 305	1 278
Isanti	1 257	4 796 343	6.7	9.3	0.1	4.0	7.5	2.3	68.0	131.8	76.3	35.3	924	904
Itasca	1 538	7 554 704	6.6	8.1	0.4	8.7	15.2	3.8	55.3	301.4	126.6	54.1	1 196	1 185
Jackson	515	1 776 829	11.8	7.0	0.2	8.4	20.7	6.0	44.4	50.6	24.7	15.9	1 544	1 531
Kanabec	867	2 925 087	5.0	6.1	0.0	4.3	35.1	1.6	43.5	90.0	33.3	14.7	920	889
Kandiyohi	2 286	9 769 471	6.3	8.2	0.4	2.9	40.7	4.1	36.3	282.7	84.2	49.6	1 170	1 089
Kittson	282	1 417 262	8.1	3.9	0.0	6.1	5.8	4.7	69.0	29.6	16.1	6.4	1 432	1 411
Koochiching	528	2 114 323	5.7	6.7	1.6	5.8	7.4	7.8	61.4	61.1	35.8	8.3	632	626
Lac qui Parle	625	1 888 050	6.9	3.8	0.0	5.1	33.9	3.0	45.7	46.7	21.4	8.4	1 176	1 141
Lake	361	1 980 601	12.9	10.1	0.3	9.4	6.4	8.7	48.8	64.0	33.4	15.7	1 454	1 414
Lake of the Woods	143	726 420	14.0	7.3	0.0	9.2	10.2	5.3	51.7	20.3	13.0	5.1	1 272	1 255
Le Sueur	871	2 940 497	8.0	8.1	0.0	4.7	11.3	5.1	60.6	96.7	50.3	31.2	1 128	1 088
Lincoln	199	603 609	18.2	11.9	0.1	15.9	1.7	6.8	38.3	21.7	9.6	8.1	1 392	1 384
Lyon	1 012	3 496 744	7.5	9.5	0.1	6.3	1.3	11.7	60.6	145.6	71.4	30.6	1 199	1 151
McLeod	1 516	6 615 440	5.8	6.3	0.2	3.2	37.7	10.6	34.8	212.6	66.7	39.1	1 084	1 063
Mahnomen	413	1 411 273	11.1	5.4	0.0	2.8	22.1	3.6	50.5	40.8	24.5	6.0	1 085	1 083
Marshall	459	1 668 424	9.8	5.5	0.5	7.6	16.1	9.7	49.9	55.9	36.6	9.4	991	982
Martin	655	3 114 449	10.3	9.8	0.1	7.4	3.2	9.6	56.8	92.7	49.5	24.0	1 170	1 158
Meeker	1 226	4 903 007	5.1	5.4	0.1	2.7	21.6	3.2	60.7	139.5	63.7	28.6	1 239	1 222
Mille Lacs	1 239	4 213 762	8.0	10.1	0.2	3.3	6.5	3.4	67.4	113.5	71.6	30.4	1 182	1 162
Morrison	1 124	4 203 099	7.6	8.2	0.9	5.8	10.1	2.5	63.7	118.8	71.3	29.8	903	875
Mower	1 542	6 255 175	7.7	8.0	0.8	4.4	8.9	12.3	56.6	166.8	93.6	36.0	915	853
Murray	420	2 070 204	5.7	4.9	0.0	4.6	33.5	2.7	42.5	54.5	22.6	10.9	1 273	1 259
Nicollet	835	3 375 650	8.8	10.9	0.1	6.1	20.8	7.8	43.0	108.0	39.0	29.6	899	839
Nobles	747	5 019 216	4.9	6.5	0.1	3.1	5.4	4.5	73.5	104.9	59.6	21.9	1 019	964
Norman	410	1 309 952	11.1	4.4	0.2	8.7	6.0	6.0	61.5	40.3	26.4	8.4	1 266	1 263
Olmsted	4 101	28 521 111	5.6	8.4	2.3	3.1	9.3	7.4	60.7	672.3	289.4	201.9	1 373	1 242
Otter Tail	2 164	8 240 552	8.0	7.4	0.2	4.7	21.9	3.4	52.3	298.8	109.1	62.1	1 083	1 068
Pennington	640	2 304 729	5.4	8.5	1.6	4.2	7.5	11.0	56.5	114.3	37.7	13.8	984	963
Pine	879	3 660 809	9.4	7.3	0.3	7.0	4.0	1.4	67.8	103.3	61.8	27.4	938	920
Pipestone	661	2 186 364	6.7	4.4	0.1	5.7	33.1	2.8	46.0	72.9	31.8	11.0	1 175	1 146
Polk	1 733	5 824 889	5.7	5.8	1.5	3.5	29.5	8.1	43.7	191.1	112.8	36.5	1 161	1 082
Pope	553	2 333 307	3.9	5.8	0.0	8.4	42.6	1.9	32.2	48.8	23.1	14.2	1 302	1 287
Ramsey	16 492	141 646 187	5.1	8.3	2.7	4.8	6.3	4.1	67.7	2 881.4	1 248.1	805.8	1 549	1 417
Red Lake	258	709 610	7.9	6.0	0.0	6.6	6.3	5.2	67.6	24.0	15.3	4.3	1 044	1 038
Redwood	739	3 232 367	9.3	5.7	0.2	4.8	7.0	5.7	65.2	101.1	39.6	20.4	1 287	1 261
Renville	704	2 316 532	18.7	8.2	0.0	9.5	12.1	4.4	43.1	88.9	34.9	21.9	1 424	1 401
Rice	2 519	10 254 560	4.8	6.6	0.7	2.9	41.2	2.9	39.9	352.9	102.9	62.2	959	916
Rock	396	1 387 361	10.8	6.2	0.1	8.3	1.0	11.6	59.9	45.4	21.6	11.5	1 203	1 152
Roseau	687	2 591 371	8.0	6.4	0.0	5.4	6.6	3.1	69.0	74.6	50.8	14.1	909	899
St. Louis	7 560	37 760 893	7.0	10.6	2.8	7.2	13.4	8.3	44.2	1 073.0	545.0	233.2	1 164	1 026
Scott	3 486	17 619 282	8.6	9.3	0.5	3.5	6.2	5.2	64.4	500.4	232.5	180.8	1 338	1 287
Sherburne	3 233	14 013 536	5.6	10.8	0.4	2.4	4.7	3.2	71.3	366.7	185.3	126.0	1 408	1 391
Sibley	636	2 194 050	9.3	7.3	0.3	6.5	27.2	1.9	46.6	76.3	33.5	18.9	1 250	1 235
Stearns	4 907	24 879 439	7.5	10.1	1.5	2.8	14.9	4.1	56.2	676.6	322.4	196.7	1 297	1 129
Steele	1 297	5 726 547	5.5	10.8	0.9	4.1	6.2	10.3	60.3	147.4	81.6	42.4	1 167	1 112
Stevens	479	1 791 149	11.2	17.4	0.6	6.2	9.0	11.6	40.3	43.2	23.3	12.2	1 258	1 229
Swift	748	2 235 013	8.5	5.5	0.0	5.7	37.9	3.6	34.8	82.8	25.2	13.2	1 379	1 363
Todd	994	3 435 036	8.2	8.5	0.0	4.5	12.5	2.3	58.8	94.8	59.3	21.3	869	840
Traverse	251	735 078	9.6	10.4	0.1	13.3	21.2	2.5	41.3	26.6	9.8	7.7	2 242	2 236
Wabasha	717	2 663 637	12.2	9.5	0.1	4.8	7.6	8.0	55.6	95.1	50.4	27.4	1 278	1 244
Wadena	723	2 230 614	6.7	2.7	0.1	5.3	11.7	4.2	66.3	67.0	41.7	12.2	887	870
Waseca	839	2 685 918	9.1	9.2	1.4	6.3	7.1	5.6	60.1	83.8	42.3	21.8	1 133	1 094
Washington	6 573	28 742 198	7.5	9.9	1.5	2.6	4.9	4.1	68.0	850.9	369.3	318.3	1 304	1 251
Watonwan	544	1 961 440	9.4	7.3	0.3	6.3	9.4	7.3	57.7	52.1	29.2	12.3	1 097	1 083
Wilkin	308	1 120 394	10.9	8.0	0.0	10.2	10.2	7.3	51.6	36.4	21.4	9.3	1 417	1 407
Winona	1 299	5 244 944	8.6	10.3	2.2	4.6	9.2	8.7	54.4	161.3	88.3	44.7	866	816
Wright	4 086	18 042 110	5.5	7.7	0.2	3.1	16.3	2.4	60.5	548.1	243.1	150.9	1 185	1 154
Yellow Medicine	412	1 492 491	12.8	9.7	0.0	10.5	8.7	6.7	48.7	72.8	27.5	13.9	1 364	1 345

1. Based on the resident population estimated as of July 1 of the year shown.

STATE County	Local government finances, 2012 (cont.)									Government employment, 2013			Presidential election,[2] 2012		
	Direct general expenditure							Debt outstanding					Percent of vote cast:		
			Percent of total for:												
	Total (mil dol)	Per capita[1] (dollars)	Education	Health and hospitals	Police protection	Public welfare	Highways	Total (mil dol)	Per capita[1] (dollars)	Federal civilian	Federal military	State and local	Democratic	Republican	All other
	185	186	187	188	189	190	191	192	193	194	195	196	197	198	199
MINNESOTA—Cont'd															
Fillmore	76.1	3 651	36.6	4.1	4.6	4.1	17.1	66.9	3 213	73	75	1 245	52.7	44.4	2.8
Freeborn	125.1	4 028	42.5	2.8	6.6	6.1	15.4	132.0	4 249	80	113	1 441	57.4	40.2	2.4
Goodhue	204.0	4 403	43.7	3.7	6.0	4.9	10.8	184.3	3 977	124	168	4 089	48.1	49.5	2.3
Grant	31.2	5 248	38.6	0.9	4.1	11.4	16.0	31.1	5 236	31	22	332	51.3	45.7	3.0
Hennepin	7 135.3	6 024	29.8	13.2	5.5	5.6	5.3	9 944.8	8 395	12 882	4 769	82 544	63.4	34.8	1.8
Houston	81.7	4 339	53.8	2.6	5.0	5.5	10.5	57.5	3 052	70	68	1 109	54.3	43.6	2.2
Hubbard	78.2	3 842	35.6	0.3	3.6	14.6	18.2	83.3	4 093	34	75	1 144	41.9	56.3	1.8
Isanti	136.1	3 558	50.4	3.4	6.9	7.7	11.0	169.3	4 426	77	139	1 879	41.1	56.5	2.4
Itasca	350.2	7 744	24.1	20.6	2.5	8.1	14.2	319.0	7 054	171	164	3 241	55.2	42.3	2.6
Jackson	50.2	4 887	33.0	4.1	3.8	7.8	19.0	50.8	4 943	33	37	688	46.6	50.8	2.6
Kanabec	84.8	5 300	27.0	37.5	2.3	6.2	8.2	63.2	3 950	37	58	1 171	44.0	52.7	3.3
Kandiyohi	300.9	7 100	20.9	38.3	5.5	4.8	6.1	333.7	7 875	145	152	3 874	46.2	51.7	2.1
Kittson	33.3	7 415	39.2	0.7	3.3	4.6	22.4	21.5	4 785	61	16	288	58.1	39.6	2.3
Koochiching	70.6	5 344	34.8	3.6	4.7	13.7	11.0	39.7	3 002	183	48	915	53.6	43.5	2.8
Lac qui Parle	48.9	6 880	33.1	26.2	3.0	4.0	16.2	28.8	4 046	35	25	685	51.5	45.6	2.9
Lake	63.2	5 838	24.4	5.5	5.8	10.5	17.5	119.8	11 076	25	39	826	59.9	37.8	2.3
Lake of the Woods	20.1	5 071	32.1	0.5	4.1	7.7	23.1	304.4	76 625	28	14	279	42.0	55.3	2.8
Le Sueur	119.9	4 333	53.4	2.4	3.8	5.4	10.2	161.8	5 845	72	101	1 317	46.6	50.9	2.5
Lincoln	25.1	4 309	25.1	0.5	6.1	11.4	20.4	39.0	6 710	27	21	262	48.5	47.7	3.8
Lyon	146.3	5 727	52.4	0.4	7.1	3.1	11.6	165.7	6 486	121	90	2 749	48.1	49.7	2.2
McLeod	206.8	5 737	26.6	34.0	4.4	4.9	10.2	191.4	5 309	80	130	1 678	39.4	57.8	2.8
Mahnomen	39.5	7 142	44.6	20.1	5.7	5.9	9.3	26.1	4 718	26	20	1 351	61.3	36.0	2.7
Marshall	64.2	6 790	36.8	0.4	2.9	5.0	21.2	37.9	4 006	54	34	573	48.8	48.2	3.0
Martin	94.4	4 613	46.0	0.5	6.6	4.8	14.2	96.9	4 732	57	74	1 229	41.0	56.3	2.7
Meeker	131.9	5 719	44.6	17.9	4.5	5.3	7.4	173.9	7 539	68	84	1 131	42.9	53.7	3.4
Mille Lacs	118.0	4 583	57.3	0.6	3.7	6.4	6.8	133.7	5 195	61	93	3 597	44.8	52.0	3.1
Morrison	121.6	3 680	48.7	1.8	3.7	7.1	14.7	122.4	3 704	422	119	1 858	39.1	58.1	2.8
Mower	168.0	4 268	46.1	1.1	4.6	8.4	11.8	1 198.8	30 447	149	142	2 420	60.5	36.9	2.6
Murray	54.4	6 337	23.7	28.8	4.7	2.0	15.6	37.9	4 418	43	31	589	48.7	48.2	3.1
Nicollet	111.3	3 380	30.7	17.7	4.8	6.8	10.6	144.3	4 383	34	111	2 883	54.2	43.7	2.1
Nobles	104.2	4 852	42.9	3.4	7.6	7.3	10.8	69.0	3 210	87	78	1 391	48.2	49.6	2.3
Norman	40.7	6 134	33.4	1.1	3.5	8.1	19.4	17.3	2 601	37	24	444	62.0	35.1	2.9
Olmsted	687.5	4 675	34.2	1.9	4.8	7.4	9.9	2 857.8	19 432	840	543	7 298	50.6	47.3	2.0
Otter Tail	312.8	5 461	45.3	8.8	3.2	5.1	10.5	310.4	5 419	217	208	3 424	42.4	55.3	2.3
Pennington	122.4	8 695	70.1	0.0	2.8	3.6	4.7	105.6	7 504	76	51	1 584	49.8	47.6	2.6
Pine	95.3	3 262	45.6	1.9	5.8	7.4	12.1	136.2	4 662	302	101	3 315	49.3	47.7	3.0
Pipestone	70.7	7 570	36.9	25.0	2.8	5.3	9.6	31.4	3 359	47	33	939	42.1	55.2	2.6
Polk	182.0	5 792	29.6	1.4	3.7	10.5	14.8	169.8	5 406	105	111	2 570	51.2	46.6	2.2
Pope	48.7	4 470	30.5	12.3	9.7	6.5	14.2	36.7	3 368	41	40	710	50.7	47.0	2.3
Ramsey	2 823.6	5 428	39.6	2.3	6.4	6.6	5.2	4 373.6	8 408	3 328	1 969	55 644	66.0	32.1	2.0
Red Lake	25.7	6 285	56.4	0.3	4.3	4.4	15.8	18.7	4 565	19	15	270	51.1	44.9	4.0
Redwood	94.9	5 987	30.0	25.7	4.1	7.3	11.4	93.1	5 876	63	57	1 983	41.6	55.2	3.2
Renville	96.1	6 251	25.3	21.0	3.3	5.9	14.5	80.0	5 207	61	55	1 029	48.0	48.6	3.4
Rice	342.7	5 285	25.9	37.7	3.6	2.9	5.8	303.1	4 673	136	211	3 500	54.7	43.2	2.2
Rock	42.6	4 461	42.5	0.6	4.4	8.4	12.8	74.6	7 811	28	34	664	41.8	55.8	2.4
Roseau	80.9	5 225	41.7	0.5	3.6	5.4	18.9	44.4	2 870	98	56	961	40.2	57.6	2.1
St. Louis	1 223.1	6 106	33.5	5.6	5.4	6.8	9.4	959.9	4 792	1 430	835	15 008	65.1	32.6	2.3
Scott	487.6	3 608	45.0	0.4	4.6	4.1	15.6	1 025.8	7 590	121	500	9 308	43.5	54.7	1.8
Sherburne	342.7	3 831	57.6	0.7	4.6	4.0	8.4	655.5	7 328	122	324	3 975	39.9	58.1	2.0
Sibley	82.9	5 484	34.0	16.4	4.2	4.8	14.5	70.1	4 636	39	55	837	38.8	58.1	3.1
Stearns	692.0	4 565	39.7	8.6	5.0	4.9	11.1	994.2	6 558	2 115	536	9 896	45.3	52.3	2.4
Steele	144.4	3 975	47.3	1.6	5.1	5.6	14.0	145.9	4 016	72	132	2 001	45.9	51.2	2.9
Stevens	43.9	4 548	36.6	0.3	5.8	5.7	19.8	77.2	7 986	79	32	1 271	49.4	48.1	2.5
Swift	86.6	9 024	19.1	41.7	2.8	4.8	8.8	45.2	4 715	55	35	877	55.4	41.6	2.9
Todd	111.4	4 544	53.4	2.6	3.5	6.4	11.8	81.6	3 330	80	88	1 394	43.1	54.1	2.8
Traverse	29.5	8 562	21.2	13.2	3.7	4.8	17.5	15.5	4 502	27	12	306	51.3	45.8	2.9
Wabasha	100.8	4 696	37.3	2.8	5.5	4.0	15.3	103.1	4 800	55	78	1 001	47.5	49.9	2.6
Wadena	92.1	6 693	61.5	1.4	3.3	12.6	6.8	28.2	2 051	51	49	1 218	40.2	57.6	2.2
Waseca	84.8	4 408	42.7	2.1	5.7	11.6	9.7	75.0	3 897	270	65	1 108	44.5	52.7	2.8
Washington	872.4	3 574	51.1	1.8	5.9	3.6	8.8	1 195.5	4 898	391	895	10 489	51.3	46.9	1.8
Watonwan	57.4	5 127	43.4	1.2	4.2	7.5	11.1	64.3	5 747	49	40	750	48.7	48.0	3.2
Wilkin	36.2	5 494	38.6	2.9	5.1	6.0	20.9	19.1	2 000	23	24	366	45.4	52.3	2.3
Winona	157.7	3 054	44.7	2.6	5.6	6.4	13.8	84.9	1 645	134	172	3 578	58.4	39.3	2.3
Wright	554.0	4 351	45.4	11.5	4.5	3.5	7.8	1 170.5	9 192	186	470	5 630	40.2	57.6	2.2
Yellow Medicine	83.2	8 190	26.8	22.5	2.0	9.0	12.3	76.0	7 477	42	36	1 512	50.6	46.3	3.1

1. Based on the resident population estimated as of July 1 of the year shown. 2.

STATE/ County code	CBSA code[1]	County type[2]	STATE County	Land area,[3] (sq km) 2010	Population, 2014: Total persons 2014	Population, 2014: Rank	Population, 2014: Per square kilometer	Population and population characteristics, 2013: Race alone or in combination, not Hispanic or Latino (percent): White	Black	American Indian, Alaska Native	Asian and Pacific Islander	Percent Hispanic or Latino[4]	Age (percent): Under 5 years	5 to 17 years	18 to 24 years	25 to 34 years	35 to 44 years	45 to 54 years
				1	2	3	4	5	6	7	8	9	10	11	12	13	14	15
28 000	...	X	MISSISSIPPI	121 531	2 994 079	X	24.6	58.3	37.7	0.8	1.3	2.9	6.6	18.0	10.5	13.0	12.4	13.2
28 001	35020	5	Adams	1 198	31 737	1 392	26.5	38.9	53.2	0.6	0.8	7.6	6.0	15.4	8.4	12.9	12.0	13.9
28 003	18420	7	Alcorn	1 036	37 380	1 241	36.1	84.5	12.7	0.6	0.5	2.7	6.1	17.6	8.2	12.2	13.2	13.4
28 005	32620	8	Amite	1 891	12 629	2 254	6.7	57.6	41.2	0.6	0.4	1.0	6.3	15.6	7.8	10.1	10.4	14.0
28 007	...	6	Attala	1 904	19 163	1 869	10.1	55.5	42.3	0.5	0.5	1.9	6.9	18.6	8.0	10.8	11.3	12.5
28 009	32820	8	Benton	1 053	8 296	2 578	7.9	60.7	36.9	0.7	0.2	2.2	5.6	17.4	7.9	11.6	12.6	14.5
28 011	17380	5	Bolivar	2 270	33 768	1 333	14.9	32.8	64.5	0.3	0.9	2.1	7.6	18.1	11.9	13.8	11.1	12.1
28 013	...	7	Calhoun	1 519	14 745	2 119	9.7	66.3	28.3	0.5	0.3	5.7	6.6	17.8	8.0	10.9	12.3	13.7
28 015	24900	9	Carroll	1 627	10 254	2 416	6.3	65.2	33.5	0.6	0.3	1.2	4.5	15.4	8.1	10.8	11.1	14.1
28 017	...	7	Chickasaw	1 300	17 313	1 961	13.3	52.5	43.5	0.5	0.5	3.9	6.9	18.1	9.6	12.0	11.7	13.6
28 019	...	9	Choctaw	1 083	8 294	2 580	7.7	68.0	30.7	0.5	0.5	1.4	5.7	17.4	8.0	10.6	11.2	14.5
28 021	46980	6	Claiborne	1 262	9 080	2 510	7.2	14.2	84.4	0.5	0.7	1.1	6.1	16.0	19.9	10.7	9.6	10.8
28 023	32940	9	Clarke	1 791	16 299	2 024	9.1	63.9	34.7	0.6	0.3	1.1	5.6	17.9	8.4	11.1	11.6	13.8
28 025	...	7	Clay	1 062	20 225	1 825	19.0	39.8	58.7	0.4	0.3	1.3	6.2	18.5	9.4	11.9	11.6	12.8
28 027	17260	5	Coahoma	1 431	24 807	1 617	17.3	23.0	75.1	0.4	0.7	1.4	8.5	19.7	11.1	12.5	10.5	12.6
28 029	27140	2	Copiah	2 013	28 797	1 465	14.3	46.0	51.1	0.5	0.6	2.8	6.7	17.3	11.1	11.9	11.1	13.6
28 031	...	8	Covington	1 072	19 442	1 855	18.1	62.2	35.7	0.4	0.5	2.1	7.1	17.8	9.1	12.3	11.7	13.0
28 033	32820	1	DeSoto	1 233	170 913	372	138.6	69.5	24.6	0.6	1.8	4.9	6.5	20.7	8.7	12.8	15.1	13.9
28 035	25620	3	Forrest	1 208	76 330	720	63.2	58.6	37.3	0.6	1.3	3.4	7.0	16.2	16.6	15.0	11.3	11.5
28 037	...	9	Franklin	1 460	7 833	2 608	5.4	63.4	35.6	0.5	0.3	1.0	5.8	18.8	7.3	10.6	11.8	13.6
28 039	...	3	George	1 240	23 303	1 672	18.8	88.6	8.8	0.8	0.4	2.3	7.2	19.1	9.4	12.5	12.9	13.7
28 041	...	8	Greene	1 846	14 326	2 145	7.8	71.4	27.5	0.6	0.3	1.1	4.7	15.4	9.4	17.0	15.4	14.4
28 043	24980	7	Grenada	1 093	21 666	1 747	19.8	56.1	42.5	0.5	0.6	1.2	6.5	17.4	9.4	11.4	12.2	14.0
28 045	25060	3	Hancock	1 227	45 949	1 049	37.4	86.8	8.7	1.3	1.5	3.6	5.6	17.0	8.3	11.4	12.0	14.5
28 047	25060	3	Harrison	1 487	199 058	327	133.9	67.6	24.5	1.0	3.8	5.4	7.2	17.2	10.6	14.5	12.3	13.4
28 049	27140	2	Hinds	2 253	243 729	272	108.2	27.3	70.6	0.4	1.0	1.6	7.0	18.6	11.8	14.4	11.8	12.7
28 051	...	6	Holmes	1 960	18 459	1 898	9.4	16.3	82.7	0.3	0.5	0.8	8.1	19.5	12.5	11.9	10.4	12.8
28 053	...	7	Humphreys	1 084	8 741	2 537	8.1	23.0	74.6	0.4	0.5	2.4	7.9	19.7	9.5	12.5	10.6	13.5
28 055	...	9	Issaquena	1 070	1 397	3 087	1.3	34.3	64.1	0.5	0.4	0.8	3.6	11.5	13.8	16.5	10.3	15.8
28 057	46180	7	Itawamba	1 380	23 527	1 660	17.0	91.6	6.8	0.4	0.4	1.4	5.9	16.5	11.3	11.1	12.4	13.5
28 059	25060	3	Jackson	1 872	141 137	449	75.4	70.3	22.5	0.9	2.8	5.3	6.2	18.3	9.0	12.9	13.0	14.2
28 061	29860	9	Jasper	1 751	16 601	2 000	9.5	46.6	52.2	0.3	0.3	1.1	6.5	16.7	8.9	10.7	11.2	13.6
28 063	...	7	Jefferson	1 347	7 599	2 633	5.6	14.2	85.2	0.3	0.2	0.4	6.6	16.2	10.4	13.6	11.7	14.2
28 065	...	8	Jefferson Davis	1 058	11 822	2 307	11.2	38.8	60.0	0.6	0.3	1.0	6.0	15.4	9.2	10.7	11.8	13.8
28 067	29860	4	Jones	1 800	68 290	780	37.9	65.7	29.3	0.8	0.6	4.4	7.3	18.4	9.5	12.6	11.7	12.7
28 069	32940	9	Kemper	1 984	10 163	2 424	5.1	35.3	60.6	4.0	0.3	0.7	4.8	16.9	12.4	11.2	12.0	12.9
28 071	37060	6	Lafayette	1 636	52 930	942	32.4	71.1	24.1	0.5	3.0	2.3	5.4	12.9	26.2	13.8	10.9	10.1
28 073	25620	3	Lamar	1 287	60 099	865	46.7	75.8	20.9	0.6	1.5	2.4	6.9	18.8	9.6	15.7	13.9	12.8
28 075	32940	5	Lauderdale	1 822	79 739	694	43.8	54.2	43.1	0.5	1.1	2.0	6.4	17.8	10.3	12.9	11.9	13.2
28 077	...	8	Lawrence	1 115	12 502	2 265	11.2	66.2	31.3	0.5	0.5	2.3	6.7	17.6	8.6	11.9	11.4	14.4
28 079	...	6	Leake	1 510	23 193	1 675	15.4	48.4	41.7	5.9	0.4	4.3	6.9	21.9	9.1	12.5	11.7	12.0
28 081	46180	5	Lee	1 165	85 246	667	73.2	68.2	29.0	0.5	1.0	2.4	7.1	19.0	8.7	13.1	12.9	13.6
28 083	24900	5	Leflore	1 535	31 422	1 402	20.5	24.6	72.4	0.4	0.8	2.5	7.7	19.4	11.4	13.8	11.7	12.0
28 085	15020	6	Lincoln	1 518	34 775	1 308	22.9	67.6	30.9	0.5	0.5	1.2	6.6	18.3	8.9	11.9	12.8	13.4
28 087	18060	5	Lowndes	1 309	59 730	870	45.6	53.5	44.1	0.5	1.1	1.8	6.6	17.6	10.8	13.4	11.8	13.3
28 089	27140	2	Madison	1 851	101 688	587	54.9	56.3	38.7	0.4	2.6	2.9	6.6	19.2	8.9	13.4	13.5	14.2
28 091	...	6	Marion	1 405	25 868	1 566	18.4	65.6	32.9	0.4	0.6	1.4	6.7	17.9	8.8	12.5	12.1	13.1
28 093	32820	1	Marshall	1 829	36 234	1 269	19.8	49.1	47.5	0.5	0.4	3.4	5.9	16.3	10.2	12.2	12.2	14.6
28 095	...	7	Monroe	1 982	36 003	1 273	18.2	68.0	30.9	0.5	0.4	1.1	5.6	17.4	8.9	11.6	12.2	13.7
28 097	...	7	Montgomery	1 054	10 400	2 404	9.9	53.0	45.5	0.4	0.5	1.2	6.0	17.2	8.8	10.7	10.7	14.6
28 099	...	7	Neshoba	1 477	29 465	1 441	19.9	60.3	22.0	16.6	0.8	1.9	7.6	20.8	8.8	11.9	12.1	12.3
28 101	...	7	Newton	1 497	21 832	1 743	14.6	63.0	30.6	5.0	0.6	1.6	7.0	18.5	10.4	11.0	12.8	12.3
28 103	...	7	Noxubee	1 800	11 115	2 346	6.2	26.9	71.9	0.5	0.4	1.0	6.8	18.9	9.9	12.0	11.2	13.1
28 105	44260	5	Oktibbeha	1 187	49 414	994	41.6	58.2	37.2	0.5	3.6	1.6	5.5	12.6	31.6	13.5	8.8	9.4
28 107	...	6	Panola	1 775	34 444	1 315	19.4	48.4	49.9	0.6	0.5	1.6	7.2	18.8	9.7	12.1	11.9	13.7
28 109	38100	6	Pearl River	2 100	55 224	913	26.3	83.2	13.3	1.3	0.8	3.1	6.3	17.5	9.3	11.1	12.1	13.7
28 111	25620	3	Perry	1 676	12 227	2 284	7.3	78.5	20.5	0.7	0.2	1.1	6.5	17.4	8.7	11.2	12.2	14.1
28 113	32620	7	Pike	1 059	40 058	1 170	37.8	45.6	52.5	0.6	0.8	1.3	7.1	19.3	9.5	11.6	11.7	12.6
28 115	46180	7	Pontotoc	1 289	30 950	1 415	24.0	78.5	15.5	0.6	0.4	6.1	6.7	19.7	8.6	13.0	12.6	14.0
28 117	...	7	Prentiss	1 075	25 428	1 589	23.7	84.1	14.8	0.4	0.4	1.4	6.6	16.8	11.0	11.7	11.8	13.5
28 119	...	6	Quitman	1 049	7 678	2 622	7.3	29.3	69.8	0.6	0.7	0.9	6.8	18.1	9.9	11.4	11.8	13.8
28 121	27140	2	Rankin	2 008	148 070	436	73.7	76.3	20.2	0.5	1.4	2.6	6.5	18.1	8.0	14.7	14.5	13.5
28 123	...	6	Scott	1 578	28 461	1 474	18.0	51.4	37.8	0.5	0.5	10.8	7.8	18.7	9.3	13.2	12.5	13.2
28 125	...	9	Sharkey	1 118	4 647	2 856	4.2	27.9	70.6	0.4	0.4	1.4	7.4	17.7	8.8	11.2	10.6	13.5
28 127	27140	2	Simpson	1 526	27 463	1 515	18.0	62.3	35.7	0.5	0.7	1.7	6.6	18.9	9.0	11.9	11.9	13.2
28 129	...	8	Smith	1 648	16 188	2 029	9.8	75.1	23.7	0.3	0.2	1.4	6.4	17.8	8.8	10.8	12.1	13.6
28 131	...	3	Stone	1 154	17 875	1 919	15.5	77.9	20.1	1.0	0.6	1.5	5.9	17.1	12.6	12.4	12.3	13.5

1. CBSA = Core Based Statistical Area. See Appendix A for explanation. See Appendix B for list of metropolitan areas with component counties. 2. County type code from the Economic Research Service of USDA Rural-Urban Continuum Codes. See Appendix A for definition. 3. Dry land or land partially or temporarily covered by water. 4. May be of any race.

Table B. States and Counties — **Population and Households**

STATE County	Population, 2013 (cont.): Age (percent) (cont.): 55 to 64 years	65 to 74 years	75 years and over	Percent female	Population change and components of change, 2000–2014: Total persons: 2000	2010	Percent change: 2000–2010	2010–2014	Components of change, 2010–2014: Births	Deaths	Net migration	Households, 2009–2013: Number	Persons per household	Percent: Family households	Female family householder[1]	One person
	16	17	18	19	20	21	22	23	24	25	26	27	28	29	30	31
MISSISSIPPI	12.3	8.0	5.9	51.4	2 844 658	2 967 297	4.3	0.9	165 775	123 715	-16 999	1 088 073	2.65	68.9	18.3	27.1
Adams	15.0	8.8	7.7	49.6	34 340	32 297	-5.9	-1.7	1 580	1 700	-436	12 087	2.54	59.0	19.9	38.8
Alcorn	12.6	10.0	6.8	51.1	34 558	37 057	7.2	0.9	1 887	1 831	296	14 679	2.50	68.1	12.1	28.6
Amite	15.7	11.5	8.6	50.9	13 599	13 131	-3.4	-3.8	579	581	-506	5 212	2.49	62.3	15.9	36.9
Attala	13.0	10.4	8.4	52.4	19 661	19 564	-0.5	-2.0	1 107	1 150	-299	7 185	2.65	66.9	19.3	30.7
Benton	13.0	10.3	7.1	50.1	8 026	8 729	8.8	-5.0	365	388	-419	3 195	2.69	66.4	13.2	32.1
Bolivar	12.2	8.1	5.2	53.5	40 633	34 145	-16.0	-1.1	2 415	1 756	-1 054	12 301	2.64	64.1	27.0	31.4
Calhoun	13.5	9.4	7.9	51.8	15 069	14 962	-0.7	-1.5	731	738	-194	5 944	2.46	65.4	14.8	31.7
Carroll	15.6	12.5	7.9	48.9	10 769	10 597	-1.6	-3.2	370	420	-320	3 757	2.72	74.0	15.2	25.0
Chickasaw	12.8	8.3	6.9	51.9	19 440	17 392	-10.5	-0.5	1 054	706	-396	6 614	2.58	68.3	19.7	28.6
Choctaw	13.7	10.6	8.3	51.5	9 758	8 547	-12.4	-3.0	362	366	-256	3 378	2.43	67.1	15.5	31.5
Claiborne	12.9	7.5	6.4	52.3	11 831	9 604	-18.8	-5.4	473	384	-633	3 190	2.84	62.0	24.8	35.7
Clarke	13.8	10.3	7.4	52.6	17 955	16 732	-6.8	-2.6	792	789	-420	6 305	2.62	73.0	17.8	25.0
Clay	13.8	8.7	7.0	53.0	21 979	20 634	-6.1	-2.0	1 029	931	-489	7 750	2.61	73.5	25.4	25.3
Coahoma	12.1	7.2	5.8	53.9	30 622	26 151	-14.6	-5.1	1 805	1 283	-1 847	9 464	2.66	68.4	32.3	28.5
Copiah	13.4	8.6	6.3	51.7	28 757	29 449	2.4	-2.2	1 589	1 311	-893	9 897	2.83	67.7	15.3	30.5
Covington	12.4	9.4	7.2	51.1	19 407	19 568	0.8	-0.7	1 153	1 013	-258	7 036	2.73	68.4	16.6	29.5
DeSoto	10.9	7.1	4.4	51.5	107 199	161 252	50.4	6.0	8 753	4 964	5 696	57 979	2.82	75.9	15.1	20.4
Forrest	10.1	6.9	5.4	52.2	72 604	74 934	3.2	1.9	4 606	3 013	-230	27 822	2.58	61.8	16.9	29.5
Franklin	14.5	9.5	8.1	51.1	8 448	8 118	-3.9	-3.5	391	377	-300	3 311	2.39	72.9	15.5	26.6
George	11.3	9.1	4.8	49.5	19 144	22 578	17.9	3.2	1 517	999	160	7 842	2.83	75.0	10.0	23.9
Greene	11.3	7.6	4.8	40.4	13 299	14 400	8.3	-0.5	555	500	-149	4 117	2.74	74.2	12.3	25.4
Grenada	13.1	9.1	6.9	52.9	23 263	21 906	-5.8	-1.1	1 119	1 153	-207	7 941	2.69	65.0	18.6	32.1
Hancock	14.3	10.4	6.6	50.5	42 967	43 929	2.2	4.4	1 930	1 774	1 762	18 145	2.43	70.5	12.6	25.0
Harrison	11.9	7.5	5.4	50.3	189 601	187 105	-1.3	6.4	11 802	7 400	7 284	72 253	2.57	66.0	17.0	27.5
Hinds	11.9	6.6	5.1	53.2	250 800	245 285	-2.2	-0.7	14 278	8 482	-7 463	87 844	2.71	65.4	24.3	29.5
Holmes	11.7	7.2	6.1	52.9	21 609	19 198	-11.2	-5.2	1 198	942	-1 217	6 511	2.81	66.3	32.8	32.5
Humphreys	12.6	7.6	6.0	52.7	11 206	9 375	-16.3	-6.8	564	423	-776	3 107	2.95	64.9	26.6	32.1
Issaquena	13.9	7.7	6.9	40.0	2 274	1 406	-38.2	-0.6	67	49	-39	461	2.38	64.0	15.0	33.8
Itawamba	12.2	9.9	7.2	51.0	22 770	23 401	2.8	0.5	1 177	1 060	-18	8 859	2.53	72.5	11.7	25.8
Jackson	12.6	8.3	5.5	50.7	131 420	139 668	6.3	1.1	6 763	5 461	249	50 007	2.77	70.0	15.3	25.3
Jasper	14.4	10.4	7.5	51.5	18 149	17 062	-6.0	-2.7	1 038	762	-748	7 015	2.38	69.9	20.7	28.3
Jefferson	13.8	7.0	6.5	50.0	9 740	7 726	-20.7	-1.7	509	318	-321	2 520	2.84	66.3	30.1	33.1
Jefferson Davis	14.5	10.9	7.7	52.1	13 962	12 487	-10.6	-5.3	624	634	-639	4 895	2.48	64.8	20.2	33.3
Jones	12.6	8.5	6.7	51.3	64 958	67 761	4.3	0.8	4 221	3 094	-530	24 677	2.69	72.8	16.3	23.7
Kemper	13.1	8.9	7.8	50.0	10 453	10 456	0.0	-2.8	377	411	-275	3 605	2.64	63.3	17.3	35.0
Lafayette	9.6	6.5	4.6	51.1	38 744	47 351	22.2	11.8	2 392	1 543	4 531	15 743	2.77	59.2	13.9	31.5
Lamar	10.8	6.8	4.5	51.8	39 070	55 658	42.5	7.9	3 446	1 569	2 455	21 678	2.60	70.0	15.0	23.0
Lauderdale	12.6	8.1	6.7	51.5	78 161	80 261	2.7	-0.7	4 415	3 556	-1 291	29 809	2.56	67.6	21.2	29.2
Lawrence	13.8	9.2	6.4	50.8	13 258	12 929	-2.5	-3.3	642	572	-487	4 830	2.63	72.1	13.3	25.4
Leake	11.8	7.9	6.2	48.0	20 940	23 805	13.7	-2.6	1 269	1 118	-758	8 069	2.77	72.2	20.4	25.8
Lee	11.6	7.9	6.0	52.1	75 755	82 910	9.4	2.8	4 924	3 929	1 248	31 898	2.59	71.1	18.3	25.4
Leflore	11.6	6.6	5.7	51.9	37 947	32 317	-14.8	-2.8	2 081	1 520	-1 472	10 887	2.77	64.7	31.2	32.8
Lincoln	13.0	8.5	6.6	52.2	33 166	34 869	5.1	-0.3	1 949	1 632	-394	13 045	2.62	75.3	19.6	22.8
Lowndes	12.5	7.8	6.2	52.4	61 586	59 779	-2.9	-0.1	3 444	2 360	-1 104	23 178	2.51	65.3	17.0	30.5
Madison	12.4	6.9	4.9	51.9	74 674	95 203	27.5	6.8	5 391	4 333	5 209	36 342	2.63	69.9	14.2	26.4
Marion	12.8	8.8	7.2	51.6	25 595	27 088	5.8	-4.5	1 468	1 480	-1 235	9 985	2.58	70.6	16.2	27.2
Marshall	14.3	8.7	5.7	50.7	34 993	37 144	6.1	-2.4	1 904	1 760	-1 063	13 050	2.67	70.7	20.4	25.6
Monroe	13.4	9.8	7.5	52.0	38 014	36 989	-2.7	-2.7	1 803	1 662	-1 078	13 960	2.60	73.1	16.9	24.7
Montgomery	13.9	10.4	7.8	52.2	12 189	10 925	-10.4	-4.8	574	612	-497	4 229	2.51	68.5	21.2	30.1
Neshoba	12.4	7.8	6.4	52.3	28 684	29 676	3.5	-0.7	1 811	1 382	-620	10 829	2.69	70.4	19.9	27.2
Newton	12.0	8.9	7.1	51.9	21 838	21 720	-0.5	0.5	1 196	1 139	23	7 931	2.64	76.8	17.0	21.6
Noxubee	13.4	8.2	6.6	51.6	12 548	11 545	-8.0	-3.7	646	514	-634	4 194	2.66	72.3	29.3	24.7
Oktibbeha	8.9	5.5	4.4	50.3	42 902	47 671	11.1	3.7	2 385	1 244	539	18 176	2.42	53.6	14.9	33.1
Panola	12.7	8.2	5.7	51.7	34 274	34 707	1.3	-0.7	2 172	1 692	-720	11 928	2.86	66.5	20.7	30.6
Pearl River	13.5	10.1	6.4	50.7	48 621	55 834	14.8	-0.9	2 754	2 501	-799	20 556	2.65	72.8	15.3	23.4
Perry	13.2	10.1	6.5	51.2	12 138	12 250	0.9	-0.2	645	521	-203	4 483	2.69	74.3	17.3	24.0
Pike	12.9	8.6	6.7	52.6	38 940	40 404	3.8	-0.9	2 455	2 066	-724	14 614	2.70	66.5	19.8	29.4
Pontotoc	11.7	7.7	6.0	50.4	26 726	29 957	12.1	3.3	1 876	1 102	219	9 937	3.01	71.8	15.9	25.1
Prentiss	12.1	9.4	7.2	50.7	25 556	25 276	-1.1	0.6	1 429	1 065	-174	9 611	2.53	71.5	17.0	26.4
Quitman	13.2	8.8	6.2	52.3	10 117	8 223	-18.7	-6.6	462	456	-584	3 114	2.53	67.0	23.8	28.7
Rankin	12.0	7.8	5.1	51.7	115 327	141 617	22.8	4.2	8 154	4 492	2 324	53 223	2.60	72.7	14.7	23.0
Scott	12.1	7.5	5.8	51.1	28 423	28 264	-0.6	0.7	1 877	1 199	-456	9 692	2.88	72.2	19.6	24.6
Sharkey	15.3	8.1	7.3	53.6	6 580	4 916	-25.3	-5.5	308	216	-353	1 725	2.75	68.3	26.1	28.7
Simpson	13.3	8.7	6.5	51.3	27 639	27 503	-0.5	-0.1	1 442	1 189	-257	9 786	2.72	71.6	15.6	26.5
Smith	13.5	9.8	7.2	51.9	16 182	16 491	1.9	-1.8	828	648	-452	6 269	2.60	74.4	17.4	24.5
Stone	12.6	8.5	5.1	49.9	13 622	17 786	30.6	0.5	864	725	-84	5 871	2.88	73.1	11.1	21.8

1. No spouse present.

STATE County	Persons in group quarters, 2014	Daytime population, 2009–2013: Number	Daytime population, 2009–2013: Employ-ment/ resi-dence ratio	Births, 2014: Total	Births, 2014: Rate[1]	Deaths, 2014: Number	Deaths, 2014: Rate[1]	Persons under 65 with no health insurance, 2013: Number	Persons under 65 with no health insurance, 2013: Percent	Medicare, 2014: Eligible for Medicare	Medicare, 2014: Enrolled in Medicare Advantage	Medicare, 2014: Enrolled in a Medicare prescription drug plan	Serious crimes known to police,[2] 2013: Total: Number	Serious crimes known to police,[2] 2013: Total: Rate[3]
	32	33	34	35	36	37	38	39	40	41	42	43	44	45
MISSISSIPPI	96 334	2 930 082	0.96	38 206	12.8	29 573	9.9	497 103	20.0	553 275	74 639	314 138	89 714	2 999
Adams	2 548	33 027	1.07	341	10.7	411	13.0	5 204	21.4	6 878	918	4 111	1 503	4 698
Alcorn	744	37 462	1.02	446	11.9	431	11.5	6 001	19.7	8 821	232	6 574	NA	NA
Amite	116	10 564	0.44	124	9.8	149	11.8	2 347	23.0	3 044	313	1 912	NA	NA
Attala	344	17 732	0.75	255	13.3	258	13.5	3 025	19.4	4 305	527	2 451	NA	NA
Benton	78	6 949	0.42	77	9.3	90	10.8	1 546	22.0	1 865	210	1 260	NA	NA
Bolivar	1 679	33 626	0.96	551	16.3	418	12.4	5 573	19.9	6 804	489	4 442	815	3 083
Calhoun	214	13 267	0.71	160	10.9	175	11.9	2 912	24.0	3 492	225	2 406	NA	NA
Carroll	379	8 252	0.31	76	7.4	103	10.0	1 879	23.7	2 569	75	1 726	NA	NA
Chickasaw	487	16 988	0.93	243	14.0	186	10.7	3 051	21.3	3 943	427	2 570	NA	NA
Choctaw	122	7 514	0.68	82	9.9	102	12.3	1 366	20.2	1 719	138	1 137	75	905
Claiborne	1 016	9 936	1.14	103	11.3	97	10.7	1 394	20.2	1 709	350	1 012	217	2 336
Clarke	52	14 139	0.59	186	11.4	181	11.1	2 740	20.5	3 914	393	2 404	NA	NA
Clay	303	19 446	0.85	238	11.8	228	11.3	3 623	21.4	4 296	467	2 748	456	2 237
Coahoma	664	26 290	1.06	396	16.0	291	11.7	4 097	19.0	4 874	278	3 525	NA	NA
Copiah	979	26 859	0.77	347	12.0	307	10.7	4 922	20.5	5 765	1 348	2 823	NA	NA
Covington	239	17 699	0.74	271	13.9	209	10.7	3 623	22.5	4 002	644	2 267	NA	NA
DeSoto	609	136 796	0.65	2 085	12.2	1 236	7.2	25 174	17.1	24 377	3 650	12 495	3 455	2 261
Forrest	3 559	87 016	1.34	1 049	13.7	728	9.5	13 754	21.4	12 580	2 237	6 647	NA	NA
Franklin	67	6 859	0.61	90	11.5	69	8.8	1 380	21.3	1 803	109	1 070	54	732
George	573	19 652	0.62	355	15.2	222	9.5	3 852	19.9	4 156	786	2 165	70	350
Greene	3 112	12 555	0.53	135	9.4	121	8.4	2 034	21.7	2 440	207	1 455	20	144
Grenada	255	22 910	1.14	248	11.4	246	11.4	3 412	19.0	5 119	537	3 286	342	1 582
Hancock	549	44 692	1.01	459	10.0	411	8.9	8 546	22.8	8 451	2 143	3 583	773	1 975
Harrison	5 410	204 926	1.16	2 769	13.9	1 704	8.6	35 499	21.4	33 520	5 194	13 494	8 480	4 322
Hinds	8 328	267 806	1.21	3 214	13.2	2 039	8.4	41 107	19.6	38 863	9 359	18 297	12 935	5 849
Holmes	906	17 438	0.73	266	14.4	247	13.4	3 195	20.6	3 832	338	2 710	NA	NA
Humphreys	82	9 034	0.92	120	13.7	116	13.3	1 593	20.7	1 840	158	1 284	NA	NA
Issaquena	305	1 342	0.86	14	10.0	9	6.4	198	22.3	161	15	110	NA	NA
Itawamba	947	19 831	0.61	297	12.6	238	10.1	3 759	20.1	5 365	205	3 747	366	1 569
Jackson	1 335	136 564	0.94	1 513	10.7	1 298	9.2	23 836	20.0	25 114	5 363	10 764	4 751	3 381
Jasper	87	15 264	0.75	259	15.6	171	10.3	2 822	21.1	3 773	496	2 229	NA	NA
Jefferson	411	7 238	0.76	127	16.7	75	9.9	1 336	21.4	1 547	214	968	53	885
Jefferson Davis	111	10 401	0.58	140	11.8	155	13.1	2 272	23.5	2 593	195	1 646	NA	NA
Jones	1 853	70 265	1.08	975	14.3	791	11.6	12 018	21.0	13 571	1 925	7 871	1 761	2 773
Kemper	917	10 168	0.94	77	7.6	100	9.8	1 879	24.4	1 995	199	1 157	97	1 057
Lafayette	6 549	50 051	1.06	597	11.3	386	7.3	8 218	20.6	6 761	462	4 410	NA	NA
Lamar	311	50 009	0.75	846	14.1	333	5.5	9 414	18.3	8 282	1 373	4 205	945	1 684
Lauderdale	3 947	85 421	1.16	1 034	13.0	817	10.2	12 026	18.5	14 401	1 285	8 269	3 288	4 099
Lawrence	0	11 100	0.64	133	10.6	133	10.6	2 147	20.5	3 104	277	1 933	NA	NA
Leake	1 921	21 842	0.78	281	12.1	282	12.2	4 812	26.5	4 245	644	2 449	NA	NA
Lee	1 060	98 387	1.40	1 134	13.3	1 003	11.8	12 694	17.5	16 130	950	10 702	NA	NA
Leflore	2 048	35 189	1.34	454	14.4	356	11.3	5 529	21.2	5 784	196	4 278	1 484	4 863
Lincoln	705	33 936	0.93	452	13.0	378	10.9	5 911	20.3	7 094	759	4 417	417	1 194
Lowndes	1 315	61 469	1.07	827	13.8	562	9.4	9 546	19.0	11 067	1 018	6 493	617	1 035
Madison	1 779	98 654	1.03	1 286	12.6	1 099	10.8	13 268	15.4	14 994	2 575	7 750	1 133	1 313
Marion	732	26 175	0.94	331	12.8	324	12.5	4 619	21.6	5 581	859	3 347	519	1 977
Marshall	1 847	30 124	0.52	446	12.3	429	11.8	6 659	22.6	7 058	1 171	3 915	NA	NA
Monroe	405	33 648	0.78	435	12.1	388	10.8	6 042	20.4	8 238	562	5 403	NA	NA
Montgomery	99	10 398	0.90	145	13.9	122	11.7	1 795	20.8	2 607	65	1 872	NA	NA
Neshoba	393	29 710	1.00	421	14.3	343	11.6	5 923	23.5	5 581	443	3 515	NA	NA
Newton	553	19 349	0.73	264	12.1	302	13.8	3 877	21.8	4 677	506	2 724	NA	NA
Noxubee	171	10 866	0.87	151	13.6	134	12.1	2 235	24.0	2 464	72	1 829	NA	NA
Oktibbeha	4 814	49 499	1.07	567	11.5	355	7.2	7 920	20.0	6 269	531	3 972	964	1 992
Panola	315	33 383	0.90	510	14.8	397	11.5	6 191	21.0	6 840	890	4 165	1 216	3 605
Pearl River	1 226	47 698	0.62	613	11.1	596	10.8	9 584	21.4	12 394	2 672	5 715	NA	NA
Perry	101	10 833	0.66	149	12.2	115	9.4	2 208	21.9	2 502	341	1 528	NA	NA
Pike	887	42 318	1.14	558	13.9	511	12.8	6 452	19.4	8 317	1 379	4 837	1 019	2 709
Pontotoc	237	28 553	0.87	467	15.1	241	7.8	5 674	21.4	5 871	515	3 787	NA	NA
Prentiss	874	23 250	0.77	325	12.8	207	8.1	4 397	21.5	5 567	175	3 909	NA	NA
Quitman	164	7 041	0.60	107	13.9	103	13.4	1 485	22.7	1 698	96	1 224	NA	NA
Rankin	5 447	134 584	0.86	1 864	12.6	1 082	7.3	18 902	15.5	24 360	4 379	11 939	1 805	1 310
Scott	228	28 901	1.06	423	14.9	303	10.6	6 376	26.2	5 331	925	3 120	398	1 767
Sharkey	108	4 875	0.99	65	14.0	45	9.7	804	20.3	1 053	78	733	NA	NA
Simpson	631	25 055	0.76	329	12.0	291	10.6	4 923	21.5	5 420	779	3 179	167	672
Smith	107	14 067	0.62	192	11.9	163	10.1	2 896	21.7	3 334	444	1 843	NA	NA
Stone	1 415	15 998	0.73	189	10.6	161	9.0	2 981	21.0	3 313	687	1 526	263	1 454

1. Per 1,000 estimated resident population. 2. Data for serious crimes have not been adjusted for underreporting; this may affect comparability between geographic areas and over time.
3. Per 100,000 population estimated by the FBI.

Table B. States and Counties — **Crime, Education, Money Income, and Poverty**

STATE County	Serious crimes known to police, 2013 (cont.)[1]		Education						Money income, 2009–2013				Income and poverty, 2013			
	Rate[2]		School enrollment and attainment, 2009–2013				Local government expenditures,[5] 2012–2013			Households				Percent below poverty level		
			Enrollment[3]		Attainment[4] (percent)											
	Violent	Property	Total	Percent private	High school graduate or less	Bachelor's degree or more	Total current spending (mil dol)	Current spending per student (dollars)	Per capita income[6] (dollars)	Median income (dollars)	Mean income (dollars)	Percent with income of $200,000 or more	Median household income (dollars)	All persons	Children under 18 years	Children 5 to 17 years in families
	46	47	48	49	50	51	52	53	54	55	56	57	58	59	60	61
MISSISSIPPI	275	2 725	812 513	12.7	49.0	20.1	4 023.6	8 130	20 618	39 031	54 132	2.1	38 191	23.9	34.0	32.4
Adams	234	4 464	7 957	10.3	55.2	17.5	35.7	9 469	17 544	27 381	42 991	1.6	31 385	30.9	44.3	41.8
Alcorn	NA	NA	8 750	7.6	56.0	17.4	46.3	7 703	19 145	33 600	46 875	1.2	33 467	24.8	31.8	29.1
Amite	NA	NA	2 620	34.8	60.6	11.6	11.1	10 290	16 977	30 750	40 299	0.7	33 571	24.1	36.8	36.6
Attala	NA	NA	4 768	14.9	55.2	16.0	28.1	7 991	18 422	31 641	47 067	1.5	31 644	26.7	37.9	37.4
Benton	NA	NA	2 080	8.1	63.1	9.9	11.5	9 145	18 597	31 060	47 177	2.0	30 198	27.8	39.6	36.4
Bolivar	235	2 849	10 609	6.8	52.2	21.2	59.2	9 146	16 462	28 599	43 223	0.8	29 622	37.7	55.8	54.9
Calhoun	NA	NA	3 440	9.9	63.9	9.5	18.8	7 352	17 034	30 000	40 832	0.6	32 656	25.8	36.3	35.9
Carroll	NA	NA	2 421	27.9	60.4	12.3	8.5	8 496	16 897	31 039	44 656	0.7	37 283	18.7	28.5	26.1
Chickasaw	NA	NA	4 460	4.8	64.7	10.0	25.2	8 267	16 677	31 061	42 007	0.9	32 525	24.4	33.2	30.8
Choctaw	36	869	2 178	11.7	55.1	12.6	14.8	9 752	17 145	29 876	41 118	0.1	32 922	25.9	37.3	34.4
Claiborne	345	1 992	3 233	7.5	49.8	18.6	16.4	9 607	12 177	23 689	34 353	0.1	25 438	40.9	52.1	52.1
Clarke	NA	NA	4 066	8.5	58.4	11.7	23.3	7 646	18 066	31 362	45 175	0.1	34 141	21.8	31.2	29.4
Clay	270	1 967	5 998	13.5	52.8	17.9	28.0	8 134	18 273	30 764	46 355	2.0	30 935	31.0	47.7	50.1
Coahoma	NA	NA	8 192	10.8	50.2	17.5	46.1	9 335	15 742	26 407	41 755	1.5	27 500	39.5	55.9	53.7
Copiah	NA	NA	7 905	15.3	53.9	13.5	36.1	7 875	18 318	35 421	50 020	1.8	32 060	29.6	42.5	41.0
Covington	NA	NA	5 051	7.3	57.9	14.2	24.4	8 002	17 241	33 381	43 775	0.5	32 999	28.2	41.1	38.2
DeSoto	183	2 077	46 996	12.9	42.0	21.6	212.5	6 488	25 176	58 505	69 296	2.0	59 043	12.0	16.4	15.4
Forrest	NA	NA	23 998	13.3	43.7	27.0	105.9	9 160	19 736	36 726	51 397	1.5	34 391	28.0	37.7	37.4
Franklin	122	610	2 024	13.9	60.0	11.3	13.4	8 900	24 234	32 372	60 452	1.8	35 963	23.1	34.4	30.3
George	35	315	5 402	9.6	60.4	10.3	28.3	6 740	20 217	43 958	55 609	1.0	43 597	18.8	25.7	24.6
Greene	94	51	3 063	4.9	65.2	7.8	17.0	7 927	14 463	36 888	46 104	0.5	38 192	23.7	25.8	23.2
Grenada	180	1 401	5 882	12.0	53.3	14.7	31.7	7 318	21 084	34 129	53 882	2.0	31 703	25.2	35.9	35.3
Hancock	89	1 886	10 512	14.8	45.3	22.0	53.9	8 377	22 621	44 522	56 211	1.2	43 870	20.2	30.5	27.9
Harrison	321	4 002	47 036	16.8	43.5	20.7	251.0	8 305	22 677	43 124	57 651	2.0	41 657	22.7	35.4	34.3
Hinds	766	5 083	77 678	16.6	40.0	27.4	340.4	8 350	20 448	37 626	54 184	2.6	34 826	29.7	40.3	40.0
Holmes	NA	NA	5 905	8.0	62.2	12.7	30.1	8 322	12 113	22 325	32 373	0.3	22 674	45.7	62.1	60.8
Humphreys	NA	NA	2 629	7.6	63.9	10.9	14.5	8 234	12 874	23 600	35 566	1.6	22 599	48.3	64.7	63.2
Issaquena	NA	NA	233	22.3	76.6	5.3	NA	NA	13 731	24 767	38 090	0.7	31 254	42.5	56.4	56.5
Itawamba	86	1 483	5 812	5.6	55.3	13.5	26.0	7 246	18 106	36 073	47 093	0.2	39 927	19.4	27.0	24.4
Jackson	241	3 140	36 418	10.4	46.0	19.6	212.7	8 736	23 879	48 943	63 341	2.7	47 813	16.4	25.9	23.1
Jasper	NA	NA	4 123	12.5	58.3	12.9	22.7	9 163	18 075	31 170	43 376	1.6	33 606	24.2	33.3	33.3
Jefferson	334	551	2 165	1.6	57.2	19.9	12.2	8 836	12 723	26 028	35 928	0.0	26 401	35.4	49.7	50.1
Jefferson Davis	NA	NA	2 988	9.4	58.3	14.4	15.6	9 714	16 216	27 186	38 419	1.0	27 754	30.1	44.3	42.7
Jones	250	2 523	16 979	10.7	49.9	16.8	91.2	7 827	19 519	38 074	51 747	2.0	36 204	21.6	32.1	30.6
Kemper	44	1 013	2 681	10.8	59.6	10.4	11.6	9 880	13 795	29 003	37 377	0.8	30 849	30.4	41.4	37.8
Lafayette	NA	NA	19 903	4.1	35.5	37.2	57.4	8 811	21 388	43 328	60 598	4.0	40 749	27.8	29.7	26.5
Lamar	64	1 620	16 517	10.9	34.2	33.1	79.0	7 850	26 345	51 154	67 740	3.6	51 337	16.4	21.8	20.4
Lauderdale	337	3 762	21 356	9.8	46.0	18.9	107.9	8 305	21 346	36 203	54 754	2.5	35 038	26.2	38.8	34.7
Lawrence	NA	NA	3 183	7.7	55.7	12.9	18.4	8 494	20 655	38 393	52 819	1.7	36 317	20.2	27.4	26.9
Leake	NA	NA	6 187	16.2	61.6	10.7	22.2	7 105	16 780	32 521	47 712	2.3	34 099	27.9	48.2	43.1
Lee	NA	NA	20 763	11.1	45.5	21.8	127.1	8 185	21 799	42 074	56 266	2.2	43 221	18.0	26.3	24.9
Leflore	590	4 273	9 973	7.8	55.9	19.0	51.4	9 057	14 307	24 480	38 516	1.4	24 704	44.8	56.2	55.8
Lincoln	52	1 142	8 876	11.2	51.3	16.8	46.3	7 756	19 566	36 498	51 084	1.2	33 632	26.9	34.8	32.5
Lowndes	62	973	16 471	13.9	48.2	21.4	79.3	8 206	20 951	37 868	51 948	1.8	38 839	23.5	36.1	34.5
Madison	102	1 211	28 874	23.2	27.3	45.8	125.5	7 901	33 170	59 904	86 579	8.5	64 657	12.7	18.2	17.2
Marion	183	1 795	6 310	12.1	60.8	13.2	34.7	8 464	18 126	29 400	46 416	0.9	32 628	27.5	40.5	37.0
Marshall	NA	NA	8 297	18.8	64.0	11.2	38.1	7 704	17 978	36 022	48 795	1.3	36 728	23.4	36.3	34.5
Monroe	NA	NA	8 302	6.3	60.4	13.1	55.2	8 027	18 167	36 308	46 272	0.9	36 264	22.8	30.9	28.6
Montgomery	NA	NA	2 455	16.3	61.3	13.1	13.5	9 191	15 523	30 466	38 478	0.3	30 128	23.7	36.6	35.3
Neshoba	NA	NA	8 236	12.3	54.3	12.6	32.9	7 256	18 693	37 050	50 176	1.6	34 719	24.9	36.8	34.5
Newton	NA	NA	5 853	10.7	49.3	14.7	31.1	8 049	18 864	39 190	50 114	1.6	36 904	22.1	32.1	30.6
Noxubee	NA	NA	3 317	16.3	65.8	11.2	17.4	9 676	12 780	24 338	34 492	0.0	26 459	38.6	50.4	50.0
Oktibbeha	112	1 881	22 699	6.8	32.9	42.6	49.3	9 523	20 202	30 987	50 835	2.9	33 594	31.2	32.7	32.8
Panola	344	3 261	8 722	12.4	57.0	14.3	51.8	8 384	18 073	35 715	48 481	1.6	33 129	25.9	39.0	37.7
Pearl River	NA	NA	14 058	13.9	51.5	13.2	71.2	8 213	20 549	42 510	53 003	1.7	41 706	23.4	34.6	32.1
Perry	NA	NA	2 854	9.6	58.7	8.2	16.4	8 479	17 183	36 124	44 991	0.6	34 771	24.0	33.1	31.8
Pike	255	2 454	10 990	12.8	54.2	15.8	56.9	8 102	18 183	34 841	47 699	1.4	30 835	28.9	42.3	41.0
Pontotoc	NA	NA	7 890	4.9	60.0	12.0	42.0	7 184	18 576	39 899	50 256	0.7	40 245	16.3	23.9	23.0
Prentiss	NA	NA	6 178	4.0	61.4	11.4	29.2	7 941	16 589	32 503	42 192	0.4	34 219	21.1	31.7	30.7
Quitman	NA	NA	2 064	13.4	57.4	13.7	11.1	9 015	13 954	22 863	35 206	0.7	26 100	43.5	58.3	57.4
Rankin	71	1 239	36 976	18.4	39.1	28.5	179.7	7 680	26 897	57 380	71 123	3.0	55 838	11.6	16.7	15.7
Scott	493	1 274	6 961	10.5	63.8	9.6	39.4	7 175	16 789	34 534	46 595	1.7	31 850	27.2	39.2	40.7
Sharkey	NA	NA	1 383	19.5	55.2	21.1	10.4	11 328	15 744	25 125	43 316	0.3	27 380	38.5	57.9	57.1
Simpson	68	604	6 877	16.4	57.7	14.7	33.4	7 897	18 314	38 362	49 202	1.1	35 039	26.9	39.9	39.1
Smith	NA	NA	3 844	12.5	61.5	13.2	22.8	7 949	20 334	34 753	51 871	2.0	36 581	20.4	30.8	29.6
Stone	77	1 377	4 280	16.8	47.7	13.6	21.2	7 748	18 576	42 963	53 564	1.3	40 294	22.4	30.9	29.4

1. Data for serious crimes have not been adjusted for underreporting; this may affect comparability between geographic areas and over time. 2. Per 100,000 population estimated by the FBI.
3. All persons 3 years old and over enrolled in nursery school through college. 4. Persons 25 years old and over. 5. Elementary and secondary education expenditures.
6. Based on population estimated by the American Community Survey, 2009–2013.

STATE County	Personal income, 2013										Earnings, 2013		
	Total (mil dol)	Percent change, 2012–2013	Per capita[1]		Wages and salaries (mil dol)	Supplements to wages and salaries; employer contributions (mil dol)		Proprietors' income (mil dol)	Dividends, interest, and rent (mil dol)	Personal transfer receipts (mil dol)	Total (mil dol)	Contributions for government social insurance (mil dol)	
			Dollars	Rank		Pension and insurance	Government social insurance					From employee and self-employed	From employer
	62	63	64	65	66	67	68	69	70	71	72	73	74
MISSISSIPPI	101 442	1.6	33 913	X	44 434	7 282	3 396	10 608	14 824	25 334	65 719	4 128	3 396
Adams	1 147	2.2	35 735	1 793	416	60	31	171	197	325	679	45	31
Alcorn	1 089	0.4	29 195	2 782	481	76	38	70	161	357	665	48	38
Amite	397	4.8	30 753	2 587	64	11	5	65	46	127	144	11	5
Attala	544	3.3	28 185	2 878	160	28	12	68	70	186	269	19	12
Benton	206	2.5	24 074	3 079	47	10	4	18	22	80	79	6	4
Bolivar	1 142	-2.6	33 540	2 168	432	75	32	132	157	367	671	40	32
Calhoun	436	3.6	29 588	2 743	113	20	9	62	51	149	203	13	9
Carroll	376	-2.6	36 204	1 712	40	7	3	16	40	99	67	7	3
Chickasaw	492	0.6	28 397	2 857	192	30	16	49	64	166	287	20	16
Choctaw	244	5.4	29 103	2 794	87	16	6	23	31	78	132	9	6
Claiborne	267	-0.3	28 878	2 818	178	40	13	12	28	115	244	15	13
Clarke	491	1.1	29 926	2 699	115	20	9	36	59	172	178	14	9
Clay	669	4.6	32 781	2 287	199	30	15	127	111	191	371	21	15
Coahoma	881	2.0	34 994	1 896	317	48	24	115	124	305	503	30	24
Copiah	766	2.0	26 473	3 008	256	50	20	69	98	281	395	27	20
Covington	598	4.9	30 774	2 583	168	31	13	102	78	178	314	19	13
DeSoto	5 951	2.1	35 374	1 842	1 830	256	140	559	590	930	2 786	179	140
Forrest	2 424	1.3	31 461	2 486	1 576	272	118	398	468	650	2 364	141	118
Franklin	231	2.3	29 104	2 793	65	13	5	14	31	82	97	7	5
George	614	2.8	26 527	3 006	167	30	13	33	79	171	243	18	13
Greene	347	3.4	24 331	3 073	67	15	5	40	35	108	127	9	5
Grenada	670	0.9	30 982	2 551	350	58	27	46	89	231	481	33	27
Hancock	1 551	0.8	34 029	2 075	729	131	58	151	309	353	1 069	67	58
Harrison	7 013	0.7	35 688	1 802	3 827	699	310	480	1 371	1 528	5 316	313	310
Hinds	9 203	-0.3	37 578	1 493	5 889	962	432	1 548	1 486	2 020	8 831	524	432
Holmes	519	-1.0	28 154	2 880	126	23	10	50	55	237	208	14	10
Humphreys	290	0.7	32 452	2 345	84	15	7	59	40	101	165	9	7
Issaquena	63	-17.1	45 199	677	6	1	0	30	8	9	38	1	0
Itawamba	750	1.0	32 024	2 409	209	34	16	53	83	230	312	24	16
Jackson	5 043	2.2	35 906	1 762	2 618	484	201	222	822	1 061	3 526	221	201
Jasper	534	3.9	32 398	2 352	158	28	12	59	68	165	256	17	12
Jefferson	214	-5.0	27 992	2 901	44	10	3	27	22	87	85	5	3
Jefferson Davis	354	5.6	29 641	2 736	60	11	5	45	39	123	121	8	5
Jones	2 412	1.7	34 973	1 900	1 203	208	87	275	314	681	1 773	111	87
Kemper	448	31.3	43 540	797	290	39	24	20	35	112	372	23	24
Lafayette	1 722	2.4	33 549	2 166	827	143	60	207	300	333	1 236	74	60
Lamar	2 100	0.8	35 707	1 798	592	87	45	72	310	343	796	54	45
Lauderdale	2 808	1.6	34 992	1 897	1 424	234	113	175	519	691	1 946	123	113
Lawrence	437	6.8	34 888	1 917	117	19	8	57	41	137	202	13	8
Leake	620	7.5	26 509	3 007	164	29	14	100	61	193	307	18	14
Lee	3 005	-0.7	35 208	1 871	2 037	282	158	277	430	658	2 753	174	158
Leflore	989	-3.5	31 300	2 510	507	90	39	129	180	330	766	45	39
Lincoln	1 016	1.9	29 195	2 782	426	63	32	99	131	314	620	43	32
Lowndes	2 210	2.1	36 882	1 613	1 270	204	97	178	360	492	1 749	107	97
Madison	5 635	3.5	56 116	186	2 388	295	175	888	962	621	3 745	224	175
Marion	821	4.1	31 376	2 496	301	45	23	102	104	266	471	31	23
Marshall	1 025	1.5	28 070	2 890	221	34	17	62	95	306	334	26	17
Monroe	1 072	0.2	29 671	2 729	372	63	29	88	140	333	553	40	29
Montgomery	318	1.4	30 095	2 675	89	16	7	23	48	116	135	10	7
Neshoba	1 135	3.6	38 459	1 378	457	74	34	247	156	266	812	46	34
Newton	639	3.6	29 484	2 754	201	37	15	57	82	218	311	21	15
Noxubee	343	7.4	30 955	2 559	80	16	6	87	38	116	189	10	6
Oktibbeha	1 454	2.0	29 653	2 735	728	144	54	106	253	306	1 032	62	54
Panola	1 035	1.3	30 081	2 678	402	65	31	131	116	311	629	41	31
Pearl River	1 658	1.1	30 112	2 671	361	68	27	105	232	514	561	45	27
Perry	300	2.1	24 717	3 064	100	15	7	10	35	116	132	10	7
Pike	1 158	1.7	28 934	2 813	495	87	38	83	161	388	702	48	38
Pontotoc	851	0.9	27 558	2 929	385	55	32	77	87	227	550	37	32
Prentiss	640	-0.3	25 193	3 049	235	41	18	23	82	231	318	24	18
Quitman	234	-5.9	30 049	2 683	41	8	3	38	26	91	90	5	3
Rankin	5 681	2.0	38 705	1 337	2 447	350	182	448	695	1 041	3 426	217	182
Scott	799	5.5	28 269	2 870	409	71	34	85	79	246	599	36	34
Sharkey	174	-3.3	36 930	1 598	41	7	3	34	24	58	85	4	3
Simpson	957	4.6	34 803	1 931	233	40	18	112	89	283	403	25	18
Smith	473	8.0	29 133	2 789	109	20	9	77	47	145	215	12	9
Stone	507	-0.9	28 129	2 883	138	24	10	13	62	166	186	14	10

1. Based on the resident population estimated as of July 1 of the year shown.

STATE County	Earnings, 2013 (cont.): Percent by selected industries: Farm	Mining	Construction	Manu-facturing	Infor-mation: professional, scientific, technical services	Retail trade	Finance, insur-ance, real estate and leasing	Health care and social assistance	Govern-ment	Social Security beneficiaries, December 2013: Number	Rate[1]	Supple-mental Security Income recipients, December 2013	Housing units, 2014: Total	Percent change, 2010–2014
	75	76	77	78	79	80	81	82	83	84	85	86	87	88
MISSISSIPPI	3.5	2.0	6.8	12.3	5.4	7.4	5.6	10.7	22.0	632 191	211	126 240	1 294 721	1.6
Adams	3.1	12.6	5.6	3.7	4.5	9.5	4.6	D	14.0	7 855	245	1 902	14 617	-0.3
Alcorn	1.3	0.0	4.5	19.4	2.5	11.1	4.6	10.8	22.2	10 295	276	1 786	17 106	0.2
Amite	12.3	2.2	6.3	8.2	D	7.7	4.4	D	13.0	3 465	269	770	6 632	0.0
Attala	2.1	0.5	15.1	10.6	3.3	11.8	4.3	D	21.0	4 925	255	1 023	9 126	0.0
Benton	9.6	0.0	4.5	9.2	D	D	D	6.9	25.4	2 165	255	517	4 195	0.2
Bolivar	14.6	0.0	3.3	13.1	D	12.0	3.2	13.5	18.7	7 975	234	3 133	14 301	1.6
Calhoun	20.3	0.0	1.6	20.1	2.3	8.3	D	D	18.0	4 030	273	784	6 923	0.1
Carroll	6.6	D	15.2	11.8	D	4.4	D	D	23.8	2 885	279	553	5 060	0.2
Chickasaw	6.5	0.0	2.6	41.6	1.7	8.1	2.7	D	14.5	4 495	260	904	7 507	-0.1
Choctaw	4.9	D	3.2	9.4	D	4.4	D	D	14.9	2 020	241	411	4 154	0.1
Claiborne	2.8	0.0	3.9	2.5	1.3	2.7	D	D	32.3	2 090	228	731	4 221	0.0
Clarke	3.7	11.1	7.7	12.3	1.9	7.1	D	D	18.9	4 580	279	789	7 874	0.0
Clay	22.3	D	5.1	11.1	3.9	8.6	3.8	D	11.6	4 890	240	1 132	9 194	0.2
Coahoma	17.1	0.0	2.3	6.7	4.5	7.4	7.6	D	18.4	5 675	226	2 227	10 750	-0.4
Copiah	5.2	2.5	3.8	28.8	D	7.4	2.7	D	19.3	6 645	231	1 516	12 113	-0.6
Covington	16.4	0.6	9.0	15.6	D	5.8	2.6	D	18.7	4 670	240	1 011	8 505	0.1
DeSoto	0.8	D	9.5	8.8	3.2	10.4	5.3	12.4	12.5	27 210	162	2 721	63 932	3.7
Forrest	0.7	0.9	5.5	6.9	4.5	8.0	5.4	17.0	28.4	14 445	188	2 944	32 602	1.0
Franklin	3.4	D	7.1	3.8	11.1	4.8	D	D	34.3	2 075	263	373	4 157	0.1
George	1.7	D	10.2	8.8	4.6	12.0	3.9	5.5	29.3	4 850	209	681	9 357	0.3
Greene	12.1	1.8	D	D	D	6.6	D	4.6	36.7	2 800	197	454	5 123	0.0
Grenada	1.3	0.0	2.0	27.2	D	10.2	4.4	D	20.7	5 950	276	1 394	10 188	0.3
Hancock	-0.1	0.6	7.7	8.1	12.0	5.2	2.9	D	34.9	9 390	206	1 309	23 604	7.9
Harrison	0.0	D	6.1	5.7	5.2	7.3	4.9	7.6	34.7	37 305	190	6 046	89 749	5.4
Hinds	0.2	4.0	3.8	2.7	8.7	5.3	10.3	14.6	29.2	44 465	181	11 133	104 082	0.6
Holmes	17.4	D	2.1	10.6	D	6.6	7.4	D	27.1	4 460	238	2 036	8 415	0.0
Humphreys	25.2	0.0	2.6	19.0	D	4.6	6.2	D	12.3	2 125	238	1 050	3 832	-0.6
Issaquena	77.9	0.0	D	0.0	D	D	D	D	8.4	190	134	64	558	-0.4
Itawamba	3.1	D	11.7	26.7	1.3	6.6	2.4	D	18.6	6 355	271	701	10 167	0.4
Jackson	0.0	0.3	12.0	35.3	5.4	4.6	2.9	6.2	18.1	28 975	207	3 434	61 115	1.7
Jasper	12.4	4.9	4.3	27.4	5.3	5.3	2.9	D	17.1	4 450	269	909	8 217	0.1
Jefferson	29.0	D	1.8	D	D	D	D	9.0	32.4	1 845	242	717	3 677	0.1
Jefferson Davis	20.9	1.4	18.3	1.0	D	6.9	D	D	23.2	2 995	251	640	5 879	0.1
Jones	3.2	15.2	7.0	18.6	3.1	5.6	3.8	4.6	18.8	15 545	226	2 793	28 638	0.8
Kemper	1.6	D	65.9	4.1	D	1.5	D	D	8.3	2 245	218	583	4 732	0.2
Lafayette	0.5	D	5.5	7.0	9.1	6.6	6.6	13.8	34.7	7 480	144	1 018	23 978	5.5
Lamar	1.7	1.3	5.8	3.3	D	15.0	6.9	20.0	14.0	9 360	159	1 151	24 261	0.8
Lauderdale	0.1	D	4.1	7.5	4.5	8.8	5.1	20.4	21.8	16 265	202	3 253	34 945	0.7
Lawrence	17.6	0.8	8.6	29.1	D	5.5	D	3.8	16.2	3 565	285	575	6 034	0.2
Leake	21.3	0.2	D	D	1.6	9.0	D	D	12.8	4 995	214	987	9 419	0.1
Lee	0.6	0.0	3.2	19.5	6.4	8.8	5.9	19.2	10.3	18 735	219	2 937	36 216	1.0
Leflore	8.2	D	7.6	10.8	5.2	6.8	3.5	8.3	27.8	6 730	213	2 773	13 162	-0.3
Lincoln	2.7	3.6	8.7	8.4	3.2	10.2	4.2	14.6	12.7	8 170	235	1 488	15 274	0.1
Lowndes	1.6	0.5	14.1	16.6	3.0	7.5	3.8	11.4	20.3	12 500	209	2 442	27 014	1.7
Madison	0.3	6.0	6.3	13.8	13.7	7.4	11.9	8.0	6.5	16 025	160	2 243	41 147	6.7
Marion	7.1	10.2	10.1	5.1	3.4	9.2	4.3	D	14.2	6 575	251	1 274	11 840	0.0
Marshall	5.4	0.0	11.8	9.9	D	8.6	6.9	D	19.0	8 100	222	1 747	15 038	1.1
Monroe	4.2	1.9	11.8	27.2	1.9	6.7	2.9	D	13.9	9 395	260	1 486	16 443	-0.1
Montgomery	5.1	0.0	5.3	2.2	3.5	8.7	D	D	24.3	2 960	281	671	5 419	4.3
Neshoba	8.5	D	30.0	3.4	1.4	6.3	2.0	D	32.8	6 500	221	1 187	12 359	0.0
Newton	11.3	D	5.7	15.6	D	7.0	2.1	D	29.3	5 280	243	896	9 371	0.0
Noxubee	34.3	D	3.7	13.8	D	6.9	D	D	19.9	2 660	240	1 002	5 167	-0.1
Oktibbeha	1.2	0.0	3.5	7.8	4.2	6.0	3.3	6.5	50.0	6 890	140	1 614	21 292	1.6
Panola	6.7	0.1	6.3	14.8	7.7	9.6	4.4	D	17.1	8 110	235	2 156	14 718	0.2
Pearl River	-0.1	0.3	10.4	9.4	D	12.8	5.5	D	28.8	13 980	254	1 968	24 552	2.6
Perry	5.4	0.4	2.2	34.3	2.1	4.7	D	9.1	17.4	3 050	252	605	5 521	0.0
Pike	1.1	1.4	2.5	13.6	3.3	12.6	5.3	8.9	27.5	9 435	236	2 322	17 891	0.2
Pontotoc	2.3	0.0	3.6	47.5	2.9	5.9	2.5	D	10.9	6 895	224	972	12 551	0.9
Prentiss	1.1	0.0	5.6	23.0	5.1	7.2	3.8	D	23.1	6 420	252	891	11 074	0.2
Quitman	33.0	D	1.0	2.9	D	3.5	4.3	D	18.3	1 880	240	756	3 595	0.2
Rankin	1.1	1.6	9.6	7.1	4.6	9.4	8.4	11.3	14.5	26 870	183	2 818	58 210	3.1
Scott	10.2	0.1	5.0	44.1	D	6.0	2.4	D	11.6	6 190	219	1 388	11 481	0.1
Sharkey	45.0	0.1	0.9	0.0	D	6.3	3.2	D	21.8	1 210	258	470	2 122	1.0
Simpson	16.3	0.7	4.7	2.1	2.7	7.7	4.8	D	18.2	6 185	225	1 320	11 934	0.0
Smith	29.7	D	2.5	24.3	2.9	2.9	D	0.8	13.3	3 905	241	694	7 244	0.1
Stone	0.2	D	2.6	17.9	3.6	9.3	3.9	D	29.2	3 795	211	550	7 238	1.1

1. Per 1,000 resident population estimated as of July 1 of the year shown.

STATE County	Housing units, 2009–2013: Occupied units: Total	Owner-occupied: Percent	Owner-occupied: Median value[1]	Median owner cost as a percent of income: With a mortgage	Median owner cost as a percent of income: Without a mortgage[2]	Renter-occupied: Median rent[3]	Renter-occupied: Median rent as a percent of income[2]	Substandard units[4] (percent)	Civilian labor force, 2014: Total	Percent change, 2013–2014	Unemployment: Total	Unemployment: Rate[5]	Civilian employment,[6] 2009–2013: Total	Percent: Management, business, science and arts	Percent: Construction, production, and maintenance occupations
	89	90	91	92	93	94	95	96	97	98	99	100	101	102	103
MISSISSIPPI	1 088 073	69.4	99 900	22.8	11.9	702	32.1	3.4	1 236 310	-2.9	96 343	7.8	1 194 436	30.8	27.5
Adams	12 087	68.0	80 900	26.6	14.0	585	34.2	2.3	11 485	-3.0	978	8.5	10 709	29.3	23.1
Alcorn	14 679	71.1	84 300	22.4	11.7	597	29.4	2.9	15 044	-2.3	1 021	6.8	14 953	31.2	27.7
Amite	5 212	85.3	70 300	27.2	13.9	629	37.5	3.6	4 478	-1.6	365	8.2	4 530	22.8	35.3
Attala	7 185	73.6	71 200	23.2	11.8	563	28.4	4.8	7 039	-3.0	655	9.3	6 849	30.1	35.0
Benton	3 195	81.7	81 200	27.4	13.8	606	50.0	4.7	3 049	-2.8	287	9.4	3 004	23.3	40.7
Bolivar	12 301	56.4	83 500	24.1	12.7	575	31.3	2.2	13 180	-4.5	1 327	10.1	12 364	31.8	24.4
Calhoun	5 944	70.5	61 500	22.2	12.3	501	29.4	1.5	6 212	-3.3	496	8.0	5 875	23.1	43.3
Carroll	3 757	83.2	68 800	17.8	16.6	604	41.3	3.4	3 387	-2.3	319	9.4	3 273	24.5	28.3
Chickasaw	6 614	73.2	64 600	26.9	11.4	501	32.4	4.8	7 163	-6.0	734	10.2	6 562	16.8	45.3
Choctaw	3 378	71.4	70 600	28.5	12.4	523	27.8	3.0	3 500	-6.6	300	8.6	2 980	29.5	37.1
Claiborne	3 190	80.0	54 500	28.0	16.1	490	37.1	3.5	3 113	-5.8	466	15.0	2 850	17.7	30.9
Clarke	6 305	84.1	59 900	23.2	13.4	613	31.2	3.9	6 232	-6.5	577	9.3	6 148	25.9	37.9
Clay	7 750	71.3	80 600	26.7	13.6	631	34.4	3.6	7 977	-5.0	1 123	14.1	7 382	25.1	32.6
Coahoma	9 464	53.3	55 600	24.7	13.8	574	30.9	4.3	9 493	-3.4	1 181	12.4	8 390	28.3	23.4
Copiah	9 897	76.3	74 100	22.4	12.2	613	29.3	1.9	11 138	-3.0	999	9.0	10 596	23.3	34.9
Covington	7 036	83.0	71 800	24.5	12.6	605	31.9	2.5	7 757	-2.5	516	6.7	7 022	21.4	39.2
DeSoto	57 979	75.1	152 600	22.0	10.0	936	27.7	2.7	79 242	-2.3	4 248	5.4	78 664	33.5	25.6
Forrest	27 822	56.5	117 500	23.3	12.4	694	34.7	2.0	32 467	-1.9	2 431	7.5	31 919	32.6	22.4
Franklin	3 311	79.6	63 700	21.2	10.4	539	31.8	4.1	2 868	-3.0	243	8.5	3 022	24.4	40.0
George	7 842	84.2	94 400	20.7	10.2	675	32.0	3.8	8 904	3.9	747	8.4	8 245	25.8	42.9
Greene	4 117	87.4	83 200	21.4	13.2	493	28.6	2.2	4 394	-1.1	401	9.1	3 847	25.1	38.5
Grenada	7 941	73.5	86 500	24.1	12.1	518	34.3	3.4	9 152	-2.1	681	7.4	8 393	26.6	36.6
Hancock	18 145	75.3	133 900	24.3	12.6	761	30.8	3.5	18 330	-3.3	1 360	7.4	18 260	30.0	27.6
Harrison	72 253	61.0	143 000	25.0	11.6	852	32.6	4.1	83 826	-3.4	5 863	7.0	82 983	28.7	23.1
Hinds	87 844	59.3	106 400	22.7	11.0	767	35.5	3.5	107 895	-2.5	7 945	7.4	104 507	32.4	20.3
Holmes	6 511	71.0	49 000	33.0	16.5	472	28.5	6.9	6 140	-2.7	973	15.8	5 774	22.7	39.2
Humphreys	3 107	54.3	63 000	27.8	15.5	544	38.8	2.4	2 576	-15.8	439	17.0	2 739	23.2	36.0
Issaquena	461	67.5	60 800	29.0	21.5	370	30.0	2.5	425	-4.5	78	18.4	320	14.4	42.8
Itawamba	8 859	79.0	79 300	21.2	11.3	617	31.1	2.6	9 764	-2.8	725	7.4	9 385	27.9	41.5
Jackson	50 007	70.8	123 300	22.9	10.8	853	31.5	3.8	58 908	-3.5	4 860	8.3	58 974	29.0	27.1
Jasper	7 015	79.3	72 700	25.7	14.2	627	25.8	2.0	6 283	-3.6	549	8.7	6 379	24.9	41.4
Jefferson	2 520	71.5	61 500	26.5	13.6	432	35.2	5.0	2 389	-3.8	396	16.6	1 979	29.8	25.2
Jefferson Davis	4 895	78.8	78 300	27.5	15.2	656	38.0	4.3	4 075	-3.3	432	10.6	4 407	24.3	36.3
Jones	24 677	73.5	84 200	22.2	11.9	641	29.2	2.5	26 472	-3.2	1 659	6.3	26 820	27.6	35.9
Kemper	3 605	76.1	65 500	26.4	15.2	442	30.9	2.7	3 765	-5.0	504	13.4	3 495	18.2	38.7
Lafayette	15 743	59.4	163 000	21.3	11.4	796	39.3	2.4	22 982	-0.2	1 425	6.2	20 889	36.4	20.1
Lamar	21 678	65.8	163 900	22.2	10.0	809	31.9	3.5	27 073	-1.7	1 407	5.2	26 721	38.3	21.5
Lauderdale	29 809	66.1	87 400	23.7	11.1	659	30.7	3.2	32 383	-6.5	2 547	7.9	32 099	31.7	23.6
Lawrence	4 830	80.0	79 600	20.1	13.7	591	26.0	5.0	4 506	-4.7	392	8.7	4 683	30.7	35.4
Leake	8 069	75.5	73 800	22.1	14.4	548	28.5	2.3	7 770	-4.3	572	7.4	8 114	27.5	37.3
Lee	31 898	70.9	108 300	22.9	11.0	638	30.4	4.9	38 580	-2.7	2 953	7.7	36 629	29.6	28.5
Leflore	10 887	50.7	69 200	24.1	14.0	564	35.7	2.9	10 490	-2.5	1 396	13.3	9 708	31.7	26.3
Lincoln	13 045	74.0	84 900	20.6	12.2	611	32.6	2.8	13 623	-2.3	926	6.8	13 286	29.7	31.2
Lowndes	23 178	62.1	115 700	23.9	10.0	693	34.4	3.4	25 097	-7.1	2 346	9.3	23 790	28.8	28.4
Madison	36 342	70.3	201 200	21.1	10.0	863	28.8	2.7	48 843	-1.9	2 657	5.4	46 506	47.7	14.4
Marion	9 985	74.7	77 900	22.6	13.9	578	34.6	4.0	9 834	-1.2	856	8.7	9 123	27.4	34.5
Marshall	13 050	79.5	83 700	24.7	14.0	691	32.2	3.1	14 350	-3.2	1 275	8.9	14 192	17.8	38.0
Monroe	13 960	77.3	78 500	22.3	12.2	567	26.9	3.1	15 318	-1.3	1 617	10.6	13 791	25.1	33.2
Montgomery	4 229	74.5	68 600	24.6	13.5	610	39.5	5.0	4 168	-4.8	404	9.7	3 664	25.5	37.9
Neshoba	10 829	73.2	75 900	22.3	11.7	592	25.2	3.2	10 700	-2.3	729	6.8	11 846	28.6	25.6
Newton	7 931	77.6	72 100	22.4	11.7	618	25.1	3.7	8 638	-3.9	582	6.7	8 548	33.5	28.6
Noxubee	4 194	71.8	59 000	31.0	15.3	501	33.0	2.1	4 003	-2.1	536	13.4	3 694	19.2	42.9
Oktibbeha	18 176	51.7	129 200	21.8	11.4	691	42.3	4.7	21 685	-2.5	1 624	7.5	19 632	43.4	16.1
Panola	11 928	76.3	77 500	22.9	13.5	667	35.2	3.0	13 343	-2.5	1 470	11.0	12 084	30.1	30.5
Pearl River	20 556	77.6	111 600	23.1	12.5	753	32.1	4.0	22 105	-3.4	1 516	6.9	21 207	31.3	29.5
Perry	4 483	84.9	81 200	21.8	11.6	668	29.5	2.4	4 156	-2.1	381	9.2	4 071	23.5	42.6
Pike	14 614	70.1	82 200	23.0	11.9	649	33.0	3.3	14 327	-2.3	1 218	8.5	14 481	26.0	32.8
Pontotoc	9 937	78.2	80 000	22.3	11.3	622	24.7	2.3	13 329	-2.6	936	7.0	12 688	26.7	37.5
Prentiss	9 611	72.8	73 200	23.3	11.8	491	29.9	2.8	10 765	-1.8	846	7.9	9 228	21.9	38.1
Quitman	3 114	68.6	49 200	31.8	12.9	538	35.3	2.5	2 740	-4.2	371	13.5	2 575	29.2	28.9
Rankin	53 223	75.5	148 900	20.5	10.0	875	28.7	7.5	69 830	-2.0	3 269	4.7	67 718	41.2	19.1
Scott	9 692	75.7	68 600	23.3	12.4	592	28.7	7.0	12 536	-1.7	697	5.6	11 371	21.7	42.7
Sharkey	1 725	64.4	64 900	23.4	10.0	488	29.7	6.0	1 776	-3.9	207	11.7	1 737	34.1	22.0
Simpson	9 786	76.0	80 800	22.9	11.5	593	26.3	5.0	10 698	-2.4	693	6.5	10 346	26.7	34.1
Smith	6 269	83.3	77 600	21.8	13.0	576	25.7	2.6	6 700	-2.3	403	6.0	6 328	26.9	37.4
Stone	5 871	82.6	107 000	23.1	10.6	690	32.4	5.9	6 266	-3.0	538	8.6	6 842	24.0	30.4

1. Specified owner-occupied units. 2. A value of 10.0 represents 10 percent or less; a value of 50.0 represents 50 percent or more. 3. Specified renter-occupied units.
4. Overcrowded or lacking complete plumbing facilities. 5. Percent of civilian labor force. 6. Persons 16 years old and over.

Table B. States and Counties — **Nonfarm Employment and Agriculture**

STATE County	Private nonfarm establishments, employment and payroll, 2013									Agriculture, 2012			
		Employment						Annual payroll		Farms			
											Percent with:		
	Number of establish-ments	Total	Health care and social assistance	Manufac-turing	Retail trade	Finance and insurance	Professional, scientific, and technical services	Total (mil dol)	Average per employee (dollars)	Number	Fewer than 50 acres	500 acres or more	Farm operators whose principal occu-pation is farming (percent)
	104	105	106	107	108	109	110	111	112	113	114	115	116
MISSISSIPPI	58 435	902 638	164 332	138 335	137 076	33 789	31 020	31 697	35 116	38 076	28.1	11.8	43.0
Adams	817	10 418	1 813	386	2 274	405	214	326	31 272	189	33.9	10.6	45.0
Alcorn	782	11 780	2 531	2 371	2 239	293	364	361	30 645	505	27.3	5.3	30.9
Amite	165	1 210	161	267	147	D	20	37	30 990	590	27.1	8.6	46.8
Attala	334	4 528	594	741	799	D	D	139	30 641	456	20.4	10.3	34.2
Benton	57	928	142	181	105	D	D	24	26 052	312	16.3	9.0	36.9
Bolivar	735	8 683	1 869	1 522	1 499	268	180	278	31 969	419	23.4	45.8	57.0
Calhoun	257	2 654	511	922	396	D	27	79	29 806	621	20.3	11.9	33.3
Carroll	103	598	D	D	76	D	D	16	27 552	503	18.1	17.7	33.6
Chickasaw	343	5 231	D	3 085	737	125	54	141	26 912	575	20.7	12.2	34.4
Choctaw	120	1 212	220	216	146	23	D	54	44 240	254	15.0	11.4	42.9
Claiborne	111	D	D	D	D	D	15	D	D	249	16.9	17.7	48.6
Clarke	229	2 520	D	594	340	111	D	94	37 340	329	32.5	4.9	47.4
Clay	356	4 090	661	698	738	122	116	141	34 516	420	20.5	12.1	45.7
Coahoma	555	6 625	1 783	773	1 045	230	232	212	31 987	273	22.0	44.3	63.0
Copiah	437	5 924	705	2 184	805	170	89	162	27 295	506	26.3	8.9	44.5
Covington	328	3 932	517	1 380	521	D	74	116	29 483	493	27.8	6.9	45.8
DeSoto	2 613	46 136	5 959	3 687	8 253	948	920	1 409	30 544	433	44.3	9.7	50.1
Forrest	1 853	31 976	8 061	3 964	4 302	1 048	1 021	1 163	36 373	359	49.0	3.9	36.5
Franklin	117	1 123	337	63	104	D	D	37	32 847	189	19.6	13.2	34.4
George	310	3 508	768	309	1 059	D	99	107	30 596	573	52.5	1.9	51.5
Greene	122	709	D	D	179	D	D	22	31 291	395	33.2	7.3	37.7
Grenada	546	8 225	1 246	2 264	1 311	221	197	253	30 742	316	17.4	14.9	41.8
Hancock	686	9 779	995	723	1 489	303	2 332	403	41 168	248	46.4	2.0	42.3
Harrison	4 114	71 566	14 045	3 045	10 973	2 599	2 418	2 545	35 558	331	66.2	1.5	36.0
Hinds	5 446	98 058	31 486	3 832	10 754	5 186	5 101	4 163	42 453	1 047	32.5	11.3	39.3
Holmes	246	2 068	434	399	437	90	43	51	24 834	531	18.1	19.0	28.2
Humphreys	154	1 751	225	D	293	64	D	48	27 283	262	21.4	35.9	50.8
Issaquena	8	65	D	NA	NA	D	NA	2	23 615	97	11.3	42.3	53.6
Itawamba	346	4 709	544	1 701	644	152	32	142	30 227	443	15.8	7.0	40.4
Jackson	2 241	43 812	5 248	D	5 113	998	1 663	2 105	48 040	409	62.3	2.4	41.6
Jasper	215	3 442	D	1 525	367	D	83	121	35 087	445	22.0	8.1	47.4
Jefferson	60	713	323	D	NA	D	NA	23	32 376	277	22.4	15.5	51.6
Jefferson Davis	152	1 020	D	19	207	34	D	58	56 491	337	23.7	6.5	57.3
Jones	1 330	24 668	3 021	D	2 897	D	445	886	35 910	927	38.2	2.9	49.6
Kemper	138	1 663	D	D	160	53	D	64	38 575	378	15.9	12.7	41.8
Lafayette	1 067	14 001	2 669	1 405	2 551	441	1 005	455	32 488	449	17.8	8.9	40.3
Lamar	1 283	16 441	3 157	149	5 010	594	691	456	27 752	424	42.0	4.5	34.2
Lauderdale	1 945	30 471	7 530	2 186	5 023	1 623	1 063	994	32 637	373	34.9	6.2	41.8
Lawrence	162	1 796	189	688	352	D	12	79	44 134	397	28.5	6.0	42.3
Leake	289	4 802	617	D	805	D	45	119	24 763	637	25.0	6.4	44.0
Lee	2 422	45 839	7 614	9 317	7 056	2 334	1 189	1 534	33 471	525	34.3	7.8	48.4
Leflore	724	12 257	2 902	2 480	1 656	379	330	368	30 004	300	14.0	43.7	54.7
Lincoln	794	10 329	1 751	1 226	1 842	339	318	358	34 681	595	30.4	5.9	39.7
Lowndes	1 494	20 302	2 615	3 641	3 501	517	547	743	36 613	413	27.4	15.7	30.3
Madison	2 897	45 064	3 511	6 033	6 885	3 125	3 368	1 793	39 799	685	32.4	14.5	32.7
Marion	588	6 120	799	580	1 202	282	180	203	33 157	552	32.2	5.8	48.7
Marshall	420	6 472	1 356	557	837	301	D	177	27 289	573	25.7	15.4	39.4
Monroe	644	7 909	1 575	2 400	1 097	230	100	260	32 922	726	25.1	13.2	40.8
Montgomery	215	2 415	D	249	504	99	28	64	26 666	345	15.7	14.8	42.3
Neshoba	507	7 940	D	D	1 265	298	158	354	44 553	677	29.1	5.0	52.1
Newton	318	3 827	695	D	642	129	D	145	37 822	562	30.1	7.7	52.3
Noxubee	195	1 708	282	499	309	D	13	49	28 505	565	21.6	20.4	42.3
Oktibbeha	846	11 180	1 644	1 143	1 927	373	408	296	26 513	402	24.6	12.7	42.8
Panola	629	8 295	1 398	1 837	1 595	319	117	254	30 587	745	14.6	16.4	37.7
Pearl River	808	7 860	1 030	553	1 984	327	385	224	28 556	813	47.6	5.3	42.6
Perry	147	1 528	240	599	239	D	D	72	47 162	310	40.3	3.5	50.3
Pike	974	12 650	2 515	2 436	2 451	381	329	375	29 673	531	35.8	4.0	48.2
Pontotoc	490	10 304	794	6 242	965	216	122	293	28 414	889	29.9	6.6	26.4
Prentiss	482	6 084	1 169	1 889	888	D	186	157	25 862	504	24.8	6.5	32.1
Quitman	107	723	D	D	108	57	D	19	26 835	347	18.7	27.7	39.2
Rankin	3 451	51 315	8 486	3 814	8 579	2 552	1 465	1 850	36 048	670	43.4	8.7	43.1
Scott	465	9 376	040	D	1 206	176	96	308	32 832	716	31.6	6.4	51.5
Sharkey	125	781	210	NA	170	D	D	23	29 647	128	16.4	50.8	61.7
Simpson	417	5 713	2 291	371	995	501	91	156	27 351	606	29.4	5.3	54.1
Smith	162	2 207	D	929	202	63	120	75	34 012	637	27.6	4.9	62.0
Stone	261	2 690	474	D	600	D	90	78	28 975	271	43.9	5.9	42.1

Agriculture, 2012 (cont.)

STATE County	Land in farms: Acreage (1,000)	Land in farms: Percent change, 2007–2012	Land in farms: Acres: Average size of farm	Land in farms: Acres: Total irrigated (1,000)	Land in farms: Acres: Total cropland (1,000)	Value of land and buildings (dollars): Average per farm	Value of land and buildings (dollars): Average per acre	Value of machinery and equipment, average per farm (dollars)	Value of products sold: Total (mil dol)	Value of products sold: Average per farm (dollars)	Value of products sold: Percent from: Crops	Value of products sold: Percent from: Livestock and poultry products	Percent of farms with sales of: $10,000 or more	Percent of farms with sales of: $100,000 or more	Government payments: Total ($1,000)	Government payments: Percent of farms
	117	118	119	120	121	122	123	124	125	126	127	128	129	130	131	132
MISSISSIPPI	10 931	-4.6	287	1 652.0	5 075.6	652 593	2 273	91 910	6 441.0	169 162	46.2	53.8	33.0	12.4	181 205	43.3
Adams	66	-5.6	349	D	20.3	757 720	2 170	73 026	9.9	52 228	85.4	14.6	18.5	4.2	1 107	38.1
Alcorn	94	-0.3	185	D	43.3	345 842	1 866	59 352	20.9	41 461	84.6	15.4	25.1	3.6	795	50.7
Amite	121	10.2	205	0.1	23.0	690 939	3 365	66 768	68.4	115 958	5.6	94.4	32.4	8.8	1 025	43.4
Attala	125	-8.6	275	0.4	29.1	495 542	1 801	48 726	23.1	50 686	54.8	45.2	22.4	4.2	1 359	52.0
Benton	82	-4.3	264	D	29.2	421 772	1 596	49 298	14.5	46 596	72.8	27.2	19.6	6.7	740	56.4
Bolivar	390	-8.8	932	247.8	362.0	2 254 100	2 419	463 976	277.0	661 122	99.9	0.1	70.9	50.1	12 645	85.0
Calhoun	175	-13.3	282	1.2	80.1	520 758	1 844	98 725	78.5	126 446	92.9	7.1	34.5	12.1	3 146	73.4
Carroll	169	-11.1	336	12.3	57.8	631 318	1 879	75 996	36.5	72 620	86.9	13.1	30.0	8.3	2 451	46.1
Chickasaw	166	-7.0	289	3.0	67.2	533 009	1 847	69 757	60.9	105 897	49.6	50.4	34.6	10.3	2 924	65.0
Choctaw	63	-12.0	250	1.0	9.0	492 768	1 973	41 854	11.4	44 945	11.1	88.9	18.9	4.3	444	49.2
Claiborne	83	-11.5	334	D	22.0	671 028	2 011	54 072	11.4	45 864	77.2	22.8	25.3	3.6	1 125	55.0
Clarke	56	-12.9	171	0.4	13.9	404 097	2 358	59 161	33.5	101 763	4.5	95.5	24.9	5.2	160	17.6
Clay	130	-8.6	310	0.8	30.8	507 521	1 639	66 540	92.3	219 655	7.8	92.2	33.3	8.3	1 554	48.6
Coahoma	261	-13.8	956	138.0	226.8	2 411 634	2 523	406 249	179.6	657 799	96.1	3.9	62.3	50.2	10 498	86.4
Copiah	116	-11.8	229	0.2	18.4	523 654	2 286	58 763	61.4	121 336	10.4	89.6	29.1	6.7	527	32.8
Covington	106	-9.0	215	0.6	24.6	631 521	2 941	97 406	203.5	412 838	3.1	96.9	46.5	22.1	617	26.4
DeSoto	119	-16.2	274	17.2	81.2	723 771	2 641	84 483	50.0	115 386	90.2	9.8	24.5	9.0	1 866	25.4
Forrest	43	-6.1	119	0.8	9.8	406 844	3 416	65 822	20.8	58 075	22.8	77.2	27.9	5.8	598	24.2
Franklin	50	6.8	266	0.0	8.8	680 487	2 562	74 143	10.5	55 667	21.7	78.3	27.5	6.3	254	39.7
George	61	-10.6	106	0.5	19.3	357 428	3 361	75 084	22.7	39 620	84.8	15.2	27.2	4.4	421	16.6
Greene	69	34.8	174	0.2	16.2	379 203	2 175	91 420	32.8	83 139	30.5	69.5	26.6	6.8	300	13.2
Grenada	88	-20.8	280	1.1	25.8	511 345	1 828	51 522	11.6	36 775	59.4	40.6	26.9	4.7	1 414	63.6
Hancock	25	-40.2	102	0.1	4.8	403 952	3 964	38 907	2.7	10 988	D	D	27.4	1.6	175	14.1
Harrison	24	12.6	73	0.1	5.6	452 586	6 199	37 532	3.4	10 417	45.8	54.2	19.6	2.1	63	6.9
Hinds	251	-3.5	240	0.5	61.8	549 542	2 292	58 127	73.4	70 106	34.0	66.0	22.0	3.2	3 055	41.2
Holmes	238	4.2	447	51.1	119.8	938 991	2 098	99 501	93.4	175 972	97.7	2.3	25.4	9.8	5 781	66.9
Humphreys	194	-0.5	740	82.7	161.4	1 633 874	2 209	292 195	132.7	506 458	87.2	12.8	55.7	42.4	5 952	84.0
Issaquena	124	2.7	1 282	19.7	75.2	2 458 216	1 917	298 340	53.3	549 691	D	D	52.6	36.1	2 396	88.7
Itawamba	95	1.7	214	0.0	30.2	429 835	2 007	59 011	17.6	39 623	67.5	32.5	29.3	5.9	786	48.8
Jackson	38	-9.3	92	0.2	14.3	347 257	3 778	60 181	14.4	35 164	87.3	12.7	22.0	3.2	277	8.8
Jasper	97	7.1	218	0.0	14.1	436 222	1 998	73 629	97.2	218 366	1.6	98.4	36.2	16.0	545	27.0
Jefferson	86	-14.7	310	0.6	29.9	655 975	2 119	67 863	31.7	114 484	46.7	53.3	32.1	10.8	815	37.5
Jefferson Davis	59	-13.2	175	0.3	10.6	347 445	1 985	54 522	36.0	106 831	4.9	95.1	30.3	7.7	460	36.5
Jones	126	14.7	136	0.4	25.5	433 357	3 189	62 438	217.0	234 063	2.2	97.8	37.6	19.2	1 212	21.6
Kemper	124	-9.1	328	0.1	18.0	569 079	1 738	52 138	20.5	54 119	9.1	90.9	31.2	4.5	619	28.6
Lafayette	109	-4.8	242	0.6	26.9	543 419	2 242	56 581	8.9	19 904	73.3	26.7	22.7	3.1	1 120	50.3
Lamar	64	-12.3	151	0.2	13.2	544 656	3 602	64 014	25.0	59 033	13.8	86.2	36.3	6.4	565	25.0
Lauderdale	69	-17.4	185	0.1	14.6	441 753	2 387	46 413	5.4	14 453	50.1	49.9	21.4	0.8	252	17.2
Lawrence	73	-9.1	183	D	18.2	492 441	2 689	75 239	79.4	199 970	7.3	92.7	40.8	10.3	804	35.5
Leake	106	-16.7	167	0.1	22.6	446 077	2 678	58 912	283.3	444 706	0.9	99.1	38.9	21.4	711	34.5
Lee	133	-9.2	253	0.4	84.7	484 651	1 913	65 162	45.0	85 766	89.3	10.7	31.0	6.9	880	39.2
Leflore	293	-6.9	977	164.1	235.8	1 970 613	2 017	381 793	241.9	806 193	78.3	21.7	55.0	41.0	7 438	81.3
Lincoln	109	-12.8	183	0.2	20.1	547 086	2 997	65 555	69.9	117 405	4.6	95.4	37.3	9.2	615	25.7
Lowndes	119	-8.3	289	4.8	57.3	613 637	2 122	89 651	43.1	104 276	62.2	37.8	33.9	12.1	1 478	47.7
Madison	203	-8.8	296	0.1	68.6	776 399	2 619	67 238	33.3	48 600	82.6	17.4	19.9	6.7	3 611	45.5
Marion	82	-11.3	148	D	18.2	438 998	2 966	75 457	97.3	176 281	2.1	97.9	28.4	13.0	1 259	37.9
Marshall	203	5.3	355	3.5	70.0	699 567	1 972	81 276	32.7	57 079	84.1	15.9	30.7	7.7	1 667	47.3
Monroe	228	14.8	314	0.5	99.6	549 209	1 749	77 127	55.2	76 070	82.2	17.8	28.0	9.6	2 655	54.8
Montgomery	97	-0.1	282	0.7	26.8	501 565	1 779	64 942	20.1	58 339	54.5	45.5	26.4	7.2	1 257	52.2
Neshoba	101	-16.0	150	0.0	20.6	461 393	3 081	79 096	246.5	364 069	0.9	99.1	43.7	21.9	249	16.2
Newton	109	-9.4	194	0.6	22.6	404 137	2 083	65 811	102.4	182 242	4.2	95.8	37.0	15.5	659	22.1
Noxubee	213	-3.8	377	17.3	105.9	815 425	2 161	147 076	140.3	248 235	48.3	51.7	49.7	31.5	2 547	59.6
Oktibbeha	105	3.3	260	0.3	21.7	573 619	2 203	56 042	15.1	37 674	15.0	85.0	24.9	4.7	912	37.8
Panola	273	1.1	366	30.4	134.8	704 463	1 924	87 615	71.9	96 451	91.6	8.4	31.3	9.8	5 745	61.9
Pearl River	118	-12.8	146	1.0	23.0	465 647	3 200	48 637	17.6	21 654	45.7	54.3	28.2	3.4	735	14.8
Perry	44	5.8	140	0.5	12.1	401 719	2 862	68 168	21.8	70 442	23.7	76.3	31.6	7.4	513	23.9
Pike	72	-1.9	136	0.1	14.6	481 913	3 552	55 004	74.4	140 021	2.3	97.7	32.8	7.7	984	38.4
Pontotoc	153	4.7	172	D	64.2	312 294	1 819	55 052	24.7	27 747	76.8	23.2	24.9	5.2	2 249	64.2
Prentiss	93	-8.1	185	0.0	38.4	290 214	1 569	45 899	15.5	30 835	83.6	16.4	23.6	5.6	966	69.4
Quitman	209	-5.3	601	68.7	155.8	1 210 934	2 014	188 674	85.1	245 130	D	D	38.6	24.5	8 654	91.4
Rankin	126	-10.3	188	0.0	28.5	561 387	2 990	65 404	111.2	165 990	8.2	91.8	32.4	12.2	829	20.4
Scott	115	-9.2	161	0.1	27.8	406 497	2 528	85 180	270.8	378 270	1.7	98.3	41.3	16.9	476	20.3
Sharkey	155	-13.5	1 214	61.0	135.2	2 782 797	2 292	455 836	108.2	844 969	96.1	3.9	61.7	45.3	3 767	88.3
Simpson	110	-6.9	181	1.2	28.2	495 135	2 739	80 403	202.4	334 068	3.4	96.6	44.2	21.5	396	16.7
Smith	108	-1.3	170	0.1	26.2	502 821	2 956	74 466	251.1	394 133	3.0	97.0	49.1	25.9	427	11.8
Stone	46	-11.9	169	0.1	7.5	615 882	3 655	58 841	10.7	39 410	D	D	32.5	2.6	298	18.1

STATE County	Water use, 2010		Wholesale trade,[1] 2007				Retail trade,[2] 2007				Real estate and rental and leasing,[2] 2007			
	Total water withdrawn (mil gal/day)	Gallons withdrawn per person per day	Number of establish-ments	Number of employees	Sales (mil dol)	Annual payroll (mil dol)	Number of establish-ments	Number of employees	Sales (mil dol)	Annual payroll (mil dol)	Number of establish-ments	Number of employees	Receipts (mil dol)	Annual payroll (mil dol)
	133	134	135	136	137	138	139	140	141	142	143	144	145	146
MISSISSIPPI	3 933.0	1 325	2 556	32 382	23 003.6	1 276.0	12 452	141 426	33 751.4	2 910.9	2 517	10 169	1 734.6	283.7
Adams	7.5	233	38	D	D	D	191	2 037	427.7	41.5	41	148	18.9	4.0
Alcorn	6.7	182	37	D	D	D	196	2 237	527.6	46.6	23	200	10.7	3.5
Amite	2.2	165	8	29	17.9	0.8	33	177	36.3	3.1	2	D	D	D
Attala	4.5	231	21	87	37.0	3.1	95	845	171.4	16.0	9	22	2.3	0.4
Benton	2.5	290	NA	NA	NA	NA	15	130	25.1	2.2	1	D	D	D
Bolivar	440.8	12 910	31	D	D	D	167	1 558	303.4	27.8	38	126	15.4	2.4
Calhoun	2.8	188	11	75	29.0	1.8	68	443	94.1	7.6	3	D	D	D
Carroll	8.0	757	3	D	D	D	21	159	24.2	1.7	2	D	D	D
Chickasaw	9.7	558	18	188	101.5	4.5	84	681	128.0	10.6	12	30	3.0	0.6
Choctaw	15.0	1 755	2	D	D	D	31	185	30.8	2.9	2	D	D	D
Claiborne	35.9	3 742	3	D	D	D	31	183	39.3	3.5	1	D	D	D
Clarke	2.8	166	6	D	D	D	51	377	58.1	4.7	5	D	D	D
Clay	4.2	203	14	D	D	D	77	634	126.0	10.7	9	39	4.5	0.8
Coahoma	164.0	6 271	26	D	D	D	127	1 112	260.3	22.7	38	111	14.1	2.4
Copiah	10.2	347	11	D	D	D	92	733	143.1	13.0	9	58	2.9	1.0
Covington	6.3	319	13	68	66.6	2.0	74	567	171.6	11.3	10	18	1.7	0.2
DeSoto	35.7	221	100	2 098	1 676.8	80.1	471	7 895	2 069.5	178.0	110	434	90.0	12.1
Forrest	18.4	245	77	858	424.1	31.1	382	4 496	2 121.6	104.1	99	D	D	D
Franklin	1.3	158	3	D	D	D	20	119	20.9	1.7	2	D	D	D
George	3.5	154	11	D	D	D	81	888	231.5	16.4	9	18	1.7	0.3
Greene	8.3	575	3	79	27.6	2.6	29	194	39.1	2.9	5	12	1.7	0.2
Grenada	11.9	545	29	D	D	D	136	1 378	377.0	31.1	26	92	16.3	2.4
Hancock	8.2	187	21	D	D	D	116	1 411	383.2	32.7	32	69	12.5	1.6
Harrison	158.3	846	156	1 618	839.7	70.4	821	11 071	2 903.2	254.4	252	968	175.6	29.3
Hinds	60.5	247	292	4 183	2 118.8	188.3	962	12 358	2 992.6	279.3	286	1 689	412.2	60.1
Holmes	36.1	1 880	10	121	31.1	2.9	81	534	114.4	8.8	14	D	D	D
Humphreys	105.1	11 214	6	35	15.1	1.2	35	298	81.4	5.2	3	D	D	D
Issaquena	34.3	24 403	2	D	D	D	NA	NA	NA	NA	NA	NA	NA	NA
Itawamba	11.4	485	10	222	59.4	7.0	80	635	135.0	12.8	2	D	D	D
Jackson	520.3	3 725	51	D	D	D	453	5 356	1 305.0	116.0	105	370	48.8	9.3
Jasper	11.1	650	11	89	89.5	3.4	42	370	68.9	7.2	4	38	5.4	0.9
Jefferson	1.2	155	1	D	D	D	13	89	18.6	1.3	2	D	D	D
Jefferson Davis	5.7	460	2	D	D	D	52	345	57.3	5.2	5	D	D	D
Jones	16.4	241	79	664	402.7	28.0	284	3 367	816.4	70.0	60	314	59.4	12.9
Kemper	2.3	218	3	D	D	D	31	176	46.7	2.9	1	D	D	D
Lafayette	5.6	118	22	D	D	D	205	2 419	507.1	48.5	54	177	25.0	3.6
Lamar	12.1	218	35	D	D	D	320	4 871	991.8	90.5	64	D	D	D
Lauderdale	11.9	148	84	1 696	1 127.6	65.7	449	5 400	1 320.6	112.8	73	294	39.3	6.1
Lawrence	37.7	2 914	3	D	D	D	43	301	46.8	5.1	2	D	D	D
Leake	5.9	249	10	93	22.7	2.6	88	799	180.4	15.4	5	12	0.6	0.2
Lee	5.2	63	159	1 859	847.9	65.3	541	6 753	1 439.5	136.4	99	511	88.6	14.7
Leflore	200.8	6 214	39	D	D	D	182	1 803	438.7	34.7	47	D	D	D
Lincoln	7.4	211	28	D	D	D	178	1 998	502.0	41.8	28	102	14.5	2.3
Lowndes	41.0	685	80	D	D	D	349	3 950	809.3	80.4	75	233	33.3	5.1
Madison	15.1	159	131	2 958	3 305.9	119.5	457	6 441	1 268.4	135.6	139	719	159.0	24.1
Marion	5.1	187	24	233	155.7	7.4	132	1 253	259.0	23.4	24	79	18.8	2.2
Marshall	4.7	126	13	68	43.5	2.3	114	886	166.4	17.0	17	47	6.4	1.1
Monroe	25.0	675	23	245	111.1	7.4	146	1 432	282.0	26.1	16	42	3.8	0.8
Montgomery	1.9	170	7	30	7.6	0.9	59	526	136.6	9.1	4	D	D	D
Neshoba	4.6	156	19	197	286.9	9.2	126	1 227	255.8	23.7	19	53	5.7	1.1
Newton	4.2	194	5	32	9.2	0.7	85	811	146.7	14.0	7	18	2.0	0.2
Noxubee	22.3	1 931	10	77	26.8	1.5	52	395	82.9	6.0	1	D	D	D
Oktibbeha	6.1	128	17	416	166.2	13.4	161	2 105	387.9	39.8	49	170	25.6	3.5
Panola	36.4	1 049	31	572	484.5	21.1	185	1 664	384.4	30.0	17	72	10.2	1.8
Pearl River	7.2	129	30	D	D	D	209	2 452	615.6	52.1	25	76	9.3	1.3
Perry	22.6	1 842	3	D	D	D	37	280	60.4	4.6	3	D	D	D
Pike	9.4	232	50	454	188.7	12.9	235	2 583	544.7	51.1	43	D	D	D
Pontotoc	4.1	137	16	155	57.5	4.3	84	886	203.6	15.3	5	D	D	D
Prentiss	3.7	148	13	43	17.8	1.0	109	763	162.0	14.7	43	96	8.1	1.3
Quitman	135.1	16 431	6	35	19.1	0.9	20	158	24.7	2.2	5	10	1.5	0.2
Rankin	19.8	140	215	3 621	2 629.6	169.1	521	8 124	2 226.2	183.0	147	646	121.9	20.6
Scott	10.6	374	21	71	41.2	1.9	125	1 156	235.1	21.0	8	30	2.5	0.6
Sharkey	69.6	14 164	13	91	64.2	3.1	23	199	31.0	2.8	7	18	2.1	0.3
Simpson	5.8	210	12	D	D	D	93	1 044	212.6	19.8	13	44	4.7	0.9
Smith	4.9	298	8	34	12.6	0.8	36	312	51.1	4.8	3	7	0.4	0.1
Stone	4.8	269	14	D	D	D	65	716	190.7	15.7	11	38	3.1	0.6

1. Merchant wholesalers, except manufacturers' sales branches and offices. 2. Employer establishments.

Table B. States and Counties — **Professional Services, Manufacturing, and Accommodation and Food Services**

STATE County	Professional, scientific, and technical services,[1] 2007				Manufacturing, 2007				Accommodation and food services, 2007			
	Number of establish-ments	Number of employees	Receipts (mil dol)	Annual payroll (mil dol)	Number of establish-ments	Number of employees	Receipts (mil dol)	Annual payroll (mil dol)	Number of establish-ments	Number of employees	Sales (mil dol)	Annual payroll (mil dol)
	147	148	149	150	151	152	153	154	155	156	157	158
MISSISSIPPI	4 751	30 855	3 971.9	1 350.3	2 598	159 235	59 869.5	5 756.6	4 817	119 626	7 045.1	1 812.3
Adams	62	248	24.6	6.6	NA	NA	NA	NA	88	1 728	98.0	22.2
Alcorn	60	298	26.6	8.6	49	2 994	944.6	122.4	70	1 157	42.5	11.0
Amite	6	D	D	D	10	599	D	21.9	4	28	1.3	0.3
Attala	23	58	5.4	1.4	23	984	319.5	27.8	26	326	13.7	3.4
Benton	2	D	D	D	NA	NA	NA	NA	NA	NA	NA	NA
Bolivar	50	219	19.7	7.1	18	1 345	287.0	48.5	44	777	31.1	7.0
Calhoun	14	50	5.8	1.6	21	876	235.3	26.9	12	90	2.5	0.6
Carroll	4	D	D	D	NA	NA	NA	NA	5	28	0.7	0.2
Chickasaw	15	47	3.5	1.1	51	2 668	427.2	79.1	19	253	11.5	2.2
Choctaw	6	17	1.5	0.6	NA	NA	NA	NA	8	43	1.7	0.3
Claiborne	7	21	1.6	0.4	NA	NA	NA	NA	12	181	4.7	1.4
Clarke	15	D	D	D	22	584	D	16.8	11	108	4.5	1.1
Clay	22	D	D	D	23	1 122	393.0	46.5	34	465	15.8	3.8
Coahoma	47	D	D	D	22	738	D	27.3	42	1 353	120.6	21.8
Copiah	24	66	6.4	1.8	26	2 644	D	D	33	484	15.7	3.8
Covington	17	82	7.5	2.5	12	1 505	D	34.9	21	359	11.2	3.2
DeSoto	175	921	77.9	28.8	133	4 822	1 663.5	208.2	260	6 230	256.8	67.1
Forrest	184	D	D	D	72	D	883.4	137.5	176	4 078	158.8	42.8
Franklin	8	36	2.9	1.3	NA	NA	NA	NA	5	D	D	D
George	18	D	D	D	NA	NA	NA	NA	27	342	13.4	3.0
Greene	4	19	1.2	0.5	NA	NA	NA	NA	4	42	1.7	0.4
Grenada	33	151	14.0	5.6	24	2 910	732.5	101.7	61	875	36.2	8.5
Hancock	93	D	D	D	32	863	D	58.5	78	1 616	133.8	33.0
Harrison	393	D	D	D	110	3 234	D	137.4	353	17 953	1 619.1	435.9
Hinds	710	D	D	D	160	5 610	1 406.2	243.1	451	9 284	403.8	107.2
Holmes	13	59	20.1	4.7	6	622	208.0	17.5	25	178	5.5	1.5
Humphreys	5	12	1.3	0.4	4	D	D	D	9	139	4.4	1.2
Issaquena	NA	NA	NA	NA	NA	NA	NA	NA	NA	NA	NA	NA
Itawamba	17	D	D	D	40	1 531	D	46.8	27	365	12.3	3.2
Jackson	203	D	D	D	82	D	D	D	227	4 167	178.0	47.2
Jasper	18	136	7.2	3.3	13	1 283	256.5	41.6	13	117	4.4	1.0
Jefferson	1	D	D	D	NA	NA	NA	NA	3	D	D	D
Jefferson Davis	13	14	3.8	1.4	NA	NA	NA	NA	9	144	6.2	1.5
Jones	97	598	55.1	16.0	72	8 571	1 760.0	265.3	105	5 520	442.8	106.5
Kemper	5	D	D	D	NA	NA	NA	NA	5	36	1.4	0.4
Lafayette	113	D	D	D	27	1 479	D	47.5	128	2 298	96.2	26.3
Lamar	102	604	72.1	22.9	28	D	D	19.7	100	2 701	103.5	30.2
Lauderdale	120	D	D	D	66	2 880	750.9	99.6	159	3 620	135.8	38.0
Lawrence	8	12	1.6	0.2	12	717	D	42.1	16	104	4.0	0.9
Leake	14	45	3.3	0.8	7	D	D	D	23	299	13.0	3.1
Lee	189	D	D	D	149	11 736	2 986.8	427.4	195	4 096	148.2	41.3
Leflore	50	D	D	D	34	D	D	D	62	1 137	51.4	13.1
Lincoln	56	469	44.0	15.4	33	1 146	275.7	45.4	58	883	41.2	9.6
Lowndes	116	617	78.4	24.7	63	3 879	2 075.5	172.6	111	2 456	88.6	23.4
Madison	323	D	D	D	75	7 495	6 471.9	320.7	228	4 619	180.6	49.6
Marion	43	185	16.0	6.7	23	950	166.3	22.0	44	529	20.1	4.6
Marshall	21	71	6.6	1.8	31	D	D	D	28	422	14.2	3.8
Monroe	40	121	8.7	2.5	53	3 144	1 472.7	130.0	51	541	21.8	4.9
Montgomery	14	27	3.7	0.7	NA	NA	NA	NA	23	229	7.3	1.8
Neshoba	19	90	8.2	3.8	14	628	192.4	23.2	42	665	24.2	5.8
Newton	17	48	2.9	1.0	21	1 693	290.8	51.2	22	356	11.2	3.0
Noxubee	6	12	0.8	0.2	18	792	198.9	26.1	11	81	4.6	1.3
Oktibbeha	73	D	D	D	29	1 506	514.3	63.9	100	2 129	77.3	20.5
Panola	29	157	15.1	3.8	41	2 083	495.3	74.2	54	866	32.6	9.2
Pearl River	63	281	22.1	9.8	36	637	D	25.3	83	1 210	43.2	10.9
Perry	6	D	D	D	10	811	D	40.9	5	34	1.2	0.4
Pike	76	D	D	D	34	2 777	D	68.1	76	1 311	50.9	13.2
Pontotoc	22	D	D	D	78	6 833	D	198.6	30	434	14.8	3.8
Prentiss	26	165	34.4	5.8	40	2 609	975.2	79.1	33	507	17.5	4.8
Quitman	4	D	D	D	NA	NA	NA	NA	5	62	1.9	0.4
Rankin	314	1 450	204.0	67.5	131	3 897	1 865.8	161.8	241	4 832	197.8	52.7
Scott	21	93	5.2	1.9	23	5 072	1 057.5	143.6	38	518	19.7	4.5
Sharkey	8	18	1.2	0.3	NA	NA	NA	NA	4	35	1.6	0.4
Simpson	27	121	8.9	2.6	NA	NA	NA	NA	37	552	20.6	5.2
Smith	14	94	8.1	1.8	13	1 052	402.6	37.5	10	73	1.8	0.5
Stone	18	D	D	D	23	616	D	23.1	27	482	18.6	4.8

1. Establishment subject to federal tax.

Table B. States and Counties — **Health Care and Social Assistance, Other Services, Nonemployer Businesses, and Residential Construction**

STATE County	Health care and social assistance, 2007				Other services, 2007				Nonemployer businesses, 2013		Value of residential construction authorized by building permits, 2014	
	Number of establish-ments	Number of employees	Receipts (mil dol)	Annual payroll (mil dol)	Number of establish-ments	Number of employees	Receipts (mil dol)	Annual payroll (mil dol)	Number	Receipts (mil dol)	New Construction ($1,000)	Number of housing units
	159	160	161	162	163	164	165	166	167	168	169	170
MISSISSIPPI	5 876	146 858	14 113.8	5 371.7	3 853	20 421	1 949.6	489.6	201 939	7 902.9	1 033 059	6 871
Adams	102	1 881	178.3	62.7	47	213	16.9	4.3	2 360	93.6	341	3
Alcorn	101	2 008	215.4	68.5	58	171	12.7	3.6	2 465	112.2	1 248	10
Amite	10	D	D	D	7	D	D	D	811	29.8	80	1
Attala	24	579	42.6	15.4	25	224	11.7	2.5	1 215	47.4	435	5
Benton	9	D	D	D	3	D	D	D	573	16.7	170	2
Bolivar	72	1 942	135.8	49.2	50	218	16.6	4.2	1 953	65.4	3 182	22
Calhoun	23	429	25.9	10.0	14	34	2.4	0.6	955	34.6	300	2
Carroll	5	D	D	D	5	D	D	D	656	25.6	NA	NA
Chickasaw	29	D	D	D	23	50	3.4	0.8	1 090	41.2	548	3
Choctaw	9	D	D	D	11	29	2.5	0.6	659	23.2	0	0
Claiborne	18	368	21.4	9.2	5	D	D	D	329	9.8	0	0
Clarke	21	402	26.3	10.1	18	D	D	D	968	37.7	0	0
Clay	27	690	57.3	22.3	23	88	8.4	2.0	1 273	42.7	867	6
Coahoma	77	1 897	179.5	61.3	36	194	8.1	2.7	1 768	52.9	372	6
Copiah	31	610	53.4	14.9	33	130	9.5	2.2	1 665	47.3	360	6
Covington	29	506	37.1	14.6	22	110	8.6	2.0	1 430	56.0	800	8
DeSoto	208	4 172	424.4	157.5	171	993	101.2	24.0	11 583	486.4	141 615	990
Forrest	188	7 667	787.3	357.7	102	747	52.0	15.4	5 162	201.6	21 062	165
Franklin	10	258	14.0	6.6	4	D	D	D	448	16.0	0	0
George	30	637	52.8	24.7	23	88	7.1	1.8	1 291	40.9	0	0
Greene	10	99	5.9	2.2	10	D	D	D	638	19.8	0	0
Grenada	69	1 053	95.7	36.1	40	113	10.8	2.5	1 337	47.7	1 971	14
Hancock	59	D	D	D	46	174	16.7	4.7	3 200	111.9	65 538	502
Harrison	437	12 887	1 498.9	570.4	289	1 778	181.3	47.3	13 979	545.9	152 231	1 125
Hinds	735	25 347	2 673.9	985.5	462	3 256	316.5	88.2	19 824	746.9	81 210	611
Holmes	33	252	17.8	6.9	18	185	9.0	2.6	1 148	33.2	649	7
Humphreys	19	262	15.8	6.5	14	41	2.5	0.6	542	16.8	0	0
Issaquena	2	D	D	D	NA	NA	NA	NA	71	2.2	182	1
Itawamba	28	D	D	D	24	64	5.1	1.2	1 287	54.2	120	1
Jackson	288	5 343	569.6	219.1	152	761	64.7	18.1	8 646	323.3	48 904	327
Jasper	14	289	16.4	7.9	14	47	3.9	1.2	887	26.7	170	1
Jefferson	12	210	14.1	5.9	4	D	D	D	491	11.1	0	0
Jefferson Davis	13	296	18.9	7.0	12	26	2.3	0.4	812	21.8	0	0
Jones	118	3 373	257.7	116.3	98	690	80.7	19.1	4 091	168.9	2 607	21
Kemper	7	175	6.2	2.8	4	D	D	D	485	11.3	NA	NA
Lafayette	107	2 270	243.9	82.9	66	402	121.4	9.9	3 634	187.9	46 410	471
Lamar	121	2 445	268.5	88.9	54	240	18.4	4.6	4 149	206.4	0	0
Lauderdale	207	8 113	919.1	320.4	139	675	59.3	14.6	4 904	170.3	22 888	118
Lawrence	20	200	13.0	4.4	10	D	D	D	691	24.4	306	5
Leake	24	521	31.2	14.9	15	43	4.1	1.2	1 144	40.1	0	0
Lee	254	7 385	910.0	337.6	143	1 055	92.7	31.7	5 659	244.2	13 659	98
Leflore	77	D	D	D	47	D	D	D	1 505	63.3	1 532	19
Lincoln	72	1 556	139.9	50.4	42	274	20.1	7.4	2 292	95.5	1 254	8
Lowndes	166	2 987	282.4	97.3	104	514	36.0	10.9	3 820	128.7	8 836	85
Madison	198	2 810	222.5	81.4	133	813	94.1	26.2	9 961	578.8	182 762	742
Marion	43	756	58.5	24.4	46	159	14.5	3.1	1 789	64.9	0	0
Marshall	24	1 149	76.2	24.6	19	D	D	D	2 557	95.9	14 001	118
Monroe	64	1 478	119.2	49.2	48	132	11.1	3.0	1 889	72.5	395	3
Montgomery	21	434	28.4	12.4	16	76	7.0	1.6	581	18.9	2 412	89
Neshoba	39	1 155	94.9	39.8	33	191	16.0	4.3	1 620	55.6	0	0
Newton	31	671	46.8	18.6	29	89	4.3	1.2	1 212	43.5	0	0
Noxubee	18	269	18.3	7.2	15	D	D	D	937	28.2	0	0
Oktibbeha	73	1 625	116.2	50.9	66	330	64.0	5.7	2 887	98.8	26 555	257
Panola	60	1 311	84.1	38.4	25	118	7.1	1.9	2 411	81.2	896	9
Pearl River	94	937	64.3	25.1	58	272	20.8	6.3	3 867	132.6	21 700	177
Perry	20	289	18.8	7.1	11	46	2.8	0.9	726	28.6	175	1
Pike	120	D	D	D	56	D	D	D	2 923	101.0	200	1
Pontotoc	39	D	D	D	32	88	6.9	1.6	1 939	73.5	1 219	25
Prentiss	39	982	51.0	18.4	32	D	D	D	1 510	47.6	1 925	14
Quitman	17	299	17.0	7.3	8	12	0.8	0.2	471	13.7	40	1
Rankin	265	7 288	705.5	276.3	214	1 210	112.5	32.6	11 639	537.0	129 807	573
Scott	46	1 040	65.6	25.7	36	141	10.6	3.0	1 517	51.0	860	4
Sharkey	12	207	15.2	5.5	9	42	1.5	0.6	377	11.3	280	2
Simpson	53	2 198	104.8	45.4	33	139	9.8	2.6	1 953	74.3	4 149	24
Smith	8	D	D	D	8	D	D	D	895	34.7	175	2
Stone	19	D	D	D	14	31	3.4	1.0	1 167	43.1	2 000	20

STATE County	Government employment and payroll, 2012									Local government finances, 2012				
			March payroll (percent of total)							General revenue				
												Taxes		
													Per capita[1] (dollars)	
	Full-time equivalent employees	March payroll (dollars)	Adminis-tration, judicial, and legal	Police and Corrections	Fire Protection	Highways and transpor-tation	Health and Welfare	Natural resources and utilities	Education and libraries	Total (mil dol)	Inter-govern-mental (mil dol)	Total (mil dol)	Total	Property
	171	172	173	174	175	176	177	178	179	180	181	182	183	184
MISSISSIPPI	X	X	X	X	X	X	X	X	X	X	X	X	X	X
Adams	1 489	4 260 491	9.2	8.0	2.4	5.1	26.3	5.5	41.4	139.6	46.8	32.7	1 016	894
Alcorn	2 243	7 489 226	3.0	3.6	1.7	1.3	54.6	4.0	31.8	263.0	70.9	24.2	650	610
Amite	299	736 289	14.3	7.8	0.1	5.8	2.2	1.8	66.9	23.6	11.3	6.5	502	498
Attala	932	2 477 820	6.6	4.7	2.3	3.4	21.1	4.4	56.3	69.8	32.7	16.3	850	818
Benton	295	719 394	10.6	6.4	0.0	3.6	0.4	1.7	76.1	18.5	13.0	3.5	406	392
Bolivar	1 582	4 628 258	5.5	13.0	0.3	4.9	0.3	3.0	72.0	119.8	63.2	35.1	1 036	985
Calhoun	797	2 771 233	3.3	2.8	0.0	1.3	49.8	1.3	39.9	46.2	18.3	8.5	575	564
Carroll	314	861 917	13.2	17.2	0.2	6.8	1.7	0.3	60.4	21.1	8.8	6.4	617	604
Chickasaw	881	2 154 461	7.6	9.3	1.7	3.6	8.8	5.2	62.6	53.0	32.3	11.7	673	613
Choctaw	408	952 647	11.6	4.1	0.2	1.9	1.6	2.0	76.1	22.8	12.4	4.5	537	521
Claiborne	496	1 465 091	5.5	6.2	1.5	4.2	22.1	1.6	57.8	34.3	20.9	6.0	640	605
Clarke	690	1 711 804	10.0	5.8	0.8	4.0	1.9	7.4	68.8	41.5	20.7	15.2	917	894
Clay	763	1 943 802	4.0	6.9	4.0	3.4	11.5	2.8	66.9	50.0	29.0	16.2	791	775
Coahoma	1 488	4 098 825	5.5	7.7	3.1	2.8	0.4	13.9	66.3	114.9	75.2	21.5	837	778
Copiah	1 481	4 154 517	5.1	5.7	0.7	2.2	11.5	2.3	72.0	103.1	56.6	17.6	609	584
Covington	1 021	2 828 948	4.9	4.0	0.1	11.3	32.9	1.7	44.1	78.2	25.0	13.0	663	643
DeSoto	5 452	16 140 720	6.4	11.9	7.2	2.5	2.2	3.5	65.3	471.9	208.5	194.3	1 169	1 065
Forrest	6 510	21 206 976	3.1	4.5	2.3	1.8	60.8	2.2	24.8	662.3	117.6	91.2	1 187	1 057
Franklin	363	888 524	9.6	4.0	0.0	5.2	1.8	1.0	78.1	35.6	14.5	5.9	746	704
George	1 085	2 865 559	4.2	7.1	0.4	2.7	30.9	0.7	53.5	89.3	31.9	12.7	553	528
Greene	532	1 305 598	6.9	3.9	0.0	3.1	15.5	1.6	67.6	37.4	20.6	9.4	654	637
Grenada	1 382	4 096 902	5.7	4.4	2.9	2.1	40.8	1.9	40.3	116.3	39.5	20.6	949	909
Hancock	1 924	6 676 661	5.8	6.9	3.4	2.2	23.0	4.5	52.3	287.9	169.1	47.6	1 052	1 011
Harrison	8 736	32 935 719	4.4	8.9	5.2	4.2	30.6	3.3	42.1	1 243.7	542.0	244.1	1 258	1 055
Hinds	10 525	28 655 948	5.9	10.5	4.8	2.2	1.5	4.8	70.4	878.7	450.7	268.0	1 078	1 017
Holmes	1 272	3 625 794	5.9	6.2	0.7	2.4	0.9	1.6	81.9	86.9	59.2	11.7	625	598
Humphreys	384	897 846	4.1	7.0	1.7	2.5	13.2	3.0	68.3	30.0	17.0	9.1	991	961
Issaquena	19	50 080	41.5	24.8	0.0	24.5	6.1	1.7	0.0	5.7	0.8	1.6	1 159	1 141
Itawamba	1 223	4 512 156	2.7	2.6	0.2	1.5	0.6	1.9	90.4	109.5	57.9	13.4	576	538
Jackson	7 975	28 632 767	3.0	5.8	2.5	2.0	45.3	2.4	38.2	857.2	237.3	174.7	1 245	1 188
Jasper	861	2 242 650	7.4	4.2	0.0	4.5	26.0	3.0	54.5	55.7	24.4	18.0	1 092	1 057
Jefferson	478	1 235 476	6.8	10.4	0.0	2.4	29.1	1.1	48.4	43.5	13.0	6.2	816	767
Jefferson Davis	567	1 467 224	8.3	4.6	0.9	4.0	30.4	1.6	49.8	39.7	17.1	8.1	672	658
Jones	4 753	12 100 544	2.7	3.7	2.3	2.1	35.5	1.9	50.3	341.0	127.5	54.3	791	752
Kemper	712	2 430 022	3.8	6.4	0.1	2.1	1.0	0.6	85.7	67.6	39.0	6.3	610	594
Lafayette	1 452	4 109 506	5.9	10.5	4.9	4.1	3.5	5.7	63.4	177.9	50.8	51.3	1 036	964
Lamar	2 053	4 821 922	4.0	6.2	0.6	4.8	0.9	0.5	81.5	123.2	59.9	53.4	924	906
Lauderdale	3 227	9 470 298	9.1	5.9	3.6	6.1	0.0	4.9	68.9	246.0	129.7	76.1	949	901
Lawrence	479	1 248 756	9.0	6.6	0.7	3.8	1.7	1.5	76.3	29.2	16.0	11.0	873	858
Leake	684	1 880 375	16.5	12.0	1.7	3.7	1.5	2.2	61.0	53.2	27.1	11.1	478	447
Lee	4 000	11 007 645	6.2	9.1	3.5	3.3	2.8	6.2	68.2	257.6	136.9	85.3	1 003	974
Leflore	2 494	8 995 576	3.1	4.0	1.8	1.7	57.3	2.3	29.6	240.0	68.2	28.3	913	861
Lincoln	1 177	3 186 542	7.5	6.9	3.7	3.9	0.6	2.4	74.6	84.1	45.5	26.5	760	721
Lowndes	2 233	7 025 354	8.5	12.2	3.9	4.4	1.2	8.3	59.4	183.3	105.0	53.8	901	845
Madison	2 936	9 496 425	7.8	11.0	5.2	3.3	1.3	2.9	67.0	279.8	105.3	131.7	1 337	1 266
Marion	1 327	2 909 454	6.2	11.0	1.8	3.7	1.7	1.0	73.2	79.0	36.5	17.5	662	635
Marshall	1 090	3 348 828	7.9	14.8	1.8	9.2	0.0	8.4	56.4	69.4	40.2	23.0	629	608
Monroe	1 425	3 622 413	13.2	8.0	3.4	7.1	1.1	4.6	60.5	97.7	48.7	27.8	764	733
Montgomery	546	1 639 820	6.9	4.5	1.6	3.8	37.3	2.7	42.6	35.2	16.1	7.1	672	642
Neshoba	938	2 330 410	5.2	9.8	3.5	4.9	0.8	6.3	69.2	84.7	35.9	14.6	489	471
Newton	1 105	3 232 369	4.5	4.7	0.6	1.9	0.9	5.5	81.6	80.7	53.7	13.3	616	581
Noxubee	657	1 978 193	6.6	1.5	0.5	2.2	28.3	0.4	59.1	39.8	18.4	8.4	752	729
Oktibbeha	1 842	5 582 328	2.8	4.7	3.1	1.1	47.2	4.4	36.2	155.8	47.9	35.8	744	726
Panola	1 433	4 200 779	4.8	10.0	2.0	2.8	2.1	3.6	74.4	97.6	58.1	28.7	832	760
Pearl River	2 574	7 161 607	5.5	5.4	1.8	2.1	8.1	3.0	73.4	183.3	100.0	38.8	702	666
Perry	466	1 122 268	9.5	5.9	0.4	5.6	1.3	2.1	74.8	33.9	18.6	9.5	788	759
Pike	2 872	9 325 024	3.8	4.6	1.6	1.6	46.9	2.2	38.5	249.1	83.4	32.7	816	780
Pontotoc	982	3 251 798	6.3	8.7	2.5	3.4	1.2	4.1	73.1	74.0	42.6	18.2	594	546
Prentiss	1 158	3 605 727	3.3	4.8	2.1	1.8	1.3	1.1	85.6	87.2	54.3	15.2	598	572
Quitman	519	1 364 995	6.8	5.4	0.1	5.5	31.8	1.2	49.1	23.7	13.9	7.2	919	878
Rankin	4 244	12 845 764	5.1	11.8	6.8	3.4	0.1	3.9	68.2	344.6	160.2	130.8	901	859
Scott	1 071	2 578 316	6.0	10.4	1.4	2.8	0.9	4.7	73.7	65.2	39.7	17.6	624	583
Sharkey	279	713 380	12.1	7.5	0.1	4.4	1.2	10.7	63.5	17.4	9.5	5.1	1 064	1 028
Simpson	898	2 221 618	6.8	8.7	0.2	5.6	1.2	1.8	73.3	56.8	33.6	17.5	639	614
Smith	568	1 449 509	9.4	8.8	0.0	4.1	1.0	2.8	73.8	37.3	21.8	10.9	667	654
Stone	1 427	5 071 678	2.8	2.3	0.5	0.8	0.4	0.4	92.7	126.2	75.9	12.5	691	645

1. Based on the resident population estimated as of July 1 of the year shown.

STATE County	Local government finances, 2012 (cont.) — Direct general expenditure — Total (mil dol)	Per capita[1] (dollars)	Percent of total for: Education	Health and hospitals	Police protection	Public welfare	Highways	Debt outstanding — Total (mil dol)	Per capita[1] (dollars)	Government employment, 2013 — Federal civilian	Federal military	State and local	Presidential election,[2] 2012 — Percent of vote cast: Democratic	Republican	All other
	185	186	187	188	189	190	191	192	193	194	195	196	197	198	199
MISSISSIPPI	X	X	X	X	X	X	X	X	X	25 524	29 259	222 452	43.0	56.2	0.8
Adams	139.6	4 345	30.8	31.5	5.2	0.2	5.9	55.9	1 739	116	178	1 793	57.5	41.8	0.7
Alcorn	255.2	6 866	20.1	53.1	2.1	0.1	2.6	317.3	8 537	96	222	3 017	27.2	71.2	1.6
Amite	19.7	1 524	56.2	1.8	6.7	0.0	13.8	0.3	25	26	77	392	43.8	55.5	0.7
Attala	75.3	3 933	38.1	28.5	2.8	0.2	5.1	32.6	1 702	54	115	1 207	41.9	57.4	0.7
Benton	19.4	2 227	67.1	0.9	4.4	0.2	12.1	3.9	444	49	51	346	48.0	50.2	1.8
Bolivar	121.4	3 582	53.7	4.8	5.9	0.2	8.4	52.7	1 553	78	196	2 874	67.2	31.8	1.0
Calhoun	49.9	3 364	39.2	32.8	3.2	0.1	5.9	14.4	971	35	88	821	35.9	63.5	0.6
Carroll	20.6	1 974	43.6	0.9	2.8	0.0	14.4	13.5	1 292	22	60	347	34.1	65.4	0.4
Chickasaw	52.1	2 994	52.7	1.8	5.1	8.9	7.0	31.3	1 795	43	102	908	50.7	48.5	0.8
Choctaw	30.5	3 651	50.2	10.5	5.3	0.1	10.2	32.0	3 838	34	50	419	35.3	63.6	1.1
Claiborne	35.4	3 783	50.8	3.0	3.9	0.2	5.8	129.3	13 835	26	49	1 641	85.9	13.7	0.4
Clarke	40.6	2 452	65.6	0.9	5.4	0.1	8.0	10.9	661	31	99	784	37.2	62.3	0.6
Clay	52.7	2 577	56.9	0.6	7.8	0.6	8.0	34.3	1 677	57	121	911	59.1	40.3	0.6
Coahoma	119.1	4 634	63.3	0.9	4.4	0.0	4.0	151.1	5 877	66	148	1 927	71.9	27.6	0.5
Copiah	112.0	3 869	65.2	13.0	4.2	0.0	7.0	26.9	930	72	168	1 638	53.2	46.2	0.6
Covington	69.3	3 537	37.9	38.8	3.9	0.1	7.3	13.5	688	66	116	1 258	40.7	58.4	0.9
DeSoto	452.7	2 723	48.5	1.1	8.4	0.0	5.1	539.6	3 246	219	1 011	6 243	30.5	68.8	0.7
Forrest	657.8	8 555	16.6	64.3	2.3	0.0	3.0	378.3	4 920	730	823	10 926	42.8	56.3	1.0
Franklin	33.3	4 206	42.1	31.8	4.6	0.0	7.5	3.6	454	57	47	612	37.0	62.1	0.9
George	87.3	3 806	33.7	44.6	2.8	0.1	6.5	28.7	1 250	40	136	1 395	16.4	82.5	1.1
Greene	39.0	2 727	52.3	0.8	6.9	16.0	9.3	7.5	522	14	67	1 161	23.6	75.3	1.1
Grenada	114.7	5 290	29.2	42.6	4.9	0.0	4.5	98.3	4 534	243	129	1 650	44.4	55.1	0.5
Hancock	284.4	6 285	23.0	16.2	2.7	0.1	4.9	96.7	2 137	2 038	718	1 980	22.1	76.3	1.6
Harrison	1 263.3	6 511	21.1	29.5	4.6	0.2	4.8	919.9	4 741	5 994	9 173	12 810	36.6	62.6	0.9
Hinds	892.8	3 591	57.8	0.8	5.7	0.3	4.2	1 035.1	4 163	4 952	1 498	35 449	69.2	30.3	0.5
Holmes	104.3	5 551	78.5	1.3	3.6	0.2	4.5	35.2	1 870	52	108	1 239	81.4	18.0	0.7
Humphreys	30.1	3 277	50.7	1.4	6.0	0.1	15.6	10.5	1 144	22	53	486	70.9	28.5	0.6
Issaquena	5.9	4 234	0.9	5.4	10.5	0.0	13.4	1.8	1 275	0	0	92	60.9	38.3	0.7
Itawamba	111.8	4 790	82.2	0.5	2.0	0.0	3.7	48.6	2 082	47	136	1 102	20.9	77.0	2.1
Jackson	885.7	6 313	30.2	41.1	3.1	0.1	3.7	521.2	3 715	940	999	8 983	32.7	66.3	1.0
Jasper	52.0	3 145	47.2	13.8	3.9	0.1	13.0	21.9	1 327	56	99	915	54.6	44.9	0.5
Jefferson	38.6	5 053	32.5	24.2	4.3	10.8	4.1	5.0	653	16	44	671	86.7	12.3	1.0
Jefferson Davis	43.5	3 615	47.4	27.4	3.9	0.0	7.0	9.1	759	21	71	655	60.4	39.0	0.6
Jones	365.6	5 326	40.2	37.4	2.4	0.8	3.6	230.8	3 362	218	405	6 970	30.2	68.9	0.9
Kemper	67.4	6 517	80.0	0.6	1.8	0.1	3.5	9.1	878	32	56	617	62.3	37.0	0.6
Lafayette	126.1	2 548	52.3	0.9	7.5	0.0	9.3	146.9	2 968	328	291	7 385	43.3	55.7	1.0
Lamar	128.5	2 224	68.5	0.7	6.9	0.2	7.3	76.2	1 319	49	353	2 370	21.6	77.4	1.1
Lauderdale	232.7	2 900	60.0	3.5	5.9	0.0	5.1	138.1	1 722	793	1 670	5 444	40.3	59.1	0.6
Lawrence	30.1	2 396	64.4	1.7	4.0	0.4	8.9	8.0	634	45	76	712	36.9	62.3	0.8
Leake	54.6	2 344	49.9	15.0	4.7	0.0	8.2	21.7	931	61	129	785	44.4	55.0	0.6
Lee	265.1	3 118	54.1	0.9	7.2	0.2	8.9	210.0	2 470	464	510	5 156	34.4	64.9	0.7
Leflore	246.7	7 972	21.8	53.9	3.5	0.0	2.9	171.6	5 546	104	179	4 046	68.1	31.4	0.5
Lincoln	82.3	2 359	58.3	1.7	7.0	0.0	9.8	29.6	848	87	206	1 652	33.6	65.7	0.7
Lowndes	180.6	3 026	47.7	0.8	6.3	0.1	7.7	210.1	3 521	834	1 726	3 306	48.1	51.0	1.0
Madison	302.7	3 074	49.9	0.4	6.9	0.1	12.3	478.1	4 855	221	595	4 430	42.0	57.5	0.5
Marion	79.2	2 994	45.6	21.5	5.3	0.0	4.2	27.0	1 020	48	154	1 442	34.0	65.4	0.6
Marshall	73.1	1 995	56.1	1.7	6.9	0.1	12.7	20.0	545	72	209	1 205	58.8	40.6	0.7
Monroe	96.6	2 653	58.9	1.2	7.3	0.4	7.6	47.3	1 299	128	216	1 484	41.0	58.2	0.8
Montgomery	37.1	3 497	42.0	24.7	4.2	0.3	9.9	11.3	1 062	30	63	654	45.7	53.8	0.6
Neshoba	87.8	2 947	41.8	32.2	3.5	0.0	5.2	30.9	1 037	84	176	6 165	27.3	72.0	0.7
Newton	81.2	3 757	66.9	1.0	5.1	0.0	5.2	11.7	539	74	128	1 987	32.7	66.8	0.6
Noxubee	40.0	3 569	46.0	25.3	3.7	0.1	6.1	6.0	537	42	66	740	76.3	23.1	0.5
Oktibbeha	178.0	3 694	32.7	38.4	3.7	0.0	4.9	104.4	2 167	243	277	9 609	49.6	49.6	0.8
Panola	102.7	2 980	56.0	1.3	6.9	0.2	7.0	38.1	1 104	106	206	2 170	52.9	46.4	0.6
Pearl River	195.3	3 533	60.8	8.4	3.0	0.1	6.4	65.6	1 186	125	326	3 117	19.2	79.7	1.1
Perry	35.3	2 921	48.4	1.5	4.7	0.1	17.1	88.9	7 358	18	73	550	27.1	71.8	1.1
Pike	242.6	6 051	34.8	43.8	2.9	0.0	2.6	84.1	2 098	113	236	3 515	51.4	47.9	0.7
Pontotoc	80.2	2 621	56.4	1.0	4.0	0.1	6.4	30.1	983	46	185	1 214	23.2	75.6	1.2
Prentiss	89.5	3 525	81.0	0.8	4.2	0.0	3.0	31.5	1 242	42	175	1 530	27.6	70.4	2.0
Quitman	33.0	4 231	64.9	0.9	4.1	0.0	8.6	7.5	959	23	46	373	67.3	32.0	0.7
Rankin	365.9	2 521	50.1	0.9	7.2	0.1	9.8	417.1	2 873	603	853	9 370	22.8	76.3	0.9
Scott	65.3	2 311	62.2	1.9	5.4	0.0	7.7	22.0	779	207	169	1 240	43.1	56.4	0.5
Sharkey	21.1	4 406	71.8	0.6	4.2	0.0	8.3	5.6	1 159	23	28	404	68.2	31.2	0.5
Simpson	63.8	2 330	55.8	1.6	3.8	2.0	6.9	28.1	1 027	42	162	1 618	38.2	60.6	1.2
Smith	36.8	2 253	63.0	1.0	5.3	0.0	13.3	9.9	606	27	97	627	23.7	75.4	0.9
Stone	142.2	7 887	79.3	0.5	3.6	0.0	2.5	30.7	1 701	55	100	1 126	27.5	71.1	1.4

1. Based on the resident population estimated as of July 1 of the year shown. 2.

STATE/ County code	CBSA code[1]	County type[2]	STATE County	Land area,[3] (sq km) 2010	Population, 2014: Total persons 2014	Population, 2014: Rank	Population, 2014: Per square kilometer	Population and population characteristics, 2013: Race alone or in combination, not Hispanic or Latino (percent): White	Black	American Indian, Alaska Native	Asian and Pacific Islander	Percent Hispanic or Latino[4]	Age (percent): Under 5 years	5 to 17 years	18 to 24 years	25 to 34 years	35 to 44 years	45 to 54 years
				1	2	3	4	5	6	7	8	9	10	11	12	13	14	15
			MISSISSIPPI—Cont'd															
28 133	26940	5	Sunflower	1 807	27 496	1 512	15.2	25.5	72.6	0.5	0.5	1.5	6.6	16.9	11.6	15.8	12.7	13.4
28 135	...	7	Tallahatchie	1 671	14 761	2 118	8.8	36.9	56.4	0.6	1.1	6.0	5.7	15.1	11.7	16.0	14.0	12.9
28 137	32820	1	Tate	1 048	28 204	1 483	26.9	66.1	31.4	0.6	0.5	2.6	6.1	18.6	11.6	11.7	11.7	13.4
28 139	...	7	Tippah	1 186	22 039	1 728	18.6	78.4	17.1	0.5	0.3	5.0	6.4	18.3	9.5	11.8	12.1	14.1
28 141	...	8	Tishomingo	1 099	19 420	1 859	17.7	94.0	3.3	0.6	0.4	2.7	5.6	16.7	8.2	10.5	12.2	14.1
28 143	32820	1	Tunica	1 178	10 598	2 390	9.0	21.8	75.2	0.5	1.0	2.4	8.6	21.2	9.7	14.1	12.8	12.5
28 145	...	7	Union	1 076	28 097	1 488	26.1	80.0	15.6	0.6	0.5	4.6	6.6	18.7	8.4	12.5	13.2	13.3
28 147	...	9	Walthall	1 046	14 859	2 110	14.2	54.1	44.1	0.8	0.4	1.7	6.1	18.9	8.3	11.3	11.6	12.7
28 149	46980	4	Warren	1 524	47 983	1 013	31.5	49.1	48.1	0.5	1.1	2.0	6.5	18.6	8.7	12.5	12.3	13.6
28 151	24740	5	Washington	1 877	48 958	1 000	26.1	26.8	71.3	0.3	0.9	1.3	7.4	19.2	9.9	12.5	11.3	13.0
28 153	...	7	Wayne	2 100	20 490	1 802	9.8	59.6	38.9	0.6	0.4	1.4	6.5	18.6	9.2	12.1	11.8	13.6
28 155	...	9	Webster	1 090	9 972	2 442	9.1	78.6	20.1	0.5	0.4	1.3	5.9	17.8	7.9	12.2	11.5	14.7
28 157	...	8	Wilkinson	1 756	9 191	2 496	5.2	29.3	70.0	0.3	0.3	0.7	6.1	15.6	9.4	14.9	11.5	13.7
28 159	...	7	Winston	1 573	18 478	1 897	11.7	51.9	46.1	1.2	0.4	1.1	6.2	17.6	8.3	11.7	11.9	13.1
28 161	...	7	Yalobusha	1 210	12 276	2 278	10.1	60.1	38.5	0.5	0.4	1.6	6.2	17.0	8.4	11.0	12.0	13.0
28 163	27140	6	Yazoo	2 390	27 817	1 502	11.6	37.1	57.1	0.5	0.7	5.4	6.8	17.5	8.9	16.1	14.3	12.9
29 000	...	X	MISSOURI	178 040	6 063 589	X	34.1	82.1	12.5	1.1	2.4	3.9	6.2	16.9	9.9	13.2	12.1	13.9
29 001	28860	7	Adair	1 469	25 602	1 580	17.4	93.7	2.2	0.7	2.6	2.3	4.9	13.7	26.6	10.6	9.1	11.1
29 003	41140	3	Andrew	1 121	17 379	1 956	15.5	96.0	1.2	0.9	0.7	2.4	5.4	17.8	8.1	10.5	12.4	14.6
29 005	...	9	Atchison	1 418	5 382	2 810	3.8	97.7	0.9	0.8	0.3	1.2	5.5	14.5	7.6	9.3	10.7	14.1
29 007	33020	6	Audrain	1 793	25 887	1 563	14.4	89.6	7.8	0.7	0.9	2.7	6.3	17.1	8.5	12.9	12.5	13.2
29 009	...	6	Barry	2 016	35 662	1 281	17.7	89.0	0.6	2.1	1.5	8.3	6.4	16.9	7.5	10.0	10.9	14.1
29 011	...	6	Barton	1 533	12 057	2 294	7.9	95.5	0.9	2.6	0.8	2.4	5.7	19.8	7.9	10.5	10.7	13.6
29 013	28140	1	Bates	2 167	16 584	2 002	7.7	96.0	1.4	1.3	0.4	2.1	5.9	18.1	7.2	11.1	10.8	14.5
29 015	...	9	Benton	1 824	18 806	1 879	10.3	96.9	0.6	1.5	0.6	1.6	4.1	13.5	5.8	7.6	9.1	13.5
29 017	16020	9	Bollinger	1 600	12 394	2 271	7.7	97.6	0.7	1.2	0.5	1.0	6.1	16.6	8.1	10.3	11.8	15.1
29 019	17860	3	Boone	1 775	172 717	366	97.3	82.9	10.7	1.0	5.0	3.2	6.0	14.6	20.9	15.3	11.3	11.3
29 021	41140	3	Buchanan	1 057	89 486	643	84.7	86.9	6.9	1.0	1.6	5.8	6.8	16.3	10.4	14.1	12.0	13.7
29 023	38740	7	Butler	1 799	42 972	1 112	23.9	91.4	6.3	1.5	1.2	1.8	6.5	17.0	8.2	12.0	11.9	13.5
29 025	28140	1	Caldwell	1 104	9 034	2 514	8.2	96.7	1.2	1.3	0.6	2.0	5.4	18.7	7.5	10.2	11.3	14.5
29 027	27620	3	Callaway	2 162	44 750	1 076	20.7	92.6	5.2	1.3	0.9	1.8	5.7	16.1	11.3	12.9	12.4	14.6
29 029	...	7	Camden	1 699	44 021	1 089	25.9	95.7	0.9	1.1	0.8	2.6	4.7	14.0	6.4	9.4	9.7	13.8
29 031	16020	5	Cape Girardeau	1 498	78 043	708	52.1	88.7	8.5	0.7	1.6	2.2	5.9	15.8	14.5	12.4	11.2	12.7
29 033	...	6	Carroll	1 799	9 043	2 512	5.0	95.9	2.9	0.8	0.7	1.3	5.7	16.9	8.1	10.0	12.0	13.4
29 035	...	9	Carter	1 314	6 258	2 739	4.8	96.3	0.9	2.1	0.5	2.1	5.9	17.6	8.4	11.2	11.2	14.5
29 037	28140	1	Cass	1 805	100 889	590	55.9	90.6	4.5	1.3	1.3	4.2	6.1	19.3	7.9	11.7	13.0	14.4
29 039	...	6	Cedar	1 229	13 952	2 174	11.4	96.7	0.5	1.7	0.7	1.9	5.4	17.5	6.6	9.4	10.3	12.7
29 041	...	9	Chariton	1 946	7 694	2 621	4.0	96.5	2.7	0.6	0.2	0.8	6.0	16.0	6.8	9.8	10.0	13.9
29 043	44180	2	Christian	1 457	82 101	680	56.3	95.3	1.2	1.3	1.1	2.7	6.6	19.7	7.6	13.0	13.7	13.6
29 045	22800	9	Clark	1 307	6 917	2 685	5.3	98.2	0.6	0.7	0.7	0.9	6.0	17.6	6.9	10.4	11.0	14.5
29 047	28140	1	Clay	1 029	233 682	278	227.1	85.1	6.6	1.2	3.1	6.3	6.7	18.6	8.2	14.3	14.1	14.0
29 049	28140	1	Clinton	1 085	20 299	1 819	18.7	95.4	2.2	1.3	0.7	2.0	6.0	18.5	7.6	10.9	12.2	14.8
29 051	27620	3	Cole	1 020	76 557	719	75.1	84.2	12.5	0.7	1.7	2.8	6.2	16.9	9.1	13.8	12.8	14.4
29 053	...	6	Cooper	1 463	17 585	1 943	12.0	90.4	8.0	1.0	0.9	1.5	5.6	16.3	10.0	13.5	11.3	13.8
29 055	...	6	Crawford	1 923	24 650	1 623	12.8	97.1	0.7	1.1	0.5	1.7	6.0	17.6	7.8	11.3	11.6	14.6
29 057	...	8	Dade	1 269	7 628	2 628	6.0	96.4	0.9	2.5	0.6	1.8	4.8	16.7	6.6	8.8	10.7	13.9
29 059	44180	2	Dallas	1 401	16 389	2 019	11.7	96.8	0.6	1.9	0.5	1.8	5.9	17.7	7.2	10.4	10.9	14.2
29 061	...	8	Daviess	1 459	8 297	2 577	5.7	97.4	1.0	0.8	0.4	1.5	6.6	19.3	8.2	9.6	11.3	12.5
29 063	41140	3	DeKalb	1 091	12 692	2 250	11.6	85.6	11.8	1.0	0.6	2.0	4.4	12.5	8.6	15.9	15.5	15.8
29 065	...	7	Dent	1 950	15 655	2 064	8.0	96.4	1.0	1.9	1.0	1.3	5.8	17.2	7.4	10.8	10.6	14.5
29 067	...	6	Douglas	2 107	13 546	2 202	6.4	97.7	0.7	1.9	0.5	1.0	5.8	15.5	6.9	9.8	9.9	14.0
29 069	28380	7	Dunklin	1 401	31 344	1 403	22.4	82.9	11.1	0.8	0.5	6.2	7.3	18.7	8.3	11.1	11.6	13.4
29 071	41180	1	Franklin	2 390	102 084	581	42.7	96.6	1.4	0.8	0.7	1.6	6.3	17.6	8.3	12.0	11.7	15.5
29 073	...	6	Gasconade	1 341	14 866	2 109	11.1	97.7	0.7	0.8	0.7	1.3	4.9	16.1	7.1	9.8	10.7	14.9
29 075	...	8	Gentry	1 273	6 826	2 697	5.4	98.2	0.9	0.5	0.4	0.8	7.0	17.2	7.9	11.0	10.4	13.6
29 077	44180	2	Greene	1 749	285 865	236	163.4	91.0	4.2	1.5	2.5	3.3	6.1	14.9	14.1	14.2	11.6	12.4
29 079	...	7	Grundy	1 127	10 197	2 422	9.0	96.3	1.1	1.1	0.7	1.9	6.4	17.3	9.2	10.9	9.7	12.8
29 081	...	7	Harrison	1 871	8 639	2 548	4.6	96.8	0.7	0.9	0.6	2.0	6.7	17.8	7.0	10.5	10.2	12.8
29 083	...	6	Henry	1 805	22 028	1 729	12.2	95.8	1.7	1.4	0.6	1.9	5.9	16.6	7.1	11.2	11.1	14.1
29 085	...	8	Hickory	1 034	9 219	2 493	8.9	97.1	0.7	1.9	0.5	1.3	4.1	13.3	5.4	7.1	8.5	13.0
29 087	...	8	Holt	1 198	4 516	2 863	3.8	97.4	0.5	1.3	0.7	0.9	5.1	14.8	6.8	9.7	11.0	14.8
29 089	...	3	Howard	1 201	10 159	2 425	8.5	92.7	6.1	1.2	0.7	1.3	6.0	16.0	12.9	11.2	10.0	13.6
29 091	48460	7	Howell	2 402	40 173	1 168	16.7	96.4	0.8	1.6	0.9	1.9	6.7	17.8	8.1	11.5	11.9	13.0
29 093	...	6	Iron	1 425	10 267	2 414	7.2	96.1	2.0	1.7	0.4	1.6	6.2	16.0	7.6	10.4	11.9	14.5
29 095	28140	1	Jackson	1 566	683 191	92	436.3	65.3	24.9	1.2	2.6	8.6	6.9	17.2	9.0	15.0	12.5	13.7

1. CBSA = Core Based Statistical Area. See Appendix A for explanation. See Appendix B for list of metropolitan areas with component counties. 2. County type code from the Economic Research Service of USDA Rural-Urban Continuum Codes. See Appendix A for definition. 3. Dry land or land partially or temporarily covered by water. 4. May be of any race.

STATE County	Population, 2013 (cont.): Age (percent) (cont.): 55 to 64 years	65 to 74 years	75 years and over	Percent female	Population change and components of change, 2000–2014: Total persons: 2000	2010	Percent change: 2000–2010	2010–2014	Components of change, 2010–2014: Births	Deaths	Net migration	Households, 2009–2013: Number	Persons per house-hold	Percent: Family house-holds	Female family house-holder[1]	One per-son
	16	17	18	19	20	21	22	23	24	25	26	27	28	29	30	31
MISSISSIPPI—Cont'd																
Sunflower	11.8	6.4	4.7	46.8	34 369	29 450	-14.3	-6.6	1 461	1 216	-2 260	8 394	2.92	70.5	29.4	27.0
Tallahatchie	11.6	7.4	5.6	44.4	14 903	15 378	3.2	-4.0	655	644	-639	4 640	2.58	70.1	27.0	26.8
Tate	12.6	8.9	5.4	51.9	25 370	28 886	13.9	-2.3	1 443	1 143	-981	9 936	2.73	70.6	15.0	25.4
Tippah	12.2	9.4	6.3	50.7	20 826	22 232	6.8	-0.9	1 080	1 061	-226	8 472	2.56	74.1	14.4	23.4
Tishomingo	13.6	11.1	8.1	51.7	19 163	19 593	2.2	-0.9	804	1 156	181	7 643	2.52	75.6	15.4	22.7
Tunica	11.3	5.9	4.0	52.1	9 227	10 778	16.8	-1.7	875	398	-636	4 116	2.53	56.9	22.8	37.7
Union	11.8	8.9	6.6	51.2	25 362	27 134	7.0	3.5	1 556	1 100	510	10 322	2.62	75.0	13.2	21.3
Walthall	13.5	9.5	8.0	51.8	15 156	15 443	1.9	-3.8	748	736	-608	5 649	2.68	63.4	12.0	33.0
Warren	13.8	8.4	5.8	52.3	49 644	48 773	-1.8	-1.6	2 654	2 088	-1 315	18 404	2.60	66.5	19.8	29.8
Washington	13.4	7.6	5.5	52.9	62 977	51 137	-18.8	-4.3	3 377	2 539	-2 988	18 123	2.75	68.5	30.6	28.5
Wayne	12.7	9.0	6.4	51.9	21 216	20 747	-2.2	-1.2	1 185	869	-587	8 105	2.52	68.6	15.4	28.6
Webster	13.4	9.3	7.2	51.1	10 294	10 253	-0.4	-2.7	544	590	-259	4 084	2.45	74.7	17.0	23.0
Wilkinson	13.9	8.2	6.6	46.8	10 312	9 878	-4.2	-7.0	490	483	-712	3 496	2.48	67.2	24.1	30.3
Winston	13.7	9.5	8.0	51.2	20 160	19 198	-4.8	-3.8	831	924	-617	7 635	2.44	68.5	19.8	28.8
Yalobusha	14.5	10.2	7.8	51.8	13 051	12 678	-2.9	-3.2	642	712	-319	4 797	2.58	68.2	16.4	30.4
Yazoo	11.1	6.6	5.7	44.7	28 149	28 065	-0.3	-0.9	1 644	1 096	-767	8 710	2.83	68.2	25.8	28.0
MISSOURI	12.9	8.4	6.6	51.0	5 595 211	5 988 927	7.0	1.2	321 112	236 479	-8 048	2 360 131	2.47	65.3	12.3	28.8
Adair	10.6	7.3	6.1	52.0	24 977	25 607	2.5	0.0	1 083	853	-200	9 648	2.31	57.0	9.1	33.7
Andrew	14.2	9.6	7.5	50.6	16 492	17 291	4.8	0.5	787	693	-38	6 691	2.55	70.0	6.3	24.8
Atchison	14.8	13.0	10.3	50.4	6 430	5 685	-11.6	-5.3	246	337	-213	2 448	2.21	62.3	6.3	32.2
Audrain	13.0	8.8	7.7	54.6	25 853	25 529	-1.3	1.4	1 422	1 230	166	9 327	2.54	68.9	10.6	26.6
Barry	14.2	11.6	8.3	50.3	34 010	35 597	4.7	0.2	1 821	1 687	-23	13 464	2.62	70.5	8.9	24.7
Barton	13.5	9.4	8.8	50.9	12 541	12 402	-1.1	-2.8	619	561	-407	5 065	2.42	72.1	7.3	24.1
Bates	13.6	10.1	8.7	50.7	16 653	17 049	2.4	-2.7	815	864	-428	6 832	2.42	66.3	9.3	29.4
Benton	18.4	16.8	11.2	49.9	17 180	19 056	10.9	-1.3	641	1 138	285	8 225	2.28	70.0	8.2	26.6
Bollinger	14.6	10.3	7.0	50.0	12 029	12 363	2.8	0.3	592	536	-1	4 758	2.57	70.1	9.9	26.7
Boone	10.5	5.7	4.4	51.6	135 454	162 642	20.1	6.2	9 015	4 264	5 242	65 649	2.38	56.9	10.1	29.1
Buchanan	12.5	7.7	6.6	49.7	85 998	89 201	3.7	0.3	5 106	3 995	-741	33 331	2.56	63.8	13.2	30.4
Butler	13.6	9.5	7.9	51.3	40 867	42 794	4.7	0.4	2 458	2 319	140	17 085	2.46	66.0	12.4	28.7
Caldwell	14.0	10.1	8.3	49.6	8 969	9 424	5.1	-4.1	381	404	-402	3 743	2.42	71.3	10.8	26.5
Callaway	13.1	8.2	5.6	48.9	40 766	44 332	8.7	0.9	2 183	1 576	-138	16 548	2.45	67.9	11.5	27.7
Camden	17.8	15.7	8.5	50.6	37 051	44 002	18.8	0.0	1 720	1 886	201	17 647	2.45	71.2	8.9	25.0
Cape Girardeau	12.4	7.9	7.2	51.7	68 693	75 674	10.2	3.1	3 877	3 020	1 418	29 411	2.47	65.5	10.4	27.4
Carroll	13.7	11.0	9.3	51.3	10 285	9 295	-9.6	-2.7	473	532	-197	3 613	2.52	68.5	9.4	28.4
Carter	14.1	10.3	6.8	51.4	5 941	6 265	5.5	-0.1	323	309	-22	2 426	2.56	62.7	10.1	32.7
Cass	12.6	8.5	6.5	51.0	82 092	99 478	21.2	1.4	5 050	3 737	43	37 307	2.65	74.1	11.2	21.4
Cedar	14.1	13.1	10.9	50.2	13 733	13 982	1.8	-0.2	701	823	162	5 970	2.29	63.9	10.0	33.9
Chariton	14.9	11.1	11.5	50.7	8 438	7 831	-7.2	-1.7	369	365	-135	2 958	2.53	66.3	7.1	31.2
Christian	11.9	8.4	5.5	51.2	54 285	77 422	42.6	6.0	4 263	2 298	2 593	29 652	2.63	76.2	9.6	19.5
Clark	14.6	10.4	8.4	49.6	7 416	7 139	-3.7	-3.1	349	335	-228	2 749	2.53	64.9	8.6	31.1
Clay	11.9	7.2	5.1	51.0	184 006	221 939	20.6	5.3	13 084	6 686	5 412	86 934	2.56	68.0	11.5	26.2
Clinton	13.6	9.0	7.4	49.5	18 979	20 743	9.3	-2.1	965	996	-438	8 089	2.50	71.8	10.5	22.7
Cole	13.2	7.7	5.9	49.5	71 397	75 990	6.4	0.8	3 919	2 549	-708	29 302	2.46	65.7	12.5	28.7
Cooper	13.2	8.6	7.6	47.5	16 670	17 601	5.6	-0.1	836	779	-94	6 568	2.43	70.6	10.8	24.8
Crawford	13.5	10.0	7.5	50.5	22 804	24 696	8.3	-0.2	1 192	1 205	-46	9 485	2.57	67.7	11.1	28.0
Dade	16.3	11.8	10.3	49.4	7 923	7 883	-0.5	-3.2	280	427	-115	3 175	2.39	68.6	11.1	29.4
Dallas	14.7	10.8	8.2	50.1	15 661	16 777	7.1	-2.3	828	748	-480	6 443	2.56	74.6	12.8	20.8
Daviess	14.0	10.9	7.6	49.7	8 016	8 433	5.2	-1.6	477	349	-249	3 151	2.61	71.7	7.0	24.5
DeKalb	11.9	8.1	7.3	37.1	11 597	12 892	11.2	-1.6	445	481	-212	3 769	2.48	67.2	8.1	30.4
Dent	13.8	11.0	8.9	50.3	14 927	15 657	4.9	0.0	742	801	65	5 858	2.63	72.0	11.6	24.1
Douglas	16.3	12.3	9.5	50.5	13 084	13 684	4.6	-1.0	612	652	-87	5 178	2.61	70.5	7.3	26.8
Dunklin	12.7	9.5	7.4	52.0	33 155	31 953	-3.6	-1.9	1 958	1 814	-732	12 882	2.42	65.0	16.5	30.4
Franklin	13.5	8.6	6.5	50.4	93 807	101 492	8.2	0.6	5 325	4 084	-675	39 263	2.56	70.6	10.2	25.1
Gasconade	15.1	11.5	10.0	50.8	15 342	15 222	-0.8	-2.3	646	859	-113	6 168	2.40	66.5	8.2	29.8
Gentry	12.8	9.5	10.6	51.4	6 861	6 738	-1.8	1.3	387	358	65	2 800	2.33	66.8	9.5	29.2
Greene	11.8	8.1	6.9	51.2	240 391	275 174	14.5	3.9	15 086	10 857	6 327	115 574	2.30	60.1	10.8	31.4
Grundy	12.7	10.8	10.2	52.3	10 432	10 261	-1.6	-0.6	607	563	-112	4 148	2.40	64.9	9.7	30.9
Harrison	13.8	10.6	10.6	50.0	8 850	8 957	1.2	-3.6	483	465	-343	3 515	2.46	66.0	6.7	29.3
Henry	14.0	11.3	8.9	51.0	21 997	22 272	1.3	-1.1	1 120	1 317	-14	9 551	2.29	64.4	9.5	30.5
Hickory	17.2	18.5	12.8	51.4	8 940	9 627	7.7	-4.2	304	586	-98	4 219	2.23	67.0	5.0	28.3
Holt	15.2	10.7	11.8	51.1	5 351	4 912	-8.2	-8.1	213	264	-347	2 218	2.10	66.4	8.5	29.9
Howard	14.0	8.9	7.5	50.3	10 212	10 144	-0.7	0.1	501	383	-94	3 825	2.46	64.8	12.3	31.5
Howell	12.9	9.9	8.2	51.1	37 238	40 400	8.5	-0.6	2 235	2 084	-349	15 796	2.52	68.9	10.7	27.7
Iron	15.0	10.7	7.7	50.7	10 697	10 630	-0.6	-3.4	452	551	-334	4 126	2.45	68.3	10.2	26.7
Jackson	12.4	7.3	6.0	51.6	654 880	674 158	2.9	1.3	40 734	25 890	-5 037	271 545	2.45	60.5	15.5	32.8

1. No spouse present.

STATE County	Persons in group quarters, 2014	Daytime population, 2009–2013: Number	Daytime population, 2009–2013: Employment/residence ratio	Births, 2014: Total	Births, 2014: Rate[1]	Deaths, 2014: Number	Deaths, 2014: Rate[1]	Persons under 65 with no health insurance, 2013: Number	Persons under 65 with no health insurance, 2013: Percent	Medicare, 2014: Eligible for Medicare	Medicare, 2014: Enrolled in Medicare Advantage	Medicare, 2014: Enrolled in a Medicare prescription drug plan	Serious crimes known to police,[2] 2013: Total: Number	Serious crimes known to police,[2] 2013: Total: Rate[3]
	32	33	34	35	36	37	38	39	40	41	42	43	44	45
MISSISSIPPI—Cont'd														
Sunflower	4 164	28 799	1.01	311	11.3	278	10.1	4 431	21.3	4 607	278	3 308	592	2 701
Tallahatchie	2 456	14 320	0.78	139	9.4	154	10.4	2 328	21.7	2 734	136	1 988	NA	NA
Tate	1 279	24 133	0.60	326	11.6	288	10.2	4 658	20.2	5 411	822	2 924	NA	NA
Tippah	287	20 828	0.85	246	11.2	222	10.1	4 034	22.0	5 145	273	3 661	64	291
Tishomingo	279	18 492	0.85	181	9.3	277	14.3	3 252	20.8	4 951	138	3 561	88	449
Tunica	104	17 650	2.59	212	20.0	88	8.3	1 639	17.4	1 727	281	1 043	226	2 175
Union	269	26 164	0.89	382	13.6	235	8.4	5 121	22.0	5 981	384	3 911	NA	NA
Walthall	127	12 955	0.56	154	10.4	181	12.2	2 950	24.1	3 240	356	2 058	NA	NA
Warren	526	50 742	1.12	632	13.2	509	10.6	7 751	19.0	8 917	1 199	4 242	1 691	3 533
Washington	812	50 960	1.02	756	15.4	655	13.4	8 612	20.3	9 819	1 310	6 034	3 274	6 636
Wayne	137	18 540	0.71	259	12.6	192	9.4	3 598	20.8	3 998	427	2 628	35	224
Webster	58	9 022	0.68	127	12.7	141	14.1	1 788	21.5	2 798	114	1 950	NA	NA
Wilkinson	1 058	9 050	0.81	107	11.6	130	14.1	1 415	20.3	1 881	241	1 221	NA	NA
Winston	469	17 887	0.83	175	9.5	228	12.3	3 141	20.9	4 356	456	2 787	129	679
Yalobusha	155	11 052	0.68	143	11.6	171	13.9	1 906	18.9	3 537	302	2 288	NA	NA
Yazoo	4 385	26 598	0.82	373	13.4	251	9.0	3 998	19.7	4 736	450	3 200	NA	NA
MISSOURI	174 872	6 047 126	1.01	74 988	12.4	56 033	9.2	761 124	15.3	1 119 836	298 510	527 160	215 803	3 570
Adair	2 905	26 429	1.08	250	9.8	190	7.4	3 241	16.7	4 301	225	2 888	796	3 105
Andrew	192	11 547	0.33	183	10.5	171	9.8	1 898	13.2	3 022	186	1 868	214	1 225
Atchison	98	5 170	0.84	51	9.5	77	14.3	609	14.7	1 414	62	927	33	601
Audrain	2 331	25 724	1.01	311	12.0	283	10.9	3 272	16.8	5 152	791	2 957	713	2 771
Barry	296	37 818	1.16	424	11.9	381	10.7	6 143	21.7	8 017	2 536	3 234	1 157	3 254
Barton	90	11 768	0.88	145	12.0	133	11.0	1 859	18.6	2 797	491	1 581	338	2 737
Bates	311	14 518	0.67	184	11.1	188	11.3	2 359	17.8	3 692	636	2 032	563	3 385
Benton	244	17 143	0.71	131	7.0	269	14.3	2 954	21.8	6 223	1 252	3 207	492	2 595
Bollinger	163	9 441	0.41	133	10.7	118	9.5	1 878	18.3	2 880	358	1 674	177	1 425
Boone	9 008	170 033	1.05	2 187	12.7	1 030	6.0	19 037	13.1	22 421	3 040	12 527	6 182	3 621
Buchanan	4 461	98 024	1.21	1 170	13.1	872	9.7	11 309	15.5	16 422	1 282	9 821	5 030	5 581
Butler	867	46 232	1.19	591	13.8	539	12.5	5 641	16.0	10 381	1 086	6 466	2 201	5 092
Caldwell	214	7 312	0.49	88	9.7	87	9.6	1 277	17.6	1 927	237	1 053	148	1 632
Callaway	3 812	38 590	0.71	520	11.6	370	8.3	4 832	13.9	8 099	1 068	4 666	1 337	3 012
Camden	774	44 535	1.04	392	8.9	451	10.2	6 253	19.0	11 397	1 518	6 272	844	1 923
Cape Girardeau	3 829	82 476	1.17	917	11.7	688	8.8	8 262	13.2	14 157	1 079	8 655	2 835	3 658
Carroll	88	8 283	0.77	116	12.8	127	14.0	1 221	16.9	2 228	287	1 384	149	1 648
Carter	40	5 711	0.79	84	13.4	75	12.0	1 093	21.0	1 577	172	984	76	1 213
Cass	1 044	78 974	0.56	1 170	11.6	884	8.8	10 341	12.2	17 528	6 177	6 160	2 195	2 184
Cedar	156	13 125	0.84	169	12.1	196	14.0	2 025	19.2	3 934	1 188	1 607	433	3 145
Chariton	213	6 806	0.72	82	10.7	100	13.0	1 007	17.4	1 888	135	1 232	152	1 999
Christian	582	58 888	0.46	978	11.9	563	6.9	10 412	15.1	14 197	5 927	4 887	1 559	1 933
Clark	90	5 734	0.57	88	12.7	69	10.0	1 036	18.6	1 559	117	1 035	56	808
Clay	2 648	201 653	0.79	3 105	13.3	1 605	6.9	23 591	11.8	36 048	7 817	17 499	10 290	4 479
Clinton	445	16 584	0.57	219	10.8	228	11.2	2 514	14.8	3 592	367	2 184	319	1 558
Cole	4 952	90 442	1.39	920	12.0	622	8.1	7 693	12.5	13 021	1 452	8 080	1 999	2 609
Cooper	1 540	15 915	0.79	200	11.4	176	10.0	2 040	15.2	3 453	602	1 935	426	2 429
Crawford	332	21 796	0.69	283	11.5	273	11.1	3 476	17.3	5 530	1 401	2 817	623	2 496
Dade	133	6 919	0.74	59	7.7	106	13.9	1 140	19.4	1 929	642	777	110	1 469
Dallas	199	14 078	0.56	191	11.7	192	11.7	2 761	20.7	3 923	1 701	1 407	377	2 237
Daviess	152	6 949	0.60	109	13.1	77	9.3	1 490	22.5	1 817	149	1 128	69	842
DeKalb	3 537	12 837	0.99	98	7.7	97	7.6	1 206	16.1	2 046	159	1 223	182	1 401
Dent	201	14 596	0.82	176	11.2	203	13.0	2 479	19.7	3 764	283	2 313	400	2 554
Douglas	123	12 017	0.66	131	9.7	163	12.0	2 238	21.2	3 320	1 400	1 192	285	2 096
Dunklin	667	30 411	0.87	436	13.9	432	13.8	4 455	17.1	7 505	832	5 096	1 233	3 869
Franklin	857	92 824	0.81	1 240	12.1	931	9.1	11 921	13.9	19 818	8 176	7 809	2 716	2 673
Gasconade	250	14 388	0.89	151	10.2	197	13.3	1 985	17.0	3 724	887	1 988	229	1 535
Gentry	177	6 329	0.84	97	14.2	89	13.0	975	18.1	1 674	76	1 159	22	323
Greene	11 256	311 965	1.26	3 581	12.5	2 562	9.0	40 334	17.4	53 183	21 339	19 134	19 002	6 714
Grundy	350	10 172	0.97	157	15.4	131	12.8	1 365	17.0	2 417	111	1 617	255	2 455
Harrison	145	8 444	0.88	119	13.8	118	13.7	1 287	18.8	2 082	109	1 443	116	1 337
Henry	233	21 486	0.93	258	11.7	289	13.1	2 776	15.8	5 891	1 251	2 976	798	3 600
Hickory	75	8 630	0.71	64	6.9	124	13.5	1 500	23.5	3 187	1 059	1 364	108	1 158
Holt	101	4 345	0.81	47	10.4	62	13.7	585	16.7	1 126	81	674	91	1 983
Howard	714	8 497	0.61	116	11.4	81	8.0	1 337	16.8	2 048	291	1 185	102	1 000
Howell	608	42 121	1.11	493	12.3	504	12.5	5 603	17.1	9 892	1 912	5 291	1 407	3 454
Iron	276	10 431	0.98	98	9.5	138	13.4	1 451	17.5	2 651	222	1 840	194	1 879
Jackson	11 221	737 423	1.20	9 537	14.0	6 218	9.1	103 638	17.8	113 740	39 216	43 322	35 129	5 169

1. Per 1,000 estimated resident population. 2. Data for serious crimes have not been adjusted for underreporting; this may affect comparability between geographic areas and over time.
3. Per 100,000 population estimated by the FBI.

STATE County	Serious crimes known to police, 2013 (cont.)[1] Rate[2] Violent	Rate[2] Property	Education: School enrollment and attainment, 2009–2013: Enrollment[3] Total	Enrollment[3] Percent private	Attainment[4] (percent) High school graduate or less	Attainment[4] (percent) Bachelor's degree or more	Local government expenditures,[5] 2012–2013: Total current spending (mil dol)	Current spending per student (dollars)	Money income, 2009–2013: Per capita income[6] (dollars)	Households: Median income (dollars)	Households: Mean income (dollars)	Households: Percent with income of $200,000 or more	Income and poverty, 2013: Median household income (dollars)	Percent below poverty level: All persons	Children under 18 years	Children 5 to 17 years in families
	46	47	48	49	50	51	52	53	54	55	56	57	58	59	60	61
MISSISSIPPI—Cont'd																
Sunflower	342	2 359	8 259	12.7	57.6	13.0	38.9	9 209	12 588	26 619	39 879	1.3	28 562	37.8	51.7	47.9
Tallahatchie	NA	NA	3 762	24.2	65.9	8.5	20.2	9 744	12 747	29 853	37 584	0.2	29 780	36.2	45.6	44.5
Tate	NA	NA	8 235	14.3	51.2	15.4	35.6	7 412	20 431	41 494	56 775	2.3	40 624	19.4	27.3	25.2
Tippah	55	237	5 495	9.3	60.8	10.3	31.9	7 702	18 493	34 636	46 322	1.1	35 908	24.4	31.6	29.9
Tishomingo	36	413	4 316	4.4	60.9	11.3	27.0	8 492	18 338	32 592	45 289	1.4	35 891	18.8	27.3	25.0
Tunica	144	2 031	2 991	12.5	53.5	15.4	23.3	10 252	15 549	31 446	39 374	0.6	30 033	32.2	48.2	47.3
Union	NA	NA	6 852	5.5	57.3	14.8	38.2	7 738	19 273	38 373	50 931	1.4	40 148	18.8	27.2	27.0
Walthall	NA	NA	4 100	7.3	62.2	12.6	20.0	8 895	16 850	31 090	43 800	1.8	30 289	25.0	42.6	38.3
Warren	278	3 255	12 921	9.5	44.8	24.7	76.7	8 800	22 362	41 025	56 783	2.3	41 883	26.2	41.3	41.5
Washington	288	6 348	14 622	11.9	53.3	18.7	83.9	8 905	16 671	28 093	44 355	2.0	28 948	34.8	51.1	48.3
Wayne	51	173	5 289	7.4	64.5	10.2	30.1	8 381	18 928	29 925	48 381	1.6	31 688	25.7	36.1	33.8
Webster	NA	NA	2 389	12.7	49.4	19.0	14.9	7 990	18 728	33 524	46 385	1.6	34 930	22.9	31.2	30.0
Wilkinson	NA	NA	1 954	15.0	65.7	11.8	12.2	9 435	18 717	33 618	49 252	0.6	26 373	35.2	42.1	41.1
Winston	163	516	4 566	17.9	54.2	15.8	24.0	8 338	18 501	30 821	44 675	0.6	30 961	29.5	41.5	38.8
Yalobusha	NA	NA	2 982	11.6	57.4	13.2	15.2	8 255	18 750	32 930	45 974	1.0	32 660	26.9	39.4	37.6
Yazoo	NA	NA	6 879	17.5	61.7	11.9	34.9	8 172	14 291	26 336	39 966	1.1	28 757	41.8	51.4	49.6
MISSOURI	433	3 137	1 557 979	19.2	44.0	26.2	8 788.6	9 597	25 649	47 380	63 756	2.9	46 905	15.8	22.2	20.5
Adair	218	2 887	10 104	8.2	46.5	27.6	27.5	8 812	19 258	34 733	49 296	1.4	35 282	24.9	24.9	22.3
Andrew	114	1 110	3 864	8.5	49.5	22.0	24.1	8 402	25 302	54 336	64 793	2.0	54 185	10.1	13.1	11.8
Atchison	0	601	1 053	13.2	53.2	21.3	10.0	12 523	24 748	44 426	55 405	2.2	43 215	13.2	16.8	15.9
Audrain	253	2 519	5 706	10.8	61.4	13.1	30.2	8 863	19 687	43 013	52 396	1.1	41 164	19.7	32.9	31.3
Barry	273	2 981	7 979	12.5	59.3	13.3	55.8	8 307	19 489	38 710	48 753	1.2	36 573	20.2	32.2	28.9
Barton	486	2 251	2 847	7.9	55.5	16.9	18.4	8 899	20 678	40 580	50 908	1.9	37 723	18.5	27.8	23.5
Bates	577	2 808	3 986	11.2	61.0	11.9	24.4	8 976	21 047	38 579	50 557	1.1	38 586	21.6	27.9	24.5
Benton	322	2 274	3 380	11.6	62.3	10.8	21.0	7 988	19 717	32 951	44 819	0.8	32 563	23.1	39.3	37.4
Bollinger	322	1 103	3 039	13.3	64.4	10.9	15.0	7 981	19 470	37 716	48 665	1.9	37 627	19.6	29.0	27.3
Boone	333	3 288	60 150	12.8	27.4	47.3	220.1	9 502	26 895	48 627	66 942	3.6	49 118	19.8	17.4	16.1
Buchanan	438	5 143	22 673	13.4	51.6	20.1	119.9	9 352	21 961	44 363	55 937	1.3	43 461	17.8	25.7	22.4
Butler	497	4 594	10 058	8.8	57.3	14.4	53.1	7 679	19 246	34 969	47 010	1.6	35 381	22.0	31.6	28.1
Caldwell	276	1 356	2 169	9.7	57.8	13.5	16.1	9 834	21 482	41 169	52 502	0.8	41 546	15.3	22.3	19.4
Callaway	286	2 726	11 479	20.2	51.7	21.1	42.4	8 721	23 171	47 964	59 626	1.9	45 573	13.8	20.1	18.1
Camden	171	1 752	8 547	9.2	46.6	20.8	51.9	9 672	23 038	43 458	54 285	1.7	41 314	18.0	32.6	30.5
Cape Girardeau	385	3 274	21 491	14.2	45.6	27.4	84.2	8 411	23 751	46 516	60 091	1.7	44 248	15.8	21.9	18.0
Carroll	133	1 515	2 118	7.2	61.0	15.6	15.1	9 885	24 073	46 002	58 957	2.0	41 279	17.7	26.2	23.9
Carter	112	1 102	1 664	6.9	53.7	13.8	11.1	8 779	18 245	30 962	44 627	2.5	30 017	23.7	36.9	36.6
Cass	160	2 024	26 424	15.9	42.9	23.3	159.9	8 591	27 463	60 350	72 731	2.5	63 031	9.2	12.7	11.5
Cedar	341	2 804	3 294	17.5	57.7	14.6	18.4	7 931	16 362	30 302	37 957	0.5	30 816	25.5	37.9	34.0
Chariton	302	1 696	1 629	18.2	64.6	11.7	11.6	10 680	19 481	39 385	48 740	0.4	40 352	16.8	22.4	21.3
Christian	171	1 762	20 834	14.6	39.1	25.9	115.4	7 878	25 134	52 838	66 571	2.7	51 394	11.4	16.4	14.7
Clark	144	664	1 628	8.4	57.5	12.0	9.2	8 629	20 279	40 204	47 853	0.5	39 712	17.5	25.6	24.3
Clay	731	3 748	59 078	16.8	35.9	30.6	389.1	9 716	29 406	60 936	74 715	3.1	60 641	10.0	12.2	10.9
Clinton	249	1 309	4 706	10.0	50.1	17.1	37.6	8 798	25 100	53 826	63 571	1.4	52 461	11.5	16.8	14.8
Cole	351	2 258	19 569	24.4	40.8	30.8	100.7	8 737	26 160	53 931	66 319	2.2	52 023	13.7	18.1	16.9
Cooper	205	2 223	4 003	14.8	53.3	18.4	22.9	9 087	22 910	45 992	59 967	1.4	44 397	15.5	22.4	20.3
Crawford	208	2 288	5 680	15.4	61.0	13.2	26.7	7 487	18 415	35 897	46 292	0.5	37 299	20.1	30.1	27.9
Dade	414	1 055	1 674	10.5	57.0	13.2	10.4	9 299	20 034	35 483	48 083	1.4	36 720	18.4	29.2	25.7
Dallas	237	2 000	3 310	18.7	64.1	14.1	22.4	8 833	18 155	40 120	47 865	0.7	37 540	21.7	33.0	30.4
Daviess	73	769	1 880	15.9	57.6	16.4	12.3	9 507	19 890	42 393	51 989	1.3	38 332	18.9	31.1	28.8
DeKalb	239	1 162	2 674	5.4	64.8	9.5	10.6	10 176	16 635	44 092	54 206	1.3	44 286	17.2	17.7	15.9
Dent	172	2 382	3 314	10.4	61.0	11.4	17.6	7 975	18 544	36 311	45 967	1.3	34 761	23.0	33.7	31.0
Douglas	235	1 861	2 965	12.3	62.6	10.5	13.8	8 710	16 404	32 130	40 191	0.5	31 289	22.5	35.8	34.8
Dunklin	292	3 578	7 421	5.8	67.3	11.4	48.7	7 961	17 990	31 304	42 579	0.9	32 050	27.0	40.0	36.5
Franklin	204	2 470	24 637	20.1	48.8	17.9	148.3	8 978	24 742	48 857	63 006	2.5	51 138	10.8	16.0	14.8
Gasconade	194	1 340	3 318	12.9	59.7	15.4	24.7	8 516	21 830	41 392	51 822	0.9	41 270	15.8	23.8	21.1
Gentry	0	323	1 452	5.6	57.9	15.3	12.0	10 413	20 534	39 192	49 397	1.0	39 265	16.1	21.8	20.8
Greene	718	5 997	75 141	16.3	38.0	28.3	313.8	8 274	23 520	40 337	55 391	2.1	38 525	20.2	25.2	22.5
Grundy	376	2 080	2 413	9.4	54.6	14.9	14.9	8 594	19 527	37 964	47 519	1.4	37 172	21.4	31.8	27.0
Harrison	69	1 268	1 831	3.5	66.1	9.6	14.1	9 305	19 468	37 739	47 826	0.9	36 229	19.0	30.4	27.7
Henry	347	3 253	4 917	10.9	55.3	14.4	26.7	8 914	22 394	39 839	51 870	1.6	39 666	18.4	28.6	25.7
Hickory	11	1 147	1 660	17.3	60.3	10.4	9.1	10 255	17 361	29 325	37 791	0.2	30 040	24.7	43.1	39.9
Holt	109	1 874	811	7.0	58.3	16.2	7.0	11 475	24 127	42 979	51 559	1.5	41 213	13.1	19.0	17.6
Howard	127	872	2 926	31.7	51.9	22.7	12.1	8 200	21 590	42 747	56 168	1.0	41 356	15.9	23.4	21.7
Howell	231	3 223	9 841	7.1	56.6	15.4	46.4	8 578	17 416	32 533	42 953	1.0	31 665	27.6	38.5	35.9
Iron	387	1 491	2 225	4.0	59.1	11.0	18.2	9 622	19 101	36 387	46 178	0.3	32 994	22.0	34.8	32.0
Jackson	721	4 448	171 481	18.1	41.2	27.6	994.3	10 282	26 062	47 015	62 955	2.7	46 802	17.2	24.3	23.2

1. Data for serious crimes have not been adjusted for underreporting; this may affect comparability between geographic areas and over time. 2. Per 100,000 population estimated by the FBI.
3. All persons 3 years old and over enrolled in nursery school through college. 4. Persons 25 years old and over. 5. Elementary and secondary education expenditures.
6. Based on population estimated by the American Community Survey, 2009–2013.

STATE County	Personal income, 2013										Earnings, 2013		
			Per capita[1]			Supplements to wages and salaries; employer contributions (mil dol)						Contributions for government social insurance (mil dol)	
	Total (mil dol)	Percent change, 2012–2013	Dollars	Rank	Wages and salaries (mil dol)	Pension and insurance	Government social insurance	Proprietors' income (mil dol)	Dividends, interest, and rent (mil dol)	Personal transfer receipts (mil dol)	Total (mil dol)	From employee and self-employed	From employer
	62	63	64	65	66	67	68	69	70	71	72	73	74
MISSISSIPPI—Cont'd													
Sunflower	844	-2.0	30 134	2 668	297	56	22	132	131	268	507	27	22
Tallahatchie	445	5.2	29 499	2 753	107	17	8	95	43	132	228	12	8
Tate	878	1.0	30 961	2 557	200	35	15	75	86	244	326	23	15
Tippah	608	1.7	27 547	2 934	200	34	16	43	79	212	293	22	16
Tishomingo	506	1.5	25 890	3 027	182	32	15	20	82	192	249	20	15
Tunica	368	1.1	34 886	1 918	364	36	31	73	55	95	505	28	31
Union	863	2.1	31 097	2 535	402	59	30	72	114	222	563	38	30
Walthall	423	6.0	28 358	2 860	85	16	7	57	49	147	164	12	7
Warren	1 798	-1.2	37 280	1 540	917	167	73	121	279	421	1 277	78	73
Washington	1 661	-0.6	33 428	2 187	655	109	51	203	268	520	1 017	61	51
Wayne	632	4.2	30 765	2 584	195	32	15	81	102	185	322	20	15
Webster	276	3.1	27 631	2 921	68	12	5	21	34	115	106	9	5
Wilkinson	239	-1.3	25 530	3 037	66	11	5	13	37	92	96	7	5
Winston	538	3.8	28 641	2 833	175	28	14	48	70	191	265	19	14
Yalobusha	390	0.2	31 525	2 473	103	19	8	30	50	144	161	13	8
Yazoo	783	-0.1	28 066	2 892	262	51	20	86	117	247	419	26	20
MISSOURI	245 771	2.2	40 663	X	124 198	22 007	9 073	22 657	44 625	47 746	177 934	10 395	9 073
Adair	796	3.4	31 120	2 532	331	77	24	78	168	200	510	29	24
Andrew	860	4.0	49 320	401	81	19	6	84	116	123	190	11	6
Atchison	254	15.4	46 601	577	54	13	4	76	46	48	147	6	4
Audrain	906	8.2	35 297	1 859	338	80	24	167	147	204	609	32	24
Barry	1 163	5.7	32 704	2 304	532	102	39	134	209	313	807	49	39
Barton	414	7.6	33 759	2 135	104	25	8	91	70	114	229	12	8
Bates	589	1.7	35 609	1 812	119	31	9	91	97	156	250	15	9
Benton	599	3.9	31 632	2 458	113	28	8	60	108	230	209	17	8
Bollinger	371	2.3	29 679	2 727	54	13	4	41	57	117	112	8	4
Boone	7 006	2.9	41 028	1 045	3 859	920	263	436	1 370	1 010	5 478	283	263
Buchanan	3 250	1.8	36 259	1 700	1 999	375	148	282	507	776	2 803	162	148
Butler	1 572	3.8	36 489	1 665	653	140	51	206	231	498	1 051	62	51
Caldwell	360	4.9	39 553	1 226	52	14	4	62	45	73	132	7	4
Callaway	1 404	3.4	31 652	2 456	583	145	42	97	237	320	867	49	42
Camden	1 556	2.3	35 467	1 825	515	94	41	165	354	412	815	55	41
Cape Girardeau	3 059	1.8	39 560	1 225	1 623	300	120	341	598	582	2 384	138	120
Carroll	386	10.2	42 293	909	79	18	6	97	74	82	200	9	6
Carter	179	2.5	28 431	2 856	42	12	3	16	29	68	74	5	3
Cass	3 767	1.4	37 430	1 517	861	174	64	191	577	705	1 290	84	64
Cedar	400	4.0	28 727	2 826	87	23	6	41	73	153	158	12	6
Chariton	323	8.5	42 336	904	58	14	4	78	69	70	153	8	4
Christian	2 785	2.7	34 432	2 002	520	110	40	226	387	537	896	61	40
Clark	251	8.5	36 258	1 702	42	12	3	59	38	58	116	6	3
Clay	9 297	2.0	40 339	1 131	4 549	733	338	910	1 204	1 422	6 530	381	338
Clinton	803	5.7	39 051	1 291	136	32	10	69	124	141	247	14	10
Cole	3 341	2.4	43 560	792	2 188	538	149	203	707	538	3 078	158	149
Cooper	583	4.8	33 034	2 246	181	39	14	75	100	133	309	17	14
Crawford	834	1.7	33 989	2 084	239	49	18	146	120	232	451	29	18
Dade	227	2.7	29 937	2 694	50	13	4	29	42	70	96	6	4
Dallas	520	1.9	31 460	2 487	70	18	5	67	86	154	160	12	5
Daviess	279	12.1	33 640	2 157	50	13	4	60	52	66	126	6	4
DeKalb	341	4.9	26 528	3 005	113	31	8	28	49	81	179	10	8
Dent	477	2.8	30 343	2 639	142	32	10	31	79	158	216	15	10
Douglas	374	2.0	27 673	2 917	72	17	6	71	56	120	167	12	6
Dunklin	1 086	4.9	34 234	2 045	288	63	23	143	144	397	517	31	23
Franklin	3 852	1.8	37 835	1 457	1 442	279	110	232	646	773	2 063	130	110
Gasconade	520	3.0	34 924	1 910	164	37	13	32	107	141	245	17	13
Gentry	265	6.2	39 078	1 284	76	16	5	44	46	70	142	7	5
Greene	10 466	1.8	36 869	1 616	6 503	1 162	482	1 156	2 033	2 150	9 303	548	482
Grundy	351	5.6	33 900	2 098	125	30	9	44	61	98	207	12	9
Harrison	313	12.7	35 815	1 778	73	19	5	67	60	85	164	8	5
Henry	787	3.7	35 659	1 806	266	65	19	61	151	231	411	26	19
Hickory	238	2.3	25 620	3 034	34	9	3	13	48	108	58	7	3
Holt	223	16.8	48 852	425	46	11	3	65	37	42	125	5	3
Howard	411	7.8	40 074	1 166	80	18	6	45	64	85	149	8	6
Howell	1 203	1.5	29 790	2 718	508	111	39	92	200	396	750	50	39
Iron	321	2.8	31 049	2 543	131	25	9	10	41	129	176	13	9
Jackson	28 536	1.4	41 965	943	19 620	3 219	1 428	3 656	4 221	5 291	27 923	1 598	1 428

1. Based on the resident population estimated as of July 1 of the year shown.

STATE County	Earnings, 2013 (cont.) Percent by selected industries: Farm	Mining	Construction	Manu-facturing	Infor-mation: professional, scientific, technical services	Retail trade	Finance, insur-ance, real estate and leasing	Health care and social assistance	Govern-ment	Social Security beneficiaries, December 2013: Number	Rate[1]	Supple-mental Security Income recipients, December 2013	Housing units, 2014: Total	Percent change, 2010–2014
	75	76	77	78	79	80	81	82	83	84	85	86	87	88
MISSISSIPPI—Cont'd														
Sunflower	23.4	0.0	2.1	3.1	D	4.6	3.2	5.5	33.4	5 545	198	2 042	9 698	0.1
Tallahatchie	32.5	0.0	3.2	1.1	D	5.6	1.7	D	19.2	3 185	212	1 279	5 533	0.1
Tate	6.5	D	6.2	8.8	D	8.9	4.1	11.5	24.6	6 110	216	929	11 165	2.0
Tippah	2.2	D	5.8	27.0	D	7.7	3.3	D	17.7	6 025	273	1 071	9 717	0.2
Tishomingo	0.8	0.0	4.9	33.5	D	7.6	3.3	D	17.2	5 820	299	742	10 312	0.2
Tunica	11.5	0.0	1.5	3.1	D	2.4	1.3	1.9	8.4	2 075	197	814	4 824	0.4
Union	2.1	0.0	3.8	36.3	D	6.2	2.5	9.8	10.8	6 975	251	914	11 789	2.3
Walthall	15.1	3.9	5.2	12.7	1.9	10.3	4.1	D	19.3	3 735	251	820	7 139	0.1
Warren	1.6	0.3	3.9	14.5	6.8	7.0	3.3	11.2	28.8	9 995	207	2 094	21 878	-0.1
Washington	13.0	D	2.6	7.7	5.3	8.1	3.6	8.4	23.9	11 485	231	4 603	21 621	-0.4
Wayne	14.1	6.4	9.8	8.8	2.3	8.3	3.5	D	18.3	4 700	229	1 094	9 213	0.0
Webster	9.6	D	4.7	11.1	D	7.3	D	D	18.6	3 220	324	600	4 805	0.0
Wilkinson	4.6	0.3	2.2	7.5	D	7.9	3.5	D	27.9	2 230	239	768	5 039	0.0
Winston	6.7	D	4.7	20.4	D	9.6	2.8	D	13.9	5 115	273	973	8 738	-0.1
Yalobusha	3.7	D	7.8	27.9	D	6.2	3.3	2.1	23.9	4 075	330	854	6 374	0.5
Yazoo	11.2	D	3.2	11.0	1.8	4.8	4.2	D	30.0	5 460	195	1 818	10 064	-0.1
MISSOURI	1.7	0.3	5.7	10.5	11.3	6.3	8.0	12.1	16.1	1 232 526	204	142 219	2 735 742	0.8
Adair	2.6	0.0	4.8	7.1	5.0	9.1	3.8	D	24.8	4 755	185	698	11 343	0.7
Andrew	18.1	D	11.1	0.7	D	10.2	3.3	D	18.1	3 380	194	219	7 282	-0.3
Atchison	43.0	0.0	2.3	1.3	3.8	4.3	2.8	7.8	12.3	1 480	272	78	2 961	-0.8
Audrain	13.2	0.0	4.1	21.5	D	8.9	3.4	D	20.9	5 655	221	571	10 798	-0.5
Barry	6.9	0.2	4.9	29.0	15.9	7.0	4.1	D	10.8	9 105	255	960	17 384	-0.8
Barton	24.9	D	6.4	5.5	D	7.5	4.8	4.7	20.4	3 190	260	338	5 568	-0.6
Bates	15.6	D	6.9	3.1	6.5	12.1	4.9	6.9	24.6	4 275	259	415	7 809	-0.4
Benton	4.5	0.0	D	6.4	2.5	11.3	9.1	9.1	25.6	6 975	369	585	14 011	-1.0
Bollinger	10.4	D	11.3	5.2	3.2	8.5	D	11.0	19.8	3 315	266	461	5 825	-0.9
Boone	0.3	0.2	5.0	4.3	7.9	7.3	7.2	11.0	37.4	23 965	140	2 676	73 174	5.2
Buchanan	1.4	D	5.5	26.4	5.6	6.7	5.2	15.5	13.7	17 845	199	2 460	38 453	0.1
Butler	6.8	0.0	5.4	12.9	5.1	9.4	4.3	18.2	19.7	11 625	270	2 501	19 649	-0.4
Caldwell	21.8	D	13.3	0.7	4.7	6.9	3.7	D	20.9	2 135	235	161	4 604	0.0
Callaway	4.1	0.4	6.3	12.3	3.6	4.2	2.6	D	22.3	9 115	205	874	18 522	0.0
Camden	-0.1	D	10.6	4.0	5.5	15.4	7.5	16.3	12.1	12 450	284	655	41 213	0.1
Cape Girardeau	1.0	0.2	5.8	12.4	6.0	8.3	4.4	26.0	13.6	15 510	200	1 604	33 025	1.3
Carroll	32.7	0.0	10.1	9.7	1.8	5.3	3.9	D	14.1	2 395	263	217	4 609	-0.5
Carter	0.2	D	D	9.3	D	9.5	D	8.2	28.8	1 865	296	348	3 243	-0.1
Cass	2.1	0.3	11.3	5.7	4.4	9.2	4.8	9.1	21.9	19 095	190	1 033	40 488	1.1
Cedar	1.6	D	9.6	7.3	3.2	11.0	4.7	10.4	27.0	4 480	321	453	7 174	-0.7
Chariton	24.1	0.0	6.0	3.1	D	6.8	6.1	5.1	13.9	1 990	260	147	4 141	-0.6
Christian	0.2	D	13.8	7.0	8.9	9.6	6.2	6.9	18.2	15 920	197	1 126	32 623	3.3
Clark	32.4	D	2.7	5.8	1.7	9.5	3.1	3.6	18.1	1 765	255	136	3 456	-0.5
Clay	0.3	0.1	7.3	14.1	17.1	6.9	4.2	7.7	14.8	38 710	168	2 501	94 966	1.1
Clinton	18.2	D	6.3	3.8	D	5.9	5.3	17.1	23.3	3 985	194	273	8 887	0.1
Cole	0.1	D	5.5	4.7	9.2	6.4	5.6	10.8	39.3	15 340	200	1 789	32 798	1.7
Cooper	15.7	D	6.3	10.1	D	7.0	5.5	7.0	20.6	3 875	220	317	7 443	-0.3
Crawford	-0.3	D	6.3	23.5	D	25.8	2.9	D	10.5	6 425	262	800	11 918	-0.3
Dade	15.7	D	5.8	9.7	D	5.7	D	2.0	23.8	2 155	285	184	3 933	-0.8
Dallas	0.5	D	D	2.9	2.7	10.3	4.3	D	21.0	4 445	269	553	7 579	-1.1
Daviess	30.9	0.0	10.9	D	D	7.1	2.7	4.0	18.3	1 990	240	143	4 183	-0.4
DeKalb	10.4	0.0	3.7	1.0	D	8.6	8.0	D	35.9	2 285	179	174	4 293	-0.8
Dent	-1.5	0.0	4.8	19.6	2.4	9.6	5.8	8.4	22.3	4 255	270	579	7 242	-0.6
Douglas	-0.8	D	8.5	15.6	D	10.5	3.1	D	14.4	3 760	279	475	6 450	-1.1
Dunklin	16.3	0.0	3.2	5.1	2.3	10.5	5.0	D	16.7	8 700	275	2 468	14 335	-0.6
Franklin	0.8	0.2	8.3	25.1	4.8	7.3	4.1	12.0	12.3	22 310	219	1 711	43 886	1.1
Gasconade	0.6	D	4.2	29.1	D	7.6	4.1	D	21.5	4 150	279	263	8 131	-0.9
Gentry	28.8	0.0	D	D	D	6.0	D	16.5	15.2	1 905	281	166	3 196	-0.4
Greene	0.1	D	4.2	10.2	8.8	8.0	7.2	19.1	13.1	57 315	202	6 698	129 146	3.0
Grundy	12.1	D	4.4	21.0	D	6.1	3.3	11.5	22.6	2 570	248	265	5 003	-0.4
Harrison	30.4	D	1.9	1.1	D	12.3	4.4	6.0	22.3	2 255	258	227	4 386	-0.5
Henry	4.9	D	5.2	17.2	2.8	9.1	5.0	9.7	25.2	6 535	296	723	10 874	-0.1
Hickory	4.0	D	D	D	D	13.5	D	8.8	28.2	3 510	378	286	6 732	-1.5
Holt	44.3	D	3.8	6.9	D	5.8	2.6	3.8	11.4	1 195	261	82	2 783	-0.8
Howard	19.7	D	4.2	10.6	2.4	7.4	D	D	14.3	2 235	218	276	4 543	-0.9
Howell	0.4	0.2	2.9	17.1	4.9	8.6	4.5	20.1	15.3	11 335	281	1 643	18 062	0.2
Iron	-1.3	D	D	2.0	1.0	7.8	2.1	D	17.4	3 015	291	574	5 279	-1.0
Jackson	0.1	0.0	6.3	6.7	19.0	4.9	11.8	11.3	16.1	123 845	182	17 339	314 701	0.8

1. Per 1,000 resident population estimated as of July 1 of the year shown.

STATE County	Housing units, 2009–2013: Occupied units: Total	Owner-occupied: Percent	Owner-occupied: Median value[1]	Median owner cost as a percent of income: With a mortgage	Median owner cost as a percent of income: Without a mortgage[2]	Renter-occupied: Median rent[3]	Renter-occupied: Median rent as a percent of income[2]	Substandard units[4] (percent)	Civilian labor force, 2014: Total	Percent change, 2013–2014	Unemployment: Total	Unemployment: Rate[5]	Civilian employment,[6] 2009–2013: Total	Percent: Management, business, science and arts	Percent: Construction, production, and maintenance occupations
	89	90	91	92	93	94	95	96	97	98	99	100	101	102	103
MISSISSIPPI—Cont'd															
Sunflower	8 394	58.6	69 500	26.7	13.1	500	30.6	4.8	8 621	-4.3	1 150	13.3	8 458	27.5	29.0
Tallahatchie	4 640	73.0	64 000	24.9	13.5	469	26.2	2.8	5 824	0.2	568	9.8	4 132	28.6	27.8
Tate	9 936	74.5	112 600	24.0	10.9	677	38.2	2.4	11 758	-1.9	1 031	8.8	11 599	27.1	30.7
Tippah	8 472	76.5	74 800	23.7	12.4	566	29.3	1.5	8 641	-1.2	738	8.5	8 344	21.6	41.3
Tishomingo	7 643	75.9	72 900	23.5	10.2	514	32.3	9.0	7 522	-2.3	594	7.9	7 403	26.1	39.5
Tunica	4 116	43.6	74 000	22.2	10.0	662	32.1	4.9	4 721	-1.6	582	12.3	4 438	23.3	17.5
Union	10 322	72.8	85 500	22.5	10.3	638	29.9	3.1	12 768	-2.5	816	6.4	11 396	22.8	39.3
Walthall	5 649	82.5	85 100	26.6	13.5	446	27.6	2.0	5 109	-3.6	495	9.7	5 492	28.5	35.7
Warren	18 404	64.9	103 600	21.4	10.0	654	32.4	4.9	20 674	-4.7	1 665	8.1	19 901	35.9	23.0
Washington	18 123	54.8	73 700	23.0	14.1	610	34.4	2.4	18 281	-4.5	2 446	13.4	17 188	33.1	22.4
Wayne	8 105	83.3	68 400	22.1	14.7	542	28.8	4.6	7 634	-3.4	701	9.2	7 639	20.2	45.4
Webster	4 084	73.6	70 900	21.4	10.3	509	34.3	4.1	3 919	-4.0	362	9.2	3 528	34.1	32.3
Wilkinson	3 496	77.5	59 400	20.9	11.7	520	35.2	3.1	2 801	-6.1	325	11.6	3 273	27.7	31.7
Winston	7 635	71.3	76 300	22.6	13.9	567	36.9	3.6	7 109	-4.0	757	10.6	7 035	29.5	29.5
Yalobusha	4 797	74.6	67 800	21.5	12.8	402	31.0	4.2	4 923	-2.1	482	9.8	4 761	26.6	41.1
Yazoo	8 710	60.0	64 100	24.7	14.5	592	37.8	2.7	9 275	-1.9	970	10.5	8 659	28.4	28.3
MISSOURI	2 360 131	68.4	137 000	21.9	11.7	727	29.7	2.1	3 058 118	1.4	186 901	6.1	2 770 617	34.5	22.3
Adair	9 648	60.2	102 600	19.0	11.3	544	35.2	1.1	11 094	-0.6	682	6.1	11 123	36.7	20.5
Andrew	6 691	76.7	127 700	20.6	10.2	692	25.9	0.9	9 990	1.2	507	5.1	8 667	31.5	26.7
Atchison	2 448	69.6	76 400	18.8	12.5	541	20.5	1.8	2 897	0.7	158	5.5	2 712	32.7	29.9
Audrain	9 327	74.2	90 500	20.8	11.4	619	24.2	3.4	11 249	0.3	624	5.5	10 774	25.6	31.3
Barry	13 464	75.9	107 500	22.6	10.4	563	26.4	2.6	14 854	-0.1	905	6.1	14 297	27.4	38.3
Barton	5 065	75.3	84 700	20.8	12.7	506	32.5	2.3	5 556	1.2	354	6.4	5 113	28.5	34.4
Bates	6 832	73.8	99 400	23.3	12.7	576	31.7	4.1	8 156	2.2	572	7.0	7 233	25.9	31.7
Benton	8 225	84.0	106 400	24.8	11.9	580	34.6	3.0	7 224	0.1	549	7.6	6 646	27.3	31.0
Bollinger	4 758	80.7	96 600	21.2	10.5	550	29.5	1.5	5 755	0.2	386	6.7	5 052	23.7	40.5
Boone	65 649	57.1	162 200	20.4	10.0	784	33.3	1.8	98 362	1.0	4 058	4.1	88 035	46.3	13.5
Buchanan	33 331	64.7	109 700	20.0	11.6	684	30.9	1.8	46 820	0.7	2 636	5.6	40 961	26.8	28.3
Butler	17 085	65.9	89 700	21.0	11.7	578	30.6	3.0	19 226	3.2	1 326	6.9	17 653	26.0	30.0
Caldwell	3 743	71.0	83 600	21.8	12.8	661	28.2	1.7	4 410	1.6	245	5.6	3 938	26.7	32.7
Callaway	16 548	76.1	124 500	21.7	10.0	632	26.5	2.6	21 734	0.7	1 217	5.6	19 967	31.6	24.9
Camden	17 647	78.2	170 200	24.1	11.3	623	28.9	1.8	18 922	0.9	1 519	8.0	18 382	31.3	22.2
Cape Girardeau	29 411	66.5	137 500	20.4	10.3	658	29.1	2.6	40 812	-0.1	2 223	5.4	36 929	31.3	22.7
Carroll	3 613	80.3	83 900	19.2	11.5	521	27.8	2.5	4 771	2.3	340	7.1	4 117	26.7	33.0
Carter	2 426	73.6	98 300	23.3	12.3	447	29.7	1.8	2 575	1.4	225	8.7	2 580	33.7	23.9
Cass	37 307	77.6	154 900	23.0	12.6	917	28.9	3.2	53 200	2.0	3 022	5.7	47 828	33.3	26.4
Cedar	5 970	70.9	88 500	24.4	13.5	638	32.5	2.0	5 900	0.6	371	6.3	4 957	29.5	28.6
Chariton	2 958	76.2	74 700	21.3	12.3	467	21.4	2.0	3 845	3.1	223	5.8	3 353	27.1	33.4
Christian	29 652	74.0	142 600	21.8	11.8	746	28.4	2.8	42 077	2.7	2 063	4.9	37 289	35.9	20.5
Clark	2 749	76.8	71 300	20.0	11.9	457	22.7	1.8	3 443	2.9	235	6.8	3 083	25.4	41.5
Clay	86 934	71.0	153 700	21.9	12.1	807	26.8	2.4	128 955	1.9	6 993	5.4	114 925	37.6	20.6
Clinton	8 089	72.6	142 900	21.7	11.4	730	24.4	1.7	10 935	1.8	639	5.8	9 817	26.7	28.2
Cole	29 302	66.8	142 400	19.1	10.0	602	24.3	1.9	39 984	0.8	1 998	5.0	37 040	39.6	17.2
Cooper	6 568	73.3	119 800	19.1	11.6	602	26.4	2.8	7 719	0.6	455	5.9	7 848	27.7	26.6
Crawford	9 485	76.0	105 100	21.3	13.1	612	35.6	2.3	10 995	1.0	851	7.7	9 681	24.0	35.4
Dade	3 175	77.1	78 200	23.0	12.8	548	26.2	5.0	3 516	2.1	209	5.9	3 236	30.4	30.3
Dallas	6 443	80.3	101 400	23.3	10.0	567	24.7	3.7	7 096	2.3	526	7.4	6 218	25.9	35.5
Daviess	3 151	76.3	104 700	24.1	12.4	572	21.5	0.7	4 060	-0.1	236	5.8	3 552	30.6	29.6
DeKalb	3 769	65.2	110 400	19.8	12.1	552	27.6	2.9	5 080	1.0	272	5.4	4 360	25.1	30.8
Dent	5 858	72.9	86 000	24.0	11.5	538	30.8	3.3	6 320	-4.3	419	6.6	5 880	23.9	30.0
Douglas	5 178	77.7	102 900	23.7	12.1	566	29.3	2.1	5 034	-0.3	377	7.5	4 924	21.6	40.0
Dunklin	12 882	61.4	67 800	20.8	12.6	508	29.6	2.7	13 190	2.0	1 154	8.7	11 585	26.3	31.6
Franklin	39 263	76.6	150 500	23.0	11.2	664	26.8	3.6	52 131	1.1	3 362	6.4	47 216	28.8	32.0
Gasconade	6 168	77.2	116 000	21.9	10.7	563	28.0	5.0	7 657	1.7	406	5.3	6 653	26.5	34.9
Gentry	2 800	72.2	80 400	20.0	12.7	501	24.9	1.7	3 657	1.8	206	5.6	2 967	32.9	27.9
Greene	115 574	59.3	128 100	21.5	10.4	679	31.5	4.2	148 077	2.6	7 160	4.8	132 328	34.0	19.1
Grundy	4 148	72.3	72 700	18.7	11.6	525	28.6	2.9	4 955	0.8	265	5.3	4 328	27.5	30.8
Harrison	3 515	74.3	71 300	20.8	13.8	552	23.8	2.2	4 017	1.4	258	6.4	3 784	26.4	31.1
Henry	9 551	73.1	95 700	22.6	12.7	615	31.2	2.4	10 145	2.9	649	6.4	9 458	26.7	33.7
Hickory	4 219	82.8	98 700	27.4	14.8	491	33.4	2.1	3 736	1.5	311	8.3	3 082	23.7	30.5
Holt	2 218	71.6	78 900	20.8	10.7	476	24.3	1.5	2 734	-0.2	134	4.9	2 321	29.7	30.6
Howard	3 825	74.0	96 400	22.0	10.1	595	29.0	1.4	5 032	2.4	270	5.4	4 381	30.9	30.2
Howell	15 796	69.7	97 700	23.0	10.4	546	30.8	3.2	16 319	-0.3	1 144	7.0	15 814	26.7	33.1
Iron	4 126	72.3	78 800	19.9	10.0	531	29.6	2.0	3 928	5.4	373	9.5	3 789	24.6	27.6
Jackson	271 545	61.1	126 800	22.5	13.0	791	31.5	2.8	359 322	2.0	25 459	7.1	320 520	35.3	19.8

1. Specified owner-occupied units. 2. A value of 10.0 represents 10 percent or less; a value of 50.0 represents 50 percent or more. 3. Specified renter-occupied units.
4. Overcrowded or lacking complete plumbing facilities. 5. Percent of civilian labor force. 6. Persons 16 years old and over.

STATE County	Private nonfarm establishments, employment and payroll, 2013									Agriculture, 2012			
		Employment						Annual payroll		Farms			
											Percent with:		
	Number of establish-ments	Total	Health care and social assistance	Manufac-turing	Retail trade	Finance and insurance	Professional, scientific, and technical services	Total (mil dol)	Average per employee (dollars)	Number	Fewer than 50 acres	500 acres or more	Farm operators whose principal occu-pation is farming (percent)
	104	105	106	107	108	109	110	111	112	113	114	115	116
MISSISSIPPI—Cont'd													
Sunflower	447	4 861	D	327	865	198	72	153	31 518	350	22.6	44.0	59.7
Tallahatchie	172	1 710	D	D	281	35	34	54	31 671	509	13.6	28.7	38.9
Tate	358	3 961	557	721	754	192	111	119	30 077	569	25.3	14.1	38.8
Tippah	343	5 098	622	1 617	629	138	122	146	28 555	691	25.2	5.4	32.0
Tishomingo	350	4 062	578	1 461	577	D	97	125	30 654	287	22.0	3.8	36.2
Tunica	217	9 548	208	D	474	D	D	265	27 723	108	7.4	62.0	64.8
Union	495	9 445	1 252	3 966	1 087	209	97	313	33 142	688	29.1	6.4	25.3
Walthall	217	1 983	240	435	386	66	21	52	26 293	684	30.7	4.8	49.9
Warren	1 017	19 620	4 057	2 943	2 554	384	719	656	33 425	238	18.5	19.7	39.9
Washington	1 154	14 531	3 027	1 003	2 923	359	357	435	29 938	284	18.7	47.5	71.1
Wayne	378	4 528	D	875	962	D	93	160	35 303	508	34.4	5.5	48.0
Webster	172	1 655	D	361	242	D	73	49	29 874	362	20.7	11.0	32.9
Wilkinson	139	1 487	355	159	293	48	14	39	26 036	198	17.7	23.7	41.4
Winston	381	4 995	696	1 435	889	D	92	152	30 486	506	27.1	9.5	40.9
Yalobusha	180	2 301	323	889	324	D	35	70	30 534	364	21.2	13.7	50.5
Yazoo	401	4 017	848	D	727	D	153	134	33 382	672	14.3	25.9	49.9
MISSOURI	150 290	2 355 336	399 510	244 754	305 270	129 953	160 562	98 487	41 814	99 171	25.5	13.7	44.2
Adair	638	8 369	2 021	622	1 495	235	686	211	25 237	822	19.6	16.7	44.0
Andrew	288	1 632	300	D	285	63	D	47	28 798	826	29.5	12.8	42.1
Atchison	202	1 301	250	D	321	D	D	37	28 151	395	12.9	36.5	66.6
Audrain	553	6 778	1 207	1 763	1 104	263	136	198	29 272	1 015	18.6	25.1	55.8
Barry	748	13 455	1 888	4 648	1 499	273	D	476	35 394	1 427	31.1	8.4	43.5
Barton	254	2 779	450	446	504	175	D	76	27 433	940	24.0	22.8	45.7
Bates	340	2 646	740	D	592	159	75	72	27 319	1 169	23.4	18.1	46.6
Benton	368	2 240	414	172	676	D	D	51	22 559	800	18.5	13.1	52.8
Bollinger	193	1 358	343	153	309	D	D	33	24 091	788	16.9	12.8	42.4
Boone	4 447	71 502	16 923	3 848	11 278	6 890	3 682	2 595	36 289	1 171	39.5	8.6	38.3
Buchanan	2 306	44 794	7 764	12 894	5 435	2 019	1 132	1 623	36 232	727	29.4	13.1	44.4
Butler	1 243	14 985	4 430	D	2 644	488	388	455	30 378	509	23.8	24.6	47.9
Caldwell	150	825	D	D	193	59	D	26	32 040	1 035	24.3	10.6	41.0
Callaway	745	11 788	2 291	1 561	1 243	339	295	434	36 797	1 417	28.4	9.7	35.5
Camden	1 403	12 282	2 254	450	3 156	446	650	358	29 180	533	16.3	12.0	42.2
Cape Girardeau	2 377	39 716	11 508	3 794	6 041	984	1 162	1 311	33 015	1 139	29.5	10.2	47.8
Carroll	232	1 808	343	188	325	112	38	55	30 634	1 112	18.4	18.2	39.8
Carter	200	922	175	180	160	45	D	20	21 268	196	23.5	17.9	45.4
Cass	1 813	18 463	2 932	2 180	3 881	619	452	548	29 676	1 495	41.1	9.2	46.3
Cedar	278	2 324	620	347	477	102	D	56	24 159	819	19.9	10.4	45.2
Chariton	205	1 279	D	D	257	83	D	36	28 515	1 120	17.1	21.3	47.8
Christian	1 650	13 075	1 462	1 420	2 685	578	968	360	27 516	1 177	36.4	5.6	43.8
Clark	140	964	D	120	228	D	11	24	24 679	673	13.5	20.8	40.9
Clay	4 784	87 124	12 785	9 974	11 073	2 552	D	4 025	46 194	578	48.8	10.2	42.6
Clinton	370	2 780	924	135	528	137	81	81	29 091	758	35.1	8.8	38.5
Cole	2 267	32 675	6 143	2 457	5 389	1 900	1 650	1 230	37 634	1 055	24.1	5.4	38.2
Cooper	400	3 905	816	D	751	146	76	101	25 985	928	16.4	17.3	42.8
Crawford	529	5 410	878	1 971	624	D	133	170	31 357	679	20.2	12.8	40.4
Dade	140	1 215	37	D	166	45	13	37	30 190	734	21.5	16.5	47.0
Dallas	265	2 358	D	D	502	121	40	44	18 667	1 188	31.7	7.6	46.8
Daviess	161	912	79	D	179	D	D	24	26 154	1 199	23.4	12.9	36.8
DeKalb	215	1 969	379	D	558	227	D	58	29 493	863	22.7	12.6	40.3
Dent	416	3 617	795	571	508	168	D	123	33 875	673	21.0	13.5	35.7
Douglas	200	2 118	267	715	442	62	33	46	21 568	984	18.6	10.9	43.2
Dunklin	756	8 908	3 217	D	1 481	272	D	191	21 462	345	22.6	42.6	63.5
Franklin	2 598	33 020	3 915	9 128	4 636	1 152	901	1 163	35 234	1 841	33.6	5.1	32.6
Gasconade	429	4 732	948	1 358	701	166	121	120	25 409	859	14.6	10.0	39.1
Gentry	198	1 737	736	D	274	58	D	49	28 268	708	20.2	16.2	40.8
Greene	8 201	137 721	27 952	12 023	18 786	7 497	6 212	5 037	36 573	1 752	48.8	4.5	43.9
Grundy	243	2 672	600	810	425	D	38	85	31 856	689	23.1	12.0	42.7
Harrison	209	1 970	514	D	622	103	23	46	23 176	1 051	18.5	17.4	42.7
Henry	574	6 537	1 693	1 208	1 102	237	120	232	35 456	894	21.8	21.5	54.7
Hickory	147	667	135	24	203	D	D	15	22 753	487	14.4	18.1	56.5
Holt	137	971	D	209	157	D	D	28	28 535	408	20.3	26.7	49.3
Howard	192	1 942	486	D	252	78	47	52	27 003	765	17.0	19.0	36.6
Howell	1 124	12 844	3 539	2 453	2 136	422	321	369	28 756	1 535	24.8	10.1	41.3
Iron	349	2 054	756	75	281	D	17	66	32 213	273	15.4	13.6	46.2
Jackson	17 072	319 751	52 482	26 085	34 614	23 624	25 414	15 018	46 968	701	57.5	5.6	38.7

STATE County	Agriculture, 2012 (cont.)															
	Land in farms					Value of land and buildings (dollars)		Value of machinery and equipment, average per farm (dollars)	Value of products sold				Percent of farms with sales of:		Government payments	
	Acreage (1,000)	Percent change, 2007–2012	Acres: Average size of farm	Acres: Total irrigated (1,000)	Acres: Total cropland (1,000)	Average per farm	Average per acre		Total (mil dol)	Average per farm (dollars)	Percent from: Crops	Percent from: Livestock and poultry products	$10,000 or more	$100,000 or more	Total ($1,000)	Percent of farms
	117	118	119	120	121	122	123	124	125	126	127	128	129	130	131	132
MISSISSIPPI—Cont'd																
Sunflower	373	-1.3	1 065	216.7	323.8	2 077 580	1 951	360 220	273.8	782 283	89.3	10.7	66.9	50.3	10 155	85.1
Tallahatchie	341	7.9	669	112.4	254.8	1 505 411	2 249	200 244	165.0	324 202	99.2	0.8	45.2	22.6	9 164	76.8
Tate	153	-2.5	269	2.2	69.6	540 237	2 008	73 946	44.4	78 025	68.7	31.3	31.1	9.3	2 745	43.8
Tippah	124	-9.9	179	0.3	37.9	291 781	1 628	51 965	22.1	31 961	66.3	33.7	20.0	2.5	932	57.3
Tishomingo	50	-12.7	173	0.7	16.6	319 711	1 852	47 373	6.1	21 167	85.7	14.3	21.6	3.8	420	52.3
Tunica	212	5.3	1 959	101.4	194.5	5 291 852	2 701	598 713	130.1	1 204 222	D	D	73.1	58.3	7 006	89.8
Union	121	-10.4	176	0.1	43.7	364 727	2 073	44 686	17.1	24 785	75.7	24.3	22.7	3.8	1 531	57.8
Walthall	118	-7.8	173	0.1	32.2	516 697	2 992	55 263	79.8	116 722	5.8	94.2	31.9	11.3	1 773	53.7
Warren	125	11.5	524	4.9	43.8	983 702	1 877	103 592	30.6	128 723	98.9	1.1	26.5	10.9	1 648	54.6
Washington	342	2.7	1 206	220.9	313.0	2 563 155	2 126	548 342	271.4	955 764	96.4	3.6	78.9	58.5	9 036	77.1
Wayne	93	8.3	184	0.5	24.0	535 941	2 914	76 234	194.0	381 982	3.5	96.5	45.9	24.6	200	13.8
Webster	81	-3.9	223	0.7	25.8	401 997	1 806	50 633	20.3	56 180	69.6	30.4	25.1	6.9	1 899	68.5
Wilkinson	103	-8.9	521	0.5	15.0	1 170 980	2 248	70 000	7.2	36 182	42.0	58.0	26.3	5.6	829	52.0
Winston	98	2.4	193	0.0	18.8	419 709	2 172	59 943	74.7	147 630	4.5	95.5	27.9	7.1	455	31.4
Yalobusha	95	-4.8	260	1.3	33.4	472 665	1 820	61 310	18.3	50 379	86.4	13.6	25.3	6.6	1 492	56.6
Yazoo	351	-1.3	522	44.8	195.4	1 096 741	2 100	118 775	151.3	225 109	92.5	7.5	34.1	16.4	9 095	74.7
MISSOURI	28 266	-2.6	285	1 180.9	15 259.3	795 444	2 791	88 960	9 164.9	92 415	49.8	50.2	46.8	12.5	323 953	41.7
Adair	273	-2.4	332	0.1	134.0	815 103	2 453	79 223	35.8	43 539	56.3	43.7	44.5	9.9	3 054	50.5
Andrew	199	-16.8	240	D	138.0	855 310	3 558	90 700	57.7	69 831	80.1	19.9	48.9	14.9	3 587	66.8
Atchison	263	-13.5	666	12.2	228.6	3 238 514	4 862	297 134	170.0	430 256	86.5	13.5	73.9	49.9	3 963	84.3
Audrain	436	2.7	430	15.1	354.0	1 643 676	3 822	172 912	151.2	148 960	59.3	40.7	62.2	26.4	5 605	66.0
Barry	268	-7.4	188	0.4	73.6	476 843	2 538	56 169	357.8	250 751	1.8	98.2	51.4	18.3	876	13.0
Barton	332	-4.9	353	11.1	224.0	743 856	2 105	126 076	120.1	127 807	61.0	39.0	56.4	23.0	4 742	59.7
Bates	448	-5.4	383	2.2	278.2	869 524	2 268	113 850	104.1	89 087	61.5	38.6	53.8	14.7	4 369	57.5
Benton	241	8.3	301	0.7	87.2	628 791	2 090	70 250	62.7	78 371	20.8	79.2	52.4	10.3	1 013	29.1
Bollinger	200	-3.7	254	6.8	79.3	511 848	2 014	58 244	31.6	40 128	52.1	47.9	44.8	7.0	1 313	42.0
Boone	241	-7.0	206	5.3	144.4	749 119	3 644	69 631	52.2	44 565	66.0	34.0	34.9	8.1	1 837	31.0
Buchanan	189	-4.5	260	D	136.1	895 721	3 451	91 761	67.5	92 891	89.6	10.4	53.1	15.4	3 153	69.1
Butler	234	-6.6	460	123.6	186.2	1 464 493	3 184	181 733	126.3	248 189	97.4	2.6	52.7	25.0	6 090	52.1
Caldwell	245	-2.2	236	D	153.0	537 488	2 275	54 284	38.9	37 541	62.4	37.6	37.4	6.6	5 312	71.0
Callaway	316	-2.1	223	5.4	160.9	728 630	3 267	79 792	84.9	59 929	40.1	59.9	40.0	8.2	2 756	40.8
Camden	139	-4.0	260	0.1	24.4	566 041	2 177	44 377	17.6	32 951	11.0	89.0	43.7	4.5	100	5.4
Cape Girardeau	253	-16.4	222	11.6	157.3	695 755	3 133	80 699	77.7	68 175	67.2	32.8	45.8	11.8	3 397	54.9
Carroll	432	7.5	388	3.5	320.9	1 216 926	3 134	121 291	130.5	117 322	85.3	14.7	48.6	16.7	7 522	80.2
Carter	74	16.3	376	D	9.6	624 724	1 663	49 066	4.6	23 520	22.7	77.3	31.6	6.1	123	12.8
Cass	319	-2.2	214	2.8	202.4	708 608	3 318	73 090	86.2	57 682	69.8	30.2	36.3	7.5	2 726	34.4
Cedar	190	-0.4	232	D	63.3	422 039	1 822	57 703	23.6	28 797	28.9	71.1	49.7	4.5	639	17.7
Chariton	406	5.7	363	3.9	282.6	1 078 481	2 973	126 969	123.8	110 555	72.1	27.9	53.2	19.3	5 823	73.5
Christian	179	-5.1	152	0.1	53.3	476 400	3 124	48 936	24.3	20 622	14.3	85.7	38.9	3.8	240	7.1
Clark	241	-8.3	358	3.2	150.9	950 793	2 654	103 065	72.1	107 064	71.9	28.1	46.5	17.7	4 399	80.8
Clay	111	-23.1	191	D	57.2	819 787	4 282	92 087	50.4	87 118	38.6	61.4	40.0	11.8	1 079	24.7
Clinton	192	-19.3	253	D	126.9	866 280	3 427	84 827	56.4	74 431	68.5	31.5	39.7	10.3	2 589	48.2
Cole	176	-2.5	167	0.9	67.5	486 792	2 913	62 366	38.4	36 372	27.4	72.6	48.5	5.5	980	30.0
Cooper	307	1.6	331	0.7	190.3	940 300	2 841	108 986	78.3	84 363	57.5	42.5	58.6	16.9	4 120	64.7
Crawford	194	3.9	286	0.0	47.6	595 339	2 080	51 605	15.2	22 392	20.5	79.5	40.4	4.6	344	12.4
Dade	246	-11.1	335	6.5	113.4	733 312	2 192	86 000	69.5	94 661	47.9	52.1	56.1	13.6	1 656	27.9
Dallas	218	-2.2	183	0.2	60.1	426 668	2 326	44 228	47.7	40 160	11.5	88.5	43.7	7.2	612	9.5
Daviess	315	-4.8	263	0.1	210.5	731 193	2 784	71 812	96.6	80 591	40.0	60.0	36.0	9.4	8 392	71.9
DeKalb	243	-6.8	281	0.0	168.3	792 630	2 817	89 886	59.9	69 447	60.8	39.2	48.0	12.4	4 479	66.9
Dent	188	6.5	279	0.4	32.1	447 679	1 602	48 750	17.3	25 779	10.7	89.3	46.2	5.1	307	9.7
Douglas	254	-0.1	258	0.4	45.2	419 160	1 624	41 030	33.3	33 851	8.8	91.2	45.3	6.8	542	8.9
Dunklin	280	-13.9	811	155.8	266.2	3 056 875	3 770	425 835	199.0	576 846	98.9	1.1	69.6	48.7	8 186	75.9
Franklin	292	-2.7	158	1.3	128.9	589 536	3 722	57 212	64.1	34 794	43.1	56.9	34.9	4.9	1 483	26.9
Gasconade	209	-1.7	243	0.4	63.7	596 109	2 451	60 327	25.9	30 207	35.7	64.3	45.4	6.2	853	39.6
Gentry	253	-8.2	358	0.0	160.4	943 222	2 636	84 585	126.6	178 880	28.1	71.9	42.4	13.3	4 831	74.0
Greene	211	-9.2	120	0.3	68.2	442 679	3 683	42 410	41.5	23 669	17.4	82.6	32.9	3.4	609	9.0
Grundy	204	-12.1	296	0.5	139.8	681 840	2 303	67 837	44.7	64 835	63.4	36.6	37.7	9.9	4 432	65.7
Harrison	401	3.2	381	0.1	264.1	951 168	2 494	96 657	76.0	72 288	77.4	22.6	41.9	12.1	8 648	77.3
Henry	358	3.6	400	D	200.2	849 449	2 124	107 462	69.9	78 166	50.1	49.9	56.6	16.2	3 752	48.2
Hickory	182	24.0	374	D	57.3	725 201	1 941	50 281	25.8	52 959	16.3	83.7	47.0	8.0	757	33.7
Holt	200	-15.4	491	19.0	166.5	1 865 299	3 799	204 819	94.9	232 583	95.9	4.1	63.5	33.3	3 139	82.8
Howard	243	-12.0	318	2.8	139.9	807 152	2 537	97 344	47.8	62 455	77.5	22.5	49.2	14.9	3 553	66.1
Howell	354	-8.2	230	0.1	58.5	433 877	1 883	51 521	53.9	35 139	4.5	95.5	41.2	5.9	829	9.6
Iron	71	1.0	258	0.5	17.3	415 751	1 610	44 161	6.0	21 967	14.8	85.2	41.0	4.0	66	5.1
Jackson	111	-20.3	158	0.3	75.1	638 655	4 037	72 385	32.5	46 408	78.2	21.8	35.1	8.8	1 036	29.7

STATE County	Water use, 2010		Wholesale trade,[1] 2007				Retail trade,[2] 2007				Real estate and rental and leasing,[2] 2007			
	Total water withdrawn (mil gal/day)	Gallons withdrawn per person per day	Number of establish-ments	Number of employees	Sales (mil dol)	Annual payroll (mil dol)	Number of establish-ments	Number of employees	Sales (mil dol)	Annual payroll (mil dol)	Number of establish-ments	Number of employees	Receipts (mil dol)	Annual payroll (mil dol)
	133	134	135	136	137	138	139	140	141	142	143	144	145	146
MISSISSIPPI—Cont'd														
Sunflower	366.4	12 441	22	D	D	D	106	913	211.3	15.8	12	36	4.7	0.7
Tallahatchie	126.0	8 193	9	85	62.4	2.7	47	265	56.8	5.1	6	9	1.4	0.1
Tate	7.4	257	13	70	18.7	2.0	93	974	237.7	20.0	16	30	2.8	0.5
Tippah	4.6	208	18	137	131.8	4.6	88	660	130.9	11.6	4	D	D	D
Tishomingo	3.2	161	20	196	54.7	4.4	82	588	112.6	10.6	12	28	5.0	0.5
Tunica	155.8	14 454	6	47	40.7	2.3	80	581	130.7	8.7	11	26	6.1	0.5
Union	3.2	118	17	173	174.7	6.1	106	998	267.3	19.4	17	45	2.8	0.6
Walthall	3.7	238	8	D	D	D	44	485	124.7	9.4	2	D	D	D
Warren	217.4	4 458	42	D	D	D	249	2 696	606.5	54.4	47	186	30.6	5.3
Washington	458.9	8 974	69	D	D	D	284	3 067	577.7	57.6	62	276	31.5	7.9
Wayne	6.0	289	27	220	221.1	12.0	89	899	178.9	16.1	8	29	3.0	0.4
Webster	1.7	165	6	13	2.0	0.4	45	289	69.6	5.7	3	D	D	D
Wilkinson	3.5	352	9	65	44.2	1.8	38	289	59.8	5.5	3	3	0.7	0.1
Winston	3.1	160	15	266	187.9	16.2	96	879	183.2	16.7	11	82	3.0	1.6
Yalobusha	3.7	288	5	17	14.1	0.6	42	328	59.7	4.6	7	6	1.0	0.1
Yazoo	44.9	1 600	20	D	D	D	92	770	230.5	15.6	21	47	5.9	0.9
MISSOURI	8 568.5	1 431	6 903	96 451	81 032.9	4 533.6	23 360	317 318	76 575.2	7 155.3	7 003	39 625	7 186.3	1 248.8
Adair	3.2	124	25	178	54.7	5.4	118	1 536	310.1	28.9	23	95	12.0	2.1
Andrew	19.7	1 140	12	77	36.9	3.0	45	362	80.0	6.4	18	D	D	D
Atchison	6.3	1 108	10	74	67.8	1.8	46	364	86.6	6.4	4	D	D	D
Audrain	13.7	537	28	D	D	D	109	1 115	247.8	21.8	18	56	5.6	1.1
Barry	19.4	545	24	331	134.8	13.8	154	1 753	413.8	35.9	33	97	11.3	2.3
Barton	14.4	1 159	11	106	76.0	3.4	55	726	135.1	12.4	7	25	2.3	0.6
Bates	3.5	207	11	104	77.4	3.2	62	540	135.4	11.6	7	D	D	D
Benton	4.8	251	11	56	18.4	1.1	79	739	174.3	13.9	19	40	6.1	0.7
Bollinger	14.0	1 129	13	D	D	D	33	327	59.6	6.2	6	D	D	D
Boone	18.7	115	125	1 422	610.4	56.7	646	11 317	3 012.3	239.7	243	D	D	D
Buchanan	78.2	877	101	1 393	1 015.5	55.4	382	5 943	1 438.7	128.5	108	462	49.9	9.7
Butler	339.5	7 933	56	D	D	D	242	2 705	634.8	52.7	38	231	24.8	6.1
Caldwell	1.2	126	6	38	21.2	1.0	29	228	34.1	3.1	2	D	D	D
Callaway	31.0	700	25	165	70.8	5.8	133	1 336	331.1	24.6	32	D	D	D
Camden	13.7	310	43	267	109.4	9.4	311	3 184	677.9	72.0	90	316	47.1	7.7
Cape Girardeau	36.5	483	125	2 111	1 792.0	77.8	445	6 137	1 353.0	122.1	115	427	63.0	9.8
Carroll	5.2	562	16	76	70.1	2.4	42	279	60.6	5.1	9	D	D	D
Carter	0.8	129	9	57	13.6	1.2	22	157	27.7	2.1	3	4	0.4	0.1
Cass	5.5	55	60	424	351.6	15.8	270	3 715	898.7	79.0	78	264	36.2	7.1
Cedar	2.0	144	8	54	13.7	1.1	63	478	119.9	8.5	12	47	5.4	1.6
Chariton	1.6	198	15	184	198.0	7.0	44	215	51.8	4.0	9	D	D	D
Christian	9.4	122	71	623	166.4	21.0	236	2 971	716.8	67.2	77	156	24.3	3.0
Clark	2.4	331	11	D	D	D	36	269	88.7	4.8	4	11	0.4	0.1
Clay	148.4	669	300	4 532	4 517.3	232.9	683	12 599	3 366.9	280.9	247	1 057	193.9	35.1
Clinton	2.6	124	11	59	96.8	1.9	64	641	147.2	13.3	17	41	5.0	0.8
Cole	9.3	122	71	2 541	706.1	76.6	359	5 504	1 203.7	115.4	73	252	44.8	6.2
Cooper	5.1	291	16	114	75.7	3.4	73	787	225.6	15.4	15	48	5.2	0.8
Crawford	3.2	128	16	201	105.2	6.6	78	726	174.3	15.0	25	105	9.7	2.1
Dade	7.9	1 006	9	305	62.4	6.9	29	165	46.9	2.9	3	2	0.3	0.1
Dallas	2.4	144	7	94	59.9	2.4	65	540	144.7	10.5	9	32	2.5	0.5
Daviess	2.1	251	10	73	41.8	1.6	39	178	45.3	3.4	1	D	D	D
DeKalb	1.0	75	7	D	D	D	38	569	128.0	10.7	16	D	D	D
Dent	32.5	2 076	7	D	D	D	56	549	124.5	11.0	19	106	3.7	1.0
Douglas	39.6	2 893	10	D	D	D	44	446	93.7	8.0	6	6	0.9	0.1
Dunklin	111.4	3 485	35	298	132.8	8.9	167	1 527	371.3	29.0	32	407	21.8	7.0
Franklin	1 018.9	10 039	97	937	386.4	36.3	422	4 955	1 326.7	112.0	95	461	34.5	8.3
Gasconade	2.2	146	18	183	63.1	5.1	80	683	146.0	12.8	16	D	D	D
Gentry	1.9	275	12	76	35.2	2.9	42	258	59.2	4.8	7	152	3.0	1.8
Greene	228.2	829	432	7 514	5 076.0	316.1	1 253	19 282	4 710.4	421.0	458	2 781	340.0	68.3
Grundy	4.2	409	5	55	76.5	2.0	51	452	88.3	7.4	8	18	2.4	0.4
Harrison	1.7	194	10	203	55.5	5.1	53	720	143.5	13.1	6	D	D	D
Henry	410.1	18 413	24	194	101.1	5.9	125	1 237	284.3	25.2	22	84	10.0	1.9
Hickory	1.4	149	2	D	D	D	32	194	50.0	3.6	3	D	D	D
Holt	17.0	3 453	9	97	84.7	3.5	20	152	35.8	2.0	3	D	D	D
Howard	9.7	955	6	81	19.3	2.3	43	312	88.1	5.7	2	D	D	D
Howell	8.2	203	46	340	180.7	11.2	260	2 356	545.8	45.5	54	151	17.5	3.6
Iron	6.9	648	4	11	1.6	0.2	48	301	65.8	5.0	9	D	D	D
Jackson	644.8	956	850	13 194	11 179.9	661.9	2 326	35 780	8 460.8	825.3	904	6 335	1 474.2	222.6

1. Merchant wholesalers, except manufacturers' sales branches and offices. 2. Employer establishments.

Table B. States and Counties — **Professional Services, Manufacturing, and Accommodation and Food Services**

STATE County	Professional, scientific, and technical services,[1] 2007				Manufacturing, 2007				Accommodation and food services, 2007			
	Number of establish-ments	Number of employees	Receipts (mil dol)	Annual payroll (mil dol)	Number of establish-ments	Number of employees	Receipts (mil dol)	Annual payroll (mil dol)	Number of establish-ments	Number of employees	Sales (mil dol)	Annual payroll (mil dol)
	147	148	149	150	151	152	153	154	155	156	157	158
MISSISSIPPI—Cont'd												
Sunflower	28	D	D	D	18	918	D	D	31	349	15.1	4.1
Tallahatchie	14	36	3.2	0.7	NA	NA	NA	NA	8	106	3.6	0.9
Tate	25	74	6.2	2.0	15	922	244.3	28.7	29	384	14.6	4.2
Tippah	18	103	7.3	2.8	37	2 635	566.2	83.9	24	291	11.8	2.9
Tishomingo	19	96	4.7	1.8	34	1 856	305.4	57.9	29	219	9.2	2.4
Tunica	7	17	2.2	0.5	NA	NA	NA	NA	34	13 817	1 308.6	349.9
Union	27	88	11.5	3.3	36	2 512	418.1	75.6	32	629	20.8	5.4
Walthall	11	22	3.0	0.7	19	684	167.3	20.7	16	D	D	D
Warren	98	885	77.8	31.7	48	4 399	1 856.7	165.7	105	4 199	384.6	71.9
Washington	91	D	D	D	47	1 994	840.3	75.2	86	1 529	93.8	20.2
Wayne	21	66	4.6	1.2	16	1 128	287.5	33.7	29	355	15.3	3.8
Webster	8	34	3.7	1.1	NA	NA	NA	NA	12	68	3.2	0.8
Wilkinson	7	22	1.3	0.3	NA	NA	NA	NA	6	71	3.4	0.8
Winston	24	87	14.5	2.1	25	1 856	483.4	76.9	28	485	16.5	4.6
Yalobusha	11	D	D	D	7	598	D	D	12	47	2.9	0.6
Yazoo	26	D	D	D	19	801	371.8	27.9	25	311	12.4	3.2
MISSOURI	13 524	130 786	19 749.8	7 454.7	6 886	295 313	110 907.6	12 996.5	12 261	241 438	11 070.6	3 109.1
Adair	40	D	D	D	14	987	D	31.6	60	1 400	38.7	11.6
Andrew	15	D	D	D	NA	NA	NA	NA	14	125	4.5	1.2
Atchison	9	D	D	D	NA	NA	NA	NA	14	189	4.5	1.1
Audrain	24	120	8.1	3.8	40	1 935	1 337.1	75.2	39	471	18.6	5.0
Barry	53	D	D	D	55	5 548	1 409.8	176.1	63	795	25.8	6.1
Barton	15	125	6.9	2.4	26	1 041	174.3	30.6	20	315	8.4	2.3
Bates	18	D	D	D	NA	NA	NA	NA	26	348	12.3	2.9
Benton	19	D	D	D	NA	NA	NA	NA	60	470	13.2	3.4
Bollinger	8	D	D	D	NA	NA	NA	NA	14	D	D	D
Boone	382	D	D	D	96	4 601	D	D	422	8 458	315.1	93.0
Buchanan	177	D	D	D	95	D	D	D	197	4 175	154.5	45.6
Butler	64	591	53.9	18.7	49	2 657	632.7	72.8	87	1 666	57.9	17.4
Caldwell	8	D	D	D	NA	NA	NA	NA	15	73	2.1	0.5
Callaway	37	161	12.2	4.3	39	918	D	33.6	60	845	33.2	9.5
Camden	85	433	53.5	14.3	54	1 117	251.1	35.5	187	3 061	157.6	47.4
Cape Girardeau	156	D	D	D	97	4 574	D	D	177	4 043	145.9	42.6
Carroll	15	D	D	D	NA	NA	NA	NA	17	170	5.5	1.5
Carter	4	D	D	D	NA	NA	NA	NA	15	107	3.5	1.0
Cass	164	D	D	D	84	1 867	483.7	64.7	143	2 343	82.4	25.4
Cedar	14	D	D	D	NA	NA	NA	NA	32	340	9.8	2.7
Chariton	11	D	D	D	NA	NA	NA	NA	10	61	2.0	0.4
Christian	137	606	52.2	16.4	106	1 327	255.6	44.9	105	1 662	59.7	18.6
Clark	9	16	0.8	0.2	NA	NA	NA	NA	10	73	2.1	0.5
Clay	464	D	D	D	219	12 349	10 903.5	773.8	389	11 292	822.1	192.9
Clinton	24	D	D	D	NA	NA	NA	NA	27	430	16.2	4.3
Cole	238	1 409	174.0	63.0	64	3 384	1 568.1	146.9	157	3 134	127.6	37.1
Cooper	22	D	D	D	16	594	155.3	20.2	39	1 070	112.7	19.2
Crawford	27	D	D	D	44	1 479	271.7	46.1	55	496	25.5	6.3
Dade	4	D	D	D	NA	NA	NA	NA	13	48	2.1	0.5
Dallas	16	D	D	D	19	562	D	11.1	23	234	8.4	2.3
Daviess	8	D	D	D	NA	NA	NA	NA	12	80	2.2	0.6
DeKalb	9	D	D	D	NA	NA	NA	NA	13	118	5.2	1.3
Dent	13	D	D	D	19	654	246.6	25.1	20	286	10.8	3.1
Douglas	9	D	D	D	15	D	D	D	13	211	7.7	2.1
Dunklin	40	107	8.7	2.2	18	626	D	D	59	739	24.9	6.5
Franklin	195	D	D	D	227	9 233	2 432.1	350.1	184	3 096	109.3	32.7
Gasconade	36	137	7.0	2.2	42	1 413	172.4	45.2	44	445	13.5	4.2
Gentry	7	D	D	D	NA	NA	NA	NA	13	112	2.0	0.6
Greene	792	D	D	D	330	14 842	3 845.4	560.0	663	14 922	578.3	170.4
Grundy	13	D	D	D	9	649	D	24.9	16	174	6.2	1.8
Harrison	11	D	D	D	NA	NA	NA	NA	19	269	11.0	2.8
Henry	40	127	9.5	2.5	34	1 426	566.6	49.7	61	718	25.0	6.8
Hickory	9	D	D	D	NA	NA	NA	NA	14	45	1.6	0.4
Holt	2	D	D	D	NA	NA	NA	NA	18	140	4.0	1.0
Howard	12	D	D	D	NA	NA	NA	NA	15	157	3.4	1.0
Howell	59	325	21.7	8.9	82	3 113	682.1	85.3	71	1 251	47.6	13.3
Iron	11	D	D	D	NA	NA	NA	NA	18	168	5.3	1.5
Jackson	2 115	D	D	D	721	29 100	8 939.0	1 337.1	1 431	29 957	1 505.8	416.6

1. Establishment subject to federal tax.

Table B. States and Counties — **Health Care and Social Assistance, Other Services, Nonemployer Businesses, and Residential Construction**

STATE County	Health care and social assistance, 2007				Other services, 2007				Nonemployer businesses, 2013		Value of residential construction authorized by building permits, 2014	
	Number of establish- ments	Number of employees	Receipts (mil dol)	Annual payroll (mil dol)	Number of establish- ments	Number of employees	Receipts (mil dol)	Annual payroll (mil dol)	Number	Receipts (mil dol)	New Construction ($1,000)	Number of housing units
	159	160	161	162	163	164	165	166	167	168	169	170
MISSISSIPPI—Cont'd												
Sunflower	44	1 198	83.5	33.4	33	176	19.6	3.9	1 440	47.9	578	7
Tallahatchie	17	353	21.6	9.3	11	31	2.5	0.7	821	21.4	196	4
Tate	35	525	43.8	16.2	23	148	10.2	3.2	1 958	69.6	9 278	45
Tippah	32	603	37.6	16.6	14	45	2.5	0.9	1 369	55.8	107	5
Tishomingo	29	581	44.2	15.6	29	110	13.2	2.0	1 102	39.8	166	2
Tunica	16	192	11.7	4.4	9	D	D	D	678	26.7	1 205	15
Union	47	977	90.9	30.7	23	99	7.6	2.3	1 840	78.8	1 781	19
Walthall	24	403	24.2	9.9	14	41	2.5	0.6	1 151	34.4	0	0
Warren	104	3 313	385.9	149.9	74	342	22.1	6.2	3 094	104.0	1 353	7
Washington	161	2 889	236.1	95.3	94	477	51.0	10.8	3 399	124.9	1 657	10
Wayne	27	646	41.6	20.9	23	73	4.4	1.5	1 304	48.4	374	2
Webster	11	412	35.5	12.4	11	26	1.9	0.6	790	28.6	110	2
Wilkinson	15	374	27.0	11.7	8	33	5.2	0.6	564	21.0	0	0
Winston	33	577	41.6	15.2	21	65	5.7	1.1	1 349	55.3	5 461	32
Yalobusha	17	317	17.1	7.7	9	15	1.2	0.3	810	27.1	304	10
Yazoo	46	617	55.9	21.9	29	83	5.8	1.6	1 552	47.9	1 089	6
MISSOURI	15 984	362 340	32 886.6	12 918.6	11 111	67 476	6 770.7	1 799.9	393 292	16 592.4	2 682 665	16 003
Adair	105	D	D	D	72	D	D	D	1 495	50.4	9 215	54
Andrew	21	D	D	D	19	D	D	D	1 207	46.3	762	4
Atchison	18	D	D	D	20	34	3.0	0.5	440	18.1	235	1
Audrain	83	1 602	112.6	47.8	46	227	18.1	5.5	1 387	59.5	165	3
Barry	77	1 193	74.3	28.8	60	192	13.5	3.4	2 306	79.9	1 755	13
Barton	30	525	26.3	11.0	19	46	4.1	0.8	905	31.1	221	2
Bates	39	725	49.6	18.9	22	D	D	D	1 205	43.5	260	1
Benton	32	262	15.0	6.0	37	90	6.3	1.4	1 422	57.1	0	0
Bollinger	20	D	D	D	16	D	D	D	729	25.8	0	0
Boone	562	15 933	1 695.8	615.7	323	D	D	D	10 871	534.1	262 282	1 414
Buchanan	288	7 250	708.8	284.3	195	1 259	108.1	37.6	4 175	160.2	16 950	95
Butler	218	3 809	413.0	129.8	78	310	22.4	5.7	2 483	117.5	1 359	25
Caldwell	12	88	5.1	2.1	13	D	D	D	625	20.7	2 589	11
Callaway	76	2 346	134.5	65.4	66	300	22.3	6.3	2 263	74.6	6 511	52
Camden	120	1 950	227.0	78.6	114	384	31.8	7.6	3 731	178.4	5 191	54
Cape Girardeau	279	9 550	972.9	354.9	162	D	D	D	5 196	213.3	33 624	187
Carroll	24	440	23.0	8.9	19	43	4.3	1.2	621	24.4	1 700	11
Carter	27	173	5.4	2.5	7	34	3.2	0.6	522	26.0	145	3
Cass	127	2 842	187.5	76.7	130	548	36.7	11.6	6 604	255.5	64 553	305
Cedar	44	674	32.5	15.0	19	34	2.2	0.6	1 054	38.6	650	6
Chariton	14	198	7.0	3.0	14	32	4.5	1.0	623	19.8	0	0
Christian	110	1 174	59.8	24.8	109	415	28.9	7.8	6 446	258.9	81 946	390
Clark	11	D	D	D	14	48	4.6	0.6	462	19.1	199	4
Clay	515	11 678	1 189.7	480.0	362	2 009	162.9	50.6	14 345	560.6	46 705	222
Clinton	56	956	70.2	27.6	28	98	6.6	1.9	1 318	45.3	4 981	28
Cole	244	5 943	612.2	230.3	238	1 584	169.1	49.2	4 729	212.7	19 398	188
Cooper	56	652	39.0	14.9	24	88	6.8	1.6	1 071	40.5	900	4
Crawford	66	896	64.6	24.2	30	120	9.6	2.3	1 526	55.1	1 965	11
Dade	14	67	3.4	1.4	11	D	D	D	495	18.7	0	0
Dallas	26	1 112	24.3	12.8	18	60	2.9	0.7	1 370	54.0	0	0
Daviess	16	109	5.6	2.1	11	41	3.8	1.2	771	37.6	200	1
DeKalb	34	D	D	D	13	54	4.4	1.3	634	27.0	331	2
Dent	51	716	35.7	14.7	21	53	3.8	0.9	936	34.2	611	6
Douglas	18	211	10.0	4.4	14	43	4.4	1.0	981	32.5	165	1
Dunklin	122	2 179	111.2	43.4	54	152	10.5	2.7	1 854	114.1	2 607	15
Franklin	216	3 558	281.7	103.4	183	796	59.8	17.4	6 608	263.4	49 973	295
Gasconade	41	587	33.8	14.9	28	85	7.4	1.7	1 184	40.4	215	3
Gentry	31	675	32.5	13.8	11	D	D	D	531	16.9	455	4
Greene	719	D	D	D	632	4 597	412.5	120.8	19 963	898.6	179 690	1 614
Grundy	28	610	46.6	15.1	27	64	5.0	1.3	707	25.0	379	4
Harrison	21	527	26.0	10.9	20	D	D	D	647	22.6	584	3
Henry	51	1 376	117.0	43.9	44	153	9.4	2.9	1 411	53.0	755	6
Hickory	7	111	5.3	2.4	5	D	D	D	681	25.8	NA	NA
Holt	12	D	D	D	7	8	1.1	0.2	422	17.0	0	0
Howard	31	377	14.2	6.7	11	D	D	D	676	21.6	80	1
Howell	157	3 094	233.5	89.4	72	283	21.7	4.9	2 944	113.0	1 418	19
Iron	105	545	30.9	10.0	36	55	3.5	0.7	502	15.4	0	0
Jackson	1 741	46 973	4 847.2	1 977.2	1 413	9 953	1 641.9	295.1	42 303	1 754.2	488 354	3 864

STATE County	Government employment and payroll, 2012									Local government finances, 2012				
			March payroll (percent of total)							General revenue				
												Taxes		
													Per capita[1] (dollars)	
	Full-time equivalent employees	March payroll (dollars)	Adminis-tration, judicial, and legal	Police and Corrections	Fire Protection	Highways and transpor-tation	Health and Welfare	Natural resources and utilities	Education and libraries	Total (mil dol)	Inter-govern-mental (mil dol)	Total (mil dol)	Total	Property
	171	172	173	174	175	176	177	178	179	180	181	182	183	184
MISSISSIPPI—Cont'd														
Sunflower	2 017	5 682 629	3.7	5.0	1.7	2.5	30.7	1.5	53.7	155.8	63.4	20.6	724	694
Tallahatchie	772	1 986 175	8.5	7.5	0.2	4.7	29.5	0.9	48.6	34.1	21.3	8.2	542	517
Tate	1 430	4 623 219	2.1	2.6	1.1	1.1	0.9	1.2	90.6	106.6	62.4	20.6	724	690
Tippah	915	2 435 046	6.8	3.3	0.2	2.1	22.7	2.8	61.0	68.1	38.2	11.3	512	467
Tishomingo	694	1 807 779	8.5	7.3	1.2	2.3	1.2	4.4	73.2	46.2	29.7	10.1	515	495
Tunica	738	1 778 465	10.4	23.6	0.0	4.7	6.1	9.7	45.3	86.8	57.0	21.4	2 043	1 507
Union	1 025	2 626 662	4.5	7.6	2.0	3.0	1.3	10.2	71.3	61.0	37.8	16.4	596	576
Walthall	518	1 141 649	3.1	5.7	0.2	3.0	2.1	0.6	83.4	45.4	21.5	8.4	559	539
Warren	1 819	5 138 472	4.6	6.1	7.5	3.0	0.3	7.0	69.2	170.1	68.3	68.7	1 429	1 171
Washington	3 566	9 118 481	5.7	7.2	2.5	3.0	32.4	4.6	43.1	298.0	98.6	52.7	1 060	977
Wayne	1 112	3 158 182	4.3	5.0	0.4	2.8	39.5	1.7	44.9	88.7	32.9	10.5	508	496
Webster	496	1 240 223	6.4	4.4	0.1	3.7	24.5	1.5	58.9	36.7	19.1	6.3	623	599
Wilkinson	427	1 032 081	12.7	10.5	0.3	7.1	2.1	3.0	61.9	56.6	14.2	5.9	630	607
Winston	620	1 506 689	8.7	16.0	2.1	4.3	1.9	2.4	64.2	46.2	24.1	11.5	602	576
Yalobusha	708	1 878 214	6.3	4.5	1.3	4.5	39.0	4.3	40.1	42.2	18.6	8.6	691	675
Yazoo	1 019	2 766 051	5.8	9.4	4.3	6.7	2.3	10.2	60.9	70.1	40.4	21.3	755	728
MISSOURI	X	X	X	X	X	X	X	X	X	X	X	X	X	X
Adair	916	2 496 611	7.3	5.8	2.8	3.2	13.2	5.6	59.0	68.7	23.1	26.9	1 051	570
Andrew	515	1 433 245	5.1	4.2	0.9	3.0	4.0	5.7	76.7	48.4	17.6	23.4	1 345	1 199
Atchison	319	829 091	7.7	5.0	0.1	22.0	10.0	5.1	49.6	22.0	10.2	9.7	1 755	1 294
Audrain	1 347	4 107 516	4.1	5.9	0.2	2.5	49.7	3.5	33.4	133.2	34.7	34.4	1 343	940
Barry	1 307	3 855 776	4.7	5.7	1.8	2.3	1.6	5.6	77.7	94.7	45.3	37.8	1 063	636
Barton	723	2 240 324	3.5	2.9	0.7	1.9	43.2	5.8	41.8	83.5	14.1	10.7	866	674
Bates	840	2 585 067	4.7	5.8	0.3	2.0	37.0	4.7	45.0	43.7	19.9	13.4	805	577
Benton	748	1 949 137	5.2	5.4	0.1	2.8	27.9	2.2	53.8	41.5	16.6	13.2	696	514
Bollinger	361	902 476	5.5	5.4	0.3	4.6	0.0	1.6	82.4	21.6	12.4	7.2	585	414
Boone	6 008	20 052 275	7.9	5.3	3.3	2.8	2.7	11.3	63.5	497.3	161.0	228.2	1 354	805
Buchanan	3 079	9 642 143	5.9	9.4	5.3	3.7	2.5	5.0	66.6	296.5	114.1	129.1	1 439	812
Butler	1 617	4 243 462	2.3	5.6	2.5	3.4	0.0	4.2	79.9	124.9	58.1	43.7	1 015	498
Caldwell	485	1 279 896	6.3	9.6	0.0	2.5	7.8	5.3	68.5	29.5	14.3	7.8	847	648
Callaway	1 265	3 154 685	6.9	9.5	2.6	4.3	5.4	8.0	63.0	88.2	36.4	34.7	782	576
Camden	1 451	4 272 326	7.8	13.4	5.1	5.6	4.2	2.2	60.3	116.5	32.4	68.3	1 557	990
Cape Girardeau	2 602	6 797 882	6.6	9.1	5.9	6.5	1.2	10.3	58.6	207.7	74.1	101.6	1 320	702
Carroll	390	1 096 814	9.3	3.7	1.4	4.2	4.3	6.6	70.1	26.7	11.7	10.0	1 101	852
Carter	278	723 988	1.6	5.8	0.0	2.9	3.2	2.5	72.4	15.4	9.6	3.9	625	446
Cass	4 195	14 748 324	5.3	6.9	4.3	2.7	12.2	4.5	63.7	380.9	126.2	139.6	1 391	927
Cedar	643	1 585 692	4.7	5.5	0.2	3.0	25.1	6.6	54.3	50.4	15.5	11.7	850	590
Chariton	295	762 719	8.8	6.7	0.2	3.7	5.8	6.0	68.4	20.7	8.4	9.5	1 240	969
Christian	2 200	6 653 224	5.3	7.1	2.0	1.8	0.2	4.7	77.8	188.4	89.3	71.0	890	611
Clark	372	840 780	6.1	5.8	0.0	4.4	21.9	7.3	53.6	21.0	7.2	6.3	911	738
Clay	12 186	43 650 964	3.1	4.3	2.0	0.8	42.4	2.3	44.6	1 333.0	239.3	340.1	1 495	1 078
Clinton	670	2 036 971	7.0	9.3	0.4	4.7	2.3	8.2	67.6	52.6	24.6	20.4	993	788
Cole	2 439	7 947 888	7.8	8.8	4.1	4.5	3.5	5.9	65.1	213.9	62.0	116.3	1 523	890
Cooper	744	2 121 619	5.8	7.9	1.4	3.1	23.2	4.8	52.9	62.0	16.7	23.7	1 353	687
Crawford	756	1 998 530	5.7	8.1	0.0	3.7	7.3	5.6	68.1	45.1	21.5	17.0	683	512
Dade	452	949 754	5.1	2.9	0.0	1.2	37.3	2.9	50.6	20.8	9.6	6.2	824	608
Dallas	463	1 037 873	7.3	5.8	0.3	5.2	0.8	2.2	78.1	31.3	18.2	10.5	627	394
Daviess	341	863 936	7.8	3.3	0.0	3.1	2.5	7.8	74.9	20.0	9.8	7.4	895	719
DeKalb	227	666 095	6.8	3.3	0.0	4.5	3.8	6.9	74.5	18.0	7.8	6.8	522	356
Dent	677	1 899 125	6.9	2.7	0.2	3.0	33.8	4.1	48.4	46.0	16.0	9.7	622	406
Douglas	383	1 073 499	10.7	2.4	0.0	4.9	5.0	5.3	70.1	32.6	12.6	16.6	1 225	824
Dunklin	1 473	3 567 888	5.4	6.8	1.4	3.0	1.6	10.3	68.2	82.8	44.0	27.3	859	614
Franklin	3 292	11 002 286	4.9	8.8	2.3	3.4	4.3	2.7	72.9	276.7	102.6	133.5	1 317	868
Gasconade	880	2 347 282	3.9	4.6	0.0	3.4	28.6	4.8	53.1	70.3	15.8	18.8	1 257	905
Gentry	345	893 935	12.0	4.7	0.4	7.4	4.6	5.3	65.1	20.8	9.7	7.8	1 144	911
Greene	10 039	36 380 689	4.7	8.2	3.7	4.6	1.4	13.2	55.1	880.5	308.6	410.2	1 462	763
Grundy	761	1 960 447	2.6	5.1	1.0	3.5	14.2	6.8	64.8	55.4	22.3	10.8	1 048	654
Harrison	594	1 570 497	5.2	2.6	0.2	3.0	37.3	7.0	42.9	43.2	13.0	10.7	1 229	806
Henry	1 267	4 585 264	3.2	3.7	1.3	1.0	61.3	2.7	26.7	117.2	50.1	23.1	1 045	588
Hickory	326	851 720	6.0	4.2	0.0	2.3	0.0	2.3	84.9	21.9	12.6	6.7	714	572
Holt	184	461 150	11.3	6.1	0.0	5.3	1.7	7.2	68.0	16.0	6.1	7.4	1 595	1 143
Howard	396	983 070	7.8	7.5	0.4	5.0	4.3	9.4	64.8	23.9	8.7	11.5	1 135	911
Howell	1 537	3 973 191	5.5	5.3	1.4	3.4	4.8	7.9	71.2	100.7	49.7	31.7	781	439
Iron	459	1 303 360	4.7	4.4	0.6	6.5	6.1	1.8	75.7	26.1	13.0	10.3	991	765
Jackson	27 447	101 433 064	7.4	14.7	9.5	6.2	0.7	5.5	54.6	3 343.9	905.1	1 696.2	2 504	1 116

1. Based on the resident population estimated as of July 1 of the year shown.

STATE County	Local government finances, 2012 (cont.)									Government employment, 2013			Presidential election,[2] 2012		
	Direct general expenditure							Debt outstanding					Percent of vote cast:		
			Percent of total for:												
	Total (mil dol)	Per capita[1] (dollars)	Educa-tion	Health and hospitals	Police protec-tion	Public welfare	High-ways	Total (mil dol)	Per capita[1] (dollars)	Federal civilian	Federal military	State and local	Demo-cratic	Republi-can	All other
	185	186	187	188	189	190	191	192	193	194	195	196	197	198	199
MISSISSIPPI—Cont'd															
Sunflower	160.1	5 631	46.7	34.5	2.9	0.1	5.4	30.8	1 085	53	143	3 695	70.0	29.0	1.0
Tallahatchie	39.2	2 596	54.2	1.1	5.0	0.0	7.9	12.7	843	36	76	960	59.1	40.1	0.7
Tate	144.1	5 057	68.2	0.5	2.9	0.0	3.0	96.6	3 389	80	163	1 573	39.2	60.1	0.8
Tippah	68.2	3 095	49.3	23.7	3.2	0.2	8.8	13.9	629	53	132	1 145	27.0	71.3	1.7
Tishomingo	53.8	2 746	50.8	1.1	4.8	0.0	7.0	25.8	1 315	58	116	892	23.3	74.2	2.5
Tunica	103.7	9 896	24.0	1.9	8.0	0.7	5.8	114.9	10 965	19	63	920	75.7	23.5	0.8
Union	59.7	2 178	65.6	1.4	6.1	0.0	5.6	32.4	1 180	50	166	1 192	24.5	74.4	1.1
Walthall	45.0	2 981	52.1	26.1	4.3	0.2	4.8	1.9	128	24	89	684	44.4	54.7	0.9
Warren	169.5	3 526	45.5	1.1	6.6	0.2	7.1	264.3	5 496	2 172	336	2 522	48.2	51.2	0.6
Washington	305.6	6 143	28.7	43.2	3.9	0.1	4.1	140.1	2 816	469	315	3 905	67.1	32.4	0.5
Wayne	70.5	3 414	47.5	34.9	3.4	0.1	5.6	14.5	700	36	123	1 298	38.8	60.6	0.6
Webster	31.4	3 130	63.8	1.3	4.6	0.0	7.8	7.1	706	31	60	434	24.7	74.6	0.7
Wilkinson	55.4	5 871	26.6	28.9	2.5	0.1	3.6	35.9	3 804	0	50	554	68.8	30.4	0.9
Winston	45.6	2 397	54.2	1.3	6.9	0.1	7.3	5.2	272	37	111	780	45.5	53.8	0.7
Yalobusha	40.4	3 257	39.3	27.4	4.0	0.0	10.5	17.9	1 447	72	74	736	46.2	53.1	0.7
Yazoo	75.1	2 663	51.5	1.3	5.5	0.3	5.8	42.6	1 510	622	142	1 497	53.3	46.1	0.6
MISSOURI	X	X	X	X	X	X	X	X	X	57 379	37 855	380 478	49.3	49.4	1.3
Adair	66.2	2 589	44.3	3.2	5.6	7.5	7.7	43.5	1 700	76	84	2 377	48.3	49.6	2.1
Andrew	36.8	2 114	65.6	3.0	5.9	1.0	6.2	25.6	1 468	33	61	686	38.1	60.1	1.9
Atchison	22.0	3 990	52.6	2.6	2.8	0.0	17.0	6.5	1 173	29	19	352	33.6	65.1	1.3
Audrain	139.4	5 440	36.1	40.4	2.1	3.8	3.0	68.4	2 669	86	82	2 421	41.1	57.2	1.7
Barry	100.1	2 815	59.9	3.2	4.9	0.0	15.0	67.2	1 892	104	125	1 588	31.6	66.6	1.7
Barton	83.6	6 780	22.2	65.7	1.4	0.0	2.7	35.3	2 861	36	43	889	24.5	74.2	1.3
Bates	44.5	2 660	58.6	0.1	9.7	6.8	7.3	46.0	2 754	56	57	1 129	39.5	58.3	2.2
Benton	41.9	2 209	51.5	5.5	3.4	22.2	5.5	22.9	1 210	97	66	952	37.9	60.2	1.9
Bollinger	21.1	1 700	73.8	1.0	4.3	0.0	7.9	3.1	248	31	43	438	29.2	68.7	2.1
Boone	580.4	3 444	44.8	3.1	4.3	0.2	6.2	2 592.5	15 382	2 492	601	28 391	55.2	43.2	1.6
Buchanan	261.5	2 915	51.6	2.2	9.4	0.7	5.3	599.9	6 688	482	321	6 451	49.1	48.9	2.0
Butler	122.1	2 837	60.0	0.0	6.4	0.0	5.4	48.6	1 129	676	149	2 845	30.7	68.1	1.3
Caldwell	28.6	3 124	59.8	1.8	3.5	5.7	7.6	9.9	1 087	35	31	613	39.7	58.2	2.1
Callaway	85.8	1 936	53.8	4.3	8.4	0.0	6.7	57.3	1 293	109	143	3 788	39.2	58.9	1.8
Camden	113.7	2 593	47.6	3.7	9.0	0.0	11.7	112.7	2 570	78	152	1 845	35.1	63.6	1.3
Cape Girardeau	211.7	2 751	54.0	0.3	5.4	0.0	9.9	197.3	2 564	379	285	5 870	32.7	66.3	1.0
Carroll	27.9	3 076	59.3	3.2	3.9	0.0	11.1	12.4	1 360	43	32	565	33.8	65.1	1.1
Carter	15.8	2 520	74.5	2.8	1.9	0.0	3.9	29.2	4 657	93	22	354	34.0	63.5	2.6
Cass	400.2	3 987	50.4	13.7	3.1	0.3	5.8	468.7	4 669	256	448	4 562	39.5	59.2	1.3
Cedar	37.7	2 733	50.1	29.0	5.1	0.0	2.8	32.6	2 361	62	49	799	32.4	66.0	1.6
Chariton	22.7	2 968	52.9	4.1	2.8	0.0	14.2	3.5	456	44	26	448	42.7	55.5	1.8
Christian	179.8	2 252	67.4	0.5	4.7	1.0	5.5	246.9	3 093	104	283	2 823	31.5	67.3	1.1
Clark	23.6	3 386	46.2	6.2	1.8	17.9	8.0	8.6	1 234	33	24	475	45.5	51.6	3.0
Clay	1 296.4	5 696	31.9	48.7	2.3	0.0	1.9	934.2	4 105	870	866	13 959	49.0	49.7	1.2
Clinton	50.6	2 467	62.4	1.9	7.3	0.0	8.9	42.6	2 078	63	71	1 051	43.5	54.6	1.9
Cole	222.3	2 911	50.1	2.6	10.7	0.0	10.0	194.9	2 552	623	282	19 380	36.0	62.9	1.0
Cooper	65.2	3 719	36.8	19.0	3.7	4.9	5.9	51.2	2 925	46	57	1 265	37.3	61.1	1.6
Crawford	44.2	1 780	63.0	8.1	3.6	0.0	5.8	29.0	1 169	34	85	934	38.8	59.6	1.7
Dade	20.9	2 758	51.9	1.1	3.6	23.8	6.9	4.0	526	28	26	530	28.8	69.6	1.6
Dallas	39.6	2 358	42.6	3.7	4.9	0.0	39.8	4.3	254	32	58	612	34.6	63.7	1.7
Daviess	19.9	2 419	62.2	3.1	3.1	0.1	12.4	10.1	1 231	33	29	493	37.0	59.8	3.2
DeKalb	17.0	1 315	62.4	3.4	4.1	0.0	6.0	6.2	478	32	33	1 275	36.1	61.7	2.2
Dent	47.9	3 058	43.1	38.7	4.1	0.0	4.2	2.6	166	56	55	873	29.9	67.8	2.3
Douglas	34.6	2 550	64.0	1.9	3.6	0.0	13.6	7.5	553	46	47	399	31.9	65.6	2.5
Dunklin	76.5	2 405	65.8	1.0	6.7	0.0	5.4	33.5	1 052	95	110	1 586	38.6	59.9	1.5
Franklin	286.0	2 820	58.5	2.0	6.4	0.0	9.3	497.8	4 909	208	357	4 407	43.1	55.5	1.4
Gasconade	55.7	3 719	45.7	31.4	2.9	0.5	4.5	60.7	4 054	47	52	1 015	37.3	61.3	1.4
Gentry	20.3	2 997	59.9	3.6	3.3	0.0	10.5	8.2	1 217	37	23	432	37.5	59.7	2.8
Greene	855.2	3 047	50.1	1.1	8.7	0.2	6.0	1 601.3	5 706	2 080	988	18 371	41.4	57.2	1.3
Grundy	48.8	4 722	61.4	3.0	2.3	10.7	6.0	28.4	2 746	62	35	970	33.3	63.4	3.2
Harrison	40.5	4 640	35.7	40.6	3.2	0.0	7.4	11.6	1 333	38	30	731	32.9	64.2	3.0
Henry	113.3	5 114	25.1	59.5	2.3	0.1	3.3	36.1	1 629	77	77	1 601	43.6	54.6	1.7
Hickory	21.4	2 275	79.2	1.5	2.4	0.0	5.9	11.7	1 244	43	33	309	42.4	55.7	1.8
Holt	15.2	3 273	49.5	0.6	2.4	0.0	13.7	0.8	182	33	10	205	30.6	68.1	1.4
Howard	22.1	2 174	53.2	3.8	5.5	0.3	6.2	33.3	3 276	34	34	462	41.9	55.8	2.3
Howell	94.2	2 317	67.7	2.1	5.1	0.0	5.1	39.4	970	107	141	2 144	33.7	64.5	1.8
Iron	27.4	2 641	71.9	1.5	3.9	0.0	5.6	10.9	1 046	17	36	619	50.1	47.3	2.5
Jackson	3 093.9	4 567	37.7	2.6	9.6	0.3	7.4	6 245.9	9 221	16 622	2 495	43 856	62.1	36.8	1.1

1. Based on the resident population estimated as of July 1 of the year shown. 2.

STATE/ County code	CBSA code[1]	County type[2]	STATE County	Land area,[3] (sq km) 2010	Population, 2014: Total persons 2014	Population, 2014: Rank	Population, 2014: Per square kilometer	Population and population characteristics, 2013: Race alone or in combination, not Hispanic or Latino (percent): White	Black	American Indian, Alaska Native	Asian and Pacific Islander	Percent Hispanic or Latino[4]	Age (percent): Under 5 years	5 to 17 years	18 to 24 years	25 to 34 years	35 to 44 years	45 to 54 years
				1	2	3	4	5	6	7	8	9	10	11	12	13	14	15
			MISSOURI—Cont'd															
29 097	27900	3	Jasper	1 654	117 543	521	71.1	87.9	2.9	2.8	1.7	7.4	7.1	18.2	9.9	13.9	12.5	12.8
29 099	41180	1	Jefferson	1 701	222 716	288	130.9	96.3	1.5	0.8	1.0	1.7	6.4	17.8	8.2	12.9	13.2	15.5
29 101	47660	4	Johnson	2 148	54 362	920	25.3	88.9	5.6	1.4	3.1	3.8	6.6	15.5	21.1	14.0	10.3	11.3
29 103	...	9	Knox	1 305	4 000	2 903	3.1	97.7	0.9	0.9	0.6	1.2	6.4	17.7	7.5	9.8	10.3	14.2
29 105	30060	6	Laclede	1 981	35 439	1 289	17.9	95.7	1.4	1.6	1.0	2.2	6.7	18.2	8.0	11.8	12.0	14.1
29 107	28140	1	Lafayette	1 628	32 688	1 369	20.1	94.2	3.0	1.2	0.9	2.6	5.8	17.7	8.3	11.1	11.7	14.5
29 109	...	6	Lawrence	1 584	38 023	1 220	24.0	91.4	0.7	1.7	0.6	7.0	6.5	19.1	7.6	11.3	12.0	13.6
29 111	39500	9	Lewis	1 308	10 138	2 430	7.8	94.3	4.1	0.8	0.6	1.7	5.9	17.1	11.9	10.8	10.5	13.5
29 113	41180	1	Lincoln	1 623	54 249	921	33.4	95.1	2.7	0.9	0.8	2.2	6.9	19.9	8.2	12.9	12.7	15.0
29 115	...	7	Linn	1 594	12 311	2 277	7.7	96.7	1.4	0.6	0.5	1.9	5.7	18.1	7.5	9.9	11.2	13.5
29 117	...	6	Livingston	1 379	15 053	2 097	10.9	94.8	3.6	0.8	0.7	1.5	5.7	15.7	8.0	12.7	12.7	13.3
29 119	22220	2	McDonald	1 397	22 800	1 697	16.3	82.1	1.8	4.5	3.0	11.5	6.8	19.7	8.5	11.7	12.5	14.4
29 121	...	7	Macon	2 075	15 479	2 074	7.5	95.5	3.2	0.9	0.9	1.2	6.0	17.9	7.2	10.5	11.0	13.1
29 123	...	7	Madison	1 280	12 368	2 275	9.7	96.4	0.8	0.8	1.1	1.9	6.2	17.1	7.9	11.2	11.7	13.8
29 125	...	8	Maries	1 365	9 013	2 518	6.6	97.5	0.8	1.2	0.5	1.2	4.8	17.4	7.4	10.6	10.9	15.0
29 127	25300	5	Marion	1 132	28 920	1 458	25.5	92.4	6.4	0.7	1.1	1.5	6.3	17.2	9.4	12.0	11.6	13.6
29 129	...	9	Mercer	1 175	3 719	2 926	3.2	98.0	0.7	0.8	0.9	0.9	5.6	18.8	7.0	9.3	10.2	14.2
29 131	...	6	Miller	1 535	25 141	1 602	16.4	96.6	1.1	1.4	0.8	1.6	5.9	17.7	7.8	11.6	11.5	14.0
29 133	...	7	Mississippi	1 066	14 232	2 150	13.4	73.3	24.9	0.6	0.4	2.0	6.7	15.6	8.4	13.8	13.2	14.0
29 135	27620	3	Moniteau	1 075	15 856	2 052	14.7	90.8	4.2	0.9	0.6	4.5	6.4	18.6	8.2	13.2	13.5	14.2
29 137	...	9	Monroe	1 677	8 707	2 539	5.2	95.4	3.6	0.8	0.6	1.0	5.2	17.4	7.2	10.0	10.6	14.2
29 139	...	8	Montgomery	1 389	11 841	2 304	8.5	96.2	2.1	0.8	0.7	1.6	6.1	16.8	7.4	10.1	10.8	14.5
29 141	...	8	Morgan	1 548	20 240	1 822	13.1	96.1	1.2	1.5	0.8	1.9	5.9	15.9	6.9	9.4	9.6	13.5
29 143	...	7	New Madrid	1 748	18 272	1 907	10.5	82.0	16.5	0.7	0.8	1.6	5.8	17.8	7.9	11.2	12.1	14.1
29 145	27900	3	Newton	1 618	58 598	880	36.2	89.6	1.5	4.0	2.7	4.9	6.4	18.3	8.8	11.2	11.6	13.8
29 147	32340	6	Nodaway	2 271	23 081	1 680	10.2	93.9	3.0	0.5	2.1	1.5	4.6	12.5	28.4	11.0	8.7	10.8
29 149	...	9	Oregon	2 046	10 911	2 364	5.3	96.4	0.8	2.6	0.7	1.4	6.0	16.2	7.5	9.1	10.2	14.2
29 151	27620	3	Osage	1 565	13 703	2 192	8.8	98.7	0.6	0.5	0.3	0.6	5.7	17.8	9.2	10.7	12.5	15.0
29 153	...	9	Ozark	1 929	9 492	2 469	4.9	97.3	0.7	1.4	0.4	1.6	4.7	14.8	6.5	8.4	9.3	13.4
29 155	...	7	Pemiscot	1 276	17 650	1 938	13.8	70.5	27.4	0.7	0.4	2.3	7.6	19.2	8.9	11.4	11.7	13.2
29 157	...	7	Perry	1 229	19 202	1 866	15.6	96.6	0.8	0.7	0.8	2.1	6.0	18.3	8.2	11.5	12.2	14.0
29 159	42740	4	Pettis	1 767	42 225	1 127	23.9	87.5	4.1	0.9	1.3	8.1	7.0	18.2	9.2	13.2	11.3	13.6
29 161	40620	5	Phelps	1 740	44 847	1 074	25.8	91.4	3.2	1.6	3.7	2.3	5.9	15.4	17.8	11.7	10.4	12.6
29 163	...	6	Pike	1 736	18 541	1 891	10.7	89.9	8.2	0.6	0.5	2.1	6.1	15.8	8.8	13.4	12.4	14.5
29 165	28140	1	Platte	1 088	94 788	617	87.1	84.9	7.0	1.1	3.7	5.6	6.3	17.9	8.3	13.2	13.8	15.0
29 167	44180	2	Polk	1 646	31 054	1 412	18.9	95.5	1.3	1.5	1.1	2.1	6.1	17.9	12.5	10.5	11.2	13.2
29 169	22780	5	Pulaski	1 417	53 436	935	37.7	73.7	13.4	1.8	4.9	10.4	7.2	15.9	22.8	18.3	11.7	9.6
29 171	...	9	Putnam	1 340	4 829	2 848	3.6	98.1	0.6	0.5	0.7	1.0	5.2	16.9	7.2	9.2	10.0	13.5
29 173	25300	9	Ralls	1 217	10 255	2 415	8.4	96.9	1.7	0.6	0.7	1.3	5.4	16.7	6.8	9.9	11.8	15.4
29 175	33620	6	Randolph	1 250	25 072	1 606	20.1	91.6	6.8	1.0	0.9	1.8	5.9	16.6	9.4	13.6	12.9	14.0
29 177	28140	1	Ray	1 473	22 949	1 688	15.6	95.5	1.9	1.1	0.6	2.2	5.6	18.3	7.8	10.7	12.0	15.3
29 179	...	9	Reynolds	2 094	6 565	2 716	3.1	97.0	1.2	1.9	0.5	1.3	5.0	16.0	6.5	10.0	10.8	14.3
29 181	...	9	Ripley	1 630	13 969	2 173	8.6	96.9	0.9	1.8	0.6	1.1	6.8	16.2	7.9	11.0	11.5	13.8
29 183	41180	1	St. Charles	1 452	379 493	178	261.4	89.8	5.3	0.6	2.9	3.0	6.2	18.5	8.7	13.1	13.3	15.0
29 185	...	8	St. Clair	1 735	9 457	2 473	5.5	96.1	1.1	1.9	0.4	2.3	5.0	14.6	6.5	8.7	10.2	14.1
29 186	...	6	Ste. Genevieve	1 293	17 914	1 918	13.9	97.7	1.1	0.8	0.5	0.9	5.4	16.8	7.9	10.5	11.5	15.5
29 187	22100	4	St. Francois	1 170	65 960	799	56.4	93.3	4.9	0.9	0.6	1.4	5.5	16.1	9.1	14.4	13.4	14.3
29 189	41180	1	St. Louis	1 315	1 001 876	43	761.9	69.6	24.5	0.6	4.5	2.7	5.8	16.7	8.9	12.6	11.8	14.3
29 195	32180	6	Saline	1 957	23 347	1 670	11.9	83.4	6.6	1.0	1.9	9.5	6.4	16.4	11.6	12.2	11.0	13.0
29 197	28860	9	Schuyler	796	4 370	2 874	5.5	98.4	0.5	0.7	0.3	0.9	5.9	19.3	8.2	9.2	11.2	13.2
29 199	...	9	Scotland	1 131	4 863	2 845	4.3	98.5	0.4	0.6	0.3	0.9	8.1	20.3	8.0	10.7	9.9	12.8
29 201	43460	5	Scott	1 088	38 903	1 200	35.8	85.6	12.3	0.9	0.6	2.2	7.0	17.3	8.7	12.2	12.0	13.7
29 203	...	9	Shannon	2 600	8 329	2 572	3.2	96.6	0.8	2.7	0.5	1.9	5.4	17.0	7.8	10.1	10.1	15.1
29 205	...	9	Shelby	1 297	6 108	2 749	4.7	97.5	1.2	0.4	0.4	1.4	6.2	17.5	7.2	10.8	10.7	13.5
29 207	...	7	Stoddard	2 132	29 867	1 432	14.0	96.7	1.4	0.9	0.4	1.5	5.6	16.3	8.3	11.5	12.2	13.8
29 209	14700	8	Stone	1 202	31 104	1 411	25.9	96.7	0.7	1.4	0.6	1.9	4.1	13.5	6.1	7.8	9.7	14.1
29 211	...	9	Sullivan	1 678	6 411	2 723	3.8	80.0	1.4	0.8	0.4	18.2	5.6	17.5	7.9	10.0	12.3	14.5
29 213	14700	6	Taney	1 638	54 230	922	33.1	91.7	1.7	1.7	1.3	5.5	6.0	15.6	10.2	11.5	11.1	13.1
29 215	...	9	Texas	3 049	25 642	1 577	8.4	93.3	4.0	1.9	0.6	2.0	5.8	15.6	8.3	11.8	11.2	14.1
29 217	...	7	Vernon	2 140	21 001	1 773	9.8	95.9	1.2	1.5	0.9	2.0	6.2	18.3	8.9	10.8	11.1	13.6
29 219	41180	1	Warren	1 110	33 253	1 348	30.0	93.7	3.0	0.9	0.8	3.1	6.3	18.0	7.5	12.0	11.5	15.1
29 221	...	1	Washington	1 968	25 077	1 605	12.7	95.7	2.7	1.1	0.5	1.2	6.0	17.3	7.9	12.2	13.2	14.9
29 223	...	9	Wayne	1 966	13 452	2 210	6.8	97.5	0.9	1.5	0.5	1.3	5.8	14.8	7.1	9.6	10.5	15.2
29 225	44180	2	Webster	1 535	36 888	1 252	24.0	96.2	1.5	1.5	0.5	1.8	6.7	20.5	7.8	11.7	12.7	14.2
29 227	...	9	Worth	691	2 073	3 044	3.0	97.4	1.3	0.6	0.6	1.2	5.7	14.9	6.9	9.3	9.1	14.8
29 229	...	6	Wright	1 766	18 291	1 906	10.4	96.7	1.0	1.5	0.6	1.7	6.4	19.0	7.6	10.6	10.5	13.9

1. CBSA = Core Based Statistical Area. See Appendix A for explanation. See Appendix B for list of metropolitan areas with component counties. 2. County type code from the Economic Research Service of USDA Rural-Urban Continuum Codes. See Appendix A for definition. 3. Dry land or land partially or temporarily covered by water. 4. May be of any race.

STATE County	Population, 2013 (cont.) Age (percent) (cont.) 55 to 64 years	65 to 74 years	75 years and over	Percent female	Population change and components of change, 2000–2014 Total persons 2000	2010	Percent change 2000–2010	2010–2014	Components of change, 2010–2014 Births	Deaths	Net migration	Households, 2009–2013 Number	Persons per household	Percent Family households	Female family householder[1]	One person
	16	17	18	19	20	21	22	23	24	25	26	27	28	29	30	31
MISSOURI—Cont'd																
Jasper	11.9	7.6	6.1	51.0	104 686	117 404	12.1	0.1	7 353	4 797	-2 516	44 849	2.55	66.1	12.7	27.1
Jefferson	13.2	8.0	4.7	50.3	198 099	218 733	10.4	1.8	11 369	7 795	188	80 812	2.69	73.1	11.2	21.8
Johnson	9.8	6.6	4.9	48.8	48 258	52 595	9.0	3.4	3 042	1 574	288	20 092	2.45	65.6	7.9	22.4
Knox	13.5	11.5	9.3	50.5	4 361	4 131	-5.3	-3.2	211	212	-141	1 724	2.33	65.0	10.8	32.5
Laclede	12.7	9.7	6.9	50.7	32 513	35 571	9.4	-0.4	1 921	1 538	-540	13 912	2.53	72.2	12.6	23.1
Lafayette	13.5	9.3	8.1	50.5	32 960	33 381	1.3	-2.1	1 622	1 476	-813	13 117	2.47	70.5	9.1	25.5
Lawrence	12.6	9.3	7.9	50.6	35 204	38 634	9.7	-1.6	2 059	1 819	-868	14 817	2.55	69.4	9.1	25.9
Lewis	12.5	9.5	8.2	49.8	10 494	10 211	-2.7	-0.7	475	429	-129	3 936	2.39	68.4	9.3	27.0
Lincoln	12.4	7.2	4.8	49.9	38 944	52 566	35.0	3.2	3 065	1 740	353	18 714	2.80	72.0	10.9	23.9
Linn	14.1	10.5	9.6	51.6	13 754	12 761	-7.2	-3.5	578	704	-319	4 854	2.56	65.4	8.3	30.7
Livingston	12.8	9.5	9.7	55.1	14 558	15 195	4.4	-0.9	687	799	-39	5 660	2.42	65.1	10.7	29.0
McDonald	12.6	8.6	5.2	49.5	21 681	23 083	6.5	-1.2	1 296	853	-704	8 221	2.76	69.2	12.4	27.9
Macon	13.7	10.9	9.7	50.8	15 762	15 566	-1.2	-0.6	753	785	-48	6 389	2.38	63.3	8.4	32.8
Madison	13.2	10.7	8.2	50.8	11 800	12 226	3.6	1.2	603	697	203	4 603	2.64	70.9	12.3	23.4
Maries	14.7	11.3	7.9	50.0	8 903	9 176	3.1	-1.8	353	413	-115	3 749	2.40	69.4	8.4	26.0
Marion	13.3	8.6	8.0	51.8	28 289	28 781	1.7	0.5	1 577	1 292	-117	11 203	2.42	68.5	13.8	26.7
Mercer	14.9	10.3	9.6	49.9	3 757	3 785	0.7	-1.7	167	169	-59	1 575	2.34	68.4	10.9	28.8
Miller	14.0	9.8	7.6	50.3	23 564	24 748	5.0	1.6	1 244	1 154	330	10 034	2.45	67.1	10.2	29.2
Mississippi	12.1	9.3	6.8	46.5	13 427	14 358	6.9	-0.9	756	795	-103	5 227	2.50	63.9	16.5	33.2
Moniteau	11.5	8.1	6.5	47.0	14 827	15 607	5.3	1.6	891	590	-44	5 464	2.61	69.9	9.4	25.8
Monroe	15.1	11.5	8.7	49.7	9 311	8 840	-5.1	-1.5	387	363	-141	3 497	2.46	65.6	8.5	30.1
Montgomery	14.5	10.5	9.2	50.5	12 136	12 236	0.8	-3.2	626	651	-379	5 091	2.31	69.2	11.6	27.0
Morgan	15.3	14.1	9.4	49.5	19 309	20 565	6.5	-1.6	1 065	1 249	-140	8 164	2.46	67.5	7.8	28.0
New Madrid	14.0	9.7	7.4	52.3	19 760	18 956	-4.1	-3.6	982	997	-636	7 423	2.47	68.2	18.1	28.1
Newton	12.9	9.9	7.2	50.4	52 636	58 114	10.4	0.8	3 137	2 536	-146	22 045	2.61	71.7	9.5	23.3
Nodaway	10.2	6.9	6.9	49.5	21 912	23 370	6.7	-1.2	958	780	-468	8 599	2.35	53.6	6.6	32.8
Oregon	15.4	12.6	8.8	51.0	10 344	10 881	5.2	0.3	545	582	46	4 572	2.37	63.6	6.8	32.0
Osage	12.8	8.7	7.6	48.0	13 062	13 878	6.2	-1.3	632	513	-306	5 168	2.63	73.5	7.7	22.3
Ozark	17.1	15.2	10.6	49.7	9 542	9 723	1.9	-2.4	387	517	-100	4 063	2.35	73.4	10.6	23.4
Pemiscot	12.6	8.3	7.0	52.6	20 047	18 296	-8.7	-3.5	1 223	975	-861	6 941	2.58	62.8	20.0	33.7
Perry	13.5	8.6	7.8	50.1	18 132	18 971	4.6	1.2	962	850	77	7 511	2.49	70.6	8.5	25.7
Pettis	12.5	7.8	7.2	50.6	39 403	42 201	7.1	0.1	2 468	1 752	-598	16 212	2.55	66.3	10.3	28.5
Phelps	11.6	8.1	6.5	47.6	39 825	45 156	13.4	-0.7	2 308	1 745	-811	16 699	2.50	64.0	9.7	28.0
Pike	12.6	9.2	7.1	45.1	18 351	18 516	0.9	0.1	934	797	-127	6 559	2.48	69.0	9.9	26.2
Platte	13.1	7.6	4.9	50.7	73 781	89 322	21.1	6.1	4 887	2 500	3 118	36 781	2.45	67.2	9.7	27.4
Polk	11.9	9.1	7.6	51.1	26 992	31 137	15.4	-0.3	1 596	1 451	-149	11 937	2.50	69.9	8.3	24.6
Pulaski	7.2	4.3	3.1	43.4	41 165	52 274	27.0	2.2	3 623	1 166	-1 286	15 747	2.74	65.0	11.2	26.8
Putnam	14.7	13.0	10.2	49.6	5 223	4 979	-4.7	-3.0	215	244	-115	2 230	2.18	63.9	8.8	33.7
Ralls	15.6	11.8	6.7	49.5	9 626	10 167	5.6	0.9	395	377	99	4 044	2.50	73.9	6.8	20.0
Randolph	12.4	8.2	6.9	47.9	24 663	25 414	3.0	-1.3	1 211	1 092	-467	8 925	2.59	67.0	13.0	27.2
Ray	13.8	9.9	6.7	50.0	23 354	23 494	0.6	-2.3	1 035	1 022	-575	8 735	2.63	72.2	9.7	24.0
Reynolds	14.5	13.1	9.8	48.7	6 689	6 696	0.1	-1.9	276	351	-114	2 664	2.44	67.0	9.5	27.6
Ripley	13.4	11.1	8.3	50.6	13 509	14 100	4.4	-0.9	763	824	-55	5 544	2.52	70.2	11.5	25.1
St. Charles	12.3	7.4	5.4	50.9	283 883	360 485	27.0	5.3	19 120	9 998	9 650	135 974	2.64	72.6	9.5	22.9
St. Clair	15.6	14.2	11.2	49.4	9 652	9 805	1.6	-3.5	396	602	-151	4 139	2.28	66.1	10.2	31.5
Ste. Genevieve	15.4	9.3	7.7	49.3	17 842	18 145	1.7	-1.3	721	795	-108	7 235	2.45	69.1	6.1	27.1
St. Francois	12.3	8.4	6.5	46.6	55 641	65 359	17.5	0.9	3 167	3 147	545	24 654	2.34	65.0	11.0	29.8
St. Louis	13.8	8.5	7.6	52.7	1 016 315	998 954	-1.7	0.3	49 523	39 761	-5 941	403 293	2.43	65.4	14.4	29.8
Saline	12.8	8.9	7.8	50.4	23 756	23 370	-1.6	-0.1	1 318	1 052	-254	8 764	2.48	65.8	14.2	28.0
Schuyler	12.8	10.5	9.7	51.2	4 170	4 431	6.3	-1.4	245	209	-89	1 773	2.45	67.1	9.4	30.9
Scotland	11.6	9.5	8.9	50.6	4 983	4 843	-2.8	0.4	327	237	-72	1 915	2.48	65.0	8.9	27.7
Scott	13.1	9.1	6.9	51.4	40 422	39 191	-3.0	-0.7	2 230	1 766	-708	15 169	2.55	71.2	14.3	23.7
Shannon	15.4	11.9	7.1	50.3	8 324	8 441	1.4	-1.3	407	363	-136	3 220	2.57	70.8	8.4	24.2
Shelby	14.3	10.2	9.6	50.3	6 799	6 373	-6.3	-4.2	291	330	-213	2 597	2.31	63.1	6.9	34.3
Stoddard	13.5	10.1	8.7	51.4	29 705	29 968	0.9	-0.3	1 529	1 610	10	12 224	2.39	67.2	11.0	28.1
Stone	17.8	16.8	10.1	51.0	28 658	32 202	12.4	-3.4	1 095	1 486	-648	13 320	2.37	72.0	7.7	23.6
Sullivan	13.7	10.3	8.2	49.2	7 219	6 714	-7.0	-4.5	368	317	-351	2 640	2.46	66.3	11.5	30.9
Taney	13.4	11.4	7.7	51.4	39 703	51 675	30.2	4.9	2 629	2 152	2 026	20 698	2.45	65.8	12.0	28.5
Texas	14.0	10.6	8.5	48.0	23 003	26 008	13.1	-1.4	1 221	1 189	-340	9 370	2.58	69.7	9.8	25.6
Vernon	13.7	9.8	7.6	51.4	20 454	21 159	3.4	-0.7	1 105	1 002	-245	7 999	2.51	65.5	10.9	29.5
Warren	13.2	9.7	6.6	50.4	24 525	32 513	32.6	2.3	1 720	1 101	115	12 572	2.57	72.3	10.3	22.4
Washington	13.6	9.2	5.8	48.5	23 344	25 195	7.9	-0.5	1 249	1 086	-263	9 199	2.61	70.8	10.3	24.7
Wayne	15.1	13.1	8.7	50.3	13 259	13 521	2.0	-0.5	633	828	129	5 589	2.37	68.5	9.9	26.6
Webster	12.2	8.4	5.9	49.1	31 045	36 202	16.6	1.9	2 174	1 286	-175	12 668	2.80	75.1	9.5	21.7
Worth	14.9	12.3	12.1	50.4	2 382	2 171	-8.9	-4.5	102	115	-79	940	2.20	65.2	7.6	26.9
Wright	13.3	10.5	8.2	50.9	17 955	18 815	4.8	-2.8	994	920	-610	7 295	2.52	69.5	10.5	26.6

1. No spouse present.

STATE County	Persons in group quarters, 2014	Daytime population, 2009–2013: Number	Daytime population, 2009–2013: Employment/residence ratio	Births, 2014: Total	Births, 2014: Rate[1]	Deaths, 2014: Number	Deaths, 2014: Rate[1]	Persons under 65 with no health insurance, 2013: Number	Persons under 65 with no health insurance, 2013: Percent	Medicare, 2014: Eligible for Medicare	Medicare, 2014: Enrolled in Medicare Advantage	Medicare, 2014: Enrolled in a Medicare prescription drug plan	Serious crimes known to police,[2] 2013: Total: Number	Serious crimes known to police,[2] 2013: Total: Rate[3]
	32	33	34	35	36	37	38	39	40	41	42	43	44	45
MISSOURI—Cont'd														
Jasper	2 478	122 746	1.11	1 733	14.7	1 083	9.2	17 542	17.8	21 278	4 519	10 751	5 978	5 212
Jefferson	1 983	167 035	0.49	2 664	12.0	1 900	8.5	25 766	13.5	37 885	14 990	14 985	4 566	2 065
Johnson	3 824	50 475	0.88	715	13.2	364	6.7	6 464	14.4	7 337	1 316	3 246	1 267	2 300
Knox	87	3 797	0.83	55	13.8	44	11.0	791	24.9	954	53	630	43	1 055
Laclede	345	35 516	1.00	443	12.5	359	10.1	4 924	16.7	7 992	3 270	2 693	1 156	3 264
Lafayette	724	28 544	0.69	378	11.6	338	10.3	3 935	14.7	6 998	1 628	3 607	538	1 686
Lawrence	559	33 384	0.68	487	12.8	424	11.2	6 167	19.7	8 340	3 035	3 253	1 482	3 849
Lewis	782	8 705	0.68	110	10.9	96	9.5	1 320	16.9	2 078	161	1 364	150	1 472
Lincoln	632	42 056	0.52	711	13.1	399	7.4	7 013	14.9	8 753	2 443	4 449	776	1 445
Linn	152	12 526	0.99	135	11.0	173	14.1	1 619	16.5	3 079	251	1 951	345	2 776
Livingston	1 613	15 917	1.14	166	11.0	177	11.8	1 750	16.1	3 230	315	2 061	343	2 281
McDonald	157	20 451	0.73	306	13.4	208	9.1	4 385	22.7	3 777	1 034	1 594	784	3 430
Macon	286	14 612	0.86	167	10.8	169	10.9	2 026	16.5	3 789	249	2 341	310	1 987
Madison	165	11 532	0.82	139	11.2	182	14.7	1 850	18.5	3 105	340	2 032	341	2 714
Maries	67	7 054	0.45	82	9.1	91	10.1	1 404	19.4	2 078	191	1 089	133	1 481
Marion	1 374	30 019	1.09	362	12.5	295	10.2	3 299	14.2	6 206	508	3 999	1 350	4 688
Mercer	51	4 087	1.22	39	10.5	23	6.2	597	20.3	863	55	523	38	1 021
Miller	271	22 316	0.75	305	12.1	263	10.5	3 782	18.4	5 055	784	2 796	614	2 466
Mississippi	1 903	13 877	0.93	170	11.9	175	12.3	1 801	17.6	2 985	183	2 087	370	2 578
Moniteau	1 371	13 691	0.70	216	13.6	147	9.3	2 240	18.3	2 737	310	1 657	229	1 463
Monroe	128	7 224	0.57	90	10.3	81	9.3	1 370	19.7	2 100	165	1 342	86	989
Montgomery	394	10 438	0.68	143	12.1	143	12.1	1 680	17.8	2 705	430	1 605	174	1 457
Morgan	302	19 083	0.80	253	12.5	275	13.6	3 469	22.6	5 714	761	3 244	497	2 484
New Madrid	332	19 437	1.10	235	12.9	224	12.3	2 366	15.7	3 834	329	2 698	343	1 990
Newton	880	57 205	0.95	718	12.3	604	10.3	9 400	19.5	11 402	2 431	5 568	2 138	3 592
Nodaway	3 623	23 285	0.99	220	9.5	173	7.5	2 457	14.7	3 564	164	2 416	378	1 610
Oregon	121	10 230	0.81	129	11.8	145	13.3	1 863	21.6	2 774	461	1 587	137	1 240
Osage	405	11 625	0.67	148	10.8	120	8.8	1 705	15.3	2 449	281	1 590	104	749
Ozark	123	8 764	0.71	94	9.9	131	13.8	1 644	23.2	2 845	738	1 226	153	1 597
Pemiscot	202	17 833	0.95	281	15.9	260	14.7	2 063	13.8	3 926	678	2 452	890	4 913
Perry	286	19 571	1.06	231	12.0	210	10.9	2 404	15.2	3 743	309	2 417	262	1 374
Pettis	851	43 876	1.09	571	13.5	387	9.2	7 112	20.2	8 178	1 066	4 540	1 924	4 535
Phelps	3 009	46 490	1.08	520	11.6	405	9.0	6 317	17.7	8 375	1 011	4 460	1 279	2 843
Pike	2 305	18 641	1.01	218	11.8	189	10.2	2 268	16.8	3 631	426	2 213	243	1 304
Platte	869	88 217	0.94	1 153	12.2	575	6.1	8 265	10.3	13 641	2 937	6 350	3 791	4 099
Polk	1 512	29 017	0.83	364	11.7	364	11.7	4 364	17.7	6 099	2 590	2 323	904	2 912
Pulaski	9 974	57 453	1.16	834	15.6	264	4.9	5 749	14.4	5 507	583	2 000	1 203	2 248
Putnam	57	4 525	0.80	51	10.6	51	10.6	797	21.3	1 253	89	887	38	771
Ralls	54	8 558	0.66	88	8.6	84	8.2	1 207	14.6	2 291	222	1 339	117	1 132
Randolph	2 455	26 040	1.08	279	11.1	255	10.2	3 044	15.9	4 933	767	2 992	718	2 832
Ray	311	18 040	0.47	238	10.4	265	11.5	2 694	14.2	4 559	602	2 655	605	2 632
Reynolds	101	7 040	1.17	60	9.1	86	13.1	911	18.1	1 657	152	1 037	69	1 034
Ripley	63	12 360	0.67	174	12.5	205	14.7	2 066	18.3	3 518	351	2 259	533	3 796
St. Charles	5 434	310 849	0.71	4 508	11.9	2 460	6.5	30 786	9.7	57 443	20 939	22 963	6 649	1 788
St. Clair	207	8 733	0.74	87	9.2	143	15.1	1 506	21.6	2 680	620	1 307	154	1 642
Ste. Genevieve	277	16 131	0.76	166	9.3	176	9.8	2 062	14.1	3 588	439	2 323	237	1 343
St. Francois	6 882	64 549	0.96	740	11.2	735	11.1	7 848	15.7	14 007	1 794	8 785	2 065	3 120
St. Louis	19 414	1 089 204	1.19	11 548	11.5	9 555	9.5	98 926	12.0	186 848	63 502	76 745	27 466	2 738
Saline	1 328	22 964	0.97	308	13.2	248	10.6	3 079	16.8	4 638	752	2 743	488	2 088
Schuyler	47	3 634	0.58	55	12.6	50	11.4	802	23.2	971	67	652	24	551
Scotland	76	4 487	0.82	78	16.0	50	10.3	809	20.3	947	48	647	48	979
Scott	559	38 549	0.96	514	13.2	440	11.3	4 766	14.6	9 190	829	6 032	1 603	4 090
Shannon	80	7 542	0.73	98	11.8	80	9.6	1 468	21.9	2 012	346	1 149	112	1 350
Shelby	198	5 746	0.81	65	10.6	65	10.6	935	19.1	1 471	118	945	62	1 000
Stoddard	691	28 692	0.90	364	12.2	380	12.7	4 054	16.9	7 313	1 012	4 526	645	2 165
Stone	300	27 368	0.62	257	8.3	366	11.8	5 032	22.1	8 975	3 139	3 674	708	2 249
Sullivan	108	6 785	1.06	89	13.9	73	11.4	1 124	21.5	1 450	100	993	98	1 506
Taney	1 747	57 992	1.25	610	11.2	500	9.2	9 623	22.9	12 391	3 808	5 079	2 211	4 138
Texas	1 899	23 889	0.79	280	10.9	260	10.1	3 790	19.9	5 519	597	3 001	549	2 129
Vernon	750	20 968	1.00	270	12.9	223	10.6	3 034	18.1	4 396	709	2 458	1 139	5 509
Warren	317	25 668	0.53	404	12.1	280	8.4	4 193	15.4	6 188	2 242	2 700	852	2 591
Washington	1 091	22 021	0.64	287	11.4	273	10.9	3 529	17.3	5 011	904	2 996	526	2 094
Wayne	133	12 080	0.73	152	11.3	207	15.4	1 988	19.1	3 587	512	2 183	309	2 308
Webster	882	30 066	0.56	528	14.3	315	8.5	6 364	20.9	7 170	3 459	2 222	797	2 187
Worth	52	1 861	0.74	26	12.5	22	10.6	308	19.6	533	16	344	37	1 796
Wright	195	17 998	0.90	229	12.5	209	11.4	3 121	20.9	4 752	1 633	2 010	427	2 296

1. Per 1,000 estimated resident population. 2. Data for serious crimes have not been adjusted for underreporting; this may affect comparability between geographic areas and over time.
3. Per 100,000 population estimated by the FBI.

Table B. States and Counties — **Crime, Education, Money Income, and Poverty**

STATE County	Serious crimes known to police, 2013 (cont.)[1] Rate[2] Violent	Serious crimes known to police, 2013 (cont.)[1] Rate[2] Property	Education: School enrollment and attainment, 2009–2013 Enrollment[3] Total	Enrollment[3] Percent private	Attainment[4] (percent) High school graduate or less	Attainment[4] (percent) Bachelor's degree or more	Local government expenditures,[5] 2012–2013 Total current spending (mil dol)	Local government expenditures,[5] 2012–2013 Current spending per student (dollars)	Money income, 2009–2013 Per capita income[6] (dollars)	Households Median income (dollars)	Households Mean income (dollars)	Households Percent with income of $200,000 or more	Income and poverty, 2013 Median household income (dollars)	Percent below poverty level All persons	Percent below poverty level Children under 18 years	Percent below poverty level Children 5 to 17 years in families
	46	47	48	49	50	51	52	53	54	55	56	57	58	59	60	61
MISSOURI—Cont'd																
Jasper	355	4 858	29 970	13.5	50.3	20.2	170.8	7 979	21 124	40 399	53 573	1.4	40 530	18.3	25.3	23.7
Jefferson	205	1 861	55 351	16.9	47.3	17.4	322.7	9 134	24 792	54 845	65 670	1.7	55 305	11.5	14.6	12.9
Johnson	123	2 176	17 998	7.7	39.9	25.6	68.0	8 833	21 547	47 223	56 038	1.2	45 011	17.7	18.9	18.2
Knox	0	1 055	859	31.3	60.1	14.8	5.3	10 488	20 946	34 481	49 505	2.3	34 894	21.3	35.5	33.3
Laclede	344	2 919	8 484	10.0	61.0	12.9	47.0	7 979	19 553	39 013	48 925	1.3	36 632	22.1	30.8	28.4
Lafayette	85	1 601	7 813	14.3	53.3	17.0	47.4	8 980	23 637	50 527	59 158	0.7	46 878	12.7	19.3	17.0
Lawrence	340	3 508	9 406	13.2	56.7	15.4	48.0	7 986	19 060	39 334	49 140	0.9	38 724	18.6	29.3	26.6
Lewis	118	1 354	2 566	33.2	58.3	12.5	13.3	8 753	19 317	42 071	49 836	0.2	41 187	17.5	26.2	23.7
Lincoln	173	1 272	14 064	16.7	55.8	14.2	73.8	8 242	22 063	52 835	60 782	1.3	54 144	11.9	17.1	16.1
Linn	386	2 390	2 910	6.4	63.9	12.7	22.0	9 465	21 015	38 250	52 897	2.0	37 773	19.6	27.3	25.6
Livingston	180	2 102	3 101	13.7	60.2	17.5	19.8	9 071	21 011	40 116	53 573	1.3	38 839	17.2	24.1	22.2
McDonald	761	2 669	6 115	8.0	56.3	10.5	30.5	8 058	17 505	37 997	46 550	1.0	35 915	20.7	32.2	29.7
Macon	205	1 782	3 478	13.5	58.2	15.3	21.5	9 346	20 054	38 443	48 208	1.3	38 110	18.8	28.2	25.1
Madison	310	2 404	2 772	8.5	62.0	7.7	18.0	8 561	17 316	35 870	44 110	0.9	33 631	21.4	33.0	31.2
Maries	212	1 270	1 873	8.1	58.9	16.5	10.7	7 810	22 026	42 566	52 066	1.2	40 404	17.5	27.4	24.4
Marion	292	4 396	7 037	21.3	53.5	18.5	43.2	8 408	21 909	42 046	55 261	1.9	40 981	16.8	24.9	23.4
Mercer	161	860	798	13.8	62.3	12.9	6.6	10 743	20 178	40 272	48 531	0.2	38 726	17.6	25.0	23.5
Miller	189	2 277	6 254	13.5	56.8	14.5	44.6	8 873	19 385	35 507	47 134	1.5	36 552	20.5	31.2	28.1
Mississippi	314	2 265	2 848	8.4	70.4	9.8	17.3	7 852	15 558	29 787	40 523	0.4	31 421	36.3	51.6	49.9
Moniteau	153	1 309	3 691	15.6	58.1	18.1	19.6	8 269	19 451	47 118	54 626	0.4	46 123	14.1	21.9	20.2
Monroe	138	851	1 912	11.5	61.2	13.1	13.7	9 050	20 331	40 657	49 071	0.4	38 940	15.7	27.2	25.1
Montgomery	84	1 373	2 779	12.8	61.7	12.1	15.5	8 936	20 991	40 236	50 553	0.8	39 750	15.3	22.6	21.4
Morgan	355	2 129	3 716	19.8	62.5	12.7	16.8	7 992	17 935	34 797	43 510	0.0	32 761	22.0	33.1	30.6
New Madrid	342	1 648	4 150	6.7	65.8	12.3	27.0	9 692	21 215	35 793	52 050	1.2	34 927	23.7	34.8	31.1
Newton	195	3 397	14 947	12.9	48.2	18.1	68.4	7 931	22 341	42 268	58 491	2.4	41 440	16.1	23.5	20.6
Nodaway	238	1 371	9 178	7.5	51.8	23.4	29.4	10 709	18 079	36 641	46 712	0.9	41 952	18.5	16.7	15.7
Oregon	181	1 059	2 276	5.0	63.9	9.8	15.9	9 012	16 331	27 743	38 256	0.6	29 464	26.4	39.7	37.1
Osage	43	706	3 477	20.1	60.0	15.4	13.7	8 336	22 629	51 408	59 116	0.3	48 990	10.1	12.3	11.1
Ozark	407	1 190	1 691	8.3	61.1	12.5	14.9	9 764	17 215	32 078	40 159	0.2	30 799	26.2	41.7	36.9
Pemiscot	878	4 035	4 789	2.9	65.7	10.0	39.4	10 834	16 881	28 889	41 682	0.9	28 664	31.4	45.4	41.4
Perry	168	1 206	4 625	26.7	62.3	14.6	21.3	8 668	23 435	47 876	58 971	2.1	53 798	12.7	17.5	16.4
Pettis	330	4 205	10 671	11.9	50.7	15.2	52.9	7 855	19 709	38 580	50 007	1.2	39 527	20.1	27.6	25.2
Phelps	318	2 525	15 260	10.5	46.9	27.2	57.3	8 850	21 173	41 964	55 260	2.0	38 930	16.4	23.0	21.2
Pike	107	1 197	3 741	15.3	65.3	10.3	22.4	8 485	18 650	39 850	51 661	0.7	39 499	19.8	27.3	26.3
Platte	696	3 403	24 530	21.3	28.9	39.2	165.1	10 596	35 143	67 721	85 629	5.5	68 411	7.7	10.0	9.0
Polk	364	2 548	8 734	24.1	54.8	18.3	46.9	8 858	19 511	39 512	51 113	1.1	38 023	20.0	28.6	26.6
Pulaski	269	1 979	15 724	13.3	41.6	21.4	81.9	9 000	20 863	49 820	57 727	0.6	49 499	15.1	17.4	17.1
Putnam	0	771	977	10.2	59.4	13.7	6.7	9 237	19 397	36 713	42 918	0.3	34 106	17.9	31.2	27.9
Ralls	97	1 036	2 156	18.9	57.9	13.3	5.7	7 765	23 299	47 969	57 422	1.4	49 393	11.4	17.4	15.5
Randolph	162	2 670	6 011	15.3	54.7	13.6	35.4	9 175	17 587	37 203	47 103	0.6	38 988	22.4	28.9	25.3
Ray	274	2 358	5 775	10.1	56.9	13.9	27.9	8 105	24 549	52 698	63 744	1.2	52 430	13.2	20.8	19.8
Reynolds	255	779	1 326	1.7	68.6	6.7	13.5	12 134	18 449	34 496	44 850	0.2	32 089	23.3	37.0	33.7
Ripley	278	3 518	3 149	8.9	64.4	10.7	18.3	7 915	16 408	32 291	40 121	0.5	30 843	23.6	39.0	37.3
St. Charles	125	1 664	101 533	27.1	32.7	35.1	568.5	9 565	31 586	71 077	83 957	4.5	70 468	6.4	8.3	7.9
St. Clair	277	1 365	1 717	10.8	66.1	12.1	12.2	8 902	17 337	31 539	40 465	0.5	30 612	26.4	38.5	34.8
Ste. Genevieve	249	1 093	4 226	22.2	57.8	10.7	20.9	11 080	22 921	48 433	56 742	0.7	48 266	12.3	17.7	15.9
St. Francois	227	2 894	14 964	12.2	54.1	14.3	88.5	8 253	18 544	37 238	48 466	1.0	37 696	20.7	28.0	26.1
St. Louis	281	2 457	269 762	29.0	30.2	40.6	1 862.2	13 436	34 795	58 910	84 730	6.8	59 284	10.9	16.2	14.9
Saline	133	1 955	6 308	26.3	57.2	17.2	31.5	8 764	19 006	39 519	48 052	0.7	38 230	18.4	28.5	28.9
Schuyler	69	482	956	10.9	62.0	9.8	5.3	8 295	18 160	34 688	44 344	0.8	36 029	21.2	34.1	30.4
Scotland	0	979	947	29.6	61.1	17.0	6.0	9 871	20 363	39 028	49 993	2.6	36 511	17.6	27.4	25.9
Scott	918	3 171	9 354	11.7	61.7	14.6	53.4	7 854	20 825	40 651	52 651	1.5	40 441	18.4	29.0	27.5
Shannon	241	1 109	1 973	6.5	61.9	11.2	17.7	9 034	16 862	31 132	42 470	0.5	26 538	31.5	50.1	45.9
Shelby	48	951	1 402	14.4	56.6	12.7	9.9	9 037	19 331	35 938	45 329	0.3	40 420	17.2	26.0	25.0
Stoddard	171	1 994	6 468	8.8	63.4	13.3	41.2	8 062	22 967	37 965	54 479	1.4	37 689	16.3	24.2	21.6
Stone	461	1 788	5 934	12.4	56.2	15.2	38.4	9 306	21 733	40 850	50 820	1.2	39 018	16.1	30.0	26.7
Sullivan	292	1 214	1 458	5.2	63.9	12.0	10.7	9 919	19 279	36 676	45 307	1.1	37 039	16.5	22.6	20.5
Taney	500	3 639	12 449	23.8	51.1	18.6	69.9	8 679	20 231	38 461	49 893	1.2	34 860	19.7	29.0	27.0
Texas	128	2 001	5 638	11.0	62.5	12.0	32.7	8 327	17 868	36 082	46 458	1.0	34 266	25.4	37.6	35.2
Vernon	416	5 093	5 151	15.5	59.1	13.2	28.5	8 834	19 734	38 679	48 913	0.9	35 090	21.5	31.0	27.7
Warren	432	2 159	7 507	19.7	51.7	16.0	39.7	8 539	24 692	50 830	64 428	2.4	52 517	11.7	18.9	16.7
Washington	191	1 903	5 704	9.8	67.9	8.4	31.5	8 470	17 703	34 702	45 903	0.8	33 491	26.2	39.2	36.4
Wayne	202	2 106	2 502	7.1	64.7	10.3	15.2	8 394	18 070	33 160	44 429	0.6	31 208	26.3	41.6	39.4
Webster	181	2 006	8 955	16.6	56.1	15.0	54.6	7 793	19 955	44 596	55 165	1.5	44 069	19.5	32.0	29.3
Worth	0	1 796	456	7.2	58.2	15.6	3.0	9 075	22 967	39 348	51 359	1.6	37 832	15.0	23.3	22.5
Wright	172	2 124	4 573	13.6	63.0	11.1	28.3	7 968	14 752	28 645	36 906	0.2	29 605	29.1	41.2	38.5

1. Data for serious crimes have not been adjusted for underreporting; this may affect comparability between geographic areas and over time. 2. Per 100,000 population estimated by the FBI.
3. All persons 3 years old and over enrolled in nursery school through college. 4. Persons 25 years old and over. 5. Elementary and secondary education expenditures.
6. Based on population estimated by the American Community Survey, 2009–2013.

STATE County	Personal income, 2013: Total (mil dol)	Personal income, 2013: Percent change, 2012–2013	Personal income, 2013: Per capita[1]: Dollars	Personal income, 2013: Per capita[1]: Rank	Personal income, 2013: Wages and salaries (mil dol)	Personal income, 2013: Supplements to wages and salaries; employer contributions (mil dol): Pension and insurance	Personal income, 2013: Supplements to wages and salaries; employer contributions (mil dol): Government social insurance	Personal income, 2013: Proprietors' income (mil dol)	Personal income, 2013: Dividends, interest, and rent (mil dol)	Personal income, 2013: Personal transfer receipts (mil dol)	Earnings, 2013: Total (mil dol)	Earnings, 2013: Contributions for government social insurance (mil dol): From employee and self-employed	Earnings, 2013: Contributions for government social insurance (mil dol): From employer
	62	63	64	65	66	67	68	69	70	71	72	73	74
MISSOURI—Cont'd													
Jasper	3 866	1.4	33 213	2 227	2 254	436	167	303	763	919	3 161	187	167
Jefferson	8 041	1.8	36 320	1 692	1 776	350	137	475	960	1 578	2 738	183	137
Johnson	1 767	4.7	32 377	2 355	768	227	64	173	363	350	1 231	58	64
Knox	160	12.0	39 240	1 262	32	8	2	47	31	35	89	4	2
Laclede	1 073	1.4	30 086	2 676	411	93	34	86	202	317	624	41	34
Lafayette	1 327	4.2	40 290	1 141	281	66	21	153	202	300	521	30	21
Lawrence	1 136	3.5	29 753	2 720	301	70	22	60	187	324	453	31	22
Lewis	345	10.7	33 996	2 081	80	19	6	66	55	79	170	8	6
Lincoln	1 735	4.0	32 206	2 386	392	86	29	121	219	388	628	40	29
Linn	435	3.4	35 167	1 876	154	31	13	53	83	121	252	16	13
Livingston	544	6.0	36 550	1 654	218	47	16	75	105	135	356	20	16
McDonald	602	1.2	26 675	2 995	222	48	16	38	75	157	323	20	16
Macon	552	5.5	35 534	1 820	158	42	11	78	99	148	289	16	11
Madison	379	2.8	30 486	2 631	111	27	8	21	63	137	168	12	8
Maries	325	5.0	36 054	1 738	42	11	3	52	50	83	108	7	3
Marion	1 086	4.9	37 568	1 495	488	93	38	114	186	283	734	43	38
Mercer	116	1.7	31 401	2 495	34	6	2	20	20	31	63	3	2
Miller	724	3.6	28 868	2 819	216	48	18	61	118	205	341	22	18
Mississippi	473	9.3	33 151	2 234	127	30	9	98	70	138	264	13	9
Moniteau	536	4.4	34 017	2 077	123	31	9	59	87	100	221	12	9
Monroe	326	16.0	37 118	1 563	64	17	5	84	53	78	170	8	5
Montgomery	431	7.4	36 002	1 745	96	22	7	61	74	109	186	11	7
Morgan	773	3.9	38 137	1 418	120	28	9	66	278	212	224	16	9
New Madrid	618	5.0	33 651	2 153	292	55	22	88	75	190	457	25	22
Newton	2 226	1.4	37 824	1 458	788	150	58	123	365	491	1 119	69	58
Nodaway	713	5.8	30 674	2 604	283	72	20	118	133	143	493	25	20
Oregon	293	1.9	26 616	3 001	76	18	7	25	45	119	127	10	7
Osage	524	3.9	38 299	1 399	121	28	9	47	83	90	204	12	9
Ozark	269	1.9	28 147	2 881	43	12	3	17	47	112	75	7	3
Pemiscot	639	2.8	35 853	1 771	193	48	14	86	80	216	342	19	14
Perry	675	5.7	35 377	1 841	347	70	26	53	101	154	496	29	26
Pettis	1 440	3.5	34 117	2 059	657	136	51	129	252	362	973	57	51
Phelps	1 524	1.4	34 018	2 076	659	164	46	73	283	375	942	54	46
Pike	604	8.2	32 351	2 360	194	48	14	76	115	148	332	18	14
Platte	4 434	2.1	47 516	508	1 869	295	140	249	693	522	2 553	149	140
Polk	914	2.6	29 523	2 750	275	68	20	54	162	269	417	27	20
Pulaski	2 147	1.4	39 952	1 176	1 214	372	116	47	456	313	1 749	74	116
Putnam	158	7.1	32 458	2 344	37	10	2	21	33	49	70	4	2
Ralls	405	11.4	39 696	1 206	150	28	11	60	60	80	249	13	11
Randolph	900	3.5	36 087	1 734	359	83	27	135	125	244	604	35	27
Ray	895	1.8	38 847	1 312	149	38	11	113	106	188	311	19	11
Reynolds	189	-0.1	28 583	2 841	65	14	5	8	30	78	92	7	5
Ripley	389	1.5	27 710	2 914	79	20	6	31	49	172	136	11	6
St. Charles	16 378	2.2	43 850	770	5 870	958	438	764	2 240	2 179	8 030	489	438
St. Clair	294	5.9	31 007	2 547	49	13	4	35	57	103	101	7	4
Ste. Genevieve	659	-1.0	37 046	1 573	241	43	18	23	144	144	325	21	18
St. Francois	1 950	1.4	29 448	2 758	750	175	56	80	279	639	1 062	69	56
St. Louis	57 266	1.0	57 183	153	33 941	4 887	2 390	4 736	14 431	7 554	45 953	2 695	2 390
Saline	942	7.8	40 522	1 111	306	69	22	183	155	243	581	29	22
Schuyler	119	5.6	27 250	2 957	19	6	1	15	22	38	41	3	1
Scotland	174	9.5	35 347	1 847	37	12	2	43	36	38	95	4	2
Scott	1 551	2.0	39 483	1 233	545	109	42	218	244	412	915	55	42
Shannon	211	3.6	25 378	3 040	37	10	3	26	34	82	75	6	3
Shelby	237	10.8	38 449	1 381	54	14	4	56	44	53	128	6	4
Stoddard	1 054	3.8	35 393	1 836	352	71	29	159	160	303	611	36	29
Stone	1 163	3.3	37 160	1 554	191	38	15	160	208	317	404	31	15
Sullivan	231	3.2	35 893	1 763	97	20	6	45	31	58	168	8	6
Taney	1 542	2.7	28 776	2 823	856	143	71	67	263	461	1 138	75	71
Texas	689	1.6	26 857	2 979	188	53	14	31	144	220	286	20	14
Vernon	698	1.6	33 310	2 203	260	66	19	73	116	200	418	23	19
Warren	1 160	2.0	35 141	1 879	246	52	19	47	178	252	364	26	19
Washington	689	1.7	27 369	2 950	153	43	11	23	69	257	230	17	11
Wayne	377	1.9	28 115	2 885	71	19	5	21	59	155	116	10	5
Webster	1 071	1.8	29 378	2 766	216	51	16	53	147	266	336	25	16
Worth	75	15.7	36 072	1 736	13	4	1	16	14	18	34	2	1
Wright	484	2.5	26 226	3 020	131	32	10	6	96	188	180	15	10

1. Based on the resident population estimated as of July 1 of the year shown.

Table B. States and Counties — **Earnings, Social Security, and Housing**

STATE County	Earnings, 2013 (cont.) — Percent by selected industries: Farm	Mining	Construction	Manu-facturing	Infor-mation: professional, scientific, technical services	Retail trade	Finance, insur-ance, real estate and leasing	Health care and social assistance	Govern-ment	Social Security beneficiaries, December 2013: Number	Rate[1]	Supple-mental Security Income recipients, December 2013	Housing units, 2014: Total	Percent change, 2010–2014
	75	76	77	78	79	80	81	82	83	84	85	86	87	88
MISSOURI—Cont'd														
Jasper	0.7	0.2	5.0	19.1	3.9	8.8	4.3	10.4	12.1	23 955	206	3 347	51 307	1.3
Jefferson	0.0	0.3	11.8	10.6	4.1	8.1	5.4	11.7	18.8	43 170	195	3 225	88 817	1.4
Johnson	3.9	D	6.5	4.2	2.1	5.5	3.4	5.0	55.6	8 140	149	684	21 776	1.2
Knox	35.8	D	3.2	7.6	4.9	3.8	3.8	2.4	14.2	1 055	259	101	2 271	-0.8
Laclede	0.9	D	4.4	34.7	2.6	11.1	4.1	10.2	13.0	9 165	257	1 184	15 760	-0.1
Lafayette	17.1	0.0	7.9	7.8	6.0	7.3	4.2	D	21.0	7 640	232	543	14 688	-0.2
Lawrence	5.4	D	6.9	17.2	3.8	8.1	3.3	D	26.3	9 400	247	955	16 542	-0.6
Lewis	31.9	D	3.4	3.3	D	6.3	D	D	16.4	2 310	228	196	4 497	-0.8
Lincoln	5.1	1.1	12.0	13.5	D	9.3	4.3	5.2	23.0	10 280	191	897	21 080	0.3
Linn	9.8	0.0	3.4	16.0	6.0	6.7	6.4	9.5	15.4	3 280	266	375	6 383	-0.7
Livingston	10.0	D	6.4	8.4	2.8	9.3	4.8	D	19.7	3 515	236	333	6 738	0.1
McDonald	2.7	D	6.0	36.7	D	8.9	2.3	3.4	16.0	4 480	198	609	9 825	-1.0
Macon	11.5	0.0	6.0	12.9	5.8	6.7	3.6	D	29.0	4 195	270	307	7 615	-0.7
Madison	2.9	D	8.4	10.5	D	10.4	D	9.2	25.5	3 595	290	566	5 930	-0.7
Maries	-0.9	0.0	D	17.1	D	9.7	D	7.4	13.6	2 345	259	197	4 565	-1.0
Marion	6.0	D	7.6	10.0	D	8.9	3.8	D	13.9	6 760	234	980	12 884	0.5
Mercer	44.0	D	3.7	0.0	D	3.6	2.8	4.8	18.4	940	255	87	2 116	-0.9
Miller	5.6	D	9.7	9.9	D	12.1	5.1	D	21.9	5 840	233	651	12 731	-0.2
Mississippi	25.3	0.0	2.1	4.5	0.8	6.7	3.3	D	19.2	3 450	242	737	5 702	-0.2
Moniteau	13.8	D	13.2	13.4	2.2	7.6	3.6	D	23.3	3 060	194	225	6 130	-0.7
Monroe	37.6	D	3.3	10.7	2.1	3.3	D	3.4	18.5	2 290	262	194	4 819	0.4
Montgomery	18.9	0.5	7.7	14.9	1.5	8.0	5.2	5.9	18.8	3 045	255	313	6 159	0.5
Morgan	15.6	D	9.5	9.4	2.3	13.3	4.5	3.8	20.0	6 495	321	600	15 382	-0.9
New Madrid	14.2	0.0	1.9	23.2	D	9.4	1.6	D	11.0	4 450	242	986	8 537	0.1
Newton	4.4	D	5.4	12.6	4.1	7.2	2.8	29.5	12.6	12 925	220	1 267	24 333	0.1
Nodaway	13.8	D	3.4	18.1	4.0	6.8	3.1	10.3	24.8	3 915	169	259	9 646	1.3
Oregon	3.1	D	2.4	8.3	D	10.6	3.1	D	19.3	3 075	280	610	5 428	-1.1
Osage	8.3	0.4	10.6	25.3	1.2	7.6	3.7	5.8	17.6	2 770	202	164	6 542	-0.8
Ozark	7.9	D	5.9	5.7	D	9.2	6.7	6.1	28.0	3 310	347	351	5 616	-0.6
Pemiscot	17.9	D	1.9	13.2	0.9	7.7	3.3	8.3	24.1	4 555	256	1 514	8 110	-0.6
Perry	4.2	D	9.1	31.1	D	6.4	4.5	D	12.6	4 280	224	390	8 598	0.4
Pettis	4.2	D	4.9	23.6	6.2	7.7	2.9	8.3	18.0	8 940	212	1 164	18 188	-0.3
Phelps	-0.2	D	3.9	6.3	3.6	8.5	3.6	13.5	39.8	9 255	206	1 152	19 766	1.2
Pike	14.7	D	7.2	5.7	4.2	11.2	2.9	6.1	26.2	4 090	220	455	7 828	-0.6
Platte	1.3	D	6.0	9.1	7.2	7.9	6.6	7.0	11.2	14 520	156	655	40 155	2.4
Polk	2.5	0.2	4.3	2.5	D	8.8	4.0	D	32.3	6 870	221	813	13 338	0.3
Pulaski	-0.1	D	2.1	D	1.8	3.0	1.6	2.3	81.1	6 440	120	803	18 760	4.8
Putnam	23.8	0.0	D	D	D	7.6	6.8	2.5	29.8	1 370	281	138	2 964	-0.6
Ralls	20.6	0.0	D	46.7	D	3.1	1.0	D	7.8	2 445	240	181	5 136	-0.9
Randolph	3.3	D	3.1	8.5	1.7	16.5	5.7	12.0	17.9	5 305	213	797	10 659	-0.5
Ray	5.3	D	8.7	8.2	4.1	11.9	5.1	D	21.6	5 040	219	329	9 965	-0.2
Reynolds	0.9	D	1.4	9.3	D	4.2	D	10.0	20.2	1 995	302	301	4 000	-0.8
Ripley	3.8	0.0	4.5	12.6	D	10.4	3.6	17.1	25.3	4 105	293	858	6 532	-1.0
St. Charles	0.4	D	8.2	12.2	11.7	8.1	10.0	10.0	12.5	61 950	166	2 644	147 221	4.4
St. Clair	14.5	D	4.8	2.3	D	9.1	3.3	8.6	27.5	2 965	312	315	5 573	-1.2
Ste. Genevieve	3.0	6.4	8.0	8.7	D	5.7	3.0	D	17.5	4 130	230	342	8 638	0.0
St. Francois	-0.1	0.5	6.4	8.1	3.1	8.8	6.5	16.9	27.7	15 945	241	2 625	29 354	3.1
St. Louis	0.0	0.4	5.6	10.2	13.2	5.8	10.3	12.5	8.5	196 690	196	17 340	438 081	0.0
Saline	17.9	0.0	2.1	19.6	D	5.3	2.6	D	16.3	5 020	216	615	10 079	-0.4
Schuyler	15.4	0.0	12.3	D	D	9.2	2.1	3.5	33.3	1 065	244	125	2 089	-0.6
Scotland	28.9	D	3.3	3.1	D	6.5	2.9	D	33.1	1 035	211	66	2 346	-1.0
Scott	5.1	D	4.9	14.4	12.6	5.0	3.9	15.5	13.5	10 315	263	1 852	17 023	0.2
Shannon	3.6	D	D	25.6	D	8.6	3.7	D	19.4	2 315	279	376	4 124	-1.0
Shelby	31.3	D	3.0	9.5	1.9	8.7	D	D	19.5	1 570	255	128	3 179	-0.8
Stoddard	15.0	0.3	5.9	22.8	2.9	7.8	4.5	D	12.3	8 230	276	1 187	13 600	-0.1
Stone	0.3	D	11.4	D	3.6	11.1	11.9	D	14.3	10 115	323	559	20 542	0.8
Sullivan	24.7	D	2.4	D	D	4.7	4.0	3.0	14.3	1 610	250	202	3 330	-0.8
Taney	0.2	0.2	4.0	2.0	4.3	11.1	5.6	D	11.8	13 795	258	1 063	30 119	3.0
Texas	1.1	0.2	4.8	15.4	3.0	8.3	3.8	5.8	34.7	6 280	245	817	11 579	-0.9
Vernon	9.7	0.7	3.4	20.9	D	6.6	5.7	D	22.0	5 000	238	699	9 467	-0.3
Warren	3.5	D	9.8	25.2	2.5	7.4	4.1	5.6	18.6	7 170	217	507	14 920	1.6
Washington	1.6	D	3.6	10.9	D	6.3	D	D	38.5	6 060	241	1 246	10 858	-1.4
Wayne	3.3	D	3.3	11.8	D	9.4	3.8	12.6	25.5	4 150	309	735	7 976	-1.3
Webster	0.8	0.3	9.0	13.2	D	11.4	4.5	D	22.6	8 215	225	826	14 480	0.4
Worth	39.1	D	D	D	D	4.8	D	2.9	22.5	680	278	45	1 271	-0.8
Wright	1.0	D	4.3	9.5	D	14.6	4.0	D	24.4	5 535	300	890	8 616	-1.0

1. Per 1,000 resident population estimated as of July 1 of the year shown.

STATE County	Housing units, 2009–2013: Occupied units: Total	Occupied units: Owner-occupied: Percent	Owner-occupied: Median value[1]	Owner-occupied: Median owner cost as a percent of income: With a mortgage	Owner-occupied: Median owner cost as a percent of income: Without a mortgage[2]	Renter-occupied: Median rent[3]	Renter-occupied: Median rent as a percent of income[2]	Sub-standard units[4] (percent)	Civilian labor force, 2014: Total	Civilian labor force, 2014: Percent change, 2013–2014	Unemployment: Total	Unemployment: Rate[5]	Civilian employment,[6] 2009–2013: Total	Percent: Management, business, science and arts	Percent: Construction, production, and maintenance occupations
	89	90	91	92	93	94	95	96	97	98	99	100	101	102	103
MISSOURI—Cont'd															
Jasper	44 849	64.5	98 300	21.2	12.4	666	29.8	1.8	57 895	0.0	3 051	5.3	52 998	28.2	27.2
Jefferson	80 812	82.6	152 100	22.5	12.0	744	28.9	2.3	116 120	1.3	7 261	6.3	105 383	28.5	27.9
Johnson	20 092	61.4	139 200	22.3	11.1	711	32.3	3.5	23 182	0.6	1 465	6.3	23 006	29.5	25.6
Knox	1 724	74.8	64 900	21.7	12.8	447	27.0	2.7	2 008	0.6	91	4.5	1 796	29.8	31.1
Laclede	13 912	70.0	96 800	23.1	11.7	601	27.1	2.4	15 919	2.3	1 279	8.0	14 680	22.3	37.0
Lafayette	13 117	74.5	117 300	19.9	11.3	625	28.3	2.4	17 256	2.1	1 017	5.9	15 483	28.4	33.0
Lawrence	14 817	72.9	93 700	23.1	12.1	606	26.0	3.7	17 545	0.8	1 028	5.9	15 986	26.3	32.6
Lewis	3 936	74.2	82 300	19.3	10.7	490	22.2	1.7	5 173	2.0	268	5.2	4 725	24.0	34.2
Lincoln	18 714	78.1	149 400	23.3	11.4	733	29.4	1.6	26 482	0.9	1 722	6.5	23 584	26.0	31.8
Linn	4 854	76.7	68 600	19.7	12.7	540	29.7	1.7	5 243	-1.0	418	8.0	5 037	28.3	31.9
Livingston	5 660	70.8	98 500	19.2	12.2	599	27.7	7.6	7 338	1.2	365	5.0	6 495	29.1	29.1
McDonald	8 221	69.5	86 300	22.3	11.6	597	26.4	2.8	10 379	4.2	593	5.7	9 271	20.9	39.8
Macon	6 389	76.8	83 600	20.2	12.3	520	27.3	1.5	7 519	1.5	458	6.1	6 707	28.9	28.2
Madison	4 603	76.1	86 100	25.1	12.1	602	31.3	2.8	5 533	-0.1	370	6.7	4 687	22.9	36.6
Maries	3 749	77.3	116 300	22.5	10.2	591	24.5	1.5	4 013	-4.4	245	6.1	3 790	28.1	34.4
Marion	11 203	68.1	102 200	19.8	11.0	589	27.6	4.6	14 685	0.5	808	5.5	12 881	30.4	28.2
Mercer	1 575	77.7	67 600	18.3	10.7	532	24.1	3.0	1 870	3.7	94	5.0	1 539	33.2	29.6
Miller	10 034	77.1	112 000	23.7	11.0	588	29.7	6.3	11 690	1.9	893	7.6	10 403	24.0	28.0
Mississippi	5 227	63.9	60 600	23.2	11.7	557	29.3	2.6	6 293	-0.1	461	7.3	5 453	23.3	30.2
Moniteau	5 464	74.6	112 100	19.8	10.0	549	25.6	1.7	7 379	1.0	439	5.9	6 546	29.4	32.3
Monroe	3 497	75.9	89 500	22.7	11.7	516	23.6	1.6	4 197	2.2	275	6.6	3 726	25.8	34.0
Montgomery	5 091	75.3	101 500	22.2	10.9	600	33.0	5.7	5 729	0.3	343	6.0	5 325	25.8	34.4
Morgan	8 164	80.1	110 500	26.3	12.4	593	32.1	1.0	8 033	2.7	682	8.5	6 699	26.9	33.8
New Madrid	7 423	62.2	75 400	19.7	11.9	497	28.0	2.7	8 474	2.5	621	7.3	7 770	27.1	31.7
Newton	22 045	74.9	107 700	21.6	11.4	614	27.3	1.6	28 893	0.0	1 538	5.3	25 995	29.4	28.1
Nodaway	8 599	55.9	101 800	20.6	10.7	583	33.3	3.0	11 732	-1.3	759	6.5	11 764	25.9	29.3
Oregon	4 572	76.1	72 400	23.9	12.9	496	30.0	0.9	4 178	1.4	309	7.4	3 865	20.9	36.6
Osage	5 168	82.2	123 100	19.2	10.0	497	22.6	5.2	7 262	0.9	336	4.6	6 707	27.9	33.0
Ozark	4 063	79.1	89 900	23.1	10.5	514	29.9	3.5	3 663	0.3	318	8.7	3 101	24.3	39.7
Pemiscot	6 941	54.9	64 300	21.5	11.7	513	32.3	1.4	7 124	0.8	644	9.0	6 503	24.4	31.1
Perry	7 511	77.8	123 100	19.5	11.5	680	27.7	3.8	10 315	1.9	557	5.4	9 176	23.8	39.3
Pettis	16 212	69.6	98 200	21.8	11.8	675	32.9	1.8	20 723	3.4	1 264	6.1	18 815	26.3	33.4
Phelps	16 699	61.3	111 700	20.7	10.0	638	31.0	2.3	20 239	1.2	1 255	6.2	19 144	35.6	21.7
Pike	6 559	74.1	90 100	20.2	12.0	552	28.9	1.8	8 197	1.5	465	5.7	7 310	24.2	32.1
Platte	36 781	64.3	184 900	21.1	11.0	862	26.9	2.5	53 699	2.0	2 746	5.1	47 815	41.3	17.7
Polk	11 937	68.2	109 800	21.3	10.5	626	31.5	3.2	14 226	2.4	888	6.2	12 594	29.6	26.3
Pulaski	15 747	53.3	121 600	21.1	10.0	934	24.7	2.2	15 336	-1.6	1 114	7.3	15 701	33.9	22.5
Putnam	2 230	74.6	100 300	23.2	17.1	523	28.5	2.0	2 530	3.0	125	4.9	2 119	32.9	36.5
Ralls	4 044	81.5	108 400	19.0	11.7	615	27.2	2.7	5 632	0.6	297	5.3	4 924	28.2	34.6
Randolph	8 925	71.4	84 600	21.3	11.9	632	28.6	1.4	10 580	0.8	719	6.8	9 918	23.8	29.8
Ray	8 735	78.1	117 600	22.1	12.3	733	28.5	4.4	11 286	1.5	763	6.8	10 190	25.8	35.0
Reynolds	2 664	77.6	86 100	22.1	11.4	500	31.1	3.3	2 703	7.5	222	8.2	2 325	24.0	40.4
Ripley	5 544	71.9	76 200	22.2	12.1	528	32.9	1.1	5 593	1.3	446	8.0	5 501	23.3	32.0
St. Charles	135 974	80.3	189 100	21.7	11.9	877	27.4	4.7	209 612	1.5	10 149	4.8	189 799	41.1	16.7
St. Clair	4 139	77.6	81 600	24.5	13.5	440	29.6	2.9	4 023	2.9	308	7.7	3 615	28.6	28.7
Ste. Genevieve	7 235	82.2	121 600	23.5	11.9	602	29.0	3.1	9 096	1.0	596	6.6	8 192	21.7	40.3
St. Francois	24 654	68.7	98 900	21.8	11.1	589	30.9	1.4	26 452	0.8	1 997	7.5	24 659	27.7	27.9
St. Louis	403 293	71.0	174 500	22.0	12.3	861	29.8	2.1	531 068	1.5	31 029	5.8	486 741	43.1	14.3
Saline	8 764	67.8	85 700	21.5	12.5	567	26.3	4.9	11 308	2.1	629	5.6	10 460	27.5	32.6
Schuyler	1 773	71.0	73 600	23.3	13.9	483	24.9	4.3	1 958	0.1	137	7.0	1 848	26.0	37.6
Scotland	1 915	78.9	70 900	24.5	12.4	411	20.6	3.8	2 423	2.2	116	4.8	2 173	31.2	34.1
Scott	15 169	69.2	96 600	18.6	10.2	586	27.5	3.1	19 971	1.0	1 311	6.6	17 818	26.0	30.9
Shannon	3 220	78.1	80 300	23.5	10.7	456	32.0	2.2	3 436	2.2	322	9.4	3 275	28.5	42.2
Shelby	2 597	71.0	71 500	22.6	12.9	450	23.3	1.7	3 076	0.7	186	6.0	2 875	27.4	33.4
Stoddard	12 224	71.7	83 800	19.4	11.0	521	28.0	1.9	13 158	0.0	999	7.6	12 135	26.6	34.2
Stone	13 320	78.6	145 000	22.9	11.7	709	29.3	3.8	13 528	-0.3	1 280	9.5	12 325	27.9	23.1
Sullivan	2 640	69.2	74 200	23.8	12.5	533	24.7	1.6	2 765	2.6	181	6.5	2 797	23.9	42.1
Taney	20 698	63.2	129 100	24.9	11.2	678	30.2	3.2	25 687	-0.2	2 463	9.6	22 601	23.4	15.9
Texas	9 370	75.3	98 000	20.9	11.7	533	29.5	2.4	9 459	-2.2	738	7.8	9 427	22.8	32.0
Vernon	7 999	69.7	83 700	22.6	11.0	608	28.8	3.0	9 856	1.0	556	5.6	9 121	28.2	27.6
Warren	12 572	79.4	151 300	22.0	12.0	726	29.4	4.2	17 053	1.3	1 058	6.2	15 323	25.8	32.4
Washington	9 199	76.3	73 000	21.2	11.1	517	26.7	2.8	10 521	0.7	896	8.5	8 902	19.4	37.1
Wayne	5 589	75.1	75 100	21.4	10.0	519	35.1	5.4	5 675	1.1	415	7.3	5 139	24.1	35.6
Webster	12 668	75.9	116 800	21.1	10.0	608	27.7	0.4	16 295	2.6	973	6.0	14 347	24.8	33.5
Worth	940	76.3	57 900	14.8	12.6	311	16.4	3.6	1 332	0.2	52	3.9	1 047	39.2	27.5
Wright	7 295	72.2	86 700	24.1	11.4	522	28.5	2.6	7 669	1.4	547	7.1	6 584	25.2	33.4

1. Specified owner-occupied units. 2. A value of 10.0 represents 10 percent or less; a value of 50.0 represents 50 percent or more. 3. Specified renter-occupied units.
4. Overcrowded or lacking complete plumbing facilities. 5. Percent of civilian labor force. 6. Persons 16 years old and over.

STATE County	Private nonfarm establishments, employment and payroll, 2013									Agriculture, 2012			
		Employment						Annual payroll		Farms			
											Percent with:		
	Number of establish-ments	Total	Health care and social assistance	Manufac-turing	Retail trade	Finance and insurance	Professional, scientific, and technical services	Total (mil dol)	Average per employee (dollars)	Number	Fewer than 50 acres	500 acres or more	Farm operators whose principal occu-pation is farming (percent)
	104	105	106	107	108	109	110	111	112	113	114	115	116
MISSOURI—Cont'd													
Jasper	2 863	49 729	8 315	8 919	7 688	1 165	1 071	1 776	35 708	1 299	34.9	7.4	39.9
Jefferson	3 961	39 960	6 690	4 209	7 060	1 290	974	1 314	32 874	705	41.3	5.4	49.1
Johnson	917	9 493	2 330	1 133	1 771	331	340	264	27 784	1 657	28.5	10.6	40.4
Knox	94	683	37	D	117	55	D	18	25 714	695	15.4	21.7	51.9
Laclede	797	10 793	1 435	3 990	1 869	322	170	313	28 982	1 398	29.2	12.1	41.3
Lafayette	689	6 016	1 077	771	1 053	261	D	166	27 656	1 174	32.1	14.6	49.2
Lawrence	702	6 852	1 296	1 414	1 287	192	145	208	30 424	1 849	40.1	7.4	41.4
Lewis	187	1 874	261	D	307	104	D	46	24 308	729	19.9	21.3	44.3
Lincoln	896	7 764	1 174	1 055	1 431	331	193	262	33 758	1 162	33.0	13.6	46.3
Linn	290	3 143	513	872	536	147	85	103	32 726	1 039	18.2	17.5	41.0
Livingston	402	4 735	888	529	1 176	203	121	143	30 255	847	20.2	16.1	42.3
McDonald	306	5 574	260	D	936	118	36	159	28 439	926	27.3	6.8	53.6
Macon	340	3 267	527	D	654	161	D	90	27 603	1 291	20.4	14.5	36.9
Madison	284	2 937	D	265	547	84	D	74	25 357	373	19.6	14.2	44.2
Maries	134	1 075	156	195	246	D	D	30	27 611	836	16.6	14.5	46.7
Marion	838	11 663	2 912	1 641	1 799	404	265	379	32 459	704	21.2	14.8	44.0
Mercer	72	407	73	D	69	D	D	11	26 725	567	11.8	21.2	40.9
Miller	656	5 944	450	491	1 753	234	230	164	27 538	1 013	17.1	10.4	42.7
Mississippi	259	2 411	424	197	478	129	D	63	26 336	205	16.6	47.3	70.7
Moniteau	328	2 679	303	D	447	116	72	78	29 026	1 089	20.4	9.5	45.5
Monroe	197	1 383	D	D	254	79	D	37	26 410	1 061	18.2	14.8	39.7
Montgomery	258	2 110	379	D	295	110	D	61	29 121	795	18.9	21.1	49.4
Morgan	477	2 969	272	528	795	121	83	65	21 776	922	24.8	8.6	47.5
New Madrid	431	5 913	817	D	1 259	167	66	216	36 559	317	11.7	56.8	74.8
Newton	1 297	20 107	6 682	2 686	2 125	592	418	677	33 677	1 578	36.8	5.1	39.4
Nodaway	485	6 672	1 031	1 181	1 069	193	121	177	26 474	1 252	23.2	18.7	46.2
Oregon	210	1 721	468	D	417	63	28	35	20 148	752	19.5	15.4	50.1
Osage	266	2 897	328	1 146	445	110	D	86	29 736	1 115	17.9	10.9	40.8
Ozark	171	900	93	D	202	79	D	19	21 052	639	13.5	20.2	52.7
Pemiscot	432	4 399	1 483	D	728	180	44	130	29 571	227	16.3	53.3	61.2
Perry	476	9 653	1 117	D	1 031	D	142	311	32 236	951	23.1	11.0	34.8
Pettis	1 002	17 656	2 954	3 486	2 384	395	1 609	538	30 460	1 311	28.1	17.5	45.9
Phelps	1 125	13 296	3 427	962	2 400	428	378	393	29 546	718	25.5	9.1	39.3
Pike	398	4 230	778	D	576	144	D	126	29 674	1 003	17.7	18.1	39.8
Platte	2 244	37 383	3 224	2 619	6 439	2 092	1 429	1 434	38 368	599	33.1	11.2	44.4
Polk	578	7 322	1 930	D	1 113	220	D	270	36 854	1 505	30.0	9.4	47.0
Pulaski	711	8 632	D	152	1 781	D	522	244	28 282	520	19.2	11.3	39.8
Putnam	84	602	D	D	202	53	22	15	25 000	649	12.2	21.1	45.6
Ralls	206	2 429	D	1 309	182	41	D	107	44 062	723	22.0	20.5	36.9
Randolph	555	7 321	1 370	999	1 164	399	100	245	33 503	818	23.0	10.9	40.3
Ray	352	2 896	613	D	638	122	92	85	29 278	1 162	27.1	9.8	50.9
Reynolds	180	1 258	225	D	122	D	D	49	38 644	363	19.0	11.8	41.6
Ripley	421	2 460	937	D	462	D	26	59	24 169	439	17.3	15.9	42.8
St. Charles	8 092	121 402	15 048	11 134	19 128	10 451	6 620	4 635	38 177	566	34.5	15.7	51.9
St. Clair	176	1 344	510	D	283	D	23	32	24 153	728	20.1	19.0	51.6
Ste. Genevieve	390	4 897	D	1 570	457	140	88	186	37 972	608	22.0	13.2	37.2
St. Francois	1 475	17 599	5 052	1 564	2 979	937	299	509	28 901	627	30.1	5.1	45.3
St. Louis	30 847	559 606	84 611	35 197	68 427	31 689	52 526	28 814	51 490	217	53.5	7.8	49.3
Saline	513	7 640	1 602	2 161	1 040	236	D	216	28 303	959	20.9	26.2	49.9
Schuyler	81	306	19	D	138	D	D	8	27 647	516	22.7	16.3	42.2
Scotland	130	813	D	67	177	43	D	21	26 442	674	19.1	19.1	46.9
Scott	1 056	14 120	3 311	2 776	1 449	429	481	457	32 331	484	32.6	20.2	49.6
Shannon	162	1 060	163	509	126	68	D	22	20 809	452	23.9	13.7	46.7
Shelby	161	1 142	94	234	D	57	D	29	25 208	709	18.6	26.4	43.2
Stoddard	713	8 512	1 773	2 457	1 336	393	D	269	31 570	907	29.4	23.3	49.1
Stone	679	3 617	427	110	813	D	108	99	27 404	601	26.1	7.8	42.3
Sullivan	116	2 042	227	D	166	60	D	65	31 847	798	12.5	25.2	46.4
Taney	1 754	23 978	2 345	476	4 858	465	380	644	26 839	414	21.5	14.0	47.8
Texas	479	4 210	923	803	686	159	72	106	25 067	1 296	18.7	14.7	51.2
Vernon	560	6 035	D	D	941	416	140	173	28 677	1 356	26.6	13.7	43.8
Warren	588	5 845	669	1 283	885	220	153	190	32 492	621	33.8	11.1	40.3
Washington	457	3 256	D	D	519	D	38	00	26 520	531	21.7	9.0	43.9
Wayne	256	1 581	310	354	334	108	D	37	23 691	411	12.4	13.9	44.8
Webster	628	4 910	495	695	1 129	246	186	139	28 245	1 837	35.6	5.7	44.3
Worth	51	229	D	42	69	D	D	6	26 367	384	15.6	16.7	40.9
Wright	404	3 460	515	432	886	D	53	86	24 770	1 246	23.0	11.9	50.2

STATE County	Agriculture, 2012 (cont.)															
	Land in farms					Value of land and buildings (dollars)			Value of products sold				Percent of farms with sales of:		Government payments	
			Acres								Percent from:					
	Acreage (1,000)	Percent change, 2007–2012	Average size of farm	Total irrigated (1,000)	Total cropland (1,000)	Average per farm	Average per acre	Value of machinery and equipment, average per farm (dollars)	Total (mil dol)	Average per farm (dollars)	Crops	Livestock and poultry products	$10,000 or more	$100,000 or more	Total ($1,000)	Percent of farms
	117	118	119	120	121	122	123	124	125	126	127	128	129	130	131	132
MISSOURI—Cont'd																
Jasper	247	-4.7	190	3.5	127.7	443 779	2 337	62 487	100.5	77 336	32.5	67.5	41.6	8.9	2 322	37.0
Jefferson	98	5.7	138	0.3	36.3	471 186	3 407	53 340	13.6	19 325	51.0	49.0	28.9	3.3	255	12.3
Johnson	391	-7.9	236	1.9	219.9	624 016	2 645	95 386	119.9	72 340	38.5	61.5	47.1	9.3	2 968	40.3
Knox	281	10.8	404	D	193.3	1 205 037	2 981	147 283	76.3	109 799	49.5	50.5	53.8	21.2	5 347	73.4
Laclede	320	10.9	229	0.2	89.6	503 814	2 200	50 168	50.4	36 045	15.1	84.9	46.4	7.4	526	10.8
Lafayette	327	-7.4	278	1.8	244.5	1 176 566	4 225	133 569	143.2	122 010	80.6	19.4	57.8	20.8	4 495	57.0
Lawrence	311	-3.6	168	2.3	118.1	431 114	2 562	62 340	204.9	110 819	7.4	92.6	45.3	10.8	1 959	18.6
Lewis	284	8.8	390	2.0	201.3	1 128 680	2 894	139 615	81.2	111 418	64.0	36.0	51.7	19.3	4 159	71.1
Lincoln	281	13.0	242	1.3	191.8	943 589	3 900	91 473	85.6	73 707	55.9	44.1	44.8	12.0	3 161	55.4
Linn	336	1.7	323	0.3	209.0	780 366	2 416	78 069	66.6	64 131	59.0	41.0	48.7	15.5	6 639	67.9
Livingston	284	-8.2	335	0.4	200.5	976 103	2 916	104 609	72.5	85 636	68.9	31.1	49.8	15.6	6 044	70.0
McDonald	187	-6.6	202	0.3	49.5	466 203	2 314	79 172	175.8	189 865	2.1	97.9	44.0	10.9	630	9.9
Macon	386	-2.1	299	0.3	214.7	740 631	2 477	78 400	66.8	51 777	53.6	46.4	41.6	10.1	6 172	58.1
Madison	107	9.0	287	D	24.1	528 405	1 840	54 603	18.4	49 201	9.8	90.2	41.8	6.7	102	13.1
Maries	241	0.4	289	0.2	59.4	563 396	1 951	60 886	35.3	42 176	13.0	87.0	53.8	6.8	435	16.1
Marion	221	-6.6	315	3.0	157.5	1 120 118	3 561	118 102	87.1	123 751	61.6	38.4	48.0	18.2	3 060	71.2
Mercer	227	12.6	400	D	119.4	887 578	2 219	93 078	102.7	181 146	18.6	81.4	40.9	12.5	3 303	67.4
Miller	248	1.2	245	1.4	62.0	544 853	2 221	58 525	103.0	101 659	4.7	95.3	51.2	11.1	549	13.7
Mississippi	245	-5.2	1 195	86.5	232.3	4 962 234	4 153	473 244	157.0	766 000	97.9	2.1	81.5	55.6	3 759	87.8
Moniteau	235	-3.2	216	0.2	99.9	582 663	2 698	67 761	173.5	159 302	9.4	90.6	57.0	13.5	2 018	37.6
Monroe	356	23.4	335	1.1	237.9	1 047 572	3 125	121 686	86.2	81 207	58.0	42.0	40.8	13.2	7 034	75.6
Montgomery	279	12.5	351	3.2	194.0	1 212 507	3 453	132 268	64.0	80 541	73.9	26.1	50.9	20.5	4 635	65.9
Morgan	198	-8.5	215	0.2	77.6	569 115	2 646	63 366	144.8	157 103	8.6	91.4	56.6	21.3	768	17.5
New Madrid	345	-9.5	1 087	196.5	332.5	4 819 981	4 435	524 943	217.1	684 994	99.9	0.1	84.2	65.6	8 243	90.9
Newton	248	0.8	157	0.3	93.4	404 596	2 577	60 035	251.5	159 393	6.0	94.0	44.3	9.5	1 034	17.3
Nodaway	424	-22.0	338	0.3	293.3	1 100 251	3 251	116 792	141.6	113 082	81.0	19.0	58.3	21.6	7 586	72.6
Oregon	254	6.0	338	0.4	35.9	525 161	1 556	53 593	34.5	45 934	3.4	96.6	45.3	6.8	955	26.7
Osage	283	-4.8	254	2.3	82.4	520 062	2 047	73 506	78.7	70 544	17.7	82.3	55.0	9.7	1 003	30.9
Ozark	229	-7.6	358	0.1	29.1	581 482	1 624	60 313	39.2	61 365	5.3	94.7	54.0	10.6	597	8.6
Pemiscot	305	-1.7	1 344	122.7	287.5	4 861 687	3 618	516 802	186.1	819 758	99.9	0.1	79.3	61.7	7 220	80.6
Perry	226	-5.2	238	D	122.0	636 469	2 673	82 989	63.4	66 614	50.1	49.9	52.2	13.4	2 226	64.9
Pettis	420	2.6	320	0.4	263.2	876 005	2 736	116 004	177.0	135 019	30.8	69.2	52.6	19.0	5 117	51.0
Phelps	157	-10.5	219	0.1	27.2	504 223	2 301	51 199	11.7	16 320	15.8	84.2	34.1	2.6	225	12.0
Pike	362	-3.1	361	3.7	226.0	1 247 957	3 461	127 424	87.4	87 094	62.9	37.1	51.7	15.3	4 506	65.7
Platte	153	-14.4	255	1.7	100.7	992 603	3 888	94 775	44.9	74 917	83.7	16.3	41.9	12.0	1 720	48.2
Polk	336	-4.0	223	1.3	102.6	461 553	2 066	49 912	85.2	56 613	10.6	89.4	49.2	10.0	859	15.3
Pulaski	112	-8.6	216	0.1	20.9	421 379	1 948	50 873	12.9	24 752	15.6	84.4	42.1	4.2	110	6.5
Putnam	293	7.3	451	D	124.7	930 538	2 063	91 116	86.1	132 669	19.3	80.7	49.3	18.3	3 373	59.5
Ralls	283	15.5	392	1.1	196.9	1 258 679	3 210	138 203	54.8	75 806	76.5	23.5	39.0	16.7	4 168	76.3
Randolph	209	-5.5	256	1.1	109.1	673 561	2 630	65 106	36.7	44 873	58.5	41.5	35.5	6.2	2 820	54.8
Ray	273	-6.4	235	7.7	174.7	641 818	2 730	86 155	74.5	64 122	71.7	28.3	41.8	10.1	3 721	53.8
Reynolds	97	-9.5	268	0.0	16.5	391 482	1 463	44 970	4.8	13 284	25.3	74.7	35.5	1.1	79	7.4
Ripley	138	0.4	314	12.1	45.1	563 134	1 794	65 385	19.1	43 583	55.8	44.2	40.5	7.3	777	26.7
St. Charles	158	1.3	279	1.1	121.0	1 184 827	4 240	119 919	62.5	110 417	84.8	15.2	53.0	20.7	1 607	55.5
St. Clair	239	-10.0	328	0.5	99.3	542 646	1 656	69 935	33.8	46 482	42.4	57.6	50.7	9.9	1 115	36.4
Ste. Genevieve	163	-13.9	267	0.2	72.3	616 641	2 305	76 181	26.6	43 755	58.6	41.4	46.9	8.7	1 492	46.4
St. Francois	116	3.4	186	0.1	32.0	466 490	2 513	46 496	14.0	22 332	32.9	67.1	36.8	2.6	343	13.1
St. Louis	30	-8.0	137	0.5	15.4	565 189	4 128	69 313	19.1	87 807	97.3	2.7	37.3	11.1	279	20.7
Saline	461	2.6	481	3.5	362.9	1 934 485	4 023	199 556	212.0	221 075	73.3	26.7	66.1	28.7	5 961	79.7
Schuyler	159	4.6	309	D	83.8	687 409	2 226	76 853	30.4	58 917	48.8	51.2	50.2	12.4	2 272	61.8
Scotland	244	5.4	362	D	158.4	1 063 616	2 936	106 022	82.2	121 938	44.7	55.3	53.9	21.5	4 627	70.0
Scott	223	-2.4	461	72.4	192.8	1 878 114	4 077	237 058	188.8	390 035	69.0	31.0	48.6	26.9	4 263	63.8
Shannon	124	11.8	274	0.0	23.0	458 142	1 670	50 407	10.5	23 197	11.5	88.5	37.4	5.8	171	6.6
Shelby	299	3.5	422	1.6	211.0	1 499 389	3 552	149 536	83.0	117 100	71.2	28.8	59.0	24.0	5 033	75.6
Stoddard	448	-2.8	494	226.7	396.3	2 169 982	4 392	245 480	315.0	347 277	81.3	18.7	49.9	26.1	11 137	73.4
Stone	118	-3.1	196	0.1	32.1	465 231	2 369	50 319	34.5	57 393	10.6	89.4	45.3	7.0	368	10.0
Sullivan	323	-3.3	405	D	158.8	751 872	1 858	87 835	149.6	187 526	12.2	87.8	46.5	14.7	5 745	61.3
Taney	116	8.8	280	0.1	18.8	549 092	1 961	49 271	11.7	28 259	10.8	89.2	38.2	4.3	209	10.1
Texas	392	10.4	303	0.1	68.0	496 529	1 641	48 862	42.0	32 416	8.8	91.2	47.4	7.5	565	10.3
Vernon	419	-8.2	309	5.4	244.4	665 520	2 156	99 091	209.0	154 128	29.8	70.2	51.6	13.6	4 561	44.8
Warren	136	-7.3	219	1.1	85.3	850 634	3 880	94 071	31.4	50 589	78.6	21.4	43.3	11.6	1 941	51.2
Washington	124	-9.7	233	0.0	24.3	447 979	1 919	44 347	11.1	20 846	20.8	79.2	37.9	4.7	106	3.6
Wayne	117	10.0	284	D	28.0	433 238	1 527	59 358	7.8	18 949	20.0	80.0	33.8	2.9	356	24.3
Webster	272	0.3	148	0.2	82.9	386 911	2 612	45 690	76.1	41 450	8.4	91.6	45.5	9.0	1 345	8.9
Worth	125	-17.6	326	D	70.0	733 870	2 254	84 737	37.1	96 646	37.1	62.9	43.2	14.1	2 824	84.1
Wright	294	3.4	236	0.2	67.2	424 095	1 797	48 860	47.2	37 913	6.9	93.1	45.8	8.7	1 041	14.4

Table B. States and Counties — **Water Use, Wholesale Trade, Retail Trade, and Real Estate**

STATE County	Water use, 2010		Wholesale trade,[1] 2007				Retail trade,[2] 2007				Real estate and rental and leasing,[2] 2007			
	Total water withdrawn (mil gal/day)	Gallons withdrawn per person per day	Number of establish-ments	Number of employees	Sales (mil dol)	Annual payroll (mil dol)	Number of establish-ments	Number of employees	Sales (mil dol)	Annual payroll (mil dol)	Number of establish-ments	Number of employees	Receipts (mil dol)	Annual payroll (mil dol)
	133	134	135	136	137	138	139	140	141	142	143	144	145	146
MISSOURI—Cont'd														
Jasper	30.8	262	140	1 528	793.4	59.1	596	8 171	1 967.4	165.8	141	654	76.4	16.1
Jefferson	829.3	3 791	143	1 438	782.8	66.2	524	6 796	1 709.8	154.1	171	592	69.1	13.5
Johnson	9.1	174	16	D	D	D	157	1 958	412.9	37.0	40	D	D	D
Knox	1.5	363	9	45	29.9	1.3	21	107	27.8	1.8	1	D	D	D
Laclede	17.8	500	28	D	D	D	192	2 059	469.7	43.6	38	99	10.7	2.0
Lafayette	5.7	170	36	277	140.6	9.1	151	1 402	301.4	25.1	23	99	5.2	1.7
Lawrence	10.7	276	25	222	63.7	5.9	138	1 257	419.5	30.9	33	95	9.4	1.3
Lewis	2.4	237	8	D	D	D	38	296	59.3	5.0	4	7	0.6	0.0
Lincoln	7.2	138	36	242	91.8	8.3	138	1 500	433.2	35.9	38	D	D	D
Linn	4.8	378	14	58	38.9	2.8	59	554	117.7	9.7	11	27	1.6	0.3
Livingston	2.5	163	20	218	86.2	7.1	85	1 124	234.5	22.3	13	54	13.3	1.2
McDonald	6.6	288	13	D	D	D	69	1 055	223.3	19.0	7	9	0.5	0.1
Macon	3.2	208	16	189	50.6	5.1	71	725	156.5	12.5	16	44	3.7	0.7
Madison	1.4	112	9	23	6.9	0.5	41	536	106.6	12.2	7	22	1.5	0.3
Maries	1.6	177	5	19	7.4	0.5	26	186	46.3	3.1	2	D	D	D
Marion	7.7	268	30	234	114.4	7.0	149	1 901	423.0	34.5	26	D	D	D
Mercer	2.2	568	2	D	D	D	12	58	20.2	0.8	NA	NA	NA	NA
Miller	4.0	160	20	122	68.9	4.1	134	1 734	451.8	39.8	60	155	27.0	4.7
Mississippi	82.6	5 753	17	176	235.2	6.7	58	458	161.5	8.4	6	24	1.5	0.3
Moniteau	3.4	218	13	219	106.3	5.5	60	490	159.7	8.6	5	D	D	D
Monroe	8.2	931	9	52	36.6	1.9	35	263	48.0	3.9	5	13	1.1	0.1
Montgomery	2.5	202	19	143	117.2	4.4	44	342	81.5	6.3	10	14	1.3	0.2
Morgan	6.5	315	18	149	22.1	2.1	101	948	191.5	18.2	24	55	7.0	1.1
New Madrid	984.5	51 936	31	432	288.0	14.3	85	1 479	509.8	28.1	12	26	2.6	0.4
Newton	9.7	167	42	1 233	491.8	33.5	203	1 925	605.7	42.4	41	181	18.7	3.1
Nodaway	3.3	139	18	D	D	D	83	1 099	206.8	17.6	22	50	6.1	0.7
Oregon	2.0	186	5	85	14.2	1.8	45	415	90.9	8.0	9	24	1.5	0.3
Osage	60.8	4 377	9	62	26.7	1.7	54	478	132.8	10.0	6	11	0.5	0.1
Ozark	14.2	1 460	8	D	D	D	33	218	46.0	3.1	7	10	1.7	0.3
Pemiscot	110.5	6 038	23	224	382.6	7.6	72	705	209.5	11.3	17	58	10.8	1.7
Perry	4.7	245	14	388	97.3	14.8	90	1 027	263.5	22.5	16	47	5.9	0.6
Pettis	9.2	217	36	418	169.4	15.6	202	2 398	547.3	50.9	54	353	38.4	9.1
Phelps	10.4	229	31	329	103.5	10.9	208	2 361	632.5	48.7	45	140	17.0	3.1
Pike	7.4	401	25	289	252.2	8.7	76	702	161.3	13.9	9	19	2.2	0.5
Platte	459.5	5 144	102	1 593	3 535.5	90.3	302	5 691	1 737.4	132.0	143	1 279	197.2	33.9
Polk	5.2	167	25	170	43.3	4.1	105	1 249	276.0	26.0	22	78	7.2	1.3
Pulaski	6.8	129	11	76	18.2	2.1	144	1 556	376.5	32.4	39	127	16.4	2.8
Putnam	1.8	364	1	D	D	D	26	152	38.6	2.8	6	21	4.8	0.3
Ralls	1.7	166	15	D	D	D	31	199	60.2	4.5	5	D	D	D
Randolph	740.2	29 127	17	D	D	D	107	1 224	293.5	24.6	26	118	19.3	2.7
Ray	6.3	266	15	152	92.2	5.0	66	695	141.7	13.1	11	27	1.2	0.3
Reynolds	5.7	851	5	30	8.3	0.6	26	150	28.7	2.4	1	D	D	D
Ripley	31.0	2 201	5	29	8.0	0.6	48	475	92.4	8.0	11	42	5.2	0.7
St. Charles	505.1	1 401	349	3 773	9 325.6	184.0	1 115	17 972	4 408.5	414.5	378	1 629	420.4	50.7
St. Clair	1.6	159	7	D	D	D	36	289	64.7	4.8	6	D	D	D
Ste. Genevieve	8.1	449	12	146	73.6	5.1	64	515	148.2	9.3	10	19	1.4	0.3
St. Francois	8.2	125	37	D	D	D	250	3 208	685.8	63.6	61	265	26.8	5.3
St. Louis	535.5	536	1 719	27 191	27 366.6	1 590.7	4 151	72 067	17 237.5	1 929.5	1 537	12 311	2 477.9	474.1
Saline	5.7	243	33	D	D	D	108	1 103	230.3	19.9	21	58	6.5	0.8
Schuyler	0.4	86	3	D	D	D	27	179	32.1	2.4	NA	NA	NA	NA
Scotland	0.9	176	6	D	D	D	31	168	39.4	3.0	3	D	D	D
Scott	104.6	2 670	57	538	252.4	16.0	190	1 515	358.4	29.1	48	D	D	D
Shannon	1.3	153	8	59	14.3	1.0	21	167	26.2	1.9	7	30	1.5	0.3
Shelby	1.8	282	12	71	30.5	2.0	35	229	49.1	3.8	4	7	0.4	0.0
Stoddard	333.0	11 112	31	230	196.3	7.0	143	1 409	436.1	29.7	23	62	5.3	1.0
Stone	4.6	144	15	35	14.2	0.8	116	1 086	222.9	21.9	53	262	26.8	5.0
Sullivan	3.6	539	2	D	D	D	28	183	45.0	3.2	3	3	0.3	0.0
Taney	33.7	651	33	199	76.0	5.7	447	4 576	833.0	84.4	137	1 343	295.8	52.2
Texas	3.8	148	22	121	50.7	3.1	92	789	167.8	13.9	12	30	2.4	0.7
Vernon	12.7	599	18	130	61.2	4.6	79	839	200.6	17.0	18	44	5.6	0.9
Warren	3.6	109	29	D	D	D	109	1 166	318.0	22.2	27	97	13.4	2.0
Washington	8.3	329	14	D	D	D	53	400	124.3	9.7	5	D	D	D
Wayne	1.4	104	8	44	29.8	1.2	46	388	65.8	6.4	2	D	D	D
Webster	4.5	123	31	146	69.5	5.3	122	1 123	294.2	23.4	23	56	5.3	0.9
Worth	0.3	134	5	14	7.7	0.4	13	64	13.2	1.0	1	D	D	D
Wright	2.9	156	16	101	31.7	1.9	99	989	237.9	19.7	18	47	4.1	0.6

1. Merchant wholesalers, except manufacturers' sales branches and offices. 2. Employer establishments.

STATE County	Professional, scientific, and technical services,[1] 2007				Manufacturing, 2007				Accommodation and food services, 2007			
	Number of establish-ments	Number of employees	Receipts (mil dol)	Annual payroll (mil dol)	Number of establish-ments	Number of employees	Receipts (mil dol)	Annual payroll (mil dol)	Number of establish-ments	Number of employees	Sales (mil dol)	Annual payroll (mil dol)
	147	148	149	150	151	152	153	154	155	156	157	158
MISSOURI—Cont'd												
Jasper	200	D	D	D	189	10 351	3 336.6	383.6	247	4 792	182.3	52.8
Jefferson	227	976	75.8	27.1	202	5 784	1 538.1	229.5	272	5 399	203.3	58.0
Johnson	70	D	D	D	36	2 030	D	D	94	1 797	56.7	16.8
Knox	8	D	D	D	NA	NA	NA	NA	5	26	0.6	0.2
Laclede	41	169	11.1	3.7	63	4 892	1 225.6	151.8	74	1 233	50.3	13.9
Lafayette	50	D	D	D	36	1 123	225.7	32.8	67	793	25.4	7.2
Lawrence	48	181	11.2	3.6	48	1 622	608.7	58.5	55	686	20.5	6.1
Lewis	7	D	D	D	NA	NA	NA	NA	12	D	D	D
Lincoln	47	190	12.6	4.5	47	1 400	528.3	68.0	66	1 037	31.1	8.7
Linn	23	82	6.6	1.9	19	1 107	166.9	37.4	21	269	9.3	2.5
Livingston	30	160	10.0	3.2	17	610	130.3	22.4	32	534	17.4	5.0
McDonald	16	43	2.3	0.8	24	2 413	D	60.7	29	265	10.0	2.5
Macon	18	79	7.2	2.8	NA	NA	NA	NA	36	486	15.2	4.2
Madison	11	D	D	D	NA	NA	NA	NA	23	278	6.7	2.0
Maries	6	D	D	D	NA	NA	NA	NA	15	154	2.6	0.7
Marion	48	D	D	D	43	1 843	D	72.9	74	1 275	41.8	12.7
Mercer	3	D	D	D	NA	NA	NA	NA	9	22	0.6	0.2
Miller	42	199	24.5	9.5	23	699	74.8	21.2	58	650	30.0	9.1
Mississippi	10	D	D	D	NA	NA	NA	NA	23	271	10.0	2.8
Moniteau	18	62	4.5	1.3	26	747	D	25.2	27	280	8.2	2.4
Monroe	8	D	D	D	10	731	D	20.3	21	139	4.4	1.1
Montgomery	12	D	D	D	19	561	121.7	18.2	16	195	6.0	2.4
Morgan	26	D	D	D	28	537	108.1	14.7	43	428	13.3	3.9
New Madrid	17	D	D	D	17	1 768	D	87.0	28	383	15.0	4.2
Newton	69	D	D	D	80	3 434	646.7	107.1	105	1 962	69.6	20.4
Nodaway	27	114	8.4	3.0	19	2 064	866.6	65.7	40	934	28.8	8.2
Oregon	11	D	D	D	NA	NA	NA	NA	11	178	5.9	1.6
Osage	10	21	1.8	0.5	31	943	433.1	33.5	23	167	4.1	1.1
Ozark	9	D	D	D	NA	NA	NA	NA	22	174	6.4	1.9
Pemiscot	17	D	D	D	12	D	D	D	34	398	14.4	3.5
Perry	28	128	9.1	4.0	38	3 339	711.6	105.7	43	599	20.2	5.8
Pettis	69	328	30.2	9.1	60	5 058	1 535.8	162.4	92	1 590	55.4	17.2
Phelps	66	371	33.0	12.0	51	1 224	454.8	51.5	106	1 893	73.6	19.1
Pike	16	77	5.4	1.6	20	722	308.9	32.8	28	318	11.3	3.0
Platte	248	1 331	180.9	60.2	65	2 816	2 077.4	128.3	198	6 301	465.6	109.4
Polk	48	182	13.4	4.5	35	697	D	17.9	54	667	23.3	5.5
Pulaski	47	D	D	D	NA	NA	NA	NA	87	2 033	74.3	32.2
Putnam	4	D	D	D	NA	NA	NA	NA	4	18	0.5	0.1
Ralls	9	D	D	D	15	1 481	D	69.9	16	127	3.6	1.1
Randolph	32	79	9.7	1.7	30	1 165	196.9	38.5	40	600	21.8	5.5
Ray	24	79	6.3	2.1	NA	NA	NA	NA	31	329	10.2	2.8
Reynolds	6	D	D	D	NA	NA	NA	NA	17	45	4.1	0.9
Ripley	10	D	D	D	NA	NA	NA	NA	12	140	5.7	1.6
St. Charles	761	D	D	D	271	15 683	6 532.8	806.9	677	14 650	537.7	161.9
St. Clair	8	D	D	D	NA	NA	NA	NA	15	88	5.4	0.9
Ste. Genevieve	22	84	6.3	2.0	32	1 678	368.5	68.7	37	411	11.4	3.3
St. Francois	88	D	D	D	65	2 228	341.8	69.5	116	D	D	D
St. Louis	3 774	42 378	6 944.0	2 652.2	1 098	54 752	22 654.6	3 285.3	2 142	50 401	2 440.7	703.9
Saline	32	99	6.7	2.0	20	1 768	803.5	62.2	41	511	15.9	5.4
Schuyler	2	D	D	D	NA	NA	NA	NA	5	19	0.4	0.1
Scotland	7	D	D	D	NA	NA	NA	NA	10	61	2.2	0.6
Scott	75	435	41.6	14.0	72	D	976.9	D	83	D	D	D
Shannon	5	D	D	D	NA	NA	NA	NA	21	125	4.4	1.2
Shelby	11	D	D	D	NA	NA	NA	NA	13	76	1.7	0.5
Stoddard	28	184	15.6	4.4	42	2 753	888.0	99.0	39	630	20.5	6.0
Stone	39	139	7.7	3.0	NA	NA	NA	NA	101	641	47.6	10.4
Sullivan	5	D	D	D	6	D	D	D	6	21	0.6	0.1
Taney	110	581	45.4	16.2	50	535	D	D	303	6 283	360.7	106.6
Texas	25	D	D	D	48	987	214.7	28.7	38	381	11.0	3.3
Vernon	29	116	9.9	3.0	28	1 135	D	45.3	40	498	18.7	4.4
Warren	33	175	15.1	5.3	44	1 039	297.4	42.7	47	658	22.4	6.1
Washington	14	D	D	D	20	512	104.2	16.5	17	401	17.3	5.2
Wayne	10	D	D	D	NA	NA	NA	NA	21	128	4.4	1.2
Webster	40	D	D	D	48	977	161.5	30.7	36	638	22.2	5.6
Worth	4	D	D	D	NA	NA	NA	NA	5	15	0.5	0.1
Wright	21	D	D	D	24	526	146.6	18.0	30	301	38.0	5.8

1. Establishment subject to federal tax.

STATE County	Health care and social assistance, 2007				Other services, 2007				Nonemployer businesses, 2013		Value of residential construction authorized by building permits, 2014	
	Number of establish- ments	Number of employees	Receipts (mil dol)	Annual payroll (mil dol)	Number of establish- ments	Number of employees	Receipts (mil dol)	Annual payroll (mil dol)	Number	Receipts (mil dol)	New Construction ($1,000)	Number of housing units
	159	160	161	162	163	164	165	166	167	168	169	170
MISSOURI—Cont'd												
Jasper	396	5 138	349.6	164.1	252	1 297	92.5	27.5	6 403	253.0	37 529	371
Jefferson	445	5 598	366.7	155.4	336	1 668	139.3	42.8	12 589	481.4	74 146	520
Johnson	112	1 779	123.5	51.0	59	D	D	D	2 946	109.4	5 759	75
Knox	8	59	2.8	1.1	13	37	3.2	0.5	357	15.7	0	0
Laclede	73	1 228	108.3	42.8	64	223	17.7	4.3	2 505	109.5	2 919	17
Lafayette	65	1 130	62.7	26.3	49	166	10.3	2.7	2 095	80.8	6 123	27
Lawrence	80	1 522	97.2	45.6	42	116	8.5	2.5	2 546	94.7	1 510	14
Lewis	18	311	10.5	5.2	11	D	D	D	633	27.5	617	7
Lincoln	65	1 291	67.9	28.8	76	276	22.2	5.4	3 304	119.8	6 482	50
Linn	34	549	30.3	12.4	29	119	8.4	1.8	948	48.9	0	0
Livingston	45	846	58.9	22.5	39	182	9.9	2.4	981	35.4	3 448	17
McDonald	26	D	D	D	18	D	D	D	1 309	49.4	290	4
Macon	37	528	31.5	12.7	36	91	7.0	1.7	1 084	41.9	200	4
Madison	29	713	27.3	13.6	20	42	3.6	0.6	744	24.5	335	5
Maries	12	167	5.7	2.6	6	D	D	D	597	22.1	0	0
Marion	105	2 778	210.2	85.6	75	352	19.4	4.8	1 677	61.4	7 459	43
Mercer	10	86	3.7	1.7	5	27	2.0	0.5	258	9.3	0	0
Miller	34	444	24.7	10.1	45	261	16.6	5.8	1 632	68.6	12 164	85
Mississippi	30	540	24.2	9.3	16	43	3.3	0.9	610	47.9	605	7
Moniteau	33	355	20.1	6.8	23	68	3.5	0.8	960	31.6	0	0
Monroe	27	251	8.6	3.2	13	28	4.2	0.5	565	21.9	190	4
Montgomery	21	357	17.0	7.2	19	72	7.5	2.1	830	38.0	3 551	20
Morgan	31	247	10.6	4.3	34	95	12.0	2.0	1 637	65.0	1 208	4
New Madrid	42	639	32.5	12.2	27	69	5.6	1.0	800	22.9	1 736	7
Newton	111	7 121	739.8	271.7	92	378	24.7	7.1	3 787	157.3	4 374	37
Nodaway	52	1 096	87.0	32.5	35	127	10.0	2.6	1 432	49.0	5 429	36
Oregon	32	358	14.2	6.8	20	37	3.9	0.7	772	29.2	215	2
Osage	21	412	15.0	6.4	14	35	4.9	0.5	913	36.6	0	0
Ozark	17	104	4.6	2.2	18	D	D	D	761	22.5	68	5
Pemiscot	47	1 256	66.8	26.9	17	101	5.3	1.6	824	28.1	318	8
Perry	53	1 036	59.5	24.7	30	D	D	D	1 220	45.4	5 584	34
Pettis	146	2 640	182.0	75.0	98	D	D	D	2 527	103.1	1 775	18
Phelps	151	3 275	288.8	101.3	86	329	22.0	5.9	2 568	88.8	13 327	114
Pike	42	744	37.7	16.5	25	79	6.8	1.1	1 127	41.9	842	12
Platte	172	2 586	221.3	89.4	165	1 057	107.2	29.4	6 798	300.6	60 987	228
Polk	78	1 895	124.5	55.0	50	138	11.8	2.2	2 339	89.5	7 440	59
Pulaski	65	1 496	131.3	52.4	65	334	20.8	7.0	1 991	70.3	8 602	72
Putnam	12	143	8.3	4.2	9	D	D	D	438	18.6	210	3
Ralls	15	189	8.6	3.8	15	89	10.2	2.0	678	27.2	0	0
Randolph	89	1 422	119.9	40.1	47	139	10.3	2.8	1 365	52.1	1 580	14
Ray	33	516	33.9	13.3	28	87	6.2	1.4	1 246	42.2	4 061	21
Reynolds	18	141	5.4	2.6	3	D	D	D	442	17.0	195	1
Ripley	41	544	20.3	10.7	15	44	3.7	0.7	854	32.3	720	6
St. Charles	738	12 709	1 145.5	439.2	596	3 813	272.6	90.1	23 420	1 001.4	509 388	2 646
St. Clair	25	512	26.2	14.2	9	D	D	D	680	23.1	335	3
Ste. Genevieve	35	769	45.9	18.9	36	151	10.5	2.9	1 064	28.7	1 044	5
St. Francois	233	4 516	300.1	121.7	108	885	33.7	10.9	3 079	107.7	12 730	130
St. Louis	3 357	78 505	7 776.5	3 129.0	2 050	16 511	1 702.5	517.0	72 436	3 630.3	348 478	1 062
Saline	69	1 467	93.4	35.5	38	113	10.3	2.8	1 218	40.9	4 950	41
Schuyler	4	D	D	D	8	D	D	D	330	14.8	639	3
Scotland	12	223	15.1	7.7	15	D	D	D	514	27.8	140	1
Scott	123	2 713	175.7	73.4	77	D	D	D	2 226	89.2	6 145	71
Shannon	20	90	4.6	2.0	5	13	1.4	0.3	757	28.0	0	0
Shelby	8	90	4.6	1.5	12	31	3.9	0.8	494	18.8	345	2
Stoddard	77	1 558	69.0	31.2	39	165	16.4	3.8	1 935	91.9	3 920	22
Stone	50	549	43.6	15.7	52	260	18.3	5.2	2 681	109.3	55 112	132
Sullivan	17	262	14.1	5.8	12	26	2.7	0.6	416	12.8	65	1
Taney	111	2 196	243.6	93.9	110	512	47.6	11.1	4 286	162.3	21 082	106
Texas	58	954	49.9	20.6	37	79	6.4	1.3	1 696	65.3	0	0
Vernon	103	1 272	87.7	30.4	38	184	14.1	4.1	1 346	57.4	1 431	20
Warren	42	517	26.6	10.7	42	153	9.1	2.9	1 982	62.3	16 420	75
Washington	55	676	39.2	15.2	23	66	4.5	1.1	1 008	34.1	70	1
Wayne	29	319	12.6	4.9	10	D	D	D	685	26.8	NA	NA
Webster	48	D	D	D	42	136	8.9	2.3	2 831	99.4	4 506	42
Worth	3	D	D	D	3	13	0.9	0.2	211	8.6	0	0
Wright	43	479	25.8	10.2	29	81	6.0	1.4	1 276	53.8	335	5

STATE County	Government employment and payroll, 2012: Full-time equivalent employees	March payroll (dollars)	March payroll (percent of total): Adminis-tration, judicial, and legal	Police and Corrections	Fire Protection	Highways and transpor-tation	Health and Welfare	Natural resources and utilities	Education and libraries	Local government finances, 2012: General revenue: Total (mil dol)	Inter-govern-mental (mil dol)	Taxes: Total (mil dol)	Per capita[1] (dollars): Total	Property
	171	172	173	174	175	176	177	178	179	180	181	182	183	184
MISSOURI—Cont'd														
Jasper	4 406	12 579 406	4.8	9.9	4.0	3.6	1.3	3.8	71.5	389.2	139.5	146.6	1 272	589
Jefferson	6 669	24 871 942	2.8	6.2	4.1	2.5	3.8	3.1	76.7	560.9	238.8	255.4	1 160	796
Johnson	2 208	7 565 488	3.1	4.7	2.1	2.3	37.3	2.7	47.4	195.3	49.7	52.6	967	584
Knox	221	492 621	7.9	5.4	0.0	7.2	22.0	5.2	52.2	12.1	5.9	4.4	1 068	756
Laclede	1 413	3 701 221	5.5	5.9	1.6	12.4	1.2	6.8	65.2	72.4	35.3	26.3	742	477
Lafayette	1 188	3 488 934	7.8	8.3	0.6	3.5	2.3	9.3	67.9	88.1	38.4	34.2	1 034	710
Lawrence	1 155	3 231 901	5.5	6.1	0.7	2.7	6.5	2.7	75.5	76.5	38.1	27.2	706	425
Lewis	450	1 137 169	6.6	5.6	0.1	4.4	19.6	4.3	58.6	29.3	13.4	9.1	892	661
Lincoln	1 917	6 064 837	5.5	7.0	1.3	2.6	24.9	0.7	57.6	159.5	58.6	49.5	928	677
Linn	590	1 568 941	6.7	5.1	0.0	4.8	4.2	7.5	69.7	39.5	19.0	13.4	1 074	641
Livingston	654	1 837 354	4.6	6.8	5.3	2.6	13.9	14.2	51.7	49.5	19.1	16.1	1 073	702
McDonald	606	1 598 982	8.5	7.8	0.1	4.5	1.5	6.0	70.3	51.8	29.8	17.6	770	427
Macon	1 039	2 633 830	3.7	3.4	0.8	3.2	42.4	2.9	43.4	92.8	45.8	29.8	1 914	1 610
Madison	682	1 827 224	2.1	3.5	0.1	2.1	44.4	2.8	42.9	25.4	13.9	8.3	667	425
Maries	323	761 125	7.6	6.0	0.0	6.9	9.4	3.4	66.1	18.2	8.6	7.6	847	638
Marion	1 348	3 816 108	4.3	7.2	3.7	3.7	10.5	8.5	58.2	94.9	33.0	39.1	1 361	752
Mercer	176	501 591	15.9	5.2	0.1	7.0	6.8	4.3	59.8	9.5	4.4	3.9	1 038	887
Miller	1 205	3 202 179	4.4	4.5	1.6	2.3	11.6	1.8	73.2	80.0	30.4	36.5	1 472	1 081
Mississippi	496	1 277 944	12.1	11.0	0.1	3.6	4.4	7.4	61.1	39.2	20.9	12.9	904	600
Moniteau	498	1 342 360	7.0	4.0	0.2	3.3	8.9	4.9	70.4	34.2	15.0	12.7	813	528
Monroe	490	1 220 603	5.4	5.4	0.3	4.2	22.2	8.5	53.6	28.8	12.5	9.7	1 109	878
Montgomery	414	1 189 713	7.9	12.4	0.0	5.3	4.0	3.0	66.0	27.1	9.4	13.0	1 088	730
Morgan	588	1 595 566	8.3	9.3	0.7	4.5	8.1	2.2	61.6	37.0	13.2	17.9	892	558
New Madrid	720	1 973 525	9.1	7.8	0.4	5.1	5.0	6.0	65.2	48.9	21.7	21.3	1 153	837
Newton	1 886	5 757 934	4.6	4.8	2.8	1.7	3.3	2.2	80.6	121.7	59.7	39.0	661	405
Nodaway	726	2 001 480	9.5	5.9	0.8	3.6	4.2	6.4	68.6	62.2	22.3	27.8	1 186	755
Oregon	416	986 254	6.1	4.7	0.0	3.9	0.0	4.8	79.9	22.3	13.8	6.1	554	379
Osage	364	958 029	5.9	4.6	2.7	4.1	8.7	5.2	68.3	23.3	8.9	9.6	696	471
Ozark	375	902 737	3.5	3.0	0.0	3.7	2.8	1.2	83.1	20.2	12.4	5.9	612	453
Pemiscot	869	2 608 472	5.8	7.8	0.7	1.4	2.9	7.8	73.3	61.3	38.4	13.9	770	506
Perry	569	1 561 790	6.3	12.2	0.0	3.8	5.0	9.4	63.2	42.8	15.7	20.2	1 064	628
Pettis	2 440	8 051 066	2.4	3.6	1.7	1.5	41.8	2.5	45.8	222.9	54.6	51.1	1 207	624
Phelps	2 804	9 025 924	2.3	3.7	1.2	1.5	51.9	4.5	33.4	301.2	46.2	39.1	869	478
Pike	681	2 031 713	2.7	3.7	0.2	0.7	28.4	3.3	60.9	45.8	18.4	20.6	1 109	754
Platte	2 626	11 215 330	4.0	6.6	2.9	2.1	4.0	1.9	78.0	290.1	82.7	172.3	1 871	1 274
Polk	1 882	6 311 305	2.0	2.0	0.1	1.6	60.7	1.1	32.3	164.9	36.7	18.1	584	439
Pulaski	1 731	5 423 451	3.5	3.9	1.1	2.3	7.4	5.5	75.3	125.6	76.5	29.6	556	371
Putnam	314	940 189	4.5	2.1	0.0	2.4	55.0	5.9	29.6	17.4	5.2	7.7	1 554	1 199
Ralls	284	692 452	21.1	12.6	0.0	13.9	2.2	4.0	41.7	13.1	5.3	6.2	600	404
Randolph	1 211	3 641 751	3.9	5.9	1.9	2.1	2.9	4.9	77.8	104.1	32.8	33.6	1 328	821
Ray	1 243	21 423 521	0.8	0.5	0.3	0.3	89.8	0.8	7.3	87.1	25.3	21.5	933	704
Reynolds	325	775 935	7.0	5.6	0.0	5.7	4.1	1.6	75.1	20.4	10.7	7.5	1 131	997
Ripley	665	1 587 309	4.3	3.8	0.5	1.9	28.8	2.6	58.2	27.1	17.6	6.3	449	337
St. Charles	12 474	44 955 774	5.7	9.4	5.0	2.8	3.2	4.3	66.6	1 191.7	344.4	666.4	1 808	1 183
St. Clair	558	1 434 103	4.2	10.9	0.0	2.8	35.5	3.2	42.1	48.9	23.1	6.2	654	535
Ste. Genevieve	472	1 571 579	6.8	13.6	0.1	3.5	5.8	7.1	62.2	37.1	12.7	20.0	1 125	724
St. Francois	2 385	7 190 551	2.7	4.3	0.6	1.6	5.1	5.3	80.0	178.1	78.4	65.4	993	571
St. Louis	35 141	147 062 201	4.5	10.0	7.3	2.5	1.6	2.8	69.6	3 629.3	1 051.6	2 133.5	2 133	1 497
Saline	749	2 090 138	7.0	10.8	3.2	5.2	6.6	26.6	39.7	61.0	25.6	21.0	898	647
Schuyler	276	469 325	6.5	3.5	0.0	3.7	25.1	6.2	54.3	12.0	5.3	3.2	735	541
Scotland	479	1 508 783	7.5	3.0	0.0	5.6	60.2	4.1	19.3	31.5	5.9	4.5	918	718
Scott	1 609	5 229 887	4.1	7.7	1.4	1.8	4.2	23.8	53.9	108.4	50.7	38.1	973	559
Shannon	529	555 611	8.1	5.1	0.0	7.2	7.0	5.1	67.1	13.2	8.0	2.9	343	223
Shelby	432	1 223 611	12.6	7.4	0.3	6.2	25.9	5.7	38.5	23.5	9.7	6.6	1 064	756
Stoddard	1 139	2 920 419	5.2	6.2	0.8	8.7	6.5	5.3	66.9	72.2	30.2	21.0	704	560
Stone	846	2 351 044	6.0	5.6	1.1	2.7	0.1	2.1	82.4	74.2	35.5	30.6	969	612
Sullivan	370	985 283	6.2	4.1	0.2	3.8	27.9	5.8	50.1	23.6	9.0	6.6	1 012	748
Taney	1 787	5 327 466	7.7	9.1	3.9	4.1	8.3	6.6	58.2	198.6	59.2	103.3	1 952	978
Texas	1 227	3 278 813	3.7	3.2	0.1	3.2	31.5	5.3	50.4	84.8	28.4	20.4	791	654
Vernon	1 038	3 438 287	4.3	4.0	1.4	1.5	36.6	4.4	47.6	48.3	21.1	19.4	934	559
Warren	943	2 742 942	5.8	9.6	2.2	1.6	5.8	4.1	68.2	70.7	27.9	32.8	1 001	734
Washington	953	2 869 920	3.5	2.5	0.3	2.7	34.5	4.9	50.7	69.6	27.6	13.6	541	368
Wayne	459	1 011 584	9.4	3.6	0.0	7.6	5.0	3.2	71.2	25.2	14.3	7.7	573	378
Webster	946	2 669 213	5.5	5.0	0.3	2.8	11.0	3.5	71.2	63.4	29.0	20.2	556	309
Worth	134	294 433	8.2	2.8	0.0	3.4	21.0	5.8	57.6	6.8	2.2	2.2	1 037	834
Wright	792	2 007 501	4.3	3.8	0.3	2.7	11.1	4.2	73.0	47.2	25.3	12.2	656	392

1. Based on the resident population estimated as of July 1 of the year shown.

STATE County	Local government finances, 2012 (cont.) — Direct general expenditure: Total (mil dol)	Direct general expenditure: Per capita[1] (dollars)	Percent of total for: Education	Percent of total for: Health and hospitals	Percent of total for: Police protection	Percent of total for: Public welfare	Percent of total for: Highways	Debt outstanding: Total (mil dol)	Debt outstanding: Per capita[1] (dollars)	Government employment, 2013: Federal civilian	Government employment, 2013: Federal military	Government employment, 2013: State and local	Presidential election,[2] 2012 — Percent of vote cast: Democratic	Percent of vote cast: Republican	Percent of vote cast: All other
	185	186	187	188	189	190	191	192	193	194	195	196	197	198	199
MISSOURI—Cont'd															
Jasper	396.9	3 443	54.1	10.7	5.4	0.1	5.6	243.6	2 113	289	432	6 823	32.8	65.9	1.3
Jefferson	583.0	2 648	64.1	2.8	6.2	0.0	7.7	577.7	2 623	283	774	8 289	50.6	48.1	1.4
Johnson	233.9	4 299	31.0	47.8	3.5	0.0	4.6	246.2	4 525	1 225	3 975	5 969	42.9	55.2	1.9
Knox	10.9	2 667	49.1	8.8	4.0	18.8	5.9	0.6	147	33	14	277	37.5	59.9	2.6
Laclede	68.0	1 919	74.1	0.0	4.7	0.0	6.3	34.1	962	80	125	1 497	32.0	66.6	1.4
Lafayette	87.7	2 650	57.3	1.7	5.6	0.1	7.0	105.1	3 177	110	118	2 113	41.6	56.9	1.5
Lawrence	78.1	2 031	67.8	0.8	3.9	5.7	6.5	98.6	2 562	210	133	1 942	30.6	67.7	1.7
Lewis	26.7	2 624	50.7	1.4	3.7	15.5	8.9	11.0	1 085	46	33	608	40.8	57.6	1.6
Lincoln	153.2	2 871	47.7	26.4	4.4	0.0	4.4	139.5	2 615	107	188	2 376	43.5	54.9	1.7
Linn	37.6	3 014	60.3	3.0	4.4	0.0	11.3	26.2	2 102	58	43	781	44.5	52.9	2.6
Livingston	59.6	3 966	50.2	2.8	4.8	8.2	7.4	28.8	1 918	76	48	1 324	37.2	60.9	1.9
McDonald	44.0	1 922	69.8	0.0	4.1	0.0	8.0	31.9	1 393	84	79	857	30.2	67.6	2.2
Macon	48.3	3 102	46.4	1.1	3.5	22.2	8.9	21.2	1 363	73	54	1 635	37.2	61.4	1.4
Madison	30.2	2 426	68.9	0.0	6.2	0.0	6.2	3.9	310	23	43	900	40.6	57.6	1.8
Maries	18.1	2 013	61.7	4.7	4.0	0.0	9.9	10.7	1 187	11	32	334	35.2	62.7	2.1
Marion	99.0	3 444	54.3	3.1	3.7	6.3	4.7	133.0	4 628	103	97	1 881	37.5	61.4	1.2
Mercer	9.9	2 650	69.6	5.6	1.5	0.0	12.0	8.6	2 310	25	13	240	29.7	66.9	3.4
Miller	78.5	3 161	59.5	4.2	3.5	6.0	5.7	46.2	1 860	48	88	1 438	30.8	67.6	1.6
Mississippi	35.3	2 466	49.4	5.6	5.4	0.6	6.5	20.3	1 418	12	44	1 038	42.0	56.6	1.4
Moniteau	32.1	2 054	63.0	5.8	3.2	0.0	6.8	31.2	1 994	46	51	1 039	31.3	67.0	1.7
Monroe	28.8	3 309	49.1	3.2	3.9	16.0	10.7	54.4	6 255	65	31	618	39.5	58.7	1.8
Montgomery	28.9	2 411	56.1	3.6	5.3	0.0	7.9	11.0	913	40	41	665	40.1	58.5	1.4
Morgan	40.7	2 025	46.7	0.1	7.7	7.9	8.7	22.0	1 093	39	70	959	39.0	59.6	1.5
New Madrid	46.5	2 517	59.4	2.4	6.4	0.0	7.6	18.4	995	56	64	960	41.6	56.8	1.6
Newton	127.6	2 161	69.8	3.0	3.0	0.5	3.4	106.0	1 794	150	205	2 622	29.3	69.4	1.3
Nodaway	59.7	2 551	52.7	3.7	4.8	0.0	11.8	64.8	2 766	88	69	2 496	44.0	54.5	1.5
Oregon	21.9	1 990	73.6	1.6	2.2	0.0	5.3	3.9	358	30	38	518	39.4	57.8	2.8
Osage	23.1	1 669	59.8	6.0	2.4	0.0	5.6	11.0	794	34	47	769	26.9	71.5	1.6
Ozark	20.7	2 155	78.4	2.7	3.2	0.1	6.5	0.7	69	21	33	433	35.4	62.3	2.3
Pemiscot	61.8	3 411	67.4	1.6	4.6	0.0	5.4	11.3	624	53	62	1 579	43.0	56.1	0.9
Perry	43.0	2 261	53.4	1.8	6.3	0.0	8.0	19.0	1 001	44	66	1 154	34.8	63.9	1.3
Pettis	213.3	5 041	37.6	44.8	2.5	0.0	4.2	106.8	2 524	132	147	3 170	38.1	60.5	1.4
Phelps	295.8	6 576	23.7	59.1	2.1	0.3	2.9	165.9	3 688	365	237	5 859	38.0	60.2	1.7
Pike	43.7	2 354	53.0	1.6	7.4	0.0	9.9	24.3	1 308	69	58	1 700	44.2	54.2	1.6
Platte	285.1	3 097	65.5	0.9	4.8	0.2	5.0	434.8	4 724	505	346	3 687	46.2	52.6	1.2
Polk	168.1	5 419	28.7	60.0	1.0	0.0	3.1	55.0	1 774	71	104	2 174	33.2	65.4	1.4
Pulaski	139.6	2 621	69.4	2.9	2.8	0.0	4.4	141.0	2 648	3 871	12 272	2 180	35.0	63.7	1.3
Putnam	17.9	3 623	40.9	1.9	1.7	18.6	8.7	7.6	1 551	21	17	451	29.7	68.0	2.3
Ralls	12.4	1 207	50.3	3.6	5.3	0.0	17.2	14.9	1 451	27	36	351	40.1	58.8	1.1
Randolph	103.6	4 090	59.4	15.6	4.7	0.0	3.9	94.5	3 731	68	80	2 135	37.5	60.8	1.7
Ray	82.9	3 594	35.4	24.2	3.6	15.3	8.2	32.9	1 426	43	80	1 350	47.4	50.6	2.0
Reynolds	20.8	3 118	70.7	4.1	2.1	0.5	3.4	4.8	719	17	23	375	43.1	54.2	2.6
Ripley	26.6	1 894	72.9	5.2	4.9	0.0	4.4	1.2	88	51	49	642	33.5	63.5	3.0
St. Charles	1 188.4	3 223	54.5	2.1	6.5	0.1	9.4	1 722.2	4 671	688	1 304	15 254	44.7	54.4	1.0
St. Clair	44.1	4 651	28.5	34.9	1.9	0.0	5.3	16.1	1 703	33	33	543	37.8	59.8	2.4
Ste. Genevieve	38.8	2 184	67.5	3.0	6.6	0.0	7.8	28.1	1 581	27	62	928	56.4	42.3	1.3
St. Francois	177.6	2 694	64.6	4.1	6.8	0.1	6.3	112.4	1 705	127	210	5 636	47.0	51.6	1.4
St. Louis	3 854.3	3 853	55.7	1.6	7.0	0.9	5.2	4 175.7	4 174	5 788	3 523	49 982	59.5	39.6	0.9
Saline	61.1	2 617	55.2	5.4	6.9	0.3	7.5	7.5	323	84	77	1 891	47.8	50.4	1.8
Schuyler	11.1	2 542	46.7	3.1	1.3	22.3	14.5	7.8	1 793	30	15	315	39.1	57.4	3.5
Scotland	35.5	7 289	17.7	58.8	1.2	11.4	5.9	18.8	3 848	21	17	591	37.8	59.5	2.7
Scott	109.3	2 794	52.1	2.0	13.1	0.0	3.9	182.4	4 661	97	137	2 138	34.7	64.1	1.1
Shannon	12.9	1 551	60.4	0.2	2.3	0.0	12.2	2.7	326	15	29	305	42.7	54.1	3.3
Shelby	24.1	3 872	42.9	4.0	2.6	27.1	7.7	6.0	969	34	21	587	33.6	65.3	1.1
Stoddard	67.4	2 263	63.7	5.5	2.6	0.0	6.1	41.2	1 384	157	103	1 299	29.4	69.2	1.4
Stone	68.6	2 173	57.5	0.0	4.0	0.0	7.1	49.4	1 566	37	109	1 128	30.7	68.0	1.3
Sullivan	22.7	3 475	48.2	30.8	2.2	0.1	5.6	9.1	1 389	47	22	438	40.9	56.0	3.1
Taney	188.6	3 561	41.8	3.4	3.9	0.0	6.1	593.9	11 215	172	183	2 225	30.8	68.0	1.1
Texas	72.4	2 804	46.8	37.3	2.0	0.1	3.4	30.6	1 185	78	84	1 911	31.4	66.5	2.1
Vernon	45.8	2 207	64.9	3.0	3.5	0.0	7.3	60.2	2 903	101	71	1 720	38.1	60.1	1.8
Warren	69.9	2 135	57.6	4.6	6.2	0.0	5.1	59.4	1 815	48	116	1 270	43.0	55.7	1.3
Washington	67.0	2 707	40.1	31.2	3.2	0.0	3.6	32.6	1 201	51	85	1 542	49.0	48.9	2.0
Wayne	23.2	1 734	66.5	1.8	4.6	0.0	10.8	24.4	1 824	73	47	551	36.4	61.5	2.1
Webster	62.8	1 727	65.3	0.3	4.1	9.7	6.4	23.5	648	76	125	1 434	34.8	63.8	1.5
Worth	7.6	3 657	53.1	2.9	3.3	20.3	3.2	1.0	466	22	0	162	36.4	60.2	3.4
Wright	48.4	2 598	61.6	0.2	2.3	10.5	5.3	14.9	799	47	64	875	30.0	67.9	2.0

1. Based on the resident population estimated as of July 1 of the year shown. 2.

STATE/ County code	CBSA code[1]	County type[2]	STATE County	Land area,[3] (sq km) 2010	Population, 2014: Total persons 2014	Population, 2014: Rank	Population, 2014: Per square kilometer	Race alone or in combination, not Hispanic or Latino (percent): White	Black	American Indian, Alaska Native	Asian and Pacific Islander	Percent Hispanic or Latino[4]	Age (percent): Under 5 years	5 to 17 years	18 to 24 years	25 to 34 years	35 to 44 years	45 to 54 years
				1	2	3	4	5	6	7	8	9	10	11	12	13	14	15
			MISSOURI—Cont'd															
29 510	41180	1	St. Louis city	160	317 419	209	1 983.9	45.2	48.8	0.9	3.7	3.7	6.7	13.6	11.1	19.2	12.7	13.1
30 000	...	X	MONTANA	376 962	1 023 579	X	2.7	89.2	0.9	7.6	1.3	3.3	6.0	16.0	9.9	12.5	11.3	13.3
30 001	...	7	Beaverhead	14 353	9 345	2 483	0.7	93.2	0.6	2.5	1.6	3.7	4.7	13.7	14.2	10.0	9.7	12.7
30 003	...	6	Big Horn	12 938	13 282	2 221	1.0	32.1	0.6	63.9	0.9	5.0	10.3	23.1	10.0	11.8	10.1	12.2
30 005	...	9	Blaine	10 949	6 619	2 711	0.6	49.8	0.5	49.2	0.4	2.1	8.8	21.4	9.0	11.6	9.9	13.1
30 007	...	9	Broadwater	3 089	5 667	2 788	1.8	95.3	0.7	2.3	0.5	2.6	5.0	16.2	6.2	9.0	11.0	15.8
30 009	13740	3	Carbon	5 306	10 399	2 405	2.0	95.9	0.5	1.7	0.6	2.3	4.2	14.7	5.9	8.8	10.8	15.2
30 011	...	9	Carter	8 653	1 169	3 100	0.1	98.0	0.2	1.2	0.3	0.8	5.6	11.5	6.3	10.6	6.8	15.4
30 013	24500	3	Cascade	6 988	82 344	678	11.8	89.2	2.3	6.1	1.9	3.9	6.8	15.9	10.3	13.7	10.6	13.0
30 015	...	8	Chouteau	10 289	5 894	2 766	0.6	77.4	0.5	21.0	0.9	2.0	5.0	19.8	8.5	10.5	10.3	12.4
30 017	...	7	Custer	9 799	12 092	2 292	1.2	94.6	0.7	2.8	0.7	2.7	6.3	15.5	8.9	12.5	10.5	13.6
30 019	...	9	Daniels	3 694	1 793	3 070	0.5	95.3	0.7	3.3	0.5	2.0	6.0	14.5	6.2	9.8	8.9	12.4
30 021	...	7	Dawson	6 143	9 518	2 467	1.5	94.7	0.8	3.0	0.6	2.6	6.4	15.3	9.5	12.8	10.9	13.3
30 023	...	7	Deer Lodge	1 908	9 150	2 500	4.8	93.1	0.8	4.4	0.8	3.1	4.1	13.0	9.4	10.1	11.9	14.5
30 025	...	9	Fallon	4 198	3 108	2 965	0.7	96.7	0.7	1.3	1.0	1.5	7.9	16.9	7.6	12.5	11.0	12.8
30 027	...	7	Fergus	11 240	11 442	2 330	1.0	96.0	0.6	2.3	0.6	2.1	4.9	15.1	6.3	10.3	10.7	13.5
30 029	28060	5	Flathead	13 177	94 924	616	7.2	95.2	0.6	2.4	1.3	2.6	5.9	16.6	7.3	11.8	11.8	13.9
30 031	14580	5	Gallatin	6 741	97 308	605	14.4	94.2	0.7	1.7	2.0	3.1	6.0	14.7	16.1	16.2	12.8	11.7
30 033	...	9	Garfield	12 109	1 309	3 094	0.1	98.5	0.5	0.9	0.2	0.8	6.7	17.1	5.1	11.2	8.8	11.6
30 035	...	7	Glacier	7 759	13 696	2 193	1.8	35.3	0.4	64.4	0.6	2.3	9.4	22.0	10.0	13.1	10.4	13.1
30 037	13740	8	Golden Valley	3 044	852	3 115	0.3	94.3	0.2	2.4	1.5	4.0	3.6	16.8	6.3	8.4	9.1	14.6
30 039	...	8	Granite	4 474	3 209	2 957	0.7	96.7	0.6	1.9	0.6	2.0	3.8	12.0	4.7	7.6	8.9	14.3
30 041	...	7	Hill	7 508	16 596	2 001	2.2	73.7	0.9	24.3	1.3	3.1	8.2	18.8	10.7	13.1	10.7	12.0
30 043	25740	9	Jefferson	4 290	11 558	2 323	2.7	95.3	0.7	3.1	0.8	2.2	4.4	17.0	6.5	8.2	10.8	16.0
30 045	...	8	Judith Basin	4 843	1 991	3 050	0.4	96.8	0.3	1.6	0.6	1.5	4.3	14.2	6.8	7.8	9.2	17.1
30 047	...	6	Lake	3 859	29 099	1 452	7.5	72.9	0.7	28.2	1.1	4.0	6.5	17.8	8.1	10.2	10.2	12.7
30 049	25740	5	Lewis and Clark	8 958	65 856	801	7.4	93.8	0.9	3.5	1.3	2.8	5.9	16.0	8.5	12.6	11.5	14.2
30 051	...	9	Liberty	3 704	2 359	3 017	0.6	98.8	0.3	1.0	0.4	0.5	5.9	15.5	8.3	11.1	9.6	14.8
30 053	...	7	Lincoln	9 357	19 125	1 870	2.0	95.5	0.5	2.6	0.9	2.7	4.7	13.8	5.6	8.5	9.9	14.2
30 055	...	9	McCone	6 846	1 694	3 073	0.2	97.3	0.6	1.5	0.6	1.2	4.2	15.2	6.4	9.5	9.8	14.0
30 057	...	9	Madison	9 292	7 820	2 611	0.8	95.5	0.8	1.5	0.6	3.1	4.0	12.3	6.0	8.7	9.9	13.9
30 059	...	9	Meagher	6 195	1 853	3 065	0.3	96.9	0.6	1.4	0.7	1.8	5.9	12.8	6.9	9.1	8.6	13.0
30 061	...	8	Mineral	3 158	4 257	2 883	1.3	94.3	0.7	3.7	1.4	2.7	4.5	13.5	5.7	8.6	9.0	13.9
30 063	33540	3	Missoula	6 717	112 684	539	16.8	92.5	1.0	4.0	2.2	2.9	5.4	14.0	15.6	15.3	11.8	11.9
30 065	...	8	Musselshell	4 838	4 589	2 859	0.9	94.7	0.6	2.5	0.6	3.2	4.9	15.4	5.8	8.4	9.9	15.3
30 067	...	7	Park	7 260	15 880	2 051	2.2	95.6	0.5	2.1	0.9	2.6	5.0	14.1	5.8	10.4	12.8	15.4
30 069	...	9	Petroleum	4 286	485	3 137	0.1	98.4	0.0	1.6	0.0	1.0	4.0	19.8	6.5	7.7	8.9	16.2
30 071	...	9	Phillips	13 313	4 192	2 886	0.3	89.0	0.9	11.3	0.8	2.2	5.9	16.2	7.4	9.2	9.0	15.6
30 073	...	7	Pondera	4 203	6 219	2 740	1.5	83.0	0.8	15.9	0.8	1.9	6.6	18.1	7.4	10.9	10.1	13.5
30 075	...	9	Powder River	8 540	1 783	3 071	0.2	96.3	0.9	2.6	0.4	1.7	2.8	14.4	7.8	8.2	8.7	16.2
30 077	...	7	Powell	6 025	6 909	2 690	1.1	91.7	1.4	5.2	0.7	2.3	4.4	11.6	8.2	12.8	12.5	16.8
30 079	...	9	Prairie	4 498	1 148	3 102	0.3	96.6	1.3	2.5	1.4	2.0	6.3	11.4	4.8	8.7	9.8	11.0
30 081	...	6	Ravalli	6 192	41 030	1 152	6.6	94.7	0.6	2.0	1.2	3.2	4.9	15.8	6.5	9.3	10.5	14.0
30 083	...	7	Richland	5 398	11 576	2 319	2.1	93.0	0.8	3.0	0.8	4.6	7.2	17.0	9.1	13.1	12.1	14.2
30 085	...	7	Roosevelt	6 099	11 332	2 337	1.9	40.3	0.5	59.5	0.8	2.0	9.5	21.5	10.3	13.3	10.4	12.1
30 087	...	9	Rosebud	12 977	9 326	2 485	0.7	61.1	0.7	35.8	1.1	4.0	8.1	20.8	8.5	11.0	10.9	12.8
30 089	...	8	Sanders	7 150	11 364	2 332	1.6	92.8	0.6	6.0	0.7	2.6	4.4	13.7	5.9	7.9	9.3	12.9
30 091	...	9	Sheridan	4 344	3 696	2 928	0.9	95.6	0.8	2.8	1.0	1.9	5.1	14.9	6.7	11.1	9.8	13.3
30 093	15580	5	Silver Bow	1 861	34 680	1 312	18.6	93.1	0.6	3.0	1.1	4.0	5.8	14.9	11.7	11.4	10.8	13.8
30 095	...	8	Stillwater	4 650	9 290	2 488	2.0	95.2	0.6	1.8	0.9	3.2	4.6	17.1	6.5	8.5	11.4	14.5
30 097	...	9	Sweet Grass	4 805	3 665	2 929	0.8	96.9	0.5	1.6	1.0	1.7	4.3	18.0	6.5	8.6	10.6	12.9
30 099	...	8	Teton	5 885	6 064	2 754	1.0	96.7	0.4	2.9	0.5	1.4	5.9	17.3	7.1	9.8	10.1	13.8
30 101	...	7	Toole	4 962	5 150	2 829	1.0	90.5	1.1	6.6	1.0	2.9	5.1	14.9	8.5	13.6	11.9	15.6
30 103	...	8	Treasure	2 531	692	3 128	0.3	94.0	0.7	3.3	0.4	3.3	5.9	10.0	5.3	9.4	6.9	14.7
30 105	...	7	Valley	12 758	7 640	2 625	0.6	87.7	0.7	10.7	1.1	2.1	5.3	17.2	7.1	9.8	10.1	13.8
30 107	...	9	Wheatland	3 686	2 102	3 040	0.6	96.6	1.1	2.1	1.1	1.7	7.0	16.3	6.6	8.9	11.8	10.4
30 109	...	9	Wibaux	2 303	1 121	3 103	0.5	95.5	0.4	1.6	1.0	2.7	3.7	16.8	7.3	8.7	9.0	14.9
30 111	13740	3	Yellowstone	6 820	155 634	411	22.8	89.7	1.3	5.1	1.3	5.1	6.5	17.1	8.7	13.8	12.1	13.3
31 000	...	X	NEBRASKA	198 974	1 881 503	X	9.5	82.5	5.4	1.3	2.6	9.9	7.0	17.9	10.1	13.5	12.0	13.0
31 001	25580	5	Adams	1 459	31 457	1 400	21.6	88.8	1.3	0.7	1.8	8.5	6.3	17.1	11.8	11.6	10.7	13.2
31 003	...	9	Antelope	2 220	6 398	2 724	2.9	96.2	0.6	0.4	0.4	3.0	6.4	16.8	6.5	10.0	8.9	13.8
31 005	...	9	Arthur	1 853	453	3 138	0.2	93.9	0.2	1.1	0.4	5.3	7.9	20.5	5.5	9.0	13.1	10.7
31 007	42420	9	Banner	1 932	764	3 123	0.4	95.1	0.5	0.8	0.0	4.2	4.3	12.1	6.1	8.8	5.9	14.0

1. CBSA = Core Based Statistical Area. See Appendix A for explanation. See Appendix B for list of metropolitan areas with component counties. 2. County type code from the Economic Research Service of USDA Rural-Urban Continuum Codes. See Appendix A for definition. 3. Dry land or land partially or temporarily covered by water. 4. May be of any race.

STATE County	Population, 2013 (cont.) Age (percent) (cont.) 55 to 64 years	65 to 74 years	75 years and over	Percent female	Population change and components of change, 2000–2014 Total persons 2000	2010	Percent change 2000–2010	2010–2014	Components of change, 2010–2014 Births	Deaths	Net migration	Households, 2009–2013 Number	Persons per house-hold	Percent Family house-holds	Female family house-holder[1]	One per-son
	16	17	18	19	20	21	22	23	24	25	26	27	28	29	30	31
MISSOURI—Cont'd																
St. Louis city	12.5	6.0	5.2	51.6	348 189	319 294	-8.3	-0.6	20 186	12 652	-9 082	140 652	2.19	46.7	18.4	43.8
MONTANA	14.7	9.3	6.9	49.8	902 195	989 415	9.7	3.5	51 465	38 383	20 502	405 525	2.39	63.1	8.9	30.1
Beaverhead	15.7	11.3	8.1	48.8	9 202	9 246	0.5	1.1	394	313	7	4 110	2.11	58.1	7.7	34.4
Big Horn	11.6	6.8	4.1	50.3	12 671	12 865	1.5	3.2	1 141	523	-185	3 444	3.70	77.2	20.4	20.3
Blaine	12.3	7.5	6.6	50.4	7 009	6 491	-7.4	2.0	462	270	-65	2 237	2.86	66.4	18.6	28.4
Broadwater	16.9	12.2	7.6	49.2	4 385	5 612	28.0	0.9	233	212	25	2 421	2.32	70.3	9.9	26.6
Carbon	18.8	13.2	8.4	49.4	9 552	10 078	5.5	3.2	340	392	372	4 322	2.32	64.6	6.8	31.1
Carter	19.3	12.7	11.8	48.9	1 360	1 160	-14.7	0.8	45	55	17	495	2.46	68.7	7.1	28.7
Cascade	13.3	8.8	7.6	49.7	80 357	81 327	1.2	1.3	5 011	3 382	-545	33 430	2.37	63.8	9.7	31.3
Chouteau	15.5	9.7	8.3	50.7	5 970	5 813	-2.6	1.4	175	233	131	2 228	2.53	71.2	11.8	25.7
Custer	14.4	9.3	9.0	50.1	11 696	11 699	0.0	3.4	661	614	340	4 986	2.28	61.7	8.0	34.8
Daniels	16.7	11.4	14.1	50.5	2 017	1 751	-13.2	2.4	72	90	47	890	1.96	57.8	4.3	37.2
Dawson	15.0	8.5	8.2	48.7	9 059	8 966	-1.0	6.2	472	426	522	3 885	2.21	68.8	8.3	27.5
Deer Lodge	17.1	11.2	8.8	46.4	9 417	9 298	-1.3	-1.5	299	521	72	3 855	2.17	59.6	7.4	36.5
Fallon	15.5	7.4	8.4	48.5	2 837	2 890	1.9	7.5	207	116	134	1 199	2.53	69.4	7.9	28.9
Fergus	16.5	12.2	10.5	49.7	11 893	11 586	-2.6	-1.2	496	671	39	4 924	2.24	59.7	4.0	36.3
Flathead	16.1	9.8	6.6	50.1	74 471	90 928	22.1	4.4	4 680	3 273	2 508	36 901	2.45	66.3	8.1	28.2
Gallatin	11.8	6.4	4.3	48.5	67 831	89 513	32.0	8.7	4 706	2 214	5 118	36 973	2.36	59.9	6.3	27.6
Garfield	17.4	13.2	8.8	50.1	1 279	1 206	-5.7	8.3	53	43	77	465	2.44	68.8	8.0	27.3
Glacier	11.2	6.2	4.6	50.7	13 247	13 399	1.1	2.2	1 062	628	-147	4 194	3.10	68.8	19.0	26.8
Golden Valley	18.9	12.5	10.0	48.4	1 042	884	-15.2	-3.6	29	43	-14	323	2.12	63.5	9.0	33.1
Granite	20.3	17.2	11.2	49.8	2 830	3 079	8.8	4.2	77	133	165	1 473	2.07	67.2	5.4	25.5
Hill	13.1	7.4	6.0	49.5	16 673	16 096	-3.5	3.1	1 244	609	-162	6 139	2.58	66.3	9.8	28.1
Jefferson	19.5	12.1	5.5	49.1	10 049	11 406	13.5	1.3	381	446	202	4 527	2.46	71.2	4.9	22.8
Judith Basin	17.9	13.0	9.7	47.9	2 329	2 072	-11.0	-3.9	65	79	-75	879	2.32	60.9	3.1	34.6
Lake	15.5	11.5	7.6	50.9	26 507	28 746	8.4	1.2	1 574	1 119	-95	11 829	2.38	65.6	11.9	28.5
Lewis and Clark	15.8	9.2	6.3	50.7	55 716	63 395	13.8	3.9	3 167	2 347	1 625	26 555	2.35	62.3	8.4	31.0
Liberty	14.9	9.1	10.8	52.0	2 158	2 339	8.4	0.9	93	92	17	847	2.53	66.4	3.4	31.5
Lincoln	19.7	15.1	8.5	49.4	18 837	19 687	4.5	-2.9	761	947	-369	8 872	2.18	60.9	6.4	34.2
McCone	18.4	11.1	11.4	49.2	1 977	1 734	-12.3	-2.3	49	67	-26	760	2.34	68.2	2.9	30.1
Madison	20.6	15.5	9.3	48.2	6 851	7 691	12.3	1.7	245	296	155	3 542	2.10	62.1	3.7	34.8
Meagher	18.5	14.5	10.6	48.9	1 932	1 891	-2.1	-2.0	88	107	-29	716	2.62	63.0	9.9	32.7
Mineral	19.3	15.8	9.8	47.7	3 884	4 223	8.7	0.8	188	182	4	1 629	2.53	59.5	7.2	32.2
Missoula	12.9	7.9	5.2	49.8	95 802	109 299	14.1	3.1	5 163	3 359	1 597	45 523	2.36	57.6	9.2	30.1
Musselshell	19.9	12.8	7.7	50.1	4 497	4 538	0.9	1.1	176	224	110	1 966	2.36	69.3	3.5	28.7
Park	17.5	11.5	7.4	50.0	15 694	15 636	-0.4	1.6	603	590	243	6 445	2.39	60.1	7.0	35.4
Petroleum	17.0	11.3	8.7	46.6	493	494	0.2	-1.8	14	15	-13	233	2.31	66.5	1.3	32.6
Phillips	16.0	10.2	10.3	50.3	4 601	4 253	-7.6	-1.4	198	218	-29	1 800	2.28	67.0	5.7	30.5
Pondera	14.1	9.6	9.6	51.2	6 424	6 153	-4.2	1.1	307	277	41	2 302	2.52	68.0	6.2	29.0
Powder River	18.1	12.1	11.7	49.5	1 858	1 743	-6.2	2.3	42	85	78	720	2.26	67.4	9.7	30.0
Powell	15.8	10.6	7.3	38.4	7 180	7 027	-2.1	-1.7	214	306	-15	2 411	2.31	63.5	9.6	29.5
Prairie	19.6	16.7	11.7	49.4	1 199	1 179	-1.7	-2.6	58	70	-21	502	2.31	65.3	6.2	32.7
Ravalli	17.2	13.2	8.8	50.3	36 070	40 212	11.5	2.0	1 621	1 757	870	16 848	2.37	65.1	8.0	29.1
Richland	14.1	7.5	5.7	47.9	9 667	9 746	0.8	18.8	619	400	1 599	4 270	2.40	64.3	6.6	31.8
Roosevelt	12.1	6.0	4.9	50.4	10 620	10 425	-1.8	8.7	961	574	511	3 264	3.21	64.4	16.9	31.7
Rosebud	14.8	8.1	4.9	49.4	9 383	9 233	-1.6	1.0	713	348	-284	3 268	2.82	69.0	11.3	27.8
Sanders	20.4	15.8	9.6	49.1	10 227	11 413	11.6	-0.4	416	517	46	5 149	2.17	65.2	6.9	29.9
Sheridan	17.7	10.0	11.2	48.8	4 105	3 384	-17.6	9.2	156	240	388	1 612	2.09	64.1	7.5	32.8
Silver Bow	14.6	9.3	7.7	49.2	34 606	34 200	-1.2	1.4	1 671	1 707	501	15 042	2.21	56.2	11.4	36.2
Stillwater	18.5	11.5	7.4	49.1	8 195	9 117	11.3	1.9	361	338	142	3 757	2.40	74.6	4.2	22.8
Sweet Grass	16.2	12.5	10.5	50.0	3 609	3 651	1.2	0.4	127	161	42	1 304	2.73	71.9	3.1	26.4
Teton	14.6	11.2	10.3	50.8	6 445	6 073	-5.8	-0.1	316	277	-51	2 303	2.52	66.9	5.2	30.1
Toole	14.9	8.1	7.4	43.9	5 267	5 324	1.1	-3.3	240	184	-239	1 927	2.30	67.9	10.6	28.6
Treasure	20.7	13.9	13.3	48.9	861	718	-16.6	-3.6	27	26	-27	332	2.14	66.9	5.1	33.1
Valley	16.1	9.9	10.7	49.7	7 675	7 369	-4.0	3.7	342	325	270	3 248	2.25	62.3	8.4	36.2
Wheatland	16.4	12.8	9.8	50.5	2 259	2 168	-4.0	-3.0	99	87	-81	817	2.50	64.3	1.1	35.1
Wibaux	16.2	10.2	13.3	49.8	1 068	1 017	-4.8	10.2	42	55	111	409	2.22	66.7	4.6	30.1
Yellowstone	13.5	8.2	6.8	51.0	129 352	147 972	14.4	5.2	8 509	5 800	4 848	61 023	2.40	63.5	10.9	29.5
NEBRASKA	12.4	7.4	6.7	50.2	1 711 263	1 826 341	6.7	3.0	109 785	63 958	10 030	725 787	2.47	65.0	9.8	28.8
Adams	13.2	8.3	7.8	49.9	31 151	31 364	0.7	0.3	1 708	1 273	-357	12 578	2.37	63.8	7.4	28.4
Antelope	15.6	10.5	11.4	50.4	7 452	6 685	-10.3	-4.3	344	295	-311	2 855	2.28	72.1	6.5	26.0
Arthur	12.7	10.7	10.0	50.9	444	460	3.6	-1.5	17	15	-6	177	2.86	64.4	11.3	33.3
Banner	17.4	17.8	13.6	47.8	819	690	-15.8	10.7	26	14	16	330	2.47	73.0	5.8	22.7

1. No spouse present.

STATE County	Persons in group quarters, 2014	Daytime population, 2009–2013: Number	Daytime population, 2009–2013: Employment/residence ratio	Births, 2014: Total	Births, 2014: Rate[1]	Deaths, 2014: Number	Deaths, 2014: Rate[1]	Persons under 65 with no health insurance, 2013: Number	Persons under 65 with no health insurance, 2013: Percent	Medicare, 2014: Eligible for Medicare	Medicare, 2014: Enrolled in Medicare Advantage	Medicare, 2014: Enrolled in a Medicare prescription drug plan	Serious crimes known to police,[2] 2013: Total: Number	Serious crimes known to police,[2] 2013: Total: Rate[3]
	32	33	34	35	36	37	38	39	40	41	42	43	44	45
MISSOURI—Cont'd														
St. Louis city	12 024	430 525	1.78	4 601	14.5	3 038	9.6	50 290	18.4	48 945	16 362	21 805	26 888	8 440
MONTANA	28 887	996 181	0.99	12 243	12.0	9 089	8.9	166 750	20.0	196 751	5 444	89 786	28 520	2 809
Beaverhead	443	9 117	0.96	92	9.8	85	9.1	1 629	22.9	2 032	224	1 015	73	774
Big Horn	137	13 177	1.05	261	19.7	136	10.2	3 311	28.5	1 711	109	795	16	121
Blaine	220	6 615	1.03	108	16.3	63	9.5	1 652	29.1	1 055	81	549	15	271
Broadwater	52	4 891	0.69	52	9.2	46	8.1	1 038	23.0	1 288	237	505	92	1 579
Carbon	53	8 498	0.68	77	7.4	79	7.6	1 903	23.6	2 430	495	1 109	102	1 000
Carter	11	1 182	0.91	8	6.8	12	10.3	257	29.2	289	21	170	1	84
Cascade	2 546	81 985	1.01	1 169	14.2	763	9.3	12 026	17.9	16 359	3 727	6 174	3 172	3 859
Chouteau	135	5 383	0.82	39	6.6	60	10.2	1 278	26.8	1 144	165	622	NA	NA
Custer	412	11 768	1.00	163	13.5	150	12.4	1 734	18.3	2 466	278	1 306	204	1 698
Daniels	41	1 808	1.03	16	8.9	18	10.0	213	16.0	438	11	309	8	442
Dawson	498	8 918	0.95	108	11.3	86	9.0	1 195	16.0	1 696	70	1 150	278	2 956
Deer Lodge	845	9 183	0.98	70	7.7	114	12.5	1 352	19.6	2 334	231	1 163	225	2 433
Fallon	34	3 203	1.07	47	15.1	27	8.7	396	15.3	521	13	354	12	389
Fergus	465	11 437	0.99	123	10.7	152	13.3	1 801	20.7	2 883	573	1 224	206	1 800
Flathead	992	91 190	0.99	1 106	11.7	786	8.3	16 196	21.0	19 564	4 251	8 222	2 645	2 864
Gallatin	3 264	91 218	0.99	1 152	11.8	539	5.5	13 867	17.0	12 272	2 302	5 050	2 090	2 266
Garfield	0	1 156	1.02	12	9.2	10	7.6	319	32.0	266	14	175	4	309
Glacier	690	13 779	1.06	245	17.9	155	11.3	3 660	29.8	1 838	58	907	164	1 182
Golden Valley	89	599	0.64	9	10.6	8	9.4	204	30.8	265	54	115	5	603
Granite	40	2 889	0.83	17	5.3	30	9.3	585	26.2	852	105	397	36	1 148
Hill	593	16 708	1.06	306	18.4	147	8.9	3 167	22.5	2 781	247	1 675	713	4 315
Jefferson	230	9 198	0.56	88	7.6	119	10.3	1 608	17.2	2 424	402	926	107	934
Judith Basin	0	1 905	0.85	16	8.0	16	8.0	409	26.4	500	127	190	11	544
Lake	585	28 104	0.93	376	12.9	287	9.9	6 672	28.6	6 358	1 099	2 859	809	2 770
Lewis and Clark	1 946	66 853	1.08	750	11.4	570	8.7	8 165	15.1	12 514	2 224	4 596	1 886	2 874
Liberty	403	2 413	1.06	19	8.1	19	8.1	413	21.9	410	11	305	NA	NA
Lincoln	209	19 502	0.99	178	9.3	234	12.2	3 441	23.4	6 278	1 653	2 694	264	1 352
McCone	19	1 707	0.91	12	7.1	13	7.7	411	31.4	316	NA	233	9	530
Madison	163	7 443	0.93	53	6.8	59	7.5	1 246	21.6	2 028	201	993	65	834
Meagher	174	1 870	0.96	17	9.2	22	11.9	383	26.6	536	NA	302	27	1 387
Mineral	22	4 018	0.86	43	10.1	34	8.0	731	23.1	1 221	214	575	1	24
Missoula	3 638	114 398	1.07	1 219	10.8	794	7.0	17 993	19.1	18 636	2 874	8 867	3 782	3 375
Musselshell	52	4 495	0.88	39	8.5	53	11.5	891	24.4	1 194	168	611	114	2 409
Park	108	14 833	0.89	141	8.9	139	8.8	2 785	22.0	3 416	545	1 649	164	1 049
Petroleum	0	616	1.30	2	4.1	2	4.1	97	24.0	91	12	47	NA	NA
Phillips	127	4 048	0.91	49	11.7	44	10.5	899	27.2	936	51	576	62	1 510
Pondera	646	5 813	0.87	71	11.4	60	9.6	1 286	25.7	1 283	208	697	45	726
Powder River	35	1 689	1.02	14	7.9	15	8.4	321	24.3	379	58	178	NA	NA
Powell	1 539	7 297	1.09	41	5.9	72	10.4	952	22.2	1 452	171	630	122	1 704
Prairie	21	1 096	0.81	16	13.9	9	7.8	205	24.4	360	40	206	1	87
Ravalli	480	36 534	0.77	378	9.2	430	10.5	7 479	23.6	10 853	2 212	4 257	562	1 405
Richland	34	10 332	1.00	167	14.4	93	8.0	1 631	16.8	1 734	NA	1 212	125	1 111
Roosevelt	185	11 074	1.11	243	21.4	168	14.8	2 647	26.7	1 522	27	886	198	1 976
Rosebud	65	9 990	1.17	173	18.6	99	10.6	1 788	22.1	1 551	157	768	65	685
Sanders	188	11 080	0.92	111	9.8	121	10.6	2 503	30.0	3 466	570	1 512	148	1 290
Sheridan	85	3 515	1.02	41	11.1	57	15.4	527	18.3	886	37	638	87	2 371
Silver Bow	998	34 135	0.99	377	10.9	399	11.5	4 851	17.4	7 146	1 015	3 553	1 419	4 097
Stillwater	112	8 737	0.90	86	9.3	82	8.8	1 199	15.9	2 000	423	913	135	1 456
Sweet Grass	45	3 776	1.08	35	9.5	34	9.3	568	20.2	837	110	424	47	1 299
Teton	461	5 871	0.93	79	13.0	62	10.2	1 091	23.1	1 404	411	603	60	988
Toole	766	5 531	1.14	51	9.9	45	8.7	741	20.0	862	58	493	148	2 842
Treasure	0	661	0.86	6	8.7	4	5.8	134	26.4	203	12	124	NA	NA
Valley	126	7 410	0.98	88	11.5	71	9.3	1 412	23.5	1 771	51	1 085	106	1 397
Wheatland	147	2 160	1.03	26	12.4	15	7.1	458	27.9	513	67	249	5	238
Wibaux	24	853	0.83	14	12.5	10	8.9	211	24.7	245	NA	172	2	185
Yellowstone	3 694	152 520	1.03	2 044	13.1	1 372	8.8	22 818	17.8	26 942	5 444	12 777	7 012	4 559
NEBRASKA	52 101	1 858 618	1.02	25 961	13.8	14 658	7.8	201 408	12.9	308 030	NA	181 940	53 915	2 885
Adams	1 472	31 655	1.02	411	13.1	303	9.6	3 189	12.6	6 265	263	4 276	1 090	3 453
Antelope	67	6 083	0.84	84	13.1	63	9.8	715	14.3	1 495	NA	1 138	19	383
Arthur	0	464	0.80	2	4.4	5	11.0	89	24.7	109	NA	74	1	202
Banner	0	661	0.62	7	9.2	4	5.2	128	24.9	218	12	131	NA	NA

1. Per 1,000 estimated resident population. 2. Data for serious crimes have not been adjusted for underreporting; this may affect comparability between geographic areas and over time.
3. Per 100,000 population estimated by the FBI.

STATE County	Serious crimes known to police, 2013 (cont.)[1] Rate[2] Violent	Serious crimes known to police, 2013 (cont.)[1] Rate[2] Property	Education: School enrollment and attainment, 2009–2013 Enrollment[3] Total	Education: School enrollment and attainment, 2009–2013 Enrollment[3] Percent private	Education: Attainment[4] (percent) High school graduate or less	Education: Attainment[4] (percent) Bachelor's degree or more	Education: Local government expenditures,[5] 2012–2013 Total current spending (mil dol)	Education: Local government expenditures,[5] 2012–2013 Current spending per student (dollars)	Money income, 2009–2013 Per capita income[6] (dollars)	Money income, 2009–2013 Households Median income (dollars)	Money income, 2009–2013 Households Mean income (dollars)	Money income, 2009–2013 Households Percent with income of $200,000 or more	Income and poverty, 2013 Median household income (dollars)	Income and poverty, 2013 Percent below poverty level All persons	Income and poverty, 2013 Percent below poverty level Children under 18 years	Income and poverty, 2013 Percent below poverty level Children 5 to 17 years in families
	46	47	48	49	50	51	52	53	54	55	56	57	58	59	60	61
MISSOURI—Cont'd																
St. Louis city	1 621	6 820	84 017	32.6	41.9	29.6	349.9	10 810	23 048	34 582	50 431	1.8	34 346	27.2	43.1	43.0
MONTANA	253	2 557	238 914	12.6	37.9	28.7	1 527.0	10 625	25 373	46 230	60 639	2.4	46 893	16.1	20.8	19.3
Beaverhead	106	668	2 677	6.3	38.0	27.2	12.9	11 077	22 872	41 614	50 612	0.6	40 054	17.1	24.7	23.2
Big Horn	30	91	3 631	3.4	49.3	15.5	37.0	15 916	15 695	39 966	53 128	1.7	38 026	27.6	36.5	34.6
Blaine	90	181	1 642	4.1	45.8	15.9	17.8	14 167	17 437	37 151	47 895	1.9	35 215	28.2	33.9	33.6
Broadwater	378	1 201	1 155	13.7	51.6	19.4	6.3	9 759	24 270	45 932	57 095	3.2	46 246	13.3	18.4	16.7
Carbon	78	922	1 862	7.3	41.0	27.6	16.8	12 184	27 599	47 831	62 104	1.8	46 413	12.6	16.5	14.4
Carter	0	84	218	21.1	45.3	16.4	2.3	18 950	24 921	39 659	56 322	2.2	39 017	15.5	22.6	24.4
Cascade	255	3 604	18 766	13.3	40.1	24.6	109.4	9 502	24 727	44 963	58 185	2.2	43 674	15.7	21.7	20.8
Chouteau	NA	NA	1 491	11.1	42.5	22.9	10.1	15 781	21 737	40 070	55 158	2.5	41 177	21.8	28.8	24.3
Custer	158	1 540	2 588	10.0	40.5	19.7	16.0	9 700	23 910	43 524	54 722	1.8	43 958	12.8	17.1	16.6
Daniels	110	331	249	14.9	36.5	22.9	3.2	12 270	31 449	46 100	61 812	2.1	51 400	9.3	10.5	10.5
Dawson	223	2 733	1 965	8.8	40.3	18.1	14.7	10 970	26 126	50 405	60 578	1.7	50 650	11.9	14.5	14.6
Deer Lodge	292	2 141	1 806	11.5	47.1	18.1	11.4	10 451	22 052	38 958	49 895	1.5	37 542	17.7	25.3	23.9
Fallon	65	324	649	4.8	49.5	16.1	9.4	17 809	28 563	51 164	69 218	3.7	59 083	7.8	10.8	11.0
Fergus	411	1 390	2 213	13.4	42.9	25.5	20.8	12 988	24 429	38 344	52 455	1.7	41 111	14.4	19.5	18.6
Flathead	257	2 608	20 099	16.3	36.9	28.4	126.6	9 340	25 790	46 581	61 661	2.9	46 885	16.7	22.4	21.3
Gallatin	176	2 091	27 740	11.3	23.7	46.0	107.3	9 172	28 939	52 833	70 089	3.6	56 680	14.0	13.0	11.7
Garfield	77	232	229	7.0	54.0	13.0	2.2	11 281	25 921	45 096	59 060	1.5	38 663	17.3	24.4	22.4
Glacier	216	966	4 344	7.6	43.8	18.4	37.3	13 673	15 604	33 519	46 178	0.9	33 648	31.0	37.9	34.6
Golden Valley	483	121	112	0.9	53.5	20.3	2.6	18 978	23 508	39 313	47 225	0.3	36 747	19.6	31.5	29.5
Granite	0	1 148	537	11.9	45.7	26.5	4.9	13 013	26 277	45 236	55 266	1.9	41 391	15.9	24.4	20.5
Hill	496	3 819	4 369	8.9	34.7	22.6	38.5	12 335	21 376	43 726	55 144	0.9	43 244	18.5	22.9	21.6
Jefferson	175	759	2 481	16.2	34.9	33.5	15.8	10 156	30 397	60 863	74 750	4.0	59 001	10.5	13.8	12.1
Judith Basin	99	445	365	2.7	40.2	29.7	4.7	18 561	24 260	41 932	53 403	0.9	41 731	14.3	20.5	18.5
Lake	479	2 291	6 504	11.4	40.8	24.8	47.9	11 018	21 521	38 019	52 079	1.3	39 219	20.3	30.7	28.6
Lewis and Clark	293	2 581	15 421	21.3	28.8	37.5	93.5	9 846	28 400	56 243	66 949	2.0	53 982	12.6	16.2	14.9
Liberty	NA	NA	358	14.5	46.8	20.6	3.1	12 725	25 522	44 493	69 271	6.3	39 073	23.0	26.7	24.4
Lincoln	184	1 168	3 744	19.2	47.7	18.3	26.3	10 767	21 719	33 333	47 027	1.9	34 926	17.6	31.3	29.2
McCone	0	530	288	3.1	51.8	18.6	2.9	11 805	27 161	46 667	61 974	2.9	41 918	15.5	21.3	18.5
Madison	154	680	1 414	18.9	36.0	32.7	13.0	15 241	33 062	47 762	70 937	4.2	44 046	12.2	17.6	16.0
Meagher	103	1 285	404	8.2	50.1	17.4	2.9	13 013	20 288	38 182	48 097	1.4	35 694	19.6	31.2	32.0
Mineral	24	0	663	10.3	56.3	12.1	8.8	14 407	19 859	33 033	45 682	2.2	36 169	18.1	31.0	28.9
Missoula	310	3 066	31 604	9.4	29.1	39.1	136.0	10 192	25 764	46 117	61 057	2.7	45 895	17.4	18.8	16.9
Musselshell	254	2 156	966	9.7	54.3	13.6	7.3	10 425	23 022	43 409	53 875	0.9	39 403	17.0	28.6	27.1
Park	205	844	3 130	17.1	37.6	33.6	22.0	11 392	24 611	42 426	55 546	2.6	42 439	13.8	18.9	17.7
Petroleum	NA	NA	100	8.0	51.6	15.4	1.4	15 337	22 714	41 705	50 959	3.4	37 276	14.8	18.3	13.9
Phillips	219	1 291	846	6.3	50.2	15.9	10.9	16 548	22 890	42 632	53 043	0.9	40 202	18.1	24.3	22.9
Pondera	97	629	1 439	13.4	42.2	20.5	13.4	14 114	22 256	41 277	57 767	1.5	40 694	20.1	28.9	26.4
Powder River	NA	NA	335	7.5	37.4	19.9	4.1	15 648	28 528	46 250	63 245	4.3	43 107	12.4	15.0	12.7
Powell	182	1 523	1 189	18.6	47.5	17.8	10.7	14 551	19 736	40 802	51 114	1.1	39 820	20.0	24.5	23.3
Prairie	0	87	173	4.0	55.0	16.9	2.0	14 180	20 644	38 036	45 275	1.0	41 843	12.7	21.2	21.6
Ravalli	165	1 240	8 380	13.6	42.1	24.5	53.1	9 519	22 872	38 688	53 430	1.9	39 487	19.8	26.1	23.9
Richland	204	907	2 071	3.8	44.1	17.7	24.5	12 555	32 036	58 112	77 099	6.1	64 171	7.7	10.1	9.9
Roosevelt	619	1 357	2 762	3.1	55.2	13.7	36.2	14 905	16 888	36 920	48 975	1.0	34 291	26.6	37.8	36.0
Rosebud	126	559	2 329	7.3	42.7	22.3	28.0	16 700	22 229	48 789	59 830	1.5	50 597	19.5	26.9	25.8
Sanders	183	1 107	2 015	22.7	53.3	16.7	19.1	13 735	19 188	32 881	42 930	0.5	34 847	21.9	31.6	30.0
Sheridan	599	1 771	751	10.3	35.2	23.4	8.6	15 610	31 378	48 667	67 392	4.0	50 292	10.4	13.1	12.0
Silver Bow	251	3 846	8 110	10.5	47.1	22.2	42.0	9 501	23 562	38 659	52 218	1.6	40 691	20.0	25.9	25.4
Stillwater	216	1 240	1 948	12.4	44.7	22.1	16.1	11 220	28 868	57 906	69 187	2.1	58 109	9.5	12.0	10.3
Sweet Grass	193	1 106	840	11.2	47.1	27.1	6.3	11 495	22 743	45 938	58 399	1.4	43 146	12.2	16.0	13.5
Teton	33	955	1 268	16.7	41.9	24.5	13.6	11 845	22 799	43 327	55 675	1.2	43 828	15.1	19.2	17.5
Toole	538	2 304	1 038	13.3	45.8	14.6	9.2	12 860	23 162	46 972	58 128	2.1	44 252	16.9	18.6	16.5
Treasure	NA	NA	119	1.7	46.4	21.3	1.5	16 591	23 948	37 105	49 875	0.9	48 282	11.3	19.1	21.7
Valley	158	1 238	1 535	6.8	45.9	17.1	16.2	13 089	25 685	47 181	57 725	1.6	45 747	13.3	18.8	17.4
Wheatland	95	143	279	14.0	57.6	19.2	4.8	14 570	17 336	31 867	44 042	0.0	32 519	19.7	30.2	30.0
Wibaux	0	185	171	16.4	47.7	19.6	2.3	14 400	27 492	41 875	59 781	2.4	43 722	11.0	17.3	14.7
Yellowstone	325	4 234	35 532	14.1	38.7	28.7	212.3	9 311	27 761	51 342	67 055	2.9	52 079	12.9	15.8	14.1
NEBRASKA	262	2 623	510 425	17.3	37.7	28.5	3 513.1	11 579	26 899	51 672	67 023	3.0	51 502	12.9	17.1	15.0
Adams	177	3 276	8 924	21.4	42.1	20.4	65.3	12 916	25 571	49 440	63 513	2.6	52 267	11.4	16.2	14.3
Antelope	60	322	1 378	10.4	48.3	16.7	23.1	20 778	25 186	43 518	58 434	2.3	48 814	12.8	18.4	17.4
Arthur	0	202	137	10.9	26.5	31.7	1.8	18 330	17 656	40 568	45 886	1.1	39 874	9.2	15.4	15.1
Banner	NA	NA	180	17.8	35.0	15.8	2.9	20 743	25 814	36 875	62 160	3.3	46 769	12.3	21.6	21.7

1. Data for serious crimes have not been adjusted for underreporting; this may affect comparability between geographic areas and over time. 2. Per 100,000 population estimated by the FBI.
3. All persons 3 years old and over enrolled in nursery school through college. 4. Persons 25 years old and over. 5. Elementary and secondary education expenditures.
6. Based on population estimated by the American Community Survey, 2009–2013.

STATE County	Personal income, 2013										Earnings, 2013		
			Per capita[1]			Supplements to wages and salaries; employer contributions (mil dol)						Contributions for government social insurance (mil dol)	
	Total (mil dol)	Percent change, 2012–2013	Dollars	Rank	Wages and salaries (mil dol)	Pension and insurance	Government social insurance	Proprietors' income (mil dol)	Dividends, interest, and rent (mil dol)	Personal transfer receipts (mil dol)	Total (mil dol)	From employee and self-employed	From employer
	62	63	64	65	66	67	68	69	70	71	72	73	74
MISSOURI—Cont'd													
St. Louis city	12 152	1.0	38 163	1 414	13 410	2 235	979	1 391	1 730	3 057	18 015	1 017	979
MONTANA	39 963	1.5	39 366	X	17 598	3 095	1 634	4 139	9 406	7 344	26 466	1 681	1 634
Beaverhead	342	3.9	36 620	1 649	129	26	11	28	97	75	194	12	11
Big Horn	374	-1.4	28 650	2 830	181	40	15	24	66	102	261	15	15
Blaine	203	-1.0	30 775	2 582	54	14	5	43	47	50	116	5	5
Broadwater	162	-0.1	28 447	2 854	45	9	4	15	39	41	73	5	4
Carbon	399	2.4	38 623	1 348	86	16	8	30	115	76	139	11	8
Carter	39	-3.4	33 215	2 225	10	2	1	7	10	8	20	1	1
Cascade	3 358	0.5	40 759	1 083	1 493	291	142	290	789	647	2 216	138	142
Chouteau	219	-6.1	37 501	1 506	44	9	4	39	70	38	96	5	4
Custer	466	2.0	39 005	1 300	224	38	20	46	96	88	329	21	20
Daniels	104	-12.1	57 872	139	24	5	2	41	21	15	71	3	2
Dawson	343	-1.9	36 339	1 684	170	28	17	19	71	65	235	16	17
Deer Lodge	311	2.6	33 298	2 207	116	22	10	13	63	85	162	12	10
Fallon	156	-0.6	50 652	344	100	13	8	25	26	18	146	9	8
Fergus	443	1.2	38 483	1 375	155	31	15	59	126	91	260	17	15
Flathead	3 614	3.2	38 832	1 315	1 509	236	149	414	922	702	2 308	156	149
Gallatin	3 852	2.3	40 670	1 091	1 846	310	172	458	992	440	2 786	169	172
Garfield	42	1.9	32 836	2 276	10	3	1	8	14	8	21	1	1
Glacier	444	-1.2	32 340	2 362	171	40	15	65	88	113	292	15	15
Golden Valley	42	1.4	48 950	419	6	2	0	5	15	8	12	1	0
Granite	109	1.9	34 728	1 945	27	6	3	12	33	27	47	4	3
Hill	658	-2.0	39 719	1 199	292	56	29	66	147	131	444	27	29
Jefferson	508	2.1	44 121	747	96	19	9	70	108	83	193	13	9
Judith Basin	88	3.1	43 553	794	16	4	1	21	26	15	42	2	1
Lake	907	2.4	31 264	2 514	277	58	25	62	245	256	423	30	25
Lewis and Clark	2 739	1.6	41 927	945	1 518	300	134	176	592	449	2 128	130	134
Liberty	94	-2.5	39 505	1 230	18	4	2	27	34	14	50	2	2
Lincoln	588	1.0	30 216	2 652	180	37	18	41	137	207	277	23	18
McCone	68	2.5	40 070	1 167	24	5	2	13	16	9	43	2	2
Madison	314	5.5	40 757	1 085	128	19	14	29	90	62	190	13	14
Meagher	67	1.8	34 424	2 005	17	3	2	5	21	20	28	2	2
Mineral	126	2.8	29 371	2 768	35	8	3	10	24	45	56	5	3
Missoula	4 181	1.7	37 397	1 520	2 156	376	204	343	953	719	3 078	196	204
Musselshell	170	1.1	36 763	1 630	63	10	5	7	43	43	85	6	5
Park	633	2.0	40 353	1 126	180	29	18	43	199	118	271	19	18
Petroleum	17	-6.7	33 300	2 206	4	1	0	4	4	3	9	0	0
Phillips	164	-3.7	39 126	1 276	48	10	4	35	40	35	97	5	4
Pondera	246	-1.3	39 682	1 207	64	12	6	49	72	50	131	8	6
Powder River	61	10.4	34 826	1 926	22	4	2	7	15	10	35	2	2
Powell	218	2.1	31 124	2 530	92	22	8	9	54	52	132	8	8
Prairie	40	-8.4	34 333	2 024	11	3	1	2	12	11	17	1	1
Ravalli	1 400	2.4	34 301	2 032	364	69	35	98	417	348	566	44	35
Richland	712	7.0	63 458	72	380	50	34	97	141	61	560	33	34
Roosevelt	374	-0.1	33 658	2 151	150	32	13	42	68	93	236	14	13
Rosebud	352	-2.0	37 748	1 469	200	43	18	21	58	71	281	16	18
Sanders	325	2.0	28 601	2 837	85	19	9	26	83	116	138	12	9
Sheridan	218	4.6	59 514	113	74	12	7	57	53	28	150	7	7
Silver Bow	1 555	2.6	45 047	685	633	116	58	371	234	289	1 178	76	58
Stillwater	392	6.3	42 018	935	207	29	16	20	86	64	273	18	16
Sweet Grass	120	5.0	32 703	2 305	74	11	6	7	47	26	98	7	6
Teton	286	1.0	47 165	542	68	14	6	48	102	47	136	8	6
Toole	256	-3.7	49 818	373	91	19	8	73	61	33	191	10	8
Treasure	34	-4.4	48 829	427	6	1	0	9	11	6	17	1	0
Valley	350	-4.6	45 829	629	122	23	12	56	91	64	214	12	12
Wheatland	69	-0.4	32 507	2 328	19	4	2	9	21	17	33	2	2
Wibaux	36	5.5	32 466	2 341	12	3	1	6	8	7	21	1	1
Yellowstone	6 573	1.4	42 635	878	3 475	528	320	540	1 392	1 043	4 863	314	320
NEBRASKA	88 114	3.4	47 157	X	41 749	7 179	3 162	14 812	16 805	12 277	66 902	3 625	3 162
Adams	1 358	0.3	42 960	844	583	106	44	195	325	236	928	51	44
Antelope	530	3.3	82 149	19	78	15	5	290	84	54	388	12	5
Arthur	16	19.4	35 808	1 780	5	1	0	1	5	3	7	0	0
Banner	41	11.6	54 032	234	8	1	1	16	5	6	26	1	1

1. Based on the resident population estimated as of July 1 of the year shown.

STATE County	Earnings, 2013 (cont.) — Percent by selected industries: Farm	Mining	Construction	Manu- facturing	Infor- mation: professional, scientific, technical services	Retail trade	Finance, insur- ance, real estate and leasing	Health care and social assistance	Govern- ment	Social Security beneficiaries, December 2013: Number	Rate[1]	Supple- mental Security Income recipients, December 2013	Housing units, 2014: Total	Percent change, 2010– 2014
	75	76	77	78	79	80	81	82	83	84	85	86	87	88
MISSOURI—Cont'd														
St. Louis city	0.0	0.0	D	8.9	16.2	1.8	8.4	15.4	15.2	54 345	171	17 297	175 355	-0.4
MONTANA	3.1	4.7	7.6	4.1	7.8	8.1	6.1	13.3	20.7	208 546	205	18 673	491 531	1.8
Beaverhead	8.7	D	6.8	1.3	3.4	7.6	6.8	D	28.2	2 200	236	122	5 254	-0.4
Big Horn	8.4	20.7	D	D	1.8	4.1	1.8	D	42.7	2 030	155	354	4 661	-0.7
Blaine	32.2	1.2	3.0	0.9	D	5.6	D	D	34.8	1 155	175	221	2 814	-1.0
Broadwater	12.4	5.0	D	D	D	6.0	D	5.8	17.8	1 365	240	81	2 697	0.0
Carbon	2.4	5.2	11.6	1.5	6.7	7.1	6.1	8.4	22.8	2 610	253	104	6 463	0.4
Carter	38.7	0.0	D	0.0	D	4.6	D	D	20.7	295	252	0	808	-0.2
Cascade	0.9	D	6.3	2.9	6.7	8.6	6.5	16.2	28.3	17 560	213	1 884	37 565	0.8
Chouteau	39.5	0.0	3.1	0.9	D	5.1	4.1	D	21.0	1 220	208	65	2 858	-0.7
Custer	4.9	D	5.3	1.1	3.5	10.0	6.6	13.2	20.1	2 565	215	251	5 622	1.1
Daniels	46.5	D	5.2	D	D	3.3	3.2	D	8.3	470	264	12	1 115	0.4
Dawson	3.7	7.3	3.4	1.3	4.7	8.7	4.2	12.9	16.7	1 665	177	95	4 359	3.0
Deer Lodge	0.1	0.0	7.6	D	6.5	5.7	2.3	24.9	30.4	2 475	267	291	5 121	0.0
Fallon	3.8	37.5	14.4	0.2	2.0	3.9	2.2	4.8	10.5	555	182	16	1 529	4.0
Fergus	9.6	0.4	13.5	5.6	3.9	8.2	5.7	D	20.1	3 005	261	185	5 809	-0.5
Flathead	0.2	1.2	9.2	7.5	6.7	9.2	8.8	16.5	13.3	20 630	222	1 362	47 362	0.8
Gallatin	1.4	0.7	12.0	4.9	12.8	10.2	7.4	9.9	18.6	12 760	135	631	44 870	6.1
Garfield	41.1	0.0	D	D	D	5.2	D	D	28.2	285	222	9	848	0.5
Glacier	14.4	5.5	3.9	0.3	1.9	6.2	D	3.7	42.9	2 000	145	585	5 327	-0.4
Golden Valley	30.9	D	D	D	D	D	D	D	24.3	275	321	18	479	0.6
Granite	2.9	2.8	8.7	3.9	D	6.4	D	D	26.1	910	291	39	2 789	-1.2
Hill	8.9	1.4	4.8	0.5	7.8	7.9	3.7	10.0	27.5	2 660	160	431	7 217	-0.5
Jefferson	1.3	D	10.9	5.7	D	13.0	7.9	6.9	21.7	2 660	231	158	5 041	-0.3
Judith Basin	51.2	D	D	D	D	2.3	D	0.5	18.0	515	256	30	1 334	-0.1
Lake	3.5	0.6	8.3	5.2	6.2	8.7	3.5	13.3	34.3	6 905	238	733	16 602	0.1
Lewis and Clark	0.3	1.2	4.9	2.1	10.3	6.5	8.4	11.7	36.6	13 600	208	1 255	30 594	1.4
Liberty	50.4	D	D	D	D	2.5	D	D	12.2	390	164	51	1 033	-1.0
Lincoln	-0.1	3.6	10.0	3.2	4.7	9.0	4.0	14.8	28.1	6 325	326	588	11 477	0.6
McCone	28.7	0.0	D	0.0	D	8.9	D	D	13.8	360	211	11	1 007	-0.2
Madison	3.9	4.0	8.3	2.3	3.3	4.7	8.0	D	13.9	2 165	281	60	6 916	-0.3
Meagher	12.3	D	D	D	D	6.7	D	D	21.2	570	298	53	1 426	-0.4
Mineral	-0.7	0.0	7.4	D	D	10.7	D	13.6	27.1	1 350	316	159	2 447	0.0
Missoula	-0.1	0.2	6.1	3.3	9.3	8.9	6.8	18.1	20.4	19 380	173	2 143	51 411	2.6
Musselshell	1.0	48.3	5.3	0.7	3.0	3.1	D	6.9	14.4	1 280	277	103	2 657	0.1
Park	3.3	0.3	7.6	6.9	6.8	8.2	5.4	11.6	14.9	3 410	218	261	9 368	-0.1
Petroleum	54.7	D	D	0.0	D	D	0.0	D	23.0	100	198	0	327	0.9
Phillips	25.4	D	D	D	D	6.3	4.0	D	21.2	1 010	242	80	2 319	-0.7
Pondera	20.9	1.5	8.2	4.0	2.5	13.3	4.4	D	13.1	1 290	206	179	2 641	-0.7
Powder River	12.8	D	D	D	D	6.4	D	1.0	23.9	375	214	10	1 013	-0.9
Powell	1.5	D	D	D	D	4.3	2.3	D	50.1	1 540	221	137	3 097	-0.3
Prairie	15.3	0.0	D	D	D	1.8	D	D	53.3	375	319	19	669	-0.6
Ravalli	-0.1	0.2	8.9	6.8	D	8.6	5.3	12.0	21.4	11 600	284	740	19 553	-0.2
Richland	7.4	17.9	10.6	4.2	6.2	4.9	4.5	D	7.7	1 855	166	113	5 010	10.1
Roosevelt	8.2	4.6	5.9	0.9	D	8.4	2.4	D	37.4	1 720	155	436	4 080	0.4
Rosebud	4.9	17.4	8.0	0.1	D	3.2	1.3	D	31.6	1 695	182	246	4 107	1.2
Sanders	1.3	3.7	8.8	5.3	3.6	8.0	3.2	13.5	24.9	3 815	336	313	6 660	-0.3
Sheridan	32.8	11.1	3.8	0.1	2.1	4.7	2.7	D	13.4	915	250	35	2 137	2.3
Silver Bow	0.0	24.4	3.0	3.9	5.6	9.4	3.3	13.9	14.7	7 845	227	964	16 811	0.6
Stillwater	0.9	D	D	5.1	3.8	3.6	1.4	D	8.5	2 150	231	82	4 812	0.2
Sweet Grass	1.2	D	7.0	2.5	1.8	4.9	4.0	0.6	15.1	895	244	17	2 129	-0.8
Teton	22.4	D	9.2	1.4	D	5.1	4.5	6.3	15.9	1 480	244	108	2 882	-0.3
Toole	20.7	15.9	D	D	D	3.7	2.5	2.3	23.8	865	168	102	2 346	0.4
Treasure	64.2	0.0	D	0.0	D	D	D	D	14.1	220	315	0	423	0.2
Valley	22.4	D	4.3	0.8	4.2	5.5	D	D	19.3	1 820	239	149	4 844	-0.7
Wheatland	7.8	0.0	11.9	7.4	D	5.2	2.7	D	21.8	470	221	53	1 193	-0.3
Wibaux	22.0	D	D	D	D	1.0	1.2	D	21.2	245	218	13	536	-0.4
Yellowstone	0.1	3.2	9.1	5.8	D	8.1	6.9	17.1	12.5	28 665	186	2 500	67 062	4.9
NEBRASKA	10.2	0.3	6.2	10.1	7.6	5.5	8.0	10.1	15.7	321 882	172	27 457	814 970	2.3
Adams	14.1	0.0	6.1	13.6	3.7	6.0	3.6	D	14.3	6 615	209	545	13 664	2.4
Antelope	45.5	D	4.0	18.5	0.7	2.5	D	3.4	5.7	1 560	242	95	3 287	0.1
Arthur	47.4	0.0	D	D	D	D	0.0	D	24.5	105	233	0	252	-0.8
Banner	69.2	0.0	D	0.0	0.0	0.0	D	D	11.9	255	328	13	365	-1.1

1. Per 1,000 resident population estimated as of July 1 of the year shown.

STATE County	Housing units, 2009–2013: Occupied units: Total	Owner-occupied: Percent	Owner-occupied: Median value[1]	Median owner cost as a percent of income: With a mortgage	Median owner cost as a percent of income: Without a mortgage[2]	Renter-occupied: Median rent[3]	Renter-occupied: Median rent as a percent of income[2]	Sub-standard units[4] (percent)	Civilian labor force, 2014: Total	Percent change, 2013–2014	Unemployment: Total	Unemployment: Rate[5]	Civilian employment,[6] 2009–2013: Total	Percent: Management, business, science and arts	Percent: Construction, production, and maintenance occupations
	89	90	91	92	93	94	95	96	97	98	99	100	101	102	103
MISSOURI—Cont'd															
St. Louis city	140 652	44.6	119 200	23.5	13.8	724	33.0	0.4	161 379	1.0	12 395	7.7	145 581	37.1	15.7
MONTANA	405 525	68.3	184 200	23.7	11.5	682	28.5	2.5	516 437	0.5	24 346	4.7	477 015	35.1	22.0
Beaverhead	4 110	64.1	173 400	21.3	11.0	562	29.3	12.5	4 903	0.7	183	3.7	4 434	41.6	21.3
Big Horn	3 444	67.4	89 300	20.7	10.1	594	23.5	2.9	5 644	-1.6	565	10.0	4 788	32.7	20.0
Blaine	2 237	65.4	76 200	21.4	11.9	429	23.0	3.6	2 456	-1.2	143	5.8	2 417	37.1	28.0
Broadwater	2 421	80.7	174 000	24.0	13.1	498	29.3	2.4	2 532	0.3	140	5.5	2 613	30.6	31.9
Carbon	4 322	76.7	205 900	22.8	13.2	729	24.4	4.2	5 446	0.4	213	3.9	5 185	34.9	27.1
Carter	495	80.4	82 400	21.1	12.0	423	18.4	3.0	685	1.3	23	3.4	643	55.8	24.0
Cascade	33 430	65.6	157 900	22.6	11.0	617	26.1	2.2	38 560	-0.1	1 679	4.4	36 775	31.9	22.5
Chouteau	2 228	62.3	114 200	22.7	10.7	428	18.7	2.8	2 619	0.7	85	3.2	2 516	39.9	18.5
Custer	4 986	68.9	112 100	19.6	10.7	543	23.1	0.6	6 614	-0.8	215	3.3	5 936	31.0	21.9
Daniels	890	75.2	96 800	18.8	12.5	530	29.8	2.8	959	2.3	30	3.1	1 026	39.4	20.5
Dawson	3 885	70.3	122 200	16.1	10.0	487	24.0	3.0	4 898	1.3	130	2.7	4 562	33.5	29.5
Deer Lodge	3 855	72.7	117 800	22.8	10.9	499	26.7	1.7	5 307	1.2	238	4.5	4 140	28.0	25.4
Fallon	1 199	72.0	106 700	16.6	10.0	489	21.7	3.6	2 098	2.4	40	1.9	1 737	31.8	34.9
Fergus	4 924	74.4	113 800	19.9	13.9	623	30.9	2.1	5 804	-1.7	253	4.4	5 553	37.3	25.3
Flathead	36 901	71.0	228 100	28.4	12.2	750	31.2	1.6	44 066	0.0	2 860	6.5	42 647	30.8	23.4
Gallatin	36 973	61.8	261 900	25.9	11.2	829	29.9	4.7	57 218	3.8	1 993	3.5	50 021	38.5	19.2
Garfield	465	76.3	113 300	23.1	11.0	513	16.4	10.7	748	-2.3	20	2.7	601	48.4	20.3
Glacier	4 194	59.5	80 200	17.8	10.3	414	22.9	5.9	5 965	-6.5	640	10.7	4 755	31.9	18.8
Golden Valley	323	79.3	89 300	24.7	12.0	719	24.2	6.7	402	0.8	19	4.7	311	32.2	39.9
Granite	1 473	76.1	200 500	23.3	11.8	617	23.5	2.6	1 541	1.9	108	7.0	1 344	35.4	28.1
Hill	6 139	67.8	122 600	20.7	10.1	516	26.1	0.9	7 902	-1.0	461	5.8	7 539	35.1	26.5
Jefferson	4 527	85.9	230 100	21.9	10.0	662	25.4	0.8	5 696	1.0	262	4.6	5 263	44.1	23.1
Judith Basin	879	75.4	106 800	19.3	12.2	463	18.5	3.6	975	-0.8	42	4.3	915	51.9	18.4
Lake	11 829	69.1	218 600	27.7	12.2	628	27.8	1.6	12 640	1.4	736	5.8	11 331	34.8	24.4
Lewis and Clark	26 555	72.3	203 600	23.5	10.3	737	27.1	5.1	35 495	0.6	1 329	3.7	32 861	46.0	14.7
Liberty	847	62.2	102 800	19.0	10.0	480	21.4	4.7	988	-1.0	31	3.1	881	45.3	20.8
Lincoln	8 872	78.4	158 200	28.0	12.7	529	26.6	2.2	8 041	-1.6	907	11.3	7 217	30.4	24.1
McCone	760	77.2	101 600	18.8	11.0	451	21.4	1.9	1 113	1.1	27	2.4	1 022	54.5	17.7
Madison	3 542	76.1	239 600	26.9	10.9	688	24.8	1.3	4 253	1.7	197	4.6	3 878	40.3	21.8
Meagher	716	71.9	115 700	30.2	12.1	608	26.3	0.6	933	-0.3	40	4.3	892	31.2	26.2
Mineral	1 629	70.9	167 300	30.3	12.8	538	32.9	2.4	1 770	-0.8	160	9.0	1 498	20.5	30.8
Missoula	45 523	58.8	237 500	24.5	12.1	755	33.5	3.7	60 284	0.9	2 702	4.5	57 234	37.4	16.4
Musselshell	1 966	78.5	106 100	21.3	11.9	578	27.2	0.9	2 405	0.7	98	4.1	2 033	27.0	33.2
Park	6 445	75.1	204 500	28.3	14.3	663	27.7	3.9	8 114	0.8	456	5.6	7 387	36.8	24.0
Petroleum	233	76.0	83 200	32.1	10.0	579	50.0	2.1	298	0.7	12	4.0	263	48.3	27.8
Phillips	1 800	76.4	86 600	18.9	10.3	484	23.5	7.1	2 014	-2.7	108	5.4	1 798	35.0	28.0
Pondera	2 302	69.1	99 000	21.5	13.1	529	22.2	2.5	2 873	-1.5	142	4.9	2 750	38.5	23.1
Powder River	720	69.9	105 200	16.5	10.0	496	19.9	2.3	1 061	-6.2	34	3.2	882	42.2	22.8
Powell	2 411	71.5	120 900	21.8	12.3	493	20.5	0.8	2 967	0.0	155	5.2	2 775	29.4	20.6
Prairie	502	86.9	69 800	21.8	10.0	487	50.0	2.8	524	0.0	23	4.4	473	39.7	30.4
Ravalli	16 848	72.9	233 700	28.2	13.6	681	31.6	1.3	18 981	0.6	1 179	6.2	17 243	32.4	25.4
Richland	4 270	69.1	153 000	16.8	10.0	665	23.4	4.5	7 335	3.2	176	2.4	5 521	28.2	34.8
Roosevelt	3 264	58.9	70 100	16.6	10.3	384	17.5	5.7	4 873	-1.6	257	5.3	3 693	34.5	22.8
Rosebud	3 268	68.5	110 900	20.2	10.2	536	15.9	5.1	4 204	-0.5	241	5.7	4 140	33.9	29.6
Sanders	5 149	76.6	166 500	30.7	12.9	620	26.7	0.4	4 694	-1.6	442	9.4	4 293	27.6	31.9
Sheridan	1 612	74.4	109 500	17.9	10.6	545	25.3	1.3	2 119	-3.0	57	2.7	1 761	36.3	21.5
Silver Bow	15 042	65.5	121 900	19.8	11.9	597	29.1	3.7	17 134	-0.8	854	5.0	15 934	30.7	22.1
Stillwater	3 757	79.9	185 900	20.6	12.6	706	21.5	2.1	5 058	-0.7	192	3.8	4 513	27.6	37.4
Sweet Grass	1 304	73.0	192 700	26.0	10.5	618	25.9	4.1	1 805	1.5	64	3.5	1 766	33.6	32.4
Teton	2 303	75.9	134 700	23.8	13.1	559	25.3	2.8	2 922	-1.6	110	3.8	2 680	42.9	21.0
Toole	1 927	63.5	106 300	19.8	10.4	533	21.3	3.3	2 375	-1.1	72	3.0	2 242	31.8	22.5
Treasure	332	70.2	67 500	25.9	13.2	625	10.0	1.7	353	-1.1	15	4.2	353	24.9	39.4
Valley	3 248	69.0	102 300	18.1	10.0	484	21.8	8.4	4 390	2.8	135	3.1	3 622	35.4	23.4
Wheatland	817	71.5	78 400	25.4	13.8	547	23.1	0.7	796	-4.0	40	5.0	742	41.6	26.1
Wibaux	409	70.9	102 700	14.5	10.0	533	24.1	1.7	553	-0.9	17	3.1	442	36.9	28.5
Yellowstone	61 023	68.8	181 500	21.8	11.2	718	28.4	1.5	80 039	0.4	2 998	3.7	77 174	33.0	22.5
NEBRASKA	725 787	67.0	128 000	21.1	12.2	706	27.2	2.3	1 022 152	0.0	33 903	3.3	948 701	35.2	23.6
Adams	12 578	69.8	98 000	19.1	10.6	627	25.6	2.7	16 915	-0.6	569	3.4	15 830	30.1	26.5
Antelope	2 855	75.2	74 300	20.8	11.5	507	27.3	0.6	3 629	-0.1	99	2.7	3 317	38.3	27.6
Arthur	177	61.6	76 400	19.4	13.3	660	18.0	2.4	218	-2.2	12	5.5	215	53.0	28.4
Banner	330	63.6	85 000	19.1	21.0	605	23.3	2.8	421	-3.9	16	3.8	415	42.4	23.4

1. Specified owner-occupied units. 2. A value of 10.0 represents 10 percent or less; a value of 50.0 represents 50 percent or more. 3. Specified renter-occupied units.
4. Overcrowded or lacking complete plumbing facilities. 5. Percent of civilian labor force. 6. Persons 16 years old and over.

STATE County	Private nonfarm establishments, employment and payroll, 2013									Agriculture, 2012			
		Employment						Annual payroll		Farms			
											Percent with:		
	Number of establish-ments	Total	Health care and social assistance	Manufac-turing	Retail trade	Finance and insurance	Professional, scientific, and technical services	Total (mil dol)	Average per employee (dollars)	Number	Fewer than 50 acres	500 acres or more	Farm operators whose principal occu-pation is farming (percent)
	104	105	106	107	108	109	110	111	112	113	114	115	116
MISSOURI—Cont'd													
St. Louis city	9 794	223 481	36 233	17 472	9 752	13 259	18 839	11 294	50 535	NA	NA	NA	NA
MONTANA	36 529	350 196	66 154	17 196	56 008	15 808	17 529	12 447	35 542	28 008	28.1	42.2	55.1
Beaverhead	344	2 295	448	40	500	D	74	65	28 300	430	32.3	41.4	56.5
Big Horn	217	2 332	565	D	346	71	D	105	44 983	527	23.3	45.2	50.5
Blaine	147	1 202	D	D	182	44	28	48	39 975	546	9.0	66.7	67.2
Broadwater	137	782	D	D	133	D	D	23	29 018	287	21.6	39.7	54.4
Carbon	412	2 190	290	D	262	D	108	57	26 169	726	24.4	32.6	57.0
Carter	34	152	D	D	NA	NA	D	4	24 783	327	6.4	83.2	76.5
Cascade	2 429	28 891	6 657	798	5 072	1 754	1 121	927	32 090	1 105	36.0	29.3	47.8
Chouteau	160	761	252	D	115	D	D	20	26 033	774	5.6	75.6	69.6
Custer	434	4 445	977	80	844	D	111	151	34 020	423	24.8	48.0	60.0
Daniels	71	D	D	D	96	39	D	D	D	338	3.8	71.3	53.8
Dawson	343	2 985	D	42	520	102	74	103	34 472	485	12.8	61.4	57.1
Deer Lodge	248	2 727	D	D	276	65	110	91	33 426	93	31.2	32.3	34.4
Fallon	159	1 293	D	D	134	D	D	76	58 659	295	14.6	62.4	60.3
Fergus	433	3 337	831	376	466	D	74	107	31 923	790	20.1	53.9	62.9
Flathead	3 872	33 284	5 592	2 474	5 545	D	1 834	1 158	34 793	1 035	60.4	6.3	49.9
Gallatin	4 962	38 950	4 622	2 711	6 979	1 362	2 638	1 351	34 674	1 163	47.7	18.6	45.0
Garfield	28	144	D	D	NA	D	D	4	24 694	297	8.8	83.2	76.8
Glacier	248	2 341	445	D	480	46	D	81	34 518	602	12.8	48.5	58.6
Golden Valley	16	D	D	D	D	D	D	2	D	157	8.9	61.1	59.2
Granite	111	524	D	29	111	D	4	16	30 729	163	15.3	52.8	56.4
Hill	536	5 444	1 479	20	1 112	232	222	163	30 019	802	8.7	59.0	53.6
Jefferson	269	1 686	237	D	185	D	D	71	42 226	401	40.4	20.7	40.6
Judith Basin	59	177	10	D	21	32	11	5	30 311	324	12.7	65.4	66.4
Lake	773	5 251	1 096	344	1 045	D	D	157	29 832	1 156	54.8	9.3	45.4
Lewis and Clark	2 210	24 645	5 673	D	3 751	1 392	1 743	899	36 487	703	59.2	17.2	36.6
Liberty	67	334	D	D	D	21	D	8	24 533	304	3.9	80.6	74.3
Lincoln	596	3 820	900	165	701	130	97	106	27 716	325	49.8	5.8	38.2
McCone	59	351	D	D	68	D	D	11	32 402	489	3.3	73.4	68.3
Madison	362	1 980	D	D	202	71	D	65	32 687	571	28.5	37.5	48.7
Meagher	72	276	D	D	D	20	D	6	23 040	136	22.8	60.3	64.7
Mineral	114	892	D	266	189	D	D	25	27 483	95	50.5	9.5	30.5
Missoula	4 177	46 400	9 127	1 494	7 678	1 976	3 140	1 502	32 363	637	58.4	10.0	38.3
Musselshell	113	914	172	D	128	30	D	45	49 684	356	13.5	43.3	58.1
Park	772	4 504	818	341	644	D	170	136	30 108	564	36.0	36.2	55.1
Petroleum	11	D	D	NA	NA	NA	D	0	D	100	6.0	78.0	78.0
Phillips	137	824	D	18	206	45	D	21	25 797	507	13.0	64.1	64.5
Pondera	172	1 396	279	D	223	83	34	44	31 240	505	14.1	59.2	62.2
Powder River	74	349	D	D	116	D	17	9	24 954	328	16.2	74.7	64.9
Powell	163	1 072	D	D	D	D	28	32	30 220	263	31.2	38.8	57.8
Prairie	39	142	D	D	24	D	D	4	25 317	186	11.3	69.4	71.5
Ravalli	1 378	8 721	1 508	825	1 452	D	512	245	28 146	1 438	69.6	5.7	47.0
Richland	573	5 810	D	475	606	142	187	300	51 582	544	12.7	67.3	64.2
Roosevelt	233	2 378	D	D	534	84	28	72	30 154	606	5.9	63.2	55.6
Rosebud	184	2 437	273	D	269	56	D	118	48 361	437	18.1	53.5	57.9
Sanders	353	2 020	502	205	314	68	38	52	25 798	492	31.1	16.3	41.3
Sheridan	186	1 073	319	1	196	83	29	29	26 725	527	2.3	67.6	66.4
Silver Bow	1 154	13 069	2 956	D	2 229	345	557	463	35 451	140	24.3	22.9	43.6
Stillwater	258	2 615	209	D	250	65	55	171	65 502	593	21.8	43.7	56.5
Sweet Grass	155	998	D	D	139	D	23	56	56 056	332	18.1	50.6	53.9
Teton	206	1 213	265	33	200	80	32	36	29 716	742	17.0	43.8	58.8
Toole	194	1 618	256	D	146	D	37	57	35 167	423	5.2	75.4	60.0
Treasure	18	61	D	NA	D	D	D	2	26 016	109	11.9	66.1	75.2
Valley	270	2 244	D	D	358	100	D	69	30 582	654	8.7	62.7	66.1
Wheatland	59	383	D	D	D	D	8	10	27 115	154	11.7	65.6	65.6
Wibaux	39	184	D	D	22	D	D	6	31 826	172	7.6	66.9	73.3
Yellowstone	5 521	68 676	13 611	3 363	10 506	3 692	3 366	2 731	39 771	1 330	48.0	21.8	46.9
NEBRASKA	52 585	830 073	121 695	91 328	108 268	60 199	88 150	33 114	39 892	49 969	23.3	37.7	59.7
Adams	973	13 290	2 587	2 363	1 944	373	292	431	32 423	567	25.9	38.8	65.1
Antelope	219	1 398	273	92	289	88	D	40	28 621	767	17.7	39.5	61.0
Arthur	10	D	NA	NA	D	D	D	1	D	85	10.6	81.2	71.8
Banner	10	D	NA	NA	NA	D	NA	1	D	193	5.2	63.7	62.7

STATE County	Agriculture, 2012 (cont.) Land in farms: Acreage (1,000)	Percent change, 2007–2012	Acres: Average size of farm	Acres: Total irrigated (1,000)	Acres: Total cropland (1,000)	Value of land and buildings (dollars): Average per farm	Average per acre	Value of machinery and equipment, average per farm (dollars)	Value of products sold: Total (mil dol)	Average per farm (dollars)	Percent from: Crops	Percent from: Livestock and poultry products	Percent of farms with sales of: $10,000 or more	$100,000 or more	Government payments: Total ($1,000)	Percent of farms
	117	118	119	120	121	122	123	124	125	126	127	128	129	130	131	132
MISSOURI—Cont'd																
St. Louis city	NA	NA	NA	NA	NA	NA	NA	NA	NA	NA	NA	NA	NA	NA	NA	NA
MONTANA	59 759	-2.7	2 134	1 903.0	17 022.2	1 674 568	785	137 611	4 230.1	151 031	53.3	46.7	50.4	26.2	209 846	44.4
Beaverhead	1 381	11.4	3 211	238.5	178.6	3 580 193	1 115	151 598	142.9	332 270	21.8	78.2	57.9	32.3	368	15.1
Big Horn	3 149	8.6	5 975	46.3	268.1	2 633 651	441	151 454	108.7	206 351	48.8	51.2	53.7	28.8	2 505	32.6
Blaine	2 204	-5.4	4 037	50.5	626.8	2 408 179	597	202 203	113.8	208 509	62.9	37.1	68.9	39.7	8 869	67.2
Broadwater	477	0.4	1 661	39.6	151.3	1 901 303	1 144	166 115	38.1	132 909	56.2	43.8	52.6	27.2	1 700	47.0
Carbon	791	-0.3	1 090	72.8	136.7	1 283 405	1 178	115 977	76.9	105 871	33.8	66.2	52.2	20.4	1 696	35.3
Carter	1 778	4.7	5 437	1.4	234.8	2 923 162	538	205 480	83.2	254 431	14.9	85.1	83.2	51.7	2 009	58.1
Cascade	1 255	-9.1	1 136	33.4	427.7	1 197 706	1 055	96 719	111.1	100 568	48.2	51.8	40.9	16.2	5 952	51.5
Chouteau	2 072	-9.0	2 677	10.4	1 260.3	2 146 671	802	225 031	186.1	240 424	85.5	14.5	66.5	50.4	16 813	81.9
Custer	2 190	3.0	5 177	30.3	139.3	2 082 525	402	132 858	109.2	258 158	19.4	80.6	59.6	35.7	1 847	40.7
Daniels	768	-10.7	2 273	4.1	536.0	1 171 905	516	259 464	95.0	281 074	91.6	8.4	55.6	37.3	5 520	85.8
Dawson	1 258	-8.7	2 594	17.2	399.4	1 163 130	448	171 186	80.4	165 701	69.0	31.0	65.4	36.9	6 390	70.9
Deer Lodge	67	-16.1	716	10.8	11.2	1 154 925	1 613	74 237	5.5	59 613	33.5	66.5	35.5	15.1	60	16.1
Fallon	980	0.1	3 321	0.9	172.1	1 456 376	439	201 753	56.4	191 095	21.4	78.6	65.1	38.0	2 136	74.2
Fergus	1 961	-19.8	2 482	12.4	592.4	2 147 954	865	155 286	145.7	184 456	49.2	50.8	64.3	39.4	6 716	55.1
Flathead	170	-32.5	164	18.2	71.3	819 700	4 994	55 080	34.7	33 504	79.6	20.4	24.2	6.9	707	16.6
Gallatin	703	-9.5	604	79.1	225.1	1 596 942	2 643	97 028	106.0	91 118	55.5	44.5	38.9	15.4	2 741	21.6
Garfield	2 191	-8.4	7 376	1.5	386.1	3 642 283	494	210 761	72.9	245 549	37.1	62.9	78.5	51.2	3 399	60.6
Glacier	1 570	-7.6	2 609	34.1	525.6	1 781 623	683	172 369	105.6	175 380	64.6	35.4	53.5	25.6	6 940	51.3
Golden Valley	708	5.4	4 511	7.0	135.4	2 545 656	564	118 675	21.4	136 242	34.9	65.1	51.0	30.6	2 347	67.5
Granite	285	-5.8	1 751	28.5	27.4	2 233 558	1 276	92 485	19.2	117 497	17.5	82.5	58.3	32.5	152	16.0
Hill	1 598	-5.8	1 992	9.4	1 168.9	1 288 555	647	196 585	164.0	204 451	84.5	15.5	56.0	37.7	17 713	74.4
Jefferson	371	-5.1	926	29.2	50.3	1 049 736	1 134	48 180	22.4	55 920	19.5	80.5	33.2	10.0	519	11.2
Judith Basin	1 034	23.4	3 193	14.0	343.2	2 852 596	893	209 031	92.6	285 664	30.8	69.2	76.2	42.6	2 905	64.5
Lake	556	-12.8	481	80.7	80.7	767 869	1 597	58 202	56.6	48 930	42.9	57.1	42.0	10.6	783	20.2
Lewis and Clark	843	-13.2	1 199	47.5	92.4	1 816 522	1 515	56 963	46.6	66 228	39.5	60.5	27.3	8.4	1 192	14.5
Liberty	898	-0.7	2 954	5.9	604.4	1 795 457	608	271 908	84.7	278 500	81.4	18.6	70.7	51.6	9 709	92.4
Lincoln	47	-8.9	145	3.5	9.8	545 972	3 753	40 302	3.5	10 665	29.1	70.9	18.8	1.8	55	3.4
McCone	1 372	-9.0	2 806	14.2	604.9	1 347 873	480	197 613	102.2	209 053	76.1	23.9	70.3	44.2	7 765	83.6
Madison	1 085	2.3	1 901	111.9	144.9	2 382 159	1 253	124 492	81.3	142 301	33.6	66.4	49.0	23.5	856	15.6
Meagher	812	0.0	5 973	36.1	69.6	5 741 787	961	168 647	39.0	286 809	24.3	75.7	61.8	40.4	533	36.8
Mineral	17	-24.7	179	0.9	4.0	798 084	4 447	32 147	1.1	11 653	23.5	76.6	10.5	2.1	23	13.7
Missoula	247	-12.3	388	16.8	19.9	1 074 215	2 769	40 830	13.6	21 355	29.8	70.2	22.1	4.6	395	9.4
Musselshell	1 018	-10.2	2 859	11.4	124.2	1 412 604	494	87 795	38.1	107 006	27.3	72.7	36.5	18.3	1 854	32.0
Park	774	1.5	1 372	57.1	110.1	3 502 195	2 552	96 943	38.5	68 239	34.1	65.9	47.3	17.4	754	17.7
Petroleum	690	7.7	6 898	11.2	158.3	3 025 110	439	211 460	31.6	316 040	39.0	61.0	77.0	52.0	1 194	69.0
Phillips	2 067	3.0	4 076	33.2	702.0	2 344 404	575	148 256	95.8	188 955	61.0	39.0	63.9	35.9	7 362	68.8
Pondera	957	1.3	1 894	65.8	568.2	1 536 014	811	209 016	113.8	225 259	73.9	26.1	67.3	41.8	8 483	76.4
Powder River	1 589	-1.9	4 843	9.9	171.7	2 666 905	551	151 963	62.4	190 296	13.0	87.0	75.9	48.2	1 530	38.7
Powell	589	-12.1	2 240	53.3	53.5	2 120 281	946	112 894	34.2	130 114	22.3	77.7	48.7	23.6	264	15.6
Prairie	769	0.2	4 135	9.2	119.3	2 331 349	564	147 817	31.2	167 710	47.9	52.1	69.4	41.9	1 749	70.4
Ravalli	235	-10.7	163	61.6	51.3	792 834	4 856	42 915	34.7	24 148	30.2	69.8	25.4	5.4	549	8.6
Richland	1 293	1.1	2 377	62.7	556.5	1 418 388	597	263 978	139.2	255 820	67.3	32.7	65.3	38.1	6 117	73.3
Roosevelt	1 240	-14.6	2 046	16.6	729.0	1 292 137	632	213 368	126.4	208 579	89.4	10.6	58.1	34.5	7 701	79.0
Rosebud	3 142	15.8	7 189	35.9	238.9	2 970 357	413	141 041	91.7	209 929	28.1	71.9	56.5	27.7	2 043	31.6
Sanders	339	-0.9	688	17.5	34.4	817 530	1 187	47 451	14.2	28 917	38.8	61.2	29.9	6.3	501	10.8
Sheridan	1 042	-2.2	1 977	9.2	696.0	1 172 598	593	315 522	129.8	246 207	88.5	11.5	62.2	44.4	7 618	88.0
Silver Bow	70	-31.0	498	4.6	4.4	781 493	1 569	76 293	4.2	30 043	18.4	81.6	30.7	7.1	5	2.9
Stillwater	809	-5.6	1 365	21.6	187.3	1 905 005	1 396	84 403	56.9	95 933	22.8	77.2	48.6	18.7	2 997	42.5
Sweet Grass	856	5.3	2 577	35.8	78.7	2 771 482	1 075	105 373	33.5	100 892	12.8	87.2	49.7	20.8	689	25.0
Teton	975	-15.4	1 314	114.8	548.9	1 381 036	1 051	159 619	140.1	188 811	58.6	41.4	56.5	32.6	8 825	73.3
Toole	1 129	1.2	2 668	6.3	747.3	1 912 251	717	212 683	102.7	242 745	79.8	20.2	65.2	46.1	11 090	85.6
Treasure	618	33.7	5 666	21.9	44.2	2 847 431	503	329 853	46.6	427 202	48.1	51.9	80.7	48.6	548	56.0
Valley	1 635	-20.7	2 499	40.4	788.4	1 240 586	496	243 817	151.5	231 596	78.6	21.4	62.7	38.2	9 013	80.0
Wheatland	874	6.3	5 675	21.7	124.4	2 906 149	512	153 864	46.8	304 071	22.7	77.3	64.9	39.0	1 520	55.2
Wibaux	545	10.7	3 171	1.5	135.7	1 483 262	468	201 831	29.3	170 174	54.3	45.7	75.0	44.8	2 282	85.5
Yellowstone	1 668	3.3	1 254	73.2	351.1	957 953	764	95 176	216.8	163 019	28.0	72.0	38.0	15.5	3 843	30.2
NEBRASKA	45 332	-0.3	907	8 296.6	21 597.4	2 159 268	2 380	230 212	23 068.8	461 661	49.3	50.7	68.5	43.0	392 428	68.7
Adams	341	11.2	601	215.3	284.3	3 170 141	5 278	359 032	418.0	737 136	62.7	37.3	69.5	53.4	5 673	67.4
Antelope	475	-8.0	619	249.7	343.9	2 634 722	4 254	283 301	535.1	697 674	47.9	52.1	74.7	55.9	8 424	73.8
Arthur	453	-0.2	5 327	12.4	29.3	2 247 882	422	174 412	31.5	370 412	29.2	70.8	90.6	57.6	308	24.7
Banner	422	6.9	2 188	15.2	191.6	1 685 534	770	178 580	113.0	585 622	21.3	78.7	68.4	36.3	3 220	77.7

STATE County	Water use, 2010		Wholesale trade,[1] 2007				Retail trade,[2] 2007				Real estate and rental and leasing,[2] 2007			
	Total water withdrawn (mil gal/day)	Gallons withdrawn per person per day	Number of establish-ments	Number of employees	Sales (mil dol)	Annual payroll (mil dol)	Number of establish-ments	Number of employees	Sales (mil dol)	Annual payroll (mil dol)	Number of establish-ments	Number of employees	Receipts (mil dol)	Annual payroll (mil dol)
	133	134	135	136	137	138	139	140	141	142	143	144	145	146
MISSOURI—Cont'd														
St. Louis city	91.5	286	522	9 422	5 042.1	462.3	1 028	11 368	2 496.7	263.5	418	2 633	606.6	94.7
MONTANA	7 645.2	7 727	1 254	12 849	8 202.8	503.4	5 258	58 883	14 686.9	1 317.8	1 892	6 410	848.3	153.3
Beaverhead	483.0	52 234	5	64	24.3	1.9	57	466	122.9	10.0	16	69	8.5	2.1
Big Horn	268.1	20 838	5	D	D	D	48	433	87.4	7.1	10	45	2.1	0.4
Blaine	236.4	36 426	9	32	27.6	0.8	25	174	44.2	3.2	4	10	0.6	0.1
Broadwater	192.4	34 284	6	27	10.3	0.5	16	157	59.2	2.9	7	8	0.6	0.3
Carbon	400.2	39 709	12	55	21.0	2.3	59	330	60.7	5.7	20	31	5.0	0.7
Carter	1.6	1 379	NA	NA	NA	NA	5	30	11.9	0.4	2	D	D	D
Cascade	166.9	2 052	118	1 077	672.0	42.5	388	5 507	1 302.3	121.0	137	378	56.3	8.3
Chouteau	42.1	7 242	12	62	38.4	1.9	19	125	44.7	2.0	6	D	D	D
Custer	151.5	12 950	17	128	75.1	4.4	67	847	199.9	16.5	14	34	3.3	0.6
Daniels	3.9	2 204	4	13	9.9	0.3	12	72	26.6	1.7	NA	NA	NA	NA
Dawson	79.0	8 810	15	157	107.6	3.5	54	506	118.3	9.6	8	20	1.5	0.3
Deer Lodge	39.6	4 259	1	D	D	D	38	264	71.5	5.9	12	32	2.5	0.5
Fallon	7.0	2 419	4	33	32.9	1.7	16	145	26.3	2.3	2	D	D	D
Fergus	50.0	4 316	15	155	400.2	5.8	76	512	135.4	10.7	19	65	4.8	1.2
Flathead	61.7	679	98	959	863.6	40.1	550	6 076	1 581.3	147.8	269	936	113.6	23.5
Gallatin	333.2	3 722	127	1 405	508.8	50.8	621	7 467	1 791.8	184.6	361	1 265	193.6	33.4
Garfield	4.5	3 706	1	D	D	D	6	63	10.2	0.8	NA	NA	NA	NA
Glacier	128.1	9 561	10	59	125.2	2.3	45	449	106.3	9.5	7	16	1.3	0.2
Golden Valley	39.6	44 830	1	D	D	D	1	D	D	D	NA	NA	NA	NA
Granite	72.0	23 368	1	D	D	D	17	120	23.8	2.0	4	3	0.1	0.1
Hill	10.8	673	26	182	190.2	5.8	87	1 020	231.1	19.5	18	49	5.4	1.0
Jefferson	91.0	7 979	8	D	D	D	26	177	39.9	2.9	7	15	0.9	0.3
Judith Basin	16.8	8 127	5	18	4.6	0.4	8	25	5.5	0.3	3	3	0.5	0.1
Lake	390.6	13 587	20	43	8.7	1.0	152	1 201	277.0	26.1	49	77	10.9	1.5
Lewis and Clark	154.1	2 430	48	445	199.6	16.9	302	4 070	972.9	94.0	98	657	83.2	14.2
Liberty	29.0	12 407	4	12	10.5	0.4	13	69	15.6	1.2	4	10	0.4	0.1
Lincoln	18.2	924	10	42	12.1	1.0	93	721	170.6	13.3	29	66	7.2	0.8
McCone	25.6	14 758	1	D	D	D	11	68	18.0	1.2	1	D	D	D
Madison	434.4	56 479	7	D	D	D	49	184	48.9	4.0	29	38	4.7	0.9
Meagher	217.2	114 839	NA	NA	NA	NA	13	69	16.4	1.1	1	D	D	D
Mineral	5.2	1 238	1	D	D	D	23	242	46.1	4.5	4	3	0.4	0.1
Missoula	85.6	783	169	1 825	860.1	69.5	587	8 668	2 179.4	194.6	227	952	126.3	21.6
Musselshell	73.5	16 197	5	11	5.0	0.3	24	140	33.6	2.6	4	6	0.7	0.1
Park	193.5	12 373	15	58	26.3	2.5	112	723	208.9	15.4	30	52	8.3	1.1
Petroleum	49.5	100 142	NA	NA	NA	NA	2	D	D	D	1	D	D	D
Phillips	244.2	57 409	7	65	80.8	1.6	27	161	34.0	3.1	3	4	0.5	0.0
Pondera	243.5	39 574	13	119	46.1	4.1	34	262	64.7	4.9	5	D	D	D
Powder River	31.4	18 038	1	D	D	D	13	87	13.8	1.3	2	D	D	D
Powell	138.4	19 695	3	D	D	D	17	168	35.0	3.1	8	13	2.0	0.3
Prairie	72.2	61 213	1	D	D	D	8	32	7.4	0.5	1	D	D	D
Ravalli	168.9	4 200	38	220	165.0	7.4	185	1 567	344.8	31.2	72	206	16.7	4.5
Richland	259.7	26 649	19	149	235.8	5.9	60	598	128.6	10.9	18	64	8.0	1.7
Roosevelt	86.4	8 289	11	41	66.3	1.4	40	359	99.9	6.5	7	29	1.1	0.2
Rosebud	195.7	21 190	1	D	D	D	32	306	53.4	4.5	6	33	3.0	0.6
Sanders	62.2	5 446	9	D	D	D	53	366	82.1	6.6	17	41	3.4	0.6
Sheridan	20.2	5 954	5	20	5.0	0.7	21	167	31.5	2.5	2	D	D	D
Silver Bow	40.7	1 191	31	D	D	D	189	2 183	504.7	44.3	45	144	14.9	3.0
Stillwater	87.0	9 540	3	9	14.2	0.5	43	308	103.2	4.5	7	10	1.6	0.2
Sweet Grass	154.1	42 205	2	D	D	D	27	170	42.7	3.1	11	16	3.3	0.4
Teton	427.0	70 308	9	D	D	D	29	220	43.9	4.4	9	21	1.7	0.3
Toole	8.6	1 619	9	114	96.3	3.6	26	202	54.8	3.8	8	17	1.5	0.2
Treasure	90.1	125 501	1	D	D	D	4	D	D	D	1	D	D	D
Valley	191.6	25 999	13	148	80.4	5.1	54	331	81.3	6.8	3	D	D	D
Wheatland	126.9	58 552	1	D	D	D	13	74	18.3	1.0	1	D	D	D
Wibaux	3.5	3 412	NA	NA	NA	NA	4	22	4.3	0.2	NA	NA	NA	NA
Yellowstone	437.5	2 956	297	4 467	2 772.5	196.0	757	10 151	2 840.7	249.2	263	907	142.3	26.5
NEBRASKA	8 036.3	4 400	2 668	32 329	24 019.9	1 323.5	7 888	108 200	26 186.6	2 230.5	2 032	9 974	1 045.5	292.0
Adams	128.1	4 083	56	783	499.7	27.1	163	1 863	360.8	34.7	54	D	D	D
Antelope	83.1	12 432	27	225	136.3	6.5	45	278	57.0	4.4	3	3	0.8	0.0
Arthur	5.5	11 935	NA	NA	NA	NA	3	7	0.9	0.1	NA	NA	NA	NA
Banner	17.5	25 333	NA	NA	NA	NA	NA	NA	NA	NA	NA	NA	NA	NA

1. Merchant wholesalers, except manufacturers' sales branches and offices. 2. Employer establishments.

STATE County	Professional, scientific, and technical services,[1] 2007				Manufacturing, 2007				Accommodation and food services, 2007			
	Number of establish-ments	Number of employees	Receipts (mil dol)	Annual payroll (mil dol)	Number of establish-ments	Number of employees	Receipts (mil dol)	Annual payroll (mil dol)	Number of establish-ments	Number of employees	Sales (mil dol)	Annual payroll (mil dol)
	147	148	149	150	151	152	153	154	155	156	157	158
MISSOURI—Cont'd												
St. Louis city	1 005	D	D	D	543	21 432	10 920.6	998.2	934	20 372	1 059.3	311.4
MONTANA	3 403	16 547	1 770.9	670.6	1 324	19 525	10 638.1	808.2	3 360	46 137	2 079.4	554.2
Beaverhead	30	78	7.3	2.0	NA	NA	NA	NA	48	408	16.1	3.9
Big Horn	15	D	D	D	NA	NA	NA	NA	27	248	13.6	3.1
Blaine	10	D	D	D	NA	NA	NA	NA	18	112	2.4	0.6
Broadwater	5	25	1.9	0.7	NA	NA	NA	NA	19	140	5.7	1.4
Carbon	31	110	13.8	4.8	NA	NA	NA	NA	50	557	18.5	5.6
Carter	3	D	D	D	NA	NA	NA	NA	1	D	D	D
Cascade	199	D	D	D	81	1 094	670.9	44.8	247	3 997	174.3	48.6
Chouteau	9	21	2.1	0.4	NA	NA	NA	NA	19	104	3.8	0.8
Custer	23	143	8.9	3.6	NA	NA	NA	NA	40	624	22.1	5.9
Daniels	4	8	0.7	0.1	NA	NA	NA	NA	7	25	1.0	0.2
Dawson	16	64	3.7	1.3	NA	NA	NA	NA	31	396	21.2	4.1
Deer Lodge	23	51	5.1	1.5	NA	NA	NA	NA	36	378	16.4	4.3
Fallon	8	D	D	D	NA	NA	NA	NA	17	99	4.0	0.7
Fergus	29	93	6.5	1.7	NA	NA	NA	NA	49	489	14.1	4.3
Flathead	380	D	D	D	177	3 464	919.4	149.7	347	4 617	232.9	63.0
Gallatin	631	2 552	301.5	113.3	188	2 425	512.6	95.2	376	6 788	325.8	89.9
Garfield	NA	NA	NA	NA	NA	NA	NA	NA	6	19	0.6	0.2
Glacier	15	D	D	D	NA	NA	NA	NA	48	265	37.6	6.4
Golden Valley	1	D	D	D	NA	NA	NA	NA	4	12	0.4	0.1
Granite	6	9	0.8	0.3	NA	NA	NA	NA	15	66	2.5	0.6
Hill	36	D	D	D	NA	NA	NA	NA	49	658	23.8	6.2
Jefferson	26	52	5.1	1.9	NA	NA	NA	NA	31	273	7.3	2.0
Judith Basin	3	D	D	D	NA	NA	NA	NA	9	34	1.3	0.3
Lake	58	D	D	D	44	654	119.8	21.8	78	817	34.7	8.0
Lewis and Clark	243	1 713	207.8	84.6	54	655	D	24.3	190	2 961	118.6	32.9
Liberty	4	7	0.8	0.1	NA	NA	NA	NA	6	24	0.8	0.2
Lincoln	42	D	D	D	NA	NA	NA	NA	66	501	26.5	6.7
McCone	1	D	D	D	NA	NA	NA	NA	5	17	0.7	0.1
Madison	21	D	D	D	NA	NA	NA	NA	65	221	15.0	4.2
Meagher	1	D	D	D	NA	NA	NA	NA	13	74	2.1	0.5
Mineral	8	41	3.0	1.2	NA	NA	NA	NA	22	139	6.7	1.6
Missoula	458	D	D	D	112	2 159	674.9	93.8	332	6 209	269.1	70.0
Musselshell	8	13	1.3	0.4	NA	NA	NA	NA	9	74	3.5	0.7
Park	62	182	20.4	6.6	NA	NA	NA	NA	120	1 083	61.9	16.9
Petroleum	1	D	D	D	NA	NA	NA	NA	3	15	0.4	0.1
Phillips	9	22	1.8	0.5	NA	NA	NA	NA	16	114	4.1	0.9
Pondera	13	43	3.4	1.2	NA	NA	NA	NA	15	168	4.2	1.1
Powder River	6	22	1.4	0.3	NA	NA	NA	NA	9	46	2.2	0.6
Powell	9	57	3.1	1.1	NA	NA	NA	NA	26	177	7.3	2.0
Prairie	2	D	D	D	NA	NA	NA	NA	5	16	0.9	0.1
Ravalli	111	D	D	D	105	1 048	130.2	38.9	105	992	36.5	10.6
Richland	35	156	20.1	6.0	NA	NA	NA	NA	37	502	19.7	4.5
Roosevelt	11	D	D	D	NA	NA	NA	NA	30	269	9.7	2.5
Rosebud	4	15	1.0	0.2	NA	NA	NA	NA	29	274	9.0	2.1
Sanders	17	41	2.5	1.0	NA	NA	NA	NA	36	313	12.2	3.5
Sheridan	8	33	1.8	0.7	NA	NA	NA	NA	17	142	4.8	1.2
Silver Bow	107	D	D	D	NA	NA	NA	NA	133	1 946	78.3	22.7
Stillwater	27	52	5.3	1.6	NA	NA	NA	NA	23	220	9.8	2.6
Sweet Grass	15	34	3.4	1.0	NA	NA	NA	NA	18	158	6.2	1.7
Teton	9	D	D	D	NA	NA	NA	NA	17	118	3.0	0.7
Toole	18	49	4.2	1.4	NA	NA	NA	NA	26	180	10.6	2.8
Treasure	2	D	D	D	NA	NA	NA	NA	2	D	D	D
Valley	18	D	D	D	NA	NA	NA	NA	29	268	11.0	3.0
Wheatland	2	D	D	D	NA	NA	NA	NA	11	55	1.6	0.3
Wibaux	4	12	0.8	0.2	NA	NA	NA	NA	5	31	1.1	0.2
Yellowstone	566	3 170	367.2	135.7	187	3 974	5 740.0	D	368	7 687	361.7	97.3
NEBRASKA	4 205	40 692	4 836.4	2 011.0	1 984	99 547	40 158.0	3 788.6	4 241	69 142	2 685.6	749.1
Adams	61	312	33.2	12.0	67	D	D	D	79	1 185	43.7	10.9
Antelope	13	22	2.4	0.6	NA	NA	NA	NA	13	98	2.4	0.6
Arthur	1	D	D	D	NA	NA	NA	NA	1	D	D	D
Banner	NA	NA	NA	NA	NA	NA	NA	NA	NA	NA	NA	NA

1. Establishment subject to federal tax.

Table B. States and Counties — **Health Care and Social Assistance, Other Services, Nonemployer Businesses, and Residential Construction**

STATE County	Health care and social assistance, 2007				Other services, 2007				Nonemployer businesses, 2013		Value of residential construction authorized by building permits, 2014	
	Number of establish-ments	Number of employees	Receipts (mil dol)	Annual payroll (mil dol)	Number of establish-ments	Number of employees	Receipts (mil dol)	Annual payroll (mil dol)	Number	Receipts (mil dol)	New Construction ($1,000)	Number of housing units
	159	160	161	162	163	164	165	166	167	168	169	170
MISSOURI—Cont'd												
St. Louis city	1 036	34 294	3 510.6	1 207.0	694	5 574	635.1	165.4	21 248	813.2	123 458	758
MONTANA	3 301	57 860	4 970.8	1 983.7	2 287	10 323	995.4	245.8	84 251	3 614.3	647 022	3 884
Beaverhead	38	382	31.4	11.9	21	65	3.8	0.8	865	33.6	391	3
Big Horn	19	D	D	D	12	23	2.3	0.6	499	16.3	300	4
Blaine	11	D	D	D	9	40	2.7	0.6	318	7.1	750	2
Broadwater	7	79	5.2	2.1	6	D	D	D	442	18.9	0	0
Carbon	26	243	13.4	6.8	16	43	2.5	0.6	1 050	46.2	1 638	9
Carter	2	D	D	D	1	D	D	D	103	5.5	30	1
Cascade	269	6 050	517.8	206.6	166	845	65.4	18.8	4 611	185.7	71 028	463
Chouteau	17	236	10.9	5.7	5	D	D	D	365	15.6	970	4
Custer	48	926	70.2	30.5	26	112	10.9	2.4	838	34.5	635	3
Daniels	5	153	7.2	3.0	5	D	D	D	140	7.2	375	1
Dawson	26	567	40.5	16.9	33	122	8.4	2.2	602	22.7	3 677	30
Deer Lodge	46	1 240	68.6	39.8	14	57	4.9	1.1	459	17.4	595	5
Fallon	5	D	D	D	10	D	D	D	329	14.8	2 520	25
Fergus	51	770	47.6	20.8	31	107	9.7	1.4	1 071	40.7	213	1
Flathead	350	5 001	471.0	166.6	222	967	80.5	21.7	9 930	438.7	75 697	233
Gallatin	349	3 634	330.0	120.5	245	1 072	133.4	30.6	11 075	512.1	225 447	1 191
Garfield	3	D	D	D	2	D	D	D	135	5.0	0	0
Glacier	18	D	D	D	20	D	D	D	687	21.7	275	1
Golden Valley	2	D	D	D	NA	NA	NA	NA	89	2.9	0	0
Granite	3	D	D	D	2	D	D	D	298	11.3	0	0
Hill	45	1 016	86.8	34.9	45	174	14.1	3.1	909	28.3	777	3
Jefferson	19	205	8.9	3.5	15	D	D	D	979	39.2	255	1
Judith Basin	5	23	0.3	0.2	1	D	D	D	197	8.0	0	0
Lake	77	1 136	84.7	36.0	45	141	10.0	2.6	2 300	88.6	2 785	15
Lewis and Clark	247	4 736	462.8	182.3	202	D	D	D	5 294	231.4	37 605	338
Liberty	2	D	D	D	2	D	D	D	145	5.5	0	0
Lincoln	50	743	48.2	21.0	39	145	12.2	2.6	1 573	56.5	172	3
McCone	3	D	D	D	3	D	D	D	174	5.9	0	0
Madison	16	142	8.5	4.0	16	35	5.7	1.0	1 005	42.6	995	4
Meagher	5	D	D	D	4	D	D	D	180	6.6	0	0
Mineral	14	139	6.7	2.9	4	D	D	D	305	9.9	786	3
Missoula	451	8 022	754.8	278.6	288	1 618	150.7	37.8	9 374	418.3	49 236	578
Musselshell	9	D	D	D	8	18	1.4	0.3	376	13.2	0	0
Park	45	702	61.1	25.4	53	221	17.3	4.9	2 097	81.4	5 429	34
Petroleum	1	D	D	D	NA	NA	NA	NA	40	1.4	0	0
Phillips	10	216	10.0	4.4	11	D	D	D	372	13.7	94	1
Pondera	20	304	16.6	7.5	11	37	2.3	0.4	432	13.6	0	0
Powder River	1	D	D	D	4	D	D	D	187	5.5	0	0
Powell	17	178	12.1	4.6	9	20	2.2	0.3	481	20.8	4 338	17
Prairie	1	D	D	D	3	D	D	D	83	2.8	0	0
Ravalli	118	1 257	80.6	32.8	86	265	21.9	5.8	4 148	171.0	1 996	15
Richland	32	687	41.9	17.9	32	98	9.4	2.2	948	52.7	17 930	164
Roosevelt	15	D	D	D	13	54	3.9	0.7	545	19.6	982	12
Rosebud	15	259	10.4	5.0	11	37	3.2	1.0	533	14.0	0	0
Sanders	34	423	25.4	11.6	18	46	5.0	0.9	1 009	38.1	0	0
Sheridan	10	224	12.3	6.7	8	D	D	D	345	19.0	680	3
Silver Bow	157	2 804	184.9	75.9	66	346	32.6	7.7	2 191	93.6	4 887	58
Stillwater	19	229	10.8	4.4	11	D	D	D	776	30.3	766	3
Sweet Grass	7	22	0.7	0.3	10	30	2.1	0.5	422	16.2	360	3
Teton	19	228	9.4	4.9	8	31	4.2	1.1	597	27.0	401	2
Toole	10	226	19.0	8.0	9	19	1.8	0.3	338	14.3	510	3
Treasure	3	D	D	D	1	D	D	D	62	2.4	0	0
Valley	19	544	34.1	13.7	21	57	4.6	1.0	559	20.7	100	1
Wheatland	3	D	D	D	4	5	0.3	0.1	152	6.8	0	0
Wibaux	3	D	D	D	NA	NA	NA	NA	91	3.5	687	5
Yellowstone	504	11 503	1 168.5	474.6	380	1 972	198.3	48.7	11 126	534.2	130 712	642
NEBRASKA	4 920	114 928	10 081.0	4 107.3	4 073	22 543	2 391.3	542.8	127 427	5 202.5	1 205 027	7 005
Adams	120	2 780	229.1	100.8	67	369	23.9	6.5	2 148	85.4	21 644	120
Antelope	16	268	18.2	6.7	19	39	3.7	0.7	623	26.0	2 378	11
Arthur	NA	NA	NA	NA	2	D	D	D	42	1.8	NA	NA
Banner	NA	NA	NA	NA	NA	NA	NA	NA	39	1.8	NA	NA

STATE County	Government employment and payroll, 2012: Full-time equivalent employees	March payroll (dollars)	March payroll (percent of total): Adminis-tration, judicial, and legal	Police and Corrections	Fire Protection	Highways and transpor-tation	Health and Welfare	Natural resources and utilities	Education and libraries	Local government finances, 2012: General revenue: Total (mil dol)	Inter-govern-mental (mil dol)	Taxes: Total (mil dol)	Per capita[1] (dollars): Total	Property
	171	172	173	174	175	176	177	178	179	180	181	182	183	184
MISSOURI—Cont'd														
St. Louis city	15 033	62 103 817	5.6	17.2	5.7	20.6	1.5	12.9	34.1	2 385.3	762.8	924.8	2 907	1 228
MONTANA	X	X	X	X	X	X	X	X	X	X	X	X	X	X
Beaverhead	518	1 862 160	5.1	4.6	0.4	2.9	54.8	1.7	29.5	66.4	12.9	10.3	1 104	1 099
Big Horn	748	2 839 698	3.5	4.0	0.0	3.4	4.1	1.1	82.8	62.2	38.7	13.7	1 049	1 040
Blaine	358	1 163 514	11.3	3.8	0.0	6.0	0.6	3.7	73.6	31.5	20.8	7.2	1 083	1 053
Broadwater	160	477 725	12.8	12.5	0.0	5.0	4.9	1.1	62.3	14.4	6.3	5.4	935	924
Carbon	377	1 229 196	11.7	8.3	1.5	6.6	1.7	4.4	62.9	33.2	13.2	15.7	1 547	1 457
Carter	67	178 052	5.5	6.2	0.0	11.1	1.6	2.3	58.2	7.1	3.5	2.6	2 229	2 201
Cascade	2 704	9 771 107	6.8	13.0	3.8	5.6	3.7	6.9	59.0	238.3	103.2	77.2	944	913
Chouteau	318	956 267	6.0	6.6	0.0	4.7	29.2	2.6	49.0	26.4	10.3	9.2	1 565	1 560
Custer	539	1 661 688	7.8	7.4	3.4	4.8	3.2	3.6	68.6	42.2	19.5	9.9	832	817
Daniels	99	271 126	13.7	7.5	0.1	5.3	5.9	3.5	61.2	10.7	3.8	5.1	2 865	1 845
Dawson	486	1 501 541	7.2	15.3	1.5	5.5	7.5	3.6	57.4	42.3	16.8	12.8	1 387	1 374
Deer Lodge	264	898 579	8.3	14.8	4.3	3.9	1.1	6.9	59.7	28.1	15.5	7.9	855	847
Fallon	190	709 670	11.6	5.6	3.4	9.5	5.9	6.1	55.5	33.9	25.4	5.0	1 645	1 614
Fergus	520	1 621 405	6.8	8.4	2.1	15.7	1.2	2.9	61.6	43.5	22.6	14.7	1 286	1 268
Flathead	2 820	10 913 778	6.6	7.4	3.2	3.5	3.5	3.7	70.8	292.8	116.8	111.5	1 216	1 179
Gallatin	2 434	9 405 208	8.1	11.0	3.8	2.9	5.0	5.6	60.7	253.4	77.2	121.2	1 309	1 215
Garfield	115	230 472	8.7	3.3	2.9	6.0	24.2	7.0	41.9	7.0	2.6	2.3	1 862	1 861
Glacier	700	2 311 773	4.2	4.6	0.0	3.2	3.2	2.5	81.1	52.7	34.1	13.8	1 008	1 004
Golden Valley	58	147 171	10.6	3.5	0.0	4.0	0.0	0.3	80.9	4.9	2.7	1.9	2 302	2 299
Granite	179	573 451	9.2	4.8	0.0	3.8	33.5	2.9	44.5	15.4	5.5	4.2	1 364	1 358
Hill	793	2 599 436	4.3	6.6	2.9	3.9	3.3	3.7	74.5	62.6	35.3	17.8	1 085	1 070
Jefferson	303	957 909	14.8	9.2	0.0	4.0	5.0	1.6	64.0	29.3	15.5	10.6	927	924
Judith Basin	121	355 407	6.9	3.6	0.0	13.7	0.1	1.1	72.7	9.7	4.7	3.9	1 915	1 915
Lake	962	3 993 744	4.2	5.9	0.2	1.6	3.5	2.9	80.7	85.3	44.4	27.2	940	933
Lewis and Clark	1 872	7 755 463	7.5	9.0	2.6	3.9	8.6	5.4	59.9	213.1	82.3	69.8	1 076	1 054
Liberty	111	316 696	12.4	8.7	0.0	7.1	6.6	4.8	58.9	8.2	3.8	3.3	1 372	1 372
Lincoln	599	1 992 630	12.4	7.4	0.5	3.8	2.7	4.3	65.2	57.6	31.7	14.9	766	754
McCone	168	326 681	15.1	4.8	0.1	1.2	1.9	4.1	42.3	8.6	3.2	4.3	2 540	2 486
Madison	459	1 488 288	7.5	4.1	0.2	3.8	40.5	2.0	39.5	41.8	10.9	17.1	2 205	2 194
Meagher	122	326 266	10.3	7.3	0.0	3.7	0.0	4.5	46.8	8.8	3.1	3.4	1 746	1 742
Mineral	297	957 709	7.9	6.9	0.3	1.9	33.5	1.3	47.5	23.2	8.6	6.0	1 442	1 403
Missoula	3 035	11 623 602	8.8	11.6	6.2	6.3	5.7	3.6	55.2	333.0	140.7	131.9	1 189	1 156
Musselshell	259	845 308	4.5	3.3	0.0	3.2	25.2	1.6	61.7	22.2	9.1	7.4	1 596	1 532
Park	528	1 727 963	10.9	8.8	4.3	3.9	4.6	4.7	62.0	50.7	22.2	18.0	1 154	1 123
Petroleum	36	121 984	11.4	0.0	0.0	5.5	0.0	6.6	74.9	4.7	3.4	0.9	1 705	1 703
Phillips	229	653 111	10.8	5.9	0.1	6.4	3.3	8.6	61.5	21.3	11.3	6.4	1 542	1 503
Pondera	212	607 909	10.4	10.1	0.2	5.9	1.8	7.3	62.5	34.1	12.3	7.0	1 132	1 127
Powder River	137	334 388	14.5	7.2	0.0	8.8	27.7	1.7	37.3	12.1	5.0	3.7	2 074	1 968
Powell	199	625 409	10.4	7.0	0.5	5.1	2.6	2.8	69.0	21.5	10.6	6.4	906	902
Prairie	95	225 508	8.2	3.7	0.0	5.1	32.5	1.7	42.7	7.5	2.4	1.9	1 617	1 608
Ravalli	1 130	3 297 468	9.0	9.9	0.2	2.5	1.0	3.9	72.3	96.2	49.5	36.0	885	874
Richland	560	1 708 186	7.9	8.6	0.2	7.8	4.4	8.1	58.4	72.7	47.2	9.4	866	853
Roosevelt	704	2 186 188	5.4	5.6	0.2	3.3	10.8	2.9	70.0	63.5	42.5	12.7	1 161	1 154
Rosebud	641	1 932 124	5.8	8.0	0.0	6.1	4.9	5.7	68.6	65.9	31.0	16.0	1 705	1 689
Sanders	390	1 112 745	8.1	9.8	0.3	5.2	3.6	1.9	69.3	33.6	16.5	12.8	1 123	1 122
Sheridan	333	1 098 598	7.7	3.6	1.6	5.2	44.9	1.5	34.4	19.8	10.2	5.6	1 551	1 542
Silver Bow	995	3 780 881	7.3	11.3	8.8	7.4	1.2	11.1	51.5	120.3	54.8	39.2	1 139	1 112
Stillwater	340	1 123 218	10.5	6.8	1.0	7.0	2.4	1.8	70.1	29.0	12.6	12.5	1 360	1 350
Sweet Grass	197	563 456	9.7	3.8	0.0	3.5	28.6	2.5	49.1	22.0	6.9	6.1	1 698	1 696
Teton	434	1 416 652	5.6	3.0	0.1	2.9	31.7	6.4	49.4	34.6	11.1	9.4	1 552	1 512
Toole	386	1 266 882	7.5	5.0	0.0	3.8	44.2	2.8	34.4	36.1	9.0	7.8	1 492	1 473
Treasure	44	114 460	17.8	4.4	0.0	4.5	6.2	7.2	53.1	3.7	1.5	1.7	2 261	2 258
Valley	402	1 205 227	6.6	9.6	0.0	6.9	3.9	4.9	66.3	36.1	17.0	11.6	1 551	1 486
Wheatland	160	440 257	19.4	6.3	0.0	12.1	3.4	4.6	49.3	9.4	4.2	4.2	1 974	1 965
Wibaux	61	199 780	22.1	5.7	0.0	16.7	2.2	0.8	52.4	6.8	4.9	1.2	1 174	1 124
Yellowstone	4 840	19 590 185	5.0	8.6	4.7	4.9	8.9	6.0	55.1	469.5	175.3	161.7	1 065	989
NEBRASKA	X	X	X	X	X	X	X	X	X	X	X	X	X	X
Adams	2 340	8 844 524	2.4	3.7	1.5	2.0	0.5	13.9	70.2	174.2	49.6	89.6	2 849	2 506
Antelope	558	1 836 977	2.9	2.2	0.0	3.6	29.5	1.6	60.0	30.0	8.2	17.8	2 718	2 366
Arthur	35	130 066	6.4	2.0	0.0	4.7	0.0	27.0	59.3	5.8	0.9	4.6	9 488	9 335
Banner	61	179 960	9.3	1.7	0.0	7.8	0.0	0.0	79.6	4.4	1.3	2.8	3 726	3 499

1. Based on the resident population estimated as of July 1 of the year shown.

STATE County	Local government finances, 2012 (cont.)									Government employment, 2013			Presidential election,[2] 2012		
	Direct general expenditure							Debt outstanding					Percent of vote cast:		
			Percent of total for:												
	Total (mil dol)	Per capita[1] (dollars)	Education	Health and hospitals	Police protection	Public welfare	Highways	Total (mil dol)	Per capita[1] (dollars)	Federal civilian	Federal military	State and local	Democratic	Republican	All other
	185	186	187	188	189	190	191	192	193	194	195	196	197	198	199
MISSOURI—Cont'd															
St. Louis city	2 326.2	7 311	33.4	1.7	10.8	0.0	1.1	3 993.6	12 552	13 924	1 670	21 315	83.7	15.5	0.8
MONTANA	X	X	X	X	X	X	X	X	X	13 076	8 299	73 423	47.3	49.5	3.2
Beaverhead	83.3	8 915	24.9	55.9	2.2	0.0	3.8	91.0	9 739	192	45	771	33.9	63.2	2.9
Big Horn	70.6	5 404	65.3	1.6	3.9	0.0	4.8	34.0	2 603	380	65	1 923	67.4	31.2	1.4
Blaine	33.0	4 932	63.3	2.3	5.1	0.0	8.2	3.4	513	188	32	496	58.2	39.0	2.8
Broadwater	14.1	2 447	49.7	2.6	9.1	0.2	5.3	4.7	809	40	28	199	31.8	65.8	2.4
Carbon	34.2	3 380	55.4	0.7	7.0	0.2	11.0	23.7	2 339	93	52	478	42.5	54.1	3.4
Carter	7.6	6 469	34.7	9.5	5.5	0.1	25.5	0.4	371	15	0	89	15.5	80.1	4.3
Cascade	242.5	2 968	53.0	1.0	9.7	1.4	5.2	90.0	1 101	1 675	3 660	4 104	49.9	47.6	2.4
Chouteau	26.7	4 530	44.1	21.5	3.3	0.0	8.4	4.1	697	33	29	427	39.2	57.1	3.7
Custer	40.6	3 415	62.2	2.4	7.6	0.1	8.1	9.5	801	192	58	896	41.6	55.9	2.5
Daniels	9.9	5 552	39.1	7.1	5.2	0.0	8.9	3.2	1 792	19	0	112	32.0	64.7	3.4
Dawson	38.5	4 159	54.9	3.1	5.4	1.0	7.1	8.2	884	31	45	740	35.9	59.5	4.5
Deer Lodge	30.1	3 259	41.6	2.0	6.6	2.8	4.8	4.9	531	85	42	843	67.0	29.6	3.4
Fallon	38.0	12 574	45.8	4.0	2.8	0.0	17.5	0.2	57	12	15	256	22.2	74.3	3.5
Fergus	44.0	3 847	53.6	2.3	4.8	0.0	11.5	9.5	831	142	55	881	31.0	65.9	3.1
Flathead	299.8	3 272	56.2	3.9	5.8	1.2	5.0	178.9	1 952	753	462	4 099	36.9	58.5	4.6
Gallatin	262.4	2 834	48.1	1.3	10.1	4.2	4.1	247.8	2 676	620	468	8 657	50.3	46.9	2.8
Garfield	7.3	5 772	36.8	2.4	2.5	23.3	14.2	0.6	450	25	0	120	15.1	82.3	2.6
Glacier	51.7	3 768	77.0	2.8	4.0	0.1	4.7	22.4	1 630	434	65	1 908	68.9	29.2	1.9
Golden Valley	4.5	5 323	65.4	0.9	4.3	0.5	4.7	0.0	5	0	0	67	25.3	69.9	4.9
Granite	15.6	5 012	35.1	0.6	6.3	26.8	7.6	2.0	654	31	16	198	35.0	59.1	5.9
Hill	62.8	3 840	76.1	0.8	4.8	0.0	3.2	16.7	1 020	166	80	1 957	54.3	42.1	3.6
Jefferson	31.9	2 799	57.0	3.8	8.3	0.0	5.0	4.6	400	41	57	701	40.7	55.8	3.5
Judith Basin	9.6	4 741	53.8	0.9	3.4	0.0	18.1	3.4	1 658	31	10	139	32.1	64.8	3.1
Lake	86.4	2 980	61.8	0.9	5.2	0.3	4.0	23.2	799	75	142	2 734	48.6	46.7	4.7
Lewis and Clark	212.2	3 270	47.9	4.1	8.6	3.1	5.3	156.7	2 415	1 921	330	8 924	52.1	45.5	2.4
Liberty	7.9	3 293	47.0	5.3	10.3	0.0	12.1	1.8	772	21	10	120	36.7	59.3	4.0
Lincoln	58.1	2 979	51.4	6.8	7.7	0.1	7.8	18.2	932	408	96	715	32.8	61.8	5.4
McCone	8.6	5 082	52.1	3.7	4.1	0.8	13.0	2.4	1 422	18	0	147	29.4	66.5	4.0
Madison	42.1	5 447	35.2	13.7	4.0	18.5	7.6	7.0	907	65	38	461	35.2	61.8	3.0
Meagher	10.9	5 666	29.5	3.3	0.7	0.0	6.7	0.3	179	23	0	110	30.8	64.6	4.6
Mineral	24.9	5 975	42.3	33.5	3.9	0.0	3.9	5.6	1 346	52	21	255	42.4	52.8	4.9
Missoula	338.7	3 052	44.0	5.5	7.0	0.8	5.2	188.8	1 701	1 338	547	9 196	61.8	35.1	3.0
Musselshell	23.0	4 926	37.1	29.7	2.1	0.0	4.3	1.8	390	15	23	252	27.6	68.6	3.9
Park	60.3	3 873	58.7	2.2	5.8	0.5	3.5	26.2	1 681	65	78	626	46.9	49.2	3.9
Petroleum	4.6	8 926	53.5	1.5	1.5	0.0	8.0	0.4	812	0	0	52	22.7	75.7	1.7
Phillips	22.5	5 449	53.5	1.7	4.2	0.0	11.5	7.9	1 903	76	20	305	30.1	67.0	2.9
Pondera	34.1	5 531	42.2	35.4	3.5	1.5	3.2	14.5	2 348	30	28	331	42.4	55.0	2.6
Powder River	12.1	6 877	33.4	1.6	5.0	22.2	16.5	0.1	69	11	0	173	20.0	77.3	2.7
Powell	23.3	3 289	58.1	0.9	6.4	0.4	8.2	1.7	234	80	27	1 024	36.3	59.8	3.9
Prairie	7.4	6 390	28.9	2.4	3.9	29.4	8.6	2.0	1 732	36	0	127	28.7	68.4	2.9
Ravalli	99.9	2 460	64.0	1.1	7.3	0.5	5.0	31.4	773	527	202	1 386	38.0	58.9	3.1
Richland	76.0	7 032	41.5	1.4	4.3	0.9	22.5	6.1	568	77	56	681	26.6	70.5	2.9
Roosevelt	58.9	5 389	63.9	10.7	5.5	0.5	4.5	9.1	836	180	55	1 509	61.8	35.5	2.7
Rosebud	68.3	7 269	51.2	7.9	4.8	0.3	4.7	257.2	27 372	235	46	1 471	50.4	46.4	3.2
Sanders	36.1	3 162	60.5	4.1	6.1	0.0	8.2	4.9	428	126	56	507	33.7	60.9	5.4
Sheridan	21.8	6 087	50.6	2.2	6.1	1.6	16.8	1.9	517	73	18	262	47.5	49.2	3.3
Silver Bow	113.4	3 297	39.5	4.4	5.9	0.1	4.1	60.4	1 757	256	203	2 296	68.8	28.4	2.8
Stillwater	30.5	3 315	64.5	0.6	4.5	0.1	6.8	2.6	287	34	46	425	32.4	64.1	3.5
Sweet Grass	22.6	6 259	30.6	0.8	5.2	32.8	6.0	1.4	398	23	18	316	26.0	71.7	2.3
Teton	35.3	5 826	43.7	23.0	0.8	4.8	5.1	8.3	1 372	53	28	420	39.5	57.3	3.2
Toole	36.4	6 970	29.7	40.6	6.4	0.0	6.6	14.4	2 766	173	22	517	34.7	62.1	3.2
Treasure	3.8	5 182	44.6	5.5	3.4	0.1	10.4	0.5	679	0	0	53	32.1	64.6	3.3
Valley	35.4	4 717	51.9	2.2	5.0	0.1	10.3	8.7	1 160	139	38	597	42.1	54.2	3.7
Wheatland	8.9	4 252	54.8	5.6	6.4	0.1	6.6	3.2	1 505	23	10	132	29.5	67.0	3.6
Wibaux	6.5	6 114	36.4	10.7	5.5	0.0	16.1	1.2	1 157	0	0	105	26.0	67.6	6.4
Yellowstone	506.3	3 333	47.8	7.1	5.8	0.2	6.1	224.5	1 478	1 698	788	7 133	45.5	51.8	2.7
NEBRASKA	X	X	X	X	X	X	X	X	X	16 532	12 799	144 108	41.6	56.5	1.9
Adams	180.4	5 735	72.7	0.4	3.1	0.2	6.2	136.0	4 322	110	114	2 238	35.5	62.5	2.1
Antelope	34.5	5 275	71.6	0.0	2.2	0.0	12.9	7.4	1 136	28	24	447	23.8	74.8	1.4
Arthur	4.1	8 356	45.4	0.2	0.8	0.0	11.7	0.0	0	0	0	47	14.8	82.5	2.7
Banner	4.4	5 725	68.1	0.3	1.3	0.0	14.7	0.0	0	0	0	68	14.9	83.7	1.4

1. Based on the resident population estimated as of July 1 of the year shown. 2.

STATE/ County code	CBSA code[1]	County type[2]	STATE County	Land area,[3] (sq km) 2010	Population, 2014: Total persons 2014	Population, 2014: Rank	Population, 2014: Per square kilometer	Population and population characteristics, 2013: Race alone or in combination, not Hispanic or Latino (percent): White	Black	American Indian, Alaska Native	Asian and Pacific Islander	Percent Hispanic or Latino[4]	Age (percent): Under 5 years	5 to 17 years	18 to 24 years	25 to 34 years	35 to 44 years	45 to 54 years
				1	2	3	4	5	6	7	8	9	10	11	12	13	14	15
			NEBRASKA—Cont'd															
31 009	...	9	Blaine	1 841	504	3 135	0.3	99.4	0.4	0.4	0.4	0.2	7.9	13.1	7.1	7.1	10.4	17.0
31 011	...	9	Boone	1 778	5 353	2 812	3.0	97.5	0.5	0.7	0.4	1.5	5.6	17.1	7.4	9.9	8.8	14.5
31 013	...	7	Box Butte	2 785	11 340	2 335	4.1	84.7	1.1	3.8	0.7	11.4	6.8	18.1	7.4	11.6	11.3	12.5
31 015	...	9	Boyd	1 398	2 033	3 046	1.5	96.2	0.3	1.3	0.9	1.8	5.5	15.4	5.8	7.7	8.4	13.3
31 017	...	9	Brown	3 163	2 941	2 980	0.9	98.1	0.7	1.0	0.3	1.1	4.6	16.8	5.8	8.3	10.0	13.6
31 019	28260	5	Buffalo	2 507	48 224	1 010	19.2	89.2	1.4	0.6	1.6	8.3	6.9	16.6	15.9	14.0	11.1	11.4
31 021	...	8	Burt	1 273	6 573	2 715	5.2	94.7	0.7	2.1	0.6	2.8	5.4	17.0	6.4	8.9	9.7	13.7
31 023	...	6	Butler	1 515	8 249	2 586	5.4	96.2	0.6	0.5	0.6	2.9	5.5	18.4	6.9	9.4	10.6	14.9
31 025	36540	2	Cass	1 444	25 524	1 583	17.7	95.8	0.8	1.0	0.8	2.9	5.9	18.7	7.2	10.6	12.2	15.3
31 027	...	9	Cedar	1 917	8 610	2 550	4.5	97.7	0.3	0.7	0.3	1.6	5.8	19.0	7.4	8.7	9.5	14.0
31 029	...	9	Chase	2 317	3 978	2 906	1.7	86.6	0.5	0.6	0.2	12.9	6.5	18.0	6.2	10.5	10.6	12.8
31 031	...	7	Cherry	15 437	5 762	2 782	0.4	92.0	0.8	6.7	0.9	2.4	5.6	16.4	6.5	10.3	11.3	13.2
31 033	...	7	Cheyenne	3 098	10 148	2 428	3.3	90.7	0.6	1.2	2.0	6.4	6.1	18.1	6.9	12.8	12.4	13.8
31 035	...	9	Clay	1 482	6 315	2 734	4.3	90.7	0.8	0.7	0.3	8.2	6.3	17.9	7.4	10.1	10.3	14.1
31 037	...	7	Colfax	1 066	10 504	2 395	9.9	54.7	1.4	0.6	0.7	43.2	8.7	20.7	8.7	12.4	11.7	13.4
31 039	...	7	Cuming	1 478	9 027	2 516	6.1	90.2	0.6	0.4	0.4	9.1	5.6	18.9	7.0	9.8	9.9	14.0
31 041	...	7	Custer	6 671	10 728	2 377	1.6	96.2	0.9	0.8	0.3	2.8	5.9	16.8	7.0	10.2	10.9	13.7
31 043	43580	3	Dakota	684	20 850	1 784	30.5	53.5	4.5	2.8	3.9	36.6	7.9	21.0	9.8	13.1	12.0	12.8
31 045	...	7	Dawes	3 617	9 042	2 513	2.5	89.0	2.3	4.7	2.8	3.7	5.2	13.3	21.8	10.6	8.9	11.1
31 047	30420	7	Dawson	2 624	24 096	1 641	9.2	62.0	4.0	0.7	1.0	33.0	7.5	20.6	8.8	12.0	12.0	12.3
31 049	...	9	Deuel	1 139	1 940	3 057	1.7	93.3	0.6	0.9	0.4	5.4	4.9	17.0	5.4	8.3	10.9	14.6
31 051	43580	3	Dixon	1 233	5 782	2 779	4.7	87.2	0.6	0.8	0.4	11.7	6.0	19.1	7.0	10.0	10.6	12.9
31 053	23340	4	Dodge	1 369	36 744	1 256	26.8	87.1	1.3	0.8	0.9	10.9	6.3	17.1	9.1	11.6	11.3	13.1
31 055	36540	2	Douglas	851	543 244	120	638.4	73.3	12.5	1.1	3.7	11.7	7.6	18.2	9.5	16.2	12.9	12.9
31 057	...	9	Dundy	2 382	1 886	3 062	0.8	91.9	1.1	1.4	0.3	7.0	4.2	18.5	6.7	8.6	11.0	12.8
31 059	...	9	Fillmore	1 490	5 661	2 790	3.8	95.0	0.8	0.6	0.5	3.6	4.9	15.8	7.3	9.6	9.2	15.1
31 061	...	9	Franklin	1 491	3 076	2 969	2.1	98.0	0.6	1.0	0.3	1.5	4.8	14.9	6.7	8.3	9.1	15.0
31 063	...	9	Frontier	2 524	2 705	2 993	1.1	97.3	0.6	0.6	0.4	2.0	4.1	16.8	11.0	9.6	9.7	12.0
31 065	...	9	Furnas	1 863	4 888	2 843	2.6	96.0	0.7	0.8	0.5	3.1	5.0	17.3	6.9	8.7	9.6	13.1
31 067	13100	6	Gage	2 205	21 663	1 748	9.8	96.3	0.9	1.1	0.8	2.0	5.8	16.7	7.4	10.0	11.0	14.6
31 069	...	9	Garden	4 414	1 911	3 061	0.4	94.1	0.9	1.3	0.2	4.7	3.9	13.2	6.4	8.3	9.4	15.2
31 071	...	9	Garfield	1 476	2 003	3 049	1.4	98.2	0.6	0.1	0.3	1.1	3.4	15.6	6.6	8.7	8.2	13.1
31 073	30420	9	Gosper	1 187	1 970	3 052	1.7	94.9	1.0	1.1	0.8	4.0	6.4	17.3	6.7	10.3	9.4	13.8
31 075	...	9	Grant	2 010	619	3 133	0.3	98.1	0.3	0.9	0.2	1.4	8.2	14.1	5.1	12.0	8.4	17.1
31 077	...	9	Greeley	1 476	2 482	3 008	1.7	97.0	0.8	0.6	0.2	1.9	5.7	18.1	6.0	9.0	9.5	13.6
31 079	24260	5	Hall	1 415	61 492	853	43.5	71.0	2.4	0.7	1.6	25.4	7.7	19.3	8.9	13.0	12.4	13.0
31 081	24260	7	Hamilton	1 406	9 135	2 501	6.5	96.4	0.6	0.5	0.5	2.8	5.8	19.0	7.5	9.9	11.6	14.0
31 083	...	9	Harlan	1 433	3 492	2 940	2.4	97.4	0.4	0.7	0.3	1.9	6.4	15.1	6.5	8.1	9.5	14.4
31 085	...	9	Hayes	1 847	933	3 110	0.5	94.8	0.7	0.3	0.5	3.9	4.8	16.2	8.3	9.8	7.0	13.1
31 087	...	9	Hitchcock	1 839	2 901	2 984	1.6	96.9	0.6	1.0	0.3	2.3	5.5	15.4	6.0	10.5	9.1	13.2
31 089	...	7	Holt	6 248	10 403	2 403	1.7	95.4	0.5	0.5	0.4	3.8	6.9	16.7	6.8	9.1	9.5	14.5
31 091	...	9	Hooker	1 868	728	3 125	0.4	97.2	0.3	2.2	0.1	1.0	5.8	14.8	5.3	7.9	10.6	10.6
31 093	24260	9	Howard	1 475	6 362	2 730	4.3	96.7	0.6	0.7	0.5	2.3	6.0	17.6	7.1	9.9	11.7	14.0
31 095	...	7	Jefferson	1 477	7 335	2 648	5.0	95.6	0.8	0.7	0.7	3.3	5.3	16.9	6.3	10.1	10.2	13.2
31 097	...	8	Johnson	974	5 185	2 825	5.3	81.6	5.9	1.3	1.7	10.1	4.9	15.0	6.8	13.9	12.6	15.6
31 099	28260	7	Kearney	1 337	6 644	2 708	5.0	94.4	0.4	0.5	0.5	4.8	6.1	18.0	6.8	10.8	11.3	14.0
31 101	...	7	Keith	2 750	8 121	2 594	3.0	92.5	0.8	0.8	0.9	6.2	4.6	16.4	6.5	9.3	10.0	14.5
31 103	...	9	Keya Paha	2 002	810	3 117	0.4	99.2	0.0	0.5	0.1	0.5	4.8	14.3	5.6	7.3	8.5	14.7
31 105	...	6	Kimball	2 465	3 713	2 927	1.5	89.6	0.7	1.5	1.5	8.2	6.2	15.8	7.1	10.3	9.6	13.2
31 107	...	9	Knox	2 871	8 482	2 559	3.0	88.3	0.7	9.5	0.7	2.4	6.1	18.1	6.3	8.2	9.3	13.3
31 109	30700	2	Lancaster	2 169	301 795	222	139.1	85.5	4.8	1.1	4.5	6.4	6.8	16.3	15.1	14.7	12.1	11.8
31 111	35820	5	Lincoln	6 641	35 815	1 278	5.4	90.0	1.2	0.9	0.9	8.0	6.5	18.1	7.7	11.9	12.1	12.8
31 113	35820	9	Logan	1 478	750	3 124	0.5	96.1	0.5	1.7	0.5	2.0	5.4	18.1	6.4	12.2	10.6	13.0
31 115	...	9	Loup	1 472	588	3 134	0.4	96.5	1.0	0.2	0.0	2.2	3.8	15.5	6.1	7.5	8.2	13.7
31 117	35820	9	McPherson	2 225	498	3 136	0.2	99.0	1.1	0.0	0.6	0.6	6.3	20.9	4.6	9.3	8.7	16.5
31 119	35740	5	Madison	1 483	35 174	1 295	23.7	82.8	1.9	1.3	1.0	14.2	7.4	17.4	10.1	12.8	10.6	13.4
31 121	24260	7	Merrick	1 256	7 766	2 614	6.2	93.9	0.7	0.8	1.5	4.1	5.9	17.8	7.5	10.7	10.8	14.6
31 123	...	9	Morrill	3 688	4 862	2 846	1.3	83.9	0.5	1.1	0.9	14.6	5.8	18.8	6.8	10.4	11.4	13.4
31 125	...	9	Nance	1 144	3 570	2 934	3.1	96.8	0.6	0.6	0.2	2.4	6.5	16.2	6.8	9.6	10.1	14.3
31 127	...	7	Nemaha	1 055	7 175	2 664	6.8	95.8	1.5	0.8	0.9	2.4	6.1	15.0	13.2	12.1	8.9	12.8
31 129	...	9	Nuckolls	1 490	4 369	2 875	2.9	96.9	0.6	0.9	0.5	2.2	4.5	16.1	5.6	9.5	9.4	13.1
31 131	...	6	Otoe	1 594	15 797	2 056	9.9	91.9	1.0	0.8	1.0	6.5	6.4	17.1	7.1	10.6	11.4	14.2
31 133	...	9	Pawnee	1 116	2 702	2 994	2.4	97.1	1.0	0.8	0.6	2.0	5.1	16.2	6.0	8.2	9.7	13.3
31 135	...	9	Perkins	2 288	2 891	2 985	1.3	95.7	0.5	0.3	0.4	3.4	6.7	17.2	5.8	10.5	10.1	13.2
31 137	...	7	Phelps	1 398	9 187	2 497	6.6	93.9	0.7	0.6	0.5	5.1	7.1	17.5	7.3	11.0	10.8	13.8
31 139	35740	9	Pierce	1 485	7 202	2 659	4.8	97.6	0.4	0.6	0.6	1.5	5.9	18.8	7.4	10.7	10.5	15.2

1. CBSA = Core Based Statistical Area. See Appendix A for explanation. See Appendix B for list of metropolitan areas with component counties. 2. County type code from the Economic Research Service of USDA Rural-Urban Continuum Codes. See Appendix A for definition. 3. Dry land or land partially or temporarily covered by water. 4. May be of any race.

STATE County	Population, 2013 (cont.): Age (percent) (cont.): 55 to 64 years	65 to 74 years	75 years and over	Percent female	Population change and components of change, 2000–2014: Total persons: 2000	2010	Percent change: 2000–2010	2010–2014	Components of change, 2010–2014: Births	Deaths	Net migration	Households, 2009–2013: Number	Persons per house-hold	Percent: Family house-holds	Female family house-holder[1]	One per-son
	16	17	18	19	20	21	22	23	24	25	26	27	28	29	30	31
NEBRASKA—Cont'd																
Blaine	15.8	13.1	8.7	48.1	583	478	-18.0	5.4	24	20	17	249	2.35	71.9	5.6	18.9
Boone	15.3	9.1	12.3	49.7	6 259	5 505	-12.0	-2.8	254	266	-132	2 242	2.38	65.9	5.4	31.4
Box Butte	16.5	8.0	7.7	50.0	12 158	11 308	-7.0	0.3	641	469	-126	4 860	2.28	62.9	9.7	34.0
Boyd	15.9	13.8	14.2	50.5	2 438	2 099	-13.9	-3.1	79	116	-29	938	2.20	60.6	3.2	36.6
Brown	16.7	11.3	12.7	51.6	3 525	3 145	-10.8	-6.4	114	154	-146	1 544	2.02	67.2	11.3	30.8
Buffalo	11.4	6.7	5.9	50.4	42 259	46 102	9.1	4.6	2 906	1 410	631	17 705	2.51	64.2	9.3	26.8
Burt	15.2	10.8	12.9	50.8	7 791	6 858	-12.0	-4.2	295	422	-161	2 899	2.29	69.0	7.6	28.6
Butler	14.2	9.5	10.7	49.4	8 767	8 395	-4.2	-1.7	396	408	-155	3 482	2.35	67.6	6.4	27.1
Cass	14.6	8.8	6.7	49.6	24 334	25 241	3.7	1.1	1 224	972	35	9 701	2.57	72.4	6.4	24.1
Cedar	14.5	9.1	12.0	49.6	9 615	8 852	-7.9	-2.7	429	420	-243	3 529	2.45	67.3	4.2	30.2
Chase	15.0	9.3	11.2	51.1	4 068	3 966	-2.5	0.3	186	198	33	1 697	2.30	68.7	8.0	27.0
Cherry	15.0	11.0	10.7	50.7	6 148	5 713	-7.1	0.9	291	245	-4	2 618	2.15	68.4	5.3	28.0
Cheyenne	13.4	7.8	8.6	50.4	9 830	9 998	1.7	1.5	535	370	-32	4 405	2.25	62.7	7.7	33.8
Clay	15.2	10.0	8.8	49.5	7 039	6 542	-7.1	-3.5	313	299	-223	2 647	2.41	69.8	7.2	27.1
Colfax	11.1	6.4	7.0	48.3	10 441	10 515	0.7	-0.1	717	318	-403	3 686	2.81	71.8	9.7	24.3
Cuming	13.5	9.3	11.9	50.2	10 203	9 139	-10.4	-1.2	453	410	-139	3 822	2.34	68.8	5.1	28.4
Custer	14.6	10.4	10.4	50.2	11 793	10 939	-7.2	-2.0	501	575	-158	4 738	2.26	66.4	6.1	29.9
Dakota	11.1	7.0	5.4	49.8	20 253	21 006	3.7	-0.7	1 591	629	-1 137	7 309	2.82	73.0	10.6	21.1
Dawes	11.9	8.6	8.7	50.3	9 060	9 182	1.3	-1.5	432	363	-211	3 709	2.15	58.0	7.7	36.9
Dawson	12.2	7.8	6.9	49.1	24 365	24 326	-0.2	-0.9	1 604	896	-914	8 774	2.73	70.9	10.9	26.0
Deuel	15.5	11.3	12.1	50.1	2 098	1 941	-7.5	-0.1	66	92	32	855	2.26	58.2	4.9	37.1
Dixon	15.3	10.4	8.8	50.1	6 339	6 000	-5.3	-3.6	295	258	-246	2 348	2.50	71.4	7.9	27.3
Dodge	12.7	9.1	9.7	50.9	36 160	36 691	1.5	0.1	2 029	1 786	-196	15 221	2.34	67.0	9.2	27.3
Douglas	11.5	6.3	5.0	50.8	463 585	517 110	11.5	5.1	35 355	15 889	7 298	204 226	2.51	61.9	12.4	31.1
Dundy	16.0	10.6	11.8	49.5	2 292	2 008	-12.4	-6.1	55	118	-53	893	2.18	71.1	4.3	23.6
Fillmore	15.3	10.5	12.3	50.5	6 634	5 890	-11.2	-3.9	237	358	-94	2 444	2.28	64.0	6.2	32.1
Franklin	16.1	12.0	13.0	49.7	3 574	3 225	-9.8	-4.6	113	155	-98	1 398	2.21	69.0	7.3	26.3
Frontier	15.9	11.1	9.8	48.7	3 099	2 756	-11.1	-1.9	95	68	-72	1 086	2.23	67.8	5.5	27.0
Furnas	16.2	11.6	11.6	50.3	5 324	4 959	-6.9	-1.4	194	279	23	2 215	2.18	63.9	6.3	34.4
Gage	14.6	9.6	10.3	50.6	22 993	22 311	-3.0	-2.9	1 029	1 179	-494	9 133	2.36	64.2	7.3	30.5
Garden	15.5	12.7	15.6	49.1	2 292	2 057	-10.3	-7.1	80	116	-107	836	2.29	70.0	6.8	28.0
Garfield	17.2	12.3	14.8	50.6	1 902	2 049	7.7	-2.2	55	136	25	864	2.21	63.2	3.7	33.8
Gosper	16.3	9.8	9.9	48.3	2 143	2 044	-4.6	-3.6	98	95	-91	767	2.57	75.1	5.9	21.9
Grant	16.7	10.1	8.4	46.0	747	614	-17.8	0.8	38	24	-11	246	2.38	71.1	8.5	28.5
Greeley	14.7	10.4	13.0	48.8	2 714	2 538	-6.5	-2.2	119	111	-67	1 011	2.44	68.1	9.1	30.8
Hall	11.8	7.3	6.6	49.8	53 534	58 607	9.5	4.9	3 887	2 174	1 172	22 168	2.64	65.9	11.1	27.0
Hamilton	14.7	9.0	8.6	49.9	9 403	9 124	-3.0	0.2	441	328	-77	3 488	2.56	73.5	7.9	22.7
Harlan	16.4	12.7	10.9	48.6	3 786	3 423	-9.6	2.0	175	179	73	1 573	2.15	63.8	5.9	35.1
Hayes	17.4	10.9	12.5	47.8	1 068	967	-9.5	-3.5	52	19	-80	477	2.39	74.0	2.1	24.5
Hitchcock	16.7	11.6	12.1	49.9	3 111	2 908	-6.5	-0.2	141	155	4	1 366	2.07	61.4	6.1	35.4
Holt	15.5	9.9	11.1	50.4	11 551	10 435	-9.7	-0.3	581	503	-110	4 469	2.29	65.5	3.9	30.3
Hooker	16.9	12.6	15.6	51.8	783	736	-6.0	-1.1	28	39	5	295	2.21	67.5	1.4	31.2
Howard	14.2	10.5	9.2	49.2	6 567	6 274	-4.5	1.4	302	255	57	2 576	2.43	68.1	5.9	28.1
Jefferson	16.0	10.7	11.4	50.4	8 333	7 547	-9.4	-2.8	345	445	-121	3 301	2.25	63.0	7.9	32.2
Johnson	13.8	8.4	9.0	41.8	4 488	5 217	16.2	-0.6	190	235	15	1 926	2.17	60.9	7.4	34.1
Kearney	14.1	9.5	9.5	51.0	6 882	6 489	-5.7	2.4	365	290	94	2 621	2.44	72.6	8.4	23.5
Keith	15.9	12.9	9.9	50.2	8 875	8 368	-5.7	-3.0	318	393	-176	3 786	2.15	64.6	7.6	29.3
Keya Paha	16.6	13.2	15.1	50.6	983	824	-16.2	-1.7	30	28	-17	354	1.97	66.7	7.9	31.4
Kimball	15.2	11.5	11.1	49.8	4 089	3 821	-6.6	-2.8	174	191	-81	1 641	2.27	63.5	6.8	35.6
Knox	15.0	10.8	12.9	51.3	9 374	8 701	-7.2	-2.5	407	494	-147	3 776	2.22	67.3	7.1	29.1
Lancaster	11.5	6.5	5.3	49.9	250 291	285 407	14.0	5.7	17 179	8 051	7 193	115 237	2.40	61.2	9.7	29.3
Lincoln	14.2	8.8	8.1	50.4	34 632	36 288	4.8	-1.3	1 861	1 471	-884	15 067	2.34	63.1	9.1	31.6
Logan	16.4	9.6	8.4	51.6	774	763	-1.4	-1.7	42	19	-35	345	2.28	66.7	4.6	29.0
Loup	20.7	15.3	9.4	50.0	712	632	-11.2	-6.4	23	18	-44	240	2.42	71.7	5.8	23.3
McPherson	14.1	9.7	9.9	50.0	533	539	1.1	-7.6	9	12	-41	169	2.24	78.7	7.7	18.9
Madison	12.9	7.4	7.8	50.4	35 226	34 876	-1.0	0.9	2 217	1 441	-498	13 867	2.44	65.6	10.4	29.4
Merrick	14.0	9.9	8.9	50.2	8 204	7 845	-4.4	-1.1	370	344	-115	3 316	2.29	69.4	8.3	23.3
Morrill	15.1	9.0	9.3	49.2	5 440	5 042	-7.3	-3.6	227	220	-226	2 037	2.37	70.1	12.4	26.9
Nance	16.0	8.9	11.6	50.3	4 038	3 735	-7.5	-4.4	178	187	-165	1 534	2.33	66.9	9.9	31.0
Nemaha	14.3	8.7	8.9	50.3	7 576	7 248	-4.3	-1.0	334	348	-20	3 001	2.23	59.2	7.1	34.7
Nuckolls	15.6	12.5	13.6	50.0	5 057	4 500	-11.0	-2.9	167	248	-32	2 119	2.08	67.2	6.7	30.3
Otoe	13.8	9.4	10.0	51.0	15 396	15 740	2.2	0.4	794	787	41	6 438	2.40	67.9	7.8	27.9
Pawnee	15.1	12.0	14.2	49.7	3 087	2 773	-10.2	-2.6	117	142	-30	1 314	2.07	58.9	5.5	36.6
Perkins	15.5	9.4	11.6	49.2	3 200	2 970	-7.2	-2.7	155	120	-113	1 262	2.30	68.5	3.2	25.3
Phelps	13.0	9.1	10.4	50.6	9 747	9 188	-5.7	0.0	475	465	-24	3 808	2.35	66.2	4.8	29.3
Pierce	13.4	8.9	9.1	49.4	7 857	7 266	-7.5	-0.9	352	276	-123	2 916	2.42	70.6	6.6	27.0

1. No spouse present.

STATE County	Persons in group quarters, 2014	Daytime population, 2009–2013: Number	Daytime population, 2009–2013: Employment/residence ratio	Births, 2014: Total	Births, 2014: Rate[1]	Deaths, 2014: Number	Deaths, 2014: Rate[1]	Persons under 65 with no health insurance, 2013: Number	Persons under 65 with no health insurance, 2013: Percent	Medicare, 2014: Eligible for Medicare	Medicare, 2014: Enrolled in Medicare Advantage	Medicare, 2014: Enrolled in a Medicare prescription drug plan	Serious crimes known to police,[2] 2013: Total: Number	Serious crimes known to police,[2] 2013: Total: Rate[3]
	32	33	34	35	36	37	38	39	40	41	42	43	44	45
NEBRASKA—Cont'd														
Blaine	0	502	0.70	6	11.9	5	9.9	110	29.5	110	NA	62	NA	NA
Boone	110	5 530	1.03	65	12.1	71	13.3	488	11.6	1 210	54	856	NA	NA
Box Butte	186	11 515	1.04	160	14.1	108	9.5	1 212	12.8	2 065	111	1 472	174	1 532
Boyd	31	2 006	0.91	16	7.9	23	11.3	254	17.5	619	NA	413	NA	NA
Brown	36	3 178	1.01	28	9.5	28	9.5	383	17.4	770	NA	496	21	702
Buffalo	2 187	47 944	1.04	699	14.5	342	7.1	4 648	11.7	7 011	619	4 357	1 124	2 341
Burt	129	5 919	0.74	71	10.8	98	14.9	651	13.1	1 714	155	1 128	NA	NA
Butler	174	7 429	0.78	100	12.1	87	10.5	727	11.1	1 794	97	1 237	56	676
Cass	293	18 615	0.48	293	11.5	228	8.9	2 080	9.8	4 541	606	2 304	335	1 332
Cedar	145	7 892	0.80	94	10.9	95	11.0	893	13.1	1 807	369	1 053	36	412
Chase	70	4 320	1.17	39	9.8	46	11.6	554	17.6	836	NA	629	50	1 217
Cherry	56	5 796	1.02	69	12.0	58	10.1	781	17.3	1 280	NA	845	45	783
Cheyenne	101	10 893	1.16	133	13.1	73	7.2	856	10.2	1 842	90	1 222	64	638
Clay	90	5 832	0.80	73	11.6	67	10.6	742	14.5	1 370	NA	975	NA	NA
Colfax	93	10 183	0.94	157	14.9	70	6.7	1 801	20.1	1 395	53	959	NA	NA
Cuming	135	8 787	0.93	115	12.7	87	9.6	1 059	15.1	2 080	122	1 494	22	243
Custer	126	10 640	0.96	126	11.7	128	11.9	1 332	15.7	2 371	NA	1 757	102	953
Dakota	255	21 472	1.05	388	18.6	123	5.9	3 587	19.8	3 077	765	1 494	322	1 563
Dawes	1 132	9 199	1.01	100	11.1	90	10.0	1 158	17.3	1 769	245	933	208	2 269
Dawson	299	24 241	1.00	387	16.1	201	8.3	3 939	19.4	3 881	503	2 517	520	2 146
Deuel	20	1 758	0.81	16	8.2	21	10.8	218	14.8	490	NA	329	22	1 108
Dixon	79	5 184	0.73	67	11.6	49	8.5	701	15.1	1 070	243	765	64	1 159
Dodge	1 251	36 147	0.97	485	13.2	403	11.0	4 122	14.3	7 731	809	4 551	833	2 341
Douglas	12 565	578 130	1.20	8 436	15.5	3 668	6.8	61 435	13.2	74 998	17 053	36 633	23 009	4 294
Dundy	35	1 985	0.99	12	6.4	23	12.2	288	19.0	454	NA	336	NA	NA
Fillmore	216	5 641	0.94	56	9.9	79	14.0	463	10.9	1 464	NA	1 043	NA	NA
Franklin	52	2 874	0.79	26	8.5	28	9.1	299	13.0	853	NA	608	17	534
Frontier	113	2 434	0.90	22	8.1	15	5.5	290	14.4	560	39	399	NA	NA
Furnas	77	4 925	1.00	49	10.0	59	12.1	526	14.2	1 280	NA	914	NA	NA
Gage	515	20 738	0.88	252	11.6	266	12.3	1 866	10.8	5 252	361	3 463	572	2 819
Garden	34	1 933	0.97	20	10.5	19	9.9	250	18.5	582	40	388	NA	NA
Garfield	46	2 001	1.06	14	7.0	27	13.5	283	19.2	482	14	348	NA	NA
Gosper	45	1 642	0.65	21	10.7	18	9.1	204	13.0	508	70	308	8	394
Grant	3	613	1.00	9	14.5	4	6.5	108	21.1	176	NA	129	NA	NA
Greeley	57	2 305	0.82	25	10.1	22	8.9	381	20.1	581	NA	381	NA	NA
Hall	1 141	64 031	1.15	924	15.0	502	8.2	8 721	16.9	9 636	858	5 868	2 759	4 522
Hamilton	118	8 382	0.84	110	12.0	81	8.9	695	9.3	1 899	90	1 295	95	1 056
Harlan	47	3 090	0.78	43	12.3	32	9.2	365	13.7	855	NA	594	NA	NA
Hayes	0	951	0.68	14	15.0	2	2.1	248	33.5	191	NA	121	NA	NA
Hitchcock	30	2 452	0.68	34	11.7	38	13.1	347	16.0	747	NA	546	29	1 003
Holt	118	10 466	1.01	137	13.2	124	11.9	1 175	14.3	2 536	NA	1 917	19	183
Hooker	28	794	1.26	7	9.6	7	9.6	85	16.1	227	NA	169	0	0
Howard	42	4 961	0.57	73	11.5	56	8.8	714	14.1	1 367	NA	933	NA	NA
Jefferson	101	7 641	1.02	83	11.3	89	12.1	723	12.4	1 902	140	1 330	NA	NA
Johnson	1 045	4 881	0.85	43	8.3	54	10.4	473	14.2	874	30	658	32	624
Kearney	85	5 940	0.83	88	13.2	58	8.7	553	10.5	1 233	51	899	102	1 570
Keith	41	8 060	0.95	76	9.4	82	10.1	867	13.9	2 078	162	1 357	170	2 076
Keya Paha	0	620	0.81	9	11.1	3	3.7	144	25.6	257	NA	184	2	250
Kimball	44	3 778	1.00	37	10.0	33	8.9	423	14.9	917	21	617	38	1 006
Knox	229	8 103	0.87	99	11.7	110	13.0	1 180	18.2	2 103	216	1 381	20	234
Lancaster	14 510	297 891	1.05	4 055	13.4	1 884	6.2	30 833	12.4	42 218	3 800	25 375	10 917	3 682
Lincoln	564	37 003	1.05	437	12.2	340	9.5	3 242	11.0	7 225	1 360	5 002	1 265	3 502
Logan	0	725	0.84	9	12.0	6	8.0	105	16.9	168	17	124	NA	NA
Loup	0	545	0.87	6	10.2	3	5.1	83	19.2	147	NA	96	NA	NA
McPherson	0	317	0.62	0	0.0	1	2.0	80	19.0	84	17	55	NA	NA
Madison	1 081	38 186	1.18	505	14.4	375	10.7	4 204	14.4	6 429	834	4 050	971	2 763
Merrick	196	6 944	0.78	88	11.3	73	9.4	839	13.5	1 726	105	1 105	90	1 158
Morrill	83	4 563	0.83	49	10.1	41	8.4	627	15.8	917	75	618	51	1 381
Nance	143	3 337	0.79	39	10.9	33	9.2	421	14.9	673	21	469	11	296
Nemaha	536	7 664	1.14	80	11.1	61	8.5	632	11.7	1 512	52	957	NA	NA
Nuckolls	54	4 143	0.85	37	8.5	61	14.0	482	14.9	1 215	34	829	NA	NA
Otoe	335	14 474	0.84	183	11.6	167	10.6	1 424	11.3	3 296	279	2 112	NA	NA
Pawnee	36	2 588	0.86	27	10.0	28	10.4	318	16.1	648	NA	461	52	1 877
Perkins	40	2 965	1.01	33	11.4	21	7.3	316	13.8	651	13	466	17	582
Phelps	250	9 797	1.13	109	11.9	95	10.3	776	10.6	2 023	11	1 538	154	1 666
Pierce	106	5 976	0.67	88	12.2	71	9.9	706	12.2	1 301	NA	956	NA	NA

1. Per 1,000 estimated resident population. 2. Data for serious crimes have not been adjusted for underreporting; this may affect comparability between geographic areas and over time.
3. Per 100,000 population estimated by the FBI.

Table B. States and Counties — **Crime, Education, Money Income, and Poverty**

STATE County	Serious crimes known to police, 2013 (cont.)[1] Rate[2] Violent	Rate[2] Property	Education: School enrollment and attainment, 2009–2013: Enrollment[3] Total	Enrollment[3] Percent private	Attainment[4] (percent) High school graduate or less	Attainment[4] (percent) Bachelor's degree or more	Local government expenditures,[5] 2012–2013: Total current spending (mil dol)	Current spending per student (dollars)	Money income, 2009–2013: Per capita income[6] (dollars)	Households: Median income (dollars)	Households: Mean income (dollars)	Households: Percent with income of $200,000 or more	Income and poverty, 2013: Median household income (dollars)	Percent below poverty level: All persons	Percent below poverty level: Children under 18 years	Percent below poverty level: Children 5 to 17 years in families
	46	47	48	49	50	51	52	53	54	55	56	57	58	59	60	61
NEBRASKA—Cont'd																
Blaine	NA	NA	172	4.1	39.8	16.0	2.3	21 575	19 141	42 917	47 630	0.4	38 323	18.0	29.7	31.7
Boone	NA	NA	1 206	16.3	53.0	13.8	12.8	15 336	25 590	45 246	60 694	3.3	50 156	9.9	13.0	11.9
Box Butte	176	1 356	2 883	6.8	45.0	17.6	23.3	11 740	25 046	46 373	57 422	1.4	54 120	12.9	18.8	17.3
Boyd	NA	NA	388	8.8	53.6	16.1	5.7	17 021	23 157	41 279	51 332	1.6	39 838	13.9	25.4	24.0
Brown	0	702	600	11.3	44.0	21.8	9.9	19 948	21 843	33 647	44 580	1.4	39 861	13.8	19.6	15.7
Buffalo	150	2 191	15 111	7.5	34.6	31.6	87.9	11 574	24 830	50 963	63 962	2.2	52 333	12.7	15.2	13.6
Burt	NA	NA	1 505	4.1	45.9	18.3	16.0	12 387	25 203	46 817	59 217	2.2	47 749	11.7	17.2	15.9
Butler	48	628	2 044	24.7	49.1	14.1	13.7	13 371	27 673	50 247	66 552	2.2	46 211	9.8	12.2	10.6
Cass	48	1 284	6 577	14.0	40.1	23.6	42.6	11 325	29 638	64 697	75 828	3.5	63 738	8.2	12.4	10.5
Cedar	0	412	2 163	25.3	50.0	16.6	17.1	15 161	25 738	48 038	63 100	2.8	56 300	9.4	13.1	11.9
Chase	170	1 047	851	1.4	46.0	18.2	10.2	12 833	28 241	45 610	65 331	2.4	52 924	9.8	12.8	11.5
Cherry	139	644	1 144	20.3	39.4	21.3	12.2	15 576	25 213	45 464	56 825	1.9	43 229	13.5	21.7	19.7
Cheyenne	NA	NA	2 346	8.5	34.5	25.3	19.5	11 674	28 296	51 529	64 016	3.0	53 430	9.9	13.7	11.9
Clay	NA	NA	1 578	6.5	47.4	17.6	19.5	13 025	23 876	46 784	58 493	1.8	50 587	11.4	17.9	17.1
Colfax	NA	NA	2 615	10.1	60.0	14.4	27.4	11 366	23 751	51 765	65 729	3.0	51 103	10.1	15.2	14.7
Cuming	0	243	2 140	28.4	51.1	17.5	19.2	12 145	24 496	47 500	58 433	1.5	50 252	9.8	13.1	11.7
Custer	56	897	2 465	9.6	43.6	21.0	25.4	14 350	24 615	44 873	56 201	1.3	44 608	13.1	19.7	18.3
Dakota	107	1 456	5 518	12.4	60.2	11.1	48.7	11 506	20 179	47 069	56 489	1.0	45 631	14.4	22.3	20.5
Dawes	120	2 149	2 713	2.6	29.4	40.6	13.7	11 899	21 137	40 359	51 271	1.7	39 507	17.5	22.3	19.2
Dawson	161	1 985	6 294	3.3	58.5	16.0	59.6	11 188	20 142	46 078	53 682	0.8	44 976	14.8	20.2	18.1
Deuel	151	957	418	2.6	39.2	21.8	7.2	16 465	27 199	44 922	58 523	1.5	48 523	12.8	23.0	20.1
Dixon	18	1 141	1 496	3.3	50.9	16.5	14.2	13 386	23 769	47 325	59 277	2.2	47 637	10.2	15.3	13.7
Dodge	149	2 192	8 692	20.5	51.2	18.7	69.3	11 902	24 588	48 626	59 038	1.6	48 671	11.3	15.1	14.0
Douglas	480	3 814	153 146	22.1	32.5	36.4	999.0	10 868	29 180	53 325	73 151	4.4	51 959	15.2	20.0	16.7
Dundy	NA	NA	381	6.6	41.5	22.2	5.8	14 708	28 502	47 431	66 016	5.2	47 098	13.6	20.6	17.5
Fillmore	NA	NA	1 331	7.5	46.5	18.2	13.5	15 045	25 460	48 464	59 178	1.8	52 606	9.0	12.9	11.8
Franklin	31	503	656	5.5	46.0	17.5	4.5	14 226	26 095	43 011	60 168	3.6	44 871	13.0	18.0	16.4
Frontier	NA	NA	662	12.7	43.1	16.5	9.1	15 588	25 262	50 227	58 516	1.5	48 258	13.4	14.6	12.2
Furnas	NA	NA	1 072	12.1	46.1	16.8	15.1	14 016	22 068	39 603	48 755	1.5	41 446	14.2	21.8	20.2
Gage	434	2 385	4 963	11.1	45.6	20.0	41.1	12 627	24 555	47 654	58 234	1.9	45 212	11.3	16.0	14.4
Garden	NA	NA	327	9.8	40.6	20.8	4.0	16 110	26 715	39 400	59 581	3.3	38 837	15.9	27.1	24.2
Garfield	NA	NA	412	7.8	55.1	13.8	4.4	12 052	22 092	41 892	48 227	1.0	40 758	12.9	19.0	16.2
Gosper	0	394	485	8.2	39.9	18.0	3.3	13 966	23 266	45 893	57 587	1.6	58 357	9.9	15.1	14.9
Grant	NA	NA	179	5.6	43.7	17.7	2.4	16 524	19 968	44 167	46 260	0.0	44 778	11.1	16.3	18.2
Greeley	NA	NA	559	16.8	49.9	15.0	7.3	16 310	23 833	44 950	55 178	1.6	42 743	13.6	19.5	17.3
Hall	238	4 284	14 964	10.4	49.6	17.1	138.3	11 398	23 380	48 712	60 255	1.9	49 750	14.9	22.2	19.6
Hamilton	11	1 045	2 315	12.5	38.0	24.1	19.3	12 168	26 715	56 065	68 413	3.3	54 663	8.8	11.7	10.8
Harlan	NA	NA	674	6.1	44.2	15.3	4.0	14 208	25 322	45 920	54 862	1.5	45 806	12.1	18.3	17.8
Hayes	NA	NA	257	2.7	39.2	19.8	2.4	20 033	23 749	49 125	57 483	3.4	51 101	14.6	25.1	23.7
Hitchcock	104	900	589	5.9	40.1	13.8	6.1	21 935	23 554	39 702	50 152	0.9	40 217	15.0	23.2	21.9
Holt	19	163	2 205	16.0	44.2	19.0	22.8	14 224	24 120	44 427	56 094	2.0	44 518	13.0	16.7	16.8
Hooker	0	0	160	5.6	36.4	24.7	2.9	16 842	20 737	39 327	47 083	1.7	39 377	9.9	12.6	12.8
Howard	NA	NA	1 497	9.0	47.4	17.8	8.9	11 760	26 770	49 088	64 704	1.8	49 496	10.9	14.8	13.8
Jefferson	NA	NA	1 702	6.0	54.3	13.5	19.8	12 583	24 777	44 843	56 039	1.7	46 252	12.7	19.8	17.4
Johnson	20	605	1 020	9.0	55.1	12.8	9.7	12 664	19 435	42 364	52 684	2.2	46 456	14.8	17.5	16.2
Kearney	139	1 431	1 521	4.4	37.9	26.4	16.3	13 001	27 796	56 466	67 561	3.5	57 823	9.2	13.4	12.4
Keith	98	1 978	1 581	14.1	42.7	20.4	20.7	18 569	25 097	41 970	55 426	0.5	42 851	13.9	22.4	18.4
Keya Paha	0	250	111	2.7	49.2	17.2	2.1	22 011	25 251	36 923	48 451	0.8	41 491	19.4	33.3	30.6
Kimball	476	529	792	5.4	47.2	16.4	6.8	12 447	24 565	42 180	55 007	1.9	45 023	13.6	19.6	17.8
Knox	0	234	1 877	10.8	50.8	17.0	22.5	14 831	25 214	42 230	56 204	2.0	41 066	15.1	21.0	19.1
Lancaster	345	3 337	88 831	17.1	29.5	36.1	435.9	10 395	27 141	51 574	67 394	3.2	52 275	14.8	16.7	14.7
Lincoln	141	3 361	9 287	15.7	41.7	19.4	57.9	10 029	26 188	48 158	62 136	2.1	52 395	12.6	17.9	16.3
Logan	NA	NA	178	7.3	38.8	19.9	2.7	12 748	22 799	44 417	53 042	0.6	48 688	10.6	14.9	13.8
Loup	NA	NA	145	3.4	49.0	12.6	1.8	20 466	21 499	38 125	51 307	1.7	41 192	16.7	29.4	25.3
McPherson	NA	NA	53	0.0	37.5	26.3	1.8	18 657	25 339	54 926	59 789	1.2	40 834	14.9	29.3	26.2
Madison	97	2 666	9 143	20.6	40.4	20.8	60.3	10 818	24 593	46 566	60 360	3.0	45 738	12.5	17.4	16.4
Merrick	39	1 119	1 800	7.8	45.4	17.0	11.6	11 821	24 639	50 859	60 368	1.2	50 317	11.1	16.3	14.9
Morrill	0	1 381	1 137	8.0	48.4	18.3	12.7	14 269	22 543	43 886	54 148	1.6	47 296	13.4	19.2	17.0
Nance	54	242	752	5.6	49.7	13.2	10.2	13 090	23 684	44 286	55 881	2.1	45 091	12.6	18.0	16.9
Nemaha	NA	NA	2 115	8.8	44.0	24.9	18.9	16 960	25 269	42 672	60 571	1.8	48 892	13.2	17.1	16.2
Nuckolls	NA	NA	872	9.6	52.1	13.7	6.1	13 324	22 448	37 594	48 490	0.8	44 139	11.6	18.8	16.6
Otoe	NA	NA	3 629	15.8	46.6	23.2	28.7	11 290	25 855	50 881	62 732	1.9	52 565	9.8	13.7	12.0
Pawnee	72	1 804	477	19.1	60.0	11.6	7.1	14 573	25 426	37 321	53 310	1.6	38 735	15.2	23.7	22.2
Perkins	68	514	610	22.1	37.1	22.3	6.3	15 649	27 931	58 625	64 759	1.7	53 893	10.0	13.4	12.6
Phelps	65	1 601	2 127	14.4	36.3	21.7	22.9	14 467	26 856	50 000	64 266	2.3	53 607	8.7	12.9	12.8
Pierce	NA	NA	1 770	17.1	46.4	18.8	15.5	12 370	24 830	51 924	61 588	1.5	50 807	9.6	12.1	10.8

1. Data for serious crimes have not been adjusted for underreporting; this may affect comparability between geographic areas and over time. 2. Per 100,000 population estimated by the FBI.
3. All persons 3 years old and over enrolled in nursery school through college. 4. Persons 25 years old and over. 5. Elementary and secondary education expenditures.
6. Based on population estimated by the American Community Survey, 2009–2013.

STATE County	Personal income, 2013										Earnings, 2013		
			Per capita[1]			Supplements to wages and salaries; employer contributions (mil dol)						Contributions for government social insurance (mil dol)	
	Total (mil dol)	Percent change, 2012–2013	Dollars	Rank	Wages and salaries (mil dol)	Pension and insurance	Government social insurance	Proprietors' income (mil dol)	Dividends, interest, and rent (mil dol)	Personal transfer receipts (mil dol)	Total (mil dol)	From employee and self-employed	From employer
	62	63	64	65	66	67	68	69	70	71	72	73	74
NEBRASKA—Cont'd													
Blaine	15	10.7	31 598	2 464	5	1	0	0	5	3	7	0	0
Boone	333	22.5	61 816	88	83	17	6	131	59	41	236	8	6
Box Butte	486	2.0	42 987	841	252	40	29	73	82	88	394	23	29
Boyd	99	1.7	48 889	423	16	5	1	39	16	22	61	2	1
Brown	143	8.6	48 719	437	43	9	3	39	30	28	93	4	3
Buffalo	2 635	-0.5	55 023	201	1 010	183	75	373	977	278	1 640	91	75
Burt	352	17.0	53 508	252	68	14	5	103	50	61	189	8	5
Butler	437	9.4	52 588	284	97	19	7	133	70	61	257	10	7
Cass	1 177	8.6	46 421	596	198	38	15	146	199	173	397	22	15
Cedar	579	23.8	66 427	62	98	20	7	275	98	57	400	11	7
Chase	236	-11.2	58 905	122	68	13	5	87	50	30	171	6	5
Cherry	253	5.6	43 768	779	74	15	5	63	56	42	157	7	5
Cheyenne	537	2.2	53 214	262	326	48	21	79	79	66	473	27	21
Clay	335	-0.3	52 381	291	106	22	7	100	54	48	235	9	7
Colfax	467	14.3	44 808	709	189	35	14	128	74	55	365	16	14
Cuming	702	18.8	77 993	25	149	26	10	379	87	64	564	19	10
Custer	532	2.0	49 305	403	164	32	12	162	90	85	370	15	12
Dakota	723	7.3	34 502	1 985	470	85	35	145	86	127	735	40	35
Dawes	303	0.1	33 292	2 209	116	27	9	33	64	66	185	11	9
Dawson	945	1.1	39 035	1 294	406	80	30	192	157	154	708	35	30
Deuel	75	-3.1	38 689	1 339	21	4	1	11	16	16	37	2	1
Dixon	272	23.0	46 537	581	62	13	4	90	41	35	170	6	4
Dodge	1 567	4.4	42 920	853	615	114	46	270	282	285	1 045	57	46
Douglas	26 863	2.0	50 000	368	16 730	2 491	1 261	4 155	5 211	3 286	24 637	1 444	1 261
Dundy	135	1.3	67 927	56	31	5	2	50	30	19	87	3	2
Fillmore	360	2.4	63 243	75	88	18	6	133	65	50	244	8	6
Franklin	142	-7.7	46 100	613	26	6	2	43	28	28	76	3	2
Frontier	142	10.8	52 445	288	30	7	2	60	20	19	99	4	2
Furnas	231	8.3	47 399	517	71	15	5	56	43	47	147	7	5
Gage	1 057	9.6	48 362	460	315	65	23	255	173	220	659	34	23
Garden	100	-2.9	52 703	278	23	5	2	31	21	20	60	2	2
Garfield	92	2.8	45 059	684	26	5	2	25	21	17	58	3	2
Gosper	113	0.4	57 438	149	19	4	1	38	21	17	61	2	1
Grant	22	3.6	34 303	2 031	7	1	1	1	8	5	10	1	1
Greeley	115	9.7	45 921	623	23	5	2	41	23	20	71	2	2
Hall	2 439	1.4	40 162	1 155	1 341	242	100	274	495	400	1 957	113	100
Hamilton	527	0.4	57 884	138	133	23	10	163	109	63	330	13	10
Harlan	171	1.5	48 777	433	30	6	2	57	31	30	95	3	2
Hayes	73	-4.7	74 472	33	9	2	1	45	9	6	56	1	1
Hitchcock	125	2.4	43 631	787	30	7	2	32	20	28	72	4	2
Holt	590	-1.1	56 457	178	166	30	12	230	89	93	438	18	12
Hooker	25	3.3	33 789	2 128	10	2	1	0	6	7	13	1	1
Howard	296	10.3	46 601	577	52	12	4	78	46	48	146	6	4
Jefferson	350	11.1	46 257	603	118	22	10	77	70	65	227	11	10
Johnson	205	13.6	39 867	1 185	58	16	4	54	29	32	132	6	4
Kearney	460	-0.6	70 278	46	86	16	6	211	59	54	319	12	6
Keith	359	2.5	44 216	741	111	21	8	84	75	68	225	12	8
Keya Paha	46	3.0	58 358	128	6	1	0	22	9	7	29	1	0
Kimball	191	-0.6	51 491	317	66	13	5	46	32	33	130	7	5
Knox	397	19.4	46 393	599	93	21	7	131	67	72	252	9	7
Lancaster	12 594	2.3	42 399	896	7 093	1 305	531	892	2 614	1 738	9 821	575	531
Lincoln	1 649	-2.7	45 730	641	732	119	73	320	261	304	1 244	72	73
Logan	39	1.6	51 257	324	7	1	0	16	5	6	25	1	0
Loup	20	10.2	34 481	1 992	4	1	0	2	5	5	7	0	0
McPherson	16	19.2	29 568	2 744	3	1	0	1	5	3	5	0	0
Madison	1 507	5.9	42 709	869	808	151	59	249	288	249	1 266	70	59
Merrick	369	5.9	47 335	524	89	17	6	99	55	63	210	9	6
Morrill	279	1.5	56 812	164	63	12	4	119	37	36	199	7	4
Nance	192	19.8	52 903	271	41	8	3	73	23	29	125	4	3
Nemaha	347	9.9	48 486	452	157	33	11	81	60	62	282	13	11
Nuckolls	230	6.4	52 037	299	47	10	3	83	36	44	143	5	3
Otoe	738	7.0	46 869	560	231	46	17	111	189	121	405	21	17
Pawnee	140	29.1	51 615	314	30	7	2	55	21	22	95	3	2
Perkins	189	2.1	64 723	69	49	10	3	78	36	21	139	5	3
Phelps	490	-0.2	53 235	261	186	38	13	133	82	75	369	16	13
Pierce	379	11.9	53 065	267	73	15	5	130	64	47	224	8	5

1. Based on the resident population estimated as of July 1 of the year shown.

STATE County	Earnings, 2013 (cont.) Percent by selected industries									Social Security beneficiaries, December 2013		Supple-mental Security Income recipients, December 2013	Housing units, 2014	
	Farm	Mining	Construction	Manu-facturing	Infor-mation: professional, scientific, technical services	Retail trade	Finance, insur-ance, real estate and leasing	Health care and social assistance	Govern-ment	Number	Rate[1]		Total	Percent change, 2010–2014
	75	76	77	78	79	80	81	82	83	84	85	86	87	88
NEBRASKA—Cont'd														
Blaine	13.6	0.0	D	0.0	0.0	D	D	D	56.1	110	229	0	323	-0.9
Boone	50.7	0.0	2.4	4.8	0.8	3.2	2.3	3.5	14.1	1 265	235	55	2 643	-0.2
Box Butte	14.1	0.0	2.2	4.7	D	3.8	2.5	3.6	15.5	1 815	160	188	5 434	-0.8
Boyd	41.9	0.0	1.7	1.0	D	2.8	3.1	4.0	15.8	630	312	28	1 375	-1.1
Brown	31.9	0.0	4.2	1.3	D	7.2	D	3.5	24.2	800	274	49	1 845	-1.0
Buffalo	5.8	0.1	4.9	20.7	4.8	7.4	4.1	14.5	14.2	7 420	154	478	19 753	3.6
Burt	44.5	0.0	4.0	4.4	D	3.1	4.0	4.5	14.2	1 835	279	102	3 462	-0.1
Butler	45.4	D	3.5	12.6	D	2.5	D	D	13.0	1 910	229	93	4 060	0.2
Cass	21.4	3.5	5.6	7.8	2.7	6.1	5.4	4.7	18.2	4 775	188	225	11 250	1.2
Cedar	56.6	D	5.0	3.2	1.6	2.8	3.0	2.3	8.5	1 905	219	60	4 132	-0.4
Chase	42.2	D	3.8	0.9	D	7.4	3.9	1.3	14.4	895	225	39	1 933	-0.7
Cherry	31.8	0.0	6.7	1.7	3.8	7.6	2.2	5.8	19.2	1 345	233	77	3 160	0.1
Cheyenne	8.4	0.5	2.2	4.1	2.6	8.2	2.2	6.2	8.7	1 960	194	123	4 961	1.5
Clay	39.9	D	5.9	9.5	D	2.6	D	3.5	17.8	1 460	229	62	2 992	-0.3
Colfax	27.9	D	D	D	1.5	2.8	1.9	D	9.6	1 515	146	85	4 140	1.0
Cuming	40.0	D	3.0	25.1	1.6	1.9	3.2	4.1	6.5	2 125	236	79	4 211	0.2
Custer	38.7	0.0	6.1	10.0	2.4	4.6	3.6	6.7	12.1	2 520	233	128	5 559	-0.4
Dakota	7.7	D	5.2	40.0	D	3.8	7.7	2.9	9.7	3 405	163	277	7 747	1.5
Dawes	5.7	D	4.7	D	2.9	12.4	3.7	11.9	33.8	1 795	197	118	4 221	-0.7
Dawson	21.0	D	2.9	23.6	3.0	5.6	3.1	D	17.1	4 245	176	328	10 136	0.1
Deuel	19.6	0.0	D	0.0	D	9.1	D	7.4	23.7	515	266	23	1 033	-1.1
Dixon	46.1	0.0	6.1	D	D	1.3	1.4	1.9	11.4	1 130	194	51	2 700	0.4
Dodge	15.7	0.1	4.1	18.1	2.7	8.3	4.1	D	16.8	8 295	227	503	16 631	0.3
Douglas	0.1	D	8.5	7.0	12.3	5.2	11.9	12.1	11.3	78 485	146	9 880	226 919	3.3
Dundy	53.3	0.0	2.9	1.0	D	2.0	1.3	2.5	14.4	510	259	25	1 115	-0.9
Fillmore	48.1	0.0	6.2	4.6	0.5	2.8	4.7	3.0	13.7	1 545	272	60	2 916	0.1
Franklin	47.5	0.0	2.8	0.0	D	4.5	D	3.1	19.6	895	290	53	1 726	-0.5
Frontier	43.2	0.0	5.1	D	D	2.2	7.0	D	15.4	585	216	26	1 570	-0.3
Furnas	36.6	0.0	3.2	4.5	6.1	3.4	D	8.2	16.6	1 370	282	78	2 711	-0.4
Gage	20.9	D	3.3	22.3	1.8	6.4	3.0	D	17.0	5 565	255	375	10 420	-0.2
Garden	51.0	0.0	D	D	D	7.5	3.1	0.6	21.0	630	331	31	1 301	-1.0
Garfield	26.4	D	5.7	5.7	2.2	5.5	D	7.5	13.7	515	253	19	1 174	-0.3
Gosper	60.0	0.0	3.5	D	D	1.0	D	0.4	12.2	505	256	13	1 279	0.9
Grant	27.1	0.0	3.5	0.0	D	10.5	D	D	30.9	180	288	0	389	-0.5
Greeley	50.8	0.0	2.8	1.6	D	D	3.7	0.4	15.4	625	252	31	1 299	-0.1
Hall	4.6	0.0	5.8	20.4	3.6	8.5	5.2	11.7	15.7	10 310	169	928	24 174	2.7
Hamilton	41.6	0.0	3.7	7.5	4.0	3.8	2.8	D	8.7	2 020	221	66	4 041	1.9
Harlan	55.5	D	1.8	0.7	D	4.2	D	D	14.1	895	255	43	2 365	-0.4
Hayes	82.5	D	D	D	D	D	D	0.2	6.2	175	180	12	509	-0.4
Hitchcock	29.1	5.8	4.7	14.1	D	2.2	0.9	0.6	18.4	810	282	49	1 736	-1.5
Holt	35.8	0.2	2.9	9.5	1.4	4.9	3.7	D	9.0	2 695	258	181	5 222	0.1
Hooker	-1.4	0.0	2.9	D	D	3.2	D	D	28.0	220	301	0	434	0.7
Howard	46.1	0.4	2.9	2.1	1.7	4.1	2.9	3.1	22.4	1 435	226	64	3 006	1.9
Jefferson	28.0	0.3	6.2	12.7	2.8	7.3	2.5	8.4	12.2	1 960	260	153	3 903	-0.4
Johnson	28.5	0.0	D	4.9	D	3.9	6.8	4.2	35.2	930	181	48	2 172	-0.9
Kearney	35.9	0.0	2.8	35.3	D	1.1	1.7	D	7.5	1 285	196	82	2 928	1.5
Keith	24.7	D	5.9	5.2	3.3	8.5	5.5	7.8	12.6	2 200	271	112	5 378	-0.8
Keya Paha	74.7	0.0	D	D	D	D	D	D	9.6	260	326	12	544	-0.9
Kimball	15.7	15.8	2.4	11.2	D	5.0	D	D	15.7	955	259	45	1 942	-1.1
Knox	49.9	0.0	2.2	2.5	D	4.3	2.5	D	18.9	2 290	268	136	4 869	1.7
Lancaster	0.9	D	5.5	8.5	9.3	6.1	10.1	13.2	22.2	43 285	146	4 717	124 817	3.3
Lincoln	13.7	D	3.8	5.4	2.9	6.3	3.4	13.6	14.6	6 360	176	717	16 609	0.2
Logan	68.9	0.0	D	D	D	0.9	D	0.5	14.0	165	216	11	395	0.0
Loup	42.8	0.0	0.8	0.0	0.0	D	D	1.1	32.9	155	267	0	436	2.6
McPherson	39.7	0.0	0.0	D	D	D	D	0.0	41.2	85	163	0	280	-1.1
Madison	8.7	D	4.4	16.0	3.5	8.0	5.3	14.6	16.5	6 870	195	548	15 119	0.7
Merrick	34.1	D	11.5	7.2	D	3.1	4.0	D	12.7	1 855	238	146	3 758	1.5
Morrill	46.1	D	1.9	1.1	D	3.8	1.6	D	14.4	1 020	209	89	2 425	-0.7
Nance	51.7	D	D	D	1.4	2.6	2.9	4.8	14.7	755	210	59	1 840	2.2
Nemaha	23.0	0.0	1.6	4.6	D	2.9	2.8	4.4	49.2	1 630	227	136	3 499	0.0
Nuckolls	47.3	0.0	D	D	D	5.0	3.5	10.5	12.0	1 270	289	67	2 450	-0.6
Otoe	19.9	0.0	5.0	18.2	2.2	6.0	3.7	D	20.4	3 405	217	215	7 069	0.6
Pawnee	52.9	D	D	12.4	0.4	2.8	2.1	2.9	16.1	680	249	37	1 603	0.9
Perkins	44.0	0.0	9.0	3.1	D	1.9	D	1.9	13.4	660	227	18	1 442	-0.6
Phelps	31.2	D	D	D	2.2	4.2	4.2	D	11.4	2 110	229	115	4 208	0.8
Pierce	47.4	0.2	5.0	3.1	1.4	3.5	3.7	5.8	8.8	1 405	196	62	3 227	0.2

1. Per 1,000 resident population estimated as of July 1 of the year shown.

STATE County	Housing units, 2009–2013: Total	Occupied units: Owner-occupied: Percent	Owner-occupied: Median value[1]	Median owner cost as a percent of income: With a mortgage	Median owner cost as a percent of income: Without a mortgage[2]	Renter-occupied: Median rent[3]	Renter-occupied: Median rent as a percent of income[2]	Sub-standard units[4] (percent)	Civilian labor force, 2014: Total	Percent change, 2013–2014	Unemployment: Total	Unemployment: Rate[5]	Civilian employment,[6] 2009–2013: Total	Percent: Management, business, science and arts	Percent: Construction, production, and maintenance occupations
	89	90	91	92	93	94	95	96	97	98	99	100	101	102	103
NEBRASKA—Cont'd															
Blaine	249	58.2	57 200	23.2	10.0	600	22.1	1.9	266	-2.6	12	4.5	290	33.8	35.9
Boone	2 242	77.0	85 000	21.4	12.3	487	16.5	4.1	3 054	-0.5	80	2.6	2 784	34.8	28.0
Box Butte	4 860	65.9	90 000	18.9	11.0	513	25.8	2.2	5 861	-2.4	180	3.1	5 521	30.8	38.9
Boyd	938	83.2	54 500	24.2	12.4	432	23.2	0.0	1 113	-1.9	37	3.3	967	41.4	26.1
Brown	1 544	69.5	58 900	24.3	14.6	451	21.0	1.1	1 435	-0.5	49	3.4	1 566	37.1	29.5
Buffalo	17 705	64.8	139 800	21.1	11.4	678	27.9	1.4	27 662	0.5	757	2.7	25 999	31.6	24.3
Burt	2 899	76.6	85 700	20.5	13.7	591	24.6	4.6	3 635	-1.2	158	4.3	3 200	33.4	23.8
Butler	3 482	75.9	99 200	19.5	11.4	588	21.7	1.8	4 854	1.0	144	3.0	4 235	30.7	36.8
Cass	9 701	79.2	146 700	22.3	13.8	775	24.2	1.5	13 416	0.3	507	3.8	12 737	33.3	26.4
Cedar	3 529	81.2	89 100	19.6	12.1	551	25.4	0.2	4 719	-0.7	114	2.4	4 508	33.1	29.3
Chase	1 697	77.1	86 000	20.9	12.4	571	17.9	0.8	2 368	-1.9	48	2.0	2 041	33.6	26.8
Cherry	2 618	67.0	95 500	21.9	11.5	483	22.4	1.7	3 456	-1.4	86	2.5	3 273	37.1	21.8
Cheyenne	4 405	66.7	104 100	18.3	12.4	580	24.4	1.7	5 825	-0.2	125	2.1	5 632	33.9	20.7
Clay	2 647	77.8	76 100	19.7	11.9	524	22.8	5.7	3 502	-0.4	116	3.3	3 222	33.2	32.7
Colfax	3 686	74.4	87 900	19.2	10.6	613	21.9	2.3	5 665	0.4	167	2.9	5 086	22.0	49.3
Cuming	3 822	70.6	88 300	19.3	10.7	591	24.3	1.7	4 977	-0.1	134	2.7	4 639	31.8	31.7
Custer	4 738	75.5	81 600	19.7	13.1	556	21.7	5.9	6 195	0.2	151	2.4	5 634	32.7	32.1
Dakota	7 309	64.4	103 300	20.8	13.1	703	28.0	1.9	11 448	0.2	608	5.3	10 390	20.9	39.3
Dawes	3 709	64.8	100 700	20.0	15.3	546	29.8	5.8	5 336	-2.1	166	3.1	4 824	34.8	18.5
Dawson	8 774	68.3	88 200	21.0	13.1	624	24.4	0.2	13 372	0.4	467	3.5	11 874	23.1	43.6
Deuel	855	77.7	67 400	19.6	12.0	604	19.9	1.9	1 093	-4.0	30	2.7	1 040	28.2	27.5
Dixon	2 348	76.8	76 300	19.2	12.3	523	23.5	2.0	3 147	0.3	106	3.4	2 929	30.6	35.5
Dodge	15 221	68.0	109 200	19.6	13.1	694	23.8	2.6	19 362	0.2	705	3.6	18 429	25.4	30.4
Douglas	204 226	62.7	143 300	21.8	12.9	790	29.2	0.0	289 144	0.5	10 587	3.7	271 014	38.9	18.2
Dundy	893	67.6	69 100	18.1	11.3	462	16.5	0.5	1 318	0.7	30	2.3	980	44.5	31.6
Fillmore	2 444	77.3	73 300	17.6	11.1	526	22.7	2.1	3 291	-0.8	79	2.4	3 087	32.8	30.1
Franklin	1 398	82.2	56 200	18.4	12.0	543	23.1	1.2	1 584	-1.3	51	3.2	1 532	34.2	30.3
Frontier	1 086	74.5	74 200	19.3	11.1	527	17.2	1.4	1 561	-2.6	43	2.8	1 330	33.3	27.2
Furnas	2 215	72.3	56 400	23.5	13.4	488	17.9	1.5	2 730	-0.4	78	2.9	2 271	33.9	29.4
Gage	9 133	72.4	101 600	20.4	12.4	610	24.7	0.7	11 150	-0.2	469	4.2	10 904	34.4	26.1
Garden	836	77.6	61 800	24.9	11.2	545	22.1	0.0	1 190	-4.0	35	2.9	990	31.0	21.8
Garfield	864	74.2	86 100	22.4	12.2	338	25.5	0.5	1 216	-1.7	32	2.6	988	24.2	36.4
Gosper	767	76.4	104 100	21.9	11.2	583	20.8	1.2	1 145	-2.1	34	3.0	1 063	23.4	29.2
Grant	246	66.3	45 600	23.8	10.0	620	20.0	0.4	416	-1.4	11	2.6	320	37.8	36.3
Greeley	1 011	80.8	57 500	21.5	12.0	493	16.6	4.1	1 290	-1.1	41	3.2	1 186	33.4	31.1
Hall	22 168	65.3	113 200	21.0	12.8	646	25.5	0.7	32 722	0.1	1 256	3.8	30 802	25.4	32.3
Hamilton	3 488	77.6	113 300	19.6	11.1	709	28.1	1.1	4 852	-0.3	143	2.9	4 638	32.8	27.0
Harlan	1 573	77.9	75 100	18.9	13.0	546	21.3	3.1	1 832	-2.0	49	2.7	1 676	31.5	30.0
Hayes	477	67.7	66 100	23.4	11.3	621	22.2	4.0	623	-4.0	18	2.9	619	40.5	35.5
Hitchcock	1 366	73.3	62 300	18.8	11.7	554	30.9	1.4	1 351	-1.2	48	3.6	1 359	34.0	32.5
Holt	4 469	74.5	90 500	19.4	13.5	543	24.4	2.0	5 995	-0.6	161	2.7	5 642	31.6	28.5
Hooker	295	85.4	63 300	21.1	16.3	761	28.6	0.5	432	-1.1	18	4.2	367	36.0	27.2
Howard	2 576	79.4	101 200	20.5	13.6	558	25.0	1.3	3 434	0.0	125	3.6	3 248	33.7	31.0
Jefferson	3 301	78.2	70 400	18.6	12.1	465	23.1	1.5	4 351	-0.3	134	3.1	3 811	30.6	27.0
Johnson	1 926	74.0	75 300	21.7	13.7	560	19.5	1.5	2 184	-0.5	85	3.9	2 085	28.8	30.7
Kearney	2 621	73.3	96 400	18.5	12.1	687	22.1	0.2	3 872	-1.2	95	2.5	3 514	29.7	31.1
Keith	3 786	70.0	91 500	19.6	14.0	601	23.6	2.0	4 708	-0.4	136	2.9	4 193	30.4	29.9
Keya Paha	354	81.4	80 000	30.0	13.3	438	25.7	2.9	617	0.7	17	2.8	422	45.0	23.7
Kimball	1 641	66.1	77 900	23.5	13.8	632	24.8	1.2	2 251	1.9	59	2.6	1 827	29.2	31.4
Knox	3 776	72.6	74 000	19.0	11.7	408	19.6	2.3	4 791	-0.7	151	3.2	4 215	32.3	30.0
Lancaster	115 237	60.1	148 600	21.2	11.1	715	29.1	1.6	170 250	0.5	4 986	2.9	155 801	38.6	19.1
Lincoln	15 067	68.6	112 800	21.2	13.8	626	25.4	3.2	18 969	-1.7	615	3.2	17 764	26.3	32.8
Logan	345	72.5	101 700	25.9	12.3	561	20.5	0.0	503	-0.4	16	3.2	400	31.0	30.8
Loup	240	71.7	71 100	30.0	10.0	480	18.9	0.0	378	-0.3	14	3.7	288	46.5	28.5
McPherson	169	69.2	142 300	19.5	11.6	620	13.6	2.8	378	1.3	11	2.9	175	32.0	37.7
Madison	13 867	66.1	109 000	19.6	11.9	571	26.5	1.1	19 454	0.2	576	3.0	18 326	28.1	29.2
Merrick	3 316	72.7	85 300	19.0	12.3	581	27.2	2.1	4 222	0.0	157	3.7	4 014	30.3	27.6
Morrill	2 037	66.5	76 300	20.2	12.5	651	24.0	2.3	2 707	-2.1	81	3.0	2 370	28.6	32.1
Nance	1 534	75.4	67 000	18.8	11.1	531	28.9	2.9	2 090	0.2	57	2.7	1 804	32.5	31.4
Nemaha	3 001	68.3	84 400	17.8	11.8	487	24.5	2.0	3 764	-2.0	151	4.0	3 426	31.8	27.0
Nuckolls	2 119	76.1	52 300	18.4	11.5	498	21.5	1.1	2 440	-1.2	70	2.9	2 136	32.1	29.7
Otoe	6 438	73.1	118 000	19.6	11.7	650	27.3	3.4	8 349	-1.5	318	3.8	8 172	30.5	30.3
Pawnee	1 314	74.9	57 200	22.3	13.4	456	25.3	0.4	1 669	-1.4	47	2.8	1 257	35.5	29.3
Perkins	1 262	75.1	88 500	17.1	11.6	590	20.6	0.3	1 861	1.7	40	2.1	1 557	43.4	27.6
Phelps	3 808	72.1	100 700	18.9	11.5	597	23.0	1.3	5 087	-0.5	135	2.7	4 664	30.4	29.2
Pierce	2 916	80.2	97 000	21.5	11.7	562	18.5	2.5	4 258	0.5	121	2.8	3 748	33.0	30.7

1. Specified owner-occupied units. 2. A value of 10.0 represents 10 percent or less; a value of 50.0 represents 50 percent or more. 3. Specified renter-occupied units.
4. Overcrowded or lacking complete plumbing facilities. 5. Percent of civilian labor force. 6. Persons 16 years old and over.

Table B. States and Counties — **Nonfarm Employment and Agriculture**

STATE County	Private nonfarm establishments, employment and payroll, 2013									Agriculture, 2012			
		Employment						Annual payroll		Farms			
											Percent with:		
	Number of establish-ments	Total	Health care and social assistance	Manufac-turing	Retail trade	Finance and insurance	Professional, scientific, and technical services	Total (mil dol)	Average per employee (dollars)	Number	Fewer than 50 acres	500 acres or more	Farm operators whose principal occu-pation is farming (percent)
	104	105	106	107	108	109	110	111	112	113	114	115	116
NEBRASKA—Cont'd													
Blaine	8	D	NA	NA	NA	D	NA	D	D	117	14.5	66.7	76.1
Boone	191	1 415	288	102	248	D	28	47	33 406	646	12.7	42.4	68.3
Box Butte	312	2 982	627	D	511	D	94	95	31 895	466	17.8	48.7	59.9
Boyd	67	380	108	D	73	36	D	9	24 405	266	14.7	56.0	59.4
Brown	129	889	184	D	283	41	D	24	26 529	328	24.1	51.2	68.3
Buffalo	1 558	21 705	3 855	3 199	3 793	643	618	725	33 384	1 046	29.4	31.4	53.2
Burt	195	1 550	199	D	157	D	D	53	33 901	560	22.9	35.0	63.0
Butler	208	2 072	364	668	D	D	D	67	32 467	840	23.8	32.5	58.2
Cass	534	3 507	D	408	628	225	131	123	34 954	731	34.1	31.1	54.2
Cedar	300	1 867	D	D	326	137	85	58	31 029	939	20.8	29.9	58.7
Chase	148	1 017	D	D	272	75	18	34	33 624	342	11.7	54.1	64.9
Cherry	230	1 793	D	D	447	D	70	43	24 037	566	14.8	70.8	80.4
Cheyenne	291	4 601	D	D	878	146	80	256	55 554	555	10.6	54.1	58.9
Clay	190	1 134	D	73	185	D	20	37	32 829	457	25.2	42.5	67.0
Colfax	253	3 542	258	D	339	97	64	126	35 524	554	22.6	30.3	66.1
Cuming	344	2 543	357	242	384	179	101	83	32 591	918	26.1	25.1	61.2
Custer	382	2 833	617	D	552	167	85	88	31 114	1 352	21.1	43.3	62.9
Dakota	428	10 407	504	D	888	D	81	378	36 335	243	35.0	28.0	42.4
Dawes	277	2 224	563	D	635	D	D	60	26 867	493	11.8	52.7	53.5
Dawson	693	9 291	1 112	3 176	1 507	276	234	295	31 741	806	24.9	39.0	64.6
Deuel	58	333	23	NA	105	D	D	9	25 736	237	14.3	51.1	58.2
Dixon	105	1 242	D	D	75	44	D	39	31 122	570	24.9	31.1	60.5
Dodge	1 013	15 180	2 614	3 129	2 483	438	187	483	31 843	767	29.6	28.3	68.3
Douglas	15 069	307 365	45 254	20 824	35 524	34 555	19 559	14 366	46 738	396	58.3	13.6	44.4
Dundy	66	338	101	22	51	15	23	12	34 666	251	8.0	59.0	55.0
Fillmore	222	1 644	274	227	221	159	22	56	33 810	472	13.1	48.5	72.5
Franklin	74	439	D	NA	105	44	D	12	26 499	338	11.2	47.9	67.8
Frontier	71	458	D	D	83	43	D	12	27 275	317	15.8	51.1	60.6
Furnas	169	1 310	368	109	193	75	19	48	36 289	389	16.7	48.3	67.1
Gage	673	7 241	1 889	1 425	1 037	214	129	210	29 047	1 263	26.6	27.4	49.6
Garden	53	410	D	D	D	24	D	9	22 598	261	20.3	51.7	69.7
Garfield	94	578	116	98	121	D	24	14	24 870	226	16.8	41.2	58.0
Gosper	61	270	D	D	29	26	D	9	31 856	260	13.1	55.0	63.1
Grant	30	90	NA	D	D	D	D	2	22 389	80	13.8	65.0	75.0
Greeley	66	337	D	D	NA	33	NA	9	28 083	389	9.0	47.8	68.9
Hall	1 812	30 339	4 450	6 998	5 039	1 201	658	985	32 470	593	29.3	34.2	59.9
Hamilton	292	2 525	342	428	296	118	89	91	35 973	572	22.7	40.2	72.0
Harlan	103	624	D	D	100	53	34	17	27 522	360	19.7	40.6	60.6
Hayes	20	67	D	D	D	D	D	1	21 478	235	8.1	60.0	67.7
Hitchcock	67	382	D	81	NA	26	NA	15	38 139	299	10.4	50.8	59.5
Holt	419	3 466	852	D	644	179	70	109	31 316	1 279	14.3	49.4	64.4
Hooker	32	D	D	D	D	D	D	4	D	82	11.0	76.8	54.9
Howard	150	949	D	D	190	D	D	28	29 022	682	26.1	29.0	59.1
Jefferson	237	2 628	D	D	482	D	49	77	29 331	627	21.9	33.2	55.5
Johnson	117	937	D	D	D	D	D	26	28 253	587	22.7	25.0	49.1
Kearney	173	1 957	D	269	D	79	D	58	29 548	344	15.1	56.1	78.5
Keith	342	2 631	D	D	585	188	125	72	27 288	388	14.7	46.4	72.2
Keya Paha	21	D	NA	NA	D	D	4	1	D	244	11.9	66.0	73.0
Kimball	129	1 017	D	D	179	D	27	36	35 379	402	9.0	52.5	52.5
Knox	264	1 625	313	36	374	153	66	39	23 934	1 080	17.5	38.1	68.3
Lancaster	8 049	127 883	22 952	11 904	17 792	10 430	8 818	4 897	38 292	1 836	51.1	14.9	34.2
Lincoln	1 049	11 311	2 439	271	2 259	503	455	363	32 078	1 168	29.8	39.2	59.2
Logan	23	77	D	D	D	D	D	2	25 039	149	22.8	46.3	63.8
Loup	8	D	NA	NA	NA	D	NA	D	D	138	12.3	49.3	62.3
McPherson	6	D	NA	NA	NA	D	NA	0	D	118	11.9	71.2	59.3
Madison	1 320	18 047	2 720	3 062	3 148	672	649	601	33 280	753	25.9	29.9	59.2
Merrick	244	1 699	D	294	201	D	D	59	34 670	492	27.8	33.7	57.1
Morrill	118	695	D	D	203	47	D	22	31 072	512	19.3	42.6	61.1
Nance	104	570	134	NA	105	50	D	13	22 714	355	22.8	34.9	64.2
Nemaha	191	1 455	325	D	250	111	D	41	28 491	451	16.0	33.3	57.6
Nuckolls	170	1 123	365	D	237	D	46	30	26 561	435	16.3	43.7	55.2
Otoe	467	5 127	D	1 509	821	199	95	160	31 219	897	29.8	29.7	40.3
Pawnee	66	519	116	D	60	48	D	15	28 736	540	12.4	34.1	52.0
Perkins	127	782	D	12	126	D	D	29	37 153	394	8.6	57.1	65.7
Phelps	330	3 908	853	D	429	154	86	134	34 244	405	16.3	54.1	72.3
Pierce	231	1 455	341	111	186	84	44	46	31 716	677	21.1	30.9	60.4

STATE County	Agriculture, 2012 (cont.) Land in farms Acreage (1,000)	Land in farms Percent change, 2007–2012	Land in farms Acres Average size of farm	Land in farms Acres Total irrigated (1,000)	Land in farms Acres Total cropland (1,000)	Value of land and buildings (dollars) Average per farm	Value of land and buildings (dollars) Average per acre	Value of machinery and equipment, average per farm (dollars)	Value of products sold Total (mil dol)	Value of products sold Average per farm (dollars)	Value of products sold Percent from: Crops	Value of products sold Percent from: Livestock and poultry products	Percent of farms with sales of: $10,000 or more	Percent of farms with sales of: $100,000 or more	Government payments Total ($1,000)	Government payments Percent of farms
	117	118	119	120	121	122	123	124	125	126	127	128	129	130	131	132
NEBRASKA—Cont'd																
Blaine	403	-9.2	3 440	7.0	32.6	1 760 274	512	95 709	34.7	296 214	16.3	83.7	76.9	39.3	293	32.5
Boone	434	7.2	672	184.7	326.9	2 964 181	4 408	289 596	453.4	701 850	42.9	57.1	83.4	59.0	5 870	78.8
Box Butte	675	0.7	1 449	141.6	337.5	1 547 721	1 068	292 384	299.3	642 170	56.3	43.7	65.2	43.3	4 279	68.2
Boyd	291	15.6	1 094	5.2	98.0	1 504 169	1 375	147 015	62.9	236 477	30.2	69.8	72.9	32.3	913	75.9
Brown	725	9.6	2 212	40.2	109.4	1 584 393	716	138 912	195.4	595 826	20.1	79.9	66.5	43.3	1 694	38.4
Buffalo	581	-5.2	555	240.8	342.3	2 074 083	3 737	226 212	395.1	377 751	68.9	31.1	67.5	40.6	8 102	64.9
Burt	310	12.7	553	37.6	278.5	2 886 561	5 216	245 725	226.9	405 252	66.2	33.8	72.3	50.4	4 598	77.0
Butler	370	3.9	441	110.8	306.6	2 179 969	4 948	258 019	276.4	329 043	66.9	33.1	67.0	42.9	6 657	78.6
Cass	345	22.8	472	3.5	304.3	2 732 765	5 792	210 464	149.3	204 291	93.9	6.1	60.7	41.6	4 746	66.5
Cedar	466	-1.7	497	139.0	371.7	2 189 874	4 408	211 296	388.7	413 987	42.0	58.0	75.6	45.4	6 256	73.7
Chase	541	-2.6	1 583	159.7	290.6	3 112 181	1 966	393 310	414.9	1 213 085	44.2	55.8	65.2	52.6	6 032	76.9
Cherry	3 757	-0.1	6 637	50.9	358.5	3 521 118	531	181 652	246.8	435 974	32.4	67.6	78.3	55.7	3 354	27.2
Cheyenne	703	-6.8	1 267	48.7	499.3	1 131 528	893	203 490	205.7	370 593	43.6	56.4	65.0	38.6	7 026	85.4
Clay	331	-9.5	723	191.7	259.1	3 712 295	5 133	386 182	355.1	776 978	59.6	40.4	77.9	58.4	5 141	73.7
Colfax	258	20.8	465	66.8	224.9	2 460 460	5 291	266 197	337.9	609 935	34.2	65.8	77.8	45.5	5 060	75.8
Cuming	363	0.8	395	52.4	312.6	2 120 511	5 364	285 514	1 081.3	1 177 889	12.9	87.1	79.3	49.3	6 797	76.8
Custer	1 504	-6.9	1 112	261.5	484.9	2 110 533	1 898	187 440	845.3	625 226	34.7	65.3	70.6	40.8	7 479	55.4
Dakota	158	-5.2	650	29.3	136.0	3 120 123	4 799	228 041	73.0	300 317	89.4	10.6	56.4	28.8	2 079	68.3
Dawes	824	-2.9	1 671	21.4	172.7	1 243 284	744	109 030	75.6	153 410	27.8	72.2	62.1	37.9	2 428	67.5
Dawson	630	-1.6	782	248.5	321.8	2 429 274	3 106	263 305	826.3	1 025 163	34.3	65.7	71.3	48.9	6 166	55.2
Deuel	277	-0.8	1 168	17.4	216.1	1 167 042	999	226 080	70.6	297 971	57.3	42.7	69.2	43.9	2 383	69.6
Dixon	299	20.3	525	24.0	226.3	2 176 037	4 148	211 812	169.1	296 716	42.0	58.0	63.0	35.4	4 695	73.7
Dodge	330	-2.5	430	118.0	305.0	2 414 327	5 611	281 532	326.0	425 043	60.7	39.3	72.2	48.9	5 602	74.3
Douglas	86	2.1	217	19.8	76.3	1 352 033	6 217	152 404	58.0	146 513	93.4	6.6	47.0	23.7	1 378	40.9
Dundy	521	-12.4	2 075	94.8	208.6	2 820 614	1 359	377 386	195.6	779 363	54.1	45.9	69.3	51.8	3 944	73.3
Fillmore	328	-9.3	696	211.0	296.4	3 835 816	5 513	473 146	334.8	709 335	78.0	22.0	84.1	68.9	5 465	81.4
Franklin	288	-1.3	851	85.8	166.2	2 527 118	2 969	260 417	119.1	352 447	87.0	13.0	78.4	48.2	3 802	81.1
Frontier	452	-4.9	1 426	53.3	174.7	2 093 385	1 468	232 278	124.6	393 145	53.1	46.9	70.7	41.0	3 205	74.4
Furnas	436	-2.3	1 120	66.4	282.7	2 622 414	2 341	282 820	181.6	466 720	54.2	45.8	69.9	44.2	5 719	82.3
Gage	534	-1.1	423	63.8	422.0	1 477 063	3 491	156 753	244.5	193 561	71.5	28.5	60.9	35.7	9 908	75.5
Garden	1 026	-2.1	3 932	35.7	149.4	2 403 636	611	180 276	113.6	435 341	33.3	66.7	65.5	44.1	1 714	70.1
Garfield	346	-5.4	1 531	22.5	70.7	1 517 035	991	146 903	64.8	286 597	34.9	65.1	74.3	42.9	1 373	48.7
Gosper	290	28.5	1 115	98.8	171.8	3 529 077	3 165	330 900	139.1	534 885	79.2	20.8	76.5	55.8	3 628	73.5
Grant	493	-0.4	6 167	1.7	41.0	3 407 063	552	136 288	29.0	362 063	D	D	71.3	53.8	226	8.8
Greeley	338	19.8	870	88.2	154.4	2 807 974	3 229	210 997	187.6	482 134	45.5	54.5	75.1	47.0	3 064	74.0
Hall	330	0.4	556	207.6	245.4	2 484 954	4 470	292 526	353.1	595 405	65.9	34.1	69.5	52.1	4 755	64.6
Hamilton	304	-4.6	532	235.5	273.2	3 430 491	6 446	346 014	353.2	617 547	77.1	22.9	77.4	62.4	5 705	77.6
Harlan	313	-10.9	869	93.3	211.8	2 677 533	3 082	261 208	223.5	620 828	56.6	43.4	67.8	44.2	2 989	68.1
Hayes	385	-15.1	1 639	57.1	186.1	2 121 255	1 294	253 677	163.4	695 383	44.9	55.1	70.2	50.2	4 320	92.8
Hitchcock	399	14.8	1 335	21.5	207.4	1 723 151	1 290	204 060	63.6	212 803	67.4	32.6	71.2	42.1	3 553	79.9
Holt	1 414	-7.7	1 106	280.2	600.5	2 314 973	2 093	217 735	636.4	497 540	51.7	48.3	77.2	43.2	7 584	53.2
Hooker	437	-4.4	5 327	3.1	15.7	2 361 890	443	104 793	17.3	210 500	10.9	89.1	81.7	35.4	897	34.1
Howard	312	12.0	458	115.4	182.5	1 350 003	2 949	186 560	246.3	361 128	45.5	54.5	71.7	39.9	3 603	70.1
Jefferson	352	8.2	562	92.8	270.7	2 206 616	3 928	230 150	219.6	350 234	62.2	37.8	66.3	39.4	5 179	74.8
Johnson	198	12.6	337	14.3	132.9	856 930	2 545	107 278	74.6	127 112	58.7	41.3	54.7	26.7	3 405	79.9
Kearney	294	-9.4	854	194.5	242.8	4 508 817	5 283	440 390	407.4	1 184 375	56.9	43.1	84.0	72.4	5 065	80.2
Keith	541	-6.9	1 395	115.3	253.9	2 593 289	1 859	276 216	228.3	588 492	60.7	39.3	65.7	44.3	3 371	67.0
Keya Paha	466	-3.7	1 909	20.1	98.0	1 480 037	775	148 684	107.1	438 848	27.2	72.8	77.9	43.0	733	40.6
Kimball	598	13.3	1 487	34.4	384.8	1 289 806	868	160 933	60.8	151 256	83.5	16.5	51.0	30.6	5 236	87.3
Knox	628	17.0	581	63.9	326.6	1 612 287	2 774	174 033	312.8	289 671	29.9	70.1	69.4	35.1	7 276	74.4
Lancaster	489	16.0	266	21.4	402.6	1 219 781	4 580	123 412	177.8	96 822	82.5	17.5	42.8	18.1	8 810	59.5
Lincoln	1 423	-11.1	1 219	239.8	432.3	1 749 910	1 436	196 783	782.7	670 087	33.8	66.2	62.2	33.0	5 832	45.5
Logan	330	-9.2	2 216	23.0	61.4	2 518 114	1 136	213 148	42.0	281 846	62.5	37.5	63.1	39.6	1 180	53.0
Loup	283	-20.2	2 051	8.2	29.3	1 519 891	741	106 181	32.1	232 406	24.2	75.8	68.8	37.7	772	58.7
McPherson	471	-13.2	3 990	7.1	20.2	1 789 517	449	88 102	30.1	255 144	19.5	80.5	70.3	39.8	167	18.6
Madison	352	11.6	467	122.0	291.0	2 250 416	4 817	236 368	303.7	403 263	49.2	50.8	71.8	40.2	7 057	69.5
Merrick	235	-5.2	478	167.4	200.2	1 833 841	3 838	280 335	275.2	559 394	58.6	41.4	66.1	47.8	4 182	72.6
Morrill	799	-11.4	1 561	128.6	240.5	1 440 148	923	169 750	345.2	674 223	33.1	66.9	68.9	45.1	3 595	69.7
Nance	208	-8.0	586	63.3	133.7	2 003 290	3 417	204 239	145.9	410 927	49.3	50.7	70.4	46.8	3 285	73.5
Nemaha	253	19.1	562	11.4	211.4	2 284 878	4 068	234 035	108.1	239 772	89.3	10.7	67.4	42.4	4 984	80.9
Nuckolls	350	13.9	804	65.2	230.4	3 033 191	3 773	259 074	168.4	387 140	81.8	18.2	82.8	54.7	4 756	79.3
Otoe	388	20.4	432	8.4	321.9	1 856 521	4 295	174 511	158.5	176 670	84.1	15.9	61.3	36.8	5 428	69.3
Pawnee	269	23.5	498	7.3	180.1	1 288 361	2 588	153 443	75.7	140 241	75.7	24.3	58.7	29.6	4 461	78.3
Perkins	557	-0.3	1 413	127.9	432.1	3 208 183	2 271	350 124	233.1	591 713	78.2	21.8	76.9	56.3	7 804	85.8
Phelps	331	-2.6	818	231.9	265.0	3 684 978	4 504	546 160	738.8	1 824 185	35.7	64.3	85.7	76.3	6 054	77.3
Pierce	329	3.9	486	130.0	260.6	2 102 468	4 324	270 908	261.2	385 832	56.4	43.6	72.8	41.1	5 154	70.3

STATE County	Water use, 2010		Wholesale trade,[1] 2007				Retail trade,[2] 2007				Real estate and rental and leasing,[2] 2007			
	Total water withdrawn (mil gal/day)	Gallons withdrawn per person per day	Number of establish-ments	Number of employees	Sales (mil dol)	Annual payroll (mil dol)	Number of establish-ments	Number of employees	Sales (mil dol)	Annual payroll (mil dol)	Number of establish-ments	Number of employees	Receipts (mil dol)	Annual payroll (mil dol)
	133	134	135	136	137	138	139	140	141	142	143	144	145	146
NEBRASKA—Cont'd														
Blaine	3.1	6 444	NA	NA	NA	NA	4	D	D	D	NA	NA	NA	NA
Boone	60.9	11 055	12	179	92.7	5.6	45	290	81.6	4.8	5	25	3.2	0.4
Box Butte	101.8	9 002	19	197	90.0	6.6	55	474	82.2	7.6	17	46	9.1	1.1
Boyd	9.1	4 350	2	D	D	D	14	120	13.2	1.0	1	D	D	D
Brown	51.1	16 232	4	50	26.3	1.4	29	226	48.1	4.0	1	D	D	D
Buffalo	230.8	5 007	66	776	659.3	33.4	250	3 653	739.9	67.8	62	210	34.1	5.1
Burt	10.6	1 550	21	183	70.4	5.2	34	146	40.6	2.8	3	10	0.3	0.1
Butler	51.2	6 100	13	107	118.8	4.5	26	402	72.3	5.9	1	D	D	D
Cass	18.4	728	18	103	99.1	3.6	74	734	183.6	13.3	24	41	3.9	0.6
Cedar	28.4	3 209	22	124	69.7	3.8	55	348	121.8	6.4	8	14	1.2	0.3
Chase	144.2	36 364	15	161	135.1	7.1	31	307	60.4	5.4	3	7	1.1	0.1
Cherry	44.7	7 826	6	D	D	D	48	468	78.3	7.6	6	7	1.2	0.2
Cheyenne	43.3	4 327	15	76	97.9	3.2	57	D	D	D	10	19	7.6	0.4
Clay	121.3	18 546	19	141	155.6	4.1	28	212	60.7	4.3	2	D	D	D
Colfax	24.1	2 294	15	99	63.6	3.9	48	400	107.6	8.6	3	4	0.2	0.1
Cuming	12.8	1 395	29	158	117.4	5.0	61	429	174.6	8.1	3	7	1.0	0.1
Custer	169.1	15 460	14	113	52.8	3.6	81	511	118.0	8.8	9	D	D	D
Dakota	7.4	350	19	D	D	D	73	878	170.3	16.5	16	D	D	D
Dawes	7.9	861	5	33	10.0	0.7	58	706	164.6	12.9	12	15	1.6	0.3
Dawson	182.7	7 511	32	403	424.7	14.1	123	1 576	345.3	32.8	22	46	4.1	0.6
Deuel	28.0	14 405	3	D	D	D	12	125	102.0	2.3	1	D	D	D
Dixon	9.6	1 597	9	D	D	D	18	219	37.1	2.5	1	D	D	D
Dodge	36.0	980	63	D	D	D	176	2 356	665.0	53.5	45	162	21.1	3.2
Douglas	386.0	746	760	10 589	6 079.8	494.7	1 863	36 151	8 109.0	805.7	719	5 588	961.6	186.2
Dundy	108.0	53 800	5	D	D	D	9	51	14.0	0.9	2	D	D	D
Fillmore	120.6	20 467	21	162	113.4	5.1	38	219	39.7	3.6	3	4	0.2	0.0
Franklin	37.5	11 622	8	68	51.2	1.8	18	117	17.3	1.7	NA	NA	NA	NA
Frontier	36.0	13 059	4	D	D	D	14	90	14.8	1.1	2	D	D	D
Furnas	32.8	6 622	12	91	88.6	2.6	35	224	50.2	4.0	3	3	0.6	0.0
Gage	24.9	1 115	32	D	D	D	118	1 164	238.1	22.4	22	69	8.1	1.3
Garden	27.9	13 578	5	D	D	D	11	72	12.4	0.9	NA	NA	NA	NA
Garfield	12.7	6 193	4	64	9.2	0.9	24	124	27.1	1.9	1	D	D	D
Gosper	57.3	28 048	5	D	D	D	7	23	2.3	0.2	4	13	4.3	0.5
Grant	2.1	3 453	4	26	8.3	0.5	6	D	D	D	NA	NA	NA	NA
Greeley	51.5	20 280	4	45	23.8	1.1	19	91	25.4	1.7	1	D	D	D
Hall	132.6	2 263	100	1 192	707.9	50.5	336	5 113	1 087.7	99.4	68	261	44.6	7.2
Hamilton	142.7	15 642	13	322	375.5	12.9	41	308	101.1	5.1	8	D	D	D
Harlan	37.2	10 876	11	55	55.1	1.4	17	96	26.0	1.8	1	D	D	D
Hayes	41.6	43 020	NA	NA	NA	NA	2	D	D	D	NA	NA	NA	NA
Hitchcock	24.6	8 473	7	28	18.7	0.5	10	D	D	D	NA	NA	NA	NA
Holt	358.2	34 327	37	395	149.3	8.6	87	716	143.2	10.3	9	25	4.2	1.1
Hooker	2.6	3 519	1	D	D	D	7	D	D	D	NA	NA	NA	NA
Howard	168.0	26 771	7	49	38.4	1.6	30	260	48.4	3.8	2	D	D	D
Jefferson	40.6	5 376	16	132	139.0	4.8	38	496	124.8	9.3	10	21	1.0	0.3
Johnson	6.9	1 326	4	D	D	D	28	144	34.4	2.5	2	D	D	D
Kearney	103.6	15 958	14	154	151.7	4.4	25	172	29.7	2.6	3	4	0.6	0.1
Keith	119.8	14 315	15	100	54.7	3.9	70	628	203.8	12.4	14	22	2.0	0.5
Keya Paha	22.1	26 796	2	D	D	D	4	D	D	D	NA	NA	NA	NA
Kimball	29.1	7 618	4	D	D	D	29	191	49.0	3.9	2	D	D	D
Knox	33.1	3 800	10	92	61.8	2.5	62	395	82.4	6.4	5	21	0.9	0.3
Lancaster	22.0	77	272	3 823	2 729.9	166.3	1 052	17 169	3 662.7	345.8	367	1 558	250.6	43.1
Lincoln	263.4	7 257	39	356	245.4	13.4	204	2 419	634.9	47.6	35	152	20.7	2.9
Logan	12.3	16 107	2	D	D	D	3	D	D	D	NA	NA	NA	NA
Loup	9.1	14 320	1	D	D	D	3	D	D	D	1	D	D	D
McPherson	6.9	12 801	NA	NA	NA	NA	3	D	D	D	NA	NA	NA	NA
Madison	40.5	1 162	65	1 797	1 880.2	61.8	230	3 067	649.7	57.8	61	D	D	D
Merrick	111.9	14 264	18	162	208.7	5.4	37	195	45.6	3.3	4	D	D	D
Morrill	213.9	42 422	13	134	48.1	4.9	24	152	46.2	2.7	2	D	D	D
Nance	36.4	9 751	5	24	35.0	0.9	18	113	22.4	1.7	2	D	D	D
Nemaha	727.0	100 304	11	56	59.9	2.1	44	305	59.3	4.7	4	10	1.0	0.1
Nuckolls	62.4	13 860	14	81	147.0	2.6	32	252	53.3	4.3	3	D	D	D
Otoe	314.8	19 998	19	139	238.0	5.4	84	858	146.8	14.1	16	48	6.0	1.1
Pawnee	4.9	1 771	2	D	D	D	13	73	14.4	1.1	1	D	D	D
Perkins	96.5	32 495	15	82	128.3	2.5	15	114	44.7	2.7	3	14	0.7	0.2
Phelps	153.9	16 748	24	285	152.0	10.1	50	385	94.5	7.8	11	34	1.5	0.3
Pierce	54.4	7 480	18	162	77.6	4.7	36	215	41.4	3.0	4	D	D	D

1. Merchant wholesalers, except manufacturers' sales branches and offices. 2. Employer establishments.

STATE County	Professional, scientific, and technical services,[1] 2007				Manufacturing, 2007				Accommodation and food services, 2007			
	Number of establish-ments	Number of employees	Receipts (mil dol)	Annual payroll (mil dol)	Number of establish-ments	Number of employees	Receipts (mil dol)	Annual payroll (mil dol)	Number of establish-ments	Number of employees	Sales (mil dol)	Annual payroll (mil dol)
	147	148	149	150	151	152	153	154	155	156	157	158
NEBRASKA—Cont'd												
Blaine	NA	NA	NA	NA	NA	NA	NA	NA	1	D	D	D
Boone	7	23	4.1	0.6	NA	NA	NA	NA	17	113	3.6	0.8
Box Butte	25	100	7.3	2.3	NA	NA	NA	NA	34	410	12.4	3.3
Boyd	3	D	D	D	NA	NA	NA	NA	5	D	D	D
Brown	6	32	2.3	0.7	NA	NA	NA	NA	11	111	2.9	0.7
Buffalo	93	527	44.2	18.6	59	4 292	D	D	137	2 585	103.1	28.3
Burt	11	62	13.5	2.5	NA	NA	NA	NA	12	68	2.0	0.4
Butler	11	98	3.7	1.8	10	612	D	D	13	60	2.0	0.4
Cass	35	D	D	D	NA	NA	NA	NA	46	537	14.2	4.1
Cedar	11	56	5.0	1.3	NA	NA	NA	NA	17	176	3.5	0.9
Chase	11	20	2.5	0.5	NA	NA	NA	NA	11	69	2.0	0.6
Cherry	14	53	5.7	1.1	NA	NA	NA	NA	21	276	9.7	2.7
Cheyenne	12	32	3.4	1.0	NA	NA	NA	NA	39	507	21.1	5.4
Clay	6	22	2.5	0.6	NA	NA	NA	NA	7	36	1.4	0.3
Colfax	9	39	3.9	0.7	6	D	D	D	16	124	3.5	0.8
Cuming	20	D	D	D	NA	NA	NA	NA	20	229	6.5	2.0
Custer	25	81	7.1	1.8	NA	NA	NA	NA	31	292	8.2	2.3
Dakota	17	D	D	D	39	D	D	D	35	499	19.2	5.6
Dawes	21	148	5.7	1.9	NA	NA	NA	NA	41	538	13.7	4.1
Dawson	60	D	D	D	31	D	D	D	57	694	24.7	6.1
Deuel	4	7	0.6	0.2	NA	NA	NA	NA	7	93	4.1	1.3
Dixon	2	D	D	D	3	D	D	D	14	35	1.9	0.3
Dodge	53	D	D	D	61	3 299	1 233.8	121.2	98	1 454	53.0	13.9
Douglas	1 631	D	D	D	513	23 258	10 012.8	961.2	1 237	25 985	1 118.9	321.6
Dundy	6	14	1.3	0.3	NA	NA	NA	NA	6	24	0.5	0.1
Fillmore	8	20	1.3	0.3	NA	NA	NA	NA	21	196	3.5	0.8
Franklin	4	18	0.8	0.3	NA	NA	NA	NA	5	20	1.0	0.2
Frontier	2	D	D	D	NA	NA	NA	NA	4	25	0.6	0.1
Furnas	9	16	1.4	0.4	NA	NA	NA	NA	14	D	D	D
Gage	30	132	11.7	3.7	44	1 994	602.6	66.8	47	580	23.4	4.8
Garden	2	D	D	D	NA	NA	NA	NA	6	D	D	D
Garfield	5	18	1.3	0.4	NA	NA	NA	NA	9	66	1.3	0.3
Gosper	3	D	D	D	NA	NA	NA	NA	4	23	1.7	0.2
Grant	1	D	D	D	NA	NA	NA	NA	2	D	D	D
Greeley	NA	NA	NA	NA	NA	NA	NA	NA	3	9	0.4	0.1
Hall	99	D	D	D	79	D	D	D	136	2 551	96.9	28.1
Hamilton	19	68	8.0	2.8	24	617	463.4	20.6	13	160	5.1	1.5
Harlan	10	25	2.3	0.6	NA	NA	NA	NA	12	82	2.8	0.6
Hayes	2	D	D	D	NA	NA	NA	NA	3	3	0.3	0.0
Hitchcock	NA	NA	NA	NA	NA	NA	NA	NA	6	19	1.0	0.2
Holt	22	72	9.3	2.6	NA	NA	NA	NA	35	333	10.2	2.4
Hooker	NA	NA	NA	NA	NA	NA	NA	NA	5	D	D	D
Howard	8	D	D	D	NA	NA	NA	NA	12	63	2.8	0.5
Jefferson	12	44	3.4	1.1	13	531	127.9	19.7	22	187	6.4	1.5
Johnson	3	8	0.6	0.1	NA	NA	NA	NA	9	78	3.1	0.7
Kearney	10	16	1.5	0.5	NA	NA	NA	NA	14	94	2.8	0.7
Keith	28	114	9.2	3.1	NA	NA	NA	NA	46	562	22.8	5.0
Keya Paha	2	D	D	D	NA	NA	NA	NA	1	D	D	D
Kimball	9	21	1.4	0.2	NA	NA	NA	NA	15	82	3.1	0.7
Knox	18	64	5.6	1.5	NA	NA	NA	NA	23	74	3.3	0.5
Lancaster	773	8 282	1 102.6	383.8	252	13 413	D	540.6	651	12 028	472.5	132.9
Lincoln	81	D	D	D	NA	NA	NA	NA	96	D	D	D
Logan	1	D	D	D	NA	NA	NA	NA	NA	NA	NA	NA
Loup	NA	NA	NA	NA	NA	NA	NA	NA	NA	NA	NA	NA
McPherson	NA	NA	NA	NA	NA	NA	NA	NA	2	D	D	D
Madison	85	D	D	D	53	D	D	D	87	1 451	48.5	14.0
Merrick	10	D	D	D	NA	NA	NA	NA	16	176	3.9	1.1
Morrill	1	D	D	D	NA	NA	NA	NA	13	82	3.2	0.7
Nance	4	13	0.4	0.2	NA	NA	NA	NA	8	25	0.8	0.2
Nemaha	14	45	3.5	1.3	NA	NA	NA	NA	23	326	7.0	2.3
Nuckolls	10	31	2.7	0.6	NA	NA	NA	NA	8	81	2.1	0.5
Otoe	26	77	8.6	2.8	12	1 395	405.4	48.3	41	612	17.0	5.1
Pawnee	4	D	D	D	NA	NA	NA	NA	6	42	0.9	0.2
Perkins	7	19	1.7	0.3	NA	NA	NA	NA	4	34	0.8	0.2
Phelps	31	110	9.3	3.8	9	D	D	D	20	297	9.1	2.3
Pierce	10	D	D	D	NA	NA	NA	NA	9	81	1.6	0.4

1. Establishment subject to federal tax.

Table B. States and Counties — Health Care and Social Assistance, Other Services, Nonemployer Businesses, and Residential Construction

STATE County	Health care and social assistance, 2007				Other services, 2007				Nonemployer businesses, 2013		Value of residential construction authorized by building permits, 2014	
	Number of establish-ments	Number of employees	Receipts (mil dol)	Annual payroll (mil dol)	Number of establish-ments	Number of employees	Receipts (mil dol)	Annual payroll (mil dol)	Number	Receipts (mil dol)	New Construction ($1,000)	Number of housing units
	159	160	161	162	163	164	165	166	167	168	169	170
NEBRASKA—Cont'd												
Blaine	NA	NA	NA	NA	NA	NA	NA	NA	45	1.6	NA	NA
Boone	16	416	24.7	11.0	10	29	2.5	0.7	519	23.5	0	0
Box Butte	27	617	40.7	17.1	35	115	9.6	2.1	696	23.1	750	1
Boyd	9	98	4.2	1.9	7	12	1.1	0.2	199	7.1	0	0
Brown	14	191	9.2	4.1	15	36	3.4	0.7	311	10.4	225	1
Buffalo	151	3 954	365.2	145.3	114	553	45.3	10.9	3 675	164.9	44 494	277
Burt	16	196	12.3	5.0	15	60	6.2	2.0	520	22.5	1 221	9
Butler	16	360	22.6	9.4	15	D	D	D	693	23.4	947	3
Cass	28	350	19.1	7.9	41	132	9.4	2.4	1 791	69.0	10 598	63
Cedar	16	108	6.0	2.1	22	52	5.7	1.3	714	34.0	1 668	9
Chase	9	176	10.0	4.7	10	45	3.0	0.7	391	24.0	195	1
Cherry	15	297	22.0	8.1	18	41	4.9	0.7	574	21.4	2 429	29
Cheyenne	19	392	39.7	12.0	28	91	9.6	1.9	657	29.7	5 824	28
Clay	11	151	4.8	2.7	11	28	1.4	0.4	535	27.9	1 688	10
Colfax	13	254	21.3	7.8	28	83	6.0	1.7	572	27.8	4 303	18
Cuming	25	404	37.6	13.4	34	156	16.4	3.0	737	39.3	3 359	14
Custer	35	684	39.2	16.7	32	60	5.5	0.9	1 118	40.0	4 139	35
Dakota	32	D	D	D	38	D	D	D	1 021	44.3	4 689	27
Dawes	30	390	27.0	11.5	26	73	4.2	1.0	648	21.0	212	1
Dawson	67	D	D	D	59	D	D	D	1 430	63.1	6 892	44
Deuel	4	D	D	D	4	22	0.5	0.2	182	12.0	0	0
Dixon	10	D	D	D	7	D	D	D	459	19.3	735	4
Dodge	109	2 771	199.9	78.0	85	381	31.3	6.5	2 266	95.1	10 930	45
Douglas	1 552	42 408	4 430.8	1 793.5	1 085	8 366	1 051.5	224.7	34 944	1 621.8	309 433	2 572
Dundy	8	152	7.8	4.1	1	D	D	D	159	6.5	0	0
Fillmore	15	290	18.1	7.4	21	71	4.3	1.0	471	23.4	3 117	15
Franklin	8	138	7.7	3.5	7	19	1.2	0.2	249	8.4	290	2
Frontier	11	87	2.7	1.1	6	D	D	D	235	9.1	1 080	3
Furnas	15	282	15.9	6.5	15	33	3.4	0.5	442	19.1	1 155	5
Gage	62	1 697	91.0	39.6	58	252	13.0	3.5	1 503	55.6	2 143	11
Garden	1	D	D	D	1	D	D	D	197	8.2	0	0
Garfield	7	100	4.6	2.1	7	29	1.8	0.4	228	8.4	875	8
Gosper	5	D	D	D	2	D	D	D	187	7.6	870	6
Grant	NA	NA	NA	NA	3	D	D	D	92	3.3	NA	NA
Greeley	4	D	D	D	4	12	1.0	0.2	237	9.8	0	0
Hall	171	3 816	320.6	125.5	158	976	68.8	16.8	3 584	154.8	35 261	216
Hamilton	18	388	17.5	7.8	25	74	8.0	2.0	835	34.4	7 786	36
Harlan	7	168	8.9	4.0	6	D	D	D	324	10.9	1 633	8
Hayes	1	D	D	D	1	D	D	D	85	3.3	0	0
Hitchcock	4	17	0.7	0.3	3	D	D	D	236	9.1	0	0
Holt	36	696	49.5	20.5	33	93	12.6	2.0	1 249	70.9	2 189	10
Hooker	2	D	D	D	3	D	D	D	91	3.6	265	3
Howard	11	D	D	D	17	62	3.6	0.9	538	17.6	4 342	28
Jefferson	14	376	23.3	9.9	20	73	3.8	0.8	458	18.9	2 580	8
Johnson	14	306	19.6	7.8	11	D	D	D	281	9.3	335	3
Kearney	15	654	22.6	10.6	13	44	4.9	1.0	472	18.0	4 645	13
Keith	30	330	26.8	10.1	26	104	7.6	2.0	762	27.8	1 868	10
Keya Paha	1	D	D	D	3	9	0.7	0.1	118	4.5	0	0
Kimball	9	D	D	D	10	26	1.4	0.4	264	10.0	0	0
Knox	20	318	15.6	6.2	13	27	1.8	0.5	660	23.6	3 970	36
Lancaster	842	21 431	1 932.6	789.3	660	4 233	546.6	118.0	19 668	749.5	283 545	1 923
Lincoln	120	D	D	D	83	D	D	D	2 199	89.1	9 934	54
Logan	1	D	D	D	2	D	D	D	74	2.2	NA	NA
Loup	NA	NA	NA	NA	1	D	D	D	82	2.6	564	5
McPherson	NA	NA	NA	NA	NA	NA	NA	NA	33	1.1	NA	NA
Madison	158	D	D	D	107	D	D	D	2 614	108.0	10 388	61
Merrick	13	D	D	D	20	40	4.6	0.9	629	24.4	4 522	24
Morrill	5	122	8.2	3.7	5	D	D	D	398	15.1	502	7
Nance	10	D	D	D	16	33	2.7	0.5	257	9.6	2 968	20
Nemaha	23	359	23.3	10.5	19	61	2.9	0.7	481	19.3	875	4
Nuckolls	16	395	18.8	9.4	20	55	3.4	0.6	363	13.6	300	2
Otoe	41	915	51.3	21.8	38	186	10.3	3.7	1 182	39.2	5 825	29
Pawnee	8	143	8.2	3.8	5	D	D	D	244	8.7	300	2
Perkins	6	211	11.2	4.6	12	D	D	D	273	12.5	0	0
Phelps	25	743	51.3	17.5	36	118	16.9	3.0	848	32.5	3 236	14
Pierce	18	D	D	D	15	D	D	D	623	27.9	3 727	23

Table B. States and Counties — **Government Employment and Payroll, and Local Government Finances**

STATE County	Government employment and payroll, 2012									Local government finances, 2012				
			March payroll (percent of total)							General revenue				
												Taxes		
													Per capita[1] (dollars)	
	Full-time equivalent employees	March payroll (dollars)	Adminis-tration, judicial, and legal	Police and Corrections	Fire Protection	Highways and transpor-tation	Health and Welfare	Natural resources and utilities	Education and libraries	Total (mil dol)	Inter-govern-mental (mil dol)	Total (mil dol)	Total	Property
	171	172	173	174	175	176	177	178	179	180	181	182	183	184
NEBRASKA—Cont'd														
Blaine	38	116 097	9.8	2.6	0.0	4.4	0.0	0.8	82.3	3.5	0.8	2.4	4 720	4 449
Boone	460	1 692 880	3.4	2.8	0.0	3.1	53.1	1.6	35.2	48.2	4.1	17.4	3 205	2 668
Box Butte	797	2 934 530	5.1	4.9	0.6	2.6	34.3	4.7	46.8	73.9	15.5	21.5	1 898	1 550
Boyd	117	356 840	12.6	1.7	0.0	16.0	0.2	10.9	57.9	9.3	3.1	5.0	2 429	2 227
Brown	260	870 487	5.2	3.3	0.0	3.3	24.0	16.3	47.5	23.9	5.2	7.5	2 470	2 176
Buffalo	1 737	6 480 217	6.2	9.5	0.9	3.9	2.1	3.9	71.0	175.2	52.8	86.9	1 830	1 377
Burt	405	1 151 444	8.6	6.4	0.0	7.3	1.0	16.5	58.3	32.4	6.0	19.8	2 978	2 657
Butler	460	1 583 569	5.4	4.9	0.0	7.3	25.9	17.6	38.5	51.3	15.3	24.0	2 892	2 645
Cass	930	3 065 349	8.2	11.0	0.0	5.1	1.0	3.6	70.6	95.9	27.6	43.8	1 744	1 516
Cedar	483	1 415 097	8.1	3.5	0.0	8.8	0.8	13.3	64.8	39.6	9.7	20.9	2 385	2 173
Chase	332	1 110 424	4.3	4.0	0.0	4.7	35.2	7.8	44.0	41.9	4.1	13.9	3 412	3 043
Cherry	255	767 776	8.8	7.8	0.0	8.5	0.8	7.7	65.2	38.3	6.2	15.0	2 611	2 227
Cheyenne	473	1 711 606	5.9	6.9	0.1	6.1	2.1	17.6	59.6	50.6	16.3	25.0	2 484	1 966
Clay	462	1 297 168	6.4	2.9	0.0	4.4	10.6	4.8	67.8	36.0	7.3	21.7	3 380	3 083
Colfax	471	1 687 680	7.1	4.2	0.1	3.4	0.0	8.5	76.2	45.8	15.6	25.2	2 364	2 089
Cuming	453	1 421 997	8.3	5.2	0.0	7.6	0.8	11.8	65.0	41.8	8.7	22.9	2 521	2 184
Custer	710	2 846 682	7.1	7.6	0.6	7.7	7.1	24.5	41.2	53.1	11.4	26.7	2 483	2 199
Dakota	972	3 563 243	6.5	7.2	0.4	2.2	0.4	6.2	75.7	80.5	44.9	26.9	1 286	955
Dawes	367	1 249 160	8.1	6.9	0.0	5.6	4.6	6.3	67.5	30.8	10.5	13.6	1 487	1 140
Dawson	1 718	5 640 576	3.0	5.6	0.0	2.6	22.8	12.1	52.5	153.2	47.5	40.1	1 657	1 368
Deuel	141	507 062	13.6	7.1	0.0	10.8	0.8	3.1	63.8	13.1	2.9	7.5	3 787	3 435
Dixon	423	1 293 730	7.0	5.2	0.0	4.4	0.1	2.3	78.0	31.8	9.3	14.9	2 525	2 324
Dodge	2 164	10 158 631	3.6	5.2	1.1	2.6	42.4	7.4	36.3	221.5	79.5	60.9	1 672	1 359
Douglas	24 079	100 381 103	3.6	9.6	4.0	3.5	4.4	25.2	48.9	2 457.4	796.5	1 177.7	2 217	1 587
Dundy	208	669 425	6.4	3.2	0.0	3.8	42.5	2.5	41.3	17.3	2.2	6.8	3 356	3 043
Fillmore	362	1 220 014	6.9	3.1	0.1	6.7	29.9	2.4	49.5	43.0	5.2	18.2	3 154	2 687
Franklin	266	1 622 165	12.8	12.9	0.0	7.6	20.4	27.8	17.9	14.4	3.0	5.2	1 628	1 517
Frontier	255	1 135 230	18.7	2.7	0.0	9.6	0.0	22.2	46.4	17.7	4.4	9.4	3 436	3 195
Furnas	443	1 409 219	6.3	2.7	0.2	3.0	18.5	17.2	51.3	28.8	8.9	13.3	2 701	2 216
Gage	894	3 582 464	6.7	7.0	2.9	7.2	0.7	19.7	53.9	82.2	27.8	39.6	1 814	1 546
Garden	214	658 334	5.9	3.2	0.9	5.3	49.9	2.8	31.7	16.1	1.9	6.4	3 289	2 928
Garfield	99	296 601	11.6	3.8	0.0	6.2	0.0	8.4	68.2	7.8	2.6	4.1	2 026	1 771
Gosper	141	396 475	7.9	4.8	0.0	10.0	27.7	9.6	37.4	12.4	1.6	6.8	3 334	3 090
Grant	58	138 009	9.1	2.9	0.0	8.9	0.0	0.0	78.7	4.2	0.6	3.2	5 083	4 808
Greeley	162	445 160	7.7	2.9	0.0	5.1	0.0	6.8	77.0	13.4	3.4	7.4	3 018	2 769
Hall	2 737	10 820 863	5.4	7.6	3.9	3.5	0.6	18.3	59.8	240.9	94.1	101.1	1 675	1 264
Hamilton	408	1 264 730	9.1	7.2	0.0	7.2	3.0	5.2	67.5	39.3	8.1	21.3	2 363	2 061
Harlan	208	554 731	9.8	4.8	0.0	6.6	36.0	7.8	31.8	21.6	4.7	5.2	1 526	1 274
Hayes	59	140 504	6.9	0.0	0.0	17.5	0.0	1.1	74.5	4.9	1.1	3.3	3 501	3 306
Hitchcock	135	502 076	5.5	9.7	0.0	8.5	0.6	32.9	42.8	12.2	2.7	6.3	2 166	1 952
Holt	457	1 501 263	9.1	4.7	0.0	9.6	2.1	8.2	65.9	52.2	11.5	29.0	2 791	2 328
Hooker	94	243 859	6.4	2.5	0.0	3.0	31.7	0.0	53.1	6.6	1.1	3.3	4 499	4 234
Howard	489	1 673 314	3.0	2.5	0.0	3.5	30.8	15.6	43.1	39.6	8.7	12.1	1 910	1 679
Jefferson	388	1 330 833	4.5	5.1	0.5	4.1	1.7	10.5	71.7	34.4	8.5	21.1	2 812	2 496
Johnson	311	1 042 290	4.4	2.9	0.0	4.2	35.4	11.8	40.5	31.4	6.4	12.0	2 329	2 119
Kearney	491	1 419 422	5.9	3.6	0.2	4.7	23.6	1.7	59.6	37.0	4.9	21.7	3 345	3 061
Keith	405	1 305 826	7.9	6.0	2.7	4.6	0.5	4.9	72.0	34.2	10.9	18.9	2 304	1 808
Keya Paha	48	112 765	9.7	2.6	0.0	8.1	0.1	0.9	76.3	3.9	0.8	2.8	3 476	3 285
Kimball	327	1 077 444	7.5	4.5	0.0	4.9	31.5	6.3	43.8	23.2	8.1	9.0	2 386	2 123
Knox	455	1 410 392	6.9	5.2	0.0	6.0	0.5	11.5	69.5	39.5	15.7	18.5	2 154	1 898
Lancaster	10 733	45 755 791	5.1	7.8	4.0	4.4	4.3	11.6	61.0	979.6	313.6	469.5	1 600	1 150
Lincoln	1 720	6 235 856	4.7	7.5	3.4	4.1	1.7	7.3	69.6	279.7	58.1	71.6	1 983	1 637
Logan	59	160 033	10.8	4.2	0.0	4.3	0.0	2.4	77.5	4.8	1.4	3.0	3 927	3 676
Loup	40	120 306	13.9	4.4	0.0	11.3	0.0	1.2	68.0	3.9	1.3	2.1	3 615	3 416
McPherson	37	88 185	16.1	0.0	0.0	8.0	0.0	0.1	75.8	3.0	0.5	2.2	4 361	4 232
Madison	1 848	7 112 436	4.2	6.2	2.5	3.0	2.2	7.2	74.5	181.2	50.7	86.6	2 472	2 061
Merrick	402	1 076 825	8.5	3.7	0.0	5.6	31.5	5.5	44.2	35.9	7.1	13.5	1 732	1 569
Morrill	306	1 053 262	7.6	5.7	0.1	4.9	0.1	9.8	68.4	37.2	13.6	10.5	2 152	1 947
Nance	276	922 483	9.8	3.4	0.0	6.6	22.8	3.9	52.2	23.2	3.7	11.8	3 167	2 896
Nemaha	407	1 469 356	4.6	3.0	0.0	3.2	23.9	9.1	55.9	43.7	12.6	14.0	1 959	1 690
Nuckolls	283	687 707	10.1	4.5	0.0	6.4	0.3	41.3	36.3	18.3	8.3	7.3	1 653	1 451
Otoe	850	2 831 957	5.7	5.8	1.1	4.0	15.2	13.1	52.1	63.3	14.6	30.7	1 948	1 590
Pawnee	199	600 056	5.0	2.2	0.0	4.6	35.8	3.6	47.4	19.2	4.6	6.3	2 267	2 041
Perkins	326	1 063 703	7.6	5.6	0.0	8.0	47.1	0.7	29.4	27.8	2.7	9.8	3 327	2 981
Phelps	471	1 581 446	8.2	8.0	0.0	6.4	0.6	7.7	68.6	46.7	11.6	24.5	2 663	2 090
Pierce	446	1 313 225	5.7	3.6	0.0	4.0	19.8	2.4	64.0	35.8	6.4	16.9	2 364	2 111

1. Based on the resident population estimated as of July 1 of the year shown.

STATE County	Local government finances, 2012 (cont.)									Government employment, 2013			Presidential election,[2] 2012		
	Direct general expenditure							Debt outstanding					Percent of vote cast:		
			Percent of total for:												
	Total (mil dol)	Per capita[1] (dollars)	Education	Health and hospitals	Police protection	Public welfare	Highways	Total (mil dol)	Per capita[1] (dollars)	Federal civilian	Federal military	State and local	Democratic	Republican	All other
	185	186	187	188	189	190	191	192	193	194	195	196	197	198	199
NEBRASKA—Cont'd															
Blaine	3.5	6 794	68.8	0.0	1.3	0.1	13.6	0.2	409	27	0	53	13.6	84.2	2.2
Boone	44.3	8 176	31.0	48.5	1.6	0.2	8.2	3.3	617	29	20	644	26.2	72.0	1.8
Box Butte	77.0	6 806	35.7	37.0	2.5	2.0	3.9	22.0	1 940	34	42	1 035	37.9	58.9	3.2
Boyd	9.7	4 699	58.5	0.6	1.5	0.2	13.1	3.5	1 709	17	0	225	22.5	75.6	1.9
Brown	24.8	8 204	40.4	26.1	2.3	0.3	10.6	32.9	10 893	20	11	411	19.8	77.1	3.1
Buffalo	185.9	3 916	56.3	0.0	5.0	0.1	9.3	209.9	4 423	134	174	3 914	30.4	67.9	1.7
Burt	33.4	5 018	48.1	0.0	2.4	7.6	14.7	21.0	3 159	30	24	549	41.7	56.3	2.0
Butler	46.9	5 656	32.0	32.2	1.7	0.4	12.1	67.8	8 175	48	31	610	31.0	66.6	2.4
Cass	93.1	3 704	51.2	0.3	3.0	4.3	10.9	110.7	4 404	66	95	1 333	39.2	58.7	2.1
Cedar	36.7	4 202	50.3	0.2	2.2	11.6	13.5	12.1	1 386	98	32	583	28.5	69.8	1.7
Chase	45.4	11 179	31.0	33.0	1.0	7.2	9.0	27.2	6 701	23	15	489	18.5	80.1	1.4
Cherry	38.0	6 630	32.1	37.2	1.7	0.3	10.5	8.0	1 401	50	22	528	19.6	77.1	3.3
Cheyenne	49.4	4 909	41.1	0.6	3.5	0.7	11.0	57.6	5 724	34	38	774	24.2	73.8	1.9
Clay	34.4	5 370	60.7	0.6	1.7	7.2	11.3	9.1	1 421	155	24	583	25.7	71.8	2.5
Colfax	46.8	4 390	67.4	0.0	2.2	0.1	9.4	40.1	3 760	69	39	615	35.1	63.0	1.9
Cuming	41.2	4 546	53.9	0.1	3.2	10.9	11.1	33.8	3 720	33	33	742	31.2	66.8	2.0
Custer	58.1	5 407	49.7	9.3	2.4	0.2	14.8	69.4	6 462	50	40	854	21.4	77.1	1.5
Dakota	78.7	3 764	62.6	0.2	7.4	0.1	7.6	134.6	6 433	84	78	1 083	46.8	51.5	1.7
Dawes	29.9	3 268	45.6	1.0	4.2	5.9	7.9	6.6	723	134	30	1 056	34.0	62.9	3.0
Dawson	147.3	6 083	43.0	30.0	3.4	0.3	4.0	105.3	4 347	102	90	2 047	30.0	68.4	1.6
Deuel	13.9	7 026	54.5	0.2	3.3	12.7	8.4	6.2	3 140	0	0	206	24.5	73.7	1.8
Dixon	37.0	6 247	66.9	0.5	2.1	6.9	10.0	11.9	2 016	40	22	421	33.9	63.9	2.3
Dodge	228.6	6 277	38.1	39.7	2.7	0.1	4.4	108.2	2 971	108	134	2 894	43.0	55.0	2.0
Douglas	2 356.0	4 435	50.4	2.4	4.8	0.7	3.5	5 801.4	10 920	5 538	2 253	34 336	51.5	46.9	1.6
Dundy	16.6	8 200	35.5	42.3	1.9	0.1	6.9	4.4	2 201	12	0	228	21.4	76.8	1.8
Fillmore	52.3	9 062	29.1	41.2	1.9	5.3	7.7	42.5	7 369	33	21	691	32.6	64.9	2.4
Franklin	15.0	4 719	33.2	32.0	1.8	0.8	12.7	4.5	1 407	20	12	311	28.5	69.5	2.0
Frontier	20.5	7 466	46.9	0.1	2.3	0.1	8.9	3.3	1 221	16	10	329	24.9	73.6	1.5
Furnas	28.2	5 750	56.4	1.0	2.4	0.6	7.4	29.1	5 927	32	18	540	23.9	74.1	2.0
Gage	86.9	3 984	52.5	1.0	5.5	0.3	9.7	60.4	2 770	95	81	1 969	44.0	53.5	2.5
Garden	15.6	7 995	28.9	43.5	2.2	0.1	10.1	6.3	3 250	17	0	259	24.9	74.2	1.0
Garfield	7.9	3 915	57.3	0.0	2.5	0.1	10.1	2.3	1 144	0	0	161	20.6	77.7	1.7
Gosper	10.9	5 386	31.3	0.1	3.2	25.6	12.4	14.3	7 034	12	0	162	24.8	74.0	1.1
Grant	3.8	6 037	69.2	0.0	2.1	0.4	9.7	0.6	886	0	0	75	11.2	86.6	2.2
Greeley	13.1	5 331	58.5	0.6	2.1	10.6	11.9	0.6	256	15	0	266	38.2	59.6	2.2
Hall	244.4	4 050	57.3	0.2	5.0	0.4	4.7	235.9	3 910	654	226	4 299	36.9	61.0	2.1
Hamilton	38.8	4 301	50.9	10.9	3.5	0.3	6.8	21.3	2 363	32	34	574	27.8	70.6	1.6
Harlan	18.5	5 430	23.7	38.1	1.7	0.1	10.0	8.8	2 568	28	13	262	22.8	75.3	2.0
Hayes	4.6	4 815	56.7	0.0	1.7	0.1	23.0	3.0	3 102	0	0	80	15.4	83.4	1.3
Hitchcock	14.2	4 921	60.3	0.0	1.9	12.2	13.1	25.6	8 853	11	11	288	25.1	72.6	2.3
Holt	51.3	4 932	45.5	0.4	1.7	4.7	17.2	22.9	2 199	46	39	774	21.9	75.3	2.8
Hooker	6.6	9 034	46.4	0.1	1.6	24.9	5.3	2.7	3 706	0	0	108	17.1	81.1	1.8
Howard	38.9	6 142	41.7	32.5	1.3	0.1	6.8	35.9	5 667	28	24	614	36.1	61.6	2.2
Jefferson	40.6	5 402	53.7	1.6	3.4	0.3	20.6	11.0	1 468	35	28	551	41.1	56.9	2.0
Johnson	34.2	6 653	29.7	38.9	1.2	0.3	9.9	24.3	4 729	36	16	802	43.3	54.1	2.6
Kearney	35.5	5 473	48.5	23.6	1.5	0.3	10.0	27.7	4 274	26	24	473	27.8	70.6	1.6
Keith	39.6	4 813	60.0	0.5	6.0	0.4	7.6	23.7	2 887	32	31	531	24.5	74.1	1.3
Keya Paha	3.8	4 669	59.2	0.1	1.4	0.2	21.0	0.1	63	0	0	72	21.6	76.7	1.7
Kimball	23.1	6 099	29.0	29.9	2.7	0.3	7.3	8.6	2 260	16	14	425	24.2	74.3	1.4
Knox	36.1	4 212	62.9	0.2	2.2	0.2	15.1	13.8	1 609	48	31	1 049	30.7	66.8	2.5
Lancaster	1 063.8	3 626	52.7	2.0	4.3	0.9	6.6	2 798.4	9 538	3 007	1 113	29 741	51.6	46.6	1.8
Lincoln	277.0	7 674	31.2	44.8	2.8	0.1	3.5	165.3	4 578	249	134	2 662	31.0	66.5	2.5
Logan	4.4	5 741	67.1	0.1	2.1	0.1	12.6	0.0	0	0	0	80	19.5	78.6	1.9
Loup	3.6	6 161	52.9	0.1	1.5	0.1	13.6	0.2	387	0	0	62	21.9	76.8	1.3
McPherson	2.7	5 281	63.8	0.0	1.7	0.0	16.4	0.2	424	0	0	41	15.4	81.9	2.7
Madison	170.2	4 860	59.2	2.5	5.3	4.1	7.9	156.1	4 457	198	130	3 565	29.5	68.7	1.8
Merrick	35.5	4 565	36.4	31.5	2.4	0.0	9.6	24.0	3 084	31	29	531	28.7	69.2	2.0
Morrill	33.2	6 781	39.2	26.6	3.3	9.2	5.8	13.5	2 752	21	18	486	23.7	73.4	2.9
Nance	23.3	6 270	46.3	24.6	3.0	0.1	9.3	5.5	1 467	16	13	371	32.2	65.4	2.5
Nemaha	44.9	6 283	42.5	30.4	2.7	0.2	5.5	29.2	4 079	30	25	1 618	35.7	61.4	2.9
Nuckolls	18.8	4 230	39.6	0.3	2.4	0.5	14.2	17.6	3 963	29	16	351	29.6	67.4	3.0
Otoe	67.1	4 260	45.5	16.1	3.2	0.1	12.3	80.0	5 710	52	58	1 287	41.1	56.9	2.0
Pawnee	19.3	6 965	36.0	32.5	1.5	0.2	10.3	5.3	1 916	24	10	285	34.9	62.1	3.0
Perkins	25.8	8 812	27.1	49.1	2.1	0.3	6.5	3.1	1 070	17	11	350	21.8	76.9	1.3
Phelps	43.9	4 769	54.3	0.1	2.5	4.2	9.8	37.5	4 071	53	34	729	23.5	75.1	1.4
Pierce	33.9	4 731	50.9	15.7	2.6	6.0	10.0	8.7	1 213	27	27	398	24.3	73.9	1.8

1. Based on the resident population estimated as of July 1 of the year shown. 2.

STATE/ County code	CBSA code[1]	County type[2]	STATE County	Land area,[3] (sq km) 2010	Population, 2014: Total persons 2014	Population, 2014: Rank	Population, 2014: Per square kilometer	Race alone or in combination, not Hispanic or Latino (percent): White	Race: Black	Race: American Indian, Alaska Native	Race: Asian and Pacific Islander	Percent Hispanic or Latino[4]	Age (percent): Under 5 years	Age: 5 to 17 years	Age: 18 to 24 years	Age: 25 to 34 years	Age: 35 to 44 years	Age: 45 to 54 years
				1	2	3	4	5	6	7	8	9	10	11	12	13	14	15
			NEBRASKA—Cont'd															
31 141	18100	5	Platte	1 746	32 666	1 370	18.7	82.8	0.7	0.6	0.7	15.8	7.5	18.7	8.5	12.0	11.3	13.6
31 143	...	9	Polk	1 135	5 271	2 816	4.6	95.8	0.4	0.7	0.5	3.6	5.6	17.9	6.2	9.1	11.3	13.8
31 145	...	7	Red Willow	1 857	10 867	2 369	5.9	93.3	1.3	1.0	0.5	4.9	6.0	16.8	9.7	11.3	10.3	13.3
31 147	...	7	Richardson	1 429	8 128	2 593	5.7	94.4	0.7	4.1	0.9	1.7	4.9	15.3	7.0	9.7	10.0	14.5
31 149	...	9	Rock	2 612	1 443	3 082	0.6	97.7	0.1	1.1	0.4	1.2	4.5	15.9	4.8	10.3	9.7	13.7
31 151	...	6	Saline	1 487	14 252	2 149	9.6	74.0	1.2	0.7	2.3	22.9	6.9	17.1	14.1	10.7	11.8	13.1
31 153	36540	2	Sarpy	619	172 193	369	278.2	85.1	5.2	0.9	3.4	8.1	8.0	20.5	8.6	15.2	14.1	13.6
31 155	36540	2	Saunders	1 943	20 919	1 780	10.8	96.6	0.8	0.7	0.7	2.1	6.3	18.7	7.2	10.5	11.0	15.8
31 157	42420	5	Scotts Bluff	1 915	36 465	1 266	19.0	74.7	0.9	1.8	0.9	22.6	6.8	17.7	8.7	12.2	11.3	12.5
31 159	30700	2	Seward	1 480	17 150	1 975	11.6	96.5	0.9	0.7	0.8	2.1	5.9	17.4	13.6	10.5	10.4	13.2
31 161	...	9	Sheridan	6 322	5 259	2 817	0.8	86.7	0.9	11.0	1.0	3.7	5.3	17.3	5.5	10.1	10.2	11.4
31 163	...	9	Sherman	1 465	3 074	2 970	2.1	97.6	0.4	0.4	0.5	1.8	5.0	16.2	5.9	7.9	9.7	13.4
31 165	42420	9	Sioux	5 353	1 303	3 095	0.2	94.6	0.5	1.9	0.1	4.5	5.4	16.8	6.1	8.5	10.1	14.2
31 167	35740	9	Stanton	1 108	6 069	2 752	5.5	93.1	1.3	1.4	0.4	5.3	6.5	19.9	7.6	11.9	11.1	14.2
31 169	...	9	Thayer	1 486	5 230	2 822	3.5	97.0	0.7	0.7	0.5	2.1	4.9	16.1	6.6	8.7	9.5	13.1
31 171	...	9	Thomas	1 847	687	3 129	0.4	96.3	0.3	0.4	0.6	3.2	8.2	14.6	6.4	11.4	11.3	9.7
31 173	...	8	Thurston	1 019	6 969	2 681	6.8	40.9	1.1	55.1	1.0	4.2	10.3	25.2	9.9	11.3	9.1	11.5
31 175	...	9	Valley	1 471	4 204	2 885	2.9	97.1	0.5	0.4	0.6	2.2	5.6	17.2	6.4	9.1	10.2	13.0
31 177	36540	2	Washington	1 010	20 258	1 821	20.1	96.1	1.2	0.6	0.7	2.5	5.5	18.4	9.0	9.9	11.4	15.9
31 179	...	6	Wayne	1 147	9 431	2 476	8.2	91.4	2.2	0.9	1.0	5.4	5.7	13.8	26.3	10.0	8.4	10.9
31 181	...	9	Webster	1 489	3 658	2 930	2.5	93.8	1.1	0.8	1.1	4.7	6.3	15.7	7.1	8.3	10.1	14.3
31 183	...	9	Wheeler	1 490	766	3 121	0.5	98.4	0.0	0.5	0.7	0.9	6.2	13.8	8.0	9.0	10.0	14.2
31 185	...	7	York	1 483	13 917	2 178	9.4	93.1	1.9	0.9	0.9	4.3	6.6	15.7	10.0	11.9	10.2	13.3
32 000	...	X	NEVADA	284 332	2 839 099	X	10.0	54.8	9.2	1.5	10.3	27.5	6.4	17.3	9.1	14.2	13.6	13.6
32 001	21980	6	Churchill	12 770	23 989	1 642	1.9	77.5	2.8	5.1	4.7	13.2	6.5	17.4	8.7	12.7	10.9	13.4
32 003	29820	1	Clark	20 439	2 069 681	14	101.3	48.8	11.7	1.0	12.1	30.0	6.6	17.6	9.2	14.7	14.3	13.5
32 005	23820	4	Douglas	1 838	47 536	1 025	25.9	83.6	1.2	2.7	3.1	11.9	4.2	14.3	6.6	9.6	9.8	14.3
32 007	21220	5	Elko	44 470	52 766	945	1.2	69.4	1.4	5.4	1.9	23.7	7.3	20.8	9.9	14.5	12.7	14.0
32 009	...	9	Esmeralda	9 277	822	3 116	0.1	74.6	3.2	5.6	1.4	18.0	3.2	12.7	5.4	11.7	10.7	13.7
32 011	21220	9	Eureka	10 815	2 018	3 047	0.2	82.8	1.4	3.0	1.3	13.4	6.4	15.9	7.9	9.7	12.5	16.9
32 013	49080	7	Humboldt	24 969	17 279	1 964	0.7	68.9	1.4	4.7	1.7	25.2	7.7	19.8	8.8	13.8	12.6	14.0
32 015	...	7	Lander	14 219	6 009	2 757	0.4	71.5	1.3	4.1	1.0	23.3	7.5	19.2	9.7	12.4	11.1	14.6
32 017	...	8	Lincoln	27 540	5 184	2 826	0.2	87.2	4.0	2.1	1.6	7.2	3.5	18.7	9.8	10.7	11.2	12.7
32 019	22280	6	Lyon	5 183	51 789	962	10.0	79.1	1.9	3.5	2.6	15.8	5.6	17.4	7.1	10.9	11.2	14.0
32 021	...	7	Mineral	9 720	4 500	2 866	0.5	68.8	5.0	15.5	3.4	10.7	6.0	12.7	8.1	10.3	8.9	13.8
32 023	37220	6	Nye	47 091	42 282	1 124	0.9	79.9	3.0	2.6	3.0	14.1	4.5	14.1	6.3	8.2	9.0	13.6
32 027	...	8	Pershing	15 635	6 698	2 704	0.4	69.1	4.4	3.9	2.1	22.5	4.4	14.6	8.5	14.3	15.1	16.7
32 029	39900	2	Storey	681	3 912	2 912	5.7	86.4	2.1	2.6	3.2	7.6	2.8	11.7	5.6	8.1	8.9	16.0
32 031	39900	2	Washoe	16 323	440 078	158	27.0	67.0	3.0	2.0	7.5	23.3	6.2	16.6	10.0	14.0	12.4	13.7
32 033	...	7	White Pine	22 988	10 034	2 435	0.4	75.6	4.9	4.8	1.7	14.8	6.4	15.1	8.2	15.0	12.1	14.6
32 510	16180	3	Carson City	375	54 522	919	145.4	70.9	2.4	2.8	3.2	22.7	5.3	15.5	8.5	12.0	11.6	14.3
33 000	...	X	NEW HAMPSHIRE	23 187	1 326 813	X	57.2	92.9	1.7	0.7	2.9	3.2	5.0	15.5	9.6	11.5	12.3	16.2
33 001	29060	4	Belknap	1 037	60 305	863	58.2	96.3	1.1	0.8	1.6	1.5	4.9	14.8	7.0	10.6	11.5	15.8
33 003	...	8	Carroll	2 411	47 399	1 026	19.7	97.0	0.8	0.9	0.9	1.4	3.8	13.3	6.5	8.5	10.3	15.8
33 005	28300	4	Cheshire	1 830	76 115	723	41.6	96.0	1.1	0.8	1.8	1.7	4.8	14.1	12.7	11.3	10.9	14.8
33 007	13620	7	Coos	4 648	31 653	1 394	6.8	96.9	0.9	1.1	0.9	1.5	4.1	13.5	6.9	9.9	11.4	15.6
33 009	17200	5	Grafton	4 426	89 658	642	20.3	93.1	1.4	1.0	4.1	2.1	4.4	13.0	13.7	11.7	10.5	14.2
33 011	31700	2	Hillsborough	2 269	405 184	169	178.6	88.2	2.8	0.6	4.2	5.8	5.6	16.6	8.8	12.6	13.1	16.5
33 013	18180	4	Merrimack	2 419	147 171	440	60.8	94.9	1.6	0.8	2.2	1.8	4.8	15.5	9.5	11.2	12.3	16.2
33 015	14460	1	Rockingham	1 799	300 621	225	167.1	94.7	1.1	0.6	2.4	2.5	4.6	16.5	7.7	10.8	12.7	17.9
33 017	14460	1	Strafford	956	125 604	495	131.4	93.7	1.7	0.7	3.6	2.1	5.2	14.5	16.1	11.9	11.8	14.6
33 019	17200	7	Sullivan	1 392	43 103	1 109	31.0	97.0	1.0	1.1	0.9	1.4	4.9	15.0	7.1	10.4	12.1	15.9
34 000	...	X	NEW JERSEY	19 047	8 938 175	X	469.3	58.8	13.6	0.5	9.8	18.9	6.0	16.7	8.9	12.8	13.3	15.2
34 001	12100	2	Atlantic	1 439	275 209	245	191.3	58.6	15.7	0.6	8.8	18.1	6.1	16.3	9.6	11.8	12.1	15.2
34 003	35620	1	Bergen	603	933 572	54	1 548.2	60.7	5.8	0.3	16.6	17.8	5.3	16.6	7.9	11.7	13.7	15.8
34 005	37980	1	Burlington	2 068	449 722	151	217.5	71.1	17.5	0.7	5.7	7.3	5.4	16.7	8.8	11.9	12.7	16.1
34 007	37980	1	Camden	573	511 038	131	891.9	60.2	19.5	0.6	6.2	15.4	6.4	17.1	8.9	13.5	12.8	14.6
34 009	36140	3	Cape May	651	95 344	614	146.5	87.4	5.1	0.5	1.5	7.0	4.9	13.1	8.3	10.1	9.6	14.5
34 011	47220	3	Cumberland	1 253	157 389	404	125.6	50.1	20.1	1.4	1.8	28.7	6.9	16.9	9.2	14.6	13.6	13.8
34 013	35620	1	Essex	327	795 723	75	2 433.4	33.8	39.9	0.6	5.6	21.6	6.7	17.5	9.5	13.6	14.3	14.6
34 015	37980	1	Gloucester	834	290 951	232	348.9	81.4	10.9	0.5	3.4	5.4	5.7	17.6	9.3	11.8	13.1	15.7
34 017	35620	1	Hudson	120	669 115	95	5 576.0	30.8	11.9	0.5	15.3	42.6	6.9	13.4	9.3	21.0	15.5	13.0
34 019	35620	1	Hunterdon	1 108	126 067	493	113.8	87.8	2.7	0.3	4.3	5.9	4.1	17.6	8.0	8.3	11.8	19.3

1. CBSA = Core Based Statistical Area. See Appendix A for explanation. See Appendix B for list of metropolitan areas with component counties. 2. County type code from the Economic Research Service of USDA Rural-Urban Continuum Codes. See Appendix A for definition. 3. Dry land or land partially or temporarily covered by water. 4. May be of any race.

STATE County	Population, 2013 (cont.) Age (percent) (cont.) 55 to 64 years	65 to 74 years	75 years and over	Percent female	Population change and components of change, 2000–2014 Total persons 2000	2010	Percent change 2000–2010	2010–2014	Components of change, 2010–2014 Births	Deaths	Net migration	Households, 2009–2013 Number	Persons per house-hold	Percent Family house-holds	Female family house-holder[1]	One per-son
	16	17	18	19	20	21	22	23	24	25	26	27	28	29	30	31
NEBRASKA—Cont'd																
Platte	13.1	7.7	7.7	49.6	31 662	32 237	1.8	1.3	2 012	1 097	-511	12 477	2.56	66.2	8.4	29.9
Polk	16.3	9.5	10.3	50.3	5 639	5 406	-4.1	-2.5	220	273	-51	2 232	2.33	69.0	6.5	27.5
Red Willow	14.0	8.7	9.9	50.1	11 448	11 055	-3.4	-1.7	532	468	-231	4 732	2.25	61.6	5.7	32.3
Richardson	15.4	10.8	12.4	50.5	9 531	8 363	-12.3	-2.8	373	471	-119	3 779	2.14	57.6	6.5	40.5
Rock	20.4	9.6	11.1	48.5	1 756	1 526	-13.1	-5.6	74	77	-105	666	2.08	58.7	2.6	39.2
Saline	11.7	7.1	7.5	48.9	13 843	14 200	2.6	0.4	821	581	-167	5 051	2.63	66.7	10.0	26.0
Sarpy	10.3	5.9	3.9	50.0	122 595	158 840	29.6	8.4	10 921	3 427	5 826	59 606	2.71	73.9	10.5	21.6
Saunders	13.7	9.1	7.8	49.3	19 830	20 780	4.8	0.7	1 044	779	-123	8 142	2.52	69.2	5.7	26.6
Scotts Bluff	13.7	8.6	8.6	51.6	36 951	36 970	0.1	-1.4	2 111	1 735	-841	14 690	2.45	65.2	12.8	28.8
Seward	12.6	8.4	7.9	48.9	16 496	16 750	1.5	2.4	829	669	224	6 165	2.51	70.5	5.5	25.2
Sheridan	16.9	11.1	12.2	50.6	6 198	5 469	-11.8	-3.8	243	292	-149	2 380	2.22	63.7	7.9	32.3
Sherman	16.0	12.0	13.9	51.1	3 318	3 152	-5.0	-2.5	129	154	-58	1 369	2.24	67.6	8.3	30.8
Sioux	17.5	9.9	11.4	49.0	1 475	1 311	-11.1	-0.6	37	25	-21	553	2.22	65.6	5.1	31.8
Stanton	13.7	7.9	7.2	49.4	6 455	6 129	-5.1	-1.0	304	172	-204	2 336	2.62	77.8	10.3	20.0
Thayer	16.1	11.0	14.0	51.5	6 055	5 228	-13.7	0.0	238	322	94	2 343	2.15	63.9	4.2	33.2
Thomas	18.3	11.2	8.9	48.5	729	647	-11.2	6.2	39	22	14	323	2.27	72.4	4.3	25.7
Thurston	10.4	6.0	6.3	50.7	7 171	6 940	-3.2	0.4	588	303	-253	2 050	3.33	71.7	21.3	24.6
Valley	14.3	12.2	11.9	50.4	4 647	4 260	-8.3	-1.3	207	235	-20	1 893	2.21	67.3	6.5	30.2
Washington	14.3	8.7	6.9	50.0	18 780	20 234	7.7	0.1	872	674	-153	7 647	2.57	70.9	7.0	26.0
Wayne	11.1	6.4	7.4	49.4	9 851	9 595	-2.6	-1.7	415	251	-308	3 401	2.41	63.7	7.2	28.7
Webster	14.7	10.8	12.6	51.3	4 061	3 812	-6.1	-4.0	150	234	-68	1 548	2.34	64.7	4.5	32.6
Wheeler	18.1	11.9	8.8	49.5	886	818	-7.7	-6.4	30	21	-48	379	2.29	57.3	3.7	39.6
York	13.9	8.7	9.8	51.0	14 598	13 665	-6.4	1.8	722	578	113	5 501	2.36	66.1	6.1	30.3
NEVADA	12.1	8.5	5.2	49.6	1 998 257	2 700 551	35.1	5.1	149 568	88 521	74 737	999 016	2.70	64.8	12.9	27.3
Churchill	13.3	10.3	6.8	49.7	23 982	24 877	3.7	-3.6	1 335	1 073	-1 165	9 253	2.61	67.7	10.8	26.8
Clark	11.4	8.0	4.8	49.8	1 375 765	1 951 269	41.8	6.1	111 857	60 256	64 729	710 058	2.75	65.0	13.8	27.0
Douglas	17.4	14.3	9.3	50.0	41 259	46 997	13.9	1.1	1 537	1 830	817	19 455	2.40	68.4	8.8	25.7
Elko	11.8	5.9	3.2	47.9	45 291	48 818	7.8	7.8	2 995	1 160	1 989	17 599	2.80	70.3	7.9	23.2
Esmeralda	17.3	13.8	11.4	42.4	971	783	-19.4	4.8	15	38	51	479	2.00	51.8	5.4	42.0
Eureka	16.4	8.6	5.7	45.8	1 651	1 987	20.4	1.6	87	49	-19	733	2.43	59.6	1.1	36.3
Humboldt	12.9	6.6	3.7	47.7	16 106	16 528	2.6	4.6	1 158	491	85	6 314	2.63	66.8	6.5	27.6
Lander	12.5	8.2	4.8	48.8	5 794	5 775	-0.3	4.1	388	128	-15	2 010	2.87	73.2	6.6	17.0
Lincoln	14.0	11.9	7.5	45.7	4 165	5 345	28.3	-3.0	167	188	-123	1 969	2.51	70.2	10.1	28.4
Lyon	14.9	12.4	6.6	49.5	34 501	51 980	50.7	-0.4	2 316	2 187	-357	19 278	2.65	68.3	9.9	24.7
Mineral	16.2	14.2	9.7	50.8	5 071	4 772	-5.9	-5.7	245	339	-184	2 147	2.13	52.0	11.8	39.5
Nye	17.2	17.1	10.0	49.5	32 485	43 946	35.3	-3.8	1 590	2 655	-661	18 046	2.38	68.8	10.0	25.4
Pershing	13.0	8.7	4.5	36.5	6 693	6 753	0.9	-0.8	250	197	-102	2 091	2.34	68.4	8.6	26.3
Storey	21.4	17.6	7.9	48.3	3 399	4 010	18.0	-2.4	76	101	-113	1 843	2.14	63.0	5.7	30.3
Washoe	13.2	8.8	5.2	49.6	339 486	421 407	24.1	4.4	22 625	14 686	10 412	163 198	2.57	62.6	11.6	28.7
White Pine	13.4	8.8	6.4	42.7	9 181	10 030	9.2	0.0	491	390	-87	3 357	2.74	59.7	6.1	36.3
Carson City	14.2	10.3	8.2	48.8	52 457	55 274	5.4	-1.4	2 436	2 753	-520	21 186	2.50	61.5	12.4	31.4
NEW HAMPSHIRE	14.6	8.9	6.5	50.6	1 235 786	1 316 470	6.5	0.8	53 225	45 357	3 013	518 245	2.47	66.8	9.5	25.7
Belknap	16.4	11.3	7.8	50.9	56 325	60 088	6.7	0.4	2 311	2 712	585	25 049	2.37	67.7	10.0	26.4
Carroll	18.2	13.8	9.9	50.5	43 666	47 818	9.5	-0.9	1 548	2 103	163	20 922	2.25	67.0	7.5	26.7
Cheshire	14.9	9.5	7.1	51.2	73 825	77 117	4.5	-1.3	2 970	2 887	-1 036	30 458	2.36	62.9	9.3	27.7
Coos	17.2	11.7	9.6	49.0	33 111	33 055	-0.2	-4.2	1 046	1 732	-722	14 531	2.15	61.5	9.4	33.0
Grafton	15.1	10.0	7.4	50.5	81 743	89 118	9.0	0.6	3 223	3 274	630	35 111	2.35	62.3	8.9	30.3
Hillsborough	13.5	7.7	5.8	50.4	380 841	400 721	5.2	1.1	18 483	12 510	-1 338	154 324	2.55	67.2	10.6	25.1
Merrimack	15.1	8.8	6.7	50.7	136 225	146 445	7.5	0.5	5 760	5 343	341	56 812	2.47	66.6	9.1	26.3
Rockingham	15.1	8.7	6.0	50.6	277 359	295 223	6.4	1.8	10 867	9 114	3 781	116 262	2.53	69.7	8.4	23.3
Strafford	12.6	7.6	5.8	51.3	112 233	123 143	9.7	2.0	5 315	3 900	1 036	46 968	2.47	65.0	10.2	24.8
Sullivan	16.3	10.6	7.7	50.5	40 458	43 742	8.1	-1.5	1 702	1 782	-427	17 808	2.40	67.6	9.0	25.2
NEW JERSEY	12.7	7.9	6.5	51.2	8 414 350	8 791 894	4.5	1.7	444 933	300 194	6 968	3 186 418	2.71	69.2	13.4	25.9
Atlantic	13.5	8.7	6.7	51.4	252 552	274 549	8.7	0.2	14 331	10 755	-2 692	101 091	2.64	67.0	15.7	27.9
Bergen	13.3	8.3	7.5	51.6	884 118	905 116	2.4	3.1	38 755	29 651	20 841	335 422	2.69	71.4	11.2	24.7
Burlington	13.2	8.2	6.9	50.8	423 394	448 734	6.0	0.2	19 084	15 884	-1 779	164 979	2.65	70.1	11.7	25.2
Camden	12.7	7.7	6.2	51.6	508 932	513 657	0.9	-0.5	27 371	19 111	-10 593	187 941	2.69	67.5	16.0	27.5
Cape May	16.3	13.0	10.4	51.2	102 326	97 265	-4.9	-2.0	3 914	5 352	-264	42 312	2.22	64.7	9.4	30.3
Cumberland	11.6	7.5	5.9	48.5	146 438	156 898	7.1	0.3	9 105	6 009	-2 388	50 676	2.86	69.9	18.3	25.1
Essex	11.6	6.7	5.5	51.9	793 633	783 969	-1.2	1.5	44 734	25 183	-7 524	277 302	2.76	65.8	20.5	29.3
Gloucester	13.1	7.9	5.8	51.5	254 673	288 288	13.2	0.9	12 897	10 145	-90	104 145	2.73	72.5	12.9	22.5
Hudson	10.2	6.0	4.7	50.2	608 975	634 266	4.2	5.5	41 669	16 423	9 789	243 875	2.61	61.6	17.2	29.3
Hunterdon	16.0	8.9	5.9	50.5	121 989	128 349	5.2	-1.0	3 897	3 541	-1 656	46 816	2.61	72.8	8.1	22.8

1. No spouse present.

STATE County	Persons in group quarters, 2014	Daytime population, 2009–2013: Number	Daytime population, 2009–2013: Employment/residence ratio	Births, 2014: Total	Births, 2014: Rate[1]	Deaths, 2014: Number	Deaths, 2014: Rate[1]	Persons under 65 with no health insurance, 2013: Number	Persons under 65 with no health insurance, 2013: Percent	Medicare, 2014: Eligible for Medicare	Medicare, 2014: Enrolled in Medicare Advantage	Medicare, 2014: Enrolled in a Medicare prescription drug plan	Serious crimes known to police,[2] 2013: Total: Number	Serious crimes known to police,[2] 2013: Total: Rate[3]
	32	33	34	35	36	37	38	39	40	41	42	43	44	45
NEBRASKA—Cont'd														
Platte	470	34 582	1.13	468	14.3	259	7.9	3 667	13.5	5 849	258	3 894	641	1 949
Polk	115	4 445	0.67	53	10.1	58	11.0	485	11.6	1 149	NA	812	65	1 224
Red Willow	377	11 487	1.09	125	11.5	121	11.1	996	11.6	2 337	12	1 672	256	2 333
Richardson	150	7 389	0.77	92	11.3	112	13.8	892	14.4	2 112	16	1 458	137	1 653
Rock	29	1 423	0.98	20	13.9	12	8.3	242	21.8	191	NA	166	2	149
Saline	1 055	14 496	1.02	185	13.0	125	8.8	1 831	16.1	2 372	17	1 696	325	2 210
Sarpy	1 146	138 119	0.71	2 550	14.8	874	5.1	13 465	8.9	20 516	3 159	8 201	2 344	1 392
Saunders	337	15 930	0.54	240	11.5	180	8.6	1 697	9.9	3 853	397	2 369	158	757
Scotts Bluff	838	37 422	1.03	474	13.0	390	10.7	4 292	14.3	7 687	816	4 895	1 095	3 025
Seward	1 351	14 939	0.77	188	11.0	144	8.4	1 189	9.1	3 057	108	2 144	145	852
Sheridan	102	4 892	0.80	55	10.5	60	11.4	757	18.9	1 273	139	683	72	1 362
Sherman	53	2 590	0.65	31	10.1	38	12.4	397	17.4	790	70	482	14	451
Sioux	0	957	0.58	8	6.1	6	4.6	183	17.8	230	13	162	NA	NA
Stanton	1	4 861	0.60	66	10.9	36	5.9	582	11.3	903	115	524	70	1 149
Thayer	133	5 342	1.07	61	11.7	82	15.7	463	12.0	1 338	NA	973	120	2 344
Thomas	2	767	1.08	8	11.6	2	2.9	117	21.2	149	11	112	NA	NA
Thurston	57	7 515	1.24	135	19.4	79	11.3	1 077	17.7	962	37	598	NA	NA
Valley	40	4 462	1.09	45	10.7	51	12.1	458	14.6	1 018	NA	721	NA	NA
Washington	526	18 316	0.82	203	10.0	161	7.9	1 367	8.2	3 602	552	2 064	179	882
Wayne	1 093	9 161	0.93	88	9.3	37	3.9	961	13.7	1 456	141	978	NA	NA
Webster	150	3 470	0.82	32	8.7	57	15.6	369	13.4	966	36	677	30	810
Wheeler	0	918	1.10	8	10.4	4	5.2	119	20.0	152	NA	104	8	999
York	778	14 801	1.15	171	12.3	135	9.7	1 193	11.2	2 903	12	2 056	240	1 738
NEVADA	36 558	2 737 437	1.01	35 153	12.4	21 702	7.6	552 362	23.2	435 234	31 377	145 972	96 001	3 441
Churchill	339	24 617	1.00	320	13.3	243	10.1	4 106	20.8	5 015	396	2 131	607	2 493
Clark	22 796	1 983 853	1.01	26 178	12.6	14 963	7.2	416 594	23.8	291 050	108 464	89 248	74 792	3 692
Douglas	230	45 716	0.94	365	7.7	469	9.9	7 207	20.2	12 685	1 044	6 405	881	1 867
Elko	788	47 880	0.91	790	15.0	319	6.0	8 930	19.1	5 520	84	2 854	1 540	2 948
Esmeralda	1	944	0.90	7	8.5	2	2.4	198	31.8	244	24	107	15	1 931
Eureka	1	5 796	6.00	24	11.9	6	3.0	245	13.9	299	NA	144	42	2 087
Humboldt	183	17 465	1.09	276	16.0	104	6.0	3 383	22.0	2 281	75	1 195	288	1 667
Lander	16	5 623	0.91	104	17.3	31	5.2	1 032	19.8	813	12	403	174	2 890
Lincoln	258	5 404	1.06	59	11.4	48	9.3	1 015	25.3	1 024	17	579	49	901
Lyon	360	45 032	0.65	517	10.0	529	10.2	10 014	24.1	12 083	2 411	4 841	1 292	2 519
Mineral	52	4 725	1.02	55	12.2	93	20.7	698	19.9	1 263	146	472	1	22
Nye	424	42 732	0.95	339	8.0	605	14.3	7 244	23.6	13 631	6 274	3 146	1 079	2 518
Pershing	1 649	6 811	1.03	67	10.0	41	6.1	1 083	25.0	914	20	513	144	2 125
Storey	5	3 232	0.55	14	3.6	12	3.1	576	19.7	1 044	167	409	125	3 178
Washoe	5 294	425 851	1.00	5 340	12.1	3 528	8.0	79 580	21.6	73 660	21 281	26 325	12 633	2 908
White Pine	1 308	10 055	1.01	118	11.8	84	8.4	1 312	17.9	1 703	14	925	108	1 070
Carson City	2 854	61 701	1.31	580	10.6	625	11.5	9 145	22.0	12 005	960	6 275	1 057	1 924
NEW HAMPSHIRE	40 523	1 279 437	0.94	12 338	9.3	10 834	8.2	139 339	12.8	259 075	17 440	135 968	31 889	2 410
Belknap	867	55 683	0.85	512	8.5	703	11.7	7 090	14.6	15 449	1 131	8 148	1 873	3 098
Carroll	534	46 574	0.95	364	7.7	534	11.3	6 358	17.6	13 412	689	7 351	1 091	2 627
Cheshire	4 342	74 280	0.93	679	8.9	643	8.4	8 489	14.1	16 291	1 164	8 656	NA	NA
Coos	1 387	31 806	0.95	248	7.8	400	12.6	3 953	16.1	9 167	246	5 379	NA	NA
Grafton	6 891	101 306	1.27	755	8.4	763	8.5	10 602	15.7	18 665	1 149	9 622	NA	NA
Hillsborough	7 937	387 340	0.93	4 241	10.5	3 036	7.5	42 957	12.5	69 424	5 545	37 136	10 223	2 676
Merrimack	6 703	149 271	1.03	1 334	9.1	1 228	8.3	15 175	12.8	29 387	2 113	14 607	2 526	2 066
Rockingham	2 459	282 615	0.91	2 591	8.6	2 175	7.2	27 034	10.7	55 473	3 748	28 261	5 452	1 900
Strafford	8 687	113 398	0.84	1 225	9.8	938	7.5	12 795	12.8	22 065	1 379	11 341	3 460	2 821
Sullivan	716	37 164	0.71	389	9.0	414	9.6	4 886	14.0	9 742	276	5 467	NA	NA
NEW JERSEY	185 527	8 564 591	0.93	103 440	11.6	71 699	8.0	1 125 347	15.0	1 475 203	226 965	848 010	193 230	2 171
Atlantic	6 216	280 966	1.05	3 315	12.0	2 637	9.6	40 449	17.6	50 989	4 740	31 488	9 354	3 388
Bergen	10 415	898 721	0.97	9 129	9.8	6 982	7.5	110 046	14.3	158 358	21 162	90 967	11 181	1 245
Burlington	12 782	433 119	0.92	4 392	9.8	3 819	8.5	35 600	9.6	80 558	13 441	44 882	8 414	1 859
Camden	7 480	475 035	0.84	6 330	12.4	4 626	9.1	62 460	14.3	87 806	16 335	49 784	17 305	3 365
Cape May	2 642	95 091	0.96	903	9.5	1 284	13.5	10 416	14.4	25 492	2 655	16 619	4 168	4 336
Cumberland	12 423	157 853	1.01	2 063	13.1	1 437	9.1	22 837	18.0	26 762	4 076	17 275	7 673	4 848
Essex	23 173	810 947	1.07	10 417	13.1	6 041	7.6	126 206	18.5	111 485	23 301	58 682	25 174	3 186
Gloucester	4 223	255 436	0.75	2 979	10.2	2 491	8.6	26 158	10.6	49 068	8 233	28 028	7 430	2 559
Hudson	9 415	595 687	0.85	9 918	14.8	4 014	6.0	133 669	22.7	77 564	17 552	40 921	13 718	2 082
Hunterdon	3 769	119 452	0.88	882	7.0	840	6.7	8 008	7.7	21 987	1 822	14 134	1 058	834

1. Per 1,000 estimated resident population. 2. Data for serious crimes have not been adjusted for underreporting; this may affect comparability between geographic areas and over time.
3. Per 100,000 population estimated by the FBI.

STATE County	Serious crimes known to police, 2013 (cont.)[1] — Rate[2] — Violent	Serious crimes known to police, 2013 (cont.)[1] — Rate[2] — Property	Education — School enrollment and attainment, 2009–2013 — Enrollment[3] — Total	Education — School enrollment and attainment, 2009–2013 — Enrollment[3] — Percent private	Education — School enrollment and attainment, 2009–2013 — Attainment[4] (percent) — High school graduate or less	Education — School enrollment and attainment, 2009–2013 — Attainment[4] (percent) — Bachelor's degree or more	Education — Local government expenditures,[5] 2012–2013 — Total current spending (mil dol)	Education — Local government expenditures,[5] 2012–2013 — Current spending per student (dollars)	Money income, 2009–2013 — Per capita income[6] (dollars)	Money income, 2009–2013 — Households — Median income (dollars)	Money income, 2009–2013 — Households — Mean income (dollars)	Money income, 2009–2013 — Households — Percent with income of $200,000 or more	Income and poverty, 2013 — Median household income (dollars)	Income and poverty, 2013 — Percent below poverty level — All persons	Income and poverty, 2013 — Percent below poverty level — Children under 18 years	Income and poverty, 2013 — Percent below poverty level — Children 5 to 17 years in families
	46	47	48	49	50	51	52	53	54	55	56	57	58	59	60	61
NEBRASKA—Cont'd																
Platte	76	1 873	8 338	24.0	42.7	18.5	57.5	12 520	24 219	51 213	61 090	1.7	52 368	10.2	14.2	14.1
Polk	0	1 224	1 259	11.5	41.4	20.3	17.4	13 966	27 639	52 848	65 331	2.5	56 618	8.9	12.1	10.7
Red Willow	118	2 214	2 554	10.1	42.1	19.5	19.6	11 321	23 320	42 345	54 298	1.5	44 826	12.2	16.7	15.4
Richardson	24	1 629	1 832	9.5	49.6	18.8	16.9	13 798	23 566	38 582	50 177	1.1	41 679	14.4	21.8	19.2
Rock	0	149	297	10.1	44.9	19.1	3.3	17 244	24 501	43 500	52 743	1.5	40 870	15.2	25.6	22.6
Saline	102	2 108	4 276	25.0	50.4	15.1	33.1	11 654	20 407	44 109	54 828	1.2	49 047	12.0	14.9	14.9
Sarpy	64	1 328	50 025	17.4	28.2	36.2	266.1	10 519	30 189	69 965	81 470	3.5	67 740	6.3	8.5	7.7
Saunders	48	709	5 381	27.6	41.5	24.4	30.8	11 188	30 039	59 870	75 270	3.9	61 174	8.7	10.9	9.6
Scotts Bluff	135	2 890	9 586	13.7	43.6	20.0	74.6	11 381	23 220	43 444	56 605	2.1	43 406	15.2	24.3	22.5
Seward	71	781	5 120	33.2	39.4	26.1	36.9	14 328	28 359	59 435	75 458	3.9	59 053	10.2	9.8	8.6
Sheridan	189	1 173	1 186	9.5	41.2	22.6	11.6	13 280	22 551	38 548	50 473	1.5	38 411	16.0	26.9	23.9
Sherman	32	419	717	1.7	50.8	17.7	6.5	13 677	24 837	41 835	55 310	1.5	41 224	13.8	20.9	19.0
Sioux	NA	NA	240	13.3	37.6	27.0	2.6	22 894	31 517	42 014	66 367	4.0	48 313	16.5	26.6	24.5
Stanton	16	1 132	1 662	12.3	41.2	17.7	5.4	11 787	23 131	51 493	59 969	0.9	54 263	8.3	12.1	11.1
Thayer	20	2 325	981	10.6	47.4	16.3	13.5	16 720	26 965	44 422	59 981	2.2	43 938	13.1	17.6	15.5
Thomas	NA	NA	132	8.3	31.2	22.7	2.0	19 206	30 116	55 089	69 950	5.0	43 247	15.5	21.8	24.2
Thurston	NA	NA	2 315	5.0	47.6	15.8	29.1	16 792	17 106	41 400	55 926	2.2	38 558	30.5	40.7	39.4
Valley	NA	NA	798	11.2	48.6	17.8	9.0	13 679	23 227	40 445	51 422	1.0	44 105	12.3	18.2	16.7
Washington	49	833	5 654	17.8	39.1	28.9	35.4	10 144	29 328	65 409	76 170	3.2	66 160	7.7	9.7	8.3
Wayne	NA	NA	3 760	3.4	33.1	33.1	26.1	17 024	24 448	52 147	65 674	3.5	49 981	13.2	13.1	12.4
Webster	54	756	882	8.2	46.9	17.2	8.0	12 750	21 423	41 045	50 400	0.8	42 305	12.4	15.1	14.4
Wheeler	0	999	173	4.0	45.4	17.5	2.2	19 138	25 898	38 807	58 940	4.7	37 495	16.0	25.5	26.5
York	14	1 723	3 355	25.6	41.5	24.9	22.4	11 903	28 207	49 633	69 146	4.1	56 687	9.8	13.7	13.2
NEVADA	603	2 838	677 081	11.0	44.1	22.4	3 622.3	8 339	26 589	52 800	69 629	3.3	51 250	15.8	22.7	21.1
Churchill	144	2 350	6 267	6.4	45.1	16.8	40.3	10 771	24 716	49 830	61 657	0.8	50 158	13.9	21.0	19.9
Clark	678	3 014	488 987	11.4	45.3	22.1	2 555.2	8 066	26 217	52 873	69 671	3.4	51 071	16.3	23.7	22.1
Douglas	140	1 727	9 821	11.8	33.1	25.7	56.5	9 207	34 123	60 100	80 273	4.6	56 613	10.2	15.8	14.4
Elko	291	2 657	13 279	8.8	44.9	16.4	93.5	9 494	28 358	70 238	78 624	4.0	71 354	9.1	12.1	11.0
Esmeralda	257	1 673	177	1.7	50.2	13.9	2.0	30 299	20 862	30 284	42 463	0.0	41 075	13.8	21.1	20.0
Eureka	398	1 690	468	10.0	45.6	24.7	7.5	27 856	28 056	64 632	69 128	0.5	66 592	8.1	9.8	9.6
Humboldt	394	1 273	4 303	8.0	53.5	12.6	34.4	9 814	26 515	59 472	70 157	2.2	66 290	10.1	14.4	13.4
Lander	781	2 110	1 396	15.3	53.0	12.0	13.7	12 508	29 800	72 742	84 580	2.5	69 658	9.8	13.2	12.9
Lincoln	74	827	1 392	14.3	49.6	16.3	12.8	13 090	22 879	40 143	58 883	1.5	44 366	14.1	20.7	18.6
Lyon	250	2 269	12 186	11.6	45.7	16.7	80.3	9 949	21 757	46 137	55 835	0.6	46 526	15.7	24.1	22.5
Mineral	0	22	768	1.8	49.0	11.0	6.9	13 814	23 146	35 017	48 778	1.2	40 496	18.3	30.2	30.7
Nye	359	2 159	8 174	10.9	52.9	12.3	55.7	10 347	21 838	39 876	52 040	0.7	42 998	18.5	31.6	30.1
Pershing	753	1 372	1 621	1.4	57.8	10.5	11.4	16 100	18 203	52 101	60 210	0.4	51 548	21.2	24.6	23.0
Storey	941	2 237	594	8.8	37.0	21.5	6.4	15 440	33 472	61 573	70 967	3.0	59 785	8.2	12.6	11.2
Washoe	369	2 539	112 144	10.1	37.7	27.3	546.5	8 408	28 670	53 040	72 369	4.0	53 565	15.1	19.6	17.6
White Pine	258	813	2 199	7.2	51.3	13.8	16.7	11 629	24 435	48 586	62 162	1.7	52 588	13.5	17.6	16.6
Carson City	242	1 682	13 305	9.2	43.9	20.1	82.4	10 502	26 264	51 957	65 041	2.1	47 476	15.4	22.9	20.4
NEW HAMPSHIRE	215	2 194	327 063	21.6	37.5	33.7	2 598.9	13 721	33 134	64 916	82 935	5.3	64 064	9.0	10.9	9.9
Belknap	225	2 873	12 614	15.2	39.9	28.0	129.1	14 829	30 518	58 654	73 577	3.2	57 568	9.3	13.6	11.6
Carroll	214	2 413	9 199	17.6	38.7	31.2	98.5	17 558	31 558	50 866	71 853	3.6	50 598	10.4	16.5	15.2
Cheshire	NA	NA	20 318	16.8	42.7	30.4	141.8	16 574	27 874	55 155	69 305	3.0	52 246	11.4	13.7	12.3
Coos	NA	NA	6 471	10.5	52.5	17.3	64.1	15 290	24 367	41 985	53 695	1.6	40 917	14.8	22.4	20.5
Grafton	NA	NA	23 859	32.4	37.3	37.7	204.8	17 955	30 738	54 912	74 661	5.1	55 131	11.1	13.4	12.1
Hillsborough	293	2 383	101 316	24.1	36.8	35.0	721.9	12 670	34 390	69 829	88 012	6.4	67 162	9.3	11.0	9.8
Merrimack	165	1 900	36 218	25.0	36.8	33.3	317.3	13 316	31 310	65 353	79 297	4.1	64 068	9.1	10.8	10.2
Rockingham	137	1 764	72 317	19.8	33.6	37.2	621.6	13 270	38 399	77 348	97 073	7.4	74 785	5.9	6.7	6.0
Strafford	245	2 576	35 755	15.6	37.3	31.8	211.6	13 328	29 369	58 825	75 335	3.7	59 290	9.8	11.5	10.9
Sullivan	NA	NA	8 996	21.2	47.4	25.6	97.3	15 730	28 582	54 463	67 957	3.2	52 114	10.4	15.0	13.5
NEW JERSEY	288	1 883	2 288 598	19.3	40.9	35.8	24 972.4	17 572	36 027	71 629	97 225	9.4	70 224	11.4	16.5	15.2
Atlantic	443	2 945	68 714	14.1	49.2	24.2	833.0	18 329	27 391	54 235	72 092	4.0	51 668	17.1	25.3	22.3
Bergen	90	1 155	230 543	22.7	33.4	45.9	2 447.9	18 298	43 347	83 794	115 950	13.6	81 615	8.1	10.6	10.1
Burlington	157	1 701	116 116	18.2	38.4	34.6	1 250.2	17 604	36 835	78 446	98 211	8.1	76 868	6.2	9.0	8.2
Camden	576	2 789	135 911	17.3	44.3	29.1	1 488.0	18 970	30 592	61 683	80 653	5.1	57 641	14.7	22.3	20.3
Cape May	258	4 078	18 909	14.6	46.5	28.7	257.1	19 903	32 948	56 494	75 629	4.4	56 520	10.8	17.9	17.8
Cumberland	537	4 311	37 904	11.3	62.8	14.3	504.4	18 695	22 524	50 750	65 150	2.4	45 850	20.1	28.4	26.5
Essex	733	2 454	218 670	17.8	45.5	32.0	2 714.2	23 340	32 181	55 095	87 252	8.9	53 358	17.7	24.9	22.5
Gloucester	119	2 440	78 863	15.7	43.7	28.4	783.8	16 092	32 600	74 524	88 964	5.7	71 137	9.4	11.4	10.6
Hudson	407	1 675	150 750	19.2	44.0	36.3	1 597.6	20 153	32 641	58 442	83 074	7.4	55 699	19.4	31.5	31.2
Hunterdon	39	795	32 709	16.9	28.7	47.6	406.8	19 151	50 349	106 143	135 249	18.5	107 203	4.1	4.2	3.6

1. Data for serious crimes have not been adjusted for underreporting; this may affect comparability between geographic areas and over time. 2. Per 100,000 population estimated by the FBI.
3. All persons 3 years old and over enrolled in nursery school through college. 4. Persons 25 years old and over. 5. Elementary and secondary education expenditures.
6. Based on population estimated by the American Community Survey, 2009–2013.

STATE County	Personal income, 2013										Earnings, 2013		
	Total (mil dol)	Percent change, 2012–2013	Per capita[1] Dollars	Per capita[1] Rank	Wages and salaries (mil dol)	Supplements to wages and salaries; employer contributions (mil dol): Pension and insurance	Supplements: Government social insurance	Proprietors' income (mil dol)	Dividends, interest, and rent (mil dol)	Personal transfer receipts (mil dol)	Total (mil dol)	Contributions for government social insurance (mil dol): From employee and self-employed	Contributions: From employer
	62	63	64	65	66	67	68	69	70	71	72	73	74
NEBRASKA—Cont'd													
Platte	1 500	5.5	46 143	612	752	148	56	303	269	197	1 259	64	56
Polk	317	4.8	60 007	105	51	11	4	135	42	40	201	6	4
Red Willow	476	-0.5	43 206	828	204	39	16	83	100	91	342	19	16
Richardson	378	12.0	46 485	592	85	18	7	92	67	77	202	10	7
Rock	81	7.0	57 344	151	19	4	1	31	19	8	55	2	1
Saline	601	8.2	41 716	970	280	53	21	117	90	97	470	23	21
Sarpy	7 443	2.7	43 957	759	3 199	618	256	189	1 177	869	4 262	242	256
Saunders	1 005	10.1	48 022	479	180	36	13	145	158	142	374	18	13
Scotts Bluff	1 502	0.2	40 773	1 082	705	124	59	252	233	295	1 140	68	59
Seward	833	3.6	48 735	435	254	45	19	130	161	111	449	23	19
Sheridan	218	1.0	41 540	989	53	12	4	50	47	43	119	5	4
Sherman	127	1.7	40 785	1 079	24	6	2	41	22	27	73	3	2
Sioux	67	3.0	51 301	322	10	2	1	24	11	7	36	1	1
Stanton	323	21.7	52 651	280	78	13	5	96	41	32	193	7	5
Thayer	299	4.1	57 654	145	101	19	7	84	69	49	211	9	7
Thomas	27	4.6	37 954	1 438	10	2	1	2	8	5	15	1	1
Thurston	330	20.4	47 906	488	122	27	9	102	48	54	260	10	9
Valley	225	1.6	53 698	246	62	14	4	75	39	39	155	6	4
Washington	1 015	5.4	50 168	362	455	79	32	103	193	129	670	37	32
Wayne	445	21.3	47 330	525	140	31	10	131	81	58	312	12	10
Webster	159	1.9	43 072	835	33	7	2	39	29	34	82	4	2
Wheeler	48	20.8	63 540	71	14	2	1	21	10	5	38	1	1
York	744	1.5	53 565	250	299	52	23	182	159	110	556	26	23
NEVADA	109 471	1.3	39 235	X	54 854	9 024	3 906	8 186	24 713	17 067	75 970	4 073	3 906
Churchill	1 143	1.2	47 484	513	388	89	30	255	198	197	763	37	30
Clark	75 957	1.4	37 457	1 515	39 842	6 202	2 853	5 875	15 542	11 984	54 772	2 957	2 853
Douglas	2 819	0.8	59 826	108	764	124	54	144	1 038	375	1 086	65	54
Elko	2 206	-0.1	42 117	927	1 130	182	76	79	310	219	1 467	75	76
Esmeralda	38	4.6	45 585	649	20	4	1	1	9	7	27	1	1
Eureka	81	-1.7	39 068	1 288	424	52	28	3	13	8	507	27	28
Humboldt	829	3.9	47 769	498	462	82	32	83	134	88	659	31	32
Lander	299	5.7	49 550	385	253	39	17	12	35	30	321	16	17
Lincoln	147	0.3	27 955	2 904	57	19	3	7	36	41	86	4	3
Lyon	1 598	1.3	30 993	2 550	456	97	33	81	320	385	667	41	33
Mineral	162	-1.0	35 073	1 888	60	16	4	8	34	48	88	5	4
Nye	1 455	-0.3	34 392	2 013	536	91	38	76	311	459	741	50	38
Pershing	195	1.0	28 386	2 858	95	25	5	7	37	37	132	6	5
Storey	141	1.6	35 723	1 795	165	25	15	8	30	30	212	12	15
Washoe	19 628	1.3	45 253	673	8 716	1 562	627	1 285	5 988	2 655	12 190	648	627
White Pine	405	-2.6	40 291	1 140	215	55	13	19	68	70	302	14	13
Carson City	2 369	0.4	43 798	774	1 269	360	76	243	609	436	1 948	85	76
NEW HAMPSHIRE	67 513	2.1	51 013	X	31 243	5 227	2 275	6 052	12 939	9 520	44 797	2 698	2 275
Belknap	2 910	2.6	48 359	461	1 024	198	77	235	773	530	1 535	99	77
Carroll	2 333	2.7	49 119	408	725	135	56	251	688	458	1 167	78	56
Cheshire	3 512	1.9	45 849	628	1 414	269	104	388	732	588	2 176	134	104
Coos	1 285	3.5	40 174	1 151	463	106	36	100	252	360	706	48	36
Grafton	4 499	2.1	50 194	360	2 767	446	209	468	1 043	687	3 891	230	209
Hillsborough	21 213	1.9	52 509	286	11 137	1 707	798	1 791	3 572	2 704	15 433	919	798
Merrimack	7 107	2.2	48 400	457	3 545	684	258	552	1 387	1 084	5 039	296	258
Rockingham	17 588	2.0	58 797	124	7 281	1 104	528	1 812	3 168	1 907	10 725	643	528
Strafford	5 231	1.8	41 984	940	2 302	460	165	296	943	842	3 224	193	165
Sullivan	1 834	2.1	42 665	872	585	115	44	158	382	359	902	59	44
NEW JERSEY	492 897	1.2	55 386	X	234 209	36 773	17 975	42 438	90 189	70 447	331 395	19 431	17 975
Atlantic	11 704	0.5	42 425	894	6 026	1 058	507	1 165	2 170	2 508	8 756	519	507
Bergen	64 306	1.0	69 495	50	28 228	4 041	2 189	6 924	13 566	6 700	41 382	2 384	2 189
Burlington	23 280	0.8	51 638	312	11 414	1 899	947	1 801	4 149	3 488	16 061	941	947
Camden	23 357	0.9	45 544	653	10 220	1 758	836	1 584	3 860	4 607	14 398	881	836
Cape May	5 172	1.1	53 932	239	1 545	321	141	453	1 372	1 111	2 459	161	141
Cumberland	5 636	0.6	35 825	1 775	2 652	559	226	457	866	1 471	3 895	235	226
Essex	43 115	0.9	54 606	214	22 457	3 806	1 687	3 888	7 851	7 073	31 839	1 821	1 687
Gloucester	13 111	0.9	45 169	680	4 588	855	391	659	1 830	2 194	6 493	402	391
Hudson	33 128	1.5	50 172	361	17 808	2 721	1 287	3 126	4 322	4 861	24 942	1 434	1 287
Hunterdon	9 535	1.3	75 523	29	2 996	456	225	890	1 956	833	4 567	268	225

1. Based on the resident population estimated as of July 1 of the year shown.

STATE County	Earnings, 2013 (cont.) — Percent by selected industries: Farm	Mining	Construction	Manu-facturing	Infor-mation: professional, scientific, technical services	Retail trade	Finance, insur-ance, real estate and leasing	Health care and social assistance	Govern-ment	Social Security beneficiaries, December 2013: Number	Rate[1]	Supple-mental Security Income recipients, December 2013	Housing units, 2014: Total	Percent change, 2010–2014
	75	76	77	78	79	80	81	82	83	84	85	86	87	88
NEBRASKA—Cont'd														
Platte	15.3	0.0	4.9	31.4	2.7	5.1	3.8	6.7	12.3	6 165	190	311	13 604	1.7
Polk	59.3	D	2.7	0.5	D	3.2	D	3.5	12.2	1 175	224	51	2 716	-0.5
Red Willow	13.0	1.4	4.4	9.7	3.5	8.5	4.9	10.8	16.5	2 450	222	156	5 280	0.2
Richardson	36.3	0.1	3.6	6.4	2.8	5.5	2.7	D	13.5	2 280	281	158	4 375	-0.4
Rock	54.0	0.0	D	D	D	2.2	D	1.0	17.0	190	134	0	909	-0.5
Saline	20.2	0.0	1.1	35.0	1.1	3.5	2.0	D	15.4	2 580	180	148	5 790	0.5
Sarpy	0.7	0.0	6.9	4.0	9.5	5.7	8.9	5.1	28.9	21 380	126	1 205	65 910	6.4
Saunders	31.6	D	9.1	4.2	D	5.3	4.3	D	20.5	3 965	190	202	9 418	2.1
Scotts Bluff	5.7	D	4.7	7.1	3.8	7.0	6.4	16.4	15.7	8 130	221	823	16 332	-0.5
Seward	22.0	0.0	5.8	16.6	2.5	3.8	3.9	D	14.6	3 150	185	137	6 997	1.8
Sheridan	36.4	D	1.7	1.4	D	6.3	D	1.9	25.5	1 360	259	72	2 905	-1.1
Sherman	51.1	0.0	1.5	0.9	D	3.3	D	4.1	17.1	850	273	28	1 939	-0.1
Sioux	81.9	0.0	0.0	0.0	D	1.1	D	D	11.0	235	178	0	821	0.7
Stanton	45.1	D	D	D	D	0.6	1.8	D	7.4	1 045	172	25	2 638	0.2
Thayer	32.7	D	4.3	21.2	0.7	2.9	3.5	2.9	15.7	1 350	260	73	2 742	0.4
Thomas	20.3	D	D	D	D	D	D	D	26.6	165	237	0	401	-0.2
Thurston	36.7	0.0	3.0	5.5	D	2.0	D	5.8	32.9	1 105	160	218	2 417	0.4
Valley	42.7	D	3.2	2.6	D	4.7	2.8	2.3	20.7	1 075	256	59	2 277	0.2
Washington	11.0	D	10.8	16.1	5.5	8.4	3.4	D	22.8	3 735	185	131	8 408	1.3
Wayne	38.4	0.0	1.8	12.1	1.5	3.0	5.0	6.9	19.9	1 500	159	77	3 841	1.7
Webster	45.9	D	D	D	D	4.7	3.5	5.4	18.2	1 045	284	92	1 902	-0.5
Wheeler	76.0	0.0	0.3	0.0	0.0	D	D	0.0	7.6	150	198	0	576	0.0
York	26.1	D	3.6	10.4	3.7	5.3	4.4	D	12.6	3 035	219	161	6 284	0.9
NEVADA	0.3	2.3	6.3	3.8	8.6	7.2	6.0	8.9	17.4	459 536	165	48 817	1 198 907	2.1
Churchill	2.7	1.8	8.6	3.5	8.1	6.6	5.6	8.3	26.0	5 320	221	480	10 686	-1.3
Clark	0.0	0.1	6.4	2.7	8.9	7.4	6.3	8.7	16.3	308 355	152	37 209	863 010	2.7
Douglas	0.5	D	6.2	11.6	7.6	7.1	6.0	8.1	15.0	12 965	275	401	23 776	0.4
Elko	1.8	21.1	7.9	1.2	3.0	6.2	1.8	5.5	17.5	5 900	112	488	20 511	4.8
Esmeralda	3.8	D	D	D	D	D	0.0	0.0	17.4	250	300	14	829	-2.7
Eureka	1.3	91.9	D	D	D	D	D	D	3.2	305	147	17	1 043	-3.1
Humboldt	6.9	35.7	7.3	2.7	D	6.0	0.8	D	16.5	2 470	142	215	7 275	2.1
Lander	2.5	64.9	D	D	D	2.5	D	0.4	12.6	900	148	77	2 628	2.1
Lincoln	3.6	D	D	D	21.7	5.0	2.1	2.7	47.8	1 055	201	71	2 730	0.0
Lyon	6.5	3.8	4.8	18.7	3.7	14.1	2.3	D	20.6	13 070	254	880	22 399	-0.7
Mineral	2.2	13.7	D	D	D	3.7	D	D	41.4	1 295	284	129	2 794	-1.3
Nye	3.7	14.8	5.1	0.9	18.8	6.9	1.5	D	16.6	14 765	349	1 027	21 783	-2.5
Pershing	7.0	40.4	D	D	D	3.8	D	D	36.0	955	139	71	2 416	-1.9
Storey	0.0	D	5.5	17.2	D	1.1	D	D	8.2	1 100	283	34	1 985	-0.3
Washoe	0.1	1.2	6.4	6.7	9.5	6.8	7.0	11.3	18.3	76 835	177	6 646	187 142	1.2
White Pine	1.7	34.7	3.6	0.3	D	3.9	1.3	D	36.5	1 775	177	140	4 436	-1.4
Carson City	0.0	D	3.2	8.8	5.6	6.6	6.1	13.8	38.8	12 220	226	918	23 464	-0.3
NEW HAMPSHIRE	0.1	0.1	6.6	12.1	11.4	8.8	9.3	12.6	13.5	278 664	211	19 507	619 856	0.8
Belknap	0.1	D	D	10.0	8.0	12.2	5.1	14.1	16.5	16 765	278	992	37 672	0.8
Carroll	-0.1	D	12.7	4.5	7.0	11.7	8.3	12.0	15.1	14 270	300	745	40 232	1.0
Cheshire	0.1	D	8.8	13.8	5.4	10.0	6.8	13.6	15.0	17 815	233	1 186	34 813	0.1
Coos	0.3	D	10.0	5.8	D	9.7	3.4	16.6	25.2	10 335	323	982	21 263	-0.3
Grafton	0.4	0.1	4.2	10.0	8.4	7.3	4.1	23.4	11.6	19 745	220	1 058	51 624	1.0
Hillsborough	0.0	0.0	5.8	14.9	15.0	8.3	11.2	11.3	10.7	74 820	185	6 876	167 418	0.8
Merrimack	0.1	0.2	6.7	8.3	7.8	8.3	8.9	14.6	22.0	31 950	217	2 316	63 643	0.2
Rockingham	0.0	0.1	7.6	10.8	13.6	9.5	8.9	9.1	9.5	58 280	195	2 406	128 444	1.4
Strafford	0.0	D	D	10.9	7.0	7.6	14.4	13.6	23.1	24 175	194	2 084	52 403	1.4
Sullivan	0.2	D	D	25.4	D	10.1	5.1	8.1	15.5	10 510	244	862	22 344	0.0
NEW JERSEY	0.1	0.1	5.3	7.6	15.3	6.2	10.0	11.2	15.7	1 548 525	174	180 354	3 591 588	1.1
Atlantic	1.0	D	6.4	1.7	6.2	7.0	4.0	14.4	23.2	55 330	200	6 818	127 375	0.6
Bergen	0.0	D	5.5	7.5	14.7	6.5	7.3	14.9	9.9	158 335	171	11 835	356 335	1.1
Burlington	0.2	D	5.7	9.0	11.1	7.1	12.1	11.6	18.3	86 375	192	5 821	177 647	1.2
Camden	0.1	D	5.5	7.5	11.2	7.1	5.3	18.0	19.2	95 145	186	16 279	206 622	0.8
Cape May	0.3	D	10.1	1.4	4.9	10.3	6.8	11.9	28.2	27 640	288	1 806	98 922	0.6
Cumberland	2.2	0.3	5.5	13.8	3.4	7.0	2.9	14.1	28.5	29 890	190	5 570	56 348	0.9
Essex	0.0	D	3.4	4.7	16.0	3.8	11.6	11.0	21.8	115 930	146	28 839	314 515	0.5
Gloucester	1.2	0.1	9.8	8.8	6.4	10.8	3.9	10.8	21.7	53 890	186	4 639	112 268	2.3
Hudson	0.0	0.0	2.5	2.5	15.8	4.8	28.0	6.2	10.0	79 905	120	22 047	277 166	2.5
Hunterdon	0.2	0.1	9.3	4.4	16.9	9.6	10.3	10.7	15.3	22 565	178	848	49 705	0.4

1. Per 1,000 resident population estimated as of July 1 of the year shown.

STATE County	Housing units, 2009–2013: Total	Occupied units: Owner-occupied: Percent	Owner-occupied: Median value[1]	Median owner cost as a percent of income: With a mortgage	Median owner cost as a percent of income: Without a mortgage[2]	Renter-occupied: Median rent[3]	Renter-occupied: Median rent as a percent of income[2]	Sub-standard units[4] (percent)	Civilian labor force, 2014: Total	Percent change, 2013–2014	Unemployment: Total	Unemployment: Rate[5]	Civilian employment,[6] 2009–2013: Total	Percent: Management, business, science and arts	Percent: Construction, production, and maintenance occupations
	89	90	91	92	93	94	95	96	97	98	99	100	101	102	103
NEBRASKA—Cont'd															
Platte	12 477	71.5	115 400	20.7	11.1	601	23.1	1.0	17 440	-2.1	519	3.0	16 808	25.6	36.5
Polk	2 232	74.3	95 200	20.6	11.3	574	21.4	0.9	2 990	-0.7	95	3.2	2 752	35.4	30.7
Red Willow	4 732	71.4	84 200	18.8	14.1	589	24.1	1.0	6 347	-1.7	165	2.6	5 507	27.9	26.7
Richardson	3 779	77.0	62 600	20.1	12.5	490	19.9	1.5	4 366	-0.9	179	4.1	3 945	31.6	29.1
Rock	666	83.0	65 200	18.3	13.0	386	12.5	2.9	883	-0.7	23	2.6	749	39.7	27.1
Saline	5 051	65.6	94 400	21.3	11.0	664	30.7	1.9	7 303	-1.7	257	3.5	6 751	30.6	34.4
Sarpy	59 606	70.6	162 400	21.4	11.4	851	26.3	0.5	90 144	0.6	2 830	3.1	83 615	40.8	17.7
Saunders	8 142	79.1	147 600	21.9	13.7	711	23.0	2.9	11 234	0.2	389	3.5	10 648	35.8	24.9
Scotts Bluff	14 690	67.7	102 600	22.4	14.6	659	29.1	0.6	18 792	-2.3	700	3.7	18 224	27.9	26.3
Seward	6 165	73.5	142 600	20.1	11.3	604	23.4	2.4	9 053	0.0	271	3.0	8 283	35.4	27.4
Sheridan	2 380	69.5	65 800	21.5	12.9	529	24.4	0.5	2 800	-0.6	85	3.0	2 588	39.8	21.5
Sherman	1 369	81.2	82 000	21.9	13.3	595	22.9	0.0	1 747	0.1	58	3.3	1 566	35.6	27.7
Sioux	553	77.4	86 500	33.5	14.1	442	15.7	1.0	800	-1.2	22	2.8	656	43.8	19.7
Stanton	2 336	81.7	98 900	21.8	10.0	584	18.2	1.1	3 590	-3.1	101	2.8	3 261	30.7	32.3
Thayer	2 343	79.6	61 200	19.5	12.1	466	21.5	0.0	3 051	-0.7	80	2.6	2 440	36.3	27.5
Thomas	323	73.7	79 200	20.0	10.3	542	18.2	10.2	428	-6.1	15	3.5	448	39.3	23.7
Thurston	2 050	67.0	68 500	17.5	11.6	475	22.5	0.1	3 063	-1.9	204	6.7	2 523	35.8	22.5
Valley	1 893	74.7	78 100	18.7	11.8	424	26.9	0.6	2 133	-0.8	63	3.0	2 256	32.4	27.0
Washington	7 647	78.1	169 700	22.3	12.4	722	27.7	2.3	11 240	0.5	362	3.2	10 790	38.6	23.9
Wayne	3 401	64.5	103 200	18.0	10.0	538	21.7	1.6	5 616	-1.6	159	2.8	5 091	34.7	25.7
Webster	1 548	79.2	67 300	19.9	13.3	505	22.8	1.1	1 750	-0.2	60	3.4	1 647	34.1	29.9
Wheeler	379	71.2	87 100	21.7	12.1	604	19.4	1.0	523	-0.8	15	2.9	505	47.5	27.3
York	5 501	69.3	108 500	19.6	11.2	600	23.0	3.0	7 498	-0.4	236	3.1	7 066	33.5	23.9
NEVADA	999 016	56.7	169 100	26.8	11.3	986	31.0	4.9	1 394 599	0.7	108 125	7.8	1 229 604	27.8	18.7
Churchill	9 253	61.9	153 300	22.8	10.9	840	27.2	5.2	10 761	-4.2	800	7.4	9 729	28.4	28.4
Clark	710 058	54.4	165 000	27.3	11.2	1 019	31.1	2.0	1 019 653	1.3	79 647	7.8	894 854	26.6	17.4
Douglas	19 455	71.8	271 400	28.3	12.2	1 028	28.7	3.7	22 323	-2.1	1 758	7.9	20 688	30.7	20.9
Elko	17 599	70.1	184 300	19.9	10.0	877	22.8	7.7	28 175	-2.7	1 544	5.5	24 761	25.3	33.0
Esmeralda	479	55.5	81 400	21.8	10.0	452	32.1	4.9	534	-2.0	24	4.5	366	25.7	45.6
Eureka	733	65.8	117 400	15.3	10.0	685	13.7	4.6	1 071	-2.3	63	5.9	799	37.7	35.8
Humboldt	6 314	70.7	147 400	18.8	10.0	741	22.5	3.7	8 969	-4.4	550	6.1	7 633	21.7	40.1
Lander	2 010	78.5	103 300	15.0	10.0	789	18.8	1.6	3 360	-5.5	217	6.5	2 513	23.6	47.8
Lincoln	1 969	62.9	140 600	22.0	11.0	542	26.9	2.5	1 944	-5.3	151	7.8	1 793	38.1	18.0
Lyon	19 278	70.3	133 400	27.5	11.8	933	30.0	5.4	22 760	-0.4	2 302	10.1	19 094	28.0	29.3
Mineral	2 147	71.7	95 500	20.4	13.2	503	21.0	2.7	1 671	-8.2	186	11.1	1 660	28.6	27.2
Nye	18 046	70.9	112 600	27.7	12.9	838	35.0	5.8	16 320	-1.4	1 550	9.5	13 846	24.5	26.3
Pershing	2 091	66.3	138 100	26.2	12.8	704	24.2	0.0	2 591	-3.8	189	7.3	2 049	29.0	37.8
Storey	1 843	93.8	167 700	29.3	10.2	715	22.3	4.8	1 890	-0.4	170	9.0	1 734	37.3	24.1
Washoe	163 198	58.0	203 300	26.7	11.9	913	31.8	2.4	222 613	0.3	16 554	7.4	201 440	32.8	18.8
White Pine	3 357	70.9	113 800	18.5	10.0	757	26.8	3.2	4 897	-1.1	293	6.0	4 021	26.3	29.1
Carson City	21 186	58.1	198 900	24.6	12.2	872	28.8	1.2	25 068	-1.5	2 128	8.5	22 624	31.3	20.1
NEW HAMPSHIRE	518 245	71.4	239 900	25.9	16.7	987	29.8	1.9	741 178	-0.1	31 959	4.3	690 769	39.3	20.1
Belknap	25 049	75.1	219 900	26.8	17.2	883	28.8	2.1	31 788	-0.7	1 314	4.1	30 505	34.7	23.1
Carroll	20 922	80.6	226 200	27.2	14.8	893	32.4	2.2	24 319	-0.6	1 034	4.3	23 177	34.0	21.0
Cheshire	30 458	71.3	195 400	26.5	18.8	937	31.8	2.1	41 642	-0.9	1 713	4.1	39 518	35.5	23.9
Coos	14 531	71.0	128 500	25.1	16.5	648	29.6	2.0	15 490	-2.9	902	5.8	14 961	29.0	26.0
Grafton	35 111	69.0	212 000	24.0	15.7	912	28.2	2.1	48 088	-0.7	1 727	3.6	45 147	42.3	18.4
Hillsborough	154 324	67.4	249 900	25.7	16.6	1 049	29.7	2.0	228 666	0.1	10 321	4.5	212 028	40.7	19.6
Merrimack	56 812	72.2	231 000	26.2	17.0	924	30.4	1.4	81 156	0.2	3 091	3.8	76 057	40.8	19.3
Rockingham	116 262	76.8	282 100	26.0	16.3	1 095	29.0	2.3	175 766	0.1	8 194	4.7	161 393	41.6	18.4
Strafford	46 968	65.6	220 600	26.8	17.5	969	31.3	1.6	70 253	0.3	2 811	4.0	66 052	36.4	20.3
Sullivan	17 808	74.1	171 700	25.0	16.6	861	29.3	3.8	24 011	-0.5	852	3.5	21 931	33.7	27.1
NEW JERSEY	3 186 418	65.6	327 100	28.1	18.7	1 172	32.2	3.9	4 518 712	-0.3	300 277	6.6	4 197 483	40.3	17.6
Atlantic	101 091	68.2	237 400	30.7	19.4	1 038	34.8	2.6	133 130	-3.0	13 817	10.4	127 482	29.1	16.4
Bergen	335 422	65.6	451 400	29.2	19.5	1 334	30.8	1.5	479 448	0.0	25 760	5.4	446 366	46.4	13.9
Burlington	164 979	77.8	252 500	26.0	17.1	1 186	31.6	2.3	232 025	-0.8	14 671	6.3	219 945	41.8	16.1
Camden	187 941	68.3	210 700	27.1	19.2	975	34.1	1.5	255 560	-1.2	19 169	7.5	239 855	38.0	18.0
Cape May	42 312	74.6	312 800	29.1	18.1	1 026	33.8	4.2	48 961	0.0	5 893	12.0	42 995	33.8	18.4
Cumberland	50 676	67.1	168 900	26.8	17.8	980	37.5	5.5	67 165	-2.9	6 629	9.9	61 872	26.5	28.0
Essex	277 302	45.9	364 800	30.6	20.3	1 055	33.1	1.3	375 861	-0.5	29 624	7.9	349 646	37.2	19.0
Gloucester	104 145	80.3	224 700	26.3	18.1	1 049	33.6	7.7	148 835	-1.2	10 581	7.1	139 549	40.2	18.4
Hudson	243 875	32.6	347 200	31.1	21.8	1 174	28.9	1.8	357 862	-0.3	23 258	6.5	325 602	38.6	19.0
Hunterdon	46 816	84.5	404 300	26.2	16.2	1 296	30.9	3.0	66 365	0.2	3 152	4.7	64 648	49.7	12.8

1. Specified owner-occupied units. 2. A value of 10.0 represents 10 percent or less; a value of 50.0 represents 50 percent or more. 3. Specified renter-occupied units.
4. Overcrowded or lacking complete plumbing facilities. 5. Percent of civilian labor force. 6. Persons 16 years old and over.

STATE County	Private nonfarm establishments, employment and payroll, 2013									Agriculture, 2012			
		Employment						Annual payroll		Farms			
											Percent with:		
	Number of establish-ments	Total	Health care and social assistance	Manufac-turing	Retail trade	Finance and insurance	Professional, scientific, and technical services	Total (mil dol)	Average per employee (dollars)	Number	Fewer than 50 acres	500 acres or more	Farm operators whose principal occu-pation is farming (percent)
	104	105	106	107	108	109	110	111	112	113	114	115	116
NEBRASKA—Cont'd													
Platte	1 012	15 574	1 387	5 238	2 172	516	415	547	35 098	942	24.3	31.0	64.9
Polk	150	906	260	D	134	54	D	26	28 754	466	23.2	39.7	66.1
Red Willow	420	3 875	588	D	921	217	126	115	29 653	405	26.7	39.0	47.4
Richardson	259	1 820	446	D	329	87	58	48	26 568	736	21.6	28.7	55.7
Rock	45	342	D	D	40	D	D	10	28 216	247	14.2	68.0	61.1
Saline	299	5 716	556	2 807	496	144	D	211	36 938	756	22.9	32.3	56.6
Sarpy	3 337	44 160	4 747	2 361	7 902	1 963	2 742	1 665	37 712	396	57.6	15.4	39.4
Saunders	524	3 681	597	473	556	208	125	114	30 934	1 204	30.4	25.1	55.8
Scotts Bluff	1 078	12 304	2 823	972	2 349	466	355	416	33 843	966	30.6	22.7	49.7
Seward	439	5 441	773	D	515	213	D	173	31 867	992	36.4	23.3	47.0
Sheridan	168	1 037	D	10	250	102	D	24	23 130	536	16.2	50.9	68.5
Sherman	81	510	D	D	92	D	D	13	25 569	414	12.1	38.9	60.9
Sioux	13	35	D	NA	D	D	D	1	29 086	354	8.2	63.6	71.2
Stanton	108	D	D	D	89	D	D	D	D	619	20.8	29.9	64.6
Thayer	208	1 962	D	D	194	117	34	75	38 037	432	15.7	44.9	63.9
Thomas	21	143	NA	D	D	D	D	5	33 189	87	14.9	70.1	66.7
Thurston	122	1 282	124	D	229	47	D	54	42 185	367	25.3	45.2	65.7
Valley	182	1 403	344	85	364	78	65	39	28 123	402	13.9	49.3	73.1
Washington	559	6 263	857	1 048	1 081	290	176	279	44 563	821	40.0	21.4	58.0
Wayne	252	3 178	473	D	356	262	78	85	26 677	518	24.7	33.0	67.0
Webster	89	657	165	NA	147	39	D	18	27 282	423	21.5	42.6	53.9
Wheeler	21	100	NA	D	NA	D	NA	2	17 530	198	17.2	56.6	67.7
York	515	5 939	967	793	954	D	128	198	33 420	541	21.1	43.4	70.6
NEVADA	60 306	1 047 657	107 580	39 608	135 128	34 963	54 071	41 601	39 708	4 137	53.2	18.9	53.0
Churchill	485	5 159	814	324	865	169	456	183	35 561	672	63.1	7.6	54.3
Clark	40 969	767 816	75 656	18 061	99 696	26 063	39 545	29 628	38 588	252	78.6	2.0	46.8
Douglas	1 596	15 974	1 277	1 835	2 190	350	850	574	35 939	255	65.1	7.5	62.4
Elko	1 098	20 724	1 438	258	2 353	298	630	1 046	50 450	552	37.0	31.5	53.4
Esmeralda	14	D	NA	D	NA	NA	D	D	D	38	23.7	31.6	63.2
Eureka	45	1 765	D	D	D	D	D	144	81 582	101	8.9	49.5	68.3
Humboldt	406	7 123	550	226	1 001	76	120	369	51 735	359	36.2	38.2	54.6
Lander	96	1 499	D	D	236	D	D	83	55 169	124	37.1	47.6	62.1
Lincoln	87	611	118	D	D	D	D	16	26 697	185	35.7	20.5	43.8
Lyon	771	10 812	499	1 932	1 265	173	316	338	31 233	462	60.0	15.4	56.1
Mineral	59	1 080	D	D	98	D	25	41	37 765	119	67.2	1.7	27.7
Nye	643	6 647	711	D	1 396	140	172	237	35 635	198	63.6	15.2	51.0
Pershing	74	1 081	D	D	D	14	D	55	50 607	154	29.2	37.7	81.8
Storey	81	571	D	D	90	D	D	13	22 581	6	100.0	0.0	0.0
Washoe	11 477	167 121	22 146	13 625	22 052	5 933	10 167	7 156	42 817	479	69.3	7.1	44.1
White Pine	185	2 639	286	D	388	43	D	142	53 733	160	40.6	26.3	43.8
Carson City	1 935	20 226	3 635	2 901	3 137	953	1 053	845	41 796	21	81.0	4.8	47.6
NEW HAMPSHIRE	37 185	551 793	87 050	67 915	97 039	24 348	30 621	24 906	45 136	4 391	55.5	3.5	48.0
Belknap	1 763	20 289	3 695	2 448	4 882	D	691	774	38 149	302	55.6	1.7	42.4
Carroll	1 834	16 624	2 786	954	3 526	440	482	524	31 538	291	53.6	3.4	52.6
Cheshire	1 905	27 313	3 981	4 369	5 760	1 427	621	1 070	39 180	407	53.6	5.7	47.4
Coos	854	9 065	2 165	701	1 735	305	127	295	32 560	293	38.2	6.5	50.2
Grafton	2 867	47 625	10 823	5 527	7 491	937	1 542	2 208	46 361	500	38.0	7.2	45.2
Hillsborough	10 764	173 304	28 199	28 142	27 944	5 679	11 439	8 534	49 243	688	64.0	1.5	50.0
Merrimack	4 031	60 018	12 171	5 609	10 204	3 479	3 575	2 500	41 649	600	55.7	3.8	49.2
Rockingham	9 422	128 330	15 318	13 010	26 625	6 422	7 689	5 792	45 134	658	69.6	0.8	48.8
Strafford	2 536	35 159	6 471	4 366	6 505	D	1 252	1 546	43 974	354	58.2	1.1	48.6
Sullivan	937	11 609	1 347	2 789	2 367	454	189	452	38 903	298	51.3	5.7	43.0
NEW JERSEY	230 281	3 492 216	553 578	221 052	445 176	198 540	307 495	195 073	55 859	9 071	71.2	3.1	49.5
Atlantic	6 495	114 051	17 643	1 549	17 239	2 922	4 889	4 042	35 436	402	69.4	2.2	61.4
Bergen	31 524	429 410	70 645	32 673	60 626	16 751	34 581	25 386	59 118	60	88.3	0.0	48.3
Burlington	10 557	179 487	25 480	15 611	24 264	17 283	17 996	9 132	50 879	838	69.5	5.0	56.4
Camden	11 449	171 022	38 412	10 789	23 846	5 050	12 151	7 626	44 590	175	81.1	1.1	50.3
Cape May	3 806	24 732	4 757	458	5 622	1 111	1 021	982	38 906	152	75.7	1.3	48.0
Cumberland	2 898	43 640	9 748	7 456	7 237	1 231	984	1 616	37 040	583	61.7	5.3	55.2
Essex	18 765	287 991	54 830	17 617	26 490	21 878	24 590	16 789	58 297	13	100.0	0.0	53.8
Gloucester	5 894	87 331	13 775	7 319	17 062	1 741	3 632	3 456	39 579	584	74.3	2.6	45.0
Hudson	12 879	211 322	26 166	7 586	22 585	35 494	12 460	14 140	66 914	0	0.0	0.0	0.0
Hunterdon	3 877	45 457	7 775	3 713	6 673	3 146	3 895	2 935	64 561	1 447	71.9	1.9	43.7

STATE County	Agriculture, 2012 (cont.) — Land in farms: Acreage (1,000)	Land in farms: Percent change, 2007–2012	Land in farms: Acres: Average size of farm	Land in farms: Acres: Total irrigated (1,000)	Land in farms: Acres: Total cropland (1,000)	Value of land and buildings (dollars): Average per farm	Value of land and buildings (dollars): Average per acre	Value of machinery and equipment, average per farm (dollars)	Value of products sold: Total (mil dol)	Value of products sold: Average per farm (dollars)	Value of products sold: Percent from: Crops	Value of products sold: Percent from: Live-stock and poultry products	Percent of farms with sales of: $10,000 or more	Percent of farms with sales of: $100,000 or more	Government payments: Total ($1,000)	Government payments: Percent of farms
	117	118	119	120	121	122	123	124	125	126	127	128	129	130	131	132
NEBRASKA—Cont'd																
Platte	426	0.1	453	194.0	351.5	2 302 510	5 088	284 312	652.1	692 256	36.3	63.7	75.7	53.7	6 298	74.1
Polk	245	-8.9	526	151.0	212.2	3 128 150	5 943	329 976	326.2	700 084	51.2	48.8	80.3	64.4	3 710	79.2
Red Willow	420	-6.0	1 036	53.1	241.6	1 651 696	1 594	224 978	180.5	445 701	45.7	54.3	64.4	37.5	3 807	61.5
Richardson	319	14.3	434	4.7	245.8	1 653 332	3 812	171 026	162.0	220 139	71.0	29.0	65.4	38.2	6 434	82.2
Rock	645	2.0	2 610	36.3	146.9	2 813 632	1 078	195 603	97.8	395 903	40.2	59.8	82.6	53.8	1 332	36.0
Saline	362	21.3	479	108.1	296.7	2 306 246	4 818	261 522	208.8	276 152	82.3	17.7	65.9	41.4	5 966	80.8
Sarpy	92	-9.0	232	10.4	82.2	1 380 134	5 959	127 424	63.6	160 553	75.4	24.6	45.5	24.5	1 340	58.1
Saunders	469	9.8	390	105.6	412.0	2 054 154	5 268	198 767	380.5	316 033	59.0	41.0	65.2	37.4	7 393	72.3
Scotts Bluff	445	23.6	461	199.2	239.7	860 445	1 867	172 940	390.1	403 791	41.2	58.8	62.1	31.2	3 579	62.3
Seward	355	6.7	358	129.9	294.3	1 799 861	5 031	216 676	308.5	311 017	59.7	40.3	59.3	34.5	6 718	71.2
Sheridan	1 534	-0.4	2 863	60.7	275.5	1 983 683	693	201 590	167.5	312 541	50.0	50.0	62.5	35.1	3 179	57.3
Sherman	281	4.1	679	71.1	127.7	1 609 171	2 369	172 713	114.2	275 754	68.3	31.7	78.7	42.8	2 093	70.5
Sioux	1 224	-5.2	3 459	39.5	94.0	1 981 486	573	151 356	146.0	412 446	20.3	79.7	74.6	44.1	1 338	46.0
Stanton	254	7.9	411	28.4	195.1	1 798 275	4 375	202 628	182.1	294 158	35.1	64.9	67.7	35.4	3 656	77.9
Thayer	326	-7.1	755	135.5	254.0	3 114 514	4 123	323 176	249.4	577 278	74.7	25.3	78.7	56.9	4 259	81.5
Thomas	368	-13.5	4 225	2.9	8.0	2 125 345	503	114 736	22.4	257 770	D	D	73.6	37.9	438	18.4
Thurston	248	24.0	675	11.9	215.9	3 406 256	5 049	284 038	197.7	538 651	47.3	52.7	72.2	57.8	3 744	80.1
Valley	349	-1.9	869	93.1	150.7	1 919 602	2 209	248 953	205.1	510 179	46.5	53.5	76.9	52.2	2 783	75.1
Washington	248	14.2	302	17.3	209.8	1 820 340	6 024	180 247	163.5	199 117	62.8	37.2	54.9	32.6	4 069	59.3
Wayne	280	1.2	540	49.8	238.4	2 363 431	4 373	235 147	203.3	392 380	45.7	54.3	75.5	43.8	3 410	77.4
Webster	302	-1.1	715	55.0	177.8	2 021 950	2 830	228 965	226.9	536 404	40.4	59.6	76.8	45.2	3 545	71.6
Wheeler	357	-0.9	1 804	39.4	90.9	2 208 793	1 225	254 586	259.8	1 312 323	13.6	86.4	74.7	51.5	1 407	52.5
York	340	-1.9	628	252.4	313.1	3 534 628	5 631	429 436	415.4	767 861	72.9	27.1	81.0	65.1	6 039	74.5
NEVADA	5 914	0.8	1 429	687.8	756.9	1 324 673	927	134 626	764.1	184 710	47.9	52.1	42.0	21.2	3 253	8.2
Churchill	197	50.0	294	53.6	56.3	713 604	2 431	110 594	89.9	133 833	34.5	65.5	44.6	18.3	414	7.3
Clark	16	-82.3	62	3.7	4.4	347 790	5 611	66 325	6.8	27 083	48.2	51.8	33.7	4.4	34	3.6
Douglas	101	10.9	396	25.6	18.6	1 141 780	2 884	76 525	D	D	D	D	36.9	12.2	D	0.8
Elko	2 127	2.0	3 853	132.2	170.4	1 908 208	495	122 257	95.6	173 221	15.3	84.7	42.4	23.6	398	6.5
Esmeralda	35	38.7	911	17.5	19.2	1 631 211	1 791	350 737	13.1	345 974	98.2	1.8	60.5	60.5	0	0.0
Eureka	639	-18.5	6 325	46.7	49.1	4 087 158	646	288 782	36.0	356 634	81.2	18.8	72.3	59.4	D	3.0
Humboldt	809	6.9	2 253	137.5	165.3	2 233 571	991	271 593	135.3	376 983	75.7	24.3	48.7	37.9	703	26.7
Lander	314	-7.4	2 532	37.2	44.6	1 880 298	743	211 121	39.3	316 581	68.9	31.1	55.6	46.8	132	15.3
Lincoln	D	D	D	22.0	22.4	1 074 735	D	145 276	23.2	125 487	60.2	39.8	41.6	21.6	34	5.9
Lyon	366	40.4	792	87.7	78.3	1 738 119	2 194	137 630	133.0	287 959	43.8	56.2	44.2	21.4	485	5.8
Mineral	D	D	D	D	D	863 597	D	38 882	0.9	7 429	56.4	43.6	25.2	0.8	0	0.0
Nye	65	-28.3	329	20.0	26.4	703 429	2 139	127 217	70.5	356 035	D	D	36.9	12.6	62	6.1
Pershing	299	22.5	1 943	52.8	57.4	1 813 416	933	262 714	62.8	407 474	52.5	47.5	63.6	42.9	779	29.2
Storey	0	D	14	D	D	550 167	38 384	29 833	D	D	D	D	0.0	0.0	0	0.0
Washoe	443	-8.9	924	15.4	13.7	752 190	814	53 073	16.5	34 543	49.6	50.4	27.8	6.7	75	4.0
White Pine	193	D	1 208	32.7	24.3	987 431	817	150 775	20.7	129 069	43.9	56.1	40.6	22.5	120	7.5
Carson City	D	D	D	D	D	665 048	D	108 429	5.8	275 476	D	D	23.8	19.0	0	0.0
NEW HAMPSHIRE	474	0.5	108	2.6	98.3	449 848	4 167	56 426	190.9	43 477	52.8	47.2	26.6	6.0	3 472	10.6
Belknap	24	2.2	79	0.3	5.7	431 990	5 462	54 798	7.8	25 712	61.2	38.8	22.2	5.0	194	7.3
Carroll	29	-8.4	101	0.2	3.9	479 337	4 751	50 859	5.5	18 801	63.2	36.8	24.1	2.7	203	9.6
Cheshire	63	31.2	156	0.1	9.2	455 386	2 928	52 337	17.3	42 582	39.6	60.4	31.4	6.9	231	7.9
Coos	57	11.6	194	0.0	12.5	462 461	2 386	65 020	14.2	48 461	34.6	65.4	28.7	6.5	200	14.7
Grafton	82	-17.6	165	0.1	17.2	489 910	2 974	61 806	29.8	59 662	19.5	80.5	28.8	8.0	753	19.8
Hillsborough	48	-5.0	69	0.7	11.1	450 385	6 495	52 282	22.5	32 759	69.8	30.2	22.8	7.0	261	6.8
Merrimack	65	0.5	108	0.6	13.7	430 238	3 974	58 167	45.3	75 443	77.7	22.3	30.5	6.8	686	13.0
Rockingham	36	7.2	55	0.3	9.0	406 448	7 428	49 995	18.4	27 964	68.9	31.1	23.7	4.6	352	7.9
Strafford	31	19.2	87	0.3	7.7	425 040	4 904	61 031	12.8	36 144	47.0	53.0	30.5	3.1	295	10.7
Sullivan	39	-9.7	131	0.1	8.3	515 507	3 937	66 409	17.3	58 091	30.8	69.2	23.5	8.1	296	9.4
NEW JERSEY	715	-2.5	79	88.4	456.8	1 008 402	12 792	81 470	1 006.9	111 006	88.5	11.5	36.1	12.3	7 596	11.4
Atlantic	29	-2.9	73	11.3	18.9	903 438	12 320	135 682	125.4	312 040	98.2	1.8	51.7	25.4	247	8.2
Bergen	1	21.7	24	0.1	0.5	1 005 933	42 148	74 700	5.2	86 600	96.3	3.7	60.0	20.0	D	1.7
Burlington	96	11.8	114	13.1	52.3	1 108 438	9 686	98 032	100.9	120 390	95.4	4.6	45.3	14.4	1 939	13.4
Camden	7	-18.5	41	2.5	4.7	513 600	12 583	67 920	16.0	91 526	99.2	0.8	32.6	12.0	20	5.7
Cape May	7	-7.8	48	2.2	4.3	557 868	11 534	51 809	8.0	52 809	93.4	6.6	40.1	10.5	D	2.0
Cumberland	65	-7.1	111	19.3	49.7	889 362	8 035	130 184	170.4	292 216	97.2	2.8	50.9	22.1	520	14.9
Essex	0	-30.4	10	0.0	0.0	624 923	63 469	61 769	1.9	148 462	D	D	69.2	38.5	0	0.0
Gloucester	43	-7.3	74	9.0	32.0	882 231	11 909	93 639	87.7	150 154	93.9	6.1	33.6	15.6	700	13.0
Hudson	0	0.0	0	0.0	0.0	0	0	0	0.0	0	0.0	0.0	0.0	0.0	0	0.0
Hunterdon	96	-4.0	66	1.2	58.3	1 088 382	16 401	59 249	67.2	46 445	85.3	14.7	26.3	5.1	724	10.8

STATE County	Water use, 2010		Wholesale trade,[1] 2007				Retail trade,[2] 2007				Real estate and rental and leasing,[2] 2007			
	Total water withdrawn (mil gal/day)	Gallons withdrawn per person per day	Number of establish-ments	Number of employees	Sales (mil dol)	Annual payroll (mil dol)	Number of establish-ments	Number of employees	Sales (mil dol)	Annual payroll (mil dol)	Number of establish-ments	Number of employees	Receipts (mil dol)	Annual payroll (mil dol)
	133	134	135	136	137	138	139	140	141	142	143	144	145	146
NEBRASKA—Cont'd														
Platte	124.5	3 861	49	529	517.8	22.9	174	2 136	494.3	41.2	38	118	19.0	2.4
Polk	65.5	12 107	9	109	103.3	3.5	24	116	35.5	2.1	2	D	D	D
Red Willow	39.9	3 608	20	244	140.9	8.3	88	789	175.9	17.3	20	59	3.8	0.7
Richardson	2.9	343	27	130	186.9	3.8	48	337	70.4	6.2	6	26	1.5	0.4
Rock	21.6	14 174	5	66	23.4	1.6	10	D	D	D	NA	NA	NA	NA
Saline	46.1	3 245	15	139	157.0	6.1	55	552	102.4	10.1	8	23	1.5	0.3
Sarpy	35.1	221	159	2 584	3 005.9	128.5	373	6 783	2 285.8	157.2	131	543	99.7	15.6
Saunders	104.3	5 020	25	145	147.8	5.1	64	570	149.0	10.7	13	17	1.1	0.3
Scotts Bluff	518.7	14 031	65	D	D	D	200	2 451	519.8	49.3	42	133	17.9	2.9
Seward	51.2	3 057	25	182	127.1	8.0	56	577	109.8	10.4	9	17	2.2	0.2
Sheridan	54.4	9 947	11	166	64.8	3.6	46	281	50.3	4.0	3	D	D	D
Sherman	45.1	14 293	3	33	11.3	0.9	15	69	35.5	1.5	1	D	D	D
Sioux	99.0	75 484	4	D	D	D	4	D	D	D	NA	NA	NA	NA
Stanton	19.0	3 105	3	D	D	D	15	136	33.0	2.7	1	D	D	D
Thayer	79.1	15 132	19	146	98.6	5.7	41	254	54.9	4.0	2	D	D	D
Thomas	1.4	2 148	2	D	D	D	4	D	D	D	1	D	D	D
Thurston	5.9	853	9	73	115.0	2.5	24	199	54.1	4.1	4	D	D	D
Valley	120.0	28 174	12	89	48.4	2.8	36	316	66.8	5.9	3	D	D	D
Washington	445.8	22 032	19	159	211.4	5.9	60	926	642.6	35.6	15	30	2.2	0.5
Wayne	15.8	1 641	11	139	51.9	3.4	44	394	79.5	6.7	7	20	1.1	0.4
Webster	42.0	11 020	15	75	58.9	2.1	20	155	23.7	1.8	1	D	D	D
Wheeler	40.5	49 450	2	D	D	D	3	D	D	D	NA	NA	NA	NA
York	138.2	10 112	32	332	239.1	12.1	77	1 045	241.3	20.8	18	39	3.9	0.5
NEVADA	2 623.1	971	2 614	36 052	19 255.9	1 698.5	8 492	139 829	37 434.0	3 691.7	4 613	31 603	6 187.3	1 106.5
Churchill	191.8	7 708	19	153	33.3	2.7	84	1 195	265.3	28.6	38	140	11.9	2.6
Clark	486.6	249	1 698	23 067	11 493.1	1 114.8	5 744	99 817	26 676.6	2 656.9	3 356	25 654	5 235.4	925.5
Douglas	111.6	2 374	57	D	D	D	198	2 817	670.4	66.1	140	539	94.0	19.5
Elko	357.1	7 314	58	D	D	D	179	2 307	791.4	57.3	39	297	26.7	5.9
Esmeralda	25.8	32 950	NA	NA	NA	NA	2	D	D	D	NA	NA	NA	NA
Eureka	306.2	154 076	NA	NA	NA	NA	6	35	16.3	1.4	NA	NA	NA	NA
Humboldt	282.4	17 086	15	140	71.5	7.5	76	1 042	333.6	24.9	11	43	5.6	0.9
Lander	164.0	28 391	3	D	D	D	22	237	55.0	4.0	3	4	0.7	0.1
Lincoln	54.1	10 123	2	D	D	D	17	247	31.1	3.0	3	19	0.8	0.2
Lyon	222.1	4 274	40	D	D	D	117	1 080	371.4	25.3	45	138	14.9	3.0
Mineral	3.1	658	2	D	D	D	11	D	D	D	3	5	0.3	0.0
Nye	63.9	1 455	16	D	D	D	135	1 554	396.8	37.9	52	141	14.5	2.9
Pershing	82.8	12 261	2	D	D	D	18	154	43.0	3.2	3	9	0.4	0.1
Storey	2.0	491	NA	NA	NA	NA	22	54	6.8	1.1	2	D	D	D
Washoe	132.9	315	602	10 370	6 317.7	461.6	1 555	25 025	6 667.4	671.0	763	D	D	D
White Pine	119.8	11 943	8	D	D	D	44	458	88.8	8.4	8	37	3.0	0.6
Carson City	17.0	307	92	D	D	D	262	3 698	991.5	99.5	147	569	73.4	16.0
NEW HAMPSHIRE	1 214.6	923	1 561	21 457	14 564.5	1 196.3	6 603	98 333	25 353.9	2 380.5	1 534	7 266	1 371.8	248.2
Belknap	9.3	155	48	D	D	D	372	5 212	1 348.7	133.2	88	399	56.6	10.2
Carroll	5.0	104	34	D	D	D	424	3 891	889.0	96.0	84	D	D	D
Cheshire	7.9	103	66	D	D	D	382	5 775	1 649.0	139.3	69	296	49.3	10.0
Coos	13.6	411	21	D	D	D	197	2 229	602.9	50.3	27	D	D	D
Grafton	12.2	137	80	D	D	D	592	8 158	1 961.3	195.5	140	582	72.8	17.5
Hillsborough	55.1	137	515	6 535	3 873.1	386.1	1 657	27 793	7 647.3	678.7	443	2 664	554.7	96.4
Merrimack	216.2	1 476	159	3 811	2 812.4	173.4	673	10 315	2 605.6	244.8	168	900	222.5	32.8
Rockingham	871.2	2 951	520	6 810	5 844.8	426.4	1 667	25 911	6 414.9	605.5	364	1 542	284.2	58.2
Strafford	19.0	154	81	856	351.1	50.2	439	6 640	1 672.9	173.9	111	428	65.7	10.6
Sullivan	5.1	117	37	D	D	D	200	2 409	562.4	63.3	40	136	16.4	3.1
NEW JERSEY	5 670.7	645	14 033	221 729	233 413.0	13 266.6	34 482	460 843	124 813.6	12 050.0	9 618	64 021	16 347.6	2 939.1
Atlantic	60.1	219	196	2 916	1 342.2	127.1	1 291	17 258	4 429.4	428.6	287	1 867	378.7	56.9
Bergen	116.3	128	3 046	40 189	66 117.9	2 584.6	4 128	55 875	16 475.0	1 768.6	1 441	7 655	2 294.7	412.7
Burlington	109.5	244	572	11 618	15 040.9	649.7	1 594	27 383	7 005.1	706.9	409	3 744	881.0	182.1
Camden	57.5	112	645	D	D	D	1 911	24 858	5 859.3	601.8	457	3 080	575.7	118.0
Cape May	79.6	818	65	561	276.1	25.3	746	6 103	1 584.9	164.8	258	836	177.1	27.0
Cumberland	58.9	375	160	D	D	D	564	7 602	1 952.7	185.4	125	540	88.3	16.2
Essex	33.2	42	1 081	17 340	12 622.5	1 116.1	2 892	30 136	7 750.6	764.8	947	5 988	1 411.3	243.8
Gloucester	72.2	251	314	8 732	8 962.5	426.2	989	17 301	4 352.5	386.0	180	D	D	D
Hudson	209.4	330	829	16 313	14 524.9	885.7	2 267	22 579	6 099.9	552.6	725	4 635	1 442.8	235.2
Hunterdon	89.7	699	157	1 283	629.5	62.0	572	6 676	2 186.6	193.2	112	407	102.1	17.6

1. Merchant wholesalers, except manufacturers' sales branches and offices. 2. Employer establishments.

STATE County	Professional, scientific, and technical services,[1] 2007				Manufacturing, 2007				Accommodation and food services, 2007			
	Number of establish-ments	Number of employees	Receipts (mil dol)	Annual payroll (mil dol)	Number of establish-ments	Number of employees	Receipts (mil dol)	Annual payroll (mil dol)	Number of establish-ments	Number of employees	Sales (mil dol)	Annual payroll (mil dol)
	147	148	149	150	151	152	153	154	155	156	157	158
NEBRASKA—Cont'd												
Platte	59	D	D	D	79	6 253	2 353.6	248.9	80	1 110	39.1	10.6
Polk	13	25	2.0	0.3	NA	NA	NA	NA	8	44	1.1	0.2
Red Willow	33	139	10.8	4.3	NA	NA	NA	NA	27	540	16.4	4.5
Richardson	16	69	3.8	1.3	NA	NA	NA	NA	23	142	4.1	1.1
Rock	1	D	D	D	NA	NA	NA	NA	3	23	0.3	0.1
Saline	17	55	4.1	1.0	19	2 907	951.8	112.2	33	340	11.3	2.8
Sarpy	255	D	D	D	79	2 573	587.7	115.2	224	4 211	160.3	47.6
Saunders	41	D	D	D	25	645	D	D	39	361	9.2	2.3
Scotts Bluff	70	D	D	D	42	D	177.9	33.7	104	1 488	52.9	14.4
Seward	31	79	9.7	2.4	20	977	D	36.8	34	438	13.5	3.4
Sheridan	9	43	3.1	0.8	NA	NA	NA	NA	18	104	2.9	0.8
Sherman	5	7	0.6	0.1	NA	NA	NA	NA	8	50	2.1	0.4
Sioux	1	D	D	D	NA	NA	NA	NA	2	D	D	D
Stanton	6	D	D	D	NA	NA	NA	NA	6	46	1.6	0.4
Thayer	7	16	1.0	0.3	NA	NA	NA	NA	16	80	1.9	0.5
Thomas	1	D	D	D	NA	NA	NA	NA	3	31	1.0	0.3
Thurston	6	D	D	D	NA	NA	NA	NA	8	D	D	D
Valley	12	65	5.1	1.7	NA	NA	NA	NA	13	110	2.7	0.7
Washington	45	418	36.6	19.4	23	1 181	724.2	54.8	40	393	12.5	3.2
Wayne	13	188	8.3	2.6	12	821	180.0	22.8	21	361	9.3	2.2
Webster	3	D	D	D	NA	NA	NA	NA	7	D	D	D
Wheeler	NA	NA	NA	NA	NA	NA	NA	NA	7	D	D	D
York	30	156	17.6	6.2	25	936	353.2	37.8	40	705	28.9	7.7
NEVADA	7 895	57 357	8 881.4	3 241.1	2 035	51 958	15 735.8	2 290.8	5 570	325 544	28 815.5	8 594.6
Churchill	36	500	38.5	23.5	NA	NA	NA	NA	52	725	33.0	8.9
Clark	5 282	43 063	6 982.5	2 498.8	1 096	26 478	7 180.7	1 086.3	3 797	266 845	24 857.8	7 431.8
Douglas	240	1 032	106.0	46.4	78	2 652	751.8	140.6	130	9 342	680.4	200.0
Elko	100	D	D	D	NA	NA	NA	NA	127	5 776	474.1	122.0
Esmeralda	1	D	D	D	NA	NA	NA	NA	2	D	D	D
Eureka	5	D	D	D	NA	NA	NA	NA	4	51	2.2	0.5
Humboldt	20	123	9.5	3.6	NA	NA	NA	NA	57	1 024	52.0	14.6
Lander	3	D	D	D	NA	NA	NA	NA	17	126	5.4	1.5
Lincoln	8	12	1.4	0.3	NA	NA	NA	NA	16	D	D	D
Lyon	52	288	24.8	10.7	101	2 171	573.6	85.1	67	798	35.0	9.5
Mineral	4	D	D	D	NA	NA	NA	NA	13	326	20.2	4.8
Nye	53	214	14.9	6.1	NA	NA	NA	NA	74	1 519	88.1	21.8
Pershing	4	8	0.6	0.2	NA	NA	NA	NA	14	226	9.2	3.3
Storey	8	12	1.5	0.3	NA	NA	NA	NA	13	93	4.8	1.5
Washoe	1 688	10 089	1 442.8	548.7	505	D	D	D	990	35 447	2 399.4	729.2
White Pine	10	D	D	D	NA	NA	NA	NA	30	472	22.0	6.5
Carson City	381	D	D	D	143	3 528	621.6	141.7	167	2 664	127.7	37.8
NEW HAMPSHIRE	3 961	29 160	3 730.8	1 570.2	2 104	81 592	18 592.4	4 196.2	3 508	55 268	2 631.0	799.8
Belknap	161	D	D	D	102	3 274	687.1	142.4	229	2 742	151.6	48.3
Carroll	145	D	D	D	86	992	213.4	35.5	304	3 900	214.9	63.8
Cheshire	150	D	D	D	150	5 483	1 095.2	258.2	161	2 643	110.3	35.0
Coos	44	D	D	D	42	1 166	295.9	43.6	117	1 747	85.7	25.0
Grafton	251	D	D	D	130	6 138	1 314.3	272.5	356	5 844	272.8	83.7
Hillsborough	1 347	D	D	D	633	31 243	7 707.6	1 944.4	875	15 987	732.3	224.9
Merrimack	456	2 625	412.7	152.0	230	7 043	1 539.6	315.1	306	4 900	223.5	68.4
Rockingham	1 101	D	D	D	475	17 081	3 912.6	801.3	832	13 262	660.7	198.6
Strafford	234	D	D	D	152	5 739	1 186.0	243.3	256	3 500	146.8	42.8
Sullivan	72	D	D	D	104	3 433	640.8	140.0	72	743	32.3	9.4
NEW JERSEY	31 040	330 133	52 442.8	23 639.9	9 250	310 606	116 608.1	16 399.3	19 526	291 327	19 993.6	5 232.4
Atlantic	648	D	D	D	140	2 974	D	113.8	862	56 370	6 093.0	1 505.4
Bergen	4 367	D	D	D	1 313	42 288	11 973.8	2 236.6	2 222	27 945	1 848.3	489.0
Burlington	1 374	D	D	D	418	20 568	6 072.3	1 150.1	907	13 306	657.0	180.6
Camden	1 613	D	D	D	486	17 283	4 150.1	819.3	1 019	13 550	678.8	185.1
Cape May	250	D	D	D	81	662	D	18.9	832	5 615	517.0	144.9
Cumberland	231	D	D	D	175	9 037	2 591.4	341.6	262	3 263	155.1	40.0
Essex	2 443	D	D	D	914	27 302	10 422.7	1 472.5	1 514	19 727	1 335.8	357.1
Gloucester	538	D	D	D	276	10 190	15 679.4	573.7	472	8 461	379.4	104.3
Hudson	1 255	D	D	D	477	9 898	2 614.2	404.6	1 297	13 289	880.7	218.3
Hunterdon	644	D	D	D	148	D	D	194.1	284	3 243	175.8	47.2

1. Establishment subject to federal tax.

Table B. States and Counties — **Health Care and Social Assistance, Other Services, Nonemployer Businesses, and Residential Construction**

STATE County	Health care and social assistance, 2007				Other services, 2007				Nonemployer businesses, 2013		Value of residential construction authorized by building permits, 2014	
	Number of establish-ments	Number of employees	Receipts (mil dol)	Annual payroll (mil dol)	Number of establish-ments	Number of employees	Receipts (mil dol)	Annual payroll (mil dol)	Number	Receipts (mil dol)	New Construction ($1,000)	Number of housing units
	159	160	161	162	163	164	165	166	167	168	169	170
NEBRASKA—Cont'd												
Platte	84	1 587	125.4	47.5	78	497	25.0	8.6	2 112	85.0	13 529	61
Polk	7	233	12.9	5.6	16	24	3.1	0.6	426	12.8	400	2
Red Willow	36	D	D	D	31	107	7.8	2.0	874	33.9	1 055	5
Richardson	22	369	24.4	9.9	22	64	4.1	0.7	636	20.6	785	4
Rock	4	D	D	D	5	11	1.1	0.3	224	9.7	175	2
Saline	29	583	31.8	14.0	26	111	6.1	1.5	784	31.8	1 721	11
Sarpy	233	3 559	246.5	105.4	206	1 307	107.8	31.8	9 443	345.2	285 653	1 276
Saunders	32	536	30.1	13.0	28	87	8.7	2.2	1 710	64.6	10 580	56
Scotts Bluff	127	2 980	274.2	115.9	97	459	29.8	9.3	2 456	97.5	4 835	29
Seward	32	744	45.5	21.7	40	139	14.5	3.1	1 255	37.8	13 644	71
Sheridan	16	192	11.7	5.1	19	47	2.9	0.5	458	16.7	71	1
Sherman	6	D	D	D	7	D	D	D	263	10.1	503	3
Sioux	NA	NA	NA	NA	2	D	D	D	114	3.1	350	3
Stanton	8	D	D	D	5	D	D	D	472	19.4	4 908	22
Thayer	11	446	23.6	10.7	20	57	7.1	1.1	419	20.4	2 039	9
Thomas	NA	NA	NA	NA	1	D	D	D	82	4.8	NA	NA
Thurston	10	361	29.4	13.2	7	30	4.1	0.9	294	10.6	680	2
Valley	21	369	21.3	9.7	14	45	4.1	0.8	409	14.3	2 325	11
Washington	37	733	47.9	21.5	35	82	7.0	2.1	1 521	62.5	14 452	71
Wayne	23	365	23.1	10.5	20	D	D	D	587	22.6	4 145	35
Webster	6	209	9.5	4.1	4	19	1.9	0.3	294	8.5	900	4
Wheeler	NA	NA	NA	NA	NA	NA	NA	NA	96	5.2	0	0
York	41	952	62.2	27.7	57	300	19.3	4.9	1 024	42.7	3 234	16
NEVADA	5 772	96 633	12 191.2	4 398.5	3 571	27 234	2 584.3	701.7	192 044	9 781.7	1 754 597	13 016
Churchill	45	862	82.8	33.3	40	160	12.6	3.7	1 130	49.3	5 677	38
Clark	3 978	67 163	8 517.4	3 017.6	2 313	18 791	1 602.5	473.7	141 658	6 992.8	1 132 984	10 036
Douglas	113	1 064	117.7	39.7	70	470	48.3	14.1	4 996	327.6	53 185	156
Elko	121	D	D	D	81	549	62.7	17.8	2 327	104.5	44 438	350
Esmeralda	NA	NA	NA	NA	1	D	D	D	59	1.7	NA	NA
Eureka	3	D	D	D	NA	NA	NA	NA	117	4.1	NA	NA
Humboldt	31	D	D	D	31	166	19.9	5.8	865	32.4	3 010	20
Lander	8	D	D	D	6	D	D	D	257	7.5	996	7
Lincoln	4	D	D	D	2	D	D	D	280	7.2	2 923	12
Lyon	47	D	D	D	38	195	22.3	4.9	2 522	112.9	27 918	140
Mineral	6	D	D	D	5	D	D	D	174	5.1	150	1
Nye	60	848	76.2	23.1	50	196	13.8	3.6	2 187	84.4	NA	NA
Pershing	10	162	14.0	6.0	6	D	D	D	206	5.2	261	2
Storey	1	D	D	D	4	D	D	D	259	10.7	685	6
Washoe	1 112	D	D	D	761	D	D	D	29 629	1 613.5	470 205	2 210
White Pine	13	337	31.8	15.1	14	65	4.6	1.7	500	17.4	486	3
Carson City	220	3 407	453.3	164.1	149	948	83.3	25.4	4 878	405.4	11 679	35
NEW HAMPSHIRE	3 492	83 717	8 085.7	3 377.8	2 886	16 153	1 574.3	457.9	101 795	5 484.4	653 428	3 403
Belknap	146	4 011	310.9	143.1	148	629	54.4	15.2	5 524	285.6	46 018	198
Carroll	138	D	D	D	113	407	34.1	9.7	5 384	271.1	55 883	197
Cheshire	166	3 980	330.1	134.0	145	933	73.0	26.8	5 837	291.1	20 181	141
Coos	105	D	D	D	72	355	26.3	8.8	2 227	88.2	10 013	56
Grafton	278	9 894	1 483.6	559.2	198	1 083	91.7	24.6	7 890	417.3	35 459	187
Hillsborough	1 020	26 771	2 503.8	1 065.3	828	5 317	501.5	155.6	27 576	1 548.7	141 652	968
Merrimack	415	11 751	1 002.1	454.0	398	1 940	280.1	63.3	10 928	544.0	61 065	312
Rockingham	803	14 595	1 324.2	540.6	702	3 817	377.6	106.8	25 514	1 529.8	198 812	875
Strafford	310	6 170	638.1	267.0	202	1 255	103.4	34.1	7 643	363.8	72 344	416
Sullivan	111	1 594	107.2	47.5	80	417	32.3	12.8	3 272	144.8	12 003	53
NEW JERSEY	25 777	503 370	51 913.7	21 313.6	19 047	105 659	11 203.7	3 003.1	629 395	36 044.8	4 069 959	28 155
Atlantic	821	16 172	1 780.0	702.6	547	3 496	270.1	81.7	15 850	764.3	125 565	722
Bergen	3 435	65 456	7 781.4	2 953.4	2 581	12 322	1 348.6	355.7	86 102	5 807.0	514 764	3 408
Burlington	1 134	21 970	2 400.1	864.6	850	4 976	384.6	128.9	26 321	1 495.8	116 105	1 000
Camden	1 580	35 383	3 701.1	1 521.5	939	6 051	479.3	157.1	28 223	1 469.1	97 816	1 506
Cape May	268	D	D	D	288	1 124	91.2	29.5	7 862	444.4	206 175	638
Cumberland	399	8 351	820.8	333.3	273	1 439	103.0	31.1	6 032	267.8	24 627	212
Essex	2 540	56 955	5 884.7	2 599.3	1 720	10 832	1 188.8	341.0	60 582	3 173.8	243 184	2 617
Gloucester	614	11 646	980.0	422.4	530	3 301	272.0	77.5	15 030	726.6	65 372	491
Hudson	1 337	24 006	2 231.5	898.1	1 118	4 826	463.3	126.1	48 782	2 194.6	794 088	4 621
Hunterdon	361	6 893	634.4	274.0	285	1 717	127.5	40.9	11 463	732.6	49 384	348

STATE County	Government employment and payroll, 2012: Full-time equivalent employees	March payroll (dollars)	March payroll (percent of total): Adminis-tration, judicial, and legal	Police and Corrections	Fire Protection	Highways and transpor-tation	Health and Welfare	Natural resources and utilities	Education and libraries	Local government finances, 2012 — General revenue: Total (mil dol)	Inter-govern-mental (mil dol)	Taxes: Total (mil dol)	Per capita[1] (dollars): Total	Property
	171	172	173	174	175	176	177	178	179	180	181	182	183	184
NEBRASKA—Cont'd														
Platte	3 477	20 266 212	1.3	2.8	0.3	1.8	0.3	79.5	13.4	163.8	34.4	61.8	1 892	1 373
Polk	420	1 380 326	5.6	2.1	0.0	3.0	15.0	11.8	58.7	37.3	5.7	21.1	3 974	3 451
Red Willow	459	1 542 403	5.5	7.0	2.8	3.6	3.4	14.8	59.2	39.4	13.2	18.3	1 666	1 234
Richardson	419	1 193 885	9.7	4.8	0.6	7.6	0.0	12.0	63.6	30.7	8.7	18.1	2 182	1 949
Rock	140	411 891	13.3	2.7	0.0	6.6	35.8	2.2	35.4	13.0	2.1	4.8	3 482	3 134
Saline	632	2 291 344	7.0	11.3	0.3	4.0	0.9	7.0	67.4	70.4	19.1	28.7	1 969	1 723
Sarpy	5 078	18 211 968	6.6	10.7	1.5	2.7	1.0	2.9	72.0	450.7	142.5	250.1	1 508	1 248
Saunders	810	2 374 236	6.4	9.1	0.3	4.5	15.3	6.0	56.4	83.3	19.9	36.4	1 747	1 563
Scotts Bluff	2 061	7 164 008	4.8	7.4	1.1	2.8	2.5	7.6	73.3	182.1	72.1	64.7	1 751	1 338
Seward	680	2 373 107	7.0	6.7	0.0	6.0	0.7	9.6	68.9	55.3	12.4	35.6	2 103	1 821
Sheridan	512	1 548 088	13.3	3.5	0.0	6.0	29.3	9.8	37.6	40.3	9.6	11.2	2 111	1 872
Sherman	144	428 471	12.6	3.9	0.0	9.3	0.2	2.5	70.1	13.6	4.9	7.3	2 338	2 074
Sioux	56	132 554	19.8	4.1	0.0	17.1	0.0	2.1	56.8	4.9	1.0	3.0	2 305	2 122
Stanton	142	497 786	10.8	7.3	0.0	12.3	0.9	19.3	48.7	13.2	4.4	6.8	1 111	1 047
Thayer	412	1 461 621	5.5	2.0	0.0	5.1	41.8	4.4	38.2	41.8	5.4	16.6	3 236	3 029
Thomas	60	133 894	17.6	0.2	0.0	4.3	2.3	11.2	63.8	4.0	0.7	2.8	4 143	3 988
Thurston	545	1 799 779	5.2	2.2	0.0	2.7	22.5	1.8	65.3	52.7	28.4	8.7	1 244	1 115
Valley	518	1 666 812	3.3	2.5	0.0	3.6	47.1	17.8	25.3	53.3	10.2	13.7	3 233	2 920
Washington	750	2 779 921	6.4	9.0	0.0	4.2	8.1	3.5	68.0	69.7	16.2	43.5	2 146	1 843
Wayne	341	1 199 613	9.9	5.1	0.0	9.4	0.0	6.2	69.3	36.1	12.9	18.5	1 940	1 746
Webster	258	1 370 728	10.8	2.2	0.0	8.5	14.9	37.0	25.2	25.0	5.9	8.3	2 228	1 836
Wheeler	43	129 479	13.7	4.4	0.0	13.0	0.0	0.4	68.2	4.3	0.9	3.2	3 984	3 805
York	557	2 016 974	7.4	11.4	2.9	4.0	1.6	20.2	51.6	58.5	16.3	32.4	2 356	1 736
NEVADA	X	X	X	X	X	X	X	X	X	X	X	X	X	X
Churchill	944	3 773 220	10.4	12.8	0.4	2.3	1.9	7.4	51.3	114.7	52.6	27.8	1 142	921
Clark	51 796	300 546 553	8.1	16.4	5.9	3.4	8.6	10.1	45.3	8 606.7	3 678.4	2 735.1	1 367	869
Douglas	1 543	6 734 261	11.5	13.8	10.6	2.6	1.1	9.0	47.4	190.9	73.5	79.1	1 682	1 414
Elko	1 843	7 360 751	11.7	10.6	2.2	3.0	2.9	4.9	62.8	202.1	112.9	62.5	1 220	871
Esmeralda	82	243 932	21.0	20.4	0.0	9.4	1.5	2.3	37.8	7.7	4.9	1.6	2 030	2 012
Eureka	151	777 513	15.5	14.0	0.0	9.5	5.9	8.6	42.4	52.6	15.1	33.5	16 737	16 592
Humboldt	805	3 278 576	10.2	13.2	0.3	2.8	19.5	2.9	48.7	119.3	53.7	33.6	1 972	1 745
Lander	301	1 258 391	12.7	11.1	0.0	4.5	25.4	3.4	42.8	97.8	10.8	72.9	12 271	11 925
Lincoln	324	1 339 919	8.9	8.4	0.1	6.3	17.9	11.0	44.6	43.9	32.2	5.0	930	812
Lyon	1 568	6 140 208	8.1	8.1	3.5	1.3	1.3	10.4	64.0	160.6	98.5	45.8	892	708
Mineral	326	1 115 225	7.2	7.3	1.2	2.2	44.5	6.8	29.7	44.0	21.3	4.5	977	861
Nye	1 197	5 104 254	15.1	13.0	3.6	2.6	5.5	2.8	53.7	149.5	78.9	54.1	1 259	1 117
Pershing	319	1 109 998	11.6	9.0	0.3	4.2	22.5	5.0	44.3	34.1	14.3	8.8	1 300	1 263
Storey	188	901 189	19.1	15.5	16.1	3.8	0.0	4.0	34.8	29.3	7.0	16.6	4 219	4 028
Washoe	13 423	56 391 305	10.3	14.1	5.5	4.2	4.2	8.5	50.6	1 707.2	748.2	591.5	1 376	997
White Pine	513	2 356 531	8.8	7.1	1.5	3.7	40.7	2.2	32.8	71.2	22.1	18.0	1 791	1 611
Carson City	1 396	6 652 347	9.5	13.4	7.3	4.2	3.5	6.4	53.3	189.1	96.1	54.9	1 001	717
NEW HAMPSHIRE	X	X	X	X	X	X	X	X	X	X	X	X	X	X
Belknap	2 709	10 085 919	5.6	9.4	4.9	3.9	5.2	2.9	67.2	286.0	77.2	174.6	2 894	2 867
Carroll	2 191	7 449 385	6.3	9.2	2.5	4.0	7.7	3.0	65.3	220.7	71.1	131.4	2 763	2 740
Cheshire	3 313	11 134 351	6.0	8.9	2.9	3.9	7.7	4.1	65.0	326.6	110.7	178.9	2 328	2 314
Coos	1 565	5 117 863	3.6	6.6	2.3	4.9	20.1	3.2	58.8	159.6	71.8	67.1	2 091	2 079
Grafton	4 014	15 506 186	5.7	9.6	3.8	4.9	5.6	2.9	66.7	413.3	113.5	253.8	2 845	2 823
Hillsborough	13 991	56 054 764	4.1	10.8	6.0	4.5	3.9	3.8	65.8	1 458.9	470.6	808.2	2 006	1 981
Merrimack	5 875	21 465 982	6.0	10.6	5.3	4.2	7.6	3.1	61.7	555.7	176.5	328.2	2 236	2 219
Rockingham	10 620	43 247 180	4.5	10.2	6.0	2.4	3.9	2.7	68.4	1 174.1	314.0	771.3	2 590	2 568
Strafford	4 327	16 109 116	5.0	11.0	4.3	2.9	5.3	4.6	64.6	465.8	153.2	257.6	2 076	2 027
Sullivan	1 670	6 151 956	5.3	6.7	2.1	4.8	8.2	3.5	67.8	169.0	64.2	91.6	2 126	2 114
NEW JERSEY	X	X	X	X	X	X	X	X	X	X	X	X	X	X
Atlantic	14 001	71 971 044	5.3	13.7	4.7	1.7	5.3	3.8	63.4	1 749.6	507.4	1 016.6	3 691	3 639
Bergen	32 531	187 619 946	3.6	14.1	2.2	2.4	3.4	3.1	69.8	4 811.6	664.9	3 480.7	3 788	3 728
Burlington	17 657	91 624 216	4.0	9.2	2.6	2.9	2.3	3.0	75.0	2 079.2	596.9	1 183.3	2 622	2 584
Camden	20 756	110 518 829	3.6	10.7	3.0	3.5	5.8	2.8	67.4	3 281.1	1 305.1	1 230.4	2 396	2 359
Cape May	5 885	27 086 618	8.8	13.8	3.3	3.6	9.4	7.3	49.4	701.1	152.6	449.5	4 667	4 561
Cumberland	7 697	36 180 326	5.2	9.1	0.8	1.2	4.3	5.3	72.5	886.9	544.0	234.1	1 483	1 435
Essex	27 848	164 987 769	6.6	19.3	7.5	1.4	6.3	6.8	50.7	4 140.4	1 433.6	2 242.3	2 846	2 712
Gloucester	12 453	61 264 381	3.9	10.6	0.6	1.8	6.9	3.4	70.7	1 465.5	472.5	747.5	2 581	2 536
Hudson	18 627	101 485 405	7.4	23.1	8.9	1.9	5.7	4.8	45.5	2 886.1	1 144.0	1 243.6	1 906	1 849
Hunterdon	5 140	25 927 699	5.8	5.6	0.8	4.7	2.2	2.5	77.1	623.8	82.1	477.9	3 762	3 722

1. Based on the resident population estimated as of July 1 of the year shown.

STATE County	Local government finances, 2012 (cont.) — Direct general expenditure: Total (mil dol)	Per capita[1] (dollars)	Percent of total for: Educa-tion	Health and hospitals	Police protec-tion	Public welfare	High-ways	Debt outstanding: Total (mil dol)	Per capita[1] (dollars)	Government employment, 2013: Federal civilian	Federal military	State and local	Presidential election,[2] 2012 — Percent of vote cast: Demo-cratic	Republi-can	All other
	185	186	187	188	189	190	191	192	193	194	195	196	197	198	199
NEBRASKA—Cont'd															
Platte	113.1	3 461	56.1	0.4	3.7	0.6	15.1	2 372.1	72 585	84	121	2 492	28.3	69.8	1.9
Polk	34.4	6 457	55.6	18.0	1.4	0.1	7.2	36.4	6 843	23	19	500	26.3	71.6	2.1
Red Willow	41.1	3 746	48.6	0.9	4.2	0.6	6.1	41.9	3 815	66	40	1 072	24.1	74.0	1.8
Richardson	30.5	3 684	56.0	0.2	3.6	0.5	13.4	14.8	1 787	36	30	560	38.1	59.0	2.8
Rock	12.2	8 902	28.5	45.3	2.3	0.2	9.0	0.5	363	0	0	208	17.4	79.9	2.7
Saline	69.9	4 800	47.6	15.1	3.0	5.7	7.4	56.7	3 893	59	50	1 430	50.9	46.4	2.7
Sarpy	475.3	2 866	55.1	0.8	7.4	0.2	4.2	984.0	5 933	3 339	6 253	6 785	41.2	57.1	1.8
Saunders	75.5	3 628	42.1	21.4	3.2	0.2	8.3	105.7	5 074	100	78	1 444	36.9	60.6	2.5
Scotts Bluff	188.1	5 089	58.5	0.3	4.2	1.6	3.8	124.2	3 361	157	136	3 067	32.2	65.9	1.9
Seward	66.4	3 923	62.3	0.1	3.8	0.8	11.4	73.7	4 351	52	59	1 108	35.9	61.7	2.4
Sheridan	37.7	7 085	31.7	24.7	2.1	9.8	6.1	9.5	1 782	23	19	641	18.4	78.8	2.7
Sherman	13.4	4 324	49.2	0.3	3.1	0.3	17.7	6.5	2 098	12	12	289	37.2	60.4	2.4
Sioux	4.8	3 666	52.8	0.0	2.8	0.0	23.8	0.0	0	12	0	79	16.0	82.4	1.6
Stanton	13.6	2 232	42.0	0.7	4.3	0.5	31.8	14.5	2 388	20	23	277	26.6	71.4	2.0
Thayer	43.3	8 429	33.8	38.7	2.7	0.2	7.2	11.5	2 243	34	19	628	32.3	65.8	1.9
Thomas	4.0	5 904	53.0	0.5	3.1	0.0	7.9	0.8	1 214	10	0	84	13.1	84.9	2.1
Thurston	60.1	8 565	48.8	36.6	1.1	0.1	3.6	70.6	10 050	218	26	1 405	52.7	45.7	1.6
Valley	51.9	12 276	20.8	38.7	0.9	0.1	4.8	58.0	13 716	31	16	633	29.1	68.4	2.5
Washington	65.2	3 221	57.9	0.1	4.7	0.2	11.9	202.8	10 013	46	74	1 607	36.0	62.3	1.8
Wayne	43.1	4 516	51.6	0.3	2.5	0.4	9.5	23.9	2 503	30	31	1 047	32.8	65.7	1.5
Webster	23.9	6 404	33.4	19.3	2.3	5.0	13.2	9.5	2 548	24	13	297	30.4	67.9	1.8
Wheeler	4.1	5 045	61.1	0.0	2.5	0.0	23.7	0.6	806	0	0	60	21.8	75.9	2.3
York	55.4	4 034	45.6	2.4	5.0	0.3	13.4	105.0	7 641	51	50	1 180	24.5	73.8	1.7
NEVADA	X	X	X	X	X	X	X	X	X	18 387	18 608	129 983	55.1	42.7	2.2
Churchill	117.7	4 831	40.0	0.3	7.9	1.8	3.2	48.9	2 005	592	771	1 293	32.9	64.4	2.6
Clark	9 171.7	4 584	29.1	8.3	9.6	2.7	7.2	21 727.8	10 860	12 515	15 775	81 774	58.5	39.5	2.0
Douglas	187.5	3 990	36.5	0.3	5.7	2.5	2.5	82.9	1 764	88	130	2 140	41.2	56.5	2.3
Elko	209.5	4 091	47.0	0.9	7.2	0.7	5.0	51.6	1 008	365	142	3 286	28.3	68.5	3.2
Esmeralda	8.2	10 566	34.9	3.8	14.2	0.4	10.2	1.0	1 279	0	0	90	23.7	69.0	7.3
Eureka	40.5	20 245	25.6	2.0	4.9	0.3	18.1	0.0	0	0	0	202	19.3	75.7	5.0
Humboldt	102.4	6 005	35.6	26.8	6.8	1.0	6.9	5.9	344	158	48	1 326	33.7	63.3	3.0
Lander	42.2	7 095	31.4	24.0	6.2	2.0	4.2	0.0	0	69	17	489	27.5	69.7	2.8
Lincoln	42.9	7 928	28.0	0.6	5.4	1.6	11.1	9.9	1 834	43	14	578	24.6	71.1	4.3
Lyon	173.5	3 380	52.1	0.6	14.8	3.1	4.1	198.7	3 872	65	142	2 010	39.8	57.6	2.6
Mineral	39.6	8 513	17.4	39.2	5.2	0.6	3.6	14.3	3 064	75	14	498	46.9	49.0	4.1
Nye	174.9	4 071	43.6	4.0	14.2	1.5	4.9	134.2	3 123	119	119	1 600	41.3	54.5	4.2
Pershing	35.1	5 199	33.9	28.5	4.8	1.5	1.5	18.6	2 751	15	14	693	36.7	58.6	4.8
Storey	27.2	6 900	26.2	0.0	10.5	0.8	8.2	58.6	14 880	0	11	226	45.6	51.6	2.9
Washoe	1 673.2	3 892	35.9	1.1	6.6	4.3	3.3	4 470.2	10 398	3 520	1 236	23 671	55.2	42.6	2.1
White Pine	67.7	6 746	27.2	38.8	5.4	1.6	6.0	14.1	1 407	205	24	1 215	32.0	63.5	4.5
Carson City	205.0	3 738	48.3	2.1	8.1	1.2	5.3	391.1	7 131	543	143	8 892	49.1	48.2	2.7
NEW HAMPSHIRE	X	X	X	X	X	X	X	X	X	7 403	4 668	82 405	54.1	44.5	1.4
Belknap	273.9	4 541	53.3	0.3	6.3	6.1	4.4	96.2	1 595	141	202	4 183	50.0	48.8	1.2
Carroll	240.5	5 057	57.3	1.0	4.6	7.3	6.0	161.9	3 404	129	160	2 909	52.4	46.1	1.5
Cheshire	326.5	4 248	59.3	0.8	4.3	5.5	5.6	178.9	2 328	155	246	5 307	63.0	35.5	1.5
Coos	150.6	4 691	46.4	1.2	3.9	16.3	6.1	37.2	1 158	363	104	2 712	58.3	40.1	1.6
Grafton	440.6	4 940	56.2	0.8	4.4	4.8	5.7	258.1	2 895	514	285	6 824	63.0	35.5	1.5
Hillsborough	1 496.1	3 713	52.0	0.6	6.1	3.8	4.7	1 157.0	2 872	3 900	1 376	18 007	51.2	47.5	1.3
Merrimack	608.7	4 147	55.4	0.5	5.3	7.4	4.5	341.5	2 327	809	482	15 359	56.3	42.5	1.3
Rockingham	1 129.6	3 793	60.9	0.4	6.4	4.0	3.7	523.7	1 758	991	1 264	13 516	49.9	48.8	1.3
Strafford	444.5	3 582	51.7	0.1	5.7	7.3	4.8	294.8	2 375	315	405	11 161	59.5	39.2	1.3
Sullivan	166.1	3 857	51.2	0.5	4.3	11.4	5.9	81.8	1 900	86	144	2 427	58.2	40.3	1.5
NEW JERSEY	X	X	X	X	X	X	X	X	X	49 510	25 222	545 485	57.3	41.7	1.0
Atlantic	1 718.6	6 240	52.7	0.6	6.1	2.1	1.7	1 314.6	4 773	2 642	963	21 168	57.0	41.9	1.1
Bergen	4 857.2	5 286	54.3	5.8	7.0	1.3	2.6	3 581.0	3 897	2 533	1 881	45 163	54.3	44.9	0.8
Burlington	2 064.4	4 574	62.3	1.5	4.2	2.2	3.1	2 370.1	5 251	5 304	6 165	24 757	58.8	40.2	1.0
Camden	3 129.5	6 094	51.5	4.2	4.5	3.4	4.0	3 660.4	7 128	2 359	1 075	30 260	67.6	31.3	1.1
Cape May	000.9	0 400	33.8	1.5	5.3	4.4	4.9	673.4	6 992	437	929	8 339	45.0	53.7	1.3
Cumberland	880.4	5 580	60.1	2.7	3.8	3.4	2.5	354.4	2 246	638	299	13 173	60.1	38.5	1.4
Essex	4 300.2	5 459	38.9	3.3	8.3	2.9	1.3	3 851.1	4 889	8 985	1 636	66 042	76.0	23.4	0.6
Gloucester	1 410.5	4 871	58.9	0.8	4.6	2.2	1.9	1 385.8	4 785	461	589	18 133	55.4	43.3	1.3
Hudson	2 833.2	4 343	33.2	3.1	8.5	2.8	1.8	3 638.2	5 577	5 541	1 483	38 421	72.9	26.2	0.9
Hunterdon	605.4	4 765	66.0	1.2	3.5	0.8	6.1	565.1	4 448	247	252	8 428	42.6	56.0	1.4

1. Based on the resident population estimated as of July 1 of the year shown. 2.

STATE/ County code	CBSA code[1]	County type[2]	STATE County	Land area,[3] (sq km) 2010	Population, 2014: Total persons 2014	Population, 2014: Rank	Population, 2014: Per square kilometer	Population and population characteristics, 2013: Race alone or in combination, not Hispanic or Latino (percent): White	Black	American Indian, Alaska Native	Asian and Pacific Islander	Percent Hispanic or Latino[4]	Age (percent): Under 5 years	5 to 17 years	18 to 24 years	25 to 34 years	35 to 44 years	45 to 54 years
				1	2	3	4	5	6	7	8	9	10	11	12	13	14	15
			NEW JERSEY—Cont'd															
34 021	45940	2	Mercer	582	371 537	183	638.4	53.9	20.3	0.5	10.9	16.2	5.8	16.2	11.2	12.7	13.4	14.8
34 023	35620	1	Middlesex	800	836 297	67	1 045.4	47.5	9.9	0.5	24.1	19.5	6.0	16.2	9.9	13.9	14.0	14.6
34 025	35620	1	Monmouth	1 214	629 279	104	518.4	77.2	7.6	0.4	6.0	10.3	5.2	17.4	8.3	10.5	12.4	16.9
34 027	35620	1	Morris	1 192	499 727	137	419.2	74.5	3.5	0.3	10.7	12.4	5.2	17.5	7.9	10.8	13.1	17.1
34 029	35620	1	Ocean	1 629	586 301	109	359.9	86.1	3.5	0.3	2.3	8.8	6.8	16.7	7.6	10.8	10.7	13.1
34 031	35620	1	Passaic	478	508 856	132	1 064.6	44.6	11.5	0.4	5.8	38.8	6.9	17.6	10.3	13.2	13.1	14.2
34 033	37980	1	Salem	860	64 715	813	75.3	77.3	14.6	0.7	1.4	7.7	5.8	16.7	8.4	11.5	11.8	15.0
34 035	35620	1	Somerset	782	332 568	199	425.3	61.1	9.5	0.3	16.7	13.9	5.5	18.1	7.5	10.8	13.9	17.2
34 037	35620	1	Sussex	1 344	144 909	443	107.8	89.0	2.3	0.4	2.6	7.0	4.8	17.3	8.4	9.7	12.5	18.0
34 039	35620	1	Union	266	552 939	118	2 078.7	44.2	21.8	0.4	5.7	29.3	6.5	17.5	8.8	13.0	14.0	15.2
34 041	10900	2	Warren	924	106 917	560	115.7	85.3	4.4	0.4	3.3	7.9	5.1	16.9	8.6	10.2	12.5	17.2
35 000	...	X	NEW MEXICO	314 161	2 085 572	X	6.6	40.6	2.3	9.3	2.0	47.3	6.7	17.7	10.1	13.3	11.7	13.0
35 001	10740	2	Bernalillo	3 007	675 551	94	224.7	42.1	3.1	4.7	3.3	48.7	6.4	16.8	9.9	15.0	12.5	13.2
35 003	...	9	Catron	17 932	3 556	2 936	0.2	77.0	1.1	4.0	0.6	19.5	3.1	11.9	4.7	6.1	6.6	11.7
35 005	40740	5	Chaves	15 709	65 878	800	4.2	42.5	1.9	1.3	1.1	54.0	7.4	20.0	10.4	12.7	10.9	12.4
35 006	24380	6	Cibola	11 757	27 349	1 519	2.3	22.4	1.3	39.5	0.9	37.2	7.0	17.4	9.8	13.8	12.3	13.1
35 007	...	7	Colfax	9 733	12 680	2 251	1.3	49.4	0.8	2.0	0.7	48.6	5.1	14.5	7.6	10.2	9.8	13.3
35 009	17580	5	Curry	3 638	50 969	973	14.0	52.2	6.4	1.3	2.3	39.8	8.8	18.6	12.7	16.5	11.2	11.1
35 011	...	9	De Baca	6 016	1 825	3 068	0.3	58.4	0.6	2.4	0.2	40.7	6.6	15.6	6.0	9.4	9.2	13.7
35 013	29740	3	Dona Ana	9 861	213 676	300	21.7	30.0	1.7	1.2	1.5	66.5	7.4	18.5	14.8	12.7	10.7	11.5
35 015	16100	5	Eddy	10 815	56 395	900	5.2	51.3	1.6	1.5	1.0	45.7	7.1	19.0	9.3	13.5	11.4	12.8
35 017	43500	7	Grant	10 261	29 096	1 453	2.8	48.6	1.1	1.6	0.9	49.2	5.4	15.6	8.5	10.1	9.6	11.5
35 019	...	7	Guadalupe	7 849	4 468	2 868	0.6	16.7	1.6	1.8	1.4	79.1	4.9	15.4	8.5	14.8	11.4	14.5
35 021	...	9	Harding	5 505	683	3 130	0.1	55.4	0.7	0.4	0.6	43.8	5.1	11.3	4.2	9.1	5.9	13.9
35 023	...	7	Hidalgo	8 901	4 560	2 861	0.5	41.6	1.0	0.7	0.9	57.0	7.3	16.9	8.8	11.3	9.5	14.2
35 025	26020	5	Lea	11 372	69 999	764	6.2	40.8	4.0	1.2	0.7	54.1	8.5	21.5	10.1	14.8	12.2	12.0
35 027	...	7	Lincoln	12 512	19 706	1 848	1.6	65.1	0.8	3.2	0.7	31.5	5.0	13.7	6.5	9.1	8.8	13.6
35 028	31060	6	Los Alamos	283	17 682	1 934	62.5	76.1	1.1	1.5	7.2	16.0	5.3	18.0	6.3	9.8	12.4	16.4
35 029	19700	6	Luna	7 680	24 673	1 621	3.2	34.0	1.1	1.2	0.8	63.5	7.0	18.5	9.2	11.0	10.0	11.5
35 031	23700	4	McKinley	14 115	74 098	738	5.2	11.5	1.3	74.3	1.2	13.8	8.9	21.5	11.5	13.4	11.5	12.4
35 033	...	8	Mora	5 002	4 592	2 858	0.9	18.3	0.5	0.6	0.4	81.2	4.4	15.0	8.0	9.2	9.8	14.6
35 035	10460	4	Otero	17 128	65 082	811	3.8	53.3	4.2	6.7	2.3	35.4	7.6	16.9	11.2	14.0	10.8	12.0
35 037	...	7	Quay	7 445	8 501	2 558	1.1	52.8	1.7	1.6	1.3	43.8	5.8	15.2	7.1	10.0	9.9	13.4
35 039	21580	6	Rio Arriba	15 179	39 777	1 178	2.6	13.8	0.6	14.2	0.7	71.4	6.8	17.5	8.7	11.5	11.7	13.7
35 041	38780	7	Roosevelt	6 339	19 536	1 851	3.1	55.9	2.3	1.8	1.5	40.0	7.7	17.7	18.4	13.2	10.5	10.2
35 043	10740	2	Sandoval	9 611	137 608	460	14.3	47.4	2.6	12.8	2.2	37.0	6.0	19.2	8.2	12.1	12.8	13.9
35 045	22140	3	San Juan	14 279	123 785	500	8.7	42.4	1.1	38.2	0.9	19.3	7.5	20.3	9.5	14.0	11.7	12.6
35 047	29780	6	San Miguel	12 214	28 239	1 482	2.3	20.1	1.4	1.4	0.9	76.8	5.2	14.9	11.0	11.3	10.7	14.1
35 049	42140	3	Santa Fe	4 945	148 164	435	30.0	44.5	1.0	3.0	1.6	51.1	5.0	14.9	7.6	11.3	12.0	14.1
35 051	...	6	Sierra	10 823	11 325	2 338	1.0	68.2	1.0	2.4	0.8	29.4	4.2	11.4	5.7	8.1	7.6	12.3
35 053	...	6	Socorro	17 215	17 310	1 963	1.0	37.5	1.3	11.5	1.6	49.5	6.4	17.1	11.8	12.0	10.4	12.8
35 055	45340	7	Taos	5 706	33 084	1 353	5.8	37.3	0.7	6.2	0.9	56.1	5.0	14.3	7.0	10.2	11.0	14.1
35 057	10740	2	Torrance	8 663	15 611	2 065	1.8	55.4	1.8	3.0	1.0	40.5	5.5	17.3	8.4	10.6	11.2	13.9
35 059	...	9	Union	9 903	4 297	2 880	0.4	55.7	2.2	1.8	0.8	40.6	4.2	14.0	8.7	15.0	12.1	14.1
35 061	10740	2	Valencia	2 761	75 817	726	27.5	35.7	1.3	4.0	0.9	59.1	6.4	18.7	9.1	11.8	11.8	14.2
36 000	...	X	NEW YORK	122 057	19 746 227	X	161.8	58.4	15.4	0.7	8.8	18.3	6.0	15.6	10.1	14.3	12.8	14.3
36 001	10580	2	Albany	1 354	308 171	218	227.6	76.3	13.4	0.6	6.4	5.5	5.0	14.0	14.4	13.2	11.3	13.9
36 003	...	7	Allegany	2 666	47 736	1 021	17.9	96.0	1.6	0.5	1.4	1.5	5.4	15.6	15.1	10.2	10.3	13.1
36 005	35620	1	Bronx	109	1 438 159	26	13 194.1	11.2	30.6	0.6	4.1	54.3	7.6	18.1	11.7	15.0	12.8	13.4
36 007	13780	2	Broome	1 828	197 349	330	108.0	87.2	6.0	0.6	4.6	3.8	5.1	14.6	13.9	11.4	10.3	14.0
36 009	36460	4	Cattaraugus	3 389	78 600	701	23.2	92.8	2.2	3.7	1.1	1.9	5.8	16.9	9.5	11.0	11.2	14.4
36 011	12180	4	Cayuga	1 791	78 823	699	44.0	92.4	5.0	0.7	0.9	2.6	5.2	15.4	8.9	12.1	11.8	15.5
36 013	27460	4	Chautauqua	2 746	132 053	477	48.1	90.0	3.2	0.9	0.9	6.8	5.3	15.7	10.7	11.2	10.9	14.1
36 015	21300	3	Chemung	1 055	87 770	652	83.2	89.2	8.0	0.7	1.8	2.8	5.9	15.9	9.3	12.2	11.7	14.4
36 017	...	6	Chenango	2 314	49 426	993	21.4	96.2	1.3	0.9	0.9	2.1	5.3	16.1	8.2	10.4	11.4	15.2
36 019	38460	5	Clinton	2 688	81 632	681	30.4	91.8	4.3	0.8	1.7	2.7	4.8	13.6	13.7	12.4	12.1	15.4
36 021	26460	6	Columbia	1 644	62 122	842	37.8	89.1	5.6	0.6	2.4	4.2	4.4	14.6	7.8	9.7	11.1	16.1
36 023	18660	4	Cortland	1 292	49 024	997	37.9	94.5	2.3	0.8	1.5	2.5	5.0	15.1	18.2	10.8	10.6	13.4
36 025	...	6	Delaware	3 736	46 581	1 033	12.5	93.6	2.2	0.7	1.2	3.5	4.7	13.7	10.4	9.4	10.1	14.5
36 027	35620	2	Dutchess	2 061	296 579	227	143.9	74.9	10.7	0.6	4.5	11.3	4.7	15.8	11.3	11.0	12.1	16.4
36 029	15380	1	Erie	2 701	922 835	56	341.7	78.3	14.0	0.9	3.5	4.9	5.3	15.5	10.3	13.1	11.3	14.5
36 031	...	6	Essex	4 647	38 679	1 204	8.3	93.5	3.0	0.8	1.0	2.8	4.1	13.4	7.6	11.7	11.6	15.5
36 033	31660	5	Franklin	4 219	51 262	970	12.2	82.7	6.3	8.0	0.9	3.3	5.2	14.6	10.6	14.3	12.4	15.3
36 035	24100	4	Fulton	1 283	54 105	923	42.2	94.6	2.4	0.6	1.0	2.7	5.2	15.7	8.3	11.5	12.1	15.5

1. CBSA = Core Based Statistical Area. See Appendix A for explanation. See Appendix B for list of metropolitan areas with component counties. 2. County type code from the Economic Research Service of USDA Rural-Urban Continuum Codes. See Appendix A for definition. 3. Dry land or land partially or temporarily covered by water. 4. May be of any race.

STATE County	Population, 2013 (cont.) Age (percent) (cont.) 55 to 64 years	65 to 74 years	75 years and over	Percent female	Population change 2000–2014 Total persons 2000	2010	Percent change 2000–2010	2010–2014	Components of change, 2010–2014 Births	Deaths	Net migration	Households, 2009–2013 Number	Persons per household	Percent Family households	Female family householder[1]	One person
	16	17	18	19	20	21	22	23	24	25	26	27	28	29	30	31
NEW JERSEY—Cont'd																
Mercer	12.5	7.3	6.2	51.0	350 761	366 513	4.5	1.1	18 427	12 052	-2 219	130 754	2.67	67.6	13.4	26.9
Middlesex	12.1	7.2	6.0	50.8	750 162	809 858	8.0	3.3	42 237	24 368	9 020	280 988	2.82	72.3	11.8	22.9
Monmouth	14.1	8.4	6.8	51.3	615 301	630 380	2.5	-0.2	26 547	22 825	-4 559	233 909	2.66	69.6	10.6	25.7
Morris	13.4	8.2	6.8	51.0	470 212	492 276	4.7	1.5	20 137	15 594	3 299	179 665	2.71	72.0	8.5	23.8
Ocean	12.6	11.1	10.6	51.9	510 916	576 567	12.8	1.7	34 591	29 840	5 213	221 774	2.58	67.2	9.7	28.8
Passaic	11.8	7.2	5.7	51.3	489 049	501 226	2.5	1.4	30 326	15 413	-7 497	162 543	3.03	72.0	18.2	24.6
Salem	14.2	9.1	7.5	51.1	64 285	66 083	2.8	-2.1	3 046	2 969	-1 471	25 003	2.58	68.4	14.2	27.2
Somerset	13.2	7.5	6.2	51.2	297 490	323 444	8.7	2.8	14 850	9 519	3 642	115 531	2.79	72.7	9.4	23.1
Sussex	15.4	8.7	5.4	50.3	144 166	149 265	3.5	-2.7	5 535	4 819	-4 587	54 746	2.67	74.2	8.7	21.0
Union	12.1	6.9	6.0	51.3	522 541	536 499	2.7	3.1	29 579	16 890	4 272	185 483	2.88	70.9	15.9	24.8
Warren	14.0	8.4	6.9	51.2	102 437	108 692	6.1	-1.6	3 811	3 771	-1 789	41 463	2.56	70.1	10.6	24.8
NEW MEXICO	12.9	8.6	6.1	50.4	1 819 046	2 059 179	13.2	1.3	115 471	70 216	-18 886	761 938	2.66	65.4	13.9	28.6
Bernalillo	12.5	7.8	5.8	50.9	556 678	662 564	19.0	2.0	35 735	22 018	-426	263 135	2.50	62.1	14.0	30.6
Catron	23.2	20.8	11.9	48.0	3 543	3 725	5.1	-4.5	103	121	-104	1 581	2.23	58.1	2.2	40.5
Chaves	11.8	7.8	6.7	50.2	61 382	65 645	6.9	0.4	4 057	2 710	-1 008	23 499	2.70	69.0	15.4	26.7
Cibola	12.9	7.8	6.0	49.0	25 595	27 213	6.3	0.5	1 777	1 056	-628	8 016	3.15	65.8	17.7	30.1
Colfax	16.9	13.0	9.6	49.0	14 189	13 750	-3.1	-7.8	529	576	-1 029	5 574	2.33	59.5	11.9	34.7
Curry	9.7	6.4	5.1	48.4	45 044	48 376	7.4	5.4	3 942	1 557	183	18 027	2.67	68.8	13.2	26.8
De Baca	16.5	12.8	10.2	50.2	2 240	2 022	-9.7	-9.7	70	99	-167	689	2.83	65.7	8.0	31.2
Dona Ana	10.8	7.7	5.9	50.7	174 682	209 233	19.8	2.1	13 060	6 284	-2 428	73 797	2.79	69.5	16.4	23.9
Eddy	12.9	7.5	6.5	49.6	51 658	53 829	4.2	4.8	3 343	2 234	1 509	19 866	2.69	68.5	12.8	26.3
Grant	15.8	13.5	10.0	50.4	31 002	29 514	-4.8	-1.4	1 357	1 446	-324	12 216	2.36	62.5	12.7	32.0
Guadalupe	12.7	9.2	8.7	42.8	4 680	4 687	0.1	-4.7	182	173	-251	1 260	3.14	65.5	12.7	29.8
Harding	20.2	13.9	16.6	47.8	810	695	-14.2	-1.7	21	32	-1	261	2.63	59.8	2.7	36.8
Hidalgo	13.4	9.9	8.8	49.2	5 932	4 894	-17.5	-6.8	235	177	-402	1 837	2.57	69.5	18.0	28.6
Lea	10.4	5.8	4.8	48.5	55 511	64 727	16.6	8.1	4 822	2 183	2 606	21 126	3.01	73.7	11.8	21.7
Lincoln	17.9	15.5	9.8	50.6	19 411	20 497	5.6	-3.9	830	784	-800	8 685	2.32	60.7	10.1	33.5
Los Alamos	15.4	9.2	7.2	49.6	18 343	17 950	-2.1	-1.5	723	488	-519	7 590	2.35	67.9	6.5	27.3
Luna	12.0	11.4	9.2	49.8	25 016	25 095	0.3	-1.7	1 677	1 196	-895	8 862	2.78	64.4	13.7	30.5
McKinley	10.5	6.0	4.3	51.8	74 798	71 492	-4.4	3.6	5 485	2 246	-574	17 427	4.10	70.1	22.4	27.1
Mora	17.8	12.4	8.9	48.5	5 180	4 881	-5.8	-5.9	181	175	-282	1 532	3.10	51.4	7.0	41.1
Otero	11.8	8.9	6.9	49.1	62 298	63 797	2.4	2.0	4 140	2 309	-468	23 945	2.60	68.8	12.9	26.7
Quay	15.6	13.6	9.5	51.4	10 155	9 041	-11.0	-6.0	483	492	-540	3 476	2.53	61.4	11.7	35.4
Rio Arriba	14.2	9.4	6.4	50.7	41 190	40 246	-2.3	-1.2	2 547	1 640	-1 256	14 783	2.68	67.0	15.9	27.5
Roosevelt	10.1	6.7	5.5	49.7	18 018	19 846	10.1	-1.6	1 179	683	-817	7 043	2.69	67.8	12.0	25.1
Sandoval	13.5	8.9	5.3	51.0	89 908	131 561	46.3	4.6	6 342	3 920	3 294	47 164	2.82	72.3	13.4	22.1
San Juan	12.1	7.0	5.4	50.4	113 801	130 044	14.3	-4.8	7 913	3 960	-10 339	40 945	3.10	73.7	16.1	22.4
San Miguel	15.1	10.8	6.9	50.6	30 126	29 393	-2.4	-3.9	1 418	1 120	-1 478	11 435	2.38	56.4	16.3	37.6
Santa Fe	16.6	11.7	6.7	51.2	129 292	144 170	11.5	2.8	5 928	4 418	2 416	61 012	2.33	58.6	11.2	34.1
Sierra	17.7	18.3	14.6	49.9	13 270	11 988	-9.7	-5.5	383	946	-84	4 350	2.68	53.7	8.9	43.9
Socorro	13.3	9.7	6.3	48.9	18 078	17 866	-1.2	-3.1	965	718	-828	5 329	3.23	61.3	13.9	34.8
Taos	17.5	12.9	8.0	50.8	29 979	32 937	9.9	0.4	1 362	1 162	-70	13 338	2.43	58.3	12.8	36.6
Torrance	16.0	11.2	6.1	47.9	16 911	16 383	-3.1	-4.7	686	592	-866	5 638	2.71	65.0	11.0	32.0
Union	12.4	10.1	9.4	42.3	4 174	4 549	9.0	-5.6	199	188	-259	1 606	2.49	65.8	11.8	30.3
Valencia	13.2	8.9	5.7	49.7	66 152	76 569	15.7	-1.0	3 797	2 513	-2 051	26 894	2.78	71.2	13.3	24.1
NEW YORK	12.5	7.9	6.6	51.5	18 976 457	19 378 102	2.1	1.9	1 023 877	638 192	-1 626	7 234 743	2.61	64.1	14.8	29.4
Albany	13.2	7.9	7.0	51.7	294 565	304 204	3.3	1.3	13 262	11 295	2 351	122 700	2.35	56.5	11.9	34.3
Allegany	13.8	9.1	7.5	49.5	49 927	48 946	-2.0	-2.5	2 063	1 924	-1 308	18 786	2.32	65.9	9.4	28.1
Bronx	10.2	6.2	4.9	52.8	1 332 650	1 385 108	3.9	3.8	92 126	39 902	1 194	474 842	2.85	65.9	31.4	29.9
Broome	13.5	8.8	8.5	51.0	200 536	200 600	0.0	-1.6	8 803	8 783	-3 084	79 763	2.37	60.7	11.4	31.9
Cattaraugus	14.7	9.2	7.4	50.5	83 955	80 317	-4.3	-2.1	3 881	3 483	-2 032	32 246	2.38	63.4	11.0	29.7
Cayuga	14.3	9.0	7.6	48.9	81 963	80 026	-2.4	-1.5	3 401	3 129	-1 465	31 311	2.41	64.6	11.0	29.0
Chautauqua	14.4	9.4	8.3	50.5	139 750	134 905	-3.5	-2.1	5 991	6 052	-2 638	54 863	2.33	62.5	12.2	30.6
Chemung	13.9	8.8	7.8	50.2	91 070	88 830	-2.5	-1.2	4 370	3 965	-1 413	35 622	2.34	62.8	12.8	30.5
Chenango	15.0	10.5	7.9	50.1	51 401	50 477	-1.8	-2.1	2 232	2 301	-999	19 829	2.49	67.2	10.7	26.3
Clinton	13.3	8.2	6.6	48.8	79 894	82 128	2.8	-0.6	3 316	2 924	-919	31 901	2.32	63.3	11.4	27.5
Columbia	16.2	11.6	8.7	49.8	63 094	63 096	0.0	-1.5	2 299	2 734	-513	25 280	2.38	64.2	11.2	28.6
Cortland	12.4	8.2	6.3	51.1	48 599	49 336	1.5	-0.6	1 967	1 809	-432	18 069	2.53	60.9	11.6	30.9
Delaware	15.9	12.3	9.0	49.7	48 055	47 980	-0.2	-2.9	1 809	2 255	-833	19 844	2.28	62.8	9.7	32.2
Dutchess	13.6	8.3	6.7	50.3	280 150	297 488	6.2	-0.3	11 561	10 119	-2 209	107 830	2.59	67.9	10.8	26.3
Erie	13.7	8.5	7.9	51.6	950 265	919 040	-3.3	0.4	42 092	40 440	3 802	380 152	2.34	60.8	13.9	32.8
Essex	15.6	11.3	9.2	48.1	38 851	39 370	1.3	-1.8	1 409	1 670	-491	15 919	2.28	62.8	8.5	31.4
Franklin	13.1	8.3	6.2	44.8	51 134	51 599	0.9	-0.6	2 207	1 935	-595	19 238	2.35	64.4	10.5	29.6
Fulton	14.2	9.6	7.9	50.5	55 073	55 531	0.8	-2.6	2 276	2 556	-1 134	22 611	2.37	65.4	13.4	27.2

1. No spouse present.

STATE County	Persons in group quarters, 2014	Daytime population, 2009–2013: Number	Daytime population, 2009–2013: Employ-ment/resi-dence ratio	Births, 2014: Total	Births, 2014: Rate[1]	Deaths, 2014: Number	Deaths, 2014: Rate[1]	Persons under 65 with no health insurance, 2013: Number	Persons under 65 with no health insurance, 2013: Percent	Medicare, 2014: Eligible for Medicare	Medicare, 2014: Enrolled in Medicare Advantage	Medicare, 2014: Enrolled in a Medicare prescription drug plan	Serious crimes known to police,[2] 2013: Total: Number	Serious crimes known to police,[2] 2013: Total: Rate[3]
	32	33	34	35	36	37	38	39	40	41	42	43	44	45
NEW JERSEY—Cont'd														
Mercer	19 387	417 258	1.28	4 278	11.5	2 862	7.7	44 180	14.6	62 062	9 070	40 143	8 877	2 404
Middlesex	23 505	799 283	0.95	9 750	11.7	5 903	7.1	101 087	14.4	122 493	18 602	68 753	14 522	1 753
Monmouth	7 278	592 136	0.87	6 161	9.8	5 434	8.6	65 392	12.4	111 134	14 314	65 013	12 440	1 975
Morris	8 786	530 630	1.14	4 655	9.3	3 691	7.4	39 695	9.6	81 970	7 744	47 503	5 220	1 043
Ocean	7 140	509 162	0.70	8 120	13.8	6 929	11.8	61 499	13.6	142 857	25 194	83 079	10 354	1 778
Passaic	11 035	462 624	0.82	7 012	13.8	3 637	7.1	89 719	20.6	76 560	14 512	42 062	12 196	2 420
Salem	1 257	61 101	0.83	692	10.7	713	11.0	6 899	12.8	13 326	1 523	8 969	1 623	2 467
Somerset	4 087	342 408	1.10	3 416	10.3	2 363	7.1	28 841	10.2	49 077	4 114	29 786	4 295	1 304
Sussex	1 742	117 386	0.59	1 240	8.6	1 168	8.1	13 354	10.8	25 082	2 292	14 909	1 505	1 023
Union	6 803	516 851	0.91	6 889	12.5	3 972	7.2	87 724	18.5	80 719	14 567	42 933	12 601	2 304
Warren	1 969	93 445	0.72	899	8.4	856	8.0	11 110	12.4	19 854	1 716	12 080	1 685	1 568
NEW MEXICO	43 150	2 066 282	1.00	26 805	12.9	16 863	8.1	381 887	21.9	364 036	113 298	139 542	90 038	4 318
Bernalillo	11 944	694 666	1.09	8 293	12.3	5 465	8.1	114 477	20.0	110 467	53 956	27 487	38 376	5 692
Catron	106	3 656	0.98	26	7.3	11	3.1	693	28.4	1 273	180	545	NA	NA
Chaves	1 786	63 509	0.92	956	14.5	615	9.3	12 541	22.9	11 492	1 454	6 757	4 034	6 153
Cibola	2 554	27 187	0.99	429	15.7	271	9.9	4 939	23.1	4 449	683	2 004	605	2 220
Colfax	408	13 596	1.02	112	8.8	139	11.0	1 920	19.5	3 319	516	1 678	299	2 488
Curry	1 485	50 504	1.05	915	18.0	354	6.9	8 809	20.3	6 977	685	4 043	2 493	5 093
De Baca	9	1 950	0.96	13	7.1	21	11.5	414	28.4	519	45	327	23	1 216
Dona Ana	4 583	206 942	0.95	2 950	13.8	1 506	7.0	45 396	25.2	34 279	10 315	13 757	6 904	3 264
Eddy	995	56 962	1.11	823	14.6	519	9.2	8 101	17.2	9 402	680	5 884	2 174	3 996
Grant	590	29 374	0.99	323	11.1	322	11.1	3 949	17.9	7 776	1 691	3 347	NA	NA
Guadalupe	572	4 714	1.07	44	9.8	43	9.6	660	20.8	959	154	577	NA	NA
Harding	0	655	0.88	4	5.9	5	7.3	119	24.5	202	20	110	NA	NA
Hidalgo	64	4 970	1.07	47	10.3	48	10.5	797	21.3	1 042	225	467	50	1 050
Lea	2 066	67 124	1.05	1 207	17.2	471	6.7	13 105	22.3	8 295	210	5 762	2 949	4 423
Lincoln	116	20 080	0.97	194	9.8	174	8.8	3 947	26.5	5 420	1 073	2 665	428	2 120
Los Alamos	94	25 765	1.88	170	9.6	105	5.9	779	5.3	3 031	209	563	NA	NA
Luna	551	24 918	0.99	409	16.6	262	10.6	5 031	26.3	6 310	1 942	2 669	1 044	4 188
McKinley	769	72 879	1.02	1 302	17.6	515	7.0	19 804	29.7	9 652	613	5 290	3 050	4 168
Mora	8	4 468	0.79	43	9.4	30	6.5	883	23.7	1 336	215	707	NA	NA
Otero	2 363	64 058	0.97	954	14.7	563	8.7	12 374	23.2	11 528	2 049	4 275	1 321	2 011
Quay	22	9 002	1.04	116	13.6	99	11.6	1 255	19.0	2 453	351	1 306	315	3 643
Rio Arriba	425	36 266	0.75	591	14.9	411	10.3	8 351	24.9	8 219	2 143	3 431	859	2 138
Roosevelt	1 080	18 812	0.86	267	13.7	164	8.4	3 908	23.7	2 771	242	1 756	NA	NA
Sandoval	761	112 666	0.63	1 470	10.7	972	7.1	20 677	17.7	23 666	10 750	5 905	2 523	1 852
San Juan	1 735	128 527	1.00	1 781	14.4	985	8.0	27 529	24.9	18 057	693	10 473	3 380	2 650
San Miguel	1 299	27 274	0.82	342	12.1	269	9.5	4 673	20.7	6 293	1 192	3 574	NA	NA
Santa Fe	2 629	147 909	1.04	1 356	9.2	1 041	7.0	27 769	23.5	31 326	9 087	12 395	2 155	1 471
Sierra	265	12 129	1.06	84	7.4	227	20.0	1 774	23.1	4 091	1 109	1 629	310	2 624
Socorro	582	17 629	0.98	208	12.0	156	9.0	3 369	23.7	3 319	767	1 411	736	4 215
Taos	471	32 784	0.99	316	9.6	283	8.6	6 398	24.5	8 081	1 658	3 882	703	2 155
Torrance	615	14 841	0.74	153	9.8	143	9.2	2 741	22.1	3 134	1 386	918	288	1 817
Union	663	4 557	1.06	49	11.4	40	9.3	625	21.7	926	46	552	45	1 027
Valencia	1 540	65 909	0.62	858	11.3	634	8.4	14 082	22.1	13 972	6 959	3 396	3 136	4 109
NEW YORK	581 178	19 820 342	1.04	240 710	12.2	154 357	7.8	2 037 979	12.4	3 304 425	1 202 651	1 363 263	435 970	2 219
Albany	17 615	376 398	1.47	3 124	10.1	2 659	8.6	21 914	8.9	55 137	22 668	21 172	9 335	3 048
Allegany	4 296	45 409	0.84	453	9.5	452	9.5	3 968	11.0	9 754	3 506	3 715	795	1 649
Bronx	44 960	1 241 643	0.70	21 446	14.9	10 082	7.0	191 922	15.6	186 324	98 525	59 740	(6)	(6)
Broome	10 740	207 085	1.09	2 059	10.4	2 085	10.6	15 312	9.9	42 528	14 878	21 245	6 692	3 388
Cattaraugus	2 597	77 545	0.94	883	11.2	803	10.2	7 397	11.5	16 936	7 591	5 745	1 766	2 227
Cayuga	4 045	71 542	0.77	790	10.0	690	8.8	6 503	10.4	15 150	3 914	6 642	1 505	1 893
Chautauqua	6 394	134 284	1.00	1 402	10.6	1 363	10.3	11 224	10.7	29 268	13 062	10 792	3 613	2 711
Chemung	4 853	90 134	1.03	1 019	11.6	939	10.7	5 948	8.6	18 882	5 944	8 201	2 199	2 470
Chenango	778	47 899	0.89	537	10.9	538	10.9	3 961	9.9	11 358	3 762	5 230	926	1 857
Clinton	6 799	81 672	0.99	761	9.3	678	8.3	6 397	10.1	16 655	2 830	8 396	1 657	2 087
Columbia	2 147	57 752	0.83	520	8.4	624	10.0	5 318	11.0	14 173	3 975	6 210	1 113	1 823
Cortland	3 854	47 282	0.91	450	9.2	409	8.3	3 461	9.0	8 722	2 036	4 209	1 064	2 145
Delaware	2 318	46 552	0.95	427	9.2	533	11.4	4 240	12.1	10 655	2 578	5 544	810	1 755
Dutchess	19 548	276 700	0.85	2 700	9.1	2 476	8.3	22 181	9.4	53 658	9 680	28 563	4 960	1 693
Erie	28 570	948 160	1.07	10 101	10.9	9 583	10.4	62 930	8.4	185 302	104 332	44 966	29 276	3 182
Essex	2 522	38 398	0.95	340	8.8	413	10.7	3 192	11.1	8 680	1 552	4 345	496	1 275
Franklin	6 256	52 360	1.04	529	10.3	471	9.2	4 941	12.9	10 287	2 160	5 668	825	1 588
Fulton	1 285	50 871	0.82	505	9.3	567	10.5	4 622	10.4	12 054	5 148	5 677	1 529	2 790

1. Per 1,000 estimated resident population. 2. Data for serious crimes have not been adjusted for underreporting; this may affect comparability between geographic areas and over time.
3. Per 100,000 population estimated by the FBI. 6. Bronx, Kings, Queens, and Richmond counties are included with New York county.

STATE County	Serious crimes known to police, 2013 (cont.)[1] — Rate[2]: Violent	Serious crimes known to police, 2013 (cont.)[1] — Rate[2]: Property	Education — School enrollment and attainment, 2009–2013 — Enrollment[3]: Total	Education — Enrollment[3]: Percent private	Education — Attainment[4] (percent): High school graduate or less	Education — Attainment[4] (percent): Bachelor's degree or more	Education — Local government expenditures,[5] 2012–2013: Total current spending (mil dol)	Education — Local government expenditures,[5] 2012–2013: Current spending per student (dollars)	Money income, 2009–2013: Per capita income[6] (dollars)	Money income, 2009–2013 — Households: Median income (dollars)	Money income, 2009–2013 — Households: Mean income (dollars)	Money income, 2009–2013 — Households: Percent with income of $200,000 or more	Income and poverty, 2013: Median household income (dollars)	Income and poverty, 2013 — Percent below poverty level: All persons	Income and poverty, 2013 — Percent below poverty level: Children under 18 years	Income and poverty, 2013 — Percent below poverty level: Children 5 to 17 years in families
	46	47	48	49	50	51	52	53	54	55	56	57	58	59	60	61
NEW JERSEY—Cont'd																
Mercer	408	1 995	103 246	23.9	38.7	38.8	1 078.0	18 652	37 465	73 480	102 738	10.9	70 575	11.8	15.4	14.9
Middlesex	151	1 603	218 243	15.6	38.1	40.1	2 050.3	16 984	34 345	79 596	97 382	8.7	76 515	9.4	12.6	12.0
Monmouth	166	1 809	163 872	21.7	33.8	41.4	1 821.9	18 026	42 749	84 526	113 380	13.1	83 424	7.8	10.3	9.7
Morris	64	979	129 987	23.6	29.5	50.0	1 385.2	17 840	48 814	98 633	132 161	17.0	99 950	4.9	5.6	5.0
Ocean	87	1 691	139 917	32.3	47.6	25.4	1 210.0	16 561	30 477	61 136	77 916	4.6	59 888	10.5	19.4	17.5
Passaic	474	1 945	136 610	13.8	53.2	25.6	1 558.9	19 440	27 152	57 654	78 880	6.1	57 426	16.6	25.2	24.6
Salem	246	2 220	15 837	13.0	52.4	20.4	199.1	17 454	28 772	59 718	73 201	3.2	58 483	15.0	23.5	21.9
Somerset	69	1 235	85 149	20.2	28.8	51.1	939.4	17 470	47 803	99 020	131 911	17.4	96 947	5.7	6.6	6.3
Sussex	41	982	37 997	19.2	37.8	32.4	444.0	19 944	37 949	87 335	101 993	8.5	85 747	6.1	7.2	6.4
Union	361	1 943	141 519	16.3	44.7	31.8	1 711.2	19 167	35 089	68 507	98 637	10.1	64 272	11.5	15.0	14.4
Warren	72	1 496	27 123	15.4	45.4	29.6	291.6	16 791	33 555	70 912	86 652	6.3	68 011	8.7	11.6	11.1
NEW MEXICO	613	3 705	565 878	10.4	42.8	25.8	2 951.6	9 012	23 763	44 927	61 682	2.9	44 026	21.4	30.1	28.5
Bernalillo	746	4 945	185 819	14.3	36.3	32.1	797.4	8 475	26 814	48 801	65 910	3.4	48 053	18.7	27.1	25.7
Catron	NA	NA	606	15.3	43.9	18.5	5.7	18 099	20 616	39 826	43 401	0.9	32 644	21.7	40.8	36.5
Chaves	534	5 619	18 688	11.1	49.0	18.4	100.8	8 520	19 492	39 131	52 652	1.1	41 388	21.2	31.2	29.1
Cibola	539	1 680	7 364	10.0	59.1	10.4	37.3	9 947	16 129	37 237	45 766	0.6	36 307	32.2	42.9	41.2
Colfax	175	2 313	2 847	6.2	47.0	19.8	22.1	11 657	21 387	37 734	47 854	1.1	37 152	20.1	32.3	28.6
Curry	582	4 510	14 133	8.3	42.3	20.4	77.4	8 070	21 259	39 871	55 088	1.5	39 186	21.1	29.8	28.4
De Baca	423	793	585	0.0	52.4	17.9	4.6	15 801	24 879	37 660	56 763	2.5	33 045	22.0	36.9	37.2
Dona Ana	316	2 948	68 291	4.5	44.5	26.6	353.6	8 696	19 565	37 933	54 043	2.1	36 831	27.0	37.6	36.4
Eddy	574	3 423	13 852	6.4	50.9	16.7	96.2	9 107	28 438	49 165	73 400	3.6	49 865	15.1	21.1	20.0
Grant	NA	NA	7 138	8.7	44.2	24.2	43.4	9 913	22 755	37 899	53 133	1.7	39 220	22.4	33.7	31.5
Guadalupe	NA	NA	1 169	9.2	63.9	11.3	9.9	13 429	14 198	29 071	41 872	1.1	29 924	25.8	35.7	33.7
Harding	NA	NA	117	2.6	45.3	21.4	3.0	36 134	25 686	34 063	65 248	7.3	37 520	15.2	23.2	25.0
Hidalgo	21	1 029	1 105	2.8	55.2	14.1	10.1	14 213	18 392	34 080	44 950	0.2	32 993	25.7	38.5	38.9
Lea	604	3 818	17 966	9.5	57.6	13.3	111.1	7 925	22 484	50 694	66 378	3.0	53 556	14.8	20.0	19.2
Lincoln	238	1 883	4 284	7.4	42.0	23.6	31.0	10 562	25 449	43 014	56 623	2.2	40 756	18.8	34.1	31.9
Los Alamos	NA	NA	4 491	10.1	14.2	63.4	37.3	10 562	51 044	106 686	119 595	13.7	110 930	4.0	4.4	3.9
Luna	782	3 406	6 171	7.4	63.1	13.8	51.6	9 424	16 114	29 282	40 890	1.3	28 040	31.2	44.1	41.7
McKinley	726	3 442	22 982	7.9	59.9	11.2	138.0	10 368	12 679	30 458	43 070	1.1	27 790	40.3	47.5	44.4
Mora	NA	NA	1 497	9.2	60.2	9.5	2.1	28 413	20 543	28 481	39 881	0.0	29 263	23.8	37.3	33.2
Otero	225	1 786	16 702	6.7	45.5	16.6	66.0	8 881	19 880	39 263	51 764	1.6	41 960	21.3	33.6	34.3
Quay	370	3 273	1 976	1.0	57.6	13.2	17.4	11 562	17 936	30 802	41 423	0.4	30 496	25.8	39.7	38.8
Rio Arriba	495	1 643	9 299	11.7	51.2	16.4	66.8	11 380	20 014	40 250	51 296	1.1	36 716	24.8	32.6	31.4
Roosevelt	NA	NA	7 025	4.9	45.5	21.1	35.6	10 037	17 477	38 764	47 906	1.2	35 322	24.6	31.5	30.8
Sandoval	208	1 644	37 481	11.4	36.3	28.3	181.9	8 646	26 924	58 017	73 865	3.8	56 190	15.3	20.9	18.2
San Juan	490	2 160	34 030	5.2	50.9	15.2	211.3	8 814	21 260	48 196	62 497	2.2	44 417	21.8	27.0	26.1
San Miguel	NA	NA	7 471	11.3	48.5	19.6	53.6	11 736	17 926	28 275	41 565	0.5	31 222	32.4	43.3	40.1
Santa Fe	144	1 327	33 781	18.8	34.2	39.7	146.9	9 052	32 298	52 917	75 165	5.7	51 697	18.1	26.9	25.7
Sierra	254	2 370	1 605	8.5	51.3	21.1	13.6	10 030	17 752	27 430	36 523	0.4	29 680	26.9	46.3	43.6
Socorro	756	3 459	5 549	5.1	53.9	19.4	25.5	11 198	18 104	34 036	52 030	2.1	32 090	27.9	43.9	41.7
Taos	328	1 827	6 889	7.2	37.6	29.5	42.0	11 052	21 333	32 637	48 501	1.5	33 021	26.2	37.5	36.0
Torrance	246	1 571	3 778	6.2	53.0	14.7	40.5	10 091	18 675	31 161	48 793	1.1	35 046	27.8	39.2	35.2
Union	23	1 004	906	7.2	59.4	17.0	8.5	14 168	18 472	38 902	46 465	0.7	37 902	20.1	24.4	24.0
Valencia	879	3 230	20 281	8.1	49.7	16.6	109.4	8 575	19 623	42 506	53 663	0.9	41 412	23.4	31.2	30.0
NEW YORK	394	1 825	5 016 964	23.8	42.0	33.2	55 065.8	19 818	32 382	58 003	84 432	7.0	57 255	16.0	22.9	22.2
Albany	324	2 723	85 195	24.0	33.8	38.8	687.6	18 866	32 328	59 394	77 687	4.2	55 778	13.7	16.1	14.5
Allegany	112	1 537	14 486	30.1	52.2	18.9	127.4	18 465	20 978	42 445	53 800	1.2	41 849	16.7	25.6	23.5
Bronx	(7)	(7)	399 023	19.3	57.6	18.1	(7)	(7)	18 171	34 388	49 421	1.5	33 079	30.7	41.6	42.3
Broome	258	3 130	54 838	8.5	43.6	26.1	472.7	17 298	24 835	45 958	60 570	2.6	45 142	17.7	25.0	23.1
Cattaraugus	146	2 081	19 177	19.8	53.9	17.2	234.2	17 351	22 049	42 603	53 652	1.4	40 936	18.9	28.7	26.7
Cayuga	160	1 733	18 003	16.0	48.9	19.6	155.8	16 019	24 702	51 581	62 027	1.7	48 976	14.2	22.2	20.6
Chautauqua	203	2 508	32 330	8.8	47.5	20.7	332.6	16 430	22 168	42 429	53 272	1.1	40 468	19.1	29.5	27.4
Chemung	170	2 300	20 237	16.2	47.2	21.5	180.4	14 937	25 329	48 804	62 523	2.4	45 337	17.0	25.5	22.6
Chenango	96	1 761	11 464	7.3	53.2	17.1	149.3	19 084	22 097	43 941	54 569	1.1	44 328	16.8	24.7	22.9
Clinton	135	1 952	20 371	8.9	51.6	22.1	208.3	18 791	24 676	50 282	63 087	2.0	45 900	15.7	20.5	18.5
Columbia	124	1 699	13 112	16.8	43.0	28.2	147.7	19 656	33 613	57 336	80 898	4.7	57 094	11.8	17.9	16.2
Cortland	103	2 042	15 425	6.5	45.4	23.5	108.9	16 441	23 179	47 151	60 268	1.4	46 163	14.6	20.7	19.0
Delaware	117	1 638	9 998	5.9	51.4	19.8	134.7	21 116	23 677	44 470	55 302	1.1	43 380	17.8	29.1	27.6
Dutchess	195	1 498	82 089	28.6	38.2	32.9	826.9	19 281	33 594	72 525	90 044	6.8	69 300	9.5	12.8	12.1
Erie	444	2 738	239 190	18.1	38.8	30.0	2 117.0	17 775	27 978	50 653	66 095	3.2	51 123	15.1	23.1	22.4
Essex	126	1 149	7 820	14.5	46.9	23.3	87.7	22 130	26 582	47 380	63 672	2.0	46 337	11.7	19.0	18.4
Franklin	106	1 483	10 608	14.8	54.1	16.5	146.6	19 142	21 575	45 667	56 804	1.7	42 672	22.4	29.0	27.1
Fulton	113	2 677	11 996	7.3	53.9	14.9	134.0	15 761	23 839	44 276	57 365	1.8	42 264	15.7	25.1	24.1

1. Data for serious crimes have not been adjusted for underreporting; this may affect comparability between geographic areas and over time. 2. Per 100,000 population estimated by the FBI.
3. All persons 3 years old and over enrolled in nursery school through college. 4. Persons 25 years old and over. 5. Elementary and secondary education expenditures.
6. Based on population estimated by the American Community Survey, 2009–2013. 7. Bronx, Kings, Queens, and Richmond counties are included with New York county.

STATE County	Personal income, 2013: Total (mil dol)	Personal income, 2013: Percent change, 2012–2013	Per capita[1]: Dollars	Per capita[1]: Rank	Wages and salaries (mil dol)	Supplements to wages and salaries; employer contributions (mil dol): Pension and insurance	Supplements to wages and salaries; employer contributions (mil dol): Government social insurance	Proprietors' income (mil dol)	Dividends, interest, and rent (mil dol)	Personal transfer receipts (mil dol)	Earnings, 2013: Total (mil dol)	Contributions for government social insurance (mil dol): From employee and self-employed	Contributions for government social insurance (mil dol): From employer
	62	63	64	65	66	67	68	69	70	71	72	73	74
NEW JERSEY—Cont'd													
Mercer	21 079	2.2	56 906	161	14 773	2 290	1 097	1 593	4 207	2 983	19 752	1 127	1 097
Middlesex	43 345	1.8	52 291	294	25 038	3 802	1 948	3 543	6 883	5 672	34 331	1 975	1 948
Monmouth	39 607	1.5	62 901	78	13 268	2 155	1 075	2 897	8 023	4 836	19 395	1 167	1 075
Morris	37 482	0.7	75 054	32	22 591	2 981	1 605	4 485	7 410	3 264	31 662	1 781	1 605
Ocean	25 212	0.9	43 214	826	6 760	1 306	582	1 724	5 068	5 912	10 371	745	582
Passaic	22 598	0.5	44 688	714	8 822	1 583	722	1 533	3 684	4 315	12 660	772	722
Salem	2 737	0.2	41 997	938	1 202	254	96	156	454	627	1 707	105	96
Somerset	25 682	1.7	77 685	26	15 327	1 925	1 042	2 593	4 957	2 043	20 887	1 177	1 042
Sussex	7 731	-0.1	52 958	270	1 713	339	143	485	1 242	1 013	2 681	174	143
Union	29 815	2.2	54 382	223	15 094	2 351	1 091	2 209	5 440	4 088	20 744	1 209	1 091
Warren	5 266	1.5	49 040	414	1 688	312	139	273	878	849	2 412	153	139
NEW MEXICO	74 996	0.5	35 965	X	35 518	6 472	2 808	5 657	13 859	16 143	50 456	3 095	2 808
Bernalillo	25 264	-0.1	37 471	1 511	14 791	2 547	1 186	1 495	4 958	4 855	20 019	1 232	1 186
Catron	125	1.9	34 729	1 944	23	7	2	26	29	36	57	3	2
Chaves	2 116	1.4	32 147	2 393	743	142	58	336	373	561	1 279	74	58
Cibola	740	-0.8	27 087	2 964	298	66	23	29	98	220	416	26	23
Colfax	487	1.4	37 211	1 545	168	37	14	77	97	134	296	17	14
Curry	2 089	3.7	41 293	1 017	940	209	87	269	375	387	1 504	72	87
De Baca	92	0.2	48 107	472	17	4	1	30	17	22	53	2	1
Dona Ana	6 750	0.9	31 620	2 462	2 721	584	216	524	1 169	1 661	4 045	245	216
Eddy	2 579	3.6	46 488	591	1 419	226	104	379	317	441	2 129	129	104
Grant	1 048	0.9	35 738	1 792	395	91	29	52	208	329	567	39	29
Guadalupe	134	2.2	29 546	2 747	41	10	3	24	18	48	77	4	3
Harding	52	6.3	75 447	30	8	2	1	23	13	6	34	1	1
Hidalgo	195	3.9	41 810	956	69	18	6	35	28	47	127	6	6
Lea	2 997	3.6	44 040	752	1 732	235	127	422	320	452	2 516	150	127
Lincoln	721	1.2	35 861	1 768	209	40	17	76	192	197	342	24	17
Los Alamos	1 109	-3.0	62 284	80	1 252	116	97	48	222	87	1 512	93	97
Luna	785	1.0	31 827	2 431	274	64	22	94	119	257	455	29	22
McKinley	1 787	-1.9	24 383	3 071	731	186	60	35	268	571	1 011	63	60
Mora	145	0.3	30 760	2 585	24	7	2	12	26	57	45	3	2
Otero	2 109	0.3	32 140	2 396	913	225	81	92	491	497	1 312	74	81
Quay	340	2.3	39 268	1 258	98	21	7	63	57	108	190	10	7
Rio Arriba	1 206	-1.4	30 106	2 672	331	79	25	71	179	389	507	35	25
Roosevelt	716	4.0	35 871	1 766	226	52	18	130	105	162	426	19	18
Sandoval	4 690	0.0	34 339	2 022	1 378	222	107	145	762	895	1 851	130	107
San Juan	4 211	-0.2	33 289	2 210	2 349	408	176	270	591	863	3 203	197	176
San Miguel	966	0.7	33 845	2 108	272	78	21	76	141	330	446	28	21
Santa Fe	6 532	0.6	44 309	739	2 788	507	209	457	1 810	1 080	3 960	250	209
Sierra	425	1.7	36 748	1 633	101	24	8	44	91	165	176	13	8
Socorro	560	-0.6	31 861	2 429	207	56	15	46	88	159	324	18	15
Taos	1 064	1.4	32 195	2 388	345	66	29	98	253	315	537	38	29
Torrance	502	-1.8	31 915	2 421	117	26	9	44	61	147	197	12	9
Union	155	10.7	35 577	1 816	46	10	4	26	31	39	86	4	4
Valencia	2 304	0.5	30 208	2 653	493	108	44	110	351	625	755	56	44
NEW YORK	1 070 236	1.1	54 462	X	565 113	102 124	40 363	101 183	206 943	185 354	808 784	42 473	40 363
Albany	16 426	2.1	53 515	251	12 182	3 366	973	1 513	3 317	2 766	18 034	889	973
Allegany	1 509	0.7	31 362	2 498	486	164	42	97	256	411	788	46	42
Bronx	46 609	1.3	32 852	2 274	12 145	2 119	1 018	3 723	5 520	14 687	19 005	1 130	1 018
Broome	7 766	0.2	39 315	1 249	3 598	1 009	298	479	1 592	1 829	5 384	296	298
Cattaraugus	3 032	0.9	38 429	1 386	1 170	366	97	202	495	835	1 834	102	97
Cayuga	3 073	0.5	38 666	1 344	1 055	298	90	231	532	664	1 673	89	90
Chautauqua	4 596	-0.1	34 533	1 978	1 809	502	158	272	823	1 302	2 741	159	158
Chemung	3 460	0.4	39 096	1 281	1 644	410	136	177	600	835	2 367	132	136
Chenango	1 909	1.8	38 571	1 362	739	209	61	125	321	465	1 135	64	61
Clinton	3 168	0.4	38 831	1 317	1 336	404	113	216	517	733	2 069	109	113
Columbia	2 932	1.4	47 101	548	808	221	69	194	684	607	1 291	74	69
Cortland	1 768	1.6	36 092	1 733	680	193	58	154	302	395	1 085	58	58
Delaware	1 737	2.0	37 186	1 549	620	199	52	160	369	433	1 031	57	52
Dutchess	14 735	0.4	49 627	381	5 710	1 302	457	638	2 785	2 413	8 108	438	457
Erie	41 850	1.1	45 496	655	20 829	4 814	1 714	3 001	7 877	8 408	30 357	1 636	1 714
Essex	1 524	1.8	39 309	1 250	563	177	48	98	341	380	886	49	48
Franklin	1 763	0.4	34 111	2 060	750	298	61	91	287	450	1 200	64	61
Fulton	2 133	1.2	39 083	1 283	661	195	56	148	343	569	1 060	63	56

1. Based on the resident population estimated as of July 1 of the year shown.

STATE County	Earnings, 2013 (cont.) — Percent by selected industries: Farm	Mining	Construction	Manu-facturing	Infor-mation: professional, scientific, technical services	Retail trade	Finance, insur-ance, real estate and leasing	Health care and social assistance	Govern-ment	Social Security beneficiaries, December 2013: Number	Rate[1]	Supple-mental Security Income recipients, December 2013	Housing units, 2014: Total	Percent change, 2010–2014
	75	76	77	78	79	80	81	82	83	84	85	86	87	88
NEW JERSEY—Cont'd														
Mercer	0.0	0.0	2.9	5.7	20.9	4.0	11.2	9.6	19.7	65 775	177	9 992	144 991	1.3
Middlesex	0.0	0.7	4.8	8.8	17.8	5.6	7.5	8.2	14.0	126 715	153	12 971	299 476	1.6
Monmouth	0.2	D	8.5	3.6	17.8	8.3	8.9	14.9	15.3	116 840	186	7 933	260 744	0.9
Morris	0.0	D	4.6	11.1	19.0	5.7	12.1	8.5	9.3	82 380	165	4 428	191 473	0.9
Ocean	0.0	0.5	9.8	3.1	7.0	10.4	5.8	18.9	22.5	153 500	263	7 065	278 639	0.2
Passaic	0.0	0.1	6.3	11.7	7.6	8.6	5.8	12.8	19.8	80 565	159	14 899	176 730	0.4
Salem	2.9	0.0	D	14.3	4.0	4.3	2.3	10.3	19.3	14 865	228	1 642	27 564	0.5
Somerset	0.0	0.2	3.5	11.6	24.4	5.4	9.8	6.3	7.4	49 865	151	3 130	126 015	2.3
Sussex	-0.2	0.2	9.3	5.7	8.8	9.6	4.1	14.0	23.3	27 260	187	1 658	62 204	0.5
Union	0.0	D	6.0	12.8	15.5	5.4	5.9	10.3	14.4	84 560	154	10 744	201 580	1.0
Warren	0.8	D	D	12.4	5.6	8.9	2.6	13.6	19.1	21 135	198	1 390	45 269	0.8
NEW MEXICO	2.8	5.7	5.9	4.3	11.4	6.7	4.7	11.2	27.3	392 306	188	64 300	912 890	1.3
Bernalillo	0.0	0.2	6.1	4.3	16.0	6.8	6.0	13.0	26.6	117 220	174	17 471	288 400	1.5
Catron	37.8	D	4.4	1.2	D	D	D	D	33.4	1 370	381	75	3 280	-0.2
Chaves	12.8	9.1	4.3	4.8	5.4	9.0	3.7	13.4	20.2	12 925	196	2 294	26 693	0.0
Cibola	2.0	D	1.8	0.6	D	7.7	1.6	D	41.1	4 910	179	987	11 086	-0.1
Colfax	17.9	1.9	5.2	1.8	2.7	7.2	4.6	5.6	29.7	3 620	277	415	10 062	0.4
Curry	14.2	D	4.1	3.2	2.6	5.1	2.4	9.3	40.1	7 445	147	1 638	20 788	3.6
De Baca	54.9	0.0	D	D	D	4.8	D	D	18.4	555	293	81	1 340	-0.3
Dona Ana	4.8	0.1	5.5	3.9	8.8	6.1	3.5	14.1	33.8	36 755	172	7 772	84 221	3.3
Eddy	1.6	35.8	7.0	4.4	D	5.1	3.1	6.6	12.7	10 620	191	1 426	23 407	3.6
Grant	2.2	25.2	4.6	0.7	2.6	6.3	2.4	7.9	35.5	8 610	294	906	14 651	-0.3
Guadalupe	29.0	D	3.0	D	D	8.7	D	10.3	29.1	1 120	246	281	2 387	-0.3
Harding	63.1	D	D	D	0.5	D	D	0.0	15.6	215	313	13	526	0.0
Hidalgo	26.1	0.0	D	D	D	4.4	D	D	46.2	1 175	254	175	2 384	-0.4
Lea	2.5	35.7	9.8	4.8	3.0	4.9	4.1	D	9.3	9 355	137	1 568	25 084	0.7
Lincoln	6.1	D	7.5	0.8	6.8	10.9	5.8	11.6	21.9	5 820	291	401	17 674	0.9
Los Alamos	0.0	0.0	1.3	0.2	73.5	0.9	2.1	3.5	8.5	2 940	165	96	8 312	-0.5
Luna	12.4	D	4.3	7.3	D	10.2	1.9	D	35.7	6 920	279	1 437	10 960	-0.4
McKinley	0.3	D	3.1	3.9	2.2	10.1	2.4	11.5	47.5	10 170	139	4 545	25 771	-0.2
Mora	18.5	D	D	D	D	5.3	1.6	D	36.5	1 475	316	352	3 223	-0.3
Otero	1.2	D	5.0	0.7	5.2	5.6	2.5	9.2	55.4	12 585	191	1 764	30 965	-0.1
Quay	29.0	0.0	4.3	D	1.4	6.4	3.1	D	25.7	2 640	304	432	5 555	-0.3
Rio Arriba	3.7	1.2	5.2	1.1	D	7.3	2.2	13.9	45.5	9 315	232	1 601	19 544	-0.5
Roosevelt	30.5	D	3.9	5.6	2.2	5.6	2.0	D	27.8	3 040	152	643	8 317	1.9
Sandoval	0.4	0.6	6.0	26.7	6.9	6.2	3.4	6.3	22.3	25 390	186	2 785	54 482	4.2
San Juan	0.4	22.8	7.9	2.4	2.5	7.2	3.3	11.1	21.2	20 465	162	4 197	49 618	0.6
San Miguel	8.3	0.2	4.5	0.7	2.2	6.5	3.0	D	47.5	7 020	245	1 867	15 540	-0.4
Santa Fe	0.1	1.3	5.2	1.3	9.3	9.1	9.4	13.4	30.2	32 270	219	2 948	71 749	0.7
Sierra	16.0	D	7.7	1.7	2.6	7.1	2.8	D	29.9	4 360	377	574	8 284	-0.9
Socorro	11.2	D	1.5	2.2	8.0	4.7	2.5	D	47.5	3 630	207	1 135	7 998	-0.8
Taos	1.2	5.6	8.1	0.9	5.8	10.2	4.9	16.8	23.1	8 650	262	1 163	20 354	0.4
Torrance	16.3	D	5.4	3.6	D	8.7	1.6	5.2	29.0	3 535	225	616	7 753	-0.6
Union	31.5	D	D	D	D	5.4	D	11.1	22.2	1 005	229	114	2 301	-0.2
Valencia	4.9	0.3	7.6	3.9	2.8	9.4	3.3	D	30.7	15 180	199	2 528	30 181	0.3
NEW YORK	0.2	0.1	4.3	4.6	16.5	5.0	18.1	10.8	16.8	3 444 200	175	698 928	8 191 040	1.0
Albany	0.0	D	5.7	3.3	11.7	5.3	7.9	10.7	36.0	58 900	192	7 998	138 253	0.4
Allegany	1.1	0.8	6.1	18.5	2.8	5.4	1.8	7.5	33.2	11 105	231	1 586	26 002	-0.5
Bronx	0.0	D	6.6	2.6	5.7	5.9	6.0	29.4	12.8	189 005	132	110 002	522 149	2.0
Broome	0.2	0.2	5.9	11.8	7.0	7.1	4.5	16.6	26.7	47 090	238	7 295	89 816	-0.8
Cattaraugus	1.2	0.7	3.3	15.9	2.9	7.8	2.9	D	36.7	19 220	243	2 729	40 971	-0.3
Cayuga	5.5	D	6.0	14.0	5.2	8.0	2.3	11.7	28.9	17 090	215	1 991	36 392	-0.3
Chautauqua	1.6	0.6	4.7	22.3	3.7	7.9	2.7	12.6	25.5	33 055	248	5 087	66 659	-0.4
Chemung	0.1	2.6	5.2	15.9	3.6	7.2	5.1	15.5	24.3	21 180	239	3 604	38 382	0.0
Chenango	2.1	D	4.2	28.4	4.7	6.3	8.6	7.5	24.5	12 760	258	1 758	24 779	0.3
Clinton	2.4	D	4.3	10.5	3.6	8.7	2.2	16.2	34.0	18 695	229	3 166	35 930	0.1
Columbia	1.5	D	7.1	7.0	6.2	7.7	4.1	17.9	26.4	15 405	247	1 729	32 838	0.2
Cortland	1.4	0.0	4.7	18.2	5.7	7.5	4.3	12.0	25.0	9 740	198	1 338	20 515	-0.2
Delaware	1.6	1.6	5.7	24.1	5.6	5.8	3.4	D	28.4	11 905	254	1 282	31 186	-0.1
Dutchess	0.1	0.2	5.4	15.5	6.4	6.6	4.1	14.7	24.9	58 040	195	5 958	119 119	0.4
Erie	0.1	0.3	4.4	11.4	9.2	6.0	8.1	12.7	21.4	202 785	220	30 307	421 127	0.3
Essex	0.0	1.1	8.2	7.5	3.8	6.9	2.8	11.2	37.3	9 565	246	1 102	25 763	0.6
Franklin	2.0	D	0.1	D	3.3	5.7	1.7	14.1	55.8	11 490	224	1 989	25 288	-0.1
Fulton	0.2	D	5.5	8.4	5.1	9.0	2.9	17.0	28.9	13 815	253	2 200	28 676	0.4

1. Per 1,000 resident population estimated as of July 1 of the year shown.

STATE County	Housing units, 2009–2013: Occupied units: Total	Owner-occupied: Percent	Owner-occupied: Median value[1]	Owner-occupied: Median owner cost as a percent of income: With a mortgage	Owner-occupied: Median owner cost as a percent of income: Without a mortgage[2]	Renter-occupied: Median rent[3]	Renter-occupied: Median rent as a percent of income[2]	Substandard units[4] (percent)	Civilian labor force, 2014: Total	Civilian labor force, 2014: Percent change, 2013–2014	Unemployment: Total	Unemployment: Rate[5]	Civilian employment,[6] 2009–2013: Total	Percent: Management, business, science and arts	Percent: Construction, production, and maintenance occupations
	89	90	91	92	93	94	95	96	97	98	99	100	101	102	103
NEW JERSEY—Cont'd															
Mercer	130 754	65.8	286 900	25.8	16.6	1 120	31.3	4.1	194 539	0.4	11 126	5.7	176 840	42.7	15.2
Middlesex	280 988	66.2	330 000	27.7	18.0	1 265	29.1	2.0	432 112	0.3	25 938	6.0	394 477	43.9	17.3
Monmouth	233 909	75.2	389 900	27.9	17.6	1 219	34.2	1.6	328 655	0.3	19 569	6.0	305 222	42.8	15.0
Morris	179 665	75.9	432 400	26.8	16.6	1 339	28.4	2.2	263 878	0.1	12 959	4.9	252 520	49.0	12.8
Ocean	221 774	81.3	268 100	29.4	20.4	1 318	38.8	10.7	265 294	-0.3	19 048	7.2	241 241	34.1	19.7
Passaic	162 543	54.3	351 000	31.3	21.8	1 159	37.8	1.7	248 437	-0.6	20 173	8.1	226 263	31.7	25.0
Salem	25 003	71.7	190 200	24.9	18.2	963	36.1	2.1	31 435	-0.6	2 592	8.2	28 790	31.9	28.3
Somerset	115 531	78.0	398 800	26.6	17.0	1 386	29.4	1.2	173 968	0.1	8 893	5.1	165 266	51.1	13.5
Sussex	54 746	84.7	285 800	28.1	17.7	1 189	37.4	8.5	78 651	-0.4	4 914	6.2	75 891	38.6	19.3
Union	185 483	60.4	362 300	29.5	20.3	1 172	32.8	1.6	279 108	-0.3	18 996	6.8	260 121	35.2	21.8
Warren	41 463	74.1	271 100	28.2	19.6	988	30.9	3.1	57 425	-0.2	3 517	6.1	52 892	36.1	20.7
NEW MEXICO	761 938	68.7	160 000	23.3	10.0	758	30.2	4.6	918 206	-0.5	60 057	6.5	876 823	35.2	20.7
Bernalillo	263 135	63.2	186 800	23.8	10.0	791	30.7	3.5	318 070	-0.6	19 441	6.1	310 525	39.6	16.6
Catron	1 581	88.5	158 900	26.5	10.0	725	29.2	4.2	1 344	0.0	96	7.1	1 181	28.7	31.2
Chaves	23 499	66.5	96 800	20.5	10.0	652	29.5	10.2	26 808	0.4	1 613	6.0	27 031	29.9	25.7
Cibola	8 016	72.4	83 800	19.1	10.0	530	29.6	2.2	8 972	-0.8	717	8.0	9 437	24.0	27.2
Colfax	5 574	67.9	117 100	26.1	10.5	582	27.5	2.2	6 280	-0.3	386	6.1	5 491	29.6	21.8
Curry	18 027	59.7	119 600	20.9	10.0	682	29.4	2.9	21 514	0.4	1 064	4.9	20 840	26.5	32.0
De Baca	689	79.7	79 200	23.8	10.0	522	22.6	4.9	778	3.7	39	5.0	667	37.5	30.3
Dona Ana	73 797	65.4	139 100	23.5	10.7	685	34.0	4.2	93 212	-0.7	6 687	7.2	86 666	32.5	21.1
Eddy	19 866	72.9	110 400	17.0	10.0	712	24.9	3.4	29 017	3.5	1 246	4.3	24 410	29.8	32.3
Grant	12 216	76.9	125 300	22.4	10.0	612	33.3	1.6	12 312	-2.5	816	6.6	10 990	35.6	22.5
Guadalupe	1 260	80.2	88 400	23.9	13.0	511	29.6	2.7	1 646	-1.6	125	7.6	1 299	29.3	20.2
Harding	261	82.4	66 300	32.5	10.0	663	31.3	3.8	325	8.7	14	4.3	263	29.3	33.5
Hidalgo	1 837	66.4	76 800	18.6	10.7	444	28.7	4.7	2 049	-3.8	145	7.1	1 893	27.7	26.0
Lea	21 126	70.0	97 200	18.2	10.0	734	23.4	7.0	30 192	3.3	1 288	4.3	27 256	25.2	37.7
Lincoln	8 685	78.8	156 300	25.3	12.0	779	25.0	0.8	9 014	-1.0	528	5.9	8 794	28.6	20.5
Los Alamos	7 590	75.4	284 500	18.3	10.0	996	20.5	4.2	8 406	-2.5	342	4.1	8 987	67.8	7.7
Luna	8 862	68.2	89 800	26.1	10.2	573	25.9	21.1	10 623	-0.2	1 917	18.0	8 699	25.7	27.5
McKinley	17 427	72.6	74 900	21.3	10.0	537	23.0	6.7	23 798	-2.6	2 340	9.8	22 600	28.1	22.5
Mora	1 532	86.9	96 200	23.6	10.4	591	28.8	3.9	2 128	-0.7	237	11.1	1 658	27.1	30.1
Otero	23 945	66.3	102 400	22.1	10.6	730	27.3	2.6	24 818	-2.8	1 513	6.1	22 303	26.7	24.1
Quay	3 476	79.0	68 900	24.6	11.6	474	26.0	5.9	3 456	0.2	214	6.2	3 144	25.9	26.0
Rio Arriba	14 783	79.2	133 300	22.4	10.0	649	27.7	5.2	16 356	-1.4	1 361	8.3	16 110	33.8	19.1
Roosevelt	7 043	60.6	111 300	21.2	10.0	687	36.0	4.9	8 094	-3.1	445	5.5	8 587	27.9	25.4
Sandoval	47 164	80.8	180 900	24.7	10.0	988	30.4	10.1	59 968	-0.6	4 257	7.1	57 547	39.4	17.6
San Juan	40 945	74.3	148 700	20.6	10.0	748	28.0	2.2	55 116	1.0	3 463	6.3	51 608	27.9	28.8
San Miguel	11 435	69.5	116 700	26.9	13.2	625	38.9	3.8	11 214	-1.3	866	7.7	10 308	31.9	18.4
Santa Fe	61 012	69.6	278 400	27.0	10.0	903	31.0	2.6	71 510	-1.6	3 843	5.4	69 113	42.1	14.5
Sierra	4 350	73.9	93 900	23.0	12.6	572	33.2	3.1	3 849	0.2	338	8.8	3 761	28.0	21.8
Socorro	5 329	71.9	122 800	24.0	11.3	556	28.8	6.2	6 449	-2.5	462	7.2	6 224	37.6	23.8
Taos	13 338	72.1	204 800	27.5	11.0	763	37.4	7.1	14 752	-1.4	1 430	9.7	13 694	36.6	17.1
Torrance	5 638	81.7	105 200	27.0	15.9	648	33.9	4.3	5 185	-0.7	495	9.5	5 281	32.7	22.9
Union	1 606	64.4	86 500	20.0	13.9	655	22.0	3.9	1 672	-0.5	85	5.1	1 682	34.1	30.6
Valencia	26 894	79.7	133 600	25.3	10.4	728	35.4	1.3	29 284	-0.9	2 248	7.7	28 774	28.0	24.9
NEW YORK	7 234 743	54.2	288 200	25.7	15.1	1 088	31.9	5.3	9 569 062	-0.7	605 041	6.3	9 062 757	38.7	16.9
Albany	122 700	59.3	209 300	22.5	12.6	904	29.1	2.9	157 291	-1.8	7 706	4.9	153 118	43.5	12.4
Allegany	18 786	73.3	69 600	20.5	14.0	595	31.1	12.2	23 344	-1.5	1 445	6.2	20 905	31.9	27.2
Bronx	474 842	19.4	374 500	32.3	13.6	1 032	34.5	1.9	606 630	0.7	59 479	9.8	541 791	23.9	18.3
Broome	79 763	66.5	107 900	20.8	13.0	678	32.3	2.9	88 320	-3.6	5 826	6.6	89 152	35.5	19.3
Cattaraugus	32 246	71.9	81 100	22.1	13.7	618	29.2	1.8	36 768	-3.0	2 529	6.9	34 977	28.0	26.7
Cayuga	31 311	72.0	106 600	20.6	13.4	660	27.4	2.0	37 714	-2.6	2 254	6.0	36 993	30.8	26.7
Chautauqua	54 863	69.1	83 500	20.1	13.9	609	30.4	1.2	57 727	-3.7	3 925	6.8	58 610	29.8	26.6
Chemung	35 622	67.4	94 300	18.6	13.0	692	30.7	2.3	38 420	-3.0	2 407	6.3	38 919	33.4	21.9
Chenango	19 829	75.6	90 600	21.6	14.2	602	28.8	2.2	23 306	-2.9	1 434	6.2	21 508	31.1	27.7
Clinton	31 901	67.7	122 900	21.2	11.9	719	31.2	1.5	36 049	-2.7	2 411	6.7	35 878	32.3	22.7
Columbia	25 280	72.4	221 600	24.7	15.5	851	27.9	2.3	31 486	-0.8	1 487	4.7	29 725	37.3	20.9
Cortland	18 069	65.9	105 700	21.7	14.0	670	28.2	3.5	23 764	-1.9	1 530	6.4	23 044	33.3	22.8
Delaware	19 844	74.6	133 200	23.1	13.4	662	29.3	2.2	20 239	-3.5	1 312	6.5	20 612	29.0	29.6
Dutchess	107 830	69.6	289 400	27.5	16.9	1 105	32.4	1.2	142 053	-2.0	7 570	5.3	142 315	39.9	17.3
Erie	380 152	65.3	124 300	20.9	13.5	724	30.4	2.8	448 222	-2.2	27 279	6.1	434 684	37.6	17.4
Essex	15 919	72.4	146 600	23.2	14.0	780	29.0	2.4	17 593	-2.5	1 212	6.9	17 594	33.8	22.7
Franklin	19 238	72.3	97 100	20.4	13.5	664	29.4	1.5	20 618	-3.9	1 502	7.3	20 025	30.1	22.1
Fulton	22 611	69.0	106 000	22.5	13.6	699	31.4	1.5	23 463	-4.8	1 793	7.6	24 254	28.0	27.0

1. Specified owner-occupied units. 2. A value of 10.0 represents 10 percent or less; a value of 50.0 represents 50 percent or more. 3. Specified renter-occupied units.
4. Overcrowded or lacking complete plumbing facilities. 5. Percent of civilian labor force. 6. Persons 16 years old and over.

STATE County	Private nonfarm establishments, employment and payroll, 2013									Agriculture, 2012			
		Employment						Annual payroll		Farms			
											Percent with:		
	Number of establish-ments	Total	Health care and social assistance	Manufac-turing	Retail trade	Finance and insurance	Professional, scientific, and technical services	Total (mil dol)	Average per employee (dollars)	Number	Fewer than 50 acres	500 acres or more	Farm operators whose principal occu-pation is farming (percent)
	104	105	106	107	108	109	110	111	112	113	114	115	116
NEW JERSEY—Cont'd													
Mercer	9 701	185 388	30 948	7 074	19 466	14 509	22 025	11 360	61 277	272	71.0	2.9	46.0
Middlesex	21 535	381 947	46 857	28 047	38 272	14 300	50 370	22 616	59 211	198	73.2	5.1	43.9
Monmouth	18 959	224 059	41 133	8 481	39 089	11 250	20 448	10 608	47 344	823	82.4	2.4	57.2
Morris	16 761	274 566	34 849	13 371	29 209	18 310	38 233	19 765	71 987	366	79.0	0.8	43.4
Ocean	12 332	131 388	32 488	5 021	27 165	3 564	6 249	4 691	35 705	178	82.0	1.7	51.1
Passaic	11 866	150 775	27 983	17 839	22 807	5 114	8 005	6 931	45 968	78	92.3	0.0	48.7
Salem	1 169	19 049	3 221	2 784	1 879	497	469	943	49 508	825	60.4	6.5	53.3
Somerset	9 925	184 467	21 472	11 840	19 086	12 847	21 769	14 224	77 109	400	71.0	3.5	33.3
Sussex	3 267	31 594	6 507	2 191	5 843	1 033	1 314	1 172	37 108	885	69.5	1.9	47.9
Union	13 669	200 810	32 825	15 849	24 827	6 074	13 737	11 259	56 068	8	100.0	0.0	37.5
Warren	2 487	30 169	5 679	3 784	5 888	647	947	1 312	43 497	784	65.3	3.2	49.4
NEW MEXICO	43 737	606 002	115 028	27 766	92 607	21 410	44 745	23 205	38 293	24 721	51.3	25.3	50.1
Bernalillo	15 800	248 438	47 531	12 511	33 875	9 684	19 041	9 494	38 214	1 006	80.9	7.4	44.2
Catron	58	393	131	D	66	D	D	9	23 226	351	14.5	40.2	63.0
Chaves	1 443	17 301	3 915	835	3 335	660	1 137	581	33 560	595	39.7	36.1	55.3
Cibola	329	5 067	1 456	D	837	100	58	174	34 399	522	54.4	26.1	44.4
Colfax	420	3 225	535	113	569	D	101	94	29 002	290	13.4	41.4	47.9
Curry	1 049	12 586	2 707	D	2 402	488	515	355	28 231	600	16.8	49.7	45.0
De Baca	45	246	D	D	50	D	D	6	24 524	203	39.9	39.4	60.1
Dona Ana	3 554	49 387	12 912	2 502	8 049	1 744	3 739	1 424	28 832	2 184	85.6	4.5	37.7
Eddy	1 335	21 750	2 743	1 349	3 013	509	860	1 068	49 081	551	41.0	31.4	56.4
Grant	619	6 921	1 625	112	1 245	201	188	236	34 098	407	30.7	33.9	45.7
Guadalupe	98	928	80	D	D	22	D	23	24 881	372	19.9	55.9	62.4
Harding	9	22	D	NA	NA	D	NA	0	15 591	202	5.4	61.4	66.8
Hidalgo	89	791	148	D	218	D	D	19	23 836	171	24.6	55.0	66.1
Lea	1 708	25 072	2 419	915	2 855	478	516	1 238	49 379	460	29.6	44.1	55.4
Lincoln	698	5 264	576	78	1 225	311	143	134	25 534	362	30.7	43.9	55.5
Los Alamos	377	D	1 033	54	406	D	D	D	D	9	100.0	0.0	88.9
Luna	387	4 194	966	D	1 048	D	83	101	24 132	190	26.3	36.8	61.6
McKinley	974	15 502	4 528	D	3 453	406	224	464	29 906	2 297	38.9	35.6	60.3
Mora	47	285	107	D	NA	D	D	7	24 154	597	31.5	19.6	61.8
Otero	960	11 709	2 124	203	2 292	330	655	328	28 026	486	49.4	22.6	48.1
Quay	235	1 944	D	46	434	104	48	46	23 802	553	13.0	53.7	52.4
Rio Arriba	554	6 249	1 922	D	1 151	214	D	210	33 675	1 892	63.4	14.3	44.2
Roosevelt	342	3 728	602	366	678	134	75	103	27 688	680	17.4	47.5	50.7
Sandoval	1 654	26 762	3 687	3 426	3 097	857	731	1 248	46 622	1 029	63.8	14.2	45.3
San Juan	2 806	39 476	6 624	2 057	6 351	962	1 222	1 764	44 698	2 628	61.7	20.8	54.2
San Miguel	441	5 828	2 997	45	958	174	114	154	26 488	877	19.4	39.9	53.5
Santa Fe	4 714	44 633	7 812	754	9 349	1 860	2 425	1 748	39 164	715	67.0	13.4	43.6
Sierra	216	2 068	588	D	453	72	37	53	25 692	256	35.9	36.3	67.6
Socorro	228	2 940	D	58	463	D	259	84	28 614	704	60.2	20.0	55.0
Taos	1 083	8 521	1 505	118	1 492	211	273	230	27 009	983	75.3	7.4	35.6
Torrance	231	1 854	D	D	470	D	42	49	26 348	589	16.1	40.7	53.0
Union	106	934	D	D	151	D	D	27	28 905	353	5.7	73.1	58.6
Valencia	893	9 904	2 005	D	2 362	313	289	247	24 905	1 607	87.4	2.7	43.1
NEW YORK	532 669	7 688 492	1 445 220	429 298	920 848	533 082	603 392	466 815	60 716	35 537	32.6	8.4	57.4
Albany	9 409	172 571	34 588	7 509	21 934	12 753	15 223	7 708	44 664	494	42.5	3.6	46.6
Allegany	812	11 455	1 943	2 304	1 341	198	242	360	31 385	784	23.3	6.9	51.8
Bronx	17 090	240 666	97 799	6 092	28 471	4 202	3 535	10 354	43 020	1	100.0	0.0	100.0
Broome	4 299	72 516	15 425	8 000	11 339	2 261	3 839	2 647	36 504	563	34.1	3.0	48.8
Cattaraugus	1 628	23 128	3 510	3 901	4 125	642	600	784	33 889	1 038	26.6	7.5	51.8
Cayuga	1 652	19 869	3 858	3 344	3 542	357	462	667	33 587	891	33.2	12.7	59.4
Chautauqua	2 906	41 950	8 493	10 026	6 432	852	1 056	1 272	30 310	1 515	35.2	4.8	54.3
Chemung	1 816	31 960	6 705	5 677	5 285	997	735	1 193	37 341	372	27.2	4.3	53.8
Chenango	922	13 383	1 902	4 136	1 804	D	357	521	38 906	828	22.9	8.1	56.3
Clinton	1 868	25 311	5 051	3 759	5 123	431	689	852	33 666	603	26.9	11.6	57.5
Columbia	1 707	15 388	4 336	1 423	2 713	450	520	547	35 545	494	42.1	9.7	61.5
Cortland	1 035	16 389	3 536	3 195	2 302	366	857	506	30 868	518	23.0	9.1	52.1
Delaware	1 062	10 364	1 757	3 268	1 604	375	199	379	36 581	704	27.7	9.5	62.2
Dutchess	7 512	92 683	18 574	7 758	14 152	3 255	7 497	4 071	43 925	678	44.5	7.2	54.3
Erie	22 535	413 072	72 432	44 177	54 129	29 070	29 153	16 936	41 001	1 044	45.3	5.1	57.4
Essex	1 162	10 365	2 508	D	1 773	D	232	341	32 918	261	29.5	11.1	55.6
Franklin	992	10 553	3 310	519	1 863	D	436	331	31 411	688	23.0	8.4	59.4
Fulton	1 182	13 847	3 222	1 856	2 252	339	305	491	35 470	211	37.0	6.6	57.3

STATE County	Agriculture, 2012 (cont.) — Land in farms — Acreage (1,000)	Land in farms — Percent change, 2007–2012	Land in farms — Acres — Average size of farm	Land in farms — Acres — Total irrigated (1,000)	Land in farms — Acres — Total cropland (1,000)	Value of land and buildings (dollars) — Average per farm	Value of land and buildings (dollars) — Average per acre	Value of machinery and equipment, average per farm (dollars)	Value of products sold — Total (mil dol)	Value of products sold — Average per farm (dollars)	Value of products sold — Percent from: Crops	Value of products sold — Percent from: Livestock and poultry products	Percent of farms with sales of: $10,000 or more	Percent of farms with sales of: $100,000 or more	Government payments — Total ($1,000)	Government payments — Percent of farms
	117	118	119	120	121	122	123	124	125	126	127	128	129	130	131	132
NEW JERSEY—Cont'd																
Mercer	20	-9.1	73	1.1	12.4	1 474 301	20 310	59 195	19.7	72 533	83.1	16.9	43.0	11.0	310	14.3
Middlesex	17	-7.8	87	2.7	12.3	1 716 202	19 686	104 551	29.3	147 732	98.6	1.4	46.0	20.2	130	15.2
Monmouth	39	-11.7	47	3.7	25.1	1 021 639	21 581	73 476	84.4	102 565	79.6	20.4	38.6	12.8	169	6.2
Morris	14	-15.1	40	0.7	7.2	914 418	23 148	75 101	28.4	77 560	95.8	4.2	33.6	8.5	61	2.2
Ocean	8	-19.0	45	0.7	2.9	691 534	15 446	55 247	11.6	64 888	84.3	15.7	41.0	11.2	112	5.6
Passaic	1	-26.6	19	0.1	0.2	581 667	31 204	58 385	3.4	44 051	92.5	7.5	26.9	6.4	D	1.3
Salem	102	5.5	123	18.1	81.2	974 698	7 895	107 623	112.0	135 749	84.0	16.0	37.5	17.6	1 386	22.2
Somerset	35	6.2	87	0.5	20.2	1 779 905	20 497	72 478	23.2	58 015	89.2	10.8	34.0	8.5	128	7.0
Sussex	61	-6.5	69	0.3	27.9	735 954	10 672	48 488	18.7	21 078	62.1	37.9	23.4	5.2	370	8.1
Union	0	-23.8	12	0.0	0.1	1 513 000	126 083	85 375	2.4	294 875	D	D	62.5	37.5	0	0.0
Warren	72	-3.6	92	1.7	46.4	942 751	10 230	77 084	91.2	116 333	59.9	40.1	31.9	11.4	773	17.3
NEW MEXICO	43 201	-0.1	1 748	680.3	1 976.7	755 185	432	60 316	2 550.1	103 157	24.2	75.8	24.4	7.0	70 588	22.3
Bernalillo	351	47.5	349	5.3	12.5	395 200	1 134	33 582	18.1	18 023	41.5	58.5	13.0	1.9	172	8.6
Catron	1 078	-27.3	3 070	5.4	3.1	1 311 014	427	62 142	12.7	36 302	1.3	98.7	27.4	8.8	613	13.7
Chaves	2 483	1.2	4 173	49.8	63.0	1 503 955	360	147 017	388.1	652 267	11.6	88.4	53.6	30.9	4 688	32.9
Cibola	1 559	5.4	2 987	D	3.9	930 634	312	37 464	D	D	D	D	14.8	1.3	500	26.1
Colfax	1 963	-8.8	6 769	10.3	23.9	2 682 179	396	76 979	35.7	123 255	6.0	94.0	47.2	17.9	918	23.1
Curry	881	-0.8	1 468	62.2	479.0	849 413	579	157 685	447.3	745 525	7.0	93.0	42.0	19.5	8 250	72.2
De Baca	1 068	-0.2	5 261	8.1	11.2	1 301 429	247	90 015	24.0	118 064	36.9	63.1	55.7	27.1	1 868	58.6
Dona Ana	660	12.0	302	76.3	93.8	540 877	1 790	75 238	351.0	160 729	47.5	52.5	23.9	8.1	1 453	9.5
Eddy	1 142	3.1	2 073	43.3	53.0	926 314	447	123 615	119.6	216 995	42.2	57.8	45.6	15.6	2 481	35.2
Grant	1 064	-12.3	2 615	4.0	8.4	980 442	375	52 437	14.5	35 732	14.3	85.7	33.2	5.9	1 329	15.0
Guadalupe	1 643	17.0	4 417	3.8	17.7	1 176 723	266	43 145	17.7	47 605	2.1	97.9	32.0	9.1	2 853	36.0
Harding	1 034	9.5	5 119	D	21.3	1 447 842	283	58 356	13.5	66 807	2.1	97.9	39.6	14.4	1 289	40.1
Hidalgo	930	-9.6	5 440	9.6	12.9	1 347 661	248	97 895	29.2	170 491	57.9	42.1	73.1	24.6	1 228	46.2
Lea	1 982	-16.2	4 309	51.6	117.0	1 461 422	339	136 552	188.9	410 709	21.6	78.4	48.0	23.0	5 045	37.8
Lincoln	1 553	-11.3	4 291	2.0	5.1	1 519 177	354	62 006	16.9	46 588	3.2	96.8	42.8	11.6	2 709	26.0
Los Alamos	0	88.9	2	D	D	28 889	15 294	6 556	D	D	D	D	0.0	0.0	0	0.0
Luna	550	-15.8	2 896	20.6	37.2	1 228 332	424	174 526	62.5	328 853	63.9	36.1	58.4	30.5	1 472	52.6
McKinley	3 023	-4.7	1 316	1.9	44.1	414 200	315	22 288	8.4	3 652	7.4	92.6	5.1	0.4	845	29.7
Mora	778	-14.9	1 303	7.6	13.3	723 692	555	45 174	11.6	19 469	9.9	90.1	21.1	3.2	1 839	18.8
Otero	1 224	8.6	2 518	6.0	D	1 057 944	420	53 058	14.6	30 113	55.0	45.0	30.2	5.3	1 183	12.1
Quay	1 518	1.9	2 745	7.0	216.2	919 353	335	76 897	36.8	66 526	6.4	93.6	33.5	10.8	6 471	71.1
Rio Arriba	1 433	-1.9	757	29.2	66.8	548 193	724	43 273	19.0	10 031	37.5	62.5	19.8	1.4	1 277	14.5
Roosevelt	1 349	-9.7	1 984	46.1	290.3	966 632	487	120 344	264.3	388 712	6.9	93.1	39.9	13.2	8 038	62.4
Sandoval	950	60.6	923	9.4	17.8	482 790	523	31 229	10.6	10 288	52.9	47.1	16.2	1.0	815	10.0
San Juan	2 580	58.2	982	85.9	115.6	341 496	348	41 084	71.3	27 135	88.9	11.1	13.3	1.2	1 023	14.0
San Miguel	2 350	4.9	2 680	4.6	22.4	1 010 876	377	43 104	18.6	21 244	5.1	94.9	21.4	2.7	1 639	16.5
Santa Fe	718	26.0	1 004	8.9	13.1	848 969	846	39 010	12.8	17 869	75.1	24.9	15.0	2.7	394	5.7
Sierra	1 250	-7.0	4 883	12.4	19.4	1 396 238	286	91 934	39.3	153 699	44.6	55.4	55.9	20.7	1 418	37.1
Socorro	1 271	-11.1	1 806	18.9	21.4	890 670	493	67 983	77.2	109 726	15.3	84.7	37.2	11.9	1 539	9.5
Taos	313	-31.4	319	14.5	24.6	373 969	1 173	30 988	8.4	8 561	41.0	59.0	10.8	1.6	440	9.0
Torrance	1 865	3.8	3 166	25.0	47.9	1 151 192	364	79 518	58.5	99 355	39.9	60.1	32.6	9.3	3 259	27.7
Union	1 967	-10.3	5 573	26.0	66.1	2 047 037	367	96 062	98.1	278 011	17.2	82.8	66.3	31.4	2 900	49.3
Valencia	670	32.4	417	23.1	23.4	392 418	942	48 432	55.8	34 701	23.8	76.2	13.8	2.6	641	6.3
NEW YORK	7 184	0.1	202	59.8	4 217.0	525 587	2 600	117 163	5 415.1	152 380	41.5	58.5	49.2	20.0	74 511	26.4
Albany	63	3.9	128	0.4	36.5	397 650	3 099	73 182	46.0	93 030	67.6	32.4	38.3	8.3	384	16.8
Allegany	150	-0.3	192	0.1	71.3	335 583	1 750	70 612	73.4	93 569	28.5	71.5	36.4	12.8	1 099	27.0
Bronx	D	D	D	D	D	D	D	D	D	D	D	D	100.0	0.0	0	0.0
Broome	80	-8.0	142	0.1	38.1	371 162	2 623	66 933	30.7	54 552	22.9	77.1	34.3	5.9	770	18.7
Cattaraugus	197	7.5	190	0.9	97.3	359 361	1 891	91 609	99.1	95 503	25.3	74.7	41.8	14.7	1 895	31.4
Cayuga	238	-4.4	268	0.4	181.7	860 439	3 215	216 304	293.5	329 376	33.8	66.2	59.1	29.6	2 791	35.8
Chautauqua	237	0.3	156	0.9	129.5	322 390	2 065	95 881	161.8	106 831	45.6	54.4	54.3	18.9	2 502	19.8
Chemung	58	-10.8	156	0.2	28.1	376 065	2 407	75 599	16.0	43 143	41.2	58.8	28.5	8.6	482	22.8
Chenango	167	-5.7	202	0.2	79.3	370 505	1 835	87 490	65.9	79 630	22.3	77.7	45.4	19.3	2 117	30.9
Clinton	147	-1.3	244	0.1	74.0	494 534	2 025	144 806	149.0	247 096	28.4	71.6	46.9	19.7	1 660	24.7
Columbia	95	-10.5	193	1.4	56.9	1 008 441	5 223	115 555	66.5	134 664	54.0	46.0	55.1	20.6	674	19.8
Cortland	115	-7.9	222	0.2	60.4	423 170	1 906	104 708	62.9	121 423	21.4	78.6	47.5	15.6	984	35.7
Delaware	146	-12.1	207	0.2	59.3	515 442	2 492	83 908	47.7	67 736	19.5	80.5	46.9	17.5	1 248	33.7
Dutchess	112	9.9	166	0.8	45.6	860 500	5 187	97 681	49.0	72 304	53.1	46.9	49.1	16.7	427	10.3
Erie	143	-4.5	137	1.9	93.8	404 428	2 959	112 551	133.1	127 535	46.3	53.7	42.2	16.4	1 863	23.9
Essex	55	9.2	210	0.1	20.0	443 410	2 110	75 100	11.7	44 862	47.6	52.4	34.1	8.0	209	13.0
Franklin	145	10.8	211	0.6	74.8	354 044	1 680	100 096	84.2	122 334	23.2	76.8	48.4	18.3	1 583	26.0
Fulton	32	-5.9	151	0.1	14.7	324 464	2 148	74 938	9.3	44 081	36.2	63.8	41.2	10.0	269	18.5

STATE County	Water use, 2010		Wholesale trade,[1] 2007				Retail trade,[2] 2007				Real estate and rental and leasing,[2] 2007			
	Total water withdrawn (mil gal/day)	Gallons withdrawn per person per day	Number of establish-ments	Number of employees	Sales (mil dol)	Annual payroll (mil dol)	Number of establish-ments	Number of employees	Sales (mil dol)	Annual payroll (mil dol)	Number of establish-ments	Number of employees	Receipts (mil dol)	Annual payroll (mil dol)
	133	134	135	136	137	138	139	140	141	142	143	144	145	146
NEW JERSEY—Cont'd														
Mercer	477.6	1 303	359	9 737	8 421.0	816.7	1 412	20 683	5 089.1	505.0	357	D	D	D
Middlesex	67.9	84	1 687	33 964	32 631.8	1 994.9	2 826	40 815	11 131.0	1 048.5	731	6 267	2 206.4	316.6
Monmouth	79.9	127	931	8 184	11 058.9	484.6	2 860	42 007	11 225.1	1 095.8	764	3 716	750.0	139.6
Morris	105.0	213	1 011	15 352	17 440.0	989.0	2 107	31 238	8 756.3	877.7	672	7 848	2 066.6	522.5
Ocean	574.6	997	453	D	D	D	1 984	27 149	7 307.4	674.0	576	2 485	460.9	83.1
Passaic	221.2	441	802	10 498	7 021.1	539.0	1 912	23 180	6 598.0	579.0	447	5 992	1 103.1	211.4
Salem	3 054.1	46 216	36	D	D	D	197	2 311	669.4	52.0	58	D	D	D
Somerset	13.6	42	528	11 335	14 634.5	863.8	1 216	19 972	5 756.0	530.3	304	1 592	453.3	63.9
Sussex	16.8	112	146	D	D	D	488	5 806	1 722.4	150.3	96	D	D	D
Union	147.8	276	908	14 610	12 948.7	823.8	2 085	25 619	7 312.1	644.5	600	3 270	988.0	135.5
Warren	26.1	240	107	D	D	D	441	6 292	1 550.6	140.4	72	D	D	D
NEW MEXICO	3 161.0	1 535	1 763	19 891	10 589.3	805.8	7 208	97 385	24 470.0	2 250.8	2 525	11 678	1 954.7	355.6
Bernalillo	149.0	225	833	12 139	6 135.0	503.5	2 253	36 900	9 396.1	903.3	1 000	5 337	898.3	155.2
Catron	20.0	5 366	NA	NA	NA	NA	13	77	7.2	0.7	3	7	0.4	0.2
Chaves	241.3	3 676	52	D	D	D	260	3 271	836.1	69.7	85	283	43.2	8.1
Cibola	11.1	408	9	35	15.9	0.8	79	850	217.4	18.8	15	40	3.7	0.7
Colfax	47.8	3 477	12	54	45.1	1.8	91	719	158.8	14.3	34	126	14.6	2.0
Curry	164.0	3 390	49	251	171.5	8.4	198	2 519	591.3	52.1	49	170	25.6	4.4
De Baca	51.8	25 628	NA	NA	NA	NA	11	63	12.4	0.9	NA	NA	NA	NA
Dona Ana	397.2	1 899	120	1 076	448.2	34.1	536	7 881	1 925.6	159.5	229	1 009	143.2	22.2
Eddy	193.5	3 594	58	D	D	D	208	2 384	562.8	51.7	39	226	30.2	7.3
Grant	46.5	1 576	19	D	D	D	132	1 257	261.4	25.4	45	121	16.4	2.6
Guadalupe	24.6	5 249	2	D	D	D	20	290	109.9	4.9	NA	NA	NA	NA
Harding	3.2	4 604	NA	NA	NA	NA	4	6	1.3	0.1	NA	NA	NA	NA
Hidalgo	61.6	12 585	2	D	D	D	36	279	113.4	4.9	1	D	D	D
Lea	175.5	2 711	90	879	376.7	40.0	213	2 759	765.9	67.6	69	617	138.6	32.7
Lincoln	23.3	1 135	8	D	D	D	150	1 162	245.6	25.1	66	175	23.4	3.7
Los Alamos	3.6	202	4	D	D	D	35	490	97.9	9.7	19	78	14.2	2.1
Luna	109.7	4 371	19	D	D	D	76	1 111	236.8	20.2	27	83	13.0	1.6
McKinley	13.8	193	45	D	D	D	262	3 778	926.4	85.1	48	162	21.7	3.0
Mora	12.7	2 600	NA	NA	NA	NA	9	58	14.1	0.9	1	D	D	D
Otero	30.1	472	25	D	D	D	193	2 385	527.8	46.2	62	246	27.8	4.2
Quay	41.6	4 597	4	9	1.7	0.2	53	450	143.9	7.2	7	20	0.7	0.2
Rio Arriba	107.1	2 660	10	D	D	D	101	1 402	313.5	32.0	24	95	10.9	1.9
Roosevelt	173.6	8 748	12	D	D	D	56	660	166.7	13.5	13	46	3.4	0.6
Sandoval	65.5	498	40	262	113.1	12.1	197	3 168	1 117.4	78.1	85	272	35.5	5.8
San Juan	343.7	2 643	146	1 454	866.4	70.4	482	6 671	1 742.0	155.5	120	879	211.5	45.2
San Miguel	38.5	1 309	9	D	D	D	103	1 187	277.2	23.4	16	60	4.4	0.8
Santa Fe	49.8	345	134	D	D	D	887	9 949	2 426.3	261.6	311	1 092	206.0	40.8
Sierra	42.8	3 567	NA	NA	NA	NA	52	375	82.8	6.9	13	36	3.3	0.5
Socorro	129.4	7 241	2	D	D	D	46	574	126.2	10.7	17	54	10.3	1.0
Taos	106.5	3 232	25	D	D	D	245	1 624	309.2	35.7	67	241	23.9	4.6
Torrance	55.6	3 396	8	42	13.7	1.2	42	562	157.5	10.5	7	36	8.7	0.9
Union	63.2	13 900	1	D	D	D	18	100	27.5	1.8	3	D	D	D
Valencia	163.6	2 136	25	110	51.6	3.3	147	2 424	571.3	52.6	50	162	21.5	3.5
NEW YORK	10 574.5	546	30 863	357 459	313 461.9	19 609.0	76 637	892 863	230 718.1	22 336.7	32 588	171 601	49 867.2	7 941.7
Albany	50.0	164	423	6 321	3 642.6	319.4	1 379	22 854	5 404.4	519.3	424	3 112	619.8	107.2
Allegany	5.7	116	20	165	51.4	4.2	157	1 457	276.7	24.7	17	62	6.8	1.5
Bronx	0.2	0	695	10 432	8 039.8	553.9	3 462	24 355	5 539.8	522.1	2 274	8 916	1 703.5	270.6
Broome	47.3	236	194	3 831	1 958.8	150.2	753	11 949	2 573.0	237.6	157	1 114	191.8	31.2
Cattaraugus	13.7	171	55	678	465.7	22.7	372	4 040	1 009.0	84.4	56	197	26.8	4.3
Cayuga	9.6	120	57	D	D	D	273	3 852	884.0	81.6	60	189	27.6	4.2
Chautauqua	436.2	3 234	99	1 610	2 621.3	60.6	555	6 699	1 364.1	133.2	87	480	66.4	12.6
Chemung	9.8	111	86	1 077	357.9	43.2	388	5 580	1 207.2	111.0	79	410	65.6	10.7
Chenango	7.7	153	28	254	126.3	10.2	188	2 203	518.2	47.4	33	84	8.1	2.1
Clinton	15.4	188	97	1 223	679.4	42.8	378	4 890	1 195.0	102.8	85	315	51.1	7.8
Columbia	8.5	134	62	D	D	D	259	2 555	638.4	62.4	69	180	22.6	3.8
Cortland	6.1	123	29	D	D	D	194	2 268	523.1	45.9	40	285	21.5	3.6
Delaware	455.5	9 493	21	361	441.0	14.7	207	1 726	389.6	36.3	35	106	13.7	2.3
Dutchess	77.9	262	228	2 069	982.3	109.1	1 095	14 632	3 599.2	356.2	387	1 844	287.9	63.2
Erie	482.8	525	1 089	20 509	19 416.1	964.4	3 360	53 571	11 217.1	1 096.8	831	6 025	929.8	172.6
Essex	22.2	564	9	95	17.9	1.9	231	1 852	429.2	39.7	35	99	16.5	2.5
Franklin	13.3	257	30	D	D	D	214	2 257	476.4	45.8	40	125	14.9	2.7
Fulton	6.4	116	67	D	D	D	199	2 338	577.1	50.9	41	152	28.4	5.0

1. Merchant wholesalers, except manufacturers' sales branches and offices. 2. Employer establishments.

Table B. States and Counties — **Professional Services, Manufacturing, and Accommodation and Food Services**

STATE County	Professional, scientific, and technical services,[1] 2007				Manufacturing, 2007				Accommodation and food services, 2007			
	Number of establish-ments	Number of employees	Receipts (mil dol)	Annual payroll (mil dol)	Number of establish-ments	Number of employees	Receipts (mil dol)	Annual payroll (mil dol)	Number of establish-ments	Number of employees	Sales (mil dol)	Annual payroll (mil dol)
	147	148	149	150	151	152	153	154	155	156	157	158
NEW JERSEY—Cont'd												
Mercer	1 646	30 900	5 790.4	2 345.3	293	9 352	D	420.1	834	12 103	695.8	197.7
Middlesex	4 053	D	D	D	847	36 047	12 207.3	1 840.4	1 614	21 554	1 275.1	337.5
Monmouth	2 754	D	D	D	511	11 717	3 468.4	538.0	1 642	21 953	1 153.5	316.0
Morris	2 796	43 496	7 752.3	3 425.8	628	22 068	7 631.7	1 181.6	1 290	18 119	1 129.8	314.1
Ocean	1 167	D	D	D	315	D	D	251.0	1 087	12 584	703.0	182.7
Passaic	1 162	D	D	D	872	22 028	5 178.3	1 042.9	905	9 296	538.7	133.2
Salem	84	D	D	D	43	3 113	1 440.4	204.7	112	1 580	82.3	21.6
Somerset	1 830	D	D	D	337	17 673	6 401.5	1 159.7	712	10 739	656.1	180.0
Sussex	379	D	D	D	128	D	D	89.0	299	3 245	172.4	46.5
Union	1 546	D	D	D	712	31 897	18 574.7	2 106.8	1 110	12 763	748.0	199.9
Warren	260	D	D	D	136	4 603	2 212.2	240.2	250	2 622	118.0	31.3
NEW MEXICO	4 789	43 001	5 975.8	2 516.7	1 574	35 409	17 122.7	1 560.5	4 090	80 415	3 734.3	1 054.8
Bernalillo	2 248	D	D	D	661	16 573	D	719.8	1 319	29 908	1 398.0	410.5
Catron	3	D	D	D	NA	NA	NA	NA	11	57	2.6	0.4
Chaves	111	780	108.2	34.2	45	1 098	661.5	37.7	121	2 306	92.4	25.0
Cibola	21	D	D	D	NA	NA	NA	NA	43	1 403	117.3	25.0
Colfax	37	D	D	D	NA	NA	NA	NA	76	1 426	56.9	17.2
Curry	76	D	D	D	28	530	D	20.6	86	1 934	68.3	17.8
De Baca	1	D	D	D	NA	NA	NA	NA	3	D	D	D
Dona Ana	315	D	D	D	141	2 349	931.9	84.2	298	5 955	238.7	64.9
Eddy	76	D	D	D	37	1 302	D	84.5	110	1 778	80.5	20.8
Grant	45	D	D	D	NA	NA	NA	NA	76	957	35.5	9.1
Guadalupe	1	D	D	D	NA	NA	NA	NA	29	373	16.7	4.5
Harding	NA	NA	NA	NA	NA	NA	NA	NA	3	16	0.3	0.1
Hidalgo	2	D	D	D	NA	NA	NA	NA	16	275	9.9	2.6
Lea	78	522	60.7	24.9	38	815	280.4	36.4	115	1 944	85.1	21.0
Lincoln	61	D	D	D	NA	NA	NA	NA	103	1 114	60.2	15.1
Los Alamos	79	D	D	D	NA	NA	NA	NA	36	467	17.7	4.8
Luna	22	D	D	D	14	759	D	21.5	57	945	36.9	8.4
McKinley	50	D	D	D	33	685	D	37.7	148	2 474	109.1	27.3
Mora	1	D	D	D	NA	NA	NA	NA	3	D	D	D
Otero	83	D	D	D	NA	NA	NA	NA	103	1 798	92.4	24.3
Quay	10	D	D	D	NA	NA	NA	NA	35	555	17.9	4.9
Rio Arriba	42	D	D	D	NA	NA	NA	NA	79	1 184	66.8	18.3
Roosevelt	19	D	D	D	NA	NA	NA	NA	26	607	17.6	5.0
Sandoval	174	D	D	D	65	5 705	D	321.5	144	3 392	150.8	45.5
San Juan	239	D	D	D	91	1 649	668.7	64.3	192	4 108	173.2	45.8
San Miguel	32	D	D	D	NA	NA	NA	NA	66	773	33.1	8.2
Santa Fe	693	D	D	D	153	980	D	34.5	398	9 203	540.4	166.3
Sierra	17	D	D	D	NA	NA	NA	NA	39	423	14.9	4.1
Socorro	25	D	D	D	NA	NA	NA	NA	47	673	24.2	6.5
Taos	125	D	D	D	NA	NA	NA	NA	173	2 330	100.1	31.3
Torrance	9	D	D	D	NA	NA	NA	NA	29	309	12.9	3.1
Union	8	D	D	D	NA	NA	NA	NA	14	178	6.6	1.6
Valencia	86	378	26.4	9.5	35	1 114	D	D	92	1 501	55.7	14.8
NEW YORK	58 087	539 635	112 045.6	41 604.5	18 629	533 835	162 720.2	24 268.0	43 791	591 653	39 813.5	10 956.3
Albany	1 142	11 543	1 773.4	706.6	256	8 253	3 351.5	417.3	957	14 776	738.9	207.1
Allegany	56	D	D	D	44	2 826	965.9	115.8	94	1 151	40.2	10.9
Bronx	631	D	D	D	393	8 668	D	315.7	1 368	10 987	743.2	180.9
Broome	327	D	D	D	210	11 107	2 525.4	D	511	7 795	326.4	92.6
Cattaraugus	104	D	D	D	91	3 972	738.7	169.0	197	4 131	264.8	62.2
Cayuga	100	641	45.6	20.3	92	3 338	1 109.9	150.7	174	1 897	76.4	19.7
Chautauqua	196	D	D	D	212	11 887	4 461.9	489.2	355	4 951	181.2	55.0
Chemung	115	D	D	D	93	6 348	1 280.8	285.8	198	3 151	123.1	35.2
Chenango	74	513	31.5	25.6	86	2 489	595.6	93.2	90	777	32.2	9.6
Clinton	128	D	D	D	88	3 873	1 599.8	155.8	187	2 627	126.6	35.6
Columbia	212	D	D	D	73	1 896	619.2	82.0	165	1 392	65.1	19.5
Cortland	86	D	D	D	65	3 201	603.7	134.6	135	2 079	84.6	21.7
Delaware	73	D	D	D	41	5 120	1 432.9	223.6	125	862	41.2	11.0
Dutchess	778	D	D	D	217	15 948	3 823.0	1 263.0	701	8 172	424.7	117.2
Erie	2 100	D	D	D	1 111	48 058	15 873.8	2 444.8	2 112	36 944	1 462.8	434.5
Essex	65	D	D	D	34	842	D	45.8	217	2 094	125.6	39.4
Franklin	75	D	D	D	NA	NA	NA	NA	113	927	42.7	11.3
Fulton	82	325	25.3	9.0	90	2 346	520.6	84.0	126	1 089	46.6	12.3

1. Establishment subject to federal tax.

Table B. States and Counties — **Health Care and Social Assistance, Other Services, Nonemployer Businesses, and Residential Construction**

STATE County	Health care and social assistance, 2007				Other services, 2007				Nonemployer businesses, 2013		Value of residential construction authorized by building permits, 2014	
	Number of establish-ments	Number of employees	Receipts (mil dol)	Annual payroll (mil dol)	Number of establish-ments	Number of employees	Receipts (mil dol)	Annual payroll (mil dol)	Number	Receipts (mil dol)	New Construction ($1,000)	Number of housing units
	159	160	161	162	163	164	165	166	167	168	169	170
NEW JERSEY—Cont'd												
Mercer	1 147	26 724	2 609.3	1 180.7	860	6 084	828.6	214.7	23 100	1 240.6	60 727	368
Middlesex	1 970	39 959	4 285.8	1 742.4	1 581	10 420	1 588.0	354.1	51 540	2 868.0	298 858	1 901
Monmouth	2 300	37 165	4 035.3	1 558.5	1 518	8 075	720.8	214.3	50 713	3 292.9	248 347	1 484
Morris	1 660	31 028	3 263.2	1 484.4	1 271	7 416	1 016.6	232.4	40 290	2 785.7	227 385	1 591
Ocean	1 497	29 082	2 698.1	1 085.8	1 065	5 305	486.8	125.2	36 987	2 081.6	557 235	2 937
Passaic	1 325	24 170	2 259.9	957.3	1 001	5 020	386.3	118.6	35 521	1 810.2	61 360	518
Salem	164	2 988	240.8	99.2	116	364	28.8	7.0	2 853	127.0	7 050	51
Somerset	1 081	19 020	2 016.6	793.7	713	4 064	574.1	130.4	25 267	1 613.1	143 108	1 310
Sussex	328	D	D	D	330	1 293	112.9	31.6	10 930	584.6	37 108	222
Union	1 526	30 202	2 934.9	1 280.0	1 218	6 401	626.3	175.7	39 104	2 221.2	162 653	1 966
Warren	290	5 884	498.8	205.5	243	1 133	106.2	29.7	6 843	343.8	29 048	244
NEW MEXICO	4 732	105 496	8 834.1	3 781.1	2 953	18 061	1 689.7	449.5	119 195	4 622.4	881 907	4 799
Bernalillo	1 713	42 659	3 957.7	1 724.2	1 089	8 015	670.7	211.2	38 835	1 551.0	259 627	1 525
Catron	5	D	D	D	4	D	D	D	357	13.3	NA	NA
Chaves	181	3 596	342.3	122.8	90	528	39.8	10.3	3 083	144.9	10 848	54
Cibola	45	1 043	70.7	34.1	22	94	7.2	1.8	1 008	27.0	NA	NA
Colfax	37	577	51.5	22.2	29	110	11.7	2.4	767	28.8	5 640	13
Curry	101	2 865	190.8	97.7	85	460	40.9	8.1	1 913	76.6	27 344	141
De Baca	5	D	D	D	4	D	D	D	102	5.3	NA	NA
Dona Ana	474	10 748	798.2	323.2	230	1 237	94.1	27.7	12 098	441.3	133 152	617
Eddy	117	2 773	225.3	88.8	85	461	40.5	9.3	2 437	129.4	43 917	336
Grant	94	1 506	116.4	49.4	57	207	14.7	4.1	1 495	40.0	928	4
Guadalupe	9	45	5.4	0.9	9	38	4.7	1.3	156	5.5	NA	NA
Harding	1	D	D	D	NA	NA	NA	NA	52	2.3	NA	NA
Hidalgo	10	102	3.8	1.6	4	D	D	D	223	8.6	NA	NA
Lea	116	2 483	199.9	74.8	100	709	134.5	23.5	3 071	185.8	39 784	276
Lincoln	48	634	54.9	24.5	42	160	16.4	3.3	1 914	72.6	15 246	59
Los Alamos	59	965	92.7	34.9	22	151	9.0	2.7	1 044	33.6	1 075	3
Luna	46	804	77.0	24.9	30	109	6.8	1.5	1 006	29.7	1 197	7
McKinley	94	4 020	292.3	155.2	83	528	35.7	9.6	4 138	80.2	1 000	4
Mora	6	230	10.0	5.6	3	D	D	D	306	7.5	NA	NA
Otero	111	2 152	174.8	70.1	66	348	19.2	5.4	3 189	104.3	0	0
Quay	27	448	31.4	13.0	21	115	13.1	2.8	353	12.6	NA	NA
Rio Arriba	95	1 808	119.6	66.0	27	134	14.4	2.8	1 899	59.6	0	0
Roosevelt	35	728	43.6	18.2	15	78	5.4	1.5	817	31.3	3 199	20
Sandoval	159	1 861	134.8	53.8	94	498	42.3	11.8	7 515	256.4	168 562	943
San Juan	265	6 274	534.2	226.2	192	1 363	170.4	37.1	5 381	230.7	35 978	173
San Miguel	84	2 532	164.2	69.9	26	92	7.4	2.0	1 422	37.8	0	0
Santa Fe	518	8 465	809.4	318.0	341	1 849	231.0	54.1	15 652	732.8	37 092	161
Sierra	21	538	33.1	15.9	20	116	7.2	2.2	694	20.6	0	0
Socorro	30	763	45.9	27.0	15	45	2.9	0.7	796	19.6	217	1
Taos	109	1 548	112.1	48.0	68	270	19.9	5.3	3 198	96.3	9 653	80
Torrance	20	361	12.4	6.4	9	23	2.3	0.5	773	23.8	NA	NA
Union	9	D	D	D	11	D	D	D	268	7.9	NA	NA
Valencia	88	2 682	113.5	56.1	60	242	20.0	5.2	3 233	105.2	8 131	75
NEW YORK	53 948	1 326 039	128 595.2	54 422.4	42 575	249 391	39 147.4	8 073.4	1 626 367	79 407.0	5 581 783	36 286
Albany	1 010	30 989	2 855.4	1 165.0	792	6 198	716.3	200.7	17 594	872.7	133 826	775
Allegany	95	1 994	106.1	50.1	73	265	17.5	3.8	2 534	86.3	7 626	64
Bronx	1 997	86 879	8 795.8	3 868.5	1 621	7 061	680.8	184.8	112 552	3 054.9	185 203	1 885
Broome	435	14 029	1 253.0	505.5	326	2 032	161.7	44.0	10 051	406.2	9 023	53
Cattaraugus	189	3 656	263.6	110.7	127	794	49.7	12.5	3 954	142.2	13 646	80
Cayuga	201	3 683	257.5	112.0	124	487	41.2	8.9	4 175	161.3	19 311	171
Chautauqua	297	8 735	581.0	235.6	255	1 558	110.3	23.3	6 994	254.9	26 261	212
Chemung	221	6 722	587.1	247.0	129	786	59.9	15.7	3 832	138.5	21 995	61
Chenango	116	1 795	134.8	55.4	77	270	21.0	6.0	2 760	107.1	10 194	204
Clinton	240	5 056	399.7	180.2	123	585	43.2	12.2	3 920	157.2	19 499	140
Columbia	170	3 928	274.7	130.3	97	395	38.3	9.8	5 809	256.3	30 349	97
Cortland	130	3 262	202.1	93.4	103	557	37.9	10.7	2 342	84.1	5 791	42
Delaware	118	2 235	146.6	55.3	83	357	59.3	8.2	3 533	126.2	11 175	77
Dutchess	908	17 764	1 631.3	682.5	614	2 577	260.9	68.7	20 656	935.1	59 488	358
Erie	2 709	73 571	6 357.2	2 520.7	1 773	13 107	1 091.7	322.8	45 745	2 038.9	307 875	1 682
Essex	137	1 755	114.9	54.8	79	374	35.7	8.7	3 044	117.4	23 610	94
Franklin	155	3 205	236.2	102.9	84	250	17.9	4.8	2 775	101.3	11 599	57
Fulton	187	3 419	228.8	106.1	87	492	37.8	12.4	2 808	100.6	12 691	72

STATE County	Government employment and payroll, 2012									Local government finances, 2012				
			March payroll (percent of total)							General revenue				
												Taxes		
													Per capita[1] (dollars)	
	Full-time equivalent employees	March payroll (dollars)	Adminis-tration, judicial, and legal	Police and Corrections	Fire Protection	Highways and transpor-tation	Health and Welfare	Natural resources and utilities	Education and libraries	Total (mil dol)	Inter-govern-mental (mil dol)	Total (mil dol)	Total	Property
	171	172	173	174	175	176	177	178	179	180	181	182	183	184
NEW JERSEY—Cont'd														
Mercer	15 352	84 285 619	4.4	12.4	3.3	2.0	4.4	4.9	64.8	2 164.5	711.0	1 168.1	3 172	3 117
Middlesex	26 592	147 425 663	4.2	13.0	2.6	1.8	4.3	3.9	68.2	3 819.6	965.9	2 247.0	2 730	2 672
Monmouth	27 427	142 190 760	5.3	14.3	0.7	3.0	5.2	3.7	66.3	3 459.7	822.0	2 117.8	3 365	3 308
Morris	19 889	108 738 326	4.6	10.9	0.8	2.8	3.7	5.8	68.0	2 618.5	372.1	1 893.1	3 801	3 744
Ocean	20 430	99 202 051	5.5	14.5	0.4	3.0	4.9	5.2	63.9	2 394.3	580.3	1 531.1	2 638	2 603
Passaic	15 817	88 473 333	5.1	16.3	5.0	2.0	8.1	4.7	57.7	2 251.4	742.8	1 305.1	2 595	2 566
Salem	3 305	15 720 003	5.8	12.2	0.0	2.4	4.8	2.4	69.6	394.8	172.3	152.1	2 313	2 287
Somerset	13 026	68 430 732	3.9	11.5	0.6	3.4	3.0	2.1	73.5	1 611.4	277.0	1 174.0	3 583	3 530
Sussex	5 561	30 640 722	5.9	8.8	0.2	3.9	3.0	1.3	75.3	772.0	189.2	484.5	3 286	3 255
Union	23 222	130 750 946	5.8	13.4	5.4	2.2	5.9	2.3	63.3	3 230.4	1 130.6	1 723.2	3 168	3 100
Warren	4 346	20 547 388	6.3	9.9	0.9	3.6	6.8	2.0	68.4	536.8	183.8	292.4	2 716	2 688
NEW MEXICO	X	X	X	X	X	X	X	X	X	X	X	X	X	X
Bernalillo	22 833	89 838 327	6.2	16.3	6.5	6.3	5.2	6.3	51.7	2 451.4	1 173.3	882.0	1 310	743
Catron	146	386 239	12.7	8.6	0.0	7.4	4.7	1.5	64.1	15.7	10.9	2.6	698	511
Chaves	2 443	7 710 245	4.6	11.3	4.7	3.4	1.7	6.7	65.0	249.1	177.0	44.9	682	436
Cibola	909	2 491 571	7.4	11.5	1.3	2.3	1.9	3.3	70.0	97.5	46.9	12.3	451	248
Colfax	652	2 023 377	9.7	9.4	4.3	3.0	9.7	10.8	51.3	63.7	33.7	19.3	1 463	839
Curry	2 120	6 374 697	3.9	9.1	4.6	2.6	2.3	2.7	74.0	176.6	105.3	49.5	991	345
De Baca	134	371 334	8.8	11.3	0.0	8.7	3.7	10.9	56.5	13.8	7.8	2.5	1 319	841
Dona Ana	7 916	26 726 295	5.8	10.4	2.7	2.6	2.1	5.9	66.7	732.8	425.3	209.7	978	447
Eddy	2 143	8 178 370	5.4	14.2	5.2	4.3	2.1	6.4	59.3	275.0	129.3	115.7	2 126	1 225
Grant	1 747	5 905 715	4.3	7.8	1.4	2.5	44.2	2.7	35.9	187.1	80.4	29.7	1 009	473
Guadalupe	390	1 120 471	7.2	4.4	2.0	4.0	2.5	2.3	74.8	29.2	18.8	6.1	1 319	617
Harding	70	190 631	18.3	3.6	0.0	12.0	4.9	3.4	55.3	10.0	6.0	3.0	4 246	2 506
Hidalgo	293	795 504	9.1	17.5	0.0	4.5	3.0	5.4	58.2	28.3	19.6	4.7	976	778
Lea	3 191	11 349 323	4.4	10.8	3.6	2.9	15.4	4.7	55.7	413.1	170.9	153.5	2 314	1 380
Lincoln	853	2 783 245	8.5	11.0	3.3	4.9	5.2	9.6	53.8	99.8	41.5	37.7	1 857	1 135
Los Alamos	1 400	5 075 436	10.8	6.3	17.0	4.7	1.3	11.9	40.5	138.8	77.2	49.3	2 712	875
Luna	1 233	3 637 272	6.8	12.9	1.8	1.9	2.6	2.4	66.6	103.9	67.8	23.4	936	513
McKinley	3 373	9 383 425	3.6	7.5	2.2	1.6	1.9	3.4	78.5	249.0	155.9	62.8	861	271
Mora	208	516 517	10.0	3.6	0.0	4.3	0.8	0.5	79.2	16.8	10.9	2.4	506	430
Otero	1 662	5 122 202	6.3	14.5	0.3	2.5	2.3	4.7	67.9	147.4	86.7	40.4	612	307
Quay	563	1 605 317	7.9	9.3	0.4	3.2	4.0	8.7	65.3	54.3	38.6	8.0	912	461
Rio Arriba	1 378	4 062 743	9.2	7.6	1.7	2.7	5.6	3.5	67.3	133.9	69.5	50.2	1 244	819
Roosevelt	849	2 598 517	4.7	9.9	3.2	3.4	1.0	3.2	73.2	65.0	40.9	14.6	714	505
Sandoval	3 959	13 152 644	7.2	11.4	4.7	3.3	1.2	5.4	66.3	399.2	201.9	135.8	1 002	605
San Juan	5 857	21 149 302	4.2	11.0	2.6	2.0	1.9	8.4	68.4	491.8	290.9	126.9	987	702
San Miguel	1 294	3 946 008	6.9	7.5	1.7	1.8	1.8	6.1	72.8	102.3	63.7	27.0	933	408
Santa Fe	4 848	18 022 225	9.3	12.0	6.4	3.8	4.1	9.6	48.1	527.4	253.9	199.3	1 361	807
Sierra	644	2 455 286	6.7	6.0	0.0	1.9	22.5	6.1	54.0	49.9	22.0	12.6	1 060	582
Socorro	721	1 882 356	6.5	9.1	3.0	3.6	4.4	6.7	63.5	61.4	43.7	9.7	551	305
Taos	1 245	3 508 311	12.0	9.6	1.7	3.3	3.5	5.5	61.6	118.8	59.8	45.9	1 400	624
Torrance	904	2 576 995	5.9	5.6	0.5	2.0	1.4	1.7	82.4	69.5	50.0	14.8	923	704
Union	203	666 897	11.2	10.4	3.2	8.9	2.6	4.7	56.6	23.5	13.2	5.9	1 327	768
Valencia	2 378	6 663 270	5.6	7.4	1.3	1.2	2.2	2.4	79.8	195.8	120.3	56.4	736	383
NEW YORK	X	X	X	X	X	X	X	X	X	X	X	X	X	X
Albany	12 459	58 755 137	5.6	15.4	3.5	2.8	8.7	5.3	57.2	1 776.2	540.6	885.9	2 900	2 024
Allegany	2 326	8 539 230	7.1	8.0	0.7	8.2	7.3	2.7	64.1	300.9	162.2	113.9	2 356	1 929
Bronx	(3)	(3)	(3)	(3)	(3)	(3)	(3)	(3)	(3)	(3)	(3)	(3)	(3)	(3)
Broome	9 618	36 733 525	4.9	8.4	2.7	4.4	10.5	3.0	64.3	1 182.8	494.6	520.5	2 628	1 756
Cattaraugus	4 623	18 563 190	6.2	8.6	1.7	8.0	12.2	3.6	59.1	526.9	273.4	184.2	2 318	1 675
Cayuga	3 237	14 564 325	6.1	8.2	3.3	5.0	9.9	3.2	63.1	427.9	185.0	169.5	2 131	1 441
Chautauqua	6 787	27 243 053	4.8	7.7	2.9	6.8	9.0	2.9	65.0	772.7	364.8	268.8	2 013	1 539
Chemung	3 853	14 858 297	5.0	9.7	2.9	4.0	13.2	3.8	59.7	476.3	219.3	175.3	1 971	1 236
Chenango	2 731	10 005 930	6.4	7.7	1.8	9.2	7.9	1.6	64.4	295.2	157.3	105.1	2 106	1 541
Clinton	3 949	16 260 748	5.3	6.0	0.9	6.0	11.3	2.6	65.0	458.8	198.9	190.2	2 329	1 643
Columbia	3 025	13 243 189	8.0	8.1	0.4	9.6	12.9	2.0	57.7	374.6	114.6	212.1	3 394	2 596
Cortland	2 146	9 594 343	7.0	14.5	2.0	8.9	10.2	5.2	50.7	258.6	118.1	110.0	2 223	1 645
Delaware	2 262	8 403 397	8.5	6.5	0.1	11.8	10.9	1.5	59.1	286.6	118.1	136.3	2 883	2 410
Dutchess	12 054	60 953 575	5.6	9.6	3.0	3.7	5.7	1.9	69.4	1 683.1	521.2	964.5	3 244	2 611
Erie	35 259	161 616 876	3.7	12.8	3.3	2.9	5.3	5.1	65.4	5 298.2	2 255.2	2 176.7	2 368	1 547
Essex	1 990	7 313 826	9.9	6.1	1.3	9.8	14.0	4.4	53.3	255.8	76.1	132.5	3 401	2 621
Franklin	2 713	9 538 618	5.8	5.4	0.9	6.2	10.0	2.2	68.0	305.3	153.8	104.0	2 008	1 575
Fulton	2 664	9 331 227	4.7	7.9	2.7	4.8	13.2	1.3	64.4	301.1	138.4	121.2	2 207	1 595

1. Based on the resident population estimated as of July 1 of the year shown. 3. Bronx, Kings, Queens, and Richmond counties are included with New York county.

STATE County	Local government finances, 2012 (cont.)									Government employment, 2013			Presidential election,[2] 2012		
	Direct general expenditure							Debt outstanding					Percent of vote cast:		
			Percent of total for:												
	Total (mil dol)	Per capita[1] (dollars)	Educa-tion	Health and hospitals	Police protec-tion	Public welfare	High-ways	Total (mil dol)	Per capita[1] (dollars)	Federal civilian	Federal military	State and local	Demo-cratic	Republi-can	All other
	185	186	187	188	189	190	191	192	193	194	195	196	197	198	199
NEW JERSEY—Cont'd															
Mercer	2 145.5	5 825	52.3	0.9	5.3	4.3	1.4	1 928.9	5 237	2 371	741	39 979	67.4	31.4	1.2
Middlesex	3 874.0	4 707	54.1	1.1	5.8	2.4	1.7	4 163.4	5 059	2 333	1 769	52 872	60.4	38.5	1.1
Monmouth	3 411.5	5 420	54.8	1.1	6.0	2.1	2.9	2 733.3	4 343	2 214	1 530	33 242	47.6	51.3	1.1
Morris	2 580.5	5 182	55.7	1.5	5.7	1.5	3.1	2 056.9	4 130	5 568	1 103	26 396	45.5	53.6	0.9
Ocean	2 437.7	4 200	51.2	0.6	6.8	3.2	3.4	2 209.0	3 805	2 973	1 352	25 233	40.2	58.6	1.3
Passaic	2 262.2	4 499	45.8	2.5	6.7	5.0	2.2	1 387.8	2 760	1 031	1 019	27 761	60.4	38.7	0.8
Salem	408.1	6 204	53.4	1.9	3.9	2.2	4.2	399.9	6 081	152	131	4 240	51.2	47.2	1.6
Somerset	1 638.3	4 999	58.6	2.0	5.3	1.0	4.6	1 441.4	4 399	1 696	671	16 284	52.5	46.4	1.1
Sussex	733.7	4 976	63.4	1.4	3.9	2.2	4.2	551.0	3 737	316	301	7 632	38.9	59.6	1.5
Union	3 281.6	6 033	53.5	2.9	6.2	1.6	1.8	2 546.6	4 681	1 490	1 116	32 126	63.7	35.5	0.9
Warren	573.8	5 330	58.0	1.8	4.0	3.5	3.9	237.2	2 203	219	217	5 836	42.2	56.2	1.7
NEW MEXICO	X	X	X	X	X	X	X	X	X	30 398	18 350	162 612	56.9	41.8	1.3
Bernalillo	2 337.5	3 471	48.0	2.0	9.0	1.6	5.0	3 333.0	4 949	14 094	5 450	54 237	60.0	38.7	1.3
Catron	17.1	4 674	36.7	2.0	4.1	0.6	7.9	9.9	2 693	103	10	229	31.4	66.2	2.4
Chaves	248.0	3 771	52.6	0.0	6.6	2.3	4.4	107.2	1 630	275	184	4 004	37.1	61.7	1.2
Cibola	102.5	3 749	38.6	30.4	2.4	3.0	2.9	41.6	1 521	330	68	2 907	64.1	34.4	1.5
Colfax	65.2	4 931	40.3	5.9	6.4	0.7	7.3	52.6	3 979	55	35	1 426	54.7	43.9	1.4
Curry	185.3	3 711	57.6	0.2	5.2	0.7	4.3	71.0	1 422	865	4 835	2 527	32.3	66.5	1.2
De Baca	13.6	7 072	35.8	17.8	4.5	0.1	4.9	5.2	2 717	14	0	186	34.4	64.8	0.9
Dona Ana	719.6	3 356	57.5	1.3	6.7	1.9	4.1	440.1	2 052	3 757	591	16 868	58.1	40.5	1.3
Eddy	252.5	4 640	47.2	2.8	8.5	1.6	5.2	120.4	2 213	633	151	3 169	36.6	62.2	1.2
Grant	196.6	6 690	26.5	40.7	4.6	2.8	2.6	102.5	3 489	206	79	3 463	59.2	39.3	1.5
Guadalupe	26.2	5 682	37.7	0.7	4.4	6.5	5.2	22.0	4 789	24	11	406	70.9	28.2	0.9
Harding	10.9	15 478	46.4	1.6	4.0	0.1	7.1	5.9	8 396	15	0	91	41.5	57.2	1.3
Hidalgo	27.3	5 693	43.1	2.0	15.9	0.6	2.6	9.5	1 987	309	13	393	50.9	48.0	1.1
Lea	416.5	6 278	45.5	12.6	5.6	1.1	7.8	219.2	3 304	88	182	3 518	27.4	71.6	1.0
Lincoln	102.5	5 048	37.3	4.2	6.6	0.5	5.9	89.0	4 382	114	55	1 122	36.5	61.9	1.7
Los Alamos	168.1	9 258	31.9	0.0	4.1	1.6	6.7	190.8	10 505	283	52	1 645	52.6	45.7	1.6
Luna	99.5	3 974	55.3	2.0	7.7	1.0	3.5	25.7	1 027	562	67	1 566	51.7	46.4	1.9
McKinley	255.3	3 497	63.0	1.1	4.0	1.8	3.8	145.8	1 997	2 519	201	5 034	71.4	27.5	1.1
Mora	17.2	3 658	55.5	0.3	2.6	0.0	3.0	10.3	2 189	41	13	262	78.6	20.6	0.8
Otero	149.2	2 258	50.7	0.5	8.4	3.1	9.6	138.3	2 094	1 842	4 527	4 496	39.6	58.8	1.6
Quay	53.7	6 124	48.7	5.9	4.7	3.6	4.1	28.0	3 197	44	24	881	38.7	59.2	2.1
Rio Arriba	130.8	3 245	54.4	0.5	4.5	1.1	2.9	101.6	2 519	335	110	4 542	75.0	24.1	0.9
Roosevelt	64.4	3 152	61.8	0.1	6.6	2.2	4.8	18.8	922	57	52	2 163	34.3	64.2	1.6
Sandoval	384.6	2 836	51.6	0.1	6.8	1.0	6.1	599.5	4 422	365	375	7 147	55.7	43.0	1.3
San Juan	551.0	4 287	55.6	3.3	6.3	1.2	4.3	2 140.3	16 652	1 546	348	9 900	38.8	59.9	1.3
San Miguel	108.9	3 769	60.5	0.3	4.2	0.7	4.8	73.4	2 539	144	75	3 772	79.7	19.1	1.1
Santa Fe	578.2	3 950	45.8	1.3	6.0	2.2	3.5	916.2	6 259	962	408	16 202	76.9	21.9	1.2
Sierra	50.5	4 245	27.8	29.9	10.1	1.0	8.1	29.4	2 475	109	31	758	42.9	55.0	2.1
Socorro	72.0	4 091	47.8	0.2	3.8	0.0	4.6	25.8	1 466	194	47	2 496	59.5	38.4	2.1
Taos	129.6	3 953	49.9	1.4	3.2	2.6	3.3	125.3	3 823	283	90	1 940	81.8	17.0	1.2
Torrance	69.7	4 348	66.8	0.8	2.8	0.8	2.9	231.1	14 425	73	42	975	44.5	53.8	1.7
Union	21.1	4 754	42.4	8.0	5.7	1.5	6.6	13.0	2 941	51	10	295	28.2	70.4	1.3
Valencia	184.9	2 413	64.8	0.5	5.8	0.6	3.4	196.9	2 570	106	207	3 992	53.2	45.5	1.4
NEW YORK	X	X	X	X	X	X	X	X	X	116 234	59 347	1 283 015	62.9	36.0	1.0
Albany	1 817.9	5 952	40.0	3.9	5.2	11.2	3.9	2 211.1	7 239	5 080	669	58 974	63.8	34.4	1.8
Allegany	309.4	6 398	47.0	2.5	1.8	9.8	11.7	294.0	6 080	117	72	3 847	38.2	60.0	1.8
Bronx	(3)	(3)	(3)	(3)	(3)	(3)	(3)	(3)	(3)	6 551	2 353	14 714	88.7	10.9	0.4
Broome	1 232.1	6 221	48.7	3.4	2.9	12.0	3.8	1 229.8	6 209	529	308	18 948	53.2	45.2	1.6
Cattaraugus	550.0	6 922	49.6	5.9	2.3	13.2	7.5	513.3	6 460	234	150	9 594	43.9	54.5	1.6
Cayuga	442.3	5 560	52.0	4.7	3.2	9.3	6.8	308.3	3 875	134	124	5 630	53.3	44.8	1.8
Chautauqua	806.8	6 042	50.1	3.0	2.9	12.8	6.0	665.7	4 985	305	208	8 720	49.6	48.6	1.8
Chemung	467.0	5 252	42.9	3.0	3.0	18.1	8.9	490.6	5 518	214	138	6 170	48.8	50.0	1.1
Chenango	297.2	5 953	57.1	3.1	1.6	8.2	7.3	216.1	4 329	91	80	3 895	48.4	49.6	2.0
Clinton	495.0	6 062	54.0	4.9	1.9	11.3	5.6	401.8	4 921	703	125	7 025	60.7	37.8	1.6
Columbia	381.3	6 100	48.0	4.5	2.2	13.2	9.0	225.4	3 607	153	99	4 291	55.9	42.5	1.6
Cortland	277.6	5 611	47.3	4.6	3.0	10.4	8.5	199.2	4 027	111	75	3 684	54.2	44.2	1.6
Delaware	281.8	5 961	44.9	3.5	1.5	9.4	12.5	208.3	4 406	126	74	4 569	46.4	51.6	2.0
Dutchess	1 642.8	5 525	55.5	3.6	3.3	7.6	4.0	1 417.6	4 768	1 193	455	19 393	53.7	45.1	1.2
Erie	5 644.5	6 141	44.0	10.5	3.7	9.5	3.2	5 158.7	5 613	8 426	1 750	66 361	58.0	40.5	1.6
Essex	273.6	7 022	36.7	6.8	1.3	10.7	9.0	306.9	7 877	330	59	3 962	55.9	42.6	1.5
Franklin	335.9	6 486	56.1	3.6	1.2	11.1	5.6	277.2	5 352	163	75	8 138	60.4	38.2	1.4
Fulton	288.3	5 250	49.7	2.7	2.5	16.8	5.0	192.0	3 496	78	88	3 811	44.5	53.7	1.8

1. Based on the resident population estimated as of July 1 of the year shown. 2. 3. Bronx, Kings, Queens, and Richmond counties are included with New York county.

STATE/ County code	CBSA code[1]	County type[2]	STATE County	Land area,[3] (sq km) 2010	Population, 2014: Total persons 2014	Population, 2014: Rank	Population, 2014: Per square kilometer	Population and population characteristics, 2013: Race alone or in combination, not Hispanic or Latino (percent): White	Black	American Indian, Alaska Native	Asian and Pacific Islander	Percent Hispanic or Latino[4]	Age (percent): Under 5 years	5 to 17 years	18 to 24 years	25 to 34 years	35 to 44 years	45 to 54 years
				1	2	3	4	5	6	7	8	9	10	11	12	13	14	15
			NEW YORK—Cont'd															
36 037	12860	4	Genesee	1 277	59 162	877	46.3	92.4	3.7	1.5	1.1	2.9	5.3	15.7	9.3	11.6	11.5	15.8
36 039	...	6	Greene	1 676	47 967	1 015	28.6	87.9	6.4	0.7	1.3	5.2	4.5	13.2	9.8	10.4	11.6	15.9
36 041	...	8	Hamilton	4 448	4 715	2 854	1.1	97.1	1.3	0.9	0.7	1.2	3.5	12.0	5.7	7.5	9.4	15.2
36 043	46540	2	Herkimer	3 656	63 744	823	17.4	96.1	1.7	0.5	0.8	2.0	5.3	15.9	9.3	10.9	11.1	14.7
36 045	48060	4	Jefferson	3 286	119 103	517	36.2	84.8	6.9	1.1	2.7	7.0	8.6	16.3	13.1	16.9	11.6	11.8
36 047	35620	1	Kings	183	2 621 793	8	14 326.7	37.1	32.1	0.6	12.4	19.5	7.4	15.9	9.7	17.8	13.8	12.4
36 049	...	6	Lewis	3 301	27 220	1 522	8.2	96.9	1.2	0.6	0.6	1.6	6.4	17.5	8.1	11.3	11.6	14.8
36 051	40380	1	Livingston	1 636	64 586	815	39.5	92.6	3.0	0.7	1.9	3.2	4.6	14.5	15.3	10.3	11.0	15.3
36 053	45060	2	Madison	1 696	72 369	748	42.7	94.7	2.2	1.0	1.3	2.0	4.7	15.9	13.2	10.3	10.9	15.4
36 055	40380	1	Monroe	1 702	749 857	84	440.6	73.7	15.7	0.6	4.2	7.9	5.7	16.0	11.0	13.4	11.6	14.3
36 057	11220	4	Montgomery	1 044	49 779	983	47.7	84.8	2.6	0.6	1.1	12.4	6.0	16.8	8.4	11.9	11.6	13.9
36 059	35620	1	Nassau	737	1 358 627	28	1 843.5	64.2	11.7	0.4	9.3	15.6	5.4	16.9	8.9	11.1	12.4	15.6
36 061	35620	1	New York	59	1 636 268	20	27 733.4	49.1	13.7	0.5	12.9	25.7	5.2	9.5	9.7	22.8	14.7	12.6
36 063	15380	1	Niagara	1 353	213 525	301	157.8	88.5	8.1	1.6	1.4	2.5	5.2	15.3	9.3	11.7	11.4	15.3
36 065	46540	2	Oneida	3 140	232 871	281	74.2	85.2	7.0	0.6	3.8	5.1	5.7	15.6	10.0	12.0	11.5	14.7
36 067	45060	2	Onondaga	2 016	468 196	145	232.2	80.5	12.1	1.3	4.1	4.5	5.8	16.3	10.8	12.9	11.5	14.6
36 069	40380	1	Ontario	1 668	109 707	548	65.8	92.2	2.9	0.6	1.7	4.1	4.9	16.2	9.5	10.5	11.4	15.6
36 071	35620	2	Orange	2 102	376 099	179	178.9	68.3	10.6	0.7	3.2	19.2	6.7	19.6	10.7	11.0	12.7	15.2
36 073	40380	1	Orleans	1 013	41 984	1 129	41.4	88.5	7.0	1.0	0.8	4.4	4.9	15.6	9.7	11.7	11.8	16.3
36 075	45060	2	Oswego	2 465	120 913	510	49.1	95.7	1.3	0.8	1.0	2.3	5.6	16.3	11.8	11.6	11.6	15.7
36 077	36580	6	Otsego	2 594	61 128	858	23.6	93.1	2.4	0.6	1.9	3.4	4.2	12.9	17.7	9.4	9.7	13.8
36 079	35620	1	Putnam	597	99 487	591	166.6	82.6	2.9	0.4	2.8	12.6	4.7	17.3	8.3	9.8	12.8	18.3
36 081	35620	1	Queens	281	2 321 580	11	8 261.9	27.8	19.1	0.8	26.3	27.9	6.2	14.2	9.2	16.3	14.4	14.2
36 083	10580	2	Rensselaer	1 690	159 774	399	94.5	86.7	7.5	0.6	2.9	4.3	5.4	15.0	11.1	13.1	12.1	14.8
36 085	35620	1	Richmond	151	473 279	144	3 134.3	64.3	10.4	0.5	8.5	17.9	5.9	16.6	9.4	12.8	13.2	14.8
36 087	35620	1	Rockland	449	323 866	206	721.3	65.0	12.1	0.4	7.1	16.8	7.6	20.2	9.3	11.4	11.4	13.7
36 089	36300	5	St. Lawrence	6 942	111 400	541	16.0	93.6	2.7	1.5	1.5	2.1	5.5	15.2	14.7	11.7	11.2	13.7
36 091	10580	2	Saratoga	2 098	224 921	286	107.2	93.1	2.1	0.5	3.0	2.8	5.2	16.3	8.4	11.7	13.3	16.1
36 093	10580	2	Schenectady	530	155 735	410	293.8	78.7	11.5	1.0	5.5	6.4	5.8	16.3	9.6	12.6	12.2	14.8
36 095	10580	2	Schoharie	1 611	31 566	1 397	19.6	94.8	1.7	0.7	1.1	3.0	4.7	14.4	11.1	9.9	11.2	15.0
36 097	...	6	Schuyler	850	18 479	1 896	21.7	96.4	1.7	0.7	0.7	1.8	4.6	14.8	8.4	10.4	11.5	15.6
36 099	42900	6	Seneca	838	34 884	1 303	41.6	90.7	5.5	0.8	1.0	3.2	5.4	15.1	9.5	12.9	11.6	14.4
36 101	18500	4	Steuben	3 602	98 394	597	27.3	95.3	2.2	0.7	1.7	1.5	5.6	16.8	8.2	11.3	11.7	14.8
36 103	35620	1	Suffolk	2 362	1 502 968	24	636.3	71.1	7.7	0.5	4.3	17.7	5.4	17.2	9.2	11.2	12.9	16.4
36 105	...	4	Sullivan	2 507	75 943	724	30.3	75.2	9.3	0.8	2.1	14.4	5.6	16.0	8.8	11.4	11.6	15.8
36 107	13780	2	Tioga	1 343	49 870	982	37.1	96.5	1.2	0.6	1.1	1.6	5.3	17.1	7.7	10.6	11.3	16.1
36 109	27060	3	Tompkins	1 229	104 691	565	85.2	81.3	5.0	0.8	11.2	4.6	4.2	11.4	27.2	13.2	9.9	10.9
36 111	28740	3	Ulster	2 912	180 445	356	62.0	82.5	6.9	0.8	2.6	9.5	4.6	14.3	10.0	11.4	12.2	15.9
36 113	24020	3	Warren	2 245	64 973	812	28.9	95.7	1.6	0.7	1.2	2.1	4.8	14.5	8.0	10.8	11.6	15.8
36 115	24020	3	Washington	2 153	62 372	840	29.0	93.9	3.4	0.6	0.8	2.4	5.0	15.0	8.7	11.7	12.5	15.7
36 117	40380	1	Wayne	1 564	92 051	631	58.9	92.2	3.9	0.6	1.0	4.0	5.6	16.8	8.2	10.7	11.9	16.2
36 119	35620	1	Westchester	1 115	972 634	47	872.3	56.9	14.3	0.4	6.6	23.3	5.7	17.4	8.7	11.4	13.2	15.3
36 121	...	6	Wyoming	1 535	41 188	1 145	26.8	90.5	5.9	0.6	0.7	3.1	4.9	14.5	8.4	13.7	13.2	16.2
36 123	40380	6	Yates	876	25 208	1 601	28.8	96.4	1.4	0.4	0.7	2.0	6.2	17.1	11.4	9.8	9.6	13.4
37 000	...	X	NORTH CAROLINA	125 920	9 943 964	X	79.0	65.9	22.3	1.7	3.0	8.9	6.2	17.0	10.0	12.9	13.3	13.9
37 001	15500	3	Alamance	1 098	155 792	409	141.9	67.5	19.7	0.8	1.8	11.8	5.8	17.1	10.3	11.6	12.9	14.3
37 003	25860	2	Alexander	673	37 392	1 240	55.6	88.6	6.4	0.6	1.3	4.3	5.1	16.4	7.7	11.1	13.4	15.2
37 005	...	9	Alleghany	609	10 879	2 368	17.9	87.9	1.8	0.6	0.8	9.9	4.2	14.3	7.3	8.8	11.3	14.4
37 007	...	1	Anson	1 376	25 765	1 570	18.7	46.5	48.9	0.9	1.3	3.5	5.1	15.7	9.4	13.2	13.1	14.3
37 009	...	9	Ashe	1 104	27 126	1 529	24.6	93.5	1.1	0.6	0.6	5.0	4.8	13.9	6.8	10.0	11.7	14.2
37 011	...	8	Avery	640	17 773	1 931	27.8	90.1	4.5	0.7	0.7	4.7	3.9	12.2	9.7	12.5	13.8	14.5
37 013	47820	6	Beaufort	2 142	47 585	1 024	22.2	66.8	25.4	0.6	0.6	7.6	5.5	15.7	7.4	10.0	11.5	13.4
37 015	...	9	Bertie	1 811	20 106	1 832	11.1	35.8	61.8	0.9	0.8	1.7	4.6	14.6	8.7	11.6	11.0	14.6
37 017	...	6	Bladen	2 264	34 657	1 313	15.3	55.8	34.9	2.7	0.5	7.4	5.2	16.7	8.4	10.6	12.0	13.7
37 019	34820	2	Brunswick	2 194	118 836	518	54.2	82.7	11.9	1.3	1.0	4.8	4.6	13.0	6.1	9.7	10.8	12.4
37 021	11700	2	Buncombe	1 701	250 539	264	147.3	85.6	7.2	1.0	1.7	6.3	5.3	14.4	8.5	13.6	13.2	13.5
37 023	25860	2	Burke	1 313	89 486	643	68.2	83.6	7.3	0.7	4.1	5.7	5.0	15.4	9.6	10.8	12.3	15.3
37 025	16740	1	Cabarrus	937	192 103	337	205.0	71.4	16.9	0.7	2.9	9.8	6.5	20.0	8.2	11.9	15.2	14.7
37 027	25860	2	Caldwell	1 221	81 484	683	66.7	89.3	5.6	0.6	0.8	4.9	5.1	16.3	8.3	10.3	13.4	15.3
37 029	21020	8	Camden	623	10 331	2 411	16.6	81.9	13.9	1.1	2.8	2.5	4.5	19.6	7.6	10.5	13.7	16.4
37 031	33980	4	Carteret	1 311	68 811	775	52.5	88.1	6.9	1.1	1.7	4.0	4.5	14.1	7.3	11.0	11.5	14.4
37 033	...	8	Caswell	1 101	23 082	1 679	21.0	62.7	34.0	0.9	0.6	3.3	4.8	14.5	8.0	10.7	12.0	15.4
37 035	25860	2	Catawba	1 033	154 534	415	149.6	78.6	9.5	0.6	4.2	8.7	5.8	17.3	8.6	11.2	13.3	14.8
37 037	20500	2	Chatham	1 767	68 698	777	38.9	72.6	13.4	0.7	1.7	12.9	5.0	15.6	6.3	9.1	12.2	14.1
37 039	...	9	Cherokee	1 180	27 141	1 528	23.0	93.7	2.0	2.9	0.9	2.8	4.5	14.0	6.5	8.7	10.7	13.2

1. CBSA = Core Based Statistical Area. See Appendix A for explanation. See Appendix B for list of metropolitan areas with component counties. 2. County type code from the Economic Research Service of USDA Rural-Urban Continuum Codes. See Appendix A for definition. 3. Dry land or land partially or temporarily covered by water. 4. May be of any race.

STATE County	Population, 2013 (cont.) Age (percent) (cont.) 55 to 64 years	65 to 74 years	75 years and over	Percent female	Population change and components of change, 2000–2014 Total persons 2000	2010	Percent change 2000–2010	2010–2014	Components of change, 2010–2014 Births	Deaths	Net migration	Households, 2009–2013 Number	Persons per house-hold	Percent Family house-holds	Female family house-holder[1]	One per-son
	16	17	18	19	20	21	22	23	24	25	26	27	28	29	30	31
NEW YORK—Cont'd																
Genesee	14.1	8.9	7.9	50.3	60 370	60 079	-0.5	-1.5	2 593	2 604	-866	23 884	2.46	66.8	10.8	26.8
Greene	15.2	11.3	8.1	47.8	48 195	49 221	2.1	-2.5	1 809	2 160	-907	18 365	2.47	64.2	10.2	29.9
Hamilton	20.9	15.5	10.3	49.7	5 379	4 836	-10.1	-2.5	153	243	-22	1 854	2.54	64.9	6.2	27.8
Herkimer	14.5	9.8	8.6	50.8	64 427	64 519	0.1	-1.2	2 760	2 800	-736	26 815	2.35	65.2	11.8	29.2
Jefferson	10.0	6.7	5.2	47.8	111 738	116 229	4.0	2.5	9 288	3 810	-2 798	45 011	2.50	68.1	12.6	25.4
Kings	10.9	6.6	5.4	52.6	2 465 326	2 504 700	1.6	4.7	180 295	68 321	6 688	916 025	2.73	63.7	20.2	28.7
Lewis	14.1	8.7	7.5	49.4	26 944	27 087	0.5	0.5	1 433	1 078	-275	10 677	2.51	70.3	9.0	24.1
Livingston	13.8	8.5	6.8	49.8	64 328	65 393	1.7	-1.0	2 235	2 210	-648	24 092	2.44	66.0	10.5	26.4
Madison	14.2	8.8	6.6	50.9	69 441	73 442	5.8	-1.5	2 962	2 561	-1 454	26 565	2.54	66.8	10.3	26.7
Monroe	13.0	8.1	6.9	51.7	735 343	744 344	1.2	0.7	35 648	27 360	-2 473	297 040	2.42	61.4	14.1	31.4
Montgomery	14.1	8.8	8.5	50.9	49 708	50 219	1.0	-0.9	2 439	2 377	-489	19 703	2.49	63.9	12.8	30.6
Nassau	13.6	8.3	7.8	51.5	1 334 544	1 339 532	0.4	1.4	59 865	46 279	7 268	441 955	2.99	76.7	12.0	19.8
New York	11.3	7.8	6.4	52.8	1 537 195	1 585 873	3.2	3.2	82 886	43 268	12 272	736 192	2.10	41.0	11.6	47.9
Niagara	14.8	9.1	7.9	51.3	219 846	216 469	-1.5	-1.4	9 124	9 849	-1 871	88 376	2.39	62.8	12.4	31.8
Oneida	13.4	8.9	8.2	50.1	235 469	234 878	-0.3	-0.9	11 155	10 524	-2 361	91 075	2.42	62.1	12.4	31.6
Onondaga	13.2	7.8	7.2	51.7	458 336	467 026	1.9	0.2	22 838	17 325	-4 016	184 855	2.43	61.6	13.8	31.4
Ontario	14.7	9.7	7.5	51.0	100 224	107 931	7.7	1.5	4 456	4 399	1 478	43 794	2.39	65.9	10.5	27.4
Orange	12.0	7.0	5.2	50.0	341 367	372 813	9.2	0.9	20 806	10 752	-6 526	125 317	2.88	71.7	12.2	23.4
Orleans	14.2	9.0	6.8	50.5	44 171	42 883	-2.9	-2.1	1 722	1 737	-890	15 725	2.51	68.4	13.3	26.7
Oswego	13.5	8.2	5.8	50.1	122 377	122 109	-0.2	-1.0	5 655	4 368	-2 396	45 325	2.57	67.5	12.1	24.7
Otsego	14.3	10.0	7.9	51.4	61 676	62 259	0.9	-1.8	2 221	2 535	-690	24 078	2.36	62.4	9.2	27.8
Putnam	14.6	8.6	5.7	50.2	95 745	99 710	4.1	-0.3	3 636	2 853	-977	34 496	2.82	76.9	10.0	19.7
Queens	12.1	7.3	6.1	51.4	2 229 379	2 230 722	0.1	4.1	129 534	60 876	24 550	778 630	2.86	67.5	16.1	26.3
Rensselaer	13.8	8.3	6.5	50.5	152 538	159 429	4.5	0.2	7 015	6 416	-166	64 242	2.39	62.3	12.7	29.0
Richmond	13.1	8.2	5.9	51.6	443 728	468 730	5.6	1.0	23 081	14 706	-3 249	164 609	2.80	73.7	14.1	23.1
Rockland	11.8	7.9	6.7	50.9	286 753	311 687	8.7	3.9	20 315	8 883	1 129	98 326	3.13	75.7	10.4	20.8
St. Lawrence	12.9	8.4	6.5	49.1	111 931	111 944	0.0	-0.5	5 252	4 348	-1 345	41 839	2.39	64.0	11.2	28.4
Saratoga	13.8	9.0	6.3	50.6	200 635	219 607	9.5	2.4	9 337	7 226	3 198	88 460	2.45	65.8	8.3	27.3
Schenectady	13.3	7.9	7.5	51.4	146 555	154 727	5.6	0.7	8 104	6 284	-750	58 059	2.59	61.2	11.9	33.4
Schoharie	15.5	10.6	7.5	50.3	31 582	32 749	3.7	-3.6	1 133	1 136	-1 136	12 820	2.40	65.7	9.3	27.6
Schuyler	15.9	10.6	8.1	49.6	19 224	18 343	-4.6	0.7	767	840	163	7 684	2.33	63.4	7.1	29.4
Seneca	14.3	9.5	7.3	47.7	33 342	35 251	5.7	-1.0	1 557	1 344	-528	13 429	2.40	62.4	10.0	30.0
Steuben	14.4	9.4	7.7	50.4	98 726	98 990	0.3	-0.6	4 699	4 093	-1 139	41 503	2.34	63.9	10.7	29.7
Suffolk	12.8	8.3	6.6	50.8	1 419 369	1 493 350	5.2	0.6	67 733	49 840	-6 907	497 347	2.95	75.3	12.1	20.4
Sullivan	14.6	9.9	6.3	48.7	73 966	77 547	4.8	-2.1	3 852	3 069	-2 236	29 531	2.46	62.6	12.7	30.5
Tioga	14.5	9.6	7.8	50.4	51 784	51 125	-1.3	-2.5	2 079	1 870	-1 419	20 202	2.49	69.9	9.9	25.8
Tompkins	11.3	6.8	5.1	50.7	96 501	101 564	5.2	3.0	3 883	2 683	1 913	38 409	2.31	52.6	7.9	32.3
Ulster	14.8	9.5	7.3	50.3	177 749	182 493	2.7	-1.1	6 885	6 779	-2 030	69 862	2.44	64.2	11.4	28.8
Warren	15.4	10.9	8.4	51.1	63 303	65 707	3.8	-1.1	2 515	2 739	-481	28 081	2.29	64.6	11.3	28.8
Washington	14.3	9.5	7.6	48.4	61 042	63 216	3.6	-1.3	2 644	2 645	-762	24 499	2.44	68.9	11.8	25.4
Wayne	14.6	9.3	6.7	50.4	93 765	93 772	0.0	-1.8	4 199	3 512	-2 292	36 399	2.51	69.7	11.0	24.6
Westchester	12.7	8.0	7.5	51.7	923 459	949 113	2.8	2.5	45 249	29 703	8 896	343 561	2.71	69.3	13.2	26.9
Wyoming	14.2	8.9	6.1	45.5	43 424	42 155	-2.9	-2.3	1 627	1 463	-1 097	15 624	2.43	67.3	9.7	27.6
Yates	14.7	10.0	7.8	51.3	24 621	25 348	3.0	-0.6	1 373	1 048	-451	9 602	2.50	70.8	10.6	23.8
NORTH CAROLINA	12.4	8.4	5.9	51.3	8 049 313	9 535 483	18.5	4.3	511 558	345 465	233 880	3 715 565	2.53	66.6	13.6	27.8
Alamance	12.4	8.6	7.1	52.2	130 800	151 131	15.5	3.0	7 452	6 442	3 445	60 139	2.46	67.5	14.1	28.3
Alexander	13.6	10.8	6.8	49.3	33 603	37 198	10.7	0.5	1 550	1 437	-92	14 101	2.57	69.1	9.9	27.2
Alleghany	16.1	13.6	10.0	50.4	10 677	11 155	4.5	-2.5	381	518	-136	4 793	2.26	70.1	8.8	25.6
Anson	13.6	9.0	6.6	48.2	25 275	26 948	6.6	-4.4	1 129	1 233	-1 090	9 686	2.52	67.6	19.4	28.4
Ashe	15.6	13.3	9.7	50.9	24 384	27 281	11.9	-0.6	1 068	1 395	114	11 839	2.26	69.3	10.9	25.2
Avery	13.7	11.3	8.5	45.5	17 167	17 797	3.7	-0.1	645	802	146	7 122	2.17	66.2	8.8	27.5
Beaufort	15.5	12.7	8.2	51.9	44 958	47 759	6.2	-0.4	2 143	2 324	-19	19 266	2.44	68.0	14.1	29.4
Bertie	15.4	10.4	9.0	50.1	19 773	21 282	7.6	-5.6	800	1 031	-1 013	7 629	2.58	65.4	18.3	31.3
Bladen	15.3	10.8	7.3	51.9	32 278	35 190	9.0	-1.5	1 530	1 666	-414	14 256	2.40	64.7	17.9	31.8
Brunswick	17.6	17.5	8.1	51.3	73 143	107 431	46.9	10.6	4 406	5 003	11 545	47 600	2.30	70.5	11.0	25.3
Buncombe	14.1	9.9	7.6	51.9	206 330	238 318	15.5	5.1	11 113	10 168	10 721	100 838	2.33	59.8	10.7	32.4
Burke	13.9	10.2	7.6	50.0	89 148	90 912	2.0	-1.6	3 660	4 245	-778	34 664	2.53	67.0	13.1	28.4
Cabarrus	11.2	7.3	4.9	51.2	131 063	178 011	35.8	7.8	9 841	6 072	9 970	64 713	2.78	72.7	11.5	23.3
Caldwell	14.1	10.5	6.8	50.6	77 415	83 029	7.3	-1.9	3 414	3 742	-1 203	31 417	2.59	66.0	11.7	30.8
Camden	13.2	9.0	5.7	50.2	6 885	9 980	45.0	3.5	385	254	199	3 580	2.79	75.5	10.7	21.0
Carteret	16.2	12.7	8.3	50.6	59 383	66 469	11.9	3.5	2 693	3 159	2 762	29 158	2.27	65.1	11.9	30.4
Caswell	15.9	11.2	7.5	49.3	23 501	23 719	0.9	2.7	001	1 117	-511	8 813	2.51	71.6	15.3	25.8
Catawba	13.2	9.4	6.4	50.9	141 685	154 358	8.9	0.1	7 576	6 540	-854	58 533	2.60	68.0	11.8	26.6
Chatham	15.0	12.9	9.7	51.8	49 329	63 505	28.7	8.2	2 645	2 625	4 411	26 017	2.46	71.1	9.5	25.1
Cherokee	17.1	15.8	9.7	51.3	24 298	27 444	12.9	-1.1	926	1 476	236	10 722	2.50	69.7	10.2	27.2

1. No spouse present.

STATE County	Persons in group quarters, 2014	Daytime population, 2009–2013		Births, 2014		Deaths, 2014		Persons under 65 with no health insurance, 2013		Medicare, 2014			Serious crimes known to police,[2] 2013	
													Total	
		Number	Employ-ment/ residence ratio	Total	Rate[1]	Number	Rate[1]	Number	Percent	Eligible for Medicare	Enrolled in Medicare Advantage	Enrolled in a Medicare prescription drug plan	Number	Rate[3]
	32	33	34	35	36	37	38	39	40	41	42	43	44	45
NEW YORK—Cont'd														
Genesee	1 985	55 676	0.85	600	10.1	611	10.3	4 826	10.0	12 130	6 629	3 139	1 447	2 411
Greene	3 355	44 837	0.79	415	8.7	508	10.6	3 811	10.5	11 043	3 411	4 539	677	1 475
Hamilton	82	4 537	0.86	35	7.4	69	14.6	460	13.0	1 444	367	727	62	1 300
Herkimer	1 435	55 056	0.67	643	10.1	667	10.5	5 650	11.0	14 047	4 944	5 945	1 190	1 982
Jefferson	6 216	121 601	1.07	2 184	18.3	916	7.7	10 236	10.3	18 603	4 415	7 475	2 370	2 008
Kings	36 319	2 256 073	0.74	42 945	16.4	16 771	6.4	336 464	14.8	339 529	135 593	143 404	[6]	[6]
Lewis	316	23 694	0.71	346	12.7	263	9.7	2 737	12.1	4 848	1 270	2 099	330	1 208
Livingston	5 991	57 382	0.74	482	7.5	505	7.8	4 496	9.1	12 160	7 139	2 876	1 067	1 649
Madison	4 647	64 233	0.73	717	9.9	573	7.9	4 934	8.7	12 981	4 173	5 016	1 146	1 589
Monroe	26 397	780 185	1.10	8 347	11.1	6 435	8.6	57 795	9.4	141 871	90 003	29 952	23 035	3 072
Montgomery	881	48 313	0.92	570	11.5	545	10.9	4 713	11.5	11 610	4 372	5 351	1 125	2 255
Nassau	21 328	1 269 404	0.88	14 060	10.3	10 952	8.1	115 073	10.3	244 084	57 590	124 620	18 468	1 364
New York	66 721	3 108 190	2.79	19 434	11.9	10 929	6.7	146 866	10.9	262 577	88 854	111 536	[6]195 910	[6]2 333
Niagara	4 254	191 706	0.75	2 114	9.9	2 324	10.9	17 892	10.2	46 455	24 218	13 055	6 582	3 063
Oneida	12 930	242 574	1.08	2 576	11.1	2 445	10.5	18 491	10.1	49 778	16 303	19 855	5 937	2 544
Onondaga	17 046	498 648	1.15	5 364	11.5	4 083	8.7	40 503	10.5	87 085	29 080	31 955	13 976	2 991
Ontario	3 376	109 420	1.02	1 066	9.7	1 012	9.2	7 719	8.8	22 810	13 153	5 036	2 082	1 952
Orange	11 481	347 783	0.85	4 968	13.2	2 622	7.0	33 616	10.5	56 659	9 029	31 890	8 531	2 273
Orleans	2 730	38 937	0.78	388	9.2	404	9.6	3 697	11.0	8 176	4 306	2 579	701	1 706
Oswego	4 969	107 491	0.72	1 313	10.9	1 037	8.6	10 157	10.2	23 087	7 572	9 795	2 659	2 185
Otsego	5 496	62 629	1.02	513	8.4	609	10.0	5 628	12.2	13 133	2 598	6 868	824	1 337
Putnam	2 582	78 671	0.57	828	8.3	680	6.8	7 566	9.1	16 714	2 872	9 734	759	777
Queens	27 712	1 906 794	0.67	30 482	13.1	15 057	6.5	380 815	19.2	325 398	138 977	122 158	[6]	[6]
Rensselaer	5 919	139 745	0.75	1 616	10.1	1 522	9.5	11 082	8.4	29 427	11 673	10 422	4 128	2 578
Richmond	7 128	393 293	0.62	5 331	11.3	3 761	7.9	40 931	10.2	80 342	31 797	29 834	[6]	[6]
Rockland	7 082	288 808	0.81	5 127	15.8	2 255	7.0	30 357	11.3	53 126	9 241	30 316	3 771	1 179
St. Lawrence	11 089	109 786	0.95	1 213	10.9	1 014	9.1	10 229	12.1	22 036	4 392	10 048	1 957	1 830
Saratoga	3 905	192 998	0.75	2 199	9.8	1 807	8.0	13 478	7.2	41 472	16 985	14 722	3 073	1 377
Schenectady	4 521	148 017	0.91	1 996	12.8	1 470	9.4	12 313	9.6	29 587	12 593	11 025	5 374	3 459
Schoharie	1 351	28 775	0.75	251	8.0	277	8.8	2 662	10.7	6 105	1 600	3 115	536	1 678
Schuyler	367	16 068	0.71	194	10.5	179	9.7	1 585	10.8	4 327	1 344	1 801	159	855
Seneca	2 856	32 903	0.84	343	9.8	312	8.9	2 767	10.3	7 073	2 971	2 616	785	2 736
Steuben	1 741	98 007	0.98	1 107	11.3	973	9.9	9 176	11.3	20 847	6 449	7 888	1 524	1 536
Suffolk	29 185	1 404 752	0.87	15 574	10.4	12 165	8.1	134 882	10.7	266 169	55 490	143 609	26 174	1 744
Sullivan	3 831	73 272	0.88	968	12.7	739	9.7	8 973	14.4	15 718	1 525	9 770	1 715	2 237
Tioga	515	42 956	0.67	517	10.4	429	8.6	3 864	9.4	10 526	3 654	4 824	635	1 261
Tompkins	13 269	113 169	1.23	948	9.1	599	5.7	9 151	11.6	14 605	2 994	6 042	NA	NA
Ulster	11 769	166 130	0.81	1 562	8.7	1 637	9.1	18 032	12.5	36 801	8 223	18 380	3 574	1 966
Warren	704	71 650	1.19	578	8.9	640	9.9	5 244	10.0	15 942	5 996	5 753	1 291	1 969
Washington	3 157	53 503	0.65	591	9.5	663	10.6	5 403	10.9	12 481	4 554	4 709	881	1 401
Wayne	1 294	80 712	0.71	980	10.6	799	8.7	7 779	10.1	20 129	11 240	5 521	1 818	1 959
Westchester	28 557	938 461	0.96	10 470	10.8	7 162	7.4	94 774	11.9	162 590	37 952	83 398	13 906	1 466
Wyoming	3 827	38 962	0.84	370	9.0	322	7.8	3 018	9.6	7 928	4 214	2 269	507	1 211
Yates	1 285	22 855	0.79	339	13.4	250	9.9	2 703	13.8	5 449	2 755	1 537	413	1 628
NORTH CAROLINA	253 987	9 653 754	1.00	120 099	12.1	83 750	8.4	1 488 551	18.1	1 731 222	496 213	781 879	341 749	3 470
Alamance	4 293	144 323	0.88	1 759	11.3	1 524	9.8	24 672	19.5	29 366	14 904	9 620	5 562	3 583
Alexander	1 282	31 629	0.66	371	9.9	345	9.2	5 111	17.4	7 989	2 053	3 724	663	1 800
Alleghany	110	10 697	0.92	88	8.1	121	11.1	2 087	25.1	3 087	974	1 445	NA	NA
Anson	2 335	25 344	0.87	252	9.8	275	10.7	3 771	19.0	5 143	905	2 937	1 041	4 748
Ashe	368	25 063	0.82	245	9.0	326	12.0	4 885	23.4	6 919	1 844	3 629	401	1 478
Avery	2 489	18 662	1.14	148	8.3	188	10.6	2 949	24.6	3 866	943	1 953	242	1 371
Beaufort	512	47 815	1.01	503	10.6	564	11.9	7 289	19.5	12 363	1 659	7 042	1 464	3 167
Bertie	1 340	20 057	0.89	175	8.7	257	12.8	2 606	17.0	5 052	422	3 483	497	2 421
Bladen	500	35 014	1.00	357	10.3	416	12.0	5 722	20.3	7 419	1 658	4 004	931	2 665
Brunswick	869	101 902	0.80	1 041	8.8	1 273	10.7	16 522	19.4	34 734	6 206	18 158	3 523	3 164
Buncombe	7 726	256 218	1.13	2 666	10.6	2 481	9.9	40 002	20.0	52 835	12 883	25 103	8 144	3 304
Burke	3 206	86 169	0.88	863	9.6	960	10.7	14 104	19.6	19 052	5 661	9 122	2 307	2 587
Cabarrus	1 409	167 419	0.82	2 319	12.1	1 451	7.6	26 594	16.4	28 556	9 007	12 255	4 219	2 258
Caldwell	965	76 077	0.80	795	9.8	875	10.7	13 150	19.5	17 543	5 935	8 260	2 641	3 227
Camden	17	7 004	0.32	91	8.8	45	4.4	1 362	15.7	1 836	169	800	66	650
Carteret	985	63 064	0.86	626	9.1	765	11.1	10 055	18.8	16 556	2 485	7 499	2 267	3 327
Caswell	1 364	18 061	0.36	213	9.2	247	10.7	3 023	17.0	5 430	2 217	2 280	495	2 139
Catawba	2 268	168 031	1.20	1 767	11.4	1 568	10.1	23 657	18.4	32 119	9 578	15 711	5 278	3 417
Chatham	778	54 442	0.63	598	8.7	667	9.7	9 853	19.3	15 307	5 543	5 933	1 425	2 129
Cherokee	440	27 093	0.98	213	7.8	324	11.9	4 458	22.1	8 259	1 871	4 011	701	2 603

1. Per 1,000 estimated resident population. 2. Data for serious crimes have not been adjusted for underreporting; this may affect comparability between geographic areas and over time.
3. Per 100,000 population estimated by the FBI. 6. Bronx, Kings, Queens, and Richmond counties are included with New York county.

STATE County	Serious crimes known to police, 2013 (cont.)[1] Rate[2] Violent	Rate[2] Property	Education: School enrollment and attainment, 2009–2013 Enrollment[3] Total	Enrollment[3] Percent private	Attainment[4] (percent) High school graduate or less	Attainment[4] (percent) Bachelor's degree or more	Local government expenditures,[5] 2012–2013 Total current spending (mil dol)	Local government expenditures,[5] 2012–2013 Current spending per student (dollars)	Money income, 2009–2013 Per capita income[6] (dollars)	Households Median income (dollars)	Households Mean income (dollars)	Households Percent with income of $200,000 or more	Income and poverty, 2013 Median household income (dollars)	Percent below poverty level All persons	Percent below poverty level Children under 18 years	Percent below poverty level Children 5 to 17 years in families
	46	47	48	49	50	51	52	53	54	55	56	57	58	59	60	61
NEW YORK—Cont'd																
Genesee	173	2 238	13 885	11.2	46.5	20.8	144.5	16 528	25 403	49 922	62 861	1.6	42 641	14.7	19.3	19.2
Greene	124	1 351	8 555	12.5	51.0	20.1	126.3	19 718	25 700	49 655	65 010	2.6	50 190	13.9	21.6	19.4
Hamilton	84	1 216	850	6.9	44.8	24.2	17.9	35 563	28 265	51 522	64 240	2.9	45 737	12.1	21.8	18.9
Herkimer	210	1 772	15 515	11.2	46.8	20.5	158.8	16 410	23 418	45 047	55 883	1.5	42 460	16.4	25.4	22.2
Jefferson	116	1 892	29 273	12.4	46.8	20.0	276.6	14 686	23 078	46 484	58 157	1.7	46 510	15.7	22.6	22.8
Kings	(7)	(7)	670 584	28.8	48.8	30.6	(7)	(7)	25 289	46 085	67 629	4.4	47 067	23.3	33.3	33.5
Lewis	88	1 121	6 097	12.7	59.1	13.6	72.2	17 019	22 942	46 840	57 419	1.2	45 926	14.8	22.9	21.6
Livingston	85	1 564	18 291	13.1	44.9	24.4	135.5	16 561	23 978	53 518	63 155	1.6	51 901	15.0	17.7	15.1
Madison	75	1 514	20 005	22.5	43.6	25.9	166.4	16 154	25 230	53 589	66 249	2.7	51 057	13.9	19.3	16.8
Monroe	358	2 715	204 350	25.2	35.4	35.8	1 969.5	18 433	28 732	52 394	70 190	3.8	51 722	15.5	22.7	22.2
Montgomery	96	2 158	11 690	14.0	53.3	16.0	117.7	15 775	23 417	44 156	57 380	1.4	43 880	17.3	28.5	26.9
Nassau	154	1 210	355 676	26.4	34.4	41.5	5 005.6	24 744	42 400	97 690	126 127	15.9	95 395	6.5	9.1	8.5
New York	(7)625	(7)1 708	335 847	45.6	26.8	58.9	(7)22 278.7	(7)22 518	62 498	69 659	130 490	17.4	71 443	19.0	26.6	28.6
Niagara	370	2 692	51 092	17.0	46.0	22.2	480.0	16 130	25 991	47 955	61 729	1.9	46 752	13.8	19.5	17.9
Oneida	228	2 316	57 560	15.2	46.0	22.4	544.8	16 112	25 103	48 729	62 437	2.5	44 031	17.6	25.6	23.8
Onondaga	319	2 672	129 293	26.5	37.0	33.1	1 178.4	16 765	28 746	54 242	70 478	3.7	52 055	15.3	21.4	20.0
Ontario	108	1 844	27 207	21.5	36.7	31.7	270.6	16 254	29 904	56 479	73 446	3.8	57 846	10.0	13.3	11.8
Orange	230	2 043	108 764	21.6	41.5	28.7	1 229.3	20 090	30 583	70 458	88 290	6.5	68 249	13.6	21.2	20.6
Orleans	134	1 572	9 586	9.7	54.9	16.4	98.3	15 265	22 255	48 502	58 931	1.3	43 876	15.7	24.7	21.1
Oswego	128	2 057	33 265	8.6	54.5	17.2	365.5	17 541	23 126	48 051	60 258	1.8	46 281	18.6	27.7	24.1
Otsego	102	1 235	17 792	16.3	44.5	26.8	139.5	18 399	24 165	47 765	60 649	2.5	47 689	17.1	21.6	19.8
Putnam	50	727	26 354	19.4	33.9	38.4	363.1	23 644	40 309	95 117	114 442	12.7	92 014	5.8	6.7	6.0
Queens	(7)	(7)	550 238	22.3	47.1	30.0	(7)	(7)	26 495	57 001	73 521	4.2	56 307	15.4	21.6	22.1
Rensselaer	293	2 285	41 980	29.0	39.6	28.6	358.4	17 715	29 987	59 432	73 410	3.5	56 643	14.0	20.7	19.6
Richmond	(7)	(7)	122 648	24.7	44.2	29.7	(7)	(7)	31 823	72 569	89 552	6.9	68 621	13.1	19.0	18.4
Rockland	123	1 056	92 782	41.0	36.4	40.4	950.9	23 595	34 591	84 951	108 126	12.3	80 132	14.8	24.6	21.9
St. Lawrence	105	1 725	31 763	24.3	49.5	20.4	275.2	17 586	22 198	43 647	57 017	1.7	43 556	21.4	29.7	27.3
Saratoga	77	1 300	54 022	19.8	32.8	37.1	472.9	15 181	35 176	69 826	86 514	5.6	69 917	7.9	9.7	8.9
Schenectady	434	3 025	38 463	17.3	40.6	29.0	418.3	16 536	28 319	56 061	70 104	3.2	53 978	14.2	23.8	23.3
Schoharie	85	1 593	7 712	7.3	50.3	19.3	88.4	19 843	26 584	53 245	65 597	2.6	49 307	13.7	18.8	17.4
Schuyler	75	779	3 908	12.5	50.1	16.9	40.4	18 409	24 173	46 976	57 460	1.1	44 080	17.9	25.8	22.0
Seneca	213	2 523	7 475	20.0	49.4	19.2	76.8	18 626	23 115	47 618	58 883	1.5	45 265	13.1	21.7	20.8
Steuben	123	1 413	22 704	11.3	47.8	20.8	266.0	17 309	25 371	47 476	60 649	2.0	46 540	15.6	24.7	21.9
Suffolk	127	1 617	391 343	15.1	40.1	32.9	5 465.5	21 944	36 945	87 763	108 316	10.8	84 940	7.5	10.1	8.8
Sullivan	223	2 014	17 572	12.9	49.2	20.9	238.8	24 259	24 963	48 089	62 802	2.8	46 928	19.4	28.3	27.4
Tioga	52	1 210	12 054	11.9	45.7	24.1	127.6	16 083	27 230	55 726	67 843	2.4	51 026	11.7	18.0	16.4
Tompkins	NA	NA	42 651	49.3	27.0	49.3	209.0	19 154	27 418	51 393	71 456	4.8	49 457	18.8	17.9	16.8
Ulster	162	1 804	43 820	13.3	40.7	29.9	527.3	21 935	30 442	58 590	76 828	4.8	56 933	12.7	17.4	15.6
Warren	81	1 888	14 033	14.1	43.1	28.0	168.1	17 987	30 351	55 904	70 421	3.2	52 552	11.3	18.9	17.7
Washington	114	1 286	13 655	10.9	55.7	18.3	152.4	16 887	24 168	52 361	61 970	1.6	48 522	15.1	21.7	20.1
Wayne	157	1 802	21 838	13.6	47.4	20.9	260.6	17 820	25 327	52 601	63 443	1.5	50 603	11.4	17.7	16.7
Westchester	229	1 237	254 646	25.4	33.9	45.4	3 463.9	23 561	47 984	81 946	130 829	16.9	83 094	9.9	13.4	13.0
Wyoming	98	1 113	8 678	11.2	53.5	14.6	72.8	16 749	22 700	51 100	59 649	0.8	51 676	11.8	16.9	15.7
Yates	55	1 572	6 086	37.0	50.3	23.2	41.7	17 728	24 457	49 335	63 666	3.0	45 509	16.5	27.3	25.2
NORTH CAROLINA	342	3 128	2 536 304	14.4	42.1	27.3	12 383.1	8 390	25 284	46 334	63 707	3.3	45 946	17.8	25.1	23.6
Alamance	382	3 201	39 864	18.9	46.6	21.7	181.0	7 914	23 166	43 043	57 240	2.3	43 001	19.8	27.1	25.3
Alexander	125	1 675	8 384	13.1	60.1	11.7	45.1	8 382	20 440	40 637	51 821	1.1	46 064	14.0	22.9	21.0
Alleghany	NA	NA	2 192	6.7	53.6	18.3	16.1	10 700	19 510	35 170	44 754	0.4	37 086	21.2	32.6	28.5
Anson	593	4 155	5 885	6.3	64.4	10.2	38.8	10 618	16 752	33 870	44 526	1.7	33 443	28.8	37.9	35.4
Ashe	74	1 405	5 438	7.3	49.8	19.5	30.8	9 299	20 838	35 951	47 902	1.3	35 155	22.4	33.2	28.8
Avery	147	1 223	3 787	23.4	48.4	20.4	22.9	10 200	21 598	36 969	53 710	3.5	34 933	20.4	31.6	28.8
Beaufort	335	2 831	10 991	7.9	51.0	18.3	62.0	8 545	21 636	40 429	51 449	1.0	39 043	20.5	32.6	31.2
Bertie	180	2 241	4 415	11.6	64.6	10.6	27.8	9 742	17 096	30 768	43 889	0.6	31 610	26.6	36.9	33.7
Bladen	177	2 488	8 907	7.8	58.0	10.5	49.6	9 486	19 154	30 164	45 090	1.3	33 971	27.1	37.4	35.9
Brunswick	202	2 962	20 485	12.6	41.3	25.1	111.2	8 939	26 839	46 438	61 517	2.2	47 799	16.1	28.1	25.6
Buncombe	240	3 064	55 472	18.2	36.5	33.8	266.7	8 885	26 159	44 713	60 714	2.8	45 738	15.7	22.0	21.3
Burke	190	2 397	20 919	8.0	53.6	16.6	112.8	8 454	19 701	37 263	49 263	1.1	36 150	20.6	31.1	27.6
Cabarrus	119	2 138	50 152	12.6	41.2	25.1	281.4	7 832	25 247	53 551	68 882	3.2	55 046	12.1	17.0	14.8
Caldwell	148	3 079	19 771	9.5	56.9	12.5	103.1	8 323	19 228	34 357	47 430	1.6	34 811	18.3	25.4	22.5
Camden	39	610	2 808	10.2	38.9	18.8	16.8	8 686	25 620	56 607	68 190	1.5	60 537	9.5	13.9	11.7
Carteret	282	3 045	14 794	9.6	39.8	23.9	76.0	8 729	27 496	46 534	61 663	2.5	46 227	15.2	24.1	23.0
Caswell	194	1 945	5 205	14.9	61.7	9.0	26.4	9 186	17 975	35 315	44 954	1.0	37 122	25.5	33.2	30.6
Catawba	267	3 150	37 635	13.4	47.8	21.0	201.7	8 157	23 232	44 332	59 226	2.3	43 777	16.5	24.9	23.8
Chatham	184	1 945	14 023	14.2	38.1	36.4	78.2	9 253	31 175	57 091	76 475	5.4	56 981	15.6	21.9	20.6
Cherokee	160	2 444	5 676	11.7	50.3	16.7	32.8	9 237	18 340	34 432	43 248	0.3	34 476	22.5	34.3	31.8

1. Data for serious crimes have not been adjusted for underreporting; this may affect comparability between geographic areas and over time. 2. Per 100,000 population estimated by the FBI.
3. All persons 3 years old and over enrolled in nursery school through college. 4. Persons 25 years old and over. 5. Elementary and secondary education expenditures.
6. Based on population estimated by the American Community Survey, 2009–2013. 7. Bronx, Kings, Queens, and Richmond counties are included with New York county.

STATE County	Personal income, 2013										Earnings, 2013		
			Per capita[1]			Supplements to wages and salaries; employer contributions (mil dol)						Contributions for government social insurance (mil dol)	
	Total (mil dol)	Percent change, 2012–2013	Dollars	Rank	Wages and salaries (mil dol)	Pension and insurance	Government social insurance	Proprietors' income (mil dol)	Dividends, interest, and rent (mil dol)	Personal transfer receipts (mil dol)	Total (mil dol)	From employee and self-employed	From employer
	62	63	64	65	66	67	68	69	70	71	72	73	74
NEW YORK—Cont'd													
Genesee	2 227	1.1	37 465	1 513	867	250	75	204	380	499	1 396	73	75
Greene	2 034	1.2	41 978	941	580	193	49	107	401	464	929	54	49
Hamilton	228	1.9	47 868	492	53	23	5	10	70	51	91	6	5
Herkimer	2 366	0.6	36 871	1 615	609	186	52	142	400	617	988	61	52
Jefferson	5 374	-0.8	44 968	690	2 669	829	253	242	1 093	865	3 993	178	253
Kings	109 663	1.1	42 306	907	22 895	4 070	1 949	5 599	15 148	26 241	34 514	2 050	1 949
Lewis	947	0.8	34 873	1 921	239	91	20	106	174	201	456	23	20
Livingston	2 337	0.4	36 117	1 727	750	274	63	196	404	503	1 282	68	63
Madison	2 724	0.6	37 628	1 485	822	224	70	186	504	545	1 302	72	70
Monroe	36 103	1.3	48 162	469	18 233	3 732	1 495	3 143	7 602	6 743	26 603	1 420	1 495
Montgomery	1 762	1.9	35 310	1 855	704	171	62	63	314	528	1 000	60	62
Nassau	98 096	0.4	72 549	39	34 729	6 608	2 768	9 215	22 896	11 628	53 320	2 776	2 768
New York	197 792	1.3	121 632	1	258 193	36 151	15 413	44 998	45 686	17 943	354 755	17 737	15 413
Niagara	8 392	1.2	39 169	1 270	2 824	735	242	292	1 395	2 016	4 092	245	242
Oneida	9 377	1.0	40 145	1 159	4 310	1 219	355	552	1 804	2 263	6 435	350	355
Onondaga	21 121	0.8	45 093	682	11 592	2 623	947	1 485	3 854	4 092	16 647	872	947
Ontario	5 098	1.0	46 723	569	2 274	503	182	405	975	912	3 364	181	182
Orange	16 446	0.7	43 788	776	6 009	1 551	507	830	2 743	2 970	8 897	465	507
Orleans	1 414	1.1	33 473	2 178	518	180	43	73	221	350	814	44	43
Oswego	4 238	0.4	34 976	1 899	1 343	434	109	153	600	1 054	2 040	117	109
Otsego	2 293	0.9	37 181	1 552	944	262	78	78	512	520	1 362	77	78
Putnam	5 875	0.2	58 955	121	1 268	295	104	244	1 018	711	1 912	108	104
Queens	103 251	2.1	44 966	691	26 515	4 479	2 245	4 801	15 977	23 295	38 039	2 218	2 245
Rensselaer	7 061	2.0	44 152	745	2 363	600	196	314	1 170	1 344	3 473	194	196
Richmond	24 259	0.6	51 328	320	4 339	761	370	920	3 552	5 330	6 391	399	370
Rockland	18 182	0.9	56 657	169	6 434	1 431	508	1 225	3 451	2 836	9 600	508	508
St. Lawrence	3 660	1.3	32 692	2 306	1 434	458	121	208	644	974	2 221	122	121
Saratoga	11 614	2.2	51 878	301	3 871	827	320	742	2 164	1 592	5 760	313	320
Schenectady	7 223	1.8	46 502	588	3 483	715	277	267	1 507	1 377	4 742	263	277
Schoharie	1 302	2.8	40 894	1 065	314	102	26	52	196	248	495	29	26
Schuyler	713	0.2	38 630	1 347	174	53	15	65	117	172	307	18	15
Seneca	1 296	0.1	36 606	1 652	489	144	40	95	226	293	767	42	40
Steuben	3 904	1.6	39 572	1 220	1 944	419	150	232	637	870	2 745	151	150
Suffolk	85 395	0.3	56 940	160	35 472	7 459	2 784	4 880	16 956	12 864	50 595	2 685	2 784
Sullivan	3 158	0.6	41 197	1 024	956	293	81	160	613	812	1 490	85	81
Tioga	2 020	0.1	40 213	1 148	623	146	50	95	340	421	914	54	50
Tompkins	4 102	0.5	39 592	1 218	2 424	474	209	236	991	609	3 343	172	209
Ulster	8 059	0.7	44 527	728	2 425	715	202	370	1 781	1 664	3 712	208	202
Warren	2 899	1.0	44 364	735	1 484	330	125	189	686	619	2 128	118	125
Washington	2 390	1.0	37 888	1 448	678	227	57	90	391	524	1 052	60	57
Wayne	3 641	0.7	39 372	1 244	1 193	389	100	137	553	815	1 820	103	100
Westchester	77 855	0.6	80 363	22	28 499	5 001	2 078	6 141	19 389	8 274	41 719	2 174	2 078
Wyoming	1 447	1.2	34 849	1 922	557	185	47	88	231	309	878	45	47
Yates	906	1.4	35 997	1 747	230	67	20	39	215	212	356	21	20
NORTH CAROLINA	380 954	1.4	38 683	X	192 772	30 963	15 008	35 381	65 159	74 869	274 124	16 532	15 008
Alamance	5 224	0.8	33 840	2 110	2 298	350	183	443	896	1 212	3 275	214	183
Alexander	1 244	2.0	33 684	2 146	290	55	25	180	163	296	549	36	25
Alleghany	362	2.0	33 058	2 243	99	20	8	44	79	113	171	12	8
Anson	702	0.8	26 821	2 984	258	57	20	84	96	251	420	26	20
Ashe	832	0.8	30 642	2 608	250	45	20	75	168	262	390	29	20
Avery	535	1.9	30 193	2 656	209	39	18	63	121	148	329	21	18
Beaufort	1 635	-1.0	34 455	1 998	590	109	46	142	316	505	887	59	46
Bertie	656	0.5	32 255	2 371	199	43	15	85	82	234	343	21	15
Bladen	1 111	0.5	31 879	2 425	437	84	34	139	127	362	695	42	34
Brunswick	4 072	2.8	35 319	1 853	1 121	199	89	321	875	1 198	1 730	130	89
Buncombe	9 283	1.6	37 443	1 516	4 784	777	378	798	2 183	2 050	6 737	424	378
Burke	2 968	0.3	33 030	2 248	1 077	212	88	419	447	777	1 796	117	88
Cabarrus	7 302	3.1	39 000	1 302	2 614	423	204	723	888	1 202	3 964	245	204
Caldwell	2 379	0.5	29 012	2 805	826	148	68	142	372	722	1 184	85	68
Camden	419	-0.4	41 169	1 031	70	11	5	40	63	73	126	7	5
Carteret	2 889	1.1	42 214	916	750	140	59	288	722	643	1 237	83	59
Caswell	795	0.7	34 288	2 035	105	25	8	38	98	224	176	15	8
Catawba	5 457	1.0	35 250	1 866	3 247	520	265	294	979	1 292	4 326	273	265
Chatham	3 564	1.4	53 336	258	524	90	42	464	796	535	1 121	76	42
Cherokee	754	1.0	27 697	2 916	251	47	20	55	139	309	373	29	20

1. Based on the resident population estimated as of July 1 of the year shown.

STATE County	Earnings, 2013 (cont.) — Percent by selected industries: Farm	Mining	Construction	Manu-facturing	Infor-mation: professional, scientific, technical services	Retail trade	Finance, insur-ance, real estate and leasing	Health care and social assistance	Govern-ment	Social Security beneficiaries, December 2013: Number	Rate[1]	Supple-mental Security Income recipients, December 2013	Housing units, 2014: Total	Percent change, 2010–2014
	75	76	77	78	79	80	81	82	83	84	85	86	87	88
NEW YORK—Cont'd														
Genesee	7.2	0.3	5.3	14.2	2.4	7.0	2.9	9.2	29.1	13 530	228	1 260	25 617	0.2
Greene	0.7	D	5.4	6.9	4.9	7.8	3.0	6.8	40.6	12 225	253	1 443	29 278	0.2
Hamilton	0.0	D	8.6	D	1.4	8.0	D	D	54.3	1 595	335	68	8 754	0.7
Herkimer	2.0	0.2	6.8	18.0	2.6	8.1	2.3	9.6	29.5	15 940	248	1 837	33 349	-0.1
Jefferson	1.4	0.1	4.4	3.7	2.6	5.8	2.0	8.7	60.3	21 200	177	2 984	58 769	1.4
Kings	0.0	D	6.4	3.1	9.0	7.7	9.1	25.9	10.0	319 740	123	143 614	1 022 498	2.2
Lewis	11.5	D	6.2	15.4	2.8	5.9	1.7	D	36.1	5 550	204	656	15 286	1.1
Livingston	4.3	D	7.2	9.1	2.9	7.7	2.4	7.9	40.8	13 500	209	1 313	27 315	1.0
Madison	2.6	D	6.6	12.8	5.1	7.1	3.8	12.3	23.6	14 325	198	1 437	31 763	0.0
Monroe	0.2	0.0	5.9	13.6	13.1	5.3	6.2	12.8	15.1	154 150	206	26 928	323 242	0.8
Montgomery	2.6	0.3	4.0	17.1	2.4	9.8	2.5	21.2	20.8	13 215	265	2 099	23 202	0.6
Nassau	0.0	0.1	5.9	3.2	15.0	7.7	9.6	17.4	17.4	252 125	186	18 542	466 928	-0.3
New York	0.0	0.1	1.4	0.8	25.2	2.9	31.6	5.0	12.2	248 185	152	79 021	867 609	2.4
Niagara	1.3	D	4.7	15.4	5.2	8.1	2.7	12.7	27.4	52 005	243	6 304	99 175	0.1
Oneida	0.6	0.1	3.3	8.1	6.5	7.7	7.7	15.6	33.0	54 545	233	8 925	103 964	-0.2
Onondaga	0.4	0.1	5.2	9.2	11.0	6.2	7.5	12.7	21.0	95 205	203	14 990	204 447	1.0
Ontario	2.3	0.1	8.3	13.5	5.7	9.4	3.7	11.5	19.2	24 790	227	2 015	49 603	2.7
Orange	0.3	0.1	4.6	5.7	7.8	9.4	3.6	14.4	32.1	62 815	168	7 397	139 669	1.9
Orleans	7.4	0.3	2.8	17.1	1.2	4.1	6.5	D	42.1	9 415	222	1 018	18 475	0.2
Oswego	1.3	0.2	5.1	11.0	2.9	7.2	2.4	11.0	31.4	26 790	220	3 477	53 694	0.2
Otsego	0.7	D	3.5	5.0	3.6	8.3	6.4	26.5	26.0	14 385	233	1 548	30 613	-0.5
Putnam	0.1	0.0	9.3	5.3	8.8	5.6	4.5	18.2	26.4	17 825	179	940	38 320	0.2
Queens	0.0	0.0	13.0	3.7	5.3	6.5	8.2	16.8	10.4	317 375	138	76 853	847 706	1.5
Rensselaer	0.3	0.3	7.2	8.3	9.8	6.0	4.3	12.9	25.4	32 305	202	4 430	71 808	0.5
Richmond	0.0	0.0	11.2	D	8.5	8.5	4.6	26.6	10.5	86 555	183	15 544	178 570	1.1
Rockland	0.0	D	6.0	9.9	10.2	6.4	6.0	13.6	22.9	54 760	171	5 936	104 525	0.4
St. Lawrence	2.2	0.2	5.4	9.2	2.7	7.7	2.1	D	36.8	25 235	225	4 105	52 229	0.2
Saratoga	0.2	D	8.1	13.0	9.7	7.3	10.1	9.2	18.5	44 745	200	3 101	101 819	3.2
Schenectady	0.0	D	3.9	13.9	21.3	5.4	3.9	13.7	20.0	32 440	209	5 415	68 122	-0.1
Schoharie	2.3	D	9.7	2.4	3.6	7.8	5.5	9.7	35.5	6 800	214	714	17 229	0.0
Schuyler	3.6	D	10.8	11.3	3.1	8.0	D	D	27.1	4 785	259	484	9 576	1.3
Seneca	2.6	D	4.6	25.8	D	8.3	2.5	D	32.0	7 925	225	842	16 213	1.1
Steuben	1.9	0.4	2.2	15.4	15.8	5.2	4.4	8.8	21.6	23 310	236	3 247	48 828	-0.1
Suffolk	0.2	0.2	7.2	8.6	10.1	6.7	9.2	11.6	22.2	285 145	190	23 244	570 418	0.1
Sullivan	0.6	0.5	4.7	4.0	3.9	6.5	5.2	19.4	35.4	17 610	229	2 973	49 629	0.9
Tioga	1.2	0.2	4.6	41.6	D	5.3	1.9	4.7	20.0	11 780	235	1 216	22 195	0.0
Tompkins	0.7	1.2	2.3	7.9	7.4	5.3	3.4	D	14.9	15 195	146	1 723	42 080	0.9
Ulster	0.7	0.2	4.8	5.7	5.6	9.3	4.3	12.7	34.3	39 925	221	4 673	83 710	0.1
Warren	0.0	0.5	7.1	11.5	7.5	8.8	5.5	16.3	16.3	17 740	272	1 771	38 993	0.7
Washington	2.3	0.4	7.5	20.2	D	6.3	1.6	6.9	39.5	14 100	225	1 702	29 018	0.6
Wayne	3.9	0.2	5.8	19.5	3.1	5.9	2.2	6.7	35.3	22 545	244	2 407	41 338	0.7
Westchester	0.0	0.1	6.2	4.5	14.8	5.6	12.8	13.0	17.4	165 000	170	18 322	369 864	-0.3
Wyoming	8.9	D	3.0	11.4	D	6.1	2.3	D	41.9	9 030	218	722	18 044	0.4
Yates	10.3	0.0	4.6	14.5	2.4	6.7	2.9	D	22.9	5 995	238	567	13 711	1.6
NORTH CAROLINA	1.2	0.1	5.2	11.7	9.5	6.2	10.7	10.1	19.9	1 907 394	194	234 362	4 452 334	2.9
Alamance	0.4	0.1	5.6	15.8	4.3	7.6	7.9	20.7	11.1	32 425	210	3 233	68 102	2.2
Alexander	6.5	D	4.1	27.1	4.4	4.4	9.1	D	18.4	8 665	234	665	16 170	-0.1
Alleghany	13.2	D	9.3	12.3	D	5.6	3.2	13.0	18.0	3 430	315	337	8 139	0.6
Anson	10.6	D	2.3	16.8	D	4.9	4.4	D	29.5	5 810	223	1 121	11 514	-0.5
Ashe	3.9	D	12.3	13.3	D	9.4	4.9	12.1	15.5	7 740	285	832	17 468	0.7
Avery	2.5	D	8.9	1.6	D	8.0	7.1	D	23.4	4 305	243	368	14 027	1.0
Beaufort	5.5	0.0	4.8	21.8	4.1	7.6	6.0	9.7	16.6	13 685	289	1 941	25 392	2.8
Bertie	19.5	D	1.6	22.2	D	2.6	D	D	20.3	5 805	284	1 331	9 745	-0.8
Bladen	10.6	0.0	2.8	35.2	1.4	3.6	6.6	D	19.3	8 535	245	1 799	17 622	-0.5
Brunswick	1.0	D	9.0	4.3	7.2	8.1	10.2	9.5	17.1	36 625	318	2 331	81 416	5.1
Buncombe	0.3	0.1	4.9	10.4	7.1	8.1	8.2	20.9	15.9	56 285	227	5 863	115 680	2.0
Burke	0.4	0.1	3.8	23.9	3.0	5.9	9.3	16.0	21.6	21 605	241	2 116	40 656	-0.5
Cabarrus	0.5	D	6.5	8.2	4.5	9.6	7.4	6.5	20.2	31 835	170	2 707	75 521	5.0
Caldwell	0.4	D	5.4	21.5	2.8	7.4	5.1	11.5	18.1	20 055	245	1 816	37 590	-0.2
Camden	20.4	0.0	4.9	1.3	D	3.6	D	D	18.8	2 005	197	145	4 146	1.0
Carteret	0.2	D	7.2	3.6	5.1	10.6	9.9	9.8	23.8	17 685	258	1 287	48 898	1.5
Caswell	7.8	D	6.3	8.4	2.3	5.2	D	D	36.9	6 190	266	828	10 607	-0.1
Catawba	0.3	D	3.3	27.0	4.5	8.0	3.9	10.8	13.1	36 095	233	3 010	67 762	-0.2
Chatham	1.8	D	8.1	11.5	9.5	4.9	17.8	10.9	12.3	15 720	235	814	29 976	4.3
Cherokee	1.4	D	D	9.6	8.8	10.6	5.2	D	21.6	9 335	344	858	17 690	1.0

1. Per 1,000 resident population estimated as of July 1 of the year shown.

STATE County	Housing units, 2009–2013: Occupied units: Total	Owner-occupied: Percent	Owner-occupied: Median value[1]	Median owner cost as a percent of income: With a mortgage	Median owner cost as a percent of income: Without a mortgage[2]	Renter-occupied: Median rent[3]	Renter-occupied: Median rent as a percent of income[2]	Substandard units[4] (percent)	Civilian labor force, 2014: Total	Civilian labor force, 2014: Percent change, 2013–2014	Unemployment: Total	Unemployment: Rate[5]	Civilian employment,[6] 2009–2013: Total	Percent: Management, business, science and arts	Percent: Construction, production, and maintenance occupations
	89	90	91	92	93	94	95	96	97	98	99	100	101	102	103
NEW YORK—Cont'd															
Genesee	23 884	72.7	105 000	21.9	14.7	716	29.4	1.6	30 085	-1.1	1 661	5.5	29 194	30.9	29.0
Greene	18 365	74.3	183 300	25.2	16.8	841	34.9	0.8	20 823	-2.0	1 395	6.7	19 927	35.6	22.6
Hamilton	1 854	83.9	164 700	23.1	12.8	610	18.7	1.9	2 443	1.1	178	7.3	2 022	31.8	22.5
Herkimer	26 815	70.5	92 500	20.3	13.9	614	28.8	2.5	29 085	-2.7	1 964	6.8	28 970	32.5	24.1
Jefferson	45 011	56.1	131 800	21.9	13.9	903	29.3	11.1	46 699	-3.0	3 569	7.6	44 668	31.1	22.7
Kings	916 025	29.8	557 100	32.8	17.0	1 149	32.7	1.9	1 222 973	1.0	94 042	7.7	1 114 135	37.0	15.5
Lewis	10 677	77.0	107 200	20.8	13.0	661	30.7	2.0	11 890	-2.5	930	7.8	11 927	27.7	34.8
Livingston	24 092	74.4	119 300	22.4	13.5	693	31.6	1.3	31 039	-2.3	1 794	5.8	30 569	35.2	25.5
Madison	26 565	75.5	121 100	22.3	14.0	724	26.7	1.6	33 428	-2.5	2 143	6.4	32 866	37.6	22.4
Monroe	297 040	65.1	136 000	22.1	13.7	810	33.4	2.8	364 745	-2.2	21 079	5.8	353 757	42.2	16.1
Montgomery	19 703	67.6	101 200	22.2	16.7	705	30.6	2.7	22 242	-3.7	1 661	7.5	21 714	30.3	28.3
Nassau	441 955	80.5	454 500	29.6	19.3	1 504	33.3	6.1	684 861	-1.4	32 650	4.8	651 746	43.1	13.9
New York	736 192	22.8	828 100	20.5	10.5	1 442	28.4	1.3	915 344	1.4	55 387	6.1	855 506	58.7	6.2
Niagara	88 376	70.4	105 200	21.2	14.3	646	31.1	1.6	102 089	-2.4	7 095	6.9	98 804	30.9	23.0
Oneida	91 075	67.2	110 500	20.5	13.3	689	29.9	1.6	103 635	-3.0	6 319	6.1	103 620	35.1	20.2
Onondaga	184 855	65.4	132 300	21.2	13.2	759	30.4	1.8	224 744	-2.7	12 510	5.6	220 116	40.6	15.9
Ontario	43 794	73.7	138 100	21.5	14.5	778	29.6	3.9	54 551	-2.1	2 865	5.3	53 208	38.3	19.8
Orange	125 317	69.2	276 900	28.0	18.3	1 133	35.5	2.6	175 742	-1.4	9 633	5.5	170 981	35.7	20.0
Orleans	15 725	77.4	91 100	23.4	17.3	634	31.0	2.2	18 165	-2.6	1 384	7.6	17 610	27.1	33.4
Oswego	45 325	72.4	93 000	21.9	13.6	719	32.8	3.1	55 142	-3.3	4 429	8.0	53 083	28.5	29.6
Otsego	24 078	73.3	137 900	22.7	14.0	775	33.8	2.0	30 248	-2.5	1 720	5.7	28 901	36.1	21.1
Putnam	34 496	83.1	372 200	28.1	17.9	1 259	34.8	9.8	50 203	-1.9	2 451	4.9	50 459	43.9	15.4
Queens	778 630	44.2	450 900	32.4	15.1	1 315	33.2	1.5	1 157 675	1.4	73 867	6.4	1 072 133	31.4	19.3
Rensselaer	64 242	65.7	178 200	23.4	14.3	858	29.1	4.1	81 533	-2.0	4 356	5.3	79 345	39.5	17.9
Richmond	164 609	68.6	441 000	28.7	15.3	1 173	32.9	6.5	222 974	1.3	16 148	7.2	206 255	38.3	17.2
Rockland	98 326	69.9	435 300	28.8	18.4	1 324	36.1	2.6	148 428	-1.1	7 600	5.1	143 224	43.1	14.2
St. Lawrence	41 839	70.8	84 400	21.3	13.6	673	31.6	0.8	47 230	-2.3	3 648	7.7	45 156	33.0	21.4
Saratoga	88 460	71.9	230 700	22.4	12.9	952	27.2	1.5	115 554	-1.8	5 371	4.6	112 301	42.9	16.4
Schenectady	58 059	67.2	166 500	23.2	14.5	835	32.4	2.1	76 221	-2.0	4 098	5.4	74 017	38.1	17.0
Schoharie	12 820	77.7	146 000	23.2	14.0	724	31.4	1.7	14 921	-2.1	992	6.6	14 693	32.2	26.0
Schuyler	7 684	78.5	94 400	21.6	13.4	597	24.9	1.8	8 578	-2.9	594	6.9	8 319	31.0	25.7
Seneca	13 429	74.5	94 400	21.9	14.0	674	29.6	2.2	15 570	-1.8	880	5.7	15 215	31.9	27.1
Steuben	41 503	71.4	86 800	20.8	12.5	644	26.2	2.6	44 267	-2.8	3 064	6.9	43 246	34.3	26.6
Suffolk	497 347	80.0	383 400	29.9	19.7	1 495	34.8	3.2	766 711	-1.5	40 793	5.3	727 484	37.8	18.9
Sullivan	29 531	65.3	172 100	27.8	16.3	843	32.6	1.4	33 318	-3.4	2 225	6.7	32 494	32.2	24.2
Tioga	20 202	79.5	108 400	20.0	12.6	626	28.3	1.7	24 033	-3.5	1 466	6.1	24 434	36.0	25.0
Tompkins	38 409	56.3	169 200	21.5	13.3	942	35.1	1.9	54 643	-2.0	2 362	4.3	49 393	51.5	13.8
Ulster	69 862	69.8	232 400	27.1	17.6	1 005	34.1	1.3	88 232	-2.1	5 096	5.8	86 111	38.9	19.2
Warren	28 081	70.8	189 400	23.5	14.0	853	30.5	2.0	32 244	-2.2	2 098	6.5	31 834	35.3	20.3
Washington	24 499	73.6	148 300	23.8	14.1	799	31.1	1.6	28 705	-1.9	1 734	6.0	28 549	27.9	30.4
Wayne	36 399	78.7	109 300	21.7	14.2	681	29.7	4.5	44 652	-2.5	2 748	6.2	43 817	33.6	28.9
Westchester	343 561	61.9	518 400	27.4	18.5	1 325	33.3	0.7	470 316	-1.2	24 097	5.1	456 825	45.5	13.4
Wyoming	15 624	75.4	100 200	21.1	12.1	602	29.9	2.8	18 411	-1.8	1 199	6.5	18 388	28.2	32.8
Yates	9 602	76.6	118 200	23.2	12.8	641	29.8	3.2	11 673	-2.0	651	5.6	11 637	31.4	26.1
NORTH CAROLINA	3 715 565	66.4	153 600	23.0	11.9	776	30.6	2.8	4 656 194	-0.5	285 815	6.1	4 234 977	35.7	22.8
Alamance	60 139	67.1	137 000	22.9	11.8	731	31.0	3.6	76 272	-1.2	4 273	5.6	69 111	31.7	26.6
Alexander	14 101	77.5	121 300	21.5	10.0	579	27.9	1.9	17 155	-1.6	951	5.5	16 124	24.4	40.0
Alleghany	4 793	76.3	156 100	24.1	13.8	552	37.5	2.1	4 346	-1.4	293	6.7	4 246	28.8	32.6
Anson	9 686	68.6	79 400	22.2	14.8	661	31.3	1.6	10 864	-0.3	760	7.0	9 708	22.0	38.9
Ashe	11 839	76.9	150 900	28.6	10.7	644	32.6	3.5	12 310	-4.0	833	6.8	11 896	27.4	33.2
Avery	7 122	76.1	140 800	29.4	10.2	675	31.4	2.3	7 606	-0.8	483	6.4	6 936	26.7	27.2
Beaufort	19 266	70.1	117 000	24.7	14.9	656	32.4	2.4	19 864	-2.6	1 425	7.2	18 970	30.6	29.6
Bertie	7 629	75.3	79 100	23.8	16.1	586	36.2	2.6	8 436	0.0	659	7.8	7 312	22.2	38.6
Bladen	14 256	67.8	81 800	24.3	16.2	593	31.4	1.9	14 229	-0.6	1 306	9.2	13 367	25.9	40.0
Brunswick	47 600	76.4	186 600	26.7	12.8	860	33.4	2.4	47 307	-0.4	3 572	7.6	42 753	30.5	24.6
Buncombe	100 838	64.5	191 200	24.0	11.6	806	29.9	2.5	127 155	-0.3	5 805	4.6	114 881	37.6	18.0
Burke	34 664	71.8	110 900	22.7	10.8	605	29.6	2.6	39 324	-1.7	2 432	6.2	36 949	28.3	29.8
Cabarrus	64 713	73.1	167 800	23.1	11.8	794	29.2	1.5	92 661	0.8	5 231	5.6	81 758	36.9	21.8
Caldwell	31 417	71.9	105 800	22.4	12.6	611	32.6	3.8	35 472	-2.2	2 505	7.1	32 936	23.7	37.0
Camden	3 580	86.4	220 200	26.3	13.7	1 030	37.7	1.6	4 441	-1.6	266	6.0	4 404	37.5	22.6
Carteret	29 158	70.2	199 200	24.8	12.9	759	29.0	1.8	30 894	-0.5	1 846	6.0	29 412	33.3	24.2
Caswell	8 813	71.8	98 900	23.2	12.3	592	36.2	2.6	9 560	-2.7	666	7.0	8 834	23.7	33.4
Catawba	58 533	71.1	133 000	21.5	10.6	674	29.5	2.1	74 388	-1.9	4 683	6.3	69 215	31.2	29.5
Chatham	26 017	79.9	211 400	23.7	11.6	774	29.2	1.9	31 582	0.2	1 481	4.7	28 895	41.0	22.6
Cherokee	10 722	82.1	145 000	26.7	11.0	589	29.7	4.9	10 957	-2.5	769	7.0	9 580	27.8	28.9

1. Specified owner-occupied units. 2. A value of 10.0 represents 10 percent or less; a value of 50.0 represents 50 percent or more. 3. Specified renter-occupied units.
4. Overcrowded or lacking complete plumbing facilities. 5. Percent of civilian labor force. 6. Persons 16 years old and over.

STATE County	Private nonfarm establishments, employment and payroll, 2013									Agriculture, 2012			
		Employment						Annual payroll		Farms			
											Percent with:		
	Number of establishments	Total	Health care and social assistance	Manufacturing	Retail trade	Finance and insurance	Professional, scientific, and technical services	Total (mil dol)	Average per employee (dollars)	Number	Fewer than 50 acres	500 acres or more	Farm operators whose principal occupation is farming (percent)
	104	105	106	107	108	109	110	111	112	113	114	115	116
NEW YORK—Cont'd													
Genesee	1 344	16 417	2 806	2 805	2 618	397	308	552	33 638	549	35.3	12.0	56.5
Greene	1 164	11 282	1 245	803	2 127	355	246	329	29 156	273	31.9	5.9	51.3
Hamilton	197	855	D	D	183	D	D	24	27 675	26	34.6	0.0	42.3
Herkimer	1 125	11 736	2 327	2 681	1 959	299	188	381	32 454	687	21.0	7.9	59.7
Jefferson	2 453	30 639	6 565	2 277	6 834	750	1 000	1 029	33 599	876	20.5	17.2	57.4
Kings	53 226	544 525	182 392	21 153	68 937	14 978	18 457	20 610	37 849	10	100.0	0.0	60.0
Lewis	529	4 737	1 094	1 137	801	D	D	162	34 212	634	18.3	12.5	60.4
Livingston	1 254	13 143	1 911	2 084	2 561	277	377	409	31 109	661	34.2	14.7	55.8
Madison	1 418	17 233	2 946	2 840	2 585	531	685	576	33 417	838	27.3	10.6	58.2
Monroe	17 458	344 253	62 686	38 338	41 843	12 092	22 245	14 657	42 575	475	54.5	10.1	66.7
Montgomery	1 075	15 337	3 886	3 346	2 469	359	249	518	33 794	659	23.2	9.3	67.2
Nassau	47 683	532 008	103 702	16 475	78 424	34 892	42 193	26 644	50 082	55	90.9	1.8	47.3
New York	105 439	2 116 201	243 950	18 931	155 122	284 733	289 232	217 576	102 814	6	100.0	0.0	0.0
Niagara	4 451	59 262	10 275	8 067	10 817	1 366	1 640	1 965	33 162	760	47.2	7.0	52.9
Oneida	4 859	86 672	19 163	9 569	11 820	6 721	3 509	3 146	36 304	1 066	25.7	8.3	56.7
Onondaga	11 764	215 260	38 657	18 216	29 223	11 603	15 247	8 982	41 728	681	44.1	8.8	54.9
Ontario	2 844	45 004	8 035	6 324	9 186	874	1 285	1 806	40 119	853	40.9	10.6	58.0
Orange	9 144	110 714	20 131	7 557	22 861	3 062	6 326	3 987	36 012	658	42.1	4.6	60.6
Orleans	646	8 024	1 231	2 419	1 145	D	115	261	32 520	487	41.9	9.2	55.2
Oswego	2 112	23 568	4 658	2 778	4 541	614	625	890	37 755	657	32.6	5.3	54.5
Otsego	1 439	19 113	6 165	907	3 300	1 157	589	695	36 364	995	26.2	6.8	57.3
Putnam	2 824	19 914	4 823	1 337	2 945	635	1 169	847	42 521	72	72.2	4.2	50.0
Queens	46 506	517 577	120 353	20 710	60 538	D	13 837	23 297	45 011	6	66.7	0.0	16.7
Rensselaer	2 985	42 626	9 406	2 764	5 599	1 277	3 429	1 701	39 899	495	34.1	8.7	52.3
Richmond	8 929	94 961	30 096	984	16 185	2 481	3 478	3 615	38 064	8	100.0	0.0	50.0
Rockland	9 425	103 462	22 570	8 415	13 703	3 445	5 269	4 538	43 860	23	82.6	0.0	65.2
St. Lawrence	1 973	26 862	6 309	2 449	5 172	721	576	934	34 779	1 303	13.7	10.8	60.2
Saratoga	5 124	65 942	8 968	6 650	10 496	4 367	3 866	2 845	43 150	583	46.5	4.5	61.9
Schenectady	3 071	49 046	11 899	4 406	7 465	2 274	D	2 100	42 811	169	41.4	3.6	46.2
Schoharie	560	5 305	957	289	1 149	D	179	175	32 913	532	22.0	6.8	62.0
Schuyler	387	4 275	D	595	673	52	D	207	48 512	393	30.8	5.3	50.4
Seneca	718	9 130	1 318	1 467	2 297	157	119	315	34 504	584	30.5	9.1	69.3
Steuben	1 813	25 922	5 973	4 534	4 593	1 044	D	1 254	48 360	1 667	19.3	11.4	51.4
Suffolk	48 689	557 995	95 503	53 039	78 845	22 175	47 076	27 802	49 825	604	70.4	1.5	69.2
Sullivan	1 939	18 129	5 282	1 290	2 760	760	616	587	32 394	321	38.6	7.2	59.5
Tioga	821	10 840	1 008	1 238	1 296	225	D	535	49 398	536	22.9	8.8	54.1
Tompkins	2 346	46 909	5 670	2 677	5 126	864	2 279	1 675	35 712	558	43.9	6.8	50.5
Ulster	4 682	44 305	8 774	3 554	8 825	2 262	1 488	1 481	33 431	486	48.4	5.1	67.3
Warren	2 341	30 701	6 576	3 870	5 815	1 191	844	1 169	38 082	117	60.7	0.0	54.7
Washington	1 063	10 161	1 683	3 097	1 738	216	227	371	36 475	851	31.1	11.6	55.6
Wayne	1 718	19 188	3 000	5 508	3 270	594	653	703	36 626	873	38.3	8.6	62.2
Westchester	31 680	377 971	78 769	11 278	50 634	22 101	25 873	23 616	62 481	131	74.8	1.5	58.8
Wyoming	787	9 408	1 187	1 851	1 424	373	367	306	32 477	713	33.0	14.9	62.8
Yates	551	5 087	973	887	756	111	117	146	28 709	919	27.1	3.6	66.6
NORTH CAROLINA	218 285	3 421 195	553 390	408 390	457 694	169 983	201 818	143 342	41 898	50 218	48.1	6.8	48.9
Alamance	3 162	50 672	8 407	8 912	8 797	1 571	1 384	1 732	34 179	732	42.5	4.6	41.7
Alexander	559	6 812	547	3 238	788	156	130	191	28 050	603	55.4	5.0	53.2
Alleghany	248	2 167	569	D	307	63	D	59	27 272	567	43.0	4.6	49.7
Anson	386	5 089	881	1 511	700	92	111	153	30 098	429	26.8	9.3	55.7
Ashe	514	5 356	1 103	1 042	1 040	191	54	158	29 428	1 140	47.6	2.1	46.4
Avery	503	4 410	765	138	754	83	59	121	27 326	483	63.1	0.8	46.2
Beaufort	1 085	12 898	2 149	2 589	2 332	417	302	429	33 237	364	39.8	21.7	50.5
Bertie	320	4 511	1 162	D	359	D	50	118	26 199	325	30.8	23.1	64.0
Bladen	507	10 469	1 251	D	852	D	D	332	31 715	492	42.3	12.4	53.3
Brunswick	2 300	23 411	3 776	D	4 508	D	662	803	34 300	254	52.8	7.1	42.9
Buncombe	7 399	101 093	20 474	10 981	16 904	2 568	4 267	3 702	36 620	1 060	64.8	0.9	51.0
Burke	1 446	21 453	4 388	7 565	2 620	389	434	702	32 735	486	58.8	1.6	50.6
Cabarrus	4 020	57 722	9 749	5 781	12 000	912	1 728	2 056	35 620	589	52.0	4.2	50.1
Caldwell	1 337	18 142	3 250	5 639	2 830	433	325	564	31 072	411	56.9	1.7	44.8
Camden	110	554	D	D	96	D	31	15	27 477	60	41.7	36.7	65.0
Carteret	1 915	17 456	3 317	844	3 949	498	467	614	20 463	125	64.0	7.2	48.8
Caswell	238	1 592	392	174	344	46	35	37	23 219	543	32.2	6.6	49.9
Catawba	4 050	75 940	11 047	20 876	9 774	1 377	1 675	2 854	37 584	698	55.6	1.7	41.8
Chatham	1 304	12 754	2 688	1 813	2 075	242	463	380	29 810	1 138	47.0	1.9	45.2
Cherokee	586	5 797	1 398	728	1 379	187	241	160	27 620	255	54.1	3.9	54.5

STATE County	Agriculture, 2012 (cont.) — Land in farms: Acreage (1,000)	Land in farms: Percent change, 2007–2012	Land in farms: Acres: Average size of farm	Land in farms: Acres: Total irrigated (1,000)	Land in farms: Acres: Total cropland (1,000)	Value of land and buildings (dollars): Average per farm	Value of land and buildings (dollars): Average per acre	Value of machinery and equipment, average per farm (dollars)	Value of products sold: Total (mil dol)	Value of products sold: Average per farm (dollars)	Value of products sold: Percent from: Crops	Value of products sold: Percent from: Livestock and poultry products	Percent of farms with sales of: $10,000 or more	Percent of farms with sales of: $100,000 or more	Government payments: Total ($1,000)	Government payments: Percent of farms
	117	118	119	120	121	122	123	124	125	126	127	128	129	130	131	132
NEW YORK—Cont'd																
Genesee	187	2.1	341	6.3	143.3	898 004	2 632	213 681	237.0	431 607	36.0	64.0	48.1	25.9	2 111	45.5
Greene	43	-3.0	157	0.7	18.7	588 198	3 736	65 901	22.4	82 022	43.5	56.5	40.3	6.2	911	23.8
Hamilton	2	361.8	80	D	0.3	145 692	1 823	28 538	0.3	13 385	D	D	19.2	7.7	0	0.0
Herkimer	140	0.2	204	0.1	76.4	393 428	1 927	92 482	70.4	102 536	25.1	74.9	57.9	21.0	1 414	32.0
Jefferson	291	10.9	332	0.3	173.5	544 535	1 640	133 429	183.6	209 551	24.7	75.3	51.6	24.1	2 974	31.5
Kings	D	D	D	0.0	D	951 000	D	15 000	2.0	199 300	D	D	60.0	40.0	0	0.0
Lewis	182	8.7	287	0.1	97.2	478 692	1 670	145 063	137.0	216 151	17.2	82.8	64.0	35.3	2 400	37.7
Livingston	195	-12.4	295	0.2	149.6	854 528	2 897	176 086	186.8	282 614	43.2	56.8	44.3	22.5	2 425	41.9
Madison	187	-0.4	224	0.8	111.0	456 792	2 042	116 047	117.7	140 489	26.4	73.6	52.0	24.7	2 231	29.2
Monroe	99	-25.8	208	0.9	79.5	737 682	3 551	142 223	90.6	190 695	89.8	10.2	46.1	19.2	1 331	21.7
Montgomery	131	5.5	199	0.2	85.9	458 426	2 299	108 599	86.8	131 701	24.8	75.2	60.8	22.8	1 523	32.0
Nassau	3	108.2	49	0.1	0.3	894 000	18 333	51 509	6.2	113 546	47.9	52.1	47.3	21.8	0	0.0
New York	D	D	D	0.0	0.0	D	D	47 000	D	D	D	D	16.7	0.0	0	0.0
Niagara	143	0.1	188	3.0	118.5	430 664	2 292	136 736	122.7	161 415	62.2	37.8	45.1	14.9	1 684	27.1
Oneida	205	6.7	192	0.2	118.7	383 145	1 991	109 238	113.2	106 181	37.3	62.7	48.2	21.7	2 155	31.5
Onondaga	150	-0.2	221	1.3	101.8	696 072	3 155	166 094	152.1	223 275	31.8	68.2	50.2	19.2	1 688	32.5
Ontario	193	-3.2	226	0.9	148.2	727 475	3 222	149 744	180.3	211 402	42.8	57.2	53.0	25.2	2 675	32.8
Orange	88	8.7	134	2.7	45.8	740 827	5 537	116 939	100.7	153 035	71.5	28.5	59.3	22.9	2 006	27.8
Orleans	135	-3.3	277	4.6	109.5	720 725	2 598	232 292	150.3	308 672	92.1	7.9	46.0	25.5	1 883	39.4
Oswego	94	-6.0	143	0.6	45.4	289 994	2 022	85 426	47.6	72 454	47.3	52.7	39.7	11.6	555	17.8
Otsego	181	2.4	182	0.2	85.5	407 769	2 245	80 409	66.8	67 096	35.6	64.4	42.7	15.8	1 391	21.8
Putnam	6	4.8	82	D	1.6	448 681	5 468	42 181	3.3	45 222	92.2	7.8	29.2	13.9	24	6.9
Queens	0	D	74	0.0	0.4	377 833	5 129	82 333	0.2	26 833	95.7	5.0	100.0	0.0	0	0.0
Rensselaer	89	4.4	179	0.6	50.6	616 113	3 436	104 002	53.1	107 204	52.9	47.1	48.3	16.0	733	30.5
Richmond	D	D	D	0.0	D	440 750	D	D	1.0	120 125	100.0	0.0	50.0	50.0	0	0.0
Rockland	1	D	23	0.1	0.2	1 980 870	86 616	71 913	1.7	75 391	96.5	3.5	56.5	21.7	0	0.0
St. Lawrence	357	2.8	274	0.6	172.1	388 063	1 417	95 682	187.4	143 794	20.7	79.3	48.3	16.7	2 569	20.7
Saratoga	79	4.2	135	0.3	43.8	647 986	4 791	109 096	80.0	137 166	24.3	75.7	43.2	12.9	613	14.2
Schenectady	20	3.9	118	0.1	9.1	406 036	3 454	77 172	4.2	24 621	70.7	29.3	36.7	5.3	101	7.1
Schoharie	98	3.0	185	0.7	55.0	421 389	2 279	86 735	39.5	74 248	39.0	61.0	49.1	13.9	1 105	31.0
Schuyler	69	4.3	176	0.2	38.0	503 155	2 857	92 982	44.5	113 160	29.1	70.9	47.6	17.6	375	16.0
Seneca	130	1.7	223	0.4	98.0	656 699	2 945	168 820	118.9	203 640	44.2	55.8	67.1	39.4	1 017	28.9
Steuben	406	9.1	243	1.2	221.7	446 421	1 834	105 887	187.2	112 301	43.4	56.6	44.6	16.4	3 112	29.8
Suffolk	36	4.6	60	11.8	23.2	696 702	11 697	138 692	239.8	397 050	85.3	14.7	63.7	32.0	790	7.1
Sullivan	54	6.8	168	0.1	22.8	617 897	3 683	74 601	27.1	84 424	15.0	85.0	44.5	13.1	274	18.1
Tioga	108	1.0	201	0.7	50.7	396 076	1 968	83 879	36.7	68 560	30.8	69.2	42.2	14.6	1 112	36.9
Tompkins	91	-16.5	163	0.3	54.4	448 507	2 757	113 717	67.4	120 772	33.7	66.3	43.7	16.1	900	25.8
Ulster	71	-5.3	147	4.2	26.1	738 835	5 042	103 237	55.9	115 019	83.0	17.0	43.0	12.6	328	10.1
Warren	10	11.4	81	0.1	1.5	325 487	3 997	58 376	D	D	D	D	28.2	11.1	D	0.9
Washington	189	-6.6	223	0.6	101.9	539 925	2 426	111 270	139.1	163 510	19.4	80.6	53.3	21.0	2 914	28.6
Wayne	179	6.3	205	1.9	126.3	508 517	2 479	166 179	205.6	235 517	72.7	27.3	60.5	31.2	2 084	27.5
Westchester	8	-9.0	59	0.1	1.5	952 855	16 102	104 863	8.8	67 176	47.6	52.4	46.6	17.6	D	2.3
Wyoming	226	3.6	317	3.4	159.5	828 938	2 617	216 229	318.5	446 711	24.5	75.5	52.7	29.3	3 057	35.1
Yates	127	0.7	138	0.6	88.1	546 444	3 956	115 875	117.0	127 336	37.6	62.4	75.1	45.8	1 081	17.1
NORTH CAROLINA	8 415	-0.7	168	174.5	4 745.0	726 944	4 338	92 882	12 588.1	250 670	34.2	65.8	37.3	16.6	120 129	28.7
Alamance	84	-4.9	114	0.9	31.8	538 171	4 715	60 452	32.9	44 986	46.8	53.2	30.3	9.2	470	17.5
Alexander	59	6.7	97	0.6	20.9	578 788	5 949	70 687	187.7	311 227	5.8	94.2	45.6	28.9	177	6.8
Alleghany	91	18.6	160	D	32.9	770 166	4 803	70 547	36.3	64 092	56.6	43.4	44.1	11.5	590	23.1
Anson	84	-7.9	195	1.1	28.3	725 956	3 725	97 247	193.9	451 900	8.7	91.3	49.4	30.3	551	36.6
Ashe	112	3.7	99	0.2	33.1	561 065	5 687	54 833	54.5	47 790	74.4	25.6	38.1	7.9	216	10.4
Avery	28	1.5	58	0.4	11.6	407 195	6 968	55 195	17.2	35 607	96.1	3.9	44.5	8.1	71	4.8
Beaufort	148	-7.5	407	2.6	129.3	1 244 750	3 056	218 201	121.6	334 074	84.7	15.3	49.2	34.6	3 011	71.7
Bertie	147	-0.4	452	4.2	95.4	1 220 674	2 703	219 246	225.2	692 822	37.4	62.6	68.9	49.2	3 200	74.8
Bladen	117	-7.7	238	4.6	52.9	784 878	3 291	106 965	308.5	627 110	19.3	80.7	46.7	26.2	1 102	38.8
Brunswick	45	3.1	179	1.2	27.4	769 642	4 302	92 492	58.2	229 197	48.0	52.0	34.3	12.6	427	24.8
Buncombe	71	-0.8	67	0.9	17.2	580 025	8 601	48 772	54.4	51 333	72.1	27.9	22.0	4.1	1 481	17.4
Burke	34	18.3	71	1.8	12.9	376 290	5 318	50 689	45.4	93 364	25.0	75.0	30.5	9.9	70	4.5
Cabarrus	66	-0.8	112	0.3	29.9	823 779	7 325	65 380	55.9	94 829	24.8	75.2	25.3	6.3	427	14.3
Caldwell	32	-1.6	78	0.4	11.8	430 625	5 521	45 667	17.8	43 294	53.7	46.3	26.0	7.3	145	6.6
Camden	49	-10.6	822	0.0	46.8	2 334 567	2 841	450 750	48.9	815 217	D	D	56.7	40.0	603	40.0
Carteret	63	13.4	503	0.2	45.5	1 653 072	3 288	92 024	29.2	233 656	98.9	1.2	33.6	15.2	363	18.4
Caswell	97	-5.1	179	1.7	24.8	514 319	2 877	64 361	34.2	63 063	51.7	48.3	29.3	8.5	946	35.4
Catawba	67	-6.7	96	0.7	29.3	519 109	5 400	59 158	67.3	96 430	29.4	70.6	32.2	9.6	447	16.0
Chatham	112	7.3	98	1.2	26.7	487 262	4 961	47 006	163.9	144 033	5.5	94.5	40.3	11.0	546	11.6
Cherokee	21	5.0	84	D	7.6	483 376	5 746	59 451	D	D	D	D	23.1	5.5	232	14.1

STATE County	Water use, 2010		Wholesale trade,[1] 2007				Retail trade,[2] 2007				Real estate and rental and leasing,[2] 2007			
	Total water withdrawn (mil gal/day)	Gallons withdrawn per person per day	Number of establish-ments	Number of employees	Sales (mil dol)	Annual payroll (mil dol)	Number of establish-ments	Number of employees	Sales (mil dol)	Annual payroll (mil dol)	Number of establish-ments	Number of employees	Receipts (mil dol)	Annual payroll (mil dol)
	133	134	135	136	137	138	139	140	141	142	143	144	145	146
NEW YORK—Cont'd														
Genesee	22.9	381	68	1 164	811.7	44.7	217	2 616	705.7	55.2	47	197	33.4	7.3
Greene	7.1	143	18	309	232.2	12.0	206	2 553	623.0	58.5	49	217	24.8	5.8
Hamilton	1.1	219	NA	NA	NA	NA	31	191	31.9	3.2	8	15	1.5	0.2
Herkimer	11.9	185	37	577	186.8	22.1	222	2 045	503.1	45.4	44	192	20.2	2.7
Jefferson	24.2	208	71	D	D	D	506	7 188	1 867.7	163.4	122	543	98.9	14.3
Kings	27.6	11	3 342	26 145	13 802.2	914.5	8 365	58 365	15 431.9	1 347.7	4 068	13 786	2 886.4	411.2
Lewis	9.2	340	12	96	33.0	3.5	77	738	175.8	13.9	12	49	4.8	1.0
Livingston	15.6	238	42	418	219.8	16.8	215	2 587	586.5	56.8	48	199	28.9	4.0
Madison	4.0	55	32	318	109.5	13.1	227	2 700	665.9	61.9	60	150	18.7	3.9
Monroe	121.9	164	809	13 783	6 778.3	728.2	2 376	40 062	8 496.1	845.7	803	6 215	1 025.4	193.7
Montgomery	10.6	211	45	D	D	D	197	2 469	621.8	52.2	27	112	13.1	3.3
Nassau	532.2	397	3 078	D	D	D	6 356	84 280	24 312.6	2 273.8	2 501	D	D	D
New York	29.4	19	8 941	99 779	108 757.4	6 717.5	11 665	134 567	38 797.5	4 490.7	9 469	68 786	28 476.7	4 350.0
Niagara	367.5	1 698	181	2 476	1 059.3	105.4	746	9 522	2 075.1	191.8	131	614	71.4	14.5
Oneida	36.3	155	176	2 098	939.4	80.7	869	12 369	2 751.0	264.4	206	822	151.8	19.7
Onondaga	109.2	234	668	12 250	17 121.5	571.3	1 776	28 722	6 363.1	613.2	629	3 439	663.2	124.4
Ontario	17.5	162	119	1 291	536.7	60.1	556	8 689	1 894.2	180.1	98	450	67.4	10.2
Orange	374.4	1 004	447	7 417	6 859.2	335.0	1 586	22 345	5 729.2	517.4	424	1 591	379.5	45.1
Orleans	7.4	171	21	259	88.6	9.2	111	1 282	262.6	25.9	19	44	9.3	1.0
Oswego	985.4	8 070	55	429	210.8	13.3	365	4 290	994.1	87.1	74	310	32.8	5.8
Otsego	7.4	119	44	D	D	D	301	3 661	932.4	86.1	47	184	26.5	3.8
Putnam	6.7	67	119	928	504.7	43.3	342	3 171	922.3	84.8	110	300	58.0	11.0
Queens	1 244.3	558	2 886	26 189	15 308.5	1 249.2	6 725	54 013	14 587.1	1 322.4	2 839	13 751	2 943.0	522.5
Rensselaer	22.1	139	100	997	1 387.7	42.1	421	5 833	1 384.4	133.0	98	481	74.1	13.1
Richmond	350.6	748	366	1 791	1 320.1	77.2	1 242	16 274	3 850.1	358.9	322	1 157	269.4	33.9
Rockland	133.3	428	508	5 549	3 228.2	282.0	1 186	14 122	3 866.8	346.8	458	1 752	406.8	51.6
St. Lawrence	23.9	214	53	463	116.1	13.2	447	5 183	1 238.8	105.9	66	289	33.0	5.8
Saratoga	39.4	179	182	2 958	2 239.4	160.4	775	11 807	4 506.4	256.4	177	988	181.6	30.5
Schenectady	40.7	263	100	1 124	601.6	44.6	498	7 600	1 664.3	161.8	117	668	114.3	21.0
Schoharie	169.7	5 183	18	126	36.0	4.7	98	1 106	268.9	23.2	21	50	6.8	1.0
Schuyler	20.7	1 131	6	D	D	D	66	713	179.9	15.8	10	43	2.9	0.7
Seneca	8.2	233	26	D	D	D	201	2 141	426.2	39.1	25	106	20.4	2.4
Steuben	17.7	178	36	D	D	D	363	4 336	1 076.9	89.5	56	249	29.4	7.5
Suffolk	604.0	404	3 039	42 142	38 208.9	2 400.2	6 750	83 958	23 319.9	2 217.8	1 813	D	D	D
Sullivan	102.6	1 322	67	714	299.1	22.3	318	3 035	815.2	71.1	156	507	66.3	10.1
Tioga	6.3	123	23	D	D	D	151	1 310	302.2	27.3	12	24	3.4	0.4
Tompkins	232.7	2 291	54	426	189.6	15.5	372	5 068	1 018.3	106.1	95	748	116.2	19.8
Ulster	458.2	2 511	150	1 607	946.5	86.5	794	9 242	2 241.1	216.3	209	676	125.2	18.4
Warren	54.2	824	72	758	342.0	32.5	452	5 899	1 382.2	138.7	86	377	67.9	10.4
Washington	32.6	516	30	246	85.1	8.5	206	1 934	485.6	43.7	20	58	4.8	1.1
Wayne	475.6	5 072	68	484	189.4	19.1	289	3 451	816.7	76.7	61	273	27.3	4.5
Westchester	2 044.6	2 154	1 419	17 179	20 059.6	1 155.2	4 058	50 195	14 205.1	1 423.2	2 162	9 027	2 373.8	416.9
Wyoming	18.8	447	30	288	297.2	11.5	144	1 463	338.0	30.6	21	72	7.7	1.7
Yates	76.6	3 024	16	136	42.7	4.4	105	690	178.9	15.2	18	105	9.6	2.4
NORTH CAROLINA	12 420.1	1 303	10 049	142 342	88 795.9	6 969.2	36 592	466 577	114 578.2	10 342.7	11 258	53 563	11 175.1	1 881.4
Alamance	23.9	158	153	1 839	655.8	73.3	631	8 251	1 968.8	168.1	135	523	83.0	14.7
Alexander	4.2	114	22	157	49.8	5.9	91	914	216.8	19.7	14	41	4.0	0.7
Alleghany	5.5	497	5	21	1.5	0.4	44	385	73.7	6.5	11	31	4.8	0.5
Anson	9.5	354	14	333	153.5	13.9	92	825	180.0	16.2	8	18	2.1	0.5
Ashe	17.5	641	15	155	55.9	4.2	117	1 176	292.4	23.5	40	83	15.7	1.8
Avery	19.9	1 120	22	132	41.6	3.9	94	1 029	197.6	20.0	35	119	13.0	3.2
Beaufort	89.9	1 882	58	487	285.4	18.1	216	2 459	573.4	49.8	39	109	12.8	2.0
Bertie	20.8	978	16	98	51.2	3.1	59	390	93.0	8.1	9	D	D	D
Bladen	93.2	2 647	22	166	174.2	5.6	98	847	196.7	15.9	14	52	6.5	1.5
Brunswick	1 384.0	12 882	74	578	206.7	20.5	392	4 264	1 004.2	90.1	214	689	113.2	22.5
Buncombe	300.6	1 261	257	2 838	1 162.9	114.1	1 205	15 865	3 597.9	342.4	427	1 534	277.8	51.2
Burke	38.9	428	65	757	289.5	27.9	277	2 689	661.2	57.0	53	164	18.2	3.4
Cabarrus	22.7	127	188	2 962	1 412.3	131.7	732	11 058	2 807.8	239.7	214	763	107.6	21.6
Caldwell	19.7	237	74	577	236.8	23.0	276	2 676	648.6	56.4	60	193	26.1	5.2
Camden	6.1	614	5	31	9.5	1.2	17	96	27.0	1.6	2	D	D	D
Carteret	10.7	160	66	577	254.3	21.1	429	4 148	979.6	91.1	134	575	70.7	14.5
Caswell	4.2	178	3	D	D	D	49	260	53.0	4.9	4	3	0.7	0.1
Catawba	1 076.7	6 975	253	6 524	4 087.3	263.5	797	10 577	2 683.1	233.9	193	700	142.2	20.2
Chatham	246.4	3 880	46	360	128.7	13.0	190	2 197	559.4	47.7	42	128	12.6	3.1
Cherokee	21.8	794	12	146	60.5	3.1	153	1 675	404.0	34.7	54	151	18.3	2.8

1. Merchant wholesalers, except manufacturers' sales branches and offices. 2. Employer establishments.

Table B. States and Counties — **Professional Services, Manufacturing, and Accommodation and Food Services**

STATE County	Professional, scientific, and technical services,[1] 2007				Manufacturing, 2007				Accommodation and food services, 2007			
	Number of establish-ments	Number of employees	Receipts (mil dol)	Annual payroll (mil dol)	Number of establish-ments	Number of employees	Receipts (mil dol)	Annual payroll (mil dol)	Number of establish-ments	Number of employees	Sales (mil dol)	Annual payroll (mil dol)
	147	148	149	150	151	152	153	154	155	156	157	158
NEW YORK—Cont'd												
Genesee	83	D	D	D	99	3 206	815.5	128.9	130	1 727	79.5	20.5
Greene	75	265	21.4	7.7	35	1 088	591.1	56.0	195	2 556	90.6	25.0
Hamilton	4	D	D	D	NA	NA	NA	NA	56	228	22.6	4.9
Herkimer	72	D	D	D	68	2 839	546.4	109.7	156	1 274	54.2	14.6
Jefferson	123	899	103.8	37.4	73	2 624	839.9	108.5	320	3 748	172.0	49.7
Kings	3 411	20 021	1 888.6	653.2	1 932	24 955	4 555.6	893.8	3 266	23 522	1 544.4	395.6
Lewis	21	D	D	D	23	1 254	511.6	54.3	68	480	18.0	4.8
Livingston	99	D	D	D	68	2 292	463.9	86.0	146	1 790	70.8	19.5
Madison	121	D	D	D	61	2 696	941.4	101.1	157	1 943	77.6	22.6
Monroe	1 947	22 172	2 654.9	1 237.9	939	49 854	16 615.4	2 345.4	1 531	24 626	1 061.3	307.5
Montgomery	67	D	D	D	74	3 483	719.5	132.6	120	1 073	42.0	12.0
Nassau	7 008	D	D	D	1 221	D	D	1 034.1	3 192	39 540	2 439.4	680.0
New York	17 114	263 221	72 850.5	26 601.0	2 731	37 037	8 315.1	1 396.0	8 583	175 329	17 182.6	4 753.4
Niagara	338	D	D	D	270	10 209	3 433.1	526.8	490	8 908	662.4	150.8
Oneida	390	D	D	D	261	10 874	3 251.8	437.3	506	5 862	260.5	74.7
Onondaga	1 214	D	D	D	482	23 308	7 251.5	1 213.7	1 112	17 535	784.3	229.2
Ontario	245	D	D	D	156	6 949	2 097.3	295.7	281	4 645	206.3	62.0
Orange	901	D	D	D	337	7 510	2 353.5	321.0	792	8 755	454.7	123.2
Orleans	37	D	D	D	36	1 853	465.2	67.5	64	652	21.3	5.9
Oswego	127	D	D	D	90	3 535	2 441.3	152.4	258	3 262	128.1	34.9
Otsego	105	D	D	D	58	919	177.8	34.9	193	2 170	121.7	31.0
Putnam	339	D	D	D	92	2 030	D	103.5	209	1 704	94.4	24.5
Queens	2 858	D	D	D	1 433	29 325	5 654.4	1 159.3	3 619	32 175	2 223.4	577.7
Rensselaer	305	D	D	D	111	3 040	D	133.8	309	3 929	171.8	47.8
Richmond	895	D	D	D	137	1 325	D	53.5	658	7 506	401.6	101.9
Rockland	1 225	D	D	D	266	10 344	13 670.4	540.7	689	7 222	435.3	121.2
St. Lawrence	122	D	D	D	82	3 601	2 141.6	180.7	247	3 033	116.6	31.5
Saratoga	589	D	D	D	132	5 287	1 783.6	274.6	487	6 869	333.5	99.7
Schenectady	288	D	D	D	120	4 317	1 702.5	207.6	293	3 421	151.8	44.1
Schoharie	36	D	D	D	NA	NA	NA	NA	64	450	21.6	5.2
Schuyler	15	D	D	D	29	D	D	D	61	387	25.5	6.8
Seneca	32	D	D	D	39	1 197	428.1	58.2	70	685	33.0	8.7
Steuben	151	D	D	D	82	6 168	1 821.2	305.7	221	2 295	103.4	27.7
Suffolk	5 588	D	D	D	2 356	64 453	19 089.7	3 021.9	3 274	39 934	2 376.4	651.5
Sullivan	171	D	D	D	52	1 129	243.8	33.5	243	2 027	120.7	33.2
Tioga	59	D	D	D	38	1 700	535.8	D	79	868	32.7	10.2
Tompkins	273	D	D	D	92	3 152	742.8	137.3	308	3 742	177.7	51.9
Ulster	455	D	D	D	202	D	D	165.3	533	6 542	321.4	103.9
Warren	180	944	94.7	37.4	74	4 240	1 130.5	170.1	418	4 956	300.0	91.2
Washington	70	252	19.0	6.4	102	3 023	832.2	132.7	111	623	25.0	6.6
Wayne	105	D	D	D	134	6 009	1 889.0	242.2	148	1 406	52.3	14.8
Westchester	4 401	27 021	4 865.8	2 046.8	697	14 835	4 122.9	669.0	2 176	25 314	1 799.3	483.6
Wyoming	51	D	D	D	54	2 185	457.0	77.6	78	692	31.1	8.5
Yates	33	D	D	D	32	844	D	30.6	55	446	24.4	6.5
NORTH CAROLINA	22 385	182 224	26 003.8	10 698.3	10 150	506 013	205 867.3	19 589.8	18 268	343 235	16 126.9	4 395.1
Alamance	233	D	D	D	236	11 733	3 163.1	445.0	281	5 080	219.4	62.8
Alexander	37	D	D	D	80	3 931	604.8	120.1	44	697	22.6	6.4
Alleghany	13	56	4.6	1.2	17	628	109.2	18.2	21	186	11.3	3.2
Anson	31	D	D	D	25	1 449	D	49.1	27	D	D	D
Ashe	25	105	4.7	2.6	22	1 122	206.3	35.3	45	634	22.6	6.5
Avery	39	117	11.1	3.1	NA	NA	NA	NA	49	604	33.6	11.9
Beaufort	91	330	25.8	9.6	56	3 317	1 215.6	147.4	80	1 450	49.9	13.1
Bertie	12	57	4.7	1.4	17	2 099	D	52.2	14	152	5.6	1.4
Bladen	31	154	18.6	4.3	31	5 738	1 530.9	164.7	41	448	23.3	5.3
Brunswick	212	D	D	D	75	2 008	D	80.1	238	3 285	150.6	42.5
Buncombe	826	D	D	D	310	11 987	3 211.7	470.5	658	13 930	684.3	203.1
Burke	125	D	D	D	158	9 740	2 271.2	307.2	126	2 637	107.7	28.0
Cabarrus	347	D	D	D	188	8 103	D	394.6	324	6 659	321.5	90.2
Caldwell	93	413	39.9	14.0	142	9 418	1 558.4	255.5	117	1 623	63.7	16.4
Camden	5	D	D	D	NA	NA	NA	NA	4	30	1.4	0.4
Carteret	164	666	65.1	24.7	76	1 488	292.2	43.4	226	3 424	151.0	45.1
Caswell	20	43	4.3	1.4	NA	NA	NA	NA	17	149	5.4	1.4
Catawba	329	1 780	202.9	70.0	465	27 597	6 291.1	935.4	358	6 654	272.1	76.2
Chatham	135	D	D	D	82	4 982	1 129.7	167.6	74	1 036	39.6	12.7
Cherokee	61	230	14.5	5.5	28	1 258	265.4	42.1	63	898	36.8	9.7

1. Establishment subject to federal tax.

STATE County	Health care and social assistance, 2007				Other services, 2007				Nonemployer businesses, 2013		Value of residential construction authorized by building permits, 2014	
	Number of establish-ments	Number of employees	Receipts (mil dol)	Annual payroll (mil dol)	Number of establish-ments	Number of employees	Receipts (mil dol)	Annual payroll (mil dol)	Number	Receipts (mil dol)	New Construction ($1,000)	Number of housing units
	159	160	161	162	163	164	165	166	167	168	169	170
NEW YORK—Cont'd												
Genesee	138	2 647	175.3	76.3	114	697	46.0	12.6	2 916	122.1	7 070	41
Greene	88	1 144	83.7	35.5	84	378	29.5	8.3	3 374	130.6	19 357	100
Hamilton	7	D	D	D	11	28	2.6	0.5	498	18.1	10 448	42
Herkimer	114	2 288	136.2	57.2	101	517	31.0	8.9	3 316	135.2	50 797	78
Jefferson	234	5 780	429.1	201.9	195	898	78.3	18.3	5 087	192.2	52 240	519
Kings	5 583	161 022	14 296.4	6 402.9	3 728	15 019	1 389.0	367.8	249 647	9 841.5	734 465	7 551
Lewis	55	855	63.8	25.6	44	158	15.2	3.2	1 737	68.0	9 290	79
Livingston	132	1 722	134.3	54.6	95	341	33.1	7.9	3 494	141.1	10 061	62
Madison	166	3 088	238.0	98.8	110	377	33.0	7.8	4 185	169.4	15 373	82
Monroe	1 842	57 096	4 771.0	2 015.8	1 188	7 877	802.1	210.9	44 014	1 967.9	227 112	1 204
Montgomery	177	3 928	341.6	131.3	93	471	34.8	9.3	2 478	86.2	7 581	46
Nassau	5 468	93 663	10 928.4	4 452.3	3 837	19 915	1 990.6	549.8	132 134	8 571.5	333 009	905
New York	7 612	221 081	26 406.6	10 594.3	8 951	77 817	22 175.4	3 558.5	219 326	16 946.2	524 215	5 380
Niagara	525	10 180	700.6	294.5	347	1 603	108.7	30.2	9 333	349.6	35 241	196
Oneida	613	19 752	1 470.7	696.7	412	3 017	192.8	57.4	11 696	455.1	25 448	158
Onondaga	1 276	34 330	3 449.0	1 451.7	875	6 075	549.0	157.6	26 955	1 226.5	136 191	956
Ontario	233	6 834	523.6	257.8	213	1 115	83.8	23.1	6 739	284.8	75 661	323
Orange	993	19 291	1 706.1	771.0	740	3 887	436.7	98.5	23 743	1 079.4	140 716	916
Orleans	92	1 541	92.8	40.8	63	198	14.5	3.3	1 802	66.7	4 009	27
Oswego	216	4 739	316.5	138.8	173	706	47.1	12.4	5 428	186.9	15 955	125
Otsego	166	5 311	528.4	232.3	109	599	83.4	10.4	4 268	162.6	27 692	181
Putnam	269	4 944	483.4	199.1	244	1 081	126.3	35.3	8 809	422.0	19 675	85
Queens	4 492	113 126	10 607.0	4 480.8	4 042	18 673	1 754.2	509.4	229 249	8 224.4	458 159	4 900
Rensselaer	364	8 983	702.4	317.7	241	1 427	143.4	43.5	8 673	325.5	33 664	241
Richmond	1 155	27 313	2 449.3	1 101.3	763	3 659	309.0	82.8	33 359	1 455.4	121 227	712
Rockland	1 129	21 162	1 829.5	815.0	688	3 019	297.1	81.4	25 962	1 479.9	71 481	483
St. Lawrence	294	6 372	455.2	200.8	147	707	55.3	14.2	4 951	171.5	17 753	172
Saratoga	500	7 674	608.5	245.7	285	1 860	145.7	45.8	14 938	696.2	202 357	969
Schenectady	451	10 861	867.2	407.5	207	1 481	128.2	33.4	8 489	325.1	33 072	228
Schoharie	62	1 202	72.4	30.4	37	182	15.4	4.0	1 844	66.2	3 778	18
Schuyler	40	828	61.1	23.0	28	134	12.6	2.7	1 117	35.8	6 497	31
Seneca	66	1 457	83.2	37.8	44	193	14.3	3.8	1 823	71.9	4 178	28
Steuben	250	5 902	447.9	194.8	152	723	55.8	12.6	5 235	191.0	11 633	86
Suffolk	4 546	85 581	8 923.6	3 788.5	3 767	17 775	1 746.8	492.8	123 386	6 672.8	750 599	1 217
Sullivan	257	4 674	361.5	155.5	163	497	165.2	14.6	5 518	219.7	40 747	238
Tioga	74	855	49.9	20.4	67	221	19.0	5.2	2 782	102.5	5 101	32
Tompkins	250	4 919	388.7	152.9	149	945	129.2	21.6	7 170	257.9	43 102	301
Ulster	520	D	D	D	316	1 559	117.0	30.2	15 868	640.6	68 499	289
Warren	259	6 492	526.3	243.7	145	743	71.0	20.9	4 651	214.8	39 685	278
Washington	106	1 424	84.5	39.5	75	286	26.8	6.9	3 710	140.8	7 477	90
Wayne	155	2 322	153.3	68.8	134	406	33.6	8.0	4 717	183.1	16 069	105
Westchester	3 543	70 365	7 454.7	3 252.3	2 733	13 610	2 092.1	482.3	92 896	6 001.0	238 056	584
Wyoming	66	1 294	84.9	37.6	60	242	19.8	5.4	2 092	81.8	4 098	34
Yates	55	D	D	D	38	130	11.8	2.3	1 880	83.8	13 785	70
NORTH CAROLINA	21 712	523 397	46 688.8	19 047.4	14 105	85 304	9 362.1	2 216.6	679 725	27 102.7	8 619 650	49 911
Alamance	335	6 483	549.1	227.9	201	1 165	93.5	27.7	9 280	335.1	85 140	606
Alexander	45	637	35.9	15.0	46	200	12.3	2.5	2 266	76.1	15 085	53
Alleghany	29	504	27.7	11.6	13	26	2.7	0.6	919	32.8	2 983	17
Anson	43	668	36.8	15.1	24	76	7.1	1.4	1 278	40.7	4 671	33
Ashe	53	1 151	64.3	30.9	34	118	10.4	2.6	2 370	90.9	15 977	75
Avery	42	1 137	75.6	27.1	34	241	15.7	5.3	1 660	55.3	20 471	44
Beaufort	140	2 810	170.8	79.7	90	363	28.7	8.3	3 243	126.6	19 540	170
Bertie	68	1 684	69.8	33.2	26	94	8.1	1.9	905	24.7	4 132	20
Bladen	73	1 375	79.3	33.1	29	136	8.7	3.3	1 781	57.5	6 894	80
Brunswick	189	2 834	213.6	88.0	103	542	41.7	10.5	9 436	363.6	414 829	1 973
Buncombe	757	20 467	2 071.2	821.5	437	2 703	222.9	64.3	23 896	951.2	279 774	1 312
Burke	205	4 028	380.6	148.4	97	357	32.3	8.0	5 098	196.5	20 755	94
Cabarrus	333	9 224	692.5	325.0	246	1 272	120.1	30.7	13 106	466.0	183 204	1 554
Caldwell	128	3 262	228.5	88.4	85	439	35.1	10.2	4 847	168.6	27 004	164
Camden	6	D	D	D	9	76	5.4	2.1	631	19.9	5 006	20
Carteret	176	3 206	234.8	97.8	143	657	52.6	14.3	6 121	240.0	52 027	230
Caswell	29	463	18.1	9.9	17	62	4.0	1.0	1 093	35.9	4 423	23
Catawba	383	9 682	953.0	378.2	255	1 587	177.8	46.5	10 209	447.0	55 364	283
Chatham	117	3 903	236.4	89.8	85	377	29.3	10.2	5 496	231.7	151 593	587
Cherokee	84	1 489	109.2	44.9	37	128	8.7	2.4	2 099	68.7	16 261	94

Table B. States and Counties — **Government Employment and Payroll, and Local Government Finances**

STATE County	Government employment and payroll, 2012									Local government finances, 2012				
			March payroll (percent of total)							General revenue				
												Taxes		
													Per capita[1] (dollars)	
	Full-time equivalent employees	March payroll (dollars)	Adminis-tration, judicial, and legal	Police and Corrections	Fire Protection	Highways and transpor-tation	Health and Welfare	Natural resources and utilities	Education and libraries	Total (mil dol)	Inter-govern-mental (mil dol)	Total (mil dol)	Total	Property
	171	172	173	174	175	176	177	178	179	180	181	182	183	184
NEW YORK—Cont'd														
Genesee	3 495	13 011 030	5.1	5.8	1.6	4.1	10.0	1.1	70.6	378.8	154.3	137.4	2 290	1 468
Greene	2 313	9 425 632	7.2	6.0	0.0	7.6	11.6	1.6	64.8	291.0	101.2	151.7	3 117	2 471
Hamilton	511	1 883 521	13.9	3.7	0.5	18.0	10.6	5.4	45.2	54.6	10.1	40.8	8 548	7 863
Herkimer	3 357	17 320 913	6.2	16.3	10.9	9.4	4.5	5.4	45.2	354.3	171.8	137.0	2 124	1 648
Jefferson	5 239	20 682 670	6.0	6.1	2.2	6.7	6.7	3.0	66.9	631.5	312.9	217.3	1 807	1 154
Kings	(3)	(3)	(3)	(3)	(3)	(3)	(3)	(3)	(3)	(3)	(3)	(3)	(3)	(3)
Lewis	1 643	6 393 465	5.3	4.0	0.1	9.3	34.1	0.3	46.2	221.0	80.0	54.5	2 001	1 591
Livingston	2 962	11 287 932	7.2	8.2	0.0	6.5	18.2	2.0	56.7	340.1	136.2	132.2	2 039	1 556
Madison	2 860	10 880 867	5.6	7.3	1.1	8.0	7.4	2.2	66.8	324.2	144.9	143.1	1 977	1 638
Monroe	32 909	147 986 255	4.0	10.2	3.5	2.4	4.8	4.9	68.8	4 246.2	1 878.0	1 825.1	2 441	1 824
Montgomery	2 237	9 439 506	8.2	8.8	2.4	6.9	5.7	2.1	64.3	270.8	126.1	103.0	2 062	1 500
Nassau	60 368	360 394 360	4.0	11.4	0.7	2.4	9.9	3.6	66.2	10 545.3	2 263.0	7 088.6	5 254	4 380
New York	(3)411 393	(3)36 392 993	(3)3.2	(3)18.6	(3)5.3	(3)14.2	(3)17.3	(3)4.7	(3)33.2	(3)89 561.8	(3)30 794.6	(3)42 487.9	(3)5 096	(3)2 183
Niagara	8 942	40 897 207	4.2	9.3	3.5	3.3	5.7	3.9	65.8	1 197.2	504.4	461.1	2 144	1 505
Oneida	10 265	43 288 880	5.1	9.3	3.3	5.7	6.1	4.4	65.3	1 243.2	607.6	466.1	1 996	1 316
Onondaga	21 333	98 896 686	3.5	9.2	2.8	3.6	6.0	5.0	68.2	2 768.2	1 213.5	1 131.6	2 424	1 706
Ontario	5 314	22 633 286	7.3	8.2	1.0	4.3	6.4	3.2	68.2	617.9	231.6	291.0	2 682	1 907
Orange	15 475	79 024 558	5.0	9.7	1.3	3.8	7.6	2.1	69.2	2 388.1	851.1	1 242.0	3 316	2 623
Orleans	1 883	7 322 413	5.8	7.3	1.3	4.6	12.9	1.4	65.5	215.9	108.4	76.5	1 785	1 393
Oswego	5 833	24 108 601	4.0	4.7	1.8	4.8	6.7	1.2	74.7	720.3	332.9	266.4	2 189	1 640
Otsego	2 867	10 320 001	6.5	5.1	1.5	9.1	12.9	1.2	62.0	319.5	134.0	135.1	2 189	1 567
Putnam	3 780	21 486 132	6.3	9.6	0.0	4.8	5.6	1.1	71.4	620.4	156.8	423.9	4 256	3 653
Queens	(3)	(3)	(3)	(3)	(3)	(3)	(3)	(3)	(3)	(3)	(3)	(3)	(3)	(3)
Rensselaer	7 740	35 240 411	5.4	10.0	1.8	3.0	10.0	3.2	65.6	935.0	383.9	372.9	2 333	1 782
Richmond	(3)	(3)	(3)	(3)	(3)	(3)	(3)	(3)	(3)	(3)	(3)	(3)	(3)	(3)
Rockland	12 621	72 071 900	6.2	11.8	0.2	3.4	10.5	3.3	63.3	2 081.2	511.7	1 307.8	4 116	3 491
St. Lawrence	5 029	19 319 273	5.7	6.1	1.0	8.5	20.0	3.1	54.2	629.7	288.6	207.1	1 845	1 390
Saratoga	8 393	36 185 319	5.4	6.8	1.4	6.5	7.0	2.5	68.7	1 010.7	328.4	547.9	2 467	1 874
Schenectady	6 336	30 200 971	4.8	10.8	2.9	3.7	8.4	3.1	64.2	840.2	334.0	398.5	2 569	1 914
Schoharie	1 588	6 242 263	7.0	4.8	0.1	8.7	8.1	2.1	67.7	198.0	92.7	86.5	2 696	2 164
Schuyler	713	2 598 532	9.7	8.4	0.0	8.0	12.3	2.8	55.9	92.6	40.4	41.0	2 213	1 616
Seneca	1 397	5 203 170	7.6	6.3	0.0	6.3	10.3	4.6	63.8	187.5	82.2	75.2	2 129	1 460
Steuben	5 430	22 838 751	6.3	4.7	1.6	6.5	9.0	2.5	68.7	603.0	285.7	219.9	2 220	1 686
Suffolk	63 444	372 480 221	4.1	12.0	1.0	2.5	5.0	2.8	71.0	10 433.2	3 062.8	6 438.8	4 295	3 385
Sullivan	3 903	18 183 844	6.0	6.2	4.1	7.1	11.7	2.9	59.7	571.4	182.8	285.0	3 711	3 207
Tioga	2 377	8 831 267	4.9	6.4	0.5	4.3	7.4	1.1	72.8	263.8	126.3	98.9	1 959	1 427
Tompkins	4 530	19 870 493	5.0	6.2	2.8	4.4	7.3	3.5	68.0	531.9	184.0	252.8	2 465	1 857
Ulster	8 282	38 442 668	5.7	7.7	1.3	4.8	8.8	1.7	68.0	1 095.2	330.4	630.3	3 467	2 848
Warren	3 395	12 916 351	7.7	10.3	0.3	8.0	7.0	4.0	60.4	411.0	122.0	230.3	3 513	2 589
Washington	3 303	11 817 292	4.2	5.9	0.6	5.8	10.6	1.3	70.1	334.5	150.3	129.8	2 063	1 703
Wayne	4 573	16 899 070	5.7	6.6	0.1	4.5	9.5	2.2	70.0	506.8	227.4	194.1	2 088	1 627
Westchester	42 725	278 687 815	4.6	13.0	4.0	2.1	14.4	4.1	55.6	8 694.6	1 905.2	4 937.7	5 135	4 223
Wyoming	1 997	7 253 253	6.6	6.7	0.7	6.2	29.3	3.6	45.9	224.2	78.4	71.1	1 698	1 279
Yates	984	3 705 476	8.7	13.4	0.2	8.3	6.2	2.9	58.0	114.7	43.0	58.3	2 300	1 770
NORTH CAROLINA	X	X	X	X	X	X	X	X	X	X	X	X	X	X
Alamance	1 005 835	17 822 770	4.1	10.8	2.8	1.7	7.8	5.8	64.0	420.3	210.4	147.7	960	694
Alexander	1 147	3 312 277	3.5	5.4	1.2	0.1	15.0	1.1	71.6	79.1	47.9	22.9	622	467
Alleghany	425	1 164 658	3.2	4.3	0.0	1.2	5.7	2.7	76.9	29.9	16.8	10.5	964	802
Anson	1 315	3 876 045	2.9	6.4	2.5	0.6	7.2	4.8	74.4	91.7	58.9	20.0	760	612
Ashe	790	2 611 411	5.6	7.1	0.0	1.1	16.3	2.1	65.4	64.2	34.4	23.7	876	672
Avery	815	1 974 739	6.6	9.8	1.1	1.1	14.1	2.6	59.8	51.3	22.8	24.5	1 387	1 109
Beaufort	2 278	5 974 850	4.5	7.2	2.1	0.6	8.3	10.0	62.5	173.8	99.8	49.9	1 050	812
Bertie	997	3 093 286	5.9	4.6	0.1	0.6	4.8	2.9	80.8	51.4	32.6	12.0	580	454
Bladen	1 399	4 935 403	2.7	6.3	0.5	0.4	11.2	2.6	74.0	133.3	64.5	29.1	834	667
Brunswick	3 900	12 967 182	6.8	10.3	1.5	1.3	19.2	7.5	47.9	393.3	118.2	177.6	1 582	1 215
Buncombe	8 896	30 002 974	4.8	8.2	3.6	1.6	11.7	7.3	59.6	751.0	306.2	322.9	1 321	936
Burke	3 144	9 746 027	4.9	6.5	1.0	0.9	9.1	5.9	70.6	228.4	129.8	66.9	739	594
Cabarrus	7 505	25 676 197	3.6	8.3	4.5	1.2	14.4	6.7	58.7	601.3	252.6	258.8	1 403	1 100
Caldwell	3 445	10 357 515	2.9	6.0	2.1	0.6	13.9	3.0	69.5	257.1	164.6	64.8	791	595
Camden	352	1 014 214	1.0	5.8	0.0	0.0	0.0	4.2	71.8	30.3	17.1	11.7	1 163	952
Carteret	2 554	7 543 452	5.4	9.0	4.8	1.2	10.1	4.3	60.9	338.2	84.6	98.9	1 462	1 061
Caswell	710	2 061 989	3.0	5.5	0.0	0.0	17.8	1.7	67.9	51.5	32.9	13.2	569	464
Catawba	7 515	27 058 433	3.4	5.6	2.5	1.6	35.0	3.0	45.2	716.3	255.5	171.8	1 113	804
Chatham	1 616	6 230 991	4.0	6.8	0.3	0.8	10.6	4.0	68.1	164.8	66.0	78.0	1 182	977
Cherokee	1 091	3 381 536	5.0	8.1	0.0	1.1	13.2	8.0	61.9	84.3	45.8	26.1	966	704

1. Based on the resident population estimated as of July 1 of the year shown. 3. Bronx, Kings, Queens, and Richmond counties are included with New York county.

STATE County	Local government finances, 2012 (cont.) — Direct general expenditure — Total (mil dol)	Per capita[1] (dollars)	Percent of total for: Education	Health and hospitals	Police protection	Public welfare	Highways	Debt outstanding — Total (mil dol)	Per capita[1] (dollars)	Government employment, 2013 — Federal civilian	Federal military	State and local	Presidential election,[2] 2012 — Percent of vote cast: Democratic	Republican	All other
	185	186	187	188	189	190	191	192	193	194	195	196	197	198	199
NEW YORK—Cont'd															
Genesee	380.9	6 350	48.2	3.3	2.6	11.4	6.0	207.2	3 454	589	94	4 929	40.1	58.5	1.5
Greene	302.4	6 212	48.5	5.4	2.1	9.8	9.4	211.7	4 350	91	74	4 161	44.1	54.0	1.8
Hamilton	53.0	11 093	36.6	5.7	1.7	2.5	16.4	24.5	5 123	18	0	688	35.9	62.8	1.3
Herkimer	352.7	5 467	56.7	3.1	1.8	9.3	8.9	252.1	3 907	101	104	4 215	44.5	53.8	1.7
Jefferson	631.0	5 247	49.6	3.4	2.6	9.2	6.9	554.7	4 612	3 279	17 670	8 295	46.8	52.0	1.2
Kings	[3]	[3]	[3]	[3]	[3]	[3]	[3]	[3]	[3]	6 498	4 375	28 562	79.4	20.0	0.6
Lewis	250.8	9 211	33.2	34.9	1.3	6.5	7.0	120.5	4 427	58	44	2 268	44.8	53.6	1.6
Livingston	328.9	5 074	44.9	5.5	2.8	18.2	7.8	282.5	4 359	129	97	6 686	45.3	53.2	1.5
Madison	345.6	4 774	52.0	4.3	2.3	7.4	8.1	456.5	6 307	130	111	4 171	49.3	48.5	2.2
Monroe	4 348.7	5 815	50.1	4.2	4.3	10.9	3.2	3 397.3	4 543	2 728	1 294	44 420	58.3	40.5	1.2
Montgomery	305.0	6 106	50.5	2.2	2.0	7.7	5.3	285.4	5 714	100	80	2 446	45.0	53.1	1.9
Nassau	11 105.9	8 231	48.3	7.2	8.7	5.9	3.1	9 302.1	6 894	5 253	2 540	73 457	53.8	45.4	0.7
New York	[3]84 366.2	[3]10 120	[3]26.6	[3]10.0	[3]6.0	[3]15.1	[3]1.9	[3]168 630.0	[3]20 227	21 637	2 835	423 779	85.7	13.5	0.8
Niagara	1 203.8	5 596	48.1	2.7	3.7	8.2	5.8	966.3	4 492	1 045	381	12 807	49.7	48.7	1.6
Oneida	1 300.4	5 568	52.4	2.6	3.1	11.0	5.5	1 381.4	5 915	2 272	411	24 075	46.1	52.2	1.6
Onondaga	3 043.0	6 518	47.4	3.2	3.3	10.4	4.6	3 160.9	6 771	4 367	857	37 528	59.3	38.9	1.8
Ontario	612.2	5 642	54.1	2.3	2.9	8.5	6.6	594.8	5 481	1 366	176	6 908	49.2	49.3	1.5
Orange	2 555.9	6 825	54.6	4.6	3.7	10.5	3.3	1 906.2	5 090	4 799	6 644	20 740	51.6	47.4	1.0
Orleans	216.3	5 050	53.5	3.8	2.2	13.7	6.1	184.0	4 295	83	65	3 870	39.9	58.6	1.5
Oswego	722.5	5 936	55.7	2.6	2.1	8.4	6.2	668.5	5 493	244	220	8 798	50.3	47.9	1.8
Otsego	326.6	5 293	47.1	2.7	1.6	14.9	9.2	292.6	4 742	129	93	4 789	52.0	46.1	1.9
Putnam	630.2	6 327	61.1	2.1	4.6	3.9	5.1	400.1	4 017	141	159	4 286	45.8	53.3	1.0
Queens	[3]	[3]	[3]	[3]	[3]	[3]	[3]	[3]	[3]	14 302	3 765	21 697	75.1	24.3	0.6
Rensselaer	989.2	6 189	51.6	3.4	3.1	13.0	3.7	809.6	5 065	368	267	10 202	53.7	44.4	1.9
Richmond	[3]	[3]	[3]	[3]	[3]	[3]	[3]	[3]	[3]	1 009	1 270	5 029	47.6	51.7	0.7
Rockland	2 333.3	7 343	45.2	11.3	4.7	6.4	4.3	1 968.4	6 195	474	516	19 840	52.6	46.7	0.6
St. Lawrence	626.2	5 579	45.3	11.0	2.3	10.4	8.4	441.9	3 937	586	279	9 329	57.5	41.1	1.4
Saratoga	1 019.1	4 588	54.8	5.8	3.1	8.2	5.3	814.5	3 667	398	2 107	11 441	50.9	47.5	1.6
Schenectady	849.4	5 476	48.9	2.4	3.7	14.9	3.5	691.5	4 458	591	257	10 147	55.3	42.6	2.0
Schoharie	201.5	6 278	47.0	3.9	1.2	7.5	15.0	132.3	4 121	80	50	2 449	41.8	56.1	2.1
Schuyler	91.9	4 963	40.6	6.3	1.9	11.2	10.5	63.1	3 409	50	30	1 158	45.7	52.8	1.5
Seneca	180.7	5 118	46.5	4.6	2.7	8.7	6.0	331.8	9 398	92	53	2 706	50.4	47.8	1.8
Steuben	616.7	6 226	58.5	3.7	1.6	11.1	8.0	529.5	5 345	991	160	6 792	40.9	57.8	1.3
Suffolk	11 000.9	7 338	53.4	3.5	5.3	5.4	3.3	9 786.8	6 528	11 549	2 682	93 031	52.6	46.6	0.9
Sullivan	549.1	7 150	46.8	4.4	2.6	12.2	8.2	363.9	4 739	178	120	5 629	54.1	44.6	1.3
Tioga	265.1	5 251	53.3	3.7	1.7	7.4	7.4	230.5	4 566	154	89	2 422	44.1	54.3	1.7
Tompkins	541.1	5 276	48.3	4.4	2.7	8.0	5.5	696.7	6 794	293	164	6 156	70.2	28.1	1.7
Ulster	1 119.8	6 160	51.1	2.0	2.8	12.1	5.4	695.1	3 823	442	299	13 143	61.0	37.4	1.7
Warren	406.2	6 198	44.0	4.8	3.3	10.1	9.1	365.7	5 580	191	107	4 544	50.6	47.9	1.5
Washington	349.4	5 552	55.7	4.3	1.6	11.5	6.6	209.9	3 336	121	98	5 019	49.5	48.7	1.7
Wayne	528.4	5 684	56.8	4.2	2.3	10.7	5.9	364.9	3 926	180	153	8 080	44.3	54.2	1.4
Westchester	8 708.4	9 055	42.2	12.9	4.6	6.4	1.7	6 138.8	6 383	4 431	1 546	55 332	63.4	35.8	0.8
Wyoming	218.6	5 217	34.6	26.6	2.8	7.6	9.3	135.9	3 244	99	62	4 095	36.1	62.3	1.6
Yates	112.7	4 445	44.0	5.8	4.2	8.7	10.8	161.3	6 365	60	39	1 170	47.6	51.3	1.0
NORTH CAROLINA	X	X	X	X	X	X	X	X	X	69 318	136 770	655 105	49.7	49.4	0.9
Alamance	427.7	2 779	50.9	3.4	8.3	5.8	1.6	182.0	1 183	215	377	6 826	44.9	54.2	0.9
Alexander	79.9	2 168	57.3	6.5	5.6	7.5	0.5	21.9	594	54	89	1 940	29.9	68.3	1.7
Alleghany	28.9	2 648	55.4	5.1	5.7	7.6	0.2	8.2	749	44	27	598	38.4	59.4	2.2
Anson	92.1	3 494	62.0	2.8	6.7	6.7	1.0	5.0	191	48	59	2 524	60.2	39.2	0.7
Ashe	66.1	2 439	50.5	2.7	5.8	13.7	1.2	26.9	992	59	67	1 150	37.3	60.6	2.2
Avery	52.4	2 970	45.9	4.8	9.0	7.8	1.8	12.6	717	46	38	1 539	27.4	71.5	1.1
Beaufort	192.0	4 042	45.1	2.4	4.2	6.6	1.0	78.5	1 653	118	118	2 746	41.1	58.5	0.4
Bertie	49.9	2 417	57.0	0.9	7.9	10.3	1.0	16.3	788	89	48	1 274	65.2	34.6	0.2
Bladen	137.6	3 942	46.1	22.2	4.7	6.1	1.2	40.6	1 164	97	86	2 458	50.7	48.7	0.6
Brunswick	396.3	3 530	32.7	9.9	9.3	4.9	1.6	543.6	4 843	419	344	4 729	40.5	58.5	1.0
Buncombe	800.5	3 274	41.8	1.9	10.0	8.4	2.1	617.7	2 527	3 213	661	13 357	56.3	42.4	1.3
Burke	231.0	2 553	56.9	2.9	7.1	6.7	0.9	69.8	771	142	217	7 449	39.8	59.0	1.2
Cabarrus	593.1	3 214	47.0	1.8	6.9	5.0	1.7	669.7	3 630	260	466	13 333	40.4	58.9	0.7
Caldwell	274.4	3 349	49.9	21.1	4.8	6.2	1.3	60.2	735	128	203	4 260	34.4	64.1	1.6
Camden	29.0	2 871	58.0	0.3	6.4	4.2	0.0	8.6	849	11	25	455	33.1	65.1	1.7
Carteret	311.1	4 600	29.2	30.1	5.8	4.1	1.4	132.7	1 963	278	420	4 628	32.2	66.9	1.0
Caswell	54.4	2 344	50.3	5.5	16.1	11.3	0.1	23.2	1 000	39	55	1 327	51.0	47.9	1.0
Catawba	685.5	4 441	36.4	32.8	4.4	5.5	1.4	324.5	2 102	350	384	9 510	36.9	61.9	1.2
Chatham	177.4	2 689	45.4	4.2	15.7	6.3	0.6	171.9	2 605	114	165	2 401	54.3	44.6	1.1
Cherokee	85.8	3 180	51.5	5.7	5.1	7.8	0.4	29.5	1 092	89	67	1 532	30.1	68.7	1.3

1. Based on the resident population estimated as of July 1 of the year shown. 2. © 2013 Election Data Services, Inc. All rights reserved. 3. Bronx, Kings, Queens, and Richmond counties are included with New York county.

STATE/ County code	CBSA code[1]	County type[2]	STATE County	Land area,[3] (sq km) 2010	Population, 2014: Total persons 2014	Population, 2014: Rank	Population, 2014: Per square kilometer	Population and population characteristics, 2013 — Race alone or in combination, not Hispanic or Latino (percent): White	Black	American Indian, Alaska Native	Asian and Pacific Islander	Percent Hispanic or Latino[4]	Age (percent): Under 5 years	5 to 17 years	18 to 24 years	25 to 34 years	35 to 44 years	45 to 54 years
				1	2	3	4	5	6	7	8	9	10	11	12	13	14	15
			NORTH CAROLINA—Cont'd															
37 041	...	7	Chowan	447	14 572	2 131	32.6	61.7	34.7	0.7	0.8	3.2	5.5	15.8	7.5	10.2	10.3	13.6
37 043	...	9	Clay	556	10 581	2 391	19.0	95.3	1.5	0.9	0.6	3.1	4.2	13.8	6.2	8.3	10.4	12.5
37 045	43140	4	Cleveland	1 202	97 076	608	80.8	75.2	21.4	0.6	1.2	3.1	5.8	16.7	9.7	10.6	12.2	14.6
37 047	...	6	Columbus	2 428	56 953	892	23.5	61.5	30.6	3.9	0.6	4.7	5.6	16.8	8.8	11.8	12.0	13.9
37 049	35100	5	Craven	1 836	104 510	566	56.9	68.6	22.5	1.0	3.3	6.9	7.2	15.5	13.3	13.4	10.5	11.4
37 051	22180	2	Cumberland	1 689	326 328	203	193.2	48.7	38.0	2.5	4.1	10.7	8.2	17.8	12.7	16.8	11.9	12.1
37 053	47260	1	Currituck	678	24 976	1 607	36.8	89.4	6.7	1.1	1.2	3.4	5.1	17.1	7.5	10.7	13.1	17.1
37 055	28620	5	Dare	993	35 104	1 297	35.4	89.4	3.4	1.0	0.9	6.9	5.3	14.4	6.5	11.6	12.5	15.3
37 057	49180	4	Davidson	1 431	164 072	387	114.7	82.6	9.7	0.8	1.6	6.6	5.5	17.3	8.0	10.8	13.3	15.4
37 059	49180	2	Davie	684	41 434	1 139	60.6	86.4	7.1	0.7	0.9	6.3	5.1	17.1	7.5	9.1	12.8	15.3
37 061	...	6	Duplin	2 114	59 882	868	28.3	53.1	25.3	0.7	0.6	21.4	6.9	18.1	8.8	11.8	12.6	13.6
37 063	20500	2	Durham	741	294 460	228	397.4	43.6	38.6	1.0	5.4	13.5	7.2	14.9	10.8	18.3	14.5	12.5
37 065	40580	3	Edgecombe	1 309	54 933	914	42.0	38.0	57.8	0.7	0.4	4.0	6.3	17.2	9.1	11.6	11.2	13.7
37 067	49180	2	Forsyth	1 057	365 298	185	345.6	59.4	26.6	0.8	2.5	12.4	6.5	17.4	10.0	12.8	12.8	14.0
37 069	39580	2	Franklin	1 273	62 860	836	49.4	64.7	27.0	1.0	0.9	7.9	5.8	17.6	8.7	11.1	13.3	15.2
37 071	16740	1	Gaston	922	211 127	303	229.0	76.5	16.4	0.9	1.7	6.2	6.2	17.1	8.8	11.8	13.8	14.7
37 073	47260	8	Gates	882	11 567	2 321	13.1	64.2	34.0	1.2	0.8	1.8	4.9	16.8	8.1	9.9	11.3	17.1
37 075	...	9	Graham	756	8 644	2 547	11.4	90.0	0.9	7.6	0.6	2.8	5.3	15.9	7.8	10.0	10.8	14.0
37 077	37080	6	Granville	1 377	58 500	881	42.5	59.8	32.2	0.8	1.0	7.5	5.1	16.5	9.3	10.8	13.9	16.1
37 079	...	3	Greene	689	21 093	1 768	30.6	48.5	36.2	0.9	0.6	14.8	5.9	16.0	8.5	13.7	14.0	14.3
37 081	24660	2	Guilford	1 672	512 119	130	306.3	54.4	34.2	1.1	5.0	7.5	6.1	16.7	11.2	13.5	13.2	13.8
37 083	40260	4	Halifax	1 875	52 970	941	28.3	40.1	53.3	4.2	1.0	2.7	5.5	16.3	9.1	10.8	11.2	14.6
37 085	20380	4	Harnett	1 541	126 666	488	82.2	65.1	22.3	1.7	2.0	11.7	7.6	19.9	9.8	15.2	13.9	12.5
37 087	11700	2	Haywood	1 434	59 471	875	41.5	94.2	1.5	1.1	0.6	3.6	4.5	14.1	7.3	10.0	11.7	14.4
37 089	11700	2	Henderson	966	111 149	545	115.1	85.4	3.9	1.0	1.5	9.8	5.0	14.9	6.5	10.1	11.8	13.3
37 091	...	7	Hertford	914	24 308	1 632	26.6	35.1	59.9	1.7	0.9	3.7	5.3	14.5	11.3	11.6	11.4	13.9
37 093	22180	2	Hoke	1 012	51 611	964	51.0	44.2	34.9	10.0	2.5	12.2	9.5	19.5	9.0	18.6	13.8	11.9
37 095	...	9	Hyde	1 587	5 676	2 787	3.6	61.4	30.2	0.8	0.5	8.0	4.3	13.8	7.0	13.4	14.1	13.7
37 097	16740	4	Iredell	1 486	166 675	382	112.2	78.4	12.6	0.7	2.7	7.2	5.7	18.5	8.5	11.2	13.8	15.7
37 099	19000	6	Jackson	1 271	40 981	1 153	32.2	83.2	2.6	9.6	1.2	5.1	4.9	12.6	19.1	11.3	10.4	11.6
37 101	39580	2	Johnston	2 049	181 423	355	88.5	70.4	16.0	0.9	1.1	13.2	6.8	20.1	8.0	11.7	15.4	14.8
37 103	35100	8	Jones	1 219	10 076	2 432	8.3	63.4	32.2	1.0	0.8	4.2	4.9	14.7	8.3	10.8	10.0	14.3
37 105	41820	4	Lee	660	59 662	872	90.4	59.3	20.0	0.9	1.4	20.0	7.1	18.9	8.8	12.6	12.8	13.3
37 107	28820	4	Lenoir	1 038	58 485	882	56.3	51.4	41.0	0.7	1.0	7.1	5.9	17.3	8.7	10.8	11.3	14.1
37 109	16740	4	Lincoln	772	79 829	693	103.4	86.4	6.2	0.7	0.9	7.1	5.3	17.0	8.0	10.4	14.1	16.2
37 111	32000	6	McDowell	1 141	44 965	1 069	39.4	89.4	4.4	0.8	1.0	5.5	5.3	15.8	7.8	11.2	13.1	14.5
37 113	...	7	Macon	1 335	33 875	1 330	25.4	90.5	1.9	0.9	0.9	6.7	4.7	14.0	7.3	9.6	9.9	13.0
37 115	11700	2	Madison	1 164	21 157	1 765	18.2	95.0	2.0	1.0	0.7	2.5	4.7	14.5	10.9	9.8	11.9	13.8
37 117	...	6	Martin	1 195	23 454	1 665	19.6	52.9	43.4	0.6	0.6	3.5	5.2	15.6	8.1	9.5	10.9	14.2
37 119	16740	1	Mecklenburg	1 357	1 012 539	41	746.2	50.8	32.0	0.9	5.7	12.6	7.1	17.7	9.5	16.5	15.5	13.6
37 121	...	9	Mitchell	573	15 311	2 080	26.7	94.0	0.9	0.8	0.6	4.7	4.6	13.8	7.3	9.9	11.7	14.3
37 123	...	6	Montgomery	1 274	27 395	1 516	21.5	64.7	19.0	0.7	1.7	15.0	6.1	17.3	8.4	10.7	12.1	13.4
37 125	38240	4	Moore	1 807	93 077	628	51.5	78.7	13.9	1.3	1.5	6.3	5.4	15.9	6.8	10.5	11.5	12.9
37 127	40580	3	Nash	1 400	94 357	619	67.4	53.2	39.4	1.1	1.1	6.6	5.8	17.1	9.1	11.0	12.6	14.6
37 129	48900	2	New Hanover	496	216 298	297	436.1	78.3	15.1	1.0	2.1	5.5	5.4	14.2	13.1	13.8	12.9	12.8
37 131	40260	9	Northampton	1 390	20 463	1 805	14.7	39.2	58.6	0.8	0.4	2.0	5.1	14.3	8.3	9.4	9.9	14.4
37 133	27340	3	Onslow	1 975	187 589	342	95.0	70.3	16.6	1.4	3.7	11.8	10.0	15.6	21.7	18.6	9.9	8.7
37 135	20500	2	Orange	1 031	140 420	450	136.2	71.9	12.6	1.0	8.5	8.4	4.8	15.7	19.0	12.4	12.1	13.2
37 137	35100	9	Pamlico	872	12 948	2 235	14.8	75.2	20.9	0.9	0.9	3.5	3.9	12.7	6.8	9.7	10.3	14.1
37 139	21020	7	Pasquotank	588	39 787	1 177	67.7	56.4	38.4	0.9	2.0	4.4	6.2	15.5	12.0	13.6	11.6	13.6
37 141	48900	2	Pender	2 253	56 250	902	25.0	75.5	17.8	1.2	1.0	6.3	5.6	16.8	8.0	11.0	13.0	14.8
37 143	21020	9	Perquimans	640	13 466	2 209	21.0	72.5	25.1	0.7	0.7	2.3	4.8	15.5	6.8	10.3	10.2	13.5
37 145	20500	2	Person	1 016	39 132	1 193	38.5	67.7	27.8	1.0	0.7	4.2	5.5	16.7	8.2	10.3	12.7	14.9
37 147	24780	3	Pitt	1 689	175 354	364	103.8	58.0	35.1	0.7	2.3	5.8	6.2	15.8	18.8	13.6	12.0	11.7
37 149	...	8	Polk	616	20 357	1 815	33.0	89.3	5.0	0.7	0.6	5.6	3.6	14.0	6.8	7.4	10.2	14.2
37 151	24660	2	Randolph	2 027	142 778	446	70.4	81.5	6.6	0.9	1.3	10.9	5.9	17.9	8.3	10.9	13.3	15.0
37 153	40460	4	Richmond	1 227	45 733	1 054	37.3	59.5	31.4	3.3	1.4	6.3	6.4	17.6	9.7	11.3	12.6	13.6
37 155	31300	4	Robeson	2 458	134 760	471	54.8	28.4	25.3	39.6	1.0	8.0	7.2	18.8	11.1	12.4	12.7	13.0
37 157	24660	2	Rockingham	1 465	91 696	633	62.6	74.4	19.6	0.9	0.9	5.9	5.1	15.9	8.0	10.2	12.6	15.4
37 159	16740	4	Rowan	1 324	138 630	457	104.7	74.5	16.7	0.8	1.4	8.0	5.7	17.2	9.2	11.7	12.5	14.5
37 161	22580	4	Rutherford	1 461	66 600	795	45.6	85.4	10.8	0.7	0.7	3.9	5.3	16.1	8.2	10.0	12.3	14.6
37 163	...	6	Sampson	2 447	64 050	819	26.2	53.6	26.8	2.3	0.7	18.0	6.5	18.4	8.6	11.4	12.9	13.6
37 165	29900	6	Scotland	826	35 576	1 282	43.1	46.6	39.7	12.1	1.1	2.7	6.5	17.4	10.0	11.5	12.4	13.3
37 167	10620	6	Stanly	1 023	60 600	862	59.2	82.8	11.8	0.6	2.1	3.9	5.6	16.3	9.3	11.3	12.5	14.6
37 169	49180	2	Stokes	1 163	46 419	1 040	39.9	92.5	4.5	0.8	0.4	2.8	4.7	15.9	7.8	9.5	12.8	16.2
37 171	34340	4	Surry	1 378	72 968	744	53.0	85.5	4.1	0.6	0.8	9.9	5.6	16.9	8.2	9.9	12.8	14.6

1. CBSA = Core Based Statistical Area. See Appendix A for explanation. See Appendix B for list of metropolitan areas with component counties. 2. County type code from the Economic Research Service of USDA Rural-Urban Continuum Codes. See Appendix A for definition. 3. Dry land or land partially or temporarily covered by water. 4. May be of any race.

STATE County	Population, 2013 (cont.) — Age (percent) (cont.) — 55 to 64 years	65 to 74 years	75 years and over	Percent female	Population change and components of change, 2000–2014 — Total persons — 2000	2010	Percent change — 2000–2010	2010–2014	Components of change, 2010–2014 — Births	Deaths	Net migration	Households, 2009–2013 — Number	Persons per household	Percent — Family households	Female family householder[1]	One person
	16	17	18	19	20	21	22	23	24	25	26	27	28	29	30	31
NORTH CAROLINA—Cont'd																
Chowan	15.5	12.0	9.5	52.3	14 526	14 793	1.8	-1.5	663	782	-113	5 945	2.42	64.4	15.4	31.9
Clay	17.1	16.9	10.6	50.6	8 775	10 587	20.6	-0.1	338	571	253	4 431	2.37	66.1	6.8	29.8
Cleveland	13.8	9.9	6.7	51.9	96 287	98 078	1.9	-1.0	4 657	4 749	-868	37 760	2.53	68.0	13.7	28.6
Columbus	13.8	10.2	7.0	50.5	54 749	58 098	6.1	-2.0	2 747	2 886	-1 084	21 758	2.52	65.7	16.9	30.6
Craven	12.1	9.3	7.3	49.3	91 436	103 505	13.2	1.0	6 818	4 119	-1 765	39 931	2.51	70.4	13.2	25.6
Cumberland	10.1	6.2	4.3	51.1	302 963	319 431	5.4	2.2	24 504	9 846	-7 943	121 226	2.55	66.9	18.5	28.0
Currituck	14.7	9.2	5.4	50.5	18 190	23 547	29.5	6.1	972	890	1 343	9 121	2.60	71.8	9.8	21.8
Dare	16.6	11.3	6.4	50.3	29 967	33 920	13.2	3.5	1 581	1 257	839	14 624	2.33	63.1	8.7	27.5
Davidson	13.3	9.7	6.6	51.0	147 246	162 878	10.6	0.7	7 269	6 897	620	64 580	2.49	69.6	12.4	26.3
Davie	14.6	10.6	8.1	51.2	34 835	41 240	18.4	0.5	1 667	1 677	198	16 234	2.52	72.5	10.6	24.0
Duplin	12.9	9.0	6.4	50.7	49 063	58 505	19.2	2.4	3 238	2 119	318	22 052	2.64	67.2	14.3	26.0
Durham	11.2	6.1	4.5	52.0	223 314	267 587	19.8	9.1	18 134	7 570	13 377	111 276	2.36	59.3	15.1	31.6
Edgecombe	14.5	9.4	6.9	53.5	55 606	56 552	1.7	-2.9	2 828	2 458	-2 043	21 021	2.60	69.1	23.1	26.5
Forsyth	12.5	7.9	6.2	52.4	306 067	350 670	14.6	4.2	19 524	12 920	8 155	140 439	2.45	63.5	14.2	31.5
Franklin	13.8	8.8	5.8	50.4	47 260	60 619	28.3	3.7	2 850	2 205	1 576	23 313	2.55	71.4	12.3	24.8
Gaston	12.9	8.6	6.1	51.6	190 365	206 086	8.3	2.4	10 752	9 140	3 358	79 450	2.57	68.4	14.9	27.2
Gates	14.7	10.5	6.7	51.1	10 516	12 197	16.0	-5.1	467	468	-582	4 459	2.67	73.7	14.4	23.5
Graham	14.5	12.5	9.1	50.6	7 993	8 861	10.9	-2.4	392	449	-170	3 462	2.49	70.0	9.5	26.0
Granville	13.7	8.9	5.9	48.9	48 498	59 916	23.5	1.7	2 394	2 024	523	19 953	2.72	71.1	14.9	26.0
Greene	13.5	8.2	5.9	45.7	18 974	21 362	12.6	-1.3	956	749	-502	7 104	2.71	70.0	17.1	28.2
Guilford	12.0	7.6	5.8	52.4	421 048	488 406	16.0	4.9	25 993	16 613	14 246	196 463	2.44	63.0	15.3	30.5
Halifax	14.5	10.0	7.9	52.3	57 370	54 691	-4.7	-3.1	2 478	2 833	-1 372	21 550	2.45	65.3	22.3	31.2
Harnett	10.2	6.6	4.3	50.6	91 025	114 678	26.0	10.5	7 620	3 753	7 942	40 677	2.83	71.5	13.4	24.7
Haywood	15.1	13.2	9.8	51.8	54 033	59 036	9.3	0.7	2 330	2 946	1 001	26 608	2.19	67.6	11.3	27.5
Henderson	14.3	13.0	10.9	51.6	89 173	106 740	19.7	4.1	4 506	5 468	5 246	45 246	2.34	67.0	8.4	28.0
Hertford	14.8	9.5	7.5	50.9	22 601	24 669	9.2	-1.4	1 012	1 111	-242	8 624	2.53	67.5	22.8	29.0
Hoke	9.7	5.1	2.9	50.7	33 646	46 952	39.5	9.9	4 027	1 295	1 815	16 161	2.96	74.7	18.2	21.6
Hyde	16.3	9.9	7.6	45.0	5 826	5 810	-0.3	-2.3	220	215	-168	2 148	2.34	69.9	19.9	26.2
Iredell	12.4	8.5	5.7	50.7	122 660	159 437	30.0	4.5	7 501	6 056	5 614	59 468	2.69	72.6	12.6	23.6
Jackson	13.2	10.7	6.3	50.8	33 121	40 271	21.6	1.8	1 648	1 398	488	15 609	2.36	62.2	11.0	30.1
Johnston	11.5	7.5	4.3	50.8	121 965	168 878	38.5	7.4	9 464	5 309	7 984	60 759	2.81	74.9	13.3	20.6
Jones	16.0	12.0	8.9	51.6	10 381	10 153	-2.2	-0.8	419	546	-79	4 151	2.42	63.1	13.9	31.9
Lee	12.2	8.3	6.0	51.0	49 040	57 866	18.0	3.1	3 518	2 189	515	21 204	2.72	69.3	14.3	26.3
Lenoir	14.5	9.8	7.6	52.2	59 648	59 495	-0.3	-1.7	2 821	2 943	-849	23 569	2.46	65.6	19.1	30.3
Lincoln	13.8	9.8	5.5	50.2	63 780	78 265	22.7	2.0	3 247	2 998	1 303	29 994	2.60	72.4	11.0	23.7
McDowell	14.4	10.4	7.5	50.0	42 151	44 996	6.7	-0.1	1 947	1 996	86	17 252	2.54	66.9	12.2	28.8
Macon	15.7	14.7	11.1	51.5	29 811	33 922	13.8	-0.1	1 399	1 753	358	15 340	2.18	66.6	10.5	28.1
Madison	15.1	11.4	7.9	50.5	19 635	20 764	5.7	1.8	794	935	542	8 207	2.41	68.7	10.3	26.7
Martin	16.5	11.6	8.3	53.1	25 593	24 505	-4.3	-4.3	1 013	1 334	-800	9 444	2.54	66.6	16.0	29.9
Mecklenburg	10.4	5.8	4.0	51.8	695 454	919 628	32.2	10.1	59 073	22 842	55 382	366 689	2.54	62.2	14.4	30.3
Mitchell	15.6	13.1	9.6	50.9	15 687	15 579	-0.7	-1.7	600	896	18	6 455	2.35	70.5	11.1	25.8
Montgomery	14.1	10.6	7.2	51.4	26 822	27 798	3.6	-1.4	1 387	1 175	-616	10 610	2.51	63.6	14.5	31.6
Moore	13.3	12.5	11.3	52.0	74 769	88 247	18.0	5.5	4 107	4 407	4 948	36 997	2.38	67.4	10.3	28.7
Nash	14.0	9.2	6.5	51.7	87 420	95 840	9.6	-1.5	4 736	4 162	-2 041	37 726	2.47	66.4	16.7	29.5
New Hanover	12.5	9.0	6.3	51.8	160 307	202 667	26.4	6.7	9 571	7 159	10 939	86 010	2.33	57.9	11.0	32.3
Northampton	16.3	12.6	9.8	51.8	22 086	22 099	0.1	-7.4	824	1 143	-1 284	8 604	2.43	64.6	21.6	32.4
Onslow	7.3	4.8	3.3	45.5	150 355	177 772	18.2	5.5	18 455	3 817	-5 177	60 071	2.76	72.9	13.1	21.9
Orange	11.9	6.7	4.2	52.4	118 227	133 801	13.2	5.0	5 370	3 172	4 387	51 403	2.45	59.8	10.0	29.9
Pamlico	17.3	14.7	10.4	48.8	12 934	13 144	1.6	-1.5	392	600	-17	5 146	2.42	71.6	10.5	26.0
Pasquotank	12.4	8.5	6.4	51.0	34 897	40 661	16.5	-2.1	2 063	1 734	-1 223	14 399	2.65	69.1	16.0	25.7
Pender	14.0	10.3	6.5	50.1	41 082	52 217	27.1	7.8	2 565	1 988	3 380	20 254	2.57	70.4	12.1	25.0
Perquimans	15.4	14.2	9.4	51.9	11 368	13 453	18.3	0.1	557	610	65	5 437	2.46	74.5	12.5	19.8
Person	14.9	9.7	7.1	51.3	35 623	39 464	10.8	-0.8	1 724	1 766	-294	15 320	2.54	67.5	15.3	27.2
Pitt	10.9	6.4	4.5	52.8	133 798	168 148	25.7	4.3	9 100	4 938	3 000	66 026	2.49	59.3	16.2	30.1
Polk	16.8	14.4	12.6	52.2	18 324	20 510	11.9	-0.7	564	1 147	446	8 788	2.28	66.6	9.9	29.2
Randolph	13.0	9.4	6.3	50.7	130 454	141 752	8.7	0.7	6 860	5 743	-28	54 350	2.59	71.4	12.9	24.8
Richmond	13.1	9.2	6.4	50.9	46 564	46 639	0.2	-1.9	2 364	2 288	-982	18 254	2.48	63.9	17.6	30.6
Robeson	12.2	7.7	4.9	51.5	123 339	134 168	8.8	0.4	8 109	5 292	-2 110	45 154	2.90	70.6	23.7	25.6
Rockingham	14.8	10.2	7.8	51.8	91 928	93 643	1.9	-2.1	3 947	4 555	-1 251	37 693	2.43	68.5	14.5	27.9
Rowan	13.2	9.2	6.8	50.7	130 340	138 428	6.2	0.1	6 599	6 448	-34	52 300	2.55	68.8	13.7	26.2
Rutherford	14.6	11.3	7.7	51.7	62 899	67 810	7.8	-1.8	2 930	3 493	-552	27 214	2.43	70.8	14.0	25.5
Sampson	12.9	8.9	6.7	50.9	60 161	63 431	5.4	1.0	3 647	2 576	-456	23 336	2.69	67.9	16.4	27.3
Scotland	13.7	9.0	6.3	50.8	35 998	36 157	0.4	-1.6	1 968	1 677	-904	13 047	2.63	67.2	24.0	29.4
Stanly	13.4	9.9	7.1	50.0	58 100	60 585	4.3	0.0	2 726	2 744	29	23 108	2.52	69.2	12.2	27.4
Stokes	14.7	10.9	7.5	51.1	44 711	47 401	6.0	-2.1	1 715	2 086	-681	18 969	2.45	72.0	10.5	25.6
Surry	13.6	10.4	8.0	51.1	71 219	73 673	3.4	-1.0	3 297	3 516	-569	29 967	2.42	67.8	12.1	28.6

1. No spouse present.

STATE County	Persons in group quarters, 2014	Daytime population, 2009–2013: Number	Daytime population, 2009–2013: Employment/residence ratio	Births, 2014: Total	Births, 2014: Rate[1]	Deaths, 2014: Number	Deaths, 2014: Rate[1]	Persons under 65 with no health insurance, 2013: Number	Persons under 65 with no health insurance, 2013: Percent	Medicare, 2014: Eligible for Medicare	Medicare, 2014: Enrolled in Medicare Advantage	Medicare, 2014: Enrolled in a Medicare prescription drug plan	Serious crimes known to police,[2] 2013: Total: Number	Serious crimes known to police,[2] 2013: Total: Rate[3]
	32	33	34	35	36	37	38	39	40	41	42	43	44	45
NORTH CAROLINA—Cont'd														
Chowan	274	14 261	0.90	151	10.4	190	13.0	2 058	18.0	3 819	357	2 253	406	2 739
Clay	92	9 648	0.74	80	7.6	145	13.7	1 679	21.9	3 312	623	1 613	274	2 569
Cleveland	2 034	93 618	0.90	1 081	11.1	1 124	11.6	13 065	16.5	21 946	4 908	12 337	2 256	2 328
Columbus	2 844	55 349	0.88	625	11.0	721	12.7	9 213	20.5	12 789	1 831	7 739	2 768	4 875
Craven	5 102	107 861	1.09	1 527	14.6	985	9.4	13 922	16.9	20 850	1 796	10 752	3 615	3 430
Cumberland	8 450	350 490	1.20	5 625	17.2	2 361	7.2	44 571	15.7	45 617	10 372	14 935	19 583	6 001
Currituck	273	18 794	0.55	231	9.2	204	8.2	3 660	17.8	4 113	437	1 874	478	1 967
Dare	135	35 932	1.09	379	10.8	289	8.2	5 839	20.4	7 285	659	3 891	1 497	4 293
Davidson	1 733	136 929	0.63	1 685	10.3	1 652	10.1	23 780	17.5	32 468	17 571	10 242	4 007	2 470
Davie	377	34 331	0.61	390	9.4	367	8.9	6 118	18.2	8 963	4 590	2 757	927	2 281
Duplin	499	56 319	0.88	726	12.1	511	8.5	13 198	26.2	9 971	1 493	5 554	492	811
Durham	12 717	330 717	1.40	4 335	14.7	1 876	6.4	43 748	17.8	38 055	10 009	17 545	12 924	4 545
Edgecombe	1 229	53 080	0.85	645	11.7	606	11.0	7 828	17.2	11 231	1 787	6 952	2 381	4 380
Forsyth	10 073	378 536	1.15	4 580	12.5	3 057	8.4	52 331	17.4	63 296	33 249	18 428	17 749	4 910
Franklin	1 675	49 217	0.53	684	10.9	555	8.8	9 986	19.3	10 349	2 885	4 839	1 248	2 105
Gaston	3 288	188 692	0.79	2 486	11.8	2 182	10.3	31 948	18.1	40 247	12 645	18 281	6 663	3 294
Gates	61	8 841	0.36	112	9.7	108	9.3	1 597	16.7	2 280	365	1 142	NA	NA
Graham	93	8 299	0.85	91	10.5	91	10.5	1 514	22.0	2 089	473	1 058	NA	NA
Granville	4 297	55 549	0.89	553	9.5	519	8.9	7 636	16.5	10 331	2 965	4 854	1 826	3 005
Greene	2 314	18 593	0.67	212	10.1	204	9.7	3 596	22.4	3 251	430	1 953	495	2 300
Guilford	15 915	547 171	1.23	6 201	12.1	4 120	8.0	76 958	18.1	84 084	40 542	26 451	19 726	3 897
Halifax	1 388	51 943	0.88	572	10.8	688	13.0	7 274	17.0	13 533	2 421	8 002	2 290	4 294
Harnett	3 315	96 288	0.53	1 845	14.6	939	7.4	20 362	18.8	17 372	3 385	8 425	3 524	2 826
Haywood	725	54 924	0.83	551	9.3	698	11.7	8 464	18.6	16 427	4 624	7 284	2 016	3 485
Henderson	1 311	103 356	0.90	1 070	9.6	1 313	11.8	16 707	20.2	29 585	7 166	14 185	2 397	2 199
Hertford	2 426	25 684	1.15	229	9.4	262	10.8	3 120	17.2	4 868	607	3 127	679	2 865
Hoke	727	39 636	0.53	935	18.1	306	5.9	9 623	20.6	5 647	1 474	2 431	684	1 321
Hyde	757	5 831	1.03	50	8.8	38	6.7	947	23.3	1 010	142	592	NA	NA
Iredell	1 290	160 021	0.98	1 764	10.6	1 473	8.8	24 998	17.8	29 013	8 959	13 025	5 160	3 143
Jackson	3 672	41 346	1.06	372	9.1	332	8.1	7 492	24.5	7 648	1 712	3 566	944	2 325
Johnston	1 770	144 626	0.64	2 208	12.2	1 314	7.2	30 034	19.3	27 207	6 092	13 702	3 809	2 201
Jones	91	8 358	0.56	88	8.7	119	11.8	1 726	21.5	2 229	281	1 245	NA	NA
Lee	1 031	61 071	1.09	827	13.9	510	8.5	10 772	21.2	10 830	2 183	5 433	835	1 409
Lenoir	1 232	62 835	1.15	653	11.2	734	12.6	9 358	19.4	13 265	1 632	8 047	2 719	4 639
Lincoln	698	66 873	0.66	746	9.3	740	9.3	12 434	18.6	14 326	3 366	7 545	1 873	2 345
McDowell	1 674	43 640	0.92	452	10.1	472	10.5	6 391	17.8	10 560	2 848	4 754	1 557	3 451
Macon	437	33 727	0.99	346	10.2	402	11.9	6 340	25.3	10 204	1 302	5 582	992	2 922
Madison	1 286	17 837	0.64	199	9.4	229	10.8	2 844	17.7	5 152	1 217	2 494	272	1 404
Martin	148	22 049	0.76	237	10.1	289	12.3	3 258	17.2	5 389	634	3 421	1 137	4 764
Mecklenburg	16 655	1 076 955	1.28	14 113	13.9	5 789	5.7	162 549	18.5	118 420	35 155	52 666	39 698	4 019
Mitchell	209	15 409	0.99	144	9.4	210	13.7	2 205	18.7	4 122	987	1 884	NA	NA
Montgomery	999	27 074	0.94	317	11.6	272	9.9	5 056	23.2	5 046	1 273	2 748	755	2 844
Moore	825	87 905	0.96	990	10.6	1 107	11.9	11 894	17.1	23 477	5 343	11 409	1 998	2 270
Nash	1 858	97 895	1.06	1 096	11.6	978	10.4	13 833	17.7	19 231	3 411	11 029	3 514	3 712
New Hanover	6 627	222 118	1.16	2 276	10.5	1 750	8.1	32 596	18.6	38 651	5 996	20 767	9 345	4 454
Northampton	626	20 227	0.80	193	9.4	274	13.4	2 538	16.2	5 254	818	3 116	527	2 906
Onslow	15 499	183 191	1.04	4 327	23.1	937	5.0	24 742	15.9	19 972	2 352	8 115	1 555	840
Orange	9 459	143 173	1.11	1 269	9.0	738	5.3	17 576	15.3	18 711	6 304	7 258	3 280	2 350
Pamlico	700	11 805	0.73	85	6.6	133	10.3	1 806	19.9	3 672	385	2 006	356	2 717
Pasquotank	2 514	40 703	1.02	470	11.8	379	9.5	5 340	17.1	7 436	919	3 701	1 182	2 906
Pender	1 089	42 544	0.51	598	10.6	490	8.7	9 087	20.2	10 960	1 822	5 868	1 065	1 951
Perquimans	73	11 132	0.53	130	9.7	137	10.2	1 770	17.1	3 617	413	1 840	212	1 555
Person	442	34 613	0.71	395	10.1	405	10.3	5 390	16.6	8 352	2 814	3 631	1 052	2 675
Pitt	6 745	171 311	1.01	2 136	12.2	1 227	7.0	26 379	17.7	25 195	3 591	13 869	6 626	3 855
Polk	353	18 518	0.76	138	6.8	281	13.8	3 199	21.6	5 713	1 096	2 969	303	1 547
Randolph	1 293	127 286	0.76	1 609	11.3	1 395	9.8	25 147	21.0	27 696	14 362	8 653	4 458	3 120
Richmond	1 069	45 278	0.92	526	11.5	536	11.7	7 748	20.2	10 692	1 355	6 235	2 695	5 764
Robeson	4 272	130 285	0.91	1 832	13.6	1 288	9.6	28 627	24.7	22 812	4 748	12 637	8 016	5 902
Rockingham	1 066	85 109	0.79	940	10.3	1 116	12.2	13 643	18.2	21 446	10 766	7 048	3 189	3 479
Rowan	4 316	131 749	0.88	1 567	11.3	1 524	11.0	21 442	19.0	28 315	10 679	10 736	4 019	3 068
Rutherford	1 205	64 268	0.87	667	10.0	845	12.7	9 946	18.5	15 585	3 016	8 669	1 802	2 857
Sampson	1 077	59 054	0.83	867	13.5	627	9.8	12 805	24.0	12 378	2 403	6 720	1 646	2 601
Scotland	2 380	37 572	1.13	448	12.6	391	11.0	5 209	18.3	7 953	1 520	4 682	1 697	4 797
Stanly	2 007	55 008	0.78	631	10.4	654	10.8	8 818	18.1	12 815	3 118	6 368	1 442	2 792
Stokes	456	37 129	0.50	398	8.6	496	10.7	6 249	16.5	9 509	5 697	2 530	1 331	2 848
Surry	894	72 508	0.97	746	10.2	829	11.4	11 974	20.2	16 581	8 498	5 629	2 291	3 107

1. Per 1,000 estimated resident population. 2. Data for serious crimes have not been adjusted for underreporting; this may affect comparability between geographic areas and over time.
3. Per 100,000 population estimated by the FBI.

STATE County	Serious crimes known to police, 2013 (cont.)[1] Rate[2]		Education: School enrollment and attainment, 2009–2013				Education: Local government expenditures,[5] 2012–2013		Money income, 2009–2013				Income and poverty, 2013			
			Enrollment[3]		Attainment[4] (percent)					Households				Percent below poverty level		
	Violent	Property	Total	Percent private	High school graduate or less	Bachelor's degree or more	Total current spending (mil dol)	Current spending per student (dollars)	Per capita income[6] (dollars)	Median income (dollars)	Mean income (dollars)	Percent with income of $200,000 or more	Median household income (dollars)	All persons	Children under 18 years	Children 5 to 17 years in families
	46	47	48	49	50	51	52	53	54	55	56	57	58	59	60	61
NORTH CAROLINA—Cont'd																
Chowan	331	2 409	3 417	11.7	54.3	20.1	25.3	10 939	19 240	34 420	47 006	0.9	39 143	22.2	36.1	32.4
Clay	187	2 381	2 436	10.6	42.0	20.6	13.4	9 685	22 081	38 828	50 277	1.0	37 078	19.3	32.9	29.0
Cleveland	163	2 165	24 971	11.2	51.9	16.3	142.1	8 910	20 062	38 989	50 235	1.3	40 528	19.6	31.0	28.2
Columbus	477	4 398	13 790	7.7	52.2	12.2	77.4	8 720	19 275	35 761	48 994	1.3	35 026	25.3	38.3	35.4
Craven	267	3 164	25 317	11.8	41.2	21.0	120.4	8 013	24 260	47 141	59 612	1.9	45 022	16.6	26.2	25.8
Cumberland	551	5 451	96 200	14.0	37.5	22.7	433.0	8 181	23 067	45 231	58 134	1.8	44 038	18.0	27.4	26.1
Currituck	119	1 848	5 592	9.0	49.2	18.4	35.3	9 020	25 854	57 159	67 597	1.1	57 577	11.7	19.1	17.5
Dare	267	4 026	7 258	11.5	32.9	30.6	54.3	10 664	30 529	55 481	70 145	3.5	52 083	11.1	19.8	19.1
Davidson	198	2 272	39 005	11.2	53.3	17.6	199.4	7 673	22 549	43 083	55 811	1.7	40 424	19.3	28.3	27.5
Davie	167	2 114	9 951	13.9	47.6	24.9	54.5	8 167	26 319	50 139	65 969	3.9	49 708	13.9	19.2	17.0
Duplin	79	732	14 308	8.5	59.0	10.4	82.2	8 638	17 122	34 433	45 057	0.8	38 106	25.4	37.0	33.3
Durham	541	4 004	78 676	27.6	30.9	45.1	343.7	10 390	29 347	51 853	71 615	4.5	52 331	17.0	22.4	22.7
Edgecombe	574	3 806	14 347	6.0	58.4	10.5	59.1	8 605	16 971	33 960	43 639	0.6	33 080	27.3	45.8	41.9
Forsyth	487	4 423	92 602	19.6	39.3	31.9	457.9	8 499	26 541	45 724	65 578	3.7	46 163	20.5	30.4	26.6
Franklin	148	1 956	14 800	16.5	51.6	17.1	70.2	8 085	21 399	41 696	54 997	1.5	39 312	18.4	25.3	23.8
Gaston	369	2 925	50 578	13.7	48.4	18.0	239.6	7 535	22 658	42 017	57 285	2.3	42 461	19.2	28.0	27.5
Gates	NA	NA	2 804	12.2	53.4	11.6	19.0	10 650	21 187	46 592	54 917	0.5	48 194	18.2	26.5	24.1
Graham	NA	NA	1 871	9.3	55.2	14.4	13.2	10 572	19 780	33 903	47 331	1.2	33 553	24.7	35.9	34.7
Granville	304	2 701	14 535	14.1	51.2	16.4	71.5	8 257	22 295	49 852	59 984	1.1	48 680	15.3	21.0	19.2
Greene	153	2 147	5 149	9.1	56.1	11.6	34.5	10 433	18 441	40 853	51 186	2.0	39 481	23.3	33.9	32.9
Guilford	421	3 476	139 009	14.4	37.8	33.2	670.1	9 035	26 461	45 431	65 044	3.5	46 093	19.2	27.4	27.7
Halifax	418	3 876	12 564	10.8	59.5	11.8	78.8	9 995	17 937	32 329	44 406	1.1	32 597	31.6	43.5	41.9
Harnett	231	2 595	35 837	18.2	46.0	18.5	149.9	7 290	20 310	44 625	56 266	1.4	45 257	18.5	24.3	21.9
Haywood	322	3 164	11 801	8.8	44.9	23.1	65.7	8 613	24 536	41 557	54 746	1.6	39 320	20.4	31.1	26.3
Henderson	161	2 037	22 065	15.2	39.1	27.7	111.2	8 199	25 670	44 815	59 839	2.1	44 561	15.5	23.9	22.9
Hertford	283	2 582	6 407	26.7	55.3	15.4	32.5	10 251	17 863	33 406	47 528	0.9	33 616	24.9	38.1	36.4
Hoke	89	1 233	13 884	14.4	44.8	17.2	67.3	8 007	18 761	45 489	54 209	0.7	43 987	23.2	31.9	31.0
Hyde	NA	NA	1 161	17.8	55.1	10.7	10.2	17 050	18 408	42 279	47 759	1.5	36 681	22.9	32.5	30.0
Iredell	247	2 896	40 074	10.2	43.7	23.9	212.4	7 786	26 467	50 329	69 338	4.0	49 983	12.7	17.6	15.7
Jackson	182	2 143	12 620	4.9	41.9	27.9	32.6	8 895	21 014	36 951	51 042	1.2	40 511	24.2	31.7	31.1
Johnston	165	2 036	46 658	11.0	46.6	20.4	273.5	8 114	22 410	49 711	61 150	1.5	50 904	16.6	21.6	19.5
Jones	NA	NA	2 081	11.3	53.3	11.1	14.4	11 722	20 105	36 213	47 031	0.9	39 602	20.7	34.8	32.7
Lee	110	1 299	14 595	10.1	47.0	20.2	82.6	8 260	21 449	44 819	56 700	1.3	48 061	17.9	26.7	25.0
Lenoir	635	4 004	15 471	8.2	52.2	14.0	76.8	8 218	19 760	35 770	47 589	1.1	34 127	21.7	34.1	32.0
Lincoln	155	2 190	18 747	10.0	46.3	19.4	89.1	7 513	25 550	48 940	65 018	3.8	50 537	14.6	20.8	18.6
McDowell	135	3 316	10 283	9.0	56.0	13.9	58.8	8 883	18 932	35 297	46 025	1.1	36 840	21.9	31.3	28.5
Macon	174	2 748	6 523	11.0	44.8	20.5	41.0	9 073	23 213	37 892	51 805	1.9	37 219	20.4	33.0	28.9
Madison	62	1 342	4 845	21.9	52.3	18.6	23.8	9 150	19 902	38 598	48 740	0.9	37 479	19.9	30.1	27.1
Martin	536	4 227	5 881	8.0	56.1	11.9	35.5	9 803	18 783	35 111	45 746	0.6	34 761	22.6	35.9	34.3
Mecklenburg	539	3 479	260 915	19.7	30.7	40.7	1 188.2	8 224	32 482	55 444	81 675	6.5	54 657	15.5	20.5	20.0
Mitchell	NA	NA	3 391	9.7	54.8	16.9	20.1	9 846	21 404	37 680	50 104	1.2	38 303	18.3	29.4	27.8
Montgomery	170	2 675	6 430	5.1	55.7	15.1	38.6	9 024	18 865	31 830	47 343	1.7	35 613	22.1	33.0	29.3
Moore	170	2 100	19 297	14.7	36.3	31.3	111.3	8 620	28 913	49 544	68 247	4.5	50 169	14.3	22.3	21.1
Nash	512	3 199	24 558	14.5	50.3	19.2	156.2	9 312	22 880	43 084	56 302	2.2	41 575	16.6	24.1	22.6
New Hanover	414	4 040	55 695	12.9	31.4	36.6	222.0	8 591	29 679	49 835	69 443	3.9	48 651	18.9	24.2	23.7
Northampton	254	2 653	4 903	11.7	62.3	9.4	24.9	10 987	17 919	31 433	42 499	0.2	31 732	29.0	42.1	39.2
Onslow	66	774	44 673	13.8	39.7	18.0	198.2	7 762	21 084	45 450	55 059	1.1	45 213	16.9	23.2	23.9
Orange	145	2 205	49 960	9.7	24.7	55.8	209.1	10 511	34 465	55 569	89 459	10.2	59 472	15.5	13.4	12.5
Pamlico	351	2 366	2 633	9.5	46.9	18.7	15.2	11 405	23 724	43 853	57 640	1.7	43 517	19.0	35.1	32.4
Pasquotank	359	2 547	11 495	9.8	44.8	20.1	52.8	8 803	22 745	46 053	61 081	2.4	40 094	21.8	33.9	30.7
Pender	167	1 784	12 145	11.7	44.6	21.7	70.6	8 058	23 526	44 524	60 435	2.8	44 949	18.3	25.5	24.4
Perquimans	147	1 409	2 856	9.3	51.4	18.4	18.0	9 746	23 809	43 709	58 255	2.0	42 504	20.9	35.1	34.9
Person	323	2 352	9 643	9.7	53.1	14.7	43.5	8 797	21 292	42 317	52 555	1.2	42 091	18.4	25.7	23.6
Pitt	461	3 395	61 698	7.9	39.6	28.1	197.0	8 282	23 029	40 718	57 292	2.7	40 940	25.4	31.1	29.8
Polk	87	1 460	3 920	5.9	42.1	26.9	26.3	10 765	24 611	44 745	55 992	1.3	43 665	14.7	26.4	23.4
Randolph	141	2 979	33 558	9.9	57.1	13.8	187.0	7 956	20 523	41 208	52 359	0.9	40 896	19.8	28.7	26.1
Richmond	464	5 300	11 869	11.4	56.9	12.4	66.7	8 473	17 236	32 384	42 891	1.1	32 825	27.3	40.8	36.9
Robeson	691	5 211	36 882	3.9	60.0	12.5	204.9	8 312	15 343	29 806	42 420	1.2	30 248	30.7	44.0	41.7
Rockingham	206	3 273	21 283	9.5	56.2	12.9	115.3	8 477	21 102	38 567	50 623	1.2	40 446	21.2	29.3	25.7
Rowan	354	2 714	33 509	16.0	52.5	17.0	171.5	8 506	20 912	41 495	53 720	1.4	41 475	18.8	27.8	27.1
Rutherford	178	2 679	15 938	9.2	49.1	17.0	80.6	8 996	19 551	36 334	47 542	1.3	35 544	23.9	34.4	33.0
Sampson	228	2 373	15 684	6.5	58.7	12.6	99.1	8 275	19 479	36 496	50 029	1.4	35 890	24.3	32.8	29.4
Scotland	749	4 048	9 733	9.9	58.0	14.3	64.7	10 310	15 079	29 592	40 473	0.5	32 314	34.1	44.1	41.1
Stanly	182	2 610	14 498	16.3	52.4	16.0	70.5	7 984	20 504	42 518	52 171	0.8	42 801	17.7	25.6	23.9
Stokes	293	2 555	9 447	10.9	59.1	13.4	60.1	8 705	21 311	42 703	52 212	1.1	44 552	14.4	20.7	18.7
Surry	209	2 898	16 219	7.9	54.6	15.0	97.5	8 432	20 219	35 641	48 859	1.3	36 221	21.3	31.0	28.7

1. Data for serious crimes have not been adjusted for underreporting; this may affect comparability between geographic areas and over time. 2. Per 100,000 population estimated by the FBI.
3. All persons 3 years old and over enrolled in nursery school through college. 4. Persons 25 years old and over. 5. Elementary and secondary education expenditures.
6. Based on population estimated by the American Community Survey, 2009–2013.

STATE County	Personal income, 2013										Earnings, 2013		
	Total (mil dol)	Percent change, 2012–2013	Per capita[1] Dollars	Per capita[1] Rank	Wages and salaries (mil dol)	Supplements to wages and salaries; employer contributions (mil dol): Pension and insurance	Supplements to wages and salaries; employer contributions (mil dol): Government social insurance	Proprietors' income (mil dol)	Dividends, interest, and rent (mil dol)	Personal transfer receipts (mil dol)	Total (mil dol)	Contributions for government social insurance (mil dol): From employee and self-employed	Contributions for government social insurance (mil dol): From employer
	62	63	64	65	66	67	68	69	70	71	72	73	74
NORTH CAROLINA—Cont'd													
Chowan	543	0.0	36 891	1 609	170	29	13	67	114	156	280	18	13
Clay	316	1.1	29 812	2 716	58	12	5	21	69	113	96	9	5
Cleveland	3 269	0.9	33 680	2 148	1 258	224	103	171	451	994	1 757	120	103
Columbus	1 760	1.8	30 745	2 589	586	114	45	173	228	615	918	61	45
Craven	4 100	-0.5	39 243	1 261	2 124	508	185	264	924	898	3 080	167	185
Cumberland	14 793	-0.3	45 394	664	8 416	2 125	772	659	3 026	2 715	11 973	575	772
Currituck	1 040	0.2	42 644	875	235	37	20	71	164	167	363	23	20
Dare	1 486	2.3	42 441	893	623	101	55	162	387	259	941	58	55
Davidson	5 917	0.7	36 208	1 709	1 585	268	129	672	778	1 340	2 653	183	129
Davie	1 612	0.5	38 785	1 320	362	60	30	105	301	344	557	41	30
Duplin	1 935	2.7	32 211	2 385	649	127	50	481	227	450	1 307	65	50
Durham	11 922	1.9	41 376	1 008	12 902	1 626	923	1 468	2 112	1 811	16 920	987	923
Edgecombe	1 610	-1.0	28 968	2 808	676	137	54	129	230	586	996	64	54
Forsyth	14 355	1.1	39 739	1 196	8 818	1 237	679	1 433	2 832	2 685	12 167	746	679
Franklin	1 986	1.0	31 897	2 422	465	85	36	193	237	451	780	52	36
Gaston	7 404	0.9	35 355	1 846	2 682	430	218	606	1 014	1 817	3 936	260	218
Gates	348	-0.7	29 879	2 708	49	11	4	33	53	92	96	6	4
Graham	236	0.7	27 017	2 969	76	14	7	20	34	87	117	9	7
Granville	1 870	1.1	32 087	2 405	871	214	68	105	291	420	1 257	75	68
Greene	629	-0.2	29 607	2 740	137	34	10	98	70	163	279	16	10
Guilford	19 941	1.1	39 362	1 245	12 884	1 858	1 000	1 459	3 646	3 626	17 202	1 045	1 000
Halifax	1 717	-0.6	32 126	2 399	578	116	45	110	276	630	850	60	45
Harnett	3 848	1.7	30 787	2 581	812	157	65	469	544	863	1 502	96	65
Haywood	2 065	1.4	34 890	1 915	605	111	47	190	402	624	955	70	47
Henderson	4 229	1.3	38 611	1 353	1 360	221	109	246	1 012	1 036	1 936	138	109
Hertford	719	0.2	29 418	2 762	338	59	26	51	99	233	474	30	26
Hoke	1 687	-0.8	32 861	2 272	273	60	23	86	187	341	442	28	23
Hyde	187	-4.5	32 729	2 296	69	14	6	35	38	43	124	6	6
Iredell	5 959	1.5	36 221	1 707	3 016	444	231	371	1 015	1 173	4 062	255	231
Jackson	1 254	2.6	30 643	2 606	536	113	41	95	251	307	786	49	41
Johnston	6 476	2.4	36 391	1 676	1 672	301	130	651	709	1 227	2 754	173	130
Jones	379	-1.6	37 067	1 571	65	12	5	46	59	99	128	8	5
Lee	1 944	-0.1	32 251	2 373	971	172	79	138	336	486	1 360	85	79
Lenoir	2 120	-0.3	35 990	1 748	1 020	200	80	216	350	622	1 517	93	80
Lincoln	2 948	0.4	36 973	1 591	783	134	65	79	399	582	1 062	73	65
McDowell	1 280	1.1	28 459	2 853	518	105	43	65	171	414	730	51	43
Macon	1 102	1.3	32 542	2 321	367	64	30	72	287	350	534	41	30
Madison	629	1.1	29 928	2 697	128	27	10	43	100	198	208	17	10
Martin	797	0.6	33 635	2 158	277	50	21	57	121	261	405	27	21
Mecklenburg	48 666	2.7	49 109	409	37 851	4 646	2 798	7 783	7 243	5 571	53 078	3 078	2 798
Mitchell	438	0.6	28 583	2 841	172	34	14	12	74	157	232	17	14
Montgomery	854	2.6	30 966	2 555	322	60	26	75	148	234	483	31	26
Moore	3 733	1.2	40 758	1 084	1 266	191	98	293	1 083	872	1 848	127	98
Nash	3 475	-0.3	36 543	1 656	1 580	277	124	269	539	858	2 249	140	124
New Hanover	8 285	2.4	38 846	1 313	4 357	703	339	1 081	1 829	1 613	6 479	392	339
Northampton	694	-2.1	33 308	2 205	181	34	15	47	106	238	276	20	15
Onslow	8 343	-0.9	45 041	686	4 289	1 220	418	248	1 826	1 123	6 175	265	418
Orange	7 346	1.0	52 339	292	3 512	780	248	429	1 650	748	4 970	275	248
Pamlico	528	-1.0	40 791	1 076	98	21	8	40	114	141	167	12	8
Pasquotank	1 243	-0.5	31 090	2 536	642	143	51	114	227	344	950	55	51
Pender	1 792	1.5	32 379	2 354	371	67	29	109	276	448	576	40	29
Perquimans	461	-1.1	33 895	2 099	69	14	5	53	98	138	142	10	5
Person	1 234	0.6	31 428	2 492	380	73	31	71	166	359	554	39	31
Pitt	6 300	0.7	36 153	1 721	3 172	631	240	384	982	1 278	4 427	259	240
Polk	844	1.9	41 372	1 010	158	29	13	63	241	201	263	20	13
Randolph	4 534	0.5	31 802	2 435	1 594	280	130	304	649	1 154	2 308	157	130
Richmond	1 353	0.8	29 159	2 785	487	95	42	77	176	514	701	49	42
Robeson	3 627	0.8	26 899	2 975	1 324	261	105	239	437	1 305	1 928	125	105
Rockingham	3 012	0.0	32 788	2 285	981	177	80	158	446	883	1 397	101	80
Rowan	4 317	0.5	31 210	2 517	1 872	339	150	118	724	1 218	2 479	166	150
Rutherford	1 894	-0.6	28 283	2 868	622	119	52	150	296	642	942	69	52
Sampson	2 150	2.0	33 509	2 174	659	120	51	328	304	569	1 158	59	51
Scotland	1 086	0.7	30 140	2 665	422	77	35	71	166	399	606	41	35
Stanly	1 998	1.5	32 948	2 262	663	118	53	138	302	522	972	66	53
Stokes	1 532	0.3	32 889	2 267	228	46	18	125	185	375	417	33	18
Surry	2 368	0.4	32 411	2 349	943	170	76	184	390	694	1 373	93	76

1. Based on the resident population estimated as of July 1 of the year shown.

STATE County	Earnings, 2013 (cont.) Percent by selected industries: Farm	Mining	Construction	Manu-facturing	Infor-mation: professional, scientific, technical services	Retail trade	Finance, insur-ance, real estate and leasing	Health care and social assistance	Govern-ment	Social Security beneficiaries, December 2013: Number	Rate[1]	Supple-mental Security Income recipients, December 2013	Housing units, 2014: Total	Percent change, 2010–2014
	75	76	77	78	79	80	81	82	83	84	85	86	87	88
NORTH CAROLINA—Cont'd														
Chowan	13.2	0.0	5.2	7.4	5.1	6.4	5.5	D	16.3	4 200	286	597	7 260	-0.4
Clay	1.0	0.0	14.8	D	D	14.9	8.6	D	26.9	3 640	343	315	7 220	1.1
Cleveland	1.5	D	5.4	22.7	2.8	8.1	4.7	D	16.7	25 085	258	3 271	43 264	-0.3
Columbus	6.0	0.0	3.6	16.1	D	7.5	6.9	14.0	20.3	14 645	256	3 163	25 908	-0.5
Craven	0.9	D	3.2	6.9	5.3	5.1	4.9	8.5	52.0	22 455	215	2 453	45 922	2.0
Cumberland	0.4	D	3.3	4.1	4.8	4.5	3.0	4.9	62.9	52 205	160	9 894	143 870	6.2
Currituck	2.4	D	9.3	0.7	D	10.1	15.4	D	17.8	4 615	189	296	15 017	3.9
Dare	0.0	D	9.5	2.8	D	12.7	15.8	5.8	19.7	7 750	222	296	34 004	1.5
Davidson	0.7	0.1	7.2	18.9	3.3	7.0	8.6	8.9	13.2	37 040	226	3 336	73 010	0.5
Davie	1.3	0.3	6.8	14.2	D	10.5	8.9	10.0	15.7	9 990	240	601	18 197	-0.2
Duplin	22.2	0.0	3.9	18.7	D	4.2	3.2	3.8	13.8	11 055	186	1 896	25 521	-0.8
Durham	0.1	D	2.2	21.7	15.9	2.9	9.4	16.1	9.3	40 055	139	6 122	128 817	7.2
Edgecombe	5.2	D	4.7	17.9	D	8.3	4.2	D	23.5	12 895	232	2 925	24 673	-0.7
Forsyth	0.1	0.0	3.6	10.4	8.2	6.9	12.2	17.1	9.8	68 720	190	7 927	160 645	2.4
Franklin	3.0	D	11.0	19.1	5.9	5.4	7.2	8.4	16.9	11 590	186	1 524	26 906	1.3
Gaston	0.1	D	4.9	22.6	4.2	8.0	7.3	16.4	13.7	45 820	219	5 496	89 915	1.4
Gates	27.7	0.0	D	D	1.7	4.6	D	3.5	27.4	2 595	222	324	5 223	0.4
Graham	0.5	0.0	22.2	D	D	5.3	3.7	5.0	21.3	2 370	272	299	5 930	0.0
Granville	1.9	D	3.6	25.0	1.6	3.6	2.8	D	44.9	11 945	205	1 479	23 231	1.8
Greene	16.8	0.0	8.5	4.0	D	4.1	4.2	7.4	34.1	3 810	180	737	8 125	-1.1
Guilford	0.1	0.1	4.8	14.1	9.5	6.5	9.5	12.1	12.2	91 170	180	11 336	223 183	2.4
Halifax	5.0	0.0	4.1	13.6	2.0	8.7	5.2	9.7	27.6	15 155	284	3 983	25 705	-0.3
Harnett	3.3	D	10.3	4.7	5.1	9.7	12.3	D	21.2	19 855	159	2 997	49 319	5.5
Haywood	1.2	D	6.1	18.4	4.3	10.6	8.6	11.3	21.0	18 110	306	1 681	35 087	0.4
Henderson	1.8	D	6.6	17.3	4.5	8.1	7.5	14.6	16.1	31 525	288	1 832	55 478	1.4
Hertford	4.9	0.0	5.3	17.2	D	6.6	3.9	D	17.3	5 495	225	1 295	10 519	-1.1
Hoke	3.9	D	8.5	25.5	D	5.2	3.7	7.5	26.0	6 660	130	1 457	20 015	9.9
Hyde	27.3	0.0	7.0	2.2	D	4.4	D	2.7	28.3	1 115	195	178	3 353	0.2
Iredell	1.1	0.1	5.4	16.9	D	7.6	4.2	9.3	12.0	32 515	197	2 539	70 298	1.9
Jackson	1.4	D	6.3	3.1	D	6.4	4.2	10.1	45.4	8 370	204	690	26 574	2.4
Johnston	2.6	0.1	10.0	18.7	4.0	8.4	9.0	6.2	18.0	30 700	172	4 170	70 082	3.5
Jones	24.9	0.0	9.6	1.0	D	3.8	D	D	19.8	2 490	244	343	4 860	0.5
Lee	1.0	0.3	4.9	34.3	D	7.5	4.9	10.4	12.9	12 210	204	1 391	24 240	0.4
Lenoir	3.7	D	7.0	21.4	4.0	6.0	8.4	8.5	21.6	14 955	254	2 706	27 242	-0.7
Lincoln	1.5	D	9.2	23.4	5.2	8.2	4.0	D	19.4	15 900	200	1 450	33 976	1.0
McDowell	0.9	0.7	4.2	37.6	D	8.3	4.3	8.7	17.5	11 880	264	1 374	20 909	0.5
Macon	0.4	0.1	9.8	6.5	10.9	11.1	6.8	14.4	17.6	11 250	333	814	25 331	0.3
Madison	2.2	D	6.5	9.9	D	6.0	3.4	D	22.7	5 665	268	817	10 684	0.7
Martin	9.0	0.0	4.5	24.6	D	7.6	6.8	D	18.4	6 190	261	1 065	11 558	-1.2
Mecklenburg	0.1	0.0	5.2	5.7	13.8	5.3	21.7	6.2	10.5	127 170	128	17 458	419 118	5.2
Mitchell	0.4	D	D	4.8	1.5	9.0	3.8	17.4	23.3	4 615	301	464	8 737	0.3
Montgomery	4.3	D	5.5	29.1	D	8.3	D	D	18.1	5 905	215	726	16 056	0.9
Moore	1.5	0.1	6.2	5.0	D	7.5	8.8	27.2	13.2	25 050	274	1 542	45 228	2.9
Nash	3.1	D	5.3	22.0	5.7	7.0	6.6	9.1	15.8	21 325	226	3 490	42 394	0.3
New Hanover	0.0	D	6.7	9.2	12.0	9.1	10.4	12.0	19.1	41 380	194	4 326	105 532	4.0
Northampton	10.3	0.0	5.8	8.9	D	14.9	D	D	22.0	5 885	283	1 270	11 539	-1.1
Onslow	0.4	D	3.0	0.8	2.0	4.0	2.5	2.9	75.4	22 510	121	2 909	76 054	11.5
Orange	0.3	D	2.0	2.0	7.6	5.0	8.6	5.6	58.0	19 050	137	1 684	56 488	1.7
Pamlico	8.8	D	7.9	3.9	4.1	8.5	6.7	D	27.1	3 930	304	319	7 592	0.8
Pasquotank	3.9	0.0	3.0	4.1	6.3	8.8	6.5	8.9	41.3	8 205	206	1 247	16 900	0.4
Pender	8.8	0.3	9.0	7.0	D	7.0	6.9	7.9	25.2	12 110	220	1 187	27 224	1.9
Perquimans	18.9	0.0	5.7	1.6	D	4.7	D	D	22.5	3 870	284	383	7 036	0.7
Person	1.8	D	6.7	15.9	3.5	8.0	6.1	9.6	18.2	9 575	244	1 094	18 173	-0.1
Pitt	1.1	D	3.9	9.9	4.5	6.7	6.4	11.9	37.2	28 185	162	5 849	76 619	2.2
Polk	3.5	0.0	6.8	5.6	D	5.2	9.3	22.7	17.1	6 185	303	319	11 462	0.3
Randolph	1.0	0.1	5.9	35.5	2.7	6.0	5.6	9.3	14.4	31 395	220	3 162	61 242	0.3
Richmond	3.2	1.1	4.7	17.5	4.7	8.9	3.5	12.9	21.6	11 440	247	2 212	20 976	1.1
Robeson	4.9	0.0	4.4	14.8	2.3	7.6	4.7	18.8	23.6	26 905	199	7 441	52 299	-0.9
Rockingham	1.2	D	5.5	25.6	D	7.8	5.3	12.2	15.9	24 500	267	3 104	43 590	-0.2
Rowan	0.7	0.4	4.9	17.6	3.4	7.2	3.2	10.1	23.0	31 510	228	3 225	60 136	-0.1
Rutherford	0.8	D	5.1	16.1	6.0	9.4	7.3	14.7	18.3	17 845	267	2 060	33 884	0.0
Sampson	28.0	0.0	3.4	13.8	2.4	5.5	3.8	5.4	19.4	14 005	218	2 298	27 097	-0.5
Scotland	3.5	D	3.5	18.9	2.5	8.0	5.3	17.2	20.5	9 225	256	2 004	15 146	-0.3
Stanly	1.9	D	7.6	18.1	2.9	8.4	7.8	13.1	18.9	14 460	238	1 409	27 247	0.5
Stokes	4.9	0.0	6.8	19.4	D	7.2	D	10.7	22.7	10 910	234	994	21 794	-0.6
Surry	2.9	0.3	14.3	11.7	D	9.4	5.7	D	17.5	18 830	258	2 050	33 556	-0.3

1. Per 1,000 resident population estimated as of July 1 of the year shown.

STATE County	Housing units, 2009–2013: Occupied units: Total	Owner-occupied: Percent	Owner-occupied: Median value[1]	Median owner cost as a percent of income: With a mortgage	Median owner cost as a percent of income: Without a mortgage[2]	Renter-occupied: Median rent[3]	Renter-occupied: Median rent as a percent of income[2]	Substandard units[4] (percent)	Civilian labor force, 2014: Total	Percent change, 2013–2014	Unemployment: Total	Unemployment: Rate[5]	Civilian employment,[6] 2009–2013: Total	Percent: Management, business, science and arts	Percent: Construction, production, and maintenance occupations
	89	90	91	92	93	94	95	96	97	98	99	100	101	102	103
NORTH CAROLINA—Cont'd															
Chowan	5 945	66.4	129 100	27.0	17.7	743	37.6	1.4	5 649	-1.0	437	7.7	5 483	35.6	25.6
Clay	4 431	80.7	154 700	23.3	12.4	615	41.5	2.5	4 033	-0.2	258	6.4	3 780	29.6	23.2
Cleveland	37 760	68.0	106 100	22.2	11.6	642	32.1	2.3	45 480	-1.9	3 248	7.1	40 381	27.7	28.0
Columbus	21 758	71.5	84 500	24.7	12.7	584	34.3	1.8	22 885	-4.7	1 907	8.3	20 679	27.0	26.2
Craven	39 931	63.6	152 400	23.5	12.7	870	31.0	2.3	40 884	-1.1	2 784	6.8	38 773	30.0	26.2
Cumberland	121 226	54.8	128 700	23.1	11.7	853	29.4	1.4	126 451	-3.0	9 832	7.8	116 226	33.0	20.8
Currituck	9 121	80.2	223 800	26.6	11.9	986	32.4	1.0	12 289	-2.0	746	6.1	11 224	27.3	28.9
Dare	14 624	70.7	293 900	29.1	13.0	998	28.9	2.6	19 822	-3.0	1 623	8.2	18 629	31.9	22.2
Davidson	64 580	73.0	134 000	22.6	11.1	637	28.5	1.4	77 923	-1.5	4 803	6.2	71 672	27.9	30.7
Davie	16 234	80.6	162 100	21.3	11.6	682	26.1	4.9	19 684	-1.0	1 113	5.7	18 133	34.2	25.8
Duplin	22 052	67.7	87 600	23.7	14.2	586	29.5	3.3	26 417	0.1	1 661	6.3	24 488	24.1	42.2
Durham	111 276	55.0	180 600	21.8	11.4	859	30.5	3.7	150 959	0.5	7 537	5.0	136 752	49.3	14.3
Edgecombe	21 021	62.9	80 600	24.0	17.2	646	32.2	3.3	23 063	-3.4	2 336	10.1	21 236	21.9	34.1
Forsyth	140 439	64.0	150 600	22.1	11.0	714	31.0	3.5	174 969	-1.1	10 247	5.9	159 115	39.5	19.3
Franklin	23 313	76.5	123 300	24.9	13.4	702	31.4	3.8	28 312	0.7	1 743	6.2	25 983	31.5	27.8
Gaston	79 450	66.8	123 600	23.0	12.2	714	31.7	3.1	100 681	0.2	6 557	6.5	89 964	29.1	28.4
Gates	4 459	79.6	150 200	24.1	14.4	803	34.2	1.8	5 188	-1.1	305	5.9	4 966	26.5	35.2
Graham	3 462	81.9	125 700	21.7	10.0	549	24.4	2.8	3 347	-4.5	431	12.9	3 161	24.5	36.4
Granville	19 953	74.9	137 100	22.6	13.0	739	27.6	6.3	27 965	-1.4	1 533	5.5	23 886	33.8	28.0
Greene	7 104	69.6	88 500	23.8	13.5	608	25.6	2.7	9 363	-0.3	584	6.2	8 637	23.3	31.0
Guilford	196 463	61.0	156 000	23.2	11.2	747	30.7	2.8	250 327	-1.6	16 015	6.4	230 344	36.2	19.8
Halifax	21 550	61.8	86 100	23.6	16.2	647	36.4	3.3	21 069	-3.0	2 011	9.5	19 123	25.9	29.5
Harnett	40 677	68.2	132 600	23.4	13.0	756	31.0	2.4	48 877	-1.3	3 520	7.2	45 118	30.3	26.7
Haywood	26 608	74.4	156 900	24.0	11.1	713	32.1	2.2	27 238	-1.0	1 511	5.5	24 861	31.4	25.4
Henderson	45 246	74.3	185 500	23.1	10.1	732	31.4	3.0	48 956	-0.1	2 369	4.8	44 332	34.6	24.6
Hertford	8 624	63.1	84 200	24.6	15.2	634	30.6	4.9	9 328	-1.6	676	7.2	8 258	31.1	26.2
Hoke	16 161	67.9	141 300	24.5	12.5	781	32.0	0.8	19 117	-2.7	1 515	7.9	16 845	28.9	25.5
Hyde	2 148	77.6	76 400	22.8	12.4	692	37.1	2.5	2 154	0.4	192	8.9	2 394	25.2	27.4
Iredell	59 468	74.1	166 700	23.0	10.6	787	31.4	2.4	79 485	0.4	4 815	6.1	70 634	33.1	28.2
Jackson	15 609	67.8	172 800	24.9	10.0	636	34.8	3.3	18 125	-1.1	1 155	6.4	17 158	30.1	18.5
Johnston	60 759	71.6	141 200	22.7	11.9	778	33.3	2.4	85 187	1.2	4 649	5.5	77 497	33.5	25.9
Jones	4 151	69.5	97 600	23.0	13.3	637	30.9	4.2	4 520	-0.1	288	6.4	4 235	28.4	32.9
Lee	21 204	69.1	131 300	22.2	12.6	686	28.5	2.8	24 749	-4.8	1 995	8.1	25 214	28.7	29.2
Lenoir	23 569	60.1	94 200	22.5	14.5	642	31.4	1.9	27 673	-2.6	1 939	7.0	23 983	27.4	30.4
Lincoln	29 994	77.1	154 600	22.1	11.0	665	30.9	2.3	39 881	0.3	2 367	5.9	35 738	30.4	29.6
McDowell	17 252	71.5	101 200	21.7	10.7	569	29.2	2.7	20 596	1.0	1 303	6.3	17 193	26.6	31.5
Macon	15 340	74.0	165 400	26.0	10.0	739	37.0	2.4	14 849	-2.0	965	6.5	12 882	28.2	22.7
Madison	8 207	74.8	161 700	25.4	10.2	619	27.7	2.3	9 366	-1.0	547	5.8	8 475	30.0	25.3
Martin	9 444	69.9	84 600	24.2	15.6	591	28.6	2.8	9 819	-2.5	752	7.7	9 154	32.5	31.3
Mecklenburg	366 689	59.5	181 900	22.6	11.7	889	29.6	3.0	540 956	1.0	31 759	5.9	470 120	41.1	16.5
Mitchell	6 455	76.5	117 300	23.7	10.2	575	35.0	4.1	6 488	-2.6	487	7.5	6 082	29.2	32.2
Montgomery	10 610	69.6	88 900	23.6	12.4	553	31.7	2.1	11 401	-2.3	727	6.4	10 373	27.1	36.6
Moore	36 997	74.1	201 600	23.0	11.2	725	28.4	3.5	37 883	0.2	2 244	5.9	33 956	36.8	19.7
Nash	37 726	64.1	117 300	23.1	13.3	751	31.1	3.2	43 775	-3.2	3 443	7.9	41 259	29.5	28.2
New Hanover	86 010	58.9	215 200	25.0	12.6	900	32.2	2.0	109 507	0.2	6 343	5.8	100 333	38.5	16.1
Northampton	8 604	72.9	80 000	24.1	16.6	622	38.6	2.2	7 943	-2.5	627	7.9	7 480	22.7	31.7
Onslow	60 071	54.8	151 700	24.6	12.5	950	31.3	2.2	63 739	-0.3	3 769	5.9	57 779	28.9	23.3
Orange	51 403	60.5	272 600	22.2	11.0	872	32.7	2.9	73 196	0.8	3 254	4.4	67 302	55.3	10.7
Pamlico	5 146	81.6	157 500	25.6	13.6	757	32.4	4.2	5 278	-0.8	345	6.5	5 077	29.5	27.7
Pasquotank	14 399	63.7	171 600	27.8	13.9	885	32.3	3.4	17 177	-2.7	1 370	8.0	17 234	30.6	23.3
Pender	20 254	77.3	155 600	24.8	13.9	757	30.7	1.2	24 990	0.1	1 722	6.9	22 453	29.7	28.4
Perquimans	5 437	77.2	170 700	27.2	14.9	738	39.2	3.1	5 095	-2.2	386	7.6	4 939	36.8	25.1
Person	15 320	71.9	118 800	23.5	11.4	622	30.6	2.6	18 113	-0.8	1 342	7.4	16 650	28.5	29.8
Pitt	66 026	54.4	134 900	22.3	14.1	716	33.2	1.7	86 461	-1.1	5 432	6.3	79 604	38.1	19.2
Polk	8 788	74.2	170 200	25.8	10.0	707	29.3	3.1	8 349	-3.3	434	5.2	7 795	27.2	31.5
Randolph	54 350	73.8	121 900	23.6	11.9	650	29.6	2.4	66 378	-2.0	4 166	6.3	62 152	26.4	34.5
Richmond	18 254	64.4	77 500	22.7	13.3	583	33.3	5.4	16 957	-3.8	1 481	8.7	16 505	25.6	32.7
Robeson	45 154	64.9	66 800	24.4	13.8	592	32.0	1.8	50 686	-2.6	4 681	9.2	47 737	25.8	34.4
Rockingham	37 693	70.6	102 900	22.1	11.6	596	30.4	2.6	41 128	-2.1	2 994	7.3	38 712	24.9	34.1
Rowan	52 300	68.8	130 200	22.7	11.9	698	30.4	3.0	62 646	0.1	4 180	6.7	56 365	28.2	30.8
Rutherford	27 214	71.4	108 600	22.5	11.8	587	29.8	4.0	25 198	-2.7	2 122	8.4	24 905	28.3	32.7
Sampson	23 336	69.2	89 200	23.6	13.3	572	29.1	3.7	29 411	-0.3	1 821	6.2	27 089	26.6	36.9
Scotland	13 047	63.6	77 100	24.8	14.8	628	39.8	2.7	11 915	-2.6	1 397	11.7	10 976	31.4	26.2
Stanly	23 108	73.2	125 100	23.2	12.8	638	30.6	2.5	28 308	-1.7	1 669	5.9	25 329	29.0	28.1
Stokes	18 969	80.4	118 100	21.1	10.1	620	30.8	3.2	21 788	-1.3	1 260	5.8	20 365	25.3	34.4
Surry	29 967	72.8	109 900	22.7	12.5	591	29.6	2.9	32 669	-1.6	1 983	6.1	30 836	28.2	31.5

1. Specified owner-occupied units. 2. A value of 10.0 represents 10 percent or less; a value of 50.0 represents 50 percent or more. 3. Specified renter-occupied units. 4. Overcrowded or lacking complete plumbing facilities. 5. Percent of civilian labor force. 6. Persons 16 years old and over.

STATE County	Private nonfarm establishments, employment and payroll, 2013									Agriculture, 2012			
		Employment						Annual payroll		Farms			
											Percent with:		
	Number of establish-ments	Total	Health care and social assistance	Manufac-turing	Retail trade	Finance and insurance	Professional, scientific, and technical services	Total (mil dol)	Average per employee (dollars)	Number	Fewer than 50 acres	500 acres or more	Farm operators whose principal occu-pation is farming (percent)
	104	105	106	107	108	109	110	111	112	113	114	115	116
NORTH CAROLINA—Cont'd													
Chowan	362	3 724	1 010	D	496	78	127	118	31 782	141	32.6	27.7	73.0
Clay	200	1 441	270	D	D	34	D	35	24 475	154	56.5	0.6	53.2
Cleveland	1 926	28 081	5 684	5 427	3 787	449	983	995	35 427	1 036	43.3	3.7	35.3
Columbus	1 011	11 496	3 140	1 905	2 183	D	221	369	32 101	731	41.6	11.4	48.2
Craven	2 144	26 984	6 491	2 736	4 433	839	1 775	970	35 953	256	45.3	14.1	59.8
Cumberland	5 664	93 550	18 722	6 626	16 220	2 466	6 001	3 151	33 681	389	41.4	10.8	45.8
Currituck	601	4 554	232	32	858	89	93	159	34 957	82	46.3	28.0	56.1
Dare	1 897	13 601	935	436	3 453	417	419	436	32 023	9	55.6	22.2	88.9
Davidson	2 754	44 013	D	9 135	4 905	813	888	1 520	34 537	1 062	54.7	1.6	45.3
Davie	782	8 145	1 058	1 312	1 302	218	227	251	30 830	640	53.4	1.9	47.2
Duplin	838	12 340	1 750	5 069	1 759	215	158	376	30 445	940	37.4	11.3	62.7
Durham	6 795	166 032	24 170	11 178	14 825	5 346	28 491	9 642	58 076	232	62.5	2.6	44.8
Edgecombe	749	12 364	2 533	2 787	1 440	184	154	403	32 616	272	34.9	19.5	52.2
Forsyth	8 233	156 291	24 178	14 380	20 504	10 100	6 746	6 939	44 398	662	65.7	1.2	50.6
Franklin	926	9 309	1 178	D	1 374	159	189	355	38 169	542	40.8	9.0	39.7
Gaston	3 900	63 311	11 951	14 015	9 170	1 183	1 308	2 184	34 501	520	54.8	1.0	39.8
Gates	120	762	D	134	178	37	D	20	26 543	182	33.5	14.3	44.0
Graham	169	1 810	260	D	231	41	D	65	35 664	107	54.2	0.0	39.3
Granville	835	12 578	2 167	4 082	1 303	310	229	423	33 666	589	37.0	5.4	50.6
Greene	245	1 958	558	130	308	39	D	50	25 606	260	31.9	18.8	62.7
Guilford	13 194	252 208	36 975	32 187	27 393	13 404	11 009	10 517	41 699	962	56.9	4.2	43.9
Halifax	992	12 123	2 974	1 924	2 302	317	218	368	30 394	341	28.2	27.3	49.3
Harnett	1 607	19 196	3 755	1 523	3 188	561	455	566	29 508	797	55.6	9.2	47.9
Haywood	1 375	13 662	2 491	1 691	2 952	442	437	424	31 001	597	58.8	2.5	42.2
Henderson	2 520	30 280	6 219	5 914	4 934	827	979	1 056	34 876	468	68.6	2.8	52.1
Hertford	498	7 269	2 054	991	1 099	D	95	247	34 003	162	37.7	24.7	64.8
Hoke	397	5 779	953	2 300	829	73	124	145	25 160	202	47.0	13.4	54.0
Hyde	168	914	D	52	123	D	D	28	31 049	158	39.9	27.8	55.1
Iredell	4 356	60 162	8 953	10 510	8 164	1 253	2 831	2 517	41 835	1 203	47.3	5.2	55.9
Jackson	925	10 727	1 931	D	1 620	189	337	325	30 258	245	59.6	0.8	44.5
Johnston	3 040	38 299	5 047	6 828	7 633	829	888	1 251	32 656	1 175	50.6	7.1	46.6
Jones	136	750	184	31	96	D	17	25	33 451	170	35.9	15.3	60.0
Lee	1 273	23 080	2 734	8 728	3 023	358	363	772	33 446	246	47.6	6.9	43.9
Lenoir	1 258	21 107	4 083	3 822	2 857	599	607	656	31 059	401	37.4	17.0	64.3
Lincoln	1 514	16 970	2 479	3 804	2 955	404	476	557	32 832	651	53.6	1.8	35.5
McDowell	726	12 874	1 728	5 728	1 591	200	150	389	30 212	334	53.6	1.5	46.1
Macon	1 071	9 047	1 592	745	1 870	336	212	273	30 170	326	62.0	0.6	42.3
Madison	301	3 058	651	360	D	44	38	74	24 147	719	49.0	1.1	38.4
Martin	440	5 258	1 290	949	927	163	105	144	27 393	357	22.1	23.5	61.6
Mecklenburg	28 715	558 911	64 301	25 427	54 144	65 990	46 379	31 324	56 046	237	64.1	2.5	47.7
Mitchell	376	3 986	871	332	889	96	D	128	32 025	286	62.9	0.3	37.1
Montgomery	478	6 291	1 010	2 275	748	D	67	193	30 749	250	44.0	6.0	63.6
Moore	2 199	28 712	8 812	1 942	4 595	876	1 387	1 038	36 167	718	51.9	3.3	47.9
Nash	2 053	34 010	5 567	D	5 151	1 405	851	1 262	37 113	430	39.8	14.9	56.5
New Hanover	6 806	84 705	15 700	4 695	14 146	2 631	5 748	3 443	40 642	50	74.0	2.0	52.0
Northampton	265	4 017	643	420	D	30	D	125	31 123	319	25.1	24.1	65.8
Onslow	2 743	34 624	5 440	1 055	7 823	1 036	1 796	926	26 748	347	48.4	7.2	54.2
Orange	3 092	38 205	12 766	951	5 871	1 870	2 199	1 598	41 818	645	54.0	2.6	47.8
Pamlico	271	2 489	569	D	394	D	D	67	27 031	80	40.0	31.3	68.8
Pasquotank	911	11 236	2 692	857	2 417	533	271	357	31 741	136	39.7	30.9	66.2
Pender	950	7 548	1 364	718	1 421	106	218	223	29 565	335	51.3	7.8	49.9
Perquimans	201	1 362	193	50	232	45	24	39	28 781	185	27.0	30.8	68.6
Person	669	7 987	1 380	1 513	1 386	179	124	265	33 220	395	36.5	12.9	50.6
Pitt	3 526	57 690	15 790	4 657	8 383	2 019	1 913	2 035	35 275	391	34.8	21.5	59.3
Polk	481	3 679	1 485	312	405	129	148	101	27 546	290	55.2	1.4	50.0
Randolph	2 540	38 343	4 985	14 070	4 130	1 094	615	1 244	32 450	1 486	46.7	2.8	48.6
Richmond	842	11 192	2 067	3 242	1 859	247	155	328	29 287	277	40.1	5.4	49.8
Robeson	1 800	30 207	7 571	6 765	4 744	1 151	523	880	29 136	941	45.2	13.2	56.3
Rockingham	1 667	22 553	3 409	6 381	3 626	481	479	734	32 535	902	44.5	3.8	46.1
Rowan	2 553	41 848	D	8 345	4 268	676	840	1 608	38 415	1 011	55.2	4.2	36.2
Rutherford	1 254	14 864	3 182	2 973	2 478	331	264	457	30 760	638	51.4	2.2	48.4
Sampson	996	13 803	2 605	3 620	2 160	247	274	428	30 982	1 067	36.3	13.0	55.2
Scotland	618	9 589	2 440	1 569	1 537	213	106	289	30 092	150	32.0	16.7	51.3
Stanly	1 299	15 830	3 240	3 277	2 653	373	292	477	30 120	664	54.7	4.8	44.3
Stokes	607	5 298	1 169	886	898	107	155	156	29 424	926	40.4	2.4	50.9
Surry	1 682	26 776	4 279	3 907	4 041	638	361	922	34 439	1 256	49.2	2.2	48.5

STATE County	Agriculture, 2012 (cont.)															
	Land in farms					Value of land and buildings (dollars)		Value of machinery and equipment, average per farm (dollars)	Value of products sold				Percent of farms with sales of:		Government payments	
	Acreage (1,000)	Percent change, 2007–2012	Acres: Average size of farm	Acres: Total irrigated (1,000)	Acres: Total cropland (1,000)	Average per farm	Average per acre		Total (mil dol)	Average per farm (dollars)	Percent from: Crops	Percent from: Livestock and poultry products	$10,000 or more	$100,000 or more	Total ($1,000)	Percent of farms
	117	118	119	120	121	122	123	124	125	126	127	128	129	130	131	132
NORTH CAROLINA—Cont'd																
Chowan	58	-22.1	412	5.0	47.5	1 307 021	3 169	343 525	70.7	501 582	81.4	18.6	70.2	46.1	1 586	72.3
Clay	12	21.7	76	0.2	4.3	380 760	4 990	38 864	3.2	20 636	80.3	19.7	20.1	2.6	209	26.6
Cleveland	117	0.9	113	0.2	47.2	463 430	4 116	58 367	127.7	123 296	17.2	82.8	30.7	11.3	834	23.6
Columbus	159	4.5	218	2.4	116.3	660 404	3 032	132 025	196.5	268 835	42.1	57.9	46.5	19.7	3 374	56.0
Craven	71	-0.4	276	0.9	51.5	853 684	3 094	150 055	55.5	216 820	68.0	32.0	43.8	25.0	1 471	55.9
Cumberland	82	-6.8	212	3.4	47.7	660 437	3 121	119 159	104.8	269 383	40.3	59.7	40.1	18.0	1 021	38.8
Currituck	35	28.2	431	0.2	32.1	1 762 451	4 088	244 244	25.9	315 537	99.9	0.1	51.2	28.0	507	48.8
Dare	D	D	D	0.0	D	1 553 333	D	159 111	1.1	125 333	D	D	44.4	22.2	D	22.2
Davidson	87	-4.6	82	0.8	40.8	504 619	6 138	56 573	54.6	51 412	39.8	60.2	25.1	7.1	616	15.6
Davie	60	-14.7	93	0.1	30.0	575 472	6 178	50 453	25.4	39 625	49.7	50.3	28.0	6.3	227	11.3
Duplin	231	-6.9	246	11.7	155.0	1 001 313	4 076	159 549	1 276.4	1 357 895	10.5	89.5	69.7	53.0	3 324	41.0
Durham	21	-20.3	90	0.4	6.5	771 086	8 578	50 358	9.4	40 517	83.1	16.9	26.7	4.7	237	23.7
Edgecombe	127	-9.4	466	5.9	90.4	1 226 103	2 634	266 243	156.0	573 618	62.9	37.1	47.1	31.6	2 479	71.3
Forsyth	40	-7.2	61	0.2	19.7	507 905	8 309	46 530	16.1	24 311	89.3	10.7	20.4	3.0	254	15.4
Franklin	117	3.6	216	3.8	59.5	921 013	4 271	108 980	81.5	150 308	69.2	30.8	31.9	12.7	1 070	36.5
Gaston	42	11.6	81	0.1	15.1	488 746	6 062	41 181	17.1	32 792	30.0	70.0	23.3	5.0	186	14.2
Gates	63	-16.5	348	3.8	45.2	1 210 253	3 480	152 918	66.8	367 126	45.9	54.1	46.7	30.8	980	70.3
Graham	7	-4.8	64	0.0	1.4	385 037	6 026	55 776	1.7	15 972	32.2	67.8	32.7	1.9	94	15.0
Granville	101	-21.5	171	2.0	27.9	703 173	4 108	50 185	22.8	38 769	84.2	15.8	28.0	7.0	1 224	47.0
Greene	101	9.8	389	2.1	69.4	1 517 792	3 900	167 331	274.0	1 053 758	27.7	72.3	66.2	44.2	2 286	73.8
Guilford	91	-6.0	94	1.5	41.7	583 445	6 185	63 998	58.2	60 500	56.2	43.8	28.3	8.8	962	14.8
Halifax	196	-0.9	574	3.5	120.4	1 362 000	2 371	216 636	128.3	376 211	67.7	32.3	42.5	30.2	6 355	73.0
Harnett	120	7.2	150	2.3	77.0	803 863	5 349	95 246	190.3	238 732	38.7	61.3	35.5	19.8	3 369	38.8
Haywood	49	-12.9	82	0.4	10.1	519 586	6 334	39 461	14.1	23 660	45.5	54.5	23.8	4.5	773	23.1
Henderson	36	-5.8	76	3.4	17.4	596 389	7 807	67 859	61.8	132 139	87.6	12.4	36.8	14.1	1 427	8.8
Hertford	83	5.6	513	5.6	53.7	1 226 611	2 393	231 747	146.4	903 531	36.8	63.2	54.3	38.9	1 813	72.2
Hoke	59	-2.7	290	0.7	37.4	929 153	3 204	113 114	96.8	479 327	26.1	73.9	44.1	22.8	855	43.6
Hyde	108	30.1	681	0.5	83.1	1 674 475	2 460	333 924	133.4	844 373	D	D	47.5	29.7	1 787	79.1
Iredell	152	10.1	127	0.9	75.4	761 847	6 014	74 110	165.9	137 929	22.4	77.6	39.7	16.2	1 528	12.6
Jackson	16	21.5	66	0.1	6.2	638 514	9 656	51 196	8.2	33 502	93.6	6.4	29.4	6.1	90	11.0
Johnston	195	0.4	166	3.6	133.7	809 586	4 883	105 065	265.2	225 684	57.9	42.1	39.1	18.5	4 347	39.2
Jones	59	-14.1	349	1.1	45.3	931 588	2 668	189 171	185.6	1 091 594	16.6	83.4	55.9	38.8	2 130	57.6
Lee	39	7.9	159	1.3	15.0	663 992	4 180	71 622	34.7	141 252	49.5	50.5	32.9	12.2	569	19.5
Lenoir	122	-11.2	304	3.7	94.2	1 027 628	3 375	183 147	312.4	778 973	31.1	68.9	62.1	44.1	3 454	64.3
Lincoln	56	-6.4	85	0.2	25.6	475 570	5 571	55 046	56.5	86 731	17.2	82.8	27.6	7.5	350	18.1
McDowell	25	8.4	75	0.2	6.1	430 174	5 770	59 126	25.2	75 392	68.3	31.7	23.1	7.5	110	5.1
Macon	23	7.3	70	0.1	5.2	530 994	7 631	48 359	5.6	17 295	36.0	64.0	20.6	1.5	91	9.8
Madison	56	-15.7	78	0.2	10.2	423 822	5 414	31 459	5.7	7 861	67.5	32.5	18.1	0.8	859	34.6
Martin	127	20.6	356	0.8	88.7	1 004 266	2 819	192 616	100.3	281 070	84.3	15.7	61.3	37.8	4 684	85.4
Mecklenburg	15	-19.3	65	0.5	5.9	1 341 371	20 591	136 338	D	D	D	D	30.4	5.9	D	5.9
Mitchell	19	-15.2	68	0.0	4.3	356 112	5 271	34 846	2.5	8 703	80.4	19.6	24.1	0.3	119	13.6
Montgomery	35	-17.6	140	1.2	9.7	574 648	4 099	95 416	122.3	489 116	7.6	92.4	48.4	30.8	162	9.6
Moore	82	3.0	115	1.6	19.2	611 519	5 325	58 081	162.4	226 213	9.3	90.7	34.8	14.3	635	10.7
Nash	141	-8.4	327	6.0	91.5	1 246 505	3 812	153 670	184.4	428 723	60.8	39.2	50.5	32.6	1 705	50.5
New Hanover	3	-34.8	58	0.1	1.2	819 980	14 231	42 980	5.4	107 060	99.0	1.0	46.0	20.0	80	14.0
Northampton	163	4.6	510	3.2	109.5	1 335 680	2 618	218 533	133.0	416 821	56.9	43.1	59.2	35.4	5 226	85.6
Onslow	58	4.4	166	1.5	38.4	634 349	3 819	115 625	187.7	540 928	15.6	84.4	46.4	30.5	1 001	38.3
Orange	57	-5.6	88	0.8	21.8	587 984	6 693	53 744	30.6	47 462	50.5	49.5	31.9	6.4	611	22.6
Pamlico	47	1.4	585	2.4	39.4	1 682 463	2 877	334 763	35.8	448 100	D	D	53.8	38.8	881	63.8
Pasquotank	72	-15.6	531	D	67.7	1 678 897	3 159	307 206	69.0	507 537	99.4	0.6	58.1	40.4	969	52.2
Pender	56	-9.4	166	1.7	30.5	704 096	4 229	93 278	173.6	518 069	19.5	80.5	40.6	25.1	1 532	33.7
Perquimans	80	17.0	433	0.9	72.4	1 405 173	3 245	296 043	98.8	534 081	59.9	40.1	78.4	60.0	1 749	75.1
Person	95	-3.3	241	2.8	49.5	916 124	3 797	106 694	41.0	103 868	88.5	11.5	33.9	15.7	851	43.5
Pitt	172	0.2	439	3.6	131.7	1 397 719	3 181	233 246	215.9	552 194	51.5	48.5	60.1	38.9	3 877	57.3
Polk	24	14.8	83	0.1	7.1	609 310	7 332	49 707	D	D	D	D	20.7	5.2	56	13.1
Randolph	157	6.4	106	1.2	57.1	505 668	4 792	63 355	236.4	159 079	10.1	89.9	35.1	14.9	961	13.1
Richmond	48	16.3	172	1.5	19.4	707 336	4 119	72 953	165.2	596 390	7.1	92.9	48.7	32.5	610	27.4
Robeson	266	-0.9	282	6.5	198.6	828 756	2 937	136 951	409.6	435 310	35.2	64.8	45.7	24.4	4 522	51.1
Rockingham	112	-4.2	124	3.4	37.2	503 050	4 045	50 227	32.8	36 368	74.3	25.7	25.5	5.7	726	27.6
Rowan	121	4.5	120	1.1	65.9	677 980	5 658	79 407	84.0	83 067	60.5	39.5	29.5	8.0	458	12.6
Rutherford	60	-9.6	93	0.2	16.1	376 525	4 035	35 348	22.8	35 751	14.3	85.7	22.7	3.9	313	14.4
Sampson	292	-9.3	273	16.3	179.3	1 086 479	3 975	186 084	1 258.8	1 179 750	17.7	82.3	66.3	46.2	3 373	53.7
Scotland	69	4.8	460	2.2	33.4	1 654 193	3 600	113 933	82.2	547 833	24.5	75.5	50.7	34.7	427	44.7
Stanly	93	-11.0	140	0.5	54.5	720 660	5 141	85 458	96.5	145 354	33.8	66.2	27.1	11.0	928	26.5
Stokes	92	0.6	99	0.5	30.8	380 308	3 847	46 631	31.4	33 949	36.4	63.6	22.2	4.2	1 065	26.6
Surry	127	10.8	101	1.1	56.3	463 494	4 588	84 900	198.9	158 387	22.9	77.1	34.1	10.7	1 293	26.1

STATE County	Water use, 2010		Wholesale trade,[1] 2007				Retail trade,[2] 2007				Real estate and rental and leasing,[2] 2007			
	Total water withdrawn (mil gal/day)	Gallons withdrawn per person per day	Number of establish-ments	Number of employees	Sales (mil dol)	Annual payroll (mil dol)	Number of establish-ments	Number of employees	Sales (mil dol)	Annual payroll (mil dol)	Number of establish-ments	Number of employees	Receipts (mil dol)	Annual payroll (mil dol)
	133	134	135	136	137	138	139	140	141	142	143	144	145	146
NORTH CAROLINA—Cont'd														
Chowan	7.0	475	12	132	38.5	3.7	64	613	136.1	11.8	22	48	7.3	0.8
Clay	1.3	119	1	D	D	D	53	377	133.7	8.6	19	D	D	D
Cleveland	43.4	442	92	1 550	1 247.0	52.1	406	3 947	928.8	83.7	66	308	50.5	7.0
Columbus	43.1	741	43	329	234.2	11.1	249	2 318	527.6	46.1	34	111	13.2	2.3
Craven	37.3	361	64	714	827.7	26.5	424	4 538	1 111.7	101.0	118	413	56.0	11.0
Cumberland	45.7	143	161	1 706	920.0	69.8	1 073	15 913	3 897.4	343.3	334	1 700	252.2	48.9
Currituck	5.6	240	15	D	D	D	149	1 102	263.9	23.7	54	676	58.8	20.8
Dare	8.7	257	40	D	D	D	475	3 467	869.1	88.5	159	1 414	127.7	48.6
Davidson	27.2	167	153	D	D	D	507	5 128	1 264.2	110.6	111	337	39.1	7.0
Davie	6.4	155	31	349	139.1	11.9	126	1 475	407.8	34.3	25	64	10.7	1.3
Duplin	38.5	658	41	418	350.2	14.5	192	1 697	412.6	33.5	29	67	6.1	0.9
Durham	33.8	126	215	8 974	7 657.3	842.9	935	14 439	3 135.3	311.5	320	1 941	375.4	76.0
Edgecombe	15.3	270	25	D	D	D	159	1 539	324.7	29.8	34	117	18.9	2.6
Forsyth	49.5	141	424	7 342	4 542.0	312.0	1 442	21 315	5 202.9	479.2	432	D	D	D
Franklin	9.5	156	37	324	178.0	14.6	138	1 245	371.8	29.8	23	65	10.7	1.4
Gaston	851.7	4 133	196	2 163	1 178.4	82.7	672	9 557	2 245.3	202.1	162	1 041	167.7	29.2
Gates	2.9	234	10	104	81.1	3.9	22	159	34.0	2.3	1	D	D	D
Graham	39.1	4 408	3	D	D	D	33	209	46.2	3.9	5	D	D	D
Granville	8.2	137	28	286	125.2	9.6	141	1 315	323.9	30.8	31	68	8.1	1.5
Greene	7.6	357	8	31	15.9	0.8	45	375	97.8	6.5	4	D	D	D
Guilford	66.0	135	1 024	14 772	11 295.4	710.0	2 004	30 247	7 252.6	718.7	690	4 564	1 455.5	147.4
Halifax	31.7	580	27	158	77.1	5.9	270	3 023	610.3	58.8	41	134	12.9	2.4
Harnett	27.7	241	46	D	D	D	270	3 148	872.0	65.4	51	D	D	D
Haywood	101.2	1 714	47	325	174.4	13.1	278	3 010	821.8	69.3	87	204	27.5	4.4
Henderson	19.4	182	115	1 173	709.9	41.9	441	5 353	1 479.2	127.7	120	346	52.3	9.3
Hertford	10.7	432	14	122	61.2	4.8	116	1 213	252.0	24.0	15	53	3.5	0.9
Hoke	26.2	559	10	94	33.1	2.7	67	512	121.7	8.1	16	23	4.3	0.5
Hyde	1.8	312	10	90	23.5	1.9	44	190	26.7	2.8	5	D	D	D
Iredell	26.0	163	228	2 420	1 275.9	116.5	647	8 360	2 288.9	201.7	219	693	119.2	22.8
Jackson	5.1	127	16	148	52.9	5.1	175	1 872	433.7	43.2	65	275	32.1	6.4
Johnston	29.7	176	111	1 055	820.9	49.7	580	7 163	1 971.7	148.1	105	477	77.7	12.2
Jones	3.7	362	10	127	41.2	4.4	29	163	31.8	2.8	1	D	D	D
Lee	11.8	204	56	1 128	672.2	43.6	251	2 966	764.5	65.2	63	197	32.0	6.0
Lenoir	29.6	498	62	D	D	D	276	3 537	842.8	80.8	54	229	28.0	4.7
Lincoln	26.9	343	73	986	436.2	38.6	248	2 683	713.8	60.8	71	181	40.8	6.0
McDowell	11.1	246	32	266	78.2	8.4	144	1 722	482.4	40.0	28	104	9.3	2.2
Macon	278.1	8 198	19	61	14.8	1.8	270	2 136	476.3	48.7	89	196	25.4	4.7
Madison	2.7	132	9	56	26.5	1.3	48	381	76.0	6.3	16	34	3.4	1.0
Martin	63.6	2 594	29	320	111.7	10.2	89	955	227.8	19.9	19	63	6.5	1.2
Mecklenburg	2 804.9	3 050	1 845	27 817	17 104.8	1 537.0	3 525	55 782	14 114.3	1 327.1	1 804	11 907	2 904.8	551.9
Mitchell	4.1	265	15	93	32.3	2.4	65	794	171.9	15.5	20	56	6.2	1.1
Montgomery	6.1	220	25	227	116.6	7.3	96	866	210.2	17.5	12	39	4.0	1.0
Moore	21.1	240	61	410	172.4	16.5	386	4 202	1 001.1	90.2	107	324	56.3	9.4
Nash	20.6	215	106	D	D	D	477	5 773	1 271.2	114.8	89	416	77.2	11.3
New Hanover	42.4	209	295	2 736	1 410.1	113.1	1 107	15 150	3 825.5	355.4	432	1 968	326.8	63.7
Northampton	21.4	970	19	425	256.1	14.5	58	435	102.0	7.6	5	15	1.0	0.2
Onslow	32.3	182	40	259	96.9	10.7	550	7 276	1 913.9	154.2	185	757	108.4	17.2
Orange	24.2	181	77	870	580.5	58.3	390	6 181	1 195.3	142.9	153	502	117.5	17.2
Pamlico	3.8	286	11	79	20.7	1.9	45	328	68.9	6.2	15	D	D	D
Pasquotank	5.3	131	34	447	148.8	13.5	217	2 750	694.3	61.8	50	D	D	D
Pender	12.6	241	34	1 166	583.9	54.7	158	1 271	331.8	26.0	57	172	20.9	5.8
Perquimans	2.9	212	11	84	32.4	2.4	37	242	69.0	5.2	9	D	D	D
Person	1 014.8	25 714	28	383	193.3	13.9	143	1 570	384.2	34.0	21	115	8.8	1.9
Pitt	28.8	171	137	1 700	898.9	70.5	668	8 846	2 176.0	188.8	201	D	D	D
Polk	2.6	126	17	146	65.0	4.9	68	506	110.3	9.5	28	87	10.0	2.2
Randolph	23.4	165	150	1 813	746.4	75.8	438	4 465	1 156.7	95.9	73	292	46.6	7.1
Richmond	18.6	399	33	D	D	D	204	2 076	424.1	40.0	34	93	11.1	1.6
Robeson	37.2	277	73	728	627.1	26.1	431	5 144	1 337.9	103.6	51	259	25.5	4.1
Rockingham	133.4	1 424	59	813	611.5	27.4	340	3 682	839.6	76.3	61	190	15.7	3.5
Rowan	197.6	1 427	111	1 570	628.6	56.4	452	4 755	1 163.8	98.1	98	293	52.2	8.8
Rutherford	11.6	170	45	D	D	D	278	2 767	640.1	59.2	61	218	29.2	6.6
Sampson	37.9	597	52	781	002.0	29.7	226	2 403	575.8	48.7	33	106	16.1	2.6
Scotland	7.3	203	18	D	D	D	153	1 711	361.7	32.9	23	81	9.4	1.9
Stanly	9.5	157	47	D	D	D	237	2 596	610.0	54.4	40	D	D	D
Stokes	1 283.4	27 076	18	73	11.7	2.2	115	893	226.5	18.4	27	D	D	D
Surry	26.5	360	69	D	D	D	350	3 963	1 054.1	82.9	73	272	32.5	6.3

1. Merchant wholesalers, except manufacturers' sales branches and offices. 2. Employer establishments.

Table B. States and Counties — Professional Services, Manufacturing, and Accommodation and Food Services

STATE County	Professional, scientific, and technical services,[1] 2007				Manufacturing, 2007				Accommodation and food services, 2007			
	Number of establish-ments	Number of employees	Receipts (mil dol)	Annual payroll (mil dol)	Number of establish-ments	Number of employees	Receipts (mil dol)	Annual payroll (mil dol)	Number of establish-ments	Number of employees	Sales (mil dol)	Annual payroll (mil dol)
	147	148	149	150	151	152	153	154	155	156	157	158
NORTH CAROLINA—Cont'd												
Chowan	23	124	11.6	4.9	25	899	341.7	29.6	28	483	19.5	5.1
Clay	16	49	3.5	1.3	NA	NA	NA	NA	15	217	7.4	2.4
Cleveland	127	752	82.0	28.9	142	7 198	2 229.8	290.6	159	2 277	96.6	25.9
Columbus	56	204	18.0	5.1	41	2 487	887.7	108.8	87	980	41.1	9.4
Craven	223	D	D	D	85	4 745	D	D	178	3 824	142.1	37.9
Cumberland	495	D	D	D	110	8 424	D	391.0	586	D	D	D
Currituck	40	128	20.3	14.7	NA	NA	NA	NA	75	512	34.5	8.5
Dare	131	681	58.9	24.1	45	636	98.4	20.3	301	3 755	248.3	77.0
Davidson	207	778	76.6	26.4	281	11 982	2 696.7	413.6	211	3 621	131.8	39.7
Davie	68	290	21.9	8.1	54	3 503	1 001.6	134.9	59	795	29.0	8.2
Duplin	59	175	14.5	5.3	33	5 747	1 621.4	158.2	76	1 215	42.2	11.1
Durham	970	D	D	D	179	12 930	9 359.6	750.8	617	12 949	729.3	202.7
Edgecombe	43	244	21.7	7.2	43	4 437	1 226.9	152.8	73	954	36.4	9.8
Forsyth	977	D	D	D	350	18 381	16 881.5	858.1	712	14 261	646.8	179.3
Franklin	73	245	28.2	10.7	54	3 150	1 034.1	150.9	46	514	21.4	6.0
Gaston	287	D	D	D	341	14 259	4 158.6	541.2	296	5 638	253.4	67.4
Gates	10	44	4.0	1.3	NA	NA	NA	NA	6	100	2.3	0.7
Graham	7	32	2.4	0.9	NA	NA	NA	NA	22	240	15.4	4.8
Granville	64	184	17.9	5.5	48	4 792	2 252.1	186.8	66	1 132	48.8	11.0
Greene	8	28	2.3	0.8	NA	NA	NA	NA	9	158	6.3	1.8
Guilford	1 533	D	D	D	746	37 752	23 940.4	1 616.0	1 114	22 829	1 044.5	295.5
Halifax	61	404	24.2	9.2	42	2 208	D	D	86	1 899	71.9	20.1
Harnett	126	509	42.7	16.9	71	2 631	464.7	96.3	121	D	D	D
Haywood	107	575	60.3	24.7	45	1 926	D	D	156	2 341	99.1	28.6
Henderson	228	D	D	D	145	6 752	2 129.6	286.6	198	3 449	170.5	47.5
Hertford	19	D	D	D	17	867	D	50.6	43	689	25.4	7.0
Hoke	33	D	D	D	16	2 137	D	59.1	23	D	D	D
Hyde	3	D	D	D	NA	NA	NA	NA	30	233	16.9	4.3
Iredell	378	2 782	321.6	112.2	285	11 898	3 167.1	446.0	332	6 039	246.7	69.9
Jackson	78	D	D	D	NA	NA	NA	NA	96	1 556	74.0	20.1
Johnston	243	1 132	109.7	43.0	125	6 409	2 418.3	284.9	268	4 718	197.2	51.1
Jones	6	D	D	D	NA	NA	NA	NA	8	31	1.2	0.3
Lee	83	742	30.8	39.5	81	9 028	3 521.6	361.8	95	1 796	67.3	17.6
Lenoir	74	459	87.6	21.0	55	4 937	1 229.1	156.0	92	1 811	69.7	19.7
Lincoln	120	601	61.6	20.2	106	5 190	2 106.0	188.7	102	1 705	65.2	17.0
McDowell	37	170	13.2	6.6	65	6 522	1 332.5	196.9	70	1 139	42.0	10.9
Macon	76	272	22.9	9.4	40	821	230.5	26.8	114	1 234	68.2	18.9
Madison	20	43	3.7	1.0	NA	NA	NA	NA	30	282	12.1	3.2
Martin	26	142	7.7	3.6	18	945	362.6	29.7	43	693	26.4	6.9
Mecklenburg	3 689	D	D	D	890	30 349	11 201.0	1 354.0	2 253	47 379	2 550.5	702.9
Mitchell	23	80	5.9	2.0	27	552	71.0	17.1	35	311	12.6	3.4
Montgomery	15	67	6.8	2.0	68	3 307	750.8	108.9	33	282	13.4	3.5
Moore	218	1 452	151.3	60.2	85	2 129	669.6	80.3	174	4 310	227.5	65.9
Nash	179	988	111.3	41.0	102	8 298	2 956.2	347.9	193	4 104	163.8	45.4
New Hanover	832	D	D	D	193	5 743	2 883.6	306.4	615	12 542	525.5	152.3
Northampton	17	39	3.3	0.9	NA	NA	NA	NA	19	142	5.2	1.6
Onslow	210	D	D	D	43	1 016	253.0	31.8	310	6 265	287.9	71.5
Orange	507	D	D	D	73	1 534	D	56.5	304	6 088	275.6	80.1
Pamlico	15	D	D	D	NA	NA	NA	NA	23	355	23.8	6.6
Pasquotank	76	455	50.5	14.9	31	720	D	29.1	93	1 931	64.8	19.0
Pender	74	D	D	D	44	1 416	D	55.4	70	892	35.5	9.3
Perquimans	14	D	D	D	NA	NA	NA	NA	16	167	5.8	1.8
Person	43	D	D	D	39	2 114	D	69.9	50	818	37.4	9.0
Pitt	310	1 750	198.5	77.0	98	6 930	D	265.8	306	7 187	293.5	79.2
Polk	40	138	13.3	4.7	21	605	153.1	17.9	38	436	15.5	4.9
Randolph	167	D	D	D	339	17 982	4 397.7	570.6	175	3 029	131.3	35.1
Richmond	57	215	16.0	5.2	50	3 690	697.3	94.5	67	960	37.7	9.5
Robeson	110	D	D	D	71	8 436	2 792.6	243.8	161	3 476	128.8	31.9
Rockingham	114	D	D	D	109	7 771	3 118.4	274.8	143	2 124	84.6	22.6
Rowan	183	1 213	90.5	35.2	200	12 036	3 724.3	428.4	195	3 283	132.1	37.0
Rutherford	74	294	21.3	6.8	75	3 936	901.9	140.1	110	1 401	60.2	16.7
Sampson	50	182	16.8	5.6	52	3 043	917.6	101.1	81	996	38.6	10.7
Scotland	35	D	D	D	39	3 122	1 061.2	119.9	48	812	32.7	8.8
Stanly	77	329	37.3	12.0	111	3 900	925.8	137.4	103	1 570	55.7	15.7
Stokes	38	147	12.5	4.6	33	1 078	D	37.3	53	775	28.7	8.0
Surry	111	435	39.1	12.2	111	5 478	1 038.0	168.5	153	2 464	84.9	24.9

1. Establishment subject to federal tax.

STATE County	Health care and social assistance, 2007				Other services, 2007				Nonemployer businesses, 2013		Value of residential construction authorized by building permits, 2014	
	Number of establish-ments	Number of employees	Receipts (mil dol)	Annual payroll (mil dol)	Number of establish-ments	Number of employees	Receipts (mil dol)	Annual payroll (mil dol)	Number	Receipts (mil dol)	New Construction ($1,000)	Number of housing units
	159	160	161	162	163	164	165	166	167	168	169	170
NORTH CAROLINA—Cont'd												
Chowan	55	1 192	83.8	35.5	22	83	6.3	1.9	936	31.7	3 377	17
Clay	23	249	13.9	6.1	11	27	2.2	0.6	1 029	32.0	12 959	43
Cleveland	234	5 819	490.3	202.6	153	638	53.0	14.4	5 366	171.2	17 443	128
Columbus	179	3 658	217.6	90.8	69	229	18.8	4.7	3 246	111.7	4 302	35
Craven	270	7 199	648.9	263.3	159	826	66.8	16.7	5 704	208.3	35 634	254
Cumberland	743	18 732	1 573.8	646.8	411	2 670	176.6	55.2	16 641	624.2	133 130	870
Currituck	27	D	D	D	41	156	13.2	4.0	1 926	92.1	71 494	241
Dare	80	D	D	D	104	469	33.4	9.9	4 925	254.4	77 959	234
Davidson	199	4 731	325.5	145.4	190	982	67.6	19.2	10 844	395.2	76 514	290
Davie	60	1 058	67.1	25.0	58	288	17.0	4.2	2 888	110.5	17 289	82
Duplin	100	2 002	108.4	48.0	56	246	19.6	6.0	3 094	115.1	8 030	48
Durham	725	22 856	2 828.6	960.5	443	4 038	664.4	153.1	20 690	721.9	259 124	1 591
Edgecombe	92	2 468	153.9	63.4	60	290	122.0	6.8	2 576	70.9	5 702	31
Forsyth	806	28 766	2 859.9	1 108.0	605	3 859	391.1	95.0	24 481	927.0	181 002	1 542
Franklin	84	D	D	D	63	191	19.9	4.8	3 812	134.7	43 001	242
Gaston	458	10 998	937.0	410.1	287	1 815	186.1	44.0	12 476	458.0	153 243	687
Gates	10	D	D	D	11	47	3.7	0.8	549	16.9	3 814	20
Graham	13	355	11.2	6.0	11	36	3.1	0.7	679	22.9	3 339	20
Granville	93	3 092	230.2	104.3	49	176	20.4	4.8	2 889	91.4	39 397	224
Greene	43	D	D	D	13	24	2.1	0.5	1 012	34.6	8 573	70
Guilford	1 240	30 287	2 861.8	1 177.0	878	5 437	740.5	148.8	37 997	1 625.9	450 433	2 339
Halifax	147	3 611	218.3	96.3	82	556	35.0	12.1	2 489	71.0	14 361	54
Harnett	164	3 567	226.1	103.5	107	465	33.0	9.3	6 172	227.9	75 834	612
Haywood	143	3 091	230.7	99.3	107	477	37.4	10.5	4 603	172.8	30 921	122
Henderson	258	6 122	487.6	204.4	177	1 007	81.9	21.7	8 532	315.0	82 522	339
Hertford	92	2 191	124.1	52.4	34	190	10.7	3.3	971	31.4	3 767	20
Hoke	70	1 927	78.2	35.9	23	117	6.2	2.0	2 177	63.7	46 465	219
Hyde	9	118	6.7	2.8	5	D	D	D	566	20.4	2 665	8
Iredell	424	8 552	821.5	326.2	275	1 666	126.0	37.4	12 432	554.1	273 211	798
Jackson	95	1 971	181.1	75.7	50	166	12.4	3.6	3 003	109.9	80 870	211
Johnston	273	D	D	D	208	934	80.2	21.0	11 251	476.1	219 625	1 280
Jones	17	340	28.1	12.4	5	16	1.3	0.4	551	18.2	1 704	10
Lee	163	2 887	196.6	80.7	96	469	32.0	9.7	3 368	136.7	16 849	71
Lenoir	199	4 574	298.0	130.7	92	624	44.7	14.6	3 177	108.4	9 237	54
Lincoln	133	2 130	166.7	69.0	119	509	39.0	10.1	5 231	193.9	62 083	374
McDowell	74	1 529	92.9	42.0	43	273	20.8	6.2	2 433	85.7	28 949	106
Macon	91	1 666	120.6	47.7	88	341	29.1	8.4	3 143	106.9	31 677	107
Madison	29	602	33.2	15.2	15	43	4.6	1.0	1 729	62.4	16 840	59
Martin	78	1 408	83.4	33.9	24	71	5.9	1.7	1 180	40.6	0	0
Mecklenburg	2 283	55 497	6 082.2	2 453.1	1 613	12 728	2 085.7	371.7	83 428	3 697.3	1 265 076	9 340
Mitchell	33	1 041	61.4	29.9	23	59	5.3	1.2	1 135	38.6	6 876	32
Montgomery	60	1 009	52.5	22.7	30	109	8.4	2.2	1 549	53.1	6 304	41
Moore	263	7 138	705.1	303.2	139	727	58.8	16.2	7 058	321.3	125 195	608
Nash	251	6 815	557.6	243.4	153	908	75.7	23.0	5 492	201.9	29 060	185
New Hanover	686	18 139	1 822.5	767.7	468	2 908	234.9	65.3	18 388	878.3	295 470	1 749
Northampton	35	782	29.4	14.3	18	44	4.0	0.8	859	28.9	5 364	17
Onslow	246	5 465	433.8	163.4	213	1 136	68.0	21.4	8 433	301.6	126 274	1 081
Orange	346	11 588	1 122.7	491.9	198	1 397	316.4	46.2	12 185	507.6	98 152	304
Pamlico	20	249	12.5	6.2	16	60	4.7	1.4	1 001	35.8	0	0
Pasquotank	134	2 919	242.3	101.8	75	459	24.8	7.8	2 432	73.8	9 759	63
Pender	75	1 036	69.8	27.3	55	222	16.9	5.4	3 911	146.5	70 203	459
Perquimans	17	D	D	D	12	49	2.6	0.9	915	28.2	5 344	26
Person	75	1 144	90.0	35.7	43	149	15.1	3.8	2 040	71.8	13 100	105
Pitt	439	D	D	D	185	1 084	108.0	21.6	10 067	378.2	113 146	905
Polk	60	1 456	89.9	38.7	30	96	13.7	2.4	1 828	73.8	20 965	67
Randolph	223	4 468	325.3	141.7	177	744	66.7	18.5	9 402	345.4	41 652	184
Richmond	104	2 119	160.5	62.8	59	D	D	D	2 001	61.8	10 018	197
Robeson	296	8 599	561.4	242.8	100	368	30.8	7.8	7 398	228.4	21 164	140
Rockingham	192	3 997	291.2	118.1	131	503	36.3	9.9	4 875	166.1	26 897	109
Rowan	241	7 413	717.6	322.1	164	987	59.9	18.8	8 794	306.5	74 392	288
Rutherford	140	3 133	214.0	89.4	79	509	34.9	10.2	4 037	157.1	21 005	130
Sampson	115	2 686	170.9	74.6	72	D	D	D	3 251	120.3	10 976	65
Scotland	120	2 664	202.4	87.2	39	D	D	D	1 742	50.5	3 816	32
Stanly	181	3 106	221.3	87.9	94	454	34.3	10.4	3 811	138.2	13 343	92
Stokes	54	1 233	69.0	30.2	48	232	17.3	5.0	2 902	103.3	19 907	135
Surry	172	3 892	303.4	119.7	103	663	52.0	16.7	4 977	205.4	15 974	73

Table B. States and Counties — **Government Employment and Payroll, and Local Government Finances**

STATE County	Government employment and payroll, 2012									Local government finances, 2012				
			March payroll (percent of total)							General revenue				
												Taxes		
													Per capita[1] (dollars)	
	Full-time equivalent employees	March payroll (dollars)	Adminis-tration, judicial, and legal	Police and Corrections	Fire Protection	Highways and transpor-tation	Health and Welfare	Natural resources and utilities	Education and libraries	Total (mil dol)	Inter-govern-mental (mil dol)	Total (mil dol)	Total	Property
	171	172	173	174	175	176	177	178	179	180	181	182	183	184
NORTH CAROLINA—Cont'd														
Chowan	470	1 457 821	1.5	4.5	1.5	0.7	1.5	4.7	79.9	47.9	24.9	15.3	1 036	830
Clay	374	1 096 838	4.9	8.6	0.1	2.1	18.6	3.2	58.6	30.3	17.7	10.0	938	759
Cleveland	5 555	17 029 077	1.4	2.7	1.1	0.6	40.8	3.7	48.8	997.0	173.6	81.7	838	665
Columbus	2 576	8 631 036	7.0	13.2	4.0	1.6	9.8	5.6	57.3	181.2	110.5	43.2	750	595
Craven	5 760	21 786 606	3.1	4.6	1.8	1.3	49.5	4.0	34.0	683.8	247.7	93.3	890	647
Cumberland	18 665	65 054 561	1.3	6.1	1.9	0.8	41.4	3.9	38.6	1 026.5	546.0	340.9	1 052	756
Currituck	1 085	3 605 883	4.2	9.0	1.4	0.2	12.9	4.4	63.7	101.1	28.3	49.2	2 044	1 156
Dare	1 891	6 914 953	10.6	12.1	4.0	0.9	18.7	6.6	40.2	195.1	51.6	121.3	3 507	2 197
Davidson	5 783	17 327 794	4.1	6.9	2.6	0.9	8.4	4.1	68.7	408.7	228.5	125.0	765	602
Davie	1 001 378	4 164 460	3.3	9.1	0.2	0.6	15.6	2.8	66.1	100.6	51.4	36.9	892	723
Duplin	2 002 596	7 169 108	4.4	6.0	0.9	1.1	11.3	3.0	71.0	166.7	96.1	42.2	702	533
Durham	9 926	33 408 797	6.2	5.0	0.4	2.0	10.8	7.2	66.1	1 014.8	394.0	460.1	1 645	1 286
Edgecombe	2 085	7 168 867	2.6	6.9	1.2	0.7	10.7	5.5	70.6	170.1	100.0	37.8	676	569
Forsyth	13 925	45 845 272	4.9	9.9	5.3	1.5	7.4	5.9	62.7	1 198.2	555.3	456.5	1 275	995
Franklin	1 848	5 584 621	4.4	7.9	0.4	0.3	14.6	2.9	65.1	141.2	69.1	51.6	840	681
Gaston	7 249	25 015 194	7.4	6.7	2.8	2.9	12.2	6.4	59.7	643.2	307.9	230.9	1 110	864
Gates	371	1 271 812	3.9	2.8	0.0	1.1	5.8	2.3	82.4	29.7	19.3	7.6	641	522
Graham	358	999 021	5.0	6.3	0.1	2.3	19.0	2.4	60.3	29.4	18.8	7.3	834	661
Granville	1 871	5 604 572	7.1	8.1	0.7	1.1	4.5	5.4	70.7	198.6	73.9	47.4	785	648
Greene	792	2 460 297	7.1	5.1	0.0	2.0	11.7	8.9	63.9	57.2	35.0	8.8	409	388
Guilford	18 710	71 857 919	4.6	10.1	4.0	2.3	6.6	6.4	63.8	1 781.8	770.6	726.5	1 450	1 146
Halifax	5 002 529	8 099 327	3.1	5.7	1.4	1.3	12.8	5.1	68.3	190.1	109.1	47.9	886	669
Harnett	3 872	13 569 140	4.6	12.1	0.4	1.1	9.2	4.4	66.9	288.8	164.5	83.5	684	544
Haywood	3 238	11 027 848	3.6	5.3	0.5	0.6	44.4	2.8	39.6	310.3	118.9	68.8	1 168	882
Henderson	4 495	15 113 386	3.5	6.2	0.7	0.5	37.6	2.5	46.9	628.0	121.4	105.7	976	755
Hertford	1 107	3 318 864	2.9	8.6	0.6	0.6	10.8	4.2	66.9	79.7	46.0	21.1	863	629
Hoke	1 946	6 883 544	2.2	5.4	0.2	1.0	6.2	1.3	80.3	121.2	74.9	31.7	626	463
Hyde	303	895 248	4.8	5.1	0.0	0.0	17.4	6.5	63.4	29.6	15.5	8.8	1 500	1 122
Iredell	5 871	18 788 013	4.4	8.0	3.5	0.6	9.3	4.8	66.7	482.4	216.0	188.6	1 159	907
Jackson	1 418	4 256 176	4.4	6.6	0.0	1.0	11.8	4.0	65.6	109.9	53.3	43.4	1 072	832
Johnston	7 756	24 977 350	2.3	4.6	1.2	0.6	24.0	3.4	62.5	698.3	273.2	164.7	942	743
Jones	494	1 149 556	4.9	6.6	0.0	0.2	13.5	4.3	66.8	28.8	17.3	6.8	664	556
Lee	3 038	10 911 112	3.3	6.5	2.0	1.2	5.3	3.7	57.7	206.8	113.6	67.5	1 130	854
Lenoir	2 634	8 323 127	3.5	7.1	2.0	2.2	10.0	8.6	63.7	209.1	121.6	56.5	955	735
Lincoln	2 462	7 572 141	4.1	8.7	1.3	1.3	14.4	4.8	63.7	182.3	86.5	68.9	868	682
McDowell	1 584	3 817 801	1.8	2.8	0.5	0.8	1.5	2.4	89.3	105.4	60.6	31.8	708	497
Macon	1 378	3 815 292	6.5	9.2	0.5	1.5	16.3	5.7	56.3	100.9	48.1	36.6	1 081	971
Madison	876	2 682 447	3.6	4.9	0.2	0.3	14.0	3.1	71.6	52.3	29.4	15.8	761	620
Martin	1 141	3 472 186	4.5	5.3	2.4	1.3	15.0	4.7	65.2	85.6	46.7	22.7	948	699
Mecklenburg	60 489	285 037 206	2.7	6.4	2.0	1.6	56.6	3.0	26.7	8 195.0	1 390.6	1 863.3	1 923	1 419
Mitchell	1 336	2 250 773	2.5	3.7	0.0	0.0	5.6	2.2	79.0	52.4	33.1	13.0	844	617
Montgomery	1 174	3 454 946	3.3	6.9	0.0	0.7	9.4	3.4	74.1	81.0	47.9	21.9	792	630
Moore	3 494	11 423 864	5.9	7.9	2.5	1.7	12.6	3.7	62.8	269.6	121.4	108.4	1 201	948
Nash	6 656	23 448 806	3.3	5.8	2.6	2.0	39.4	6.2	39.5	555.5	191.0	99.1	1 035	775
New Hanover	11 962	45 527 134	2.5	6.8	2.5	1.2	49.3	4.7	29.7	1 468.2	274.1	326.8	1 562	1 109
Northampton	777	2 301 803	10.7	8.8	0.0	0.6	20.3	6.4	49.8	67.1	36.8	21.0	982	870
Onslow	5 873	18 455 158	3.9	7.0	1.9	1.2	10.7	4.8	66.2	585.4	209.5	152.5	832	536
Orange	5 385	18 675 410	6.4	8.5	3.1	3.3	8.9	7.6	55.3	495.0	178.9	247.0	1 791	1 537
Pamlico	537	1 656 218	4.6	6.6	0.2	0.4	9.9	5.9	70.1	42.4	25.2	12.6	965	785
Pasquotank	3 546	11 505 340	5.8	3.9	1.2	1.0	34.4	2.5	33.1	251.3	70.2	38.8	955	676
Pender	1 621	5 227 407	6.3	8.7	1.1	0.4	9.8	2.7	65.8	149.8	76.0	58.2	1 074	864
Perquimans	396	1 289 198	8.5	2.8	0.0	0.0	8.3	6.7	68.4	34.0	18.9	10.8	795	634
Person	1 548	5 009 176	3.6	7.9	2.5	1.2	11.6	4.6	65.6	119.0	63.0	39.6	1 007	800
Pitt	6 107	20 619 861	3.8	8.9	3.2	2.0	4.2	10.9	60.2	555.7	265.7	167.7	972	677
Polk	5 000 658	2 004 992	5.0	7.0	0.0	2.3	8.7	5.2	70.0	53.2	24.8	21.2	1 045	877
Randolph	4 527	16 669 167	4.3	8.3	2.7	1.2	7.8	3.4	68.3	345.4	185.5	117.9	828	644
Richmond	2 132	5 122 800	4.4	8.9	2.0	1.6	14.1	4.9	62.7	142.5	82.7	39.5	848	648
Robeson	1 006 145	18 365 522	4.4	13.6	1.4	1.1	12.5	5.8	59.7	414.1	250.9	103.1	761	522
Rockingham	3 543	11 125 272	5.5	9.4	2.7	1.5	10.3	3.0	62.8	267.2	141.9	84.2	908	715
Rowan	5 594	16 509 444	3.8	6.2	1.8	1.2	7.6	4.3	71.8	395.5	204.5	128.5	930	719
Rutherford	3 135	8 814 742	3.6	6.0	1.3	1.0	9.8	3.6	57.5	200.1	101.7	53.6	796	593
Sampson	2 002 770	7 777 872	2.8	6.0	0.4	0.4	11.9	2.4	71.5	212.9	127.6	48.5	759	539
Scotland	1 728	5 628 337	3.5	5.7	0.4	0.9	9.5	5.0	72.9	112.7	68.9	30.4	843	662
Stanly	2 443	7 501 977	4.3	7.7	2.6	2.1	13.1	6.3	62.1	184.7	101.2	51.9	857	641
Stokes	1 636	4 531 305	4.4	6.7	2.3	0.1	12.8	2.1	70.0	122.3	78.2	33.7	720	593
Surry	3 820	12 472 258	2.4	4.5	0.8	0.5	33.1	2.1	53.9	321.4	128.8	65.4	889	603

1. Based on the resident population estimated as of July 1 of the year shown.

STATE County	Local government finances, 2012 (cont.) — Direct general expenditure: Total (mil dol)	Per capita[1] (dollars)	Percent of total for: Educa-tion	Health and hospitals	Police protec-tion	Public welfare	High-ways	Debt outstanding: Total (mil dol)	Per capita[1] (dollars)	Government employment, 2013: Federal civilian	Federal military	State and local	Presidential election,[2] 2012 — Percent of vote cast: Demo-cratic	Republi-can	All other
	185	186	187	188	189	190	191	192	193	194	195	196	197	198	199
NORTH CAROLINA—Cont'd															
Chowan	47.4	3 208	53.9	0.4	10.6	6.8	2.3	21.8	1 475	31	36	866	49.1	50.2	0.7
Clay	30.1	2 831	45.1	6.7	10.1	14.8	0.1	11.8	1 114	19	26	495	31.3	66.9	1.8
Cleveland	561.2	5 758	30.2	48.9	3.5	3.9	0.5	167.5	1 719	170	238	5 627	39.6	59.5	0.9
Columbus	177.1	3 072	58.4	4.6	6.2	8.6	0.7	63.1	1 095	118	136	3 707	45.6	53.5	0.9
Craven	658.8	6 288	21.8	54.9	3.8	3.5	0.8	179.3	1 712	5 388	9 386	7 080	43.4	55.8	0.8
Cumberland	1 088.1	3 358	50.4	3.7	7.9	6.3	1.3	508.0	1 568	14 693	50 200	23 305	58.5	40.9	0.6
Currituck	92.8	3 854	37.2	6.0	8.8	4.4	0.1	60.9	2 529	36	61	1 133	33.7	65.2	1.2
Dare	214.0	6 189	25.3	7.8	9.4	3.9	1.4	229.3	6 632	237	199	2 825	44.7	54.0	1.3
Davidson	418.5	2 563	60.4	2.9	6.7	5.2	1.1	214.7	1 315	162	405	6 537	32.7	66.2	1.1
Davie	101.9	2 459	54.9	7.3	7.9	6.1	0.9	31.0	749	62	103	1 600	30.3	68.6	1.0
Duplin	161.0	2 681	57.6	5.6	6.5	7.2	1.1	40.0	667	135	149	3 300	45.0	54.4	0.6
Durham	1 130.0	4 041	36.7	5.4	7.7	4.9	2.8	1 199.0	4 288	5 802	867	14 939	75.6	23.6	0.8
Edgecombe	174.9	3 125	52.2	4.1	6.7	12.0	1.1	31.7	567	206	137	4 335	67.1	32.6	0.3
Forsyth	1 295.8	3 618	44.3	6.0	8.5	3.9	2.2	1 426.9	3 984	1 591	915	18 928	54.8	44.3	0.8
Franklin	146.8	2 389	50.6	6.0	5.3	7.7	1.0	126.9	2 064	77	152	2 373	49.1	49.8	1.1
Gaston	705.2	3 389	45.5	9.1	9.5	5.7	2.2	453.5	2 180	330	517	9 420	37.2	62.2	0.6
Gates	29.2	2 457	67.6	0.6	4.9	6.5	0.1	8.9	752	25	29	530	52.2	47.0	0.8
Graham	26.4	3 040	48.5	6.1	10.0	8.9	1.3	9.5	1 093	32	22	473	30.3	67.7	2.0
Granville	202.2	3 345	38.7	26.8	6.4	4.7	0.7	131.9	2 182	1 485	135	6 946	52.9	46.3	0.8
Greene	57.7	2 693	65.9	4.7	3.8	7.2	0.7	25.4	1 185	33	47	1 873	46.8	52.7	0.4
Guilford	1 919.4	3 832	43.8	4.5	7.5	4.2	2.9	2 139.4	4 271	3 913	1 287	30 209	58.8	40.4	0.8
Halifax	185.9	3 442	51.7	6.0	5.5	8.7	1.6	112.0	2 073	124	130	4 375	64.0	35.7	0.3
Harnett	319.1	2 613	48.6	4.3	6.4	3.5	1.3	272.9	2 234	107	311	5 601	41.2	57.9	0.8
Haywood	325.8	5 531	28.2	47.8	4.0	5.8	1.3	100.5	1 706	118	147	3 829	45.4	53.1	1.5
Henderson	411.4	3 800	31.5	38.2	5.0	4.9	1.3	200.9	1 856	191	271	5 268	38.9	59.9	1.2
Hertford	78.3	3 203	52.5	7.5	6.9	8.5	1.0	105.4	4 314	61	55	1 643	70.5	29.0	0.5
Hoke	115.8	2 291	61.0	2.2	4.8	7.7	0.8	96.8	1 915	53	127	2 142	59.0	40.3	0.7
Hyde	31.1	5 313	35.0	17.4	4.4	5.8	0.0	21.2	3 614	43	12	664	50.3	49.1	0.6
Iredell	484.3	2 977	49.9	1.9	7.8	5.0	2.0	564.7	3 470	247	410	8 562	37.3	61.7	1.0
Jackson	117.6	2 908	51.0	4.9	4.2	6.3	0.6	47.1	1 164	53	94	7 353	52.0	46.6	1.5
Johnston	707.4	4 044	42.4	30.3	4.0	3.6	1.0	672.2	3 843	209	441	8 909	37.7	61.4	0.8
Jones	28.7	2 798	50.8	6.3	6.8	10.5	0.5	4.3	418	21	25	483	45.5	53.9	0.6
Lee	211.6	3 544	60.3	1.6	7.1	4.8	1.1	152.3	2 550	151	148	3 203	45.3	53.7	1.0
Lenoir	226.0	3 816	45.8	3.1	5.0	6.3	0.8	200.6	3 387	199	145	6 093	49.7	49.8	0.4
Lincoln	184.5	2 326	52.4	5.8	7.2	7.4	0.6	203.5	2 566	99	198	3 689	32.7	66.0	1.3
McDowell	115.5	2 567	60.9	1.8	4.8	9.3	1.1	20.1	447	76	108	2 548	35.7	62.7	1.5
Macon	106.3	3 138	46.9	3.4	10.5	5.7	2.0	49.0	1 446	173	84	1 656	38.4	59.9	1.7
Madison	53.5	2 579	46.9	5.8	7.8	10.1	0.9	10.7	515	62	50	933	48.4	50.0	1.6
Martin	89.4	3 730	50.1	10.1	7.7	7.3	1.2	36.3	1 513	46	59	1 568	52.1	47.5	0.4
Mecklenburg	7 529.3	7 770	17.3	51.9	4.4	2.3	1.8	7 935.0	8 189	5 535	2 551	67 661	61.8	37.4	0.7
Mitchell	54.4	3 537	64.7	2.0	5.5	8.9	0.2	3.0	192	48	38	1 139	28.5	70.1	1.4
Montgomery	78.0	2 820	58.5	5.5	7.0	5.5	1.1	28.8	1 042	48	66	1 709	43.9	54.9	1.2
Moore	304.5	3 372	46.2	2.7	12.1	4.3	1.8	140.3	1 553	139	233	4 473	38.9	60.3	0.9
Nash	589.1	6 155	29.3	42.9	4.8	3.1	1.6	113.0	1 181	187	233	6 077	49.0	50.4	0.6
New Hanover	1 459.0	6 973	21.3	49.4	4.8	2.5	1.1	1 476.2	7 055	894	721	18 504	48.8	50.2	1.0
Northampton	68.1	3 176	37.6	9.0	6.4	10.1	1.8	37.7	1 759	41	51	1 187	65.0	34.6	0.4
Onslow	563.2	3 073	38.6	24.7	6.7	6.5	1.0	439.4	2 398	7 156	47 603	8 016	38.8	60.3	0.8
Orange	485.2	3 518	44.0	6.5	6.9	6.2	1.4	328.7	2 383	223	366	38 751	71.8	27.1	1.1
Pamlico	43.2	3 303	51.1	3.1	4.3	7.4	0.9	13.7	1 044	27	56	900	42.3	57.0	0.8
Pasquotank	254.1	6 261	28.0	49.1	4.4	3.4	1.2	135.3	3 334	731	823	5 141	56.5	42.8	0.7
Pender	152.0	2 804	46.6	4.9	6.0	6.5	0.6	184.1	3 396	92	164	2 481	41.7	57.3	0.9
Perquimans	34.1	2 515	51.3	2.5	8.3	7.0	1.1	30.1	2 218	33	34	625	42.6	56.6	0.8
Person	126.4	3 218	53.5	5.5	6.7	8.5	0.7	200.1	5 097	51	97	1 926	45.3	53.8	0.8
Pitt	557.6	3 232	46.8	1.8	9.9	5.2	2.1	400.7	2 322	454	461	24 379	54.1	45.3	0.6
Polk	49.0	2 420	52.7	2.7	8.4	8.4	1.3	16.1	796	39	50	868	41.6	56.7	1.7
Randolph	349.0	2 450	59.5	2.6	7.6	5.8	1.4	147.2	1 033	202	354	6 200	28.2	70.5	1.3
Richmond	150.1	3 220	56.1	3.4	6.8	7.0	1.1	48.8	1 047	78	113	3 080	50.3	48.8	1.0
Robeson	429.7	3 171	54.2	4.0	5.7	7.6	1.3	103.7	765	270	328	8 633	56.5	42.7	0.8
Rockingham	263.7	2 844	53.2	2.0	6.8	7.4	2.1	167.2	1 803	145	227	4 209	41.5	57.4	1.1
Rowan	420.9	3 046	54.8	2.5	6.5	5.4	1.5	263.4	1 906	2 279	336	6 886	38.0	60.8	1.2
Rutherford	191.7	2 848	53.0	6.6	6.5	6.8	1.1	113.5	1 685	101	165	3 490	33.6	65.4	1.1
Sampson	232.7	3 639	52.4	12.1	4.0	0.9	0.7	122.1	1 909	108	158	4 201	45.5	53.9	0.6
Scotland	112.8	3 125	56.5	1.8	7.2	8.7	1.5	27.4	758	43	84	2 353	57.3	42.2	0.4
Stanly	179.1	2 956	54.3	4.3	6.6	5.6	1.2	61.7	1 019	140	147	3 522	31.1	67.8	1.0
Stokes	117.6	2 514	64.2	4.7	5.2	6.5	0.4	62.1	1 328	67	116	1 905	31.6	66.6	1.7
Surry	324.4	4 410	40.1	37.5	3.8	3.5	0.8	112.5	1 530	158	181	4 595	35.5	63.4	1.1

1. Based on the resident population estimated as of July 1 of the year shown. 2.

STATE/ County code	CBSA code[1]	County type[2]	STATE County	Land area,[3] (sq km) 2010	Population, 2014: Total persons 2014	Population, 2014: Rank	Population, 2014: Per square kilometer	Population and population characteristics, 2013: Race alone or in combination, not Hispanic or Latino (percent): White	Black	American Indian, Alaska Native	Asian and Pacific Islander	Percent Hispanic or Latino[4]	Age (percent): Under 5 years	5 to 17 years	18 to 24 years	25 to 34 years	35 to 44 years	45 to 54 years
				1	2	3	4	5	6	7	8	9	10	11	12	13	14	15
			NORTH CAROLINA—Cont'd															
37 173	...	8	Swain	1 368	14 274	2 148	10.4	67.8	1.9	29.2	1.0	4.4	6.4	16.3	9.4	11.2	11.7	13.5
37 175	14820	6	Transylvania	980	33 045	1 355	33.7	92.0	4.8	1.0	0.8	3.1	4.1	12.7	8.4	8.6	10.0	12.7
37 177	28620	9	Tyrrell	1 008	4 115	2 895	4.1	54.7	36.9	0.5	2.6	6.8	5.3	13.0	8.5	14.0	12.1	14.5
37 179	16740	1	Union	1 636	218 568	293	133.6	75.1	12.4	0.7	2.4	10.9	6.3	22.8	8.4	9.8	15.3	15.9
37 181	25780	4	Vance	657	44 614	1 080	67.9	42.2	50.5	0.5	0.8	7.0	6.6	17.5	9.7	10.9	12.0	13.5
37 183	39580	2	Wake	2 163	998 691	44	461.7	62.9	21.6	0.8	6.8	9.9	6.7	18.6	9.5	14.8	15.7	14.5
37 185	...	8	Warren	1 110	20 231	1 823	18.2	39.2	51.9	5.8	0.6	4.0	4.7	14.6	8.2	10.8	10.6	14.0
37 187	...	7	Washington	902	12 570	2 259	13.9	46.6	49.3	0.5	0.6	4.2	5.3	16.4	8.3	8.8	10.5	13.9
37 189	14380	6	Watauga	810	52 560	951	64.9	93.3	2.2	0.9	1.4	3.5	3.5	9.9	30.4	10.8	9.3	10.6
37 191	24140	3	Wayne	1 432	124 456	499	86.9	56.3	32.3	0.8	1.9	10.7	6.8	17.4	10.6	13.1	12.1	13.4
37 193	35900	6	Wilkes	1 954	68 838	774	35.2	89.4	4.8	0.6	0.6	5.7	5.0	16.4	7.6	10.1	12.4	14.7
37 195	48980	4	Wilson	954	81 401	684	85.3	49.8	39.5	0.6	1.3	10.0	6.4	17.4	9.1	11.5	12.2	13.8
37 197	49180	2	Yadkin	867	37 792	1 230	43.6	85.9	3.6	0.5	0.4	10.5	5.4	16.7	8.0	10.2	12.8	15.5
37 199	...	8	Yancey	810	17 614	1 942	21.7	93.7	1.4	0.7	0.4	4.7	4.8	14.7	7.1	9.3	12.2	14.0
38 000	...	X	NORTH DAKOTA	178 711	739 482	X	4.1	88.9	2.2	6.1	1.7	2.9	6.7	15.7	12.8	14.4	11.0	12.6
38 001	...	9	Adams	2 558	2 384	3 013	0.9	97.1	1.0	1.8	0.9	0.9	5.0	13.5	6.3	10.0	8.9	14.3
38 003	...	6	Barnes	3 863	11 144	2 344	2.9	95.0	1.7	1.5	1.6	1.6	5.2	15.2	10.3	11.0	10.1	13.4
38 005	...	9	Benson	3 597	6 833	2 694	1.9	44.5	0.5	54.7	0.6	1.8	10.1	24.1	9.2	11.2	9.2	11.9
38 007	...	9	Billings	2 976	901	3 113	0.3	96.8	0.0	0.7	1.5	1.2	4.6	12.5	8.0	14.9	10.8	14.9
38 009	...	9	Bottineau	4 321	6 650	2 707	1.5	94.7	1.2	3.6	0.8	1.8	6.4	14.3	9.6	10.2	9.5	13.2
38 011	...	9	Bowman	3 009	3 247	2 955	1.1	94.0	0.6	1.3	0.3	4.6	6.7	17.3	6.8	11.6	9.9	11.9
38 013	...	9	Burke	2 858	2 245	3 030	0.8	95.1	1.0	1.7	0.7	2.7	7.4	15.9	7.6	12.7	9.3	14.0
38 015	13900	3	Burleigh	4 229	90 503	639	21.4	92.7	1.4	4.7	1.0	1.6	6.6	16.0	10.4	14.8	12.0	13.2
38 017	22020	3	Cass	4 571	167 005	381	36.5	90.9	3.7	1.9	3.0	2.3	6.8	15.1	16.2	17.0	12.2	11.5
38 019	...	9	Cavalier	3 856	3 855	2 917	1.0	97.2	0.6	1.7	0.4	1.0	5.2	14.7	6.5	8.5	8.8	14.3
38 021	...	9	Dickey	2 930	5 150	2 829	1.8	95.0	1.0	1.4	0.8	3.1	5.9	17.1	9.8	9.9	10.0	12.2
38 023	...	9	Divide	3 265	2 432	3 010	0.7	95.2	1.0	1.2	0.8	3.1	5.4	14.2	7.4	11.1	8.5	13.7
38 025	...	9	Dunn	5 202	4 399	2 873	0.8	86.5	1.0	10.7	0.8	2.9	6.1	16.1	8.8	13.7	10.8	15.2
38 027	...	9	Eddy	1 632	2 377	3 014	1.5	93.1	0.7	4.0	0.6	3.1	5.2	16.6	6.4	9.8	9.3	13.9
38 029	...	8	Emmons	3 912	3 422	2 944	0.9	98.0	0.6	1.0	0.3	1.1	4.2	16.3	6.5	6.0	9.4	14.1
38 031	...	9	Foster	1 646	3 362	2 948	2.0	97.4	0.7	1.2	0.3	1.2	4.9	16.4	7.6	9.3	10.9	14.5
38 033	...	9	Golden Valley	2 592	1 825	3 068	0.7	95.7	0.9	1.1	0.3	2.8	5.9	17.8	7.3	10.6	10.9	12.0
38 035	24220	3	Grand Forks	3 720	70 138	763	18.9	88.6	3.5	3.5	3.0	3.7	6.6	13.6	22.9	14.9	9.7	10.7
38 037	...	8	Grant	4 297	2 361	3 016	0.5	97.1	0.6	2.4	0.6	1.0	5.6	12.9	5.9	8.1	8.9	14.1
38 039	...	9	Griggs	1 836	2 319	3 022	1.3	98.0	0.3	0.6	0.3	0.7	4.8	13.1	5.9	8.1	8.3	12.7
38 041	...	9	Hettinger	2 932	2 660	2 998	0.9	94.4	1.2	3.8	0.5	1.9	5.9	16.1	7.1	10.7	9.6	13.3
38 043	...	8	Kidder	3 500	2 424	3 012	0.7	94.6	0.5	0.5	0.9	4.0	5.1	15.7	6.7	9.9	10.1	14.2
38 045	...	9	LaMoure	2 968	4 149	2 892	1.4	98.3	0.5	0.7	0.2	0.9	4.9	15.8	6.0	8.5	9.8	13.3
38 047	...	9	Logan	2 571	1 944	3 056	0.8	98.3	0.6	0.8	0.5	0.8	5.1	15.7	6.4	7.3	9.7	13.9
38 049	33500	9	McHenry	4 854	5 988	2 759	1.2	96.1	0.7	1.2	0.5	2.6	6.2	16.7	7.2	11.7	10.7	13.9
38 051	...	9	McIntosh	2 525	2 801	2 987	1.1	96.8	0.6	1.1	0.5	1.8	5.4	13.5	5.4	8.4	7.5	13.7
38 053	...	9	McKenzie	7 149	10 996	2 359	1.5	78.9	1.0	16.3	0.7	4.8	8.0	20.0	9.5	15.2	11.7	13.5
38 055	...	8	McLean	5 467	9 578	2 465	1.8	91.1	0.6	7.6	0.3	2.0	5.8	15.5	6.2	10.0	10.3	13.5
38 057	...	6	Mercer	2 701	8 746	2 536	3.2	95.1	0.7	2.6	0.6	2.1	6.2	15.7	6.3	11.3	9.9	16.6
38 059	13900	3	Morton	4 989	29 822	1 433	6.0	93.0	1.1	4.4	0.8	2.4	6.6	16.6	8.1	14.6	11.9	13.8
38 061	...	9	Mountrail	4 728	9 782	2 458	2.1	67.1	1.0	28.5	0.7	5.3	8.1	16.6	10.4	15.0	11.9	13.9
38 063	...	8	Nelson	2 543	3 045	2 972	1.2	96.1	0.8	2.3	0.3	1.9	4.9	13.7	6.0	8.7	8.5	14.1
38 065	13900	8	Oliver	1 871	1 850	3 066	1.0	95.1	0.5	2.9	0.5	1.9	6.2	16.8	6.1	9.8	9.3	15.3
38 067	...	9	Pembina	2 897	7 128	2 668	2.5	94.4	0.7	2.8	0.5	2.9	5.2	15.5	6.1	10.5	9.9	13.9
38 069	...	7	Pierce	2 638	4 404	2 872	1.7	93.7	0.7	4.9	0.2	1.4	6.1	15.8	7.3	9.8	10.1	13.5
38 071	...	7	Ramsey	3 074	11 564	2 322	3.8	88.3	0.9	10.5	0.9	2.2	6.8	15.4	9.5	11.7	10.1	14.1
38 073	...	8	Ransom	2 233	5 446	2 809	2.4	96.9	0.8	1.3	0.7	1.5	5.7	17.5	6.9	9.5	11.2	14.0
38 075	33500	9	Renville	2 272	2 587	3 002	1.1	96.7	1.2	1.2	0.4	2.0	6.3	15.9	8.4	11.0	10.1	14.8
38 077	47420	6	Richland	3 719	16 432	2 012	4.4	93.9	1.2	2.9	1.0	2.4	5.4	16.0	14.6	10.6	9.6	13.8
38 079	...	9	Rolette	2 339	14 616	2 129	6.2	22.4	0.6	77.7	0.3	1.5	10.2	23.1	10.0	12.2	10.9	12.9
38 081	...	9	Sargent	2 224	3 931	2 908	1.8	95.3	0.6	1.5	0.7	2.6	5.4	15.5	7.8	9.9	10.5	14.9
38 083	...	9	Sheridan	2 518	1 326	3 093	0.5	97.0	0.3	2.2	0.5	1.6	2.9	12.8	6.1	8.5	7.8	13.8
38 085	13900	8	Sioux	2 834	4 422	2 871	1.6	16.9	0.7	81.2	0.5	3.5	12.0	25.4	10.8	13.0	11.3	12.6
38 087	...	9	Slope	3 147	765	3 122	0.2	96.1	0.4	1.3	0.0	2.5	6.8	15.2	5.8	10.2	8.1	15.6
38 089	19860	7	Stark	3 457	30 372	1 420	8.8	92.2	1.7	1.8	1.8	3.9	7.2	15.6	11.8	16.5	10.6	13.0
38 091	...	8	Steele	1 845	1 955	3 053	1.1	97.6	0.3	1.6	0.1	1.1	5.3	15.2	6.1	9.2	9.6	14.3
38 093	27420	7	Stutsman	5 754	21 129	1 767	3.7	94.8	1.3	2.2	1.0	2.0	5.4	14.9	10.4	12.3	10.9	13.8
38 095	...	9	Towner	2 654	2 310	3 025	0.9	94.9	0.6	4.5	0.5	1.0	5.9	14.2	6.1	8.6	8.1	15.8
38 097	...	8	Traill	2 232	8 082	2 595	3.6	95.0	1.1	1.7	0.6	3.0	6.3	15.6	10.8	10.2	10.3	13.8
38 099	...	6	Walsh	3 320	10 970	2 362	3.3	87.1	0.6	2.0	0.6	10.8	6.0	16.5	7.4	10.3	9.8	14.3

1. CBSA = Core Based Statistical Area. See Appendix A for explanation. See Appendix B for list of metropolitan areas with component counties. 2. County type code from the Economic Research Service of USDA Rural-Urban Continuum Codes. See Appendix A for definition. 3. Dry land or land partially or temporarily covered by water. 4. May be of any race.

STATE County	Population, 2013 (cont.)				Population change and components of change, 2000–2014							Households, 2009–2013				
	Age (percent) (cont.)				Total persons		Percent change		Components of change, 2010–2014					Percent		
	55 to 64 years	65 to 74 years	75 years and over	Percent female	2000	2010	2000–2010	2010–2014	Births	Deaths	Net migration	Number	Persons per house-hold	Family house-holds	Female family house-holder[1]	One per-son
	16	17	18	19	20	21	22	23	24	25	26	27	28	29	30	31
NORTH CAROLINA—Cont'd																
Swain	13.5	11.0	7.1	51.7	12 968	13 981	7.8	2.1	820	784	252	5 368	2.56	65.9	12.4	27.6
Transylvania	15.3	15.5	12.6	51.8	29 334	33 090	12.8	-0.1	1 120	1 654	543	13 981	2.26	65.4	8.0	30.5
Tyrrell	13.7	10.3	8.5	46.6	4 149	4 407	6.2	-6.6	175	172	-285	1 480	2.48	72.4	15.6	26.4
Union	10.6	7.0	4.0	50.6	123 677	201 292	62.8	8.6	10 144	5 180	12 026	68 211	2.98	80.6	10.6	15.9
Vance	13.8	9.2	6.7	53.3	42 954	45 422	5.7	-1.8	2 463	2 067	-1 204	16 640	2.66	66.7	21.6	29.8
Wake	10.5	5.9	3.8	51.3	627 846	900 993	43.5	10.8	53 073	19 788	63 182	348 627	2.60	66.5	11.5	26.7
Warren	16.1	11.9	9.0	49.1	19 972	20 972	5.0	-3.5	773	969	-511	7 731	2.59	66.5	17.7	28.9
Washington	16.4	11.3	9.1	52.7	13 723	13 228	-3.6	-4.9	562	663	-552	5 056	2.53	63.3	17.2	34.2
Watauga	11.8	8.2	5.4	50.0	42 695	51 079	19.6	2.9	1 492	1 407	1 467	20 909	2.20	52.7	7.1	27.8
Wayne	12.5	8.1	6.0	50.8	113 329	122 623	8.2	1.5	7 328	4 815	-597	47 330	2.54	68.1	17.6	26.9
Wilkes	14.4	11.2	8.2	50.7	65 632	69 340	5.6	-0.7	2 863	3 149	-290	27 512	2.48	70.3	11.0	25.9
Wilson	13.5	9.2	6.8	52.4	73 814	81 234	10.1	0.2	4 104	3 521	-499	31 690	2.51	67.1	16.8	28.7
Yadkin	13.7	10.3	7.5	50.5	36 348	38 406	5.7	-1.6	1 701	1 688	-601	14 926	2.53	69.8	9.7	27.8
Yancey	15.1	13.1	9.8	50.8	17 774	17 818	0.2	-1.1	724	918	15	7 278	2.41	70.9	7.9	25.9
NORTH DAKOTA	12.5	7.2	7.0	48.9	642 200	672 591	4.7	9.9	42 376	25 140	48 867	287 270	2.31	61.1	7.8	31.2
Adams	17.3	11.4	13.1	51.7	2 593	2 343	-9.6	1.7	106	109	40	1 101	2.05	67.1	3.6	27.5
Barnes	14.7	9.9	10.0	49.8	11 775	11 066	-6.0	0.7	506	558	132	4 871	2.15	62.8	5.7	29.8
Benson	12.1	6.7	5.5	48.7	6 964	6 660	-4.4	2.6	623	307	-149	2 291	2.92	70.1	19.7	26.3
Billings	17.0	8.8	8.6	46.3	888	783	-11.8	15.1	43	12	94	350	2.38	65.1	2.6	34.3
Bottineau	15.9	11.7	9.3	47.6	7 149	6 429	-10.1	3.4	289	320	254	3 028	2.06	60.6	4.9	34.6
Bowman	16.0	9.6	10.2	48.7	3 242	3 151	-2.8	3.0	176	192	131	1 354	2.28	64.2	3.5	32.0
Burke	15.2	9.7	8.2	46.8	2 242	1 968	-12.2	14.1	134	87	222	1 007	2.07	59.7	4.9	36.0
Burleigh	12.9	7.4	6.7	50.5	69 416	81 308	17.1	11.3	5 042	2 796	6 732	34 703	2.34	63.6	8.5	29.4
Cass	10.7	5.4	5.1	49.3	123 138	149 778	21.6	11.5	10 033	3 883	10 839	65 816	2.27	55.1	7.4	33.3
Cavalier	16.1	12.7	13.2	49.2	4 831	3 993	-17.3	-3.5	170	218	-65	1 754	2.19	66.5	1.7	31.2
Dickey	12.9	10.5	11.8	50.4	5 757	5 289	-8.1	-2.6	222	300	-67	2 178	2.27	60.7	4.4	35.4
Divide	16.1	11.1	12.4	47.9	2 283	2 071	-9.3	17.4	106	103	364	1 035	2.02	63.7	2.3	28.6
Dunn	14.9	7.1	7.3	47.1	3 600	3 536	-1.8	24.4	214	146	792	1 438	2.55	69.1	4.9	24.1
Eddy	15.8	10.3	12.8	50.4	2 757	2 385	-13.5	-0.3	111	189	77	1 104	2.07	57.1	9.6	37.4
Emmons	15.9	12.7	15.0	49.2	4 331	3 550	-18.0	-3.6	111	206	-28	1 634	2.11	61.4	3.9	37.3
Foster	14.2	9.2	13.1	50.4	3 759	3 343	-11.1	0.6	136	168	65	1 555	2.11	67.7	8.9	29.6
Golden Valley	16.6	8.7	10.1	49.5	1 924	1 680	-12.7	8.6	85	72	128	754	2.16	52.1	5.3	45.4
Grand Forks	10.7	5.9	5.0	48.4	66 109	66 861	1.1	4.9	4 075	1 985	1 136	27 465	2.28	54.9	7.7	34.0
Grant	17.2	14.1	13.3	48.6	2 841	2 394	-15.7	-1.4	107	116	-13	1 113	2.08	60.1	3.1	35.8
Griggs	18.4	14.2	14.4	49.0	2 754	2 420	-12.1	-4.2	83	157	-17	1 149	2.00	62.6	5.6	34.3
Hettinger	13.2	10.8	13.2	52.1	2 715	2 477	-8.8	7.4	128	147	191	1 097	2.20	68.7	5.4	28.1
Kidder	17.3	10.0	11.0	49.1	2 753	2 435	-11.6	-0.5	117	65	-46	1 146	2.11	73.9	2.6	24.8
LaMoure	16.3	10.9	14.5	48.7	4 701	4 139	-12.0	0.2	173	183	27	1 955	2.08	62.5	3.8	34.8
Logan	14.6	12.6	14.5	49.5	2 308	1 990	-13.8	-2.3	83	97	-34	827	2.28	66.1	3.9	33.0
McHenry	14.2	9.5	9.8	47.1	5 987	5 395	-9.9	11.0	289	243	535	2 573	2.14	61.8	7.0	33.9
McIntosh	13.9	12.3	19.9	51.0	3 390	2 809	-17.1	-0.3	122	225	90	1 308	2.04	62.7	4.6	34.1
McKenzie	12.2	5.6	4.3	47.1	5 737	6 360	10.9	72.9	542	225	4 217	2 666	2.71	70.6	10.2	23.6
McLean	17.5	12.2	9.0	48.8	9 311	8 962	-3.7	6.9	478	453	620	4 021	2.23	67.0	5.6	30.0
Mercer	16.9	9.3	7.8	48.5	8 644	8 424	-2.5	3.8	416	327	237	3 650	2.28	65.6	5.9	31.4
Morton	13.6	8.0	6.8	49.6	25 303	27 471	8.6	8.6	1 778	1 106	1 635	11 416	2.39	68.0	7.9	25.9
Mountrail	12.7	6.4	5.0	45.3	6 631	7 673	15.7	27.5	646	323	1 733	3 069	2.63	71.9	13.3	24.7
Nelson	16.6	13.6	14.0	49.1	3 715	3 126	-15.9	-2.6	129	241	33	1 474	2.03	60.6	5.6	37.4
Oliver	19.3	10.1	7.2	48.5	2 065	1 846	-10.6	0.2	86	44	-40	753	2.44	75.4	4.4	21.2
Pembina	17.6	10.0	11.3	48.9	8 585	7 413	-13.7	-3.8	314	361	-243	3 328	2.14	64.2	5.9	32.2
Pierce	14.4	10.0	13.0	49.3	4 675	4 357	-6.8	1.1	213	271	109	1 983	2.08	61.0	3.9	36.4
Ramsey	14.2	9.1	9.1	49.8	12 066	11 451	-5.1	1.0	654	549	35	4 826	2.28	57.3	8.6	36.5
Ransom	14.8	8.8	11.6	49.1	5 890	5 457	-7.4	-0.2	264	307	48	2 283	2.32	61.3	4.0	35.8
Renville	14.4	9.0	10.0	47.7	2 610	2 470	-5.4	4.7	128	103	89	1 041	2.36	69.9	4.4	27.4
Richland	14.2	7.4	8.4	48.6	17 998	16 321	-9.3	0.7	716	545	-67	6 614	2.28	64.5	6.6	29.3
Rolette	10.7	6.0	4.1	50.6	13 674	13 937	1.9	4.9	1 275	638	37	4 750	2.95	72.6	23.1	25.4
Sargent	16.7	10.9	8.5	46.9	4 366	3 829	-12.3	2.7	154	134	93	1 741	2.20	65.7	5.6	29.2
Sheridan	17.9	15.3	15.0	49.6	1 710	1 321	-22.7	0.4	53	43	-9	614	2.14	70.8	3.6	27.9
Sioux	7.5	4.7	2.8	49.9	4 044	4 153	2.7	6.5	409	236	95	1 116	3.76	72.8	28.8	24.2
Slope	18.7	9.7	9.7	45.7	767	727	-5.2	5.2	38	11	13	296	2.49	73.0	7.1	23.0
Stark	11.7	6.1	7.5	48.0	22 636	24 199	6.9	25.5	1 676	942	5 358	10 439	2.37	62.6	6.8	28.1
Steele	16.3	11.7	12.1	[illegible]	2 250	1 975	-12.5	-1.0	83	63	-59	890	2.22	66.9	4.9	29.2
Stutsman	15.1	8.2	9.0	48.8	21 908	21 100	-3.7	0.1	978	998	64	8 873	2.18	61.6	9.2	32.2
Towner	17.0	11.4	12.9	48.5	2 876	2 246	-21.9	2.8	111	116	59	1 034	2.17	64.6	7.2	33.9
Traill	14.1	8.9	9.8	49.5	8 477	8 121	-4.2	-0.5	402	373	-74	3 306	2.35	59.4	5.9	35.4
Walsh	14.9	10.2	10.5	49.2	12 389	11 119	-10.3	-1.3	582	556	-146	4 948	2.16	62.9	7.0	33.6

1. No spouse present.

STATE County	Persons in group quarters, 2014	Daytime population, 2009–2013: Number	Daytime population, 2009–2013: Employment/residence ratio	Births, 2014: Total	Births, 2014: Rate[1]	Deaths, 2014: Number	Deaths, 2014: Rate[1]	Persons under 65 with no health insurance, 2013: Number	Persons under 65 with no health insurance, 2013: Percent	Medicare, 2014: Eligible for Medicare	Medicare, 2014: Enrolled in Medicare Advantage	Medicare, 2014: Enrolled in a Medicare prescription drug plan	Serious crimes known to police,[2] 2013: Total: Number	Serious crimes known to police,[2] 2013: Total: Rate[3]
	32	33	34	35	36	37	38	39	40	41	42	43	44	45
NORTH CAROLINA—Cont'd														
Swain	237	14 975	1.19	195	13.7	199	13.9	2 598	22.5	3 534	440	1 675	306	2 150
Transylvania	1 040	31 277	0.88	260	7.9	384	11.6	4 657	20.2	9 338	2 263	4 505	662	2 014
Tyrrell	516	4 322	1.04	40	9.7	36	8.7	695	24.5	805	96	501	58	1 341
Union	2 268	175 096	0.67	2 384	10.9	1 239	5.7	29 966	16.1	27 858	6 697	13 379	4 732	2 266
Vance	802	44 618	0.97	567	12.7	507	11.4	6 719	18.0	9 863	2 893	4 871	2 761	6 109
Wake	20 638	950 429	1.05	12 545	12.6	4 963	5.0	122 976	14.4	116 624	35 020	48 501	24 644	2 539
Warren	1 027	18 357	0.65	176	8.7	244	12.1	3 099	20.2	4 326	1 161	2 238	615	3 125
Washington	151	12 987	1.01	131	10.4	152	12.1	1 728	17.1	3 198	380	2 098	301	2 383
Watauga	5 885	54 640	1.13	344	6.5	341	6.5	7 342	18.6	8 259	2 181	3 755	774	1 479
Wayne	2 996	120 459	0.94	1 749	14.1	1 217	9.8	18 981	18.2	22 111	3 923	10 788	4 578	3 744
Wilkes	965	66 272	0.89	670	9.7	777	11.3	11 323	20.5	16 832	6 899	6 570	1 908	2 744
Wilson	1 568	85 528	1.12	925	11.4	875	10.7	13 587	20.1	17 462	2 460	10 273	3 085	3 856
Yadkin	303	32 816	0.66	405	10.7	411	10.9	6 295	20.2	8 233	4 652	2 372	1 016	2 801
Yancey	174	15 803	0.72	167	9.5	200	11.4	2 754	20.4	5 126	1 358	2 291	119	675
NORTH DAKOTA	26 637	719 212	1.08	10 780	14.6	5 879	8.0	74 043	12.3	116 703	1 624	76 440	17 102	2 364
Adams	67	2 278	0.96	33	13.8	23	9.6	270	15.2	642	65	480	10	426
Barnes	544	10 827	0.96	126	11.3	124	11.1	963	11.2	2 481	399	1 701	215	1 915
Benson	16	6 654	0.97	159	23.3	68	10.0	1 171	19.2	1 031	62	681	18	260
Billings	9	927	1.11	12	13.3	3	3.3	125	17.3	151	NA	95	18	1 844
Bottineau	235	6 283	0.92	66	9.9	76	11.4	790	15.4	1 554	41	1 064	101	1 492
Bowman	38	3 219	1.03	45	13.9	35	10.8	375	14.6	679	74	501	31	942
Burke	2	2 038	0.95	39	17.4	22	9.8	247	13.1	476	NA	328	38	1 656
Burleigh	3 368	86 298	1.05	1 252	13.8	665	7.3	7 373	10.0	14 508	3 018	9 537	2 160	2 427
Cass	5 681	167 668	1.15	2 508	15.0	984	5.9	15 645	11.1	20 496	3 846	11 883	4 503	2 789
Cavalier	70	3 786	0.91	37	9.6	43	11.2	352	12.2	1 053	109	775	37	921
Dickey	274	5 141	0.95	62	12.0	66	12.8	565	14.4	1 134	128	808	26	484
Divide	70	2 247	1.08	29	11.9	17	7.0	221	12.5	523	NA	372	8	343
Dunn	129	4 140	1.19	63	14.3	16	3.6	595	16.6	664	81	441	41	975
Eddy	88	2 133	0.79	31	13.0	44	18.5	268	14.6	601	76	438	15	622
Emmons	52	3 413	0.93	27	7.9	45	13.2	480	19.2	978	255	700	40	1 128
Foster	49	3 499	1.08	35	10.4	39	11.6	307	11.8	769	125	580	NA	NA
Golden Valley	52	1 704	1.01	23	12.6	9	4.9	253	17.8	366	NA	258	10	530
Grand Forks	4 119	71 066	1.10	988	14.1	459	6.5	7 037	12.2	9 126	1 359	5 467	1 773	2 568
Grant	18	2 301	0.94	25	10.6	34	14.4	428	24.9	666	139	472	5	212
Griggs	46	2 351	0.98	20	8.6	36	15.5	224	13.7	658	103	427	5	209
Hettinger	168	2 412	0.89	33	12.4	26	9.8	294	15.5	640	105	481	26	987
Kidder	0	2 227	0.85	31	12.8	11	4.5	342	17.9	575	186	405	27	1 094
LaMoure	84	4 036	0.95	47	11.3	43	10.4	421	13.6	1 030	196	745	13	310
Logan	69	1 914	0.94	22	11.3	18	9.3	304	21.8	531	138	380	17	876
McHenry	47	4 620	0.64	77	12.9	59	9.9	813	17.1	1 267	197	856	45	743
McIntosh	114	2 838	1.04	30	10.7	52	18.6	335	18.1	903	220	679	2	72
McKenzie	148	9 451	1.58	182	16.6	53	4.8	1 148	13.5	979	NA	642	235	2 672
McLean	148	8 946	0.95	121	12.6	100	10.4	1 059	14.2	2 224	338	1 501	101	1 050
Mercer	126	9 267	1.19	102	11.7	73	8.3	762	10.7	1 614	258	1 040	90	1 036
Morton	625	23 273	0.70	456	15.3	240	8.0	2 942	12.0	5 148	1 154	3 481	773	2 678
Mountrail	557	10 105	1.44	173	17.7	73	7.5	1 429	17.0	1 309	NA	824	188	2 023
Nelson	80	2 948	0.90	30	9.9	51	16.7	297	13.4	930	23	624	29	926
Oliver	2	2 240	1.47	25	13.5	5	2.7	253	16.4	389	80	268	10	533
Pembina	155	7 758	1.12	72	10.1	91	12.8	719	12.8	1 662	211	1 106	54	732
Pierce	257	4 466	1.03	56	12.7	60	13.6	499	15.2	1 014	306	712	70	1 526
Ramsey	466	11 900	1.07	142	12.3	119	10.3	1 313	14.3	2 431	33	1 680	377	3 194
Ransom	180	5 350	0.95	61	11.2	78	14.3	512	11.8	1 177	127	847	41	737
Renville	55	2 352	0.88	29	11.2	22	8.5	242	11.5	515	NA	369	23	870
Richland	1 078	15 956	0.96	195	11.9	131	8.0	1 496	11.6	2 890	564	1 885	268	1 623
Rolette	123	13 983	0.96	294	20.1	179	12.2	2 839	21.4	1 908	36	1 111	37	250
Sargent	39	4 751	1.45	43	10.9	35	8.9	314	10.1	841	68	612	19	474
Sheridan	1	1 186	0.81	18	13.6	6	4.5	203	22.5	408	68	300	18	1 410
Sioux	44	4 988	1.58	103	23.3	78	17.6	758	18.4	419	19	218	0	0
Slope	0	684	0.86	10	13.1	2	2.6	80	13.1	166	NA	110	2	255
Stark	730	27 343	1.12	452	14.9	236	7.8	2 469	10.4	4 217	519	3 087	727	2 576
Steele	0	1 783	0.81	19	9.7	9	4.6	176	11.9	429	50	286	5	245
Stutsman	1 683	21 761	1.07	239	11.3	224	10.6	1 950	12.2	4 401	1 132	2 845	481	2 257
Towner	35	2 227	0.95	33	14.3	23	10.0	246	14.1	624	NA	439	9	375
Traill	356	7 643	0.88	95	11.8	89	11.0	706	11.0	1 574	212	1 027	50	608
Walsh	329	11 200	1.02	150	13.7	136	12.4	1 290	14.8	2 495	289	1 830	211	1 874

1. Per 1,000 estimated resident population. 2. Data for serious crimes have not been adjusted for underreporting; this may affect comparability between geographic areas and over time.
3. Per 100,000 population estimated by the FBI.

STATE County	Serious crimes known to police, 2013 (cont.)[1]		Education						Money income, 2009–2013				Income and poverty, 2013			
	Rate[2]		School enrollment and attainment, 2009–2013				Local government expenditures,[5] 2012–2013			Households				Percent below poverty level		
			Enrollment[3]		Attainment[4] (percent)											
	Violent	Property	Total	Percent private	High school graduate or less	Bachelor's degree or more	Total current spending (mil dol)	Current spending per student (dollars)	Per capita income[6] (dollars)	Median income (dollars)	Mean income (dollars)	Percent with income of $200,000 or more	Median household income (dollars)	All persons	Children under 18 years	Children 5 to 17 years in families
	46	47	48	49	50	51	52	53	54	55	56	57	58	59	60	61
NORTH CAROLINA—Cont'd																
Swain	337	1 813	3 165	8.4	49.5	16.3	19.5	9 375	19 626	36 094	47 954	0.8	34 552	23.2	34.9	34.7
Transylvania	131	1 883	7 114	22.7	40.2	27.6	35.8	9 961	23 757	41 781	54 006	1.6	40 578	15.6	29.7	27.3
Tyrrell	162	1 179	950	4.9	64.9	8.4	8.6	14 391	16 658	34 216	45 278	0.5	32 642	27.2	38.9	39.6
Union	225	2 042	62 028	16.6	38.1	31.8	319.6	7 861	28 894	65 892	85 939	6.5	63 912	10.3	14.4	13.3
Vance	648	5 461	11 682	9.9	60.8	11.4	63.5	8 892	17 905	34 987	45 831	1.2	35 565	27.3	40.3	36.3
Wake	232	2 307	275 007	18.0	25.3	48.0	1 175.7	7 788	33 166	66 006	86 702	6.8	65 433	10.9	14.5	13.4
Warren	188	2 937	4 284	10.6	58.5	13.5	26.4	10 683	19 052	34 285	48 143	1.2	33 767	27.2	39.8	37.8
Washington	372	2 011	3 064	13.8	59.4	11.7	19.1	10 537	18 779	34 936	45 728	0.9	31 596	25.5	40.3	38.0
Watauga	119	1 361	21 364	6.0	31.3	37.9	42.6	9 369	21 854	34 293	53 048	2.3	38 380	27.3	21.3	19.5
Wayne	366	3 379	32 491	11.9	47.5	16.4	153.4	7 765	21 557	41 731	53 695	1.3	41 526	20.8	32.1	31.1
Wilkes	213	2 531	15 094	9.3	58.5	12.5	84.0	8 091	19 029	33 159	46 995	1.7	35 895	23.1	31.5	27.2
Wilson	364	3 492	20 346	16.2	53.4	17.9	101.1	8 057	20 972	39 204	52 193	1.4	40 772	20.9	33.7	30.7
Yadkin	276	2 525	8 263	7.2	56.8	13.1	48.7	8 297	22 726	40 371	56 415	2.4	40 998	18.9	27.1	24.0
Yancey	57	618	3 704	18.2	50.6	17.9	21.8	9 361	20 257	38 579	48 096	1.0	35 866	21.3	30.8	28.7
NORTH DAKOTA	270	2 094	174 205	11.7	36.3	27.2	1 214.6	11 980	29 732	53 741	70 235	3.6	56 800	11.6	12.4	11.3
Adams	43	383	334	10.2	44.1	23.2	3.6	12 633	31 502	47 798	64 949	3.7	44 833	10.2	13.7	12.7
Barnes	143	1 773	2 674	6.8	43.6	26.2	15.8	14 133	31 721	50 274	72 587	4.2	52 035	10.9	12.2	10.1
Benson	29	231	1 819	3.2	52.2	11.6	17.2	15 908	18 162	36 491	52 107	1.9	42 326	30.2	37.7	34.8
Billings	102	1 742	132	0.0	48.3	21.6	2.3	32 222	37 972	57 083	87 124	6.0	74 636	8.2	6.8	6.5
Bottineau	89	1 403	1 268	7.8	39.4	20.9	12.6	15 306	31 969	51 667	69 530	3.6	61 279	10.0	12.3	11.5
Bowman	61	881	571	4.0	44.7	20.7	7.6	12 666	32 045	56 964	75 180	3.4	60 429	8.0	8.3	7.5
Burke	44	1 613	429	6.1	47.8	17.4	4.9	15 408	32 908	53 693	68 838	3.1	60 416	9.5	11.2	11.2
Burleigh	258	2 169	20 852	22.1	30.3	33.2	127.0	10 533	32 876	61 811	78 200	3.9	63 503	8.3	9.2	8.8
Cass	316	2 472	45 526	12.4	25.9	37.2	239.9	11 149	30 529	52 590	70 508	4.1	53 077	13.2	11.2	9.7
Cavalier	0	921	721	21.5	42.0	16.4	6.3	14 349	32 028	55 904	71 718	3.0	53 577	8.6	11.5	10.4
Dickey	56	428	1 280	20.5	43.6	23.6	8.2	9 803	24 644	47 359	57 909	2.4	52 414	12.2	14.0	12.3
Divide	43	300	247	13.8	42.8	21.8	4.4	12 968	36 303	55 057	80 491	4.9	63 616	9.0	15.0	14.2
Dunn	71	903	731	10.9	42.8	17.9	8.1	16 669	33 788	60 500	84 928	7.5	69 914	9.6	12.5	11.2
Eddy	83	539	475	1.5	41.7	20.1	5.3	14 732	27 323	44 250	57 278	1.4	46 875	10.0	11.5	9.8
Emmons	0	1 128	685	6.1	52.4	14.4	7.5	13 181	27 690	38 477	59 407	3.5	43 438	13.9	14.5	12.3
Foster	NA	NA	668	2.7	47.0	19.6	5.4	9 828	33 063	50 677	72 423	4.2	55 172	8.3	9.0	7.8
Golden Valley	106	424	438	0.9	37.2	18.3	4.9	15 451	26 113	36 100	55 529	1.1	48 103	11.7	17.0	15.8
Grand Forks	256	2 311	23 036	6.8	31.7	32.6	102.5	11 796	27 026	46 745	64 247	3.6	49 697	15.1	12.0	11.2
Grant	0	212	462	4.1	50.9	16.4	3.5	14 139	28 129	41 694	61 754	3.6	45 908	15.1	20.5	19.2
Griggs	83	125	378	6.3	51.9	14.8	5.7	15 304	27 197	45 542	56 464	1.4	50 570	9.4	10.4	9.3
Hettinger	38	949	492	9.1	46.6	17.3	6.2	13 872	27 910	47 743	64 321	5.0	60 171	10.5	12.7	11.3
Kidder	203	891	492	1.6	47.4	19.4	4.9	12 207	28 904	50 000	62 740	3.3	47 390	13.1	17.0	15.4
LaMoure	71	238	705	13.0	43.2	21.5	10.7	13 636	31 989	53 691	69 159	3.5	55 388	9.6	10.3	8.9
Logan	0	876	433	3.5	57.3	13.0	4.9	13 300	27 887	49 076	67 320	2.5	48 520	11.9	13.9	12.5
McHenry	0	743	1 054	13.1	50.4	16.3	12.3	13 328	28 331	45 343	61 525	3.1	49 078	11.1	14.3	12.9
McIntosh	0	72	410	2.7	54.7	18.6	5.4	13 574	25 427	36 066	53 464	2.8	40 540	15.2	17.2	16.1
McKenzie	364	2 308	1 729	11.5	38.2	22.3	15.5	12 925	33 078	64 866	88 187	6.8	75 699	9.9	12.7	10.8
McLean	125	925	1 782	4.6	43.1	17.5	19.4	11 919	30 992	53 565	69 339	3.2	53 604	10.6	13.0	11.8
Mercer	115	921	1 708	2.3	42.0	20.5	14.5	11 269	31 767	66 534	73 367	2.7	70 150	7.1	7.9	7.4
Morton	239	2 439	6 359	16.8	39.0	24.1	47.4	11 084	29 389	60 065	72 203	3.2	59 650	8.3	11.4	10.4
Mountrail	237	1 786	1 929	7.7	39.6	18.3	20.4	12 524	33 803	68 722	87 085	7.2	65 546	11.5	15.2	14.5
Nelson	96	830	544	8.8	39.7	21.0	6.6	14 513	30 432	49 839	63 595	2.0	55 915	9.6	12.2	11.1
Oliver	160	373	355	8.5	43.0	16.4	3.0	14 765	32 253	71 250	81 201	1.9	66 082	10.4	17.3	16.2
Pembina	41	691	1 430	7.6	47.1	19.2	14.4	13 683	27 817	49 846	60 590	2.1	53 983	8.4	9.3	8.3
Pierce	218	1 308	717	8.2	52.2	12.4	7.6	12 915	23 491	42 975	51 785	1.6	44 585	12.3	13.3	11.7
Ramsey	203	2 991	2 682	7.5	40.3	21.0	25.6	14 260	28 081	48 604	64 215	2.8	49 299	13.0	17.4	17.3
Ransom	90	647	1 264	2.1	48.0	16.5	10.2	10 846	26 137	49 788	60 622	1.9	58 578	8.8	9.7	8.5
Renville	0	870	511	8.4	36.3	17.2	9.0	14 763	31 178	60 847	73 423	3.1	61 533	7.6	9.9	9.2
Richland	61	1 562	4 299	7.6	37.5	20.8	30.4	13 266	27 713	53 759	66 994	2.6	54 312	10.6	10.8	9.3
Rolette	34	216	2 534	1.7	40.5	19.9	39.4	13 125	15 502	31 336	45 135	1.1	34 836	29.6	33.4	28.6
Sargent	0	474	809	3.1	46.5	17.9	8.6	13 314	29 950	53 381	67 368	3.3	58 672	6.5	7.4	6.9
Sheridan	78	1 331	209	10.5	53.8	16.0	2.1	19 046	29 219	43 250	58 189	2.3	43 346	16.5	23.4	19.2
Sioux	0	0	1 386	6.5	44.8	17.7	9.7	22 901	15 478	36 111	56 657	1.7	34 491	37.3	43.0	41.7
Slope	0	255	133	4.5	45.6	22.5	0.6	37 563	30 586	61 667	72 350	4.4	59 852	9.1	8.3	7.7
Stark	280	2 296	6 257	14.5	41.8	24.7	39.8	10 998	31 412	62 559	75 471	3.6	69 566	8.7	7.7	7.3
Steele	98	147	387	2.8	39.0	20.3	3.7	16 652	31 455	55 735	70 614	2.4	65 730	7.3	11.5	10.1
Stutsman	239	2 018	6 003	20.2	47.9	23.7	38.6	13 323	27 351	50 120	63 656	2.4	50 941	12.1	13.5	12.0
Towner	42	334	467	1.1	38.0	21.8	3.1	11 732	33 357	55 521	70 942	5.1	55 199	10.5	15.2	14.2
Traill	36	571	2 092	4.3	34.7	28.9	17.0	12 678	27 098	48 767	64 184	1.7	57 006	9.3	9.2	8.4
Walsh	240	1 634	2 187	6.9	48.8	18.3	25.4	13 748	29 072	48 592	64 605	2.3	48 301	11.2	13.4	11.8

1. Data for serious crimes have not been adjusted for underreporting; this may affect comparability between geographic areas and over time. 2. Per 100,000 population estimated by the FBI.
3. All persons 3 years old and over enrolled in nursery school through college. 4. Persons 25 years old and over. 5. Elementary and secondary education expenditures.
6. Based on population estimated by the American Community Survey, 2009–2013.

STATE County	Personal income, 2013										Earnings, 2013		
			Per capita[1]			Supplements to wages and salaries; employer contributions (mil dol)						Contributions for government social insurance (mil dol)	
	Total (mil dol)	Percent change, 2012–2013	Dollars	Rank	Wages and salaries (mil dol)	Pension and insurance	Government social insurance	Proprietors' income (mil dol)	Dividends, interest, and rent (mil dol)	Personal transfer receipts (mil dol)	Total (mil dol)	From employee and self-employed	From employer
	62	63	64	65	66	67	68	69	70	71	72	73	74
NORTH CAROLINA—Cont'd													
Swain	421	1.7	29 914	2 701	208	38	17	13	75	142	276	19	17
Transylvania	1 073	1.2	32 605	2 310	288	50	23	72	331	326	432	34	23
Tyrrell	123	-3.8	29 911	2 702	36	8	3	13	18	36	60	4	3
Union	8 386	1.5	39 417	1 241	2 357	382	188	582	1 065	1 130	3 508	214	188
Vance	1 415	-0.3	31 583	2 469	507	94	40	89	211	470	729	49	40
Wake	44 912	3.0	46 097	614	26 410	3 552	1 979	4 408	7 274	4 798	36 348	2 130	1 979
Warren	552	0.5	26 831	2 983	125	26	9	27	88	194	187	15	9
Washington	417	0.0	32 782	2 286	108	23	8	43	65	152	183	12	8
Watauga	1 651	1.6	31 520	2 474	776	149	59	137	374	312	1 121	69	59
Wayne	4 213	0.1	33 815	2 123	1 858	385	153	238	732	1 045	2 633	153	153
Wilkes	2 382	1.0	34 509	1 983	737	147	57	191	382	689	1 132	77	57
Wilson	2 938	0.9	35 972	1 751	1 666	292	129	213	429	775	2 299	141	129
Yadkin	1 278	0.4	33 610	2 162	348	59	29	116	191	331	553	37	29
Yancey	496	0.8	28 221	2 875	122	24	10	27	94	184	183	16	10
NORTH DAKOTA	38 472	-2.6	53 182	X	21 707	2 832	1 670	4 363	7 589	4 764	30 572	1 779	1 670
Adams	106	-22.8	44 974	689	39	5	3	23	19	22	70	4	3
Barnes	528	-16.9	47 179	540	192	30	16	90	126	93	328	21	16
Benson	252	-21.2	36 609	1 651	85	18	7	58	42	62	167	8	7
Billings	83	-0.9	94 519	7	27	4	2	10	17	5	44	2	2
Bottineau	366	-20.0	54 266	226	117	19	9	75	90	59	220	12	9
Bowman	190	-2.1	59 241	119	89	11	6	29	48	25	135	8	6
Burke	131	-11.5	56 805	165	57	9	4	3	41	16	73	5	4
Burleigh	4 388	3.6	49 601	383	2 624	355	202	373	878	562	3 554	218	202
Cass	8 140	1.4	49 991	370	5 061	657	387	1 126	1 647	841	7 231	430	387
Cavalier	210	-19.4	53 834	241	64	10	5	50	55	36	129	7	5
Dickey	266	-29.8	50 642	345	78	11	6	61	70	46	156	8	6
Divide	160	-5.8	69 160	52	57	8	5	25	47	18	94	5	5
Dunn	403	11.2	96 913	6	227	21	15	40	68	26	303	17	15
Eddy	102	-23.6	42 353	900	27	4	2	21	19	24	55	3	2
Emmons	135	-33.1	38 713	1 334	35	6	3	27	35	33	71	4	3
Foster	167	-23.3	49 467	391	71	10	6	22	50	27	108	6	6
Golden Valley	75	-7.0	40 906	1 063	29	4	2	7	23	11	42	3	2
Grand Forks	2 990	-0.9	43 218	825	1 763	298	141	263	664	404	2 465	138	141
Grant	102	-33.7	42 943	849	22	4	2	23	20	22	51	3	2
Griggs	118	-20.8	51 238	326	36	6	3	23	29	24	67	4	3
Hettinger	109	-14.9	40 934	1 060	30	5	2	13	31	22	51	3	2
Kidder	114	-11.1	47 121	545	25	4	2	35	23	22	67	3	2
LaMoure	220	-35.0	52 800	275	58	9	4	50	64	34	121	6	4
Logan	104	-31.6	53 506	253	21	4	2	37	23	19	63	3	2
McHenry	245	-11.8	41 434	1 002	58	11	5	38	48	45	112	6	5
McIntosh	129	-15.3	46 842	561	38	6	3	29	31	33	75	4	3
McKenzie	840	19.0	90 173	9	697	66	54	52	156	44	869	50	54
McLean	474	-9.4	49 810	375	177	30	14	27	105	83	248	16	14
Mercer	424	3.1	49 361	399	310	55	26	14	76	60	405	24	26
Morton	1 200	-0.2	41 405	1 004	503	74	44	16	206	202	637	41	44
Mountrail	850	8.5	90 614	8	464	48	35	31	149	62	578	34	35
Nelson	146	-12.4	47 206	538	37	6	3	26	35	38	72	4	3
Oliver	104	-8.8	55 420	195	56	9	5	14	18	13	84	4	5
Pembina	416	-6.9	57 923	136	167	25	14	86	109	60	291	13	14
Pierce	190	-11.1	42 646	874	68	10	5	41	42	39	125	7	5
Ramsey	499	-7.1	43 229	824	222	36	18	67	100	99	343	21	18
Ransom	264	-16.5	47 770	497	81	13	7	59	52	49	160	8	7
Renville	147	-13.1	56 365	182	45	6	3	30	36	21	83	4	3
Richland	709	-19.8	43 394	812	321	48	25	82	181	108	476	27	25
Rolette	437	-3.1	29 971	2 691	160	42	13	48	63	146	262	15	13
Sargent	199	-25.4	51 119	330	117	17	9	32	56	27	176	9	9
Sheridan	53	-31.5	40 495	1 115	8	2	1	13	13	14	23	1	1
Sioux	110	-4.7	24 879	3 058	68	16	5	6	14	39	95	5	5
Slope	57	-10.2	74 389	34	21	2	1	18	16	6	43	1	1
Stark	2 082	8.4	73 800	37	1 364	129	97	253	302	166	1 843	110	97
Steele	106	-34.6	53 918	240	30	4	2	24	32	13	62	3	2
Stutsman	980	-10.4	46 411	597	428	66	34	175	208	168	703	44	34
Towner	123	-19.8	53 004	268	27	5	2	42	26	23	76	3	2
Traill	395	-14.7	47 897	490	139	21	11	39	102	67	211	12	11
Walsh	548	-5.5	49 312	402	195	30	16	93	148	96	334	19	16

1. Based on the resident population estimated as of July 1 of the year shown.

STATE County	Earnings, 2013 (cont.) — Percent by selected industries: Farm	Mining	Construction	Manu-facturing	Infor-mation: professional, scientific, technical services	Retail trade	Finance, insur-ance, real estate and leasing	Health care and social assistance	Govern-ment	Social Security beneficiaries, December 2013: Number	Rate[1]	Supple-mental Security Income recipients, December 2013	Housing units, 2014: Total	Percent change, 2010–2014
	75	76	77	78	79	80	81	82	83	84	85	86	87	88
NORTH CAROLINA—Cont'd														
Swain	0.4	0.0	D	7.4	1.4	5.9	2.1	D	46.2	4 030	288	348	8 793	0.8
Transylvania	1.1	D	9.2	4.6	D	9.8	6.1	17.7	18.4	10 030	305	606	19 355	1.0
Tyrrell	13.2	0.0	5.8	5.2	D	6.8	D	D	37.6	870	212	140	2 058	-0.5
Union	3.1	D	12.2	18.5	4.9	7.4	7.3	4.6	16.4	30 425	143	2 333	76 520	5.0
Vance	4.5	D	3.4	12.2	D	10.4	4.9	16.3	19.0	11 090	248	2 307	19 959	-0.6
Wake	0.1	0.2	5.8	7.3	19.1	5.5	12.1	8.9	14.8	121 810	125	12 161	402 020	8.1
Warren	7.7	0.0	4.2	8.7	D	4.5	D	6.7	36.0	4 810	235	953	11 731	-0.7
Washington	15.9	0.0	1.9	14.2	D	6.2	5.9	D	27.5	3 535	277	674	6 426	-0.9
Watauga	0.2	D	5.7	2.1	4.9	9.1	7.3	17.2	31.3	8 740	167	658	32 957	2.6
Wayne	4.0	D	5.8	11.6	3.3	6.8	4.5	11.7	33.4	24 865	200	4 691	53 213	0.5
Wilkes	6.1	D	3.8	16.4	D	7.6	5.8	6.6	19.9	19 405	281	2 178	33 038	-0.1
Wilson	2.7	D	7.4	29.8	4.3	5.9	6.2	6.7	15.5	19 370	237	3 156	35 669	0.4
Yadkin	9.8	0.0	7.5	19.2	4.8	5.1	6.9	5.6	13.9	9 275	244	795	17 235	-0.6
Yancey	0.6	D	12.2	8.5	3.4	9.2	4.9	D	22.7	5 640	321	665	11 049	0.2
NORTH DAKOTA	5.2	10.0	9.7	5.1	6.2	6.0	7.0	10.1	15.6	123 363	170	8 350	350 560	10.4
Adams	26.9	D	6.2	2.4	D	9.2	2.9	25.1	9.4	675	285	16	1 385	0.6
Barnes	10.0	D	9.7	11.6	4.0	5.4	4.2	10.7	16.9	2 685	241	150	5 743	0.7
Benson	29.5	0.0	7.3	D	D	1.8	D	0.8	42.8	1 220	177	195	2 995	1.5
Billings	13.5	D	5.0	D	0.4	D	D	0.0	22.9	145	163	0	534	10.3
Bottineau	18.7	14.7	7.2	2.9	D	5.9	3.7	D	15.7	1 660	247	52	4 423	1.9
Bowman	11.9	19.0	14.7	1.0	2.4	4.9	D	8.6	9.4	725	226	23	1 739	3.3
Burke	-11.1	D	9.1	0.0	D	D	3.9	0.7	26.5	490	214	13	1 416	5.7
Burleigh	0.2	1.4	8.4	2.1	8.6	7.5	7.7	19.0	20.7	15 250	172	862	39 998	11.9
Cass	2.0	0.1	8.2	7.9	10.5	7.1	13.0	13.2	12.2	21 460	131	1 770	75 125	10.6
Cavalier	25.0	D	11.2	0.7	D	5.0	D	6.2	10.4	1 110	286	36	2 330	0.9
Dickey	31.6	0.0	3.7	7.6	D	5.9	D	D	9.3	1 190	227	56	2 649	0.5
Divide	17.6	D	9.5	0.6	D	3.5	2.5	D	12.2	545	235	19	1 476	11.5
Dunn	7.0	41.5	D	D	D	1.6	1.6	D	4.9	655	157	32	2 296	7.7
Eddy	31.7	3.2	D	D	D	4.0	D	14.4	14.5	620	258	34	1 338	1.1
Emmons	27.7	0.0	10.0	0.3	D	6.8	D	10.7	16.5	1 075	309	33	2 115	1.4
Foster	14.0	D	7.8	D	D	7.4	3.8	11.7	12.2	815	242	30	1 814	0.7
Golden Valley	4.6	9.3	D	D	D	5.2	5.6	10.8	18.6	365	201	14	1 005	3.9
Grand Forks	4.0	0.5	7.3	3.9	5.3	8.8	4.8	16.4	29.6	9 555	138	746	31 341	6.8
Grant	37.7	0.0	2.6	5.3	D	2.7	3.7	12.7	13.9	700	295	27	1 708	1.1
Griggs	20.2	0.0	8.0	11.9	D	4.8	D	8.5	12.9	690	301	23	1 463	0.1
Hettinger	15.1	D	8.3	3.3	D	3.3	5.8	6.7	18.4	700	262	18	1 429	1.1
Kidder	50.8	D	4.1	0.2	D	2.8	D	1.8	12.1	605	249	31	1 690	1.0
LaMoure	29.4	0.0	4.5	2.9	0.9	5.4	D	3.1	14.3	1 050	254	49	2 257	0.8
Logan	45.2	0.0	7.6	D	D	3.0	D	D	11.1	555	287	17	1 157	1.1
McHenry	26.4	D	D	D	3.9	2.4	3.1	3.1	18.2	1 290	218	56	3 084	4.6
McIntosh	37.7	0.0	2.8	5.4	D	4.5	3.3	15.9	11.1	970	351	42	1 859	0.1
McKenzie	1.0	21.9	23.8	0.1	D	2.1	3.1	D	9.9	1 035	111	47	3 760	21.7
McLean	2.2	D	11.2	2.0	D	3.5	3.7	D	16.6	2 400	253	101	5 927	6.0
Mercer	-1.4	D	16.2	D	2.5	3.5	2.0	D	6.3	1 810	211	64	4 672	5.0
Morton	2.4	1.0	9.5	11.1	11.2	8.0	4.7	D	13.8	5 390	186	316	13 875	14.9
Mountrail	0.5	25.2	D	D	D	4.0	1.9	2.0	6.8	1 395	149	88	4 784	16.1
Nelson	31.4	0.0	5.8	2.0	D	2.0	D	D	16.2	1 015	330	31	1 944	0.9
Oliver	13.7	D	14.3	1.1	D	D	D	D	5.8	420	225	18	922	1.9
Pembina	30.6	0.2	8.3	13.0	D	3.8	D	4.0	18.2	1 755	245	78	3 879	0.5
Pierce	21.9	0.0	D	D	2.2	5.9	D	D	10.9	1 085	247	44	2 222	1.0
Ramsey	7.0	D	7.9	3.9	4.2	9.6	9.3	D	22.9	2 610	226	202	5 777	2.9
Ransom	32.7	D	5.1	8.5	1.6	5.3	3.7	9.1	14.8	1 255	229	58	2 674	0.7
Renville	23.4	28.6	4.0	4.0	D	1.4	D	4.2	12.6	575	220	14	1 407	1.5
Richland	11.8	D	8.1	24.4	3.7	5.0	2.8	D	19.9	3 040	186	156	7 653	2.0
Rolette	9.2	D	7.0	3.4	0.5	6.0	D	D	59.9	2 135	146	841	5 501	2.4
Sargent	19.4	D	3.8	D	D	2.8	D	1.2	7.8	900	232	26	2 060	2.8
Sheridan	48.4	0.0	2.1	D	D	D	D	D	17.6	430	327	22	898	0.4
Sioux	5.7	0.0	1.5	0.0	D	D	0.0	D	86.2	505	114	231	1 330	1.4
Slope	46.1	D	0.7	0.0	0.0	0.0	0.0	0.0	3.0	165	217	0	437	0.2
Stark	2.3	30.6	9.8	4.8	4.8	4.8	5.2	4.7	6.6	4 450	157	244	13 745	28.0
Steele	40.5	0.0	10.8	9.1	D	4.0	D	D	10.0	475	242	0	1 189	1.5
Stutsman	6.2	D	5.4	11.5	3.9	6.8	4.9	D	16.1	4 655	221	404	10 069	2.1
Towner	49.8	0.0	D	D	D	2.1	D	D	9.4	655	285	19	1 450	0.1
Traill	15.8	D	4.5	12.4	1.9	3.1	4.4	D	17.8	1 720	210	51	3 809	0.8
Walsh	18.5	D	5.7	8.9	3.6	3.8	8.2	D	16.6	2 705	244	123	5 579	1.5

1. Per 1,000 resident population estimated as of July 1 of the year shown.

STATE County	Housing units, 2009–2013: Occupied units: Total	Owner-occupied: Percent	Owner-occupied: Median value[1]	Median owner cost as a percent of income: With a mortgage	Median owner cost as a percent of income: Without a mortgage[2]	Renter-occupied: Median rent[3]	Renter-occupied: Median rent as a percent of income[2]	Sub-standard units[4] (percent)	Civilian labor force, 2014: Total	Civilian labor force, 2014: Percent change, 2013–2014	Unemployment: Total	Unemployment: Rate[5]	Civilian employment,[6] 2009–2013: Total	Percent: Management, business, science and arts	Percent: Construction, production, and maintenance occupations
	89	90	91	92	93	94	95	96	97	98	99	100	101	102	103
NORTH CAROLINA—Cont'd															
Swain	5 368	74.9	132 500	22.7	10.0	584	31.7	1.4	6 363	-3.3	564	8.9	5 314	29.5	21.2
Transylvania	13 981	76.3	171 600	23.4	10.0	659	31.7	0.2	13 239	-1.1	768	5.8	13 459	31.7	23.0
Tyrrell	1 480	75.4	107 100	26.1	15.7	643	23.8	2.5	1 529	-1.4	146	9.5	1 464	15.2	40.8
Union	68 211	82.1	194 300	22.4	11.4	851	31.3	4.3	106 780	1.3	5 462	5.1	94 325	38.3	21.2
Vance	16 640	62.5	99 600	23.8	13.6	666	35.3	2.7	17 897	-1.0	1 641	9.2	17 527	23.8	28.6
Wake	348 627	65.2	229 000	21.3	10.0	913	28.4	3.3	517 101	1.4	24 628	4.8	468 289	49.5	12.7
Warren	7 731	70.6	98 300	26.4	15.2	681	33.0	1.2	7 225	-0.8	629	8.7	7 122	24.1	29.7
Washington	5 056	72.3	89 000	23.0	16.3	585	39.3	1.2	5 013	-5.2	473	9.4	4 183	26.6	35.6
Watauga	20 909	54.9	228 700	24.2	10.7	819	50.0	3.4	26 826	-0.3	1 377	5.1	24 913	32.8	15.6
Wayne	47 330	60.7	108 600	22.2	11.8	694	30.6	3.2	53 587	-1.9	3 363	6.3	50 744	29.4	30.9
Wilkes	27 512	73.9	111 700	24.4	12.6	573	33.5	3.4	29 274	-2.0	1 910	6.5	26 403	25.5	30.7
Wilson	31 690	60.9	111 500	24.9	14.4	738	32.8	3.1	37 397	-1.7	3 469	9.3	34 392	29.3	28.1
Yadkin	14 926	77.6	121 100	23.1	12.5	593	26.9	4.0	17 585	-1.2	956	5.4	16 353	28.4	33.5
Yancey	7 278	76.9	135 100	23.5	11.2	615	25.7	1.5	7 452	-4.6	491	6.6	7 189	27.7	32.8
NORTH DAKOTA	287 270	66.1	132 400	19.2	10.0	645	25.3	1.6	416 367	2.4	11 503	2.8	371 612	34.6	24.9
Adams	1 101	73.5	106 300	17.5	10.4	464	20.4	1.2	1 108	1.2	32	2.9	1 330	43.7	27.4
Barnes	4 871	70.1	87 900	18.5	10.1	491	23.6	10.1	5 585	-1.4	181	3.2	5 848	33.1	27.6
Benson	2 291	64.5	52 800	18.7	11.2	407	19.6	2.3	2 476	-0.9	168	6.8	2 550	36.1	27.1
Billings	350	78.0	108 900	20.0	10.0	632	10.0	1.1	498	4.6	15	3.0	476	34.5	38.0
Bottineau	3 028	76.9	84 200	15.9	10.0	559	24.4	0.7	3 227	0.9	118	3.7	3 215	31.6	28.6
Bowman	1 354	77.2	115 100	17.5	10.0	581	17.1	2.1	1 893	-4.4	35	1.8	1 683	31.9	31.0
Burke	1 007	67.6	77 900	14.8	10.0	607	22.7	1.4	1 277	-4.1	36	2.8	1 079	30.8	33.3
Burleigh	34 703	71.2	172 800	19.8	10.4	676	24.5	1.5	47 920	0.7	1 202	2.5	47 129	37.1	21.2
Cass	65 816	53.4	158 900	21.0	10.1	674	26.4	0.2	93 540	1.8	2 332	2.5	90 433	38.3	20.7
Cavalier	1 754	84.7	68 700	13.9	10.0	450	22.8	0.5	1 988	-0.3	62	3.1	1 926	43.4	27.0
Dickey	2 178	72.5	76 700	19.4	10.0	486	19.5	0.7	2 578	-1.3	56	2.2	2 642	35.1	26.5
Divide	1 035	85.2	72 200	16.6	10.0	457	20.8	1.9	1 815	5.5	28	1.5	1 246	41.0	24.6
Dunn	1 438	82.3	104 800	13.4	10.0	537	17.5	0.1	4 325	4.3	55	1.3	1 934	31.8	35.6
Eddy	1 104	74.4	58 800	18.5	10.0	405	15.1	1.2	1 265	2.8	75	5.9	1 207	44.5	26.9
Emmons	1 634	80.9	70 200	19.2	12.2	391	21.8	0.7	1 553	-0.3	92	5.9	1 644	38.6	25.0
Foster	1 555	73.8	88 700	16.5	10.0	465	34.1	5.6	1 636	1.4	52	3.2	1 742	33.8	32.3
Golden Valley	754	72.3	83 800	18.3	10.2	475	30.9	1.1	962	1.7	21	2.2	876	35.3	24.7
Grand Forks	27 465	52.6	152 100	20.5	10.6	682	30.0	1.3	37 387	-0.2	1 069	2.9	37 138	35.0	20.6
Grant	1 113	76.2	67 200	19.4	12.3	434	21.8	0.5	1 285	3.5	38	3.0	1 224	43.4	25.7
Griggs	1 149	76.3	61 900	17.3	10.0	422	21.8	2.9	1 175	-0.1	29	2.5	1 188	36.7	26.3
Hettinger	1 097	83.1	74 400	16.7	10.0	432	20.3	0.3	1 485	4.6	34	2.3	1 166	39.8	27.8
Kidder	1 146	77.0	71 500	20.1	10.0	508	25.0	0.6	1 227	3.6	53	4.3	1 334	44.1	27.2
LaMoure	1 955	80.2	76 500	19.3	10.0	504	24.3	0.5	2 219	2.1	58	2.6	2 109	41.4	26.9
Logan	827	84.2	58 600	17.4	10.2	615	29.1	2.3	902	1.0	29	3.2	884	38.5	25.6
McHenry	2 573	77.5	77 300	19.2	10.0	487	20.5	0.5	3 186	1.2	144	4.5	2 731	30.0	34.8
McIntosh	1 308	83.7	55 600	20.5	11.8	472	20.8	3.4	1 235	0.1	39	3.2	1 292	35.6	26.6
McKenzie	2 666	67.1	123 800	13.4	10.0	571	17.1	0.9	9 130	19.5	133	1.5	3 668	35.0	30.0
McLean	4 021	77.5	117 000	17.2	10.0	480	20.7	0.9	4 852	2.0	204	4.2	4 392	35.3	26.9
Mercer	3 650	82.9	113 600	16.3	10.0	523	21.9	1.2	4 192	-0.5	170	4.1	4 330	27.4	31.6
Morton	11 416	79.3	147 900	20.5	10.0	661	26.0	4.6	16 032	1.1	539	3.4	15 698	34.1	23.7
Mountrail	3 069	72.2	89 400	15.0	10.0	640	19.2	0.4	9 030	12.7	118	1.3	4 364	29.8	29.3
Nelson	1 474	82.7	54 000	16.5	10.0	427	21.9	0.8	1 522	0.9	60	3.9	1 563	37.4	27.0
Oliver	753	86.3	98 900	15.3	10.0	512	20.2	0.8	919	2.6	57	6.2	864	34.7	30.3
Pembina	3 328	77.1	72 200	17.0	10.4	521	23.8	0.2	3 596	0.3	211	5.9	3 623	30.9	30.2
Pierce	1 983	72.3	83 100	18.8	12.9	615	27.8	2.4	1 809	-0.3	80	4.4	2 116	29.2	31.4
Ramsey	4 826	64.6	89 600	17.6	10.0	504	20.2	1.0	5 734	-0.7	210	3.7	6 128	32.3	22.2
Ransom	2 283	69.6	87 400	19.3	10.0	552	22.7	1.0	2 695	-0.4	81	3.0	2 721	29.0	40.8
Renville	1 041	78.9	95 200	16.2	10.0	568	18.6	1.2	1 395	2.5	38	2.7	1 296	36.3	29.6
Richland	6 614	72.6	101 800	19.1	10.0	477	23.4	6.6	8 556	-0.3	269	3.1	8 567	30.3	31.3
Rolette	4 750	70.2	63 400	16.3	12.0	379	24.4	0.3	4 857	-1.9	571	11.8	4 873	36.5	20.5
Sargent	1 741	77.3	72 500	19.0	10.0	526	20.9	0.5	2 164	1.8	51	2.4	2 012	33.1	39.3
Sheridan	614	86.5	58 300	23.3	10.5	382	19.5	13.5	664	2.0	38	5.7	692	39.2	26.7
Sioux	1 116	44.6	70 700	15.2	10.0	443	14.9	3.4	1 347	2.0	64	4.8	1 281	41.5	15.0
Slope	296	86.8	61 100	12.6	10.0	806	32.5	2.4	480	-1.8	11	2.3	395	49.4	30.1
Stark	10 439	72.7	166 200	17.8	10.0	706	25.4	1.3	21 558	9.1	351	1.6	14 562	28.6	32.3
Steele	890	75.1	73 700	15.9	10.0	424	19.3	0.3	1 000	-0.2	24	2.4	1 058	36.1	32.1
Stutsman	8 873	69.8	98 600	17.9	10.0	578	26.0	1.1	10 577	0.2	302	2.9	11 107	32.2	26.8
Towner	1 034	80.7	60 600	17.0	10.0	407	24.4	0.8	1 192	2.8	46	3.9	1 212	47.7	17.7
Traill	3 306	74.0	94 400	19.3	11.4	521	23.8	1.0	4 448	-0.4	123	2.8	4 199	31.1	29.3
Walsh	4 948	76.3	68 100	17.3	10.0	502	24.5	1.4	5 577	0.5	270	4.8	5 747	31.2	31.9

1. Specified owner-occupied units. 2. A value of 10.0 represents 10 percent or less; a value of 50.0 represents 50 percent or more. 3. Specified renter-occupied units.
4. Overcrowded or lacking complete plumbing facilities. 5. Percent of civilian labor force. 6. Persons 16 years old and over.

STATE County	Private nonfarm establishments, employment and payroll, 2013									Agriculture, 2012			
		Employment						Annual payroll		Farms			
											Percent with:		
	Number of establish-ments	Total	Health care and social assistance	Manufac-turing	Retail trade	Finance and insurance	Professional, scientific, and technical services	Total (mil dol)	Average per employee (dollars)	Number	Fewer than 50 acres	500 acres or more	Farm operators whose principal occu-pation is farming (percent)
	104	105	106	107	108	109	110	111	112	113	114	115	116
NORTH CAROLINA—Cont'd													
Swain	362	3 186	D	D	530	71	D	92	28 720	94	62.8	1.1	26.6
Transylvania	790	7 049	1 478	460	1 456	212	198	208	29 463	221	63.8	2.3	46.6
Tyrrell	78	432	27	D	136	19	6	11	26 100	78	21.8	28.2	57.7
Union	4 097	47 496	5 466	9 858	6 786	913	1 309	1 707	35 945	1 059	55.6	6.8	53.0
Vance	844	12 682	2 460	1 631	2 195	257	253	396	31 218	242	36.4	10.7	36.8
Wake	26 040	409 573	54 355	12 787	52 566	21 003	47 005	19 511	47 638	783	57.0	4.5	49.0
Warren	262	2 198	570	D	351	D	81	53	24 268	256	34.0	11.7	42.6
Washington	242	2 975	683	D	427	68	D	105	35 442	156	25.6	30.1	59.0
Watauga	1 562	16 384	3 568	609	3 470	339	654	488	29 756	609	49.4	2.0	44.7
Wayne	2 135	33 406	7 132	5 787	5 786	1 126	787	1 093	32 719	563	40.1	18.1	60.9
Wilkes	1 219	17 838	2 999	4 097	2 430	380	419	574	32 166	972	44.9	3.9	50.6
Wilson	1 737	32 323	4 825	8 372	3 908	D	707	1 268	39 235	297	42.4	17.8	61.3
Yadkin	587	8 582	1 019	2 414	756	140	206	255	29 747	952	55.6	2.7	44.9
Yancey	327	3 039	462	680	594	81	90	91	29 783	450	57.3	0.7	31.1
NORTH DAKOTA	24 088	342 747	59 341	23 441	48 790	16 925	14 063	15 560	45 397	30 961	11.0	48.8	56.6
Adams	105	774	D	D	168	D	D	27	34 273	392	12.8	48.7	60.2
Barnes	372	3 973	1 095	626	468	146	83	122	30 825	855	11.6	40.6	52.4
Benson	99	1 132	D	D	D	D	D	35	30 976	563	6.9	54.2	64.5
Billings	64	D	NA	D	14	D	4	20	D	197	4.6	68.5	68.0
Bottineau	278	1 878	265	94	339	136	D	78	41 763	863	8.5	41.7	48.8
Bowman	157	1 171	58	45	215	D	D	54	45 713	348	8.6	55.5	54.3
Burke	97	581	21	NA	97	34	D	28	47 807	488	6.4	47.3	54.3
Burleigh	2 951	46 571	11 551	944	7 054	2 162	2 298	1 994	42 808	1 014	23.1	34.7	42.3
Cass	5 179	97 100	16 787	8 652	12 833	7 552	5 034	4 113	42 356	968	21.0	49.8	66.3
Cavalier	171	1 239	213	D	226	94	D	44	35 884	667	7.5	57.1	63.4
Dickey	223	1 816	406	213	321	D	29	54	30 007	543	11.0	45.7	53.8
Divide	120	872	D	9	80	35	18	42	47 615	452	5.5	54.4	54.6
Dunn	192	2 319	D	D	175	D	D	139	60 042	628	13.1	56.5	66.1
Eddy	78	473	216	D	69	D	D	14	29 721	331	8.8	50.2	46.2
Emmons	123	784	225	D	103	51	D	22	28 313	609	6.6	58.1	55.2
Foster	140	1 388	319	D	266	59	7	53	38 115	310	10.3	49.7	61.0
Golden Valley	79	478	D	NA	D	D	D	17	35 431	251	7.2	58.6	62.2
Grand Forks	1 900	32 196	6 920	1 830	5 874	992	1 531	1 141	35 452	970	12.3	35.8	62.7
Grant	73	444	175	76	32	D	D	13	29 140	508	8.3	59.4	65.2
Griggs	102	709	D	D	57	31	D	23	32 750	456	6.6	45.8	52.9
Hettinger	97	465	D	D	74	55	D	15	32 972	494	5.9	50.4	54.9
Kidder	66	482	D	5	78	40	D	16	32 384	559	6.4	54.2	49.7
LaMoure	154	980	155	52	D	D	D	35	35 649	642	8.6	49.2	59.0
Logan	69	451	D	D	37	30	D	12	27 257	379	7.4	56.2	58.3
McHenry	129	734	D	D	D	48	D	28	37 512	911	9.2	48.8	64.8
McIntosh	116	871	325	D	126	D	D	25	29 240	471	7.4	51.4	59.7
McKenzie	458	4 348	242	D	290	123	230	310	71 382	574	10.5	59.4	61.1
McLean	255	2 419	444	D	278	137	17	124	51 158	868	7.3	51.6	51.6
Mercer	242	D	471	45	536	116	52	D	D	422	12.3	46.2	54.3
Morton	823	9 475	1 684	895	1 268	371	D	432	45 615	887	20.3	47.9	55.2
Mountrail	361	3 764	222	D	570	D	89	242	64 388	670	4.6	57.9	66.4
Nelson	127	847	265	D	98	59	D	23	27 044	603	6.8	35.8	36.5
Oliver	48	571	D	D	D	11	D	40	70 623	290	13.4	48.3	53.4
Pembina	282	2 582	D	590	404	120	32	94	36 472	584	12.3	45.0	62.3
Pierce	162	1 457	D	D	301	D	D	50	34 195	521	7.5	53.7	58.3
Ramsey	424	4 374	856	D	950	257	57	141	32 250	573	11.0	48.5	51.5
Ransom	194	1 757	413	386	273	D	52	55	31 398	548	11.7	36.3	48.7
Renville	108	754	D	D	D	D	D	25	33 764	304	8.2	68.1	73.4
Richland	533	6 269	596	1 863	900	155	209	218	34 839	854	15.6	47.9	64.3
Rolette	208	2 466	549	D	500	104	D	70	28 487	649	9.1	38.8	48.8
Sargent	124	2 190	63	D	138	44	21	102	46 406	537	6.5	45.4	55.9
Sheridan	46	170	D	D	D	D	D	5	31 541	370	7.8	53.5	54.6
Sioux	28	950	D	D	D	D	D	27	28 196	176	10.8	67.0	66.5
Slope	20	110	NA	NA	NA	NA	NA	10	90 382	221	9.5	62.4	62.0
Stark	1 184	16 249	1 916	691	2 120	451	447	947	58 288	837	20.2	39.1	48.6
Steele	59	507	D	169	D	52	D	21	40 686	355	8.7	52.4	63.1
Stutsman	664	9 258	2 713	816	1 407	429	216	314	33 899	1 028	10.1	49.8	55.2
Towner	84	467	D	D	D	56	23	15	31 448	529	7.2	62.4	61.1
Traill	301	2 716	D	335	347	161	34	97	35 550	468	17.3	48.3	63.7
Walsh	405	3 609	708	571	574	170	87	123	34 023	962	13.7	38.9	47.3

STATE County	Agriculture, 2012 (cont.)															
	Land in farms					Value of land and buildings (dollars)		Value of machinery and equipment, average per farm (dollars)	Value of products sold				Percent of farms with sales of:		Government payments	
			Acres								Percent from:					
	Acreage (1,000)	Percent change, 2007–2012	Average size of farm	Total irrigated (1,000)	Total cropland (1,000)	Average per farm	Average per acre		Total (mil dol)	Average per farm (dollars)	Crops	Livestock and poultry products	$10,000 or more	$100,000 or more	Total ($1,000)	Percent of farms
	117	118	119	120	121	122	123	124	125	126	127	128	129	130	131	132
NORTH CAROLINA—Cont'd																
Swain	D	D	D	0.0	D	349 085	D	37 309	0.7	7 202	48.3	51.7	16.0	1.1	17	10.6
Transylvania	18	11.7	81	0.4	6.6	716 964	8 838	43 715	20.4	92 131	81.5	18.5	34.8	11.3	200	12.7
Tyrrell	65	19.9	828	0.0	57.8	2 107 192	2 545	343 936	59.6	763 474	D	D	62.8	42.3	772	83.3
Union	202	13.2	190	0.4	148.3	1 075 361	5 647	112 638	535.8	505 977	24.0	76.0	43.6	25.9	1 807	17.4
Vance	55	-0.4	227	1.6	19.5	784 640	3 460	79 628	17.3	71 463	97.7	2.3	26.4	11.2	446	45.9
Wake	84	-0.9	108	3.2	44.4	1 029 967	9 575	68 049	65.2	83 324	94.1	5.9	33.0	9.6	848	24.8
Warren	66	-9.6	257	0.8	26.0	657 488	2 562	60 867	25.6	100 156	53.7	46.3	37.9	14.5	678	57.4
Washington	91	-5.7	586	4.4	75.9	1 767 526	3 017	301 814	68.4	438 237	95.5	4.5	52.6	35.9	1 639	76.3
Watauga	56	21.8	92	0.0	14.5	684 361	7 474	51 750	15.3	25 108	38.4	61.6	34.5	5.1	222	22.5
Wayne	191	9.1	340	4.8	146.8	1 400 607	4 124	199 504	577.2	1 025 265	27.4	72.6	61.5	44.8	2 943	56.5
Wilkes	111	1.0	114	0.1	36.2	553 577	4 842	80 330	284.9	293 140	6.6	93.4	42.1	19.1	329	6.6
Wilson	111	6.4	375	1.4	86.4	1 431 529	3 817	266 391	179.6	604 822	84.3	15.7	46.5	30.6	1 876	62.3
Yadkin	100	-4.5	106	0.5	53.5	555 887	5 267	68 082	124.7	130 956	26.8	73.2	33.8	12.3	921	25.7
Yancey	31	-7.3	69	0.1	6.2	446 533	6 482	28 402	5.7	12 758	71.8	28.2	23.8	2.7	532	23.3
NORTH DAKOTA	39 263	-1.0	1 268	218.4	27 147.2	1 808 801	1 426	300 285	10 950.7	353 693	88.3	11.7	59.0	40.6	381 710	80.1
Adams	601	-4.1	1 534	D	380.0	1 236 143	806	192 020	107.5	274 329	77.3	22.7	54.1	36.7	4 734	81.9
Barnes	937	3.3	1 096	1.7	836.5	2 449 174	2 235	342 849	376.4	440 175	97.5	2.5	54.9	39.5	11 719	83.6
Benson	802	5.6	1 425	1.2	644.4	1 841 764	1 293	354 654	240.6	427 405	92.7	7.3	62.0	46.0	7 551	83.5
Billings	722	-0.3	3 666	0.0	131.3	2 888 964	788	226 416	36.7	186 127	48.1	51.9	78.7	41.1	1 365	68.5
Bottineau	899	-12.6	1 042	D	773.0	1 408 030	1 351	275 319	254.0	294 359	95.1	4.9	53.3	34.9	9 818	83.4
Bowman	730	1.3	2 099	1.5	372.6	1 577 514	752	251 733	111.4	320 164	54.1	45.9	61.5	41.4	4 005	80.2
Burke	595	4.3	1 219	D	434.6	1 023 576	839	247 330	105.1	215 455	91.7	8.3	50.4	32.4	5 413	86.9
Burleigh	951	8.1	938	4.6	494.7	1 320 447	1 408	162 938	179.6	177 132	72.9	27.1	50.2	23.6	5 300	53.9
Cass	1 107	6.6	1 144	9.3	1 044.5	3 277 384	2 865	455 639	567.1	585 855	96.8	3.2	68.0	54.3	14 691	78.3
Cavalier	940	7.7	1 410	0.0	871.5	2 681 525	1 902	456 447	334.5	501 547	98.2	1.8	65.1	54.4	15 805	92.2
Dickey	633	-9.2	1 166	16.3	481.1	2 629 105	2 254	359 029	266.8	491 398	88.2	11.8	57.8	43.1	10 047	79.4
Divide	565	-20.2	1 250	2.4	419.2	807 018	646	241 810	93.8	207 496	90.9	9.1	55.1	38.3	4 848	90.5
Dunn	1 031	-1.2	1 642	0.4	374.3	1 498 726	913	250 261	124.8	198 707	60.6	39.4	72.3	39.3	3 189	70.9
Eddy	396	5.1	1 196	0.2	288.7	1 600 341	1 338	283 166	105.1	317 538	90.2	9.8	52.0	37.2	4 696	87.9
Emmons	744	-14.7	1 222	3.9	443.9	1 439 232	1 178	269 821	171.3	281 255	80.9	19.1	62.7	47.0	5 117	87.8
Foster	374	-6.5	1 206	2.6	314.3	2 254 016	1 868	422 081	169.4	546 484	80.4	19.6	65.5	51.3	4 700	78.4
Golden Valley	562	-1.4	2 241	D	242.6	1 887 992	843	258 785	59.6	237 327	73.3	26.7	63.3	38.2	4 251	79.7
Grand Forks	816	-1.1	842	18.9	749.2	1 768 300	2 101	322 178	428.8	442 023	94.8	5.2	51.3	39.3	11 254	90.9
Grant	1 050	-0.8	2 067	2.4	504.0	1 904 955	922	235 537	157.1	309 232	70.3	29.7	68.1	45.9	5 753	84.8
Griggs	445	9.7	977	2.8	342.4	1 781 884	1 824	254 471	127.8	280 325	91.5	8.5	53.7	35.5	8 891	88.4
Hettinger	716	1.1	1 449	0.0	558.5	1 624 585	1 121	263 455	159.0	321 927	91.4	8.6	49.4	34.4	8 615	88.7
Kidder	780	3.6	1 396	15.0	429.8	1 290 878	925	198 445	148.3	265 326	72.2	27.8	59.9	40.4	4 079	84.6
LaMoure	726	5.5	1 131	7.4	611.3	2 445 422	2 163	342 617	292.4	455 500	88.9	11.1	63.6	50.9	7 967	85.7
Logan	572	-1.0	1 508	1.5	333.3	1 541 950	1 022	285 359	172.1	454 087	50.0	50.0	63.1	48.3	3 296	90.0
McHenry	1 061	-2.0	1 165	1.2	624.8	1 047 299	899	161 514	198.2	217 581	72.3	27.7	56.4	34.7	8 289	77.9
McIntosh	590	7.3	1 252	D	397.2	1 472 964	1 176	214 769	139.8	296 754	75.3	24.7	66.7	42.7	3 350	79.6
McKenzie	1 064	-1.0	1 854	19.9	425.6	1 366 373	737	246 225	114.4	199 387	69.0	31.0	62.9	38.5	4 116	70.0
McLean	1 113	-4.3	1 282	7.4	838.7	1 681 880	1 312	307 744	293.4	338 025	92.3	7.7	62.2	41.6	11 766	82.8
Mercer	503	-1.3	1 192	1.4	231.0	1 135 981	953	188 306	76.7	181 765	73.3	26.7	65.6	32.5	2 572	70.9
Morton	1 220	4.7	1 375	7.6	549.1	1 405 868	1 022	208 989	225.2	253 934	67.6	32.4	62.8	34.6	5 558	62.0
Mountrail	964	-7.0	1 438	0.2	578.8	1 308 849	910	278 960	154.9	231 166	86.8	13.2	60.3	37.0	7 195	77.0
Nelson	560	1.9	929	2.1	474.9	1 092 551	1 175	230 488	145.8	241 725	93.3	6.7	37.3	24.5	9 207	95.5
Oliver	395	4.4	1 360	5.9	165.1	1 388 955	1 021	192 590	85.5	294 810	60.2	39.8	74.8	39.3	2 057	75.2
Pembina	692	6.6	1 185	5.7	632.8	3 054 467	2 577	574 476	406.0	695 164	98.7	1.3	60.3	44.9	8 554	77.7
Pierce	598	2.9	1 148	1.0	479.8	1 180 380	1 028	257 340	142.1	272 649	90.5	9.5	55.9	41.8	6 473	90.6
Ramsey	698	-2.3	1 219	D	622.7	1 696 558	1 392	394 349	236.1	412 005	96.7	3.3	51.0	41.2	10 448	85.3
Ransom	502	-4.9	915	14.8	339.3	1 673 436	1 828	213 192	179.3	327 126	85.4	14.6	50.2	32.5	9 311	81.6
Renville	500	-9.8	1 645	0.0	445.8	2 659 974	1 617	536 164	156.4	514 605	97.8	2.2	80.6	66.1	6 902	84.2
Richland	869	-4.1	1 017	3.7	788.5	3 021 842	2 970	437 697	535.7	627 234	95.1	4.9	67.7	54.3	15 676	82.2
Rolette	534	-5.9	823	D	365.5	925 470	1 124	187 112	107.9	166 301	90.8	9.2	50.7	24.8	5 631	68.1
Sargent	513	1.5	955	13.7	432.5	2 265 119	2 372	338 054	243.4	453 311	90.3	9.7	55.5	45.8	9 185	87.2
Sheridan	514	2.7	1 388	D	347.3	1 297 773	935	230 697	107.8	291 295	91.1	8.9	53.8	38.9	4 293	82.7
Sioux	573	-21.5	3 256	D	155.9	2 912 585	894	265 188	62.7	356 421	47.1	52.9	71.6	52.3	1 476	58.5
Slope	674	-12.3	3 051	D	245.0	2 603 290	853	329 502	67.6	305 688	72.0	28.0	64.3	41.6	3 166	72.4
Stark	830	-0.9	991	0.8	498.8	1 345 419	1 358	207 119	152.6	182 298	77.8	22.2	52.9	27.4	4 741	66.3
Steele	426	5.9	1 200	6.0	397.0	2 218 885	1 850	483 662	210.6	593 158	98.3	1.7	63.7	57.2	6 646	94.6
Stutsman	1 303	9.2	1 267	8.2	1 030.6	2 212 500	1 746	385 059	464.6	451 914	90.0	10.0	60.1	41.3	13 278	78.3
Towner	645	6.3	1 220	0.4	573.3	1 565 902	1 283	320 216	196.8	372 049	91.2	8.8	60.5	53.1	7 528	87.1
Traill	548	0.8	1 170	2.0	526.2	3 395 635	2 901	477 162	308.8	659 887	99.3	0.7	68.2	54.9	8 804	80.6
Walsh	802	0.9	834	3.4	714.5	1 982 913	2 377	308 740	424.0	440 783	98.3	1.7	49.7	37.8	14 445	87.1

STATE County	Water use, 2010		Wholesale trade,[1] 2007				Retail trade,[2] 2007				Real estate and rental and leasing,[2] 2007			
	Total water withdrawn (mil gal/day)	Gallons withdrawn per person per day	Number of establish-ments	Number of employees	Sales (mil dol)	Annual payroll (mil dol)	Number of establish-ments	Number of employees	Sales (mil dol)	Annual payroll (mil dol)	Number of establish-ments	Number of employees	Receipts (mil dol)	Annual payroll (mil dol)
	133	134	135	136	137	138	139	140	141	142	143	144	145	146
NORTH CAROLINA—Cont'd														
Swain	15.0	1 073	7	23	2.3	0.4	104	619	112.3	10.1	19	45	5.4	0.8
Transylvania	811.1	24 513	11	D	D	D	122	1 331	266.2	27.0	59	173	19.8	4.6
Tyrrell	0.6	134	2	D	D	D	19	143	30.7	2.0	1	D	D	D
Union	42.2	210	264	2 640	1 232.8	112.2	515	6 568	1 699.8	148.6	179	530	100.8	17.6
Vance	9.8	216	30	D	D	D	190	2 242	582.1	48.3	45	164	22.9	3.9
Wake	114.5	127	1 059	15 635	11 334.3	918.8	3 181	49 828	12 598.1	1 162.4	1 374	7 297	1 901.6	324.0
Warren	2.6	123	8	32	17.7	0.9	53	340	62.9	6.2	6	30	3.4	0.6
Washington	5.8	438	13	111	83.2	3.4	52	467	107.7	8.6	5	10	1.1	0.2
Watauga	11.0	215	47	343	169.3	15.6	343	3 588	795.2	79.3	145	505	59.3	11.5
Wayne	34.3	280	102	1 843	1 094.5	71.2	501	5 759	1 388.0	113.7	70	288	35.3	6.6
Wilkes	14.3	206	43	546	260.6	16.6	226	2 503	759.3	50.0	57	229	52.4	8.6
Wilson	26.0	320	93	1 060	728.8	48.9	370	4 130	1 058.6	89.8	70	193	29.9	4.4
Yadkin	15.3	399	24	169	101.2	5.9	127	897	238.6	16.8	13	D	D	D
Yancey	12.8	716	9	32	7.1	0.7	64	592	149.1	12.3	13	30	3.0	0.7
NORTH DAKOTA	1 147.1	1 705	1 332	14 866	13 099.3	627.1	3 361	44 054	10 527.3	891.4	770	3 748	668.8	96.0
Adams	0.5	222	8	46	31.0	1.3	19	147	30.7	2.5	2	D	D	D
Barnes	2.2	194	25	115	142.6	4.5	57	536	147.8	10.6	7	D	D	D
Benson	2.1	321	13	83	125.1	3.1	18	104	20.1	1.2	2	D	D	D
Billings	2.1	2 669	1	D	D	D	10	5	1.2	0.1	NA	NA	NA	NA
Bottineau	3.2	496	16	95	135.0	3.6	47	317	57.0	5.2	10	12	0.6	0.1
Bowman	2.1	673	9	66	80.7	2.4	25	197	63.5	4.2	2	D	D	D
Burke	1.1	549	7	39	131.0	1.4	14	51	17.9	0.8	2	D	D	D
Burleigh	16.2	199	132	1 613	889.1	71.9	385	6 713	1 401.0	134.8	110	365	53.8	8.4
Cass	17.2	115	335	D	D	D	663	12 008	2 885.6	256.5	268	1 630	226.4	45.8
Cavalier	0.9	215	13	116	261.5	4.9	33	186	83.2	4.1	1	D	D	D
Dickey	7.6	1 431	13	109	151.7	3.7	46	308	78.1	6.0	2	D	D	D
Divide	2.2	1 067	5	56	21.3	0.6	12	74	11.8	0.9	5	D	D	D
Dunn	3.0	834	5	22	6.5	0.6	13	106	39.3	2.2	1	D	D	D
Eddy	2.0	818	4	19	21.0	0.7	14	86	32.5	1.8	2	D	D	D
Emmons	5.7	1 606	8	65	46.8	1.7	19	104	26.8	2.3	NA	NA	NA	NA
Foster	1.8	523	15	113	101.7	4.9	27	251	80.7	5.1	2	D	D	D
Golden Valley	0.6	339	5	120	89.0	5.0	14	86	49.9	1.3	NA	NA	NA	NA
Grand Forks	17.5	262	89	1 169	734.3	49.4	336	5 844	1 238.2	114.6	58	422	58.8	9.2
Grant	9.6	3 989	6	20	27.3	0.5	13	47	12.4	0.9	3	3	0.4	0.0
Griggs	3.1	1 269	9	62	38.0	2.3	11	48	11.2	1.0	NA	NA	NA	NA
Hettinger	0.3	113	4	D	D	D	16	104	46.9	1.9	3	D	D	D
Kidder	13.9	5 696	3	15	10.5	0.4	10	68	28.0	1.1	4	9	0.8	0.1
LaMoure	5.3	1 285	14	124	137.8	5.6	24	157	37.2	2.3	2	D	D	D
Logan	2.8	1 392	7	52	62.4	1.8	9	41	21.5	1.0	1	D	D	D
McHenry	22.0	4 085	5	D	D	D	20	128	37.1	2.4	6	D	D	D
McIntosh	0.9	313	9	59	53.3	1.7	26	165	48.5	3.4	3	9	1.0	0.1
McKenzie	37.7	5 925	11	83	94.9	3.7	21	155	36.8	2.7	4	D	D	D
McLean	21.6	2 407	16	123	208.0	5.5	38	290	52.8	4.2	4	8	0.2	0.0
Mercer	372.6	44 230	5	D	D	D	43	393	85.7	7.0	6	6	0.4	0.0
Morton	51.2	1 865	39	283	238.1	9.2	94	1 105	342.1	27.2	33	75	13.6	1.5
Mountrail	3.4	446	11	80	110.9	2.8	39	322	118.9	6.1	3	8	0.3	0.1
Nelson	1.0	326	12	84	138.2	3.5	21	94	24.4	1.5	4	6	0.2	0.0
Oliver	433.1	234 588	1	D	D	D	4	34	10.0	0.7	NA	NA	NA	NA
Pembina	2.1	286	34	286	367.9	9.1	51	480	90.0	8.3	3	2	0.2	0.0
Pierce	1.3	287	11	100	85.9	2.8	28	286	85.7	5.2	2	D	D	D
Ramsey	0.3	26	26	212	266.3	8.0	85	886	234.3	20.1	5	11	0.7	0.1
Ransom	10.6	1 933	8	96	142.5	4.3	33	303	53.9	5.0	3	D	D	D
Renville	1.4	579	13	D	D	D	11	71	23.8	1.4	3	D	D	D
Richland	6.2	379	40	D	D	D	70	718	205.0	14.7	15	49	5.0	0.9
Rolette	2.1	149	10	100	85.8	2.5	45	476	107.1	9.1	1	D	D	D
Sargent	4.5	1 183	14	101	152.9	3.6	22	141	27.6	2.1	4	9	1.8	0.2
Sheridan	0.4	310	5	21	22.9	0.7	4	11	4.3	0.2	3	3	0.1	0.0
Sioux	0.7	166	NA	NA	NA	NA	7	63	13.2	0.7	NA	NA	NA	NA
Slope	6.1	8 391	NA	NA	NA	NA	NA	NA	NA	NA	NA	NA	NA	NA
Stark	3.2	132	46	D	D	D	160	1 686	403.4	33.8	23	76	11.4	1.9
Steele	0.8	400	6	39	159.8	1.9	9	72	25.9	1.6	2	D	D	D
Stutsman	9.1	430	33	D	D	D	123	1 275	309.7	24.8	23	142	10.6	1.3
Towner	0.5	205	7	D	D	D	13	60	7.2	0.9	2	D	D	D
Traill	1.1	132	31	238	275.7	9.1	41	310	72.5	5.6	9	27	1.4	0.3
Walsh	1.0	92	31	285	296.2	10.6	70	592	98.8	9.2	11	19	0.9	0.2

1. Merchant wholesalers, except manufacturers' sales branches and offices. 2. Employer establishments.

STATE County	Professional, scientific, and technical services,[1] 2007				Manufacturing, 2007				Accommodation and food services, 2007			
	Number of establish-ments	Number of employees	Receipts (mil dol)	Annual payroll (mil dol)	Number of establish-ments	Number of employees	Receipts (mil dol)	Annual payroll (mil dol)	Number of establish-ments	Number of employees	Sales (mil dol)	Annual payroll (mil dol)
	147	148	149	150	151	152	153	154	155	156	157	158
NORTH CAROLINA—Cont'd												
Swain	11	60	2.5	1.6	NA	NA	NA	NA	99	2 857	561.6	68.9
Transylvania	69	D	D	D	32	532	71.9	18.2	84	1 132	62.8	18.4
Tyrrell	3	D	D	D	NA	NA	NA	NA	5	D	D	D
Union	352	1 204	140.3	48.1	249	11 264	D	459.4	246	D	D	D
Vance	45	206	16.7	7.7	42	1 916	639.2	68.4	69	1 363	53.9	15.3
Wake	4 064	34 994	5 389.2	2 217.3	631	17 932	14 091.7	827.9	1 773	36 260	1 726.6	480.0
Warren	17	55	3.7	1.0	NA	NA	NA	NA	18	120	5.7	1.6
Washington	10	85	5.4	1.6	14	1 499	727.9	D	24	376	13.5	3.5
Watauga	160	D	D	D	54	862	129.8	26.6	159	3 289	131.4	41.8
Wayne	143	825	65.7	22.8	84	6 147	1 474.8	221.7	197	3 485	132.1	36.2
Wilkes	92	461	38.9	15.2	98	5 839	1 503.3	173.5	104	1 569	62.1	17.2
Wilson	112	D	D	D	100	8 193	8 357.1	336.3	131	2 582	112.8	28.7
Yadkin	40	247	19.4	7.6	43	1 856	D	65.2	66	883	33.6	9.2
Yancey	25	86	5.6	2.4	17	655	127.4	21.1	22	291	10.5	3.0
NORTH DAKOTA	1 432	9 707	1 110.7	416.9	767	26 361	11 349.8	991.4	1 840	30 307	1 214.2	337.8
Adams	4	D	D	D	NA	NA	NA	NA	9	D	D	D
Barnes	21	94	5.4	3.7	14	691	339.8	22.4	35	439	12.1	3.2
Benson	6	21	1.8	0.8	NA	NA	NA	NA	14	39	2.1	0.4
Billings	1	D	D	D	NA	NA	NA	NA	9	76	13.5	3.2
Bottineau	14	57	4.0	1.7	NA	NA	NA	NA	32	152	6.9	1.5
Bowman	8	28	3.4	1.2	NA	NA	NA	NA	15	95	3.9	0.9
Burke	3	D	D	D	NA	NA	NA	NA	9	59	3.3	0.5
Burleigh	260	D	D	D	73	2 089	D	85.3	173	4 405	170.1	50.3
Cass	412	D	D	D	201	8 266	2 480.1	310.9	363	8 796	341.2	101.0
Cavalier	7	12	1.0	0.4	NA	NA	NA	NA	18	103	3.1	0.7
Dickey	9	36	1.8	0.6	NA	NA	NA	NA	19	168	4.8	1.0
Divide	5	11	1.1	0.2	NA	NA	NA	NA	7	D	D	D
Dunn	1	D	D	D	NA	NA	NA	NA	8	D	D	D
Eddy	5	14	1.3	0.4	NA	NA	NA	NA	8	D	D	D
Emmons	11	148	2.0	1.2	NA	NA	NA	NA	14	D	D	D
Foster	8	12	0.8	0.2	NA	NA	NA	NA	11	130	3.7	1.1
Golden Valley	4	17	1.0	0.3	NA	NA	NA	NA	7	26	1.0	0.2
Grand Forks	118	D	D	D	55	2 762	565.3	85.8	186	4 180	141.1	41.2
Grant	3	7	0.5	0.1	NA	NA	NA	NA	7	D	D	D
Griggs	9	57	3.4	1.2	NA	NA	NA	NA	9	D	D	D
Hettinger	4	D	D	D	NA	NA	NA	NA	6	30	1.2	0.2
Kidder	4	D	D	D	NA	NA	NA	NA	7	D	D	D
LaMoure	3	D	D	D	NA	NA	NA	NA	15	86	2.6	0.6
Logan	2	D	D	D	NA	NA	NA	NA	7	52	1.1	0.2
McHenry	3	D	D	D	NA	NA	NA	NA	10	30	1.0	0.2
McIntosh	9	19	1.5	0.4	NA	NA	NA	NA	12	61	2.1	0.4
McKenzie	13	27	5.0	1.2	NA	NA	NA	NA	17	97	3.5	0.8
McLean	6	18	1.4	0.3	NA	NA	NA	NA	34	160	7.2	1.4
Mercer	11	39	3.5	1.1	NA	NA	NA	NA	34	277	8.2	2.1
Morton	52	D	D	D	39	919	D	43.4	50	717	26.1	7.3
Mountrail	6	D	D	D	NA	NA	NA	NA	21	102	4.8	0.9
Nelson	3	6	0.3	0.1	NA	NA	NA	NA	13	69	2.0	0.5
Oliver	3	D	D	D	NA	NA	NA	NA	2	D	D	D
Pembina	12	23	4.4	0.7	21	707	486.5	28.8	24	177	5.6	1.3
Pierce	11	33	2.5	0.9	NA	NA	NA	NA	15	118	3.0	0.8
Ramsey	19	47	4.5	1.5	NA	NA	NA	NA	45	656	21.7	6.0
Ransom	16	45	3.3	0.9	NA	NA	NA	NA	18	146	4.3	1.1
Renville	6	D	D	D	NA	NA	NA	NA	11	29	1.0	0.2
Richland	24	D	D	D	34	1 788	941.6	73.8	47	1 096	84.6	18.1
Rolette	6	12	0.6	0.2	NA	NA	NA	NA	21	429	36.1	10.5
Sargent	7	15	0.8	0.3	9	D	D	D	14	74	2.2	0.5
Sheridan	1	D	D	D	NA	NA	NA	NA	5	23	0.6	0.2
Sioux	NA	NA	NA	NA	NA	NA	NA	NA	6	D	D	D
Slope	NA	NA	NA	NA	NA	NA	NA	NA	2	D	D	D
Stark	51	D	D	D	33	1 170	270.6	46.9	71	1 089	40.9	11.5
Steele	3	8	0.3	0.1	NA	NA	NA	NA	5	14	0.6	0.1
Stutsman	30	171	12.2	6.1	21	867	230.4	30.4	62	802	30.2	8.6
Towner	6	20	1.7	0.3	NA	NA	NA	NA	8	D	D	D
Traill	10	38	2.4	1.2	NA	NA	NA	NA	30	233	7.0	1.8
Walsh	27	91	6.8	2.0	7	582	D	D	42	281	9.2	2.2

1. Establishment subject to federal tax.

STATE County	Health care and social assistance, 2007				Other services, 2007				Nonemployer businesses, 2013		Value of residential construction authorized by building permits, 2014	
	Number of establish-ments	Number of employees	Receipts (mil dol)	Annual payroll (mil dol)	Number of establish-ments	Number of employees	Receipts (mil dol)	Annual payroll (mil dol)	Number	Receipts (mil dol)	New Construction ($1,000)	Number of housing units
	159	160	161	162	163	164	165	166	167	168	169	170
NORTH CAROLINA—Cont'd												
Swain	33	734	66.1	30.1	22	77	14.7	1.9	1 261	40.4	10 549	50
Transylvania	75	1 508	129.0	49.3	49	260	19.8	5.8	2 892	105.9	27 235	65
Tyrrell	7	D	D	D	8	44	4.0	1.5	264	10.4	65	1
Union	245	5 091	406.8	165.8	279	1 143	102.8	30.0	15 681	677.2	272 184	1 425
Vance	105	2 901	199.7	80.9	52	236	17.8	5.0	2 346	91.4	4 317	26
Wake	2 244	46 079	4 446.4	1 865.0	1 598	12 238	1 416.0	382.4	76 044	3 434.4	1 691 319	10 125
Warren	27	313	17.8	7.7	15	D	D	D	970	34.0	5 908	30
Washington	36	818	36.9	17.9	13	43	4.6	1.3	606	19.5	717	8
Watauga	141	3 151	479.3	119.2	75	395	23.8	7.9	4 596	197.7	62 802	243
Wayne	294	7 587	573.0	248.6	159	949	70.0	20.5	5 815	222.2	40 390	257
Wilkes	149	2 955	184.8	80.4	71	456	24.3	9.3	4 408	166.7	19 840	92
Wilson	183	4 655	332.9	143.5	116	660	43.2	14.7	4 480	163.1	33 136	182
Yadkin	51	1 200	55.8	25.5	38	170	10.5	2.6	2 358	84.2	6 342	36
Yancey	33	527	25.1	11.8	18	78	6.2	1.8	1 591	52.4	6 344	51
NORTH DAKOTA	1 748	52 197	3 906.9	1 716.1	1 708	9 261	746.0	199.3	51 879	2 614.4	1 636 051	12 178
Adams	13	330	20.4	11.6	12	24	2.0	0.4	215	7.7	4 096	33
Barnes	39	1 076	41.5	21.3	33	127	7.2	2.0	883	48.2	10 904	76
Benson	5	D	D	D	2	D	D	D	321	10.3	195	1
Billings	NA	NA	NA	NA	2	D	D	D	103	5.4	2 671	12
Bottineau	8	297	13.1	6.3	12	40	3.7	0.6	683	30.2	600	3
Bowman	11	216	12.1	5.9	12	27	2.3	0.4	282	14.5	1 313	7
Burke	2	D	D	D	4	9	1.1	0.2	230	13.0	1 024	5
Burleigh	236	8 903	742.0	330.0	256	1 700	150.7	42.5	6 982	370.9	177 353	1 254
Cass	427	13 903	1 348.8	549.8	368	D	D	D	11 239	649.6	379 549	3 207
Cavalier	11	267	11.8	5.9	17	54	2.7	0.6	361	13.1	3 500	11
Dickey	23	363	20.2	8.9	18	60	4.2	0.9	401	13.2	793	3
Divide	8	D	D	D	7	D	D	D	230	11.8	2 510	24
Dunn	6	D	D	D	5	D	D	D	317	25.0	13 945	113
Eddy	8	199	8.2	4.7	12	32	3.8	0.7	194	8.5	1 050	9
Emmons	11	200	8.8	3.8	8	D	D	D	278	10.4	1 800	10
Foster	13	239	18.6	8.7	11	30	1.6	0.4	271	10.2	800	4
Golden Valley	5	D	D	D	8	D	D	D	180	7.4	5 177	23
Grand Forks	154	6 143	522.1	221.1	153	D	D	D	3 920	181.8	129 271	931
Grant	7	212	9.4	4.6	4	D	D	D	200	7.6	265	2
Griggs	3	D	D	D	4	D	D	D	198	8.8	300	2
Hettinger	7	98	5.0	2.1	10	22	1.5	0.3	208	8.3	700	3
Kidder	6	105	3.6	2.0	1	D	D	D	247	10.3	0	0
LaMoure	11	118	4.7	3.0	14	49	3.5	0.7	354	14.2	580	1
Logan	7	97	3.3	1.6	7	D	D	D	171	8.3	340	2
McHenry	6	D	D	D	7	D	D	D	399	16.5	5 309	27
McIntosh	10	351	15.3	8.5	8	D	D	D	274	9.6	500	1
McKenzie	6	D	D	D	17	43	2.4	0.7	695	46.9	172 462	1 692
McLean	14	453	20.2	11.0	23	58	3.7	0.8	692	25.3	26 089	158
Mercer	17	395	22.9	10.6	14	55	3.3	0.9	607	16.3	3 792	14
Morton	41	1 197	49.4	28.3	51	265	27.0	7.4	2 190	106.7	74 635	509
Mountrail	14	297	11.8	6.5	14	53	4.1	1.4	692	43.4	23 943	153
Nelson	10	D	D	D	13	34	2.8	0.5	286	10.0	340	3
Oliver	3	D	D	D	2	D	D	D	134	4.6	2 347	8
Pembina	19	367	15.9	6.6	19	47	3.3	0.7	545	21.0	0	0
Pierce	11	363	18.3	9.2	14	59	3.1	0.7	380	15.1	1 248	4
Ramsey	48	1 056	49.8	22.6	28	122	7.5	1.8	897	41.5	4 732	31
Ransom	26	364	21.5	9.6	21	89	5.1	1.2	375	14.7	1 255	5
Renville	5	D	D	D	3	D	D	D	170	6.7	1 235	8
Richland	47	D	D	D	35	D	D	D	1 107	50.8	5 141	25
Rolette	23	610	56.0	21.9	14	24	2.3	0.5	655	18.6	350	1
Sargent	5	80	3.1	1.8	12	40	4.1	0.7	290	10.3	4 127	22
Sheridan	1	D	D	D	3	D	D	D	116	4.8	121	2
Sioux	1	D	D	D	3	D	D	D	119	3.7	0	0
Slope	NA	NA	NA	NA	2	D	D	D	58	2.8	0	0
Stark	75	1 879	98.7	47.5	72	D	D	D	2 546	158.8	117 586	627
Steele	2	D	D	D	3	5	0.5	0.1	130	4.4	1 260	6
Stutsman	69	2 315	113.4	58.1	61	318	18.0	5.5	1 391	56.7	9 079	43
Towner	3	D	D	D	6	D	D	D	237	9.5	0	0
Traill	21	589	26.2	13.1	22	53	4.9	0.8	564	21.8	2 849	11
Walsh	31	707	34.7	17.0	34	95	7.0	1.9	765	33.8	2 492	11

STATE County	Government employment and payroll, 2012									Local government finances, 2012				
			March payroll (percent of total)							General revenue				
												Taxes		
													Per capita[1] (dollars)	
	Full-time equivalent employees	March payroll (dollars)	Adminis-tration, judicial, and legal	Police and Corrections	Fire Protection	Highways and transpor-tation	Health and Welfare	Natural resources and utilities	Education and libraries	Total (mil dol)	Inter-govern-mental (mil dol)	Total (mil dol)	Total	Property
	171	172	173	174	175	176	177	178	179	180	181	182	183	184
NORTH CAROLINA—Cont'd														
Swain	570	1 634 935	2.8	6.9	0.0	0.2	15.2	3.5	58.7	39.0	24.0	8.3	586	366
Transylvania	1 211	3 349 488	5.1	9.9	0.5	1.7	16.3	4.8	52.7	82.0	34.9	38.2	1 162	930
Tyrrell	212	788 126	5.4	5.1	0.0	0.3	6.1	4.4	76.8	19.0	12.0	4.7	1 091	930
Union	6 960	22 437 486	4.7	8.5	1.4	0.7	5.2	5.8	72.3	593.9	274.3	239.3	1 148	942
Vance	2 151	6 716 262	3.1	6.3	2.9	1.8	9.0	3.0	71.8	166.4	101.2	37.4	828	618
Wake	31 235	120 436 016	3.6	9.3	3.7	3.7	7.3	6.6	61.6	3 180.9	1 227.2	1 366.9	1 436	1 077
Warren	682	2 143 055	2.8	7.9	0.0	0.0	10.7	3.8	61.2	57.4	29.8	20.1	976	845
Washington	551	1 546 357	6.0	8.2	0.0	0.4	15.3	5.7	59.9	40.0	25.2	10.3	805	588
Watauga	1 481	4 632 704	6.0	11.0	2.1	4.5	13.2	7.1	47.6	137.3	56.5	63.0	1 214	855
Wayne	5 237	14 176 474	3.0	6.2	2.1	1.3	9.2	6.0	66.2	346.7	199.6	101.5	817	585
Wilkes	3 431	10 259 077	2.0	4.8	0.3	0.9	32.4	1.6	56.6	184.5	95.3	58.2	840	635
Wilson	3 417	11 244 041	5.5	9.5	3.3	2.4	11.6	11.2	53.8	288.2	140.0	90.5	1 105	863
Yadkin	1 268	3 737 818	3.9	5.9	0.1	0.5	11.5	3.0	70.9	88.3	50.5	29.0	763	624
Yancey	773	2 283 963	4.6	6.2	0.2	1.0	23.0	3.1	60.9	45.5	25.0	17.2	973	798
NORTH DAKOTA	X	X	X	X	X	X	X	X	X	X	X	X	X	X
Adams	92	255 672	10.2	8.6	0.0	6.4	7.5	3.3	62.1	8.2	3.6	3.0	1 313	1 054
Barnes	418	1 392 699	15.6	9.1	0.5	3.9	5.1	9.8	55.6	66.9	40.2	17.6	1 597	1 448
Benson	305	941 315	6.1	1.3	0.6	5.7	5.8	1.7	78.6	27.9	19.5	4.6	683	672
Billings	71	278 902	16.6	9.9	1.1	28.8	4.2	4.9	31.5	14.4	10.4	1.7	1 884	1 457
Bottineau	258	801 858	8.7	5.1	0.1	7.5	5.5	8.6	64.2	29.2	15.4	8.8	1 337	1 194
Bowman	154	498 076	10.9	6.0	0.1	7.5	7.8	4.7	63.1	25.9	15.6	5.2	1 630	1 395
Burke	132	476 712	12.0	4.9	0.0	8.5	2.8	2.4	67.3	11.4	4.8	4.8	2 215	1 096
Burleigh	2 640	9 881 026	4.2	8.2	4.2	3.6	6.6	9.1	61.0	347.2	171.6	100.7	1 174	925
Cass	4 659	18 693 995	4.8	9.4	2.9	4.9	9.6	7.5	60.1	694.2	293.1	246.4	1 578	1 145
Cavalier	150	482 792	10.3	7.1	0.0	7.2	5.9	7.5	58.4	17.1	7.4	6.7	1 688	1 662
Dickey	177	602 013	11.3	6.4	0.0	5.8	12.2	3.2	59.7	28.7	12.8	9.2	1 751	1 617
Divide	112	399 142	14.1	7.5	0.0	19.6	4.6	5.6	47.0	17.6	9.2	3.7	1 673	1 505
Dunn	163	514 670	8.7	4.7	0.8	11.8	6.5	2.4	65.0	27.2	19.0	3.9	992	865
Eddy	101	291 076	9.8	5.2	0.0	6.4	5.8	4.1	67.8	12.9	6.6	3.2	1 370	1 257
Emmons	160	461 725	8.9	3.7	0.1	7.4	1.9	9.4	68.6	16.2	7.3	6.2	1 777	1 711
Foster	109	345 480	14.5	2.4	0.1	5.2	6.9	1.6	67.7	14.4	6.3	5.0	1 462	1 302
Golden Valley	168	598 525	4.4	2.4	0.0	4.3	3.1	1.4	83.6	12.6	6.8	3.5	1 923	1 846
Grand Forks	2 414	9 092 121	5.6	9.8	3.4	6.3	6.5	11.9	54.2	280.6	106.1	94.4	1 399	1 054
Grant	103	251 784	10.0	5.5	0.0	9.2	10.7	3.2	60.2	8.5	3.8	3.4	1 448	1 414
Griggs	112	363 293	9.3	4.3	0.0	8.1	9.0	2.0	65.6	13.5	5.4	5.3	2 241	2 176
Hettinger	147	439 881	7.5	2.1	0.1	8.1	4.0	22.4	54.8	15.0	6.5	5.4	2 133	1 985
Kidder	100	305 849	4.8	4.8	0.0	1.6	8.6	4.8	75.3	16.0	7.8	3.7	1 533	1 484
LaMoure	228	740 715	7.4	3.3	0.0	6.3	2.2	19.6	60.3	63.8	47.3	9.5	2 316	2 252
Logan	83	243 512	4.2	4.7	0.0	5.7	6.1	5.0	73.3	10.5	5.6	3.9	2 040	2 023
McHenry	239	766 397	8.6	2.6	0.1	4.2	4.4	4.0	74.9	20.6	10.3	7.3	1 263	1 225
McIntosh	139	432 649	7.6	5.1	0.1	10.8	4.4	16.0	55.9	10.7	5.5	3.7	1 328	1 289
McKenzie	313	1 128 904	9.9	9.8	0.0	9.8	6.5	4.0	57.4	54.1	24.6	7.4	930	751
McLean	438	1 374 148	6.7	7.0	0.0	5.7	12.1	3.3	64.5	43.6	23.1	11.4	1 229	1 093
Mercer	347	1 135 199	9.4	9.5	0.0	9.4	2.8	4.7	62.2	34.8	17.4	9.3	1 093	917
Morton	946	3 200 962	5.4	9.1	1.2	7.7	8.1	5.9	61.5	106.1	48.2	35.2	1 253	1 139
Mountrail	385	1 261 569	8.3	7.4	0.0	8.6	6.2	3.5	65.1	85.8	57.9	12.5	1 434	1 307
Nelson	146	457 045	9.7	3.0	0.0	8.5	4.7	8.9	63.6	17.3	8.0	6.7	2 183	2 144
Oliver	76	233 042	14.9	6.8	0.0	9.6	2.9	7.5	56.4	9.0	3.8	3.7	2 018	1 749
Pembina	393	1 633 628	6.4	4.3	0.0	3.1	4.1	45.4	36.2	40.0	15.7	16.1	2 221	2 125
Pierce	154	464 990	7.2	8.4	0.0	4.1	5.0	3.6	69.5	21.3	8.8	5.5	1 245	1 151
Ramsey	543	1 755 199	7.3	12.7	1.3	4.3	10.4	5.8	57.4	84.1	57.8	15.4	1 331	1 034
Ransom	223	692 010	8.7	4.1	0.8	4.5	6.6	5.2	68.5	23.4	12.3	7.8	1 436	1 220
Renville	140	452 741	8.2	6.0	0.0	8.7	3.5	2.3	70.0	19.2	9.5	5.9	2 288	2 255
Richland	582	2 019 868	4.8	9.7	0.0	6.5	9.5	7.4	61.0	75.6	33.2	29.0	1 787	1 613
Rolette	726	2 856 302	1.9	2.3	0.2	1.2	3.8	2.8	87.6	53.9	43.3	5.9	409	382
Sargent	167	536 100	9.7	3.9	0.0	3.3	5.4	6.8	70.4	21.4	9.5	8.1	2 073	2 002
Sheridan	59	160 666	12.8	0.0	0.0	8.5	0.2	3.7	73.9	5.6	2.2	2.9	2 255	2 229
Sioux	129	394 909	4.4	0.8	1.7	4.0	0.3	1.7	86.3	11.5	9.3	1.5	349	348
Slope	36	114 876	15.1	4.2	0.0	6.9	0.2	2.1	68.6	5.2	3.3	1.0	1 297	1 208
Stark	970	3 430 314	4.3	17.8	1.0	4.4	10.3	9.5	51.8	103.5	43.2	33.0	1 232	836
Steele	76	279 013	12.8	4.5	0.1	2.6	1.4	2.1	76.4	12.4	4.6	4.9	2 441	2 369
Stutsman	738	2 551 998	5.2	10.8	0.9	5.8	9.7	7.6	58.2	88.6	38.8	29.6	1 413	1 195
Towner	120	341 158	12.4	5.1	0.0	10.5	3.7	3.7	63.4	10.1	3.9	3.9	1 695	1 626
Traill	299	1 042 936	6.6	4.5	0.0	5.7	5.6	2.7	74.1	35.7	16.3	11.8	1 468	1 367
Walsh	425	1 396 845	7.5	5.6	0.0	5.1	6.2	9.3	63.8	46.8	22.8	16.0	1 451	1 295

1. Based on the resident population estimated as of July 1 of the year shown.

STATE County	Local government finances, 2012 (cont.)									Government employment, 2013			Presidential election,[2] 2012		
	Direct general expenditure							Debt outstanding					Percent of vote cast:		
			Percent of total for:												
	Total (mil dol)	Per capita[1] (dollars)	Education	Health and hospitals	Police protection	Public welfare	Highways	Total (mil dol)	Per capita[1] (dollars)	Federal civilian	Federal military	State and local	Democratic	Republican	All other
	185	186	187	188	189	190	191	192	193	194	195	196	197	198	199
NORTH CAROLINA—Cont'd															
Swain	40.3	2 852	47.4	5.4	7.2	14.3	0.2	10.7	758	199	35	2 284	48.4	50.0	1.6
Transylvania	80.6	2 453	45.7	4.8	9.9	7.4	1.1	13.0	395	132	80	1 374	43.0	55.6	1.4
Tyrrell	18.9	4 355	54.4	1.2	9.5	7.3	0.7	10.3	2 385	22	0	460	48.8	50.3	0.9
Union	614.4	2 946	53.1	2.0	6.1	4.7	1.0	748.0	3 587	238	528	10 206	36.2	62.9	0.9
Vance	164.7	3 650	56.0	9.8	6.5	7.1	0.6	48.5	1 074	85	110	2 753	63.1	36.4	0.5
Wake	3 282.9	3 448	42.3	4.0	6.5	3.3	2.2	9 085.4	9 542	5 131	2 945	76 422	56.7	42.3	1.0
Warren	54.2	2 635	50.1	5.1	10.5	10.6	0.3	7.2	348	31	49	1 344	69.5	30.0	0.5
Washington	43.9	3 443	43.6	0.4	7.2	13.8	1.5	7.6	594	27	31	1 011	58.1	41.4	0.6
Watauga	128.3	2 473	32.3	4.5	9.1	5.1	3.7	134.7	2 596	101	120	6 194	51.3	47.0	1.7
Wayne	344.7	2 774	55.1	4.8	6.3	6.3	1.4	151.3	1 217	1 241	4 818	8 264	45.4	54.0	0.5
Wilkes	183.3	2 645	60.4	4.2	5.5	7.8	0.6	49.6	715	180	171	4 290	30.1	68.3	1.7
Wilson	278.4	3 401	41.7	5.4	8.2	8.1	1.5	192.4	2 351	155	201	6 239	52.8	46.7	0.4
Yadkin	87.9	2 308	57.4	4.6	6.9	10.0	0.9	50.3	1 322	66	95	1 444	26.4	72.4	1.2
Yancey	44.5	2 522	51.4	2.5	6.4	10.3	0.6	14.3	810	30	44	853	46.2	51.9	1.9
NORTH DAKOTA	X	X	X	X	X	X	X	X	X	9 198	11 893	65 139	44.6	53.3	2.1
Adams	8.2	3 529	45.9	0.0	4.8	3.9	18.8	0.1	33	16	16	133	34.2	62.0	3.8
Barnes	64.0	5 811	34.3	4.3	8.8	3.5	21.8	18.2	1 650	75	73	1 052	48.1	49.6	2.2
Benson	27.4	4 053	65.7	0.2	1.4	3.3	17.2	0.6	85	160	47	1 374	66.1	32.6	1.3
Billings	17.0	18 828	14.4	6.5	9.0	0.0	56.2	0.1	133	53	0	125	22.8	75.2	2.0
Bottineau	32.3	4 914	41.2	2.2	4.2	0.0	32.5	11.5	1 748	79	45	619	39.4	58.6	2.0
Bowman	21.3	6 655	38.7	2.4	2.9	1.6	30.5	1.3	409	23	22	237	29.1	67.5	3.4
Burke	10.7	4 949	47.9	0.4	2.6	2.0	26.1	0.1	67	101	16	162	30.3	67.9	1.8
Burleigh	313.0	3 649	41.6	1.2	5.7	1.7	12.7	181.5	2 116	1 067	590	10 264	37.3	60.9	1.7
Cass	703.9	4 508	39.9	0.1	5.6	3.0	13.2	1 204.5	7 713	2 236	1 112	11 809	52.7	45.6	1.7
Cavalier	16.8	4 263	40.9	2.0	4.3	4.3	23.7	11.4	2 878	38	26	206	43.7	53.0	3.4
Dickey	36.5	6 935	38.3	1.4	3.0	1.6	13.3	34.3	6 520	23	34	297	39.8	58.2	1.9
Divide	23.6	10 577	21.6	1.5	4.6	0.7	33.8	0.9	389	32	15	157	41.0	55.7	3.3
Dunn	24.7	6 221	37.5	0.0	3.7	1.5	33.1	0.3	74	15	28	265	32.1	65.7	2.3
Eddy	13.4	5 660	43.4	0.1	4.4	2.5	14.8	1.6	686	22	16	159	50.0	47.0	2.9
Emmons	14.9	4 274	52.4	1.3	1.9	2.0	14.2	3.8	1 081	24	24	223	29.7	67.0	3.3
Foster	13.8	4 065	45.3	1.9	3.7	2.8	14.1	10.6	3 116	25	23	223	41.6	55.4	3.0
Golden Valley	12.7	7 062	41.7	1.5	3.3	2.2	17.1	4.6	2 568	10	12	178	24.0	73.4	2.6
Grand Forks	251.5	3 728	47.0	1.0	5.1	1.4	4.7	705.5	10 456	1 084	2 052	9 690	51.7	46.6	1.7
Grant	8.1	3 453	49.5	18.0	2.5	2.6	12.7	1.2	524	24	16	140	21.1	44.2	34.8
Griggs	13.1	5 527	43.9	3.5	2.8	2.9	21.9	3.7	1 562	18	16	187	45.5	51.9	2.6
Hettinger	16.2	6 357	49.8	0.0	2.6	2.3	14.4	1.9	738	21	17	185	30.1	66.2	3.6
Kidder	15.9	6 560	32.7	24.9	1.7	1.4	20.1	2.4	973	21	17	161	34.4	61.2	4.4
LaMoure	23.0	5 581	54.0	0.0	2.5	2.6	15.6	7.0	1 691	43	28	291	38.7	58.5	2.8
Logan	8.8	4 566	63.4	1.0	2.8	0.2	13.9	1.7	867	17	13	136	28.3	68.7	3.0
McHenry	20.8	3 592	61.0	0.0	2.3	2.7	13.3	1.0	180	51	40	365	40.6	56.9	2.5
McIntosh	10.1	3 663	56.1	1.5	2.9	2.7	15.9	1.7	619	18	18	176	37.8	59.8	2.4
McKenzie	61.8	7 738	29.9	3.0	3.5	1.3	31.4	15.2	1 897	45	63	1 485	34.4	64.1	1.5
McLean	38.0	4 086	53.6	1.4	4.7	3.8	12.0	18.4	1 973	119	65	711	39.4	58.4	2.2
Mercer	37.5	4 418	49.3	0.5	5.7	1.3	17.4	59.3	6 990	38	58	531	33.6	63.4	3.0
Morton	106.7	3 797	49.8	2.5	5.2	2.3	6.9	103.5	3 685	97	196	1 589	38.3	59.3	2.4
Mountrail	86.5	9 907	36.3	0.5	1.9	1.2	37.1	26.9	3 081	42	61	637	50.3	47.9	1.9
Nelson	16.3	5 277	44.9	2.6	2.2	1.3	18.7	14.3	4 644	26	21	222	51.8	45.7	2.6
Oliver	7.8	4 256	42.5	0.0	3.8	0.0	8.3	20.2	10 993	0	13	100	31.9	65.6	2.5
Pembina	37.7	5 190	45.2	0.5	3.9	2.4	8.5	14.9	2 043	242	74	537	45.2	52.1	2.8
Pierce	24.3	5 462	53.5	2.7	4.5	1.9	9.5	4.3	974	21	29	250	37.0	60.8	2.2
Ramsey	75.8	6 569	35.0	0.9	2.9	2.1	20.4	33.0	2 865	170	76	1 348	48.6	49.6	1.8
Ransom	25.2	4 634	45.6	1.6	2.9	1.7	12.3	21.6	3 965	39	37	487	56.4	41.0	2.6
Renville	20.6	8 041	40.3	0.1	2.1	0.0	28.2	3.6	1 387	19	18	199	37.5	59.4	3.1
Richland	75.3	4 645	43.3	4.4	4.5	1.9	13.1	88.9	5 482	68	111	1 874	46.4	51.6	2.0
Rolette	53.3	3 703	79.0	1.4	2.2	2.2	5.1	6.0	419	914	100	1 990	75.1	23.0	1.9
Sargent	19.0	4 886	48.6	1.5	1.7	2.4	13.8	11.5	2 940	40	27	248	57.9	40.4	1.8
Sheridan	5.5	4 306	39.7	1.2	1.7	1.0	20.2	0.2	179	12	0	94	28.5	69.1	2.4
Sioux	11.0	2 521	85.3	0.0	0.5	4.1	5.3	3.0	686	237	30	1 332	83.1	15.6	1.3
Slope	3.6	4 734	14.2	2.9	4.4	0.0	33.2	0.4	538	0	0	35	25.8	72.3	1.9
Stark	96.5	3 605	41.6	0.0	4.4	3.4	11.2	19.1	712	172	187	2 128	34.3	63.5	2.2
Steele	11.3	5 664	42.7	0.0	2.8	4.2	26.4	5.7	2 876	16	14	111	59.5	39.1	1.4
Stutsman	83.3	3 978	42.4	3.2	5.0	2.2	13.9	57.9	2 766	190	134	1 876	41.5	56.2	2.3
Towner	8.9	3 844	45.7	5.0	3.3	2.3	18.6	2.2	931	23	16	122	51.9	44.8	3.3
Traill	35.4	4 390	54.9	0.9	3.8	2.9	12.5	42.5	5 269	37	54	831	52.9	45.7	1.5
Walsh	51.9	4 703	54.4	1.3	4.4	2.5	9.7	23.8	2 156	61	74	1 112	47.6	49.5	2.9

1. Based on the resident population estimated as of July 1 of the year shown. 2.

STATE/ County code	CBSA code[1]	County type[2]	STATE County	Land area,[3] (sq km) 2010	Population, 2014: Total persons 2014	Population, 2014: Rank	Population, 2014: Per square kilometer	Race alone or in combination, not Hispanic or Latino (percent): White	Black	American Indian, Alaska Native	Asian and Pacific Islander	Percent Hispanic or Latino[4]	Age (percent): Under 5 years	5 to 17 years	18 to 24 years	25 to 34 years	35 to 44 years	45 to 54 years
				1	2	3	4	5	6	7	8	9	10	11	12	13	14	15
			NORTH DAKOTA—Cont'd															
38 101	33500	5	Ward	5 214	69 384	772	13.3	88.1	4.3	3.2	2.1	4.8	7.6	15.3	15.9	17.2	11.2	11.1
38 103	...	9	Wells	3 292	4 192	2 886	1.3	98.2	0.5	1.2	0.3	0.9	5.4	13.5	6.3	7.8	8.5	15.4
38 105	48780	7	Williams	5 380	32 130	1 382	6.0	90.0	1.5	5.6	1.1	4.4	7.6	17.0	10.7	17.5	11.8	13.2
39 000	...	X	OHIO	105 829	11 594 163	X	109.6	82.2	13.4	0.7	2.3	3.4	6.0	16.9	9.6	12.6	12.2	14.1
39 001	...	6	Adams	1 512	28 129	1 487	18.6	98.0	1.0	1.2	0.3	0.9	6.1	18.2	7.7	10.9	12.8	14.3
39 003	30620	3	Allen	1 042	105 040	564	100.8	84.1	14.0	0.6	1.2	2.7	6.1	17.3	10.8	11.8	11.5	13.4
39 005	11740	4	Ashland	1 095	53 035	940	48.4	97.1	1.3	0.5	0.9	1.1	5.8	17.3	10.5	11.1	11.3	13.4
39 007	11780	4	Ashtabula	1 818	99 175	594	54.6	92.0	4.7	0.8	0.7	3.7	5.8	17.0	8.1	11.1	12.1	14.8
39 009	11900	4	Athens	1 304	64 713	814	49.6	91.9	3.6	1.0	3.9	1.8	4.0	11.2	30.6	12.4	9.6	10.5
39 011	47540	4	Auglaize	1 040	45 841	1 051	44.1	97.4	0.9	0.5	0.8	1.4	6.3	18.2	7.8	10.9	11.8	14.6
39 013	48540	3	Belmont	1 378	69 461	770	50.4	94.5	4.8	0.6	0.6	0.8	5.0	14.1	8.3	12.2	12.0	14.2
39 015	17140	1	Brown	1 269	44 116	1 087	34.8	97.8	1.4	0.7	0.4	0.8	5.9	17.8	7.9	11.1	12.5	14.9
39 017	17140	1	Butler	1 210	374 158	181	309.2	85.1	8.8	0.6	3.2	4.3	6.3	18.1	12.0	11.9	12.4	14.1
39 019	15940	2	Carroll	1 022	28 187	1 484	27.6	97.7	1.1	0.8	0.4	1.1	4.9	16.9	7.3	9.9	11.7	15.2
39 021	46500	6	Champaign	1 110	39 128	1 194	35.3	95.5	3.3	1.0	0.7	1.4	5.8	17.9	8.7	10.9	12.4	14.9
39 023	44220	3	Clark	1 029	136 554	462	132.7	87.2	10.5	0.9	1.1	3.0	5.9	17.1	8.5	11.4	11.6	13.9
39 025	17140	1	Clermont	1 171	201 560	320	172.1	95.6	1.9	0.6	1.5	1.7	6.1	18.4	8.0	12.1	13.0	15.2
39 027	48940	6	Clinton	1 058	41 835	1 131	39.5	95.3	3.4	0.8	0.8	1.6	6.4	17.8	9.3	11.7	12.0	14.3
39 029	41400	4	Columbiana	1 378	105 686	562	76.7	95.7	3.0	0.6	0.6	1.4	5.3	15.6	7.7	11.1	12.5	14.8
39 031	18740	6	Coshocton	1 461	36 516	1 264	25.0	97.4	1.8	0.6	0.5	0.9	6.1	17.4	7.8	11.3	11.6	14.0
39 033	15340	4	Crawford	1 041	42 480	1 119	40.8	97.0	1.6	0.5	0.6	1.4	5.5	16.8	7.8	10.6	12.1	14.0
39 035	17460	1	Cuyahoga	1 184	1 259 828	30	1 064.0	62.1	30.6	0.6	3.4	5.2	5.8	16.0	9.1	12.9	11.8	14.3
39 037	24820	6	Darke	1 549	52 196	953	33.7	97.5	1.1	0.5	0.5	1.4	6.2	18.4	7.5	10.4	11.7	14.2
39 039	19580	4	Defiance	1 066	38 510	1 207	36.1	88.0	2.4	0.6	0.6	9.6	6.0	17.9	9.1	11.5	11.9	13.2
39 041	18140	1	Delaware	1 148	189 113	341	164.7	89.0	4.2	0.5	5.7	2.3	6.3	21.6	7.2	10.3	16.1	15.5
39 043	41780	3	Erie	652	75 828	725	116.3	86.8	10.2	0.8	0.9	3.8	5.2	15.9	8.0	10.8	11.2	14.6
39 045	18140	1	Fairfield	1 306	150 381	426	115.1	89.8	7.6	0.8	1.8	1.9	5.7	19.1	8.4	11.7	13.5	14.9
39 047	47920	6	Fayette	1 052	28 800	1 464	27.4	95.0	3.3	0.7	1.0	1.8	6.3	17.6	8.1	11.5	12.7	14.0
39 049	18140	1	Franklin	1 378	1 231 393	33	893.6	68.8	23.2	0.9	5.0	5.0	7.2	16.5	10.7	17.4	13.4	13.0
39 051	45780	2	Fulton	1 050	42 580	1 116	40.6	90.7	0.9	0.5	0.6	8.2	6.1	18.4	8.1	10.8	11.9	14.6
39 053	38580	6	Gallia	1 208	30 397	1 419	25.2	95.4	3.4	1.0	0.7	1.2	6.1	17.0	8.7	11.6	11.9	13.9
39 055	17460	1	Geauga	1 036	94 295	620	91.0	96.6	1.7	0.4	1.0	1.3	5.0	19.5	7.9	7.9	10.9	15.9
39 057	19380	2	Greene	1 072	163 820	389	152.8	86.8	8.4	0.9	3.9	2.6	5.5	15.4	13.1	13.0	10.9	13.6
39 059	15740	6	Guernsey	1 353	39 590	1 183	29.3	96.8	2.6	0.8	0.6	1.0	5.9	17.0	8.1	11.2	11.8	14.3
39 061	17140	1	Hamilton	1 051	806 631	74	767.5	68.8	27.1	0.6	2.8	2.8	6.6	16.7	9.9	14.3	11.7	13.8
39 063	22300	4	Hancock	1 376	75 337	730	54.8	91.4	2.4	0.5	2.1	5.0	6.0	16.7	10.0	12.8	11.8	14.0
39 065	...	6	Hardin	1 218	31 796	1 390	26.1	96.7	1.6	0.6	1.0	1.5	5.8	17.2	16.1	10.2	11.6	12.4
39 067	...	6	Harrison	1 042	15 543	2 070	14.9	96.7	3.1	0.6	0.5	0.8	5.1	15.8	7.3	10.0	11.1	14.8
39 069	...	6	Henry	1 077	27 937	1 496	25.9	91.4	0.9	0.6	0.6	7.3	6.0	18.0	8.0	11.1	11.8	14.0
39 071	...	6	Highland	1 432	43 045	1 110	30.1	97.1	2.3	0.8	0.5	0.8	6.2	18.5	7.8	11.3	12.5	13.8
39 073	18140	6	Hocking	1 091	28 725	1 467	26.3	98.0	1.1	0.9	0.4	0.8	5.6	17.7	7.7	10.7	12.6	14.6
39 075	...	7	Holmes	1 094	43 898	1 092	40.1	98.4	0.6	0.3	0.3	0.9	9.2	24.4	9.9	11.9	11.0	11.2
39 077	35940	4	Huron	1 273	58 714	879	46.1	92.4	1.8	0.7	0.6	5.9	6.2	18.9	8.4	11.3	12.4	14.3
39 079	27160	7	Jackson	1 089	32 748	1 364	30.1	97.5	1.2	1.1	0.5	1.0	6.1	17.9	8.0	12.2	12.8	13.6
39 081	48260	3	Jefferson	1 058	67 694	787	64.0	92.6	6.6	0.6	0.7	1.3	4.8	14.8	9.8	10.2	11.3	14.1
39 083	34540	4	Knox	1 361	61 167	856	44.9	96.7	1.5	0.6	1.1	1.4	5.9	17.3	11.8	10.8	11.3	13.5
39 085	17460	1	Lake	589	229 230	283	389.2	91.2	4.4	0.4	1.6	3.8	5.1	16.2	7.8	11.4	12.0	15.2
39 087	26580	2	Lawrence	1 174	61 623	849	52.5	96.3	3.0	0.7	0.6	0.8	5.6	17.1	8.1	11.7	12.9	14.3
39 089	18140	1	Licking	1 768	169 390	376	95.8	93.6	4.7	0.8	1.2	1.6	6.1	17.8	9.1	11.3	12.7	14.9
39 091	13340	4	Logan	1 187	45 507	1 060	38.3	95.8	3.0	0.7	1.1	1.4	6.1	18.2	7.7	11.0	12.1	14.5
39 093	17460	1	Lorain	1 272	304 216	220	239.2	81.8	9.4	0.8	1.5	8.9	5.7	17.3	8.8	10.9	12.6	14.8
39 095	45780	2	Lucas	883	435 286	160	493.0	72.5	20.6	0.8	2.1	6.5	6.3	16.9	10.4	13.2	12.0	13.6
39 097	18140	1	Madison	1 207	43 918	1 091	36.4	91.0	7.2	0.7	1.0	1.6	5.3	16.1	8.5	13.2	14.7	15.7
39 099	49660	2	Mahoning	1 066	233 204	280	218.8	78.6	16.2	0.7	1.1	5.1	5.1	15.6	8.7	11.0	11.5	13.9
39 101	32020	4	Marion	1 046	65 720	802	62.8	90.6	7.2	0.6	0.8	2.3	5.8	15.4	8.9	12.7	12.9	15.0
39 103	17460	1	Medina	1 091	176 029	361	161.3	95.5	1.8	0.5	1.5	1.9	5.4	18.6	7.5	10.5	13.3	16.0
39 105	...	6	Meigs	1 114	23 331	1 671	20.9	98.1	1.4	0.7	0.4	0.5	5.6	16.7	7.3	11.6	12.3	14.4
39 107	16380	7	Mercer	1 198	40 831	1 158	34.1	97.1	0.8	0.5	0.9	1.7	6.7	18.9	8.2	11.1	11.0	13.6
39 109	19380	2	Miami	1 053	103 900	569	98.7	94.8	3.3	0.6	1.6	1.5	5.8	17.5	7.8	11.4	12.4	14.4
39 111	...	8	Monroe	1 180	14 465	2 136	12.3	98.6	1.0	0.8	0.3	0.5	5.2	15.7	6.9	10.2	11.3	14.3
39 113	19380	2	Montgomery	1 195	533 116	123	446.1	74.4	22.2	0.8	2.6	2.5	6.1	16.3	9.9	13.0	11.6	13.7
39 115	...	6	Morgan	1 079	14 843	2 113	13.8	95.6	4.8	1.5	0.7	0.8	5.1	17.0	7.8	10.5	11.3	14.8
39 117	18140	1	Morrow	1 052	35 152	1 296	33.4	97.6	1.1	0.7	0.6	1.3	6.0	18.7	7.6	10.5	13.0	14.8
39 119	49780	4	Muskingum	1 721	85 818	665	49.9	94.6	5.7	0.9	0.7	0.9	6.1	17.4	8.6	11.6	12.0	14.1
39 121	...	6	Noble	1 031	14 363	2 141	13.9	96.2	3.1	0.7	0.4	0.4	5.2	13.4	6.3	9.3	8.9	13.9

1. CBSA = Core Based Statistical Area. See Appendix A for explanation. See Appendix B for list of metropolitan areas with component counties. 2. County type code from the Economic Research Service of USDA Rural-Urban Continuum Codes. See Appendix A for definition. 3. Dry land or land partially or temporarily covered by water. 4. May be of any race.

STATE County	Population, 2013 (cont.): Age (percent) (cont.): 55 to 64 years	65 to 74 years	75 years and over	Percent female	Population change and components of change, 2000–2014: Total persons: 2000	2010	Percent change: 2000–2010	2010–2014	Components of change, 2010–2014: Births	Deaths	Net migration	Households, 2009–2013: Number	Persons per house-hold	Percent: Family house-holds	Female family house-holder[1]	One per-son
	16	17	18	19	20	21	22	23	24	25	26	27	28	29	30	31
NORTH DAKOTA—Cont'd																
Ward	10.0	5.8	5.8	47.3	58 795	61 675	4.9	12.5	4 780	2 062	4 948	25 173	2.44	62.9	9.0	28.7
Wells	15.6	12.5	15.0	50.3	5 102	4 207	-17.5	-0.4	164	299	131	1 949	2.10	67.2	6.6	31.8
Williams	11.9	5.0	5.2	46.1	19 761	22 398	13.3	43.5	2 023	930	8 521	10 411	2.34	62.3	7.0	28.8
OHIO	13.4	8.3	6.8	51.1	11 353 140	11 536 504	1.6	0.5	586 295	471 142	-50 959	4 557 655	2.47	64.7	12.9	29.6
Adams	13.9	9.4	6.7	50.8	27 330	28 550	4.5	-1.5	1 479	1 377	-507	10 816	2.59	71.5	12.4	24.7
Allen	13.5	8.3	7.3	49.7	108 473	106 331	-2.0	-1.2	5 438	4 524	-2 185	40 552	2.51	66.9	14.9	28.4
Ashland	13.6	9.3	7.6	51.0	52 523	53 139	1.2	-0.2	2 605	2 286	-424	20 207	2.52	70.7	8.6	24.3
Ashtabula	14.4	9.5	7.4	49.8	102 728	101 497	-1.2	-2.3	4 727	4 809	-2 163	38 952	2.50	65.9	12.1	28.1
Athens	10.6	6.5	4.5	50.2	62 223	64 757	4.1	-0.1	2 400	2 082	-391	22 181	2.49	55.0	9.5	30.8
Auglaize	13.9	8.4	8.0	50.4	46 611	45 949	-1.4	-0.2	2 244	2 017	-419	18 241	2.49	69.6	8.0	26.5
Belmont	15.6	9.7	8.8	49.2	70 226	70 400	0.2	-1.3	2 900	3 801	78	28 329	2.33	64.8	9.7	31.1
Brown	13.8	9.4	6.8	50.5	42 285	44 846	6.1	-1.6	2 183	1 937	-964	16 380	2.69	72.9	11.7	23.2
Butler	12.5	7.3	5.5	51.0	332 807	368 130	10.6	1.6	19 493	12 822	-684	134 612	2.66	70.3	12.4	23.8
Carroll	15.4	11.0	7.7	50.0	28 836	28 836	0.0	-2.3	1 146	1 202	-558	11 107	2.54	70.7	7.5	24.0
Champaign	13.4	9.4	6.5	50.3	38 890	40 097	3.1	-2.4	1 798	1 601	-1 175	15 014	2.60	72.3	10.5	23.5
Clark	14.1	9.7	7.8	51.4	144 742	138 333	-4.4	-1.3	6 796	6 974	-1 543	54 963	2.45	65.2	14.0	28.8
Clermont	13.7	8.2	5.3	50.8	177 977	197 363	10.9	2.1	10 062	6 645	776	73 728	2.67	71.9	10.3	23.3
Clinton	13.7	8.5	6.3	50.7	40 543	42 040	3.7	-0.5	2 119	1 825	-488	15 969	2.56	71.0	10.8	24.6
Columbiana	15.2	9.9	7.9	49.6	112 075	107 841	-3.8	-2.0	4 640	4 924	-1 756	42 095	2.45	67.8	10.7	26.7
Coshocton	14.4	9.7	7.8	50.4	36 655	36 901	0.7	-1.0	1 836	1 612	-595	14 495	2.51	70.0	11.3	26.1
Crawford	14.2	10.2	8.8	51.5	46 966	43 784	-6.8	-3.0	2 023	2 067	-1 180	17 655	2.42	67.1	10.4	28.6
Cuyahoga	13.9	8.3	7.9	52.4	1 393 978	1 280 122	-8.2	-1.6	63 260	57 530	-24 649	534 476	2.33	58.0	16.2	36.6
Darke	13.4	9.9	8.3	50.8	53 309	52 959	-0.7	-1.4	2 550	2 372	-967	20 776	2.50	68.1	8.8	28.0
Defiance	14.1	9.1	7.3	50.6	39 500	39 037	-1.2	-1.3	1 899	1 659	-781	15 203	2.51	71.7	11.5	23.7
Delaware	11.8	6.8	4.3	50.5	109 989	174 214	58.4	8.6	8 955	4 025	9 688	64 208	2.73	76.5	7.8	19.5
Erie	15.3	10.6	8.4	51.2	79 551	77 079	-3.1	-1.6	3 314	3 784	-734	31 972	2.35	65.7	11.9	29.4
Fairfield	12.7	8.2	5.8	50.2	122 759	146 156	19.1	2.9	7 006	4 912	1 966	54 309	2.66	72.2	11.2	22.7
Fayette	13.6	9.3	6.9	50.8	28 433	29 030	2.1	-0.8	1 574	1 411	-403	11 514	2.46	66.2	13.4	28.2
Franklin	11.2	6.1	4.5	51.3	1 068 978	1 163 414	8.8	5.8	77 487	37 635	28 855	468 295	2.47	58.3	14.1	32.7
Fulton	14.5	8.5	7.0	50.8	42 084	42 698	1.5	-0.3	2 036	1 687	-580	16 285	2.59	74.0	8.1	23.5
Gallia	14.0	9.7	7.2	50.7	31 069	30 934	-0.4	-1.7	1 558	1 491	-597	11 576	2.59	71.3	10.7	24.9
Geauga	15.4	10.0	7.5	50.7	90 895	93 389	2.7	0.9	3 981	3 218	100	34 621	2.68	74.4	8.3	21.7
Greene	13.4	8.4	6.7	50.9	147 886	161 573	9.3	1.4	7 489	5 585	339	62 836	2.44	66.6	11.0	27.6
Guernsey	14.5	9.8	7.5	50.8	40 792	40 087	-1.7	-1.2	1 937	1 833	-528	15 690	2.51	68.4	11.8	26.8
Hamilton	13.0	7.4	6.6	51.8	845 303	802 374	-5.1	0.5	46 746	32 377	-8 966	327 914	2.39	59.5	15.2	34.1
Hancock	13.2	8.5	7.0	51.0	71 295	74 782	4.9	0.7	3 784	2 887	-341	30 610	2.40	65.7	10.8	29.3
Hardin	12.2	8.2	6.4	50.5	31 945	32 058	0.4	-0.8	1 609	1 317	-560	11 504	2.57	67.4	11.5	28.3
Harrison	16.5	10.9	8.5	50.6	15 856	15 864	0.1	-2.0	661	868	-103	6 395	2.43	68.8	9.4	26.5
Henry	14.0	8.7	8.3	50.4	29 210	28 215	-3.4	-1.0	1 444	1 128	-713	11 006	2.51	69.6	9.1	25.1
Highland	13.3	9.5	7.1	51.0	40 875	43 589	6.6	-1.2	2 195	1 981	-753	16 918	2.54	69.1	12.3	26.4
Hocking	14.4	10.0	6.7	50.5	28 241	29 380	4.0	-2.2	1 334	1 238	-570	11 478	2.49	69.4	11.1	26.6
Holmes	10.2	6.6	5.6	50.1	38 943	42 366	8.8	3.6	3 443	1 243	-660	12 467	3.37	79.8	6.2	17.9
Huron	13.5	8.6	6.4	50.7	59 487	59 626	0.2	-1.5	3 047	2 374	-1 563	22 361	2.62	70.6	11.0	23.6
Jackson	14.0	8.9	6.4	50.9	32 641	33 225	1.8	-1.4	1 737	1 643	-560	13 288	2.46	66.8	14.2	28.4
Jefferson	15.8	10.3	8.8	51.7	73 894	69 709	-5.7	-2.9	2 707	4 078	-508	28 326	2.35	65.9	11.9	29.8
Knox	13.4	9.0	7.0	50.9	54 500	60 921	11.8	0.4	3 140	2 599	-319	22 583	2.54	69.5	8.9	25.4
Lake	14.8	9.6	7.8	51.1	227 511	230 041	1.1	-0.4	9 543	9 891	-326	94 048	2.41	65.3	10.8	29.4
Lawrence	13.6	9.7	7.0	51.2	62 319	62 450	0.2	-1.3	3 006	2 972	-794	24 009	2.57	68.6	14.2	27.2
Licking	13.3	8.8	6.0	51.1	145 491	166 492	14.4	1.7	8 287	6 278	914	64 009	2.55	70.4	10.5	24.5
Logan	14.2	9.2	7.0	50.8	46 005	45 858	-0.3	-0.8	2 294	2 020	-618	18 143	2.49	69.3	11.9	25.0
Lorain	14.0	8.9	6.9	50.7	284 664	301 356	5.9	0.9	14 336	12 007	443	116 705	2.50	68.8	13.8	26.5
Lucas	13.3	7.8	6.4	51.5	455 054	441 815	-2.9	-1.5	24 267	18 335	-12 196	178 101	2.41	60.6	15.9	32.8
Madison	12.8	7.9	5.8	45.8	40 213	43 435	8.0	1.1	1 827	1 631	316	14 611	2.59	70.0	9.4	25.7
Mahoning	15.3	9.5	9.3	51.4	257 555	238 823	-7.3	-2.4	10 062	12 821	-2 449	98 201	2.34	62.8	14.9	32.8
Marion	13.9	8.6	6.9	46.9	66 217	66 501	0.4	-1.2	3 321	2 897	-1 118	24 578	2.44	68.7	11.7	26.5
Medina	13.8	8.8	6.1	50.6	151 095	172 332	14.1	2.1	7 384	5 800	2 018	65 499	2.62	73.8	8.8	21.4
Meigs	14.9	9.7	7.4	50.9	23 072	23 770	3.0	-1.9	1 043	1 088	-382	9 560	2.45	68.8	11.5	26.0
Mercer	14.0	8.5	8.0	49.9	40 924	40 814	-0.3	0.0	2 197	1 671	-531	15 851	2.55	72.2	7.8	23.9
Miami	13.9	9.7	7.2	50.8	98 868	102 506	3.7	1.4	4 772	4 150	793	41 239	2.47	68.1	10.6	26.4
Monroe	15.3	12.2	8.9	49.8	15 180	14 642	-3.5	-1.2	664	750	-141	6 111	2.37	69.7	8.3	26.1
Montgomery	13.2	8.7	7.6	51.9	559 062	535 153	-4.3	-0.4	28 422	23 901	-5 805	222 578	2.32	60.6	15.3	34.0
Morgan	14.7	10.4	8.4	50.3	14 897	15 054	1.1	-1.4	637	658	-167	6 204	2.39	71.8	10.8	24.3
Morrow	14.2	9.0	6.3	50.0	31 628	34 827	10.1	0.9	1 684	1 295	-93	12 940	2.67	75.4	9.1	20.0
Muskingum	13.7	8.9	7.5	51.5	84 585	86 074	1.8	-0.3	4 334	3 941	-528	33 976	2.47	67.6	14.0	26.5
Noble	19.9	14.5	8.6	41.7	14 058	14 645	4.2	-1.9	563	506	-350	4 883	2.47	70.4	10.0	28.1

1. No spouse present.

STATE County	Persons in group quarters, 2014	Daytime population, 2009–2013		Births, 2014		Deaths, 2014		Persons under 65 with no health insurance, 2013		Medicare, 2014			Serious crimes known to police,[2] 2013	
													Total	
		Number	Employment/ residence ratio	Total	Rate[1]	Number	Rate[1]	Number	Percent	Eligible for Medicare	Enrolled in Medicare Advantage	Enrolled in a Medicare prescription drug plan	Number	Rate[3]
	32	33	34	35	36	37	38	39	40	41	42	43	44	45
NORTH DAKOTA—Cont'd														
Ward	3 354	66 392	1.07	1 209	17.4	496	7.1	7 037	12.3	8 910	1 073	5 826	1 341	1 998
Wells	103	4 297	1.04	41	9.8	46	11.0	389	12.9	1 194	37	921	40	912
Williams	554	30 942	1.43	610	19.0	207	6.4	2 719	10.3	3 333	13	2 295	1 533	5 315
OHIO	311 030	11 558 632	1.00	137 999	11.9	111 233	9.6	1 246 964	13.0	2 123 783	824 953	1 057 777	371 852	3 214
Adams	338	25 759	0.73	336	11.9	320	11.4	3 535	15.1	6 030	1 815	3 740	381	1 345
Allen	6 082	112 788	1.15	1 288	12.3	1 063	10.1	10 741	12.8	20 515	5 394	13 280	3 897	3 711
Ashland	2 126	50 390	0.88	612	11.5	549	10.4	5 760	13.7	10 387	3 967	5 396	908	1 717
Ashtabula	3 458	93 930	0.83	1 091	11.0	1 092	11.0	11 738	14.6	21 514	5 484	12 724	NA	NA
Athens	9 105	65 431	1.02	582	9.0	466	7.2	7 810	16.1	9 465	3 286	6 493	1 507	2 345
Auglaize	525	43 113	0.87	513	11.2	479	10.4	3 807	10.0	8 439	2 114	5 735	NA	NA
Belmont	3 874	64 022	0.79	693	10.0	835	12.0	7 191	13.4	15 405	7 245	7 138	732	1 070
Brown	575	36 252	0.53	510	11.6	465	10.5	5 280	14.3	9 003	3 514	4 687	279	659
Butler	11 203	348 748	0.88	4 572	12.2	3 186	8.5	38 543	12.3	59 883	24 094	28 810	15 054	4 184
Carroll	405	23 411	0.56	264	9.4	281	10.0	3 413	15.0	5 968	2 692	2 504	335	1 172
Champaign	793	34 280	0.67	423	10.8	376	9.6	3 892	12.0	7 472	3 166	4 540	827	2 094
Clark	2 829	128 210	0.83	1 567	11.5	1 631	11.9	15 102	13.6	28 802	13 585	14 141	6 465	4 724
Clermont	1 717	161 834	0.61	2 357	11.7	1 574	7.8	18 194	10.6	33 862	14 504	14 901	5 494	2 764
Clinton	1 073	42 765	1.04	495	11.8	427	10.2	4 520	13.0	7 968	2 807	4 352	870	2 073
Columbiana	3 943	93 832	0.70	1 095	10.4	1 140	10.8	12 653	15.1	22 963	8 344	11 132	834	834
Coshocton	428	34 405	0.84	426	11.7	369	10.1	4 814	16.0	7 709	2 114	4 733	689	1 871
Crawford	579	40 393	0.83	469	11.0	460	10.8	4 638	13.5	10 034	2 826	6 211	1 618	3 795
Cuyahoga	29 620	1 408 424	1.24	14 801	11.7	13 316	10.6	138 430	13.3	241 155	94 709	114 718	41 193	3 755
Darke	606	48 891	0.83	594	11.4	579	11.1	5 741	13.5	11 017	3 067	5 811	1 013	2 077
Defiance	756	37 767	0.93	430	11.2	396	10.3	4 043	12.8	7 920	1 759	5 683	677	1 752
Delaware	2 350	161 790	0.82	2 119	11.2	1 019	5.4	11 898	7.4	24 313	10 170	12 566	2 780	1 555
Erie	1 677	77 511	1.03	783	10.3	870	11.5	7 893	13.0	17 255	3 974	11 627	1 793	2 358
Fairfield	3 413	122 631	0.64	1 647	11.0	1 233	8.2	13 435	10.8	25 603	12 042	11 312	3 701	2 870
Fayette	593	29 201	1.02	377	13.1	300	10.4	3 306	13.8	5 831	2 436	3 122	1 344	4 652
Franklin	27 326	1 295 394	1.20	18 595	15.1	9 197	7.5	155 985	14.7	162 162	71 141	79 260	55 759	4 616
Fulton	391	40 342	0.89	457	10.7	411	9.7	4 291	12.1	8 081	2 501	5 012	554	1 449
Gallia	933	31 886	1.09	364	12.0	345	11.3	3 493	14.1	6 476	1 714	4 214	933	3 054
Geauga	864	83 467	0.77	956	10.1	757	8.0	10 271	13.4	18 136	6 408	9 118	708	846
Greene	8 757	166 882	1.06	1 757	10.7	1 350	8.2	14 594	11.2	28 054	10 707	10 255	4 528	2 785
Guernsey	510	39 182	0.95	455	11.5	443	11.2	4 599	14.1	8 760	2 668	5 135	643	1 633
Hamilton	20 407	922 240	1.32	11 009	13.6	7 718	9.6	89 594	13.2	136 461	52 628	59 254	35 463	4 576
Hancock	1 560	83 779	1.24	903	12.0	654	8.7	7 347	11.8	13 580	3 700	8 553	1 742	2 435
Hardin	2 151	28 820	0.76	373	11.7	319	10.0	3 343	13.4	5 712	1 424	3 673	730	2 314
Harrison	232	13 537	0.65	161	10.4	205	13.2	1 750	14.0	3 475	1 279	2 014	104	668
Henry	346	25 588	0.80	346	12.4	239	8.6	2 762	12.0	5 554	1 352	3 902	578	2 157
Highland	484	38 997	0.73	502	11.7	462	10.7	5 441	15.1	8 839	2 764	5 024	966	2 265
Hocking	312	24 733	0.63	308	10.7	290	10.1	3 324	14.0	5 995	1 721	3 598	406	1 386
Holmes	765	44 635	1.10	822	18.7	316	7.2	9 151	24.2	4 574	1 819	2 075	346	804
Huron	578	55 900	0.87	706	12.0	541	9.2	7 192	14.5	11 235	2 461	7 361	NA	NA
Jackson	325	31 667	0.89	409	12.5	352	10.7	3 788	13.7	6 937	1 722	4 462	744	2 260
Jefferson	2 361	65 144	0.87	650	9.6	939	13.9	6 827	12.9	16 156	5 649	8 539	NA	NA
Knox	3 562	56 373	0.83	763	12.5	600	9.8	6 799	14.1	11 668	3 842	6 775	1 647	2 712
Lake	2 772	209 305	0.82	2 204	9.6	2 366	10.3	21 569	11.5	47 183	18 076	22 303	3 507	1 726
Lawrence	669	51 779	0.55	702	11.4	693	11.2	6 871	13.4	13 971	2 959	8 083	1 181	1 930
Licking	3 417	148 393	0.76	1 948	11.5	1 505	8.9	16 573	11.8	30 829	12 675	13 743	5 140	3 189
Logan	450	44 769	0.95	536	11.8	496	10.9	5 113	13.5	8 959	2 545	5 656	1 132	2 616
Lorain	8 763	271 916	0.78	3 340	11.0	2 794	9.2	30 008	12.2	58 358	19 238	32 566	NA	NA
Lucas	10 133	458 461	1.10	5 742	13.2	4 365	10.0	52 552	14.3	78 310	30 253	42 252	13 520	3 268
Madison	5 103	40 707	0.86	441	10.0	370	8.4	3 964	12.2	7 101	3 609	3 544	999	2 341
Mahoning	7 883	237 781	1.01	2 369	10.2	2 957	12.7	23 341	12.6	52 384	24 820	23 865	8 181	3 505
Marion	6 109	66 317	1.00	769	11.7	688	10.5	6 900	13.8	13 207	4 401	7 316	3 353	5 057
Medina	1 198	146 410	0.68	1 732	9.8	1 352	7.7	14 487	9.9	30 825	12 377	14 520	1 746	1 005
Meigs	212	19 375	0.49	239	10.2	258	11.1	2 892	14.9	5 114	1 288	3 356	323	1 433
Mercer	439	38 392	0.88	516	12.6	377	9.2	3 891	11.6	7 745	2 112	5 113	624	1 522
Miami	1 055	97 620	0.89	1 106	10.6	966	9.3	10 222	12.0	20 639	7 663	9 864	2 710	2 743
Monroe	165	13 964	0.88	161	11.1	199	13.8	1 564	13.7	3 641	1 635	1 815	70	573
Montgomery	14 820	557 363	1.09	6 708	12.6	5 632	10.6	60 645	13.9	103 894	47 579	40 156	21 056	4 005
Morgan	188	12 630	0.58	153	10.3	141	9.5	1 836	15.2	3 133	1 085	1 868	73	490
Morrow	366	27 175	0.49	385	11.0	302	8.6	4 008	13.6	6 326	2 156	3 529	532	1 518
Muskingum	1 743	85 283	0.98	973	11.3	925	10.8	9 489	13.4	18 503	5 513	10 801	2 968	3 449
Noble	2 734	13 714	0.77	112	7.8	126	8.8	1 319	13.7	2 414	851	1 514	NA	NA

1. Per 1,000 estimated resident population. 2. Data for serious crimes have not been adjusted for underreporting; this may affect comparability between geographic areas and over time.
3. Per 100,000 population estimated by the FBI.

Table B. States and Counties — **Crime, Education, Money Income, and Poverty**

STATE County	Serious crimes known to police, 2013 (cont.)[1] Rate[2] Violent	Serious crimes Rate[2] Property	Education: School enrollment and attainment, 2009–2013 Enrollment[3] Total	Enrollment[3] Percent private	Attainment[4] (percent) High school graduate or less	Attainment[4] (percent) Bachelor's degree or more	Local government expenditures,[5] 2012–2013 Total current spending (mil dol)	Current spending per student (dollars)	Money income, 2009–2013 Per capita income[6] (dollars)	Households Median income (dollars)	Households Mean income (dollars)	Households Percent with income of $200,000 or more	Income and poverty, 2013 Median household income (dollars)	Percent below poverty level All persons	Children under 18 years	Children 5 to 17 years in families
	46	47	48	49	50	51	52	53	54	55	56	57	58	59	60	61
NORTH DAKOTA—Cont'd																
Ward	218	1 781	15 300	9.2	35.5	25.9	106.3	11 118	28 557	56 580	70 301	3.0	56 192	8.9	9.9	9.5
Wells	23	889	676	9.8	48.8	19.3	7.4	13 286	29 301	44 132	61 156	3.4	54 251	10.3	11.5	10.6
Williams	444	4 871	5 144	10.7	40.4	19.9	51.1	12 417	38 738	76 210	93 329	7.0	84 237	7.8	9.0	8.2
OHIO	286	2 927	3 038 471	18.1	46.2	25.2	19 171.9	11 197	26 046	48 308	64 449	3.0	48 138	15.9	22.7	20.8
Adams	56	1 288	6 443	8.4	67.4	10.6	45.4	9 301	18 235	35 678	45 859	0.4	37 259	24.1	35.2	32.6
Allen	379	3 332	29 270	18.8	51.5	17.2	161.7	11 172	22 295	42 823	56 189	1.8	43 274	16.1	22.9	21.1
Ashland	44	1 674	13 999	31.7	56.3	19.3	91.7	10 664	21 940	46 548	57 197	1.4	48 196	12.9	19.8	18.0
Ashtabula	NA	NA	23 859	12.6	60.0	12.6	153.9	10 704	20 011	40 516	50 023	0.7	40 899	18.9	29.2	26.0
Athens	87	2 258	28 922	3.5	43.8	28.2	99.1	13 355	17 019	33 823	46 791	1.4	35 783	31.0	29.5	28.1
Auglaize	NA	NA	11 190	10.6	52.4	17.1	79.9	10 137	25 323	52 239	63 293	1.5	54 010	9.7	13.7	12.5
Belmont	64	1 005	14 760	12.2	56.0	14.4	82.0	9 585	22 380	41 534	53 195	1.5	39 264	16.8	25.2	23.9
Brown	12	647	10 412	7.9	65.7	11.0	74.1	10 296	21 206	44 341	55 432	1.9	43 050	17.8	25.7	21.7
Butler	388	3 797	105 793	13.6	45.2	27.4	617.7	10 950	26 813	56 610	71 993	3.3	55 992	13.3	17.4	15.1
Carroll	178	994	6 255	11.9	64.0	11.0	31.5	9 317	21 783	43 779	54 849	1.0	44 622	15.5	23.5	21.0
Champaign	109	1 985	10 057	18.7	57.0	17.0	75.7	10 456	23 358	49 157	60 528	1.9	48 516	12.0	18.5	16.8
Clark	348	4 376	34 993	18.8	51.1	17.6	217.1	10 699	22 780	43 136	56 049	1.3	44 029	18.2	28.3	26.8
Clermont	95	2 670	50 005	18.8	47.1	25.6	266.2	9 836	28 761	60 365	75 825	3.9	61 398	9.7	14.1	13.4
Clinton	76	1 997	11 097	15.8	56.4	14.5	70.6	8 699	22 026	46 048	56 558	1.5	46 541	17.3	25.3	24.0
Columbiana	55	779	23 655	11.8	60.7	12.6	156.2	10 881	21 575	42 300	53 654	1.4	41 996	17.8	27.4	25.3
Coshocton	76	1 795	7 974	14.9	63.2	12.3	52.5	10 680	20 526	41 274	51 136	0.8	39 496	14.4	24.8	22.8
Crawford	129	3 666	9 918	15.7	59.5	11.8	67.3	10 051	21 478	40 783	51 782	1.0	38 421	18.2	27.1	24.6
Cuyahoga	613	3 142	328 878	25.9	41.1	29.7	2 288.5	14 915	27 423	43 804	63 539	3.6	43 653	19.2	28.1	26.4
Darke	96	1 980	12 456	11.4	61.6	11.9	82.2	9 613	22 511	43 425	56 065	1.6	43 465	14.6	21.2	20.6
Defiance	93	1 659	9 865	17.7	55.0	16.5	59.0	9 263	22 739	47 593	57 654	1.3	48 971	11.4	17.3	15.7
Delaware	72	1 483	52 381	22.6	24.6	50.5	282.3	10 095	40 189	89 757	110 852	11.0	89 016	5.6	6.4	5.9
Erie	125	2 233	17 788	14.9	50.3	21.0	173.3	14 711	26 135	46 498	61 916	2.4	46 495	15.0	22.7	21.3
Fairfield	181	2 689	40 173	16.6	43.3	26.0	235.3	9 689	27 031	58 786	71 763	2.8	56 697	11.8	15.3	13.6
Fayette	163	4 489	6 474	9.9	62.0	13.7	42.2	9 039	20 603	37 619	50 683	1.8	40 031	17.9	28.2	24.8
Franklin	407	4 208	332 926	16.9	36.0	36.4	2 255.2	13 463	28 283	50 877	69 197	4.0	51 456	17.7	25.4	24.5
Fulton	76	1 373	11 227	13.7	52.3	16.3	113.9	14 887	24 771	52 856	64 226	1.5	51 454	10.8	14.5	13.0
Gallia	79	2 975	7 529	14.0	60.3	15.2	60.6	13 851	21 168	39 226	54 833	1.3	39 447	20.3	33.2	30.9
Geauga	44	802	23 664	26.0	36.6	35.9	140.3	12 172	34 455	67 663	92 481	7.7	69 078	7.4	10.3	9.4
Greene	106	2 679	51 102	21.7	34.6	36.0	236.3	11 076	30 040	58 080	75 764	4.1	60 093	12.8	15.7	14.4
Guernsey	99	1 534	9 198	14.3	58.2	12.9	58.3	12 056	20 537	38 841	50 388	1.0	39 760	22.6	33.9	31.6
Hamilton	461	4 115	217 176	25.2	38.7	33.7	1 333.6	13 313	29 681	48 593	70 632	4.8	47 123	18.7	25.8	22.9
Hancock	113	2 322	19 976	23.1	44.5	25.7	141.8	10 351	26 139	49 589	63 169	2.7	48 729	12.6	16.2	15.0
Hardin	114	2 200	9 511	31.6	63.1	13.4	44.2	10 239	19 626	40 415	51 886	1.0	42 474	15.7	22.2	19.8
Harrison	6	661	3 214	8.0	63.5	9.2	15.7	10 087	21 029	39 002	50 896	1.3	40 343	16.5	26.1	24.2
Henry	75	2 083	7 178	13.3	55.2	13.8	64.0	14 373	23 347	49 439	58 759	1.0	51 105	11.2	15.6	14.5
Highland	77	2 188	10 561	8.4	60.5	11.4	69.1	9 119	19 348	39 091	48 468	0.8	40 419	21.2	33.2	31.2
Hocking	27	1 359	7 210	8.6	58.8	12.7	39.6	9 928	21 037	42 089	53 061	0.7	42 376	16.2	26.8	24.4
Holmes	19	785	9 243	37.0	77.0	8.5	41.5	9 763	17 177	45 477	56 607	1.4	49 118	12.4	20.2	19.1
Huron	NA	NA	15 277	14.4	59.9	13.1	107.2	9 655	22 257	49 404	57 894	1.1	44 825	14.6	21.6	20.5
Jackson	91	2 169	7 782	11.9	62.5	15.2	49.4	9 497	19 405	36 356	47 537	1.1	37 823	21.4	30.1	27.1
Jefferson	NA	NA	16 150	22.1	54.8	14.7	99.3	10 760	22 324	40 577	52 864	1.7	38 074	18.4	26.7	24.1
Knox	72	2 640	15 826	30.7	53.2	21.2	88.4	11 374	23 878	49 750	62 500	2.2	47 053	14.5	22.3	20.7
Lake	164	1 562	55 141	18.6	43.2	24.9	380.8	11 682	29 132	56 018	70 236	2.8	55 477	9.4	13.1	12.2
Lawrence	113	1 818	14 748	9.5	59.2	14.9	125.1	12 805	21 365	41 552	53 143	1.0	41 137	20.6	28.5	26.9
Licking	207	2 982	44 401	18.4	49.1	21.9	287.8	11 008	26 716	55 114	68 701	2.7	54 909	11.2	17.1	14.7
Logan	129	2 487	10 564	11.9	62.4	14.8	82.1	12 396	22 878	47 542	57 199	1.4	50 077	13.2	18.7	15.3
Lorain	NA	NA	79 751	20.2	45.7	22.2	452.7	10 683	26 030	51 816	65 972	2.7	52 762	14.6	22.6	20.6
Lucas	738	2 529	121 200	17.9	44.3	23.4	687.5	13 243	23 885	41 556	57 207	2.5	40 751	21.6	29.7	27.3
Madison	70	2 271	10 499	13.7	54.1	17.6	74.8	11 340	24 014	54 956	69 267	2.9	54 039	12.2	17.9	16.9
Mahoning	291	3 213	57 446	14.0	51.2	20.8	380.1	12 511	23 975	41 058	56 335	2.0	41 076	18.0	26.8	23.9
Marion	267	4 790	14 648	10.6	57.8	12.4	127.2	13 902	20 624	42 572	54 751	1.0	42 862	16.3	24.2	21.9
Medina	39	967	45 496	16.3	39.3	29.6	267.2	9 751	30 707	65 951	80 696	4.4	66 720	6.6	8.9	7.9
Meigs	75	1 358	5 243	11.0	60.4	12.2	35.7	10 592	18 816	35 469	45 737	0.2	40 023	20.6	31.4	28.3
Mercer	54	1 469	9 957	7.5	57.4	16.2	88.2	10 825	24 157	52 535	62 288	1.7	55 110	9.4	11.7	10.7
Miami	83	2 660	24 804	13.0	49.8	19.7	173.4	11 320	25 369	52 040	62 385	1.7	51 892	10.1	15.8	14.3
Monroe	25	549	2 935	13.5	64.5	10.4	26.8	10 815	21 487	40 573	50 706	0.9	41 000	16.7	25.5	24.2
Montgomery	357	3 647	150 199	22.2	40.8	24.6	841.7	12 128	24 997	43 401	58 719	2.4	43 103	18.8	28.7	26.1
Morgan	74	416	3 358	7.8	60.7	10.5	21.0	10 270	21 027	37 865	51 300	1.5	36 057	22.8	33.1	30.4
Morrow	49	1 469	8 515	16.0	58.0	14.1	50.0	9 512	22 228	51 484	60 066	0.5	49 980	13.3	21.9	20.3
Muskingum	189	3 260	21 724	13.7	57.3	14.2	172.2	11 901	20 775	40 524	51 460	0.9	40 399	20.6	30.3	28.0
Noble	NA	NA	2 719	8.4	70.3	9.7	18.3	10 876	18 853	38 290	46 315	0.1	42 425	17.3	21.7	20.8

1. Data for serious crimes have not been adjusted for underreporting; this may affect comparability between geographic areas and over time. 2. Per 100,000 population estimated by the FBI.
3. All persons 3 years old and over enrolled in nursery school through college. 4. Persons 25 years old and over. 5. Elementary and secondary education expenditures.
6. Based on population estimated by the American Community Survey, 2009–2013.

STATE County	Personal income, 2013										Earnings, 2013		
			Per capita[1]			Supplements to wages and salaries; employer contributions (mil dol)						Contributions for government social insurance (mil dol)	
	Total (mil dol)	Percent change, 2012–2013	Dollars	Rank	Wages and salaries (mil dol)	Pension and insurance	Government social insurance	Proprietors' income (mil dol)	Dividends, interest, and rent (mil dol)	Personal transfer receipts (mil dol)	Total (mil dol)	From employee and self-employed	From employer
	62	63	64	65	66	67	68	69	70	71	72	73	74
NORTH DAKOTA—Cont'd													
Ward	3 594	1.3	52 861	273	2 032	306	171	301	647	392	2 810	159	171
Wells	265	-21.6	63 124	77	62	10	6	94	61	43	171	7	6
Williams	3 430	5.6	115 897	2	2 979	228	204	131	432	154	3 542	205	204
OHIO	474 973	2.2	41 049	X	244 388	45 093	18 293	40 182	73 616	93 599	347 956	19 261	18 293
Adams	803	3.2	28 563	2 844	211	56	15	77	100	280	360	23	15
Allen	3 625	2.5	34 428	2 003	2 154	429	169	312	604	909	3 064	171	169
Ashland	1 678	2.3	31 625	2 459	676	138	53	134	257	389	1 000	59	53
Ashtabula	3 267	2.6	32 736	2 294	1 136	249	92	190	431	990	1 667	103	92
Athens	1 938	1.6	29 955	2 692	843	267	47	111	323	484	1 268	52	47
Auglaize	1 975	2.4	43 000	840	807	155	63	137	400	325	1 161	64	63
Belmont	2 494	5.5	35 851	1 772	932	183	68	210	379	638	1 392	85	68
Brown	1 402	1.9	31 683	2 451	309	80	23	141	164	381	552	34	23
Butler	14 593	1.6	39 304	1 252	6 662	1 198	503	1 300	2 034	2 645	9 662	538	503
Carroll	863	2.2	30 512	2 628	286	54	23	112	134	235	475	29	23
Champaign	1 361	5.3	34 498	1 987	436	89	33	132	174	304	690	40	33
Clark	5 087	1.4	37 361	1 528	1 915	380	149	296	737	1 296	2 740	165	149
Clermont	7 812	2.0	39 019	1 296	2 369	424	181	685	1 017	1 413	3 659	215	181
Clinton	1 443	2.1	34 414	2 007	658	139	51	189	209	336	1 038	56	51
Columbiana	3 520	2.7	33 237	2 221	1 127	247	89	223	519	960	1 686	105	89
Coshocton	1 239	6.0	33 699	2 143	444	96	35	181	163	330	757	44	35
Crawford	1 440	0.8	33 642	2 156	494	108	39	131	217	412	772	46	39
Cuyahoga	59 739	1.7	47 294	530	39 383	6 574	2 932	7 086	10 310	11 438	55 975	3 076	2 932
Darke	1 964	2.3	37 503	1 504	678	138	55	221	326	412	1 091	63	55
Defiance	1 396	3.5	36 232	1 704	678	125	54	145	182	313	1 001	57	54
Delaware	12 451	3.6	67 309	59	4 468	703	319	1 028	1 582	957	6 517	358	319
Erie	3 201	1.2	42 097	931	1 380	282	109	370	541	684	2 141	120	109
Fairfield	5 550	3.0	37 282	1 538	1 542	313	118	429	820	1 039	2 401	139	118
Fayette	1 085	4.4	37 669	1 476	395	79	31	135	136	271	640	34	31
Franklin	52 741	3.2	43 506	800	37 800	6 973	2 660	5 121	7 649	8 332	52 553	2 652	2 660
Fulton	1 597	2.2	37 597	1 491	689	137	55	203	239	311	1 083	58	55
Gallia	1 034	0.5	33 758	2 136	447	108	34	72	136	331	660	38	34
Geauga	5 203	1.5	55 367	197	1 398	255	112	348	986	628	2 113	123	112
Greene	6 690	1.3	40 992	1 052	3 827	912	296	491	1 257	1 128	5 527	282	296
Guernsey	1 354	4.4	34 168	2 052	580	124	44	88	195	388	836	50	44
Hamilton	40 415	1.4	50 235	357	29 438	4 590	2 147	3 805	7 938	6 443	39 980	2 221	2 147
Hancock	3 262	4.6	43 046	837	2 037	351	155	323	449	540	2 865	160	155
Hardin	991	4.5	31 330	2 504	320	72	25	107	129	234	524	28	25
Harrison	493	1.9	31 585	2 468	170	35	13	21	70	148	239	16	13
Henry	1 061	2.7	37 786	1 465	445	94	36	119	144	221	695	36	36
Highland	1 262	2.1	29 140	2 788	360	93	27	108	177	385	588	34	27
Hocking	914	1.5	31 869	2 427	225	58	16	54	126	270	353	21	16
Holmes	1 329	5.9	30 489	2 630	645	122	53	344	194	192	1 165	60	53
Huron	1 938	2.6	32 910	2 263	893	170	79	157	287	471	1 300	76	79
Jackson	1 007	1.7	30 714	2 596	374	82	30	69	124	321	554	34	30
Jefferson	2 346	1.8	34 514	1 982	852	185	68	129	322	708	1 234	79	68
Knox	2 170	3.1	35 680	1 803	861	162	68	162	311	514	1 253	74	68
Lake	9 990	1.8	43 462	805	4 195	805	323	486	1 380	1 824	5 808	335	323
Lawrence	1 997	0.6	32 250	2 374	427	107	33	68	233	650	635	43	33
Licking	6 738	2.1	40 019	1 171	2 107	412	161	376	910	1 247	3 056	179	161
Logan	1 750	3.8	38 471	1 376	842	149	66	173	235	355	1 230	71	66
Lorain	11 731	2.1	38 738	1 328	4 225	845	326	505	1 621	2 462	5 900	346	326
Lucas	16 846	1.7	38 604	1 355	9 539	1 800	727	1 702	2 427	3 947	13 766	753	727
Madison	1 636	3.3	37 807	1 460	618	134	44	192	221	285	988	49	44
Mahoning	9 067	1.2	38 770	1 323	3 833	762	300	1 033	1 529	2 341	5 927	345	300
Marion	2 262	1.6	34 316	2 028	971	220	75	216	277	579	1 481	81	75
Medina	7 792	2.4	44 547	725	2 460	466	190	459	1 064	1 134	3 575	209	190
Meigs	648	1.8	27 569	2 927	118	32	9	39	76	228	197	14	9
Mercer	1 689	5.2	41 405	1 004	701	144	54	185	295	276	1 084	57	54
Miami	4 179	1.8	40 397	1 121	1 616	313	126	221	645	801	2 277	133	126
Monroe	468	2.4	32 122	2 400	139	33	11	30	60	135	214	14	11
Montgomery	21 514	1.4	40 150	1 158	11 624	2 118	894	1 442	3 840	4 785	16 078	907	894
Morgan	403	3.7	27 007	2 970	90	22	7	33	56	130	151	10	7
Morrow	1 156	3.3	33 007	2 251	192	49	13	90	125	264	345	20	13
Muskingum	2 888	2.2	33 885	2 102	1 260	263	96	161	421	795	1 780	105	96
Noble	393	17.8	26 833	2 981	164	37	11	24	48	98	236	13	11

1. Based on the resident population estimated as of July 1 of the year shown.

STATE County	Earnings, 2013 (cont.) Percent by selected industries: Farm	Mining	Construction	Manu-facturing	Infor-mation: professional, scientific, technical services	Retail trade	Finance, insur-ance, real estate and leasing	Health care and social assistance	Govern-ment	Social Security beneficiaries, December 2013: Number	Rate[1]	Supple-mental Security Income recipients, December 2013	Housing units, 2014: Total	Percent change, 2010–2014
	75	76	77	78	79	80	81	82	83	84	85	86	87	88
NORTH DAKOTA—Cont'd														
Ward	1.7	7.4	11.6	1.4	5.0	7.7	5.9	10.8	26.0	9 140	134	560	31 717	18.6
Wells	48.1	D	3.4	1.2	0.9	D	3.7	D	7.3	1 210	289	52	2 500	0.8
Williams	0.3	41.4	13.4	1.1	3.8	3.4	5.1	2.4	3.3	3 635	123	209	16 411	56.8
OHIO	0.7	0.7	5.1	14.4	9.2	6.1	8.2	12.9	15.6	2 239 797	194	311 195	5 146 933	0.4
Adams	1.3	D	8.5	15.5	2.9	9.5	3.7	D	23.2	6 620	235	1 737	12 818	-1.2
Allen	1.7	D	4.7	23.0	3.8	7.0	3.4	19.2	13.3	22 325	212	3 104	44 840	-0.4
Ashland	1.2	0.3	6.7	19.7	D	7.0	D	D	15.3	11 130	210	782	22 085	-0.3
Ashtabula	0.9	1.0	5.9	25.5	3.4	7.3	3.3	14.7	16.2	22 815	229	3 237	45 853	-0.5
Athens	0.3	D	3.9	D	4.3	7.6	3.5	12.4	51.5	9 285	144	2 519	26 188	-0.8
Auglaize	5.6	D	5.1	42.2	D	5.3	2.7	8.6	11.7	8 915	194	518	19 640	0.3
Belmont	0.3	17.7	6.8	3.8	D	10.2	8.6	12.4	15.8	16 720	240	2 230	32 155	-0.9
Brown	4.5	D	D	7.6	3.3	7.1	3.4	D	20.5	10 125	229	1 257	19 380	0.4
Butler	0.1	D	7.0	16.7	4.0	7.6	10.3	10.3	13.5	64 110	173	7 304	149 270	0.7
Carroll	4.3	3.5	21.8	17.3	D	6.4	2.6	6.1	11.1	6 545	232	615	13 592	-0.8
Champaign	6.8	D	5.1	35.7	4.5	5.5	3.2	D	15.8	8 105	205	624	16 676	-0.5
Clark	1.8	0.2	4.0	15.8	D	7.0	8.2	14.3	15.9	30 440	223	3 993	61 192	-0.4
Clermont	0.4	D	7.6	10.2	10.5	9.3	10.8	9.1	13.5	36 605	183	3 214	82 030	1.7
Clinton	4.9	D	3.0	22.3	3.4	6.0	5.0	D	14.1	8 625	206	977	18 056	-0.4
Columbiana	1.0	0.9	6.0	19.0	2.5	10.1	3.7	14.6	18.7	25 000	236	3 202	46 667	-0.9
Coshocton	2.7	7.3	4.8	22.2	D	6.6	2.9	10.3	11.8	8 455	230	948	16 356	-1.1
Crawford	7.9	D	4.4	22.5	4.4	6.3	6.7	D	14.7	10 910	255	1 175	20 002	-0.8
Cuyahoga	0.0	D	3.8	10.5	12.7	4.4	11.4	15.1	13.3	249 170	197	51 173	618 803	-0.5
Darke	4.6	D	9.2	24.3	D	6.4	5.2	11.0	11.6	11 915	228	870	22 700	-0.1
Defiance	4.0	0.0	3.7	32.9	3.4	9.3	5.3	D	12.1	8 755	227	771	16 711	-0.1
Delaware	0.3	D	3.7	7.7	11.9	6.4	15.4	6.5	8.2	23 960	129	1 186	69 650	4.9
Erie	0.4	D	4.0	19.5	3.0	7.0	4.1	13.2	16.3	18 120	238	1 599	37 707	-0.4
Fairfield	1.6	0.3	7.7	12.5	4.5	9.1	6.1	15.2	17.8	27 115	182	2 546	59 693	1.7
Fayette	8.8	0.0	5.4	15.2	D	11.7	5.7	D	16.3	6 490	225	1 003	12 677	-0.1
Franklin	0.0	0.4	4.6	5.4	12.9	5.6	11.8	10.9	20.0	165 275	136	32 444	541 069	2.6
Fulton	5.7	D	8.0	33.5	D	5.8	2.6	8.9	13.1	8 625	203	483	17 365	-0.2
Gallia	0.6	D	3.2	5.6	D	7.7	5.0	D	16.3	7 045	230	1 610	13 778	-1.1
Geauga	0.3	D	11.7	22.4	5.2	7.8	4.3	9.6	12.2	17 950	191	815	36 747	0.5
Greene	0.7	D	3.0	4.5	15.8	5.9	4.6	6.1	46.8	27 875	171	2 179	69 161	1.4
Guernsey	0.7	3.4	10.0	21.5	5.0	7.7	3.5	13.8	16.8	9 590	242	1 555	19 091	-0.5
Hamilton	0.0	D	4.5	10.7	12.9	4.2	10.0	13.8	10.1	142 355	177	24 211	376 928	-0.1
Hancock	1.8	D	3.6	27.9	4.4	6.2	2.9	9.9	7.5	14 695	194	1 106	33 273	0.3
Hardin	13.7	0.0	3.0	23.6	2.2	5.7	3.1	D	15.0	6 300	198	683	13 103	0.0
Harrison	1.3	19.9	17.2	10.4	D	3.3	D	7.9	15.9	3 805	244	527	8 084	-1.1
Henry	8.4	D	6.9	31.7	D	6.2	3.6	8.2	17.2	5 935	212	360	11 917	-0.4
Highland	6.7	0.4	6.3	19.3	D	9.7	5.4	9.8	23.8	9 820	227	1 432	19 222	-0.8
Hocking	0.4	D	9.1	14.2	2.5	7.6	6.3	8.4	30.7	6 640	232	1 029	13 311	-0.8
Holmes	2.9	1.2	17.8	30.2	D	7.5	3.1	D	8.1	4 725	108	402	13 598	-0.5
Huron	3.7	D	9.9	28.4	3.0	5.4	3.5	10.4	12.0	12 095	205	1 189	25 133	-0.3
Jackson	0.5	1.9	6.4	29.9	2.2	8.8	3.4	10.3	16.5	7 535	230	1 652	14 555	-0.2
Jefferson	0.3	D	D	7.1	4.3	7.7	3.3	D	14.9	17 740	261	2 653	32 526	-0.9
Knox	1.2	0.7	8.9	30.5	3.2	6.7	D	11.4	12.9	12 500	205	1 225	25 438	1.3
Lake	0.7	D	5.5	28.4	5.0	7.6	4.3	10.3	13.3	49 005	213	2 738	101 712	0.5
Lawrence	0.3	0.0	10.2	5.4	3.2	10.0	3.6	16.5	26.8	14 935	241	3 706	27 391	-0.8
Licking	1.3	0.5	7.1	13.7	6.5	9.8	8.5	11.7	16.6	32 690	194	3 271	69 968	1.0
Logan	1.9	0.2	4.1	40.8	3.4	4.7	2.7	7.8	10.8	9 610	211	823	23 154	-0.1
Lorain	0.7	0.0	5.2	23.7	4.2	7.9	4.3	11.5	18.3	61 465	203	7 158	128 724	1.3
Lucas	0.1	0.1	5.6	15.2	7.9	6.9	6.0	18.0	15.7	83 155	190	17 791	202 107	-0.3
Madison	8.4	D	5.6	20.4	D	5.6	2.4	D	21.7	7 405	171	647	15 936	0.0
Mahoning	0.2	0.8	6.6	11.2	5.9	7.9	9.2	16.1	15.7	56 445	241	8 716	111 341	-0.4
Marion	3.4	D	3.6	26.6	6.4	6.7	3.4	15.6	16.9	14 215	216	2 270	27 773	-0.2
Medina	0.3	0.2	8.7	16.1	6.1	8.9	5.6	9.4	12.8	31 980	183	1 493	70 606	2.1
Meigs	5.6	8.1	7.8	3.4	D	10.6	3.7	D	29.2	5 500	234	1 288	11 025	-1.5
Mercer	7.8	D	7.3	30.9	D	7.4	4.5	5.7	14.4	8 260	203	456	17 666	0.2
Miami	1.9	D	5.2	29.0	D	7.4	3.5	9.2	13.3	22 130	214	1 709	44 261	0.0
Monroe	1.8	8.3	8.0	D	1.7	6.6	4.6	D	18.5	3 985	273	562	7 476	-1.2
Montgomery	0.1	0.0	4.4	11.8	12.0	5.2	7.4	18.8	16.4	109 355	204	16 362	254 402	-0.1
Morgan	1.7	D	5.5	21.0	D	7.0	3.4	10.2	23.8	3 435	230	543	7 828	-0.8
Morrow	10.8	0.5	8.2	17.0	D	6.2	3.7	D	25.6	6 975	199	675	14 104	-0.4
Muskingum	0.8	3.5	4.0	10.4	4.4	9.3	1.2	21.4	17.0	20 440	239	3 317	37 775	-0.8
Noble	0.8	D	30.8	3.3	2.6	3.9	D	4.8	26.2	2 700	186	306	6 037	-0.3

1. Per 1,000 resident population estimated as of July 1 of the year shown.

STATE County	Housing units, 2009–2013								Civilian labor force, 2014				Civilian employment,[6] 2009–2013		
	Occupied units										Unemployment			Percent	
		Owner-occupied				Renter-occupied									
				Median owner cost as a percent of income											
	Total	Percent	Median value[1]	With a mortgage	Without a mortgage[2]	Median rent[3]	Median rent as a percent of income[2]	Substandard units[4] (percent)	Total	Percent change, 2013–2014	Total	Rate[5]	Total	Management, business, science and arts	Construction, production, and maintenance occupations
	89	90	91	92	93	94	95	96	97	98	99	100	101	102	103
NORTH DAKOTA—Cont'd															
Ward	25 173	63.7	155 800	19.7	10.0	749	26.1	1.8	34 869	0.3	942	2.7	33 103	29.2	26.7
Wells	1 949	76.7	65 700	16.7	10.0	434	19.7	2.0	2 118	0.9	101	4.8	2 056	33.4	28.0
Williams	10 411	69.4	151 400	14.2	10.0	649	18.8	3.0	32 308	8.8	384	1.2	13 959	26.8	34.7
OHIO	4 557 655	67.5	130 800	22.5	12.7	718	30.1	1.7	5 719 472	-0.1	327 969	5.7	5 266 386	34.4	23.2
Adams	10 816	73.2	92 900	24.0	13.2	531	32.9	1.9	10 450	-2.5	951	9.1	10 159	28.0	34.2
Allen	40 552	68.6	105 000	21.3	12.2	647	32.8	2.8	48 461	-2.3	2 773	5.7	46 107	26.9	27.6
Ashland	20 207	74.7	122 100	23.1	12.7	674	26.1	2.2	25 599	0.1	1 497	5.8	23 445	29.3	29.5
Ashtabula	38 952	72.5	110 800	23.1	13.5	616	33.5	2.4	45 155	-2.1	3 179	7.0	41 319	24.1	34.0
Athens	22 181	56.6	115 500	22.1	12.1	689	43.8	1.4	27 216	-1.2	1 859	6.8	26 873	34.9	17.5
Auglaize	18 241	74.6	129 400	21.2	11.5	657	24.8	0.8	24 197	0.8	1 029	4.3	22 339	29.9	35.1
Belmont	28 329	74.6	88 500	20.2	11.5	533	26.7	2.0	31 752	-0.8	2 098	6.6	29 613	26.1	28.9
Brown	16 380	77.6	116 300	24.1	14.0	667	29.0	2.0	19 899	-1.0	1 431	7.2	18 235	25.5	31.8
Butler	134 612	70.4	157 400	22.3	12.5	798	31.5	3.8	186 764	0.1	10 050	5.4	174 017	35.5	21.3
Carroll	11 107	78.8	110 400	23.3	11.7	589	28.5	1.2	13 645	-0.6	817	6.0	12 303	25.4	36.4
Champaign	15 014	74.3	124 600	22.5	12.5	688	29.4	2.0	19 957	-0.5	993	5.0	17 251	29.9	33.4
Clark	54 963	67.0	106 400	21.5	12.3	662	31.7	1.2	65 345	-1.1	3 644	5.6	58 521	29.0	27.3
Clermont	73 728	75.2	154 500	21.8	12.6	754	28.4	2.0	102 806	0.1	5 471	5.3	95 259	35.7	22.6
Clinton	15 969	66.8	118 600	23.3	12.7	668	29.5	1.6	16 870	-1.5	1 284	7.6	18 579	26.8	30.2
Columbiana	42 095	72.6	96 000	21.3	11.3	589	27.8	1.7	50 048	-1.2	3 200	6.4	45 608	25.4	32.3
Coshocton	14 495	73.9	93 300	22.1	10.8	564	26.8	1.0	16 166	-1.4	1 178	7.3	15 328	23.9	38.6
Crawford	17 655	69.9	87 300	22.7	11.9	643	28.1	1.5	19 857	0.5	1 294	6.5	17 582	25.4	34.1
Cuyahoga	534 476	60.9	125 700	23.8	14.5	732	31.8	1.5	624 344	0.4	39 921	6.4	573 033	38.2	17.7
Darke	20 776	74.4	110 600	21.8	12.1	585	27.1	1.7	26 295	-0.6	1 363	5.2	23 211	24.9	38.1
Defiance	15 203	75.8	106 100	20.7	12.2	632	27.7	1.1	18 964	-0.1	1 021	5.4	17 508	26.6	34.2
Delaware	64 208	82.3	246 300	22.5	12.0	883	27.2	1.2	99 524	1.2	3 988	4.0	90 140	51.4	12.5
Erie	31 972	69.0	135 200	22.5	13.4	696	27.3	1.8	37 885	-1.9	2 361	6.2	35 483	29.6	25.5
Fairfield	54 309	72.8	163 700	22.4	11.3	774	30.4	2.1	74 869	0.9	3 777	5.0	68 659	35.7	21.1
Fayette	11 514	62.4	107 000	24.4	13.3	696	32.3	2.5	14 201	-1.3	817	5.8	12 341	24.3	29.2
Franklin	468 295	55.1	150 800	22.7	13.0	819	29.5	2.1	645 990	0.9	30 750	4.8	588 930	40.6	16.1
Fulton	16 285	80.1	128 900	22.4	13.0	668	27.9	2.0	22 301	-0.9	1 304	5.8	20 136	28.6	34.2
Gallia	11 576	76.3	95 500	22.4	12.8	580	25.6	2.0	12 415	-0.9	935	7.5	11 815	30.1	29.9
Geauga	34 621	86.6	224 700	23.9	13.0	802	26.8	1.0	49 400	0.4	2 534	5.1	45 015	38.8	21.8
Greene	62 836	67.8	158 000	21.9	12.1	834	29.1	2.0	79 466	-0.2	4 122	5.2	74 495	43.5	17.0
Guernsey	15 690	73.7	94 000	22.8	11.6	570	31.4	1.8	18 865	1.6	1 258	6.7	16 270	26.0	32.6
Hamilton	327 914	59.5	144 400	22.6	13.1	698	31.2	0.5	404 116	0.2	21 571	5.3	377 526	39.4	16.7
Hancock	30 610	70.7	127 800	20.8	11.4	652	28.0	2.7	40 601	0.8	1 789	4.4	36 682	34.3	28.8
Hardin	11 504	70.1	95 600	21.5	12.6	645	30.2	2.3	15 172	1.4	849	5.6	13 473	24.4	33.5
Harrison	6 395	76.7	83 500	21.6	11.6	577	32.1	1.3	7 380	1.0	439	5.9	6 571	21.5	37.3
Henry	11 006	79.4	114 000	22.0	13.8	673	26.0	2.2	13 737	-2.2	865	6.3	13 125	27.1	36.6
Highland	16 918	70.9	101 800	24.4	12.2	631	30.2	2.6	17 263	-1.6	1 318	7.6	16 537	25.0	39.8
Hocking	11 478	76.2	109 800	21.9	12.0	584	31.2	5.0	13 314	0.7	835	6.3	12 489	28.5	31.6
Holmes	12 467	76.0	151 400	22.3	10.3	564	20.8	2.1	19 839	-1.2	777	3.9	17 777	20.6	45.5
Huron	22 361	72.9	118 800	22.1	11.9	619	27.6	2.6	27 872	-3.0	2 211	7.9	26 640	24.3	37.2
Jackson	13 288	67.2	89 600	22.2	14.2	609	28.9	1.3	13 209	-3.0	1 135	8.6	12 867	29.9	34.2
Jefferson	28 326	73.0	86 400	19.9	12.0	575	28.6	2.0	29 840	-2.7	2 387	8.0	28 745	27.5	27.6
Knox	22 583	71.4	133 500	22.4	12.7	681	30.0	1.2	31 071	2.0	1 621	5.2	27 954	31.0	29.2
Lake	94 048	75.0	151 300	23.0	13.2	806	28.8	2.1	126 134	0.4	7 122	5.6	115 645	34.6	22.9
Lawrence	24 009	73.3	97 200	21.5	12.0	618	29.1	1.7	25 783	-1.4	1 683	6.5	24 406	29.8	28.1
Licking	64 009	72.9	149 500	22.5	12.5	732	29.5	2.6	87 242	0.6	4 463	5.1	80 210	33.3	22.7
Logan	18 143	74.1	118 600	21.6	14.2	700	28.4	1.5	23 097	0.0	1 138	4.9	19 898	27.0	36.6
Lorain	116 705	71.6	140 700	22.6	12.8	733	31.0	1.2	151 304	0.2	9 998	6.6	136 639	33.1	24.1
Lucas	178 101	62.2	108 700	22.9	13.5	649	31.7	2.0	209 116	-1.0	13 238	6.3	191 164	31.9	23.4
Madison	14 611	71.4	144 100	22.3	13.1	741	27.6	1.2	20 432	0.7	956	4.7	18 828	28.1	29.1
Mahoning	98 201	69.8	95 800	22.1	12.8	616	31.8	1.7	108 098	-1.5	7 117	6.6	101 374	30.7	23.7
Marion	24 578	69.1	98 600	21.3	12.5	702	30.9	1.4	27 876	-1.1	1 649	5.9	26 609	26.5	34.6
Medina	65 499	79.6	181 000	22.4	11.8	821	28.6	1.9	95 308	0.4	4 916	5.2	86 808	37.1	21.8
Meigs	9 560	79.5	82 600	22.2	12.4	566	31.5	1.4	9 138	-3.1	819	9.0	8 440	25.4	34.3
Mercer	15 851	79.1	124 200	21.3	11.2	644	28.0	1.6	22 654	0.9	851	3.8	20 030	25.3	38.1
Miami	41 239	71.2	133 700	22.0	11.2	711	27.3	2.0	51 844	-0.2	2 759	5.3	48 458	30.5	30.9
Monroe	6 111	79.0	89 100	19.6	10.0	506	26.2	1.6	5 964	-8.4	646	10.8	5 667	24.5	39.4
Montgomery	222 578	62.0	112 800	23.0	14.0	723	31.5	2.2	250 307	-0.6	15 106	6.0	234 563	34.9	20.3
Morgan	6 204	77.3	89 000	22.1	10.0	550	34.6	2.6	6 691	-0.3	519	7.8	5 829	25.9	35.9
Morrow	12 940	82.2	127 400	23.3	12.8	652	31.0	1.8	16 948	0.2	977	5.8	15 523	25.9	37.6
Muskingum	33 976	68.3	108 500	22.2	13.1	624	29.7	2.8	39 208	-2.2	2 754	7.0	37 050	25.8	28.6
Noble	4 883	80.3	77 300	23.6	10.0	581	33.8	1.3	5 085	-4.1	386	7.6	4 005	23.7	39.1

1. Specified owner-occupied units. 2. A value of 10.0 represents 10 percent or less; a value of 50.0 represents 50 percent or more. 3. Specified renter-occupied units.
4. Overcrowded or lacking complete plumbing facilities. 5. Percent of civilian labor force. 6. Persons 16 years old and over.

Table B. States and Counties — **Nonfarm Employment and Agriculture**

STATE County	Private nonfarm establishments, employment and payroll, 2013									Agriculture, 2012			
		Employment						Annual payroll		Farms			
											Percent with:		
	Number of establish-ments	Total	Health care and social assistance	Manufac-turing	Retail trade	Finance and insurance	Professional, scientific, and technical services	Total (mil dol)	Average per employee (dollars)	Number	Fewer than 50 acres	500 acres or more	Farm operators whose principal occu-pation is farming (percent)
	104	105	106	107	108	109	110	111	112	113	114	115	116
NORTH DAKOTA—Cont'd													
Ward	2 055	28 507	4 717	542	6 003	1 016	826	1 241	43 517	961	15.3	47.9	60.1
Wells	189	1 430	489	D	226	79	D	41	28 976	543	8.1	50.8	56.9
Williams	1 432	22 543	1 395	254	2 075	400	654	1 588	70 444	758	8.8	52.1	52.4
OHIO	250 117	4 587 136	815 279	632 722	553 457	252 885	234 066	195 631	42 648	75 462	41.1	8.3	43.9
Adams	372	4 098	1 110	D	901	162	93	139	33 962	1 351	38.0	4.2	37.2
Allen	2 463	46 512	12 431	7 051	6 062	1 193	961	1 724	37 074	904	38.8	11.8	42.9
Ashland	1 026	15 094	2 391	3 588	1 991	322	D	512	33 918	1 034	36.4	5.4	46.8
Ashtabula	1 938	24 877	5 581	6 050	3 704	562	540	828	33 265	1 099	41.6	6.7	46.8
Athens	1 045	12 743	3 356	237	2 714	D	604	362	28 394	722	31.2	3.3	37.8
Auglaize	964	18 696	2 524	8 024	2 045	357	424	705	37 691	1 040	34.6	9.8	42.5
Belmont	1 489	19 307	4 652	911	3 958	798	530	601	31 116	700	27.1	4.9	42.1
Brown	542	6 112	1 523	649	974	183	124	187	30 533	1 379	40.4	5.7	39.7
Butler	6 982	123 695	15 574	16 935	16 964	8 354	3 208	5 140	41 550	865	51.0	6.6	43.9
Carroll	468	5 394	830	1 662	746	78	106	160	29 590	733	33.2	5.5	40.9
Champaign	594	9 033	988	3 600	989	199	258	339	37 477	873	46.0	11.6	46.2
Clark	2 364	43 251	9 816	5 750	5 570	2 679	1 250	1 487	34 376	785	53.2	11.3	49.6
Clermont	3 521	46 448	5 211	4 552	9 174	2 305	2 897	1 742	37 507	822	60.1	5.0	38.6
Clinton	720	13 484	1 754	2 797	1 530	408	D	509	37 733	759	42.2	15.5	53.1
Columbiana	2 055	26 849	5 721	5 870	4 027	767	431	822	30 605	1 045	44.7	4.5	42.0
Coshocton	638	9 174	2 005	2 347	1 314	239	137	321	34 958	1 122	32.6	5.4	40.6
Crawford	847	12 326	2 411	4 050	1 277	681	477	411	33 372	634	33.1	18.6	50.9
Cuyahoga	32 989	667 847	140 231	69 703	61 963	46 156	40 663	32 661	48 904	114	87.7	0.0	40.4
Darke	1 164	15 722	2 252	5 177	1 967	568	291	562	35 734	1 693	41.8	10.8	41.2
Defiance	807	13 565	2 422	3 271	2 277	595	235	523	38 557	1 030	37.5	12.1	38.5
Delaware	4 144	75 839	6 705	5 896	11 077	14 990	3 486	3 723	49 091	755	56.4	9.9	43.8
Erie	1 859	29 932	5 069	6 469	4 704	616	636	1 061	35 459	345	42.9	12.2	48.1
Fairfield	2 571	33 635	6 603	4 496	6 695	865	951	1 078	32 035	1 184	51.2	8.2	43.2
Fayette	581	9 535	1 335	1 667	2 547	164	72	286	30 004	504	35.5	24.2	56.5
Franklin	27 088	599 369	103 694	29 347	64 890	57 089	38 667	28 165	46 991	388	62.9	8.2	40.5
Fulton	939	14 806	2 283	6 397	1 674	356	241	560	37 805	825	42.4	13.3	42.8
Gallia	556	8 775	D	450	1 371	342	79	333	37 931	957	34.6	2.7	39.0
Geauga	2 755	27 828	4 172	7 476	3 689	728	1 091	1 143	41 090	959	55.2	2.2	49.8
Greene	3 020	48 115	6 495	3 296	9 128	1 172	9 404	1 907	39 641	800	61.6	9.0	39.4
Guernsey	834	12 844	2 763	2 776	1 755	D	D	432	33 598	1 228	36.6	1.6	34.6
Hamilton	20 884	456 696	84 173	39 177	44 025	32 473	38 366	23 739	51 981	295	67.1	3.1	42.4
Hancock	1 706	39 791	5 120	10 707	4 210	602	815	1 714	43 087	831	32.7	15.4	45.5
Hardin	459	6 920	704	1 873	880	206	87	213	30 723	793	31.3	14.1	52.2
Harrison	268	2 828	600	344	270	59	D	123	43 325	444	26.6	6.8	46.2
Henry	566	8 234	1 334	2 971	949	274	80	319	38 758	848	33.1	15.7	47.9
Highland	674	8 156	1 621	1 636	1 579	542	129	265	32 439	1 412	38.3	7.9	45.1
Hocking	467	5 003	1 038	804	786	177	78	139	27 724	367	38.4	3.0	40.9
Holmes	1 137	17 128	1 573	6 478	1 966	330	268	525	30 664	1 969	36.7	2.4	50.0
Huron	1 136	16 927	2 778	5 423	2 014	433	417	628	37 108	865	38.7	12.7	47.1
Jackson	583	8 859	1 376	3 145	1 390	281	151	266	30 038	526	32.3	4.9	41.8
Jefferson	1 281	19 193	4 755	1 288	3 032	411	303	620	32 285	493	26.0	4.1	39.4
Knox	1 063	18 844	3 055	4 875	2 133	439	341	809	42 937	1 374	45.8	5.5	44.6
Lake	6 083	85 433	11 266	19 123	12 883	2 079	3 056	3 543	41 474	214	70.6	1.4	55.6
Lawrence	808	10 105	2 702	846	1 931	279	272	306	30 273	592	26.2	1.9	41.9
Licking	2 892	46 523	7 253	7 593	7 126	3 843	1 822	1 699	36 510	1 484	51.1	5.7	39.8
Logan	860	15 705	2 033	D	1 645	279	809	636	40 492	868	40.4	12.3	39.2
Lorain	5 533	83 106	14 328	16 280	13 297	1 965	3 374	3 216	38 693	768	52.7	6.0	46.4
Lucas	9 599	197 276	38 867	18 335	23 543	5 860	9 185	7 696	39 012	330	52.7	12.4	58.2
Madison	675	11 429	1 350	3 122	1 744	D	D	406	35 531	699	40.1	21.9	53.2
Mahoning	5 572	87 382	20 212	8 938	12 410	2 406	3 592	3 055	34 957	578	44.5	4.2	48.3
Marion	1 130	21 005	4 457	6 017	2 783	429	304	741	35 260	578	34.1	16.6	41.9
Medina	3 992	50 938	7 260	8 860	8 559	2 475	1 987	1 955	38 373	920	63.0	4.0	50.2
Meigs	298	2 406	517	64	539	128	D	63	26 067	588	27.0	3.2	53.2
Mercer	950	15 273	2 139	4 107	1 962	593	284	524	34 279	1 208	35.3	12.0	45.0
Miami	2 117	36 572	4 780	11 342	4 473	770	1 016	1 322	36 136	1 068	54.6	10.0	41.8
Monroe	254	3 379	D	D	406	D	46	148	43 866	823	26.5	2.8	41.9
Montgomery	11 473	224 561	51 110	26 303	25 944	10 673	12 172	9 481	42 222	770	63.8	6.6	42.7
Morgan	164	1 879	368	625	293	83	31	55	29 337	510	22.2	5.5	39.4
Morrow	383	3 655	891	D	467	D	147	114	31 151	824	43.9	8.7	43.0
Muskingum	1 736	27 530	7 135	2 738	4 591	719	433	985	35 795	1 259	35.3	4.8	38.4
Noble	217	1 910	377	295	269	84	D	51	26 877	595	27.2	4.2	33.3

STATE County	Agriculture, 2012 (cont.)															
	Land in farms					Value of land and buildings (dollars)			Value of products sold				Percent of farms with sales of:		Government payments	
			Acres								Percent from:					
	Acreage (1,000)	Percent change, 2007–2012	Average size of farm	Total irrigated (1,000)	Total cropland (1,000)	Average per farm	Average per acre	Value of machinery and equipment, average per farm (dollars)	Total (mil dol)	Average per farm (dollars)	Crops	Livestock and poultry products	$10,000 or more	$100,000 or more	Total ($1,000)	Percent of farms
	117	118	119	120	121	122	123	124	125	126	127	128	129	130	131	132
NORTH DAKOTA—Cont'd																
Ward	1 073	0.7	1 117	0.2	829.4	1 716 400	1 537	298 381	274.5	285 596	93.3	6.7	62.7	39.2	9 875	71.4
Wells	738	-2.5	1 359	0.8	622.3	2 198 269	1 617	364 245	272.0	500 842	95.1	4.9	58.2	44.6	7 746	85.6
Williams	1 063	-7.1	1 403	15.6	739.1	1 044 598	745	289 881	178.7	235 756	93.8	6.2	59.4	36.7	6 315	72.2
OHIO	13 961	0.0	185	46.6	10 748.6	894 933	4 837	116 896	10 064.1	133 366	65.6	34.4	47.4	20.3	228 858	45.9
Adams	172	-6.3	128	0.2	84.4	365 260	2 862	59 237	38.9	28 798	68.6	31.4	33.6	6.6	2 316	55.4
Allen	183	-2.2	203	D	163.0	1 070 715	5 284	144 872	144.1	159 393	76.2	23.8	61.7	30.3	3 593	74.4
Ashland	153	1.6	148	0.2	110.9	677 328	4 578	93 800	103.6	100 214	53.0	47.0	52.5	17.5	2 061	45.4
Ashtabula	166	2.6	151	0.2	109.0	494 527	3 275	114 303	82.3	74 846	74.4	25.6	38.8	13.2	1 609	28.7
Athens	90	10.1	125	0.1	28.0	348 506	2 781	47 575	9.5	13 224	57.2	42.8	21.3	2.1	320	16.8
Auglaize	210	-1.5	202	0.0	191.5	1 220 936	6 044	176 234	190.6	183 235	60.6	39.4	66.1	34.0	5 338	77.1
Belmont	113	-12.3	162	0.0	35.0	540 911	3 344	59 970	20.1	28 764	21.9	78.1	37.4	4.1	613	9.7
Brown	206	-14.1	150	0.1	139.3	539 260	3 602	89 819	82.6	59 891	88.5	11.5	41.8	12.2	3 795	57.9
Butler	146	14.8	169	0.3	116.4	986 918	5 845	107 817	65.0	75 191	80.4	19.6	36.6	12.4	2 379	32.4
Carroll	106	-9.1	145	0.4	58.4	539 031	3 718	86 621	39.2	53 478	51.6	48.4	40.5	10.2	989	28.0
Champaign	190	-7.2	218	3.7	164.9	1 166 636	5 359	147 490	130.4	149 386	86.6	13.4	49.7	24.6	3 854	56.2
Clark	174	-1.7	222	1.6	149.8	1 141 031	5 138	147 288	145.1	184 896	80.4	19.6	45.1	23.8	2 754	47.6
Clermont	121	15.7	147	0.2	88.5	752 370	5 106	83 123	58.0	70 583	93.3	6.7	25.5	8.4	1 264	29.7
Clinton	208	-4.7	274	0.1	187.7	1 360 628	4 962	172 278	163.8	215 867	90.5	9.5	60.1	34.8	3 825	63.8
Columbiana	128	-2.4	122	0.3	81.7	594 740	4 861	98 871	99.3	95 020	38.4	61.6	45.0	15.4	1 509	24.8
Coshocton	170	-0.8	151	0.6	88.7	518 983	3 430	87 948	81.7	72 781	39.9	60.1	39.2	13.4	1 530	30.7
Crawford	240	9.3	379	0.1	221.9	1 772 235	4 681	250 994	193.1	304 645	74.0	26.0	67.2	43.7	4 734	75.6
Cuyahoga	3	-10.4	23	0.1	0.6	391 509	17 113	56 079	10.2	89 605	98.5	1.5	25.4	8.8	12	3.5
Darke	340	-3.0	201	1.1	311.6	1 425 144	7 097	175 760	559.5	330 475	32.2	67.8	65.2	32.9	6 902	69.5
Defiance	225	-3.4	219	0.0	198.1	980 354	4 483	116 630	113.5	110 232	75.9	24.1	48.4	21.8	6 297	85.8
Delaware	141	2.0	187	0.8	123.4	1 108 061	5 937	144 164	121.9	161 464	88.5	11.5	45.0	20.5	2 396	45.2
Erie	83	-0.9	242	0.4	71.9	1 137 035	4 708	184 907	88.2	255 583	92.2	7.8	56.8	31.6	1 343	55.1
Fairfield	207	16.3	175	0.3	162.9	833 232	4 773	114 217	105.8	89 394	79.4	20.6	36.5	15.8	3 782	48.0
Fayette	197	-10.0	390	0.0	180.6	2 134 145	5 473	226 067	143.5	284 808	87.9	12.1	59.9	39.3	4 144	73.0
Franklin	62	4.1	160	0.3	53.5	983 101	6 151	118 101	48.2	124 299	96.2	3.8	44.8	17.5	853	37.9
Fulton	195	6.2	237	0.5	179.6	1 315 518	5 556	166 076	175.7	213 023	69.4	30.6	60.7	35.4	4 204	67.3
Gallia	116	-0.9	121	0.2	34.6	393 862	3 254	51 183	15.1	15 827	51.6	48.4	22.6	2.9	734	23.6
Geauga	67	18.1	70	0.3	32.7	494 216	7 094	47 118	43.6	45 477	41.0	59.0	40.0	9.1	345	5.6
Greene	146	-10.3	182	0.6	124.7	1 095 626	6 012	120 653	95.9	119 883	90.7	9.3	39.6	17.1	2 173	46.6
Guernsey	144	4.5	117	0.0	51.7	336 147	2 871	49 570	21.5	17 502	36.6	63.4	24.9	2.9	291	10.2
Hamilton	22	1.5	73	0.2	10.0	533 654	7 282	73 278	23.6	80 153	61.3	38.7	32.5	10.5	257	13.2
Hancock	230	-7.1	277	0.0	212.8	1 310 924	4 731	164 752	160.2	192 834	91.7	8.3	71.2	41.2	4 142	77.1
Hardin	248	-3.5	313	0.4	222.6	1 527 226	4 887	171 834	272.5	343 571	53.8	46.2	61.9	34.6	4 779	72.1
Harrison	95	2.2	215	0.0	38.1	645 957	3 007	68 225	18.2	41 081	42.6	57.4	32.9	7.9	245	14.4
Henry	236	1.6	278	0.6	221.4	1 570 350	5 645	170 375	155.5	183 383	91.6	8.4	72.3	36.0	4 449	85.6
Highland	265	-2.0	187	0.2	197.7	677 928	3 619	97 353	128.6	91 069	82.6	17.4	43.9	16.3	6 128	62.6
Hocking	38	-9.3	104	0.0	14.0	372 025	3 585	44 937	5.3	14 450	80.2	19.8	22.9	2.7	212	19.3
Holmes	221	17.7	112	0.3	124.1	653 282	5 822	64 655	204.9	104 045	20.9	79.1	59.6	24.3	1 796	12.9
Huron	238	8.6	275	3.2	208.7	1 235 467	4 485	165 143	190.7	220 421	81.0	19.0	55.8	32.1	3 680	57.9
Jackson	72	-0.3	136	0.1	27.2	321 939	2 362	58 485	10.7	20 293	44.2	55.8	29.3	5.9	525	32.3
Jefferson	68	-1.6	139	0.0	25.9	381 974	2 755	68 801	7.8	15 880	48.4	51.6	30.2	3.4	218	19.9
Knox	186	-6.2	135	0.1	128.7	647 124	4 779	91 124	121.4	88 386	66.0	34.0	42.4	15.0	2 491	35.7
Lake	17	6.6	80	1.9	8.6	604 140	7 550	111 075	81.8	382 351	99.4	0.6	48.1	17.8	23	8.9
Lawrence	65	-1.8	109	0.1	17.0	266 258	2 441	50 843	4.8	8 189	57.3	42.7	15.7	1.5	366	18.2
Licking	224	-0.8	151	0.2	161.4	738 829	4 894	103 000	194.8	131 270	52.2	47.8	36.8	12.1	2 331	25.5
Logan	213	5.8	245	0.3	177.7	1 221 374	4 979	135 014	147.9	170 409	82.6	17.4	49.5	23.4	4 046	58.8
Lorain	123	-1.1	160	1.4	102.7	750 453	4 698	125 251	179.1	233 203	89.7	10.3	51.8	20.6	1 519	41.5
Lucas	63	0.2	191	1.5	59.7	1 103 406	5 778	138 709	66.2	200 521	95.2	4.8	58.2	31.8	964	55.2
Madison	263	6.2	377	0.1	244.2	1 917 923	5 092	202 773	193.8	277 230	79.4	20.6	58.4	39.9	5 148	66.0
Mahoning	75	17.0	130	0.9	54.5	644 289	4 968	119 341	65.4	113 234	45.9	54.1	48.1	19.9	847	32.9
Marion	189	-8.5	327	D	174.8	1 562 507	4 773	199 900	151.4	261 990	74.2	25.8	55.0	32.0	4 497	73.5
Medina	95	-0.5	103	0.6	72.4	656 848	6 363	94 628	60.5	65 797	70.1	29.9	37.1	11.6	1 274	20.8
Meigs	76	-2.5	129	0.3	24.6	312 980	2 428	53 207	14.5	24 622	66.8	33.2	29.1	4.3	748	17.9
Mercer	273	-6.8	226	0.1	248.7	1 775 939	7 854	213 011	596.4	493 681	25.7	74.3	76.3	49.7	7 650	79.1
Miami	184	-6.5	173	2.3	164.8	983 794	5 703	103 808	110.0	102 998	91.9	8.1	51.2	21.7	3 147	59.2
Monroe	111	11.9	135	0.0	29.7	311 759	2 308	58 011	13.7	16 612	32.4	67.6	23.2	2.6	264	6.3
Montgomery	124	11.8	161	1.2	104.7	944 147	5 858	111 271	76.8	99 695	84.6	15.4	38.8	13.0	1 656	44.4
Morgan	95	-6.9	187	0.0	30.0	448 463	2 403	64 149	12.2	23 975	41.5	58.5	34.1	5.1	370	22.7
Morrow	168	1.6	204	0.2	139.2	952 987	4 682	131 218	131.7	159 848	70.9	29.1	50.7	20.0	2 689	43.8
Muskingum	173	4.1	138	0.1	79.2	449 031	3 263	70 551	58.1	46 149	51.8	48.2	34.4	7.8	1 298	24.1
Noble	86	-3.6	145	0.1	28.8	368 677	2 547	55 652	9.8	16 403	37.1	62.9	31.9	2.2	78	4.9

STATE County	Water use, 2010		Wholesale trade,[1] 2007				Retail trade,[2] 2007				Real estate and rental and leasing,[2] 2007			
	Total water withdrawn (mil gal/day)	Gallons withdrawn per person per day	Number of establish-ments	Number of employees	Sales (mil dol)	Annual payroll (mil dol)	Number of establish-ments	Number of employees	Sales (mil dol)	Annual payroll (mil dol)	Number of establish-ments	Number of employees	Receipts (mil dol)	Annual payroll (mil dol)
	133	134	135	136	137	138	139	140	141	142	143	144	145	146
NORTH DAKOTA—Cont'd														
Ward	7.7	125	86	1 139	1 379.7	48.4	294	4 738	1 119.0	96.4	70	D	D	D
Wells	1.0	226	18	166	184.6	5.6	35	212	64.0	3.9	3	D	D	D
Williams	21.1	942	58	618	442.6	28.2	119	1 400	403.3	30.7	38	223	93.1	12.3
OHIO	9 442.8	819	12 591	192 403	135 575.3	8 914.0	40 075	591 237	138 816.0	12 729.5	10 973	67 048	15 011.3	2 339.2
Adams	588.8	20 622	9	62	21.1	1.5	86	941	210.3	18.1	14	52	3.8	1.2
Allen	34.6	325	135	D	D	D	464	6 950	1 577.5	133.6	105	481	67.1	12.2
Ashland	5.6	105	38	494	206.2	20.8	174	2 094	418.6	41.9	33	136	11.8	3.1
Ashtabula	189.6	1 868	59	D	D	D	384	4 298	1 077.6	84.7	82	260	24.1	5.3
Athens	9.5	147	31	D	D	D	210	2 784	563.2	53.8	73	265	35.3	5.5
Auglaize	10.8	234	43	D	D	D	188	2 451	493.8	45.5	43	141	16.0	3.0
Belmont	179.5	2 550	43	D	D	D	331	4 544	888.8	83.4	48	272	29.8	5.5
Brown	4.8	107	20	107	55.0	3.0	104	1 103	262.3	20.4	18	65	5.0	1.1
Butler	131.6	357	453	9 364	7 337.0	461.8	981	16 941	4 876.2	400.2	309	1 717	345.3	53.6
Carroll	3.1	107	18	208	104.2	6.7	79	767	163.6	15.3	11	42	5.0	0.8
Champaign	9.4	233	33	242	146.4	8.3	119	1 204	287.6	23.3	24	71	6.8	1.3
Clark	25.8	187	95	D	D	D	460	6 625	1 398.7	131.7	101	485	64.0	10.9
Clermont	384.0	1 946	151	1 870	1 036.0	96.4	574	10 087	2 439.6	211.8	161	776	99.1	21.4
Clinton	4.1	98	31	D	D	D	142	1 945	450.9	39.6	29	125	12.4	3.2
Columbiana	10.3	96	93	D	D	D	386	4 544	1 064.2	93.7	61	274	29.4	6.6
Coshocton	147.3	3 993	19	D	D	D	121	1 291	259.2	24.1	20	48	3.7	0.7
Crawford	5.5	125	34	D	D	D	150	1 370	338.7	28.8	26	83	8.2	1.5
Cuyahoga	466.0	364	2 116	34 314	18 894.4	1 783.4	4 767	65 431	14 478.9	1 428.9	1 585	15 316	5 925.5	709.0
Darke	8.5	161	58	D	D	D	190	2 166	447.2	44.7	38	200	16.9	6.3
Defiance	11.2	286	41	D	D	D	176	2 624	559.5	50.4	28	115	15.0	2.1
Delaware	28.3	162	145	1 979	998.5	95.4	575	10 155	2 331.4	213.5	168	677	114.1	20.4
Erie	34.2	443	64	D	D	D	351	5 086	1 034.9	101.8	79	360	40.9	8.8
Fairfield	14.6	100	82	D	D	D	441	6 485	1 360.6	129.2	135	493	62.7	11.8
Fayette	4.2	146	26	D	D	D	199	2 495	610.7	45.4	24	102	21.6	2.0
Franklin	177.8	153	1 288	26 610	22 138.4	1 251.1	3 785	71 503	19 403.6	1 758.9	1 558	10 816	2 221.5	414.0
Fulton	4.5	104	44	416	238.8	15.8	168	1 614	405.9	36.5	26	94	8.0	1.6
Gallia	1 109.4	35 863	19	D	D	D	139	1 509	356.0	30.2	21	78	7.6	1.7
Geauga	9.8	105	138	955	424.6	52.7	320	4 005	916.7	88.8	84	347	43.3	9.3
Greene	15.6	97	73	1 126	1 275.5	46.9	540	9 938	2 029.3	193.0	136	540	93.5	13.9
Guernsey	6.5	163	29	D	D	D	169	1 911	468.3	37.2	41	235	22.1	4.5
Hamilton	382.5	477	1 199	19 282	13 030.3	993.2	3 148	49 028	10 629.5	1 082.2	1 066	7 462	1 577.4	296.1
Hancock	19.2	257	71	D	D	D	316	4 752	1 092.8	97.8	68	504	55.9	13.2
Hardin	4.6	143	17	105	112.7	3.7	91	962	193.0	18.7	15	36	4.8	1.0
Harrison	1.3	83	11	117	42.8	5.3	43	323	52.9	4.9	4	102	3.0	1.2
Henry	11.7	413	33	350	317.9	11.9	92	989	268.0	20.0	19	70	14.4	1.7
Highland	3.4	78	15	166	79.8	3.6	143	1 767	370.5	35.3	27	83	8.7	1.7
Hocking	3.0	101	7	D	D	D	85	1 027	218.9	20.2	29	91	7.4	1.7
Holmes	6.4	151	51	658	240.9	18.8	155	1 663	360.3	35.1	16	43	5.3	0.8
Huron	7.1	120	54	D	D	D	203	2 294	550.3	46.2	43	143	18.6	4.1
Jackson	2.3	70	19	131	50.1	4.5	129	1 483	336.1	29.1	26	101	10.0	2.0
Jefferson	1 734.0	24 875	55	D	D	D	271	3 523	721.5	68.3	47	237	27.3	5.0
Knox	9.0	147	38	362	130.8	11.2	192	2 397	541.9	47.6	49	164	16.6	3.6
Lake	818.4	3 558	336	3 443	1 867.8	164.5	866	14 140	3 460.9	314.5	227	1 178	182.9	30.4
Lawrence	9.4	150	20	D	D	D	179	2 312	508.8	44.5	26	87	9.4	1.6
Licking	19.9	119	114	1 769	1 141.4	70.9	466	7 144	1 774.7	145.2	108	536	62.9	13.7
Logan	6.1	134	31	1 117	399.6	41.2	161	1 914	420.7	40.3	38	176	33.1	4.3
Lorain	464.5	1 541	262	2 745	1 822.7	120.2	895	14 057	3 225.5	286.4	222	860	120.8	21.2
Lucas	685.3	1 551	514	7 283	4 943.6	319.4	1 649	25 392	5 830.0	548.2	452	2 854	961.5	103.5
Madison	7.0	162	29	D	D	D	122	1 839	958.6	41.6	33	84	11.5	2.0
Mahoning	7.4	31	278	4 344	1 858.8	172.5	1 026	13 896	3 025.7	281.4	199	1 337	156.7	33.1
Marion	12.4	186	42	598	338.1	21.5	203	2 997	674.8	62.5	59	224	28.5	6.2
Medina	9.7	56	233	2 592	1 303.4	116.6	548	8 390	2 113.4	185.9	140	501	71.5	12.2
Meigs	9.0	379	7	41	11.4	1.0	75	561	124.2	9.5	5	D	D	D
Mercer	8.9	218	56	1 112	655.7	39.5	174	1 876	394.4	40.1	34	187	14.1	2.7
Miami	16.5	161	90	1 551	4 168.9	79.6	354	4 699	1 080.5	101.0	92	323	48.5	8.1
Monroe	2.9	107	9	47	22.8	2.1	51	370	62.6	5.8	1	D	D	D
Montgomery	141.2	264	592	8 419	3 766.7	387.5	1 778	27 154	6 844.6	588.6	576	3 882	564.5	128.9
Morgan	1.7	114	5	D	D	D	28	225	52.3	3.8	4	D	D	D
Morrow	3.4	99	14	D	D	D	58	644	167.9	10.1	13	29	2.6	0.4
Muskingum	16.5	192	55	884	2 222.1	37.7	385	5 125	1 125.7	96.6	71	309	46.8	8.3
Noble	1.3	89	8	36	6.2	0.8	37	324	103.3	6.3	1	D	D	D

1. Merchant wholesalers, except manufacturers' sales branches and offices. 2. Employer establishments.

STATE County	Professional, scientific, and technical services,[1] 2007				Manufacturing, 2007				Accommodation and food services, 2007			
	Number of establish-ments	Number of employees	Receipts (mil dol)	Annual payroll (mil dol)	Number of establish-ments	Number of employees	Receipts (mil dol)	Annual payroll (mil dol)	Number of establish-ments	Number of employees	Sales (mil dol)	Annual payroll (mil dol)
	147	148	149	150	151	152	153	154	155	156	157	158
NORTH DAKOTA—Cont'd												
Ward	104	D	D	D	54	623	D	19.9	150	2 891	106.7	30.0
Wells	10	19	0.9	0.3	NA	NA	NA	NA	17	107	3.0	0.8
Williams	61	217	22.9	8.3	NA	NA	NA	NA	66	913	36.6	10.7
OHIO	24 963	224 265	32 285.4	12 304.2	16 237	760 267	295 890.9	35 485.5	23 959	436 598	17 779.9	5 078.5
Adams	27	87	5.8	1.6	35	694	133.9	28.1	43	523	19.0	5.1
Allen	170	D	D	D	136	8 661	10 009.0	475.9	219	4 469	173.2	47.4
Ashland	67	984	128.0	36.1	93	4 140	1 017.4	164.5	101	1 572	55.6	17.7
Ashtabula	114	D	D	D	161	7 218	2 201.4	296.4	219	2 745	110.6	29.7
Athens	70	D	D	D	NA	NA	NA	NA	145	2 712	81.0	23.2
Auglaize	65	400	46.1	14.1	88	7 835	2 550.6	349.6	87	1 193	42.9	11.2
Belmont	103	568	50.3	18.4	53	1 279	500.9	53.0	128	2 517	91.2	26.8
Brown	29	D	D	D	29	736	74.2	27.6	69	794	29.3	7.5
Butler	605	D	D	D	440	21 082	11 362.0	1 035.6	630	13 512	531.1	154.3
Carroll	27	D	D	D	49	1 700	344.6	63.8	43	566	18.9	5.9
Champaign	40	D	D	D	46	3 238	1 050.2	151.4	60	717	25.9	6.5
Clark	163	D	D	D	182	7 164	2 494.3	299.2	241	4 574	173.1	49.6
Clermont	376	D	D	D	183	5 777	1 250.6	258.1	285	6 271	239.5	71.3
Clinton	46	D	D	D	47	3 877	1 025.4	165.6	81	1 390	62.2	15.0
Columbiana	126	D	D	D	197	6 535	1 572.1	239.5	189	2 561	87.5	25.6
Coshocton	35	320	16.5	8.4	52	2 947	1 222.9	129.2	49	633	22.7	6.4
Crawford	44	409	26.8	11.1	93	4 989	1 470.9	182.8	90	1 106	39.1	10.5
Cuyahoga	4 341	41 689	6 487.8	2 543.7	2 172	82 169	23 131.7	4 156.8	3 089	54 151	2 499.2	691.0
Darke	69	313	25.3	8.8	82	4 404	1 517.1	185.6	97	1 088	43.7	11.5
Defiance	50	D	D	D	53	3 940	1 048.4	281.8	81	1 194	41.3	11.2
Delaware	496	D	D	D	133	6 065	2 314.5	282.2	361	8 335	344.2	103.5
Erie	132	D	D	D	110	7 149	2 329.9	344.9	279	5 661	254.7	69.0
Fairfield	187	D	D	D	131	4 804	1 061.6	210.4	228	4 636	169.5	50.3
Fayette	29	D	D	D	33	2 795	975.5	112.5	58	942	38.9	10.7
Franklin	3 545	D	D	D	925	35 625	14 289.4	1 605.8	2 664	56 718	2 596.3	744.2
Fulton	49	313	19.1	6.6	112	9 086	3 330.4	358.4	75	987	34.7	9.3
Gallia	26	90	6.3	1.7	NA	NA	NA	NA	50	883	33.3	9.2
Geauga	332	D	D	D	209	11 444	2 964.4	460.0	190	2 615	94.1	26.5
Greene	428	D	D	D	106	3 881	924.1	176.9	319	7 229	283.3	86.4
Guernsey	45	271	32.0	10.5	61	3 169	1 403.2	119.8	94	1 659	67.0	18.4
Hamilton	2 601	D	D	D	1 155	58 305	25 048.9	3 058.2	1 933	39 897	1 788.4	522.8
Hancock	128	947	81.3	34.7	105	10 975	3 757.2	498.2	172	3 619	130.6	38.4
Hardin	22	95	6.3	2.1	35	2 052	560.5	79.9	51	917	29.5	10.4
Harrison	16	37	2.3	0.6	18	740	165.2	24.3	29	211	6.6	1.5
Henry	20	107	10.5	2.4	46	3 770	2 284.3	162.1	51	609	17.8	5.1
Highland	44	143	10.1	3.2	43	2 879	643.0	102.7	54	958	36.1	9.3
Hocking	24	72	4.3	1.7	23	964	261.5	36.3	66	1 006	40.2	11.2
Holmes	39	291	31.3	10.7	265	6 123	1 366.4	190.0	58	1 057	36.4	12.0
Huron	81	377	27.1	11.0	104	7 206	2 375.8	284.2	108	1 450	51.7	14.4
Jackson	34	185	10.9	3.2	38	4 015	2 083.9	115.7	52	1 087	35.5	10.6
Jefferson	90	D	D	D	37	2 938	D	167.9	157	1 884	66.3	18.1
Knox	66	275	29.5	7.1	75	4 551	1 914.0	244.6	91	1 472	53.0	14.2
Lake	612	D	D	D	688	19 820	5 220.9	887.6	561	9 339	390.8	105.4
Lawrence	44	D	D	D	39	835	D	32.1	68	1 066	41.2	11.1
Licking	252	D	D	D	162	8 610	3 351.8	375.6	284	5 123	194.2	54.7
Logan	50	D	D	D	50	6 042	D	351.6	104	1 333	55.7	14.3
Lorain	469	D	D	D	408	18 330	8 305.3	976.6	565	8 530	326.6	88.0
Lucas	911	D	D	D	560	21 793	20 075.5	1 275.0	1 026	19 773	728.6	211.7
Madison	44	D	D	D	46	2 949	994.6	131.8	66	1 038	38.4	12.0
Mahoning	465	D	D	D	385	9 874	2 475.1	376.4	544	9 489	340.7	96.4
Marion	72	D	D	D	77	7 737	3 409.2	305.4	119	2 051	79.1	22.6
Medina	409	2 246	229.9	91.4	297	9 403	2 558.8	395.6	309	5 106	186.1	53.0
Meigs	20	66	4.6	1.3	NA	NA	NA	NA	31	500	15.3	4.6
Mercer	47	319	31.6	12.5	76	3 926	927.9	149.4	79	1 223	39.4	11.3
Miami	162	D	D	D	241	9 924	2 807.3	420.5	181	3 438	127.6	37.5
Monroe	15	66	5.9	2.4	13	D	D	D	21	123	4.3	1.0
Montgomery	1 213	14 942	2 031.9	829.3	811	34 993	14 049.2	1 607.2	1 112	22 069	882.7	259.0
Morgan	11	29	2.1	0.5	NA	NA	NA	NA	19	264	5.8	2.0
Morrow	32	D	D	D	32	1 150	D	D	36	381	14.0	3.5
Muskingum	103	D	D	D	86	5 131	1 134.2	188.0	194	3 276	124.0	35.9
Noble	11	32	3.5	1.3	NA	NA	NA	NA	23	187	7.3	2.0

1. Establishment subject to federal tax.

STATE County	Health care and social assistance, 2007				Other services, 2007				Nonemployer businesses, 2013		Value of residential construction authorized by building permits, 2014	
	Number of establish-ments	Number of employees	Receipts (mil dol)	Annual payroll (mil dol)	Number of establish-ments	Number of employees	Receipts (mil dol)	Annual payroll (mil dol)	Number	Receipts (mil dol)	New Construction ($1,000)	Number of housing units
	159	160	161	162	163	164	165	166	167	168	169	170
NORTH DAKOTA—Cont'd												
Ward	145	4 360	345.9	154.2	142	804	60.2	14.9	4 266	211.6	106 454	854
Wells	15	431	17.8	8.2	18	63	3.8	0.8	364	19.3	300	6
Williams	59	1 432	91.6	40.6	67	300	32.1	7.7	2 467	140.7	329 669	2 221
OHIO	27 965	741 194	65 882.5	27 621.4	20 349	135 272	13 047.5	3 463.9	745 540	31 388.8	3 753 786	19 872
Adams	50	1 037	62.0	25.1	34	90	7.4	1.9	1 982	69.0	224	2
Allen	330	11 408	999.0	417.5	213	1 448	93.3	27.9	5 373	210.0	10 975	61
Ashland	120	2 082	157.8	61.9	88	601	40.6	12.3	3 304	146.6	7 785	48
Ashtabula	224	5 839	408.3	160.8	165	656	44.9	10.3	6 288	240.5	14 862	91
Athens	132	2 593	205.9	84.2	92	453	26.1	7.0	3 238	100.5	19 843	93
Auglaize	94	1 995	147.5	53.5	91	583	38.4	11.5	2 700	107.9	13 851	74
Belmont	180	4 237	294.3	125.5	134	648	35.1	9.4	3 243	123.6	508	5
Brown	50	1 563	104.1	41.4	52	182	12.5	3.4	2 774	103.6	9 560	60
Butler	720	15 799	1 313.6	535.8	541	3 726	354.1	101.3	21 401	898.9	156 704	866
Carroll	42	753	37.9	17.0	38	206	12.0	2.9	1 955	82.5	80	1
Champaign	48	2 077	87.8	43.6	62	335	15.3	4.1	2 201	84.0	4 729	29
Clark	319	8 186	619.8	258.2	237	1 402	188.1	38.4	6 735	230.7	11 313	53
Clermont	299	5 104	392.2	165.2	289	1 734	158.3	44.1	12 944	549.1	69 311	389
Clinton	95	2 151	205.3	80.6	72	328	34.1	7.9	2 728	103.9	4 860	23
Columbiana	288	5 808	384.5	150.6	186	1 007	73.0	18.6	6 000	238.3	2 311	16
Coshocton	81	1 979	132.3	52.6	61	253	22.6	4.7	2 261	84.3	340	3
Crawford	106	2 166	148.3	58.0	80	362	27.6	6.6	2 286	83.4	1 898	11
Cuyahoga	3 734	125 281	12 200.2	5 313.6	2 652	19 545	2 112.5	553.2	88 494	3 879.3	184 863	719
Darke	75	2 098	138.9	57.8	102	445	27.1	6.9	3 482	137.8	10 186	38
Defiance	84	2 208	196.0	68.9	71	446	31.5	7.6	2 162	82.1	4 187	22
Delaware	313	4 655	420.9	171.9	239	1 914	339.1	69.1	15 548	832.7	197 711	914
Erie	195	4 986	434.3	162.8	155	815	49.6	14.5	4 687	181.0	14 820	57
Fairfield	303	5 804	488.6	207.0	181	1 121	102.5	31.8	10 180	413.5	77 683	349
Fayette	62	1 289	87.9	36.6	44	213	13.1	3.6	1 508	53.0	4 421	22
Franklin	3 020	84 476	8 383.5	3 503.0	2 217	18 766	2 208.7	582.1	87 914	3 840.9	811 638	5 058
Fulton	96	2 174	147.7	58.5	80	274	25.2	6.2	2 960	123.4	8 411	43
Gallia	64	2 853	219.5	89.5	41	180	12.5	3.6	1 906	71.0	175	3
Geauga	239	3 737	301.3	141.0	204	1 142	105.0	33.0	10 614	577.5	61 770	154
Greene	316	5 995	488.2	198.0	221	1 261	95.4	29.9	9 451	358.6	100 247	250
Guernsey	126	2 427	186.0	69.5	71	304	23.6	4.9	2 387	105.8	6 494	54
Hamilton	2 455	80 329	7 905.8	3 420.9	1 585	11 594	1 292.8	325.3	54 764	2 504.8	237 253	1 590
Hancock	190	4 688	443.2	165.7	146	824	77.7	21.1	4 256	179.8	26 417	92
Hardin	38	581	47.0	15.9	40	151	10.5	2.3	1 564	62.9	2 764	17
Harrison	32	603	31.4	13.7	18	59	3.1	1.0	869	38.9	0	0
Henry	54	1 190	74.9	32.2	51	312	18.6	5.2	1 627	65.1	4 230	20
Highland	87	1 656	120.8	47.8	48	210	13.9	3.0	2 998	122.2	735	8
Hocking	44	956	62.4	24.2	42	162	14.1	3.2	1 897	67.9	1 709	15
Holmes	52	1 317	99.8	34.0	42	198	17.5	4.5	4 966	286.2	510	4
Huron	103	2 460	202.1	85.0	103	523	39.8	10.3	3 095	129.9	6 910	40
Jackson	56	1 099	115.7	43.2	52	179	15.7	3.4	1 680	58.6	12 159	57
Jefferson	161	4 454	333.9	139.7	119	627	37.2	10.5	3 002	96.1	1 834	21
Knox	124	2 475	191.6	75.8	88	591	37.7	10.9	4 720	203.6	20 543	119
Lake	558	10 822	900.8	358.1	527	3 432	252.8	76.9	14 944	644.0	108 414	567
Lawrence	112	2 226	101.3	48.4	68	271	21.7	6.1	2 876	97.3	744	6
Licking	243	6 550	476.2	212.4	222	1 766	267.4	63.7	11 470	461.3	51 595	248
Logan	89	1 988	150.1	60.1	81	516	66.0	10.9	2 777	108.2	10 534	56
Lorain	613	13 174	1 097.1	440.0	510	3 049	252.6	68.6	16 810	648.8	160 689	824
Lucas	1 272	40 299	3 669.6	1 580.7	796	5 652	509.1	131.0	24 064	1 015.3	100 244	814
Madison	67	1 103	78.5	30.0	42	188	9.9	2.8	2 698	111.8	9 008	44
Mahoning	792	15 765	1 334.0	516.8	418	2 914	216.6	61.1	15 440	613.2	30 908	135
Marion	158	4 318	356.2	157.7	115	652	43.2	11.7	3 133	105.9	11 244	94
Medina	376	6 790	475.2	207.0	302	1 636	114.7	34.9	12 767	574.0	131 799	636
Meigs	41	532	28.4	11.6	15	52	4.5	1.0	1 183	36.2	1 635	9
Mercer	79	1 611	102.7	42.0	95	430	37.7	9.3	2 675	115.4	15 145	65
Miami	195	D	D	D	177	953	76.1	19.4	6 579	244.9	38 356	148
Monroe	18	203	11.5	4.4	24	83	5.5	1.3	1 035	37.3	0	0
Montgomery	1 505	47 348	4 928.7	1 955.0	954	6 992	738.6	202.7	31 748	1 240.7	80 247	381
Morgan	15	250	14.2	5.5	17	44	2.9	0.8	864	27.7	1 635	5
Morrow	45	902	60.2	20.7	24	79	7.7	1.9	2 619	113.1	5 332	27
Muskingum	220	6 095	498.6	219.4	171	1 233	81.4	23.2	5 150	193.6	3 235	50
Noble	19	433	20.2	8.2	15	37	2.5	0.4	812	32.1	3 878	29

STATE County	Government employment and payroll, 2012									Local government finances, 2012				
			March payroll (percent of total)							General revenue				
												Taxes		
													Per capita[1] (dollars)	
	Full-time equivalent employees	March payroll (dollars)	Adminis-tration, judicial, and legal	Police and Corrections	Fire Protection	Highways and transpor-tation	Health and Welfare	Natural resources and utilities	Education and libraries	Total (mil dol)	Inter-govern-mental (mil dol)	Total (mil dol)	Total	Property
	171	172	173	174	175	176	177	178	179	180	181	182	183	184
NORTH DAKOTA—Cont'd														
Ward	2 136	7 851 589	4.3	7.5	2.8	4.2	5.4	5.7	68.4	241.7	117.3	80.2	1 238	819
Wells	201	657 258	11.8	3.8	0.0	9.3	11.4	5.1	54.7	18.7	8.8	6.5	1 519	1 436
Williams	864	3 064 820	7.6	11.5	0.1	4.9	6.8	4.6	59.1	140.3	49.9	59.7	2 236	1 126
OHIO	X	X	X	X	X	X	X	X	X	X	X	X	X	X
Adams	1 309	4 554 288	8.6	6.3	1.2	4.8	20.7	12.5	44.5	95.0	57.8	28.2	996	856
Allen	4 029	14 917 726	8.3	9.1	4.8	3.4	9.8	5.8	55.9	394.8	197.5	125.6	1 195	774
Ashland	1 952	6 407 247	7.9	9.8	3.4	8.4	11.1	4.1	54.7	148.8	65.0	62.1	1 172	812
Ashtabula	3 445	13 283 345	8.6	8.3	6.3	6.3	10.0	5.8	52.9	379.5	210.8	114.5	1 141	880
Athens	2 322	8 135 468	7.7	8.6	2.5	4.0	14.9	8.3	53.4	218.6	106.3	74.7	1 161	793
Auglaize	1 848	6 837 964	8.1	11.1	3.6	6.2	9.8	11.2	48.9	165.8	68.7	63.4	1 383	791
Belmont	2 607	9 128 313	8.1	10.6	2.1	10.5	11.9	10.3	46.0	191.0	101.3	63.6	913	616
Brown	1 467	5 037 757	10.7	6.4	1.0	3.0	3.9	4.5	68.2	139.2	79.2	35.6	803	573
Butler	12 086	48 616 602	7.6	9.8	5.5	2.6	6.4	6.6	59.8	1 333.8	510.2	553.1	1 493	1 108
Carroll	814	2 533 284	12.9	4.6	0.1	10.7	12.6	3.6	53.6	67.3	39.5	18.9	663	541
Champaign	1 507	5 457 874	8.0	11.9	3.0	4.5	7.3	4.2	60.0	133.3	67.8	46.2	1 167	749
Clark	5 386	19 627 638	7.6	10.0	4.2	2.3	8.2	4.4	57.6	501.3	270.1	168.3	1 227	774
Clermont	5 289	20 437 759	7.0	10.5	7.4	2.9	8.3	2.8	59.9	577.6	246.3	251.2	1 262	1 074
Clinton	1 809	5 888 599	9.0	8.5	2.2	3.7	8.2	6.6	60.3	157.7	71.7	54.0	1 288	849
Columbiana	3 495	11 243 471	8.0	8.4	2.1	5.7	10.5	5.6	58.7	309.6	171.8	94.5	887	570
Coshocton	1 280	4 337 624	6.8	5.0	9.6	5.4	10.8	3.0	57.6	122.4	67.8	38.8	1 056	791
Crawford	1 254	4 325 266	5.9	4.7	3.6	1.8	1.1	5.5	77.2	151.9	72.7	51.8	1 209	747
Cuyahoga	62 490	287 120 691	6.2	10.3	5.0	6.7	17.9	8.2	44.0	8 188.0	2 777.4	3 498.3	2 765	1 595
Darke	1 735	6 310 491	7.2	9.5	3.5	3.8	9.0	4.8	60.8	161.4	77.3	60.1	1 145	652
Defiance	1 658	5 904 403	6.0	5.9	1.8	3.6	22.5	5.1	51.1	159.4	60.4	46.4	1 200	722
Delaware	5 621	21 810 855	6.5	8.3	8.6	3.5	6.9	3.8	60.6	594.5	125.1	379.4	2 096	1 582
Erie	3 210	12 237 910	9.9	7.7	6.1	3.6	6.5	6.6	58.0	347.1	131.6	140.7	1 841	1 302
Fairfield	4 930	17 614 468	7.6	7.4	6.0	3.4	7.0	5.5	62.0	533.2	218.0	227.0	1 539	972
Fayette	1 569	5 994 441	8.4	7.6	3.1	4.0	30.8	6.0	35.4	151.4	51.3	42.0	1 454	900
Franklin	43 936	204 420 126	7.5	12.0	8.0	4.8	6.8	5.9	53.0	6 852.6	2 645.8	3 248.5	2 717	1 632
Fulton	1 714	6 275 872	9.2	6.4	2.8	7.9	4.5	5.4	60.4	175.3	77.4	66.6	1 566	1 017
Gallia	1 230	4 310 190	10.5	5.0	0.3	10.5	8.6	3.8	60.0	121.8	67.0	35.1	1 144	879
Geauga	2 853	10 934 381	6.8	10.3	1.9	6.2	6.6	5.0	60.8	321.0	103.8	177.1	1 890	1 605
Greene	5 165	20 150 214	7.8	10.0	5.1	2.9	8.5	4.8	58.8	586.4	206.6	277.8	1 698	1 294
Guernsey	1 477	4 435 295	10.2	6.1	1.9	6.0	6.7	6.6	52.4	132.8	73.2	38.5	968	624
Hamilton	30 330	130 350 382	7.8	13.0	8.0	5.1	7.5	8.7	47.8	4 236.2	1 499.4	1 927.5	2 403	1 479
Hancock	2 432	8 819 684	8.0	8.9	4.5	4.6	9.6	8.0	55.4	271.6	110.7	109.9	1 453	890
Hardin	1 423	4 258 899	9.1	8.7	1.2	4.7	11.9	3.6	57.1	110.9	55.5	32.7	1 034	564
Harrison	710	1 856 484	14.6	4.5	0.0	15.6	8.0	4.7	51.0	49.7	28.0	13.6	864	670
Henry	1 481	5 408 211	10.0	3.9	0.9	3.5	8.5	11.1	57.7	117.5	56.0	44.6	1 592	1 074
Highland	2 293	6 286 414	5.2	4.7	1.8	3.3	31.1	2.7	50.4	172.7	76.0	41.2	959	563
Hocking	914	2 885 727	10.2	5.6	1.4	5.5	5.2	3.2	67.0	114.8	42.6	28.6	978	747
Holmes	1 321	4 844 879	5.9	5.2	1.1	8.0	34.0	1.8	43.4	120.7	39.0	36.0	838	671
Huron	2 467	10 437 634	6.6	7.8	2.4	4.1	4.3	21.4	48.4	200.0	86.9	77.4	1 306	715
Jackson	1 363	4 190 837	9.9	7.6	2.0	7.6	8.5	6.5	56.1	108.3	64.9	23.7	718	505
Jefferson	2 754	8 388 400	8.2	12.7	2.8	7.2	11.7	7.8	48.7	279.5	143.1	76.7	1 121	730
Knox	2 080	6 852 809	7.4	6.9	4.1	5.9	8.2	4.9	60.0	183.1	81.3	75.5	1 244	918
Lake	9 604	40 201 055	7.4	10.0	6.0	4.6	9.6	6.7	54.4	980.1	328.7	481.4	2 097	1 489
Lawrence	2 540	8 380 560	7.9	7.5	1.5	3.4	6.7	4.8	67.2	216.7	128.7	37.7	607	431
Licking	5 717	20 737 584	8.7	10.0	5.7	3.6	5.5	4.6	60.9	579.7	236.0	255.6	1 525	1 041
Logan	1 959	6 311 962	5.8	5.7	2.0	5.4	16.7	4.0	58.9	181.6	83.8	65.2	1 434	1 028
Lorain	11 564	45 174 817	6.2	9.7	3.8	2.9	8.7	7.0	60.5	1 201.2	540.9	467.7	1 551	1 088
Lucas	14 739	62 111 336	9.0	11.4	8.7	4.8	10.1	5.0	50.5	2 086.3	910.4	780.9	1 783	1 087
Madison	1 659	6 453 004	10.2	8.0	6.0	3.9	8.2	4.3	57.6	145.7	58.9	62.4	1 448	1 020
Mahoning	8 773	31 345 985	6.1	10.6	3.5	4.0	7.9	7.9	58.9	868.3	433.7	320.4	1 363	887
Marion	2 295	8 158 244	7.0	10.0	5.7	2.9	9.1	2.6	60.7	238.0	129.7	65.6	990	651
Medina	5 924	23 018 921	7.1	9.8	2.3	4.3	7.5	6.6	61.1	592.1	209.5	282.6	1 627	1 274
Meigs	1 067	3 103 267	7.9	7.6	0.0	6.4	10.2	11.3	53.7	74.8	52.2	14.0	593	473
Mercer	1 924	6 814 130	6.9	4.9	1.1	2.5	23.6	3.3	56.9	205.3	75.3	58.0	1 418	907
Miami	3 473	13 601 040	7.3	8.3	2.8	3.5	7.7	7.6	59.9	385.2	159.1	157.7	1 531	850
Monroe	802	1 932 268	10.9	3.9	0.2	9.0	13.4	7.6	53.8	74.7	47.7	17.9	1 229	1 062
Montgomery	22 502	93 151 363	7.9	9.7	4.7	6.0	8.0	8.2	54.1	2 605.5	1 042.9	1 055.0	1 974	1 302
Morgan	442	1 318 311	13.5	4.8	0.0	6.2	1.1	3.1	69.8	48.1	33.5	10.1	676	539
Morrow	1 452	4 922 890	11.2	5.3	0.3	5.8	24.4	1.2	49.4	129.7	48.6	32.8	939	663
Muskingum	3 889	12 275 435	6.0	8.2	2.0	4.2	10.5	5.2	60.2	370.0	202.8	113.8	1 324	918
Noble	445	1 384 468	17.5	1.9	0.0	7.5	11.4	15.2	45.8	48.2	22.3	17.2	1 183	1 099

1. Based on the resident population estimated as of July 1 of the year shown.

STATE County	Local government finances, 2012 (cont.)									Government employment, 2013			Presidential election,[2] 2012		
	Direct general expenditure							Debt outstanding					Percent of vote cast:		
			Percent of total for:												
	Total (mil dol)	Per capita[1] (dollars)	Educa-tion	Health and hospitals	Police protec-tion	Public welfare	High-ways	Total (mil dol)	Per capita[1] (dollars)	Federal civilian	Federal military	State and local	Demo-cratic	Republi-can	All other
	185	186	187	188	189	190	191	192	193	194	195	196	197	198	199
NORTH DAKOTA—Cont'd															
Ward	230.0	3 550	57.5	0.3	5.1	2.2	10.8	95.7	1 477	1 158	5 871	4 243	39.6	58.8	1.6
Wells	18.0	4 209	46.4	1.9	3.5	4.3	18.7	9.3	2 176	27	28	264	35.4	61.8	2.9
Williams	130.1	4 872	37.2	3.2	4.7	0.9	16.5	127.0	4 757	80	200	1 969	31.2	67.1	1.7
OHIO	X	X	X	X	X	X	X	X	X	76 666	36 168	681 086	51.5	46.9	1.6
Adams	85.9	3 030	56.6	4.4	3.7	6.7	8.9	48.9	1 726	69	72	1 457	36.6	60.7	2.7
Allen	385.4	3 665	49.5	5.4	6.9	4.3	6.7	180.7	1 719	324	258	5 860	38.8	59.6	1.6
Ashland	147.7	2 789	50.7	9.1	6.1	3.4	7.9	51.1	966	94	131	2 387	37.0	60.2	2.8
Ashtabula	389.2	3 877	53.0	7.0	3.8	6.1	7.1	243.8	2 429	187	268	4 392	55.8	42.2	2.0
Athens	231.8	3 605	47.4	7.2	2.6	14.9	4.9	68.3	1 062	247	156	10 129	66.6	31.3	2.0
Auglaize	176.4	3 848	52.8	1.4	5.8	4.8	6.3	154.1	3 362	83	117	2 250	28.6	69.8	1.5
Belmont	186.0	2 669	48.0	6.2	2.5	6.5	6.8	55.5	797	158	171	3 805	50.3	47.6	2.1
Brown	134.7	3 035	63.4	3.5	6.0	3.2	5.5	58.8	1 325	84	113	1 851	37.3	60.6	2.1
Butler	1 326.8	3 580	50.2	3.7	7.9	4.7	5.8	1 987.8	5 364	575	950	19 742	38.0	60.6	1.4
Carroll	59.8	2 092	47.0	8.7	3.5	6.9	10.6	17.3	605	45	72	943	46.0	50.9	3.1
Champaign	144.3	3 648	59.7	3.7	3.5	3.9	6.6	60.2	1 522	67	100	1 810	39.1	59.0	1.9
Clark	474.6	3 459	49.3	5.8	5.9	6.2	3.3	206.0	1 502	545	348	6 544	47.9	50.4	1.8
Clermont	582.2	2 924	49.6	6.2	6.8	6.0	5.4	332.6	1 671	277	513	7 272	33.1	65.5	1.4
Clinton	150.9	3 602	49.6	3.5	5.9	5.2	7.7	60.1	1 434	126	106	2 280	34.0	64.3	1.8
Columbiana	314.7	2 954	56.2	3.2	5.1	8.9	6.3	123.5	1 160	591	265	4 585	45.1	52.8	2.1
Coshocton	116.3	3 163	50.7	9.0	6.0	6.2	9.6	60.1	1 634	68	94	1 494	45.6	51.4	3.0
Crawford	163.0	3 804	50.5	4.3	4.1	5.0	8.0	99.7	2 328	83	109	1 780	39.1	58.2	2.7
Cuyahoga	8 005.7	6 328	36.6	14.5	5.9	3.6	2.9	11 286.9	8 922	15 939	3 631	77 218	68.9	30.0	1.1
Darke	165.9	3 160	56.8	4.8	5.9	4.6	7.2	76.5	1 457	105	134	2 109	30.9	67.0	2.1
Defiance	164.9	4 263	38.1	17.8	4.2	3.1	5.7	96.2	2 486	87	98	1 952	43.8	54.2	2.0
Delaware	580.7	3 207	51.8	3.6	4.6	2.2	6.9	734.5	4 057	214	472	7 220	39.7	59.3	1.1
Erie	360.9	4 724	52.1	2.5	5.2	3.9	4.2	232.7	3 046	312	193	4 985	56.1	42.3	1.6
Fairfield	537.8	3 647	55.2	5.3	4.9	3.9	3.7	791.1	5 364	233	400	6 401	40.7	57.8	1.6
Fayette	143.4	4 966	32.8	26.1	3.8	3.7	4.5	83.9	2 906	52	73	1 720	37.6	60.7	1.6
Franklin	6 511.1	5 446	38.1	3.0	6.3	6.0	4.2	8 029.0	6 716	12 875	3 532	116 102	59.7	39.0	1.3
Fulton	197.2	4 637	67.2	2.5	4.2	2.4	4.5	104.1	2 450	92	109	2 528	45.1	53.2	1.7
Gallia	123.5	4 023	57.7	2.3	5.6	5.4	6.2	74.2	2 416	84	77	1 771	35.9	61.9	2.2
Geauga	314.3	3 355	48.5	9.3	6.8	2.6	8.8	302.2	3 225	104	242	4 061	41.6	56.9	1.5
Greene	655.1	4 004	53.0	4.0	6.4	4.0	4.8	524.5	3 206	13 873	3 161	11 087	40.1	58.5	1.3
Guernsey	125.8	3 159	48.1	3.5	4.9	8.6	7.9	38.7	973	119	101	2 227	44.0	53.1	2.9
Hamilton	4 409.2	5 497	37.9	6.8	6.8	4.4	3.4	5 717.7	7 129	8 755	2 139	47 292	53.0	46.0	1.0
Hancock	295.5	3 905	53.3	7.9	3.8	2.7	4.3	240.6	3 180	148	192	3 254	37.5	60.6	1.9
Hardin	110.3	3 489	43.3	1.9	7.5	10.6	8.3	59.1	1 869	66	76	1 450	38.2	59.1	2.7
Harrison	46.0	2 927	48.6	1.1	3.7	9.2	14.1	4.8	305	50	40	700	47.3	49.7	3.0
Henry	116.8	4 166	57.4	9.8	4.3	0.3	7.0	51.0	1 819	69	72	2 024	42.6	55.5	1.9
Highland	157.5	3 663	45.3	24.8	5.4	4.0	5.4	55.6	1 293	95	111	2 340	35.7	62.1	2.2
Hocking	118.1	4 036	34.2	34.9	4.9	5.2	5.5	21.9	748	44	73	1 741	48.3	49.1	2.6
Holmes	122.6	2 851	35.9	29.5	3.5	5.1	8.0	35.7	830	62	111	1 551	28.3	69.5	2.3
Huron	227.6	3 839	59.2	1.8	3.8	5.5	5.6	177.4	2 992	138	151	2 446	47.2	50.4	2.4
Jackson	103.5	3 142	55.6	4.5	4.9	6.5	7.1	74.9	2 274	66	84	1 478	38.6	58.7	2.7
Jefferson	274.2	4 010	48.3	6.7	5.3	3.8	7.4	154.1	2 253	171	171	3 161	49.1	48.9	2.1
Knox	190.4	3 137	48.2	3.8	2.8	3.7	12.6	94.4	1 554	102	148	2 599	39.0	58.9	2.0
Lake	960.6	4 184	51.1	7.4	6.8	2.5	5.5	411.1	1 790	448	616	11 145	49.6	48.7	1.7
Lawrence	214.4	3 452	60.9	5.7	3.5	4.9	4.0	51.1	822	128	158	3 003	41.4	56.7	1.9
Licking	578.6	3 453	56.4	0.8	6.3	6.5	4.5	386.9	2 309	363	439	7 430	41.2	57.0	1.8
Logan	185.1	4 071	51.9	5.6	4.3	4.6	6.6	117.8	2 592	119	117	2 121	35.7	62.3	1.9
Lorain	1 206.9	4 003	55.2	4.3	5.8	3.9	4.7	1 730.7	5 741	1 110	784	14 285	58.1	40.2	1.7
Lucas	1 896.4	4 330	37.6	9.4	7.1	4.9	3.8	2 289.2	5 226	1 958	1 200	27 690	65.0	33.5	1.5
Madison	152.8	3 549	60.2	4.9	4.6	3.8	5.7	137.1	3 184	74	99	3 025	37.4	60.8	1.8
Mahoning	851.8	3 622	47.9	5.8	7.8	3.8	4.3	531.9	2 262	1 223	598	13 253	62.2	35.6	2.1
Marion	232.6	3 512	58.7	1.2	4.1	2.2	4.0	316.2	4 773	110	178	3 776	44.4	53.3	2.4
Medina	715.8	4 121	54.5	3.6	4.6	2.1	11.9	431.2	2 483	309	477	6 711	45.2	53.3	1.5
Meigs	70.8	3 002	53.3	2.8	2.8	10.1	10.2	25.4	1 075	64	60	1 053	39.5	58.1	2.4
Mercer	196.0	4 794	46.2	26.1	3.3	3.1	7.9	89.2	2 183	96	104	2 671	27.5	71.0	1.5
Miami	405.1	3 930	56.7	3.4	6.0	3.1	5.3	280.3	2 720	186	267	4 618	34.8	63.3	1.9
Monroe	83.7	5 754	66.8	2.8	2.6	8.8	8.9	2.9	200	47	37	755	53.1	43.9	3.0
Montgomery	2 652.7	4 965	44.5	3.0	6.4	8.6	5.3	2 338.6	4 377	4 214	4 120	27 334	52.4	46.2	1.4
Morgan	43.8	2 938	48.1	4.6	5.2	8.6	11.1	11.3	760	41	38	640	44.9	52.1	3.1
Morrow	139.5	3 994	47.5	22.8	1.4	3.0	5.3	60.5	1 733	47	90	1 536	37.1	60.5	2.4
Muskingum	340.0	3 956	54.4	3.3	4.9	6.1	6.4	122.4	1 424	220	218	5 221	45.4	52.6	2.0
Noble	36.8	2 523	50.8	2.9	4.1	7.6	14.3	3.0	208	24	31	948	40.1	55.9	4.0

1. Based on the resident population estimated as of July 1 of the year shown. 2.

STATE/ County code	CBSA code[1]	County type[2]	STATE County	Land area,[3] (sq km) 2010	Population, 2014: Total persons 2014	Population, 2014: Rank	Population, 2014: Per square kilometer	Race alone or in combination, not Hispanic or Latino (percent): White	Black	American Indian, Alaska Native	Asian and Pacific Islander	Percent Hispanic or Latino[4]	Age (percent): Under 5 years	5 to 17 years	18 to 24 years	25 to 34 years	35 to 44 years	45 to 54 years
				1	2	3	4	5	6	7	8	9	10	11	12	13	14	15
			OHIO—Cont'd															
39 123	38840	2	Ottawa	660	41 154	1 148	62.4	93.8	1.5	0.5	0.5	4.8	4.5	15.3	7.0	9.2	10.8	15.0
39 125	...	6	Paulding	1 079	18 989	1 876	17.6	94.0	1.5	0.7	0.5	4.5	6.0	18.4	7.8	10.9	11.8	14.6
39 127	18140	6	Perry	1 057	35 812	1 279	33.9	98.4	0.9	1.1	0.3	0.7	6.1	18.5	8.3	11.5	12.6	14.8
39 129	18140	1	Pickaway	1 298	56 876	894	43.8	94.4	4.3	0.7	0.7	1.3	5.3	17.0	9.2	12.8	14.1	14.8
39 131	...	7	Pike	1 140	28 256	1 481	24.8	97.3	1.7	1.3	0.5	0.8	6.0	18.0	8.2	11.2	12.7	14.7
39 133	10420	2	Portage	1 262	161 882	392	128.3	92.1	5.3	0.7	2.1	1.6	4.5	14.8	17.8	10.9	11.0	13.9
39 135	...	2	Preble	1 098	41 586	1 135	37.9	97.9	1.0	0.7	0.8	0.7	5.5	17.9	7.6	11.1	12.1	14.6
39 137	...	6	Putnam	1 250	34 171	1 323	27.3	93.5	0.6	0.3	0.4	5.8	6.8	18.8	8.4	11.0	11.4	14.7
39 139	31900	3	Richland	1 283	121 942	505	95.0	88.3	10.2	0.7	1.0	1.7	5.6	16.3	8.6	11.7	12.0	14.0
39 141	17060	4	Ross	1 785	77 159	714	43.2	91.9	7.4	1.1	0.8	1.1	5.5	16.5	8.1	12.6	13.8	15.4
39 143	23380	4	Sandusky	1 058	60 179	864	56.9	87.1	4.1	0.6	0.5	9.5	6.0	17.5	7.9	11.4	12.0	14.4
39 145	39020	4	Scioto	1 580	77 258	713	48.9	95.2	3.4	1.3	0.6	1.2	5.7	16.4	9.6	12.5	12.6	13.4
39 147	45660	4	Seneca	1 427	55 669	909	39.0	92.1	3.4	0.5	0.8	4.7	5.4	17.2	10.9	11.4	11.4	13.6
39 149	43380	4	Shelby	1 056	48 951	1 001	46.4	95.0	3.3	0.5	1.3	1.5	6.5	19.9	8.2	11.1	12.3	14.6
39 151	15940	2	Stark	1 490	375 736	180	252.2	89.4	9.1	0.8	1.2	1.8	5.5	16.6	9.0	11.4	11.7	14.2
39 153	10420	2	Summit	1 069	541 943	121	507.0	80.8	15.8	0.7	3.1	1.8	5.7	16.2	9.1	12.5	12.1	14.5
39 155	49660	2	Trumbull	1 601	205 175	313	128.2	89.3	9.4	0.6	0.8	1.6	5.2	16.0	8.2	10.8	11.6	14.3
39 157	35420	4	Tuscarawas	1 470	92 788	629	63.1	96.4	1.3	0.6	0.6	2.2	5.9	17.1	7.8	11.5	11.9	14.0
39 159	18140	1	Union	1 118	53 776	932	48.1	92.9	3.1	0.6	3.3	1.4	5.9	20.0	8.1	12.4	15.8	15.6
39 161	46780	6	Van Wert	1 060	28 462	1 473	26.9	95.8	1.6	0.4	0.5	2.8	5.7	17.7	7.9	11.1	11.7	13.9
39 163	...	9	Vinton	1 068	13 234	2 224	12.4	98.1	0.9	1.0	0.4	0.8	5.3	17.8	8.4	10.8	12.8	15.3
39 165	17140	1	Warren	1 039	221 659	289	213.3	89.5	3.9	0.5	5.1	2.4	6.1	20.2	7.5	11.4	14.5	15.8
39 167	31930	3	Washington	1 637	61 213	855	37.4	96.9	1.8	0.9	1.0	1.0	4.9	15.2	9.2	10.9	11.6	14.3
39 169	49300	4	Wayne	1 437	115 537	530	80.4	95.8	2.3	0.6	1.1	1.6	6.6	18.2	10.0	11.3	11.5	13.4
39 171	...	7	Williams	1 090	37 291	1 244	34.2	94.2	1.5	0.5	0.7	4.0	5.7	17.5	7.9	11.4	11.9	14.5
39 173	45780	2	Wood	1 599	129 590	480	81.0	90.4	3.2	0.6	2.1	5.1	5.4	15.4	17.5	12.1	11.3	12.5
39 175	...	7	Wyandot	1 054	22 353	1 715	21.2	96.3	0.7	0.5	0.8	2.6	5.7	17.9	7.6	11.4	12.2	13.9
40 000	...	X	OKLAHOMA	177 660	3 878 051	X	21.8	72.4	8.7	12.3	2.6	9.6	6.9	17.7	10.2	13.7	12.1	12.9
40 001	...	6	Adair	1 485	22 186	1 724	14.9	51.9	0.9	50.7	0.8	5.8	6.6	20.3	9.0	11.6	12.5	13.8
40 003	...	9	Alfalfa	2 244	5 790	2 777	2.6	87.0	4.8	4.8	0.5	5.1	5.1	14.1	6.4	11.0	14.8	16.9
40 005	...	7	Atoka	2 527	13 796	2 185	5.5	78.4	4.8	19.4	0.8	3.4	6.3	16.7	8.2	12.4	12.0	13.4
40 007	...	9	Beaver	4 700	5 486	2 806	1.2	75.9	1.3	2.3	0.3	22.1	6.1	19.2	7.7	11.1	11.2	14.3
40 009	21120	7	Beckham	2 336	23 691	1 654	10.1	78.4	4.9	4.2	1.1	13.7	8.0	17.3	9.7	16.0	12.4	13.0
40 011	...	6	Blaine	2 405	9 917	2 444	4.1	78.6	4.2	11.3	0.8	8.9	7.2	18.1	8.2	10.6	10.4	13.2
40 013	20460	6	Bryan	2 343	44 486	1 083	19.0	79.2	2.4	18.9	1.0	5.3	6.6	16.7	10.8	13.2	11.7	12.1
40 015	...	6	Caddo	3 311	29 317	1 445	8.9	62.9	4.2	26.4	0.7	11.2	7.2	18.3	8.7	13.2	11.7	13.4
40 017	36420	1	Canadian	2 322	129 582	481	55.8	81.8	3.5	7.1	3.7	7.8	6.9	19.7	7.9	14.6	14.2	13.3
40 019	11620	5	Carter	2 129	48 821	1 004	22.9	76.2	8.6	13.4	1.5	6.4	6.7	18.6	8.2	12.6	12.5	13.3
40 021	45140	6	Cherokee	1 941	48 341	1 008	24.9	58.0	2.2	41.3	1.0	6.5	6.5	17.0	15.0	12.0	11.0	11.9
40 023	...	7	Choctaw	1 995	15 161	2 090	7.6	68.4	12.6	21.3	0.8	3.5	6.2	17.9	7.8	10.6	10.9	13.1
40 025	...	9	Cimarron	4 752	2 294	3 026	0.5	78.4	1.1	2.0	0.4	20.1	6.2	17.8	6.0	10.7	10.1	12.3
40 027	36420	1	Cleveland	1 395	269 908	249	193.5	78.7	5.9	7.8	5.1	7.8	6.0	16.6	15.0	15.2	12.5	12.3
40 029	...	9	Coal	1 338	5 807	2 773	4.3	79.0	1.8	23.5	0.5	3.5	6.6	18.1	8.8	9.4	10.9	12.6
40 031	30020	3	Comanche	2 769	125 033	498	45.2	62.3	19.0	7.6	4.6	12.5	7.5	17.0	13.4	16.7	12.2	12.2
40 033	30020	6	Cotton	1 639	6 150	2 745	3.8	82.2	3.2	11.9	0.9	6.6	5.5	17.8	8.4	10.7	11.5	14.3
40 035	...	6	Craig	1 972	14 582	2 130	7.4	73.2	4.3	27.1	1.3	3.0	5.3	16.5	8.3	11.2	12.2	15.1
40 037	46140	2	Creek	2 461	70 632	759	28.7	83.3	3.3	15.3	0.8	3.7	6.2	18.0	8.2	11.5	12.0	14.0
40 039	48220	7	Custer	2 561	29 500	1 440	11.5	73.3	3.6	8.1	1.8	16.2	7.5	16.7	17.6	14.1	10.0	10.9
40 041	...	6	Delaware	1 912	41 446	1 138	21.7	72.5	0.7	29.8	1.4	3.2	4.8	16.7	7.3	9.5	10.8	13.4
40 043	...	9	Dewey	2 589	4 914	2 841	1.9	86.9	1.3	7.7	1.2	5.9	6.6	18.8	7.4	10.6	10.6	13.4
40 045	...	9	Ellis	3 190	4 150	2 891	1.3	89.3	1.2	3.2	0.5	7.5	5.2	18.4	6.7	9.5	11.3	13.0
40 047	21420	5	Garfield	2 741	63 091	830	23.0	80.9	4.3	4.3	3.7	10.4	7.5	18.1	9.2	13.9	11.1	12.5
40 049	...	6	Garvin	2 077	27 561	1 510	13.3	81.7	3.3	11.6	0.8	7.2	6.6	18.0	7.9	12.1	12.0	12.8
40 051	36420	1	Grady	2 850	53 854	930	18.9	86.4	3.2	8.8	0.8	5.1	6.1	18.5	8.6	12.4	12.5	14.1
40 053	...	9	Grant	2 592	4 501	2 865	1.7	92.0	2.2	3.8	0.5	3.8	6.0	17.2	7.1	10.1	10.5	14.6
40 055	...	7	Greer	1 656	6 151	2 744	3.7	79.2	8.1	4.2	0.5	10.6	4.9	14.7	8.2	16.1	12.7	14.0
40 057	...	9	Harmon	1 391	2 798	2 988	2.0	63.4	8.6	3.4	0.8	26.7	7.4	17.6	8.0	12.1	10.3	12.9
40 059	...	9	Harper	2 691	3 812	2 920	1.4	79.4	0.6	1.8	0.4	19.2	6.9	18.2	7.1	12.1	10.4	13.9
40 061	...	6	Haskell	1 493	12 896	2 240	8.6	78.6	1.2	22.2	1.0	3.8	6.3	18.1	8.2	11.5	11.2	12.6
40 063	...	7	Hughes	2 084	13 806	2 183	6.6	71.7	6.5	23.8	0.6	4.4	5.4	16.3	8.4	13.1	12.4	12.8
40 065	11060	5	Jackson	2 079	25 998	1 560	12.5	67.1	8.3	3.4	2.3	22.1	7.8	17.7	11.2	14.5	11.3	12.4
40 067	...	8	Jefferson	1 965	6 292	2 735	3.2	83.4	1.8	9.5	0.8	9.0	6.4	17.2	7.4	10.6	11.2	13.4
40 069	...	7	Johnston	1 665	11 103	2 347	6.7	78.5	2.8	21.1	0.7	4.3	6.2	17.3	9.8	11.3	11.3	13.3
40 071	38620	5	Kay	2 382	45 478	1 061	19.1	80.7	2.9	13.3	1.0	7.0	7.1	18.0	9.1	11.6	10.9	12.6
40 073	...	6	Kingfisher	2 326	15 532	2 071	6.7	80.6	1.8	5.2	0.6	14.5	6.9	19.4	8.0	11.8	11.8	14.2

1. CBSA = Core Based Statistical Area. See Appendix A for explanation. See Appendix B for list of metropolitan areas with component counties. 2. County type code from the Economic Research Service of USDA Rural-Urban Continuum Codes. See Appendix A for definition. 3. Dry land or land partially or temporarily covered by water. 4. May be of any race.

STATE County	Population, 2013 (cont.) Age (percent) (cont.) 55 to 64 years	65 to 74 years	75 years and over	Percent female	Population change and components of change, 2000–2014 Total persons 2000	2010	Percent change 2000–2010	2010–2014	Components of change, 2010–2014 Births	Deaths	Net migration	Households, 2009–2013 Number	Persons per household	Percent Family households	Female family householder[1]	One person
	16	17	18	19	20	21	22	23	24	25	26	27	28	29	30	31
OHIO—Cont'd																
Ottawa	17.0	12.4	8.8	50.5	40 985	41 428	1.1	-0.7	1 508	2 020	173	17 614	2.30	69.3	8.5	26.7
Paulding	14.3	9.4	6.9	50.2	20 293	19 614	-3.3	-3.2	935	836	-728	7 730	2.50	70.3	8.4	25.9
Perry	13.7	8.9	5.6	49.9	34 078	36 058	5.8	-0.7	1 729	1 514	-450	13 793	2.59	72.7	12.2	23.8
Pickaway	12.5	8.4	6.0	47.3	52 727	55 698	5.6	2.1	2 572	2 147	750	19 167	2.69	74.2	10.7	21.3
Pike	13.4	9.0	6.8	50.1	27 695	28 709	3.7	-1.6	1 435	1 389	-480	10 859	2.59	69.9	14.9	25.1
Portage	13.1	8.2	5.8	51.2	152 061	161 419	6.2	0.3	5 981	5 656	202	60 992	2.57	66.1	11.7	25.7
Preble	14.4	9.5	7.2	50.4	42 337	42 270	-0.2	-1.6	1 875	1 879	-648	16 238	2.56	71.7	11.1	24.0
Putnam	13.8	7.7	7.4	50.0	34 726	34 499	-0.7	-1.0	1 911	1 298	-974	13 022	2.61	74.0	7.1	22.4
Richland	14.0	9.5	8.2	49.5	128 852	124 475	-3.4	-2.0	5 970	5 610	-2 815	48 458	2.40	64.3	12.9	31.4
Ross	13.6	8.6	6.0	47.4	73 345	78 064	6.4	-1.2	3 529	3 405	-956	28 308	2.53	67.8	12.4	26.9
Sandusky	14.4	9.0	7.6	50.7	61 792	60 944	-1.4	-1.3	2 973	2 541	-1 157	23 906	2.46	68.8	11.2	26.8
Scioto	13.5	8.9	7.5	50.7	79 195	79 499	0.4	-2.8	3 767	3 887	-2 051	29 452	2.56	65.1	11.2	29.5
Seneca	14.2	8.3	7.5	50.0	58 683	56 745	-3.3	-1.9	2 385	2 471	-1 004	21 651	2.47	69.8	11.9	24.9
Shelby	13.3	8.0	6.3	49.9	47 910	49 423	3.2	-1.0	2 659	1 756	-1 355	18 311	2.66	72.4	9.8	22.8
Stark	14.3	9.3	8.0	51.5	378 098	375 586	-0.7	0.0	17 344	16 902	245	150 003	2.44	66.1	12.2	29.0
Summit	14.1	8.5	7.3	51.6	542 899	541 781	-0.2	0.0	26 247	23 384	-2 093	220 375	2.42	62.8	13.1	31.5
Trumbull	15.1	10.2	8.6	51.3	225 116	210 312	-6.6	-2.4	8 822	10 479	-3 112	86 246	2.37	64.5	13.4	30.9
Tuscarawas	14.3	9.3	8.3	50.6	90 914	92 582	1.8	0.2	4 646	4 129	-289	36 149	2.53	69.4	10.1	26.2
Union	11.3	6.5	4.4	52.4	40 909	52 300	27.8	2.9	2 511	1 336	281	18 216	2.72	73.5	9.6	22.4
Van Wert	14.0	9.5	8.4	51.1	29 659	28 744	-3.1	-1.0	1 354	1 246	-429	11 442	2.47	69.3	9.4	27.2
Vinton	14.5	9.1	6.0	50.0	12 806	13 435	4.9	-1.5	650	594	-232	5 191	2.56	70.8	13.0	24.9
Warren	12.1	7.3	5.2	49.7	158 383	212 693	34.3	4.1	10 367	6 456	4 748	76 546	2.74	76.3	8.4	19.5
Washington	15.1	10.5	8.2	51.0	63 251	61 778	-2.3	-0.9	2 598	2 964	-90	25 029	2.39	65.6	9.4	29.4
Wayne	13.3	8.7	7.1	50.5	111 564	114 520	2.6	0.9	6 420	4 484	-848	42 487	2.61	70.7	9.1	25.2
Williams	14.0	9.3	7.8	50.3	39 188	37 642	-3.9	-0.9	1 831	1 582	-565	14 947	2.44	68.0	9.7	27.1
Wood	12.5	7.4	6.0	50.9	121 065	125 488	3.7	3.3	5 721	4 204	2 410	49 086	2.45	63.8	9.5	27.5
Wyandot	13.8	9.0	8.5	50.5	22 908	22 615	-1.3	-1.2	1 130	981	-393	9 284	2.39	66.1	9.5	28.3
OKLAHOMA	12.2	8.1	6.1	50.5	3 450 654	3 751 351	8.7	3.4	224 135	157 577	58 870	1 444 081	2.55	66.6	12.4	28.1
Adair	12.1	8.6	5.6	50.0	21 038	22 683	7.8	-2.2	1 265	1 009	-759	8 046	2.76	74.2	16.0	23.7
Alfalfa	13.6	9.6	8.6	40.4	6 105	5 642	-7.6	2.6	244	282	205	2 031	2.27	64.0	7.4	30.6
Atoka	13.5	10.3	7.1	48.2	13 879	14 182	2.2	-2.7	630	553	-418	5 303	2.40	71.7	16.3	25.8
Beaver	13.7	9.3	7.5	49.6	5 857	5 636	-3.8	-2.7	230	175	-194	2 108	2.62	73.1	5.6	23.6
Beckham	11.4	6.4	5.7	46.5	19 799	22 119	11.7	7.1	1 544	1 001	1 014	7 755	2.68	68.0	14.2	26.9
Blaine	14.2	9.6	8.4	50.7	11 976	11 943	-0.3	-17.0	669	484	-2 400	3 815	2.18	66.1	13.5	29.6
Bryan	12.1	9.9	6.9	51.2	36 534	42 416	16.1	4.9	2 557	1 914	1 391	16 575	2.53	64.5	12.7	29.5
Caddo	12.2	8.6	6.6	48.2	30 150	29 600	-1.8	-1.0	1 714	1 486	-477	10 230	2.71	69.6	13.4	25.4
Canadian	11.5	7.2	4.6	50.4	87 697	115 541	31.8	12.2	7 006	3 642	10 368	41 876	2.80	74.5	10.0	21.5
Carter	12.7	8.7	6.7	51.2	45 621	47 557	4.2	2.3	2 729	2 529	895	17 411	2.70	66.5	12.1	29.4
Cherokee	11.8	8.8	5.9	50.7	42 521	46 987	10.5	2.9	2 640	2 008	700	16 875	2.68	65.9	12.5	29.2
Choctaw	14.0	11.3	8.1	51.3	15 342	15 205	-0.9	-0.3	831	832	-40	6 043	2.48	64.7	15.0	33.4
Cimarron	14.3	11.4	11.0	50.4	3 148	2 475	-21.4	-7.3	107	105	-191	1 067	2.25	67.5	11.9	28.2
Cleveland	11.0	6.9	4.6	50.1	208 016	255 755	22.9	5.5	12 982	7 685	8 406	96 701	2.58	66.4	10.7	26.0
Coal	13.8	10.8	9.0	51.4	6 031	5 925	-1.8	-2.0	280	333	-78	2 328	2.51	66.8	12.8	30.3
Comanche	10.2	6.1	4.7	48.1	114 996	124 098	7.9	0.8	8 527	4 095	-3 547	44 251	2.59	66.3	15.6	27.7
Cotton	13.9	10.0	7.8	50.0	6 614	6 193	-6.4	-0.7	308	342	-20	2 345	2.58	69.6	10.6	27.3
Craig	12.9	10.6	7.9	49.2	14 950	15 029	0.5	-2.9	687	879	-264	5 603	2.46	67.6	10.8	29.2
Creek	13.6	9.8	6.7	50.6	67 367	69 967	3.9	1.0	3 691	3 518	414	26 296	2.64	71.9	10.8	25.0
Custer	10.3	6.7	6.3	50.1	26 142	27 469	5.1	7.4	1 954	1 213	1 269	10 562	2.51	65.7	9.6	24.7
Delaware	15.1	13.8	8.6	50.7	37 077	41 487	11.9	-0.1	1 616	2 155	533	16 589	2.47	69.8	9.4	26.2
Dewey	13.4	10.6	8.6	50.8	4 743	4 810	1.4	2.2	242	298	147	1 830	2.57	68.6	7.0	28.4
Ellis	15.8	10.7	9.4	51.1	4 075	4 151	1.9	0.0	190	207	11	1 734	2.32	69.1	7.0	29.5
Garfield	12.4	7.9	7.4	50.3	57 813	60 580	4.8	4.1	4 048	2 844	1 355	23 508	2.52	67.6	12.8	28.2
Garvin	13.5	9.5	7.7	50.8	27 210	27 576	1.3	-0.1	1 561	1 572	24	10 294	2.62	68.7	11.9	27.2
Grady	13.1	8.8	5.9	50.2	45 516	52 431	15.2	2.7	2 596	2 203	1 073	19 762	2.64	75.0	10.2	22.2
Grant	13.9	10.0	10.5	50.8	5 144	4 527	-12.0	-0.6	214	252	16	1 951	2.27	66.5	7.7	30.5
Greer	11.2	9.0	9.3	43.1	6 061	6 239	2.9	-1.4	280	318	-57	2 246	2.24	62.9	6.7	34.3
Harmon	12.9	9.3	9.5	51.4	3 283	2 922	-11.0	-4.2	150	138	-142	1 106	2.50	70.3	15.1	26.9
Harper	13.5	8.1	9.7	50.1	3 562	3 685	3.5	3.4	212	218	135	1 492	2.45	69.0	6.9	28.6
Haskell	13.1	11.2	7.9	50.1	11 792	12 769	8.3	1.0	633	585	141	4 713	2.70	66.8	10.4	27.9
Hughes	13.0	10.2	8.3	46.3	14 154	14 003	-1.1	-1.4	593	760	-34	4 920	2.47	68.3	13.1	29.2
Jackson	11.5	7.5	6.0	50.2	28 439	26 446	-7.0	-1.7	1 943	1 008	-1 382	10 455	2.44	67.2	11.8	26.0
Jefferson	14.6	10.8	8.3	49.7	6 818	6 472	-5.1	-2.8	321	375	-130	2 456	2.56	70.7	10.9	26.4
Johnston	13.3	10.1	7.4	51.2	10 513	10 957	4.2	1.3	552	620	227	4 248	2.51	67.1	14.1	30.3
Kay	13.0	9.4	8.3	50.5	48 080	46 562	-3.2	-2.3	2 724	2 321	-1 395	18 357	2.46	65.1	11.3	30.0
Kingfisher	12.6	7.9	7.3	50.5	13 926	15 034	8.0	3.3	865	615	235	5 733	2.59	72.3	10.3	25.1

1. No spouse present.

STATE County	Persons in group quarters, 2014	Daytime population, 2009–2013 Number	Daytime population, 2009–2013 Employment/residence ratio	Births, 2014 Total	Births, 2014 Rate[1]	Deaths, 2014 Number	Deaths, 2014 Rate[1]	Persons under 65 with no health insurance, 2013 Number	Persons under 65 with no health insurance, 2013 Percent	Medicare, 2014 Eligible for Medicare	Medicare, 2014 Enrolled in Medicare Advantage	Medicare, 2014 Enrolled in a Medicare prescription drug plan	Serious crimes known to police,[2] 2013 Total Number	Serious crimes known to police,[2] 2013 Total Rate[3]
	32	33	34	35	36	37	38	39	40	41	42	43	44	45
OHIO—Cont'd														
Ottawa	495	37 291	0.78	351	8.5	486	11.8	3 836	12.0	10 237	3 124	6 362	596	1 698
Paulding	85	16 264	0.62	208	11.0	180	9.5	2 140	13.4	3 907	1 015	2 476	255	1 353
Perry	307	28 926	0.50	388	10.8	363	10.1	4 483	14.6	6 935	1 972	3 951	419	1 202
Pickaway	4 891	48 902	0.69	623	11.0	535	9.4	5 554	12.7	10 060	4 476	4 864	1 827	3 221
Pike	496	29 597	1.10	327	11.6	347	12.3	3 255	13.7	6 142	1 424	3 867	410	1 441
Portage	7 862	145 405	0.77	1 369	8.5	1 329	8.2	15 656	12.0	27 645	12 525	13 558	2 984	2 005
Preble	386	35 282	0.64	440	10.6	419	10.1	4 478	13.0	8 242	3 374	3 918	805	1 931
Putnam	303	28 763	0.68	450	13.2	320	9.4	2 884	10.1	6 026	1 361	4 530	233	709
Richland	7 234	124 157	1.02	1 413	11.6	1 313	10.8	13 008	13.8	26 356	6 747	15 959	5 895	4 852
Ross	5 855	77 631	0.99	828	10.7	785	10.2	7 880	13.0	14 841	5 319	7 622	3 704	4 787
Sandusky	901	59 509	0.96	687	11.4	589	9.8	6 415	12.9	12 201	3 299	7 642	1 423	2 813
Scioto	3 300	76 271	0.90	867	11.2	885	11.5	9 050	14.5	16 142	3 547	10 575	2 541	3 246
Seneca	2 670	51 197	0.79	532	9.6	549	9.9	5 820	13.0	11 270	2 354	7 532	NA	NA
Shelby	589	53 234	1.18	617	12.6	405	8.3	4 659	11.1	8 566	2 591	5 039	1 565	3 204
Stark	9 098	369 386	0.96	4 106	10.9	3 910	10.4	38 395	12.6	78 642	38 522	30 027	11 399	3 072
Summit	10 349	557 542	1.06	6 235	11.5	5 595	10.3	56 550	12.6	101 732	49 288	43 213	18 058	3 624
Trumbull	4 003	199 643	0.89	2 070	10.1	2 407	11.7	23 978	14.5	47 586	22 164	21 419	6 178	3 070
Tuscarawas	1 251	88 190	0.89	1 098	11.8	970	10.5	10 880	14.4	18 914	8 095	8 315	1 038	1 143
Union	2 940	58 192	1.23	588	10.9	317	5.9	4 097	9.2	7 068	2 889	3 690	674	1 273
Van Wert	396	26 954	0.86	325	11.4	296	10.4	2 904	12.6	5 979	1 628	3 510	661	2 293
Vinton	68	10 904	0.50	165	12.5	150	11.3	1 639	14.6	2 412	655	1 590	241	1 825
Warren	5 769	200 463	0.85	2 396	10.8	1 636	7.4	16 852	9.1	31 832	13 431	14 376	3 506	1 626
Washington	1 756	60 704	0.96	623	10.2	693	11.3	6 766	14.0	13 772	2 822	8 511	673	1 104
Wayne	3 484	111 238	0.93	1 501	13.0	1 055	9.1	13 773	14.7	21 069	8 818	10 258	2 066	1 898
Williams	990	37 809	1.01	430	11.5	369	9.9	3 695	12.2	7 693	2 380	4 710	NA	NA
Wood	7 150	129 058	1.03	1 370	10.6	1 011	7.8	11 874	11.3	21 036	8 385	11 856	2 172	1 903
Wyandot	251	20 422	0.80	276	12.3	243	10.9	2 270	12.4	4 574	1 305	2 963	162	853
OKLAHOMA	110 052	3 774 415	0.99	53 091	13.7	37 703	9.7	662 280	20.6	668 902	102 043	337 967	143 046	3 715
Adair	92	20 806	0.80	342	15.4	274	12.4	5 095	26.6	4 149	152	2 488	448	2 015
Alfalfa	1 054	5 568	0.95	69	11.9	51	8.8	719	18.9	1 113	40	758	56	982
Atoka	750	12 926	0.77	130	9.4	110	8.0	2 796	26.0	2 935	174	1 863	229	1 633
Beaver	43	4 891	0.73	55	10.0	42	7.7	1 062	23.1	998	24	636	87	1 554
Beckham	1 921	24 672	1.20	378	16.0	255	10.8	3 678	19.4	3 511	162	2 332	551	2 340
Blaine	107	10 441	1.07	173	17.4	104	10.5	1 839	23.2	2 025	76	1 394	214	2 185
Bryan	1 134	41 651	0.92	624	14.0	505	11.4	8 496	23.6	8 369	512	4 884	1 664	3 795
Caddo	1 932	27 822	0.83	359	12.2	360	12.3	5 955	25.5	5 605	175	3 491	607	2 036
Canadian	2 488	92 549	0.53	1 705	13.2	893	6.9	16 582	15.2	17 658	4 421	7 500	4 820	3 848
Carter	913	51 022	1.16	673	13.8	617	12.6	8 186	20.1	9 659	698	6 076	2 639	5 447
Cherokee	2 009	45 012	0.87	595	12.3	464	9.6	10 303	25.9	8 487	700	4 594	1 493	3 066
Choctaw	172	14 907	0.95	196	12.9	206	13.6	2 680	22.3	3 567	221	2 183	196	1 286
Cimarron	7	2 299	0.88	26	11.3	20	8.7	540	30.0	602	NA	417	19	801
Cleveland	10 545	218 868	0.67	3 060	11.3	1 849	6.9	37 610	16.4	37 298	6 678	16 701	10 158	3 765
Coal	61	5 478	0.80	59	10.2	73	12.6	1 225	26.1	1 176	65	658	40	666
Comanche	10 312	128 964	1.08	1 861	14.9	1 020	8.2	18 851	18.5	16 903	734	6 855	6 371	5 006
Cotton	48	5 428	0.73	85	13.8	82	13.3	1 084	21.4	1 291	47	718	41	664
Craig	1 050	15 347	1.08	158	10.8	218	14.9	2 499	22.0	3 594	282	2 128	168	1 142
Creek	1 062	61 715	0.71	859	12.2	865	12.2	11 535	19.7	14 427	4 405	6 247	1 515	2 130
Custer	1 516	28 094	1.00	468	15.9	283	9.6	5 520	22.7	4 321	232	2 782	634	2 185
Delaware	356	36 799	0.71	420	10.1	520	12.5	8 180	25.5	9 693	1 178	5 115	559	1 344
Dewey	93	4 723	0.96	63	12.8	75	15.3	827	21.4	1 067	32	688	61	1 273
Ellis	46	3 991	0.93	49	11.8	49	11.8	574	17.3	861	79	516	59	1 437
Garfield	1 801	62 256	1.05	960	15.2	648	10.3	9 630	18.6	11 316	610	7 171	2 739	4 446
Garvin	317	28 053	1.06	377	13.7	323	11.7	5 019	22.4	5 895	383	3 820	782	2 861
Grady	1 082	44 656	0.65	603	11.2	486	9.0	8 311	18.5	9 315	1 158	5 118	1 226	2 289
Grant	73	4 183	0.84	55	12.2	49	10.9	623	17.4	985	39	673	24	530
Greer	1 146	5 619	0.76	73	11.9	61	9.9	737	18.6	1 276	21	867	69	1 137
Harmon	100	2 803	0.91	39	13.9	31	11.1	550	24.4	620	23	424	134	4 597
Harper	41	3 592	0.94	52	13.6	71	18.6	759	24.4	723	12	516	7	190
Haskell	78	12 121	0.84	164	12.7	138	10.7	2 794	26.5	3 096	236	1 754	192	1 470
Hughes	1 565	13 038	0.83	137	9.9	171	12.4	2 572	26.0	3 118	227	1 784	118	853
Jackson	718	26 842	1.05	468	18.0	204	7.8	4 396	20.0	4 138	138	2 144	910	3 463
Jefferson	144	5 713	0.71	76	12.1	84	13.4	1 278	25.0	1 457	79	951	88	1 378
Johnston	292	10 431	0.86	133	12.0	162	14.6	2 035	23.1	2 390	123	1 512	121	1 095
Kay	1 273	47 421	1.07	647	14.2	553	12.2	7 740	21.0	9 956	881	6 320	1 794	3 914
Kingfisher	155	14 287	0.89	226	14.6	132	8.5	2 908	22.6	2 714	186	1 906	217	1 442

1. Per 1,000 estimated resident population. 2. Data for serious crimes have not been adjusted for underreporting; this may affect comparability between geographic areas and over time.
3. Per 100,000 population estimated by the FBI.

STATE County	Serious crimes known to police, 2013 (cont.)[1]		Education						Money income, 2009–2013				Income and poverty, 2013			
	Rate[2]		School enrollment and attainment, 2009–2013				Local government expenditures,[5] 2012–2013			Households				Percent below poverty level		
			Enrollment[3]		Attainment[4] (percent)											
	Violent	Property	Total	Percent private	High school graduate or less	Bachelor's degree or more	Total current spending (mil dol)	Current spending per student (dollars)	Per capita income[6] (dollars)	Median income (dollars)	Mean income (dollars)	Percent with income of $200,000 or more	Median household income (dollars)	All persons	Children under 18 years	Children 5 to 17 years in families
	46	47	48	49	50	51	52	53	54	55	56	57	58	59	60	61
OHIO—Cont'd																
Ottawa	97	1 601	8 840	13.0	48.0	20.3	73.0	11 313	27 979	53 202	65 723	2.2	51 787	10.4	14.8	13.6
Paulding	53	1 300	4 712	10.2	61.7	12.1	35.2	11 617	22 714	44 861	57 147	1.7	46 921	12.3	18.6	16.8
Perry	52	1 151	9 109	9.2	63.2	10.2	62.8	10 894	19 372	41 446	50 003	1.1	41 586	17.8	27.1	25.3
Pickaway	78	3 144	13 761	10.8	59.1	16.1	95.5	10 157	23 851	54 003	67 287	2.0	52 666	13.6	19.0	17.5
Pike	25	1 416	6 774	6.2	66.8	12.2	64.1	13 373	20 071	42 165	51 535	0.9	41 092	24.3	36.0	32.0
Portage	88	1 917	50 460	9.7	47.8	25.1	248.3	11 065	25 332	52 697	65 457	2.2	52 576	16.9	18.4	16.3
Preble	77	1 855	10 410	9.4	58.2	11.3	65.4	10 076	23 374	48 405	59 273	1.3	47 251	13.1	19.8	17.4
Putnam	49	660	9 029	11.2	51.0	19.9	61.7	10 415	25 481	61 192	67 868	1.8	60 562	7.2	9.2	8.5
Richland	197	4 655	28 741	19.2	55.8	14.9	200.6	13 157	21 932	41 835	54 211	1.2	40 210	17.6	25.6	22.9
Ross	204	4 583	18 747	9.0	59.7	13.7	125.9	11 242	21 310	43 264	56 902	1.9	42 730	19.4	28.1	26.7
Sandusky	243	2 569	15 104	16.9	52.2	13.7	92.5	10 919	22 799	46 140	56 439	1.2	46 800	12.9	19.5	18.3
Scioto	124	3 122	19 659	9.0	57.5	14.2	129.9	11 067	19 437	35 379	49 798	1.5	36 682	24.5	32.1	29.6
Seneca	NA	NA	14 960	24.6	56.2	15.3	68.0	12 081	22 075	43 764	56 020	1.5	47 121	13.9	20.3	18.3
Shelby	94	3 110	13 059	11.5	58.1	14.5	82.9	9 650	24 028	50 427	63 549	2.1	51 529	10.0	14.9	13.4
Stark	275	2 796	97 045	16.4	50.1	21.1	574.5	10 143	24 453	45 641	59 807	2.2	45 199	15.4	23.1	20.5
Summit	378	3 246	141 232	16.5	42.1	29.6	862.9	11 886	27 818	49 669	66 568	3.6	49 353	14.8	20.6	20.0
Trumbull	234	2 836	46 725	12.0	56.9	17.0	330.4	11 438	22 568	42 880	53 566	1.3	41 951	18.7	32.3	31.6
Tuscarawas	54	1 089	21 616	11.1	61.5	15.2	151.8	9 877	21 966	43 739	54 561	1.3	44 121	14.3	21.7	21.3
Union	34	1 239	13 818	11.8	45.2	27.0	75.0	9 714	28 852	65 086	81 415	4.5	68 650	7.8	9.5	8.2
Van Wert	87	2 206	7 028	16.4	57.4	15.4	54.6	11 197	22 790	45 355	55 992	1.0	47 169	13.3	17.6	15.8
Vinton	121	1 704	3 372	5.0	67.1	8.5	24.3	10 693	18 101	36 705	46 110	0.3	37 842	22.2	35.1	32.1
Warren	63	1 564	59 801	19.3	35.3	37.9	363.8	10 140	33 172	72 487	92 522	7.7	75 041	7.3	8.8	7.7
Washington	77	1 027	14 151	20.2	54.4	16.0	86.4	10 659	23 496	42 834	56 439	2.0	41 236	16.3	22.3	20.0
Wayne	76	1 822	28 965	22.9	57.1	20.0	181.4	11 631	23 061	49 135	61 230	1.9	49 580	13.1	20.1	18.8
Williams	NA	NA	9 149	12.0	58.8	12.8	57.4	10 088	21 350	43 089	52 988	1.1	45 510	12.1	18.8	17.0
Wood	76	1 827	42 002	9.6	38.8	29.5	214.2	12 749	26 326	52 069	66 861	2.4	52 578	13.0	12.7	11.6
Wyandot	37	816	5 487	11.0	60.3	12.0	32.4	9 325	22 382	44 448	54 131	1.0	46 568	11.2	14.8	13.6
OKLAHOMA	441	3 274	987 913	11.0	45.4	23.5	5 176.3	7 672	24 208	45 339	61 481	2.7	45 724	16.7	23.8	21.7
Adair	288	1 727	5 960	3.4	62.8	12.7	42.1	8 985	15 116	32 556	41 049	0.3	31 997	30.4	40.5	38.1
Alfalfa	88	894	1 042	7.0	51.4	21.4	10.3	11 589	22 488	44 811	58 102	2.7	50 190	15.9	19.4	17.9
Atoka	100	1 534	3 183	6.6	59.2	14.2	21.1	9 263	17 842	37 012	48 691	1.5	34 973	20.8	29.4	26.5
Beaver	125	1 429	1 370	4.7	54.6	17.9	12.0	10 802	26 109	51 422	69 174	3.6	55 279	10.4	15.3	13.8
Beckham	183	2 157	4 599	7.3	56.6	16.4	28.6	7 069	23 959	48 989	67 935	3.7	49 578	15.9	20.7	19.8
Blaine	235	1 951	2 190	2.2	54.7	17.0	18.4	9 850	20 242	44 206	55 195	2.0	41 276	16.8	26.0	24.8
Bryan	436	3 359	10 532	5.1	51.7	20.1	59.9	8 022	20 524	38 897	51 352	1.6	36 601	19.2	27.6	27.0
Caddo	299	1 738	6 995	3.6	58.1	13.7	45.5	8 479	17 858	39 267	49 431	1.0	37 298	21.1	29.6	26.7
Canadian	443	3 405	32 176	10.0	37.7	25.3	167.2	6 840	27 552	63 629	75 889	3.3	63 889	7.3	10.8	9.4
Carter	890	4 557	11 934	15.2	56.7	17.1	74.0	7 955	21 476	41 401	55 599	2.0	43 030	17.3	23.5	22.6
Cherokee	234	2 832	13 970	7.2	44.3	24.5	62.9	8 392	18 582	37 260	48 090	0.8	36 643	22.0	32.6	29.5
Choctaw	105	1 181	3 449	3.6	59.9	14.0	21.5	8 095	17 739	30 201	42 455	0.8	30 972	27.3	40.2	38.2
Cimarron	42	759	522	11.7	52.9	18.5	5.3	12 073	23 514	38 301	54 092	2.1	39 617	17.5	28.7	26.6
Cleveland	316	3 449	81 229	10.1	35.2	31.4	313.0	7 152	26 920	54 989	70 566	3.1	54 865	12.7	15.3	14.0
Coal	33	632	1 353	10.7	63.9	13.3	12.8	10 531	19 752	34 867	48 619	0.8	35 538	18.1	26.8	23.7
Comanche	746	4 260	32 871	5.9	45.3	19.9	172.3	7 587	22 363	46 036	58 541	2.1	42 733	20.2	28.5	27.5
Cotton	16	648	1 471	9.1	56.0	14.7	9.6	8 807	21 452	46 317	54 814	0.6	40 608	16.1	23.5	20.9
Craig	54	1 088	3 249	6.7	57.4	12.5	24.0	8 251	19 820	39 236	49 888	0.8	36 932	19.9	27.9	23.3
Creek	200	1 930	16 624	8.8	54.5	15.3	97.5	7 473	22 327	43 026	57 489	2.3	44 608	14.9	21.2	18.8
Custer	217	1 968	8 671	4.9	47.8	27.8	40.1	7 685	23 261	44 972	60 337	2.1	47 399	15.1	18.6	18.4
Delaware	118	1 226	8 367	6.4	54.4	16.1	53.8	7 981	21 109	36 588	51 471	1.7	36 225	22.0	35.0	31.0
Dewey	21	1 252	1 113	3.7	54.0	19.5	11.6	10 951	24 860	46 488	63 107	3.8	49 308	12.4	17.9	15.3
Ellis	122	1 315	875	2.1	45.9	23.9	10.7	12 445	27 183	47 344	64 070	3.4	49 804	11.9	17.2	14.7
Garfield	393	4 054	14 938	12.8	49.5	21.7	83.5	7 632	24 177	44 530	59 952	2.5	47 961	13.7	20.5	19.1
Garvin	282	2 580	5 558	6.9	60.1	15.4	43.3	8 024	21 285	38 245	54 387	2.3	38 414	19.8	24.7	22.4
Grady	359	1 931	13 241	6.9	51.8	16.8	66.8	7 144	23 500	49 637	60 983	2.0	48 671	13.0	17.9	15.8
Grant	22	508	975	5.6	46.3	22.1	8.9	10 924	27 469	46 625	62 883	2.7	51 119	12.4	18.4	16.5
Greer	99	1 038	1 158	1.6	57.0	14.4	8.0	8 432	17 969	39 900	48 155	1.7	34 806	21.7	31.1	27.8
Harmon	137	4 460	630	4.9	53.2	17.8	4.8	8 673	18 582	26 688	47 857	2.0	31 707	23.5	32.9	32.7
Harper	27	163	832	8.5	58.0	16.1	7.0	9 102	22 675	46 117	54 235	0.4	45 395	10.1	14.4	13.9
Haskell	138	1 332	2 920	3.6	60.3	11.4	19.9	8 484	18 896	35 334	46 471	1.3	35 045	22.3	32.2	29.2
Hughes	65	788	2 868	1.8	61.0	10.9	21.5	8 982	18 268	34 619	49 692	2.4	34 656	22.5	31.5	28.9
Jackson	228	3 235	6 748	8.2	43.3	20.1	39.2	7 653	22 925	42 824	56 485	1.5	41 147	17.3	26.0	25.5
Jefferson	188	1 190	1 361	2.4	65.4	11.2	11.3	9 671	19 042	34 701	46 751	0.9	31 916	21.7	30.5	28.7
Johnston	443	651	2 860	7.9	51.3	17.7	16.4	8 376	19 967	36 192	49 524	1.4	35 171	20.5	27.9	23.6
Kay	415	3 500	11 306	7.6	48.0	19.5	67.9	8 044	22 207	41 012	54 399	2.0	41 098	19.6	28.2	25.7
Kingfisher	60	1 382	4 008	8.8	49.6	18.2	28.6	8 344	25 773	54 666	65 389	2.1	54 982	10.4	14.5	13.5

1. Data for serious crimes have not been adjusted for underreporting; this may affect comparability between geographic areas and over time. 2. Per 100,000 population estimated by the FBI.
3. All persons 3 years old and over enrolled in nursery school through college. 4. Persons 25 years old and over. 5. Elementary and secondary education expenditures.
6. Based on population estimated by the American Community Survey, 2009–2013.

STATE County	Personal income, 2013										Earnings, 2013		
			Per capita[1]			Supplements to wages and salaries; employer contributions (mil dol)						Contributions for government social insurance (mil dol)	
	Total (mil dol)	Percent change, 2012–2013	Dollars	Rank	Wages and salaries (mil dol)	Pension and insurance	Government social insurance	Proprietors' income (mil dol)	Dividends, interest, and rent (mil dol)	Personal transfer receipts (mil dol)	Total (mil dol)	From employee and self-employed	From employer
	62	63	64	65	66	67	68	69	70	71	72	73	74
OHIO—Cont'd													
Ottawa	1 759	1.6	42 752	866	571	125	45	124	299	398	865	52	45
Paulding	644	1.6	33 452	2 184	172	41	13	54	96	151	280	15	13
Perry	975	2.9	27 085	2 965	225	54	17	31	114	309	325	22	17
Pickaway	1 976	2.5	35 093	1 885	590	154	40	146	241	419	929	47	40
Pike	968	8.4	34 107	2 064	459	85	36	100	107	304	681	40	36
Portage	6 300	1.8	38 448	1 383	2 336	553	160	401	896	1 168	3 449	176	160
Preble	1 470	1.8	35 232	1 868	380	82	29	95	195	340	586	35	29
Putnam	1 369	2.9	40 161	1 156	429	87	34	153	188	227	703	38	34
Richland	4 016	1.5	32 979	2 255	1 918	410	151	180	622	1 084	2 659	155	151
Ross	2 533	2.3	32 512	2 327	1 169	261	89	134	316	677	1 652	91	89
Sandusky	2 161	3.5	35 952	1 755	1 029	223	84	135	288	499	1 471	83	84
Scioto	2 399	0.0	30 691	2 600	887	218	68	108	324	846	1 281	75	68
Seneca	1 883	3.1	33 668	2 150	685	153	54	132	271	477	1 024	59	54
Shelby	1 822	3.3	37 030	1 578	1 235	216	98	145	285	332	1 694	93	98
Stark	14 659	3.0	39 046	1 293	6 535	1 229	517	1 216	2 280	3 252	9 497	556	517
Summit	23 853	1.9	44 024	753	12 538	2 248	936	1 664	3 703	4 443	17 387	982	936
Trumbull	7 055	1.0	34 173	2 051	2 862	563	229	364	1 132	1 990	4 018	251	229
Tuscarawas	3 151	3.6	34 000	2 079	1 311	282	104	193	481	749	1 889	111	104
Union	2 152	3.0	40 372	1 124	1 691	265	126	90	237	291	2 173	119	126
Van Wert	1 103	4.4	38 745	1 326	396	84	32	93	148	231	605	33	32
Vinton	356	-1.1	26 832	2 982	78	23	5	14	53	126	119	8	5
Warren	10 131	1.9	46 226	608	3 794	661	283	489	1 344	1 272	5 227	295	283
Washington	2 274	1.8	37 094	1 566	1 055	213	83	144	344	546	1 495	89	83
Wayne	3 907	3.5	33 952	2 089	1 903	378	145	279	632	800	2 705	152	145
Williams	1 321	2.8	35 223	1 869	636	136	52	121	189	301	945	53	52
Wood	5 033	1.8	38 936	1 310	2 700	541	208	343	752	857	3 791	199	208
Wyandot	825	4.4	36 750	1 632	343	71	27	103	120	168	543	28	27
OKLAHOMA	161 188	2.0	41 861	X	72 479	11 804	5 805	24 611	28 130	29 176	114 699	6 165	5 805
Adair	510	1.6	22 964	3 091	162	37	14	43	62	203	256	16	14
Alfalfa	243	-5.4	41 497	994	79	15	6	37	65	39	137	7	6
Atoka	408	1.7	29 389	2 764	114	23	9	70	57	127	215	13	9
Beaver	267	-0.1	47 943	486	80	15	6	68	53	33	168	7	6
Beckham	1 057	3.4	44 707	713	599	74	46	205	163	150	925	49	46
Blaine	360	-2.2	37 038	1 575	113	21	9	50	84	84	192	11	9
Bryan	1 394	3.5	31 514	2 475	563	97	44	91	210	384	795	49	44
Caddo	884	-0.3	29 859	2 710	270	60	21	78	161	239	428	26	21
Canadian	5 334	3.1	42 296	908	1 304	208	105	306	732	701	1 923	115	105
Carter	2 046	2.3	42 189	917	1 000	163	80	299	365	430	1 543	86	80
Cherokee	1 466	1.3	30 536	2 621	537	95	41	125	238	406	798	46	41
Choctaw	464	1.7	30 816	2 576	147	30	12	38	63	177	227	15	12
Cimarron	99	-9.9	42 320	905	26	4	2	28	18	21	60	2	2
Cleveland	10 525	2.5	39 078	1 284	3 174	560	252	903	1 893	1 593	4 889	274	252
Coal	180	-1.5	30 722	2 593	41	8	3	21	28	55	73	5	3
Comanche	4 754	1.3	38 052	1 426	2 377	562	215	222	938	914	3 376	167	215
Cotton	237	-2.8	38 515	1 370	50	12	4	24	40	51	90	5	4
Craig	502	-0.1	34 235	2 044	200	41	16	59	84	146	316	19	16
Creek	2 508	1.3	35 587	1 815	775	126	66	279	434	608	1 244	77	66
Custer	1 230	1.2	41 876	951	591	93	46	144	289	193	874	48	46
Delaware	1 373	1.9	33 185	2 230	283	51	24	125	247	378	483	33	24
Dewey	259	5.1	53 445	254	88	14	8	57	48	35	166	8	8
Ellis	227	1.4	54 357	225	62	11	5	55	54	28	133	6	5
Garfield	2 853	1.8	45 812	631	1 332	218	105	287	648	510	1 942	108	105
Garvin	1 047	1.7	38 321	1 396	437	74	36	128	155	271	674	40	36
Grady	1 892	2.2	35 240	1 867	502	82	41	228	310	382	853	50	41
Grant	218	-5.7	48 067	477	71	11	5	45	47	34	133	7	5
Greer	177	-1.8	28 673	2 828	44	9	4	14	29	57	70	5	4
Harmon	106	5.9	36 896	1 605	31	6	2	19	19	28	59	3	2
Harper	141	-2.2	37 098	1 564	44	8	3	13	42	26	69	4	3
Haskell	441	0.8	33 804	2 127	115	20	11	67	57	133	212	12	11
Hughes	439	1.9	31 747	2 440	120	22	10	68	65	134	220	13	10
Jackson	942	-0.7	36 126	1 726	430	105	37	84	203	208	656	33	37
Jefferson	182	0.4	28 323	2 863	42	9	3	19	31	61	74	5	3
Johnston	358	0.9	32 619	2 309	99	20	8	46	47	116	173	10	8
Kay	1 786	1.2	39 146	1 274	807	125	66	225	360	413	1 223	72	66
Kingfisher	686	0.7	44 903	695	271	43	21	119	124	104	453	23	21

1. Based on the resident population estimated as of July 1 of the year shown.

STATE County	Earnings, 2013 (cont.) — Percent by selected industries: Farm	Mining	Construction	Manu-facturing	Infor-mation: professional, scientific, technical services	Retail trade	Finance, insur-ance, real estate and leasing	Health care and social assistance	Govern-ment	Social Security beneficiaries, December 2013: Number	Rate[1]	Supple-mental Security Income recipients, December 2013	Housing units, 2014: Total	Percent change, 2010–2014
	75	76	77	78	79	80	81	82	83	84	85	86	87	88
OHIO—Cont'd														
Ottawa	1.6	D	5.7	17.5	D	7.1	4.9	9.0	16.1	10 760	261	513	28 014	0.4
Paulding	17.4	0.3	4.4	23.5	1.7	5.9	3.1	D	21.9	4 360	227	391	8 692	-0.7
Perry	1.9	4.6	16.5	12.8	2.2	7.5	2.7	D	26.4	7 715	215	1 326	15 126	-0.6
Pickaway	7.1	D	6.1	21.9	D	5.9	3.3	D	28.1	10 750	190	1 290	21 159	-0.5
Pike	1.6	D	9.0	5.5	D	4.9	2.2	10.6	12.6	6 670	235	1 893	12 530	0.4
Portage	0.2	1.5	4.9	20.4	4.5	6.5	4.2	5.3	28.8	28 840	179	2 384	68 046	0.8
Preble	9.3	D	4.3	33.4	D	7.6	3.1	D	17.2	8 970	215	700	17 846	-0.2
Putnam	10.4	D	8.9	34.4	2.3	5.4	3.4	5.4	12.9	6 495	190	329	13 782	0.4
Richland	0.4	0.0	5.5	22.0	4.8	8.1	4.3	14.5	18.8	28 340	232	3 368	54 275	-0.6
Ross	2.4	0.1	2.8	19.8	3.0	7.2	2.8	18.3	27.7	15 960	206	2 945	31 793	-1.1
Sandusky	2.3	D	7.4	37.1	2.3	6.3	4.0	D	13.2	13 110	218	1 167	26 222	-0.6
Scioto	0.3	D	4.5	8.2	4.5	8.0	3.4	26.1	25.7	16 755	215	5 346	34 086	-0.2
Seneca	5.2	0.8	6.9	21.5	3.2	7.5	D	9.4	15.9	12 210	219	1 063	23 932	-0.8
Shelby	3.3	0.0	7.0	48.1	D	4.3	2.1	D	9.2	9 275	189	828	20 190	0.1
Stark	0.2	2.6	6.2	19.7	5.2	7.1	6.4	16.7	12.7	83 565	223	9 325	165 555	0.2
Summit	0.0	0.1	4.6	12.4	9.1	6.7	6.7	15.6	12.4	105 725	195	14 301	245 155	0.0
Trumbull	0.2	0.3	5.2	24.2	3.0	8.3	4.1	13.6	15.5	52 310	253	6 244	95 471	-0.7
Tuscarawas	0.8	3.0	5.8	24.4	4.0	8.0	3.8	12.4	15.5	20 250	218	1 972	39 981	-0.6
Union	0.8	D	2.7	40.4	15.0	3.4	1.9	3.2	10.6	7 445	139	507	19 975	2.9
Van Wert	9.1	D	4.4	28.3	D	5.8	8.8	11.8	13.5	6 530	229	508	12 688	0.6
Vinton	0.9	D	7.1	21.5	D	3.9	5.4	D	30.0	2 725	205	641	6 197	-1.5
Warren	0.3	0.0	4.9	16.0	9.3	7.5	10.0	9.2	12.3	33 420	152	1 952	83 583	3.5
Washington	0.4	3.5	7.9	19.4	4.1	7.0	4.9	18.3	11.8	14 880	242	1 926	28 052	-1.1
Wayne	1.6	3.1	5.8	31.5	3.5	6.1	4.3	D	15.3	21 895	190	1 884	45 998	0.3
Williams	4.2	0.4	3.8	41.6	D	5.8	2.3	10.4	12.7	8 240	220	588	16 545	-0.7
Wood	1.8	0.1	6.0	27.3	4.3	5.2	4.0	7.2	18.9	21 230	164	1 518	53 840	0.9
Wyandot	13.9	1.7	8.8	33.9	D	5.1	3.1	D	14.3	4 930	219	316	9 874	0.0
OKLAHOMA	1.0	12.8	6.4	9.2	6.8	6.4	6.0	9.6	18.5	741 822	193	97 616	1 699 438	2.1
Adair	6.8	D	4.0	24.0	1.6	6.7	2.6	9.9	28.2	4 915	221	937	9 219	0.8
Alfalfa	5.2	26.2	D	D	D	5.9	4.3	2.8	18.7	1 225	211	88	2 746	-0.6
Atoka	0.5	6.1	5.9	4.6	D	12.4	4.7	D	26.9	3 405	247	573	6 343	0.5
Beaver	21.6	18.9	D	D	D	2.0	D	D	14.0	1 050	190	58	2 661	-0.3
Beckham	1.0	31.8	10.8	3.2	D	10.0	6.4	D	6.1	3 955	168	599	10 020	3.9
Blaine	8.2	7.9	6.1	14.0	3.8	6.3	D	5.3	18.9	2 235	228	258	5 179	-0.3
Bryan	1.6	2.0	4.5	6.5	5.9	6.1	3.2	12.7	34.5	9 535	216	1 645	19 913	1.7
Caddo	6.0	6.1	7.0	1.1	4.6	8.0	3.9	D	33.2	6 295	213	984	13 178	0.3
Canadian	0.2	11.1	9.2	14.5	4.7	7.7	5.8	5.7	17.7	18 870	150	1 249	47 130	2.9
Carter	0.0	16.2	6.5	16.5	4.9	7.5	4.6	11.3	11.4	11 210	230	1 632	21 495	1.6
Cherokee	5.1	0.5	5.5	1.4	2.0	7.9	3.8	8.0	49.7	9 730	203	1 587	21 692	1.1
Choctaw	1.7	D	5.4	2.6	3.2	7.4	3.1	13.1	28.1	4 065	270	911	7 522	0.0
Cimarron	44.0	D	D	D	D	4.0	3.4	D	16.7	635	273	36	1 575	-0.8
Cleveland	0.2	2.8	9.4	5.6	8.9	9.1	5.7	9.4	29.2	40 390	150	3 522	110 355	5.3
Coal	2.8	10.5	6.0	3.5	D	7.9	D	9.8	25.8	1 315	226	244	2 803	-0.2
Comanche	0.0	D	4.0	8.4	3.6	5.8	3.8	5.4	55.3	19 230	154	3 173	51 651	1.8
Cotton	12.2	3.4	3.7	D	D	2.6	3.7	3.8	45.0	1 435	233	136	3 010	-0.2
Craig	2.7	D	3.9	7.0	D	9.0	3.9	8.3	28.1	3 880	265	629	6 729	-0.3
Creek	0.5	6.9	13.2	20.9	D	6.5	4.4	9.3	14.4	16 380	232	1 762	30 013	0.8
Custer	0.6	17.7	5.4	11.1	4.5	7.0	4.8	D	16.3	4 770	163	542	12 466	2.1
Delaware	5.1	D	10.2	7.6	D	9.2	5.0	D	24.3	10 835	262	1 312	24 882	0.3
Dewey	2.1	24.8	26.7	2.7	4.9	4.8	D	2.2	11.3	1 170	243	65	2 439	-0.2
Ellis	6.6	28.1	2.2	0.2	D	5.1	D	3.0	15.3	940	227	40	2 276	-0.4
Garfield	2.0	15.9	6.3	7.5	6.7	6.5	4.2	10.6	17.5	12 330	197	1 339	26 832	0.0
Garvin	0.8	18.7	12.4	12.5	3.1	8.3	3.4	D	13.5	6 795	248	847	12 805	-0.2
Grady	1.7	16.6	11.9	8.6	4.2	8.3	5.2	D	16.5	10 545	197	1 320	22 492	1.2
Grant	10.6	28.1	11.5	0.4	D	2.8	D	2.6	11.6	1 075	238	62	2 480	-0.2
Greer	13.4	D	1.7	D	D	6.2	D	13.8	39.8	1 455	236	207	2 734	-0.1
Harmon	29.7	0.3	D	D	D	3.8	D	3.4	23.7	710	247	155	1 544	0.0
Harper	23.1	9.8	D	D	D	4.1	5.1	3.4	28.3	795	207	48	1 893	-0.8
Haskell	9.0	12.7	6.9	7.2	D	7.8	1.9	20.8	14.9	3 505	270	554	6 042	0.2
Hughes	12.5	19.5	4.9	5.0	2.8	6.2	D	D	20.9	3 580	260	485	6 246	1.0
Jackson	5.3	0.3	2.8	6.7	3.2	6.9	3.3	4.1	51.5	4 620	176	742	12 137	0.5
Jefferson	14.4	6.6	D	D	D	8.7	6.5	D	27.0	1 630	256	215	3 390	0.4
Johnston	7.7	9.0	3.2	12.5	D	5.2	D	13.9	27.6	2 715	246	460	5 141	0.3
Kay	1.6	6.6	10.2	10.8	D	8.0	4.0	8.2	16.1	11 205	247	1 067	21 592	-0.5
Kingfisher	7.4	29.2	5.4	6.1	10.4	5.9	3.7	D	8.8	2 980	194	184	6 464	0.9

1. Per 1,000 resident population estimated as of July 1 of the year shown.

STATE County	Housing units, 2009–2013								Civilian labor force, 2014				Civilian employment,[6] 2009–2013		
	Occupied units										Unemployment			Percent	
		Owner-occupied				Renter-occupied									
				Median owner cost as a percent of income											
	Total	Percent	Median value[1]	With a mortgage	Without a mortgage[2]	Median rent[3]	Median rent as a percent of income[2]	Substandard units[4] (percent)	Total	Percent change, 2013–2014	Total	Rate[5]	Total	Management, business, science and arts	Construction, production, and maintenance occupations
	89	90	91	92	93	94	95	96	97	98	99	100	101	102	103
OHIO—Cont'd															
Ottawa	17 614	80.5	136 000	22.6	12.6	716	30.3	1.4	21 775	-1.1	1 621	7.4	19 348	28.7	30.5
Paulding	7 730	78.1	92 300	20.6	10.8	582	29.0	3.1	9 097	0.7	487	5.4	8 360	23.2	41.6
Perry	13 793	70.5	93 100	22.0	11.9	583	30.4	2.1	16 087	-0.1	1 151	7.2	14 595	24.9	34.5
Pickaway	19 167	74.6	149 200	22.7	12.4	732	28.7	3.5	25 879	0.6	1 438	5.6	23 643	31.1	27.1
Pike	10 859	71.9	96 200	22.7	12.1	676	36.1	1.3	10 448	-3.2	940	9.0	9 940	30.9	32.2
Portage	60 992	68.2	150 300	22.1	12.7	802	32.8	1.1	87 776	-0.1	5 107	5.8	81 747	30.1	25.4
Preble	16 238	77.7	116 700	23.4	13.7	717	28.6	1.1	21 283	-0.4	1 197	5.6	19 298	24.8	35.0
Putnam	13 022	84.1	133 500	19.5	10.0	650	22.7	1.2	18 680	-0.9	839	4.5	17 822	31.5	36.2
Richland	48 458	69.2	103 500	22.0	11.7	608	27.3	2.7	54 719	-0.6	3 503	6.4	51 586	27.3	29.3
Ross	28 308	72.5	111 100	21.1	12.2	641	30.7	1.1	33 661	0.3	2 130	6.3	29 158	26.9	31.8
Sandusky	23 906	75.8	110 400	22.1	12.4	613	28.9	1.9	31 203	-1.3	1 757	5.6	28 145	25.1	37.8
Scioto	29 452	69.6	88 200	21.1	13.0	553	33.1	1.0	29 928	-1.6	2 592	8.7	28 135	33.1	23.7
Seneca	21 651	72.4	97 900	19.9	12.0	619	27.1	2.0	27 289	-0.6	1 530	5.6	25 092	24.8	37.1
Shelby	18 311	74.6	123 400	21.6	12.2	689	28.3	1.3	23 709	-0.4	1 191	5.0	22 577	27.0	38.1
Stark	150 003	70.0	122 400	21.9	12.2	666	29.4	1.3	188 619	-0.5	10 751	5.7	169 366	31.3	24.3
Summit	220 375	67.9	135 600	22.3	12.9	741	30.9	1.4	271 591	0.0	15 719	5.8	254 129	36.8	20.2
Trumbull	86 246	72.3	97 400	22.1	12.5	625	30.7	1.6	92 919	-1.7	6 532	7.0	86 531	27.1	29.2
Tuscarawas	36 149	72.9	108 700	21.5	12.0	622	28.9	1.0	45 247	0.3	2 460	5.4	41 620	26.7	32.6
Union	18 216	75.8	171 800	23.0	13.9	810	26.1	1.2	26 913	0.9	1 170	4.3	24 638	36.6	25.9
Van Wert	11 442	79.0	88 600	20.7	10.8	618	27.5	4.5	14 429	1.3	697	4.8	13 010	25.8	38.5
Vinton	5 191	76.4	75 700	22.2	11.6	617	33.7	1.0	5 543	-0.8	437	7.9	5 115	25.5	38.4
Warren	76 546	77.9	188 500	21.9	12.2	919	27.5	1.5	110 718	0.6	5 360	4.8	102 259	43.5	16.4
Washington	25 029	75.3	108 600	21.0	10.3	591	29.5	2.9	28 195	-0.6	1 750	6.2	25 842	29.1	27.8
Wayne	42 487	73.2	135 300	22.3	11.2	665	27.5	1.3	59 250	-0.3	2 716	4.6	53 700	29.0	31.4
Williams	14 947	75.3	98 600	22.3	12.6	625	29.8	1.1	18 779	0.4	1 013	5.4	16 413	23.1	41.0
Wood	49 086	67.6	149 500	21.8	12.7	718	29.4	0.5	68 919	-0.5	3 556	5.2	62 241	35.8	23.4
Wyandot	9 284	71.2	103 500	20.6	10.2	598	25.6	4.4	12 473	0.7	540	4.3	10 970	24.2	40.2
OKLAHOMA	1 444 081	67.1	112 800	21.1	10.9	699	28.7	3.1	1 784 035	-1.1	80 203	4.5	1 686 404	32.7	24.9
Adair	8 046	70.8	75 300	22.3	11.0	518	27.6	0.7	8 052	-2.2	613	7.6	8 346	23.7	39.6
Alfalfa	2 031	77.1	62 600	16.2	10.0	544	23.4	3.0	3 046	3.7	77	2.5	2 186	36.4	28.6
Atoka	5 303	75.1	79 800	21.6	11.5	548	27.7	0.5	4 776	-2.8	292	6.1	5 096	31.9	31.8
Beaver	2 108	73.8	86 200	19.5	10.0	600	15.0	2.0	3 136	3.6	86	2.7	2 717	31.6	35.7
Beckham	7 755	60.9	103 400	19.3	10.0	675	20.2	2.5	12 588	-0.1	358	2.8	9 687	25.0	36.4
Blaine	3 815	72.5	68 000	17.2	11.4	536	24.0	3.9	4 478	3.6	155	3.5	3 826	32.8	20.6
Bryan	16 575	63.3	88 900	19.6	11.4	639	27.8	4.2	17 710	-0.2	863	4.9	18 295	28.5	26.7
Caddo	10 230	70.8	74 900	18.7	10.7	534	24.8	1.8	10 979	-3.6	602	5.5	10 716	27.5	32.3
Canadian	41 876	77.3	139 200	20.9	10.2	856	26.1	2.8	64 407	-0.6	2 297	3.6	59 129	36.1	20.3
Carter	17 411	69.0	90 600	20.7	10.1	634	25.3	3.7	21 761	-1.3	974	4.5	20 118	27.6	29.4
Cherokee	16 875	66.5	103 900	21.4	10.4	576	29.1	3.1	18 297	-2.4	1 090	6.0	19 139	32.5	24.6
Choctaw	6 043	73.6	71 600	22.0	10.5	550	29.1	3.3	5 723	-4.1	465	8.1	5 443	26.2	33.7
Cimarron	1 067	71.8	64 700	17.9	10.0	374	20.2	2.6	1 277	3.5	37	2.9	1 171	38.9	30.6
Cleveland	96 701	67.4	141 300	21.1	10.5	806	30.3	5.9	135 994	-0.8	4 970	3.7	128 217	38.8	18.1
Coal	2 328	72.9	68 400	20.8	10.7	474	25.2	2.8	2 281	1.2	156	6.8	2 306	26.7	36.6
Comanche	44 251	56.6	111 700	20.8	10.3	752	27.1	2.8	48 746	-2.8	2 322	4.8	47 907	31.7	24.9
Cotton	2 345	74.4	74 600	19.7	11.2	619	24.6	3.0	2 821	-1.5	130	4.6	2 692	31.5	29.0
Craig	5 603	78.8	86 800	20.7	10.8	587	25.4	3.7	5 999	-4.0	335	5.6	6 135	27.0	28.6
Creek	26 296	74.8	105 800	22.3	11.0	668	26.4	4.2	30 954	-1.0	1 543	5.0	29 528	27.2	32.1
Custer	10 562	62.8	110 600	19.6	10.2	570	27.2	3.6	15 823	-1.3	492	3.1	13 861	32.3	28.2
Delaware	16 589	77.8	105 200	25.2	12.2	601	27.4	2.6	16 917	-0.5	982	5.8	16 187	27.5	29.6
Dewey	1 830	76.3	77 400	16.8	11.7	611	17.2	1.6	2 376	-8.5	75	3.2	2 018	31.6	37.1
Ellis	1 734	77.7	75 900	16.0	10.6	625	19.6	3.3	2 342	0.3	71	3.0	1 913	38.7	29.3
Garfield	23 508	66.9	89 400	20.5	10.1	647	23.8	2.3	29 313	-0.5	1 048	3.6	27 265	26.1	30.9
Garvin	10 294	73.5	83 800	21.0	11.6	597	24.5	2.8	12 553	0.7	512	4.1	10 894	26.5	34.4
Grady	19 762	76.3	108 400	20.8	10.0	633	25.0	0.9	25 415	-0.5	1 012	4.0	23 922	30.4	29.6
Grant	1 951	75.8	62 800	18.2	10.0	578	19.4	2.9	2 774	4.2	75	2.7	2 129	33.8	31.9
Greer	2 246	67.0	63 000	19.1	12.2	609	24.0	1.3	2 032	1.5	96	4.7	2 361	34.2	22.4
Harmon	1 106	65.0	43 400	16.7	11.4	504	37.7	1.2	1 281	-5.1	52	4.1	1 003	37.6	23.1
Harper	1 492	80.5	68 500	17.1	10.0	508	24.0	2.7	1 958	2.0	55	2.8	1 833	27.8	36.8
Haskell	4 713	74.2	78 000	21.2	10.3	574	28.5	2.3	4 311	-3.3	310	7.2	4 578	26.0	37.9
Hughes	4 920	76.9	66 200	19.7	11.8	577	29.7	4.2	5 631	-2.0	395	7.0	4 766	27.4	33.0
Jackson	10 455	61.8	87 400	20.0	11.4	673	25.8	3.5	10 536	-2.8	462	4.4	11 009	28.9	28.1
Jefferson	2 456	75.2	59 500	21.2	12.1	433	25.1	3.4	2 574	-0.4	121	4.7	2 552	25.4	32.2
Johnston	4 248	71.8	77 200	19.2	11.2	517	28.5	3.6	3 562	-0.6	249	7.0	3 938	32.7	34.9
Kay	18 357	69.9	75 700	19.8	11.3	600	26.0	2.0	19 196	-4.0	1 091	5.7	20 003	28.6	28.8
Kingfisher	5 733	77.2	115 000	18.3	10.8	665	24.3	2.6	7 866	1.0	244	3.1	7 307	30.0	33.7

1. Specified owner-occupied units. 2. A value of 10.0 represents 10 percent or less; a value of 50.0 represents 50 percent or more. 3. Specified renter-occupied units.
4. Overcrowded or lacking complete plumbing facilities. 5. Percent of civilian labor force. 6. Persons 16 years old and over.

STATE County	Private nonfarm establishments, employment and payroll, 2013									Agriculture, 2012			
		Employment						Annual payroll		Farms			
											Percent with:		
	Number of establish- ments	Total	Health care and social assistance	Manufac- turing	Retail trade	Finance and insurance	Professional, scientific, and technical services	Total (mil dol)	Average per employee (dollars)	Number	Fewer than 50 acres	500 acres or more	Farm operators whose principal occu- pation is farming (percent)
	104	105	106	107	108	109	110	111	112	113	114	115	116
OHIO—Cont'd													
Ottawa	1 019	10 444	1 801	1 994	1 372	323	162	416	39 849	620	45.2	8.4	40.5
Paulding	299	3 729	623	1 328	385	100	67	113	30 219	676	34.8	18.2	39.8
Perry	424	3 786	753	756	642	180	D	111	29 204	699	39.1	4.9	29.3
Pickaway	785	11 143	2 311	2 266	1 372	303	424	421	37 816	803	39.6	18.3	52.3
Pike	411	8 049	1 558	1 414	924	195	D	386	48 008	490	27.6	5.3	38.0
Portage	2 969	44 275	5 813	9 990	7 496	734	1 210	1 598	36 094	847	56.6	3.0	42.9
Preble	646	8 448	1 134	2 834	1 241	246	191	286	33 886	1 088	45.9	11.9	41.8
Putnam	728	9 470	966	3 428	1 092	300	180	324	34 266	1 272	27.6	12.2	40.8
Richland	2 639	42 940	7 748	8 033	6 394	1 126	933	1 370	31 906	1 010	37.2	5.0	52.0
Ross	1 218	22 202	5 988	4 182	3 700	511	478	985	44 385	980	35.1	9.0	48.1
Sandusky	1 305	22 149	3 493	8 435	2 456	D	394	834	37 645	737	36.9	14.8	47.2
Scioto	1 279	17 459	6 160	1 509	2 851	445	565	544	31 154	689	39.2	4.9	40.3
Seneca	1 140	16 520	2 689	3 773	2 069	399	392	521	31 553	1 113	28.4	14.7	41.3
Shelby	982	23 185	1 991	11 283	1 824	332	393	1 050	45 286	986	32.4	11.1	41.3
Stark	8 291	139 224	28 598	24 924	20 227	6 440	4 115	4 881	35 059	1 168	56.1	3.3	46.5
Summit	13 388	240 741	44 041	28 811	30 648	9 914	15 312	10 502	43 622	304	72.4	1.6	41.4
Trumbull	4 135	67 464	11 259	14 739	9 842	1 631	1 512	2 629	38 964	888	41.6	4.2	46.7
Tuscarawas	2 143	30 197	5 405	7 940	4 506	693	895	1 024	33 919	1 014	39.2	4.7	41.3
Union	1 004	31 616	1 773	5 560	1 891	363	2 965	1 374	43 468	995	48.2	11.1	44.5
Van Wert	545	9 398	1 517	3 315	1 188	753	142	333	35 425	655	29.2	23.1	55.7
Vinton	137	1 601	403	372	201	D	D	43	27 037	226	25.7	3.5	36.3
Warren	3 928	73 166	9 788	9 563	9 582	4 978	3 946	3 489	47 687	942	67.3	4.7	42.3
Washington	1 414	21 494	4 804	3 523	2 864	737	644	835	38 854	1 122	31.0	2.7	48.7
Wayne	2 448	37 488	5 367	11 042	4 736	1 205	1 574	1 422	37 945	1 928	41.7	5.2	52.0
Williams	801	14 180	2 064	6 462	1 291	247	231	504	35 564	984	35.6	9.8	37.5
Wood	2 722	49 483	4 974	11 148	6 117	823	1 875	2 034	41 108	1 091	42.4	13.7	44.6
Wyandot	497	7 799	760	3 333	768	254	93	272	34 912	593	32.2	21.2	42.2
OKLAHOMA	91 717	1 325 927	215 114	133 191	175 150	58 032	68 636	54 713	41 264	80 245	25.0	19.0	42.1
Adair	219	2 960	552	D	533	D	56	87	29 342	1 129	26.5	10.5	43.8
Alfalfa	130	833	D	D	187	69	D	25	30 543	645	6.8	41.4	55.5
Atoka	270	2 343	424	227	477	D	45	64	27 132	1 103	17.9	16.1	37.0
Beaver	167	1 375	D	D	103	52	38	57	41 793	965	6.1	40.3	32.7
Beckham	894	11 117	1 139	D	1 765	295	357	516	46 375	1 016	15.0	28.0	33.0
Blaine	289	2 349	397	D	307	147	D	74	31 367	798	8.5	35.5	54.1
Bryan	750	10 107	2 079	1 071	1 537	583	361	298	29 509	1 484	23.9	13.9	40.9
Caddo	458	4 609	696	51	834	206	324	147	31 808	1 461	12.3	26.7	46.5
Canadian	2 458	25 835	2 663	2 797	3 712	858	D	982	38 023	1 307	32.8	19.3	47.1
Carter	1 560	20 531	3 430	3 304	2 920	689	664	766	37 326	1 321	22.6	15.7	34.1
Cherokee	728	8 857	2 595	114	1 783	322	129	247	27 839	1 233	29.4	8.5	38.8
Choctaw	261	3 157	1 123	D	D	115	86	81	25 748	965	18.4	18.7	50.3
Cimarron	73	369	D	D	84	32	9	9	23 314	554	3.4	52.0	49.6
Cleveland	5 529	69 588	12 822	3 737	11 226	2 409	3 680	2 320	33 345	1 081	53.6	4.8	45.1
Coal	84	786	223	D	163	D	D	22	27 802	571	16.5	23.1	43.1
Comanche	2 180	31 596	6 216	3 315	5 470	1 621	792	1 025	32 434	1 107	22.6	23.7	43.8
Cotton	75	1 042	60	D	95	40	D	33	31 441	500	11.4	37.0	51.4
Craig	341	4 081	1 245	484	658	209	D	127	31 178	1 263	21.9	13.9	43.9
Creek	1 382	16 456	2 101	4 476	2 002	472	342	640	38 896	1 777	39.0	6.9	31.6
Custer	920	10 688	1 622	1 148	1 851	360	312	416	38 902	877	15.7	36.7	41.7
Delaware	730	7 129	1 301	552	1 470	268	149	199	27 933	1 345	27.7	8.0	46.4
Dewey	148	890	D	30	224	59	28	31	34 552	743	7.1	41.6	40.5
Ellis	103	1 130	169	D	205	47	32	47	41 794	760	5.3	39.7	42.2
Garfield	1 710	22 698	4 113	2 126	3 613	780	545	825	36 335	1 098	16.8	31.5	46.8
Garvin	706	7 727	1 156	1 074	1 187	275	190	297	38 441	1 498	25.3	15.3	36.5
Grady	1 101	11 524	1 770	1 639	1 534	426	368	372	32 246	1 666	26.8	17.6	45.3
Grant	123	1 108	116	D	157	74	17	47	42 607	801	8.1	36.6	50.1
Greer	94	703	218	D	148	D	19	20	28 088	498	5.4	38.6	40.2
Harmon	52	419	127	D	D	D	D	12	29 778	366	4.6	43.7	44.3
Harper	103	673	137	D	135	D	34	20	30 321	532	4.7	49.1	46.1
Haskell	225	2 614	D	D	469	63	52	75	28 710	864	19.8	14.5	46.9
Hughes	226	2 421	788	D	461	70	35	81	25 176	921	15.4	20.7	47.8
Jackson	535	7 637	D	D	1 278	266	117	250	32 787	694	16.7	34.6	44.2
Jefferson	105	751	D	41	123	85	D	24	32 162	417	8.4	42.0	48.2
Johnston	180	1 755	487	D	241	D	36	56	31 928	645	18.0	16.3	42.6
Kay	1 129	15 048	2 190	2 928	2 203	466	410	531	35 309	993	22.7	25.0	43.5
Kingfisher	476	5 564	571	D	592	195	D	242	43 504	1 021	13.0	33.7	49.8

STATE County	Agriculture, 2012 (cont.) — Land in farms: Acreage (1,000)	Land in farms: Percent change, 2007–2012	Land in farms: Acres: Average size of farm	Land in farms: Acres: Total irrigated (1,000)	Land in farms: Acres: Total cropland (1,000)	Value of land and buildings (dollars): Average per farm	Value of land and buildings (dollars): Average per acre	Value of machinery and equipment, average per farm (dollars)	Value of products sold: Total (mil dol)	Value of products sold: Average per farm (dollars)	Value of products sold: Percent from: Crops	Value of products sold: Percent from: Livestock and poultry products	Percent of farms with sales of: $10,000 or more	Percent of farms with sales of: $100,000 or more	Government payments: Total ($1,000)	Government payments: Percent of farms
	117	118	119	120	121	122	123	124	125	126	127	128	129	130	131	132
OHIO—Cont'd																
Ottawa	113	-2.1	182	1.5	103.6	863 753	4 753	119 450	79.1	127 503	98.5	1.5	59.5	26.8	2 390	74.0
Paulding	221	-13.6	327	0.0	205.3	1 583 920	4 848	188 343	187.2	276 864	55.0	45.0	57.8	27.5	5 581	86.1
Perry	107	9.5	153	0.0	67.8	556 103	3 625	82 957	37.1	53 074	82.3	17.7	31.3	7.2	866	21.3
Pickaway	294	1.7	366	0.8	265.8	1 752 654	4 792	200 377	172.3	214 609	78.8	21.2	51.4	28.0	6 106	64.8
Pike	97	20.8	199	0.7	53.2	631 647	3 176	71 429	26.9	54 855	85.3	14.7	35.5	8.4	992	35.7
Portage	83	0.7	98	0.4	58.7	511 001	5 195	78 929	43.7	51 571	73.7	26.3	32.9	7.8	618	18.5
Preble	224	-2.8	206	0.2	195.1	1 083 226	5 256	148 121	154.8	142 302	65.9	34.1	50.6	24.9	4 689	55.9
Putnam	306	0.6	240	0.6	287.2	1 208 173	5 029	175 040	243.2	191 203	74.8	25.2	78.0	41.4	5 606	84.4
Richland	161	9.6	159	0.1	120.3	789 172	4 962	110 557	128.7	127 408	51.7	48.3	55.0	29.5	1 806	32.5
Ross	222	-0.9	226	D	153.7	816 043	3 607	92 039	79.8	81 432	87.5	12.5	35.5	14.3	6 567	57.1
Sandusky	181	0.1	246	0.8	166.3	1 159 189	4 709	160 579	135.3	183 525	93.5	6.5	65.9	37.9	3 636	76.5
Scioto	94	-7.5	137	0.1	42.0	385 210	2 813	67 393	22.2	32 229	63.5	36.5	25.5	6.1	995	25.5
Seneca	291	7.8	261	0.2	258.1	1 272 024	4 873	163 428	174.6	156 848	85.0	15.0	69.7	33.2	4 919	80.8
Shelby	206	-5.4	209	0.0	183.2	1 245 277	5 952	149 865	207.9	210 807	59.5	40.5	68.6	37.9	3 948	77.1
Stark	136	-1.7	116	0.5	105.4	640 866	5 514	101 840	130.7	111 895	50.6	49.4	46.0	16.5	1 693	26.5
Summit	17	9.1	54	0.3	9.6	459 954	8 451	59 490	11.3	37 118	86.7	13.3	32.2	7.6	112	8.2
Trumbull	114	-9.0	128	0.1	77.5	514 001	4 007	112 287	66.5	74 841	72.0	28.0	44.7	14.8	1 117	30.4
Tuscarawas	138	-3.2	136	0.0	78.4	521 749	3 831	95 939	92.3	91 066	25.6	74.4	38.4	12.5	1 562	25.1
Union	242	10.6	243	0.2	216.6	1 248 834	5 136	151 144	169.0	169 875	84.5	15.5	48.0	22.9	4 372	58.6
Van Wert	227	-7.8	347	0.8	214.8	2 177 867	6 276	212 111	209.7	320 087	73.0	27.0	78.0	48.7	5 103	85.0
Vinton	33	-9.3	148	0.0	11.8	358 668	2 427	42 867	4.7	20 805	82.4	17.6	27.9	2.7	195	35.8
Warren	107	13.0	113	0.7	80.2	809 270	7 150	85 670	66.7	70 815	91.1	8.9	30.7	10.1	1 061	24.3
Washington	139	12.0	124	1.8	49.5	331 367	2 676	58 988	30.5	27 165	59.2	40.8	30.7	5.4	1 152	22.1
Wayne	272	9.4	141	0.8	209.6	878 912	6 238	113 697	381.0	197 614	27.2	72.8	64.0	28.8	4 320	29.2
Williams	208	-2.1	211	1.3	181.6	809 134	3 828	101 897	126.0	128 026	66.2	33.8	44.0	20.6	5 771	79.3
Wood	268	-2.8	246	1.0	252.2	1 429 592	5 821	162 243	227.7	208 712	85.0	15.0	63.2	34.8	5 520	80.8
Wyandot	221	0.6	372	0.0	202.0	1 872 809	5 029	211 556	196.7	331 749	66.8	33.2	63.1	38.1	4 364	86.0
OKLAHOMA	34 356	-2.1	428	479.8	11 279.0	573 858	1 340	74 209	7 129.6	88 848	26.3	73.7	40.8	10.0	256 845	37.1
Adair	252	1.1	223	0.2	44.5	441 987	1 979	56 876	164.2	145 455	1.5	98.5	41.5	10.7	1 278	20.4
Alfalfa	545	0.4	845	1.3	326.6	1 201 132	1 421	186 451	168.5	261 298	36.7	63.3	72.1	34.3	5 814	82.8
Atoka	353	-13.5	320	0.1	59.9	447 024	1 396	52 142	24.5	22 249	17.1	82.9	35.4	2.8	1 311	23.5
Beaver	1 116	-1.2	1 156	24.6	351.9	772 084	668	100 918	187.0	193 772	17.6	82.4	37.8	15.8	7 765	74.1
Beckham	568	9.3	559	6.2	159.8	617 433	1 105	74 880	44.3	43 574	43.5	56.5	35.2	9.1	5 558	66.4
Blaine	522	-10.9	654	3.1	247.1	778 357	1 190	124 377	138.2	173 231	30.2	69.8	65.3	21.2	4 901	77.8
Bryan	441	-10.1	297	8.1	111.8	526 677	1 771	56 929	60.9	41 060	31.9	68.1	40.2	6.3	1 971	26.3
Caddo	708	-5.6	484	30.3	276.1	647 626	1 337	93 927	128.9	88 215	46.9	53.1	54.2	15.2	9 454	61.7
Canadian	501	-1.6	383	10.0	253.8	737 861	1 926	107 595	145.8	111 524	35.7	64.3	44.0	16.1	4 250	42.1
Carter	457	13.3	346	1.1	79.5	545 662	1 579	53 157	33.0	24 953	17.0	83.0	30.2	4.6	1 055	14.8
Cherokee	236	-4.2	191	1.1	46.0	453 732	2 370	56 633	138.7	112 483	75.8	24.2	33.4	3.6	1 083	15.0
Choctaw	330	1.3	342	1.1	63.2	503 597	1 471	63 712	47.5	49 178	13.2	86.8	44.7	8.1	1 810	29.3
Cimarron	1 157	10.8	2 089	39.4	426.9	1 055 505	505	132 971	376.7	679 890	17.4	82.6	46.8	29.8	9 997	86.6
Cleveland	134	-16.3	124	1.4	36.1	386 582	3 125	42 396	14.9	13 764	44.7	55.3	19.7	2.2	585	12.1
Coal	274	1.6	479	0.4	45.1	603 704	1 260	65 790	22.4	39 282	18.5	81.5	43.8	8.4	856	20.0
Comanche	463	-6.9	418	0.7	137.1	577 613	1 381	62 284	47.4	42 794	35.9	64.1	40.3	9.5	2 995	43.9
Cotton	400	9.0	800	0.1	185.5	900 322	1 126	122 376	64.4	128 862	46.0	54.0	61.0	24.2	5 699	79.0
Craig	462	1.1	366	D	110.9	582 744	1 592	61 639	97.3	77 075	11.9	88.1	51.1	8.4	1 725	33.9
Creek	347	-8.1	195	0.4	71.1	349 067	1 788	43 752	23.5	13 238	19.0	81.0	23.5	2.1	384	8.3
Custer	623	9.5	710	8.2	254.9	951 593	1 340	134 592	103.2	117 636	48.3	51.7	58.6	20.4	6 729	69.3
Delaware	283	-8.3	211	0.1	62.4	488 390	2 319	62 352	254.4	189 144	1.8	98.2	48.9	13.8	1 183	27.9
Dewey	625	6.1	841	2.4	165.1	852 131	1 013	90 935	42.0	56 580	49.7	50.3	51.4	13.3	5 420	76.6
Ellis	758	5.6	998	8.7	168.7	796 726	798	83 476	119.8	157 616	11.0	89.0	45.5	15.3	4 705	74.5
Garfield	666	0.4	607	8.4	433.0	870 574	1 434	146 813	151.8	138 239	61.8	38.2	64.4	24.7	9 317	69.1
Garvin	463	-7.5	309	1.1	111.0	488 585	1 580	72 700	44.9	29 975	38.2	61.8	39.6	6.3	2 210	32.0
Grady	583	-4.1	350	14.3	182.7	563 619	1 610	77 691	138.9	83 344	21.0	79.0	40.3	9.8	3 014	33.0
Grant	582	-8.0	727	1.3	409.2	992 482	1 365	152 116	96.9	120 953	73.4	26.6	58.9	24.2	8 734	87.3
Greer	402	7.0	806	3.7	142.9	690 175	856	99 878	32.7	65 681	61.5	38.5	54.0	17.1	4 991	84.5
Harmon	341	5.7	931	25.2	167.1	886 842	953	143 131	53.6	146 579	51.7	48.3	48.1	20.8	4 837	86.6
Harper	618	0.1	1 161	5.9	201.9	884 026	761	78 647	148.7	279 560	9.4	90.6	47.4	20.1	5 563	82.0
Haskell	256	-11.8	296	0.5	46.7	448 627	1 514	60 922	98.8	114 407	2.5	97.5	45.7	10.6	810	23.4
Hughes	436	-1.1	474	1.8	64.0	590 418	1 247	68 746	90.2	97 958	6.1	93.9	41.4	7.5	2 392	36.4
Jackson	479	0.9	690	14.1	295.6	690 865	1 001	154 581	53.2	76 591	78.7	21.3	45.5	20.3	7 021	77.2
Jefferson	475	3.3	1 140	0.1	79.3	1 153 223	1 011	87 902	82.4	197 511	7.5	92.5	63.3	24.0	1 921	59.7
Johnston	284	-15.1	440	0.5	40.9	591 054	1 344	55 721	21.6	33 541	17.6	82.4	42.5	4.8	766	33.6
Kay	484	-1.6	488	1.8	307.1	659 226	1 352	109 617	86.7	87 312	66.5	33.5	54.7	17.3	8 096	67.4
Kingfisher	568	0.2	556	9.1	327.5	757 269	1 362	135 742	161.8	158 497	39.2	60.8	65.2	27.9	4 945	69.9

Table B. States and Counties — **Water Use, Wholesale Trade, Retail Trade, and Real Estate**

STATE County	Water use, 2010		Wholesale trade,[1] 2007				Retail trade,[2] 2007				Real estate and rental and leasing,[2] 2007			
	Total water withdrawn (mil gal/day)	Gallons withdrawn per person per day	Number of establish- ments	Number of employees	Sales (mil dol)	Annual payroll (mil dol)	Number of establish- ments	Number of employees	Sales (mil dol)	Annual payroll (mil dol)	Number of establish- ments	Number of employees	Receipts (mil dol)	Annual payroll (mil dol)
	133	134	135	136	137	138	139	140	141	142	143	144	145	146
OHIO—Cont'd														
Ottawa	37.1	896	27	156	71.8	5.3	168	1 623	461.2	40.9	56	175	15.6	4.2
Paulding	2.6	132	17	147	115.5	5.4	53	450	97.3	7.7	6	48	7.0	0.7
Perry	2.7	75	16	134	85.4	3.7	83	644	136.1	11.0	15	39	3.3	0.5
Pickaway	23.4	420	34	D	D	D	136	1 521	416.4	33.0	30	93	12.5	1.8
Pike	7.6	263	17	119	30.1	3.2	86	872	197.0	18.1	14	75	10.7	1.8
Portage	50.5	313	155	3 035	1 875.5	173.6	469	6 734	1 657.4	143.7	128	511	84.6	14.0
Preble	5.0	118	23	240	147.5	7.9	109	1 500	443.1	34.3	26	82	4.8	1.1
Putnam	6.1	178	33	244	172.3	8.5	111	1 225	252.3	22.4	11	33	2.6	0.8
Richland	17.0	137	127	2 113	1 010.6	76.7	497	7 387	1 489.5	145.8	108	571	59.2	12.3
Ross	40.9	524	47	456	226.6	17.5	260	3 640	831.2	73.4	54	165	26.6	3.6
Sandusky	14.7	241	50	D	D	D	220	2 801	598.0	58.8	35	166	13.9	2.6
Scioto	11.8	149	34	D	D	D	277	3 038	700.7	63.1	45	243	20.5	4.8
Seneca	6.5	115	55	D	D	D	184	2 086	458.8	46.8	36	114	9.9	1.8
Shelby	8.0	161	49	D	D	D	147	1 991	432.5	42.7	32	107	17.4	2.9
Stark	45.2	120	373	5 489	2 630.6	232.4	1 384	21 952	4 963.7	474.3	325	1 569	207.8	36.6
Summit	24.3	45	847	13 957	7 063.5	674.3	1 883	30 797	7 384.2	694.2	503	2 855	465.8	85.0
Trumbull	176.8	840	179	D	D	D	771	10 690	2 318.4	204.0	163	1 205	175.7	35.1
Tuscarawas	38.8	419	90	714	251.1	20.2	399	4 730	1 077.4	94.8	73	365	46.8	7.7
Union	14.3	272	67	925	1 881.7	43.8	129	2 022	479.1	49.9	46	148	26.0	4.4
Van Wert	6.5	226	28	229	127.0	9.4	101	1 234	242.8	25.0	13	128	10.5	1.5
Vinton	0.8	61	5	D	D	D	33	223	43.3	3.3	3	3	0.4	0.0
Warren	23.4	110	184	3 170	2 006.8	169.3	566	8 735	1 862.6	178.0	171	800	123.9	25.5
Washington	777.3	12 582	71	D	D	D	256	2 962	658.4	58.4	45	198	34.6	6.4
Wayne	16.6	145	124	D	D	D	409	5 123	1 110.2	109.3	82	279	48.0	7.5
Williams	4.9	130	41	461	229.2	14.7	143	1 575	333.9	29.5	30	97	18.2	2.7
Wood	11.7	94	177	2 923	1 505.1	126.0	434	6 632	1 522.5	125.5	118	657	135.0	21.6
Wyandot	7.4	328	28	295	210.6	9.9	71	922	190.2	15.8	14	37	4.3	1.1
OKLAHOMA	3 168.2	845	3 917	52 262	48 074.7	2 312.2	13 554	170 984	43 095.4	3 610.4	4 003	24 887	3 852.3	806.2
Adair	10.3	452	7	D	D	D	52	528	108.4	8.2	8	D	D	D
Alfalfa	8.2	1 456	10	53	23.3	1.5	25	145	33.3	2.4	2	D	D	D
Atoka	24.4	1 721	10	41	33.1	1.1	51	528	136.9	10.6	8	12	1.3	0.2
Beaver	42.0	7 452	8	13	9.5	0.4	20	103	22.0	1.5	4	D	D	D
Beckham	11.2	508	26	246	146.7	9.2	141	1 480	523.6	30.6	36	248	57.7	13.7
Blaine	10.3	863	13	105	135.3	3.2	53	290	74.6	4.0	7	22	4.0	0.7
Bryan	13.9	327	31	D	D	D	132	1 523	318.8	26.6	24	91	9.2	1.8
Caddo	65.9	2 227	23	237	70.1	5.1	113	970	234.4	15.6	10	22	2.1	0.4
Canadian	15.3	132	88	D	D	D	260	3 385	1 110.7	74.0	119	645	105.4	26.1
Carter	438.1	9 212	67	686	590.4	24.2	248	2 695	686.9	56.1	61	D	D	D
Cherokee	9.6	203	18	D	D	D	137	1 620	332.5	28.5	35	135	20.8	2.0
Choctaw	9.4	617	6	25	15.2	0.7	46	485	118.9	9.5	7	37	1.6	0.5
Cimarron	55.4	22 347	6	20	24.9	0.6	17	91	33.2	1.5	NA	NA	NA	NA
Cleveland	39.1	153	136	1 719	671.5	65.8	723	10 355	2 522.3	217.5	309	1 336	233.5	39.6
Coal	3.3	552	2	D	D	D	24	133	38.1	2.5	NA	NA	NA	NA
Comanche	25.4	204	56	D	D	D	435	5 540	1 206.8	108.0	135	484	66.7	10.9
Cotton	6.8	1 095	1	D	D	D	15	126	33.5	1.6	1	D	D	D
Craig	2.0	134	14	201	87.0	5.1	60	663	191.7	14.7	8	D	D	D
Creek	216.7	3 096	66	997	384.5	43.4	179	2 339	518.3	42.5	49	138	18.1	3.2
Custer	9.0	327	33	325	270.9	13.1	155	1 547	407.5	29.1	38	213	45.7	13.9
Delaware	7.2	174	20	80	47.1	2.8	133	1 238	292.6	25.4	26	184	46.5	7.1
Dewey	30.0	6 239	7	25	20.4	0.7	34	216	43.4	2.9	2	D	D	D
Ellis	23.3	5 602	5	D	D	D	24	136	41.2	2.5	1	D	D	D
Garfield	9.8	162	76	D	D	D	259	3 293	737.1	68.1	72	342	43.8	8.7
Garvin	44.6	1 617	27	179	95.8	6.6	121	1 137	331.6	22.2	15	50	13.6	2.5
Grady	37.1	707	53	550	198.9	19.2	167	1 657	440.1	35.6	40	140	17.7	3.5
Grant	15.3	3 369	11	39	29.6	1.0	12	148	54.7	3.2	NA	NA	NA	NA
Greer	4.5	723	3	12	4.0	0.2	16	179	28.1	2.5	3	6	0.8	0.1
Harmon	31.0	10 620	3	D	D	D	15	80	17.7	1.2	3	D	D	D
Harper	9.0	2 432	3	D	D	D	17	117	21.0	1.7	2	D	D	D
Haskell	5.0	388	6	D	D	D	36	425	131.0	9.2	3	11	0.5	0.1
Hughes	9.3	664	7	25	7.9	0.6	52	300	87.5	6.1	7	D	D	D
Jackson	74.2	2 805	23	D	D	D	115	1 365	350.2	28.6	18	83	11.3	1.8
Jefferson	12.3	1 904	1	D	D	D	28	152	34.8	2.6	3	2	0.3	0.1
Johnston	4.6	418	8	D	D	D	44	262	74.9	5.3	3	7	0.6	0.1
Kay	46.5	998	49	407	305.1	13.7	205	2 351	576.4	45.6	47	158	20.8	3.0
Kingfisher	10.3	683	27	388	429.2	16.3	64	549	185.2	12.0	9	79	10.9	1.9

1. Merchant wholesalers, except manufacturers' sales branches and offices. 2. Employer establishments.

Table B. States and Counties — **Professional Services, Manufacturing, and Accommodation and Food Services**

STATE County	Professional, scientific, and technical services,[1] 2007				Manufacturing, 2007				Accommodation and food services, 2007			
	Number of establish-ments	Number of employees	Receipts (mil dol)	Annual payroll (mil dol)	Number of establish-ments	Number of employees	Receipts (mil dol)	Annual payroll (mil dol)	Number of establish-ments	Number of employees	Sales (mil dol)	Annual payroll (mil dol)
	147	148	149	150	151	152	153	154	155	156	157	158
OHIO—Cont'd												
Ottawa	53	D	D	D	52	2 560	762.7	127.2	173	1 635	101.4	27.2
Paulding	12	44	4.4	1.2	37	1 755	388.7	56.9	34	305	7.9	2.1
Perry	27	106	6.8	3.5	25	933	124.5	31.4	45	369	13.8	3.7
Pickaway	59	D	D	D	37	2 342	D	D	73	1 033	40.0	10.8
Pike	21	136	21.4	7.3	30	1 781	620.8	57.6	51	738	31.5	8.4
Portage	253	D	D	D	263	11 370	2 969.6	484.1	297	4 583	187.7	51.5
Preble	45	D	D	D	56	3 248	1 070.3	155.5	65	940	32.2	9.6
Putnam	36	203	20.4	7.3	50	3 304	1 985.0	133.2	67	1 022	23.2	7.2
Richland	194	1 044	110.4	41.0	192	11 080	3 563.7	555.3	277	4 802	178.9	52.5
Ross	82	D	D	D	43	4 135	2 522.2	232.5	121	2 466	90.2	26.1
Sandusky	88	D	D	D	121	9 457	3 373.1	382.1	131	1 853	76.3	19.6
Scioto	81	D	D	D	52	1 874	927.1	65.7	150	2 160	84.8	23.2
Seneca	76	334	21.6	7.6	85	5 777	1 408.8	227.8	111	1 640	46.5	13.9
Shelby	62	339	33.0	16.6	147	15 057	6 238.4	707.2	81	1 351	55.2	14.0
Stark	739	D	D	D	542	27 177	10 387.4	1 175.2	784	13 705	518.0	153.6
Summit	1 618	D	D	D	925	32 483	9 275.5	1 470.3	1 231	22 475	885.0	253.4
Trumbull	300	D	D	D	262	18 808	8 841.0	1 138.4	434	6 588	245.2	68.7
Tuscarawas	142	D	D	D	224	9 223	2 206.5	380.1	215	3 448	114.4	36.4
Union	92	1 863	520.2	149.5	57	8 296	D	559.4	78	1 297	51.4	14.4
Van Wert	42	D	D	D	44	3 604	1 072.3	138.2	48	734	25.5	7.0
Vinton	7	D	D	D	21	592	106.5	19.2	17	69	2.8	0.6
Warren	439	D	D	D	222	13 472	4 111.2	572.2	345	8 227	329.8	99.7
Washington	99	D	D	D	96	4 374	2 563.7	217.1	120	2 065	83.7	22.8
Wayne	155	935	221.8	39.5	250	11 456	2 896.5	467.3	163	3 204	111.0	31.6
Williams	33	192	14.4	4.5	138	7 558	3 376.8	296.4	75	1 012	33.7	9.2
Wood	238	D	D	D	203	16 126	4 416.4	797.4	293	5 767	191.1	57.2
Wyandot	27	142	10.3	3.9	41	2 644	791.2	101.2	52	681	21.8	5.4
OKLAHOMA	9 128	D	D	D	3 964	142 351	60 681.4	5 971.2	6 900	129 159	5 106.6	1 401.3
Adair	13	D	D	D	13	1 314	414.4	41.1	15	269	6.1	1.8
Alfalfa	9	41	3.1	0.9	NA	NA	NA	NA	6	39	1.2	0.3
Atoka	13	46	3.2	0.9	NA	NA	NA	NA	28	317	13.9	2.9
Beaver	17	33	3.1	0.7	NA	NA	NA	NA	7	55	1.2	0.4
Beckham	70	317	32.5	12.1	NA	NA	NA	NA	69	895	39.2	9.7
Blaine	25	72	9.2	2.1	NA	NA	NA	NA	21	190	8.9	1.6
Bryan	61	944	87.3	48.4	38	1 102	238.2	35.2	62	1 089	40.4	10.6
Caddo	40	205	14.1	7.3	NA	NA	NA	NA	43	447	13.1	3.2
Canadian	214	663	67.6	21.1	75	3 234	1 192.9	132.5	146	2 623	102.2	26.3
Carter	118	D	D	D	49	2 993	D	167.2	86	1 979	68.1	20.7
Cherokee	50	134	11.3	3.5	NA	NA	NA	NA	84	1 092	42.1	11.2
Choctaw	19	D	D	D	NA	NA	NA	NA	28	337	10.9	2.7
Cimarron	4	12	1.5	0.2	NA	NA	NA	NA	11	79	3.4	0.7
Cleveland	613	D	D	D	151	3 299	1 223.0	138.1	447	10 104	391.8	108.8
Coal	2	D	D	D	NA	NA	NA	NA	4	70	2.2	0.7
Comanche	175	D	D	D	48	3 549	1 232.4	171.0	204	4 330	154.5	46.4
Cotton	7	12	0.7	0.3	NA	NA	NA	NA	8	D	D	D
Craig	21	83	9.2	3.2	16	783	139.0	26.4	28	374	14.8	4.0
Creek	106	320	25.6	8.0	133	4 257	1 204.4	178.6	83	1 181	43.4	11.0
Custer	72	D	D	D	33	1 346	533.9	45.2	67	1 053	41.5	11.0
Delaware	45	D	D	D	26	540	102.2	18.5	62	738	27.1	7.8
Dewey	9	98	8.2	2.6	NA	NA	NA	NA	4	24	1.2	0.2
Ellis	11	32	4.0	0.7	NA	NA	NA	NA	7	D	D	D
Garfield	128	559	58.4	20.1	68	2 356	1 097.7	75.9	115	1 848	74.4	19.1
Garvin	50	157	11.8	4.1	31	954	D	42.6	40	583	20.3	5.4
Grady	78	D	D	D	59	1 616	419.7	54.6	51	1 092	38.4	9.9
Grant	7	27	1.6	0.5	NA	NA	NA	NA	6	17	0.6	0.1
Greer	5	12	0.6	0.2	NA	NA	NA	NA	5	51	1.7	0.4
Harmon	4	D	D	D	NA	NA	NA	NA	3	D	D	D
Harper	8	30	3.6	1.1	NA	NA	NA	NA	3	D	D	D
Haskell	23	58	4.5	1.3	NA	NA	NA	NA	15	138	6.0	1.1
Hughes	14	40	2.6	0.8	NA	NA	NA	NA	18	237	9.3	2.1
Jackson	41	D	D	D	14	961	357.0	32.6	49	1 106	41.0	10.3
Jefferson	7	28	3.2	0.5	NA	NA	NA	NA	9	D	D	D
Johnston	11	20	1.9	0.8	NA	NA	NA	NA	11	106	3.1	0.9
Kay	96	523	46.1	17.9	72	4 415	D	189.3	100	1 688	61.5	15.4
Kingfisher	25	126	7.4	2.5	NA	NA	NA	NA	28	D	D	D

1. Establishment subject to federal tax.

STATE County	Health care and social assistance, 2007				Other services, 2007				Nonemployer businesses, 2013		Value of residential construction authorized by building permits, 2014	
	Number of establish-ments	Number of employees	Receipts (mil dol)	Annual payroll (mil dol)	Number of establish-ments	Number of employees	Receipts (mil dol)	Annual payroll (mil dol)	Number	Receipts (mil dol)	New Construction ($1,000)	Number of housing units
	159	160	161	162	163	164	165	166	167	168	169	170
OHIO—Cont'd												
Ottawa	81	1 637	110.7	45.6	88	343	29.7	8.0	2 905	122.0	26 271	94
Paulding	34	698	42.7	15.8	20	74	6.2	1.6	1 096	40.4	1 036	10
Perry	54	635	35.1	17.3	36	156	9.1	2.3	2 120	71.6	4 341	28
Pickaway	95	2 475	169.4	69.8	52	197	12.7	4.0	3 263	124.6	4 217	25
Pike	54	1 517	108.2	38.6	27	92	8.9	1.8	1 446	49.9	9 113	49
Portage	241	5 264	393.7	166.5	248	1 440	99.7	32.6	9 938	409.2	51 291	292
Preble	56	D	D	D	58	211	17.2	4.8	2 448	95.0	4 310	27
Putnam	60	839	39.3	19.8	58	311	21.6	5.9	1 975	79.1	11 807	47
Richland	354	7 670	663.5	263.1	238	1 533	109.3	29.3	6 815	264.6	12 430	61
Ross	156	5 154	523.2	252.8	96	524	31.0	8.7	3 887	139.0	5 734	55
Sandusky	152	3 553	255.6	97.1	115	796	44.3	14.1	3 178	115.2	3 319	20
Scioto	227	6 224	459.5	192.9	92	374	31.7	6.9	3 951	119.6	3 429	151
Seneca	158	2 914	170.9	73.5	109	500	33.9	8.3	2 902	104.3	3 288	27
Shelby	91	1 953	160.7	61.2	71	510	35.2	10.4	2 767	110.9	9 256	41
Stark	993	26 783	2 133.6	922.1	734	4 997	421.9	118.4	23 301	936.1	107 274	550
Summit	1 506	40 278	3 667.9	1 497.1	1 137	7 859	748.5	201.0	37 149	1 563.6	130 149	471
Trumbull	581	12 548	1 071.0	422.7	352	2 030	169.6	45.8	12 465	517.6	16 079	88
Tuscarawas	201	4 721	317.9	130.1	198	1 262	111.7	28.6	5 897	251.4	9 573	59
Union	81	1 684	128.4	53.5	75	579	46.8	15.6	3 430	152.3	91 174	336
Van Wert	63	1 826	108.9	46.4	52	270	18.6	3.7	1 566	65.8	4 538	24
Vinton	15	259	11.0	5.9	8	24	1.9	0.4	697	22.4	0	0
Warren	359	5 727	414.5	179.5	240	1 775	131.8	46.7	15 102	703.2	256 158	1 301
Washington	155	4 309	327.5	129.5	122	575	43.8	11.0	3 750	150.0	3 876	40
Wayne	221	5 004	347.5	147.0	168	907	73.3	19.6	8 752	386.9	36 785	184
Williams	69	1 680	147.8	63.1	66	337	25.7	5.8	2 198	85.6	5 500	29
Wood	249	4 637	338.3	145.9	212	1 461	123.4	36.4	7 401	305.0	48 437	218
Wyandot	41	803	50.6	21.0	57	286	21.4	5.4	1 353	53.5	2 937	16
OKLAHOMA	10 332	200 777	18 363.2	6 825.0	5 541	31 654	3 318.1	758.8	266 444	12 381.9	2 457 497	14 179
Adair	20	417	25.7	10.5	16	32	2.8	0.5	1 378	44.2	4 816	25
Alfalfa	9	136	4.3	2.0	8	D	D	D	383	18.1	0	0
Atoka	23	400	21.8	8.9	15	60	4.3	0.9	1 059	46.6	305	2
Beaver	6	77	5.1	1.8	9	D	D	D	481	19.9	0	0
Beckham	94	1 175	97.0	35.4	34	D	D	D	1 857	124.3	6 139	29
Blaine	29	397	17.0	7.4	16	25	2.5	0.3	673	28.4	700	6
Bryan	118	2 034	160.5	59.8	41	205	17.1	5.0	2 834	131.1	8 911	87
Caddo	44	693	28.0	13.3	25	90	9.8	2.4	1 532	69.6	1 805	12
Canadian	197	2 602	171.1	68.3	146	685	65.2	14.4	9 333	425.4	67 473	265
Carter	207	D	D	D	86	775	146.3	25.7	3 368	155.5	10 890	71
Cherokee	105	2 168	177.3	75.2	45	351	16.9	4.5	2 716	111.5	6 830	63
Choctaw	38	995	57.6	21.8	13	71	3.8	0.8	951	42.1	0	0
Cimarron	4	D	D	D	4	D	D	D	213	10.3	0	0
Cleveland	652	10 521	826.9	355.0	284	1 582	299.8	39.2	19 586	875.7	256 448	1 743
Coal	9	231	9.2	4.6	5	14	2.2	0.2	456	17.8	0	0
Comanche	274	6 219	580.1	223.7	170	879	63.3	15.2	4 610	185.0	19 739	113
Cotton	13	116	5.0	2.6	7	26	2.1	0.5	319	12.8	104	1
Craig	57	1 077	57.8	31.0	20	72	9.0	2.5	937	35.7	600	5
Creek	121	1 874	101.1	42.7	82	271	25.8	6.0	4 673	201.8	16 511	108
Custer	100	1 416	93.7	42.8	48	328	28.9	8.2	2 115	100.6	10 210	44
Delaware	77	1 238	98.6	37.7	52	261	18.3	4.8	2 780	121.8	5 440	36
Dewey	6	D	D	D	8	30	3.1	0.4	505	26.5	0	0
Ellis	9	186	14.7	5.1	11	D	D	D	356	16.9	60	1
Garfield	213	3 989	367.5	133.1	129	581	49.7	12.7	4 191	181.2	16 130	69
Garvin	65	1 101	61.4	25.3	28	137	17.6	2.3	2 093	105.3	2 772	33
Grady	82	1 524	110.5	46.8	67	265	18.5	5.0	3 520	169.7	19 381	100
Grant	7	103	4.6	2.0	4	D	D	D	332	14.1	465	6
Greer	13	204	14.8	4.9	6	D	D	D	313	11.2	90	1
Harmon	6	110	8.5	3.0	5	D	D	D	159	7.3	NA	NA
Harper	7	116	4.7	2.2	9	D	D	D	319	14.0	0	0
Haskell	35	915	48.8	19.5	13	41	3.1	0.7	1 046	44.2	2 666	25
Hughes	36	685	24.0	10.0	7	D	D	D	740	32.1	426	2
Jackson	56	1 399	96.7	40.1	40	190	13.1	2.9	1 369	51.6	11 549	27
Jefferson	8	70	3.5	1.3	3	D	D	D	410	17.5	0	8
Johnston	24	462	25.9	9.4	6	D	D	D	665	22.0	405	5
Kay	153	2 093	170.2	55.7	86	348	28.7	7.5	2 592	100.2	7 552	71
Kingfisher	42	586	29.0	11.3	30	92	8.7	2.0	1 516	79.7	5 999	27

STATE County	Government employment and payroll, 2012: Full-time equivalent employees	March payroll (dollars)	March payroll (percent of total): Adminis-tration, judicial, and legal	Police and Corrections	Fire Protection	Highways and transpor-tation	Health and Welfare	Natural resources and utilities	Education and libraries	Local government finances, 2012: General revenue: Total (mil dol)	Inter-govern-mental (mil dol)	Taxes: Total (mil dol)	Per capita[1] (dollars): Total	Property
	171	172	173	174	175	176	177	178	179	180	181	182	183	184
OHIO—Cont'd														
Ottawa	1 807	6 970 433	8.9	9.2	2.9	11.6	10.2	7.2	48.1	169.9	58.3	72.2	1 746	1 408
Paulding	840	2 899 437	7.0	5.4	0.3	5.0	30.9	2.1	47.9	78.4	30.7	20.4	1 057	705
Perry	1 584	4 562 693	8.5	5.7	0.8	9.1	10.2	4.3	60.2	119.5	77.0	27.9	775	640
Pickaway	2 330	14 643 979	43.7	3.1	0.9	1.5	14.8	1.6	34.2	261.8	90.0	68.3	1 211	848
Pike	1 231	4 378 557	9.2	6.9	1.1	6.4	9.9	6.4	59.2	142.7	70.7	26.2	920	694
Portage	6 776	25 510 983	5.9	7.0	4.0	6.3	23.8	3.4	48.7	675.5	218.5	230.1	1 425	1 010
Preble	1 714	6 190 256	11.3	8.4	1.2	8.8	6.9	4.8	52.3	137.6	66.2	50.4	1 204	713
Putnam	1 034	3 725 218	9.3	7.5	0.0	5.3	1.5	3.8	72.3	126.1	61.7	46.9	1 371	814
Richland	5 091	18 513 991	8.5	9.4	5.0	4.1	11.2	8.3	52.0	473.0	237.7	163.9	1 336	864
Ross	2 848	9 604 595	8.8	6.4	2.9	4.7	10.0	4.2	62.4	240.8	134.0	79.9	1 032	625
Sandusky	2 171	7 625 048	7.2	8.4	1.7	3.5	12.3	6.5	58.8	231.5	116.4	82.4	1 362	773
Scioto	2 809	9 457 558	7.1	6.9	2.7	3.9	7.6	6.7	64.1	259.9	167.7	61.3	781	581
Seneca	1 825	6 110 506	9.4	11.2	4.5	4.6	9.9	4.4	55.0	195.7	93.8	60.1	1 073	657
Shelby	1 460	5 397 171	6.3	6.1	4.3	3.0	5.5	5.6	68.3	184.8	82.0	67.4	1 370	761
Stark	11 531	42 201 589	4.3	6.8	4.8	4.1	1.9	6.1	71.3	1 313.7	628.2	474.7	1 266	949
Summit	20 065	81 863 137	7.5	10.7	5.8	4.7	7.7	7.2	54.5	2 401.2	877.7	1 094.2	2 023	1 303
Trumbull	7 911	27 957 859	8.3	9.9	5.3	3.3	10.3	6.6	55.2	724.1	366.6	245.2	1 182	844
Tuscarawas	3 307	11 310 698	8.3	7.0	2.8	5.4	6.0	9.0	58.9	309.5	126.6	106.5	1 152	825
Union	2 131	8 121 953	6.0	5.6	3.5	2.1	30.6	3.2	47.7	262.5	68.5	90.7	1 720	1 149
Van Wert	1 050	4 217 502	8.6	7.4	2.1	8.6	3.4	13.7	52.1	118.7	67.2	36.2	1 260	753
Vinton	591	1 697 854	7.1	2.3	0.0	6.1	13.7	1.9	66.2	47.0	34.8	7.8	590	511
Warren	5 863	22 314 741	4.2	7.3	6.2	2.1	0.6	3.3	75.2	748.9	233.0	383.6	1 766	1 359
Washington	2 326	7 490 510	7.9	9.4	3.2	6.0	8.9	3.7	59.9	189.5	93.8	66.4	1 080	769
Wayne	4 495	16 994 820	7.3	7.8	2.6	5.0	22.5	5.7	48.6	484.9	177.5	144.9	1 261	926
Williams	1 758	5 321 575	7.9	5.7	0.7	4.6	15.8	10.1	54.0	135.0	55.5	50.2	1 339	733
Wood	4 470	17 275 956	8.6	10.8	3.6	3.3	9.2	6.1	56.1	532.6	184.0	232.7	1 815	1 163
Wyandot	1 084	3 936 981	8.9	7.2	0.8	3.5	33.2	5.1	40.6	97.2	30.4	25.4	1 124	531
OKLAHOMA	X	X	X	X	X	X	X	X	X	X	X	X	X	X
Adair	986	2 539 434	3.7	4.1	0.2	2.8	2.6	7.8	77.6	58.2	42.9	7.8	352	205
Alfalfa	248	605 307	12.0	6.9	0.5	12.8	1.7	4.7	59.3	13.7	4.5	6.9	1 225	981
Atoka	901	3 031 357	2.1	2.9	0.0	0.7	13.5	14.8	65.5	69.1	37.2	9.2	658	295
Beaver	349	1 030 481	7.5	3.5	0.0	11.8	12.7	7.2	56.4	23.3	11.7	9.1	1 626	1 124
Beckham	996	2 808 433	5.1	8.4	3.6	5.8	2.7	8.0	63.2	78.3	28.3	36.4	1 577	607
Blaine	619	1 556 580	6.7	6.5	0.9	6.6	23.9	4.9	49.9	45.9	14.5	14.0	1 429	639
Bryan	1 434	4 012 582	7.3	9.9	3.7	4.8	3.9	6.2	62.9	108.1	53.8	36.2	833	407
Caddo	1 563	4 548 760	3.7	5.7	1.7	6.2	8.5	8.8	64.8	96.6	61.1	21.0	708	392
Canadian	3 819	11 398 884	4.8	10.1	3.4	2.2	6.5	2.2	69.3	291.7	123.9	127.1	1 037	614
Carter	1 811	5 386 589	5.3	10.5	3.1	4.9	1.1	6.3	67.9	152.0	61.4	59.3	1 233	591
Cherokee	2 005	6 302 718	3.9	5.1	1.3	3.4	35.5	5.3	44.2	165.4	56.2	22.0	457	230
Choctaw	795	2 289 614	6.3	3.7	1.7	3.9	19.7	5.9	57.8	37.7	23.4	8.9	588	233
Cimarron	196	450 099	9.5	5.4	0.0	14.3	1.7	5.6	54.3	9.9	3.7	3.1	1 291	950
Cleveland	9 950	35 955 536	3.3	6.4	4.0	1.7	32.0	2.8	48.9	893.3	214.7	278.1	1 047	619
Coal	319	840 600	8.4	5.3	4.4	7.5	6.5	3.4	64.6	24.3	13.0	8.5	1 425	897
Comanche	6 240	22 060 234	3.6	5.7	3.0	2.1	37.2	3.2	44.6	505.2	159.3	103.2	817	354
Cotton	263	656 798	7.9	5.3	1.5	6.9	1.4	7.9	66.9	18.1	12.3	3.0	492	352
Craig	859	2 734 367	4.9	5.6	1.6	5.0	35.0	3.8	42.2	46.2	23.2	13.9	943	509
Creek	2 475	7 871 373	5.1	6.6	4.0	2.5	1.9	5.1	74.1	169.5	81.2	61.8	874	489
Custer	1 316	3 555 785	5.3	7.5	2.4	3.8	17.0	5.5	56.6	88.8	32.3	37.3	1 306	656
Delaware	1 264	3 298 724	6.6	7.0	0.4	4.1	1.2	4.6	74.6	80.2	42.1	28.6	690	467
Dewey	334	940 532	8.5	5.7	0.5	11.7	14.3	4.1	54.3	35.1	7.3	21.9	4 581	2 207
Ellis	243	705 922	9.0	9.1	0.0	18.9	2.9	2.2	56.6	31.4	7.5	8.4	2 051	1 616
Garfield	2 242	6 971 075	5.4	9.4	5.9	4.5	1.4	5.0	66.7	176.9	68.5	75.4	1 232	577
Garvin	1 260	3 212 232	6.5	6.6	2.1	5.0	14.9	6.4	57.8	92.3	43.7	25.1	920	451
Grady	1 921	5 776 643	3.4	5.2	3.6	3.2	26.9	2.4	54.3	157.9	56.1	41.4	779	442
Grant	233	634 768	12.0	7.0	0.1	21.2	0.0	6.1	53.1	15.2	6.4	5.9	1 313	1 043
Greer	288	950 821	5.8	5.3	2.0	1.0	29.5	6.4	48.4	16.6	9.5	2.9	481	285
Harmon	242	611 023	7.5	4.4	0.0	5.4	40.8	2.6	38.3	7.4	4.3	1.9	648	388
Harper	266	708 452	8.7	5.5	0.0	9.6	26.4	4.5	45.3	14.8	7.0	5.9	1 592	1 096
Haskell	614	1 704 293	4.5	5.0	0.0	5.1	27.6	1.6	53.4	31.8	20.1	7.0	543	274
Hughes	768	2 037 752	4.4	2.9	0.8	3.3	28.1	3.9	55.8	38.4	20.3	12.6	908	604
Jackson	1 759	6 015 452	3.3	4.6	2.2	1.8	47.3	5.6	33.9	146.2	38.1	20.7	788	304
Jefferson	350	958 729	7.0	3.6	0.7	3.6	15.4	11.0	58.0	49.9	41.2	3.0	470	281
Johnston	410	1 050 719	7.1	6.5	0.6	3.4	2.9	5.1	73.6	22.7	13.6	6.2	561	357
Kay	2 026	5 686 908	6.0	8.0	6.7	4.3	2.5	9.9	60.6	149.2	58.1	50.8	1 108	557
Kingfisher	634	1 825 978	7.8	7.8	3.3	9.1	1.5	4.9	65.1	48.4	22.2	18.8	1 254	825

1. Based on the resident population estimated as of July 1 of the year shown.

STATE County	Local government finances, 2012 (cont.)									Government employment, 2013			Presidential election,[2] 2012		
	Direct general expenditure							Debt outstanding					Percent of vote cast:		
			Percent of total for:												
	Total (mil dol)	Per capita[1] (dollars)	Education	Health and hospitals	Police protection	Public welfare	Highways	Total (mil dol)	Per capita[1] (dollars)	Federal civilian	Federal military	State and local	Democratic	Republican	All other
	185	186	187	188	189	190	191	192	193	194	195	196	197	198	199
OHIO—Cont'd															
Ottawa	183.7	4 444	50.5	4.7	6.9	9.8	7.3	162.5	3 930	166	150	2 046	52.2	46.0	1.7
Paulding	83.9	4 350	53.2	21.6	2.3	1.9	7.4	20.8	1 079	48	50	1 076	42.6	54.4	2.9
Perry	127.1	3 530	59.9	5.5	4.7	7.4	7.0	19.6	543	60	92	1 546	47.1	50.1	2.7
Pickaway	245.9	4 360	42.1	29.7	3.7	2.8	4.2	155.1	2 750	86	133	3 792	38.3	60.0	1.8
Pike	136.0	4 775	54.3	20.5	2.3	3.4	5.2	25.3	889	78	72	1 364	48.2	49.3	2.5
Portage	676.4	4 190	37.6	28.6	4.0	3.4	4.1	295.0	1 827	297	409	15 555	53.5	44.5	2.0
Preble	135.2	3 229	56.4	4.3	5.3	6.0	7.0	22.8	546	73	107	1 817	33.3	64.6	2.1
Putnam	148.9	4 353	62.5	3.1	4.2	4.4	6.0	72.4	2 117	70	87	1 555	28.3	70.0	1.8
Richland	480.9	3 920	52.3	8.7	5.0	4.8	5.5	209.0	1 703	554	298	7 241	42.1	55.7	2.2
Ross	234.3	3 026	58.4	0.5	5.1	7.8	4.6	264.6	3 418	1 611	186	4 905	45.4	52.6	2.0
Sandusky	231.1	3 819	59.9	4.6	7.5	4.6	4.8	105.5	1 744	109	153	3 204	51.4	46.7	1.9
Scioto	262.2	3 341	61.1	5.0	1.9	4.1	4.6	211.5	2 694	170	193	5 381	45.8	52.2	2.0
Seneca	196.2	3 502	52.9	6.1	6.7	3.7	7.6	729.9	13 029	120	138	2 640	47.7	50.4	2.0
Shelby	185.3	3 769	51.8	0.7	3.4	11.7	9.7	191.1	3 887	72	126	2 421	30.9	67.3	1.8
Stark	1 278.7	3 411	55.1	4.6	5.7	5.0	5.4	444.1	1 185	981	975	18 074	51.7	46.3	2.0
Summit	2 276.4	4 209	43.9	4.8	5.6	4.3	3.4	4 224.1	7 811	1 958	1 398	29 663	57.6	41.1	1.3
Trumbull	736.8	3 552	53.3	5.9	6.4	5.6	3.7	248.1	1 196	505	552	9 330	60.0	37.6	2.4
Tuscarawas	292.0	3 160	50.0	4.4	5.1	6.3	5.1	119.9	1 297	242	236	4 844	50.1	47.6	2.3
Union	256.7	4 870	31.4	31.2	3.9	1.4	6.7	364.0	6 906	63	134	3 264	35.1	63.2	1.7
Van Wert	130.4	4 536	67.9	0.9	3.8	2.9	7.3	64.6	2 247	52	73	1 381	35.3	62.6	2.1
Vinton	47.0	3 548	53.9	4.2	3.0	10.0	10.2	7.8	588	23	34	638	43.6	53.5	2.9
Warren	743.8	3 424	50.7	0.4	7.2	6.1	4.8	599.3	2 759	265	579	9 479	31.4	67.5	1.1
Washington	192.0	3 124	48.4	9.0	6.4	6.0	9.1	94.7	1 541	210	154	2 774	41.3	56.9	1.8
Wayne	466.4	4 061	44.9	24.0	3.9	6.3	4.1	103.7	903	253	290	6 586	41.6	56.3	2.1
Williams	124.0	3 304	51.6	1.0	5.4	10.9	7.1	67.6	1 801	75	94	2 089	44.4	53.7	1.9
Wood	538.0	4 197	50.7	2.8	4.6	11.9	5.6	402.7	3 142	210	333	11 852	52.7	45.6	1.7
Wyandot	101.5	4 489	33.1	34.8	4.5	8.4	7.7	18.8	830	56	57	1 356	40.6	57.1	2.2
OKLAHOMA	X	X	X	X	X	X	X	X	X	47 221	35 621	286 659	34.4	65.6	0.0
Adair	58.1	2 606	75.3	1.7	3.3	0.0	6.3	8.0	359	37	86	1 546	30.7	69.3	0.0
Alfalfa	13.7	2 424	57.6	1.3	4.0	0.0	1.2	6.6	1 158	34	19	519	16.9	83.1	0.0
Atoka	56.5	4 036	38.0	13.0	4.0	0.0	9.5	27.1	1 931	38	51	1 178	28.1	71.9	0.0
Beaver	21.3	3 811	59.5	6.4	2.9	0.1	14.8	3.5	632	33	21	473	10.8	89.2	0.0
Beckham	65.5	2 839	44.5	3.2	6.9	0.0	8.4	42.2	1 830	48	84	1 060	22.0	78.0	0.0
Blaine	43.3	4 420	45.4	22.1	2.7	0.0	10.7	12.1	1 232	56	37	809	24.6	75.4	0.0
Bryan	107.3	2 473	57.5	3.2	6.5	0.0	4.5	150.1	3 458	99	167	5 612	32.2	67.8	0.0
Caddo	102.4	3 449	54.1	1.6	3.8	0.0	12.2	21.8	736	564	107	2 414	34.7	65.3	0.0
Canadian	275.3	2 246	65.8	0.4	5.8	0.0	4.1	217.3	1 773	578	548	5 533	23.9	76.1	0.0
Carter	138.7	2 885	55.4	3.2	6.9	0.0	8.9	72.9	1 517	96	186	3 349	29.7	70.3	0.0
Cherokee	168.8	3 505	38.7	45.6	2.0	0.0	2.6	38.5	800	282	178	7 559	43.9	56.1	0.0
Choctaw	38.5	2 537	57.0	7.0	5.1	0.5	14.4	11.0	728	44	58	1 397	33.3	66.7	0.0
Cimarron	9.8	4 126	56.2	20.2	2.6	0.0	5.2	1.3	527	15	0	256	12.0	88.0	0.0
Cleveland	909.8	3 425	38.7	32.5	4.4	0.0	4.9	703.2	2 647	711	1 069	22 596	38.0	62.0	0.0
Coal	24.2	4 050	54.5	2.2	3.3	0.0	16.0	1.2	199	16	22	392	26.4	73.6	0.0
Comanche	515.7	4 080	36.9	40.3	4.3	0.0	3.0	244.6	1 935	4 322	12 293	9 865	41.2	58.8	0.0
Cotton	18.1	2 940	59.1	0.3	2.7	0.0	14.7	9.2	1 490	25	24	898	27.8	72.2	0.0
Craig	47.8	3 238	66.7	1.2	4.4	0.0	10.2	13.5	915	56	53	1 729	35.0	65.0	0.0
Creek	169.8	2 404	59.1	3.0	5.7	0.0	7.1	161.0	2 279	236	269	3 124	29.2	70.8	0.0
Custer	81.3	2 850	57.0	0.1	7.9	0.0	10.2	57.0	1 999	172	108	2 694	25.3	74.7	0.0
Delaware	80.1	1 934	71.5	1.7	5.9	0.0	2.4	56.3	1 357	78	159	2 532	33.1	66.9	0.0
Dewey	31.7	6 636	49.7	0.2	2.9	9.2	14.3	8.2	1 718	30	18	376	15.7	84.3	0.0
Ellis	30.2	7 367	36.1	47.3	0.6	0.0	4.4	13.0	3 179	23	16	373	14.8	85.2	0.0
Garfield	196.4	3 209	47.9	2.4	5.3	0.1	7.4	189.6	3 098	449	1 481	3 596	24.5	75.5	0.0
Garvin	89.3	3 271	48.3	13.4	4.7	0.0	8.8	23.0	841	81	105	1 805	28.2	71.8	0.0
Grady	154.9	2 916	45.5	28.8	4.1	0.0	7.2	30.5	575	85	204	2 554	26.6	73.4	0.0
Grant	14.3	3 176	61.0	1.3	3.6	0.0	8.2	4.8	1 069	33	17	317	21.9	78.1	0.0
Greer	17.2	2 824	46.1	10.9	6.9	0.0	14.6	3.8	617	26	19	544	26.8	73.2	0.0
Harmon	8.0	2 738	65.6	4.3	8.1	0.0	0.4	0.3	109	20	11	293	30.6	69.4	0.0
Harper	17.7	4 809	42.7	7.9	3.9	0.0	26.2	2.4	653	21	15	395	14.1	85.9	0.0
Haskell	31.5	2 434	63.9	0.9	4.0	0.2	11.6	2.2	171	57	50	601	31.5	68.5	0.0
Hughes	38.5	2 780	61.1	1.7	3.7	0.0	13.2	24.0	1 755	30	47	980	35.3	64.7	0.0
Jackson	175.1	6 672	28.3	40.8	3.6	0.0	5.4	32.6	1 243	1 346	1 441	2 452	25.2	74.8	0.0
Jefferson	21.5	3 367	52.8	2.1	2.8	0.0	12.1	30.4	4 768	29	24	396	32.8	67.2	0.0
Johnston	21.5	1 952	72.5	4.2	4.8	0.0	3.1	3.8	343	46	41	1 008	31.6	68.4	0.0
Kay	166.0	3 621	41.7	1.9	7.4	0.0	9.5	127.9	2 790	111	172	4 116	29.2	70.8	0.0
Kingfisher	52.9	3 526	63.6	1.6	4.5	0.0	9.8	16.6	1 106	43	59	826	15.8	84.2	0.0

1. Based on the resident population estimated as of July 1 of the year shown. 2.

STATE/ County code	CBSA code[1]	County type[2]	STATE County	Land area,[3] (sq km) 2010	Population, 2014: Total persons 2014	Population, 2014: Rank	Population, 2014: Per square kilometer	Race alone or in combination, not Hispanic or Latino (percent): White	Race: Black	Race: American Indian, Alaska Native	Race: Asian and Pacific Islander	Percent Hispanic or Latino[4]	Age (percent): Under 5 years	5 to 17 years	18 to 24 years	25 to 34 years	35 to 44 years	45 to 54 years
				1	2	3	4	5	6	7	8	9	10	11	12	13	14	15
			OKLAHOMA—Cont'd															
40 075	...	6	Kiowa	2 629	9 336	2 484	3.6	78.7	5.3	8.6	0.9	10.0	5.9	17.7	7.5	11.3	10.4	14.1
40 077	...	7	Latimer	1 870	10 693	2 381	5.7	75.1	1.8	26.7	0.8	3.4	6.4	16.0	10.8	11.1	10.4	13.2
40 079	22900	2	Le Flore	4 116	49 761	984	12.1	77.8	2.9	17.3	0.9	6.8	6.0	18.1	8.7	12.1	12.0	13.7
40 081	36420	1	Lincoln	2 466	34 619	1 314	14.0	88.3	2.5	10.7	0.7	2.9	5.9	18.5	7.9	10.5	11.6	14.6
40 083	36420	1	Logan	1 927	45 276	1 064	23.5	81.4	10.1	6.0	1.1	5.5	6.1	18.0	10.9	11.4	12.3	13.6
40 085	...	9	Love	1 331	9 773	2 459	7.3	77.1	3.0	9.4	0.9	14.2	6.7	18.4	8.0	11.3	11.2	13.2
40 087	36420	1	McClain	1 478	37 313	1 243	25.2	84.6	1.4	10.6	0.9	7.5	6.4	19.8	7.9	11.6	12.9	14.3
40 089	...	7	McCurtain	4 791	33 050	1 354	6.9	70.1	10.0	19.9	1.5	5.1	7.1	18.5	8.5	11.2	11.6	13.4
40 091	...	6	McIntosh	1 602	20 088	1 833	12.5	75.7	4.5	23.9	0.8	2.5	5.0	15.2	6.9	9.4	10.1	13.4
40 093	...	9	Major	2 473	7 750	2 617	3.1	87.4	1.7	3.2	1.0	8.8	7.2	17.2	7.4	11.3	10.2	13.8
40 095	...	6	Marshall	961	16 182	2 031	16.8	72.6	2.3	14.3	0.6	15.7	6.2	17.3	7.5	10.4	10.9	13.2
40 097	...	6	Mayes	1 697	40 816	1 159	24.1	74.7	0.9	29.6	0.7	3.2	6.3	18.3	8.3	11.5	11.8	13.5
40 099	...	7	Murray	1 079	13 803	2 184	12.8	80.2	2.5	17.4	0.8	5.5	5.9	18.0	7.4	11.4	11.5	13.2
40 101	34780	4	Muskogee	2 099	69 966	765	33.3	64.4	12.8	24.3	1.0	5.6	7.1	17.5	9.2	12.9	12.0	12.9
40 103	...	6	Noble	1 896	11 494	2 328	6.1	86.2	2.7	11.2	0.9	3.1	6.1	18.0	7.3	11.8	11.5	14.3
40 105	...	6	Nowata	1 465	10 524	2 394	7.2	75.9	3.3	26.5	0.6	2.9	5.7	17.5	8.3	11.1	11.1	14.2
40 107	...	6	Okfuskee	1 602	12 186	2 288	7.6	67.9	8.8	24.7	0.9	4.2	7.5	16.7	7.9	12.3	12.5	14.2
40 109	36420	1	Oklahoma	1 836	766 215	79	417.3	62.0	17.0	5.8	4.0	15.9	7.8	17.7	9.8	15.8	12.4	12.5
40 111	46140	2	Okmulgee	1 806	39 095	1 196	21.6	70.5	10.5	22.9	0.8	3.6	6.2	17.8	10.2	11.6	11.0	13.2
40 113	46140	2	Osage	5 818	47 981	1 014	8.2	70.4	12.3	20.3	0.7	3.3	5.4	17.8	7.8	11.0	11.4	14.4
40 115	33060	6	Ottawa	1 219	32 105	1 383	26.3	73.7	1.6	25.2	2.1	4.9	6.9	17.8	10.3	11.2	11.5	12.4
40 117	46140	2	Pawnee	1 471	16 401	2 017	11.1	83.5	1.5	17.4	0.6	2.6	6.0	18.1	7.9	10.5	11.8	13.7
40 119	44660	4	Payne	1 773	80 264	690	45.3	82.8	4.8	8.3	4.9	4.3	5.8	13.7	27.8	13.5	9.4	9.5
40 121	32540	5	Pittsburg	3 381	44 626	1 078	13.2	77.5	4.6	20.2	0.8	4.5	6.2	16.1	8.2	13.0	11.9	13.6
40 123	10220	7	Pontotoc	1 866	38 005	1 221	20.4	74.5	3.7	23.4	1.3	4.4	7.3	16.5	12.2	13.7	11.1	12.3
40 125	43060	4	Pottawatomie	2 040	71 811	754	35.2	79.0	4.2	16.9	1.3	4.7	6.8	17.6	10.0	12.7	12.2	13.2
40 127	...	9	Pushmataha	3 615	11 125	2 345	3.1	78.4	1.5	22.2	0.6	3.1	5.8	16.0	7.6	10.6	10.1	14.3
40 129	...	9	Roger Mills	2 956	3 761	2 923	1.3	87.2	1.2	7.1	0.6	6.0	6.9	18.3	6.2	12.5	10.6	12.9
40 131	46140	2	Rogers	1 750	89 815	641	51.3	80.8	1.7	20.0	1.6	4.1	5.7	19.1	9.1	11.5	12.5	14.5
40 133	...	7	Seminole	1 639	25 421	1 590	15.5	72.1	6.3	23.5	0.8	4.5	6.5	18.9	9.0	11.1	11.2	13.6
40 135	22900	2	Sequoyah	1 744	41 358	1 141	23.7	73.3	2.5	28.6	0.9	3.7	5.8	18.5	8.5	11.2	12.5	14.2
40 137	20340	4	Stephens	2 254	44 493	1 082	19.7	85.5	2.8	8.6	0.9	6.7	6.3	17.6	8.0	12.1	11.3	13.2
40 139	25100	7	Texas	5 287	21 853	1 742	4.1	48.3	3.0	1.6	2.5	45.7	8.1	19.8	11.7	14.4	13.4	12.0
40 141	...	6	Tillman	2 256	7 628	2 628	3.4	64.2	8.3	4.9	0.8	24.7	6.4	17.9	8.4	11.6	11.0	13.5
40 143	46140	2	Tulsa	1 477	629 598	103	426.3	68.9	12.0	9.8	3.3	11.6	7.4	18.1	9.4	14.6	12.9	12.9
40 145	46140	2	Wagoner	1 454	75 702	727	52.1	79.3	4.8	15.8	2.0	5.3	6.3	19.4	7.7	12.5	13.3	13.7
40 147	12780	4	Washington	1 076	51 937	960	48.3	79.9	3.7	14.9	2.1	5.6	6.4	17.2	8.5	11.9	11.2	12.8
40 149	...	7	Washita	2 598	11 547	2 325	4.4	86.5	1.6	4.6	0.5	9.4	6.4	19.3	7.8	13.1	10.8	13.3
40 151	...	7	Woods	3 332	9 288	2 489	2.8	87.1	3.9	3.8	1.5	5.9	6.2	13.2	18.0	13.8	9.6	11.3
40 153	49260	7	Woodward	3 218	21 529	1 753	6.7	82.8	2.3	4.1	1.1	11.7	7.5	17.9	9.0	15.1	12.5	12.9
41 000	...	X	OREGON	248 608	3 970 239	X	16.0	80.3	2.5	2.4	5.8	12.3	5.9	16.0	9.3	13.6	13.0	13.1
41 001	...	7	Baker	7 947	16 059	2 038	2.0	93.9	1.0	2.4	1.1	3.7	5.1	14.3	6.8	10.3	9.7	13.0
41 003	18700	3	Benton	1 751	86 316	663	49.3	85.4	1.6	1.6	7.9	7.0	4.2	12.7	23.4	12.3	10.0	10.8
41 005	38900	1	Clackamas	4 844	394 972	174	81.5	86.1	1.4	1.6	5.7	8.1	5.3	17.2	8.1	11.5	12.8	14.7
41 007	11820	4	Clatsop	2 147	37 474	1 238	17.5	88.7	1.0	2.2	2.5	8.0	5.4	14.3	8.6	12.0	10.9	13.1
41 009	38900	1	Columbia	1 703	49 459	992	29.0	92.3	1.0	2.9	2.3	4.6	5.2	17.4	7.5	10.6	12.6	14.6
41 011	18300	5	Coos	4 134	62 475	838	15.1	89.8	0.9	5.1	2.2	5.9	5.0	13.6	7.3	10.7	9.9	13.2
41 013	39260	6	Crook	7 716	20 998	1 774	2.7	90.5	0.5	2.3	1.0	7.4	4.4	15.1	6.6	9.1	11.0	13.3
41 015	15060	7	Curry	4 215	22 335	1 716	5.3	90.4	0.7	4.1	1.5	6.3	4.3	11.4	5.7	8.1	8.6	12.7
41 017	13460	3	Deschutes	7 817	170 388	373	21.8	90.0	0.8	1.7	2.0	7.7	5.4	16.4	7.1	12.3	13.1	13.4
41 019	40700	4	Douglas	13 043	106 972	559	8.2	91.6	0.7	3.5	2.0	5.1	5.1	14.5	7.4	10.3	10.2	13.1
41 021	...	9	Gilliam	3 120	1 932	3 058	0.6	91.3	0.6	2.1	1.5	6.1	5.4	13.5	6.0	8.7	10.0	14.6
41 023	...	9	Grant	11 729	7 180	2 663	0.6	94.3	0.7	2.7	1.1	3.5	4.7	14.0	5.8	8.9	9.1	12.8
41 025	...	7	Harney	26 245	7 126	2 669	0.3	90.9	1.0	5.2	1.2	4.6	4.9	15.6	7.5	9.5	10.8	13.2
41 027	26220	6	Hood River	1 352	22 885	1 693	16.9	66.9	0.7	1.6	2.6	30.3	6.5	18.6	8.1	12.4	13.0	14.3
41 029	32780	3	Jackson	7 209	210 287	305	29.2	85.0	1.2	2.4	2.5	11.7	5.8	15.5	8.4	11.8	11.2	12.8
41 031	...	6	Jefferson	4 612	22 192	1 722	4.8	62.3	0.9	17.8	1.6	19.3	7.1	18.0	8.1	10.8	11.0	13.0
41 033	24420	4	Josephine	4 247	83 599	670	19.7	90.4	0.8	2.9	1.9	6.8	4.9	14.8	7.1	9.7	10.1	12.8
41 035	28900	5	Klamath	15 387	65 455	805	4.3	82.8	1.3	5.8	1.9	11.7	6.0	15.6	9.3	11.3	10.9	13.0
41 037	...	7	Lake	21 080	7 838	2 607	0.4	88.7	1.2	3.7	1.8	7.7	4.1	13.9	6.3	9.9	11.7	14.2
41 039	21660	2	Lane	11 793	358 337	188	30.4	87.0	1.7	2.7	4.4	8.0	4.9	14.2	13.4	12.4	11.5	12.4
41 041	35440	4	Lincoln	2 538	46 406	1 041	18.3	86.5	1.0	5.3	2.2	8.3	4.9	12.3	6.6	10.1	10.1	12.7
41 043	10540	4	Linn	5 931	119 356	516	20.1	88.9	0.9	2.6	2.1	8.2	6.3	17.2	8.3	12.6	11.9	13.0
41 045	36620	6	Malheur	25 609	30 359	1 422	1.2	63.5	1.5	1.7	2.2	32.6	7.1	18.1	10.0	13.1	12.1	12.1
41 047	41420	2	Marion	3 062	326 110	204	106.5	69.8	1.6	2.1	3.8	25.4	7.0	18.7	10.1	13.5	12.4	12.4

1. CBSA = Core Based Statistical Area. See Appendix A for explanation. See Appendix B for list of metropolitan areas with component counties. 2. County type code from the Economic Research Service of USDA Rural-Urban Continuum Codes. See Appendix A for definition. 3. Dry land or land partially or temporarily covered by water. 4. May be of any race.

STATE County	Population, 2013 (cont.) — Age (percent) (cont.) — 55 to 64 years	65 to 74 years	75 years and over	Percent female	Population change and components of change, 2000–2014 — Total persons — 2000	2010	Percent change — 2000–2010	2010–2014	Components of change, 2010–2014 — Births	Deaths	Net migration	Households, 2009–2013 — Number	Persons per house-hold	Percent — Family house-holds	Female family house-holder[1]	One per-son
	16	17	18	19	20	21	22	23	24	25	26	27	28	29	30	31
OKLAHOMA—Cont'd																
Kiowa	14.4	10.6	8.2	50.6	10 227	9 446	-7.6	-1.2	509	528	-66	3 886	2.35	65.2	14.5	30.6
Latimer	13.0	10.6	8.5	49.1	10 692	11 154	4.3	-4.1	523	469	-519	4 160	2.53	71.5	11.5	25.6
Le Flore	13.1	9.6	6.8	50.0	48 109	50 384	4.7	-1.2	2 487	2 496	-621	18 412	2.63	68.8	12.2	27.2
Lincoln	14.0	10.1	6.8	50.2	32 080	34 273	6.8	1.0	1 651	1 451	101	13 256	2.55	71.1	11.4	24.8
Logan	13.1	8.7	5.9	50.6	33 924	41 848	23.4	8.2	1 980	1 437	2 624	14 927	2.75	72.6	9.3	24.5
Love	13.1	10.8	7.2	50.4	8 831	9 423	6.7	3.7	567	476	262	3 378	2.78	75.8	10.4	21.3
McClain	12.7	8.8	5.5	50.3	27 740	34 506	24.4	8.1	1 814	1 299	2 263	12 749	2.74	76.1	8.5	20.7
McCurtain	13.0	9.7	6.9	51.0	34 402	33 151	-3.6	-0.3	1 951	1 609	-409	13 078	2.49	70.6	15.3	26.8
McIntosh	15.0	14.4	10.5	50.5	19 456	20 252	4.1	-0.8	848	1 380	268	8 092	2.48	68.2	9.8	27.5
Major	14.0	9.8	9.1	51.0	7 545	7 527	-0.2	3.0	441	327	128	3 084	2.43	69.6	6.7	27.2
Marshall	14.0	12.1	8.5	50.3	13 184	15 840	20.1	2.2	845	730	228	5 970	2.62	65.0	8.9	30.7
Mayes	13.6	10.0	6.6	50.3	38 369	41 259	7.5	-1.1	2 155	2 089	-491	15 896	2.55	71.3	10.9	25.2
Murray	13.8	10.6	8.1	49.8	12 623	13 488	6.9	2.3	637	767	407	5 121	2.58	69.4	9.7	24.7
Muskogee	12.7	8.8	6.8	51.1	69 451	70 990	2.2	-1.4	4 097	3 782	-1 366	26 802	2.51	66.7	14.3	28.6
Noble	13.6	9.7	7.7	50.7	11 411	11 561	1.3	-0.6	559	537	-81	4 565	2.47	73.8	11.5	24.0
Nowata	13.6	10.4	8.1	50.9	10 569	10 536	-0.3	-0.1	501	548	54	4 050	2.56	71.2	10.0	26.0
Okfuskee	12.2	9.9	6.7	46.9	11 814	12 191	3.2	0.0	718	659	-62	4 246	2.59	70.9	14.6	25.5
Oklahoma	11.7	6.9	5.4	51.0	660 448	718 633	8.8	6.6	52 082	28 464	23 908	285 320	2.52	62.0	13.9	31.6
Okmulgee	13.3	9.4	7.3	50.5	39 685	40 069	1.0	-2.4	2 159	2 185	-933	15 124	2.55	66.2	14.2	30.0
Osage	14.4	10.6	7.2	49.7	44 437	47 472	6.8	1.1	1 861	1 970	403	18 512	2.50	71.3	11.7	24.8
Ottawa	12.4	10.0	7.7	51.0	33 194	31 848	-4.1	0.8	1 885	1 889	203	12 134	2.55	69.0	13.2	27.1
Pawnee	14.6	10.4	7.1	50.2	16 612	16 577	-0.2	-1.1	846	831	-169	6 341	2.59	70.1	11.3	25.8
Payne	9.2	6.1	4.9	48.8	68 190	77 350	13.4	3.8	3 904	2 303	1 329	30 010	2.33	55.2	8.6	30.4
Pittsburg	13.4	10.1	7.5	49.1	43 953	45 837	4.3	-2.6	2 324	2 456	-925	18 456	2.32	65.8	12.4	29.2
Pontotoc	11.4	8.7	6.9	51.2	35 143	37 492	6.7	1.4	2 288	1 893	148	14 793	2.47	65.5	14.2	28.3
Pottawatomie	12.0	8.9	6.4	52.3	65 521	69 442	6.0	3.4	3 960	3 282	1 708	25 658	2.60	70.5	13.0	26.3
Pushmataha	13.9	12.7	9.1	51.0	11 667	11 572	-0.8	-3.9	523	647	-319	4 900	2.30	61.1	12.9	34.8
Roger Mills	13.7	10.1	8.8	50.3	3 436	3 647	6.1	3.1	194	135	17	1 305	2.82	69.8	7.0	25.7
Rogers	12.6	8.9	6.1	50.2	70 641	86 905	23.0	3.3	4 141	3 237	1 909	32 693	2.65	76.4	9.8	20.0
Seminole	12.8	9.6	7.3	50.8	24 894	25 482	2.4	-0.2	1 440	1 374	-87	9 327	2.66	69.9	15.5	26.7
Sequoyah	12.8	10.0	6.5	50.7	38 972	42 391	8.8	-2.5	1 804	1 989	-905	15 624	2.65	72.5	13.8	23.6
Stephens	13.7	9.4	8.4	51.3	43 182	45 048	4.3	-1.2	2 333	2 307	-578	17 690	2.51	67.4	9.9	29.7
Texas	10.4	5.6	4.7	47.1	20 107	20 640	2.7	5.9	1 490	537	251	7 180	2.87	73.4	10.1	21.9
Tillman	13.2	9.9	8.1	49.7	9 287	7 992	-13.9	-4.6	431	361	-409	3 013	2.50	68.2	12.4	29.3
Tulsa	12.0	7.1	5.6	51.3	563 299	603 403	7.1	4.3	39 929	23 620	10 232	241 915	2.48	63.6	13.6	30.6
Wagoner	12.8	9.2	5.0	50.7	57 491	73 085	27.1	3.6	3 799	2 540	1 302	27 016	2.73	76.5	10.3	19.9
Washington	13.5	9.5	8.9	51.4	48 996	50 976	4.0	1.9	2 683	2 519	836	21 332	2.37	66.5	11.2	29.3
Washita	12.7	8.4	8.1	50.3	11 508	11 629	1.1	-0.7	609	611	-52	4 630	2.48	72.7	10.3	24.2
Woods	11.3	8.1	8.5	46.5	9 089	8 878	-2.3	4.6	452	416	355	3 439	2.27	56.6	7.6	35.1
Woodward	11.4	7.8	6.0	47.0	18 486	20 081	8.6	7.2	1 380	853	895	7 382	2.63	67.4	8.8	28.4
OREGON	13.7	9.0	6.5	50.5	3 421 399	3 831 074	12.0	3.6	191 586	139 246	85 464	1 516 456	2.49	63.8	10.6	27.8
Baker	16.6	14.0	10.3	49.3	16 741	16 134	-3.6	-0.5	725	845	101	7 120	2.18	64.6	8.6	30.5
Benton	12.8	7.8	5.8	49.8	78 153	85 579	9.5	0.9	3 100	2 267	-118	33 384	2.42	56.0	7.6	29.3
Clackamas	14.9	9.3	6.3	50.8	338 391	375 992	11.1	5.0	16 713	13 055	14 735	146 527	2.58	69.6	9.8	24.2
Clatsop	17.1	11.3	7.4	50.6	35 630	37 039	4.0	1.2	1 778	1 592	268	15 749	2.30	62.7	10.8	30.7
Columbia	15.6	10.3	6.1	50.2	43 560	49 351	13.3	0.2	2 010	1 699	-205	19 069	2.57	72.0	10.5	22.9
Coos	17.0	13.3	10.0	50.8	62 779	63 043	0.4	-0.9	2 619	3 648	434	26 072	2.36	61.0	9.8	31.5
Crook	16.9	14.5	9.1	50.5	19 182	20 978	9.4	0.1	736	932	200	8 880	2.33	68.0	8.1	26.1
Curry	19.0	17.5	12.8	50.8	21 137	22 364	5.8	-0.1	789	1 455	638	10 355	2.13	59.5	6.4	33.2
Deschutes	14.8	10.8	6.7	50.7	115 367	157 733	36.7	8.0	7 188	5 548	10 860	64 568	2.47	67.1	8.9	24.8
Douglas	16.2	13.0	10.2	50.7	100 399	107 667	7.2	-0.6	4 572	5 783	633	43 846	2.41	66.6	10.6	26.2
Gilliam	18.5	12.4	10.8	49.3	1 915	1 871	-2.3	3.3	81	77	54	883	2.15	60.2	8.6	36.5
Grant	18.5	14.7	11.6	50.2	7 935	7 445	-6.2	-3.6	257	328	-197	3 319	2.17	64.1	7.1	30.5
Harney	16.9	12.7	8.9	49.3	7 609	7 422	-2.5	-4.0	321	335	-277	3 113	2.29	69.3	8.9	27.8
Hood River	13.3	7.3	6.3	49.8	20 411	22 346	9.5	2.4	1 219	694	17	8 144	2.62	67.0	7.5	24.3
Jackson	15.0	11.0	8.5	51.3	181 269	203 206	12.1	3.5	9 870	9 291	6 211	83 140	2.42	64.9	11.7	28.4
Jefferson	14.2	11.1	6.7	49.8	19 009	21 720	14.3	2.2	1 224	781	15	7 882	2.62	69.9	13.3	23.1
Josephine	16.2	13.8	10.5	51.3	75 726	82 713	9.2	1.1	3 404	4 875	2 357	34 390	2.37	64.0	10.0	30.2
Klamath	15.1	11.0	7.7	50.0	63 775	66 380	4.1	-1.4	3 332	3 066	-1 066	27 378	2.38	66.9	11.9	26.6
Lake	17.2	13.5	9.2	46.9	7 422	7 895	6.4	-0.7	298	330	-33	3 566	2.09	60.2	5.5	33.0
Lane	14.4	9.7	7.1	50.9	322 959	351 715	8.9	1.9	14 750	13 030	5 092	144 912	2.38	59.5	10.7	28.8
Lincoln	19.5	14.7	9.1	51.4	44 479	46 034	3.5	0.8	1 864	2 398	1 033	20 913	2.17	62.4	9.6	31.1
Linn	13.9	9.7	7.1	50.5	103 069	116 672	13.2	2.3	6 101	4 819	1 351	44 722	2.60	69.0	11.3	24.0
Malheur	11.8	8.4	7.3	45.7	31 615	31 313	-1.0	-3.0	1 828	1 197	-1 635	10 136	2.69	67.9	11.8	28.0
Marion	12.1	7.9	6.1	50.1	284 834	315 335	10.7	3.4	18 578	11 041	3 183	113 285	2.72	69.1	13.1	25.6

1. No spouse present.

STATE County	Persons in group quarters, 2014	Daytime population, 2009–2013: Number	Daytime population, 2009–2013: Employment/residence ratio	Births, 2014: Total	Births, 2014: Rate[1]	Deaths, 2014: Number	Deaths, 2014: Rate[1]	Persons under 65 with no health insurance, 2013: Number	Persons under 65 with no health insurance, 2013: Percent	Medicare, 2014: Eligible for Medicare	Medicare, 2014: Enrolled in Medicare Advantage	Medicare, 2014: Enrolled in a Medicare prescription drug plan	Serious crimes known to police,[2] 2013: Total: Number	Serious crimes known to police,[2] 2013: Total: Rate[3]
	32	33	34	35	36	37	38	39	40	41	42	43	44	45
OKLAHOMA—Cont'd														
Kiowa	171	8 629	0.81	136	14.6	120	12.9	1 717	23.0	2 245	132	1 425	220	2 362
Latimer	574	11 019	1.00	118	11.0	102	9.5	1 876	22.4	2 392	156	1 328	88	798
Le Flore	1 616	46 667	0.81	667	13.4	658	13.2	10 722	26.6	10 399	1 324	5 587	1 201	2 407
Lincoln	386	28 978	0.63	389	11.2	323	9.3	5 859	20.7	6 867	1 080	3 167	717	2 091
Logan	2 174	33 078	0.48	457	10.1	340	7.5	6 821	18.7	7 136	1 247	3 515	836	1 882
Love	88	10 769	1.32	140	14.3	115	11.8	1 872	23.5	2 128	112	1 376	182	1 888
McClain	194	28 871	0.61	429	11.5	297	8.0	6 107	19.6	6 439	708	3 253	1 199	3 324
McCurtain	454	32 833	0.97	480	14.5	416	12.6	6 277	23.0	7 116	570	4 414	944	2 830
McIntosh	345	18 726	0.77	193	9.6	324	16.1	3 821	25.0	5 772	393	3 463	491	2 364
Major	77	7 111	0.86	109	14.1	68	8.8	1 199	19.3	1 613	45	1 112	99	1 273
Marshall	329	14 913	0.84	215	13.3	139	8.6	3 218	25.5	3 685	229	2 323	233	1 451
Mayes	566	38 404	0.83	507	12.4	512	12.5	7 447	22.0	8 426	1 166	4 439	673	1 629
Murray	313	12 743	0.86	147	10.6	187	13.5	2 208	20.1	2 985	138	1 862	260	1 888
Muskogee	3 524	72 953	1.08	924	13.2	891	12.7	13 219	23.4	14 651	1 280	7 802	2 673	3 779
Noble	273	10 942	0.88	124	10.8	114	9.9	1 629	17.2	2 365	99	1 571	181	1 566
Nowata	157	8 861	0.58	127	12.1	132	12.5	1 983	23.3	2 452	162	1 416	108	1 010
Okfuskee	1 228	11 216	0.74	141	11.6	152	12.5	2 329	24.7	2 516	235	1 475	318	2 553
Oklahoma	14 899	836 936	1.31	12 342	16.1	6 699	8.7	141 562	21.8	114 961	25 297	50 796	39 792	5 291
Okmulgee	1 374	36 666	0.79	498	12.7	516	13.2	6 864	21.6	8 646	1 033	4 702	999	2 521
Osage	1 504	39 038	0.55	408	8.5	518	10.8	7 637	20.0	8 745	1 767	4 219	1 131	2 342
Ottawa	968	31 769	0.98	471	14.7	498	15.5	5 768	22.3	7 627	649	4 300	716	2 203
Pawnee	194	14 085	0.63	195	11.9	172	10.5	2 825	20.8	3 666	365	2 042	211	1 278
Payne	7 770	79 193	1.04	914	11.4	540	6.7	12 887	20.5	10 664	366	6 826	1 509	1 909
Pittsburg	2 431	46 581	1.06	545	12.2	564	12.6	7 750	22.2	9 661	645	4 862	1 392	3 094
Pontotoc	1 696	39 527	1.11	517	13.6	495	13.0	6 482	21.0	7 462	508	4 205	1 327	3 469
Pottawatomie	3 053	67 276	0.90	900	12.5	786	10.9	11 213	19.4	13 966	2 356	6 196	2 781	3 892
Pushmataha	110	10 751	0.84	120	10.8	157	14.1	2 349	26.8	3 018	245	1 726	157	1 410
Roger Mills	11	3 845	1.08	43	11.4	23	6.1	610	20.2	713	11	472	51	1 329
Rogers	1 216	74 449	0.67	986	11.0	784	8.7	12 203	16.2	15 581	4 489	6 491	1 339	1 501
Seminole	581	24 667	0.92	334	13.1	329	12.9	4 766	23.0	5 262	528	2 987	729	2 852
Sequoyah	464	37 079	0.69	526	12.7	522	12.6	8 343	24.3	9 091	1 353	4 722	1 027	2 490
Stephens	540	44 041	0.95	555	12.5	525	11.8	7 263	19.8	9 524	947	5 320	1 762	3 927
Texas	572	20 859	0.97	391	17.9	132	6.0	4 960	25.8	2 501	144	1 498	355	1 626
Tillman	267	7 176	0.77	100	13.1	71	9.3	1 439	23.7	1 704	87	1 108	212	2 716
Tulsa	9 870	672 724	1.22	9 404	14.9	5 703	9.1	106 255	19.8	99 791	29 445	43 324	29 863	4 821
Wagoner	319	53 092	0.36	895	11.8	625	8.3	12 856	19.8	12 435	3 684	5 115	1 639	2 159
Washington	798	51 947	1.03	616	11.9	621	12.0	8 357	20.1	11 239	882	6 765	1 125	2 161
Washita	206	10 083	0.68	154	13.3	147	12.7	1 933	20.0	2 108	91	1 382	168	1 438
Woods	1 004	9 506	1.15	112	12.1	96	10.3	1 085	16.3	1 621	87	1 158	119	1 344
Woodward	1 240	21 424	1.10	345	16.0	242	11.2	3 380	19.8	3 421	140	2 239	670	3 216
OREGON	86 917	3 912 948	1.03	45 209	11.4	33 295	8.4	560 442	17.2	731 167	318 457	238 704	134 721	3 428
Baker	410	15 964	0.99	177	11.0	199	12.4	1 996	16.9	4 507	194	2 595	493	3 103
Benton	4 472	86 758	1.02	729	8.4	526	6.1	9 451	13.5	13 617	6 077	4 986	2 326	2 675
Clackamas	2 911	351 750	0.84	4 049	10.3	3 192	8.1	44 789	13.8	70 568	41 895	14 421	9 560	2 535
Clatsop	897	38 408	1.07	421	11.2	395	10.5	5 459	18.3	8 467	1 868	3 883	1 450	3 870
Columbia	372	40 207	0.54	469	9.5	440	8.9	5 808	14.2	10 163	5 152	2 595	672	1 361
Coos	1 225	63 054	1.01	620	9.9	857	13.7	8 646	18.3	17 766	1 794	9 813	2 250	3 748
Crook	215	20 038	0.89	172	8.2	221	10.5	2 863	18.0	5 814	1 301	2 572	469	2 263
Curry	318	22 041	0.96	191	8.6	340	15.2	2 857	18.4	7 868	793	4 175	406	1 921
Deschutes	1 214	160 861	1.00	1 707	10.0	1 304	7.7	25 407	18.7	35 503	10 493	15 493	4 678	2 849
Douglas	1 741	106 744	0.99	1 081	10.1	1 330	12.4	14 237	17.4	29 833	9 352	11 278	2 309	2 153
Gilliam	21	2 009	1.11	22	11.4	21	10.9	237	15.9	484	12	265	20	1 007
Grant	95	7 423	1.02	59	8.2	76	10.6	1 047	19.6	2 040	363	922	71	974
Harney	153	7 343	1.01	79	11.1	70	9.8	1 206	22.0	1 808	101	1 119	123	1 716
Hood River	791	22 919	1.04	296	12.9	159	6.9	4 272	22.0	3 675	882	1 622	266	1 172
Jackson	3 554	205 229	1.00	2 316	11.0	2 172	10.3	32 868	19.8	48 833	15 399	19 138	8 966	4 312
Jefferson	898	20 287	0.85	278	12.5	201	9.1	4 210	24.3	4 663	1 150	2 090	556	2 547
Josephine	1 544	81 297	0.95	826	9.9	1 119	13.4	10 724	17.1	23 843	9 057	8 168	3 514	4 225
Klamath	1 057	65 699	0.98	771	11.8	724	11.1	10 731	20.3	15 221	3 271	6 976	1 870	2 872
Lake	465	8 017	1.05	71	9.1	80	10.2	1 228	21.7	2 015	131	1 011	NA	NA
Lane	7 827	354 531	1.01	3 488	9.7	3 304	9.2	53 281	18.3	73 232	35 956	22 355	13 192	3 736
Lincoln	810	46 267	1.01	448	9.7	543	11.7	7 329	20.9	13 539	2 655	6 485	1 712	3 697
Linn	1 196	112 904	0.90	1 412	11.8	1 186	9.9	15 655	15.9	25 010	12 455	7 469	4 116	3 454
Malheur	3 373	34 270	1.32	414	13.6	260	8.6	4 920	21.7	5 694	505	3 515	1 042	3 818
Marion	10 674	325 945	1.06	4 321	13.3	2 669	8.2	51 067	19.0	55 495	31 513	14 234	11 457	3 557

1. Per 1,000 estimated resident population. 2. Data for serious crimes have not been adjusted for underreporting; this may affect comparability between geographic areas and over time.
3. Per 100,000 population estimated by the FBI.

STATE County	Serious crimes known to police, 2013 (cont.)[1] Rate[2] Violent	Property	Education: School enrollment and attainment, 2009–2013: Enrollment[3] Total	Percent private	Attainment[4] (percent) High school graduate or less	Bachelor's degree or more	Local government expenditures,[5] 2012–2013: Total current spending (mil dol)	Current spending per student (dollars)	Money income, 2009–2013: Per capita income[6] (dollars)	Households: Median income (dollars)	Mean income (dollars)	Percent with income of $200,000 or more	Income and poverty, 2013: Median household income (dollars)	Percent below poverty level: All persons	Children under 18 years	Children 5 to 17 years in families
	46	47	48	49	50	51	52	53	54	55	56	57	58	59	60	61
OKLAHOMA—Cont'd																
Kiowa	150	2 212	2 100	7.6	51.7	17.2	14.6	8 821	23 576	36 281	55 157	2.2	34 611	21.5	30.3	26.5
Latimer	172	626	2 851	6.5	50.0	13.8	12.0	8 721	22 603	40 970	56 641	2.4	36 177	19.2	27.4	26.2
Le Flore	214	2 193	11 971	3.9	57.7	12.9	80.4	7 915	18 141	36 542	47 265	0.6	35 122	24.3	30.8	27.3
Lincoln	181	1 910	8 157	8.5	55.9	12.5	41.0	7 302	21 888	42 668	55 432	1.5	42 378	15.8	23.6	20.9
Logan	104	1 779	11 634	10.8	42.6	24.5	35.1	7 552	25 620	53 591	71 079	4.4	57 490	12.8	16.8	15.7
Love	197	1 691	2 089	9.5	60.0	14.4	13.1	7 609	19 910	43 260	52 980	2.1	46 154	14.7	23.7	21.3
McClain	150	3 174	8 893	6.0	49.0	20.4	50.6	6 888	25 293	54 426	67 432	2.4	57 784	10.0	14.8	13.5
McCurtain	264	2 566	8 012	6.6	59.7	13.9	59.2	8 645	17 615	31 790	43 655	1.0	31 319	25.4	36.4	33.4
McIntosh	183	2 181	4 034	5.8	56.6	13.0	27.7	8 264	19 100	36 096	45 519	1.0	38 094	18.8	31.0	28.4
Major	116	1 157	1 630	7.3	55.0	16.6	9.1	8 201	27 168	49 905	66 158	3.5	52 226	12.0	16.0	15.0
Marshall	100	1 351	3 670	6.8	56.4	14.4	23.0	7 658	19 583	37 319	48 976	1.1	38 055	19.2	29.4	27.6
Mayes	249	1 380	9 946	5.6	53.8	15.3	59.0	8 057	20 585	42 751	51 604	0.6	41 142	20.0	29.4	27.2
Murray	225	1 663	2 938	3.3	56.9	19.0	17.8	7 042	21 870	44 151	54 907	1.7	49 816	15.1	21.8	19.4
Muskogee	582	3 196	17 798	7.5	48.0	17.9	104.0	7 588	19 868	38 502	50 490	1.3	38 574	19.9	29.9	27.2
Noble	95	1 471	2 824	1.2	48.3	21.5	18.3	8 545	21 947	44 842	54 977	0.9	47 028	13.4	19.7	17.8
Nowata	187	823	2 631	5.8	57.3	13.8	15.2	8 099	19 256	39 430	47 771	0.9	40 563	18.2	27.4	24.5
Okfuskee	161	2 393	2 704	6.5	59.2	11.1	28.6	6 472	16 528	35 170	45 600	0.7	34 982	25.3	32.8	30.9
Oklahoma	646	4 644	195 256	14.4	39.7	29.6	941.3	7 441	26 561	45 215	65 932	3.8	45 988	17.5	26.2	24.4
Okmulgee	189	2 332	9 992	4.6	52.2	13.9	54.3	7 880	19 753	39 156	49 368	1.1	36 588	19.7	29.1	26.4
Osage	273	2 069	11 742	9.2	53.0	16.1	34.8	9 060	22 353	44 195	56 573	1.1	49 999	14.0	21.9	19.8
Ottawa	225	1 978	7 819	5.6	52.0	13.9	47.0	7 711	18 331	36 473	46 561	0.8	35 921	22.6	33.1	31.1
Pawnee	176	1 103	3 917	9.8	54.9	17.0	20.0	7 531	21 220	44 375	53 782	1.3	42 967	15.4	23.6	21.3
Payne	140	1 768	31 973	4.5	37.6	35.9	87.6	8 145	20 868	36 812	52 971	2.3	39 609	23.0	22.3	20.2
Pittsburg	220	2 874	9 705	9.1	53.3	15.3	67.3	8 530	21 966	41 252	54 086	1.9	41 105	18.1	25.3	23.0
Pontotoc	549	2 920	9 859	8.1	45.0	28.0	59.3	8 372	22 381	41 881	54 746	1.9	40 479	20.5	26.5	25.8
Pottawatomie	349	3 544	17 824	13.4	50.5	17.6	99.2	7 470	20 937	42 764	55 172	1.8	44 405	19.0	27.3	26.7
Pushmataha	162	1 249	2 262	5.9	58.9	11.6	20.6	8 916	18 542	29 897	41 462	0.9	32 352	24.4	38.8	36.4
Roger Mills	78	1 251	875	3.9	45.5	19.7	12.4	14 792	27 326	53 885	73 099	4.6	53 962	12.2	18.3	17.2
Rogers	179	1 322	23 617	13.4	42.6	23.0	107.5	7 562	27 365	58 525	72 464	2.8	55 865	9.2	12.5	11.3
Seminole	141	2 711	6 397	4.6	54.6	14.1	43.3	8 417	18 321	33 819	47 483	1.4	34 731	23.7	35.4	31.1
Sequoyah	225	2 264	10 195	5.6	59.3	13.3	68.1	7 906	18 131	35 742	46 588	1.0	33 912	25.0	34.5	29.9
Stephens	234	3 693	10 354	7.5	55.0	17.4	60.9	7 374	23 038	43 885	56 974	1.9	45 607	15.9	22.0	19.9
Texas	179	1 447	5 518	6.2	57.1	18.8	36.7	8 208	22 064	49 901	63 618	1.6	46 914	13.7	19.0	18.1
Tillman	372	2 344	1 899	3.9	61.4	16.0	14.6	9 253	18 035	36 354	45 599	0.5	35 054	22.1	31.4	29.5
Tulsa	696	4 125	160 402	18.4	37.6	29.7	883.1	7 643	27 676	48 181	68 209	3.9	48 082	15.7	23.1	20.4
Wagoner	196	1 963	19 894	11.3	45.1	21.6	45.7	6 768	24 874	55 723	67 199	1.8	53 098	11.5	15.9	14.3
Washington	194	1 967	11 761	12.1	44.5	25.2	60.9	7 385	27 053	48 687	64 237	3.0	46 836	13.8	20.2	18.4
Washita	163	1 276	2 754	9.1	54.1	18.0	18.6	8 357	23 811	46 686	59 618	1.9	46 742	15.6	21.3	19.4
Woods	56	1 288	2 437	10.3	43.2	27.1	14.1	10 708	26 022	51 619	63 850	1.9	48 583	14.4	17.5	17.6
Woodward	226	2 990	4 431	7.9	53.1	17.8	29.0	7 610	24 922	51 867	64 791	2.8	54 158	14.6	18.1	15.9
OREGON	254	3 174	967 820	14.7	35.2	29.7	5 557.8	9 543	26 809	50 229	66 666	3.3	50 228	16.5	21.6	19.3
Baker	189	2 914	3 351	12.3	41.7	20.9	23.7	9 675	23 234	41 500	51 265	1.8	42 200	14.5	24.7	24.8
Benton	120	2 555	32 817	7.7	20.8	50.0	81.2	9 368	26 738	48 604	66 438	3.7	50 714	20.8	14.6	13.0
Clackamas	87	2 448	92 472	16.2	31.3	31.8	537.6	9 246	32 781	64 352	83 873	5.4	66 514	9.7	11.3	8.9
Clatsop	144	3 725	8 378	10.7	35.1	23.2	51.8	10 368	25 680	44 683	59 841	2.1	43 048	16.7	24.4	21.9
Columbia	67	1 294	11 355	12.2	43.5	18.1	69.5	8 861	26 271	54 968	66 733	2.1	55 222	11.8	17.2	14.5
Coos	152	3 596	11 715	9.8	43.5	18.0	98.0	10 367	22 239	37 940	51 146	1.5	37 583	19.6	30.1	25.4
Crook	198	2 065	4 392	12.1	51.1	14.5	29.7	9 386	20 883	38 795	48 674	0.7	43 343	17.4	28.3	24.0
Curry	99	1 821	3 450	8.8	39.4	20.7	22.8	9 708	23 972	39 516	50 650	0.9	37 175	18.7	28.0	25.9
Deschutes	222	2 628	38 364	12.6	29.6	31.0	235.4	9 490	27 524	50 209	66 924	3.2	49 427	15.2	20.1	17.7
Douglas	190	1 963	22 946	10.3	44.5	16.1	148.4	10 353	21 870	40 524	51 987	1.4	40 243	19.5	28.6	24.4
Gilliam	0	1 007	344	7.8	44.4	14.7	6.9	23 646	25 320	44 743	54 528	0.8	50 027	11.9	19.7	19.8
Grant	14	960	1 416	9.7	43.5	20.5	13.8	15 354	23 828	35 051	51 458	2.7	40 569	18.0	29.0	26.7
Harney	70	1 647	1 612	8.5	49.9	15.6	16.2	15 383	20 865	38 113	47 882	0.5	37 041	18.1	28.0	25.6
Hood River	141	1 031	5 384	6.5	42.6	30.5	44.8	10 818	25 181	56 725	67 538	2.7	50 891	14.8	21.4	19.0
Jackson	339	3 973	45 610	12.4	38.2	24.8	279.8	9 729	24 378	44 005	58 441	2.1	43 393	18.7	26.7	24.0
Jefferson	124	2 424	5 055	6.8	48.3	17.3	42.2	11 583	21 593	43 373	57 497	1.7	41 107	21.8	33.9	31.7
Josephine	164	4 062	16 539	8.9	43.5	17.0	99.3	9 292	21 791	37 733	51 368	1.6	37 619	19.4	30.7	25.2
Klamath	213	2 659	15 833	10.7	44.2	19.7	94.6	9 942	21 489	39 627	51 421	1.4	37 542	18.2	26.8	25.6
Lake	NA	NA	1 427	4.2	49.6	18.6	14.0	11 623	22 056	33 611	47 734	0.5	37 856	20.9	29.0	24.9
Lane	171	3 565	96 437	11.3	34.1	27.7	443.9	9 761	24 224	42 931	57 848	2.1	43 778	21.1	24.4	21.1
Lincoln	272	3 425	7 886	12.0	30.7	24.4	52.7	10 019	25 194	42 005	55 042	1.4	39 801	20.1	33.0	30.1
Linn	81	3 373	29 042	10.1	42.4	16.9	197.8	8 945	21 500	46 939	54 960	0.9	44 941	19.0	26.3	23.0
Malheur	253	3 566	8 295	10.5	50.4	13.1	58.0	11 145	16 352	35 578	47 558	1.4	34 565	29.4	38.8	34.4
Marion	228	3 329	83 951	15.3	43.2	21.2	586.5	9 867	22 001	46 885	60 071	1.8	46 919	18.8	27.9	26.3

1. Data for serious crimes have not been adjusted for underreporting; this may affect comparability between geographic areas and over time. 2. Per 100,000 population estimated by the FBI.
3. All persons 3 years old and over enrolled in nursery school through college. 4. Persons 25 years old and over. 5. Elementary and secondary education expenditures.
6. Based on population estimated by the American Community Survey, 2009–2013.

STATE County	Personal income, 2013										Earnings, 2013		
	Total (mil dol)	Percent change, 2012–2013	Per capita[1] Dollars	Per capita[1] Rank	Wages and salaries (mil dol)	Supplements to wages and salaries; employer contributions (mil dol): Pension and insurance	Supplements to wages and salaries; employer contributions (mil dol): Government social insurance	Proprietors' income (mil dol)	Dividends, interest, and rent (mil dol)	Personal transfer receipts (mil dol)	Total (mil dol)	Contributions for government social insurance (mil dol): From employee and self-employed	Contributions for government social insurance (mil dol): From employer
	62	63	64	65	66	67	68	69	70	71	72	73	74
OKLAHOMA—Cont'd													
Kiowa	310	-1.6	33 197	2 228	86	18	7	37	57	92	149	9	7
Latimer	385	-1.5	35 704	1 799	145	30	12	32	61	115	219	13	12
Le Flore	1 456	0.5	29 250	2 777	511	91	44	127	191	472	773	49	44
Lincoln	1 158	1.8	33 699	2 143	257	45	20	117	169	267	440	28	20
Logan	1 908	3.2	42 944	848	255	43	21	415	265	291	734	36	21
Love	413	2.8	42 383	899	155	37	12	15	55	86	218	13	12
McClain	1 719	3.1	47 087	551	329	52	27	82	216	260	489	31	27
McCurtain	990	2.4	29 934	2 695	383	70	36	121	119	332	610	36	36
McIntosh	658	1.5	32 116	2 402	133	25	11	57	104	243	226	18	11
Major	344	2.6	44 839	704	114	19	9	67	60	58	209	10	9
Marshall	508	2.1	31 782	2 437	162	28	14	56	87	150	260	17	14
Mayes	1 292	1.1	31 653	2 455	496	87	43	98	211	363	724	45	43
Murray	541	1.5	39 452	1 238	207	45	16	42	88	124	310	18	16
Muskogee	2 406	1.7	34 223	2 047	1 219	241	103	181	381	692	1 744	103	103
Noble	401	0.6	35 071	1 889	194	33	15	24	82	92	267	16	15
Nowata	335	2.5	31 699	2 449	60	12	5	28	52	96	104	8	5
Okfuskee	327	2.6	26 426	3 011	78	17	6	37	53	115	138	9	6
Oklahoma	35 899	2.8	47 533	507	23 181	3 618	1 813	7 089	6 309	5 329	35 702	1 841	1 813
Okmulgee	1 242	1.5	31 498	2 480	382	72	31	72	178	391	557	38	31
Osage	1 934	1.4	40 312	1 136	294	53	24	301	227	359	672	37	24
Ottawa	1 062	0.2	32 950	2 261	390	71	31	73	175	321	566	36	31
Pawnee	553	1.5	33 519	2 172	142	28	12	45	89	151	227	15	12
Payne	2 937	2.3	37 146	1 558	1 355	273	104	413	565	458	2 144	112	104
Pittsburg	1 584	-3.3	35 430	1 831	699	139	58	133	301	395	1 029	61	58
Pontotoc	1 436	1.6	37 807	1 460	669	129	53	138	264	344	989	56	53
Pottawatomie	2 574	2.2	36 170	1 717	801	133	65	258	456	581	1 258	76	65
Pushmataha	346	-0.1	30 826	2 573	85	19	7	36	59	126	148	10	7
Roger Mills	175	-2.6	46 789	566	45	9	3	18	66	24	75	4	3
Rogers	3 660	1.7	41 106	1 040	1 255	197	108	370	553	630	1 930	111	108
Seminole	839	1.2	33 009	2 250	277	52	23	88	149	245	440	27	23
Sequoyah	1 229	0.4	29 827	2 714	268	56	23	103	182	404	450	31	23
Stephens	2 083	2.4	46 376	600	724	105	57	551	327	385	1 437	74	57
Texas	828	-0.6	37 505	1 503	392	67	29	153	133	102	641	28	29
Tillman	275	6.6	35 719	1 796	75	16	6	51	54	71	147	7	6
Tulsa	32 890	2.4	52 843	274	17 398	2 449	1 399	7 812	6 121	4 339	29 057	1 471	1 399
Wagoner	2 691	1.5	35 552	1 818	358	61	30	70	336	502	519	41	30
Washington	2 376	2.3	46 072	615	1 123	170	82	314	518	428	1 689	97	82
Washita	411	-4.5	35 156	1 878	93	17	7	34	83	84	150	9	7
Woods	396	-1.9	43 782	777	163	31	12	38	120	60	244	14	12
Woodward	1 018	4.0	47 972	484	547	76	42	224	150	128	889	45	42
OREGON	156 605	2.3	39 848	X	80 432	12 686	7 127	11 622	30 847	30 731	111 867	6 933	7 127
Baker	542	2.8	33 840	2 110	180	39	17	36	136	161	272	18	17
Benton	3 507	1.3	40 502	1 114	1 700	335	145	235	886	495	2 416	144	145
Clackamas	19 201	2.1	49 453	392	7 073	986	640	1 373	3 839	2 521	10 072	636	640
Clatsop	1 415	2.4	37 989	1 432	635	112	60	122	286	345	929	58	60
Columbia	1 759	1.9	35 654	1 808	376	72	36	57	266	422	541	41	36
Coos	2 198	2.6	35 291	1 862	798	164	76	160	440	714	1 198	82	76
Crook	692	3.3	33 234	2 222	255	45	23	48	152	213	372	27	23
Curry	775	1.8	34 675	1 958	220	43	21	57	208	267	341	26	21
Deschutes	6 548	4.1	39 456	1 237	2 595	420	246	723	1 679	1 382	3 984	258	246
Douglas	3 617	2.3	33 821	2 121	1 331	257	126	234	741	1 168	1 950	138	126
Gilliam	77	5.2	39 716	1 200	33	7	3	9	19	17	52	3	3
Grant	244	1.9	33 459	2 180	85	23	8	10	60	71	126	9	8
Harney	240	3.5	33 536	2 170	81	22	7	19	55	70	129	8	7
Hood River	871	2.0	38 428	1 387	437	70	42	56	212	151	605	34	42
Jackson	7 687	3.1	36 861	1 617	3 107	537	293	648	1 759	1 928	4 585	305	293
Jefferson	662	2.0	31 323	2 507	227	52	21	33	115	207	333	21	21
Josephine	2 655	1.9	31 869	2 427	799	144	78	186	587	946	1 207	94	78
Klamath	2 124	2.5	32 220	2 382	820	160	77	131	425	671	1 189	79	77
Lake	286	2.9	36 526	1 658	89	23	8	43	67	73	164	9	8
Lane	13 048	2.1	36 630	1 648	5 785	1 027	534	876	2 798	3 031	8 221	533	534
Lincoln	1 719	2.3	37 079	1 569	619	116	58	142	398	473	936	64	58
Linn	3 739	1.7	31 483	2 484	1 650	280	156	174	661	1 140	2 261	151	156
Malheur	882	3.7	28 954	2 809	439	94	40	93	170	271	666	38	40
Marion	11 485	2.7	35 489	1 823	5 658	1 075	505	902	1 970	2 706	8 140	490	505

1. Based on the resident population estimated as of July 1 of the year shown.

STATE County	Earnings, 2013 (cont.) — Percent by selected industries: Farm	Mining	Construction	Manu-facturing	Infor-mation: professional, scientific, technical services	Retail trade	Finance, insur-ance, real estate and leasing	Health care and social assistance	Govern-ment	Social Security beneficiaries, December 2013: Number	Rate[1]	Supple-mental Security Income recipients, December 2013	Housing units, 2014: Total	Percent change, 2010–2014
	75	76	77	78	79	80	81	82	83	84	85	86	87	88
OKLAHOMA—Cont'd														
Kiowa	13.6	10.6	D	D	D	6.9	4.7	7.8	24.6	2 460	262	355	5 179	-0.7
Latimer	2.5	13.5	15.9	D	D	4.0	1.8	4.7	25.1	2 845	265	375	4 979	0.0
Le Flore	5.1	12.5	7.6	7.1	D	7.3	3.3	D	30.9	11 745	236	2 092	21 690	1.1
Lincoln	1.1	D	12.8	9.7	3.1	8.0	8.7	D	18.6	7 790	227	803	15 221	0.1
Logan	0.3	22.4	11.5	4.0	D	6.7	9.9	8.0	9.4	7 770	175	763	17 258	0.4
Love	0.7	D	2.2	2.2	D	4.4	2.3	D	61.6	2 345	241	243	4 533	-0.1
McClain	1.7	9.8	16.7	3.0	5.1	13.1	4.4	6.9	19.5	7 115	195	559	14 771	5.5
McCurtain	6.9	D	5.2	21.6	D	7.9	2.6	D	19.2	8 290	250	1 622	15 578	0.3
McIntosh	-0.2	3.2	7.5	2.1	D	17.9	4.8	12.9	24.5	6 750	330	784	13 426	0.6
Major	12.2	30.3	7.7	4.8	2.5	5.1	D	3.0	10.2	1 750	228	101	3 662	-0.2
Marshall	1.9	3.4	2.8	30.5	3.5	7.0	5.5	8.9	15.0	4 055	254	454	10 032	0.3
Mayes	2.3	2.4	13.1	23.5	D	9.8	2.6	D	20.2	9 655	236	1 212	19 245	0.0
Murray	-0.4	5.3	6.8	6.7	D	6.6	2.9	D	44.1	3 355	245	343	6 776	0.4
Muskogee	0.7	0.5	6.0	14.6	2.9	7.1	3.7	D	33.1	16 595	236	2 929	30 907	0.0
Noble	2.3	2.2	2.6	D	D	3.9	3.4	D	21.6	2 615	230	243	5 321	-0.4
Nowata	3.8	6.9	7.6	14.6	3.1	4.6	4.9	11.3	21.8	2 740	260	266	4 818	-0.2
Okfuskee	7.2	7.6	7.1	5.0	D	6.8	D	10.9	38.1	2 810	229	574	5 300	0.3
Oklahoma	0.1	15.2	4.4	6.3	7.9	5.7	7.3	11.3	18.3	123 795	164	19 465	330 153	3.2
Okmulgee	1.6	3.0	8.3	19.4	2.9	8.0	3.6	D	31.8	9 895	251	1 636	17 818	-0.4
Osage	4.8	21.0	11.7	5.5	D	6.0	2.9	4.1	21.3	10 120	211	1 141	21 444	1.4
Ottawa	4.3	1.8	3.2	11.0	1.8	7.3	3.1	D	40.2	8 855	274	1 383	14 053	0.0
Pawnee	1.8	D	3.8	3.4	11.5	8.1	3.6	7.9	25.9	4 245	257	433	7 726	-0.3
Payne	0.2	11.2	6.0	5.5	4.6	8.7	4.0	4.6	39.0	11 720	148	1 284	35 208	3.6
Pittsburg	0.9	9.9	7.0	9.0	D	7.9	3.4	D	34.5	10 665	238	1 508	22 876	1.1
Pontotoc	0.3	7.2	4.7	7.0	6.4	5.9	4.8	11.4	37.3	8 280	217	1 261	16 684	0.5
Pottawatomie	1.3	7.0	6.2	12.6	D	7.7	4.0	10.5	22.5	15 550	218	2 013	29 642	1.7
Pushmataha	0.5	D	6.9	3.0	D	9.0	5.0	15.2	30.2	3 470	309	600	6 113	0.0
Roger Mills	5.9	14.5	D	D	4.5	5.0	D	0.6	28.0	755	202	80	1 901	-0.2
Rogers	0.3	1.2	18.0	24.0	D	5.0	3.5	6.4	18.4	17 380	195	1 344	36 370	3.4
Seminole	0.7	D	5.4	13.9	1.8	6.4	2.9	D	22.2	6 095	239	1 099	11 661	0.2
Sequoyah	2.5	1.5	5.6	1.2	5.8	13.2	4.4	D	32.5	10 590	256	1 991	18 844	1.0
Stephens	0.3	D	4.6	11.9	D	6.7	5.2	7.9	7.6	10 715	238	1 093	20 689	0.2
Texas	18.9	4.9	4.3	19.6	7.8	4.9	2.9	2.4	13.3	2 750	125	184	8 174	-0.4
Tillman	26.2	0.9	D	D	D	3.3	D	3.0	24.1	1 915	249	316	4 051	-0.6
Tulsa	0.0	13.6	6.3	11.4	9.1	5.6	7.2	10.6	7.0	108 305	174	14 454	277 004	3.2
Wagoner	0.7	0.6	13.5	25.3	2.8	8.6	3.4	D	19.9	14 155	187	1 250	30 773	3.6
Washington	0.2	36.8	3.4	5.2	4.5	5.6	3.9	D	7.3	12 635	245	1 080	23 633	0.8
Washita	7.4	20.5	6.4	2.7	4.4	5.8	6.4	4.3	24.5	2 360	201	220	5 461	-0.3
Woods	2.2	32.8	4.4	2.8	D	6.9	5.7	D	21.4	1 665	185	104	4 448	-0.7
Woodward	2.0	37.0	9.7	4.8	2.1	5.1	3.8	4.9	9.4	3 755	177	292	8 927	1.0
OREGON	1.4	0.2	5.8	12.7	10.0	6.8	6.2	12.4	17.1	777 832	198	83 264	1 700 549	1.5
Baker	7.3	D	4.0	9.4	4.8	8.6	3.2	13.4	25.3	4 895	304	449	8 821	-0.1
Benton	0.9	0.1	3.1	12.1	11.5	5.3	3.0	14.9	30.4	14 175	165	961	37 107	2.4
Clackamas	1.3	0.0	8.1	13.9	11.3	7.5	7.5	13.3	10.4	74 095	191	5 152	160 781	2.4
Clatsop	1.8	D	5.3	15.8	D	9.7	3.3	13.7	20.1	9 360	252	774	21 801	1.2
Columbia	0.6	0.8	7.7	17.2	D	8.4	4.9	8.5	21.8	11 370	231	957	20 664	-0.2
Coos	1.8	0.2	4.4	8.6	4.1	8.9	3.4	11.4	29.5	19 275	309	2 240	30 393	-0.7
Crook	-1.3	0.1	7.1	9.3	7.0	5.1	2.0	9.7	21.3	6 335	305	452	10 319	1.1
Curry	3.9	D	6.8	10.2	4.8	11.3	4.1	D	21.0	8 365	375	583	12 607	0.0
Deschutes	-0.4	0.1	9.3	6.3	11.7	9.4	7.4	18.2	14.4	37 930	229	2 213	82 414	2.8
Douglas	0.0	0.5	4.6	16.3	4.4	7.5	3.6	13.3	23.9	32 715	306	3 107	48 929	0.0
Gilliam	22.1	0.0	6.0	D	D	2.5	D	2.8	22.6	505	261	32	1 147	-0.8
Grant	0.4	D	5.6	5.8	D	6.7	D	D	48.8	2 225	306	167	4 304	-0.9
Harney	10.7	0.0	D	D	D	8.0	2.2	5.8	47.8	2 005	280	217	3 795	-1.0
Hood River	8.8	0.0	3.8	12.1	12.6	7.4	2.5	14.4	13.2	3 980	175	264	9 506	2.5
Jackson	0.2	0.1	7.6	9.2	6.7	10.8	5.0	18.4	15.6	52 270	251	4 590	91 919	1.1
Jefferson	6.6	D	1.8	15.2	D	5.5	1.9	8.9	40.6	5 145	236	548	9 767	-0.5
Josephine	-0.4	D	6.0	10.5	4.5	12.0	5.6	19.7	15.6	26 110	314	2 623	38 022	0.1
Klamath	2.9	D	4.3	8.3	D	9.3	3.3	14.5	25.1	16 600	252	1 968	32 763	0.0
Lake	20.0	D	3.7	6.5	3.4	5.4	2.0	D	38.8	2 190	279	248	4 401	-0.9
Lane	0.3	0.2	5.5	10.6	8.7	9.0	5.6	16.3	20.0	77 830	219	8 769	157 899	1.1
Lincoln	3.5	D	5.6	8.3	4.1	10.5	3.9	11.4	25.4	14 480	313	1 308	30 700	0.3
Linn	2.4	D	6.2	23.3	3.2	7.1	2.9	11.0	16.6	27 440	231	3 253	49 300	1.0
Malheur	11.1	D	2.2	5.5	D	9.4	2.5	12.5	20.0	6 360	200	912	11 617	-0.6
Marion	2.8	0.2	6.1	6.1	5.2	7.1	5.2	16.2	30.3	59 795	186	7 816	122 449	1.2

1. Per 1,000 resident population estimated as of July 1 of the year shown.

STATE County	Housing units, 2009–2013: Occupied units: Total	Owner-occupied: Percent	Owner-occupied: Median value[1]	Median owner cost as a percent of income: With a mortgage	Median owner cost as a percent of income: Without a mortgage[2]	Renter-occupied: Median rent[3]	Renter-occupied: Median rent as a percent of income[2]	Substandard units[4] (percent)	Civilian labor force, 2014: Total	Percent change, 2013–2014	Unemployment: Total	Unemployment: Rate[5]	Civilian employment,[6] 2009–2013: Total	Percent: Management, business, science and arts	Percent: Construction, production, and maintenance occupations
	89	90	91	92	93	94	95	96	97	98	99	100	101	102	103
OKLAHOMA—Cont'd															
Kiowa	3 886	68.0	56 600	18.1	11.1	491	25.7	5.2	4 021	-3.2	165	4.1	3 947	27.7	32.6
Latimer	4 160	69.3	71 200	18.3	10.0	475	24.8	3.6	3 964	-4.5	298	7.5	4 039	30.4	32.8
Le Flore	18 412	74.1	80 100	22.2	11.9	554	26.9	4.0	19 283	-2.7	1 341	7.0	18 229	24.9	33.2
Lincoln	13 256	76.6	92 600	19.5	10.0	556	30.6	3.2	15 430	-0.3	699	4.5	14 630	27.2	32.7
Logan	14 927	78.6	135 700	21.0	10.3	659	26.0	3.9	20 674	-0.4	828	4.0	19 151	33.6	23.7
Love	3 378	75.8	80 500	20.0	11.2	593	23.9	3.0	5 345	1.7	195	3.6	4 079	26.3	32.9
McClain	12 749	81.8	139 300	21.1	10.7	673	26.9	4.7	17 798	-0.2	660	3.7	16 366	31.1	25.8
McCurtain	13 078	68.1	71 500	20.7	11.0	551	28.3	3.0	14 156	-1.2	1 126	8.0	12 527	23.8	37.6
McIntosh	8 092	79.8	79 600	22.2	10.8	574	31.2	2.5	6 969	-5.4	620	8.9	7 070	29.1	29.1
Major	3 084	75.6	85 300	18.3	10.0	495	20.9	4.7	4 324	4.6	114	2.6	3 649	25.9	37.9
Marshall	5 970	79.3	83 700	20.2	11.0	586	26.5	4.2	6 895	-1.0	332	4.8	6 192	21.1	35.3
Mayes	15 896	75.2	96 200	20.9	10.9	604	26.8	3.5	18 554	-1.7	916	4.9	16 653	29.6	31.9
Murray	5 121	73.3	82 200	19.9	10.0	616	22.9	2.7	6 485	0.1	273	4.2	5 995	28.6	25.0
Muskogee	26 802	67.4	92 200	21.3	11.1	624	33.1	2.8	28 988	-2.5	1 678	5.8	27 835	28.1	28.4
Noble	4 565	72.8	85 200	19.6	10.8	600	31.4	3.0	5 505	0.5	202	3.7	5 288	34.2	28.2
Nowata	4 050	81.2	74 300	18.9	12.3	553	27.6	4.0	4 739	-1.8	290	6.1	4 171	26.4	35.4
Okfuskee	4 246	73.6	69 300	21.7	10.0	483	30.5	3.1	4 455	0.7	267	6.0	4 100	28.0	31.7
Oklahoma	285 320	59.9	126 500	21.8	11.4	748	30.4	2.3	365 832	-0.8	15 352	4.2	342 697	35.2	20.7
Okmulgee	15 124	69.7	77 100	21.1	11.8	580	25.3	3.0	16 152	-0.7	1 089	6.7	15 195	28.2	28.7
Osage	18 512	79.0	93 900	20.4	11.6	599	25.7	4.7	21 013	-0.6	1 083	5.2	19 896	28.4	32.0
Ottawa	12 134	72.8	81 000	21.7	11.0	595	29.3	3.5	13 663	-3.3	905	6.6	13 090	26.1	28.0
Pawnee	6 341	76.5	83 500	20.5	10.8	622	28.9	2.8	7 365	-0.4	389	5.3	6 990	27.4	34.5
Payne	30 010	50.9	130 800	21.8	10.3	686	36.9	3.6	38 126	1.5	1 420	3.7	37 095	37.5	20.5
Pittsburg	18 456	72.0	86 800	19.1	10.3	647	30.5	4.2	16 989	-5.6	1 040	6.1	18 409	27.7	27.8
Pontotoc	14 793	66.6	99 100	21.2	10.0	626	29.4	3.0	17 619	-0.9	769	4.4	17 630	34.2	23.1
Pottawatomie	25 658	71.9	96 400	20.3	10.3	654	29.4	4.2	31 853	-0.9	1 511	4.7	29 188	31.3	26.7
Pushmataha	4 900	74.1	71 000	20.9	12.3	514	30.5	2.2	4 680	-0.7	345	7.4	4 259	31.9	28.3
Roger Mills	1 305	78.8	81 300	18.3	10.0	567	16.1	2.8	1 777	-5.4	51	2.9	1 622	30.9	35.1
Rogers	32 693	78.9	143 600	20.7	10.0	786	26.5	3.7	43 412	-1.0	1 826	4.2	41 358	32.7	27.8
Seminole	9 327	73.9	70 500	21.8	10.0	512	29.1	4.3	9 452	-2.9	643	6.8	9 388	27.6	31.2
Sequoyah	15 624	71.5	85 800	21.2	11.7	609	30.6	2.5	16 566	-2.1	1 161	7.0	15 796	26.1	31.0
Stephens	17 690	70.8	89 300	19.9	10.9	618	26.4	8.3	19 958	-3.2	910	4.6	18 645	29.5	29.9
Texas	7 180	64.6	89 000	19.5	10.0	632	21.7	2.1	9 281	-0.2	346	3.7	10 478	24.3	40.9
Tillman	3 013	73.5	52 800	20.7	12.4	544	25.2	3.1	3 271	-3.0	154	4.7	3 162	29.8	29.9
Tulsa	241 915	60.9	134 100	21.4	11.4	749	29.1	2.7	308 610	-0.9	13 295	4.3	292 199	35.4	21.3
Wagoner	27 016	82.5	138 400	21.3	10.8	758	29.4	1.7	35 639	-0.9	1 508	4.2	33 687	31.0	26.5
Washington	21 332	72.9	111 000	19.9	10.3	638	25.1	2.5	24 277	-1.5	1 036	4.3	22 558	34.6	23.6
Washita	4 630	70.7	76 500	16.9	10.0	640	19.4	1.4	5 576	-0.1	193	3.5	5 027	31.6	33.0
Woods	3 439	66.2	80 700	15.5	10.0	578	21.8	2.9	5 193	1.0	141	2.7	4 304	32.9	24.4
Woodward	7 382	71.8	104 300	17.7	10.0	618	21.6	3.6	10 671	-0.6	329	3.1	9 617	28.5	35.2
OREGON	1 516 456	62.0	238 000	26.2	12.8	875	32.2	3.4	1 942 025	1.6	134 956	6.9	1 736 894	36.5	21.0
Baker	7 120	67.0	147 700	22.9	12.2	625	29.8	2.2	6 742	-0.9	576	8.5	6 446	35.3	22.1
Benton	33 384	57.9	270 500	23.7	10.2	816	40.0	3.0	44 024	1.2	2 341	5.3	40 197	48.3	13.9
Clackamas	146 527	68.8	300 600	26.8	12.9	983	30.4	3.7	200 522	1.8	12 601	6.3	178 142	37.6	20.2
Clatsop	15 749	62.7	256 500	27.6	13.1	812	32.8	2.3	18 118	1.4	1 205	6.7	16 779	27.7	25.6
Columbia	19 069	73.9	213 200	24.5	12.2	785	33.7	2.3	22 639	1.6	1 902	8.4	20 412	29.6	30.9
Coos	26 072	66.1	177 000	26.3	14.1	720	34.0	3.5	26 260	-0.4	2 404	9.2	23 722	28.2	24.4
Crook	8 880	70.5	173 000	29.2	11.8	748	33.7	3.5	9 045	1.4	911	10.1	7 677	23.8	25.3
Curry	10 355	67.8	230 100	30.6	11.7	797	32.2	2.9	8 690	0.4	900	10.4	8 021	26.0	22.4
Deschutes	64 568	65.5	249 500	28.3	13.0	922	32.6	2.9	80 907	3.5	6 384	7.9	69 789	36.2	19.3
Douglas	43 846	68.8	171 300	26.1	12.6	768	31.3	1.8	44 224	0.1	4 164	9.4	39 764	28.3	27.6
Gilliam	883	63.3	116 400	21.9	11.8	691	24.4	1.7	841	-0.4	67	8.0	887	22.1	44.6
Grant	3 319	70.4	136 400	25.9	12.2	619	25.6	4.1	3 185	-0.3	343	10.8	2 924	31.5	23.8
Harney	3 113	64.9	112 300	21.5	10.3	560	26.9	4.0	3 336	0.2	328	9.8	3 083	36.6	27.1
Hood River	8 144	66.1	321 700	28.3	12.0	791	27.2	3.4	14 024	2.0	767	5.5	11 323	34.2	28.9
Jackson	83 140	62.2	225 100	28.5	13.9	875	36.6	4.4	97 104	1.2	8 356	8.6	85 665	32.7	20.8
Jefferson	7 882	65.4	165 900	27.4	12.3	722	25.9	3.1	9 397	1.9	848	9.0	7 871	23.3	30.6
Josephine	34 390	66.2	220 900	28.1	12.1	798	36.3	3.6	32 925	2.2	3 175	9.6	28 546	29.1	23.7
Klamath	27 378	65.8	155 000	24.8	11.0	726	34.6	2.3	28 638	-0.9	2 767	9.7	26 299	30.2	26.7
Lake	3 566	66.2	144 100	24.0	12.4	551	29.5	2.4	3 522	1.5	345	9.8	3 285	33.8	26.7
Lane	144 912	59.6	218 900	26.5	12.8	841	34.7	3.2	169 465	1.2	11 980	7.1	153 594	34.5	20.2
Lincoln	20 913	65.5	237 200	27.3	13.6	827	30.6	3.0	20 671	0.2	1 645	8.0	19 870	28.4	20.4
Linn	44 722	66.8	173 600	25.5	12.2	798	31.6	5.8	54 020	1.0	4 520	8.4	48 173	27.5	29.6
Malheur	10 136	61.6	132 600	23.6	11.5	601	36.0	5.6	12 151	-1.7	996	8.2	10 773	28.9	29.8
Marion	113 285	60.3	192 200	26.6	12.8	789	32.0	8.4	149 448	1.5	11 189	7.5	133 339	30.4	25.8

1. Specified owner-occupied units. 2. A value of 10.0 represents 10 percent or less; a value of 50.0 represents 50 percent or more. 3. Specified renter-occupied units.
4. Overcrowded or lacking complete plumbing facilities. 5. Percent of civilian labor force. 6. Persons 16 years old and over.

STATE County	Private nonfarm establishments, employment and payroll, 2013									Agriculture, 2012			
		Employment						Annual payroll		Farms			
											Percent with:		
	Number of establish-ments	Total	Health care and social assistance	Manufac-turing	Retail trade	Finance and insurance	Professional, scientific, and technical services	Total (mil dol)	Average per employee (dollars)	Number	Fewer than 50 acres	500 acres or more	Farm operators whose principal occu-pation is farming (percent)
	104	105	106	107	108	109	110	111	112	113	114	115	116
OKLAHOMA—Cont'd													
Kiowa	193	1 701	513	D	275	97	D	50	29 414	667	9.0	44.8	53.2
Latimer	166	1 871	404	D	276	68	65	63	33 842	691	27.2	13.9	36.3
Le Flore	806	8 408	2 822	406	1 566	398	282	260	30 894	1 843	32.2	8.4	48.0
Lincoln	571	5 510	D	805	721	424	113	184	33 382	2 121	26.0	10.6	43.9
Logan	786	6 375	1 153	405	1 041	213	183	172	26 936	1 203	27.2	14.8	37.1
Love	157	4 317	123	D	120	D	48	123	28 563	621	22.9	15.5	45.7
McClain	803	7 322	922	370	1 453	269	263	242	33 101	1 239	39.9	12.2	38.7
McCurtain	573	8 434	1 696	2 472	1 155	244	97	246	29 176	1 577	28.0	8.1	39.9
McIntosh	360	3 281	856	92	905	141	124	91	27 811	1 018	25.8	9.4	36.7
Major	260	2 297	D	D	277	76	47	110	47 681	901	13.7	32.6	45.3
Marshall	290	3 801	538	1 191	621	D	102	122	31 986	525	26.5	15.6	40.8
Mayes	799	9 773	1 134	2 754	1 608	312	340	368	37 681	1 551	36.6	7.7	42.5
Murray	291	2 996	504	347	613	154	96	95	31 561	470	22.1	17.0	37.4
Muskogee	1 436	22 139	5 625	3 640	3 187	628	534	810	36 572	1 735	34.2	8.4	46.0
Noble	216	3 748	387	D	329	143	D	157	41 993	828	15.5	27.5	39.4
Nowata	160	1 359	337	248	141	62	D	38	27 807	889	22.5	14.3	44.2
Okfuskee	165	2 260	D	D	204	D	D	64	28 328	881	18.5	15.7	39.5
Oklahoma	22 949	365 176	57 466	20 953	44 374	18 444	24 363	16 667	45 642	1 180	56.6	5.7	44.4
Okmulgee	679	7 669	2 262	1 449	1 414	303	174	228	29 665	1 329	32.3	10.8	44.6
Osage	580	6 029	698	296	823	157	114	191	31 698	1 325	28.5	25.6	47.8
Ottawa	592	8 878	1 405	D	975	272	271	254	28 592	1 020	36.4	7.9	38.6
Pawnee	268	2 528	522	229	384	D	D	105	41 427	813	21.4	18.2	31.5
Payne	1 761	22 120	3 518	1 518	4 098	881	1 214	696	31 454	1 466	34.9	10.5	34.1
Pittsburg	963	11 476	2 492	1 177	2 087	432	375	383	33 417	1 567	27.1	15.8	39.8
Pontotoc	978	12 651	3 546	1 155	1 766	990	356	404	31 895	1 313	26.9	10.1	38.2
Pottawatomie	1 312	18 571	2 974	2 900	2 869	681	717	561	30 209	1 643	32.0	9.6	39.6
Pushmataha	190	1 909	797	115	308	D	D	47	24 559	732	15.4	15.8	47.0
Roger Mills	86	545	D	D	88	D	D	21	38 257	678	9.9	42.6	49.6
Rogers	1 702	25 729	2 960	7 036	2 536	757	795	1 189	46 198	1 733	47.8	8.1	33.8
Seminole	469	5 783	1 017	743	813	234	106	190	32 855	1 054	20.7	10.5	36.2
Sequoyah	572	6 972	2 438	D	1 173	353	120	160	22 997	1 204	37.7	6.9	42.6
Stephens	1 080	13 229	2 162	2 114	2 131	612	531	464	35 072	1 286	23.6	17.1	33.0
Texas	488	7 660	505	D	934	246	D	316	41 278	1 024	8.4	42.6	38.7
Tillman	143	1 264	272	D	169	68	23	38	29 895	556	8.1	44.4	52.2
Tulsa	18 583	322 777	50 122	36 954	37 521	15 212	20 227	15 060	46 657	1 036	57.6	3.8	40.0
Wagoner	919	8 705	789	2 253	1 483	276	214	296	33 987	1 090	44.7	7.5	35.0
Washington	1 192	19 631	3 074	1 042	2 405	742	1 456	937	47 725	811	37.5	9.5	41.2
Washita	238	1 580	267	D	311	87	D	50	31 709	973	12.3	36.2	50.5
Woods	284	2 796	D	D	472	157	78	105	37 497	751	13.6	41.9	52.2
Woodward	809	8 905	1 052	508	1 246	322	210	412	46 217	882	15.3	33.9	39.1
OREGON	108 527	1 396 563	218 688	151 532	190 891	58 985	84 411	61 062	43 723	35 439	61.5	10.6	49.9
Baker	521	3 896	681	497	760	122	182	122	31 322	645	31.0	28.7	60.5
Benton	2 081	25 350	5 478	3 002	3 530	592	2 069	1 096	43 217	886	71.4	5.6	46.3
Clackamas	11 118	132 173	18 317	16 197	18 623	5 521	8 179	5 852	44 278	3 745	81.4	1.1	41.1
Clatsop	1 445	13 529	1 971	D	2 636	267	334	458	33 867	199	55.3	2.5	45.7
Columbia	905	7 705	1 541	1 303	1 367	280	243	229	29 775	751	69.9	2.4	45.7
Coos	1 569	17 480	3 665	1 340	2 878	460	818	602	34 448	654	41.4	9.5	56.9
Crook	479	3 780	473	792	590	87	137	124	32 751	551	49.9	16.7	51.0
Curry	660	5 077	1 005	672	961	157	105	154	30 373	197	37.6	21.3	60.4
Deschutes	6 078	53 397	9 692	3 949	9 670	1 774	2 651	1 965	36 804	1 283	78.9	3.0	44.0
Douglas	2 411	27 741	4 882	3 880	4 479	818	832	958	34 547	1 927	50.9	8.1	48.3
Gilliam	72	755	78	NA	74	D	D	26	34 874	170	4.1	77.6	63.5
Grant	236	1 379	D	D	210	D	72	44	31 882	398	28.1	36.9	54.3
Harney	185	1 200	326	D	266	50	D	36	30 122	497	21.5	42.3	57.1
Hood River	975	9 506	1 742	1 113	1 354	172	423	272	28 569	554	74.9	0.5	56.7
Jackson	5 861	66 354	13 098	5 980	11 692	2 450	2 415	2 303	34 709	1 722	72.1	2.4	56.2
Jefferson	358	3 581	D	924	513	62	58	118	32 948	474	42.2	18.4	53.2
Josephine	1 899	20 079	4 585	2 340	4 120	594	568	612	30 483	617	76.3	0.6	55.8
Klamath	1 530	16 433	3 042	1 939	3 002	1 018	630	573	34 845	955	38.7	19.4	63.7
Lake	191	1 163	288	219	158	23	D	39	33 318	373	21.4	40.2	70.2
Lane	9 538	117 026	21 572	12 753	18 846	5 316	5 247	4 215	36 016	2 660	73.9	2.9	44.5
Lincoln	1 562	13 527	D	861	2 802	D	320	414	30 633	362	63.3	3.9	48.3
Linn	2 437	32 742	4 765	6 643	4 611	886	853	1 217	37 169	2 083	64.8	6.7	48.7
Malheur	712	8 023	1 603	D	1 831	200	196	222	27 708	1 113	33.9	20.8	64.1
Marion	7 685	95 058	18 300	9 016	15 546	3 464	3 920	3 287	34 581	2 567	72.5	5.6	47.1

STATE County	Agriculture, 2012 (cont.) — Land in farms — Acreage (1,000)	Land in farms — Percent change, 2007–2012	Land in farms — Acres — Average size of farm	Land in farms — Acres — Total irrigated (1,000)	Land in farms — Acres — Total cropland (1,000)	Value of land and buildings (dollars) — Average per farm	Value of land and buildings (dollars) — Average per acre	Value of machinery and equipment, average per farm (dollars)	Value of products sold — Total (mil dol)	Value of products sold — Average per farm (dollars)	Value of products sold — Percent from: Crops	Value of products sold — Percent from: Livestock and poultry products	Percent of farms with sales of: $10,000 or more	Percent of farms with sales of: $100,000 or more	Government payments — Total ($1,000)	Government payments — Percent of farms
	117	118	119	120	121	122	123	124	125	126	127	128	129	130	131	132
OKLAHOMA—Cont'd																
Kiowa	593	5.1	890	2.7	302.3	854 510	961	144 499	107.8	161 627	59.1	40.9	61.3	28.0	8 081	79.2
Latimer	221	3.3	319	0.1	38.2	425 538	1 333	56 986	24.6	35 570	8.5	91.5	34.6	4.6	1 268	15.8
Le Flore	395	-15.3	214	6.1	103.7	425 397	1 985	57 896	287.3	155 883	6.6	93.4	38.0	12.0	2 522	25.6
Lincoln	454	-6.9	214	0.8	106.5	369 323	1 724	54 060	38.7	18 260	26.8	73.2	31.7	3.2	1 147	16.3
Logan	367	-9.0	305	1.1	133.7	575 341	1 884	63 051	44.0	36 563	47.2	52.8	37.2	5.5	2 181	38.3
Love	219	-16.2	353	1.1	48.8	611 282	1 730	56 594	23.9	38 472	19.5	80.5	40.7	7.4	1 234	29.0
McClain	283	-16.1	228	1.7	78.9	466 267	2 043	61 161	48.5	39 117	26.2	73.8	32.6	7.7	1 349	24.8
McCurtain	317	-6.8	201	1.5	70.3	349 785	1 742	57 386	163.1	103 452	7.2	92.8	36.6	7.8	1 573	24.0
McIntosh	236	-4.4	232	0.2	58.1	357 114	1 541	52 882	22.3	21 872	13.1	86.9	37.7	3.6	672	23.3
Major	537	3.8	596	10.1	217.0	668 974	1 122	95 212	105.4	116 986	39.2	60.8	59.4	20.3	3 795	65.7
Marshall	192	21.6	365	0.7	41.8	610 888	1 672	64 185	18.4	34 983	20.8	79.2	37.0	5.3	830	24.0
Mayes	285	-9.0	184	0.4	85.2	388 246	2 112	56 484	76.0	48 985	8.0	92.0	37.0	6.8	1 628	24.2
Murray	208	5.6	443	0.0	24.3	613 813	1 386	65 602	28.0	59 557	8.2	91.8	36.6	4.9	709	33.0
Muskogee	350	-6.5	202	7.3	120.2	356 096	1 765	55 445	50.6	29 140	42.3	57.7	33.9	4.0	2 161	29.6
Noble	443	-5.2	535	1.9	193.3	762 217	1 425	79 824	61.3	73 995	48.4	51.6	51.1	16.2	4 809	64.4
Nowata	292	-17.6	329	0.1	64.8	544 327	1 657	53 998	40.0	45 009	12.3	87.7	46.1	5.5	1 267	31.7
Okfuskee	320	7.0	363	0.7	60.1	463 053	1 276	57 190	34.7	39 373	13.3	86.7	39.7	5.3	922	26.4
Oklahoma	144	-9.8	122	2.3	47.9	378 664	3 099	43 969	20.4	17 300	71.0	29.0	19.7	3.6	502	14.4
Okmulgee	300	2.0	226	0.7	78.0	406 784	1 801	51 241	27.1	20 421	27.7	72.3	30.5	3.8	908	21.6
Osage	1 217	-5.7	918	1.3	131.4	968 906	1 055	58 483	121.5	91 682	6.2	93.8	42.9	11.2	4 433	23.2
Ottawa	193	-18.8	189	0.2	87.9	436 945	2 306	76 215	117.6	115 291	43.1	56.9	39.0	7.8	1 622	25.5
Pawnee	286	-3.9	352	0.0	52.2	468 352	1 331	55 888	26.7	32 864	14.6	85.4	37.8	7.4	1 400	30.3
Payne	350	-2.0	239	0.4	105.1	451 118	1 891	52 108	34.1	23 231	26.5	73.5	33.4	4.1	1 737	23.5
Pittsburg	524	-4.3	334	1.8	95.6	454 824	1 361	54 429	41.6	26 535	15.7	84.3	35.4	4.8	1 898	16.1
Pontotoc	325	-14.4	247	0.9	69.0	434 772	1 759	49 674	36.0	27 438	17.6	82.3	34.4	2.4	1 242	16.4
Pottawatomie	335	-15.1	204	0.9	86.9	358 388	1 756	52 875	35.4	21 523	24.0	76.0	26.0	2.7	1 346	14.2
Pushmataha	297	2.4	406	D	37.9	462 504	1 138	44 060	14.6	19 939	9.7	90.3	36.9	4.4	2 454	23.9
Roger Mills	719	0.0	1 061	5.3	117.5	1 093 820	1 031	96 844	46.0	67 827	28.1	71.9	47.8	14.0	4 532	58.1
Rogers	302	-18.7	174	1.0	71.8	429 069	2 464	44 947	66.4	38 290	11.7	88.3	31.2	4.5	1 186	15.5
Seminole	243	-3.0	231	0.2	48.0	325 588	1 411	46 705	38.1	36 162	10.4	89.6	29.9	2.2	875	20.8
Sequoyah	215	-7.3	179	3.3	63.8	357 679	2 002	52 061	55.5	46 084	23.0	77.0	31.2	3.9	1 620	9.1
Stephens	481	2.3	374	0.1	75.9	474 056	1 268	58 719	42.2	32 782	12.5	87.5	35.1	5.8	2 539	29.9
Texas	1 287	6.7	1 257	153.0	678.8	1 005 370	800	180 940	1 013.9	990 157	15.0	85.0	42.1	19.9	12 943	78.5
Tillman	541	16.7	974	10.6	290.0	977 950	1 004	163 739	102.4	184 257	53.7	46.3	62.4	25.7	6 753	79.0
Tulsa	106	-19.0	103	4.7	42.7	372 738	3 635	35 707	21.0	20 313	70.3	29.7	23.9	2.9	692	10.0
Wagoner	199	-24.3	182	4.0	78.6	443 074	2 428	53 862	33.8	31 050	57.8	42.2	31.1	4.7	1 257	26.2
Washington	231	1.9	285	D	55.6	476 007	1 672	50 665	37.4	46 086	19.2	80.8	35.4	7.5	590	22.3
Washita	633	7.2	651	7.0	343.6	780 371	1 199	136 291	114.7	117 867	54.3	45.7	64.5	23.2	10 153	80.5
Woods	808	-3.0	1 077	2.8	231.1	1 167 659	1 085	114 887	82.5	109 875	43.0	57.0	55.7	23.7	4 609	71.0
Woodward	715	-8.7	810	4.6	149.9	898 007	1 108	85 655	116.5	132 078	13.4	86.6	46.1	13.4	4 264	56.5
OREGON	16 302	-0.6	460	1 629.7	4 690.4	865 613	1 882	90 222	4 883.7	137 805	66.5	33.5	35.6	13.1	85 840	15.1
Baker	711	-0.1	1 102	100.9	107.5	1 117 372	1 014	118 667	93.3	144 583	49.4	50.6	52.2	21.6	1 883	25.7
Benton	124	8.2	140	11.3	68.2	830 059	5 932	68 867	103.3	116 597	78.2	21.8	28.6	10.4	486	6.4
Clackamas	163	-11.0	43	22.2	84.0	585 754	13 486	53 573	325.2	86 833	76.7	23.3	27.5	7.1	607	3.8
Clatsop	16	-22.7	82	0.7	5.3	456 739	5 548	53 940	11.5	58 010	12.3	87.7	22.1	6.0	50	6.0
Columbia	57	-1.9	75	1.9	18.0	414 475	5 493	41 466	39.4	52 413	D	D	17.6	1.6	232	4.1
Coos	157	8.1	241	11.2	20.9	776 687	3 225	60 953	50.4	77 018	21.5	78.6	43.6	12.2	678	10.7
Crook	823	8.0	1 493	61.9	57.0	1 357 530	909	76 437	42.3	76 766	32.1	67.9	38.3	9.4	554	9.3
Curry	63	-14.8	322	3.2	5.2	1 095 939	3 408	71 112	21.4	108 411	44.9	55.1	53.8	19.3	524	17.3
Deschutes	131	1.3	102	34.0	28.9	716 430	7 015	52 158	20.6	16 033	54.1	45.9	22.1	2.4	241	3.4
Douglas	382	-3.7	198	14.6	49.2	611 961	3 084	44 231	64.8	33 629	36.3	63.7	27.3	4.7	730	5.3
Gilliam	723	-1.4	4 255	6.5	331.7	2 117 900	498	293 047	44.1	259 141	84.6	15.4	50.6	40.0	7 931	90.0
Grant	656	-13.8	1 649	31.6	96.4	1 326 967	805	79 166	25.4	63 719	22.3	77.7	50.8	14.8	900	14.8
Harney	1 505	3.0	3 029	165.7	223.0	1 660 966	548	163 302	88.9	178 966	41.7	58.3	55.7	30.0	1 414	24.9
Hood River	26	-4.2	47	14.1	16.3	885 421	19 000	90 121	77.1	139 200	D	D	49.8	26.9	777	13.4
Jackson	214	-12.3	124	36.5	32.8	582 023	4 682	40 415	64.1	37 240	57.6	42.4	25.7	3.4	252	3.8
Jefferson	817	15.2	1 724	41.1	62.9	1 104 840	641	154 973	65.0	137 198	72.7	27.3	40.7	19.4	1 182	32.7
Josephine	28	-25.1	46	9.0	8.4	460 319	10 052	35 806	18.8	30 481	D	D	25.0	4.7	129	2.9
Klamath	650	-3.7	681	159.9	205.2	1 004 853	1 475	136 301	181.5	190 037	56.5	43.5	48.7	21.8	1 951	21.4
Lake	657	-5.2	1 762	148.9	131.1	1 791 244	1 017	171 150	85.6	229 614	52.6	47.4	61.7	33.8	716	20.6
Lane	220	-10.6	83	19.3	100.0	563 427	6 824	49 734	142.5	53 574	74.6	25.4	23.5	5.6	575	5.1
Lincoln	30	-3.1	83	0.4	5.1	400 392	4 795	35 680	5.5	15 293	30.6	69.4	22.7	1.7	93	3.6
Linn	331	-12.0	159	28.7	227.5	769 891	4 840	89 696	241.2	115 812	77.1	22.9	31.3	11.7	882	6.8
Malheur	1 077	-8.0	967	183.0	204.8	1 136 094	1 174	174 964	359.3	322 829	50.7	49.3	68.3	32.6	2 574	40.2
Marion	286	-7.0	111	84.9	213.8	885 406	7 942	130 593	592.9	230 953	81.5	18.5	41.0	17.7	1 583	9.8

STATE County	Water use, 2010		Wholesale trade,[1] 2007				Retail trade,[2] 2007				Real estate and rental and leasing,[2] 2007			
	Total water withdrawn (mil gal/day)	Gallons withdrawn per person per day	Number of establish-ments	Number of employees	Sales (mil dol)	Annual payroll (mil dol)	Number of establish-ments	Number of employees	Sales (mil dol)	Annual payroll (mil dol)	Number of establish-ments	Number of employees	Receipts (mil dol)	Annual payroll (mil dol)
	133	134	135	136	137	138	139	140	141	142	143	144	145	146
OKLAHOMA—Cont'd														
Kiowa	13.8	1 456	11	67	56.8	2.2	44	283	55.4	5.0	7	14	2.0	0.3
Latimer	2.9	261	7	105	90.3	3.6	24	248	40.5	4.0	5	43	17.1	2.7
Le Flore	23.7	470	22	D	D	D	140	1 531	376.3	28.7	15	176	24.6	7.3
Lincoln	21.3	620	22	138	85.5	5.3	87	609	161.9	11.3	14	D	D	D
Logan	11.2	267	22	D	D	D	95	878	275.6	19.9	32	D	D	D
Love	5.5	585	4	24	8.9	0.9	26	181	56.4	4.0	3	D	D	D
McClain	8.1	234	17	D	D	D	108	1 453	413.0	32.3	29	94	19.3	2.7
McCurtain	9.9	298	27	114	95.7	3.8	116	1 075	261.1	20.9	16	76	6.8	1.4
McIntosh	5.0	246	7	30	9.6	0.7	74	820	266.4	14.6	11	28	2.0	0.3
Major	17.3	2 300	9	71	39.5	2.2	40	313	78.8	5.0	7	23	2.3	0.5
Marshall	7.2	452	10	D	D	D	52	567	126.8	11.2	8	25	2.9	0.6
Mayes	111.1	2 692	28	402	301.4	19.2	160	1 490	414.6	31.2	22	46	5.1	0.8
Murray	21.3	1 577	5	87	42.2	3.5	50	627	193.6	13.4	8	119	12.9	4.1
Muskogee	48.0	677	65	994	580.7	49.8	287	3 468	904.0	71.7	66	548	45.6	10.3
Noble	35.6	3 079	6	37	28.0	0.9	30	315	86.8	6.2	6	25	1.7	0.2
Nowata	51.1	4 845	8	50	16.3	1.6	23	145	24.9	2.6	8	22	1.4	0.5
Okfuskee	5.8	479	4	17	2.8	0.2	29	199	64.6	3.5	2	D	D	D
Oklahoma	131.1	182	1 126	18 070	27 232.3	809.9	2 951	42 806	10 760.0	980.9	1 107	8 218	1 238.5	294.4
Okmulgee	18.9	471	20	125	42.1	4.6	128	1 286	329.5	25.9	19	D	D	D
Osage	19.1	402	17	D	D	D	98	769	172.1	12.9	18	D	D	D
Ottawa	4.9	152	24	D	D	D	98	1 206	287.6	24.9	27	106	9.3	2.3
Pawnee	13.3	800	8	D	D	D	45	366	82.5	6.3	10	D	D	D
Payne	11.9	153	41	D	D	D	307	3 890	818.4	74.3	76	247	33.8	5.1
Pittsburg	17.3	377	32	373	230.0	10.5	189	2 198	606.9	43.6	51	202	33.8	5.6
Pontotoc	152.5	4 066	47	D	D	D	170	1 813	409.0	34.0	38	148	21.8	3.8
Pottawatomie	22.9	330	33	D	D	D	253	2 824	682.3	55.9	47	203	23.7	4.2
Pushmataha	1.3	110	8	62	10.7	1.6	52	385	74.8	5.3	1	D	D	D
Roger Mills	7.8	2 137	1	D	D	D	20	124	42.8	2.4	NA	NA	NA	NA
Rogers	90.3	1 039	59	1 075	921.9	47.3	210	2 575	663.8	58.0	72	392	64.2	6.9
Seminole	342.0	13 423	14	73	85.1	3.1	78	800	192.6	16.7	14	48	5.2	0.9
Sequoyah	10.4	244	13	D	D	D	115	1 258	362.4	23.5	16	43	3.4	0.6
Stephens	137.0	3 040	42	D	D	D	210	2 076	495.1	40.4	27	107	11.0	1.7
Texas	301.9	14 629	27	D	D	D	80	814	182.6	15.7	12	D	D	D
Tillman	11.4	1 431	8	94	56.8	3.0	30	231	35.8	2.4	1	D	D	D
Tulsa	15.4	26	1 045	16 244	10 026.2	838.5	2 386	37 579	9 580.7	830.1	970	8 195	1 347.7	274.3
Wagoner	14.1	192	34	208	107.6	9.1	106	1 039	276.4	20.7	31	80	17.1	1.5
Washington	11.6	228	28	D	D	D	198	2 531	626.4	53.3	47	D	D	D
Washita	9.1	780	11	113	38.7	3.4	40	249	76.4	4.4	7	77	9.6	2.3
Woods	11.3	1 277	15	362	69.0	7.1	57	491	99.8	7.9	10	20	1.0	0.1
Woodward	24.4	1 217	40	330	140.6	9.5	120	1 238	337.4	25.8	28	132	16.8	4.4
OREGON	6 734.5	1 758	4 806	67 040	51 910.8	3 215.5	14 991	204 793	50 370.9	4 916.3	6 391	30 978	5 077.2	950.3
Baker	496.0	30 744	15	81	19.1	2.6	92	747	155.5	15.0	22	45	7.3	1.2
Benton	38.8	454	48	537	387.1	21.2	275	3 559	685.2	73.0	119	543	58.1	11.3
Clackamas	299.2	796	598	8 273	5 292.4	386.7	1 269	19 910	5 095.8	496.5	693	2 795	563.1	98.3
Clatsop	65.5	1 769	24	184	75.5	7.6	303	2 717	604.5	60.4	68	363	38.1	8.2
Columbia	39.5	801	25	122	96.8	6.6	132	1 563	357.4	33.8	41	112	15.0	2.5
Coos	27.5	435	41	426	260.8	15.3	290	3 298	716.0	79.5	69	274	33.4	6.2
Crook	225.6	10 755	19	160	100.5	5.1	80	632	139.9	13.3	36	92	6.9	1.7
Curry	21.2	948	15	D	D	D	105	1 188	227.0	23.4	59	107	12.7	2.0
Deschutes	157.5	998	234	2 089	1 222.6	93.9	867	10 952	2 809.1	271.9	452	1 782	229.7	48.2
Douglas	72.3	671	69	D	D	D	441	5 113	1 169.2	107.6	150	493	55.4	10.5
Gilliam	18.9	10 086	4	20	31.6	0.8	15	63	13.5	1.0	NA	NA	NA	NA
Grant	130.8	17 574	4	D	D	D	47	286	72.5	6.1	14	D	D	D
Harney	422.9	56 975	4	11	3.0	0.5	31	330	87.6	7.4	16	36	10.7	0.6
Hood River	83.1	3 718	33	754	224.4	25.8	146	1 393	293.7	32.9	36	62	9.3	1.5
Jackson	392.4	1 931	230	2 304	1 047.1	90.9	991	12 243	3 422.4	290.1	360	1 563	205.4	36.5
Jefferson	172.1	7 925	19	154	192.4	6.2	69	667	165.3	15.3	19	D	D	D
Josephine	30.2	365	60	D	D	D	347	4 549	1 024.3	107.4	110	450	47.1	9.5
Klamath	661.6	9 967	62	D	D	D	271	3 311	788.4	73.8	89	356	44.1	7.6
Lake	465.5	58 958	9	92	40.3	3.6	35	205	52.1	4.7	13	D	D	D
Lane	224.2	637	444	5 530	2 889.2	242.0	1 403	20 408	4 452.2	456.9	569	2 554	380.1	59.6
Lincoln	28.9	627	29	171	48.4	6.4	349	3 069	559.6	61.3	96	461	55.9	9.3
Linn	122.6	1 051	126	1 577	956.9	59.9	355	4 708	1 159.0	108.4	114	470	55.0	9.7
Malheur	616.4	19 684	38	D	D	D	143	2 095	484.6	46.7	37	103	10.7	1.7
Marion	281.5	893	312	3 806	3 461.7	161.2	1 109	16 819	4 016.6	399.2	485	2 686	337.4	66.2

1. Merchant wholesalers, except manufacturers' sales branches and offices. 2. Employer establishments.

STATE County	Professional, scientific, and technical services,[1] 2007				Manufacturing, 2007				Accommodation and food services, 2007			
	Number of establish-ments	Number of employees	Receipts (mil dol)	Annual payroll (mil dol)	Number of establish-ments	Number of employees	Receipts (mil dol)	Annual payroll (mil dol)	Number of establish-ments	Number of employees	Sales (mil dol)	Annual payroll (mil dol)
	147	148	149	150	151	152	153	154	155	156	157	158
OKLAHOMA—Cont'd												
Kiowa	15	32	2.8	0.7	NA	NA	NA	NA	19	192	6.4	2.3
Latimer	15	41	3.0	0.9	NA	NA	NA	NA	10	125	5.1	1.2
Le Flore	56	D	D	D	35	740	147.5	D	49	675	25.8	6.7
Lincoln	46	D	D	D	23	599	198.2	22.1	40	557	19.6	5.4
Logan	43	138	12.9	4.3	NA	NA	NA	NA	53	655	27.9	7.4
Love	16	D	D	D	NA	NA	NA	NA	12	134	5.3	1.4
McClain	59	224	22.8	6.4	NA	NA	NA	NA	53	721	30.8	8.0
McCurtain	30	371	14.1	8.5	27	2 178	1 361.7	89.3	39	577	21.7	5.1
McIntosh	30	114	10.7	4.0	NA	NA	NA	NA	35	366	15.5	3.4
Major	18	38	3.6	1.0	NA	NA	NA	NA	12	120	3.6	0.9
Marshall	21	78	5.0	2.0	21	1 228	207.7	43.7	30	329	12.2	3.4
Mayes	59	277	16.1	6.9	64	3 085	944.0	130.1	70	989	36.0	9.0
Murray	23	83	7.2	2.9	NA	NA	NA	NA	28	278	14.0	3.8
Muskogee	107	D	D	D	69	3 455	1 167.5	153.0	129	2 484	88.1	22.8
Noble	13	35	1.9	0.6	10	D	D	D	17	186	7.1	1.8
Nowata	10	37	4.7	0.8	NA	NA	NA	NA	11	140	4.0	1.2
Okfuskee	7	18	1.2	0.5	NA	NA	NA	NA	11	113	2.3	0.6
Oklahoma	2 783	D	D	D	770	23 255	7 039.4	908.1	1 638	36 363	1 500.9	422.5
Okmulgee	38	166	9.8	3.5	38	971	363.2	43.3	56	829	29.5	7.8
Osage	49	144	12.0	3.4	NA	NA	NA	NA	44	606	18.2	4.8
Ottawa	39	D	D	D	51	1 581	379.1	58.9	59	778	28.0	8.0
Pawnee	25	70	5.9	1.7	NA	NA	NA	NA	21	289	10.4	2.7
Payne	158	D	D	D	69	2 305	1 065.3	84.8	154	3 263	117.8	31.2
Pittsburg	82	D	D	D	24	797	223.8	31.9	85	1 430	64.5	13.5
Pontotoc	88	D	D	D	48	1 648	501.3	52.6	62	1 204	47.1	13.7
Pottawatomie	104	D	D	D	62	3 105	1 024.3	130.3	125	2 706	98.9	26.8
Pushmataha	13	82	10.5	2.1	NA	NA	NA	NA	12	159	4.7	1.2
Roger Mills	6	12	0.5	0.1	NA	NA	NA	NA	9	60	1.9	0.4
Rogers	129	570	49.1	19.3	145	7 179	2 856.0	335.5	96	1 756	62.4	17.1
Seminole	27	89	6.5	1.9	24	679	124.7	24.7	33	536	17.7	4.6
Sequoyah	40	147	12.0	4.1	23	616	272.3	D	61	797	34.9	9.1
Stephens	71	389	31.8	10.8	71	2 625	1 084.9	117.8	84	956	38.8	9.7
Texas	34	D	D	D	12	D	D	D	47	720	24.4	6.1
Tillman	11	35	2.2	1.0	NA	NA	NA	NA	10	81	2.7	0.7
Tulsa	2 398	16 682	2 403.2	894.7	998	39 890	16 400.1	1 834.9	1 452	29 323	1 226.5	347.3
Wagoner	70	199	22.0	6.4	76	2 040	561.4	74.7	57	912	30.7	8.7
Washington	90	D	D	D	51	1 462	353.5	58.1	114	1 889	72.5	17.9
Washita	16	48	7.3	2.0	NA	NA	NA	NA	15	113	3.3	0.9
Woods	24	64	4.1	1.2	NA	NA	NA	NA	23	262	10.4	2.3
Woodward	54	D	D	D	NA	NA	NA	NA	52	797	34.2	8.9
OREGON	11 363	83 190	9 750.4	4 869.5	5 717	183 953	66 880.7	8 138.9	10 241	150 538	7 555.8	2 152.9
Baker	40	D	D	D	27	605	138.0	20.5	58	558	25.7	6.9
Benton	282	D	D	D	92	4 322	590.5	209.8	206	3 197	134.0	37.2
Clackamas	1 234	D	D	D	619	17 625	5 668.2	841.4	775	12 928	607.4	176.9
Clatsop	90	317	22.4	8.1	56	1 868	683.6	92.0	248	3 078	160.6	45.4
Columbia	69	D	D	D	59	2 020	826.2	95.4	97	1 005	44.2	11.8
Coos	117	D	D	D	81	1 652	279.1	53.5	187	2 021	83.5	23.3
Crook	35	D	D	D	41	1 245	209.9	42.5	48	517	22.7	6.4
Curry	39	130	9.5	3.2	21	644	190.7	30.1	113	1 073	56.2	13.7
Deschutes	650	D	D	D	299	5 359	897.4	201.7	504	8 078	416.4	121.1
Douglas	179	D	D	D	132	6 439	1 506.4	236.6	301	4 331	228.4	62.9
Gilliam	1	D	D	D	NA	NA	NA	NA	8	66	1.5	0.5
Grant	19	D	D	D	NA	NA	NA	NA	25	162	6.6	1.9
Harney	11	D	D	D	NA	NA	NA	NA	27	211	11.1	2.6
Hood River	108	401	54.3	17.0	58	1 200	245.7	38.6	88	1 371	55.7	17.7
Jackson	491	D	D	D	324	6 115	2 037.5	228.8	590	7 946	372.9	108.9
Jefferson	24	76	4.7	1.9	20	1 501	242.9	50.7	45	798	45.8	13.3
Josephine	134	D	D	D	127	3 127	471.3	105.0	205	2 493	108.9	33.0
Klamath	118	D	D	D	75	2 360	539.7	92.5	176	2 259	103.0	28.9
Lake	10	D	D	D	NA	NA	NA	NA	27	159	7.2	1.7
Lane	988	5 097	554.6	217.5	606	20 273	6 219.9	853.6	920	13 385	607.7	171.5
Lincoln	102	D	D	D	57	1 108	582.7	58.0	292	4 035	205.4	59.9
Linn	170	D	D	D	198	7 814	2 737.6	393.7	200	2 746	125.4	33.1
Malheur	45	D	D	D	36	1 237	D	42.8	84	1 077	45.3	12.7
Marion	720	3 958	416.3	163.9	380	10 724	2 845.4	367.2	652	D	D	D

1. Establishment subject to federal tax.

Table B. States and Counties — **Health Care and Social Assistance, Other Services, Nonemployer Businesses, and Residential Construction**

STATE County	Health care and social assistance, 2007				Other services, 2007				Nonemployer businesses, 2013		Value of residential construction authorized by building permits, 2014	
	Number of establish-ments	Number of employees	Receipts (mil dol)	Annual payroll (mil dol)	Number of establish-ments	Number of employees	Receipts (mil dol)	Annual payroll (mil dol)	Number	Receipts (mil dol)	New Construction ($1,000)	Number of housing units
	159	160	161	162	163	164	165	166	167	168	169	170
OKLAHOMA—Cont'd												
Kiowa	28	562	24.3	11.9	11	D	D	D	627	24.7	40	1
Latimer	25	368	21.0	8.5	6	D	D	D	746	29.7	65	1
Le Flore	83	2 121	125.4	52.5	47	208	17.8	4.5	2 974	123.1	8 143	77
Lincoln	53	679	35.2	14.2	22	74	7.0	1.7	2 451	115.8	2 564	14
Logan	52	1 253	69.4	30.4	48	157	13.4	2.9	3 620	159.0	2 630	16
Love	10	D	D	D	5	58	2.9	0.9	636	25.8	0	0
McClain	59	802	51.2	21.4	44	124	8.9	2.5	3 199	157.1	45 814	222
McCurtain	69	1 380	73.5	30.1	31	202	12.0	3.2	2 178	97.1	1 048	8
McIntosh	51	760	36.8	14.8	24	87	8.5	1.6	1 370	57.6	4 662	35
Major	14	297	12.9	6.6	11	D	D	D	693	31.0	133	4
Marshall	28	527	35.1	13.9	9	25	2.3	0.6	1 064	45.3	1 153	6
Mayes	80	939	60.0	24.5	53	144	9.6	2.7	2 569	99.4	2 500	17
Murray	31	735	38.4	17.2	17	50	3.0	0.6	853	38.0	2 454	12
Muskogee	204	5 438	384.1	180.9	95	525	35.5	10.5	3 803	161.4	4 224	22
Noble	18	365	21.0	9.0	11	49	3.4	0.8	800	28.4	215	2
Nowata	17	307	12.4	5.6	12	27	2.2	0.5	684	25.6	770	12
Okfuskee	40	432	28.1	10.9	4	D	D	D	711	28.7	0	0
Oklahoma	2 737	55 697	6 769.4	2 187.6	1 423	10 026	936.1	253.2	58 063	2 962.6	1 062 572	5 510
Okmulgee	140	2 352	159.6	68.4	40	147	11.2	2.7	2 228	86.2	30	1
Osage	50	D	D	D	29	76	5.9	1.3	2 927	122.2	21 233	124
Ottawa	77	1 537	101.7	45.9	36	139	9.6	2.2	1 833	66.0	503	8
Pawnee	32	D	D	D	12	38	2.9	0.6	975	39.7	160	1
Payne	175	3 518	266.5	103.7	128	813	170.0	17.8	4 790	205.1	35 688	303
Pittsburg	112	2 647	187.7	81.2	55	272	22.7	6.3	2 589	108.0	10 929	73
Pontotoc	142	3 131	253.4	92.6	52	247	17.7	4.4	2 809	121.2	8 870	106
Pottawatomie	160	2 846	216.8	79.4	67	322	22.1	6.5	4 231	191.6	14 728	83
Pushmataha	22	701	33.9	15.5	6	25	1.8	0.3	765	26.6	0	0
Roger Mills	5	D	D	D	5	D	D	D	379	22.6	143	1
Rogers	172	2 431	186.6	80.4	82	353	36.0	9.0	6 260	281.9	76 667	505
Seminole	49	1 081	63.1	22.9	21	81	7.7	1.9	1 434	56.4	653	5
Sequoyah	77	1 737	70.5	32.7	33	88	6.8	2.0	2 685	108.6	7 813	70
Stephens	104	1 988	136.6	52.6	66	530	67.0	11.5	3 065	152.9	5 963	36
Texas	44	D	D	D	32	161	11.4	2.3	1 292	54.6	1 195	9
Tillman	18	282	15.3	6.2	11	36	1.7	0.5	448	12.8	68	1
Tulsa	2 035	44 983	4 548.0	1 765.5	1 197	7 646	833.4	205.9	46 906	2 340.2	572 068	3 464
Wagoner	72	713	45.0	19.9	60	141	11.4	2.8	5 077	213.2	55 245	330
Washington	167	3 108	237.6	98.9	80	611	85.0	15.0	3 163	133.0	18 019	91
Washita	16	335	18.7	7.5	16	46	3.6	0.8	843	41.6	0	0
Woods	21	357	18.0	8.9	19	64	5.7	1.0	792	34.5	150	1
Woodward	84	1 194	76.0	31.7	43	204	27.2	5.6	1 532	80.9	3 970	23
OREGON	11 261	192 233	20 159.6	7 895.9	6 888	39 129	4 462.4	1 090.6	260 438	11 910.7	16 514 119	104
Baker	50	D	D	D	41	108	12.1	2.2	1 094	33.7	3 977	18
Benton	229	4 356	504.0	201.1	128	855	158.3	22.7	5 510	221.7	86 019	451
Clackamas	963	15 229	1 702.2	665.4	660	3 437	314.4	95.4	28 103	1 509.4	400 222	1 480
Clatsop	132	1 627	144.1	62.7	84	522	32.2	9.3	2 684	120.9	25 815	102
Columbia	107	826	54.7	20.8	63	218	15.4	4.5	2 587	105.4	24 114	106
Coos	236	3 508	329.8	126.1	92	481	59.7	11.1	3 520	140.4	5 278	30
Crook	33	540	47.3	18.4	38	168	11.4	3.3	1 387	57.5	21 546	85
Curry	98	865	61.8	23.0	34	134	10.3	2.5	1 790	77.7	9 515	42
Deschutes	543	8 144	974.3	351.5	322	1 761	169.5	46.5	15 397	737.8	325 824	1 330
Douglas	313	5 280	511.0	215.0	150	757	84.4	17.7	5 697	230.2	39 698	166
Gilliam	7	D	D	D	4	D	D	D	100	2.3	NA	NA
Grant	21	D	D	D	20	48	3.4	0.8	492	18.4	NA	NA
Harney	20	D	D	D	10	35	2.1	0.7	531	16.6	405	2
Hood River	95	1 595	107.6	43.6	47	229	20.7	6.4	1 788	84.3	20 816	88
Jackson	627	11 160	1 173.9	434.7	357	2 107	182.0	56.9	16 219	712.7	166 991	747
Jefferson	21	D	D	D	25	125	8.9	2.4	974	40.8	10 458	39
Josephine	251	4 055	356.7	128.0	131	605	40.6	12.5	5 578	236.4	34 689	149
Klamath	223	3 021	286.0	113.0	119	570	40.2	11.6	3 353	136.4	17 197	75
Lake	15	270	18.4	8.1	15	20	2.2	0.5	478	19.6	1 813	9
Lane	993	18 660	1 947.8	735.6	684	3 684	516.8	95.3	22 051	927.6	240 005	1 316
Lincoln	106	1 583	155.8	62.7	107	475	30.8	8.8	3 278	163.8	29 113	144
Linn	214	3 654	320.4	126.2	149	1 075	112.6	34.9	5 715	227.9	77 351	393
Malheur	102	1 403	116.3	45.0	62	D	D	D	1 329	55.5	6 715	29
Marion	911	15 212	1 453.0	599.2	514	2 628	214.1	64.3	15 789	718.8	165 945	698

STATE County	Government employment and payroll, 2012									Local government finances, 2012				
			March payroll (percent of total)							General revenue				
												Taxes		
													Per capita[1] (dollars)	
	Full-time equivalent employees	March payroll (dollars)	Adminis-tration, judicial, and legal	Police and Corrections	Fire Protection	Highways and transpor-tation	Health and Welfare	Natural resources and utilities	Education and libraries	Total (mil dol)	Inter-govern-mental (mil dol)	Total (mil dol)	Total	Property
	171	172	173	174	175	176	177	178	179	180	181	182	183	184
OKLAHOMA—Cont'd														
Kiowa	554	1 581 546	4.8	5.3	0.8	4.5	36.0	6.1	41.7	28.0	15.7	7.6	812	529
Latimer	754	2 593 866	3.2	2.1	0.0	3.7	15.7	2.1	72.9	31.9	13.6	7.0	636	318
Le Flore	1 864	5 014 735	3.3	6.0	0.4	3.5	3.6	5.5	75.8	125.0	71.3	28.8	578	300
Lincoln	1 059	2 802 834	6.5	7.7	1.4	5.3	0.3	7.8	70.0	71.7	38.3	21.4	627	358
Logan	875	2 347 456	7.2	7.5	3.8	5.0	0.6	6.6	67.9	60.0	30.1	18.4	421	259
Love	481	1 481 165	6.9	3.8	0.0	3.5	40.8	1.2	43.6	19.3	11.3	5.6	581	387
McClain	1 466	3 975 638	5.5	7.7	3.1	4.0	13.2	3.3	60.7	113.4	39.8	57.3	1 609	1 149
McCurtain	1 454	3 983 530	2.5	5.7	1.1	5.2	4.9	5.0	74.7	93.6	55.4	21.0	632	354
McIntosh	617	1 761 398	8.2	6.9	0.0	2.0	1.7	6.5	74.4	51.2	28.1	16.0	778	358
Major	407	1 118 428	9.8	3.5	0.5	9.3	27.6	2.4	45.6	26.8	10.8	7.7	1 002	610
Marshall	530	1 477 680	5.8	6.2	1.0	4.3	3.0	4.0	74.8	36.0	20.4	10.5	660	446
Mayes	1 472	4 043 970	8.9	5.6	0.7	3.0	3.2	7.1	70.0	95.9	51.9	32.6	792	421
Murray	655	1 707 493	6.8	7.5	3.1	2.3	19.7	11.8	48.5	44.1	24.1	10.4	762	306
Muskogee	3 141	8 727 804	4.0	8.5	4.5	4.3	6.8	5.1	65.6	275.3	85.7	75.6	1 071	547
Noble	622	1 661 200	5.9	6.7	2.5	6.0	18.5	6.1	53.2	44.6	16.7	14.0	1 213	863
Nowata	422	1 000 994	6.4	5.5	1.0	6.4	3.0	5.6	71.4	24.0	14.4	5.9	556	321
Okfuskee	460	1 098 562	3.9	6.1	0.0	6.2	0.9	3.6	76.5	34.2	24.4	6.6	531	326
Oklahoma	24 286	88 713 472	5.8	14.1	10.2	3.4	2.9	6.5	56.5	2 544.3	761.2	1 182.3	1 594	722
Okmulgee	1 552	4 277 777	5.1	5.1	2.9	3.2	3.2	5.9	73.4	89.1	52.5	23.2	586	272
Osage	1 130	2 941 818	9.3	7.0	1.1	14.2	11.3	6.8	48.8	74.5	39.5	19.7	410	229
Ottawa	1 421	4 097 793	5.8	5.3	2.3	2.7	1.7	8.0	73.0	80.7	44.3	21.1	654	269
Pawnee	597	1 604 091	5.8	5.4	1.0	3.9	18.9	7.0	56.7	35.2	20.6	8.5	514	277
Payne	3 634	11 234 115	4.8	7.5	4.2	1.9	31.7	8.2	40.1	192.3	66.9	89.1	1 137	592
Pittsburg	2 380	5 927 369	5.7	11.0	5.4	4.2	4.8	9.9	55.6	254.4	76.4	76.1	1 689	1 039
Pontotoc	1 436	4 130 846	4.3	6.5	3.1	5.4	2.1	5.4	70.4	103.9	50.5	34.4	905	337
Pottawatomie	2 336	6 720 266	6.0	7.2	4.0	2.8	0.1	7.4	71.9	167.8	93.6	52.1	737	301
Pushmataha	607	1 521 960	2.8	3.2	1.8	5.1	17.4	5.2	63.2	38.1	21.2	5.6	504	248
Roger Mills	256	746 029	12.5	6.7	0.0	25.4	12.9	5.1	34.8	20.6	10.5	6.4	1 687	1 138
Rogers	2 835	7 580 674	6.2	6.2	5.0	5.0	1.0	15.1	60.3	197.1	79.1	87.2	986	621
Seminole	1 164	2 881 448	5.7	5.9	2.6	4.0	1.0	5.8	73.2	80.4	47.5	19.7	772	340
Sequoyah	1 722	4 751 418	4.1	6.5	0.8	2.8	13.0	2.9	69.8	115.2	65.1	22.1	534	266
Stephens	1 530	4 875 145	5.7	8.9	3.8	3.6	0.3	5.9	70.1	109.2	51.3	39.9	891	426
Texas	1 138	3 387 767	5.5	7.8	2.0	6.4	23.7	3.4	50.3	93.1	28.0	34.4	1 601	1 035
Tillman	545	1 405 251	6.0	9.3	2.4	4.7	24.1	6.9	45.0	21.8	14.4	3.8	490	335
Tulsa	23 532	78 482 436	5.7	10.6	6.5	3.9	2.1	5.2	62.5	2 206.7	679.3	1 020.7	1 663	890
Wagoner	1 330	3 590 004	7.0	7.2	2.6	4.0	2.4	9.2	64.5	85.8	39.9	34.9	465	232
Washington	1 747	5 123 970	4.5	9.2	5.9	3.5	2.6	6.6	65.7	123.9	52.2	47.3	915	518
Washita	621	1 807 048	6.4	5.9	0.7	7.4	8.9	3.3	66.3	43.9	25.8	12.0	1 030	518
Woods	575	1 537 398	8.0	4.6	2.6	8.1	31.6	4.9	39.0	38.5	13.1	16.6	1 883	804
Woodward	891	2 568 486	5.9	8.6	3.5	5.0	7.2	4.7	61.8	69.5	25.7	32.5	1 583	708
OREGON	X	X	X	X	X	X	X	X	X	X	X	X	X	X
Baker	487	1 718 138	10.0	12.3	6.0	4.4	2.9	7.2	54.6	56.2	31.8	15.5	977	900
Benton	1 834	7 923 562	9.3	13.4	6.2	3.8	7.4	9.4	45.7	259.6	93.0	115.4	1 335	1 185
Clackamas	10 411	44 609 746	8.2	11.7	6.1	3.3	4.7	6.1	57.9	1 431.7	520.8	623.0	1 623	1 458
Clatsop	1 540	5 672 121	8.9	12.5	2.7	5.7	8.3	8.9	49.7	172.7	53.4	71.3	1 912	1 596
Columbia	1 444	6 022 192	7.2	9.3	8.1	2.1	0.4	16.3	52.3	192.4	87.9	59.7	1 211	1 123
Coos	3 079	13 113 856	2.7	5.5	1.8	2.4	45.7	3.7	37.5	386.2	116.4	74.2	1 187	1 048
Crook	584	2 274 092	9.3	15.0	2.6	3.8	3.7	7.2	51.7	72.1	28.3	22.8	1 099	940
Curry	803	3 143 734	7.1	10.1	0.4	5.5	38.6	5.6	31.1	90.5	25.4	26.9	1 211	1 076
Deschutes	4 773	21 188 503	8.1	12.1	5.4	2.6	5.0	7.0	55.3	649.0	217.1	283.8	1 749	1 579
Douglas	3 555	13 196 754	6.3	8.9	6.6	3.1	10.3	6.1	57.1	374.6	196.1	94.6	883	829
Gilliam	145	510 580	18.3	7.1	1.3	10.8	8.3	8.3	45.2	24.4	3.8	15.2	7 770	6 077
Grant	485	1 961 339	5.0	4.3	0.1	3.5	41.5	3.5	38.1	55.0	23.8	7.9	1 083	1 049
Harney	427	1 530 704	6.7	5.9	0.4	3.5	37.4	2.0	42.0	51.3	21.5	7.2	998	925
Hood River	639	2 757 629	6.9	8.8	4.6	6.5	3.0	12.1	54.2	95.2	38.6	26.4	1 171	1 023
Jackson	4 931	20 369 335	9.1	14.6	6.5	6.1	5.2	6.8	50.0	668.0	291.3	260.8	1 263	1 068
Jefferson	1 028	3 923 905	4.1	6.5	1.3	1.7	29.3	8.4	46.4	112.4	50.4	24.0	1 101	997
Josephine	2 192	8 995 230	6.6	12.9	2.5	3.4	1.3	3.1	68.4	243.6	119.9	70.8	854	781
Klamath	1 819	7 192 100	5.9	8.2	6.2	6.2	7.0	7.1	56.2	234.1	125.3	59.4	901	796
Lake	460	1 602 079	5.2	5.5	1.6	6.9	38.3	7.3	33.1	51.6	18.7	10.7	1 372	1 263
Lane	11 647	50 155 119	7.2	10.9	5.2	6.9	4.1	11.4	48.1	1 390.4	585.1	463.2	1 306	1 120
Lincoln	1 465	6 826 571	10.2	14.7	2.9	4.9	8.2	27.9	29.0	200.9	55.6	104.1	2 255	1 881
Linn	3 984	16 207 525	6.1	11.2	5.6	4.0	5.1	4.9	61.9	447.9	223.4	146.4	1 237	1 133
Malheur	1 459	4 992 780	4.9	8.6	1.3	2.7	8.2	7.2	66.0	146.8	85.7	25.2	821	712
Marion	12 046	53 396 211	5.2	8.9	3.6	3.2	3.6	3.7	69.6	1 311.4	678.7	400.1	1 250	1 131

1. Based on the resident population estimated as of July 1 of the year shown.

STATE County	Local government finances, 2012 (cont.)									Government employment, 2013			Presidential election,[2] 2012		
	Direct general expenditure							Debt outstanding					Percent of vote cast:		
			Percent of total for:												
	Total (mil dol)	Per capita[1] (dollars)	Educa-tion	Health and hospitals	Police protec-tion	Public welfare	High-ways	Total (mil dol)	Per capita[1] (dollars)	Federal civilian	Federal military	State and local	Demo-cratic	Republi-can	All other
	185	186	187	188	189	190	191	192	193	194	195	196	197	198	199
OKLAHOMA—Cont'd															
Kiowa	28.9	3 103	50.8	1.7	5.1	0.0	11.2	18.6	1 994	45	36	719	32.6	67.4	0.0
Latimer	33.5	3 038	45.3	21.6	2.5	0.0	11.1	4.0	365	25	40	1 217	31.5	68.5	0.0
Le Flore	128.2	2 571	63.3	5.2	3.9	0.1	7.2	41.9	840	170	187	4 592	30.7	69.3	0.0
Lincoln	69.8	2 043	62.1	1.0	6.3	0.0	9.1	22.4	656	78	132	1 703	25.1	74.9	0.0
Logan	60.7	1 390	56.3	2.5	8.0	0.0	8.8	34.1	782	63	164	1 310	31.3	68.7	0.0
Love	22.3	2 329	73.8	2.7	1.9	0.0	7.2	4.8	506	22	37	2 770	32.7	67.3	0.0
McClain	115.0	3 229	69.2	1.7	5.3	0.0	6.8	54.5	1 531	65	141	1 685	24.1	75.9	0.0
McCurtain	89.7	2 703	65.8	3.0	3.2	0.0	7.5	40.6	1 222	131	126	2 362	26.5	73.5	0.0
McIntosh	48.8	2 370	65.3	1.5	5.7	0.0	9.6	27.7	1 344	34	78	1 160	40.4	59.6	0.0
Major	27.0	3 519	43.6	21.9	3.4	0.2	15.4	8.4	1 096	28	29	433	14.8	85.2	0.0
Marshall	35.6	2 234	67.7	3.5	3.9	0.0	4.1	8.2	513	22	61	777	30.6	69.4	0.0
Mayes	94.4	2 293	68.5	1.3	6.4	0.0	6.3	46.9	1 140	62	156	2 391	36.0	64.0	0.0
Murray	43.2	3 162	41.5	28.0	3.6	0.0	4.3	20.9	1 532	65	52	2 759	29.8	70.2	0.0
Muskogee	284.3	4 027	38.4	31.9	3.5	0.0	3.0	95.6	1 354	2 876	260	6 393	42.5	57.5	0.0
Noble	44.7	3 877	46.3	20.3	3.8	0.0	12.0	32.4	2 812	34	43	1 268	23.2	76.8	0.0
Nowata	24.4	2 295	64.3	0.0	4.0	0.0	11.1	7.8	734	27	40	487	31.8	68.2	0.0
Okfuskee	34.0	2 753	77.0	0.0	2.3	0.0	10.3	17.9	1 449	25	43	1 100	35.9	64.1	0.0
Oklahoma	2 264.8	3 053	44.4	0.4	10.3	0.2	5.6	2 878.7	3 881	26 046	9 315	58 156	41.6	58.4	0.0
Okmulgee	89.9	2 270	65.7	0.5	4.7	0.0	7.2	96.2	2 428	122	147	3 398	41.5	58.5	0.0
Osage	73.9	1 543	50.5	8.5	2.4	0.8	12.7	17.6	367	174	201	2 680	38.1	61.9	0.0
Ottawa	87.3	2 709	53.9	2.6	5.3	0.0	11.8	33.9	1 051	98	121	5 469	38.2	61.8	0.0
Pawnee	33.0	2 003	61.8	3.2	3.7	0.0	10.4	20.5	1 247	230	63	919	31.3	68.7	0.0
Payne	185.3	2 363	48.5	0.4	11.8	0.1	8.4	115.8	1 477	253	285	14 510	36.5	63.5	0.0
Pittsburg	209.1	4 642	32.4	36.3	4.6	0.0	4.1	129.8	2 882	1 696	167	3 964	31.7	68.3	0.0
Pontotoc	100.3	2 643	61.6	0.6	5.6	0.0	7.3	22.3	586	160	141	6 429	31.6	68.4	0.0
Pottawatomie	171.7	2 427	59.2	0.4	6.1	0.0	8.2	62.2	879	140	265	6 123	30.8	69.2	0.0
Pushmataha	38.0	3 395	55.0	22.5	3.5	0.2	8.3	9.5	847	28	43	924	28.3	71.7	0.0
Roger Mills	21.1	5 590	33.6	1.3	3.6	0.0	42.2	0.7	196	35	14	355	16.0	84.0	0.0
Rogers	198.7	2 249	54.8	0.9	4.1	0.0	9.8	136.5	1 544	428	340	6 216	28.0	72.0	0.0
Seminole	79.1	3 109	54.5	1.3	3.6	0.0	6.2	27.2	1 070	153	96	1 946	34.7	65.3	0.0
Sequoyah	115.1	2 781	61.2	12.8	4.0	0.7	4.6	67.9	1 639	127	176	3 034	32.0	68.0	0.0
Stephens	108.9	2 432	55.9	0.5	5.5	0.0	9.4	48.1	1 074	78	172	2 036	24.0	76.0	0.0
Texas	98.3	4 570	36.3	26.0	2.2	0.1	7.6	39.3	1 829	74	83	1 711	14.7	85.3	0.0
Tillman	23.0	2 944	65.1	1.9	5.6	0.0	12.8	6.9	884	33	29	740	32.2	67.8	0.0
Tulsa	2 175.2	3 544	44.8	4.4	6.3	0.8	7.9	3 349.0	5 456	3 294	2 411	30 979	37.8	62.2	0.0
Wagoner	88.4	1 178	62.5	2.4	6.7	0.0	8.5	84.6	1 128	67	310	1 889	29.1	70.9	0.0
Washington	127.7	2 473	49.2	0.7	6.0	0.0	8.3	98.7	1 911	92	197	2 441	27.7	72.3	0.0
Washita	39.5	3 402	50.0	0.3	4.5	0.0	20.5	17.5	1 502	36	44	714	22.0	78.0	0.0
Woods	34.4	3 894	39.3	5.7	3.4	0.0	14.9	7.3	829	28	31	1 115	22.3	77.7	0.0
Woodward	71.3	3 469	43.9	1.0	6.2	0.0	7.9	53.7	2 613	84	77	1 612	17.4	82.6	0.0
OREGON	X	X	X	X	X	X	X	X	X	27 606	12 151	236 918	56.7	40.4	2.9
Baker	54.2	3 408	42.8	7.5	5.5	1.6	8.5	12.0	754	219	43	876	32.0	64.4	3.7
Benton	259.2	2 999	46.3	7.4	9.6	0.0	4.2	233.8	2 705	529	264	10 653	64.3	32.8	2.8
Clackamas	1 519.2	3 958	45.7	4.4	7.2	1.0	4.3	2 524.7	6 577	1 065	1 139	13 799	53.9	43.6	2.5
Clatsop	169.8	4 551	35.4	2.0	7.8	5.6	4.9	220.8	5 921	207	527	2 372	57.7	38.8	3.5
Columbia	192.3	3 902	51.6	1.9	4.3	0.2	3.0	214.6	4 353	67	136	1 727	54.1	42.0	3.9
Coos	396.6	6 341	32.9	41.8	2.9	0.1	2.5	240.2	3 841	324	409	4 784	46.5	49.6	3.9
Crook	64.9	3 132	41.4	3.3	7.3	0.2	6.7	59.1	2 852	305	57	839	35.1	61.5	3.4
Curry	101.4	4 557	23.1	33.1	4.3	2.7	5.0	92.8	4 173	84	103	985	42.4	53.9	3.7
Deschutes	663.5	4 089	49.1	3.5	7.4	0.4	5.0	1 093.2	6 736	867	457	7 482	48.7	49.0	2.4
Douglas	388.7	3 627	47.5	11.2	5.7	0.2	5.6	258.0	2 407	1 367	335	5 989	38.3	58.4	3.2
Gilliam	26.0	13 296	30.4	4.8	3.1	0.9	11.5	62.9	32 197	10	0	210	38.7	58.4	2.9
Grant	58.7	8 019	29.3	28.9	3.0	0.6	14.1	17.9	2 444	266	20	685	25.7	71.2	3.0
Harney	51.9	7 203	32.1	38.3	1.6	0.5	8.2	34.0	4 719	244	19	724	25.8	70.5	3.7
Hood River	99.3	4 399	46.3	2.2	2.8	0.6	8.1	98.9	4 381	107	61	1 096	64.1	33.2	2.7
Jackson	678.0	3 285	42.6	5.3	8.6	0.0	6.1	887.0	4 297	1 686	570	8 760	48.6	48.5	2.9
Jefferson	108.0	4 966	39.6	27.4	3.8	0.4	3.9	71.9	3 306	132	58	2 229	44.3	52.9	2.8
Josephine	253.3	3 055	59.6	2.9	7.1	0.1	5.0	145.0	1 748	249	227	2 742	41.4	54.6	4.0
Klamath	233.2	3 538	47.7	4.6	6.8	0.2	7.6	72.7	1 103	886	193	3 783	31.9	65.0	3.1
Lake	52.0	6 689	27.7	39.5	2.5	0.3	10.2	44.6	5 745	213	20	720	25.9	71.5	2.5
Lane	1 390.2	3 921	44.2	5.1	6.9	2.2	4.3	1 580.1	4 457	1 598	1 054	23 620	62.3	34.9	2.8
Lincoln	229.9	4 981	36.4	6.6	7.4	0.1	6.6	316.8	6 864	353	206	3 294	59.7	36.8	3.5
Linn	449.1	3 794	51.6	3.6	6.2	0.4	4.4	449.9	3 801	307	327	5 845	42.6	54.0	3.4
Malheur	157.2	5 132	62.3	4.3	3.4	0.2	3.8	62.8	2 050	217	76	2 906	28.3	68.6	3.1
Marion	1 325.2	4 141	57.0	3.6	5.0	0.2	4.6	1 931.4	6 036	1 300	874	31 516	49.6	47.4	3.0

1. Based on the resident population estimated as of July 1 of the year shown.

2.

STATE/ County code	CBSA code[1]	County type[2]	STATE County	Land area,[3] (sq km) 2010	Population, 2014: Total persons 2014	Population, 2014: Rank	Population, 2014: Per square kilometer	Race alone or in combination, not Hispanic or Latino (percent): White	Black	American Indian, Alaska Native	Asian and Pacific Islander	Percent Hispanic or Latino[4]	Age (percent): Under 5 years	5 to 17 years	18 to 24 years	25 to 34 years	35 to 44 years	45 to 54 years
				1	2	3	4	5	6	7	8	9	10	11	12	13	14	15
			OREGON—Cont'd															
41 049	25840	6	Morrow	5 262	11 187	2 340	2.1	63.4	1.0	2.0	1.3	34.2	7.3	20.6	8.7	11.1	11.9	12.6
41 051	38900	1	Multnomah	1 117	776 712	76	695.4	75.1	6.6	1.9	9.4	11.1	6.0	13.9	8.7	18.5	16.0	12.9
41 053	41420	2	Polk	1 919	77 916	710	40.6	82.3	1.3	3.2	3.5	13.0	5.9	17.6	13.0	11.0	11.4	11.9
41 055	...	9	Sherman	2 133	1 710	3 072	0.8	91.5	0.8	2.0	0.5	6.9	4.2	14.8	6.3	9.9	10.0	14.7
41 057	...	6	Tillamook	2 856	25 342	1 597	8.9	87.5	0.7	2.3	1.9	9.8	5.4	13.8	6.8	10.2	10.3	13.0
41 059	25840	5	Umatilla	8 328	76 705	716	9.2	69.8	1.1	4.3	1.6	25.1	7.1	18.9	9.6	13.4	12.5	12.5
41 061	29260	7	Union	5 275	25 691	1 573	4.9	91.7	1.0	2.2	3.0	4.4	6.1	16.0	12.6	11.2	10.0	11.6
41 063	...	9	Wallowa	8 149	6 820	2 699	0.8	95.5	1.1	1.6	1.1	2.7	5.0	13.4	4.7	9.8	8.9	13.1
41 065	45520	6	Wasco	6 168	25 515	1 585	4.1	78.0	0.9	4.7	2.1	16.4	6.0	16.3	8.2	11.9	11.1	12.4
41 067	38900	1	Washington	1 876	562 998	111	300.1	71.6	2.6	1.3	12.1	16.1	6.7	17.9	8.3	15.3	15.1	13.6
41 069	...	9	Wheeler	4 441	1 375	3 091	0.3	92.5	1.3	3.2	1.9	4.8	4.6	13.0	5.5	7.5	7.9	12.0
41 071	38900	1	Yamhill	1 854	101 758	584	54.9	80.6	1.3	2.4	2.9	15.3	5.9	17.7	10.9	12.0	12.6	13.0
42 000	...	X	PENNSYLVANIA	115 883	12 787 209	X	110.3	79.7	11.5	0.5	3.5	6.3	5.6	15.7	9.7	12.6	12.0	14.4
42 001	23900	4	Adams	1 343	101 714	586	75.7	91.0	2.1	0.5	1.0	6.5	5.2	15.8	9.9	10.3	11.8	15.1
42 003	38300	1	Allegheny	1 891	1 231 255	34	651.1	81.5	14.3	0.5	3.7	1.8	5.2	13.9	9.5	14.5	11.5	13.9
42 005	38300	1	Armstrong	1 692	67 785	786	40.1	98.1	1.3	0.3	0.4	0.7	4.9	14.9	7.3	10.5	11.9	15.3
42 007	38300	1	Beaver	1 126	169 392	375	150.4	91.7	7.5	0.4	0.8	1.4	5.1	14.7	8.1	11.2	11.1	15.1
42 009	...	6	Bedford	2 622	48 946	1 002	18.7	97.9	1.0	0.4	0.5	1.1	5.0	15.9	7.3	10.0	12.0	15.2
42 011	39740	2	Berks	2 218	413 691	166	186.5	76.1	5.0	0.4	1.8	18.1	5.9	17.1	10.1	11.6	12.1	14.8
42 013	11020	3	Blair	1 362	125 955	494	92.5	96.3	2.5	0.4	0.9	1.1	5.5	15.1	9.2	11.2	11.8	13.8
42 015	42380	6	Bradford	2 972	61 784	846	20.8	97.2	0.9	0.7	0.8	1.4	5.9	16.4	7.5	10.5	11.0	15.0
42 017	37980	1	Bucks	1 565	626 685	106	400.4	87.0	4.3	0.4	4.9	4.7	5.1	16.7	7.8	10.9	12.1	16.5
42 019	38300	1	Butler	2 042	185 943	345	91.1	96.3	1.6	0.4	1.4	1.3	5.0	16.1	9.1	10.8	12.3	15.8
42 021	27780	3	Cambria	1 783	137 732	458	77.2	94.0	4.5	0.3	0.8	1.6	4.9	14.3	9.5	10.6	11.5	14.0
42 023	...	7	Cameron	1 026	4 805	2 850	4.7	98.2	0.9	0.6	0.6	0.7	4.3	13.2	7.1	9.3	10.4	15.6
42 025	10900	2	Carbon	988	64 441	816	65.2	93.8	2.0	0.5	0.8	3.9	4.8	15.3	6.9	10.8	12.2	15.6
42 027	44300	3	Centre	2 875	158 742	402	55.2	88.6	3.7	0.4	6.1	2.6	4.1	11.4	26.8	13.0	10.3	11.5
42 029	37980	1	Chester	1 944	512 784	129	263.8	82.4	6.7	0.5	5.0	7.0	5.8	17.9	9.1	11.3	12.8	15.7
42 031	...	6	Clarion	1 556	38 821	1 202	24.9	97.5	1.4	0.5	0.8	0.7	5.2	13.9	14.9	10.5	10.7	13.4
42 033	20180	4	Clearfield	2 965	81 191	687	27.4	94.2	2.6	0.4	0.9	2.7	4.7	14.3	8.1	11.7	13.0	15.5
42 035	30820	6	Clinton	2 300	39 745	1 180	17.3	96.1	2.1	0.4	0.9	1.3	5.6	14.9	16.4	10.4	10.7	12.5
42 037	14100	4	Columbia	1 251	67 122	791	53.7	94.5	2.2	0.5	1.3	2.5	4.6	13.5	16.5	10.3	11.0	13.5
42 039	32740	4	Crawford	2 622	87 175	659	33.2	96.3	2.4	0.5	0.8	1.2	5.4	16.1	9.5	10.7	11.4	14.2
42 041	25420	2	Cumberland	1 413	243 762	271	172.5	89.6	4.2	0.5	4.2	3.3	5.2	15.1	10.2	12.8	12.4	14.3
42 043	25420	2	Dauphin	1 360	271 453	248	199.6	71.1	18.9	0.6	4.1	7.9	6.2	16.4	8.4	13.6	12.2	14.4
42 045	37980	1	Delaware	476	562 960	112	1 182.7	70.8	21.3	0.6	5.8	3.4	6.1	16.5	10.5	12.5	11.9	14.4
42 047	...	7	Elk	2 143	31 194	1 407	14.6	98.3	0.7	0.4	0.6	0.8	4.8	15.2	6.9	9.7	11.7	16.3
42 049	21500	2	Erie	2 070	278 443	241	134.5	87.7	8.3	0.5	1.7	3.7	5.8	16.1	11.2	12.6	11.4	13.7
42 051	38300	1	Fayette	2 047	134 086	472	65.5	93.8	5.6	0.5	0.6	1.0	5.0	14.7	7.8	11.2	12.2	14.7
42 053	...	9	Forest	1 106	7 518	2 638	6.8	75.3	18.7	0.5	0.4	5.8	1.7	7.0	10.9	17.5	12.4	14.8
42 055	16540	4	Franklin	2 000	152 892	422	76.4	90.8	4.2	0.5	1.4	4.8	6.2	17.0	7.9	11.7	12.5	13.9
42 057	...	8	Fulton	1 133	14 632	2 128	12.9	97.4	1.7	0.6	0.3	1.1	5.1	16.3	7.6	10.2	12.8	15.0
42 059	...	6	Greene	1 492	37 843	1 228	25.4	94.8	3.6	0.7	0.6	1.3	5.0	14.3	10.1	11.8	13.1	14.2
42 061	26500	6	Huntingdon	2 265	45 750	1 053	20.2	92.2	5.9	0.3	0.8	1.7	4.6	14.4	9.7	12.3	12.6	14.5
42 063	26860	4	Indiana	2 142	87 706	655	40.9	94.9	3.0	0.4	1.3	1.3	4.9	13.6	17.2	10.7	10.1	13.0
42 065	...	7	Jefferson	1 690	44 638	1 077	26.4	98.4	0.8	0.5	0.4	0.7	5.8	15.5	8.1	11.0	11.3	14.5
42 067	...	6	Juniata	1 014	24 796	1 618	24.5	96.0	1.0	0.3	0.6	2.9	5.8	17.0	7.3	11.0	11.6	14.3
42 069	42540	2	Lackawanna	1 189	212 719	302	178.9	89.4	3.2	0.4	2.4	5.9	5.3	14.8	9.9	12.1	11.5	14.1
42 071	29540	2	Lancaster	2 444	533 320	122	218.2	84.9	4.2	0.4	2.4	9.5	6.6	17.6	9.6	12.4	11.6	13.6
42 073	35260	4	Lawrence	928	88 771	645	95.7	94.2	5.1	0.4	0.7	1.2	5.2	15.4	8.4	10.4	11.5	14.2
42 075	30140	3	Lebanon	937	136 359	463	145.5	85.9	2.4	0.4	1.5	10.8	6.3	16.6	8.5	11.4	11.9	14.0
42 077	10900	2	Lehigh	894	357 823	189	400.2	70.5	6.2	0.4	3.7	20.7	5.9	16.9	9.1	12.6	12.5	14.5
42 079	42540	2	Luzerne	2 306	318 829	208	138.3	86.9	4.0	0.3	1.4	8.5	5.1	14.7	9.4	11.7	12.0	14.6
42 081	48700	3	Lycoming	3 182	116 508	527	36.6	92.9	5.7	0.5	1.0	1.6	5.5	14.9	10.4	12.4	11.3	14.2
42 083	14620	7	McKean	2 536	42 554	1 117	16.8	94.6	3.0	0.6	0.8	2.0	5.2	15.3	9.3	11.6	12.5	14.3
42 085	49660	2	Mercer	1 742	114 884	532	65.9	92.2	6.7	0.5	1.0	1.3	4.9	15.6	9.9	10.2	11.1	14.3
42 087	30380	4	Mifflin	1 065	46 552	1 034	43.7	97.5	1.2	0.4	0.7	1.3	5.9	16.7	7.4	10.8	11.4	14.2
42 089	20700	4	Monroe	1 575	166 314	383	105.6	70.4	13.7	0.8	2.8	14.2	4.6	17.1	11.0	9.9	11.7	16.8
42 091	37980	1	Montgomery	1 251	816 857	72	653.0	79.2	9.8	0.4	7.7	4.6	5.7	16.5	7.9	12.4	12.8	15.2
42 093	14100	6	Montour	337	18 641	1 883	55.3	93.5	2.0	0.4	2.8	2.1	5.9	14.7	7.4	12.8	10.6	14.7
42 095	10900	2	Northampton	957	300 654	224	314.2	80.5	5.8	0.4	3.2	11.7	5.0	15.8	10.1	11.3	12.1	14.9
42 097	44980	4	Northumberland	1 187	93 944	622	79.1	94.3	2.7	0.4	0.6	2.9	5.3	14.7	7.7	12.0	11.9	14.5
42 099	25420	2	Perry	1 428	45 634	1 057	32.0	96.9	1.2	0.5	0.7	1.6	5.9	16.3	8.0	11.1	12.5	15.5
42 101	37980	1	Philadelphia	347	1 560 297	23	4 496.5	37.7	42.8	0.8	7.4	13.2	7.0	15.2	11.9	17.7	12.2	12.4
42 103	35620	1	Pike	1 411	56 191	903	39.8	83.2	6.1	0.8	1.5	9.8	3.9	16.7	8.0	8.4	11.3	17.2

1. CBSA = Core Based Statistical Area. See Appendix A for explanation. See Appendix B for list of metropolitan areas with component counties. 2. County type code from the Economic Research Service of USDA Rural-Urban Continuum Codes. See Appendix A for definition. 3. Dry land or land partially or temporarily covered by water. 4. May be of any race.

STATE County	Population, 2013 (cont.): Age (percent) (cont.): 55 to 64 years	65 to 74 years	75 years and over	Percent female	Population change and components of change, 2000–2014: Total persons: 2000	2010	Percent change: 2000–2010	2010–2014	Components of change, 2010–2014: Births	Deaths	Net migration	Households, 2009–2013: Number	Persons per household	Percent: Family households	Female family householder[1]	One person
	16	17	18	19	20	21	22	23	24	25	26	27	28	29	30	31
OREGON—Cont'd																
Morrow	13.7	8.3	5.8	48.7	10 995	11 173	1.6	0.1	670	338	-337	3 741	2.98	75.1	11.3	21.1
Multnomah	12.3	6.8	4.8	50.6	660 486	735 334	11.3	5.6	40 078	23 556	24 582	305 939	2.39	54.3	10.8	33.2
Polk	12.8	9.2	7.2	51.7	62 380	75 403	20.9	3.3	3 687	2 696	1 416	28 239	2.62	69.2	10.0	22.9
Sherman	16.1	13.1	10.9	50.2	1 934	1 765	-8.7	-3.1	69	52	-76	827	2.24	58.5	6.8	32.6
Tillamook	18.0	13.5	9.1	49.7	24 262	25 250	4.1	0.4	1 052	1 182	325	10 236	2.40	64.2	8.7	29.4
Umatilla	12.3	7.8	5.9	47.8	70 548	75 889	7.6	1.1	4 657	2 601	-1 164	26 744	2.70	68.9	13.8	25.9
Union	14.5	10.1	8.0	50.9	24 530	25 748	5.0	-0.2	1 281	1 097	-185	10 235	2.43	66.1	8.0	25.7
Wallowa	19.3	14.5	11.3	51.2	7 226	7 008	-3.0	-2.7	248	330	-92	2 996	2.27	61.6	9.6	35.3
Wasco	14.8	10.7	8.6	50.4	23 791	25 213	6.0	1.2	1 247	1 227	272	9 612	2.39	67.5	11.9	27.1
Washington	11.6	6.7	4.7	50.7	445 342	529 710	18.9	6.3	30 486	12 759	15 363	201 771	2.64	67.1	10.1	25.3
Wheeler	17.3	19.3	13.0	49.7	1 547	1 441	-6.9	-4.6	42	72	-32	625	2.00	65.6	5.3	32.8
Yamhill	12.8	8.4	6.7	50.1	84 992	99 193	16.7	2.6	4 703	3 442	1 141	34 138	2.77	73.1	10.7	21.8
PENNSYLVANIA	13.6	8.7	7.7	51.1	12 281 054	12 702 379	3.4	0.7	604 903	539 878	29 004	4 958 427	2.48	64.8	11.9	29.5
Adams	14.2	9.8	7.8	50.8	91 292	101 407	11.1	0.3	4 265	3 967	-195	38 141	2.55	72.1	9.3	23.0
Allegheny	14.3	8.6	8.5	51.9	1 281 666	1 223 348	-4.6	0.6	55 668	57 820	12 588	526 004	2.26	57.9	11.8	35.4
Armstrong	15.6	10.4	9.3	50.5	72 392	68 941	-4.8	-1.7	2 936	3 626	-404	28 525	2.37	68.1	9.8	28.2
Beaver	15.3	9.8	9.6	51.5	181 412	170 539	-6.0	-0.7	7 297	8 702	568	70 867	2.35	66.0	11.6	29.8
Bedford	14.6	10.9	9.2	50.2	49 984	49 762	-0.4	-1.7	2 070	2 234	-654	20 198	2.42	70.1	9.5	26.5
Berks	12.9	8.3	7.3	50.8	373 638	411 442	10.1	0.5	20 544	15 526	-2 363	153 897	2.59	68.7	11.9	25.0
Blair	14.6	9.8	9.1	51.3	129 144	127 089	-1.6	-0.9	5 714	6 751	-197	51 433	2.40	64.8	11.3	30.1
Bradford	14.6	10.7	8.3	50.5	62 761	62 622	-0.2	-1.3	3 109	2 868	-1 027	24 213	2.55	69.1	9.7	26.0
Bucks	14.6	8.8	7.4	51.0	597 635	625 249	4.6	0.2	24 951	23 301	-306	230 366	2.68	71.9	9.4	23.8
Butler	14.5	8.9	7.6	50.7	174 083	183 862	5.6	1.1	7 490	7 813	2 263	73 213	2.45	68.4	8.5	26.4
Cambria	15.5	10.0	9.7	50.4	152 598	143 679	-5.8	-4.1	5 715	7 676	-3 851	58 208	2.31	64.0	10.9	31.3
Cameron	17.2	12.6	10.2	50.4	5 974	5 085	-14.9	-5.5	201	283	-188	2 144	2.29	62.5	8.0	32.2
Carbon	15.2	10.7	8.5	50.5	58 802	65 249	11.0	-1.2	2 444	3 307	96	25 903	2.48	69.0	11.3	25.5
Centre	10.6	6.7	5.6	47.9	135 758	153 990	13.4	3.1	5 505	4 027	3 329	57 197	2.40	57.0	6.3	27.4
Chester	13.3	8.0	6.2	50.8	433 501	498 886	15.1	2.7	23 431	15 721	6 042	184 788	2.64	70.6	8.4	23.8
Clarion	13.9	9.6	8.1	51.2	41 765	39 988	-4.3	-2.9	1 658	1 782	-1 033	15 776	2.40	64.0	8.5	27.6
Clearfield	14.1	10.0	8.7	48.1	83 382	81 642	-2.1	-0.6	3 136	3 948	408	32 192	2.38	66.8	9.6	29.3
Clinton	12.5	9.2	7.7	51.1	37 914	39 238	3.5	1.3	1 781	1 653	385	15 067	2.45	64.4	10.7	28.4
Columbia	13.6	9.3	7.8	51.8	64 151	67 295	4.9	-0.3	2 663	2 853	41	26 225	2.40	63.7	9.9	27.1
Crawford	14.8	10.2	7.7	51.0	90 366	88 765	-1.8	-1.8	3 982	4 084	-1 332	34 831	2.43	66.1	10.0	28.6
Cumberland	13.4	8.9	7.7	50.7	213 674	235 406	10.2	3.5	10 768	9 228	6 799	95 286	2.35	64.7	8.4	29.5
Dauphin	13.9	8.2	6.7	51.6	251 798	268 100	6.5	1.3	14 543	10 258	-420	108 831	2.41	62.4	13.3	31.2
Delaware	13.2	7.5	7.3	52.0	550 864	558 979	1.5	0.8	28 548	22 959	-498	204 771	2.62	66.9	14.4	28.3
Elk	15.5	10.1	9.9	49.9	35 112	31 946	-9.0	-2.4	1 290	1 638	-375	13 478	2.33	66.2	10.8	31.1
Erie	13.8	8.2	7.1	50.7	280 843	280 566	-0.1	-0.8	13 450	11 673	-3 533	109 675	2.44	63.6	12.7	30.2
Fayette	15.4	10.1	8.9	50.8	148 644	136 606	-8.1	-1.8	5 722	7 665	-432	54 363	2.42	64.7	12.2	30.6
Forest	14.7	13.1	7.8	33.1	4 946	7 716	56.0	-2.6	152	345	-21	2 001	2.37	59.4	7.4	34.7
Franklin	13.0	9.6	8.2	51.1	129 313	149 618	15.7	2.2	7 870	6 044	1 352	58 273	2.54	68.2	9.3	27.1
Fulton	13.9	11.4	7.7	49.7	14 261	14 845	4.1	-1.4	662	556	-276	5 965	2.47	70.9	8.5	23.6
Greene	14.8	9.4	7.3	48.2	40 672	38 686	-4.9	-2.2	1 566	1 893	-499	14 417	2.36	66.0	10.9	27.8
Huntingdon	13.9	10.3	7.7	46.8	45 586	45 913	0.7	-0.6	1 766	1 931	-93	17 193	2.37	68.2	8.8	28.4
Indiana	13.7	9.0	7.8	50.2	89 605	88 880	-0.8	-1.3	3 693	3 728	-1 091	34 310	2.42	63.7	8.6	27.9
Jefferson	14.6	9.9	9.2	50.3	45 932	45 200	-1.6	-1.2	2 148	2 366	-329	18 503	2.39	66.4	9.9	29.5
Juniata	13.4	10.5	9.0	50.1	22 821	24 636	8.0	0.6	1 121	1 057	-55	9 248	2.64	71.2	8.2	24.0
Lackawanna	13.9	9.5	8.9	51.7	213 295	214 437	0.5	-0.8	9 162	11 168	564	85 769	2.40	63.4	12.5	31.4
Lancaster	12.6	8.3	7.7	51.1	470 658	519 445	10.4	2.7	29 773	19 622	3 521	194 082	2.62	70.5	8.9	24.2
Lawrence	15.3	9.7	9.9	51.7	94 643	91 108	-3.7	-2.6	4 055	4 670	-1 650	36 823	2.39	67.3	12.6	29.0
Lebanon	13.4	9.5	8.6	51.1	120 327	133 568	11.0	2.1	7 029	5 977	1 744	52 023	2.52	69.8	10.2	25.7
Lehigh	12.8	8.2	7.5	51.3	312 090	349 497	12.0	2.3	17 481	13 893	4 682	133 289	2.57	67.5	12.9	26.8
Luzerne	13.9	9.7	9.0	50.8	319 250	320 918	0.5	-0.7	13 289	16 749	1 915	130 880	2.36	63.6	13.4	31.8
Lycoming	14.1	9.0	8.2	50.8	120 044	116 111	-3.3	0.3	5 424	5 331	431	46 046	2.42	64.8	10.5	28.1
McKean	14.1	9.4	8.4	48.8	45 936	43 450	-5.4	-2.1	1 732	2 231	-359	17 450	2.31	65.7	12.3	29.9
Mercer	14.6	9.8	9.6	50.9	120 293	116 638	-3.0	-1.5	4 802	5 896	-698	46 187	2.36	66.1	11.6	30.1
Mifflin	13.6	10.8	9.2	50.9	46 486	46 682	0.4	-0.3	2 429	2 177	-347	18 711	2.46	67.4	11.2	27.1
Monroe	14.4	8.7	5.8	50.6	138 687	169 842	22.5	-2.1	6 069	5 732	-3 752	58 875	2.81	73.9	13.0	20.2
Montgomery	13.4	8.3	7.8	51.4	750 097	799 874	6.6	2.1	38 234	30 857	10 021	307 488	2.55	67.9	9.2	27.0
Montour	14.7	9.3	10.0	52.1	18 236	18 267	0.2	2.0	952	891	301	7 233	2.44	66.2	8.7	30.0
Northampton	13.7	8.9	8.1	51.0	267 066	297 735	11.5	1.0	12 707	11 029	1 992	112 189	2.56	69.1	11.1	25.1
Northumberland	14.6	10.2	9.2	49.9	94 556	94 528	0.0	-0.6	4 162	4 879	299	39 348	2.28	65.5	11.3	29.8
Perry	15.4	9.2	6.1	49.7	43 602	45 969	5.4	-0.7	2 370	1 752	-916	18 173	2.49	71.9	9.3	21.7
Philadelphia	11.2	6.7	5.7	52.7	1 517 550	1 526 006	0.6	2.2	98 698	61 716	-1 231	580 017	2.56	53.3	20.4	39.4
Pike	15.1	12.0	7.5	49.9	46 302	57 369	23.9	-2.0	1 682	1 853	-1 183	21 581	2.63	72.0	10.0	23.7

1. No spouse present.

STATE County	Persons in group quarters, 2014	Daytime population, 2009–2013: Number	Daytime population, 2009–2013: Employment/residence ratio	Births, 2014: Total	Births, 2014: Rate[1]	Deaths, 2014: Number	Deaths, 2014: Rate[1]	Persons under 65 with no health insurance, 2013: Number	Persons under 65 with no health insurance, 2013: Percent	Medicare, 2014: Eligible for Medicare	Medicare, 2014: Enrolled in Medicare Advantage	Medicare, 2014: Enrolled in a Medicare prescription drug plan	Serious crimes known to police,[2] 2013: Total: Number	Serious crimes known to police,[2] 2013: Total: Rate[3]
	32	33	34	35	36	37	38	39	40	41	42	43	44	45
OREGON—Cont'd														
Morrow	23	10 979	0.95	153	13.7	85	7.6	1 962	20.2	1 866	239	967	284	2 516
Multnomah	19 554	845 072	1.26	9 406	12.1	5 741	7.4	115 321	17.3	109 548	61 989	26 421	39 975	5 201
Polk	1 914	64 885	0.65	860	11.0	643	8.3	10 545	16.9	14 978	8 729	3 761	2 370	3 086
Sherman	0	2 058	1.26	15	8.8	13	7.6	251	19.2	479	76	224	31	1 798
Tillamook	463	25 308	1.00	254	10.0	276	10.9	4 218	22.0	6 946	1 600	3 134	510	2 011
Umatilla	4 042	76 192	1.00	1 109	14.5	626	8.2	12 569	20.1	12 698	1 651	6 890	2 496	3 258
Union	732	25 585	0.99	297	11.6	257	10.0	3 560	17.4	5 555	554	3 552	610	2 362
Wallowa	108	6 861	0.98	58	8.5	62	9.1	931	18.5	2 105	100	1 290	NA	NA
Wasco	741	25 948	1.06	300	11.8	272	10.7	4 421	21.7	5 592	1 291	2 507	876	3 418
Washington	7 058	536 871	0.99	7 253	12.9	3 147	5.6	72 264	14.9	73 409	41 073	17 346	10 671	1 924
Wheeler	27	1 258	0.94	8	5.8	9	6.5	215	23.1	457	86	206	25	1 761
Yamhill	6 022	91 966	0.82	1 079	10.6	776	7.6	13 898	17.3	17 876	8 700	5 226	2 312	2 293
PENNSYLVANIA	430 836	12 670 852	0.99	142 032	11.1	128 600	10.1	1 203 230	11.6	2 503 511	994 744	1 013 792	306 089	2 396
Adams	4 019	86 996	0.71	974	9.6	931	9.2	9 962	12.4	21 301	6 261	9 014	1 372	1 352
Allegheny	36 814	1 319 457	1.16	13 231	10.7	13 743	11.2	96 840	9.8	247 192	153 327	51 641	29 838	2 425
Armstrong	650	58 765	0.67	702	10.4	880	13.0	6 420	11.8	15 902	10 275	4 119	598	877
Beaver	3 290	150 405	0.74	1 731	10.2	2 084	12.3	13 203	9.8	39 916	25 611	7 743	3 994	2 374
Bedford	551	45 468	0.81	478	9.8	519	10.6	4 927	12.7	12 186	5 844	4 100	590	1 234
Berks	11 817	391 262	0.89	4 838	11.7	3 692	8.9	41 629	12.3	77 202	26 183	35 593	8 929	2 177
Blair	3 727	132 490	1.10	1 327	10.5	1 627	12.9	10 999	10.9	29 303	14 496	10 529	2 435	1 916
Bradford	578	63 889	1.05	739	12.0	702	11.4	6 427	12.8	14 018	3 593	8 158	1 095	1 743
Bucks	8 079	569 376	0.82	5 838	9.3	5 672	9.1	43 854	8.5	121 021	38 173	54 837	12 115	1 932
Butler	5 398	184 573	1.00	1 753	9.4	1 862	10.0	12 917	8.6	36 666	20 681	7 899	2 579	1 393
Cambria	6 492	140 353	0.96	1 300	9.4	1 771	12.9	11 055	10.4	34 474	20 943	10 114	2 799	1 987
Cameron	92	4 988	0.99	54	11.2	64	13.3	449	11.9	1 426	346	894	69	1 410
Carbon	699	53 918	0.60	562	8.7	768	11.9	6 349	12.2	14 710	2 749	8 358	1 479	2 279
Centre	19 455	162 194	1.11	1 325	8.3	979	6.2	13 841	11.6	21 666	9 978	8 498	2 291	1 474
Chester	13 532	494 857	0.97	5 497	10.7	3 807	7.4	37 365	8.8	81 982	18 390	42 779	7 407	1 460
Clarion	1 423	38 021	0.90	376	9.7	423	10.9	3 741	12.1	8 581	2 562	4 318	618	1 563
Clearfield	5 759	80 609	0.97	741	9.1	922	11.4	7 796	12.7	18 446	6 962	8 598	1 812	2 237
Clinton	2 664	37 345	0.87	419	10.5	383	9.6	4 181	13.7	8 103	3 318	4 073	691	1 746
Columbia	4 358	65 833	0.96	636	9.5	683	10.2	5 760	11.1	13 657	5 455	6 141	1 363	2 043
Crawford	3 892	85 328	0.92	933	10.7	930	10.7	9 369	13.7	19 909	6 042	10 282	1 420	1 629
Cumberland	12 775	248 489	1.09	2 582	10.6	2 148	8.8	18 222	9.6	46 868	17 979	19 441	3 864	1 614
Dauphin	6 785	317 727	1.38	3 416	12.6	2 430	9.0	27 261	12.0	49 905	23 197	20 014	7 678	2 844
Delaware	22 558	513 031	0.82	6 669	11.8	5 401	9.6	48 504	10.6	98 307	26 803	46 154	15 404	2 744
Elk	355	31 512	0.98	311	10.0	373	12.0	2 412	9.6	7 731	1 377	4 683	623	1 982
Erie	12 891	285 360	1.04	3 108	11.2	2 730	9.8	24 756	10.9	54 287	24 149	20 663	7 361	2 625
Fayette	4 236	124 687	0.78	1 322	9.9	1 820	13.6	13 336	12.5	33 544	18 671	10 701	3 665	2 725
Forest	2 503	8 245	1.32	35	4.7	73	9.7	536	15.0	1 581	504	801	109	1 424
Franklin	2 569	141 050	0.86	1 824	11.9	1 500	9.8	16 646	13.5	32 386	7 353	15 833	3 192	2 105
Fulton	122	13 563	0.81	156	10.7	137	9.4	1 442	12.3	3 519	719	1 885	232	1 575
Greene	3 091	40 044	1.11	348	9.2	435	11.5	2 895	10.1	7 751	3 729	2 875	758	2 001
Huntingdon	4 888	42 505	0.82	414	9.0	474	10.4	3 876	11.8	9 910	3 497	5 447	650	1 415
Indiana	5 717	87 548	0.98	883	10.1	869	9.9	9 115	13.4	17 526	10 467	5 046	1 464	1 664
Jefferson	774	42 518	0.87	491	11.0	519	11.6	4 681	13.0	10 620	3 663	4 936	653	1 465
Juniata	292	21 333	0.69	250	10.1	254	10.2	2 788	14.1	5 042	2 207	2 361	258	1 032
Lackawanna	8 233	216 459	1.02	2 113	9.9	2 573	12.1	18 688	11.1	48 494	12 640	25 932	4 465	2 083
Lancaster	12 933	509 374	0.94	7 067	13.3	4 774	9.0	60 893	14.0	99 193	35 036	44 437	10 750	2 033
Lawrence	2 087	84 491	0.85	979	11.0	1 089	12.3	7 807	11.1	21 493	12 333	6 064	2 407	2 712
Lebanon	3 675	124 637	0.85	1 630	12.0	1 424	10.4	13 650	12.6	28 585	10 763	11 015	2 718	2 003
Lehigh	8 931	365 174	1.08	4 101	11.5	3 237	9.0	38 140	13.0	67 058	20 897	31 808	10 326	2 894
Luzerne	11 906	321 176	1.00	3 097	9.7	4 011	12.6	31 356	12.5	71 153	16 921	37 987	8 736	2 723
Lycoming	5 456	118 499	1.04	1 288	11.1	1 297	11.1	10 435	11.3	24 473	7 699	13 520	2 744	2 337
McKean	3 210	42 246	0.94	375	8.8	512	12.0	3 724	11.4	9 827	1 988	5 558	787	1 829
Mercer	6 788	117 890	1.04	1 140	9.9	1 440	12.5	10 015	11.5	27 635	12 579	10 727	2 608	2 262
Mifflin	559	44 307	0.87	581	12.5	506	10.9	5 015	13.5	11 011	4 641	5 045	927	1 981
Monroe	3 816	157 112	0.84	1 413	8.5	1 443	8.7	19 406	14.0	29 592	5 095	15 738	4 744	2 819
Montgomery	22 077	866 385	1.15	8 923	10.9	7 466	9.1	55 144	8.3	145 796	39 367	71 744	16 145	1 992
Montour	844	24 737	1.77	222	11.9	211	11.3	1 305	9.0	4 052	1 936	1 800	306	1 666
Northampton	10 792	273 213	0.82	3 068	10.2	2 818	9.4	27 186	11.3	60 860	16 076	30 206	6 219	2 076
Northumberland	3 715	84 400	0.75	994	10.6	1 080	11.5	9 078	12.4	21 826	7 408	11 285	1 560	1 653
Perry	657	33 335	0.44	539	11.8	415	9.1	4 972	13.0	8 964	4 020	3 715	842	1 929
Philadelphia	57 774	1 650 072	1.19	23 145	14.8	14 868	9.5	217 971	16.5	244 699	103 945	90 374	70 546	4 542
Pike	478	47 267	0.57	414	7.4	460	8.2	5 820	12.9	12 517	1 306	7 558	1 117	1 969

1. Per 1,000 estimated resident population. 2. Data for serious crimes have not been adjusted for underreporting; this may affect comparability between geographic areas and over time.
3. Per 100,000 population estimated by the FBI.

STATE County	Serious crimes known to police, 2013 (cont.)[1] — Rate[2] — Violent	Serious crimes — Rate[2] — Property	Education — School enrollment and attainment, 2009–2013 — Enrollment[3] — Total	Enrollment[3] — Percent private	Attainment[4] (percent) — High school graduate or less	Attainment[4] (percent) — Bachelor's degree or more	Local government expenditures,[5] 2012–2013 — Total current spending (mil dol)	Local government expenditures — Current spending per student (dollars)	Money income, 2009–2013 — Per capita income[6] (dollars)	Households — Median income (dollars)	Households — Mean income (dollars)	Households — Percent with income of $200,000 or more	Income and poverty, 2013 — Median household income (dollars)	Percent below poverty level — All persons	Percent below poverty level — Children under 18 years	Percent below poverty level — Children 5 to 17 years in families
	46	47	48	49	50	51	52	53	54	55	56	57	58	59	60	61
OREGON—Cont'd																
Morrow	142	2 374	2 956	5.2	58.1	9.7	23.5	9 611	20 663	49 940	59 763	1.1	51 289	16.8	24.5	22.7
Multnomah	474	4 727	185 408	19.4	29.5	39.9	998.2	10 779	30 475	52 511	72 045	4.5	53 624	18.2	23.0	22.3
Polk	264	2 822	21 935	11.6	36.1	29.0	59.0	9 056	24 426	52 808	64 566	2.0	51 224	18.3	21.8	19.7
Sherman	116	1 682	377	16.7	41.8	16.5	3.6	14 618	24 314	42 639	54 652	2.2	52 679	17.1	23.7	21.5
Tillamook	110	1 901	4 971	12.2	46.3	20.7	38.5	12 078	22 452	43 676	52 723	1.8	41 584	16.6	26.1	23.5
Umatilla	167	3 091	19 777	6.1	47.3	15.5	146.7	10 655	20 836	48 389	58 270	1.7	47 053	17.1	22.8	18.8
Union	139	2 223	6 571	12.6	43.0	22.5	35.5	9 425	22 684	42 542	55 370	2.4	41 331	19.4	24.7	21.7
Wallowa	NA	NA	1 282	12.5	40.8	24.0	14.1	16 756	23 131	41 994	51 265	1.3	42 751	15.1	26.3	23.7
Wasco	86	3 332	5 669	9.4	42.9	20.1	39.9	11 205	22 844	43 765	59 468	2.4	42 461	17.2	25.9	23.0
Washington	133	1 791	143 343	17.7	28.4	39.4	792.5	9 192	31 078	64 180	81 240	5.2	63 632	10.9	13.8	12.1
Wheeler	493	1 268	207	20.3	48.1	16.8	4.4	13 813	24 575	37 974	48 656	1.0	33 065	22.6	39.1	35.8
Yamhill	136	2 157	27 253	25.5	43.3	22.5	153.3	9 212	24 290	54 535	67 930	2.6	57 427	14.3	18.6	16.8
PENNSYLVANIA	335	2 061	3 149 036	24.2	48.4	27.5	24 371.8	13 864	28 502	52 548	71 088	4.2	52 005	13.7	19.2	17.5
Adams	98	1 255	24 623	29.0	56.0	20.4	276.2	20 032	27 284	59 492	71 406	2.7	57 725	9.5	14.7	12.2
Allegheny	392	2 033	297 896	25.8	38.1	35.9	2 286.7	15 859	31 593	51 366	72 043	4.6	51 400	13.5	18.5	17.4
Armstrong	92	784	13 562	12.7	61.5	14.6	115.1	15 328	23 661	45 241	56 086	1.5	42 927	14.7	20.2	18.3
Beaver	273	2 101	36 825	18.2	48.9	21.9	313.3	13 956	26 258	49 217	61 794	1.9	49 215	11.3	16.3	15.0
Bedford	171	1 062	9 975	15.1	65.7	12.6	87.7	12 522	22 259	43 290	53 380	1.1	48 003	13.5	20.2	18.4
Berks	298	1 879	106 920	17.0	54.8	22.3	944.1	13 729	26 723	55 170	69 790	3.3	55 634	14.0	21.2	19.4
Blair	209	1 707	27 324	14.1	58.6	18.4	229.4	13 023	23 875	42 992	57 056	2.2	41 756	16.2	24.3	21.3
Bradford	180	1 563	13 129	11.6	60.5	17.1	130.7	13 539	23 667	46 963	59 331	2.2	49 117	13.5	20.2	18.4
Bucks	107	1 825	154 354	24.7	38.6	35.8	1 385.5	16 018	37 466	76 555	99 402	9.0	73 662	6.4	8.4	7.4
Butler	93	1 299	47 202	16.1	43.7	30.5	312.2	11 345	30 957	58 230	76 864	4.5	58 430	9.4	9.9	9.3
Cambria	190	1 797	31 936	21.1	57.9	18.3	228.6	12 404	22 659	41 730	53 656	1.4	40 930	16.2	23.2	20.5
Cameron	123	1 288	912	9.4	64.7	14.2	9.7	14 007	22 747	41 410	50 552	0.7	37 891	14.6	22.8	21.7
Carbon	234	2 045	13 746	13.8	58.6	15.1	119.4	13 449	24 861	48 900	60 992	1.3	44 338	14.1	22.2	19.1
Centre	95	1 380	61 039	7.8	39.6	40.4	193.1	14 954	25 545	50 336	67 209	3.7	52 559	18.4	13.6	12.5
Chester	134	1 327	136 747	26.4	30.9	48.5	1 158.3	16 651	42 210	86 050	113 472	13.0	83 775	7.0	8.4	7.9
Clarion	157	1 407	10 253	8.3	59.7	18.5	97.9	16 625	21 902	42 389	54 043	1.8	40 043	18.7	21.9	19.8
Clearfield	264	1 973	15 935	11.9	63.5	13.5	169.1	14 639	21 273	41 030	51 133	1.0	39 912	16.5	23.5	20.7
Clinton	93	1 652	11 069	9.1	59.7	17.0	58.1	13 462	21 875	42 184	54 824	0.9	44 887	14.2	21.9	20.7
Columbia	174	1 869	19 138	8.1	57.7	20.7	82.6	13 085	23 681	44 807	59 128	1.8	45 564	17.1	20.2	19.0
Crawford	75	1 554	20 299	23.5	59.0	18.7	149.7	13 018	21 741	42 504	53 953	1.4	43 793	14.4	22.6	20.5
Cumberland	84	1 531	59 014	22.5	43.6	32.5	350.5	13 693	31 791	60 826	77 712	4.4	60 134	8.6	11.5	10.1
Dauphin	410	2 434	64 760	17.9	46.6	28.5	486.6	13 724	29 234	54 066	70 586	3.8	53 480	13.8	20.4	19.2
Delaware	490	2 254	155 652	34.5	40.5	35.0	1 132.2	16 337	33 179	64 041	87 921	7.2	64 186	10.9	14.2	13.0
Elk	108	1 874	6 632	27.1	61.1	14.9	43.2	11 536	23 738	45 767	54 840	1.4	46 388	9.8	13.9	12.3
Erie	246	2 378	72 719	24.6	50.9	24.8	502.3	13 085	24 189	45 202	60 020	2.4	44 223	17.9	26.9	24.5
Fayette	207	2 518	26 988	12.0	64.0	14.0	217.4	12 606	20 884	39 115	50 182	1.1	37 929	19.2	30.4	28.5
Forest	235	1 189	1 023	23.9	68.8	7.8	10.4	19 796	13 646	36 556	42 867	0.2	38 087	24.5	38.0	31.5
Franklin	152	1 953	33 328	17.8	58.1	19.3	250.5	10 985	25 741	52 637	64 593	1.9	53 913	11.8	17.4	16.1
Fulton	190	1 385	3 149	12.7	67.0	11.8	28.8	13 047	23 201	48 461	56 993	1.1	46 032	12.5	18.1	16.5
Greene	187	1 813	7 937	21.8	63.7	15.5	76.6	14 597	21 819	44 388	57 301	1.1	45 156	16.3	22.5	20.8
Huntingdon	157	1 258	9 355	24.3	64.7	13.5	64.4	11 460	20 739	44 183	53 205	0.9	42 479	14.8	21.3	18.7
Indiana	329	1 336	24 726	8.9	56.3	21.9	167.2	16 972	22 933	43 997	57 196	2.0	44 504	14.7	20.0	17.7
Jefferson	159	1 305	9 210	12.4	63.9	13.2	72.7	14 997	21 300	41 262	50 827	0.9	41 637	15.5	24.0	21.6
Juniata	88	944	5 230	21.3	70.1	11.8	28.7	9 677	21 628	46 163	55 545	0.8	46 183	11.8	17.5	16.2
Lackawanna	190	1 893	52 108	33.8	49.0	25.7	350.4	12 588	25 594	46 044	62 023	2.6	44 926	14.8	20.8	20.0
Lancaster	171	1 862	127 259	26.1	54.7	24.2	949.3	13 988	26 496	56 483	70 236	3.1	56 766	10.5	15.3	14.6
Lawrence	335	2 377	19 850	16.4	56.5	19.6	158.1	12 702	22 906	43 546	54 792	1.4	43 199	13.8	20.9	19.7
Lebanon	178	1 825	30 835	23.4	59.2	19.4	221.1	11 553	27 074	54 818	68 089	2.7	54 952	11.2	16.0	14.2
Lehigh	238	2 656	86 741	22.5	46.9	28.1	712.0	14 619	27 923	54 923	71 910	4.0	53 722	14.2	22.2	20.9
Luzerne	257	2 466	72 271	21.8	51.6	21.0	551.7	12 548	24 793	44 402	58 948	2.4	44 734	16.1	26.8	24.1
Lycoming	165	2 171	27 264	14.9	54.7	18.8	222.2	13 719	22 987	45 430	56 502	1.7	46 663	14.0	20.0	18.9
McKean	318	1 511	10 071	14.3	59.7	15.1	98.7	15 646	22 426	41 834	51 971	1.2	41 653	19.0	27.8	24.4
Mercer	251	2 011	27 064	25.1	55.4	20.5	256.6	15 933	22 831	44 301	56 097	1.6	43 936	14.1	22.2	20.9
Mifflin	169	1 813	9 024	22.0	67.9	11.5	94.0	17 759	20 794	40 384	50 754	1.5	42 567	14.5	24.4	21.9
Monroe	367	2 451	46 768	15.5	47.3	23.8	435.0	15 532	25 494	57 408	70 696	2.9	55 273	12.0	16.7	15.0
Montgomery	168	1 824	205 997	31.6	32.0	45.5	1 775.8	16 934	41 472	79 183	106 495	10.8	77 021	6.8	8.2	7.5
Montour	376	1 291	3 845	17.1	51.5	26.8	29.3	12 455	29 600	51 482	72 055	4.8	53 329	10.3	16.3	15.6
Northampton	157	1 920	76 564	27.7	46.6	26.6	633.3	14 826	29 266	60 097	75 813	4.0	59 605	10.1	12.8	11.7
Northumberland	214	1 439	18 157	17.7	65.5	14.0	190.8	15 952	22 478	41 208	53 173	1.2	41 078	14.7	23.1	21.5
Perry	257	1 672	9 413	15.5	60.1	15.5	76.5	12 245	26 048	57 375	65 232	1.3	56 544	10.2	16.1	14.7
Philadelphia	1 100	3 442	421 991	34.0	53.3	23.9	2 905.9	20 194	22 279	37 192	54 367	2.5	36 918	26.0	36.3	34.3
Pike	132	1 837	13 848	12.5	45.2	22.5	118.3	14 046	27 691	59 340	71 441	2.3	60 168	10.4	15.8	13.0

1. Data for serious crimes have not been adjusted for underreporting; this may affect comparability between geographic areas and over time. 2. Per 100,000 population estimated by the FBI.
3. All persons 3 years old and over enrolled in nursery school through college. 4. Persons 25 years old and over. 5. Elementary and secondary education expenditures.
6. Based on population estimated by the American Community Survey, 2009–2013.

STATE County	Personal income, 2013 Total (mil dol)	Percent change, 2012–2013	Per capita[1] Dollars	Per capita[1] Rank	Wages and salaries (mil dol)	Supplements to wages and salaries; employer contributions (mil dol) Pension and insurance	Supplements to wages and salaries; employer contributions (mil dol) Government social insurance	Proprietors' income (mil dol)	Dividends, interest, and rent (mil dol)	Personal transfer receipts (mil dol)	Earnings, 2013 Total (mil dol)	Contributions for government social insurance (mil dol) From employee and self-employed	Contributions for government social insurance (mil dol) From employer
	62	63	64	65	66	67	68	69	70	71	72	73	74
OREGON—Cont'd													
Morrow	500	5.5	44 079	749	229	41	21	131	56	80	422	16	21
Multnomah	33 376	2.2	43 564	791	24 609	3 738	2 163	3 525	6 455	5 234	34 035	2 012	2 163
Polk	2 567	2.7	33 421	2 189	623	130	57	85	500	585	895	63	57
Sherman	100	-2.4	57 738	141	32	8	3	26	18	19	70	3	3
Tillamook	932	2.8	36 806	1 622	303	59	28	81	217	257	471	31	28
Umatilla	2 581	0.5	33 643	2 155	1 156	220	112	240	431	609	1 729	99	112
Union	892	1.8	34 792	1 933	366	74	36	66	175	240	541	34	36
Wallowa	264	2.5	38 755	1 324	77	18	7	32	71	75	134	9	7
Wasco	943	2.0	37 002	1 585	417	74	38	70	178	235	599	36	38
Washington	24 840	2.1	44 757	712	16 316	1 985	1 317	841	4 159	3 176	20 459	1 250	1 317
Wheeler	46	3.7	32 969	2 257	9	2	1	5	12	14	16	1	1
Yamhill	3 594	1.3	35 677	1 804	1 300	234	123	152	645	764	1 809	114	123
PENNSYLVANIA	590 171	1.4	46 202	X	285 598	53 238	22 491	52 782	103 002	112 900	414 108	24 276	22 491
Adams	3 699	1.5	36 428	1 672	1 307	276	111	260	685	772	1 954	121	111
Allegheny	65 527	1.7	53 208	263	39 881	6 466	3 052	7 601	11 462	11 199	56 999	3 281	3 052
Armstrong	2 547	1.4	37 391	1 521	742	171	61	297	385	682	1 271	83	61
Beaver	7 031	1.5	41 331	1 013	2 300	529	191	305	1 016	1 724	3 326	221	191
Bedford	1 702	0.8	34 689	1 953	560	126	48	194	271	454	927	60	48
Berks	17 121	1.1	41 403	1 006	7 694	1 592	622	1 171	2 935	3 495	11 079	655	622
Blair	4 821	1.3	38 169	1 413	2 313	515	201	275	861	1 271	3 304	206	201
Bradford	2 395	-0.4	38 430	1 385	1 083	224	85	175	405	543	1 567	97	85
Bucks	36 348	0.9	57 973	135	12 792	2 207	1 029	3 141	6 713	4 934	19 170	1 122	1 029
Butler	9 180	1.7	49 496	387	4 196	815	334	487	1 692	1 499	5 832	346	334
Cambria	5 082	-0.1	36 173	1 716	2 078	477	173	301	826	1 517	3 029	199	173
Cameron	186	3.3	38 105	1 420	80	19	7	10	38	59	116	8	7
Carbon	2 375	2.9	36 660	1 644	581	147	50	275	385	598	1 053	68	50
Centre	6 510	2.3	41 894	948	3 313	1 276	253	474	1 238	896	5 315	266	253
Chester	33 694	1.4	66 136	65	16 672	2 501	1 200	3 724	6 476	3 358	24 097	1 341	1 200
Clarion	1 448	1.4	36 987	1 588	488	140	41	135	275	382	804	49	41
Clearfield	2 841	0.9	34 999	1 894	1 134	265	96	203	457	783	1 699	109	96
Clinton	1 418	1.6	35 491	1 822	543	144	45	114	209	336	846	52	45
Columbia	2 259	1.0	33 815	2 123	921	239	79	176	409	558	1 415	87	79
Crawford	3 032	1.5	34 702	1 950	1 155	264	99	250	479	831	1 767	112	99
Cumberland	11 399	1.8	47 258	533	6 304	1 203	512	698	2 248	1 809	8 717	504	512
Dauphin	12 299	2.8	45 396	663	9 293	2 052	719	837	2 034	2 295	12 901	716	719
Delaware	30 328	0.9	53 966	236	12 382	2 100	948	1 868	5 541	4 836	17 298	1 020	948
Elk	1 253	0.9	39 790	1 192	582	133	51	67	217	318	833	52	51
Erie	10 575	0.8	37 729	1 472	5 172	1 135	426	544	1 825	2 579	7 277	438	426
Fayette	4 820	1.4	35 704	1 799	1 488	354	129	339	749	1 504	2 310	160	129
Forest	201	2.1	26 290	3 019	94	33	8	16	44	63	150	9	8
Franklin	5 684	1.6	37 377	1 527	2 286	493	196	345	1 114	1 190	3 319	202	196
Fulton	518	1.5	35 308	1 857	203	46	17	38	92	131	304	19	17
Greene	1 582	2.1	41 820	955	913	171	69	102	211	361	1 255	76	69
Huntingdon	1 471	1.2	32 200	2 387	461	126	39	78	245	405	704	47	39
Indiana	3 424	0.9	39 018	1 297	1 526	382	119	409	536	763	2 435	140	119
Jefferson	1 571	0.2	34 939	1 907	583	129	50	118	269	447	880	58	50
Juniata	836	2.4	33 754	2 138	208	47	18	122	142	199	396	24	18
Lackawanna	8 863	1.0	41 428	1 003	3 864	801	327	587	1 659	2 156	5 580	344	327
Lancaster	21 775	1.9	41 116	1 039	9 658	1 806	791	2 206	4 273	3 942	14 462	844	791
Lawrence	3 295	0.6	36 888	1 612	1 185	256	99	229	590	942	1 768	118	99
Lebanon	5 690	1.4	41 994	939	1 968	459	163	341	989	1 113	2 931	178	163
Lehigh	15 587	1.7	43 897	767	9 172	1 624	712	1 124	2 787	2 962	12 633	740	712
Luzerne	12 683	0.9	39 621	1 215	5 684	1 216	484	750	2 210	3 118	8 134	502	484
Lycoming	4 534	0.5	38 832	1 315	2 260	495	184	249	826	994	3 189	194	184
McKean	1 612	-0.9	37 501	1 506	668	162	55	140	251	416	1 025	63	55
Mercer	4 121	0.8	35 774	1 787	1 886	401	157	185	709	1 164	2 630	170	157
Mifflin	1 543	2.3	33 109	2 238	572	130	49	140	228	448	890	58	49
Monroe	5 671	1.0	33 930	2 095	2 275	549	191	277	889	1 241	3 292	199	191
Montgomery	56 907	1.1	70 050	49	31 797	4 615	2 383	6 489	11 384	6 157	45 285	2 543	2 383
Montour	890	3.1	48 013	480	1 081	208	67	151	143	158	1 508	83	67
Northampton	13 010	1.6	43 398	811	4 858	970	404	583	2 324	2 512	6 815	424	404
Northumberland	3 525	1.9	37 468	1 512	1 045	252	90	167	613	914	1 553	105	90
Perry	1 742	1.0	38 224	1 407	254	71	21	109	262	364	456	32	21
Philadelphia	65 473	2.3	42 155	922	40 176	7 036	3 109	9 901	8 557	16 751	60 221	3 379	3 109
Pike	2 218	0.6	39 188	1 265	356	96	31	122	378	475	605	44	31

1. Based on the resident population estimated as of July 1 of the year shown.

STATE County	Earnings, 2013 (cont.): Percent by selected industries: Farm	Mining	Construction	Manu-facturing	Infor-mation: professional, scientific, technical services	Retail trade	Finance, insur-ance, real estate and leasing	Health care and social assistance	Govern-ment	Social Security beneficiaries, December 2013: Number	Rate[1]	Supple-mental Security Income recipients, December 2013	Housing units, 2014: Total	Percent change, 2010–2014
	75	76	77	78	79	80	81	82	83	84	85	86	87	88
OREGON—Cont'd														
Morrow	37.4	0.1	2.5	20.5	D	1.4	1.1	1.6	11.6	2 025	180	212	4 447	0.1
Multnomah	0.1	D	5.5	7.3	14.6	5.1	8.2	11.3	17.4	112 315	147	20 121	330 768	1.8
Polk	5.0	D	5.5	10.4	D	5.3	2.6	12.0	32.5	16 175	211	1 385	30 607	1.0
Sherman	37.5	0.0	D	D	D	D	D	0.6	33.2	505	294	31	906	-1.3
Tillamook	8.5	D	6.3	13.3	2.9	7.4	3.2	10.7	23.7	7 580	299	508	18 463	0.6
Umatilla	8.9	0.1	4.1	8.5	3.6	6.6	2.6	10.2	25.1	13 600	177	1 693	29 700	0.0
Union	5.8	0.0	4.6	12.9	3.6	8.7	3.0	15.5	24.6	5 935	232	598	11 477	-0.1
Wallowa	12.7	0.0	6.3	4.1	3.8	7.7	5.3	7.3	28.4	2 285	336	156	4 075	-0.8
Wasco	10.2	D	4.4	5.4	7.2	10.4	2.6	20.1	22.3	6 020	236	644	11 390	-0.8
Washington	0.5	0.1	5.2	25.9	10.1	5.7	6.1	8.1	7.3	76 320	137	6 785	218 881	3.0
Wheeler	27.2	0.0	D	D	D	D	D	D	32.0	485	347	30	888	-0.8
Yamhill	4.4	D	5.9	23.4	4.4	7.0	3.9	12.7	15.4	19 135	190	1 498	37 522	1.1
PENNSYLVANIA	0.4	1.3	5.7	10.3	13.3	5.7	8.3	13.9	14.0	2 697 111	211	379 194	5 590 373	0.4
Adams	2.0	D	7.8	19.4	5.3	7.2	3.8	D	16.2	22 915	226	1 177	41 281	1.1
Allegheny	0.0	2.2	5.4	6.1	15.1	5.0	10.7	14.2	9.8	263 685	214	36 537	589 709	0.1
Armstrong	-0.2	17.4	6.1	11.7	4.6	7.4	3.0	14.2	15.3	17 785	261	2 230	32 384	-0.4
Beaver	-0.2	0.9	5.0	16.4	7.6	7.5	3.1	14.9	16.9	43 570	256	5 058	78 381	0.2
Bedford	3.8	D	12.8	11.7	D	9.3	2.8	8.1	15.3	13 365	272	1 375	24 013	0.2
Berks	0.8	0.1	6.0	19.5	7.4	7.6	4.9	13.5	14.4	83 670	202	10 609	164 822	0.0
Blair	0.7	D	4.9	12.8	6.3	8.4	3.1	19.9	16.7	29 860	236	4 916	56 064	-0.4
Bradford	1.3	9.6	4.5	16.7	4.1	6.3	5.0	19.9	13.4	15 695	252	1 906	30 129	0.5
Bucks	0.0	0.2	10.0	11.5	13.2	7.7	6.5	13.2	10.7	126 265	202	7 259	246 842	0.4
Butler	0.0	1.5	6.0	16.8	8.1	7.1	4.5	9.6	14.6	40 210	217	3 406	80 358	2.8
Cambria	0.8	1.4	4.2	7.8	8.1	7.8	5.8	22.0	18.1	37 975	273	5 171	65 240	-0.6
Cameron	0.8	D	2.0	48.2	D	2.8	D	4.8	21.6	1 540	315	142	4 400	-1.2
Carbon	0.1	0.2	4.9	10.7	21.5	7.4	3.3	15.7	16.6	16 695	258	1 393	34 398	0.3
Centre	0.0	0.9	4.4	5.5	8.3	5.4	3.8	9.6	50.3	22 880	145	1 514	65 107	2.9
Chester	0.7	0.4	4.9	7.8	20.9	5.6	15.7	9.0	8.3	84 310	165	4 241	195 644	1.7
Clarion	0.9	8.7	6.5	10.1	3.4	7.9	3.3	13.9	27.7	9 585	245	1 272	19 879	-0.4
Clearfield	-0.1	4.3	4.2	9.0	3.6	8.4	3.5	19.9	19.0	20 600	252	2 720	38 565	-0.2
Clinton	1.3	2.9	7.4	23.2	D	6.5	2.3	D	24.3	8 920	224	1 116	18 993	-0.5
Columbia	0.3	0.1	6.5	20.6	5.5	8.5	3.3	12.6	22.7	15 170	226	1 478	29 595	0.3
Crawford	2.0	1.4	4.3	25.0	4.0	7.2	3.1	16.4	16.3	21 910	251	3 115	44 373	-0.7
Cumberland	0.5	D	4.2	6.0	11.2	6.1	10.3	12.7	17.2	48 770	202	2 641	102 907	2.9
Dauphin	0.2	0.1	4.3	7.8	7.7	4.0	8.6	14.7	25.4	54 020	199	7 623	121 802	1.2
Delaware	0.0	D	6.1	9.6	11.3	5.6	11.3	13.4	11.7	103 760	185	12 612	221 921	-0.4
Elk	0.6	1.1	4.0	47.0	2.5	5.1	2.2	12.1	10.4	8 680	276	750	17 521	-0.4
Erie	0.4	0.2	4.1	22.0	4.9	6.9	7.5	17.1	16.6	60 935	218	11 500	119 816	0.6
Fayette	0.1	4.4	7.8	9.4	4.7	9.3	2.6	15.7	19.6	37 255	276	8 823	62 878	0.2
Forest	4.5	8.8	D	D	D	2.0	D	12.1	52.7	1 785	235	167	8 675	-1.0
Franklin	2.3	0.1	4.7	18.9	4.9	7.1	3.2	15.1	18.6	34 515	227	2 729	64 125	1.4
Fulton	1.4	D	10.4	39.1	D	4.2	2.2	10.5	14.9	3 810	259	389	7 106	-0.2
Greene	-0.5	D	8.6	1.6	3.9	4.8	2.6	D	15.1	8 735	231	1 863	16 421	-0.2
Huntingdon	1.2	D	6.4	10.9	2.6	6.5	4.2	D	30.6	11 035	241	1 248	22 397	0.1
Indiana	1.1	15.3	7.5	5.3	3.3	7.1	3.4	9.3	21.3	19 555	222	2 549	38 618	1.0
Jefferson	0.3	10.2	4.9	23.6	3.9	6.6	2.5	15.1	14.4	11 670	259	1 477	22 418	-0.1
Juniata	8.5	D	10.9	26.5	D	6.7	3.7	D	12.1	5 545	224	498	11 005	0.2
Lackawanna	0.1	0.3	5.4	10.3	8.1	8.4	7.5	17.9	14.2	53 245	249	6 787	96 640	-0.2
Lancaster	2.2	0.2	10.4	16.5	7.3	7.2	6.2	13.8	10.2	105 865	200	10 166	206 404	1.7
Lawrence	0.7	D	11.8	14.8	5.1	6.8	5.9	15.1	14.9	23 860	267	3 549	40 745	-0.6
Lebanon	2.4	0.0	4.9	17.9	5.4	7.5	2.9	13.3	20.8	30 850	227	2 490	56 209	1.1
Lehigh	0.1	D	4.6	10.0	7.6	5.6	5.4	20.2	10.1	73 190	206	10 716	143 377	0.5
Luzerne	0.0	0.5	4.8	11.5	7.1	7.6	6.0	14.8	16.2	78 445	245	10 227	148 243	-0.3
Lycoming	0.4	6.8	6.0	16.5	5.1	6.6	4.5	13.8	18.6	26 940	231	3 407	52 598	0.2
McKean	-0.2	16.8	4.6	21.9	2.7	5.4	2.1	12.3	16.5	11 125	260	1 748	21 042	-0.9
Mercer	0.7	1.9	4.1	21.4	D	8.2	5.8	18.3	13.8	30 575	265	4 272	51 615	-0.2
Mifflin	2.2	0.0	6.2	26.4	2.5	8.9	3.4	16.3	13.3	12 160	260	1 644	21 518	-0.1
Monroe	0.0	0.1	4.3	14.6	4.4	8.5	3.3	11.9	28.3	33 830	202	3 019	80 685	0.4
Montgomery	0.0	0.1	7.5	9.6	21.3	5.0	12.9	12.2	6.9	150 500	185	8 387	327 451	0.5
Montour	0.7	D	3.4	1.9	4.8	2.1	2.0	D	6.6	4 385	237	474	8 034	0.9
Northampton	0.3	0.1	5.5	15.1	8.5	6.7	6.8	10.2	16.0	65 955	220	6 048	121 143	0.6
Northumberland	2.3	0.8	5.7	17.9	4.0	6.5	3.0	12.4	18.7	24 200	257	2 962	44 937	-0.4
Perry	8.8	D	12.1	5.4	3.6	8.7	4.6	7.8	26.5	9 810	215	777	20 497	0.4
Philadelphia	0.0	0.0	1.9	3.0	23.4	3.0	9.0	15.7	16.6	255 215	161	112 075	670 401	0.0
Pike	0.0	0.5	7.0	1.7	7.7	10.1	4.6	8.3	31.4	14 075	249	757	38 538	0.5

1. Per 1,000 resident population estimated as of July 1 of the year shown.

STATE County	Housing units, 2009–2013: Occupied units: Total	Owner-occupied: Percent	Owner-occupied: Median value[1]	Median owner cost as a percent of income: With a mortgage	Median owner cost as a percent of income: Without a mortgage[2]	Renter-occupied: Median rent[3]	Renter-occupied: Median rent as a percent of income[2]	Substandard units[4] (percent)	Civilian labor force, 2014: Total	Civilian labor force, 2014: Percent change, 2013–2014	Unemployment: Total	Unemployment: Rate[5]	Civilian employment,[6] 2009–2013: Total	Percent: Management, business, science and arts	Percent: Construction, production, and maintenance occupations
	89	90	91	92	93	94	95	96	97	98	99	100	101	102	103
OREGON—Cont'd															
Morrow	3 741	73.2	119 800	20.9	10.7	665	32.1	3.7	5 557	0.3	393	7.1	4 770	24.9	44.0
Multnomah	305 939	54.2	271 600	26.2	14.3	913	32.5	2.9	420 520	2.0	25 468	6.1	377 598	42.3	17.0
Polk	28 239	65.4	217 400	25.2	12.2	793	30.9	2.3	35 359	2.1	2 459	7.0	31 829	35.6	21.1
Sherman	827	64.9	135 400	22.0	11.9	752	26.8	1.8	878	1.7	66	7.5	780	38.1	26.7
Tillamook	10 236	69.9	226 500	28.1	12.5	771	29.9	5.7	11 167	2.3	781	7.0	10 374	27.1	30.4
Umatilla	26 744	63.8	142 700	21.8	10.9	668	26.9	2.7	35 389	0.4	2 801	7.9	32 047	26.6	32.4
Union	10 235	63.4	156 600	21.8	11.6	664	33.3	1.5	11 743	-0.1	872	7.4	10 800	30.4	23.5
Wallowa	2 996	73.9	199 900	24.7	14.1	674	30.7	2.5	3 227	0.2	328	10.2	2 843	37.5	21.2
Wasco	9 612	64.9	181 600	24.8	12.4	757	33.2	3.3	13 620	-0.7	912	6.7	10 661	27.5	28.3
Washington	201 771	61.0	282 400	25.0	12.1	976	29.5	2.2	293 632	2.2	16 805	5.7	263 823	43.2	16.9
Wheeler	625	72.0	123 700	25.6	12.7	556	21.9	2.8	735	0.1	47	6.4	571	36.3	30.5
Yamhill	34 138	68.8	224 900	26.6	12.6	902	32.0	2.1	50 300	1.8	3 308	6.6	44 217	31.2	27.2
PENNSYLVANIA	4 958 427	69.8	164 700	23.1	13.6	813	30.1	1.7	6 378 495	-1.0	369 962	5.8	5 914 876	36.2	21.8
Adams	38 141	76.7	198 200	24.6	13.1	820	29.7	1.0	54 997	-0.6	2 472	4.5	51 121	29.3	31.6
Allegheny	526 004	65.5	122 400	20.7	13.3	751	28.7	1.3	644 822	-1.0	34 303	5.3	600 384	42.6	14.8
Armstrong	28 525	76.5	94 100	20.6	12.4	588	27.6	1.2	33 219	-1.3	2 136	6.4	30 794	26.3	32.9
Beaver	70 867	73.4	115 400	21.2	13.3	623	28.4	1.9	86 031	-0.6	5 538	6.4	79 501	32.3	24.1
Bedford	20 198	79.8	120 200	22.2	12.7	593	27.9	2.1	24 139	-2.4	1 577	6.5	22 152	24.5	35.3
Berks	153 897	72.0	170 600	24.1	14.9	832	31.6	1.1	210 590	-0.4	11 525	5.5	194 775	31.2	27.4
Blair	51 433	72.4	106 500	20.1	12.5	615	29.0	2.7	60 764	-1.2	3 420	5.6	57 741	30.2	24.8
Bradford	24 213	74.9	119 900	21.5	12.5	641	27.7	1.2	31 489	-1.2	1 679	5.3	27 154	28.7	33.7
Bucks	230 366	78.0	309 900	25.3	15.1	1 107	31.0	1.2	335 628	-0.5	17 472	5.2	318 687	41.7	18.0
Butler	73 213	76.8	169 700	21.3	12.0	739	29.0	0.8	96 927	-1.0	4 882	5.0	90 214	35.4	22.7
Cambria	58 208	73.9	87 100	20.0	13.4	550	27.7	0.4	62 959	-2.6	4 363	6.9	59 839	31.6	24.9
Cameron	2 144	71.5	69 500	20.4	12.2	493	24.8	1.2	2 280	-3.3	160	7.0	2 238	26.6	41.4
Carbon	25 903	78.9	146 700	25.5	14.2	757	31.4	3.3	31 712	-1.6	2 205	7.0	28 748	26.0	30.5
Centre	57 197	59.6	192 600	22.0	11.6	872	35.7	1.7	77 752	-0.3	3 219	4.1	72 760	43.4	17.0
Chester	184 788	75.7	325 200	23.8	13.9	1 166	28.9	2.1	272 270	-0.4	11 245	4.1	256 131	47.6	15.2
Clarion	15 776	70.9	106 200	19.8	11.2	591	32.3	1.4	18 327	-1.8	1 141	6.2	17 225	28.8	29.4
Clearfield	32 192	76.8	85 100	22.0	14.0	580	29.1	1.6	36 576	-3.1	2 580	7.1	34 675	25.9	32.0
Clinton	15 067	71.7	110 900	22.4	14.7	637	28.7	1.2	18 875	-2.1	1 358	7.2	17 102	24.2	31.6
Columbia	26 225	69.6	135 000	21.5	13.9	679	31.3	3.0	34 175	-3.3	2 057	6.0	31 011	30.1	28.3
Crawford	34 831	73.7	102 700	22.6	13.2	590	27.9	1.4	41 128	-1.5	2 354	5.7	37 596	29.7	30.4
Cumberland	95 286	71.1	184 500	22.1	12.2	854	27.1	1.7	125 124	-0.5	5 570	4.5	118 172	39.2	18.9
Dauphin	108 831	64.4	158 800	22.3	12.4	839	27.8	1.4	139 418	-0.8	7 371	5.3	131 933	38.1	18.5
Delaware	204 771	70.6	234 100	24.6	15.1	964	32.4	0.5	290 026	-0.2	15 933	5.5	265 554	42.0	16.2
Elk	13 478	80.3	92 100	19.6	12.1	556	26.6	1.7	16 311	-0.9	828	5.1	14 835	22.3	43.1
Erie	109 675	67.5	115 100	21.2	12.4	660	31.4	1.8	134 343	-1.2	8 231	6.1	127 586	32.8	24.0
Fayette	54 363	72.8	84 200	20.9	12.8	570	27.5	2.0	58 560	-1.8	4 461	7.6	53 743	25.8	29.5
Forest	2 001	83.1	83 600	23.5	11.6	501	27.5	1.9	1 927	-2.4	153	7.9	1 788	20.6	26.2
Franklin	58 273	73.0	177 500	23.7	12.2	772	28.0	2.1	76 085	-0.6	4 023	5.3	69 682	32.1	28.5
Fulton	5 965	77.4	159 300	24.0	11.6	611	23.9	1.1	7 248	-1.9	493	6.8	6 508	23.5	37.1
Greene	14 417	73.0	89 400	18.8	11.6	597	31.4	1.9	18 395	-1.9	1 002	5.4	15 108	28.5	31.2
Huntingdon	17 193	76.5	115 000	21.8	12.6	543	25.7	3.0	19 734	-2.8	1 526	7.7	18 677	28.4	31.5
Indiana	34 310	71.6	103 000	20.5	12.0	656	32.3	2.3	43 193	-2.0	2 549	5.9	39 071	28.2	29.4
Jefferson	18 503	74.5	86 800	21.1	11.5	566	27.3	2.4	20 742	-1.6	1 306	6.3	19 566	24.4	36.0
Juniata	9 248	76.4	138 200	23.3	12.1	571	25.2	1.2	11 764	-2.2	655	5.6	11 105	25.1	39.9
Lackawanna	85 769	66.8	144 100	23.3	15.0	679	27.8	2.0	106 676	-0.9	6 988	6.6	98 620	34.3	22.0
Lancaster	194 082	69.5	188 200	23.9	12.8	875	31.0	1.8	270 239	0.1	12 349	4.6	252 661	32.3	27.6
Lawrence	36 823	75.3	96 700	21.9	13.6	621	30.9	2.0	42 610	-1.0	2 646	6.2	39 853	30.0	26.7
Lebanon	52 023	72.0	164 300	22.9	12.7	739	27.7	2.0	70 020	-1.0	3 421	4.9	64 365	30.2	27.4
Lehigh	133 289	67.5	196 600	24.4	14.2	914	32.6	1.4	181 598	-0.9	10 967	6.0	164 359	35.8	22.1
Luzerne	130 880	67.8	121 000	22.3	14.6	665	29.1	1.8	158 634	-1.3	11 508	7.3	145 639	30.5	24.9
Lycoming	46 046	70.0	131 000	22.9	14.0	675	28.7	0.9	61 303	-0.9	3 721	6.1	53 771	29.0	28.6
McKean	17 450	73.2	72 700	19.8	12.0	599	31.0	1.9	19 264	-2.0	1 208	6.3	17 840	29.0	31.3
Mercer	46 187	74.5	104 600	21.7	12.7	613	29.4	3.8	52 892	-1.7	3 140	5.9	49 167	30.3	25.9
Mifflin	18 711	73.6	95 700	23.4	13.9	597	27.4	1.8	21 032	-1.5	1 312	6.2	19 137	25.0	36.0
Monroe	58 875	80.0	191 800	28.6	16.5	990	33.6	1.2	79 673	-2.4	5 919	7.4	75 532	33.7	22.0
Montgomery	307 488	73.2	292 600	23.8	14.2	1 128	29.0	1.3	434 429	-0.3	20 051	4.6	411 991	48.5	14.2
Montour	7 233	73.8	153 200	20.5	12.5	703	25.3	2.4	9 232	-2.6	424	4.6	8 398	38.8	22.6
Northampton	112 189	73.1	212 100	24.6	15.0	923	31.0	1.3	154 841	-0.6	9 149	5.9	140 891	34.3	23.5
Northumberland	39 348	71.3	98 200	21.2	13.5	589	27.3	2.2	43 945	-1.7	2 894	6.6	41 105	26.7	30.9
Perry	18 173	79.5	158 400	23.4	12.0	704	24.7	3.0	24 040	-1.1	1 238	5.1	22 842	28.0	31.3
Philadelphia	580 017	53.3	142 500	25.4	15.3	893	34.5	1.2	689 205	-1.3	55 169	8.0	619 094	35.5	16.6
Pike	21 581	84.2	193 100	26.8	14.4	1 071	36.9	1.9	25 390	-1.7	1 863	7.3	24 011	31.5	23.1

1. Specified owner-occupied units. 2. A value of 10.0 represents 10 percent or less; a value of 50.0 represents 50 percent or more. 3. Specified renter-occupied units.
4. Overcrowded or lacking complete plumbing facilities. 5. Percent of civilian labor force. 6. Persons 16 years old and over.

Table B. States and Counties — **Nonfarm Employment and Agriculture**

STATE County	Private nonfarm establishments, employment and payroll, 2013: Number of establish-ments	Employment: Total	Employment: Health care and social assistance	Employment: Manufac-turing	Employment: Retail trade	Employment: Finance and insurance	Employment: Professional, scientific, and technical services	Annual payroll: Total (mil dol)	Annual payroll: Average per employee (dollars)	Agriculture, 2012: Farms: Number	Farms: Percent with: Fewer than 50 acres	Farms: Percent with: 500 acres or more	Farm operators whose principal occu-pation is farming (percent)
	104	105	106	107	108	109	110	111	112	113	114	115	116
OREGON—Cont'd													
Morrow	179	2 725	D	1 490	71	D	7	122	44 793	401	27.7	51.9	63.1
Multnomah	25 361	390 372	58 621	32 549	39 078	19 418	30 676	19 076	48 865	598	84.8	1.7	44.5
Polk	1 336	12 758	2 515	1 520	1 489	256	401	387	30 346	1 143	66.0	5.2	52.2
Sherman	52	426	D	NA	D	D	D	14	34 016	186	5.4	76.3	73.7
Tillamook	704	6 371	D	1 270	1 046	152	118	200	31 435	280	45.4	3.2	68.2
Umatilla	1 533	21 299	3 057	2 651	2 959	490	817	692	32 508	1 603	49.0	25.0	49.0
Union	750	6 991	1 391	1 206	1 348	218	225	224	32 015	829	46.4	18.2	46.9
Wallowa	356	1 535	380	82	288	D	84	49	32 021	522	37.0	27.4	47.9
Wasco	704	7 080	1 755	361	1 469	209	261	231	32 630	670	39.4	24.2	52.1
Washington	14 380	236 283	25 657	28 047	29 090	11 769	19 744	13 726	58 090	1 643	74.4	3.0	44.7
Wheeler	29	150	D	NA	NA	D	NA	3	18 453	153	10.5	51.0	58.8
Yamhill	2 315	25 887	4 305	5 841	3 418	683	624	946	36 563	2 028	73.7	3.8	47.0
PENNSYLVANIA	297 692	5 180 805	960 789	539 575	655 853	265 897	320 473	237 620	45 866	59 309	39.3	4.1	51.7
Adams	1 902	27 938	4 428	5 798	3 280	532	533	930	33 277	1 188	48.2	6.3	50.9
Allegheny	33 583	696 023	131 104	36 833	74 245	47 734	57 345	34 733	49 903	428	50.7	0.9	41.6
Armstrong	1 339	14 471	3 453	1 530	2 263	672	391	481	33 265	783	25.0	6.1	42.0
Beaver	3 430	49 161	10 053	7 533	7 144	896	2 522	1 829	37 201	646	45.2	1.9	47.5
Bedford	1 043	13 299	1 736	2 144	2 295	327	204	422	31 751	1 210	25.0	6.5	50.6
Berks	8 246	148 933	25 075	29 883	20 780	5 993	6 703	6 331	42 508	2 039	47.8	3.5	61.4
Blair	3 212	52 021	12 007	6 725	8 913	1 710	1 703	1 812	34 827	525	35.8	5.9	58.5
Bradford	1 394	19 556	4 751	3 431	2 876	691	568	764	39 086	1 629	25.8	7.6	45.8
Bucks	18 930	245 793	38 508	25 212	37 769	8 921	19 197	10 719	43 611	827	71.1	2.7	51.3
Butler	4 766	79 977	12 558	12 389	11 362	2 204	6 665	3 464	43 311	1 061	39.9	4.1	45.6
Cambria	3 337	48 133	12 313	4 595	7 165	2 143	2 532	1 607	33 394	551	33.4	5.6	37.4
Cameron	113	1 579	204	924	145	D	D	53	33 327	36	25.0	11.1	50.0
Carbon	1 134	13 291	3 040	1 295	2 126	309	201	373	28 050	195	46.2	2.6	37.4
Centre	3 252	44 783	8 227	3 990	8 120	1 312	3 128	1 556	34 737	1 192	40.1	4.8	57.4
Chester	13 950	239 228	33 318	15 124	28 162	24 199	22 891	14 906	62 309	1 730	57.1	2.5	60.7
Clarion	937	10 918	2 815	1 449	1 770	287	270	321	29 369	652	22.1	6.3	39.3
Clearfield	2 004	26 252	5 792	2 759	4 930	626	597	873	33 236	533	34.3	4.3	45.0
Clinton	759	10 950	1 272	D	1 785	D	228	368	33 617	469	37.1	3.8	51.0
Columbia	1 373	22 851	3 925	5 179	3 424	577	932	793	34 694	944	37.3	4.6	39.8
Crawford	2 031	27 581	5 194	7 145	3 815	509	857	873	31 645	1 351	31.1	6.0	51.5
Cumberland	5 733	114 225	15 612	7 546	15 994	9 258	7 225	4 768	41 743	1 415	47.0	3.5	53.1
Dauphin	6 728	142 209	32 969	7 003	15 531	9 853	6 939	6 450	45 357	811	49.0	2.7	44.9
Delaware	12 628	210 571	38 799	13 340	24 853	13 609	12 140	11 493	54 581	76	64.5	0.0	48.7
Elk	881	13 828	1 925	6 582	1 419	D	296	502	36 280	271	45.4	1.5	33.6
Erie	6 229	113 617	24 201	21 565	16 143	D	3 649	4 096	36 047	1 422	41.2	4.1	48.7
Fayette	2 679	35 252	7 348	3 137	6 209	612	1 028	1 118	31 719	941	34.0	3.4	47.8
Forest	101	1 068	D	210	100	D	D	33	31 224	56	25.0	3.6	41.1
Franklin	3 022	47 802	7 710	8 448	7 317	1 143	1 768	1 709	35 749	1 596	35.9	6.3	60.8
Fulton	274	D	D	D	387	81	D	D	D	656	22.6	5.2	38.6
Greene	756	14 579	1 415	356	2 505	313	218	719	49 324	876	27.2	3.3	40.4
Huntingdon	821	9 809	1 848	1 461	1 407	437	269	293	29 895	833	25.1	7.1	45.9
Indiana	1 902	25 453	3 100	2 265	5 145	D	963	989	38 868	1 166	38.0	3.9	50.2
Jefferson	1 159	13 465	2 881	3 483	1 766	261	423	448	33 277	577	25.0	5.7	51.5
Juniata	460	5 385	731	1 963	572	241	53	154	28 595	737	42.3	3.0	47.6
Lackawanna	5 402	96 226	22 209	8 789	13 394	5 401	5 097	3 215	33 409	303	25.1	1.3	43.6
Lancaster	12 266	213 446	35 200	33 732	30 036	7 022	9 925	8 334	39 047	5 657	44.1	1.3	72.2
Lawrence	1 975	26 783	6 873	3 853	3 400	1 242	772	900	33 596	659	33.4	3.6	50.4
Lebanon	2 634	43 681	8 241	8 163	6 889	873	1 112	1 520	34 800	1 219	48.2	2.3	58.9
Lehigh	8 437	165 363	37 185	16 438	21 154	6 142	6 301	7 868	47 581	486	58.8	5.8	56.2
Luzerne	7 175	129 227	24 498	17 010	18 492	4 918	6 405	4 696	36 341	556	38.8	3.6	42.3
Lycoming	2 850	46 696	8 560	7 834	7 502	1 432	1 630	1 684	36 053	1 207	32.4	3.7	44.0
McKean	1 062	14 014	2 655	3 514	1 750	D	211	515	36 720	290	37.2	3.1	36.9
Mercer	2 806	45 046	10 742	7 804	7 320	1 414	811	1 472	32 688	1 185	32.3	4.1	45.1
Mifflin	948	13 983	3 235	D	2 064	350	157	477	34 124	808	35.4	2.1	49.0
Monroe	3 360	44 388	6 627	D	8 954	988	1 276	1 546	34 822	283	53.0	2.5	55.1
Montgomery	25 988	480 721	75 949	38 767	58 016	34 785	44 176	27 527	57 262	596	75.2	1.0	55.0
Montour	458	14 458	7 334	D	692	D	482	930	64 328	459	43.1	1.5	45.3
Northampton	6 208	96 900	12 678	10 864	13 551	4 531	4 301	3 907	40 319	498	62.9	6.0	50.6
Northumberland	1 657	23 134	5 511	3 817	3 051	590	482	797	34 437	847	43.0	6.5	54.7
Perry	777	6 249	1 078	632	1 128	255	212	160	25 584	889	32.6	4.8	50.6
Philadelphia	27 239	582 474	144 014	21 177	50 039	29 723	45 332	31 026	53 267	22	81.8	0.0	45.5
Pike	888	7 756	929	170	1 905	D	211	197	25 360	50	46.0	14.0	34.0

STATE County	Agriculture, 2012 (cont.) — Land in farms: Acreage (1,000)	Land in farms: Percent change, 2007–2012	Land in farms: Acres: Average size of farm	Land in farms: Acres: Total irrigated (1,000)	Land in farms: Acres: Total cropland (1,000)	Value of land and buildings (dollars): Average per farm	Value of land and buildings (dollars): Average per acre	Value of machinery and equipment, average per farm (dollars)	Value of products sold: Total (mil dol)	Value of products sold: Average per farm (dollars)	Value of products sold: Percent from: Crops	Value of products sold: Percent from: Livestock and poultry products	Percent of farms with sales of: $10,000 or more	Percent of farms with sales of: $100,000 or more	Government payments: Total ($1,000)	Government payments: Percent of farms
	117	118	119	120	121	122	123	124	125	126	127	128	129	130	131	132
OREGON—Cont'd																
Morrow	1 165	5.5	2 906	65.6	486.4	2 762 863	951	302 516	568.1	1 416 736	34.3	65.7	50.4	34.9	11 900	61.1
Multnomah	30	5.2	50	4.6	17.4	598 075	11 928	72 756	68.9	115 278	D	D	30.1	9.5	242	6.0
Polk	145	-13.1	127	20.4	101.0	777 650	6 141	85 558	149.8	131 099	77.6	22.4	33.3	12.8	912	16.1
Sherman	514	-0.1	2 762	2.2	365.1	1 645 672	596	308 538	54.5	292 914	D	D	61.8	44.6	8 820	93.5
Tillamook	37	-3.3	131	7.1	14.5	817 064	6 259	115 754	117.1	418 361	2.6	97.4	53.6	38.6	1 553	34.3
Umatilla	1 308	-9.6	816	147.8	769.7	1 332 795	1 633	163 995	423.3	264 089	87.9	12.1	42.1	22.2	18 381	40.8
Union	412	-15.6	497	49.0	119.2	768 875	1 548	101 823	68.4	82 473	75.0	25.0	39.0	12.2	2 713	30.0
Wallowa	453	-14.3	867	38.0	88.5	1 094 554	1 263	101 395	46.6	89 310	47.5	52.5	45.8	20.5	2 746	38.5
Wasco	1 427	50.3	2 130	50.6	210.0	1 605 100	753	118 193	89.8	134 005	88.7	11.3	41.3	18.4	6 871	39.3
Washington	136	6.1	83	20.3	82.0	774 189	9 371	81 491	238.0	144 840	94.7	5.3	38.5	12.8	1 544	15.0
Wheeler	649	-14.3	4 242	10.4	24.8	2 749 542	648	97 634	14.2	92 536	22.9	77.1	45.1	19.6	748	26.1
Yamhill	177	-1.9	87	22.1	108.5	801 316	9 162	76 411	280.9	138 487	78.9	21.1	32.8	10.8	2 466	16.2
PENNSYLVANIA	7 704	-1.3	130	39.0	4 546.1	704 712	5 425	89 730	7 400.8	124 783	37.6	62.4	48.1	19.9	86 359	27.0
Adams	171	-1.9	144	2.2	125.6	898 623	6 232	113 572	201.7	169 817	56.5	43.5	48.6	19.2	1 818	28.5
Allegheny	35	-8.4	81	0.2	14.1	428 841	5 269	53 269	10.4	24 292	84.2	15.8	31.3	5.1	41	7.9
Armstrong	129	5.6	165	0.2	66.6	474 018	2 875	83 686	35.9	45 800	56.3	43.7	42.1	9.2	924	24.8
Beaver	56	-16.8	86	0.2	28.5	415 333	4 809	67 373	20.9	32 373	52.0	48.0	32.8	6.0	500	16.1
Bedford	210	-0.6	173	0.1	104.3	640 069	3 692	95 976	122.8	101 504	29.7	70.3	48.1	21.7	1 863	29.4
Berks	234	5.2	115	1.6	182.3	1 015 554	8 859	120 253	528.7	259 299	42.6	57.4	58.5	30.2	3 646	28.3
Blair	90	3.1	172	0.3	63.3	783 611	4 565	106 916	107.7	205 145	16.2	83.8	54.1	29.0	1 416	32.6
Bradford	308	15.5	189	0.2	163.3	700 259	3 704	89 510	128.8	79 063	22.6	77.4	43.1	15.3	6 994	43.0
Bucks	64	-15.6	77	0.8	48.0	950 716	12 280	89 245	62.4	75 475	75.1	24.9	41.0	13.7	579	13.7
Butler	136	4.9	128	0.6	77.1	609 486	4 747	89 819	52.9	49 863	69.6	30.4	41.3	10.0	1 502	26.6
Cambria	77	-12.6	140	0.1	45.4	457 327	3 277	82 508	32.6	59 240	55.5	44.5	42.3	8.5	775	31.9
Cameron	6	22.1	173	0.0	1.6	337 472	1 955	55 528	0.7	19 222	45.4	54.6	44.4	0.0	55	38.9
Carbon	21	5.6	109	0.2	13.4	710 523	6 547	99 005	9.3	47 892	91.4	8.6	46.7	8.2	191	42.1
Centre	162	9.1	136	1.1	84.9	736 207	5 416	86 739	91.6	76 830	34.3	65.7	47.2	20.0	1 985	30.3
Chester	164	-1.4	95	1.2	107.1	1 242 743	13 070	110 712	660.7	381 933	81.0	19.0	52.6	27.7	1 631	15.8
Clarion	116	-12.2	178	0.1	60.5	524 998	2 951	75 406	36.1	55 423	55.7	44.3	41.7	10.3	960	33.3
Clearfield	69	10.4	130	0.1	34.8	344 137	2 649	68 355	13.7	25 687	53.2	46.8	36.4	6.9	392	21.6
Clinton	53	-6.9	112	0.8	29.1	608 542	5 414	85 166	60.6	129 122	20.2	79.8	57.1	31.8	951	29.2
Columbia	123	0.1	130	0.6	85.1	610 161	4 693	89 506	74.4	78 762	65.5	34.5	40.7	13.8	2 088	48.9
Crawford	228	-1.9	169	0.3	130.3	475 734	2 822	91 693	116.1	85 918	44.3	55.7	46.3	15.4	2 095	26.6
Cumberland	155	-1.6	109	1.6	119.7	853 018	7 793	95 594	195.4	138 061	30.4	69.6	55.3	26.6	1 997	28.5
Dauphin	129	44.5	160	0.7	60.0	724 409	4 541	94 716	122.6	151 158	23.4	76.6	49.3	20.1	724	27.1
Delaware	5	8.3	62	0.1	1.2	857 868	13 799	57 684	9.8	128 697	99.0	1.0	32.9	6.6	D	2.6
Elk	23	-29.4	87	0.0	9.7	296 376	3 420	49 461	4.2	15 605	47.6	52.4	30.6	2.2	66	8.5
Erie	169	-2.6	119	0.9	96.2	407 705	3 438	75 158	91.7	64 469	76.5	23.5	41.5	12.8	1 693	20.5
Fayette	113	-19.8	120	0.0	55.2	398 345	3 321	66 763	27.0	28 717	52.6	47.4	31.6	5.3	588	17.7
Forest	8	-22.8	148	0.0	2.5	356 125	2 408	69 071	1.8	32 500	38.8	61.2	35.7	5.4	25	17.9
Franklin	265	9.0	166	2.8	201.8	1 101 504	6 646	133 634	413.8	259 277	21.6	78.4	66.3	40.4	4 302	34.1
Fulton	112	8.4	171	0.1	61.1	622 541	3 639	84 477	53.0	80 755	24.7	75.3	41.9	12.0	1 033	53.5
Greene	112	-25.2	128	D	36.3	385 629	3 007	66 540	14.6	16 637	39.3	60.7	28.3	2.2	189	7.2
Huntingdon	158	6.8	190	0.8	77.2	728 200	3 832	89 801	93.5	112 249	19.5	80.5	42.3	14.4	2 274	35.4
Indiana	154	-18.1	132	D	85.4	369 054	2 799	70 768	67.3	57 725	58.4	41.6	38.3	9.9	1 078	22.7
Jefferson	91	4.9	158	0.1	53.2	410 645	2 596	71 778	27.7	48 057	44.9	55.1	44.5	10.2	436	16.1
Juniata	91	-6.8	124	0.3	53.8	622 389	5 039	92 383	101.4	137 639	14.1	85.9	51.4	24.6	1 913	44.6
Lackawanna	33	-17.6	108	0.1	16.1	529 017	4 894	68 812	13.2	43 687	71.2	28.8	32.0	7.3	127	17.5
Lancaster	439	3.3	78	6.1	332.0	973 388	12 529	101 987	1 475.0	260 731	17.7	82.3	74.2	48.4	5 843	18.4
Lawrence	80	-12.9	122	0.1	46.8	501 196	4 105	84 781	38.5	58 451	53.5	46.5	48.7	10.3	652	25.9
Lebanon	121	7.0	100	1.5	97.4	1 052 028	10 562	122 164	348.9	286 245	13.1	86.9	64.1	37.6	2 250	26.6
Lehigh	76	-9.8	157	0.8	63.2	1 308 144	8 329	109 327	90.8	186 899	69.6	30.4	51.4	14.4	701	25.3
Luzerne	61	-8.5	110	0.3	34.4	491 933	4 489	67 198	21.0	37 757	82.2	17.8	31.7	9.2	970	41.4
Lycoming	158	-1.2	131	0.6	79.7	559 934	4 265	73 065	72.2	59 819	53.8	46.2	41.6	13.2	2 246	39.1
McKean	36	-12.5	125	0.0	13.2	258 072	2 062	49 907	5.0	17 076	49.3	50.7	31.4	4.5	192	24.5
Mercer	163	-5.1	138	0.1	97.7	470 815	3 420	88 056	82.7	69 747	56.5	43.5	47.8	14.8	1 376	29.9
Mifflin	91	-3.8	112	0.1	53.2	550 040	4 908	76 090	94.0	116 365	17.7	82.3	55.6	24.8	1 361	26.6
Monroe	26	-9.2	94	0.1	13.0	735 583	7 861	71 198	11.0	38 777	66.8	33.2	35.7	8.5	174	15.5
Montgomery	31	-26.6	52	0.8	18.7	725 669	14 051	52 896	25.6	42 943	71.9	28.1	39.8	8.1	293	10.6
Montour	43	-13.5	95	0.1	29.6	519 508	5 483	62 275	47.4	103 322	60.1	39.9	44.2	17.6	678	36.4
Northampton	66	-3.7	132	0.3	55.6	1 084 882	8 218	115 108	43.5	87 341	82.9	17.1	44.6	16.9	845	23.3
Northumberland	130	-12.3	153	1.4	92.8	748 819	4 898	101 762	154.3	182 218	37.0	63.0	54.0	24.7	2 014	43.1
Perry	135	-6.4	152	0.3	81.3	767 425	5 051	104 962	140.4	157 931	19.7	80.3	52.2	25.5	1 816	36.2
Philadelphia	0	8.8	13	0.0	0.1	587 318	45 337	29 864	0.8	34 909	94.7	5.2	50.0	9.1	0	0.0
Pike	28	2.5	565	0.0	3.4	1 037 120	1 835	55 680	3.0	59 300	91.3	8.7	40.0	10.0	D	6.0

STATE County	Water use, 2010		Wholesale trade,[1] 2007				Retail trade,[2] 2007				Real estate and rental and leasing,[2] 2007			
	Total water withdrawn (mil gal/day)	Gallons withdrawn per person per day	Number of establish-ments	Number of employees	Sales (mil dol)	Annual payroll (mil dol)	Number of establish-ments	Number of employees	Sales (mil dol)	Annual payroll (mil dol)	Number of establish-ments	Number of employees	Receipts (mil dol)	Annual payroll (mil dol)
	133	134	135	136	137	138	139	140	141	142	143	144	145	146
OREGON—Cont'd														
Morrow	412.1	36 879	12	67	49.4	2.6	16	80	17.4	1.6	10	12	1.2	0.2
Multnomah	58.3	79	1 271	22 685	22 043.8	1 114.4	2 945	40 269	9 868.5	1 035.5	1 491	9 735	1 770.9	366.4
Polk	42.6	565	33	206	70.3	7.4	150	1 728	375.1	39.0	71	238	21.7	3.6
Sherman	11.3	6 380	4	25	12.0	1.0	10	119	56.0	2.2	1	D	D	D
Tillamook	47.5	1 882	17	134	31.0	3.1	121	1 118	224.9	23.0	34	116	11.0	2.5
Umatilla	383.3	5 051	64	733	284.5	27.6	263	3 024	763.6	71.6	68	224	24.3	4.5
Union	206.1	8 006	20	D	D	D	125	1 483	333.8	32.7	20	86	9.5	1.9
Wallowa	138.6	19 773	2	D	D	D	56	376	82.7	7.5	22	51	5.3	1.0
Wasco	125.6	4 982	23	D	D	D	133	1 749	381.9	39.5	45	85	9.8	1.6
Washington	103.5	195	813	12 907	11 021.8	793.3	1 718	31 456	8 754.4	792.4	843	4 645	992.7	165.9
Wheeler	35.9	24 892	1	D	D	D	7	27	10.4	0.7	2	D	D	D
Yamhill	75.7	763	84	699	396.8	27.5	282	3 509	951.1	84.9	117	331	42.7	7.6
PENNSYLVANIA	8 134.9	640	13 161	200 151	142 859.2	10 100.7	46 532	672 042	166 842.8	14 862.3	9 904	68 954	13 602.6	2 611.8
Adams	20.2	199	62	D	D	D	376	3 798	832.4	79.9	52	230	42.8	5.9
Allegheny	641.5	524	1 600	21 032	18 141.6	1 090.2	4 795	76 658	20 075.4	1 643.2	1 273	9 972	2 000.7	387.3
Armstrong	180.4	2 617	32	D	D	D	221	2 352	532.1	48.4	27	281	29.5	9.7
Beaver	432.3	2 535	107	1 504	1 180.1	64.0	571	7 902	1 555.3	143.4	91	424	74.0	12.5
Bedford	17.8	358	41	387	295.5	13.0	209	2 165	581.6	43.1	16	164	45.2	4.8
Berks	57.1	139	375	6 306	4 417.6	306.7	1 327	20 433	4 953.2	466.8	273	1 384	210.2	39.4
Blair	22.8	179	123	2 160	1 511.2	87.6	619	9 366	2 038.7	179.6	82	393	66.7	10.3
Bradford	11.9	191	44	D	D	D	286	2 941	727.8	59.9	26	62	9.3	1.2
Bucks	182.4	292	1 167	14 880	9 859.6	803.5	2 551	41 993	13 089.8	1 020.0	608	3 671	787.7	145.9
Butler	15.7	85	237	3 604	2 580.2	171.0	719	10 950	2 527.3	224.8	141	630	125.2	17.6
Cambria	27.1	189	123	1 362	582.5	44.2	588	7 207	1 626.5	137.9	99	584	65.8	16.7
Cameron	0.8	157	2	D	D	D	18	208	29.6	2.8	NA	NA	NA	NA
Carbon	25.1	385	19	137	35.8	5.7	198	2 301	483.9	48.2	36	117	17.5	3.7
Centre	45.4	295	92	1 091	572.3	70.9	548	8 014	1 604.3	151.0	129	922	184.7	26.2
Chester	191.4	384	769	9 902	8 571.4	771.3	1 610	30 395	11 338.4	923.5	479	D	D	D
Clarion	5.1	126	38	669	287.4	20.4	203	2 147	421.1	42.0	18	50	8.7	1.1
Clearfield	304.3	3 727	66	D	D	D	368	4 677	1 150.1	91.9	39	275	26.4	6.1
Clinton	16.9	430	17	D	D	D	139	1 862	520.7	36.8	26	140	14.6	2.6
Columbia	10.4	155	42	461	109.9	16.0	274	3 692	826.2	71.3	58	206	30.7	5.6
Crawford	14.0	157	76	442	146.7	14.5	329	3 948	877.3	86.8	51	197	24.6	4.2
Cumberland	33.0	140	228	3 165	3 657.8	134.6	907	15 471	3 684.9	333.7	218	1 352	288.3	50.4
Dauphin	100.4	374	277	9 815	6 456.6	493.7	1 064	16 695	3 869.5	361.3	227	2 010	515.1	72.8
Delaware	782.2	1 399	548	7 021	4 220.0	470.4	1 861	26 462	6 358.4	617.2	449	5 011	1 168.9	196.0
Elk	21.6	676	30	226	69.9	7.8	130	1 536	291.2	26.0	13	44	4.2	0.6
Erie	49.4	176	279	3 118	1 157.2	124.0	1 051	15 831	3 428.4	314.5	187	1 115	135.3	25.9
Fayette	45.1	330	106	1 042	528.1	40.6	514	6 849	1 535.5	134.9	79	394	54.6	8.9
Forest	2.0	264	1	D	D	D	20	75	19.3	1.5	2	D	D	D
Franklin	19.1	127	120	D	D	D	503	7 526	1 750.0	160.6	92	485	71.2	13.7
Fulton	2.9	193	14	237	215.3	9.8	48	390	101.4	7.7	4	D	D	D
Greene	35.7	922	20	375	191.1	11.3	134	1 541	432.8	29.6	11	D	D	D
Huntingdon	14.0	306	25	D	D	D	154	1 600	363.2	31.0	17	59	7.7	1.0
Indiana	59.8	673	63	693	492.3	27.0	336	5 039	1 279.0	102.9	49	248	23.9	5.5
Jefferson	4.7	105	46	445	235.4	16.4	183	1 927	477.4	35.0	24	100	14.7	2.4
Juniata	3.8	154	21	169	69.8	7.3	81	785	197.6	14.2	10	D	D	D
Lackawanna	52.1	243	258	4 248	3 127.6	160.5	991	14 196	3 178.8	281.9	158	913	119.1	22.3
Lancaster	78.2	151	604	10 635	6 333.6	435.7	2 000	30 083	6 542.3	644.4	348	2 223	420.1	74.3
Lawrence	100.3	1 101	91	D	D	D	313	4 208	949.6	90.6	46	290	23.1	5.6
Lebanon	14.6	109	104	3 250	2 802.6	122.3	451	6 611	1 488.6	144.1	68	271	43.5	7.3
Lehigh	50.9	146	429	D	D	D	1 273	20 590	5 081.2	466.6	314	1 860	329.1	58.8
Luzerne	85.3	266	309	5 139	2 174.7	206.4	1 279	18 777	5 223.7	389.9	226	1 687	264.5	49.6
Lycoming	16.0	138	116	1 933	701.9	62.0	519	6 968	1 458.4	130.8	94	444	80.7	11.4
McKean	12.9	298	31	D	D	D	176	1 917	422.3	37.9	22	D	D	D
Mercer	30.6	263	91	D	D	D	555	7 229	1 441.6	140.5	85	394	65.8	10.3
Mifflin	9.3	199	48	D	D	D	187	2 415	526.1	48.8	21	78	13.9	1.8
Monroe	33.1	195	98	D	D	D	688	9 091	2 014.9	190.0	166	583	84.7	14.8
Montgomery	114.8	143	1 367	20 029	12 012.4	1 249.2	3 458	58 150	15 151.3	1 443.8	1 062	9 282	2 287.0	478.4
Montour	18.8	1 030	11	131	177.0	5.8	69	690	156.9	14.3	8	29	4.3	0.6
Northampton	267.2	897	245	3 915	9 815.9	174.0	908	13 201	3 405.0	302.0	187	D	D	D
Northumberland	22.9	242	47	795	587.5	33.8	318	3 286	797.0	66.7	45	193	19.5	4.7
Perry	3.9	85	20	141	85.1	5.4	154	1 537	393.4	30.1	17	68	4.4	0.7
Philadelphia	374.8	246	1 067	18 338	11 566.1	956.3	4 420	50 225	11 167.8	1 158.1	1 088	9 813	1 956.1	433.9
Pike	4.6	79	22	D	D	D	131	1 946	401.1	43.2	50	D	D	D

1. Merchant wholesalers, except manufacturers' sales branches and offices. 2. Employer establishments.

STATE County	Professional, scientific, and technical services,[1] 2007				Manufacturing, 2007				Accommodation and food services, 2007			
	Number of establish-ments	Number of employees	Receipts (mil dol)	Annual payroll (mil dol)	Number of establish-ments	Number of employees	Receipts (mil dol)	Annual payroll (mil dol)	Number of establish-ments	Number of employees	Sales (mil dol)	Annual payroll (mil dol)
	147	148	149	150	151	152	153	154	155	156	157	158
OREGON—Cont'd												
Morrow	4	D	D	D	10	774	D	D	18	162	7.1	1.7
Multnomah	3 324	D	D	D	1 153	37 545	10 527.6	1 668.5	2 472	38 415	2 048.6	604.2
Polk	106	312	29.3	8.6	68	2 059	416.7	70.8	121	D	D	D
Sherman	1	D	D	D	NA	NA	NA	NA	8	87	5.9	1.3
Tillamook	38	156	13.0	4.8	29	1 509	633.8	59.1	124	1 033	53.7	15.7
Umatilla	97	D	D	D	69	3 335	D	D	166	2 721	159.4	40.4
Union	60	236	19.3	7.1	33	1 450	337.1	56.4	65	831	32.9	9.0
Wallowa	22	73	6.4	2.1	NA	NA	NA	NA	42	224	7.4	1.9
Wasco	55	196	17.2	6.8	NA	NA	NA	NA	72	896	47.6	13.5
Washington	1 773	D	D	D	770	32 506	24 049.0	1 759.9	1 085	17 125	849.4	249.8
Wheeler	NA	NA	NA	NA	NA	NA	NA	NA	6	14	0.6	0.1
Yamhill	207	D	D	D	205	6 265	1 885.8	291.9	186	2 305	98.9	28.4
PENNSYLVANIA	29 534	292 791	45 888.3	18 184.2	15 406	650 804	234 840.4	29 433.0	26 910	420 209	19 625.4	5 454.0
Adams	135	D	D	D	126	8 038	2 498.3	297.9	206	4 098	160.1	46.1
Allegheny	3 954	D	D	D	1 198	43 118	15 725.2	2 149.5	3 153	56 803	2 540.3	735.1
Armstrong	76	D	D	D	78	2 086	370.9	75.0	103	1 227	39.5	10.1
Beaver	243	D	D	D	191	7 749	4 708.8	344.4	315	4 355	156.3	42.3
Bedford	52	D	D	D	69	2 286	728.7	81.8	104	1 402	70.3	19.4
Berks	735	6 289	1 449.0	389.4	550	32 597	8 461.8	1 487.9	715	11 030	446.0	124.4
Blair	228	D	D	D	139	7 282	1 931.2	285.6	274	4 841	178.9	52.0
Bradford	80	D	D	D	69	4 787	1 772.4	198.6	108	1 206	48.8	13.1
Bucks	2 375	D	D	D	1 129	31 813	9 316.3	1 484.6	1 307	19 756	970.2	258.4
Butler	411	D	D	D	294	14 408	5 362.0	750.1	361	6 949	269.5	74.9
Cambria	221	D	D	D	146	5 409	1 439.8	199.6	307	4 135	156.0	40.9
Cameron	6	17	1.2	0.5	26	1 180	213.8	48.8	14	96	2.8	0.6
Carbon	70	D	D	D	56	2 450	514.3	95.1	127	1 491	104.7	21.7
Centre	376	D	D	D	150	4 341	1 216.5	181.0	301	5 961	240.1	68.8
Chester	2 310	20 064	3 947.2	1 610.7	572	18 981	6 753.0	985.9	907	15 286	783.2	221.0
Clarion	36	D	D	D	46	2 716	586.6	92.7	103	1 315	51.2	13.0
Clearfield	100	D	D	D	112	3 213	D	108.8	177	2 316	88.0	22.5
Clinton	40	182	15.4	4.8	46	2 730	1 215.0	104.5	82	998	43.2	11.5
Columbia	92	843	50.1	27.7	90	6 569	D	245.6	152	2 252	90.6	25.1
Crawford	124	D	D	D	282	7 686	1 632.6	308.8	199	2 438	90.1	26.7
Cumberland	614	D	D	D	200	10 191	3 472.6	404.8	520	9 519	402.7	116.0
Dauphin	720	D	D	D	215	9 794	D	446.3	668	12 489	676.8	194.8
Delaware	1 603	D	D	D	425	16 122	19 060.4	1 158.3	1 028	15 048	779.5	206.2
Elk	36	193	9.0	3.3	139	6 932	1 616.5	280.7	76	634	24.1	5.3
Erie	416	D	D	D	505	24 441	6 890.8	1 190.2	646	10 728	428.1	114.6
Fayette	154	D	D	D	128	3 757	1 161.4	153.0	270	5 432	246.9	78.3
Forest	3	D	D	D	NA	NA	NA	NA	25	145	8.4	2.1
Franklin	227	D	D	D	222	10 149	3 244.4	412.7	278	3 837	164.5	45.5
Fulton	12	41	2.6	0.8	19	D	D	D	23	206	9.9	2.4
Greene	46	D	D	D	25	D	D	D	73	908	36.8	10.2
Huntingdon	49	D	D	D	45	D	D	85.0	86	898	40.4	10.7
Indiana	112	D	D	D	105	3 316	D	120.8	166	2 740	92.4	24.4
Jefferson	66	D	D	D	101	4 415	953.5	171.7	91	908	32.3	8.1
Juniata	20	64	3.2	0.7	54	2 047	392.0	63.6	34	506	14.6	4.5
Lackawanna	472	D	D	D	267	11 834	D	439.1	546	8 601	360.5	99.6
Lancaster	939	D	D	D	920	40 077	13 269.9	1 735.9	935	17 060	763.9	221.2
Lawrence	119	D	D	D	147	3 840	1 745.2	183.6	177	2 325	73.4	21.3
Lebanon	193	D	D	D	213	9 655	2 393.6	363.3	241	3 075	125.3	35.3
Lehigh	763	D	D	D	419	18 331	7 031.6	835.6	740	11 730	546.3	148.6
Luzerne	594	D	D	D	352	17 955	5 708.3	727.4	763	10 586	442.9	119.8
Lycoming	183	1 367	102.9	39.6	183	10 240	3 358.2	408.7	277	3 721	147.9	40.0
McKean	65	D	D	D	56	4 029	1 394.4	160.6	112	1 055	40.9	10.5
Mercer	172	D	D	D	193	8 929	3 463.6	365.1	271	4 434	166.8	48.8
Mifflin	34	D	D	D	91	3 899	950.4	162.2	80	1 055	36.1	10.3
Monroe	340	1 671	198.0	53.9	131	5 322	2 656.5	317.4	386	7 491	394.4	113.0
Montgomery	3 697	45 686	7 015.0	3 370.4	1 110	51 179	20 398.8	2 848.2	1 769	27 834	1 478.0	409.4
Montour	32	444	32.4	25.9	18	950	D	55.4	42	734	27.5	7.5
Northampton	594	D	D	D	340	13 197	3 923.1	608.1	646	8 637	384.8	103.8
Northumberland	99	520	39.6	13.0	105	6 048	1 420.5	226.3	170	1 443	54.5	13.9
Perry	56	D	D	D	35	741	D	25.0	76	490	21.7	5.0
Philadelphia	2 703	44 302	9 243.3	3 533.1	946	32 672	18 069.4	1 396.7	3 396	48 552	3 051.4	837.9
Pike	80	D	D	D	NA	NA	NA	NA	98	1 300	75.8	17.6

1. Establishment subject to federal tax.

Table B. States and Counties — **Health Care and Social Assistance, Other Services, Nonemployer Businesses, and Residential Construction**

STATE County	Health care and social assistance, 2007				Other services, 2007				Nonemployer businesses, 2013		Value of residential construction authorized by building permits, 2014	
	Number of establish-ments	Number of employees	Receipts (mil dol)	Annual payroll (mil dol)	Number of establish-ments	Number of employees	Receipts (mil dol)	Annual payroll (mil dol)	Number	Receipts (mil dol)	New Construction ($1,000)	Number of housing units
	159	160	161	162	163	164	165	166	167	168	169	170
OREGON—Cont'd												
Morrow	14	119	11.2	4.8	11	32	2.2	0.7	506	22.5	3 660	16
Multnomah	2 601	53 379	6 135.2	2 471.3	1 726	11 789	1 748.2	367.3	62 224	2 937.5	791 689	5 090
Polk	136	2 127	127.1	56.4	82	248	21.8	5.9	3 911	154.2	39 888	246
Sherman	3	19	0.2	0.1	1	D	D	D	108	4.2	NA	NA
Tillamook	57	739	73.7	28.6	46	212	15.6	3.9	1 831	78.5	19 913	82
Umatilla	176	2 641	240.9	94.7	103	435	33.4	10.3	3 399	144.6	17 387	93
Union	93	1 185	95.8	38.1	51	168	13.3	3.2	1 553	59.3	15 724	86
Wallowa	33	345	24.2	10.1	20	72	8.6	1.7	758	31.7	4 324	23
Wasco	80	1 708	137.4	58.1	43	179	15.2	4.1	1 262	46.5	NA	NA
Washington	1 514	23 384	2 575.1	967.1	823	5 172	497.9	165.1	33 720	1 591.8	542 708	3 030
Wheeler	3	D	D	D	2	D	D	D	141	6.0	NA	NA
Yamhill	241	3 852	342.7	131.0	124	541	45.5	13.4	5 581	237.9	78 048	376
PENNSYLVANIA	35 156	874 743	81 977.9	33 431.6	25 316	154 379	17 622.1	3 932.7	778 528	37 039.3	4 714 443	25 059
Adams	185	3 887	313.4	130.3	165	1 004	81.8	20.2	6 356	268.5	60 304	272
Allegheny	4 262	122 200	12 649.6	4 896.5	2 985	19 550	2 504.6	520.9	74 402	3 471.7	461 426	2 343
Armstrong	187	3 226	201.5	90.4	101	428	33.0	7.2	3 490	145.4	6 627	45
Beaver	462	9 722	707.9	319.0	343	1 506	101.6	28.4	8 495	328.2	29 051	141
Bedford	117	1 558	121.2	45.9	97	373	23.8	5.8	3 245	143.3	10 945	66
Berks	799	21 887	2 014.4	848.1	781	4 670	398.8	108.0	23 771	1 094.0	71 145	458
Blair	403	10 162	909.5	373.1	299	1 686	115.7	33.5	6 055	284.4	17 545	100
Bradford	151	4 300	465.5	174.1	118	521	31.0	7.9	3 580	146.6	13 376	77
Bucks	1 925	37 382	3 395.7	1 381.8	1 395	8 612	709.3	229.6	49 858	2 794.9	138 828	778
Butler	538	11 344	839.5	338.5	370	2 184	230.6	48.0	11 475	554.8	155 802	624
Cambria	545	11 825	872.0	383.6	320	1 590	114.3	28.9	6 190	237.1	11 445	61
Cameron	19	D	D	D	12	58	2.6	0.6	242	7.6	0	0
Carbon	153	2 525	180.6	78.6	94	352	26.4	6.6	3 280	133.2	14 457	70
Centre	332	6 543	549.7	238.6	228	1 270	100.7	27.6	9 288	444.9	101 610	511
Chester	1 343	29 982	2 692.4	1 136.2	977	6 655	1 590.1	229.8	39 966	2 349.8	247 147	1 459
Clarion	141	2 411	155.7	62.5	85	393	36.9	7.1	2 443	111.7	55 354	422
Clearfield	248	5 584	449.8	185.9	162	945	63.1	17.4	4 181	169.9	16 805	126
Clinton	80	1 208	90.9	36.0	56	270	23.0	3.8	1 859	72.6	5 413	38
Columbia	165	D	D	D	115	683	49.7	14.2	3 181	133.9	15 752	79
Crawford	270	5 084	377.9	156.5	177	867	60.3	16.1	5 380	223.3	15 157	73
Cumberland	602	14 452	1 308.1	541.9	539	3 906	387.1	102.6	14 747	713.6	155 050	879
Dauphin	810	28 300	2 611.3	1 119.7	681	4 904	598.9	167.0	15 201	669.0	102 696	651
Delaware	1 545	38 693	3 531.7	1 521.9	1 055	6 909	1 240.3	197.9	38 838	1 988.6	96 133	435
Elk	124	2 206	134.3	63.1	78	353	23.8	4.9	1 606	63.2	7 631	55
Erie	893	21 880	1 847.7	783.0	563	3 529	242.4	70.2	13 801	567.3	43 914	321
Fayette	410	7 904	526.2	234.4	234	1 061	91.0	21.2	6 146	248.2	45 102	193
Forest	8	D	D	D	6	18	1.0	0.2	310	11.4	187	4
Franklin	307	7 302	640.1	267.8	297	1 653	121.0	33.1	8 745	362.0	56 284	356
Fulton	27	542	34.2	15.5	31	103	7.1	1.8	950	44.0	3 471	26
Greene	109	1 540	121.0	46.4	68	274	22.5	6.0	1 558	63.1	10 294	66
Huntingdon	103	1 660	111.2	44.5	69	239	14.8	3.6	2 491	103.1	12 158	65
Indiana	259	4 492	319.7	135.2	174	868	76.5	20.1	4 969	223.0	10 599	54
Jefferson	161	3 304	179.1	77.6	99	440	28.8	7.1	2 961	127.2	11 573	74
Juniata	29	501	29.9	10.8	29	101	11.5	2.9	1 769	87.0	5 446	34
Lackawanna	708	18 457	1 560.5	641.5	400	2 264	181.5	52.3	11 625	576.8	405 945	2 009
Lancaster	1 062	32 573	2 878.0	1 163.1	1 042	6 812	587.2	157.1	39 855	2 035.5	196 565	1 109
Lawrence	256	5 749	392.9	166.1	183	789	56.7	15.6	4 826	204.9	7 206	41
Lebanon	266	7 662	626.6	286.9	233	1 059	93.0	25.2	7 968	360.9	52 952	348
Lehigh	1 111	32 364	3 486.0	1 402.0	715	4 637	451.0	121.5	21 126	899.7	103 182	773
Luzerne	983	23 418	1 986.6	809.9	582	2 996	231.0	58.1	16 441	798.2	48 987	252
Lycoming	285	8 065	675.8	272.5	244	1 521	150.1	33.0	6 204	268.6	36 448	214
McKean	165	2 857	191.3	87.7	104	404	26.1	6.1	2 130	84.9	5 035	28
Mercer	395	10 499	750.1	314.8	260	1 319	87.8	23.5	6 338	271.4	15 926	90
Mifflin	115	2 731	210.0	90.3	71	250	19.9	4.7	2 609	112.3	8 710	56
Monroe	367	6 064	537.3	221.1	308	1 590	119.9	36.2	9 813	444.6	38 574	153
Montgomery	2 746	62 216	6 560.8	2 613.6	1 933	12 597	1 506.0	352.9	66 225	4 058.2	256 177	1 752
Montour	63	D	D	D	33	170	18.8	5.0	1 047	41.6	6 567	34
Northampton	749	11 498	979.1	394.3	545	3 094	224.8	70.6	17 157	813.3	115 219	714
Northumberland	199	3 853	241.3	103.8	151	809	44.5	12.4	4 462	207.8	13 816	68
Perry	73	565	40.9	13.2	70	241	17.4	4.0	2 822	115.8	16 990	72
Philadelphia	3 600	131 738	14 539.8	5 888.7	2 466	17 806	2 843.4	574.6	80 370	2 946.1	879 066	3 973
Pike	89	D	D	D	102	701	56.6	16.3	3 736	165.5	24 246	85

STATE County	Government employment and payroll, 2012: Full-time equivalent employees	Government employment and payroll, 2012: March payroll (dollars)	March payroll (percent of total): Adminis-tration, judicial, and legal	March payroll (percent of total): Police and Corrections	March payroll (percent of total): Fire Protection	March payroll (percent of total): Highways and transpor-tation	March payroll (percent of total): Health and Welfare	March payroll (percent of total): Natural resources and utilities	March payroll (percent of total): Education and libraries	Local government finances, 2012, General revenue: Total (mil dol)	General revenue: Inter-govern-mental (mil dol)	Taxes: Total (mil dol)	Taxes, Per capita[1] (dollars): Total	Taxes, Per capita[1] (dollars): Property
	171	172	173	174	175	176	177	178	179	180	181	182	183	184
OREGON—Cont'd														
Morrow	611	2 174 057	7.8	9.3	1.6	5.2	17.4	6.6	45.7	79.1	31.3	21.7	1 928	1 801
Multnomah	29 478	148 927 675	7.5	11.9	4.2	13.6	6.4	9.0	42.8	4 680.8	1 700.4	1 856.1	2 445	1 660
Polk	1 230	4 842 625	12.3	13.6	2.4	1.9	8.6	6.6	52.1	138.5	77.6	42.1	552	500
Sherman	121	446 146	20.7	9.6	8.8	9.9	11.4	7.5	29.5	23.4	4.3	6.6	3 808	3 775
Tillamook	1 081	4 310 792	8.6	7.5	1.5	5.0	4.7	26.1	44.4	116.8	36.6	46.1	1 822	1 701
Umatilla	2 519	9 346 604	6.6	11.0	3.9	3.0	1.9	7.4	65.3	307.6	163.2	86.2	1 122	1 020
Union	750	2 655 712	8.7	12.0	2.8	4.4	0.9	8.8	60.1	87.0	50.9	20.7	802	722
Wallowa	382	1 406 470	6.1	5.5	0.3	3.8	43.8	3.1	36.5	46.2	14.1	8.6	1 262	1 113
Wasco	982	3 676 060	6.9	6.4	4.7	3.8	3.2	15.2	58.1	115.4	52.3	37.4	1 468	1 319
Washington	14 620	63 993 061	6.8	11.2	6.7	2.5	2.0	7.5	60.1	1 882.7	665.8	834.1	1 523	1 366
Wheeler	106	329 289	21.3	2.9	0.0	9.3	0.0	7.4	57.6	8.1	5.1	1.6	1 126	1 092
Yamhill	2 820	11 200 226	7.7	9.1	4.6	1.7	6.0	8.9	59.7	320.3	146.1	104.5	1 043	942
PENNSYLVANIA	X	X	X	X	X	X	X	X	X	X	X	X	X	X
Adams	2 548	9 790 732	7.8	9.5	0.9	2.6	2.1	3.4	73.2	374.0	165.8	167.3	1 648	1 256
Allegheny	43 945	195 375 705	6.5	12.8	2.4	11.5	5.4	5.9	53.8	6 769.1	2 823.5	2 739.2	2 228	1 525
Armstrong	2 222	7 529 691	6.9	7.0	0.0	4.1	6.8	5.5	68.9	227.1	114.7	81.0	1 185	1 004
Beaver	5 422	21 094 763	6.4	10.1	0.3	4.8	6.7	6.8	64.1	785.3	350.5	233.6	1 372	1 124
Bedford	1 369	4 444 835	5.3	5.6	0.8	4.2	1.7	5.0	77.4	128.7	70.2	45.3	918	675
Berks	14 566	69 528 665	6.1	16.3	5.1	2.6	4.7	5.3	58.7	2 039.3	792.5	835.6	2 021	1 642
Blair	4 030	13 533 958	4.8	8.4	2.3	5.0	8.5	7.0	62.6	402.4	214.5	126.2	993	707
Bradford	2 246	8 350 493	7.8	4.9	0.5	5.3	11.4	1.9	67.4	247.1	119.2	78.6	1 252	972
Bucks	18 333	88 124 851	6.0	11.7	0.6	4.0	4.0	3.9	68.9	2 731.2	688.4	1 517.1	2 419	2 074
Butler	4 890	20 031 417	6.5	6.1	0.5	3.3	5.6	4.7	72.2	629.8	252.7	262.6	1 420	1 090
Cambria	4 484	15 273 184	8.2	8.3	1.4	5.9	5.7	6.0	63.9	555.1	293.7	143.3	1 012	781
Cameron	214	664 238	8.3	4.9	0.0	5.0	7.5	2.5	70.2	17.3	9.0	6.0	1 223	1 052
Carbon	2 113	7 282 054	7.7	9.6	0.0	3.5	11.6	5.7	60.5	211.1	71.9	108.6	1 671	1 438
Centre	3 965	14 048 206	7.5	8.6	0.0	7.9	9.9	5.8	58.3	455.2	154.4	216.4	1 394	1 018
Chester	13 231	61 935 244	7.1	9.3	0.2	2.2	4.5	2.8	71.3	2 107.9	567.4	1 254.5	2 476	2 063
Clarion	1 226	4 224 897	6.3	6.9	0.0	3.1	1.8	3.0	78.3	155.3	103.3	39.4	993	773
Clearfield	2 608	9 251 789	4.9	5.4	0.0	3.3	1.6	4.7	78.9	261.5	141.7	88.1	1 086	853
Clinton	1 129	4 364 621	9.8	5.9	2.2	2.6	11.0	7.0	59.8	138.0	54.0	44.3	1 121	835
Columbia	1 917	7 059 353	6.5	11.0	0.0	3.3	2.0	3.1	73.5	197.2	86.4	83.5	1 248	914
Crawford	2 501	8 880 019	8.6	8.3	1.6	5.0	10.3	5.8	59.4	270.2	125.4	98.7	1 127	906
Cumberland	7 023	27 433 306	6.6	8.7	0.0	2.7	6.7	4.9	68.9	914.8	308.3	434.2	1 820	1 330
Dauphin	10 041	42 265 280	7.7	13.4	1.0	4.7	1.7	5.4	64.3	1 441.8	522.5	527.9	1 958	1 407
Delaware	18 047	76 207 314	10.5	9.6	1.0	2.0	6.2	4.1	65.6	2 712.5	932.9	1 199.8	2 138	1 938
Elk	1 009	3 366 414	8.9	6.3	0.0	12.9	2.6	6.2	61.7	108.1	52.0	37.3	1 181	901
Erie	8 523	32 472 819	5.3	9.7	2.6	5.6	3.9	6.0	65.7	1 197.6	616.5	364.0	1 297	1 046
Fayette	3 546	14 568 652	6.8	9.1	0.4	5.2	7.7	9.3	61.2	411.7	262.1	104.7	772	570
Forest	197	632 875	20.3	3.4	0.0	3.6	5.7	3.9	62.0	19.5	9.4	7.5	980	863
Franklin	3 820	13 644 359	7.7	8.8	1.7	2.3	9.1	6.1	63.5	415.1	130.8	191.4	1 265	978
Fulton	454	1 468 178	11.3	2.6	0.0	2.5	0.0	2.1	81.0	47.4	25.7	16.4	1 112	912
Greene	1 301	4 613 569	10.4	5.2	0.0	6.2	4.1	7.8	65.3	144.0	67.6	57.8	1 518	1 258
Huntingdon	1 125	3 453 282	9.3	7.1	0.0	3.2	3.8	5.2	70.1	118.4	66.3	38.4	837	613
Indiana	2 289	9 093 274	6.9	6.4	0.1	4.5	4.9	5.1	70.9	313.8	170.3	97.7	1 107	879
Jefferson	1 211	4 334 856	6.6	7.0	0.0	4.9	1.4	6.4	72.3	125.7	68.4	38.4	858	661
Juniata	563	1 993 044	11.0	5.3	1.3	2.6	0.1	1.9	75.5	49.2	23.8	21.6	867	690
Lackawanna	6 361	25 493 690	6.8	11.8	3.2	4.1	6.5	6.5	59.1	757.3	291.3	324.8	1 515	1 101
Lancaster	12 622	54 624 168	5.9	11.7	0.8	2.8	3.4	3.5	70.9	1 833.2	668.6	843.7	1 601	1 327
Lawrence	2 433	9 509 559	8.0	8.4	1.5	4.9	1.0	3.8	71.8	318.9	174.0	106.5	1 185	905
Lebanon	4 116	14 939 586	6.1	9.0	1.7	2.8	9.0	5.5	65.4	485.8	160.6	191.5	1 416	1 136
Lehigh	11 303	49 829 858	7.3	10.7	1.9	4.5	9.3	4.5	60.4	1 670.5	674.3	669.0	1 883	1 523
Luzerne	9 404	36 055 331	7.5	12.5	3.5	3.7	4.7	5.2	62.1	1 080.5	466.5	439.6	1 369	1 039
Lycoming	3 615	14 906 594	7.7	7.9	1.8	4.3	2.7	6.0	68.7	451.3	198.0	155.7	1 329	953
McKean	1 616	5 647 554	6.9	7.4	1.5	4.5	8.7	8.2	62.2	167.7	97.2	44.6	1 033	829
Mercer	3 570	12 446 506	8.5	9.8	1.2	3.2	1.2	4.2	70.1	402.4	216.5	133.0	1 150	861
Mifflin	1 135	4 324 228	8.8	6.8	1.1	5.0	2.7	9.1	64.8	153.4	81.3	46.8	1 002	733
Monroe	5 957	25 067 544	5.7	4.3	0.0	5.4	1.6	1.5	80.9	719.0	225.3	441.5	2 616	2 404
Montgomery	23 690	112 151 487	6.4	12.2	0.4	2.4	5.0	4.0	68.6	3 430.1	888.0	2 054.1	2 541	2 087
Montour	515	1 746 307	6.4	6.4	0.0	4.4	0.9	6.3	73.4	92.9	26.6	26.3	1 431	915
Northampton	10 782	47 706 434	7.1	11.9	1.8	2.5	7.7	4.9	61.8	1 411.9	496.8	671.7	2 244	1 804
Northumberland	3 162	10 304 053	9.0	7.6	0.0	3.1	16.2	4.4	59.0	273.2	137.2	88.2	934	631
Perry	1 241	4 130 390	6.3	5.0	0.0	3.3	5.0	1.5	77.8	139.6	62.3	60.0	1 312	977
Philadelphia	60 937	311 591 353	8.6	18.6	4.6	16.9	6.0	8.1	36.4	11 133.9	5 530.3	4 080.0	2 636	743
Pike	1 166	4 430 795	9.4	13.5	0.0	2.5	4.3	1.7	67.0	128.4	48.7	71.2	1 252	1 185

1. Based on the resident population estimated as of July 1 of the year shown.

STATE County	Local government finances, 2012 (cont.) — Direct general expenditure: Total (mil dol)	Per capita[1] (dollars)	Percent of total for: Educa-tion	Health and hospitals	Police protec-tion	Public welfare	High-ways	Debt outstanding: Total (mil dol)	Per capita[1] (dollars)	Government employment, 2013: Federal civilian	Federal military	State and local	Presidential election,[2] 2012 — Percent of vote cast: Demo-cratic	Republi-can	All other
	185	186	187	188	189	190	191	192	193	194	195	196	197	198	199
OREGON—Cont'd															
Morrow	78.1	6 947	32.8	11.0	4.6	0.3	5.8	136.8	12 168	57	37	736	34.7	61.8	3.4
Multnomah	4 425.0	5 828	31.5	4.6	5.2	4.0	6.5	7 864.7	10 358	12 308	2 465	57 603	76.7	20.6	2.7
Polk	140.8	1 844	43.0	8.4	8.3	1.0	5.6	271.5	3 556	72	208	5 047	48.4	48.9	2.6
Sherman	18.9	10 932	20.7	4.0	4.0	1.4	11.8	3.5	2 023	130	0	183	36.8	60.6	2.7
Tillamook	118.4	4 684	38.3	7.8	3.6	0.3	5.5	166.8	6 595	107	107	1 622	53.2	43.3	3.5
Umatilla	311.2	4 051	58.5	1.4	4.4	0.0	4.1	422.0	5 493	513	203	6 253	37.2	59.8	3.1
Union	90.0	3 495	44.0	3.4	5.7	0.4	5.1	30.5	1 185	224	69	2 037	36.6	60.2	3.2
Wallowa	44.0	6 453	31.6	33.8	3.6	0.8	8.6	38.3	5 620	95	19	515	33.4	63.5	3.1
Wasco	106.5	4 180	48.5	2.2	4.8	0.4	4.4	159.3	6 251	289	69	1 675	51.9	44.8	3.3
Washington	1 940.6	3 543	44.5	2.9	7.1	0.0	5.6	2 532.1	4 623	707	1 522	19 833	59.8	37.7	2.5
Wheeler	9.5	6 659	47.9	0.8	2.6	1.5	12.0	2.0	1 419	0	0	103	34.6	61.3	4.1
Yamhill	320.3	3 195	49.5	5.9	5.8	0.1	3.1	445.1	4 439	467	263	3 669	47.8	49.1	3.1
PENNSYLVANIA	X	X	X	X	X	X	X	X	X	97 070	36 241	654 389	54.7	44.3	1.0
Adams	458.0	4 513	68.9	3.6	1.4	3.2	2.7	405.6	3 997	739	261	3 454	39.6	59.2	1.1
Allegheny	6 640.6	5 402	42.9	7.9	4.6	4.6	3.0	13 494.2	10 977	12 568	3 654	52 998	57.3	41.8	0.9
Armstrong	246.9	3 609	57.6	1.5	1.2	7.5	5.0	239.3	3 498	186	180	2 707	37.0	61.6	1.3
Beaver	789.6	4 638	46.6	3.5	3.0	14.1	3.9	1 928.6	11 328	291	448	7 978	47.9	50.8	1.3
Bedford	155.3	3 148	66.4	0.0	0.4	2.0	4.8	224.7	4 556	110	130	2 156	27.0	71.8	1.2
Berks	2 024.3	4 896	54.5	3.4	4.1	7.2	2.8	3 478.7	8 413	934	1 077	21 670	53.9	44.7	1.4
Blair	409.0	3 217	49.0	3.1	3.0	8.6	3.9	474.2	3 730	961	329	7 719	37.3	61.6	1.1
Bradford	244.7	3 898	54.4	2.0	1.6	7.3	6.2	751.2	11 963	205	165	3 022	40.0	58.4	1.6
Bucks	2 875.9	4 586	57.6	0.8	5.5	7.0	4.5	3 960.3	6 316	1 107	1 677	22 358	53.8	45.1	1.1
Butler	656.7	3 550	51.5	4.2	2.4	9.5	4.4	1 305.0	7 055	2 813	487	8 684	35.7	63.1	1.2
Cambria	571.5	4 037	49.2	3.2	5.7	14.0	3.6	641.5	4 531	969	384	7 385	49.4	48.7	1.9
Cameron	19.1	3 864	59.4	3.8	1.2	2.5	5.9	30.2	6 117	13	13	394	39.2	58.9	1.9
Carbon	219.0	3 370	60.5	0.1	2.6	4.4	3.4	265.0	4 076	103	171	2 574	50.0	48.1	1.9
Centre	453.5	2 923	51.0	2.2	3.5	7.9	6.1	486.7	3 136	442	447	46 951	55.4	43.5	1.1
Chester	2 204.4	4 352	57.7	5.2	3.8	3.4	3.3	2 995.8	5 914	2 544	1 332	23 124	54.2	45.0	0.8
Clarion	168.8	4 258	67.2	3.0	1.9	2.5	3.4	87.7	2 213	103	101	3 457	38.0	60.4	1.5
Clearfield	261.5	3 221	66.6	0.0	3.5	3.1	4.8	310.5	3 824	244	204	4 675	43.0	55.2	1.8
Clinton	137.3	3 474	41.4	0.3	1.3	4.6	4.0	99.3	2 514	131	102	3 043	48.0	50.7	1.3
Columbia	207.5	3 102	63.6	0.0	3.1	3.7	4.7	212.5	3 176	148	168	5 129	47.1	51.6	1.3
Crawford	281.4	3 212	48.8	2.8	1.9	9.1	5.8	238.2	2 719	262	224	3 974	44.0	54.4	1.6
Cumberland	1 033.3	4 330	58.9	3.0	2.8	6.7	2.5	1 275.7	5 346	4 618	1 373	12 367	42.6	56.3	1.1
Dauphin	1 554.4	5 764	46.5	4.7	3.9	9.1	2.6	2 450.3	9 087	2 553	759	40 152	54.0	45.0	1.0
Delaware	2 744.1	4 891	50.1	2.1	4.9	11.1	2.0	4 601.2	8 200	1 980	1 473	23 452	60.2	38.8	1.0
Elk	92.2	2 921	46.8	0.2	2.8	1.8	8.2	287.8	9 123	109	83	1 288	51.1	46.8	2.1
Erie	1 203.4	4 288	44.0	5.6	2.7	14.2	3.5	1 705.3	6 076	1 509	765	16 029	59.3	39.4	1.2
Fayette	427.6	3 152	56.8	10.4	1.2	3.1	3.6	909.8	6 706	352	351	6 110	49.2	49.6	1.2
Forest	20.2	2 638	52.6	4.6	0.8	4.0	10.1	11.6	1 515	63	14	918	42.5	55.9	1.6
Franklin	452.7	2 992	54.1	4.1	1.9	5.5	4.8	619.1	4 092	2 453	406	6 193	33.3	65.8	0.9
Fulton	47.5	3 214	61.6	0.0	3.7	4.3	4.1	65.3	4 419	28	39	724	25.0	73.6	1.4
Greene	138.0	3 624	59.6	4.6	1.0	1.6	6.1	149.4	3 923	130	93	2 485	49.0	49.4	1.6
Huntingdon	134.9	2 937	57.1	1.3	1.8	2.3	5.0	147.7	3 216	122	110	2 950	35.5	63.0	1.4
Indiana	303.7	3 442	61.2	0.1	1.0	6.1	4.2	387.8	4 396	201	226	7 416	45.7	52.9	1.4
Jefferson	139.0	3 104	60.2	0.0	1.5	3.9	5.0	213.5	4 770	100	118	1 874	34.3	64.1	1.6
Juniata	46.0	1 848	65.2	0.1	0.9	2.6	5.4	13.7	550	71	65	686	31.6	66.8	1.6
Lackawanna	820.1	3 824	47.2	0.3	3.9	6.6	3.0	968.6	4 516	953	559	10 016	62.6	36.6	0.8
Lancaster	2 018.4	3 831	55.1	5.4	4.3	5.1	3.3	3 447.0	6 543	1 209	1 383	19 281	43.7	55.5	0.9
Lawrence	334.2	3 719	50.8	2.1	3.0	11.6	4.1	469.7	5 226	217	233	3 601	46.8	51.9	1.3
Lebanon	507.4	3 752	47.7	2.2	2.9	15.0	5.1	705.4	5 215	2 829	354	5 424	40.0	58.9	1.2
Lehigh	1 756.6	4 945	46.2	3.6	3.3	11.2	2.9	3 948.1	11 114	815	957	16 338	57.1	41.6	1.3
Luzerne	1 193.5	3 718	54.0	0.4	3.0	3.8	4.8	1 386.1	4 318	3 056	850	14 627	53.6	45.2	1.2
Lycoming	560.5	4 783	43.8	0.0	2.2	3.1	4.4	997.6	8 514	365	299	8 913	37.3	61.5	1.2
McKean	182.4	4 229	57.8	3.7	2.0	4.1	3.6	130.5	3 026	409	106	2 029	40.5	57.8	1.6
Mercer	435.3	3 764	63.5	2.3	3.0	2.6	3.9	444.6	3 844	245	308	5 156	49.1	49.4	1.6
Mifflin	166.3	3 555	61.5	4.0	1.7	0.4	3.1	218.1	4 664	88	123	1 749	32.6	66.2	1.2
Monroe	739.9	4 384	67.9	0.1	3.0	3.9	2.5	1 201.0	7 115	3 756	467	8 521	57.6	41.3	1.0
Montgomery	3 494.4	4 322	56.9	1.9	5.0	6.2	3.6	4 364.3	5 398	2 693	2 278	33 692	60.0	39.2	0.8
Montour	79.5	4 333	44.5	0.0	1.9	1.3	3.0	805.8	40 000	33	47	1 442	41.9	57.0	1.1
Northampton	1 501.3	5 017	49.8	3.1	4.0	11.6	2.7	2 550.6	8 523	1 091	776	13 778	55.5	43.2	1.3
Northumberland	266.3	2 820	54.3	3.8	5.1	7.1	3.9	255.4	2 704	166	245	4 249	42.2	56.0	1.7
Perry	128.6	2 813	61.7	2.5	0.8	7.4	4.3	107.1	2 343	79	120	1 838	32.4	66.1	1.5
Philadelphia	9 802.9	6 334	34.2	13.8	6.2	5.8	1.1	18 737.5	12 107	30 666	5 193	73 834	83.1	16.3	0.6
Pike	135.9	2 388	49.0	0.4	1.9	5.8	3.9	42.8	752	212	150	2 351	47.3	51.5	1.1

1. Based on the resident population estimated as of July 1 of the year shown. 2.

STATE/ County code	CBSA code[1]	County type[2]	STATE County	Land area,[3] (sq km) 2010	Population, 2014: Total persons 2014	Population, 2014: Rank	Population, 2014: Per square kilometer	Population and population characteristics, 2013 — Race alone or in combination, not Hispanic or Latino (percent): White	Black	American Indian, Alaska Native	Asian and Pacific Islander	Percent Hispanic or Latino[4]	Age (percent): Under 5 years	5 to 17 years	18 to 24 years	25 to 34 years	35 to 44 years	45 to 54 years
				1	2	3	4	5	6	7	8	9	10	11	12	13	14	15
			PENNSYLVANIA—Cont'd															
42 105	...	9	Potter	2 801	17 206	1 971	6.1	97.8	0.7	0.6	0.5	1.1	5.6	16.0	7.4	9.7	10.6	14.2
42 107	39060	4	Schuylkill	2 017	145 797	442	72.3	93.0	3.2	0.4	0.8	3.4	4.9	14.8	7.5	11.7	12.8	15.0
42 109	42780	7	Snyder	851	40 323	1 165	47.4	96.3	1.4	0.4	0.8	1.9	5.2	16.5	12.1	11.0	11.6	13.8
42 111	43740	4	Somerset	2 783	76 218	721	27.4	95.6	2.8	0.3	0.5	1.3	4.4	14.1	7.4	11.3	12.4	15.0
42 113	...	8	Sullivan	1 165	6 339	2 731	5.4	94.7	3.2	0.7	0.5	1.7	3.7	9.5	9.6	8.7	9.1	15.1
42 115	...	6	Susquehanna	2 133	41 920	1 130	19.7	97.3	0.8	0.5	0.6	1.7	4.8	15.1	7.6	9.9	10.8	16.1
42 117	...	6	Tioga	2 936	42 274	1 125	14.4	97.1	1.2	0.6	0.7	1.3	5.4	14.5	11.0	10.8	10.7	14.1
42 119	30260	4	Union	818	44 874	1 073	54.9	85.5	7.6	0.6	1.8	5.7	4.3	13.7	13.2	13.7	13.7	13.7
42 121	36340	4	Venango	1 746	53 529	934	30.7	97.0	1.8	0.5	0.7	1.1	5.3	15.2	7.5	10.3	11.2	14.8
42 123	47620	6	Warren	2 290	40 703	1 161	17.8	98.0	0.8	0.5	0.7	0.9	4.9	14.9	7.3	10.3	11.0	15.3
42 125	38300	1	Washington	2 220	208 187	308	93.8	94.5	4.1	0.5	1.1	1.4	5.0	14.9	8.8	10.5	11.9	15.0
42 127	...	6	Wayne	1 879	51 401	968	27.4	92.1	3.5	0.5	0.8	4.0	4.1	14.0	7.3	10.6	11.8	16.0
42 129	38300	1	Westmoreland	2 661	359 320	187	135.0	95.5	3.3	0.4	1.1	1.0	4.6	14.4	7.9	10.2	11.5	15.4
42 131	42540	2	Wyoming	1 029	28 131	1 486	27.3	96.7	1.2	0.6	0.7	1.8	5.1	15.6	8.9	10.9	11.8	14.6
42 133	49620	2	York	2 342	440 755	156	188.2	86.7	6.4	0.5	1.8	6.3	5.8	16.8	8.5	11.9	12.8	15.2
44 000	...	X	RHODE ISLAND	2 678	1 055 173	X	394.0	76.9	6.6	1.0	3.9	13.6	5.2	15.2	11.2	12.9	12.0	14.8
44 001	39300	1	Bristol	63	49 060	996	778.7	94.8	1.4	0.6	2.3	2.3	4.0	15.8	10.8	9.6	11.0	15.8
44 003	39300	1	Kent	436	165 128	384	378.7	91.8	2.1	0.8	3.0	4.0	4.8	14.8	7.6	12.2	12.6	16.1
44 005	39300	1	Newport	265	82 358	677	310.8	89.1	4.6	1.0	2.7	5.1	4.5	14.4	9.4	11.4	11.7	14.9
44 007	39300	1	Providence	1 061	631 974	102	595.6	66.8	9.4	1.1	4.7	20.2	5.8	15.4	11.7	14.3	12.4	14.1
44 009	39300	1	Washington	853	126 653	489	148.5	93.1	1.9	1.4	2.5	2.8	3.9	14.6	14.7	8.7	10.2	15.5
45 000	...	X	SOUTH CAROLINA	77 857	4 832 482	X	62.1	65.2	28.3	0.8	1.9	5.3	6.1	16.5	10.2	12.9	12.5	13.6
45 001	24940	6	Abbeville	1 270	24 965	1 609	19.7	70.0	28.8	0.7	0.6	1.2	5.6	16.3	10.0	9.6	11.4	13.7
45 003	12260	2	Aiken	2 774	164 753	386	59.4	68.7	25.6	1.0	1.3	5.2	5.9	16.4	8.9	12.5	11.5	14.0
45 005	...	6	Allendale	1 057	9 695	2 462	9.2	24.0	72.8	0.5	0.6	2.8	5.3	14.6	9.4	14.2	12.5	14.0
45 007	24860	3	Anderson	1 853	192 810	336	104.1	79.3	17.2	0.6	1.1	3.3	6.1	17.4	8.6	11.4	12.6	14.1
45 009	...	7	Bamberg	1 019	15 182	2 087	14.9	36.4	61.4	0.7	0.6	1.8	5.2	15.4	14.6	9.3	10.3	13.0
45 011	...	6	Barnwell	1 420	21 959	1 733	15.5	52.7	44.7	0.9	0.9	2.3	6.8	18.3	9.0	11.0	11.4	14.1
45 013	25940	5	Beaufort	1 493	175 852	363	117.8	68.2	19.5	0.6	1.8	11.6	5.9	14.2	9.8	11.9	10.6	11.0
45 015	16700	2	Berkeley	2 846	198 205	329	69.6	66.3	25.6	1.2	3.4	6.1	7.0	17.5	10.6	14.6	13.2	13.6
45 017	17900	2	Calhoun	987	14 878	2 108	15.1	54.2	42.3	0.8	0.6	3.2	5.4	15.3	8.1	10.1	11.1	14.9
45 019	16700	2	Charleston	2 373	381 015	177	160.6	64.3	29.2	0.7	2.1	5.2	6.2	14.1	10.5	17.1	12.3	13.0
45 021	23500	4	Cherokee	1 017	56 024	905	55.1	74.7	21.2	0.7	0.8	4.0	6.5	17.5	9.7	11.6	12.9	14.0
45 023	16740	6	Chester	1 504	32 337	1 378	21.5	60.3	37.8	1.0	0.7	1.7	6.3	16.8	8.7	11.1	11.9	14.6
45 025	...	6	Chesterfield	2 070	46 125	1 046	22.3	62.9	33.1	1.0	0.7	3.8	5.8	17.4	8.9	11.0	12.7	14.8
45 027	...	6	Clarendon	1 572	34 113	1 325	21.7	47.8	48.7	0.5	0.8	3.0	5.1	15.6	10.6	10.9	10.5	13.2
45 029	...	6	Colleton	2 736	37 771	1 232	13.8	57.5	39.1	1.2	0.7	2.9	6.2	17.0	8.3	10.9	11.1	14.1
45 031	22500	3	Darlington	1 453	67 799	785	46.7	56.3	41.6	0.7	0.7	1.9	5.9	17.3	9.4	10.7	12.4	13.8
45 033	...	6	Dillon	1 049	31 127	1 410	29.7	48.6	47.1	3.0	0.6	2.5	7.0	18.7	9.3	11.7	11.8	13.7
45 035	16700	2	Dorchester	1 485	148 469	433	100.0	67.0	26.8	1.3	2.7	4.7	6.6	19.4	8.8	13.8	13.7	14.8
45 037	12260	2	Edgefield	1 296	26 553	1 546	20.5	57.2	36.9	0.6	0.7	5.6	3.9	15.4	9.1	12.7	13.6	15.4
45 039	17900	2	Fairfield	1 777	22 976	1 686	12.9	38.9	59.2	0.6	0.5	1.9	5.2	15.8	8.7	10.0	11.2	15.3
45 041	22500	3	Florence	2 072	139 231	455	67.2	54.0	42.3	0.7	1.7	2.4	6.6	17.7	9.6	12.5	12.6	13.5
45 043	23860	4	Georgetown	2 107	60 773	860	28.8	63.5	32.9	0.5	0.8	3.0	4.9	15.4	7.3	9.2	10.7	13.0
45 045	24860	2	Greenville	2 033	482 752	142	237.5	70.8	18.9	0.6	2.6	8.7	6.6	17.1	9.5	13.4	13.4	13.9
45 047	24940	4	Greenwood	1 178	69 520	768	59.0	61.4	32.2	0.5	1.2	5.7	6.4	16.8	10.5	12.2	12.0	13.2
45 049	...	6	Hampton	1 450	20 405	1 811	14.1	42.3	53.6	0.6	0.8	3.8	5.7	16.9	9.1	12.5	13.0	13.9
45 051	34820	3	Horry	2 937	298 832	226	101.7	78.7	14.3	1.0	1.7	6.1	5.3	14.3	8.8	12.2	11.9	13.2
45 053	25940	6	Jasper	1 697	27 170	1 526	16.0	40.4	45.1	0.5	1.0	14.0	6.4	16.0	10.3	14.0	12.6	14.0
45 055	17900	2	Kershaw	1 882	63 161	829	33.6	70.1	25.4	0.7	0.9	4.2	6.1	17.7	7.9	11.3	12.2	14.6
45 057	16740	4	Lancaster	1 422	83 160	674	58.5	71.2	23.6	0.6	1.0	4.8	5.8	16.1	7.7	11.9	13.5	13.5
45 059	24860	2	Laurens	1 849	66 533	796	36.0	69.5	26.3	0.6	0.6	4.2	6.1	16.5	9.9	11.0	12.2	14.2
45 061	...	6	Lee	1 062	18 343	1 904	17.3	34.3	63.3	0.5	0.6	2.1	4.9	15.8	10.3	13.7	11.1	14.2
45 063	17900	2	Lexington	1 810	277 888	242	153.5	77.5	15.5	0.9	2.1	5.7	6.3	17.5	8.5	13.1	13.4	14.5
45 065	...	8	McCormick	930	9 846	2 451	10.6	49.2	49.6	0.4	0.5	1.2	3.4	9.7	6.2	11.3	10.7	13.7
45 067	...	6	Marion	1 267	31 933	1 386	25.2	40.3	56.1	0.9	0.9	2.9	6.3	17.2	8.9	11.2	11.6	13.0
45 069	13500	6	Marlboro	1 242	27 924	1 497	22.5	41.3	51.6	5.1	0.7	3.1	5.4	15.2	8.8	14.5	13.4	14.7
45 071	35140	6	Newberry	1 632	37 783	1 231	23.2	61.2	31.2	0.6	0.8	7.4	5.9	16.1	10.2	11.1	11.5	13.6
45 073	42860	6	Oconee	1 622	75 192	733	46.4	86.5	8.4	0.7	1.0	4.8	5.5	15.0	8.4	10.6	11.2	13.3
45 075	36700	4	Orangeburg	2 865	90 090	640	31.4	34.4	62.4	1.0	1.2	2.1	6.4	16.2	11.9	11.5	10.5	13.3
45 077	24860	2	Pickens	1 286	120 368	513	93.6	87.9	7.4	0.6	2.1	3.4	5.0	14.7	18.6	11.1	11.1	12.9
45 079	17900	2	Richland	1 961	401 566	171	204.8	45.8	47.1	0.8	3.3	5.0	6.0	16.1	16.1	14.8	12.5	12.6
45 081	17900	2	Saluda	1 173	20 026	1 834	17.1	58.8	26.3	0.5	0.5	14.8	6.4	16.3	8.3	12.4	12.1	13.4
45 083	43900	2	Spartanburg	2 093	293 542	230	140.2	70.6	21.5	0.6	2.6	6.2	6.4	17.5	9.9	12.2	12.7	14.0

1. CBSA = Core Based Statistical Area. See Appendix A for explanation. See Appendix B for list of metropolitan areas with component counties. 2. County type code from the Economic Research Service of USDA Rural-Urban Continuum Codes. See Appendix A for definition. 3. Dry land or land partially or temporarily covered by water. 4. May be of any race.

STATE County	Population, 2013 (cont.)				Population change and components of change, 2000–2014							Households, 2009–2013				
	Age (percent) (cont.)				Total persons		Percent change		Components of change, 2010–2014					Percent		
	55 to 64 years	65 to 74 years	75 years and over	Percent female	2000	2010	2000–2010	2010–2014	Births	Deaths	Net migration	Number	Persons per house-hold	Family house-holds	Female family house-holder[1]	One per-son
	16	17	18	19	20	21	22	23	24	25	26	27	28	29	30	31
PENNSYLVANIA—Cont'd																
Potter	15.4	11.8	9.2	49.9	18 080	17 457	-3.4	-1.4	831	862	-187	7 077	2.44	67.8	8.7	28.0
Schuylkill	14.3	9.8	9.1	49.0	150 336	148 289	-1.4	-1.7	5 839	7 981	-116	59 658	2.36	65.7	11.3	29.2
Snyder	13.3	9.0	7.5	50.6	37 546	39 702	5.7	1.6	1 911	1 470	220	14 397	2.60	72.4	8.9	22.4
Somerset	15.4	10.3	9.6	48.3	80 023	77 742	-2.9	-2.0	2 872	3 881	-417	29 791	2.45	69.2	7.8	27.1
Sullivan	17.9	14.6	11.9	48.1	6 556	6 428	-2.0	-1.4	211	469	157	2 402	2.50	63.6	5.5	32.7
Susquehanna	16.2	11.4	8.2	49.7	42 238	43 356	2.6	-3.3	1 685	1 859	-1 313	17 163	2.48	68.6	9.8	26.0
Tioga	14.3	10.9	8.3	50.6	41 373	41 981	1.5	0.7	2 018	1 835	126	17 058	2.37	68.9	10.0	25.3
Union	11.8	8.2	7.6	44.7	41 624	44 947	8.0	-0.2	1 718	1 590	-165	15 062	2.37	68.1	9.2	24.4
Venango	16.4	10.5	8.9	50.9	57 565	54 984	-4.5	-2.6	2 401	2 805	-1 041	22 547	2.36	67.1	11.3	28.9
Warren	16.1	11.0	9.2	49.9	43 863	41 815	-4.7	-2.7	1 713	2 111	-650	17 257	2.35	65.0	8.3	30.3
Washington	15.3	9.8	8.7	51.1	202 897	207 820	2.4	0.2	8 429	10 482	2 619	84 098	2.41	66.1	10.1	28.8
Wayne	16.2	12.1	8.1	47.2	47 722	52 822	10.7	-2.7	1 732	2 453	-888	19 558	2.48	68.5	8.5	26.9
Westmoreland	15.8	10.6	9.5	51.1	369 993	365 169	-1.3	-1.6	13 346	18 423	-262	152 109	2.34	66.8	10.5	28.9
Wyoming	15.1	11.0	7.0	49.9	28 080	28 276	0.7	-0.5	1 229	1 256	-103	10 992	2.49	68.1	10.0	25.6
York	13.5	8.7	6.8	50.6	381 751	434 972	13.9	1.3	20 979	15 895	991	167 592	2.55	70.3	10.9	24.5
RHODE ISLAND	13.3	8.2	7.3	51.6	1 048 319	1 052 567	0.4	0.2	46 520	40 353	-3 441	410 058	2.46	62.7	13.7	30.4
Bristol	14.6	9.4	9.1	51.9	50 648	49 875	-1.5	-1.6	1 487	2 051	-290	19 174	2.42	67.3	9.2	27.1
Kent	14.8	9.1	8.0	51.7	167 090	166 158	-0.6	-0.6	6 719	7 264	-327	68 880	2.38	62.5	10.4	31.6
Newport	15.0	10.5	8.3	51.0	85 433	82 888	-3.0	-0.9	3 064	2 893	-848	34 774	2.28	61.6	9.9	31.5
Providence	12.2	7.2	6.8	51.5	621 602	626 667	0.8	0.8	31 297	23 683	-2 015	237 800	2.52	61.8	16.4	31.0
Washington	15.2	9.8	7.4	51.6	123 546	126 979	2.8	-0.3	3 953	4 462	39	49 430	2.44	66.2	9.6	26.7
SOUTH CAROLINA	13.0	9.2	6.0	51.3	4 012 012	4 625 364	15.3	4.5	244 058	182 009	139 545	1 780 251	2.55	67.3	15.2	27.5
Abbeville	14.9	11.0	7.7	51.4	26 167	25 417	-2.9	-1.8	1 093	1 136	-396	9 809	2.49	67.5	13.6	28.3
Aiken	13.9	10.0	6.9	51.5	142 552	160 099	12.3	2.9	7 894	6 824	3 416	63 388	2.50	67.8	15.1	28.6
Allendale	14.5	9.7	5.8	46.0	11 211	10 419	-7.1	-6.9	443	448	-705	3 424	2.63	65.9	23.8	30.8
Anderson	13.1	9.8	6.9	51.7	165 740	187 126	12.9	3.0	9 512	8 353	4 380	73 296	2.53	70.5	13.8	26.1
Bamberg	14.6	10.0	7.5	52.3	16 658	15 987	-4.0	-5.0	679	754	-697	5 883	2.47	63.4	18.8	34.7
Barnwell	13.9	9.2	6.3	52.3	23 478	22 621	-3.7	-2.9	1 307	1 100	-883	8 416	2.63	68.3	20.4	27.9
Beaufort	13.3	14.4	8.9	50.7	120 937	162 233	34.1	8.4	8 809	5 725	10 118	64 417	2.46	69.5	10.0	25.5
Berkeley	11.7	7.7	4.0	50.0	142 651	177 843	24.7	11.4	10 974	5 065	13 696	65 392	2.77	71.2	13.6	23.6
Calhoun	16.0	11.8	7.1	51.3	15 185	15 175	-0.1	-2.0	626	717	-232	6 163	2.43	71.2	17.3	26.3
Charleston	12.7	8.4	5.7	51.6	309 969	350 209	13.0	8.8	20 392	12 432	21 924	143 717	2.41	58.4	14.0	32.2
Cherokee	12.9	9.0	5.8	51.4	52 537	55 342	5.3	1.0	2 873	2 480	266	20 762	2.63	68.3	16.6	28.1
Chester	14.4	9.7	6.5	51.7	34 068	33 140	-2.7	-2.4	1 726	1 593	-920	12 368	2.63	68.8	20.3	28.6
Chesterfield	13.8	9.6	5.9	51.3	42 768	46 734	9.3	-1.3	2 217	2 064	-787	17 622	2.60	68.3	17.0	29.1
Clarendon	15.0	11.9	7.2	50.8	32 502	34 971	7.6	-2.4	1 512	1 532	-786	12 690	2.60	69.2	20.0	28.1
Colleton	14.5	10.9	7.0	52.2	38 264	38 892	1.6	-2.9	1 928	2 038	-1 044	14 905	2.55	69.9	20.1	26.7
Darlington	14.5	9.7	6.3	52.7	67 394	68 681	1.9	-1.3	3 400	3 389	-785	26 609	2.52	69.6	19.4	27.6
Dillon	13.3	8.6	5.8	52.7	30 722	32 062	4.4	-2.9	1 865	1 542	-1 265	11 744	2.66	69.2	22.6	27.3
Dorchester	11.8	7.1	4.0	51.2	96 413	136 555	41.6	8.7	7 767	3 833	7 545	50 321	2.74	73.3	15.6	23.1
Edgefield	14.7	9.7	5.6	46.1	24 595	26 985	9.7	-1.6	930	834	-569	9 108	2.62	71.1	15.5	25.8
Fairfield	16.6	10.6	6.7	52.2	23 454	23 956	2.1	-4.1	984	1 192	-746	9 408	2.46	66.4	19.2	30.9
Florence	13.0	8.7	5.7	53.0	125 761	136 885	8.8	1.7	7 643	6 107	947	51 332	2.61	69.1	19.9	26.7
Georgetown	16.2	14.5	8.7	52.3	55 797	60 158	7.8	1.0	2 570	2 950	864	23 115	2.58	69.1	15.2	26.7
Greenville	12.2	8.2	5.7	51.4	379 616	451 225	18.9	7.0	25 986	16 133	21 025	175 149	2.56	67.2	13.3	28.3
Greenwood	12.4	9.1	7.3	53.2	66 271	69 661	5.1	-0.2	3 817	2 952	-1 004	27 004	2.49	67.0	17.4	28.6
Hampton	13.5	9.2	6.1	48.5	21 386	21 090	-1.4	-3.2	969	874	-754	7 470	2.60	70.6	19.8	26.5
Horry	14.7	12.5	7.1	51.4	196 629	269 291	37.0	11.0	13 036	11 827	27 195	113 490	2.42	65.4	12.1	27.4
Jasper	12.4	8.7	5.5	48.3	20 678	24 777	19.8	9.7	1 373	926	1 834	8 563	2.86	66.8	17.3	27.7
Kershaw	14.3	9.6	6.3	51.5	52 647	61 697	17.2	2.6	3 039	2 678	1 219	24 084	2.55	72.6	16.0	24.2
Lancaster	13.3	11.5	6.5	50.9	61 351	76 652	24.9	8.5	3 828	3 226	5 579	28 956	2.64	70.8	16.5	25.6
Laurens	13.7	9.6	6.8	51.5	69 567	66 537	-4.4	0.0	3 311	3 316	34	25 184	2.54	71.8	18.1	24.8
Lee	14.3	9.2	6.5	47.9	20 119	19 220	-4.5	-4.6	776	961	-737	6 737	2.54	64.9	24.6	32.1
Lexington	13.0	8.4	5.3	51.2	216 014	262 391	21.5	5.9	13 907	9 327	10 597	103 742	2.54	68.4	13.3	25.8
McCormick	16.4	19.0	9.7	45.3	9 958	10 233	2.8	-3.8	230	503	-115	4 069	2.15	71.1	14.8	25.5
Marion	15.3	10.0	6.5	53.8	35 466	33 062	-6.8	-3.4	1 695	1 820	-990	12 049	2.69	70.0	25.2	26.4
Marlboro	13.3	9.1	5.7	46.7	28 818	28 933	0.4	-3.5	1 296	1 345	-943	9 779	2.58	65.9	21.0	31.0
Newberry	14.1	10.4	7.1	51.1	36 108	37 508	3.9	0.7	1 832	1 740	171	14 254	2.55	70.1	16.8	24.9
Oconee	15.0	12.7	8.2	50.6	66 215	74 273	12.2	1.2	3 364	3 547	1 149	30 106	2.45	69.8	12.7	26.1
Orangeburg	13.6	9.8	6.8	53.0	91 582	92 501	1.0	-2.6	4 853	4 362	-2 831	34 180	2.59	66.1	21.3	30.4
Pickens	11.8	8.8	6.1	50.2	110 757	119 224	7.6	1.0	5 050	4 607	650	43 971	2.54	65.3	9.1	26.2
Richland	11.1	6.4	4.4	51.4	320 677	384 504	19.9	4.4	20 607	11 828	8 190	143 874	2.50	60.9	17.2	31.6
Saluda	13.5	10.4	7.3	49.5	19 181	19 875	3.6	0.8	1 043	800	-70	7 020	2.79	70.1	13.1	26.0
Spartanburg	12.7	8.7	5.9	51.5	253 791	284 307	12.0	3.2	15 234	11 817	5 856	107 350	2.60	70.1	15.5	25.7

1. No spouse present.

STATE County	Persons in group quarters, 2014	Daytime population, 2009–2013: Number	Daytime population, 2009–2013: Employment/residence ratio	Births, 2014: Total	Births, 2014: Rate[1]	Deaths, 2014: Number	Deaths, 2014: Rate[1]	Persons under 65 with no health insurance, 2013: Number	Persons under 65 with no health insurance, 2013: Percent	Medicare, 2014: Eligible for Medicare	Medicare, 2014: Enrolled in Medicare Advantage	Medicare, 2014: Enrolled in a Medicare prescription drug plan	Serious crimes known to police,[2] 2013: Total: Number	Serious crimes known to police,[2] 2013: Total: Rate[3]
	32	33	34	35	36	37	38	39	40	41	42	43	44	45
PENNSYLVANIA—Cont'd														
Potter	217	17 473	1.00	195	11.3	204	11.9	1 918	14.0	4 325	1 198	2 225	208	1 182
Schuylkill	7 072	137 127	0.83	1 330	9.1	1 835	12.6	13 479	11.9	34 018	9 554	17 706	2 627	1 806
Snyder	2 468	38 873	0.95	480	11.9	346	8.6	4 389	14.1	7 712	3 407	3 946	674	1 701
Somerset	4 945	72 720	0.86	679	8.9	934	12.3	7 666	13.4	18 158	10 396	5 604	983	1 282
Sullivan	435	5 940	0.81	48	7.6	101	15.9	786	17.1	1 766	494	994	89	1 375
Susquehanna	282	36 361	0.65	398	9.5	415	9.9	4 798	14.2	9 710	2 009	5 464	460	1 148
Tioga	1 848	41 325	0.95	489	11.6	445	10.5	4 065	12.5	9 774	2 282	5 134	594	1 390
Union	8 814	47 288	1.14	409	9.1	392	8.7	3 560	12.2	7 614	2 712	3 772	447	995
Venango	1 300	53 148	0.94	568	10.6	654	12.2	5 178	12.1	13 361	4 485	6 779	835	1 546
Warren	785	40 070	0.93	406	10.0	508	12.5	3 778	11.7	9 755	1 799	5 870	710	1 735
Washington	5 667	198 173	0.90	1 986	9.5	2 484	11.9	15 880	9.6	47 213	29 022	11 272	3 999	1 939
Wayne	3 883	49 047	0.85	397	7.7	550	10.7	4 967	13.1	12 754	1 835	7 637	869	1 684
Westmoreland	6 977	338 536	0.85	3 113	8.7	4 409	12.3	26 240	9.3	84 743	55 617	18 078	5 703	1 581
Wyoming	627	28 026	0.99	276	9.8	307	10.9	2 582	11.5	6 043	1 878	2 773	520	1 853
York	8 740	402 232	0.84	4 906	11.1	3 787	8.6	39 785	10.9	82 699	27 902	33 497	8 921	2 035
RHODE ISLAND	41 534	1 031 616	0.96	10 918	10.3	9 543	9.0	118 371	13.8	200 967	69 573	81 167	28 383	2 699
Bristol	2 752	40 696	0.64	348	7.1	503	10.3	4 147	10.8	10 535	4 056	3 707	822	1 677
Kent	1 506	156 090	0.88	1 577	9.6	1 691	10.2	13 907	10.2	35 189	13 367	13 057	3 525	2 139
Newport	3 147	85 988	1.08	715	8.7	700	8.5	7 086	10.9	17 859	4 171	7 269	2 015	2 460
Providence	27 306	631 497	1.01	7 350	11.6	5 549	8.8	83 892	16.2	111 384	40 358	46 254	19 890	3 157
Washington	6 823	117 345	0.85	928	7.3	1 100	8.7	9 340	9.4	26 000	7 621	10 880	2 070	1 645
SOUTH CAROLINA	136 745	4 643 519	0.98	57 401	11.9	44 230	9.2	729 643	18.6	916 057	204 112	444 725	197 327	4 133
Abbeville	917	21 480	0.59	250	10.0	251	10.1	3 602	18.3	5 753	1 676	2 675	825	3 283
Aiken	2 454	159 277	0.96	1 758	10.7	1 648	10.0	22 991	17.1	33 446	6 798	17 022	6 615	4 027
Allendale	1 372	10 394	1.07	88	9.1	102	10.5	1 231	17.5	1 970	720	837	271	2 733
Anderson	2 799	176 121	0.84	2 228	11.6	1 994	10.3	27 314	17.4	40 696	11 944	19 198	11 931	6 291
Bamberg	1 250	15 236	0.90	151	9.9	181	11.9	2 191	18.6	3 229	890	1 567	686	4 350
Barnwell	285	21 668	0.91	313	14.3	287	13.1	3 047	16.5	4 214	1 069	2 195	1 067	4 812
Beaufort	5 022	169 379	1.06	2 077	11.8	1 401	8.0	27 652	21.9	41 995	6 586	22 341	5 622	3 297
Berkeley	3 596	157 725	0.68	2 632	13.3	1 276	6.4	30 792	18.4	28 923	5 780	10 431	6 434	3 317
Calhoun	155	11 783	0.47	140	9.4	180	12.1	2 221	18.3	3 303	860	1 622	539	3 719
Charleston	10 555	415 248	1.33	4 841	12.7	3 056	8.0	59 013	19.1	62 847	10 942	27 877	13 141	3 548
Cherokee	832	53 826	0.91	659	11.8	559	10.0	9 432	20.0	11 594	3 490	5 505	663	1 184
Chester	218	29 142	0.69	407	12.6	403	12.5	4 907	18.1	7 085	1 594	3 683	1 355	4 168
Chesterfield	872	44 179	0.87	517	11.2	508	11.0	7 641	19.7	9 116	1 404	5 344	1 761	3 818
Clarendon	1 543	32 302	0.79	366	10.7	363	10.6	5 410	20.7	8 112	1 899	4 009	1 558	4 540
Colleton	388	34 694	0.74	444	11.8	534	14.1	6 943	22.5	8 885	2 181	3 929	1 879	4 934
Darlington	1 371	64 032	0.84	791	11.7	813	12.0	10 205	18.2	14 080	2 251	8 287	3 787	5 547
Dillon	449	30 396	0.88	441	14.2	361	11.6	5 470	20.7	6 047	1 253	3 396	2 115	6 743
Dorchester	1 992	113 557	0.58	1 863	12.5	958	6.5	21 389	16.9	22 572	4 357	8 562	5 362	3 754
Edgefield	3 047	23 474	0.67	322	12.1	226	8.5	3 566	18.2	4 823	1 154	2 224	465	1 771
Fairfield	398	20 930	0.71	221	9.6	279	12.1	3 323	17.6	4 911	1 314	2 340	944	4 051
Florence	3 360	146 433	1.16	1 794	12.9	1 441	10.3	18 029	15.6	26 451	3 174	15 837	6 538	4 750
Georgetown	557	59 986	0.99	600	9.9	741	12.2	9 857	21.5	17 095	3 024	8 836	2 109	3 493
Greenville	11 798	491 040	1.15	6 197	12.8	3 898	8.1	75 770	19.1	83 703	24 792	38 406	19 334	4 073
Greenwood	2 575	71 508	1.07	893	12.8	752	10.8	10 855	19.4	14 559	3 207	7 189	3 652	5 211
Hampton	1 577	19 391	0.80	217	10.6	227	11.1	2 774	17.5	4 024	931	1 903	727	4 025
Horry	2 954	279 099	1.02	3 064	10.3	2 905	9.7	56 132	24.4	71 488	11 019	36 913	15 895	5 534
Jasper	1 438	22 586	0.74	309	11.4	221	8.1	5 811	27.2	4 524	1 160	2 028	784	2 986
Kershaw	402	54 671	0.72	710	11.2	678	10.7	10 148	19.4	12 646	2 256	6 540	1 714	2 745
Lancaster	2 143	69 802	0.73	927	11.1	797	9.6	12 019	18.8	18 065	2 846	10 493	3 190	3 978
Laurens	2 397	60 956	0.79	749	11.3	804	12.1	10 113	18.9	14 934	4 408	6 949	2 885	4 343
Lee	2 009	16 282	0.57	185	10.1	257	14.0	2 766	20.3	3 848	805	2 154	754	4 062
Lexington	2 321	250 994	0.88	3 273	11.8	2 202	7.9	37 620	16.1	45 652	8 743	23 513	8 237	3 033
McCormick	1 285	9 460	0.78	50	5.1	128	13.0	974	16.8	3 283	972	1 556	200	2 022
Marion	199	29 445	0.73	369	11.6	439	13.7	4 780	17.9	7 079	1 238	4 093	2 033	6 269
Marlboro	3 320	27 619	0.90	301	10.8	326	11.7	4 012	19.3	5 922	1 176	3 305	1 519	5 419
Newberry	1 176	36 674	0.95	424	11.2	409	10.8	5 968	19.9	8 216	1 959	4 155	1 033	2 736
Oconee	793	73 369	0.96	770	10.2	854	11.4	11 584	19.7	19 407	4 332	9 886	2 601	3 466
Orangeburg	3 133	91 683	1.00	1 077	12.0	1 065	11.8	14 110	19.4	18 627	5 346	8 785	5 260	5 775
Pickens	6 613	110 126	0.81	1 168	9.7	1 099	9.1	17 589	18.4	23 317	7 467	10 408	4 868	4 045
Richland	30 026	430 038	1.22	4 860	12.1	2 956	7.4	52 441	16.2	55 753	10 407	26 276	21 268	5 339
Saluda	267	17 271	0.67	241	12.0	183	9.1	3 931	23.9	4 054	963	2 028	478	2 392
Spartanburg	8 206	291 286	1.04	3 584	12.2	2 840	9.7	47 362	19.6	57 489	19 968	24 945	10 507	3 612

1. Per 1,000 estimated resident population. 2. Data for serious crimes have not been adjusted for underreporting; this may affect comparability between geographic areas and over time.
3. Per 100,000 population estimated by the FBI.

STATE County	Serious crimes known to police, 2013 (cont.)[1] Rate[2] Violent	Rate[2] Property	Education: School enrollment and attainment, 2009–2013: Enrollment[3] Total	Enrollment[3] Percent private	Attainment[4] (percent) High school graduate or less	Attainment[4] (percent) Bachelor's degree or more	Local government expenditures,[5] 2012–2013: Total current spending (mil dol)	Current spending per student (dollars)	Money income, 2009–2013: Per capita income[6] (dollars)	Households: Median income (dollars)	Households: Mean income (dollars)	Households: Percent with income of $200,000 or more	Income and poverty, 2013: Median household income (dollars)	Percent below poverty level: All persons	Children under 18 years	Children 5 to 17 years in families
	46	47	48	49	50	51	52	53	54	55	56	57	58	59	60	61
PENNSYLVANIA—Cont'd																
Potter	119	1 062	3 711	10.4	62.1	14.6	34.1	13 602	22 564	41 547	54 414	1.7	39 781	15.4	24.0	21.5
Schuylkill	180	1 626	29 619	14.2	62.2	14.3	236.7	13 596	23 021	45 012	55 789	1.3	41 514	13.6	19.8	18.3
Snyder	250	1 451	10 038	34.9	63.4	16.7	57.4	11 633	23 088	46 513	61 711	2.4	45 558	12.0	19.2	17.4
Somerset	108	1 174	14 653	14.8	64.3	14.5	127.4	13 119	22 192	43 597	55 211	1.6	42 712	12.7	19.4	16.3
Sullivan	77	1 298	974	12.0	61.2	14.0	11.8	18 792	22 923	40 964	52 772	1.2	41 668	14.3	21.9	21.4
Susquehanna	125	1 023	8 848	14.8	59.0	16.5	98.9	14 800	24 477	48 231	59 569	1.7	49 244	14.4	21.5	18.7
Tioga	133	1 256	9 990	12.5	55.6	19.1	70.9	12 796	22 621	44 187	55 262	1.5	45 052	13.2	18.6	17.9
Union	91	904	11 923	46.0	57.0	21.2	52.7	13 257	22 259	48 528	63 968	3.7	49 488	13.5	16.4	14.8
Venango	87	1 459	11 424	14.5	60.9	15.4	86.2	13 852	22 060	41 977	51 915	0.7	41 736	15.8	25.0	23.0
Warren	249	1 486	8 303	16.8	57.5	17.9	59.2	12 711	24 179	43 764	57 053	1.4	42 043	14.2	23.1	20.9
Washington	189	1 751	48 243	17.7	49.9	25.6	387.1	13 733	28 433	53 693	68 847	3.6	54 919	10.9	14.2	12.9
Wayne	134	1 551	10 092	15.6	55.1	19.2	77.4	15 432	24 005	49 313	60 840	1.9	45 807	11.8	18.8	16.6
Westmoreland	182	1 399	79 387	18.2	47.7	25.3	609.7	12 534	28 051	50 736	65 904	2.9	51 412	10.7	15.9	13.5
Wyoming	228	1 625	6 267	21.3	58.3	17.4	55.1	14 571	24 195	48 482	60 530	1.8	47 012	11.3	16.8	15.7
York	224	1 811	103 887	20.0	53.4	22.0	849.3	13 141	28 132	58 745	71 782	3.1	56 963	10.8	16.9	14.6
RHODE ISLAND	257	2 442	275 804	26.0	42.0	31.3	2 127.8	14 415	30 469	56 361	75 749	4.8	55 015	14.7	22.0	20.2
Bristol	55	1 622	13 621	38.9	32.8	43.7	103.7	15 239	38 893	71 238	99 689	9.1	68 415	8.2	9.1	7.8
Kent	117	2 022	38 157	20.7	39.3	30.0	361.2	16 196	33 814	62 279	79 741	4.2	63 232	8.1	11.3	10.1
Newport	190	2 269	20 052	32.4	30.2	44.7	162.4	16 492	40 293	71 713	93 357	7.9	67 291	10.1	13.4	11.7
Providence	347	2 810	167 595	28.1	47.5	26.4	1 230.7	15 033	26 308	49 297	66 395	3.6	47 642	18.6	28.5	26.9
Washington	91	1 554	36 379	13.8	30.6	43.5	269.9	17 316	37 023	72 138	93 512	7.4	69 267	9.6	10.5	9.1
SOUTH CAROLINA	508	3 624	1 198 974	14.6	45.4	25.1	6 981.8	9 514	23 943	44 779	60 601	2.6	44 310	18.5	27.3	25.2
Abbeville	318	2 965	6 130	20.8	56.6	12.2	27.5	8 676	18 134	35 947	45 632	0.3	36 187	20.3	28.4	26.2
Aiken	331	3 696	39 099	12.1	46.7	24.0	208.6	8 451	24 769	44 509	60 728	2.5	43 876	18.3	28.6	26.7
Allendale	595	2 138	2 207	7.1	62.2	15.0	19.4	14 597	13 334	25 252	37 189	1.0	25 753	42.4	56.1	53.3
Anderson	608	5 682	46 460	14.0	50.2	19.3	262.8	8 394	22 081	41 579	55 713	1.7	41 591	16.7	24.3	21.8
Bamberg	577	3 773	4 480	16.5	50.5	17.5	26.0	11 590	18 902	31 483	47 786	1.1	30 762	30.7	43.0	39.9
Barnwell	636	4 176	6 081	11.6	59.4	11.2	42.3	10 071	18 862	35 231	47 861	0.5	31 899	25.0	38.6	34.6
Beaufort	520	2 777	35 165	17.0	33.1	37.6	229.0	11 201	32 503	57 316	80 008	6.3	56 354	14.1	23.9	21.8
Berkeley	299	3 018	48 210	15.6	45.0	21.3	268.8	8 686	24 165	52 427	64 596	2.2	50 794	15.7	24.4	23.6
Calhoun	421	3 298	3 387	18.9	54.9	16.9	18.1	10 549	23 023	40 704	55 479	1.8	40 593	19.7	30.6	28.8
Charleston	385	3 163	91 607	18.7	33.0	39.4	510.3	11 441	30 158	50 792	72 569	5.1	51 206	17.4	25.8	25.4
Cherokee	182	1 002	13 875	12.4	60.2	14.3	81.2	8 993	18 240	34 202	46 702	1.1	37 726	24.3	36.5	29.3
Chester	551	3 618	7 594	10.0	60.9	12.4	54.1	9 800	18 098	33 103	45 683	0.7	36 523	21.6	32.9	30.1
Chesterfield	412	3 406	10 919	6.8	63.7	12.6	67.9	9 086	17 140	31 252	42 640	0.5	33 591	26.5	37.0	33.5
Clarendon	516	4 024	7 862	15.2	60.3	13.0	47.0	9 220	17 665	31 410	45 609	1.6	30 096	27.3	40.6	38.0
Colleton	654	4 280	9 300	10.5	56.6	14.7	56.3	9 188	18 769	33 233	47 044	1.2	33 817	24.0	39.3	36.7
Darlington	584	4 962	16 943	13.6	57.7	17.0	92.6	9 021	20 105	36 323	50 535	1.7	34 209	28.2	39.2	36.2
Dillon	1 020	5 723	7 468	8.2	69.0	8.2	48.4	8 155	14 988	28 817	39 244	0.5	33 696	27.1	42.9	39.9
Dorchester	387	3 368	39 062	16.7	39.9	24.5	228.5	8 808	24 495	53 857	65 457	2.3	55 193	13.3	18.6	17.8
Edgefield	145	1 626	6 312	9.3	56.6	17.2	35.9	10 224	20 753	43 861	57 414	1.1	44 862	19.7	27.1	24.0
Fairfield	554	3 497	5 081	13.7	58.2	15.5	41.8	13 816	20 257	36 120	48 165	1.3	35 531	23.1	34.8	32.0
Florence	421	4 329	36 706	14.2	50.7	21.3	215.8	9 287	22 432	41 910	57 895	2.4	41 028	20.1	28.7	26.1
Georgetown	451	3 043	13 172	9.1	47.8	22.7	100.4	10 321	24 437	40 131	60 198	3.2	41 213	21.3	37.9	32.3
Greenville	600	3 473	117 411	22.9	40.3	31.2	620.2	8 421	26 643	49 022	67 633	3.5	49 476	16.2	24.5	22.8
Greenwood	739	4 472	17 857	6.5	49.6	22.1	102.8	8 733	21 053	36 540	52 446	1.7	37 217	25.6	34.7	33.3
Hampton	620	3 405	4 823	10.1	62.8	11.4	39.2	11 419	19 332	34 233	48 479	1.4	32 941	27.3	36.9	34.9
Horry	598	4 936	59 752	8.4	44.4	22.7	413.3	10 333	24 002	42 431	56 988	2.1	41 808	19.1	31.3	29.7
Jasper	244	2 743	5 951	13.5	61.5	12.5	37.1	12 748	17 350	36 413	46 044	1.2	34 852	27.2	40.3	36.9
Kershaw	442	2 303	14 994	9.3	49.6	19.3	90.2	8 675	22 638	43 765	57 561	2.0	44 787	16.3	25.8	24.5
Lancaster	489	3 490	17 539	8.7	51.9	18.7	103.3	8 753	21 003	42 217	53 222	1.5	40 837	18.8	24.6	23.4
Laurens	620	3 723	15 642	15.4	57.8	14.5	81.7	9 128	19 153	37 383	48 125	0.9	36 771	23.0	35.1	31.7
Lee	533	3 529	4 254	14.9	65.5	9.1	21.9	9 754	14 740	27 373	39 486	0.1	30 972	32.8	44.2	38.9
Lexington	325	2 708	68 541	13.5	39.3	28.7	372.1	9 819	26 886	54 061	67 779	2.7	53 880	12.8	18.8	16.2
McCormick	273	1 749	1 532	12.1	49.8	18.2	11.6	14 146	22 150	40 028	54 877	1.7	38 186	21.9	37.8	36.9
Marion	734	5 535	8 076	9.9	61.4	13.6	51.4	9 869	16 531	29 149	41 719	0.6	28 520	30.7	53.5	49.5
Marlboro	978	4 442	6 523	4.9	70.7	8.7	41.0	9 514	14 577	28 297	39 077	0.8	31 185	31.3	40.8	39.2
Newberry	352	2 384	8 916	14.7	55.2	18.9	59.5	10 060	21 591	41 718	54 951	1.9	37 890	19.8	28.4	25.4
Oconee	554	2 912	16 902	10.0	50.4	21.7	109.1	10 330	23 904	41 394	57 692	2.0	42 077	16.8	27.7	24.1
Orangeburg	604	5 171	25 022	14.6	56.2	18.6	154.1	11 087	17 687	34 110	45 181	0.8	32 180	25.7	38.3	35.9
Pickens	301	3 744	39 165	9.9	18.0	23.0	131.1	7 832	21 182	41 788	55 504	2.0	42 400	10.7	21.7	19.5
Richland	784	4 555	123 903	16.2	32.7	36.1	780.5	11 626	25 763	48 359	65 720	3.2	47 492	18.6	24.6	21.3
Saluda	415	1 977	4 083	11.0	63.8	12.4	20.7	9 467	19 725	38 514	50 955	1.6	40 366	22.1	33.0	30.7
Spartanburg	465	3 147	74 211	15.3	48.6	21.3	456.7	9 742	21 889	42 919	56 606	1.8	42 638	18.7	26.9	25.8

1. Data for serious crimes have not been adjusted for underreporting; this may affect comparability between geographic areas and over time. 2. Per 100,000 population estimated by the FBI.
3. All persons 3 years old and over enrolled in nursery school through college. 4. Persons 25 years old and over. 5. Elementary and secondary education expenditures.
6. Based on population estimated by the American Community Survey, 2009–2013.

STATE County	Personal income, 2013										Earnings, 2013		
			Per capita[1]			Supplements to wages and salaries; employer contributions (mil dol)						Contributions for government social insurance (mil dol)	
	Total (mil dol)	Percent change, 2012–2013	Dollars	Rank	Wages and salaries (mil dol)	Pension and insurance	Government social insurance	Proprietors' income (mil dol)	Dividends, interest, and rent (mil dol)	Personal transfer receipts (mil dol)	Total (mil dol)	From employee and self-employed	From employer
	62	63	64	65	66	67	68	69	70	71	72	73	74
PENNSYLVANIA—Cont'd													
Potter	635	1.5	36 268	1 698	212	55	17	92	111	171	377	23	17
Schuylkill	5 263	1.0	35 820	1 776	1 910	448	163	284	894	1 429	2 805	183	163
Snyder	1 350	1.8	33 863	2 106	505	118	45	113	237	383	781	48	45
Somerset	2 708	0.3	35 384	1 839	917	226	77	217	493	712	1 436	94	77
Sullivan	232	0.9	36 527	1 657	59	16	5	12	56	70	92	7	5
Susquehanna	1 527	0.5	36 110	1 729	398	92	32	135	313	357	656	44	32
Tioga	1 441	1.6	33 942	2 092	536	139	43	73	274	371	792	51	43
Union	1 568	2.6	34 957	1 904	688	154	59	142	290	284	1 042	60	59
Venango	1 937	-0.1	35 940	1 757	730	188	61	91	312	622	1 070	70	61
Warren	1 551	1.7	37 940	1 441	579	141	47	127	278	392	894	57	47
Washington	10 285	1.3	49 399	396	4 564	807	357	696	1 683	1 950	6 423	396	357
Wayne	1 896	1.1	36 787	1 626	557	137	47	110	405	481	850	57	47
Westmoreland	16 409	1.4	45 275	671	5 597	1 128	465	856	2 671	3 470	8 046	523	465
Wyoming	1 063	0.5	37 965	1 436	454	90	37	30	203	237	611	39	37
York	17 989	1.5	40 979	1 054	7 807	1 555	642	906	3 225	3 352	10 911	656	642
RHODE ISLAND	49 410	1.7	46 989	X	23 429	4 030	1 936	3 965	9 083	9 515	33 360	2 208	1 936
Bristol	2 925	1.7	59 418	114	591	111	51	197	687	384	951	71	51
Kent	8 233	1.5	49 889	371	3 555	584	302	468	1 363	1 489	4 910	337	302
Newport	4 653	1.6	56 472	176	2 162	434	192	239	1 244	698	3 027	189	192
Providence	26 764	1.8	42 577	884	14 743	2 404	1 193	2 582	4 263	5 939	20 922	1 377	1 193
Washington	6 835	1.7	54 132	230	2 378	497	197	479	1 526	1 005	3 551	234	197
SOUTH CAROLINA	171 088	2.5	35 831	X	81 434	14 191	6 415	13 105	28 705	37 988	115 145	7 188	6 415
Abbeville	748	2.5	29 902	2 703	213	45	19	50	92	235	327	25	19
Aiken	5 754	-0.2	35 047	1 891	2 831	447	216	425	926	1 391	3 919	255	216
Allendale	266	1.0	26 991	2 972	142	28	10	20	37	94	199	12	10
Anderson	6 256	2.4	32 818	2 279	2 414	432	193	409	890	1 605	3 448	235	193
Bamberg	433	0.7	28 040	2 896	138	31	11	41	56	161	221	14	11
Barnwell	590	-0.3	26 662	2 997	183	39	15	37	80	215	276	19	15
Beaufort	7 507	2.0	43 688	784	2 832	541	237	511	2 602	1 441	4 121	254	237
Berkeley	6 686	2.7	34 462	1 995	2 167	353	164	644	846	1 222	3 329	209	164
Calhoun	580	2.2	38 540	1 367	192	38	15	78	75	140	323	20	15
Charleston	17 405	2.3	46 686	570	11 155	1 963	874	2 651	3 844	2 582	16 643	945	874
Cherokee	1 643	3.4	29 401	2 763	690	120	58	165	191	485	1 033	65	58
Chester	1 012	2.6	31 050	2 542	337	63	27	54	130	303	481	34	27
Chesterfield	1 244	3.9	26 939	2 974	514	95	43	70	148	405	722	50	43
Clarendon	940	2.0	27 358	2 951	230	50	18	78	142	341	376	28	18
Colleton	1 191	2.3	31 505	2 477	349	68	28	78	178	374	523	38	28
Darlington	2 114	1.4	31 122	2 531	931	161	71	98	280	626	1 261	85	71
Dillon	777	0.5	24 872	3 059	274	53	23	47	92	280	396	28	23
Dorchester	5 076	3.6	34 913	1 912	1 161	208	93	54	665	972	1 515	105	93
Edgefield	956	1.5	36 148	1 722	218	44	18	25	123	196	305	21	18
Fairfield	682	1.7	29 500	2 752	440	83	34	28	90	228	585	37	34
Florence	5 032	2.8	36 377	1 679	2 680	466	206	358	718	1 266	3 710	231	206
Georgetown	2 397	2.1	39 655	1 211	870	150	69	206	569	653	1 295	90	69
Greenville	19 093	2.8	40 257	1 143	11 686	1 711	912	1 587	2 851	3 354	15 896	976	912
Greenwood	2 266	0.9	32 495	2 334	1 137	229	88	122	381	638	1 577	101	88
Hampton	574	-0.4	28 118	2 884	196	40	15	41	83	181	293	20	15
Horry	8 924	3.5	30 810	2 578	3 913	629	326	626	1 725	2 563	5 495	378	326
Jasper	761	4.4	28 593	2 839	278	50	22	54	73	195	404	27	22
Kershaw	2 239	2.7	35 819	1 777	635	123	51	167	292	513	977	65	51
Lancaster	2 481	6.9	30 834	2 572	920	156	70	193	364	704	1 338	93	70
Laurens	2 151	5.7	32 477	2 339	752	135	61	43	258	693	991	73	61
Lee	540	0.6	29 460	2 756	128	27	10	51	61	186	216	14	10
Lexington	10 390	2.6	37 956	1 437	4 332	753	335	825	1 596	1 850	6 245	385	335
McCormick	294	1.4	29 551	2 746	59	15	5	9	72	120	87	9	5
Marion	849	1.8	26 470	3 009	232	47	19	104	105	310	401	30	19
Marlboro	750	3.3	26 784	2 987	316	59	25	37	95	255	437	30	25
Newberry	1 223	2.6	32 595	2 311	478	93	38	47	189	341	656	44	38
Oconee	2 603	2.8	34 684	1 954	1 050	212	81	130	494	714	1 473	99	81
Orangeburg	2 825	1.4	31 067	2 538	1 163	224	94	159	375	879	1 641	108	94
Pickens	3 581	1.8	29 887	2 704	1 390	272	108	155	580	938	1 925	131	108
Richland	15 310	2.8	38 346	1 394	10 240	1 915	795	890	2 542	2 765	13 839	786	795
Saluda	733	3.6	36 460	1 671	133	30	10	31	76	169	203	14	10
Spartanburg	10 033	2.2	34 482	1 991	5 593	903	437	963	1 611	2 291	7 896	500	437

1. Based on the resident population estimated as of July 1 of the year shown.

STATE County	Earnings, 2013 (cont.) — Percent by selected industries: Farm	Mining	Construction	Manu-facturing	Infor-mation: professional, scientific, technical services	Retail trade	Finance, insur-ance, real estate and leasing	Health care and social assistance	Govern-ment	Social Security beneficiaries, December 2013: Number	Rate[1]	Supple-mental Security Income recipients, December 2013	Housing units, 2014: Total	Percent change, 2010–2014
	75	76	77	78	79	80	81	82	83	84	85	86	87	88
PENNSYLVANIA—Cont'd														
Potter	1.0	0.6	6.7	9.7	22.2	5.2	3.5	D	17.3	4 885	279	501	12 843	-0.7
Schuylkill	1.2	2.3	4.3	22.0	4.2	6.7	3.0	13.9	18.7	38 115	260	3 919	69 072	-0.4
Snyder	4.3	D	5.2	23.0	3.3	11.3	3.0	D	19.5	8 565	214	640	16 127	0.6
Somerset	1.5	6.2	5.3	10.5	5.0	7.3	4.3	12.9	21.4	20 085	262	2 386	37 945	-0.4
Sullivan	0.0	D	D	D	D	7.5	D	D	27.4	1 930	304	130	6 300	-0.1
Susquehanna	0.5	15.8	16.8	4.1	4.3	7.3	4.0	7.6	18.9	10 735	254	915	23 024	0.2
Tioga	0.1	6.3	4.4	14.4	4.7	8.1	4.3	D	23.9	10 775	254	1 154	21 492	0.6
Union	3.7	D	5.3	6.9	2.9	5.7	3.7	D	23.8	8 360	187	531	17 064	0.4
Venango	1.9	1.6	3.1	25.6	2.5	7.6	3.0	14.2	21.9	15 175	281	2 203	27 269	-0.7
Warren	0.0	7.4	3.4	17.4	3.7	7.4	5.4	14.0	16.1	11 020	269	1 025	23 375	-0.8
Washington	-0.2	7.4	11.6	11.0	7.9	5.4	6.4	11.4	10.8	51 740	249	5 489	93 912	1.0
Wayne	0.0	0.6	10.2	3.1	9.1	9.8	4.9	14.6	27.8	14 240	276	1 065	31 864	0.7
Westmoreland	0.2	2.7	7.4	15.3	7.2	8.0	4.0	12.5	14.3	93 585	259	8 918	168 255	0.0
Wyoming	-0.7	8.0	5.8	31.3	D	6.6	2.2	D	12.1	6 990	248	636	13 314	0.5
York	0.4	0.3	8.0	19.6	7.8	6.5	4.1	13.3	14.6	90 015	205	8 673	180 653	1.1
RHODE ISLAND	0.1	D	5.2	8.8	10.8	5.7	10.2	14.9	17.5	214 095	203	33 133	462 625	-0.2
Bristol	0.0	0.0	6.0	D	6.5	5.0	5.7	14.0	18.2	10 955	222	700	20 803	-0.2
Kent	0.0	D	5.2	10.7	9.9	8.9	10.1	15.8	13.8	38 130	231	3 494	73 595	-0.1
Newport	0.2	D	4.2	D	11.7	5.4	4.9	7.9	37.4	18 240	221	1 396	41 861	0.2
Providence	0.0	0.0	5.4	7.1	11.8	4.5	12.2	16.0	14.5	119 600	190	26 017	263 473	-0.5
Washington	0.3	0.2	4.9	16.4	6.7	8.6	4.3	13.1	22.9	27 170	215	1 526	62 893	1.1
SOUTH CAROLINA	0.6	0.1	5.5	13.9	8.6	7.3	8.3	9.3	21.1	1 014 683	213	118 384	2 188 129	2.4
Abbeville	-0.2	0.0	6.3	29.9	4.0	4.6	2.9	D	23.0	6 400	256	750	12 002	-0.6
Aiken	-0.3	0.2	10.2	13.6	11.0	5.8	5.5	7.5	12.3	37 270	227	4 228	74 032	2.5
Allendale	6.0	0.0	D	29.6	D	2.9	D	D	28.7	2 270	231	642	4 433	-1.2
Anderson	0.2	0.1	5.9	23.4	3.9	9.4	4.5	7.9	20.6	46 260	243	4 313	85 449	0.8
Bamberg	9.2	0.0	2.2	18.2	D	5.9	D	7.4	22.3	3 665	237	752	7 621	-1.2
Barnwell	4.5	0.0	4.0	26.0	D	9.2	1.6	D	26.5	4 950	223	1 082	10 378	-1.0
Beaufort	0.9	0.1	6.4	1.1	7.5	8.1	8.5	8.7	34.2	42 825	250	2 056	94 287	1.4
Berkeley	0.1	D	8.7	15.3	20.7	7.0	5.0	3.5	16.7	32 090	166	3 348	77 272	5.3
Calhoun	6.3	0.0	13.2	30.1	2.2	3.0	2.9	D	11.8	3 755	249	492	7 298	-0.5
Charleston	0.0	0.0	5.3	7.8	10.4	6.6	12.8	10.2	24.8	66 290	178	7 654	178 050	4.8
Cherokee	9.7	D	4.1	33.5	1.7	6.8	3.0	D	12.2	13 590	244	1 668	23 986	-0.1
Chester	2.9	0.0	6.3	33.1	4.0	5.6	2.5	D	18.0	8 265	254	1 157	14 603	-0.7
Chesterfield	1.0	0.6	4.0	38.5	2.7	6.6	2.1	8.1	14.4	10 580	229	1 692	21 281	-0.9
Clarendon	6.9	0.0	4.3	4.8	6.9	11.5	3.5	6.8	34.4	9 105	266	1 738	17 387	-0.4
Colleton	2.3	D	5.9	7.4	D	9.2	6.0	14.4	20.6	10 130	268	1 771	19 707	-1.0
Darlington	1.4	0.0	4.0	27.9	2.3	6.3	2.7	9.9	12.6	16 210	239	2 995	30 214	-0.3
Dillon	3.7	0.0	2.2	20.5	D	10.5	3.9	D	19.7	7 040	225	1 713	13 573	-1.2
Dorchester	0.4	D	5.3	20.2	4.1	9.3	3.7	8.4	21.6	24 730	170	2 531	57 688	4.5
Edgefield	4.0	0.0	3.9	14.4	1.3	6.5	2.4	D	33.5	5 370	204	677	10 617	0.6
Fairfield	1.2	D	2.2	26.7	D	4.2	1.0	D	13.7	5 555	240	908	11 646	-0.3
Florence	0.5	D	3.6	11.5	7.3	8.1	14.7	13.1	20.0	29 695	215	5 719	59 088	0.7
Georgetown	0.0	0.2	7.6	13.3	6.1	8.7	6.6	11.6	22.9	18 855	312	1 675	34 056	1.1
Greenville	0.0	0.0	5.3	14.2	12.3	6.1	8.5	9.7	11.8	91 680	193	9 149	200 831	2.7
Greenwood	0.2	D	3.8	24.4	3.5	6.9	3.7	11.7	25.2	16 290	234	1 838	31 125	0.2
Hampton	2.8	0.0	4.2	13.6	D	7.7	D	D	30.4	4 615	226	861	9 031	-1.2
Horry	-0.1	0.1	7.4	3.4	6.5	11.9	12.2	10.7	17.1	77 625	268	5 800	193 090	3.8
Jasper	0.4	0.0	12.3	3.0	D	18.2	5.3	13.2	19.0	4 970	186	692	10 890	5.7
Kershaw	3.5	1.4	7.4	21.6	4.0	10.1	8.2	6.5	18.9	14 395	230	1 540	28 012	1.9
Lancaster	0.8	0.0	3.6	15.2	20.1	12.3	4.6	12.0	14.3	19 770	246	1 657	34 103	4.3
Laurens	-1.5	D	3.2	35.2	4.3	5.9	2.1	D	20.5	17 230	260	2 199	30 617	-0.3
Lee	14.2	0.0	4.2	12.9	D	6.2	D	11.8	27.1	4 455	242	1 032	7 678	-1.3
Lexington	0.3	0.1	7.6	10.6	6.4	9.1	6.8	7.2	19.3	50 075	183	4 445	118 642	4.1
McCormick	1.5	0.0	D	11.0	D	4.4	D	D	49.0	3 470	349	315	5 468	0.3
Marion	1.3	D	5.5	9.3	D	13.9	6.7	19.2	19.2	8 355	261	1 778	14 794	-1.1
Marlboro	4.7	D	2.4	33.1	8.6	6.4	1.8	D	24.5	6 915	247	1 523	11 950	-1.0
Newberry	1.2	0.0	5.9	39.0	D	6.7	2.1	D	18.9	9 155	244	997	17 977	0.3
Oconee	2.5	D	4.9	28.0	D	6.4	3.1	6.7	15.8	21 425	286	1 514	39 128	0.9
Orangeburg	2.0	0.0	4.4	22.2	2.5	9.9	3.9	7.0	26.9	21 355	235	4 036	42 184	-0.8
Pickens	0.0	D	4.6	18.8	4.6	9.4	4.2	8.6	33.6	26 115	219	2 134	52 121	1.7
Richland	0.0	D	3.6	5.5	11.4	5.1	11.4	11.2	30.9	61 295	154	8 414	166 973	3.2
Saluda	10.8	0.0	3.4	34.8	D	5.1	2.0	3.7	23.1	4 520	225	529	9 200	-0.2
Spartanburg	0.2	0.1	5.5	24.8	5.4	6.2	6.9	8.2	15.8	64 535	222	7 390	124 505	1.5

1. Per 1,000 resident population estimated as of July 1 of the year shown.

STATE County	Housing units, 2009–2013: Occupied units: Total	Owner-occupied: Percent	Owner-occupied: Median value[1]	Median owner cost as a percent of income: With a mortgage	Median owner cost as a percent of income: Without a mortgage[2]	Renter-occupied: Median rent[3]	Renter-occupied: Median rent as a percent of income[2]	Substandard units[4] (percent)	Civilian labor force, 2014: Total	Civilian labor force, 2014: Percent change, 2013–2014	Unemployment: Total	Unemployment: Rate[5]	Civilian employment,[6] 2009–2013: Total	Percent: Management, business, science and arts	Percent: Construction, production, and maintenance occupations
	89	90	91	92	93	94	95	96	97	98	99	100	101	102	103
PENNSYLVANIA—Cont'd															
Potter	7 077	76.8	96 500	22.6	13.3	587	29.7	1.2	7 604	-1.9	549	7.2	7 087	29.0	36.4
Schuylkill	59 658	75.1	93 500	22.2	14.6	608	27.3	2.6	68 732	-2.1	4 776	6.9	63 799	27.7	32.2
Snyder	14 397	76.7	133 700	22.4	12.5	660	26.2	1.1	19 804	0.3	1 012	5.1	18 708	26.0	32.2
Somerset	29 791	78.9	98 400	22.0	13.0	555	25.8	1.7	34 777	-2.7	2 497	7.2	33 213	28.0	32.0
Sullivan	2 402	83.1	137 000	23.4	14.0	517	29.7	1.3	3 008	-1.6	184	6.1	2 571	25.5	36.7
Susquehanna	17 163	78.2	139 000	22.8	14.0	681	29.8	1.6	21 404	-4.1	1 244	5.8	19 381	27.1	33.4
Tioga	17 058	74.3	116 000	22.7	13.6	674	29.4	1.7	20 386	-4.1	1 396	6.8	18 250	29.7	32.1
Union	15 062	73.3	154 300	23.8	12.9	706	29.5	1.2	19 132	-0.1	946	4.9	17 450	33.6	25.1
Venango	22 547	74.6	81 000	20.3	11.4	581	29.4	1.8	24 613	-2.6	1 451	5.9	24 131	27.8	30.4
Warren	17 257	77.0	88 700	19.9	12.0	584	27.7	1.1	20 078	-1.7	1 054	5.2	18 604	30.1	31.5
Washington	84 098	76.1	143 600	20.0	11.5	643	27.9	1.2	105 860	-1.1	6 046	5.7	98 327	33.3	23.5
Wayne	19 558	79.7	179 900	27.0	13.5	760	33.1	0.8	22 262	-1.8	1 398	6.3	21 591	27.2	28.3
Westmoreland	152 109	76.3	133 600	20.5	12.7	637	27.3	2.1	184 190	-1.2	10 437	5.7	172 147	34.0	24.6
Wyoming	10 992	77.6	155 100	23.1	14.2	674	27.7	1.3	14 142	-1.5	952	6.7	13 029	25.2	34.7
York	167 592	75.1	174 200	24.0	14.4	820	29.5	1.4	229 957	-1.0	12 268	5.3	214 136	31.9	27.4
RHODE ISLAND	410 058	61.2	247 400	26.5	15.8	918	30.6	2.2	553 332	-0.6	42 430	7.7	509 865	36.9	18.6
Bristol	19 174	72.4	341 000	26.1	17.5	922	31.7	1.3	26 256	-0.1	1 691	6.4	24 482	48.8	13.4
Kent	68 880	71.4	220 200	26.1	16.2	981	30.2	0.9	91 195	-0.7	6 560	7.2	84 810	36.4	19.0
Newport	34 774	62.6	355 800	25.7	14.5	1 144	28.1	2.9	44 106	-0.2	2 949	6.7	40 969	43.7	13.7
Providence	237 800	54.3	224 100	27.0	16.3	882	31.2	1.0	322 238	-0.8	26 367	8.2	294 690	33.6	20.3
Washington	49 430	74.5	321 900	25.7	14.4	1 020	29.5	2.2	69 539	-0.4	4 864	7.0	64 914	43.5	15.3
SOUTH CAROLINA	1 780 251	69.1	137 400	22.8	11.4	768	31.5	2.3	2 197 587	0.8	141 451	6.4	2 003 023	32.5	23.8
Abbeville	9 809	76.4	91 200	22.4	13.0	629	36.4	2.0	10 457	-0.3	799	7.6	9 341	26.6	35.8
Aiken	63 388	73.3	124 600	21.2	10.4	705	30.3	3.2	72 669	0.6	4 673	6.4	67 203	34.8	25.7
Allendale	3 424	63.5	65 400	22.9	15.7	564	33.6	2.4	2 890	-6.1	351	12.1	2 740	27.1	33.9
Anderson	73 296	72.9	123 400	21.7	10.4	655	32.4	3.7	85 879	0.6	5 066	5.9	78 375	29.8	28.8
Bamberg	5 883	75.9	74 700	20.1	14.7	567	34.0	4.5	5 577	0.4	647	11.6	5 773	26.2	29.4
Barnwell	8 416	74.6	72 400	24.2	12.7	625	36.5	3.0	8 705	0.3	837	9.6	8 071	26.2	36.6
Beaufort	64 417	71.4	275 500	28.2	12.0	1 039	30.5	1.9	68 502	2.3	3 877	5.7	66 992	32.0	17.9
Berkeley	65 392	70.3	150 400	23.4	11.8	960	31.0	2.2	89 661	1.5	5 335	6.0	79 771	31.0	26.4
Calhoun	6 163	80.1	100 600	20.3	13.3	674	33.4	1.7	6 917	0.3	550	8.0	6 387	27.6	36.1
Charleston	143 717	60.6	236 100	25.9	13.4	950	34.0	3.7	189 718	1.6	9 756	5.1	172 528	38.4	17.5
Cherokee	20 762	66.9	83 600	21.4	11.2	615	28.6	2.3	23 475	-0.6	1 938	8.3	21 070	25.5	35.3
Chester	12 368	75.6	82 500	22.3	12.0	606	35.3	2.1	13 608	0.0	1 297	9.5	12 271	20.6	37.8
Chesterfield	17 622	69.8	79 400	22.8	10.9	592	36.8	2.9	21 096	1.0	1 454	6.9	18 255	23.2	36.4
Clarendon	12 690	72.9	85 900	24.5	12.1	584	32.1	3.0	12 909	-0.1	1 096	8.5	11 466	28.4	29.1
Colleton	14 905	74.4	89 900	27.0	13.5	702	32.3	2.4	16 660	2.4	1 266	7.6	14 555	24.8	31.1
Darlington	26 609	69.7	87 200	20.6	11.5	601	32.2	5.2	29 503	-1.5	2 345	7.9	26 608	27.9	28.6
Dillon	11 744	63.7	64 400	24.2	12.8	546	29.9	1.7	12 512	-1.5	1 208	9.7	10 943	19.1	35.1
Dorchester	50 321	70.7	167 400	24.7	11.7	957	31.0	3.6	69 376	1.7	4 020	5.8	62 557	34.3	22.7
Edgefield	9 108	78.2	109 500	20.0	13.0	597	31.2	1.4	10 512	0.6	708	6.7	9 910	25.2	36.5
Fairfield	9 408	73.6	91 900	23.9	12.9	633	30.9	2.3	10 015	-0.4	862	8.6	9 345	24.8	33.9
Florence	51 332	65.8	114 900	20.8	10.6	647	29.2	2.1	63 830	-1.2	4 633	7.3	57 422	33.6	21.3
Georgetown	23 115	77.8	158 800	28.3	13.6	803	33.6	1.8	24 859	2.6	2 054	8.3	22 522	28.9	24.3
Greenville	175 149	67.0	153 600	21.4	10.0	747	29.1	3.0	231 979	1.1	12 319	5.3	208 962	36.6	21.3
Greenwood	27 004	66.0	104 900	20.8	10.5	637	32.8	4.3	31 392	0.0	2 180	6.9	27 939	30.0	30.2
Hampton	7 470	75.9	79 400	22.8	16.7	633	29.2	4.2	8 299	-0.1	641	7.7	7 530	25.5	31.2
Horry	113 490	69.5	159 600	26.3	11.9	833	35.3	3.7	132 999	0.6	9 662	7.3	123 595	27.6	17.4
Jasper	8 563	71.0	90 200	28.9	13.3	758	32.2	1.7	11 307	1.6	644	5.7	10 922	21.5	29.3
Kershaw	24 084	76.1	116 000	23.3	10.9	679	25.9	2.0	27 917	0.7	1 764	6.3	25 916	29.7	28.1
Lancaster	28 956	75.0	142 200	23.6	11.4	654	32.2	2.8	34 382	0.7	2 491	7.2	30 547	26.2	27.8
Laurens	25 184	71.7	81 800	21.1	10.5	663	32.8	3.6	29 779	0.3	2 062	6.9	27 279	22.7	36.4
Lee	6 737	73.2	65 000	24.5	12.9	561	30.2	1.5	6 406	-2.0	582	9.1	6 311	25.5	28.5
Lexington	103 742	74.3	140 100	20.8	10.0	820	29.6	0.4	138 534	1.3	7 061	5.1	128 218	36.1	21.7
McCormick	4 069	79.3	112 500	25.6	11.4	514	31.5	2.1	3 516	0.7	277	7.9	3 164	22.5	32.1
Marion	12 049	67.1	77 800	24.1	13.8	544	37.3	3.3	12 819	-1.4	1 343	10.5	12 130	25.8	30.6
Marlboro	9 779	66.1	58 200	23.2	14.0	590	31.1	2.0	9 944	-5.0	1 053	10.6	9 080	20.8	39.8
Newberry	14 254	71.5	107 400	21.5	11.8	637	30.6	2.2	18 297	2.5	1 041	5.7	15 958	27.8	33.0
Oconee	30 106	75.2	136 300	23.0	10.1	665	31.9	2.7	33 963	2.8	2 154	6.3	28 577	31.4	27.4
Orangeburg	34 180	68.2	84 700	23.3	13.3	661	32.9	2.0	38 070	-0.8	4 292	11.3	34 399	28.6	28.4
Pickens	43 971	69.3	123 900	21.3	10.0	713	34.5	1.7	54 686	0.7	3 385	6.2	50 215	33.7	25.3
Richland	143 874	60.7	149 800	22.4	10.9	849	32.6	3.3	191 663	1.0	11 564	6.0	176 185	39.2	15.4
Saluda	7 020	72.8	90 400	21.3	12.8	589	23.1	2.5	8 629	1.3	490	5.7	7 993	23.4	40.7
Spartanburg	107 350	69.6	121 300	21.7	10.2	686	30.8	2.9	134 890	0.1	8 517	6.3	123 556	30.4	27.6

1. Specified owner-occupied units. 2. A value of 10.0 represents 10 percent or less; a value of 50.0 represents 50 percent or more. 3. Specified renter-occupied units. 4. Overcrowded or lacking complete plumbing facilities. 5. Percent of civilian labor force. 6. Persons 16 years old and over.

Table B. States and Counties — **Nonfarm Employment and Agriculture**

STATE County	Private nonfarm establishments, employment and payroll, 2013									Agriculture, 2012			
		Employment						Annual payroll		Farms			
											Percent with:		
	Number of establish- ments	Total	Health care and social assistance	Manufac- turing	Retail trade	Finance and insurance	Professional, scientific, and technical services	Total (mil dol)	Average per employee (dollars)	Number	Fewer than 50 acres	500 acres or more	Farm operators whose principal occu- pation is farming (percent)
	104	105	106	107	108	109	110	111	112	113	114	115	116
PENNSYLVANIA—Cont'd													
Potter	349	4 212	970	519	530	D	152	155	36 710	442	23.8	9.3	55.9
Schuylkill	2 804	40 381	7 356	9 181	5 696	960	1 129	1 379	34 157	791	41.5	5.4	49.7
Snyder	861	14 441	1 414	3 627	2 993	292	183	385	26 655	933	46.7	2.9	47.9
Somerset	1 702	18 776	3 481	2 699	2 624	695	613	645	34 339	1 140	22.5	7.2	48.3
Sullivan	160	1 233	486	D	D	24	D	30	24 027	179	24.6	8.9	50.3
Susquehanna	887	7 097	1 124	610	1 193	228	206	219	30 898	1 005	29.7	5.5	51.0
Tioga	890	11 332	1 951	2 269	1 992	384	378	375	33 070	1 125	21.0	7.0	49.5
Union	879	14 919	3 913	1 381	1 564	375	331	498	33 384	613	37.8	2.3	61.5
Venango	1 205	16 494	3 403	4 008	2 678	446	400	541	32 774	464	33.0	5.4	48.1
Warren	952	13 988	3 045	2 963	2 197	D	275	498	35 619	602	34.7	4.5	39.0
Washington	5 037	82 272	13 382	9 269	8 555	1 535	3 287	4 121	50 086	1 915	36.1	1.8	44.6
Wayne	1 311	12 236	2 526	631	2 496	466	314	380	31 095	711	24.9	4.1	50.4
Westmoreland	8 669	123 087	20 462	19 790	18 629	2 939	6 017	4 657	37 837	1 274	37.3	3.1	46.2
Wyoming	646	11 026	637	D	1 318	214	279	676	61 318	508	30.9	3.1	46.1
York	8 578	159 069	22 976	31 332	22 130	3 675	5 342	6 263	39 374	2 171	56.6	4.4	48.9
RHODE ISLAND	28 026	408 489	86 042	37 438	47 348	24 198	22 047	17 784	43 535	1 243	71.1	0.9	49.8
Bristol	1 231	12 710	3 333	1 470	1 352	233	426	419	32 966	42	73.8	0.0	57.1
Kent	4 638	68 044	11 497	6 208	10 715	5 281	4 446	2 796	41 093	126	65.9	1.6	41.3
Newport	2 710	29 934	4 952	1 270	4 028	1 458	2 973	1 162	38 834	214	72.4	0.9	55.6
Providence	15 524	254 490	58 118	22 004	24 671	15 895	12 055	11 486	45 134	425	73.2	0.2	45.6
Washington	3 723	40 756	8 062	6 485	6 582	971	1 664	1 759	43 168	436	69.7	1.4	52.8
SOUTH CAROLINA	101 545	1 583 213	218 379	214 541	223 958	67 543	81 697	59 301	37 456	25 266	44.1	8.1	41.0
Abbeville	335	4 387	434	2 072	427	D	43	141	32 057	574	32.2	5.9	34.1
Aiken	2 674	47 188	6 371	6 745	6 624	1 152	D	2 144	45 442	1 102	46.5	4.6	33.9
Allendale	125	1 628	D	848	131	D	28	67	41 187	141	22.0	27.0	54.6
Anderson	3 650	54 617	8 087	10 705	8 617	1 088	1 721	1 916	35 079	1 498	50.9	2.9	35.6
Bamberg	262	3 069	554	784	470	106	60	86	28 146	315	19.4	15.6	40.3
Barnwell	353	4 756	615	1 832	782	129	D	155	32 524	397	36.5	11.8	44.6
Beaufort	4 800	49 929	7 214	515	9 291	1 938	3 093	1 602	32 094	137	56.9	16.1	39.4
Berkeley	2 722	39 368	2 417	4 959	6 332	921	2 842	1 686	42 821	373	57.4	9.7	45.8
Calhoun	238	3 373	362	1 382	236	40	47	146	43 141	412	31.1	14.3	45.4
Charleston	12 138	183 068	29 402	13 730	26 263	5 974	15 407	7 439	40 633	359	64.1	3.6	42.9
Cherokee	975	16 743	1 127	5 599	2 702	311	174	514	30 678	490	43.1	3.9	31.4
Chester	527	6 709	D	2 426	891	153	129	233	34 793	477	33.5	8.6	39.8
Chesterfield	691	12 171	1 687	4 886	1 241	218	77	423	34 731	717	36.8	7.9	34.0
Clarendon	477	5 454	D	613	1 256	244	68	142	26 078	422	29.6	17.1	55.2
Colleton	730	7 380	1 365	692	1 619	276	228	232	31 457	530	40.4	13.0	42.1
Darlington	1 101	18 394	2 496	2 998	2 221	412	252	853	46 355	385	36.9	20.0	46.2
Dillon	478	8 647	1 160	2 047	1 144	197	D	199	22 999	228	21.1	24.6	46.5
Dorchester	2 113	24 523	2 765	4 792	3 798	687	825	794	32 366	411	48.7	7.5	46.7
Edgefield	312	4 455	504	1 183	385	59	46	137	30 739	389	40.1	9.0	36.2
Fairfield	290	4 676	646	767	570	63	D	256	54 824	194	32.5	10.3	40.2
Florence	3 051	55 467	13 193	5 668	8 554	4 868	2 271	1 924	34 696	632	33.4	11.1	44.3
Georgetown	1 762	17 817	3 616	1 926	2 817	519	739	610	34 234	209	39.7	13.9	44.0
Greenville	12 255	212 945	24 395	27 238	25 269	8 099	15 102	8 515	39 985	1 101	62.7	1.4	33.9
Greenwood	1 350	22 463	4 531	5 557	3 388	512	1 176	793	35 289	476	44.1	4.6	49.6
Hampton	340	3 405	502	664	690	119	94	113	33 118	323	28.5	18.6	46.1
Horry	8 213	98 267	10 654	2 537	21 139	3 522	3 227	2 721	27 688	938	44.1	9.8	50.5
Jasper	560	5 842	1 037	220	1 466	D	133	197	33 805	115	40.9	23.5	65.2
Kershaw	1 082	14 796	2 211	3 243	2 211	501	360	506	34 168	483	44.7	6.8	39.3
Lancaster	1 230	16 615	2 294	1 801	2 769	693	469	685	41 235	577	47.1	4.0	47.1
Laurens	935	16 339	2 012	6 296	1 612	423	D	557	34 086	826	40.0	5.3	35.4
Lee	189	1 769	252	D	409	77	D	48	26 892	386	26.2	16.8	45.3
Lexington	6 168	92 583	12 990	8 885	15 703	2 838	3 363	3 236	34 953	1 011	56.2	3.8	42.0
McCormick	88	960	206	288	104	23	D	28	29 382	93	24.7	21.5	35.5
Marion	506	6 965	674	767	1 040	209	62	166	23 858	275	40.7	17.1	41.8
Marlboro	328	4 791	968	1 979	776	120	55	150	31 279	224	26.8	20.1	44.6
Newberry	710	10 824	1 252	4 525	1 345	D	147	356	32 925	594	36.2	7.7	38.9
Oconee	1 440	19 710	2 779	5 202	2 845	436	456	778	39 438	884	60.7	1.7	39.3
Orangeburg	1 650	25 573	4 016	6 835	4 008	701	368	849	33 185	1 056	34.2	12.7	42.2
Pickens	2 003	26 257	3 662	4 836	4 463	682	892	776	29 565	727	69.6	1.1	44.0
Richland	8 660	155 345	26 514	10 179	18 212	17 983	11 308	6 329	40 744	398	52.0	4.5	38.9
Saluda	250	3 396	419	D	359	49	D	97	28 496	587	30.7	9.2	44.6
Spartanburg	6 141	118 348	14 205	25 991	13 891	2 125	4 991	4 772	40 323	1 338	57.6	1.4	43.7

STATE County	Agriculture, 2012 (cont.) — Land in farms: Acreage (1,000)	Land in farms: Percent change, 2007–2012	Land in farms — Acres: Average size of farm	Acres: Total irrigated (1,000)	Acres: Total cropland (1,000)	Value of land and buildings (dollars): Average per farm	Value of land and buildings (dollars): Average per acre	Value of machinery and equipment, average per farm (dollars)	Value of products sold: Total (mil dol)	Value of products sold: Average per farm (dollars)	Percent from: Crops	Percent from: Livestock and poultry products	Percent of farms with sales of: $10,000 or more	Percent of farms with sales of: $100,000 or more	Government payments: Total ($1,000)	Government payments: Percent of farms
	117	118	119	120	121	122	123	124	125	126	127	128	129	130	131	132
PENNSYLVANIA—Cont'd																
Potter	97	9.3	219	0.0	42.0	601 247	2 749	87 593	35.5	80 204	31.7	68.3	36.2	12.9	1 364	52.0
Schuylkill	106	-10.8	134	1.7	72.1	860 377	6 436	105 598	165.9	209 675	46.3	53.7	47.0	21.0	1 486	42.7
Snyder	91	-9.0	98	0.8	59.7	568 781	5 820	67 891	165.5	177 377	16.4	83.6	56.2	24.9	1 273	25.3
Somerset	215	3.8	188	0.1	119.4	495 161	2 631	91 144	104.2	91 411	26.0	74.0	52.8	21.1	1 602	30.9
Sullivan	37	34.7	209	0.0	15.4	645 698	3 084	97 117	9.5	53 168	26.7	73.3	33.5	8.9	461	43.6
Susquehanna	166	5.2	166	0.1	73.7	675 315	4 079	80 360	43.3	43 106	20.7	79.3	35.2	11.3	1 585	35.2
Tioga	205	11.4	182	0.2	109.0	626 933	3 438	78 940	80.3	71 340	26.5	73.5	43.6	13.3	2 590	42.0
Union	93	46.2	152	0.1	52.7	820 065	5 391	101 024	136.0	221 811	19.1	80.9	73.2	45.0	713	27.2
Venango	62	-5.0	133	0.0	29.0	410 136	3 093	81 901	15.8	33 998	64.5	35.5	39.2	6.7	489	22.8
Warren	82	-17.2	137	0.1	27.6	321 166	2 346	63 495	20.7	34 464	32.9	67.1	28.9	6.6	464	15.9
Washington	206	-2.5	107	0.8	86.4	489 897	4 558	68 244	35.4	18 492	53.1	46.9	28.1	2.7	841	10.9
Wayne	113	21.6	159	0.1	43.2	592 875	3 730	76 821	32.4	45 502	21.0	79.0	43.5	11.4	696	20.0
Westmoreland	143	-14.6	112	0.4	81.9	534 291	4 758	92 900	48.6	38 155	55.6	44.4	37.1	7.1	1 118	25.3
Wyoming	69	-11.8	135	0.1	32.4	542 844	4 011	79 911	14.6	28 772	57.3	42.7	32.7	7.7	633	31.7
York	262	-10.4	121	0.8	195.0	910 957	7 547	87 005	234.1	107 814	62.9	37.1	45.3	16.5	2 746	22.2
RHODE ISLAND	70	2.6	56	4.0	22.6	786 093	14 041	56 065	59.7	47 990	82.1	17.9	35.7	8.7	2 345	15.3
Bristol	D	D	D	0.1	1.1	977 024	D	52 190	2.7	63 548	80.4	19.5	47.6	16.7	D	2.4
Kent	D	D	D	0.2	1.9	790 095	D	39 087	4.4	34 548	80.4	19.6	38.1	7.9	D	7.9
Newport	12	13.9	54	0.5	6.5	1 201 720	22 248	63 850	14.6	68 365	83.1	16.9	47.2	12.6	390	22.4
Providence	D	D	D	0.6	4.9	600 586	D	41 569	14.1	33 127	77.8	22.2	31.3	5.2	949	17.9
Washington	27	10.8	63	2.6	8.2	743 369	11 870	71 654	23.9	54 865	84.6	15.4	32.6	9.6	936	12.6
SOUTH CAROLINA	4 971	1.7	197	159.2	1 967.3	586 518	2 981	72 400	3 040.1	120 323	42.6	57.4	27.0	8.6	46 616	26.9
Abbeville	92	0.9	160	D	23.7	444 972	2 775	52 261	9.6	16 786	31.0	69.0	26.1	1.2	631	19.9
Aiken	154	-3.1	140	1.3	55.8	532 257	3 800	54 850	96.3	87 426	16.3	83.7	26.9	7.1	892	16.1
Allendale	124	-0.7	882	6.5	39.1	1 949 496	2 211	94 773	25.6	181 532	89.3	10.7	27.0	12.8	946	68.8
Anderson	159	-8.1	106	0.6	46.5	463 880	4 367	51 636	62.8	41 918	D	D	23.5	4.3	779	12.3
Bamberg	93	-25.9	294	7.4	36.6	650 460	2 215	93 587	37.2	118 187	69.9	30.1	36.5	15.6	1 408	67.9
Barnwell	88	-5.2	221	4.4	37.5	539 234	2 437	79 058	48.4	121 867	D	D	29.5	13.9	1 091	48.9
Beaufort	42	-14.6	308	3.2	6.4	1 041 226	3 382	99 153	D	D	D	D	32.1	6.6	51	10.9
Berkeley	75	42.4	201	0.4	19.5	718 094	3 568	54 810	6.9	18 413	87.5	12.5	27.1	4.3	388	18.8
Calhoun	118	7.1	287	14.9	64.5	802 779	2 794	154 303	79.7	193 354	69.6	30.4	40.0	19.4	1 632	45.9
Charleston	35	-15.0	99	1.6	8.8	615 329	6 234	49 072	D	D	D	D	28.1	5.8	76	4.7
Cherokee	65	3.0	132	D	16.6	399 810	3 033	43 643	24.0	49 078	40.7	59.3	20.8	2.0	625	15.9
Chester	96	-14.6	200	0.5	19.0	564 608	2 820	65 338	42.6	89 329	D	D	29.8	6.1	376	10.3
Chesterfield	131	-6.8	183	1.2	42.4	500 552	2 739	59 743	121.2	169 050	D	D	23.2	7.8	1 047	37.1
Clarendon	174	12.3	412	8.5	98.1	758 033	1 840	152 725	139.6	330 829	53.2	46.8	42.2	20.1	1 972	68.7
Colleton	188	7.4	354	2.8	45.9	955 200	2 697	90 266	33.6	63 330	95.4	4.6	28.7	6.6	707	36.2
Darlington	177	2.4	459	7.3	113.7	1 132 418	2 465	182 395	129.2	335 509	58.4	41.6	45.7	26.5	2 806	47.3
Dillon	107	1.7	468	1.3	75.2	1 218 289	2 602	169 167	132.2	579 724	38.6	61.4	43.4	28.1	2 245	69.3
Dorchester	75	14.6	181	2.1	34.5	623 706	3 440	74 095	50.0	121 572	47.1	52.9	28.5	10.7	853	29.2
Edgefield	81	6.4	210	6.0	20.9	619 203	2 955	80 298	44.7	114 854	73.3	26.7	23.7	5.1	540	24.2
Fairfield	45	-14.2	229	D	7.3	640 268	2 791	51 732	30.9	159 237	5.0	95.0	26.8	6.7	137	9.8
Florence	156	-1.7	247	1.8	94.3	546 794	2 215	91 321	54.0	85 517	98.4	1.6	35.1	11.6	2 303	49.8
Georgetown	66	15.1	318	0.5	12.4	747 407	2 354	71 541	12.8	61 287	98.3	1.7	23.0	8.6	313	56.5
Greenville	73	0.3	66	1.6	20.6	430 060	6 498	38 996	16.6	15 044	81.7	18.4	15.8	1.7	180	5.3
Greenwood	86	21.0	180	0.2	12.7	432 540	2 407	46 794	6.7	14 023	33.3	66.7	23.3	1.7	311	11.1
Hampton	139	9.7	431	6.3	51.7	1 032 814	2 398	85 718	34.6	107 266	98.8	1.2	31.6	13.3	1 584	64.4
Horry	178	8.5	189	5.6	108.0	571 035	3 016	93 665	101.3	107 988	78.6	21.4	31.4	14.0	2 149	45.7
Jasper	69	31.6	597	D	8.7	1 620 974	2 717	69 043	6.4	55 626	93.5	6.5	26.1	5.2	60	17.4
Kershaw	83	-3.1	172	1.1	16.7	524 702	3 058	60 770	147.2	304 687	3.3	96.7	23.6	10.8	499	16.6
Lancaster	65	-0.2	113	0.3	14.0	443 986	3 936	45 899	78.0	135 208	4.5	95.5	24.4	7.5	86	8.8
Laurens	123	-5.7	148	0.7	35.0	503 297	3 389	47 098	40.9	49 530	D	D	28.8	4.8	1 085	15.0
Lee	142	1.0	369	7.4	93.2	835 806	2 265	151 886	118.6	307 225	51.3	48.7	31.6	18.9	2 289	66.8
Lexington	108	19.2	107	10.7	49.0	424 407	3 984	64 111	164.6	162 818	25.9	74.1	27.2	10.1	660	13.2
McCormick	30	20.5	323	D	3.6	570 806	1 767	42 785	5.2	55 946	22.6	77.4	21.5	5.4	155	32.3
Marion	80	15.4	292	1.1	44.5	679 087	2 328	107 269	40.6	147 815	69.8	30.2	29.5	14.2	931	66.5
Marlboro	113	-7.5	506	2.7	71.1	1 096 866	2 169	123 723	61.8	276 063	73.5	26.5	33.0	23.2	2 154	62.5
Newberry	104	3.7	176	0.8	31.7	476 949	2 711	66 958	139.5	234 891	D	D	31.1	7.2	1 004	22.2
Oconee	68	-4.0	77	0.3	15.4	407 562	5 308	49 633	121.4	137 313	5.0	95.0	21.4	7.9	382	6.3
Orangeburg	283	-1.5	268	25.4	152.9	677 763	2 528	124 560	231.5	219 264	53.8	46.2	33.3	16.3	3 506	43.9
Pickens	45	-12.3	62	0.8	13.0	344 880	5 575	41 396	8.4	11 611	66.3	33.7	12.5	1.0	167	4.0
Richland	61	3.5	153	2.0	31.1	536 626	3 511	68 653	30.0	75 472	76.9	23.1	24.6	5.8	507	10.1
Saluda	108	-1.7	184	4.4	29.6	524 673	2 853	81 700	126.3	215 130	21.8	78.2	37.0	11.6	750	25.6
Spartanburg	102	-7.3	76	1.9	37.7	377 862	4 964	38 547	34.6	25 829	56.6	43.4	18.1	2.2	833	8.1

STATE County	Water use, 2010		Wholesale trade,[1] 2007				Retail trade,[2] 2007				Real estate and rental and leasing,[2] 2007			
	Total water withdrawn (mil gal/day)	Gallons withdrawn per person per day	Number of establish-ments	Number of employees	Sales (mil dol)	Annual payroll (mil dol)	Number of establish-ments	Number of employees	Sales (mil dol)	Annual payroll (mil dol)	Number of establish-ments	Number of employees	Receipts (mil dol)	Annual payroll (mil dol)
	133	134	135	136	137	138	139	140	141	142	143	144	145	146
PENNSYLVANIA—Cont'd														
Potter	6.3	358	8	44	19.0	0.9	77	611	138.4	13.3	9	D	D	D
Schuylkill	36.7	247	111	1 946	1 070.2	69.4	542	6 085	1 317.9	116.0	69	349	52.4	7.6
Snyder	276.6	6 967	33	462	191.2	17.9	197	2 774	566.3	51.9	16	72	8.6	1.8
Somerset	29.7	382	76	D	D	D	288	3 146	764.7	63.1	50	186	21.4	4.7
Sullivan	0.6	95	3	D	D	D	27	234	45.0	3.9	4	D	D	D
Susquehanna	4.4	102	40	385	215.8	11.1	153	1 399	403.6	27.2	17	D	D	D
Tioga	8.0	190	22	362	201.8	11.7	166	1 867	413.5	33.9	22	64	8.6	1.6
Union	6.4	142	29	D	D	D	136	1 658	372.1	32.7	26	158	23.1	4.2
Venango	8.2	149	48	D	D	D	219	2 754	594.2	51.7	27	111	9.8	2.0
Warren	14.0	334	23	D	D	D	156	2 468	485.3	70.4	17	67	8.5	1.5
Washington	357.6	1 721	226	3 427	2 454.7	182.4	688	9 027	2 283.2	192.3	150	1 109	214.6	42.2
Wayne	5.8	110	34	333	112.0	11.7	251	2 925	692.3	64.6	37	132	19.1	3.4
Westmoreland	40.0	110	353	7 050	5 390.5	288.0	1 350	18 320	4 154.7	368.1	255	1 118	178.8	29.9
Wyoming	13.1	464	16	397	95.2	17.2	113	1 156	288.6	22.9	9	28	1.9	0.3
York	2 641.2	6 072	371	6 539	3 822.9	299.4	1 344	21 762	4 942.7	455.6	285	2 158	294.5	75.5
RHODE ISLAND	375.5	357	1 277	18 128	9 182.8	914.9	4 080	50 865	12 286.5	1 215.4	1 233	6 493	1 462.8	227.2
Bristol	1.6	32	52	399	227.4	18.9	154	1 362	295.7	31.8	45	124	24.8	4.2
Kent	4.0	24	251	2 688	1 381.3	132.7	756	12 020	3 242.9	302.7	219	1 573	272.6	57.0
Newport	11.7	142	75	407	264.0	18.4	471	4 251	1 096.2	111.0	126	702	102.1	24.1
Providence	330.8	528	771	12 496	5 856.9	563.2	2 117	25 827	5 924.9	582.2	674	3 676	982.7	130.0
Washington	27.4	216	128	2 138	1 453.2	181.7	582	7 405	1 726.7	187.7	169	418	80.6	11.9
SOUTH CAROLINA	6 782.2	1 466	4 323	58 524	40 498.0	2 599.4	18 886	231 685	54 298.4	4 878.1	5 473	30 417	5 194.1	989.8
Abbeville	4.4	172	9	D	D	D	59	385	71.9	6.1	6	D	D	D
Aiken	207.9	1 298	75	D	D	D	548	7 076	1 599.8	133.8	141	529	92.9	11.6
Allendale	12.8	1 229	6	D	D	D	33	231	32.6	3.3	1	D	D	D
Anderson	266.7	1 425	183	D	D	D	755	8 901	2 004.7	178.1	140	502	97.1	14.2
Bamberg	5.4	337	7	D	D	D	57	506	102.8	10.6	3	D	D	D
Barnwell	5.6	247	3	D	D	D	85	859	169.1	15.5	13	D	D	D
Beaufort	24.4	150	113	607	298.2	30.7	831	9 776	2 255.1	219.3	458	3 902	452.0	146.7
Berkeley	571.4	3 213	127	2 367	1 766.5	109.9	417	6 328	1 552.3	136.7	145	913	147.3	27.9
Calhoun	91.5	6 031	9	146	144.5	4.9	44	292	66.8	4.1	8	35	7.6	1.0
Charleston	53.5	153	456	6 015	3 267.4	282.6	2 079	27 439	6 321.0	628.8	781	3 982	734.2	133.9
Cherokee	11.5	208	23	D	D	D	249	2 817	718.1	50.5	38	134	19.3	2.5
Chester	5.3	160	13	D	D	D	103	902	210.9	16.0	19	D	D	D
Chesterfield	9.7	207	30	377	150.3	11.9	163	1 354	298.1	26.0	22	70	8.4	1.7
Clarendon	6.4	183	17	191	54.8	5.8	130	1 399	296.4	24.0	14	41	5.9	1.2
Colleton	12.3	316	26	D	D	D	181	1 858	419.7	35.6	55	184	32.6	4.5
Darlington	216.8	3 156	59	426	226.1	15.7	251	2 548	527.5	45.6	31	129	78.6	3.4
Dillon	5.6	174	18	511	300.1	17.6	136	1 331	381.7	22.1	20	55	7.1	1.0
Dorchester	33.6	246	66	467	170.2	19.3	303	4 078	879.5	75.8	118	317	54.4	8.0
Edgefield	11.4	422	10	D	D	D	65	444	120.3	8.7	8	33	2.2	0.6
Fairfield	772.0	32 227	10	D	D	D	65	652	216.2	12.6	15	32	4.7	0.8
Florence	42.8	313	162	2 645	1 358.7	102.6	776	9 415	2 237.9	187.5	139	686	104.0	17.8
Georgetown	833.2	13 850	34	D	D	D	331	3 181	702.2	67.4	124	424	60.0	13.1
Greenville	41.7	93	735	10 557	11 581.9	554.2	1 836	25 425	6 036.6	561.9	618	3 268	752.1	121.6
Greenwood	13.0	186	46	476	271.2	17.7	301	3 710	774.3	74.2	64	189	26.3	5.0
Hampton	8.3	394	9	144	92.0	7.4	105	759	150.7	12.7	10	123	8.5	3.1
Horry	141.7	526	256	2 237	907.6	82.2	1 810	21 072	4 967.2	459.4	708	5 839	829.9	187.4
Jasper	29.2	1 178	30	342	145.1	13.4	104	1 489	400.8	38.0	23	73	14.1	3.4
Kershaw	11.2	182	22	D	D	D	199	2 472	577.7	45.4	42	96	13.2	2.5
Lancaster	20.5	268	40	D	D	D	236	2 447	587.9	48.7	39	D	D	D
Laurens	7.3	109	33	225	67.0	9.4	191	1 585	370.1	29.2	31	75	9.4	1.7
Lee	3.9	203	14	98	49.6	3.2	49	416	154.6	6.9	7	18	3.7	0.5
Lexington	257.7	982	289	6 123	3 588.4	280.6	1 057	15 882	3 666.1	330.3	249	1 180	218.4	33.2
McCormick	1.5	149	1	D	D	D	30	144	34.8	2.3	6	D	D	D
Marion	4.5	135	21	144	104.4	4.7	143	1 316	269.9	25.6	15	69	6.4	1.5
Marlboro	32.7	1 130	14	D	D	D	99	824	159.0	13.1	16	42	3.9	0.6
Newberry	9.3	247	28	D	D	D	155	1 543	369.9	30.4	24	82	20.6	2.2
Oconee	2 537.7	34 167	43	D	D	D	281	3 107	743.5	67.0	86	253	40.0	7.7
Orangeburg	32.4	351	68	801	405.7	25.0	419	4 494	1 007.0	85.1	55	226	24.6	5.4
Pickens	48.8	409	69	588	253.2	23.4	359	4 451	1 153.5	99.3	86	337	60.5	9.1
Richland	78.0	203	372	6 129	3 150.7	274.8	1 376	19 518	4 367.7	420.7	467	3 828	845.8	134.4
Saluda	6.1	308	8	D	D	D	49	323	73.4	6.1	5	8	0.6	0.1
Spartanburg	42.1	148	440	6 437	5 482.0	278.5	1 089	13 937	3 638.4	309.0	279	1 279	220.8	45.1

1. Merchant wholesalers, except manufacturers' sales branches and offices. 2. Employer establishments.

STATE County	Professional, scientific, and technical services,[1] 2007				Manufacturing, 2007				Accommodation and food services, 2007			
	Number of establish-ments	Number of employees	Receipts (mil dol)	Annual payroll (mil dol)	Number of establish-ments	Number of employees	Receipts (mil dol)	Annual payroll (mil dol)	Number of establish-ments	Number of employees	Sales (mil dol)	Annual payroll (mil dol)
	147	148	149	150	151	152	153	154	155	156	157	158
PENNSYLVANIA—Cont'd												
Potter	27	139	19.5	9.9	24	847	205.9	27.4	44	237	10.6	2.3
Schuylkill	156	D	D	D	199	10 211	3 043.4	397.8	283	2 971	135.8	34.2
Snyder	46	232	20.6	8.3	70	5 014	D	175.0	85	1 423	54.0	15.6
Somerset	99	D	D	D	131	3 933	955.5	146.0	167	2 204	81.4	22.4
Sullivan	9	D	D	D	NA	NA	NA	NA	25	120	6.8	1.4
Susquehanna	51	243	17.2	5.0	68	785	115.7	24.8	84	691	32.1	7.8
Tioga	52	251	20.1	8.4	43	2 220	463.1	75.2	99	1 048	40.0	9.8
Union	78	334	27.5	9.6	37	2 086	D	78.8	95	2 094	80.2	23.4
Venango	63	D	D	D	88	4 097	1 113.0	187.8	105	1 407	44.3	12.6
Warren	52	D	D	D	67	2 932	D	129.5	85	870	35.0	8.8
Washington	401	D	D	D	263	9 565	3 672.9	430.6	384	6 106	233.7	64.3
Wayne	105	D	D	D	66	727	115.0	24.7	172	2 482	187.8	54.9
Westmoreland	751	D	D	D	603	21 064	7 077.0	907.1	762	12 797	454.3	129.6
Wyoming	41	D	D	D	30	2 737	D	71.9	60	571	22.3	6.1
York	726	5 437	620.4	240.9	600	38 016	11 957.4	1 669.8	736	13 112	527.9	146.4
RHODE ISLAND	3 096	22 732	2 777.8	1 173.9	1 831	53 718	12 061.5	2 374.8	2 926	44 426	2 148.7	622.1
Bristol	119	D	D	D	105	2 573	496.5	106.2	126	1 694	68.3	19.2
Kent	521	2 701	336.1	123.1	284	11 531	3 039.1	562.5	459	8 862	398.6	116.0
Newport	321	D	D	D	86	2 796	346.1	181.9	366	5 148	343.0	103.6
Providence	1 780	D	D	D	1 195	29 601	6 422.9	1 177.0	1 527	23 350	1 065.9	303.8
Washington	355	1 442	208.5	75.4	161	7 217	1 757.0	347.3	448	5 372	272.8	79.5
SOUTH CAROLINA	9 459	74 372	9 343.3	3 622.6	4 335	242 153	93 977.5	10 061.5	9 291	182 899	8 383.5	2 311.0
Abbeville	14	D	D	D	31	2 098	657.5	67.3	32	329	11.0	2.9
Aiken	236	D	D	D	96	7 853	3 959.3	375.4	238	4 608	172.9	46.1
Allendale	10	39	4.7	1.6	7	920	385.4	33.0	8	86	2.9	0.6
Anderson	288	D	D	D	222	12 655	4 886.3	495.2	350	6 420	235.8	64.5
Bamberg	19	45	4.7	1.1	22	913	D	28.0	21	286	9.4	2.5
Barnwell	24	157	16.0	4.8	21	2 635	681.3	85.3	28	471	14.7	3.8
Beaufort	563	D	D	D	90	1 092	223.4	35.8	458	9 686	530.5	174.2
Berkeley	206	D	D	D	98	5 794	5 527.3	322.0	208	3 935	161.2	42.2
Calhoun	12	52	4.8	1.3	17	1 057	D	D	9	113	4.1	1.0
Charleston	1 449	D	D	D	302	10 706	5 338.1	479.6	1 045	24 504	1 382.7	377.1
Cherokee	51	D	D	D	62	6 205	2 484.9	208.7	97	1 833	68.2	18.2
Chester	28	D	D	D	51	3 002	1 407.5	132.6	42	616	25.2	6.5
Chesterfield	25	77	7.3	1.8	54	4 663	1 361.0	166.1	76	803	30.5	7.5
Clarendon	22	122	15.9	8.2	18	1 147	291.4	37.0	66	778	29.8	7.2
Colleton	53	250	26.4	7.4	32	1 583	245.2	48.8	71	1 146	56.0	12.1
Darlington	67	D	D	D	66	4 742	2 433.4	212.9	88	1 230	53.9	13.7
Dillon	21	76	5.5	1.5	24	2 687	432.6	65.3	58	867	31.6	8.3
Dorchester	166	D	D	D	93	5 543	2 361.4	240.2	153	2 811	104.0	29.3
Edgefield	15	D	D	D	20	1 112	343.9	37.7	25	262	7.9	2.3
Fairfield	25	70	5.3	2.1	16	D	263.2	42.4	22	261	8.9	2.4
Florence	220	D	D	D	116	7 150	2 885.4	333.4	286	5 943	250.0	68.0
Georgetown	189	D	D	D	47	2 206	1 046.2	116.7	169	2 982	136.6	40.5
Greenville	1 441	13 561	2 034.0	790.8	605	29 758	10 821.4	1 244.5	1 005	19 205	817.8	232.7
Greenwood	118	D	D	D	71	7 950	2 821.1	342.0	124	2 484	86.1	24.2
Hampton	21	D	D	D	15	878	280.3	36.9	43	459	17.6	4.3
Horry	660	D	D	D	168	4 103	894.8	166.8	1 178	25 931	1 483.8	396.2
Jasper	26	D	D	D	23	515	76.4	16.2	56	679	32.4	8.1
Kershaw	90	472	41.7	14.1	68	3 696	1 419.1	161.8	95	1 386	52.2	13.6
Lancaster	73	457	58.8	20.2	68	2 473	1 247.6	103.7	93	1 331	56.3	12.9
Laurens	35	181	11.1	6.4	95	5 523	1 562.3	201.4	80	1 512	53.7	13.2
Lee	9	52	3.4	1.7	NA	NA	NA	NA	19	284	10.7	2.5
Lexington	551	D	D	D	219	9 772	3 465.7	404.4	489	10 726	434.5	123.1
McCormick	6	D	D	D	NA	NA	NA	NA	13	73	2.0	0.6
Marion	28	73	5.9	2.1	29	1 846	367.7	58.0	46	859	31.2	7.8
Marlboro	14	D	D	D	24	2 808	989.8	95.9	31	336	13.4	3.2
Newberry	41	138	11.2	4.7	46	4 931	1 277.5	159.0	61	827	30.4	7.3
Oconee	129	D	D	D	79	4 971	1 546.4	219.7	113	1 581	62.8	15.8
Orangeburg	95	D	D	D	83	6 962	2 597.9	284.9	177	3 686	152.2	36.8
Pickens	135	791	102.7	28.7	125	5 999	1 460.0	226.2	219	3 727	142.9	36.5
Richland	1 207	D	D	D	248	13 434	6 109.8	625.7	779	16 632	733.6	210.8
Saluda	12	43	2.1	1.0	NA	NA	NA	NA	17	95	4.3	1.1
Spartanburg	467	D	D	D	462	26 108	11 731.8	1 204.9	528	10 002	411.5	113.6

1. Establishment subject to federal tax.

STATE County	Health care and social assistance, 2007				Other services, 2007				Nonemployer businesses, 2013		Value of residential construction authorized by building permits, 2014	
	Number of establish-ments	Number of employees	Receipts (mil dol)	Annual payroll (mil dol)	Number of establish-ments	Number of employees	Receipts (mil dol)	Annual payroll (mil dol)	Number	Receipts (mil dol)	New Construction ($1,000)	Number of housing units
	159	160	161	162	163	164	165	166	167	168	169	170
PENNSYLVANIA—Cont'd												
Potter	42	959	78.9	36.6	25	112	7.9	1.8	1 263	50.6	1 275	10
Schuylkill	329	8 127	582.5	249.2	257	1 183	88.5	22.8	6 645	311.9	22 999	134
Snyder	71	873	91.6	31.2	68	299	24.2	5.7	2 887	133.5	10 425	51
Somerset	190	3 365	255.4	98.5	154	653	44.4	10.6	4 552	182.6	11 371	57
Sullivan	16	D	D	D	14	36	2.8	0.5	484	21.5	2 722	17
Susquehanna	58	1 150	66.1	30.2	71	276	20.3	4.6	3 180	159.9	12 287	57
Tioga	102	1 718	120.4	48.4	61	237	17.5	3.5	2 535	107.5	14 998	79
Union	127	3 445	295.0	119.2	61	263	20.9	4.1	2 658	132.0	14 099	57
Venango	175	3 506	275.1	106.9	118	568	47.7	11.9	2 905	108.0	8 834	41
Warren	111	2 982	206.3	94.5	83	528	24.5	6.4	2 174	92.7	2 890	19
Washington	667	11 459	1 051.3	428.0	408	2 500	208.2	64.5	12 102	631.7	108 396	453
Wayne	121	2 206	164.1	62.8	115	734	49.3	15.0	3 840	180.0	23 061	110
Westmoreland	1 208	18 721	1 494.6	612.9	838	4 651	586.3	92.4	20 906	916.4	94 763	391
Wyoming	70	1 134	74.3	31.2	52	207	17.3	4.3	1 819	78.7	7 018	40
York	925	20 265	1 931.3	790.7	746	5 098	582.7	115.6	24 995	1 139.8	138 969	816
RHODE ISLAND	3 274	81 947	7 161.4	3 091.6	2 382	14 379	1 449.0	373.1	73 758	3 335.3	195 030	952
Bristol	125	2 477	122.6	61.2	109	508	38.2	10.9	4 166	201.2	8 502	30
Kent	560	11 848	1 044.5	404.2	404	2 163	261.2	52.9	11 127	543.1	22 050	144
Newport	248	4 372	328.4	140.2	205	1 192	111.3	33.0	7 428	361.5	39 761	185
Providence	1 929	55 833	5 104.0	2 241.1	1 377	9 041	908.3	243.3	39 945	1 700.6	51 498	342
Washington	412	7 417	562.0	244.9	287	1 475	130.0	32.9	11 092	528.9	73 220	251
SOUTH CAROLINA	9 291	200 216	20 408.6	7 761.4	7 088	45 520	3 901.6	1 127.5	308 746	12 771.1	5 424 387	27 537
Abbeville	31	662	51.4	20.1	26	67	5.4	1.1	1 393	47.5	7 290	41
Aiken	294	5 266	409.6	149.4	199	1 171	94.2	22.0	9 909	353.4	126 450	678
Allendale	14	D	D	D	12	D	D	D	482	11.8	2 300	27
Anderson	362	8 112	786.0	301.2	244	1 871	154.5	55.0	11 711	446.8	149 019	863
Bamberg	38	731	60.2	24.8	24	D	D	D	762	19.9	1 754	10
Barnwell	45	588	41.2	17.5	26	100	10.4	2.4	1 389	37.4	2 303	37
Beaufort	386	6 365	642.3	230.6	308	3 068	238.0	84.7	14 067	729.5	459 800	1 197
Berkeley	189	1 837	109.4	42.3	168	880	63.2	18.6	11 146	435.3	358 411	1 977
Calhoun	25	D	D	D	14	59	4.4	1.0	889	32.6	4 967	28
Charleston	1 172	27 107	3 473.9	1 178.0	808	5 844	526.7	158.5	33 229	1 737.7	630 520	3 123
Cherokee	81	1 272	123.5	43.5	76	324	31.3	6.5	2 444	77.5	12 293	143
Chester	47	D	D	D	37	112	8.0	2.2	1 545	55.2	4 666	26
Chesterfield	71	1 480	110.1	45.2	51	169	12.7	3.6	2 260	76.4	5 650	50
Clarendon	48	D	D	D	36	163	11.2	3.4	2 077	71.6	11 466	97
Colleton	69	1 254	116.6	43.1	45	155	12.7	3.1	2 824	99.9	8 508	37
Darlington	91	2 494	206.3	84.5	85	353	28.5	7.1	3 749	117.3	17 410	99
Dillon	40	1 072	90.3	34.8	40	94	8.1	1.8	1 531	46.5	1 977	19
Dorchester	197	2 586	233.9	88.1	183	831	62.9	19.0	8 650	319.5	224 302	1 055
Edgefield	23	513	24.6	10.7	23	88	10.8	2.4	1 346	45.0	14 008	71
Fairfield	38	748	44.5	20.1	13	47	4.2	1.0	1 330	40.2	8 899	64
Florence	346	11 564	1 326.6	490.1	206	1 439	126.8	33.5	8 618	323.8	39 465	280
Georgetown	203	2 044	196.3	80.6	118	628	41.3	12.4	5 087	215.6	68 963	296
Greenville	1 015	23 581	2 447.5	997.9	750	5 475	472.2	148.4	33 938	1 531.2	605 227	3 094
Greenwood	146	4 589	530.7	197.4	88	619	39.9	10.0	3 843	130.7	16 139	162
Hampton	33	486	35.2	14.8	28	134	8.6	2.1	1 139	35.3	1 237	9
Horry	611	9 079	976.0	358.7	512	3 110	265.6	65.3	21 976	986.3	541 816	3 473
Jasper	40	679	58.0	22.5	36	139	10.6	3.0	1 451	67.1	55 305	229
Kershaw	93	1 990	179.3	74.3	92	374	26.1	7.0	3 895	146.4	35 713	262
Lancaster	114	D	D	D	104	434	55.0	13.9	4 893	178.3	317 389	1 063
Laurens	88	2 025	149.6	58.9	58	416	22.2	9.5	3 148	101.4	14 090	88
Lee	32	406	17.5	7.9	17	87	6.0	1.3	871	23.7	966	9
Lexington	498	10 985	869.5	379.9	487	2 989	252.0	79.3	18 292	754.1	368 316	1 412
McCormick	7	D	D	D	6	D	D	D	511	15.2	5 416	24
Marion	72	D	D	D	37	139	9.5	2.5	1 604	52.1	2 586	15
Marlboro	51	942	68.5	28.0	20	67	4.1	1.1	934	25.6	1 217	9
Newberry	55	1 125	84.0	32.3	60	281	21.9	6.3	1 805	60.6	11 959	59
Oconee	144	2 853	264.0	105.4	99	613	40.1	11.7	4 474	165.4	72 080	243
Orangeburg	225	3 525	326.0	128.6	134	606	44.5	13.3	4 912	154.8	5 554	41
Pickens	195	3 134	291.7	105.9	144	767	108.9	18.6	7 094	287.1	101 422	434
Richland	919	24 686	2 939.7	1 122.2	701	5 188	511.3	144.2	25 311	1 081.2	253 911	2 275
Saluda	23	D	D	D	20	54	5.3	0.9	899	34.5	5 042	26
Spartanburg	510	13 349	1 287.4	520.8	433	2 920	283.9	69.8	17 533	750.2	174 769	1 090

STATE County	Government employment and payroll, 2012									Local government finances, 2012				
			March payroll (percent of total)							General revenue				
												Taxes		
													Per capita[1] (dollars)	
	Full-time equivalent employees	March payroll (dollars)	Adminis-tration, judicial, and legal	Police and Corrections	Fire Protection	Highways and transpor-tation	Health and Welfare	Natural resources and utilities	Education and libraries	Total (mil dol)	Inter-govern-mental (mil dol)	Total (mil dol)	Total	Property
	171	172	173	174	175	176	177	178	179	180	181	182	183	184
PENNSYLVANIA—Cont'd														
Potter	590	2 437 639	12.0	6.7	1.0	7.4	0.9	10.0	61.5	73.9	41.6	21.8	1 241	1 052
Schuylkill	4 186	15 090 961	8.1	8.5	0.1	3.8	7.3	7.1	64.1	485.2	233.0	166.2	1 130	842
Snyder	1 018	3 558 017	6.3	8.1	0.0	2.9	3.5	3.8	74.2	107.4	42.7	49.5	1 247	859
Somerset	2 210	7 165 165	8.8	4.3	0.0	5.7	1.8	4.2	70.6	225.8	112.7	81.2	1 055	857
Sullivan	201	742 784	15.2	1.7	1.1	5.2	3.8	5.3	67.2	22.1	7.8	11.8	1 822	1 657
Susquehanna	1 464	5 097 993	5.6	5.6	0.6	4.5	1.7	2.4	79.2	139.9	73.6	54.2	1 268	1 138
Tioga	1 450	4 927 182	7.0	6.0	0.6	3.5	10.4	7.0	64.2	150.3	76.5	54.9	1 290	1 005
Union	883	3 323 742	9.7	6.0	0.0	3.9	4.3	8.9	66.1	157.6	75.7	51.5	1 145	812
Venango	2 052	6 987 537	7.7	7.9	3.0	3.8	5.2	5.7	65.4	196.8	112.6	57.2	1 053	811
Warren	1 409	4 668 630	8.7	7.2	1.1	5.4	17.0	2.6	57.5	113.1	58.7	41.3	1 004	762
Washington	5 853	22 585 416	6.8	9.1	1.4	4.1	7.0	4.9	65.0	790.8	371.8	291.3	1 396	1 069
Wayne	2 592	9 809 084	4.6	4.1	0.0	2.0	28.2	1.9	57.7	212.3	71.7	119.1	2 293	2 175
Westmoreland	10 354	41 162 785	6.1	8.6	0.9	4.3	6.4	9.3	63.6	1 302.8	557.8	500.8	1 378	1 099
Wyoming	947	3 123 745	15.3	5.7	0.0	2.7	0.3	2.0	71.4	97.3	46.7	41.6	1 479	1 225
York	12 293	50 416 660	6.7	12.2	1.5	2.7	6.3	3.6	64.5	1 771.5	572.5	787.5	1 799	1 467
RHODE ISLAND	X	X	X	X	X	X	X	X	X	X	X	X	X	X
Bristol	1 397	7 178 253	3.0	7.9	2.0	3.0	1.9	4.4	77.5	205.0	41.5	148.0	3 011	2 942
Kent	4 694	24 743 968	2.8	9.9	10.7	2.0	1.3	3.7	68.1	624.4	144.3	407.2	2 470	2 403
Newport	2 527	11 716 139	5.0	10.6	9.2	2.6	0.2	5.5	65.4	364.6	76.1	229.2	2 793	2 650
Providence	17 322	86 400 418	3.8	11.7	9.5	2.0	0.4	5.9	66.0	2 313.9	791.5	1 215.6	1 935	1 896
Washington	4 199	20 282 486	4.3	9.4	3.8	3.0	1.3	3.8	73.7	552.3	102.2	401.4	3 187	3 138
SOUTH CAROLINA	X	X	X	X	X	X	X	X	X	X	X	X	X	X
Abbeville	815	2 384 457	7.4	9.5	1.1	1.8	7.5	8.4	63.9	60.8	30.4	21.1	840	689
Aiken	4 376	15 335 939	9.0	9.9	1.0	4.3	3.0	6.2	65.7	401.1	181.9	160.3	984	738
Allendale	625	1 746 281	7.6	6.7	0.0	2.9	29.6	2.5	49.5	29.1	16.4	9.0	902	790
Anderson	5 484	17 493 225	6.4	10.0	1.2	2.0	1.3	5.3	72.7	476.2	210.0	176.3	931	827
Bamberg	819	2 552 389	7.1	5.8	0.6	1.4	37.3	0.9	45.9	39.6	22.1	13.7	867	775
Barnwell	1 118	3 299 448	5.3	8.6	0.4	1.1	16.7	7.6	59.3	70.5	38.2	23.1	1 038	893
Beaufort	5 616	22 420 841	6.5	9.3	6.0	1.7	27.9	4.2	42.3	768.1	132.7	391.8	2 332	1 843
Berkeley	4 857	15 229 373	6.7	8.6	2.0	1.9	2.3	2.1	74.3	476.5	201.9	143.2	755	670
Calhoun	495	1 790 689	3.0	5.0	0.5	1.8	4.1	1.1	81.6	33.4	14.6	15.0	1 004	980
Charleston	13 396	47 281 757	9.0	15.4	8.8	3.6	4.8	11.4	43.8	1 612.3	402.2	924.2	2 531	1 581
Cherokee	1 933	5 953 218	3.7	7.2	1.7	1.1	6.9	7.7	68.8	146.3	65.3	61.5	1 104	806
Chester	1 174	3 574 024	8.6	9.3	2.2	0.6	4.9	8.2	64.8	79.0	35.9	29.6	909	770
Chesterfield	1 558	4 244 462	5.6	8.8	0.8	1.2	1.7	2.9	77.8	100.3	53.6	36.7	796	594
Clarendon	1 529	4 986 545	5.1	7.6	1.8	1.2	37.8	2.0	42.4	136.5	40.9	33.6	977	747
Colleton	1 758	4 967 648	10.1	9.9	7.4	1.9	2.9	2.2	63.4	116.4	49.6	49.9	1 307	1 182
Darlington	2 194	6 310 138	4.5	9.9	1.9	2.4	4.0	4.0	70.6	151.5	78.7	44.0	646	554
Dillon	1 167	2 987 274	6.2	10.5	1.5	1.1	5.2	3.0	70.1	74.9	42.2	21.2	675	561
Dorchester	4 560	14 338 815	6.9	8.6	2.2	1.2	2.7	4.6	73.0	360.3	155.5	139.0	976	789
Edgefield	1 053	2 997 459	5.4	8.0	0.1	1.3	20.4	4.5	59.7	56.1	29.4	18.1	688	606
Fairfield	1 055	3 207 938	8.3	8.3	1.2	2.5	4.8	5.3	67.8	73.7	26.6	41.9	1 793	1 684
Florence	4 772	15 317 333	6.1	8.9	1.8	2.8	7.2	5.8	66.2	387.1	172.1	134.7	976	696
Georgetown	2 430	7 765 625	7.3	7.7	6.1	2.1	3.9	7.3	63.7	209.0	63.2	106.1	1 762	1 609
Greenville	21 594	81 147 575	3.3	5.4	3.5	1.1	44.4	4.7	36.9	2 639.7	456.3	485.5	1 038	884
Greenwood	2 547	7 901 666	5.9	7.9	1.9	1.7	4.3	10.3	62.2	563.0	100.6	69.9	1 002	786
Hampton	938	2 724 640	7.1	11.8	1.3	1.6	5.2	2.5	69.3	58.5	31.0	21.3	1 028	897
Horry	9 820	34 724 743	8.4	11.7	5.0	3.5	2.7	7.6	58.9	1 161.7	254.9	609.6	2 160	1 278
Jasper	809	2 603 546	11.5	13.8	11.9	2.4	1.3	2.1	56.6	69.7	25.2	37.2	1 441	1 298
Kershaw	2 730	9 680 043	3.3	4.0	1.9	0.5	41.5	2.8	45.5	255.3	130.9	56.4	904	774
Lancaster	2 327	7 452 417	5.3	8.0	1.9	1.0	4.2	8.2	68.9	189.5	79.8	80.0	1 012	782
Laurens	2 310	7 353 314	3.4	6.7	2.3	0.9	31.0	8.0	45.9	214.0	83.0	50.0	755	651
Lee	612	1 602 678	12.0	8.7	1.3	2.9	9.6	3.4	62.1	41.4	23.3	12.5	672	517
Lexington	14 886	59 502 218	2.4	4.2	1.3	0.5	41.6	2.7	46.6	1 461.3	374.4	370.5	1 370	1 163
McCormick	304	811 090	7.2	12.7	0.0	1.9	8.7	11.9	53.4	21.6	7.9	10.9	1 095	1 058
Marion	1 230	3 302 618	5.6	10.1	1.2	1.8	3.5	3.5	72.9	78.2	42.6	22.7	700	520
Marlboro	985	2 122 399	9.2	11.9	1.6	1.6	3.1	6.4	62.6	68.7	37.5	16.6	591	514
Newberry	1 757	5 725 610	5.0	8.2	1.1	1.3	25.7	9.1	48.9	109.3	44.6	46.1	1 227	1 069
Oconee	2 527	8 134 083	7.1	8.0	2.1	2.9	2.0	10.1	66.8	184.8	66.5	95.0	1 272	1 175
Orangeburg	4 563	16 266 007	3.4	5.4	0.2	1.1	46.5	2.7	38.9	425.4	101.6	103.8	1 135	920
Pickens	3 247	10 077 389	5.7	8.6	2.0	3.3	4.7	5.9	66.7	262.7	109.4	112.3	939	722
Richland	13 444	45 241 826	6.4	9.8	3.8	1.6	2.7	7.7	65.0	1 390.8	394.8	589.3	1 496	1 309
Saluda	474	1 331 037	7.6	11.4	2.9	2.3	1.5	2.7	69.2	35.8	16.8	14.0	705	629
Spartanburg	14 164	55 750 441	3.2	4.9	1.6	0.6	47.1	3.9	37.9	1 488.8	350.6	322.9	1 118	988

1. Based on the resident population estimated as of July 1 of the year shown.

STATE County	Local government finances, 2012 (cont.) — Direct general expenditure: Total (mil dol)	Per capita[1] (dollars)	Percent of total for: Education	Health and hospitals	Police protection	Public welfare	Highways	Debt outstanding: Total (mil dol)	Per capita[1] (dollars)	Government employment, 2013: Federal civilian	Federal military	State and local	Presidential election,[2] 2012 — Percent of vote cast: Democratic	Republican	All other
	185	186	187	188	189	190	191	192	193	194	195	196	197	198	199
PENNSYLVANIA—Cont'd															
Potter	70.3	3 999	50.7	1.3	1.0	9.1	10.6	81.5	4 636	42	46	1 036	30.6	68.1	1.3
Schuylkill	520.8	3 541	55.0	1.5	2.5	6.8	4.7	555.0	3 774	606	374	7 262	44.9	53.5	1.6
Snyder	122.1	3 077	62.0	2.4	4.4	0.0	4.2	222.5	5 610	93	101	2 166	34.8	64.0	1.3
Somerset	213.0	2 768	61.0	0.1	2.5	5.7	5.5	286.3	3 720	185	192	4 313	36.6	61.7	1.7
Sullivan	25.1	3 889	63.1	2.1	0.7	2.7	8.5	9.0	1 396	19	16	378	39.5	59.0	1.5
Susquehanna	148.2	3 471	72.6	0.9	1.4	2.1	5.8	59.8	1 401	105	112	1 823	43.5	55.1	1.4
Tioga	137.5	3 229	52.4	0.0	1.2	10.9	7.3	119.5	2 807	143	109	2 945	35.5	63.0	1.5
Union	203.9	4 535	63.4	1.3	1.3	2.6	2.9	249.6	5 553	1 537	95	1 424	42.1	56.7	1.2
Venango	206.3	3 800	58.4	2.1	1.5	7.2	5.3	271.4	5 001	96	141	3 409	39.6	58.9	1.5
Warren	109.9	2 672	58.9	0.5	2.9	0.7	5.6	93.3	2 267	161	107	1 904	46.1	52.3	1.6
Washington	804.7	3 855	54.3	1.5	2.6	11.8	4.2	903.0	4 326	438	573	9 887	47.0	51.8	1.2
Wayne	210.9	4 059	64.5	2.4	0.7	4.4	3.0	262.7	5 056	518	128	2 505	43.3	55.6	1.1
Westmoreland	1 328.7	3 656	53.4	2.5	2.9	10.3	4.0	1 848.5	5 087	802	967	14 837	41.1	57.8	1.1
Wyoming	92.1	3 276	63.0	0.1	3.2	5.3	6.8	54.9	1 953	56	73	1 120	45.6	53.2	1.3
York	1 790.5	4 089	47.4	3.5	3.3	9.2	2.6	2 454.1	5 605	4 225	1 330	16 445	42.7	56.3	1.1
RHODE ISLAND	X	X	X	X	X	X	X	X	X	10 197	7 548	54 032	63.3	35.0	1.7
Bristol	201.6	4 102	66.6	0.2	4.1	0.1	4.2	147.6	3 004	87	237	2 003	62.6	35.9	1.5
Kent	593.7	3 601	58.4	0.1	6.4	0.5	2.8	449.3	2 725	724	809	7 435	57.7	40.5	1.8
Newport	357.9	4 363	48.4	2.1	8.0	0.4	3.0	203.9	2 486	4 503	2 846	3 339	60.9	37.6	1.6
Providence	2 229.9	3 549	53.2	0.2	8.2	0.1	2.8	1 836.7	2 923	4 302	3 039	29 390	66.9	31.5	1.6
Washington	532.3	4 226	67.5	0.5	5.4	0.4	3.5	302.1	2 398	581	617	11 865	59.0	39.2	1.8
SOUTH CAROLINA	X	X	X	X	X	X	X	X	X	32 658	54 937	311 585	44.9	53.9	1.2
Abbeville	59.7	2 377	50.1	3.0	7.7	0.0	1.3	24.7	985	37	101	1 385	41.8	56.9	1.3
Aiken	373.4	2 294	57.5	1.3	7.7	0.1	2.4	155.5	955	708	677	7 297	37.4	61.4	1.2
Allendale	27.5	2 758	69.3	1.7	5.0	0.0	1.5	14.8	1 477	18	36	1 194	75.3	23.5	1.2
Anderson	483.1	2 551	63.5	0.3	6.2	0.2	2.1	1 327.5	7 010	310	787	11 643	32.7	66.0	1.3
Bamberg	61.7	3 917	76.9	0.2	5.2	0.0	0.8	38.4	2 439	31	59	1 019	65.0	33.9	1.2
Barnwell	71.5	3 218	57.8	0.4	6.7	0.2	2.1	37.0	1 667	49	91	1 465	50.3	48.7	1.0
Beaufort	752.2	4 476	32.2	19.6	6.0	1.1	2.3	1 451.5	8 637	2 380	10 442	7 475	44.1	54.9	0.9
Berkeley	500.4	2 637	57.1	1.2	5.3	0.4	2.8	2 158.7	11 375	944	812	7 763	42.8	55.9	1.3
Calhoun	36.1	2 418	56.3	3.7	6.6	1.8	1.0	42.7	2 864	24	62	796	51.3	47.8	0.9
Charleston	1 363.0	3 733	36.6	1.0	11.9	0.2	4.7	2 857.4	7 825	9 160	11 572	36 812	53.5	45.2	1.2
Cherokee	132.3	2 378	65.3	1.5	6.6	5.1	2.3	1 423.8	25 579	102	230	2 161	34.7	64.1	1.2
Chester	89.7	2 756	62.9	3.1	5.0	0.0	0.4	59.0	1 811	58	135	1 585	53.5	45.2	1.3
Chesterfield	104.7	2 271	63.2	0.0	8.7	0.0	2.6	194.8	4 224	84	189	2 009	47.9	50.9	1.2
Clarendon	138.9	4 044	34.7	40.8	4.1	0.0	1.0	88.7	2 583	56	137	2 276	55.8	43.5	0.8
Colleton	127.8	3 350	47.8	0.7	8.0	0.8	3.0	141.2	3 701	91	165	2 023	49.7	49.2	1.0
Darlington	148.0	2 173	64.2	0.4	7.0	0.0	2.0	103.9	1 525	145	278	2 934	49.4	49.6	1.0
Dillon	76.7	2 441	64.6	0.3	6.0	3.0	2.1	10.2	324	81	129	1 474	55.2	43.8	1.0
Dorchester	349.2	2 451	64.0	1.4	6.0	0.0	7.4	507.4	3 561	184	601	5 953	41.6	57.1	1.3
Edgefield	58.3	2 211	67.5	2.4	6.3	0.5	2.0	25.9	981	396	98	1 278	44.1	55.0	1.0
Fairfield	86.5	3 704	53.6	6.2	5.9	0.0	1.7	21.4	917	37	95	1 567	65.3	33.7	1.0
Florence	382.5	2 773	59.5	5.9	6.5	0.2	1.7	270.2	1 958	604	590	12 253	48.0	51.2	0.9
Georgetown	194.2	3 227	56.8	1.4	5.1	0.6	2.7	502.9	8 355	115	288	4 630	46.9	52.1	1.0
Greenville	2 628.6	5 621	23.1	51.4	2.7	0.2	1.1	3 479.0	7 440	1 808	1 998	28 223	37.2	61.0	1.8
Greenwood	506.5	7 261	23.9	58.7	2.1	0.0	0.7	466.2	6 684	142	280	6 923	41.6	57.3	1.1
Hampton	68.8	3 318	69.0	2.5	7.3	0.9	1.8	31.5	1 522	336	79	1 189	62.2	36.8	1.0
Horry	1 100.1	3 897	39.1	12.4	5.6	0.1	5.5	1 603.2	5 679	588	1 203	14 850	37.1	61.7	1.3
Jasper	67.2	2 600	51.4	0.2	8.9	0.4	1.9	79.1	3 062	53	105	1 358	60.9	38.0	1.1
Kershaw	253.6	4 068	36.7	41.9	2.8	0.2	1.0	291.1	4 669	105	260	3 296	40.1	58.8	1.0
Lancaster	185.7	2 347	54.7	4.0	5.6	0.0	2.8	219.5	2 775	88	328	3 499	42.0	56.8	1.2
Laurens	231.7	3 499	34.1	32.5	3.9	0.1	2.1	194.1	2 931	99	270	3 755	40.2	58.3	1.4
Lee	37.3	1 999	57.1	4.7	6.6	0.1	2.1	54.1	2 902	31	68	1 173	65.1	33.6	1.3
Lexington	1 529.8	5 658	44.1	37.4	3.3	0.0	0.9	1 531.8	5 665	602	1 136	18 080	30.4	68.4	1.1
McCormick	18.6	1 873	57.9	5.8	5.0	0.0	2.0	32.0	3 218	75	36	771	52.7	46.6	0.8
Marion	79.9	2 460	61.3	1.8	8.6	0.0	2.4	5.2	159	66	136	1 553	63.3	35.7	1.0
Marlboro	80.0	2 841	65.4	1.7	6.2	2.2	0.0	67.2	2 386	348	103	1 526	62.5	36.7	0.8
Newberry	116.7	3 107	49.9	1.3	5.2	0.5	1.6	134.2	3 573	84	152	2 265	40.6	58.2	1.2
Oconee	188.2	2 522	59.7	0.5	7.2	0.2	3.1	171.5	2 298	134	310	4 043	30.5	68.0	1.6
Orangeburg	436.4	4 771	34.3	43.8	4.1	0.1	3.6	296.9	3 246	198	373	6 972	68.6	30.5	0.9
Pickens	329.4	2 752	64.3	1.5	5.1	0.1	3.3	469.0	3 919	180	485	9 201	25.9	72.1	2.0
Richland	1 388.2	3 525	44.0	0.2	4.6	0.1	1.1	5 237.8	13 300	9 280	11 606	44 534	64.0	35.1	0.9
Saluda	34.3	1 725	55.3	2.1	7.5	0.1	2.3	31.1	1 565	32	83	931	38.6	60.3	1.0
Spartanburg	1 501.9	5 202	32.3	48.4	2.8	0.4	1.0	1 018.7	3 528	467	1 187	19 380	38.4	60.0	1.5

1. Based on the resident population estimated as of July 1 of the year shown. 2.

Table B. States and Counties — **Land Area and Population**

STATE/ County code	CBSA code[1]	County type[2]	STATE County	Land area,[3] (sq km) 2010	Population, 2014: Total persons 2014	Population, 2014: Rank	Population, 2014: Per square kilometer	Race alone or in combination, not Hispanic or Latino (percent): White	Black	American Indian, Alaska Native	Asian and Pacific Islander	Percent Hispanic or Latino[4]	Age (percent): Under 5 years	5 to 17 years	18 to 24 years	25 to 34 years	35 to 44 years	45 to 54 years
				1	2	3	4	5	6	7	8	9	10	11	12	13	14	15
			SOUTH CAROLINA—Cont'd															
45 085	44940	3	Sumter	1 723	107 919	557	62.6	47.9	47.4	0.8	1.9	3.7	7.1	17.6	11.3	13.2	11.4	13.2
45 087	43900	6	Union	1 332	27 876	1 499	20.9	66.9	32.3	0.5	0.5	1.1	5.4	16.4	8.1	10.2	12.3	14.7
45 089	...	6	Williamsburg	2 419	32 695	1 368	13.5	31.9	65.6	0.6	0.5	2.2	5.5	16.5	8.8	11.5	12.0	13.5
45 091	16740	1	York	1 763	245 346	270	139.2	73.4	20.1	1.3	2.1	4.9	6.4	18.6	9.0	12.1	14.2	14.7
46 000	...	X	SOUTH DAKOTA	196 350	853 175	X	4.3	85.1	2.4	9.6	1.6	3.4	7.1	17.5	10.1	13.2	11.2	13.0
46 003	...	9	Aurora	1 835	2 745	2 990	1.5	93.0	0.5	2.4	0.8	4.2	6.7	19.8	6.4	10.2	10.0	12.8
46 005	26700	7	Beadle	3 260	18 169	1 912	5.6	82.9	1.9	1.5	6.0	8.9	8.2	17.0	8.2	12.2	9.9	13.9
46 007	...	9	Bennett	3 068	3 430	2 943	1.1	37.7	0.9	62.0	1.1	3.3	10.2	23.5	10.5	11.4	9.6	12.3
46 009	...	9	Bon Homme	1 460	7 023	2 674	4.8	89.2	1.4	8.2	0.5	2.2	4.6	14.8	8.5	13.0	11.9	14.5
46 011	15100	7	Brookings	2 052	33 314	1 346	16.2	92.2	1.6	1.8	3.3	2.4	6.0	13.5	28.7	13.1	9.3	9.5
46 013	10100	5	Brown	4 437	38 408	1 213	8.7	91.6	1.8	3.9	2.0	2.3	6.7	16.7	9.9	13.5	11.0	13.2
46 015	...	9	Brule	2 117	5 309	2 814	2.5	88.1	0.9	11.1	0.6	2.4	7.1	18.7	7.2	11.1	10.9	14.0
46 017	...	9	Buffalo	1 221	2 077	3 043	1.7	19.2	1.1	78.5	0.4	2.5	13.0	26.7	10.2	14.0	10.3	9.8
46 019	...	6	Butte	5 827	10 298	2 412	1.8	93.6	1.0	3.4	0.7	3.5	6.4	17.9	7.7	11.4	10.0	13.6
46 021	...	9	Campbell	1 900	1 386	3 090	0.7	97.5	0.4	1.0	0.4	1.4	3.7	12.4	6.7	7.0	7.3	20.4
46 023	...	9	Charles Mix	2 842	9 287	2 490	3.3	65.9	0.7	33.0	0.7	2.3	8.7	20.7	8.1	10.1	9.7	12.7
46 025	...	9	Clark	2 480	3 645	2 931	1.5	96.8	1.0	0.5	0.2	2.3	7.9	15.2	6.6	10.8	9.7	12.7
46 027	46820	6	Clay	1 068	13 932	2 175	13.0	90.7	2.2	4.1	2.5	2.6	5.6	12.1	31.7	12.8	8.4	9.0
46 029	47980	7	Codington	1 783	27 938	1 495	15.7	94.6	1.0	2.8	1.0	1.8	7.1	17.3	9.2	12.8	11.8	13.5
46 031	...	9	Corson	6 396	4 182	2 889	0.7	33.6	0.7	64.1	0.8	3.8	8.7	25.2	9.3	12.7	10.5	12.6
46 033	39660	8	Custer	4 033	8 445	2 562	2.1	92.5	1.0	4.5	0.9	2.9	4.2	13.3	4.9	8.4	8.9	15.1
46 035	33580	7	Davison	1 128	19 885	1 843	17.6	93.6	1.3	3.3	1.0	2.2	6.4	16.8	10.5	12.7	10.8	12.8
46 037	...	9	Day	2 662	5 588	2 796	2.1	88.7	0.7	9.7	0.6	2.0	5.6	16.3	6.3	9.7	9.1	12.9
46 039	...	9	Deuel	1 613	4 312	2 879	2.7	95.4	1.2	0.8	0.4	3.1	6.0	16.9	6.9	9.9	10.7	14.3
46 041	...	9	Dewey	5 963	5 662	2 789	0.9	25.7	0.7	73.9	0.4	2.9	11.2	23.4	10.2	12.8	10.4	13.0
46 043	...	9	Douglas	1 118	2 973	2 979	2.7	95.6	0.8	2.3	0.3	1.8	6.0	16.6	6.7	8.9	8.9	13.4
46 045	10100	9	Edmunds	2 916	3 983	2 905	1.4	97.0	0.5	1.1	0.4	1.9	5.6	18.0	7.1	9.4	9.9	14.2
46 047	...	7	Fall River	4 506	6 845	2 692	1.5	88.4	1.5	8.6	1.0	3.3	3.4	13.9	6.3	7.8	9.6	14.0
46 049	...	9	Faulk	2 543	2 357	3 018	0.9	98.2	0.5	0.8	0.4	1.0	6.1	16.6	7.2	9.2	8.5	14.1
46 051	...	7	Grant	1 765	7 241	2 657	4.1	95.2	0.7	1.4	0.6	3.0	5.7	16.9	7.1	9.3	10.7	15.1
46 053	...	9	Gregory	2 629	4 217	2 884	1.6	90.5	0.9	8.7	0.8	1.4	5.8	16.8	6.1	8.7	10.1	12.6
46 055	...	8	Haakon	4 689	1 847	3 067	0.4	95.0	1.7	4.2	1.2	1.3	6.2	15.8	5.6	9.3	10.1	12.3
46 057	...	9	Hamlin	1 314	5 989	2 758	4.6	95.7	0.7	0.9	0.3	3.2	9.0	21.7	7.6	10.5	10.3	11.9
46 059	...	9	Hand	3 721	3 345	2 950	0.9	97.9	0.3	1.1	0.5	1.1	5.1	15.4	7.0	9.1	8.5	14.8
46 061	33580	8	Hanson	1 125	3 419	2 945	3.0	98.4	0.3	0.7	0.4	0.7	9.5	22.8	6.8	9.8	11.7	12.5
46 063	...	9	Harding	6 919	1 250	3 099	0.2	95.0	0.9	2.7	0.4	2.5	7.1	14.4	7.6	13.2	10.7	14.6
46 065	38180	7	Hughes	1 921	17 642	1 940	9.2	85.4	1.7	11.5	1.0	2.6	7.0	16.6	7.6	13.9	11.7	14.4
46 067	...	8	Hutchinson	2 105	7 200	2 661	3.4	96.1	1.0	1.5	0.4	1.9	6.3	17.1	6.5	8.6	10.6	12.7
46 069	...	9	Hyde	2 229	1 396	3 088	0.6	89.1	0.8	10.0	0.8	1.1	5.3	15.7	7.5	10.4	8.1	12.9
46 071	...	8	Jackson	4 828	3 274	2 952	0.7	47.1	1.3	53.4	0.8	2.0	10.0	23.3	9.3	10.9	9.8	12.8
46 073	...	9	Jerauld	1 363	2 007	3 048	1.5	93.7	0.4	0.8	0.4	5.4	6.8	16.1	5.0	10.6	9.5	11.7
46 075	...	9	Jones	2 511	975	3 108	0.4	92.4	1.6	5.3	1.3	2.3	6.4	14.9	5.9	9.6	10.7	14.6
46 077	...	9	Kingsbury	2 155	5 075	2 834	2.4	96.6	0.8	1.2	0.6	2.0	6.6	15.5	6.4	10.0	9.6	14.4
46 079	...	6	Lake	1 459	12 368	2 275	8.5	94.9	1.3	1.6	1.1	2.3	5.5	14.6	11.2	10.5	9.4	13.2
46 081	43940	6	Lawrence	2 072	24 657	1 622	11.9	92.5	1.6	3.3	1.1	3.4	4.7	14.0	13.5	11.8	10.1	12.7
46 083	43620	3	Lincoln	1 495	51 548	966	34.5	95.2	1.8	1.0	1.6	1.8	8.6	20.8	6.7	16.2	14.8	12.3
46 085	...	9	Lyman	4 253	3 877	2 913	0.9	60.0	1.1	38.8	0.7	2.0	7.9	20.7	8.7	11.8	10.2	12.6
46 087	43620	3	McCook	1 487	5 649	2 791	3.8	95.5	0.6	0.8	0.5	3.2	6.9	19.0	6.9	10.1	10.8	14.0
46 089	...	9	McPherson	2 944	2 429	3 011	0.8	97.6	0.5	0.8	0.5	1.2	5.4	16.2	5.8	7.2	9.4	12.8
46 091	...	9	Marshall	2 171	4 683	2 855	2.2	83.9	1.4	8.5	0.4	7.0	6.0	16.0	8.0	12.0	9.9	13.0
46 093	39660	3	Meade	8 990	26 951	1 537	3.0	90.3	2.5	4.2	1.6	4.1	6.5	17.6	11.2	14.1	10.9	12.7
46 095	...	9	Mellette	3 386	2 100	3 041	0.6	45.4	1.2	54.9	0.9	2.7	8.8	21.4	10.0	9.5	9.6	12.8
46 097	...	8	Miner	1 477	2 316	3 023	1.6	96.5	0.9	0.8	0.6	2.3	5.6	18.3	6.5	9.1	9.3	14.7
46 099	43620	3	Minnehaha	2 091	182 882	352	87.5	86.6	5.4	3.3	2.2	4.6	7.7	17.3	9.7	15.9	12.4	13.4
46 101	...	8	Moody	1 345	6 367	2 729	4.7	82.1	1.5	14.8	1.6	2.7	7.2	18.2	7.7	11.0	10.4	14.6
46 103	39660	3	Pennington	7 191	108 242	554	15.1	83.4	2.4	11.1	1.9	4.6	7.0	17.0	9.1	14.1	11.4	13.0
46 105	...	9	Perkins	7 435	3 033	2 974	0.4	96.9	0.5	2.1	0.4	1.1	5.2	16.1	6.3	9.5	9.4	14.1
46 107	...	9	Potter	2 230	2 340	3 020	1.0	96.4	0.6	1.9	0.5	1.5	5.6	15.4	5.8	8.9	8.2	13.3
46 109	...	9	Roberts	2 852	10 374	2 406	3.6	62.5	0.7	37.4	0.6	1.9	8.4	19.7	8.1	9.7	9.9	12.5
46 111	...	9	Sanborn	1 475	2 336	3 021	1.6	96.9	0.5	1.4	0.4	2.2	5.3	15.7	6.7	12.0	9.5	14.1
46 113	...	7	Shannon	5 423	14 218	2 152	2.6	6.1	0.4	91.6	0.3	3.0	11.6	26.6	12.3	14.2	10.7	10.5
46 115	...	7	Spink	3 895	6 598	2 714	1.7	96.0	0.9	2.0	0.3	1.9	5.8	18.5	7.6	10.5	9.2	13.9
46 117	38180	9	Stanley	3 741	2 983	2 978	0.8	89.2	1.4	10.1	0.3	1.4	5.9	17.9	7.0	11.9	12.0	13.3
46 119	38180	9	Sully	2 608	1 438	3 083	0.6	94.9	1.6	2.7	0.1	2.3	4.9	17.3	6.7	10.2	9.9	15.4
46 121	...	9	Todd	3 596	9 882	2 447	2.7	12.2	0.6	85.4	0.5	3.3	13.0	27.3	10.9	13.8	10.2	9.3

1. CBSA = Core Based Statistical Area. See Appendix A for explanation. See Appendix B for list of metropolitan areas with component counties. 2. County type code from the Economic Research Service of USDA Rural-Urban Continuum Codes. See Appendix A for definition. 3. Dry land or land partially or temporarily covered by water. 4. May be of any race.

STATE County	Population, 2013 (cont.): Age (percent) (cont.): 55 to 64 years	65 to 74 years	75 years and over	Percent female	Population change and components of change, 2000–2014: Total persons: 2000	2010	Percent change: 2000–2010	2010–2014	Components of change, 2010–2014: Births	Deaths	Net migration	Households, 2009–2013: Number	Persons per household	Percent: Family households	Female family householder[1]	One person
	16	17	18	19	20	21	22	23	24	25	26	27	28	29	30	31
SOUTH CAROLINA—Cont'd																
Sumter	12.0	8.0	6.1	51.6	104 646	107 456	2.7	0.4	6 500	4 233	-1 786	39 373	2.66	68.9	19.1	27.4
Union	14.6	10.4	7.8	52.5	29 881	28 961	-3.1	-3.8	1 291	1 568	-788	11 854	2.37	66.6	17.5	30.4
Williamsburg	15.3	10.1	6.9	51.4	37 217	34 423	-7.5	-5.0	1 445	1 751	-1 418	11 621	2.76	65.3	21.2	31.9
York	12.3	7.9	4.8	51.7	164 614	226 073	37.3	8.5	12 432	7 760	14 141	86 483	2.62	71.4	12.9	23.9
SOUTH DAKOTA	13.0	7.8	7.2	49.8	754 844	814 180	7.9	4.8	51 014	30 398	18 038	323 136	2.45	64.8	9.7	29.2
Aurora	14.1	9.3	10.7	48.4	3 058	2 710	-11.4	1.3	152	116	10	1 102	2.36	67.2	4.2	28.4
Beadle	13.8	7.9	8.8	49.4	17 023	17 398	2.2	4.4	1 336	828	287	7 343	2.32	60.1	9.0	34.4
Bennett	10.9	5.4	6.3	51.8	3 574	3 431	-4.0	0.0	298	123	-162	1 059	3.18	73.9	21.2	21.8
Bon Homme	13.2	8.6	10.9	41.8	7 260	7 070	-2.6	-0.6	287	309	-18	2 501	2.29	66.3	4.7	29.8
Brookings	9.7	5.4	4.9	49.1	28 220	31 965	13.3	4.2	1 690	831	502	11 979	2.38	58.1	6.8	30.3
Brown	13.0	7.5	8.4	51.0	35 460	36 531	3.0	5.1	2 056	1 577	1 423	15 590	2.27	61.0	8.5	33.6
Brule	14.2	7.6	9.3	51.0	5 364	5 255	-2.0	1.0	315	233	-31	2 094	2.32	71.0	12.2	24.3
Buffalo	8.5	4.8	2.6	50.7	2 032	1 912	-5.9	8.6	228	79	22	542	3.62	78.8	29.5	17.9
Butte	15.4	9.8	7.9	49.7	9 094	10 110	11.2	1.9	532	434	70	4 015	2.51	61.8	6.6	33.0
Campbell	17.1	11.7	13.6	47.6	1 782	1 466	-17.7	-5.5	48	54	-57	679	2.09	61.3	3.7	37.3
Charles Mix	12.1	8.8	9.2	50.4	9 350	9 129	-2.4	1.7	675	373	-131	3 191	2.74	64.4	11.7	32.7
Clark	15.5	10.0	11.5	49.4	4 143	3 691	-10.9	-1.2	206	205	-58	1 431	2.33	61.3	4.2	35.7
Clay	9.7	5.6	5.0	50.8	13 537	13 864	2.4	0.5	650	396	-196	5 145	2.25	50.7	5.4	31.0
Codington	13.0	7.7	7.6	50.0	25 897	27 227	5.1	2.6	1 611	991	117	11 566	2.33	59.4	8.2	33.6
Corson	10.2	6.1	4.6	48.8	4 181	4 050	-3.1	3.3	371	200	-50	1 185	3.44	72.8	18.2	21.0
Custer	21.5	14.7	9.0	49.9	7 275	8 216	12.9	2.8	308	330	248	3 731	2.12	65.3	5.3	30.6
Davison	13.0	7.7	9.5	50.3	18 741	19 504	4.1	2.0	1 115	838	125	8 471	2.21	61.4	6.4	33.5
Day	16.3	11.6	12.1	49.2	6 267	5 710	-8.9	-2.1	282	336	-69	2 511	2.19	63.6	10.0	34.5
Deuel	14.7	10.3	10.3	48.2	4 498	4 364	-3.0	-1.2	196	161	-82	1 789	2.41	68.1	5.5	29.0
Dewey	8.9	5.5	4.5	51.1	5 972	5 301	-11.2	6.8	607	294	51	1 687	3.17	68.2	23.8	25.1
Douglas	15.0	10.4	14.0	49.9	3 458	3 002	-13.2	-1.0	155	175	-21	1 258	2.31	69.6	5.2	26.6
Edmunds	14.9	10.0	10.9	49.3	4 367	4 071	-6.8	-2.2	189	199	-54	1 589	2.32	63.8	5.0	32.3
Fall River	19.1	14.1	11.8	49.0	7 453	7 094	-4.8	-3.5	239	448	-58	3 138	2.11	57.2	9.4	38.5
Faulk	15.1	9.9	13.5	49.4	2 640	2 364	-10.5	-0.3	113	97	-28	930	2.30	62.6	3.5	30.9
Grant	15.4	9.9	9.9	48.9	7 847	7 356	-6.3	-1.6	331	332	-107	3 159	2.24	68.5	6.5	27.8
Gregory	15.8	11.5	12.6	49.3	4 792	4 271	-10.9	-1.3	183	259	36	1 986	2.11	62.1	7.3	34.6
Haakon	17.3	11.7	11.6	49.7	2 196	1 937	-11.8	-4.6	85	92	-84	807	2.34	69.5	4.5	27.3
Hamlin	11.6	8.5	8.7	49.7	5 540	5 903	6.6	1.5	493	303	-114	2 041	2.79	71.0	4.1	24.0
Hand	15.1	9.7	15.3	49.7	3 741	3 431	-8.3	-2.5	150	173	-70	1 429	2.36	67.2	5.5	29.7
Hanson	13.1	10.0	3.8	48.5	3 139	3 331	6.1	2.6	220	74	-56	1 037	3.00	73.9	4.1	23.8
Harding	16.8	8.5	7.1	46.4	1 353	1 255	-7.2	-0.4	56	35	-36	527	2.39	70.2	3.6	26.0
Hughes	14.3	7.8	6.7	51.3	16 481	17 022	3.3	3.6	1 010	580	193	6 992	2.33	61.8	6.7	35.1
Hutchinson	14.2	9.3	14.8	50.8	8 075	7 343	-9.1	-1.9	362	456	-53	2 937	2.27	66.5	6.7	31.6
Hyde	16.2	10.4	13.4	48.9	1 671	1 420	-15.0	-1.7	55	65	-9	549	2.46	63.9	6.9	33.3
Jackson	10.7	6.7	6.7	49.6	2 930	3 031	3.4	8.0	302	131	72	1 056	2.89	72.0	7.6	22.6
Jerauld	16.0	11.5	12.8	50.0	2 295	2 071	-9.8	-3.1	101	106	-63	882	2.28	72.6	10.0	24.6
Jones	16.6	9.6	11.8	53.4	1 193	1 006	-15.7	-3.1	46	38	-48	438	2.24	60.0	6.8	40.0
Kingsbury	15.8	9.7	11.9	49.2	5 815	5 148	-11.5	-1.4	247	290	-38	2 311	2.16	68.5	3.5	27.2
Lake	16.6	10.9	8.2	48.7	11 276	11 200	-0.7	10.4	556	445	1 021	4 655	2.32	63.0	7.9	31.9
Lawrence	15.6	9.4	8.1	50.4	21 802	24 097	10.5	2.3	989	897	430	10 597	2.16	60.0	8.3	32.1
Lincoln	10.7	5.6	4.3	50.5	24 131	44 828	85.8	15.0	3 400	842	4 036	17 250	2.68	74.5	9.1	20.4
Lyman	13.0	8.9	6.2	47.3	3 895	3 755	-3.6	3.2	301	127	-59	1 423	2.66	66.3	12.4	29.1
McCook	13.2	9.5	9.7	49.7	5 832	5 618	-3.7	0.6	308	322	21	2 186	2.46	68.8	6.1	27.2
McPherson	14.4	11.6	17.3	51.0	2 904	2 459	-15.3	-1.2	102	135	-4	1 045	2.07	66.1	8.0	32.8
Marshall	15.7	10.5	9.0	45.4	4 576	4 656	1.7	0.6	244	238	25	1 683	2.62	61.7	6.2	33.3
Meade	14.2	7.8	5.1	48.0	24 253	25 434	4.9	5.9	1 391	730	842	10 083	2.49	71.5	9.7	23.7
Mellette	12.6	7.8	7.4	47.2	2 083	2 048	-1.7	2.5	133	87	-1	698	2.92	73.5	24.9	22.5
Miner	15.0	9.2	12.3	49.4	2 884	2 389	-17.2	-3.1	98	134	-33	1 053	2.18	60.1	7.7	35.8
Minnehaha	11.8	6.5	5.4	49.9	148 281	169 468	14.3	7.9	11 950	5 476	6 807	67 623	2.48	64.4	11.2	28.6
Moody	14.4	8.8	7.7	49.5	6 595	6 486	-1.7	-1.8	394	205	-288	2 686	2.34	71.8	10.4	25.4
Pennington	13.4	8.0	6.9	50.0	88 565	100 948	14.0	7.2	6 533	3 381	4 030	40 723	2.45	64.7	11.2	28.1
Perkins	15.9	11.2	12.3	48.6	3 363	2 982	-11.3	1.7	130	173	80	1 364	2.09	58.7	3.6	39.0
Potter	16.4	12.1	14.2	51.0	2 693	2 329	-13.5	0.5	100	147	52	1 051	2.13	63.0	6.7	34.9
Roberts	13.5	9.6	8.6	49.9	10 016	10 149	1.3	2.2	776	455	-93	3 646	2.71	71.5	11.2	24.2
Sanborn	17.3	8.7	10.6	47.3	2 675	2 355	-12.0	-0.8	132	116	-28	1 051	2.15	61.9	5.3	32.1
Shannon	7.4	4.2	2.5	51.5	12 466	13 586	0.0	4.7	1 407	627	-221	2 007	4.70	82.0	43.3	15.1
Spink	14.9	9.1	10.5	49.6	7 454	6 415	-13.9	2.9	343	313	153	2 624	2.36	63.5	5.8	32.6
Stanley	15.0	10.5	6.4	48.7	2 772	2 966	7.0	0.6	167	64	-85	1 273	2.32	62.7	9.7	30.5
Sully	17.2	9.2	9.3	47.0	1 556	1 373	-11.8	4.7	64	35	42	606	2.33	65.5	5.4	28.9
Todd	8.6	4.1	2.7	51.0	9 050	9 612	6.2	2.8	1 170	480	-429	2 680	3.62	75.5	36.7	21.9

1. No spouse present.

STATE County	Persons in group quarters, 2014	Daytime population, 2009–2013		Births, 2014		Deaths, 2014		Persons under 65 with no health insurance, 2013		Medicare, 2014			Serious crimes known to police,[2] 2013	
													Total	
		Number	Employ-ment/ resi-dence ratio	Total	Rate[1]	Number	Rate[1]	Number	Percent	Eligible for Medicare	Enrolled in Medicare Advantage	Enrolled in a Medicare prescription drug plan	Number	Rate[3]
	32	33	34	35	36	37	38	39	40	41	42	43	44	45
SOUTH CAROLINA—Cont'd														
Sumter	2 784	107 436	1.00	1 529	14.2	1 006	9.3	15 777	17.5	19 542	3 191	9 325	4 662	4 289
Union	456	26 441	0.79	299	10.7	369	13.2	3 872	17.1	7 162	2 261	3 248	1 100	3 904
Williamsburg	1 479	32 194	0.84	319	9.8	405	12.4	4 963	19.0	7 343	1 968	3 699	889	2 651
York	3 962	212 886	0.83	2 983	12.2	1 848	7.5	32 044	15.6	38 273	8 337	19 211	6 741	2 829
SOUTH DAKOTA	33 981	828 363	1.01	12 217	14.3	6 893	8.1	89 614	12.8	153 418	0	91 040	18 851	2 231
Aurora	96	2 664	0.96	36	13.1	24	8.7	306	14.6	569	96	401	26	937
Beadle	620	17 726	1.01	342	18.8	191	10.5	2 326	15.6	3 444	685	2 230	418	2 324
Bennett	37	3 331	0.91	68	19.8	26	7.6	578	18.8	471	14	297	52	1 505
Bon Homme	1 544	6 573	0.83	69	9.8	69	9.8	618	14.1	1 481	181	996	3	42
Brookings	3 592	33 070	1.04	410	12.3	189	5.7	3 320	12.6	3 924	636	2 486	209	632
Brown	1 365	38 217	1.06	497	12.9	357	9.3	3 069	9.9	6 858	645	4 658	761	2 094
Brule	132	5 467	1.07	79	14.9	46	8.7	734	16.7	921	132	599	NA	NA
Buffalo	3	1 949	0.97	51	24.6	29	14.0	362	19.1	202	NA	111	NA	NA
Butte	111	8 641	0.68	127	12.3	96	9.3	1 368	16.2	1 988	434	1 002	159	1 539
Campbell	0	1 326	0.84	11	7.9	4	2.9	135	13.6	372	54	263	7	507
Charles Mix	589	9 381	1.05	164	17.7	98	10.6	1 434	19.4	1 809	162	1 301	107	1 327
Clark	489	3 455	0.90	49	13.4	43	11.8	396	14.1	771	215	547	14	392
Clay	2 241	13 617	0.95	150	10.8	81	5.8	1 484	14.2	1 811	282	1 213	323	2 255
Codington	381	28 433	1.07	377	13.5	217	7.8	2 677	11.4	5 020	1 609	3 312	727	2 604
Corson	1	3 950	0.89	93	22.2	53	12.7	782	20.7	524	17	331	19	463
Custer	254	7 644	0.82	69	8.2	72	8.5	911	14.5	2 159	336	1 014	107	1 271
Davison	769	20 981	1.13	264	13.3	172	8.6	1 805	11.4	3 890	465	2 813	549	2 746
Day	139	5 417	0.91	68	12.2	85	15.2	674	15.9	1 444	286	980	NA	NA
Deuel	50	4 064	0.87	43	10.0	30	7.0	431	12.7	1 013	286	649	21	475
Dewey	19	5 755	1.18	150	26.5	89	15.7	1 080	21.3	762	22	441	9	159
Douglas	178	2 987	0.99	38	12.8	34	11.4	343	15.2	748	115	561	2	67
Edmunds	420	3 551	0.77	49	12.3	40	10.0	351	11.1	863	92	638	0	0
Fall River	197	7 233	1.08	55	8.0	97	14.2	738	15.0	2 218	255	907	NA	NA
Faulk	497	2 324	0.96	26	11.0	17	7.2	216	11.9	535	15	403	6	250
Grant	104	7 549	1.06	80	11.0	85	11.7	757	13.1	1 713	567	1 078	NA	NA
Gregory	44	4 118	0.93	43	10.2	55	13.0	543	17.0	1 107	175	768	NA	NA
Haakon	36	1 985	1.04	16	8.7	13	7.0	221	15.3	419	50	290	NA	NA
Hamlin	245	5 054	0.69	125	20.9	71	11.9	670	13.7	1 023	286	689	36	604
Hand	61	3 381	0.97	33	9.9	34	10.2	307	12.1	813	61	625	17	500
Hanson	520	2 502	0.46	51	14.9	11	3.2	390	13.4	1 361	149	733	6	176
Harding	29	1 483	1.22	14	11.2	4	3.2	170	16.4	206	24	120	5	371
Hughes	772	18 118	1.09	240	13.6	150	8.5	1 585	11.0	3 000	266	1 876	512	2 892
Hutchinson	832	6 712	0.85	94	13.1	102	14.2	724	13.6	1 893	416	1 407	17	237
Hyde	38	1 456	1.09	12	8.6	10	7.2	178	16.9	324	19	218	NA	NA
Jackson	42	3 091	0.98	71	21.7	28	8.6	603	21.5	474	35	290	NA	NA
Jerauld	176	2 307	1.25	22	11.0	15	7.5	229	14.8	634	72	416	1	49
Jones	0	950	0.94	10	10.3	6	6.2	152	19.5	218	24	139	NA	NA
Kingsbury	203	4 694	0.82	52	10.2	65	12.8	482	12.3	1 240	177	841	NA	NA
Lake	874	11 288	0.96	133	10.8	110	8.9	997	10.8	3 174	434	1 861	NA	NA
Lawrence	1 073	23 957	0.97	246	10.0	203	8.2	2 529	12.8	5 116	963	2 574	558	2 265
Lincoln	284	35 493	0.56	812	15.8	187	3.6	3 081	6.9	5 616	1 254	3 236	1 152	2 317
Lyman	36	3 692	0.93	66	17.0	14	3.6	706	21.6	660	61	404	NA	NA
McCook	312	4 798	0.72	74	13.1	69	12.2	507	11.2	1 125	173	747	62	1 098
McPherson	347	2 349	0.93	26	10.7	27	11.1	267	15.4	715	47	524	2	82
Marshall	373	4 425	0.89	59	12.6	46	9.8	668	17.5	977	91	654	50	1 061
Meade	797	21 386	0.66	342	12.7	184	6.8	3 215	14.0	4 728	848	2 049	276	1 044
Mellette	49	1 874	0.75	30	14.3	10	4.8	368	20.9	329	18	216	20	936
Miner	80	2 237	0.90	23	9.9	27	11.7	211	11.6	564	46	394	4	172
Minnehaha	6 272	189 924	1.18	2 898	15.8	1 290	7.1	18 283	11.9	29 687	5 923	17 104	5 196	2 920
Moody	164	5 786	0.80	93	14.6	50	7.9	772	14.5	1 241	207	766	80	1 235
Pennington	2 566	107 871	1.10	1 552	14.3	792	7.3	11 784	13.4	20 930	3 557	9 978	3 595	3 389
Perkins	65	2 902	0.97	31	10.2	25	8.2	441	19.2	751	94	512	14	455
Potter	63	2 319	1.00	25	10.7	31	13.2	236	13.5	676	22	438	7	294
Roberts	281	10 092	0.97	186	17.9	97	9.4	1 461	17.5	2 022	328	1 217	87	835
Sanborn	174	2 012	0.72	33	14.1	23	9.8	302	16.2	465	56	324	NA	NA
Shannon	91	14 569	1.23	347	24.4	164	11.5	2 255	16.9	1 259	11	605	0	0
Spink	404	6 441	0.97	84	12.7	72	10.9	588	11.4	1 509	143	1 082	48	714
Stanley	0	2 467	0.71	33	11.1	5	1.7	376	15.2	576	55	334	9	301
Sully	0	1 324	0.88	14	9.7	7	4.9	176	15.1	306	25	183	5	343
Todd	28	10 135	1.13	270	27.3	132	13.4	1 451	15.4	872	NA	479	NA	NA

1. Per 1,000 estimated resident population. 2. Data for serious crimes have not been adjusted for underreporting; this may affect comparability between geographic areas and over time.
3. Per 100,000 population estimated by the FBI.

STATE County	Serious crimes known to police, 2013 (cont.)[1]		Education						Money income, 2009–2013				Income and poverty, 2013			
	Rate[2]		School enrollment and attainment, 2009–2013				Local government expenditures,[5] 2012–2013			Households				Percent below poverty level		
			Enrollment[3]		Attainment[4] (percent)											
	Violent	Property	Total	Percent private	High school graduate or less	Bachelor's degree or more	Total current spending (mil dol)	Current spending per student (dollars)	Per capita income[6] (dollars)	Median income (dollars)	Mean income (dollars)	Percent with income of $200,000 or more	Median household income (dollars)	All persons	Children under 18 years	Children 5 to 17 years in families
	46	47	48	49	50	51	52	53	54	55	56	57	58	59	60	61
SOUTH CAROLINA—Cont'd																
Sumter	673	3 615	29 158	16.5	48.3	19.2	143.8	8 563	20 340	41 366	53 133	1.4	39 182	20.8	33.6	32.3
Union	504	3 400	6 607	8.7	59.4	12.9	35.8	8 648	19 037	32 556	44 480	0.7	34 042	18.7	30.0	27.0
Williamsburg	355	2 296	9 001	12.4	62.4	12.2	49.2	10 642	14 845	25 849	38 787	0.6	29 391	33.4	49.3	44.1
York	420	2 409	61 991	11.0	40.7	28.5	372.9	9 214	26 553	53 740	69 888	3.4	54 927	12.7	17.2	15.3
SOUTH DAKOTA	316	1 915	215 275	13.0	41.5	26.2	1 118.9	8 470	25 740	49 495	64 133	2.9	49 200	14.0	18.6	17.3
Aurora	144	793	630	7.9	52.9	16.7	6.4	10 991	23 504	46 667	58 113	2.3	46 493	10.8	16.6	15.3
Beadle	317	2 007	3 950	16.6	50.5	18.6	22.6	8 509	24 025	42 196	56 946	1.8	43 682	16.5	22.1	22.0
Bennett	666	839	1 070	8.8	49.0	15.9	5.6	11 486	16 275	37 607	53 392	3.0	35 083	35.5	48.7	45.2
Bon Homme	0	42	1 389	5.5	50.7	17.9	10.8	9 564	20 941	40 980	56 762	2.6	45 803	14.9	17.7	16.2
Brookings	48	584	13 548	4.5	32.1	40.2	35.9	8 427	23 105	46 896	59 474	2.0	51 893	13.6	12.0	11.3
Brown	237	1 858	9 612	17.5	42.7	26.9	40.4	7 647	27 138	51 398	63 138	3.0	50 047	10.6	12.3	11.3
Brule	NA	NA	1 144	16.1	48.7	22.3	11.3	9 673	21 928	45 284	54 369	1.8	45 878	13.9	19.7	18.4
Buffalo	NA	NA	580	20.2	64.0	9.1	NA	NA	11 405	30 962	40 446	0.0	21 572	41.0	47.5	47.0
Butte	165	1 374	2 386	19.2	48.3	16.9	13.6	7 856	21 744	41 332	52 168	1.8	41 413	14.3	20.8	19.0
Campbell	72	435	277	9.7	58.5	16.5	1.4	11 913	24 152	35 729	51 346	1.8	47 579	9.8	11.7	11.5
Charles Mix	211	1 116	2 494	18.4	50.8	16.6	18.7	10 971	19 030	40 102	51 258	2.4	37 996	24.3	34.9	32.5
Clark	56	336	722	3.9	50.0	18.7	5.6	9 045	27 878	49 055	70 699	4.5	45 592	12.0	21.3	20.8
Clay	272	1 983	6 615	4.7	33.3	41.6	10.4	8 604	20 595	38 173	52 783	1.6	41 970	20.8	19.4	17.8
Codington	251	2 353	6 859	11.2	46.5	21.9	34.1	7 596	25 582	47 214	60 840	3.3	49 022	10.1	12.2	11.0
Corson	24	438	1 292	2.2	50.4	13.8	12.6	14 742	14 262	30 880	48 590	1.8	31 418	43.0	53.4	46.7
Custer	83	1 188	1 416	11.0	36.3	27.7	8.0	9 207	28 356	50 074	62 229	2.3	51 326	10.8	18.1	16.6
Davison	320	2 426	4 740	20.1	39.8	26.1	25.4	8 172	24 597	48 341	57 137	1.1	47 506	12.6	15.0	14.0
Day	NA	NA	1 164	10.3	51.4	16.4	6.4	8 767	23 126	39 761	50 009	1.2	44 188	14.3	20.3	18.6
Deuel	68	407	917	4.7	50.2	20.1	4.2	7 789	27 525	51 632	65 983	3.2	52 527	9.2	13.0	12.1
Dewey	18	142	1 617	1.9	55.0	14.8	5.0	14 451	15 558	30 710	48 562	2.6	34 389	28.7	35.4	36.4
Douglas	0	67	586	15.4	57.0	16.7	3.3	10 209	28 323	49 200	67 689	5.9	48 344	11.0	14.5	13.8
Edmunds	0	0	828	16.3	46.9	22.2	6.2	9 532	25 775	49 831	61 867	2.1	51 352	10.9	15.5	14.0
Fall River	NA	NA	1 121	6.7	41.9	22.4	11.7	10 405	23 624	37 667	49 595	0.7	39 552	14.6	23.6	20.3
Faulk	0	250	524	28.8	50.7	18.4	3.0	9 199	23 069	41 453	58 214	3.4	50 092	11.6	20.9	20.2
Grant	NA	NA	1 488	12.1	57.4	15.9	10.5	9 022	24 554	48 896	57 229	1.0	51 065	10.5	14.2	13.3
Gregory	NA	NA	820	4.6	52.1	17.0	7.7	10 586	23 041	36 719	49 859	2.1	35 589	17.6	25.5	22.8
Haakon	NA	NA	411	4.4	42.3	20.2	2.7	8 947	25 754	47 198	61 437	3.6	45 456	12.2	15.8	15.3
Hamlin	34	571	1 470	10.5	52.7	18.2	11.8	9 073	25 233	55 563	69 746	3.7	56 860	10.3	13.5	13.3
Hand	29	471	688	12.5	51.3	18.3	4.2	9 664	26 027	47 679	58 789	2.7	50 737	9.3	11.7	10.6
Hanson	59	117	955	22.9	48.4	22.6	3.0	7 002	23 197	55 815	70 435	2.4	57 800	8.9	13.7	13.3
Harding	74	297	335	7.8	36.4	35.1	2.7	15 056	22 247	44 353	56 244	3.0	43 860	11.7	17.9	19.2
Hughes	356	2 536	3 712	10.2	34.6	32.0	19.3	7 389	30 284	59 338	73 760	2.9	57 538	10.3	14.1	12.5
Hutchinson	0	237	1 586	10.4	49.1	25.2	13.3	9 377	26 110	42 451	62 538	4.0	44 958	13.1	18.3	16.9
Hyde	NA	NA	258	1.2	54.1	20.4	2.8	10 249	26 195	47 813	61 374	1.5	47 072	11.0	13.1	12.0
Jackson	NA	NA	932	2.7	40.9	17.4	4.1	10 960	20 319	46 224	57 549	3.9	35 387	30.2	44.5	40.9
Jerauld	0	49	466	11.4	54.6	15.4	3.2	10 016	26 590	46 591	61 668	2.5	48 126	14.5	24.3	23.7
Jones	NA	NA	226	13.3	46.9	15.8	2.0	11 131	23 377	44 808	53 688	1.4	45 095	13.4	20.7	20.4
Kingsbury	NA	NA	990	7.2	47.4	21.3	10.0	9 443	27 485	51 373	62 439	1.9	50 045	9.7	14.0	14.2
Lake	NA	NA	3 426	6.7	42.3	27.7	16.9	8 404	27 015	48 936	64 068	2.6	53 116	12.3	13.5	12.3
Lawrence	89	2 176	6 226	6.6	38.6	29.1	24.3	8 243	27 498	43 273	61 413	2.8	42 867	14.9	18.9	16.1
Lincoln	229	2 088	13 044	19.6	27.9	39.4	47.4	7 354	34 839	74 751	91 946	5.6	78 567	4.3	5.2	4.9
Lyman	NA	NA	979	6.6	47.9	19.4	5.3	13 610	20 586	47 596	56 662	1.3	40 057	21.7	31.5	29.8
McCook	18	1 080	1 300	16.4	44.4	22.1	11.4	9 540	26 505	52 703	68 528	1.8	53 478	9.6	11.7	11.2
McPherson	0	82	413	8.7	49.6	18.4	4.2	11 510	22 596	37 240	51 185	1.8	38 222	14.9	23.2	21.0
Marshall	233	828	1 118	9.7	45.1	19.6	5.9	8 282	24 205	46 597	64 691	3.6	49 254	12.5	19.9	19.0
Meade	121	923	6 408	9.2	41.7	19.6	21.4	7 620	25 375	49 324	62 891	2.6	50 711	10.6	15.7	14.4
Mellette	140	796	634	0.9	48.8	16.8	4.9	11 007	15 760	35 109	45 431	0.9	33 460	32.7	47.9	44.7
Miner	43	129	521	6.5	50.3	21.7	5.6	9 921	31 288	48 477	70 272	3.2	45 787	12.2	15.5	14.0
Minnehaha	334	2 586	44 289	19.1	38.8	29.2	237.1	7 705	26 380	52 345	65 796	2.8	52 382	11.0	13.6	13.1
Moody	201	1 035	1 517	5.1	44.4	24.1	8.2	8 992	27 682	51 791	67 423	3.6	53 712	10.9	15.0	15.1
Pennington	470	2 919	26 580	13.3	36.4	27.8	146.0	8 290	27 000	50 833	66 585	3.2	48 886	15.4	22.1	20.2
Perkins	65	390	517	17.2	51.7	17.9	4.8	12 466	25 751	38 362	55 751	4.0	40 042	14.4	18.7	17.0
Potter	84	210	435	9.9	52.7	18.5	3.9	10 624	26 180	44 556	56 886	2.4	50 887	10.3	14.8	13.7
Roberts	288	547	2 545	3.4	51.1	16.5	16.8	10 725	22 670	47 191	60 679	2.3	44 626	19.7	27.4	25.8
Sanborn	NA	NA	420	16.0	55.0	16.4	1.8	8 944	25 823	48 384	58 497	2.0	46 936	13.1	18.3	17.0
Shannon	0	0	4 905	6.5	50.9	11.8	22.5	15 645	8 768	25 648	36 393	0.9	28 512	55.1	53.4	50.9
Spink	74	639	1 505	9.0	49.9	19.7	12.0	9 280	27 757	48 911	69 845	1.6	50 271	11.3	11.0	13.2
Stanley	0	301	576	8.0	41.1	27.4	4.7	10 497	30 933	54 620	71 038	3.5	57 188	8.8	14.1	12.9
Sully	69	275	308	11.4	44.9	30.9	3.3	12 373	30 218	54 524	68 721	2.6	57 620	6.3	7.2	6.5
Todd	NA	NA	3 685	4.3	47.8	12.4	23.8	11 547	10 575	31 934	37 575	0.4	30 549	44.0	51.1	48.9

1. Data for serious crimes have not been adjusted for underreporting; this may affect comparability between geographic areas and over time. 2. Per 100,000 population estimated by the FBI.
3. All persons 3 years old and over enrolled in nursery school through college. 4. Persons 25 years old and over. 5. Elementary and secondary education expenditures.
6. Based on population estimated by the American Community Survey, 2009–2013.

STATE County	Personal income, 2013: Total (mil dol)	Personal income, 2013: Percent change, 2012–2013	Per capita[1]: Dollars	Per capita[1]: Rank	Wages and salaries (mil dol)	Supplements to wages and salaries; employer contributions (mil dol): Pension and insurance	Supplements: Government social insurance	Proprietors' income (mil dol)	Dividends, interest, and rent (mil dol)	Personal transfer receipts (mil dol)	Earnings, 2013: Total (mil dol)	Contributions for government social insurance (mil dol): From employee and self-employed	Contributions: From employer
	62	63	64	65	66	67	68	69	70	71	72	73	74
SOUTH CAROLINA—Cont'd													
Sumter	3 602	1.9	33 310	2 203	1 775	396	153	184	693	939	2 508	143	153
Union	825	3.0	29 448	2 758	252	50	21	37	96	285	360	28	21
Williamsburg	971	1.7	29 376	2 767	364	83	29	64	115	335	540	36	29
York	8 782	1.7	36 688	1 640	3 450	562	269	457	1 202	1 557	4 738	300	269
SOUTH DAKOTA	38 897	2.1	46 039	X	16 170	2 802	1 200	7 605	8 448	5 586	27 777	1 499	1 200
Aurora	161	20.3	59 360	118	29	6	2	77	24	17	114	3	2
Beadle	878	3.2	48 570	446	314	56	24	215	192	123	609	32	24
Bennett	112	-3.5	32 384	2 353	27	8	2	21	18	29	58	2	2
Bon Homme	286	4.8	40 661	1 092	57	14	4	102	54	46	178	7	4
Brookings	1 413	1.0	42 862	857	677	158	50	177	357	147	1 062	57	50
Brown	1 930	-2.4	50 911	335	811	138	61	397	470	238	1 407	78	61
Brule	259	11.8	48 279	464	63	12	5	102	45	35	182	7	5
Buffalo	46	-3.7	22 959	3 092	20	5	2	8	7	18	35	2	2
Butte	330	2.5	31 946	2 418	94	17	7	53	73	65	172	11	7
Campbell	75	-4.8	56 406	180	14	3	1	32	15	10	50	2	1
Charles Mix	396	6.6	42 891	855	105	23	8	131	79	75	268	11	8
Clark	203	9.3	56 199	185	34	7	3	83	48	24	126	4	3
Clay	681	7.6	48 901	422	205	56	15	233	99	80	509	22	15
Codington	1 229	1.5	44 120	748	585	98	44	169	303	174	895	53	44
Corson	134	-11.3	31 799	2 436	31	8	2	35	21	32	75	3	2
Custer	307	1.0	36 205	1 710	80	18	6	34	81	63	139	10	6
Davison	936	0.6	47 233	534	446	73	34	176	213	137	728	43	34
Day	253	-7.8	45 199	677	62	12	5	66	61	49	145	7	5
Deuel	213	4.3	49 404	395	60	11	5	58	42	32	134	6	5
Dewey	190	-4.7	34 090	2 065	78	20	6	26	33	50	130	7	6
Douglas	171	7.9	56 597	172	40	7	3	78	26	22	127	4	3
Edmunds	256	2.8	63 315	74	49	9	3	96	55	26	157	5	3
Fall River	277	0.1	40 553	1 105	98	23	9	18	81	74	149	10	9
Faulk	114	-21.1	47 617	504	23	4	2	38	26	19	68	2	2
Grant	359	0.3	49 251	405	149	24	11	74	86	53	257	14	11
Gregory	197	15.8	46 485	592	46	9	3	69	39	37	128	5	3
Haakon	90	-4.9	47 714	499	27	5	2	26	21	13	61	3	2
Hamlin	261	-1.2	43 732	782	61	12	4	69	56	32	146	6	4
Hand	208	4.1	61 385	90	45	8	3	94	37	23	151	4	3
Hanson	212	4.7	62 132	84	21	4	2	68	59	36	94	4	2
Harding	57	0.7	44 811	708	22	4	2	7	19	6	34	2	2
Hughes	854	2.7	48 804	429	417	94	30	132	190	103	673	36	30
Hutchinson	403	13.0	56 401	181	85	15	6	170	73	56	276	10	6
Hyde	70	7.6	50 253	356	21	4	2	18	20	10	45	2	2
Jackson	78	-15.5	24 147	3 075	22	6	2	13	15	23	43	2	2
Jerauld	141	12.4	68 030	55	51	9	4	62	23	18	125	5	4
Jones	53	-7.3	53 418	255	14	3	1	19	12	7	36	1	1
Kingsbury	276	0.0	54 574	215	62	12	5	98	50	39	177	7	5
Lake	586	1.9	48 585	445	172	35	13	142	135	94	363	19	13
Lawrence	928	1.7	37 250	1 543	374	64	28	96	270	170	563	37	28
Lincoln	3 040	3.5	60 972	95	792	107	58	353	551	179	1 310	72	58
Lyman	201	10.9	51 707	308	44	10	3	82	34	28	139	4	3
McCook	304	12.5	53 729	244	48	9	3	133	43	37	194	7	3
McPherson	111	-10.3	45 209	676	19	4	1	30	34	19	55	2	1
Marshall	197	-8.7	41 462	997	60	10	4	57	48	31	131	6	4
Meade	1 215	2.0	44 684	715	270	65	21	353	239	159	709	40	21
Mellette	66	-12.5	31 590	2 466	10	3	1	19	9	17	32	1	1
Miner	142	24.9	60 958	96	22	4	2	68	22	17	97	2	2
Minnehaha	8 075	2.6	44 949	693	5 218	750	381	1 443	1 578	1 095	7 792	465	381
Moody	346	2.0	54 058	232	83	16	6	93	73	40	198	8	6
Pennington	4 479	0.9	42 346	903	2 285	402	176	181	1 223	796	3 044	186	176
Perkins	98	-8.3	32 129	2 398	34	8	3	12	27	23	57	4	3
Potter	199	0.8	83 252	16	29	5	2	99	51	19	135	5	2
Roberts	408	-11.7	39 796	1 191	112	26	8	95	83	79	242	11	8
Sanborn	100	15.5	42 966	843	22	5	2	23	19	14	51	2	2
Shannon	301	-2.1	21 324	3 103	144	39	11	8	30	138	202	11	11
Spink	425	-6.2	64 332	70	84	19	6	175	78	72	284	9	6
Stanley	175	15.8	58 563	127	48	8	4	35	43	16	94	4	4
Sully	153	3.6	106 547	3	23	3	2	83	29	8	111	2	2
Todd	228	-3.4	22 832	3 095	101	26	7	16	27	86	150	8	7

1. Based on the resident population estimated as of July 1 of the year shown.

STATE County	Earnings, 2013 (cont.) — Percent by selected industries: Farm	Mining	Construction	Manu-facturing	Infor-mation: professional, scientific, technical services	Retail trade	Finance, insur-ance, real estate and leasing	Health care and social assistance	Govern-ment	Social Security beneficiaries, December 2013: Number	Rate[1]	Supple-mental Security Income recipients, December 2013	Housing units, 2014: Total	Percent change, 2010–2014
	75	76	77	78	79	80	81	82	83	84	85	86	87	88
SOUTH CAROLINA—Cont'd														
Sumter	0.9	0.0	6.2	13.9	3.9	5.5	3.0	11.2	39.1	22 390	207	4 195	47 029	2.2
Union	3.2	D	2.8	23.7	D	7.3	4.5	D	28.3	8 385	300	1 028	14 015	-1.0
Williamsburg	3.8	0.0	4.1	32.1	D	4.8	D	D	23.7	8 485	257	2 034	15 176	-1.2
York	0.7	0.0	4.6	15.6	8.4	8.4	10.1	10.0	14.4	42 280	177	3 723	98 856	4.9
SOUTH DAKOTA	13.0	0.3	5.8	9.5	5.3	6.7	10.4	12.9	15.9	162 695	192	14 833	376 319	3.5
Aurora	59.9	0.0	D	D	D	2.6	D	8.5	7.6	600	221	20	1 332	0.6
Beadle	15.3	D	5.3	20.2	2.1	5.7	9.0	D	12.5	3 615	198	402	8 386	1.0
Bennett	33.2	0.0	7.7	D	D	6.0	D	D	31.7	515	149	167	1 257	-0.5
Bon Homme	41.2	0.0	3.7	3.7	2.0	4.5	6.3	D	16.2	1 550	221	78	2 946	0.5
Brookings	6.8	D	4.8	26.1	3.4	5.4	5.2	3.8	26.8	4 090	124	252	13 823	5.2
Brown	9.7	D	6.5	14.1	4.2	7.5	8.6	14.4	12.3	7 115	186	508	17 568	5.2
Brule	43.2	D	5.4	0.4	2.8	5.9	2.7	7.2	10.4	985	183	90	2 485	2.1
Buffalo	26.3	0.0	D	0.0	D	D	D	D	65.4	240	118	119	608	-0.2
Butte	8.1	D	12.5	3.5	D	10.0	D	7.6	15.8	2 180	211	198	4 682	1.3
Campbell	60.6	0.0	D	D	D	3.3	D	1.3	6.4	395	293	19	977	-0.3
Charles Mix	37.4	0.0	4.8	1.7	2.1	4.6	3.2	D	21.7	1 915	208	284	3 853	0.1
Clark	57.5	0.0	7.0	4.6	D	3.1	D	3.1	7.6	815	225	67	1 811	5.9
Clay	21.0	D	4.1	9.1	3.1	4.6	2.9	7.5	31.7	1 875	135	164	5 795	2.8
Codington	5.6	0.1	6.7	20.0	4.6	8.9	8.3	12.8	12.9	5 490	197	357	12 723	2.6
Corson	47.3	0.0	0.8	0.0	1.2	1.2	D	D	37.4	590	139	238	1 534	-0.4
Custer	0.1	1.9	12.8	0.6	3.1	6.6	4.1	D	30.3	2 245	267	113	4 870	5.2
Davison	6.4	D	6.8	20.8	6.3	9.8	5.9	13.2	9.9	4 190	211	349	9 248	4.5
Day	38.8	0.0	6.2	6.9	D	5.4	D	5.8	13.0	1 570	280	90	3 668	1.0
Deuel	28.2	0.0	14.5	12.3	D	4.0	2.4	4.6	7.6	1 100	256	36	2 215	0.5
Dewey	9.2	D	3.9	D	D	7.7	3.9	D	59.1	890	159	389	1 998	-0.2
Douglas	56.0	D	4.4	3.1	D	2.1	D	D	5.7	755	250	37	1 439	0.0
Edmunds	48.5	0.0	3.8	3.5	1.5	4.9	5.7	D	9.5	890	221	37	2 012	2.3
Fall River	11.2	0.7	2.3	1.4	2.9	4.5	2.0	D	41.6	2 250	329	177	4 169	-0.5
Faulk	55.2	0.0	3.0	D	1.9	3.0	2.7	D	9.0	545	229	52	1 153	1.5
Grant	18.5	0.7	10.3	17.2	1.9	5.5	7.1	D	6.7	1 810	248	89	3 552	0.7
Gregory	44.0	D	6.1	0.4	1.5	6.8	5.2	D	9.7	1 160	274	98	2 506	0.1
Haakon	30.4	0.0	D	D	8.0	6.1	3.7	D	9.6	425	225	0	1 009	-0.4
Hamlin	46.9	0.0	7.5	D	D	4.3	2.8	2.7	14.1	1 105	186	62	2 832	2.6
Hand	59.7	0.0	2.8	0.9	D	2.8	D	D	6.9	855	252	47	1 812	-0.2
Hanson	60.3	D	7.5	5.2	D	1.5	4.5	D	8.1	1 510	443	57	1 179	0.2
Harding	13.8	D	27.9	0.0	D	3.3	D	D	16.3	215	170	0	733	0.3
Hughes	8.6	D	3.3	0.6	6.3	7.3	8.7	10.3	38.6	3 200	183	329	7 791	2.2
Hutchinson	51.3	0.0	3.1	3.9	1.1	4.0	3.8	D	6.9	1 975	275	114	3 351	0.0
Hyde	43.3	0.0	D	D	D	4.2	D	D	19.5	330	238	19	703	-0.7
Jackson	25.7	0.0	D	D	D	5.4	D	D	40.8	510	158	139	1 189	-0.3
Jerauld	41.7	0.0	D	D	D	2.1	1.7	D	4.0	645	313	46	1 070	0.0
Jones	46.5	0.0	2.2	D	D	8.1	2.3	1.2	15.7	235	236	11	600	1.9
Kingsbury	47.4	0.0	4.1	9.8	D	3.2	D	4.8	7.5	1 305	257	63	2 730	0.4
Lake	20.0	D	6.1	18.4	4.3	7.0	3.4	7.2	16.0	3 305	274	138	5 659	1.8
Lawrence	0.5	D	7.8	4.5	4.9	10.5	7.7	13.5	17.7	5 375	216	332	13 347	4.6
Lincoln	10.1	0.0	8.6	11.7	D	6.5	17.7	11.7	5.4	5 795	116	194	19 055	6.6
Lyman	58.7	0.0	D	D	D	5.8	1.1	0.2	23.5	745	192	82	1 720	0.9
McCook	43.6	0.0	2.9	D	3.0	3.0	2.7	4.7	6.6	1 205	213	65	2 495	0.2
McPherson	56.4	0.1	1.2	3.2	D	3.2	6.3	6.2	11.9	730	299	64	1 422	0.3
Marshall	36.8	D	8.2	14.2	D	4.0	D	D	11.6	1 035	218	84	2 570	1.4
Meade	1.5	D	11.7	1.9	7.1	5.2	15.8	7.3	25.9	5 125	193	329	11 498	4.4
Mellette	53.9	0.0	D	0.0	D	D	D	0.9	28.5	345	166	119	835	-0.4
Miner	69.2	0.0	D	1.6	D	2.0	D	4.2	7.6	575	246	35	1 327	1.5
Minnehaha	1.0	D	5.4	7.7	8.2	7.4	19.3	19.4	9.6	31 460	175	2 840	76 120	6.4
Moody	42.4	0.0	10.1	6.8	D	1.9	D	D	16.5	1 305	203	57	2 837	0.5
Pennington	0.6	0.1	6.5	4.6	6.4	8.7	6.9	19.3	24.1	22 250	209	1 999	46 804	4.1
Perkins	7.8	0.0	9.8	D	2.5	8.8	D	7.8	19.7	795	262	56	1 731	-0.5
Potter	31.8	0.0	3.3	1.8	D	40.8	D	D	5.3	675	285	18	1 497	-0.2
Roberts	31.2	D	4.1	6.0	1.8	4.2	D	6.8	30.2	2 245	218	229	4 934	0.6
Sanborn	45.7	0.0	D	D	D	2.1	D	D	12.8	540	232	26	1 185	1.1
Shannon	2.4	0.0	2.5	D	1.6	D	D	1.8	79.9	1 485	105	1 133	3 580	-0.4
Spink	54.7	0.0	4.1	4.4	0.9	2.2	3.4	D	16.2	1 565	237	186	3 167	0.9
Stanley	25.2	D	29.6	D	D	5.5	D	D	10.8	600	201	19	1 449	4.5
Sully	76.5	0.0	D	D	D	2.5	1.9	D	5.1	320	219	0	868	2.7
Todd	10.4	0.0	1.2	D	D	3.5	D	D	72.4	1 025	103	595	3 132	-0.3

1. Per 1,000 resident population estimated as of July 1 of the year shown.

STATE County	Housing units, 2009–2013: Occupied units: Total	Owner-occupied: Percent	Owner-occupied: Median value[1]	Median owner cost as a percent of income: With a mortgage	Median owner cost as a percent of income: Without a mortgage[2]	Renter-occupied: Median rent[3]	Renter-occupied: Median rent as a percent of income[2]	Substandard units[4] (percent)	Civilian labor force, 2014: Total	Percent change, 2013–2014	Unemployment: Total	Unemployment: Rate[5]	Civilian employment,[6] 2009–2013: Total	Percent: Management, business, science and arts	Percent: Construction, production, and maintenance occupations
	89	90	91	92	93	94	95	96	97	98	99	100	101	102	103
SOUTH CAROLINA—Cont'd															
Sumter	39 373	65.4	107 300	21.2	11.6	726	28.5	1.9	43 964	0.0	3 223	7.3	41 056	29.5	28.0
Union	11 854	73.1	74 000	20.8	13.1	610	31.0	2.9	11 498	-1.6	985	8.6	10 641	23.6	36.4
Williamsburg	11 621	74.3	67 100	26.7	14.4	576	33.5	1.9	12 712	0.7	1 261	9.9	10 932	23.2	30.4
York	86 483	71.6	159 300	21.9	10.0	796	29.5	1.5	120 614	1.4	7 690	6.4	107 813	36.1	21.8
SOUTH DAKOTA	323 136	68.0	132 400	21.4	10.9	632	26.3	2.7	448 201	0.7	15 228	3.4	418 991	34.5	23.4
Aurora	1 102	80.6	68 800	17.4	11.1	582	19.4	5.0	1 616	-2.0	41	2.5	1 400	32.6	28.4
Beadle	7 343	64.8	87 500	18.5	11.2	523	25.3	15.0	9 452	-0.5	293	3.1	9 088	27.4	32.4
Bennett	1 059	52.4	54 300	24.5	10.7	464	23.7	3.4	1 132	-0.5	63	5.6	1 095	40.5	20.5
Bon Homme	2 501	77.6	69 700	19.7	10.4	419	26.1	1.2	3 000	-0.3	85	2.8	2 861	42.2	21.6
Brookings	11 979	58.0	147 400	22.2	10.7	659	29.1	0.9	18 185	2.1	569	3.1	17 990	33.3	28.5
Brown	15 590	70.2	133 900	20.2	12.0	559	23.7	1.6	21 036	0.2	608	2.9	20 096	32.9	24.6
Brule	2 094	70.1	92 500	21.8	12.3	513	20.0	16.8	2 592	-0.7	84	3.2	2 529	36.7	21.6
Buffalo	542	37.3	38 800	18.3	14.4	545	17.5	1.9	727	-2.2	57	7.8	598	33.9	23.4
Butte	4 015	72.0	111 900	23.6	11.9	530	26.9	0.7	5 086	0.7	173	3.4	4 903	26.1	32.2
Campbell	679	78.9	52 100	19.8	12.0	475	27.9	4.5	835	-1.1	28	3.4	703	40.1	23.2
Charles Mix	3 191	70.8	74 500	20.2	11.1	471	24.2	2.6	4 053	1.2	153	3.8	3 898	33.6	24.3
Clark	1 431	78.9	69 000	20.1	10.0	545	22.4	1.5	1 987	0.2	77	3.9	1 764	33.9	29.6
Clay	5 145	55.8	133 800	20.8	11.5	640	36.7	1.8	7 137	0.5	245	3.4	7 350	39.0	17.9
Codington	11 566	69.5	134 800	21.5	12.1	606	25.8	14.2	15 423	-0.4	507	3.3	14 870	27.2	27.9
Corson	1 185	52.9	48 900	12.9	14.6	421	20.7	2.2	1 505	-0.5	89	5.9	1 222	44.8	21.8
Custer	3 731	80.0	192 000	24.1	12.9	577	24.2	1.6	4 039	0.3	180	4.5	3 688	43.4	19.8
Davison	8 471	62.5	123 300	20.1	10.3	595	24.4	2.9	11 331	0.7	317	2.8	10 519	34.1	24.7
Day	2 511	70.5	76 800	22.3	12.0	505	26.4	1.9	2 906	-0.7	153	5.3	2 695	32.9	26.9
Deuel	1 789	85.0	93 700	18.9	10.0	436	20.4	9.4	2 337	-2.0	125	5.3	2 283	32.2	32.9
Dewey	1 687	58.2	57 500	18.9	12.4	438	25.3	0.3	2 358	-2.8	342	14.5	1 869	44.6	19.8
Douglas	1 258	78.5	70 900	17.1	10.0	545	26.3	0.3	1 741	1.9	51	2.9	1 519	38.2	27.0
Edmunds	1 589	78.2	84 000	18.9	10.0	572	24.6	2.2	2 293	0.2	56	2.4	2 168	35.7	28.9
Fall River	3 138	67.1	89 700	23.2	11.5	513	29.0	4.4	3 026	-0.6	140	4.6	2 964	31.6	21.4
Faulk	930	78.6	65 200	21.0	10.0	444	24.3	1.4	1 156	-0.8	36	3.1	1 144	40.7	24.6
Grant	3 159	76.6	100 500	23.5	10.0	463	24.0	2.6	4 745	1.9	169	3.6	3 951	29.4	29.3
Gregory	1 986	71.2	58 400	21.0	11.5	470	29.8	1.2	2 086	-0.9	71	3.4	1 928	40.4	20.4
Haakon	807	77.6	74 400	20.9	10.0	620	19.6	5.6	1 096	1.1	30	2.7	938	45.5	17.9
Hamlin	2 041	77.7	108 100	20.4	10.0	523	24.0	1.4	3 158	1.1	108	3.4	2 833	31.7	34.3
Hand	1 429	73.5	86 400	21.5	10.1	467	24.1	2.5	1 832	0.0	47	2.6	1 677	33.8	26.8
Hanson	1 037	83.5	102 700	23.7	12.5	560	19.8	0.9	1 815	0.3	63	3.5	1 638	36.1	29.7
Harding	527	74.2	69 400	19.8	10.2	434	20.6	1.9	781	0.6	19	2.4	692	43.6	33.1
Hughes	6 992	67.4	160 900	20.8	10.0	568	25.4	1.4	10 008	0.8	258	2.6	9 475	43.0	14.3
Hutchinson	2 937	77.2	71 000	19.7	11.8	538	26.2	2.0	3 665	-0.2	105	2.9	3 659	38.6	25.8
Hyde	549	76.3	68 700	16.3	11.5	467	20.0	10.8	703	-2.4	20	2.8	751	40.2	25.6
Jackson	1 056	62.7	52 600	19.4	10.0	433	14.4	2.3	1 316	0.2	71	5.4	1 234	46.8	21.7
Jerauld	882	72.7	69 900	20.4	11.0	517	17.3	0.9	1 217	1.6	31	2.5	1 017	32.2	31.9
Jones	438	75.1	67 600	18.3	11.5	464	32.5	1.5	622	0.2	22	3.5	493	32.7	21.9
Kingsbury	2 311	76.9	82 000	17.9	10.6	455	19.8	0.2	2 928	1.3	86	2.9	2 546	35.1	30.0
Lake	4 655	72.5	118 500	20.5	11.2	517	24.7	2.0	6 280	-0.7	224	3.6	6 261	30.1	26.2
Lawrence	10 597	64.8	167 100	24.4	11.5	593	27.0	0.9	12 700	0.0	444	3.5	12 793	29.6	22.3
Lincoln	17 250	77.0	184 900	21.4	10.0	837	25.4	7.9	29 100	1.8	698	2.4	25 912	44.6	18.1
Lyman	1 423	65.6	74 200	17.5	10.0	449	14.8	2.5	1 817	-2.5	77	4.2	1 716	43.4	18.1
McCook	2 186	80.1	101 100	19.4	10.7	531	23.9	2.4	3 211	1.2	85	2.6	2 935	36.4	26.3
McPherson	1 045	74.7	55 800	20.7	11.4	100	11.4	2.1	1 142	0.4	44	3.9	1 120	42.6	21.7
Marshall	1 683	73.0	93 200	19.0	11.9	510	24.5	3.6	2 542	-0.3	104	4.1	2 278	31.0	29.5
Meade	10 083	72.2	157 100	23.9	13.3	728	30.6	10.5	13 636	0.6	447	3.3	12 669	29.4	25.4
Mellette	698	66.8	54 100	20.0	10.0	429	15.7	0.8	824	-1.4	50	6.1	804	44.4	26.1
Miner	1 053	76.6	63 000	17.7	12.6	463	21.0	2.2	1 243	0.4	40	3.2	1 219	40.9	27.7
Minnehaha	67 623	64.4	149 600	21.7	10.0	693	26.7	1.9	104 575	1.8	3 117	3.0	95 431	32.5	21.9
Moody	2 686	70.7	101 000	20.2	10.9	530	19.5	2.1	3 979	-0.7	164	4.1	3 496	38.7	28.4
Pennington	40 723	65.4	156 100	23.1	11.9	756	28.5	2.0	53 691	0.7	1 813	3.4	51 212	34.0	20.0
Perkins	1 364	71.2	56 700	19.8	10.2	409	19.4	0.1	1 557	1.2	52	3.3	1 460	40.5	27.4
Potter	1 051	81.4	60 000	17.3	13.0	592	25.0	2.7	1 213	0.7	41	3.4	1 194	32.7	31.0
Roberts	3 646	69.8	83 000	19.8	10.4	481	24.2	2.0	4 912	1.3	232	4.7	4 386	35.7	23.9
Sanborn	1 051	73.7	68 200	18.8	10.0	511	19.1	36.7	1 259	-2.8	32	2.5	1 252	31.8	34.0
Shannon	2 867	52.5	19 900	13.6	13.0	408	17.1	0.9	3 642	-1.1	479	13.2	3 257	40.0	17.2
Spink	2 624	73.7	64 000	17.2	10.0	491	23.1	3.0	3 398	1.6	120	3.5	3 053	34.8	25.7
Stanley	1 273	78.7	110 900	20.4	13.1	649	27.6	2.3	1 879	1.0	48	2.6	1 749	38.6	26.4
Sully	606	72.4	88 200	22.3	10.0	607	12.6	19.4	892	0.8	25	2.8	786	40.6	30.8
Todd	2 680	46.5	40 200	28.4	10.0	447	19.9	4.6	3 093	-2.9	268	8.7	2 774	35.1	20.0

1. Specified owner-occupied units. 2. A value of 10.0 represents 10 percent or less; a value of 50.0 represents 50 percent or more. 3. Specified renter-occupied units.
4. Overcrowded or lacking complete plumbing facilities. 5. Percent of civilian labor force. 6. Persons 16 years old and over.

STATE County	Private nonfarm establishments, employment and payroll, 2013: Number of establishments	Employment: Total	Employment: Health care and social assistance	Employment: Manufacturing	Employment: Retail trade	Employment: Finance and insurance	Employment: Professional, scientific, and technical services	Annual payroll: Total (mil dol)	Annual payroll: Average per employee (dollars)	Agriculture, 2012: Farms: Number	Farms: Percent with: Fewer than 50 acres	Farms: Percent with: 500 acres or more	Farm operators whose principal occupation is farming (percent)
	104	105	106	107	108	109	110	111	112	113	114	115	116
SOUTH CAROLINA—Cont'd													
Sumter	1 777	29 965	5 641	5 614	4 499	820	719	968	32 319	515	44.3	14.2	45.8
Union	449	5 968	D	1 465	942	200	D	188	31 461	264	33.0	7.2	33.7
Williamsburg	490	6 578	811	D	840	165	101	238	36 170	679	28.9	15.8	38.3
York	4 548	68 940	8 723	8 957	9 607	4 728	2 523	2 704	39 228	1 004	48.3	4.7	35.8
SOUTH DAKOTA	26 021	340 485	65 548	43 702	50 992	26 758	11 268	12 355	36 287	31 989	19.6	43.6	58.9
Aurora	90	613	D	D	D	48	D	18	30 016	442	12.2	47.5	60.6
Beadle	558	7 105	1 473	1 715	1 138	364	126	211	29 645	754	19.4	43.4	55.6
Bennett	63	678	191	D	137	D	D	17	24 984	219	7.3	68.5	68.0
Bon Homme	176	1 166	375	128	205	74	D	30	25 419	671	20.3	38.3	54.7
Brookings	869	13 353	1 513	4 497	1 764	586	590	449	33 638	1 023	31.7	23.9	46.2
Brown	1 267	18 422	2 891	3 217	2 988	935	525	637	34 551	1 056	23.6	38.9	57.4
Brule	225	1 799	465	24	275	72	51	48	26 737	407	21.4	47.2	61.9
Buffalo	11	172	D	D	NA	NA	D	4	22 651	78	7.7	66.7	75.6
Butte	312	2 259	D	162	424	84	86	68	30 016	659	21.1	35.2	57.7
Campbell	56	269	22	D	D	D	9	9	33 253	242	7.9	56.6	63.2
Charles Mix	272	2 357	514	87	431	117	D	60	25 312	759	14.1	45.1	67.2
Clark	114	621	D	D	78	D	D	19	31 032	597	11.6	48.1	58.1
Clay	301	3 383	735	D	813	78	55	73	21 695	461	27.1	37.3	64.4
Codington	1 115	14 275	1 715	3 424	2 654	798	266	473	33 100	713	30.9	29.6	44.6
Corson	34	175	17	NA	NA	D	NA	6	31 594	323	6.5	73.7	79.3
Custer	274	1 314	237	D	257	D	D	44	33 736	446	33.0	32.5	54.3
Davison	733	11 383	2 292	1 804	2 034	322	381	365	32 046	427	26.5	31.1	48.2
Day	175	1 494	302	260	266	D	D	43	28 786	693	14.0	35.9	46.0
Deuel	138	1 768	150	D	109	D	D	82	46 273	664	26.5	28.6	53.6
Dewey	84	582	D	D	87	104	D	19	32 002	342	14.6	65.2	55.6
Douglas	104	845	D	108	126	33	D	23	27 199	434	15.0	42.9	72.4
Edmunds	129	872	176	D	129	52	D	29	33 420	422	9.7	60.7	62.6
Fall River	205	2 491	1 531	D	245	D	55	128	51 212	327	18.7	51.1	64.5
Faulk	72	428	D	D	70	D	D	14	32 318	280	6.4	70.7	75.4
Grant	279	3 044	389	573	524	D	50	108	35 473	618	22.0	39.6	64.6
Gregory	187	1 113	315	35	246	D	35	29	25 844	505	10.1	52.3	65.3
Haakon	79	610	D	D	82	D	D	18	30 252	287	2.8	72.8	73.2
Hamlin	176	1 093	157	D	146	D	27	35	32 182	489	28.6	30.3	52.8
Hand	125	1 027	222	47	206	60	29	31	30 044	415	6.5	64.6	68.7
Hanson	68	307	D	D	D	30	D	10	33 365	370	16.8	44.1	60.0
Harding	42	373	D	NA	27	D	D	20	54 284	250	5.6	80.4	79.2
Hughes	654	6 408	1 137	D	1 323	527	300	209	32 650	338	33.1	34.3	50.0
Hutchinson	243	2 157	671	280	324	109	D	62	28 870	802	16.5	40.5	60.3
Hyde	45	497	D	NA	80	D	D	16	32 052	207	11.6	63.8	81.2
Jackson	51	249	D	D	110	D	D	6	23 265	299	7.7	70.6	70.6
Jerauld	81	D	D	D	D	32	D	D	D	233	18.5	46.4	49.8
Jones	52	274	D	NA	90	D	D	8	28 281	163	4.3	72.4	73.0
Kingsbury	166	1 345	209	400	144	116	D	46	34 385	518	14.9	45.8	64.1
Lake	363	3 723	637	880	501	123	D	120	32 356	502	29.1	30.3	51.6
Lawrence	1 008	9 211	D	496	1 401	276	298	270	29 282	312	28.8	17.9	42.0
Lincoln	1 294	13 719	2 212	2 641	1 616	1 219	491	540	39 379	899	34.8	27.5	50.3
Lyman	78	670	D	NA	280	31	D	14	20 231	430	6.3	62.3	53.7
McCook	181	907	235	5	158	43	D	25	27 752	568	25.0	37.5	53.5
McPherson	77	359	D	D	66	53	D	9	24 616	398	12.6	54.0	60.6
Marshall	150	1 186	D	386	183	D	D	39	32 607	518	14.5	41.5	53.7
Meade	703	5 090	D	295	622	175	203	215	42 247	891	21.2	50.4	56.9
Mellette	23	D	D	NA	D	D	D	3	D	229	3.1	76.4	83.8
Miner	75	495	123	29	D	D	D	15	30 083	486	17.5	36.8	55.6
Minnehaha	5 516	113 513	D	10 967	14 825	13 478	4 033	4 624	40 738	1 157	39.7	23.2	52.0
Moody	160	1 716	D	382	181	D	D	56	32 902	513	29.2	25.7	63.0
Pennington	3 654	46 130	9 070	2 369	8 464	3 230	1 937	1 614	34 979	599	24.5	38.4	52.1
Perkins	128	735	137	D	105	46	9	22	29 796	437	8.9	72.3	69.6
Potter	108	769	D	50	96	D	D	28	36 299	247	11.3	56.3	68.0
Roberts	230	2 182	567	229	380	99	D	57	26 264	876	19.2	35.0	54.3
Sanborn	61	452	D	D	46	D	22	10	29 055	402	10.2	41.5	47.0
Shannon	66	1 845	297	D	214	D	D	54	29 222	174	4.6	69.5	77.0
Spink	188	1 290	330	94	D	85	D	44	34 260	675	11.4	56.7	67.0
Stanley	110	1 065	17	D	137	38	D	35	32 682	183	7.1	71.0	66.1
Sully	67	329	5	D	95	D	D	11	34 951	191	6.3	66.0	72.8
Todd	55	1 192	D	D	233	D	D	38	32 045	231	10.4	63.2	70.6

STATE County	Agriculture, 2012 (cont.)															
	Land in farms					Value of land and buildings (dollars)		Value of machinery and equipment, average per farm (dollars)	Value of products sold				Percent of farms with sales of:		Government payments	
	Acreage (1,000)	Percent change, 2007–2012	Acres: Average size of farm	Acres: Total irrigated (1,000)	Acres: Total cropland (1,000)	Average per farm	Average per acre		Total (mil dol)	Average per farm (dollars)	Percent from: Crops	Percent from: Livestock and poultry products	$10,000 or more	$100,000 or more	Total ($1,000)	Percent of farms
	117	118	119	120	121	122	123	124	125	126	127	128	129	130	131	132
SOUTH CAROLINA—Cont'd																
Sumter	176	14.7	342	8.9	69.5	792 967	2 320	105 033	130.5	253 379	36.9	63.1	27.2	10.9	1 870	57.3
Union	47	4.0	179	0.1	9.0	394 534	2 201	43 322	15.3	58 121	12.3	87.7	29.5	1.9	303	14.4
Williamsburg	224	7.2	331	0.8	91.8	689 383	2 086	83 346	61.8	91 032	83.2	16.8	29.9	12.8	2 763	60.1
York	124	-0.2	123	0.7	38.1	621 009	5 031	48 627	96.8	96 452	D	D	23.4	4.1	572	14.6
SOUTH DAKOTA	43 257	-0.9	1 352	378.7	19 147.3	2 281 027	1 687	241 373	10 170.2	317 929	59.7	40.3	65.0	40.7	283 797	71.3
Aurora	442	21.2	1 000	D	267.7	2 361 032	2 361	226 367	127.3	287 910	53.6	46.4	71.7	45.5	3 875	81.4
Beadle	794	3.1	1 053	11.2	576.9	3 014 625	2 864	295 423	300.2	398 088	63.3	36.7	66.3	46.9	7 071	74.9
Bennett	606	-19.5	2 769	6.6	178.6	1 564 995	565	198 361	62.2	283 799	35.8	64.2	76.7	51.1	2 139	73.5
Bon Homme	352	13.9	524	6.6	277.2	1 529 963	2 920	189 478	107.9	160 744	38.3	61.7	66.0	30.3	4 954	86.3
Brookings	449	-2.9	439	16.9	327.4	1 870 065	4 261	195 803	312.5	305 506	51.9	48.1	52.9	29.9	7 038	68.3
Brown	1 079	-0.6	1 022	6.4	854.5	2 980 409	2 917	318 692	520.6	493 029	88.9	11.1	56.9	40.7	17 500	66.3
Brule	514	-0.9	1 263	3.7	263.9	2 876 440	2 278	244 592	150.9	370 715	51.0	49.0	70.0	42.8	2 702	68.8
Buffalo	296	-5.1	3 797	6.3	87.0	4 488 474	1 182	380 705	45.7	585 256	50.3	49.7	70.5	50.0	912	78.2
Butte	1 135	-0.5	1 722	45.4	116.8	1 066 480	619	99 675	75.4	114 340	23.0	77.0	67.2	26.1	3 255	46.7
Campbell	360	-10.1	1 489	2.3	211.0	1 898 711	1 275	321 665	98.9	408 607	62.8	37.2	71.1	51.7	2 928	85.5
Charles Mix	692	4.8	912	15.3	448.9	2 146 680	2 353	264 441	227.9	300 271	45.2	54.8	70.2	44.9	5 433	87.7
Clark	609	19.7	1 020	7.3	401.3	2 584 074	2 534	297 191	249.4	417 714	64.0	36.0	66.2	51.1	5 326	83.9
Clay	259	-3.0	561	20.8	237.6	2 481 560	4 422	279 267	96.8	210 037	82.3	17.7	64.2	46.6	4 323	79.4
Codington	369	0.6	518	4.3	255.9	1 389 913	2 684	168 854	172.4	241 811	62.8	37.2	56.2	33.4	3 757	62.6
Corson	1 242	-3.2	3 846	D	346.4	2 514 418	654	240 712	117.1	362 492	50.9	49.1	86.4	60.4	3 165	66.3
Custer	623	3.7	1 397	3.1	46.9	1 600 944	1 146	76 119	26.0	58 325	11.0	89.0	47.8	15.7	1 285	19.7
Davison	275	-1.5	645	1.7	210.2	2 187 288	3 393	215 440	78.8	184 515	63.7	36.3	55.7	31.4	2 594	65.6
Day	570	0.5	823	0.3	395.0	1 571 924	1 911	211 440	189.7	273 775	83.5	16.5	51.7	32.5	6 718	78.6
Deuel	342	7.8	515	1.1	207.6	1 519 508	2 951	183 530	177.8	267 700	52.5	47.5	54.2	32.2	4 206	78.2
Dewey	1 182	-18.5	3 455	0.0	214.4	1 979 599	573	171 526	69.3	202 535	42.2	57.8	76.9	44.7	4 224	64.9
Douglas	270	19.8	622	2.1	192.3	1 774 048	2 854	210 823	117.5	270 668	35.4	64.6	81.1	50.5	2 807	79.3
Edmunds	697	6.1	1 652	1.0	492.8	3 620 645	2 192	451 389	271.4	643 123	68.7	31.3	74.2	58.3	5 097	81.5
Fall River	1 089	14.6	3 330	7.5	63.8	1 714 394	515	112 138	116.9	357 364	5.5	94.5	59.3	30.3	1 885	40.4
Faulk	616	0.2	2 199	0.5	382.8	4 275 536	1 945	559 368	216.3	772 596	72.3	27.7	83.9	66.4	5 575	87.9
Grant	429	17.9	694	3.4	290.7	2 075 218	2 992	261 960	240.8	389 675	56.4	43.6	66.0	48.1	4 517	70.6
Gregory	635	-3.0	1 257	0.5	239.1	1 534 659	1 221	156 531	94.1	186 410	42.4	57.6	73.5	37.4	2 245	79.4
Haakon	1 133	-1.5	3 949	0.1	324.6	2 375 324	601	186 188	77.1	268 700	43.0	57.0	75.6	50.2	4 539	73.5
Hamlin	311	0.4	636	7.9	241.7	2 272 331	3 572	285 902	188.2	384 920	66.3	33.7	59.1	39.9	4 136	74.8
Hand	905	0.7	2 181	4.5	565.6	4 161 320	1 908	431 607	284.4	685 390	69.6	30.4	77.1	58.1	5 362	85.3
Hanson	274	25.1	741	1.1	212.2	2 773 749	3 745	316 603	110.7	299 054	60.7	39.3	67.6	46.8	2 701	75.1
Harding	1 467	-8.1	5 869	0.7	179.7	2 465 216	420	212 876	70.4	281 628	24.3	75.7	80.0	55.6	2 729	61.6
Hughes	431	4.8	1 275	9.8	269.5	2 502 944	1 963	213 530	107.3	317 577	81.2	18.8	54.7	32.8	3 532	62.1
Hutchinson	513	0.7	640	4.0	409.7	2 103 788	3 287	263 249	186.2	232 226	38.3	61.7	69.1	38.4	7 192	85.2
Hyde	515	7.0	2 486	0.3	216.3	3 454 498	1 390	317 135	94.3	455 705	66.9	33.1	80.7	57.5	2 441	75.4
Jackson	1 158	-2.2	3 873	0.6	176.6	3 077 278	795	179 492	51.9	173 619	34.6	65.4	71.2	41.8	2 083	58.2
Jerauld	333	1.3	1 428	1.4	181.6	2 811 747	1 968	300 974	99.3	426 206	62.4	37.6	67.8	40.8	2 191	73.4
Jones	612	17.9	3 757	0.7	210.1	2 730 785	727	235 785	65.3	400 319	61.5	38.5	74.8	58.3	2 535	81.0
Kingsbury	521	9.1	1 006	2.1	382.3	3 338 884	3 319	324 201	278.3	537 182	63.0	37.0	75.3	55.8	5 135	74.9
Lake	262	-16.9	521	1.8	207.3	2 128 008	4 081	237 606	168.8	336 323	66.6	33.4	56.6	41.8	3 352	75.5
Lawrence	159	18.9	509	2.7	29.7	722 071	1 419	76 962	19.1	61 064	12.7	87.3	41.0	11.9	315	22.1
Lincoln	366	9.8	407	2.9	329.9	2 211 686	5 440	198 632	172.3	191 619	60.0	40.0	61.4	33.1	6 946	71.4
Lyman	1 029	5.3	2 392	8.7	456.4	2 398 733	1 003	253 705	136.8	318 044	69.5	30.5	65.6	47.0	6 670	81.6
McCook	363	-0.1	639	D	299.5	2 713 745	4 248	278 900	157.0	276 347	61.6	38.4	65.0	40.1	3 979	72.9
McPherson	573	10.5	1 439	1.3	286.8	2 201 472	1 530	274 035	159.4	400 425	53.1	46.9	71.4	42.0	3 081	76.9
Marshall	532	-0.4	1 027	D	316.0	2 296 672	2 235	328 147	306.8	592 357	47.6	52.4	58.7	39.6	8 084	82.2
Meade	2 033	-8.0	2 281	4.0	349.8	1 537 875	674	117 736	116.4	130 688	21.8	78.2	60.3	28.5	4 935	42.4
Mellette	699	-4.2	3 051	D	117.4	2 181 253	715	174 258	46.2	201 799	30.1	69.9	82.5	52.8	1 048	65.1
Miner	357	19.1	735	D	231.5	2 361 718	3 212	260 222	123.7	254 517	60.6	39.4	57.4	40.1	4 341	82.5
Minnehaha	408	-3.2	353	1.7	322.4	1 814 344	5 146	191 197	270.2	233 576	60.8	39.2	56.3	34.4	5 753	67.2
Moody	254	-13.3	496	3.2	208.8	2 525 815	5 094	216 696	215.0	419 047	61.1	38.9	59.8	40.7	4 100	76.2
Pennington	1 074	-9.4	1 793	5.8	222.8	1 253 793	699	110 694	65.7	109 760	45.0	55.0	55.9	23.7	2 942	30.7
Perkins	1 631	-10.8	3 732	0.2	393.2	2 007 828	538	177 826	125.0	286 087	34.6	65.4	77.6	51.5	4 913	77.1
Potter	538	4.1	2 178	D	357.3	4 354 235	1 999	489 332	157.0	635 684	89.5	10.5	70.9	54.7	3 783	78.1
Roberts	623	5.1	711	2.3	429.3	1 800 643	2 531	225 765	251.2	286 725	79.7	20.3	57.1	36.6	9 142	79.2
Sanborn	360	13.2	896	D	221.8	2 130 490	2 377	270 057	118.8	295 401	58.4	41.6	60.9	39.8	3 561	78.1
Shannon	1 101	-17.4	6 329	0.5	97.8	2 910 178	460	155 874	32.3	185 563	27.0	73.0	77.0	36.8	1 772	45.4
Spink	945	4.1	1 400	19.2	714.7	4 166 481	2 976	425 689	447.6	663 096	74.7	25.3	72.3	56.4	12 003	87.4
Stanley	791	-14.1	4 323	0.2	219.4	3 968 497	918	248 842	64.0	349 896	63.7	36.3	77.6	50.3	2 309	62.3
Sully	628	3.2	3 289	24.6	501.0	5 131 304	1 560	595 026	225.6	1 181 042	82.7	17.3	77.5	61.3	3 981	77.0
Todd	860	-1.1	3 723	7.2	125.2	1 902 965	511	163 303	59.7	258 268	26.7	73.3	72.3	42.4	398	37.2

STATE County	Water use, 2010		Wholesale trade,[1] 2007				Retail trade,[2] 2007				Real estate and rental and leasing,[2] 2007			
	Total water withdrawn (mil gal/day)	Gallons withdrawn per person per day	Number of establish-ments	Number of employees	Sales (mil dol)	Annual payroll (mil dol)	Number of establish-ments	Number of employees	Sales (mil dol)	Annual payroll (mil dol)	Number of establish-ments	Number of employees	Receipts (mil dol)	Annual payroll (mil dol)
	133	134	135	136	137	138	139	140	141	142	143	144	145	146
SOUTH CAROLINA—Cont'd														
Sumter	23.5	219	73	D	D	D	417	4 919	1 021.5	91.8	87	308	36.7	6.8
Union	4.7	161	15	D	D	D	107	885	192.2	16.9	14	37	3.7	0.7
Williamsburg	5.4	155	19	237	102.5	7.5	124	995	224.6	16.9	14	46	3.9	0.9
York	217.1	960	222	2 949	2 150.1	141.9	689	8 200	2 172.7	179.1	229	825	113.7	21.4
SOUTH DAKOTA	625.8	769	1 248	13 402	11 400.5	550.8	4 172	50 842	12 266.2	1 045.3	888	3 844	523.9	90.3
Aurora	0.8	284	5	22	19.2	0.6	15	86	38.1	1.3	2	D	D	D
Beadle	5.7	329	25	D	D	D	97	1 262	245.8	23.2	31	108	12.4	1.3
Bennett	26.2	7 648	1	D	D	D	15	118	24.0	1.9	NA	NA	NA	NA
Bon Homme	6.9	976	11	87	43.2	2.0	38	231	40.7	3.4	3	6	0.2	0.0
Brookings	17.0	532	30	D	D	D	118	1 729	338.2	30.7	38	151	14.4	3.4
Brown	8.8	241	78	863	1 471.6	34.6	209	2 980	692.2	65.4	55	264	39.3	5.8
Brule	3.9	742	11	70	46.8	2.7	42	320	78.5	5.0	2	D	D	D
Buffalo	15.4	8 044	NA	NA	NA	NA	2	D	D	D	1	D	D	D
Butte	17.2	1 698	9	67	29.1	2.2	46	386	108.9	8.9	11	D	D	D
Campbell	15.8	10 764	5	D	D	D	5	21	3.9	0.2	1	D	D	D
Charles Mix	19.9	2 178	15	113	73.1	3.2	60	428	82.1	6.2	3	5	1.0	0.1
Clark	8.2	2 208	8	50	64.3	2.0	16	82	21.0	1.6	1	D	D	D
Clay	5.5	397	10	D	D	D	45	772	140.1	12.2	14	75	5.3	0.6
Codington	12.8	469	62	536	344.0	22.7	201	2 602	560.7	51.7	40	D	D	D
Corson	1.8	447	4	D	D	D	7	59	10.6	0.9	NA	NA	NA	NA
Custer	12.5	1 525	4	D	D	D	30	228	51.5	5.1	9	17	2.8	0.3
Davison	1.6	80	33	393	407.0	17.7	135	2 055	436.2	38.6	27	D	D	D
Day	8.5	1 490	11	128	97.1	4.4	35	245	51.0	3.9	5	D	D	D
Deuel	2.9	671	3	D	D	D	24	142	36.4	2.6	1	D	D	D
Dewey	1.1	208	7	39	12.5	1.1	20	132	23.8	1.5	2	D	D	D
Douglas	4.3	1 419	6	D	D	D	16	113	22.5	1.9	2	D	D	D
Edmunds	3.0	747	12	119	196.3	4.5	24	159	39.7	2.7	3	10	0.1	0.0
Fall River	7.1	1 001	3	20	3.6	0.4	40	338	68.7	5.4	6	32	3.0	0.2
Faulk	0.9	389	8	49	72.7	1.2	13	75	20.3	1.7	1	D	D	D
Grant	20.4	2 766	11	114	122.8	5.2	48	500	99.8	9.3	10	29	2.7	0.3
Gregory	3.1	716	10	41	27.3	0.8	38	277	53.0	4.5	1	D	D	D
Haakon	6.3	3 242	6	31	54.6	1.0	15	106	23.9	1.7	1	D	D	D
Hamlin	1.6	276	8	90	80.7	4.5	24	147	49.1	3.1	1	D	D	D
Hand	1.1	329	11	107	76.5	3.7	24	150	30.3	2.7	NA	NA	NA	NA
Hanson	1.6	477	6	D	D	D	5	45	6.0	0.5	2	D	D	D
Harding	0.8	622	NA	NA	NA	NA	6	36	8.7	0.5	NA	NA	NA	NA
Hughes	46.8	2 752	22	227	250.1	6.9	120	1 409	262.3	27.8	31	134	6.8	1.1
Hutchinson	1.9	261	24	237	321.5	7.2	48	338	74.0	5.7	3	4	0.4	0.1
Hyde	0.8	528	NA	NA	NA	NA	10	116	37.5	2.0	2	D	D	D
Jackson	2.1	683	2	D	D	D	15	114	29.1	2.0	NA	NA	NA	NA
Jerauld	1.2	594	8	D	D	D	11	79	20.5	1.5	2	D	D	D
Jones	2.7	2 674	2	D	D	D	13	99	23.0	1.9	NA	NA	NA	NA
Kingsbury	6.1	1 189	6	82	103.3	3.6	30	155	34.1	2.6	2	D	D	D
Lake	8.0	716	12	215	225.0	8.6	54	516	134.7	10.4	15	44	2.3	0.5
Lawrence	23.1	959	23	D	D	D	148	1 532	435.1	35.0	61	197	19.8	4.4
Lincoln	5.4	120	47	355	337.8	14.4	115	1 241	444.4	33.9	34	D	D	D
Lyman	5.5	1 475	5	D	D	D	19	278	69.0	4.3	1	D	D	D
McCook	1.6	287	10	59	41.4	1.7	26	152	43.5	3.0	5	D	D	D
McPherson	1.4	582	3	D	D	D	16	60	15.7	1.0	3	3	0.2	0.0
Marshall	8.8	1 881	11	75	38.1	2.1	27	177	48.2	3.1	1	D	D	D
Meade	10.3	403	21	88	39.2	3.6	86	702	194.3	15.1	29	94	15.6	1.5
Mellette	4.5	2 202	2	D	D	D	6	47	9.3	0.7	NA	NA	NA	NA
Miner	0.5	213	5	D	D	D	13	64	10.7	0.9	NA	NA	NA	NA
Minnehaha	34.2	202	322	4 798	3 023.5	224.1	851	14 984	3 823.8	329.4	205	1 263	204.2	36.8
Moody	4.4	680	7	32	16.5	1.0	20	180	38.3	3.2	2	D	D	D
Pennington	51.8	513	155	1 934	1 007.2	75.1	600	7 902	1 967.8	178.9	158	677	112.7	16.5
Perkins	1.6	550	4	D	D	D	26	144	28.2	2.7	1	D	D	D
Potter	5.0	2 130	7	59	52.0	2.3	21	169	26.8	2.0	2	D	D	D
Roberts	8.8	862	16	108	211.1	3.4	51	384	81.0	6.0	1	D	D	D
Sanborn	0.7	301	7	75	51.0	3.4	7	65	6.7	0.5	NA	NA	NA	NA
Shannon	0.9	67	NA	NA	NA	NA	15	194	39.2	2.4	1	D	D	D
Spink	18.3	2 846	10	127	248.3	5.6	30	199	41.1	3.6	3	7	0.4	0.0
Stanley	4.5	1 514	4	D	D	D	19	114	30.7	2.3	3	3	0.3	0.1
Sully	27.2	19 825	2	D	D	D	13	86	31.3	1.7	1	D	D	D
Todd	39.4	4 097	1	D	D	D	21	241	39.5	2.9	NA	NA	NA	NA

1. Merchant wholesalers, except manufacturers' sales branches and offices. 2. Employer establishments.

Table B. States and Counties — **Professional Services, Manufacturing, and Accommodation and Food Services**

STATE County	Professional, scientific, and technical services,[1] 2007				Manufacturing, 2007				Accommodation and food services, 2007			
	Number of establish-ments	Number of employees	Receipts (mil dol)	Annual payroll (mil dol)	Number of establish-ments	Number of employees	Receipts (mil dol)	Annual payroll (mil dol)	Number of establish-ments	Number of employees	Sales (mil dol)	Annual payroll (mil dol)
	147	148	149	150	151	152	153	154	155	156	157	158
SOUTH CAROLINA—Cont'd												
Sumter	139	D	D	D	82	7 707	1 922.0	253.3	149	3 173	109.4	29.8
Union	25	192	6.9	2.2	31	2 062	488.4	72.4	32	554	18.5	4.9
Williamsburg	31	117	10.1	3.9	35	2 811	1 398.1	93.0	29	404	12.8	3.1
York	403	D	D	D	233	10 096	3 621.2	457.8	365	6 983	285.8	78.0
SOUTH DAKOTA	1 735	10 073	1 093.4	385.9	1 052	40 961	13 051.1	1 539.3	2 426	36 710	1 622.8	436.2
Aurora	5	25	2.2	0.4	NA	NA	NA	NA	11	D	D	D
Beadle	24	D	D	D	32	1 140	298.6	32.3	54	609	20.8	5.4
Bennett	4	9	0.3	0.1	NA	NA	NA	NA	8	57	1.8	0.4
Bon Homme	8	13	1.5	0.3	NA	NA	NA	NA	15	80	2.3	0.5
Brookings	64	350	33.7	12.4	42	5 104	2 265.7	210.4	76	1 636	53.2	14.1
Brown	85	419	41.1	15.3	37	D	D	D	116	1 989	74.1	19.8
Brule	13	33	2.3	0.8	NA	NA	NA	NA	26	252	9.9	2.4
Buffalo	NA	NA	NA	NA	NA	NA	NA	NA	1	D	D	D
Butte	23	67	5.7	1.9	NA	NA	NA	NA	32	261	8.5	2.2
Campbell	3	7	0.2	0.1	NA	NA	NA	NA	7	D	D	D
Charles Mix	13	47	4.3	1.0	NA	NA	NA	NA	26	453	18.2	6.7
Clark	6	19	1.6	0.3	NA	NA	NA	NA	7	47	1.6	0.4
Clay	18	D	D	D	NA	NA	NA	NA	44	703	19.3	5.2
Codington	64	D	D	D	73	D	D	D	88	1 873	75.6	22.1
Corson	NA	NA	NA	NA	NA	NA	NA	NA	3	5	0.1	0.0
Custer	15	40	2.4	0.9	NA	NA	NA	NA	58	281	27.8	7.3
Davison	44	D	D	D	45	1 717	D	68.7	69	1 211	45.6	13.5
Day	8	31	1.9	0.7	NA	NA	NA	NA	21	146	4.3	1.2
Deuel	4	D	D	D	NA	NA	NA	NA	15	60	2.5	0.5
Dewey	4	D	D	D	NA	NA	NA	NA	7	D	D	D
Douglas	6	13	0.9	0.2	NA	NA	NA	NA	10	D	D	D
Edmunds	6	19	2.2	0.7	NA	NA	NA	NA	15	81	1.9	0.4
Fall River	19	72	3.7	1.2	NA	NA	NA	NA	41	248	10.0	2.6
Faulk	2	D	D	D	NA	NA	NA	NA	9	D	D	D
Grant	18	64	4.5	1.4	13	531	634.2	20.6	30	297	9.1	2.4
Gregory	8	25	2.3	0.5	NA	NA	NA	NA	19	102	2.8	0.7
Haakon	7	12	1.2	0.4	NA	NA	NA	NA	9	D	D	D
Hamlin	2	D	D	D	NA	NA	NA	NA	15	77	2.3	0.5
Hand	11	23	2.3	0.8	NA	NA	NA	NA	14	56	2.7	0.5
Hanson	3	D	D	D	NA	NA	NA	NA	3	23	0.4	0.1
Harding	1	D	D	D	NA	NA	NA	NA	3	15	0.9	0.1
Hughes	61	248	29.9	9.5	NA	NA	NA	NA	55	935	35.1	9.4
Hutchinson	10	28	1.8	0.7	NA	NA	NA	NA	17	135	3.9	0.8
Hyde	3	D	D	D	NA	NA	NA	NA	1	D	D	D
Jackson	1	D	D	D	NA	NA	NA	NA	13	30	1.9	0.5
Jerauld	6	10	1.2	0.2	1	D	D	D	7	D	D	D
Jones	3	D	D	D	NA	NA	NA	NA	13	70	3.7	1.1
Kingsbury	9	21	2.7	0.5	NA	NA	NA	NA	17	106	3.7	0.9
Lake	30	143	22.1	4.4	26	935	342.9	35.0	45	471	14.3	3.7
Lawrence	62	250	21.7	7.4	44	D	D	17.3	140	2 623	221.7	42.6
Lincoln	64	D	D	D	67	1 630	D	59.2	45	840	27.6	8.0
Lyman	2	D	D	D	NA	NA	NA	NA	19	249	15.9	3.4
McCook	12	D	D	D	NA	NA	NA	NA	21	91	3.4	0.6
McPherson	4	7	0.4	0.1	NA	NA	NA	NA	7	D	D	D
Marshall	13	28	2.1	0.6	NA	NA	NA	NA	17	90	4.4	1.1
Meade	38	D	D	D	NA	NA	NA	NA	71	557	33.4	8.2
Mellette	2	D	D	D	NA	NA	NA	NA	4	D	D	D
Miner	3	19	0.9	0.4	NA	NA	NA	NA	8	D	D	D
Minnehaha	469	D	D	D	184	11 483	3 518.8	475.0	426	9 651	389.9	118.4
Moody	10	21	1.1	0.4	NA	NA	NA	NA	17	D	D	D
Pennington	288	D	D	D	119	2 893	678.3	D	341	5 981	286.5	80.6
Perkins	4	12	0.6	0.1	NA	NA	NA	NA	7	D	D	D
Potter	3	9	0.5	0.1	NA	NA	NA	NA	12	81	4.2	0.8
Roberts	12	D	D	D	NA	NA	NA	NA	28	221	7.2	1.7
Sanborn	5	13	1.6	0.4	NA	NA	NA	NA	7	28	1.1	0.2
Shannon	2	D	D	D	NA	NA	NA	NA	8	343	18.1	6.1
Spink	4	21	2.0	0.6	NA	NA	NA	NA	16	143	4.6	1.4
Stanley	4	36	2.2	0.7	NA	NA	NA	NA	12	166	5.4	1.3
Sully	2	D	D	D	NA	NA	NA	NA	9	54	2.0	0.5
Todd	NA	NA	NA	NA	NA	NA	NA	NA	4	24	1.7	0.4

1. Establishment subject to federal tax.

Table B. States and Counties — **Health Care and Social Assistance, Other Services, Nonemployer Businesses, and Residential Construction**

STATE County	Health care and social assistance, 2007				Other services, 2007				Nonemployer businesses, 2013		Value of residential construction authorized by building permits, 2014	
	Number of establish-ments	Number of employees	Receipts (mil dol)	Annual payroll (mil dol)	Number of establish-ments	Number of employees	Receipts (mil dol)	Annual payroll (mil dol)	Number	Receipts (mil dol)	New Construction ($1,000)	Number of housing units
	159	160	161	162	163	164	165	166	167	168	169	170
SOUTH CAROLINA—Cont'd												
Sumter	180	4 812	469.3	172.7	152	1 141	69.7	21.7	6 023	200.9	36 844	289
Union	38	843	67.2	27.3	36	130	7.0	2.4	1 104	30.5	2 763	14
Williamsburg	51	827	49.6	20.3	47	216	9.9	3.1	1 714	46.4	2 178	17
York	341	7 680	718.6	271.7	285	1 897	155.7	47.3	14 944	571.7	632 028	2 982
SOUTH DAKOTA	2 241	56 480	4 767.2	2 038.8	1 815	8 518	749.6	181.9	62 414	2 811.7	689 248	4 722
Aurora	9	D	D	D	5	D	D	D	239	8.3	610	3
Beadle	55	1 392	77.8	34.6	54	230	14.4	3.9	1 067	46.9	4 111	23
Bennett	5	D	D	D	4	D	D	D	166	5.1	140	1
Bon Homme	22	454	20.9	9.1	11	27	1.9	0.4	478	18.7	4 167	20
Brookings	67	1 209	62.3	28.9	69	307	49.5	7.2	1 996	84.9	28 190	205
Brown	153	3 178	275.0	99.1	89	467	31.6	8.1	2 759	135.0	13 101	145
Brule	21	378	21.3	9.1	17	61	6.6	1.3	475	19.6	5 540	29
Buffalo	3	D	D	D	NA	NA	NA	NA	42	0.5	NA	NA
Butte	21	137	9.2	3.9	25	79	6.2	1.6	887	35.6	3 690	22
Campbell	4	D	D	D	2	D	D	D	136	7.4	389	2
Charles Mix	25	495	22.8	10.2	26	81	7.8	1.7	671	21.0	1 090	6
Clark	8	114	5.0	2.1	7	D	D	D	285	10.2	4 402	13
Clay	30	D	D	D	24	155	31.3	2.6	796	32.8	4 330	48
Codington	85	1 592	157.0	49.1	86	386	29.0	6.7	2 116	86.2	19 396	149
Corson	5	16	0.8	0.3	NA	NA	NA	NA	168	4.4	0	0
Custer	15	52	3.1	1.4	13	75	5.6	1.7	888	36.5	14 172	86
Davison	92	D	D	D	55	D	D	D	1 362	57.2	5 384	33
Day	21	327	13.6	5.6	13	37	2.7	0.6	493	19.7	7 711	44
Deuel	7	210	8.8	4.1	5	22	1.2	0.3	379	15.0	300	1
Dewey	14	176	21.1	7.7	6	12	1.0	0.4	256	10.1	107	2
Douglas	8	231	10.8	5.1	8	D	D	D	254	10.4	1 145	7
Edmunds	12	199	9.7	4.0	7	19	1.9	0.3	379	18.5	2 925	15
Fall River	21	593	65.4	34.0	20	62	4.5	1.0	578	21.7	640	3
Faulk	5	D	D	D	8	D	D	D	201	9.6	1 005	5
Grant	21	260	13.5	4.9	21	75	6.2	1.4	667	26.5	3 206	32
Gregory	17	266	17.2	7.6	12	D	D	D	462	17.2	1 530	10
Haakon	6	D	D	D	3	D	D	D	197	8.7	70	1
Hamlin	11	182	5.6	2.4	7	17	1.0	0.3	434	16.3	3 579	26
Hand	8	208	8.5	4.2	10	D	D	D	306	13.1	2 738	11
Hanson	2	D	D	D	3	D	D	D	305	10.9	1 000	7
Harding	5	D	D	D	2	D	D	D	186	6.7	747	6
Hughes	52	D	D	D	92	382	55.6	11.0	1 510	63.9	13 229	118
Hutchinson	19	684	33.3	15.0	14	40	3.7	0.7	568	17.9	3 983	22
Hyde	4	D	D	D	2	D	D	D	112	4.7	0	0
Jackson	1	D	D	D	1	D	D	D	179	4.7	0	0
Jerauld	6	D	D	D	6	D	D	D	148	6.0	325	1
Jones	3	D	D	D	1	D	D	D	123	5.0	296	8
Kingsbury	16	274	12.2	6.0	10	33	3.4	0.7	495	21.6	3 710	19
Lake	34	623	34.1	15.3	23	126	5.5	3.2	1 002	42.1	6 924	31
Lawrence	68	1 002	71.9	30.2	67	233	17.2	4.5	2 366	108.7	44 000	220
Lincoln	95	1 906	189.0	75.1	53	223	21.5	5.9	4 227	223.2	38 801	261
Lyman	3	D	D	D	1	D	D	D	247	9.3	1 306	9
McCook	22	240	11.9	5.1	9	D	D	D	462	23.3	6 497	35
McPherson	8	58	3.0	1.0	7	33	1.5	0.3	208	7.3	350	2
Marshall	13	177	9.4	3.8	8	28	2.5	0.5	339	17.9	5 137	19
Meade	37	D	D	D	45	128	18.0	3.2	2 169	89.1	17 982	121
Mellette	3	D	D	D	1	D	D	D	98	3.9	254	2
Miner	8	D	D	D	5	D	D	D	201	9.1	574	6
Minnehaha	459	19 818	1 859.2	861.9	380	2 417	200.5	55.5	12 586	640.7	257 954	2 019
Moody	15	184	9.5	4.2	6	40	4.4	1.5	437	18.6	3 676	13
Pennington	328	D	D	D	259	1 546	127.6	34.5	7 812	358.3	75 262	464
Perkins	13	D	D	D	18	42	3.0	0.9	258	10.6	0	0
Potter	13	168	8.1	3.5	10	27	1.7	0.3	259	13.4	430	3
Roberts	21	472	24.2	10.8	18	53	2.7	0.8	582	21.5	5 998	28
Sanborn	5	D	D	D	4	D	D	D	185	6.3	1 325	8
Shannon	12	320	27.4	10.6	7	D	D	D	326	5.6	NA	NA
Spink	16	274	14.9	7.1	9	16	1.2	0.3	501	23.7	4 855	24
Stanley	3	D	D	D	7	21	1.0	0.2	315	16.0	4 026	18
Sully	2	D	D	D	3	0	0.2	0.1	166	6.5	1 878	9
Todd	8	D	D	D	NA	NA	NA	NA	201	3.7	0	0

STATE County	Government employment and payroll, 2012: Full-time equivalent employees	Government employment and payroll, 2012: March payroll (dollars)	March payroll (percent of total): Adminis-tration, judicial, and legal	March payroll (percent of total): Police and Corrections	March payroll (percent of total): Fire Protection	March payroll (percent of total): Highways and transpor-tation	March payroll (percent of total): Health and Welfare	March payroll (percent of total): Natural resources and utilities	March payroll (percent of total): Education and libraries	Local government finances, 2012, General revenue: Total (mil dol)	General revenue: Inter-govern-mental (mil dol)	Taxes: Total (mil dol)	Taxes: Per capita[1] (dollars): Total	Taxes: Per capita[1] (dollars): Property
	171	172	173	174	175	176	177	178	179	180	181	182	183	184
SOUTH CAROLINA—Cont'd														
Sumter	6 341	17 021 292	4.2	6.1	1.7	1.8	1.6	3.3	80.4	271.8	124.5	114.5	1 060	719
Union	1 425	4 994 326	5.2	7.0	0.2	1.0	39.3	5.0	41.2	156.7	60.9	39.0	1 380	1 287
Williamsburg	1 213	3 312 602	4.2	7.9	1.6	5.2	5.0	3.6	71.8	89.9	50.4	26.4	785	649
York	6 735	24 865 548	7.3	9.2	2.7	1.3	1.7	7.5	67.9	705.5	262.8	328.3	1 399	1 188
SOUTH DAKOTA	X	X	X	X	X	X	X	X	X	X	X	X	X	X
Aurora	140	322 496	9.8	3.3	0.0	8.6	1.1	1.5	66.8	11.3	4.4	5.5	2 022	1 782
Beadle	584	1 871 207	6.9	12.0	1.9	6.5	2.6	6.6	60.1	58.6	17.5	28.6	1 609	1 176
Bennett	147	346 133	7.8	7.3	0.0	5.0	1.7	2.9	72.7	11.6	7.6	3.2	943	754
Bon Homme	246	662 539	7.1	6.3	0.0	9.5	0.7	8.4	67.8	20.1	7.9	9.7	1 383	1 174
Brookings	1 332	4 813 095	7.8	6.0	0.3	3.2	25.9	9.5	35.5	157.9	19.7	49.9	1 530	1 086
Brown	1 246	3 689 884	7.8	11.6	5.1	6.3	2.4	10.7	55.2	123.6	32.4	67.9	1 819	1 288
Brule	271	673 549	6.8	6.7	0.0	5.9	4.3	5.0	71.0	23.2	8.9	9.4	1 779	1 325
Buffalo	8	22 528	50.6	21.1	0.0	22.9	5.5	0.0	0.0	0.8	0.4	0.4	192	185
Butte	371	1 001 042	7.3	7.8	0.0	4.9	3.0	11.2	62.8	30.3	11.5	12.6	1 233	945
Campbell	48	126 932	22.4	4.9	0.0	20.2	1.5	5.8	43.7	4.7	1.5	2.4	1 718	1 442
Charles Mix	442	1 244 510	5.7	6.5	0.0	4.7	3.0	7.5	71.5	43.1	25.6	13.6	1 477	1 206
Clark	179	456 728	7.7	2.5	0.0	10.5	1.0	1.7	74.5	13.4	3.7	8.2	2 276	2 032
Clay	330	1 043 813	10.4	13.3	0.4	5.7	5.0	14.2	48.1	31.3	7.5	16.6	1 174	904
Codington	1 090	3 894 294	3.6	7.6	3.8	3.8	1.7	14.6	62.8	104.2	32.6	43.8	1 587	1 028
Corson	271	904 657	3.0	2.6	0.0	2.6	0.1	2.2	88.7	21.6	17.7	2.5	623	555
Custer	232	684 633	12.9	6.8	0.0	6.7	2.7	5.5	65.3	24.6	3.9	16.5	1 973	1 606
Davison	843	2 644 986	5.7	9.5	3.2	6.0	2.9	7.3	64.6	80.5	25.5	35.2	1 779	1 145
Day	198	482 927	10.0	8.0	0.0	11.7	0.7	5.9	61.4	17.2	6.4	8.5	1 510	1 240
Deuel	127	393 062	16.5	8.2	0.0	17.0	0.4	1.9	51.5	10.7	2.3	7.0	1 607	1 351
Dewey	249	617 513	9.8	3.1	0.0	5.4	0.5	3.0	76.8	18.8	15.2	2.6	474	405
Douglas	103	390 547	16.4	4.6	0.0	12.5	2.5	2.3	56.5	11.6	4.6	5.2	1 737	1 444
Edmunds	292	715 008	7.1	3.1	0.0	7.8	38.4	2.4	38.6	22.4	5.8	9.6	2 374	2 086
Fall River	314	938 839	8.8	7.6	0.0	7.0	1.0	10.3	60.3	26.8	9.4	11.3	1 614	1 321
Faulk	160	527 286	5.6	4.5	0.5	2.3	56.7	2.0	27.9	16.8	4.1	5.1	2 160	1 927
Grant	245	716 131	9.0	6.4	0.0	8.2	1.2	3.8	68.1	23.2	5.9	13.7	1 887	1 505
Gregory	203	581 904	10.2	4.7	0.0	9.2	1.1	2.4	71.6	14.3	5.6	7.1	1 664	1 354
Haakon	81	213 827	13.1	5.5	0.0	16.5	0.4	2.6	58.3	6.5	2.3	3.6	1 879	1 523
Hamlin	251	731 928	6.3	2.3	0.0	5.0	20.2	5.1	60.7	25.7	8.6	10.9	1 835	1 641
Hand	128	359 355	11.0	4.7	0.0	11.4	0.2	8.6	63.0	11.0	2.9	6.5	1 921	1 624
Hanson	122	328 179	9.5	3.1	0.0	9.0	0.2	1.6	71.2	10.7	3.6	5.8	1 710	1 577
Harding	80	208 002	15.2	4.0	0.0	10.1	0.3	2.9	63.3	10.2	6.4	3.1	2 343	2 124
Hughes	626	1 983 352	7.7	12.8	0.3	6.2	2.7	9.5	57.1	62.6	25.1	25.5	1 463	989
Hutchinson	312	1 009 609	5.2	3.1	0.0	6.2	0.4	1.3	82.1	25.8	8.2	14.2	1 970	1 677
Hyde	72	227 594	10.2	2.5	0.0	8.4	0.0	1.6	77.3	7.5	1.8	4.3	2 988	2 608
Jackson	115	288 915	10.3	3.2	0.0	5.1	1.0	2.8	74.9	7.4	4.2	2.7	835	680
Jerauld	90	237 116	13.3	5.9	0.0	10.4	1.6	8.1	58.2	8.7	2.5	4.4	2 169	1 851
Jones	52	131 432	19.8	7.6	0.0	10.4	0.0	7.8	54.5	4.5	1.4	2.5	2 475	1 992
Kingsbury	244	603 141	5.3	3.1	0.0	8.6	0.5	3.3	72.9	19.8	5.2	12.1	2 312	2 048
Lake	462	1 563 214	5.5	6.2	2.0	5.6	2.5	13.5	62.4	39.3	10.2	19.2	1 628	1 310
Lawrence	692	2 469 903	12.9	15.3	0.3	6.8	1.3	10.2	51.2	81.2	20.9	45.9	1 883	1 338
Lincoln	1 033	2 768 370	9.1	4.4	0.0	3.8	0.9	2.0	77.7	90.9	26.1	51.6	1 069	947
Lyman	133	337 375	11.7	3.3	0.0	7.7	3.0	3.7	67.3	10.3	4.3	4.8	1 278	913
McCook	186	538 315	9.8	4.8	0.0	8.7	1.8	2.2	71.0	17.3	5.5	9.8	1 740	1 508
McPherson	123	336 878	14.7	3.6	0.0	5.4	0.4	2.0	72.6	9.5	2.9	5.6	2 295	1 958
Marshall	176	472 048	9.8	7.5	0.0	9.0	0.7	2.0	69.8	18.3	6.1	9.2	1 978	1 696
Meade	671	2 100 253	11.4	12.6	0.3	4.8	2.3	5.9	59.2	71.1	19.6	32.1	1 233	1 036
Mellette	114	303 196	8.5	5.7	0.0	4.1	0.4	0.8	78.5	7.4	5.3	1.6	750	650
Miner	106	326 794	11.4	7.0	0.0	13.4	1.2	6.7	59.0	10.3	2.7	6.3	2 717	2 393
Minnehaha	5 678	21 221 355	6.2	10.8	4.4	3.8	2.4	6.0	65.2	616.7	171.2	329.3	1 882	1 201
Moody	202	536 978	10.4	8.8	0.0	7.4	2.5	6.9	57.6	17.4	5.8	9.2	1 422	1 220
Pennington	4 148	12 984 488	4.9	10.8	1.8	2.6	2.5	4.4	67.5	388.6	116.3	197.4	1 891	1 300
Perkins	118	328 373	10.9	5.6	0.1	9.6	2.5	6.3	62.1	12.4	5.3	5.7	1 878	1 506
Potter	120	307 306	11.7	3.9	0.0	9.7	0.1	2.7	67.9	9.5	3.0	5.6	2 367	2 004
Roberts	404	1 039 666	5.9	3.7	0.0	5.7	2.4	2.0	77.9	33.8	13.8	12.6	1 220	986
Sanborn	116	293 325	10.3	3.6	0.0	17.9	1.1	1.1	64.9	9.9	3.4	5.4	2 323	2 120
Shannon	423	1 199 764	0.8	0.3	0.0	0.8	0.1	0.1	98.0	32.0	30.4	0.8	60	34
Spink	406	1 160 424	5.6	3.5	0.0	5.0	32.9	2.4	50.2	35.9	9.8	13.7	2 078	1 808
Stanley	129	372 565	10.6	5.4	0.0	9.7	1.2	9.7	61.3	12.9	5.5	6.2	2 082	1 623
Sully	83	220 042	14.4	4.9	0.0	19.2	0.0	3.4	56.8	8.2	1.3	6.2	4 370	3 985
Todd	452	1 136 660	0.9	0.9	0.0	1.9	0.0	0.5	95.5	33.5	29.5	2.7	275	165

1. Based on the resident population estimated as of July 1 of the year shown.

STATE County	Local government finances, 2012 (cont.) — Direct general expenditure — Total (mil dol)	Per capita[1] (dollars)	Percent of total for: Education	Health and hospitals	Police protection	Public welfare	Highways	Debt outstanding — Total (mil dol)	Per capita[1] (dollars)	Government employment, 2013 — Federal civilian	Federal military	State and local	Presidential election,[2] 2012 — Percent of vote cast: Democratic	Republican	All other
	185	186	187	188	189	190	191	192	193	194	195	196	197	198	199
SOUTH CAROLINA—Cont'd															
Sumter	256.2	2 371	55.2	1.2	7.1	0.3	2.5	245.3	2 270	1 491	5 933	5 569	57.3	41.9	0.8
Union	153.8	5 444	47.1	30.4	4.0	0.0	1.3	64.7	2 291	71	115	1 881	43.8	55.0	1.2
Williamsburg	98.8	2 939	50.1	2.9	6.6	0.2	2.4	85.8	2 551	364	132	1 893	68.6	30.4	1.0
York	690.0	2 941	56.4	0.2	5.6	0.3	5.3	1 179.4	5 026	402	985	11 728	40.5	58.2	1.4
SOUTH DAKOTA	X	X	X	X	X	X	X	X	X	11 151	8 283	64 473	44.7	53.2	2.1
Aurora	10.8	3 945	58.5	0.4	3.0	0.2	16.5	1.6	575	21	16	197	43.8	53.1	3.1
Beadle	52.6	2 962	43.9	0.4	4.7	0.5	16.7	29.0	1 634	291	106	978	45.3	52.6	2.2
Bennett	9.4	2 748	64.2	0.1	4.4	0.1	6.8	1.2	356	26	21	355	46.1	50.8	3.1
Bon Homme	17.7	2 516	62.3	1.6	3.0	0.2	15.6	31.0	4 403	27	33	582	43.1	53.9	3.0
Brookings	154.9	4 746	25.5	21.6	2.6	0.2	6.1	90.0	2 758	149	183	5 774	51.7	46.1	2.2
Brown	117.1	3 136	36.3	1.3	5.8	0.9	19.9	125.1	3 352	502	223	2 682	51.9	46.3	1.8
Brule	20.0	3 782	59.2	3.2	3.6	0.4	11.2	7.8	1 479	34	32	350	39.6	57.7	2.7
Buffalo	0.8	373	0.0	0.1	9.4	0.1	48.9	0.0	0	146	12	309	73.3	25.2	1.5
Butte	26.8	2 623	51.6	0.6	5.1	0.1	7.2	14.4	1 409	50	62	574	30.7	66.3	3.0
Campbell	4.2	2 981	36.0	0.6	4.6	0.0	22.5	0.4	298	0	0	75	28.5	69.2	2.3
Charles Mix	36.8	3 989	58.4	1.9	2.5	0.1	9.6	8.3	898	182	52	1 087	45.4	53.0	1.6
Clark	12.5	3 493	42.0	1.9	2.9	0.4	29.1	4.5	1 242	25	19	234	42.8	54.9	2.3
Clay	28.7	2 034	37.0	1.5	8.1	0.3	17.6	30.7	2 172	35	73	3 397	61.0	36.8	2.2
Codington	112.1	4 060	54.8	0.3	6.8	0.1	7.1	80.3	2 910	184	166	1 962	45.9	52.3	1.8
Corson	23.4	5 738	86.2	0.1	2.0	0.0	5.0	0.0	0	68	26	578	59.5	38.1	2.4
Custer	27.8	3 331	34.7	5.4	4.4	0.4	11.1	31.7	3 801	192	50	528	32.7	64.5	2.7
Davison	79.9	4 042	50.0	4.3	4.8	0.5	9.4	39.7	2 006	113	115	1 280	42.0	56.0	2.0
Day	17.9	3 188	37.1	0.7	3.2	0.3	29.6	10.3	1 840	61	33	378	55.7	42.8	1.5
Deuel	11.0	2 511	38.7	3.1	3.5	0.4	20.6	3.8	861	24	26	236	47.5	49.1	3.4
Dewey	20.6	3 719	81.8	0.2	1.5	0.0	11.1	1.0	189	388	34	1 152	65.8	32.6	1.6
Douglas	13.1	4 408	29.4	0.6	2.1	0.1	14.6	4.2	1 429	24	17	168	24.1	73.6	2.2
Edmunds	19.8	4 926	31.7	14.2	1.7	12.6	18.5	5.7	1 415	20	22	338	39.5	58.4	2.1
Fall River	27.6	3 962	45.4	2.5	5.3	0.5	9.0	13.8	1 973	473	40	539	35.1	61.6	3.2
Faulk	15.6	6 550	19.0	49.2	1.5	0.1	14.5	9.5	4 005	20	11	131	35.7	62.0	2.3
Grant	24.5	3 375	44.5	0.6	3.4	0.2	18.1	33.2	4 576	32	43	349	46.6	50.9	2.4
Gregory	13.6	3 189	55.3	0.9	3.5	0.2	17.9	4.1	966	31	25	256	34.3	63.3	2.4
Haakon	5.9	3 054	42.6	5.8	5.5	0.1	21.5	1.1	586	16	11	102	16.2	81.4	2.3
Hamlin	22.8	3 851	49.4	1.4	2.0	13.5	15.0	12.1	2 042	27	35	475	37.4	59.6	3.0
Hand	10.6	3 130	41.2	0.5	4.5	0.1	26.1	19.0	5 596	18	20	209	35.7	62.0	2.3
Hanson	11.6	3 434	65.3	0.5	1.6	0.3	16.2	6.0	1 773	0	17	191	39.5	58.7	1.8
Harding	10.1	7 661	50.7	0.5	2.4	0.4	25.4	8.7	6 600	24	0	101	18.4	78.3	3.3
Hughes	62.3	3 568	31.3	0.8	5.8	0.2	8.1	67.4	3 862	281	101	3 666	35.9	62.6	1.6
Hutchinson	27.0	3 751	58.0	0.4	2.3	0.4	18.5	16.9	2 349	42	38	417	34.4	63.3	2.2
Hyde	6.9	4 834	48.1	0.3	2.2	0.2	22.1	3.4	2 354	0	0	187	28.8	69.7	1.5
Jackson	6.7	2 101	64.9	0.5	3.6	0.1	11.3	0.1	43	114	19	213	38.4	59.0	2.6
Jerauld	8.5	4 170	41.2	4.0	3.2	0.4	21.3	7.5	3 682	11	11	121	49.0	49.4	1.5
Jones	4.6	4 509	46.3	0.5	2.9	0.0	21.7	0.2	192	0	0	134	23.4	73.8	2.7
Kingsbury	18.6	3 559	52.1	0.8	2.8	0.4	20.1	7.7	1 482	37	29	266	45.9	51.5	2.6
Lake	36.5	3 105	51.8	0.5	4.3	0.3	14.7	90.9	7 721	58	68	1 164	49.3	48.6	2.1
Lawrence	77.3	3 170	35.3	0.4	7.0	0.2	6.3	116.0	4 753	170	144	1 805	40.9	56.3	2.8
Lincoln	90.3	1 871	58.4	0.4	3.1	0.3	11.9	267.9	5 547	47	301	1 356	41.6	56.8	1.6
Lyman	9.2	2 439	55.2	0.9	3.3	0.2	15.6	1.7	440	89	23	679	43.3	54.5	2.3
McCook	15.8	2 821	51.5	2.0	4.3	1.1	18.5	9.6	1 716	30	32	268	41.4	55.9	2.7
McPherson	9.4	3 852	48.9	0.7	3.2	0.2	24.6	1.4	581	11	13	150	32.1	66.5	1.4
Marshall	17.1	3 652	35.5	1.2	4.5	1.6	22.5	18.4	3 939	23	27	331	57.6	41.1	1.4
Meade	75.4	2 895	52.2	1.6	5.1	0.0	8.9	43.4	1 666	1 352	162	1 385	32.3	64.8	2.9
Mellette	6.7	3 182	72.5	0.9	4.5	0.0	7.6	0.1	43	13	12	234	44.2	52.8	3.0
Miner	10.4	4 490	36.7	2.2	3.5	0.3	27.2	3.8	1 655	17	14	155	49.7	47.4	3.0
Minnehaha	640.2	3 657	45.9	1.7	5.7	0.6	9.2	652.2	3 726	2 453	1 111	8 299	49.5	48.7	1.8
Moody	17.2	2 661	47.1	1.8	6.6	1.5	18.2	8.8	1 373	114	38	652	51.1	46.3	2.6
Pennington	412.8	3 956	45.6	1.3	6.0	0.5	8.9	401.2	3 844	1 511	3 927	6 101	38.5	59.6	1.9
Perkins	12.2	4 029	44.2	1.4	4.2	1.5	18.1	0.6	203	25	18	237	29.6	65.4	5.0
Potter	9.5	4 047	43.5	2.0	3.4	0.0	20.1	1.6	667	17	14	156	33.5	65.1	1.5
Roberts	30.3	2 938	57.6	0.5	2.8	0.1	10.2	9.6	930	197	60	1 339	58.9	39.3	1.8
Sanborn	8.5	3 645	45.3	1.1	3.8	0.1	31.4	2.8	1 215	10	10	154	41.4	55.4	3.1
Shannon	33.5	2 386	97.4	0.1	0.3	0.0	1.0	0.0	1	618	85	2 434	88.7	9.9	1.4
Spink	34.6	5 228	34.4	27.8	3.5	0.4	14.0	21.8	3 298	44	38	954	47.4	50.8	1.8
Stanley	13.1	4 413	38.6	0.8	6.2	0.1	30.5	9.4	3 157	0	18	194	32.8	65.5	1.7
Sully	7.0	4 938	44.2	0.2	5.0	0.4	25.5	3.3	2 332	10	0	123	28.0	69.7	2.3
Todd	28.4	2 854	92.0	0.1	0.7	0.0	2.9	1.4	137	277	60	1 994	78.1	20.2	1.7

1. Based on the resident population estimated as of July 1 of the year shown. 2.

STATE/ County code	CBSA code[1]	County type[2]	STATE County	Land area,[3] (sq km) 2010	Population, 2014: Total persons 2014	Rank	Per square kilometer	Population and population characteristics, 2013 — Race alone or in combination, not Hispanic or Latino (percent): White	Black	American Indian, Alaska Native	Asian and Pacific Islander	Percent Hispanic or Latino[4]	Age (percent): Under 5 years	5 to 17 years	18 to 24 years	25 to 34 years	35 to 44 years	45 to 54 years
				1	2	3	4	5	6	7	8	9	10	11	12	13	14	15
			SOUTH DAKOTA—Cont'd															
46 123	...	7	Tripp	4 176	5 512	2 801	1.3	84.3	0.7	14.9	0.6	1.7	6.1	16.3	7.9	9.3	10.0	14.6
46 125	43620	3	Turner	1 598	8 272	2 582	5.2	96.4	0.7	1.2	0.4	2.2	6.1	17.5	6.5	10.0	11.3	14.1
46 127	43580	3	Union	1 193	15 029	2 100	12.6	93.6	1.6	1.3	1.6	3.2	6.3	19.3	7.6	11.0	12.2	14.3
46 129	...	7	Walworth	1 835	5 511	2 802	3.0	84.1	0.9	16.0	0.5	1.5	6.0	16.4	6.2	10.5	9.6	12.9
46 135	49460	7	Yankton	1 350	22 684	1 702	16.8	91.6	2.3	3.4	0.9	3.2	5.8	15.7	8.6	12.8	11.9	14.4
46 137	...	9	Ziebach	5 080	2 826	2 986	0.6	27.0	1.1	70.9	0.6	3.7	7.3	29.4	10.6	12.0	11.4	14.1
47 000	...	X	TENNESSEE	106 798	6 549 352	X	61.3	76.3	17.6	0.8	2.0	4.9	6.2	16.8	9.7	13.0	13.0	13.9
47 001	28940	2	Anderson	873	75 528	729	86.5	91.9	5.1	0.9	1.5	2.4	5.3	15.8	8.1	11.1	12.2	14.4
47 003	43180	6	Bedford	1 227	46 627	1 032	38.0	79.4	8.6	0.7	1.3	11.7	6.8	19.5	8.8	12.1	13.2	13.5
47 005	...	7	Benton	1 021	16 145	2 034	15.8	94.4	2.9	1.1	0.8	2.1	5.3	14.6	7.2	9.5	11.4	14.6
47 007	...	8	Bledsoe	1 053	13 931	2 176	13.2	93.1	4.4	1.0	0.4	2.1	4.2	15.2	7.9	10.9	13.6	16.0
47 009	28940	2	Blount	1 447	126 339	491	87.3	92.9	3.5	0.9	1.2	3.0	5.2	16.2	8.3	11.1	12.7	14.8
47 011	17420	3	Bradley	851	102 975	575	121.0	88.8	5.1	0.8	1.4	5.4	5.7	16.7	10.3	12.5	13.0	14.1
47 013	28940	6	Campbell	1 244	39 918	1 174	32.1	97.6	0.7	1.0	0.5	1.3	5.3	15.9	8.1	10.5	13.0	14.4
47 015	34980	1	Cannon	688	13 757	2 188	20.0	96.3	2.1	0.9	0.5	1.6	5.1	15.7	8.1	11.4	12.6	15.4
47 017	...	6	Carroll	1 552	28 370	1 477	18.3	86.4	11.5	0.9	0.5	2.3	6.0	15.7	10.2	10.2	11.5	13.9
47 019	27740	3	Carter	884	56 886	893	64.4	96.3	1.9	0.7	0.5	1.6	5.1	14.3	8.7	11.6	12.4	14.4
47 021	34980	1	Cheatham	783	39 764	1 179	50.8	94.9	2.1	0.9	0.7	2.6	5.6	18.1	8.1	11.5	13.9	16.4
47 023	27180	3	Chester	740	17 379	1 956	23.5	87.6	10.2	1.0	0.6	2.4	5.0	17.2	14.3	11.0	11.8	12.6
47 025	...	6	Claiborne	1 126	31 592	1 396	28.1	97.0	1.4	1.0	0.8	1.0	4.8	14.8	9.6	11.5	12.6	14.2
47 027	...	8	Clay	613	7 765	2 615	12.7	96.4	2.1	0.8	0.3	1.6	5.4	14.9	7.1	9.0	11.6	14.8
47 029	35460	6	Cocke	1 126	35 374	1 290	31.4	95.1	2.6	1.1	0.5	2.1	5.3	15.8	7.7	10.2	12.4	14.9
47 031	46100	4	Coffee	1 111	53 623	933	48.3	91.2	4.6	0.8	1.3	3.9	6.0	18.0	8.4	11.8	12.1	14.2
47 033	27180	8	Crockett	688	14 668	2 126	21.3	76.9	13.8	0.6	0.4	9.5	5.8	18.4	8.1	11.8	11.9	14.3
47 035	18900	7	Cumberland	1 764	57 985	884	32.9	95.9	0.7	0.9	0.7	2.7	5.0	13.5	6.7	9.1	10.2	12.6
47 037	34980	1	Davidson	1 305	668 347	96	512.1	58.9	28.6	0.8	4.0	9.9	7.0	14.6	10.6	19.0	13.7	12.8
47 039	...	9	Decatur	865	11 666	2 314	13.5	93.2	3.5	0.8	0.7	3.0	4.7	15.5	7.4	10.2	11.5	13.5
47 041	...	6	DeKalb	788	19 268	1 864	24.5	90.6	1.9	0.7	0.5	7.3	5.7	16.9	8.0	11.7	12.3	14.5
47 043	34980	1	Dickson	1 269	50 575	978	39.9	91.8	5.1	0.9	0.8	3.1	6.0	17.6	8.3	12.0	13.2	15.0
47 045	20540	5	Dyer	1 327	37 935	1 224	28.6	81.7	15.3	0.7	0.8	3.0	6.5	17.7	8.6	11.4	12.7	14.1
47 047	32820	1	Fayette	1 825	39 011	1 198	21.4	68.9	28.0	0.7	0.8	2.5	5.5	15.9	6.9	10.9	12.2	14.6
47 049	...	9	Fentress	1 291	17 855	1 924	13.8	97.9	0.5	0.9	0.4	1.2	5.0	17.2	7.6	9.7	12.1	14.5
47 051	46100	6	Franklin	1 436	41 402	1 140	28.8	90.9	5.7	1.2	1.2	2.7	4.9	16.3	10.6	10.0	11.8	13.6
47 053	...	4	Gibson	1 561	49 472	991	31.7	78.6	19.1	0.6	0.5	2.4	6.3	18.1	8.0	11.6	12.4	13.8
47 055	...	6	Giles	1 582	28 853	1 461	18.2	87.0	11.3	1.0	0.8	1.8	5.4	15.8	8.6	10.7	11.5	15.0
47 057	28940	3	Grainger	727	22 864	1 694	31.4	96.3	1.0	0.7	0.3	2.7	5.1	16.1	7.7	10.1	13.1	15.3
47 059	24620	6	Greene	1 611	68 335	779	42.4	94.4	2.6	0.7	0.7	2.7	4.7	15.5	8.4	10.3	12.6	14.6
47 061	...	8	Grundy	934	13 425	2 214	14.4	97.6	0.8	1.2	0.3	1.1	5.5	16.5	7.9	10.7	12.0	13.6
47 063	34100	3	Hamblen	417	63 036	832	151.2	83.8	4.9	0.7	1.3	11.0	6.3	17.2	8.1	11.6	13.1	14.0
47 065	16860	2	Hamilton	1 405	351 220	193	250.0	73.0	20.4	0.8	2.5	4.9	5.9	15.4	9.9	13.4	12.7	13.6
47 067	...	8	Hancock	576	6 657	2 706	11.6	98.6	0.8	1.0	0.4	0.4	5.1	15.3	7.4	11.3	12.0	14.0
47 069	...	6	Hardeman	1 730	25 965	1 561	15.0	56.1	41.9	0.6	0.8	1.6	5.1	15.0	9.3	14.3	12.8	14.7
47 071	...	6	Hardin	1 495	25 870	1 565	17.3	93.6	4.3	0.9	0.7	1.9	5.4	15.6	7.7	9.9	11.9	14.3
47 073	28700	3	Hawkins	1 261	56 735	898	45.0	96.6	1.9	0.8	0.7	1.3	5.1	16.2	7.6	10.3	13.0	15.0
47 075	...	6	Haywood	1 381	18 185	1 910	13.2	45.9	50.1	0.4	0.3	4.1	5.7	18.2	8.6	11.5	11.4	14.4
47 077	...	6	Henderson	1 347	28 009	1 491	20.8	89.4	8.9	0.6	0.6	2.2	5.9	17.7	8.2	11.6	12.8	14.5
47 079	37540	7	Henry	1 456	32 204	1 380	22.1	88.9	9.0	0.8	0.6	2.2	5.2	15.7	7.3	10.2	11.5	14.2
47 081	34980	1	Hickman	1 586	24 384	1 631	15.4	92.3	5.4	1.1	0.5	2.0	5.5	16.3	8.4	12.4	13.3	15.3
47 083	...	8	Houston	519	8 267	2 583	15.9	94.1	3.8	1.0	0.8	2.2	5.2	16.8	8.1	10.6	12.0	13.7
47 085	...	6	Humphreys	1 375	18 135	1 914	13.2	94.4	3.3	0.9	0.6	2.0	5.6	16.4	8.0	10.5	12.4	14.2
47 087	18260	8	Jackson	799	11 568	2 320	14.5	97.2	0.8	1.1	0.3	1.7	4.7	14.8	7.7	9.3	12.0	15.1
47 089	34100	3	Jefferson	710	52 677	948	74.2	93.5	2.8	0.8	0.7	3.5	5.3	15.8	9.5	10.6	12.2	14.7
47 091	...	6	Johnson	773	17 859	1 923	23.1	95.5	2.7	0.7	0.4	1.7	4.4	13.2	7.7	11.8	13.8	14.9
47 093	28940	2	Knox	1 316	448 644	152	340.9	85.0	9.8	0.8	2.6	3.7	5.9	15.7	12.3	13.4	12.8	13.5
47 095	...	9	Lake	429	7 631	2 627	17.8	69.5	29.1	0.8	0.4	2.0	4.7	11.7	10.7	17.5	15.2	13.7
47 097	...	6	Lauderdale	1 222	27 382	1 518	22.4	61.5	35.5	0.9	1.0	2.4	5.8	17.5	9.6	14.3	13.4	14.1
47 099	29980	6	Lawrence	1 598	42 274	1 125	26.5	95.7	2.3	1.0	0.6	1.8	6.8	18.0	8.3	11.0	12.1	13.9
47 101	...	6	Lewis	731	11 906	2 302	16.3	94.8	2.7	0.9	0.8	2.0	5.6	16.8	7.9	10.4	12.4	13.6
47 103	...	6	Lincoln	1 477	33 637	1 338	22.8	89.0	7.6	1.3	0.7	3.1	5.6	17.2	7.8	10.9	11.8	14.8
47 105	28940	2	Loudon	594	50 771	977	85.5	89.7	1.8	0.7	0.9	7.8	5.2	14.9	7.0	9.8	11.2	13.2
47 107	11940	4	McMinn	1 114	52 626	950	47.2	91.9	4.7	1.2	1.0	3.1	5.6	16.1	8.7	10.5	12.4	14.4
47 109	...	6	McNairy	1 458	26 267	1 551	18.0	91.5	6.7	0.8	0.4	1.9	5.9	16.9	8.0	10.5	12.2	13.7
47 111	34980	1	Macon	795	23 003	1 685	28.9	93.6	0.9	0.7	0.6	5.1	7.1	17.6	8.8	11.6	12.8	14.2
47 113	27180	3	Madison	1 443	98 178	600	68.0	58.2	37.8	0.5	1.4	3.5	6.6	16.6	11.4	12.5	12.0	13.7
47 115	16860	2	Marion	1 290	28 407	1 476	22.0	93.6	4.6	1.0	0.7	1.5	5.1	16.3	7.9	11.0	12.4	14.5

1. CBSA = Core Based Statistical Area. See Appendix A for explanation. See Appendix B for list of metropolitan areas with component counties. 2. County type code from the Economic Research Service of USDA Rural-Urban Continuum Codes. See Appendix A for definition. 3. Dry land or land partially or temporarily covered by water. 4. May be of any race.

STATE County	Population, 2013 (cont.): Age (percent) (cont.): 55 to 64 years	65 to 74 years	75 years and over	Percent female	Population change and components of change, 2000–2014: Total persons: 2000	2010	Percent change: 2000–2010	2010–2014	Components of change, 2010–2014: Births	Deaths	Net migration	Households, 2009–2013: Number	Persons per house-hold	Percent: Family house-holds	Female family house-holder[1]	One per-son
	16	17	18	19	20	21	22	23	24	25	26	27	28	29	30	31
SOUTH DAKOTA—Cont'd																
Tripp	14.2	9.9	11.7	50.6	6 430	5 644	-12.2	-2.3	279	277	-122	2 530	2.15	65.3	8.9	30.9
Turner	14.7	9.6	10.3	49.7	8 849	8 347	-5.7	-0.9	383	405	-51	3 461	2.36	69.3	6.0	26.9
Union	14.4	8.5	6.6	49.5	12 584	14 399	14.4	4.4	719	463	371	5 758	2.51	66.7	6.7	29.6
Walworth	14.6	11.2	12.5	50.7	5 974	5 438	-9.0	1.3	278	321	125	2 342	2.26	62.6	6.7	35.0
Yankton	13.8	8.6	8.5	48.1	21 652	22 438	3.6	1.1	1 099	889	46	8 698	2.34	63.3	7.9	28.9
Ziebach	8.2	4.0	3.0	50.4	2 519	2 801	11.2	0.9	178	53	-92	803	3.51	78.0	29.4	18.3
TENNESSEE	12.8	8.7	6.0	51.2	5 689 283	6 346 105	11.5	3.2	339 088	258 632	121 745	2 475 195	2.52	66.8	13.4	28.1
Anderson	14.6	10.1	8.4	51.5	71 330	75 129	5.3	0.5	3 461	3 746	786	30 548	2.43	66.2	12.7	29.5
Bedford	11.9	8.7	5.5	50.6	37 586	45 058	19.9	3.5	2 638	1 831	746	16 402	2.73	73.7	11.2	21.8
Benton	15.3	13.4	8.6	50.6	16 537	16 489	-0.3	-2.1	675	1 028	4	6 892	2.35	65.9	10.5	30.6
Bledsoe	14.6	11.0	6.6	45.7	12 367	12 876	4.1	8.3	510	534	974	4 556	2.55	70.4	9.9	24.6
Blount	14.0	10.6	7.3	51.5	105 823	123 010	16.2	2.7	5 386	5 198	3 056	48 728	2.50	69.4	10.4	26.3
Bradley	12.3	9.1	6.2	51.3	87 965	98 963	12.5	4.1	4 919	3 961	2 994	37 603	2.59	68.8	12.4	26.6
Campbell	14.1	11.4	7.4	51.3	39 854	40 716	2.2	-2.0	1 746	2 188	-291	15 959	2.51	68.9	13.4	27.3
Cannon	13.8	10.1	7.7	50.6	12 826	13 801	7.6	-0.3	622	639	-28	5 383	2.53	72.2	14.5	24.3
Carroll	13.3	11.0	8.1	51.3	29 475	28 522	-3.2	-0.5	1 377	1 656	169	11 022	2.50	66.6	10.3	30.9
Carter	14.3	11.2	7.9	51.1	56 742	57 424	1.2	-0.9	2 291	2 797	-46	24 079	2.32	67.3	11.8	29.1
Cheatham	13.8	8.1	4.4	50.2	35 912	39 105	8.9	1.7	1 852	1 489	266	14 421	2.70	74.1	9.8	20.9
Chester	12.0	9.1	7.1	52.1	15 540	17 131	10.2	1.4	777	684	132	5 936	2.68	72.9	14.5	24.8
Claiborne	14.6	11.0	7.0	51.2	29 862	32 213	7.9	-1.9	1 287	1 766	-131	12 553	2.46	66.8	12.2	30.1
Clay	14.6	13.7	9.0	51.0	7 976	7 861	-1.4	-1.2	372	481	-18	3 281	2.35	73.1	9.3	24.5
Cocke	15.1	11.6	7.0	51.6	33 565	35 662	6.2	-0.8	1 631	1 924	83	14 917	2.36	68.5	13.7	27.3
Coffee	12.8	9.5	7.1	51.4	48 014	52 796	10.0	1.6	2 697	2 690	879	21 019	2.49	67.0	13.2	28.7
Crockett	12.5	9.6	7.6	52.2	14 532	14 586	0.4	0.6	774	720	40	5 619	2.55	70.1	14.6	26.4
Cumberland	14.5	16.8	11.6	51.2	46 802	56 053	19.8	3.4	2 428	3 170	2 551	23 764	2.35	68.4	8.1	27.9
Davidson	11.4	6.2	4.7	51.7	569 891	626 681	10.0	6.7	41 231	21 557	22 263	256 745	2.39	55.7	14.6	35.7
Decatur	14.7	12.8	9.6	50.8	11 731	11 757	0.2	-0.7	432	740	219	5 066	2.26	68.6	14.2	28.6
DeKalb	13.9	10.3	6.6	50.4	17 423	18 723	7.5	2.9	975	987	573	7 037	2.62	70.2	11.0	26.0
Dickson	13.1	8.6	6.0	50.8	43 156	49 666	15.1	1.9	2 481	2 026	449	18 647	2.65	74.3	14.2	22.0
Dyer	12.9	9.5	6.5	51.6	37 279	38 335	2.8	-1.0	2 074	1 789	-684	15 100	2.49	72.1	15.5	23.9
Fayette	16.2	11.0	6.8	50.3	28 806	38 413	33.4	1.6	1 806	1 510	231	14 535	2.62	76.1	12.1	20.8
Fentress	14.6	12.4	7.1	51.0	16 625	17 959	8.0	-0.6	790	984	95	7 348	2.42	67.4	12.0	27.9
Franklin	14.1	10.9	7.9	51.4	39 270	41 052	4.5	0.9	1 702	1 961	632	16 067	2.42	71.1	12.4	23.6
Gibson	12.4	9.3	8.1	52.4	48 152	49 683	3.2	-0.4	2 597	2 794	0	19 205	2.53	68.0	14.3	29.0
Giles	14.5	10.9	7.5	51.0	29 447	29 485	0.1	-2.1	1 224	1 407	-413	11 766	2.42	69.2	13.6	26.8
Grainger	14.6	11.5	6.4	49.9	20 659	22 657	9.7	0.9	942	1 076	364	9 003	2.50	68.7	8.5	27.0
Greene	14.5	11.6	7.8	50.9	62 909	68 831	9.4	-0.7	2 525	3 536	533	28 677	2.33	69.3	11.7	26.0
Grundy	13.7	12.4	7.6	50.6	14 332	13 703	-4.4	-2.1	618	801	-120	5 359	2.51	67.0	12.2	29.1
Hamblen	12.4	10.2	7.2	51.2	58 128	62 544	7.6	0.8	3 361	2 916	96	24 315	2.55	69.7	13.4	26.4
Hamilton	13.5	8.8	6.9	51.8	307 896	336 463	9.3	4.4	17 546	14 115	11 473	135 496	2.45	65.0	13.2	29.8
Hancock	16.6	10.6	7.6	50.7	6 786	6 819	0.5	-2.4	316	409	-62	2 835	2.32	65.5	16.2	31.9
Hardeman	13.1	9.3	6.5	45.5	28 105	27 253	-3.0	-4.7	1 150	1 156	-1 284	8 690	2.69	68.5	18.7	28.4
Hardin	14.9	11.8	8.5	51.5	25 578	26 026	1.8	-0.6	1 158	1 409	155	9 934	2.58	66.9	11.2	28.9
Hawkins	14.3	11.5	7.2	51.0	53 563	56 833	6.1	-0.2	2 410	2 807	263	23 348	2.41	70.9	11.1	25.8
Haywood	14.7	8.8	6.6	53.4	19 797	18 787	-5.1	-3.2	960	822	-789	7 099	2.58	63.7	18.9	32.6
Henderson	13.1	9.8	6.4	51.8	25 522	27 769	8.8	0.8	1 376	1 271	116	10 930	2.53	71.6	12.2	26.0
Henry	14.8	12.4	8.7	51.5	31 115	32 330	3.9	-0.4	1 375	1 916	427	13 473	2.35	66.5	10.5	30.5
Hickman	13.4	9.3	6.2	47.4	22 295	24 690	10.7	-1.3	1 136	1 109	-353	8 846	2.59	71.4	9.6	25.2
Houston	14.4	11.3	7.9	50.5	8 088	8 426	4.2	-1.9	346	396	-96	3 423	2.39	67.0	9.6	27.7
Humphreys	14.3	10.9	7.7	50.4	17 929	18 538	3.4	-2.2	895	975	-305	7 396	2.46	68.2	10.2	27.7
Jackson	16.1	12.7	7.5	49.9	10 984	11 638	6.0	-0.6	466	610	74	4 493	2.52	68.3	12.8	28.0
Jefferson	13.5	11.6	6.7	50.9	44 294	51 407	16.1	2.1	2 254	2 434	1 160	19 797	2.53	69.8	11.2	25.7
Johnson	14.0	12.4	7.8	46.4	17 499	18 244	4.3	-2.1	588	847	-148	6 921	2.36	70.1	10.0	27.1
Knox	12.4	8.1	6.0	51.4	382 032	432 226	13.1	3.8	22 169	17 153	11 304	181 100	2.35	60.2	9.9	33.7
Lake	12.2	8.2	6.2	36.6	7 954	7 832	-1.5	-2.6	290	398	-91	2 201	2.41	63.3	19.5	34.1
Lauderdale	11.9	8.1	5.2	47.6	27 101	27 815	2.6	-1.6	1 323	1 140	-591	9 686	2.58	69.1	20.2	26.9
Lawrence	12.7	10.0	7.3	51.1	39 926	41 869	4.9	1.0	2 349	2 094	201	15 862	2.62	70.5	10.2	26.5
Lewis	15.4	10.7	7.2	50.9	11 367	12 161	7.0	-2.1	566	535	-276	4 750	2.49	67.9	9.0	27.3
Lincoln	14.1	10.1	7.7	51.1	31 340	33 361	6.4	0.8	1 553	1 689	431	13 438	2.45	69.8	11.8	26.2
Loudon	14.8	14.7	9.2	51.1	39 086	48 556	24.2	4.6	2 301	2 367	2 210	19 543	2.49	74.6	8.6	22.6
McMinn	13.0	10.0	7.5	51.2	40 015	52 266	6.0	0.7	2 099	2 040	003	20 313	2.53	70.4	10.5	28.4
McNairy	13.7	11.4	7.6	51.0	24 653	26 075	5.8	0.7	1 272	1 411	319	9 736	2.64	68.3	10.1	29.3
Macon	12.7	9.1	6.1	51.3	20 386	22 248	9.1	3.4	1 321	1 113	543	8 544	2.59	72.7	12.3	22.7
Madison	12.9	8.2	6.2	52.6	91 837	98 294	7.0	-0.1	5 437	3 860	-1 599	35 713	2.64	66.4	16.3	30.0
Marion	14.9	11.0	6.8	50.8	27 776	28 237	1.7	0.6	1 265	1 396	350	11 226	2.49	69.7	13.0	26.8

1. No spouse present.

STATE County	Persons in group quarters, 2014	Daytime population, 2009–2013: Number	Daytime population, 2009–2013: Employment/residence ratio	Births, 2014: Total	Births, 2014: Rate[1]	Deaths, 2014: Number	Deaths, 2014: Rate[1]	Persons under 65 with no health insurance, 2013: Number	Persons under 65 with no health insurance, 2013: Percent	Medicare, 2014: Eligible for Medicare	Medicare, 2014: Enrolled in Medicare Advantage	Medicare, 2014: Enrolled in a Medicare prescription drug plan	Serious crimes known to police,[2] 2013: Total: Number	Serious crimes known to police,[2] 2013: Total: Rate[3]
	32	33	34	35	36	37	38	39	40	41	42	43	44	45
SOUTH DAKOTA—Cont'd														
Tripp	131	5 451	0.96	67	12.2	63	11.4	779	18.4	1 300	102	938	25	457
Turner	153	6 636	0.60	86	10.4	88	10.6	849	12.8	1 760	427	1 148	63	754
Union	89	15 841	1.18	167	11.1	90	6.0	1 017	8.1	2 723	533	1 602	116	887
Walworth	152	5 303	0.93	66	12.0	69	12.5	599	14.3	1 470	59	973	68	1 236
Yankton	2 297	24 092	1.14	264	11.6	191	8.4	2 016	11.8	4 490	761	2 970	499	2 188
Ziebach	0	2 543	0.68	42	14.9	19	6.7	530	19.9	155	NA	85	5	172
TENNESSEE	154 597	6 441 658	1.01	80 172	12.2	61 664	9.4	876 189	16.2	1 212 463	396 026	499 946	244 993	3 771
Anderson	1 183	90 968	1.52	820	10.9	862	11.4	8 199	13.5	17 196	6 113	5 665	1 445	1 912
Bedford	545	42 608	0.85	629	13.5	415	8.9	8 468	21.7	8 285	2 314	3 619	1 026	2 242
Benton	162	15 468	0.84	154	9.5	254	15.7	2 273	18.0	4 549	818	2 620	282	1 726
Bledsoe	2 049	11 391	0.65	118	8.5	131	9.4	1 989	20.9	2 764	677	1 219	141	1 103
Blount	2 040	115 468	0.85	1 284	10.2	1 196	9.5	15 008	14.8	27 608	10 817	8 478	2 996	2 404
Bradley	2 747	98 866	0.97	1 181	11.5	954	9.3	14 840	17.7	20 827	7 414	8 225	3 920	3 847
Campbell	519	37 305	0.76	409	10.2	549	13.8	5 396	16.7	10 195	4 665	3 659	1 505	3 728
Cannon	164	10 810	0.44	152	11.0	127	9.2	1 841	16.4	3 004	884	1 350	191	1 381
Carroll	1 080	25 750	0.74	324	11.4	374	13.2	3 526	16.0	7 208	1 276	4 116	712	2 509
Carter	1 438	47 291	0.56	505	8.9	710	12.5	8 044	17.7	13 886	6 501	4 100	1 554	2 707
Cheatham	283	30 023	0.49	451	11.3	353	8.9	4 976	14.5	6 745	2 826	2 245	1 031	2 619
Chester	1 290	14 531	0.63	182	10.5	150	8.6	2 097	15.7	3 572	615	2 035	342	1 990
Claiborne	1 259	29 296	0.78	295	9.3	411	13.0	4 089	16.5	8 072	3 508	3 164	782	2 475
Clay	96	7 052	0.73	92	11.8	98	12.6	1 106	18.5	2 015	321	1 219	100	1 275
Cocke	294	32 228	0.74	387	10.9	450	12.7	4 897	17.1	9 234	4 062	3 205	1 478	4 154
Coffee	557	56 223	1.15	637	11.9	614	11.5	7 311	16.6	11 567	2 674	5 482	1 675	3 136
Crockett	194	12 738	0.69	195	13.3	173	11.8	2 378	19.8	3 192	387	1 980	362	2 470
Cumberland	636	56 132	0.98	572	9.9	765	13.2	7 721	18.9	19 308	3 753	10 395	2 244	3 913
Davidson	25 841	741 549	1.33	9 886	14.8	5 301	7.9	103 814	18.5	89 590	36 480	31 133	33 104	5 048
Decatur	213	10 749	0.79	104	8.9	175	15.0	1 594	17.8	3 371	602	1 863	308	2 641
DeKalb	298	18 166	0.91	230	11.9	213	11.1	3 111	19.8	4 179	1 775	1 556	530	2 793
Dickson	617	45 245	0.78	562	11.1	444	8.8	6 854	16.1	9 386	3 250	3 776	1 655	3 268
Dyer	516	38 877	1.04	482	12.7	427	11.3	4 411	13.9	8 187	1 057	5 073	1 820	4 756
Fayette	422	30 030	0.50	415	10.6	390	10.0	4 580	14.6	8 497	1 964	3 880	637	1 643
Fentress	132	16 549	0.76	188	10.5	240	13.4	2 578	18.0	4 961	773	3 063	453	2 523
Franklin	1 950	38 497	0.84	411	9.9	428	10.3	4 979	15.7	9 620	2 202	4 513	905	2 222
Gibson	991	45 328	0.78	599	12.1	640	12.9	6 280	15.5	11 188	1 665	6 824	1 459	2 939
Giles	610	27 681	0.87	281	9.7	337	11.7	3 669	16.0	6 787	1 199	3 581	678	2 338
Grainger	151	18 546	0.50	220	9.6	255	11.2	3 378	18.2	5 444	2 719	1 720	467	2 055
Greene	1 752	67 544	0.96	583	8.5	825	12.1	9 380	17.4	17 897	7 250	6 346	1 957	2 841
Grundy	180	12 229	0.69	137	10.2	173	12.9	1 978	18.5	3 580	997	1 642	413	3 028
Hamblen	918	67 755	1.20	776	12.3	672	10.7	10 437	20.2	14 062	5 434	5 516	2 414	3 841
Hamilton	10 298	381 297	1.26	4 208	12.0	3 409	9.7	43 983	15.4	65 661	21 781	27 922	17 845	5 118
Hancock	149	5 992	0.63	80	12.0	92	13.8	887	16.6	1 329	552	533	178	2 660
Hardeman	3 818	25 863	0.88	256	9.9	282	10.9	2 817	15.2	5 586	998	3 135	812	3 081
Hardin	371	24 959	0.89	263	10.2	338	13.1	3 708	18.0	6 985	1 032	4 202	945	3 642
Hawkins	456	48 100	0.60	590	10.4	695	12.2	7 029	15.3	14 534	8 050	3 985	1 394	2 465
Haywood	174	17 325	0.83	232	12.8	213	11.7	2 458	16.1	3 828	822	2 086	805	4 450
Henderson	218	26 010	0.83	318	11.4	292	10.4	3 535	15.2	5 662	1 165	3 097	953	3 387
Henry	491	32 352	1.00	316	9.8	471	14.6	4 336	17.3	8 502	1 286	4 844	1 143	3 531
Hickman	1 510	19 586	0.47	270	11.1	250	10.3	3 386	17.7	4 761	1 699	2 007	410	1 706
Houston	177	7 081	0.57	77	9.3	86	10.4	1 140	17.2	1 749	373	949	112	1 332
Humphreys	205	18 493	1.01	216	11.9	225	12.4	2 440	16.6	4 265	851	2 359	330	1 814
Jackson	177	9 744	0.53	117	10.1	151	13.1	1 640	18.1	2 957	608	1 662	192	1 687
Jefferson	1 727	45 010	0.68	520	9.9	601	11.4	6 859	16.7	12 237	5 062	4 358	1 444	2 751
Johnson	1 811	17 038	0.81	124	6.9	207	11.6	2 279	18.0	4 787	1 892	1 729	379	2 099
Knox	12 164	464 728	1.13	5 295	11.8	4 084	9.1	51 950	14.0	78 272	31 272	27 364	19 149	4 308
Lake	2 499	7 867	1.05	64	8.4	96	12.6	647	15.1	1 265	115	913	136	1 777
Lauderdale	2 691	26 845	0.89	303	11.1	262	9.6	3 281	15.4	5 060	1 027	2 756	1 021	3 682
Lawrence	407	38 563	0.80	546	12.9	476	11.3	5 690	16.5	9 674	1 719	5 575	1 455	3 452
Lewis	217	10 517	0.65	150	12.6	122	10.2	1 881	19.4	2 580	655	1 244	313	2 647
Lincoln	283	29 585	0.73	380	11.3	374	11.1	4 339	15.8	7 605	1 852	3 435	957	2 852
Loudon	480	45 379	0.80	565	11.1	534	10.5	6 809	17.9	13 944	5 494	4 896	941	1 875
McMinn	950	51 152	0.94	559	10.6	605	11.5	7 122	16.9	12 141	3 551	5 496	2 291	4 361
McNairy	313	24 295	0.80	303	11.5	325	12.4	3 617	17.2	6 738	997	4 006	628	2 393
Macon	269	19 521	0.67	315	13.7	259	11.3	3 640	19.1	4 622	1 415	2 265	387	1 713
Madison	4 424	113 225	1.36	1 281	13.0	907	9.2	11 891	14.7	18 296	3 229	10 021	5 222	5 282
Marion	250	25 231	0.73	304	10.7	328	11.5	3 475	15.0	6 614	2 125	3 061	695	2 453

1. Per 1,000 estimated resident population. 2. Data for serious crimes have not been adjusted for underreporting; this may affect comparability between geographic areas and over time.
3. Per 100,000 population estimated by the FBI.

Table B. States and Counties — **Crime, Education, Money Income, and Poverty**

STATE County	Serious crimes known to police, 2013 (cont.)[1] Rate[2]		Education: School enrollment and attainment, 2009–2013				Education: Local government expenditures,[5] 2012–2013		Money income, 2009–2013				Income and poverty, 2013			
			Enrollment[3]		Attainment[4] (percent)					Households				Percent below poverty level		
	Violent	Property	Total	Percent private	High school graduate or less	Bachelor's degree or more	Total current spending (mil dol)	Current spending per student (dollars)	Per capita income[6] (dollars)	Median income (dollars)	Mean income (dollars)	Percent with income of $200,000 or more	Median household income (dollars)	All persons	Children under 18 years	Children 5 to 17 years in families
	46	47	48	49	50	51	52	53	54	55	56	57	58	59	60	61
SOUTH DAKOTA—Cont'd																
Tripp	110	347	1 096	3.2	46.7	21.2	8.1	8 483	23 270	39 324	52 616	2.6	40 975	19.6	27.0	24.5
Turner	72	683	1 823	8.6	49.3	19.4	13.6	8 782	25 406	51 925	60 529	1.5	53 115	10.6	13.2	12.0
Union	61	825	3 839	16.0	37.7	32.2	24.7	8 605	36 167	63 468	88 641	7.6	66 831	7.0	7.9	7.0
Walworth	127	1 109	1 193	6.7	49.6	21.8	7.6	8 798	25 915	41 826	57 989	2.2	41 030	14.5	19.5	18.0
Yankton	202	1 986	5 142	20.3	43.8	26.4	22.9	7 395	27 268	52 578	67 645	3.2	46 599	13.0	14.9	13.5
Ziebach	0	172	1 013	4.4	52.4	14.7	9.9	14 640	12 339	32 708	41 373	0.0	30 465	48.7	55.4	38.8
TENNESSEE	591	3 181	1 590 507	17.0	48.7	23.8	8 221.1	8 208	24 409	44 298	61 291	2.9	44 268	17.8	26.5	24.3
Anderson	177	1 735	16 018	12.6	49.9	23.5	121.7	9 935	24 561	43 620	58 962	2.1	42 365	19.7	29.8	28.9
Bedford	354	1 888	10 864	10.9	64.7	12.3	58.2	7 066	19 303	40 759	51 860	1.0	42 288	18.6	27.7	25.0
Benton	178	1 549	3 104	7.0	66.2	10.3	19.5	8 483	18 456	33 033	42 506	0.7	35 559	21.3	35.6	33.0
Bledsoe	102	1 002	2 755	14.8	67.5	9.3	16.4	8 065	15 747	33 443	43 916	1.2	35 715	25.5	36.3	31.6
Blount	307	2 097	27 626	14.4	49.8	20.8	154.8	8 464	23 788	45 991	58 629	2.0	45 348	14.9	20.3	17.5
Bradley	484	3 363	25 589	22.4	51.2	18.5	120.3	7 581	21 649	41 083	55 437	1.5	42 665	18.6	27.5	23.0
Campbell	240	3 488	8 162	12.6	71.1	9.5	42.9	7 282	16 812	31 943	41 117	0.6	32 325	23.9	35.7	31.9
Cannon	166	1 215	2 715	8.5	65.5	13.0	15.8	7 446	20 566	40 689	51 773	0.7	40 809	18.3	25.2	22.9
Carroll	183	2 326	6 641	15.1	61.0	15.4	37.2	7 835	18 330	35 049	46 059	1.1	35 929	19.9	27.0	27.1
Carter	226	2 481	12 546	13.8	59.0	15.8	66.7	8 122	19 018	31 842	44 056	1.0	32 773	23.0	34.0	32.2
Cheatham	269	2 350	9 605	14.5	54.6	18.9	47.4	7 101	23 459	52 446	62 520	1.7	52 544	13.3	20.3	18.2
Chester	262	1 728	4 892	28.3	55.1	15.5	19.3	6 864	18 817	41 875	51 939	1.7	40 779	19.4	27.1	23.4
Claiborne	443	2 032	7 503	27.2	67.1	13.3	38.6	8 185	18 583	33 229	44 737	1.4	32 775	22.9	30.9	28.3
Clay	89	1 186	1 307	3.4	70.8	12.9	9.0	8 242	16 867	29 727	39 283	0.1	30 587	24.8	39.7	36.9
Cocke	601	3 552	6 125	5.0	69.4	9.5	44.7	8 026	17 476	30 573	41 028	0.8	30 950	24.7	41.1	37.2
Coffee	346	2 790	12 475	7.9	56.5	18.0	82.9	8 804	20 357	37 618	50 853	1.5	43 375	19.8	29.9	26.4
Crockett	478	1 992	3 286	9.2	66.7	11.9	22.0	7 189	18 664	36 066	47 281	1.3	37 085	19.3	27.7	25.1
Cumberland	356	3 557	9 839	9.9	57.3	17.4	54.0	7 210	21 141	37 188	49 004	1.6	36 163	18.2	29.1	26.5
Davidson	1 047	4 001	160 853	31.3	37.8	35.9	810.7	9 800	28 467	47 335	67 515	4.2	47 239	17.8	29.4	29.0
Decatur	454	2 187	2 369	7.3	62.5	14.2	12.2	7 210	25 368	36 258	58 176	4.1	36 213	24.1	32.9	28.2
DeKalb	163	2 630	3 952	6.4	65.7	13.3	21.9	7 219	21 606	37 482	55 876	2.6	37 392	21.9	33.6	31.3
Dickson	373	2 895	11 631	11.5	60.3	14.2	64.3	7 606	21 547	44 318	55 814	1.8	44 991	15.0	22.6	20.3
Dyer	862	3 894	9 152	7.7	57.4	18.1	54.5	7 997	21 208	38 953	52 950	1.6	40 158	18.7	28.6	26.5
Fayette	266	1 377	8 433	34.4	50.8	21.5	30.4	7 966	28 201	56 618	73 151	4.5	56 058	14.7	21.0	20.3
Fentress	200	2 322	3 579	4.0	72.1	11.1	18.4	7 706	16 454	29 192	39 402	0.7	31 065	22.6	37.0	32.7
Franklin	319	1 902	10 523	22.8	56.2	18.4	46.9	8 002	22 398	42 904	55 962	2.0	41 477	19.0	25.4	22.2
Gibson	620	2 318	12 069	9.4	55.5	16.5	69.9	7 559	20 402	38 343	51 056	1.5	40 083	18.0	27.2	25.4
Giles	324	2 014	6 812	17.4	61.0	14.6	32.7	8 067	19 998	38 495	48 102	1.0	39 880	17.8	24.9	23.0
Grainger	132	1 923	4 739	10.0	68.8	10.5	26.5	7 253	17 933	32 364	44 119	1.3	35 301	19.0	29.1	26.7
Greene	292	2 549	13 793	10.1	60.9	15.5	78.6	7 721	19 801	35 545	47 257	1.1	35 980	19.6	29.8	26.6
Grundy	601	2 427	2 813	7.0	72.5	10.0	18.4	7 970	15 683	26 814	39 259	0.5	26 101	28.9	38.3	36.7
Hamblen	348	3 493	13 975	8.8	58.7	16.0	76.0	7 400	21 261	39 596	53 326	1.7	38 807	20.5	29.1	25.8
Hamilton	628	4 491	84 916	22.0	41.3	27.2	375.3	8 587	27 229	46 702	66 470	3.6	47 373	16.9	25.8	23.2
Hancock	194	2 466	1 394	10.1	70.4	9.0	9.3	9 558	14 326	23 892	33 256	0.4	26 000	31.5	45.2	42.4
Hardeman	474	2 607	5 443	13.9	67.0	9.8	33.7	8 302	14 975	30 973	42 498	0.3	34 766	24.7	32.4	30.7
Hardin	355	3 288	5 130	14.1	66.6	11.2	30.3	8 153	20 127	33 622	50 103	2.3	36 154	24.1	36.1	33.1
Hawkins	200	2 265	12 037	8.3	62.2	12.7	65.1	8 014	20 662	37 357	49 569	1.0	36 102	21.2	31.3	28.5
Haywood	901	3 549	4 757	7.0	65.3	11.4	27.6	8 156	18 714	34 542	46 312	1.1	34 557	23.1	35.1	31.2
Henderson	515	2 871	6 553	8.7	60.5	13.1	37.3	7 569	20 449	38 280	51 376	1.4	40 960	19.4	27.6	24.7
Henry	294	3 238	6 899	9.6	61.4	16.0	39.7	8 004	22 239	36 950	52 405	2.1	37 327	20.8	32.9	30.3
Hickman	287	1 419	5 293	12.0	66.3	12.0	28.9	7 832	18 383	39 581	50 262	0.8	33 816	23.2	33.2	29.4
Houston	333	999	1 942	5.1	66.4	9.7	10.9	7 667	18 539	35 271	44 691	0.4	37 743	20.2	30.8	27.3
Humphreys	242	1 572	3 992	5.5	60.3	12.4	23.5	7 547	22 183	42 846	53 990	1.0	41 954	17.0	27.2	25.3
Jackson	220	1 467	2 141	3.7	70.6	9.9	12.7	8 032	18 387	33 386	44 782	1.1	33 158	26.3	39.9	37.7
Jefferson	271	2 480	11 701	17.3	58.7	13.6	55.7	7 376	20 619	39 745	52 000	1.0	40 490	16.4	26.5	24.2
Johnson	515	1 584	3 175	13.1	70.8	9.0	20.6	8 862	16 470	29 609	40 212	0.6	30 652	28.1	38.3	33.9
Knox	456	3 852	111 661	17.2	35.9	34.3	462.4	7 848	28 136	47 694	66 713	3.8	49 105	16.3	20.3	19.3
Lake	274	1 502	1 439	14.2	72.9	7.0	7.6	7 941	12 042	27 115	40 559	1.1	28 391	39.0	44.9	42.0
Lauderdale	772	2 910	6 775	6.1	69.1	10.4	37.1	7 845	15 758	32 326	43 437	1.0	32 169	27.7	36.1	32.4
Lawrence	550	2 902	9 925	12.5	63.7	12.0	52.6	7 682	19 136	37 368	49 619	1.1	39 532	17.9	27.4	25.3
Lewis	431	2 216	2 436	8.6	62.7	11.7	13.6	6 958	17 751	34 397	44 382	0.9	35 097	21.3	31.2	29.1
Lincoln	399	2 453	7 589	15.4	59.6	15.5	40.1	7 279	21 811	41 571	52 863	1.5	41 453	18.0	26.7	24.5
Loudon	145	1 730	9 241	12.9	47.2	25.2	56.4	7 622	27 045	51 074	66 537	3.2	53 230	14.2	24.8	20.7
McMinn	468	3 893	11 573	15.3	60.5	14.3	60.9	7 447	19 744	39 410	49 112	0.8	40 543	16.9	24.6	22.1
McNairy	302	2 062	5 077	10.0	65.7	11.0	30.5	7 508	18 428	33 452	40 712	1.0	34 598	19.4	28.7	26.6
Macon	279	1 434	4 883	5.0	70.0	8.4	25.1	6 520	17 009	35 306	44 551	0.5	35 432	21.3	32.6	30.2
Madison	1 033	4 250	27 221	27.3	47.7	24.6	114.4	8 557	23 283	41 617	59 617	3.1	40 750	21.1	30.4	26.3
Marion	385	2 068	6 368	14.8	59.7	15.4	34.7	7 481	21 399	41 268	52 576	1.2	42 128	16.4	26.4	24.2

1. Data for serious crimes have not been adjusted for underreporting; this may affect comparability between geographic areas and over time. 2. Per 100,000 population estimated by the FBI.
3. All persons 3 years old and over enrolled in nursery school through college. 4. Persons 25 years old and over. 5. Elementary and secondary education expenditures.
6. Based on population estimated by the American Community Survey, 2009–2013.

STATE County	Personal income, 2013										Earnings, 2013		
	Total (mil dol)	Percent change, 2012–2013	Per capita[1]		Wages and salaries (mil dol)	Supplements to wages and salaries; employer contributions (mil dol)		Proprietors' income (mil dol)	Dividends, interest, and rent (mil dol)	Personal transfer receipts (mil dol)	Total (mil dol)	Contributions for government social insurance (mil dol)	
			Dollars	Rank		Pension and insurance	Government social insurance					From employee and self-employed	From employer
	62	63	64	65	66	67	68	69	70	71	72	73	74
SOUTH DAKOTA—Cont'd													
Tripp	258	9.6	46 960	556	72	13	5	83	50	47	173	8	5
Turner	491	12.4	58 706	126	71	14	5	194	60	58	284	11	5
Union	1 073	6.0	72 387	40	439	59	29	237	298	86	765	40	29
Walworth	233	1.9	42 143	925	74	14	6	40	65	47	134	8	6
Yankton	892	5.0	39 308	1 251	464	82	35	95	195	154	676	39	35
Ziebach	62	-8.0	21 848	3 098	13	3	1	14	10	16	30	1	1
TENNESSEE	256 969	2.1	39 558	X	124 018	21 188	8 887	34 202	36 710	53 284	188 296	10 942	8 887
Anderson	2 957	1.7	39 148	1 273	2 098	316	154	527	435	692	3 095	180	154
Bedford	1 575	3.3	34 315	2 029	653	137	49	161	227	357	1 000	59	49
Benton	502	1.6	30 800	2 579	127	32	10	38	86	185	207	16	10
Bledsoe	349	2.5	27 162	2 961	58	21	4	21	41	112	103	8	4
Blount	4 417	1.9	35 310	1 855	1 950	349	143	451	706	1 013	2 894	179	143
Bradley	3 645	2.6	35 791	1 783	1 581	300	120	644	453	848	2 644	155	120
Campbell	1 237	2.2	30 734	2 590	323	72	25	88	162	466	508	38	25
Cannon	448	2.1	32 501	2 332	69	18	5	61	65	127	152	11	5
Carroll	965	2.0	33 856	2 107	267	58	21	107	114	349	453	29	21
Carter	1 751	1.1	30 544	2 619	363	82	27	168	255	583	640	48	27
Cheatham	1 406	1.6	35 594	1 814	306	72	22	169	153	280	569	35	22
Chester	549	1.9	31 718	2 445	118	29	9	66	61	154	222	15	9
Claiborne	943	1.1	29 883	2 706	300	68	23	46	128	346	437	32	23
Clay	237	1.1	30 476	2 633	50	13	4	42	30	82	110	8	4
Cocke	976	2.0	27 508	2 935	269	61	20	53	122	373	403	32	20
Coffee	1 988	1.8	37 260	1 542	1 001	182	74	297	280	508	1 556	91	74
Crockett	544	6.0	37 290	1 536	146	33	11	125	61	153	315	17	11
Cumberland	1 868	2.2	32 505	2 329	567	112	43	173	381	662	895	69	43
Davidson	33 750	3.1	51 245	325	23 252	3 266	1 633	9 706	4 620	4 517	37 857	2 019	1 633
Decatur	414	1.4	35 540	1 819	136	29	10	44	51	151	219	15	10
DeKalb	627	2.0	32 734	2 295	201	42	15	80	92	172	337	21	15
Dickson	1 661	1.4	33 039	2 245	566	109	43	163	200	412	882	55	43
Dyer	1 415	3.6	37 032	1 576	552	122	42	248	182	396	964	54	42
Fayette	1 973	4.4	50 988	331	329	66	24	414	236	316	833	45	24
Fentress	563	5.8	31 427	2 493	162	34	12	74	64	211	282	20	12
Franklin	1 378	4.2	33 513	2 173	374	82	29	120	206	383	605	40	29
Gibson	1 647	3.3	33 294	2 208	482	110	37	248	209	549	877	53	37
Giles	988	3.6	34 364	2 020	343	68	26	88	146	292	525	34	26
Grainger	694	1.1	30 558	2 617	117	29	9	43	82	213	198	17	9
Greene	2 343	2.5	34 324	2 027	901	178	70	101	293	970	1 251	86	70
Grundy	380	1.8	28 170	2 879	69	20	5	39	44	151	133	11	5
Hamblen	2 000	1.5	31 716	2 446	1 100	210	81	153	268	574	1 544	96	81
Hamilton	14 767	1.8	42 352	902	8 795	1 527	640	1 802	2 385	2 851	12 764	731	640
Hancock	147	1.7	21 970	3 097	26	9	2	4	19	69	41	4	2
Hardeman	765	3.3	29 082	2 796	260	60	20	78	89	251	417	26	20
Hardin	943	1.7	36 203	1 713	306	64	22	114	148	312	507	33	22
Hawkins	1 734	0.6	30 521	2 625	457	101	35	67	214	562	659	52	35
Haywood	674	7.0	36 970	1 592	200	47	15	137	73	181	400	19	15
Henderson	817	-1.3	29 125	2 790	280	56	22	73	120	248	430	28	22
Henry	1 182	6.7	36 706	1 638	389	92	30	174	216	350	686	41	30
Hickman	639	1.1	26 313	3 017	118	33	9	37	72	213	196	15	9
Houston	261	-0.7	31 456	2 488	48	14	4	19	36	90	85	6	4
Humphreys	645	3.7	35 345	1 848	271	59	20	40	93	186	390	25	20
Jackson	389	3.0	33 807	2 126	52	14	4	105	40	122	176	11	4
Jefferson	1 574	1.3	30 193	2 656	492	97	37	101	249	478	727	52	37
Johnson	487	2.6	27 077	2 966	148	37	11	27	74	182	223	17	11
Knox	18 466	2.2	41 533	990	10 196	1 698	736	2 298	2 774	3 215	14 928	858	736
Lake	187	6.8	24 152	3 074	55	18	4	13	26	83	90	5	4
Lauderdale	693	1.0	24 945	3 054	206	53	16	66	94	244	341	21	16
Lawrence	1 206	3.4	28 715	2 827	339	76	26	146	160	403	588	39	26
Lewis	327	3.6	27 318	2 954	75	20	6	32	39	115	132	9	6
Lincoln	1 177	1.8	34 996	1 895	331	76	24	91	170	309	522	34	24
Loudon	1 996	1.6	39 561	1 224	557	101	41	89	413	488	788	56	41
McMinn	1 620	0.7	30 948	2 562	672	125	53	136	213	494	987	66	53
McNairy	739	1.5	28 287	2 867	187	50	15	49	90	281	301	22	15
Macon	703	1.5	30 978	2 552	147	37	11	86	88	208	281	18	11
Madison	3 850	1.5	38 998	1 304	2 238	451	163	447	573	863	3 299	185	163
Marion	929	1.4	32 746	2 293	254	56	19	56	118	270	385	27	19

1. Based on the resident population estimated as of July 1 of the year shown.

Table B. States and Counties — **Earnings, Social Security, and Housing**

STATE County	Earnings, 2013 (cont.) — Percent by selected industries: Farm	Mining	Construction	Manu-facturing	Information: professional, scientific, technical services	Retail trade	Finance, insurance, real estate and leasing	Health care and social assistance	Govern-ment	Social Security beneficiaries, December 2013: Number	Rate[1]	Supple-mental Security Income recipients, December 2013	Housing units, 2014: Total	Percent change, 2010–2014
	75	76	77	78	79	80	81	82	83	84	85	86	87	88
SOUTH DAKOTA—Cont'd														
Tripp	37.0	0.0	4.5	2.0	3.1	7.6	D	D	10.9	1 365	248	152	3 068	-0.1
Turner	41.9	D	4.7	19.9	2.2	1.9	D	D	6.0	1 825	218	76	3 991	1.3
Union	13.6	0.0	2.1	17.9	5.5	3.2	9.5	12.2	5.0	2 865	194	98	6 658	6.0
Walworth	17.4	D	4.4	0.8	D	9.8	4.3	D	13.8	1 510	274	125	2 998	-0.2
Yankton	12.5	D	3.0	23.2	D	6.4	5.0	15.2	15.9	4 775	211	373	9 779	1.3
Ziebach	50.6	0.0	1.7	D	D	D	D	D	29.4	170	60	78	984	-0.3
TENNESSEE	0.4	0.2	6.2	12.0	8.7	6.9	7.8	15.3	14.6	1 348 004	207	183 784	2 869 323	2.0
Anderson	-0.1	0.2	6.3	27.3	23.3	4.1	3.8	8.7	12.1	19 145	254	2 330	34 747	0.1
Bedford	-0.5	D	8.3	35.8	D	6.0	4.8	D	12.0	9 460	206	1 077	18 547	1.0
Benton	-0.2	D	5.7	14.2	D	10.1	5.8	D	27.1	5 270	324	592	8 977	0.0
Bledsoe	-3.1	D	11.6	1.9	D	5.7	3.8	5.6	51.8	2 865	208	451	5 690	-0.5
Blount	-0.2	D	12.5	17.8	3.8	8.2	6.5	7.3	16.0	30 325	243	2 819	55 893	1.1
Bradley	-0.1	D	5.6	21.7	3.3	6.6	3.9	D	10.4	23 425	230	2 677	42 414	2.5
Campbell	-0.6	D	10.1	14.2	2.5	10.4	5.9	D	20.9	11 595	288	2 770	20 331	1.8
Cannon	1.7	D	16.8	7.4	D	6.1	D	D	21.2	3 415	248	443	6 053	0.3
Carroll	10.5	D	4.0	9.5	D	6.0	5.8	D	18.7	7 985	280	987	13 181	0.1
Carter	-0.6	D	12.7	9.1	3.5	11.3	5.3	D	21.4	15 835	276	2 334	27 836	0.3
Cheatham	0.4	D	D	23.6	D	6.8	3.6	D	15.3	7 715	196	732	15 794	0.8
Chester	2.9	0.0	D	9.6	D	8.3	5.1	D	22.2	4 145	239	495	7 022	0.6
Claiborne	-1.6	5.5	3.8	18.4	D	6.3	5.8	D	23.3	9 320	295	1 960	15 009	1.0
Clay	-3.0	D	5.6	7.6	D	7.6	4.1	D	21.2	2 310	297	385	4 253	-0.7
Cocke	0.3	D	D	23.7	1.7	10.6	3.5	D	25.3	10 565	299	2 067	17 363	-0.5
Coffee	0.9	0.0	5.2	16.5	25.4	6.3	3.4	10.8	13.9	13 170	247	1 587	23 565	0.6
Crockett	11.9	0.0	5.7	24.0	2.4	12.1	5.6	D	14.0	3 565	244	433	6 399	-0.4
Cumberland	-2.3	1.4	7.9	14.0	D	11.2	5.2	15.3	14.5	21 190	369	1 755	28 639	1.7
Davidson	0.0	0.2	5.0	4.1	13.3	5.0	9.5	25.4	9.1	96 090	146	15 595	292 895	3.1
Decatur	-0.1	D	6.3	11.1	D	6.6	D	28.7	16.1	3 885	333	495	6 835	-0.5
DeKalb	2.9	0.0	D	23.0	13.6	5.7	2.9	D	16.5	4 795	251	682	9 434	0.3
Dickson	-1.0	D	10.3	21.7	3.3	9.6	4.4	12.9	16.1	10 525	210	1 158	21 076	1.3
Dyer	7.2	0.0	11.3	22.7	D	7.6	4.7	10.7	15.6	9 455	248	1 572	16 785	0.5
Fayette	7.0	D	6.5	21.4	D	10.5	9.0	D	10.7	9 090	234	1 310	16 231	3.6
Fentress	0.0	D	9.6	5.2	2.4	10.5	4.8	22.0	15.1	5 745	321	1 151	8 931	-0.3
Franklin	3.8	1.0	5.6	17.0	D	8.6	3.5	D	18.9	10 675	258	1 027	18 956	1.4
Gibson	9.1	0.0	7.2	17.1	3.5	9.4	6.5	D	19.1	12 750	258	1 642	22 379	1.7
Giles	-0.2	D	8.6	30.0	D	7.9	3.6	D	14.6	7 600	264	833	13 836	-0.1
Grainger	-3.2	D	12.0	23.5	D	7.4	D	4.3	26.3	6 245	275	1 063	10 854	-0.3
Greene	-1.5	D	4.5	25.6	2.6	9.4	4.1	D	17.5	20 045	294	2 584	32 162	0.4
Grundy	-0.5	D	8.5	9.8	D	10.8	4.3	11.1	29.1	4 175	310	831	6 372	-0.4
Hamblen	0.5	D	4.4	30.1	2.9	8.4	3.1	13.2	13.4	15 950	253	1 986	27 024	0.2
Hamilton	0.0	D	6.5	13.2	7.8	7.0	9.0	12.4	16.4	70 930	203	8 590	154 643	2.3
Hancock	0.1	0.0	D	3.7	D	9.4	D	15.1	53.0	1 515	227	467	3 604	-0.6
Hardeman	6.3	0.0	4.6	24.0	D	4.8	D	D	23.5	6 435	245	1 375	10 853	0.0
Hardin	1.6	D	6.6	27.8	5.7	9.2	5.5	D	17.9	8 010	308	1 268	13 982	0.3
Hawkins	-1.1	D	3.3	36.3	D	6.2	2.5	D	20.6	16 980	299	2 214	26 839	-0.1
Haywood	24.8	0.0	3.1	22.6	D	4.7	3.6	5.3	17.0	4 350	239	1 022	8 407	1.1
Henderson	2.7	0.0	4.8	19.9	1.9	8.5	8.8	7.8	17.9	6 600	236	924	12 817	0.2
Henry	8.3	D	5.8	18.5	2.9	8.7	5.5	7.3	21.7	9 540	297	960	17 003	-0.3
Hickman	-1.1	0.0	D	12.4	D	5.4	2.5	D	32.4	5 510	228	712	10 271	-0.4
Houston	-3.0	0.0	D	12.9	D	7.3	3.6	17.4	30.7	1 980	239	273	4 170	-0.4
Humphreys	-1.6	D	7.0	33.1	8.2	5.4	2.5	D	21.1	4 865	267	502	8 875	0.1
Jackson	-0.7	0.3	13.7	7.6	D	6.3	D	D	15.5	3 380	293	533	5 822	-0.4
Jefferson	-0.7	D	D	17.9	D	8.0	4.0	D	17.1	13 875	265	1 416	23 635	0.6
Johnson	-0.3	D	5.2	21.9	D	5.6	3.5	9.3	25.4	5 355	298	879	8 914	-0.5
Knox	-0.1	0.1	6.5	5.4	11.3	8.0	8.0	16.4	15.0	83 915	189	10 068	198 917	2.0
Lake	14.2	0.0	D	D	D	4.1	1.4	9.5	50.9	1 415	184	340	2 607	0.3
Lauderdale	11.9	0.0	2.5	18.4	D	6.0	4.6	7.5	28.4	5 815	211	1 259	11 286	0.3
Lawrence	5.2	D	6.3	16.8	3.9	9.9	3.7	D	19.3	11 140	265	1 294	18 145	-0.2
Lewis	-1.7	0.0	6.0	8.3	2.9	13.6	2.0	D	24.8	3 055	256	358	5 451	-0.3
Lincoln	-0.9	D	7.1	26.4	3.6	9.1	4.3	4.3	22.9	8 385	250	834	15 346	0.7
Loudon	2.4	D	7.2	20.8	6.4	8.5	4.8	8.1	16.0	14 910	296	899	22 245	2.4
McMinn	-0.9	D	6.0	36.5	D	8.0	5.0	D	13.1	13 565	259	1 723	23 249	-0.4
McNairy	2.2	0.0	5.5	20.4	1.9	7.7	2.5	D	24.2	7 715	295	1 178	11 982	0.4
Macon	5.0	0.0	8.6	9.6	D	13.3	6.5	D	20.9	5 465	241	834	9 966	1.1
Madison	1.0	D	8.5	16.6	4.0	7.5	4.3	13.2	22.6	20 330	206	3 344	42 685	1.9
Marion	-0.1	D	5.5	24.5	D	10.5	2.9	10.2	18.9	7 460	263	1 087	13 039	0.7

1. Per 1,000 resident population estimated as of July 1 of the year shown.

STATE County	Housing units, 2009–2013: Occupied units: Total	Owner-occupied: Percent	Owner-occupied: Median value[1]	Median owner cost as a percent of income: With a mortgage	Median owner cost as a percent of income: Without a mortgage[2]	Renter-occupied: Median rent[3]	Renter-occupied: Median rent as a percent of income[2]	Substandard units[4] (percent)	Civilian labor force, 2014: Total	Percent change, 2013–2014	Unemployment: Total	Unemployment: Rate[5]	Civilian employment,[6] 2009–2013: Total	Percent: Management, business, science and arts	Percent: Construction, production, and maintenance occupations
	89	90	91	92	93	94	95	96	97	98	99	100	101	102	103
SOUTH DAKOTA—Cont'd															
Tripp	2 530	68.7	72 200	19.3	11.2	580	30.6	1.6	3 128	0.8	100	3.2	2 947	45.3	25.8
Turner	3 461	78.5	93 200	22.6	11.3	573	22.8	0.7	4 792	1.4	137	2.9	4 389	31.7	30.2
Union	5 758	75.2	150 300	19.0	10.0	745	21.6	0.9	7 973	0.9	295	3.7	7 214	39.2	22.1
Walworth	2 342	64.2	73 000	20.0	10.8	473	24.7	1.0	2 393	1.3	126	5.3	2 635	34.5	24.5
Yankton	8 698	71.8	126 700	19.7	10.0	549	28.3	13.7	11 398	-1.2	342	3.0	11 101	31.3	25.5
Ziebach	803	51.7	70 100	17.8	11.8	454	29.1	1.7	1 014	-1.9	59	5.8	900	49.0	21.6
TENNESSEE	2 475 195	67.8	139 200	23.1	11.1	742	30.9	2.3	3 011 495	-2.3	200 633	6.7	2 806 948	33.5	24.0
Anderson	30 548	68.5	127 000	21.6	10.6	687	29.2	5.7	33 091	-2.2	2 261	6.8	31 140	34.5	22.1
Bedford	16 402	70.0	114 600	23.1	12.2	670	30.8	4.2	19 349	-3.6	1 430	7.4	18 815	25.3	38.9
Benton	6 892	78.7	80 100	23.9	11.4	496	38.5	4.7	6 680	-3.4	598	9.0	5 874	24.0	36.9
Bledsoe	4 556	79.8	106 100	25.1	11.1	507	32.4	1.4	4 201	-3.5	366	8.7	4 274	23.5	38.7
Blount	48 728	73.3	163 900	23.2	10.3	720	29.9	3.1	58 296	-2.0	3 508	6.0	54 861	31.5	24.3
Bradley	37 603	67.0	138 900	23.1	10.6	689	32.6	1.6	48 032	-3.1	2 978	6.2	42 229	28.5	28.3
Campbell	15 959	69.2	91 500	22.5	12.1	522	30.7	2.2	14 857	-2.9	1 390	9.4	13 743	24.3	34.0
Cannon	5 383	77.2	116 400	26.3	11.9	613	24.1	2.1	5 832	-1.4	362	6.2	5 414	24.3	35.2
Carroll	11 022	75.8	80 500	22.0	11.8	526	31.4	2.3	12 465	-5.3	1 262	10.1	10 734	30.2	33.7
Carter	24 079	72.3	101 100	22.3	12.0	537	31.1	2.0	23 873	-3.9	1 817	7.6	23 512	28.4	27.6
Cheatham	14 421	81.0	152 900	24.4	11.1	885	36.2	1.7	19 825	-1.0	1 092	5.5	18 452	30.6	27.9
Chester	5 936	72.6	102 300	21.9	11.0	616	29.4	1.4	8 037	-3.3	564	7.0	7 210	29.8	31.9
Claiborne	12 553	75.0	94 900	22.9	10.8	504	31.3	2.2	12 594	-3.6	1 095	8.7	11 962	27.5	33.2
Clay	3 281	77.7	96 400	21.8	13.1	516	28.2	3.7	2 966	-4.6	274	9.2	2 882	23.2	32.7
Cocke	14 917	70.5	99 700	24.5	10.9	509	30.7	3.6	14 483	-3.7	1 317	9.1	13 477	21.2	34.2
Coffee	21 019	67.8	116 900	23.9	12.0	642	31.1	3.0	24 462	-0.1	1 542	6.3	21 322	31.1	28.7
Crockett	5 619	68.3	85 700	23.1	12.4	644	30.6	1.5	6 784	-3.8	533	7.9	6 050	27.7	33.5
Cumberland	23 764	78.4	142 200	23.8	10.4	608	30.5	2.7	22 882	-2.8	1 835	8.0	19 981	28.5	29.8
Davidson	256 745	54.7	167 500	24.2	11.2	837	30.2	2.8	353 770	-0.6	17 882	5.1	322 971	39.1	16.7
Decatur	5 066	77.2	83 100	21.4	10.1	515	31.1	2.1	4 735	-7.2	456	9.6	4 624	31.9	29.7
DeKalb	7 037	72.6	115 100	21.8	10.0	535	24.9	1.7	7 331	-4.8	584	8.0	7 607	26.6	37.1
Dickson	18 647	73.6	138 500	23.5	11.2	765	32.8	2.3	23 597	-1.2	1 471	6.2	21 770	28.4	30.0
Dyer	15 100	63.5	99 500	21.8	12.2	615	29.7	2.1	16 513	-3.6	1 380	8.4	16 093	29.0	33.1
Fayette	14 535	80.8	175 100	23.9	10.0	649	27.2	2.8	17 589	-3.6	1 315	7.5	17 042	33.3	26.1
Fentress	7 348	76.5	93 300	24.7	12.7	510	32.4	0.9	7 096	-4.5	593	8.4	6 112	28.4	35.0
Franklin	16 067	76.6	104 800	22.8	11.2	632	25.6	2.1	19 561	-0.7	1 200	6.1	16 403	31.6	32.4
Gibson	19 205	72.7	87 700	23.7	11.9	585	29.5	1.9	21 130	-4.7	1 907	9.0	19 821	28.6	29.3
Giles	11 766	72.7	100 000	22.2	11.7	576	35.0	2.6	14 210	0.5	896	6.3	11 915	29.1	33.7
Grainger	9 003	81.0	91 400	23.8	12.0	556	32.8	2.4	9 153	-3.2	751	8.2	8 464	23.5	40.8
Greene	28 677	72.7	110 800	23.4	10.4	558	28.4	3.9	29 540	-3.1	2 442	8.3	27 756	29.3	32.2
Grundy	5 359	77.6	80 100	26.0	13.5	483	28.6	1.5	5 064	-5.1	475	9.4	4 686	23.9	35.3
Hamblen	24 315	69.6	125 000	22.6	11.2	627	31.0	2.0	26 295	-2.7	1 921	7.3	25 344	26.0	35.0
Hamilton	135 496	64.9	154 200	21.8	10.8	741	30.4	4.4	163 306	-3.4	10 314	6.3	158 786	37.4	20.0
Hancock	2 835	74.7	75 900	26.1	14.4	365	28.4	3.0	2 058	-4.5	205	10.0	2 054	23.8	39.7
Hardeman	8 690	70.2	86 300	27.3	12.4	593	36.7	2.3	9 510	-3.1	898	9.4	8 356	23.9	34.0
Hardin	9 934	77.9	98 000	24.4	12.0	574	29.5	1.2	10 426	-5.4	942	9.0	9 575	23.2	35.4
Hawkins	23 348	76.9	108 900	22.1	11.4	581	27.7	4.8	23 798	-3.8	1 730	7.3	22 295	28.2	35.3
Haywood	7 099	60.8	94 500	24.2	12.1	625	32.6	2.6	7 715	-5.1	765	9.9	7 326	23.5	36.3
Henderson	10 930	75.7	94 400	21.7	10.9	589	28.8	2.0	12 127	-4.7	1 063	8.8	11 371	25.7	34.5
Henry	13 473	73.2	91 300	22.2	10.2	599	28.4	4.6	13 818	-3.9	1 137	8.2	12 384	26.6	30.5
Hickman	8 846	77.9	100 400	23.7	10.0	647	32.4	3.9	10 356	-1.7	687	6.6	9 640	24.8	34.5
Houston	3 423	70.1	87 300	20.5	13.3	574	29.1	1.4	3 290	-2.5	327	9.9	3 082	19.1	45.4
Humphreys	7 396	77.8	108 000	22.2	11.4	585	22.8	1.4	8 236	-5.1	659	8.0	7 483	25.2	38.2
Jackson	4 493	79.9	102 900	28.4	12.6	484	31.7	2.0	4 426	-3.4	387	8.7	3 903	27.7	39.7
Jefferson	19 797	74.5	121 800	23.7	11.3	629	26.3	5.7	22 784	-2.7	1 709	7.5	21 881	26.0	30.8
Johnson	6 921	75.9	101 200	25.9	11.7	506	29.1	1.4	7 075	-3.9	493	7.0	6 071	25.8	36.5
Knox	181 100	65.2	157 400	22.1	10.6	769	30.7	3.6	223 824	-1.9	12 267	5.5	210 719	39.8	16.4
Lake	2 201	55.4	72 700	22.5	12.1	427	29.9	2.9	2 109	-3.6	195	9.2	1 811	17.3	29.7
Lauderdale	9 686	63.6	77 600	24.5	12.4	606	29.0	3.6	9 812	-4.4	971	9.9	9 089	24.1	32.4
Lawrence	15 862	75.4	97 900	22.8	11.7	541	28.8	1.3	17 575	-3.4	1 445	8.2	16 992	23.7	35.8
Lewis	4 750	74.4	94 400	23.8	12.6	596	27.3	1.1	4 869	-2.8	438	9.0	4 484	26.3	31.0
Lincoln	13 438	76.2	109 400	22.5	11.2	582	27.8	2.2	15 235	-2.4	814	5.3	14 380	26.3	35.0
Loudon	19 543	76.8	177 600	22.2	10.0	757	28.2	1.6	21 647	-2.3	1 441	6.7	19 872	29.5	27.9
McMinn	20 313	74.7	119 000	22.3	10.5	598	31.0	2.7	22 230	-3.1	1 692	7.6	20 880	25.4	39.0
McNairy	9 736	73.5	86 100	23.2	12.3	539	29.7	3.8	8 944	-4.4	944	10.6	9 118	26.3	40.2
Macon	8 544	73.1	97 900	23.5	12.3	495	24.6	2.0	9 893	-2.0	643	6.5	8 965	23.1	40.6
Madison	35 713	66.3	112 700	23.2	11.1	739	36.5	2.6	46 229	-3.1	3 189	6.9	41 893	33.1	23.0
Marion	11 226	73.8	118 900	22.9	10.2	597	31.8	2.9	11 596	-3.7	918	7.9	11 262	27.1	33.5

1. Specified owner-occupied units. 2. A value of 10.0 represents 10 percent or less; a value of 50.0 represents 50 percent or more. 3. Specified renter-occupied units.
4. Overcrowded or lacking complete plumbing facilities. 5. Percent of civilian labor force. 6. Persons 16 years old and over.

STATE County	Private nonfarm establishments, employment and payroll, 2013: Number of establish-ments	Employment: Total	Employment: Health care and social assistance	Employment: Manufac-turing	Employment: Retail trade	Employment: Finance and insurance	Employment: Professional, scientific, and technical services	Annual payroll: Total (mil dol)	Annual payroll: Average per employee (dollars)	Agriculture, 2012: Farms: Number	Farms: Percent with: Fewer than 50 acres	Farms: Percent with: 500 acres or more	Farm operators whose principal occu-pation is farming (percent)
	104	105	106	107	108	109	110	111	112	113	114	115	116
SOUTH DAKOTA—Cont'd													
Tripp	211	1 565	398	D	383	D	53	47	30 210	629	12.6	58.8	65.5
Turner	261	1 607	401	185	266	75	47	48	29 685	794	26.4	30.6	57.4
Union	497	8 302	998	1 674	444	869	186	389	46 882	527	24.5	37.6	63.6
Walworth	215	2 017	378	D	393	81	86	59	29 286	256	18.0	48.8	60.5
Yankton	730	10 970	2 005	2 947	1 708	707	227	367	33 465	692	23.0	34.0	57.2
Ziebach	43	268	59	D	D	D	D	7	27 257	240	8.8	75.0	72.5
TENNESSEE	130 819	2 394 068	389 848	299 961	310 904	110 322	101 423	99 011	41 357	68 050	39.4	5.5	41.8
Anderson	1 526	39 455	3 674	D	3 354	1 103	9 329	2 163	54 825	441	52.4	1.4	34.0
Bedford	765	11 876	1 029	3 602	1 445	451	227	414	34 832	1 411	36.2	7.6	47.1
Benton	308	3 253	676	674	599	142	51	86	26 500	463	24.8	6.7	43.4
Bledsoe	98	474	90	54	D	44	6	16	33 943	579	28.5	5.4	40.6
Blount	2 263	38 321	6 750	D	5 612	2 101	1 393	1 415	36 916	980	52.0	2.7	45.6
Bradley	1 881	37 734	4 864	7 751	4 733	1 578	841	1 379	36 535	807	50.7	4.2	40.8
Campbell	577	7 598	2 388	1 378	1 413	263	107	218	28 665	370	41.9	1.4	41.9
Cannon	172	1 474	380	289	205	45	27	43	29 447	717	36.7	3.6	43.1
Carroll	437	6 526	1 713	866	846	254	101	188	28 748	732	31.3	7.9	40.2
Carter	686	8 547	1 727	1 044	1 728	315	139	236	27 610	493	51.7	1.6	37.7
Cheatham	538	5 638	630	D	816	154	116	204	36 117	415	38.8	2.9	46.5
Chester	238	3 072	362	417	440	104	D	79	25 785	391	32.5	4.3	26.6
Claiborne	416	7 026	1 187	1 957	789	254	124	222	31 597	945	36.3	3.6	40.2
Clay	100	1 148	D	D	D	31	D	30	26 297	424	23.6	7.8	47.2
Cocke	484	6 036	871	1 596	1 350	218	104	182	30 201	625	39.8	1.0	44.6
Coffee	1 210	20 471	2 985	4 204	2 928	766	661	771	37 639	895	47.4	7.9	36.0
Crockett	213	1 709	479	D	252	87	37	60	34 841	369	35.8	17.6	45.3
Cumberland	1 084	14 490	2 978	2 472	2 591	468	317	442	30 514	764	39.4	7.5	36.8
Davidson	18 333	396 610	75 555	19 365	38 148	19 611	24 161	19 304	48 673	360	49.2	2.2	40.8
Decatur	208	2 984	1 088	454	318	80	51	108	36 317	405	22.2	7.2	40.7
DeKalb	292	4 137	511	1 908	512	85	88	134	32 293	637	37.2	4.9	38.8
Dickson	897	12 790	2 045	3 233	2 196	448	189	414	32 369	1 143	36.7	3.8	33.8
Dyer	792	12 300	2 049	3 663	2 127	463	181	414	33 633	449	34.5	22.5	50.6
Fayette	588	6 926	595	2 094	936	D	D	275	39 650	745	33.0	12.8	41.3
Fentress	239	3 474	1 546	281	597	180	43	96	27 596	536	38.4	6.5	45.5
Franklin	663	10 475	1 489	2 852	1 413	241	163	378	36 097	861	48.0	5.3	40.0
Gibson	917	10 941	1 909	2 043	2 056	366	200	325	29 689	830	40.0	13.3	40.8
Giles	543	7 280	881	2 409	1 238	262	133	253	34 770	1 692	28.9	4.4	40.7
Grainger	220	2 403	216	1 101	374	D	D	67	27 747	885	40.7	0.8	43.3
Greene	1 096	21 597	4 147	5 650	2 833	609	280	673	31 155	2 529	49.8	1.4	46.9
Grundy	165	1 520	383	395	289	D	D	35	23 164	278	42.1	2.5	34.5
Hamblen	1 291	25 882	3 977	8 662	3 793	545	329	890	34 373	569	49.4	1.9	48.7
Hamilton	8 712	178 107	25 930	25 908	19 822	12 371	7 788	7 051	39 591	561	53.8	3.2	39.2
Hancock	47	383	177	NA	99	D	D	12	32 050	457	28.9	4.4	40.0
Hardeman	367	5 316	1 166	D	611	164	D	168	31 639	579	24.2	11.2	31.6
Hardin	500	6 873	1 188	1 985	1 247	180	101	233	33 973	589	29.2	11.9	37.4
Hawkins	590	9 342	1 412	3 691	1 324	229	95	299	31 962	1 437	42.7	1.3	45.4
Haywood	307	4 764	477	D	603	162	D	168	35 233	413	31.2	19.9	44.8
Henderson	482	6 238	927	1 475	1 087	D	95	182	29 214	844	24.6	6.5	32.0
Henry	700	8 602	1 390	1 596	1 601	333	257	255	29 630	826	30.4	10.8	41.3
Hickman	243	2 134	497	D	299	D	D	63	29 756	639	27.4	8.1	39.7
Houston	109	1 067	D	206	161	35	D	28	26 554	338	29.9	6.8	47.9
Humphreys	337	4 170	649	1 275	580	D	77	176	42 224	598	30.3	12.0	36.8
Jackson	90	972	D	D	111	30	D	34	35 477	499	32.5	5.6	38.7
Jefferson	651	10 691	1 167	1 786	1 770	257	135	345	32 226	981	45.9	1.4	43.7
Johnson	243	2 863	618	564	386	113	50	102	35 605	476	45.0	1.9	37.0
Knox	10 971	205 667	34 241	11 288	30 092	10 207	9 285	8 020	38 993	912	55.8	1.0	45.5
Lake	74	637	D	NA	NA	14	D	15	24 267	60	16.7	41.7	58.3
Lauderdale	307	4 708	648	990	700	174	D	141	29 964	457	34.4	15.5	37.4
Lawrence	702	8 374	1 368	1 597	1 587	242	192	234	27 969	1 559	36.4	5.6	42.3
Lewis	194	1 861	517	284	422	64	45	47	25 049	222	40.5	5.9	44.6
Lincoln	568	7 372	865	2 469	1 375	225	138	246	33 419	1 595	33.1	6.1	37.6
Loudon	907	12 520	1 573	3 102	1 854	317	358	436	34 811	685	49.5	2.3	41.3
McMinn	884	13 929	1 815	4 778	2 083	508	294	501	35 934	1 043	44.8	3.9	44.1
McNairy	396	4 557	812	1 084	631	116	79	134	29 350	658	26.0	5.9	38.4
Macon	327	3 294	658	790	709	D	62	98	29 832	879	33.8	3.2	43.2
Madison	2 537	50 444	11 861	8 441	6 855	1 219	1 243	1 783	35 351	592	31.3	10.0	46.8
Marion	414	5 303	817	1 438	1 098	166	70	166	31 290	280	33.2	8.6	41.4

STATE County	Agriculture, 2012 (cont.)															
	Land in farms					Value of land and buildings (dollars)		Value of machinery and equipment, average per farm (dollars)	Value of products sold				Percent of farms with sales of:		Government payments	
	Acreage (1,000)	Percent change, 2007–2012	Acres: Average size of farm	Acres: Total irrigated (1,000)	Acres: Total cropland (1,000)	Average per farm	Average per acre		Total (mil dol)	Average per farm (dollars)	Percent from: Crops	Percent from: Livestock and poultry products	$10,000 or more	$100,000 or more	Total ($1,000)	Percent of farms
	117	118	119	120	121	122	123	124	125	126	127	128	129	130	131	132
SOUTH DAKOTA—Cont'd																
Tripp	1 019	0.5	1 620	2.7	477.8	1 810 404	1 118	224 453	229.0	364 110	37.8	62.2	74.6	49.9	5 336	83.1
Turner	384	3.5	484	18.3	329.3	2 089 242	4 316	248 820	182.2	229 447	55.4	44.6	67.3	36.3	5 690	72.5
Union	288	3.4	547	41.4	259.3	2 743 670	5 012	281 402	158.4	300 653	67.2	32.8	70.2	45.2	4 998	80.8
Walworth	445	0.1	1 737	1.9	245.7	2 572 492	1 481	343 938	117.8	460 305	75.6	24.4	62.1	47.3	3 077	78.1
Yankton	328	1.7	474	15.5	265.0	1 962 231	4 142	221 565	117.4	169 691	48.4	51.6	62.4	33.1	4 604	81.5
Ziebach	1 108	4.7	4 618	0.0	175.6	2 194 488	475	163 100	49.8	207 504	38.7	61.3	75.0	42.9	2 580	56.7
TENNESSEE	10 868	-0.9	160	146.4	5 329.7	569 416	3 565	69 244	3 611.0	53 065	57.8	42.2	30.2	6.1	67 665	23.8
Anderson	36	-10.7	81	0.1	10.2	475 961	5 856	61 673	3.6	8 102	21.2	78.8	13.2	1.6	36	7.3
Bedford	232	0.5	165	0.5	88.6	629 255	3 821	62 006	107.3	76 062	9.8	90.2	37.7	8.9	811	18.9
Benton	88	21.2	190	0.0	38.5	425 503	2 241	67 212	10.8	23 348	67.9	32.1	29.4	3.9	606	39.1
Bledsoe	102	11.1	177	0.8	42.6	619 174	3 506	74 772	42.7	73 789	24.9	75.1	42.3	11.2	96	10.5
Blount	101	2.4	103	0.6	42.8	700 027	6 811	59 394	17.0	17 341	36.6	63.4	28.7	3.4	234	11.1
Bradley	87	-9.4	107	0.1	28.6	583 543	5 439	57 476	115.7	143 376	5.5	94.5	30.1	11.3	217	8.7
Campbell	33	-2.0	91	0.1	11.5	338 165	3 736	58 478	3.3	9 041	22.3	77.7	18.9	1.1	50	9.2
Cannon	96	-17.5	134	0.1	38.5	415 745	3 097	55 290	21.1	29 431	49.3	50.7	27.3	5.7	381	14.1
Carroll	178	-1.0	243	2.0	121.4	595 486	2 450	92 384	62.2	84 956	95.1	4.9	25.4	6.7	2 510	50.3
Carter	40	2.3	82	0.0	12.4	427 787	5 238	49 771	8.6	17 377	18.9	81.1	24.1	2.8	95	13.4
Cheatham	52	-17.0	126	0.2	20.8	539 161	4 270	71 566	11.4	27 436	73.7	26.3	30.1	6.3	155	18.3
Chester	61	-15.1	156	0.5	28.1	300 294	1 928	52 100	10.0	25 683	80.8	19.2	25.1	4.6	404	48.8
Claiborne	121	-2.6	129	0.0	34.4	394 144	3 066	52 611	18.7	19 773	12.1	87.9	25.0	1.7	380	31.2
Clay	80	2.5	188	0.0	27.3	522 627	2 779	67 042	36.3	85 526	12.0	88.0	44.3	9.0	373	24.3
Cocke	61	-4.8	98	0.8	20.4	358 320	3 668	49 451	27.9	44 584	36.7	63.3	22.4	2.7	189	16.6
Coffee	145	3.5	162	2.6	79.0	572 818	3 540	80 251	60.8	67 884	64.7	35.3	32.5	10.1	1 075	22.3
Crockett	131	-12.5	354	4.2	112.1	1 003 241	2 836	150 220	62.1	168 247	95.5	4.5	48.2	22.0	2 946	69.1
Cumberland	129	5.3	169	0.1	49.5	643 314	3 807	70 047	34.1	44 685	37.9	62.1	29.7	5.0	264	10.2
Davidson	35	-15.8	97	0.4	11.3	601 725	6 221	58 703	D	D	D	D	16.1	1.1	55	4.2
Decatur	77	1.2	191	0.0	25.0	410 128	2 150	60 484	8.1	20 037	55.6	44.4	30.1	2.5	301	34.3
DeKalb	90	-6.0	141	1.0	33.5	451 124	3 209	64 680	62.7	98 447	91.4	8.6	31.4	5.2	154	17.9
Dickson	149	6.7	130	0.2	46.1	432 552	3 329	52 872	14.0	12 209	40.0	60.0	23.6	1.7	153	11.6
Dyer	212	-11.3	471	16.5	188.3	1 182 490	2 508	188 944	108.4	241 408	94.9	5.1	51.4	26.9	2 426	63.3
Fayette	229	0.7	307	5.3	147.4	965 636	3 141	113 322	75.3	101 050	90.2	9.8	26.8	9.1	2 515	44.0
Fentress	91	7.7	169	0.0	26.3	543 444	3 207	70 149	41.0	76 515	8.9	91.1	41.4	9.5	400	17.4
Franklin	125	-13.1	146	1.9	74.8	567 243	3 897	82 614	81.4	94 565	43.9	56.1	37.0	10.9	683	23.9
Gibson	286	-0.2	345	5.0	250.2	1 065 437	3 090	153 169	145.2	174 923	94.6	5.4	39.2	16.6	4 101	62.3
Giles	270	3.3	160	2.4	88.4	468 997	2 938	62 255	45.8	27 075	36.8	63.2	32.8	3.3	955	19.3
Grainger	85	-7.2	96	0.4	25.8	366 236	3 803	49 200	18.9	21 367	57.7	42.3	27.2	2.4	233	22.4
Greene	226	-1.4	89	0.4	90.8	362 074	4 052	56 139	85.6	33 859	15.3	84.7	26.9	3.6	1 135	23.6
Grundy	33	-22.5	119	0.5	14.2	340 791	2 864	50 061	17.7	63 507	48.4	51.6	33.5	6.8	61	9.7
Hamblen	59	-15.2	103	D	27.3	484 123	4 682	60 812	29.0	51 051	38.3	61.7	28.8	3.7	313	13.5
Hamilton	52	-4.2	93	0.1	19.7	527 171	5 654	57 647	12.4	22 182	16.9	83.1	19.6	2.9	114	5.7
Hancock	64	6.2	141	D	15.6	323 665	2 297	44 394	5.5	11 993	10.3	89.7	28.7	1.5	162	28.2
Hardeman	154	4.0	266	1.1	78.2	678 563	2 554	73 984	30.3	52 252	87.2	12.8	22.3	6.0	1 411	50.4
Hardin	126	15.0	214	1.9	59.9	542 166	2 531	66 596	22.1	37 554	81.7	18.3	31.2	6.3	849	39.0
Hawkins	133	-11.7	93	0.2	42.3	326 872	3 522	45 740	18.1	12 602	36.4	63.6	20.9	1.1	451	26.8
Haywood	219	2.4	531	14.2	197.0	1 916 540	3 608	210 751	125.6	304 107	98.6	1.4	40.7	23.0	3 018	70.0
Henderson	162	-1.9	192	0.1	79.8	424 276	2 207	64 594	35.3	41 831	73.9	26.1	31.4	5.9	1 264	50.4
Henry	205	5.8	248	4.4	131.6	688 305	2 779	98 464	91.6	110 849	62.1	37.9	36.3	14.8	2 181	48.8
Hickman	121	7.7	189	0.4	39.3	452 828	2 394	56 521	12.9	20 233	50.4	49.6	32.1	2.7	291	20.3
Houston	50	6.6	149	D	11.8	337 740	2 269	57 231	9.0	26 521	4.9	95.1	26.3	7.4	94	12.4
Humphreys	123	4.3	207	0.3	40.8	587 381	2 844	66 271	15.3	25 517	56.4	43.6	28.9	4.2	343	12.2
Jackson	74	-2.5	148	0.0	19.5	427 545	2 894	46 649	5.0	9 928	47.5	52.5	17.2	1.0	452	23.8
Jefferson	96	-5.9	97	0.5	37.7	526 143	5 400	55 272	30.7	31 318	15.3	84.7	26.7	3.3	441	16.3
Johnson	47	8.8	100	0.0	16.1	474 284	4 764	55 954	9.1	19 046	24.0	76.0	29.6	3.6	226	21.2
Knox	65	-21.2	72	0.2	24.5	549 549	7 670	49 402	14.6	16 035	59.3	40.7	17.5	1.0	241	10.0
Lake	80	-5.2	1 329	15.4	78.1	4 373 900	3 291	611 450	51.8	863 000	99.8	0.2	83.3	51.7	868	90.0
Lauderdale	201	4.5	439	13.2	172.5	1 373 934	3 127	155 593	97.3	212 827	97.2	2.8	32.6	17.5	2 290	65.4
Lawrence	236	-1.1	151	0.8	105.5	400 664	2 649	55 580	65.3	41 875	51.0	49.0	34.3	5.6	1 223	23.8
Lewis	31	-13.6	138	0.1	9.6	360 077	2 602	44 788	3.1	13 860	15.8	84.2	27.0	4.5	46	14.4
Lincoln	266	1.9	167	4.0	108.2	562 043	3 371	70 241	110.5	69 283	33.5	66.5	37.2	6.7	1 066	17.5
Loudon	69	-9.9	101	0.1	33.1	549 140	5 422	77 477	77.5	113 093	77.3	22.7	24.7	4.2	177	17.7
McMinn	122	-0.1	117	0.2	48.2	480 752	4 098	61 846	37.9	36 379	12.1	87.9	24.7	4.0	473	13.0
McNairy	130	5.9	198	D	61.5	426 061	2 157	58 903	23.0	35 026	87.3	12.7	23.9	4.0	929	47.7
Macon	122	-4.6	139	0.2	47.6	474 719	3 424	56 597	44.7	50 857	59.8	40.2	33.0	7.4	869	34.6
Madison	166	-6.3	280	7.9	117.9	706 385	2 520	101 103	66.0	111 552	94.4	5.6	30.9	11.0	2 288	61.8
Marion	51	0.3	181	0.1	22.0	533 475	2 942	88 682	13.1	46 918	46.3	53.7	33.6	8.2	183	11.8

Table B. States and Counties — **Water Use, Wholesale Trade, Retail Trade, and Real Estate**

STATE County	Water use, 2010		Wholesale trade,[1] 2007				Retail trade,[2] 2007				Real estate and rental and leasing,[2] 2007			
	Total water withdrawn (mil gal/day)	Gallons withdrawn per person per day	Number of establish-ments	Number of employees	Sales (mil dol)	Annual payroll (mil dol)	Number of establish-ments	Number of employees	Sales (mil dol)	Annual payroll (mil dol)	Number of establish-ments	Number of employees	Receipts (mil dol)	Annual payroll (mil dol)
	133	134	135	136	137	138	139	140	141	142	143	144	145	146
SOUTH DAKOTA—Cont'd														
Tripp	11.5	2 032	12	142	70.4	4.2	48	411	88.4	7.3	5	4	0.7	0.1
Turner	4.4	524	17	119	166.6	4.1	43	302	52.4	4.4	1	D	D	D
Union	6.8	472	24	D	D	D	46	541	304.2	12.4	17	36	8.0	1.6
Walworth	13.5	2 473	9	69	107.0	2.6	49	411	74.8	6.0	4	13	0.8	0.1
Yankton	19.3	859	32	D	D	D	138	1 559	293.0	29.5	22	87	8.3	1.5
Ziebach	0.5	168	3	D	D	D	4	D	D	D	NA	NA	NA	NA
TENNESSEE	7 696.6	1 213	6 282	99 238	80 116.5	4 593.4	24 234	320 739	77 547.3	7 244.6	6 087	37 737	6 950.4	1 243.0
Anderson	307.7	4 096	37	269	208.3	11.8	268	3 457	907.8	78.4	64	309	42.3	7.3
Bedford	16.0	354	25	D	D	D	156	1 508	340.6	31.6	29	156	23.1	4.7
Benton	2.5	149	10	82	35.2	2.5	69	644	136.8	12.0	9	25	2.4	0.4
Bledsoe	3.1	238	3	9	3.4	0.2	21	134	30.5	2.0	2	D	D	D
Blount	16.0	130	80	1 069	898.0	49.1	407	6 236	1 551.1	152.4	93	354	70.0	9.9
Bradley	19.0	192	60	D	D	D	396	4 673	1 164.6	107.3	82	461	88.0	12.4
Campbell	4.7	115	20	329	134.4	8.7	147	1 562	361.8	31.5	18	123	11.1	2.2
Cannon	2.0	143	4	D	D	D	33	268	53.6	5.6	7	22	2.6	0.2
Carroll	5.6	198	15	280	71.8	7.0	104	950	188.9	16.7	16	44	7.1	0.9
Carter	20.2	351	13	76	35.0	3.3	154	1 806	461.3	37.4	29	100	12.5	1.9
Cheatham	4.4	112	17	59	33.8	2.0	80	1 010	238.8	20.1	19	49	8.7	1.1
Chester	1.9	110	12	66	24.4	1.7	55	450	117.7	9.9	7	22	1.6	0.3
Claiborne	4.3	132	11	77	26.0	2.0	93	820	155.9	14.4	24	75	16.5	1.6
Clay	13.7	1 744	3	D	D	D	25	149	37.3	2.9	7	28	2.3	0.9
Cocke	6.9	193	9	D	D	D	122	1 430	326.9	28.0	24	119	8.5	2.0
Coffee	9.3	176	41	425	196.6	17.4	272	3 148	790.8	68.5	45	184	21.3	3.8
Crockett	4.3	298	11	158	112.1	5.9	48	262	65.0	4.2	3	6	1.0	0.1
Cumberland	8.3	147	37	D	D	D	252	2 531	597.0	51.9	56	279	32.5	6.2
Davidson	163.4	261	1 009	20 028	11 942.6	983.6	2 795	42 241	10 581.8	1 046.2	934	6 617	1 588.0	252.2
Decatur	2.2	189	3	D	D	D	56	433	98.9	9.8	5	6	0.4	0.1
DeKalb	3.1	164	7	47	8.5	1.5	63	551	119.4	10.8	10	22	2.5	0.4
Dickson	6.2	125	26	413	327.9	17.1	198	2 394	605.9	51.8	36	130	18.7	2.3
Dyer	13.5	352	41	315	252.5	11.1	191	2 187	514.1	47.7	36	89	15.1	3.2
Fayette	6.9	179	27	161	74.4	6.3	82	580	126.6	11.8	23	49	5.8	0.8
Fentress	2.3	130	3	D	D	D	68	687	140.5	13.0	6	101	15.2	3.1
Franklin	41.1	1 000	18	D	D	D	156	1 471	343.6	31.4	21	98	11.4	2.0
Gibson	8.6	173	39	D	D	D	207	2 054	439.0	38.8	32	101	11.5	2.5
Giles	5.4	181	22	311	112.9	13.4	126	1 300	313.3	27.1	15	73	6.4	1.4
Grainger	4.4	195	5	37	8.6	0.5	53	371	79.5	5.9	6	13	1.1	0.2
Greene	12.6	184	42	D	D	D	217	2 900	682.0	61.1	41	156	23.6	3.4
Grundy	2.6	187	3	D	D	D	49	324	67.5	5.5	3	17	1.0	0.1
Hamblen	10.0	161	59	1 370	591.7	57.0	307	4 199	1 055.0	91.8	57	268	41.6	6.3
Hamilton	1 968.0	5 849	497	5 989	2 958.5	268.0	1 500	20 722	4 865.7	467.7	403	2 354	367.5	100.3
Hancock	0.7	103	1	D	D	D	18	182	24.4	2.9	2	D	D	D
Hardeman	4.2	155	19	148	42.1	3.6	80	723	158.8	13.7	6	32	2.7	0.6
Hardin	29.4	1 128	22	124	79.7	4.7	130	1 129	313.7	25.9	24	59	8.4	1.7
Hawkins	355.5	6 255	14	D	D	D	124	1 356	286.9	24.7	26	75	6.8	1.5
Haywood	7.6	407	18	91	74.2	2.7	61	676	180.6	12.6	10	29	2.4	0.7
Henderson	4.0	145	19	135	31.8	3.6	116	1 082	279.6	21.7	11	24	3.6	0.5
Henry	5.7	177	32	D	D	D	163	1 658	404.2	35.9	26	83	10.0	1.7
Hickman	3.3	134	10	D	D	D	52	296	76.9	6.1	10	D	D	D
Houston	1.4	171	NA	NA	NA	NA	26	156	33.4	2.7	3	8	0.9	0.2
Humphreys	737.3	39 775	12	138	57.2	4.4	69	635	181.9	12.6	10	37	2.0	0.6
Jackson	1.1	97	5	37	7.2	0.9	26	116	27.8	1.7	1	D	D	D
Jefferson	8.2	160	17	101	35.3	3.9	145	1 650	554.3	35.6	34	106	11.2	1.5
Johnson	2.8	152	3	D	D	D	56	453	93.2	7.9	17	39	3.9	0.4
Knox	71.8	166	699	10 084	7 402.5	474.4	1 904	33 315	8 209.4	794.3	542	3 195	624.4	103.4
Lake	5.3	679	4	D	D	D	23	103	19.5	1.9	3	9	0.8	0.1
Lauderdale	6.7	239	19	520	829.7	23.5	82	809	151.8	14.3	16	34	4.5	1.0
Lawrence	6.6	157	39	D	D	D	181	1 587	381.0	33.5	26	95	9.3	1.7
Lewis	2.1	169	5	D	D	D	49	460	132.8	9.2	7	21	2.1	0.4
Lincoln	9.5	286	22	244	147.5	8.7	148	1 396	366.5	31.8	22	110	10.6	2.6
Loudon	18.2	374	44	610	360.6	17.1	141	1 714	435.6	35.3	36	104	15.8	2.4
McMinn	68.9	1 318	33	D	D	D	201	2 334	561.3	49.6	30	106	15.9	2.2
McNairy	4.2	160	13	99	45.7	5.2	107	788	194.7	14.0	11	54	10.3	1.4
Macon	3.5	155	10	111	30.4	2.5	72	738	167.3	15.0	20	39	4.4	0.5
Madison	16.6	168	154	2 008	1 160.4	84.0	509	7 057	1 696.5	153.0	108	765	101.1	19.3
Marion	4.0	142	23	D	D	D	109	1 194	286.6	24.1	14	32	2.8	0.5

1. Merchant wholesalers, except manufacturers' sales branches and offices. 2. Employer establishments.

STATE County	Professional, scientific, and technical services,[1] 2007				Manufacturing, 2007				Accommodation and food services, 2007			
	Number of establishments	Number of employees	Receipts (mil dol)	Annual payroll (mil dol)	Number of establishments	Number of employees	Receipts (mil dol)	Annual payroll (mil dol)	Number of establishments	Number of employees	Sales (mil dol)	Annual payroll (mil dol)
	147	148	149	150	151	152	153	154	155	156	157	158
SOUTH DAKOTA—Cont'd												
Tripp	16	53	6.1	1.5	NA	NA	NA	NA	25	208	8.1	2.0
Turner	11	D	D	D	NA	NA	NA	NA	18	90	2.2	0.5
Union	36	D	D	D	26	D	D	55.7	40	459	19.7	4.2
Walworth	16	101	7.1	2.2	NA	NA	NA	NA	31	370	19.8	5.3
Yankton	42	205	23.2	7.8	30	2 710	635.2	91.7	71	1 068	34.5	9.2
Ziebach	NA	NA	NA	NA	NA	NA	NA	NA	2	D	D	D
TENNESSEE	11 278	D	D	D	6 752	369 165	140 447.8	15 165.6	11 592	239 379	10 626.8	3 009.2
Anderson	219	D	D	D	114	9 827	1 911.2	543.9	126	3 030	126.6	35.9
Bedford	49	252	21.3	6.7	54	4 805	1 047.3	177.0	58	863	35.3	9.5
Benton	20	55	4.2	1.2	21	629	82.3	17.3	30	395	13.3	3.0
Bledsoe	5	D	D	D	NA	NA	NA	NA	10	107	3.5	0.8
Blount	186	D	D	D	125	7 527	5 312.3	375.7	209	4 739	208.5	63.7
Bradley	151	D	D	D	131	9 540	D	D	164	3 211	130.5	35.7
Campbell	28	120	10.9	4.0	39	1 737	333.9	64.2	54	901	35.4	9.3
Cannon	11	D	D	D	NA	NA	NA	NA	10	190	7.1	1.6
Carroll	28	D	D	D	37	1 640	767.0	58.6	39	448	15.4	3.6
Carter	41	D	D	D	42	1 880	296.7	D	67	1 151	41.9	12.1
Cheatham	47	161	18.8	5.3	37	2 198	754.9	86.3	44	580	23.3	5.6
Chester	16	D	D	D	NA	NA	NA	NA	21	293	11.6	3.3
Claiborne	22	83	6.0	2.1	35	2 880	436.2	79.4	27	576	21.6	5.9
Clay	5	D	D	D	NA	NA	NA	NA	11	73	4.0	1.0
Cocke	28	D	D	D	38	1 542	601.3	64.8	67	998	44.3	12.4
Coffee	87	D	D	D	77	5 036	D	201.5	102	2 204	79.3	23.3
Crockett	10	35	6.6	1.3	NA	NA	NA	NA	10	122	7.0	1.2
Cumberland	74	307	26.5	8.8	56	2 163	468.9	80.9	91	1 297	61.7	16.0
Davidson	1 912	23 798	2 943.3	1 285.4	633	23 715	7 347.2	999.0	1 605	38 979	2 203.0	626.4
Decatur	18	84	9.2	1.5	27	765	D	24.0	21	176	6.0	1.5
DeKalb	26	97	6.8	2.7	29	2 873	743.8	97.4	28	307	12.1	3.1
Dickson	59	244	23.9	8.7	56	3 805	876.6	141.8	95	1 527	60.5	17.7
Dyer	48	D	D	D	45	5 251	1 647.0	189.0	70	1 107	42.8	11.4
Fayette	40	261	17.2	8.0	49	2 337	889.8	92.7	39	355	12.6	3.3
Fentress	17	75	4.8	1.0	NA	NA	NA	NA	23	272	8.2	2.2
Franklin	43	D	D	D	46	D	3 187.1	D	51	971	28.0	8.7
Gibson	53	247	17.7	5.6	68	3 910	977.4	147.6	71	879	30.8	7.8
Giles	32	130	10.7	3.6	48	2 710	1 004.2	99.5	49	632	24.9	5.8
Grainger	10	D	D	D	29	912	171.3	28.5	13	150	6.1	1.1
Greene	83	D	D	D	109	6 613	1 814.0	225.1	100	1 681	62.0	18.0
Grundy	10	D	D	D	NA	NA	NA	NA	15	262	9.8	2.4
Hamblen	80	D	D	D	117	12 923	3 214.0	453.8	107	2 342	91.3	26.3
Hamilton	783	D	D	D	478	26 947	8 040.6	1 125.0	763	15 719	663.3	196.0
Hancock	3	D	D	D	NA	NA	NA	NA	3	42	1.4	0.3
Hardeman	11	42	4.2	0.8	27	1 913	423.7	54.8	32	370	15.6	3.7
Hardin	33	96	7.0	2.4	43	1 678	691.8	80.9	52	626	28.7	7.6
Hawkins	35	103	9.6	2.5	49	4 154	1 148.7	144.2	62	852	31.7	8.9
Haywood	19	D	D	D	21	2 761	631.5	89.4	35	414	13.9	3.6
Henderson	31	222	8.7	2.8	42	1 588	566.7	59.5	38	579	20.9	5.6
Henry	42	239	16.0	7.0	46	1 695	D	D	64	1 054	29.4	8.4
Hickman	10	37	3.3	1.0	35	666	D	21.0	27	219	7.1	1.8
Houston	5	D	D	D	NA	NA	NA	NA	13	93	2.7	0.7
Humphreys	18	73	6.7	3.0	23	1 301	1 052.9	81.1	40	441	17.8	4.1
Jackson	6	D	D	D	NA	NA	NA	NA	11	78	2.6	0.7
Jefferson	40	264	14.6	6.1	48	2 682	862.9	84.0	72	1 329	48.3	13.6
Johnson	15	36	3.9	1.1	18	603	118.2	22.4	25	210	6.6	1.9
Knox	1 265	D	D	D	452	14 456	4 470.9	601.7	890	21 308	919.2	273.6
Lake	4	D	D	D	NA	NA	NA	NA	13	174	5.9	1.6
Lauderdale	18	30	3.4	0.9	16	2 281	372.9	70.0	20	318	9.7	3.0
Lawrence	45	231	18.3	6.1	55	2 015	D	67.9	51	1 007	37.4	9.1
Lewis	16	D	D	D	NA	NA	NA	NA	18	232	8.0	2.2
Lincoln	41	148	15.9	4.1	42	2 680	D	87.5	45	649	26.2	5.6
Loudon	57	D	D	D	57	3 361	1 502.3	144.5	71	1 325	50.8	16.1
McMinn	53	D	D	D	73	6 792	2 381.0	317.2	83	1 499	57.5	16.4
McNairy	19	D	D	D	44	1 903	420.9	68.5	37	472	13.1	3.9
Macon	23	67	5.6	1.7	34	917	D	29.6	23	282	11.9	2.7
Madison	190	D	D	D	116	9 613	D	D	214	5 487	204.9	55.2
Marion	27	D	D	D	26	1 089	D	37.0	57	786	32.7	9.1

1. Establishment subject to federal tax.

STATE County	Health care and social assistance, 2007				Other services, 2007				Nonemployer businesses, 2013		Value of residential construction authorized by building permits, 2014	
	Number of establish-ments	Number of employees	Receipts (mil dol)	Annual payroll (mil dol)	Number of establish-ments	Number of employees	Receipts (mil dol)	Annual payroll (mil dol)	Number	Receipts (mil dol)	New Construction ($1,000)	Number of housing units
	159	160	161	162	163	164	165	166	167	168	169	170
SOUTH DAKOTA—Cont'd												
Tripp	24	416	23.8	10.0	14	35	3.0	0.7	550	23.8	500	6
Turner	23	456	19.7	10.0	14	D	D	D	759	30.6	3 577	15
Union	49	D	D	D	32	147	8.4	2.8	1 301	75.9	34 063	189
Walworth	11	363	21.1	9.1	19	82	4.9	1.4	478	18.7	2 165	9
Yankton	67	1 777	158.2	65.2	57	231	16.6	3.9	1 562	63.9	14 757	88
Ziebach	2	D	D	D	1	D	D	D	54	1.4	NA	NA
TENNESSEE	14 267	337 741	33 799.9	13 093.2	8 811	62 425	6 338.7	1 681.0	470 330	20 612.6	4 550 319	27 632
Anderson	189	4 039	374.3	150.2	130	683	158.7	17.7	4 421	183.2	24 824	173
Bedford	86	1 078	72.8	28.3	46	196	17.7	4.6	2 856	118.1	26 773	171
Benton	40	784	38.6	14.9	21	80	6.0	2.0	1 039	32.8	0	0
Bledsoe	11	126	6.5	2.8	2	D	D	D	793	28.5	NA	NA
Blount	219	5 817	466.8	199.2	182	962	84.2	27.1	8 431	354.0	85 704	608
Bradley	229	4 355	364.9	139.7	112	D	D	D	6 689	333.6	56 545	547
Campbell	55	1 720	121.5	49.7	36	159	13.6	3.1	2 393	88.0	16 468	151
Cannon	15	D	D	D	14	D	D	D	944	35.7	1 388	11
Carroll	63	1 482	92.8	36.8	32	106	9.0	2.6	1 573	53.5	845	5
Carter	83	1 825	125.0	48.0	51	D	D	D	3 246	116.7	6 238	51
Cheatham	44	D	D	D	27	70	5.6	1.5	3 234	136.3	18 128	107
Chester	24	377	24.3	12.7	17	45	4.5	0.9	1 016	42.1	780	8
Claiborne	39	1 367	72.7	34.4	31	138	13.2	4.3	1 938	76.3	14 213	125
Clay	11	D	D	D	7	13	1.3	0.3	699	20.9	NA	NA
Cocke	37	655	54.5	24.5	20	D	D	D	2 185	64.5	60	1
Coffee	202	2 650	246.7	85.2	82	600	60.4	18.3	3 452	136.9	16 949	129
Crockett	28	462	28.4	11.9	17	37	3.4	0.6	932	36.4	426	2
Cumberland	128	2 705	202.3	82.7	58	614	37.3	10.2	4 398	175.5	33 329	246
Davidson	1 805	55 649	7 038.6	2 486.9	1 351	13 834	1 315.2	434.2	60 225	3 059.3	989 199	6 413
Decatur	22	945	64.5	29.9	19	68	7.8	1.9	839	32.0	0	0
DeKalb	34	560	43.4	15.6	23	124	10.7	3.3	1 283	49.0	919	7
Dickson	118	1 857	190.8	69.2	54	291	27.0	7.9	3 590	144.1	32 930	202
Dyer	116	1 698	162.5	56.8	52	209	15.3	4.3	2 385	89.3	6 749	56
Fayette	51	649	48.4	18.8	43	150	11.8	3.4	3 202	152.6	62 526	235
Fentress	31	839	60.7	24.8	18	47	5.3	0.9	1 464	66.4	0	0
Franklin	90	D	D	D	38	D	D	D	2 565	91.4	16 529	110
Gibson	109	1 808	115.3	43.3	54	262	19.6	5.7	2 809	110.5	18 486	108
Giles	70	862	69.5	25.0	31	129	10.5	2.3	1 742	76.0	705	5
Grainger	12	D	D	D	16	72	5.9	1.4	1 470	56.9	431	2
Greene	142	3 580	255.9	100.8	75	451	32.0	8.8	4 027	143.9	15 004	94
Grundy	15	288	15.9	7.7	11	18	2.2	0.4	1 193	42.5	909	3
Hamblen	177	4 036	343.4	131.7	82	406	28.0	7.5	3 564	151.5	10 123	53
Hamilton	1 040	24 700	2 639.2	1 019.6	624	5 007	487.4	130.9	23 640	1 147.9	261 564	2 036
Hancock	6	154	9.1	3.7	5	D	D	D	438	9.9	0	0
Hardeman	41	1 453	77.6	38.1	25	50	5.0	1.2	1 465	46.6	2 970	23
Hardin	52	961	62.3	25.5	21	80	6.6	1.8	1 780	69.9	614	8
Hawkins	50	1 350	87.7	35.9	41	D	D	D	2 956	96.1	1 767	11
Haywood	29	D	D	D	27	D	D	D	1 095	41.6	2 256	18
Henderson	45	651	50.1	18.2	39	139	11.2	3.0	1 806	66.5	247	1
Henry	78	1 536	123.0	47.8	52	257	12.4	3.9	2 177	90.5	1 124	13
Hickman	35	580	41.6	16.2	22	D	D	D	1 669	57.4	228	3
Houston	15	361	22.4	9.2	7	D	D	D	510	19.2	299	1
Humphreys	31	560	34.4	13.0	27	118	8.0	2.9	1 126	40.1	1 282	10
Jackson	7	D	D	D	3	D	D	D	794	24.9	NA	NA
Jefferson	56	D	D	D	50	173	13.6	4.3	3 051	112.6	26 153	98
Johnson	20	371	22.5	10.1	16	34	2.6	0.6	1 060	35.0	200	1
Knox	1 200	30 846	3 184.9	1 259.7	760	5 638	513.6	159.1	33 182	1 688.0	294 011	1 912
Lake	9	D	D	D	7	D	D	D	351	8.0	321	6
Lauderdale	31	845	36.7	15.2	16	82	6.1	1.9	1 305	47.4	1 458	14
Lawrence	78	1 133	90.6	31.6	41	129	8.8	2.5	2 823	115.8	1 604	10
Lewis	27	445	22.0	8.7	15	57	3.5	1.0	893	38.9	452	5
Lincoln	69	933	63.6	25.0	47	155	12.3	3.4	2 329	91.7	370	3
Loudon	85	D	D	D	54	D	D	D	3 319	148.2	52 101	200
McMinn	100	1 932	158.2	56.3	52	258	16.0	4.6	2 951	113.6	2 181	24
McNairy	43	758	52.9	21.8	27	76	8.0	1.9	1 656	68.5	1 252	11
Macon	36	521	33.0	12.7	23	89	7.4	2.2	1 664	62.8	716	6
Madison	304	10 656	1 030.8	435.5	143	948	71.3	26.0	6 474	282.0	39 732	195
Marion	48	D	D	D	31	D	D	D	1 654	71.9	13 874	74

Table B. States and Counties — Government Employment and Payroll, and Local Government Finances

STATE County	Government employment and payroll, 2012									Local government finances, 2012				
			March payroll (percent of total)							General revenue				
												Taxes		
													Per capita[1] (dollars)	
	Full-time equivalent employees	March payroll (dollars)	Adminis- tration, judicial, and legal	Police and Corrections	Fire Protection	Highways and transpor- tation	Health and Welfare	Natural resources and utilities	Education and libraries	Total (mil dol)	Inter- govern- mental (mil dol)	Total (mil dol)	Total	Property
	171	172	173	174	175	176	177	178	179	180	181	182	183	184
SOUTH DAKOTA—Cont'd														
Tripp	313	855 393	8.1	15.4	0.0	7.0	3.8	9.9	55.0	19.6	5.9	10.3	1 882	1 410
Turner	279	817 829	8.0	3.7	0.0	8.8	0.3	5.1	73.1	26.4	8.0	14.2	1 711	1 477
Union	512	1 673 489	7.8	8.7	0.3	5.6	0.6	5.0	68.1	61.5	22.0	30.6	2 059	1 752
Walworth	221	589 011	7.5	16.1	0.1	6.5	1.9	2.6	64.6	20.6	9.1	7.9	1 440	1 024
Yankton	681	2 403 085	7.3	8.7	0.5	6.7	3.4	8.0	64.3	65.0	16.6	35.8	1 586	1 147
Ziebach	95	280 194	7.1	2.1	0.0	3.4	0.6	0.4	86.0	6.0	4.4	1.4	474	432
TENNESSEE	X	X	X	X	X	X	X	X	X	X	X	X	X	X
Anderson	3 051	10 709 572	8.9	7.5	4.2	3.4	1.7	10.8	62.8	221.7	89.4	94.0	1 246	741
Bedford	2 341	6 860 633	3.8	5.9	2.6	2.3	32.4	8.2	44.3	114.2	59.7	38.4	842	542
Benton	474	1 606 363	5.8	8.8	0.2	3.6	4.0	12.7	63.7	37.9	21.5	12.7	775	443
Bledsoe	594	1 386 704	5.7	6.0	0.0	3.7	3.2	3.2	63.4	34.4	25.2	6.2	483	381
Blount	6 070	20 455 931	4.4	6.6	1.8	2.2	37.0	5.4	41.5	528.9	111.3	129.7	1 044	749
Bradley	3 454	10 166 787	4.0	11.4	6.6	3.1	10.6	1.9	61.3	246.4	112.5	81.3	804	494
Campbell	1 510	4 358 532	4.9	7.7	2.4	5.5	4.9	19.0	54.0	98.1	55.2	27.6	684	390
Cannon	555	1 372 374	3.7	6.2	1.4	2.5	4.5	3.9	73.3	29.2	18.5	7.5	546	395
Carroll	1 139	3 140 304	5.3	9.1	1.3	4.5	0.7	12.9	62.8	71.5	41.1	18.0	635	428
Carter	1 973	5 071 600	5.5	8.9	2.0	4.0	1.2	9.8	68.0	111.1	63.2	34.7	606	404
Cheatham	1 170	3 416 461	8.9	8.5	1.2	3.8	4.2	5.4	66.2	87.0	44.5	32.3	824	545
Chester	583	1 479 520	6.9	10.4	1.3	4.6	3.5	4.5	63.6	35.4	21.8	9.2	537	327
Claiborne	1 693	4 650 708	4.4	4.7	0.0	1.8	36.9	4.7	46.4	101.7	41.7	19.7	620	402
Clay	346	836 185	8.5	6.7	0.0	5.7	8.6	7.4	60.8	19.6	11.9	5.0	642	405
Cocke	1 225	3 330 780	5.4	6.8	3.2	4.8	1.6	3.4	73.7	82.1	45.4	25.0	704	410
Coffee	2 224	6 075 717	5.2	8.5	3.3	2.4	3.8	13.4	59.9	153.4	61.5	58.5	1 099	624
Crockett	563	1 474 498	6.0	8.0	0.1	3.9	5.1	5.6	69.5	39.4	25.3	9.5	647	455
Cumberland	1 971	4 871 298	10.5	9.2	1.5	7.6	3.6	6.6	59.6	116.9	58.5	44.1	773	397
Davidson	22 627	87 554 648	6.2	13.1	7.2	2.6	9.0	12.5	47.7	2 674.3	751.4	1 227.6	1 894	1 220
Decatur	576	1 686 615	5.4	7.1	0.0	3.3	24.4	5.4	52.2	40.6	17.7	8.4	718	421
DeKalb	735	1 938 173	2.6	5.5	0.0	2.8	3.4	27.2	58.1	43.2	24.6	12.8	677	446
Dickson	1 972	5 546 728	7.3	6.8	2.6	2.4	3.9	17.9	57.6	141.4	60.1	55.8	1 108	644
Dyer	1 460	4 541 888	6.2	11.6	5.0	4.0	2.4	8.4	60.7	128.0	69.8	34.0	890	593
Fayette	1 075	2 824 788	9.0	14.5	2.4	0.3	4.2	5.6	62.7	63.0	30.1	24.0	622	428
Fentress	636	1 503 203	9.4	7.6	0.0	4.8	9.5	5.6	62.4	35.7	20.4	10.5	583	350
Franklin	1 139	3 326 510	2.9	9.5	1.7	3.7	1.6	11.4	69.2	91.2	43.8	33.8	829	597
Gibson	1 945	5 303 575	3.3	10.5	3.0	4.3	1.1	8.6	68.2	134.8	75.7	35.9	723	550
Giles	1 369	3 634 496	12.1	7.4	0.5	8.8	4.0	4.5	61.5	61.4	31.0	24.0	827	523
Grainger	662	1 667 581	3.5	8.8	0.0	0.6	5.1	2.8	78.1	45.9	30.1	11.3	496	384
Greene	2 317	6 964 692	4.1	9.6	2.3	3.1	6.4	13.2	60.6	142.8	69.9	48.8	709	420
Grundy	608	1 426 124	5.2	4.3	0.0	3.5	2.0	5.6	77.2	32.3	23.7	6.9	507	359
Hamblen	1 973	6 233 306	5.6	9.2	4.7	2.5	1.7	12.8	60.0	162.1	67.7	63.4	1 011	537
Hamilton	14 734	56 385 621	6.4	7.3	3.0	3.5	37.2	11.3	30.7	1 780.1	395.6	494.7	1 432	1 127
Hancock	347	800 025	10.1	7.0	0.2	6.6	20.3	2.7	53.2	20.3	13.2	2.7	407	312
Hardeman	1 079	2 839 972	5.5	9.2	1.0	3.5	5.9	11.2	62.9	64.6	37.7	18.1	684	425
Hardin	1 366	3 651 007	4.5	6.1	0.3	2.3	39.7	2.3	43.0	104.2	34.3	23.2	893	480
Hawkins	2 067	6 744 656	3.8	5.3	0.4	2.2	8.6	5.8	73.1	111.4	61.3	40.6	717	506
Haywood	942	2 633 709	7.9	9.5	3.1	3.5	5.1	9.8	55.4	60.5	32.7	17.9	982	679
Henderson	1 113	2 867 377	7.3	13.1	1.5	3.4	1.2	16.3	56.3	63.0	35.8	20.0	714	394
Henry	1 119	3 290 953	5.3	9.3	2.1	1.8	1.8	14.7	63.3	150.2	42.7	24.7	765	442
Hickman	1 002	2 269 272	16.1	6.3	0.5	2.3	4.1	5.8	61.1	54.5	34.7	13.4	554	369
Houston	381	990 105	9.2	11.3	0.4	5.4	8.2	5.2	59.0	21.6	14.5	4.9	585	382
Humphreys	1 002	3 913 409	14.1	4.3	0.1	2.3	9.0	4.1	63.2	46.8	26.1	15.5	851	526
Jackson	425	1 046 407	9.7	7.7	0.0	7.2	3.9	4.7	66.8	24.4	16.5	5.7	497	349
Jefferson	1 433	4 289 878	5.4	8.6	1.0	4.2	5.2	9.0	66.5	126.4	54.0	43.3	829	545
Johnson	620	1 243 277	8.2	8.9	0.0	5.0	2.1	6.1	68.5	37.2	23.2	8.9	494	360
Knox	13 135	45 220 953	5.5	12.5	2.9	3.2	3.7	15.3	55.2	1 270.2	389.9	630.9	1 430	810
Lake	321	873 740	15.6	15.9	0.2	6.0	4.5	10.1	47.6	18.1	11.6	3.5	457	287
Lauderdale	1 033	2 753 225	7.4	11.7	2.0	4.8	4.6	4.1	64.7	70.8	41.8	18.4	664	441
Lawrence	1 270	4 176 846	6.6	9.0	1.9	3.7	3.6	13.3	60.8	96.9	50.8	33.0	783	468
Lewis	515	1 074 509	10.9	12.0	0.6	6.6	1.4	6.6	61.8	31.6	21.1	6.6	554	298
Lincoln	1 457	3 836 126	5.1	6.7	1.8	3.0	1.0	26.5	54.5	110.1	39.6	20.1	599	348
Loudon	1 628	5 601 296	4.4	6.8	2.4	2.3	1.4	30.5	50.4	114.9	46.7	47.0	944	641
McMinn	2 013	6 789 227	4.8	5.9	1.4	2.2	24.9	7.7	47.8	109.5	59.5	34.1	651	417
McNairy	1 044	2 736 738	6.7	5.8	0.7	3.7	0.6	11.6	68.0	61.0	40.2	14.3	547	361
Macon	840	2 132 533	7.7	8.1	1.0	0.1	5.9	5.3	70.4	49.3	29.8	13.4	597	355
Madison	7 853	28 936 219	2.2	6.4	2.6	1.2	64.3	4.4	18.6	921.0	113.3	137.5	1 393	781
Marion	942	2 790 775	7.6	7.6	0.6	2.9	2.4	9.1	69.0	67.8	35.6	24.6	870	523

1. Based on the resident population estimated as of July 1 of the year shown.

STATE County	Local government finances, 2012 (cont.) — Direct general expenditure — Total (mil dol)	Per capita[1] (dollars)	Percent of total for: Education	Health and hospitals	Police protection	Public welfare	Highways	Debt outstanding — Total (mil dol)	Per capita[1] (dollars)	Government employment, 2013 — Federal civilian	Federal military	State and local	Presidential election,[2] 2012 — Percent of vote cast: Democratic	Republican	All other
	185	186	187	188	189	190	191	192	193	194	195	196	197	198	199
SOUTH DAKOTA—Cont'd															
Tripp	20.4	3 717	42.1	1.5	4.2	0.3	17.5	16.4	2 990	28	33	364	32.2	65.5	2.3
Turner	25.7	3 093	49.0	0.7	4.4	0.2	18.6	21.3	2 563	29	50	404	38.6	58.3	3.1
Union	61.7	4 151	39.7	0.2	4.0	0.0	10.5	55.2	3 718	47	89	745	42.1	56.0	1.9
Walworth	18.8	3 440	49.6	0.6	5.7	0.1	11.1	8.2	1 510	27	33	387	34.8	62.9	2.2
Yankton	61.7	2 730	45.1	1.7	5.7	0.5	12.7	62.1	2 746	194	124	1 682	47.7	49.7	2.5
Ziebach	6.0	2 081	73.9	0.5	2.6	0.0	10.9	0.0	0	0	17	156	62.2	35.0	2.8
TENNESSEE	X	X	X	X	X	X	X	X	X	49 929	22 273	374 444	41.8	56.9	1.3
Anderson	264.4	3 506	58.7	2.4	7.0	0.0	3.3	316.3	4 194	948	244	4 241	36.1	62.3	1.6
Bedford	117.2	2 572	51.0	2.6	5.8	0.2	4.7	126.0	2 764	60	147	2 361	32.4	65.9	1.7
Benton	36.9	2 254	60.4	2.4	7.0	0.3	8.6	25.4	1 550	51	52	1 001	40.8	57.0	2.1
Bledsoe	29.7	2 318	58.9	3.4	3.8	0.3	6.6	28.6	2 232	17	38	1 024	31.7	66.2	2.1
Blount	501.3	4 037	31.7	37.6	3.9	0.0	2.2	1 376.5	11 085	254	422	7 551	29.5	68.9	1.6
Bradley	234.0	2 314	53.1	8.4	7.2	0.1	4.8	222.5	2 200	203	322	4 692	24.5	74.2	1.3
Campbell	109.0	2 696	46.6	2.9	5.5	0.1	5.8	125.9	3 115	79	129	1 985	30.6	67.6	1.8
Cannon	28.5	2 064	58.3	3.3	7.4	0.4	8.5	13.9	1 008	28	44	615	36.9	60.9	2.3
Carroll	72.3	2 547	58.4	0.4	6.1	0.2	7.2	63.9	2 250	81	89	1 538	34.2	64.0	1.8
Carter	118.2	2 060	67.1	0.7	5.7	0.0	4.3	105.8	1 845	77	181	2 568	25.7	72.8	1.5
Cheatham	93.0	2 367	69.6	2.1	5.4	0.3	4.2	61.6	1 568	70	127	1 498	33.5	65.1	1.4
Chester	35.0	2 039	59.3	1.0	5.7	0.4	11.6	19.6	1 140	31	52	1 007	27.8	71.0	1.2
Claiborne	96.3	3 036	42.5	32.9	3.7	0.0	3.6	69.4	2 188	55	98	2 002	29.5	68.9	1.6
Clay	20.9	2 663	48.6	6.1	6.2	0.2	10.9	14.3	1 818	42	25	442	41.7	56.0	2.3
Cocke	89.1	2 504	59.3	1.2	4.9	0.0	6.9	71.6	2 014	63	114	1 907	26.8	71.7	1.6
Coffee	162.9	3 060	57.5	2.0	5.5	0.1	4.0	222.3	4 176	462	226	3 187	34.3	63.7	2.0
Crockett	40.8	2 791	61.9	3.1	4.8	0.9	7.7	29.0	1 982	34	47	854	32.6	66.2	1.3
Cumberland	113.1	1 983	49.3	6.2	5.6	0.0	4.0	134.0	2 349	102	184	2 327	30.7	67.8	1.5
Davidson	2 727.2	4 207	31.0	8.4	7.3	1.2	1.6	6 313.0	9 738	7 877	2 510	38 256	59.9	38.9	1.2
Decatur	37.9	3 249	38.3	26.2	3.3	0.3	5.7	26.0	2 228	25	37	759	32.9	65.1	2.0
DeKalb	40.9	2 165	55.5	3.0	7.5	0.1	5.8	23.6	1 246	35	61	971	40.1	57.8	2.1
Dickson	126.9	2 520	53.8	2.4	7.4	0.0	4.2	145.3	2 885	85	162	2 464	38.5	59.8	1.7
Dyer	131.4	3 436	50.7	0.2	7.3	0.6	6.4	99.2	2 594	99	122	2 727	30.5	68.2	1.2
Fayette	62.3	1 611	54.0	3.2	7.9	0.0	9.2	51.2	1 325	54	124	1 505	35.8	63.2	1.0
Fentress	35.1	1 954	57.6	4.3	4.7	0.6	7.7	14.5	810	36	58	807	27.2	71.1	1.8
Franklin	85.2	2 091	56.5	0.5	7.5	0.1	5.2	83.2	2 040	128	127	1 998	37.9	60.5	1.6
Gibson	141.6	2 854	58.9	2.2	5.8	0.4	6.0	112.6	2 270	150	158	2 943	34.8	63.6	1.6
Giles	61.6	2 118	59.8	4.3	3.0	0.1	8.6	25.0	859	68	91	1 425	39.5	59.0	1.5
Grainger	44.5	1 960	64.7	3.7	4.6	0.0	7.6	29.5	1 301	48	73	1 020	27.5	70.6	1.9
Greene	138.3	2 009	61.2	3.2	5.4	0.0	7.0	106.4	1 546	220	216	3 445	28.8	69.5	1.7
Grundy	31.5	2 310	69.9	0.6	3.4	0.2	7.5	12.0	880	20	43	784	42.6	55.3	2.1
Hamblen	158.5	2 526	53.0	0.6	6.2	0.2	4.7	224.6	3 579	177	202	3 557	30.0	68.4	1.6
Hamilton	1 693.1	4 900	23.2	34.8	4.9	0.9	2.5	1 512.3	4 377	6 114	1 169	21 578	43.6	55.4	1.1
Hancock	20.0	2 979	49.9	15.8	3.9	0.2	7.0	17.1	2 543	0	21	466	27.0	70.9	2.2
Hardeman	62.6	2 361	60.6	2.7	6.6	0.1	7.3	28.4	1 071	57	73	1 845	52.7	46.5	0.8
Hardin	104.9	4 042	36.7	35.8	2.7	2.7	4.6	72.4	2 789	103	83	1 689	27.8	70.5	1.6
Hawkins	108.4	1 915	66.6	0.9	4.8	0.3	4.8	126.4	2 234	165	182	2 289	28.2	70.1	1.7
Haywood	64.2	3 520	54.9	2.6	5.5	0.0	5.8	26.7	1 465	98	58	1 129	60.3	39.0	0.8
Henderson	60.8	2 170	65.5	0.2	6.4	0.1	5.4	92.9	3 314	55	90	1 337	27.9	70.8	1.3
Henry	154.5	4 776	27.8	50.9	2.8	0.0	4.3	81.7	2 525	109	137	2 500	38.0	60.4	1.6
Hickman	52.0	2 151	60.6	3.4	4.7	0.0	9.9	46.4	1 921	51	74	1 196	41.9	56.3	1.8
Houston	20.6	2 448	57.1	4.4	4.1	0.4	9.8	13.7	1 623	21	26	564	50.0	47.9	2.0
Humphreys	43.2	2 363	55.4	1.0	7.3	0.0	8.5	7.4	405	277	58	1 048	47.5	50.4	2.1
Jackson	23.3	2 034	61.8	2.9	4.3	0.2	9.2	4.9	428	25	37	541	49.4	48.5	2.0
Jefferson	135.7	2 600	53.6	3.3	4.7	9.4	4.4	112.4	2 153	111	166	2 289	27.9	70.6	1.4
Johnson	35.0	1 933	61.4	0.7	5.0	0.2	7.3	18.8	1 038	37	52	1 062	27.9	70.1	2.0
Knox	1 174.3	2 661	40.8	2.1	7.9	0.2	2.6	2 290.6	5 191	3 603	1 483	30 405	37.7	60.7	1.5
Lake	17.1	2 221	49.1	3.9	6.9	0.5	10.4	23.7	3 088	15	17	902	45.8	52.5	1.7
Lauderdale	69.4	2 504	56.8	2.7	7.3	0.6	7.8	45.4	1 639	53	81	1 920	46.3	52.8	0.9
Lawrence	93.3	2 217	57.9	3.0	6.7	0.0	7.8	110.6	2 628	115	135	1 949	32.2	66.0	1.8
Lewis	31.4	2 639	46.3	0.6	5.1	0.1	5.8	17.0	1 431	29	38	675	37.3	61.0	1.6
Lincoln	111.8	3 338	38.2	35.1	4.0	0.0	4.7	92.5	2 760	47	108	2 217	28.1	70.3	1.6
Loudon	111.4	2 238	57.9	0.6	7.1	0.2	4.5	662.5	13 305	140	162	1 913	27.3	71.3	1.4
McMinn	110.6	2 110	58.7	0.9	5.3	0.0	5.6	28.0	534	95	166	2 132	29.5	69.1	1.4
McNairy	55.7	2 129	62.1	0.2	4.9	0.0	6.8	28.4	1 086	75	84	1 408	30.0	68.5	1.5
Macon	53.2	2 366	60.7	4.0	6.0	0.1	7.6	27.7	1 232	37	73	1 183	28.0	69.9	2.1
Madison	890.5	9 027	13.8	63.1	3.2	0.0	1.8	1 017.8	10 317	430	307	11 608	46.1	53.1	0.8
Marion	61.4	2 169	58.5	0.8	8.3	0.0	5.6	57.5	2 034	62	91	1 324	39.4	59.0	1.6

1. Based on the resident population estimated as of July 1 of the year shown. 2.

STATE/ County code	CBSA code[1]	County type[2]	STATE County	Land area,[3] (sq km) 2010	Population, 2014: Total persons 2014	Population, 2014: Rank	Population, 2014: Per square kilometer	Race alone or in combination, not Hispanic or Latino (percent): White	Black	American Indian, Alaska Native	Asian and Pacific Islander	Percent Hispanic or Latino[4]	Age (percent): Under 5 years	5 to 17 years	18 to 24 years	25 to 34 years	35 to 44 years	45 to 54 years
				1	2	3	4	5	6	7	8	9	10	11	12	13	14	15
			TENNESSEE—Cont'd															
47 117	30280	6	Marshall	972	31 269	1 404	32.2	87.6	7.5	0.8	0.8	4.8	5.9	18.1	8.2	11.7	13.4	14.5
47 119	34980	4	Maury	1 588	85 515	666	53.9	81.6	13.1	0.7	1.1	5.2	6.8	17.0	8.0	13.3	12.7	13.8
47 121	...	8	Meigs	505	11 701	2 310	23.2	95.8	1.9	1.1	0.5	1.8	4.7	15.7	7.3	10.2	12.9	15.2
47 123	...	6	Monroe	1 646	45 233	1 066	27.5	93.2	2.6	1.3	0.7	3.7	5.3	16.5	8.0	10.6	12.2	13.9
47 125	17300	3	Montgomery	1 396	189 961	340	136.1	69.0	20.5	1.3	3.9	9.2	8.7	18.5	11.9	18.7	13.3	11.5
47 127	46100	9	Moore	335	6 319	2 733	18.9	95.1	2.9	0.8	0.7	1.6	3.9	16.9	7.1	9.6	13.0	14.4
47 129	28940	6	Morgan	1 352	21 660	1 749	16.0	94.3	4.3	1.0	0.4	1.2	4.3	15.4	8.5	13.1	14.5	15.1
47 131	46460	7	Obion	1 411	30 941	1 416	21.9	85.1	11.5	0.5	0.5	3.6	5.6	16.6	8.0	11.1	12.4	13.7
47 133	18260	7	Overton	1 123	22 028	1 729	19.6	97.5	1.1	0.8	0.5	1.2	5.7	17.1	7.7	10.1	12.7	13.7
47 135	...	8	Perry	1 074	7 822	2 609	7.3	94.6	3.0	1.4	0.5	2.2	5.7	16.5	7.9	10.3	11.2	13.1
47 137	...	9	Pickett	422	5 124	2 832	12.1	98.2	0.3	0.7	0.2	1.3	4.1	15.2	6.0	9.0	10.5	14.3
47 139	17420	3	Polk	1 126	16 730	1 998	14.9	97.0	0.9	1.3	0.4	1.7	4.8	16.5	7.7	9.7	13.5	15.1
47 141	18260	4	Putnam	1 039	74 165	737	71.4	90.4	2.7	0.7	1.6	5.7	5.9	15.5	15.1	12.0	11.5	12.5
47 143	19420	6	Rhea	817	32 641	1 371	40.0	92.7	2.7	1.0	0.7	4.2	5.7	17.6	9.5	10.9	12.1	13.6
47 145	28940	4	Roane	934	52 748	946	56.5	94.7	3.3	1.1	0.9	1.6	4.6	15.4	7.3	9.4	11.8	15.0
47 147	34980	1	Robertson	1 234	68 079	783	55.2	85.6	8.2	0.8	0.8	6.0	6.8	18.6	7.9	12.6	13.2	15.1
47 149	34980	1	Rutherford	1 604	288 906	233	180.1	76.2	14.4	0.7	3.8	7.0	6.7	18.7	13.1	14.5	14.5	13.2
47 151	...	6	Scott	1 379	21 987	1 731	15.9	98.5	0.5	0.8	0.4	0.7	6.2	18.3	8.5	11.6	13.5	14.1
47 153	16860	2	Sequatchie	689	14 704	2 123	21.3	95.3	0.9	0.9	0.5	3.5	5.6	16.6	7.7	10.5	12.9	14.0
47 155	42940	4	Sevier	1 535	95 110	615	62.0	92.1	1.3	0.9	1.3	5.5	5.6	15.8	8.4	11.4	12.8	14.5
47 157	32820	1	Shelby	1 977	938 803	51	474.9	38.6	53.3	0.6	2.9	5.9	7.2	18.4	10.4	14.2	12.9	13.4
47 159	34980	1	Smith	814	19 009	1 874	23.4	94.4	2.7	1.0	0.4	2.7	5.9	17.9	7.9	11.5	12.3	15.8
47 161	...	3	Stewart	1 190	13 279	2 222	11.2	93.9	2.6	1.5	1.4	2.3	5.0	16.8	7.7	10.2	12.0	15.5
47 163	28700	3	Sullivan	1 071	157 047	405	146.6	95.0	2.8	0.7	0.9	1.7	5.0	15.0	7.9	10.5	12.5	14.6
47 165	34980	1	Sumner	1 371	172 706	367	126.0	87.5	7.4	0.7	1.7	4.2	6.0	18.4	8.0	12.0	13.8	14.9
47 167	32820	1	Tipton	1 187	61 623	849	51.9	77.9	19.3	1.0	1.1	2.4	6.2	19.8	9.1	12.1	13.2	14.9
47 169	34980	1	Trousdale	296	8 002	2 598	27.0	87.2	10.4	1.0	0.4	2.8	5.8	17.2	8.5	11.6	12.6	14.7
47 171	27740	3	Unicoi	482	17 963	1 916	37.3	94.8	0.7	0.8	0.3	4.2	4.4	15.1	6.9	10.3	12.2	14.6
47 173	28940	2	Union	579	19 113	1 871	33.0	97.9	0.5	1.0	0.4	1.4	6.2	17.0	7.7	11.4	12.3	15.4
47 175	...	9	Van Buren	708	5 633	2 792	8.0	97.7	1.1	0.7	0.3	1.2	4.5	15.0	7.2	9.3	12.4	14.1
47 177	32660	6	Warren	1 121	39 969	1 172	35.7	87.7	3.7	0.7	0.7	8.4	6.1	17.8	7.9	11.7	13.2	14.0
47 179	27740	3	Washington	846	126 242	492	149.2	91.1	4.9	0.7	1.7	3.1	5.2	14.6	12.5	12.2	12.7	13.5
47 181	...	8	Wayne	1 901	16 913	1 983	8.9	91.7	6.4	0.8	0.4	1.7	4.1	14.2	8.6	13.6	13.6	14.9
47 183	32280	7	Weakley	1 503	34 373	1 318	22.9	88.3	8.5	0.7	1.4	2.3	5.3	14.2	17.6	10.6	10.8	12.6
47 185	...	7	White	976	26 301	1 550	26.9	95.3	2.6	0.9	0.6	2.1	5.9	16.3	7.7	11.3	11.9	14.0
47 187	34980	1	Williamson	1 509	205 226	312	136.0	87.1	4.9	0.5	4.1	4.7	5.9	22.4	7.1	9.4	15.1	16.3
47 189	34980	1	Wilson	1 478	125 376	496	84.8	88.1	7.3	0.8	1.8	3.6	5.9	18.4	7.7	11.2	14.1	15.5
48 000	...	X	TEXAS	676 587	26 956 958	X	39.8	45.2	12.3	0.7	4.8	38.3	7.3	19.3	10.3	14.5	13.5	13.0
48 001	37300	5	Anderson	2 752	57 627	887	20.9	61.3	21.4	0.7	0.9	16.9	5.2	14.1	8.1	15.8	16.1	15.3
48 003	11380	6	Andrews	3 887	17 477	1 947	4.5	43.7	1.9	1.0	0.8	53.4	8.9	21.4	9.9	14.9	12.0	12.6
48 005	31260	5	Angelina	2 066	87 750	654	42.5	62.9	15.5	0.6	1.2	20.8	7.0	19.3	9.4	12.5	12.3	13.1
48 007	18580	2	Aransas	653	24 972	1 608	38.2	69.8	1.8	1.2	2.4	26.2	4.7	14.0	7.3	9.5	9.5	13.0
48 009	48660	3	Archer	2 339	8 811	2 529	3.8	89.9	1.0	1.4	0.6	8.5	3.8	18.6	8.0	9.0	11.5	16.4
48 011	11100	3	Armstrong	2 355	1 955	3 053	0.8	88.1	1.6	1.6	0.2	9.5	5.4	16.7	7.2	9.7	12.1	12.4
48 013	41700	1	Atascosa	3 159	47 774	1 020	15.1	35.9	1.0	0.7	0.5	62.6	7.4	20.9	8.9	12.4	12.2	12.8
48 015	26420	1	Austin	1 674	29 114	1 451	17.4	64.7	9.5	0.7	0.7	25.5	6.3	18.0	8.2	10.2	11.6	13.9
48 017	...	7	Bailey	2 141	6 910	2 688	3.2	37.1	1.3	0.4	0.5	61.4	9.4	21.7	8.9	12.1	11.0	11.2
48 019	41700	1	Bandera	2 049	20 892	1 782	10.2	80.7	1.0	1.3	0.7	17.4	4.2	13.5	6.2	7.9	9.4	16.3
48 021	12420	1	Bastrop	2 300	78 069	707	33.9	57.0	7.9	1.0	1.2	34.1	6.2	19.5	8.1	11.5	12.8	14.9
48 023	...	6	Baylor	2 247	3 592	2 933	1.6	84.4	3.3	0.7	0.4	12.5	5.7	15.2	7.2	9.5	10.1	12.8
48 025	13300	4	Bee	2 280	32 863	1 360	14.4	33.7	8.3	0.5	0.8	57.5	5.9	15.6	11.7	17.1	14.5	13.7
48 027	28660	2	Bell	2 722	329 140	202	120.9	51.7	22.5	1.2	5.1	23.2	8.8	19.0	12.5	17.4	12.4	11.3
48 029	41700	1	Bexar	3 211	1 855 866	18	578.0	30.7	7.7	0.6	3.3	59.0	7.3	19.1	10.9	15.4	13.3	12.6
48 031	...	8	Blanco	1 837	10 812	2 373	5.9	78.0	1.4	1.1	0.7	19.9	4.5	15.7	6.4	8.5	10.8	14.8
48 033	...	9	Borden	2 324	652	3 131	0.3	82.6	0.8	1.6	0.2	15.5	4.9	16.3	6.8	9.7	12.7	14.3
48 035	...	6	Bosque	2 546	17 780	1 929	7.0	80.6	2.3	1.0	0.6	16.7	5.3	16.5	7.0	9.0	10.5	13.7
48 037	45500	3	Bowie	2 292	93 275	624	40.7	67.0	25.1	1.3	1.4	7.2	6.4	17.6	9.1	13.4	13.0	13.4
48 039	26420	1	Brazoria	3 516	338 124	198	96.2	52.0	13.4	0.7	6.5	28.9	7.3	19.7	8.6	13.8	14.7	14.1
48 041	17780	3	Brazos	1 516	209 152	306	138.0	59.0	11.2	0.6	6.1	24.3	6.3	14.3	28.9	15.4	10.2	9.2
48 043	...	7	Brewster	16 016	9 173	2 499	0.6	53.9	1.6	1.1	1.2	43.5	6.2	14.0	8.4	14.1	11.2	12.7
48 045	...	9	Briscoe	2 331	1 536	3 079	0.7	70.3	2.9	0.8	0.4	26.9	5.9	16.5	6.0	9.6	11.5	13.5
48 047	...	6	Brooks	2 443	7 194	2 662	2.9	8.6	0.6	0.2	0.9	90.2	9.3	19.2	9.9	11.8	9.3	11.6
48 049	15220	5	Brown	2 446	37 653	1 234	15.4	74.8	3.9	1.1	0.8	20.7	5.7	17.3	8.9	11.9	11.4	12.9
48 051	17780	3	Burleson	1 707	17 253	1 966	10.1	67.5	12.9	0.8	0.5	19.6	5.9	16.9	7.6	10.3	10.6	14.6
48 053	...	6	Burnet	2 575	44 943	1 071	17.5	75.6	2.3	1.0	0.8	21.1	5.4	16.8	7.8	10.5	10.8	13.4

1. CBSA = Core Based Statistical Area. See Appendix A for explanation. See Appendix B for list of metropolitan areas with component counties. 2. County type code from the Economic Research Service of USDA Rural-Urban Continuum Codes. See Appendix A for definition. 3. Dry land or land partially or temporarily covered by water. 4. May be of any race.

STATE County	Population, 2013 (cont.): Age (percent) (cont.): 55 to 64 years	65 to 74 years	75 years and over	Percent female	Population change and components of change, 2000–2014: Total persons: 2000	2010	Percent change: 2000–2010	2010–2014	Components of change, 2010–2014: Births	Deaths	Net migration	Households, 2009–2013: Number	Persons per house-hold	Percent: Family house-holds	Female family house-holder[1]	One per-son
	16	17	18	19	20	21	22	23	24	25	26	27	28	29	30	31
TENNESSEE—Cont'd																
Marshall	13.5	9.1	5.7	50.9	26 767	30 617	14.4	2.1	1 523	1 268	379	11 578	2.63	71.4	12.7	24.9
Maury	14.0	8.5	6.0	51.6	69 498	80 956	16.5	5.6	4 646	3 361	3 203	32 144	2.51	68.2	13.9	27.3
Meigs	15.1	12.7	6.3	50.2	11 086	11 753	6.0	-0.4	447	589	105	4 776	2.42	71.4	12.9	23.5
Monroe	14.5	12.1	6.7	50.5	38 961	44 519	14.3	1.6	1 992	2 070	780	17 523	2.52	73.3	9.0	23.3
Montgomery	8.8	5.1	3.4	50.2	134 768	172 331	27.9	10.2	14 330	4 759	7 757	64 026	2.72	72.2	14.7	22.0
Moore	14.7	12.2	8.2	50.9	5 740	6 362	10.8	-0.7	197	263	29	2 416	2.58	70.8	9.1	23.1
Morgan	13.7	9.4	6.0	44.7	19 757	21 987	11.3	-1.5	781	913	-193	7 455	2.55	71.8	11.5	24.0
Obion	14.1	10.7	7.7	51.7	32 450	31 807	-2.0	-2.7	1 527	1 657	-707	12 462	2.49	70.2	15.3	25.7
Overton	14.2	11.4	7.4	50.8	20 118	22 083	9.8	-0.3	1 019	1 221	136	8 815	2.48	71.4	7.5	26.0
Perry	15.3	12.2	7.9	49.5	7 631	7 915	3.7	-1.2	376	407	-92	3 187	2.42	65.3	11.5	30.0
Pickett	16.0	14.7	10.1	50.2	4 945	5 077	2.7	0.9	157	260	134	2 388	2.09	80.9	12.3	17.0
Polk	14.2	11.4	7.2	50.5	16 050	16 825	4.8	-0.6	633	902	154	6 740	2.44	70.8	10.2	24.6
Putnam	11.8	9.2	6.7	50.6	62 315	72 321	16.1	2.5	3 761	2 995	1 089	28 980	2.40	63.3	11.6	28.4
Rhea	13.4	10.5	6.6	50.8	28 400	31 809	12.0	2.6	1 599	1 460	705	12 096	2.58	69.2	14.2	25.0
Roane	16.0	12.1	8.6	50.8	51 910	54 181	4.4	-2.6	2 057	2 816	-550	22 117	2.40	67.6	10.3	27.8
Robertson	12.7	7.9	5.1	50.7	54 433	66 283	21.8	2.7	3 879	2 584	475	24 136	2.73	73.3	13.2	22.4
Rutherford	10.1	5.7	3.6	50.7	182 023	262 604	44.3	10.0	15 603	6 896	16 995	96 731	2.73	69.3	12.1	22.9
Scott	12.8	9.3	5.8	50.8	21 127	22 228	5.2	-1.1	1 109	1 122	-213	8 206	2.67	66.1	10.6	28.9
Sequatchie	14.3	11.8	6.6	50.8	11 370	14 112	24.1	4.1	572	640	646	5 616	2.52	72.0	12.3	26.3
Sevier	14.3	10.8	6.4	50.9	71 170	89 889	26.3	5.8	4 389	3 842	4 532	36 815	2.45	72.4	11.6	22.2
Shelby	12.2	6.5	4.7	52.3	897 472	927 644	3.4	1.2	58 886	32 669	-14 404	343 517	2.66	64.5	20.8	30.5
Smith	13.6	9.5	5.5	50.3	17 712	19 166	8.2	-0.8	883	904	-133	7 263	2.61	70.8	9.5	26.6
Stewart	14.4	11.4	7.1	49.8	12 370	13 324	7.7	-0.3	582	674	59	5 292	2.49	71.2	10.4	25.5
Sullivan	14.5	11.4	8.6	51.6	153 048	156 823	2.5	0.1	6 728	8 128	1 837	66 239	2.32	67.5	11.9	28.3
Sumner	12.6	8.7	5.5	51.2	130 449	160 645	23.1	7.5	8 185	5 798	9 224	60 835	2.67	75.1	12.5	21.1
Tipton	12.1	7.7	4.8	50.6	51 271	61 081	19.1	0.9	3 140	2 270	-414	21 574	2.80	76.3	17.2	20.3
Trousdale	14.2	9.5	5.8	50.7	7 259	7 870	8.4	1.7	360	339	112	2 899	2.66	69.1	11.7	22.8
Unicoi	15.2	12.0	9.2	50.8	17 667	18 313	3.7	-1.9	681	1 042	25	7 601	2.33	66.2	8.5	31.7
Union	14.1	10.2	5.7	50.5	17 808	19 109	7.3	0.0	1 008	826	-184	7 406	2.57	69.5	12.1	25.9
Van Buren	17.2	12.9	7.4	50.6	5 508	5 548	0.7	1.5	224	209	66	2 097	2.61	71.1	13.1	25.0
Warren	12.9	9.7	6.7	50.6	38 276	39 839	4.1	0.3	1 960	1 888	84	15 366	2.55	67.3	12.0	29.4
Washington	13.0	9.6	6.8	51.1	107 198	122 979	14.7	2.7	5 786	5 360	2 813	51 771	2.30	64.0	11.4	29.1
Wayne	13.3	10.4	7.4	44.9	16 842	17 021	1.1	-0.6	691	825	15	6 093	2.43	72.2	8.8	24.5
Weakley	12.3	9.1	7.4	51.2	34 895	35 021	0.4	-1.9	1 494	1 516	-583	13 797	2.34	66.0	12.4	26.4
White	14.0	11.0	7.8	51.0	23 102	25 841	11.9	1.8	1 220	1 464	700	9 729	2.63	69.4	10.3	28.0
Williamson	12.7	6.8	4.4	51.3	126 638	183 182	44.7	12.0	8 432	4 150	17 503	66 364	2.84	78.9	7.7	18.8
Wilson	13.1	8.9	5.1	51.0	88 809	113 993	28.4	10.0	5 809	3 881	9 162	42 800	2.70	74.0	12.0	22.0
TEXAS	10.9	6.6	4.6	50.3	20 851 820	25 145 561	20.6	7.2	1 626 353	733 219	905 754	8 886 471	2.82	69.8	14.3	24.8
Anderson	12.0	8.0	5.5	39.2	55 109	58 458	6.1	-1.4	2 465	2 623	-637	16 378	2.86	70.5	13.5	26.5
Andrews	10.3	5.4	4.6	49.3	13 004	14 786	13.7	18.2	1 271	464	1 871	5 217	2.97	75.0	10.2	22.8
Angelina	11.9	8.1	6.5	51.1	80 130	86 771	8.3	1.1	5 151	3 602	-546	30 668	2.73	73.3	15.4	23.4
Aransas	15.7	15.8	10.5	50.6	22 497	23 158	2.9	7.8	1 072	1 411	1 983	9 834	2.36	68.3	9.1	27.0
Archer	14.9	10.0	7.8	50.0	8 854	9 054	2.3	-2.7	288	287	-228	3 342	2.62	76.7	4.8	20.1
Armstrong	15.3	12.1	9.1	50.7	2 148	1 901	-11.5	2.8	101	107	56	647	2.63	80.4	6.3	18.4
Atascosa	11.6	8.1	5.6	50.3	38 628	44 911	16.3	6.4	2 724	1 642	1 778	15 095	3.00	78.4	14.7	18.4
Austin	14.5	10.3	7.0	50.3	23 590	28 417	20.5	2.5	1 477	1 116	364	10 615	2.67	70.8	9.3	26.7
Bailey	11.0	7.6	7.0	48.8	6 594	7 165	8.7	-3.6	503	239	-545	2 358	2.98	76.6	11.5	20.9
Bandera	18.6	15.1	8.8	50.6	17 645	20 485	16.1	2.0	693	794	494	8 405	2.40	67.3	6.2	28.9
Bastrop	13.8	8.3	5.0	49.0	57 733	74 171	28.5	5.3	3 700	2 536	2 596	25 432	2.85	73.4	11.0	22.4
Baylor	14.4	13.3	11.7	51.7	4 093	3 726	-9.0	-3.6	165	253	-30	1 798	2.01	56.3	6.4	42.3
Bee	10.3	6.4	4.8	40.1	32 359	31 861	-1.5	3.1	1 585	1 021	467	8 539	2.86	68.7	17.1	26.9
Bell	9.0	5.6	3.9	50.0	237 974	310 235	30.4	6.1	26 631	8 108	205	104 049	2.95	72.3	16.1	23.6
Bexar	10.4	6.3	4.7	50.8	1 392 931	1 714 773	23.1	8.2	111 813	50 499	78 142	604 698	2.84	67.9	16.4	26.5
Blanco	17.9	13.5	7.9	49.5	8 418	10 497	24.7	3.1	369	455	382	4 036	2.58	69.4	9.6	26.9
Borden	14.1	10.0	11.1	48.2	729	641	-12.1	1.7	25	17	7	225	2.88	84.9	8.4	14.7
Bosque	14.8	13.5	9.8	50.6	17 204	18 212	5.9	-2.4	790	1 000	-238	7 012	2.51	71.3	9.2	25.6
Bowie	12.1	8.6	6.5	49.6	89 306	92 565	3.6	0.8	5 180	4 157	-232	33 808	2.60	68.4	16.3	28.0
Brazoria	11.3	6.4	4.1	49.2	241 767	313 166	29.5	8.0	19 626	8 801	13 847	107 717	2.86	74.3	12.7	21.8
Brazos	7.7	4.6	3.5	49.4	152 415	194 851	27.8	7.3	11 113	3 816	6 850	70 239	2.61	55.8	11.8	26.9
Brewster	15.4	11.4	6.8	50.0	8 866	9 232	4.1	-0.6	495	303	-266	4 152	2.10	54.5	6.5	37.6
Briscoe	13.1	12.4	11.5	51.1	1 790	1 637	-8.5	-6.2	52	66	-92	605	2.67	72.9	12.6	24.6
Brooks	11.2	9.9	7.9	50.1	7 976	7 223	-9.4	-0.4	546	352	-230	2 439	2.89	68.2	20.3	30.5
Brown	13.0	10.8	8.1	50.4	37 674	38 106	1.1	-1.2	1 772	1 983	-214	13 405	2.68	70.9	12.0	25.3
Burleson	15.2	10.0	8.9	50.6	16 470	17 187	4.4	0.4	797	782	54	6 258	2.71	71.2	10.5	27.3
Burnet	14.7	11.9	8.8	50.9	34 147	42 750	25.2	5.2	1 978	1 799	1 891	16 588	2.57	72.3	12.6	24.0

1. No spouse present.

STATE County	Persons in group quarters, 2014	Daytime population, 2009–2013		Births, 2014		Deaths, 2014		Persons under 65 with no health insurance, 2013		Medicare, 2014			Serious crimes known to police,[2] 2013	
													Total	
		Number	Employ-ment/resi-dence ratio	Total	Rate[1]	Number	Rate[1]	Number	Percent	Eligible for Medicare	Enrolled in Medicare Advantage	Enrolled in a Medicare prescription drug plan	Number	Rate[3]
	32	33	34	35	36	37	38	39	40	41	42	43	44	45
TENNESSEE—Cont'd														
Marshall	359	28 667	0.83	351	11.2	314	10.0	4 635	17.6	5 960	1 756	2 528	558	1 801
Maury	1 010	76 484	0.85	1 080	12.6	863	10.1	11 139	15.7	16 211	4 317	7 933	2 666	3 238
Meigs	128	9 712	0.47	103	8.8	130	11.1	1 582	17.0	2 866	967	1 178	364	3 114
Monroe	500	42 005	0.82	456	10.1	494	10.9	6 399	17.6	11 247	4 389	4 118	1 646	3 629
Montgomery	3 416	157 325	0.74	3 478	18.3	1 169	6.2	23 207	14.1	20 831	4 376	6 984	5 870	3 114
Moore	104	5 176	0.60	45	7.1	44	7.0	752	15.1	1 300	227	643	92	1 451
Morgan	2 370	18 446	0.50	178	8.2	225	10.4	2 574	16.1	4 932	2 158	1 622	442	2 015
Obion	461	32 106	1.04	361	11.7	402	13.0	4 174	16.6	7 385	895	4 939	1 040	3 332
Overton	286	19 221	0.64	226	10.3	302	13.7	2 961	16.7	5 363	912	3 076	366	1 646
Perry	123	7 402	0.83	84	10.7	90	11.5	1 193	19.2	1 994	570	954	125	1 593
Pickett	74	4 477	0.72	31	6.0	47	9.2	731	19.2	1 472	233	922	35	684
Polk	244	13 810	0.54	152	9.1	203	12.1	2 284	17.0	4 015	1 051	1 931	364	2 186
Putnam	2 543	79 194	1.22	879	11.9	710	9.6	11 078	18.6	15 113	2 797	7 999	2 960	4 026
Rhea	924	34 040	1.17	362	11.1	357	10.9	4 272	16.3	7 104	1 686	3 758	698	2 154
Roane	646	48 934	0.77	470	8.9	678	12.9	5 704	13.7	13 603	4 876	4 852	1 522	2 856
Robertson	703	56 779	0.67	915	13.4	580	8.5	9 318	16.1	11 467	4 646	4 145	1 679	2 500
Rutherford	5 110	253 101	0.87	3 691	12.8	1 670	5.8	40 084	16.1	34 201	12 424	11 911	8 414	3 023
Scott	264	20 787	0.81	264	12.0	267	12.1	2 983	16.1	4 954	1 636	2 364	497	2 242
Sequatchie	188	12 405	0.63	113	7.7	164	11.2	1 906	16.1	3 705	958	1 854	442	3 040
Sevier	982	91 160	1.00	1 035	10.9	913	9.6	17 046	22.2	20 444	8 786	6 520	3 719	3 982
Shelby	18 336	1 007 755	1.18	13 734	14.6	8 019	8.5	141 723	17.4	134 779	33 487	60 097	57 931	6 126
Smith	159	16 878	0.70	199	10.5	193	10.2	2 377	14.8	3 669	1 047	1 675	358	1 874
Stewart	92	11 719	0.67	139	10.5	168	12.7	1 776	16.4	3 040	569	1 377	235	1 768
Sullivan	2 632	165 168	1.13	1 606	10.2	1 788	11.4	18 438	14.9	39 896	22 040	10 011	5 624	3 585
Sumner	1 252	140 190	0.69	1 959	11.3	1 478	8.6	19 988	13.9	29 251	12 482	10 229	2 922	1 740
Tipton	963	47 385	0.46	737	12.0	570	9.2	7 326	13.9	9 917	2 092	4 337	1 927	3 111
Trousdale	130	6 507	0.59	79	9.9	68	8.5	1 181	18.0	1 646	593	687	148	1 902
Unicoi	405	17 727	0.92	154	8.6	254	14.1	2 320	16.4	4 912	2 068	1 652	258	1 414
Union	152	15 555	0.44	246	12.9	199	10.4	2 842	17.8	4 233	2 239	1 272	610	3 185
Van Buren	94	4 611	0.56	51	9.1	35	6.2	797	18.2	1 482	283	855	104	1 836
Warren	580	39 068	0.95	450	11.3	428	10.7	6 716	20.3	8 707	2 074	4 453	1 189	2 982
Washington	4 440	131 569	1.14	1 397	11.1	1 195	9.5	15 653	15.5	26 540	11 113	8 153	4 003	3 182
Wayne	2 149	15 840	0.80	187	11.1	206	12.2	2 203	18.5	3 757	735	2 091	180	1 058
Weakley	2 247	31 644	0.78	342	9.9	344	10.0	4 254	15.9	7 004	850	4 495	710	2 043
White	382	24 108	0.81	287	10.9	313	11.9	3 519	16.7	6 372	1 469	3 301	897	3 425
Williamson	1 153	204 287	1.17	2 019	9.8	1 017	5.0	15 517	8.9	26 068	8 989	9 853	2 552	1 301
Wilson	1 340	101 765	0.72	1 399	11.2	977	7.8	13 492	13.1	21 393	7 622	8 015	2 683	2 225
TEXAS	595 855	25 628 656	1.00	386 786	14.3	178 395	6.6	5 696 712	24.8	3 548 772	321 299	544 340	969 732	3 667
Anderson	14 224	57 897	0.98	571	9.9	643	11.2	8 859	23.9	9 475	2 207	5 394	1 787	3 063
Andrews	81	14 757	0.88	336	19.2	87	5.0	3 691	24.6	1 992	339	1 161	521	3 130
Angelina	2 978	87 764	1.02	1 202	13.7	878	10.0	18 203	25.1	16 004	3 983	8 324	3 235	3 668
Aransas	455	21 499	0.76	266	10.7	341	13.7	4 801	27.2	6 897	2 459	2 768	1 116	4 623
Archer	55	7 055	0.56	71	8.1	62	7.0	1 731	24.4	1 750	216	1 056	77	1 112
Armstrong	55	1 354	0.50	28	14.3	20	10.2	420	27.7	424	59	251	39	1 982
Atascosa	377	40 429	0.71	648	13.6	402	8.4	9 900	24.5	7 713	2 961	2 811	1 288	2 732
Austin	216	26 934	0.87	346	11.9	261	9.0	5 931	25.0	5 486	1 094	2 971	520	1 805
Bailey	106	6 631	0.85	120	17.4	40	5.8	1 978	33.0	1 057	129	715	90	1 259
Bandera	320	16 416	0.50	159	7.6	194	9.3	3 875	25.1	5 199	1 105	2 033	283	1 372
Bastrop	2 407	60 550	0.56	907	11.6	634	8.1	17 227	27.1	12 450	2 788	5 926	1 711	2 275
Baylor	60	3 682	1.00	45	12.5	48	13.4	745	27.5	1 024	143	655	120	3 327
Bee	7 629	31 948	0.97	380	11.6	215	6.5	4 831	22.3	4 301	1 395	2 000	524	1 594
Bell	8 174	328 559	1.09	6 211	18.9	1 983	6.0	54 514	18.9	40 185	11 548	11 038	11 016	3 372
Bexar	41 987	1 802 164	1.06	26 856	14.5	12 444	6.7	353 005	22.3	254 044	100 970	66 177	100 964	5 564
Blanco	105	9 713	0.82	78	7.2	96	8.9	2 399	28.6	2 448	433	1 131	157	1 461
Borden	0	574	0.73	8	12.3	4	6.1	82	16.4	124	16	75	18	2 956
Bosque	317	15 519	0.63	185	10.4	217	12.2	3 724	27.4	4 472	1 358	2 103	206	1 135
Bowie	6 206	99 627	1.18	1 245	13.3	968	10.4	14 598	19.8	17 894	3 307	8 095	4 110	4 387
Brazoria	10 353	274 145	0.69	4 689	13.9	2 205	6.5	57 377	20.2	41 500	12 617	18 204	6 929	2 102
Brazos	13 862	200 207	1.03	2 634	12.6	973	4.7	37 862	21.8	19 504	3 322	8 059	6 156	3 030
Brewster	45	9 278	1.01	116	12.6	52	5.7	1 813	24.0	1 927	451	987	140	1 494
Briscoe	0	1 477	0.80	8	5.2	7	4.6	459	39.3	416	66	262	19	1 229
Brooks	65	7 702	1.21	120	16.7	82	11.4	1 469	24.9	1 599	516	839	149	2 075
Brown	1 743	38 864	1.06	417	11.1	443	11.8	6 722	22.7	8 508	1 435	5 176	1 191	3 144
Burleson	174	15 336	0.72	187	10.8	182	10.5	3 861	27.9	3 796	886	1 676	216	1 242
Burnet	1 710	40 677	0.86	467	10.4	421	9.4	9 135	27.2	10 646	2 345	5 404	963	2 254

1. Per 1,000 estimated resident population. 2. Data for serious crimes have not been adjusted for underreporting; this may affect comparability between geographic areas and over time.
3. Per 100,000 population estimated by the FBI.

STATE County	Serious crimes known to police, 2013 (cont.)[1] Rate[2] Violent	Serious crimes known to police, 2013 (cont.)[1] Rate[2] Property	Education: School enrollment and attainment, 2009–2013: Enrollment[3] Total	Education: Enrollment[3] Percent private	Education: Attainment[4] (percent) High school graduate or less	Education: Attainment[4] (percent) Bachelor's degree or more	Education: Local government expenditures,[5] 2012–2013 Total current spending (mil dol)	Education: Local government expenditures,[5] 2012–2013 Current spending per student (dollars)	Money income, 2009–2013: Per capita income[6] (dollars)	Money income, 2009–2013: Households Median income (dollars)	Money income, 2009–2013: Households Mean income (dollars)	Money income, 2009–2013: Households Percent with income of $200,000 or more	Income and poverty, 2013: Median household income (dollars)	Income and poverty, 2013: Percent below poverty level All persons	Income and poverty, 2013: Percent below poverty level Children under 18 years	Income and poverty, 2013: Percent below poverty level Children 5 to 17 years in families
	46	47	48	49	50	51	52	53	54	55	56	57	58	59	60	61
TENNESSEE Cont'd																
Marshall	374	1 426	6 854	11.2	60.8	13.1	40.6	7 580	20 739	42 291	53 781	1.3	42 363	14.6	23.2	21.7
Maury	587	2 651	18 340	16.9	52.3	17.4	93.2	7 783	22 766	45 336	56 723	2.1	46 497	13.8	21.9	20.8
Meigs	394	2 721	2 286	6.3	65.0	8.2	14.3	7 942	19 403	35 150	47 335	0.3	37 874	19.7	30.8	26.9
Monroe	415	3 215	9 164	10.3	64.2	10.5	54.1	7 535	19 643	37 595	50 122	1.4	38 061	19.7	29.7	26.7
Montgomery	474	2 640	52 354	11.7	40.6	23.5	242.8	7 928	22 380	49 617	59 872	1.6	51 059	14.9	21.4	19.8
Moore	79	1 372	1 500	7.0	56.8	14.6	8.4	8 264	23 307	46 170	60 357	1.2	50 802	13.1	21.9	19.3
Morgan	205	1 810	4 065	7.8	72.8	7.4	25.3	7 619	17 747	37 631	50 628	1.0	38 027	24.0	33.1	29.7
Obion	359	2 973	7 294	8.5	60.7	14.2	42.0	8 006	20 900	39 467	50 723	1.4	34 469	20.4	28.7	27.6
Overton	193	1 452	4 753	6.1	65.9	12.6	25.6	7 462	18 347	34 604	45 929	1.0	35 457	20.4	29.2	26.8
Perry	357	1 236	1 724	11.8	66.2	13.7	9.9	8 524	17 214	32 845	40 807	0.2	33 017	22.2	35.1	32.5
Pickett	0	684	838	0.7	62.4	13.0	5.8	7 687	21 942	35 184	50 496	1.9	32 398	19.5	30.2	26.6
Polk	138	2 047	3 597	9.6	63.9	11.1	20.8	7 832	20 274	39 074	49 751	1.3	37 375	19.7	29.1	25.7
Putnam	375	3 650	19 566	5.5	54.5	22.9	87.6	7 906	20 517	33 709	50 455	1.8	35 554	26.7	35.6	32.4
Rhea	272	1 882	7 378	12.7	62.7	12.6	38.3	7 239	18 952	36 741	48 446	1.5	38 860	19.6	28.4	26.1
Roane	285	2 570	10 601	8.7	53.5	17.3	60.1	8 411	23 936	42 223	56 562	1.8	42 037	18.1	28.0	25.3
Robertson	412	2 088	16 642	17.1	54.8	17.1	83.2	7 227	23 809	52 792	63 475	1.8	51 093	12.1	18.8	17.1
Rutherford	461	2 562	80 657	11.4	40.1	28.3	363.5	7 635	25 077	55 401	67 993	2.3	57 056	12.3	15.5	13.9
Scott	262	1 980	5 463	3.1	69.1	10.3	32.2	7 295	17 121	28 401	44 071	0.8	27 749	29.5	39.1	35.9
Sequatchie	433	2 607	3 110	8.0	61.6	13.5	16.3	7 003	20 899	36 434	51 981	1.4	46 460	18.1	30.7	29.0
Sevier	278	3 704	18 280	10.7	55.7	15.0	123.4	8 419	22 242	43 649	55 249	1.3	40 444	16.5	27.6	25.9
Shelby	1 240	4 886	263 895	19.6	41.0	29.0	1 461.3	9 480	25 549	46 250	66 828	4.0	45 067	21.6	34.7	32.3
Smith	246	1 628	4 533	10.2	66.1	11.1	24.0	7 431	21 153	42 383	54 798	1.7	43 689	16.9	24.3	22.7
Stewart	346	1 422	3 277	7.4	56.5	11.7	18.3	8 258	21 701	39 781	53 098	1.0	43 513	17.2	26.6	23.5
Sullivan	428	3 156	33 627	13.9	51.6	20.5	191.6	8 669	23 850	39 479	55 603	2.3	40 385	18.0	27.9	25.2
Sumner	223	1 517	41 717	14.2	45.1	23.7	211.4	7 430	27 795	55 509	73 367	4.0	56 077	11.0	15.7	14.1
Tipton	526	2 585	16 607	10.5	52.5	15.1	87.5	7 402	23 054	52 423	64 270	1.5	53 183	14.4	21.9	19.7
Trousdale	257	1 645	1 949	9.0	66.3	12.9	9.0	7 049	20 491	43 034	54 255	2.8	41 286	17.0	28.0	24.6
Unicoi	362	1 053	3 689	5.4	63.2	12.9	19.7	7 483	20 152	32 292	46 705	1.2	36 568	17.6	28.9	25.3
Union	292	2 892	4 133	10.5	72.6	8.2	37.4	6 315	17 426	34 399	43 713	0.8	35 255	22.1	35.6	33.2
Van Buren	177	1 660	1 091	21.7	74.1	10.4	6.8	8 633	19 450	33 547	47 837	0.8	37 393	17.7	29.0	26.8
Warren	311	2 671	9 035	12.0	66.7	12.1	50.3	7 591	19 531	34 641	48 369	1.6	36 327	20.3	29.0	25.1
Washington	348	2 834	33 112	10.4	43.3	29.3	135.6	8 072	25 355	42 075	59 475	3.0	41 542	17.7	23.5	22.2
Wayne	229	829	3 168	3.6	70.1	7.9	19.9	7 945	17 706	33 198	44 705	0.6	33 318	22.0	30.9	27.5
Weakley	222	1 822	10 891	4.6	55.5	20.1	33.5	7 396	19 547	35 273	48 420	1.4	34 809	21.0	26.0	24.3
White	206	3 219	5 330	10.6	69.2	11.0	28.8	7 020	18 205	34 474	45 641	1.0	34 320	19.7	28.5	26.7
Williamson	136	1 165	55 249	24.1	22.6	52.8	310.0	8 339	41 292	89 779	116 204	14.0	93 241	5.5	6.7	6.0
Wilson	279	1 947	28 832	19.6	44.7	26.0	147.0	7 347	27 864	60 390	73 773	3.4	59 655	10.8	15.0	13.2
TEXAS	408	3 258	7 257 378	10.9	44.1	26.7	40 962.5	8 299	26 019	51 900	72 474	4.7	51 714	17.5	25.0	23.8
Anderson	293	2 770	12 642	6.7	60.0	10.9	74.1	8 890	18 495	40 653	57 503	2.6	41 279	22.4	27.7	26.9
Andrews	613	2 517	4 215	7.0	56.6	14.2	29.0	8 021	27 429	57 825	79 133	5.4	62 781	11.4	15.3	14.5
Angelina	316	3 352	22 883	5.7	52.9	15.0	140.1	8 256	20 982	41 354	57 776	1.8	41 804	21.5	33.1	31.2
Aransas	257	4 366	4 177	9.1	45.8	21.7	31.1	9 814	26 953	42 476	63 206	3.2	41 666	20.7	37.6	34.2
Archer	101	1 011	2 181	6.1	48.8	20.0	16.2	8 731	27 800	56 452	72 020	3.7	56 805	10.1	14.5	12.2
Armstrong	203	1 778	402	4.7	34.5	24.7	4.0	10 801	26 823	61 635	69 887	0.9	52 122	11.0	15.5	15.0
Atascosa	176	2 556	12 377	7.8	61.4	14.1	79.9	8 895	20 193	47 543	61 084	2.0	46 631	17.8	28.3	27.0
Austin	253	1 552	7 120	13.0	49.9	18.6	47.7	8 534	25 884	53 265	66 651	3.4	52 042	13.6	20.4	19.3
Bailey	126	1 133	2 024	4.3	64.1	11.1	13.3	8 893	18 676	46 139	53 322	0.9	37 626	19.9	31.5	30.2
Bandera	116	1 256	4 042	10.3	43.4	21.9	25.3	9 320	25 364	49 215	60 416	2.2	50 334	16.2	27.6	24.2
Bastrop	318	1 957	17 795	9.5	51.7	16.3	129.2	8 372	23 342	51 750	64 884	2.2	50 151	18.7	27.2	25.0
Baylor	499	2 828	760	1.4	47.8	24.1	5.5	9 368	28 021	33 445	56 046	2.1	34 563	19.5	32.3	30.2
Bee	176	1 417	6 847	11.1	60.4	8.2	42.4	8 670	16 848	43 690	58 379	4.2	41 804	25.1	31.2	30.0
Bell	364	3 008	93 151	11.4	40.1	21.7	527.5	7 955	22 857	50 060	63 108	2.2	50 223	15.1	21.5	22.6
Bexar	532	5 032	515 589	13.8	42.3	26.3	2 685.3	8 334	24 253	50 112	67 186	3.6	49 655	17.4	23.9	23.0
Blanco	223	1 238	2 223	10.6	43.6	26.8	18.0	10 732	26 781	49 487	67 829	3.0	54 914	12.7	20.8	18.8
Borden	328	2 627	150	0.0	43.8	32.1	4.6	19 310	50 042	71 607	136 472	8.0	60 443	10.5	15.6	15.4
Bosque	39	1 096	4 006	5.5	52.2	15.4	24.1	10 496	23 992	44 742	60 537	2.7	42 864	17.0	27.2	25.0
Bowie	490	3 897	23 039	7.2	48.0	19.0	153.5	8 527	22 911	42 346	59 571	2.8	41 657	21.4	31.3	31.3
Brazoria	191	1 911	87 551	10.1	40.1	27.5	481.6	7 588	29 081	67 603	83 852	5.3	66 337	11.8	15.3	14.8
Brazos	387	2 643	85 864	5.3	35.9	38.8	220.7	8 235	21 720	38 310	58 789	3.7	39 732	27.6	27.1	26.5
Brewster	149	1 345	2 359	10.1	36.0	36.1	14.8	11 723	27 796	40 477	63 244	2.9	39 106	14.9	23.5	23.4
Briscoe	65	1 164	312	6.1	51.1	17.8	4.4	10 870	20 697	36 250	50 552	1.3	40 235	17.1	20.4	27.3
Brooks	209	1 866	1 555	2.3	67.6	10.8	17.0	11 019	14 345	21 865	38 628	0.4	27 644	31.9	46.7	46.8
Brown	267	2 877	9 376	13.0	54.9	16.0	58.2	8 765	21 236	39 776	55 684	2.3	38 636	18.6	29.3	26.8
Burleson	161	1 081	3 938	10.4	60.3	11.6	25.4	8 965	21 529	45 651	56 682	1.6	45 732	17.5	28.8	26.0
Burnet	215	2 039	9 329	10.0	47.4	21.9	64.1	8 831	24 998	48 115	62 463	2.9	49 286	14.9	25.9	23.6

1. Data for serious crimes have not been adjusted for underreporting; this may affect comparability between geographic areas and over time. 2. Per 100,000 population estimated by the FBI.
3. All persons 3 years old and over enrolled in nursery school through college. 4. Persons 25 years old and over. 5. Elementary and secondary education expenditures.
6. Based on population estimated by the American Community Survey, 2009–2013.

STATE County	Personal income, 2013										Earnings, 2013		
			Per capita[1]			Supplements to wages and salaries; employer contributions (mil dol)						Contributions for government social insurance (mil dol)	
	Total (mil dol)	Percent change, 2012–2013	Dollars	Rank	Wages and salaries (mil dol)	Pension and insurance	Government social insurance	Proprietors' income (mil dol)	Dividends, interest, and rent (mil dol)	Personal transfer receipts (mil dol)	Total (mil dol)	From employee and self-employed	From employer
	62	63	64	65	66	67	68	69	70	71	72	73	74
TENNESSEE—Cont'd													
Marshall	866	2.6	27 825	2 907	279	64	21	72	135	240	436	29	21
Maury	2 803	4.5	33 464	2 179	1 290	250	97	278	386	686	1 914	115	97
Meigs	386	2.5	33 167	2 232	73	20	5	60	49	116	158	11	5
Monroe	1 279	1.8	28 259	2 871	475	100	37	94	174	431	706	49	37
Montgomery	7 677	0.0	41 695	973	1 755	362	130	598	1 302	1 185	2 845	159	130
Moore	244	0.8	38 775	1 322	74	24	5	3	32	54	107	7	5
Morgan	585	1.0	26 690	2 994	112	32	8	68	61	194	220	16	8
Obion	1 071	6.8	34 404	2 010	362	73	27	152	182	315	613	36	27
Overton	604	1.5	27 379	2 949	157	40	12	53	81	206	262	19	12
Perry	234	1.5	29 791	2 717	57	15	5	23	35	90	99	7	5
Pickett	151	2.7	29 663	2 732	29	8	2	11	27	59	50	4	2
Polk	478	-0.3	28 630	2 834	75	21	6	16	59	154	118	10	6
Putnam	2 579	2.7	35 078	1 887	1 204	274	88	254	510	639	1 820	107	88
Rhea	918	1.5	28 221	2 875	437	102	35	48	115	313	622	40	35
Roane	1 950	0.5	36 768	1 629	995	155	68	63	283	574	1 281	85	68
Robertson	2 547	6.6	37 800	1 463	784	174	59	247	264	497	1 264	73	59
Rutherford	9 868	2.9	35 113	1 881	4 980	903	366	1 198	1 138	1 526	7 448	413	366
Scott	557	2.7	25 322	3 045	175	46	14	38	60	230	273	20	14
Sequatchie	510	3.0	34 766	1 938	83	23	6	28	61	148	140	11	6
Sevier	3 245	2.1	34 684	1 954	1 241	213	97	336	476	748	1 888	120	97
Shelby	40 595	0.7	43 210	827	25 695	3 978	1 771	5 048	5 806	7 220	36 492	2 042	1 771
Smith	656	2.2	34 371	2 017	193	42	15	71	101	160	321	20	15
Stewart	476	0.5	35 660	1 805	128	34	10	26	80	134	198	13	10
Sullivan	5 806	0.5	37 074	1 570	3 158	592	223	394	930	1 554	4 367	276	223
Sumner	6 738	2.1	39 894	1 183	1 887	341	141	402	919	1 209	2 771	175	141
Tipton	2 312	0.7	37 535	1 500	392	88	29	150	234	463	659	42	29
Trousdale	377	3.6	48 149	470	48	13	4	177	28	75	242	12	4
Unicoi	596	0.2	32 987	2 254	235	52	19	26	82	222	332	23	19
Union	532	0.9	27 844	2 906	77	21	6	19	64	173	123	12	6
Van Buren	169	1.8	30 294	2 643	28	8	2	13	22	63	52	4	2
Warren	1 180	3.5	29 532	2 749	495	96	38	74	191	380	703	46	38
Washington	4 694	0.7	37 387	1 522	2 323	478	168	299	748	1 067	3 269	196	168
Wayne	435	3.4	25 695	3 031	135	38	10	19	59	166	202	14	10
Weakley	1 170	5.3	33 975	2 088	388	105	28	161	176	337	681	37	28
White	726	1.2	27 653	2 920	227	50	18	64	100	258	359	26	18
Williamson	13 812	3.2	69 439	51	6 486	805	420	2 159	2 043	896	9 871	540	420
Wilson	5 035	2.7	41 288	1 018	1 561	255	113	413	650	839	2 341	144	113
TEXAS	1 160 079	2.9	43 862	X	591 469	83 445	40 288	173 546	190 441	168 168	888 748	44 382	40 288
Anderson	1 742	1.5	30 065	2 679	791	135	54	200	275	440	1 180	63	54
Andrews	840	6.7	49 997	369	446	59	29	149	88	93	682	33	29
Angelina	3 158	-1.2	36 112	1 728	1 426	238	98	317	579	795	2 080	114	98
Aransas	1 147	2.7	47 075	552	239	38	17	77	345	267	371	25	17
Archer	465	1.5	53 578	248	82	15	5	90	69	68	192	9	5
Armstrong	91	5.7	46 513	586	13	3	1	15	19	18	32	1	1
Atascosa	1 698	2.6	36 060	1 737	588	88	40	201	251	351	917	50	40
Austin	1 256	1.6	43 550	795	480	69	34	140	282	218	723	39	34
Bailey	269	2.4	37 877	1 450	90	18	6	60	55	52	174	6	6
Bandera	871	2.0	42 262	912	106	20	7	68	231	179	200	13	7
Bastrop	2 392	3.5	31 552	2 472	567	107	39	173	417	495	887	52	39
Baylor	146	3.0	40 331	1 133	40	8	3	24	27	44	75	4	3
Bee	1 021	5.4	31 135	2 527	407	73	26	123	157	224	629	31	26
Bell	12 844	-0.3	39 298	1 253	7 290	1 717	623	767	2 528	2 250	10 396	466	623
Bexar	70 896	2.7	39 005	1 300	38 465	6 245	2 772	8 951	13 410	12 431	56 433	2 823	2 772
Blanco	580	4.3	54 051	233	114	20	8	155	135	80	296	13	8
Borden	39	-0.5	61 289	91	7	2	0	6	13	4	14	0	0
Bosque	658	2.5	36 838	1 619	127	27	8	53	150	172	215	14	8
Bowie	3 367	-1.2	36 016	1 744	1 611	314	118	232	725	809	2 274	124	118
Brazoria	13 788	2.1	41 751	964	4 933	781	336	822	1 767	1 852	6 873	364	336
Brazos	6 550	3.0	32 241	2 377	3 558	697	223	434	1 455	906	4 912	227	223
Brewster	377	2.3	40 558	1 104	157	31	10	30	97	69	228	12	10
Briscoe	67	22.3	43 606	789	12	2	1	21	12	14	36	1	1
Brooks	239	0.4	33 003	2 252	108	23	8	12	31	95	151	9	8
Brown	1 274	2.6	33 760	2 132	526	95	38	108	216	387	766	45	38
Burleson	693	1.9	40 348	1 128	210	30	14	75	113	151	329	19	14
Burnet	2 075	2.5	47 354	519	508	81	34	286	682	380	910	50	34

1. Based on the resident population estimated as of July 1 of the year shown.

STATE County	Earnings, 2013 (cont.) — Percent by selected industries: Farm	Mining	Construction	Manu-facturing	Infor-mation: professional, scientific, technical services	Retail trade	Finance, insur-ance, real estate and leasing	Health care and social assistance	Govern-ment	Social Security beneficiaries, December 2013: Number	Rate[1]	Supple-mental Security Income recipients, December 2013	Housing units, 2014: Total	Percent change, 2010–2014
	75	76	77	78	79	80	81	82	83	84	85	86	87	88
TENNESSEE—Cont'd														
Marshall	-1.6	D	7.7	30.7	3.0	8.7	4.3	4.5	21.9	6 800	219	714	13 276	1.2
Maury	0.0	D	6.9	17.8	4.6	7.1	8.9	11.2	20.5	17 950	215	1 777	35 945	2.0
Meigs	-2.4	D	13.1	27.4	D	4.6	D	3.7	18.2	3 270	281	482	5 664	0.6
Monroe	-0.4	0.0	3.6	38.9	2.9	8.3	2.8	8.0	14.8	12 660	280	1 770	20 845	0.3
Montgomery	1.0	D	10.0	9.9	6.4	9.6	6.3	11.4	22.1	24 090	130	3 258	76 987	9.8
Moore	-3.8	D	4.6	D	D	D	1.5	D	34.1	1 470	233	85	2 967	1.8
Morgan	-1.5	D	7.9	7.6	D	5.5	D	D	32.5	5 770	266	866	8 889	-0.3
Obion	12.2	D	5.9	15.1	D	10.9	5.5	8.8	15.1	8 440	271	1 038	14 582	-0.5
Overton	-1.4	1.5	9.2	17.5	2.6	8.4	5.7	13.7	23.0	6 205	282	812	10 255	-0.4
Perry	-2.1	1.8	5.3	19.0	D	7.3	D	D	24.1	2 255	287	252	4 574	-0.5
Pickett	-2.6	D	D	5.0	D	12.1	6.0	14.4	27.6	1 650	325	211	3 455	-0.2
Polk	1.0	D	5.2	9.5	D	9.4	3.8	D	36.9	4 570	274	578	8 370	4.7
Putnam	-0.4	0.2	5.9	14.2	5.4	9.1	6.4	10.8	27.8	17 065	232	1 928	32 824	2.9
Rhea	-0.2	0.3	4.0	26.3	1.9	5.2	2.3	D	40.7	8 095	249	1 163	14 431	0.5
Roane	-0.4	D	3.1	5.0	45.3	6.1	1.5	6.8	16.7	15 220	287	1 783	25 573	-0.6
Robertson	4.9	D	8.8	27.5	2.4	7.2	3.8	5.3	16.5	13 045	194	1 318	26 450	1.4
Rutherford	0.0	D	6.2	25.1	5.7	6.5	6.6	11.9	15.6	38 450	137	3 804	109 535	6.4
Scott	-1.0	3.8	7.6	22.1	2.3	9.0	3.1	D	26.6	5 695	259	1 494	9 864	-0.5
Sequatchie	0.8	4.2	5.0	7.1	D	10.0	8.6	D	32.6	4 145	283	590	6 386	0.3
Sevier	-0.2	D	6.6	3.8	3.3	12.7	9.6	5.4	16.0	23 005	246	1 998	56 271	0.6
Shelby	0.1	0.0	4.9	9.3	6.0	6.2	8.8	12.4	14.5	148 590	158	33 650	403 365	1.3
Smith	0.6	D	D	22.3	1.8	6.1	4.3	D	17.6	4 310	226	548	8 574	0.5
Stewart	-0.1	0.0	13.1	10.9	D	4.3	5.7	5.0	50.0	3 555	266	441	6 758	-0.3
Sullivan	-0.2	D	7.9	27.1	5.3	7.1	4.2	18.1	10.5	44 715	285	4 831	74 115	0.5
Sumner	0.1	D	10.8	15.1	7.3	7.5	5.6	12.6	15.6	32 455	192	2 629	68 062	3.2
Tipton	5.6	D	10.7	16.7	D	8.5	3.1	D	23.5	11 460	186	1 693	23 437	1.0
Trousdale	-0.3	0.1	D	4.7	D	10.9	13.0	15.9	11.0	1 895	243	272	3 409	1.2
Unicoi	0.0	D	6.4	35.6	D	4.5	1.6	5.9	18.7	5 215	288	626	8 845	0.2
Union	-3.4	D	D	16.9	D	9.3	D	4.6	34.9	4 910	257	897	9 085	1.4
Van Buren	-4.7	D	10.0	19.9	D	D	D	D	38.1	1 740	313	236	2 650	-0.5
Warren	1.2	0.0	5.6	30.9	3.3	7.4	3.5	11.4	15.5	9 945	249	1 539	17 826	0.0
Washington	0.0	0.1	4.4	8.8	6.5	8.1	6.3	22.2	23.4	29 085	232	3 093	58 889	2.9
Wayne	0.9	D	2.2	9.9	D	5.8	4.8	12.2	38.9	4 360	257	499	7 247	-0.5
Weakley	10.9	1.5	2.4	6.4	D	5.5	12.6	D	28.2	7 825	227	964	15 531	0.2
White	-1.6	D	5.7	23.0	D	9.6	3.1	11.8	16.8	7 270	277	941	11 592	0.7
Williamson	0.0	D	5.7	1.5	17.8	6.6	14.9	19.0	6.4	26 690	134	1 074	73 793	7.7
Wilson	-0.6	D	D	12.1	D	13.8	5.9	9.3	12.5	23 315	191	1 754	48 766	7.0
TEXAS	0.5	9.0	7.4	9.3	11.3	5.8	7.9	8.9	14.1	3 756 420	142	666 258	10 426 080	4.5
Anderson	0.5	6.7	4.5	2.5	5.3	6.8	5.1	12.8	24.5	10 200	176	1 376	20 137	0.1
Andrews	2.1	37.1	12.1	3.4	D	3.5	5.6	D	11.0	2 130	127	278	6 041	3.9
Angelina	-0.1	2.4	5.5	13.7	5.3	8.0	4.1	19.6	16.7	17 865	204	3 187	36 202	1.7
Aransas	-0.2	D	10.0	1.0	7.4	13.3	6.6	D	14.5	7 455	308	758	15 677	2.1
Archer	2.9	39.9	3.8	2.8	D	4.0	D	1.3	14.7	1 860	213	148	4 130	0.6
Armstrong	36.6	0.0	6.3	0.0	4.8	1.3	D	D	19.4	460	235	22	901	-0.3
Atascosa	0.4	17.3	18.9	2.7	3.2	7.7	7.1	D	13.4	8 510	181	1 658	17 843	1.2
Austin	0.5	3.6	12.1	17.6	9.8	11.1	5.3	3.5	12.3	5 795	201	526	13 002	0.6
Bailey	31.2	0.0	2.8	4.4	4.6	3.8	3.0	2.3	16.0	1 175	166	165	2 783	0.0
Bandera	-0.4	D	14.9	1.0	8.6	6.7	6.8	D	19.5	5 585	271	360	11 599	0.3
Bastrop	0.0	3.8	11.7	6.9	4.5	11.1	4.2	7.0	25.6	13 350	175	1 747	29 592	0.9
Baylor	18.6	D	5.7	0.9	D	5.3	D	20.9	15.0	1 090	302	126	2 653	-0.5
Bee	2.5	20.4	6.2	2.3	6.2	10.8	2.7	D	26.6	4 700	143	1 059	10 656	0.1
Bell	0.1	D	5.6	3.6	4.4	4.9	2.6	11.7	53.5	44 415	136	7 415	133 786	6.6
Bexar	0.0	2.8	6.9	4.5	10.4	6.7	11.2	10.8	22.7	273 000	150	56 062	678 122	2.3
Blanco	1.8	2.5	21.7	3.6	D	4.7	8.4	D	10.0	2 495	235	144	5 678	2.7
Borden	38.2	D	1.0	D	D	D	0.0	D	31.9	140	219	6	385	0.0
Bosque	3.2	1.2	13.6	12.3	4.1	6.6	5.4	D	26.5	4 740	265	407	9 633	0.1
Bowie	0.2	0.6	4.1	3.9	4.0	8.6	7.7	19.9	28.9	19 295	206	4 194	39 137	1.7
Brazoria	0.3	3.4	16.2	23.4	5.7	6.6	4.0	6.3	14.2	44 595	135	5 361	126 268	6.7
Brazos	0.1	4.0	5.8	5.7	8.2	7.4	4.5	10.3	37.5	20 220	99	3 467	83 500	7.5
Brewster	1.2	1.3	5.3	0.9	9.7	5.8	5.6	D	36.6	1 945	209	208	5 429	0.9
Briscoe	55.4	0.3	D	D	1.4	4.0	D	D	13.7	425	275	43	953	0.0
Brooks	-1.5	17.8	3.9	0.0	D	6.3	D	6.0	42.0	1 740	241	585	3 232	-0.2
Brown	0.2	2.3	6.2	22.4	2.9	9.8	4.5	D	18.5	9 190	242	1 282	18 468	1.0
Burleson	3.1	26.0	9.3	5.0	D	11.3	3.5	D	11.7	4 015	234	520	8 904	0.8
Burnet	-0.2	2.0	15.2	8.2	7.1	9.6	8.3	9.8	14.3	11 020	248	722	21 495	3.0

1. Per 1,000 resident population estimated as of July 1 of the year shown.

STATE County	Housing units, 2009–2013: Occupied units: Total	Owner-occupied: Percent	Owner-occupied: Median value[1]	Median owner cost as a percent of income: With a mortgage	Median owner cost as a percent of income: Without a mortgage[2]	Renter-occupied: Median rent[3]	Renter-occupied: Median rent as a percent of income[2]	Substandard units[4] (percent)	Civilian labor force, 2014: Total	Percent change, 2013–2014	Unemployment: Total	Unemployment: Rate[5]	Civilian employment,[6] 2009–2013: Total	Percent: Management, business, science and arts	Percent: Construction, production, and maintenance occupations
	89	90	91	92	93	94	95	96	97	98	99	100	101	102	103
TENNESSEE—Cont'd															
Marshall	11 578	74.7	105 900	21.7	11.9	653	29.3	2.3	14 360	-0.2	923	6.4	13 188	25.6	35.1
Maury	32 144	70.3	136 300	23.3	11.3	657	30.9	4.8	40 655	-1.0	2 495	6.1	36 927	31.6	25.0
Meigs	4 776	80.1	101 800	24.3	10.0	630	24.1	2.3	4 852	-3.8	418	8.6	3 993	20.1	49.3
Monroe	17 523	73.6	115 300	23.0	11.1	601	31.2	2.4	18 913	-2.1	1 454	7.7	16 568	22.6	36.8
Montgomery	64 026	61.2	141 800	22.6	10.3	836	28.6	2.9	76 102	-2.1	5 120	6.7	70 015	30.9	24.6
Moore	2 416	83.7	135 200	21.1	10.9	672	22.7	2.9	3 289	-1.5	169	5.1	3 033	27.9	33.6
Morgan	7 455	80.6	90 700	21.6	12.3	626	26.2	0.8	7 874	-2.6	692	8.8	7 270	24.7	32.0
Obion	12 462	68.4	89 100	21.0	11.7	575	30.1	3.4	12 929	-5.7	1 229	9.5	12 391	25.5	33.3
Overton	8 815	79.9	91 900	22.0	11.9	533	27.4	3.6	9 089	-4.6	722	7.9	8 122	25.6	36.6
Perry	3 187	74.6	86 800	25.1	10.0	526	29.7	2.0	3 029	-3.2	251	8.3	2 788	28.9	31.6
Pickett	2 388	80.2	96 300	21.9	10.0	469	29.1	3.0	2 281	-2.2	201	8.8	2 238	37.5	30.7
Polk	6 740	79.4	109 300	23.7	11.2	615	28.4	2.2	7 286	-3.4	584	8.0	6 403	23.1	35.2
Putnam	28 980	63.1	135 100	23.3	11.3	599	37.6	2.9	31 832	-2.3	2 183	6.9	29 428	33.3	22.6
Rhea	12 096	70.3	104 400	24.0	10.7	565	30.5	1.9	13 155	-1.9	1 117	8.5	12 174	23.7	39.5
Roane	22 117	74.4	120 300	21.8	11.2	662	29.3	1.7	22 640	-2.5	1 686	7.4	21 494	29.6	27.7
Robertson	24 136	76.7	153 100	23.8	11.8	775	26.3	2.4	33 390	-1.0	1 900	5.7	30 751	31.0	30.2
Rutherford	96 731	67.6	159 100	22.4	10.0	863	30.3	1.3	146 720	-0.6	7 736	5.3	132 056	34.4	22.9
Scott	8 206	77.5	81 500	24.1	13.5	515	35.2	6.2	8 198	-4.8	964	11.8	7 475	24.7	34.8
Sequatchie	5 616	73.7	119 300	21.8	10.0	605	29.7	2.8	5 711	-3.6	425	7.4	5 459	28.4	32.8
Sevier	36 815	66.8	159 400	23.2	10.0	715	28.3	3.3	48 433	-1.6	3 474	7.2	44 114	23.8	19.8
Shelby	343 517	59.2	132 700	24.3	12.7	842	34.4	2.8	427 588	-3.1	33 582	7.9	415 223	34.8	21.1
Smith	7 263	73.6	113 800	22.1	10.0	551	34.1	1.4	8 424	-1.3	530	6.3	7 830	24.6	35.2
Stewart	5 292	78.7	118 900	21.8	11.4	612	32.3	1.6	5 217	-2.6	481	9.2	4 774	31.5	30.3
Sullivan	66 239	74.1	121 700	21.4	10.4	605	30.3	1.8	69 466	-3.3	4 647	6.7	65 652	30.6	24.5
Sumner	60 835	72.9	176 600	23.6	10.5	840	28.9	1.5	85 191	-0.7	4 494	5.3	77 587	35.0	21.4
Tipton	21 574	74.0	139 100	22.1	10.9	752	29.8	0.4	27 158	-3.2	2 264	8.3	26 217	31.0	29.7
Trousdale	2 899	75.4	115 500	25.3	11.1	605	27.3	1.7	3 617	-1.3	256	7.1	3 330	26.7	27.4
Unicoi	7 601	75.1	115 900	23.0	10.9	568	29.8	3.2	7 125	-4.0	642	9.0	6 908	27.8	32.7
Union	7 406	81.7	95 800	24.7	10.0	516	31.0	3.2	7 205	-2.8	552	7.7	6 765	22.7	38.0
Van Buren	2 097	85.4	77 400	21.3	11.5	484	34.6	2.4	2 098	-4.7	202	9.6	2 246	26.0	34.0
Warren	15 366	69.9	92 400	22.2	11.0	554	26.7	1.2	17 153	-2.7	1 203	7.0	15 799	24.4	35.1
Washington	51 771	66.1	145 300	22.4	10.0	662	30.6	0.5	57 121	-3.2	3 630	6.4	56 237	36.9	19.0
Wayne	6 093	82.6	74 700	22.6	11.1	484	25.8	1.4	6 438	-1.9	566	8.8	5 846	25.1	34.2
Weakley	13 797	65.6	88 400	19.5	12.1	566	29.3	2.8	15 844	-4.5	1 364	8.6	14 281	31.5	28.4
White	9 729	74.2	98 000	23.4	11.0	584	31.8	1.1	11 419	-4.3	858	7.5	10 006	24.1	39.1
Williamson	66 364	81.3	334 900	22.3	10.0	1 078	29.3	1.6	101 242	-0.4	4 604	4.5	91 041	54.0	9.7
Wilson	42 800	79.2	190 100	22.9	10.0	864	32.5	4.8	61 274	-0.7	3 249	5.3	55 107	35.1	20.7
TEXAS	8 886 471	63.3	128 900	22.5	12.0	851	29.6	5.5	13 111 548	1.6	663 997	5.1	11 569 041	34.6	22.8
Anderson	16 378	70.4	82 000	21.4	13.0	715	31.3	7.0	21 800	-1.5	1 044	4.8	19 921	24.2	26.8
Andrews	5 217	78.1	88 600	18.9	10.3	769	23.9	4.6	9 587	4.1	281	2.9	7 048	25.0	40.3
Angelina	30 668	66.7	84 800	20.8	11.9	735	29.6	4.4	38 124	0.1	1 986	5.2	35 765	27.3	28.3
Aransas	9 834	73.3	130 900	26.4	14.1	814	31.6	2.2	10 219	1.2	559	5.5	9 106	29.9	26.1
Archer	3 342	80.6	100 300	18.9	11.2	642	27.4	2.5	4 232	-0.3	192	4.5	4 164	33.6	31.3
Armstrong	647	78.4	94 100	17.9	10.0	768	21.3	9.4	1 017	0.7	33	3.2	848	41.3	25.1
Atascosa	15 095	74.3	82 900	20.5	12.1	720	24.7	3.7	20 630	1.5	1 003	4.9	18 453	26.9	34.0
Austin	10 615	76.1	150 000	24.0	12.0	811	24.9	13.2	14 467	2.0	677	4.7	12 939	31.9	31.2
Bailey	2 358	65.2	56 500	21.6	10.0	757	22.2	1.7	3 028	-1.0	155	5.1	3 252	29.1	30.5
Bandera	8 405	80.3	143 600	22.0	12.7	796	29.7	4.8	9 246	1.6	435	4.7	8 520	39.1	22.4
Bastrop	25 432	78.2	117 700	23.6	12.3	871	30.6	2.7	36 886	2.4	1 768	4.8	32 720	30.6	27.2
Baylor	1 798	73.0	72 800	22.1	14.9	446	22.7	6.8	1 651	-1.6	71	4.3	1 458	32.3	33.1
Bee	8 539	65.4	73 000	19.3	13.3	741	25.6	2.8	10 958	-3.5	625	5.7	10 161	19.9	30.3
Bell	104 049	56.7	122 600	22.2	11.2	860	28.8	5.0	135 833	0.0	7 893	5.8	120 538	31.7	21.3
Bexar	604 698	59.7	123 700	22.3	11.5	839	29.6	5.8	872 682	1.7	40 565	4.6	782 973	34.3	19.3
Blanco	4 036	79.2	162 500	22.1	13.1	749	28.2	0.4	5 684	2.2	208	3.7	4 784	33.1	26.1
Borden	225	66.7	100 000	10.8	10.0	775	22.5	4.1	427	2.2	13	3.0	283	55.8	19.8
Bosque	7 012	76.9	90 800	21.4	12.0	608	24.2	2.8	8 168	0.7	424	5.2	7 176	30.3	28.2
Bowie	33 808	66.8	95 100	20.4	11.5	697	29.9	4.5	39 921	-1.9	2 509	6.3	37 470	29.2	25.3
Brazoria	107 717	73.9	148 000	21.2	10.7	865	27.0	4.5	168 400	2.1	8 480	5.0	147 349	40.4	23.1
Brazos	70 239	46.0	151 400	21.8	11.5	853	44.0	5.7	104 564	1.3	4 088	3.9	93 151	39.4	18.2
Brewster	4 152	60.7	111 000	19.4	10.0	606	22.5	2.5	4 141	-0.7	193	4.7	4 564	39.9	17.9
Briscoe	605	78.8	51 600	19.0	10.0	543	28.7	6.1	653	3.5	28	4.3	705	34.9	38.7
Brooks	2 439	69.3	47 300	17.3	13.8	415	30.9	1.8	2 702	-2.3	205	7.6	2 327	20.5	22.5
Brown	13 405	71.3	87 600	21.5	12.4	616	30.7	4.7	16 020	0.2	819	5.1	15 112	28.2	26.6
Burleson	6 258	79.1	87 800	19.6	10.0	673	28.1	3.6	7 790	0.8	365	4.7	7 057	27.2	29.4
Burnet	16 588	73.2	152 600	24.3	13.3	806	29.1	5.5	21 598	3.5	914	4.2	18 497	27.1	25.8

1. Specified owner-occupied units. 2. A value of 10.0 represents 10 percent or less; a value of 50.0 represents 50 percent or more. 3. Specified renter-occupied units.
4. Overcrowded or lacking complete plumbing facilities. 5. Percent of civilian labor force. 6. Persons 16 years old and over.

STATE County	Private nonfarm establishments, employment and payroll, 2013									Agriculture, 2012			
		Employment						Annual payroll		Farms			
											Percent with:		
	Number of establish-ments	Total	Health care and social assistance	Manufac-turing	Retail trade	Finance and insurance	Professional, scientific, and technical services	Total (mil dol)	Average per employee (dollars)	Number	Fewer than 50 acres	500 acres or more	Farm operators whose principal occu-pation is farming (percent)
	104	105	106	107	108	109	110	111	112	113	114	115	116
TENNESSEE—Cont'd													
Marshall	477	6 872	696	2 618	1 047	194	D	240	34 995	1 025	34.4	5.4	50.4
Maury	1 665	24 671	5 577	D	4 053	1 689	562	958	38 845	1 513	39.4	6.3	40.0
Meigs	110	1 441	100	818	222	D	D	49	34 242	317	28.7	5.4	39.1
Monroe	702	10 694	1 299	4 522	1 574	363	193	347	32 404	872	42.0	4.0	48.2
Montgomery	2 662	40 738	7 372	5 727	8 161	1 318	1 763	1 292	31 710	783	38.6	7.8	34.4
Moore	64	D	157	D	74	24	D	D	D	358	32.1	7.8	45.3
Morgan	159	1 649	426	350	242	D	D	54	32 923	413	32.9	4.4	48.9
Obion	642	9 456	1 253	2 705	1 705	409	114	278	29 351	568	32.6	16.5	57.0
Overton	286	3 534	764	818	505	D	87	110	30 996	922	39.6	4.1	32.9
Perry	118	1 525	423	618	191	51	D	46	29 867	246	19.5	6.1	40.2
Pickett	82	602	139	76	94	D	8	18	29 429	316	34.2	3.5	30.4
Polk	210	1 456	D	D	309	63	9	41	27 883	255	45.5	6.7	58.0
Putnam	1 734	27 314	5 647	4 035	4 771	1 028	552	862	31 575	898	46.1	3.1	33.9
Rhea	495	8 052	1 029	3 254	1 182	209	77	243	30 159	411	40.1	5.6	44.8
Roane	717	8 315	1 967	1 051	1 687	220	556	227	27 275	519	45.9	1.2	34.9
Robertson	1 060	16 984	1 887	5 846	2 266	386	207	592	34 855	1 180	46.6	6.6	45.3
Rutherford	4 670	96 226	11 811	14 207	13 023	3 731	2 697	3 868	40 195	1 327	46.5	4.6	41.8
Scott	317	3 462	785	897	645	139	35	101	29 278	302	30.8	3.0	43.4
Sequatchie	179	1 850	469	141	475	D	49	47	25 672	188	39.4	8.5	38.8
Sevier	2 546	34 813	2 182	1 176	7 626	934	712	872	25 043	603	40.1	1.3	41.3
Shelby	19 417	427 802	68 779	25 053	48 707	16 855	15 612	20 323	47 505	411	53.3	7.8	42.1
Smith	264	3 690	519	1 020	602	115	D	129	34 906	850	24.4	4.4	45.1
Stewart	147	1 354	199	D	271	57	D	40	29 679	350	28.0	7.1	38.6
Sullivan	3 298	65 497	12 815	D	8 266	1 928	1 932	2 740	41 841	1 074	58.0	1.8	34.8
Sumner	2 935	39 769	5 443	6 490	5 781	1 522	2 022	1 463	36 786	1 355	48.6	4.1	40.7
Tipton	694	8 470	1 433	1 645	1 627	275	119	265	31 268	520	44.6	10.6	42.9
Trousdale	119	1 056	232	D	215	61	D	27	25 589	290	32.8	4.5	37.6
Unicoi	248	4 053	779	1 618	490	81	17	148	36 477	93	60.2	0.0	31.2
Union	191	1 747	D	612	363	48	D	46	26 293	408	38.0	1.5	42.4
Van Buren	40	494	D	D	D	19	D	14	27 451	245	42.0	5.7	55.1
Warren	712	9 911	1 475	3 260	1 588	321	D	319	32 214	1 122	41.5	6.3	50.4
Washington	2 783	50 828	14 148	4 347	8 537	2 552	2 850	1 792	35 254	1 312	55.6	2.1	49.0
Wayne	199	2 440	417	642	308	171	D	70	28 871	664	19.4	7.7	35.2
Weakley	576	7 248	1 655	1 356	1 129	225	111	189	26 134	861	33.7	12.8	45.5
White	366	5 128	796	1 950	800	123	34	169	32 933	927	38.9	5.0	38.9
Williamson	6 227	100 666	11 620	2 112	13 291	11 669	8 304	5 853	58 138	1 160	46.5	3.5	43.6
Wilson	2 399	33 048	3 869	2 866	5 598	1 098	944	1 204	36 440	1 473	37.4	3.7	41.8
TEXAS	547 190	9 663 567	1 360 812	789 812	1 206 760	491 299	647 105	468 417	48 472	248 809	37.7	15.8	42.1
Anderson	916	11 848	2 193	D	1 964	332	226	431	36 412	2 001	38.3	6.5	39.4
Andrews	408	5 388	D	D	466	113	142	279	51 828	169	37.3	39.1	30.8
Angelina	1 869	30 445	7 812	4 871	4 758	863	1 026	1 070	35 139	975	47.5	3.3	39.8
Aransas	507	4 091	510	30	1 005	160	120	110	26 911	100	49.0	8.0	34.0
Archer	197	1 642	254	D	119	22	D	61	37 371	531	17.1	36.2	47.1
Armstrong	34	223	D	NA	D	D	D	6	27 704	281	5.7	55.5	45.9
Atascosa	713	10 392	1 264	195	1 855	D	212	501	48 203	1 987	29.8	15.0	37.4
Austin	604	8 114	694	1 918	999	268	196	307	37 784	2 098	38.5	7.2	36.1
Bailey	145	1 530	262	D	243	D	34	52	33 984	494	9.5	39.3	46.6
Bandera	365	2 942	375	D	305	D	107	76	25 906	1 002	36.3	17.9	45.7
Bastrop	1 135	12 107	1 741	1 008	2 724	349	440	376	31 085	2 083	40.2	6.7	49.0
Baylor	112	909	D	D	105	40	25	20	21 787	277	7.6	38.3	58.1
Bee	474	5 505	1 251	D	1 104	D	129	192	34 876	974	31.6	16.9	45.2
Bell	4 876	85 507	22 350	5 686	13 428	3 021	3 687	3 210	37 541	2 533	50.8	6.3	34.2
Bexar	33 910	676 165	107 221	31 779	85 380	59 522	41 340	28 460	42 090	2 457	56.8	4.8	41.4
Blanco	260	1 793	161	D	220	80	D	70	39 187	792	29.8	24.6	41.7
Borden	6	D	NA	NA	NA	NA	D	D	D	114	7.0	58.8	50.9
Bosque	298	2 525	583	508	424	D	54	82	32 356	1 265	26.1	17.9	41.6
Bowie	2 192	31 596	6 921	1 912	6 331	1 322	784	1 023	32 383	1 619	44.4	6.9	40.4
Brazoria	5 122	80 192	8 076	12 880	13 961	2 140	2 675	3 654	45 561	3 091	61.8	8.6	36.4
Brazos	3 991	57 295	8 090	4 698	10 291	1 632	2 768	1 895	33 067	1 412	40.0	7.5	34.7
Brewster	270	2 436	525	33	383	D	50	61	25 140	202	17.3	52.5	51.0
Briscoe	39	129	D	D	D	22	D	4	31 953	282	5.0	44.7	46.5
Brooks	131	1 571	D	NA	317	D	D	43	27 311	374	19.5	21.7	43.3
Brown	925	12 964	3 766	2 295	1 910	415	218	379	29 229	1 918	33.7	13.5	36.5
Burleson	328	3 199	298	404	656	118	141	120	37 639	1 429	30.9	10.6	49.1
Burnet	1 107	10 414	1 341	954	2 093	383	272	351	33 709	1 481	36.5	12.5	35.6

STATE County	Agriculture, 2012 (cont.)															
	Land in farms					Value of land and buildings (dollars)		Value of machinery and equipment, average per farm (dollars)	Value of products sold				Percent of farms with sales of:		Government payments	
	Acreage (1,000)	Percent change, 2007–2012	Acres: Average size of farm	Acres: Total irrigated (1,000)	Acres: Total cropland (1,000)	Average per farm	Average per acre		Total (mil dol)	Average per farm (dollars)	Percent from: Crops	Percent from: Livestock and poultry products	$10,000 or more	$100,000 or more	Total ($1,000)	Percent of farms
	117	118	119	120	121	122	123	124	125	126	127	128	129	130	131	132
TENNESSEE—Cont'd																
Marshall	162	6.9	158	0.0	62.5	477 125	3 017	54 191	38.7	37 764	12.0	88.0	32.5	6.8	534	20.7
Maury	242	7.1	160	0.5	90.1	584 794	3 649	59 194	43.3	28 632	36.7	63.3	29.1	4.0	886	16.1
Meigs	53	7.7	167	0.1	20.0	587 246	3 520	57 767	6.9	21 647	19.3	80.7	30.9	3.8	153	19.6
Monroe	111	19.5	127	0.1	48.1	571 742	4 507	62 169	33.1	37 969	22.4	77.6	26.3	6.4	282	13.9
Montgomery	147	-2.7	188	0.7	77.1	811 156	4 310	79 954	47.3	60 350	77.0	23.0	35.0	8.9	1 031	31.5
Moore	59	13.3	164	0.0	14.8	578 542	3 528	69 791	22.6	63 045	D	D	38.0	9.8	128	13.4
Morgan	55	4.0	134	0.0	19.5	460 262	3 427	57 613	15.1	36 567	7.8	92.2	24.9	3.9	70	6.3
Obion	253	0.4	445	6.1	211.8	1 418 014	3 186	191 794	141.0	248 166	72.5	27.5	48.9	23.1	3 270	65.7
Overton	123	7.2	133	0.1	36.1	433 815	3 250	49 648	16.4	17 787	19.3	80.7	31.0	2.9	345	17.8
Perry	48	-6.3	194	0.0	13.8	384 012	1 981	41 463	2.4	9 951	33.9	66.1	26.0	1.6	155	31.3
Pickett	42	10.2	132	0.0	14.5	384 127	2 905	53 035	12.0	37 842	9.2	90.8	36.7	3.8	144	23.4
Polk	36	9.8	139	0.1	16.3	623 392	4 470	73 286	38.0	149 188	9.0	91.0	35.7	16.1	180	11.8
Putnam	96	-7.7	107	D	31.4	461 269	4 329	51 198	11.5	12 845	23.2	76.8	24.9	2.3	236	13.6
Rhea	58	2.7	140	0.8	24.4	490 925	3 499	56 000	16.8	40 886	55.2	44.8	28.5	4.4	194	16.3
Roane	47	-10.7	90	0.0	14.0	460 058	5 085	48 503	4.9	9 357	21.0	79.0	21.0	0.8	70	9.2
Robertson	209	-8.0	177	2.3	140.7	862 760	4 869	106 988	134.9	114 306	83.8	16.2	37.9	13.5	1 789	31.5
Rutherford	176	7.2	133	0.7	70.4	647 736	4 878	58 704	28.4	21 424	54.3	45.7	26.5	3.1	691	11.8
Scott	39	25.9	130	D	14.9	366 026	2 824	54 722	4.3	14 189	10.1	89.9	11.3	0.7	56	9.3
Sequatchie	31	7.0	163	D	10.0	528 037	3 236	72 968	7.0	37 404	15.1	84.9	31.9	8.0	66	17.0
Sevier	56	-1.6	92	0.0	17.1	545 836	5 926	48 391	5.3	8 713	22.1	77.9	24.0	0.7	61	13.8
Shelby	82	-11.3	199	4.3	60.4	913 324	4 586	77 803	31.8	77 387	94.2	5.8	26.3	8.0	733	22.9
Smith	130	2.0	153	0.2	36.8	405 628	2 658	52 353	18.9	22 205	40.3	59.7	32.2	3.3	507	19.5
Stewart	61	9.5	173	0.2	20.7	455 657	2 629	73 034	8.2	23 537	68.6	31.4	27.4	3.4	176	22.6
Sullivan	85	3.4	79	0.1	31.7	436 682	5 526	46 955	17.8	16 535	9.8	90.2	20.5	2.2	254	16.3
Sumner	167	-8.9	123	0.2	68.7	600 046	4 864	57 937	47.2	34 830	51.7	48.3	27.4	5.4	1 321	22.0
Tipton	155	-8.7	299	5.7	127.3	887 075	2 967	121 448	67.6	130 064	96.8	3.2	33.1	13.3	2 213	44.0
Trousdale	41	-6.2	142	0.1	13.9	548 321	3 854	65 507	8.2	28 259	36.4	63.6	41.4	4.5	90	24.1
Unicoi	5	14.4	58	D	1.9	321 409	5 511	32 602	D	D	D	D	9.7	2.2	7	7.5
Union	45	-1.5	111	0.0	12.8	320 044	2 887	57 931	3.3	8 039	14.1	85.9	20.8	0.7	183	17.6
Van Buren	37	6.1	151	D	11.0	561 576	3 721	60 033	5.6	22 727	17.5	82.5	29.4	3.3	221	20.0
Warren	163	1.7	146	5.4	83.7	519 646	3 569	73 327	88.2	78 595	79.6	20.4	48.1	13.3	531	13.9
Washington	112	-5.8	85	0.9	49.4	546 271	6 417	67 845	38.6	29 405	33.5	66.5	28.3	5.3	381	22.4
Wayne	133	15.7	201	0.2	36.7	404 798	2 014	52 301	22.3	33 581	15.1	84.9	39.8	4.7	533	20.3
Weakley	254	-0.6	295	3.2	203.8	878 358	2 976	140 220	129.6	150 479	66.0	34.0	42.5	19.0	2 897	51.8
White	122	-7.6	131	0.1	39.6	494 409	3 766	60 759	25.4	27 435	14.9	85.1	41.3	2.7	344	16.5
Williamson	139	-14.3	120	0.5	52.4	882 452	7 376	54 664	23.6	20 338	46.1	53.9	24.7	3.8	254	12.2
Wilson	188	-2.4	128	0.2	57.2	566 389	4 432	47 804	18.4	12 470	16.5	83.5	27.6	1.5	423	11.3
TEXAS	130 153	-0.2	523	4 489.2	29 147.5	876 614	1 676	72 180	25 375.6	101 988	29.0	71.0	29.7	7.0	643 993	21.1
Anderson	375	8.4	187	0.9	70.3	458 514	2 446	50 885	44.6	22 278	30.6	69.4	24.5	2.6	835	5.3
Andrews	752	-7.0	4 450	5.0	71.5	1 459 077	328	91 710	12.6	74 426	46.3	53.7	24.3	12.4	1 436	34.9
Angelina	117	1.5	120	0.2	21.7	378 739	3 157	45 106	46.4	47 639	9.2	90.8	24.3	3.3	168	2.6
Aransas	40	-21.8	398	0.0	2.6	679 110	1 704	43 180	1.1	10 750	18.4	81.6	14.0	2.0	93	24.0
Archer	541	6.7	1 020	0.2	115.6	1 002 917	984	87 567	76.8	144 674	16.6	83.4	53.5	21.8	2 480	40.7
Armstrong	434	-15.9	1 545	4.6	143.0	1 623 819	1 051	116 189	19.2	68 349	42.1	57.9	38.8	16.7	2 637	76.2
Atascosa	665	3.4	335	26.7	108.1	655 914	1 959	57 840	85.0	42 778	32.7	67.3	25.2	4.1	1 512	16.8
Austin	370	10.8	176	4.3	71.2	720 469	4 086	48 374	43.5	20 754	40.1	59.9	32.1	3.1	1 256	12.1
Bailey	472	-1.0	955	48.5	307.7	768 374	805	162 789	292.4	592 000	10.9	89.1	38.3	21.9	8 049	80.4
Bandera	402	22.2	402	0.6	34.1	1 082 003	2 694	42 303	11.2	11 166	11.3	88.7	16.3	0.8	455	7.1
Bastrop	388	-3.6	186	2.9	60.3	695 536	3 738	49 157	35.3	16 955	33.7	66.3	26.0	2.7	1 678	12.0
Baylor	544	-0.6	1 963	1.9	146.8	2 039 458	1 039	143 347	44.7	161 509	33.2	66.8	57.0	24.2	2 780	77.6
Bee	539	-1.7	553	5.1	70.4	1 032 344	1 866	56 745	26.0	26 739	38.2	61.8	25.6	4.4	1 051	17.9
Bell	421	-2.5	166	3.1	170.5	509 341	3 062	64 187	84.9	33 510	69.0	31.0	22.5	3.8	2 125	16.3
Bexar	343	-19.5	140	8.3	89.1	597 423	4 281	44 547	72.4	29 462	75.6	24.4	17.1	2.7	706	10.0
Blanco	364	-8.0	460	0.5	22.1	2 172 696	4 728	46 035	19.1	24 172	47.3	52.7	27.4	1.8	481	9.3
Borden	464	6.7	4 073	5.0	63.1	2 381 579	585	242 132	9.4	82 781	56.6	43.4	36.8	16.7	1 527	74.6
Bosque	570	3.4	450	0.7	70.3	1 089 916	2 420	55 434	78.3	61 894	64.1	35.9	31.9	5.2	466	11.2
Bowie	273	-6.4	169	5.9	77.8	382 695	2 269	51 216	66.0	40 780	21.2	78.8	29.4	5.4	1 209	13.1
Brazoria	631	19.3	204	20.4	175.9	619 773	3 036	59 444	118.2	38 252	60.5	39.5	21.8	3.5	4 831	9.4
Brazos	299	8.5	212	7.3	41.9	798 834	3 771	53 654	95.0	67 278	13.1	86.9	26.3	4.2	1 409	8.6
Brewster	1 913	9.5	9 469	0.5	47.1	4 436 252	469	85 431	9.9	49 025	10.5	89.5	31.2	12.4	1 041	15.8
Briscoe	524	-4.1	1 859	22.8	139.6	1 550 957	834	128 057	20.4	72 465	62.6	37.4	36.5	20.2	3 481	84.4
Brooks	573	4.4	1 532	1.1	26.0	1 628 016	1 063	53 329	50.8	135 743	1.1	98.9	26.7	2.9	320	25.4
Brown	595	6.3	310	3.5	84.6	635 187	2 046	45 413	40.7	21 209	18.5	81.5	22.1	2.1	1 191	18.0
Burleson	335	-7.1	235	19.6	81.2	674 186	2 873	67 470	90.1	63 022	38.1	61.9	32.7	5.6	1 432	10.9
Burnet	485	0.6	328	1.7	44.7	1 089 307	3 324	42 226	14.7	9 935	25.3	74.7	19.4	1.6	588	6.6

STATE County	Water use, 2010		Wholesale trade,[1] 2007				Retail trade,[2] 2007				Real estate and rental and leasing,[2] 2007			
	Total water withdrawn (mil gal/day)	Gallons withdrawn per person per day	Number of establish-ments	Number of employees	Sales (mil dol)	Annual payroll (mil dol)	Number of establish-ments	Number of employees	Sales (mil dol)	Annual payroll (mil dol)	Number of establish-ments	Number of employees	Receipts (mil dol)	Annual payroll (mil dol)
	133	134	135	136	137	138	139	140	141	142	143	144	145	146
TENNESSEE—Cont'd														
Marshall	4.8	155	10	D	D	D	122	1 176	269.7	24.3	19	53	5.9	0.7
Maury	13.4	165	58	649	245.1	29.4	333	3 824	898.3	81.1	89	355	56.8	9.8
Meigs	1.5	130	2	D	D	D	22	149	29.8	2.7	2	D	D	D
Monroe	10.2	228	28	315	173.4	8.6	150	1 695	453.0	37.9	28	88	9.6	1.5
Montgomery	25.4	148	72	629	345.5	26.3	522	8 016	1 877.6	180.3	145	577	110.7	15.3
Moore	1.7	270	1	D	D	D	11	85	16.3	1.2	NA	NA	NA	NA
Morgan	2.4	108	6	D	D	D	40	300	58.5	4.6	3	D	D	D
Obion	8.9	281	39	D	D	D	158	1 767	403.5	37.0	24	76	8.2	1.5
Overton	3.0	134	9	70	46.7	2.6	66	457	110.7	8.0	7	D	D	D
Perry	1.9	239	2	D	D	D	24	144	24.3	1.9	5	D	D	D
Pickett	0.9	177	2	D	D	D	24	115	23.6	2.1	1	D	D	D
Polk	4.7	276	3	D	D	D	48	297	67.7	6.1	8	17	1.7	0.4
Putnam	15.5	215	70	745	465.7	30.8	379	4 766	1 193.0	106.6	72	241	40.3	5.5
Rhea	24.9	781	10	73	17.9	2.0	108	1 097	250.8	21.0	20	89	8.2	1.3
Roane	272.2	5 023	20	D	D	D	157	1 852	436.4	39.2	33	487	36.0	11.4
Robertson	9.7	146	52	742	779.4	20.7	183	2 433	627.8	53.8	52	148	19.9	2.9
Rutherford	38.8	148	232	5 472	6 226.3	256.0	758	11 262	2 804.3	250.1	212	1 110	381.8	29.8
Scott	2.7	122	8	54	28.4	1.1	83	771	159.6	14.5	8	24	3.9	0.5
Sequatchie	1.4	96	11	D	D	D	47	441	105.3	8.1	15	59	5.9	0.8
Sevier	13.4	149	40	D	D	D	750	8 050	1 641.1	170.8	198	2 343	462.4	77.6
Shelby	646.3	697	1 271	26 595	29 636.0	1 384.8	3 300	49 554	11 932.9	1 177.7	1 044	8 375	1 532.0	329.3
Smith	2.8	144	12	66	52.5	1.6	66	598	117.8	13.9	11	34	3.6	0.6
Stewart	1 291.4	96 924	4	D	D	D	34	233	63.7	5.6	4	33	1.8	0.2
Sullivan	512.0	3 265	183	2 207	1 055.3	99.4	622	8 148	2 026.3	183.8	132	649	108.4	17.1
Sumner	622.2	3 873	134	2 007	1 634.9	81.8	428	5 565	1 300.1	121.9	152	801	182.0	30.0
Tipton	9.1	148	24	253	241.9	7.3	164	1 690	404.2	33.0	27	115	11.8	2.1
Trousdale	1.2	155	2	D	D	D	27	203	41.7	3.4	1	D	D	D
Unicoi	6.2	336	8	D	D	D	44	514	119.5	10.1	6	22	2.2	0.7
Union	1.8	94	11	40	6.6	0.8	37	297	60.5	5.0	9	54	3.6	0.9
Van Buren	1.4	243	NA	NA	NA	NA	7	35	9.2	0.4	6	26	1.2	0.5
Warren	10.6	266	36	D	D	D	179	1 834	373.7	38.8	22	59	8.3	1.3
Washington	23.3	190	135	2 000	1 090.8	70.6	551	8 257	1 869.1	169.3	127	957	114.1	17.8
Wayne	2.3	135	7	52	38.0	1.3	50	347	66.6	5.4	5	D	D	D
Weakley	5.4	153	32	D	D	D	120	1 256	265.4	22.5	20	68	7.8	1.4
White	4.4	168	11	88	28.9	2.8	81	793	195.4	17.7	11	52	3.5	0.9
Williamson	4.1	23	211	2 340	2 756.0	151.2	783	13 038	3 307.0	306.4	277	2 658	406.2	84.2
Wilson	17.0	149	80	1 298	967.9	62.5	394	4 621	1 165.0	103.4	115	541	85.9	16.1
TEXAS	24 796.7	986	27 066	386 370	424 238.2	20 260.6	78 795	1 138 440	311 334.8	26 395.2	26 593	173 745	36 399.2	7 067.2
Anderson	28.7	491	33	409	365.3	16.8	183	1 958	495.5	42.5	36	149	53.3	6.1
Andrews	64.0	4 329	12	D	D	D	36	314	98.3	7.5	12	70	12.9	4.7
Angelina	15.2	175	63	D	D	D	356	5 086	1 174.1	106.3	75	359	49.1	9.6
Aransas	0.7	29	10	32	13.5	1.0	95	1 125	241.5	23.5	37	152	14.3	2.7
Archer	7.0	768	13	52	43.4	2.3	23	91	39.4	2.0	4	D	D	D
Armstrong	4.7	2 462	1	D	D	D	4	24	2.4	0.2	NA	NA	NA	NA
Atascosa	41.2	917	22	187	69.4	6.3	124	1 499	362.9	30.4	25	86	11.9	1.6
Austin	7.0	246	18	D	D	D	95	878	234.2	19.8	22	54	9.1	1.7
Bailey	65.2	9 096	20	137	69.9	4.4	27	229	41.7	3.6	1	D	D	D
Bandera	3.4	165	5	18	1.4	0.5	56	359	76.5	6.4	14	38	5.8	0.8
Bastrop	223.3	3 011	33	198	51.6	8.0	167	2 069	684.7	48.1	52	173	18.6	4.1
Baylor	6.0	1 602	8	48	33.8	1.7	16	107	27.1	1.3	3	D	D	D
Bee	8.5	266	7	D	D	D	82	1 071	247.1	23.4	25	87	10.8	2.6
Bell	73.6	237	125	2 933	4 202.7	125.3	924	12 506	3 350.0	283.0	308	1 501	209.4	40.3
Bexar	1 342.1	783	1 427	22 636	12 232.1	1 042.4	4 737	81 409	22 815.3	1 891.9	1 793	12 057	2 215.6	425.7
Blanco	2.2	212	10	D	D	D	30	213	50.6	3.6	7	D	D	D
Borden	6.7	10 374	NA	NA	NA	NA	1	D	D	D	NA	NA	NA	NA
Bosque	9.7	533	12	70	28.4	2.7	55	457	106.5	9.2	10	13	2.0	0.3
Bowie	16.0	173	104	D	D	D	487	6 447	1 535.4	141.3	102	483	67.3	11.5
Brazoria	856.3	2 734	181	1 572	841.9	74.6	743	11 791	2 958.8	265.3	252	1 604	366.6	61.3
Brazos	67.9	349	111	1 498	779.6	56.5	646	9 149	2 119.1	189.9	226	1 102	190.3	32.4
Brewster	3.7	403	9	58	20.3	1.1	00	470	86.8	8.9	23	61	5.6	1.1
Briscoe	20.0	16 359	3	20	5.4	0.3	8	27	6.7	0.4	NA	NA	NA	NA
Brooks	3.3	457	2	D	D	D	25	345	81.6	6.9	1	D	D	D
Brown	16.0	420	40	392	171.0	13.0	196	1 973	512.5	41.0	40	116	16.1	2.8
Burleson	29.3	1 705	17	D	D	D	49	501	183.8	12.0	5	16	2.2	0.5
Burnet	16.9	396	31	163	81.9	7.4	195	2 139	639.5	51.6	57	295	26.6	6.9

1. Merchant wholesalers, except manufacturers' sales branches and offices. 2. Employer establishments.

Table B. States and Counties — Professional Services, Manufacturing, and Accommodation and Food Services

STATE County	Professional, scientific, and technical services,[1] 2007				Manufacturing, 2007				Accommodation and food services, 2007			
	Number of establish-ments	Number of employees	Receipts (mil dol)	Annual payroll (mil dol)	Number of establish-ments	Number of employees	Receipts (mil dol)	Annual payroll (mil dol)	Number of establish-ments	Number of employees	Sales (mil dol)	Annual payroll (mil dol)
	147	148	149	150	151	152	153	154	155	156	157	158
TENNESSEE—Cont'd												
Marshall	28	93	6.8	1.9	52	3 821	1 490.1	145.0	37	518	21.1	5.2
Maury	108	D	D	D	82	4 575	D	312.3	144	2 835	97.3	28.3
Meigs	3	D	D	D	14	770	253.0	28.8	6	46	2.0	0.6
Monroe	48	160	12.2	5.7	72	5 246	1 386.2	189.2	81	1 224	41.0	11.3
Montgomery	160	D	D	D	70	6 052	D	D	300	6 151	245.2	64.7
Moore	2	D	D	D	NA	NA	NA	NA	8	48	1.4	0.5
Morgan	10	D	D	D	NA	NA	NA	NA	8	105	3.5	1.1
Obion	34	D	D	D	43	5 506	D	D	65	D	D	D
Overton	22	D	D	D	35	1 101	D	32.3	25	317	13.3	3.3
Perry	3	D	D	D	12	1 042	170.0	30.1	6	D	D	D
Pickett	5	D	D	D	NA	NA	NA	NA	9	67	3.1	0.5
Polk	11	D	D	D	NA	NA	NA	NA	23	175	8.8	2.4
Putnam	139	D	D	D	112	6 106	1 384.0	203.1	154	3 387	138.0	38.5
Rhea	38	97	8.6	3.1	33	4 705	894.7	149.7	45	761	26.9	6.9
Roane	60	182	19.6	6.9	23	1 440	369.7	54.9	66	1 304	46.0	12.7
Robertson	56	D	D	D	84	6 281	1 667.5	211.8	83	1 669	60.7	17.3
Rutherford	325	D	D	D	203	18 166	11 304.8	901.6	417	9 745	387.0	111.2
Scott	16	68	6.4	4.3	44	1 499	401.7	46.8	29	410	14.6	3.9
Sequatchie	12	D	D	D	13	749	D	19.2	23	244	9.4	2.5
Sevier	162	703	65.8	24.1	82	1 448	341.5	50.4	517	10 254	611.9	169.6
Shelby	1 913	16 716	2 230.2	920.2	704	31 108	17 969.7	1 490.7	1 724	39 318	1 788.0	501.5
Smith	16	47	5.2	1.5	27	1 387	D	49.2	20	347	12.4	3.2
Stewart	7	D	D	D	NA	NA	NA	NA	19	164	6.1	1.6
Sullivan	252	1 726	214.8	68.6	157	15 632	5 463.6	742.7	312	6 590	255.1	70.1
Sumner	219	D	D	D	213	7 023	1 741.4	273.0	217	4 053	155.5	45.0
Tipton	39	D	D	D	36	2 080	774.2	81.5	61	846	29.8	7.5
Trousdale	8	44	2.7	1.1	NA	NA	NA	NA	10	114	4.6	1.3
Unicoi	13	D	D	D	25	2 100	348.6	D	27	361	13.0	3.3
Union	9	D	D	D	23	615	125.6	20.5	12	198	5.7	1.2
Van Buren	2	D	D	D	NA	NA	NA	NA	1	D	D	D
Warren	38	121	12.7	3.1	67	3 140	852.3	144.5	52	803	28.8	7.8
Washington	231	D	D	D	145	6 166	1 577.7	214.1	254	6 361	247.1	74.9
Wayne	8	D	D	D	27	736	109.9	20.5	20	193	8.5	2.1
Weakley	25	D	D	D	36	1 680	D	D	58	D	D	D
White	22	64	4.9	1.5	45	2 118	552.2	66.4	28	398	16.8	5.2
Williamson	782	D	D	D	126	3 524	1 106.8	129.5	366	8 329	383.5	109.9
Wilson	185	D	D	D	111	6 274	D	273.8	179	3 640	147.3	43.5
TEXAS	57 373	534 386	90 668.7	35 376.4	21 115	893 842	593 541.5	42 835.7	43 509	866 189	42 054.6	11 502.3
Anderson	79	258	25.1	7.2	NA	NA	NA	NA	69	1 046	48.6	11.9
Andrews	19	62	9.1	2.5	NA	NA	NA	NA	23	340	14.9	3.3
Angelina	155	688	81.9	28.9	75	6 343	1 291.4	217.7	133	2 748	112.6	31.5
Aransas	39	D	D	D	NA	NA	NA	NA	84	1 089	48.8	13.4
Archer	6	D	D	D	NA	NA	NA	NA	7	38	1.4	0.4
Armstrong	1	D	D	D	NA	NA	NA	NA	6	16	0.6	0.2
Atascosa	34	264	25.9	5.5	NA	NA	NA	NA	66	904	32.2	8.5
Austin	57	D	D	D	39	2 222	D	D	46	568	25.0	6.2
Bailey	12	45	4.5	1.4	NA	NA	NA	NA	10	185	7.0	1.9
Bandera	32	D	D	D	NA	NA	NA	NA	55	499	23.2	5.8
Bastrop	84	340	33.8	11.9	64	1 068	238.6	37.7	97	2 015	115.1	33.1
Baylor	6	26	1.2	0.5	NA	NA	NA	NA	7	95	3.2	0.9
Bee	40	D	D	D	NA	NA	NA	NA	52	711	25.5	7.0
Bell	342	D	D	D	136	7 028	1 925.0	246.6	500	9 329	401.4	104.9
Bexar	3 625	D	D	D	986	35 502	12 305.1	1 366.0	3 207	75 006	3 829.0	1 073.1
Blanco	27	103	9.3	3.6	NA	NA	NA	NA	32	225	9.4	2.9
Borden	1	D	D	D	NA	NA	NA	NA	NA	NA	NA	NA
Bosque	22	84	7.7	2.5	NA	NA	NA	NA	20	104	5.3	1.2
Bowie	169	D	D	D	65	2 579	1 729.2	103.9	166	3 668	166.5	49.4
Brazoria	411	D	D	D	225	13 787	31 048.1	1 020.4	383	7 330	313.5	85.2
Brazos	388	D	D	D	111	4 881	979.4	167.5	368	8 497	340.3	91.4
Brewster	22	59	5.8	1.3	NA	NA	NA	NA	48	630	25.4	7.1
Briscoe	NA	NA	NA	NA	NA	NA	NA	NA	4	17	0.3	0.1
Brooks	12	23	2.0	0.5	NA	NA	NA	NA	28	326	14.2	4.1
Brown	54	184	16.8	4.9	41	3 100	1 249.4	125.4	87	1 374	49.9	13.7
Burleson	19	D	D	D	NA	NA	NA	NA	36	338	12.8	3.2
Burnet	82	335	31.5	12.5	57	924	D	49.7	102	1 386	74.4	21.6

1. Establishment subject to federal tax.

Table B. States and Counties — **Health Care and Social Assistance, Other Services, Nonemployer Businesses, and Residential Construction**

STATE County	Health care and social assistance, 2007				Other services, 2007				Nonemployer businesses, 2013		Value of residential construction authorized by building permits, 2014	
	Number of establish- ments	Number of employees	Receipts (mil dol)	Annual payroll (mil dol)	Number of establish- ments	Number of employees	Receipts (mil dol)	Annual payroll (mil dol)	Number	Receipts (mil dol)	New Construction ($1,000)	Number of housing units
	159	160	161	162	163	164	165	166	167	168	169	170
TENNESSEE—Cont'd												
Marshall	61	725	48.0	17.6	29	D	D	D	1 895	73.1	17 417	102
Maury	205	5 346	450.4	191.8	105	631	55.6	15.6	5 629	229.6	125 153	784
Meigs	7	D	D	D	5	8	0.7	0.2	689	29.4	9 463	45
Monroe	61	1 200	82.6	31.9	39	147	10.0	2.9	2 641	110.8	3 564	61
Montgomery	270	D	D	D	189	1 066	72.9	20.9	9 026	410.6	173 647	1 446
Moore	11	D	D	D	4	D	D	D	447	18.1	4 956	27
Morgan	17	399	21.9	9.4	10	21	4.3	1.0	1 173	35.9	0	0
Obion	89	D	D	D	47	D	D	D	1 879	61.2	2 547	11
Overton	34	D	D	D	15	D	D	D	1 755	66.6	120	3
Perry	17	367	20.0	8.1	6	46	1.0	0.3	570	22.0	0	0
Pickett	5	D	D	D	5	D	D	D	471	20.9	NA	NA
Polk	20	395	28.7	11.6	9	D	D	D	1 045	39.2	25 578	142
Putnam	214	4 527	428.2	151.4	117	591	47.0	13.3	5 733	244.8	50 994	424
Rhea	65	831	49.5	22.4	24	90	6.5	1.8	1 646	52.6	10 860	62
Roane	88	1 812	118.1	51.2	43	172	14.9	4.0	3 085	111.7	778	7
Robertson	107	1 606	145.3	52.0	79	297	24.3	6.1	4 804	214.5	37 881	243
Rutherford	447	9 041	1 019.4	424.6	285	2 300	227.1	69.6	18 296	842.6	373 025	2 744
Scott	42	719	52.3	22.0	21	107	8.3	2.5	1 339	58.7	120	3
Sequatchie	22	D	D	D	12	D	D	D	990	32.1	655	7
Sevier	134	1 672	136.2	46.3	152	884	72.3	19.5	7 588	348.4	10 689	60
Shelby	2 166	62 091	6 542.5	2 623.9	1 349	12 280	1 807.9	356.1	77 761	2 772.7	259 660	1 516
Smith	33	632	55.0	21.1	22	69	5.0	1.6	1 303	53.1	9 251	66
Stewart	15	D	D	D	8	22	2.0	0.5	796	29.5	775	18
Sullivan	446	12 705	1 354.3	507.3	253	D	D	D	9 395	392.4	49 658	249
Sumner	313	5 031	518.5	196.1	202	1 110	96.1	22.8	13 529	636.1	168 104	869
Tipton	85	1 224	96.6	35.4	45	198	14.0	3.8	3 876	120.2	20 529	138
Trousdale	21	254	19.7	6.7	7	D	D	D	574	26.0	5 689	45
Unicoi	27	681	41.5	17.4	21	D	D	D	777	29.3	200	1
Union	12	D	D	D	17	D	D	D	1 234	47.5	8 906	50
Van Buren	4	D	D	D	2	D	D	D	366	12.3	NA	NA
Warren	92	1 571	137.2	44.4	52	194	14.0	4.5	2 862	114.9	7 731	52
Washington	319	10 712	1 168.4	459.6	195	1 042	73.8	22.8	7 661	346.9	82 553	654
Wayne	29	236	12.8	5.1	10	28	4.6	0.7	968	32.7	200	1
Weakley	74	1 527	111.8	46.0	38	D	D	D	1 672	68.6	5 454	33
White	39	740	61.0	22.1	24	71	6.9	1.9	1 923	79.4	468	6
Williamson	616	10 109	1 089.7	493.9	312	2 111	177.7	52.9	22 194	1 455.3	622 855	1 902
Wilson	230	3 596	306.6	114.5	131	616	48.4	13.2	9 973	479.3	296 853	1 549
TEXAS	54 991	1 166 613	113 830.2	43 118.2	34 462	253 503	25 778.5	6 993.6	2 039 732	98 800.7	26 295 841	166 982
Anderson	135	2 083	188.4	67.2	53	319	17.2	7.4	2 875	125.6	232	2
Andrews	20	433	35.3	14.6	22	277	40.5	10.7	1 149	71.2	16 964	155
Angelina	270	7 552	517.1	207.1	129	732	120.8	17.8	5 041	253.9	12 920	76
Aransas	42	522	42.3	12.7	49	153	11.9	3.1	2 471	119.3	25 067	169
Archer	12	D	D	D	10	22	1.4	0.4	868	44.1	740	9
Armstrong	4	D	D	D	2	D	D	D	157	6.5	0	0
Atascosa	85	1 000	93.5	32.8	44	222	18.3	4.9	3 149	143.7	12 717	69
Austin	32	590	31.3	14.6	33	110	9.8	2.4	2 573	129.7	4 482	27
Bailey	16	199	13.5	5.0	19	62	3.8	0.9	357	17.7	0	0
Bandera	20	247	17.7	5.9	30	92	8.1	1.8	2 132	96.4	120	1
Bastrop	89	1 648	97.1	43.5	81	332	30.4	7.6	5 561	227.4	19 256	167
Baylor	14	535	13.2	6.7	17	39	4.3	0.6	250	14.2	0	0
Bee	49	868	63.7	28.0	41	178	13.6	3.2	1 524	58.2	1 203	11
Bell	476	18 504	1 979.2	802.1	401	2 418	173.8	50.9	15 232	642.6	326 073	1 989
Bexar	4 094	99 461	9 820.8	3 564.2	2 505	18 260	1 516.2	428.4	120 595	5 437.6	1 020 999	6 959
Blanco	18	128	6.6	2.9	19	58	5.1	1.1	1 239	57.4	2 359	35
Borden	NA	NA	NA	NA	NA	NA	NA	NA	57	3.5	NA	NA
Bosque	19	588	43.2	18.1	26	97	9.6	1.7	1 401	57.8	265	3
Bowie	304	6 810	654.9	261.4	153	940	72.8	20.8	4 969	218.9	8 435	95
Brazoria	501	7 074	500.6	206.8	341	2 203	207.4	65.3	22 189	929.9	581 093	3 476
Brazos	389	7 161	872.8	287.0	260	1 859	359.3	42.4	11 044	544.4	254 325	1 786
Brewster	20	434	33.5	14.0	20	83	5.4	1.4	939	29.0	1 356	11
Briscoe	1	D	D	D	2	D	D	D	137	5.4	NA	NA
Brooks	18	707	15.2	8.1	12	D	D	D	534	13.9	0	0
Brown	124	3 034	194.7	73.1	72	417	25.9	7.4	2 464	98.5	3 822	31
Burleson	18	258	21.6	9.0	24	100	8.3	1.8	1 317	55.1	1 068	8
Burnet	113	1 250	102.6	37.7	72	286	21.1	6.0	4 662	253.5	59 698	261

STATE County	Government employment and payroll, 2012: Full-time equivalent employees	Government employment and payroll, 2012: March payroll (dollars)	March payroll (percent of total): Administration, judicial, and legal	March payroll (percent of total): Police and Corrections	March payroll (percent of total): Fire Protection	March payroll (percent of total): Highways and transportation	March payroll (percent of total): Health and Welfare	March payroll (percent of total): Natural resources and utilities	March payroll (percent of total): Education and libraries	Local government finances, 2012, General revenue: Total (mil dol)	General revenue: Intergovernmental (mil dol)	Taxes: Total (mil dol)	Taxes, Per capita[1] (dollars): Total	Taxes, Per capita[1] (dollars): Property
	171	172	173	174	175	176	177	178	179	180	181	182	183	184
TENNESSEE—Cont'd														
Marshall	1 203	3 538 766	7.5	9.0	3.9	2.6	5.0	17.4	52.4	86.1	36.7	29.2	947	612
Maury	4 616	17 056 047	3.2	6.1	2.9	2.0	47.4	6.3	30.7	499.9	86.1	89.0	1 086	702
Meigs	438	942 766	9.9	10.0	0.1	7.3	3.2	2.3	67.2	24.7	17.0	5.2	441	333
Monroe	1 373	3 993 045	7.7	8.8	1.3	3.3	4.4	9.7	64.2	96.5	51.5	31.4	696	447
Montgomery	6 061	19 419 026	4.6	11.0	3.6	3.7	5.7	6.1	63.4	519.4	202.5	207.0	1 122	681
Moore	237	724 102	2.2	14.7	0.1	9.4	3.2	8.5	61.9	15.5	8.0	5.6	884	707
Morgan	796	1 965 391	7.2	7.4	0.0	4.6	5.8	5.4	68.9	42.3	28.2	10.4	475	387
Obion	1 057	3 471 219	8.5	14.0	3.5	4.1	0.4	7.6	60.8	80.5	42.6	24.7	789	436
Overton	829	2 041 789	5.5	9.1	0.7	4.4	6.6	7.0	65.6	46.5	30.0	11.5	520	304
Perry	339	836 675	10.6	3.6	0.0	5.3	3.5	5.7	67.5	22.6	13.7	5.6	716	537
Pickett	180	540 892	11.1	15.0	0.6	9.3	3.5	4.7	55.8	13.0	8.2	3.4	670	349
Polk	595	1 517 421	15.7	1.5	0.0	7.2	2.1	5.6	67.4	36.3	22.3	11.2	674	514
Putnam	4 261	15 613 316	2.1	4.8	1.2	1.6	55.8	4.6	27.7	418.9	71.7	81.6	1 114	597
Rhea	1 269	3 661 964	5.1	6.0	0.8	2.6	18.6	8.5	54.3	86.8	39.8	20.0	621	367
Roane	1 700	6 055 393	5.5	6.7	3.8	2.6	1.3	17.4	61.6	147.3	59.5	50.7	948	593
Robertson	2 143	5 842 234	11.7	12.9	2.0	4.7	1.8	7.6	58.5	164.1	73.4	70.3	1 050	658
Rutherford	8 751	29 120 491	7.0	11.2	3.9	1.2	3.2	8.8	62.0	738.4	270.4	325.5	1 186	718
Scott	1 044	2 569 027	6.5	7.4	0.9	5.4	5.6	10.3	62.6	56.6	33.7	12.4	560	370
Sequatchie	429	1 170 657	6.1	8.5	0.0	0.5	5.6	7.1	71.3	32.3	19.5	9.3	645	457
Sevier	3 747	12 103 289	4.1	9.3	3.0	4.0	3.5	8.2	62.6	359.9	83.9	186.0	2 010	703
Shelby	39 378	138 123 866	7.0	15.4	7.3	4.6	11.4	14.4	38.1	4 311.3	1 448.6	1 719.3	1 828	1 235
Smith	725	1 800 266	8.4	11.3	0.6	6.1	2.0	7.1	61.0	45.3	25.5	13.2	693	395
Stewart	498	1 358 521	8.2	10.6	0.2	5.1	5.7	3.5	65.2	36.1	23.5	9.2	693	470
Sullivan	5 719	18 566 959	5.4	9.7	3.3	4.6	4.4	5.7	64.8	404.7	154.7	177.3	1 131	800
Sumner	5 626	16 827 689	5.9	10.4	4.6	1.7	3.7	8.6	63.7	406.0	171.8	163.0	981	658
Tipton	2 180	6 476 685	4.4	8.2	2.1	2.7	0.9	8.0	72.1	146.0	87.1	41.2	668	453
Trousdale	275	758 540	10.0	16.9	0.0	0.0	4.0	1.1	68.0	18.5	11.4	4.6	596	490
Unicoi	819	2 543 400	3.6	3.8	1.5	4.4	24.1	4.2	48.7	63.6	21.5	9.0	495	392
Union	593	1 652 593	8.9	6.9	0.0	4.2	0.9	6.7	72.2	47.6	34.6	8.9	466	312
Van Buren	275	698 479	8.3	7.1	1.3	19.0	5.9	2.5	55.9	13.1	8.7	3.1	554	397
Warren	1 148	3 625 874	6.8	9.9	2.3	1.1	6.3	13.7	58.4	97.8	53.6	31.0	779	452
Washington	4 114	12 590 200	5.8	10.1	3.4	7.7	2.2	15.3	53.6	294.8	106.3	133.5	1 068	712
Wayne	611	1 515 515	5.5	10.2	0.2	4.9	1.5	4.4	71.7	45.0	23.8	10.1	595	364
Weakley	1 333	3 550 802	5.6	11.2	2.3	5.4	9.1	13.8	50.6	73.0	37.4	20.2	579	318
White	908	2 433 483	6.9	8.8	0.8	3.2	3.5	9.7	65.1	53.2	31.7	14.3	548	338
Williamson	8 184	27 964 745	5.4	6.5	3.3	2.0	20.1	5.4	55.8	754.7	175.6	348.2	1 805	1 175
Wilson	3 881	11 949 351	7.0	10.1	4.4	3.3	1.0	8.4	64.6	281.9	110.9	131.1	1 102	707
TEXAS	X	X	X	X	X	X	X	X	X	X	X	X	X	X
Anderson	1 888	5 360 452	8.0	11.5	3.0	3.1	0.6	3.8	69.2	124.5	47.1	61.2	1 052	867
Andrews	1 090	4 021 801	5.8	6.7	0.0	2.3	33.8	5.1	46.1	121.7	9.4	81.6	5 063	4 756
Angelina	4 483	13 382 100	4.8	8.0	2.7	2.0	11.2	3.8	66.5	300.9	135.8	97.6	1 114	832
Aransas	888	2 584 176	9.4	13.5	0.0	5.1	2.4	5.8	61.2	78.8	13.5	50.4	2 117	1 856
Archer	436	1 231 876	8.0	6.2	0.0	2.7	1.6	4.3	76.7	26.8	10.9	12.0	1 378	1 224
Armstrong	112	284 475	10.7	2.6	0.0	2.6	2.2	3.2	77.2	9.5	3.3	3.2	1 666	1 480
Atascosa	2 208	6 519 286	5.0	7.2	0.0	2.0	13.3	3.4	67.8	191.3	123.7	49.0	1 056	822
Austin	1 209	3 635 525	7.8	10.5	0.0	3.4	2.6	5.7	69.1	87.7	23.7	51.5	1 801	1 613
Bailey	547	1 435 208	5.2	6.9	0.0	2.6	29.6	1.9	53.0	36.8	12.6	9.8	1 375	1 158
Bandera	640	2 084 125	8.5	10.8	0.2	3.9	4.1	2.5	68.5	46.4	8.5	32.2	1 567	1 462
Bastrop	2 838	9 520 485	5.2	12.2	0.0	2.3	0.8	3.0	76.0	243.4	86.4	112.0	1 498	1 314
Baylor	318	889 487	6.6	4.2	0.0	2.8	45.1	5.7	34.2	22.6	4.9	3.9	1 085	880
Bee	1 435	4 453 164	5.0	5.5	1.3	2.9	4.8	5.0	74.6	114.4	63.6	30.2	930	752
Bell	16 055	50 764 685	4.5	8.6	3.4	1.9	2.7	4.5	73.5	1 144.1	497.9	378.1	1 171	912
Bexar	76 821	296 304 428	4.1	8.7	3.4	4.0	10.0	11.6	57.2	7 217.6	2 547.6	2 991.4	1 675	1 345
Blanco	357	1 339 398	8.8	7.8	0.0	1.9	0.2	3.3	77.7	39.5	6.7	29.4	2 761	2 644
Borden	74	200 651	18.7	3.1	0.0	8.2	0.0	0.5	68.4	14.0	2.2	11.3	18 268	18 188
Bosque	689	2 029 654	8.4	7.1	0.0	2.6	0.4	2.1	77.7	47.1	20.0	22.7	1 253	1 100
Bowie	4 233	13 543 434	5.4	7.5	2.7	2.3	0.7	7.1	73.2	292.7	128.5	118.6	1 273	993
Brazoria	12 753	42 706 512	5.9	10.5	0.7	2.7	5.3	4.6	69.2	1 184.7	316.7	617.5	1 901	1 646
Brazos	7 250	22 942 099	8.3	13.0	5.1	4.6	3.7	12.3	47.5	549.9	134.9	310.5	1 547	1 241
Brewster	439	1 264 854	9.4	14.2	0.0	3.7	0.7	6.1	63.5	31.3	14.9	12.8	1 373	1 071
Briscoe	68	181 356	19.1	3.9	0.0	5.1	1.2	13.9	56.0	4.9	1.8	2.3	1 491	1 329
Brooks	470	1 100 857	8.0	8.1	0.4	3.7	1.2	7.4	70.9	40.5	15.5	18.6	2 598	2 321
Brown	1 839	5 391 982	6.8	9.8	2.3	3.3	10.4	7.5	59.2	125.8	54.0	52.8	1 397	1 099
Burleson	707	1 886 727	9.3	7.8	0.0	4.3	0.7	3.5	74.3	46.7	14.9	26.1	1 507	1 240
Burnet	1 778	6 073 530	9.9	14.7	4.3	2.7	0.2	7.3	59.5	155.5	24.4	99.6	2 293	2 003

1. Based on the resident population estimated as of July 1 of the year shown.

STATE County	Local government finances, 2012 (cont.) — Direct general expenditure: Total (mil dol)	Per capita[1] (dollars)	Percent of total for: Education	Health and hospitals	Police protection	Public welfare	Highways	Debt outstanding: Total (mil dol)	Per capita[1] (dollars)	Government employment, 2013: Federal civilian	Federal military	State and local	Presidential election,[2] 2012 — Percent of vote cast: Democratic	Republican	All other
	185	186	187	188	189	190	191	192	193	194	195	196	197	198	199
TENNESSEE—Cont'd															
Marshall	82.9	2 684	52.1	3.0	8.4	0.2	5.3	93.9	3 039	58	100	1 662	38.3	59.8	1.9
Maury	491.1	5 990	19.6	56.1	3.7	0.0	3.1	294.5	3 592	172	269	6 360	38.7	60.1	1.2
Meigs	23.1	1 979	63.8	2.5	5.7	0.5	8.0	7.5	637	28	37	487	32.4	66.0	1.6
Monroe	104.4	2 314	64.5	4.7	5.5	0.1	5.1	101.6	2 250	91	145	1 897	30.1	68.5	1.4
Montgomery	461.9	2 504	57.1	3.0	7.0	0.0	4.1	4 359.0	23 630	1 196	617	8 865	45.5	53.4	1.1
Moore	15.3	2 419	59.1	2.9	4.2	0.1	11.9	10.0	1 582	0	20	820	29.8	68.1	2.1
Morgan	41.9	1 911	64.0	5.8	4.0	0.4	6.2	30.5	1 389	36	63	1 298	28.9	69.1	2.0
Obion	81.3	2 595	55.8	0.3	6.3	3.1	8.4	30.1	960	110	99	1 582	32.2	66.3	1.6
Overton	44.3	1 997	60.0	3.6	4.9	0.1	6.9	44.2	1 992	40	71	1 288	42.3	55.6	2.2
Perry	21.2	2 699	47.8	5.5	4.8	0.0	8.5	8.1	1 031	16	25	438	44.3	53.2	2.5
Pickett	13.0	2 545	48.4	5.3	3.9	0.0	10.4	3.4	663	0	16	286	32.0	66.9	1.2
Polk	34.7	2 079	61.1	2.7	6.5	0.1	8.0	19.5	1 171	63	53	751	32.7	65.6	1.7
Putnam	420.4	5 740	22.0	57.2	3.4	0.0	2.3	286.9	3 919	234	234	8 183	35.7	62.6	1.7
Rhea	100.3	3 111	50.3	17.1	4.9	0.0	5.3	141.2	4 378	1 264	102	1 672	26.2	72.4	1.4
Roane	135.7	2 538	58.0	2.9	4.6	0.2	4.6	117.8	2 203	463	170	3 195	31.0	67.3	1.7
Robertson	151.2	2 259	56.5	3.0	9.4	0.0	4.9	198.9	2 971	80	216	3 636	33.7	64.8	1.4
Rutherford	715.7	2 608	53.2	2.1	8.2	1.5	4.4	983.5	3 583	2 669	909	14 980	39.8	58.9	1.4
Scott	55.5	2 502	62.9	3.9	4.5	2.5	6.6	69.2	3 121	88	70	1 418	25.4	72.7	1.9
Sequatchie	28.3	1 960	60.8	3.3	6.5	0.0	5.5	20.7	1 434	12	47	918	31.6	66.4	2.0
Sevier	377.1	4 076	36.1	2.9	5.4	0.1	6.1	1 420.7	15 357	335	300	4 480	25.3	73.4	1.2
Shelby	4 592.5	4 882	44.5	8.2	8.9	1.1	2.0	5 549.0	5 898	14 090	3 878	55 110	63.4	36.0	0.6
Smith	46.3	2 421	56.5	3.9	7.0	0.1	6.8	37.3	1 955	117	61	944	38.7	58.9	2.4
Stewart	34.1	2 565	59.2	4.6	6.3	0.0	7.3	35.9	2 697	500	43	668	44.9	53.7	1.5
Sullivan	439.1	2 801	49.3	2.5	6.5	0.0	4.1	464.0	2 959	484	500	7 696	28.7	70.0	1.3
Sumner	387.5	2 333	56.0	2.5	7.6	0.1	4.7	365.1	2 198	465	543	7 200	32.0	66.9	1.2
Tipton	139.6	2 263	63.6	0.7	6.7	0.1	6.6	67.3	1 091	95	196	2 637	31.3	67.8	0.9
Trousdale	20.8	2 672	57.7	2.4	6.2	0.2	9.5	0.0	0	35	25	475	45.5	52.1	2.3
Unicoi	70.8	3 884	31.1	44.7	3.2	0.3	5.1	50.1	2 748	68	57	1 098	29.2	69.4	1.5
Union	45.7	2 387	70.7	3.8	4.1	0.2	4.9	34.2	1 787	22	61	850	28.6	69.8	1.6
Van Buren	17.4	3 085	70.1	3.3	3.6	0.0	8.9	9.0	1 604	0	18	371	38.5	58.7	2.9
Warren	107.0	2 687	60.0	3.5	4.8	0.0	5.4	47.1	1 181	86	128	1 852	38.3	59.5	2.2
Washington	308.7	2 467	44.9	1.3	7.5	0.5	5.7	609.5	4 872	2 572	431	9 264	32.5	66.0	1.4
Wayne	44.4	2 612	47.4	0.4	4.4	17.6	6.9	31.8	1 874	30	48	1 618	24.5	73.7	1.7
Weakley	68.4	1 967	54.8	0.5	6.6	11.4	8.3	23.7	682	115	108	3 716	33.6	64.7	1.7
White	50.7	1 943	60.1	2.7	5.8	0.3	5.6	21.8	835	48	84	1 328	35.0	63.3	1.8
Williamson	720.3	3 734	44.7	20.8	4.0	0.0	4.3	886.6	4 596	427	642	9 997	29.8	69.3	1.0
Wilson	304.2	2 557	61.0	0.4	7.4	0.0	4.9	398.5	3 350	186	391	4 774	31.1	67.6	1.3
TEXAS	X	X	X	X	X	X	X	X	X	197 794	177 742	1 598 375	43.7	55.5	0.9
Anderson	133.7	2 297	64.2	0.2	4.5	0.4	4.2	165.8	2 850	121	93	5 486	27.8	71.4	0.8
Andrews	109.9	6 817	50.8	29.4	3.5	0.0	1.1	185.6	11 518	14	35	1 216	17.1	82.4	0.5
Angelina	307.3	3 509	57.1	10.2	4.5	0.3	4.2	395.7	4 517	341	180	6 676	32.2	67.1	0.7
Aransas	80.8	3 391	53.6	1.1	9.5	1.2	4.4	116.6	4 897	18	51	1 027	30.7	68.4	0.8
Archer	26.8	3 072	60.0	1.1	6.2	0.4	7.7	257.0	29 423	19	72	499	17.0	82.4	0.7
Armstrong	8.5	4 369	44.7	28.9	3.6	0.2	4.8	4.2	2 172	0	0	133	12.9	86.5	0.6
Atascosa	210.7	4 536	43.4	9.8	2.8	0.8	23.3	433.1	9 325	53	99	2 412	44.4	55.0	0.6
Austin	84.2	2 944	55.5	4.8	7.5	0.0	7.6	104.0	3 635	77	61	1 657	24.1	75.0	1.0
Bailey	34.7	4 873	39.4	36.7	4.8	0.0	3.9	50.9	7 137	22	15	597	29.4	69.9	0.7
Bandera	43.7	2 128	59.1	2.9	6.1	0.5	5.8	35.4	1 721	13	43	739	24.2	74.6	1.2
Bastrop	242.4	3 242	50.0	11.5	5.2	0.6	5.9	413.3	5 529	381	155	3 527	45.1	53.3	1.6
Baylor	20.8	5 731	29.9	49.2	3.4	0.6	3.5	3.0	829	17	0	238	22.3	76.8	0.9
Bee	111.6	3 432	71.0	1.4	3.1	1.8	2.5	62.7	1 928	35	53	3 307	44.7	54.8	0.5
Bell	1 144.2	3 542	60.4	2.5	4.9	0.5	2.7	1 912.0	5 919	10 580	41 612	19 805	44.7	54.5	0.8
Bexar	7 362.8	4 123	44.0	14.4	5.4	2.0	2.3	18 461.5	10 338	34 751	34 838	104 389	52.4	46.8	0.7
Blanco	38.6	3 621	55.5	0.1	3.6	0.0	9.2	37.3	3 505	60	22	495	29.7	69.2	1.1
Borden	23.8	38 584	84.8	0.0	0.6	0.1	3.3	22.5	36 494	0	0	86	11.1	87.5	1.4
Bosque	45.2	2 493	68.1	0.1	4.3	0.7	4.0	30.9	1 705	66	37	1 116	23.5	75.4	1.1
Bowie	279.8	3 004	63.0	0.3	4.7	0.4	5.3	243.0	2 609	4 247	200	6 253	30.7	68.7	0.6
Brazoria	1 133.2	3 489	48.6	5.5	5.0	0.2	6.1	3 469.8	10 684	448	743	17 555	34.8	64.3	0.9
Brazos	577.4	2 877	45.4	2.3	6.2	0.4	5.6	1 281.3	6 385	753	471	33 007	34.9	63.9	1.2
Brewster	31.8	3 412	50.6	3.2	7.7	0.4	0.8	9.3	995	286	20	990	50.5	47.6	1.9
Briscoe	3.7	2 339	51.9	0.1	4.3	0.0	11.3	7.8	4 998	10	0	108	24.7	74.3	1.0
Brooks	42.3	5 904	45.4	2.3	10.2	0.3	5.0	40.3	5 626	313	15	534	75.7	24.1	0.3
Brown	120.7	3 191	51.3	7.8	5.5	0.5	4.3	150.8	3 986	128	77	2 608	18.8	80.3	0.9
Burleson	42.2	2 441	59.8	0.6	4.9	0.0	11.0	23.6	1 367	45	36	783	30.8	68.2	1.0
Burnet	148.6	3 420	46.0	1.6	5.8	0.4	3.8	219.9	5 061	80	90	2 319	27.3	71.4	1.3

1. Based on the resident population estimated as of July 1 of the year shown. 2.

STATE/ County code	CBSA code[1]	County type[2]	STATE County	Land area,[3] (sq km) 2010	Population, 2014: Total persons 2014	Population, 2014: Rank	Population, 2014: Per square kilometer	Race alone or in combination, not Hispanic or Latino (percent): White	Black	American Indian, Alaska Native	Asian and Pacific Islander	Percent Hispanic or Latino[4]	Age (percent): Under 5 years	5 to 17 years	18 to 24 years	25 to 34 years	35 to 44 years	45 to 54 years
				1	2	3	4	5	6	7	8	9	10	11	12	13	14	15
			TEXAS—Cont'd															
48 055	12420	1	Caldwell	1 412	39 810	1 175	28.2	43.5	6.8	0.7	1.1	48.9	5.9	18.7	11.9	12.8	12.5	13.2
48 057	38920	3	Calhoun	1 313	21 797	1 744	16.6	44.7	2.8	0.6	5.0	47.7	6.5	18.7	9.4	12.2	11.3	13.3
48 059	10180	3	Callahan	2 329	13 513	2 206	5.8	88.6	1.9	1.2	0.9	8.8	5.3	17.1	7.2	10.5	11.3	14.2
48 061	15180	2	Cameron	2 307	420 392	164	182.2	10.3	0.4	0.2	0.8	88.3	8.8	23.3	10.7	12.2	12.7	11.0
48 063	...	6	Camp	507	12 621	2 256	24.9	59.2	17.5	0.9	1.1	23.0	6.4	19.6	9.0	10.8	11.4	12.3
48 065	11100	3	Carson	2 383	6 013	2 756	2.5	88.2	1.3	1.7	0.6	9.6	5.9	19.3	7.0	10.6	10.9	14.4
48 067	...	6	Cass	2 427	30 261	1 425	12.5	77.5	17.8	1.0	0.7	4.3	5.7	16.7	7.6	10.1	11.5	13.6
48 069	...	6	Castro	2 317	7 781	2 613	3.4	34.8	2.2	0.5	0.5	62.4	9.2	21.9	9.0	11.3	11.1	12.0
48 071	26420	1	Chambers	1 547	38 145	1 217	24.7	69.9	8.2	0.8	1.4	20.4	6.8	20.9	8.6	12.7	14.2	14.3
48 073	27380	6	Cherokee	2 727	50 902	975	18.7	63.0	15.1	0.8	0.7	21.7	6.9	18.8	9.6	11.4	12.2	12.8
48 075	...	7	Childress	1 804	7 089	2 671	3.9	59.6	10.2	0.9	1.0	29.4	5.8	14.6	12.5	19.1	11.8	10.8
48 077	48660	3	Clay	2 820	10 370	2 408	3.7	92.3	1.3	2.1	0.6	5.2	4.9	16.9	7.0	9.2	11.2	14.8
48 079	...	9	Cochran	2 008	2 935	2 981	1.5	38.8	4.2	0.8	0.6	56.7	8.5	20.3	9.2	12.3	9.8	13.5
48 081	...	8	Coke	2 361	3 254	2 954	1.4	76.6	1.2	1.2	0.6	21.4	5.2	14.6	6.7	8.8	8.7	14.7
48 083	...	6	Coleman	3 268	8 430	2 565	2.6	79.1	3.0	1.1	0.7	17.4	5.7	16.0	6.6	8.6	11.2	13.6
48 085	19100	1	Collin	2 179	885 241	60	406.3	63.1	9.7	0.9	13.4	14.9	6.7	20.9	7.9	13.0	16.7	15.2
48 087	...	9	Collingsworth	2 379	3 017	2 976	1.3	61.8	5.3	1.7	0.5	32.1	7.7	21.0	7.7	12.2	9.6	12.7
48 089	...	6	Colorado	2 487	20 719	1 791	8.3	58.9	12.7	0.4	0.8	27.8	5.8	17.3	8.2	10.1	10.2	13.5
48 091	41700	1	Comal	1 449	123 694	501	85.4	70.6	2.2	0.9	1.3	26.1	5.6	17.5	7.7	10.6	12.1	14.6
48 093	...	7	Comanche	2 429	13 550	2 201	5.6	72.1	0.6	0.9	0.4	26.8	6.2	16.7	7.8	9.2	10.4	13.1
48 095	...	8	Concho	2 548	4 050	2 899	1.6	42.9	1.8	0.6	0.7	53.7	3.7	9.6	7.1	17.6	19.3	15.2
48 097	23620	6	Cooke	2 266	38 761	1 203	17.1	78.6	3.6	1.5	1.2	16.7	6.5	17.8	9.0	11.4	10.7	13.4
48 099	28660	2	Coryell	2 725	75 562	728	27.7	63.1	17.9	1.4	4.0	17.1	7.5	18.1	12.6	19.5	14.6	11.3
48 101	...	9	Cottle	2 332	1 415	3 084	0.6	66.0	10.0	0.7	0.2	23.9	4.5	17.3	7.1	9.5	8.6	13.8
48 103	...	6	Crane	2 033	4 950	2 840	2.4	35.7	3.2	1.0	0.5	60.3	8.0	21.1	10.5	13.2	11.4	13.7
48 105	...	7	Crockett	7 271	3 812	2 920	0.5	34.3	0.6	0.6	0.8	64.8	7.7	18.9	7.9	12.2	11.7	13.3
48 107	31180	3	Crosby	2 332	5 899	2 765	2.5	41.9	4.2	0.6	0.2	53.8	7.3	20.7	8.1	10.4	11.0	12.1
48 109	...	9	Culberson	9 875	2 266	3 028	0.2	23.5	1.5	1.4	1.5	73.0	7.1	18.0	9.2	11.1	11.0	13.6
48 111	...	7	Dallam	3 893	7 135	2 667	1.8	54.5	2.1	1.3	1.0	42.5	9.4	22.1	9.6	14.2	12.6	12.7
48 113	19100	1	Dallas	2 257	2 518 638	9	1 115.9	32.7	22.8	0.7	6.1	38.9	7.8	19.3	9.8	16.1	14.2	13.1
48 115	29500	7	Dawson	2 332	13 372	2 217	5.7	38.0	6.7	0.6	0.6	57.1	6.9	17.3	11.0	17.6	11.8	11.3
48 117	25820	6	Deaf Smith	3 877	19 195	1 867	5.0	28.1	1.3	0.6	0.6	69.9	9.3	22.6	10.0	12.9	11.7	11.2
48 119	...	1	Delta	665	5 238	2 819	7.9	83.5	8.5	2.4	1.2	7.0	5.5	16.6	7.4	10.6	10.4	13.1
48 121	19100	1	Denton	2 275	753 363	83	331.1	64.3	9.7	1.0	8.2	18.9	6.8	19.7	9.8	15.0	16.0	14.5
48 123	...	6	DeWitt	2 354	20 684	1 792	8.8	56.8	9.2	0.5	0.5	33.8	6.2	16.0	7.4	11.5	12.1	14.1
48 125	...	8	Dickens	2 335	2 218	3 031	0.9	63.9	5.3	1.2	0.8	29.6	5.9	13.7	8.2	13.7	13.2	11.5
48 127	...	6	Dimmit	3 442	11 089	2 351	3.2	12.8	1.2	0.2	0.6	85.1	8.0	22.1	9.7	11.7	11.1	11.7
48 129	...	8	Donley	2 401	3 543	2 938	1.5	83.9	5.0	1.2	0.7	10.3	5.4	13.9	14.5	9.9	9.1	11.6
48 131	...	7	Duval	4 645	11 533	2 326	2.5	10.2	1.0	0.3	0.2	88.8	7.4	18.6	10.8	11.6	11.5	12.6
48 133	...	6	Eastland	2 400	18 176	1 911	7.6	81.0	2.5	1.1	0.7	15.8	5.7	16.2	10.4	10.7	9.9	12.7
48 135	36220	3	Ector	2 325	153 904	418	66.2	38.1	4.5	0.8	1.1	56.4	8.9	20.7	11.2	15.8	12.0	11.7
48 137	...	9	Edwards	5 485	1 879	3 063	0.3	44.1	0.7	0.8	0.2	54.7	5.8	15.4	6.7	9.8	9.4	11.5
48 139	19100	1	Ellis	2 423	159 317	401	65.8	65.3	9.4	0.9	1.0	24.5	6.6	20.9	9.4	12.2	13.4	14.1
48 141	21340	2	El Paso	2 623	833 487	68	317.8	14.2	3.4	0.5	1.6	80.8	8.2	20.7	11.8	14.1	12.7	11.9
48 143	44500	7	Erath	2 805	40 147	1 169	14.3	77.0	1.8	1.0	1.0	20.0	6.1	15.2	21.4	12.0	10.2	11.2
48 145	47380	6	Falls	1 983	16 989	1 980	8.6	52.7	24.8	0.7	0.7	22.5	6.1	15.0	9.2	14.0	11.8	14.4
48 147	...	6	Fannin	2 307	33 752	1 335	14.6	81.4	7.5	1.9	0.8	10.1	5.4	15.8	8.8	12.0	12.1	14.4
48 149	...	6	Fayette	2 461	24 833	1 615	10.1	73.5	6.8	0.5	0.4	19.6	5.3	16.1	6.9	9.2	9.9	13.8
48 151	...	8	Fisher	2 328	3 831	2 919	1.6	68.5	3.5	1.1	0.3	27.7	4.6	15.8	8.6	8.5	11.2	13.4
48 153	...	6	Floyd	2 570	5 949	2 763	2.3	40.6	3.4	0.4	0.3	55.7	7.5	20.0	8.9	10.4	11.0	12.1
48 155	...	9	Foard	1 824	1 275	3 098	0.7	76.7	5.5	0.6	0.8	17.5	5.2	15.4	7.0	8.8	9.4	15.3
48 157	26420	1	Fort Bend	2 231	685 345	91	307.2	36.9	21.1	0.5	19.2	23.9	6.9	21.4	8.4	12.4	15.3	14.6
48 159	...	8	Franklin	737	10 600	2 389	14.4	81.1	4.8	1.2	0.9	13.4	6.1	18.4	7.4	10.7	10.4	13.3
48 161	...	7	Freestone	2 273	19 762	1 846	8.7	68.2	16.6	0.9	0.7	14.6	6.0	16.9	7.3	11.4	13.4	13.7
48 163	...	6	Frio	2 936	18 531	1 893	6.3	16.5	3.3	0.4	2.3	77.5	7.0	17.1	13.2	17.6	12.6	11.5
48 165	...	7	Gaines	3 891	19 425	1 857	5.0	59.0	1.9	0.6	0.5	38.6	10.0	25.0	9.9	13.6	11.3	11.9
48 167	26420	1	Galveston	980	314 198	212	320.6	59.7	13.7	0.8	3.9	23.4	6.5	18.2	9.0	13.1	13.0	14.7
48 169	...	6	Garza	2 314	6 435	2 721	2.8	44.7	6.6	0.6	0.3	47.6	5.1	13.4	13.9	19.3	12.0	13.8
48 171	23240	7	Gillespie	2 741	25 520	1 584	9.3	77.5	0.5	0.7	0.7	21.3	4.9	14.7	6.6	8.6	9.3	12.5
48 173	13700	8	Glasscock	2 332	1 291	3 097	0.6	65.1	1.7	0.6	0.2	32.7	6.6	19.9	8.7	9.4	15.2	13.1
48 175	47020	3	Goliad	2 207	7 549	2 637	3.4	59.3	5.0	0.8	0.4	35.4	4.6	16.8	8.0	9.1	10.3	14.6
48 177	...	6	Gonzales	2 763	20 462	1 806	7.4	43.9	6.7	0.4	0.5	49.3	7.3	19.7	8.8	11.8	11.3	12.9
48 179	37420	6	Gray	2 398	23 044	1 683	9.6	67.6	5.4	1.5	0.8	26.4	7.2	18.1	8.2	13.6	12.8	13.1
48 181	43300	3	Grayson	2 416	123 534	502	51.1	79.3	6.7	2.3	1.6	12.2	6.2	17.6	9.0	11.7	11.6	13.8
48 183	30980	3	Gregg	708	123 204	503	174.0	60.9	20.6	0.9	1.6	17.5	7.6	18.1	10.4	13.7	12.0	12.6
48 185	...	6	Grimes	2 040	27 172	1 525	13.3	60.4	16.5	0.9	0.6	22.6	5.4	16.5	8.6	12.5	12.4	14.7

1. CBSA = Core Based Statistical Area. See Appendix A for explanation. See Appendix B for list of metropolitan areas with component counties. 2. County type code from the Economic Research Service of USDA Rural-Urban Continuum Codes. See Appendix A for definition. 3. Dry land or land partially or temporarily covered by water. 4. May be of any race.

STATE County	Population, 2013 (cont.) Age (percent) (cont.) 55 to 64 years	65 to 74 years	75 years and over	Percent female	Population change and components of change, 2000–2014 Total persons 2000	2010	Percent change 2000–2010	2010–2014	Components of change, 2010–2014 Births	Deaths	Net migration	Households, 2009–2013 Number	Persons per house-hold	Percent Family house-holds	Female family house-holder[1]	One per-son
	16	17	18	19	20	21	22	23	24	25	26	27	28	29	30	31
TEXAS—Cont'd																
Caldwell	12.0	7.5	5.5	49.5	32 194	38 066	18.2	4.6	2 014	1 187	923	11 593	3.02	67.8	14.4	25.9
Calhoun	12.6	8.9	6.9	49.0	20 647	21 381	3.6	1.9	1 198	858	68	7 870	2.70	73.9	13.0	21.8
Callahan	14.7	11.0	8.7	50.9	12 905	13 544	5.0	-0.2	537	702	139	5 201	2.58	66.1	9.1	30.7
Cameron	9.4	6.7	5.3	51.7	335 227	406 220	21.2	3.5	31 690	10 285	-7 350	117 836	3.46	79.9	20.9	17.6
Camp	13.4	9.4	7.5	51.0	11 549	12 401	7.4	1.8	777	590	78	4 475	2.74	73.1	14.2	25.2
Carson	14.9	9.4	7.7	49.7	6 516	6 182	-5.1	-2.7	251	278	-119	2 337	2.60	76.0	7.0	21.4
Cass	14.0	12.1	8.7	51.5	30 438	30 464	0.1	-0.7	1 477	1 716	-75	11 836	2.52	67.0	13.2	29.2
Castro	11.9	6.9	6.7	48.2	8 285	8 062	-2.7	-3.5	561	207	-621	2 588	3.07	72.4	12.8	23.9
Chambers	12.0	7.0	3.7	49.6	26 031	35 096	34.8	8.7	1 956	1 065	2 113	12 147	2.90	81.0	6.2	15.6
Cherokee	12.4	9.1	6.7	49.1	46 659	50 845	9.0	0.1	3 093	2 074	-856	17 422	2.76	73.6	15.3	23.1
Childress	10.2	7.9	7.3	40.8	7 688	7 041	-8.4	0.7	319	265	-5	2 374	2.36	68.5	6.2	26.1
Clay	16.1	11.6	8.3	50.1	11 006	10 752	-2.3	-3.6	380	483	-280	4 216	2.51	71.5	7.1	25.5
Cochran	11.5	7.4	7.5	51.4	3 730	3 127	-16.2	-6.1	213	89	-321	1 039	2.85	73.1	8.2	23.9
Coke	15.0	14.3	12.1	51.5	3 864	3 320	-14.1	-2.0	119	207	15	1 436	2.16	65.1	8.6	33.3
Coleman	15.1	12.7	10.5	50.3	9 235	8 895	-3.7	-5.2	404	510	-367	3 478	2.48	72.2	12.4	25.5
Collin	10.3	6.0	3.3	50.8	491 675	782 341	59.1	13.2	44 314	14 587	71 342	289 752	2.79	74.0	10.0	21.3
Collingsworth	11.9	9.0	8.2	50.9	3 206	3 057	-4.6	-1.3	197	160	-78	1 174	2.54	64.8	9.0	33.6
Colorado	15.0	10.8	9.4	50.0	20 390	20 874	2.4	-0.7	1 034	1 131	-64	8 079	2.52	70.4	10.5	27.6
Comal	15.0	10.3	6.7	50.7	78 021	108 472	39.0	14.0	5 584	4 182	13 288	41 954	2.64	74.4	10.0	21.4
Comanche	13.9	12.9	9.9	50.6	14 026	13 974	-0.4	-3.0	698	689	-421	5 162	2.64	66.7	9.0	30.6
Concho	12.2	8.6	6.7	30.9	3 966	4 087	3.1	-0.9	108	120	-29	857	3.29	77.2	11.2	21.7
Cooke	13.9	9.7	7.5	50.5	36 363	38 437	5.7	0.8	2 219	1 678	-188	14 466	2.61	71.7	10.9	24.3
Coryell	7.9	5.2	3.3	50.3	74 978	75 388	0.5	0.2	4 217	1 651	-2 493	20 416	3.17	77.5	15.4	19.2
Cottle	14.7	13.9	10.7	52.8	1 904	1 505	-21.0	-6.0	55	88	-61	709	2.16	74.0	13.3	23.0
Crane	10.4	6.6	5.2	50.4	3 996	4 375	9.5	13.1	314	145	407	1 571	2.79	73.4	7.8	21.6
Crockett	13.7	8.4	6.4	50.6	4 099	3 719	-9.3	2.5	238	144	12	1 375	2.73	76.1	6.8	16.4
Crosby	12.3	10.1	7.9	50.9	7 072	6 059	-14.3	-2.6	313	274	-190	2 164	2.75	74.2	12.5	22.4
Culberson	14.1	8.4	7.5	51.7	2 975	2 398	-19.4	-5.5	117	55	-192	838	2.75	67.8	13.1	30.4
Dallam	10.5	5.5	3.3	48.2	6 222	6 703	7.7	6.4	608	158	-35	2 375	2.86	71.5	17.1	25.9
Dallas	10.2	5.5	3.9	50.6	2 218 899	2 368 139	6.7	6.4	164 939	62 685	51 182	858 332	2.77	65.3	16.0	28.7
Dawson	9.8	7.5	6.8	43.0	14 985	13 833	-7.7	-3.3	807	571	-714	4 414	2.63	70.1	12.7	28.1
Deaf Smith	10.6	6.0	5.6	50.5	18 561	19 372	4.4	-0.9	1 463	619	-1 021	6 191	3.07	73.7	12.5	23.8
Delta	14.6	13.2	8.6	50.5	5 327	5 231	-1.8	0.1	247	310	53	1 929	2.67	69.4	11.8	27.7
Denton	10.0	5.4	2.9	50.7	432 976	662 614	53.0	13.7	39 581	12 659	62 384	243 394	2.78	71.1	10.8	22.2
DeWitt	13.9	9.7	9.2	48.0	20 013	20 097	0.4	2.9	1 036	1 012	521	6 948	2.66	67.0	13.1	31.2
Dickens	13.6	10.7	9.6	42.9	2 762	2 444	-11.5	-9.2	93	105	-217	913	2.28	65.9	11.0	32.6
Dimmit	11.4	7.9	6.3	51.0	10 248	9 996	-2.5	10.9	773	341	674	3 542	2.86	69.8	20.3	28.5
Donley	14.0	11.5	10.1	50.9	3 828	3 677	-3.9	-5.0	143	209	-116	1 280	2.60	68.3	13.4	28.9
Duval	10.4	9.4	7.6	48.1	13 120	11 782	-10.2	-2.1	720	551	-429	3 901	2.84	69.2	17.5	27.5
Eastland	13.6	11.6	9.3	50.9	18 297	18 583	1.6	-2.2	820	1 012	-190	6 872	2.55	63.6	10.8	32.0
Ector	10.0	5.5	4.2	49.8	121 123	137 130	13.2	12.2	11 401	4 890	10 226	49 962	2.80	70.1	16.3	24.9
Edwards	16.9	14.8	9.7	50.1	2 162	2 002	-7.4	-6.1	94	67	-155	838	2.45	65.3	8.5	33.8
Ellis	12.0	7.2	4.3	50.6	111 360	149 610	34.3	6.5	8 331	4 507	5 802	51 016	2.95	79.2	12.2	17.3
El Paso	9.7	6.0	4.9	51.0	679 622	800 647	17.8	4.1	58 209	20 423	-4 865	255 573	3.13	75.5	20.1	21.4
Erath	10.4	7.6	5.9	50.7	33 001	37 890	14.8	6.0	2 043	1 284	1 386	14 383	2.57	62.4	10.1	27.4
Falls	12.9	8.9	7.7	52.5	18 576	17 866	-3.8	-4.9	845	730	-987	5 600	2.84	63.9	16.1	33.1
Fannin	13.4	10.4	7.7	47.0	31 242	33 915	8.6	-0.5	1 398	1 681	81	11 814	2.63	71.3	11.6	24.8
Fayette	15.5	12.3	10.9	50.9	21 804	24 554	12.6	1.1	999	1 241	497	9 999	2.41	67.6	6.5	29.2
Fisher	14.7	12.1	11.1	50.4	4 344	3 974	-8.5	-3.6	144	206	-63	1 518	2.54	68.6	8.6	29.1
Floyd	12.0	9.2	8.9	50.3	7 771	6 446	-17.1	-7.7	362	270	-598	2 457	2.55	72.9	12.0	25.2
Foard	13.5	12.9	12.3	52.4	1 622	1 336	-17.6	-4.6	57	78	-38	491	2.23	58.9	9.6	38.7
Fort Bend	11.9	5.8	3.1	50.8	354 452	585 375	65.1	17.2	34 534	10 877	75 041	191 406	3.15	82.9	12.3	14.7
Franklin	13.7	11.4	8.6	50.8	9 458	10 605	12.1	0.0	461	460	9	4 304	2.43	69.4	10.4	25.9
Freestone	13.5	10.1	7.7	47.9	17 867	19 816	10.9	-0.3	962	908	-100	7 251	2.51	69.3	13.6	28.0
Frio	9.6	6.5	4.9	41.5	16 252	17 217	5.9	7.6	1 069	508	769	4 805	3.09	76.4	19.0	17.7
Gaines	8.6	5.1	4.5	49.2	14 467	17 526	21.1	10.8	1 548	472	757	5 437	3.29	76.5	8.6	20.3
Galveston	13.1	7.4	5.0	50.5	250 158	291 309	16.5	7.9	16 703	9 984	15 882	110 032	2.65	69.2	13.0	25.5
Garza	10.7	6.2	5.5	36.1	4 872	6 461	32.6	-0.4	258	231	-62	1 588	2.54	69.9	16.9	26.9
Gillespie	15.5	14.5	13.5	51.8	20 814	24 837	19.3	2.7	1 037	1 458	1 034	10 655	2.30	67.4	9.6	29.2
Glasscock	13.1	8.3	5.7	46.7	1 406	1 226	-12.8	5.3	53	27	39	409	2.84	76.3	3.4	22.0
Goliad	16.2	11.5	8.8	49.5	6 928	7 210	4.1	4.7	281	292	332	3 028	2.35	73.5	10.8	23.7
Gonzales	12.5	8.8	7.0	49.5	18 628	19 807	6.3	3.3	1 194	816	280	6 638	2.95	70.0	15.4	27.0
Gray	11.5	7.9	7.5	47.6	22 744	22 535	-0.9	2.3	1 437	1 033	96	8 388	2.50	67.2	10.8	30.0
Grayson	13.3	9.6	7.1	51.2	110 595	120 877	9.3	2.2	6 372	5 605	1 901	46 559	2.55	69.7	13.6	25.3
Gregg	11.7	7.4	6.6	51.0	111 379	121 730	9.3	1.2	8 100	5 227	-1 431	45 292	2.61	67.8	14.8	28.0
Grimes	14.3	9.5	6.1	45.5	23 552	26 604	13.0	2.3	1 275	1 113	415	8 848	2.65	69.6	16.2	27.1

1. No spouse present.

STATE County	Persons in group quarters, 2014	Daytime population, 2009–2013: Number	Daytime population, 2009–2013: Employment/residence ratio	Births, 2014: Total	Births, 2014: Rate[1]	Deaths, 2014: Number	Deaths, 2014: Rate[1]	Persons under 65 with no health insurance, 2013: Number	Persons under 65 with no health insurance, 2013: Percent	Medicare, 2014: Eligible for Medicare	Medicare, 2014: Enrolled in Medicare Advantage	Medicare, 2014: Enrolled in a Medicare prescription drug plan	Serious crimes known to police,[2] 2013: Total: Number	Serious crimes known to police,[2] 2013: Total: Rate[3]
	32	33	34	35	36	37	38	39	40	41	42	43	44	45
TEXAS—Cont'd														
Caldwell	3 378	31 893	0.57	471	11.8	290	7.3	8 344	25.5	6 235	1 408	3 181	872	2 229
Calhoun	251	24 767	1.38	280	12.8	205	9.4	4 365	23.9	3 875	439	1 946	518	2 639
Callahan	72	10 724	0.48	134	9.9	171	12.7	2 657	24.5	3 018	602	1 600	164	1 208
Cameron	3 881	408 583	0.98	7 277	17.3	2 505	6.0	127 645	35.2	55 008	19 740	25 583	15 746	3 750
Camp	79	11 786	0.87	193	15.3	117	9.3	2 951	28.7	2 589	590	1 382	426	3 404
Carson	27	5 096	0.65	54	9.0	61	10.1	972	19.6	1 102	194	615	54	874
Cass	355	27 368	0.74	353	11.7	410	13.5	5 014	21.0	7 245	1 711	3 747	969	3 209
Castro	56	7 553	0.85	126	16.2	47	6.0	2 551	37.0	1 142	99	741	211	2 568
Chambers	229	32 986	0.83	479	12.6	235	6.2	6 378	19.6	5 148	1 327	2 257	1 011	2 758
Cherokee	2 895	47 982	0.85	725	14.2	487	9.6	11 672	29.0	9 688	2 426	5 514	1 378	2 685
Childress	1 460	7 321	1.10	66	9.3	59	8.3	959	21.0	1 268	256	798	NA	NA
Clay	71	7 678	0.40	96	9.3	116	11.2	1 822	21.8	2 346	305	1 324	102	970
Cochran	78	3 018	0.95	51	17.4	11	3.7	846	33.5	533	91	319	119	3 927
Coke	43	2 898	0.73	27	8.3	43	13.2	616	26.2	862	156	514	21	653
Coleman	43	8 196	0.83	91	10.8	108	12.8	1 731	26.4	2 278	328	1 368	234	2 708
Collin	4 360	762 729	0.88	10 488	11.8	3 756	4.2	124 520	16.2	90 117	21 975	41 650	17 875	2 093
Collingsworth	47	2 812	0.81	43	14.3	26	8.6	908	35.7	585	75	394	0	0
Colorado	366	20 295	0.95	242	11.7	258	12.5	4 314	26.3	4 693	519	2 931	338	1 631
Comal	1 219	107 150	0.90	1 412	11.4	965	7.8	19 830	20.4	25 004	6 391	9 901	2 992	2 566
Comanche	157	12 839	0.80	155	11.4	172	12.7	3 356	32.0	3 360	581	1 924	308	2 240
Concho	1 624	4 126	1.05	22	5.4	32	7.9	485	26.5	633	111	388	14	350
Cooke	690	37 294	0.93	539	13.9	411	10.6	7 945	25.4	7 363	1 319	4 210	NA	NA
Coryell	11 578	66 931	0.70	955	12.6	391	5.2	11 835	20.3	8 427	1 923	2 244	1 501	1 922
Cottle	0	1 421	0.82	10	7.1	16	11.3	382	34.9	433	86	286	5	336
Crane	91	4 426	0.97	90	18.2	27	5.5	1 022	24.5	626	98	363	40	861
Crockett	49	3 988	1.08	56	14.7	21	5.5	855	26.5	630	73	394	NA	NA
Crosby	67	5 552	0.80	65	11.0	51	8.6	1 404	28.8	1 242	320	706	58	939
Culberson	12	2 385	1.04	29	12.8	13	5.7	599	31.5	465	70	317	15	662
Dallam	40	7 091	1.07	146	20.5	27	3.8	2 153	33.7	916	115	501	164	2 307
Dallas	32 963	2 738 281	1.29	38 722	15.4	15 446	6.1	650 012	29.4	285 359	81 263	129 648	102 159	4 101
Dawson	1 649	13 776	1.00	191	14.3	129	9.6	2 566	26.5	2 291	362	1 433	507	3 719
Deaf Smith	380	19 813	1.06	346	18.0	172	9.0	4 922	29.3	2 657	406	1 606	611	3 147
Delta	67	4 241	0.48	55	10.5	60	11.5	1 104	27.1	1 283	168	724	83	1 542
Denton	10 673	558 868	0.63	9 592	12.7	3 240	4.3	113 662	17.3	72 578	19 122	32 895	14 709	2 040
DeWitt	1 837	19 952	0.96	257	12.4	210	10.2	3 221	21.4	4 273	560	2 771	630	3 045
Dickens	315	2 363	0.98	22	9.9	21	9.5	457	30.3	510	92	315	12	524
Dimmit	94	13 329	1.80	213	19.2	80	7.2	2 194	23.7	1 800	507	1 008	458	4 299
Donley	295	3 338	0.81	39	11.0	46	13.0	748	29.7	843	130	524	44	1 227
Duval	573	11 219	0.88	161	14.0	140	12.1	2 198	24.1	2 279	666	1 241	433	3 681
Eastland	882	18 143	0.96	169	9.3	235	12.9	3 821	27.7	4 309	856	2 425	514	2 918
Ector	2 280	140 806	0.99	2 911	18.9	1 177	7.6	33 718	25.4	17 806	3 198	9 816	7 496	5 084
Edwards	5	2 015	0.94	18	9.6	12	6.4	499	35.3	520	81	279	47	2 387
Ellis	1 768	129 251	0.68	1 943	12.2	1 117	7.0	30 377	22.3	22 459	4 855	10 697	3 458	2 230
El Paso	15 918	810 234	0.99	13 494	16.2	4 925	5.9	221 287	30.7	113 014	53 288	33 026	21 096	2 515
Erath	3 280	38 588	0.99	484	12.1	315	7.8	9 792	30.8	5 916	1 177	3 021	841	2 104
Falls	1 816	15 361	0.62	199	11.7	160	9.4	3 293	26.1	3 251	953	1 403	112	725
Fannin	3 125	29 755	0.69	320	9.5	404	12.0	6 360	25.4	7 137	1 140	3 729	456	1 455
Fayette	455	23 512	0.90	224	9.0	300	12.1	4 923	26.1	6 082	908	3 592	313	1 259
Fisher	22	3 452	0.73	33	8.6	55	14.4	695	23.6	924	181	559	110	2 874
Floyd	34	5 831	0.81	83	14.0	57	9.6	1 453	28.6	1 212	287	765	147	2 304
Foard	30	1 102	0.93	14	11.0	14	11.0	291	30.5	341	45	226	7	538
Fort Bend	4 953	476 404	0.54	8 621	12.6	2 855	4.2	104 861	17.8	66 386	21 130	27 108	12 454	1 939
Franklin	94	10 352	0.94	107	10.1	118	11.1	2 203	26.0	2 324	472	1 375	131	1 224
Freestone	1 606	18 786	0.89	226	11.4	197	10.0	3 807	25.9	3 691	651	2 193	353	1 811
Frio	3 339	19 085	1.25	266	14.4	125	6.7	2 981	23.4	2 426	659	1 505	411	2 290
Gaines	86	17 488	0.93	379	19.5	122	6.3	5 780	34.0	1 885	263	1 199	296	1 577
Galveston	4 836	267 471	0.79	3 972	12.6	2 513	8.0	52 604	19.9	46 592	11 546	20 219	10 342	3 397
Garza	2 142	6 724	1.21	54	8.4	49	7.6	875	25.1	816	218	447	51	794
Gillespie	326	24 862	0.99	251	9.8	350	13.7	5 087	28.0	7 372	1 170	4 158	376	1 483
Glasscock	0	1 379	1.40	12	9.3	6	4.6	221	20.7	198	21	122	9	706
Goliad	106	5 985	0.58	72	9.5	62	8.2	1 157	19.7	1 524	259	898	123	1 657
Gonzales	321	20 436	1.06	277	13.5	194	9.5	5 180	30.7	3 710	613	2 239	681	3 370
Gray	1 606	22 771	1.00	355	15.4	239	10.4	4 544	25.3	4 028	610	2 257	995	4 279
Grayson	2 213	117 071	0.92	1 497	12.1	1 290	10.4	23 205	23.1	24 902	4 577	12 647	3 387	2 783
Gregg	4 326	142 839	1.38	1 898	15.4	1 267	10.3	24 786	24.1	21 767	4 757	11 793	5 219	4 229
Grimes	3 037	24 695	0.79	306	11.3	235	8.6	5 498	27.4	4 779	1 074	2 315	571	2 119

1. Per 1,000 estimated resident population. 2. Data for serious crimes have not been adjusted for underreporting; this may affect comparability between geographic areas and over time.
3. Per 100,000 population estimated by the FBI.

Table B. States and Counties — **Crime, Education, Money Income, and Poverty**

STATE County	Serious crimes known to police, 2013 (cont.)[1] Rate[2] Violent	Property	Education: School enrollment and attainment, 2009–2013 Enrollment[3] Total	Percent private	Attainment[4] (percent) High school graduate or less	Bachelor's degree or more	Local government expenditures,[5] 2012–2013 Total current spending (mil dol)	Current spending per student (dollars)	Money income, 2009–2013 Per capita income[6] (dollars)	Households Median income (dollars)	Mean income (dollars)	Percent with income of $200,000 or more	Income and poverty, 2013 Median household income (dollars)	Percent below poverty level All persons	Children under 18 years	Children 5 to 17 years in families
	46	47	48	49	50	51	52	53	54	55	56	57	58	59	60	61
TEXAS—Cont'd																
Caldwell	314	1 915	10 101	8.6	58.6	15.7	53.6	8 126	19 673	44 152	58 073	2.6	46 021	17.2	26.0	25.1
Calhoun	448	2 191	5 255	6.0	55.6	15.7	34.9	8 209	23 381	47 027	61 307	2.9	51 004	18.1	28.9	26.4
Callahan	52	1 157	3 143	12.9	48.8	14.7	22.3	9 142	22 855	44 902	56 996	2.1	42 138	14.3	23.5	21.4
Cameron	239	3 510	128 449	4.5	60.4	15.4	912.1	9 142	14 710	33 179	48 645	1.8	33 905	32.4	44.6	42.0
Camp	320	3 085	3 188	3.9	55.2	15.2	30.1	11 929	19 176	37 079	50 786	1.5	37 941	18.1	33.5	30.6
Carson	162	712	1 580	3.0	42.9	21.5	13.3	10 205	26 827	65 026	70 048	2.4	59 252	8.5	11.7	10.5
Cass	295	2 914	6 850	4.8	56.9	13.0	51.1	9 042	20 104	35 598	47 736	0.8	37 546	21.8	31.6	27.6
Castro	195	2 373	2 156	3.8	66.6	12.8	16.7	9 616	19 708	36 402	55 985	1.3	40 689	19.6	30.4	29.8
Chambers	221	2 537	9 443	6.2	45.4	18.0	69.0	9 679	30 140	72 489	87 586	4.6	74 915	10.5	14.6	14.1
Cherokee	374	2 310	12 829	8.3	57.3	15.1	86.0	7 993	18 801	38 378	52 916	1.6	37 735	23.6	37.0	33.1
Childress	NA	NA	1 553	12.4	55.1	18.6	10.0	8 812	20 248	47 532	61 349	3.4	33 919	25.5	32.8	31.3
Clay	57	913	2 318	9.7	49.3	18.2	17.2	10 467	25 867	53 776	65 207	1.9	50 336	13.0	20.3	18.5
Cochran	264	3 663	762	4.5	65.5	12.4	12.1	15 506	17 371	38 650	50 020	1.4	37 242	23.6	35.1	33.3
Coke	31	622	657	2.1	49.5	17.4	5.9	11 631	26 407	40 795	58 388	2.9	38 866	14.4	23.2	22.3
Coleman	174	2 534	1 584	1.9	57.6	15.0	13.1	10 003	18 967	31 373	45 799	1.2	33 014	22.8	37.0	34.5
Collin	148	1 945	236 755	13.7	22.2	49.3	1 418.7	7 958	37 839	82 762	104 541	10.1	81 315	7.9	9.9	9.0
Collingsworth	0	0	727	5.8	49.6	18.9	5.6	9 423	22 847	41 576	56 849	4.3	35 389	21.4	36.9	33.7
Colorado	169	1 462	4 314	14.7	57.3	16.9	32.3	9 215	24 348	45 146	60 123	2.6	42 438	16.9	24.8	23.5
Comal	237	2 330	26 679	13.9	35.1	33.3	198.9	7 424	32 980	65 839	86 641	6.3	70 322	10.5	15.6	14.2
Comanche	182	2 058	2 884	5.8	56.0	18.9	21.0	9 441	19 268	36 020	48 056	1.2	35 434	20.3	32.3	30.7
Concho	100	250	596	6.5	69.2	10.8	4.8	9 901	19 976	51 411	64 052	1.9	39 035	26.9	28.7	28.2
Cooke	NA	NA	9 439	10.8	47.2	19.5	54.3	8 738	25 186	50 067	65 508	3.2	53 565	15.5	24.1	22.9
Coryell	151	1 771	21 896	8.8	44.2	15.1	93.6	8 023	19 357	49 819	60 412	1.4	50 161	14.8	21.3	20.7
Cottle	135	202	304	5.3	54.1	16.1	2.9	13 114	21 089	34 639	45 451	1.3	32 292	21.9	35.8	31.7
Crane	108	753	1 307	2.0	59.7	13.6	13.5	12 637	22 291	50 417	64 451	2.0	58 901	10.1	13.1	12.7
Crockett	NA	NA	694	3.5	61.3	11.1	9.9	12 346	23 872	50 475	63 908	0.7	50 243	13.9	20.2	19.5
Crosby	146	793	1 514	6.5	61.4	13.8	15.7	12 378	18 959	38 187	52 802	2.1	35 443	27.3	43.3	40.2
Culberson	132	530	554	1.1	67.0	16.5	5.5	12 734	16 227	37 105	43 572	0.7	32 945	24.7	36.0	34.6
Dallam	492	1 815	1 825	13.2	60.2	10.4	16.6	8 737	19 752	40 895	53 757	1.5	42 378	14.1	20.6	20.0
Dallas	439	3 661	657 540	13.4	45.7	28.6	3 577.5	8 157	26 816	49 481	72 851	5.0	47 902	19.5	29.5	28.7
Dawson	337	3 382	3 134	3.8	64.1	9.4	28.5	10 980	17 677	39 714	53 254	2.1	38 333	23.8	30.7	30.3
Deaf Smith	319	2 828	5 466	5.4	62.2	15.6	36.0	8 139	17 532	41 444	53 531	0.9	37 991	21.5	31.3	30.2
Delta	19	1 524	1 228	4.9	51.2	16.2	7.0	9 063	20 150	40 375	50 840	0.9	37 985	19.2	30.7	28.1
Denton	177	1 863	215 359	12.2	27.2	40.5	966.1	8 204	33 855	74 155	93 375	7.7	75 099	8.9	11.0	10.1
DeWitt	546	2 499	4 222	5.6	61.3	12.4	33.6	11 403	23 720	46 454	64 244	3.4	45 937	18.5	28.4	26.2
Dickens	131	393	388	5.2	54.8	13.5	5.2	12 935	20 578	38 401	50 727	1.4	35 491	23.2	35.5	34.0
Dimmit	422	3 876	2 762	5.9	64.4	9.2	22.8	9 338	17 516	36 681	49 135	1.0	35 801	27.0	39.0	37.5
Donley	139	1 087	1 029	15.5	48.2	16.7	6.6	11 241	21 904	42 411	54 362	2.3	34 861	19.7	32.1	31.2
Duval	765	2 916	2 615	4.5	67.4	6.8	25.9	10 199	20 181	34 131	55 068	2.3	35 118	25.6	35.7	33.9
Eastland	159	2 759	4 360	9.0	53.6	16.0	27.4	9 101	21 125	34 914	52 767	2.0	39 959	17.3	29.9	28.5
Ector	806	4 277	38 706	8.9	55.7	13.5	219.9	7 418	24 247	51 466	66 858	3.0	53 752	15.3	21.9	19.6
Edwards	203	2 184	357	0.0	54.0	24.2	7.5	14 247	22 015	43 839	50 827	0.5	35 339	23.0	38.3	37.2
Ellis	129	2 101	44 463	11.3	46.3	20.7	253.4	7 857	25 662	61 952	75 119	3.8	59 257	13.1	18.7	17.3
El Paso	341	2 174	264 351	7.0	50.0	20.7	1 520.3	8 554	18 379	40 157	55 486	2.1	39 748	22.7	31.2	31.9
Erath	120	1 984	13 030	4.7	45.5	24.3	46.3	8 305	21 670	39 586	55 672	2.7	40 346	21.8	25.4	24.2
Falls	123	602	4 258	5.7	63.8	10.7	26.7	11 344	16 486	32 908	45 122	0.6	34 376	25.2	33.4	32.9
Fannin	147	1 308	7 470	7.2	54.4	15.0	50.2	9 080	20 337	44 355	55 003	1.3	42 392	19.0	25.1	23.3
Fayette	133	1 127	5 253	12.4	56.4	16.8	35.0	9 467	27 032	48 015	64 245	4.0	50 938	11.2	18.4	17.1
Fisher	444	2 429	901	5.2	54.4	15.2	6.5	11 775	22 709	42 125	56 026	0.9	40 691	17.2	26.7	24.0
Floyd	251	2 053	1 680	4.7	56.7	17.1	14.5	11 005	21 655	42 279	56 985	2.6	36 534	20.5	34.0	32.3
Foard	230	307	227	2.6	49.2	21.8	2.7	12 393	20 202	33 750	43 873	0.0	33 484	17.8	28.7	27.6
Fort Bend	255	1 685	190 575	14.6	29.9	41.4	1 254.9	7 541	34 084	85 297	106 472	11.3	87 901	8.9	12.2	11.3
Franklin	140	1 084	2 385	9.9	48.9	20.3	13.7	8 461	28 189	45 523	70 331	4.2	41 497	18.3	29.8	26.5
Freestone	164	1 647	4 610	3.1	55.7	11.7	38.8	10 661	22 876	44 502	59 729	2.3	44 408	16.3	22.8	21.4
Frio	106	2 184	4 460	6.0	70.8	6.5	32.0	9 908	15 863	35 849	54 163	1.8	35 405	31.0	35.9	34.7
Gaines	144	1 433	4 752	20.8	67.4	11.9	42.9	12 770	21 572	52 910	69 647	3.8	49 661	15.1	21.4	20.4
Galveston	235	3 163	81 062	8.9	38.6	28.5	605.6	7 850	30 926	61 877	81 683	6.2	60 210	14.2	20.2	19.7
Garza	47	747	1 276	7.9	65.6	9.5	10.1	12 389	16 175	47 540	61 445	4.7	47 134	28.2	29.0	27.6
Gillespie	59	1 424	4 719	15.4	41.2	29.2	33.6	9 328	30 117	53 668	70 458	4.2	50 443	13.0	22.4	21.1
Glasscock	0	706	292	7.2	49.8	18.8	5.7	19 599	31 135	69 107	89 143	6.6	65 789	9.4	16.0	15.4
Goliad	108	1 549	1 505	3.6	47.2	14.2	13.8	10 063	30 031	50 923	71 155	4.0	48 458	14.9	24.9	22.2
Gonzales	614	2 757	5 051	12.5	61.6	14.5	37.8	9 168	20 288	39 248	56 244	2.5	37 051	22.0	30.7	28.8
Gray	821	3 458	5 169	9.4	52.5	13.5	34.1	8 337	21 738	43 504	57 796	1.5	48 623	14.9	18.5	17.3
Grayson	207	2 516	29 876	11.5	45.2	19.6	184.2	8 670	24 003	46 429	60 855	2.7	44 596	16.4	21.9	20.5
Gregg	483	3 746	31 399	10.2	45.1	19.9	213.1	8 859	24 064	45 525	62 581	2.8	46 501	17.0	24.5	22.3
Grimes	378	1 740	6 054	6.7	58.7	11.1	41.9	9 619	20 307	43 994	59 127	2.4	44 486	19.5	26.9	23.8

1. Data for serious crimes have not been adjusted for underreporting; this may affect comparability between geographic areas and over time. 2. Per 100,000 population estimated by the FBI.
3. All persons 3 years old and over enrolled in nursery school through college. 4. Persons 25 years old and over. 5. Elementary and secondary education expenditures.
6. Based on population estimated by the American Community Survey, 2009–2013.

STATE County	Personal income, 2013										Earnings, 2013		
	Total (mil dol)	Percent change, 2012–2013	Per capita[1]		Wages and salaries (mil dol)	Supplements to wages and salaries; employer contributions (mil dol)		Proprietors' income (mil dol)	Dividends, interest, and rent (mil dol)	Personal transfer receipts (mil dol)	Total (mil dol)	Contributions for government social insurance (mil dol)	
			Dollars	Rank		Pension and insurance	Government social insurance					From employee and self-employed	From employer
	62	63	64	65	66	67	68	69	70	71	72	73	74
TEXAS—Cont'd													
Caldwell	1 157	3.0	29 483	2 755	313	54	22	107	217	289	496	29	22
Calhoun	782	1.8	35 858	1 770	628	108	43	89	127	174	868	45	43
Callahan	499	2.4	36 892	1 607	83	15	5	36	88	121	139	9	5
Cameron	10 349	2.1	24 802	3 062	4 285	880	308	836	1 368	3 271	6 308	339	308
Camp	440	2.6	35 458	1 828	147	26	10	48	74	114	231	13	10
Carson	286	6.3	47 640	503	338	33	23	64	40	40	458	23	23
Cass	1 030	-0.2	33 946	2 090	268	53	18	111	176	332	450	28	18
Castro	331	-11.2	41 188	1 026	87	14	6	117	39	59	224	6	6
Chambers	2 006	1.9	54 496	220	783	118	54	67	232	228	1 021	55	54
Cherokee	1 623	1.3	31 893	2 423	534	105	35	169	281	467	843	46	35
Childress	203	12.3	28 561	2 845	78	19	5	34	37	56	136	6	5
Clay	537	0.8	51 237	327	55	11	3	119	86	94	189	9	3
Cochran	129	10.7	42 759	864	31	7	2	40	18	27	80	2	2
Coke	119	0.8	36 991	1 587	23	6	1	12	26	33	42	3	1
Coleman	310	0.2	36 322	1 691	65	14	4	38	75	100	121	8	4
Collin	47 458	3.6	55 520	194	20 371	2 353	1 357	5 954	7 207	3 374	30 036	1 500	1 357
Collingsworth	138	11.3	44 534	727	34	6	2	24	35	32	66	3	2
Colorado	914	1.8	44 021	754	283	45	20	94	202	207	443	25	20
Comal	5 742	4.6	48 466	454	1 745	245	123	463	1 286	931	2 577	145	123
Comanche	504	2.6	37 013	1 584	119	24	8	81	111	137	232	12	8
Concho	116	6.1	28 814	2 820	34	6	2	18	24	29	60	3	2
Cooke	2 262	1.8	58 815	123	785	113	54	536	435	324	1 489	70	54
Coryell	2 812	-1.5	36 900	1 602	529	117	34	107	652	458	787	39	34
Cottle	60	0.3	41 652	981	16	3	1	7	12	18	28	2	1
Crane	219	4.0	45 803	633	117	18	7	35	22	27	177	9	7
Crockett	155	5.4	40 585	1 101	65	12	4	14	35	25	95	5	4
Crosby	298	16.9	49 814	374	53	10	4	102	37	64	169	5	4
Culberson	85	5.9	37 359	1 529	40	8	3	9	13	22	60	3	3
Dallam	349	8.2	49 518	386	159	22	12	167	37	47	360	13	12
Dallas	120 638	2.5	48 638	442	95 503	11 232	6 518	26 994	19 790	14 250	140 247	6 927	6 518
Dawson	480	10.7	34 782	1 936	176	32	11	91	95	114	310	13	11
Deaf Smith	698	-3.8	36 401	1 674	277	46	18	158	111	140	499	20	18
Delta	163	2.8	31 172	2 522	31	9	2	9	26	54	51	3	2
Denton	33 237	3.4	45 605	647	9 280	1 300	641	1 922	4 703	3 085	13 143	683	641
DeWitt	941	3.9	45 919	624	309	55	20	107	274	201	490	26	20
Dickens	77	4.2	33 780	2 129	19	4	1	13	16	24	37	2	1
Dimmit	478	7.1	43 890	769	266	44	18	29	74	100	357	19	18
Donley	153	21.5	43 555	793	48	9	3	26	20	35	86	4	3
Duval	470	4.0	40 347	1 129	180	31	13	32	46	138	255	15	13
Eastland	1 283	4.4	70 322	45	343	55	24	457	263	204	879	38	24
Ector	6 598	4.2	44 168	744	4 175	490	278	680	807	892	5 623	294	278
Edwards	67	-1.1	35 384	1 839	16	4	1	7	19	20	28	2	1
Ellis	5 867	2.4	37 616	1 487	1 757	286	128	397	719	944	2 568	142	128
El Paso	25 788	1.2	31 156	2 524	12 178	2 599	934	2 680	4 295	5 731	18 390	904	934
Erath	1 301	2.3	32 800	2 282	501	93	34	132	246	272	761	37	34
Falls	560	2.2	32 019	2 410	124	31	8	77	81	170	239	12	8
Fannin	1 102	3.6	32 728	2 297	259	58	18	99	174	320	434	26	18
Fayette	1 125	1.7	45 338	667	364	61	24	84	329	241	534	31	24
Fisher	185	29.1	48 096	474	35	7	2	50	31	40	94	3	2
Floyd	278	6.8	44 677	717	64	12	4	100	33	60	180	5	4
Foard	46	0.6	35 656	1 807	9	2	1	6	8	16	18	1	1
Fort Bend	35 043	3.9	53 717	245	8 689	1 086	572	2 953	4 658	2 630	13 300	675	572
Franklin	391	2.8	36 679	1 641	108	17	8	64	86	94	197	11	8
Freestone	717	1.5	36 516	1 660	272	48	19	100	139	159	439	24	19
Frio	587	4.0	32 501	2 332	289	44	19	43	75	129	395	21	19
Gaines	699	4.9	36 931	1 597	281	45	19	177	89	95	521	21	19
Galveston	14 476	2.2	47 186	539	4 611	903	300	840	2 700	2 138	6 654	336	300
Garza	390	8.8	61 667	89	77	12	5	246	34	41	341	12	5
Gillespie	1 383	1.6	54 527	217	336	54	24	118	626	248	532	32	24
Glasscock	98	13.9	78 659	24	16	3	1	26	37	6	46	1	1
Goliad	269	3.1	36 019	1 743	62	12	4	17	71	65	95	6	4
Gonzales	755	4.9	37 183	1 550	250	45	16	83	180	166	393	20	16
Gray	1 055	2.4	45 773	636	450	69	30	221	183	173	770	37	30
Grayson	4 417	3.4	36 098	1 730	1 852	277	128	276	762	1 105	2 533	148	128
Gregg	5 897	2.8	47 934	487	3 751	480	270	1 114	1 011	1 068	5 615	288	270
Grimes	935	1.2	34 808	1 929	386	65	26	84	165	198	561	30	26

1. Based on the resident population estimated as of July 1 of the year shown.

STATE County	Earnings, 2013 (cont.) — Percent by selected industries: Farm	Mining	Construction	Manufacturing	Information: professional, scientific, technical services	Retail trade	Finance, insurance, real estate and leasing	Health care and social assistance	Government	Social Security beneficiaries, December 2013: Number	Rate[1]	Supplemental Security Income recipients, December 2013	Housing units, 2014: Total	Percent change, 2010–2014
	75	76	77	78	79	80	81	82	83	84	85	86	87	88
TEXAS—Cont'd														
Caldwell	0.7	8.2	11.2	6.7	2.9	8.6	5.8	11.8	18.3	6 735	172	1 034	13 834	0.6
Calhoun	1.4	1.7	18.7	45.5	D	5.2	2.8	2.3	8.6	4 235	194	596	11 737	2.9
Callahan	0.9	8.6	18.0	5.6	2.6	11.0	4.1	5.7	23.0	3 280	243	341	6 586	0.6
Cameron	0.9	0.1	4.2	5.2	3.9	9.1	4.4	20.6	28.3	60 040	144	23 153	146 182	3.0
Camp	4.4	D	9.7	2.9	D	8.6	6.5	D	12.5	2 815	227	427	5 671	0.3
Carson	9.5	2.0	D	D	D	1.8	D	D	4.4	1 185	198	60	2 771	-0.5
Cass	1.8	3.5	6.7	21.4	2.8	8.3	3.6	D	17.9	8 085	266	1 135	14 407	0.2
Castro	54.0	D	1.2	1.3	D	4.0	2.0	1.0	12.4	1 250	156	159	3 184	0.6
Chambers	1.3	6.7	16.3	29.6	D	3.4	5.2	D	11.0	5 810	156	587	14 418	8.5
Cherokee	4.7	3.8	7.9	12.5	D	5.9	4.8	D	23.9	10 575	207	1 594	20 977	0.6
Childress	17.8	D	D	D	3.8	8.2	3.8	4.9	39.9	1 335	189	171	2 865	-0.6
Clay	1.9	29.2	7.6	5.9	D	6.4	4.9	D	13.2	2 610	250	199	5 149	0.0
Cochran	46.5	D	D	0.0	D	3.3	D	2.0	21.4	615	205	116	1 357	-0.2
Coke	3.1	17.6	10.3	2.8	D	6.7	D	2.2	30.7	885	275	64	2 663	-0.1
Coleman	-0.5	9.7	10.1	2.2	D	9.3	7.8	D	22.2	2 500	293	283	5 527	-0.3
Collin	0.1	2.7	6.0	9.2	19.7	6.6	12.0	9.7	8.8	89 215	104	7 495	327 567	8.8
Collingsworth	30.3	0.0	D	D	D	2.5	D	D	15.6	655	212	89	1 609	-0.4
Colorado	1.0	5.4	11.5	20.2	D	7.4	5.5	D	12.1	4 895	236	515	10 551	0.2
Comal	0.0	1.7	13.3	7.2	6.2	11.2	5.1	10.1	12.5	25 565	215	1 396	51 427	9.2
Comanche	10.9	1.7	7.2	2.6	7.8	9.7	4.2	5.0	19.7	3 665	270	375	7 265	0.6
Concho	20.2	D	D	D	D	2.5	D	8.1	20.4	700	170	75	1 641	0.2
Cooke	0.4	37.0	6.6	15.0	D	4.7	3.2	D	10.3	7 750	201	700	16 690	0.5
Coryell	0.2	D	9.3	2.3	7.8	7.4	5.4	D	43.6	9 565	125	1 211	26 032	3.4
Cottle	24.9	0.3	D	D	D	7.1	D	4.2	22.3	460	319	53	960	-0.8
Crane	0.3	D	D	D	D	3.0	D	3.0	11.6	675	142	109	1 662	1.8
Crockett	0.3	42.1	D	D	D	5.7	3.5	0.9	19.9	685	182	54	1 869	0.2
Crosby	58.6	2.2	D	D	D	5.9	1.8	D	12.6	1 325	221	199	2 910	0.3
Culberson	11.9	D	D	D	D	11.9	D	D	32.9	505	221	121	1 153	1.4
Dallam	25.4	D	9.3	9.9	4.5	3.3	6.4	1.2	4.3	960	136	86	2 896	2.4
Dallas	0.0	5.4	6.0	7.9	16.8	4.7	13.4	9.0	8.9	298 625	120	64 439	974 457	3.3
Dawson	19.8	12.4	4.7	1.5	1.8	12.4	2.9	D	24.2	2 465	186	451	5 202	-0.3
Deaf Smith	23.2	D	4.6	16.1	3.2	6.0	3.7	2.2	13.1	2 830	147	440	7 061	-0.2
Delta	5.5	0.0	D	D	D	2.3	3.3	D	27.1	1 400	269	186	2 466	0.3
Denton	0.1	1.7	7.6	8.7	11.5	7.8	7.6	10.9	16.1	74 030	102	6 046	280 409	9.5
DeWitt	0.8	15.2	8.0	12.2	4.1	6.6	10.5	D	21.7	4 575	223	602	9 170	-0.1
Dickens	31.0	D	D	D	D	4.3	D	1.3	19.4	590	258	62	1 282	0.0
Dimmit	-0.1	32.5	9.4	1.5	D	4.2	2.6	D	22.6	2 010	184	673	4 357	0.2
Donley	22.5	D	D	D	2.4	5.3	2.5	4.3	20.5	885	247	69	2 135	-0.3
Duval	-0.5	26.8	D	D	D	2.9	D	3.6	24.6	2 520	217	672	5 534	0.2
Eastland	-0.4	48.4	8.3	4.0	1.7	3.3	D	D	10.4	4 665	256	569	10 251	-0.1
Ector	0.1	22.5	11.8	7.9	4.0	6.1	4.7	5.3	10.2	19 540	131	3 680	56 500	6.5
Edwards	3.9	D	D	D	D	12.4	D	D	36.2	520	277	94	1 608	0.1
Ellis	0.4	0.5	10.1	26.1	3.6	7.8	3.4	6.7	14.6	23 810	152	2 674	57 041	4.9
El Paso	0.0	0.1	6.9	6.1	5.1	7.4	5.1	10.1	36.9	118 975	143	30 044	286 659	6.0
Erath	6.8	1.4	8.5	11.5	4.6	7.7	3.9	9.9	22.0	6 135	153	660	17 460	2.8
Falls	7.6	D	5.4	3.6	D	8.8	3.1	8.2	33.5	3 535	204	785	7 723	0.0
Fannin	1.6	2.2	7.7	6.4	2.9	8.5	4.6	9.3	34.8	7 695	229	871	14 228	0.3
Fayette	0.5	8.7	7.4	8.5	4.8	10.0	7.3	8.7	17.8	6 280	253	455	13 869	0.0
Fisher	48.8	D	D	D	D	2.2	3.8	2.4	16.5	985	257	100	2 205	-0.3
Floyd	52.5	D	1.6	2.1	D	3.3	D	2.5	14.6	1 305	209	172	2 993	-0.4
Foard	24.2	0.0	D	D	D	7.8	D	D	23.0	360	283	36	789	0.0
Fort Bend	0.3	6.6	15.9	13.2	9.0	7.1	5.8	8.2	10.1	65 025	99	10 460	223 983	13.8
Franklin	4.0	D	9.3	D	D	4.8	6.1	18.4	10.9	2 535	239	271	5 784	0.2
Freestone	-0.6	25.1	15.0	1.6	3.0	7.5	2.8	D	16.4	3 890	198	401	9 290	0.3
Frio	3.8	20.5	4.7	0.9	D	5.1	3.9	D	18.1	2 610	144	739	5 894	0.8
Gaines	13.7	23.9	12.5	1.5	1.4	6.8	2.4	D	13.6	2 035	107	344	6 356	0.9
Galveston	0.0	1.6	7.5	13.8	6.5	7.3	7.2	6.9	27.8	49 260	160	6 625	139 612	5.4
Garza	6.3	55.2	6.7	1.5	D	1.8	2.8	D	6.3	865	135	120	2 223	-0.6
Gillespie	0.4	1.5	14.8	8.4	5.4	11.0	5.9	17.7	11.7	7 605	300	291	12 911	1.0
Glasscock	48.1	D	D	D	D	D	D	D	13.9	190	153	11	581	0.2
Goliad	0.4	13.6	7.1	2.9	D	5.5	2.7	D	23.4	1 680	225	205	3 714	0.1
Gonzales	12.6	9.7	3.2	13.2	2.8	6.8	3.4	D	19.0	4 000	198	572	8 796	0.0
Gray	5.7	25.3	6.3	18.5	2.6	5.4	2.7	5.4	10.0	4 435	193	383	10 101	-0.6
Grayson	0.5	0.9	9.3	18.3	4.3	8.1	6.4	17.5	13.4	26 605	217	2 986	54 309	1.3
Gregg	0.0	16.8	11.0	10.7	7.1	7.3	4.4	11.0	7.2	23 625	192	4 128	51 413	3.8
Grimes	0.1	1.9	6.4	30.6	D	5.3	4.6	D	18.5	5 240	195	743	10 980	0.7

1. Per 1,000 resident population estimated as of July 1 of the year shown.

STATE County	Housing units, 2009–2013: Occupied units: Total	Owner-occupied: Percent	Owner-occupied: Median value[1]	Median owner cost as a percent of income: With a mortgage	Median owner cost as a percent of income: Without a mortgage[2]	Renter-occupied: Median rent[3]	Renter-occupied: Median rent as a percent of income[2]	Substandard units[4] (percent)	Civilian labor force, 2014: Total	Percent change, 2013–2014	Unemployment: Total	Unemployment: Rate[5]	Civilian employment,[6] 2009–2013: Total	Percent: Management, business, science and arts	Percent: Construction, production, and maintenance occupations
	89	90	91	92	93	94	95	96	97	98	99	100	101	102	103
TEXAS—Cont'd															
Caldwell	11 593	66.6	104 000	23.1	12.9	737	30.7	6.4	17 572	2.3	897	5.1	15 463	25.5	30.6
Calhoun	7 870	71.0	98 100	19.8	11.2	729	27.4	4.2	11 091	1.9	536	4.8	8 897	25.9	37.3
Callahan	5 201	82.1	74 300	19.2	12.0	626	25.5	12.6	5 950	0.3	260	4.4	5 490	27.2	28.8
Cameron	117 836	67.2	78 300	25.3	13.1	639	32.0	8.6	167 645	0.0	13 870	8.3	141 863	27.7	22.2
Camp	4 475	67.0	103 100	23.3	12.7	629	27.6	2.1	5 244	-5.2	316	6.0	4 884	27.5	34.3
Carson	2 337	89.3	87 700	17.1	10.0	599	18.0	4.4	3 199	0.3	107	3.3	3 008	32.1	32.5
Cass	11 836	71.7	77 400	20.8	11.7	514	30.2	7.5	12 402	-1.9	944	7.6	11 629	22.0	32.8
Castro	2 588	68.7	68 500	27.1	14.4	678	30.6	3.0	3 868	1.8	156	4.0	3 386	22.8	41.2
Chambers	12 147	82.9	144 900	19.0	11.5	862	21.6	5.9	17 803	1.5	1 012	5.7	15 469	36.1	35.7
Cherokee	17 422	71.8	76 300	21.9	13.1	645	28.9	0.4	21 378	-1.1	1 249	5.8	19 617	25.1	31.7
Childress	2 374	72.8	62 700	14.8	12.7	669	35.8	2.6	2 899	-1.6	106	3.7	2 825	31.1	16.6
Clay	4 216	85.2	81 600	19.9	10.3	649	21.9	8.1	5 131	-0.6	234	4.6	5 009	30.8	28.4
Cochran	1 039	79.4	35 500	20.1	10.0	446	18.4	2.1	1 421	1.0	73	5.1	1 107	22.5	47.3
Coke	1 436	73.2	70 400	21.2	10.0	436	26.3	1.7	1 475	0.8	62	4.2	1 448	39.2	24.7
Coleman	3 478	67.9	60 900	25.5	12.4	489	26.6	2.4	3 179	0.4	190	6.0	3 264	27.5	33.3
Collin	289 752	68.2	206 100	22.2	11.2	1 063	27.0	2.1	471 554	2.6	21 277	4.5	415 734	51.3	11.0
Collingsworth	1 174	78.5	66 400	18.5	12.1	613	22.7	3.1	1 281	4.9	53	4.1	1 314	34.1	31.1
Colorado	8 079	77.3	109 600	22.1	12.2	602	23.4	4.3	10 461	3.2	462	4.4	9 021	29.9	32.7
Comal	41 954	76.1	205 000	21.8	10.5	942	28.5	6.6	58 965	1.4	2 671	4.5	51 981	38.3	19.7
Comanche	5 162	77.0	73 700	22.6	12.3	513	26.8	3.2	5 615	-1.0	271	4.8	4 899	32.3	31.6
Concho	857	79.1	76 100	15.8	10.0	417	26.7	5.2	1 423	-2.5	43	3.0	1 237	34.3	34.8
Cooke	14 466	69.5	117 100	21.2	12.7	743	27.1	3.0	20 722	0.8	796	3.8	17 728	27.2	31.2
Coryell	20 416	57.3	97 400	20.1	10.0	905	26.5	1.1	25 294	-0.3	1 517	6.0	23 074	29.7	21.5
Cottle	709	72.4	41 400	22.9	11.5	458	20.4	4.8	667	6.4	38	5.7	721	29.5	18.0
Crane	1 571	75.8	66 800	16.9	10.0	614	23.2	4.6	2 059	-1.7	80	3.9	1 743	23.6	41.8
Crockett	1 375	69.2	56 200	21.0	10.0	531	13.9	8.0	1 936	2.5	74	3.8	1 810	19.1	39.5
Crosby	2 164	67.2	55 400	19.7	11.2	576	26.3	6.8	2 796	0.6	128	4.6	2 506	29.9	29.4
Culberson	838	63.4	46 600	20.6	14.9	561	30.4	4.5	1 016	-0.7	42	4.1	1 000	24.9	21.7
Dallam	2 375	61.3	70 700	22.9	10.0	709	24.5	7.0	3 816	-2.5	115	3.0	3 375	25.7	39.2
Dallas	858 332	52.5	128 300	24.5	13.0	883	29.4	3.1	1 268 571	2.4	67 908	5.4	1 136 764	32.9	24.1
Dawson	4 414	73.6	55 700	19.8	11.6	536	25.8	6.6	5 008	-0.2	250	5.0	4 659	24.9	30.3
Deaf Smith	6 191	65.3	80 200	21.2	11.6	643	25.8	2.5	9 156	-0.4	333	3.6	7 982	25.8	40.7
Delta	1 929	83.0	71 600	19.6	12.8	636	41.5	2.6	2 707	2.3	162	6.0	1 928	29.5	31.3
Denton	243 394	65.5	184 100	21.8	12.0	944	28.2	5.0	412 700	2.7	18 160	4.4	362 095	43.0	15.0
DeWitt	6 948	78.0	80 700	19.8	10.0	610	26.5	2.1	10 092	3.6	384	3.8	8 100	25.2	34.1
Dickens	913	76.8	48 400	16.7	12.7	439	17.0	6.0	756	-2.1	48	6.3	893	35.4	28.0
Dimmit	3 542	69.8	49 900	21.2	12.2	600	23.6	4.2	7 689	13.0	291	3.8	3 882	19.7	32.7
Donley	1 280	76.7	61 100	20.5	11.7	556	22.5	11.0	1 626	-18.5	79	4.9	1 499	35.6	22.1
Duval	3 901	72.5	52 700	22.7	13.5	632	19.2	5.7	5 626	1.2	312	5.5	4 626	16.1	37.5
Eastland	6 872	75.1	61 200	23.9	11.8	550	25.0	6.9	8 452	-1.3	408	4.8	7 325	28.2	31.1
Ector	49 962	65.7	91 200	19.0	10.0	789	25.2	5.5	83 057	5.1	2 817	3.4	65 574	22.7	33.8
Edwards	838	91.6	70 500	15.6	13.3	575	18.1	3.9	866	-4.4	38	4.4	942	27.4	32.2
Ellis	51 016	74.6	137 500	22.0	12.3	884	30.0	7.6	79 731	2.3	3 877	4.9	71 863	31.6	26.1
El Paso	255 573	61.7	111 800	23.6	11.5	720	30.4	4.3	347 884	-0.4	22 644	6.5	316 765	29.5	22.8
Erath	14 383	59.9	111 100	21.6	11.3	659	35.0	4.0	20 223	1.5	847	4.2	18 851	29.3	29.1
Falls	5 600	72.0	60 800	21.3	13.2	563	27.4	3.7	6 785	-0.5	378	5.6	6 405	24.6	32.0
Fannin	11 814	74.6	92 600	22.1	13.1	682	33.1	2.0	15 479	0.7	842	5.4	13 627	29.3	30.5
Fayette	9 999	76.4	130 300	19.4	12.4	658	23.1	4.2	13 237	4.2	453	3.4	11 751	26.9	32.5
Fisher	1 518	71.1	62 200	18.7	11.7	550	21.2	5.2	1 879	-0.7	86	4.6	1 759	28.2	33.8
Floyd	2 457	69.3	61 200	17.2	11.5	579	29.1	2.2	3 101	-1.1	218	7.0	2 856	28.2	33.5
Foard	491	69.5	37 500	23.8	14.4	480	29.4	3.5	585	0.9	25	4.3	422	45.0	19.9
Fort Bend	191 406	78.7	183 600	22.7	11.6	1 167	27.2	3.2	341 733	2.2	15 348	4.5	290 579	47.7	15.0
Franklin	4 304	77.0	92 800	22.5	10.0	581	24.4	3.4	4 745	0.9	242	5.1	4 577	28.2	27.9
Freestone	7 251	79.4	76 900	19.2	12.1	642	25.9	14.9	7 760	-1.6	441	5.7	7 999	27.9	33.2
Frio	4 805	65.8	62 900	24.4	12.3	649	23.9	8.4	10 417	11.7	366	3.5	6 353	16.8	29.3
Gaines	5 437	76.9	93 000	18.5	10.0	657	19.9	3.7	9 398	5.0	302	3.2	7 390	24.9	43.6
Galveston	110 032	68.7	148 600	22.0	12.0	900	31.3	3.3	159 108	1.8	8 806	5.5	138 501	39.9	21.2
Garza	1 588	75.9	72 000	15.8	10.9	540	23.2	2.7	2 287	1.8	80	3.5	1 807	30.3	25.6
Gillespie	10 655	74.7	216 600	24.3	12.1	867	30.3	2.4	12 563	0.7	448	3.6	11 678	32.5	24.2
Glasscock	409	69.2	119 100	14.3	10.0	1 016	10.0	3.1	779	4.3	21	2.7	515	36.1	36.5
Goliad	3 028	81.1	111 600	14.6	10.3	643	27.4	10.9	3 596	1.3	146	4.1	3 123	30.0	33.5
Gonzales	6 638	69.5	77 500	21.8	12.3	545	25.4	3.5	9 941	4.1	387	3.9	8 291	23.4	36.5
Gray	8 388	74.4	68 000	19.2	11.2	615	27.7	3.0	9 856	0.4	401	4.1	9 095	24.9	34.7
Grayson	46 559	67.4	104 500	22.7	12.6	768	28.9	3.8	60 948	0.3	2 943	4.8	52 673	30.8	25.7
Gregg	45 292	62.4	121 300	21.0	11.3	748	28.9	5.8	62 036	0.4	2 980	4.8	55 001	27.9	28.3
Grimes	8 848	76.3	92 900	21.8	12.0	602	24.9	3.6	11 911	0.4	568	4.8	9 786	24.6	34.0

1. Specified owner-occupied units. 2. A value of 10.0 represents 10 percent or less; a value of 50.0 represents 50 percent or more. 3. Specified renter-occupied units.
4. Overcrowded or lacking complete plumbing facilities. 5. Percent of civilian labor force. 6. Persons 16 years old and over.

STATE County	Private nonfarm establishments, employment and payroll, 2013									Agriculture, 2012			
		Employment						Annual payroll		Farms			
											Percent with:		
	Number of establish-ments	Total	Health care and social assistance	Manufac-turing	Retail trade	Finance and insurance	Professional, scientific, and technical services	Total (mil dol)	Average per employee (dollars)	Number	Fewer than 50 acres	500 acres or more	Farm operators whose principal occu-pation is farming (percent)
	104	105	106	107	108	109	110	111	112	113	114	115	116
TEXAS—Cont'd													
Caldwell	549	6 080	1 245	862	1 181	173	116	185	30 414	1 623	42.7	8.3	40.1
Calhoun	430	8 029	592	D	1 018	185	614	473	58 918	264	29.2	31.4	46.6
Callahan	207	1 414	127	123	342	58	68	44	31 244	992	27.6	21.3	43.3
Cameron	6 306	99 190	30 767	4 935	17 561	3 433	2 447	2 570	25 912	1 305	66.3	11.5	45.4
Camp	215	2 201	D	177	378	97	D	78	35 502	487	40.0	6.2	41.3
Carson	116	679	D	D	136	D	12	30	44 143	386	15.5	46.6	51.0
Cass	502	5 225	868	1 185	896	199	156	194	37 124	1 024	29.6	5.2	43.1
Castro	177	1 088	D	D	202	54	97	33	30 377	532	9.0	51.5	54.3
Chambers	544	10 370	528	D	599	111	198	604	58 235	734	56.0	17.7	39.6
Cherokee	777	11 106	2 382	2 463	1 347	332	214	350	31 485	1 574	34.2	6.5	46.9
Childress	160	1 512	382	NA	345	66	43	40	26 778	383	5.2	34.5	41.3
Clay	124	862	169	D	227	D	11	23	26 819	861	16.4	27.1	43.4
Cochran	52	297	102	D	D	D	D	10	34 269	288	4.9	47.6	51.7
Coke	66	241	D	D	72	D	D	7	27 137	443	9.3	40.6	44.9
Coleman	218	1 444	356	D	280	80	47	38	26 226	906	10.9	36.5	46.7
Collin	19 906	336 461	40 211	17 511	45 960	38 922	35 693	19 046	56 608	2 264	64.9	4.4	33.0
Collingsworth	60	487	D	D	70	D	D	15	30 565	383	6.3	41.3	45.2
Colorado	551	6 014	805	1 621	967	177	109	196	32 571	1 575	28.3	13.0	48.6
Comal	3 093	40 920	5 833	3 324	6 041	955	1 318	1 498	36 611	1 104	44.8	9.3	36.9
Comanche	263	2 417	635	D	472	144	87	70	28 838	1 435	26.8	18.6	50.6
Concho	46	734	162	D	79	D	D	24	32 608	401	5.7	51.4	56.9
Cooke	890	13 373	1 164	3 105	1 790	366	210	557	41 663	1 946	40.0	10.9	42.2
Coryell	708	9 983	1 235	428	1 945	429	857	256	25 650	1 308	31.3	16.8	42.3
Cottle	27	154	D	D	NA	D	NA	3	19 617	264	6.4	44.7	32.2
Crane	92	1 186	D	D	113	D	D	66	56 028	27	29.6	66.7	51.9
Crockett	126	1 337	26	D	D	D	D	59	44 485	216	4.2	68.1	63.4
Crosby	98	640	142	D	125	D	9	22	34 859	431	8.6	43.4	51.0
Culberson	52	570	D	D	206	D	D	14	24 512	77	9.1	75.3	68.8
Dallam	208	1 653	50	59	D	73	68	59	35 820	371	5.9	62.3	59.0
Dallas	62 501	1 322 022	157 701	93 736	118 056	96 887	127 754	74 896	56 653	839	68.2	5.0	39.7
Dawson	277	2 818	D	143	657	125	60	102	36 064	596	7.2	42.8	55.0
Deaf Smith	399	5 131	529	1 546	696	192	129	185	36 083	621	11.3	55.2	64.6
Delta	60	528	D	D	35	D	19	9	16 447	529	33.1	10.2	41.2
Denton	12 517	182 916	22 551	12 117	26 939	12 782	8 961	7 431	40 624	3 203	73.2	3.8	34.9
DeWitt	441	5 159	1 088	566	669	262	112	181	35 000	1 711	24.1	14.0	45.7
Dickens	42	250	24	NA	58	D	D	8	30 800	437	4.8	34.3	35.5
Dimmit	234	5 806	416	57	480	D	D	313	53 892	367	23.2	35.7	36.8
Donley	85	492	103	D	103	16	D	10	20 319	380	8.9	29.7	44.5
Duval	163	2 533	370	D	233	50	22	112	44 169	1 436	11.0	25.0	45.5
Eastland	472	5 395	904	518	814	135	448	210	38 948	1 174	17.3	18.6	33.6
Ector	3 582	62 316	6 992	4 552	8 348	1 426	1 610	3 184	51 088	264	70.5	14.4	28.8
Edwards	37	182	D	D	99	D	D	4	22 033	419	6.4	50.6	51.1
Ellis	2 614	36 269	3 476	9 377	5 500	917	749	1 268	34 969	2 264	48.4	8.2	40.8
El Paso	13 814	221 264	39 507	14 173	37 264	6 611	9 466	6 706	30 309	657	81.6	7.6	39.7
Erath	915	11 608	1 592	2 518	1 801	346	319	378	32 567	2 161	30.2	13.7	44.6
Falls	223	1 771	464	D	438	71	32	48	26 928	1 263	26.5	13.2	53.4
Fannin	454	4 708	1 153	667	881	159	108	156	33 060	2 515	41.4	8.5	43.2
Fayette	734	6 827	1 079	943	1 190	254	212	224	32 753	2 822	30.8	6.7	41.5
Fisher	70	555	126	D	D	50	D	22	39 171	588	8.5	38.4	38.6
Floyd	157	1 017	269	66	124	58	D	31	30 792	589	7.3	39.4	39.9
Foard	27	156	49	D	D	D	D	3	19 718	194	8.8	42.3	46.4
Fort Bend	10 791	138 739	19 570	13 435	24 452	4 099	9 278	6 152	44 346	1 286	46.6	9.7	47.1
Franklin	168	5 741	D	D	292	100	D	101	17 666	520	28.1	12.1	47.5
Freestone	349	3 926	D	D	481	D	75	155	39 568	1 517	30.3	11.8	45.6
Frio	314	5 060	690	49	655	116	D	243	48 033	651	20.0	35.3	50.8
Gaines	391	3 803	D	D	417	94	D	176	46 165	644	10.6	50.2	55.9
Galveston	5 378	81 745	14 447	5 996	12 247	3 800	6 693	3 272	40 031	612	63.2	8.7	45.4
Garza	124	1 372	D	21	203	D	D	48	34 851	277	8.7	46.9	43.7
Gillespie	915	8 418	1 568	687	1 531	272	298	251	29 853	1 847	30.5	19.9	41.5
Glasscock	23	236	NA	D	D	D	D	12	51 746	186	4.3	70.4	59.7
Goliad	115	831	D	D	106	D	28	32	39 031	1 175	27.9	17.2	44.4
Gonzales	410	4 849	700	1 469	727	177	101	102	33 478	1 674	23.1	18.9	46.1
Gray	625	7 124	954	D	1 071	225	231	300	42 079	417	15.3	47.7	35.7
Grayson	2 513	39 572	8 535	6 508	6 012	2 391	883	1 337	33 792	2 562	50.8	5.6	44.1
Gregg	4 097	67 669	10 445	9 805	9 318	2 022	2 505	2 794	41 295	527	59.0	4.2	42.9
Grimes	405	6 010	381	2 452	686	178	148	250	41 567	1 683	37.3	10.5	39.7

STATE County	Agriculture, 2012 (cont.): Land in farms: Acreage (1,000)	Land in farms: Percent change, 2007–2012	Land in farms: Acres: Average size of farm	Land in farms: Acres: Total irrigated (1,000)	Land in farms: Acres: Total cropland (1,000)	Value of land and buildings (dollars): Average per farm	Value of land and buildings (dollars): Average per acre	Value of machinery and equipment, average per farm (dollars)	Value of products sold: Total (mil dol)	Value of products sold: Average per farm (dollars)	Value of products sold: Percent from: Crops	Value of products sold: Percent from: Livestock and poultry products	Percent of farms with sales of: $10,000 or more	Percent of farms with sales of: $100,000 or more	Government payments: Total ($1,000)	Government payments: Percent of farms
	117	118	119	120	121	122	123	124	125	126	127	128	129	130	131	132
TEXAS—Cont'd																
Caldwell	310	1.9	191	0.6	55.9	632 375	3 306	45 283	62.9	38 779	17.8	82.2	22.2	2.7	1 076	10.2
Calhoun	184	-20.1	697	5.8	60.5	1 223 477	1 755	114 295	42.1	159 489	67.2	32.8	49.2	20.5	1 664	46.2
Callahan	563	5.7	568	0.7	87.2	857 079	1 510	49 690	29.9	30 142	19.5	80.5	28.7	4.9	1 943	26.1
Cameron	310	-11.4	237	112.3	209.2	697 056	2 937	84 762	160.4	122 916	91.9	8.1	32.1	13.3	4 851	45.4
Camp	78	14.1	161	0.7	20.4	418 072	2 602	73 626	137.7	282 686	2.2	97.8	37.8	9.0	118	5.5
Carson	485	-9.8	1 256	49.4	269.8	1 156 262	920	200 505	83.0	214 990	61.0	39.0	44.8	23.8	5 875	75.1
Cass	168	-5.1	164	0.2	38.9	337 149	2 060	50 023	67.6	66 010	7.8	92.2	27.3	5.1	128	4.1
Castro	548	-3.4	1 030	154.9	411.0	1 131 530	1 098	323 836	1 312.1	2 466 429	11.9	88.1	62.0	45.5	10 759	80.5
Chambers	254	-5.1	346	15.2	92.8	690 097	1 996	80 785	25.6	34 868	58.8	41.2	27.1	7.9	3 018	17.2
Cherokee	301	2.4	191	1.4	67.8	472 935	2 470	58 168	134.0	85 123	66.9	33.1	34.1	5.7	736	3.9
Childress	444	11.1	1 159	9.2	142.1	891 243	769	90 394	19.9	51 883	65.5	34.5	38.6	11.2	3 104	80.4
Clay	633	-4.4	735	1.7	99.2	1 158 323	1 577	71 052	79.8	92 695	15.6	84.4	48.0	13.0	2 098	34.5
Cochran	449	-8.2	1 558	67.8	268.5	1 048 688	673	204 642	100.8	349 955	D	D	35.8	25.3	7 287	87.2
Coke	484	-1.4	1 093	1.0	49.0	1 141 964	1 045	62 172	7.0	15 826	29.4	70.6	26.0	3.4	967	34.5
Coleman	726	3.8	801	1.0	135.5	1 210 947	1 512	68 786	28.4	31 320	40.1	59.9	41.3	7.5	2 499	49.2
Collin	313	7.6	138	6.2	136.6	732 661	5 303	45 315	77.8	34 369	65.3	34.7	19.2	3.4	1 307	7.2
Collingsworth	495	-3.5	1 292	27.3	164.1	1 075 068	832	152 681	43.1	112 556	69.4	30.6	47.3	18.8	4 307	79.6
Colorado	485	-8.0	308	20.1	136.2	1 019 175	3 309	68 878	68.0	43 162	65.4	34.6	35.9	7.6	4 361	17.0
Comal	205	6.5	186	0.4	14.1	974 562	5 248	42 853	D	D	D	D	14.5	0.5	131	5.2
Comanche	517	-10.7	360	18.1	133.8	865 152	2 401	69 521	158.1	110 199	16.9	83.1	42.4	8.4	1 563	21.0
Concho	502	-9.0	1 251	2.1	106.6	1 979 873	1 583	117 608	22.8	56 933	62.3	37.7	54.6	13.2	3 244	67.8
Cooke	504	10.6	259	0.4	132.4	845 941	3 267	60 599	63.3	32 538	29.2	70.8	36.9	7.1	1 361	19.2
Coryell	463	-5.2	354	0.4	85.8	861 112	2 432	52 811	68.6	52 408	23.6	76.4	30.2	5.0	959	16.1
Cottle	565	5.6	2 139	2.9	98.4	1 323 023	619	96 019	15.9	60 246	33.5	66.5	33.3	9.1	2 297	81.4
Crane	239	-36.3	8 858	D	D	5 228 185	590	51 926	1.4	52 222	1.6	98.4	55.6	14.8	56	14.8
Crockett	1 546	-3.5	7 158	0.1	8.0	4 508 931	630	78 523	13.9	64 324	0.3	99.7	46.3	16.7	2 214	33.3
Crosby	558	1.0	1 296	111.7	299.6	1 107 218	855	231 005	71.6	166 100	93.9	6.1	53.1	36.2	7 549	88.6
Culberson	1 618	17.8	21 013	6.0	64.5	7 180 273	342	134 844	13.7	178 364	48.1	51.9	57.1	28.6	680	27.3
Dallam	852	-9.1	2 296	175.6	388.4	2 164 833	943	330 364	651.7	1 756 642	25.5	74.5	55.3	40.7	7 262	76.8
Dallas	84	-4.8	100	1.4	35.9	460 257	4 611	52 857	44.5	53 026	85.9	14.1	17.8	4.4	280	6.9
Dawson	558	-1.8	936	61.2	481.2	738 569	789	188 577	73.1	122 700	97.0	3.0	38.9	23.0	11 185	91.9
Deaf Smith	924	-2.4	1 487	119.9	606.7	1 470 176	989	259 588	1 379.1	2 220 734	5.8	94.2	50.4	37.5	13 023	78.9
Delta	131	-1.2	248	D	65.0	452 815	1 826	60 987	29.3	55 475	53.6	46.4	40.8	5.3	801	33.8
Denton	384	9.5	120	3.3	131.9	731 687	6 111	52 478	137.0	42 771	25.8	74.2	18.1	3.2	1 210	7.6
DeWitt	536	-2.3	314	0.6	49.7	819 210	2 613	61 814	61.4	35 856	12.4	87.6	40.9	4.7	1 068	10.0
Dickens	573	-0.3	1 310	13.4	128.3	958 899	732	87 062	18.5	42 394	43.7	56.3	31.1	8.5	3 468	78.9
Dimmit	677	-4.4	1 845	4.8	44.3	2 875 932	1 559	62 379	35.2	95 956	24.3	75.7	25.9	6.5	730	14.4
Donley	585	-0.7	1 540	14.9	68.0	1 659 213	1 078	89 887	95.1	250 337	14.1	85.9	36.3	12.9	2 000	63.4
Duval	960	-6.0	668	D	60.0	872 009	1 305	38 103	14.8	10 309	6.5	93.5	20.5	1.3	2 814	37.0
Eastland	504	-3.2	429	8.9	91.5	852 450	1 987	56 647	27.9	23 744	30.5	69.5	36.4	4.5	1 428	24.0
Ector	429	1.2	1 624	0.8	3.6	786 019	484	48 008	2.2	8 296	28.9	71.1	16.3	1.5	211	5.3
Edwards	970	-2.7	2 315	1.1	13.0	2 907 783	1 256	48 630	8.2	19 485	7.4	92.6	28.9	5.5	2 070	25.8
Ellis	474	7.0	209	0.4	224.4	665 859	3 181	73 345	91.4	40 367	73.7	26.3	24.1	4.5	2 825	24.3
El Paso	209	24.2	319	24.9	53.3	617 767	1 938	93 251	45.5	69 308	87.0	13.0	25.7	9.4	768	9.3
Erath	608	-2.5	281	12.3	124.4	903 801	3 215	72 397	256.4	118 670	7.2	92.8	32.2	7.2	1 814	8.5
Falls	383	-14.1	303	5.1	174.3	589 978	1 947	82 715	135.3	107 123	40.7	59.3	41.3	12.2	4 706	29.1
Fannin	514	8.4	204	1.2	200.0	523 141	2 561	54 400	71.1	28 287	56.0	44.0	28.2	4.9	2 381	20.3
Fayette	492	-13.0	174	1.1	95.4	738 387	4 235	49 415	66.4	23 515	20.8	79.2	32.0	2.3	1 428	15.1
Fisher	495	-9.2	842	2.6	210.1	911 269	1 083	109 594	31.1	52 872	64.8	35.2	36.6	11.9	4 632	78.7
Floyd	582	-7.3	988	96.7	392.9	1 131 611	1 145	188 253	282.7	480 039	D	D	37.0	21.2	9 002	89.8
Foard	368	-2.0	1 898	1.9	98.2	1 401 794	739	100 098	13.8	71 273	44.8	55.2	47.4	22.7	1 505	69.6
Fort Bend	339	-11.4	264	10.3	135.9	1 080 498	4 095	75 835	103.8	80 705	88.5	11.5	36.2	10.7	4 101	29.2
Franklin	113	-15.4	217	0.8	27.9	623 454	2 869	67 423	86.0	165 339	4.4	95.6	48.1	14.6	171	7.3
Freestone	421	5.4	278	0.4	47.1	583 104	2 100	56 028	44.1	29 059	13.1	86.9	30.5	4.1	433	6.7
Frio	713	10.5	1 096	60.5	152.9	2 238 931	2 043	113 647	183.7	282 138	59.4	40.6	35.9	16.0	2 765	26.3
Gaines	775	-18.2	1 203	227.0	570.6	1 167 174	970	255 823	180.5	280 233	97.2	2.8	53.4	38.4	17 390	83.5
Galveston	90	-13.4	146	0.4	17.6	527 309	3 604	49 598	D	D	D	D	24.3	1.0	756	8.3
Garza	456	-11.1	1 645	8.1	82.1	1 141 856	694	92 982	12.4	44 711	70.4	29.6	35.7	13.4	2 696	74.4
Gillespie	652	-0.1	353	1.9	66.4	1 504 356	4 260	41 480	46.1	24 981	24.5	75.5	28.0	3.1	1 901	20.8
Glasscock	434	-9.6	2 332	25.3	134.7	2 086 946	895	302 559	25.9	139 129	89.3	10.7	51.1	30.6	5 362	69.4
Goliad	495	5.4	421	0.7	33.0	871 038	2 068	55 077	19.4	16 549	19.6	80.4	29.7	3.8	751	9.4
Gonzales	610	-6.8	364	7.8	69.0	1 176 904	3 231	69 381	517.8	309 295	4.5	95.5	44.0	11.6	1 202	12.7
Gray	515	1.1	1 235	21.6	161.2	1 096 012	888	129 902	207.7	498 026	11.7	88.3	42.9	16.1	3 299	61.4
Grayson	431	7.7	168	3.5	176.4	632 363	3 757	58 110	91.9	35 889	72.7	27.3	24.6	4.3	1 948	14.2
Gregg	48	6.3	91	0.4	8.2	353 905	3 881	45 812	3.6	6 844	37.3	62.7	15.7	0.8	41	0.8
Grimes	417	-4.6	248	1.6	56.7	957 864	3 865	59 447	48.1	28 551	23.0	77.0	31.0	3.7	755	5.8

Table B. States and Counties — **Water Use, Wholesale Trade, Retail Trade, and Real Estate**

STATE County	Water use, 2010: Total water withdrawn (mil gal/day)	Water use, 2010: Gallons withdrawn per person per day	Wholesale trade,[1] 2007: Number of establish-ments	Wholesale trade,[1] 2007: Number of employees	Wholesale trade,[1] 2007: Sales (mil dol)	Wholesale trade,[1] 2007: Annual payroll (mil dol)	Retail trade,[2] 2007: Number of establish-ments	Retail trade,[2] 2007: Number of employees	Retail trade,[2] 2007: Sales (mil dol)	Retail trade,[2] 2007: Annual payroll (mil dol)	Real estate and rental and leasing,[2] 2007: Number of establish-ments	Real estate and rental and leasing,[2] 2007: Number of employees	Real estate and rental and leasing,[2] 2007: Receipts (mil dol)	Real estate and rental and leasing,[2] 2007: Annual payroll (mil dol)
	133	134	135	136	137	138	139	140	141	142	143	144	145	146
TEXAS—Cont'd														
Caldwell	21.6	567	18	89	26.4	2.8	84	997	298.3	21.3	26	135	15.4	2.9
Calhoun	49.6	2 319	16	D	D	D	69	972	322.2	26.1	14	D	D	D
Callahan	2.7	200	16	61	20.5	1.5	39	340	118.9	6.6	10	33	3.1	0.7
Cameron	281.5	693	341	3 704	1 516.6	96.3	1 230	17 667	3 911.7	340.0	341	1 593	169.4	30.0
Camp	4.3	344	8	62	33.5	2.3	46	389	96.9	7.4	8	D	D	D
Carson	80.6	13 044	5	D	D	D	23	130	49.7	2.9	1	D	D	D
Cass	33.2	1 091	20	184	155.0	7.2	98	888	216.8	17.7	20	51	6.6	0.9
Castro	324.4	40 237	14	109	154.6	3.7	36	196	40.0	2.9	3	D	D	D
Chambers	265.5	7 565	30	308	137.2	11.8	81	757	274.9	15.0	16	102	44.4	4.1
Cherokee	68.1	1 339	31	D	D	D	143	1 468	363.2	28.7	36	141	10.5	2.0
Childress	9.3	1 318	7	68	31.4	2.2	28	361	75.5	6.6	8	18	1.8	0.3
Clay	5.4	500	8	26	5.4	0.6	29	226	77.6	6.0	6	D	D	D
Cochran	65.9	21 059	4	17	12.0	0.6	13	68	26.9	1.4	NA	NA	NA	NA
Coke	34.8	10 491	1	D	D	D	12	71	24.5	1.3	NA	NA	NA	NA
Coleman	52.6	5 915	7	38	16.2	1.2	34	230	47.9	4.1	11	21	3.4	0.4
Collin	327.8	419	735	10 505	9 374.9	733.2	2 287	41 634	12 350.8	1 038.1	886	5 430	1 054.0	228.6
Collingsworth	44.5	14 540	3	D	D	D	13	77	17.2	1.7	1	D	D	D
Colorado	143.7	6 886	32	254	136.8	7.7	108	942	226.8	19.0	21	D	D	D
Comal	44.4	410	103	1 045	960.6	48.9	379	5 003	1 539.7	123.8	143	643	89.4	15.5
Comanche	28.4	2 033	24	157	83.1	4.6	54	457	117.8	8.7	8	27	2.3	0.4
Concho	7.8	1 899	2	D	D	D	13	100	17.7	1.2	2	D	D	D
Cooke	12.4	323	38	365	99.8	12.2	181	1 935	499.7	42.9	31	99	24.1	2.3
Coryell	3.7	49	17	80	34.3	3.5	140	1 752	442.6	36.7	51	153	16.9	2.7
Cottle	2.0	1 336	NA	NA	NA	NA	7	50	12.7	0.9	NA	NA	NA	NA
Crane	23.5	5 365	4	17	23.2	0.8	14	109	47.8	2.5	NA	NA	NA	NA
Crockett	11.7	3 154	4	D	D	D	27	262	58.9	4.2	3	D	D	D
Crosby	74.7	12 327	11	149	119.4	8.4	21	126	23.8	2.2	3	D	D	D
Culberson	39.2	16 351	2	D	D	D	19	221	106.2	3.6	2	D	D	D
Dallam	329.6	49 172	18	281	311.1	9.8	33	178	85.4	4.6	9	21	3.0	0.3
Dallas	307.4	130	3 935	72 986	58 165.1	4 220.6	7 719	118 275	33 177.2	3 063.0	3 505	36 320	8 668.8	1 992.1
Dawson	79.0	5 712	19	110	91.3	3.1	48	583	148.4	11.4	8	19	1.4	0.2
Deaf Smith	173.9	8 978	34	D	D	D	66	744	224.2	15.9	18	71	5.4	1.0
Delta	2.6	501	2	D	D	D	14	57	26.4	1.4	3	14	2.2	0.6
Denton	166.3	251	472	9 066	12 359.0	466.0	1 519	25 683	7 668.3	600.8	564	2 757	519.2	93.1
DeWitt	6.6	326	15	83	30.5	2.7	71	692	159.9	14.0	12	87	10.6	2.9
Dickens	8.8	3 588	NA	NA	NA	NA	11	73	11.3	0.9	1	D	D	D
Dimmit	11.2	1 116	4	D	D	D	26	330	74.8	6.6	6	D	D	D
Donley	26.8	7 289	2	D	D	D	23	123	29.2	2.2	3	D	D	D
Duval	9.3	789	8	64	17.5	2.6	27	188	49.6	2.8	4	D	D	D
Eastland	9.8	527	12	153	180.8	8.8	99	895	259.7	18.1	17	39	6.1	1.0
Ector	60.2	439	286	4 048	2 004.3	219.0	476	6 660	2 090.6	167.6	157	1 383	338.4	74.3
Edwards	0.9	455	1	D	D	D	6	53	11.7	0.6	1	D	D	D
Ellis	23.4	156	100	716	279.2	30.4	376	4 725	1 323.1	107.3	114	374	58.7	9.4
El Paso	277.5	347	911	8 442	5 002.5	303.1	2 334	33 948	8 460.9	683.1	672	3 599	629.2	106.8
Erath	16.1	425	38	D	D	D	156	1 912	445.0	39.7	43	124	17.7	3.3
Falls	10.9	611	13	79	53.1	2.3	44	330	71.6	6.0	12	32	5.3	0.5
Fannin	55.1	1 624	11	D	D	D	85	874	297.3	25.3	16	97	7.7	2.6
Fayette	24.7	1 005	29	376	158.7	15.8	133	1 041	262.0	23.8	33	94	20.3	2.4
Fisher	7.8	1 968	1	D	D	D	14	64	12.0	1.0	1	D	D	D
Floyd	93.3	14 469	15	113	65.6	4.1	24	137	40.0	2.6	3	D	D	D
Foard	2.9	2 141	5	D	D	D	6	25	7.0	0.5	NA	NA	NA	NA
Fort Bend	995.3	1 700	526	5 754	6 615.3	275.2	1 213	19 344	5 306.2	442.9	392	1 546	337.8	56.0
Franklin	5.4	505	4	21	4.8	0.8	32	304	87.9	5.7	9	24	4.3	1.1
Freestone	816.1	41 182	11	71	41.6	3.1	66	605	254.3	14.3	16	122	23.9	4.5
Frio	56.4	3 276	11	66	31.5	3.2	50	472	107.6	9.2	9	65	6.0	2.0
Gaines	333.6	19 037	18	290	169.3	12.8	46	393	82.6	7.7	9	28	4.8	1.0
Galveston	57.3	197	191	1 715	1 761.6	69.2	860	10 790	2 750.3	246.1	265	1 197	221.1	33.8
Garza	14.3	2 219	5	23	10.0	1.3	20	152	35.0	2.0	4	D	D	D
Gillespie	7.4	297	35	224	100.4	6.1	170	1 592	311.1	33.5	35	109	14.0	2.3
Glasscock	56.7	46 215	2	D	D	D	2	D	D	D	NA	NA	NA	NA
Goliad	391.7	54 325	3	D	D	D	24	149	37.3	2.2	4	D	D	D
Gonzales	19.5	985	21	188	90.2	7.3	83	682	179.2	13.4	16	33	3.4	0.5
Gray	24.6	1 093	31	D	D	D	104	D	D	D	29	192	29.1	7.8
Grayson	22.3	185	103	1 004	651.7	33.1	497	6 333	1 594.7	140.4	114	456	69.9	11.1
Gregg	90.4	743	239	3 138	1 401.5	129.5	701	9 168	2 405.2	220.9	182	1 333	290.8	56.4
Grimes	308.2	11 585	20	216	142.5	9.1	60	597	157.3	11.3	14	41	9.8	1.3

1. Merchant wholesalers, except manufacturers' sales branches and offices. 2. Employer establishments.

STATE County	Professional, scientific, and technical services,[1] 2007				Manufacturing, 2007				Accommodation and food services, 2007			
	Number of establish-ments	Number of employees	Receipts (mil dol)	Annual payroll (mil dol)	Number of establish-ments	Number of employees	Receipts (mil dol)	Annual payroll (mil dol)	Number of establish-ments	Number of employees	Sales (mil dol)	Annual payroll (mil dol)
	147	148	149	150	151	152	153	154	155	156	157	158
TEXAS—Cont'd												
Caldwell	27	D	D	D	18	615	89.8	13.9	54	672	28.2	7.2
Calhoun	31	D	D	D	17	D	D	D	60	514	21.1	5.3
Callahan	13	D	D	D	NA	NA	NA	NA	16	220	7.6	2.1
Cameron	474	D	D	D	221	D	D	D	643	12 287	503.1	131.4
Camp	16	39	4.9	1.6	NA	NA	NA	NA	15	202	7.5	1.9
Carson	6	D	D	D	NA	NA	NA	NA	12	65	1.8	0.5
Cass	26	97	8.8	2.8	30	1 339	644.7	68.9	37	432	17.5	4.2
Castro	10	29	3.5	1.0	NA	NA	NA	NA	11	76	2.4	0.6
Chambers	37	349	30.1	14.6	23	D	D	131.2	50	804	31.4	8.4
Cherokee	45	170	14.8	4.0	75	3 431	552.5	90.1	66	959	36.5	9.9
Childress	9	32	4.9	1.3	NA	NA	NA	NA	24	358	11.7	3.2
Clay	9	D	D	D	NA	NA	NA	NA	9	111	2.6	0.9
Cochran	3	4	0.2	0.1	NA	NA	NA	NA	4	15	0.3	0.1
Coke	3	D	D	D	NA	NA	NA	NA	6	D	D	D
Coleman	14	39	3.0	0.7	NA	NA	NA	NA	21	166	5.1	1.3
Collin	2 581	D	D	D	420	20 823	7 433.8	1 175.1	1 290	27 578	1 380.4	392.5
Collingsworth	6	D	D	D	NA	NA	NA	NA	8	41	1.4	0.4
Colorado	46	144	13.4	4.4	28	1 155	307.3	38.3	43	570	21.7	5.9
Comal	251	1 268	112.1	38.3	106	3 475	1 093.7	128.6	255	4 362	184.4	48.5
Comanche	22	67	6.1	1.3	NA	NA	NA	NA	17	D	D	D
Concho	2	D	D	D	NA	NA	NA	NA	6	50	4.3	0.9
Cooke	65	290	37.4	14.7	75	3 439	579.7	128.9	84	1 322	52.6	13.9
Coryell	56	D	D	D	19	504	D	D	74	1 231	45.4	11.3
Cottle	1	D	D	D	NA	NA	NA	NA	4	D	D	D
Crane	2	D	D	D	NA	NA	NA	NA	5	33	1.0	0.2
Crockett	6	13	1.0	0.3	NA	NA	NA	NA	18	153	8.3	1.7
Crosby	4	8	0.5	0.2	NA	NA	NA	NA	5	D	D	D
Culberson	1	D	D	D	NA	NA	NA	NA	19	239	10.3	2.4
Dallam	14	56	6.7	1.8	NA	NA	NA	NA	26	295	12.5	2.7
Dallas	8 664	110 830	21 051.4	8 025.1	2 706	133 063	39 047.0	6 512.8	4 753	102 354	5 705.1	1 600.9
Dawson	19	58	7.0	2.3	NA	NA	NA	NA	26	279	12.5	3.2
Deaf Smith	22	93	11.4	2.5	31	1 104	470.8	35.7	33	377	17.3	3.8
Delta	2	D	D	D	NA	NA	NA	NA	3	D	D	D
Denton	1 372	6 160	1 012.6	306.7	363	11 406	4 008.3	476.3	909	17 865	797.9	219.5
DeWitt	29	113	8.4	3.1	28	835	110.4	25.5	43	464	14.9	3.9
Dickens	2	D	D	D	NA	NA	NA	NA	6	27	0.9	0.3
Dimmit	7	20	1.6	0.3	NA	NA	NA	NA	19	253	8.3	2.9
Donley	6	20	2.3	0.4	NA	NA	NA	NA	12	105	3.7	0.8
Duval	6	10	1.0	0.3	NA	NA	NA	NA	13	55	3.7	0.7
Eastland	29	109	9.1	3.3	22	608	135.5	22.6	44	427	17.7	4.3
Ector	224	D	D	D	240	4 814	2 049.7	222.0	245	5 213	228.6	59.4
Edwards	2	D	D	D	NA	NA	NA	NA	5	D	D	D
Ellis	164	D	D	D	178	9 369	4 080.6	416.0	185	2 828	126.6	34.4
El Paso	1 151	D	D	D	588	16 091	14 423.5	617.6	1 269	24 563	1 031.3	268.5
Erath	68	355	31.3	11.9	40	2 577	849.3	108.1	81	1 489	55.4	15.9
Falls	8	26	4.1	0.7	NA	NA	NA	NA	20	D	D	D
Fannin	30	120	8.6	2.9	37	531	135.9	17.2	37	464	18.5	5.3
Fayette	60	205	17.1	5.6	40	1 024	277.8	36.3	67	782	32.0	8.4
Fisher	4	D	D	D	NA	NA	NA	NA	2	D	D	D
Floyd	10	19	1.3	0.4	NA	NA	NA	NA	11	42	1.8	0.4
Foard	2	D	D	D	NA	NA	NA	NA	3	D	D	D
Fort Bend	1 154	D	D	D	344	15 306	4 986.6	771.0	657	12 354	583.4	158.9
Franklin	13	28	2.8	1.0	NA	NA	NA	NA	18	180	6.5	2.2
Freestone	30	118	9.7	3.4	NA	NA	NA	NA	25	480	22.5	5.8
Frio	11	46	2.4	1.1	NA	NA	NA	NA	24	232	7.4	2.1
Gaines	10	53	4.1	2.0	NA	NA	NA	NA	27	249	9.5	2.1
Galveston	502	2 262	319.0	122.0	158	6 061	23 480.8	519.4	589	12 643	591.0	160.0
Garza	4	7	0.5	0.2	NA	NA	NA	NA	15	157	6.2	1.7
Gillespie	79	253	25.6	7.9	50	620	88.3	20.7	88	1 220	52.2	15.9
Glasscock	2	D	D	D	NA	NA	NA	NA	NA	NA	NA	NA
Goliad	12	D	D	D	NA	NA	NA	NA	12	97	3.9	1.1
Gonzales	38	109	10.4	2.9	22	1 416	444.7	48.1	38	399	17.4	4.5
Gray	46	D	D	D	22	D	683.7	74.3	41	D	D	D
Grayson	220	1 086	92.5	34.5	132	6 148	2 542.8	293.7	226	4 001	167.7	48.6
Gregg	340	D	D	D	184	10 510	4 234.0	456.9	294	6 063	246.7	71.9
Grimes	24	134	13.2	3.4	28	2 194	892.6	93.9	31	259	12.5	3.0

1. Establishment subject to federal tax.

Table B. States and Counties — **Health Care and Social Assistance, Other Services, Nonemployer Businesses, and Residential Construction**

STATE County	Health care and social assistance, 2007				Other services, 2007				Nonemployer businesses, 2013		Value of residential construction authorized by building permits, 2014	
	Number of establish-ments	Number of employees	Receipts (mil dol)	Annual payroll (mil dol)	Number of establish-ments	Number of employees	Receipts (mil dol)	Annual payroll (mil dol)	Number	Receipts (mil dol)	New Construction ($1,000)	Number of housing units
	159	160	161	162	163	164	165	166	167	168	169	170
TEXAS—Cont'd												
Caldwell	60	1 137	75.1	31.8	33	104	7.4	1.8	2 489	114.8	9 650	98
Calhoun	30	634	42.4	16.8	38	192	20.2	5.4	1 420	65.6	15 845	81
Callahan	10	115	4.0	1.8	12	45	3.5	0.9	1 166	48.4	959	5
Cameron	925	27 384	1 711.7	686.6	424	2 214	140.9	36.3	29 992	1 122.6	138 336	1 417
Camp	31	401	31.8	10.7	12	37	5.4	0.9	784	30.3	635	10
Carson	3	D	D	D	9	D	D	D	406	13.7	833	3
Cass	49	1 305	70.8	29.2	38	303	31.2	5.6	1 741	73.5	808	11
Castro	8	D	D	D	16	50	5.5	1.1	431	21.0	0	0
Chambers	34	638	36.5	15.8	30	182	16.3	5.6	2 499	117.5	74 758	377
Cherokee	88	2 576	163.2	77.3	53	188	13.4	3.9	3 077	136.0	570	6
Childress	20	363	28.5	10.8	9	25	2.2	0.5	339	12.8	0	0
Clay	13	D	D	D	10	36	1.6	0.4	773	35.8	568	5
Cochran	7	D	D	D	3	D	D	D	176	7.1	213	1
Coke	NA	NA	NA	NA	6	D	D	D	293	9.3	0	0
Coleman	20	357	17.6	8.7	14	43	3.2	0.7	755	39.0	0	0
Collin	2 014	24 679	3 179.0	1 127.8	878	6 502	493.2	154.1	75 827	4 076.5	2 389 272	10 635
Collingsworth	8	177	8.2	3.7	6	17	1.0	0.1	200	8.0	0	0
Colorado	34	837	60.1	24.0	33	151	10.5	2.9	1 824	84.0	853	10
Comal	271	3 624	323.2	130.3	197	1 392	78.5	44.0	11 588	625.0	410 539	2 075
Comanche	24	555	33.9	13.9	17	57	4.0	0.9	974	35.0	423	3
Concho	6	107	5.8	2.6	1	D	D	D	218	7.1	NA	NA
Cooke	85	1 158	90.7	35.2	62	417	29.3	8.7	3 333	182.0	4 466	25
Coryell	56	D	D	D	76	516	52.9	13.2	2 640	109.5	18 638	146
Cottle	4	44	1.6	0.7	2	D	D	D	132	3.6	0	0
Crane	8	159	9.5	4.5	2	D	D	D	288	13.2	20	1
Crockett	4	24	0.9	0.5	8	20	1.0	0.2	320	13.1	NA	NA
Crosby	11	D	D	D	8	D	D	D	362	15.0	335	5
Culberson	4	D	D	D	1	D	D	D	187	8.3	85	1
Dallam	12	D	D	D	21	47	9.2	1.2	498	33.7	3 121	20
Dallas	6 140	127 611	15 499.3	6 007.4	3 633	32 949	4 299.4	1 068.5	210 881	11 381.6	2 030 691	14 360
Dawson	20	352	35.8	9.6	19	77	5.2	1.5	678	26.8	1 446	7
Deaf Smith	24	492	31.4	11.6	37	168	14.2	3.3	1 166	65.6	837	10
Delta	6	289	6.4	3.1	5	D	D	D	355	12.6	431	2
Denton	1 199	16 986	1 795.5	641.2	674	4 360	369.5	112.8	59 107	2 971.2	1 031 067	3 565
DeWitt	41	1 007	62.3	25.3	39	159	12.5	3.2	1 520	81.9	766	5
Dickens	6	28	0.7	0.4	2	D	D	D	170	4.2	NA	NA
Dimmit	29	403	23.4	11.1	11	D	D	D	737	29.9	1 301	5
Donley	7	37	4.7	1.4	5	14	1.4	0.3	236	9.3	213	1
Duval	10	520	16.5	9.3	6	45	7.2	1.7	753	31.7	NA	NA
Eastland	38	1 038	42.7	22.7	34	156	10.9	3.1	1 396	58.8	0	0
Ector	300	6 988	644.3	248.5	246	2 115	283.6	64.3	10 328	628.6	108 454	556
Edwards	3	D	D	D	4	D	D	D	187	8.1	NA	NA
Ellis	214	3 320	254.6	99.6	157	863	55.1	16.6	12 541	589.8	190 698	1 096
El Paso	1 345	34 489	3 057.1	1 096.2	916	6 163	402.6	125.2	53 783	2 220.5	439 382	3 043
Erath	75	1 916	150.0	53.5	70	405	33.5	8.2	2 823	140.8	8 297	85
Falls	24	484	31.1	12.4	18	48	2.8	0.8	907	36.2	170	3
Fannin	55	1 291	117.6	48.0	36	D	D	D	2 251	95.6	1 116	27
Fayette	62	1 053	78.5	30.5	56	237	15.7	4.0	2 365	103.9	1 231	6
Fisher	6	151	10.0	4.0	7	17	1.1	0.2	222	8.6	0	0
Floyd	22	273	16.8	6.7	15	47	2.4	0.6	355	11.4	480	6
Foard	5	49	2.0	0.8	4	D	D	D	114	5.1	NA	NA
Fort Bend	993	12 302	1 197.4	443.3	518	3 251	318.1	89.4	57 132	2 860.1	1 158 820	9 268
Franklin	21	4 888	83.1	46.0	19	75	6.2	1.5	774	40.1	178	1
Freestone	31	550	37.6	13.2	29	117	9.8	1.7	1 202	51.1	785	7
Frio	29	474	27.9	10.6	15	45	2.9	0.7	984	40.9	799	11
Gaines	13	D	D	D	34	186	36.3	4.9	1 600	106.9	2 393	15
Galveston	526	14 414	1 219.8	484.8	422	2 658	336.9	70.9	21 630	1 017.0	567 297	3 006
Garza	13	D	D	D	5	D	D	D	342	17.4	0	0
Gillespie	86	1 533	119.2	51.8	54	249	25.6	5.9	3 320	153.1	7 738	39
Glasscock	NA	NA	NA	NA	NA	NA	NA	NA	125	6.5	NA	NA
Goliad	12	129	6.3	3.0	8	23	1.8	0.3	558	20.0	NA	NA
Gonzales	24	648	37.8	16.9	25	106	8.5	2.2	1 222	55.0	4 360	35
Gray	59	929	73.7	27.2	48	198	17.6	4.5	1 308	67.9	770	3
Grayson	382	8 254	706.2	279.6	165	820	59.1	16.6	8 927	396.8	32 590	271
Gregg	426	9 705	943.9	336.1	261	1 827	189.8	52.1	8 933	474.1	39 534	266
Grimes	22	266	19.3	9.9	23	80	7.0	1.9	1 892	88.7	1 615	15

STATE County	Government employment and payroll, 2012: Full-time equivalent employees	March payroll (dollars)	March payroll (percent of total): Adminis-tration, judicial, and legal	Police and Corrections	Fire Protection	Highways and transpor-tation	Health and Welfare	Natural resources and utilities	Education and libraries	Local government finances, 2012 — General revenue: Total (mil dol)	Inter-govern-mental (mil dol)	Taxes: Total (mil dol)	Per capita[1] (dollars): Total	Property
	171	172	173	174	175	176	177	178	179	180	181	182	183	184
TEXAS—Cont'd														
Caldwell	1 295	4 627 444	7.7	8.7	1.9	2.0	2.0	4.0	73.2	94.8	42.5	38.1	983	834
Calhoun	989	2 883 600	7.4	10.3	2.1	7.4	2.5	3.0	65.2	113.6	11.0	59.8	2 767	2 477
Callahan	610	1 550 184	5.1	6.1	0.1	2.1	0.9	3.3	80.5	36.2	16.2	14.8	1 095	992
Cameron	21 552	67 816 703	3.9	8.4	2.8	2.4	1.6	5.2	74.0	1 662.8	982.8	420.5	1 012	795
Camp	508	1 428 009	4.7	3.7	0.0	2.7	0.0	6.7	81.7	31.5	14.9	13.1	1 056	885
Carson	384	1 061 435	13.7	2.8	0.0	2.8	2.7	4.8	64.8	23.9	6.1	15.1	2 453	2 374
Cass	1 554	4 198 540	6.2	6.2	1.2	1.7	13.0	3.1	67.7	95.7	40.0	32.1	1 064	938
Castro	547	1 382 117	5.7	6.3	0.0	3.1	22.6	2.8	59.3	40.7	18.5	9.6	1 182	1 099
Chambers	1 626	5 773 846	8.8	6.1	0.0	3.1	10.0	6.3	64.8	164.5	34.4	100.6	2 780	2 551
Cherokee	1 869	5 488 563	6.6	9.7	2.3	2.5	5.7	2.1	69.7	129.7	67.3	48.0	938	770
Childress	583	1 738 210	4.7	11.1	1.6	1.8	46.8	4.4	29.0	62.7	9.4	6.1	867	753
Clay	559	1 694 976	3.7	2.8	0.0	4.0	14.3	8.9	63.3	47.0	12.1	16.9	1 605	1 445
Cochran	322	904 022	9.5	5.0	0.0	3.0	15.4	3.4	63.0	25.0	7.6	15.4	5 071	4 948
Coke	281	838 152	5.9	2.3	0.0	2.1	28.4	5.7	54.6	19.7	5.9	9.5	2 954	2 830
Coleman	629	1 691 631	4.4	5.0	0.9	13.7	19.1	6.3	48.7	34.6	18.7	11.3	1 301	1 096
Collin	28 433	113 769 771	4.6	8.7	4.4	3.5	1.7	4.9	69.6	3 611.2	681.0	1 995.2	2 390	2 038
Collingsworth	212	542 831	8.4	5.4	0.0	4.5	10.4	2.8	67.4	13.8	5.2	4.4	1 449	1 266
Colorado	861	2 596 959	7.5	9.0	0.0	6.1	1.1	3.8	71.4	68.4	17.2	35.5	1 716	1 501
Comal	4 722	16 455 274	5.9	10.7	5.6	2.4	1.7	4.9	65.1	413.5	81.4	279.4	2 443	2 055
Comanche	808	2 419 843	5.0	9.4	3.7	2.4	31.9	1.8	45.5	44.9	19.7	15.0	1 088	940
Concho	164	494 362	12.1	5.4	0.0	4.2	27.0	5.6	44.3	14.7	3.5	6.1	1 522	1 335
Cooke	2 150	7 756 968	4.6	7.0	2.3	2.2	22.1	3.1	58.0	192.9	53.2	71.4	1 846	1 489
Coryell	2 637	8 819 482	4.6	7.6	1.9	0.9	12.3	2.8	67.6	181.4	80.4	52.0	674	538
Cottle	98	244 407	17.9	5.3	0.0	6.5	0.0	11.3	51.6	5.8	2.0	2.8	1 867	1 769
Crane	326	1 145 731	9.6	10.7	0.0	1.4	1.7	18.9	57.2	40.3	6.9	31.6	6 922	6 690
Crockett	357	1 200 438	6.5	5.5	0.5	4.8	18.8	4.6	54.0	42.3	5.4	32.0	8 555	8 552
Crosby	396	1 113 076	6.6	6.1	0.0	1.6	0.7	8.5	76.2	24.3	14.0	7.8	1 271	1 153
Culberson	191	571 285	13.3	8.3	0.0	6.0	1.7	9.4	60.5	20.8	4.5	8.8	3 852	3 344
Dallam	459	1 265 633	7.6	10.7	0.5	2.5	1.7	3.2	73.1	27.7	8.8	15.1	2 154	1 701
Dallas	105 099	440 691 940	4.7	11.6	5.3	7.3	14.2	4.5	50.8	12 510.2	3 260.1	5 736.3	2 338	1 792
Dawson	1 027	2 968 415	3.1	5.5	0.8	1.9	24.1	9.3	55.0	56.2	16.2	34.3	2 514	2 311
Deaf Smith	1 045	3 343 534	6.0	8.2	0.3	2.5	18.1	3.3	61.2	124.1	26.6	28.5	1 470	1 181
Delta	249	617 205	10.2	5.7	0.1	0.9	0.0	6.2	76.6	18.1	9.8	6.9	1 304	1 174
Denton	21 018	80 654 351	6.5	9.2	4.5	1.3	2.5	6.0	68.8	2 022.8	459.3	1 266.0	1 790	1 527
DeWitt	1 484	4 135 234	4.5	4.4	0.5	2.2	24.6	3.4	59.6	97.2	42.1	29.7	1 450	1 280
Dickens	132	357 360	9.4	5.8	0.0	5.1	0.0	3.9	70.5	10.8	3.0	6.0	2 586	2 419
Dimmit	818	1 945 225	7.2	5.4	0.0	1.0	23.0	4.5	58.2	46.5	21.1	19.9	1 904	1 452
Donley	386	1 127 365	14.0	2.9	0.0	2.0	12.1	7.2	61.3	18.4	8.5	4.9	1 371	1 208
Duval	1 069	2 869 544	5.5	8.4	0.0	5.8	26.4	3.4	49.4	84.6	22.4	23.2	1 983	1 875
Eastland	1 310	3 783 362	4.4	5.2	0.7	1.4	13.7	3.5	70.8	84.5	34.9	24.4	1 322	1 079
Ector	6 915	26 339 816	4.0	7.3	3.2	1.3	27.3	2.1	53.3	690.5	140.4	269.5	1 867	1 389
Edwards	196	461 967	5.6	6.6	0.5	3.6	2.2	2.7	77.7	11.0	3.0	7.2	3 657	3 565
Ellis	6 187	19 866 741	5.2	9.5	4.1	1.8	0.8	3.8	73.5	481.2	162.1	262.5	1 705	1 483
El Paso	38 262	139 590 880	4.5	10.3	3.7	3.1	8.1	3.0	65.5	3 339.7	1 610.5	1 090.4	1 318	1 018
Erath	1 440	4 169 914	6.4	10.7	3.0	2.6	13.7	4.5	57.7	97.3	38.9	48.4	1 230	1 006
Falls	755	2 249 164	5.5	10.4	1.3	2.6	0.2	6.9	72.4	45.7	26.5	12.5	711	588
Fannin	1 308	3 305 390	7.2	6.5	4.5	3.2	0.4	4.6	72.9	79.2	36.7	29.9	885	758
Fayette	1 047	3 070 054	8.5	11.9	0.0	5.3	5.8	7.8	59.5	68.3	15.9	38.4	1 557	1 347
Fisher	274	819 484	9.8	4.3	0.0	4.0	33.9	2.2	42.7	20.3	6.0	7.5	1 949	1 549
Floyd	494	1 401 943	6.0	6.3	0.0	3.0	29.3	3.2	52.2	29.3	12.8	7.3	1 148	1 016
Foard	109	252 340	7.9	2.2	0.0	27.8	2.3	4.6	52.5	6.5	3.6	2.6	1 980	1 699
Fort Bend	16 162	56 081 173	6.1	10.9	2.4	2.1	1.2	2.8	73.5	1 700.0	419.7	1 031.0	1 644	1 484
Franklin	376	1 062 026	10.1	8.0	0.0	4.2	0.1	6.2	71.2	29.0	7.2	17.8	1 676	1 502
Freestone	870	2 743 049	6.9	7.9	0.0	2.8	1.7	3.3	77.1	162.3	33.5	110.1	5 642	5 300
Frio	734	2 179 421	2.5	6.3	0.0	4.5	0.2	6.1	79.7	65.4	34.3	19.5	1 102	928
Gaines	1 152	3 808 818	1.9	4.1	0.0	3.9	20.6	2.9	66.0	125.0	15.5	87.9	4 775	4 628
Galveston	16 441	61 971 543	4.8	11.2	1.9	2.4	3.8	5.1	69.9	1 645.8	615.8	806.4	2 684	2 330
Garza	293	892 400	9.4	14.2	0.0	2.3	1.8	3.0	68.2	25.0	4.6	15.2	2 373	2 062
Gillespie	1 151	3 952 390	6.0	8.2	0.8	2.5	3.0	27.3	49.9	76.0	11.8	50.4	2 005	1 655
Glasscock	71	223 571	6.0	3.1	0.0	7.3	0.0	3.2	74.8	20.5	1.8	16.3	12 932	12 861
Goliad	327	1 001 812	9.8	6.6	0.0	4.9	0.3	2.6	69.7	27.2	7.6	18.0	2 453	2 250
Gonzales	1 193	3 267 421	6.8	6.0	0.5	2.5	24.1	5.5	54.2	101.3	40.1	26.2	1 309	1 024
Gray	994	2 974 220	9.1	9.3	4.4	4.3	1.5	4.0	66.4	72.0	21.7	36.7	1 599	1 291
Grayson	5 248	18 290 717	5.6	9.2	3.5	2.7	4.2	4.8	69.0	414.8	144.6	188.3	1 544	1 271
Gregg	5 913	19 287 172	4.5	10.7	5.5	1.7	6.6	4.4	64.2	499.5	162.8	256.1	2 088	1 490
Grimes	917	2 789 960	7.3	9.4	0.7	2.4	1.2	2.1	74.4	77.3	25.0	42.7	1 594	1 464

1. Based on the resident population estimated as of July 1 of the year shown.

STATE County	Local government finances, 2012 (cont.)									Government employment, 2013			Presidential election,[2] 2012		
	Direct general expenditure							Debt outstanding					Percent of vote cast:		
			Percent of total for:												
	Total (mil dol)	Per capita[1] (dollars)	Educa-tion	Health and hospitals	Police protec-tion	Public welfare	High-ways	Total (mil dol)	Per capita[1] (dollars)	Federal civilian	Federal military	State and local	Demo-cratic	Republi-can	All other
	185	186	187	188	189	190	191	192	193	194	195	196	197	198	199
TEXAS—Cont'd															
Caldwell	103.3	2 667	49.6	3.3	5.2	0.3	3.5	64.6	1 669	57	76	1 627	46.4	52.4	1.2
Calhoun	106.7	4 938	37.9	23.7	4.3	0.2	4.4	73.3	3 392	34	107	1 320	39.7	59.7	0.6
Callahan	33.7	2 494	68.1	0.5	5.7	0.0	2.9	34.4	2 546	45	28	609	18.6	80.3	1.1
Cameron	1 613.4	3 883	61.9	0.8	4.4	0.5	3.7	1 801.3	4 335	3 164	991	27 261	64.1	35.3	0.7
Camp	30.6	2 461	71.8	0.2	3.9	0.1	5.5	43.1	3 459	32	26	585	38.0	61.3	0.8
Carson	23.0	3 741	59.9	1.1	2.8	0.0	5.0	34.1	5 539	14	13	422	13.6	85.5	0.9
Cass	91.1	3 021	59.3	15.9	3.7	0.3	2.8	50.0	1 659	62	63	1 623	29.5	69.9	0.7
Castro	33.2	4 069	51.2	27.7	4.5	0.0	3.7	20.0	2 445	19	17	614	31.4	68.2	0.4
Chambers	168.5	4 656	51.2	9.0	4.2	0.4	4.6	360.8	9 968	56	77	1 879	24.0	75.1	0.9
Cherokee	167.4	3 268	66.5	4.9	3.9	0.1	4.5	85.5	1 669	71	102	4 021	28.1	71.2	0.7
Childress	54.2	7 712	18.8	64.6	2.7	0.0	2.7	6.3	898	22	12	1 071	21.6	77.6	0.7
Clay	46.1	4 377	39.2	17.7	2.7	0.1	5.6	119.9	11 385	23	22	507	20.3	78.9	0.8
Cochran	27.0	8 873	69.4	12.8	3.0	0.0	3.8	0.1	27	11	0	329	26.9	71.7	1.4
Coke	16.5	5 122	42.6	0.1	3.0	32.6	4.0	24.2	7 483	11	0	346	19.1	79.8	1.1
Coleman	34.1	3 930	44.6	22.9	4.1	0.1	3.7	15.9	1 837	42	18	558	17.4	81.3	1.3
Collin	4 140.4	4 961	43.1	0.7	3.6	0.1	8.6	16 872.8	20 216	1 400	1 876	41 661	36.8	62.3	0.9
Collingsworth	16.5	5 436	37.3	43.5	4.4	0.0	1.5	12.6	4 138	19	0	210	19.6	78.9	1.5
Colorado	71.5	3 453	50.2	14.9	5.5	0.1	5.4	63.0	3 042	46	43	984	30.0	69.4	0.6
Comal	446.0	3 899	56.1	0.9	6.3	0.6	5.0	943.7	8 251	170	248	5 477	25.7	73.2	1.1
Comanche	42.2	3 069	50.8	15.3	4.6	0.2	5.8	30.9	2 246	45	28	1 024	25.6	73.1	1.3
Concho	12.3	3 067	36.9	29.2	4.3	0.0	4.1	3.9	977	25	0	222	23.9	74.9	1.2
Cooke	191.9	4 961	48.0	22.9	5.0	0.1	3.7	159.4	4 119	55	80	2 826	20.3	79.0	0.7
Coryell	215.6	2 792	43.6	12.0	4.0	0.3	22.6	217.4	2 815	189	526	5 780	36.1	63.0	0.9
Cottle	5.4	3 651	50.1	1.6	2.9	0.1	3.3	1.4	940	0	0	138	26.5	72.2	1.3
Crane	40.9	8 956	77.6	0.0	3.1	0.0	1.6	6.3	1 384	0	10	362	21.9	77.0	1.1
Crockett	42.8	11 437	63.2	0.7	1.7	0.8	5.5	6.0	1 614	0	0	410	33.1	66.4	0.5
Crosby	24.1	3 941	70.8	0.1	3.8	1.1	3.7	0.5	83	15	13	470	35.7	63.8	0.5
Culberson	18.7	8 167	29.9	32.6	5.7	0.0	3.2	2.8	1 224	88	0	213	64.8	33.9	1.3
Dallam	28.3	4 044	60.6	0.3	5.2	0.0	6.8	30.2	4 320	15	15	286	19.0	79.9	1.1
Dallas	11 949.9	4 870	37.6	17.2	5.8	0.7	2.6	27 138.7	11 060	25 874	6 138	139 641	57.3	42.0	0.7
Dawson	56.4	4 132	73.5	0.6	3.9	0.1	3.1	165.8	12 154	52	25	1 347	28.1	70.9	0.9
Deaf Smith	135.2	6 983	26.5	25.1	2.4	0.1	2.8	2 436.8	125 866	45	40	1 283	26.3	73.1	0.7
Delta	15.4	2 898	62.3	0.0	6.5	0.3	5.4	19.5	3 660	16	11	320	26.9	72.2	0.8
Denton	2 006.9	2 837	52.0	1.7	5.6	0.1	6.2	6 231.1	8 810	1 615	1 564	31 733	37.5	61.6	0.9
DeWitt	94.1	4 596	46.6	28.3	3.1	0.2	3.8	56.7	2 773	31	40	2 142	25.9	73.8	0.3
Dickens	13.9	5 980	66.7	0.3	4.5	0.0	7.7	7.5	3 235	12	0	160	24.1	75.1	0.8
Dimmit	42.2	4 036	66.0	0.3	4.0	0.0	3.8	95.0	9 081	285	23	951	75.0	24.4	0.6
Donley	19.7	5 489	76.6	0.0	1.8	2.7	1.6	21.5	5 966	11	0	405	17.2	81.3	1.5
Duval	69.0	5 890	36.6	35.9	4.0	0.7	3.7	59.2	5 053	153	23	1 001	74.8	24.4	0.8
Eastland	81.8	4 441	62.6	14.7	2.7	0.2	2.9	42.9	2 328	50	339	1 439	19.5	79.4	1.1
Ector	691.3	4 790	36.3	40.0	3.5	0.0	2.4	385.4	2 670	149	311	9 109	25.6	73.6	0.8
Edwards	10.4	5 270	76.7	0.0	6.7	0.0	2.3	2.5	1 271	23	0	146	33.4	65.0	1.5
Ellis	446.9	2 903	57.1	0.3	6.0	0.3	3.9	1 320.0	8 573	213	327	6 732	28.5	70.7	0.8
El Paso	3 257.4	3 937	52.3	15.6	4.9	0.4	0.9	4 034.1	4 876	12 828	28 915	54 564	65.9	33.4	0.8
Erath	86.0	2 188	55.2	1.6	7.4	0.4	5.3	109.6	2 786	73	84	3 600	22.3	76.8	0.9
Falls	44.4	2 519	65.6	1.1	5.3	0.8	6.2	13.4	762	407	33	1 222	39.7	59.4	0.8
Fannin	76.7	2 268	61.1	2.7	7.1	0.7	5.8	54.2	1 601	690	65	1 873	29.6	69.2	1.2
Fayette	68.1	2 756	56.7	3.7	5.9	0.8	7.7	47.6	1 928	65	52	1 502	28.1	70.8	1.1
Fisher	21.3	5 529	41.6	30.6	4.6	0.1	5.1	3.0	779	20	0	314	38.5	60.7	0.8
Floyd	29.6	4 646	49.4	29.9	3.4	0.0	1.0	5.9	923	27	13	497	29.0	70.8	0.3
Foard	4.6	3 531	56.3	4.7	6.8	0.2	7.6	0.1	79	0	0	93	36.8	60.8	2.4
Fort Bend	1 722.6	2 746	46.9	0.7	4.7	0.3	7.2	5 183.8	8 264	736	1 407	21 273	48.5	50.9	0.6
Franklin	25.1	2 364	51.5	0.1	5.6	0.4	9.6	29.4	2 760	18	22	417	23.1	75.5	1.4
Freestone	159.6	8 177	39.9	10.8	11.9	0.0	12.6	91.4	4 681	33	38	1 453	27.9	71.4	0.7
Frio	58.9	3 327	54.3	3.8	5.2	0.0	3.8	93.0	5 256	99	31	1 237	59.2	40.5	0.3
Gaines	132.6	7 199	63.4	14.7	1.8	0.0	4.5	120.9	6 566	25	40	1 350	16.0	83.2	0.8
Galveston	1 667.3	5 549	43.5	4.3	5.0	0.5	5.1	3 060.4	10 185	905	1 049	25 365	39.8	59.3	0.9
Garza	22.3	3 480	59.5	0.1	9.6	0.7	5.7	14.9	2 330	13	0	372	21.4	77.5	1.1
Gillespie	76.0	3 023	58.0	2.8	9.2	0.3	5.1	26.7	1 061	44	53	1 094	20.9	77.5	1.6
Glasscock	21.4	16 992	83.0	6.7	0.3	0.0	0.7	8.1	6 411	0	0	130	9.3	90.1	0.5
Goliad	22.9	3 113	65.5	4.1	7.2	0.8	7.3	16.0	2 182	18	16	441	36.4	62.0	0.8
Gonzales	101.6	5 069	39.0	28.7	5.0	0.0	3.6	43.0	2 146	01	42	1 404	34.5	64.8	0.7
Gray	70.1	3 049	52.0	0.4	5.0	0.2	5.4	80.6	3 506	43	45	1 534	14.2	85.1	0.7
Grayson	423.3	3 471	54.8	3.3	5.1	0.0	6.0	717.6	5 885	319	255	6 114	30.6	68.5	1.0
Gregg	514.7	4 196	54.4	5.9	5.3	0.0	4.4	916.0	7 468	323	253	7 096	30.9	68.5	0.6
Grimes	84.3	3 146	51.8	0.3	3.8	0.0	6.3	95.1	3 549	47	50	1 861	32.5	66.8	0.7

1. Based on the resident population estimated as of July 1 of the year shown. 2.

STATE/ County code	CBSA code[1]	County type[2]	STATE County	Land area,[3] (sq km) 2010	Population, 2014: Total persons 2014	Population, 2014: Rank	Population, 2014: Per square kilometer	Race alone or in combination, not Hispanic or Latino (percent): White	Race: Black	Race: American Indian, Alaska Native	Race: Asian and Pacific Islander	Percent Hispanic or Latino[4]	Age (percent): Under 5 years	Age: 5 to 17 years	Age: 18 to 24 years	Age: 25 to 34 years	Age: 35 to 44 years	Age: 45 to 54 years
				1	2	3	4	5	6	7	8	9	10	11	12	13	14	15
			TEXAS—Cont'd															
48 187	41700	1	Guadalupe	1 842	147 250	439	79.9	54.4	7.7	0.8	2.4	36.6	6.5	20.0	9.1	12.4	13.9	14.4
48 189	38380	4	Hale	2 602	34 720	1 310	13.3	36.1	5.4	0.6	0.6	58.0	8.2	20.1	11.7	13.7	11.6	12.1
48 191	...	9	Hall	2 288	3 147	2 963	1.4	57.5	7.6	0.8	0.2	34.7	5.7	19.5	7.5	9.0	9.8	12.4
48 193	...	6	Hamilton	2 165	8 199	2 589	3.8	87.1	1.0	0.8	0.7	11.3	5.5	15.8	6.5	9.3	10.4	12.6
48 195	...	7	Hansford	2 382	5 509	2 804	2.3	53.3	0.9	0.5	0.4	45.8	7.1	22.3	8.9	11.2	11.8	13.1
48 197	...	7	Hardeman	1 800	3 928	2 909	2.2	71.8	6.8	1.1	0.7	21.5	6.3	17.3	6.6	10.9	11.8	12.6
48 199	13140	2	Hardin	2 307	55 621	910	24.1	88.0	6.1	0.8	0.9	5.2	6.4	18.7	8.1	12.4	12.5	13.9
48 201	26420	1	Harris	4 412	4 441 370	3	1 006.7	32.9	19.1	0.5	7.2	41.4	7.9	19.5	10.0	16.1	14.3	12.8
48 203	32220	4	Harrison	2 331	67 336	790	28.9	64.8	22.6	0.9	0.9	12.0	6.7	18.6	10.2	12.0	11.9	13.1
48 205	...	9	Hartley	3 787	6 089	2 750	1.6	66.6	7.5	0.7	0.8	25.0	5.2	15.6	5.8	14.8	18.1	16.3
48 207	...	6	Haskell	2 339	5 769	2 781	2.5	70.0	4.2	1.0	1.2	25.0	5.2	14.9	8.3	11.7	11.4	13.3
48 209	12420	1	Hays	1 756	185 025	347	105.4	58.1	3.9	0.8	1.9	36.6	6.3	17.7	17.7	13.8	12.7	11.8
48 211	...	9	Hemphill	2 347	4 180	2 890	1.8	66.4	0.6	1.1	0.9	31.8	8.6	22.3	8.1	13.2	11.9	12.8
48 213	11980	4	Henderson	2 263	79 290	696	35.0	80.6	6.9	1.2	0.8	11.8	5.6	16.7	8.1	10.4	11.0	13.4
48 215	32580	2	Hidalgo	4 069	831 073	70	204.2	7.4	0.5	0.1	1.1	90.7	9.7	24.3	11.1	13.3	13.1	10.4
48 217	...	6	Hill	2 483	34 848	1 304	14.0	73.1	7.2	0.8	0.7	19.4	6.2	17.9	8.0	10.9	10.7	13.0
48 219	30220	6	Hockley	2 353	23 577	1 656	10.0	49.4	3.9	0.7	0.5	46.3	7.4	19.3	12.7	13.0	10.6	12.3
48 221	19100	4	Hood	1 089	53 921	928	49.5	86.8	1.0	1.2	0.9	11.2	5.2	15.5	7.0	10.3	10.0	13.2
48 223	44860	6	Hopkins	1 987	35 921	1 276	18.1	75.6	7.8	1.0	0.9	16.2	6.9	18.5	8.3	11.7	11.8	13.3
48 225	...	7	Houston	3 188	22 741	1 700	7.1	62.6	26.1	0.7	0.8	10.9	5.1	14.1	7.7	11.6	12.3	14.7
48 227	13700	5	Howard	2 333	36 651	1 260	15.7	52.8	6.4	1.0	1.3	39.3	6.0	15.9	11.1	14.6	12.0	16.3
48 229	21340	8	Hudspeth	11 839	3 211	2 956	0.3	20.3	1.2	0.7	0.6	78.2	6.6	19.4	9.5	10.4	10.8	13.4
48 231	19100	1	Hunt	2 176	88 493	647	40.7	75.3	8.7	1.5	1.5	14.5	6.3	17.9	9.6	12.0	11.9	14.3
48 233	14420	6	Hutchinson	2 298	21 773	1 745	9.5	73.6	3.1	2.3	0.8	22.0	7.3	19.2	8.1	12.2	12.2	12.5
48 235	41660	3	Irion	2 724	1 574	3 078	0.6	70.7	2.4	0.8	0.7	27.0	6.1	16.3	8.2	11.0	9.7	15.9
48 237	...	6	Jack	2 359	8 855	2 524	3.8	79.1	4.4	0.9	0.6	15.8	6.0	15.7	9.9	13.1	12.7	14.9
48 239	...	6	Jackson	2 148	14 739	2 121	6.9	61.1	7.3	0.7	0.8	30.9	7.0	19.3	8.1	12.2	11.0	12.6
48 241	...	6	Jasper	2 432	35 552	1 285	14.6	76.1	17.1	0.8	1.0	6.4	6.7	17.7	8.0	11.2	11.1	13.6
48 243	...	9	Jeff Davis	5 865	2 204	3 034	0.4	64.0	1.4	1.1	0.9	34.7	2.8	11.5	5.5	8.0	8.3	14.2
48 245	13140	2	Jefferson	2 270	252 235	263	111.1	43.8	34.2	0.7	4.0	18.4	6.8	16.9	10.4	14.6	12.3	13.6
48 247	...	6	Jim Hogg	2 943	5 255	2 818	1.8	6.6	0.6	0.4	0.6	92.3	8.9	20.6	8.2	12.4	10.9	11.7
48 249	10860	4	Jim Wells	2 240	41 353	1 142	18.5	19.5	0.7	0.4	0.5	79.3	7.9	20.5	9.9	12.8	11.5	12.1
48 251	19100	1	Johnson	1 877	157 456	403	83.9	76.1	3.3	1.1	1.5	19.4	6.6	19.9	8.8	12.6	13.1	14.2
48 253	10180	3	Jones	2 405	19 936	1 838	8.3	60.9	12.1	0.7	0.7	26.1	4.7	13.3	9.9	16.5	14.9	14.8
48 255	...	6	Karnes	1 936	14 906	2 106	7.7	39.5	8.8	0.5	0.4	52.2	5.6	15.1	10.4	17.2	13.1	13.0
48 257	19100	1	Kaufman	2 022	111 236	544	55.0	69.3	11.0	1.1	1.4	18.8	7.0	20.9	8.1	12.7	14.1	13.9
48 259	41700	1	Kendall	1 716	38 880	1 201	22.7	76.1	1.1	0.9	1.3	21.9	5.1	18.7	7.6	9.2	11.5	15.0
48 261	28780	9	Kenedy	3 777	400	3 139	0.1	20.6	2.2	1.5	0.7	74.7	6.8	15.3	8.5	17.0	9.0	12.6
48 263	...	9	Kent	2 337	785	3 120	0.3	80.9	1.4	1.4	0.4	17.1	3.7	19.1	3.8	9.3	9.3	13.1
48 265	28500	4	Kerr	2 858	50 562	979	17.7	71.6	2.0	1.0	1.2	25.3	5.1	14.4	8.5	9.4	9.1	12.6
48 267	...	7	Kimble	3 240	4 438	2 869	1.4	72.6	0.4	0.8	1.1	25.7	4.6	14.3	6.5	9.1	9.9	12.6
48 269	...	9	King	2 359	262	3 140	0.1	82.8	1.1	2.1	1.1	17.2	8.4	14.4	4.9	11.2	14.0	14.7
48 271	...	9	Kinney	3 523	3 526	2 939	1.0	40.8	1.6	0.9	0.5	56.4	4.9	14.8	8.6	11.4	11.3	10.8
48 273	28780	4	Kleberg	2 283	32 190	1 381	14.1	22.6	3.9	0.4	2.5	71.3	7.3	17.5	20.8	13.6	9.8	9.6
48 275	...	9	Knox	2 203	3 858	2 916	1.8	61.3	5.9	0.7	0.6	32.8	7.4	18.2	7.0	10.7	10.8	12.4
48 277	37580	4	Lamar	2 350	49 523	987	21.1	77.6	14.3	2.5	1.1	7.1	6.6	17.1	9.1	11.3	11.6	13.4
48 279	...	6	Lamb	2 632	13 574	2 199	5.2	41.3	4.6	0.7	0.3	53.9	8.5	20.4	8.6	11.4	10.7	12.8
48 281	28660	2	Lampasas	1 846	20 156	1 830	10.9	75.6	4.3	1.7	2.2	18.7	5.9	17.8	7.9	10.8	12.3	14.5
48 283	...	6	La Salle	3 851	7 474	2 642	1.9	14.1	0.7	0.6	0.3	84.1	6.6	14.1	18.2	17.3	10.8	11.2
48 285	...	6	Lavaca	2 512	19 721	1 847	7.9	75.3	7.0	0.5	0.6	17.5	6.0	17.5	7.2	9.7	10.3	13.1
48 287	...	6	Lee	1 629	16 742	1 997	10.3	65.1	11.4	0.6	0.9	23.2	5.7	17.6	8.7	10.8	11.3	14.5
48 289	...	8	Leon	2 779	16 861	1 989	6.1	77.6	7.6	0.8	1.0	14.1	6.6	15.8	6.9	10.0	9.7	13.4
48 291	26420	1	Liberty	3 000	78 117	706	26.0	68.6	11.1	1.0	0.9	19.7	6.8	18.2	9.5	13.3	13.2	14.1
48 293	...	6	Limestone	2 345	23 524	1 661	10.0	61.6	17.9	0.7	0.7	20.3	6.4	16.8	8.9	12.7	11.6	12.9
48 295	...	9	Lipscomb	2 414	3 553	2 937	1.5	66.4	1.3	1.4	0.8	31.7	6.7	21.0	8.1	13.7	10.9	13.3
48 297	...	6	Live Oak	2 693	12 091	2 293	4.5	57.6	4.4	0.9	0.9	36.9	5.0	14.5	8.4	13.5	11.7	13.8
48 299	...	7	Llano	2 419	19 510	1 852	8.1	88.6	1.3	1.0	0.8	9.3	4.2	11.5	5.2	7.5	8.0	12.0
48 301	...	9	Loving	1 733	86	3 142	0.0	78.9	0.0	3.2	0.0	16.5	9.5	17.9	2.1	16.8	5.3	20.0
48 303	31180	3	Lubbock	2 320	293 974	229	126.7	56.8	7.6	0.7	2.7	33.3	6.9	17.3	17.3	14.5	10.9	11.2
48 305	31180	6	Lynn	2 310	5 771	2 780	2.5	50.1	2.6	0.7	0.4	47.1	7.0	19.9	7.8	11.0	10.9	14.4
48 307	...	7	McCulloch	2 760	8 199	2 589	3.0	65.8	2.3	0.6	0.6	31.6	6.4	17.5	7.1	10.0	10.7	12.4
48 309	47380	3	McLennan	2 686	243 441	274	90.6	59.1	15.0	0.7	2.0	24.7	7.1	17.8	14.9	12.9	11.1	12.0
48 311	...	8	McMullen	2 951	805	3 118	0.3	61.4	1.3	1.0	0.5	36.3	3.9	16.2	6.2	9.0	10.5	15.4
48 313	...	6	Madison	1 207	13 861	2 182	11.5	57.8	20.2	0.6	1.0	21.7	5.7	15.6	11.9	17.4	13.0	11.0
48 315	...	8	Marion	986	10 149	2 427	10.3	72.9	22.6	1.8	1.1	3.8	4.6	14.0	6.4	9.5	9.9	15.9
48 317	33260	6	Martin	2 370	5 460	2 808	2.3	52.6	2.0	0.6	0.9	44.9	8.2	21.3	9.8	13.7	11.3	13.2

1. CBSA = Core Based Statistical Area. See Appendix A for explanation. See Appendix B for list of metropolitan areas with component counties. 2. County type code from the Economic Research Service of USDA Rural-Urban Continuum Codes. See Appendix A for definition. 3. Dry land or land partially or temporarily covered by water. 4. May be of any race.

Table B. States and Counties — **Population and Households**

STATE County	Population, 2013 (cont.): Age (percent) (cont.): 55 to 64 years	65 to 74 years	75 years and over	Percent female	Population change and components of change, 2000–2014: Total persons: 2000	2010	Percent change: 2000–2010	2010–2014	Components of change, 2010–2014: Births	Deaths	Net migration	Households, 2009–2013: Number	Persons per house-hold	Percent: Family house-holds	Female family house-holder[1]	One per-son
	16	17	18	19	20	21	22	23	24	25	26	27	28	29	30	31
TEXAS—Cont'd																
Guadalupe	11.1	7.5	5.2	50.7	89 023	131 533	47.8	11.9	7 262	3 788	11 850	46 409	2.89	76.3	12.7	20.2
Hale	10.1	6.6	5.8	48.1	36 602	36 273	-0.9	-4.3	2 326	1 286	-2 642	11 624	2.84	73.8	16.1	23.2
Hall	13.1	12.2	10.8	50.8	3 782	3 353	-11.3	-6.1	147	179	-172	1 177	2.76	65.6	10.0	30.5
Hamilton	14.2	13.3	12.3	50.6	8 229	8 517	3.5	-3.7	380	554	-139	3 029	2.68	70.2	7.4	28.2
Hansford	11.6	7.5	6.6	49.1	5 369	5 613	4.5	-1.9	338	196	-238	1 983	2.77	73.5	7.9	23.2
Hardeman	14.9	10.9	8.8	48.9	4 724	4 139	-12.4	-5.1	167	159	-231	1 745	2.32	62.6	12.9	32.6
Hardin	13.1	8.8	5.9	50.6	48 073	54 635	13.7	1.8	2 927	2 227	346	20 633	2.64	73.6	11.7	22.8
Harris	10.4	5.5	3.5	50.1	3 400 578	4 092 459	20.3	8.5	286 753	99 111	163 579	1 434 694	2.89	68.6	15.5	25.8
Harrison	13.0	8.5	6.0	51.1	62 110	65 631	5.7	2.6	3 576	2 554	747	23 415	2.76	73.6	15.4	22.7
Hartley	10.0	7.9	6.4	38.5	5 537	6 062	9.5	0.4	254	132	-115	1 748	2.61	74.0	3.9	23.2
Haskell	13.6	10.6	11.0	47.4	6 093	5 899	-3.2	-2.2	197	353	22	2 425	2.17	68.9	10.2	29.9
Hays	10.4	6.1	3.5	50.2	97 589	157 107	61.0	17.8	8 966	3 572	21 845	56 459	2.77	64.5	9.3	23.9
Hemphill	10.8	6.7	5.6	49.4	3 351	3 807	13.6	9.8	288	133	226	1 440	2.71	73.3	8.9	25.4
Henderson	14.3	12.0	8.5	51.1	73 277	78 532	7.2	1.0	3 804	4 142	1 164	29 732	2.60	69.0	11.7	25.8
Hidalgo	8.0	5.6	4.5	51.0	569 463	774 769	36.1	7.3	68 625	16 186	3 373	217 691	3.60	81.9	19.9	15.6
Hill	13.6	11.2	8.5	51.0	32 321	35 089	8.6	-0.7	1 762	1 617	-345	13 395	2.54	68.4	10.3	27.6
Hockley	11.2	7.6	5.9	50.6	22 716	22 935	1.0	2.8	1 446	854	45	7 973	2.81	74.7	12.2	21.8
Hood	15.2	13.7	9.9	50.7	41 100	51 182	24.5	5.4	2 428	2 496	2 785	20 758	2.46	70.4	8.0	25.4
Hopkins	12.8	9.5	7.2	50.6	31 960	35 161	10.0	2.2	1 990	1 565	283	13 303	2.60	74.8	11.6	21.4
Houston	13.9	11.2	9.5	46.8	23 185	23 732	2.4	-4.2	1 016	1 283	-719	7 889	2.64	66.1	13.3	32.0
Howard	11.6	6.7	5.9	43.4	33 627	35 012	4.1	4.7	1 899	1 597	1 306	11 010	2.69	65.8	14.1	30.1
Hudspeth	13.9	9.9	6.1	50.0	3 344	3 476	3.9	-7.6	190	70	-394	1 096	2.92	72.4	17.1	27.1
Hunt	12.9	9.0	6.2	50.7	76 596	86 129	12.4	2.7	4 515	3 580	1 452	30 756	2.73	69.4	11.0	26.2
Hutchinson	13.7	7.8	6.8	50.2	23 857	22 150	-7.2	-2.1	1 293	967	-795	8 374	2.59	64.7	13.1	32.6
Irion	14.5	10.9	7.4	48.9	1 771	1 599	-9.7	-1.6	71	52	-41	654	2.45	75.5	9.9	22.8
Jack	11.7	9.3	6.8	44.2	8 763	9 044	3.2	-2.1	409	354	-245	2 972	2.62	68.4	8.5	25.5
Jackson	13.1	8.8	7.8	50.3	14 391	14 075	-2.2	4.7	813	591	433	5 212	2.69	69.8	10.8	25.9
Jasper	13.9	10.3	7.5	50.7	35 604	35 710	0.3	-0.4	1 910	1 697	-344	13 095	2.66	70.1	13.5	27.0
Jeff Davis	21.2	18.1	10.4	49.4	2 207	2 342	6.1	-5.9	63	80	-129	989	2.27	70.1	5.3	28.2
Jefferson	12.3	7.0	6.2	48.9	252 051	252 273	0.1	0.0	14 703	10 101	-4 567	92 634	2.55	64.2	17.5	31.3
Jim Hogg	11.3	9.8	6.2	50.2	5 281	5 300	0.4	-0.8	384	223	-216	1 805	2.90	73.2	13.7	25.8
Jim Wells	11.4	7.8	6.0	50.6	39 326	40 838	3.8	1.3	2 707	1 702	-494	13 728	2.96	75.9	18.7	22.0
Johnson	11.9	7.9	5.0	50.0	126 811	150 934	19.0	4.3	8 326	5 128	3 364	52 044	2.87	76.6	10.1	19.5
Jones	11.5	8.0	6.3	37.8	20 785	20 202	-2.8	-1.3	772	765	-256	5 641	2.33	65.0	10.4	31.7
Karnes	11.4	7.2	7.0	41.1	15 446	14 824	-4.0	0.6	678	641	40	4 497	2.54	71.2	14.7	26.6
Kaufman	11.7	7.2	4.3	50.9	71 313	103 350	44.9	7.6	6 113	3 522	5 121	34 922	2.97	78.3	12.9	18.1
Kendall	14.6	10.8	7.7	51.1	23 743	33 410	40.7	16.4	1 447	1 372	5 246	12 760	2.70	77.3	7.6	19.7
Kenedy	14.6	8.5	7.8	49.3	414	416	0.5	-3.8	22	4	-40	159	3.28	76.7	14.5	23.3
Kent	13.0	14.1	14.5	51.3	859	808	-5.9	-2.8	31	55	7	401	2.15	64.1	8.5	34.4
Kerr	14.6	13.7	12.6	51.7	43 653	49 625	13.7	1.9	2 090	2 936	1 668	20 357	2.35	65.9	11.6	29.9
Kimble	16.9	14.8	11.2	50.5	4 468	4 607	3.1	-3.7	170	216	-104	1 895	2.37	66.6	9.4	28.0
King	16.5	8.8	7.0	49.1	356	286	-19.7	-8.4	9	3	-29	126	2.53	69.8	2.4	21.4
Kinney	13.1	12.9	12.1	44.4	3 379	3 598	6.5	-2.0	139	143	-60	1 195	2.81	67.4	7.3	30.2
Kleberg	9.2	7.0	5.2	49.0	31 549	32 061	1.6	0.4	2 070	1 024	-906	11 241	2.68	68.4	17.2	21.0
Knox	12.4	9.9	11.2	50.8	4 253	3 719	-12.6	3.7	216	224	149	1 557	2.31	61.2	13.2	35.7
Lamar	12.8	10.4	7.7	51.7	48 499	49 793	2.7	-0.5	2 765	2 585	-473	19 416	2.50	69.8	12.9	26.9
Lamb	11.5	8.1	8.1	49.8	14 709	13 977	-5.0	-2.9	837	657	-593	4 803	2.85	70.2	12.1	26.3
Lampasas	13.5	10.2	7.1	50.6	17 762	19 677	10.8	2.4	976	781	252	7 289	2.68	74.2	9.5	21.3
La Salle	8.7	8.0	5.2	41.3	5 866	6 886	17.4	8.5	413	194	347	1 864	3.29	64.2	18.8	30.5
Lavaca	14.3	11.3	10.5	51.1	19 210	19 263	0.3	2.4	928	1 018	551	7 711	2.45	71.5	8.4	26.4
Lee	14.3	9.4	7.7	49.6	15 657	16 612	6.1	0.8	813	623	-53	6 078	2.63	70.5	7.3	25.1
Leon	14.7	13.5	9.4	50.1	15 335	16 801	9.6	0.4	910	915	53	6 349	2.63	72.3	12.9	22.8
Liberty	12.4	7.8	4.7	50.9	70 154	75 643	7.8	3.3	4 412	3 032	1 094	24 844	2.82	74.6	13.6	21.2
Limestone	13.4	10.0	7.3	48.4	22 051	23 384	6.0	0.6	1 284	1 060	-34	7 929	2.72	71.3	12.4	26.1
Lipscomb	12.3	7.3	6.5	48.6	3 057	3 302	8.0	7.6	187	111	178	1 115	2.99	71.1	5.7	24.8
Live Oak	13.5	11.2	8.4	46.0	12 309	11 531	-6.3	4.9	521	467	529	3 882	2.58	73.2	11.6	24.6
Llano	18.4	18.6	14.6	51.8	17 044	19 301	13.2	1.1	667	1 229	690	8 519	2.23	62.3	7.9	34.4
Loving	18.9	7.4	2.1	46.3	67	82	22.4	4.9	5	3	2	33	2.64	51.5	9.1	39.4
Lubbock	10.3	6.3	5.3	50.5	242 628	278 831	14.9	5.4	16 939	9 564	7 600	105 277	2.57	62.6	14.0	28.1
Lynn	12.9	8.5	7.6	49.7	6 550	5 915	-9.7	-2.4	326	193	-270	2 179	2.63	74.6	16.3	21.8
McCulloch	14.5	11.8	9.6	50.5	8 205	8 283	1.0	-1.0	407	475	-10	2 967	2.75	66.0	6.6	32.0
McLennan	11.2	7.0	6.1	51.2	213 517	234 906	10.0	3.6	14 623	8 453	2 512	84 862	2.60	66.9	15.4	26.1
McMullen	16.1	9.8	12.8	49.5	851	707	-16.9	13.9	34	39	102	254	2.43	60.6	4.7	37.0
Madison	10.7	8.4	6.4	42.2	12 940	13 664	5.6	1.4	654	512	45	3 743	2.72	69.8	13.0	27.4
Marion	17.0	13.7	9.1	50.9	10 941	10 546	-3.6	-3.7	420	634	-192	4 563	2.26	65.6	12.0	31.0
Martin	10.4	7.4	4.8	49.5	4 746	4 799	1.1	13.8	381	167	441	1 555	3.13	74.3	11.3	23.1

1. No spouse present.

STATE County	Persons in group quarters, 2014	Daytime population, 2009–2013: Number	Daytime population, 2009–2013: Employment/residence ratio	Births, 2014: Total	Births, 2014: Rate[1]	Deaths, 2014: Number	Deaths, 2014: Rate[1]	Persons under 65 with no health insurance, 2013: Number	Persons under 65 with no health insurance, 2013: Percent	Medicare, 2014: Eligible for Medicare	Medicare, 2014: Enrolled in Medicare Advantage	Medicare, 2014: Enrolled in a Medicare prescription drug plan	Serious crimes known to police,[2] 2013: Total: Number	Serious crimes known to police,[2] 2013: Total: Rate[3]
	32	33	34	35	36	37	38	39	40	41	42	43	44	45
TEXAS—Cont'd														
Guadalupe	1 888	111 226	0.61	1 782	12.1	944	6.4	25 698	20.9	21 307	5 366	7 710	3 198	2 236
Hale	2 930	37 138	1.07	516	14.9	306	8.8	7 484	26.2	5 250	1 027	3 015	1 111	3 040
Hall	44	3 161	0.87	31	9.9	29	9.2	925	37.4	774	107	486	41	1 247
Hamilton	235	8 238	0.94	87	10.6	117	14.3	1 732	28.2	2 151	666	1 063	165	2 377
Hansford	59	5 219	0.87	81	14.7	35	6.4	1 314	27.7	878	80	564	52	943
Hardeman	21	3 917	0.89	38	9.7	36	9.2	837	26.1	914	138	587	131	3 214
Hardin	378	43 641	0.52	689	12.4	518	9.3	8 781	18.7	10 054	3 452	4 354	981	1 766
Harris	46 461	4 473 814	1.15	68 468	15.4	24 648	5.5	1 071 270	27.5	461 285	172 288	171 337	209 248	4 842
Harrison	2 315	62 538	0.86	818	12.1	628	9.3	12 199	22.1	11 875	2 455	6 101	1 862	2 726
Hartley	1 432	6 397	1.14	63	10.3	30	4.9	908	23.8	663	81	422	93	1 500
Haskell	534	5 624	0.88	50	8.7	64	11.1	999	24.3	1 351	240	890	58	978
Hays	7 803	144 570	0.75	2 192	11.8	870	4.7	32 280	21.3	21 433	5 423	10 064	3 926	2 264
Hemphill	30	4 593	1.35	71	17.0	24	5.7	901	24.9	543	49	332	81	1 930
Henderson	1 328	70 223	0.72	871	11.0	992	12.5	16 299	26.5	19 013	4 502	9 854	2 318	2 922
Hidalgo	7 268	779 001	0.96	16 120	19.4	4 060	4.9	276 623	38.2	89 877	29 108	47 640	32 558	3 974
Hill	823	31 091	0.72	396	11.4	376	10.8	7 516	27.4	7 900	1 721	4 106	865	2 453
Hockley	727	22 328	0.92	361	15.3	201	8.5	4 631	23.6	3 683	834	2 098	761	3 274
Hood	793	46 344	0.75	594	11.0	595	11.0	9 143	22.9	13 890	3 284	7 049	1 119	2 132
Hopkins	436	34 306	0.93	448	12.5	354	9.9	8 301	28.2	7 094	831	4 311	418	1 171
Houston	2 734	23 145	0.97	251	11.0	302	13.3	4 220	27.0	4 893	910	2 888	572	2 479
Howard	6 124	35 579	1.02	482	13.2	354	9.7	5 339	20.7	5 126	801	2 730	1 545	4 329
Hudspeth	86	3 593	1.17	38	11.8	7	2.2	997	37.0	589	203	259	26	787
Hunt	2 272	82 814	0.90	1 043	11.8	877	9.9	19 032	26.4	16 137	2 314	8 565	2 884	3 342
Hutchinson	146	22 588	1.07	309	14.2	210	9.6	4 286	23.2	3 776	540	2 197	801	3 987
Irion	0	1 682	1.10	17	10.8	8	5.1	277	21.2	316	37	175	36	2 297
Jack	1 091	9 001	1.00	89	10.1	72	8.1	1 772	27.7	1 579	240	953	212	2 354
Jackson	217	14 016	0.97	206	14.0	125	8.5	2 700	22.4	2 684	474	1 416	197	1 370
Jasper	942	34 832	0.92	427	12.0	393	11.1	6 506	22.8	7 588	1 903	4 009	1 068	2 958
Jeff Davis	88	2 484	1.18	9	4.1	24	10.9	499	32.8	611	108	306	20	868
Jefferson	16 092	279 900	1.28	3 444	13.7	2 474	9.8	48 617	23.8	41 177	13 606	19 114	12 175	4 819
Jim Hogg	16	5 411	1.07	88	16.7	50	9.5	1 172	26.8	923	211	567	26	495
Jim Wells	356	42 996	1.11	636	15.4	379	9.2	7 968	22.3	7 185	2 827	3 095	1 968	4 662
Johnson	2 677	128 459	0.64	1 981	12.6	1 233	7.8	32 070	24.2	25 424	10 388	9 593	3 521	2 274
Jones	5 293	19 228	0.84	185	9.3	172	8.6	3 173	26.2	3 156	567	1 849	553	2 768
Karnes	2 646	16 455	1.32	171	11.5	162	10.9	1 929	19.1	2 602	438	1 597	453	2 935
Kaufman	1 285	86 871	0.61	1 482	13.3	862	7.7	21 847	23.0	16 370	4 255	7 785	2 340	2 163
Kendall	542	32 753	0.86	370	9.5	345	8.9	6 243	20.5	8 013	1 893	3 301	620	1 680
Kenedy	0	826	2.56	7	17.5	0	0.0	71	20.5	50	11	29	13	2 968
Kent	39	961	1.10	6	7.6	16	20.4	152	27.1	180	34	106	14	1 643
Kerr	1 960	49 877	1.01	496	9.8	687	13.6	9 096	25.7	14 483	2 016	7 357	1 108	2 214
Kimble	44	4 159	0.81	43	9.7	50	11.3	1 043	31.6	1 167	187	682	59	1 291
King	0	308	0.94	1	3.8	0	0.0	44	18.4	29	NA	21	2	733
Kinney	332	3 435	0.87	30	8.5	37	10.5	608	25.9	883	198	404	NA	NA
Kleberg	2 079	31 761	0.98	487	15.1	229	7.1	6 540	24.9	4 666	1 767	1 500	1 249	3 886
Knox	105	3 878	1.10	53	13.7	47	12.2	922	31.5	843	114	577	37	967
Lamar	702	50 281	1.03	628	12.7	650	13.1	10 074	25.1	10 908	976	6 748	1 849	3 697
Lamb	184	13 660	0.95	176	13.0	148	10.9	3 375	29.5	2 582	535	1 585	417	3 183
Lampasas	221	16 527	0.59	227	11.3	170	8.4	4 381	26.4	4 400	1 099	1 594	462	2 405
La Salle	1 625	8 285	1.66	106	14.2	40	5.4	1 228	25.6	1 091	323	596	50	693
Lavaca	410	17 706	0.81	227	11.5	245	12.4	3 548	23.4	4 770	633	3 022	303	1 544
Lee	509	15 193	0.81	196	11.7	140	8.4	3 531	26.4	3 247	714	1 608	394	2 364
Leon	104	17 281	1.08	222	13.2	219	13.0	3 658	28.5	4 709	999	2 491	263	1 558
Liberty	4 963	66 811	0.66	1 059	13.6	748	9.6	16 335	26.1	11 943	4 223	4 811	2 794	3 622
Limestone	1 599	23 870	1.05	293	12.5	253	10.8	4 381	24.4	4 738	1 070	2 774	727	3 063
Lipscomb	35	3 245	0.92	46	12.9	22	6.2	900	30.2	551	54	319	29	814
Live Oak	1 155	12 319	1.18	133	11.0	108	8.9	1 908	22.5	1 859	478	990	278	2 366
Llano	177	18 073	0.85	164	8.4	291	14.9	3 283	25.4	6 168	1 360	3 224	446	2 338
Loving	0	410	6.13	0	0.0	0	0.0	15	17.7	14	NA	NA	NA	NA
Lubbock	11 452	284 601	1.01	4 026	13.7	2 357	8.0	55 849	22.7	40 602	12 158	20 645	14 604	5 056
Lynn	43	5 048	0.69	78	13.5	32	5.5	1 244	26.2	1 056	225	662	82	1 421
McCulloch	96	8 469	1.05	92	11.2	111	13.5	1 774	27.3	1 976	214	1 219	177	2 113
McLennan	9 671	243 552	1.06	3 445	14.2	2 043	8.4	46 793	23.2	38 743	10 649	18 081	9 256	3 902
McMullen	0	1 394	3.21	8	9.9	11	13.7	106	18.1	165	42	85	40	5 450
Madison	2 611	14 466	1.19	159	11.5	120	8.7	2 646	28.4	2 247	490	1 264	249	1 816
Marion	157	8 822	0.57	98	9.7	135	13.3	1 993	25.5	2 771	633	1 382	416	4 038
Martin	48	5 229	1.14	106	19.4	36	6.6	1 149	24.9	753	105	451	96	1 880

1. Per 1,000 estimated resident population. 2. Data for serious crimes have not been adjusted for underreporting; this may affect comparability between geographic areas and over time.
3. Per 100,000 population estimated by the FBI.

STATE County	Serious crimes known to police, 2013 (cont.)[1] Rate[2] Violent	Rate[2] Property	Education: School enrollment and attainment, 2009–2013: Enrollment[3] Total	Enrollment[3] Percent private	Attainment[4] (percent) High school graduate or less	Attainment[4] (percent) Bachelor's degree or more	Local government expenditures,[5] 2012–2013: Total current spending (mil dol)	Current spending per student (dollars)	Money income, 2009–2013: Per capita income[6] (dollars)	Households: Median income (dollars)	Households: Mean income (dollars)	Households: Percent with income of $200,000 or more	Income and poverty, 2013: Median household income (dollars)	Percent below poverty level: All persons	Children under 18 years	Children 5 to 17 years in families
	46	47	48	49	50	51	52	53	54	55	56	57	58	59	60	61
TEXAS—Cont'd																
Guadalupe	178	2 058	39 251	12.2	42.6	24.6	176.5	7 337	26 184	61 958	74 698	2.9	59 288	11.0	16.3	14.9
Hale	189	2 851	10 106	13.3	61.7	13.2	63.8	8 321	18 004	41 191	52 909	2.0	39 209	22.3	31.6	30.4
Hall	243	1 003	828	3.7	56.3	14.1	6.0	11 129	19 004	33 006	50 470	2.0	30 380	21.9	38.0	33.7
Hamilton	216	2 161	1 621	4.8	52.7	17.8	13.8	9 229	23 067	40 655	57 045	2.5	39 448	17.9	29.9	28.6
Hansford	73	870	1 536	4.6	53.7	21.8	16.3	11 381	23 969	49 150	65 097	3.1	52 207	12.3	18.0	16.3
Hardeman	25	3 189	728	6.0	56.4	18.6	9.6	13 105	19 829	36 377	46 058	0.7	36 726	18.7	31.1	29.9
Hardin	148	1 618	13 606	10.5	52.0	15.6	85.8	8 073	25 559	53 013	67 142	2.5	52 037	12.0	17.8	16.6
Harris	712	4 131	1 187 325	10.7	44.8	28.4	6 029.3	8 132	27 899	53 137	78 347	6.2	52 533	18.4	26.7	25.8
Harrison	315	2 411	17 198	14.1	50.0	17.8	107.8	8 329	23 236	45 675	62 689	2.7	43 777	18.7	25.8	24.9
Hartley	290	1 210	1 279	24.6	57.2	20.6	4.1	11 140	24 566	65 750	82 232	4.5	64 558	10.1	10.1	9.4
Haskell	101	876	1 025	4.0	63.0	12.2	10.4	11 019	22 223	36 857	52 752	2.9	34 473	23.5	36.1	35.2
Hays	278	1 985	58 048	7.3	32.1	36.7	246.1	7 955	26 873	58 651	75 630	4.9	59 260	14.3	15.1	14.0
Hemphill	119	1 811	1 109	5.2	49.6	19.6	9.6	9 825	29 544	56 379	78 121	4.3	69 124	8.1	11.3	10.8
Henderson	325	2 596	17 574	7.8	53.5	14.4	85.2	8 236	21 995	40 900	55 596	1.9	39 069	21.8	37.3	34.2
Hidalgo	286	3 688	261 217	5.1	62.2	15.9	1 868.5	9 112	14 222	34 146	49 152	1.7	34 607	34.0	44.5	42.5
Hill	199	2 254	8 288	6.5	52.0	14.8	62.1	9 551	21 182	40 769	54 398	1.5	40 253	17.9	28.6	25.6
Hockley	391	2 882	6 917	5.4	49.7	17.4	51.3	10 414	21 984	50 565	62 744	2.1	50 047	17.7	24.4	22.5
Hood	135	1 996	10 380	13.4	42.0	24.1	66.7	8 898	30 046	55 754	73 595	3.7	59 053	14.1	22.4	19.6
Hopkins	123	1 048	8 133	7.2	55.4	15.7	56.1	8 536	21 606	43 657	56 708	2.1	41 863	18.7	29.0	27.0
Houston	156	2 323	4 814	6.5	56.8	14.8	29.5	9 852	19 090	33 119	51 250	1.8	34 777	24.8	34.8	32.5
Howard	502	3 827	8 368	6.3	55.0	12.1	47.3	8 257	19 965	45 612	59 625	1.6	46 636	17.9	24.9	23.5
Hudspeth	30	756	860	1.6	71.1	10.1	9.3	13 055	14 142	22 545	35 900	1.0	31 354	32.0	45.7	44.6
Hunt	386	2 956	22 960	8.9	52.5	16.6	121.1	8 745	22 341	44 858	59 468	2.2	44 361	17.9	25.5	23.6
Hutchinson	781	3 206	5 833	6.7	51.0	13.5	38.0	8 885	23 383	44 731	57 482	1.6	50 060	15.5	22.4	20.4
Irion	64	2 234	374	7.2	60.8	13.0	3.9	12 807	28 055	50 357	70 331	4.7	58 826	8.8	13.1	12.4
Jack	233	2 121	1 935	8.3	57.9	10.7	14.2	11 651	24 325	49 038	72 242	3.4	50 168	17.0	21.0	19.5
Jackson	111	1 259	3 458	8.4	53.2	17.9	29.0	8 434	23 418	49 528	62 419	1.9	48 338	12.7	20.8	19.7
Jasper	324	2 634	8 304	11.8	58.7	11.2	57.3	8 799	20 254	40 417	52 965	1.0	39 414	20.8	30.1	28.9
Jeff Davis	130	738	383	3.1	38.3	35.3	5.2	15 198	26 958	49 056	62 408	1.7	44 234	13.0	26.6	26.0
Jefferson	710	4 109	63 350	9.1	50.8	17.8	383.9	9 380	23 236	42 568	60 345	3.2	42 099	22.7	31.4	30.2
Jim Hogg	57	438	1 135	0.5	67.1	10.9	10.9	9 766	19 212	36 121	50 522	3.3	35 854	24.0	34.2	33.2
Jim Wells	576	4 086	11 034	6.2	60.2	11.1	74.4	8 614	20 452	40 585	59 017	2.5	41 249	22.4	31.9	30.1
Johnson	171	2 103	40 274	13.1	49.9	16.7	257.8	8 056	24 816	57 535	71 092	2.7	55 960	12.9	18.5	17.4
Jones	310	2 458	3 537	7.0	64.8	8.9	27.9	10 459	14 827	41 297	51 489	1.5	40 621	24.7	30.2	28.1
Karnes	104	2 832	2 962	7.1	64.6	11.2	23.1	9 668	19 899	42 862	64 495	4.0	43 413	23.2	29.1	27.3
Kaufman	220	1 943	28 868	9.9	48.7	17.6	192.5	7 565	24 954	61 194	72 755	2.9	61 004	11.7	17.6	15.7
Kendall	81	1 599	8 913	15.5	30.3	39.7	64.7	7 883	35 827	73 410	97 207	8.8	75 860	8.5	13.0	11.5
Kenedy	913	2 055	145	0.0	64.4	10.6	2.2	26 639	15 157	43 438	46 419	0.0	38 088	18.6	30.7	30.6
Kent	352	1 291	154	0.6	47.0	23.1	3.3	23 069	24 839	46 875	58 112	1.7	41 038	14.7	23.7	19.9
Kerr	154	2 061	10 254	18.3	41.3	28.2	56.9	8 452	26 334	43 601	62 039	3.4	42 456	15.9	29.2	27.3
Kimble	175	1 116	714	2.8	56.5	17.6	5.7	8 370	27 502	43 424	62 266	3.1	38 019	21.6	37.7	36.0
King	0	733	52	0.0	52.5	20.5	3.6	37 375	29 836	65 000	71 656	3.2	56 680	9.8	10.8	12.2
Kinney	NA	NA	650	0.6	57.2	14.6	6.2	9 921	16 700	33 257	43 969	0.0	41 271	19.3	24.3	22.8
Kleberg	373	3 513	11 376	4.4	48.0	23.6	49.6	9 496	18 918	40 566	54 032	1.7	39 261	23.9	29.9	29.6
Knox	52	915	809	0.2	60.5	12.5	8.5	11 193	19 396	34 295	45 280	0.5	34 419	21.9	36.8	35.7
Lamar	404	3 293	12 533	7.5	51.2	16.5	75.5	8 740	21 468	40 104	53 879	2.1	37 593	18.3	28.8	26.6
Lamb	313	2 870	3 717	4.1	60.1	14.0	30.6	9 747	18 744	36 727	51 163	1.7	36 717	20.9	31.7	30.3
Lampasas	130	2 275	4 516	4.3	42.0	19.8	32.4	8 697	23 423	49 277	63 021	1.6	48 746	14.8	26.2	24.2
La Salle	83	610	1 605	2.9	74.6	5.1	14.7	11 395	13 307	26 756	43 305	1.2	35 491	27.5	35.6	36.8
Lavaca	143	1 401	4 041	16.1	60.7	16.3	33.6	8 718	24 299	44 149	60 095	2.8	43 827	12.5	18.8	17.6
Lee	204	2 160	4 109	12.2	55.8	15.7	26.9	8 942	25 123	51 534	66 209	2.9	52 088	13.6	19.7	18.5
Leon	136	1 421	3 215	2.7	52.7	14.8	31.5	10 302	24 170	44 452	60 933	3.4	43 617	16.7	26.4	26.7
Liberty	414	3 209	18 272	7.8	62.1	8.8	119.2	8 105	19 740	47 228	58 984	1.8	46 176	20.3	26.1	24.5
Limestone	240	2 823	4 984	5.5	58.4	12.4	38.8	9 452	19 352	38 823	52 550	1.1	36 537	21.4	30.2	30.2
Lipscomb	168	646	802	5.4	51.5	21.5	10.3	11 981	29 017	57 978	82 374	4.9	56 484	10.8	15.3	14.2
Live Oak	315	2 051	2 279	4.0	55.3	14.3	18.2	10 397	21 016	42 829	56 637	1.5	49 726	17.6	25.6	24.0
Llano	105	2 233	3 138	12.0	40.0	25.4	18.8	10 280	33 634	44 094	73 286	5.3	45 669	15.5	30.0	28.9
Loving	NA	NA	8	0.0	75.0	7.9	NA	NA	34 068	68 750	71 148	0.0	44 407	12.6	19.2	17.6
Lubbock	679	4 378	96 460	9.3	40.9	27.9	409.4	8 605	23 773	44 397	61 958	3.3	46 223	17.8	25.2	23.7
Lynn	208	1 213	1 417	10.2	57.7	17.7	15.4	11 846	21 639	44 375	57 439	2.2	37 678	19.5	30.4	28.0
McCulloch	107	2 006	1 614	4.6	57.7	15.0	15.7	10 134	20 677	39 194	53 367	2.2	38 408	21.2	35.0	32.5
McLennan	360	3 542	73 529	23.3	46.0	21.7	378.1	8 891	21 660	41 922	58 161	2.3	41 066	20.9	27.7	26.4
McMullen	817	4 632	114	0.0	53.6	6.8	4.1	16 631	27 375	39 500	62 696	1.6	56 686	8.7	15.9	14.5
Madison	233	1 582	3 204	7.0	59.1	12.5	21.5	8 307	15 131	41 732	52 961	1.3	37 460	22.9	30.2	28.8
Marion	592	3 446	1 948	11.6	56.9	12.2	11.5	9 221	20 337	31 967	46 107	1.7	36 090	24.4	39.4	37.2
Martin	78	1 801	1 339	3.8	64.2	10.9	12.6	11 776	20 859	42 607	60 063	1.7	50 004	13.0	19.9	18.7

1. Data for serious crimes have not been adjusted for underreporting; this may affect comparability between geographic areas and over time. 2. Per 100,000 population estimated by the FBI.
3. All persons 3 years old and over enrolled in nursery school through college. 4. Persons 25 years old and over. 5. Elementary and secondary education expenditures.
6. Based on population estimated by the American Community Survey, 2009–2013.

STATE County	Personal income, 2013										Earnings, 2013		
	Total (mil dol)	Percent change, 2012–2013	Per capita[1]		Wages and salaries (mil dol)	Supplements to wages and salaries; employer contributions (mil dol)		Proprietors' income (mil dol)	Dividends, interest, and rent (mil dol)	Personal transfer receipts (mil dol)	Total (mil dol)	Contributions for government social insurance (mil dol)	
			Dollars	Rank		Pension and insurance	Government social insurance					From employee and self-employed	From employer
	62	63	64	65	66	67	68	69	70	71	72	73	74
TEXAS—Cont'd													
Guadalupe	5 784	2.9	40 399	1 120	1 290	211	90	209	958	915	1 800	105	90
Hale	1 059	0.6	29 606	2 741	432	75	31	164	171	269	702	33	31
Hall	133	26.4	41 184	1 028	30	6	2	50	23	34	88	3	2
Hamilton	316	1.8	37 972	1 435	84	16	6	25	81	89	131	8	6
Hansford	310	-5.5	55 742	192	110	18	7	106	54	35	242	7	7
Hardeman	150	4.8	37 303	1 535	39	8	3	16	29	44	66	4	3
Hardin	2 252	0.0	40 638	1 094	535	85	39	227	307	455	886	51	39
Harris	230 463	3.6	53 141	265	150 997	17 929	9 785	53 864	32 034	24 021	232 576	11 243	9 785
Harrison	3 170	2.2	47 391	518	1 315	201	90	436	446	547	2 041	106	90
Hartley	311	-5.3	50 931	333	86	16	5	85	49	21	192	5	5
Haskell	230	11.4	39 164	1 272	57	11	4	57	39	60	129	6	4
Hays	6 148	5.5	34 927	1 909	2 045	352	140	562	1 088	884	3 098	156	140
Hemphill	323	0.5	77 681	27	130	19	8	70	99	19	228	10	8
Henderson	2 787	1.6	35 429	1 832	555	105	39	253	487	804	951	63	39
Hidalgo	18 828	2.6	23 073	3 089	7 782	1 535	543	2 405	2 185	5 613	12 265	624	543
Hill	1 239	2.2	35 572	1 817	320	60	22	116	233	340	519	31	22
Hockley	1 184	7.5	50 312	354	518	74	35	259	135	193	885	40	35
Hood	2 384	2.5	45 061	683	703	92	48	143	585	490	986	63	48
Hopkins	1 251	3.4	35 172	1 875	492	79	34	120	224	298	724	40	34
Houston	753	2.4	32 863	2 271	293	47	18	35	161	232	393	24	18
Howard	1 341	2.7	37 092	1 567	583	117	41	215	219	260	955	47	41
Hudspeth	103	-3.2	31 118	2 534	59	16	4	10	18	23	90	4	4
Hunt	3 002	3.0	34 491	1 989	1 282	250	85	194	415	730	1 812	99	85
Hutchinson	916	1.3	41 967	942	499	91	35	82	143	166	706	37	35
Irion	88	2.9	54 776	210	48	6	3	12	21	11	69	4	3
Jack	439	6.8	48 985	417	167	23	11	90	64	65	292	15	11
Jackson	542	3.3	37 136	1 560	229	37	15	47	93	126	329	18	15
Jasper	1 233	-0.1	34 573	1 974	402	71	28	134	182	359	635	37	28
Jeff Davis	89	0.1	39 670	1 209	25	5	2	9	26	18	41	2	2
Jefferson	10 084	0.0	39 958	1 175	6 203	1 087	438	803	2 039	2 208	8 531	451	438
Jim Hogg	206	2.0	39 276	1 257	82	19	6	9	26	52	117	7	6
Jim Wells	1 871	0.3	44 885	697	1 018	125	66	223	183	427	1 432	77	66
Johnson	5 621	2.4	36 336	1 685	1 792	283	125	503	782	1 111	2 703	151	125
Jones	638	5.6	32 145	2 394	202	45	12	84	94	157	343	16	12
Karnes	582	7.7	38 597	1 357	207	39	13	63	147	128	322	17	13
Kaufman	3 944	2.8	36 325	1 689	1 078	181	75	314	425	692	1 648	91	75
Kendall	2 447	3.3	64 797	68	541	77	37	114	769	269	769	44	37
Kenedy	27	4.5	65 500	66	40	4	2	3	5	2	49	2	2
Kent	32	1.3	40 164	1 154	10	3	1	2	10	9	16	1	1
Kerr	2 343	1.6	46 898	559	666	112	47	254	884	491	1 079	63	47
Kimble	177	-0.2	39 572	1 220	56	10	3	19	50	45	88	5	3
King	15	17.2	52 095	297	9	1	0	1	3	1	12	0	0
Kinney	116	-0.9	32 329	2 363	36	10	3	1	30	34	50	3	3
Kleberg	1 198	1.6	37 334	1 533	518	116	37	82	187	264	753	37	37
Knox	149	8.5	39 505	1 230	53	9	3	28	22	42	94	4	3
Lamar	1 804	2.6	36 509	1 661	769	125	55	228	300	511	1 176	65	55
Lamb	448	4.7	32 489	2 337	154	28	11	75	63	119	268	12	11
Lampasas	1 071	0.1	52 983	269	149	28	10	68	219	209	255	15	10
La Salle	301	15.0	40 858	1 072	210	25	13	24	55	49	272	15	13
Lavaca	852	2.2	43 525	799	228	39	15	81	212	205	364	22	15
Lee	737	0.6	44 324	738	317	48	21	55	117	134	439	24	21
Leon	661	2.4	39 468	1 236	262	38	18	54	148	176	372	23	18
Liberty	2 830	1.9	36 799	1 624	718	118	49	250	297	614	1 135	63	49
Limestone	810	2.0	34 746	1 942	318	69	20	65	118	246	472	25	20
Lipscomb	181	1.9	51 805	304	59	10	4	30	57	19	103	4	4
Live Oak	545	4.6	45 926	622	214	42	14	74	95	82	345	17	14
Llano	803	2.1	41 275	1 020	156	25	11	30	271	214	222	18	11
Loving	4	16.1	40 358	1 125	1	0	0	0	0	1	2	0	0
Lubbock	11 084	3.4	38 311	1 397	5 206	875	349	1 282	2 232	1 996	7 712	383	349
Lynn	266	26.8	46 496	589	51	11	3	94	39	49	160	4	3
McCulloch	360	1.9	43 200	829	142	23	10	59	71	86	234	12	10
McLennan	8 743	1.7	36 205	1 710	4 411	714	311	671	1 571	1 839	6 108	330	311
McMullen	55	8.6	71 840	41	30	5	2	3	21	5	40	2	2
Madison	424	5.4	30 731	2 591	162	27	11	42	79	111	240	12	11
Marion	360	2.2	35 216	1 870	63	13	5	29	61	116	110	8	5
Martin	259	11.7	48 843	426	77	14	5	47	60	36	144	6	5

1. Based on the resident population estimated as of July 1 of the year shown.

STATE County	Earnings, 2013 (cont.) Percent by selected industries: Farm	Mining	Construction	Manufacturing	Information: professional, scientific, technical services	Retail trade	Finance, insurance, real estate and leasing	Health care and social assistance	Government	Social Security beneficiaries, December 2013: Number	Rate[1]	Supplemental Security Income recipients, December 2013	Housing units, 2014: Total	Percent change, 2010–2014
	75	76	77	78	79	80	81	82	83	84	85	86	87	88
TEXAS—Cont'd														
Guadalupe	0.5	1.3	8.1	22.5	4.5	7.9	4.3	6.5	19.0	22 920	160	2 185	53 973	7.9
Hale	12.9	D	3.9	8.6	2.6	9.3	3.1	D	17.8	5 710	159	937	13 502	-0.3
Hall	51.2	0.0	D	D	D	2.8	3.6	3.5	13.3	845	262	88	1 936	-0.4
Hamilton	5.3	D	13.8	7.3	3.6	12.6	3.1	8.5	25.7	2 335	283	176	4 561	-0.1
Hansford	40.6	21.0	3.8	1.3	D	2.5	D	0.9	12.2	915	166	57	2 332	-0.3
Hardeman	14.0	3.9	D	D	D	6.4	5.4	4.2	30.9	990	247	131	2 404	-0.5
Hardin	-0.5	8.8	17.2	7.1	6.1	9.4	4.0	11.9	12.2	11 105	200	1 242	23 480	3.9
Harris	0.0	15.1	7.5	9.7	13.3	4.1	6.6	6.6	8.2	478 575	110	105 122	1 682 870	5.2
Harrison	-0.2	25.2	5.9	22.5	4.3	4.8	6.3	D	8.5	12 985	193	2 203	28 021	1.1
Hartley	47.2	D	8.7	0.2	D	2.2	D	D	22.1	605	100	29	1 987	2.1
Haskell	28.2	11.3	D	D	D	8.4	D	8.7	15.5	1 455	247	180	3 440	-0.1
Hays	0.0	0.9	11.0	9.0	7.6	11.9	4.9	9.3	22.3	22 015	125	1 894	70 731	19.0
Hemphill	8.0	27.7	9.4	1.0	4.3	3.8	9.1	1.3	9.5	530	128	27	1 683	3.3
Henderson	0.6	5.4	10.1	11.0	5.5	10.8	5.0	D	17.6	20 620	262	2 500	39 973	1.0
Hidalgo	0.8	2.4	5.4	2.7	4.2	10.5	4.4	19.4	25.4	98 885	121	42 920	261 184	5.2
Hill	3.0	2.6	17.2	8.2	4.9	10.5	3.1	D	20.8	8 560	246	997	16 132	0.1
Hockley	11.5	37.3	6.5	3.0	D	3.2	2.1	D	10.8	4 005	170	573	9 291	0.0
Hood	-0.3	29.3	7.2	4.8	5.9	8.7	6.8	7.3	10.9	14 235	269	762	25 506	2.2
Hopkins	2.7	3.4	10.7	12.1	D	8.9	4.6	6.8	15.7	7 665	216	1 000	15 221	1.3
Houston	-0.4	5.5	4.8	10.1	10.8	5.8	9.4	7.7	21.6	5 350	235	885	11 548	0.1
Howard	1.9	20.8	5.9	10.9	2.9	5.1	3.1	D	23.7	5 705	157	885	13 117	-0.1
Hudspeth	12.8	D	D	D	D	2.3	D	0.9	70.3	620	188	188	1 529	0.1
Hunt	0.1	0.4	5.1	37.1	3.0	7.5	3.1	6.4	20.8	17 665	202	2 597	36 909	0.6
Hutchinson	1.5	28.1	15.0	17.9	D	4.3	1.9	D	10.9	4 205	193	404	10 585	-0.4
Irion	1.4	62.6	D	D	D	D	D	D	8.0	350	218	24	856	0.0
Jack	-2.0	55.7	7.0	1.3	D	1.9	1.9	3.0	9.9	1 720	193	149	4 109	0.3
Jackson	3.0	12.2	D	D	6.0	4.7	2.4	D	15.8	2 970	203	324	6 591	0.0
Jasper	0.6	2.6	13.0	18.8	D	8.3	4.6	D	16.1	8 485	238	1 344	16 871	0.4
Jeff Davis	12.4	D	D	D	D	3.2	D	9.7	36.2	650	291	37	1 616	0.2
Jefferson	0.1	0.8	12.8	22.7	8.5	6.8	3.6	11.1	13.6	45 785	181	9 256	107 234	2.7
Jim Hogg	0.0	7.3	2.6	2.3	D	6.9	D	D	45.6	1 000	191	300	2 445	0.2
Jim Wells	1.1	42.6	2.8	3.9	2.4	4.8	5.4	D	8.2	8 135	195	1 900	16 220	0.4
Johnson	0.3	7.0	11.1	15.6	4.9	7.9	3.9	7.6	14.2	26 980	174	3 123	59 037	4.1
Jones	8.6	20.4	5.2	3.4	1.6	3.9	4.2	2.5	34.8	3 480	173	435	7 402	-0.2
Karnes	2.4	15.7	4.0	5.9	D	4.5	3.2	3.1	25.7	2 775	188	443	5 813	2.9
Kaufman	-0.1	1.4	11.2	14.1	D	8.4	4.2	7.1	20.1	18 025	166	2 182	39 192	2.3
Kendall	-0.4	1.9	12.8	6.1	12.1	14.1	8.7	9.2	13.7	8 040	215	324	15 011	6.8
Kenedy	11.4	D	0.0	0.0	D	D	D	D	9.2	65	157	10	233	0.0
Kent	19.4	0.0	D	0.0	D	D	D	11.8	44.9	190	237	17	552	0.0
Kerr	0.2	3.2	10.5	5.2	6.9	12.2	6.1	15.8	18.1	15 050	301	1 004	24 001	0.7
Kimble	2.5	D	10.0	3.8	D	9.3	19.5	2.7	19.9	1 255	281	132	3 369	-0.1
King	23.2	0.4	0.0	0.0	D	0.0	D	0.0	30.6	30	110	0	186	0.0
Kinney	0.7	0.0	D	D	D	D	D	1.4	66.0	945	261	125	1 939	-0.1
Kleberg	3.0	8.2	3.5	2.1	D	6.8	4.3	8.5	40.8	5 020	156	1 179	13 249	3.6
Knox	23.9	21.7	D	D	D	5.0	D	2.1	21.2	885	234	135	2 044	0.0
Lamar	0.3	0.4	12.5	25.7	D	8.1	4.4	13.7	13.3	11 920	242	2 004	22 582	0.5
Lamb	26.5	0.3	3.9	8.7	D	6.1	D	3.9	17.8	2 780	202	445	6 102	-0.4
Lampasas	-0.4	0.9	12.2	9.2	3.3	20.6	5.5	D	20.0	4 665	231	433	9 001	3.2
La Salle	1.5	54.6	8.5	0.0	D	1.6	0.7	D	17.2	1 200	162	335	2 878	4.8
Lavaca	-0.1	10.0	7.3	21.5	3.9	7.4	5.3	D	12.9	5 115	262	405	10 362	0.2
Lee	-0.1	13.8	28.0	6.5	4.5	4.4	6.1	D	14.8	3 445	208	330	7 599	1.4
Leon	4.0	16.3	21.2	17.4	2.5	4.5	4.1	1.3	11.7	5 015	300	445	9 537	0.3
Liberty	0.4	6.4	10.0	13.4	D	9.3	3.7	9.8	19.1	13 490	175	2 225	29 505	2.6
Limestone	0.9	9.9	3.8	9.1	1.8	6.5	4.2	10.4	31.3	5 205	222	914	10 555	0.2
Lipscomb	20.5	16.9	D	D	D	1.8	D	0.2	16.9	555	160	29	1 510	-0.1
Live Oak	-0.1	38.9	D	D	D	3.6	5.0	1.9	16.1	1 975	166	254	6 106	0.7
Llano	-2.5	1.0	10.3	3.9	3.5	6.5	8.8	D	19.6	6 465	333	373	14 734	3.2
Loving	1.7	5.2	D	D	0.0	D	0.0	0.0	52.1	15	146	0	50	0.0
Lubbock	1.5	2.0	6.9	3.5	7.7	9.0	7.8	15.3	23.0	43 410	150	6 608	121 098	5.2
Lynn	60.1	0.6	1.4	1.1	D	1.9	D	0.9	15.6	1 145	201	160	2 675	0.0
McCulloch	0.6	16.3	3.5	12.1	1.6	7.4	2.9	5.3	13.1	2 090	253	331	4 282	-0.5
McLennan	0.2	0.5	7.3	18.4	D	6.3	8.5	11.4	16.4	42 025	174	7 220	97 280	2.3
McMullen	4.1	39.0	D	0.0	D	D	D	D	18.2	170	220	9	486	0.2
Madison	14.0	D	14.6	2.1	3.8	12.0	3.4	6.3	24.5	2 535	183	307	5 182	1.7
Marion	-1.4	D	4.7	14.9	D	11.0	D	D	18.0	2 935	287	513	6 245	0.5
Martin	22.2	D	D	D	D	4.8	D	D	16.9	790	149	109	1 863	0.6

1. Per 1,000 resident population estimated as of July 1 of the year shown.

STATE County	Housing units, 2009–2013: Occupied units: Total	Owner-occupied: Percent	Owner-occupied: Median value[1]	Median owner cost as a percent of income: With a mortgage	Median owner cost as a percent of income: Without a mortgage[2]	Renter-occupied: Median rent[3]	Renter-occupied: Median rent as a percent of income[2]	Substandard units[4] (percent)	Civilian labor force, 2014: Total	Percent change, 2013–2014	Unemployment: Total	Unemployment: Rate[5]	Civilian employment,[6] 2009–2013: Total	Percent: Management, business, science and arts	Percent: Construction, production, and maintenance occupations
	89	90	91	92	93	94	95	96	97	98	99	100	101	102	103
TEXAS—Cont'd															
Guadalupe	46 409	77.8	156 000	21.8	11.4	859	27.0	7.1	71 566	1.7	3 065	4.3	63 328	34.5	22.6
Hale	11 624	63.9	70 800	19.5	10.0	585	26.3	3.1	13 772	-7.3	1 289	9.4	14 704	23.7	34.5
Hall	1 177	67.4	42 700	18.7	12.1	488	29.7	3.0	1 280	-1.2	80	6.3	1 201	29.5	30.5
Hamilton	3 029	73.4	91 500	21.4	14.6	626	24.9	4.9	3 593	-1.2	167	4.6	3 138	26.0	28.5
Hansford	1 983	76.7	72 900	16.8	10.0	611	26.8	4.6	3 287	4.6	85	2.6	2 668	27.6	38.1
Hardeman	1 745	69.6	46 800	19.6	10.4	513	32.5	2.9	1 652	-3.0	83	5.0	1 568	33.5	26.2
Hardin	20 633	78.5	100 400	18.5	10.6	805	24.9	6.7	25 581	0.9	1 587	6.2	23 734	31.1	30.4
Harris	1 434 694	56.5	131 400	23.1	12.0	880	30.0	4.0	2 251 628	2.0	110 802	4.9	1 970 541	34.2	24.5
Harrison	23 415	73.3	108 700	20.3	11.0	682	26.1	4.1	32 409	0.0	1 767	5.5	28 644	28.0	30.6
Hartley	1 748	66.1	143 700	18.3	10.0	717	26.5	3.2	2 880	-2.1	74	2.6	2 300	37.8	22.8
Haskell	2 425	74.0	45 200	18.9	10.7	412	26.5	3.9	2 700	-0.8	108	4.0	2 288	31.1	26.6
Hays	56 459	66.8	175 600	23.9	12.2	930	39.4	4.0	92 604	2.6	3 905	4.2	78 384	38.4	17.2
Hemphill	1 440	74.7	97 800	19.8	10.0	591	18.8	3.4	2 567	3.3	62	2.4	1 852	24.8	35.9
Henderson	29 732	74.8	87 800	23.6	13.6	709	32.0	15.1	35 125	1.3	1 942	5.5	30 609	25.8	29.2
Hidalgo	217 691	68.4	78 100	24.7	13.2	641	33.5	4.5	334 457	0.6	29 029	8.7	285 985	25.8	23.8
Hill	13 395	72.1	83 400	23.0	13.1	647	27.6	4.4	15 947	-0.5	841	5.3	14 397	26.0	30.9
Hockley	7 973	69.7	79 300	17.7	10.0	670	24.0	2.8	12 138	1.4	472	3.9	10 435	26.8	31.9
Hood	20 758	77.4	150 900	22.9	11.2	849	30.3	4.2	24 400	1.2	1 185	4.9	21 873	35.9	24.8
Hopkins	13 303	72.5	94 000	22.0	11.9	684	30.1	4.3	17 581	1.4	823	4.7	14 975	29.7	30.5
Houston	7 889	71.2	74 300	20.2	14.5	612	32.9	3.1	9 757	-1.7	512	5.2	7 925	27.6	27.7
Howard	11 010	67.8	65 900	17.9	10.6	693	26.1	12.6	13 687	0.5	600	4.4	13 015	25.6	27.0
Hudspeth	1 096	82.3	41 400	38.1	17.5	580	32.5	5.4	1 310	1.0	80	6.1	1 193	24.1	32.0
Hunt	30 756	69.8	93 500	21.7	12.8	746	33.8	3.0	39 024	1.9	2 244	5.8	35 473	30.4	28.6
Hutchinson	8 374	78.0	63 300	17.7	10.2	634	25.2	2.6	10 554	7.6	462	4.4	9 414	23.4	34.0
Irion	654	75.4	76 100	17.5	11.8	787	28.1	2.9	867	1.4	32	3.7	793	34.6	34.7
Jack	2 972	77.4	76 700	17.5	10.1	737	28.9	3.4	4 381	8.9	165	3.8	3 330	23.4	39.1
Jackson	5 212	77.7	84 400	19.5	11.8	687	20.6	4.1	7 683	2.9	300	3.9	6 185	28.8	34.8
Jasper	13 095	78.4	82 200	20.6	10.0	672	32.7	7.1	14 624	0.5	1 182	8.1	12 791	23.9	32.7
Jeff Davis	989	74.7	104 300	18.4	10.0	881	16.7	3.7	1 172	0.4	43	3.7	1 023	37.0	30.2
Jefferson	92 634	64.1	96 200	21.4	12.0	726	30.7	5.5	111 452	-0.1	9 186	8.2	101 918	28.6	27.0
Jim Hogg	1 805	76.7	50 700	20.8	11.9	614	26.9	6.6	2 275	-2.5	132	5.8	2 138	20.9	41.0
Jim Wells	13 728	72.7	69 000	20.3	12.5	698	28.4	4.6	20 248	0.2	1 053	5.2	16 631	27.0	28.6
Johnson	52 044	75.4	113 900	20.9	12.4	882	27.0	2.9	74 914	1.3	3 729	5.0	67 592	30.3	29.7
Jones	5 641	80.2	61 500	18.4	13.2	512	25.5	9.1	5 892	0.4	321	5.4	5 345	27.5	29.0
Karnes	4 497	72.3	75 000	18.1	11.0	631	30.6	4.7	6 247	10.6	236	3.8	4 870	29.8	27.6
Kaufman	34 922	77.8	129 500	23.7	13.2	887	29.3	4.3	53 886	2.4	2 745	5.1	48 164	33.0	25.0
Kendall	12 760	74.5	274 400	23.7	11.5	981	28.0	12.6	18 649	1.8	747	4.0	16 049	46.3	15.9
Kenedy	159	28.9	56 200	0.0	10.0	617	36.2	4.0	349	17.1	10	2.9	194	28.9	29.4
Kent	401	74.8	64 300	14.6	10.5	529	41.7	5.1	525	-1.5	17	3.2	472	40.0	27.8
Kerr	20 357	68.8	150 700	23.3	12.7	776	28.9	1.8	21 628	0.3	940	4.3	20 633	32.9	19.2
Kimble	1 895	74.5	85 100	19.3	12.9	511	29.8	11.9	2 165	-0.3	83	3.8	2 175	30.8	29.9
King	126	42.1	91 000	23.3	16.9	706	14.5	4.8	231	-3.8	10	4.3	210	39.5	37.6
Kinney	1 195	82.0	65 800	20.4	13.6	393	34.8	7.4	1 223	0.4	87	7.1	1 167	24.6	28.4
Kleberg	11 241	57.1	74 500	22.9	10.0	703	29.5	4.2	15 424	-0.5	830	5.4	13 437	32.6	23.6
Knox	1 557	65.9	40 900	17.9	10.9	461	28.5	4.3	1 745	-0.8	75	4.3	1 533	28.8	32.2
Lamar	19 416	65.2	85 300	19.5	12.4	632	29.2	4.4	22 250	-0.5	1 354	6.1	21 377	26.9	29.7
Lamb	4 803	71.4	56 900	19.5	11.9	614	25.0	2.6	6 214	0.7	357	5.7	5 666	26.0	33.4
Lampasas	7 289	74.9	129 100	20.0	13.9	737	28.8	10.4	9 126	-0.4	508	5.6	8 238	28.4	32.1
La Salle	1 864	71.1	48 200	23.7	14.3	348	28.7	6.5	4 599	9.7	141	3.1	2 090	19.7	39.5
Lavaca	7 711	79.5	92 800	19.6	10.2	598	19.0	4.9	9 075	-2.1	354	3.9	8 806	31.1	34.4
Lee	6 078	76.7	118 400	21.1	12.4	661	22.2	5.1	9 332	1.7	374	4.0	7 458	26.4	29.4
Leon	6 349	83.9	90 300	20.5	13.3	570	27.8	7.3	7 182	2.8	383	5.3	6 637	28.1	35.5
Liberty	24 844	78.1	84 400	21.9	12.1	731	26.1	4.2	31 466	1.2	2 176	6.9	27 532	22.3	37.2
Limestone	7 929	75.2	83 200	21.5	13.5	673	26.5	3.0	9 282	-2.5	537	5.8	9 376	29.4	29.8
Lipscomb	1 115	70.9	89 400	15.4	10.0	632	15.8	5.9	1 743	0.9	58	3.3	1 608	32.8	42.0
Live Oak	3 882	81.8	85 500	19.6	12.3	682	27.3	1.1	6 278	3.7	218	3.5	3 981	30.3	28.6
Llano	8 519	78.0	159 000	22.9	13.5	708	27.7	0.0	8 154	0.2	420	5.2	7 574	29.1	19.1
Loving	33	48.5	86 000	0.0	11.3	750	35.0	4.1	80	5.3	4	5.0	63	20.6	20.6
Lubbock	105 277	58.5	108 700	21.4	11.7	786	33.4	2.6	148 679	0.5	5 805	3.9	136 680	33.2	19.8
Lynn	2 179	71.4	70 200	19.1	10.3	594	30.7	5.9	2 899	1.0	126	4.3	2 652	27.9	31.1
McCulloch	2 967	76.7	69 300	21.7	13.1	617	30.2	3.7	4 110	-4.2	175	4.3	3 568	22.2	34.8
McLennan	84 862	59.6	108 300	22.4	12.5	762	32.8	0.0	112 604	0.0	5 726	5.1	105 573	31.6	24.0
McMullen	254	81.1	63 200	18.2	11.0	625	12.7	6.0	1 117	26.1	19	1.7	373	20.6	29.5
Madison	3 743	71.7	94 200	23.2	11.6	677	23.4	1.1	5 075	4.9	247	4.9	4 222	26.8	26.9
Marion	4 563	74.9	72 900	22.5	12.3	569	29.0	4.1	4 511	-0.7	286	6.3	3 985	24.1	32.6
Martin	1 555	74.8	72 200	20.1	11.7	559	22.9	2.8	2 703	5.5	91	3.4	2 046	23.3	41.0

1. Specified owner-occupied units. 2. A value of 10.0 represents 10 percent or less; a value of 50.0 represents 50 percent or more. 3. Specified renter-occupied units.
4. Overcrowded or lacking complete plumbing facilities. 5. Percent of civilian labor force. 6. Persons 16 years old and over.

STATE County	Private nonfarm establishments, employment and payroll, 2013									Agriculture, 2012			
		Employment						Annual payroll		Farms			
											Percent with:		
	Number of establish-ments	Total	Health care and social assistance	Manufac-turing	Retail trade	Finance and insurance	Professional, scientific, and technical services	Total (mil dol)	Average per employee (dollars)	Number	Fewer than 50 acres	500 acres or more	Farm operators whose principal occu-pation is farming (percent)
	104	105	106	107	108	109	110	111	112	113	114	115	116
TEXAS—Cont'd													
Guadalupe	1 880	27 160	3 123	5 275	4 283	573	619	998	36 757	2 241	48.3	6.1	35.7
Hale	716	9 615	1 293	1 114	1 485	321	172	314	32 651	899	11.7	39.6	48.8
Hall	74	522	D	D	92	D	D	16	30 975	390	3.8	44.1	39.5
Hamilton	209	1 936	516	215	353	49	D	59	30 637	1 001	17.1	21.8	42.2
Hansford	154	1 515	D	D	185	96	38	98	64 371	263	5.7	62.7	70.0
Hardeman	84	718	173	D	D	34	D	24	33 377	357	8.4	42.0	37.5
Hardin	806	8 945	884	716	2 097	274	289	339	37 927	660	64.8	4.1	33.2
Harris	95 376	1 971 437	241 179	171 706	198 165	79 661	181 462	124 068	62 933	2 207	70.1	4.5	35.0
Harrison	1 322	20 657	1 798	4 656	2 111	978	990	807	39 080	1 298	43.4	7.1	41.1
Hartley	119	1 209	D	D	D	33	35	45	36 830	255	6.7	65.5	64.7
Haskell	146	1 124	150	D	315	60	40	29	25 380	503	8.7	40.4	50.1
Hays	3 545	44 874	6 016	3 815	11 263	913	1 974	1 403	31 267	1 439	52.1	6.5	34.3
Hemphill	172	1 710	156	D	181	D	24	79	46 392	232	12.1	58.6	55.6
Henderson	1 274	12 921	2 211	1 682	2 648	422	730	392	30 311	1 961	45.2	6.2	42.4
Hidalgo	11 678	178 553	55 082	6 909	35 943	6 490	5 127	4 734	26 515	2 161	57.9	14.7	51.4
Hill	626	7 148	1 247	926	1 546	194	135	214	29 871	1 884	34.6	11.0	43.6
Hockley	517	7 038	1 306	D	868	239	D	337	47 840	781	14.7	34.1	45.6
Hood	1 211	12 439	2 118	430	2 634	455	407	444	35 690	1 286	57.1	6.8	42.8
Hopkins	751	10 113	1 380	1 822	1 649	434	246	344	33 978	2 113	31.5	8.8	42.0
Houston	354	3 538	766	548	642	150	D	116	32 778	1 505	23.3	13.2	49.9
Howard	697	9 370	1 592	753	1 381	270	206	359	38 286	475	21.3	34.3	48.8
Hudspeth	33	250	D	D	D	D	D	9	37 148	167	13.2	53.9	60.5
Hunt	1 366	21 394	3 177	6 878	3 512	435	442	923	43 148	4 206	58.7	3.6	31.9
Hutchinson	483	6 409	459	1 656	842	161	D	333	51 979	247	27.1	38.9	44.1
Irion	58	616	D	NA	D	D	D	39	63 281	155	22.6	52.3	43.9
Jack	227	2 284	190	D	192	38	47	99	43 391	864	17.1	23.8	42.0
Jackson	298	4 557	327	D	578	106	D	204	44 668	811	23.7	25.2	45.3
Jasper	623	9 194	2 220	D	1 431	275	244	298	32 383	894	59.5	2.0	36.9
Jeff Davis	56	382	84	NA	44	D	D	10	26 283	84	16.7	69.0	57.1
Jefferson	5 623	100 836	16 585	14 117	14 065	2 502	4 747	4 765	47 254	764	48.0	18.3	45.5
Jim Hogg	95	1 369	D	68	187	49	D	39	28 484	263	15.2	45.2	39.2
Jim Wells	940	16 131	4 488	627	1 752	384	286	661	41 008	1 047	32.7	16.0	33.5
Johnson	2 631	35 000	3 503	5 216	5 068	818	1 059	1 317	37 625	3 023	61.4	4.3	35.6
Jones	279	2 571	663	D	238	111	D	90	35 134	1 014	25.0	20.9	37.6
Karnes	303	3 634	481	409	507	102	D	152	41 911	1 288	17.5	13.1	45.6
Kaufman	1 703	21 734	3 261	3 867	3 581	620	532	754	34 698	3 041	59.3	4.2	38.5
Kendall	1 112	10 932	1 576	1 016	2 203	D	737	403	36 828	1 387	42.4	13.6	39.3
Kenedy	13	107	NA	NA	NA	NA	D	6	54 841	28	0.0	89.3	67.9
Kent	17	D	D	NA	NA	D	NA	D	D	194	8.8	44.3	31.4
Kerr	1 383	15 135	3 787	464	2 859	573	695	516	34 102	1 034	28.9	20.6	38.9
Kimble	134	905	D	D	274	D	D	24	26 535	602	15.4	48.2	46.7
King	NA	NA	NA	NA	NA	NA	NA	NA	NA	59	0.0	59.3	23.7
Kinney	38	367	D	NA	NA	NA	D	9	25 632	196	12.8	57.1	43.4
Kleberg	567	7 685	1 939	D	1 615	324	145	224	29 131	401	50.9	10.2	37.7
Knox	98	707	134	NA	122	D	D	28	39 560	228	8.8	47.4	56.1
Lamar	1 187	15 563	3 124	3 567	2 445	525	340	557	35 761	1 843	32.0	11.7	34.6
Lamb	245	2 536	D	D	386	D	D	94	36 883	933	10.1	37.3	52.3
Lampasas	386	3 613	678	D	691	114	D	97	26 921	1 017	37.0	17.2	46.3
La Salle	125	1 856	72	NA	211	D	D	111	59 683	446	11.9	44.6	42.2
Lavaca	486	5 370	981	1 402	792	300	D	187	34 734	2 617	29.8	7.7	40.7
Lee	421	5 426	275	370	632	227	105	225	41 414	1 807	33.8	7.2	35.0
Leon	362	4 251	162	706	569	115	59	217	51 064	1 962	30.3	11.6	52.2
Liberty	1 031	12 382	1 744	1 576	2 486	323	342	490	39 583	1 470	50.7	7.6	46.0
Limestone	407	5 460	1 068	983	956	238	78	173	31 661	1 526	24.1	14.2	50.4
Lipscomb	95	872	D	D	D	64	11	36	40 802	277	6.5	56.0	46.2
Live Oak	283	3 996	D	D	391	101	159	189	47 283	892	13.5	28.5	42.3
Llano	434	3 529	568	69	529	178	106	98	27 839	740	25.8	31.6	42.7
Loving	2	D	NA	NA	NA	D	NA	D	D	10	0.0	100.0	80.0
Lubbock	6 918	107 329	21 693	5 129	17 259	5 375	4 012	3 542	33 004	1 116	36.0	26.8	45.6
Lynn	85	632	143	D	74	63	12	23	36 979	455	8.6	49.5	60.4
McCulloch	217	2 489	261	D	456	102	D	87	34 769	619	13.1	00.0	46.2
McLennan	5 022	96 751	17 168	14 449	11 460	4 583	2 596	3 326	34 382	3 278	55.3	5.8	38.8
McMullen	36	424	D	D	77	D	D	23	53 769	238	7.1	64.3	50.4
Madison	224	2 826	D	42	727	88	76	90	31 970	970	28.8	10.4	45.8
Marion	154	1 357	378	197	201	32	15	41	30 112	247	34.8	6.1	34.8
Martin	99	1 104	D	D	152	D	D	53	47 680	414	13.5	42.3	57.0

STATE County	Agriculture, 2012 (cont.)															
	Land in farms					Value of land and buildings (dollars)			Value of products sold				Percent of farms with sales of:		Government payments	
			Acres								Percent from:					
	Acreage (1,000)	Percent change, 2007–2012	Average size of farm	Total irrigated (1,000)	Total cropland (1,000)	Average per farm	Average per acre	Value of machinery and equipment, average per farm (dollars)	Total (mil dol)	Average per farm (dollars)	Crops	Live-stock and poultry products	$10,000 or more	$100,000 or more	Total ($1,000)	Percent of farms
	117	118	119	120	121	122	123	124	125	126	127	128	129	130	131	132
TEXAS—Cont'd																
Guadalupe	383	-0.5	171	1.9	112.1	614 506	3 595	50 088	61.6	27 484	49.2	50.8	25.0	4.0	2 230	12.2
Hale	641	8.8	713	202.2	479.7	844 726	1 185	232 068	409.9	455 984	31.5	68.5	47.2	30.4	15 250	85.4
Hall	509	-4.6	1 305	27.8	186.3	1 006 900	771	121 005	24.8	63 464	74.3	25.7	36.2	13.3	4 834	83.8
Hamilton	446	-5.3	445	0.6	75.6	1 105 527	2 482	58 377	55.8	55 772	19.2	80.8	40.4	6.8	1 233	23.7
Hansford	567	-3.2	2 155	98.1	294.4	1 994 289	925	403 190	783.2	2 977 973	14.1	85.9	74.1	50.2	4 906	81.7
Hardeman	355	-4.2	993	4.5	130.9	869 655	875	82 580	25.4	71 042	36.1	63.9	45.7	8.7	2 043	80.1
Hardin	69	-24.9	104	1.7	22.7	320 964	3 092	62 642	D	D	D	D	18.0	2.0	414	2.1
Harris	236	-8.7	107	5.9	59.9	572 259	5 342	45 283	65.2	29 538	72.8	27.2	20.8	3.4	1 072	6.2
Harrison	200	-0.6	154	0.5	40.9	437 530	2 845	50 800	19.0	14 631	26.2	73.8	23.5	1.9	274	3.3
Hartley	903	-0.9	3 541	155.5	270.3	3 557 855	1 005	348 706	1 180.9	4 630 969	16.4	83.6	68.2	60.0	4 317	72.5
Haskell	567	14.6	1 128	27.5	298.5	834 078	740	144 797	38.7	76 881	74.0	26.0	42.1	16.5	5 201	84.9
Hays	245	4.0	170	1.0	30.3	1 055 578	6 200	33 647	15.0	10 403	48.9	51.1	12.7	1.5	469	4.5
Hemphill	576	4.9	2 482	3.2	39.8	1 837 310	740	115 043	110.6	476 517	2.7	97.3	46.1	19.8	1 293	50.4
Henderson	346	8.5	176	1.4	81.9	525 054	2 979	50 080	49.5	25 253	35.0	65.0	26.8	3.0	193	1.8
Hidalgo	795	10.0	368	183.6	465.6	1 117 900	3 038	115 296	452.8	209 517	91.7	8.3	33.2	14.2	9 106	20.0
Hill	504	-4.0	268	0.9	231.9	602 704	2 252	72 047	119.9	63 662	67.1	32.9	33.4	8.1	3 921	28.7
Hockley	484	-0.1	619	106.9	400.1	643 108	1 038	182 472	78.7	100 790	89.1	10.9	37.5	20.0	10 093	81.6
Hood	224	9.0	174	2.8	43.3	712 228	4 085	52 253	18.7	14 574	45.7	54.3	20.5	2.2	162	5.8
Hopkins	423	8.2	200	1.3	127.7	442 861	2 214	64 010	205.9	97 466	6.3	93.7	40.3	9.8	1 817	9.2
Houston	468	6.2	311	6.0	83.6	697 706	2 244	55 639	49.6	32 944	28.1	71.9	34.7	4.9	1 461	14.6
Howard	498	-4.7	1 049	4.2	161.9	796 236	759	88 682	13.9	29 187	33.5	66.5	18.7	4.8	4 460	62.1
Hudspeth	2 251	-0.3	13 480	18.1	48.3	7 586 677	563	134 042	34.5	206 455	71.7	28.3	65.3	22.2	1 323	35.9
Hunt	455	17.0	108	5.4	180.3	330 262	3 056	41 054	69.3	16 485	64.6	35.4	18.7	1.9	1 324	8.4
Hutchinson	521	-6.5	2 109	35.1	97.8	1 606 478	762	154 777	55.9	226 219	57.5	42.5	39.3	21.9	1 984	30.4
Irion	496	-20.6	3 201	0.7	10.7	3 005 394	939	70 394	7.5	48 148	10.3	89.7	47.1	9.7	904	25.8
Jack	528	-8.4	611	0.4	35.8	1 195 220	1 956	55 066	22.5	26 042	10.1	89.9	35.3	5.9	751	11.9
Jackson	442	-10.3	545	13.1	151.8	1 151 591	2 114	118 181	101.8	125 568	72.7	27.3	48.3	16.5	6 538	36.6
Jasper	88	-8.1	99	0.4	16.3	310 437	3 149	49 808	10.1	11 263	55.8	44.2	18.2	0.7	26	1.3
Jeff Davis	1 255	-9.8	14 941	0.1	3.6	7 177 381	480	76 583	D	D	D	D	38.1	23.8	792	26.2
Jefferson	354	6.2	463	22.4	112.7	767 829	1 657	88 914	38.0	49 778	56.8	43.2	31.8	10.1	3 631	22.3
Jim Hogg	645	0.7	2 452	D	9.6	3 272 540	1 335	58 118	11.1	42 323	D	D	36.1	6.1	1 349	33.1
Jim Wells	504	8.9	481	4.8	192.0	878 878	1 827	85 848	82.9	79 137	42.5	57.5	25.5	4.8	2 904	22.5
Johnson	429	29.5	142	2.4	119.9	578 482	4 077	50 827	78.9	26 083	25.3	74.7	20.4	2.8	834	6.3
Jones	563	-1.8	555	3.6	301.9	617 260	1 112	88 348	43.3	42 685	68.6	31.4	29.2	8.4	5 627	53.7
Karnes	465	11.3	361	0.9	82.7	937 215	2 598	66 483	27.6	21 428	38.8	61.2	32.2	3.4	1 683	18.9
Kaufman	449	6.5	148	1.4	130.5	502 007	3 399	42 963	59.0	19 395	34.4	65.6	19.8	2.3	637	2.8
Kendall	370	8.0	267	0.9	27.5	1 277 133	4 788	32 921	12.5	9 034	16.9	83.1	19.3	1.2	835	6.3
Kenedy	916	0.8	32 728	0.7	3.1	21 522 643	658	288 179	23.7	845 964	D	D	75.0	28.6	44	10.7
Kent	563	-0.8	2 903	1.1	39.3	2 479 716	854	68 263	D	D	D	D	31.4	10.8	1 687	74.2
Kerr	582	-5.1	563	1.9	44.2	1 483 207	2 634	38 048	10.8	10 448	12.2	87.8	18.3	1.6	597	7.6
Kimble	694	12.0	1 153	8.5	15.5	2 044 718	1 773	53 435	D	D	D	D	23.8	2.8	2 269	26.4
King	418	-23.0	7 078	D	23.4	4 304 051	608	122 169	6.6	111 661	D	D	37.3	15.3	748	78.0
Kinney	577	-4.1	2 943	1.2	16.6	3 539 699	1 203	48 612	4.7	24 031	24.7	75.3	32.1	5.1	903	20.9
Kleberg	484	-2.9	1 207	0.1	71.2	2 274 983	1 884	79 327	61.8	154 157	D	D	25.4	4.7	1 570	27.9
Knox	451	-8.7	1 976	21.6	189.7	1 528 439	773	192 219	59.0	258 829	32.4	67.6	64.5	27.2	3 240	82.0
Lamar	497	-4.7	269	7.0	175.8	582 745	2 163	67 187	84.9	46 058	47.7	52.3	36.2	6.5	5 129	25.7
Lamb	616	-2.9	661	179.5	469.1	764 255	1 157	226 869	575.3	616 598	20.3	79.7	46.5	30.3	14 489	85.7
Lampasas	445	6.9	437	0.2	50.3	1 097 964	2 511	49 163	16.1	15 867	18.1	81.9	25.6	3.0	530	11.1
La Salle	635	-2.2	1 423	7.0	44.0	2 777 861	1 952	69 648	18.7	41 890	63.9	36.1	28.0	6.5	1 007	15.9
Lavaca	547	-3.5	209	4.3	80.8	612 201	2 931	46 957	61.9	23 655	20.3	79.7	36.4	3.3	1 440	10.4
Lee	318	-2.3	176	0.9	44.1	563 382	3 199	42 538	38.6	21 340	33.4	66.6	31.0	1.8	935	11.9
Leon	594	4.4	303	0.8	74.0	759 197	2 506	63 997	148.7	75 810	6.7	93.3	32.8	4.6	1 172	6.9
Liberty	287	-3.7	195	5.2	101.1	488 804	2 505	70 376	34.9	23 768	42.1	57.9	22.9	3.3	1 494	6.1
Limestone	487	-3.8	319	0.3	80.9	603 233	1 891	55 660	48.3	31 641	25.6	74.4	38.2	5.0	2 192	15.3
Lipscomb	591	3.5	2 135	23.3	118.4	1 725 505	808	137 588	52.7	190 188	16.9	83.1	44.8	23.5	2 756	75.1
Live Oak	541	7.9	606	0.7	55.7	1 161 267	1 916	63 307	17.9	20 082	15.8	84.2	34.9	4.5	1 774	26.2
Llano	528	-2.0	714	0.8	21.3	1 930 442	2 705	51 043	13.8	18 600	10.4	89.6	32.2	3.2	890	12.3
Loving	380	-11.1	37 952	0.0	0.6	7 543 900	199	74 000	0.9	91 200	0.0	100.0	90.0	30.0	136	60.0
Lubbock	503	-2.6	450	155.5	423.8	834 394	1 853	174 972	174.8	156 631	54.8	45.2	39.0	22.0	10 896	61.6
Lynn	472	-4.4	1 038	71.6	406.7	933 648	900	261 402	67.6	148 560	97.3	2.7	55.6	32.3	9 808	90.1
McCulloch	614	0.3	992	0.9	90.1	1 838 354	1 852	79 971	22.6	36 454	38.2	61.8	36.7	9.5	3 014	39.9
McLennan	554	4.5	169	3.5	244.0	437 533	2 591	54 417	183.1	55 852	40.9	59.1	21.2	4.5	3 662	17.3
McMullen	517	2.2	2 174	D	19.3	3 055 197	1 405	85 521	8.3	35 025	5.2	94.8	31.5	7.6	239	8.0
Madison	291	6.7	300	2.3	35.3	840 584	2 799	79 825	82.9	85 423	D	D	33.5	4.4	1 087	10.6
Marion	40	-5.1	162	0.2	8.3	361 308	2 224	40 939	3.4	13 563	16.5	83.5	16.6	0.8	62	4.9
Martin	454	-0.9	1 096	17.1	279.6	1 130 809	1 032	160 903	20.3	48 949	88.8	11.2	26.1	13.8	5 158	80.9

STATE County	Water use, 2010: Total water withdrawn (mil gal/day)	Water use, 2010: Gallons withdrawn per person per day	Wholesale trade,[1] 2007: Number of establishments	Wholesale trade,[1] 2007: Number of employees	Wholesale trade,[1] 2007: Sales (mil dol)	Wholesale trade,[1] 2007: Annual payroll (mil dol)	Retail trade,[2] 2007: Number of establishments	Retail trade,[2] 2007: Number of employees	Retail trade,[2] 2007: Sales (mil dol)	Retail trade,[2] 2007: Annual payroll (mil dol)	Real estate and rental and leasing,[2] 2007: Number of establishments	Real estate and rental and leasing,[2] 2007: Number of employees	Real estate and rental and leasing,[2] 2007: Receipts (mil dol)	Real estate and rental and leasing,[2] 2007: Annual payroll (mil dol)
	133	134	135	136	137	138	139	140	141	142	143	144	145	146
TEXAS—Cont'd														
Guadalupe	61.1	465	85	1 519	822.1	66.5	281	3 718	1 026.1	83.1	88	401	53.9	10.2
Hale	208.4	5 744	55	D	D	D	129	1 490	325.1	26.8	29	77	10.7	1.8
Hall	30.9	9 219	3	D	D	D	17	88	23.2	1.3	1	D	D	D
Hamilton	2.5	298	8	85	44.8	3.3	59	365	78.6	7.0	3	D	D	D
Hansford	119.6	21 302	18	101	89.3	3.5	23	188	60.1	3.5	2	D	D	D
Hardeman	6.1	1 476	4	16	18.6	0.6	16	116	22.2	1.7	1	D	D	D
Hardin	6.5	119	17	115	35.9	3.9	147	2 170	612.4	51.5	26	70	5.5	0.9
Harris	443.8	108	6 086	98 893	205 478.8	5 991.8	12 342	183 618	51 899.1	4 543.5	5 047	40 175	9 714.3	1 786.5
Harrison	32.5	495	56	469	303.6	22.7	207	2 144	603.9	48.9	46	170	24.3	4.7
Hartley	311.1	51 321	5	39	41.9	2.0	9	176	34.1	2.6	5	20	1.8	0.5
Haskell	33.3	5 640	2	D	D	D	29	212	59.2	3.8	3	D	D	D
Hays	19.7	125	110	925	451.2	37.4	556	8 797	1 954.7	171.3	178	666	124.9	20.0
Hemphill	8.6	2 267	16	88	63.5	4.1	21	119	39.2	2.9	4	28	4.2	0.9
Henderson	37.6	478	38	D	D	D	245	2 819	657.4	59.7	55	206	28.4	4.5
Hidalgo	470.2	607	670	7 808	4 301.1	257.5	2 132	32 803	7 898.8	635.3	491	2 289	366.9	53.2
Hill	7.5	212	17	82	41.6	2.3	197	1 742	400.3	31.4	29	110	17.3	1.9
Hockley	126.9	5 533	28	D	D	D	73	971	201.7	16.3	13	41	2.9	0.9
Hood	25.6	501	40	278	95.5	11.5	214	2 513	730.0	60.2	64	D	D	D
Hopkins	37.7	1 073	37	D	D	D	155	1 702	447.7	35.3	30	86	12.6	1.8
Houston	10.1	426	13	119	39.1	3.4	67	707	159.3	13.2	9	39	4.9	0.8
Howard	29.6	846	23	173	88.5	6.9	121	1 297	341.2	27.6	39	183	36.5	3.5
Hudspeth	120.0	34 508	1	D	D	D	13	53	12.5	0.5	2	D	D	D
Hunt	17.2	200	45	463	263.4	15.0	262	3 554	931.3	85.6	82	328	40.0	6.5
Hutchinson	94.4	4 260	22	D	D	D	78	835	210.8	16.0	13	83	32.3	3.5
Irion	3.7	2 289	1	D	D	D	4	D	D	D	NA	NA	NA	NA
Jack	6.1	679	8	80	112.3	4.1	32	200	34.1	3.2	10	21	2.9	0.6
Jackson	90.4	6 419	16	113	67.0	4.0	52	508	133.5	9.7	10	D	D	D
Jasper	44.7	1 251	31	215	123.3	7.0	153	1 563	371.0	32.2	20	59	6.5	1.0
Jeff Davis	2.7	1 170	1	D	D	D	6	39	7.1	0.8	2	D	D	D
Jefferson	242.7	962	267	4 147	2 852.5	196.1	1 050	14 764	3 973.1	339.4	289	1 562	333.1	54.7
Jim Hogg	0.8	158	3	D	D	D	30	262	61.6	3.8	2	D	D	D
Jim Wells	7.0	171	36	422	193.4	20.3	148	1 645	462.4	34.7	42	389	85.1	21.3
Johnson	25.3	168	117	1 210	536.2	50.2	355	4 679	1 269.6	108.0	109	369	70.7	12.4
Jones	15.6	770	19	111	379.0	4.0	51	446	163.3	9.8	9	21	1.4	0.2
Karnes	5.1	344	7	57	40.7	2.3	50	443	101.8	8.8	6	13	3.9	0.2
Kaufman	59.6	577	69	690	443.1	25.8	305	3 493	943.8	79.6	57	199	26.0	4.3
Kendall	4.9	148	46	284	285.3	12.3	152	1 977	808.1	55.7	60	222	46.4	8.6
Kenedy	1.3	3 005	NA	NA	NA	NA	NA	NA	NA	NA	NA	NA	NA	NA
Kent	16.8	20 792	NA	NA	NA	NA	4	D	D	D	NA	NA	NA	NA
Kerr	10.1	203	39	D	D	D	227	2 888	719.9	68.4	89	279	39.5	6.4
Kimble	17.0	3 679	3	14	0.1	0.0	37	267	78.7	4.6	5	D	D	D
King	4.1	14 231	NA	NA	NA	NA	NA	NA	NA	NA	NA	NA	NA	NA
Kinney	2.2	620	2	D	D	D	8	59	8.1	0.7	1	D	D	D
Kleberg	3.2	100	3	D	D	D	116	1 985	657.1	47.9	32	111	10.7	1.8
Knox	26.9	7 220	15	89	41.6	2.5	18	193	34.3	1.9	1	D	D	D
Lamar	29.2	587	42	D	D	D	230	2 627	637.6	55.5	44	148	20.8	3.3
Lamb	184.9	13 231	18	152	84.2	6.2	51	350	95.8	6.5	4	D	D	D
Lampasas	3.5	176	5	25	11.5	0.9	61	644	207.1	14.4	18	50	5.7	2.0
La Salle	6.8	985	NA	NA	NA	NA	19	162	79.9	2.5	5	D	D	D
Lavaca	10.3	535	21	627	221.2	16.5	89	789	172.0	15.7	12	D	D	D
Lee	8.6	515	21	210	58.2	6.7	77	760	162.6	14.4	17	90	21.0	3.6
Leon	6.0	354	15	244	92.3	8.3	76	593	159.9	10.1	18	54	12.4	1.8
Liberty	56.6	748	36	293	151.5	9.6	207	2 602	653.0	58.1	40	279	50.5	9.2
Limestone	30.6	1 307	12	66	27.4	2.4	90	1 043	268.3	21.4	10	42	2.6	0.6
Lipscomb	30.2	9 140	5	66	47.2	2.1	18	65	24.5	0.9	1	D	D	D
Live Oak	5.3	455	9	52	25.3	1.6	41	378	112.7	6.9	7	D	D	D
Llano	74.5	3 859	12	235	94.9	8.9	81	459	113.0	9.1	28	82	42.2	7.2
Loving	2.1	26 098	NA	NA	NA	NA	NA	NA	NA	NA	NA	NA	NA	NA
Lubbock	131.7	472	376	4 888	3 707.4	212.8	1 043	16 793	3 924.9	346.3	380	D	D	D
Lynn	54.5	9 214	6	D	D	D	14	88	19.7	1.7	4	6	0.4	0.1
McCulloch	12.3	1 485	8	53	31.1	1.4	40	391	104.3	7.7	7	D	D	D
McLennan	73.7	314	243	3 197	4 606.2	120.0	872	11 703	2 942.6	248.7	211	1 408	281.7	54.3
McMullen	1.8	2 546	NA	NA	NA	NA	4	D	D	D	NA	NA	NA	NA
Madison	4.3	312	7	32	31.9	0.9	35	477	178.9	11.2	13	35	14.2	0.9
Marion	9.9	937	4	9	5.5	0.3	38	221	66.3	5.0	5	D	D	D
Martin	38.5	8 029	4	28	24.4	1.2	18	135	45.4	2.9	NA	NA	NA	NA

1. Merchant wholesalers, except manufacturers' sales branches and offices. 2. Employer establishments.

STATE County	Professional, scientific, and technical services,[1] 2007				Manufacturing, 2007				Accommodation and food services, 2007			
	Number of establish-ments	Number of employees	Receipts (mil dol)	Annual payroll (mil dol)	Number of establish-ments	Number of employees	Receipts (mil dol)	Annual payroll (mil dol)	Number of establish-ments	Number of employees	Sales (mil dol)	Annual payroll (mil dol)
	147	148	149	150	151	152	153	154	155	156	157	158
TEXAS—Cont'd												
Guadalupe	126	411	33.7	13.0	119	7 311	2 154.1	312.4	158	2 690	116.5	33.1
Hale	49	D	D	D	25	2 720	D	83.0	71	1 050	40.3	10.9
Hall	3	D	D	D	NA	NA	NA	NA	8	79	1.8	0.5
Hamilton	16	45	4.2	0.8	NA	NA	NA	NA	18	160	6.0	1.8
Hansford	8	36	6.0	1.7	NA	NA	NA	NA	13	95	3.1	0.6
Hardeman	3	6	0.4	0.1	NA	NA	NA	NA	14	128	3.4	1.1
Hardin	53	D	D	D	34	795	D	32.4	63	1 023	37.2	10.3
Harris	12 246	D	D	D	4 215	168 354	169 275.1	8 937.2	7 132	147 118	7 874.7	2 104.9
Harrison	113	671	90.9	34.0	85	4 505	1 564.3	150.9	91	1 579	64.0	16.7
Hartley	5	D	D	D	NA	NA	NA	NA	4	32	1.0	0.2
Haskell	7	25	0.8	0.2	NA	NA	NA	NA	14	115	4.7	1.1
Hays	310	1 899	141.7	53.4	135	3 692	1 081.8	154.0	286	5 739	235.3	66.8
Hemphill	10	19	4.0	1.0	NA	NA	NA	NA	10	98	4.1	1.1
Henderson	101	343	42.2	12.1	55	1 411	201.9	48.1	124	1 632	63.1	18.0
Hidalgo	793	D	D	D	276	6 007	1 503.2	183.5	896	17 219	758.0	186.5
Hill	39	142	14.4	4.4	42	832	153.6	25.9	67	1 053	44.3	12.1
Hockley	24	185	8.4	9.2	NA	NA	NA	NA	40	559	19.8	5.6
Hood	113	383	43.0	15.1	40	D	D	D	91	1 564	61.9	17.5
Hopkins	53	258	28.0	9.9	39	1 564	923.1	60.2	53	865	29.2	8.6
Houston	29	103	8.9	2.5	19	840	265.4	32.0	35	413	18.7	4.8
Howard	48	193	15.1	5.4	22	890	2 449.6	44.9	70	1 022	42.5	10.8
Hudspeth	1	D	D	D	NA	NA	NA	NA	5	34	2.0	0.4
Hunt	91	D	D	D	85	14 100	3 134.4	D	115	D	D	D
Hutchinson	29	117	14.6	4.5	23	1 832	D	145.2	46	539	21.1	5.4
Irion	3	D	D	D	NA	NA	NA	NA	1	D	D	D
Jack	13	48	5.3	2.2	NA	NA	NA	NA	16	144	6.5	1.9
Jackson	23	64	5.9	1.9	10	D	D	D	21	219	9.9	2.3
Jasper	45	170	18.7	4.2	21	1 708	725.6	104.7	54	794	32.6	7.7
Jeff Davis	1	D	D	D	NA	NA	NA	NA	10	148	7.1	1.9
Jefferson	527	D	D	D	215	15 460	D	997.3	419	9 143	387.5	110.1
Jim Hogg	3	11	0.3	0.2	NA	NA	NA	NA	9	102	3.6	1.1
Jim Wells	40	155	18.2	5.6	NA	NA	NA	NA	76	1 177	46.1	12.0
Johnson	190	749	78.9	25.0	173	5 314	1 441.4	230.2	189	3 086	126.4	33.3
Jones	10	D	D	D	NA	NA	NA	NA	15	137	4.6	1.3
Karnes	16	63	4.4	1.1	NA	NA	NA	NA	25	235	8.6	2.3
Kaufman	122	D	D	D	108	D	1 172.6	148.1	142	2 240	93.7	26.5
Kendall	121	551	59.7	24.7	32	814	180.9	27.3	83	1 229	55.8	17.1
Kenedy	1	D	D	D	NA	NA	NA	NA	NA	NA	NA	NA
Kent	NA	NA	NA	NA	NA	NA	NA	NA	2	D	D	D
Kerr	150	685	58.2	24.1	44	784	161.8	31.8	122	1 958	97.6	28.3
Kimble	10	16	1.0	0.3	NA	NA	NA	NA	22	184	8.2	2.2
King	NA	NA	NA	NA	NA	NA	NA	NA	NA	NA	NA	NA
Kinney	NA	NA	NA	NA	NA	NA	NA	NA	4	19	1.1	0.2
Kleberg	35	D	D	D	NA	NA	NA	NA	70	1 160	43.2	11.9
Knox	4	D	D	D	NA	NA	NA	NA	6	33	1.4	0.3
Lamar	62	D	D	D	59	4 501	2 411.6	192.5	87	1 413	61.1	16.8
Lamb	18	41	3.1	1.0	10	D	D	D	25	188	7.0	1.8
Lampasas	29	D	D	D	NA	NA	NA	NA	36	380	16.1	4.0
La Salle	NA	NA	NA	NA	NA	NA	NA	NA	11	127	5.3	1.3
Lavaca	32	74	6.5	1.6	35	1 701	238.2	45.2	25	249	9.1	2.4
Lee	23	102	7.8	2.9	19	503	128.5	17.8	28	283	13.2	3.0
Leon	29	76	7.7	1.8	20	501	D	34.8	25	263	13.1	2.8
Liberty	83	D	D	D	33	D	D	D	88	1 294	48.9	13.1
Limestone	33	147	11.0	5.2	18	1 073	210.8	35.3	40	395	18.2	4.1
Lipscomb	5	21	2.1	0.7	NA	NA	NA	NA	5	D	D	D
Live Oak	24	59	6.4	2.4	NA	NA	NA	NA	24	345	11.7	2.8
Llano	40	148	14.6	5.1	NA	NA	NA	NA	50	1 017	61.1	21.3
Loving	NA	NA	NA	NA	NA	NA	NA	NA	1	D	D	D
Lubbock	581	3 402	374.1	128.5	255	D	D	D	582	D	D	D
Lynn	6	17	0.8	0.3	NA	NA	NA	NA	5	27	0.8	0.2
McCulloch	18	76	5.6	2.2	NA	NA	NA	NA	22	243	8.8	2.1
McLennan	352	D	D	D	255	13 971	5 888.9	550.4	468	9 123	375.3	100.9
McMullen	1	D	D	D	NA	NA	NA	NA	1	D	D	D
Madison	16	242	12.5	3.3	NA	NA	NA	NA	26	326	13.1	3.2
Marion	8	18	1.3	0.7	NA	NA	NA	NA	22	154	5.8	1.5
Martin	6	12	0.9	0.4	NA	NA	NA	NA	3	D	D	D

1. Establishment subject to federal tax.

Table B. States and Counties — **Health Care and Social Assistance, Other Services, Nonemployer Businesses, and Residential Construction**

STATE County	Health care and social assistance, 2007				Other services, 2007				Nonemployer businesses, 2013		Value of residential construction authorized by building permits, 2014	
	Number of establish-ments	Number of employees	Receipts (mil dol)	Annual payroll (mil dol)	Number of establish-ments	Number of employees	Receipts (mil dol)	Annual payroll (mil dol)	Number	Receipts (mil dol)	New Construction ($1,000)	Number of housing units
	159	160	161	162	163	164	165	166	167	168	169	170
TEXAS—Cont'd												
Guadalupe	169	2 773	207.8	83.7	135	739	55.0	15.6	8 867	378.2	182 138	765
Hale	78	1 101	81.5	28.9	56	329	19.2	6.7	1 978	83.3	1 911	8
Hall	7	31	1.6	0.7	6	11	3.3	0.5	192	8.3	0	0
Hamilton	23	447	28.3	12.7	18	42	3.7	0.9	726	34.2	150	1
Hansford	5	D	D	D	16	75	5.8	1.8	505	22.4	2 819	17
Hardeman	14	231	14.9	6.0	11	39	3.1	0.7	260	12.2	0	0
Hardin	76	1 426	62.9	32.3	47	291	27.0	7.7	3 523	127.5	16 022	117
Harris	9 464	205 171	23 069.3	8 823.8	5 961	54 568	6 434.3	1 777.1	367 449	18 502.2	5 358 419	40 060
Harrison	107	1 714	133.0	46.3	91	754	71.9	27.3	4 348	201.4	11 080	79
Hartley	5	D	D	D	8	32	3.8	0.7	336	22.7	NA	NA
Haskell	15	224	11.5	4.5	12	28	2.2	0.5	437	13.4	75	2
Hays	267	4 674	354.5	138.2	183	973	95.1	25.5	13 750	616.9	366 638	2 305
Hemphill	8	177	10.4	4.1	12	D	D	D	380	20.3	950	6
Henderson	134	2 665	222.5	80.9	81	360	26.5	7.1	6 009	283.8	11 310	68
Hidalgo	1 655	44 931	2 877.2	1 137.1	573	3 257	238.5	61.9	66 167	2 411.8	372 000	3 473
Hill	48	951	66.8	24.6	43	155	21.0	4.0	2 250	101.2	490	6
Hockley	37	839	73.4	20.1	24	133	15.7	3.2	1 297	64.7	3 707	15
Hood	116	1 591	141.6	54.4	85	503	26.3	8.8	4 968	246.4	21 632	121
Hopkins	64	1 136	82.6	31.8	46	177	14.9	3.8	2 639	120.7	899	8
Houston	37	613	44.6	15.9	28	139	13.8	3.8	1 329	50.9	272	5
Howard	80	2 276	215.7	93.4	50	266	18.8	5.5	1 600	83.2	3 694	33
Hudspeth	1	D	D	D	2	D	D	D	238	5.8	NA	NA
Hunt	161	2 871	245.4	102.5	97	D	D	D	6 037	266.1	10 541	66
Hutchinson	45	481	32.0	14.6	38	240	25.4	6.6	1 107	45.9	0	0
Irion	1	D	D	D	2	D	D	D	199	13.6	NA	NA
Jack	11	184	10.4	4.4	8	15	2.9	0.4	754	47.5	338	5
Jackson	18	309	18.1	7.8	25	90	6.2	1.3	1 005	44.6	4 216	18
Jasper	76	3 505	149.9	51.2	45	158	12.5	3.1	2 448	104.0	748	8
Jeff Davis	5	D	D	D	7	D	D	D	249	7.9	NA	NA
Jefferson	849	17 840	1 618.2	580.6	404	3 012	265.8	73.0	14 983	654.6	122 735	1 061
Jim Hogg	8	488	8.4	4.6	4	D	D	D	392	11.7	NA	NA
Jim Wells	105	3 981	170.6	84.9	74	480	41.5	12.9	2 901	137.4	3 499	26
Johnson	190	3 530	234.8	93.3	173	1 046	82.0	29.2	11 416	524.4	153 498	960
Jones	27	675	29.9	14.3	21	65	4.1	1.2	1 195	52.5	350	1
Karnes	32	386	24.5	10.7	15	53	2.6	0.6	970	44.9	13 451	78
Kaufman	139	3 213	198.6	86.8	113	747	50.3	23.5	9 203	412.6	40 688	219
Kendall	101	975	72.6	29.4	65	358	27.6	9.0	4 656	282.7	85 658	380
Kenedy	NA	NA	NA	NA	1	D	D	D	16	0.4	NA	NA
Kent	1	D	D	D	NA	NA	NA	NA	64	2.7	NA	NA
Kerr	173	3 825	305.3	143.8	106	654	53.8	14.3	5 077	251.3	31 241	91
Kimble	10	144	8.4	3.8	6	32	1.5	0.5	590	15.5	427	5
King	NA	NA	NA	NA	NA	NA	NA	NA	0	0.0	NA	NA
Kinney	2	D	D	D	4	D	D	D	184	7.5	216	1
Kleberg	69	1 466	78.0	37.6	51	D	D	D	1 517	54.4	5 809	36
Knox	8	147	7.8	3.2	13	D	D	D	249	10.9	NA	NA
Lamar	180	3 332	297.7	102.7	84	390	27.3	7.3	3 748	151.5	4 073	43
Lamb	26	383	22.5	10.6	14	42	2.9	0.6	716	27.6	659	7
Lampasas	26	D	D	D	27	149	13.0	2.9	1 376	58.9	7 754	236
La Salle	11	99	6.1	2.5	6	D	D	D	592	20.8	1 612	24
Lavaca	50	900	57.6	21.7	44	162	11.5	2.2	1 705	74.9	858	11
Lee	29	309	17.4	7.7	29	99	8.9	2.4	1 296	51.8	410	3
Leon	18	146	8.0	3.3	22	127	8.8	2.3	1 444	67.3	NA	NA
Liberty	101	1 881	154.1	52.9	69	293	27.5	5.9	4 662	201.3	36 093	300
Limestone	45	893	66.9	25.1	18	87	7.1	1.5	1 326	49.2	560	4
Lipscomb	1	D	D	D	4	D	D	D	318	13.3	1 039	6
Live Oak	12	D	D	D	21	66	5.6	1.1	1 025	49.0	1 154	12
Llano	34	791	49.5	23.8	31	79	8.2	1.7	2 037	100.0	58 026	202
Loving	NA	NA	NA	NA	NA	NA	NA	NA	12	0.3	NA	NA
Lubbock	813	D	D	D	473	D	D	D	19 619	997.3	292 030	2 128
Lynn	7	124	5.7	2.7	4	19	1.0	0.2	352	11.0	300	3
McCulloch	22	290	19.5	7.7	17	58	4.0	0.9	713	21.8	0	0
McLennan	525	15 510	1 219.3	504.2	394	2 615	244.7	64.2	13 846	617.7	199 067	1 468
McMullen	1	D	D	D	NA	NA	NA	NA	111	4.4	NA	NA
Madison	17	265	20.5	7.6	16	71	6.2	1.6	960	41.0	614	4
Marion	15	D	D	D	14	30	2.3	0.5	715	26.0	291	2
Martin	10	168	9.5	5.1	7	17	2.0	0.4	383	21.9	420	3

STATE County	Government employment and payroll, 2012									Local government finances, 2012				
			March payroll (percent of total)							General revenue				
												Taxes		
													Per capita[1] (dollars)	
	Full-time equivalent employees	March payroll (dollars)	Adminis-tration, judicial, and legal	Police and Corrections	Fire Protection	Highways and transpor-tation	Health and Welfare	Natural resources and utilities	Education and libraries	Total (mil dol)	Inter-govern-mental (mil dol)	Total (mil dol)	Total	Property
	171	172	173	174	175	176	177	178	179	180	181	182	183	184
TEXAS—Cont'd														
Guadalupe	4 848	17 546 517	6.1	10.0	2.4	1.9	15.8	3.7	58.3	422.8	109.1	182.6	1 306	1 097
Hale	1 782	7 262 318	4.1	6.3	2.1	1.0	6.9	2.2	76.9	114.8	52.3	44.9	1 233	1 018
Hall	222	559 195	7.2	8.3	0.0	3.6	2.3	5.4	72.7	14.8	8.2	4.0	1 202	1 007
Hamilton	539	1 700 689	4.8	3.1	0.0	3.4	41.0	2.4	45.4	45.9	10.7	12.7	1 528	1 340
Hansford	494	1 557 868	4.9	2.9	0.1	2.2	32.4	1.8	53.8	31.7	6.9	19.4	3 509	3 267
Hardeman	417	1 303 943	5.8	4.2	0.7	1.9	46.4	3.2	37.5	42.6	8.4	16.1	3 932	3 714
Hardin	2 150	6 172 176	6.7	7.8	0.0	2.1	0.7	3.2	78.4	141.1	61.5	64.0	1 160	1 008
Harris	166 045	659 443 824	4.4	11.0	3.4	5.0	8.8	2.9	62.2	19 260.3	5 471.7	9 235.2	2 171	1 765
Harrison	2 833	8 500 249	3.8	8.6	2.9	1.9	0.3	3.6	77.3	193.7	50.6	119.6	1 773	1 592
Hartley	92	266 990	18.2	0.7	0.0	0.0	0.4	1.3	72.8	11.2	1.1	8.7	1 410	1 297
Haskell	331	767 433	9.1	5.5	0.1	3.6	22.4	5.8	53.3	22.1	9.1	7.4	1 260	1 097
Hays	7 053	24 108 223	5.6	10.9	2.6	1.5	6.6	5.7	64.1	545.5	162.4	287.7	1 703	1 398
Hemphill	358	1 141 524	8.4	5.9	0.0	4.6	27.8	4.3	48.3	47.6	3.4	36.2	8 863	8 415
Henderson	2 818	8 513 766	7.2	8.3	1.6	1.5	0.2	3.2	76.9	203.3	68.1	103.6	1 309	1 130
Hidalgo	39 042	129 583 687	3.7	6.7	1.7	1.6	2.9	3.9	78.6	3 159.2	1 926.2	864.1	1 071	868
Hill	1 782	5 391 972	5.2	8.8	1.2	2.0	0.1	2.7	79.5	122.0	52.4	48.3	1 376	1 175
Hockley	1 746	5 964 084	3.8	4.6	0.6	1.5	0.5	1.6	86.7	146.0	48.8	70.9	3 073	2 862
Hood	1 577	5 364 527	10.6	11.6	0.3	2.2	0.8	4.5	68.5	134.0	27.6	93.9	1 804	1 536
Hopkins	1 924	6 315 574	4.5	5.5	2.0	2.2	35.9	2.7	46.4	157.4	43.9	43.8	1 235	1 002
Houston	827	2 210 644	8.8	8.8	0.6	3.0	1.9	5.5	70.3	60.8	24.7	26.3	1 135	940
Howard	2 006	6 202 628	4.2	6.9	2.7	2.0	15.7	7.1	59.9	146.9	52.2	61.9	1 747	1 467
Hudspeth	286	780 976	7.7	13.3	0.0	2.9	1.1	7.6	67.2	19.0	10.0	7.0	2 108	2 025
Hunt	4 073	13 501 049	5.0	7.3	2.3	1.6	26.3	8.0	48.4	331.7	94.9	108.8	1 250	1 039
Hutchinson	1 204	3 868 672	7.3	8.9	2.7	2.5	1.7	5.0	70.3	90.0	30.2	42.4	1 935	1 693
Irion	111	320 492	16.7	8.2	0.0	4.3	0.8	7.7	60.9	14.0	1.4	12.0	7 598	7 380
Jack	453	1 551 359	5.7	9.9	0.3	1.9	21.3	3.8	56.6	35.4	3.7	28.0	3 118	2 834
Jackson	834	2 725 347	5.8	6.2	1.3	2.4	17.9	11.4	54.8	75.0	21.3	27.7	1 942	1 729
Jasper	1 516	4 363 997	5.7	7.7	0.0	3.0	2.1	6.7	72.0	103.2	47.1	43.9	1 222	1 064
Jeff Davis	113	390 447	7.2	8.1	0.0	0.0	1.2	1.2	81.3	9.9	6.7	3.0	1 289	1 181
Jefferson	10 830	41 244 326	6.6	14.9	6.1	3.8	6.0	8.0	53.1	1 149.2	304.3	568.5	2 258	1 850
Jim Hogg	316	819 818	7.4	11.3	0.9	0.2	7.1	5.0	62.8	22.9	9.1	11.0	2 095	1 786
Jim Wells	1 854	5 562 478	7.3	10.0	2.6	4.3	1.8	3.2	68.8	136.7	63.1	61.1	1 463	914
Johnson	6 428	20 663 672	6.4	10.8	3.7	2.3	0.9	4.4	69.6	540.8	136.3	306.3	1 996	1 658
Jones	1 148	3 124 966	5.6	5.9	0.0	1.6	32.6	5.2	48.8	55.2	25.7	15.1	754	677
Karnes	676	1 956 116	5.9	7.8	0.1	2.4	17.7	3.7	62.1	49.9	22.4	22.9	1 501	1 339
Kaufman	4 535	15 218 689	4.8	9.9	1.3	2.3	10.1	6.4	64.2	385.5	158.1	186.8	1 750	1 528
Kendall	1 662	5 537 436	9.0	8.0	1.1	3.0	1.6	5.5	70.6	133.9	20.6	100.2	2 786	2 470
Kenedy	35	84 678	6.2	3.9	0.0	0.0	0.5	0.4	86.0	11.6	0.2	10.5	24 369	24 346
Kent	75	243 441	11.6	3.7	0.1	21.1	0.0	2.6	60.8	8.5	1.3	6.8	8 151	8 082
Kerr	1 700	5 612 578	8.7	13.7	6.0	3.2	1.3	4.7	60.4	120.6	27.6	78.6	1 580	1 286
Kimble	171	555 031	11.3	14.1	0.0	6.0	2.2	4.9	60.8	13.0	3.2	6.7	1 472	1 379
King	59	195 445	17.5	2.0	0.0	2.6	0.0	0.5	77.5	9.5	1.7	7.1	25 620	25 616
Kinney	195	518 153	13.2	15.7	0.0	1.2	4.8	4.1	59.5	14.4	8.6	3.8	1 046	948
Kleberg	1 554	3 973 033	8.5	14.3	3.3	6.7	4.0	5.3	56.2	170.5	58.0	63.5	1 984	1 710
Knox	325	851 631	7.1	3.5	0.0	2.7	26.8	6.9	52.1	19.7	7.7	5.6	1 486	1 218
Lamar	2 237	7 154 454	5.0	8.6	0.2	1.3	0.9	4.5	77.8	165.7	68.1	68.9	1 384	1 087
Lamb	779	2 277 980	7.5	10.4	1.2	3.2	3.0	4.3	70.1	61.1	24.1	21.0	1 499	1 349
Lampasas	821	2 377 321	5.2	9.7	1.6	2.7	0.6	3.2	72.8	53.7	20.4	26.9	1 339	1 135
La Salle	315	950 554	9.0	9.5	0.0	3.2	0.2	4.1	71.9	22.1	6.6	13.4	1 887	1 739
Lavaca	808	2 421 042	9.6	8.5	3.3	4.6	17.2	10.0	41.0	73.1	14.0	28.2	1 446	1 296
Lee	700	2 033 290	5.6	8.6	0.0	3.2	0.0	4.3	74.9	49.3	14.2	29.5	1 776	1 564
Leon	757	2 170 423	7.7	7.0	0.0	3.1	1.2	2.4	78.4	47.5	14.0	28.8	1 714	1 601
Liberty	2 976	8 829 594	6.7	8.2	1.1	2.8	0.4	3.1	76.8	210.0	86.8	98.0	1 280	1 101
Limestone	1 302	3 748 599	6.3	12.5	1.9	3.5	15.2	4.0	56.2	116.3	27.5	51.1	2 165	1 970
Lipscomb	247	785 351	10.0	5.2	0.0	6.1	4.3	3.8	69.9	21.9	4.9	15.8	4 530	4 351
Live Oak	529	1 441 098	7.4	10.9	0.0	3.7	1.5	5.4	67.2	34.0	9.9	21.0	1 801	1 538
Llano	637	1 790 590	16.6	12.9	0.0	4.0	0.3	8.5	56.3	64.8	6.8	51.0	2 670	2 571
Loving	12	46 971	59.5	22.6	0.0	14.3	0.0	3.6	0.0	4.4	0.6	3.4	48 366	47 718
Lubbock	12 902	47 474 349	4.7	10.5	4.4	1.1	28.6	5.7	43.9	1 264.7	335.5	406.2	1 421	1 107
Lynn	453	1 252 881	5.2	5.1	0.0	1.3	20.1	4.2	62.8	30.1	12.7	8.8	1 516	1 374
McCulloch	585	1 662 784	6.4	5.5	1.5	2.1	23.0	8.4	50.7	33.3	13.2	11.4	1 371	1 168
McLennan	10 401	35 092 132	5.7	11.4	3.1	2.0	4.5	8.6	63.6	1 172.8	436.4	367.8	1 541	1 222
McMullen	82	296 876	20.7	8.4	0.0	8.2	1.7	1.9	58.1	10.8	0.8	9.1	12 590	12 296
Madison	473	1 465 387	9.1	5.4	0.0	2.2	0.6	3.0	77.1	37.7	16.3	14.6	1 066	920
Marion	304	892 993	8.9	7.6	0.0	4.1	0.5	2.4	76.0	19.4	6.6	11.1	1 074	952
Martin	332	1 249 120	9.9	4.5	0.0	9.6	23.0	3.5	48.5	39.6	3.4	28.7	5 722	5 575

1. Based on the resident population estimated as of July 1 of the year shown.

STATE County	Local government finances, 2012 (cont.)									Government employment, 2013			Presidential election,[2] 2012		
	Direct general expenditure							Debt outstanding					Percent of vote cast:		
			Percent of total for:												
	Total (mil dol)	Per capita[1] (dollars)	Education	Health and hospitals	Police protection	Public welfare	Highways	Total (mil dol)	Per capita[1] (dollars)	Federal civilian	Federal military	State and local	Democratic	Republican	All other
	185	186	187	188	189	190	191	192	193	194	195	196	197	198	199
TEXAS—Cont'd															
Guadalupe	411.4	2 942	44.3	19.5	5.0	0.8	3.8	852.5	6 096	193	299	5 682	34.0	65.0	0.9
Hale	116.3	3 196	62.2	9.1	7.7	0.6	2.8	79.2	2 177	88	70	2 352	27.2	72.1	0.6
Hall	13.5	4 104	66.2	1.9	3.1	0.1	5.0	0.2	72	17	0	261	25.6	73.6	0.8
Hamilton	41.2	4 960	31.5	48.5	2.0	0.3	2.3	24.5	2 949	25	17	686	22.8	76.1	1.0
Hansford	29.9	5 415	58.4	21.3	2.2	0.0	2.5	26.3	4 772	17	12	592	11.4	87.9	0.7
Hardeman	52.1	12 765	19.2	41.9	2.9	17.5	2.7	3.2	781	16	0	413	23.4	75.2	1.4
Hardin	129.3	2 342	65.3	0.6	6.8	0.5	3.7	120.4	2 181	72	116	2 241	19.0	80.2	0.8
Harris	18 773.0	4 413	44.4	10.5	5.7	0.1	4.8	54 673.5	12 853	24 611	10 043	234 737	50.4	48.8	0.7
Harrison	211.9	3 142	59.8	0.1	4.4	0.4	3.4	272.1	4 034	122	137	3 204	34.0	65.4	0.6
Hartley	10.5	1 709	39.9	0.0	7.7	0.2	15.4	0.2	32	0	10	875	12.6	86.2	1.2
Haskell	22.2	3 760	53.2	17.8	3.7	0.0	7.7	2.3	395	24	11	406	33.0	65.6	1.4
Hays	604.2	3 575	42.7	5.8	5.4	0.3	6.3	1 700.9	10 065	191	399	11 763	48.1	50.2	1.7
Hemphill	40.3	9 878	51.7	16.2	2.1	0.1	5.1	11.9	2 915	0	0	408	13.8	85.7	0.6
Henderson	213.8	2 703	68.0	1.9	5.3	0.0	3.7	147.7	1 868	84	165	3 218	27.3	71.9	0.8
Hidalgo	3 161.8	3 920	67.1	2.0	3.8	0.5	2.9	3 738.4	4 635	3 777	1 814	50 344	69.0	30.3	0.7
Hill	125.8	3 583	69.5	0.2	4.8	0.9	4.9	161.8	4 607	91	72	2 207	28.9	70.2	0.9
Hockley	161.5	7 000	72.9	0.5	2.3	0.2	2.4	78.0	3 383	43	48	1 902	23.5	75.8	0.7
Hood	131.2	2 521	60.0	0.3	6.6	0.1	3.8	144.0	2 767	90	110	1 891	22.5	76.6	0.9
Hopkins	166.2	4 685	40.6	33.8	3.5	0.0	3.4	140.0	3 947	74	74	2 241	27.3	72.0	0.7
Houston	60.7	2 619	51.0	8.0	6.2	0.1	5.3	62.1	2 682	75	43	1 622	30.8	68.1	1.1
Howard	188.2	5 315	65.7	10.8	3.1	0.2	2.0	576.8	16 289	918	64	2 667	26.3	72.5	1.2
Hudspeth	19.7	5 893	49.6	0.3	7.1	0.2	7.3	2.3	676	363	0	295	47.9	51.0	1.1
Hunt	326.3	3 747	36.3	30.6	4.6	0.2	2.6	436.0	5 007	252	254	6 905	29.1	69.7	1.2
Hutchinson	107.0	4 880	47.7	23.7	4.7	0.1	2.3	102.9	4 693	69	46	1 487	15.1	84.0	0.9
Irion	11.6	7 395	70.4	0.2	3.8	0.0	4.9	6.1	3 865	0	0	115	20.1	78.8	1.1
Jack	45.5	5 070	74.2	0.0	3.7	0.0	2.4	80.2	8 928	17	17	563	15.5	83.6	0.8
Jackson	78.6	5 513	49.1	25.8	3.2	0.1	3.9	106.4	7 462	30	30	1 021	25.7	73.6	0.7
Jasper	96.3	2 680	59.7	2.7	8.6	0.0	5.7	89.0	2 478	79	73	2 004	28.6	70.6	0.8
Jeff Davis	9.6	4 176	59.9	0.4	3.0	0.1	0.2	0.3	132	24	0	249	37.9	60.6	1.5
Jefferson	1 153.5	4 581	41.4	4.2	7.0	0.6	5.6	5 050.2	20 055	1 938	760	16 160	50.8	48.6	0.6
Jim Hogg	22.0	4 186	44.7	0.9	5.9	2.1	11.8	5.1	979	264	11	375	73.6	26.0	0.4
Jim Wells	136.5	3 268	62.9	0.3	5.4	0.2	3.5	108.5	2 599	76	112	2 186	57.8	41.7	0.6
Johnson	466.6	3 041	55.2	0.5	6.0	0.3	3.6	1 105.1	7 202	224	322	6 910	25.8	73.3	0.9
Jones	52.9	2 651	52.3	25.3	1.5	0.0	3.3	40.8	2 041	72	34	2 354	26.3	72.4	1.3
Karnes	43.7	2 867	55.3	6.6	2.9	0.5	5.2	10.2	671	61	26	1 530	38.9	60.4	0.7
Kaufman	387.6	3 631	51.9	6.6	4.1	0.3	7.0	686.1	6 427	178	228	6 224	31.8	67.5	0.7
Kendall	128.4	3 571	58.1	1.2	6.7	0.2	4.5	314.6	8 750	49	79	1 662	21.5	77.5	1.1
Kenedy	11.2	25 935	97.1	0.0	0.4	0.0	0.5	2.3	5 397	0	0	91	53.5	46.5	0.0
Kent	8.2	9 762	93.8	0.1	0.5	0.0	0.6	0.0	11	0	0	194	22.1	76.3	1.6
Kerr	109.6	2 202	53.6	0.5	9.0	0.7	3.7	92.9	1 865	518	103	2 702	24.7	74.3	1.0
Kimble	12.1	2 660	49.4	6.6	3.6	0.0	5.0	15.9	3 487	13	0	356	18.6	80.7	0.8
King	6.3	22 880	69.2	0.0	1.3	0.0	7.6	6.0	21 884	0	0	66	4.9	92.6	2.5
Kinney	13.4	3 722	44.0	4.4	9.1	0.6	3.6	2.9	792	155	0	296	40.8	58.5	0.7
Kleberg	174.6	5 453	30.3	33.2	3.9	0.0	12.4	115.3	3 599	963	428	3 911	53.2	46.0	0.8
Knox	18.2	4 797	47.6	28.6	3.0	0.3	3.7	1.1	293	27	0	413	26.8	72.1	1.1
Lamar	164.5	3 303	65.4	1.9	5.1	1.8	4.5	148.6	2 982	146	104	2 950	28.6	70.5	0.9
Lamb	58.4	4 171	54.5	18.7	5.0	0.0	4.5	16.0	1 139	36	29	982	25.5	73.9	0.6
Lampasas	51.3	2 552	61.5	0.3	7.0	0.3	5.8	67.4	3 353	42	42	982	24.9	74.0	1.0
La Salle	18.2	2 554	68.9	0.1	1.4	0.3	5.5	31.9	4 493	124	12	633	59.2	40.2	0.6
Lavaca	68.8	3 532	36.2	22.8	5.2	0.2	7.3	31.6	1 625	53	41	915	22.7	76.5	0.7
Lee	48.0	2 889	56.5	0.5	6.1	0.7	6.6	75.0	4 518	23	34	1 226	31.4	67.6	1.0
Leon	49.2	2 929	78.9	0.0	2.9	0.1	4.5	50.5	3 005	44	35	829	20.1	79.1	0.8
Liberty	200.4	2 617	61.0	0.6	5.8	0.5	5.2	218.2	2 850	115	152	4 219	27.7	71.4	0.9
Limestone	124.3	5 268	41.5	12.6	11.7	0.3	4.7	91.4	3 877	50	46	3 064	32.9	66.4	0.7
Lipscomb	21.7	6 247	73.2	0.5	3.5	0.1	5.7	7.8	2 241	18	0	379	12.3	87.0	0.6
Live Oak	41.2	3 535	63.8	0.2	3.3	0.0	5.5	61.8	5 297	259	23	589	25.1	74.1	0.8
Llano	64.4	3 376	59.1	0.1	6.5	0.0	4.8	33.0	1 727	29	41	782	23.4	75.6	1.0
Loving	1.8	25 817	0.0	0.0	11.2	0.0	10.5	0.0	0	0	0	18	15.2	84.8	0.0
Lubbock	1 336.0	4 675	34.3	32.4	4.8	0.0	2.2	2 306.4	8 071	1 290	646	25 841	31.3	68.0	0.8
Lynn	28.7	4 967	57.9	19.6	4.2	0.0	3.2	5.0	865	23	12	528	29.6	69.6	0.8
McCulloch	37.3	4 484	41.7	24.2	3.9	0.0	4.2	38.1	4 581	27	17	621	24.2	75.2	0.6
McLennan	1 142.6	4 787	41.4	2.5	5.0	0.0	1.6	11 590.0	48 553	2 801	587	14 123	37.7	61.6	0.8
McMullen	9.6	13 263	74.2	0.8	4.8	0.2	7.4	23.3	32 058	0	0	138	24.6	74.5	0.9
Madison	33.7	2 466	63.1	0.8	7.5	2.9	5.7	33.0	2 410	17	24	1 157	28.1	71.0	0.9
Marion	19.4	1 875	65.3	1.5	8.2	0.0	7.5	15.3	1 483	38	21	387	38.7	60.4	1.0
Martin	116.9	23 298	19.8	76.2	0.5	0.0	0.4	67.3	13 408	12	11	423	18.3	81.0	0.7

1. Based on the resident population estimated as of July 1 of the year shown. 2.

STATE/ County code	CBSA code[1]	County type[2]	STATE County	Land area,[3] (sq km) 2010	Population, 2014: Total persons 2014	Population, 2014: Rank	Population, 2014: Per square kilometer	Race alone or in combination, not Hispanic or Latino (percent): White	Black	American Indian, Alaska Native	Asian and Pacific Islander	Percent Hispanic or Latino[4]	Age (percent): Under 5 years	5 to 17 years	18 to 24 years	25 to 34 years	35 to 44 years	45 to 54 years
				1	2	3	4	5	6	7	8	9	10	11	12	13	14	15
			TEXAS—Cont'd															
48 319	...	9	Mason	2 406	4 071	2 897	1.7	75.8	0.9	0.6	0.3	23.0	3.9	17.7	5.9	8.1	9.5	12.5
48 321	13060	4	Matagorda	2 850	36 519	1 263	12.8	47.0	11.0	0.7	2.3	40.0	7.0	18.3	9.2	11.8	10.8	13.7
48 323	20580	5	Maverick	3 313	57 023	891	17.2	3.3	0.3	1.0	0.4	94.1	8.8	23.7	11.4	12.4	12.1	11.0
48 325	41700	1	Medina	3 433	47 894	1 018	14.0	45.9	2.5	0.7	0.9	50.7	5.7	18.8	10.0	11.5	11.6	14.4
48 327	...	8	Menard	2 336	2 147	3 037	0.9	62.8	1.4	0.5	0.2	35.5	4.2	13.8	6.1	9.1	7.7	13.4
48 329	33260	3	Midland	2 332	155 830	408	66.8	50.9	6.6	0.8	1.7	40.9	8.3	19.3	10.3	16.4	11.9	12.3
48 331	...	6	Milam	2 634	24 256	1 634	9.2	64.9	9.8	0.7	0.7	24.8	6.3	18.8	8.1	9.8	10.8	13.3
48 333	...	9	Mills	1 938	4 870	2 844	2.5	81.1	1.1	0.7	0.5	17.6	5.2	17.3	7.3	8.0	10.0	12.6
48 335	...	7	Mitchell	2 360	9 076	2 511	3.8	48.9	11.7	0.8	0.6	40.4	5.1	14.1	13.2	17.7	14.0	12.0
48 337	...	6	Montague	2 411	19 416	1 860	8.1	87.7	0.9	1.4	0.7	10.5	6.0	16.9	7.4	10.5	10.8	13.8
48 339	26420	1	Montgomery	2 698	518 947	127	192.3	70.7	4.9	0.8	3.1	21.9	6.9	20.1	8.4	12.6	13.9	14.2
48 341	20300	6	Moore	2 330	22 148	1 725	9.5	36.6	2.5	0.9	8.0	52.7	9.0	22.5	10.3	14.0	12.1	11.8
48 343	...	6	Morris	653	12 743	2 247	19.5	67.4	23.5	1.3	0.8	8.8	6.2	16.9	8.2	11.1	10.7	12.4
48 345	...	8	Motley	2 563	1 153	3 101	0.4	80.9	2.0	0.9	0.7	15.8	3.5	16.8	4.8	11.0	8.9	11.8
48 347	34860	5	Nacogdoches	2 452	65 301	808	26.6	61.6	18.6	0.9	1.7	18.5	7.1	16.2	20.5	11.8	9.9	10.9
48 349	18620	4	Navarro	2 615	48 195	1 011	18.4	59.5	14.0	0.7	1.8	25.1	7.2	19.4	8.9	11.4	12.0	13.2
48 351	13140	8	Newton	2 418	14 138	2 159	5.8	74.6	21.3	1.3	0.8	3.4	5.7	16.5	9.1	11.3	11.8	14.3
48 353	45020	6	Nolan	2 362	15 093	2 093	6.4	59.3	5.2	0.6	0.6	35.2	6.3	19.0	9.1	11.9	11.2	12.3
48 355	18580	2	Nueces	2 172	356 221	191	164.0	32.2	3.9	0.6	2.2	61.8	6.8	18.6	10.3	14.4	12.2	12.9
48 357	...	7	Ochiltree	2 377	10 758	2 376	4.5	47.1	0.8	1.0	0.7	51.5	9.0	22.8	9.4	13.5	12.9	12.2
48 359	11100	8	Oldham	3 886	2 070	3 045	0.5	80.0	3.9	1.2	1.1	14.9	3.9	26.3	7.1	11.1	12.4	13.4
48 361	13140	2	Orange	864	83 433	671	96.6	83.3	8.9	1.0	1.4	6.7	6.6	18.0	8.9	12.4	12.2	14.1
48 363	33420	6	Palo Pinto	2 465	28 096	1 489	11.4	77.0	2.7	0.9	0.9	19.6	6.5	17.9	8.5	10.8	11.3	13.4
48 365	...	6	Panola	2 077	23 769	1 649	11.4	74.4	16.3	1.0	0.7	8.8	6.5	17.7	8.8	12.1	11.5	12.8
48 367	19100	1	Parker	2 340	123 164	504	52.6	85.5	2.3	1.4	1.0	11.3	5.7	18.7	8.8	11.3	12.6	15.5
48 369	...	7	Parmer	2 281	9 908	2 445	4.3	36.9	1.3	0.4	0.4	61.4	8.3	21.2	10.0	13.1	11.4	12.6
48 371	...	7	Pecos	12 338	15 893	2 048	1.3	27.4	3.9	0.6	1.1	67.4	7.6	16.6	9.3	15.3	13.7	14.1
48 373	...	6	Polk	2 738	46 079	1 048	16.8	72.6	11.5	2.2	0.9	14.0	5.5	15.2	7.8	11.5	11.6	13.6
48 375	11100	3	Potter	2 353	121 627	506	51.7	48.5	10.7	0.9	4.8	36.6	8.2	19.3	9.7	15.3	12.5	12.7
48 377	...	7	Presidio	9 985	6 976	2 680	0.7	15.4	1.1	0.6	1.5	81.3	6.7	19.8	8.7	10.5	11.4	11.1
48 379	...	8	Rains	594	11 032	2 356	18.6	87.5	3.2	1.4	1.1	8.2	4.9	15.8	6.8	8.9	10.9	14.1
48 381	11100	3	Randall	2 361	128 220	484	54.3	76.5	3.1	1.0	2.0	18.7	6.7	17.9	10.3	14.7	12.4	12.5
48 383	...	6	Reagan	3 044	3 755	2 925	1.2	32.0	2.5	0.5	0.5	64.8	7.9	22.2	9.2	13.1	12.5	13.5
48 385	...	9	Real	1 811	3 371	2 947	1.9	70.8	1.1	1.7	0.8	27.1	5.3	12.1	7.3	7.4	9.0	13.6
48 387	...	6	Red River	2 685	12 446	2 268	4.6	74.7	17.6	1.6	0.5	7.0	5.2	15.3	7.3	9.9	10.9	13.9
48 389	37780	7	Reeves	6 826	14 349	2 142	2.1	19.4	5.0	0.3	1.0	73.9	6.0	16.2	12.6	15.7	14.9	12.8
48 391	...	6	Refugio	1 995	7 302	2 653	3.7	44.4	6.3	0.7	0.8	49.0	6.1	17.3	8.9	9.6	10.6	13.5
48 393	...	9	Roberts	2 393	928	3 111	0.4	85.2	1.9	1.4	0.7	12.0	5.2	18.9	6.3	13.6	9.5	13.4
48 395	17780	3	Robertson	2 216	16 500	2 008	7.4	59.4	20.9	0.7	0.9	19.2	6.6	17.6	8.6	11.2	10.7	13.4
48 397	19100	1	Rockwall	329	87 809	650	266.9	74.3	6.4	0.9	3.3	16.7	6.3	22.1	7.7	11.3	15.3	15.0
48 399	...	6	Runnels	2 722	10 416	2 402	3.8	63.4	2.3	0.8	0.6	33.6	5.8	18.4	7.4	10.6	10.4	12.9
48 401	30980	3	Rusk	2 393	53 923	927	22.5	66.0	17.9	0.9	0.7	15.6	6.6	16.6	9.2	13.4	12.7	13.8
48 403	...	9	Sabine	1 273	10 350	2 409	8.1	87.9	7.9	1.1	0.6	3.8	4.1	14.4	6.5	8.2	8.8	13.1
48 405	...	9	San Augustine	1 374	8 610	2 550	6.3	69.9	23.0	0.7	0.6	7.0	5.9	14.8	7.1	9.1	9.6	14.0
48 407	...	1	San Jacinto	1 474	27 099	1 531	18.4	76.8	10.7	1.2	0.8	12.0	5.5	17.0	8.0	9.8	10.8	14.0
48 409	18580	2	San Patricio	1 796	66 915	794	37.3	41.6	2.0	0.7	1.3	55.3	7.2	20.3	9.5	12.7	12.1	13.0
48 411	...	7	San Saba	2 940	5 622	2 794	1.9	66.8	3.6	1.0	0.5	30.5	5.4	14.8	10.2	14.8	8.8	11.4
48 413	...	8	Schleicher	3 395	3 162	2 960	0.9	47.2	1.9	0.3	0.3	51.1	6.0	22.0	7.9	13.0	11.4	11.9
48 415	43660	7	Scurry	2 345	17 328	1 959	7.4	56.0	5.1	0.6	0.8	38.6	7.4	18.0	9.9	14.1	11.9	13.2
48 417	...	8	Shackelford	2 368	3 343	2 951	1.4	87.6	1.4	0.9	0.7	10.8	5.4	18.2	8.0	9.8	11.3	14.3
48 419	...	6	Shelby	2 061	25 515	1 585	12.4	64.3	17.5	0.6	0.9	17.5	7.2	19.4	8.8	11.5	12.0	13.1
48 421	...	9	Sherman	2 391	3 084	2 968	1.3	56.2	0.9	0.8	0.5	42.4	7.2	21.3	8.8	10.9	12.8	14.4
48 423	46340	3	Smith	2 387	218 842	292	91.7	62.5	18.1	0.8	1.7	18.3	7.0	18.1	10.3	13.3	11.8	12.4
48 425	19100	8	Somervell	483	8 694	2 542	18.0	78.5	1.5	1.5	1.0	19.2	4.9	19.3	8.5	10.1	12.2	14.1
48 427	40100	4	Starr	3 168	62 955	834	19.9	3.9	0.1	0.1	0.3	95.0	10.1	23.2	11.7	12.6	12.4	10.8
48 429	...	7	Stephens	2 322	9 405	2 479	4.1	74.4	2.5	0.8	0.6	22.2	5.5	16.9	9.4	12.3	10.7	13.2
48 431	...	8	Sterling	2 392	1 339	3 092	0.6	61.2	2.1	1.4	0.2	36.7	5.4	19.1	6.7	14.6	9.9	13.8
48 433	...	8	Stonewall	2 373	1 403	3 085	0.6	79.7	4.2	0.9	0.8	15.7	5.2	16.8	6.9	9.1	9.1	14.0
48 435	...	7	Sutton	3 766	3 972	2 907	1.1	38.2	0.5	0.2	0.3	61.1	7.6	18.1	9.5	11.2	11.5	13.6
48 437	...	6	Swisher	2 306	7 581	2 636	3.3	50.1	7.4	0.9	0.3	42.1	7.1	18.9	9.1	13.4	10.5	12.0
48 439	19100	1	Tarrant	2 237	1 945 360	15	869.6	51.6	16.0	0.9	5.8	27.5	7.4	19.9	9.5	14.7	14.0	13.8
48 441	10180	3	Taylor	2 371	135 143	468	57.0	67.6	7.9	0.9	2.4	23.2	7.3	17.1	15.2	14.1	10.4	11.5
48 443	...	9	Terrell	6 107	927	3 112	0.2	46.8	1.2	1.6	3.7	47.7	6.2	13.3	6.2	13.1	12.3	11.0
48 445	...	6	Terry	2 302	12 739	2 248	5.5	42.1	4.5	0.5	0.4	53.0	7.8	19.0	9.9	14.1	10.8	12.9
48 447	...	9	Throckmorton	2 363	1 608	3 077	0.7	86.9	1.0	1.1	0.5	11.2	4.3	17.3	6.6	10.1	9.1	13.8
48 449	34420	7	Titus	1 052	32 506	1 374	30.9	48.3	10.0	0.7	1.0	40.8	8.2	21.3	10.2	12.2	12.4	12.3

1. CBSA = Core Based Statistical Area. See Appendix A for explanation. See Appendix B for list of metropolitan areas with component counties. 2. County type code from the Economic Research Service of USDA Rural-Urban Continuum Codes. See Appendix A for definition. 3. Dry land or land partially or temporarily covered by water. 4. May be of any race.

STATE County	Population, 2013 (cont.) Age (percent) (cont.) 55 to 64 years	65 to 74 years	75 years and over	Percent female	Population change and components of change, 2000–2014 Total persons 2000	2010	Percent change 2000–2010	2010–2014	Components of change, 2010–2014 Births	Deaths	Net migration	Households, 2009–2013 Number	Persons per household	Percent Family households	Female family householder[1]	One person
	16	17	18	19	20	21	22	23	24	25	26	27	28	29	30	31
TEXAS—Cont'd																
Mason	15.7	15.5	11.1	50.3	3 738	4 012	7.3	1.5	159	190	94	1 699	2.37	71.8	4.9	25.8
Matagorda	13.7	8.7	6.7	50.1	37 957	36 702	-3.3	-0.5	2 219	1 490	-861	13 260	2.72	71.2	15.7	25.7
Maverick	9.4	6.3	4.8	50.5	47 297	54 258	14.7	5.1	4 545	1 485	-282	15 714	3.45	82.4	20.2	16.3
Medina	12.9	8.8	6.2	48.4	39 304	46 006	17.1	4.1	2 212	1 574	1 253	15 284	2.86	79.1	12.5	17.4
Menard	16.3	16.1	13.2	49.9	2 360	2 242	-5.0	-4.2	74	134	-21	871	2.49	66.6	17.3	31.6
Midland	11.3	5.3	5.0	50.1	116 009	136 872	18.0	13.8	10 558	4 323	12 454	50 644	2.78	71.6	13.3	23.3
Milam	13.8	10.4	8.7	50.6	24 238	24 757	2.1	-2.0	1 297	1 152	-663	9 330	2.58	67.1	11.0	29.4
Mills	15.1	13.2	11.2	50.6	5 151	4 936	-4.2	-1.3	181	256	9	1 817	2.59	72.9	4.5	25.5
Mitchell	10.3	7.3	6.1	38.5	9 698	9 403	-3.0	-3.5	427	372	-369	2 748	2.53	69.9	10.8	28.0
Montague	13.8	11.7	9.2	50.5	19 117	19 719	3.1	-1.5	988	1 124	-130	8 038	2.41	69.0	10.6	27.9
Montgomery	12.2	7.4	4.3	50.4	293 768	455 746	55.1	13.9	27 488	13 171	47 351	163 462	2.87	74.2	10.6	21.4
Moore	10.1	5.9	4.4	48.0	20 121	21 904	8.9	1.1	1 733	540	-961	6 820	3.20	77.4	13.2	18.3
Morris	14.2	10.9	9.5	51.9	13 048	12 934	-0.9	-1.5	685	679	-201	4 949	2.56	71.8	17.9	27.0
Motley	15.4	15.1	12.7	48.1	1 426	1 210	-15.1	-4.7	38	66	-37	433	2.73	59.6	3.0	37.4
Nacogdoches	11.0	7.2	5.4	52.1	59 203	64 524	9.0	1.2	3 804	2 320	-767	23 586	2.52	62.6	14.0	31.2
Navarro	12.4	9.1	6.4	50.5	45 124	47 735	5.8	0.8	2 886	2 053	-489	17 466	2.68	72.1	15.8	23.6
Newton	14.0	10.5	6.8	48.5	15 072	14 445	-4.2	-2.1	598	655	-250	4 865	2.87	68.1	11.4	28.5
Nolan	13.2	9.4	7.6	49.8	15 802	15 216	-3.7	-0.8	833	747	-243	5 527	2.65	65.6	15.3	28.5
Nueces	12.0	7.3	5.5	50.8	313 645	340 223	8.5	4.7	20 355	11 560	7 364	123 915	2.72	67.9	16.9	25.6
Ochiltree	10.0	5.7	4.5	48.6	9 006	10 223	13.5	5.2	739	335	121	3 736	2.78	77.2	10.7	18.5
Oldham	12.4	7.5	5.9	49.2	2 185	2 052	-6.1	0.9	89	58	-15	748	2.35	65.5	9.2	32.2
Orange	13.0	8.4	6.4	50.4	84 966	81 837	-3.7	2.0	4 565	3 797	907	31 162	2.62	70.7	12.6	25.5
Palo Pinto	13.7	10.8	7.1	51.0	27 026	28 111	4.0	-0.1	1 605	1 288	-326	10 491	2.64	68.5	13.1	27.3
Panola	14.0	9.5	7.1	50.5	22 756	23 796	4.6	-0.1	1 238	1 178	-89	8 873	2.63	71.9	13.5	24.9
Parker	13.3	8.9	5.4	49.5	88 495	116 927	32.1	5.3	5 587	4 074	4 480	42 322	2.72	74.9	8.4	21.5
Parmer	10.9	7.0	5.4	48.3	10 016	10 269	2.5	-3.5	656	298	-714	3 215	3.12	77.2	13.1	18.0
Pecos	11.1	7.1	5.2	43.3	16 809	15 507	-7.7	2.5	948	466	-76	4 588	2.89	68.8	11.9	28.1
Polk	15.0	12.6	7.3	46.5	41 133	45 413	10.4	1.5	2 083	2 568	1 070	16 980	2.44	71.1	15.7	25.2
Potter	10.9	6.2	5.2	48.6	113 546	121 073	6.6	0.5	8 716	4 890	-3 292	42 751	2.72	64.9	16.2	29.9
Presidio	11.7	10.8	9.4	50.2	7 304	7 818	7.0	-10.8	484	189	-1 142	2 616	2.88	69.2	15.1	28.3
Rains	15.5	14.2	8.9	49.6	9 139	10 914	19.4	1.1	433	513	204	4 232	2.57	71.2	14.1	25.7
Randall	12.3	7.6	5.7	51.0	104 312	120 725	15.7	6.2	6 944	4 083	4 595	48 080	2.52	68.4	10.5	25.7
Reagan	11.2	5.6	4.7	47.9	3 326	3 367	1.2	11.5	239	84	234	1 178	2.87	78.3	7.3	17.1
Real	17.6	16.0	11.7	50.5	3 047	3 309	8.6	1.9	137	207	142	1 127	2.89	76.3	13.7	20.4
Red River	14.8	12.7	10.0	51.7	14 314	12 860	-10.2	-3.2	568	753	-227	5 052	2.47	65.6	13.7	31.1
Reeves	9.7	6.7	5.6	39.8	13 137	13 783	4.9	4.1	723	416	259	3 542	3.31	70.4	15.5	24.3
Refugio	13.1	11.4	9.5	50.3	7 828	7 383	-5.7	-1.1	358	337	-99	2 818	2.50	72.5	15.1	23.9
Roberts	13.0	12.3	7.9	51.1	887	929	4.7	-0.1	44	39	-10	374	2.75	80.7	5.3	19.3
Robertson	13.9	10.1	7.9	50.6	16 000	16 622	3.9	-0.7	882	756	-232	5 851	2.79	70.8	17.4	26.1
Rockwall	11.2	6.9	4.3	50.9	43 080	78 337	81.8	12.1	4 106	2 011	7 228	26 820	2.99	81.4	10.1	15.5
Runnels	13.8	11.0	9.8	50.2	11 495	10 501	-8.6	-0.8	466	588	20	3 818	2.67	75.8	16.4	23.2
Rusk	12.8	8.6	6.4	47.1	47 372	53 330	12.6	1.1	2 836	2 261	-14	17 772	2.73	70.5	13.3	26.2
Sabine	16.3	17.3	11.4	51.0	10 469	10 834	3.5	-4.5	380	680	-224	4 161	2.52	63.0	10.8	33.2
San Augustine	15.1	13.5	11.0	51.3	8 946	8 865	-0.9	-2.9	440	563	-120	3 275	2.63	62.9	14.4	32.4
San Jacinto	15.7	11.9	7.4	49.7	22 246	26 384	18.6	2.7	1 143	1 134	716	9 425	2.81	78.0	12.8	19.3
San Patricio	11.4	8.1	5.7	50.0	67 138	64 804	-3.5	3.3	3 952	2 596	708	22 147	2.91	76.2	15.9	20.0
San Saba	13.4	12.0	9.2	45.3	6 186	6 131	-0.9	-8.3	283	282	-512	2 035	2.67	67.0	10.4	30.7
Schleicher	12.9	8.9	6.1	49.3	2 935	3 461	17.9	-8.6	158	95	-372	1 078	3.05	75.5	14.7	23.5
Scurry	11.8	7.0	6.6	46.0	16 361	16 921	3.4	2.4	1 122	718	4	5 846	2.60	74.7	15.7	23.3
Shackelford	14.5	9.6	8.8	51.3	3 302	3 378	2.3	-1.0	149	126	-49	1 445	2.29	68.2	10.4	28.6
Shelby	12.2	9.0	6.9	50.4	25 224	25 448	0.9	0.3	1 504	1 168	-239	9 781	2.59	69.3	14.5	26.4
Sherman	10.8	7.8	6.1	47.9	3 186	3 034	-4.8	1.6	163	99	-5	949	3.15	75.8	4.8	20.2
Smith	11.9	8.4	6.8	51.7	174 706	209 714	20.0	4.4	12 721	8 222	4 534	78 459	2.64	68.5	13.9	26.2
Somervell	13.6	9.7	7.5	51.0	6 809	8 490	24.7	2.4	382	339	140	3 193	2.58	72.1	8.6	25.4
Starr	8.3	6.3	4.7	51.3	53 597	60 968	13.8	3.3	5 786	1 617	-2 217	15 949	3.81	84.2	23.3	14.6
Stephens	13.3	10.4	8.4	47.9	9 674	9 630	-0.5	-2.3	427	460	-172	3 509	2.50	71.2	10.7	26.4
Sterling	13.7	8.0	8.7	46.9	1 393	1 143	-17.9	17.1	50	60	199	458	2.88	80.8	9.4	17.7
Stonewall	14.0	11.0	13.9	51.2	1 693	1 490	-12.0	-5.8	51	85	-61	578	2.27	63.7	5.5	32.9
Sutton	12.8	8.7	7.0	49.5	4 077	4 128	1.3	-3.8	225	129	-268	1 445	2.79	75.4	10.9	19.9
Swisher	11.4	8.8	8.6	47.1	8 378	7 854	-6.3	-3.5	462	303	-419	2 604	2.75	70.1	9.2	27.0
Tarrant	10.7	5.9	4.0	51.0	1 446 219	1 809 034	25.1	7.5	117 734	48 438	65 806	659 736	2.77	69.3	14.3	25.6
Taylor	10.6	7.2	6.5	51.2	126 555	131 506	3.9	2.8	8 625	5 307	249	49 304	2.56	65.4	13.0	28.3
Terrell	14.7	12.8	10.4	47.4	1 081	984	-9.0	-5.8	47	41	-68	403	2.08	57.3	6.2	36.2
Terry	10.9	7.9	6.7	47.3	12 761	12 651	-0.9	0.7	828	496	-222	4 067	2.83	67.0	14.4	30.3
Throckmorton	13.6	12.8	12.5	51.2	1 850	1 641	-11.3	-2.0	63	67	-37	758	2.11	64.4	7.7	34.6
Titus	10.5	7.2	5.5	50.6	28 118	32 334	15.0	0.5	2 115	1 093	-825	10 725	2.98	74.4	13.4	21.9

1. No spouse present.

STATE County	Persons in group quarters, 2014	Daytime population, 2009–2013: Number	Daytime population, 2009–2013: Employment/residence ratio	Births, 2014: Total	Births, 2014: Rate[1]	Deaths, 2014: Number	Deaths, 2014: Rate[1]	Persons under 65 with no health insurance, 2013: Number	Persons under 65 with no health insurance, 2013: Percent	Medicare, 2014: Eligible for Medicare	Medicare, 2014: Enrolled in Medicare Advantage	Medicare, 2014: Enrolled in a Medicare prescription drug plan	Serious crimes known to police,[2] 2013: Total: Number	Serious crimes known to police,[2] 2013: Total: Rate[3]
	32	33	34	35	36	37	38	39	40	41	42	43	44	45
TEXAS—Cont'd														
Mason	3	3 859	0.90	41	10.1	46	11.3	1 192	39.5	1 134	168	709	42	1 046
Matagorda	387	35 398	0.92	516	14.1	358	9.8	7 843	25.6	6 469	1 425	3 379	1 247	3 403
Maverick	997	52 774	0.89	1 111	19.5	349	6.1	16 433	33.8	8 937	2 527	4 791	1 410	2 522
Medina	2 369	39 106	0.60	524	10.9	399	8.3	8 988	23.6	8 086	2 663	2 905	573	1 245
Menard	40	2 227	1.02	20	9.3	17	7.9	529	35.1	611	88	354	5	222
Midland	1 689	150 445	1.12	2 701	17.3	1 044	6.7	29 255	21.8	17 498	2 929	9 906	4 451	2 954
Milam	408	22 320	0.76	304	12.5	254	10.5	4 756	24.7	5 372	1 892	2 031	581	2 413
Mills	150	4 698	0.90	39	8.0	60	12.3	1 248	34.3	1 267	391	641	32	666
Mitchell	2 055	9 055	0.88	104	11.5	74	8.2	1 388	23.9	1 399	238	861	196	2 096
Montague	269	18 013	0.79	228	11.7	267	13.8	3 795	24.8	4 726	557	2 850	549	2 802
Montgomery	3 462	422 061	0.77	6 643	12.8	3 336	6.4	91 939	21.1	69 399	23 783	28 062	9 655	1 947
Moore	143	22 991	1.09	408	18.4	128	5.8	5 777	29.2	2 393	283	1 451	518	2 520
Morris	145	12 775	0.98	162	12.7	137	10.8	2 575	25.4	3 432	963	1 711	404	3 157
Motley	0	1 192	1.02	10	8.7	12	10.4	265	30.6	334	60	204	12	996
Nacogdoches	4 993	64 863	0.99	870	13.3	545	8.3	14 176	27.2	10 279	1 826	5 939	1 981	2 966
Navarro	855	46 387	0.92	678	14.1	505	10.5	10 965	27.4	9 467	1 695	5 325	1 835	3 930
Newton	724	12 016	0.54	135	9.5	172	12.2	2 463	22.4	2 529	631	1 351	122	860
Nolan	413	15 519	1.07	207	13.7	180	11.9	2 809	23.0	3 010	496	1 861	657	4 414
Nueces	5 928	354 957	1.07	4 928	13.8	2 768	7.8	71 060	23.5	53 491	24 960	15 733	17 842	5 074
Ochiltree	54	11 331	1.19	176	16.4	78	7.3	2 897	30.1	1 214	91	742	106	967
Oldham	279	2 238	1.21	23	11.1	9	4.3	330	21.0	378	69	219	27	1 304
Orange	639	74 503	0.77	1 113	13.3	903	10.8	12 994	18.5	16 010	5 170	7 601	2 545	3 042
Palo Pinto	271	26 073	0.83	383	13.6	318	11.3	6 684	29.4	5 603	747	3 072	989	3 546
Panola	380	24 082	1.02	283	11.9	268	11.3	4 314	22.0	4 623	822	2 633	792	3 273
Parker	1 691	99 333	0.64	1 368	11.1	1 000	8.1	20 104	19.9	20 242	4 345	9 086	2 126	1 757
Parmer	74	11 058	1.20	162	16.4	45	4.5	2 746	31.7	1 378	79	883	95	932
Pecos	2 080	16 212	1.10	222	14.0	95	6.0	3 096	26.4	2 177	393	1 297	451	2 871
Polk	4 399	44 075	0.90	506	11.0	625	13.6	8 741	26.8	17 124	4 004	7 748	1 147	2 498
Potter	6 851	143 382	1.41	2 027	16.7	1 136	9.3	27 958	27.4	17 165	3 120	9 618	5 462	4 435
Presidio	0	7 568	1.00	102	14.6	52	7.5	1 969	34.3	1 758	251	1 054	23	309
Rains	69	9 143	0.59	105	9.5	113	10.2	2 411	28.4	2 727	474	1 516	220	2 001
Randall	2 276	99 730	0.62	1 661	13.0	986	7.7	18 368	17.1	19 378	3 558	10 856	4 797	3 779
Reagan	33	3 823	1.23	61	16.2	15	4.0	943	29.4	426	56	248	2	57
Real	71	3 386	1.04	30	8.9	48	14.2	732	30.6	1 083	146	569	16	470
Red River	178	10 767	0.57	133	10.7	178	14.3	2 638	27.5	3 288	402	2 005	293	2 308
Reeves	3 127	14 798	1.22	183	12.8	104	7.2	2 316	25.3	2 064	230	1 394	263	1 898
Refugio	106	6 961	0.88	82	11.2	64	8.8	1 273	22.3	1 709	336	968	109	1 501
Roberts	0	873	0.67	10	10.8	8	8.6	106	16.1	166	34	101	19	2 273
Robertson	181	16 009	0.91	207	12.5	153	9.3	3 743	28.0	3 414	691	1 624	368	2 217
Rockwall	778	71 026	0.73	982	11.2	471	5.4	13 478	18.0	11 283	2 505	5 386	1 181	1 393
Runnels	188	9 741	0.83	95	9.1	132	12.7	2 156	26.7	2 420	227	1 598	185	1 767
Rusk	5 478	48 165	0.75	652	12.1	525	9.7	10 335	25.4	9 054	1 936	4 964	1 679	3 082
Sabine	79	10 065	0.81	88	8.5	142	13.7	1 783	24.2	3 301	564	1 772	194	2 037
San Augustine	229	8 565	0.88	107	12.4	117	13.6	1 693	25.8	2 371	535	1 283	132	1 491
San Jacinto	128	20 938	0.40	270	10.0	254	9.4	5 853	27.2	5 550	1 844	2 499	727	2 646
San Patricio	674	58 387	0.75	955	14.3	564	8.4	12 303	21.8	11 857	5 405	3 877	2 188	3 304
San Saba	401	5 704	0.85	66	11.7	61	10.9	1 340	32.5	1 358	282	709	102	1 705
Schleicher	1	3 030	0.80	39	12.3	21	6.6	740	27.3	527	76	304	15	468
Scurry	1 654	17 604	1.08	268	15.5	160	9.2	3 072	23.0	2 767	448	1 791	690	3 999
Shackelford	34	3 430	1.04	43	12.9	33	9.9	691	25.2	675	96	430	23	683
Shelby	174	24 896	0.93	357	14.0	301	11.8	6 308	29.2	4 933	978	2 899	611	2 321
Sherman	28	2 985	0.95	36	11.7	15	4.9	891	33.7	354	40	220	26	838
Smith	4 272	218 679	1.07	3 005	13.7	1 951	8.9	45 409	25.3	39 578	8 388	21 320	7 015	3 258
Somervell	294	9 379	1.23	95	10.9	88	10.1	1 626	22.8	1 579	401	854	101	1 166
Starr	817	59 077	0.88	1 343	21.3	369	5.9	18 794	34.6	8 736	1 545	6 030	1 176	1 896
Stephens	680	9 354	0.96	101	10.7	89	9.5	1 974	28.2	1 925	326	1 170	141	1 490
Sterling	35	1 442	1.13	12	9.0	17	12.7	197	19.8	231	38	156	12	988
Stonewall	25	1 374	1.02	16	11.4	13	9.3	305	28.4	361	33	219	18	1 221
Sutton	13	4 349	1.16	57	14.4	23	5.8	871	26.0	662	26	448	23	585
Swisher	644	7 208	0.78	98	12.9	66	8.7	1 602	27.7	1 518	161	998	105	1 325
Tarrant	22 186	1 832 993	0.98	27 965	14.4	11 954	6.1	394 842	23.2	227 934	88 136	80 492	76 929	4 032
Taylor	5 118	136 553	1.06	2 032	15.0	1 312	9.7	24 786	22.2	22 263	4 219	11 947	5 365	3 987
Terrell	0	898	1.16	10	10.8	7	7.6	242	35.0	236	40	121	9	1 008
Terry	1 096	12 165	0.90	198	15.5	120	9.4	2 889	29.4	2 093	568	1 154	298	2 355
Throckmorton	14	1 531	0.87	16	10.0	10	6.2	375	31.4	393	43	269	22	1 377
Titus	522	35 211	1.22	493	15.2	248	7.6	8 616	30.7	4 761	917	2 685	965	2 935

1. Per 1,000 estimated resident population. 2. Data for serious crimes have not been adjusted for underreporting; this may affect comparability between geographic areas and over time.
3. Per 100,000 population estimated by the FBI.

Table B. States and Counties — **Crime, Education, Money Income, and Poverty**

STATE County	Serious crimes known to police, 2013 (cont.)[1]		Education						Money income, 2009–2013				Income and poverty, 2013			
	Rate[2]		School enrollment and attainment, 2009–2013				Local government expenditures,[5] 2012–2013			Households				Percent below poverty level		
			Enrollment[3]		Attainment[4] (percent)											
	Violent	Property	Total	Percent private	High school graduate or less	Bachelor's degree or more	Total current spending (mil dol)	Current spending per student (dollars)	Per capita income[6] (dollars)	Median income (dollars)	Mean income (dollars)	Percent with income of $200,000 or more	Median household income (dollars)	All persons	Children under 18 years	Children 5 to 17 years in families
	46	47	48	49	50	51	52	53	54	55	56	57	58	59	60	61
TEXAS—Cont'd																
Mason	25	1 021	743	10.8	45.4	26.5	7.2	9 999	27 504	46 865	64 844	4.4	42 087	15.2	28.0	23.9
Matagorda	322	3 081	8 846	10.0	58.9	14.5	69.8	9 964	23 389	43 096	61 600	2.2	42 036	20.4	32.7	31.3
Maverick	175	2 347	17 985	3.6	66.0	12.2	125.5	8 318	13 668	31 395	45 003	0.8	32 073	24.4	34.8	34.7
Medina	115	1 129	12 389	9.4	48.6	20.0	76.6	8 226	22 413	55 326	66 999	2.7	53 714	18.0	26.3	24.8
Menard	0	222	686	0.3	54.2	18.8	4.5	13 212	18 253	31 215	46 357	2.1	31 390	23.7	41.9	38.9
Midland	287	2 667	38 529	14.7	41.4	24.4	211.9	8 407	33 672	62 993	92 173	7.7	71 151	10.5	15.8	14.9
Milam	183	2 230	5 720	6.8	58.3	14.4	41.0	8 940	21 248	37 391	53 907	2.1	40 120	17.4	28.3	26.5
Mills	146	520	1 151	7.3	48.6	21.9	10.8	12 738	22 651	44 213	57 451	3.5	40 318	17.2	29.8	27.0
Mitchell	396	1 701	2 302	5.9	58.0	8.3	16.1	11 020	15 936	42 045	53 732	1.0	47 677	22.3	25.8	24.5
Montague	153	2 649	4 303	9.2	49.7	16.6	30.6	9 010	24 699	44 231	58 210	2.8	41 516	15.9	24.4	22.8
Montgomery	156	1 790	128 969	12.5	38.6	30.7	685.7	7 241	32 911	67 766	91 996	8.7	69 317	11.8	16.5	15.5
Moore	379	2 140	6 464	4.0	62.1	13.2	44.5	8 544	19 770	51 181	60 490	1.5	46 991	14.9	22.7	22.4
Morris	352	2 806	2 833	5.7	52.8	13.1	20.2	9 081	20 045	37 849	50 816	1.8	36 366	21.0	31.1	28.3
Motley	83	913	312	16.7	48.9	18.1	2.7	14 564	18 828	35 845	45 776	0.0	37 159	19.6	34.3	29.9
Nacogdoches	249	2 718	21 865	4.0	48.3	24.3	90.4	8 312	20 362	36 777	53 826	2.2	36 775	26.4	33.3	32.0
Navarro	343	3 588	12 393	5.6	54.4	16.5	79.5	8 141	20 327	40 795	54 594	2.3	38 423	23.3	33.5	31.0
Newton	113	747	3 018	7.5	63.3	7.5	20.3	9 970	20 431	37 246	54 256	2.6	38 544	19.4	31.6	28.7
Nolan	578	3 836	3 801	4.2	55.7	12.5	31.7	10 231	19 002	36 806	49 136	1.4	35 846	21.5	31.9	28.7
Nueces	584	4 491	92 554	8.7	47.3	20.0	518.7	8 418	23 671	47 057	63 155	2.7	48 324	18.2	26.2	24.7
Ochiltree	137	830	2 815	7.9	62.8	15.3	19.6	8 157	23 382	49 964	65 354	2.5	60 650	10.6	15.6	14.9
Oldham	48	1 255	621	5.5	37.4	31.3	13.5	15 021	22 519	48 929	64 087	2.0	52 431	14.2	34.4	24.9
Orange	341	2 702	19 869	7.9	54.0	13.0	126.2	8 283	24 736	49 507	64 337	2.3	51 340	15.1	22.5	21.0
Palo Pinto	208	3 338	6 183	7.3	56.2	15.1	44.5	8 494	23 655	41 670	61 106	2.9	39 660	17.6	27.5	25.1
Panola	289	2 984	5 464	6.5	53.1	11.8	39.7	10 050	26 525	52 453	67 278	2.7	49 792	13.3	20.2	18.8
Parker	83	1 674	29 707	13.0	38.9	25.0	157.2	8 126	30 692	64 515	83 779	5.8	61 199	11.8	16.4	15.1
Parmer	88	844	2 764	8.7	62.2	16.2	23.5	9 589	19 304	44 943	58 244	1.9	41 784	14.9	22.6	21.7
Pecos	376	2 495	3 418	3.7	64.8	12.7	31.6	10 309	20 245	47 019	60 857	1.3	43 766	18.1	23.7	24.3
Polk	316	2 182	9 483	9.0	58.3	11.3	62.5	8 951	19 498	37 855	51 631	1.8	39 833	18.3	31.0	29.5
Potter	588	3 847	32 769	7.7	51.3	15.6	306.3	8 160	19 861	37 951	53 469	1.7	37 366	22.1	32.3	30.0
Presidio	54	255	1 703	1.9	63.8	23.6	22.6	12 757	16 175	29 634	41 029	0.2	32 766	23.3	34.5	35.1
Rains	209	1 792	2 245	8.3	58.2	11.0	13.6	8 192	21 946	44 478	54 117	0.6	42 183	18.0	30.7	27.9
Randall	504	3 275	34 448	7.7	32.4	30.2	88.9	9 635	29 124	58 529	73 175	3.6	60 439	11.0	14.2	13.0
Reagan	0	57	907	5.3	72.5	10.6	9.9	11 166	26 633	61 250	73 704	3.7	61 724	9.9	13.3	12.9
Real	0	470	613	2.4	52.9	19.5	2.5	9 511	17 931	33 885	43 174	0.0	34 556	21.6	39.1	42.9
Red River	410	1 898	2 703	9.0	60.8	14.5	23.3	10 420	19 014	31 712	44 574	1.5	31 409	19.7	30.0	28.3
Reeves	180	1 717	2 759	1.1	67.3	10.5	25.7	10 538	15 467	40 571	50 428	0.2	37 053	27.4	32.5	31.3
Refugio	207	1 295	1 530	2.0	55.3	11.2	17.0	12 190	23 174	44 548	59 721	1.8	45 214	16.1	25.7	25.2
Roberts	0	2 273	204	0.5	39.7	33.2	2.9	13 391	36 172	67 321	91 779	5.9	70 127	8.7	14.9	13.7
Robertson	361	1 855	4 073	8.4	60.9	15.8	40.7	12 615	21 709	40 601	57 183	3.2	40 631	22.8	35.0	34.7
Rockwall	84	1 309	23 807	13.8	31.1	36.5	152.8	7 878	34 617	86 119	101 545	7.7	92 466	6.6	9.1	8.0
Runnels	124	1 643	2 407	2.0	62.0	14.9	20.5	9 892	20 235	37 667	52 030	1.5	36 769	18.7	30.0	27.9
Rusk	356	2 726	11 988	9.8	53.8	13.8	68.8	8 547	21 640	45 752	61 263	2.8	44 349	21.5	27.6	26.3
Sabine	294	1 743	1 784	2.5	59.8	13.4	14.4	9 111	18 762	32 963	44 110	1.0	37 576	18.0	30.0	27.7
San Augustine	169	1 322	1 862	6.2	61.0	12.4	9.0	10 917	18 695	28 390	43 623	2.1	32 140	23.4	39.5	38.8
San Jacinto	255	2 391	5 816	4.3	61.0	12.0	30.7	8 740	24 733	46 107	66 614	4.3	42 320	22.8	33.6	30.9
San Patricio	302	3 002	17 104	6.1	52.5	14.7	126.8	8 677	23 373	50 657	65 869	3.1	46 781	16.2	23.7	22.6
San Saba	167	1 538	1 271	1.3	55.0	13.1	10.0	10 209	18 009	37 743	45 900	1.9	36 030	22.7	37.0	35.7
Schleicher	0	468	991	2.7	53.1	21.9	6.3	10 699	24 787	50 648	67 121	5.2	50 402	13.7	20.1	17.2
Scurry	527	3 472	4 408	4.4	50.7	14.4	32.5	9 875	22 860	47 513	66 140	3.3	53 219	15.0	21.1	20.6
Shackelford	148	534	767	8.0	45.5	25.4	7.0	11 117	25 436	47 277	59 343	3.4	51 116	14.7	22.2	19.2
Shelby	368	1 952	5 875	5.7	60.2	13.7	53.1	9 379	21 126	37 081	54 120	2.6	36 565	21.0	32.3	32.5
Sherman	161	677	857	13.2	51.8	20.0	8.2	8 479	21 936	48 185	65 961	2.8	48 054	12.6	18.4	16.8
Smith	279	2 978	58 251	10.5	41.2	24.5	272.8	8 242	25 626	47 432	67 397	3.8	47 711	16.8	25.3	22.3
Somervell	115	1 050	2 282	3.4	40.5	29.0	19.3	11 415	28 134	55 269	73 071	7.1	56 282	11.5	18.2	16.6
Starr	314	1 582	19 838	2.8	76.9	8.6	167.6	9 519	11 584	24 927	39 359	0.8	25 408	36.3	51.2	50.1
Stephens	159	1 332	2 107	4.7	53.9	15.6	12.2	8 371	20 535	41 728	53 201	2.1	43 779	19.9	31.4	28.9
Sterling	247	741	315	1.3	54.3	22.3	3.3	12 333	20 157	50 543	57 151	2.0	57 266	12.9	21.1	19.4
Stonewall	136	1 085	312	0.0	55.2	20.2	3.1	12 071	24 063	42 429	56 407	3.3	42 158	15.8	24.5	22.7
Sutton	229	356	1 125	1.0	53.2	17.9	11.8	12 664	27 721	53 806	75 644	6.5	59 098	13.0	18.5	18.7
Swisher	177	1 148	1 724	7.7	58.0	16.3	16.2	10 205	17 880	36 753	50 690	1.7	35 601	21.0	30.7	29.0
Tarrant	409	3 622	529 114	13.9	39.3	29.5	2 726.9	7 941	28 266	56 853	77 161	5.0	56 906	15.2	21.5	19.7
Taylor	365	3 622	38 154	26.4	43.4	24.4	196.8	8 489	23 141	44 891	59 514	2.2	44 081	17.0	24.9	22.6
Terrell	0	1 008	104	0.0	54.1	17.4	2.9	25 284	31 578	39 479	59 774	2.0	36 712	18.6	28.6	28.8
Terry	340	2 015	3 436	2.4	58.1	15.5	24.2	10 090	21 201	37 679	59 877	2.8	37 489	22.4	32.7	31.2
Throckmorton	125	1 252	289	10.7	50.0	19.8	3.7	11 879	24 086	39 286	51 575	2.1	41 582	15.1	23.7	20.5
Titus	216	2 719	9 207	5.3	54.8	13.8	57.3	8 005	19 356	42 939	57 624	1.8	40 501	20.8	32.8	32.8

1. Data for serious crimes have not been adjusted for underreporting; this may affect comparability between geographic areas and over time. 2. Per 100,000 population estimated by the FBI.
3. All persons 3 years old and over enrolled in nursery school through college. 4. Persons 25 years old and over. 5. Elementary and secondary education expenditures.
6. Based on population estimated by the American Community Survey, 2009–2013.

STATE County	Personal income, 2013: Total (mil dol)	Percent change, 2012–2013	Per capita[1]: Dollars	Per capita[1]: Rank	Wages and salaries (mil dol)	Supplements to wages and salaries; employer contributions (mil dol): Pension and insurance	Supplements: Government social insurance	Proprietors' income (mil dol)	Dividends, interest, and rent (mil dol)	Personal transfer receipts (mil dol)	Earnings, 2013: Total (mil dol)	Contributions for government social insurance (mil dol): From employee and self-employed	Contributions: From employer
	62	63	64	65	66	67	68	69	70	71	72	73	74
TEXAS—Cont'd													
Mason	155	3.2	37 500	1 508	38	8	2	22	44	38	70	4	2
Matagorda	1 296	3.0	35 426	1 834	520	100	34	109	215	315	765	40	34
Maverick	1 311	2.8	23 440	3 085	536	128	38	122	117	456	824	45	38
Medina	1 719	2.4	36 259	1 700	317	62	20	126	296	366	525	30	20
Menard	66	-0.8	30 524	2 624	13	3	1	4	16	22	21	2	1
Midland	13 314	5.1	87 897	11	5 566	664	363	5 028	1 752	810	11 620	498	363
Milam	912	1.8	37 727	1 474	264	41	17	116	148	249	439	25	17
Mills	188	3.7	38 274	1 404	44	9	3	18	52	53	74	4	3
Mitchell	291	5.6	30 950	2 561	97	22	6	49	53	69	174	8	6
Montague	976	4.9	50 047	366	236	38	15	163	186	196	452	24	15
Montgomery	26 550	3.0	53 192	264	7 991	1 021	534	2 264	4 305	2 768	11 810	623	534
Moore	795	-0.6	35 924	1 761	427	84	28	118	95	118	657	30	28
Morris	478	0.7	37 281	1 539	242	39	18	55	68	152	355	21	18
Motley	46	4.6	38 574	1 361	11	2	1	10	8	12	24	1	1
Nacogdoches	2 064	1.6	31 592	2 465	781	148	53	201	434	516	1 183	62	53
Navarro	1 777	2.6	36 985	1 589	610	113	43	178	332	460	944	52	43
Newton	425	-1.0	30 049	2 683	53	13	4	15	52	122	85	7	4
Nolan	572	2.9	38 072	1 424	240	43	16	61	115	149	361	19	16
Nueces	14 842	3.3	42 151	924	7 523	1 254	540	2 477	2 318	2 769	11 794	584	540
Ochiltree	591	2.9	54 671	212	284	36	18	162	79	51	500	22	18
Oldham	111	-2.1	52 776	276	38	6	3	33	22	12	80	2	3
Orange	3 313	-0.2	39 941	1 177	1 101	186	76	172	513	787	1 535	90	76
Palo Pinto	1 083	2.0	38 820	1 318	359	59	24	117	207	245	559	31	24
Panola	1 092	3.8	45 738	640	497	70	34	158	166	209	758	40	34
Parker	5 568	6.3	45 856	627	1 352	195	92	575	903	790	2 214	119	92
Parmer	384	-2.7	38 530	1 368	201	32	13	89	59	62	335	13	13
Pecos	498	0.4	31 723	2 444	263	46	16	41	72	103	366	18	16
Polk	1 908	1.7	41 659	979	403	74	27	119	541	656	623	47	27
Potter	4 345	2.3	35 712	1 797	3 339	560	241	1 130	648	962	5 269	253	241
Presidio	246	0.8	34 222	2 048	111	23	8	20	50	60	162	8	8
Rains	360	3.1	32 531	2 324	56	11	4	35	57	103	107	7	4
Randall	5 495	1.6	43 444	807	1 220	171	78	263	1 029	695	1 733	103	78
Reagan	172	5.3	47 777	496	117	17	8	33	21	20	174	8	8
Real	112	3.2	33 319	2 200	20	4	1	7	33	40	32	3	1
Red River	425	0.4	34 111	2 060	82	18	6	18	88	159	123	9	6
Reeves	358	3.3	25 630	3 033	150	32	9	25	54	99	215	11	9
Refugio	339	1.4	46 429	595	116	18	7	35	64	78	177	10	7
Roberts	45	1.3	53 953	237	8	2	0	3	10	5	13	1	0
Robertson	687	5.5	41 656	980	169	31	11	115	124	161	326	16	11
Rockwall	4 550	3.3	53 379	257	914	135	64	325	647	422	1 438	76	64
Runnels	356	5.7	34 548	1 976	104	21	7	52	67	103	185	10	7
Rusk	1 852	2.0	34 541	1 977	647	101	44	154	278	419	947	54	44
Sabine	356	-3.0	34 370	2 018	76	15	5	27	82	140	123	9	5
San Augustine	277	0.5	31 590	2 466	53	13	4	23	47	117	92	6	4
San Jacinto	925	0.4	34 441	2 000	79	17	5	41	126	243	141	12	5
San Patricio	2 748	2.2	41 545	987	961	171	71	133	417	570	1 336	73	71
San Saba	196	1.7	32 590	2 312	47	10	3	28	46	55	88	5	3
Schleicher	124	7.4	38 755	1 324	49	8	3	13	23	23	74	4	3
Scurry	980	10.4	56 643	170	479	61	29	227	152	127	796	38	29
Shackelford	294	6.8	87 115	12	99	13	6	132	33	29	250	10	6
Shelby	924	1.5	35 812	1 779	294	52	21	150	148	248	516	27	21
Sherman	150	-19.4	48 489	451	32	6	2	63	21	15	103	2	2
Smith	9 199	2.2	42 573	885	4 137	610	290	1 533	1 900	1 726	6 571	339	290
Somervell	361	2.3	41 667	977	221	45	14	33	63	65	312	16	14
Starr	1 289	2.8	20 811	3 105	436	122	30	104	124	522	692	38	30
Stephens	503	2.5	54 430	222	130	25	9	201	67	87	365	15	9
Sterling	69	6.7	56 435	179	28	5	2	4	29	9	39	2	2
Stonewall	76	2.8	53 240	260	21	5	1	8	24	18	35	2	1
Sutton	277	4.8	69 100	54	181	21	12	36	45	30	250	13	12
Swisher	266	-1.7	34 329	2 026	66	15	4	75	44	60	160	5	4
Tarrant	84 906	2.7	44 417	732	42 325	6 026	3 023	12 069	12 937	10 564	63 444	3 181	3 023
Taylor	5 606	2.8	41 800	959	2 547	446	190	710	1 235	1 069	3 893	196	190
Terrell	44	0.3	48 375	459	20	4	2	0	8	10	26	1	2
Terry	478	4.7	37 535	1 500	152	26	10	106	64	107	293	12	10
Throckmorton	83	-2.9	51 733	306	16	4	1	20	16	19	41	2	1
Titus	967	0.5	29 680	2 726	527	103	38	90	151	243	757	39	38

1. Based on the resident population estimated as of July 1 of the year shown.

STATE County	Earnings, 2013 (cont.) — Percent by selected industries: Farm	Mining	Construction	Manu-facturing	Infor-mation: professional, scientific, technical services	Retail trade	Finance, insur-ance, real estate and leasing	Health care and social assistance	Govern-ment	Social Security beneficiaries, December 2013: Number	Rate[1]	Supple-mental Security Income recipients, December 2013	Housing units, 2014: Total	Percent change, 2010–2014
	75	76	77	78	79	80	81	82	83	84	85	86	87	88
TEXAS—Cont'd														
Mason	0.1	D	6.7	2.7	D	4.7	9.6	5.2	18.3	1 140	275	83	2 747	0.5
Matagorda	5.2	4.8	7.8	2.6	4.7	5.5	3.7	6.3	16.3	7 105	194	1 156	19 013	1.1
Maverick	1.3	1.2	3.6	3.8	2.5	9.3	2.7	D	40.5	9 820	174	3 838	18 034	3.3
Medina	2.7	7.3	9.2	1.2	4.9	9.1	5.4	4.5	27.8	8 715	184	1 212	18 080	0.5
Menard	-8.4	D	13.8	D	D	10.2	8.4	3.3	39.5	650	303	65	1 702	0.0
Midland	0.0	54.9	3.9	4.4	5.2	3.3	3.7	3.2	4.8	18 615	123	2 271	57 999	6.7
Milam	4.9	3.4	16.6	13.2	2.4	5.4	4.4	10.4	13.8	5 795	240	854	11 374	0.6
Mills	2.5	0.2	7.0	4.3	D	15.1	5.4	13.2	21.2	1 335	273	126	2 849	0.1
Mitchell	13.9	19.3	D	D	D	6.3	D	3.2	34.4	1 535	171	224	4 049	-0.4
Montague	-0.9	40.3	7.3	4.5	4.5	6.0	5.1	D	13.8	5 160	266	442	10 154	0.2
Montgomery	0.1	13.8	9.7	8.8	10.6	7.3	6.1	8.3	11.6	71 920	144	7 416	195 381	10.0
Moore	8.3	5.4	D	D	D	5.3	2.1	D	13.6	2 555	115	308	7 983	1.3
Morris	1.0	D	2.1	51.7	13.2	2.5	D	2.5	8.8	3 690	289	544	6 020	-0.1
Motley	35.8	0.0	5.0	6.0	D	6.7	D	D	20.5	350	293	30	779	0.0
Nacogdoches	1.9	1.2	9.1	12.5	3.7	8.7	5.4	13.0	25.5	11 120	171	2 008	27 960	2.0
Navarro	0.9	3.3	11.5	18.0	2.8	7.0	4.9	10.5	19.2	10 355	215	1 735	20 459	1.1
Newton	-3.4	1.9	5.9	9.6	D	7.0	D	12.0	32.2	2 820	198	601	7 157	0.2
Nolan	2.4	11.3	6.8	13.4	3.4	8.3	3.7	D	23.2	3 215	213	548	7 112	-0.6
Nueces	1.0	14.0	11.4	7.2	6.1	5.7	4.4	12.1	16.8	58 175	165	13 275	145 670	3.3
Ochiltree	6.6	50.3	7.2	0.7	3.0	4.1	2.1	1.2	7.6	1 315	123	121	4 057	-0.1
Oldham	45.4	D	D	D	D	1.2	D	D	19.1	385	183	28	846	0.6
Orange	1.7	3.1	9.7	32.8	3.7	7.7	4.1	4.8	14.7	18 100	218	2 548	36 080	2.2
Palo Pinto	0.0	16.1	5.7	21.9	D	7.5	3.7	3.8	17.2	6 200	222	768	15 311	0.6
Panola	0.8	22.7	20.4	5.6	3.9	4.8	2.6	D	9.7	5 035	211	689	10 972	0.5
Parker	0.4	15.2	11.9	7.9	5.9	8.8	4.7	7.8	12.4	21 435	178	1 529	47 807	2.5
Parmer	31.0	D	D	D	D	2.1	D	D	11.8	1 470	147	142	3 785	-0.4
Pecos	2.9	23.1	6.4	0.4	1.0	6.8	3.8	2.9	28.8	2 305	147	412	5 596	0.2
Polk	0.3	1.7	7.9	11.6	5.0	11.5	4.2	9.0	23.5	18 785	410	1 718	23 934	5.5
Potter	0.1	4.7	5.9	9.3	8.3	7.1	6.8	15.1	17.5	18 565	152	3 313	49 045	3.8
Presidio	20.3	D	D	D	D	4.6	1.7	D	46.0	1 730	238	708	3 824	0.0
Rains	1.9	D	16.3	4.7	D	10.8	D	D	20.3	2 950	268	264	5 285	0.3
Randall	3.6	1.2	9.1	5.6	6.4	10.7	4.8	8.4	12.7	19 580	155	1 182	53 497	3.7
Reagan	6.2	38.6	D	D	0.8	1.6	D	0.3	10.7	465	128	52	1 379	0.5
Real	1.2	D	10.6	4.0	D	8.7	D	11.8	26.6	1 170	351	144	2 597	-0.1
Red River	0.9	5.2	11.6	9.4	D	5.4	6.3	15.5	26.0	3 615	289	540	6 855	0.4
Reeves	2.3	15.4	2.1	0.2	1.8	8.3	2.8	3.2	40.6	2 240	159	488	4 624	-0.3
Refugio	5.5	33.7	9.6	0.1	D	4.9	8.7	D	19.8	1 840	253	238	3 718	-0.2
Roberts	13.3	D	D	0.0	D	D	D	0.0	35.2	175	190	0	439	0.0
Robertson	4.3	28.8	12.8	1.7	D	5.0	3.2	3.7	15.9	3 650	222	686	8 541	0.7
Rockwall	-0.3	0.8	10.4	6.6	9.6	10.7	6.6	17.2	13.8	11 685	137	717	30 626	9.6
Runnels	11.8	5.5	7.1	18.8	D	5.6	3.5	6.8	20.9	2 600	252	332	5 272	-0.5
Rusk	1.0	21.8	11.7	7.6	D	5.6	3.9	6.2	12.5	9 970	185	1 374	21 366	0.8
Sabine	1.8	10.6	7.7	16.8	D	7.6	3.9	D	19.1	3 645	351	360	8 009	0.3
San Augustine	8.7	D	6.5	2.7	D	7.7	3.2	13.9	22.8	2 570	294	441	5 348	0.1
San Jacinto	-1.6	1.7	10.7	4.9	7.7	6.2	4.4	4.2	29.8	5 990	223	933	13 138	-0.3
San Patricio	2.5	7.6	19.7	13.7	4.3	5.7	2.1	4.5	25.2	12 930	195	2 371	27 016	1.9
San Saba	2.1	D	4.4	3.9	D	9.0	D	4.8	27.3	1 445	253	161	3 168	-0.3
Schleicher	6.9	29.3	D	D	D	1.6	D	4.2	16.7	545	170	64	1 492	0.2
Scurry	3.1	51.0	4.0	1.6	2.3	3.7	1.8	D	11.3	2 975	172	345	7 199	3.4
Shackelford	1.3	78.8	D	D	D	1.3	D	D	4.5	695	206	64	1 755	0.1
Shelby	4.9	10.5	10.8	19.6	4.0	7.7	3.9	5.3	13.4	5 490	212	1 022	11 924	0.4
Sherman	59.4	D	D	D	D	2.3	D	1.4	13.1	355	115	19	1 282	2.4
Smith	0.2	14.5	4.7	6.3	8.0	8.5	5.5	21.3	11.6	42 045	194	5 406	88 440	1.3
Somervell	0.2	D	5.1	0.8	D	2.5	D	D	14.9	1 630	189	126	3 714	1.1
Starr	0.7	3.4	4.5	0.4	1.4	9.2	2.0	D	45.6	9 540	153	5 073	19 625	0.5
Stephens	0.0	58.3	6.6	5.3	2.1	2.9	4.2	3.6	9.7	2 105	225	244	4 926	-0.2
Sterling	-0.4	47.8	D	D	2.0	2.5	D	D	17.0	245	199	28	615	0.0
Stonewall	5.0	19.6	D	D	D	4.3	D	D	31.3	390	273	19	928	0.0
Sutton	-1.3	41.3	6.4	3.2	D	2.1	D	D	9.5	705	176	71	2 023	-0.4
Swisher	42.4	D	1.7	2.6	D	4.8	2.4	D	22.6	1 605	207	165	3 207	-0.4
Tarrant	0.0	6.6	6.7	12.6	8.3	6.1	8.3	9.7	11.8	238 805	125	35 947	739 329	3.4
Taylor	0.0	9.4	6.7	3.2	6.2	6.9	7.1	14.3	22.6	23 935	179	3 799	56 716	1.7
Terrell	2.9	D	D	0.0	D	3.1	D	D	54.0	230	254	22	700	0.0
Terry	25.1	14.8	2.3	2.9	D	12.8	D	D	18.8	2 205	173	390	4 860	0.7
Throckmorton	10.0	41.4	D	D	D	1.3	D	5.3	18.5	425	266	29	1 079	0.0
Titus	0.8	3.9	4.6	29.5	2.0	9.2	4.1	6.8	19.8	5 155	158	775	12 071	0.1

1. Per 1,000 resident population estimated as of July 1 of the year shown.

STATE County	Housing units, 2009–2013: Occupied units: Total	Owner-occupied: Percent	Owner-occupied: Median value[1]	Median owner cost as a percent of income: With a mortgage	Median owner cost as a percent of income: Without a mortgage[2]	Renter-occupied: Median rent[3]	Renter-occupied: Median rent as a percent of income[2]	Substandard units[4] (percent)	Civilian labor force, 2014: Total	Civilian labor force, 2014: Percent change, 2013–2014	Unemployment: Total	Unemployment: Rate[5]	Civilian employment,[6] 2009–2013: Total	Percent: Management, business, science and arts	Percent: Construction, production, and maintenance occupations
	89	90	91	92	93	94	95	96	97	98	99	100	101	102	103
TEXAS—Cont'd															
Mason	1 699	83.0	170 100	18.8	12.9	363	27.4	4.7	1 940	-1.3	90	4.6	1 841	33.7	27.3
Matagorda	13 260	70.2	92 000	19.0	11.5	658	27.4	15.2	16 892	-0.1	1 320	7.8	15 845	23.1	36.1
Maverick	15 714	71.1	86 300	27.6	13.8	546	30.2	5.5	23 520	-0.9	2 560	10.9	19 497	21.6	27.2
Medina	15 284	78.1	112 900	20.3	11.7	672	26.5	2.9	20 742	1.7	1 001	4.8	18 731	32.6	24.9
Menard	871	72.1	56 400	28.3	13.1	540	31.8	4.4	901	-2.4	42	4.7	844	20.5	23.2
Midland	50 644	67.7	148 600	20.1	10.0	950	26.8	3.1	91 588	6.0	2 601	2.8	70 837	32.1	26.4
Milam	9 330	68.4	78 400	22.4	12.4	670	28.1	1.9	10 244	1.0	632	6.2	9 459	27.5	29.7
Mills	1 817	80.1	104 100	25.0	11.1	491	19.7	0.5	2 064	-0.7	91	4.4	1 899	34.2	29.1
Mitchell	2 748	74.6	45 800	19.7	10.6	553	19.4	3.2	2 923	1.2	131	4.5	2 836	26.8	35.3
Montague	8 038	75.6	86 000	22.0	12.6	652	32.0	4.8	10 406	0.0	408	3.9	8 211	31.1	33.7
Montgomery	163 462	72.9	166 200	22.0	11.6	965	28.1	8.8	252 448	2.1	11 032	4.4	217 925	37.3	22.3
Moore	6 820	72.8	85 600	18.6	10.0	627	22.2	4.0	11 395	-0.8	398	3.5	10 577	21.2	42.5
Morris	4 949	74.2	69 900	20.5	11.6	575	26.8	5.3	5 676	-3.1	435	7.7	4 768	29.7	31.8
Motley	433	66.3	59 800	20.4	13.7	529	35.0	4.8	492	-2.4	22	4.5	442	40.7	28.5
Nacogdoches	23 586	58.1	101 700	20.9	10.9	684	32.0	5.6	28 817	-1.7	1 550	5.4	27 325	32.0	26.6
Navarro	17 466	67.8	79 500	23.5	13.0	697	29.6	3.0	23 435	-0.2	1 228	5.2	20 191	24.6	33.5
Newton	4 865	76.8	77 500	24.0	10.0	522	24.8	2.6	5 621	0.0	460	8.2	5 192	23.8	32.8
Nolan	5 527	69.7	52 200	18.7	11.5	522	24.4	4.9	7 122	1.8	306	4.3	6 473	25.4	28.6
Nueces	123 915	58.6	110 300	23.0	12.5	840	30.3	6.6	170 802	1.1	8 582	5.0	154 603	28.9	25.0
Ochiltree	3 736	70.0	80 100	16.2	10.0	679	21.6	1.5	5 645	3.6	170	3.0	4 708	21.2	42.2
Oldham	748	72.6	83 700	23.2	10.2	635	34.6	2.7	971	0.7	36	3.7	864	39.1	22.9
Orange	31 162	76.0	91 900	20.1	10.0	722	25.9	4.6	38 114	0.1	3 029	7.9	34 797	27.9	32.8
Palo Pinto	10 491	71.6	85 200	21.4	12.5	735	31.1	3.8	13 450	0.1	687	5.1	11 782	28.4	33.0
Panola	8 873	81.4	83 900	18.8	10.0	653	22.2	3.3	12 939	1.2	620	4.8	10 004	24.2	39.3
Parker	42 322	79.2	152 900	21.0	12.2	883	27.8	5.2	59 755	1.4	2 708	4.5	53 613	36.2	25.3
Parmer	3 215	71.2	86 400	23.1	10.0	617	20.2	3.2	5 161	1.4	161	3.1	4 702	23.0	42.3
Pecos	4 588	65.4	64 300	15.8	10.0	607	22.7	6.2	6 870	2.1	286	4.2	6 308	21.6	34.3
Polk	16 980	79.6	78 600	23.0	12.1	640	29.8	5.9	17 343	-0.5	1 117	6.4	15 149	25.3	30.0
Potter	42 751	58.5	85 900	22.4	11.4	688	30.7	7.1	57 734	0.0	2 278	3.9	53 895	25.1	29.6
Presidio	2 616	71.9	48 500	18.8	10.9	348	20.9	2.6	3 466	-8.0	402	11.6	2 765	28.9	22.7
Rains	4 232	81.4	96 300	21.6	13.4	664	26.6	2.7	5 470	2.1	270	4.9	4 511	27.2	31.2
Randall	48 080	69.1	141 900	19.9	11.0	769	28.4	5.6	68 926	0.2	2 371	3.4	62 760	37.0	18.7
Reagan	1 178	72.5	66 200	15.3	10.1	707	14.2	2.0	2 052	4.4	64	3.1	1 670	24.7	46.9
Real	1 127	76.8	102 200	23.8	13.3	761	28.2	2.6	1 066	0.4	64	6.0	974	37.8	27.8
Red River	5 052	70.8	69 200	19.6	13.7	526	28.3	5.6	4 966	-3.7	388	7.8	4 641	25.5	36.5
Reeves	3 542	75.0	40 100	17.2	11.5	546	24.5	4.6	5 823	2.7	239	4.1	4 799	23.6	26.2
Refugio	2 818	77.6	66 300	18.6	11.1	544	27.7	1.1	3 648	2.0	157	4.3	3 150	23.8	28.4
Roberts	374	90.1	104 600	17.0	10.0	729	16.7	4.4	443	-1.8	15	3.4	501	39.1	20.0
Robertson	5 851	71.2	77 400	20.7	11.7	572	32.6	3.0	7 356	0.7	385	5.2	6 608	28.7	28.0
Rockwall	26 820	83.6	187 800	22.9	13.3	1 219	26.2	1.6	43 404	2.3	1 935	4.5	38 354	44.9	16.7
Runnels	3 818	73.3	59 100	18.9	12.6	519	23.8	3.5	5 070	1.4	210	4.1	4 343	28.2	32.0
Rusk	17 772	76.0	93 000	18.6	10.4	649	25.2	3.6	24 468	0.3	1 198	4.9	21 720	26.4	34.9
Sabine	4 161	87.2	69 300	21.7	12.8	521	31.0	2.0	3 599	0.8	378	10.5	3 036	26.0	37.8
San Augustine	3 275	77.7	68 100	20.2	13.5	474	31.0	3.7	2 844	-3.4	274	9.6	2 566	22.3	39.1
San Jacinto	9 425	83.0	88 200	23.9	10.8	685	25.6	7.5	11 478	-0.1	661	5.8	9 792	26.1	36.5
San Patricio	22 147	68.6	89 800	21.3	12.3	788	28.1	2.7	31 155	1.2	1 926	6.2	27 964	28.3	28.0
San Saba	2 035	79.4	71 300	21.0	11.1	436	32.4	7.4	2 256	-1.2	104	4.6	2 363	25.2	36.4
Schleicher	1 078	73.8	86 400	17.2	10.0	500	19.4	5.6	1 802	-0.4	54	3.0	1 486	30.0	30.6
Scurry	5 846	71.9	87 200	18.5	10.4	688	27.1	3.0	8 659	0.7	290	3.3	7 214	25.6	34.2
Shackelford	1 445	75.1	66 200	20.6	12.7	532	21.9	3.6	2 443	5.9	67	2.7	1 551	35.7	25.7
Shelby	9 781	71.7	72 000	20.1	10.9	568	28.8	5.3	11 678	0.1	680	5.8	10 666	23.8	40.6
Sherman	949	80.2	81 900	19.7	10.6	633	19.7	4.7	1 520	2.3	49	3.2	1 358	31.3	36.9
Smith	78 459	67.0	120 800	22.1	12.0	828	31.0	3.7	102 952	0.9	5 330	5.2	94 807	33.5	23.0
Somervell	3 193	73.8	139 900	19.8	13.4	773	26.0	13.8	4 221	1.4	212	5.0	3 815	40.8	29.0
Starr	15 949	78.3	62 900	27.1	13.9	484	35.8	1.9	26 234	-0.7	3 544	13.5	20 273	20.5	27.3
Stephens	3 509	75.1	72 400	23.6	13.2	577	27.2	6.8	4 313	2.1	186	4.3	3 682	27.6	33.5
Sterling	458	66.2	71 900	18.2	10.1	602	38.3	3.3	805	6.6	22	2.7	650	30.8	36.8
Stonewall	578	78.7	49 900	21.0	10.3	335	34.2	3.3	717	1.0	28	3.9	557	37.9	26.6
Sutton	1 445	65.1	80 700	25.3	10.2	651	14.6	4.0	2 076	0.1	73	3.5	1 812	22.0	47.8
Swisher	2 604	73.1	62 600	17.9	13.1	586	33.4	4.5	2 909	-2.2	179	6.2	2 856	28.1	29.9
Tarrant	659 736	61.7	136 400	22.6	12.5	881	29.7	2.7	998 520	1.4	49 734	5.0	886 038	35.8	21.8
Taylor	49 304	60.8	95 800	20.2	11.7	755	30.0	0.0	65 174	0.4	2 739	4.2	59 530	30.6	20.6
Terrell	403	72.2	57 000	13.0	11.1	704	13.8	4.3	506	-3.8	21	4.2	379	22.7	28.2
Terry	4 067	72.2	64 900	17.6	11.0	573	31.7	4.5	5 608	1.0	245	4.4	4 809	36.2	26.5
Throckmorton	758	72.7	57 500	18.5	12.7	444	30.4	11.1	838	5.0	33	3.9	750	27.9	30.9
Titus	10 725	71.8	91 600	21.0	11.2	608	26.3	3.8	13 075	-0.3	822	6.3	13 571	22.3	42.1

1. Specified owner-occupied units. 2. A value of 10.0 represents 10 percent or less; a value of 50.0 represents 50 percent or more. 3. Specified renter-occupied units.
4. Overcrowded or lacking complete plumbing facilities. 5. Percent of civilian labor force. 6. Persons 16 years old and over.

STATE County	Private nonfarm establishments, employment and payroll, 2013									Agriculture, 2012			
		Employment						Annual payroll		Farms			
											Percent with:		
	Number of establish-ments	Total	Health care and social assistance	Manufac-turing	Retail trade	Finance and insurance	Professional, scientific, and technical services	Total (mil dol)	Average per employee (dollars)	Number	Fewer than 50 acres	500 acres or more	Farm operators whose principal occu-pation is farming (percent)
	104	105	106	107	108	109	110	111	112	113	114	115	116
TEXAS—Cont'd													
Mason	134	828	145	45	138	45	D	23	28 175	640	11.1	43.4	48.9
Matagorda	730	7 902	1 366	589	1 345	234	144	388	49 046	856	28.5	27.9	47.7
Maverick	771	11 360	3 527	579	2 521	368	D	274	24 092	294	53.4	20.4	34.4
Medina	687	6 548	953	D	1 203	D	D	196	30 009	1 976	31.9	15.9	50.2
Menard	39	D	D	D	48	D	D	4	D	325	14.5	45.2	48.6
Midland	4 977	79 755	6 856	3 129	8 842	2 051	4 545	4 786	60 014	540	47.6	19.8	24.3
Milam	398	4 168	1 010	202	643	D	136	156	37 328	1 909	32.6	12.2	44.9
Mills	109	876	172	81	210	54	D	23	26 083	870	20.3	26.0	43.1
Mitchell	143	1 601	D	D	311	54	D	60	37 630	482	12.2	25.9	32.2
Montague	420	4 722	689	319	681	183	127	172	36 457	1 454	26.2	15.3	39.8
Montgomery	9 945	136 265	15 615	10 678	22 312	4 826	9 260	7 410	54 379	1 601	63.1	3.7	30.7
Moore	460	8 332	D	4 007	813	164	93	324	38 944	261	10.0	58.2	64.8
Morris	235	4 183	220	D	303	129	92	200	47 837	412	34.7	8.7	50.0
Motley	27	130	D	D	D	D	D	3	21 469	224	3.6	53.1	39.3
Nacogdoches	1 301	17 763	3 217	3 518	2 867	560	452	532	29 934	1 196	28.6	7.6	43.0
Navarro	940	13 346	2 568	2 802	2 079	404	291	444	33 296	2 573	41.0	9.2	47.6
Newton	130	1 115	325	68	199	34	D	30	26 690	450	57.8	2.2	31.3
Nolan	339	4 277	606	896	738	143	77	150	35 154	478	15.1	32.4	39.7
Nueces	7 868	133 037	26 451	7 493	17 943	3 992	5 588	5 407	40 642	754	43.4	21.1	36.3
Ochiltree	374	4 176	D	46	386	145	213	235	56 239	348	8.3	54.3	51.1
Oldham	38	505	D	D	NA	D	D	17	32 735	159	7.5	64.8	46.5
Orange	1 361	19 530	1 434	5 357	3 204	550	515	885	45 312	671	79.7	3.9	43.7
Palo Pinto	627	6 702	849	1 435	1 070	164	269	231	34 522	1 329	42.2	15.6	32.7
Panola	487	7 664	672	883	872	180	215	360	47 021	1 079	34.6	10.1	43.4
Parker	2 379	26 889	2 886	2 329	5 005	642	909	1 030	38 296	4 370	66.1	3.5	35.3
Parmer	207	3 383	D	D	162	86	D	129	38 080	570	8.6	47.9	59.3
Pecos	337	4 625	475	13	721	150	D	231	49 839	291	13.1	67.7	45.0
Polk	712	8 333	1 389	D	1 750	343	246	267	32 088	738	40.2	8.5	48.6
Potter	3 630	60 849	12 608	D	8 995	4 256	2 026	2 308	37 926	258	35.3	31.4	38.0
Presidio	130	1 000	D	D	208	68	D	28	27 713	162	8.6	63.6	45.1
Rains	158	1 310	127	D	411	D	D	33	25 072	682	47.5	7.9	44.7
Randall	2 397	32 194	4 041	1 347	5 368	1 199	782	1 207	37 477	892	30.5	27.4	36.4
Reagan	115	1 313	D	D	66	D	D	70	53 113	135	5.2	71.9	51.1
Real	78	541	178	D	55	D	D	14	25 566	241	19.9	40.7	44.4
Red River	169	1 375	350	284	250	87	27	41	29 973	1 139	22.3	17.1	45.7
Reeves	214	2 337	D	D	418	25	43	91	38 799	240	11.7	51.7	43.3
Refugio	150	1 744	268	D	298	D	D	86	49 538	259	31.3	35.9	43.2
Roberts	14	D	NA	NA	NA	NA	D	5	D	107	2.8	73.8	58.9
Robertson	278	2 740	358	D	363	86	38	135	49 336	1 520	28.7	12.0	49.5
Rockwall	1 885	20 809	3 537	1 245	4 229	616	1 155	698	33 554	440	71.8	6.4	35.7
Runnels	231	2 355	D	555	468	132	29	71	30 248	925	12.4	29.6	45.8
Rusk	834	12 017	1 513	D	1 433	D	845	506	42 138	1 390	30.9	7.8	35.1
Sabine	171	1 310	310	D	337	72	D	45	34 431	201	36.3	4.5	46.8
San Augustine	129	1 165	387	D	239	D	8	34	29 308	305	23.3	9.8	52.5
San Jacinto	196	1 014	123	108	229	D	D	32	31 840	791	48.5	2.8	44.6
San Patricio	1 044	15 936	1 755	D	2 474	D	506	683	42 854	701	47.9	21.8	41.8
San Saba	147	804	177	45	208	24	36	20	24 641	744	19.9	33.7	48.8
Schleicher	54	508	D	D	56	24	D	22	42 746	310	10.6	60.6	44.8
Scurry	434	5 743	485	100	777	126	155	301	52 471	677	16.4	32.9	39.0
Shackelford	129	1 445	D	184	86	D	10	86	59 683	233	7.7	47.6	43.3
Shelby	523	7 005	751	2 150	1 017	441	D	225	32 181	1 048	26.4	8.3	53.3
Sherman	61	449	D	D	D	31	D	23	50 871	313	5.8	59.1	48.6
Smith	5 668	89 369	21 520	7 284	12 210	4 973	4 261	3 505	39 222	2 961	54.8	3.0	45.3
Somervell	195	3 482	499	D	212	D	D	176	50 580	350	38.6	14.0	37.7
Starr	557	9 955	5 691	D	1 843	D	121	181	18 221	1 165	16.8	26.3	39.5
Stephens	255	2 276	325	361	337	104	D	88	38 666	452	7.3	40.9	30.3
Sterling	46	406	D	D	D	D	D	25	61 020	73	4.1	80.8	56.2
Stonewall	48	426	D	NA	D	D	D	16	38 451	356	5.3	45.5	34.0
Sutton	139	1 268	D	D	153	D	26	53	41 838	218	6.9	71.1	54.1
Swisher	148	1 043	D	100	143	55	D	28	26 781	565	9.6	46.5	54.2
Tarrant	38 782	729 252	91 321	77 330	96 177	41 210	39 268	33 070	45 348	1 278	74.0	3.0	28.7
Taylor	3 370	50 910	11 544	2 368	8 280	2 753	1 921	1 779	33 006	1 149	29.8	19.1	38.7
Terrell	16	74	D	NA	D	D	D	3	43 257	86	0.0	86.0	57.0
Terry	235	2 423	444	D	458	100	D	86	35 440	630	11.4	37.5	55.7
Throckmorton	49	270	119	D	D	D	D	7	27 193	275	5.5	49.1	49.1
Titus	634	13 703	2 131	5 634	1 807	439	146	434	31 665	801	35.8	5.7	37.5

STATE County	Agriculture, 2012 (cont.) Land in farms Acreage (1,000)	Land in farms Percent change, 2007–2012	Land in farms Acres Average size of farm	Land in farms Acres Total irrigated (1,000)	Land in farms Acres Total cropland (1,000)	Value of land and buildings (dollars) Average per farm	Value of land and buildings (dollars) Average per acre	Value of machinery and equipment, average per farm (dollars)	Value of products sold Total (mil dol)	Value of products sold Average per farm (dollars)	Value of products sold Percent from: Crops	Value of products sold Percent from: Livestock and poultry products	Percent of farms with sales of: $10,000 or more	Percent of farms with sales of: $100,000 or more	Government payments Total ($1,000)	Government payments Percent of farms
	117	118	119	120	121	122	123	124	125	126	127	128	129	130	131	132
TEXAS—Cont'd																
Mason	551	2.8	861	3.0	28.9	2 039 833	2 368	59 491	51.4	80 389	9.7	90.3	43.8	8.4	1 749	32.5
Matagorda	568	-1.7	664	32.7	177.0	1 315 683	1 983	126 209	129.7	151 522	59.4	40.6	48.7	16.2	5 271	34.6
Maverick	541	14.2	1 840	13.0	13.8	2 169 796	1 179	59 840	32.6	110 912	8.0	92.0	24.1	8.5	410	7.5
Medina	834	11.4	422	51.4	141.4	1 095 775	2 598	66 329	115.5	58 461	56.2	43.8	28.5	7.2	3 298	19.4
Menard	537	9.2	1 651	1.5	20.7	2 408 895	1 459	54 991	9.6	29 646	13.0	87.0	42.8	7.1	1 249	30.8
Midland	404	-11.4	749	10.7	62.4	1 072 641	1 432	83 080	17.2	31 876	65.7	34.3	17.6	5.0	1 866	23.5
Milam	528	-2.0	277	2.5	143.0	990 114	3 581	65 371	144.7	75 814	26.6	73.4	33.1	7.2	3 451	22.0
Mills	471	-0.6	542	3.3	57.5	1 204 675	2 223	58 645	43.0	49 462	12.6	87.4	40.9	4.8	1 277	22.2
Mitchell	573	-0.3	1 189	4.2	146.7	938 568	789	84 627	21.2	43 956	61.0	39.0	24.1	8.7	7 078	77.8
Montague	489	-3.7	336	0.6	74.0	840 349	2 500	59 290	44.9	30 902	18.7	81.3	32.9	5.7	1 034	14.4
Montgomery	155	-8.6	97	1.2	31.6	573 034	5 905	48 231	23.8	14 888	48.2	51.8	18.4	2.4	227	3.4
Moore	524	-5.4	2 006	122.4	263.6	1 884 521	939	303 854	605.0	2 318 107	19.4	80.6	57.1	39.8	6 010	68.6
Morris	92	7.2	223	0.0	18.1	468 248	2 100	55 663	46.9	113 922	4.9	95.1	41.3	10.4	99	9.2
Motley	595	3.6	2 658	4.2	65.8	1 960 781	738	69 571	12.8	57 143	24.5	75.5	42.0	15.2	1 767	74.6
Nacogdoches	265	-0.1	221	0.3	43.7	558 234	2 521	73 452	322.4	269 544	1.8	98.2	37.0	11.8	595	7.3
Navarro	558	-4.9	217	0.9	146.1	445 243	2 053	57 970	66.4	25 798	47.3	52.7	27.4	3.5	2 633	13.6
Newton	59	-0.8	131	0.0	8.9	261 813	2 004	54 300	2.9	6 551	35.4	64.7	17.1	0.7	D	0.7
Nolan	465	-13.9	973	3.3	118.2	1 093 607	1 124	81 916	23.8	49 847	52.0	48.0	26.2	7.5	3 074	57.3
Nueces	524	2.9	695	0.4	362.6	1 076 476	1 549	160 967	84.9	112 557	92.2	7.8	33.2	12.9	5 340	34.7
Ochiltree	545	-6.0	1 565	48.2	304.6	1 566 761	1 001	223 842	424.6	1 220 129	14.6	85.4	59.2	33.0	6 098	77.3
Oldham	830	-5.7	5 223	3.4	94.8	3 082 126	590	134 522	113.0	710 415	2.4	97.6	45.9	27.0	2 473	81.8
Orange	53	-17.2	79	0.4	6.7	261 493	3 323	47 335	4.3	6 461	44.2	55.8	11.3	0.9	112	1.5
Palo Pinto	593	7.6	446	0.7	55.4	1 074 703	2 407	51 951	53.8	40 472	18.4	81.6	24.8	4.0	489	6.5
Panola	227	4.4	211	0.7	38.6	442 762	2 101	66 066	93.3	86 466	6.0	94.0	34.5	5.8	156	4.7
Parker	494	12.0	113	2.2	93.9	567 100	5 012	49 848	74.3	17 000	20.8	79.2	17.3	2.5	294	2.4
Parmer	554	-1.3	971	163.0	444.7	1 010 667	1 040	277 575	1 329.5	2 332 523	9.9	90.1	59.3	42.1	11 381	83.3
Pecos	2 948	1.4	10 130	13.9	63.7	5 133 601	507	136 553	47.5	163 127	58.1	41.9	47.1	17.5	2 077	33.3
Polk	139	5.7	189	0.4	23.2	515 232	2 732	57 919	7.8	10 618	30.7	69.3	25.2	1.5	106	2.4
Potter	569	-0.8	2 204	3.1	54.2	1 208 547	548	66 465	21.0	81 287	7.7	92.3	29.5	12.0	1 092	22.1
Presidio	1 656	6.1	10 219	0.6	24.5	4 712 426	461	101 093	D	D	D	D	34.6	13.6	555	21.6
Rains	117	19.7	171	0.2	34.3	432 129	2 522	43 035	15.3	22 361	31.2	68.8	26.5	4.7	329	6.5
Randall	571	-0.7	640	15.9	250.8	642 873	1 004	77 600	540.3	605 734	2.9	97.1	29.8	10.0	5 003	42.9
Reagan	699	2.2	5 174	12.1	46.7	2 516 941	486	233 267	11.1	82 259	64.3	35.7	50.4	22.2	1 681	63.0
Real	321	-13.9	1 330	0.5	5.5	1 966 274	1 478	38 465	1.6	6 842	12.2	87.8	14.5	0.4	270	15.8
Red River	449	-0.2	394	2.8	94.7	654 453	1 662	73 917	53.5	46 997	26.5	73.5	42.0	7.5	1 949	18.9
Reeves	1 236	18.8	5 149	10.6	98.2	1 384 817	269	85 475	54.2	225 858	20.0	80.0	33.8	15.4	2 698	58.3
Refugio	475	-3.2	1 833	1.2	86.5	1 673 463	913	151 490	43.0	166 201	76.1	23.9	46.3	18.1	1 669	33.6
Roberts	562	15.9	5 257	6.3	49.3	3 455 290	657	143 140	16.4	153 271	31.5	68.5	57.0	31.8	1 122	57.9
Robertson	468	2.7	308	19.7	107.9	736 551	2 394	70 166	136.4	89 766	24.3	75.7	37.0	6.3	2 945	13.7
Rockwall	45	21.3	103	0.1	14.1	602 114	5 836	38 743	4.1	9 348	48.8	51.2	14.3	1.1	63	2.7
Runnels	666	1.5	720	4.5	247.9	931 382	1 294	89 466	47.4	51 272	62.3	37.7	42.8	10.9	6 002	68.8
Rusk	274	-8.8	197	0.4	47.5	431 437	2 186	58 886	75.3	54 175	25.6	74.4	24.7	3.3	295	2.4
Sabine	29	-8.5	144	0.2	4.6	392 557	2 718	84 005	14.7	73 274	3.8	96.2	31.3	3.0	22	9.0
San Augustine	73	0.3	239	0.0	8.9	552 167	2 310	122 351	63.2	207 262	2.0	98.0	42.6	11.1	25	6.2
San Jacinto	112	17.2	141	0.5	24.3	400 991	2 835	54 541	8.5	10 783	27.9	72.1	19.3	1.4	110	1.6
San Patricio	374	1.2	534	5.6	247.7	852 438	1 597	189 071	86.2	122 989	79.2	20.8	32.5	14.6	3 794	36.9
San Saba	671	-6.5	902	3.6	53.2	2 198 733	2 438	66 862	30.0	40 351	31.1	68.9	43.1	8.9	1 166	18.8
Schleicher	834	4.1	2 689	1.4	32.5	2 490 152	926	79 410	13.6	43 903	20.6	79.4	46.1	10.6	2 325	46.8
Scurry	494	-4.8	730	3.7	206.4	620 700	850	98 991	29.0	42 876	44.9	55.1	23.3	7.4	4 295	69.3
Shackelford	505	-8.5	2 168	D	55.0	2 371 000	1 093	83 609	22.3	95 854	11.6	88.4	54.5	15.9	1 604	53.2
Shelby	197	-0.3	188	1.8	36.4	550 712	2 927	92 111	473.3	451 610	2.1	97.9	46.6	21.6	334	3.9
Sherman	583	-0.2	1 863	126.6	339.1	2 006 652	1 077	378 847	590.4	1 886 121	21.9	78.1	46.3	37.7	6 153	83.1
Smith	302	0.0	102	2.5	77.1	386 589	3 786	43 300	76.8	25 934	77.5	22.5	18.6	2.6	189	1.8
Somervell	91	10.6	261	0.1	12.3	1 016 549	3 894	47 343	4.3	12 294	27.5	72.5	22.0	2.3	42	5.4
Starr	669	2.4	574	8.6	131.3	1 015 723	1 770	66 303	108.5	93 173	25.0	75.0	23.5	4.4	4 099	40.3
Stephens	517	20.4	1 143	D	54.4	1 599 708	1 399	58 681	9.2	20 392	11.6	88.4	37.6	3.1	777	30.3
Sterling	585	1.2	8 015	0.6	12.7	4 225 370	527	140 699	D	D	D	D	71.2	27.4	712	39.7
Stonewall	473	-2.6	1 328	0.7	79.5	955 171	719	52 202	47.4	133 275	5.3	94.7	35.4	6.2	2 288	80.9
Sutton	911	1.8	4 179	1.3	11.0	3 946 307	944	77 894	10.9	49 872	4.6	95.5	45.9	15.1	1 066	26.6
Swisher	546	-3.1	966	65.3	351.1	888 986	921	164 150	586.8	1 038 602	7.6	92.4	45.7	21.2	10 082	86.9
Tarrant	146	-5.6	114	0.9	38.0	722 473	6 339	54 282	34.6	27 076	72.8	27.2	18.0	4.1	109	2.8
Taylor	579	-0.1	504	1.1	158.9	570 210	1 132	55 372	37.6	32 746	27.7	72.3	23.8	4.1	3 600	37.7
Terrell	1 101	-15.5	12 800	0.3	2.0	4 976 860	389	57 116	3.1	35 686	D	D	39.5	9.3	507	22.1
Terry	442	-11.0	702	98.2	377.0	799 537	1 139	189 140	125.8	199 687	70.2	29.8	46.2	27.9	13 162	88.6
Throckmorton	508	-11.5	1 847	D	107.6	2 215 240	1 199	84 844	24.8	90 316	35.1	64.9	54.2	11.6	1 749	60.0
Titus	147	-11.9	183	D	31.1	471 061	2 575	53 954	81.2	101 401	4.5	95.5	35.3	6.1	112	7.6

STATE County	Water use, 2010		Wholesale trade,[1] 2007				Retail trade,[2] 2007				Real estate and rental and leasing,[2] 2007			
	Total water withdrawn (mil gal/day)	Gallons withdrawn per person per day	Number of establish-ments	Number of employees	Sales (mil dol)	Annual payroll (mil dol)	Number of establish-ments	Number of employees	Sales (mil dol)	Annual payroll (mil dol)	Number of establish-ments	Number of employees	Receipts (mil dol)	Annual payroll (mil dol)
	133	134	135	136	137	138	139	140	141	142	143	144	145	146
TEXAS—Cont'd														
Mason	5.2	1 306	9	65	41.3	1.6	27	137	29.0	2.1	5	6	2.7	0.2
Matagorda	210.5	5 736	31	D	D	D	157	1 428	313.9	26.8	36	286	30.2	10.8
Maverick	56.2	1 035	32	D	D	D	184	2 327	504.8	41.7	34	84	15.1	1.9
Medina	52.7	1 145	19	170	189.9	5.1	110	1 179	360.1	25.6	28	66	6.6	1.0
Menard	2.8	1 240	4	40	6.7	0.6	11	56	16.3	0.8	1	D	D	D
Midland	35.3	258	259	3 334	2 411.7	162.2	551	7 744	2 276.7	183.9	227	1 418	270.7	56.8
Milam	45.7	1 844	25	171	87.3	6.6	72	705	181.4	14.3	16	66	9.3	2.1
Mills	5.2	1 062	5	D	D	D	29	235	70.4	4.7	2	D	D	D
Mitchell	18.0	1 911	4	14	3.4	0.4	31	266	55.8	4.6	2	D	D	D
Montague	10.9	554	26	91	38.6	3.5	73	782	213.7	15.9	14	32	2.9	0.4
Montgomery	89.2	196	426	4 234	6 399.3	198.6	1 263	19 489	5 260.1	433.1	390	2 045	340.9	63.9
Moore	156.4	7 139	22	D	D	D	72	889	217.9	17.5	13	49	5.9	0.9
Morris	29.4	2 270	11	332	138.9	13.6	41	339	70.3	5.8	7	22	2.9	0.5
Motley	6.4	5 322	3	D	D	D	6	28	5.2	0.5	NA	NA	NA	NA
Nacogdoches	16.1	250	44	D	D	D	244	2 819	691.2	61.4	44	142	19.4	3.2
Navarro	51.2	1 073	26	415	285.7	13.8	184	2 168	471.8	41.1	45	139	19.8	3.3
Newton	6.2	429	6	46	10.0	1.1	23	174	50.9	2.5	2	D	D	D
Nolan	11.3	743	17	D	D	D	64	804	179.7	13.7	10	34	4.7	0.6
Nueces	235.0	691	399	4 448	2 978.5	207.0	1 174	16 877	4 314.5	365.5	432	2 613	415.5	79.1
Ochiltree	58.5	5 721	27	295	139.2	14.9	49	442	97.4	7.5	14	105	28.6	5.2
Oldham	5.8	2 836	1	D	D	D	9	50	16.8	0.9	NA	NA	NA	NA
Orange	411.3	5 026	39	235	114.4	12.1	270	3 207	852.0	62.9	58	179	36.3	4.4
Palo Pinto	50.4	1 794	18	D	D	D	124	1 135	272.7	23.0	29	102	14.0	2.4
Panola	17.4	733	22	152	80.0	4.0	89	825	222.0	15.3	27	122	21.3	3.0
Parker	22.6	193	95	692	524.2	25.3	309	4 566	1 517.8	113.9	95	312	55.9	8.3
Parmer	239.6	23 332	30	181	224.9	5.3	29	167	39.5	3.0	6	D	D	D
Pecos	145.1	9 356	9	108	117.0	4.2	68	702	154.0	11.8	9	24	3.8	0.6
Polk	558.9	12 308	22	101	51.1	3.7	120	1 721	445.4	37.0	32	100	9.2	2.3
Potter	5.6	46	179	2 786	2 064.1	117.3	579	8 653	2 490.0	183.4	159	D	D	D
Presidio	5.3	682	3	9	3.2	0.2	34	229	42.5	3.1	3	D	D	D
Rains	2.2	202	4	D	D	D	33	289	93.9	6.5	5	88	1.7	0.6
Randall	26.8	222	76	D	D	D	346	5 080	1 465.5	122.4	133	D	D	D
Reagan	25.6	7 594	3	25	4.4	1.0	18	98	23.7	1.8	1	D	D	D
Real	1.0	311	4	D	D	D	15	38	9.4	0.7	4	10	1.0	0.1
Red River	7.1	550	7	32	15.1	0.9	43	297	61.2	5.3	8	10	2.3	0.2
Reeves	56.9	4 129	8	D	D	D	34	446	113.2	7.8	6	17	1.4	0.3
Refugio	12.0	1 624	5	32	18.0	1.3	24	231	62.0	3.8	9	51	5.6	1.4
Roberts	21.1	22 680	NA	NA	NA	NA	2	D	D	D	NA	NA	NA	NA
Robertson	433.8	26 099	2	D	D	D	53	420	115.2	7.8	10	32	9.7	1.6
Rockwall	0.6	7	63	D	D	D	222	3 272	946.3	73.8	61	218	38.9	6.6
Runnels	7.8	743	8	41	24.6	1.2	51	480	128.4	11.5	3	D	D	D
Rusk	1 594.9	29 906	21	205	99.8	7.8	141	1 423	354.3	28.4	24	81	10.1	1.8
Sabine	2.2	202	NA	NA	NA	NA	35	237	51.9	4.0	4	D	D	D
San Augustine	3.1	350	5	36	6.4	0.9	28	247	70.1	4.1	3	D	D	D
San Jacinto	2.9	109	3	D	D	D	31	230	54.7	4.4	8	29	5.1	0.5
San Patricio	11.4	176	32	232	135.2	8.8	180	2 265	621.6	51.6	72	247	31.5	4.8
San Saba	7.0	1 137	12	96	18.1	2.9	38	232	60.5	4.3	4	D	D	D
Schleicher	2.7	766	6	30	13.1	0.9	10	71	10.4	1.0	NA	NA	NA	NA
Scurry	38.9	2 297	28	D	D	D	59	674	199.6	13.7	21	139	19.4	4.2
Shackelford	1.8	524	5	16	4.1	0.3	18	103	14.8	1.5	3	14	0.5	0.2
Shelby	13.5	530	12	81	97.6	4.8	95	1 106	246.5	21.2	13	38	4.0	0.6
Sherman	213.9	70 501	8	D	D	D	10	49	10.1	0.8	NA	NA	NA	NA
Smith	30.8	147	242	2 216	922.1	97.5	855	12 347	3 110.1	287.8	229	1 447	204.5	41.3
Somervell	2 043.9	240 736	7	32	14.8	1.3	37	259	55.2	4.7	8	D	D	D
Starr	26.2	429	14	D	D	D	134	1 878	445.3	31.2	10	32	3.2	0.7
Stephens	36.8	3 826	9	28	21.4	0.9	36	369	78.8	7.9	6	26	3.5	0.5
Sterling	2.0	1 724	2	D	D	D	5	D	D	D	NA	NA	NA	NA
Stonewall	2.5	1 698	2	D	D	D	10	42	8.6	0.6	2	D	D	D
Sutton	3.2	766	6	53	29.3	3.3	25	147	41.9	2.6	6	47	7.1	1.5
Swisher	104.4	13 296	14	130	42.4	3.1	22	164	35.2	2.6	6	D	D	D
Tarrant	286.1	158	1 932	32 231	25 801.5	1 571.5	5 539	89 503	24 931.4	2 192.6	1 827	11 200	2 770.0	432.7
Taylor	3.6	27	135	1 540	1 079.7	58.0	579	8 333	2 063.3	181.8	160	637	133.6	19.4
Terrell	1.5	1 514	1	D	D	D	4	12	3.9	0.3	NA	NA	NA	NA
Terry	132.5	10 473	18	187	87.3	7.7	42	478	133.7	9.3	12	73	7.6	3.1
Throckmorton	1.4	853	4	11	3.4	0.4	6	22	6.8	0.4	NA	NA	NA	NA
Titus	1 950.7	60 330	29	D	D	D	148	1 782	425.1	39.1	29	84	11.6	1.8

1. Merchant wholesalers, except manufacturers' sales branches and offices. 2. Employer establishments.

Table B. States and Counties — **Professional Services, Manufacturing, and Accommodation and Food Services**

STATE County	Professional, scientific, and technical services,[1] 2007				Manufacturing, 2007				Accommodation and food services, 2007			
	Number of establish-ments	Number of employees	Receipts (mil dol)	Annual payroll (mil dol)	Number of establish-ments	Number of employees	Receipts (mil dol)	Annual payroll (mil dol)	Number of establish-ments	Number of employees	Sales (mil dol)	Annual payroll (mil dol)
	147	148	149	150	151	152	153	154	155	156	157	158
TEXAS—Cont'd												
Mason	12	43	3.2	0.9	NA	NA	NA	NA	11	147	3.7	1.4
Matagorda	51	177	15.6	4.8	27	604	D	43.6	77	1 023	38.8	10.0
Maverick	39	D	D	D	NA	NA	NA	NA	64	1 126	48.5	11.3
Medina	58	320	20.0	7.3	30	554	75.3	12.2	73	771	29.8	8.4
Menard	3	4	0.6	0.1	NA	NA	NA	NA	5	D	D	D
Midland	436	D	D	D	140	2 366	533.8	95.2	254	5 324	259.2	69.3
Milam	32	200	14.8	6.8	15	1 521	D	D	38	481	17.7	4.4
Mills	8	20	2.1	0.4	NA	NA	NA	NA	10	64	2.1	0.6
Mitchell	7	25	4.3	0.7	NA	NA	NA	NA	13	140	3.7	0.9
Montague	44	131	12.5	4.0	NA	NA	NA	NA	24	323	10.9	3.0
Montgomery	1 101	D	D	D	373	11 265	3 667.0	522.7	621	14 471	728.6	196.7
Moore	24	90	10.1	3.3	17	D	D	D	43	548	23.0	5.1
Morris	11	95	9.3	3.9	18	2 675	1 140.4	125.1	21	229	8.8	2.2
Motley	NA	NA	NA	NA	NA	NA	NA	NA	3	9	0.3	0.0
Nacogdoches	92	D	D	D	64	4 034	1 418.9	126.1	108	2 253	87.8	23.2
Navarro	60	370	19.1	7.0	57	3 149	758.5	103.4	64	932	42.7	11.2
Newton	4	7	1.4	0.4	NA	NA	NA	NA	6	40	1.9	0.4
Nolan	27	97	10.6	3.0	13	866	224.9	35.0	39	537	16.8	4.3
Nueces	785	D	D	D	215	8 284	D	508.2	811	15 167	662.0	186.1
Ochiltree	21	169	18.6	9.2	NA	NA	NA	NA	19	217	9.2	2.1
Oldham	2	D	D	D	NA	NA	NA	NA	11	39	2.9	0.8
Orange	89	D	D	D	85	5 308	D	339.7	128	2 060	85.3	21.6
Palo Pinto	44	178	16.7	4.6	36	1 283	307.2	44.0	70	891	44.9	11.5
Panola	39	211	21.2	5.9	19	947	264.0	29.0	31	461	18.3	4.8
Parker	173	D	D	D	135	2 814	550.4	104.1	156	2 502	110.4	29.7
Parmer	14	37	3.1	0.7	4	D	D	D	9	56	1.8	0.4
Pecos	17	123	3.7	4.6	NA	NA	NA	NA	34	529	24.3	5.3
Polk	56	268	30.2	8.2	23	D	98.5	17.2	54	833	33.4	8.1
Potter	291	D	D	D	134	D	D	D	338	6 829	326.0	85.8
Presidio	4	10	0.7	0.2	NA	NA	NA	NA	27	153	5.0	1.3
Rains	8	180	4.5	2.3	NA	NA	NA	NA	15	163	6.2	1.7
Randall	187	D	D	D	73	D	D	D	171	3 442	131.9	35.3
Reagan	6	7	0.6	0.1	NA	NA	NA	NA	8	58	2.2	0.4
Real	7	21	2.0	0.7	NA	NA	NA	NA	13	41	3.7	0.7
Red River	7	20	2.2	0.7	16	634	101.8	18.3	14	D	D	D
Reeves	15	D	D	D	NA	NA	NA	NA	26	297	12.4	3.4
Refugio	7	11	1.2	0.3	NA	NA	NA	NA	16	D	D	D
Roberts	2	D	D	D	NA	NA	NA	NA	2	D	D	D
Robertson	11	D	D	D	NA	NA	NA	NA	23	303	15.2	3.4
Rockwall	185	D	D	D	68	D	301.3	D	124	2 500	105.9	30.4
Runnels	12	72	10.6	3.4	17	959	207.0	35.9	21	168	5.6	1.4
Rusk	58	D	D	D	35	1 484	D	46.9	55	666	29.7	7.8
Sabine	8	20	1.7	0.4	NA	NA	NA	NA	12	89	3.3	0.8
San Augustine	10	23	1.6	0.5	NA	NA	NA	NA	6	41	1.4	0.3
San Jacinto	17	D	D	D	NA	NA	NA	NA	9	115	4.0	1.4
San Patricio	83	D	D	D	33	1 586	D	D	135	2 042	77.6	19.2
San Saba	15	33	2.4	0.6	NA	NA	NA	NA	17	94	4.1	0.9
Schleicher	3	8	0.8	0.1	NA	NA	NA	NA	3	21	0.3	0.1
Scurry	25	137	13.6	4.9	NA	NA	NA	NA	47	517	20.6	5.9
Shackelford	6	10	1.5	0.3	NA	NA	NA	NA	7	61	1.9	0.6
Shelby	29	102	15.8	2.9	25	2 242	552.0	69.2	24	304	14.9	3.4
Sherman	2	D	D	D	NA	NA	NA	NA	3	D	D	D
Smith	548	D	D	D	224	10 737	5 423.5	474.5	339	7 563	337.3	93.6
Somervell	15	26	4.2	1.2	NA	NA	NA	NA	27	437	23.1	7.1
Starr	20	75	5.1	1.6	NA	NA	NA	NA	44	578	26.2	6.0
Stephens	22	101	20.7	3.0	NA	NA	NA	NA	20	193	6.2	1.8
Sterling	2	D	D	D	NA	NA	NA	NA	3	D	D	D
Stonewall	2	D	D	D	NA	NA	NA	NA	2	D	D	D
Sutton	10	24	2.1	0.6	NA	NA	NA	NA	18	229	9.7	2.5
Swisher	7	24	1.3	0.6	NA	NA	NA	NA	13	142	4.0	1.1
Tarrant	4 064	D	D	D	1 789	100 996	43 337.5	5 192.3	3 141	73 070	3 763.5	1 035.3
Taylor	276	D	D	D	99	2 341	D	D	286	6 524	246.2	69.0
Terrell	2	D	D	D	NA	NA	NA	NA	2	D	D	D
Terry	14	60	4.1	1.1	NA	NA	NA	NA	25	237	9.9	2.6
Throckmorton	2	D	D	D	NA	NA	NA	NA	4	D	D	D
Titus	33	135	11.8	3.8	41	5 696	1 291.5	164.4	56	1 030	40.7	11.6

1. Establishment subject to federal tax.

STATE County	Health care and social assistance, 2007				Other services, 2007				Nonemployer businesses, 2013		Value of residential construction authorized by building permits, 2014	
	Number of establish-ments	Number of employees	Receipts (mil dol)	Annual payroll (mil dol)	Number of establish-ments	Number of employees	Receipts (mil dol)	Annual payroll (mil dol)	Number	Receipts (mil dol)	New Construction ($1,000)	Number of housing units
	159	160	161	162	163	164	165	166	167	168	169	170
TEXAS—Cont'd												
Mason	10	119	5.4	2.7	9	24	1.2	0.2	566	19.8	993	4
Matagorda	65	1 248	111.1	37.0	69	331	35.5	12.4	2 561	110.3	25 226	222
Maverick	85	D	D	D	31	116	8.7	1.8	4 427	154.2	9 610	99
Medina	58	655	45.5	17.9	45	187	15.3	4.2	3 142	138.3	3 403	49
Menard	1	D	D	D	3	D	D	D	263	11.8	NA	NA
Midland	359	5 999	697.2	241.4	255	2 469	287.0	65.5	14 947	1 135.6	235 573	1 553
Milam	43	901	46.0	22.8	35	145	12.5	2.6	1 568	65.5	238	10
Mills	13	238	9.4	5.0	10	D	D	D	426	16.2	NA	NA
Mitchell	7	D	D	D	11	31	2.0	0.4	458	18.8	861	5
Montague	35	747	45.4	19.6	34	102	8.0	1.9	1 886	102.2	0	0
Montgomery	771	12 641	1 617.6	531.2	515	4 034	322.1	102.0	41 229	2 416.9	1 466 718	7 145
Moore	43	592	40.8	17.6	40	127	9.1	2.1	1 013	59.1	2 566	16
Morris	21	D	D	D	22	76	10.5	2.6	797	28.5	160	1
Motley	3	D	D	D	5	D	D	D	124	4.1	NA	NA
Nacogdoches	196	3 849	361.3	125.5	95	469	31.8	8.4	3 830	167.0	7 445	68
Navarro	87	1 687	111.9	46.7	60	220	18.5	4.3	3 141	140.1	3 211	23
Newton	10	301	11.6	5.7	5	D	D	D	626	21.3	0	0
Nolan	38	645	40.2	17.7	21	93	9.3	2.3	985	38.9	0	0
Nueces	1 014	24 413	2 103.8	808.8	571	4 159	454.4	120.5	22 777	1 023.4	306 270	2 452
Ochiltree	19	287	22.3	6.7	21	100	7.4	1.9	785	42.7	1 625	7
Oldham	2	D	D	D	3	D	D	D	169	6.9	0	0
Orange	142	1 666	146.0	54.4	95	755	115.9	20.8	4 665	172.7	45 117	428
Palo Pinto	52	D	D	D	40	D	D	D	2 076	107.0	1 064	5
Panola	47	710	52.6	17.5	32	164	17.7	3.3	1 537	77.2	2 615	14
Parker	171	D	D	D	137	773	59.9	15.7	11 363	639.3	79 809	382
Parmer	9	94	7.8	3.2	16	45	4.0	0.9	480	25.4	600	13
Pecos	17	464	35.1	13.7	25	171	9.2	2.4	898	31.8	753	7
Polk	59	1 013	81.4	29.3	55	338	21.9	5.7	3 507	166.3	95 387	469
Potter	469	12 140	1 391.8	482.7	258	1 942	218.0	44.0	7 985	422.8	164 302	853
Presidio	2	D	D	D	7	D	D	D	746	21.6	630	9
Rains	6	22	1.2	0.4	10	D	D	D	816	33.2	790	5
Randall	220	2 528	233.1	73.0	161	913	75.5	18.9	9 873	462.4	8 714	62
Reagan	4	D	D	D	6	D	D	D	346	20.5	1 086	19
Real	11	146	6.3	3.2	1	D	D	D	440	18.7	0	0
Red River	21	437	34.5	12.0	15	44	2.6	0.7	862	40.1	629	8
Reeves	15	271	21.0	8.4	12	D	D	D	564	24.4	540	3
Refugio	9	235	17.8	6.2	8	31	1.6	0.4	498	22.6	1 667	22
Roberts	NA	NA	NA	NA	NA	NA	NA	NA	76	3.6	NA	NA
Robertson	23	331	14.9	6.9	27	74	6.4	1.4	1 209	50.1	1 383	9
Rockwall	175	2 455	238.8	100.4	83	607	44.0	14.7	8 134	449.1	278 667	965
Runnels	18	327	17.7	7.2	14	31	2.7	0.7	821	29.8	900	4
Rusk	65	1 145	95.5	34.2	46	266	19.7	6.0	3 057	140.8	278	3
Sabine	13	171	11.8	5.1	13	40	2.8	0.9	711	27.5	0	0
San Augustine	19	472	21.1	9.1	9	23	1.3	0.3	516	19.0	0	0
San Jacinto	12	111	6.0	2.6	15	40	3.4	0.7	1 744	70.1	186	2
San Patricio	96	1 415	95.9	38.1	78	391	25.7	7.1	4 259	191.3	43 763	243
San Saba	13	227	8.9	4.6	9	30	2.2	0.5	591	19.6	0	0
Schleicher	4	D	D	D	5	D	D	D	273	12.7	150	1
Scurry	23	503	38.7	14.3	34	226	25.8	6.2	1 105	55.9	1 200	8
Shackelford	5	71	3.8	1.8	5	D	D	D	469	26.0	NA	NA
Shelby	36	637	39.4	16.5	31	D	D	D	1 669	83.6	1 389	15
Sherman	1	D	D	D	4	D	D	D	229	10.5	848	10
Smith	636	19 044	2 002.7	784.8	334	2 556	192.7	71.9	17 017	857.9	112 256	389
Somervell	21	449	31.2	13.2	11	28	2.6	0.7	707	36.2	3 082	18
Starr	67	4 455	134.6	68.3	26	90	4.0	0.9	6 579	176.9	NA	NA
Stephens	24	358	18.1	8.4	15	57	3.6	1.2	850	56.5	0	0
Sterling	3	D	D	D	1	D	D	D	186	6.0	NA	NA
Stonewall	4	130	6.4	2.9	5	D	D	D	152	5.2	NA	NA
Sutton	4	82	8.6	2.3	10	35	3.6	0.6	402	15.9	0	0
Swisher	13	249	12.2	5.5	10	30	1.7	0.5	465	15.6	0	0
Tarrant	3 999	75 845	8 750.6	3 062.5	2 408	19 973	1 777.8	505.0	151 025	6 950.0	1 536 130	8 985
Taylor	377	11 521	833.6	333.5	249	1 554	147.9	31.0	9 461	455.2	57 115	278
Terrell	1	D	D	D	2	D	D	D	84	2.7	NA	NA
Terry	20	601	28.0	11.0	19	79	4.5	1.4	606	25.5	366	3
Throckmorton	4	69	3.2	1.6	3	D	D	D	204	10.9	NA	NA
Titus	86	1 907	144.5	62.0	39	227	16.5	6.7	1 636	69.5	2 606	22

STATE County	Government employment and payroll, 2012									Local government finances, 2012				
			March payroll (percent of total)							General revenue				
												Taxes		
													Per capita[1] (dollars)	
	Full-time equivalent employees	March payroll (dollars)	Adminis-tration, judicial, and legal	Police and Corrections	Fire Protection	Highways and transpor-tation	Health and Welfare	Natural resources and utilities	Education and libraries	Total (mil dol)	Inter-govern-mental (mil dol)	Total (mil dol)	Total	Property
	171	172	173	174	175	176	177	178	179	180	181	182	183	184
TEXAS—Cont'd														
Mason	187	574 614	8.5	5.1	0.0	5.6	6.2	8.5	64.4	12.7	4.9	6.2	1 550	1 351
Matagorda	1 950	6 092 071	4.5	8.9	0.0	2.4	17.9	4.6	60.5	272.8	55.1	91.7	2 509	2 321
Maverick	3 274	9 420 323	4.8	5.7	1.7	2.4	2.2	3.5	79.0	215.5	121.7	45.7	826	606
Medina	2 042	6 076 041	4.7	6.4	0.0	2.1	11.3	4.7	68.9	144.1	64.8	47.3	1 012	893
Menard	160	407 534	7.5	8.8	0.0	1.5	18.9	3.1	58.6	9.7	3.2	4.0	1 788	1 631
Midland	6 743	26 604 150	5.0	7.8	4.1	1.5	30.2	1.5	47.9	761.2	127.7	334.2	2 279	1 657
Milam	1 010	3 486 020	6.1	8.9	0.2	4.0	1.5	3.6	74.9	75.2	30.4	35.9	1 485	1 337
Mills	267	764 983	7.7	3.6	0.0	3.0	2.7	4.7	78.1	16.6	9.4	5.5	1 135	994
Mitchell	583	1 683 044	7.8	5.5	0.2	3.5	33.1	3.1	46.1	46.4	10.5	19.0	2 033	1 894
Montague	1 080	3 133 643	3.8	5.6	1.7	2.8	25.9	4.1	52.2	89.9	35.1	30.6	1 565	1 349
Montgomery	15 517	53 618 969	5.3	8.9	4.3	1.6	4.2	3.6	70.3	1 469.3	416.6	880.8	1 816	1 602
Moore	1 387	4 297 575	5.7	7.6	1.6	2.0	18.7	4.0	59.3	101.2	21.6	47.4	2 125	1 879
Morris	525	1 489 068	7.2	8.0	0.0	2.6	0.2	4.5	77.3	33.3	11.9	17.9	1 399	1 218
Motley	53	139 031	14.8	3.4	0.0	11.8	4.1	2.8	61.5	4.2	1.7	2.0	1 659	1 542
Nacogdoches	3 209	11 081 415	3.8	5.6	2.6	0.8	27.6	2.8	56.3	249.0	82.9	70.1	1 062	894
Navarro	2 582	8 615 927	4.3	7.4	1.8	2.3	3.2	3.1	74.7	198.0	85.4	69.3	1 444	1 208
Newton	492	1 402 695	9.9	5.3	0.0	3.1	1.3	4.5	74.9	46.4	14.2	18.8	1 321	1 309
Nolan	1 074	3 200 019	5.7	6.5	2.3	1.6	30.0	3.7	48.4	92.2	25.3	33.8	2 265	1 854
Nueces	15 002	50 012 628	4.7	10.3	4.3	5.0	3.5	5.4	62.9	1 333.3	434.9	623.4	1 793	1 377
Ochiltree	750	1 938 537	5.3	7.0	1.8	3.2	23.4	3.9	53.5	38.3	10.0	24.3	2 264	1 986
Oldham	268	808 206	6.5	4.6	0.0	1.8	0.0	1.4	85.2	17.9	9.3	4.2	2 028	1 796
Orange	3 533	11 142 459	7.8	12.4	2.2	3.6	1.2	10.2	61.9	284.3	105.6	118.8	1 432	1 208
Palo Pinto	1 439	4 512 709	5.6	7.4	0.8	3.8	30.1	2.6	48.2	125.0	32.7	53.6	1 926	1 663
Panola	1 035	3 674 945	5.9	7.4	0.6	4.5	0.6	2.7	77.7	119.5	26.6	78.0	3 248	3 005
Parker	3 910	13 841 811	8.1	6.9	2.5	2.7	2.3	3.6	72.3	342.4	84.3	203.7	1 701	1 506
Parmer	674	1 770 342	9.3	9.6	0.0	4.1	7.1	4.4	65.0	56.5	17.4	22.7	2 231	2 142
Pecos	928	3 033 599	8.3	7.8	0.0	4.3	11.7	7.2	58.4	127.5	16.7	76.1	4 873	4 588
Polk	1 509	6 360 260	11.3	19.6	0.1	3.8	2.1	6.1	56.0	118.9	38.8	47.9	1 049	878
Potter	8 893	30 669 359	4.8	10.2	6.1	3.0	6.5	3.7	64.1	740.4	307.7	290.5	2 375	1 650
Presidio	514	1 310 951	9.3	7.0	0.0	3.7	6.0	5.4	67.8	35.4	22.2	7.8	1 041	903
Rains	490	1 074 762	8.2	7.5	0.0	2.1	0.3	4.6	75.7	30.7	11.0	16.4	1 498	1 297
Randall	1 728	5 466 299	10.7	21.4	1.0	1.7	0.6	1.5	61.9	119.8	28.9	76.8	614	566
Reagan	366	1 075 023	9.6	7.2	0.4	4.0	23.8	3.8	50.1	44.4	3.9	33.4	9 618	8 897
Real	97	286 334	19.1	8.8	0.0	5.7	12.5	1.5	51.9	7.4	1.1	5.5	1 637	1 475
Red River	579	1 522 449	5.6	7.7	1.5	3.4	0.0	3.7	77.9	37.1	22.5	10.9	857	736
Reeves	1 448	3 858 596	5.2	36.7	1.3	1.5	16.8	4.5	33.4	149.1	13.2	27.3	1 981	1 689
Refugio	551	1 642 349	7.4	7.5	0.7	4.5	25.8	3.6	49.3	40.3	10.7	21.9	3 017	2 809
Roberts	81	227 300	16.9	8.7	0.0	5.2	2.4	7.8	59.0	9.8	1.4	7.9	9 265	8 938
Robertson	905	2 580 494	9.2	10.0	0.0	3.8	0.5	5.5	69.4	85.5	23.3	56.6	3 421	3 199
Rockwall	3 263	11 181 638	8.8	10.5	1.2	0.8	0.1	2.9	74.8	283.0	72.7	179.3	2 159	1 870
Runnels	671	2 087 986	8.8	8.8	0.6	3.6	22.7	8.6	45.9	42.1	20.2	12.8	1 230	1 099
Rusk	1 692	6 115 196	8.9	12.8	1.3	2.9	0.5	7.7	64.0	130.2	38.5	76.0	1 407	1 267
Sabine	470	1 232 799	8.2	5.9	0.0	2.1	12.7	6.2	63.1	31.3	14.1	9.8	938	790
San Augustine	376	978 889	9.7	7.9	0.0	4.2	0.9	5.0	71.7	33.0	20.0	10.7	1 214	1 066
San Jacinto	778	2 008 317	6.5	5.3	0.1	3.0	0.8	1.6	81.9	49.7	19.2	26.2	965	899
San Patricio	3 506	9 765 866	4.9	8.3	1.0	2.9	7.6	7.3	67.8	239.0	100.4	101.3	1 544	1 330
San Saba	434	1 149 764	5.8	3.1	0.0	36.7	1.6	5.8	45.2	25.2	16.5	6.7	1 112	1 001
Schleicher	239	526 633	7.5	4.0	0.0	5.0	19.5	5.6	57.3	13.1	4.2	6.5	2 000	1 918
Scurry	995	3 410 030	6.1	6.6	1.3	2.1	20.3	2.2	60.2	121.2	28.5	57.3	3 345	2 945
Shackelford	207	556 026	10.6	6.6	0.0	5.6	3.6	4.5	68.0	12.7	3.6	7.4	2 193	1 913
Shelby	1 249	3 791 323	5.4	6.0	0.5	2.4	0.0	3.4	81.5	78.9	40.8	30.6	1 176	971
Sherman	266	825 372	8.9	3.5	0.0	4.4	16.5	9.6	54.1	17.5	2.5	11.5	3 752	3 455
Smith	8 764	29 028 100	7.6	10.8	2.8	1.5	6.8	3.6	65.8	648.3	207.0	325.4	1 515	1 170
Somervell	476	1 533 907	6.3	9.3	0.2	6.9	1.2	3.4	65.6	85.7	11.9	48.2	5 603	5 421
Starr	4 112	12 165 296	5.7	7.0	1.5	2.0	8.1	2.5	71.6	268.0	173.1	50.8	825	734
Stephens	543	1 467 714	8.2	6.9	1.9	2.5	26.7	3.6	48.8	27.8	5.2	19.3	2 044	1 781
Sterling	86	271 999	21.3	6.6	0.0	4.1	0.0	5.7	60.3	15.5	4.1	9.5	8 008	7 790
Stonewall	209	553 406	6.8	2.8	0.0	10.2	50.6	1.9	26.7	13.8	2.1	5.9	3 967	3 683
Sutton	312	1 080 664	8.3	4.9	0.0	4.6	23.3	3.3	51.3	24.7	7.3	14.2	3 596	3 274
Swisher	403	1 118 598	6.5	7.0	0.0	2.6	0.9	4.3	77.3	36.9	14.7	7.6	964	823
Tarrant	76 274	291 509 259	6.4	12.5	4.8	1.5	9.8	4.8	58.6	7 673.3	2 064.9	3 815.1	2 029	1 629
Taylor	5 091	16 346 681	6.1	13.5	5.9	1.9	5.4	4.7	60.8	427.2	176.5	186.9	1 401	997
Terrell	108	366 799	22.2	0.0	0.0	7.7	5.5	4.7	44.6	12.5	1.9	9.9	10 751	10 482
Terry	926	2 466 610	5.9	8.0	1.0	2.6	26.1	3.6	51.2	56.3	12.9	26.6	2 108	1 903
Throckmorton	113	346 336	4.5	0.0	0.0	1.3	25.5	5.9	62.6	9.8	3.2	3.9	2 462	2 280
Titus	2 456	7 751 640	2.6	4.2	1.3	1.2	29.0	2.5	58.4	124.8	50.8	52.8	1 617	1 410

1. Based on the resident population estimated as of July 1 of the year shown.

STATE County	Local government finances, 2012 (cont.) — Direct general expenditure: Total (mil dol)	Per capita[1] (dollars)	Percent of total for: Education	Health and hospitals	Police protection	Public welfare	Highways	Debt outstanding: Total (mil dol)	Per capita[1] (dollars)	Government employment, 2013: Federal civilian	Federal military	State and local	Presidential election,[2] 2012 — Percent of vote cast: Democratic	Republican	All other
	185	186	187	188	189	190	191	192	193	194	195	196	197	198	199
TEXAS—Cont'd															
Mason	11.2	2 787	63.4	2.7	6.9	0.1	5.9	3.4	853	14	0	275	25.7	72.8	1.5
Matagorda	250.1	6 844	32.2	45.6	2.8	0.0	2.5	242.4	6 631	80	77	2 303	35.9	63.3	0.8
Maverick	219.2	3 958	56.6	2.8	3.8	0.0	8.5	215.3	3 888	911	116	4 838	78.2	21.2	0.6
Medina	151.4	3 238	58.2	13.0	3.7	0.4	3.0	135.1	2 888	58	95	2 857	32.7	66.6	0.7
Menard	9.9	4 437	46.2	0.0	6.1	23.8	3.2	1.6	696	0	0	199	29.0	69.9	1.1
Midland	747.6	5 098	34.2	40.2	3.6	0.0	1.3	587.4	4 005	512	317	7 945	21.0	78.2	0.8
Milam	70.4	2 914	62.9	2.6	4.1	0.6	7.3	71.3	2 950	50	50	1 166	36.4	62.4	1.1
Mills	17.5	3 633	61.9	2.4	3.5	0.4	4.0	5.4	1 116	16	10	337	18.3	80.5	1.2
Mitchell	47.8	5 118	43.4	36.9	2.7	0.1	3.9	37.5	4 017	21	15	1 128	24.1	74.7	1.2
Montague	91.2	4 662	32.2	41.0	3.2	0.2	3.8	35.2	1 798	44	41	1 333	20.1	78.6	1.4
Montgomery	1 474.0	3 039	50.5	6.5	5.6	0.1	4.0	4 045.0	8 339	767	1 052	23 994	23.3	75.9	0.8
Moore	95.6	4 283	47.6	26.8	5.1	0.1	0.9	47.9	2 146	64	47	1 596	20.7	78.8	0.6
Morris	30.0	2 343	68.2	0.1	4.2	0.6	3.3	10.3	804	25	27	651	39.2	60.2	0.7
Motley	4.0	3 301	70.6	4.0	1.7	0.1	5.8	0.1	49	0	0	99	11.3	87.9	0.8
Nacogdoches	257.8	3 903	37.6	34.4	3.9	0.9	1.9	196.8	2 981	140	130	5 297	35.9	63.4	0.7
Navarro	194.1	4 045	64.8	2.1	5.7	0.3	4.2	235.6	4 910	97	100	3 592	33.1	66.2	0.7
Newton	45.7	3 222	44.4	0.0	8.1	1.7	3.7	33.4	2 356	26	28	594	33.3	65.5	1.2
Nolan	90.3	6 050	47.2	28.5	3.6	0.0	3.1	76.3	5 116	43	31	1 596	30.0	68.8	1.1
Nueces	1 384.5	3 982	48.2	4.5	6.3	0.1	3.8	2 805.4	8 069	6 496	2 882	21 381	47.3	51.8	0.9
Ochiltree	30.1	2 806	68.7	0.5	3.5	0.0	4.9	31.4	2 924	21	23	761	7.8	91.7	0.5
Oldham	17.7	8 594	83.4	0.0	4.2	0.0	2.0	4.6	2 220	0	0	280	11.1	88.4	0.5
Orange	269.5	3 248	46.6	0.7	7.3	0.2	3.2	736.8	8 880	96	174	4 108	26.0	73.1	0.9
Palo Pinto	119.5	4 289	40.7	32.3	3.8	0.0	3.5	91.1	3 271	55	58	1 752	25.3	73.4	1.3
Panola	120.9	5 033	70.2	0.4	3.5	0.2	6.0	54.6	2 272	72	50	1 337	25.3	74.2	0.5
Parker	370.5	3 095	53.1	7.2	4.5	0.0	11.8	720.3	6 017	154	251	4 869	21.9	77.1	1.0
Parmer	51.6	5 067	48.1	20.9	4.1	4.3	4.2	28.1	2 758	63	21	812	19.4	80.0	0.7
Pecos	125.4	8 031	44.7	24.0	3.2	0.0	4.0	74.8	4 792	51	29	1 866	36.8	61.8	1.3
Polk	109.6	2 400	62.3	0.6	6.0	0.2	7.5	278.0	6 089	90	88	2 914	30.9	68.1	0.9
Potter	749.2	6 124	53.7	5.1	5.8	0.0	2.4	762.3	6 231	1 905	400	12 997	29.8	69.2	1.0
Presidio	41.0	5 442	67.0	0.7	1.8	0.0	1.4	21.5	2 854	368	15	678	71.3	27.8	0.9
Rains	31.1	2 840	44.9	2.6	3.6	0.5	6.4	25.3	2 316	22	23	456	24.7	74.3	1.0
Randall	116.9	935	49.6	1.1	7.6	0.1	3.1	128.5	1 027	173	263	4 138	18.3	80.9	0.8
Reagan	38.8	11 153	53.5	17.4	3.8	0.3	7.7	32.0	9 222	0	0	366	19.8	80.0	0.2
Real	6.9	2 039	48.7	0.5	9.4	2.4	11.7	0.3	75	0	0	210	23.0	76.0	0.9
Red River	37.7	2 968	74.1	0.1	2.9	1.4	1.5	18.4	1 453	36	26	709	30.5	68.5	1.0
Reeves	138.8	10 063	21.0	12.8	3.3	0.0	1.6	136.0	9 859	76	23	1 582	52.2	47.0	0.8
Refugio	40.6	5 594	55.7	13.7	4.6	0.0	5.7	20.5	2 822	37	15	667	42.4	56.9	0.7
Roberts	9.1	10 678	90.1	0.4	2.2	0.0	2.1	0.7	768	0	0	96	7.9	92.1	0.0
Robertson	89.0	5 381	81.1	0.1	3.4	0.3	3.2	84.0	5 080	46	35	1 035	39.9	59.3	0.8
Rockwall	297.5	3 584	49.5	0.4	5.7	0.2	5.2	881.6	10 619	90	179	3 346	26.5	72.7	0.9
Runnels	43.0	4 112	51.2	23.8	1.8	0.0	4.7	11.5	1 101	37	21	796	18.6	80.6	0.7
Rusk	130.1	2 408	66.3	0.4	4.6	0.1	6.1	181.9	3 368	67	102	2 342	26.6	72.9	0.5
Sabine	29.1	2 787	50.7	22.5	5.3	0.0	6.3	11.3	1 081	48	22	460	22.1	76.9	1.0
San Augustine	28.0	3 179	73.4	1.6	6.1	0.0	0.7	34.8	3 949	19	18	427	35.7	63.0	1.2
San Jacinto	46.2	1 704	66.1	0.2	5.1	0.5	6.7	34.4	1 269	23	57	896	30.4	68.7	1.0
San Patricio	237.2	3 616	57.1	6.5	5.8	0.3	3.2	231.1	3 524	91	1 680	3 844	41.4	58.0	0.6
San Saba	18.5	3 087	57.6	1.7	4.5	1.1	6.8	15.9	2 642	20	11	495	19.8	79.0	1.2
Schleicher	13.7	4 190	45.0	27.0	0.7	0.0	3.4	34.9	10 699	11	0	266	24.8	74.4	0.8
Scurry	113.5	6 628	57.4	17.4	3.7	0.1	3.7	74.5	4 348	32	33	1 613	19.5	79.3	1.2
Shackelford	11.4	3 400	61.4	4.1	6.5	0.0	5.6	0.9	262	13	0	221	13.8	85.3	0.9
Shelby	75.6	2 905	71.6	0.6	5.1	0.0	6.1	42.1	1 619	76	54	1 298	27.6	71.9	0.5
Sherman	18.7	6 099	54.0	15.6	4.5	0.0	6.0	3.1	1 017	0	0	283	12.5	86.7	0.9
Smith	645.1	3 003	55.0	5.1	5.6	0.2	3.4	1 145.0	5 330	726	481	12 677	29.8	69.4	0.8
Somervell	86.1	10 008	49.0	29.8	3.5	0.5	3.8	65.4	7 610	12	18	882	22.6	75.8	1.6
Starr	254.5	4 130	66.2	11.4	3.9	0.0	3.6	277.9	4 510	734	129	5 026	84.5	15.2	0.3
Stephens	27.4	2 898	46.7	2.5	5.2	0.1	3.9	19.2	2 029	18	18	685	17.8	81.4	0.9
Sterling	17.5	14 668	64.5	1.9	2.1	15.3	2.0	10.2	8 554	0	0	156	15.7	84.0	0.3
Stonewall	23.1	15 635	13.2	76.1	1.3	0.0	2.7	0.1	57	10	0	224	28.0	71.3	0.7
Sutton	22.3	5 656	62.2	17.0	3.3	0.1	3.4	1.6	405	0	0	425	24.1	75.3	0.5
Swisher	30.7	3 895	48.7	32.1	4.0	0.0	0.8	3.2	409	26	15	734	32.1	66.4	1.5
Tarrant	7 651.9	4 070	42.5	12.1	6.9	0.1	3.7	19 647.2	10 450	15 028	5 136	93 434	40.7	55.4	0.8
Taylor	402.0	3 012	53.5	4.7	7.8	0.6	3.1	260.9	1 977	1 085	4 641	8 406	26.8	72.3	0.9
Terrell	12.1	13 215	63.5	3.9	7.6	0.0	8.3	21.1	22 972	70	0	131	35.8	62.2	1.9
Terry	59.1	4 683	48.8	27.3	3.7	0.4	3.1	17.6	1 397	24	25	1 076	32.2	67.3	0.5
Throckmorton	9.9	6 177	38.7	32.3	0.8	0.0	11.7	0.2	137	10	0	175	19.8	80.1	0.1
Titus	127.0	3 889	67.0	0.4	4.2	0.1	6.4	228.1	6 985	90	68	2 880	34.0	65.2	0.8

1. Based on the resident population estimated as of July 1 of the year shown. 2.

STATE/ County code	CBSA code[1]	County type[2]	STATE County	Land area,[3] (sq km) 2010	Population, 2014: Total persons 2014	Population, 2014: Rank	Population, 2014: Per square kilometer	Race alone or in combination, not Hispanic or Latino (percent): White	Black	American Indian, Alaska Native	Asian and Pacific Islander	Percent Hispanic or Latino[4]	Age (percent): Under 5 years	5 to 17 years	18 to 24 years	25 to 34 years	35 to 44 years	45 to 54 years
				1	2	3	4	5	6	7	8	9	10	11	12	13	14	15
			TEXAS—Cont'd															
48 451	41660	3	Tom Green	3 942	116 608	525	29.6	57.1	4.5	0.8	1.8	37.3	6.8	16.7	13.1	15.1	10.5	11.8
48 453	12420	1	Travis	2 565	1 151 145	36	448.8	51.6	8.7	0.7	7.0	33.8	7.0	16.3	10.5	19.6	15.7	12.6
48 455	26660	8	Trinity	1 796	14 224	2 151	7.9	80.3	10.2	1.1	0.7	9.2	4.9	15.4	6.8	9.5	10.0	13.3
48 457	...	6	Tyler	2 394	21 418	1 756	8.9	80.6	11.6	1.1	0.5	7.4	5.2	14.3	8.8	13.2	11.3	13.1
48 459	30980	3	Upshur	1 510	40 354	1 163	26.7	82.9	9.5	1.4	0.7	7.4	6.3	17.7	8.1	11.4	11.3	14.2
48 461	...	8	Upton	3 215	3 454	2 942	1.1	45.5	2.1	1.4	0.3	51.8	8.0	20.4	7.4	13.4	11.1	12.3
48 463	46620	7	Uvalde	4 020	27 117	1 530	6.7	28.7	0.8	0.4	0.7	69.9	7.6	20.4	10.9	11.8	11.5	11.3
48 465	19620	5	Val Verde	8 145	48 974	999	6.0	17.6	1.5	0.4	0.9	79.4	8.3	20.9	11.1	13.7	12.0	11.2
48 467	...	6	Van Zandt	2 182	52 910	944	24.2	85.9	3.4	1.4	0.6	10.0	5.5	17.9	7.6	10.0	11.5	13.9
48 469	47020	3	Victoria	2 285	91 081	635	39.9	47.5	6.5	0.5	1.4	44.9	7.2	18.8	9.4	13.7	11.6	12.7
48 471	26660	4	Walker	2 031	69 789	766	34.4	58.7	22.8	0.7	1.4	17.4	4.3	11.4	20.0	14.5	13.3	14.3
48 473	26420	1	Waller	1 330	46 820	1 030	35.2	44.5	25.5	0.7	0.9	29.3	6.5	17.5	20.5	9.9	10.5	12.4
48 475	...	6	Ward	2 164	11 625	2 316	5.4	44.4	4.5	1.0	0.7	50.4	7.7	20.2	9.5	13.3	11.2	12.5
48 477	14780	6	Washington	1 564	34 438	1 316	22.0	65.9	17.8	0.5	1.8	14.9	6.0	15.5	11.0	10.4	10.6	13.1
48 479	29700	3	Webb	8 706	266 673	252	30.6	3.8	0.3	0.1	0.6	94.8	9.9	24.5	11.5	13.5	13.4	11.0
48 481	20900	4	Wharton	2 813	41 168	1 146	14.6	46.8	13.8	0.4	0.6	39.0	6.8	19.4	9.2	12.2	11.1	13.0
48 483	...	9	Wheeler	2 369	5 714	2 785	2.4	70.0	3.3	1.0	0.7	26.7	6.9	19.2	8.1	12.1	11.4	12.0
48 485	48660	3	Wichita	1 626	132 355	476	81.4	68.9	11.0	1.4	2.9	17.8	6.7	16.3	13.7	14.9	11.1	12.3
48 487	46900	6	Wilbarger	2 514	12 973	2 233	5.2	62.3	8.7	1.4	1.3	27.7	6.7	17.2	9.8	12.7	10.8	13.2
48 489	39700	6	Willacy	1 530	21 903	1 739	14.3	9.9	2.0	0.2	0.7	87.3	6.6	18.6	13.4	15.3	13.0	11.0
48 491	12420	1	Williamson	2 896	489 250	139	168.9	64.1	6.9	0.8	6.5	23.8	7.1	20.5	7.8	14.1	16.5	13.6
48 493	41700	1	Wilson	2 082	46 402	1 042	22.3	58.8	1.8	0.8	0.6	38.8	5.6	19.4	8.2	10.7	12.6	15.4
48 495	...	6	Winkler	2 178	7 821	2 610	3.6	39.9	2.2	0.8	0.5	57.2	8.2	22.2	9.3	13.0	11.9	13.5
48 497	19100	1	Wise	2 342	61 638	848	26.3	79.4	1.6	1.3	0.7	18.1	6.5	18.9	8.3	12.0	12.3	15.1
48 499	...	6	Wood	1 671	42 852	1 114	25.6	84.8	5.2	1.1	0.7	9.3	4.9	14.9	7.7	8.9	9.5	12.6
48 501	...	7	Yoakum	2 071	8 286	2 581	4.0	35.9	1.4	0.6	0.5	62.5	9.1	22.9	9.2	12.9	11.1	12.5
48 503	...	6	Young	2 368	18 350	1 903	7.7	80.2	1.8	1.0	0.7	17.4	6.6	17.4	7.7	11.1	10.9	13.2
48 505	49820	6	Zapata	2 586	14 319	2 147	5.5	5.9	0.3	0.2	0.2	93.7	10.3	23.5	10.8	13.3	11.8	10.4
48 507	...	7	Zavala	3 360	12 267	2 279	3.7	6.5	0.5	0.2	0.1	92.4	8.8	21.7	12.4	12.2	11.1	10.9
49 000	...	X	UTAH	212 818	2 942 902	X	13.8	81.4	1.5	1.4	4.3	13.4	8.8	22.2	11.5	15.2	12.8	10.5
49 001	...	9	Beaver	6 708	6 461	2 720	1.0	87.0	0.5	1.1	2.0	10.4	8.5	24.0	8.4	11.4	11.8	10.5
49 003	36260	4	Box Elder	14 881	51 518	967	3.5	88.9	0.6	1.3	1.7	8.9	8.8	24.1	8.8	12.8	12.1	11.2
49 005	30860	3	Cache	3 017	118 343	519	39.2	86.0	0.9	0.9	3.4	10.2	9.4	21.8	18.9	14.6	10.9	8.6
49 007	39220	7	Carbon	3 829	20 660	1 793	5.4	84.6	0.8	1.6	1.4	12.9	7.9	19.2	9.5	13.3	11.2	11.1
49 009	...	8	Daggett	1 805	1 117	3 104	0.6	94.0	1.0	1.2	0.8	4.2	4.7	18.9	6.0	12.6	11.4	11.5
49 011	36260	2	Davis	774	329 692	201	426.0	87.0	1.8	0.8	3.9	8.8	9.2	24.4	9.4	14.7	13.4	10.8
49 013	...	6	Duchesne	8 394	20 380	1 813	2.4	87.5	0.7	5.0	1.3	7.8	10.4	23.9	9.1	15.0	11.5	10.0
49 015	...	9	Emery	11 557	10 631	2 386	0.9	92.1	0.6	1.0	0.8	6.4	8.0	23.4	7.3	12.1	11.2	11.2
49 017	...	9	Garfield	13 404	5 024	2 836	0.4	91.4	0.7	2.1	1.5	5.4	6.1	19.5	7.2	11.1	10.4	12.0
49 019	...	7	Grand	9 509	9 429	2 477	1.0	84.8	1.1	4.3	1.7	9.8	6.8	15.8	6.9	13.2	12.8	13.6
49 021	16260	4	Iron	8 538	47 269	1 027	5.5	88.0	0.8	2.5	2.2	8.1	8.6	20.5	16.6	13.3	10.8	9.3
49 023	39340	2	Juab	8 786	10 486	2 397	1.2	93.8	0.6	1.3	0.9	4.5	9.2	25.8	8.8	12.0	12.7	10.3
49 025	...	6	Kane	10 335	7 254	2 654	0.7	93.1	0.6	2.4	1.0	4.2	6.0	17.4	7.0	11.1	9.5	11.4
49 027	...	7	Millard	17 023	12 606	2 257	0.7	84.7	0.6	1.3	1.2	13.3	8.4	23.0	8.0	11.1	10.7	11.0
49 029	36260	2	Morgan	1 578	10 608	2 388	6.7	96.0	0.5	0.6	0.9	2.9	8.5	26.3	8.2	10.1	12.8	11.9
49 031	...	9	Piute	1 963	1 484	3 081	0.8	90.7	0.4	0.9	0.7	8.0	3.7	23.2	6.0	7.7	9.5	10.5
49 033	...	8	Rich	2 665	2 293	3 027	0.9	94.8	0.3	1.0	0.4	4.4	7.6	22.9	7.1	10.2	10.8	10.5
49 035	41620	2	Salt Lake	1 923	1 091 742	39	567.7	75.0	2.1	1.1	6.4	17.6	8.2	20.3	10.0	16.8	13.9	11.5
49 037	...	7	San Juan	20 254	15 251	2 083	0.8	48.7	0.8	46.7	0.9	4.9	8.1	24.2	10.5	11.4	11.3	11.9
49 039	...	6	Sanpete	4 118	28 477	1 472	6.9	87.3	1.1	1.4	2.0	9.5	6.6	21.2	16.2	12.0	11.5	10.0
49 041	...	7	Sevier	4 948	20 773	1 788	4.2	93.3	0.5	1.5	0.9	4.8	7.4	23.5	7.9	12.1	11.9	10.9
49 043	44920	2	Summit	4 848	39 105	1 195	8.1	86.3	0.6	0.6	2.3	11.3	6.2	20.4	7.8	12.3	14.2	15.9
49 045	41620	2	Tooele	17 978	61 598	851	3.4	85.2	1.1	1.5	2.0	11.9	8.8	26.1	8.3	13.7	14.8	11.1
49 047	46860	7	Uintah	11 602	36 867	1 254	3.2	83.8	0.7	8.0	1.4	7.9	9.9	23.6	9.3	16.1	12.3	10.2
49 049	39340	2	Utah	5 189	560 974	113	108.1	85.5	0.9	0.9	3.9	11.0	10.4	24.6	16.7	14.8	11.9	8.2
49 051	25720	6	Wasatch	3 045	27 714	1 507	9.1	85.4	0.5	0.7	1.6	12.9	8.2	25.2	8.0	12.6	14.4	11.9
49 053	41100	3	Washington	6 284	151 948	423	24.2	86.9	0.9	1.6	2.5	9.9	7.6	21.2	8.9	12.6	10.7	9.5
49 055	...	9	Wayne	6 373	2 723	2 992	0.4	93.2	0.7	0.7	1.3	5.4	6.2	21.6	7.1	9.3	11.1	12.0
49 057	36260	2	Weber	1 492	240 475	276	161.2	79.2	1.7	1.1	2.6	17.4	8.3	21.0	10.0	15.5	12.7	11.4
50 000	...	X	VERMONT	23 871	626 562	X	26.2	95.4	1.6	1.1	1.9	1.7	4.9	14.7	10.7	11.5	11.6	15.1
50 001	...	6	Addison	1 985	37 009	1 249	18.6	95.3	1.4	0.9	2.3	2.0	4.3	14.2	13.7	9.3	11.4	15.2
50 003	13540	6	Bennington	1 748	36 445	1 267	20.8	96.3	1.3	0.8	1.2	1.7	4.8	14.8	9.2	9.4	10.4	15.2
50 005	...	7	Caledonia	1 681	30 981	1 413	18.4	96.7	0.9	1.3	1.1	1.3	4.9	15.9	9.7	10.6	11.5	14.3

1. CBSA = Core Based Statistical Area. See Appendix A for explanation. See Appendix B for list of metropolitan areas with component counties. 2. County type code from the Economic Research Service of USDA Rural-Urban Continuum Codes. See Appendix A for definition. 3. Dry land or land partially or temporarily covered by water. 4. May be of any race.

STATE County	Population, 2013 (cont.): Age (percent) (cont.): 55 to 64 years	65 to 74 years	75 years and over	Percent female	Population change and components of change, 2000–2014: Total persons: 2000	2010	Percent change: 2000–2010	2010–2014	Components of change, 2010–2014: Births	Deaths	Net migration	Households, 2009–2013: Number	Persons per household	Percent: Family households	Female family householder[1]	One person
	16	17	18	19	20	21	22	23	24	25	26	27	28	29	30	31
TEXAS—Cont'd																
Tom Green	11.6	7.7	6.7	50.5	104 010	110 224	6.0	5.8	6 497	4 188	4 125	42 286	2.50	66.3	13.3	27.9
Travis	10.1	4.9	3.2	49.5	812 280	1 024 266	26.1	12.4	67 000	20 786	78 623	411 876	2.53	57.6	11.5	30.4
Trinity	16.0	13.8	10.1	51.6	13 779	14 585	5.8	-3.1	554	888	-127	5 091	2.81	66.5	7.9	31.6
Tyler	13.8	11.8	8.5	46.1	20 871	21 766	4.3	-1.6	950	1 071	-202	8 224	2.37	69.8	11.8	26.4
Upshur	14.1	9.9	7.0	50.5	35 291	39 309	11.4	2.6	2 036	1 779	837	14 286	2.73	72.8	11.0	23.8
Upton	13.5	7.2	6.7	49.1	3 404	3 355	-1.4	3.1	216	128	25	1 218	2.67	74.2	10.2	22.4
Uvalde	10.8	8.6	7.1	50.9	25 926	26 405	1.8	2.7	1 694	1 062	100	8 619	3.01	72.4	15.7	23.6
Val Verde	9.5	7.5	5.9	49.4	44 856	48 879	9.0	0.2	3 696	1 503	-2 146	15 082	3.14	76.9	13.6	20.7
Van Zandt	14.0	11.3	8.3	51.0	48 140	52 579	9.2	0.6	2 432	2 654	609	19 064	2.71	69.9	10.1	26.4
Victoria	12.3	7.9	6.3	51.0	84 088	86 793	3.2	4.9	5 470	3 194	2 060	32 072	2.71	71.9	16.5	23.7
Walker	11.0	6.7	4.5	41.4	61 758	67 861	9.9	2.8	2 555	2 071	1 461	20 558	2.26	59.3	13.8	28.5
Waller	11.3	7.1	4.4	50.3	32 663	43 205	32.3	8.3	2 439	1 161	2 254	13 601	2.97	72.3	13.9	20.3
Ward	11.3	7.7	6.6	50.3	10 909	10 658	-2.3	9.1	713	441	703	3 938	2.69	67.0	15.9	30.6
Washington	14.0	10.2	9.2	50.6	30 373	33 718	11.0	2.2	1 752	1 561	500	12 244	2.61	70.0	14.1	26.9
Webb	7.9	4.9	3.5	51.0	193 117	250 304	29.6	6.5	23 165	5 185	-1 504	67 372	3.74	82.9	22.7	14.2
Wharton	12.9	8.1	7.3	50.8	41 188	41 280	0.2	-0.3	2 309	1 766	-635	14 517	2.80	67.4	13.6	30.0
Wheeler	13.2	9.7	7.4	49.4	5 284	5 410	2.4	5.6	312	273	265	2 319	2.35	69.3	9.2	25.9
Wichita	11.5	7.1	6.5	48.4	131 664	131 500	-0.1	0.5	7 564	5 500	-1 375	48 305	2.45	65.2	13.5	29.5
Wilbarger	13.1	9.2	7.4	50.9	14 676	13 535	-7.8	-4.2	730	625	-636	5 161	2.44	65.5	13.1	30.0
Willacy	9.8	7.0	5.4	45.2	20 082	22 134	10.2	-1.0	1 365	666	-942	5 499	3.59	79.9	23.0	17.9
Williamson	10.0	6.5	4.0	50.8	249 967	422 679	69.1	15.8	25 911	8 792	48 071	154 948	2.82	73.1	10.3	21.7
Wilson	13.7	8.5	5.8	49.9	32 408	42 918	32.4	8.1	2 072	1 466	2 821	15 157	2.85	80.6	10.8	15.7
Winkler	10.7	6.4	4.8	48.5	7 173	7 110	-0.9	10.0	525	228	406	2 709	2.63	69.2	14.0	27.4
Wise	12.8	8.8	5.2	49.7	48 793	59 127	21.2	4.2	3 224	2 074	1 333	20 487	2.88	77.8	9.9	18.9
Wood	15.1	15.7	10.8	51.0	36 752	41 964	14.2	2.1	1 755	2 519	1 592	15 800	2.56	70.2	9.7	25.8
Yoakum	10.3	6.8	5.2	50.3	7 322	7 879	7.6	5.2	608	237	26	2 654	3.00	80.7	10.8	17.5
Young	13.9	9.9	9.2	50.6	17 943	18 550	3.4	-1.1	980	1 070	-106	7 186	2.52	70.2	9.4	26.4
Zapata	8.7	6.7	4.5	49.6	12 182	14 018	15.1	2.1	1 234	363	-578	4 460	3.17	83.5	22.2	15.2
Zavala	10.4	7.0	5.5	50.2	11 600	11 677	0.7	5.1	889	351	28	3 654	3.15	72.4	23.8	24.6
UTAH	9.3	5.6	4.1	49.7	2 233 169	2 763 885	23.8	6.5	218 387	64 878	25 597	886 770	3.12	75.1	9.7	19.4
Beaver	12.0	7.6	5.7	48.3	6 005	6 629	10.4	-2.5	490	200	-478	2 112	2.98	74.5	10.4	24.1
Box Elder	10.3	6.4	5.6	49.2	42 745	49 975	16.9	3.1	3 699	1 395	-773	16 207	3.07	81.6	8.3	16.3
Cache	7.6	4.6	3.7	50.2	91 391	112 656	23.3	5.0	10 198	2 037	-2 569	35 375	3.12	75.4	8.5	16.4
Carbon	13.2	8.1	6.5	50.4	20 422	21 403	4.8	-3.5	1 338	921	-1 158	7 764	2.64	68.3	9.7	27.1
Daggett	14.7	12.5	7.5	44.6	921	1 059	15.0	5.3	45	18	29	305	2.37	63.9	4.3	31.8
Davis	9.1	5.1	3.9	49.7	238 994	306 479	28.2	7.6	24 596	6 304	4 836	95 238	3.25	80.9	8.9	15.8
Duchesne	9.5	6.3	4.5	49.2	14 371	18 607	29.5	9.5	1 837	531	423	6 850	2.74	80.2	8.7	17.5
Emery	12.8	8.5	5.5	49.1	10 860	10 976	1.1	-3.1	677	355	-668	3 598	3.01	77.9	8.4	19.0
Garfield	15.0	10.9	7.7	47.9	4 735	5 172	9.2	-2.9	263	185	-237	1 890	2.62	69.3	7.5	25.8
Grand	15.6	9.0	6.3	49.9	8 485	9 225	8.7	2.2	556	315	-53	3 633	2.51	54.1	5.9	39.9
Iron	9.7	6.8	4.4	50.0	33 779	46 163	36.7	2.4	3 599	1 177	-1 326	15 435	2.93	71.5	9.1	21.3
Juab	9.8	6.4	4.9	48.9	8 238	10 246	24.4	2.3	786	303	-263	3 016	3.37	85.6	10.0	13.3
Kane	16.2	13.5	8.0	49.7	6 046	7 125	17.8	1.8	350	281	40	3 077	2.30	65.4	4.5	27.7
Millard	12.1	8.7	7.1	48.9	12 405	12 503	0.8	0.8	818	407	-342	4 101	3.02	76.1	10.0	20.1
Morgan	10.6	7.1	4.3	49.3	7 129	9 469	32.8	12.0	664	202	679	2 860	3.39	87.5	4.1	11.5
Piute	14.7	13.9	10.7	48.5	1 435	1 556	8.4	-4.7	54	56	-92	570	3.07	71.4	5.8	26.5
Rich	13.6	10.4	6.8	49.5	1 961	2 264	15.5	1.3	143	49	-69	664	3.41	80.6	9.2	16.6
Salt Lake	9.9	5.5	3.9	49.7	898 387	1 029 655	14.6	6.0	76 461	25 028	11 493	344 089	3.01	70.5	10.8	22.9
San Juan	10.7	7.3	4.6	50.0	14 413	14 746	2.3	3.4	1 036	391	-137	4 216	3.42	73.0	14.5	24.0
Sanpete	9.8	7.4	5.1	47.7	22 763	27 822	22.2	2.4	1 710	746	-312	7 781	3.22	75.3	6.6	19.5
Sevier	10.9	8.7	6.8	49.1	18 842	20 802	10.4	-0.1	1 248	777	-489	7 146	2.82	75.0	7.7	23.6
Summit	14.0	6.7	2.5	48.7	29 736	36 324	22.2	7.7	1 872	560	1 507	13 627	2.72	72.5	8.0	20.0
Tooele	9.0	5.0	3.2	49.5	40 735	58 218	42.9	5.8	4 217	1 327	506	18 281	3.20	80.1	11.0	16.7
Uintah	9.4	5.2	4.0	49.1	25 224	32 588	29.2	13.1	2 889	856	2 223	11 007	3.04	75.8	9.7	19.8
Utah	6.5	4.0	3.0	49.7	368 536	516 564	40.2	8.6	50 715	8 688	2 426	143 005	3.61	81.9	8.1	12.3
Wasatch	10.3	6.1	3.2	48.7	15 215	23 530	54.7	17.8	1 689	470	2 907	7 602	3.21	80.6	8.2	17.1
Washington	10.7	10.3	8.6	50.6	90 354	138 115	52.9	10.0	9 484	4 623	8 510	46 826	2.99	76.3	9.4	19.3
Wayne	14.6	11.2	6.8	49.8	2 509	2 778	10.7	-2.0	129	92	-102	970	2.80	78.4	2.7	16.7
Weber	10.2	6.1	4.8	49.8	196 533	231 236	17.7	4.0	16 824	6 584	-914	79 525	2.90	73.6	11.6	21.2
VERMONT	15.2	9.5	6.9	50.7	608 827	625 741	2.8	0.1	25 598	22 735	-1 653	257 004	2.34	62.8	9.2	28.4
Addison	15.7	9.5	6.7	50.1	35 974	36 821	2.4	0.5	1 335	1 271	121	14 164	2.40	67.3	10.4	25.0
Bennington	15.7	11.1	9.5	51.6	36 994	37 125	0.4	-1.8	1 399	1 815	-264	15 442	2.29	65.1	10.7	29.3
Caledonia	16.0	9.9	7.2	50.1	29 702	31 227	5.1	-0.8	1 227	1 256	-176	12 491	2.40	63.9	10.2	29.0

1. No spouse present.

STATE County	Persons in group quarters, 2014	Daytime population, 2009–2013: Number	Daytime population, 2009–2013: Employment/residence ratio	Births, 2014: Total	Births, 2014: Rate[1]	Deaths, 2014: Number	Deaths, 2014: Rate[1]	Persons under 65 with no health insurance, 2013: Number	Persons under 65 with no health insurance, 2013: Percent	Medicare, 2014: Eligible for Medicare	Medicare, 2014: Enrolled in Medicare Advantage	Medicare, 2014: Enrolled in a Medicare prescription drug plan	Serious crimes known to police,[2] 2013: Total: Number	Serious crimes known to police,[2] 2013: Total: Rate[3]
	32	33	34	35	36	37	38	39	40	41	42	43	44	45
TEXAS—Cont'd														
Tom Green	5 277	112 395	1.01	1 533	13.1	1 009	8.7	21 488	22.9	19 597	3 534	10 933	4 326	3 773
Travis	23 294	1 169 912	1.19	16 026	13.9	5 191	4.5	211 116	21.0	112 040	26 674	54 343	49 517	4 422
Trinity	139	13 130	0.72	115	8.1	200	14.1	2 905	26.6	4 054	936	2 221	326	2 285
Tyler	2 419	19 856	0.75	230	10.7	236	11.0	3 588	23.6	4 677	1 009	2 439	359	1 674
Upshur	514	31 990	0.52	472	11.7	398	9.9	7 679	23.4	7 914	1 988	3 881	1 224	3 122
Upton	61	3 570	1.18	56	16.2	14	4.1	757	26.5	551	95	314	19	581
Uvalde	536	26 791	1.02	403	14.9	257	9.5	6 296	28.2	5 020	1 232	2 758	1 262	4 680
Val Verde	1 960	47 924	0.96	866	17.7	348	7.1	12 008	29.7	7 907	1 703	3 896	968	1 983
Van Zandt	617	44 281	0.60	582	11.0	609	11.5	10 939	26.1	11 437	2 544	6 090	955	1 867
Victoria	1 728	89 890	1.05	1 321	14.5	772	8.5	17 600	23.1	15 745	3 406	8 793	3 529	3 901
Walker	17 508	69 558	1.07	598	8.6	532	7.6	11 069	24.7	8 652	2 488	4 805	1 681	2 444
Waller	4 175	40 138	0.79	595	12.7	295	6.3	10 362	28.6	5 617	1 575	2 383	899	2 004
Ward	126	10 709	0.97	184	15.8	80	6.9	2 199	23.1	1 913	361	1 096	441	4 004
Washington	1 955	35 258	1.10	401	11.6	356	10.3	6 268	24.1	7 408	1 217	4 329	707	2 058
Webb	3 529	255 550	1.01	5 457	20.5	1 211	4.5	82 557	34.9	28 464	5 160	16 034	12 012	4 568
Wharton	425	39 208	0.89	542	13.2	407	9.9	9 091	26.3	7 461	1 255	4 446	1 154	2 785
Wheeler	38	6 602	1.41	82	14.4	68	11.9	1 338	28.3	1 056	111	643	113	1 973
Wichita	12 265	135 873	1.07	1 762	13.3	1 306	9.9	22 911	22.2	22 399	2 872	12 186	5 681	4 301
Wilbarger	619	13 774	1.07	174	13.4	133	10.3	2 671	24.9	2 584	490	1 655	422	3 189
Willacy	3 290	21 273	0.86	314	14.3	169	7.7	4 701	29.5	3 298	1 071	1 817	908	4 107
Williamson	5 398	381 501	0.72	6 186	12.6	2 222	4.5	70 737	17.0	58 166	15 786	26 510	8 705	1 858
Wilson	533	32 734	0.45	529	11.4	357	7.7	7 636	19.8	7 197	2 299	2 366	696	1 547
Winkler	97	6 783	0.85	139	17.8	35	4.5	1 739	26.2	1 061	169	609	110	1 477
Wise	980	54 696	0.80	771	12.5	512	8.3	12 005	23.3	9 803	2 287	4 873	907	1 484
Wood	1 438	39 578	0.84	413	9.6	595	13.9	8 080	26.7	12 659	2 832	6 659	1 118	2 649
Yoakum	56	8 525	1.15	157	18.9	47	5.7	2 009	28.0	1 155	145	750	126	1 539
Young	279	18 265	0.98	240	13.1	241	13.1	3 996	27.3	4 105	259	2 699	539	2 938
Zapata	30	13 972	0.96	282	19.7	105	7.3	4 392	34.6	1 824	229	1 116	525	3 640
Zavala	411	11 323	0.87	217	17.7	87	7.1	2 728	26.8	1 940	686	1 014	209	1 728
UTAH	44 655	2 812 842	1.00	51 447	17.5	15 306	5.2	393 119	15.3	335 480	92 582	108 487	92 084	3 174
Beaver	36	6 529	1.00	112	17.3	46	7.1	1 028	18.6	1 063	180	603	31	552
Box Elder	339	48 261	0.91	862	16.7	319	6.2	5 605	12.7	7 230	2 523	2 336	1 279	2 693
Cache	3 590	113 433	0.99	2 368	20.0	494	4.2	14 946	14.5	11 528	4 994	3 227	1 524	1 302
Carbon	400	21 403	1.02	297	14.4	190	9.2	2 240	12.8	3 905	311	2 335	782	3 980
Daggett	63	836	1.03	11	9.8	1	0.9	138	16.5	208	46	69	14	1 266
Davis	3 092	282 775	0.79	5 863	17.8	1 509	4.6	31 382	10.8	34 345	11 451	7 888	6 903	2 154
Duchesne	297	19 642	1.07	473	23.2	110	5.4	2 906	16.2	2 731	563	1 211	683	3 489
Emery	43	10 691	0.95	144	13.5	87	8.2	1 327	14.4	1 799	311	835	177	1 611
Garfield	179	5 126	1.00	59	11.7	36	7.2	800	20.2	989	NA	545	NA	NA
Grand	143	9 669	1.09	122	12.9	69	7.3	1 716	21.9	1 737	21	1 017	343	3 650
Iron	825	45 375	0.94	811	17.2	274	5.8	7 981	19.7	6 487	1 668	2 635	1 124	2 381
Juab	122	9 299	0.77	183	17.5	84	8.0	1 313	14.5	1 418	41	837	237	2 272
Kane	240	7 412	1.08	77	10.6	67	9.2	838	15.4	1 645	25	904	113	1 550
Millard	122	12 399	0.97	196	15.5	92	7.3	2 097	19.9	2 103	26	1 345	241	1 903
Morgan	0	7 647	0.50	166	15.6	36	3.4	890	9.9	1 313	410	278	39	391
Piute	37	1 705	0.85	10	6.7	9	6.1	268	24.6	390	34	229	23	1 508
Rich	1	2 263	0.98	25	10.9	11	4.8	337	17.9	367	77	151	40	1 751
Salt Lake	14 348	1 121 501	1.15	18 083	16.6	6 011	5.5	161 311	16.7	122 067	48 813	37 268	53 513	4 952
San Juan	361	14 690	0.98	266	17.4	105	6.9	2 748	21.1	1 853	18	1 198	212	1 403
Sanpete	2 644	26 424	0.85	409	14.4	161	5.7	4 392	19.7	4 083	74	2 383	400	1 609
Sevier	302	21 219	1.05	266	12.8	171	8.2	2 655	15.3	3 653	55	2 452	552	2 641
Summit	116	40 787	1.18	434	11.1	135	3.5	5 040	14.4	4 373	1 322	1 646	818	2 110
Tooele	355	51 022	0.68	989	16.1	299	4.9	6 913	12.5	6 287	1 468	1 757	1 827	3 010
Uintah	206	34 390	1.05	719	19.5	205	5.6	5 388	16.7	3 622	909	1 430	772	2 176
Utah	12 087	508 615	0.91	11 961	21.3	2 048	3.7	69 041	13.8	45 945	17 734	14 106	10 781	1 956
Wasatch	249	20 643	0.65	422	15.2	109	3.9	4 500	19.0	2 919	961	1 030	267	1 027
Washington	1 923	141 545	0.99	2 188	14.4	1 094	7.2	22 756	19.4	29 271	8 495	11 035	3 132	2 161
Wayne	9	2 795	1.03	27	9.9	25	9.2	445	19.9	552	15	316	26	947
Weber	2 526	224 746	0.91	3 904	16.2	1 509	6.3	32 120	15.3	31 597	10 416	7 421	7 879	3 288
VERMONT	25 356	623 833	0.99	6 006	9.6	5 238	8.4	43 850	8.7	129 182	9 259	79 577	14 634	2 335
Addison	2 857	33 427	0.82	324	8.8	296	8.0	2 526	8.9	7 040	642	4 129	574	1 561
Bennington	1 476	38 601	1.10	341	9.4	431	11.8	2 625	9.4	9 012	641	6 026	810	2 213
Caledonia	1 346	29 359	0.88	279	9.0	277	8.9	2 437	9.8	6 710	462	4 119	681	2 188

1. Per 1,000 estimated resident population. 2. Data for serious crimes have not been adjusted for underreporting; this may affect comparability between geographic areas and over time.
3. Per 100,000 population estimated by the FBI.

STATE County	Serious crimes known to police, 2013 (cont.)[1] Rate[2] Violent	Rate[2] Property	Education: School enrollment and attainment, 2009–2013 Enrollment[3] Total	Enrollment[3] Percent private	Attainment[4] (percent) High school graduate or less	Attainment[4] (percent) Bachelor's degree or more	Local government expenditures,[5] 2012–2013 Total current spending (mil dol)	Current spending per student (dollars)	Money income, 2009–2013 Per capita income[6] (dollars)	Households Median income (dollars)	Households Mean income (dollars)	Households Percent with income of $200,000 or more	Income and poverty, 2013 Median household income (dollars)	Percent below poverty level All persons	Children under 18 years	Children 5 to 17 years in families
	46	47	48	49	50	51	52	53	54	55	56	57	58	59	60	61
TEXAS—Cont'd																
Tom Green	266	3 507	28 858	8.0	48.2	21.6	153.1	8 568	23 712	44 545	60 289	2.6	45 405	14.5	22.4	22.2
Travis	324	4 099	300 272	13.4	29.9	44.9	1 355.7	9 261	33 206	58 025	83 635	7.3	60 372	15.9	21.0	20.7
Trinity	280	2 004	2 784	2.9	64.3	9.9	22.5	9 591	18 730	34 555	45 929	0.8	33 447	20.9	33.7	31.1
Tyler	233	1 440	4 209	6.4	57.7	11.8	33.6	9 420	19 612	39 940	50 347	0.8	40 986	20.9	28.2	27.3
Upshur	288	2 833	9 400	9.2	52.7	13.3	63.2	8 876	22 483	46 600	60 293	2.6	46 489	18.1	25.9	26.1
Upton	0	581	789	3.5	60.7	11.5	12.1	15 233	22 953	51 750	62 183	1.6	54 549	13.8	20.0	19.5
Uvalde	445	4 235	8 107	5.0	54.3	14.5	52.5	8 814	17 479	34 902	50 346	2.3	35 813	24.8	39.4	37.7
Val Verde	170	1 813	12 834	5.7	61.3	15.3	87.1	8 184	17 867	40 450	53 573	1.3	38 645	23.9	32.3	31.9
Van Zandt	184	1 684	11 805	12.6	56.3	13.5	80.0	8 224	21 920	43 439	55 700	1.6	43 220	16.2	26.1	23.0
Victoria	529	3 371	22 120	13.0	49.7	16.3	129.9	8 368	24 700	50 364	65 685	2.6	51 544	15.8	23.8	23.0
Walker	379	2 065	19 581	5.8	53.2	17.9	66.8	9 232	16 330	37 617	54 039	2.2	40 092	25.5	28.6	27.0
Waller	230	1 775	15 009	18.9	56.5	19.0	81.0	8 657	22 412	50 097	66 978	3.7	49 326	19.4	26.4	23.9
Ward	554	3 450	2 658	3.2	61.3	12.5	20.0	8 786	22 278	42 568	55 699	2.2	51 026	13.7	20.1	18.8
Washington	306	1 752	7 670	8.4	48.4	23.5	45.1	8 467	23 070	44 858	59 313	2.0	49 472	14.2	21.8	21.7
Webb	431	4 138	87 959	4.3	57.7	17.2	557.4	8 189	14 553	39 449	52 392	1.8	38 652	30.6	40.6	39.5
Wharton	384	2 401	10 256	9.1	58.3	14.6	70.6	8 618	20 310	40 411	53 780	1.7	42 862	18.7	28.2	26.2
Wheeler	122	1 851	1 141	4.1	50.8	18.4	15.3	13 047	30 097	51 766	73 822	4.8	51 922	13.1	19.3	18.4
Wichita	376	3 926	33 723	8.6	47.6	20.1	175.0	8 218	22 905	45 086	59 872	2.2	43 473	19.5	27.8	24.9
Wilbarger	295	2 894	3 235	6.6	51.5	16.5	21.5	8 787	20 373	41 658	52 356	0.8	37 840	17.5	26.5	26.4
Willacy	977	3 130	5 961	4.0	69.8	8.8	49.2	10 738	11 313	25 886	36 994	0.4	28 945	43.1	49.8	50.1
Williamson	133	1 725	126 763	13.0	28.6	38.0	837.0	7 933	31 070	71 803	85 658	4.8	71 252	7.8	9.7	9.1
Wilson	113	1 434	11 372	11.4	50.2	18.0	72.0	8 433	27 238	64 571	76 400	2.9	60 844	11.3	16.3	14.4
Winkler	322	1 155	1 788	4.8	59.6	9.6	21.9	12 417	23 629	48 992	62 957	2.2	54 294	14.5	20.8	19.5
Wise	157	1 327	14 688	5.6	53.3	16.1	83.1	9 215	25 663	56 005	71 828	3.1	58 392	11.3	16.3	15.3
Wood	137	2 512	8 422	10.6	52.5	17.0	53.8	8 603	23 129	43 649	58 085	2.6	45 763	15.7	28.2	26.0
Yoakum	134	1 405	2 269	7.5	57.6	15.0	22.5	10 523	21 389	49 340	63 068	2.3	57 995	12.6	17.4	16.9
Young	142	2 796	4 013	7.8	55.0	16.7	31.1	8 821	26 979	44 429	66 175	2.9	44 372	18.2	25.1	23.2
Zapata	603	3 037	4 205	1.5	71.3	8.5	33.3	9 257	16 671	31 109	48 300	0.8	34 506	29.5	42.9	41.7
Zavala	91	1 637	3 375	2.6	63.4	9.4	25.6	10 025	12 828	25 625	37 281	1.3	25 291	33.4	45.0	44.2
UTAH	224	2 950	921 482	14.2	32.7	30.3	3 768.0	6 555	23 873	58 821	73 717	3.6	59 715	12.6	14.6	13.6
Beaver	107	445	1 905	3.3	46.8	17.0	13.0	8 324	19 415	46 660	57 558	1.4	46 138	10.6	14.0	12.9
Box Elder	219	2 474	15 566	10.5	40.6	21.2	72.1	6 448	21 720	57 292	66 577	1.8	60 372	10.4	13.0	12.6
Cache	56	1 247	45 271	7.7	29.0	36.9	139.4	6 261	20 074	49 506	63 297	2.2	49 556	14.2	14.2	13.6
Carbon	260	3 720	5 812	6.2	42.6	12.6	30.2	8 498	20 155	44 724	53 620	0.6	44 594	16.1	20.2	18.5
Daggett	0	1 266	133	9.0	48.6	18.8	3.1	14 389	22 811	46 917	59 115	2.3	53 080	7.5	8.3	7.0
Davis	120	2 034	103 598	9.4	26.8	34.1	441.4	6 289	26 035	69 707	83 588	4.1	70 456	8.2	9.7	8.7
Duchesne	521	2 968	5 242	5.6	48.5	16.0	34.6	7 061	23 411	57 683	67 241	1.9	61 386	10.5	12.2	12.0
Emery	91	1 520	2 751	4.9	42.1	12.5	23.2	9 713	20 137	52 763	59 137	0.7	52 070	13.0	17.4	16.2
Garfield	NA	NA	1 302	4.5	39.0	20.1	9.2	9 161	21 989	45 357	57 515	1.8	43 798	12.0	18.5	16.5
Grand	298	3 352	1 950	11.9	33.1	25.2	13.8	9 378	23 558	45 888	54 513	1.5	42 368	14.8	23.4	22.8
Iron	294	2 087	16 392	7.7	34.5	26.4	59.9	6 880	17 839	42 369	52 316	1.9	43 439	19.4	23.7	23.5
Juab	67	2 205	3 319	3.6	45.5	14.6	18.3	7 160	18 108	55 247	60 981	1.3	51 942	12.3	17.3	16.3
Kane	261	1 289	1 484	5.7	32.0	25.3	12.6	10 174	24 154	48 540	59 024	2.0	46 350	12.3	20.0	18.6
Millard	261	1 642	3 389	3.2	43.9	19.0	26.4	9 036	19 972	49 238	59 241	1.5	51 424	13.7	20.4	19.3
Morgan	40	350	3 213	11.3	28.8	33.4	15.1	5 839	26 274	80 337	89 626	5.7	83 496	5.4	6.3	5.9
Piute	328	1 180	556	6.1	50.9	17.0	4.4	12 590	16 959	38 500	46 444	0.4	37 897	21.8	39.6	32.3
Rich	131	1 619	608	16.0	42.5	17.0	6.3	13 072	24 258	50 000	74 796	2.1	54 640	11.2	16.1	14.9
Salt Lake	368	4 583	317 817	13.2	34.2	31.0	1 290.6	6 906	26 103	60 555	77 055	4.3	61 716	12.7	15.9	14.9
San Juan	205	1 198	4 608	7.1	50.1	18.4	33.6	10 586	15 476	40 492	49 831	1.0	40 327	27.6	30.6	27.5
Sanpete	60	1 549	9 944	12.5	39.2	20.8	45.5	7 948	17 811	48 369	60 561	2.5	45 338	18.2	21.6	20.0
Sevier	134	2 507	6 103	4.9	43.0	16.4	32.4	6 685	19 115	46 229	55 016	1.2	49 877	13.7	19.1	16.9
Summit	173	1 937	10 024	14.2	23.5	48.7	71.8	10 205	42 462	83 336	115 805	14.4	81 907	7.6	9.6	8.2
Tooele	184	2 825	19 737	11.1	38.9	20.4	91.8	6 454	22 252	61 412	70 968	1.7	59 400	9.1	11.5	10.6
Uintah	203	1 973	9 475	9.5	49.8	16.2	50.0	6 674	23 805	62 067	71 948	2.9	62 028	10.8	13.2	12.5
Utah	72	1 885	212 064	25.2	23.5	36.5	696.8	5 893	20 774	60 196	74 495	3.5	60 069	13.8	12.1	10.9
Wasatch	131	896	7 396	10.4	30.1	33.4	42.4	7 420	25 777	65 050	80 532	5.8	64 423	8.2	11.0	9.8
Washington	144	2 017	42 694	11.0	34.4	26.4	182.0	6 673	21 472	49 279	62 386	2.5	50 378	15.4	21.4	20.7
Wayne	146	801	801	7.4	32.8	25.2	5.3	9 558	19 858	41 458	53 405	1.3	38 945	15.9	25.3	22.6
Weber	237	3 051	68 328	8.4	40.2	22.7	303.1	6 950	23 106	54 974	66 810	2.3	54 055	13.3	17.2	16.4
VERMONT	121	2 214	153 287	20.0	39.4	34.8	1 531.5	16 377	29 167	54 267	69 716	3.4	52 511	12.3	15.2	13.3
Addison	117	1 444	9 880	33.9	41.6	35.6	85.7	17 642	28 722	57 565	72 372	3.3	54 683	10.5	13.2	11.3
Bennington	109	2 104	8 455	27.6	40.9	32.3	84.6	16 369	29 196	50 221	68 321	3.9	48 290	15.1	21.2	18.9
Caledonia	177	2 011	7 216	21.0	46.0	26.6	77.9	18 305	23 584	45 395	57 426	1.5	43 011	14.3	19.7	17.1

1. Data for serious crimes have not been adjusted for underreporting; this may affect comparability between geographic areas and over time. 2. Per 100,000 population estimated by the FBI.
3. All persons 3 years old and over enrolled in nursery school through college. 4. Persons 25 years old and over. 5. Elementary and secondary education expenditures.
6. Based on population estimated by the American Community Survey, 2009–2013.

STATE County	Personal income, 2013										Earnings, 2013		
	Total (mil dol)	Percent change, 2012–2013	Per capita[1] Dollars	Per capita[1] Rank	Wages and salaries (mil dol)	Supplements to wages and salaries; employer contributions (mil dol): Pension and insurance	Supplements to wages and salaries; employer contributions (mil dol): Government social insurance	Proprietors' income (mil dol)	Dividends, interest, and rent (mil dol)	Personal transfer receipts (mil dol)	Total (mil dol)	Contributions for government social insurance (mil dol): From employee and self-employed	Contributions for government social insurance (mil dol): From employer
	62	63	64	65	66	67	68	69	70	71	72	73	74
TEXAS—Cont'd													
Tom Green	4 751	2.8	41 329	1 014	1 963	355	142	498	1 167	883	2 958	152	142
Travis	54 436	2.8	48 562	447	36 674	4 903	2 429	7 085	12 443	5 158	51 091	2 497	2 429
Trinity	453	2.4	31 502	2 478	76	15	5	26	72	165	122	10	5
Tyler	657	0.2	30 602	2 611	137	31	9	34	90	203	211	14	9
Upshur	1 569	2.3	39 349	1 246	275	53	19	114	191	348	461	29	19
Upton	206	7.9	61 179	93	103	17	7	30	30	25	156	7	7
Uvalde	1 058	1.7	39 286	1 256	324	68	22	86	331	264	500	27	22
Val Verde	1 563	-0.3	32 137	2 397	701	169	58	119	257	356	1 046	54	58
Van Zandt	1 935	1.7	36 878	1 614	356	63	24	103	277	485	546	36	24
Victoria	4 235	5.0	47 041	553	1 881	272	128	681	692	720	2 962	151	128
Walker	1 931	2.4	28 055	2 893	872	213	50	109	366	404	1 245	57	50
Waller	1 429	2.2	31 605	2 463	737	117	48	75	201	286	976	51	48
Ward	521	4.6	46 347	601	258	34	16	81	69	82	389	20	16
Washington	1 721	1.9	50 396	349	588	101	39	306	420	328	1 034	52	39
Webb	7 114	2.1	27 102	2 963	3 346	650	236	899	901	1 686	5 131	254	236
Wharton	1 672	1.7	40 559	1 103	561	93	38	194	308	350	886	45	38
Wheeler	314	1.4	54 538	216	107	18	7	52	91	50	183	8	7
Wichita	5 291	1.5	40 066	1 168	2 297	442	173	836	1 181	1 066	3 748	183	173
Wilbarger	533	3.0	40 628	1 096	240	58	14	60	94	129	373	17	14
Willacy	596	0.8	27 196	2 959	138	26	9	51	53	207	225	13	9
Williamson	20 153	3.5	42 786	863	7 446	888	487	1 081	3 344	2 132	9 902	543	487
Wilson	1 833	6.6	40 351	1 127	255	50	17	81	294	306	402	24	17
Winkler	327	5.1	43 004	839	170	23	11	25	44	54	229	12	11
Wise	2 500	2.4	41 019	1 046	1 084	160	73	357	368	392	1 674	86	73
Wood	1 448	2.3	34 231	2 046	336	63	24	83	303	486	507	38	24
Yoakum	452	1.8	55 226	199	232	34	15	131	50	52	413	17	15
Young	941	3.0	51 282	323	290	53	19	275	166	178	637	30	19
Zapata	435	2.4	30 223	2 651	269	40	18	56	54	102	383	20	18
Zavala	264	2.0	21 747	3 100	90	19	6	17	32	111	132	8	6
UTAH	106 289	3.7	36 640	X	57 480	10 337	4 615	9 457	19 241	14 489	81 888	4 673	4 615
Beaver	216	9.4	33 497	2 175	117	21	10	12	38	43	161	8	10
Box Elder	1 649	3.8	32 461	2 342	709	129	59	119	277	268	1 016	60	59
Cache	3 642	3.6	31 149	2 525	1 753	405	141	279	797	528	2 576	142	141
Carbon	714	-0.1	33 999	2 080	362	71	29	37	106	172	500	31	29
Daggett	43	2.1	38 510	1 371	15	4	1	15	10	7	36	2	1
Davis	12 359	3.8	38 372	1 392	4 939	1 045	411	981	2 032	1 381	7 377	407	411
Duchesne	856	3.3	42 170	920	457	84	35	55	138	106	631	37	35
Emery	301	1.0	27 995	2 900	161	37	13	9	45	70	220	14	13
Garfield	159	3.5	31 307	2 509	69	15	7	4	36	34	96	6	7
Grand	380	3.2	40 545	1 108	158	31	14	43	112	64	246	14	14
Iron	1 249	3.1	26 699	2 992	503	121	41	107	254	284	771	45	41
Juab	276	2.5	26 633	2 998	123	24	11	17	36	61	174	10	11
Kane	262	3.1	36 134	1 723	99	20	8	21	55	54	149	9	8
Millard	424	8.9	33 496	2 176	186	43	14	56	70	80	300	15	14
Morgan	391	4.9	38 422	1 388	77	14	6	23	78	41	120	7	6
Piute	41	6.1	27 394	2 945	9	2	1	4	8	14	15	1	1
Rich	87	9.6	38 030	1 428	21	5	2	11	22	12	39	2	2
Salt Lake	45 553	3.5	42 189	917	30 644	5 192	2 423	4 518	8 072	5 521	42 777	2 424	2 423
San Juan	361	5.5	24 128	3 076	173	39	13	11	64	91	236	14	13
Sanpete	699	3.7	24 738	3 063	228	60	18	76	121	167	382	21	18
Sevier	617	3.1	29 604	2 742	278	60	23	38	115	145	398	25	23
Summit	3 177	3.1	82 558	18	951	129	81	343	921	152	1 503	82	81
Tooele	1 831	3.3	30 135	2 666	748	143	59	56	248	263	1 006	59	59
Uintah	1 164	1.3	32 728	2 297	740	117	57	76	168	146	989	58	57
Utah	15 975	5.1	28 946	2 810	8 154	1 379	654	1 743	2 453	2 267	11 930	676	654
Wasatch	807	4.6	30 519	2 627	252	46	20	47	214	103	366	22	20
Washington	4 423	4.5	29 928	2 697	1 756	330	149	332	1 123	1 037	2 567	167	149
Wayne	83	7.4	30 151	2 663	29	7	2	7	23	18	45	3	2
Weber	8 549	3.0	35 844	1 774	3 769	766	313	416	1 606	1 361	5 263	310	313
VERMONT	28 501	2.5	45 483	X	13 207	2 440	1 112	2 354	5 471	5 746	19 113	1 220	1 112
Addison	1 541	2.8	41 890	949	601	106	51	165	307	266	923	58	51
Bennington	1 657	2.1	45 199	677	694	125	61	139	400	368	1 019	69	61
Caledonia	1 151	2.0	36 929	1 599	422	86	37	128	206	275	673	45	37

1. Based on the resident population estimated as of July 1 of the year shown.

Table B. States and Counties — **Earnings, Social Security, and Housing**

STATE County	Earnings, 2013 (cont.) — Percent by selected industries: Farm	Mining	Construction	Manu-facturing	Infor-mation: professional, scientific, technical services	Retail trade	Finance, insur-ance, real estate and leasing	Health care and social assistance	Govern-ment	Social Security beneficiaries, December 2013: Number	Rate[1]	Supple-mental Security Income recipients, December 2013	Housing units, 2014: Total	Percent change, 2010–2014
	75	76	77	78	79	80	81	82	83	84	85	86	87	88
TEXAS—Cont'd														
Tom Green	1.0	7.2	5.4	9.9	D	7.1	5.7	14.2	24.0	21 150	184	2 957	47 698	2.4
Travis	0.0	2.1	5.9	8.8	21.0	5.2	9.4	8.7	17.3	113 885	101	18 409	474 929	7.6
Trinity	-0.8	D	7.4	9.4	D	7.2	D	D	24.2	4 435	308	642	8 747	0.4
Tyler	3.3	1.7	4.1	4.2	3.0	9.5	D	7.0	39.4	5 220	243	705	10 604	0.2
Upshur	-0.3	5.6	11.0	4.3	18.7	6.2	4.1	D	18.3	8 850	222	1 178	16 750	0.8
Upton	4.6	46.4	6.3	0.0	D	D	0.6	0.4	17.5	595	177	79	1 549	0.2
Uvalde	2.8	2.2	5.4	4.1	D	10.7	4.1	D	32.1	5 360	199	1 188	11 017	1.9
Val Verde	-0.1	D	3.6	7.8	2.1	9.7	3.6	8.9	46.0	8 255	168	2 415	18 803	0.8
Van Zandt	5.7	2.0	13.1	8.0	4.3	8.6	4.2	8.3	20.2	12 700	242	1 230	22 876	0.3
Victoria	0.1	17.0	7.2	8.1	3.9	11.6	6.0	13.4	11.8	16 945	188	2 684	36 032	1.7
Walker	1.0	0.8	3.6	5.2	4.2	7.2	3.2	7.9	55.6	9 110	131	1 291	24 937	3.7
Waller	1.3	4.0	7.7	27.4	7.4	6.0	2.4	3.0	21.9	5 935	130	862	16 122	1.7
Ward	0.0	46.3	6.4	2.5	5.2	4.4	5.6	1.7	10.9	2 040	181	307	4 734	0.9
Washington	0.3	4.9	6.3	33.6	3.9	7.3	6.6	6.3	15.0	7 645	224	913	15 702	1.2
Webb	0.1	8.2	3.1	0.6	4.1	8.3	4.2	10.6	27.3	30 765	117	12 604	78 048	6.2
Wharton	7.2	13.7	5.0	9.2	3.1	8.7	5.6	7.8	15.5	7 955	193	1 148	17 371	1.4
Wheeler	10.9	25.9	D	D	D	5.1	3.6	2.5	15.0	1 160	202	87	2 715	-0.5
Wichita	0.2	14.9	3.7	9.9	4.9	6.8	4.9	13.3	24.8	24 335	184	3 958	56 040	0.9
Wilbarger	4.2	2.7	2.9	17.4	2.5	9.0	3.5	2.7	38.2	2 835	216	418	6 275	-0.7
Willacy	11.9	D	2.1	0.6	D	7.1	3.8	8.0	27.3	3 645	166	1 411	7 118	1.1
Williamson	0.3	1.0	8.2	9.7	8.5	7.9	7.3	8.6	12.1	59 370	126	4 114	175 677	7.9
Wilson	1.1	7.8	13.0	4.3	5.1	13.5	3.7	D	27.2	7 685	169	745	16 991	1.3
Winkler	0.4	36.5	D	D	D	3.1	10.1	0.8	14.4	1 185	155	240	3 010	-0.6
Wise	-0.2	28.5	8.3	8.5	2.3	6.4	3.1	5.4	12.9	10 590	174	793	23 946	0.7
Wood	1.9	5.1	7.4	12.7	5.7	11.3	5.9	D	18.2	13 395	315	986	20 941	0.4
Yoakum	14.2	40.2	9.4	2.1	1.0	2.0	1.7	D	10.1	1 240	152	145	3 000	0.7
Young	0.0	39.2	5.0	13.1	3.5	4.7	4.3	5.0	10.8	4 380	239	520	8 657	0.4
Zapata	0.4	41.0	D	D	0.7	3.4	2.1	2.3	17.4	1 970	137	623	6 226	0.4
Zavala	6.8	0.8	D	D	D	5.1	D	D	26.9	2 195	180	844	4 304	0.5
UTAH	0.4	1.8	7.2	10.3	11.7	7.6	8.6	8.7	17.7	356 984	123	31 093	1 022 537	4.4
Beaver	19.7	7.7	8.3	3.2	D	5.6	D	D	23.2	1 120	173	78	2 927	0.7
Box Elder	5.2	0.5	6.4	36.1	D	6.2	2.4	6.2	13.3	7 985	157	516	18 097	4.4
Cache	1.5	0.2	5.2	24.1	8.3	6.8	4.4	10.6	22.6	12 300	105	833	39 368	6.3
Carbon	0.1	D	5.9	4.5	D	8.8	2.6	D	20.7	4 325	207	482	9 617	0.7
Daggett	-0.4	D	D	D	D	D	D	2.5	34.0	235	208	0	1 154	1.1
Davis	0.1	D	9.6	11.1	10.7	6.6	5.4	7.7	29.9	35 790	111	2 441	103 628	6.2
Duchesne	-0.3	34.3	9.3	1.8	3.4	4.8	2.1	3.6	16.4	3 090	154	307	9 800	3.2
Emery	0.1	D	11.2	0.6	D	5.1	D	D	19.7	2 100	196	134	4 500	0.2
Garfield	-2.1	D	3.6	1.9	D	6.0	1.7	D	33.2	1 085	214	44	3 818	2.5
Grand	-0.7	D	8.7	0.8	D	11.3	4.4	6.4	23.1	1 860	199	139	5 111	6.1
Iron	3.1	0.6	4.7	9.3	3.5	8.4	7.9	9.4	29.2	7 190	154	601	20 083	2.1
Juab	3.5	2.1	14.4	22.6	D	3.8	2.2	D	18.8	1 565	152	108	3 557	1.6
Kane	0.1	D	3.2	D	2.5	6.0	9.1	2.8	26.2	1 800	249	68	5 866	0.9
Millard	19.2	2.6	1.9	4.8	D	5.1	1.9	D	18.4	2 335	185	127	4 926	-0.3
Morgan	0.9	D	22.7	11.4	D	4.7	5.1	D	18.3	1 320	129	45	3 306	10.0
Piute	24.3	0.0	D	0.0	D	D	D	D	41.2	460	302	22	910	1.2
Rich	18.2	D	11.7	D	D	4.1	D	D	27.9	395	174	0	2 920	3.0
Salt Lake	0.0	1.2	6.2	9.3	12.9	7.8	11.2	8.0	15.5	128 870	119	13 389	376 456	3.4
San Juan	-0.2	12.2	13.3	2.9	D	2.9	1.2	14.5	35.9	2 050	137	576	5 835	1.8
Sanpete	7.9	2.6	6.4	10.6	D	6.0	3.7	7.2	31.9	4 560	161	321	10 415	0.3
Sevier	1.9	8.3	4.3	5.9	3.8	10.4	2.8	9.9	21.2	4 165	200	308	8 513	0.8
Summit	0.7	1.2	8.0	4.0	10.0	8.7	14.3	6.0	10.0	4 335	113	109	27 215	2.5
Tooele	0.5	1.0	6.4	11.5	D	5.1	1.9	8.1	28.1	6 760	111	683	20 369	4.7
Uintah	0.5	31.0	7.5	1.0	4.6	5.7	4.8	4.2	16.6	4 010	112	338	13 176	10.1
Utah	0.5	0.2	8.6	10.0	18.4	7.7	5.9	9.5	13.0	50 610	92	4 416	157 455	6.1
Wasatch	-0.2	D	17.2	3.6	8.2	9.0	5.3	7.9	21.5	3 050	115	113	11 613	9.8
Washington	-0.1	0.4	10.3	5.0	6.6	10.3	6.7	17.0	16.1	30 960	210	1 244	62 434	8.1
Wayne	13.9	D	10.7	D	D	4.1	D	D	31.2	615	225	27	1 619	1.8
Weber	0.0	D	6.3	16.0	5.3	7.9	6.3	12.6	23.2	32 045	134	3 608	87 849	1.9
VERMONT	1.0	0.2	7.3	11.7	9.3	7.7	6.2	14.3	19.2	138 418	221	15 741	325 789	1.0
Addison	5.1	0.2	8.3	15.0	D	8.9	3.6	13.2	12.3	7 365	200	610	16 941	1.1
Bennington	0.1	D	6.8	15.3	D	11.1	5.4	16.3	13.3	9 690	264	1 204	20 935	0.1
Caledonia	0.9	0.2	10.4	12.3	6.3	10.1	4.1	14.7	18.2	7 285	234	998	16 032	0.6

1. Per 1,000 resident population estimated as of July 1 of the year shown.

Table B. States and Counties — **Housing, Labor Force, and Employment**

STATE County	Housing units, 2009–2013: Occupied units: Total	Owner-occupied: Percent	Owner-occupied: Median value[1]	Median owner cost as a percent of income: With a mortgage	Median owner cost as a percent of income: Without a mortgage[2]	Renter-occupied: Median rent[3]	Renter-occupied: Median rent as a percent of income[2]	Substandard units[4] (percent)	Civilian labor force, 2014: Total	Percent change, 2013–2014	Unemployment: Total	Unemployment: Rate[5]	Civilian employment,[6] 2009–2013: Total	Percent: Management, business, science and arts	Percent: Construction, production, and maintenance occupations
	89	90	91	92	93	94	95	96	97	98	99	100	101	102	103
TEXAS—Cont'd															
Tom Green	42 286	64.2	99 000	20.9	11.8	721	29.1	4.8	54 752	0.6	2 211	4.0	49 948	29.9	23.7
Travis	411 876	51.8	219 200	23.5	12.5	988	30.9	3.4	649 426	2.7	26 104	4.0	561 181	45.1	14.7
Trinity	5 091	81.4	80 100	23.7	13.8	616	30.1	6.1	5 600	0.4	335	6.0	4 940	24.6	26.1
Tyler	8 224	82.6	75 100	20.1	12.0	610	26.8	6.2	7 621	0.0	610	8.0	7 189	25.7	32.1
Upshur	14 286	78.3	89 400	19.6	10.2	672	24.1	6.5	18 659	0.3	950	5.1	16 463	25.3	34.0
Upton	1 218	73.9	48 500	15.6	10.0	598	25.0	10.1	1 869	8.9	59	3.2	1 434	21.8	41.9
Uvalde	8 619	71.1	68 600	21.8	12.5	613	30.8	7.1	11 706	-2.4	670	5.7	10 291	27.5	29.2
Val Verde	15 082	66.7	91 900	22.2	13.2	649	28.9	3.9	19 610	-0.5	1 116	5.7	18 595	24.7	24.2
Van Zandt	19 064	77.9	96 900	22.0	12.6	679	32.3	4.3	24 071	0.6	1 263	5.2	21 275	27.6	31.5
Victoria	32 072	65.4	110 200	21.4	11.8	745	29.1	2.1	46 553	1.2	1 929	4.1	40 638	28.2	27.6
Walker	20 558	57.0	109 900	20.8	12.2	730	39.9	5.4	23 290	0.4	1 252	5.4	21 957	30.9	18.3
Waller	13 601	67.9	133 400	24.4	12.2	807	29.3	4.2	21 272	1.7	1 070	5.0	18 570	29.1	27.5
Ward	3 938	72.2	57 300	15.4	11.1	563	21.6	2.5	6 004	8.4	210	3.5	4 566	20.0	37.7
Washington	12 244	69.2	147 800	24.6	11.8	756	28.8	17.4	15 898	0.7	723	4.5	14 484	30.2	29.8
Webb	67 372	64.0	108 800	26.8	14.7	742	33.8	5.0	111 815	0.9	5 674	5.1	96 201	25.4	23.1
Wharton	14 517	68.0	95 600	21.2	13.7	657	30.8	5.0	21 768	0.8	1 019	4.7	18 260	26.6	34.1
Wheeler	2 319	72.5	76 600	19.2	10.0	668	25.4	2.7	3 129	-0.6	111	3.5	2 645	31.2	33.4
Wichita	48 305	62.4	89 800	21.6	13.0	730	28.2	5.0	57 054	-0.9	2 778	4.9	55 454	30.8	23.6
Wilbarger	5 161	68.3	62 000	19.4	12.5	559	23.9	8.7	5 382	-7.2	265	4.9	5 908	27.3	25.9
Willacy	5 499	77.9	48 800	21.5	14.1	563	39.3	2.7	7 250	-2.7	895	12.3	5 462	23.0	23.3
Williamson	154 948	68.6	178 900	22.7	11.9	1 050	27.9	4.6	254 484	2.8	10 945	4.3	216 214	45.1	15.2
Wilson	15 157	84.9	143 500	20.9	11.2	782	26.3	5.4	22 692	1.8	935	4.1	20 372	31.7	27.9
Winkler	2 709	80.4	45 100	15.6	10.0	575	18.0	3.1	3 369	1.0	143	4.2	3 165	22.0	42.4
Wise	20 487	80.6	121 900	22.0	12.5	840	26.8	2.9	28 873	1.3	1 387	4.8	25 962	27.7	31.7
Wood	15 800	81.1	99 900	24.1	12.4	699	27.1	9.8	16 781	0.1	991	5.9	15 497	28.1	29.7
Yoakum	2 654	80.0	71 100	17.0	10.0	542	25.4	1.9	4 334	2.5	131	3.0	3 486	24.1	46.0
Young	7 186	71.8	84 300	16.1	11.9	633	26.4	14.9	8 749	1.7	357	4.1	8 413	24.4	30.2
Zapata	4 460	79.1	55 700	20.5	10.7	560	50.0	9.4	7 022	-1.0	364	5.2	5 263	20.8	33.6
Zavala	3 654	68.6	39 900	23.4	14.8	411	37.3	5.0	3 852	-4.2	476	12.4	3 991	27.3	31.0
UTAH	886 770	70.1	212 800	24.0	10.0	856	29.5	3.9	1 431 104	1.5	54 158	3.8	1 275 709	36.3	21.4
Beaver	2 112	77.7	144 800	19.8	10.3	699	37.5	2.2	2 968	-2.0	117	3.9	2 674	27.1	31.3
Box Elder	16 207	79.3	166 100	22.6	10.0	641	23.4	4.0	23 557	1.4	907	3.9	21 554	31.2	33.2
Cache	35 375	64.5	189 100	23.6	10.0	677	28.3	2.4	58 894	1.7	1 891	3.2	53 076	36.7	23.0
Carbon	7 764	69.5	122 700	20.9	10.4	605	27.2	1.0	8 701	-3.1	450	5.2	8 957	26.6	31.4
Daggett	305	74.1	162 500	19.4	12.2	838	23.1	2.7	430	-0.2	18	4.2	248	23.4	26.6
Davis	95 238	77.7	222 600	22.9	10.0	883	28.5	4.8	155 339	1.5	5 530	3.6	140 712	40.7	18.8
Duchesne	6 850	75.9	168 000	21.7	10.0	768	25.8	2.9	9 602	3.0	345	3.6	7 645	28.8	37.8
Emery	3 598	81.6	122 500	18.1	10.0	638	27.8	2.6	4 613	-2.4	241	5.2	4 393	25.2	40.6
Garfield	1 890	78.3	154 300	22.9	10.0	580	21.1	4.1	2 726	-2.3	235	8.6	2 311	30.9	22.4
Grand	3 633	68.0	218 800	26.5	10.0	749	28.1	3.8	5 515	0.7	344	6.2	4 752	26.7	19.4
Iron	15 435	62.8	168 300	26.7	10.0	643	30.6	5.2	19 950	2.6	893	4.5	18 722	32.6	22.7
Juab	3 016	80.3	162 600	22.6	10.0	757	22.8	5.3	4 817	2.3	195	4.0	4 392	25.8	33.1
Kane	3 077	78.9	162 300	21.8	10.0	796	25.8	5.4	3 581	2.8	164	4.6	3 176	33.8	21.7
Millard	4 101	74.2	132 800	20.2	10.0	576	24.9	1.4	6 009	1.5	212	3.5	5 353	24.2	38.8
Morgan	2 860	89.2	264 400	24.6	10.0	762	27.1	3.3	4 587	1.5	154	3.4	4 088	40.3	24.5
Piute	570	83.5	152 800	21.2	10.0	625	30.0	1.2	462	-4.7	31	6.7	618	38.5	21.8
Rich	664	83.4	156 600	21.3	10.0	633	34.3	4.3	1 002	1.6	37	3.7	871	33.8	36.7
Salt Lake	344 089	67.3	232 100	24.3	10.0	895	30.4	14.5	577 571	1.1	21 173	3.7	511 735	36.6	20.3
San Juan	4 216	81.2	127 400	21.6	10.0	541	22.3	3.6	5 614	-1.6	421	7.5	4 937	32.6	27.8
Sanpete	7 781	76.2	164 100	22.8	10.0	605	23.9	4.3	11 078	-0.1	503	4.5	10 256	33.1	27.8
Sevier	7 146	79.0	151 400	22.9	10.0	658	23.8	2.6	9 278	-0.2	415	4.5	8 279	27.7	30.4
Summit	13 627	74.4	485 700	25.0	10.0	1 239	29.4	2.9	22 608	2.3	759	3.4	19 498	42.6	16.2
Tooele	18 281	75.2	177 500	23.0	10.0	821	26.3	4.2	28 911	1.2	1 371	4.7	25 376	33.4	26.6
Uintah	11 007	75.0	187 900	22.9	10.0	931	23.7	4.4	15 926	1.4	563	3.5	14 438	25.7	34.6
Utah	143 005	67.9	222 100	24.6	10.0	864	30.7	4.3	255 571	2.5	8 902	3.5	225 875	39.8	17.6
Wasatch	7 602	75.5	307 600	26.5	10.0	987	34.0	3.8	12 716	3.9	465	3.7	11 169	34.9	20.7
Washington	46 826	69.1	212 900	28.8	10.0	938	31.5	3.8	61 496	3.3	2 654	4.3	53 702	31.4	20.9
Wayne	970	83.9	173 500	24.8	10.3	571	19.5	3.1	1 386	0.1	130	9.4	1 252	32.6	21.2
Weber	79 525	71.6	170 000	23.4	10.0	779	27.8	2.2	116 198	1.2	5 038	4.3	105 650	31.3	26.7
VERMONT	257 004	71.0	216 800	25.3	16.6	875	31.1	2.0	348 868	-0.7	14 305	4.1	324 350	39.9	20.6
Addison	14 164	74.1	234 500	25.7	17.6	877	29.8	2.9	20 982	0.4	818	3.9	19 166	41.0	25.2
Bennington	15 442	70.6	214 800	26.4	17.7	848	30.9	3.4	19 052	-1.3	912	4.8	17 936	36.1	21.5
Caledonia	12 491	73.4	164 300	24.3	17.1	683	34.3	1.4	15 549	-1.6	781	5.0	15 233	34.7	24.0

1. Specified owner-occupied units. 2. A value of 10.0 represents 10 percent or less; a value of 50.0 represents 50 percent or more. 3. Specified renter-occupied units.
4. Overcrowded or lacking complete plumbing facilities. 5. Percent of civilian labor force. 6. Persons 16 years old and over.

STATE County	Private nonfarm establishments, employment and payroll, 2013									Agriculture, 2012			
		Employment						Annual payroll		Farms			
											Percent with:		
	Number of establish- ments	Total	Health care and social assistance	Manufac- turing	Retail trade	Finance and insurance	Professional, scientific, and technical services	Total (mil dol)	Average per employee (dollars)	Number	Fewer than 50 acres	500 acres or more	Farm operators whose principal occu- pation is farming (percent)
	104	105	106	107	108	109	110	111	112	113	114	115	116
TEXAS—Cont'd													
Tom Green	2 738	39 341	7 621	3 287	6 339	1 500	1 484	1 363	34 647	1 203	44.1	20.3	40.1
Travis	31 086	514 749	60 644	28 312	57 426	25 182	59 923	27 262	52 961	1 132	51.7	8.0	42.7
Trinity	182	1 766	332	184	309	D	40	49	27 567	604	32.0	6.6	39.6
Tyler	258	2 384	548	D	769	D	49	61	25 719	727	46.9	4.4	41.8
Upshur	464	4 409	638	325	744	228	418	145	32 943	1 754	46.9	3.5	33.2
Upton	86	1 127	D	NA	64	D	D	62	54 580	101	8.9	68.3	47.5
Uvalde	622	6 964	1 489	417	1 488	248	205	184	26 409	640	17.7	33.9	49.8
Val Verde	765	10 352	3 048	471	2 103	458	194	242	23 383	421	40.9	35.2	42.5
Van Zandt	836	7 950	1 142	703	1 476	238	259	253	31 826	2 915	49.6	5.0	43.6
Victoria	2 373	34 376	6 434	2 162	5 878	1 145	997	1 473	42 836	1 533	41.6	12.1	41.6
Walker	946	11 331	2 044	979	2 422	401	490	326	28 807	1 560	55.5	6.7	43.3
Waller	699	10 266	1 032	2 954	924	D	322	455	44 299	1 927	59.2	5.6	41.7
Ward	299	3 748	229	D	318	D	D	209	55 894	93	30.1	33.3	26.9
Washington	882	12 488	1 661	3 197	2 088	764	341	422	33 827	2 697	42.7	4.2	35.8
Webb	5 091	71 445	14 226	622	13 352	2 633	1 894	2 005	28 063	696	15.1	48.6	48.6
Wharton	982	11 541	1 910	1 698	2 075	412	257	401	34 777	1 553	31.6	21.6	51.6
Wheeler	200	1 764	D	D	258	D	D	66	37 557	551	8.3	39.2	37.0
Wichita	3 150	45 010	10 858	4 667	7 519	1 900	1 233	1 530	33 992	639	40.2	15.5	38.3
Wilbarger	297	3 632	504	D	D	D	61	116	31 894	424	18.6	33.0	43.6
Willacy	191	2 331	333	D	D	84	D	61	26 160	321	47.0	26.2	50.2
Williamson	8 908	137 138	16 734	7 966	22 334	7 402	11 761	6 812	49 674	2 542	48.3	9.3	43.2
Wilson	601	5 631	1 062	368	1 253	D	194	173	30 662	2 444	38.1	7.2	38.4
Winkler	170	1 540	D	D	210	58	D	77	49 788	43	30.2	60.5	32.6
Wise	1 269	18 868	2 733	1 717	2 254	387	278	828	43 877	3 095	54.2	6.4	37.6
Wood	800	8 057	1 453	881	1 373	331	704	249	30 862	1 465	44.6	4.9	47.4
Yoakum	184	2 548	D	D	222	80	D	138	54 141	339	5.0	58.1	50.1
Young	589	5 955	1 084	921	866	262	123	214	35 920	795	21.0	25.5	39.4
Zapata	163	2 218	246	D	284	87	D	92	41 478	449	9.4	49.9	49.4
Zavala	109	1 880	D	D	241	48	D	42	22 110	287	7.3	54.7	46.7
UTAH	71 887	1 101 557	127 970	112 234	137 665	56 886	87 039	45 172	41 008	18 027	57.9	12.3	38.5
Beaver	159	1 595	D	107	438	40	12	45	28 168	277	43.3	20.9	66.1
Box Elder	982	16 393	1 511	D	1 587	289	203	761	46 410	1 235	45.6	21.6	41.0
Cache	3 041	38 782	5 130	11 404	5 502	1 124	2 813	1 226	31 613	1 217	51.5	10.4	39.9
Carbon	513	6 338	867	379	1 091	D	104	257	40 594	319	63.3	13.8	46.7
Daggett	23	74	NA	NA	NA	NA	D	3	36 878	51	37.3	21.6	31.4
Davis	6 499	75 584	9 687	9 684	13 291	2 392	7 307	2 693	35 633	493	79.9	2.4	32.9
Duchesne	739	7 164	1 139	238	798	113	199	316	44 140	1 058	39.0	13.7	35.4
Emery	187	2 605	144	D	535	51	113	127	48 577	587	48.9	12.4	42.9
Garfield	153	1 182	D	D	D	17	D	35	29 695	279	42.3	12.2	43.0
Grand	445	3 520	D	D	712	66	103	96	27 249	81	60.5	13.6	51.9
Iron	1 204	11 013	1 719	1 494	1 956	424	419	305	27 729	509	39.3	24.6	45.0
Juab	188	2 084	D	437	308	D	323	66	31 543	353	33.1	22.1	28.3
Kane	249	2 128	217	D	346	83	D	67	31 309	183	33.3	24.6	39.9
Millard	241	2 813	238	500	559	D	91	121	43 106	728	29.3	30.2	49.9
Morgan	235	1 452	140	D	159	D	96	56	38 875	301	59.8	10.6	37.5
Piute	24	73	D	NA	NA	D	NA	2	21 096	123	23.6	15.4	54.5
Rich	81	385	D	D	D	D	D	13	32 569	158	29.1	54.4	61.4
Salt Lake	29 886	524 284	60 655	46 411	57 483	38 218	41 657	24 365	46 474	630	89.8	3.0	29.2
San Juan	258	2 588	608	D	319	D	D	85	32 820	746	53.8	22.8	54.7
Sanpete	398	4 537	893	719	826	143	D	128	28 172	901	52.5	13.1	38.5
Sevier	515	5 948	777	D	1 313	135	111	191	32 129	674	60.8	6.4	38.9
Summit	2 144	26 100	1 090	D	4 166	D	1 062	825	31 594	618	62.0	11.2	33.0
Tooele	758	11 037	1 349	1 693	1 778	166	1 507	430	38 978	476	60.1	14.5	31.3
Uintah	1 166	11 090	707	284	1 686	203	540	540	48 734	1 231	55.5	8.0	32.8
Utah	11 374	170 323	21 578	16 556	22 995	5 011	13 061	6 435	37 778	2 462	78.9	3.8	30.5
Wasatch	807	5 345	555	231	1 054	156	347	168	31 417	450	76.9	5.1	32.4
Washington	4 195	40 096	7 143	2 406	7 666	1 465	1 770	1 259	31 397	579	63.0	13.1	43.5
Wayne	81	632	D	D	104	D	D	17	26 900	187	29.4	10.2	48.1
Weber	5 007	75 494	10 491	11 582	10 811	3 807	7 188	2 575	34 108	1 121	79.8	3.1	36.1
VERMONT	21 119	262 474	46 343	30 480	37 633	9 071	22 480	10 074	38 381	7 338	39.2	7.3	51.5
Addison	1 139	12 178	2 254	1 397	1 755	326	389	462	37 953	814	37.0	14.7	60.6
Bennington	1 403	15 194	2 968	2 559	2 930	338	386	534	35 142	305	48.9	3.9	46.6
Caledonia	944	9 094	1 759	1 575	1 604	313	331	321	35 244	560	38.8	5.7	47.1

STATE County	Agriculture, 2012 (cont.) Land in farms Acreage (1,000)	Land in farms Percent change, 2007–2012	Land in farms Acres Average size of farm	Land in farms Acres Total irrigated (1,000)	Land in farms Acres Total cropland (1,000)	Value of land and buildings (dollars) Average per farm	Value of land and buildings (dollars) Average per acre	Value of machinery and equipment, average per farm (dollars)	Value of products sold Total (mil dol)	Value of products sold Average per farm (dollars)	Value of products sold Percent from: Crops	Value of products sold Percent from: Livestock and poultry products	Percent of farms with sales of: $10,000 or more	Percent of farms with sales of: $100,000 or more	Government payments Total ($1,000)	Government payments Percent of farms
	117	118	119	120	121	122	123	124	125	126	127	128	129	130	131	132
TEXAS—Cont'd																
Tom Green	957	3.6	795	31.1	168.2	906 863	1 140	87 951	131.4	109 257	24.8	75.2	26.9	9.4	5 161	25.4
Travis	253	-3.7	223	1.8	61.2	856 591	3 837	55 964	41.7	36 809	82.0	18.0	24.6	6.6	1 130	16.8
Trinity	111	2.1	184	0.2	17.9	427 030	2 318	57 775	7.1	11 672	24.1	75.9	31.1	1.3	161	7.3
Tyler	91	7.6	125	0.6	16.4	364 713	2 924	58 297	19.1	26 333	74.7	25.3	21.7	1.1	43	2.9
Upshur	202	2.1	115	0.4	43.1	330 283	2 863	43 263	60.6	34 526	7.6	92.4	21.8	3.2	298	2.7
Upton	686	8.2	6 794	8.9	46.1	3 991 644	587	142 505	12.7	125 584	63.6	36.4	54.5	34.7	1 495	41.6
Uvalde	977	-1.3	1 527	49.5	139.8	3 052 314	1 999	102 739	112.5	175 742	55.0	45.0	33.6	14.1	2 447	28.1
Val Verde	1 497	0.2	3 556	0.4	8.1	2 028 570	570	39 625	10.7	25 297	3.8	96.2	20.9	6.9	1 146	10.0
Van Zandt	371	-10.9	127	2.4	100.6	405 667	3 191	47 770	94.3	32 360	50.1	49.9	25.7	3.2	887	2.9
Victoria	438	-11.3	286	3.3	80.2	654 921	2 293	54 768	47.6	31 020	58.4	41.6	27.5	4.3	2 451	18.2
Walker	281	25.2	180	0.5	38.6	598 604	3 329	52 780	34.5	22 124	53.8	46.2	16.9	2.1	533	2.8
Waller	315	16.2	163	10.1	79.9	1 020 860	6 245	64 387	91.7	47 575	76.8	23.2	25.1	4.5	2 172	14.7
Ward	392	-9.5	4 211	0.2	5.9	1 560 022	370	53 290	1.8	19 054	6.5	93.5	19.4	3.2	214	18.3
Washington	369	9.0	137	1.4	89.4	758 889	5 549	51 747	45.7	16 955	24.9	75.1	25.9	1.9	914	8.4
Webb	2 098	13.1	3 015	2.6	25.2	3 265 045	1 083	57 487	30.3	43 476	2.8	97.2	31.2	7.0	1 169	14.1
Wharton	661	7.3	425	71.6	391.6	1 080 889	2 541	159 701	373.6	240 591	72.5	27.5	49.5	22.0	13 724	52.9
Wheeler	519	-11.0	942	11.2	99.6	773 481	821	83 860	111.2	201 826	8.2	91.8	40.8	10.2	2 651	61.0
Wichita	367	10.9	574	3.0	117.1	684 844	1 193	80 674	37.9	59 362	51.6	48.4	35.1	9.5	2 069	33.5
Wilbarger	587	-4.3	1 385	15.7	196.6	1 384 455	1 000	143 679	47.2	111 425	66.5	33.5	50.2	18.9	3 593	71.9
Willacy	336	-0.6	1 047	21.1	192.1	1 913 025	1 827	165 358	82.6	257 215	94.9	5.1	40.8	23.1	3 370	60.7
Williamson	559	3.1	220	1.3	211.6	853 775	3 885	61 058	129.6	51 002	57.8	42.2	25.5	6.7	3 659	26.2
Wilson	440	-5.9	180	12.4	103.3	537 404	2 987	50 097	102.1	41 775	27.3	72.7	27.5	3.0	1 988	20.7
Winkler	533	0.1	12 406	D	D	4 500 116	363	95 000	3.4	79 907	D	D	41.9	18.6	D	7.0
Wise	487	10.0	157	2.8	114.3	600 404	3 815	52 997	49.9	16 112	32.9	67.1	23.1	2.6	1 079	7.5
Wood	227	-2.8	155	1.6	52.5	442 703	2 853	57 063	105.9	72 270	6.2	93.8	27.2	5.3	267	3.3
Yoakum	488	10.1	1 441	90.4	265.9	1 166 307	809	247 257	80.0	236 012	91.6	8.4	47.2	32.4	7 563	81.7
Young	524	-0.7	659	0.2	97.8	911 345	1 384	68 309	23.7	29 801	33.8	66.2	33.8	5.2	1 385	30.1
Zapata	563	22.6	1 254	1.8	13.0	1 465 744	1 169	50 205	11.8	26 238	38.7	61.3	32.7	4.2	932	17.4
Zavala	693	-7.9	2 414	29.4	96.0	3 705 300	1 535	109 195	72.7	253 359	39.9	60.1	32.8	18.5	1 427	31.4
UTAH	10 974	-1.1	609	1 104.3	1 645.9	888 886	1 460	84 528	1 816.1	100 746	31.6	68.4	37.2	11.0	23 898	15.4
Beaver	190	20.0	686	37.6	37.1	1 370 004	1 997	140 502	288.5	1 041 520	7.5	92.5	57.8	33.6	419	31.4
Box Elder	1 171	-11.3	948	102.9	328.6	1 140 029	1 203	129 594	169.5	137 284	45.0	55.0	47.4	21.0	7 453	40.5
Cache	269	6.7	221	76.3	137.2	778 555	3 529	96 619	142.9	117 407	26.3	73.7	43.9	14.9	2 456	33.7
Carbon	241	11.6	754	11.1	20.9	918 621	1 218	59 596	9.0	28 248	27.0	73.0	31.3	5.3	239	5.6
Daggett	D	D	D	7.3	6.9	824 255	D	91 882	2.3	45 529	33.5	66.5	45.1	13.7	44	7.8
Davis	55	11.6	112	13.8	13.0	723 596	6 484	66 773	36.8	74 564	85.9	14.1	29.8	8.3	178	7.3
Duchesne	1 089	1.1	1 029	100.9	78.2	856 720	833	92 628	57.1	53 992	33.2	66.8	47.0	11.2	455	8.4
Emery	156	-23.7	266	51.7	41.6	452 336	1 700	65 775	14.1	23 978	36.2	63.8	37.8	6.0	306	16.7
Garfield	92	11.8	328	19.6	17.6	746 086	2 274	57 297	12.0	43 165	30.0	70.0	47.7	8.2	113	7.9
Grand	D	D	D	4.2	6.3	1 571 889	D	100 469	3.9	47 815	58.5	41.5	45.7	14.8	28	11.1
Iron	532	8.2	1 046	61.6	77.6	1 973 149	1 886	141 428	136.7	268 658	39.1	60.9	47.9	21.2	714	12.8
Juab	243	-6.7	688	20.5	47.9	825 640	1 200	86 938	28.4	80 331	40.7	59.3	45.6	11.6	997	35.4
Kane	125	10.6	685	4.0	4.5	966 694	1 410	50 333	4.7	25 590	16.8	83.2	43.2	2.7	214	10.4
Millard	577	1.9	793	115.2	151.6	1 114 356	1 405	200 816	180.6	248 110	41.4	58.6	64.3	27.6	2 312	38.3
Morgan	229	-24.1	760	9.0	15.8	1 196 671	1 575	63 116	20.4	67 648	16.7	83.3	36.5	12.6	71	10.0
Piute	38	-10.7	308	13.9	15.0	901 667	2 931	124 073	16.9	137 797	10.9	89.1	52.8	15.4	101	11.4
Rich	409	12.6	2 591	66.0	77.2	2 606 139	1 006	155 513	32.8	207 753	13.6	86.4	65.2	40.5	597	18.4
Salt Lake	78	-27.3	124	6.8	13.5	586 952	4 731	55 016	21.5	34 160	65.3	34.7	21.3	5.9	80	2.4
San Juan	1 609	4.0	2 157	4.3	113.0	805 649	374	43 488	13.4	17 906	32.6	67.4	16.6	5.2	1 543	23.9
Sanpete	284	-8.7	316	68.9	74.9	679 514	2 153	95 179	147.4	163 604	14.8	85.2	41.6	15.0	1 682	15.5
Sevier	122	-34.1	181	40.2	44.6	548 010	3 019	79 190	63.0	93 399	31.6	68.4	37.1	10.5	452	12.9
Summit	270	-34.9	437	20.8	25.2	996 972	2 281	51 511	24.2	39 079	13.0	87.0	34.0	7.0	154	2.4
Tooele	347	37.2	729	23.0	40.2	870 779	1 194	80 141	40.4	84 845	28.2	71.8	33.8	8.6	170	6.9
Uintah	D	D	D	69.0	62.5	930 444	D	75 442	46.6	37 877	45.7	54.3	33.5	6.3	653	6.6
Utah	343	-0.7	139	75.2	109.5	742 896	5 331	68 401	222.6	90 427	44.1	55.9	29.4	6.2	1 123	7.6
Wasatch	149	126.3	332	12.4	17.4	1 266 053	3 818	53 662	12.2	27 069	26.0	74.0	21.3	3.6	200	3.1
Washington	148	-15.0	256	14.8	20.2	934 487	3 656	50 485	12.6	21 843	51.1	48.9	29.2	5.5	210	7.8
Wayne	42	-6.3	227	15.7	15.3	914 588	4 037	78 561	15.7	84 144	19.3	80.7	62.6	14.4	500	35.3
Weber	117	10.5	105	37.7	32.9	609 955	5 823	60 135	39.9	35 568	41.9	58.1	23.5	4.4	436	8.0
VERMONT	1 252	1.5	171	3.6	488.3	546 627	3 205	86 935	776.1	105 765	22.9	77.1	40.6	15.1	13 930	21.3
Addison	208	11.1	256	0.3	126.8	779 307	3 044	130 227	185.5	227 928	15.3	84.7	47.1	21.4	3 796	32.7
Bennington	41	13.1	136	0.3	11.2	566 646	4 176	81 639	15.1	49 420	52.4	47.6	34.1	7.5	261	10.5
Caledonia	82	-0.1	146	0.1	29.1	464 918	3 182	76 234	37.2	66 509	18.1	81.9	40.4	13.6	628	15.7

Table B. States and Counties — **Water Use, Wholesale Trade, Retail Trade, and Real Estate**

STATE County	Water use, 2010		Wholesale trade,[1] 2007				Retail trade,[2] 2007				Real estate and rental and leasing,[2] 2007			
	Total water withdrawn (mil gal/day)	Gallons withdrawn per person per day	Number of establish-ments	Number of employees	Sales (mil dol)	Annual payroll (mil dol)	Number of establish-ments	Number of employees	Sales (mil dol)	Annual payroll (mil dol)	Number of establish-ments	Number of employees	Receipts (mil dol)	Annual payroll (mil dol)
	133	134	135	136	137	138	139	140	141	142	143	144	145	146
TEXAS—Cont'd														
Tom Green	55.9	507	119	D	D	D	448	D	D	D	135	631	76.0	15.8
Travis	293.3	286	1 129	19 691	14 119.8	1 362.7	3 352	52 883	13 879.5	1 341.0	1 776	12 622	2 423.6	501.6
Trinity	2.2	152	4	93	34.0	3.8	44	316	57.0	4.4	6	29	1.4	0.3
Tyler	5.1	236	7	55	70.5	4.5	56	596	115.0	10.2	3	D	D	D
Upshur	23.6	600	12	171	58.4	3.5	100	835	216.7	15.5	11	23	1.9	0.2
Upton	21.9	6 513	5	29	21.8	1.4	10	69	16.7	0.9	2	D	D	D
Uvalde	55.7	2 109	27	214	120.7	7.3	109	1 350	322.2	27.1	32	88	10.6	1.8
Val Verde	13.1	268	23	127	39.3	3.7	169	2 172	524.4	41.4	26	92	11.3	2.1
Van Zandt	11.3	216	29	209	50.1	7.4	150	1 543	410.5	30.7	35	101	26.9	1.6
Victoria	65.0	748	104	1 284	651.1	54.6	403	5 951	1 434.3	129.2	124	869	162.2	36.1
Walker	12.3	181	32	D	D	D	155	2 300	626.3	47.2	51	261	68.1	8.6
Waller	26.9	623	43	788	451.6	30.6	103	1 589	593.1	46.2	23	70	8.5	1.6
Ward	18.9	1 776	9	305	52.0	8.3	37	291	94.6	6.1	11	79	20.9	4.2
Washington	6.7	198	28	D	D	D	148	1 964	509.9	44.2	46	202	35.2	5.8
Webb	43.5	174	351	2 519	1 472.1	79.2	819	12 864	2 913.5	235.4	205	724	119.6	18.9
Wharton	223.6	5 416	53	808	541.1	32.6	179	1 961	466.7	43.6	40	169	37.9	6.8
Wheeler	17.9	3 303	8	55	25.8	1.4	30	200	46.1	3.2	5	12	0.7	0.1
Wichita	71.1	540	155	1 396	548.0	52.3	537	7 577	1 715.9	156.9	179	832	99.2	19.2
Wilbarger	34.8	2 567	15	D	D	D	55	674	170.2	12.8	9	28	2.6	0.5
Willacy	41.7	1 883	6	D	D	D	38	468	122.9	9.2	12	32	2.4	0.5
Williamson	64.1	152	307	2 913	1 525.2	153.3	1 188	21 116	9 918.0	525.2	399	1 732	363.2	60.2
Wilson	21.5	501	18	98	49.0	2.5	74	820	180.5	16.9	13	43	4.2	0.6
Winkler	14.5	2 032	7	42	29.1	2.0	25	167	40.3	3.0	5	50	7.6	1.7
Wise	68.4	1 157	55	506	418.4	23.8	162	2 002	565.3	49.6	39	365	63.5	17.4
Wood	53.0	1 262	38	268	137.0	7.4	142	1 448	383.5	30.7	36	154	21.6	3.2
Yoakum	211.9	26 888	17	160	51.2	6.8	27	169	37.0	3.3	5	D	D	D
Young	58.0	3 126	25	198	86.2	9.1	74	834	185.2	17.0	22	60	45.4	1.9
Zapata	7.4	527	3	D	D	D	37	318	62.1	4.3	7	18	2.8	0.5
Zavala	39.5	3 381	2	D	D	D	19	202	33.3	3.1	NA	NA	NA	NA
UTAH	4 463.8	1 615	3 043	43 900	25 417.4	2 012.0	8 984	142 266	36 574.2	3 240.7	4 886	20 413	3 390.8	617.4
Beaver	101.3	15 274	NA	NA	NA	NA	32	312	89.7	4.7	3	3	0.3	0.1
Box Elder	405.3	8 109	30	D	D	D	135	1 790	447.4	34.5	48	88	12.0	1.7
Cache	289.5	2 570	110	796	361.6	29.3	398	5 347	1 095.1	96.9	191	D	D	D
Carbon	41.3	1 929	29	D	D	D	98	1 271	298.9	25.4	17	63	13.1	1.5
Daggett	19.0	17 951	NA	NA	NA	NA	5	D	D	D	NA	NA	NA	NA
Davis	84.1	274	218	D	D	D	780	13 393	3 217.7	286.7	404	1 120	174.1	27.5
Duchesne	328.3	17 641	18	138	54.7	4.7	69	795	216.0	16.7	25	87	27.8	3.4
Emery	130.6	11 894	3	3	1.0	0.1	44	503	128.6	8.0	3	D	D	D
Garfield	64.5	12 477	2	D	D	D	22	134	22.9	1.8	10	13	1.9	0.4
Grand	17.1	1 857	12	84	19.7	3.2	76	661	159.9	14.7	36	106	16.2	2.6
Iron	210.1	4 551	40	D	D	D	191	2 274	652.2	48.4	96	203	35.0	4.5
Juab	56.1	5 478	5	43	19.3	1.3	34	318	112.2	4.8	2	D	D	D
Kane	17.6	2 466	5	10	3.8	0.3	49	351	72.1	6.2	22	53	6.8	1.0
Millard	291.1	23 281	11	62	23.2	1.9	65	566	125.1	9.1	3	5	0.5	0.1
Morgan	36.0	3 802	6	D	D	D	23	184	42.7	3.4	9	D	D	D
Piute	46.6	29 929	1	D	D	D	7	D	D	D	NA	NA	NA	NA
Rich	143.9	63 556	NA	NA	NA	NA	9	56	11.5	0.9	11	67	6.8	1.8
Salt Lake	410.8	399	1 649	28 039	16 956.4	1 350.3	3 424	60 133	16 758.7	1 510.5	2 085	11 470	2 022.2	384.1
San Juan	29.1	1 975	4	D	D	D	37	378	44.6	4.4	2	D	D	D
Sanpete	181.7	6 532	12	58	31.2	1.4	88	956	196.9	16.9	22	274	14.3	5.5
Sevier	143.9	6 916	14	126	112.0	4.2	108	1 312	324.6	27.4	10	65	5.2	1.4
Summit	70.9	1 952	57	322	165.8	11.7	294	3 224	659.9	64.7	270	1 214	221.5	41.6
Tooele	186.0	3 194	14	71	73.6	5.1	100	1 773	503.6	37.1	35	91	13.5	1.8
Uintah	274.6	8 426	44	D	D	D	135	1 703	461.4	37.0	75	364	138.5	19.2
Utah	366.1	709	406	6 033	2 425.0	275.6	1 357	23 988	5 772.2	518.3	753	D	D	D
Wasatch	56.3	2 391	12	D	D	D	80	1 253	228.4	27.1	46	134	12.3	2.5
Washington	122.2	885	146	1 260	510.8	48.3	593	8 035	2 087.8	185.9	367	856	122.0	20.0
Wayne	69.8	25 133	NA	NA	NA	NA	17	101	27.8	1.5	2	D	D	D
Weber	270.2	1 169	195	2 790	2 218.2	111.3	714	11 422	2 810.6	217.6	330	D	D	D
VERMONT	430.5	688	762	9 852	5 121.7	424.8	3 852	40 416	9 310.1	938.7	797	3 395	497.3	95.9
Addison	7.5	203	32	216	101.4	8.0	212	2 139	464.8	53.2	38	D	D	D
Bennington	5.3	142	31	D	D	D	338	3 415	833.0	82.6	64	230	35.2	6.8
Caledonia	4.0	128	26	212	66.2	10.1	188	1 743	412.7	39.7	26	81	14.2	2.6

1. Merchant wholesalers, except manufacturers' sales branches and offices. 2. Employer establishments.

Table B. States and Counties — **Professional Services, Manufacturing, and Accommodation and Food Services**

STATE County	Professional, scientific, and technical services,[1] 2007				Manufacturing, 2007				Accommodation and food services, 2007			
	Number of establish-ments	Number of employees	Receipts (mil dol)	Annual payroll (mil dol)	Number of establish-ments	Number of employees	Receipts (mil dol)	Annual payroll (mil dol)	Number of establish-ments	Number of employees	Sales (mil dol)	Annual payroll (mil dol)
	147	148	149	150	151	152	153	154	155	156	157	158
TEXAS—Cont'd												
Tom Green	185	D	D	D	120	D	D	D	209	D	D	D
Travis	4 745	D	D	D	768	35 731	28 294.7	1 827.7	2 277	52 877	2 833.7	797.8
Trinity	11	42	2.8	0.9	NA	NA	NA	NA	16	195	11.9	2.0
Tyler	16	60	5.0	1.4	NA	NA	NA	NA	21	225	9.8	2.1
Upshur	38	D	D	D	31	512	D	18.5	31	587	20.2	6.6
Upton	3	D	D	D	NA	NA	NA	NA	9	D	D	D
Uvalde	43	149	13.1	4.3	23	630	203.7	23.2	75	1 014	39.9	10.9
Val Verde	44	D	D	D	NA	NA	NA	NA	88	1 436	59.0	15.5
Van Zandt	52	212	25.6	8.0	35	645	119.9	24.8	64	839	32.9	9.4
Victoria	155	D	D	D	78	D	D	D	170	3 166	130.8	35.4
Walker	84	499	35.3	10.8	39	1 043	D	40.5	95	1 960	73.8	19.9
Waller	54	285	52.7	17.7	65	2 352	D	111.0	41	642	24.7	5.9
Ward	13	40	3.1	1.2	NA	NA	NA	NA	20	218	8.9	1.8
Washington	59	265	32.5	9.2	46	2 782	762.8	108.0	76	1 024	41.3	11.9
Webb	309	D	D	D	89	914	242.4	30.7	360	7 489	317.3	86.5
Wharton	59	304	34.8	13.6	47	3 941	464.0	56.6	76	1 160	45.9	12.1
Wheeler	10	30	2.7	0.9	NA	NA	NA	NA	19	197	9.3	2.3
Wichita	237	D	D	D	142	6 047	1 492.5	262.7	290	6 626	254.8	79.7
Wilbarger	22	85	5.4	1.5	9	D	D	31.9	33	368	16.1	4.2
Willacy	9	D	D	D	NA	NA	NA	NA	26	287	13.2	2.6
Williamson	886	D	D	D	269	6 524	1 647.6	312.5	636	12 187	583.6	156.5
Wilson	37	D	D	D	NA	NA	NA	NA	47	553	20.8	5.6
Winkler	9	15	4.0	0.5	NA	NA	NA	NA	9	85	4.7	1.0
Wise	78	D	D	D	76	1 728	376.5	72.3	93	1 356	59.3	16.6
Wood	66	221	20.2	6.2	44	1 026	708.0	41.2	66	761	30.4	8.3
Yoakum	6	14	1.5	0.4	NA	NA	NA	NA	18	147	6.0	1.4
Young	34	117	11.4	4.1	23	973	301.4	41.1	40	481	17.7	5.0
Zapata	6	19	1.4	0.3	NA	NA	NA	NA	22	212	9.4	2.0
Zavala	5	19	1.4	0.3	NA	NA	NA	NA	16	108	4.6	1.1
UTAH	8 203	67 426	8 197.7	3 157.3	3 368	123 249	42 431.7	5 508.5	4 541	91 808	3 980.6	1 148.6
Beaver	5	11	1.3	0.3	NA	NA	NA	NA	25	310	12.8	3.2
Box Elder	63	D	D	D	78	10 869	3 150.9	D	70	1 171	36.8	11.9
Cache	351	D	D	D	214	10 326	D	405.8	135	2 727	95.2	29.5
Carbon	39	D	D	D	NA	NA	NA	NA	40	763	26.2	6.8
Daggett	3	D	D	D	NA	NA	NA	NA	8	67	6.4	1.8
Davis	791	D	D	D	273	9 914	4 985.2	D	368	7 425	274.3	76.9
Duchesne	37	88	11.4	3.5	NA	NA	NA	NA	30	374	13.6	3.8
Emery	11	71	5.0	1.8	NA	NA	NA	NA	25	245	10.8	2.7
Garfield	5	D	D	D	NA	NA	NA	NA	43	460	49.3	12.1
Grand	33	157	14.3	5.3	NA	NA	NA	NA	80	1 369	68.2	19.9
Iron	116	D	D	D	72	1 665	736.0	59.4	101	1 618	59.6	16.9
Juab	14	277	25.2	9.7	NA	NA	NA	NA	21	223	7.2	1.8
Kane	18	27	2.9	0.9	NA	NA	NA	NA	42	404	20.9	6.1
Millard	5	D	D	D	NA	NA	NA	NA	26	342	11.6	3.2
Morgan	25	D	D	D	NA	NA	NA	NA	11	142	5.7	1.3
Piute	1	D	D	D	NA	NA	NA	NA	7	D	D	D
Rich	3	D	D	D	NA	NA	NA	NA	12	65	3.7	0.9
Salt Lake	3 763	D	D	D	1 483	51 595	18 860.5	2 351.7	1 826	40 212	1 874.6	556.6
San Juan	10	D	D	D	NA	NA	NA	NA	61	D	D	D
Sanpete	20	224	8.7	3.1	NA	NA	NA	NA	32	363	8.3	2.4
Sevier	37	134	14.3	5.8	NA	NA	NA	NA	45	828	24.7	7.2
Summit	293	896	130.5	44.8	NA	NA	NA	NA	167	4 907	228.9	70.4
Tooele	55	D	D	D	39	D	D	D	55	931	35.2	8.8
Uintah	104	324	44.6	14.3	NA	NA	NA	NA	64	1 005	46.5	11.1
Utah	1 428	16 469	1 328.9	499.4	522	D	D	D	543	11 712	451.7	128.4
Wasatch	76	346	37.0	12.8	NA	NA	NA	NA	43	722	38.8	9.1
Washington	432	D	D	D	154	3 225	609.6	117.4	279	5 631	254.5	74.5
Wayne	3	D	D	D	NA	NA	NA	NA	24	117	7.7	1.8
Weber	462	D	D	D	244	12 066	D	494.1	358	7 107	261.2	70.9
VERMONT	2 100	16 346	1 615.6	649.5	1 108	35 571	10 751.5	1 650.1	1 942	31 176	1 367.6	427.9
Addison	115	390	42.5	17.3	57	1 948	539.0	93.0	83	971	48.2	16.2
Bennington	125	407	53.7	16.5	75	2 443	571.6	97.4	152	2 316	106.7	33.0
Caledonia	66	D	D	D	60	2 120	339.1	70.8	73	712	29.9	8.4

1. Establishment subject to federal tax.

Table B. States and Counties — **Health Care and Social Assistance, Other Services, Nonemployer Businesses, and Residential Construction**

STATE County	Health care and social assistance, 2007				Other services, 2007				Nonemployer businesses, 2013		Value of residential construction authorized by building permits, 2014	
	Number of establish-ments	Number of employees	Receipts (mil dol)	Annual payroll (mil dol)	Number of establish-ments	Number of employees	Receipts (mil dol)	Annual payroll (mil dol)	Number	Receipts (mil dol)	New Construction ($1,000)	Number of housing units
	159	160	161	162	163	164	165	166	167	168	169	170
TEXAS—Cont'd												
Tom Green	259	D	D	D	212	D	D	D	7 901	337.8	69 568	629
Travis	2 549	48 334	5 562.7	2 156.3	1 930	18 213	2 025.4	609.7	101 952	5 576.0	1 850 112	12 673
Trinity	22	314	20.8	8.4	20	85	5.2	1.1	893	31.1	455	6
Tyler	22	479	27.0	11.8	11	42	3.6	0.9	1 092	45.1	130	1
Upshur	43	602	41.1	16.9	31	96	11.6	2.4	2 725	121.8	2 372	21
Upton	7	D	D	D	1	D	D	D	283	14.7	177	1
Uvalde	58	1 392	90.5	40.0	35	208	14.2	4.1	2 554	112.2	1 241	13
Val Verde	83	2 891	127.5	53.8	49	257	16.5	3.4	2 735	91.1	7 829	63
Van Zandt	82	1 209	67.2	29.5	57	255	22.6	6.0	4 076	178.0	6 253	89
Victoria	322	6 266	586.9	233.1	166	1 202	112.2	33.1	5 993	279.9	85 491	835
Walker	101	2 028	133.5	56.2	64	384	23.1	6.3	3 745	145.4	22 744	222
Waller	43	678	38.4	17.4	50	185	16.9	4.3	3 205	161.0	3 104	82
Ward	13	242	14.8	7.2	17	74	8.9	2.1	681	36.7	2 204	19
Washington	81	1 825	104.7	42.6	52	281	17.9	5.1	2 870	130.7	8 693	85
Webb	441	12 142	723.4	284.3	257	1 465	124.3	28.6	22 688	1 027.2	186 839	1 719
Wharton	63	2 282	165.5	56.7	74	291	20.7	5.3	3 039	122.6	2 757	19
Wheeler	14	227	13.3	6.2	8	19	1.8	0.4	508	23.5	0	0
Wichita	374	10 412	823.4	329.8	264	1 486	141.7	34.9	7 730	378.4	22 827	143
Wilbarger	35	D	D	D	23	126	6.1	1.8	707	24.9	285	2
Willacy	32	1 199	53.1	27.9	17	D	D	D	1 327	38.2	12 611	98
Williamson	748	9 836	926.3	368.7	518	3 892	305.6	101.9	34 913	1 521.0	990 304	4 706
Wilson	51	1 206	65.5	28.8	42	112	13.3	1.9	3 248	161.4	6 550	34
Winkler	11	139	9.2	3.7	11	D	D	D	503	32.3	0	0
Wise	104	D	D	D	70	383	30.9	8.5	4 858	276.7	7 279	46
Wood	73	1 004	76.3	27.4	53	245	16.4	4.4	3 430	146.8	854	19
Yoakum	5	D	D	D	9	48	4.5	1.0	464	21.1	1 968	14
Young	59	950	65.9	26.9	39	126	9.4	2.7	1 999	133.2	3 858	35
Zapata	14	325	8.6	3.8	6	D	D	D	1 405	57.8	NA	NA
Zavala	12	542	14.4	6.9	3	D	D	D	909	24.9	1 253	11
UTAH	6 392	112 646	10 860.4	4 156.2	4 141	26 236	2 356.1	653.1	201 838	8 913.5	3 360 911	17 510
Beaver	16	232	17.8	5.8	8	D	D	D	470	12.9	3 029	16
Box Elder	109	1 128	93.0	31.2	59	D	D	D	2 975	110.5	31 365	164
Cache	299	D	D	D	161	D	D	D	7 934	281.2	109 733	749
Carbon	76	933	82.1	24.3	52	D	D	D	1 047	32.8	10 117	66
Daggett	1	D	D	D	NA	NA	NA	NA	77	2.2	1 539	7
Davis	584	8 030	679.7	262.5	363	2 225	161.9	47.1	21 103	888.8	324 454	1 512
Duchesne	46	1 048	87.8	31.9	34	137	13.5	3.3	1 416	67.2	31 679	137
Emery	14	D	D	D	10	D	D	D	582	13.8	1 839	10
Garfield	7	170	13.1	4.8	2	D	D	D	467	12.4	7 028	42
Grand	22	249	21.4	8.5	21	55	4.5	1.2	1 022	44.2	15 859	89
Iron	108	1 434	123.3	42.3	69	394	25.3	6.8	3 271	107.6	38 855	238
Juab	21	D	D	D	8	D	D	D	712	30.3	9 293	38
Kane	15	166	15.5	3.9	14	D	D	D	669	25.1	3 122	15
Millard	24	D	D	D	14	46	9.6	1.2	770	27.4	5 252	28
Morgan	10	49	3.0	0.8	9	61	3.4	1.2	910	35.8	25 619	83
Piute	1	D	D	D	1	D	D	D	109	5.0	1 508	10
Rich	2	D	D	D	8	D	D	D	240	8.4	5 419	21
Salt Lake	2 644	53 465	5 733.1	2 203.6	1 907	13 222	1 262.1	355.0	76 464	3 716.8	864 159	4 943
San Juan	27	D	D	D	8	D	D	D	748	25.1	3 582	21
Sanpete	47	830	54.2	22.9	27	D	D	D	1 685	59.5	4 506	37
Sevier	48	694	51.0	19.5	25	133	13.4	4.9	1 369	54.2	9 191	45
Summit	108	D	D	D	95	868	98.8	22.3	5 615	356.4	114 490	286
Tooele	92	D	D	D	57	269	20.7	6.0	2 661	84.4	71 881	375
Uintah	57	598	62.7	18.5	64	297	39.7	9.0	1 776	86.0	61 164	322
Utah	1 014	D	D	D	539	D	D	D	40 259	1 665.7	954 586	5 257
Wasatch	43	464	39.7	13.6	42	D	D	D	2 522	110.9	176 224	436
Washington	393	6 648	628.5	250.2	198	1 116	95.0	27.4	12 017	549.6	309 143	1 628
Wayne	4	D	D	D	3	D	D	D	287	10.4	2 982	16
Weber	560	10 314	914.5	357.4	343	2 171	160.9	48.8	12 661	488.9	163 202	919
VERMONT	2 176	41 917	3 537.1	1 495.3	1 629	7 269	798.6	182.9	59 446	2 431.9	281 490	1 546
Addison	125	1 840	126.7	55.6	88	344	55.3	8.5	3 780	139.6	20 897	101
Bennington	166	2 867	238.3	103.6	97	441	29.7	8.0	3 637	152.7	12 300	35
Caledonia	105	1 763	124.0	55.5	72	252	20.3	5.1	2 964	113.9	10 225	49

Table B. States and Counties — **Government Employment and Payroll, and Local Government Finances**

STATE County	Government employment and payroll, 2012: Full-time equivalent employees	Government employment and payroll, 2012: March payroll (dollars)	March payroll (percent of total): Adminis-tration, judicial, and legal	March payroll (percent of total): Police and Corrections	March payroll (percent of total): Fire Protection	March payroll (percent of total): Highways and transpor-tation	March payroll (percent of total): Health and Welfare	March payroll (percent of total): Natural resources and utilities	March payroll (percent of total): Education and libraries	Local government finances, 2012: General revenue: Total (mil dol)	General revenue: Inter-govern-mental (mil dol)	Taxes: Total (mil dol)	Taxes: Per capita[1] (dollars): Total	Taxes: Per capita[1] (dollars): Property
	171	172	173	174	175	176	177	178	179	180	181	182	183	184
TEXAS—Cont'd														
Tom Green	4 430	11 842 865	8.7	16.5	6.7	1.4	3.6	6.1	55.2	321.7	125.9	138.0	1 218	917
Travis	45 034	190 376 191	8.0	14.8	5.4	4.1	5.1	18.3	42.4	4 794.7	942.7	2 689.4	2 455	2 026
Trinity	657	1 816 086	6.2	7.0	0.0	3.0	19.3	2.2	60.4	42.8	22.8	13.7	954	889
Tyler	945	2 527 612	9.2	3.5	0.0	3.0	16.0	2.8	65.4	63.8	23.6	34.9	1 625	1 538
Upshur	1 527	4 228 679	4.9	8.6	0.6	1.7	0.1	2.3	81.6	91.7	43.7	38.4	961	866
Upton	396	1 316 616	8.8	8.6	0.0	3.5	31.5	4.4	42.2	64.5	4.8	53.2	16 191	16 022
Uvalde	2 058	6 807 776	3.6	5.1	0.2	1.9	25.8	2.2	60.5	171.9	70.8	36.8	1 374	1 094
Val Verde	2 194	5 580 787	14.3	6.2	5.3	3.0	2.4	6.1	61.0	177.1	111.3	44.7	918	690
Van Zandt	1 960	5 471 112	4.9	6.7	0.3	1.8	0.4	2.9	82.3	133.5	67.2	50.0	953	821
Victoria	5 364	18 189 328	3.7	10.4	3.1	1.8	31.4	3.0	46.0	455.8	105.2	155.9	1 746	1 294
Walker	1 980	6 982 834	14.0	12.7	0.8	2.6	1.0	18.0	43.7	157.3	53.4	61.8	904	699
Waller	1 643	5 642 929	7.6	7.4	0.3	2.5	0.1	3.3	77.2	129.4	49.0	69.2	1 560	1 448
Ward	559	1 720 115	12.0	13.3	0.1	4.4	3.1	7.7	57.1	58.5	9.0	35.1	3 231	2 922
Washington	2 307	7 486 978	4.8	5.4	0.9	1.6	2.0	4.0	80.0	171.2	48.3	57.0	1 671	1 323
Webb	14 741	48 977 584	5.1	9.2	5.1	3.0	3.0	3.7	70.4	1 245.0	614.2	391.8	1 512	1 216
Wharton	3 171	11 435 949	2.9	4.7	1.0	2.5	19.8	1.5	66.6	188.9	70.3	71.4	1 729	1 485
Wheeler	514	1 406 670	6.6	3.2	0.0	2.3	33.3	2.8	49.5	54.5	8.1	36.6	6 498	6 236
Wichita	5 729	18 326 731	6.5	14.8	7.0	2.9	9.1	5.0	51.8	380.0	131.8	178.0	1 353	1 020
Wilbarger	1 195	3 537 696	3.1	4.1	2.6	1.8	21.1	2.8	64.1	75.4	29.4	23.4	1 765	1 490
Willacy	988	3 020 755	5.5	5.6	0.0	2.6	0.6	4.5	80.4	77.1	48.6	20.8	941	793
Williamson	16 819	59 733 376	3.1	6.7	3.0	0.5	4.4	2.8	78.5	1 670.1	418.9	1 031.8	2 262	1 950
Wilson	1 799	5 521 367	3.9	4.2	0.0	1.3	11.3	8.0	71.0	127.9	49.4	47.4	1 067	977
Winkler	465	1 871 237	6.8	7.5	0.0	1.6	15.1	4.2	63.8	57.9	10.9	36.9	5 029	4 658
Wise	2 052	6 283 194	8.7	7.9	0.7	4.7	0.0	3.9	72.0	189.8	35.2	132.2	2 187	1 913
Wood	1 347	3 686 462	6.7	10.8	0.5	4.1	1.5	3.8	72.4	92.1	31.3	50.5	1 202	1 071
Yoakum	719	2 354 261	7.1	8.7	0.1	3.1	26.1	3.9	50.3	97.6	9.0	68.0	8 426	8 230
Young	1 189	3 441 113	4.9	6.9	1.2	1.6	33.2	3.4	47.6	89.6	22.2	26.3	1 434	1 181
Zapata	901	2 905 195	13.0	4.2	3.8	4.8	1.0	3.6	68.4	76.6	24.7	47.2	3 300	3 261
Zavala	676	1 796 547	3.7	8.4	0.0	2.9	3.4	5.7	71.6	42.2	30.7	7.7	641	557
UTAH	X	X	X	X	X	X	X	X	X	X	X	X	X	X
Beaver	339	1 182 302	5.5	2.7	0.0	0.6	31.1	8.3	50.7	51.1	10.9	13.4	2 054	1 709
Box Elder	1 701	4 888 324	8.2	9.3	0.8	3.1	2.0	5.8	69.8	163.1	71.5	66.7	1 329	1 068
Cache	3 328	10 972 734	7.5	7.4	2.7	3.6	8.3	6.1	61.3	309.3	134.5	108.6	940	578
Carbon	959	3 089 135	8.6	9.2	0.6	4.8	13.4	11.0	49.4	77.6	27.1	32.7	1 540	1 152
Daggett	101	367 263	17.3	30.4	0.1	4.2	2.7	2.2	42.0	12.0	5.2	2.8	2 550	2 139
Davis	10 391	37 610 946	5.6	7.5	2.5	1.4	4.5	5.5	72.1	900.2	374.8	329.2	1 042	745
Duchesne	667	2 048 894	10.0	11.8	0.7	5.0	1.5	5.8	63.0	84.8	40.2	33.0	1 715	1 314
Emery	466	1 718 363	11.2	10.6	0.0	4.9	2.1	8.1	62.3	62.8	21.5	29.4	2 685	2 355
Garfield	208	742 442	11.2	13.2	0.0	8.1	3.9	3.0	59.1	29.9	14.5	10.4	2 048	1 146
Grand	491	1 568 944	14.6	13.1	0.9	6.9	12.1	8.6	39.6	48.0	15.0	23.4	2 503	1 486
Iron	1 282	4 462 404	8.5	11.6	1.0	3.6	3.5	5.1	64.5	132.5	51.2	58.7	1 257	954
Juab	437	1 313 251	9.2	9.3	0.0	4.6	1.1	6.7	66.9	40.9	23.8	12.2	1 178	963
Kane	440	1 479 423	9.0	11.3	0.3	3.4	34.0	2.0	37.7	48.6	12.0	21.3	2 951	1 982
Millard	516	1 988 139	9.7	11.9	0.0	5.8	2.6	6.2	62.0	68.1	23.0	25.6	2 037	1 792
Morgan	299	975 455	9.6	3.4	0.9	2.2	0.0	4.1	79.3	26.9	11.8	11.1	1 126	946
Piute	89	242 632	8.4	6.3	0.0	5.8	1.4	1.1	68.5	7.9	5.5	1.6	1 026	813
Rich	110	395 515	10.7	7.4	1.1	3.8	1.8	4.6	67.9	13.2	5.2	6.2	2 714	2 297
Salt Lake	34 230	125 577 298	7.2	10.3	5.3	9.8	5.0	8.9	51.0	3 731.7	1 299.6	1 519.3	1 428	1 028
San Juan	708	2 586 369	5.3	6.4	0.5	6.1	20.5	1.9	57.4	84.2	52.5	14.9	994	908
Sanpete	1 157	3 481 157	6.7	6.0	0.2	1.8	18.6	4.4	59.7	95.1	43.9	20.5	734	527
Sevier	746	2 317 397	8.0	11.6	0.2	2.5	2.9	7.4	65.4	75.7	42.9	22.0	1 059	746
Summit	1 737	6 591 640	8.6	7.7	9.0	7.8	2.4	12.1	48.0	236.3	39.4	155.2	4 084	3 100
Tooele	2 049	6 240 915	9.0	10.6	1.0	2.9	5.1	6.2	64.3	202.7	99.2	53.2	888	639
Uintah	1 239	3 713 017	11.2	10.8	0.4	5.2	9.6	10.8	46.9	155.8	52.9	70.7	2 048	1 456
Utah	14 037	52 266 547	6.3	8.0	2.5	1.4	4.9	8.4	66.6	1 574.6	646.3	574.1	1 062	718
Wasatch	952	3 521 146	10.0	7.9	0.0	2.6	6.3	11.3	55.4	122.6	39.4	52.8	2 091	1 673
Washington	4 130	14 492 173	7.3	10.1	1.7	2.6	6.5	13.4	56.5	453.7	154.1	197.8	1 366	972
Wayne	114	391 098	6.2	5.1	0.5	6.5	3.8	4.8	70.9	13.2	9.5	2.6	961	721
Weber	7 494	26 228 893	6.1	11.2	4.3	1.7	7.0	6.9	60.7	668.4	249.5	273.1	1 154	796
VERMONT	X	X	X	X	X	X	X	X	X	X	X	X	X	X
Addison	1 255	4 519 763	4.3	2.9	0.0	5.3	0.9	2.2	84.0	127.5	92.7	23.2	632	604
Bennington	948	3 568 427	6.0	7.7	0.1	5.9	0.6	5.2	74.2	128.5	92.0	25.4	692	657
Caledonia	1 032	3 333 702	5.5	3.4	1.1	8.2	0.9	4.6	76.0	108.5	81.8	18.1	580	578

1. Based on the resident population estimated as of July 1 of the year shown.

STATE County	Local government finances, 2012 (cont.)									Government employment, 2013			Presidential election,[2] 2012		
	Direct general expenditure							Debt outstanding					Percent of vote cast:		
			Percent of total for:												
	Total (mil dol)	Per capita[1] (dollars)	Education	Health and hospitals	Police protection	Public welfare	Highways	Total (mil dol)	Per capita[1] (dollars)	Federal civilian	Federal military	State and local	Democratic	Republican	All other
	185	186	187	188	189	190	191	192	193	194	195	196	197	198	199
TEXAS—Cont'd															
Tom Green	347.3	3 066	51.9	3.4	5.7	0.2	2.7	583.9	5 155	1 269	3 323	7 425	28.7	70.4	0.9
Travis	4 740.6	4 327	38.8	6.7	7.4	0.8	6.5	15 845.5	14 463	10 704	2 550	119 210	63.9	34.4	1.7
Trinity	41.5	2 899	53.9	9.1	1.8	0.5	4.9	18.1	1 265	25	30	606	31.7	67.4	0.9
Tyler	60.2	2 805	57.5	0.1	4.6	0.3	5.4	43.0	2 002	49	40	1 652	27.4	71.4	1.3
Upshur	91.6	2 291	72.4	0.0	4.3	0.1	3.6	89.1	2 229	55	83	1 664	25.0	74.0	1.0
Upton	68.5	20 851	78.3	16.8	0.3	0.1	0.7	15.4	4 703	0	0	499	24.1	75.0	0.9
Uvalde	177.9	6 652	45.7	29.2	4.7	0.7	3.6	95.4	3 566	241	56	2 509	47.1	52.4	0.6
Val Verde	202.3	4 154	44.6	1.1	4.3	0.6	18.1	196.2	4 027	2 182	1 456	2 741	54.5	44.9	0.7
Van Zandt	133.6	2 548	65.3	0.2	3.7	0.1	5.1	143.4	2 735	84	110	2 276	22.1	77.1	0.8
Victoria	447.8	5 016	35.0	30.9	5.7	0.0	7.0	427.6	4 790	196	194	6 236	32.8	66.4	0.7
Walker	336.2	4 914	20.8	2.8	2.4	0.0	2.2	2 119.8	30 987	133	138	12 310	38.3	60.7	1.0
Waller	122.5	2 761	63.3	0.0	5.3	0.2	5.2	201.4	4 540	55	96	4 198	46.1	53.3	0.6
Ward	50.2	4 618	39.7	22.1	5.2	0.5	5.1	27.1	2 491	14	24	791	25.0	74.0	1.0
Washington	177.9	5 218	67.6	1.5	3.7	0.2	9.5	209.7	6 151	77	68	2 957	28.1	70.8	1.2
Webb	1 204.4	4 647	58.3	1.3	6.0	0.4	1.5	1 569.6	6 056	3 385	549	18 217	71.4	28.0	0.5
Wharton	212.0	5 136	49.9	27.3	4.1	0.3	4.0	112.7	2 730	84	86	2 693	34.2	65.4	0.3
Wheeler	47.3	8 406	62.3	25.4	2.4	0.0	1.9	10.4	1 840	19	12	569	14.0	85.4	0.6
Wichita	367.1	2 790	48.2	3.9	7.6	0.8	4.0	311.8	2 370	1 954	5 346	8 811	30.2	69.0	0.8
Wilbarger	85.1	6 421	56.2	22.2	2.7	0.1	3.2	25.5	1 920	37	27	2 973	26.5	72.8	0.7
Willacy	71.7	3 250	69.9	2.0	3.8	0.0	3.5	245.2	11 115	27	39	1 236	69.5	29.7	0.8
Williamson	1 761.9	3 862	55.5	3.1	4.1	0.1	8.7	4 547.8	9 968	594	986	20 347	42.7	55.8	1.5
Wilson	123.3	2 779	58.0	17.0	2.5	0.0	3.5	291.4	6 568	73	95	2 163	32.8	66.6	0.6
Winkler	63.1	8 609	59.5	14.6	3.7	0.3	1.7	83.7	11 417	0	16	607	23.5	75.2	1.3
Wise	185.9	3 076	52.9	1.7	4.7	0.4	8.7	328.2	5 430	105	128	3 687	21.7	77.4	0.9
Wood	83.7	1 992	65.3	0.6	6.3	0.2	7.2	54.2	1 291	90	87	1 744	22.5	76.8	0.7
Yoakum	112.1	13 883	63.5	19.3	2.1	0.0	3.3	58.6	7 256	15	17	803	18.3	80.9	0.8
Young	85.3	4 653	35.5	36.5	4.0	0.1	3.6	63.6	3 466	38	38	1 400	17.8	81.3	0.8
Zapata	71.8	5 023	53.0	1.7	6.5	2.5	10.2	53.7	3 754	163	30	927	67.7	32.1	0.3
Zavala	39.0	3 260	64.7	0.8	4.7	0.6	3.1	27.4	2 292	11	25	843	84.2	15.4	0.4
UTAH	X	X	X	X	X	X	X	X	X	34 606	16 432	192 194	34.4	62.6	3.0
Beaver	56.0	8 618	45.5	16.6	4.4	0.1	4.4	64.4	9 900	43	28	685	21.6	75.8	2.6
Box Elder	160.8	3 204	53.7	1.5	5.9	0.0	5.0	153.6	3 061	200	222	2 449	17.4	79.9	2.7
Cache	279.8	2 422	51.7	4.7	6.0	0.3	5.2	189.4	1 640	342	498	10 621	24.9	70.5	4.6
Carbon	97.8	4 605	33.6	5.7	8.9	1.4	15.4	82.2	3 869	160	89	1 841	44.6	52.6	2.8
Daggett	10.8	9 932	41.8	0.6	12.0	0.0	4.4	7.7	7 049	53	0	153	29.8	67.7	2.5
Davis	883.2	2 797	54.5	3.5	5.9	0.7	2.9	783.9	2 482	12 356	4 956	13 847	27.5	69.7	2.8
Duchesne	87.6	4 553	62.9	1.4	3.7	0.6	5.4	67.8	3 525	74	87	1 981	15.9	81.6	2.5
Emery	55.4	5 071	43.3	1.6	9.6	0.2	10.6	197.2	18 039	55	47	852	21.9	75.5	2.6
Garfield	23.9	4 686	43.6	2.6	4.9	0.2	12.7	15.3	3 013	167	21	386	18.8	79.2	2.0
Grand	44.6	4 784	31.4	1.2	9.8	0.7	9.0	75.2	8 066	248	40	750	50.7	45.9	3.4
Iron	125.1	2 675	48.9	0.6	7.6	0.2	7.1	124.1	2 655	303	200	3 884	19.8	76.1	4.1
Juab	41.3	3 997	42.5	0.6	7.1	0.0	6.0	46.1	4 459	30	45	709	20.5	74.2	5.3
Kane	51.0	7 056	25.3	22.9	3.7	0.0	6.3	44.9	6 214	99	31	618	27.1	70.1	2.7
Millard	53.8	4 280	54.0	3.6	7.9	0.0	7.1	9.5	752	89	55	932	16.0	77.1	6.9
Morgan	30.5	3 110	65.1	1.3	3.6	0.0	3.2	31.7	3 228	11	44	438	16.6	79.6	3.9
Piute	8.4	5 526	63.5	0.9	6.3	0.0	8.4	7.6	5 012	0	0	132	17.7	79.6	2.8
Rich	11.4	5 038	56.3	0.8	5.5	2.9	8.5	10.7	4 710	10	10	189	15.3	82.6	2.1
Salt Lake	3 568.5	3 354	42.8	1.1	5.6	2.0	5.4	7 237.3	6 803	10 229	4 881	88 301	48.7	48.6	2.8
San Juan	80.3	5 367	48.8	16.3	2.8	0.1	14.7	21.4	1 432	159	64	1 440	46.9	51.4	1.7
Sanpete	90.3	3 237	50.5	20.9	4.6	0.0	3.0	121.5	4 352	77	111	2 468	18.6	76.0	5.4
Sevier	69.0	3 318	48.6	2.0	9.0	0.0	7.7	54.0	2 596	192	89	1 460	17.0	79.9	3.2
Summit	247.7	6 518	32.0	2.0	5.3	0.0	14.4	271.7	7 150	56	167	2 530	56.7	41.4	1.9
Tooele	205.1	3 426	44.3	2.1	5.5	2.9	3.0	186.1	3 109	1 416	390	2 551	33.6	63.4	2.9
Uintah	172.6	4 998	36.6	3.9	4.3	4.9	15.3	199.3	5 772	362	154	2 542	14.4	83.2	2.4
Utah	1 425.3	2 637	52.2	4.1	6.0	0.1	5.2	2 402.3	4 445	918	2 363	27 856	18.8	77.7	3.5
Wasatch	116.2	4 598	37.8	2.6	4.5	0.1	8.0	196.8	7 787	46	114	1 240	33.9	63.7	2.4
Washington	401.3	2 771	50.1	0.8	7.7	0.0	6.0	585.2	4 041	564	636	7 148	21.9	75.3	2.8
Wayne	11.3	4 138	49.8	0.3	9.5	0.0	14.9	0.8	300	85	12	185	25.5	71.5	3.0
Weber	687.2	2 904	45.7	2.1	6.6	3.6	2.8	686.2	2 900	6 256	1 067	14 006	35.0	62.5	2.5
VERMONT	X	X	X	X	X	X	X	X	X	6 588	4 402	47 851	67.5	30.4	2.1
Addison	134.4	3 658	71.2	0.1	2.3	0.1	11.8	60.1	1 636	107	242	1 770	68.6	29.5	1.9
Bennington	140.1	3 818	69.0	0.2	4.4	0.3	12.1	38.6	1 051	156	251	2 015	65.5	32.1	2.5
Caledonia	107.7	3 461	66.7	0.1	3.0	0.0	14.0	33.2	1 066	94	212	2 049	60.4	37.2	2.4

1. Based on the resident population estimated as of July 1 of the year shown. 2.

STATE/ County code	CBSA code[1]	County type[2]	STATE County	Land area,[3] (sq km) 2010	Population, 2014: Total persons 2014	Population, 2014: Rank	Population, 2014: Per square kilometer	Population and population characteristics, 2013: Race alone or in combination, not Hispanic or Latino (percent): White	Race: Black	Race: American Indian, Alaska Native	Race: Asian and Pacific Islander	Percent Hispanic or Latino[4]	Age (percent): Under 5 years	Age: 5 to 17 years	Age: 18 to 24 years	Age: 25 to 34 years	Age: 35 to 44 years	Age: 45 to 54 years
				1	2	3	4	5	6	7	8	9	10	11	12	13	14	15
			VERMONT—Cont'd															
50 007	15540	3	Chittenden	1 390	160 531	397	115.5	92.3	2.8	0.8	4.0	2.0	4.8	14.0	16.0	13.6	11.9	14.1
50 009	13620	9	Essex	1 719	6 125	2 747	3.6	97.4	0.7	1.4	0.6	1.3	4.4	13.2	6.3	8.7	11.0	16.3
50 011	15540	3	Franklin	1 641	48 642	1 007	29.6	96.5	1.0	2.4	0.9	1.4	6.1	17.3	7.9	11.9	13.3	16.0
50 013	15540	3	Grand Isle	212	6 994	2 679	33.0	96.4	1.2	2.8	0.8	1.5	4.7	14.4	7.2	9.9	11.3	16.9
50 015	...	8	Lamoille	1 188	25 082	1 604	21.1	96.6	1.3	1.3	1.0	1.5	5.4	15.9	9.6	12.2	13.1	15.0
50 017	17200	9	Orange	1 779	28 859	1 460	16.2	97.4	1.0	1.2	0.8	1.2	4.9	15.0	8.3	10.6	11.3	16.0
50 019	...	7	Orleans	1 796	27 082	1 533	15.1	97.1	1.1	1.3	0.7	1.3	4.9	15.6	7.4	10.8	11.7	14.1
50 021	40860	5	Rutland	2 408	60 086	866	25.0	97.2	0.9	0.8	1.0	1.3	4.6	13.9	9.5	10.6	10.8	15.6
50 023	12740	4	Washington	1 780	58 998	878	33.1	96.1	1.3	1.0	1.4	1.9	5.0	14.8	9.2	11.0	12.5	15.4
50 025	...	6	Windham	2 034	43 714	1 095	21.5	95.5	1.7	1.1	1.5	2.0	4.5	14.4	8.3	10.7	10.7	15.6
50 027	17200	7	Windsor	2 511	56 014	906	22.3	96.7	1.0	1.0	1.3	1.4	4.6	14.3	6.6	11.2	10.9	15.4
51 000	...	X	VIRGINIA	102 279	8 326 289	X	81.4	65.7	20.2	0.8	7.2	8.6	6.2	16.4	10.0	14.1	13.2	14.4
51 001	...	7	Accomack	1 164	33 021	1 356	28.4	62.3	28.3	0.8	0.9	9.1	6.2	14.9	7.4	10.6	10.4	13.8
51 003	16820	3	Albemarle	1 867	104 489	567	56.0	79.8	10.6	0.6	5.6	5.7	5.5	15.6	11.6	13.1	11.6	13.4
51 005	...	6	Alleghany	1 154	15 820	2 054	13.7	93.1	5.7	0.6	0.6	1.5	4.5	15.2	7.5	9.0	11.0	14.4
51 007	40060	1	Amelia	920	12 855	2 244	14.0	74.0	23.1	0.8	0.7	3.0	5.2	15.8	7.6	11.1	11.5	15.9
51 009	31340	3	Amherst	1 227	32 041	1 385	26.1	77.5	20.0	1.5	1.1	2.1	5.1	15.0	10.1	10.3	11.4	15.3
51 011	31340	3	Appomattox	864	15 279	2 082	17.7	78.3	21.1	0.5	0.6	1.2	6.1	15.8	7.6	11.7	11.7	14.4
51 013	47900	1	Arlington	67	226 908	284	3 386.7	65.9	9.1	0.7	11.5	15.5	6.0	10.7	7.7	28.0	16.4	12.3
51 015	44420	4	Augusta	2 505	73 862	741	29.5	92.7	4.7	0.6	0.8	2.4	4.4	15.6	8.0	10.8	12.2	15.6
51 017	...	9	Bath	1 371	4 563	2 860	3.3	93.3	5.2	0.6	0.5	1.6	3.6	12.8	7.6	8.7	11.1	16.3
51 019	31340	3	Bedford	1 968	76 583	718	38.9	89.6	7.6	0.7	1.4	1.8	4.5	16.3	7.6	9.1	12.0	16.0
51 021	...	8	Bland	927	6 625	2 710	7.1	95.3	3.9	0.4	0.5	0.6	4.1	13.3	6.9	11.3	15.0	15.1
51 023	40220	2	Botetourt	1 402	33 100	1 351	23.6	94.4	3.7	0.6	0.9	1.5	4.0	16.5	6.9	8.6	11.7	16.5
51 025	...	6	Brunswick	1 466	16 498	2 009	11.3	41.7	56.4	0.5	0.6	1.9	4.3	13.7	9.1	13.7	12.2	14.1
51 027	...	9	Buchanan	1 302	23 106	1 678	17.7	96.2	3.1	0.3	0.4	0.5	4.5	13.5	7.6	12.0	12.7	15.5
51 029	16820	8	Buckingham	1 501	16 913	1 983	11.3	62.5	35.8	0.6	0.7	2.1	5.3	13.7	8.3	13.2	13.5	15.6
51 031	31340	3	Campbell	1 305	54 885	915	42.1	82.3	15.4	0.8	1.4	2.0	4.9	15.5	9.1	12.1	12.3	14.6
51 033	40060	1	Caroline	1 366	29 778	1 434	21.8	66.2	29.6	1.5	1.6	4.0	6.7	16.7	7.6	13.6	13.0	14.8
51 035	...	6	Carroll	1 229	29 621	1 438	24.1	95.5	1.1	0.5	0.3	3.2	4.5	15.1	7.1	9.5	12.5	14.9
51 036	40060	1	Charles City	473	7 023	2 674	14.8	43.5	48.4	8.0	1.3	1.7	3.3	13.1	7.2	10.4	10.5	17.7
51 037	...	8	Charlotte	1 231	12 225	2 285	9.9	68.0	29.9	0.7	0.4	2.1	5.6	16.4	8.1	9.7	10.8	14.7
51 041	40060	1	Chesterfield	1 096	332 499	200	303.4	65.7	23.8	0.8	4.4	7.7	5.9	18.8	9.3	11.7	13.8	15.0
51 043	47900	1	Clarke	456	14 423	2 139	31.6	89.5	6.3	1.0	1.6	3.9	5.1	16.3	7.5	9.1	10.6	18.1
51 045	40220	2	Craig	853	5 234	2 820	6.1	98.4	0.5	0.4	0.4	1.0	4.3	15.1	7.6	8.8	12.0	16.2
51 047	47900	6	Culpeper	982	49 166	995	50.1	74.0	16.8	0.8	2.0	9.0	6.6	18.8	8.2	12.1	13.2	15.2
51 049	...	1	Cumberland	770	9 827	2 452	12.8	64.7	33.1	1.1	0.8	2.4	5.5	15.4	8.8	11.1	11.2	15.1
51 051	13720	9	Dickenson	856	15 308	2 081	17.9	98.6	0.6	0.4	0.2	0.7	5.3	15.4	7.3	11.7	12.7	14.3
51 053	40060	1	Dinwiddie	1 305	27 859	1 501	21.3	64.0	32.9	0.7	1.0	2.9	4.6	15.8	9.2	11.4	12.5	16.5
51 057	...	8	Essex	666	11 103	2 347	16.7	56.8	39.4	1.0	1.4	3.3	5.5	15.1	8.2	10.9	10.9	14.8
51 059	47900	1	Fairfax	1 013	1 137 538	37	1 122.9	55.4	10.2	0.6	20.7	16.2	6.7	17.3	8.1	14.5	14.7	15.2
51 061	47900	1	Fauquier	1 677	68 248	781	40.7	83.2	9.1	0.8	2.2	6.9	5.7	18.5	7.9	10.3	12.3	17.1
51 063	13980	8	Floyd	985	15 578	2 068	15.8	94.9	2.2	0.7	0.7	2.6	5.0	15.7	6.6	9.9	12.3	14.9
51 065	16820	3	Fluvanna	741	26 092	1 557	35.2	80.4	16.4	0.7	1.2	3.3	5.4	16.3	7.1	11.6	13.6	15.0
51 067	40220	2	Franklin	1 788	56 358	901	31.5	88.5	8.8	0.5	0.7	2.7	4.9	14.9	9.0	9.5	11.0	15.0
51 069	49020	3	Frederick	1 071	82 377	676	76.9	86.8	5.3	0.6	1.9	7.1	5.8	18.0	8.3	11.9	13.1	15.7
51 071	13980	3	Giles	921	16 815	1 995	18.3	96.4	2.0	0.5	0.6	1.4	5.2	15.8	7.6	10.2	12.8	14.6
51 073	47260	1	Gloucester	564	37 141	1 247	65.9	87.3	9.2	1.1	1.5	2.9	5.1	15.4	8.1	11.1	11.8	16.6
51 075	40060	1	Goochland	729	21 936	1 737	30.1	78.4	18.3	0.7	1.7	2.2	4.0	15.2	6.4	8.4	12.8	17.6
51 077	...	9	Grayson	1 145	15 093	2 093	13.2	94.7	2.6	0.6	0.3	2.8	4.2	13.7	7.1	9.1	11.7	14.7
51 079	16820	3	Greene	405	19 031	1 872	47.0	86.8	7.8	0.8	2.0	4.6	6.5	17.8	7.1	11.8	13.1	15.4
51 081	...	6	Greensville	765	11 681	2 313	15.3	38.4	59.2	0.5	0.7	2.0	5.0	12.1	8.9	14.8	15.1	16.0
51 083	...	6	Halifax	2 118	35 200	1 294	16.6	61.0	36.9	0.6	0.7	1.9	4.9	16.1	7.6	9.6	11.0	13.7
51 085	40060	1	Hanover	1 214	101 918	582	84.0	86.1	10.1	0.8	2.0	2.5	4.7	18.5	9.0	9.4	12.7	16.6
51 087	40060	1	Henrico	605	321 924	207	532.1	57.3	30.5	0.8	8.3	5.3	6.3	17.3	8.3	14.4	13.6	14.4
51 089	32300	4	Henry	990	52 081	956	52.6	72.2	22.7	0.6	0.8	5.2	5.1	14.9	7.3	10.1	11.3	15.3
51 091	...	9	Highland	1 075	2 248	3 029	2.1	97.7	0.7	0.2	0.4	1.2	3.0	9.8	6.2	6.7	8.8	14.9
51 093	47260	1	Isle of Wight	817	36 007	1 271	44.1	72.1	24.7	0.9	1.7	2.4	4.8	16.3	7.8	10.0	11.8	17.3
51 095	47260	1	James City	369	72 583	747	196.7	78.3	14.4	0.8	3.6	5.3	5.1	16.0	7.5	10.1	11.1	14.0
51 097	...	1	King and Queen	816	7 175	2 664	8.8	67.6	27.9	2.3	0.7	3.4	4.2	14.8	7.8	10.2	11.2	15.2
51 099	...	8	King George	465	25 371	1 595	54.6	76.8	18.4	1.2	2.5	4.2	7.0	19.6	8.6	12.8	13.3	15.8
51 101	40060	1	King William	710	16 186	2 030	22.8	78.0	18.5	2.1	1.4	2.3	6.0	17.8	7.4	12.7	13.2	15.6
51 103	...	9	Lancaster	345	11 044	2 353	32.0	69.4	28.7	0.5	0.8	1.7	3.8	11.7	6.1	7.4	7.8	12.2
51 105	...	8	Lee	1 128	24 951	1 610	22.1	93.7	4.1	0.7	0.5	1.8	5.2	14.3	7.4	12.8	13.7	14.0
51 107	47900	1	Loudoun	1 335	363 050	186	271.9	62.9	8.3	0.6	18.4	13.1	7.9	21.8	6.8	13.1	17.8	15.8

1. CBSA = Core Based Statistical Area. See Appendix A for explanation. See Appendix B for list of metropolitan areas with component counties. 2. County type code from the Economic Research Service of USDA Rural-Urban Continuum Codes. See Appendix A for definition. 3. Dry land or land partially or temporarily covered by water. 4. May be of any race.

STATE County	Population, 2013 (cont.): Age (percent) (cont.): 55 to 64 years	65 to 74 years	75 years and over	Percent female	Population change and components of change, 2000–2014: Total persons: 2000	2010	Percent change: 2000–2010	2010–2014	Components of change, 2010–2014: Births	Deaths	Net migration	Households, 2009–2013: Number	Persons per house-hold	Percent: Family house-holds	Female family house-holder[1]	One per-son
	16	17	18	19	20	21	22	23	24	25	26	27	28	29	30	31
VERMONT—Cont'd																
Chittenden	12.8	7.2	5.6	51.1	146 571	156 545	6.8	2.5	6 676	4 219	1 556	62 587	2.37	60.0	8.5	28.0
Essex	17.8	13.6	8.7	49.3	6 459	6 306	-2.4	-2.9	218	223	-180	2 774	2.26	64.6	11.1	28.6
Franklin	14.1	7.9	5.5	50.4	45 417	47 746	5.1	1.9	2 445	1 546	60	18 616	2.55	69.2	9.2	23.2
Grand Isle	18.9	11.3	5.4	50.4	6 901	6 970	1.0	0.3	248	237	30	3 023	2.31	70.9	7.7	24.3
Lamoille	14.0	8.7	6.1	50.1	23 233	24 475	5.3	2.5	1 105	809	323	10 046	2.38	60.5	8.3	29.0
Orange	17.0	10.3	6.7	50.2	28 226	28 936	2.5	-0.3	1 155	1 014	-187	11 962	2.36	66.4	9.2	26.2
Orleans	15.8	11.6	8.1	49.7	26 277	27 231	3.6	-0.5	1 149	1 232	-55	11 043	2.39	63.3	9.4	28.8
Rutland	16.3	10.8	7.8	50.7	63 400	61 642	-2.8	-2.5	2 327	2 716	-1 110	25 754	2.29	63.0	9.1	29.0
Washington	15.8	9.3	7.1	50.5	58 039	59 534	2.6	-0.9	2 456	2 200	-780	24 661	2.31	61.3	9.3	30.2
Windham	17.4	10.9	7.5	50.8	44 216	44 513	0.7	-1.8	1 749	1 803	-696	19 417	2.19	59.5	9.6	31.7
Windsor	16.9	11.6	8.4	51.0	57 418	56 670	-1.3	-1.2	2 109	2 394	-295	25 024	2.21	61.9	9.2	30.2
VIRGINIA	12.4	7.9	5.5	50.8	7 078 515	8 001 024	13.0	4.1	437 406	259 805	145 072	3 022 739	2.60	67.4	12.3	26.4
Accomack	15.8	12.1	8.7	51.5	38 305	33 164	-13.4	-0.4	1 768	1 874	-33	14 333	2.25	64.7	13.0	29.9
Albemarle	13.2	8.6	7.4	52.2	79 236	98 970	24.9	5.5	4 554	3 214	3 931	37 964	2.47	64.5	8.5	29.6
Alleghany	14.8	13.7	9.9	50.8	17 215	16 250	25.7	-2.7	520	990	-28	6 773	2.35	67.3	7.2	28.7
Amelia	15.3	11.0	6.5	51.2	11 400	12 690	11.3	1.3	591	532	85	4 808	2.62	75.3	12.5	20.8
Amherst	14.6	10.6	7.6	52.3	31 894	32 353	1.4	-1.0	1 388	1 452	-208	12 680	2.44	67.6	14.7	28.0
Appomattox	14.2	11.1	7.5	51.6	13 705	14 973	9.3	2.0	751	634	179	5 803	2.58	73.6	12.5	22.8
Arlington	9.8	5.5	3.6	49.9	189 453	207 627	9.6	9.3	13 396	3 995	9 629	94 454	2.24	46.1	6.1	40.5
Augusta	14.7	11.1	7.6	49.5	65 615	73 750	12.4	0.2	2 546	2 850	236	27 999	2.50	73.3	9.3	23.3
Bath	15.4	14.4	10.1	50.0	5 048	4 731	-6.3	-3.5	167	255	-73	2 101	2.17	64.5	7.0	32.2
Bedford	15.8	11.5	7.3	50.7	60 371	68 676	13.8	2.3	2 747	3 135	2 085	27 233	2.53	73.1	8.3	22.5
Bland	15.2	11.8	7.3	44.9	6 871	6 824	-0.7	-2.9	207	363	-35	2 480	2.37	71.5	12.5	26.4
Botetourt	16.6	11.6	7.6	50.5	30 496	33 148	8.7	-0.1	960	1 282	206	12 825	2.55	78.3	8.4	18.8
Brunswick	14.6	10.1	8.2	47.2	18 419	17 434	-5.3	-5.4	629	824	-739	5 826	2.55	67.7	17.2	29.0
Buchanan	15.6	11.5	7.0	48.9	26 978	24 098	-10.7	-4.1	872	1 161	-701	9 485	2.41	70.8	12.3	25.3
Buckingham	14.3	9.9	6.3	45.1	15 623	17 146	9.7	-1.3	711	661	-292	5 817	2.34	72.7	18.3	23.4
Campbell	13.9	10.2	7.4	51.6	51 078	54 842	7.4	0.1	2 104	2 150	101	21 774	2.50	71.0	13.2	24.8
Caroline	12.9	9.0	5.7	50.8	22 121	28 545	29.0	4.3	1 654	1 060	575	10 680	2.56	73.2	15.7	21.0
Carroll	15.3	12.5	8.7	50.3	29 245	30 042	2.7	-1.4	1 048	1 512	86	12 572	2.36	68.5	9.9	28.8
Charles City	17.8	12.5	7.5	51.1	6 926	7 256	4.8	-3.2	212	333	-125	2 850	2.53	65.6	14.0	30.2
Charlotte	14.8	11.2	8.8	50.6	12 472	12 586	0.9	-2.8	594	660	-264	4 751	2.59	69.8	15.4	25.8
Chesterfield	13.1	7.7	4.5	51.9	259 903	316 236	21.7	5.1	15 677	8 820	9 306	113 637	2.78	73.2	12.7	22.7
Clarke	15.7	10.1	7.6	50.2	12 652	14 034	10.9	2.8	607	634	440	5 580	2.49	73.4	8.8	19.5
Craig	15.7	12.3	8.0	50.2	5 091	5 190	1.9	1.2	171	205	73	2 122	2.43	69.4	7.1	27.3
Culpeper	12.5	8.2	5.3	49.6	34 262	46 689	36.3	5.3	2 701	1 577	1 323	16 039	2.84	74.6	11.0	20.9
Cumberland	14.2	11.4	7.3	51.5	9 017	10 052	11.5	-2.3	434	380	-266	4 049	2.44	67.3	14.2	28.1
Dickenson	15.1	11.2	6.9	49.4	16 395	15 903	-3.0	-3.7	706	865	-420	6 352	2.44	71.3	12.4	26.0
Dinwiddie	14.2	9.6	6.2	50.9	24 533	28 001	14.1	-0.5	1 021	1 038	-149	9 932	2.73	72.9	16.3	23.2
Essex	14.7	11.6	8.2	52.8	9 989	11 151	11.6	-0.4	552	532	-70	4 286	2.57	63.8	9.9	29.8
Fairfax	12.4	6.8	4.3	50.5	969 749	1 081 726	11.5	5.2	63 935	20 500	13 242	389 908	2.80	71.1	9.1	22.7
Fauquier	13.9	8.8	5.6	50.6	55 139	65 203	18.3	4.6	3 106	2 151	1 907	23 130	2.84	74.4	8.4	20.5
Floyd	15.8	12.1	7.8	49.9	13 874	15 279	10.1	1.9	626	605	270	6 086	2.51	67.8	7.2	26.3
Fluvanna	13.5	10.4	7.2	54.3	20 047	25 691	28.2	1.5	1 135	820	52	9 462	2.60	73.3	10.1	22.7
Franklin	15.5	12.6	7.6	50.7	47 286	56 159	18.8	0.3	2 182	2 378	435	23 358	2.34	72.2	9.9	23.8
Frederick	12.6	8.8	5.9	50.3	59 209	78 305	32.3	5.2	3 926	2 459	2 638	29 172	2.68	74.2	9.9	19.4
Giles	14.3	11.7	7.9	51.0	16 657	17 286	3.8	-2.7	745	869	-331	7 167	2.37	67.3	12.9	28.6
Gloucester	15.2	10.2	6.6	50.6	34 780	36 858	6.0	0.8	1 493	1 471	205	13 889	2.63	73.9	10.9	21.4
Goochland	17.0	12.1	6.5	50.4	16 863	21 717	28.8	1.1	701	693	160	8 058	2.40	79.3	6.2	18.2
Grayson	16.2	13.1	10.2	51.1	17 917	15 533	-13.3	-2.8	592	921	-139	6 618	2.30	66.2	11.9	29.6
Greene	12.9	10.0	5.4	50.6	15 244	18 403	20.7	3.4	928	606	277	6 897	2.67	72.1	9.8	20.9
Greensville	13.3	8.8	5.7	38.6	11 560	12 243	5.9	-4.6	581	467	-709	3 389	2.48	75.1	20.8	21.0
Halifax	15.5	12.3	9.3	52.1	37 355	36 241	-3.0	-2.9	1 460	1 981	-475	14 770	2.38	65.4	16.4	32.7
Hanover	14.1	8.9	6.2	51.0	86 320	99 863	15.7	2.1	3 754	3 460	1 732	36 927	2.65	75.7	9.6	20.2
Henrico	12.4	7.3	6.1	52.8	262 300	306 935	17.0	4.9	16 759	10 678	9 071	123 683	2.49	64.7	15.1	29.4
Henry	14.8	12.0	9.2	51.7	57 930	54 151	-6.5	-3.8	2 038	2 952	-1 201	22 690	2.33	67.8	14.7	29.6
Highland	21.4	17.9	11.4	50.7	2 536	2 321	-8.5	-3.1	61	111	-32	1 006	2.26	75.2	8.0	22.0
Isle of Wight	15.4	10.1	6.6	51.3	29 728	35 270	18.6	2.1	1 341	1 432	806	13 560	2.59	75.2	10.6	21.7
James City	13.8	12.7	9.7	51.7	48 102	67 009	39.3	7.7	3 050	2 619	4 656	26 883	2.50	71.9	10.4	23.5
King and Queen	16.6	12.0	8.1	50.1	6 630	6 945	4.8	3.3	261	280	215	2 863	2.45	70.3	8.5	26.4
King George	11.6	7.2	4.2	40.5	16 803	23 584	40.4	7.0	1 347	619	1 019	8 314	2.86	72.6	10.0	21.7
King William	13.5	8.5	5.3	51.3	13 146	15 935	21.2	1.6	801	539	4	5 998	2.65	76.4	13.1	20.3
Lancaster	16.8	17.8	16.4	53.4	11 567	11 391	-1.5	-3.1	364	838	83	5 182	2.14	60.6	10.4	37.4
Lee	14.5	11.0	7.2	47.8	23 589	25 587	8.5	-2.5	1 076	1 203	-577	9 653	2.49	68.4	11.0	29.0
Loudoun	9.2	4.7	2.9	50.4	169 599	312 311	84.1	16.2	21 269	4 619	33 419	106 997	3.04	77.7	8.7	17.1

1. No spouse present.

STATE County	Persons in group quarters, 2014	Daytime population, 2009–2013: Number	Daytime population, 2009–2013: Employment/residence ratio	Births, 2014: Total	Births, 2014: Rate[1]	Deaths, 2014: Number	Deaths, 2014: Rate[1]	Persons under 65 with no health insurance, 2013: Number	Persons under 65 with no health insurance, 2013: Percent	Medicare, 2014: Eligible for Medicare	Medicare, 2014: Enrolled in Medicare Advantage	Medicare, 2014: Enrolled in a Medicare prescription drug plan	Serious crimes known to police,[2] 2013: Total: Number	Serious crimes known to police,[2] 2013: Total: Rate[3]
	32	33	34	35	36	37	38	39	40	41	42	43	44	45
VERMONT—Cont'd														
Chittenden	9 807	171 844	1.17	1 610	10.0	1 008	6.3	9 840	7.6	26 163	2 074	15 393	4 267	2 680
Essex	16	4 943	0.51	47	7.7	53	8.7	655	13.6	1 869	126	1 141	51	821
Franklin	529	41 882	0.75	569	11.7	350	7.2	3 464	8.4	7 869	603	4 963	879	1 816
Grand Isle	0	4 804	0.40	57	8.1	48	6.9	554	9.6	1 730	175	944	93	1 329
Lamoille	694	23 849	0.94	254	10.1	180	7.2	2 072	10.0	4 636	307	2 890	328	1 306
Orange	715	23 836	0.65	257	8.9	238	8.2	2 214	9.5	6 072	278	3 606	381	1 317
Orleans	818	26 799	0.97	272	10.0	279	10.3	2 350	11.1	6 796	438	4 308	563	2 078
Rutland	2 323	60 904	0.99	545	9.1	627	10.4	4 206	8.9	14 939	945	10 267	2 011	3 327
Washington	2 414	62 886	1.11	550	9.3	516	8.7	3 580	7.5	12 257	850	6 974	1 192	2 004
Windham	1 463	47 074	1.13	410	9.4	404	9.2	3 394	9.8	10 137	648	6 403	1 265	2 884
Windsor	898	53 625	0.90	491	8.8	531	9.5	3 932	8.9	13 952	1 070	8 414	996	1 775
VIRGINIA	240 917	8 005 562	0.98	103 597	12.4	62 485	7.5	970 614	14.0	1 324 380	233 918	594 095	186 859	2 262
Accomack	429	31 687	0.89	377	11.4	424	12.8	5 352	20.5	8 225	1 081	4 469	564	1 685
Albemarle	6 163	108 604	1.17	1 080	10.3	800	7.7	10 378	12.9	17 411	1 850	9 700	2 128	2 055
Alleghany	281	16 454	1.03	117	7.4	253	16.0	1 678	13.6	4 403	709	2 728	224	1 377
Amelia	128	10 144	0.53	144	11.2	119	9.3	1 847	17.6	2 812	634	1 349	127	992
Amherst	1 666	26 596	0.61	315	9.8	361	11.3	4 018	16.0	7 263	1 098	4 296	440	1 351
Appomattox	56	11 945	0.51	182	11.9	150	9.8	2 074	16.7	3 626	530	2 187	115	757
Arlington	3 047	268 406	1.39	3 238	14.3	991	4.4	21 092	10.5	21 807	2 169	7 443	4 572	2 026
Augusta	2 426	68 278	0.84	612	8.3	705	9.5	8 373	14.5	16 072	2 335	9 265	833	1 127
Bath	53	4 377	0.86	39	8.5	54	11.8	572	16.4	1 259	130	797	36	776
Bedford	555	50 831	0.44	644	8.4	762	9.9	7 705	13.6	16 019	2 820	8 772	696	994
Bland	683	6 175	0.74	45	6.8	84	12.7	676	14.0	1 708	341	931	73	1 085
Botetourt	278	26 684	0.60	224	6.8	313	9.5	2 890	11.0	7 769	1 732	3 864	277	834
Brunswick	1 838	15 060	0.64	140	8.5	213	12.9	2 037	17.1	3 792	717	2 108	150	887
Buchanan	1 143	24 716	1.11	197	8.5	270	11.7	2 804	15.3	7 274	2 785	3 853	507	2 125
Buckingham	2 124	15 681	0.73	172	10.2	148	8.8	2 329	18.8	3 321	615	1 701	204	1 192
Campbell	468	48 703	0.75	483	8.8	507	9.2	6 834	15.1	11 818	1 770	7 096	821	1 482
Caroline	513	21 603	0.45	401	13.5	260	8.7	3 865	15.7	5 216	877	2 258	422	1 447
Carroll	337	26 372	0.71	253	8.5	380	12.8	4 492	19.0	7 639	1 044	4 768	466	1 560
Charles City	0	5 769	0.57	55	7.8	78	11.1	1 169	20.4	1 685	406	821	31	434
Charlotte	175	10 748	0.64	141	11.5	159	13.0	1 875	19.1	3 235	460	1 924	93	751
Chesterfield	4 756	278 843	0.73	3 756	11.3	2 148	6.5	35 280	12.5	50 159	10 808	22 273	6 768	2 071
Clarke	255	11 424	0.60	151	10.5	140	9.7	1 391	12.0	2 778	270	1 373	217	1 502
Craig	9	4 004	0.45	43	8.2	58	11.1	681	16.4	1 285	272	614	20	382
Culpeper	1 537	42 842	0.79	658	13.4	381	7.7	6 650	16.4	8 159	1 232	3 772	841	1 738
Cumberland	37	7 055	0.31	95	9.7	95	9.7	1 442	18.0	2 112	449	1 054	101	1 030
Dickenson	445	15 052	0.86	156	10.2	186	12.2	1 933	15.6	4 690	1 595	2 277	221	1 412
Dinwiddie	853	23 020	0.59	239	8.6	258	9.3	3 350	14.5	5 357	1 012	2 484	447	1 593
Essex	190	10 329	0.83	126	11.3	111	10.0	1 557	17.2	2 670	441	1 430	244	2 163
Fairfax	10 134	1 103 843	1.00	14 942	13.1	5 123	4.5	121 857	12.3	131 795	15 699	40 912	17 153	1 515
Fauquier	389	57 328	0.74	729	10.7	557	8.2	6 938	12.2	10 854	1 007	4 742	825	1 230
Floyd	85	12 398	0.57	145	9.3	157	10.1	2 198	17.6	3 703	723	1 949	153	990
Fluvanna	1 281	18 896	0.41	250	9.6	187	7.2	2 799	13.9	5 224	680	2 726	226	866
Franklin	1 500	48 515	0.68	511	9.1	584	10.4	7 545	17.2	13 446	3 509	6 681	813	1 436
Frederick	1 037	70 569	0.77	945	11.5	605	7.3	9 852	14.4	13 860	1 502	6 895	1 514	1 867
Giles	136	15 416	0.77	174	10.3	196	11.7	2 021	14.8	4 369	1 130	2 233	272	1 614
Gloucester	389	29 562	0.59	353	9.5	385	10.4	4 281	14.1	7 597	1 177	3 198	717	1 940
Goochland	996	23 801	1.24	169	7.7	166	7.6	1 207	7.3	4 798	910	2 503	176	828
Grayson	178	13 196	0.64	155	10.3	192	12.7	2 141	18.3	4 406	481	2 676	185	1 223
Greene	137	13 573	0.43	221	11.6	136	7.1	2 702	17.1	3 268	449	1 640	289	1 527
Greensville	3 040	12 405	1.09	131	11.2	114	9.8	1 003	14.1	2 301	724	1 455	107	910
Halifax	757	35 545	0.97	350	9.9	484	13.8	4 448	16.2	9 174	1 201	5 756	856	2 389
Hanover	1 863	91 446	0.82	896	8.8	788	7.7	8 443	10.1	17 951	3 784	8 851	1 380	1 364
Henrico	2 500	319 427	1.05	3 966	12.3	2 570	8.0	38 330	14.0	49 625	11 744	23 039	8 409	2 643
Henry	566	49 351	0.80	468	9.0	699	13.4	7 587	18.3	14 894	4 055	8 648	1 611	3 056
Highland	0	2 137	0.86	15	6.7	23	10.2	421	26.7	706	67	410	8	358
Isle of Wight	310	28 510	0.60	319	8.9	339	9.4	3 540	12.0	7 162	1 531	3 110	520	1 464
James City	1 041	64 235	0.87	724	10.0	614	8.5	6 532	12.2	17 566	1 955	7 701	971	1 393
King and Queen	0	5 118	0.40	55	7.7	63	8.8	1 084	19.0	1 610	261	867	81	1 142
King George	301	24 908	1.06	326	12.8	150	5.9	2 333	10.7	3 322	317	1 085	414	1 666
King William	72	12 278	0.53	192	11.9	118	7.3	1 982	14.3	2 907	397	1 699	135	843
Lancaster	185	11 841	1.11	84	7.6	187	16.9	1 113	15.3	4 094	530	2 255	53	472
Lee	1 750	22 939	0.68	243	9.7	305	12.2	2 972	15.5	6 297	2 022	2 846	605	2 371
Loudoun	1 340	297 023	0.83	5 095	14.0	1 186	3.3	29 193	9.1	29 065	3 472	11 126	3 896	1 129

1. Per 1,000 estimated resident population. 2. Data for serious crimes have not been adjusted for underreporting; this may affect comparability between geographic areas and over time.
3. Per 100,000 population estimated by the FBI.

STATE County	Serious crimes known to police, 2013 (cont.)[1] Rate[2]		Education: School enrollment and attainment, 2009–2013				Education: Local government expenditures,[5] 2012–2013		Money income, 2009–2013				Income and poverty, 2013			
			Enrollment[3]		Attainment[4] (percent)					Households				Percent below poverty level		
	Violent	Property	Total	Percent private	High school graduate or less	Bachelor's degree or more	Total current spending (mil dol)	Current spending per student (dollars)	Per capita income[6] (dollars)	Median income (dollars)	Mean income (dollars)	Percent with income of $200,000 or more	Median household income (dollars)	All persons	Children under 18 years	Children 5 to 17 years in families
	46	47	48	49	50	51	52	53	54	55	56	57	58	59	60	61
VERMONT—Cont'd																
Chittenden	117	2 563	46 360	18.6	27.7	47.4	373.0	17 095	33 281	63 989	81 779	5.5	62 618	10.1	10.1	8.4
Essex	32	789	1 220	11.9	59.8	14.7	14.7	17 137	20 887	35 916	46 494	1.1	36 140	18.1	26.3	23.6
Franklin	165	1 651	11 025	10.3	48.8	23.7	110.8	14 232	27 398	56 240	69 784	2.5	55 912	11.8	15.7	13.8
Grand Isle	29	1 301	1 530	16.5	40.1	30.3	12.2	12 537	33 159	59 509	78 635	5.9	57 559	9.7	14.4	12.9
Lamoille	44	1 262	5 621	8.9	38.5	36.4	60.6	16 746	27 157	52 686	65 629	3.7	46 742	12.3	15.8	14.1
Orange	48	1 268	6 442	15.9	44.2	29.9	69.9	16 931	27 289	52 480	65 350	2.5	51 348	13.0	17.2	15.3
Orleans	159	1 919	5 408	10.1	53.9	21.3	69.9	17 112	22 303	41 953	52 730	1.5	40 522	15.0	21.9	19.2
Rutland	180	3 147	14 252	15.2	45.4	28.0	148.6	17 713	26 205	49 271	61 402	2.0	45 757	13.5	17.4	14.8
Washington	79	1 925	14 180	26.7	36.2	38.1	142.1	16 888	29 761	57 281	70 028	3.1	52 619	12.6	14.0	12.9
Windham	180	2 704	9 792	29.6	40.3	33.5	121.9	18 716	28 867	50 234	65 094	2.3	46 642	14.7	19.4	17.2
Windsor	105	1 670	11 906	20.4	40.1	34.0	150.7	18 616	30 932	52 460	69 545	3.5	51 218	11.2	14.2	12.7
VIRGINIA	196	2 066	2 141 410	16.9	37.7	35.2	13 945.9	10 960	33 493	63 907	87 094	7.6	62 745	11.7	15.7	14.4
Accomack	108	1 578	6 304	15.8	60.2	17.2	51.3	10 001	22 703	39 328	51 733	2.0	38 064	19.3	29.4	29.0
Albemarle	133	1 922	30 595	16.8	26.6	52.2	224.5	12 832	37 239	67 725	96 212	9.0	70 032	9.5	11.6	10.2
Alleghany	135	1 241	3 407	15.4	54.1	16.4	28.3	10 741	24 162	44 848	56 514	1.4	44 983	13.7	20.9	18.7
Amelia	70	922	2 421	10.2	57.5	14.0	15.2	8 518	25 100	52 885	66 164	2.1	52 055	12.1	18.2	17.2
Amherst	107	1 243	7 517	21.9	55.6	17.4	43.0	9 680	22 580	44 945	55 151	0.7	47 268	14.2	20.8	18.7
Appomattox	53	704	3 478	18.1	56.0	15.0	20.1	8 744	23 636	50 167	58 082	1.2	44 062	16.2	24.0	22.9
Arlington	162	1 864	45 449	29.8	15.8	71.7	439.0	19 472	62 018	103 208	134 933	18.8	101 533	8.5	11.2	11.3
Augusta	130	997	14 843	17.3	57.3	19.9	100.2	9 319	25 519	52 027	65 647	2.0	54 834	8.9	12.9	11.5
Bath	43	733	803	27.8	50.5	20.2	9.6	14 873	28 704	51 365	65 393	0.9	42 951	11.7	17.9	15.9
Bedford	44	950	16 411	19.3	45.0	25.0	(7)92.5	(7)8 803	28 697	57 596	71 640	3.6	56 888	8.9	12.3	10.6
Bland	74	1 011	1 221	9.8	56.3	14.7	8.3	9 324	18 501	42 139	49 452	1.0	41 939	15.0	20.2	17.3
Botetourt	48	786	7 611	15.9	43.7	24.9	49.3	9 933	32 490	65 935	83 266	5.1	61 005	7.4	10.0	8.6
Brunswick	95	792	3 778	18.5	61.6	12.2	22.1	11 191	16 060	36 293	45 167	0.5	37 800	21.7	28.9	25.7
Buchanan	193	1 932	4 636	9.2	66.6	8.3	38.5	11 743	17 489	29 848	41 760	0.7	31 621	24.4	32.8	29.4
Buckingham	193	999	3 232	16.9	66.0	11.9	21.0	9 921	17 167	38 648	50 806	0.5	39 538	22.8	28.4	26.3
Campbell	143	1 340	13 173	24.5	52.7	17.1	75.0	8 936	23 231	47 162	57 272	1.1	47 982	13.3	18.7	17.1
Caroline	120	1 327	6 206	9.6	56.5	16.8	39.9	9 198	25 718	57 218	69 132	2.4	55 760	14.5	21.0	19.6
Carroll	124	1 437	6 139	9.7	57.3	12.8	42.2	9 682	19 385	32 853	44 975	0.3	36 218	16.5	25.6	21.6
Charles City	126	308	1 357	10.4	64.8	13.9	10.5	13 723	26 198	48 428	61 804	2.3	48 394	12.2	19.6	17.1
Charlotte	129	622	2 803	6.4	59.8	15.6	23.2	11 326	18 762	33 015	44 916	1.6	35 715	19.7	27.6	26.1
Chesterfield	127	1 944	91 264	14.4	34.2	36.3	533.4	9 062	32 572	72 088	89 034	6.1	67 454	8.0	10.8	9.6
Clarke	55	1 447	3 322	22.0	40.4	31.3	21.7	10 547	38 748	77 597	100 014	9.4	74 384	7.9	9.9	8.8
Craig	153	229	1 272	14.7	53.1	14.6	7.1	10 291	21 498	47 806	53 067	0.0	45 527	12.9	21.7	19.4
Culpeper	149	1 589	11 857	15.9	50.4	22.6	73.6	9 373	27 379	64 423	77 786	3.2	63 876	10.1	15.2	13.7
Cumberland	153	877	2 189	8.1	62.3	14.0	14.1	9 922	21 540	40 557	52 933	1.2	41 799	18.2	27.8	25.9
Dickenson	166	1 246	3 077	7.1	63.1	10.5	24.5	10 242	18 215	33 318	43 144	0.5	33 386	21.8	27.5	24.5
Dinwiddie	203	1 390	6 289	8.1	60.3	12.8	41.1	9 242	23 781	52 027	62 851	1.1	51 864	14.5	20.2	19.6
Essex	186	1 977	2 262	13.4	60.6	14.7	16.1	10 083	21 532	44 885	54 339	1.2	44 427	15.5	26.1	26.1
Fairfax	96	1 419	300 562	20.3	21.6	58.6	(8)2 485.0	(8)13 756	50 532	110 292	139 967	20.3	110 658	6.0	7.7	7.1
Fauquier	98	1 131	17 762	18.0	36.2	33.2	127.2	11 496	39 600	88 409	110 372	10.8	82 705	7.0	8.8	7.5
Floyd	78	913	2 912	29.8	55.2	16.0	17.8	8 731	21 816	44 618	53 012	1.8	41 652	14.2	21.1	19.4
Fluvanna	84	782	5 814	16.0	42.7	28.8	34.6	9 161	30 881	68 288	82 333	4.3	63 117	8.2	10.5	9.3
Franklin	152	1 284	12 222	20.8	51.1	19.1	73.5	9 776	24 557	45 624	59 126	2.0	48 070	14.4	22.6	20.9
Frederick	94	1 773	19 872	19.1	44.3	27.5	(9)185.8	(9)10 683	30 112	68 424	80 885	4.3	68 166	7.9	11.6	10.5
Giles	113	1 502	3 510	11.2	56.7	16.6	23.0	9 379	23 485	45 141	55 461	2.4	43 504	13.3	17.8	15.8
Gloucester	108	1 832	8 745	14.2	43.6	22.0	66.7	9 795	28 673	60 519	73 961	3.2	58 824	10.6	16.0	14.5
Goochland	24	805	4 490	33.0	37.9	38.0	25.8	10 990	45 039	80 976	122 696	13.5	76 843	7.5	9.5	8.3
Grayson	99	1 124	2 747	4.1	62.5	10.9	21.3	11 482	20 591	30 710	45 543	1.0	33 302	18.3	29.1	26.2
Greene	90	1 438	4 011	17.0	50.8	24.1	29.8	9 926	26 998	59 358	70 762	1.6	59 730	11.5	16.6	14.3
Greensville	153	757	1 931	9.3	70.0	7.2	(10)25.1	(10)9 847	16 380	39 697	55 316	1.9	38 036	26.3	28.7	28.3
Halifax	237	2 152	7 761	11.1	56.0	15.2	54.9	9 610	20 929	34 659	49 141	1.7	35 553	22.2	28.9	24.7
Hanover	124	1 241	27 262	18.4	35.6	35.5	167.2	9 099	33 540	75 070	90 159	6.3	77 316	5.6	6.8	5.9
Henrico	186	2 456	81 073	16.6	32.9	39.7	449.9	8 982	33 115	61 048	81 457	5.8	60 050	11.3	14.6	12.4
Henry	347	2 709	11 400	9.9	57.5	11.2	68.3	9 152	19 852	34 984	46 065	1.1	36 066	18.5	29.5	27.8
Highland	45	313	267	31.1	62.5	20.9	3.6	17 756	26 372	49 625	59 675	1.5	38 314	14.6	24.3	21.9
Isle of Wight	138	1 326	8 658	18.9	42.6	25.5	55.1	9 900	30 903	63 942	79 223	4.4	62 495	10.6	14.0	12.6
James City	85	1 309	16 735	15.4	28.5	45.8	(11)120.0	(11)10 885	39 133	76 960	96 875	7.4	75 806	7.5	11.2	9.9
King and Queen	212	931	1 140	23.9	59.8	14.1	11.7	12 898	23 868	48 372	57 938	2.2	44 697	13.4	21.1	18.4
King George	125	1 541	6 286	15.5	37.8	31.1	36.0	8 454	34 234	81 753	95 682	8.0	78 180	7.9	10.8	9.7
King William	56	787	3 989	13.1	51.0	19.2	29.4	9 862	26 040	62 070	69 838	1.4	61 183	9.1	13.3	12.1
Lancaster	116	357	1 815	10.7	42.2	28.3	14.7	11 062	30 737	49 248	64 740	2.8	46 578	15.2	28.4	26.5
Lee	169	2 202	5 344	10.4	58.8	11.7	35.2	10 295	16 664	31 308	40 743	0.8	32 092	29.0	38.6	35.6
Loudoun	85	1 043	99 843	18.2	20.4	57.9	854.5	12 528	46 565	122 238	140 174	19.8	117 680	3.8	4.1	3.7

1. Data for serious crimes have not been adjusted for underreporting; this may affect comparability between geographic areas and over time. 2. Per 100,000 population estimated by the FBI.
3. All persons 3 years old and over enrolled in nursery school through college. 4. Persons 25 years old and over. 5. Elementary and secondary education expenditures.
6. Based on population estimated by the American Community Survey, 2009–2013. 7. Bedford city is included with Bedford county. 8. Fairfax city is included with Fairfax county.
9. Winchester city is included with Frederick county. 10. Emporia city is included with Greensville county. 11. Williamsburg city is included with James City county.

STATE County	Personal income, 2013: Total (mil dol)	Personal income, 2013: Percent change, 2012–2013	Personal income, 2013: Per capita[1]: Dollars	Personal income, 2013: Per capita[1]: Rank	Personal income, 2013: Wages and salaries (mil dol)	Personal income, 2013: Supplements to wages and salaries; employer contributions (mil dol): Pension and insurance	Personal income, 2013: Supplements to wages and salaries; employer contributions (mil dol): Government social insurance	Personal income, 2013: Proprietors' income (mil dol)	Personal income, 2013: Dividends, interest, and rent (mil dol)	Personal income, 2013: Personal transfer receipts (mil dol)	Earnings, 2013: Total (mil dol)	Earnings, 2013: Contributions for government social insurance (mil dol): From employee and self-employed	Earnings, 2013: Contributions for government social insurance (mil dol): From employer
	62	63	64	65	66	67	68	69	70	71	72	73	74
VERMONT—Cont'd													
Chittenden	7 846	2.5	49 184	406	5 067	853	416	629	1 541	1 187	6 964	426	416
Essex	191	2.6	30 686	2 602	38	10	3	20	32	57	71	6	3
Franklin	2 157	2.6	44 657	719	730	159	62	191	260	357	1 142	69	62
Grand Isle	330	0.4	47 220	535	38	9	3	25	73	53	76	6	3
Lamoille	1 103	2.8	44 006	756	421	75	38	118	233	199	651	42	38
Orange	1 148	2.3	39 699	1 204	294	64	25	99	208	235	481	33	25
Orleans	1 061	2.4	39 055	1 290	372	78	34	112	197	309	595	40	34
Rutland	2 754	2.5	45 433	659	1 130	226	98	134	458	851	1 588	107	98
Washington	2 912	2.9	49 084	412	1 517	290	123	206	537	611	2 137	133	123
Windham	1 948	2.6	44 407	733	920	169	79	169	419	442	1 337	87	79
Windsor	2 704	1.9	48 233	466	964	188	83	220	603	534	1 456	98	83
VIRGINIA	403 425	1.2	48 838	X	210 552	33 650	15 560	27 371	82 869	53 440	287 133	16 782	15 560
Accomack	1 247	2.3	37 628	1 485	477	99	36	91	296	320	703	44	36
Albemarle	(3)7 764	(3)2.1	(3)52 693	(3)279	(3)4 574	(3)849	(3)328	(3)914	(3)2 253	(3)852	(3)6 665	(3)377	(3)328
Alleghany	(4)749	(4)-3.9	(4)34 078	(4)2 068	(4)341	(4)60	(4)26	(4)35	(4)141	(4)231	(4)462	(4)33	(4)26
Amelia	480	2.1	37 634	1 484	94	16	7	46	76	104	163	12	7
Amherst	1 086	0.7	33 760	2 132	333	68	25	49	184	272	475	34	25
Appomattox	518	1.4	33 941	2 093	99	21	7	30	77	136	157	13	7
Arlington	18 608	0.6	82 736	17	15 123	2 379	1 112	1 424	3 716	913	20 039	1 085	1 112
Augusta	(5)4 502	(5)2.4	(5)37 664	(5)1 478	(5)1 862	(5)337	(5)139	(5)356	(5)985	(5)958	(5)2 694	(5)175	(5)139
Bath	215	3.5	46 684	571	90	14	7	2	71	45	113	8	7
Bedford	(6)3 206	(6)1.5	(6)42 314	(6)906	(6)705	(6)119	(6)54	(6)179	(6)609	(6)607	(6)1 058	(6)79	(6)54
Bland	221	1.3	32 802	2 281	84	20	6	7	37	59	118	8	6
Botetourt	1 540	1.0	46 664	572	412	69	32	82	284	254	595	42	32
Brunswick	505	2.6	29 760	2 719	149	30	11	25	81	175	215	16	11
Buchanan	871	0.2	36 897	1 604	381	64	28	173	98	283	646	45	28
Buckingham	461	2.0	26 877	2 977	124	28	9	45	75	126	205	15	9
Campbell	(7)4 469	(7)2.2	(7)33 538	(7)2 169	(7)3 066	(7)462	(7)229	(7)209	(7)921	(7)1 228	(7)3 965	(7)250	(7)229
Caroline	1 111	2.1	37 920	1 444	220	49	17	77	159	204	363	24	17
Carroll	(8)1 156	(8)2.1	(8)31 320	(8)2 508	(8)381	(8)75	(8)30	(8)72	(8)188	(8)400	(8)558	(8)42	(8)30
Charles City	249	0.1	34 947	1 905	63	11	5	21	53	59	100	7	5
Charlotte	385	3.2	31 285	2 512	93	22	7	38	73	121	159	12	7
Chesterfield	15 342	2.8	46 810	564	5 944	931	440	880	2 708	1 938	8 195	498	440
Clarke	630	-0.4	43 913	765	180	26	13	35	179	91	255	17	13
Craig	180	1.3	34 465	1 994	25	5	2	9	32	46	41	4	2
Culpeper	1 840	2.1	37 943	1 440	649	116	49	127	327	307	940	59	49
Cumberland	345	2.8	35 028	1 892	42	10	3	16	53	83	71	6	3
Dickenson	462	-0.9	29 828	2 713	165	30	12	21	58	190	228	19	12
Dinwiddie	(9)3 172	(9)1.7	(9)40 629	(9)1 095	(9)1 222	(9)227	(9)93	(9)75	(9)567	(9)880	(9)1 617	(9)105	(9)93
Essex	407	2.7	36 244	1 703	137	24	10	30	86	103	201	13	10
Fairfax	(10)83 835	(10)0.5	(10)71 752	(10)42	(10)53 987	(10)6 339	(10)3 700	(10)8 647	(10)17 786	(10)5 003	(10)72 673	(10)4 140	(10)3 700
Fauquier	3 818	0.4	56 814	163	1 018	160	75	278	819	373	1 531	93	75
Floyd	483	1.9	31 126	2 528	97	19	7	36	96	129	159	13	7
Fluvanna	1 072	1.4	41 278	1 019	168	35	13	22	198	172	238	19	13
Franklin	1 993	1.3	35 374	1 842	486	88	38	71	430	472	682	53	38
Frederick	(11)4 384	(11)3.0	(11)40 394	(11)1 123	(11)2 354	(11)378	(11)178	(11)283	(11)876	(11)664	(11)3 193	(11)193	(11)178
Giles	544	0.5	32 119	2 401	195	39	15	14	97	162	263	20	15
Gloucester	1 554	0.9	42 189	917	320	65	24	50	324	274	459	32	24
Goochland	1 599	0.9	73 930	35	1 024	112	64	164	498	168	1 363	82	64
Grayson	415	2.0	27 381	2 948	75	18	6	10	84	156	108	12	6
Greene	792	1.8	42 112	929	125	22	9	32	117	118	189	14	9
Greensville	(12)449	(12)-0.5	(12)25 686	(12)3 032	(12)262	(12)56	(12)20	(12)15	(12)73	(12)153	(12)352	(12)23	(12)20
Halifax	1 177	3.3	33 259	2 216	448	89	34	82	233	344	653	45	34
Hanover	5 002	1.3	49 368	398	2 010	293	153	388	932	617	2 844	175	153
Henrico	15 128	1.5	47 482	514	9 918	1 295	723	804	3 379	1 947	12 741	762	723
Henry	(13)2 160	(13)1.0	(13)32 546	(13)2 320	(13)844	(13)156	(13)67	(13)98	(13)462	(13)713	(13)1 164	(13)89	(13)67
Highland	91	2.5	41 185	1 027	17	4	1	5	35	22	26	2	1
Isle of Wight	1 632	0.4	45 759	638	513	76	33	87	281	273	710	47	33
James City	(14)4 592	(14)2.0	(14)53 571	(14)249	(14)1 614	(14)276	(14)120	(14)311	(14)1 398	(14)673	(14)2 320	(14)145	(14)120
King and Queen	249	2.3	34 935	1 908	39	8	3	35	39	59	85	6	3
King George	1 042	1.2	41 791	961	811	198	65	82	220	124	1 157	61	65
King William	655	1.3	40 690	1 088	156	25	12	22	105	108	215	15	12
Lancaster	585	1.0	52 504	287	171	28	13	33	240	130	245	18	13
Lee	706	-1.3	28 030	2 897	176	42	14	48	109	264	280	23	14
Loudoun	20 886	1.9	59 729	111	9 534	1 224	665	927	3 018	1 036	12 350	709	665

1. Based on the resident population estimated as of July 1 of the year shown. 3. Charlottesville city is included with Albemarle county. 4. Covington city is included with Alleghany county. 5. Staunton and Waynesboro cities are included with Augusta county. 6. Bedford city is included with Bedford county. 7. Lynchburg city is included with Campbell county. 8. Galax city is included with Carroll county. 9. Petersburg and Colonial Heights cities are included with Dinwiddie county. 10. Fairfax city and Falls Church city are included with Fairfax county. 11. Winchester city is included with Frederick county. 12. Emporia city is included with Greensville county. 13. Martinsville city is included with Henry county. 14. Williamsburg city is included with James City county.

STATE County	Earnings, 2013 (cont.) — Percent by selected industries: Farm	Mining	Construction	Manu-facturing	Infor-mation: professional, scientific, technical services	Retail trade	Finance, insur-ance, real estate and leasing	Health care and social assistance	Govern-ment	Social Security beneficiaries, December 2013: Number	Rate[1]	Supple-mental Security Income recipients, December 2013	Housing units, 2014: Total	Percent change, 2010–2014
	75	76	77	78	79	80	81	82	83	84	85	86	87	88
VERMONT—Cont'd														
Chittenden	0.1	D	6.5	13.1	13.7	6.6	7.0	14.8	18.0	27 470	172	2 999	67 271	2.4
Essex	3.3	D	6.7	9.0	D	5.2	D	D	34.9	2 070	334	226	5 040	0.4
Franklin	4.4	D	6.1	16.4	D	9.9	2.6	12.0	27.5	8 615	178	1 248	21 988	1.8
Grand Isle	3.9	0.0	16.2	2.8	D	8.4	4.5	D	22.4	1 810	259	145	5 106	1.1
Lamoille	1.2	D	10.1	4.7	8.9	7.9	5.7	14.1	15.7	4 935	197	501	13 148	1.4
Orange	2.1	0.2	12.1	6.9	7.2	6.6	D	D	23.1	6 590	228	682	14 916	0.5
Orleans	3.9	D	9.6	11.0	D	9.0	4.7	15.9	20.9	7 375	271	1 059	16 560	2.5
Rutland	0.6	1.6	6.7	15.3	4.7	8.9	3.8	17.3	17.5	16 265	269	2 072	33 761	0.0
Washington	0.3	0.3	5.2	6.4	7.2	7.1	12.6	11.0	26.1	13 305	225	1 526	30 119	0.6
Windham	0.4	D	9.0	10.2	D	7.4	4.8	13.5	12.9	10 875	248	1 188	29 826	0.3
Windsor	0.2	0.2	7.9	7.7	11.1	6.3	4.4	14.7	24.2	14 770	263	1 283	34 146	0.1
VIRGINIA	0.2	0.5	5.3	5.8	20.7	5.2	7.0	8.8	23.7	1 384 419	167	153 632	3 446 471	2.4
Accomack	6.7	0.0	4.3	17.4	11.0	5.7	3.4	D	26.9	9 040	274	1 107	21 069	0.3
Albemarle	[3]-0.2	[3]0.9	[3]4.6	[3]D	[3]13.6	[3]5.0	[3]8.4	[3]9.8	[3]33.8	17 295	168	860	43 924	4.3
Alleghany	[4]-0.4	[4]D	[4]6.2	[4]D	[4]D	[4]6.8	[4]D	[4]12.0	[4]18.0	4 625	287	485	8 048	-0.4
Amelia	3.8	D	15.1	6.4	D	11.2	D	D	16.1	3 090	243	314	5 427	1.2
Amherst	-0.7	0.0	7.7	19.7	3.3	6.7	2.7	D	30.6	8 030	249	828	14 082	0.8
Appomattox	-2.2	D	16.4	2.3	3.6	12.2	4.6	D	26.4	4 025	264	554	7 081	2.3
Arlington	0.0	D	1.6	D	30.2	1.9	6.6	3.4	33.0	18 465	82	2 109	110 601	4.9
Augusta	[5]1.5	[5]D	[5]D	[5]17.8	[5]7.2	[5]7.1	[5]3.6	[5]D	[5]17.5	17 690	240	956	31 798	2.0
Bath	-0.5	0.0	7.0	1.4	8.6	2.0	3.0	11.2	17.0	1 340	291	90	3 296	0.9
Bedford	[6]-1.4	[6]0.0	[6]10.1	[6]12.4	[6]D	[6]7.6	[6]7.0	[6]10.2	[6]14.7	17 260	228	1 074	35 779	2.7
Bland	0.3	D	3.3	35.4	D	D	D	12.0	26.6	1 865	279	131	3 262	-0.1
Botetourt	-0.5	D	8.5	21.0	5.4	D	4.3	6.0	13.1	8 040	243	450	14 704	1.0
Brunswick	3.9	D	6.6	6.4	D	5.0	2.8	D	24.4	4 250	255	694	8 164	0.0
Buchanan	-0.2	50.2	5.3	3.8	D	3.7	1.9	4.8	12.4	8 635	367	1 751	11 443	-1.1
Buckingham	1.4	D	10.0	2.6	4.2	5.7	2.2	10.6	34.1	3 680	215	523	7 282	0.6
Campbell	[7]-0.1	[7]D	[7]D	[7]20.5	[7]12.1	[7]6.5	[7]6.5	[7]15.2	[7]10.2	13 420	245	1 311	25 295	2.1
Caroline	0.9	D	9.0	4.3	D	5.0	3.7	D	28.6	5 680	194	491	11 998	2.3
Carroll	[8]-0.3	[8]0.0	[8]D	[8]17.3	[8]4.2	[8]11.3	[8]3.5	[8]D	[8]22.2	8 540	286	804	16 608	0.2
Charles City	5.4	1.1	14.0	16.2	D	D	D	2.0	18.3	1 845	260	133	3 304	2.3
Charlotte	6.3	D	4.5	12.6	D	5.7	D	D	29.4	3 660	297	554	6 290	0.3
Chesterfield	0.0	D	7.9	9.3	D	8.6	7.9	10.3	16.6	53 605	163	4 099	126 436	3.2
Clarke	-2.0	D	12.7	11.9	14.7	4.0	4.9	D	15.9	2 850	199	125	6 277	0.7
Craig	-0.9	0.0	8.7	D	D	6.6	7.9	8.9	28.4	1 440	277	128	2 866	2.2
Culpeper	0.1	0.4	8.3	8.9	11.9	8.4	3.5	13.8	21.6	8 790	181	799	18 115	2.6
Cumberland	18.0	0.1	7.4	8.4	D	6.8	D	D	30.5	2 400	244	307	4 662	0.7
Dickenson	-0.9	40.1	7.5	0.9	D	5.8	D	D	18.0	5 535	358	1 038	7 514	-0.8
Dinwiddie	[9]0.5	[9]D	[9]4.6	[9]11.8	[9]D	[9]11.2	[9]D	[9]D	[9]25.1	5 975	214	810	11 578	1.4
Essex	5.3	0.0	4.2	9.3	D	12.3	8.9	17.7	15.1	2 970	265	335	5 796	0.7
Fairfax	[10]0.0	[10]0.1	[10]4.5	[10]0.7	[10]40.2	[10]3.8	[10]7.4	[10]5.8	[10]15.7	115 830	102	10 888	410 287	0.6
Fauquier	-0.6	D	12.7	3.1	15.8	8.2	6.9	11.2	20.6	10 960	163	562	26 226	2.3
Floyd	1.4	D	9.6	10.0	D	7.3	6.8	D	19.8	3 950	254	328	7 915	1.6
Fluvanna	-0.9	D	9.3	2.3	3.5	4.3	2.7	D	31.7	5 475	211	267	10 661	2.6
Franklin	0.8	D	10.2	18.7	3.5	9.3	4.4	D	17.5	14 580	259	1 226	29 471	0.5
Frederick	[11]-0.2	[11]D	[11]D	[11]14.7	[11]5.2	[11]9.4	[11]5.3	[11]18.3	[11]17.6	14 565	179	874	32 400	3.4
Giles	-1.1	0.0	D	31.8	9.3	7.8	2.4	8.4	15.9	4 860	287	562	8 334	0.2
Gloucester	0.7	D	8.4	2.4	5.0	12.5	4.3	15.6	28.6	8 045	218	628	16 151	1.9
Goochland	-0.2	D	5.9	1.6	4.6	1.9	D	2.3	5.5	4 875	225	222	8 900	3.4
Grayson	-1.3	D	2.9	15.6	1.5	5.6	9.2	D	36.2	4 970	327	488	9 155	0.0
Greene	0.6	D	10.1	2.4	12.6	11.4	2.9	D	23.9	3 535	188	252	7 991	6.4
Greensville	[12]1.1	[12]D	[12]1.6	[12]24.4	[12]D	[12]5.6	[12]D	[12]16.1	[12]28.9	2 665	227	408	4 126	0.9
Halifax	5.1	D	5.5	17.0	2.6	6.3	2.6	15.4	16.7	10 445	295	1 649	18 080	0.4
Hanover	0.2	1.2	12.1	7.2	6.5	9.1	5.1	12.9	10.1	18 850	186	830	39 863	3.9
Henrico	0.0	0.3	5.2	3.9	14.7	6.3	18.5	12.8	9.6	52 925	166	5 058	135 002	1.7
Henry	[13]0.3	[13]D	[13]D	[13]19.8	[13]D	[13]10.0	[13]3.5	[13]13.6	[13]17.4	16 790	320	1 564	26 101	-0.6
Highland	-1.7	0.0	12.8	D	D	5.0	D	6.1	30.3	745	336	24	1 856	1.2
Isle of Wight	1.0	0.1	4.1	24.9	D	4.8	4.0	D	12.8	7 750	217	553	15 065	3.0
James City	[14]0.0	[14]D	[14]D	[14]D	[14]D	[14]6.6	[14]D	[14]D	[14]22.4	17 520	247	552	31 742	5.6
King and Queen	7.4	D	11.7	5.7	D	2.7	D	D	18.9	1 740	244	145	3 445	0.9
King George	-0.1	D	3.0	0.3	20.1	1.9	2.1	1.6	63.2	3 320	133	258	9 781	3.2
King William	3.9	1.1	6.4	29.8	D	13.4	3.7	D	18.4	3 305	205	216	6 675	2.4
Lancaster	0.0	0.0	8.5	2.0	9.7	9.2	10.8	23.1	11.6	4 290	386	275	7 591	2.5
Lee	-1.2	7.3	8.1	1.6	D	8.8	2.9	D	35.1	7 325	291	1 848	11 715	-0.3
Loudoun	0.0	D	8.8	5.7	29.7	5.2	5.3	5.9	14.2	27 140	77	1 793	123 150	12.5

1. Per 1,000 resident population estimated as of July 1 of the year shown. 3. Charlottesville city is included with Albemarle county. 4. Covington city is included with Alleghany county. 5. Staunton and Waynesboro cities are included with Augusta county. 6. Bedford city is included with Bedford county. 7. Lynchburg city is included with Campbell county. 8. Galax city is included with Carroll county. 9. Petersburg and Colonial Heights cities are included with Dinwiddie county. 10. Fairfax city and Falls Church city are included with Fairfax county. 11. Winchester city is included with Frederick county. 12. Emporia city is included with Greensville county. 13. Martinsville city is included with Henry county. 14. Williamsburg city is included with James City county.

STATE County	Housing units, 2009–2013: Occupied units: Total	Owner-occupied: Percent	Owner-occupied: Median value[1]	Median owner cost as a percent of income: With a mortgage	Median owner cost as a percent of income: Without a mortgage[2]	Renter-occupied: Median rent[3]	Renter-occupied: Median rent as a percent of income[2]	Substandard units[4] (percent)	Civilian labor force, 2014: Total	Percent change, 2013–2014	Unemployment: Total	Unemployment: Rate[5]	Civilian employment,[6] 2009–2013: Total	Percent: Management, business, science and arts	Percent: Construction, production, and maintenance occupations
	89	90	91	92	93	94	95	96	97	98	99	100	101	102	103
VERMONT—Cont'd															
Chittenden	62 587	65.1	267 500	24.6	14.3	1 026	32.6	1.9	94 810	-0.4	2 969	3.1	86 895	46.3	13.9
Essex	2 774	81.0	122 200	25.6	16.8	679	35.1	2.0	2 857	-0.4	194	6.8	2 801	28.3	33.9
Franklin	18 616	76.1	204 400	25.0	15.7	861	32.2	1.6	27 362	-0.7	1 123	4.1	25 041	34.3	26.6
Grand Isle	3 023	81.2	254 300	25.9	16.8	871	30.6	2.1	4 063	-0.4	191	4.7	3 727	35.0	21.2
Lamoille	10 046	71.3	218 800	27.7	17.8	869	29.5	2.7	13 916	0.0	722	5.2	13 051	38.0	21.1
Orange	11 962	81.5	183 900	25.1	16.1	825	32.8	2.4	16 035	-1.2	623	3.9	15 079	38.9	22.8
Orleans	11 043	77.4	156 300	26.0	17.4	692	32.7	1.8	13 885	0.0	889	6.4	12 404	30.3	29.8
Rutland	25 754	69.7	176 800	24.6	17.1	789	30.7	1.7	32 010	-1.1	1 554	4.9	30 233	34.4	23.6
Washington	24 661	73.1	205 000	24.5	16.9	840	28.8	2.3	34 369	-0.7	1 386	4.0	31 476	42.8	17.8
Windham	19 417	69.4	206 800	27.4	17.4	789	29.5	2.0	23 874	-1.1	1 013	4.2	22 715	39.5	22.5
Windsor	25 024	69.8	216 300	26.2	18.2	852	29.2	4.5	30 100	-0.9	1 127	3.7	28 593	40.2	21.5
VIRGINIA	3 022 739	67.3	244 600	23.8	10.9	1 087	30.1	2.3	4 261 175	0.4	220 070	5.2	3 885 351	42.3	18.1
Accomack	14 333	69.5	153 600	23.7	12.5	734	26.6	1.0	16 024	-1.3	1 040	6.5	14 611	29.6	31.9
Albemarle	37 964	66.1	319 200	22.3	10.7	1 106	29.7	1.6	54 006	2.6	2 375	4.4	46 563	53.5	12.5
Alleghany	6 773	79.9	114 600	19.5	11.3	521	27.4	1.9	7 282	-3.4	439	6.0	6 853	31.2	31.3
Amelia	4 808	79.9	180 700	25.1	10.8	738	28.5	1.5	6 242	0.9	328	5.3	5 540	26.2	28.4
Amherst	12 680	74.1	148 700	22.7	10.1	671	24.9	1.5	15 888	0.4	861	5.4	14 823	28.3	27.1
Appomattox	5 803	80.2	145 400	22.0	10.0	609	36.5	2.8	7 188	0.2	407	5.7	6 536	28.7	32.4
Arlington	94 454	45.2	584 600	22.0	10.3	1 733	26.0	1.8	145 962	0.4	4 680	3.2	136 432	66.8	6.2
Augusta	27 999	80.9	194 600	23.3	10.9	743	27.2	3.5	37 065	0.2	1 736	4.7	33 710	30.0	29.6
Bath	2 101	76.2	152 600	19.0	12.7	764	21.5	1.4	2 634	2.0	117	4.4	2 389	21.8	31.3
Bedford	27 233	85.0	195 400	22.3	10.0	763	29.4	1.1	38 497	0.5	1 960	5.1	33 116	34.3	26.7
Bland	2 480	82.5	95 200	22.4	10.5	540	27.2	2.1	2 903	0.7	174	6.0	2 448	29.7	27.9
Botetourt	12 825	88.1	213 100	22.7	10.0	788	23.5	1.7	17 829	0.9	862	4.8	16 210	38.1	22.3
Brunswick	5 826	72.2	105 600	24.8	11.9	617	37.5	2.1	6 516	-2.4	536	8.2	6 144	22.6	27.0
Buchanan	9 485	78.6	68 200	24.2	10.2	596	38.8	3.5	7 874	-3.7	816	10.4	7 325	23.8	35.7
Buckingham	5 817	76.0	128 800	25.5	11.3	708	26.3	1.4	6 516	1.6	429	6.6	5 561	28.2	21.3
Campbell	21 774	76.0	150 300	22.2	10.0	685	28.5	2.0	27 112	0.4	1 435	5.3	25 262	31.8	29.7
Caroline	10 680	80.1	188 400	24.5	11.7	1 025	29.6	1.8	14 731	0.8	902	6.1	13 015	29.6	26.1
Carroll	12 572	78.7	102 900	23.1	11.3	532	29.7	1.9	13 228	-0.5	893	6.8	12 589	22.2	38.4
Charles City	2 850	80.5	147 500	23.5	10.4	824	29.6	3.8	3 819	0.7	221	5.8	3 419	23.5	35.9
Charlotte	4 751	73.0	98 900	24.9	12.8	556	30.9	1.3	5 331	0.1	359	6.7	5 079	24.0	34.7
Chesterfield	113 637	77.0	226 500	23.1	10.2	1 077	30.1	0.9	177 328	1.3	9 042	5.1	158 600	42.5	16.8
Clarke	5 580	79.7	342 500	24.1	10.0	1 022	25.7	0.0	7 642	0.0	330	4.3	7 090	43.8	19.0
Craig	2 122	84.4	136 500	24.8	10.0	553	23.5	2.2	2 473	0.4	155	6.3	2 200	28.4	28.0
Culpeper	16 039	73.0	250 600	25.9	10.0	1 021	32.4	4.3	23 463	0.1	1 163	5.0	21 623	35.4	22.0
Cumberland	4 049	77.4	142 400	25.0	11.8	838	29.0	3.5	4 531	0.4	275	6.1	4 297	26.9	26.1
Dickenson	6 352	78.1	75 700	20.1	10.4	517	40.3	0.9	5 239	-1.9	519	9.9	5 046	25.7	30.7
Dinwiddie	9 932	76.6	165 300	24.6	11.1	905	26.9	1.8	13 659	0.7	869	6.4	12 204	27.6	32.7
Essex	4 286	76.2	160 800	26.3	12.8	825	29.1	3.2	5 773	1.3	367	6.4	5 183	20.0	26.9
Fairfax	389 908	69.0	476 600	22.6	10.0	1 687	28.3	1.4	627 615	0.3	25 617	4.1	591 741	55.9	9.9
Fauquier	23 130	80.1	350 600	24.5	10.7	1 138	27.1	1.9	36 018	0.1	1 625	4.5	33 340	43.9	19.0
Floyd	6 086	77.6	144 700	23.6	10.0	540	17.3	1.9	8 433	0.3	387	4.6	7 278	29.2	33.3
Fluvanna	9 462	85.5	225 700	24.0	11.4	1 254	28.8	2.4	13 402	2.6	572	4.3	11 866	41.0	15.6
Franklin	23 358	78.0	163 700	24.0	10.0	655	29.5	2.6	27 446	0.7	1 454	5.3	24 560	31.4	29.5
Frederick	29 172	78.3	226 900	23.4	11.5	1 084	29.5	2.6	44 689	1.0	2 079	4.7	38 932	39.3	22.5
Giles	7 167	75.9	105 300	21.0	10.0	578	25.2	1.0	8 273	0.5	499	6.0	7 393	30.0	35.7
Gloucester	13 889	82.9	228 700	24.7	10.4	817	26.9	0.5	19 392	0.1	940	4.8	17 788	31.7	25.9
Goochland	8 058	90.2	338 500	23.9	10.0	982	25.1	0.8	10 533	1.3	500	4.7	9 557	50.5	14.8
Grayson	6 618	77.7	97 900	24.3	10.0	555	29.7	1.3	7 120	1.4	551	7.7	6 178	22.4	38.2
Greene	6 897	79.0	237 500	24.6	10.0	1 007	28.4	2.8	9 954	2.5	433	4.4	8 692	33.7	22.2
Greensville	3 389	75.8	99 600	22.8	13.8	720	33.2	1.7	4 279	-2.1	287	6.7	3 635	18.0	33.9
Halifax	14 770	72.3	106 600	22.6	12.6	568	35.1	0.8	15 675	-1.4	1 224	7.8	14 159	30.0	29.5
Hanover	36 927	83.4	262 000	22.9	11.2	1 016	30.1	1.7	56 243	1.3	2 548	4.5	51 039	44.0	16.7
Henrico	123 683	65.2	219 900	23.4	10.2	1 008	29.7	2.4	176 843	1.4	8 962	5.1	158 342	42.9	14.2
Henry	22 690	74.6	94 600	22.5	11.3	586	28.2	1.3	22 926	-2.2	1 769	7.7	21 382	24.4	32.1
Highland	1 006	86.3	171 700	23.9	10.0	490	20.2	2.1	1 434	0.8	55	3.8	1 083	33.7	34.5
Isle of Wight	13 560	80.6	249 600	24.5	11.8	951	32.1	1.0	18 903	0.0	996	5.3	17 080	36.0	25.3
James City	26 883	76.2	327 100	24.0	10.0	1 153	31.4	1.6	33 836	0.2	1 679	5.0	30 185	45.2	12.9
King and Queen	2 863	76.2	154 200	24.2	10.0	851	23.7	1.5	3 653	0.2	211	5.8	3 338	24.6	40.0
King George	8 314	73.5	278 900	22.0	10.0	1 109	26.7	0.9	12 184	1.6	641	5.3	11 257	44.9	16.9
King William	5 998	83.1	199 700	25.1	10.0	1 012	37.8	2.3	8 828	1.3	457	5.2	7 922	26.9	31.1
Lancaster	5 182	79.2	233 400	26.7	11.6	850	30.0	4.5	5 416	0.1	410	7.6	4 811	29.0	21.8
Lee	9 653	74.3	74 300	22.7	10.4	482	33.0	2.0	8 902	-4.6	729	8.2	8 196	27.0	28.3
Loudoun	106 997	77.7	437 700	24.4	10.0	1 654	28.2	1.8	192 351	0.5	8 082	4.2	173 426	56.5	9.9

1. Specified owner-occupied units. 2. A value of 10.0 represents 10 percent or less; a value of 50.0 represents 50 percent or more. 3. Specified renter-occupied units.
4. Overcrowded or lacking complete plumbing facilities. 5. Percent of civilian labor force. 6. Persons 16 years old and over.

STATE County	Private nonfarm establishments, employment and payroll, 2013										Agriculture, 2012			
		Employment							Annual payroll		Farms			
												Percent with:		
	Number of establish-ments	Total	Health care and social assistance	Manufac-turing	Retail trade	Finance and insurance	Professional, scientific, and technical services	Total (mil dol)	Average per employee (dollars)	Number	Fewer than 50 acres	500 acres or more	Farm operators whose principal occu-pation is farming (percent)
	104	105	106	107	108	109	110	111	112	113	114	115	116
VERMONT—Cont'd													
Chittenden	5 523	89 448	15 346	9 406	12 449	3 135	10 509	3 953	44 192	587	50.4	3.9	50.6
Essex	116	494	D	D	85	D	15	14	28 081	93	26.9	18.3	47.3
Franklin	1 020	12 038	2 763	2 650	2 073	300	233	439	36 484	736	28.3	12.1	54.5
Grand Isle	180	624	45	44	153	16	D	21	32 941	121	44.6	7.4	59.5
Lamoille	944	10 592	1 631	459	1 406	222	385	314	29 610	349	42.4	6.9	36.1
Orange	766	6 169	1 525	679	923	D	331	221	35 800	748	38.2	4.0	49.9
Orleans	793	8 190	1 783	D	1 309	208	150	253	30 925	638	31.7	9.7	60.3
Rutland	2 166	24 163	4 759	3 360	4 059	586	643	869	35 982	640	38.4	7.0	47.8
Washington	2 217	25 548	4 008	2 913	3 860	2 204	988	1 048	41 034	532	40.0	3.2	50.4
Windham	1 726	21 909	3 388	1 866	2 405	572	478	746	34 062	447	46.1	4.7	52.3
Windsor	2 043	19 669	4 030	2 216	2 622	529	972	762	38 723	768	42.1	4.7	48.7
VIRGINIA	193 907	3 131 723	416 774	232 762	415 557	160 979	438 370	154 472	49 325	46 030	38.6	7.7	45.1
Accomack	760	8 779	1 105	D	1 409	243	454	247	28 149	226	46.0	15.5	63.7
Albemarle	2 569	37 158	6 803	2 743	5 775	D	3 076	1 742	46 885	946	38.1	8.0	41.4
Alleghany	243	2 471	785	317	D	D	25	86	34 916	207	25.6	6.8	32.4
Amelia	258	1 804	D	193	212	32	48	50	27 831	407	30.5	9.3	44.5
Amherst	588	6 347	744	1 276	1 139	142	252	196	30 917	426	27.9	10.1	39.0
Appomattox	285	2 268	456	101	646	D	D	55	24 449	410	21.0	10.5	43.4
Arlington	6 219	132 556	8 722	220	9 430	3 267	41 664	9 776	73 751	6	100.0	0.0	50.0
Augusta	1 409	19 300	4 189	4 261	1 955	264	446	735	38 103	1 706	42.3	6.2	48.8
Bath	128	1 454	D	43	79	D	D	47	32 010	116	17.2	15.5	45.7
Bedford	1 353	11 923	1 162	2 538	1 815	305	677	427	35 791	1 369	34.2	5.0	42.7
Bland	78	1 293	D	D	61	13	D	54	42 131	362	23.2	9.1	44.8
Botetourt	725	9 682	715	2 263	851	189	229	375	38 734	584	33.0	6.5	46.7
Brunswick	260	2 451	202	165	324	45	D	68	27 670	312	19.6	10.3	44.6
Buchanan	442	6 464	615	247	841	D	236	286	44 191	103	46.6	2.9	33.0
Buckingham	252	1 849	D	89	281	32	92	60	32 604	391	24.0	13.0	52.9
Campbell	1 157	13 576	1 011	2 533	1 969	403	760	503	37 061	761	28.1	8.9	37.2
Caroline	374	3 717	301	260	549	D	285	132	35 416	221	38.5	12.2	45.2
Carroll	412	4 205	611	831	784	85	D	107	25 526	980	34.3	6.5	39.2
Charles City	141	1 496	D	317	59	D	D	55	36 638	79	43.0	16.5	58.2
Charlotte	232	1 731	272	387	223	D	D	49	28 306	518	26.8	11.4	42.9
Chesterfield	6 919	102 530	11 463	9 747	16 878	5 567	7 045	4 287	41 816	197	56.3	2.5	44.7
Clarke	355	2 981	444	D	235	D	149	129	43 229	477	47.2	4.4	46.5
Craig	57	329	D	D	98	27	D	9	26 708	207	27.5	9.7	51.7
Culpeper	990	11 884	2 108	1 207	2 233	250	783	472	39 711	731	45.7	8.1	40.9
Cumberland	142	888	97	D	216	18	D	25	28 713	262	30.2	11.1	52.7
Dickenson	202	2 213	372	D	415	70	D	98	44 381	147	48.3	4.8	51.7
Dinwiddie	350	4 699	311	707	498	134	D	191	40 664	383	32.6	9.1	45.4
Essex	297	3 497	614	641	840	124	93	98	27 951	98	36.7	26.5	43.9
Fairfax	29 556	584 523	51 550	6 153	50 341	29 572	196 409	42 358	72 465	148	77.7	2.0	34.5
Fauquier	1 809	17 008	2 705	914	2 709	666	1 650	698	41 021	1 258	48.2	7.8	43.6
Floyd	307	2 057	344	367	324	D	47	53	25 702	863	29.9	6.7	48.2
Fluvanna	386	2 433	220	139	327	55	D	75	30 635	303	36.0	6.6	43.2
Franklin	1 161	12 040	1 313	2 603	1 876	254	306	324	26 902	1 023	30.7	6.6	45.2
Frederick	1 442	21 853	1 613	4 501	3 507	D	688	843	38 563	681	45.1	5.9	36.9
Giles	284	3 672	468	932	700	D	D	137	37 427	378	27.0	5.3	40.2
Gloucester	871	6 985	1 309	195	1 962	254	277	187	26 776	136	62.5	8.8	39.0
Goochland	638	17 205	570	D	551	D	387	1 373	79 802	315	52.1	6.0	41.0
Grayson	167	1 753	D	826	162	D	D	47	27 021	764	34.6	7.6	44.2
Greene	322	2 381	204	D	720	46	D	66	27 551	216	34.7	4.6	50.0
Greensville	96	1 776	D	D	184	D	D	52	29 306	151	29.1	19.2	38.4
Halifax	711	10 121	1 898	1 931	1 388	197	149	338	33 382	935	17.9	9.7	44.0
Hanover	3 077	42 300	4 875	3 634	6 022	675	1 371	1 523	36 009	600	53.2	5.7	51.8
Henrico	8 868	163 041	23 139	5 001	22 298	22 461	13 094	7 880	48 331	117	58.1	3.4	41.9
Henry	833	10 895	836	2 889	1 461	283	280	322	29 537	290	35.2	2.8	26.2
Highland	86	361	55	D	41	D	9	9	23 579	261	14.2	22.6	51.0
Isle of Wight	638	7 885	750	D	897	206	290	353	44 832	213	47.4	20.7	51.2
James City	1 651	26 035	4 514	1 729	3 751	550	1 371	900	34 579	83	61.4	1.2	28.9
King and Queen	103	664	D	D	20	D	24	22	33 798	127	40.2	13.4	66.1
King George	468	5 582	322	D	727	164	2 499	316	56 586	160	40.6	8.1	38.1
King William	307	2 840	315	D	416	100	143	130	45 747	135	37.0	18.5	50.4
Lancaster	469	4 187	1 147	178	776	283	324	147	35 184	61	39.3	8.2	45.9
Lee	286	3 197	688	99	959	176	59	83	26 104	1 012	38.7	3.6	37.2
Loudoun	8 987	134 845	10 339	D	18 396	4 143	19 378	7 534	55 869	1 396	69.0	3.4	37.0

STATE County	Agriculture, 2012 (cont.) — Land in farms: Acreage (1,000)	Land in farms: Percent change, 2007–2012	Land in farms — Acres: Average size of farm	Acres: Total irrigated (1,000)	Acres: Total cropland (1,000)	Value of land and buildings (dollars): Average per farm	Value of land and buildings (dollars): Average per acre	Value of machinery and equipment, average per farm (dollars)	Value of products sold: Total (mil dol)	Value of products sold: Average per farm (dollars)	Percent from: Crops	Percent from: Livestock and poultry products	Percent of farms with sales of: $10,000 or more	Percent of farms with sales of: $100,000 or more	Government payments: Total ($1,000)	Government payments: Percent of farms
	117	118	119	120	121	122	123	124	125	126	127	128	129	130	131	132
VERMONT—Cont'd																
Chittenden	74	-11.8	125	0.5	25.9	538 598	4 297	75 608	42.2	71 951	47.0	53.0	40.9	12.3	609	21.8
Essex	25	-4.6	274	0.0	8.0	510 731	1 863	95 505	11.7	125 280	33.9	66.1	47.3	19.4	124	31.2
Franklin	186	3.5	253	0.6	80.2	708 868	2 801	145 685	184.4	250 497	17.1	82.9	55.8	31.4	2 937	34.2
Grand Isle	19	11.0	157	0.1	13.8	598 289	3 806	103 231	19.1	157 579	29.6	70.4	53.7	26.4	458	27.3
Lamoille	52	4.7	149	0.1	12.6	544 129	3 645	73 444	21.3	61 129	44.6	55.4	37.8	12.3	362	18.3
Orange	105	3.5	141	0.2	33.2	435 761	3 097	65 348	53.5	71 578	25.2	74.8	35.7	13.9	730	15.8
Orleans	130	0.1	204	0.2	52.5	497 260	2 432	90 815	99.3	155 655	14.4	85.6	48.6	20.5	1 342	24.3
Rutland	108	-16.9	170	0.2	36.5	460 703	2 718	73 945	30.8	48 114	33.2	66.8	36.9	10.2	1 131	25.9
Washington	67	10.4	127	0.2	21.1	508 002	4 013	70 991	27.1	50 972	25.9	74.1	35.3	8.8	535	14.5
Windham	51	0.0	114	0.5	14.0	454 076	3 998	64 159	26.4	59 116	43.0	57.0	36.9	8.5	499	17.4
Windsor	101	5.6	132	0.2	23.6	500 858	3 795	58 762	22.4	29 188	34.8	65.2	27.2	7.2	517	9.6
VIRGINIA	8 302	2.4	180	68.7	2 990.6	776 719	4 306	72 555	3 753.3	81 540	36.2	63.8	37.9	9.6	82 318	23.2
Accomack	77	-17.5	342	5.4	64.3	1 254 991	3 665	153 013	172.2	761 934	34.7	65.3	68.1	39.4	2 020	44.2
Albemarle	169	6.7	179	1.5	46.6	1 563 048	8 756	61 092	31.0	32 780	62.8	37.2	32.2	4.2	377	9.2
Alleghany	37	28.0	179	0.0	8.1	554 908	3 108	53 285	2.9	14 227	D	D	28.0	1.0	11	10.1
Amelia	88	-3.5	217	0.4	28.2	664 813	3 065	77 044	99.8	245 288	13.0	87.0	37.6	13.5	1 496	42.8
Amherst	99	11.9	232	D	19.4	846 944	3 646	60 845	9.3	21 758	35.2	64.8	35.4	2.6	175	10.6
Appomattox	96	26.9	235	0.1	28.7	668 800	2 847	63 924	12.6	30 788	35.1	64.9	42.0	7.8	367	30.0
Arlington	0	0.0	6	D	D	322 667	53 778	10 000	0.0	3 000	D	D	0.0	0.0	0	0.0
Augusta	260	-9.1	152	3.3	89.6	953 997	6 256	79 364	232.1	136 059	11.9	88.1	49.1	15.1	1 677	18.2
Bath	41	7.6	356	0.0	10.0	1 484 267	4 166	63 353	6.1	52 216	22.1	77.9	44.8	12.9	31	13.8
Bedford	207	-2.7	151	0.1	59.1	668 345	4 430	58 744	28.3	20 660	24.6	75.4	33.9	2.8	897	11.8
Bland	77	-4.1	214	D	14.1	690 022	3 225	64 199	9.3	25 785	13.1	86.9	44.2	5.2	179	18.8
Botetourt	89	1.6	153	0.1	26.2	668 360	4 370	69 147	18.7	32 027	32.4	67.6	34.1	6.0	397	15.8
Brunswick	90	3.6	288	1.3	25.2	601 074	2 088	73 490	25.7	82 349	67.1	32.9	32.7	7.7	1 243	52.9
Buchanan	10	2.4	93	D	0.8	245 175	2 642	29 864	0.5	4 651	46.3	53.7	8.7	0.0	166	23.3
Buckingham	84	8.6	215	0.0	24.5	660 348	3 077	66 338	39.9	101 997	16.2	83.8	40.9	10.2	215	19.9
Campbell	151	7.4	198	0.3	44.1	591 091	2 985	60 756	24.2	31 846	26.8	73.2	36.7	5.4	895	28.8
Caroline	56	1.5	255	2.0	37.8	1 052 570	4 128	114 928	20.4	92 172	96.6	3.4	29.9	13.1	1 149	24.9
Carroll	140	13.6	143	1.1	41.5	488 210	3 406	53 584	43.4	44 305	25.7	74.3	44.6	7.2	359	13.5
Charles City	31	13.4	395	1.4	21.4	1 482 443	3 756	221 367	23.7	299 747	D	D	40.5	24.1	744	30.4
Charlotte	149	19.0	288	0.8	41.0	654 878	2 271	58 116	21.7	41 849	51.2	48.8	40.5	7.1	1 200	34.4
Chesterfield	20	-7.3	101	0.1	6.9	539 970	5 329	73 452	6.4	32 487	59.4	40.6	18.8	6.6	259	13.7
Clarke	67	-1.4	140	0.2	27.6	1 105 929	7 880	59 356	25.9	54 333	33.1	66.9	33.5	7.3	235	10.5
Craig	47	12.0	225	0.0	9.9	714 005	3 170	76 580	4.9	23 604	26.6	73.4	43.5	2.4	106	18.4
Culpeper	126	13.5	173	0.6	58.0	1 115 272	6 450	80 141	42.8	58 534	59.9	40.1	36.3	7.3	1 059	14.5
Cumberland	57	0.6	218	0.0	15.6	782 668	3 588	66 351	44.9	171 260	8.6	91.4	37.8	11.8	377	27.9
Dickenson	15	4.9	102	0.0	2.6	303 755	2 967	43 837	0.8	5 313	21.4	78.7	16.3	0.0	72	8.8
Dinwiddie	89	13.2	233	1.2	39.0	699 723	3 003	73 689	24.8	64 747	82.3	17.7	36.3	6.3	2 425	49.3
Essex	57	6.3	579	D	38.7	1 761 745	3 045	258 112	22.8	232 418	98.5	1.5	44.9	29.6	873	48.0
Fairfax	8	11.7	53	0.1	1.4	804 507	15 156	42 581	3.4	23 243	94.0	6.0	19.6	2.7	26	6.8
Fauquier	228	2.6	181	0.4	82.2	1 439 924	7 935	73 037	53.9	42 884	40.0	60.0	32.6	6.4	865	9.9
Floyd	145	12.2	168	0.2	41.5	607 145	3 622	59 109	34.7	40 210	41.4	58.6	40.7	4.6	320	8.1
Fluvanna	47	-3.7	155	0.1	13.6	791 934	5 097	55 584	4.7	15 584	62.8	37.2	29.7	2.3	123	14.9
Franklin	165	-1.2	161	0.9	58.2	570 110	3 544	76 026	65.4	63 971	22.5	77.5	34.3	8.5	1 084	17.9
Frederick	101	2.5	148	0.2	39.7	872 966	5 903	57 128	34.3	50 389	72.5	27.5	34.4	5.4	398	5.6
Giles	66	0.1	173	0.0	12.2	458 352	2 642	53 362	8.1	21 402	20.0	80.0	35.4	5.0	55	3.2
Gloucester	20	-11.6	149	0.0	13.7	750 375	5 027	96 426	11.3	82 890	94.8	5.2	31.6	12.5	421	18.4
Goochland	50	-15.4	159	0.0	19.5	868 708	5 457	61 886	16.6	52 578	50.2	49.8	23.5	4.4	291	9.5
Grayson	132	-3.5	173	0.0	27.9	724 361	4 195	55 518	31.6	41 408	18.9	81.1	42.8	6.9	419	23.8
Greene	27	-12.0	126	0.0	7.6	868 801	6 880	62 347	9.9	45 759	15.9	84.1	34.7	4.2	40	22.7
Greensville	58	19.5	386	0.2	31.9	782 781	2 029	109 563	21.3	140 775	96.8	3.2	29.8	15.9	1 359	63.6
Halifax	212	9.2	226	2.2	61.5	520 118	2 298	77 607	36.5	39 065	63.4	36.6	35.2	7.8	3 737	53.7
Hanover	94	2.7	157	3.3	55.2	874 698	5 566	82 075	55.3	92 120	85.0	15.0	34.2	8.7	1 370	10.8
Henrico	13	-35.9	110	D	9.5	724 744	6 578	59 342	9.4	80 094	98.4	1.6	24.8	11.1	130	13.7
Henry	43	-15.4	148	0.1	9.3	400 117	2 700	50 052	D	D	D	D	27.2	2.8	177	13.1
Highland	93	21.3	357	0.0	11.6	1 205 379	3 380	69 057	30.1	115 199	4.5	95.5	61.7	18.4	252	13.4
Isle of Wight	76	3.0	355	0.7	50.0	1 262 986	3 556	165 127	45.6	214 202	72.4	27.6	49.8	22.5	1 689	51.2
James City	6	-4.9	67	0.0	3.0	585 530	8 766	72 687	D	D	D	D	36.1	1.2	94	12.0
King and Queen	42	-21.0	331	D	29.0	1 020 906	3 089	132 559	17.3	136 567	D	D	35.4	16.5	1 051	32.3
King George	24	-33.8	152	0.4	10.1	764 544	5 033	57 250	3.8	23 788	83.7	16.3	29.4	5.6	174	33.8
King William	54	16.3	397	1.1	28.6	1 481 511	3 734	107 889	16.6	123 296	84.4	15.6	32.6	17.8	735	18.5
Lancaster	11	-24.1	175	D	7.4	802 885	4 579	112 082	4.9	79 738	96.4	3.6	50.8	13.1	278	42.6
Lee	117	-0.5	116	0.1	30.4	255 115	2 202	47 907	18.2	18 026	23.8	76.2	30.8	3.3	1 007	44.5
Loudoun	135	-5.4	97	0.6	56.2	1 156 476	11 977	56 777	37.1	26 577	70.3	29.7	23.4	3.2	497	8.0

STATE County	Water use, 2010		Wholesale trade,[1] 2007				Retail trade,[2] 2007				Real estate and rental and leasing,[2] 2007			
	Total water withdrawn (mil gal/day)	Gallons withdrawn per person per day	Number of establish-ments	Number of employees	Sales (mil dol)	Annual payroll (mil dol)	Number of establish-ments	Number of employees	Sales (mil dol)	Annual payroll (mil dol)	Number of establish-ments	Number of employees	Receipts (mil dol)	Annual payroll (mil dol)
	133	134	135	136	137	138	139	140	141	142	143	144	145	146
VERMONT—Cont'd														
Chittenden	18.0	115	260	3 812	2 392.5	192.8	907	12 646	2 740.9	292.5	244	1 548	256.4	46.4
Essex	0.7	103	2	D	D	D	19	86	15.0	1.0	1	D	D	D
Franklin	7.4	156	42	667	413.3	23.2	222	2 022	545.3	42.6	30	111	10.1	2.0
Grand Isle	4.0	574	6	15	9.1	0.3	32	176	39.5	3.4	6	15	2.0	0.4
Lamoille	2.6	107	28	D	D	D	185	1 532	313.5	32.2	35	106	24.4	4.2
Orange	2.8	97	25	D	D	D	115	1 019	237.2	22.3	23	D	D	D
Orleans	3.8	138	31	299	73.4	9.4	157	1 351	324.1	31.3	23	89	12.7	2.3
Rutland	9.7	157	79	800	267.6	29.2	450	4 556	1 084.9	103.3	80	303	33.4	6.9
Washington	6.2	104	88	D	D	D	390	3 974	946.6	95.2	68	242	27.4	6.4
Windham	349.8	7 858	52	1 541	867.1	63.9	300	2 896	660.7	69.0	71	246	28.4	5.7
Windsor	8.9	157	60	749	327.7	31.0	337	2 861	691.7	70.3	88	D	D	D
VIRGINIA	7 648.0	956	6 502	98 304	60 513.4	4 787.4	29 633	431 634	105 663.3	9 991.9	9 475	60 502	12 636.8	2 408.7
Accomack	15.2	458	30	135	59.4	4.4	184	1 288	298.0	25.6	37	126	15.6	2.8
Albemarle	19.2	194	72	1 329	530.6	68.3	367	6 496	1 689.3	168.6	163	1 023	136.3	29.6
Alleghany	43.1	2 649	4	26	2.2	0.6	50	597	123.1	11.5	6	17	1.7	0.3
Amelia	7.9	623	5	150	55.4	6.2	30	236	68.0	4.8	10	17	1.6	0.3
Amherst	17.0	525	14	306	161.9	10.1	104	1 319	311.8	26.7	21	52	5.2	0.9
Appomattox	1.5	100	8	70	16.8	2.7	61	529	107.2	9.7	11	35	5.7	0.7
Arlington	0.3	1	89	1 289	453.2	94.4	641	10 702	2 482.9	275.4	326	3 620	1 333.9	243.0
Augusta	40.2	545	45	899	306.3	32.9	205	2 310	636.3	51.5	58	178	26.9	4.1
Bath	109.1	23 063	3	6	1.5	0.1	25	123	21.0	1.6	10	43	8.0	1.8
Bedford	21.6	314	48	393	369.0	13.3	182	2 048	466.5	44.9	77	160	20.8	5.1
Bland	2.9	422	5	D	D	D	20	114	38.4	1.8	1	D	D	D
Botetourt	8.7	261	34	D	D	D	87	833	247.8	16.2	23	D	D	D
Brunswick	28.4	1 629	7	46	42.0	1.9	51	377	74.6	6.3	4	11	0.9	0.1
Buchanan	0.9	36	23	229	189.8	9.3	93	750	143.9	12.6	10	30	4.4	0.8
Buckingham	2.3	136	11	76	21.5	2.1	41	284	68.7	5.5	5	10	1.0	0.1
Campbell	7.4	135	40	584	249.4	23.3	217	2 060	511.8	43.0	58	151	19.2	2.9
Caroline	9.0	314	10	59	21.2	1.9	61	760	365.9	13.7	15	43	5.5	0.6
Carroll	2.4	81	19	113	33.6	2.4	97	775	203.0	13.7	18	43	3.7	1.0
Charles City	0.9	127	7	D	D	D	10	58	10.9	2.0	4	31	5.3	1.1
Charlotte	1.5	118	6	29	10.1	1.0	36	261	62.1	4.8	6	16	0.5	0.2
Chesterfield	897.5	2 838	297	3 719	1 561.2	189.2	987	19 112	4 615.9	423.1	327	1 563	307.5	58.4
Clarke	1.9	133	14	D	D	D	41	299	91.6	5.5	15	38	3.6	0.6
Craig	3.1	588	1	D	D	D	10	116	15.8	1.7	2	D	D	D
Culpeper	5.1	109	32	D	D	D	170	2 282	547.4	50.9	38	D	D	D
Cumberland	5.9	587	5	D	D	D	31	260	46.1	5.2	3	8	0.5	0.1
Dickenson	4.8	300	6	18	8.3	0.5	61	519	122.8	9.0	4	6	0.7	0.2
Dinwiddie	2.1	76	14	335	267.0	15.4	63	529	114.9	9.7	6	18	1.9	0.5
Essex	2.0	182	5	33	8.5	1.1	65	1 007	224.6	23.0	10	37	4.9	1.2
Fairfax	14.9	14	837	14 481	13 299.5	1 136.9	2 976	53 158	14 002.4	1 444.8	1 461	11 691	3 549.6	644.9
Fauquier	6.6	101	39	D	D	D	248	2 989	853.1	78.8	84	270	36.8	9.5
Floyd	1.8	116	9	29	25.9	1.0	46	355	72.4	6.3	5	15	2.9	0.2
Fluvanna	118.8	4 625	9	61	10.4	2.3	37	326	79.4	6.8	25	39	7.0	1.3
Franklin	5.6	99	42	558	473.6	29.6	204	2 047	444.5	43.4	75	215	27.2	5.7
Frederick	16.2	206	85	1 746	632.2	78.3	193	3 291	1 120.7	83.0	53	D	D	D
Giles	149.0	8 619	7	37	18.9	1.9	74	742	172.4	14.4	8	22	4.5	0.6
Gloucester	3.5	95	23	D	D	D	145	2 107	500.1	45.9	51	162	15.9	2.8
Goochland	2.0	93	31	215	97.4	9.3	64	593	184.0	15.3	22	117	14.5	4.2
Grayson	1.9	123	5	D	D	D	34	230	47.5	3.6	7	11	1.0	0.2
Greene	1.7	95	9	79	24.6	4.2	48	371	96.0	9.6	8	30	2.5	0.6
Greensville	1.8	146	4	D	D	D	27	187	101.9	3.1	2	D	D	D
Halifax	18.5	510	21	260	133.7	8.7	141	1 474	324.1	29.4	31	143	11.8	2.1
Hanover	8.5	85	232	4 834	3 405.9	219.4	373	5 829	1 706.4	150.8	137	579	114.8	20.2
Henrico	31.0	101	377	7 248	6 197.3	368.7	1 321	23 829	6 737.2	565.7	449	3 800	724.7	135.6
Henry	11.4	211	40	714	527.7	19.9	199	1 623	437.0	33.7	26	116	13.3	2.5
Highland	9.3	4 020	1	D	D	D	24	54	8.9	0.7	1	D	D	D
Isle of Wight	23.9	678	20	192	148.2	9.6	109	1 034	212.7	19.0	37	118	16.5	3.1
James City	14.3	213	40	422	140.1	17.4	297	3 636	658.8	77.2	94	554	101.2	19.1
King and Queen	2.0	285	4	32	22.0	1.3	11	36	16.2	0.8	3	3	0.4	0.1
King George	3.9	165	9	43	8.2	1.3	50	464	155.0	10.4	19	69	11.2	1.5
King William	22.9	1 438	12	57	30.7	2.0	51	497	126.0	10.0	15	50	4.9	0.9
Lancaster	1.3	115	17	116	49.3	3.1	97	782	166.6	16.7	27	52	8.2	2.3
Lee	3.7	144	13	60	27.5	1.4	82	905	171.6	15.2	12	19	2.2	0.4
Loudoun	22.5	72	227	2 901	1 492.0	175.2	954	16 811	4 469.5	432.0	328	1 621	401.1	67.2

1. Merchant wholesalers, except manufacturers' sales branches and offices. 2. Employer establishments.

STATE County	Professional, scientific, and technical services,[1] 2007				Manufacturing, 2007				Accommodation and food services, 2007			
	Number of establish-ments	Number of employees	Receipts (mil dol)	Annual payroll (mil dol)	Number of establish-ments	Number of employees	Receipts (mil dol)	Annual payroll (mil dol)	Number of establish-ments	Number of employees	Sales (mil dol)	Annual payroll (mil dol)
	147	148	149	150	151	152	153	154	155	156	157	158
VERMONT—Cont'd												
Chittenden	713	5 579	920.1	347.2	207	12 224	4 823.5	713.8	421	7 330	360.8	104.9
Essex	5	D	D	D	12	574	62.8	17.7	18	128	3.1	1.0
Franklin	60	637	39.6	15.7	54	D	D	111.2	104	903	39.6	11.4
Grand Isle	23	38	4.0	1.4	NA	NA	NA	NA	23	52	6.5	1.8
Lamoille	96	367	42.8	16.8	NA	NA	NA	NA	113	3 837	174.2	59.5
Orange	79	D	D	D	56	846	161.9	29.2	54	556	26.2	8.1
Orleans	50	D	D	D	36	1 199	D	D	68	1 002	36.3	11.3
Rutland	185	D	D	D	111	3 885	640.8	178.5	235	3 190	124.4	37.1
Washington	244	D	D	D	131	2 690	1 011.9	103.5	172	2 907	119.0	38.2
Windham	140	667	65.4	25.1	111	2 163	375.1	89.2	232	3 861	138.4	47.5
Windsor	199	D	D	D	138	2 306	406.5	89.2	194	3 411	154.4	49.4
VIRGINIA	27 078	376 172	66 543.7	26 936.8	5 777	277 456	92 417.8	12 169.6	15 765	302 446	15 340.5	4 273.0
Accomack	71	955	187.0	50.7	28	D	526.2	67.4	105	1 005	48.1	13.0
Albemarle	288	D	D	D	64	1 487	307.1	60.2	148	2 454	120.2	36.1
Alleghany	12	26	3.4	0.4	10	642	D	21.5	22	302	11.0	3.5
Amelia	14	47	3.2	1.0	NA	NA	NA	NA	9	122	3.8	0.8
Amherst	37	153	11.1	3.8	41	1 573	554.2	68.2	40	583	23.8	6.6
Appomattox	15	D	D	D	15	572	D	16.0	15	195	7.3	1.9
Arlington	1 585	34 964	7 990.5	2 819.1	NA	NA	NA	NA	596	14 421	1 164.0	304.7
Augusta	71	D	D	D	68	4 655	1 582.6	195.5	80	1 271	57.1	14.5
Bath	11	D	D	D	NA	NA	NA	NA	17	D	D	D
Bedford	152	810	82.7	28.1	60	2 098	785.4	102.7	59	585	27.9	8.6
Bland	3	D	D	D	9	589	192.1	23.5	4	D	D	D
Botetourt	62	284	27.3	10.9	33	2 444	883.9	D	47	D	D	D
Brunswick	20	60	3.9	1.5	19	578	96.5	16.3	16	258	8.8	2.8
Buchanan	30	250	12.4	4.8	NA	NA	NA	NA	21	337	12.1	3.3
Buckingham	12	72	11.4	3.4	NA	NA	NA	NA	7	D	D	D
Campbell	80	713	79.1	39.0	67	3 798	1 527.6	170.8	57	901	32.7	9.0
Caroline	34	175	10.9	5.0	NA	NA	NA	NA	24	271	14.7	3.5
Carroll	27	D	D	D	22	1 190	236.8	27.7	37	532	23.3	5.2
Charles City	5	23	4.4	1.0	NA	NA	NA	NA	5	D	D	D
Charlotte	12	D	D	D	16	615	91.9	19.8	7	81	2.7	0.9
Chesterfield	758	7 220	726.3	357.6	189	10 511	3 850.0	574.4	510	10 924	491.5	133.5
Clarke	50	D	D	D	20	1 223	228.3	47.0	20	160	9.0	2.4
Craig	4	D	D	D	NA	NA	NA	NA	4	D	D	D
Culpeper	94	D	D	D	40	D	D	D	65	942	45.3	12.3
Cumberland	4	D	D	D	NA	NA	NA	NA	5	50	1.2	0.4
Dickenson	13	D	D	D	NA	NA	NA	NA	18	181	5.2	1.4
Dinwiddie	15	47	3.0	1.2	16	934	645.7	52.6	17	315	13.8	3.1
Essex	23	D	D	D	15	530	56.9	12.7	31	522	19.4	5.9
Fairfax	7 447	169 544	32 423.1	13 770.6	440	9 872	2 052.7	454.7	2 035	38 874	2 705.7	718.7
Fauquier	269	D	D	D	50	854	159.6	36.8	117	2 144	104.4	33.6
Floyd	22	D	D	D	NA	NA	NA	NA	23	209	6.6	2.0
Fluvanna	42	99	9.7	3.9	NA	NA	NA	NA	17	349	11.9	3.9
Franklin	93	286	21.4	8.0	59	3 462	D	118.9	68	961	40.3	10.8
Frederick	103	D	D	D	86	5 423	2 578.7	214.0	103	2 074	86.7	25.0
Giles	9	D	D	D	15	959	D	47.8	24	289	12.5	3.7
Gloucester	70	D	D	D	NA	NA	NA	NA	63	1 070	40.1	11.9
Goochland	68	233	26.8	11.5	NA	NA	NA	NA	36	280	15.8	4.8
Grayson	5	D	D	D	17	557	93.4	18.2	14	D	D	D
Greene	23	D	D	D	NA	NA	NA	NA	18	209	10.0	2.9
Greensville	1	D	D	D	7	D	248.7	29.9	15	243	14.1	3.3
Halifax	44	D	D	D	40	1 985	620.1	79.1	62	839	31.2	8.4
Hanover	284	1 672	216.1	84.1	143	3 702	926.3	149.8	170	2 915	137.0	39.1
Henrico	1 060	D	D	D	209	9 569	3 265.0	458.3	656	14 769	685.8	192.0
Henry	36	D	D	D	79	5 479	1 097.9	169.8	70	984	38.4	10.0
Highland	5	D	D	D	NA	NA	NA	NA	6	D	D	D
Isle of Wight	47	248	19.7	7.5	21	D	D	D	48	795	33.0	9.3
James City	226	D	D	D	34	2 364	1 567.2	117.0	118	3 273	164.4	47.8
King and Queen	6	19	1.4	0.5	NA	NA	NA	NA	2	D	D	D
King George	93	D	D	D	NA	NA	NA	NA	36	339	14.7	3.7
King William	27	155	11.2	4.5	NA	NA	NA	NA	15	216	7.5	1.9
Lancaster	59	242	23.7	9.5	NA	NA	NA	NA	43	461	16.0	4.9
Lee	19	D	D	D	NA	NA	NA	NA	19	336	8.6	2.3
Loudoun	1 765	D	D	D	157	5 266	1 400.2	322.6	526	10 275	610.2	173.3

1. Establishment subject to federal tax.

Table B. States and Counties — **Health Care and Social Assistance, Other Services, Nonemployer Businesses, and Residential Construction**

STATE County	Health care and social assistance, 2007				Other services, 2007				Nonemployer businesses, 2013		Value of residential construction authorized by building permits, 2014	
	Number of establish-ments	Number of employees	Receipts (mil dol)	Annual payroll (mil dol)	Number of establish-ments	Number of employees	Receipts (mil dol)	Annual payroll (mil dol)	Number	Receipts (mil dol)	New Construction ($1,000)	Number of housing units
	159	160	161	162	163	164	165	166	167	168	169	170
VERMONT—Cont'd												
Chittenden	558	13 272	1 316.5	514.9	402	2 035	174.5	54.8	13 650	665.5	92 325	533
Essex	10	D	D	D	8	39	6.0	0.5	540	19.7	1 542	9
Franklin	113	2 413	169.5	74.0	71	289	19.0	5.2	3 693	150.5	25 325	152
Grand Isle	12	69	2.9	1.2	12	15	2.2	0.5	707	30.3	4 485	21
Lamoille	81	D	D	D	75	317	125.7	7.8	2 751	111.9	12 668	66
Orange	76	1 188	89.8	41.5	56	219	23.4	5.7	2 956	113.8	8 112	39
Orleans	73	1 705	129.5	51.4	70	230	21.0	4.4	2 541	97.7	15 981	200
Rutland	226	4 434	370.4	155.8	176	773	60.8	16.3	5 016	173.1	9 109	50
Washington	236	4 379	318.6	143.2	226	1 030	120.0	32.5	6 007	228.3	29 511	127
Windham	197	2 850	214.3	93.1	129	576	55.2	14.0	5 101	188.8	21 792	91
Windsor	198	3 736	327.4	158.4	147	709	85.5	19.8	6 103	246.0	17 218	73
VIRGINIA	17 540	371 067	37 522.0	14 962.4	15 072	111 129	16 498.2	3 915.1	536 067	23 086.5	4 655 664	28 682
Accomack	60	1 229	63.6	26.3	60	368	25.8	8.0	2 306	92.4	8 486	67
Albemarle	262	4 140	493.7	194.5	144	1 431	299.4	59.9	8 591	415.9	112 612	404
Alleghany	45	864	82.1	28.9	19	89	7.3	1.6	641	22.7	2 628	17
Amelia	22	314	17.3	8.1	22	62	4.5	1.5	824	30.6	8 631	40
Amherst	42	D	D	D	63	166	12.4	3.3	1 522	46.7	7 855	50
Appomattox	22	D	D	D	17	56	4.2	1.1	820	25.5	8 787	62
Arlington	451	6 844	1 089.9	314.5	612	10 109	2 803.2	629.2	17 539	857.8	216 776	2 160
Augusta	103	3 817	394.1	139.2	85	479	39.7	12.1	4 359	205.5	53 658	418
Bath	7	D	D	D	7	D	D	D	332	10.2	367	4
Bedford	87	D	D	D	83	378	22.9	7.3	4 549	175.8	69 967	420
Bland	7	57	8.0	2.2	7	20	3.3	0.5	321	10.4	1 944	13
Botetourt	43	D	D	D	52	D	D	D	2 259	83.9	16 959	75
Brunswick	13	190	8.7	4.4	20	D	D	D	666	24.5	0	0
Buchanan	45	762	57.7	22.2	29	139	10.6	2.9	811	29.2	1 050	9
Buckingham	16	354	12.1	8.9	12	59	8.8	1.9	707	27.0	4 489	34
Campbell	76	913	40.8	18.5	84	428	34.3	9.7	2 776	89.7	37 266	297
Caroline	20	271	19.5	9.5	31	193	15.1	4.3	1 584	53.5	10 949	73
Carroll	35	586	30.9	13.7	26	76	8.1	2.2	1 661	54.4	8 870	52
Charles City	4	D	D	D	12	34	3.1	0.7	363	11.0	2 905	18
Charlotte	22	232	13.9	6.1	15	29	3.2	0.5	662	23.5	1 820	13
Chesterfield	668	9 348	867.4	385.7	471	3 356	329.6	81.4	20 411	831.6	223 508	1 622
Clarke	20	D	D	D	31	98	11.2	2.6	1 292	55.7	9 484	34
Craig	4	D	D	D	2	D	D	D	293	9.6	3 120	18
Culpeper	63	1 703	163.2	68.6	77	558	50.3	16.8	3 337	147.4	51 124	215
Cumberland	14	D	D	D	6	24	1.3	0.4	526	20.6	2 716	20
Dickenson	25	387	23.9	9.8	17	D	D	D	440	12.6	886	8
Dinwiddie	21	314	14.3	6.2	36	177	13.7	7.3	1 201	41.9	6 645	42
Essex	33	621	54.1	18.3	22	D	D	D	771	32.8	2 610	16
Fairfax	2 599	41 062	4 494.5	1 837.0	1 879	17 014	2 856.0	738.2	97 330	4 992.4	302 407	2 249
Fauquier	135	2 365	241.9	98.8	128	858	70.5	24.1	5 671	273.3	53 350	267
Floyd	18	D	D	D	21	65	6.3	1.5	1 258	38.8	10 037	49
Fluvanna	21	D	D	D	24	D	D	D	1 631	50.5	17 154	94
Franklin	62	D	D	D	94	282	22.8	5.7	3 690	131.5	29 298	112
Frederick	76	1 364	100.9	45.9	90	518	53.5	15.2	5 206	208.9	91 403	436
Giles	30	542	48.4	17.5	27	D	D	D	849	27.6	2 219	16
Gloucester	64	1 201	82.8	33.1	75	320	24.0	6.6	2 345	82.4	27 193	140
Goochland	33	D	D	D	38	378	38.0	17.6	1 969	107.7	35 652	127
Grayson	12	D	D	D	13	D	D	D	1 037	28.9	3 924	28
Greene	10	D	D	D	27	D	D	D	1 281	41.8	16 055	116
Greensville	3	D	D	D	6	D	D	D	375	8.9	1 425	14
Halifax	83	1 562	140.4	57.7	69	284	24.8	4.8	1 696	60.8	10 101	64
Hanover	218	4 557	531.6	184.8	253	1 493	138.0	43.1	7 514	322.3	105 755	522
Henrico	904	21 906	2 351.1	905.8	657	4 832	750.1	151.6	21 238	918.0	121 790	693
Henry	46	798	41.8	17.7	66	316	24.0	6.7	2 322	73.0	5 173	28
Highland	6	D	D	D	9	D	D	D	265	6.2	2 349	12
Isle of Wight	44	463	34.4	14.6	53	212	14.6	4.9	2 066	75.7	29 439	131
James City	151	2 000	194.7	75.0	98	475	33.2	10.5	4 882	215.3	125 769	709
King and Queen	5	D	D	D	8	13	1.5	0.3	392	13.9	2 529	13
King George	20	242	17.6	7.0	33	123	9.2	2.7	1 345	45.1	23 076	104
King William	23	307	16.4	7.9	37	110	11.0	2.6	1 039	42.7	11 030	74
Lancaster	41	1 063	84.9	37.9	44	169	12.6	4.1	1 033	43.5	5 634	32
Lee	33	640	53.1	21.8	21	78	5.8	1.5	1 093	32.6	2 435	16
Loudoun	596	7 622	813.8	330.8	480	3 824	485.0	126.6	27 410	1 353.5	648 864	3 480

STATE County	Government employment and payroll, 2012									Local government finances, 2012				
			March payroll (percent of total)							General revenue				
												Taxes		
													Per capita[1] (dollars)	
	Full-time equivalent employees	March payroll (dollars)	Adminis-tration, judicial, and legal	Police and Corrections	Fire Protection	Highways and transpor-tation	Health and Welfare	Natural resources and utilities	Education and libraries	Total (mil dol)	Inter-govern-mental (mil dol)	Total (mil dol)	Total	Property
	171	172	173	174	175	176	177	178	179	180	181	182	183	184
VERMONT—Cont'd														
Chittenden	6 092	25 796 817	4.3	6.7	2.8	6.4	0.8	8.4	68.8	648.3	401.0	117.0	738	613
Essex	227	673 088	8.5	1.1	0.0	5.4	1.1	1.2	82.3	22.3	16.5	3.7	588	586
Franklin	1 780	6 015 525	5.6	3.3	0.4	4.9	1.2	3.1	80.8	156.8	118.8	21.4	443	432
Grand Isle	201	726 392	10.7	0.0	0.0	6.8	2.7	2.1	76.7	25.5	17.3	7.2	1 026	1 022
Lamoille	1 075	3 560 151	5.3	4.1	0.1	5.4	1.5	5.9	77.1	94.8	63.4	20.8	832	792
Orange	1 252	3 813 072	7.2	1.2	0.1	5.8	0.2	0.5	84.5	109.1	85.0	17.9	618	616
Orleans	1 359	3 619 393	5.7	2.4	0.1	7.1	0.3	1.7	82.4	103.1	75.1	19.7	725	721
Rutland	2 343	8 318 234	5.3	3.7	1.6	7.2	0.7	4.0	76.9	234.3	164.7	46.5	764	726
Washington	2 492	8 165 965	5.6	4.3	2.3	5.1	1.2	3.5	77.0	224.6	150.4	42.0	707	701
Windham	1 877	6 583 583	5.5	4.5	2.2	6.1	1.0	3.8	75.7	202.3	137.1	44.4	1 010	989
Windsor	2 421	8 862 072	5.4	5.6	2.7	6.6	1.1	3.8	74.2	247.7	169.7	49.6	883	878
VIRGINIA	X	X	X	X	X	X	X	X	X	X	X	X	X	X
Accomack	1 352	3 776 224	8.2	7.7	0.6	0.7	9.6	1.0	70.7	104.5	55.5	39.6	1 188	876
Albemarle	3 014	10 671 438	7.3	10.3	3.1	1.0	4.5	4.6	65.3	368.6	114.7	187.5	1 833	1 375
Alleghany	689	2 172 894	9.7	10.5	0.3	0.7	8.8	8.3	59.0	58.7	31.2	19.1	1 178	989
Amelia	422	1 273 101	3.9	5.8	0.0	0.0	1.9	1.5	85.8	26.8	15.3	8.2	645	518
Amherst	989	3 067 237	5.7	5.9	0.0	0.0	5.8	6.4	73.5	75.6	42.9	26.1	807	633
Appomattox	535	1 345 618	8.3	5.6	2.3	0.0	7.7	3.3	71.1	37.2	20.5	13.3	878	716
Arlington	9 317	49 809 798	6.9	10.3	4.2	20.3	7.8	5.4	41.2	2 574.1	624.2	861.8	3 899	3 016
Augusta	2 388	6 901 173	5.3	10.5	2.9	0.7	5.8	1.4	72.4	160.8	85.2	60.8	826	604
Bath	219	806 860	8.1	6.7	0.0	0.0	0.7	2.2	80.7	19.6	4.6	14.0	3 000	2 445
Bedford	2 625	7 051 188	4.0	20.1	0.0	0.0	9.1	1.8	63.5	181.5	95.3	61.4	882	750
Bland	206	534 449	5.2	7.3	0.0	0.0	2.6	3.3	70.3	17.5	11.4	4.6	690	588
Botetourt	1 128	3 464 230	7.8	10.1	0.0	0.0	5.0	2.6	72.5	84.1	39.8	37.2	1 122	904
Brunswick	651	1 620 721	7.3	12.5	0.0	0.2	9.0	1.7	67.5	39.3	24.2	10.4	610	490
Buchanan	834	2 368 397	7.1	6.9	0.7	1.0	4.4	1.1	76.6	101.0	43.8	50.0	2 095	742
Buckingham	544	1 683 523	4.7	32.1	0.0	0.0	2.0	2.6	57.1	44.0	28.4	13.4	782	682
Campbell	1 839	5 409 816	5.0	6.0	1.2	0.4	4.4	1.8	78.6	131.1	70.6	44.2	801	613
Caroline	918	2 716 780	8.5	9.8	2.1	0.0	5.6	2.6	68.0	76.7	35.1	35.8	1 236	1 010
Carroll	1 015	2 970 573	6.2	5.3	1.8	0.4	12.0	2.7	68.4	74.0	35.3	24.9	836	659
Charles City	243	709 888	11.5	6.6	0.0	0.0	0.0	4.7	70.0	21.2	9.1	8.1	1 137	1 012
Charlotte	499	1 413 313	6.4	8.9	0.0	0.1	7.7	2.4	72.2	35.7	24.5	8.0	646	537
Chesterfield	12 105	41 117 167	7.5	9.1	5.5	0.2	7.4	4.0	62.3	1 045.1	437.5	443.8	1 370	1 103
Clarke	531	1 954 739	5.8	7.2	0.0	1.3	3.8	2.9	72.3	48.5	15.8	21.7	1 516	1 292
Craig	169	483 380	9.9	7.8	0.0	0.0	5.9	2.1	74.4	13.0	8.1	3.8	730	626
Culpeper	1 841	5 945 989	8.3	10.6	0.9	1.1	9.5	4.7	63.2	142.8	61.0	63.9	1 333	1 025
Cumberland	297	961 120	9.9	8.2	0.0	0.0	1.6	1.1	72.0	23.9	13.9	8.8	889	758
Dickenson	610	1 668 965	6.7	7.4	0.0	0.0	4.2	7.9	70.6	68.6	37.7	20.1	1 282	855
Dinwiddie	890	2 870 612	6.8	7.8	0.3	0.0	11.1	3.2	67.5	79.3	43.7	31.3	1 119	925
Essex	422	1 333 678	8.5	8.1	3.2	2.6	2.1	8.3	64.6	32.1	12.9	16.4	1 462	1 109
Fairfax	43 275	208 710 868	5.3	8.1	5.1	0.4	7.2	5.9	62.9	5 025.9	1 140.8	3 142.7	2 810	2 292
Fauquier	2 840	9 833 163	6.6	9.0	2.5	0.7	3.2	5.4	69.2	232.3	78.6	133.9	2 012	1 727
Floyd	421	1 524 813	5.3	6.1	0.0	0.0	3.6	2.2	81.6	27.7	14.4	11.9	771	609
Fluvanna	723	2 499 361	7.1	4.3	0.0	0.0	3.5	1.7	78.2	61.3	29.9	28.7	1 105	989
Franklin	1 773	5 802 144	5.5	5.8	2.1	0.7	4.3	1.4	79.1	131.8	64.9	58.9	1 044	833
Frederick	3 183	9 479 873	6.7	10.3	3.6	0.6	2.4	2.0	72.9	235.3	97.7	114.5	1 425	1 069
Giles	586	1 588 082	11.1	11.9	0.0	1.6	2.9	6.0	64.6	54.9	29.9	17.0	1 002	801
Gloucester	1 208	3 733 992	8.5	8.9	0.0	0.0	3.3	3.6	71.8	99.1	42.2	45.2	1 224	938
Goochland	541	1 850 764	13.7	7.7	3.4	0.0	1.5	3.0	67.1	56.0	13.5	37.7	1 768	1 342
Grayson	541	1 324 989	8.4	7.8	0.0	0.3	3.4	2.6	76.5	36.9	21.4	11.7	771	658
Greene	657	1 764 870	6.8	4.8	0.0	2.2	0.6	0.4	80.2	51.3	25.0	19.5	1 040	871
Greensville	571	1 743 841	9.5	15.1	0.0	0.0	1.0	4.8	67.5	48.9	30.7	8.1	686	540
Halifax	1 547	3 858 184	6.4	5.9	1.6	1.0	5.8	2.5	75.9	111.3	60.8	33.7	940	669
Hanover	4 522	15 814 948	6.9	13.8	4.2	0.4	5.6	3.8	63.1	349.4	131.9	160.0	1 590	1 262
Henrico	11 822	42 600 655	5.0	12.2	6.3	3.6	7.0	2.9	59.3	1 060.7	406.5	484.0	1 537	1 115
Henry	1 709	4 761 002	6.5	7.7	0.9	0.0	9.6	0.7	71.0	124.5	75.9	32.9	620	403
Highland	101	285 647	13.1	13.3	0.0	0.0	5.6	0.9	63.7	8.1	4.2	3.1	1 401	1 221
Isle of Wight	1 226	4 460 998	6.8	4.8	1.2	1.8	1.9	2.5	75.6	106.3	46.2	51.6	1 459	1 145
James City	3 104	11 075 839	5.4	9.6	5.6	1.6	3.8	10.2	60.5	257.6	89.5	138.2	2 003	1 605
King and Queen	300	906 918	6.2	30.6	0.0	0.0	0.5	0.0	57.6	23.5	13.1	6.2	884	787
King George	1 018	3 118 233	7.1	5.5	4.7	0.0	3.5	3.8	73.7	80.3	31.9	31.4	1 282	770
King William	608	1 988 526	5.8	6.3	0.6	0.6	2.4	1.7	79.0	49.7	22.6	23.3	1 459	1 282
Lancaster	380	818 567	17.4	17.6	0.0	0.5	6.5	2.5	53.6	32.1	11.5	18.8	1 669	1 337
Lee	981	2 345 408	5.5	6.0	0.0	0.7	1.6	1.9	83.8	61.5	44.1	13.2	519	363
Loudoun	13 775	59 560 641	6.5	6.9	4.6	0.5	5.4	3.9	70.0	1 546.7	373.1	1 012.0	3 004	2 472

1. Based on the resident population estimated as of July 1 of the year shown.

STATE County	Local government finances, 2012 (cont.) — Direct general expenditure: Total (mil dol)	Per capita[1] (dollars)	Percent of total for: Educa-tion	Health and hospitals	Police protec-tion	Public welfare	High-ways	Debt outstanding: Total (mil dol)	Per capita[1] (dollars)	Government employment, 2013: Federal civilian	Federal military	State and local	Presidential election,[2] 2012 — Percent of vote cast: Demo-cratic	Republi-can	All other
	185	186	187	188	189	190	191	192	193	194	195	196	197	198	199
VERMONT—Cont'd															
Chittenden	643.2	4 058	61.0	0.2	5.1	0.1	5.6	564.9	3 564	2 354	1 145	14 650	71.4	26.7	1.9
Essex	23.3	3 739	69.1	0.2	1.7	0.1	14.9	1.6	258	93	44	292	55.9	41.4	2.7
Franklin	162.7	3 374	75.1	0.6	4.0	0.0	8.1	53.3	1 106	1 367	340	2 921	61.4	36.6	2.0
Grand Isle	24.7	3 541	70.6	0.0	3.4	0.1	10.5	14.7	2 098	18	50	297	63.1	34.9	2.0
Lamoille	96.7	3 874	66.5	0.9	8.2	0.2	8.6	76.2	3 054	61	174	1 595	70.4	27.7	1.9
Orange	114.2	3 950	75.9	0.6	1.8	0.1	10.2	35.3	1 220	76	201	2 012	64.6	33.2	2.2
Orleans	106.7	3 935	76.0	0.3	1.8	0.0	9.3	33.0	1 219	233	188	1 842	62.6	35.1	2.3
Rutland	244.1	4 010	70.6	0.1	3.7	0.0	7.9	67.5	1 108	294	416	4 247	61.2	36.6	2.1
Washington	229.0	3 852	62.5	0.9	3.6	0.1	11.1	117.9	1 983	258	435	7 681	69.3	28.4	2.3
Windham	233.0	5 297	58.8	0.2	2.3	0.2	13.5	108.8	2 474	144	302	2 882	73.0	24.9	2.1
Windsor	275.6	4 903	62.8	0.8	3.4	0.0	12.6	98.2	1 746	1 333	402	3 598	68.8	29.1	2.0
VIRGINIA	X	X	X	X	X	X	X	X	X	193 383	140 677	534 725	52.6	46.3	1.0
Accomack	93.0	2 789	51.9	1.1	4.4	4.8	1.7	62.8	1 884	636	273	2 226	48.7	50.1	1.2
Albemarle	356.2	3 484	49.8	9.7	4.8	4.1	0.2	444.7	4 349	(3)1 241	(3)907	(3)27 803	58.4	40.4	1.2
Alleghany	59.6	3 670	51.9	0.6	5.0	6.2	1.3	32.8	2 020	(4)66	(4)70	(4)1 597	48.2	50.4	1.4
Amelia	26.9	2 108	60.3	2.6	6.3	6.1	1.7	4.0	313	25	41	450	38.1	60.8	1.1
Amherst	71.6	2 212	62.9	0.8	7.1	6.1	0.1	27.2	840	44	98	2 749	41.5	57.6	0.9
Appomattox	35.6	2 351	57.9	1.0	6.3	6.5	0.0	34.6	2 285	49	49	766	34.6	64.3	1.1
Arlington	2 639.2	11 940	16.7	1.1	2.2	3.0	2.0	8 672.6	39 235	30 199	9 157	11 790	71.7	27.1	1.2
Augusta	170.0	2 308	65.1	0.6	3.9	8.2	0.9	103.4	1 404	(5)256	(5)376	(5)8 494	29.5	69.4	1.2
Bath	17.3	3 728	54.1	1.3	5.9	4.2	0.0	9.3	1 990	30	15	357	42.9	55.5	1.6
Bedford	182.3	2 619	49.8	0.5	3.6	8.7	0.1	152.7	2 194	(6)119	(6)242	(6)2 964	30.7	68.2	1.1
Bland	15.8	2 338	54.4	0.9	6.4	8.4	6.8	5.0	743	13	19	608	29.2	68.6	2.2
Botetourt	82.4	2 486	63.3	0.6	6.0	3.8	0.0	55.7	1 681	53	105	1 360	32.7	65.9	1.4
Brunswick	41.2	2 421	57.0	0.6	6.4	7.4	0.2	19.3	1 133	41	48	1 118	62.8	36.4	0.8
Buchanan	84.4	3 538	45.9	0.7	4.7	11.2	11.3	12.4	520	65	72	1 569	46.5	52.0	1.5
Buckingham	45.4	2 658	45.9	1.1	3.9	6.2	0.1	68.7	4 022	28	48	1 271	49.9	49.0	1.1
Campbell	128.3	2 326	59.4	5.8	4.7	7.0	2.3	58.2	1 055	(7)363	(7)432	(7)6 997	31.3	67.6	1.1
Caroline	67.8	2 338	54.8	0.4	8.4	6.1	3.4	132.8	4 584	444	104	1 202	55.4	43.5	1.1
Carroll	84.4	2 829	57.3	7.7	4.7	6.3	0.7	59.6	1 996	(8)93	(8)117	(8)2 441	32.7	65.1	2.2
Charles City	20.4	2 844	63.8	0.5	3.9	5.3	0.0	2.7	382	17	23	328	68.3	31.0	0.7
Charlotte	37.5	3 022	59.8	2.5	5.0	11.4	0.1	6.2	500	38	39	953	43.9	54.8	1.3
Chesterfield	985.4	3 043	54.6	5.0	6.6	4.1	1.2	716.3	2 212	3 048	1 083	17 906	45.8	53.3	0.8
Clarke	61.0	4 259	55.3	0.7	3.6	3.6	0.4	147.7	10 315	32	45	709	46.5	51.7	1.8
Craig	12.6	2 425	55.8	1.3	6.8	12.8	0.3	4.1	793	14	17	235	33.5	64.7	1.9
Culpeper	140.4	2 931	53.3	0.9	7.6	9.8	2.8	122.9	2 566	203	151	3 294	44.6	54.3	1.2
Cumberland	23.1	2 345	63.3	1.2	6.5	4.8	0.0	44.0	4 466	10	32	441	47.7	51.2	1.1
Dickenson	61.5	3 918	45.4	5.6	3.7	9.6	1.7	13.6	869	36	48	895	48.5	49.2	2.2
Dinwiddie	72.2	2 580	60.9	3.9	5.4	4.8	0.1	113.2	4 044	(9)233	(9)249	(9)6 709	48.4	50.6	0.9
Essex	34.5	3 071	57.7	0.0	5.0	9.0	1.4	48.6	4 329	17	36	535	54.7	44.4	1.0
Fairfax	4 854.2	4 340	51.6	4.1	4.6	6.0	2.1	5 037.1	4 503	(10)45 942	(10)9 680	(10)60 469	60.1	38.9	0.9
Fauquier	242.3	3 641	59.7	0.4	7.0	4.2	1.2	187.2	2 813	613	215	3 773	42.7	56.2	1.1
Floyd	26.9	1 751	66.1	2.5	5.5	3.9	0.0	15.6	1 013	46	51	606	39.1	59.1	1.8
Fluvanna	74.8	2 882	70.0	0.8	3.4	6.6	0.3	91.0	3 506	29	79	1 264	48.6	50.4	1.0
Franklin	130.9	2 320	61.7	0.5	4.3	7.9	1.1	36.2	641	98	177	2 345	37.9	60.7	1.5
Frederick	220.1	2 740	72.6	0.5	5.1	2.7	0.1	196.2	2 443	(11)1 841	(11)359	(11)5 991	38.6	59.9	1.5
Giles	49.2	2 909	47.4	0.4	7.2	7.5	2.9	61.0	3 603	36	54	876	40.9	57.2	1.8
Gloucester	94.6	2 564	65.7	1.1	5.1	5.2	0.1	62.6	1 698	83	117	2 379	36.0	62.9	1.1
Goochland	45.4	2 128	55.2	1.1	5.8	4.2	0.5	133.0	6 229	36	66	1 319	38.3	60.8	0.8
Grayson	35.4	2 329	60.0	0.4	6.1	6.7	0.3	38.8	2 555	27	48	873	34.3	62.9	2.8
Greene	53.8	2 869	65.7	0.8	5.7	5.5	1.9	57.6	3 067	34	60	828	38.4	60.3	1.3
Greensville	52.0	4 385	49.3	0.3	4.8	5.4	0.4	56.1	4 732	(12)35	(12)45	(12)2 000	63.9	35.4	0.7
Halifax	113.2	3 157	52.4	10.5	5.0	6.6	2.0	72.1	2 012	85	111	2 129	48.2	51.0	0.7
Hanover	342.5	3 403	52.1	0.4	6.9	6.6	1.7	364.1	3 617	148	321	4 761	32.8	66.4	0.8
Henrico	1 095.4	3 478	45.2	3.0	6.3	2.5	4.7	980.8	3 114	2 136	1 017	16 746	55.7	43.5	0.8
Henry	127.8	2 414	68.2	0.9	4.2	6.1	0.0	28.3	534	(13)132	(13)211	(13)3 869	44.1	54.6	1.3
Highland	7.7	3 440	49.1	2.3	7.9	4.4	7.0	0.7	311	11	0	158	38.0	59.8	2.2
Isle of Wight	103.6	2 926	49.8	4.9	5.6	3.1	1.0	149.3	4 218	87	114	1 495	42.9	56.3	0.8
James City	260.7	3 781	54.2	6.4	4.7	1.9	0.0	269.9	3 914	(14)229	(14)382	(14)8 441	44.9	54.2	0.9
King and Queen	25.3	3 591	43.8	0.8	5.0	7.9	0.0	5.0	707	0	23	283	51.8	47.6	0.6
King George	72.4	2 957	53.1	0.9	9.0	6.0	0.1	190.9	7 793	4 531	618	1 026	42.7	56.2	1.1
King William	48.1	3 007	64.8	0.3	6.0	3.6	0.6	39.7	2 483	25	52	732	39.9	59.2	0.9
Lancaster	31.1	2 771	52.2	1.4	6.6	6.9	0.5	18.4	1 636	37	35	520	46.6	52.6	0.8
Lee	59.5	2 335	64.3	1.3	5.4	10.3	0.9	7.4	290	425	76	1 158	34.9	63.1	2.0
Loudoun	1 488.4	4 418	60.1	2.4	5.3	2.4	1.9	1 679.5	4 985	4 068	1 122	18 457	53.7	45.4	0.9

1. Based on the resident population estimated as of July 1 of the year shown. 2. © 2013 Election Data Services, Inc. All rights reserved. 3. Charlottesville city is included with Albemarle county. 4. Covington city is included with Alleghany county. 5. Staunton and Waynesboro cities are included with Augusta county. 6. Bedford city is included with Bedford county. 7. Lynchburg city is included with Campbell county. 8. Galax city is included with Carroll county. 9. Petersburg and Colonial Heights cities are included with Dinwiddie county. 10. Fairfax city and Falls Church city are included with Fairfax county. 11. Winchester city is included with Frederick county. 12. Emporia city is included with Greensville county. 13. Martinsville city is included with Henry county. 14. Williamsburg city is included with James City county.

STATE/ County code	CBSA code[1]	County type[2]	STATE County	Land area,[3] (sq km) 2010	Population, 2014: Total persons 2014	Population, 2014: Rank	Population, 2014: Per square kilometer	Race alone or in combination, not Hispanic or Latino (percent): White	Black	American Indian, Alaska Native	Asian and Pacific Islander	Percent Hispanic or Latino[4]	Age (percent): Under 5 years	5 to 17 years	18 to 24 years	25 to 34 years	35 to 44 years	45 to 54 years
				1	2	3	4	5	6	7	8	9	10	11	12	13	14	15
			VIRGINIA—Cont'd															
51 109	...	1	Louisa	1 285	34 348	1 319	26.7	79.5	18.3	0.9	0.9	2.5	5.6	15.2	7.3	11.2	12.1	16.1
51 111	...	9	Lunenburg	1 118	12 466	2 267	11.2	61.7	34.4	0.8	0.6	4.1	4.6	14.0	7.8	11.4	12.3	14.9
51 113	...	8	Madison	831	13 157	2 228	15.8	87.4	10.8	0.9	1.1	2.1	5.1	16.2	7.5	9.9	10.8	15.3
51 115	47260	1	Mathews	223	8 836	2 526	39.6	88.2	9.8	1.1	1.1	2.0	3.8	13.4	6.7	7.5	9.6	14.4
51 117	...	7	Mecklenburg	1 620	31 192	1 408	19.3	61.2	35.7	0.7	1.4	2.6	4.8	14.5	7.2	9.8	10.7	14.1
51 119	...	8	Middlesex	337	10 696	2 380	31.7	79.3	18.7	0.9	0.8	2.0	4.2	11.4	6.5	8.8	8.7	14.5
51 121	13980	3	Montgomery	1 002	97 244	606	97.0	87.1	4.6	0.6	6.9	2.9	4.5	11.3	29.7	13.7	10.4	10.1
51 125	16820	3	Nelson	1 220	14 850	2 112	12.2	83.2	13.3	0.8	1.0	3.5	4.6	14.3	6.5	9.4	10.0	14.4
51 127	40060	1	New Kent	543	20 021	1 835	36.9	81.8	14.4	1.9	1.8	2.4	5.0	16.4	7.6	10.9	13.3	16.5
51 131	...	9	Northampton	548	12 121	2 290	22.1	55.5	36.1	0.7	1.2	8.2	5.8	13.8	7.3	10.1	9.4	13.1
51 133	...	9	Northumberland	495	12 251	2 282	24.7	71.1	25.3	0.6	0.7	3.4	3.8	11.8	5.9	7.6	7.5	13.0
51 135	...	6	Nottoway	814	15 579	2 067	19.1	56.3	39.5	0.8	0.7	4.1	5.9	13.9	8.7	13.4	11.9	15.0
51 137	...	6	Orange	883	35 026	1 300	39.7	81.6	14.1	0.9	1.8	4.1	5.9	16.3	7.2	11.2	12.1	14.6
51 139	...	6	Page	805	23 848	1 647	29.6	95.5	2.5	0.5	0.7	1.8	5.0	15.4	7.7	10.7	12.3	15.3
51 141	...	8	Patrick	1 251	18 264	1 908	14.6	90.7	6.5	0.6	0.5	2.7	4.3	14.1	6.5	8.7	12.3	15.2
51 143	19260	3	Pittsylvania	2 510	62 383	839	24.9	75.2	22.3	0.6	0.6	2.4	4.4	15.6	7.4	9.9	11.9	15.8
51 145	40060	1	Powhatan	674	28 449	1 475	42.2	84.1	13.4	0.6	0.9	2.0	4.0	15.7	8.3	10.1	14.2	17.9
51 147	...	6	Prince Edward	906	23 074	1 681	25.5	63.7	33.2	0.7	1.5	2.4	4.3	12.3	26.5	10.1	8.7	11.3
51 149	40060	1	Prince George	687	37 333	1 242	54.3	58.6	32.7	1.3	3.0	7.2	5.1	16.1	9.5	15.4	15.3	14.6
51 153	47900	1	Prince William	871	446 094	153	512.2	49.8	21.8	0.9	9.9	21.4	8.0	20.4	8.9	14.6	15.4	14.8
51 155	13980	3	Pulaski	828	34 322	1 320	41.5	92.5	6.1	0.6	0.9	1.4	4.8	13.6	7.7	10.7	13.2	14.8
51 157	47900	8	Rappahannock	690	7 361	2 646	10.7	90.8	5.7	0.8	1.2	3.5	3.9	14.8	7.0	8.5	10.1	15.7
51 159	...	9	Richmond	496	8 902	2 522	17.9	62.6	31.1	0.7	0.9	6.2	4.0	13.0	7.6	13.8	13.2	16.1
51 161	40220	2	Roanoke	649	93 785	623	144.5	88.7	6.2	0.6	3.6	2.6	4.8	16.3	8.0	10.2	12.7	14.6
51 163	...	6	Rockbridge	1 548	22 327	1 717	14.4	94.6	3.3	1.1	0.9	1.4	3.9	13.7	7.2	9.8	10.8	14.8
51 165	25500	3	Rockingham	2 199	78 171	705	35.5	91.4	2.4	0.5	1.0	5.9	5.5	17.2	9.2	11.1	11.8	14.2
51 167	...	6	Russell	1 227	28 023	1 490	22.8	97.6	1.2	0.4	0.3	1.1	5.1	14.5	7.8	11.1	12.8	14.9
51 169	28700	3	Scott	1 387	22 384	1 712	16.1	97.5	1.1	0.6	0.3	1.3	4.9	14.0	7.4	10.9	12.4	14.7
51 171	...	6	Shenandoah	1 318	43 021	1 111	32.6	90.5	2.7	0.7	0.9	6.5	5.6	15.9	7.4	11.2	11.5	14.5
51 173	...	6	Smyth	1 168	31 555	1 398	27.0	95.4	2.7	0.5	0.6	1.8	4.9	15.2	8.3	10.5	12.7	14.5
51 175	...	6	Southampton	1 552	18 059	1 915	11.6	61.6	37.1	0.7	0.7	1.3	4.4	15.0	7.8	10.1	11.6	18.2
51 177	47900	1	Spotsylvania	1 040	129 188	482	124.2	73.6	16.8	0.9	3.5	8.2	6.2	19.8	9.0	12.4	13.6	15.7
51 179	47900	1	Stafford	697	139 992	451	200.8	68.9	18.6	1.1	4.5	10.5	6.4	20.6	10.4	13.0	13.9	16.5
51 181	...	1	Surry	722	6 790	2 700	9.4	52.9	45.3	0.8	0.8	1.7	4.6	14.3	8.0	10.6	9.7	17.8
51 183	40060	1	Sussex	1 270	11 767	2 309	9.3	39.7	57.8	0.6	0.6	2.3	4.6	11.5	10.1	16.5	12.8	15.2
51 185	14140	7	Tazewell	1 344	43 452	1 102	32.3	94.8	4.0	0.5	0.9	0.8	4.8	14.8	8.2	11.5	12.6	14.0
51 187	47900	1	Warren	553	38 987	1 199	70.5	89.5	6.0	0.9	1.5	4.0	5.7	17.2	9.0	11.7	12.5	16.3
51 191	28700	3	Washington	1 453	54 729	916	37.7	96.4	1.8	0.5	0.6	1.4	5.0	14.4	8.2	10.7	12.2	14.8
51 193	...	7	Westmoreland	594	17 477	1 947	29.4	65.4	28.3	1.1	1.2	6.1	5.2	13.6	7.9	10.4	9.6	14.0
51 195	13720	7	Wise	1 044	39 935	1 173	38.3	92.9	5.8	0.5	0.6	1.2	5.3	14.9	10.8	13.2	13.1	13.5
51 197	...	6	Wythe	1 196	29 121	1 450	24.3	95.2	3.6	0.5	0.8	1.1	5.1	15.2	7.4	10.9	13.0	14.6
51 199	47260	1	York	271	66 342	797	244.8	75.5	14.1	1.0	7.0	5.6	5.4	19.0	9.5	11.3	12.3	16.1
	...		Independent cities															
51 510	47900	1	Alexandria city	39	150 575	425	3 860.9	54.6	22.3	0.8	8.1	16.9	7.5	10.2	6.2	24.0	18.1	13.3
51 515	31340	3	Bedford city	NA	NA	NA	NA	NA	NA	NA	NA	NA	NA	NA	NA	NA	NA	NA
51 520	28700	3	Bristol city	34	17 184	1 973	505.4	91.2	6.9	0.7	1.2	1.7	4.4	15.6	8.4	12.4	12.3	13.9
51 530	...	6	Buena Vista city	17	6 603	2 713	388.4	90.5	6.2	1.7	1.4	2.2	6.3	15.3	14.7	12.0	10.1	12.5
51 540	16820	3	Charlottesville city	27	45 593	1 058	1 688.6	69.0	20.2	0.7	8.0	4.8	5.6	9.8	23.4	20.6	11.1	10.3
51 550	47260	1	Chesapeake city	883	233 371	279	264.3	61.7	30.7	1.0	4.6	5.0	6.3	18.4	9.4	13.9	13.1	15.2
51 570	40060	1	Colonial Heights city	19	17 731	1 932	933.2	78.9	13.5	0.9	4.0	4.7	6.7	16.3	8.9	11.7	11.3	13.2
51 580	...	6	Covington city	14	5 802	2 774	414.4	83.2	13.9	0.9	1.2	3.1	6.3	15.7	8.3	11.3	11.8	14.8
51 590	19260	3	Danville city	111	42 444	1 120	382.4	46.4	49.9	0.6	1.5	3.1	6.8	15.3	9.7	11.8	10.1	12.8
51 595	...	6	Emporia city	18	5 462	2 807	303.4	30.7	63.3	0.4	1.2	5.4	4.8	19.3	9.3	12.7	11.5	13.2
51 600	47900	1	Fairfax city	16	24 483	1 626	1 530.2	62.6	5.8	0.9	16.8	16.4	7.9	14.4	8.6	14.6	12.8	14.0
51 610	47900	1	Falls Church city	5	13 601	2 197	2 720.2	75.9	5.7	0.8	11.5	9.7	7.1	18.9	6.7	12.7	15.0	15.5
51 620	...	6	Franklin city	21	8 526	2 556	406.0	40.3	57.3	1.0	1.4	2.2	8.2	17.2	8.5	11.9	10.2	12.9
51 630	47900	1	Fredericksburg city	27	28 350	1 478	1 050.0	62.4	24.9	1.0	4.1	11.2	7.2	13.1	21.4	16.5	11.8	11.1
51 640	...	6	Galax city	21	7 014	2 678	334.0	79.0	7.1	0.5	0.8	14.2	7.2	16.4	8.0	10.8	11.4	12.6
51 650	47260	1	Hampton city	133	136 879	461	1 029.2	42.9	50.5	1.4	3.5	5.1	6.2	15.6	12.5	15.1	11.1	13.8
51 660	25500	3	Harrisonburg city	45	52 478	952	1 166.2	70.8	7.7	0.5	4.9	18.2	5.2	10.7	36.3	15.0	9.4	8.2
51 670	40060	1	Hopewell city	27	22 196	1 721	822.1	53.7	39.5	1.0	1.8	6.8	7.4	17.5	8.8	14.2	11.5	13.5
51 678	...	6	Lexington city	6	7 311	2 652	1 218.5	83.7	10.3	0.9	3.4	3.9	3.2	8.0	45.7	8.8	6.1	6.1
51 680	31340	3	Lynchburg city	127	79 047	698	622.4	64.9	29.7	0.8	3.5	3.3	6.3	13.4	24.3	12.8	9.0	10.2
51 683	47900	1	Manassas city	26	42 081	1 128	1 618.5	47.0	15.5	0.8	6.6	32.9	8.4	18.9	9.8	16.9	14.6	13.7

1. CBSA = Core Based Statistical Area. See Appendix A for explanation. See Appendix B for list of metropolitan areas with component counties. 2. County type code from the Economic Research Service of USDA Rural-Urban Continuum Codes. See Appendix A for definition. 3. Dry land or land partially or temporarily covered by water. 4. May be of any race.

STATE County	Population, 2013 (cont.): Age (percent) (cont.): 55 to 64 years	Population, 2013 (cont.): Age (percent) (cont.): 65 to 74 years	Population, 2013 (cont.): Age (percent) (cont.): 75 years and over	Population, 2013 (cont.): Percent female	Population change and components of change, 2000–2014: Total persons: 2000	Population change and components of change, 2000–2014: Total persons: 2010	Population change and components of change, 2000–2014: Percent change: 2000–2010	Population change and components of change, 2000–2014: Percent change: 2010–2014	Components of change, 2010–2014: Births	Components of change, 2010–2014: Deaths	Components of change, 2010–2014: Net migration	Households, 2009–2013: Number	Households, 2009–2013: Persons per household	Households, 2009–2013: Percent: Family households	Households, 2009–2013: Percent: Female family householder[1]	Households, 2009–2013: Percent: One person
	16	17	18	19	20	21	22	23	24	25	26	27	28	29	30	31
VIRGINIA—Cont'd																
Louisa	15.6	10.8	6.0	50.8	25 627	33 153	29.4	3.4	1 598	1 228	724	13 046	2.55	72.0	10.4	22.8
Lunenburg	15.9	11.2	8.0	46.9	13 146	12 914	-1.8	-3.5	472	620	-309	4 572	2.48	66.3	12.4	30.1
Madison	15.3	11.5	8.3	51.5	12 520	13 308	6.3	-1.1	549	540	-171	5 024	2.60	70.2	9.5	23.3
Mathews	17.1	15.6	11.7	51.7	9 207	8 978	-2.5	-1.6	277	465	72	3 856	2.29	74.7	10.7	23.0
Mecklenburg	15.8	13.1	10.0	51.8	32 380	32 727	1.1	-4.7	1 230	1 845	-915	12 650	2.42	62.7	13.1	33.9
Middlesex	17.4	17.1	11.3	50.3	9 932	10 959	10.3	-2.4	378	605	-36	4 400	2.39	67.9	8.3	29.4
Montgomery	9.6	6.2	4.6	48.1	83 629	94 392	12.9	3.0	3 880	2 529	1 570	34 789	2.44	55.2	7.7	27.3
Nelson	18.2	14.0	8.7	51.0	14 445	15 020	4.0	-1.1	559	742	52	6 404	2.31	65.0	15.6	30.2
New Kent	15.9	10.0	4.5	49.2	13 462	18 429	36.9	8.6	780	579	1 362	6 886	2.65	76.8	9.7	19.4
Northampton	16.7	13.0	10.9	52.2	13 093	12 389	-5.4	-2.2	614	795	-101	5 149	2.32	58.0	13.4	36.1
Northumberland	17.0	19.9	13.6	50.6	12 259	12 330	0.6	-0.6	393	720	255	5 691	2.16	66.6	9.7	29.0
Nottoway	13.2	10.0	8.0	46.5	15 725	15 853	0.8	-1.7	747	845	-183	5 673	2.61	65.6	13.2	29.7
Orange	13.3	11.2	8.2	50.9	25 881	33 481	29.4	4.8	1 652	1 412	1 376	12 621	2.65	74.7	11.5	21.3
Page	14.2	11.2	8.2	50.6	23 177	24 042	3.7	-0.9	988	1 170	-30	9 623	2.47	71.8	12.8	22.8
Patrick	15.4	13.9	9.7	50.7	19 407	18 490	-4.7	-1.2	620	1 071	232	7 846	2.32	66.1	11.3	30.1
Pittsylvania	15.6	11.7	7.8	51.0	61 745	63 506	2.9	-1.7	2 106	2 955	-293	26 092	2.38	70.4	12.4	26.4
Powhatan	14.9	10.1	4.9	46.2	22 377	28 046	25.3	1.4	983	808	188	9 544	2.61	78.9	8.7	18.1
Prince Edward	11.5	8.1	7.2	50.7	19 720	23 368	18.5	-1.2	878	880	-298	7 453	2.48	65.9	15.2	28.4
Prince George	12.0	7.5	4.4	44.9	33 047	35 725	8.1	4.5	1 426	960	1 136	10 848	2.92	82.5	10.9	16.0
Prince William	10.0	5.2	2.7	50.2	280 813	402 002	43.2	11.0	28 869	6 840	21 872	132 442	3.11	77.8	12.2	17.5
Pulaski	15.3	12.0	7.9	50.0	35 127	34 872	-0.7	-1.5	1 342	1 786	-23	14 875	2.28	68.2	12.6	27.9
Rappahannock	17.3	14.1	8.5	50.6	6 983	7 373	5.6	-1.9	241	293	-86	3 261	2.27	65.2	3.9	29.2
Richmond	13.2	9.7	9.4	44.2	8 809	9 254	5.1	-3.8	304	399	-257	2 853	2.56	65.8	13.7	28.7
Roanoke	14.4	10.5	8.5	52.1	85 778	92 376	7.7	1.5	3 522	4 010	1 765	37 928	2.39	68.2	9.8	27.9
Rockbridge	16.2	12.9	10.6	50.5	20 808	22 307	7.2	0.1	700	998	245	9 234	2.40	68.1	7.7	27.8
Rockingham	13.5	9.4	8.0	51.1	67 725	76 314	12.7	2.4	3 496	2 910	1 085	29 440	2.56	71.5	10.0	23.7
Russell	15.6	10.7	7.4	51.1	30 308	28 897	-4.7	-3.0	1 166	1 491	-485	11 191	2.53	68.7	10.1	27.9
Scott	14.8	11.8	9.1	49.8	23 403	23 177	-1.0	-3.4	840	1 243	-401	9 692	2.32	70.9	10.2	26.8
Shenandoah	14.1	11.2	8.7	51.2	35 075	41 993	19.7	2.4	2 006	1 887	936	17 397	2.40	70.2	9.6	25.3
Smyth	14.6	10.8	8.6	51.0	33 081	32 208	-2.6	-2.0	1 318	1 800	-142	12 650	2.47	68.5	12.0	27.4
Southampton	15.5	10.0	7.3	48.3	17 482	18 570	6.2	-2.9	582	806	-322	6 708	2.52	71.1	16.3	24.8
Spotsylvania	11.8	7.2	4.5	50.9	90 395	122 397	35.4	5.3	6 537	3 274	3 097	41 709	2.97	79.0	13.1	17.0
Stafford	10.5	5.5	3.1	49.7	92 446	128 961	39.5	8.6	7 171	2 706	6 483	42 178	3.04	81.3	10.9	15.1
Surry	16.6	11.2	7.2	50.3	6 829	7 058	3.4	-3.9	251	282	-233	2 602	2.66	71.3	13.7	25.4
Sussex	13.6	9.0	6.8	40.6	12 504	12 087	-3.3	-2.6	437	554	-207	3 704	2.19	62.0	16.4	32.3
Tazewell	15.6	10.6	7.9	50.3	44 598	45 078	1.1	-3.6	1 915	2 692	-836	18 294	2.37	69.6	10.3	26.7
Warren	13.4	8.6	5.5	50.2	31 584	37 575	19.0	4.2	1 932	1 480	1 082	14 387	2.58	70.5	11.9	23.4
Washington	15.1	11.5	8.0	50.7	51 103	54 876	7.4	-0.3	2 271	2 631	238	22 755	2.34	68.3	11.1	27.1
Westmoreland	16.4	13.5	9.3	51.3	16 718	17 454	4.4	0.1	795	820	45	7 130	2.44	62.3	11.9	32.6
Wise	14.1	9.1	6.2	48.2	40 123	41 452	3.3	-3.7	1 805	2 039	-1 357	15 406	2.48	68.2	13.5	27.7
Wythe	14.7	11.1	8.0	51.1	27 599	29 235	5.9	-0.4	1 245	1 450	115	11 656	2.48	68.5	11.0	27.4
York	12.5	8.4	5.6	50.8	56 297	65 464	16.3	1.8	2 512	1 641	196	24 071	2.69	79.4	11.9	17.5
Independent cities																
Alexandria city	10.8	6.0	3.8	51.4	128 283	139 966	9.1	7.5	11 556	3 081	2 143	65 369	2.17	47.2	7.9	43.0
Bedford city	NA	NA	NA	NA	6 299	6 222	-1.2	NA	NA	NA	NA	2 800	2.07	60.4	19.3	37.3
Bristol city	13.5	10.3	9.3	52.9	17 367	17 835	2.7	-3.7	651	1 030	-248	7 674	2.25	62.7	17.0	32.8
Buena Vista city	12.4	9.8	7.1	52.9	6 349	6 650	4.7	-0.7	364	295	-125	2 738	2.29	62.8	13.1	32.4
Charlottesville city	9.9	5.3	4.1	51.5	45 049	43 475	-3.5	5.0	2 404	1 094	800	17 443	2.33	42.1	9.4	37.9
Chesapeake city	12.2	6.9	4.6	51.2	199 184	222 209	11.6	5.0	11 957	6 892	6 114	79 421	2.77	74.9	14.7	21.0
Colonial Heights city	11.9	9.8	10.1	53.5	16 897	17 411	3.0	1.8	1 134	876	77	7 017	2.46	63.8	14.1	29.8
Covington city	13.1	10.5	8.0	50.8	6 303	5 961	-5.4	-2.6	393	291	-293	2 545	2.29	53.5	14.6	42.0
Danville city	14.3	9.7	9.6	54.2	48 411	43 055	-11.1	-1.4	2 483	2 956	-225	18 659	2.22	59.4	19.6	36.7
Emporia city	12.3	8.6	8.4	53.6	5 665	5 927	4.6	-7.8	146	375	-245	2 488	2.23	60.1	22.9	35.7
Fairfax city	12.4	8.2	7.0	50.8	21 498	22 565	5.0	8.6	2 177	747	381	8 492	2.65	67.9	9.3	21.5
Falls Church city	13.4	6.3	4.4	50.9	10 377	12 332	18.8	10.7	715	267	893	5 020	2.53	61.6	9.6	32.2
Franklin city	13.6	9.2	8.1	54.8	8 346	8 582	2.8	-0.4	675	517	-198	3 551	2.37	64.3	24.7	32.2
Fredericksburg city	9.1	5.2	4.4	54.3	19 279	24 286	26.0	18.0	1 789	748	3 120	9 779	2.38	52.9	16.6	38.0
Galax city	13.6	10.0	10.0	53.1	6 837	7 042	3.0	-0.4	501	417	-137	3 018	2.21	57.2	15.4	38.8
Hampton city	12.4	7.6	5.7	51.9	146 437	137 436	-6.1	-0.5	7 642	4 883	-3 328	52 511	2.52	63.5	17.3	30.7
Harrisonburg city	7.2	3.9	4.0	52.3	40 468	48 914	20.9	7.3	2 434	1 009	1 952	15 701	2.70	51.8	9.8	21.6
Hopewell city	11.5	8.4	7.1	53.3	22 354	22 591	1.1	-1.7	1 538	1 130	-810	8 766	2.53	60.5	22.2	34.8
Lexington city	7.9	6.6	7.6	44.2	6 867	7 042	2.5	3.9	321	227	143	1 709	2.05	50.0	10.4	42.8
Lynchburg city	10.0	6.9	7.0	53.0	65 269	75 568	15.8	4.5	4 682	3 284	1 983	28 556	2.35	56.2	14.0	35.7
Manassas city	10.3	4.7	2.8	49.4	35 135	37 821	7.6	11.2	3 126	733	1 834	12 072	3.24	75.0	14.7	19.7

1. No spouse present.

STATE County	Persons in group quarters, 2014	Daytime population, 2009–2013 Number	Daytime population, 2009–2013 Employment/residence ratio	Births, 2014 Total	Births, 2014 Rate[1]	Deaths, 2014 Number	Deaths, 2014 Rate[1]	Persons under 65 with no health insurance, 2013 Number	Persons under 65 with no health insurance, 2013 Percent	Medicare, 2014 Eligible for Medicare	Medicare, 2014 Enrolled in Medicare Advantage	Medicare, 2014 Enrolled in a Medicare prescription drug plan	Serious crimes known to police,[2] 2013 Total Number	Serious crimes known to police,[2] 2013 Total Rate[3]
	32	33	34	35	36	37	38	39	40	41	42	43	44	45
VIRGINIA—Cont'd														
Louisa	211	27 421	0.62	386	11.2	312	9.1	4 845	17.2	6 895	1 204	3 317	621	1 850
Lunenburg	975	11 194	0.64	107	8.6	151	12.1	1 735	19.0	2 890	426	1 530	125	999
Madison	193	9 998	0.48	126	9.6	118	9.0	1 817	17.2	2 717	373	1 448	130	985
Mathews	86	7 134	0.54	68	7.7	113	12.8	1 003	15.6	2 654	348	1 275	104	1 171
Mecklenburg	920	33 423	1.10	281	9.0	447	14.3	4 330	18.2	8 806	1 438	5 222	604	1 916
Middlesex	383	9 814	0.77	89	8.3	132	12.3	1 199	16.1	3 357	522	1 857	118	1 092
Montgomery	9 430	101 362	1.15	940	9.7	591	6.1	11 763	15.3	12 603	2 229	6 934	1 768	1 849
Nelson	102	12 514	0.62	130	8.8	150	10.1	1 997	17.4	4 125	550	2 187	217	1 466
New Kent	551	13 192	0.41	185	9.2	120	6.0	2 109	13.1	3 628	622	1 672	234	1 205
Northampton	260	12 626	1.06	132	10.9	206	17.0	1 909	20.9	3 336	541	1 928	212	1 737
Northumberland	0	10 775	0.68	86	7.0	174	14.2	1 517	18.7	4 538	511	2 225	133	1 074
Nottoway	1 864	16 244	1.06	183	11.7	200	12.8	1 915	16.9	3 507	644	1 963	318	2 006
Orange	602	27 663	0.56	383	10.9	309	8.8	4 478	16.3	8 003	1 000	3 682	439	1 270
Page	194	20 165	0.62	235	9.9	272	11.4	3 254	16.9	5 752	656	3 228	463	1 937
Patrick	263	17 048	0.80	138	7.6	236	12.9	2 499	17.8	4 967	1 214	2 735	324	1 753
Pittsylvania	1 046	51 625	0.57	512	8.2	695	11.1	7 632	15.4	15 031	2 540	9 284	631	1 007
Powhatan	2 210	22 076	0.51	239	8.4	212	7.5	2 927	13.5	5 145	1 014	2 590	254	900
Prince Edward	4 152	24 940	1.20	200	8.7	210	9.1	2 596	16.6	4 344	809	2 375	494	2 123
Prince George	4 672	42 328	1.39	339	9.1	239	6.4	3 518	12.6	5 272	669	2 109	418	1 115
Prince William	2 628	331 251	0.60	6 913	15.5	1 700	3.8	57 986	14.5	39 722	6 356	12 226	7 340	1 670
Pulaski	1 148	33 769	0.93	335	9.8	413	12.0	3 946	14.7	8 650	1 578	4 600	1 057	3 038
Rappahannock	35	6 428	0.71	58	7.9	67	9.1	1 115	19.4	1 840	132	923	5	67
Richmond	1 581	9 196	1.02	74	8.3	93	10.4	1 076	18.8	1 805	322	910	72	799
Roanoke	2 179	83 468	0.79	821	8.8	918	9.8	8 633	11.7	21 404	3 988	11 360	1 704	1 827
Rockbridge	175	19 899	0.75	169	7.6	224	10.0	2 756	16.2	5 574	964	3 108	313	1 392
Rockingham	1 657	72 803	0.89	810	10.4	701	9.0	10 235	16.3	15 566	2 406	8 931	736	945
Russell	434	25 973	0.74	283	10.1	350	12.5	3 661	15.8	7 591	2 278	4 269	470	1 656
Scott	706	19 790	0.63	189	8.4	289	12.9	2 605	14.9	6 412	3 073	2 271	381	1 677
Shenandoah	427	37 048	0.73	476	11.1	442	10.3	5 691	16.7	9 677	1 070	5 121	599	1 398
Smyth	774	31 745	0.98	299	9.5	439	13.9	3 824	15.1	8 583	1 730	4 855	650	2 054
Southampton	1 611	14 455	0.51	133	7.4	187	10.4	2 174	15.9	3 809	616	2 151	334	1 816
Spotsylvania	524	99 470	0.58	1 531	11.9	810	6.3	15 084	13.5	17 478	2 028	7 136	2 424	1 910
Stafford	3 769	106 839	0.61	1 720	12.3	659	4.7	12 504	10.4	14 164	1 250	4 815	2 218	1 628
Surry	0	6 056	0.73	58	8.5	45	6.6	805	14.6	1 476	339	627	81	1 193
Sussex	2 650	12 330	1.09	98	8.3	133	11.3	1 205	16.1	2 253	468	1 151	150	1 251
Tazewell	1 806	45 030	1.02	449	10.3	611	14.1	5 745	16.6	11 658	3 220	6 444	1 054	2 392
Warren	788	33 009	0.74	485	12.4	338	8.7	5 121	15.7	6 589	611	3 317	870	2 269
Washington	1 630	54 467	0.99	598	10.9	603	11.0	6 641	15.4	14 146	4 323	6 593	1 209	2 181
Westmoreland	70	14 805	0.62	190	10.9	197	11.3	2 497	18.4	4 555	580	2 002	293	1 665
Wise	2 926	44 532	1.24	432	10.8	470	11.8	4 902	15.3	10 125	3 362	4 440	1 197	2 934
Wythe	260	29 217	1.00	290	10.0	359	12.3	3 837	16.1	7 253	1 400	4 039	423	1 442
York	647	58 442	0.77	595	9.0	435	6.6	5 641	10.1	10 498	1 200	3 605	1 372	2 059
Independent cities														
Alexandria city	1 830	152 493	1.10	2 795	18.6	738	4.9	19 018	14.4	15 752	1 534	5 365	3 239	2 181
Bedford city	NA	8 929	2.13	NA	NA	NA	NA	665	14.1	1 706	302	956	250	4 242
Bristol city	225	22 297	1.67	94	5.5	242	14.1	2 080	14.9	4 417	1 696	1 762	605	3 430
Buena Vista city	435	6 058	0.79	86	13.0	72	10.9	825	15.9	1 420	297	769	67	993
Charlottesville city	2 417	59 052	1.74	597	13.1	284	6.2	6 862	17.9	5 819	776	3 333	92 262	3 655
Chesapeake city	4 388	211 698	0.87	2 877	12.3	1 705	7.3	23 665	11.9	32 794	5 882	11 736	6 979	3 027
Colonial Heights city	171	18 866	1.17	274	15.5	189	10.7	1 955	13.9	4 042	524	1 696	792	4 512
Covington city	75	5 458	0.82	94	16.2	65	11.2	705	15.0	1 683	246	976	112	1 956
Danville city	1 639	52 155	1.57	593	14.0	689	16.2	5 080	15.0	11 075	1 718	7 264	2 192	5 082
Emporia city	246	6 619	1.39	32	5.9	77	14.1	700	15.1	1 206	179	362	260	4 567
Fairfax city	521	47 823	3.03	585	23.9	202	8.3	2 745	13.7	3 638	437	1 173	422	1 773
Falls Church city	42	15 819	1.43	205	15.1	73	5.4	793	6.7	1 694	183	553	252	1 864
Franklin city	129	9 642	1.36	166	19.5	103	12.1	1 056	14.8	1 864	293	1 095	481	5 646
Fredericksburg city	2 787	38 576	2.05	445	15.7	211	7.4	3 580	15.7	3 672	408	1 730	1 256	4 421
Galax city	378	8 256	1.47	116	16.5	80	11.4	1 040	18.5	1 956	123	1 327	292	4 250
Hampton city	4 190	139 301	1.04	1 837	13.4	1 212	8.9	16 465	14.3	23 049	4 807	7 496	4 775	3 487
Harrisonburg city	7 387	59 756	1.46	601	11.5	220	4.2	8 755	21.7	5 018	552	3 027	1 475	2 849
Hopewell city	237	21 371	0.88	358	16.1	284	12.8	2 981	15.8	4 293	766	1 885	884	3 963
Lexington city	2 705	9 559	2.23	89	12.2	44	6.0	590	17.0	1 565	160	954	66	944
Lynchburg city	10 296	99 891	1.73	1 113	14.1	729	9.2	9 279	16.0	14 167	1 891	8 725	2 311	2 972
Manassas city	46	41 600	1.11	771	18.3	163	3.9	7 762	20.3	4 005	628	1 597	969	2 334

1. Per 1,000 estimated resident population. 2. Data for serious crimes have not been adjusted for underreporting; this may affect comparability between geographic areas and over time.
3. Per 100,000 population estimated by the FBI.

STATE County	Serious crimes known to police, 2013 (cont.)[1] Rate[2] Violent	Rate[2] Property	Education: School enrollment and attainment, 2009–2013 Enrollment[3] Total	Enrollment[3] Percent private	Attainment[4] (percent) High school graduate or less	Attainment[4] (percent) Bachelor's degree or more	Local government expenditures,[5] 2012–2013 Total current spending (mil dol)	Local government expenditures Current spending per student (dollars)	Money income, 2009–2013 Per capita income[6] (dollars)	Households Median income (dollars)	Households Mean income (dollars)	Households Percent with income of $200,000 or more	Income and poverty, 2013 Median household income (dollars)	Percent below poverty level All persons	Percent below poverty level Children under 18 years	Percent below poverty level Children 5 to 17 years in families
	46	47	48	49	50	51	52	53	54	55	56	57	58	59	60	61
VIRGINIA—Cont'd																
Louisa	131	1 719	6 755	14.8	57.0	18.8	49.7	10 512	26 956	54 518	67 940	2.5	53 170	11.7	17.7	16.0
Lunenburg	128	871	2 657	13.9	65.0	11.9	16.0	10 110	17 630	35 237	46 742	1.2	37 712	21.4	29.5	26.6
Madison	91	894	3 004	15.2	53.2	21.8	18.3	9 677	27 296	53 459	70 176	2.1	51 805	12.7	18.5	16.4
Mathews	34	1 138	1 766	8.6	45.7	27.2	11.8	9 976	31 342	55 192	71 419	3.6	55 128	10.5	18.2	16.5
Mecklenburg	266	1 650	6 535	8.8	58.4	13.7	40.5	8 668	20 056	36 261	47 574	1.4	38 439	17.1	28.4	25.7
Middlesex	93	1 000	1 894	12.7	41.0	27.4	NA	NA	30 531	53 309	72 035	5.1	47 399	15.5	26.6	25.0
Montgomery	110	1 739	41 268	7.1	33.3	42.4	96.2	9 878	23 548	45 543	61 901	4.1	46 024	23.4	18.3	16.1
Nelson	115	1 351	2 850	14.5	51.7	26.7	23.8	11 965	26 059	48 789	59 058	1.7	45 990	15.8	23.1	21.2
New Kent	180	1 025	4 535	13.5	44.8	23.2	26.1	8 689	32 068	70 618	84 927	5.0	72 150	6.7	9.9	8.9
Northampton	139	1 597	2 118	18.4	57.1	20.2	20.2	11 740	23 473	33 635	54 333	4.2	36 211	22.4	34.3	32.9
Northumberland	153	921	1 908	7.0	45.4	22.1	15.0	10 200	28 568	51 342	61 767	2.5	49 054	16.1	31.0	28.3
Nottoway	177	1 830	3 414	13.6	64.6	12.0	21.7	9 251	19 337	36 607	47 964	0.7	34 805	23.5	29.3	29.1
Orange	61	1 209	7 454	14.3	49.0	22.2	47.4	9 131	27 655	60 287	72 146	3.1	60 829	10.4	15.5	14.6
Page	88	1 849	4 749	9.2	66.9	11.4	33.3	9 186	22 355	42 906	55 185	1.4	41 070	15.3	22.3	19.8
Patrick	108	1 645	3 864	8.1	58.4	10.7	24.5	9 254	18 860	34 864	43 184	0.5	34 654	19.4	28.2	24.5
Pittsylvania	89	918	14 310	13.3	56.7	13.7	80.0	8 597	21 583	42 143	51 805	0.6	40 608	15.2	21.3	18.0
Powhatan	67	833	6 492	16.2	42.5	27.6	41.7	9 660	31 252	76 548	91 089	5.6	74 820	7.7	9.2	8.1
Prince Edward	185	1 938	8 441	19.8	56.5	21.9	25.2	10 852	17 208	37 436	50 327	0.7	39 077	23.5	29.3	27.2
Prince George	117	998	9 040	9.8	48.4	17.9	58.7	9 133	24 434	63 074	73 633	2.4	65 625	12.9	14.8	14.8
Prince William	162	1 508	124 823	15.9	32.1	38.1	859.5	10 249	37 401	98 071	114 894	12.9	93 671	7.0	10.0	8.8
Pulaski	250	2 788	6 888	7.3	50.9	16.2	44.8	9 907	23 987	44 312	55 276	1.6	43 555	15.7	22.3	19.5
Rappahannock	27	40	1 568	18.0	43.0	32.4	11.5	12 558	36 505	56 438	84 194	6.7	60 945	10.3	17.7	15.8
Richmond	67	733	1 788	3.5	66.0	12.3	13.4	11 409	20 875	47 083	61 382	1.9	42 738	20.3	25.8	23.3
Roanoke	165	1 662	22 220	17.3	35.8	33.1	132.0	9 186	31 728	60 795	76 344	4.0	57 663	7.7	9.8	9.2
Rockbridge	71	1 321	4 036	14.9	53.9	23.2	29.5	10 494	25 638	48 313	61 157	3.5	46 882	13.6	18.3	15.5
Rockingham	81	864	18 414	21.6	56.2	23.4	(7)180.3	(7)10 607	27 298	52 195	70 779	3.0	55 636	9.6	14.5	12.6
Russell	152	1 505	5 581	10.7	62.4	10.5	39.9	9 058	19 735	33 872	47 520	0.8	36 107	18.8	26.2	23.8
Scott	145	1 531	4 076	8.6	63.7	10.9	33.9	8 662	21 485	38 355	50 337	1.1	38 336	18.4	26.5	23.9
Shenandoah	138	1 260	8 821	12.5	54.8	19.8	64.8	10 494	25 134	49 625	60 794	1.5	47 874	11.6	18.0	16.7
Smyth	180	1 874	6 523	6.9	59.1	15.0	45.6	9 404	20 837	37 239	48 631	1.1	37 475	17.3	25.9	22.3
Southampton	147	1 669	4 245	11.5	56.2	13.6	28.6	9 890	22 433	46 150	59 728	1.9	46 547	16.7	22.5	20.2
Spotsylvania	195	1 714	34 603	13.0	42.9	28.2	234.5	9 866	31 360	78 345	91 480	5.5	73 112	7.7	10.4	9.1
Stafford	130	1 498	39 903	13.6	32.2	36.2	266.9	9 718	36 574	97 110	111 080	11.3	93 014	6.4	8.1	7.1
Surry	133	1 060	1 562	27.0	56.0	16.7	15.2	16 891	22 600	47 292	55 722	0.1	50 554	13.6	20.2	18.8
Sussex	117	1 134	2 348	15.7	68.0	10.3	18.1	15 876	16 546	39 635	50 034	0.3	38 948	24.0	30.4	28.8
Tazewell	116	2 276	9 094	11.3	57.7	12.9	56.7	8 768	21 358	35 693	50 995	1.8	38 336	17.5	22.9	21.3
Warren	130	2 139	9 356	23.4	53.3	20.5	49.0	8 912	28 889	61 610	74 985	3.7	56 291	12.0	17.0	15.6
Washington	121	2 060	11 631	20.4	49.7	22.3	73.7	9 981	25 109	41 897	59 616	2.3	42 242	14.9	21.2	18.7
Westmoreland	182	1 484	3 588	6.9	59.0	14.9	25.0	10 705	25 245	49 157	59 172	1.2	45 927	15.3	28.5	27.0
Wise	233	2 701	9 069	6.5	59.8	13.1	58.1	9 515	19 107	36 218	48 795	1.1	37 490	19.3	27.8	25.7
Wythe	123	1 320	6 086	6.2	54.5	15.0	39.9	9 123	23 219	41 275	54 474	1.8	41 168	15.1	21.6	20.3
York	126	1 933	19 109	11.8	25.7	42.0	119.5	9 619	36 373	82 073	98 020	7.1	78 327	6.0	7.4	6.6
Independent cities																
Alexandria city	174	2 007	29 281	27.4	21.0	61.4	233.1	17 789	54 608	85 706	115 642	13.5	85 562	8.8	15.3	18.1
Bedford city	204	4 038	1 257	21.6	46.4	25.0	(8)	(8)	22 322	35 593	45 977	0.6	38 162	20.2	31.0	26.0
Bristol city	334	3 095	3 992	17.8	52.9	19.6	25.7	10 905	18 820	32 221	42 160	0.5	35 167	21.6	36.4	31.3
Buena Vista city	133	860	1 898	21.3	61.5	14.9	9.4	8 897	18 453	36 591	44 970	0.0	36 915	17.2	24.1	22.8
Charlottesville city	356	3 299	17 838	8.8	34.0	49.9	(9)	(9)	27 268	44 601	65 182	4.8	45 320	22.9	23.7	25.3
Chesapeake city	321	2 705	64 248	14.9	35.7	29.3	414.5	10 460	29 905	69 743	83 155	4.8	66 516	9.6	12.6	11.4
Colonial Heights city	251	4 261	4 190	5.2	48.2	20.5	33.3	11 764	27 610	50 835	66 214	1.6	49 715	10.8	17.2	17.0
Covington city	122	1 834	1 220	0.7	58.8	8.3	10.3	10 448	20 160	34 319	44 006	0.4	33 904	16.9	24.8	23.1
Danville city	352	4 730	10 500	16.2	51.3	17.2	68.8	10 811	19 626	30 786	44 161	1.4	30 940	25.0	39.1	37.5
Emporia city	439	4 128	1 257	9.1	59.5	16.0	(10)	(10)	19 710	32 155	45 684	1.1	32 676	26.0	41.6	38.0
Fairfax city	109	1 664	6 154	17.3	24.1	51.9	(11)	(11)	44 345	97 242	119 855	15.8	89 507	7.3	7.9	8.5
Falls Church city	178	1 687	3 731	25.3	13.3	74.4	38.9	17 101	59 088	120 000	146 599	23.1	117 452	3.0	3.4	2.9
Franklin city	411	5 235	2 289	9.0	46.7	20.6	15.7	12 436	19 588	31 928	46 527	2.3	36 326	21.9	36.6	36.8
Fredericksburg city	405	4 016	8 374	10.5	35.3	35.1	40.3	11 985	27 222	47 040	67 031	4.2	48 152	17.5	23.0	21.7
Galax city	175	4 076	1 476	9.8	57.4	14.5	13.5	10 231	21 769	30 325	48 697	2.2	33 737	22.8	36.7	35.2
Hampton city	214	3 273	38 959	20.9	38.3	22.5	211.9	9 925	25 247	50 705	62 293	1.8	45 293	15.6	22.3	21.0
Harrisonburg city	205	2 645	23 955	5.1	43.9	35.1	(7)	(7)	17 080	38 048	51 742	1.6	37 588	29.3	23.4	22.2
Hopewell city	448	3 515	4 954	8.4	61.6	10.2	43.0	10 223	20 388	37 033	40 022	0.8	39 440	22.6	34.3	31.4
Lexington city	57	886	4 347	23.7	41.5	41.7	4.8	9 079	14 763	36 505	53 050	3.4	41 521	24.3	14.7	12.5
Lynchburg city	426	2 546	28 013	53.9	40.1	31.2	91.2	10 630	21 440	38 138	54 266	2.4	39 918	22.6	30.0	28.0
Manassas city	294	2 040	11 231	17.5	43.2	28.7	89.8	12 343	28 752	71 036	88 790	6.4	70 133	10.1	16.7	15.9

1. Data for serious crimes have not been adjusted for underreporting; this may affect comparability between geographic areas and over time. 2. Per 100,000 population estimated by the FBI. 3. All persons 3 years old and over enrolled in nursery school through college. 4. Persons 25 years old and over. 5. Elementary and secondary education expenditures. 6. Based on population estimated by the American Community Survey, 2009–2013. 7. Harrisonburg city is included with Rockingham county. 8. Bedford city is included with Bedford county. 9. Charlottesville city is included with Albemarle county. 10. Emporia city is included with Greensville county. 11. Fairfax city is included with Fairfax county.

STATE County	Personal income, 2013: Total (mil dol)	Percent change, 2012–2013	Per capita[1]: Dollars	Per capita[1]: Rank	Wages and salaries (mil dol)	Supplements to wages and salaries; employer contributions (mil dol): Pension and insurance	Supplements to wages and salaries; employer contributions (mil dol): Government social insurance	Proprietors' income (mil dol)	Dividends, interest, and rent (mil dol)	Personal transfer receipts (mil dol)	Earnings, 2013: Total (mil dol)	Contributions for government social insurance (mil dol): From employee and self-employed	Contributions for government social insurance (mil dol): From employer
	62	63	64	65	66	67	68	69	70	71	72	73	74
VIRGINIA—Cont'd													
Louisa	1 555	2.6	45 808	632	426	80	31	297	217	247	834	51	31
Lunenburg	379	1.8	30 243	2 649	91	19	7	20	74	112	137	10	7
Madison	531	3.4	40 197	1 149	108	20	8	53	116	93	189	13	8
Mathews	498	0.6	56 000	187	45	9	3	40	140	94	98	8	3
Mecklenburg	1 054	-0.9	33 534	2 171	384	72	30	57	229	322	542	40	30
Middlesex	489	2.2	45 460	658	112	24	8	24	156	116	168	13	8
Montgomery	[3]3 534	[3]2.0	[3]31 168	[3]2 523	[3]2 015	[3]446	[3]148	[3]169	[3]812	[3]593	[3]2 778	[3]162	[3]148
Nelson	676	1.6	45 680	644	126	25	9	22	177	142	182	15	9
New Kent	775	2.1	39 707	1 203	148	28	11	28	146	122	215	15	11
Northampton	498	1.4	41 088	1 041	166	29	12	66	121	133	274	15	12
Northumberland	568	1.7	46 521	585	91	17	7	32	218	138	146	13	7
Nottoway	542	2.5	34 339	2 022	206	53	16	20	103	167	295	20	16
Orange	1 323	2.9	38 149	1 416	356	64	26	37	315	278	484	34	26
Page	771	2.7	32 359	2 358	171	36	14	59	162	202	280	20	14
Patrick	518	0.9	28 196	2 877	149	31	12	30	95	176	221	18	12
Pittsylvania	[4]3 502	[4]1.5	[4]33 244	[4]2 219	[4]1 367	[4]246	[4]106	[4]189	[4]649	[4]1 036	[4]1 908	[4]136	[4]106
Powhatan	1 334	1.3	47 214	536	358	64	25	67	226	172	515	33	25
Prince Edward	562	1.2	24 667	3 065	310	63	24	7	117	173	404	27	24
Prince George	[5]2 468	[5]1.3	[5]41 545	[5]987	[5]1 743	[5]467	[5]154	[5]77	[5]493	[5]444	[5]2 441	[5]120	[5]154
Prince William	[6]22 717	[6]1.1	[6]45 760	[6]637	[6]7 642	[6]1 309	[6]587	[6]979	[6]3 666	[6]1 952	[6]10 517	[6]595	[6]587
Pulaski	1 241	0.9	35 976	1 750	500	89	40	39	202	335	668	47	40
Rappahannock	366	1.5	49 002	416	72	11	4	40	116	55	128	9	4
Richmond	263	2.0	29 379	2 765	104	22	7	17	64	69	150	10	7
Roanoke	[7]5 159	[7]1.9	[7]43 418	[7]809	[7]2 695	[7]458	[7]204	[7]354	[7]1 200	[7]938	[7]3 711	[7]232	[7]204
Rockbridge	[8]1 260	[8]1.0	[8]34 846	[8]1 923	[8]476	[8]89	[8]38	[8]59	[8]351	[8]296	[8]661	[8]46	[8]38
Rockingham	[9]4 412	[9]2.4	[9]34 166	[9]2 053	[9]2 421	[9]432	[9]179	[9]384	[9]939	[9]747	[9]3 415	[9]200	[9]179
Russell	844	-0.5	29 850	2 711	276	52	22	33	128	297	383	31	22
Scott	658	0.0	29 051	2 802	159	32	12	13	102	234	216	21	12
Shenandoah	1 551	2.6	36 328	1 688	471	87	36	134	343	329	728	49	36
Smyth	977	1.8	30 866	2 569	429	88	34	35	157	318	586	42	34
Southampton	[10]937	[10]-2.3	[10]35 020	[10]1 893	[10]287	[10]62	[10]21	[10]41	[10]205	[10]245	[10]411	[10]27	[10]21
Spotsylvania	[11]6 622	[11]1.0	[11]42 593	[11]883	[11]2 388	[11]371	[11]176	[11]340	[11]1 271	[11]880	[11]3 275	[11]199	[11]176
Stafford	6 070	1.1	44 378	734	2 188	432	169	147	1 136	626	2 936	165	169
Surry	250	-2.1	36 891	1 609	158	38	11	6	40	55	214	13	11
Sussex	358	-2.7	30 280	2 646	142	30	11	8	60	97	190	12	11
Tazewell	1 527	-0.6	34 619	1 968	579	111	44	69	285	467	803	58	44
Warren	1 544	1.1	39 907	1 180	527	85	40	63	250	252	715	46	40
Washington	[12]2 674	[12]-0.5	[12]37 018	[12]1 582	[12]1 200	[12]219	[12]91	[12]318	[12]519	[12]685	[12]1 827	[12]121	[12]91
Westmoreland	719	1.9	40 848	1 073	114	23	8	29	183	162	173	14	8
Wise	[13]1 382	[13]-3.2	[13]30 973	[13]2 553	[13]647	[13]131	[13]48	[13]76	[13]204	[13]501	[13]902	[13]63	[13]48
Wythe	911	1.2	31 032	2 546	389	79	30	28	159	270	526	37	30
York	[14]4 053	[14]1.3	[14]51 718	[14]307	[14]937	[14]177	[14]74	[14]198	[14]941	[14]470	[14]1 385	[14]84	[14]74
Independent cities													
Alexandria city	12 072	0.5	81 078	21	7 176	1 095	542	565	2 592	662	9 378	521	542
Bedford city	[15]	[15]	[15]	[15]	[15]	[15]	[15]	[15]	[15]	[15]	[15]	[15]	[15]
Bristol city	[12]	[12]	[12]	[12]	[12]	[12]	[12]	[12]	[12]	[12]	[12]	[12]	[12]
Buena Vista city	[8]	[8]	[8]	[8]	[8]	[8]	[8]	[8]	[8]	[8]	[8]	[8]	[8]
Charlottesville city	[16]	[16]	[16]	[16]	[16]	[16]	[16]	[16]	[16]	[16]	[16]	[16]	[16]
Chesapeake city	10 275	0.7	44 562	723	4 192	669	318	425	1 911	1 400	5 604	335	318
Colonial Heights city	[17]	[17]	[17]	[17]	[17]	[17]	[17]	[17]	[17]	[17]	[17]	[17]	[17]
Covington city	[18]	[18]	[18]	[18]	[18]	[18]	[18]	[18]	[18]	[18]	[18]	[18]	[18]
Danville city	[4]	[4]	[4]	[4]	[4]	[4]	[4]	[4]	[4]	[4]	[4]	[4]	[4]
Emporia city	[19]	[19]	[19]	[19]	[19]	[19]	[19]	[19]	[19]	[19]	[19]	[19]	[19]
Fairfax city	[20]	[20]	[20]	[20]	[20]	[20]	[20]	[20]	[20]	[20]	[20]	[20]	[20]
Falls Church city	[20]	[20]	[20]	[20]	[20]	[20]	[20]	[20]	[20]	[20]	[20]	[20]	[20]
Franklin city	[10]	[10]	[10]	[10]	[10]	[10]	[10]	[10]	[10]	[10]	[10]	[10]	[10]
Fredericksburg city	[11]	[11]	[11]	[11]	[11]	[11]	[11]	[11]	[11]	[11]	[11]	[11]	[11]
Galax city	[21]	[21]	[21]	[21]	[21]	[21]	[21]	[21]	[21]	[21]	[21]	[21]	[21]
Hampton city	5 872	1.3	42 958	845	3 066	681	254	162	1 154	1 106	4 163	229	254
Harrisonburg city	[9]	[9]	[9]	[9]	[9]	[9]	[9]	[9]	[9]	[9]	[9]	[9]	[9]
Hopewell city	[5]	[5]	[5]	[5]	[5]	[5]	[5]	[5]	[5]	[5]	[5]	[5]	[5]
Lexington city	[8]	[8]	[8]	[8]	[8]	[8]	[8]	[8]	[8]	[8]	[8]	[8]	[8]
Lynchburg city	[22]	[22]	[22]	[22]	[22]	[22]	[22]	[22]	[22]	[22]	[22]	[22]	[22]
Manassas city	[6]	[6]	[6]	[6]	[6]	[6]	[6]	[6]	[6]	[6]	[6]	[6]	[6]

1. Based on the resident population estimated as of July 1 of the year shown. 3. Radford city is included with Montgomery county. 4. Danville city is included with Pittsylvania county. 5. Hopewell city is included with Prince George county. 6. Manassas and Manassas Park cities are included with Prince William county. 7. Salem city is included with Roanoke county. 8. Buena Vista and Lexington cities are included with Rockbridge county. 9. Harrisonburg city is included with Rockingham county. 10. Franklin city is included with Southhampton county. 11. Fredericksburg city is included with Spotsylvania county. 12. Bristol city included with Washington county. 13. Norton city is included with Wise county. 14. Poquoson city is included with York county. 15. Bedford city is included with Bedford county. 16. Charlottesville city is included with Albemarle county. 17. Petersburg and Colonial Heights cities are included with Dinwiddie county. 18. Covington city is included with Alleghany county. 19. Emporia city is included with Greensville county. 20. Fairfax city and Falls Church city are included with Fairfax county. 21. Galax city is included with Carroll county. 22. Lynchburg city is included with Campbell county.

STATE County	Earnings, 2013 (cont.)									Social Security beneficiaries, December 2013		Supple-mental Security Income recipients, December 2013	Housing units, 2014	
	Percent by selected industries													
	Farm	Mining	Construction	Manu-facturing	Infor-mation: professional, scientific, technical services	Retail trade	Finance, insur-ance, real estate and leasing	Health care and social assistance	Govern-ment	Number	Rate[1]		Total	Percent change, 2010–2014
	75	76	77	78	79	80	81	82	83	84	85	86	87	88
VIRGINIA—Cont'd														
Louisa	-0.5	D	9.0	11.7	D	5.5	7.4	3.0	9.7	7 505	221	669	16 807	2.8
Lunenburg	5.6	0.0	6.5	10.1	D	5.6	D	8.3	29.5	3 130	250	451	5 935	0.0
Madison	-0.2	0.0	10.7	7.8	D	24.3	D	D	17.1	2 980	226	221	6 006	1.2
Mathews	0.5	0.1	11.2	4.1	D	7.1	D	D	21.3	2 780	312	138	5 720	0.9
Mecklenburg	1.6	D	5.9	9.3	5.3	8.9	4.2	16.1	17.8	9 815	313	1 293	18 686	0.5
Middlesex	1.6	0.1	8.5	5.2	D	7.0	4.9	D	30.2	3 575	332	223	7 230	1.4
Montgomery	[3]0.0	[3]0.1	[3]D	[3]15.4	[3]D	[3]5.8	[3]3.9	[3]8.8	[3]39.2	13 465	139	1 235	39 217	1.7
Nelson	0.2	D	7.7	10.7	7.6	4.5	4.7	D	20.5	4 345	294	356	10 043	1.1
New Kent	0.8	0.0	24.5	3.5	4.2	6.3	2.6	D	25.1	3 930	202	176	7 898	8.3
Northampton	23.3	0.0	3.1	5.8	D	4.8	D	19.0	19.2	3 560	295	644	7 322	0.3
Northumberland	4.0	D	11.9	20.8	D	6.6	4.0	3.4	17.9	4 610	377	256	9 120	1.4
Nottoway	2.0	D	3.5	5.4	2.6	5.9	2.8	D	50.4	3 795	242	600	6 717	1.0
Orange	3.6	D	5.5	11.9	D	7.7	8.6	4.1	23.2	8 430	243	542	14 871	1.9
Page	10.7	0.0	7.6	10.5	D	8.0	3.8	D	24.0	6 390	269	584	11 648	0.4
Patrick	1.4	0.0	4.2	25.3	6.5	7.4	D	12.5	18.2	5 545	303	536	10 100	0.2
Pittsylvania	[4]2.0	[4]D	[4]4.3	[4]21.8	[4]3.5	[4]8.8	[4]3.6	[4]14.3	[4]17.9	17 215	275	2 019	31 435	0.4
Powhatan	0.6	D	15.1	2.5	6.5	4.2	22.8	3.2	27.2	5 445	193	251	10 375	3.3
Prince Edward	0.7	D	3.4	1.3	2.7	10.0	3.2	D	32.7	4 745	208	888	9 289	1.6
Prince George	[5]0.0	[5]0.0	[5]D	[5]11.2	[5]D	[5]2.1	[5]D	[5]D	[5]63.6	5 880	158	490	12 281	1.9
Prince William	[6]-0.1	[6]D	[6]D	[6]3.7	[6]D	[6]8.6	[6]3.6	[6]D	[6]29.6	39 235	89	3 698	144 787	5.6
Pulaski	0.1	D	3.3	39.8	D	7.7	2.3	D	17.6	9 640	279	953	17 263	0.2
Rappahannock	-5.9	0.0	13.4	2.1	37.6	5.8	5.1	D	15.4	1 885	253	75	3 950	1.3
Richmond	4.0	0.0	6.9	4.7	D	4.8	D	D	35.3	1 930	216	229	3 905	1.4
Roanoke	[7]0.0	[7]0.3	[7]D	[7]17.4	[7]8.2	[7]6.3	[7]8.0	[7]D	[7]16.3	21 430	229	1 198	40 588	1.3
Rockbridge	[8]-0.5	[8]D	[8]5.8	[8]14.3	[8]D	[8]7.4	[8]D	[8]8.0	[8]23.1	6 020	270	493	11 268	1.0
Rockingham	[9]4.2	[9]D	[9]6.2	[9]18.0	[9]7.3	[9]6.8	[9]4.1	[9]11.7	[9]17.7	16 645	214	959	34 540	2.6
Russell	-0.4	8.4	8.3	1.6	12.5	7.7	4.4	D	20.4	8 755	310	1 457	13 405	-0.6
Scott	-2.3	0.0	2.7	18.6	D	9.9	D	13.3	28.0	7 260	321	1 212	11 868	-0.4
Shenandoah	1.4	D	6.4	24.3	7.3	6.8	3.9	8.4	15.7	10 490	246	652	21 067	0.9
Smyth	0.0	D	5.4	33.0	D	6.5	2.2	D	24.8	9 790	308	1 311	15 340	-0.6
Southampton	[10]6.5	[10]D	[10]3.5	[10]7.4	[10]D	[10]8.3	[10]D	[10]16.5	[10]31.9	4 205	231	476	7 552	0.9
Spotsylvania	[11]-0.2	[11]D	[11]6.8	[11]D	[11]10.9	[11]12.0	[11]5.6	[11]20.6	[11]17.4	18 350	144	1 255	46 242	2.1
Stafford	-0.1	D	5.7	1.5	12.0	5.6	13.6	5.6	40.1	14 240	104	955	46 526	5.8
Surry	-0.5	0.0	D	2.4	2.2	D	0.8	D	14.3	1 665	245	165	3 503	1.6
Sussex	5.2	D	3.3	2.5	D	5.4	1.3	D	40.8	2 570	218	442	4 717	0.5
Tazewell	0.1	9.3	4.9	9.8	4.5	12.0	4.5	D	19.7	13 075	296	1 948	20 677	-0.7
Warren	-0.9	0.0	16.9	9.4	3.7	7.6	4.0	10.6	15.7	7 285	189	624	16 123	1.0
Washington	[12]-0.1	[12]12.4	[12]D	[12]16.3	[12]4.2	[12]8.2	[12]3.8	[12]10.1	[12]15.3	15 755	288	1 594	25 725	0.5
Westmoreland	5.9	0.0	7.7	12.0	D	6.9	6.2	5.0	24.8	4 745	270	434	10 790	1.6
Wise	[13]-0.1	[13]17.3	[13]2.9	[13]2.4	[13]5.2	[13]9.0	[13]2.6	[13]14.3	[13]26.2	11 940	294	2 460	17 844	-0.6
Wythe	-0.3	0.9	3.9	23.5	3.2	11.1	3.7	12.1	22.8	8 220	280	773	14 189	0.8
York	[14]0.2	[14]0.4	[14]11.1	[14]D	[14]D	[14]8.8	[14]D	[14]5.8	[14]29.8	10 635	161	423	27 258	2.1
Independent cities														
Alexandria city	0.0	D	2.3	D	29.1	3.9	5.4	4.5	32.7	13 565	91	1 566	75 329	4.0
Bedford city	(15)	(15)	(15)	(15)	(15)	(15)	(15)	(15)	(15)	1 770	(15)	247	NA	NA
Bristol city	(12)	(12)	(12)	(12)	(12)	(12)	(12)	(12)	(12)	4 990	286	851	8 820	-0.1
Buena Vista city	(8)	(8)	(8)	(8)	(8)	(8)	(8)	(8)	(8)	1 585	237	198	2 920	-0.6
Charlottesville city	(16)	(16)	(16)	(16)	(16)	(16)	(16)	(16)	(16)	6 015	133	971	20 291	5.7
Chesapeake city	0.1	0.1	10.0	5.8	14.5	9.0	5.3	6.8	18.9	34 735	151	3 401	88 110	5.9
Colonial Heights city	(17)	(17)	(17)	(17)	(17)	(17)	(17)	(17)	(17)	4 300	243	342	7 803	-0.4
Covington city	(18)	(18)	(18)	(18)	(18)	(18)	(18)	(18)	(18)	1 875	321	273	3 039	-0.8
Danville city	(4)	(4)	(4)	(4)	(4)	(4)	(4)	(4)	(4)	12 365	289	2 520	22 345	-0.4
Emporia city	(19)	(19)	(19)	(19)	(19)	(19)	(19)	(19)	(19)	1 315	236	387	2 608	1.7
Fairfax city	(20)	(20)	(20)	(20)	(20)	(20)	(20)	(20)	(20)	3 320	137	238	8 810	1.6
Falls Church city	(20)	(20)	(20)	(20)	(20)	(20)	(20)	(20)	(20)	1 420	105	97	5 496	0.4
Franklin city	(10)	(10)	(10)	(10)	(10)	(10)	(10)	(10)	(10)	2 065	239	478	3 871	-0.5
Fredericksburg city	(11)	(11)	(11)	(11)	(11)	(11)	(11)	(11)	(11)	3 765	135	520	11 469	10.6
Galax city	(21)	(21)	(21)	(21)	(21)	(21)	(21)	(21)	(21)	2 160	308	343	3 232	-0.6
Hampton city	0.0	0.0	3.3	3.6	D	5.1	2.4	9.0	48.2	25 155	184	3 246	60 326	1.2
Harrisonburg city	(9)	(9)	(9)	(9)	(9)	(9)	(9)	(9)	(9)	5 250	102	747	18 065	3.6
Hopewell city	(5)	(5)	(5)	(5)	(5)	(5)	(5)	(5)	(5)	4 870	219	975	10 255	1.3
Lexington city	(8)	(8)	(8)	(8)	(8)	(8)	(8)	(8)	(8)	1 555	215	99	2 528	-0.6
Lynchburg city	(22)	(22)	(22)	(22)	(22)	(22)	(22)	(22)	(22)	15 405	198	2 474	32 349	1.0
Manassas city	(6)	(6)	(6)	(6)	(6)	(6)	(6)	(6)	(6)	3 950	95	402	13 381	1.9

1. Per 1,000 resident population estimated as of July 1 of the year shown. 3. Radford city is included with Montgomery county. 4. Danville city is included with Pittsylvania county. 5. Hopewell city is included with Prince George county. 6. Manassas and Manassas Park cities are included with Prince William county. 7. Salem city is included with Roanoke county. 8. Buena Vista and Lexington cities are included with Rockbridge county. 9. Harrisonburg city is included with Rockingham county. 10. Franklin city is included with Southhampton county. 11. Fredericksburg city is included with Spotsylvania county. 12. Bristol city included with Washington county. 13. Norton city is included with Wise county. 14. Poquoson city is included with York county. 15. Bedford city is included with Bedford county. 16. Charlottesville city is included with Albemarle county. 17. Petersburg and Colonial Heights cities are included with Dinwiddie county. 18. Covington city is included with Alleghany county. 19. Emporia city is included with Greensville county. 20. Fairfax city and Falls Church city are included with Fairfax county. 21. Galax city is included with Carroll county. 22. Lynchburg city is included with Campbell county.

STATE County	Housing units, 2009–2013: Occupied units: Total	Owner-occupied: Percent	Owner-occupied: Median value[1]	Median owner cost as a percent of income: With a mortgage	Median owner cost as a percent of income: Without a mortgage[2]	Renter-occupied: Median rent[3]	Renter-occupied: Median rent as a percent of income[2]	Substandard units[4] (percent)	Civilian labor force, 2014: Total	Percent change, 2013–2014	Unemployment: Total	Unemployment: Rate[5]	Civilian employment,[6] 2009–2013: Total	Percent: Management, business, science and arts	Percent: Construction, production, and maintenance occupations
	89	90	91	92	93	94	95	96	97	98	99	100	101	102	103
VIRGINIA—Cont'd															
Louisa	13 046	79.9	197 700	23.8	11.2	954	28.2	3.2	18 515	2.3	937	5.1	15 858	32.4	27.8
Lunenburg	4 572	75.3	100 400	25.0	12.5	681	37.7	1.9	5 378	0.7	320	6.0	4 507	26.9	26.9
Madison	5 024	80.3	240 900	25.4	12.1	854	33.0	1.6	7 309	1.0	294	4.0	6 359	31.4	25.6
Mathews	3 856	79.8	238 500	23.4	10.0	970	34.0	3.0	4 177	0.1	194	4.6	3 873	36.4	26.8
Mecklenburg	12 650	73.4	120 900	25.3	13.4	657	30.9	1.0	12 679	-1.0	982	7.7	12 356	27.9	26.8
Middlesex	4 400	82.0	247 100	24.5	10.2	770	29.1	1.0	5 066	-1.2	257	5.1	4 531	33.1	24.0
Montgomery	34 789	54.6	200 200	21.5	10.0	830	39.1	3.4	50 249	1.0	2 536	5.0	44 758	45.3	14.5
Nelson	6 404	75.8	192 900	26.2	10.0	709	24.9	1.9	7 519	2.0	364	4.8	6 569	34.2	24.1
New Kent	6 886	89.0	253 700	24.3	11.7	996	25.9	2.0	10 944	1.2	494	4.5	9 650	36.3	24.0
Northampton	5 149	68.6	168 800	23.9	13.7	672	28.9	2.0	6 080	0.6	452	7.4	5 007	34.0	30.1
Northumberland	5 691	85.0	239 000	30.9	11.3	803	34.5	2.3	5 671	-0.6	400	7.1	5 095	29.9	24.3
Nottoway	5 673	64.8	137 600	24.6	12.4	802	35.5	2.3	7 100	0.2	385	5.4	6 041	23.5	26.1
Orange	12 621	75.9	230 500	24.6	10.0	862	29.0	1.5	16 234	0.5	848	5.2	14 709	32.8	28.5
Page	9 623	72.0	180 200	23.4	12.5	695	30.8	2.1	11 922	-0.5	963	8.1	10 281	26.1	30.1
Patrick	7 846	77.0	110 500	23.5	11.0	527	29.2	2.1	7 764	-0.4	505	6.5	7 058	24.4	38.0
Pittsylvania	26 092	79.7	109 600	22.7	11.4	616	29.0	0.6	30 418	-0.2	1 916	6.3	27 492	25.8	34.9
Powhatan	9 544	88.7	269 700	23.2	10.4	1 040	31.9	3.9	13 761	1.2	623	4.5	12 562	39.6	18.9
Prince Edward	7 453	65.2	153 400	23.4	10.1	760	33.3	0.9	9 831	-1.8	771	7.8	8 983	29.5	22.5
Prince George	10 848	71.9	199 600	21.7	10.0	1 182	29.0	3.0	14 925	1.1	927	6.2	13 177	36.5	23.9
Prince William	132 442	72.1	321 400	23.7	10.0	1 477	30.4	1.7	232 150	0.3	11 151	4.8	212 154	43.6	16.4
Pulaski	14 875	72.7	133 900	21.9	10.0	591	29.8	1.7	16 871	-0.1	1 009	6.0	15 203	28.2	30.2
Rappahannock	3 261	78.3	394 800	25.9	13.8	966	28.9	1.3	3 925	0.0	183	4.7	3 630	37.8	21.5
Richmond	2 853	74.9	155 700	23.7	10.2	716	26.1	1.1	4 019	1.6	223	5.5	3 148	27.4	29.5
Roanoke	37 928	76.7	193 700	22.4	10.0	826	25.6	2.4	50 391	0.9	2 284	4.5	45 873	41.9	17.4
Rockbridge	9 234	73.2	179 500	25.2	10.2	695	29.3	3.2	10 241	-1.9	550	5.4	9 976	29.6	30.1
Rockingham	29 440	76.8	195 300	23.9	10.0	817	27.4	1.3	40 800	0.2	1 878	4.6	37 317	30.2	30.0
Russell	11 191	78.2	91 100	23.0	10.1	531	35.5	2.5	11 307	-2.8	901	8.0	10 707	26.9	35.1
Scott	9 692	77.0	91 000	19.1	10.0	496	28.7	1.8	9 998	-0.4	585	5.9	8 856	23.0	34.5
Shenandoah	17 397	70.5	205 300	24.3	11.1	782	30.7	1.4	21 300	1.5	1 063	5.0	19 741	26.9	33.3
Smyth	12 650	70.8	91 200	20.5	11.1	559	27.4	2.5	13 422	0.1	1 041	7.8	13 238	29.1	31.8
Southampton	6 708	71.8	150 000	23.4	11.7	734	31.2	1.3	9 157	-1.2	459	5.0	8 203	27.6	32.4
Spotsylvania	41 709	77.5	249 100	23.7	10.0	1 285	30.7	1.8	64 372	0.2	3 422	5.3	59 922	39.0	18.1
Stafford	42 178	76.9	299 300	23.7	10.0	1 428	30.7	3.9	66 378	0.2	3 483	5.2	61 307	45.8	15.1
Surry	2 602	79.9	161 600	23.6	12.2	687	24.8	1.1	3 684	1.3	224	6.1	3 266	21.1	37.4
Sussex	3 704	70.2	118 000	23.4	12.2	681	28.7	1.1	4 161	-0.5	309	7.4	3 514	22.0	31.6
Tazewell	18 294	73.0	88 000	21.5	11.6	560	28.7	2.1	17 303	-2.2	1 390	8.0	16 889	28.4	29.3
Warren	14 387	72.5	219 000	23.5	11.3	960	31.9	1.7	20 128	0.1	1 113	5.5	18 648	32.3	26.9
Washington	22 755	75.8	131 500	21.9	11.1	626	26.1	3.2	27 983	0.3	1 603	5.7	24 549	33.9	25.9
Westmoreland	7 130	77.9	180 900	24.8	11.7	873	31.1	2.1	9 073	-0.4	574	6.3	7 407	28.1	28.7
Wise	15 406	70.8	83 900	18.7	10.3	616	34.0	1.4	14 415	-4.5	1 351	9.4	14 455	27.6	30.5
Wythe	11 656	73.7	112 100	21.3	10.0	612	27.2	1.2	13 859	-1.1	885	6.4	13 158	28.1	30.6
York	24 071	75.1	316 800	22.8	10.1	1 349	29.2	3.4	31 977	0.2	1 603	5.0	29 359	49.0	15.6
Independent cities															
Alexandria city	65 369	43.3	476 700	22.4	11.5	1 501	28.1	0.0	94 209	0.4	3 528	3.7	88 419	58.0	8.6
Bedford city	2 800	58.7	146 400	23.7	15.9	636	38.5	1.4	NA	NA	NA	NA	2 672	35.3	20.4
Bristol city	7 674	58.6	110 800	23.9	12.9	623	28.6	1.8	7 870	0.3	502	6.4	7 074	29.1	20.4
Buena Vista city	2 738	66.1	118 900	23.6	11.3	637	36.8	1.6	3 313	-0.2	191	5.8	3 094	20.0	38.8
Charlottesville city	17 443	40.5	293 000	24.4	13.7	993	32.7	2.3	24 106	2.8	1 031	4.3	21 130	50.6	10.9
Chesapeake city	79 421	72.5	261 600	26.5	12.8	1 160	31.1	2.2	116 496	-0.1	6 134	5.3	105 110	39.8	19.9
Colonial Heights city	7 017	64.0	181 300	24.2	11.0	881	27.4	1.7	8 773	1.1	503	5.7	7 910	32.7	20.5
Covington city	2 545	72.9	66 900	26.6	12.4	641	27.4	2.2	2 505	-2.5	201	8.0	2 327	21.1	36.8
Danville city	18 659	54.4	87 800	23.3	12.2	589	31.6	2.3	19 714	-0.7	1 710	8.7	16 623	28.9	26.8
Emporia city	2 488	45.5	104 000	29.4	18.2	629	28.7	1.6	2 334	-2.2	192	8.2	2 179	31.1	27.7
Fairfax city	8 492	68.4	456 700	21.8	10.0	1 666	32.2	2.1	13 212	0.6	537	4.1	12 295	50.7	11.5
Falls Church city	5 020	59.4	660 900	21.5	11.6	1 588	27.5	3.1	7 884	0.4	283	3.6	7 238	68.7	4.3
Franklin city	3 551	42.5	186 700	26.9	15.5	746	39.6	1.4	3 620	-2.1	286	7.9	3 253	30.9	23.3
Fredericksburg city	9 779	38.1	314 300	23.2	11.7	1 045	33.1	3.3	13 814	0.2	827	6.0	12 127	40.0	12.9
Galax city	3 018	65.1	112 900	25.2	12.1	520	28.8	7.2	2 998	-0.8	216	7.2	2 791	25.4	33.5
Hampton city	52 511	60.1	195 400	25.5	13.1	998	35.2	5.4	65 819	-0.2	4 406	6.7	59 948	33.0	22.2
Harrisonburg city	15 701	36.2	208 100	22.1	10.9	852	34.3	2.8	24 121	0.2	1 466	6.1	21 844	31.6	22.8
Hopewell city	8 766	50.4	139 400	26.1	12.0	820	29.1	2.2	9 744	1.0	844	8.7	8 691	23.5	29.1
Lexington city	1 709	55.5	262 700	24.3	13.5	795	35.9	2.4	2 227	-1.5	177	7.9	2 039	41.5	6.7
Lynchburg city	28 556	52.7	145 800	23.2	12.0	735	33.6	6.9	35 955	0.4	2 283	6.3	32 753	36.2	15.3
Manassas city	12 072	65.2	245 000	23.3	13.9	1 328	34.5	2.2	22 330	0.2	1 103	4.9	20 228	32.8	22.0

1. Specified owner-occupied units. 2. A value of 10.0 represents 10 percent or less; a value of 50.0 represents 50 percent or more. 3. Specified renter-occupied units.
4. Overcrowded or lacking complete plumbing facilities. 5. Percent of civilian labor force. 6. Persons 16 years old and over.

STATE County	Private nonfarm establishments, employment and payroll, 2013									Agriculture, 2012			
		Employment						Annual payroll		Farms			
											Percent with:		
	Number of establish-ments	Total	Health care and social assistance	Manufac-turing	Retail trade	Finance and insurance	Professional, scientific, and technical services	Total (mil dol)	Average per employee (dollars)	Number	Fewer than 50 acres	500 acres or more	Farm operators whose principal occu-pation is farming (percent)
	104	105	106	107	108	109	110	111	112	113	114	115	116
VIRGINIA—Cont'd													
Louisa	539	6 385	281	1 203	1 062	118	159	289	45 325	485	39.6	8.2	40.6
Lunenburg	177	1 511	256	431	213	D	47	48	31 557	371	20.2	9.7	46.9
Madison	273	2 640	D	233	892	24	54	81	30 693	522	36.2	10.3	49.6
Mathews	169	1 068	179	D	215	21	D	23	21 696	55	72.7	5.5	47.3
Mecklenburg	786	9 447	1 685	1 394	1 714	275	279	271	28 694	527	20.5	12.0	44.8
Middlesex	323	2 138	390	D	485	61	155	58	26 908	73	43.8	12.3	61.6
Montgomery	1 935	28 942	3 965	5 098	4 988	842	2 131	1 021	35 291	603	39.5	6.6	39.6
Nelson	378	3 062	237	391	299	63	138	79	25 784	455	29.0	5.9	36.0
New Kent	339	2 726	662	110	434	23	D	77	28 330	137	52.6	5.1	49.6
Northampton	317	2 832	814	D	476	65	57	83	29 199	147	40.8	24.5	57.1
Northumberland	334	1 682	85	340	312	69	79	54	31 888	98	39.8	27.6	64.3
Nottoway	293	3 712	D	379	614	119	126	94	25 440	356	31.2	6.5	56.2
Orange	657	5 984	426	884	968	147	299	206	34 379	547	35.5	7.5	47.5
Page	410	3 954	505	D	732	D	172	113	28 535	545	45.0	5.3	56.7
Patrick	294	3 760	616	1 330	576	84	D	101	26 755	566	35.5	3.7	40.6
Pittsylvania	816	8 074	1 196	1 877	841	119	170	234	28 996	1 354	25.2	10.1	56.6
Powhatan	650	4 426	265	121	729	132	242	152	34 379	250	42.0	5.2	48.4
Prince Edward	540	6 580	1 644	127	1 454	194	114	192	29 161	413	28.8	8.5	32.4
Prince George	466	7 999	237	817	841	97	747	296	37 008	167	32.9	9.6	59.3
Prince William	7 386	94 198	9 139	1 504	21 705	2 066	10 214	3 711	39 400	330	68.2	4.8	53.0
Pulaski	606	10 917	989	4 535	1 600	168	D	384	35 147	445	38.7	11.5	42.2
Rappahannock	183	1 012	46	37	165	11	83	31	30 960	397	46.6	7.3	51.9
Richmond	176	1 920	769	127	244	46	D	51	26 563	90	34.4	21.1	54.4
Roanoke	2 015	28 903	5 161	2 992	3 626	4 222	1 369	1 061	36 702	280	52.9	4.3	44.3
Rockbridge	434	4 390	286	D	1 283	83	D	117	26 617	833	28.3	8.5	42.4
Rockingham	1 429	26 765	4 520	7 334	1 801	389	524	1 073	40 087	1 902	43.2	2.8	54.6
Russell	483	5 758	1 218	D	938	218	D	201	34 950	995	34.8	7.1	41.5
Scott	298	3 350	569	774	644	D	D	110	32 959	1 292	33.7	3.0	41.4
Shenandoah	870	11 204	1 383	3 146	1 615	304	287	358	31 988	980	45.7	4.9	50.1
Smyth	517	9 011	2 260	2 892	1 206	153	D	282	31 280	792	40.8	9.2	41.2
Southampton	226	1 746	D	498	241	21	D	52	29 955	335	26.3	31.6	60.0
Spotsylvania	2 329	27 727	2 944	1 595	7 062	561	2 331	1 019	36 764	369	56.9	5.4	43.6
Stafford	2 144	29 297	3 436	825	4 777	D	3 738	1 141	38 942	215	62.3	1.4	41.9
Surry	74	D	11	D	47	D	D	D	D	127	43.3	21.3	50.4
Sussex	191	1 991	379	D	319	D	D	62	31 135	123	29.3	26.8	61.8
Tazewell	1 088	13 482	2 373	1 356	3 378	638	430	432	32 025	584	31.8	15.6	43.5
Warren	776	9 701	1 294	924	1 703	230	283	313	32 258	346	58.1	5.8	43.1
Washington	1 176	16 890	2 511	3 854	3 331	D	690	587	34 749	1 602	48.3	4.2	39.7
Westmoreland	324	2 399	203	589	409	77	159	61	25 519	152	18.4	21.7	50.7
Wise	773	10 295	1 524	182	2 173	236	430	386	37 494	165	49.7	6.1	32.7
Wythe	689	9 454	1 251	2 009	2 129	228	203	313	33 067	952	34.2	8.3	47.8
York	1 407	16 731	1 807	241	3 847	424	1 431	513	30 649	47	63.8	2.1	70.2
Independent cities													
Alexandria city	4 640	83 411	7 937	1 118	7 526	2 914	18 295	4 832	57 928	NA	NA	NA	NA
Bedford city	315	3 824	879	654	732	126	117	113	29 530	NA	NA	NA	NA
Bristol city	621	11 042	656	1 469	1 998	340	226	470	42 551	NA	NA	NA	NA
Buena Vista city	112	1 926	138	1 036	89	37	23	68	35 480	NA	NA	NA	NA
Charlottesville city	2 013	31 317	8 953	514	3 735	777	2 455	1 517	48 425	NA	NA	NA	NA
Chesapeake city	5 328	86 962	9 474	4 032	15 086	3 877	7 846	3 366	38 709	253	71.1	8.7	44.7
Colonial Heights city	660	9 689	1 566	D	3 435	273	451	226	23 366	NA	NA	NA	NA
Covington city	228	3 880	176	D	D	93	50	183	47 197	NA	NA	NA	NA
Danville city	1 330	24 043	5 326	4 509	4 288	883	593	781	32 502	NA	NA	NA	NA
Emporia city	236	3 930	1 183	D	D	D	76	110	27 868	NA	NA	NA	NA
Fairfax city	2 207	29 657	3 671	166	5 802	1 254	6 694	1 515	51 080	NA	NA	NA	NA
Falls Church city	865	9 487	1 633	D	1 051	200	1 410	419	44 159	NA	NA	NA	NA
Franklin city	289	3 583	1 222	37	1 048	194	D	97	27 038	NA	NA	NA	NA
Fredericksburg city	1 313	20 593	5 609	260	4 192	610	1 558	792	38 446	NA	NA	NA	NA
Galax city	300	5 076	1 579	840	1 176	116	D	124	24 343	NA	NA	NA	NA
Hampton city	2 376	40 712	7 932	2 392	6 773	1 066	4 008	1 549	38 059	NA	NA	NA	NA
Harrisonburg city	1 559	20 777	2 894	2 193	5 510	892	868	704	29 608	NA	NA	NA	NA
Hopewell city	415	5 985	1 225	D	622	123	D	298	49 766	NA	NA	NA	NA
Lexington city	287	3 828	656	D	407	105	120	138	36 064	NA	NA	NA	NA
Lynchburg city	2 196	55 822	10 104	8 654	7 961	2 870	3 496	2 306	41 303	NA	NA	NA	NA
Manassas city	1 416	21 046	3 487	3 903	2 637	437	3 206	1 210	57 475	NA	NA	NA	NA

STATE County	Agriculture, 2012 (cont.) — Land in farms: Acreage (1,000)	Land in farms: Percent change, 2007–2012	Land in farms: Acres: Average size of farm	Land in farms: Acres: Total irrigated (1,000)	Land in farms: Acres: Total cropland (1,000)	Value of land and buildings (dollars): Average per farm	Value of land and buildings (dollars): Average per acre	Value of machinery and equipment, average per farm (dollars)	Value of products sold: Total (mil dol)	Value of products sold: Average per farm (dollars)	Value of products sold: Percent from: Crops	Value of products sold: Percent from: Livestock and poultry products	Percent of farms with sales of: $10,000 or more	Percent of farms with sales of: $100,000 or more	Government payments: Total ($1,000)	Government payments: Percent of farms
	117	118	119	120	121	122	123	124	125	126	127	128	129	130	131	132
VIRGINIA—Cont'd																
Louisa	80	2.2	165	0.3	30.1	946 557	5 723	61 971	14.5	29 928	46.9	53.1	36.3	6.0	784	24.5
Lunenburg	83	-0.6	223	0.4	27.7	530 593	2 380	77 668	18.5	49 846	73.2	26.8	33.7	7.3	1 085	33.4
Madison	107	4.1	205	0.1	40.1	1 294 623	6 316	74 799	29.0	55 517	39.8	60.2	51.1	9.2	389	18.2
Mathews	5	5.3	84	0.0	3.2	523 182	6 193	57 909	2.4	43 691	93.0	6.9	32.7	7.3	67	12.7
Mecklenburg	145	-7.5	276	2.8	50.8	710 928	2 575	100 488	42.9	81 395	82.5	17.5	35.9	11.6	1 229	35.5
Middlesex	19	8.3	263	0.5	13.7	1 013 082	3 855	139 068	11.3	154 233	92.5	7.5	38.4	19.2	384	39.7
Montgomery	107	20.0	178	0.3	31.6	867 716	4 878	68 212	23.7	39 315	28.2	71.8	34.7	6.6	219	12.1
Nelson	80	9.3	176	0.9	22.4	805 229	4 581	63 396	15.8	34 741	65.6	34.4	40.7	4.4	116	10.5
New Kent	20	-3.2	144	D	10.5	794 927	5 525	58 759	7.0	51 117	95.9	4.1	24.1	8.0	381	19.0
Northampton	56	-12.1	381	6.3	42.8	1 646 782	4 319	259 687	93.1	633 054	66.0	34.0	73.5	47.6	1 892	50.3
Northumberland	43	-2.5	442	0.0	33.5	1 324 908	3 001	220 061	21.4	217 929	98.3	1.7	60.2	33.7	1 104	60.2
Nottoway	62	-5.7	173	0.1	22.6	539 621	3 120	75 242	48.7	136 778	12.7	87.3	34.6	9.6	413	29.8
Orange	105	0.2	192	0.6	40.5	1 292 497	6 746	95 737	90.6	165 589	71.7	28.3	42.6	9.3	1 081	16.5
Page	71	10.5	131	1.0	28.2	767 554	5 881	84 549	141.1	258 894	4.4	95.6	51.6	25.3	472	17.2
Patrick	79	-1.1	140	0.1	22.9	466 200	3 336	52 781	16.5	29 125	45.3	54.7	36.2	3.0	555	19.6
Pittsylvania	287	4.7	212	3.7	100.4	515 637	2 430	80 956	86.9	64 211	42.5	57.5	38.3	10.0	3 886	36.0
Powhatan	32	7.7	128	0.1	10.6	735 120	5 729	48 592	10.0	40 036	39.1	60.9	25.2	4.0	128	16.0
Prince Edward	79	-4.1	191	0.1	19.7	612 015	3 203	58 479	16.5	39 993	11.6	88.4	29.5	4.8	641	51.6
Prince George	37	-18.2	220	0.0	19.0	922 305	4 202	102 784	10.8	64 449	91.8	8.2	34.7	11.4	903	47.9
Prince William	36	8.6	108	1.0	19.0	953 252	8 827	70 982	12.0	36 467	48.3	51.7	26.1	7.0	240	8.5
Pulaski	97	28.0	217	0.0	26.7	667 404	3 074	78 555	28.1	63 234	8.5	91.5	44.0	7.9	337	11.0
Rappahannock	63	-3.5	158	0.1	17.3	1 335 914	8 443	54 128	9.3	23 378	39.5	60.5	33.0	7.6	147	9.1
Richmond	32	-13.3	360	0.1	22.3	1 036 744	2 882	158 744	15.5	171 856	94.7	5.3	55.6	26.7	684	63.3
Roanoke	31	7.8	112	0.1	7.6	480 689	4 275	47 568	4.1	14 786	D	D	20.0	3.2	13	8.6
Rockbridge	168	21.7	202	0.1	42.1	868 321	4 296	57 385	31.8	38 148	21.9	78.1	41.3	5.3	649	14.3
Rockingham	222	-4.7	117	5.6	100.5	823 606	7 055	88 252	659.0	346 475	7.2	92.8	58.4	35.0	2 741	15.9
Russell	188	23.8	189	0.0	34.0	409 282	2 171	53 826	32.2	32 326	9.1	90.9	36.3	7.2	2 525	32.9
Scott	158	2.9	123	0.1	33.4	254 430	2 076	48 673	14.1	10 892	30.1	69.9	25.3	1.3	999	38.0
Shenandoah	134	-5.5	136	0.7	52.7	760 234	5 580	74 039	128.8	131 394	15.1	84.9	43.2	15.0	1 242	13.7
Smyth	167	30.9	210	0.0	34.3	586 822	2 789	64 580	58.0	73 184	6.6	93.4	43.4	13.8	760	38.1
Southampton	154	-4.8	459	3.2	94.3	1 224 988	2 668	183 934	79.2	236 310	84.6	15.4	53.7	31.9	6 268	75.8
Spotsylvania	42	-19.2	114	0.1	18.7	700 862	6 130	85 612	11.0	29 800	36.4	63.6	27.4	3.3	331	16.0
Stafford	15	-23.0	71	0.0	6.6	650 702	9 168	59 926	2.7	12 740	49.0	51.0	22.3	1.4	71	11.2
Surry	45	9.8	355	1.2	34.0	1 272 142	3 581	126 425	27.7	218 291	69.9	30.1	53.5	23.6	1 198	46.5
Sussex	64	-13.4	522	1.4	39.4	1 189 211	2 277	199 992	37.3	303 065	D	D	56.1	26.8	2 190	71.5
Tazewell	150	-2.3	257	0.0	29.1	569 505	2 215	63 351	27.0	46 267	7.2	92.8	42.3	10.8	572	21.2
Warren	48	0.8	139	0.0	15.8	990 098	7 138	60 844	5.7	16 572	37.4	62.6	24.6	2.6	40	3.2
Washington	192	-3.4	120	0.2	54.2	471 998	3 936	51 363	76.5	47 753	8.7	91.3	35.3	8.1	4 522	38.1
Westmoreland	59	-7.2	391	1.6	36.0	1 396 757	3 576	161 632	35.8	235 250	85.9	14.1	65.8	32.2	1 184	52.6
Wise	26	16.9	157	0.0	3.5	432 818	2 756	42 079	D	D	D	D	20.0	0.6	25	6.1
Wythe	174	9.4	183	0.1	49.5	619 529	3 386	69 486	51.4	54 034	13.0	87.0	47.7	10.7	840	20.7
York	3	116.4	60	0.0	D	298 723	4 991	77 489	2.4	50 830	86.9	13.1	29.8	10.6	5	6.4
Independent cities																
Alexandria city	NA	NA	NA	NA	NA	NA	NA	NA	NA	NA	NA	NA	NA	NA	NA	NA
Bedford city	NA	NA	NA	NA	NA	NA	NA	NA	NA	NA	NA	NA	NA	NA	NA	NA
Bristol city	NA	NA	NA	NA	NA	NA	NA	NA	NA	NA	NA	NA	NA	NA	NA	NA
Buena Vista city	NA	NA	NA	NA	NA	NA	NA	NA	NA	NA	NA	NA	NA	NA	NA	NA
Charlottesville city	NA	NA	NA	NA	NA	NA	NA	NA	NA	NA	NA	NA	NA	NA	NA	NA
Chesapeake city	45	-11.7	178	0.3	37.0	776 672	4 355	98 379	40.5	160 028	D	D	33.2	13.8	570	24.1
Colonial Heights city	NA	NA	NA	NA	NA	NA	NA	NA	NA	NA	NA	NA	NA	NA	NA	NA
Covington city	NA	NA	NA	NA	NA	NA	NA	NA	NA	NA	NA	NA	NA	NA	NA	NA
Danville city	NA	NA	NA	NA	NA	NA	NA	NA	NA	NA	NA	NA	NA	NA	NA	NA
Emporia city	NA	NA	NA	NA	NA	NA	NA	NA	NA	NA	NA	NA	NA	NA	NA	NA
Fairfax city	NA	NA	NA	NA	NA	NA	NA	NA	NA	NA	NA	NA	NA	NA	NA	NA
Falls Church city	NA	NA	NA	NA	NA	NA	NA	NA	NA	NA	NA	NA	NA	NA	NA	NA
Franklin city	NA	NA	NA	NA	NA	NA	NA	NA	NA	NA	NA	NA	NA	NA	NA	NA
Fredericksburg city	NA	NA	NA	NA	NA	NA	NA	NA	NA	NA	NA	NA	NA	NA	NA	NA
Galax city	NA	NA	NA	NA	NA	NA	NA	NA	NA	NA	NA	NA	NA	NA	NA	NA
Hampton city	NA	NA	NA	NA	NA	NA	NA	NA	NA	NA	NA	NA	NA	NA	NA	NA
Harrisonburg city	NA	NA	NA	NA	NA	NA	NA	NA	NA	NA	NA	NA	NA	NA	NA	NA
Hopewell city	NA	NA	NA	NA	NA	NA	NA	NA	NA	NA	NA	NA	NA	NA	NA	NA
Lexington city	NA	NA	NA	NA	NA	NA	NA	NA	NA	NA	NA	NA	NA	NA	NA	NA
Lynchburg city	NA	NA	NA	NA	NA	NA	NA	NA	NA	NA	NA	NA	NA	NA	NA	NA
Manassas city	NA	NA	NA	NA	NA	NA	NA	NA	NA	NA	NA	NA	NA	NA	NA	NA

STATE County	Water use, 2010		Wholesale trade,[1] 2007				Retail trade,[2] 2007				Real estate and rental and leasing,[2] 2007			
	Total water withdrawn (mil gal/day)	Gallons withdrawn per person per day	Number of establish-ments	Number of employees	Sales (mil dol)	Annual payroll (mil dol)	Number of establish-ments	Number of employees	Sales (mil dol)	Annual payroll (mil dol)	Number of establish-ments	Number of employees	Receipts (mil dol)	Annual payroll (mil dol)
	133	134	135	136	137	138	139	140	141	142	143	144	145	146
VIRGINIA—Cont'd														
Louisa	1 823.7	55 010	13	216	102.9	10.4	71	601	153.8	11.4	22	106	25.1	4.8
Lunenburg	5.2	406	5	144	45.7	3.1	43	300	54.7	5.4	4	6	1.2	0.1
Madison	2.5	185	9	32	8.7	0.9	52	504	112.9	11.3	6	21	1.9	0.2
Mathews	2.1	231	6	D	D	D	35	268	59.4	5.3	16	D	D	D
Mecklenburg	7.9	241	36	256	74.7	6.0	180	1 822	406.3	34.1	39	155	15.9	3.7
Middlesex	1.9	171	19	162	31.5	5.7	65	460	94.5	9.9	23	50	5.4	1.0
Montgomery	33.1	350	49	368	97.3	14.2	357	5 195	1 102.6	109.8	96	499	83.4	13.8
Nelson	5.9	395	5	7	6.7	0.2	58	345	75.6	6.1	17	51	6.6	1.6
New Kent	30.0	1 628	6	D	D	D	37	395	135.2	7.9	20	36	4.5	0.9
Northampton	4.2	335	16	149	59.3	3.4	80	681	135.1	11.7	16	41	5.9	0.8
Northumberland	4.2	340	13	76	29.7	2.1	52	421	90.2	7.9	18	44	6.0	0.6
Nottoway	2.4	149	12	125	80.2	3.2	65	754	137.3	14.5	8	25	2.1	0.5
Orange	5.6	166	12	219	212.2	12.1	112	1 031	280.3	23.4	29	59	6.7	1.7
Page	4.0	166	8	60	9.6	1.6	78	773	167.4	15.0	14	53	9.4	1.6
Patrick	3.4	183	6	46	19.0	1.7	49	559	148.6	11.5	11	18	2.2	0.2
Pittsylvania	7.6	119	33	648	247.6	15.6	157	1 083	269.3	19.5	20	84	5.7	1.2
Powhatan	4.3	153	28	158	46.6	6.1	75	604	159.3	15.5	26	76	11.2	2.3
Prince Edward	4.9	209	20	148	43.1	4.6	121	1 473	350.6	30.3	21	88	9.7	1.6
Prince George	17.4	487	20	718	502.6	24.1	61	559	197.8	13.5	19	58	5.3	1.2
Prince William	66.2	165	159	2 119	1 750.6	112.7	1 119	19 373	4 948.9	465.4	334	1 417	284.8	46.3
Pulaski	6.8	194	15	136	39.2	4.5	122	1 498	317.3	30.7	25	81	8.8	1.4
Rappahannock	0.8	110	2	D	D	D	30	142	21.9	3.0	10	10	1.2	0.2
Richmond	0.8	84	12	D	D	D	43	301	75.6	6.3	10	40	1.5	0.4
Roanoke	17.2	186	99	1 023	504.7	43.5	293	3 973	835.7	86.9	110	491	70.0	13.9
Rockbridge	5.0	226	11	92	32.7	3.0	82	1 253	338.4	25.3	15	33	2.8	0.5
Rockingham	38.0	498	61	990	539.9	41.6	225	1 985	455.5	42.0	47	939	104.3	28.7
Russell	11.5	399	21	82	36.5	2.0	94	966	255.6	20.6	10	39	3.5	0.7
Scott	2.2	94	8	D	D	D	90	837	197.2	14.4	9	D	D	D
Shenandoah	30.5	727	22	312	347.2	11.6	164	1 875	494.2	37.6	32	169	15.3	2.6
Smyth	19.8	614	14	130	52.7	4.2	127	1 337	300.3	28.4	18	88	7.9	2.4
Southampton	8.6	461	14	117	70.5	4.2	37	267	57.9	4.8	8	21	2.3	0.5
Spotsylvania	13.9	113	66	845	430.4	38.0	416	7 219	2 148.5	177.8	106	645	73.8	19.6
Stafford	13.7	106	60	1 370	1 249.9	60.4	267	3 737	930.3	84.8	95	376	69.5	11.0
Surry	1 908.5	270 397	1	D	D	D	14	56	12.6	1.0	3	D	D	D
Sussex	2.1	171	10	D	D	D	50	314	68.9	6.0	6	13	1.7	0.3
Tazewell	5.0	110	63	D	D	D	240	3 396	811.8	67.0	57	265	23.2	5.4
Warren	11.4	303	13	88	18.7	2.5	134	1 311	369.6	30.2	31	135	12.5	2.7
Washington	59.9	1 091	43	417	279.6	20.7	230	2 940	701.6	59.0	48	131	15.4	3.1
Westmoreland	4.8	273	13	79	38.9	2.8	47	479	100.4	9.3	21	57	4.7	1.2
Wise	5.3	127	35	512	496.1	22.6	205	2 077	438.6	38.0	26	80	23.0	2.6
Wythe	16.6	567	19	318	105.5	10.8	160	2 130	908.1	45.4	32	235	21.4	4.8
York	781.4	11 936	49	262	149.7	8.9	243	3 759	852.2	84.2	71	267	36.0	7.1
Independent cities														
Alexandria city	0.0	0	91	1 262	525.7	65.2	528	8 052	2 353.8	232.5	229	2 484	811.8	127.1
Bedford city	0.0	0	4	85	28.9	2.7	56	553	124.9	10.7	14	44	5.1	1.0
Bristol city	0.0	0	34	883	318.8	28.8	172	1 884	343.5	34.2	27	D	D	D
Buena Vista city	0.2	24	1	D	D	D	25	162	30.6	3.1	6	18	0.7	0.2
Charlottesville city	0.2	4	55	473	203.4	20.4	349	3 880	699.4	78.1	98	557	86.5	19.7
Chesapeake city	544.0	2 448	239	3 428	2 123.3	156.1	869	16 523	3 977.8	345.5	273	1 355	274.7	49.0
Colonial Heights city	0.0	1	8	86	28.4	2.6	204	4 064	761.1	71.4	26	134	22.6	4.5
Covington city	2.0	330	5	38	13.0	1.1	70	491	104.6	9.5	10	21	1.8	0.4
Danville city	7.2	168	55	462	204.1	18.8	330	4 395	892.2	81.8	66	332	41.4	8.8
Emporia city	0.0	7	4	D	D	D	64	705	131.6	13.2	15	50	5.0	0.9
Fairfax city	0.1	5	48	265	192.3	13.0	289	6 460	1 884.0	178.4	80	241	36.0	9.8
Falls Church city	0.0	2	16	D	D	D	104	1 129	288.0	35.4	30	195	58.1	6.3
Franklin city	1.1	122	6	50	25.5	1.4	63	900	186.3	19.5	17	65	8.0	1.6
Fredericksburg city	0.3	14	32	D	D	D	280	4 436	1 052.1	94.6	77	403	70.0	15.4
Galax city	1.9	275	5	48	36.9	1.6	78	1 085	227.5	22.5	13	62	10.3	1.5
Hampton city	0.3	2	60	800	288.9	33.5	436	7 295	1 805.7	162.3	115	873	113.0	24.2
Harrisonburg city	0.4	8	66	1 030	378.5	42.7	376	6 265	1 465.3	158.1	80	346	68.3	8.8
Hopewell city	130.5	5 775	12	130	58.1	8.8	84	696	173.9	15.1	22	98	19.3	3.2
Lexington city	0.0	0	3	6	1.9	0.2	48	447	86.8	9.8	21	50	6.1	1.2
Lynchburg city	0.2	2	82	1 125	541.5	43.2	419	7 266	1 665.1	151.2	107	466	72.4	15.3
Manassas city	0.1	2	44	D	D	D	187	2 635	921.2	85.3	59	230	41.7	8.3

1. Merchant wholesalers, except manufacturers' sales branches and offices. 2. Employer establishments.

STATE County	Professional, scientific, and technical services,[1] 2007				Manufacturing, 2007				Accommodation and food services, 2007			
	Number of establish-ments	Number of employees	Receipts (mil dol)	Annual payroll (mil dol)	Number of establish-ments	Number of employees	Receipts (mil dol)	Annual payroll (mil dol)	Number of establish-ments	Number of employees	Sales (mil dol)	Annual payroll (mil dol)
	147	148	149	150	151	152	153	154	155	156	157	158
VIRGINIA—Cont'd												
Louisa	55	188	19.2	7.0	34	1 377	435.9	62.1	22	357	13.9	3.8
Lunenburg	10	D	D	D	8	778	D	21.6	10	D	D	D
Madison	31	D	D	D	NA	NA	NA	NA	16	210	10.1	3.0
Mathews	22	54	3.7	1.6	NA	NA	NA	NA	15	D	D	D
Mecklenburg	48	295	21.7	8.1	31	1 847	281.0	47.7	76	1 111	43.5	12.5
Middlesex	30	130	7.8	3.8	NA	NA	NA	NA	23	255	8.7	2.6
Montgomery	234	D	D	D	55	3 097	838.1	141.9	187	4 037	148.3	44.8
Nelson	39	D	D	D	NA	NA	NA	NA	20	152	6.2	1.6
New Kent	20	52	3.0	1.1	NA	NA	NA	NA	23	211	9.7	2.2
Northampton	22	D	D	D	9	D	D	D	37	494	23.6	7.3
Northumberland	29	D	D	D	23	595	D	17.5	20	116	5.2	1.4
Nottoway	23	125	7.5	2.7	NA	NA	NA	NA	27	379	11.1	3.0
Orange	70	311	34.0	13.0	21	947	222.2	36.0	51	668	26.0	7.1
Page	27	194	11.4	4.9	15	868	204.1	23.2	57	679	35.4	9.2
Patrick	17	D	D	D	42	1 823	248.5	51.1	22	152	6.6	1.5
Pittsylvania	49	D	D	D	53	2 441	752.1	81.3	43	449	15.3	4.3
Powhatan	56	185	20.1	8.9	NA	NA	NA	NA	29	384	17.6	4.0
Prince Edward	30	D	D	D	NA	NA	NA	NA	51	994	40.0	11.1
Prince George	36	144	18.4	7.2	22	1 330	783.8	61.0	28	426	23.1	4.9
Prince William	918	D	D	D	120	2 548	563.6	121.6	568	10 617	537.9	148.4
Pulaski	47	D	D	D	49	6 611	2 797.1	305.5	70	917	40.7	10.0
Rappahannock	31	D	D	D	NA	NA	NA	NA	16	253	20.0	5.5
Richmond	13	D	D	D	NA	NA	NA	NA	11	D	D	D
Roanoke	190	D	D	D	67	3 769	896.1	155.4	128	2 668	112.7	32.7
Rockbridge	26	93	8.2	2.9	27	1 221	326.0	39.0	59	875	49.2	13.7
Rockingham	83	D	D	D	87	7 288	5 437.5	296.8	82	2 042	62.1	27.0
Russell	34	D	D	D	15	1 219	192.9	28.0	34	420	15.6	4.2
Scott	23	94	5.6	1.7	8	768	451.5	30.0	21	315	11.6	3.4
Shenandoah	77	D	D	D	39	5 034	1 058.1	160.9	71	1 157	50.1	15.0
Smyth	34	D	D	D	47	3 870	777.2	138.7	53	679	24.1	6.6
Southampton	11	D	D	D	14	1 917	831.4	112.2	9	D	D	D
Spotsylvania	217	1 387	228.3	78.2	64	2 164	496.4	88.8	190	3 542	169.8	47.9
Stafford	284	D	D	D	46	727	140.8	25.3	179	3 324	140.3	38.8
Surry	5	20	1.9	0.5	NA	NA	NA	NA	2	D	D	D
Sussex	8	D	D	D	NA	NA	NA	NA	14	284	15.7	4.0
Tazewell	71	D	D	D	61	1 485	354.5	D	59	1 368	52.2	15.0
Warren	77	477	36.6	17.4	24	1 002	D	41.2	67	837	41.3	11.4
Washington	110	742	49.6	24.7	74	4 862	1 359.5	171.4	91	1 505	59.2	16.7
Westmoreland	28	130	13.7	7.1	14	573	199.6	19.1	35	426	14.2	4.1
Wise	50	383	39.3	13.7	NA	NA	NA	NA	58	1 040	40.1	10.4
Wythe	42	149	16.8	6.2	44	2 009	567.4	73.2	76	1 385	63.2	17.5
York	153	1 461	184.8	74.2	39	592	D	31.7	134	3 614	187.4	50.9
Independent cities												
Alexandria city	1 166	D	D	D	88	1 483	284.5	56.3	355	6 961	471.7	135.1
Bedford city	31	D	D	D	23	1 204	D	40.3	26	442	15.4	4.7
Bristol city	43	276	21.2	11.6	32	1 673	659.8	62.1	82	2 053	76.6	23.1
Buena Vista city	8	D	D	D	15	988	202.8	37.4	13	D	D	D
Charlottesville city	290	D	D	D	51	1 589	677.1	79.1	261	5 617	303.6	85.8
Chesapeake city	485	D	D	D	139	4 487	1 437.1	200.1	431	8 991	369.8	105.5
Colonial Heights city	56	466	31.4	12.6	NA	NA	NA	NA	81	1 768	76.1	19.5
Covington city	21	D	D	D	8	D	D	D	21	D	D	D
Danville city	76	D	D	D	43	4 485	1 275.9	212.7	140	2 741	110.3	30.0
Emporia city	17	D	D	D	11	1 074	311.5	34.5	25	566	24.2	7.0
Fairfax city	655	D	D	D	NA	NA	NA	NA	150	2 521	140.3	36.8
Falls Church city	158	D	D	D	14	D	D	D	101	872	56.3	14.6
Franklin city	16	D	D	D	NA	NA	NA	NA	27	802	22.6	6.7
Fredericksburg city	166	D	D	D	NA	NA	NA	NA	178	4 003	171.6	53.4
Galax city	23	157	12.2	4.7	17	1 935	204.1	40.4	38	632	22.5	6.9
Hampton city	280	D	D	D	77	2 790	522.4	122.0	233	5 888	233.6	69.2
Harrisonburg city	150	D	D	D	47	2 824	746.3	103.1	175	4 284	168.6	46.7
Hopewell city	34	328	27.8	15.8	14	1 297	1 496.0	98.0	56	923	47.8	11.9
Lexington city	28	D	D	D	NA	NA	NA	NA	52	655	31.3	7.8
Lynchburg city	203	D	D	D	96	9 486	2 801.6	500.1	234	5 226	190.0	58.3
Manassas city	218	D	D	D	41	4 038	1 408.7	340.5	101	1 307	75.6	19.0

1. Establishment subject to federal tax.

STATE County	Health care and social assistance, 2007				Other services, 2007				Nonemployer businesses, 2013		Value of residential construction authorized by building permits, 2014	
	Number of establish-ments	Number of employees	Receipts (mil dol)	Annual payroll (mil dol)	Number of establish-ments	Number of employees	Receipts (mil dol)	Annual payroll (mil dol)	Number	Receipts (mil dol)	New Construction ($1,000)	Number of housing units
	159	160	161	162	163	164	165	166	167	168	169	170
VIRGINIA—Cont'd												
Louisa	23	D	D	D	45	232	16.8	4.8	2 112	76.6	35 820	168
Lunenburg	17	237	9.3	4.2	16	D	D	D	550	20.1	2 698	13
Madison	23	318	13.8	6.0	19	64	7.6	2.6	1 085	36.2	7 410	31
Mathews	11	D	D	D	12	D	D	D	824	30.5	5 788	25
Mecklenburg	75	1 807	149.4	58.5	71	328	21.1	5.8	1 626	61.9	11 422	60
Middlesex	20	D	D	D	36	108	7.5	2.2	971	40.6	8 153	39
Montgomery	213	4 007	427.0	162.2	159	816	249.3	18.0	4 825	198.4	46 302	233
Nelson	19	230	13.3	6.2	24	135	10.0	3.8	1 247	46.5	14 449	52
New Kent	18	D	D	D	28	103	8.9	3.3	1 427	54.2	27 868	162
Northampton	42	1 041	83.2	34.6	24	60	5.1	1.1	991	36.4	9 755	50
Northumberland	10	47	2.3	0.8	29	94	5.9	1.5	1 067	40.0	11 920	55
Nottoway	24	826	39.6	22.0	39	131	10.9	3.3	656	15.2	3 893	27
Orange	42	283	17.9	6.9	54	332	35.2	10.4	2 261	80.9	18 825	86
Page	34	522	36.3	15.9	38	118	8.4	2.4	1 385	46.7	4 633	39
Patrick	25	602	29.2	13.4	17	49	4.1	1.2	1 065	35.8	3 771	31
Pittsylvania	57	655	30.7	13.9	67	300	19.0	5.0	2 948	93.2	15 252	73
Powhatan	28	250	15.3	6.9	44	153	17.7	6.0	1 972	89.6	51 925	191
Prince Edward	78	1 677	106.9	48.8	38	157	18.5	3.3	916	29.2	6 058	52
Prince George	15	D	D	D	33	125	9.1	3.4	1 369	41.9	9 153	66
Prince William	530	7 037	690.9	267.2	500	3 204	512.8	96.7	30 436	1 176.6	228 852	1 225
Pulaski	67	1 356	89.9	40.0	50	210	17.7	5.1	1 478	45.5	10 659	45
Rappahannock	8	D	D	D	11	37	3.0	0.9	934	46.7	10 452	22
Richmond	19	797	27.3	13.6	12	66	6.6	2.1	545	17.1	2 979	26
Roanoke	238	4 618	340.9	163.7	163	824	68.4	21.3	5 430	214.8	32 611	219
Rockbridge	32	197	15.0	5.4	29	93	8.5	2.0	1 487	54.6	9 836	44
Rockingham	85	1 625	86.1	36.1	104	508	39.3	12.2	5 431	212.3	52 471	252
Russell	50	865	61.3	25.5	30	91	6.7	2.1	1 173	33.8	3 803	30
Scott	40	D	D	D	18	D	D	D	955	26.8	1 485	15
Shenandoah	69	D	D	D	90	363	31.5	7.6	2 851	99.4	15 391	87
Smyth	62	2 205	141.3	70.6	44	183	17.0	4.3	1 484	48.0	5 507	26
Southampton	9	D	D	D	18	D	D	D	838	26.7	4 064	28
Spotsylvania	176	2 198	135.5	58.7	177	1 020	91.7	27.7	7 557	285.8	95 985	375
Stafford	146	1 939	129.0	59.4	193	1 203	99.5	32.9	7 623	295.6	192 023	772
Surry	3	D	D	D	1	D	D	D	309	9.0	4 163	25
Sussex	14	D	D	D	16	94	6.0	1.8	438	13.9	2 123	20
Tazewell	149	2 424	187.5	77.1	92	595	55.8	15.6	2 108	69.5	4 658	26
Warren	55	D	D	D	77	525	36.1	11.9	2 497	99.1	19 156	87
Washington	143	2 092	197.7	76.1	73	357	22.1	7.6	3 375	114.3	11 590	55
Westmoreland	18	287	10.5	5.4	32	109	6.2	1.5	1 166	32.2	8 174	64
Wise	82	1 601	101.3	38.9	70	D	D	D	1 508	45.3	3 006	14
Wythe	70	1 283	92.5	37.2	51	275	21.2	5.3	1 501	53.6	9 166	79
York	94	1 620	176.7	67.1	138	702	47.5	16.3	3 479	130.8	36 235	432
Independent cities												
Alexandria city	397	6 347	909.3	332.6	591	9 336	2 436.1	524.5	13 472	645.3	170 552	1 324
Bedford city	44	D	D	D	36	268	21.3	7.3	387	10.4	NA	NA
Bristol city	47	D	D	D	48	D	D	D	993	37.6	900	10
Buena Vista city	15	318	15.9	8.6	7	D	D	D	304	9.8	0	0
Charlottesville city	190	10 090	1 339.7	449.4	165	1 389	295.9	42.8	3 768	210.4	30 030	173
Chesapeake city	469	7 730	746.9	298.9	404	3 023	333.8	91.6	12 540	467.0	182 896	886
Colonial Heights city	84	1 275	94.0	46.2	55	361	26.9	8.8	890	32.6	1 694	13
Covington city	20	232	8.0	3.6	19	D	D	D	243	9.1	150	1
Danville city	208	4 620	407.1	161.8	126	620	53.0	13.4	2 251	70.5	1 638	12
Emporia city	35	923	70.3	27.7	21	78	6.7	1.7	256	8.3	746	13
Fairfax city	221	3 303	269.8	121.2	181	1 155	132.0	39.9	2 866	208.3	7 183	54
Falls Church city	101	D	D	D	86	536	68.2	19.7	1 332	89.3	108 237	547
Franklin city	53	933	76.1	29.4	32	205	14.5	3.8	434	11.5	297	3
Fredericksburg city	212	5 813	824.6	293.8	106	947	60.1	21.3	1 742	97.0	5 648	23
Galax city	49	1 451	115.3	49.9	22	84	7.0	2.0	413	13.3	150	1
Hampton city	243	6 619	660.4	300.7	191	1 177	96.6	29.1	6 191	181.8	7 007	160
Harrisonburg city	160	4 724	403.1	193.2	133	725	79.2	18.1	2 446	110.6	14 080	152
Hopewell city	61	D	D	D	42	303	42.2	6.9	796	23.0	10 409	90
Lexington city	47	759	69.7	24.1	30	228	29.2	6.5	459	17.3	799	8
Lynchburg city	261	8 776	828.1	355.5	175	1 058	80.3	24.4	3 870	137.3	17 863	92
Manassas city	179	3 373	357.5	175.1	132	803	75.2	22.1	3 034	139.6	17 617	125

Table B. States and Counties — **Government Employment and Payroll, and Local Government Finances**

STATE County	Government employment and payroll, 2012: Full-time equivalent employees	March payroll (dollars)	March payroll (percent of total): Adminis-tration, judicial, and legal	Police and Corrections	Fire Protection	Highways and transpor-tation	Health and Welfare	Natural resources and utilities	Education and libraries	Local government finances, 2012: General revenue: Total (mil dol)	Inter-govern-mental (mil dol)	Taxes: Total (mil dol)	Per capita[1] (dollars): Total	Property
	171	172	173	174	175	176	177	178	179	180	181	182	183	184
VIRGINIA—Cont'd														
Louisa	1 124	3 411 101	8.2	6.8	4.2	0.0	1.1	4.9	73.3	96.7	33.7	53.8	1 609	1 418
Lunenburg	403	1 190 954	9.0	11.5	0.0	0.0	2.3	2.4	72.9	33.1	20.6	9.9	790	676
Madison	403	1 326 277	10.7	6.4	0.0	0.0	5.8	0.3	69.8	34.3	15.7	16.2	1 227	1 036
Mathews	358	848 780	8.9	7.2	0.0	0.0	5.4	0.0	74.9	23.0	9.7	12.1	1 364	1 166
Mecklenburg	1 375	3 603 811	7.0	12.8	0.2	1.1	10.7	2.6	62.8	94.5	47.2	37.6	1 185	856
Middlesex	280	843 355	10.1	15.3	0.0	0.0	3.5	0.8	70.3	25.5	8.9	15.3	1 409	1 212
Montgomery	2 699	8 781 181	9.0	11.9	0.5	4.6	2.7	5.5	61.5	255.0	103.6	112.5	1 182	829
Nelson	457	1 391 646	8.9	4.1	0.0	0.0	1.6	0.5	80.1	45.2	17.7	23.6	1 590	1 346
New Kent	638	2 123 526	10.3	8.3	5.3	0.3	4.1	7.3	63.1	52.7	21.7	26.8	1 400	1 195
Northampton	850	3 278 000	5.0	9.0	0.0	20.1	6.5	3.2	55.2	101.7	23.0	21.3	1 740	1 417
Northumberland	358	1 244 110	8.2	7.7	0.0	0.0	4.8	0.9	77.1	28.9	10.2	17.4	1 407	1 269
Nottoway	548	1 646 561	8.1	8.7	0.0	2.8	5.9	4.4	67.2	39.4	23.9	10.3	650	454
Orange	1 173	3 380 570	7.0	14.3	3.2	1.7	2.2	2.9	67.7	89.1	37.1	42.7	1 247	997
Page	878	2 456 816	8.1	13.4	0.0	0.6	1.8	3.8	71.0	65.3	32.2	27.2	1 138	890
Patrick	695	1 689 450	5.6	12.0	0.0	0.0	4.5	0.8	75.3	43.9	24.0	14.5	784	617
Pittsylvania	1 563	4 924 209	5.8	7.5	0.1	0.5	1.4	1.2	80.6	127.9	84.1	37.6	599	478
Powhatan	855	2 784 066	7.2	7.7	0.5	0.0	3.4	1.3	77.9	69.7	28.5	38.3	1 361	1 230
Prince Edward	701	2 116 144	10.4	10.6	0.3	3.1	2.0	3.4	66.4	54.6	29.8	19.8	852	490
Prince George	1 519	5 308 620	5.9	28.6	0.9	0.0	2.5	1.5	58.6	118.9	72.6	36.1	976	765
Prince William	15 485	68 447 361	3.7	8.8	4.5	3.3	4.4	3.5	69.0	1 578.6	659.7	752.7	1 749	1 412
Pulaski	1 288	4 175 730	6.1	8.3	0.9	1.1	3.6	5.9	68.5	117.9	56.3	35.2	1 013	707
Rappahannock	256	760 848	9.7	11.1	0.0	0.0	6.5	0.8	68.9	20.6	4.6	14.7	1 978	1 804
Richmond	326	1 099 371	6.8	32.6	0.0	0.0	0.6	2.6	56.3	32.9	20.4	9.1	1 002	790
Roanoke	3 729	13 158 244	7.7	7.6	6.2	0.3	4.8	9.4	62.7	353.7	116.0	158.3	1 704	1 275
Rockbridge	661	1 852 653	7.0	8.7	0.0	0.3	5.5	2.1	74.0	71.1	30.7	29.1	1 299	943
Rockingham	2 706	8 346 966	7.1	8.4	3.0	0.8	4.8	4.5	70.2	227.8	108.4	83.5	1 079	895
Russell	1 094	4 018 658	3.7	6.4	0.2	1.1	0.2	2.5	83.0	73.8	48.1	20.2	710	482
Scott	721	2 170 415	5.9	6.0	0.0	0.8	3.3	2.2	79.1	62.5	41.3	16.4	722	496
Shenandoah	1 504	4 472 709	7.1	9.2	3.6	1.5	4.6	6.2	65.6	123.4	60.3	48.9	1 149	882
Smyth	1 259	3 570 921	6.6	8.1	0.4	1.0	11.3	5.6	65.4	92.2	58.8	22.8	718	494
Southampton	717	2 092 925	8.4	10.2	0.0	0.2	6.0	3.3	70.4	53.2	26.3	21.4	1 162	1 013
Spotsylvania	3 637	13 506 224	7.0	5.7	4.9	0.0	3.5	3.8	72.0	382.7	163.4	188.0	1 496	1 158
Stafford	4 475	17 648 377	6.1	5.1	2.8	0.2	2.7	4.7	77.1	448.6	192.3	213.9	1 592	1 307
Surry	386	1 034 084	6.2	6.4	0.0	0.0	0.8	3.6	77.4	29.5	7.5	21.1	3 078	2 927
Sussex	423	1 312 782	12.9	14.1	0.0	0.2	7.5	2.3	61.1	40.7	22.0	10.1	843	685
Tazewell	1 644	4 416 984	7.8	8.5	0.4	2.1	7.4	4.0	67.6	142.1	75.0	40.0	903	580
Warren	1 201	3 547 039	8.8	13.4	0.9	2.4	2.5	5.2	65.3	103.2	45.3	48.1	1 264	942
Washington	2 294	6 382 778	4.2	19.7	0.0	2.6	2.7	7.4	62.3	154.9	83.7	51.1	926	645
Westmoreland	590	1 733 294	11.3	10.8	0.0	0.5	7.2	2.7	66.0	47.8	21.1	21.6	1 230	999
Wise	1 524	4 814 554	7.6	7.5	0.1	1.5	2.6	6.1	72.2	146.0	82.3	52.0	1 271	712
Wythe	1 424	3 649 638	5.6	26.2	0.3	2.6	1.1	5.5	55.4	100.6	52.2	30.2	1 032	628
York	2 630	9 095 299	7.9	5.3	7.7	0.0	3.3	2.6	66.6	226.0	92.7	107.0	1 618	1 182
Independent cities														
Alexandria city	5 221	27 072 935	10.0	12.5	7.7	2.6	11.9	7.2	44.7	658.7	76.2	498.6	3 408	2 503
Bedford city	151	496 858	12.0	19.7	1.8	11.7	7.9	19.2	15.0	21.6	9.7	7.6	1 271	841
Bristol city	765	2 448 312	7.6	15.4	6.1	3.8	8.9	3.5	53.6	72.5	36.3	26.8	1 519	788
Buena Vista city	329	965 276	10.8	5.3	0.0	3.3	1.3	7.0	71.5	22.5	12.2	6.9	1 023	765
Charlottesville city	2 284	8 528 975	9.8	5.8	3.3	6.0	4.6	8.3	55.8	212.5	76.7	93.0	2 116	1 314
Chesapeake city	11 013	41 054 055	4.1	9.2	5.0	1.7	24.6	3.7	49.6	1 127.4	370.1	422.6	1 850	1 301
Colonial Heights city	802	3 016 516	7.0	9.3	9.1	2.9	0.6	5.1	64.2	74.5	26.0	40.1	2 297	1 225
Covington city	279	921 554	6.6	10.3	0.0	0.0	7.9	9.3	65.9	26.1	10.0	11.0	1 904	1 291
Danville city	2 451	7 816 325	9.2	11.3	5.7	3.0	4.1	10.7	51.6	173.3	85.4	50.7	1 180	635
Emporia city	121	358 410	26.1	32.7	0.8	10.3	9.0	14.9	0.0	22.4	7.1	10.4	1 814	786
Fairfax city	414	2 320 342	17.7	23.1	21.4	10.9	3.8	13.9	0.0	121.0	20.6	87.1	3 711	2 469
Falls Church city	720	3 347 248	12.1	9.0	0.2	2.9	0.5	11.6	62.0	84.9	11.0	58.9	4 454	3 374
Franklin city	602	1 874 981	4.7	34.1	3.4	2.6	4.5	7.4	40.0	43.1	23.9	11.8	1 389	766
Fredericksburg city	1 610	5 694 248	7.8	27.8	4.3	5.6	3.2	3.1	44.2	149.0	48.1	67.8	2 483	1 244
Galax city	414	1 172 160	3.5	10.4	0.0	4.3	9.1	11.5	57.5	25.9	13.1	8.9	1 283	595
Hampton city	6 125	20 173 326	6.9	11.1	6.0	1.0	6.7	5.9	61.4	526.3	220.7	218.7	1 599	1 068
Harrisonburg city	1 474	5 157 943	4.1	7.6	6.7	5.8	3.6	11.7	53.6	162.1	48.7	63.4	1 244	631
Hopewell city	1 107	3 758 446	8.1	8.6	4.7	2.5	4.1	11.7	58.7	102.8	47.0	32.3	1 448	1 059
Lexington city	273	881 406	8.8	24.4	4.0	7.7	2.1	13.4	30.0	22.6	6.6	7.8	1 109	687
Lynchburg city	3 057	9 313 489	8.7	9.6	8.0	2.9	7.1	8.5	52.5	265.1	109.0	117.5	1 524	905
Manassas city	1 551	7 149 920	5.0	8.7	4.1	2.5	2.9	8.2	67.1	180.9	61.7	83.5	2 055	1 564

1. Based on the resident population estimated as of July 1 of the year shown.

STATE County	Local government finances, 2012 (cont.) — Direct general expenditure — Total (mil dol)	Per capita[1] (dollars)	Percent of total for: Education	Health and hospitals	Police protection	Public welfare	Highways	Debt outstanding — Total (mil dol)	Per capita[1] (dollars)	Government employment, 2013 — Federal civilian	Federal military	State and local	Presidential election,[2] 2012 — Percent of vote cast: Democratic	Republican	All other
	185	186	187	188	189	190	191	192	193	194	195	196	197	198	199
VIRGINIA—Cont'd															
Louisa	99.6	2 980	58.3	1.2	5.3	6.6	0.3	25.5	763	56	109	1 514	45.5	53.3	1.3
Lunenburg	35.6	2 826	62.6	1.1	5.0	6.7	2.1	26.9	2 134	20	37	771	47.8	51.3	0.8
Madison	32.1	2 431	58.6	4.5	8.2	11.2	0.0	15.3	1 157	67	42	544	42.7	56.1	1.2
Mathews	20.3	2 283	58.0	0.8	7.8	7.9	0.7	9.8	1 108	22	69	357	35.6	63.5	0.9
Mecklenburg	89.8	2 829	48.3	6.5	7.0	4.6	2.7	33.6	1 059	121	98	1 802	47.3	51.8	0.9
Middlesex	23.8	2 198	52.5	2.0	5.6	6.1	0.0	22.7	2 100	20	33	1 016	39.8	59.0	1.2
Montgomery	258.1	2 711	48.5	0.4	8.4	3.5	4.9	475.3	4 993	(3)356	(3)388	(3)16 909	51.7	46.8	1.5
Nelson	40.8	2 750	59.8	0.5	7.1	4.4	0.7	45.5	3 068	43	47	666	54.0	44.8	1.2
New Kent	49.4	2 579	54.5	1.0	4.6	4.2	0.0	60.4	3 152	40	61	910	35.0	63.9	1.1
Northampton	81.1	6 632	27.6	1.0	3.1	3.3	15.7	159.5	13 045	35	66	932	57.7	41.2	1.1
Northumberland	27.3	2 213	57.8	1.2	7.1	6.9	1.7	42.0	3 401	29	39	458	44.7	54.6	0.7
Nottoway	38.9	2 460	57.3	0.4	7.7	6.1	2.3	16.5	1 044	340	57	2 456	48.8	50.1	1.1
Orange	87.3	2 548	55.7	0.6	6.4	3.0	2.0	124.0	3 620	52	110	2 207	45.0	53.8	1.2
Page	66.1	2 765	55.3	0.9	7.9	5.0	2.0	77.1	3 228	193	76	1 119	40.8	58.1	1.1
Patrick	36.7	1 989	67.6	1.0	5.6	2.7	0.2	44.5	2 411	47	58	804	33.7	64.4	1.9
Pittsylvania	127.3	2 026	65.4	0.5	5.2	7.6	0.3	112.9	1 797	(4)210	(4)332	(4)6 558	37.5	61.5	0.9
Powhatan	65.5	2 328	65.3	0.3	6.2	5.1	0.0	103.3	3 675	45	84	2 388	29.3	69.8	0.9
Prince Edward	54.4	2 342	50.0	0.5	7.0	7.1	5.6	67.7	2 914	81	60	2 270	54.3	44.5	1.2
Prince George	134.6	3 644	45.1	2.0	4.5	2.6	0.3	173.0	4 684	(5)5 343	(5)9 032	(5)3 087	44.5	54.7	0.8
Prince William	1 678.9	3 902	57.5	1.9	5.9	2.5	1.6	1 440.8	3 349	(6)7 950	(6)7 532	(6)22 840	57.5	41.6	0.9
Pulaski	110.5	3 181	43.4	0.7	5.8	9.2	2.0	71.9	2 069	37	107	2 424	39.3	58.9	1.8
Rappahannock	21.0	2 817	57.1	0.7	5.0	4.4	0.0	10.8	1 446	22	24	328	47.8	50.6	1.7
Richmond	32.3	3 565	42.0	0.6	4.9	5.4	0.1	11.6	1 280	33	26	887	43.2	55.9	0.9
Roanoke	397.1	4 275	42.0	6.5	5.5	3.6	0.2	497.3	5 353	(7)2 265	(7)370	(7)6 750	38.9	60.0	1.2
Rockbridge	69.2	3 088	45.1	10.9	3.4	9.5	0.0	67.1	2 995	(8)92	(8)143	(8)2 665	42.6	56.2	1.1
Rockingham	234.6	3 031	52.1	2.8	3.5	11.4	1.3	200.1	2 585	(9)338	(9)390	(9)10 591	31.4	67.4	1.2
Russell	71.0	2 495	57.5	0.7	4.1	8.4	6.4	22.5	790	63	90	1 394	42.9	55.6	1.5
Scott	60.2	2 640	60.3	0.7	6.9	7.1	1.4	30.5	1 339	56	71	1 142	27.6	70.7	1.7
Shenandoah	116.2	2 729	54.8	0.6	6.7	6.1	3.0	146.9	3 449	127	136	2 020	36.0	62.5	1.6
Smyth	94.6	2 984	50.5	0.9	6.6	10.5	2.3	141.0	4 444	75	99	2 861	34.5	63.5	2.0
Southampton	56.0	3 044	56.1	0.8	3.6	3.8	0.2	67.3	3 657	(10)70	(10)81	(10)2 529	48.5	50.5	0.9
Spotsylvania	378.7	3 013	60.7	0.4	4.3	4.3	2.1	483.9	3 850	(11)355	(11)490	(11)9 297	46.0	52.9	1.0
Stafford	443.1	3 298	62.9	0.3	5.0	3.4	1.5	601.1	4 474	4 094	1 906	6 285	46.4	52.7	0.9
Surry	27.8	4 061	61.1	1.2	4.9	7.5	0.0	16.2	2 369	10	22	521	60.7	38.5	0.8
Sussex	39.1	3 269	58.6	0.5	7.2	7.5	0.1	26.7	2 229	54	30	1 304	61.6	37.8	0.7
Tazewell	136.7	3 088	44.7	17.2	6.0	6.5	4.1	52.5	1 186	71	136	3 397	32.8	65.7	1.5
Warren	120.1	3 155	38.6	12.5	13.4	5.4	1.5	214.6	5 637	184	122	1 721	43.4	55.1	1.6
Washington	172.4	3 125	41.6	10.5	5.9	3.9	1.1	101.3	1 835	(12)244	(12)230	(12)4 763	32.9	65.6	1.5
Westmoreland	49.6	2 832	53.8	0.8	8.0	6.1	1.5	23.2	1 322	54	56	830	54.6	44.4	1.0
Wise	142.7	3 487	49.3	6.0	6.1	9.8	4.4	186.8	4 565	(13)236	(13)134	(13)4 276	35.3	63.0	1.6
Wythe	103.2	3 530	39.8	0.1	5.8	6.6	2.0	150.9	5 159	85	94	2 387	32.9	65.7	1.4
York	226.9	3 430	55.6	0.6	4.0	2.9	0.0	176.3	2 665	(14)1 062	(14)1 562	(14)3 654	40.4	58.5	1.1
Independent cities															
Alexandria city	692.1	4 731	34.7	6.0	9.7	6.4	3.7	714.3	4 882	14 626	1 353	8 222	71.7	27.3	1.0
Bedford city	20.8	3 494	28.9	2.1	12.2	1.0	12.3	31.1	5 208	(15)	(15)	(15)	44.2	54.8	1.1
Bristol city	80.9	4 578	41.9	3.1	10.9	5.1	11.6	60.4	3 418	(12)	(12)	(12)	36.2	62.2	1.6
Buena Vista city	21.2	3 164	51.2	2.1	6.2	6.2	4.2	43.1	6 424	(8)	(8)	(8)	45.7	52.9	1.4
Charlottesville city	227.5	5 176	31.3	8.0	7.2	11.1	6.4	151.8	3 454	(16)	(16)	(16)	78.4	20.3	1.3
Chesapeake city	1 112.4	4 870	42.2	24.6	3.6	2.6	4.4	886.9	3 883	1 137	1 636	14 931	50.2	48.9	0.8
Colonial Heights city	69.5	3 974	51.8	0.0	5.3	0.6	4.6	61.6	3 526	(17)	(17)	(17)	29.0	69.6	1.4
Covington city	33.2	5 752	46.0	0.3	7.1	5.4	4.1	55.3	9 583	(18)	(18)	(18)	55.4	43.3	1.3
Danville city	179.2	4 169	41.3	2.3	5.5	4.2	5.7	156.0	3 628	(4)	(4)	(4)	59.1	40.0	0.8
Emporia city	22.3	3 882	17.9	1.2	14.0	1.4	4.2	14.6	2 551	(19)	(19)	(19)	65.0	34.3	0.7
Fairfax city	112.7	4 804	34.1	0.9	9.6	1.5	4.8	321.3	13 695	(20)	(20)	(20)	57.7	41.2	1.2
Falls Church city	76.6	5 787	47.6	0.3	8.2	2.3	6.9	97.9	7 399	(20)	(20)	(20)	69.6	29.2	1.3
Franklin city	51.8	6 072	32.0	0.5	5.3	3.8	4.2	22.8	2 673	(10)	(10)	(10)	63.7	35.6	0.7
Fredericksburg city	158.1	5 789	24.4	0.5	4.5	4.2	4.1	451.1	16 521	(11)	(11)	(11)	63.6	35.3	1.1
Galax city	28.7	4 153	45.2	0.7	8.9	5.8	7.1	10.9	1 575	(21)	(21)	(21)	43.8	54.8	1.4
Hampton city	524.9	3 836	44.8	0.8	5.1	5.6	1.2	438.4	3 204	7 211	7 893	9 425	60.1	30.1	0.8
Harrisonburg city	165.9	3 255	39.0	0.7	4.7	1.8	11.4	529.2	10 380	(9)	(9)	(9)	57.5	41.2	1.2
Hopewell city	116.0	5 192	43.8	0.5	4.4	5.9	3.4	114.6	5 128	(5)	(5)	(5)	55.5	43.6	0.9
Lexington city	28.1	4 013	24.4	2.6	5.2	2.6	4.3	34.5	4 926	(8)	(8)	(8)	62.2	36.9	0.9
Lynchburg city	262.8	3 408	36.6	0.8	6.5	7.2	2.8	337.4	4 375	(22)	(22)	(22)	47.4	51.4	1.3
Manassas city	169.8	4 182	54.0	2.2	7.8	0.7	6.2	130.5	3 213	(6)	(6)	(6)	55.2	43.8	1.0

1. Based on the resident population estimated as of July 1 of the year shown. 2. © 2013 Election Data Services, Inc. All rights reserved. 3. Radford city is included with Montgomery county. 4. Danville city is included with Pittsylvania county. 5. Hopewell city is included with Prince George county. 6. Manassas and Manassas Park cities are included with Prince William county. 7. Salem city is included with Roanoke county. 8. Buena Vista and Lexington cities are included with Rockbridge county. 9. Harrisonburg city is included with Rockingham county. 10. Franklin city is included with Southhampton county. 11. Fredericksburg city is included with Spotsylvania county. 12. Bristol city included with Washington county. 13. Norton city is included with Wise county. 14. Poquoson city is included with York county. 15. Bedford city is included with Bedford county. 16. Charlottesville city is included with Albemarle county. 17. Petersburg and Colonial Heights cities are included with Dinwiddie county. 18. Covington city is included with Alleghany county. 19. Emporia city is included with Greensville county. 20. Fairfax city and Falls Church city are included with Fairfax county. 21. Galax city is included with Carroll county. 22. Lynchburg city is included with Campbell county.

STATE/ County code	CBSA code[1]	County type[2]	STATE County	Land area,[3] (sq km) 2010	Population, 2014: Total persons 2014	Population, 2014: Rank	Population, 2014: Per square kilometer	Race alone or in combination, not Hispanic or Latino (percent): White	Black	American Indian, Alaska Native	Asian and Pacific Islander	Percent Hispanic or Latino[4]	Age (percent): Under 5 years	5 to 17 years	18 to 24 years	25 to 34 years	35 to 44 years	45 to 54 years
				1	2	3	4	5	6	7	8	9	10	11	12	13	14	15
			VIRGINIA—Cont'd															
51 685	47900	1	Manassas Park city	7	15 174	2 088	2 167.7	42.0	14.8	0.9	10.7	36.3	7.7	19.4	8.3	18.9	16.6	13.8
51 690	32300	4	Martinsville city	28	13 711	2 191	489.7	49.7	45.8	0.6	1.3	4.5	7.5	15.1	7.6	10.8	11.1	14.6
51 700	47260	1	Newport News city	178	182 965	351	1 027.9	48.1	41.7	1.2	4.4	8.2	7.4	16.2	13.1	16.7	11.6	12.9
51 710	47260	1	Norfolk city	140	245 428	269	1 753.1	46.7	43.2	1.3	5.0	7.3	6.8	13.4	19.1	18.6	11.1	11.2
51 720	13720	7	Norton city	19	4 031	2 901	212.2	89.1	8.4	0.7	1.8	2.5	5.6	16.4	10.2	13.9	11.5	13.5
51 730	40060	1	Petersburg city	59	32 701	1 367	554.3	17.3	77.9	0.9	1.6	4.3	7.9	13.6	10.8	14.0	10.1	14.5
51 735	47260	1	Poquoson city	40	12 048	2 295	301.2	93.8	1.6	0.8	3.0	2.2	3.7	18.5	8.6	8.9	12.2	16.6
51 740	47260	1	Portsmouth city	87	96 004	612	1 103.5	41.6	54.1	1.2	2.1	3.6	7.5	16.0	10.3	16.3	11.4	12.9
51 750	13980	3	Radford city	26	17 646	1 939	678.7	85.7	10.1	0.6	2.8	3.0	3.7	9.5	43.5	11.4	8.4	7.7
51 760	40060	1	Richmond city	155	217 853	295	1 405.5	41.5	50.2	0.8	3.1	6.3	6.4	12.1	14.5	20.1	11.5	12.2
51 770	40220	2	Roanoke city	110	99 428	592	903.9	63.5	30.0	0.7	2.6	5.8	7.2	14.7	8.7	15.3	12.5	13.7
51 775	40220	2	Salem city	37	25 483	1 587	688.7	87.7	8.1	0.6	2.3	2.9	5.2	14.7	13.5	11.4	11.1	13.3
51 790	44420	4	Staunton city	52	24 538	1 625	471.9	84.0	13.7	0.7	1.4	2.6	5.7	13.0	10.6	13.0	11.2	12.7
51 800	47260	1	Suffolk city	1 036	86 806	660	83.8	51.8	43.5	0.8	2.5	3.5	6.5	18.7	8.4	12.9	13.4	15.3
51 810	47260	1	Virginia Beach city	645	450 980	150	699.2	66.4	20.6	1.0	8.3	7.4	6.7	16.4	10.5	16.4	12.9	13.9
51 820	44420	4	Waynesboro city	39	21 366	1 759	547.8	80.8	13.2	0.9	1.5	6.6	7.5	16.5	8.0	13.9	11.7	12.9
51 830	47260	1	Williamsburg city	23	14 691	2 124	638.7	72.4	15.9	0.8	6.6	7.4	3.1	7.5	36.4	13.5	7.5	8.0
51 840	49020	3	Winchester city	24	27 543	1 511	1 147.6	70.8	12.4	0.7	3.0	15.8	6.8	16.2	11.0	14.7	11.9	13.1
53 000	...	X	WASHINGTON	172 119	7 061 530	X	41.0	74.4	4.8	2.5	10.5	11.9	6.4	16.5	9.6	14.3	13.1	13.6
53 001	36830	6	Adams	4 986	19 179	1 868	3.8	36.9	0.6	0.7	1.1	61.4	10.7	24.3	10.3	12.4	12.1	10.4
53 003	30300	3	Asotin	1 648	22 189	1 723	13.5	93.2	1.1	2.5	1.6	3.7	5.5	15.6	7.8	11.7	10.8	13.3
53 005	28420	3	Benton	4 404	186 486	344	42.3	75.0	2.0	1.6	3.9	19.9	7.3	19.5	9.0	13.5	12.1	13.1
53 007	48300	3	Chelan	7 564	74 588	735	9.9	70.4	0.8	1.6	1.6	27.1	7.0	17.5	8.7	12.0	10.9	13.1
53 009	38820	5	Clallam	4 502	72 715	746	16.2	86.8	1.4	6.6	3.0	5.7	4.6	13.2	7.2	10.5	9.5	12.1
53 011	38900	1	Clark	1 629	451 008	149	276.9	83.7	3.0	1.8	6.9	8.4	6.5	19.2	8.4	12.6	13.6	13.9
53 013	47460	6	Columbia	2 250	3 985	2 904	1.8	90.7	1.0	2.3	1.7	6.2	3.8	15.4	6.1	8.8	9.6	13.6
53 015	31020	3	Cowlitz	2 953	102 133	580	34.6	87.8	1.3	3.0	2.8	8.2	5.9	17.2	8.2	11.1	11.8	13.6
53 017	48300	3	Douglas	4 712	39 804	1 176	8.4	67.7	0.7	1.6	1.6	30.1	7.0	19.5	8.7	11.9	11.9	12.8
53 019	...	9	Ferry	5 706	7 667	2 624	1.3	78.6	1.3	19.0	1.9	3.8	4.6	14.1	8.6	9.3	9.6	13.0
53 021	28420	3	Franklin	3 217	87 809	650	27.3	43.9	2.5	1.0	2.7	51.4	10.2	23.5	9.7	16.4	13.2	10.5
53 023	...	8	Garfield	1 841	2 215	3 033	1.2	93.4	0.6	0.8	2.2	4.5	4.3	15.9	5.9	9.6	10.4	12.6
53 025	34180	4	Grant	6 940	93 147	625	13.4	57.8	1.3	1.7	1.5	39.3	8.8	21.7	9.8	13.2	11.7	11.6
53 027	10140	4	Grays Harbor	4 926	70 818	758	14.4	83.0	1.8	6.1	2.7	9.6	5.6	15.5	8.1	11.9	11.5	13.7
53 029	36020	4	Island	540	79 275	697	146.8	84.7	3.5	2.0	7.3	6.7	5.6	13.6	9.2	12.4	10.0	12.2
53 031	...	6	Jefferson	4 672	30 228	1 426	6.5	91.4	1.4	3.8	3.1	3.3	3.4	10.4	5.4	8.1	8.7	12.5
53 033	42660	1	King	5 479	2 079 967	13	379.6	66.9	7.6	1.7	19.2	9.3	6.2	14.9	8.8	16.7	15.0	14.2
53 035	14740	3	Kitsap	1 023	254 183	261	248.5	82.5	4.0	2.9	9.1	7.0	5.7	15.5	10.6	13.3	11.3	13.9
53 037	21260	6	Kittitas	5 950	42 522	1 118	7.1	87.2	1.5	2.0	3.5	8.4	5.0	13.0	22.5	11.7	9.8	11.3
53 039	...	6	Klickitat	4 847	20 861	1 783	4.3	84.5	0.8	3.6	1.6	12.0	5.1	15.9	6.8	9.6	11.6	13.6
53 041	16500	4	Lewis	6 223	75 128	734	12.1	87.3	1.2	2.8	1.9	9.4	5.9	16.4	8.3	11.2	11.3	13.4
53 043	...	8	Lincoln	5 984	10 250	2 417	1.7	94.0	0.9	3.0	1.6	2.9	4.8	16.6	6.3	8.4	10.2	13.2
53 045	43220	6	Mason	2 485	60 711	861	24.4	85.2	1.8	5.1	2.9	8.6	5.3	14.2	7.6	11.3	11.2	13.4
53 047	...	6	Okanogan	13 644	41 290	1 144	3.0	69.2	1.0	12.2	1.4	18.8	6.5	16.9	7.3	10.4	11.0	12.6
53 049	...	7	Pacific	2 416	20 561	1 799	8.5	86.0	1.0	4.2	3.1	8.8	4.7	12.6	6.3	8.8	9.1	12.6
53 051	44060	8	Pend Oreille	3 626	12 985	2 232	3.6	91.3	1.2	5.1	1.4	3.4	4.6	15.9	6.8	7.6	9.8	14.2
53 053	42660	1	Pierce	4 324	831 928	69	192.4	74.1	9.1	2.6	10.8	9.9	6.9	17.3	9.9	14.8	12.9	13.8
53 055	...	9	San Juan	450	16 015	2 040	35.6	91.6	1.0	1.7	2.1	5.8	3.0	11.4	5.2	8.2	9.3	13.7
53 057	34580	3	Skagit	4 484	120 365	514	26.8	77.8	1.1	2.8	3.0	17.6	6.2	16.4	8.4	12.1	11.4	13.0
53 059	38900	1	Skamania	4 288	11 340	2 335	2.6	91.0	1.2	3.0	1.8	5.7	4.6	16.3	6.8	9.7	12.2	16.0
53 061	42660	1	Snohomish	5 406	759 583	81	140.5	76.2	3.7	2.2	12.4	9.5	6.3	17.1	8.8	14.2	14.0	15.2
53 063	44060	2	Spokane	4 568	484 318	141	106.0	89.0	2.9	2.6	4.0	5.0	6.2	16.4	10.6	14.1	11.9	13.3
53 065	44060	6	Stevens	6 417	43 650	1 099	6.8	90.0	0.9	7.2	1.6	3.3	5.1	17.4	7.1	8.3	10.6	14.0
53 067	36500	3	Thurston	1 870	265 851	255	142.2	81.2	4.4	2.7	8.7	8.1	6.1	16.2	9.0	14.2	12.9	13.3
53 069	...	8	Wahkiakum	682	4 067	2 898	6.0	93.9	1.2	2.7	1.5	3.7	3.6	14.2	5.5	7.4	9.0	12.3
53 071	47460	4	Walla Walla	3 290	59 844	869	18.2	74.7	2.2	1.6	2.7	20.9	5.8	16.1	13.8	12.3	11.1	12.1
53 073	13380	3	Whatcom	5 457	208 351	307	38.2	83.3	1.8	3.8	6.0	8.6	5.6	14.7	15.0	12.7	11.6	12.4
53 075	39420	4	Whitman	5 592	46 827	1 029	8.4	83.9	2.9	1.5	10.1	5.3	4.5	10.5	37.2	13.4	8.0	8.3
53 077	49420	3	Yakima	11 125	247 687	267	22.3	47.2	1.2	4.6	1.8	47.0	8.5	21.4	10.2	13.0	11.9	11.7
54 000	...	X	WEST VIRGINIA	62 259	1 850 326	X	29.7	94.1	4.3	0.7	1.1	1.4	5.5	15.1	9.3	11.8	12.5	13.9
54 001	...	7	Barbour	883	16 766	1 996	19.0	97.6	1.5	1.2	0.5	0.7	5.2	15.7	11.1	10.4	11.9	13.9
54 003	25180	3	Berkeley	832	110 497	546	132.8	87.7	8.7	0.8	1.6	3.9	6.3	18.0	7.8	13.4	13.9	14.8
54 005	16620	2	Boone	1 299	23 714	1 651	18.3	98.5	1.0	0.4	0.2	0.5	6.2	16.8	7.4	10.4	14.1	13.6
54 007	...	8	Braxton	1 323	14 463	2 137	10.9	98.3	1.0	0.7	0.4	0.6	5.3	14.6	7.6	10.7	12.1	14.3

1. CBSA = Core Based Statistical Area. See Appendix A for explanation. See Appendix B for list of metropolitan areas with component counties. 2. County type code from the Economic Research Service of USDA Rural-Urban Continuum Codes. See Appendix A for definition. 3. Dry land or land partially or temporarily covered by water. 4. May be of any race.

STATE County	Population, 2013 (cont.): Age (percent) (cont.): 55 to 64 years	Population, 2013 (cont.): Age (percent) (cont.): 65 to 74 years	Population, 2013 (cont.): Age (percent) (cont.): 75 years and over	Population, 2013 (cont.): Percent female	Population change and components of change, 2000–2014: Total persons: 2000	Total persons: 2010	Percent change: 2000–2010	Percent change: 2010–2014	Components of change, 2010–2014: Births	Components of change, 2010–2014: Deaths	Components of change, 2010–2014: Net migration	Households, 2009–2013: Number	Households, 2009–2013: Persons per household	Percent: Family households	Percent: Female family householder[1]	Percent: One person
	16	17	18	19	20	21	22	23	24	25	26	27	28	29	30	31
VIRGINIA—Cont'd																
Manassas Park city	8.4	4.3	2.5	48.8	10 290	14 273	38.7	6.6	342	137	650	4 435	3.41	75.1	15.0	21.6
Martinsville city	13.1	10.4	9.8	54.3	15 416	13 821	-10.3	-0.8	940	932	-171	5 995	2.22	56.8	20.5	39.3
Newport News city	10.8	6.3	5.0	51.6	180 150	180 719	0.3	1.1	12 580	5 972	-4 457	69 211	2.50	63.2	18.4	30.3
Norfolk city	10.0	5.3	4.4	47.8	234 403	242 803	3.6	1.1	15 986	8 150	-5 061	85 557	2.59	57.8	17.9	32.6
Norton city	14.6	7.7	6.5	53.2	3 904	3 958	1.4	2.2	249	152	-9	1 706	2.31	52.9	15.0	38.0
Petersburg city	13.9	8.3	6.7	53.5	33 740	32 420	-3.9	0.9	2 851	1 721	-886	12 456	2.53	58.5	26.4	34.7
Poquoson city	13.8	10.7	7.1	50.3	11 566	12 150	5.0	-0.9	379	413	-86	4 591	2.62	74.5	8.6	22.7
Portsmouth city	12.0	7.3	6.3	51.9	100 565	95 535	-5.0	0.5	6 622	4 411	-1 644	36 690	2.52	64.6	22.1	29.7
Radford city	7.8	4.2	3.8	52.6	15 859	16 408	3.5	7.5	625	372	948	5 516	2.49	43.7	10.1	35.1
Richmond city	12.0	6.2	5.2	52.4	197 790	204 214	3.2	6.7	12 505	8 080	9 040	84 833	2.33	47.5	18.8	40.2
Roanoke city	13.3	7.8	6.8	52.1	94 911	97 032	2.2	2.6	6 345	5 043	1 243	42 494	2.24	54.4	17.9	38.8
Salem city	13.9	8.9	7.9	52.2	24 747	24 802	0.2	2.6	1 206	1 220	593	9 908	2.32	62.8	11.6	29.6
Staunton city	13.6	10.5	9.7	55.0	23 853	23 746	-0.4	3.3	1 333	1 424	878	10 495	2.15	56.6	12.6	38.6
Suffolk city	12.2	7.5	5.1	51.7	63 677	84 585	32.8	2.6	4 703	3 093	581	30 492	2.75	73.4	16.5	22.6
Virginia Beach city	11.3	6.9	5.0	50.9	425 257	437 994	3.0	3.0	26 387	12 192	-1 066	164 944	2.62	68.3	14.0	24.2
Waynesboro city	12.3	9.3	7.9	52.7	19 520	21 006	7.6	1.6	1 401	1 022	-82	8 708	2.41	61.7	14.4	32.2
Williamsburg city	8.9	8.4	6.8	53.4	11 998	14 068	17.3	7.4	366	433	969	4 391	2.29	51.8	9.3	38.4
Winchester city	11.9	7.6	6.8	50.6	23 585	26 203	11.1	5.1	1 692	1 126	781	10 393	2.46	54.5	13.3	35.4
WASHINGTON	12.9	8.0	5.6	50.0	5 894 121	6 724 540	14.1	5.0	370 520	214 584	179 873	2 629 126	2.54	64.6	10.2	27.7
Adams	9.6	5.8	4.4	49.2	16 428	18 728	14.0	2.4	1 710	480	-773	5 738	3.22	79.4	11.0	17.8
Asotin	15.0	11.3	9.0	51.9	20 551	21 623	5.2	2.6	1 016	981	528	9 058	2.37	63.7	10.1	31.6
Benton	12.6	7.6	5.3	49.9	142 475	175 177	23.0	6.5	10 859	5 301	5 559	65 675	2.70	69.2	11.2	25.7
Chelan	13.9	9.3	7.7	50.1	66 616	72 453	8.8	2.9	3 979	2 733	853	27 220	2.63	68.7	9.5	25.8
Clallam	16.8	14.5	11.5	50.3	64 525	71 404	10.7	1.8	2 814	3 922	2 270	30 814	2.28	60.9	8.8	31.7
Clark	12.7	8.1	5.1	50.6	345 238	425 363	23.2	6.0	23 054	12 987	15 023	158 855	2.70	69.3	11.1	24.2
Columbia	17.2	14.5	11.0	50.5	4 064	4 078	0.3	-2.3	147	200	-40	1 651	2.39	67.0	11.3	25.6
Cowlitz	14.4	10.4	7.2	50.4	92 948	102 410	10.2	-0.3	5 007	4 418	-848	39 602	2.55	67.5	11.5	25.8
Douglas	12.9	8.9	6.5	49.6	32 603	38 431	17.9	3.6	2 193	1 284	470	13 976	2.75	74.8	9.6	19.2
Ferry	19.3	14.0	7.4	48.2	7 260	7 551	4.0	1.5	285	354	183	2 951	2.48	67.4	11.7	28.7
Franklin	8.8	4.7	3.0	47.8	49 347	78 163	58.4	12.3	7 105	1 582	3 968	23 445	3.42	76.9	15.0	18.0
Garfield	18.4	11.7	11.2	51.2	2 397	2 266	-5.5	-2.3	77	119	-2	970	2.27	67.3	4.0	28.0
Grant	10.7	7.3	5.1	49.3	74 698	89 120	19.3	4.5	6 692	2 842	360	30 012	2.96	72.4	12.3	23.4
Grays Harbor	15.6	10.9	7.3	48.6	67 194	72 797	8.3	-2.7	3 376	3 369	-1 867	27 396	2.52	64.1	10.8	29.3
Island	15.5	13.0	8.5	50.3	71 558	78 506	9.7	1.0	3 768	2 674	-434	33 096	2.33	68.3	7.8	26.6
Jefferson	21.0	19.3	11.2	50.6	25 953	29 872	15.1	1.2	827	1 441	963	13 801	2.10	57.9	6.2	34.8
King	12.2	6.8	5.1	50.0	1 737 034	1 931 249	11.2	7.7	106 045	52 307	95 774	802 606	2.42	59.0	8.8	31.2
Kitsap	14.3	9.4	5.9	49.1	231 969	251 133	8.3	1.2	12 439	8 519	-1 158	97 622	2.51	67.8	9.6	25.5
Kittitas	12.3	8.9	5.5	49.6	33 362	40 915	22.6	3.9	1 750	1 216	1 089	16 538	2.35	57.1	6.8	29.1
Klickitat	17.2	12.8	7.4	49.6	19 161	20 318	6.0	2.7	880	765	448	8 019	2.53	68.4	8.4	26.6
Lewis	14.7	11.1	7.9	50.0	68 600	75 455	10.0	-0.4	3 717	3 431	-656	29 527	2.52	66.5	10.6	28.1
Lincoln	17.5	13.1	9.8	49.8	10 184	10 570	3.8	-3.0	405	486	-211	4 457	2.32	67.4	6.4	28.4
Mason	16.3	12.5	8.1	48.3	49 405	60 699	22.9	0.0	2 721	2 636	63	23 358	2.53	67.1	8.6	25.9
Okanogan	16.0	11.8	7.6	49.5	39 564	41 120	3.9	0.4	2 325	1 795	-309	15 980	2.48	68.1	9.4	26.9
Pacific	18.4	16.6	10.8	50.0	20 984	20 920	-0.3	-1.7	839	1 265	88	9 366	2.19	62.3	7.8	32.5
Pend Oreille	18.8	14.6	7.7	49.0	11 732	13 001	10.8	-0.1	493	614	128	5 484	2.34	67.2	13.0	26.6
Pierce	12.1	7.2	5.1	50.3	700 820	795 225	13.5	4.6	47 496	25 306	14 072	300 623	2.62	67.3	12.0	26.0
San Juan	21.5	17.8	10.1	51.7	14 077	15 769	12.0	1.6	347	529	435	7 753	2.01	62.0	9.0	30.9
Skagit	14.3	10.5	7.6	50.4	102 979	116 901	13.5	3.0	6 156	4 695	1 856	45 293	2.56	68.6	11.1	25.0
Skamania	17.7	10.6	6.1	49.2	9 872	11 066	12.1	2.5	438	322	196	4 452	2.48	67.2	8.7	27.8
Snohomish	12.9	7.0	4.7	49.9	606 024	713 335	17.7	6.5	39 070	20 424	27 172	268 722	2.66	68.0	10.4	24.9
Spokane	13.2	8.2	6.2	50.5	417 939	471 221	12.7	2.8	25 301	17 604	5 235	187 572	2.44	63.2	10.8	29.1
Stevens	17.6	12.7	7.3	49.9	40 066	43 531	8.6	0.3	1 866	1 793	113	17 684	2.44	68.8	7.8	25.1
Thurston	13.7	8.7	5.9	51.0	207 355	252 264	21.7	5.4	13 167	8 353	8 739	100 801	2.50	66.3	11.0	26.4
Wahkiakum	18.1	19.0	10.9	50.3	3 824	3 978	4.0	2.2	129	198	161	1 715	2.28	63.9	6.6	33.1
Walla Walla	12.6	8.3	7.8	49.1	55 180	58 781	6.5	1.8	2 901	2 291	400	21 677	2.49	64.1	11.1	30.7
Whatcom	13.0	8.8	6.1	50.4	166 814	201 140	20.6	3.6	9 620	6 361	3 992	79 314	2.50	61.8	9.5	27.6
Whitman	8.3	5.4	4.4	49.1	40 740	44 776	9.9	4.6	1 919	1 044	1 147	16 624	2.35	49.6	6.9	31.3
Yakima	10.7	7.0	5.4	49.8	222 581	243 231	9.3	1.8	17 587	7 943	-5 114	79 679	3.02	73.1	15.4	21.9
WEST VIRGINIA	14.7	9.9	7.4	50.6	1 808 344	1 852 994	2.5	-0.1	87 357	92 030	3 010	741 390	2.43	65.2	11.2	20.0
Barbour	14.0	10.3	7.5	51.2	15 557	16 589	6.6	1.1	770	791	196	6 099	2.65	70.5	10.0	26.6
Berkeley	12.9	8.1	4.7	50.6	75 905	104 169	37.2	6.1	5 818	3 812	4 227	40 447	2.59	70.3	12.5	24.9
Boone	15.9	9.4	6.3	50.4	25 535	24 629	-3.5	-3.7	1 171	1 285	-765	9 559	2.55	71.8	11.5	25.1
Braxton	15.9	11.5	8.0	49.6	14 702	14 523	-1.2	-0.4	696	708	-50	5 780	2.42	66.5	7.7	29.4

1. No spouse present.

STATE County	Persons in group quarters, 2014	Daytime population, 2009–2013		Births, 2014		Deaths, 2014		Persons under 65 with no health insurance, 2013		Medicare, 2014			Serious crimes known to police,[2] 2013	
		Number	Employment/ residence ratio	Total	Rate[1]	Number	Rate[1]	Number	Percent	Eligible for Medicare	Enrolled in Medicare Advantage	Enrolled in a Medicare prescription drug plan	Total Number	Total Rate[3]
	32	33	34	35	36	37	38	39	40	41	42	43	44	45
VIRGINIA—Cont'd														
Manassas Park city	6	10 320	0.40	18	1.2	36	2.4	3 400	22.7	1 074	170	439	220	1 347
Martinsville city	377	17 124	1.68	200	14.6	202	14.7	1 770	16.3	3 806	832	2 554	557	4 045
Newport News city	8 430	200 790	1.22	2 910	15.9	1 435	7.8	23 199	15.0	25 790	6 008	9 086	6 397	3 533
Norfolk city	32 590	306 157	1.50	3 764	15.3	2 030	8.3	32 361	17.0	30 355	7 049	10 892	12 293	4 971
Norton city	68	4 904	1.52	49	12.2	23	5.7	421	12.1	1 192	302	589	203	4 942
Petersburg city	1 058	35 192	1.24	676	20.7	435	13.3	4 543	16.5	6 974	1 600	2 926	1 271	3 991
Poquoson city	51	8 607	0.40	93	7.7	87	7.2	953	9.7	2 381	250	785	154	1 272
Portsmouth city	3 065	106 838	1.25	1 532	16.0	1 037	10.8	12 269	15.2	17 183	4 012	5 538	5 979	6 163
Radford city	3 207	16 154	0.92	160	9.1	78	4.4	2 185	17.0	1 989	371	1 111	503	2 992
Richmond city	13 337	275 464	1.70	2 945	13.5	1 959	9.0	36 416	20.2	31 332	9 330	13 439	10 059	4 726
Roanoke city	2 125	124 507	1.61	1 513	15.2	1 166	11.7	14 796	17.7	19 508	5 070	9 115	4 907	5 011
Salem city	1 993	35 540	1.90	297	11.7	291	11.4	2 606	13.4	5 797	1 074	3 037	629	2 509
Staunton city	1 538	25 305	1.12	318	13.0	305	12.4	2 642	14.3	6 023	644	3 626	652	2 716
Suffolk city	1 102	74 544	0.74	1 105	12.7	731	8.4	9 144	12.4	14 014	2 734	5 955	2 860	3 346
Virginia Beach city	9 405	409 072	0.86	6 217	13.8	3 015	6.7	51 106	13.2	62 315	9 467	21 650	12 007	2 664
Waynesboro city	192	21 077	1.00	311	14.6	212	9.9	2 856	16.2	4 675	678	2 782	736	3 476
Williamsburg city	4 379	23 105	2.44	89	6.1	109	7.4	1 436	16.5	2 315	326	1 095	221	1 420
Winchester city	879	38 417	1.97	366	13.3	246	8.9	4 323	19.1	4 866	486	2 630	1 097	4 039
WASHINGTON	140 967	6 772 180	0.98	87 995	12.5	52 257	7.4	942 751	15.9	1 155 293	285 415	413 829	278 815	3 999
Adams	162	18 724	0.99	392	20.4	113	5.9	4 159	24.4	2 270	315	1 216	790	4 129
Asotin	174	19 287	0.72	246	11.1	237	10.7	2 591	14.7	5 646	853	2 921	813	3 692
Benton	1 426	180 469	1.02	2 583	13.9	1 276	6.8	26 061	16.4	29 326	3 834	15 553	4 813	2 602
Chelan	928	78 244	1.16	926	12.4	651	8.7	12 808	21.0	14 986	2 881	6 727	1 820	2 451
Clallam	1 877	70 885	0.97	656	9.0	941	12.9	9 571	18.2	22 621	1 773	11 783	2 418	3 349
Clark	3 434	388 199	0.76	5 377	11.9	3 204	7.1	58 280	15.2	72 373	37 807	16 267	11 442	2 580
Columbia	75	3 920	0.93	30	7.5	40	10.0	499	16.7	1 179	37	656	216	5 441
Cowlitz	1 207	100 199	0.95	1 135	11.1	1 051	10.3	14 186	17.0	23 089	10 434	6 967	4 430	4 336
Douglas	190	32 677	0.64	503	12.6	297	7.5	7 590	22.8	6 886	1 254	3 102	902	2 269
Ferry	253	7 497	0.94	66	8.6	76	9.9	1 428	23.6	1 969	53	1 021	68	874
Franklin	2 855	78 656	0.90	1 613	18.4	404	4.6	17 714	23.0	8 537	902	4 730	2 050	2 316
Garfield	36	2 115	0.86	19	8.6	20	9.0	256	14.7	595	NA	357	54	2 430
Grant	1 244	91 870	1.05	1 557	16.7	654	7.0	18 148	22.8	13 962	1 992	7 073	4 315	4 763
Grays Harbor	2 715	70 332	0.93	777	11.0	793	11.2	12 192	21.7	16 761	1 109	9 379	2 397	3 351
Island	1 678	70 733	0.77	858	10.8	628	7.9	8 596	14.3	19 095	5 400	6 007	1 420	1 784
Jefferson	631	29 267	0.94	190	6.3	328	10.9	3 678	17.9	10 640	525	5 648	708	2 366
King	38 148	2 133 109	1.16	25 547	12.3	12 750	6.1	242 657	13.7	281 151	94 906	99 464	91 696	4 500
Kitsap	8 764	243 091	0.92	2 895	11.4	2 094	8.2	28 297	13.6	46 689	9 216	14 767	8 131	3 165
Kittitas	2 249	39 697	0.91	412	9.7	274	6.4	6 538	19.3	7 098	460	3 446	1 392	3 312
Klickitat	198	20 091	0.94	207	9.9	178	8.5	3 276	19.7	5 230	304	2 828	340	1 629
Lewis	948	73 797	0.94	846	11.3	791	10.5	10 966	18.1	18 130	5 416	6 967	2 012	2 699
Lincoln	94	10 025	0.89	92	9.0	112	10.9	1 212	15.3	2 740	34	1 567	166	1 592
Mason	2 524	55 412	0.76	647	10.7	611	10.1	9 231	20.1	14 898	2 728	6 195	2 158	3 535
Okanogan	640	41 198	1.00	528	12.8	431	10.4	8 695	26.2	9 587	708	4 981	1 032	2 492
Pacific	277	20 264	0.93	191	9.3	305	14.8	3 086	20.8	6 797	133	4 070	463	2 255
Pend Oreille	98	12 458	0.88	120	9.2	141	10.9	1 688	16.8	3 521	358	1 586	451	3 463
Pierce	16 672	761 823	0.88	11 291	13.6	6 382	7.7	104 841	14.8	128 825	36 689	40 609	37 228	4 541
San Juan	187	15 749	1.00	82	5.1	114	7.1	2 483	21.9	4 834	1 089	2 169	219	1 378
Skagit	1 627	118 649	1.02	1 458	12.1	1 116	9.3	18 026	18.6	25 859	7 784	9 573	5 390	4 529
Skamania	25	9 335	0.60	106	9.3	78	6.9	1 468	15.7	2 130	295	964	126	1 119
Snohomish	10 437	653 255	0.80	9 477	12.5	5 130	6.8	94 528	14.5	105 920	46 641	28 247	24 848	3 352
Spokane	14 702	482 780	1.04	6 062	12.5	4 295	8.9	66 196	16.5	88 426	30 187	28 487	31 217	6 525
Stevens	266	39 388	0.74	433	9.9	425	9.7	6 620	19.0	10 804	1 379	4 886	852	1 950
Thurston	4 051	242 343	0.88	3 157	11.9	2 010	7.6	30 695	13.9	48 168	15 882	12 768	7 538	2 889
Wahkiakum	48	3 731	0.79	33	8.1	48	11.8	535	18.9	1 296	292	543	31	772
Walla Walla	4 566	61 552	1.10	693	11.6	571	9.5	8 456	18.4	11 498	1 298	5 629	2 148	3 594
Whatcom	5 939	199 143	0.96	2 257	10.8	1 518	7.3	31 984	18.7	38 009	13 088	13 352	6 841	3 302
Whitman	6 141	48 279	1.14	481	10.3	232	5.0	5 743	16.0	5 294	96	2 609	842	1 805
Yakima	3 481	243 937	0.99	4 052	16.4	1 938	7.8	57 774	27.0	38 454	7 406	18 715	9 112	3 664
WEST VIRGINIA	49 490	1 836 328	0.98	20 466	11.1	21 735	11.7	254 093	17.1	412 831	107 485	196 041	44 581	2 404
Barbour	776	14 228	0.62	192	11.5	193	11.5	2 549	19.5	3 677	787	1 874	106	644
Berkeley	869	89 577	0.65	1 408	12.7	931	8.4	15 040	16.1	18 344	3 330	7 881	2 752	2 553
Boone	131	25 986	1.19	242	10.2	290	12.2	3 135	15.5	5 643	1 443	2 575	351	1 752
Braxton	335	14 049	0.91	170	11.8	172	11.9	2 258	19.9	3 329	976	1 467	158	1 311

1. Per 1,000 estimated resident population. 2. Data for serious crimes have not been adjusted for underreporting; this may affect comparability between geographic areas and over time.
3. Per 100,000 population estimated by the FBI.

STATE County	Serious crimes known to police, 2013 (cont.)[1] Rate[2] Violent	Serious crimes known to police, 2013 (cont.)[1] Rate[2] Property	Education: School enrollment and attainment, 2009–2013 Enrollment[3] Total	Education: Enrollment[3] Percent private	Education: Attainment[4] (percent) High school graduate or less	Education: Attainment[4] (percent) Bachelor's degree or more	Education: Local government expenditures,[5] 2012–2013 Total current spending (mil dol)	Education: Local government expenditures,[5] 2012–2013 Current spending per student (dollars)	Money income, 2009–2013: Per capita income[6] (dollars)	Money income, 2009–2013: Households Median income (dollars)	Money income, 2009–2013: Households Mean income (dollars)	Money income, 2009–2013: Households Percent with income of $200,000 or more	Income and poverty, 2013: Median household income (dollars)	Income and poverty, 2013: Percent below poverty level All persons	Income and poverty, 2013: Percent below poverty level Children under 18 years	Income and poverty, 2013: Percent below poverty level Children 5 to 17 years in families
	46	47	48	49	50	51	52	53	54	55	56	57	58	59	60	61
VIRGINIA—Cont'd																
Manassas Park city	98	1 249	4 231	12.4	42.8	26.0	31.6	10 132	26 944	71 227	84 836	4.9	71 742	8.4	13.7	12.4
Martinsville city	407	3 638	3 147	14.8	51.2	16.7	23.9	10 514	19 900	28 116	43 951	2.4	31 046	25.8	38.1	37.8
Newport News city	440	3 093	52 027	14.7	39.7	23.9	308.1	10 345	25 310	51 027	63 190	2.3	47 421	17.5	27.1	26.7
Norfolk city	579	4 392	67 618	12.0	41.0	25.3	349.6	10 639	24 659	44 747	61 027	2.7	42 949	23.3	33.0	33.1
Norton city	268	4 674	1 033	3.9	41.5	20.5	7.3	8 230	22 699	39 416	51 647	1.1	32 303	22.0	36.5	32.6
Petersburg city	518	3 473	6 285	8.7	60.8	14.9	47.8	10 771	18 936	34 424	44 794	1.0	32 623	28.1	46.9	51.8
Poquoson city	140	1 131	3 213	9.5	31.0	37.2	20.5	9 415	38 444	81 892	101 891	9.4	82 815	5.5	6.3	5.2
Portsmouth city	612	5 551	24 974	14.8	47.6	19.5	154.3	10 116	23 138	46 166	57 509	1.9	43 041	20.9	33.2	33.7
Radford city	529	2 463	9 304	4.8	33.2	32.1	14.8	9 443	16 181	30 714	44 190	1.1	34 635	31.3	20.5	18.8
Richmond city	623	4 104	56 167	18.9	41.5	34.8	307.9	13 019	27 184	40 496	62 652	4.0	39 249	25.4	37.8	36.6
Roanoke city	469	4 542	21 254	12.1	48.0	23.6	156.2	11 728	23 295	38 145	51 447	1.5	37 223	23.3	36.5	35.6
Salem city	96	2 414	7 143	30.3	41.0	30.8	40.1	10 420	26 661	48 733	65 861	4.5	47 837	10.1	14.1	13.1
Staunton city	208	2 508	5 261	30.4	47.5	28.0	30.3	11 245	24 753	38 501	55 109	2.3	39 712	15.8	24.5	24.1
Suffolk city	318	3 028	24 611	19.6	41.9	26.2	138.7	9 620	29 135	66 085	78 717	4.1	59 468	11.5	17.3	15.3
Virginia Beach city	164	2 500	119 912	17.3	29.5	32.9	746.5	10 625	31 934	65 219	82 870	4.7	62 509	9.0	13.2	11.4
Waynesboro city	217	3 259	4 859	9.6	56.1	19.1	31.9	9 832	22 872	44 847	53 942	1.8	42 434	16.7	26.2	24.9
Williamsburg city	161	1 259	7 208	4.0	27.4	49.8	(7)	(7)	23 127	48 616	70 092	4.7	47 880	21.1	25.7	24.5
Winchester city	331	3 707	6 546	23.5	46.1	28.6	(8)	(8)	26 060	44 200	63 698	4.1	43 943	14.1	23.9	22.2
WASHINGTON	289	3 710	1 709 975	15.1	33.5	31.9	10 226.1	9 672	30 742	59 478	77 827	4.9	58 431	14.1	18.6	17.6
Adams	376	3 752	5 079	6.0	59.4	14.0	46.0	10 188	16 940	43 926	53 434	1.0	45 171	17.6	23.7	23.4
Asotin	241	3 451	5 161	11.1	44.5	17.8	33.3	10 040	24 659	43 175	57 828	2.0	42 842	16.8	25.8	23.2
Benton	224	2 378	46 582	9.5	35.8	28.9	301.2	8 894	28 583	60 485	76 295	3.9	59 264	13.2	18.2	17.1
Chelan	156	2 295	17 141	10.7	46.8	23.9	131.2	10 047	25 893	51 354	67 130	3.4	50 033	16.0	23.0	21.8
Clallam	259	3 090	13 760	13.8	35.9	24.2	95.0	8 974	25 865	46 033	57 686	1.9	46 531	17.5	24.8	22.9
Clark	202	2 378	114 849	12.7	35.0	26.0	716.7	9 204	27 681	58 225	73 835	3.7	57 886	12.6	17.4	16.1
Columbia	76	5 365	722	8.3	41.8	17.2	5.7	11 654	23 814	42 519	56 380	2.6	42 332	17.0	26.0	22.3
Cowlitz	355	3 981	23 958	12.0	43.2	15.4	156.7	9 254	23 557	47 596	59 363	1.7	48 447	15.9	23.1	21.1
Douglas	101	2 169	9 821	7.2	47.2	17.3	75.5	9 746	22 467	51 908	62 390	1.9	49 293	14.4	23.7	22.0
Ferry	193	681	1 575	9.7	46.4	16.1	13.0	13 068	20 052	37 571	48 286	0.9	38 302	22.1	33.1	28.5
Franklin	218	2 098	24 242	8.7	54.8	15.0	170.4	9 342	19 503	55 177	64 031	2.0	52 720	17.1	24.0	24.1
Garfield	135	2 295	437	2.5	33.6	22.7	4.1	12 542	26 954	51 548	60 766	2.1	46 157	15.1	25.3	22.1
Grant	278	4 485	23 890	6.8	52.3	14.6	180.4	9 661	19 738	45 949	56 655	1.7	46 065	18.4	24.5	22.9
Grays Harbor	172	3 179	15 653	7.5	46.1	14.1	113.0	10 896	21 828	42 405	54 910	1.1	41 791	19.4	28.2	26.6
Island	92	1 692	16 709	16.2	29.2	31.7	70.5	8 691	30 941	58 455	72 743	3.2	53 306	10.9	15.1	14.6
Jefferson	237	2 129	4 769	11.2	27.6	36.5	29.3	10 066	28 266	46 320	59 603	3.1	47 709	13.6	23.8	22.1
King	315	4 184	481 070	19.5	24.9	46.6	2 509.6	10 005	39 911	71 811	96 523	9.1	71 779	12.4	15.7	15.1
Kitsap	271	2 894	59 844	14.2	29.8	29.5	356.6	9 822	31 769	62 413	79 284	4.1	62 516	11.4	15.0	13.5
Kittitas	126	3 186	14 156	7.7	37.0	33.6	46.6	9 577	22 796	42 982	55 189	1.2	47 287	19.0	18.6	17.7
Klickitat	77	1 553	4 350	12.2	43.5	19.5	34.5	10 706	22 229	41 694	54 681	1.5	47 960	15.9	25.0	22.5
Lewis	182	2 517	17 343	13.2	46.6	14.0	116.7	9 807	22 212	42 860	54 362	1.0	41 325	18.9	26.3	24.1
Lincoln	96	1 496	2 226	12.4	41.0	20.3	27.8	13 725	25 816	47 195	60 579	2.8	47 895	14.1	19.9	18.4
Mason	197	3 339	12 087	8.6	41.8	17.3	78.9	9 896	23 542	48 755	58 805	1.2	46 886	18.2	27.8	26.4
Okanogan	186	2 306	8 455	11.0	50.9	16.5	80.0	8 613	20 735	40 368	50 707	1.4	39 014	21.7	30.8	29.8
Pacific	170	2 085	3 715	6.8	44.2	17.8	34.1	10 346	23 888	39 830	52 391	1.7	35 703	19.0	28.1	27.0
Pend Oreille	131	3 332	2 564	13.4	43.2	17.8	18.2	11 175	23 167	40 567	53 674	2.4	44 882	18.8	31.1	27.8
Pierce	445	4 096	204 920	15.8	38.5	24.0	1 252.4	9 826	28 223	59 204	73 455	3.4	57 619	14.1	19.3	18.4
San Juan	94	1 283	2 571	22.4	22.7	45.1	20.1	11 048	37 719	53 376	77 078	5.9	56 667	10.4	18.1	16.7
Skagit	213	4 317	26 677	11.2	37.5	23.6	197.5	10 426	27 065	55 925	68 155	2.3	52 525	16.3	21.5	20.4
Skamania	169	951	2 265	16.0	38.0	20.8	12.1	10 076	28 449	53 712	68 003	3.1	52 967	13.0	20.6	18.4
Snohomish	190	3 162	181 101	14.1	33.3	28.9	1 214.7	9 426	31 349	68 381	82 005	4.3	67 443	11.2	14.5	12.2
Spokane	375	6 149	125 180	19.3	33.2	28.4	719.6	9 851	25 661	49 233	63 422	2.9	47 577	17.0	20.2	19.5
Stevens	96	1 854	9 834	12.8	42.1	18.6	69.8	10 854	21 986	41 742	53 866	1.3	43 675	16.5	26.9	24.0
Thurston	200	2 689	63 941	13.5	30.3	32.3	385.2	9 472	29 744	62 229	73 982	3.1	59 877	12.5	16.3	15.6
Wahkiakum	75	698	795	9.4	42.5	14.3	4.4	10 112	22 334	41 815	49 994	1.2	46 659	14.9	27.0	24.2
Walla Walla	196	3 399	16 544	26.3	34.8	26.0	89.8	9 945	23 809	46 597	62 443	2.6	46 294	17.3	22.6	22.3
Whatcom	203	3 100	57 237	12.7	31.5	31.9	253.3	9 366	26 530	51 939	65 929	2.6	51 119	16.4	17.1	15.9
Whitman	150	1 655	23 680	4.2	22.2	48.9	52.8	11 632	21 208	36 257	55 906	3.3	42 702	26.4	16.6	15.3
Yakima	293	3 371	65 072	8.8	55.8	15.5	509.4	9 783	19 433	43 506	57 404	1.7	41 918	21.1	29.0	28.3
WEST VIRGINIA	300	2 104	418 150	10.7	56.9	18.3	3 183.4	11 132	22 966	41 043	55 308	2.0	41 195	18.4	26.3	23.9
Barbour	201	444	3 974	20.5	68.7	11.6	25.0	10 348	17 876	37 327	45 570	0.7	35 558	21.4	30.1	26.6
Berkeley	191	2 362	26 063	13.9	52.2	19.8	191.3	10 527	26 264	53 515	67 346	2.2	54 010	13.2	18.8	16.7
Boone	170	1 582	4 861	4.5	70.9	8.5	59.3	13 099	21 627	42 156	53 992	1.0	38 098	22.5	30.3	27.0
Braxton	199	1 112	2 647	5.0	69.6	11.2	22.5	10 420	18 635	31 848	44 556	1.3	35 296	22.3	31.9	28.6

1. Data for serious crimes have not been adjusted for underreporting; this may affect comparability between geographic areas and over time. 2. Per 100,000 population estimated by the FBI.
3. All persons 3 years old and over enrolled in nursery school through college. 4. Persons 25 years old and over. 5. Elementary and secondary education expenditures.
6. Based on population estimated by the American Community Survey, 2009–2013. 7. Williamsburg city is included with James City county. 8. Winchester city is included with Frederick county.

STATE County	Personal income, 2013										Earnings, 2013		
	Total (mil dol)	Percent change, 2012–2013	Per capita[1]		Wages and salaries (mil dol)	Supplements to wages and salaries; employer contributions (mil dol)		Proprietors' income (mil dol)	Dividends, interest, and rent (mil dol)	Personal transfer receipts (mil dol)	Total (mil dol)	Contributions for government social insurance (mil dol)	
			Dollars	Rank		Pension and insurance	Government social insurance					From employee and self-employed	From employer
	62	63	64	65	66	67	68	69	70	71	72	73	74
VIRGINIA—Cont'd													
Manassas Park city	(3)	(3)	(3)	(3)	(3)	(3)	(3)	(3)	(3)	(3)	(3)	(3)	(3)
Martinsville city	(4)	(4)	(4)	(4)	(4)	(4)	(4)	(4)	(4)	(4)	(4)	(4)	(4)
Newport News city	6 892	2.0	37 862	1 451	5 431	1 107	423	227	1 504	1 325	7 189	394	423
Norfolk city	9 602	0.7	39 009	1 299	9 806	2 198	836	658	2 306	1 766	13 498	672	836
Norton city	(5)	(5)	(5)	(5)	(5)	(5)	(5)	(5)	(5)	(5)	(5)	(5)	(5)
Petersburg city	(6)	(6)	(6)	(6)	(6)	(6)	(6)	(6)	(6)	(6)	(6)	(6)	(6)
Poquoson city	(7)	(7)	(7)	(7)	(7)	(7)	(7)	(7)	(7)	(7)	(7)	(7)	(7)
Portsmouth city	3 756	1.5	39 047	1 292	2 669	704	225	185	767	863	3 783	200	225
Radford city	(8)	(8)	(8)	(8)	(8)	(8)	(8)	(8)	(8)	(8)	(8)	(8)	(8)
Richmond city	9 779	1.9	45 672	645	8 718	1 494	623	918	2 432	1 761	11 754	666	623
Roanoke city	4 239	2.1	43 053	836	3 198	505	255	247	900	950	4 205	255	255
Salem city	(9)	(9)	(9)	(9)	(9)	(9)	(9)	(9)	(9)	(9)	(9)	(9)	(9)
Staunton city	(10)	(10)	(10)	(10)	(10)	(10)	(10)	(10)	(10)	(10)	(10)	(10)	(10)
Suffolk city	3 579	0.4	41 749	965	1 336	222	100	158	700	624	1 815	112	100
Virginia Beach city	22 721	0.7	50 662	342	8 391	1 544	661	1 508	5 284	2 800	12 104	679	661
Waynesboro city	(10)	(10)	(10)	(10)	(10)	(10)	(10)	(10)	(10)	(10)	(10)	(10)	(10)
Williamsburg city	(11)	(11)	(11)	(11)	(11)	(11)	(11)	(11)	(11)	(11)	(11)	(11)	(11)
Winchester city	(12)	(12)	(12)	(12)	(12)	(12)	(12)	(12)	(12)	(12)	(12)	(12)	(12)
WASHINGTON	332 655	2.5	47 717	X	170 790	26 554	15 085	25 279	69 758	50 993	237 707	13 761	15 085
Adams	782	2.7	40 993	1 051	267	49	26	133	214	142	475	20	26
Asotin	842	2.4	38 078	1 422	198	40	19	66	204	226	323	23	19
Benton	7 702	1.1	41 746	966	4 104	632	377	648	1 405	1 311	5 762	324	377
Chelan	3 154	2.4	42 635	878	1 510	258	148	262	778	644	2 177	122	148
Clallam	2 935	1.9	40 586	1 100	876	193	85	209	928	787	1 362	94	85
Clark	18 004	3.6	40 567	1 102	6 546	1 072	615	1 082	3 740	3 128	9 315	580	615
Columbia	177	2.5	43 818	772	50	12	4	17	40	46	83	5	4
Cowlitz	3 667	3.1	36 002	1 745	1 665	270	163	256	652	1 020	2 353	154	163
Douglas	1 285	1.3	32 556	2 318	384	72	36	32	289	288	524	31	36
Ferry	230	2.4	30 114	2 670	65	18	6	9	50	83	98	7	6
Franklin	2 645	2.2	30 534	2 622	1 218	215	121	320	419	528	1 874	92	121
Garfield	82	-5.1	36 332	1 686	31	10	3	-1	22	22	43	3	3
Grant	3 190	3.6	34 717	1 949	1 410	265	136	423	545	709	2 234	104	136
Grays Harbor	2 338	0.8	32 892	2 265	856	175	85	117	464	749	1 232	82	85
Island	3 413	1.2	43 306	817	955	253	96	156	1 150	698	1 459	85	96
Jefferson	1 417	2.0	47 111	546	299	65	28	54	516	345	446	34	28
King	128 331	3.2	62 770	79	85 817	10 874	7 089	12 813	27 308	12 487	116 593	6 709	7 089
Kitsap	11 564	1.1	45 533	654	4 471	1 066	422	471	3 102	1 914	6 430	359	422
Kittitas	1 578	3.1	37 775	1 467	534	120	51	112	431	303	817	47	51
Klickitat	925	-0.7	44 340	737	320	55	30	114	206	216	520	31	30
Lewis	2 509	2.3	33 424	2 188	930	180	95	108	500	769	1 313	89	95
Lincoln	440	5.7	42 746	868	123	27	11	52	113	103	213	11	11
Mason	2 083	2.1	34 425	2 004	527	120	51	83	513	588	781	56	51
Okanogan	1 611	1.4	39 103	1 279	521	116	50	244	332	408	931	49	50
Pacific	768	2.9	37 481	1 510	226	50	22	32	192	263	330	24	22
Pend Oreille	434	1.5	33 682	2 147	123	30	11	8	98	142	173	12	11
Pierce	36 054	1.7	43 982	758	15 277	2 972	1 482	2 170	6 688	6 251	21 901	1 224	1 482
San Juan	932	1.0	58 718	125	192	33	19	62	470	143	306	22	19
Skagit	5 101	3.0	42 927	852	2 052	402	198	293	1 307	1 057	2 946	176	198
Skamania	436	1.4	38 681	1 340	78	17	8	10	97	88	112	8	8
Snohomish	34 859	2.0	46 733	568	15 231	2 493	1 360	1 281	5 403	4 585	20 365	1 203	1 360
Spokane	18 559	2.4	38 712	1 335	9 456	1 603	892	1 001	4 047	4 002	12 952	785	892
Stevens	1 358	2.4	31 262	2 515	368	80	36	53	292	432	537	40	36
Thurston	11 671	2.1	44 481	729	4 745	965	426	602	2 460	2 035	6 736	394	426
Wahkiakum	140	2.5	34 552	1 975	28	7	3	5	37	44	42	4	3
Walla Walla	2 302	1.4	38 663	1 345	1 078	204	98	214	519	485	1 593	86	98
Whatcom	8 476	2.7	41 076	1 043	3 699	664	345	668	2 062	1 529	5 375	317	345
Whitman	1 647	1.6	35 356	1 845	772	227	67	175	406	263	1 241	59	67
Yakima	9 016	1.5	36 497	1 664	3 793	649	372	924	1 760	2 159	5 738	299	372
WEST VIRGINIA	65 889	1.0	35 533	X	29 521	6 035	2 333	5 028	9 368	17 640	42 917	2 750	2 333
Barbour	466	1.8	27 759	2 911	127	28	10	32	62	150	196	15	10
Berkeley	3 567	0.8	32 816	2 280	1 322	308	109	213	468	705	1 952	119	109
Boone	727	-0.3	29 999	2 687	396	71	29	46	74	252	541	37	29
Braxton	400	0.3	27 602	2 924	128	30	10	25	52	134	193	14	10

1. Based on the resident population estimated as of July 1 of the year shown. 3. Manassas and Manassas Park cities are included with Prince William county. 4. Martinsville city is included with Henry county. 5. Norton city is included with Wise county. 6. Petersburg and Colonial Heights cities are included with Dinwiddie county. 7. Poquoson city is included with York county. 8. Radford city is included with Montgomery county. 9. Salem city is included with Roanoke county. 10. Staunton and Waynesboro cities are included with Augusta county. 11. Williamsburg city is included with James City county. 12. Winchester city is included with Frederick county.

STATE County	Earnings, 2013 (cont.) — Percent by selected industries: Farm	Mining	Construction	Manu-facturing	Infor-mation: professional, scientific, technical services	Retail trade	Finance, insur-ance, real estate and leasing	Health care and social assistance	Govern-ment	Social Security beneficiaries, December 2013: Number	Rate[1]	Supple-mental Security Income recipients, December 2013	Housing units, 2014: Total	Percent change, 2010–2014
	75	76	77	78	79	80	81	82	83	84	85	86	87	88
VIRGINIA—Cont'd														
Manassas Park city	(3)	(3)	(3)	(3)	(3)	(3)	(3)	(3)	(3)	1 170	76	142	4 900	0.1
Martinsville city	(4)	(4)	(4)	(4)	(4)	(4)	(4)	(4)	(4)	4 485	326	737	7 162	-0.6
Newport News city	0.0	D	2.8	31.8	7.5	4.4	3.2	9.7	26.3	28 100	154	4 610	77 384	1.4
Norfolk city	0.0	D	2.1	3.3	9.6	2.9	5.0	10.3	48.1	32 845	134	7 302	96 665	1.7
Norton city	(5)	(5)	(5)	(5)	(5)	(5)	(5)	(5)	(5)	1 400	349	323	1 938	-0.1
Petersburg city	(6)	(6)	(6)	(6)	(6)	(6)	(6)	(6)	(6)	7 730	237	2 303	16 448	0.7
Poquoson city	(7)	(7)	(7)	(7)	(7)	(7)	(7)	(7)	(7)	2 410	199	67	4 749	0.4
Portsmouth city	0.0	0.0	4.4	3.6	3.6	2.4	1.6	10.0	58.9	18 325	191	3 861	41 068	0.6
Radford city	(8)	(8)	(8)	(8)	(8)	(8)	(8)	(8)	(8)	2 220	128	269	6 558	2.1
Richmond city	0.0	D	3.4	4.5	D	2.3	7.9	12.4	26.8	33 940	158	9 503	100 107	1.8
Roanoke city	0.0	D	D	6.5	7.8	6.8	6.9	22.9	13.2	20 745	210	4 492	47 378	0.0
Salem city	(9)	(9)	(9)	(9)	(9)	(9)	(9)	(9)	(9)	6 080	240	449	10 854	0.1
Staunton city	(10)	(10)	(10)	(10)	(10)	(10)	(10)	(10)	(10)	6 545	269	580	11 753	0.1
Suffolk city	1.0	D	4.9	8.7	15.6	6.1	4.4	13.2	23.7	15 130	176	2 296	35 195	6.5
Virginia Beach city	0.1	D	7.2	2.9	11.4	6.5	11.5	10.6	28.7	65 630	146	5 279	182 131	2.4
Waynesboro city	(10)	(10)	(10)	(10)	(10)	(10)	(10)	(10)	(10)	5 160	243	556	10 030	3.2
Williamsburg city	(11)	(11)	(11)	(11)	(11)	(11)	(11)	(11)	(11)	2 360	160	146	4 978	1.3
Winchester city	(12)	(12)	(12)	(12)	(12)	(12)	(12)	(12)	(12)	5 255	191	654	11 917	0.4
WASHINGTON	1.4	0.1	5.9	11.1	16.3	6.7	6.0	10.1	19.5	1 197 824	172	150 239	2 963 141	2.7
Adams	28.0	0.0	2.1	13.2	1.3	4.4	1.4	D	18.3	2 515	132	320	6 295	0.8
Asotin	1.5	D	9.4	5.1	4.8	13.0	4.9	D	19.8	6 140	278	723	9 843	-0.3
Benton	5.4	D	6.6	5.5	18.9	5.9	3.5	10.0	17.7	30 985	168	3 613	72 309	5.4
Chelan	7.8	0.1	5.9	6.4	4.8	7.7	3.9	17.6	20.7	16 040	217	1 519	36 243	2.2
Clallam	-0.1	0.1	5.5	7.3	4.6	9.3	3.0	8.6	37.1	23 675	328	1 932	35 806	0.6
Clark	-0.1	D	8.5	9.6	10.3	7.0	6.0	14.3	18.7	76 265	172	8 396	172 762	3.2
Columbia	21.4	D	4.2	3.8	1.8	4.2	1.7	D	35.2	1 270	315	153	2 120	-0.7
Cowlitz	-0.1	1.0	12.4	23.0	3.5	6.7	2.9	13.0	15.2	25 650	252	3 732	43 510	0.1
Douglas	14.6	0.0	5.5	5.0	5.9	9.3	2.2	7.0	32.2	7 345	186	568	16 226	1.4
Ferry	0.1	D	D	D	D	D	1.7	D	54.1	2 225	290	296	4 410	0.2
Franklin	15.7	D	6.4	8.6	2.1	6.6	2.1	6.9	21.1	9 130	105	1 800	26 440	8.3
Garfield	-1.1	0.0	D	0.0	D	5.0	1.3	1.6	72.3	610	271	42	1 223	-0.8
Grant	23.2	D	4.0	13.8	2.0	5.5	2.4	5.0	25.2	15 210	165	2 180	35 499	1.2
Grays Harbor	0.9	D	5.9	13.4	4.2	7.9	3.4	10.8	30.9	18 445	260	2 910	35 258	0.3
Island	0.2	0.1	4.7	3.0	D	6.3	2.6	5.3	58.0	19 990	254	1 031	40 685	1.1
Jefferson	0.0	D	7.6	9.8	7.4	7.8	4.1	7.7	34.4	10 880	362	625	17 947	1.0
King	0.0	0.0	5.2	9.7	26.1	6.5	7.2	8.2	12.3	274 195	134	38 309	880 462	3.4
Kitsap	0.0	0.1	4.9	1.9	7.2	6.1	3.1	11.0	52.8	47 255	187	5 227	109 327	1.8
Kittitas	3.6	D	9.0	3.5	4.7	8.4	3.7	5.9	37.1	7 560	181	531	22 553	3.0
Klickitat	5.8	D	4.3	5.7	18.3	2.9	2.3	3.0	20.0	5 675	272	592	9 952	1.7
Lewis	1.2	0.7	5.0	14.5	3.5	10.0	2.4	13.7	22.8	20 000	266	2 547	34 095	0.1
Lincoln	27.6	0.0	5.7	0.5	4.2	4.1	1.7	D	31.9	2 940	286	222	5 839	1.1
Mason	0.4	D	5.2	12.1	D	7.9	3.2	5.7	43.3	16 215	268	1 588	32 632	0.4
Okanogan	17.9	2.2	4.3	1.8	4.9	8.4	4.0	6.4	30.3	10 495	255	1 325	22 431	0.8
Pacific	1.2	D	6.4	11.4	3.0	6.6	4.4	D	36.9	7 420	363	696	15 737	1.2
Pend Oreille	-0.6	5.3	3.4	12.7	3.3	4.3	1.6	D	55.6	3 835	297	521	8 012	1.0
Pierce	0.1	0.1	6.9	6.2	4.6	6.1	5.0	14.8	34.9	135 925	166	19 514	332 712	2.3
San Juan	-0.8	D	14.6	D	D	8.9	5.1	6.7	17.1	4 790	302	141	13 721	3.1
Skagit	3.5	0.1	8.6	15.5	5.0	9.3	5.0	8.1	24.9	27 140	229	2 460	51 870	0.8
Skamania	-1.5	D	6.1	13.3	6.7	5.4	1.9	D	37.3	2 330	207	251	5 653	0.4
Snohomish	0.1	0.1	6.6	34.2	7.7	6.5	5.6	8.4	15.5	109 365	147	12 218	297 734	3.9
Spokane	0.0	0.1	6.0	8.0	7.8	7.7	7.9	17.2	20.1	92 485	193	13 866	206 115	2.3
Stevens	-0.9	0.8	5.4	13.4	D	8.0	2.8	14.6	30.9	11 830	272	1 322	21 141	-0.1
Thurston	0.4	0.0	4.8	3.5	6.0	6.7	4.1	12.6	40.4	51 880	198	5 286	111 807	3.4
Wahkiakum	-1.5	0.0	9.3	3.9	6.5	D	2.9	D	32.0	1 370	339	92	2 070	0.1
Walla Walla	11.5	D	3.7	14.8	4.1	5.5	4.0	14.9	24.1	11 880	199	1 383	23 898	1.9
Whatcom	2.8	0.2	8.5	13.6	9.7	8.4	4.8	11.6	19.3	39 250	190	4 369	92 466	2.0
Whitman	9.2	D	2.3	14.9	2.2	4.3	1.6	5.7	47.0	5 570	119	418	19 964	3.3
Yakima	14.5	0.1	4.4	8.2	3.1	6.9	3.2	14.1	19.0	42 050	170	7 521	86 374	1.1
WEST VIRGINIA	0.0	8.7	6.7	8.7	7.2	7.1	4.8	14.8	20.6	460 494	248	79 136	884 605	0.3
Barbour	-0.7	D	10.1	D	3.6	6.1	2.7	D	19.4	4 195	250	875	7 835	-0.2
Berkeley	0.3	D	6.0	5.2	10.7	6.3	3.9	12.7	35.6	20 260	186	2 209	46 205	3.2
Boone	0.0	47.7	1.5	0.9	D	4.7	D	4.4	16.5	6 665	277	1 438	11 030	-0.4
Braxton	-0.5	1.7	8.4	9.4	3.3	13.9	3.3	15.0	22.7	3 720	258	780	7 372	-0.6

1. Per 1,000 resident population estimated as of July 1 of the year shown. 3. Manassas and Manassas Park cities are included with Prince William county. 4. Martinsville city is included with Henry county. 5. Norton city is included with Wise county. 6. Petersburg and Colonial Heights cities are included with Dinwiddie county. 7. Poquoson city is included with York county. 8. Radford city is included with Montgomery county. 9. Salem city is included with Roanoke county. 10. Staunton and Waynesboro cities are included with Augusta county. 11. Williamsburg city is included with James City county. 12. Winchester city is included with Frederick county.

STATE County	Housing units, 2009–2013								Civilian labor force, 2014				Civilian employment,[6] 2009–2013		
	Occupied units										Unemployment			Percent	
		Owner-occupied				Renter-occupied									
				Median owner cost as a percent of income											
	Total	Percent	Median value[1]	With a mortgage	Without a mortgage[2]	Median rent[3]	Median rent as a percent of income[2]	Substandard units[4] (percent)	Total	Percent change, 2013–2014	Total	Rate[5]	Total	Management, business, science and arts	Construction, production, and maintenance occupations
	89	90	91	92	93	94	95	96	97	98	99	100	101	102	103
VIRGINIA—Cont'd															
Manassas Park city	4 435	63.7	213 300	29.1	13.2	1 469	28.3	1.6	8 831	0.1	400	4.5	7 964	28.7	25.6
Martinsville city	5 995	53.7	86 800	24.2	13.6	558	37.2	2.7	5 559	-2.7	553	9.9	4 940	26.7	27.8
Newport News city	69 211	51.4	200 100	25.1	12.7	974	30.7	2.9	90 692	0.1	5 645	6.2	82 503	32.8	22.2
Norfolk city	85 557	44.5	202 800	27.9	14.2	948	33.4	1.7	112 971	0.0	7 182	6.4	102 347	31.5	22.5
Norton city	1 706	52.7	88 000	20.5	10.0	596	28.6	2.7	1 812	-3.4	142	7.8	1 841	32.4	20.3
Petersburg city	12 456	45.7	122 500	25.0	13.0	833	33.8	0.4	13 909	0.8	1 481	10.6	11 912	25.9	23.5
Poquoson city	4 591	81.8	302 400	22.6	13.0	1 237	28.0	2.9	6 364	0.1	288	4.5	5 837	48.3	17.8
Portsmouth city	36 690	57.2	175 600	27.7	15.6	953	33.5	0.0	45 364	-0.3	3 236	7.1	40 961	29.9	23.5
Radford city	5 516	46.2	144 000	21.8	12.6	718	44.1	3.3	8 411	0.7	558	6.6	7 284	33.6	13.6
Richmond city	84 833	43.1	196 400	26.8	14.9	883	33.7	2.1	111 992	1.2	6 858	6.1	98 453	38.9	15.2
Roanoke city	42 494	54.8	134 700	25.3	13.5	697	29.8	1.8	50 175	0.6	2 945	5.9	44 903	31.6	21.6
Salem city	9 908	66.6	170 300	23.4	12.3	809	28.9	3.6	13 166	0.7	672	5.1	11 864	36.9	15.7
Staunton city	10 495	57.7	169 400	23.8	11.7	704	37.6	2.3	12 010	0.3	620	5.2	10 913	33.9	20.1
Suffolk city	30 492	73.4	242 000	26.8	12.3	986	32.4	1.3	42 076	0.0	2 428	5.8	38 160	38.9	23.1
Virginia Beach city	164 944	64.2	267 600	26.7	12.6	1 235	31.4	2.2	231 784	0.1	11 442	4.9	211 587	39.3	17.3
Waynesboro city	8 708	58.2	165 600	23.4	13.1	771	31.3	1.0	10 071	0.2	538	5.3	9 232	29.1	21.4
Williamsburg city	4 391	44.7	311 800	27.5	10.5	1 068	32.1	3.3	6 891	-0.1	488	7.1	5 988	44.3	11.6
Winchester city	10 393	48.6	224 100	24.4	12.3	900	34.0	13.4	14 501	0.8	726	5.0	12 483	33.1	20.7
WASHINGTON	2 629 126	63.2	262 100	25.7	12.1	973	30.4	3.3	3 488 183	0.8	217 821	6.2	3 149 730	38.6	20.7
Adams	5 738	65.9	133 600	24.5	10.0	628	28.1	2.8	8 547	1.8	664	7.8	7 475	23.0	46.5
Asotin	9 058	67.5	173 600	24.5	10.2	674	29.4	3.1	9 735	-1.1	582	6.0	9 123	29.3	24.3
Benton	65 675	68.1	176 700	19.6	10.0	805	27.9	3.7	89 990	-0.1	6 892	7.7	81 261	37.7	23.6
Chelan	27 220	65.2	254 500	25.4	10.1	762	26.2	2.5	40 960	1.7	2 603	6.4	33 030	30.2	30.1
Clallam	30 814	69.8	222 200	26.8	11.3	802	31.5	3.0	26 939	-1.2	2 316	8.6	26 762	30.1	23.2
Clark	158 855	65.0	232 500	25.8	11.8	941	30.9	2.4	208 909	-0.4	16 404	7.9	190 101	35.2	22.8
Columbia	1 651	73.6	147 900	25.0	13.1	638	41.3	3.1	1 764	-0.5	136	7.7	1 638	31.1	22.3
Cowlitz	39 602	66.2	181 500	24.7	12.1	747	35.3	7.6	44 048	1.7	3 697	8.4	39 944	26.9	30.1
Douglas	13 976	71.0	205 100	23.9	11.2	771	27.5	5.0	19 278	2.4	1 388	7.2	17 504	22.2	38.3
Ferry	2 951	72.0	156 300	24.3	10.0	573	29.0	10.0	2 470	-0.5	289	11.7	2 323	28.4	33.0
Franklin	23 445	67.0	161 600	22.2	10.0	737	29.1	3.4	38 238	0.1	3 237	8.5	34 019	23.2	40.2
Garfield	970	76.4	139 500	20.9	10.7	717	17.7	6.8	959	-2.8	65	6.8	978	36.1	23.0
Grant	30 012	60.5	154 700	23.0	10.0	672	27.0	3.7	44 650	1.7	3 417	7.7	36 639	24.8	37.9
Grays Harbor	27 396	69.3	157 600	25.6	11.5	707	29.9	1.3	27 411	-2.3	2 840	10.4	26 548	24.0	28.5
Island	33 096	69.5	292 100	28.3	11.9	1 069	29.5	2.9	31 678	-0.1	2 176	6.9	31 452	35.5	22.1
Jefferson	13 801	73.2	284 100	28.7	13.0	838	35.0	3.3	11 160	-1.9	917	8.2	11 408	32.0	21.0
King	802 606	58.2	377 300	25.7	13.1	1 131	29.2	2.4	1 158 224	1.8	53 298	4.6	1 030 515	48.5	14.6
Kitsap	97 622	67.4	268 200	25.4	11.7	1 035	30.9	3.6	113 148	-0.1	7 123	6.3	106 880	37.7	20.3
Kittitas	16 538	56.8	244 700	27.2	12.3	796	39.2	4.8	20 003	-0.7	1 424	7.1	18 504	35.7	21.5
Klickitat	8 019	69.8	194 700	27.5	10.8	805	30.1	3.5	9 721	-0.6	809	8.3	7 835	32.4	29.9
Lewis	29 527	68.6	180 200	24.8	12.1	781	31.3	3.4	31 011	-0.8	2 862	9.2	29 116	25.6	30.9
Lincoln	4 457	77.9	155 700	24.5	10.3	615	26.4	3.3	5 048	-0.6	306	6.1	4 325	34.4	25.5
Mason	23 358	77.9	210 200	27.5	11.4	869	34.3	6.3	23 292	0.0	1 988	8.5	21 823	28.0	27.1
Okanogan	15 980	68.2	160 800	22.9	10.4	631	29.7	3.5	21 256	1.5	1 568	7.4	16 332	31.5	27.8
Pacific	9 366	72.9	162 000	23.9	13.7	720	29.7	3.4	8 056	0.7	816	10.1	7 745	30.4	30.3
Pend Oreille	5 484	75.1	186 400	25.4	10.1	785	37.3	3.0	4 623	-1.4	476	10.3	4 242	31.9	27.0
Pierce	300 623	61.5	240 400	26.9	13.0	997	31.5	6.1	383 905	0.2	27 672	7.2	352 966	33.1	22.9
San Juan	7 753	71.5	472 900	31.5	11.5	957	31.7	4.1	7 657	-2.4	399	5.2	7 715	36.4	21.5
Skagit	45 293	67.6	261 400	27.2	12.7	952	32.3	3.6	56 596	0.1	4 164	7.4	50 520	31.6	24.9
Skamania	4 452	73.8	248 200	25.2	10.7	702	25.7	3.0	4 978	-0.7	434	8.7	4 549	37.2	26.7
Snohomish	268 722	66.8	292 500	27.4	13.0	1 102	30.3	1.8	395 313	1.7	20 328	5.1	352 047	36.8	21.7
Spokane	187 572	63.9	184 700	24.1	11.3	764	32.3	4.4	225 031	-0.7	16 080	7.1	210 375	35.4	18.6
Stevens	17 684	77.5	173 500	26.4	11.7	659	29.6	2.5	17 562	-0.6	1 659	9.4	16 339	32.4	26.7
Thurston	100 801	66.8	244 900	25.7	11.8	1 021	30.5	1.5	123 119	0.6	8 184	6.6	115 107	39.3	17.5
Wahkiakum	1 715	75.9	195 600	23.6	12.2	625	50.0	3.6	1 359	4.5	135	9.9	1 305	28.2	36.5
Walla Walla	21 677	61.7	195 200	24.1	12.0	697	31.1	2.5	28 297	-0.4	1 844	6.5	25 460	35.2	21.3
Whatcom	79 314	63.0	277 000	26.0	12.3	890	33.3	0.7	101 872	0.1	6 769	6.6	96 145	33.9	21.9
Whitman	16 624	46.2	182 300	21.2	10.0	697	44.8	8.2	22 059	-0.4	1 214	5.5	20 816	48.0	12.0
Yakima	79 679	62.2	156 300	24.0	11.5	746	32.3	1.1	119 318	0.6	10 648	8.9	98 864	25.3	35.3
WEST VIRGINIA	741 390	73.4	98 500	19.6	10.0	611	29.2	1.8	790 035	-1.2	51 508	6.5	755 632	31.3	25.4
Barbour	6 099	77.2	87 900	19.4	10.0	502	27.8	2.8	6 667	-0.6	448	6.7	6 433	21.5	30.9
Berkeley	40 447	75.2	165 000	24.0	10.0	832	30.4	3.0	52 117	-0.9	2 748	5.3	47 595	31.7	27.1
Boone	9 559	77.0	77 600	18.4	10.0	519	28.8	4.6	8 495	-2.0	762	9.0	8 198	28.5	33.2
Braxton	5 780	76.9	80 400	18.0	10.0	486	29.3	1.4	5 286	-0.9	485	9.2	5 182	23.5	32.3

1. Specified owner-occupied units. 2. A value of 10.0 represents 10 percent or less; a value of 50.0 represents 50 percent or more. 3. Specified renter-occupied units.
4. Overcrowded or lacking complete plumbing facilities. 5. Percent of civilian labor force. 6. Persons 16 years old and over.

STATE County	Private nonfarm establishments, employment and payroll, 2013									Agriculture, 2012			
		Employment						Annual payroll		Farms			
											Percent with:		
	Number of establish-ments	Total	Health care and social assistance	Manufac-turing	Retail trade	Finance and insurance	Professional, scientific, and technical services	Total (mil dol)	Average per employee (dollars)	Number	Fewer than 50 acres	500 acres or more	Farm operators whose principal occu-pation is farming (percent)
	104	105	106	107	108	109	110	111	112	113	114	115	116
VIRGINIA—Cont'd													
Manassas Park city	321	3 012	D	D	232	26	117	132	43 841	NA	NA	NA	NA
Martinsville city	576	9 141	2 263	D	1 577	241	218	268	29 278	NA	NA	NA	NA
Newport News city	3 721	86 291	13 430	D	10 003	1 673	5 034	4 072	47 191	NA	NA	NA	NA
Norfolk city	5 386	106 493	18 373	6 286	12 457	4 802	11 001	4 586	43 066	NA	NA	NA	NA
Norton city	240	4 446	1 283	D	849	D	169	151	34 018	NA	NA	NA	NA
Petersburg city	713	13 700	5 822	D	1 403	206	162	456	33 298	NA	NA	NA	NA
Poquoson city	214	1 311	154	D	291	D	D	32	24 241	NA	NA	NA	NA
Portsmouth city	1 696	27 079	7 032	2 015	3 082	542	1 291	999	36 883	NA	NA	NA	NA
Radford city	314	4 693	495	D	556	D	186	180	38 412	NA	NA	NA	NA
Richmond city	6 000	122 120	26 754	5 923	9 157	11 026	12 661	6 444	52 764	NA	NA	NA	NA
Roanoke city	3 180	66 575	13 206	4 194	9 887	3 613	3 252	2 751	41 315	NA	NA	NA	NA
Salem city	969	18 587	4 662	3 395	2 068	641	519	835	44 930	NA	NA	NA	NA
Staunton city	757	10 578	3 033	431	1 902	399	269	288	27 261	NA	NA	NA	NA
Suffolk city	1 492	20 921	4 450	1 970	3 505	837	1 014	808	38 631	308	57.8	10.7	56.2
Virginia Beach city	10 720	149 848	17 976	5 821	22 218	12 585	14 760	5 666	37 814	187	64.7	7.0	48.1
Waynesboro city	610	9 424	831	1 671	2 210	D	311	309	32 781	NA	NA	NA	NA
Williamsburg city	513	9 728	636	D	1 939	179	118	256	26 289	NA	NA	NA	NA
Winchester city	1 307	23 778	6 843	1 894	4 126	605	1 024	952	40 023	NA	NA	NA	NA
WASHINGTON	176 815	2 444 098	375 679	246 382	312 494	98 936	193 509	130 765	53 502	37 249	63.2	11.0	47.4
Adams	357	4 267	D	D	600	81	52	157	36 856	713	17.8	46.6	54.8
Asotin	431	4 559	1 056	314	1 082	171	230	143	31 429	185	35.1	40.0	60.5
Benton	4 013	61 436	10 296	4 186	9 224	1 681	8 135	2 933	47 743	1 509	76.0	7.8	44.8
Chelan	2 432	26 065	5 357	1 806	4 116	877	926	1 027	39 409	890	72.2	2.9	55.7
Clallam	2 057	17 145	3 881	1 568	3 443	511	821	573	33 404	536	79.7	0.6	45.9
Clark	9 723	114 145	20 129	12 856	15 941	4 768	7 863	4 982	43 649	1 929	86.3	0.5	35.4
Columbia	133	763	175	D	D	20	D	24	31 974	308	23.1	37.7	42.5
Cowlitz	2 159	29 580	5 303	6 155	4 670	883	723	1 286	43 461	492	72.4	2.8	46.7
Douglas	675	6 454	971	333	1 608	179	185	190	29 413	849	43.0	25.9	55.9
Ferry	133	953	D	D	147	D	D	57	60 291	255	27.8	16.1	52.2
Franklin	1 406	17 565	1 773	2 712	2 890	374	472	660	37 586	883	37.5	27.2	62.7
Garfield	44	315	D	NA	54	12	D	10	31 971	211	15.6	51.2	56.9
Grant	1 742	19 611	2 955	3 875	3 245	512	504	750	38 247	1 552	31.2	25.9	66.6
Grays Harbor	1 662	15 693	2 716	2 272	2 842	D	424	573	36 540	557	63.9	4.7	44.7
Island	1 687	11 378	2 364	674	2 123	447	558	370	32 509	377	80.6	0.8	46.7
Jefferson	1 028	6 365	1 320	622	972	153	285	217	34 130	221	64.7	0.9	49.3
King	64 171	1 051 249	136 471	77 390	101 087	43 971	98 628	71 031	67 568	1 837	90.5	0.4	44.3
Kitsap	5 598	55 664	11 749	1 847	10 646	2 003	4 739	2 047	36 769	706	94.9	0.1	44.6
Kittitas	1 149	10 225	1 594	653	1 603	194	236	282	27 561	1 006	66.4	6.7	48.9
Klickitat	529	3 414	563	D	308	D	298	135	39 679	760	44.5	22.8	51.7
Lewis	1 809	18 458	3 206	2 985	3 613	386	482	651	35 290	1 647	63.8	2.1	41.0
Lincoln	257	1 515	D	D	295	77	98	59	39 197	897	16.7	48.6	54.3
Mason	988	9 450	1 788	1 099	1 568	373	243	325	34 408	377	83.8	1.9	40.6
Okanogan	1 120	8 128	1 807	473	1 864	218	448	241	29 607	1 449	52.3	11.5	48.5
Pacific	595	3 717	620	627	523	207	D	120	32 169	330	61.8	6.1	45.8
Pend Oreille	217	1 620	402	D	254	53	61	62	38 056	288	45.5	4.2	37.8
Pierce	16 584	227 238	44 022	16 885	33 497	9 634	9 096	9 435	41 522	1 478	85.3	0.3	47.0
San Juan	939	4 062	333	154	623	128	218	147	36 099	274	73.0	1.5	52.9
Skagit	3 351	38 170	7 241	5 278	6 865	1 549	1 561	1 585	41 534	1 074	73.0	4.4	48.0
Skamania	196	1 414	138	D	141	22	D	41	28 900	144	75.0	0.0	45.8
Snohomish	17 213	228 568	28 896	58 064	33 455	8 598	10 504	11 210	49 046	1 438	82.3	1.2	35.5
Spokane	12 217	172 432	33 505	14 227	25 280	10 588	8 961	7 006	40 631	2 501	59.7	9.2	41.5
Stevens	859	6 701	1 570	958	1 219	223	224	223	33 229	1 148	44.3	11.1	46.7
Thurston	5 840	64 870	13 091	2 559	12 085	2 516	4 980	2 428	37 435	1 336	79.3	2.0	30.7
Wahkiakum	84	456	D	D	74	D	D	14	29 954	109	50.5	1.8	50.5
Walla Walla	1 345	18 854	3 835	D	2 270	D	446	654	34 667	943	53.0	24.0	48.4
Whatcom	6 218	69 793	9 524	9 765	11 343	2 264	3 346	2 803	40 169	1 702	74.7	2.5	45.4
Whitman	828	9 777	1 930	D	1 291	221	276	354	36 209	1 195	21.5	45.4	59.5
Yakima	4 606	62 573	13 210	7 960	9 526	1 567	1 882	2 270	36 275	3 143	73.9	5.5	51.9
WEST VIRGINIA	37 573	575 987	130 136	40 176	86 476	17 000	25 000	21 499	37 325	21 489	28.3	5.8	42.6
Barbour	235	3 005	800	125	343	77	106	74	24 514	513	22.4	6.0	41.1
Berkeley	1 574	23 149	5 469	2 280	4 007	600	966	823	35 562	676	57.5	3.7	34.5
Boone	291	6 678	811	D	774	125	98	314	47 043	19	21.1	0.0	73.7
Braxton	257	3 053	949	D	598	D	D	88	28 933	386	16.6	12.2	50.3

STATE County	Agriculture, 2012 (cont.) — Land in farms — Acreage (1,000)	Land in farms — Percent change, 2007–2012	Land in farms — Acres — Average size of farm	Land in farms — Acres — Total irrigated (1,000)	Land in farms — Acres — Total cropland (1,000)	Value of land and buildings (dollars) — Average per farm	Value of land and buildings (dollars) — Average per acre	Value of machinery and equipment, average per farm (dollars)	Value of products sold — Total (mil dol)	Value of products sold — Average per farm (dollars)	Value of products sold — Percent from: — Crops	Value of products sold — Percent from: — Livestock and poultry products	Percent of farms with sales of: — $10,000 or more	Percent of farms with sales of: — $100,000 or more	Government payments — Total ($1,000)	Government payments — Percent of farms
	117	118	119	120	121	122	123	124	125	126	127	128	129	130	131	132
VIRGINIA—Cont'd																
Manassas Park city	NA	NA	NA	NA	NA	NA	NA	NA	NA	NA	NA	NA	NA	NA	NA	NA
Martinsville city	NA	NA	NA	NA	NA	NA	NA	NA	NA	NA	NA	NA	NA	NA	NA	NA
Newport News city	NA	NA	NA	NA	NA	NA	NA	NA	NA	NA	NA	NA	NA	NA	NA	NA
Norfolk city	NA	NA	NA	NA	NA	NA	NA	NA	NA	NA	NA	NA	NA	NA	NA	NA
Norton city	NA	NA	NA	NA	NA	NA	NA	NA	NA	NA	NA	NA	NA	NA	NA	NA
Petersburg city	NA	NA	NA	NA	NA	NA	NA	NA	NA	NA	NA	NA	NA	NA	NA	NA
Poquoson city	NA	NA	NA	NA	NA	NA	NA	NA	NA	NA	NA	NA	NA	NA	NA	NA
Portsmouth city	NA	NA	NA	NA	NA	NA	NA	NA	NA	NA	NA	NA	NA	NA	NA	NA
Radford city	NA	NA	NA	NA	NA	NA	NA	NA	NA	NA	NA	NA	NA	NA	NA	NA
Richmond city	NA	NA	NA	NA	NA	NA	NA	NA	NA	NA	NA	NA	NA	NA	NA	NA
Roanoke city	NA	NA	NA	NA	NA	NA	NA	NA	NA	NA	NA	NA	NA	NA	NA	NA
Salem city	NA	NA	NA	NA	NA	NA	NA	NA	NA	NA	NA	NA	NA	NA	NA	NA
Staunton city	NA	NA	NA	NA	NA	NA	NA	NA	NA	NA	NA	NA	NA	NA	NA	NA
Suffolk city	69	-3.0	225	0.4	50.9	1 016 494	4 521	155 899	62.5	202 760	94.4	5.6	37.3	15.6	2 466	47.4
Virginia Beach city	26	-1.8	140	0.2	21.2	744 428	5 317	93 203	17.7	94 631	95.0	5.0	36.9	13.9	373	23.0
Waynesboro city	NA	NA	NA	NA	NA	NA	NA	NA	NA	NA	NA	NA	NA	NA	NA	NA
Williamsburg city	NA	NA	NA	NA	NA	NA	NA	NA	NA	NA	NA	NA	NA	NA	NA	NA
Winchester city	NA	NA	NA	NA	NA	NA	NA	NA	NA	NA	NA	NA	NA	NA	NA	NA
WASHINGTON	14 748	-1.5	396	1 633.6	7 526.7	910 249	2 299	98 588	9 120.7	244 859	71.2	28.8	34.2	16.4	159 269	19.4
Adams	1 037	-5.6	1 454	127.0	815.0	1 790 387	1 231	252 728	430.2	603 303	79.0	21.0	50.5	39.4	15 567	68.2
Asotin	263	-3.9	1 423	0.5	84.3	1 210 465	851	103 357	20.5	110 854	79.9	20.2	40.5	25.4	2 504	49.2
Benton	704	11.2	466	197.3	519.1	1 276 306	2 738	127 966	923.2	611 771	D	D	34.5	15.0	6 225	10.9
Chelan	76	-19.2	85	22.8	31.5	746 306	8 760	64 446	206.5	231 999	98.2	1.8	65.6	33.7	658	7.0
Clallam	24	3.6	44	4.2	8.1	549 722	12 464	36 032	10.6	19 866	38.8	61.1	16.6	3.9	47	2.2
Clark	75	-4.6	39	3.7	29.0	490 328	12 652	38 798	50.9	26 367	37.1	62.9	16.4	2.6	293	2.4
Columbia	297	-5.1	966	4.1	184.5	1 038 701	1 076	177 896	57.7	187 442	93.4	6.6	39.3	24.0	5 273	73.4
Cowlitz	39	27.1	79	7.6	18.6	689 236	8 693	67 535	28.8	58 482	D	D	19.5	6.9	44	1.6
Douglas	814	-7.8	959	18.3	545.4	976 847	1 019	130 582	199.0	234 442	98.4	1.6	55.2	35.7	12 940	48.5
Ferry	792	5.7	3 107	2.8	19.4	1 320 859	425	55 478	5.3	20 906	54.0	46.0	28.2	7.5	159	13.3
Franklin	625	2.6	708	207.2	452.2	2 071 813	2 927	302 318	740.0	838 068	68.0	32.0	60.6	46.2	8 142	38.7
Garfield	308	0.1	1 462	0.8	187.5	1 384 441	947	153 076	48.2	228 474	92.0	8.0	50.7	37.0	4 878	80.6
Grant	964	-11.4	621	428.2	720.0	2 128 600	3 428	291 085	1 762.3	1 135 499	75.6	24.4	63.0	47.1	11 429	38.5
Grays Harbor	119	0.1	214	8.6	22.8	450 820	2 102	66 575	31.4	56 289	53.3	46.7	22.6	6.8	186	5.4
Island	15	-13.8	40	1.6	7.4	575 838	14 236	41 111	11.5	30 416	28.6	71.4	24.1	3.4	56	4.2
Jefferson	16	22.3	70	1.2	4.2	643 059	9 136	36 900	7.7	34 647	22.7	77.3	33.0	7.2	94	9.0
King	47	-5.2	25	4.1	19.7	545 036	21 432	39 027	120.7	65 732	36.4	63.6	22.8	4.6	791	4.0
Kitsap	10	-34.2	14	0.5	2.5	377 215	26 446	27 010	5.3	7 513	70.0	30.0	14.3	1.4	30	2.5
Kittitas	183	-4.2	182	66.9	68.3	804 841	4 421	77 593	68.9	68 500	68.4	31.6	35.5	12.2	875	10.3
Klickitat	551	-8.3	725	21.7	192.3	1 033 424	1 425	83 599	72.4	95 246	80.3	19.7	31.6	11.4	4 275	37.8
Lewis	133	1.0	81	8.2	54.3	507 676	6 294	48 523	132.3	80 345	22.0	78.0	24.0	6.3	879	6.8
Lincoln	1 115	2.3	1 243	34.7	808.5	1 383 491	1 113	173 996	183.2	204 285	94.7	5.3	46.5	33.8	20 307	77.6
Mason	24	-5.7	63	0.8	4.8	522 432	8 295	40 891	40.8	108 247	6.2	93.8	24.7	8.8	57	2.1
Okanogan	1 205	0.0	832	51.7	129.2	1 103 226	1 326	73 568	287.1	198 150	87.0	13.0	42.1	21.0	2 383	9.5
Pacific	52	-15.5	158	2.5	13.0	546 279	3 456	60 573	36.8	111 461	20.2	79.8	43.3	16.1	305	9.4
Pend Oreille	44	-20.8	151	0.9	15.3	462 514	3 054	45 521	4.0	13 729	58.5	41.5	15.3	2.4	27	2.8
Pierce	49	3.8	33	2.8	11.5	476 152	14 222	35 548	90.9	61 524	26.3	73.7	17.9	3.0	96	1.3
San Juan	16	-27.0	57	0.3	5.5	756 471	13 228	28 427	4.2	15 493	60.8	39.2	33.9	2.9	41	3.6
Skagit	107	-1.8	99	19.2	66.8	752 365	7 585	118 998	272.3	253 515	73.8	26.2	29.1	12.2	1 442	11.1
Skamania	6	18.3	45	0.4	1.3	456 965	10 166	36 611	5.5	38 458	27.7	72.3	25.0	6.9	0	0.0
Snohomish	71	-7.8	49	5.3	29.1	791 114	16 054	40 122	139.5	97 000	45.3	54.7	21.8	6.5	620	4.9
Spokane	537	-14.2	215	10.3	369.6	611 087	2 844	72 631	149.8	59 880	88.7	11.3	25.6	9.3	7 355	24.7
Stevens	527	-0.7	459	6.7	88.8	722 020	1 572	49 637	36.3	31 660	47.9	52.1	32.3	7.3	926	12.6
Thurston	77	-4.9	57	5.3	23.1	498 439	8 689	40 468	122.4	91 634	39.9	60.1	19.5	5.2	267	2.4
Wahkiakum	10	-20.5	88	0.0	2.7	411 376	4 692	38 826	3.5	31 991	8.3	91.7	31.2	7.3	92	11.9
Walla Walla	645	-5.5	684	91.1	565.8	1 426 922	2 086	175 634	437.4	463 795	D	D	42.2	23.5	12 372	45.2
Whatcom	116	12.9	68	35.5	78.7	786 343	11 554	80 437	357.3	209 937	33.5	66.5	31.2	15.5	3 425	17.6
Whitman	1 275	0.3	1 067	4.3	1 020.0	1 490 631	1 397	214 180	370.8	310 294	95.0	5.0	50.5	40.4	28 405	77.9
Yakima	1 780	8.0	566	224.4	306.9	1 021 212	1 803	118 874	1 645.5	523 548	65.0	35.0	45.7	22.4	5 804	11.5
WEST VIRGINIA	3 607	-2.5	168	2.1	804.0	413 407	2 463	50 020	806.8	37 544	17.2	82.8	25.3	4.0	7 034	10.2
Barbour	85	-6.9	165	0.0	19.2	323 021	1 955	52 060	6.6	12 930	17.5	82.5	28.8	1.9	109	8.2
Berkeley	70	-6.7	104	0.1	33.3	596 855	5 757	53 351	30.5	45 185	78.5	21.5	25.7	4.7	374	14.5
Boone	2	-2.9	117	0.0	0.1	203 895	1 736	26 526	0.0	2 526	43.8	56.3	5.3	0.0	D	10.5
Braxton	89	11.9	230	0.0	14.7	376 614	1 635	40 829	4.9	12 586	20.0	80.0	27.7	1.3	147	9.3

STATE County	Water use, 2010		Wholesale trade,[1] 2007				Retail trade,[2] 2007				Real estate and rental and leasing,[2] 2007			
	Total water withdrawn (mil gal/day)	Gallons withdrawn per person per day	Number of establish-ments	Number of employees	Sales (mil dol)	Annual payroll (mil dol)	Number of establish-ments	Number of employees	Sales (mil dol)	Annual payroll (mil dol)	Number of establish-ments	Number of employees	Receipts (mil dol)	Annual payroll (mil dol)
	133	134	135	136	137	138	139	140	141	142	143	144	145	146
VIRGINIA—Cont'd														
Manassas Park city	0.0	1	17	D	D	D	33	403	158.0	12.2	5	63	8.9	1.7
Martinsville city	0.0	0	22	D	D	D	117	1 748	316.9	34.0	36	141	22.5	3.3
Newport News city	28.6	158	116	1 470	902.0	68.5	727	10 894	2 431.3	233.8	273	2 884	374.2	84.2
Norfolk city	1.0	4	250	8 577	3 280.4	247.2	975	13 764	2 724.1	293.5	324	2 898	385.8	98.3
Norton city	0.8	200	8	54	94.2	2.5	61	886	283.8	20.0	9	15	3.8	0.6
Petersburg city	0.1	3	29	647	356.1	19.0	155	1 569	324.2	37.5	36	192	21.4	4.6
Poquoson city	0.0	0	4	D	D	D	23	331	54.7	5.5	14	34	4.6	0.7
Portsmouth city	1.4	15	48	611	173.6	27.4	296	3 428	682.1	75.7	93	383	48.6	8.5
Radford city	2.1	128	9	57	30.3	2.3	47	575	109.7	11.7	24	90	10.6	2.3
Richmond city	65.6	321	289	4 408	2 843.3	231.1	883	9 029	1 922.8	211.6	302	2 361	636.4	126.2
Roanoke city	5.3	54	198	3 098	2 233.6	130.4	588	9 765	2 039.8	215.4	161	1 274	188.6	33.5
Salem city	4.6	187	65	1 074	621.2	54.0	156	2 163	537.8	50.3	40	210	31.9	5.2
Staunton city	0.2	10	20	238	68.3	7.3	165	2 026	447.5	43.9	45	222	23.9	8.0
Suffolk city	82.8	979	50	1 105	715.8	55.7	228	3 174	820.3	70.4	74	287	44.5	10.6
Virginia Beach city	1.7	4	374	5 069	2 835.1	207.4	1 625	25 639	5 579.9	568.5	717	6 190	830.7	197.8
Waynesboro city	6.0	286	17	327	113.2	15.8	127	1 842	386.6	38.7	36	111	11.4	2.3
Williamsburg city	1.0	70	4	D	D	D	114	1 913	323.0	39.5	28	150	49.1	5.4
Winchester city	0.1	4	30	D	D	D	307	4 695	998.7	101.1	76	329	63.3	12.0
WASHINGTON	4 955.8	737	8 181	111 294	76 791.0	5 557.6	23 075	328 053	92 968.5	8 585.3	10 480	51 196	10 467.3	1 818.7
Adams	217.3	11 602	32	530	574.2	19.1	60	587	144.8	12.0	12	D	D	D
Asotin	4.9	227	12	D	D	D	57	764	208.9	20.6	24	81	6.7	1.2
Benton	415.5	2 372	103	1 062	755.4	42.6	579	8 702	2 122.0	205.5	211	1 020	197.8	30.5
Chelan	68.6	947	98	2 025	788.3	71.4	399	4 401	1 022.0	107.1	122	535	71.6	13.5
Clallam	21.0	294	53	D	D	D	306	3 678	838.3	92.9	118	356	39.9	8.4
Clark	134.1	315	398	3 778	4 238.1	213.4	1 036	16 868	4 170.0	401.5	509	2 600	386.6	88.1
Columbia	8.4	2 048	20	48	30.8	1.4	23	136	28.9	2.3	5	5	0.8	0.1
Cowlitz	146.6	1 431	78	1 136	1 415.8	51.8	360	5 018	1 219.7	117.1	117	442	54.3	9.7
Douglas	35.2	915	39	469	127.4	13.6	106	1 583	413.6	38.3	24	93	14.8	2.1
Ferry	6.3	837	1	D	D	D	25	213	35.0	3.7	3	D	D	D
Franklin	479.3	6 132	100	1 291	1 028.0	51.2	183	2 775	788.5	74.8	59	256	46.9	6.7
Garfield	3.0	1 337	8	120	70.5	3.7	12	56	11.7	1.0	NA	NA	NA	NA
Grant	1 074.9	12 061	107	1 415	599.6	49.9	306	3 137	777.5	73.9	88	180	29.6	3.9
Grays Harbor	34.3	471	54	D	D	D	293	3 214	768.6	79.2	93	332	35.6	7.1
Island	9.0	115	42	D	D	D	246	2 411	519.9	58.4	123	349	51.4	8.4
Jefferson	5.6	187	22	119	51.1	4.9	159	1 201	210.9	24.7	55	159	21.5	3.2
King	259.7	134	3 444	53 288	41 042.7	3 092.0	6 976	106 600	37 153.9	2 985.0	4 090	24 282	5 961.1	1 049.6
Kitsap	32.1	128	150	1 011	553.1	41.7	840	11 918	2 936.2	301.3	392	1 332	224.2	37.3
Kittitas	132.0	3 227	37	D	D	D	168	1 817	472.7	41.0	63	240	26.7	5.2
Klickitat	40.6	1 997	14	91	25.8	2.8	55	370	65.7	6.6	21	37	5.4	0.7
Lewis	39.2	519	71	D	D	D	355	3 853	910.6	92.6	86	380	40.6	8.8
Lincoln	32.3	3 057	40	160	133.2	6.7	48	292	91.6	8.0	9	11	1.8	0.2
Mason	43.8	722	33	D	D	D	153	1 846	420.2	44.5	58	299	32.0	6.7
Okanogan	98.7	2 400	40	590	224.4	15.7	205	1 780	417.2	39.9	59	143	15.9	2.6
Pacific	9.2	441	7	D	D	D	116	620	114.5	14.8	27	82	7.2	1.4
Pend Oreille	4.0	308	5	6	1.7	0.2	38	296	66.6	5.3	13	D	D	D
Pierce	197.2	248	704	11 348	6 090.5	468.5	2 306	35 815	9 741.6	952.3	1 094	5 695	970.6	161.2
San Juan	1.8	113	19	D	D	D	119	777	155.3	21.6	71	148	20.8	3.2
Skagit	45.3	388	124	1 557	698.0	61.2	616	7 788	2 134.8	200.4	181	653	105.5	18.3
Skamania	23.1	2 083	4	7	2.4	0.3	22	161	26.0	2.6	8	8	1.3	0.2
Snohomish	201.9	283	783	7 873	6 708.4	400.3	2 267	34 313	9 057.1	930.4	1 003	3 977	766.8	134.1
Spokane	185.1	393	655	9 341	5 354.3	394.8	1 712	26 853	6 741.2	697.7	662	3 426	630.3	105.1
Stevens	29.9	688	25	205	47.2	5.6	137	1 230	281.6	27.9	36	125	16.6	2.3
Thurston	52.3	207	177	1 766	1 003.4	78.8	822	12 136	3 103.0	313.2	323	1 234	238.8	31.6
Wahkiakum	0.7	173	NA	NA	NA	NA	14	50	11.7	0.9	5	D	D	D
Walla Walla	160.2	2 725	55	555	257.5	18.8	212	2 551	534.1	59.7	64	215	26.3	5.3
Whatcom	85.5	425	306	3 294	1 373.6	144.5	851	11 100	2 556.0	263.5	352	1 254	240.2	33.3
Whitman	8.9	199	70	520	388.9	21.4	113	1 243	271.1	23.6	45	205	19.6	3.4
Yakima	608.4	2 501	251	D	D	D	780	9 900	2 425.6	239.5	255	977	151.6	23.7
WEST VIRGINIA	3 533.0	1 907	1 372	16 790	11 036.5	656.0	7 047	92 227	20 538.8	1 776.5	1 586	7 055	1 171.0	175.3
Barbour	2.1	128	7	D	D	D	43	340	75.0	5.8	4	8	1.2	0.2
Berkeley	28.8	276	42	878	573.5	42.7	278	3 536	886.4	74.2	93	339	40.3	6.8
Boone	3.0	123	10	D	D	D	81	959	190.6	16.3	8	16	1.8	0.4
Braxton	2.3	160	10	120	57.4	4.9	83	687	219.6	14.2	6	29	3.2	0.7

1. Merchant wholesalers, except manufacturers' sales branches and offices. 2. Employer establishments.

STATE County	Professional, scientific, and technical services,[1] 2007				Manufacturing, 2007				Accommodation and food services, 2007			
	Number of establish-ments	Number of employees	Receipts (mil dol)	Annual payroll (mil dol)	Number of establish-ments	Number of employees	Receipts (mil dol)	Annual payroll (mil dol)	Number of establish-ments	Number of employees	Sales (mil dol)	Annual payroll (mil dol)
	147	148	149	150	151	152	153	154	155	156	157	158
VIRGINIA—Cont'd												
Manassas Park city	19	D	D	D	NA	NA	NA	NA	14	91	5.3	1.6
Martinsville city	45	200	16.5	8.0	24	1 157	201.4	36.7	51	875	28.7	7.9
Newport News city	345	D	D	D	107	24 155	4 702.7	1 216.0	384	7 660	329.1	89.9
Norfolk city	653	D	D	D	166	7 448	1 280.8	300.0	551	11 667	505.0	140.2
Norton city	22	D	D	D	9	D	D	D	25	464	17.3	4.9
Petersburg city	35	D	D	D	42	2 114	595.9	102.1	70	864	36.6	9.7
Poquoson city	21	95	6.7	2.2	NA	NA	NA	NA	19	290	9.2	2.6
Portsmouth city	144	D	D	D	63	2 360	652.9	105.2	169	2 513	106.2	28.8
Radford city	28	D	D	D	25	1 610	D	68.6	39	923	36.2	8.8
Richmond city	826	10 582	1 682.7	785.0	224	9 341	10 192.1	545.8	547	10 136	476.8	143.5
Roanoke city	321	D	D	D	115	4 544	1 582.4	182.7	294	6 162	267.2	83.3
Salem city	74	D	D	D	69	3 736	984.0	170.7	87	1 897	67.9	20.7
Staunton city	60	342	33.5	14.2	27	546	101.4	20.7	85	1 706	65.5	20.7
Suffolk city	122	D	D	D	48	2 362	1 307.8	109.7	121	1 981	72.8	20.2
Virginia Beach city	1 310	D	D	D	243	6 544	1 806.5	236.9	1 134	21 694	1 074.2	294.9
Waynesboro city	43	D	D	D	35	2 218	759.9	86.0	64	1 148	48.9	13.5
Williamsburg city	34	168	13.7	6.8	NA	NA	NA	NA	134	3 984	239.6	72.7
Winchester city	147	D	D	D	30	D	D	D	123	2 343	104.6	29.5
WASHINGTON	19 242	150 367	23 394.7	9 778.0	7 650	269 851	112 053.3	13 274.5	15 893	233 235	12 389.4	3 618.1
Adams	15	D	D	D	13	1 042	442.2	D	29	322	14.8	4.1
Asotin	31	D	D	D	NA	NA	NA	NA	39	591	23.0	7.4
Benton	397	D	D	D	139	3 740	D	166.4	338	5 248	238.0	69.6
Chelan	190	D	D	D	103	1 870	D	D	271	3 245	171.2	51.0
Clallam	163	D	D	D	76	1 491	470.4	72.7	227	2 376	105.7	31.6
Clark	1 066	D	D	D	457	14 492	D	D	701	10 681	493.3	143.2
Columbia	8	D	D	D	NA	NA	NA	NA	13	67	2.7	0.5
Cowlitz	150	D	D	D	128	7 001	2 914.7	356.7	215	2 782	124.0	36.2
Douglas	36	D	D	D	NA	NA	NA	NA	56	835	30.4	9.4
Ferry	11	D	D	D	NA	NA	NA	NA	13	67	2.1	0.5
Franklin	73	D	D	D	51	2 235	D	75.3	109	1 386	67.7	19.5
Garfield	3	D	D	D	NA	NA	NA	NA	3	19	0.5	0.1
Grant	113	460	43.7	14.7	68	3 528	993.0	139.9	187	1 942	95.8	27.4
Grays Harbor	94	D	D	D	84	3 158	1 056.9	132.5	238	2 234	111.0	31.7
Island	191	D	D	D	51	710	D	27.9	176	1 980	77.6	22.8
Jefferson	95	D	D	D	82	770	209.5	33.6	114	1 110	48.7	15.1
King	9 050	D	D	D	2 485	95 136	37 390.8	5 067.7	5 516	90 130	5 478.9	1 611.9
Kitsap	716	D	D	D	163	2 154	D	78.3	505	7 483	392.8	117.4
Kittitas	73	D	D	D	26	892	81.1	21.8	160	2 165	84.4	28.0
Klickitat	55	D	D	D	31	740	D	37.2	51	332	16.1	4.8
Lewis	123	D	D	D	132	3 757	1 109.1	153.6	192	2 040	96.2	26.6
Lincoln	13	86	7.6	4.3	NA	NA	NA	NA	24	88	4.0	1.0
Mason	76	D	D	D	57	1 695	D	59.0	111	1 684	115.4	33.9
Okanogan	74	D	D	D	NA	NA	NA	NA	128	1 122	49.0	14.5
Pacific	37	131	11.2	4.0	35	941	138.7	24.5	114	737	37.2	8.8
Pend Oreille	16	72	6.7	2.5	14	606	D	D	32	192	9.2	2.5
Pierce	1 386	D	D	D	668	20 326	4 958.6	894.2	1 578	24 076	1 172.5	332.7
San Juan	112	D	D	D	NA	NA	NA	NA	97	735	63.3	17.9
Skagit	305	D	D	D	205	6 387	8 918.2	294.5	347	4 734	251.0	74.1
Skamania	25	D	D	D	NA	NA	NA	NA	24	644	28.5	12.5
Snohomish	1 503	D	D	D	871	50 214	22 552.3	2 847.5	1 521	19 961	1 049.8	294.9
Spokane	1 231	8 631	1 157.2	432.4	589	17 412	3 895.4	730.7	993	17 046	780.2	232.2
Stevens	57	180	17.0	6.4	46	1 374	383.6	52.6	89	689	27.7	7.6
Thurston	598	D	D	D	189	3 118	870.1	120.7	497	7 612	346.7	102.7
Wahkiakum	6	D	D	D	NA	NA	NA	NA	12	60	1.8	0.7
Walla Walla	105	D	D	D	114	3 094	2 155.5	138.4	120	1 723	75.8	22.9
Whatcom	670	3 562	419.2	163.4	334	10 165	11 809.7	467.2	505	8 461	407.9	116.2
Whitman	55	246	20.9	7.6	27	1 248	D	D	121	1 349	49.0	13.5
Yakima	320	D	D	D	255	8 696	2 686.1	304.4	427	5 287	245.6	70.8
WEST VIRGINIA	2 906	20 766	2 341.1	857.5	1 413	59 981	25 080.6	2 645.8	3 650	61 711	2 553.3	712.8
Barbour	19	85	7.0	2.5	NA	NA	NA	NA	25	289	9.9	2.8
Berkeley	131	D	D	D	45	D	D	D	179	2 777	156.4	35.9
Boone	19	D	D	D	NA	NA	NA	NA	24	349	13.2	3.8
Braxton	12	39	2.6	0.9	NA	NA	NA	NA	37	495	16.8	4.8

1. Establishment subject to federal tax.

Table B. States and Counties — **Health Care and Social Assistance, Other Services, Nonemployer Businesses, and Residential Construction**

STATE County	Health care and social assistance, 2007				Other services, 2007				Nonemployer businesses, 2013		Value of residential construction authorized by building permits, 2014	
	Number of establish-ments	Number of employees	Receipts (mil dol)	Annual payroll (mil dol)	Number of establish-ments	Number of employees	Receipts (mil dol)	Annual payroll (mil dol)	Number	Receipts (mil dol)	New Construction ($1,000)	Number of housing units
	159	160	161	162	163	164	165	166	167	168	169	170
VIRGINIA—Cont'd												
Manassas Park city	3	D	D	D	45	223	25.0	7.7	1 109	45.1	2 050	11
Martinsville city	120	1 182	115.8	42.8	50	190	16.9	3.4	727	31.1	95	1
Newport News city	384	12 477	1 114.9	486.6	316	2 165	161.4	52.0	8 306	292.2	19 582	330
Norfolk city	543	19 046	2 097.9	833.8	448	3 670	470.1	117.0	11 529	464.4	62 419	650
Norton city	41	1 305	129.3	51.7	21	108	5.2	3.5	219	6.7	0	0
Petersburg city	121	3 782	324.7	136.8	85	562	46.0	13.3	1 187	38.3	1 145	8
Poquoson city	13	D	D	D	26	D	D	D	785	31.5	4 298	24
Portsmouth city	218	7 247	635.9	271.9	175	1 535	122.3	41.0	4 518	127.9	29 789	153
Radford city	42	520	36.8	16.3	25	D	D	D	611	28.5	1 830	10
Richmond city	641	24 371	2 530.9	1 052.8	577	4 024	535.3	122.0	13 688	573.9	58 844	551
Roanoke city	318	11 059	1 301.2	448.7	271	2 009	155.7	45.9	5 307	239.9	5 918	49
Salem city	98	5 127	596.1	259.9	103	657	37.9	15.0	1 393	57.1	5 148	38
Staunton city	97	2 054	140.2	69.9	68	387	26.9	8.9	1 497	65.2	12 766	137
Suffolk city	142	3 165	347.0	128.6	97	586	116.2	11.4	4 742	169.4	56 647	348
Virginia Beach city	933	15 592	1 547.4	617.9	897	5 832	633.2	125.9	27 597	1 329.8	158 800	1 208
Waynesboro city	52	715	44.0	16.4	60	397	38.4	11.5	1 007	39.4	6 962	48
Williamsburg city	46	1 580	118.5	77.4	26	335	65.0	11.7	827	37.9	28 521	258
Winchester city	236	5 527	637.1	278.1	86	576	43.9	14.6	1 930	115.5	3 220	23
WASHINGTON	18 474	345 161	35 886.4	14 349.6	12 324	71 213	8 920.8	2 030.0	413 446	19 922.5	7 016 518	33 898
Adams	26	636	59.9	25.3	25	85	6.3	1.3	715	42.3	6 622	50
Asotin	50	835	84.3	26.7	30	123	8.2	2.1	1 061	39.9	7 028	35
Benton	498	8 313	812.5	315.2	238	1 300	103.9	30.9	8 291	356.7	247 517	942
Chelan	208	D	D	D	165	663	60.2	14.1	4 453	200.5	56 834	304
Clallam	258	3 757	291.6	122.1	155	672	50.2	15.5	4 335	152.8	35 527	160
Clark	933	D	D	D	635	3 111	362.0	80.8	26 337	1 301.8	510 344	2 240
Columbia	12	183	11.9	5.6	14	56	7.1	2.0	209	6.7	1 628	7
Cowlitz	249	5 122	487.3	198.6	146	894	75.9	22.8	4 100	174.9	36 202	178
Douglas	53	D	D	D	39	143	9.6	2.5	1 648	56.6	33 573	156
Ferry	15	D	D	D	7	D	D	D	368	10.5	1 384	10
Franklin	115	1 477	140.0	59.3	87	508	47.4	13.6	3 139	139.9	80 005	322
Garfield	6	D	D	D	1	D	D	D	137	4.7	439	3
Grant	133	2 721	236.8	99.9	128	526	36.1	9.4	3 566	169.0	51 986	264
Grays Harbor	205	2 691	236.1	90.8	121	575	38.2	10.5	3 071	123.2	27 643	142
Island	188	2 273	176.6	76.6	99	432	33.2	10.7	5 613	212.5	62 991	252
Jefferson	104	1 284	103.5	44.2	93	342	27.7	8.7	2 975	97.8	25 505	121
King	6 535	122 486	14 324.2	5 614.7	4 508	28 932	5 137.7	935.6	151 561	8 395.1	2 880 007	14 703
Kitsap	659	12 424	1 169.6	482.9	392	2 004	157.5	48.0	13 526	579.1	138 312	598
Kittitas	98	1 407	99.1	41.4	77	327	26.7	7.3	2 363	109.5	64 532	283
Klickitat	35	575	45.3	20.5	33	116	8.8	2.2	1 378	67.6	15 608	83
Lewis	178	3 000	271.4	115.9	126	521	44.5	11.5	3 497	136.6	22 593	164
Lincoln	17	443	31.8	14.3	19	50	5.5	1.2	648	24.6	5 309	30
Mason	101	1 611	141.5	51.2	85	353	23.5	7.0	2 790	97.7	27 731	108
Okanogan	122	1 971	133.9	59.4	77	246	26.7	4.7	2 294	85.9	25 612	165
Pacific	50	748	51.5	21.8	46	149	10.8	2.7	1 313	56.5	10 624	63
Pend Oreille	22	D	D	D	14	34	3.3	0.6	721	21.1	10 666	42
Pierce	1 880	42 047	4 395.2	1 781.3	1 301	8 493	803.1	251.2	38 934	1 807.2	827 177	3 777
San Juan	62	410	26.2	10.2	56	172	27.7	4.6	2 461	102.9	24 884	109
Skagit	342	6 346	614.5	241.6	237	1 158	94.1	27.6	7 287	345.2	55 927	274
Skamania	15	D	D	D	10	18	1.6	0.4	636	22.5	6 268	34
Snohomish	1 656	24 552	2 423.9	980.0	1 144	6 150	523.3	170.6	41 212	1 852.9	762 072	3 473
Spokane	1 424	33 424	3 273.7	1 325.9	863	5 436	479.1	132.2	27 632	1 188.1	355 146	1 839
Stevens	84	1 452	109.5	47.3	60	176	15.7	4.1	2 529	86.7	16 363	79
Thurston	710	11 596	1 238.4	447.6	464	2 812	273.7	88.2	13 931	572.3	242 844	1 003
Wahkiakum	8	D	D	D	4	D	D	D	305	10.4	1 728	11
Walla Walla	164	3 939	387.3	160.0	79	454	34.6	7.9	3 088	124.6	38 927	207
Whatcom	636	9 730	862.9	348.7	390	2 155	207.5	59.0	14 229	670.8	178 949	1 007
Whitman	86	1 633	127.4	53.4	59	221	13.7	3.9	1 962	64.5	30 223	218
Yakima	537	11 636	1 119.8	441.2	297	1 767	132.9	33.9	9 131	411.2	89 789	442
WEST VIRGINIA	4 860	114 663	9 874.7	3 828.9	2 927	16 527	1 550.2	388.3	88 202	3 272.3	395 354	2 677
Barbour	29	736	36.3	14.3	14	34	2.7	0.5	703	19.2	1 800	30
Berkeley	194	D	D	D	133	643	51.0	15.1	5 456	212.4	105 997	701
Boone	41	693	35.4	14.5	22	145	10.4	4.2	735	20.7	1 662	16
Braxton	20	918	36.1	14.3	17	74	8.3	2.2	594	17.7	0	0

STATE County	Government employment and payroll, 2012: Full-time equivalent employees	Government employment and payroll, 2012: March payroll (dollars)	March payroll (percent of total): Adminis-tration, judicial, and legal	March payroll (percent of total): Police and Corrections	March payroll (percent of total): Fire Protection	March payroll (percent of total): Highways and transpor-tation	March payroll (percent of total): Health and Welfare	March payroll (percent of total): Natural resources and utilities	March payroll (percent of total): Education and libraries	Local government finances, 2012, General revenue: Total (mil dol)	General revenue: Inter-govern-mental (mil dol)	Taxes: Total (mil dol)	Taxes, Per capita[1] (dollars): Total	Taxes, Per capita[1] (dollars): Property
	171	172	173	174	175	176	177	178	179	180	181	182	183	184
VIRGINIA—Cont'd														
Manassas Park city	547	2 174 966	6.3	8.6	5.6	0.7	1.8	6.3	67.3	58.7	24.8	25.4	1 608	1 293
Martinsville city	769	2 241 998	9.4	13.6	4.4	3.9	2.0	9.5	54.3	58.0	32.0	15.8	1 148	628
Newport News city	8 482	34 753 223	6.1	10.1	4.5	2.1	4.5	9.1	62.7	786.5	332.1	322.2	1 783	1 269
Norfolk city	14 612	55 628 038	4.8	10.3	4.2	8.7	8.6	7.9	54.2	1 422.2	577.3	416.3	1 694	1 029
Norton city	226	662 054	8.5	13.0	0.5	4.4	8.7	6.7	55.1	22.2	11.9	7.7	1 884	632
Petersburg city	1 476	4 759 064	5.8	19.4	8.6	4.3	5.8	7.7	45.6	126.3	70.3	45.2	1 415	1 044
Poquoson city	447	1 474 638	7.0	6.8	6.8	3.3	0.8	2.3	70.5	38.2	15.0	19.1	1 576	1 340
Portsmouth city	4 358	16 114 476	6.2	15.8	6.6	0.8	6.9	6.3	55.4	449.4	234.6	161.2	1 671	1 219
Radford city	450	1 533 350	9.5	10.2	2.3	3.6	4.7	13.6	53.1	37.9	20.4	11.1	664	455
Richmond city	8 977	34 059 020	8.8	19.1	5.9	2.9	6.0	10.3	41.5	1 102.8	456.7	412.6	1 962	1 249
Roanoke city	3 900	14 209 461	8.0	12.7	8.2	3.3	6.2	4.1	55.6	398.1	176.5	172.9	1 774	1 086
Salem city	1 239	4 093 202	12.6	9.6	6.7	6.7	2.4	12.1	49.5	108.5	42.3	49.5	1 982	1 301
Staunton city	1 131	3 120 624	7.9	23.4	4.4	2.5	1.7	5.3	51.1	82.8	39.3	32.3	1 349	839
Suffolk city	3 558	11 946 187	10.3	7.7	9.6	2.9	4.4	6.4	58.0	305.1	145.8	134.5	1 579	1 162
Virginia Beach city	19 058	68 439 433	3.5	9.0	3.4	0.3	6.4	12.4	57.0	1 816.6	615.1	810.1	1 812	1 218
Waynesboro city	795	2 593 698	8.5	8.2	4.6	3.4	1.3	8.3	60.2	77.5	33.4	33.2	1 574	946
Williamsburg city	407	1 404 121	11.0	37.6	9.6	3.3	4.2	10.1	21.2	46.8	11.2	29.9	1 971	766
Winchester city	1 491	5 190 139	6.6	22.4	6.4	2.6	4.2	6.7	49.4	137.9	46.7	61.6	2 292	1 298
WASHINGTON	X	X	X	X	X	X	X	X	X	X	X	X	X	X
Adams	1 040	3 937 847	5.7	6.6	0.8	5.5	21.8	10.0	47.7	141.3	72.5	24.1	1 269	906
Asotin	728	2 891 078	6.7	8.1	3.6	6.7	12.3	6.0	54.9	69.3	39.9	19.3	881	674
Benton	7 559	41 657 634	4.9	6.8	3.2	4.4	13.0	32.6	34.0	876.0	367.1	242.6	1 330	745
Chelan	3 427	16 843 859	4.7	6.8	2.3	5.4	9.3	32.8	36.9	368.1	151.3	114.2	1 550	1 003
Clallam	3 439	16 962 339	5.9	7.8	3.5	5.3	38.0	11.5	26.0	416.5	135.2	89.7	1 249	834
Clark	11 478	56 406 570	6.0	8.5	5.1	6.1	1.9	9.2	59.4	1 575.0	717.2	576.6	1 316	967
Columbia	318	1 186 883	10.8	5.9	1.0	8.9	38.0	7.4	25.7	32.7	11.4	6.7	1 687	1 352
Cowlitz	3 301	15 112 407	7.8	11.6	3.0	7.2	3.7	14.2	51.3	420.9	170.2	127.1	1 246	848
Douglas	1 297	6 128 626	5.0	6.0	1.5	6.7	0.5	26.3	52.5	145.0	88.5	39.7	1 008	759
Ferry	420	1 474 156	7.4	5.9	0.4	5.7	31.9	8.5	39.8	44.5	24.8	5.0	651	505
Franklin	2 593	11 637 558	6.0	7.6	3.3	4.6	0.0	14.4	62.8	318.4	176.1	82.9	965	615
Garfield	229	842 190	7.7	6.5	0.9	9.8	47.5	1.7	24.6	29.1	16.3	3.5	1 591	960
Grant	4 837	22 986 238	4.1	5.2	1.2	2.7	20.7	28.8	35.5	555.0	232.9	128.7	1 403	1 005
Grays Harbor	2 841	12 751 235	7.3	9.1	6.2	10.1	5.9	14.9	44.7	305.6	124.6	95.4	1 330	817
Island	2 321	11 320 614	5.9	5.9	5.9	8.0	32.6	3.6	36.8	280.9	92.9	87.2	1 101	776
Jefferson	1 311	6 130 951	7.9	5.4	5.8	9.2	41.3	2.8	26.6	158.5	38.9	46.4	1 556	1 102
King	65 821	388 288 446	8.0	10.3	5.9	13.1	13.5	13.9	33.3	12 411.3	3 474.5	5 105.6	2 543	1 381
Kitsap	6 732	32 797 634	7.2	7.7	9.1	6.6	1.0	9.5	56.8	1 053.2	532.7	344.8	1 352	960
Kittitas	1 664	7 365 807	8.8	8.2	3.6	3.8	32.4	9.0	32.4	197.1	81.5	58.9	1 412	1 006
Klickitat	1 119	4 905 212	5.9	6.8	0.4	4.5	31.9	13.1	35.6	136.0	44.1	27.2	1 316	1 015
Lewis	2 603	11 808 449	7.8	9.5	3.2	6.0	10.1	11.8	47.1	268.0	123.6	81.1	1 072	750
Lincoln	806	3 420 386	7.1	4.6	0.1	8.4	38.7	1.4	38.6	95.2	44.6	15.2	1 458	1 199
Mason	2 164	10 240 656	6.6	6.6	4.0	5.9	26.0	11.1	37.8	268.3	97.3	72.6	1 193	869
Okanogan	1 848	8 014 386	6.5	8.2	0.5	3.7	30.9	10.5	38.5	228.9	90.9	42.6	1 031	722
Pacific	1 032	5 269 056	8.5	7.3	3.7	6.5	27.8	11.0	33.1	126.6	42.8	31.2	1 518	1 146
Pend Oreille	786	3 517 534	6.4	5.1	0.4	3.4	34.6	21.7	26.3	81.4	36.0	10.4	799	627
Pierce	23 934	131 701 698	8.7	9.5	9.2	8.4	2.7	12.1	47.1	3 300.2	1 329.7	1 234.7	1 521	1 076
San Juan	551	2 448 595	14.0	7.8	3.9	9.0	9.8	11.9	39.1	76.6	25.1	34.7	2 196	1 573
Skagit	5 963	27 675 332	5.4	5.4	2.0	4.5	41.5	4.7	33.8	852.8	275.6	199.6	1 688	1 157
Skamania	390	1 668 143	14.8	12.9	0.3	6.4	8.7	12.8	38.8	36.0	20.0	8.7	781	588
Snohomish	19 389	108 720 406	6.9	9.4	6.5	8.0	5.4	13.4	47.9	2 865.2	1 091.9	1 077.6	1 470	1 030
Spokane	13 368	67 439 060	9.4	11.5	7.6	7.3	3.7	7.0	51.9	1 818.7	806.0	639.3	1 344	862
Stevens	1 254	5 040 095	8.1	7.4	1.3	6.3	7.8	4.7	61.9	143.8	97.8	31.2	717	541
Thurston	7 290	36 403 899	10.9	9.6	5.9	9.3	2.0	8.9	51.8	946.4	372.7	391.6	1 516	997
Wahkiakum	161	658 898	16.0	9.8	0.1	7.0	12.6	16.9	31.8	27.2	18.9	3.6	909	651
Walla Walla	1 801	7 900 373	8.1	11.4	5.9	6.2	5.5	3.9	55.3	236.4	107.1	76.1	1 281	877
Whatcom	5 120	25 193 563	10.0	10.9	7.5	8.7	1.8	7.1	50.4	696.1	261.3	292.4	1 424	871
Whitman	1 636	7 215 336	5.6	5.7	3.5	8.0	37.2	2.3	36.4	210.9	64.2	44.8	961	644
Yakima	8 019	34 900 911	7.0	10.7	3.2	2.8	3.3	5.9	66.0	970.4	601.4	232.4	941	607
WEST VIRGINIA	X	X	X	X	X	X	X	X	X	X	X	X	X	X
Barbour	525	1 593 938	6.5	3.2	0.0	1.0	6.3	5.7	74.1	35.3	22.1	6.7	408	324
Berkeley	3 583	11 743 879	4.1	3.5	2.1	0.6	1.2	4.4	82.8	263.0	125.8	97.1	907	806
Boone	1 129	3 935 149	4.3	3.0	1.1	0.8	17.5	1.2	69.9	102.4	38.1	37.4	1 528	1 483
Braxton	464	1 418 168	6.8	3.5	5.0	0.8	1.9	4.6	76.8	34.7	20.6	7.6	528	481

1. Based on the resident population estimated as of July 1 of the year shown.

STATE County	Local government finances, 2012 (cont.)									Government employment, 2013			Presidential election,[2] 2012		
	Direct general expenditure							Debt outstanding					Percent of vote cast:		
			Percent of total for:												
	Total (mil dol)	Per capita[1] (dollars)	Educa-tion	Health and hospitals	Police protec-tion	Public welfare	High-ways	Total (mil dol)	Per capita[1] (dollars)	Federal civilian	Federal military	State and local	Demo-cratic	Republi-can	All other
	185	186	187	188	189	190	191	192	193	194	195	196	197	198	199
VIRGINIA—Cont'd															
Manassas Park city	60.1	3 803	52.0	0.2	7.5	2.3	0.9	123.4	7 811	(3)	(3)	(3)	59.5	39.5	1.0
Martinsville city	59.6	4 339	42.2	0.5	6.3	0.5	5.7	35.1	2 555	(4)	(4)	(4)	63.5	35.4	1.1
Newport News city	820.9	4 542	41.6	8.3	5.6	5.0	3.9	1 041.2	5 761	5 825	6 935	11 401	63.9	35.3	0.8
Norfolk city	1 457.9	5 932	43.5	5.0	4.7	5.2	3.6	2 294.3	9 335	14 792	42 273	20 955	71.0	28.1	0.9
Norton city	20.8	5 109	39.7	0.5	9.9	6.6	7.9	19.6	4 823	(5)	(5)	(5)	49.1	49.2	1.7
Petersburg city	134.0	4 190	38.8	1.0	8.8	11.1	4.6	60.3	1 887	(6)	(6)	(6)	88.6	10.2	1.2
Poquoson city	38.6	3 191	55.1	1.5	6.4	1.1	7.3	56.8	4 694	(7)	(7)	(7)	24.7	74.0	1.2
Portsmouth city	543.5	5 633	31.4	2.0	6.5	4.7	1.3	647.6	6 713	12 868	6 487	6 235	69.3	30.0	0.8
Radford city	44.5	2 667	45.2	0.5	8.1	5.6	5.3	28.4	1 701	(8)	(8)	(8)	54.0	44.5	1.5
Richmond city	1 081.3	5 141	30.1	4.3	8.5	1.5	3.8	1 910.6	9 085	5 095	1 233	37 141	79.1	20.0	0.9
Roanoke city	391.0	4 011	38.2	0.8	5.9	14.8	3.4	597.7	6 132	1 574	336	6 997	61.2	37.8	1.1
Salem city	120.6	4 828	38.5	0.7	5.3	1.5	4.9	167.0	6 689	(9)	(9)	(9)	41.6	57.1	1.2
Staunton city	94.0	3 928	32.9	8.4	5.8	5.6	5.2	98.6	4 122	(10)	(10)	(10)	50.6	48.4	1.1
Suffolk city	324.3	3 808	45.2	0.2	6.3	4.4	6.8	654.0	7 677	807	472	4 704	56.2	43.0	0.7
Virginia Beach city	2 062.0	4 613	40.8	2.6	4.3	3.3	4.2	2 582.9	5 778	6 596	18 474	22 815	49.1	49.8	1.0
Waynesboro city	75.1	3 556	42.8	0.6	5.0	4.9	6.7	92.3	4 374	(10)	(10)	(10)	44.1	54.3	1.6
Williamsburg city	53.2	3 510	14.0	0.9	7.4	3.7	3.5	32.4	2 134	(11)	(11)	(11)	63.8	34.7	1.6
Winchester city	131.6	4 897	37.2	0.9	5.5	5.5	4.3	337.1	12 539	(12)	(12)	(12)	52.0	46.7	1.3
WASHINGTON	X	X	X	X	X	X	X	X	X	71 772	80 410	470 315	57.7	40.5	1.9
Adams	135.7	7 140	46.3	18.1	2.6	0.0	5.7	62.9	3 309	34	53	1 508	31.9	66.3	1.7
Asotin	68.8	3 142	46.9	7.4	5.3	0.0	7.3	21.9	1 003	42	61	1 138	42.3	55.7	1.9
Benton	835.7	4 582	38.0	28.0	4.0	0.0	3.3	6 728.4	36 888	756	524	11 678	36.1	62.2	1.8
Chelan	345.4	4 688	41.8	14.6	4.2	0.0	5.4	1 594.5	21 638	614	203	5 860	43.1	55.1	1.8
Clallam	403.3	5 612	25.3	39.7	3.3	0.0	3.6	172.3	2 398	437	538	6 826	50.5	47.2	2.2
Clark	1 525.7	3 481	51.0	3.7	4.0	0.5	5.8	2 123.7	4 845	3 144	1 271	20 758	52.2	46.1	1.7
Columbia	29.1	7 286	21.7	37.4	4.2	0.0	7.5	17.2	4 300	65	11	421	30.8	67.3	1.9
Cowlitz	424.6	4 163	38.6	3.9	5.4	0.0	4.9	609.4	5 974	225	281	5 400	54.4	43.2	2.4
Douglas	142.5	3 622	59.9	8.3	5.1	0.0	6.7	350.0	8 893	237	109	1 876	38.5	59.8	1.7
Ferry	39.2	5 090	46.3	22.7	2.6	0.0	9.2	9.5	1 236	155	21	734	41.9	54.7	3.4
Franklin	294.3	3 429	60.6	1.4	3.9	0.0	4.7	315.8	3 679	486	233	5 547	37.4	61.1	1.5
Garfield	32.0	14 354	37.5	23.0	2.9	0.0	17.9	7.7	3 442	134	0	341	28.0	70.5	1.5
Grant	519.5	5 664	37.4	28.7	3.4	0.6	4.6	1 451.0	15 819	734	252	7 337	35.0	62.5	2.5
Grays Harbor	303.0	4 227	38.5	9.5	5.7	0.2	6.2	405.8	5 660	192	232	6 030	56.0	41.5	2.5
Island	257.0	3 246	28.7	33.0	3.3	0.2	7.4	171.2	2 163	1 399	5 870	3 116	52.3	46.1	1.6
Jefferson	155.4	5 205	19.1	39.9	3.6	0.3	5.2	145.8	4 885	173	94	2 008	66.3	31.7	2.0
King	11 212.0	5 585	28.9	12.4	5.0	1.2	5.5	22 389.4	11 153	20 465	6 939	149 474	70.3	28.2	1.5
Kitsap	1 054.5	4 135	42.3	4.6	3.5	0.0	3.5	748.5	2 935	16 522	10 765	12 643	55.2	42.9	1.9
Kittitas	186.9	4 485	26.5	30.6	4.7	0.0	6.5	110.8	2 658	147	119	4 687	44.9	53.0	2.1
Klickitat	118.4	5 721	34.2	32.3	3.9	0.0	8.0	215.9	10 431	93	58	1 582	48.8	48.6	2.5
Lewis	254.6	3 367	47.6	10.3	5.3	0.0	6.3	343.9	4 547	223	207	4 758	39.3	58.4	2.3
Lincoln	96.3	9 226	34.5	30.0	2.8	0.0	10.9	34.2	3 279	60	28	1 220	34.0	63.6	2.4
Mason	257.4	4 232	32.2	26.8	3.0	0.0	4.3	295.3	4 854	71	161	5 330	53.2	44.5	2.3
Okanogan	207.5	5 027	35.7	32.4	4.0	0.1	3.7	126.1	3 056	449	113	4 190	45.1	52.2	2.7
Pacific	123.7	6 010	30.5	32.4	3.3	0.0	4.1	113.3	5 509	57	168	1 701	55.7	41.6	2.6
Pend Oreille	75.9	5 850	25.2	33.2	3.2	0.1	6.9	158.1	12 178	105	36	1 378	39.1	56.7	4.2
Pierce	3 273.5	4 033	43.7	2.1	5.8	0.6	5.6	4 565.2	5 624	12 363	38 405	44 366	55.2	43.0	1.8
San Juan	74.8	4 726	30.2	8.5	3.4	0.3	9.8	34.2	2 159	58	44	787	70.0	28.1	1.9
Skagit	797.6	6 747	26.4	43.2	2.9	0.1	3.4	556.4	4 706	373	326	10 816	53.8	44.2	2.1
Skamania	41.2	3 682	35.3	7.8	6.4	0.2	7.2	16.3	1 455	127	31	509	51.3	46.0	2.7
Snohomish	2 730.6	3 725	42.2	8.8	4.8	0.6	4.4	3 753.7	5 121	2 134	6 395	35 072	58.5	39.6	2.0
Spokane	1 872.4	3 936	45.5	5.1	5.4	0.2	4.0	1 560.2	3 280	4 467	4 247	30 447	48.2	49.3	2.5
Stevens	148.2	3 405	61.9	5.5	3.5	0.0	7.0	45.9	1 055	330	120	2 562	38.0	58.8	3.2
Thurston	952.8	3 688	42.4	5.4	4.0	0.0	7.1	917.5	3 552	872	775	34 556	59.9	38.2	1.9
Wahkiakum	25.9	6 484	20.6	41.0	3.8	0.0	7.9	4.8	1 207	13	11	241	48.9	48.2	3.0
Walla Walla	228.3	3 844	45.7	5.8	5.9	0.0	7.1	249.9	4 207	1 188	155	4 319	40.8	57.4	1.9
Whatcom	644.4	3 139	42.5	4.3	6.1	0.0	5.7	595.5	2 901	1 369	625	14 043	58.0	40.1	1.9
Whitman	199.6	4 282	27.1	40.8	3.9	0.3	4.7	87.2	1 870	229	124	9 296	51.6	46.1	2.4
Yakima	1 052.2	4 260	60.9	3.2	4.2	0.8	4.9	606.3	2 455	1 230	799	15 760	43.9	54.4	1.7
WEST VIRGINIA	X	X	X	X	X	X	X	X	X	23 397	9 419	125 347	42.6	55.7	1.7
Barbour	38.2	2 315	63.0	3.6	3.6	0.0	1.0	23.1	1 402	38	80	709	38.8	59.1	2.1
Berkeley	274.3	2 561	76.5	0.5	4.5	0.0	0.7	319.3	2 981	3 854	594	4 814	42.9	55.9	1.2
Boone	117.1	4 784	50.3	15.4	4.9	0.2	0.5	11.7	479	71	120	1 641	54.1	43.4	2.5
Braxton	39.8	2 754	58.6	1.2	2.1	0.0	0.5	106.5	7 361	55	70	892	50.0	48.6	1.4

1. Based on the resident population estimated as of July 1 of the year shown. 2. 3. Manassas and Manassas Park cities are included with Prince William county. 4. Martinsville city is included with Henry county. 5. Norton city is included with Wise county. 6. Petersburg and Colonial Heights cities are included with Dinwiddie county. 7. Poquoson city is included with York county. 8. Radford city is included with Montgomery county. 9. Salem city is included with Roanoke county. 10. Staunton and Waynesboro cities are included with Augusta county. 11. Williamsburg city is included with James City county. 12. Winchester city is included with Frederick county.

STATE/ County code	CBSA code[1]	County type[2]	STATE County	Land area,[3] (sq km) 2010	Population, 2014: Total persons 2014	Population, 2014: Rank	Population, 2014: Per square kilometer	Population and population characteristics, 2013: Race alone or in combination, not Hispanic or Latino (percent): White	Race alone or in combination, not Hispanic or Latino (percent): Black	Race alone or in combination, not Hispanic or Latino (percent): American Indian, Alaska Native	Race alone or in combination, not Hispanic or Latino (percent): Asian and Pacific Islander	Percent Hispanic or Latino[4]	Age (percent): Under 5 years	Age (percent): 5 to 17 years	Age (percent): 18 to 24 years	Age (percent): 25 to 34 years	Age (percent): 35 to 44 years	Age (percent): 45 to 54 years
				1	2	3	4	5	6	7	8	9	10	11	12	13	14	15
			WEST VIRGINIA—Cont'd															
54 009	48260	3	Brooke	231	23 530	1 658	101.9	97.2	2.0	0.5	0.6	0.8	4.0	14.3	9.9	9.3	11.6	14.2
54 011	26580	2	Cabell	728	97 109	607	133.4	92.3	6.2	0.8	1.5	1.3	5.9	13.9	13.1	13.2	11.8	12.3
54 013	...	8	Calhoun	723	7 513	2 639	10.4	98.0	0.6	0.8	0.4	1.2	5.6	14.6	6.2	10.7	11.6	14.8
54 015	16620	2	Clay	886	8 941	2 521	10.1	98.9	0.6	0.8	0.2	0.5	6.3	16.8	7.3	10.1	12.1	14.4
54 017	17220	9	Doddridge	828	8 391	2 568	10.1	97.0	2.0	0.9	0.4	0.8	4.0	14.5	9.3	11.1	12.9	15.7
54 019	13220	6	Fayette	1 713	45 132	1 067	26.3	93.9	5.2	0.7	0.4	1.0	6.0	14.8	7.6	11.3	12.6	13.8
54 021	...	9	Gilmer	877	8 618	2 549	9.8	80.7	12.8	1.3	0.9	6.0	4.1	9.9	14.6	15.9	14.9	13.8
54 023	...	6	Grant	1 236	11 687	2 311	9.5	97.6	1.1	0.5	0.3	1.3	5.1	14.9	7.2	9.9	11.9	14.7
54 025	...	7	Greenbrier	2 641	35 450	1 288	13.4	95.2	3.6	0.9	0.6	1.3	5.0	14.6	7.3	11.3	11.3	14.1
54 027	49020	3	Hampshire	1 658	23 483	1 662	14.2	97.2	1.5	0.6	0.5	1.2	4.7	15.8	7.3	10.1	12.6	15.2
54 029	48260	3	Hancock	214	30 112	1 427	140.7	95.9	3.3	0.6	0.5	1.2	5.0	15.0	6.8	10.1	12.4	14.6
54 031	...	8	Hardy	1 508	13 923	2 177	9.2	93.1	2.9	0.6	1.1	3.3	5.0	15.4	7.4	10.2	12.5	15.4
54 033	17220	5	Harrison	1 077	68 761	776	63.8	96.0	2.4	0.8	0.8	1.5	5.9	15.7	7.6	12.1	12.6	14.5
54 035	...	6	Jackson	1 203	29 126	1 449	24.2	98.3	0.9	0.6	0.4	0.7	5.4	16.3	7.7	10.8	12.4	14.4
54 037	47900	1	Jefferson	543	55 713	908	102.6	85.9	7.8	1.0	2.3	5.4	5.7	17.3	9.4	11.4	13.5	15.9
54 039	16620	2	Kanawha	2 335	190 223	339	81.5	90.1	8.8	0.8	1.5	1.0	5.5	14.9	8.0	12.3	12.4	13.9
54 041	...	7	Lewis	997	16 414	2 015	16.5	98.0	1.1	0.7	0.5	0.9	5.8	14.8	7.5	11.3	12.6	14.5
54 043	26580	2	Lincoln	1 132	21 561	1 752	19.0	98.9	0.4	0.5	0.3	0.6	5.9	16.5	7.4	10.9	13.4	14.3
54 045	30880	6	Logan	1 175	35 348	1 291	30.1	96.7	2.4	0.5	0.4	0.9	5.7	14.9	7.7	11.3	14.0	13.3
54 047	...	7	McDowell	1 382	20 448	1 808	14.8	90.0	9.6	0.6	0.3	0.6	5.8	14.4	7.4	11.2	12.5	14.2
54 049	21900	4	Marion	800	56 803	896	71.0	94.5	4.3	0.7	0.8	1.2	5.8	14.0	11.2	11.6	12.3	13.0
54 051	48540	3	Marshall	791	32 416	1 376	41.0	97.7	1.1	0.6	0.6	1.0	4.9	15.1	7.8	10.5	12.2	14.2
54 053	38580	6	Mason	1 116	27 016	1 536	24.2	97.9	1.3	0.6	0.6	0.6	5.1	16.0	7.4	11.2	12.3	14.3
54 055	14140	5	Mercer	1 085	61 785	845	56.9	92.1	7.1	0.7	0.8	1.0	6.2	14.6	8.9	11.3	12.0	12.8
54 057	19060	3	Mineral	849	27 578	1 509	32.5	95.5	3.8	0.5	0.6	0.9	5.3	14.9	9.8	10.4	11.9	14.2
54 059	...	6	Mingo	1 096	25 716	1 571	23.5	97.1	2.4	0.4	0.5	0.5	6.0	15.8	7.4	12.1	13.2	14.7
54 061	34060	3	Monongalia	933	103 463	574	110.9	90.9	4.7	0.5	3.7	1.9	5.0	10.9	24.2	16.9	11.0	10.8
54 063	...	8	Monroe	1 224	13 582	2 198	11.1	98.0	1.2	1.0	0.5	0.8	5.3	15.2	6.8	9.8	11.7	14.1
54 065	...	3	Morgan	593	17 453	1 950	29.4	97.4	1.3	0.8	0.7	1.2	4.4	15.3	6.8	9.2	12.2	15.6
54 067	...	6	Nicholas	1 675	25 827	1 568	15.4	98.2	0.6	1.0	0.5	0.7	5.8	15.1	7.6	10.8	12.4	14.2
54 069	48540	3	Ohio	274	43 328	1 105	158.1	94.4	4.9	0.6	1.2	0.9	5.1	13.9	11.0	11.0	11.0	13.4
54 071	...	8	Pendleton	1 803	7 371	2 645	4.1	95.9	2.9	0.7	0.4	1.3	4.9	13.2	8.1	9.4	9.7	14.3
54 073	...	3	Pleasants	337	7 634	2 626	22.7	97.3	1.7	0.8	0.3	0.9	4.2	15.1	8.3	11.0	13.6	15.6
54 075	...	9	Pocahontas	2 435	8 662	2 545	3.6	97.2	1.3	0.8	0.4	1.4	4.9	12.6	6.6	10.7	11.1	15.3
54 077	34060	3	Preston	1 680	33 788	1 332	20.1	97.5	1.5	0.6	0.3	0.8	5.2	14.3	7.3	13.4	13.2	14.7
54 079	26580	2	Putnam	895	56 770	897	63.4	96.8	1.6	0.6	1.1	1.0	5.7	17.6	6.8	11.4	13.8	14.5
54 081	13220	4	Raleigh	1 568	78 241	704	49.9	89.3	8.9	0.9	1.3	1.4	6.1	15.0	7.8	12.5	13.4	12.7
54 083	21180	7	Randolph	2 693	29 429	1 442	10.9	97.1	1.9	0.7	0.5	0.8	5.1	14.2	8.4	12.0	12.0	14.5
54 085	...	8	Ritchie	1 171	10 011	2 438	8.5	98.6	0.6	0.6	0.3	0.8	4.9	15.9	7.1	10.1	11.8	15.2
54 087	...	6	Roane	1 252	14 664	2 127	11.7	98.2	0.7	0.7	0.5	0.9	5.4	16.1	7.1	10.0	12.4	14.1
54 089	...	7	Summers	934	13 417	2 215	14.4	92.8	5.6	1.0	0.5	1.7	4.4	13.0	6.5	11.5	13.1	14.5
54 091	17220	6	Taylor	447	17 069	1 977	38.2	97.3	1.6	0.7	0.6	0.9	5.4	15.0	7.5	11.8	13.1	14.9
54 093	...	9	Tucker	1 085	6 927	2 684	6.4	98.3	0.7	0.7	0.3	0.8	4.1	13.4	7.7	9.8	11.6	15.7
54 095	...	6	Tyler	664	9 098	2 508	13.7	98.6	0.5	0.5	0.3	0.7	4.6	15.3	7.4	9.1	12.0	15.0
54 097	...	7	Upshur	919	24 731	1 619	26.9	97.3	1.4	0.6	0.6	1.1	5.5	15.0	11.4	11.1	11.7	13.4
54 099	26580	2	Wayne	1 310	41 122	1 151	31.4	98.4	0.7	0.7	0.4	0.6	4.9	16.5	8.1	11.1	13.0	14.1
54 101	...	9	Webster	1 433	8 834	2 528	6.2	98.8	0.8	0.6	0.5	0.5	5.8	14.1	7.3	9.6	12.1	14.3
54 103	...	6	Wetzel	927	15 988	2 042	17.2	98.5	0.7	0.4	0.5	0.7	5.2	15.1	7.8	9.6	11.8	14.6
54 105	37620	3	Wirt	602	5 845	2 768	9.7	98.5	0.8	0.8	0.3	0.8	5.3	15.8	7.0	10.1	12.1	16.3
54 107	37620	3	Wood	949	86 237	664	90.9	96.9	1.9	0.7	0.9	0.9	5.7	15.8	7.8	11.4	12.3	14.6
54 109	...	7	Wyoming	1 294	22 598	1 703	17.5	98.5	1.1	0.6	0.3	0.5	5.5	15.9	7.5	10.1	13.5	13.7
55 000	...	X	WISCONSIN	140 268	5 757 564	X	41.0	83.9	7.0	1.4	2.9	6.3	6.0	16.8	9.7	12.8	12.1	14.5
55 001	...	8	Adams	1 672	20 215	1 829	12.1	91.6	3.4	1.4	0.8	3.8	3.5	11.7	5.7	10.0	10.2	14.7
55 003	...	7	Ashland	2 707	16 103	2 035	5.9	86.6	0.9	12.8	0.8	2.1	6.1	16.5	9.4	11.1	10.4	14.3
55 005	...	6	Barron	2 234	45 455	1 062	20.3	95.2	1.4	1.3	1.0	2.3	6.0	15.7	7.3	11.2	11.2	14.3
55 007	...	8	Bayfield	3 828	14 985	2 103	3.9	87.9	0.9	11.7	0.7	1.4	4.3	14.1	5.9	8.2	9.8	15.0
55 009	24580	2	Brown	1 372	256 670	259	187.1	84.4	3.1	3.1	3.4	7.8	6.8	17.7	9.5	13.9	12.5	14.7
55 011	...	8	Buffalo	1 740	13 188	2 225	7.6	97.1	0.6	0.7	0.4	2.0	5.4	15.9	7.1	10.4	10.8	15.5
55 013	...	8	Burnett	2 129	15 328	2 079	7.2	92.6	1.1	6.3	0.8	1.5	4.5	14.0	6.0	8.1	9.3	14.7
55 015	11540	3	Calumet	824	49 491	989	60.1	92.9	1.0	0.8	2.6	3.8	6.3	19.4	7.4	11.1	13.8	16.3
55 017	20740	3	Chippewa	2 612	63 460	825	24.3	95.1	1.9	0.9	1.7	1.4	5.9	17.0	7.4	12.8	12.4	15.0
55 019	...	8	Clark	3 133	34 423	1 317	11.0	94.4	0.6	0.8	0.7	4.1	8.3	21.3	7.5	10.3	10.7	13.3
55 021	31540	2	Columbia	1 983	56 615	899	28.6	94.6	1.7	0.9	0.9	2.8	5.5	17.1	7.1	11.6	12.9	15.7
55 023	...	7	Crawford	1 478	16 392	2 018	11.1	96.2	2.1	0.6	0.8	1.1	4.9	16.2	7.2	10.6	10.3	15.1
55 025	31540	2	Dane	3 101	516 284	128	166.5	83.1	6.3	0.7	6.0	6.2	6.0	15.2	13.5	15.9	12.9	13.1

1. CBSA = Core Based Statistical Area. See Appendix A for explanation. See Appendix B for list of metropolitan areas with component counties. 2. County type code from the Economic Research Service of USDA Rural-Urban Continuum Codes. See Appendix A for definition. 3. Dry land or land partially or temporarily covered by water. 4. May be of any race.

STATE County	Population, 2013 (cont.): Age (percent) (cont.): 55 to 64 years	65 to 74 years	75 years and over	Percent female	Population change and components of change, 2000–2014: Total persons: 2000	2010	Percent change: 2000–2010	2010–2014	Components of change, 2010–2014: Births	Deaths	Net migration	Households, 2009–2013: Number	Persons per household	Percent: Family households	Female family householder[1]	One person
	16	17	18	19	20	21	22	23	24	25	26	27	28	29	30	31
WEST VIRGINIA—Cont'd																
Brooke	16.1	10.7	9.9	51.2	25 447	24 069	-5.4	-2.2	762	1 422	81	9 968	2.30	65.4	12.0	30.6
Cabell	13.1	9.1	7.6	51.3	96 784	96 319	-0.5	0.8	5 216	4 730	540	40 144	2.32	60.2	13.4	32.9
Calhoun	16.3	11.6	8.5	49.8	7 582	7 627	0.6	-1.5	311	369	-62	3 141	2.41	66.9	10.0	29.3
Clay	14.8	10.6	7.6	50.0	10 330	9 386	-9.1	-4.7	485	461	-504	3 435	2.70	70.9	7.7	25.5
Doddridge	15.7	10.5	6.3	45.9	7 403	8 202	10.8	2.3	287	341	217	2 778	2.80	69.5	11.4	26.6
Fayette	15.8	10.1	8.0	49.6	47 579	46 039	-3.2	-2.0	2 291	2 763	-397	17 250	2.54	66.7	14.2	28.6
Gilmer	12.1	7.6	6.9	39.7	7 160	8 693	21.4	-0.9	275	298	-49	2 590	2.49	62.4	7.9	29.6
Grant	15.2	12.6	8.5	50.4	11 299	11 937	5.6	-2.1	479	545	-192	4 449	2.64	67.9	7.8	26.7
Greenbrier	15.8	11.9	8.8	50.8	34 453	35 480	3.0	-0.1	1 612	2 039	380	15 409	2.27	64.9	12.1	30.2
Hampshire	15.3	11.9	7.0	49.3	20 203	23 964	18.6	-2.0	936	1 062	-353	10 570	2.19	44.1	8.0	53.3
Hancock	16.3	10.3	9.4	51.7	32 667	30 676	-6.1	-1.8	1 281	1 711	-117	12 890	2.34	66.3	12.4	30.0
Hardy	14.8	11.8	7.5	49.6	12 669	14 025	10.7	-0.7	609	633	-103	5 020	2.76	61.6	8.4	35.2
Harrison	14.3	9.6	7.7	51.1	68 652	69 099	0.7	-0.5	3 364	3 643	52	27 599	2.47	67.1	12.7	29.1
Jackson	14.3	10.0	8.7	50.8	28 000	29 211	4.3	-0.3	1 350	1 452	66	11 459	2.53	68.2	11.1	27.3
Jefferson	13.3	8.6	4.9	50.6	42 190	53 498	26.8	4.1	2 535	1 883	1 521	19 889	2.65	70.6	10.2	22.7
Kanawha	15.4	9.7	8.0	51.9	200 073	193 063	-3.5	-1.5	9 336	10 269	-1 594	82 756	2.29	61.4	12.4	33.2
Lewis	14.5	11.0	7.9	50.4	16 919	16 372	-3.2	0.3	822	915	116	6 451	2.50	67.3	10.5	28.0
Lincoln	15.0	9.9	6.7	50.3	22 108	21 720	-1.8	-0.7	1 125	1 185	-121	8 416	2.57	72.6	13.0	25.2
Logan	16.6	9.7	6.7	50.2	37 710	36 743	-2.6	-3.8	1 835	2 189	-1 034	14 699	2.43	70.7	13.4	24.4
McDowell	17.1	10.1	7.5	50.6	27 329	22 113	-19.1	-7.5	1 147	1 510	-1 274	8 229	2.54	65.5	13.1	29.8
Marion	14.4	9.9	7.9	51.0	56 598	56 418	-0.3	0.7	2 761	2 766	449	22 593	2.45	65.3	12.1	28.9
Marshall	16.2	10.8	8.2	50.9	35 519	33 107	-6.8	-2.1	1 390	1 714	-338	14 042	2.30	66.9	9.9	28.9
Mason	15.1	10.6	8.0	51.8	25 957	27 324	5.3	-1.1	1 200	1 384	-142	10 609	2.50	68.8	13.0	27.0
Mercer	15.4	10.6	8.4	52.1	62 980	62 264	-1.1	-0.8	3 292	3 776	102	25 641	2.38	64.9	11.2	30.9
Mineral	14.3	11.6	7.5	50.3	27 078	28 212	4.2	-2.2	1 252	1 395	-479	11 180	2.44	55.9	10.7	41.8
Mingo	15.8	9.2	5.8	50.9	28 253	26 839	-5.0	-4.2	1 516	1 550	-1 041	10 827	2.43	70.1	12.9	26.7
Monongalia	10.7	6.0	4.5	48.5	81 866	96 189	17.5	7.6	4 397	2 709	5 512	36 449	2.50	52.5	8.0	35.8
Monroe	15.3	13.1	8.8	50.5	14 583	13 502	-7.4	0.6	595	678	185	5 648	2.38	71.4	12.1	24.1
Morgan	16.3	12.0	8.2	50.4	14 943	17 541	17.4	-0.5	577	870	255	7 343	2.37	52.7	6.9	43.1
Nicholas	15.7	11.1	7.4	50.8	26 562	26 233	-1.2	-1.5	1 286	1 446	-238	10 657	2.44	73.4	9.1	23.5
Ohio	15.4	9.7	9.4	52.1	47 427	44 443	-6.3	-2.5	2 103	2 474	-598	18 553	2.25	58.4	11.2	37.1
Pendleton	16.4	12.4	11.5	48.9	8 196	7 695	-6.1	-4.2	314	376	-238	3 274	2.27	63.9	7.7	31.0
Pleasants	14.1	10.7	7.4	46.4	7 514	7 605	1.2	0.4	272	402	161	2 747	2.58	71.2	7.4	24.8
Pocahontas	17.2	12.6	9.0	48.5	9 131	8 719	-4.5	-0.7	349	445	35	3 694	2.26	65.5	6.3	29.8
Preston	14.9	9.9	7.0	48.5	29 334	33 520	14.3	0.8	1 451	1 412	232	12 697	2.48	69.6	7.6	25.5
Putnam	14.4	9.5	6.3	50.8	51 589	55 486	7.6	2.3	2 467	2 265	966	21 391	2.61	74.8	10.6	20.9
Raleigh	15.0	9.8	7.7	50.0	79 220	78 859	-0.5	-0.8	4 169	4 318	-464	31 364	2.40	66.6	11.9	28.8
Randolph	14.4	11.5	7.9	48.4	28 262	29 405	4.0	0.1	1 353	1 512	192	11 163	2.45	67.4	10.3	30.5
Ritchie	15.6	11.5	7.9	50.3	10 343	10 449	1.0	-4.2	390	561	-252	4 032	2.54	64.5	9.6	32.7
Roane	16.0	11.3	7.7	50.5	15 446	14 926	-3.4	-1.8	702	771	-168	5 975	2.46	66.6	12.1	29.1
Summers	16.7	11.4	9.0	55.1	12 999	13 927	7.1	-3.7	486	735	-240	5 350	2.36	69.2	8.5	29.0
Taylor	14.9	10.0	7.5	49.4	16 089	16 895	5.0	1.0	755	827	274	6 878	2.38	70.8	12.6	25.5
Tucker	15.8	12.6	9.2	49.3	7 321	7 141	-2.5	-3.0	260	406	-72	3 050	2.27	68.4	7.8	27.8
Tyler	16.6	11.3	8.7	51.0	9 592	9 208	-4.0	-1.2	392	510	9	3 712	2.43	69.7	10.3	27.5
Upshur	14.1	10.4	7.4	50.6	23 404	24 254	3.6	2.0	1 205	1 120	396	9 011	2.55	68.0	9.8	27.4
Wayne	14.3	10.4	7.5	51.2	42 903	42 481	-1.0	-3.2	1 615	1 992	-994	16 555	2.52	66.3	12.0	30.2
Webster	16.5	12.2	8.1	50.1	9 719	9 154	-5.8	-3.5	421	509	-263	3 928	2.30	70.2	10.4	24.8
Wetzel	14.8	11.8	9.2	50.7	17 693	16 583	-6.3	-3.6	694	989	-291	6 903	2.36	65.6	11.1	30.5
Wirt	15.5	11.4	6.4	49.7	5 873	5 717	-2.7	2.2	249	234	103	2 427	2.39	65.6	11.8	25.0
Wood	14.4	10.3	7.7	51.7	87 986	86 956	-1.2	-0.8	3 905	4 382	-133	35 569	2.41	65.5	10.3	30.0
Wyoming	17.0	10.1	6.6	50.4	25 708	23 796	-7.4	-5.1	1 026	1 486	-691	9 101	2.57	70.6	10.2	26.2
WISCONSIN	13.3	8.1	6.7	50.3	5 363 675	5 686 986	6.0	1.2	285 690	203 329	-11 288	2 288 332	2.43	64.2	10.1	28.8
Adams	17.9	16.0	10.3	46.4	18 643	20 875	12.0	-3.2	561	995	-205	8 278	2.34	65.6	6.4	29.1
Ashland	14.9	9.4	7.8	49.9	16 866	16 157	-4.2	-0.3	771	761	-88	6 775	2.27	60.4	10.0	33.6
Barron	14.7	10.7	8.9	50.3	44 963	45 870	2.0	-0.9	2 255	2 095	-541	19 168	2.36	66.4	8.4	28.5
Bayfield	19.7	14.2	8.9	48.9	15 013	15 014	0.0	-0.2	556	709	124	6 964	2.14	64.6	6.4	29.3
Brown	12.4	7.0	5.7	50.4	226 778	248 007	9.4	3.5	14 493	7 401	1 773	98 962	2.46	65.5	10.6	28.1
Buffalo	15.4	10.5	9.0	49.1	13 804	13 587	-1.6	-2.9	588	554	-430	5 777	2.30	65.9	8.0	29.4
Burnett	17.7	14.9	10.6	49.2	15 674	15 457	-1.4	-0.8	567	676	9	7 354	2.07	64.4	8.2	28.6
Calumet	12.8	7.1	5.7	49.9	40 631	48 971	20.5	1.1	2 414	1 318	-629	18 381	2.67	74.6	7.0	20.8
Chippewa	13.7	8.7	7.0	48.2	55 195	62 415	13.1	1.5	3 109	2 155	31	24 456	2.48	67.4	8.6	26.2
Clark	12.6	8.0	7.9	49.4	33 557	34 690	3.4	-0.8	2 423	1 389	-1 310	13 036	2.61	69.1	7.6	26.2
Columbia	14.2	8.9	7.0	49.4	52 468	56 833	8.3	-0.4	2 579	2 166	-664	22 735	2.42	68.2	9.4	26.2
Crawford	15.7	11.5	8.6	48.5	17 243	16 644	-3.5	-1.5	678	746	-167	6 772	2.33	64.3	7.5	31.0
Dane	12.0	6.6	4.9	50.4	426 526	488 073	14.4	5.8	25 836	12 616	14 614	206 982	2.33	57.7	8.5	31.1

1. No spouse present.

Table B. States and Counties — **Population, Vital Statistics, Medicare, and Crime**

STATE County	Persons in group quarters, 2014	Daytime population, 2009–2013 Number	Daytime population, 2009–2013 Employment/residence ratio	Births, 2014 Total	Births, 2014 Rate[1]	Deaths, 2014 Number	Deaths, 2014 Rate[1]	Persons under 65 with no health insurance, 2013 Number	Persons under 65 with no health insurance, 2013 Percent	Medicare, 2014 Eligible for Medicare	Medicare, 2014 Enrolled in Medicare Advantage	Medicare, 2014 Enrolled in a Medicare prescription drug plan	Serious crimes known to police,[2] 2013 Total Number	Serious crimes known to police,[2] 2013 Total Rate[3]
	32	33	34	35	36	37	38	39	40	41	42	43	44	45
WEST VIRGINIA—Cont'd														
Brooke	872	22 070	0.81	174	7.4	308	13.1	2 673	14.9	5 691	1 927	2 562	213	1 076
Cabell	3 916	109 431	1.32	1 262	13.0	1 101	11.3	13 870	17.9	20 734	6 057	8 979	3 517	3 622
Calhoun	22	6 765	0.67	62	8.3	75	10.0	1 205	20.0	2 028	357	1 128	NA	NA
Clay	74	8 371	0.69	111	12.4	111	12.4	1 396	18.5	2 411	756	1 130	NA	NA
Doddridge	855	6 681	0.48	70	8.3	71	8.5	1 130	18.4	1 536	404	629	NA	NA
Fayette	1 837	42 974	0.81	507	11.2	674	14.9	6 804	19.0	10 583	2 731	4 855	964	2 263
Gilmer	2 181	8 657	0.99	61	7.1	73	8.5	1 035	19.9	1 371	381	665	NA	NA
Grant	126	11 440	0.92	110	9.4	120	10.3	1 760	19.1	2 961	600	1 520	71	783
Greenbrier	616	36 947	1.10	403	11.4	480	13.5	5 604	20.1	9 240	1 863	4 731	408	1 137
Hampshire	520	19 648	0.55	215	9.2	238	10.1	4 156	22.4	5 233	914	2 625	262	1 127
Hancock	226	29 456	0.92	298	9.9	420	13.9	3 901	16.1	7 403	1 718	3 773	318	1 093
Hardy	58	14 048	1.02	147	10.6	155	11.1	2 261	20.2	3 181	636	1 566	98	725
Harrison	841	75 676	1.23	781	11.4	866	12.6	9 300	16.5	15 515	3 639	7 617	1 345	2 092
Jackson	180	26 998	0.80	318	10.9	338	11.6	3 982	16.9	6 895	1 561	2 948	276	945
Jefferson	1 323	46 315	0.70	579	10.4	446	8.0	7 298	15.9	9 272	1 607	3 576	708	1 414
Kanawha	3 178	212 085	1.23	2 189	11.5	2 450	12.9	23 616	15.3	44 088	13 778	19 444	6 360	3 453
Lewis	248	16 948	1.08	193	11.8	233	14.2	2 230	17.0	4 190	1 259	1 828	216	1 321
Lincoln	66	18 034	0.47	258	12.0	285	13.2	3 341	18.6	5 040	1 554	2 392	NA	NA
Logan	667	37 768	1.12	418	11.8	489	13.8	5 051	17.1	8 732	2 454	4 323	660	2 015
McDowell	375	22 365	1.15	272	13.3	341	16.7	3 435	20.2	5 817	1 713	3 310	317	1 838
Marion	1 340	52 811	0.85	625	11.0	682	12.0	7 523	16.5	12 741	3 384	6 578	591	1 184
Marshall	524	31 072	0.87	344	10.6	386	11.9	4 268	16.6	6 863	2 746	3 242	663	2 232
Mason	635	25 044	0.77	283	10.5	332	12.3	3 345	15.6	6 332	1 302	3 174	292	1 182
Mercer	1 111	61 891	0.98	763	12.3	892	14.4	8 988	18.2	15 910	3 936	8 421	1 686	2 768
Mineral	666	25 130	0.73	288	10.4	334	12.1	3 641	16.8	6 416	861	3 686	495	1 881
Mingo	85	25 456	0.87	356	13.8	362	14.1	3 927	17.9	6 828	1 926	3 472	320	1 333
Monongalia	7 366	110 305	1.25	1 070	10.3	650	6.3	13 851	16.5	12 518	3 773	5 431	2 003	2 058
Monroe	57	10 808	0.47	145	10.7	152	11.2	2 210	21.1	3 554	753	1 827	149	1 109
Morgan	123	14 462	0.54	133	7.6	205	11.7	2 822	20.3	4 128	643	1 927	174	1 066
Nicholas	162	25 805	0.96	303	11.7	335	13.0	3 825	18.2	6 744	2 155	3 045	506	2 094
Ohio	2 525	54 093	1.49	516	11.9	585	13.5	5 006	15.1	10 473	4 307	4 148	1 123	2 763
Pendleton	208	6 592	0.69	66	9.0	66	9.0	1 159	20.8	2 062	422	1 053	NA	NA
Pleasants	623	7 927	1.12	70	9.2	77	10.1	805	14.3	1 647	444	818	50	870
Pocahontas	318	8 767	1.01	84	9.7	117	13.5	1 429	21.8	2 229	479	1 084	92	1 205
Preston	2 296	28 561	0.63	321	9.5	339	10.0	4 827	18.7	6 970	1 642	3 448	321	1 146
Putnam	249	51 723	0.82	557	9.8	555	9.8	6 358	13.5	11 328	3 554	4 790	846	1 520
Raleigh	3 653	80 783	1.06	972	12.4	1 037	13.3	10 369	16.9	19 028	4 300	9 149	2 998	3 872
Randolph	2 333	30 357	1.08	333	11.3	363	12.3	4 012	18.4	6 877	1 403	3 519	604	2 057
Ritchie	106	10 263	0.99	92	9.2	137	13.7	1 667	20.6	2 628	586	1 334	95	1 048
Roane	98	13 202	0.66	170	11.6	175	11.9	2 273	19.2	3 896	1 093	1 732	208	1 424
Summers	1 295	12 074	0.61	107	8.0	146	10.9	1 820	18.9	3 362	752	1 781	139	1 017
Taylor	511	13 662	0.52	180	10.5	185	10.8	2 377	17.6	3 530	701	1 825	32	188
Tucker	146	6 615	0.85	60	8.7	111	16.0	1 054	19.8	1 736	495	871	NA	NA
Tyler	67	8 288	0.73	98	10.8	109	12.0	1 287	18.0	2 244	683	1 121	120	1 469
Upshur	1 217	24 260	0.99	289	11.7	265	10.7	3 445	18.0	5 375	1 615	2 289	404	1 647
Wayne	246	37 490	0.70	384	9.3	494	12.0	6 024	17.8	9 741	2 582	4 288	796	2 101
Webster	58	8 339	0.75	95	10.8	114	12.9	1 314	18.5	2 508	737	1 360	NA	NA
Wetzel	124	16 961	1.10	156	9.8	237	14.8	2 163	17.0	3 960	1 445	1 856	66	461
Wirt	0	4 588	0.42	63	10.8	44	7.5	920	19.0	1 455	336	790	107	1 821
Wood	1 000	89 755	1.08	878	10.2	1 037	12.0	10 983	15.7	20 881	4 195	11 415	2 368	2 832
Wyoming	56	22 727	0.89	225	10.0	352	15.6	3 373	17.7	5 953	1 790	3 169	489	2 336
WISCONSIN	148 985	5 657 351	0.98	66 735	11.6	47 602	8.3	505 168	10.6	1 031 874	368 067	424 032	141 649	2 467
Adams	1 312	17 751	0.61	139	6.9	236	11.7	1 850	13.4	6 123	1 357	2 839	648	3 140
Ashland	615	17 131	1.15	186	11.6	171	10.6	1 593	12.4	3 684	1 055	1 562	516	3 236
Barron	628	45 807	1.00	523	11.5	454	10.0	4 129	11.3	10 728	3 678	4 385	NA	NA
Bayfield	109	13 155	0.71	142	9.5	183	12.2	1 725	14.9	4 150	1 338	1 603	236	1 559
Brown	6 536	270 041	1.16	3 417	13.3	1 684	6.6	23 016	10.6	40 084	19 315	11 790	5 551	2 179
Buffalo	96	11 154	0.66	141	10.7	120	9.1	1 201	11.3	3 008	597	1 370	88	832
Burnett	134	14 286	0.81	131	8.5	156	10.2	1 600	14.1	4 794	1 519	1 951	740	4 813
Calumet	182	37 790	0.55	558	11.3	338	6.8	3 231	7.5	7 038	4 313	1 522	577	1 157
Chippewa	2 614	58 955	0.88	725	11.4	537	8.5	5 308	10.4	12 063	3 535	5 120	938	1 486
Clark	486	31 908	0.83	544	15.8	317	9.2	5 549	19.3	6 239	2 913	1 729	278	809
Columbia	1 431	49 180	0.74	603	10.7	498	8.8	4 047	8.7	10 960	3 011	5 694	903	1 599
Crawford	765	17 073	1.07	168	10.2	170	10.4	1 332	10.7	3 940	1 238	1 836	NA	NA
Dane	12 857	532 130	1.13	6 167	11.9	3 007	5.8	39 043	8.9	71 756	15 488	41 053	13 760	2 712

1. Per 1,000 estimated resident population. 2. Data for serious crimes have not been adjusted for underreporting; this may affect comparability between geographic areas and over time.
3. Per 100,000 population estimated by the FBI.

STATE County	Serious crimes known to police, 2013 (cont.)[1] Rate[2] Violent	Property	Education: School enrollment and attainment, 2009–2013: Enrollment[3] Total	Per-cent private	Attainment[4] (percent) High school grad-uate or less	Bach-elor's degree or more	Local government expenditures,[5] 2012–2013: Total current spending (mil dol)	Current spend-ing per student (dollars)	Money income, 2009–2013: Per capita income[6] (dollars)	Households: Median income (dollars)	Mean income (dollars)	Percent with income of $200,000 or more	Income and poverty, 2013: Median house-hold income (dollars)	Percent below poverty level: All per-sons	Children under 18 years	Children 5 to 17 years in families
	46	47	48	49	50	51	52	53	54	55	56	57	58	59	60	61
WEST VIRGINIA—Cont'd																
Brooke	96	980	5 287	17.3	54.8	17.0	38.1	11 425	22 815	42 493	53 839	1.4	43 719	14.7	23.0	19.7
Cabell	187	3 435	25 227	11.1	46.5	25.8	143.4	11 046	23 647	38 374	54 882	2.6	37 628	23.4	32.0	32.1
Calhoun	NA	NA	1 550	1.3	73.4	10.2	11.1	10 288	18 053	31 679	41 379	0.3	31 946	21.0	31.2	29.2
Clay	NA	NA	2 161	1.1	70.8	8.1	22.5	10 915	16 740	31 613	42 094	0.3	32 640	23.6	35.7	31.4
Doddridge	NA	NA	1 585	7.7	65.6	12.4	16.6	14 276	17 334	34 817	43 448	1.1	39 399	18.1	28.0	23.8
Fayette	293	1 969	9 273	10.5	64.3	11.6	76.9	11 191	18 685	33 771	45 845	0.8	33 720	22.6	30.3	28.5
Gilmer	NA	NA	2 351	18.4	58.2	16.6	10.8	11 410	17 870	38 442	50 923	1.2	35 344	31.1	30.0	29.2
Grant	110	673	2 469	6.7	72.2	10.9	18.9	10 264	20 193	41 368	49 155	0.6	38 268	16.7	25.9	23.6
Greenbrier	61	1 076	7 375	9.0	59.3	17.1	60.2	11 517	21 720	37 895	49 479	2.1	37 218	17.7	25.1	23.0
Hampshire	353	774	5 076	12.2	75.1	8.2	36.1	10 320	17 734	27 766	37 576	0.2	37 444	16.9	27.7	25.1
Hancock	83	1 011	6 125	10.2	56.4	15.7	47.0	11 188	23 261	38 522	53 795	1.9	40 249	14.6	23.0	20.2
Hardy	251	473	2 956	8.5	68.4	9.5	22.7	9 661	19 032	32 723	44 178	0.8	36 053	18.0	26.1	24.4
Harrison	238	1 854	14 833	8.9	53.6	19.8	143.9	13 158	23 309	43 183	56 286	1.7	42 197	16.1	22.9	20.1
Jackson	264	682	6 364	6.5	55.8	15.8	54.4	10 947	22 527	40 376	54 932	1.7	38 640	18.1	26.0	22.8
Jefferson	144	1 271	14 663	14.0	44.4	27.6	100.1	11 171	29 605	65 304	79 459	4.5	64 916	11.3	14.9	13.0
Kanawha	445	3 008	40 611	13.8	49.7	25.0	319.1	11 176	28 174	46 085	64 113	3.6	45 858	15.3	24.1	21.1
Lewis	165	1 156	2 965	13.7	63.7	15.6	28.7	10 917	21 175	36 199	50 645	2.2	38 462	17.4	26.1	25.0
Lincoln	NA	NA	4 183	4.0	68.9	8.2	44.0	11 783	18 458	35 487	46 300	0.5	35 524	23.7	34.6	30.7
Logan	482	1 533	6 861	4.3	66.0	9.2	69.2	10 762	19 901	36 999	49 275	0.8	35 773	22.2	30.2	28.2
McDowell	348	1 490	3 558	6.5	79.1	5.8	50.1	14 178	14 093	22 252	34 504	0.6	25 205	36.5	47.7	44.5
Marion	258	926	12 983	10.9	53.5	20.3	90.1	11 123	23 229	42 152	55 123	1.3	41 705	15.3	23.2	22.0
Marshall	310	1 922	7 163	9.4	59.0	14.2	59.2	12 615	24 329	40 681	56 681	1.5	41 583	16.9	24.9	22.9
Mason	89	1 093	5 973	8.0	62.3	10.0	47.9	11 087	20 622	38 411	50 642	1.1	36 454	22.3	30.1	28.5
Mercer	297	2 471	13 831	11.5	57.5	17.7	105.3	10 888	20 391	34 842	47 981	1.2	34 320	26.7	40.9	37.3
Mineral	228	1 653	6 114	6.2	61.7	13.2	49.0	11 535	19 788	31 163	44 144	0.9	38 320	16.4	24.4	22.2
Mingo	313	1 021	5 476	4.4	67.8	10.7	54.6	12 295	20 609	35 955	49 772	0.9	32 431	24.9	34.3	31.9
Monongalia	299	1 759	36 428	5.2	39.7	38.1	123.5	11 197	25 846	44 173	63 740	4.2	47 281	19.2	16.9	15.6
Monroe	126	982	2 525	9.2	67.2	13.7	19.8	10 673	20 294	41 234	48 859	0.3	36 787	17.3	26.0	23.2
Morgan	202	863	3 371	8.9	65.4	15.8	28.6	11 107	22 312	36 046	49 762	1.2	42 719	15.4	23.1	20.2
Nicholas	633	1 461	5 179	6.6	65.1	14.1	46.7	11 567	23 209	40 064	58 570	3.2	38 451	18.6	26.9	25.1
Ohio	534	2 229	10 903	23.9	44.5	29.1	67.8	12 368	26 135	41 025	60 176	2.8	41 009	15.3	22.5	20.4
Pendleton	NA	NA	1 271	5.5	66.1	13.0	13.4	13 286	21 253	34 175	47 280	1.1	36 868	18.0	26.8	23.7
Pleasants	174	696	1 572	6.6	59.6	10.5	16.1	12 916	21 312	41 859	54 055	0.5	43 172	15.0	20.3	17.3
Pocahontas	131	1 074	1 434	6.6	60.9	16.4	14.7	12 992	20 373	33 779	46 263	1.1	32 199	19.2	31.1	29.2
Preston	193	953	6 293	10.3	64.4	12.6	45.1	9 859	21 457	45 413	54 654	1.4	42 187	17.0	24.8	22.4
Putnam	230	1 290	12 340	12.5	48.2	24.0	108.2	11 049	27 957	54 854	71 078	3.5	56 102	11.0	14.6	13.0
Raleigh	382	3 490	16 534	15.7	58.6	17.0	139.1	11 056	21 837	40 758	53 456	1.3	39 998	20.2	28.7	25.9
Randolph	453	1 604	5 751	16.0	63.8	19.1	47.3	11 072	19 595	37 276	48 414	0.7	35 458	18.5	27.7	25.8
Ritchie	166	883	2 143	5.6	65.2	10.6	17.6	11 389	17 843	35 769	42 675	0.1	38 147	19.1	29.0	26.1
Roane	199	1 226	2 846	4.5	72.8	10.3	25.1	10 222	17 341	28 513	41 423	0.9	35 982	23.1	34.3	31.8
Summers	44	973	2 522	8.5	63.8	12.7	16.9	10 794	17 416	33 784	42 958	0.3	31 051	22.6	35.4	32.7
Taylor	18	170	3 533	6.8	60.7	15.5	25.4	10 528	20 848	39 536	51 153	1.6	38 720	17.2	24.9	23.3
Tucker	NA	NA	1 250	8.3	62.6	15.4	12.8	12 417	21 126	37 635	47 907	0.7	37 591	16.3	25.9	24.0
Tyler	343	1 126	1 693	4.6	65.6	9.4	17.4	12 677	20 704	39 206	48 917	1.3	39 401	17.9	26.1	23.7
Upshur	77	1 569	5 980	22.8	64.7	15.4	41.1	10 668	19 498	39 381	49 512	0.9	37 676	20.6	27.7	25.7
Wayne	190	1 911	9 743	4.5	62.4	11.5	78.9	10 506	19 497	36 964	46 781	1.1	38 676	20.0	30.9	27.8
Webster	NA	NA	1 509	6.6	73.1	8.6	16.3	10 893	17 937	27 645	41 294	1.0	31 805	27.1	42.3	39.6
Wetzel	49	413	3 126	5.4	65.7	10.2	34.2	12 128	21 653	37 969	51 306	1.1	39 444	19.7	28.0	25.7
Wirt	255	1 565	1 139	8.6	62.0	10.9	11.1	10 772	21 852	34 702	51 111	1.9	37 132	21.3	31.8	28.5
Wood	299	2 533	19 642	11.8	48.1	18.4	149.9	11 238	24 042	42 287	56 945	1.9	41 205	17.9	28.9	26.2
Wyoming	597	1 739	4 865	5.8	72.2	8.7	48.7	11 405	18 377	34 454	45 785	0.4	34 525	24.3	33.2	29.6
WISCONSIN	278	2 189	1 498 269	16.8	42.4	26.8	9 685.4	11 071	27 523	52 413	67 448	2.9	51 474	13.5	18.4	16.8
Adams	276	2 864	3 525	9.3	56.8	12.1	19.8	11 808	22 196	44 897	52 953	0.8	43 814	15.1	28.0	24.7
Ashland	289	2 948	3 899	20.6	44.0	21.7	30.8	11 658	21 115	38 550	49 144	1.2	37 909	18.1	26.8	25.6
Barron	NA	NA	9 855	10.1	51.9	16.2	90.6	11 566	23 337	44 054	54 999	1.5	44 086	13.5	20.1	18.0
Bayfield	178	1 381	2 877	11.7	38.8	28.5	22.7	14 975	25 377	44 944	55 701	1.4	45 466	13.9	25.5	22.0
Brown	239	1 940	68 283	15.7	41.8	26.8	452.1	10 439	27 787	53 119	69 336	3.4	51 956	12.1	15.9	14.4
Buffalo	0	832	2 998	11.5	53.6	17.2	22.9	10 928	24 500	47 384	56 868	1.3	48 418	12.0	16.7	15.7
Burnett	176	4 637	2 851	10.9	50.5	16.7	28.2	11 270	22 843	39 564	49 058	1.2	41 388	14.3	23.5	21.2
Calumet	102	1 055	12 790	16.4	44.3	27.6	39.3	10 084	28 907	65 130	76 949	3.1	66 657	6.4	8.3	7.7
Chippewa	97	1 390	14 116	12.0	48.7	18.6	94.7	10 724	24 628	50 551	61 199	1.5	49 491	11.5	15.5	14.6
Clark	11	765	7 021	21.7	61.9	11.0	54.0	10 903	20 754	43 276	54 296	1.7	42 477	14.5	22.5	21.6
Columbia	184	1 415	13 470	12.0	44.4	21.3	94.7	10 693	28 273	57 922	69 463	2.4	57 613	9.2	12.9	11.3
Crawford	NA	NA	3 876	13.1	53.7	15.4	33.7	12 184	22 549	42 235	53 451	1.6	41 598	14.3	20.9	19.1
Dane	236	2 476	148 888	12.1	25.4	46.6	851.4	11 439	33 712	61 721	79 847	4.7	60 326	13.7	13.6	12.7

1. Data for serious crimes have not been adjusted for underreporting; this may affect comparability between geographic areas and over time. 2. Per 100,000 population estimated by the FBI.
3. All persons 3 years old and over enrolled in nursery school through college. 4. Persons 25 years old and over. 5. Elementary and secondary education expenditures.
6. Based on population estimated by the American Community Survey, 2009–2013.

STATE County	Personal income, 2013: Total (mil dol)	Personal income, 2013: Percent change, 2012–2013	Per capita[1]: Dollars	Per capita[1]: Rank	Wages and salaries (mil dol)	Supplements to wages and salaries; employer contributions (mil dol): Pension and insurance	Supplements to wages and salaries; employer contributions (mil dol): Government social insurance	Proprietors' income (mil dol)	Dividends, interest, and rent (mil dol)	Personal transfer receipts (mil dol)	Earnings, 2013: Total (mil dol)	Contributions for government social insurance (mil dol): From employee and self-employed	Contributions for government social insurance (mil dol): From employer
	62	63	64	65	66	67	68	69	70	71	72	73	74
WEST VIRGINIA—Cont'd													
Brooke	828	2.0	34 882	1 919	301	65	25	81	122	226	473	32	25
Cabell	3 475	0.8	35 779	1 786	2 194	427	178	224	581	981	3 023	186	178
Calhoun	196	3.0	25 889	3 028	64	13	5	14	24	78	96	8	5
Clay	231	0.4	24 944	3 055	52	12	4	11	26	88	79	7	4
Doddridge	198	6.8	23 704	3 083	56	12	4	17	29	50	89	7	4
Fayette	1 365	-1.2	29 945	2 693	440	96	34	87	162	489	657	47	34
Gilmer	213	1.2	24 509	3 068	90	26	7	10	32	66	133	8	7
Grant	391	3.2	33 217	2 224	169	37	14	40	56	116	259	17	14
Greenbrier	1 216	1.2	34 126	2 056	488	97	42	123	179	383	749	50	42
Hampshire	628	2.0	26 799	2 985	132	32	11	47	97	188	222	17	11
Hancock	979	1.6	32 306	2 365	395	88	33	19	147	308	535	37	33
Hardy	412	4.1	29 567	2 745	178	42	16	28	62	108	264	17	16
Harrison	2 974	3.4	43 120	833	1 632	353	128	354	434	639	2 467	146	128
Jackson	850	1.8	29 146	2 787	302	62	24	61	112	269	449	32	24
Jefferson	2 200	0.0	39 939	1 178	605	117	50	106	350	356	879	55	50
Kanawha	8 572	0.5	44 817	707	4 874	927	373	1 071	1 217	2 041	7 246	433	373
Lewis	633	1.6	38 491	1 374	358	65	27	44	93	155	493	31	27
Lincoln	568	0.2	26 339	3 014	151	28	11	15	62	192	206	18	11
Logan	1 199	-3.0	33 317	2 201	511	95	39	26	138	458	671	48	39
McDowell	590	-2.7	28 280	2 869	283	58	22	12	69	258	374	28	22
Marion	2 232	1.9	39 249	1 260	916	174	70	171	313	533	1 331	86	70
Marshall	1 364	6.0	42 016	936	608	116	45	258	161	289	1 027	62	45
Mason	737	0.1	27 176	2 960	258	64	20	28	85	266	369	26	20
Mercer	2 097	0.4	33 836	2 114	790	163	66	142	300	753	1 160	82	66
Mineral	968	0.7	34 944	1 906	310	72	25	48	119	270	456	31	25
Mingo	773	-5.2	29 864	2 709	394	72	32	27	82	311	524	38	32
Monongalia	4 045	3.1	39 550	1 228	2 600	545	195	343	617	670	3 683	205	195
Monroe	385	0.6	28 582	2 843	74	21	6	20	50	122	121	11	6
Morgan	602	-0.1	34 401	2 011	94	21	8	32	87	164	155	13	8
Nicholas	831	-2.2	31 989	2 412	306	62	24	74	111	271	467	33	24
Ohio	1 766	1.0	40 397	1 121	1 144	226	90	41	395	475	1 500	93	90
Pendleton	257	1.3	34 370	2 018	63	16	5	24	50	74	108	7	5
Pleasants	270	3.8	35 652	1 809	129	32	10	26	35	86	198	12	10
Pocahontas	288	2.6	33 214	2 226	94	21	9	27	51	104	152	10	9
Preston	1 031	1.9	30 463	2 635	289	67	24	72	143	271	451	32	24
Putnam	2 430	0.5	42 903	854	1 012	174	81	166	279	428	1 433	90	81
Raleigh	3 098	-0.6	39 293	1 255	1 408	274	111	301	433	858	2 095	133	111
Randolph	973	3.0	33 074	2 241	391	87	33	78	130	307	588	39	33
Ritchie	345	3.2	34 236	2 043	141	29	12	25	45	100	207	14	12
Roane	411	2.0	28 067	2 891	116	25	9	21	58	153	172	14	9
Summers	361	1.6	26 620	3 000	81	18	7	11	52	155	117	11	7
Taylor	503	3.1	29 622	2 739	131	28	11	18	71	143	188	14	11
Tucker	223	2.8	31 950	2 416	72	18	6	13	35	73	109	8	6
Tyler	274	2.1	30 425	2 636	101	25	8	8	46	86	142	10	8
Upshur	753	0.4	30 527	2 623	309	62	25	72	98	205	468	31	25
Wayne	1 336	0.3	32 245	2 375	419	100	34	63	148	348	617	44	34
Webster	232	0.0	26 139	3 022	81	18	6	9	36	97	114	9	6
Wetzel	550	1.2	33 921	2 096	156	34	13	14	91	178	217	17	13
Wirt	137	1.7	23 148	3 088	19	5	2	7	18	51	33	4	2
Wood	3 056	1.7	35 296	1 860	1 517	327	122	171	514	865	2 138	138	122
Wyoming	683	-1.9	29 691	2 725	249	48	19	15	67	243	331	26	19
WISCONSIN	248 335	2.1	43 244	X	124 777	25 310	9 954	18 264	44 614	42 217	178 305	10 539	9 954
Adams	812	3.9	39 628	1 213	155	41	13	153	126	218	363	23	13
Ashland	583	2.0	36 391	1 676	311	80	26	48	98	153	465	28	26
Barron	1 763	2.7	38 597	1 357	742	186	63	172	316	409	1 163	69	63
Bayfield	574	2.7	37 850	1 454	119	40	10	39	136	146	208	15	10
Brown	10 991	2.0	43 171	831	7 067	1 337	554	933	2 007	1 566	9 890	574	554
Buffalo	599	1.4	44 853	701	150	39	12	115	102	108	315	17	12
Burnett	603	2.6	39 340	1 247	157	49	13	56	119	166	276	19	13
Calumet	2 349	1.1	47 348	521	476	100	40	192	296	247	808	48	40
Chippewa	2 415	1.6	38 250	1 405	895	206	74	272	394	484	1 448	86	74
Clark	1 178	3.1	34 041	2 072	376	95	32	179	199	247	681	38	32
Columbia	2 549	1.9	44 988	688	864	200	74	274	436	389	1 411	83	74
Crawford	607	3.9	37 018	1 582	264	61	23	55	105	140	403	25	23
Dane	26 181	4.1	51 341	319	15 943	3 430	1 222	1 711	5 100	2 888	22 306	1 247	1 222

1. Based on the resident population estimated as of July 1 of the year shown.

STATE County	Earnings, 2013 (cont.) — Percent by selected industries									Social Security beneficiaries, December 2013		Supple-mental Security Income recipients, December 2013	Housing units, 2014	
	Farm	Mining	Construction	Manu-facturing	Infor-mation: professional, scientific, technical services	Retail trade	Finance, insur-ance, real estate and leasing	Health care and social assistance	Govern-ment	Number	Rate[1]		Total	Percent change, 2010–2014
	75	76	77	78	79	80	81	82	83	84	85	86	87	88
WEST VIRGINIA—Cont'd														
Brooke	-0.1	D	D	28.5	2.0	7.6	2.8	D	10.1	6 475	273	623	10 903	-0.6
Cabell	-0.1	1.4	5.9	11.4	6.2	8.3	4.6	26.0	16.2	22 170	228	4 312	46 456	0.6
Calhoun	-1.9	D	37.1	0.8	D	5.0	D	D	16.9	2 240	297	617	3 952	-0.3
Clay	-0.8	D	9.9	2.8	D	7.0	D	14.3	32.5	2 805	305	749	4 574	0.0
Doddridge	-2.2	29.6	D	D	1.8	7.9	3.8	5.3	28.0	1 730	206	256	3 927	-0.5
Fayette	-0.1	9.9	4.5	8.7	4.1	9.0	2.8	D	26.4	12 245	269	2 612	21 520	-0.5
Gilmer	-1.9	D	5.7	6.4	D	3.5	D	D	47.4	1 620	187	321	3 475	0.7
Grant	1.7	10.4	14.2	6.6	D	4.9	3.0	7.7	17.6	3 275	278	401	6 468	1.6
Greenbrier	1.0	5.8	4.7	5.8	5.0	9.3	3.1	19.2	17.6	10 160	284	1 405	19 129	0.8
Hampshire	0.8	D	10.9	4.5	D	7.4	5.8	D	29.4	5 885	251	758	13 773	0.6
Hancock	-0.1	D	2.6	39.6	4.3	4.7	4.1	7.1	13.4	8 380	277	835	14 431	-0.7
Hardy	3.3	0.0	3.0	D	3.1	7.1	3.4	D	14.9	3 630	260	452	8 137	0.7
Harrison	-0.2	8.6	7.6	5.0	9.7	6.8	4.4	12.6	25.3	17 120	248	2 918	31 550	0.4
Jackson	-1.5	D	9.3	24.1	5.8	9.0	4.6	D	16.6	7 760	266	1 304	13 262	-0.3
Jefferson	0.6	D	5.7	6.7	8.5	6.3	4.4	7.3	25.9	9 740	177	831	22 564	2.4
Kanawha	0.0	5.6	6.1	4.7	11.6	5.9	8.5	17.7	18.0	49 125	257	7 462	92 420	-0.2
Lewis	-0.4	37.7	5.2	1.8	1.5	5.9	4.0	D	15.2	4 660	283	939	7 916	-0.5
Lincoln	-0.2	D	15.0	0.5	3.6	4.8	1.2	8.4	22.3	5 825	271	1 784	9 818	-0.7
Logan	0.0	D	2.6	4.8	4.9	9.2	2.2	D	17.1	10 335	287	2 457	16 710	-0.2
McDowell	0.0	D	3.8	0.3	D	5.1	2.2	D	28.8	6 800	326	2 936	11 188	-1.2
Marion	-0.1	D	6.2	5.4	9.7	8.2	5.3	8.6	18.6	13 990	246	2 033	26 338	-0.5
Marshall	-0.5	27.1	5.3	23.5	D	4.7	2.2	7.1	9.2	7 725	237	941	15 824	-0.6
Mason	1.4	D	D	D	2.8	5.5	3.2	D	20.9	7 200	265	1 290	12 945	-0.5
Mercer	-0.2	4.5	5.6	5.3	4.9	10.2	3.7	17.0	23.0	17 510	283	3 768	29 825	-1.0
Mineral	-0.1	0.3	6.4	30.9	10.3	7.4	5.8	D	18.1	6 670	241	763	13 101	0.5
Mingo	0.0	43.2	5.1	3.6	2.9	3.2	1.8	6.8	13.4	7 910	305	2 813	12 633	-0.5
Monongalia	-0.1	2.9	6.1	9.8	8.1	5.3	3.6	19.2	26.9	13 515	132	1 733	44 494	2.9
Monroe	-3.5	0.0	10.7	22.4	D	4.7	D	7.9	37.7	4 015	297	502	7 570	-0.4
Morgan	-1.1	D	7.8	11.8	3.7	8.2	5.2	15.6	23.1	4 520	259	348	9 832	0.8
Nicholas	-0.3	18.1	3.8	9.9	3.4	12.9	2.0	D	21.1	7 670	295	1 332	13 000	-0.5
Ohio	-0.1	D	D	4.6	10.4	8.1	5.6	22.3	14.1	11 475	262	1 410	21 080	-0.4
Pendleton	10.4	D	D	D	3.5	5.9	D	D	35.1	2 290	308	219	5 167	0.7
Pleasants	-0.2	D	6.3	21.5	3.5	3.5	D	6.5	15.3	1 910	251	269	3 376	-0.4
Pocahontas	0.6	D	5.3	8.8	D	7.2	4.3	D	25.6	2 510	289	309	8 834	-0.2
Preston	-0.9	0.7	20.1	7.5	4.0	6.9	3.6	D	32.8	7 785	231	1 199	15 044	-0.4
Putnam	0.2	0.5	18.0	12.0	6.5	5.9	7.9	7.6	9.6	12 560	222	1 282	23 765	1.4
Raleigh	-0.1	19.5	4.7	2.8	6.1	8.5	3.0	16.7	18.3	21 595	275	3 644	36 015	0.2
Randolph	0.1	3.3	6.1	11.4	D	9.6	4.5	D	19.6	7 590	257	1 312	14 178	-0.1
Ritchie	-1.2	25.7	12.1	22.8	6.1	4.9	2.7	D	12.0	3 010	299	534	5 810	-0.6
Roane	-3.0	D	12.7	5.0	3.4	10.6	5.7	D	18.8	4 450	304	1 056	7 403	0.7
Summers	0.6	0.0	6.3	0.9	D	7.1	3.5	14.2	28.2	3 475	257	831	7 673	-0.1
Taylor	0.2	D	6.1	D	D	10.4	D	D	28.9	3 715	219	705	7 510	-0.4
Tucker	0.2	D	12.1	13.4	D	5.7	5.9	10.5	27.2	1 875	270	212	5 359	0.2
Tyler	-0.6	3.4	4.5	41.3	D	3.8	D	10.7	19.3	2 555	284	359	4 983	-0.4
Upshur	-0.1	9.8	11.6	9.0	5.3	10.1	3.3	D	14.3	5 975	242	1 091	11 165	0.6
Wayne	0.0	D	4.3	6.9	2.5	4.9	1.3	D	35.8	10 745	259	2 473	19 225	0.0
Webster	-0.2	D	1.3	6.8	D	4.5	D	7.9	25.8	2 790	314	764	5 405	-0.4
Wetzel	-0.2	5.9	15.2	2.8	3.7	14.0	3.5	D	26.3	4 515	279	803	8 146	-0.3
Wirt	0.1	D	D	D	D	7.6	D	10.7	39.7	1 700	289	386	3 228	-0.1
Wood	-0.3	0.8	7.6	12.7	5.0	10.0	6.6	16.3	20.4	23 255	269	3 740	40 245	0.1
Wyoming	0.0	47.0	2.7	1.5	D	5.7	1.3	D	18.4	7 175	313	1 741	10 817	-1.3
WISCONSIN	1.8	0.2	5.2	18.6	7.7	6.0	7.4	12.4	15.8	1 134 358	198	116 715	2 648 317	0.9
Adams	12.1	0.0	6.5	6.3	D	5.6	D	5.0	20.8	6 960	339	518	17 393	-0.2
Ashland	1.2	0.0	8.7	13.7	3.7	6.9	2.7	D	25.1	4 175	260	417	9 618	-0.4
Barron	5.1	1.1	5.5	23.5	2.8	8.9	3.2	10.5	20.0	11 890	261	958	23 665	0.2
Bayfield	1.9	0.0	8.7	3.5	D	7.9	3.6	D	37.9	4 605	304	301	13 146	1.1
Brown	1.0	0.1	5.3	17.1	7.3	5.6	9.1	12.9	12.5	44 535	175	4 615	107 305	2.8
Buffalo	12.8	D	6.1	4.2	D	11.3	3.5	D	16.1	3 355	252	197	6 683	0.3
Burnett	3.1	D	7.4	19.6	2.8	6.8	2.2	D	31.8	5 295	346	284	15 428	1.0
Calumet	6.7	D	7.7	26.5	D	6.8	6.6	D	11.3	7 945	160	422	19 985	1.5
Chippewa	4.1	1.1	8.1	24.4	3.0	9.9	2.5	10.1	15.9	13 465	213	1 147	27 673	1.8
Clark	12.4	D	9.1	22.1	D	6.3	2.2	D	17.0	6 910	200	495	15 038	-0.3
Columbia	4.6	D	8.2	26.2	2.7	6.4	2.7	9.6	16.4	12 000	212	609	26 159	0.1
Crawford	5.6	D	3.8	23.1	D	16.6	2.8	D	15.5	4 410	269	323	8 834	0.4
Dane	0.9	0.1	5.3	8.0	14.9	5.1	10.6	10.5	24.2	76 035	149	7 394	222 374	2.9

1. Per 1,000 resident population estimated as of July 1 of the year shown.

STATE County	Housing units, 2009–2013: Occupied units: Total	Owner-occupied: Percent	Owner-occupied: Median value[1]	Median owner cost as a percent of income: With a mortgage	Median owner cost as a percent of income: Without a mortgage[2]	Renter-occupied: Median rent[3]	Renter-occupied: Median rent as a percent of income[2]	Substandard units[4] (percent)	Civilian labor force, 2014: Total	Civilian labor force, 2014: Percent change, 2013–2014	Unemployment: Total	Unemployment: Rate[5]	Civilian employment,[6] 2009–2013: Total	Percent: Management, business, science and arts	Percent: Construction, production, and maintenance occupations
	89	90	91	92	93	94	95	96	97	98	99	100	101	102	103
WEST VIRGINIA—Cont'd															
Brooke	9 968	75.6	82 300	17.6	10.0	570	25.9	1.3	10 234	-1.6	741	7.2	10 119	28.1	26.3
Cabell	40 144	61.4	105 400	19.4	10.0	638	32.1	2.3	42 096	-0.9	2 305	5.5	40 858	36.5	15.5
Calhoun	3 141	79.4	75 900	17.6	10.0	477	32.7	2.0	2 954	2.4	280	9.5	2 677	23.1	37.6
Clay	3 435	82.7	84 500	20.3	10.0	403	29.4	2.5	3 389	-2.8	360	10.6	3 207	25.6	36.5
Doddridge	2 778	82.8	80 700	19.9	10.0	544	33.6	1.7	3 684	4.5	181	4.9	2 915	23.9	36.0
Fayette	17 250	76.7	72 000	19.3	11.0	561	27.2	2.3	16 654	-2.1	1 379	8.3	15 640	24.3	27.7
Gilmer	2 590	77.1	72 500	16.2	10.0	549	29.6	0.6	2 759	0.2	175	6.3	2 876	29.9	25.7
Grant	4 449	79.1	112 900	23.4	10.0	555	23.6	2.8	5 860	-2.5	440	7.5	5 260	22.4	42.0
Greenbrier	15 409	74.4	96 700	20.9	10.0	625	29.6	1.2	15 254	-1.5	1 040	6.8	14 499	29.0	27.8
Hampshire	10 570	53.8	123 800	24.9	10.4	504	28.3	0.9	9 556	-0.2	573	6.0	9 158	17.2	39.2
Hancock	12 890	75.5	84 700	19.2	10.6	605	28.9	1.9	13 246	-1.3	1 046	7.9	13 003	28.1	28.8
Hardy	5 020	77.4	123 100	25.0	10.6	543	27.5	2.2	5 360	-1.4	422	7.9	5 737	19.1	44.5
Harrison	27 599	74.3	94 600	18.1	10.0	615	31.7	3.0	32 016	0.6	1 702	5.3	29 626	32.4	23.7
Jackson	11 459	77.7	101 800	18.3	10.0	562	28.8	2.1	11 917	-1.1	792	6.6	11 140	31.5	28.2
Jefferson	19 889	75.1	214 400	24.3	11.6	899	26.9	1.3	27 042	-1.4	1 208	4.5	26 523	38.8	18.9
Kanawha	82 756	71.0	101 600	19.0	10.0	671	26.6	2.4	88 299	-1.4	5 189	5.9	87 528	37.3	18.0
Lewis	6 451	71.6	91 400	18.4	10.0	507	27.8	3.0	7 249	-1.6	451	6.2	6 528	25.6	30.6
Lincoln	8 416	78.7	76 700	18.3	10.0	558	36.5	1.7	7 501	-0.7	707	9.4	7 048	22.2	35.2
Logan	14 699	73.8	77 600	19.0	10.0	532	23.6	3.1	11 959	-3.4	1 231	10.3	11 584	27.0	33.7
McDowell	8 229	77.4	35 000	19.4	11.0	475	42.2	2.0	5 825	-5.9	754	12.9	4 837	23.9	32.3
Marion	22 593	76.1	91 500	18.0	11.2	661	29.5	1.2	26 487	-1.1	1 570	5.9	25 482	30.8	24.3
Marshall	14 042	76.5	86 000	18.9	10.0	517	26.7	2.5	14 287	-0.3	1 084	7.6	13 604	25.2	30.5
Mason	10 609	79.5	83 900	19.8	10.0	521	30.5	1.8	10 213	-3.5	956	9.4	10 029	24.1	33.1
Mercer	25 641	72.2	79 400	20.0	10.0	574	33.7	1.5	22 418	-3.2	1 672	7.5	23 155	30.6	23.2
Mineral	11 180	62.8	114 800	20.8	10.8	516	29.3	3.6	11 792	-0.5	850	7.2	10 796	27.7	29.1
Mingo	10 827	77.7	69 000	18.7	10.0	518	26.9	1.1	7 823	-7.9	922	11.8	8 541	28.8	35.5
Monongalia	36 449	57.0	161 800	18.0	10.0	715	33.4	3.7	50 074	-0.1	2 194	4.4	47 571	41.7	16.7
Monroe	5 648	82.5	102 200	18.8	10.0	564	22.4	1.6	5 618	-1.2	323	5.7	5 337	27.1	35.0
Morgan	7 343	65.0	161 200	23.4	12.8	680	27.6	2.6	7 411	-0.4	422	5.7	6 757	26.9	34.8
Nicholas	10 657	80.3	75 500	18.2	10.0	536	28.8	1.2	10 139	-2.4	908	9.0	10 088	26.6	30.9
Ohio	18 553	70.1	98 700	18.4	10.0	532	30.1	2.7	21 206	-0.8	1 171	5.5	20 604	33.6	19.2
Pendleton	3 274	77.3	90 600	21.8	10.0	589	23.3	1.3	3 511	-2.0	166	4.7	3 202	21.1	41.3
Pleasants	2 747	83.7	97 300	18.0	10.0	412	26.1	2.1	2 988	3.1	210	7.0	2 839	24.4	34.2
Pocahontas	3 694	81.8	104 500	23.1	10.0	578	28.7	1.8	3 570	-0.9	306	8.6	3 516	30.7	29.9
Preston	12 697	80.1	106 300	19.2	10.0	557	25.4	0.6	14 576	-0.5	844	5.8	14 070	24.4	33.9
Putnam	21 391	84.7	142 900	18.8	10.0	703	28.3	0.9	25 811	-0.7	1 425	5.5	24 901	37.6	20.3
Raleigh	31 364	73.1	93 900	19.0	10.5	603	26.5	2.3	31 201	-2.0	2 204	7.1	29 562	31.1	25.4
Randolph	11 163	75.2	99 000	21.4	10.0	534	33.9	0.9	11 849	-0.7	838	7.1	11 566	28.8	24.3
Ritchie	4 032	79.0	73 400	20.4	10.0	515	30.0	2.0	4 642	1.8	282	6.1	3 720	25.2	34.9
Roane	5 975	75.7	81 900	20.5	10.0	467	30.4	3.0	5 329	-0.7	525	9.9	4 857	24.3	31.7
Summers	5 350	79.6	79 600	19.5	10.0	469	28.9	1.0	4 513	-1.0	318	7.0	4 583	26.8	32.4
Taylor	6 878	77.6	89 900	19.7	10.3	509	27.5	1.5	7 792	0.3	410	5.3	6 880	29.5	31.1
Tucker	3 050	80.0	105 000	19.7	11.2	525	25.0	1.8	3 379	3.0	217	6.4	3 069	32.4	29.6
Tyler	3 712	80.8	78 700	17.8	10.0	499	28.4	1.5	3 594	-1.0	321	8.9	3 179	21.6	30.6
Upshur	9 011	77.2	100 500	19.7	10.0	566	27.4	2.1	9 482	-1.4	630	6.6	9 482	29.5	29.2
Wayne	16 555	78.0	79 500	18.8	10.0	569	33.7	2.7	15 946	-0.8	1 078	6.8	15 562	26.6	26.0
Webster	3 928	78.0	64 100	24.6	10.0	455	35.0	2.6	3 445	-2.2	296	8.6	3 018	16.1	40.3
Wetzel	6 903	79.3	79 000	17.8	10.0	494	32.4	4.5	7 282	-0.3	749	10.3	5 610	22.8	36.5
Wirt	2 427	83.3	73 100	17.6	10.0	494	21.6	1.8	2 282	-1.7	216	9.5	2 093	25.1	39.4
Wood	35 569	73.1	106 400	19.8	10.0	604	29.7	3.3	37 941	-1.5	2 230	5.9	36 957	31.7	23.5
Wyoming	9 101	82.0	57 500	16.0	10.0	525	28.8	1.7	8 024	-3.3	755	9.4	6 831	26.0	38.3
WISCONSIN	2 288 332	68.1	167 100	23.7	13.8	759	29.3	2.1	3 093 918	0.3	170 385	5.5	2 839 636	33.9	25.3
Adams	8 278	85.3	135 600	26.2	16.0	670	28.1	3.6	8 610	-1.4	755	8.8	7 759	21.6	32.3
Ashland	6 775	70.9	107 400	23.5	14.6	545	28.4	1.6	8 075	-1.1	613	7.6	7 330	29.1	28.0
Barron	19 168	72.5	134 900	24.4	14.8	630	27.9	2.8	23 457	-0.9	1 424	6.1	22 144	28.2	33.1
Bayfield	6 964	82.0	158 600	24.2	14.8	543	26.4	2.4	7 678	-1.1	732	9.5	6 739	34.6	26.6
Brown	98 962	66.3	158 700	22.4	13.0	699	27.4	2.0	138 840	0.4	6 842	4.9	126 640	33.1	24.7
Buffalo	5 777	76.3	140 900	24.8	14.5	624	27.5	2.8	6 538	-0.4	372	5.7	6 936	31.3	34.8
Burnett	7 354	79.4	147 600	29.2	15.0	580	29.3	1.5	7 511	0.2	600	8.0	6 426	26.3	31.2
Calumet	18 381	81.5	164 300	21.4	12.6	679	25.4	1.4	27 452	0.8	1 167	4.3	25 816	33.7	31.0
Chippewa	24 456	72.5	147 700	22.8	12.3	696	28.5	4.5	33 126	0.2	1 819	5.5	30 382	28.9	31.0
Clark	13 036	78.1	111 700	23.7	13.8	579	25.5	1.5	16 984	-1.0	942	5.5	15 753	27.3	38.7
Columbia	22 735	75.6	175 000	24.3	13.7	742	27.7	2.2	31 594	1.0	1 666	5.3	29 145	30.7	28.7
Crawford	6 772	74.9	121 100	23.2	14.2	571	28.3	2.0	8 082	-0.6	569	7.0	7 673	25.5	34.1
Dane	206 982	59.5	228 800	24.0	12.4	895	30.2	1.7	305 878	1.4	11 484	3.8	279 118	47.9	13.8

1. Specified owner-occupied units. 2. A value of 10.0 represents 10 percent or less; a value of 50.0 represents 50 percent or more. 3. Specified renter-occupied units.
4. Overcrowded or lacking complete plumbing facilities. 5. Percent of civilian labor force. 6. Persons 16 years old and over.

STATE County	Private nonfarm establishments, employment and payroll, 2013									Agriculture, 2012			
		Employment						Annual payroll		Farms			
											Percent with:		
	Number of establish-ments	Total	Health care and social assistance	Manufac-turing	Retail trade	Finance and insurance	Professional, scientific, and technical services	Total (mil dol)	Average per employee (dollars)	Number	Fewer than 50 acres	500 acres or more	Farm operators whose principal occu-pation is farming (percent)
	104	105	106	107	108	109	110	111	112	113	114	115	116
WEST VIRGINIA—Cont'd													
Brooke	404	7 330	2 007	1 755	887	132	95	261	35 635	96	29.2	8.3	45.8
Cabell	2 482	46 449	12 854	4 371	6 864	1 213	2 121	1 711	36 828	383	33.2	2.9	31.6
Calhoun	109	1 074	D	D	139	D	D	41	38 421	227	16.7	8.8	35.7
Clay	98	885	308	D	D	D	D	25	28 592	114	20.2	3.5	34.2
Doddridge	70	D	D	D	92	44	D	D	D	352	19.6	5.4	49.4
Fayette	777	8 393	2 065	622	1 617	231	D	290	34 500	232	39.7	1.3	40.1
Gilmer	127	1 310	259	D	165	D	63	38	29 149	235	9.4	11.1	46.4
Grant	243	2 657	813	313	349	103	47	91	34 073	486	24.5	12.1	45.7
Greenbrier	958	10 895	2 957	762	2 032	D	305	334	30 674	819	29.9	10.4	40.2
Hampshire	335	2 663	842	154	468	181	80	72	26 952	798	40.6	8.8	43.4
Hancock	580	9 706	1 182	3 009	1 026	293	461	316	32 536	96	47.9	1.0	30.2
Hardy	253	4 686	412	2 593	589	197	49	134	28 511	494	33.8	13.4	52.8
Harrison	1 834	27 961	6 432	1 762	4 797	599	2 033	1 099	39 314	778	26.2	4.4	34.8
Jackson	514	6 685	1 161	D	1 132	D	226	251	37 509	732	24.2	3.6	41.7
Jefferson	826	13 502	1 164	840	1 838	D	349	416	30 803	501	51.7	5.6	50.7
Kanawha	5 185	87 931	19 103	3 007	11 647	4 856	6 087	3 604	40 988	210	34.8	1.0	41.0
Lewis	392	5 622	D	D	1 122	100	55	205	36 401	476	20.6	5.5	42.9
Lincoln	201	2 218	D	D	357	D	D	83	37 311	149	14.8	4.0	47.7
Logan	658	10 322	1 970	575	1 794	D	263	464	44 961	11	54.5	9.1	45.5
McDowell	267	3 046	862	D	600	D	D	108	35 444	11	72.7	9.1	54.5
Marion	1 223	18 104	3 062	1 112	2 370	469	1 170	710	39 231	557	34.1	0.9	53.5
Marshall	510	9 559	1 584	502	1 265	D	265	395	41 372	682	23.3	1.6	43.5
Mason	327	4 457	1 097	D	607	117	71	178	39 866	875	26.2	4.0	38.9
Mercer	1 304	18 552	4 804	1 247	3 433	496	575	602	32 454	400	30.8	3.5	40.8
Mineral	449	6 154	1 184	D	1 015	134	D	234	38 097	429	34.3	7.5	33.3
Mingo	418	5 084	713	208	454	178	230	197	38 829	20	70.0	10.0	55.0
Monongalia	2 248	44 269	14 129	3 712	6 286	764	2 293	1 696	38 319	458	26.4	2.6	34.3
Monroe	177	1 417	325	D	115	49	D	46	32 412	796	27.4	7.8	41.7
Morgan	226	1 975	577	D	382	D	D	56	28 438	196	42.9	2.0	46.9
Nicholas	567	7 735	1 725	753	1 518	D	221	286	36 939	393	31.3	5.1	52.2
Ohio	1 416	27 606	6 909	1 261	3 311	D	1 820	934	33 828	197	26.4	5.1	38.1
Pendleton	131	1 157	334	156	192	67	D	31	26 517	556	17.3	16.2	51.8
Pleasants	112	2 103	240	514	154	70	D	91	43 229	150	27.3	5.3	44.0
Pocahontas	209	2 936	386	263	320	44	D	62	21 031	389	18.5	14.7	44.7
Preston	534	4 465	1 147	523	886	167	131	133	29 732	1 084	26.2	3.6	46.1
Putnam	1 218	16 900	1 795	2 126	2 351	479	782	706	41 795	544	28.9	1.5	41.9
Raleigh	1 826	30 251	7 395	1 010	5 272	515	860	1 196	39 541	332	44.9	2.4	51.5
Randolph	686	9 451	2 782	1 178	1 440	254	250	270	28 516	405	27.7	10.9	44.2
Ritchie	209	2 438	D	D	294	82	131	92	37 884	428	17.5	7.7	42.1
Roane	247	2 405	D	217	497	101	59	77	31 812	575	15.5	7.1	45.2
Summers	160	1 397	412	D	255	D	D	39	27 830	345	21.4	3.8	43.5
Taylor	229	2 416	598	D	474	37	D	85	35 329	404	36.4	4.2	40.1
Tucker	174	2 053	281	D	248	41	D	55	26 942	162	20.4	9.9	52.5
Tyler	108	1 534	293	D	127	D	D	70	45 615	286	18.9	5.2	44.1
Upshur	538	6 680	1 659	701	757	118	219	229	34 319	456	27.9	4.8	42.3
Wayne	529	7 220	D	623	1 061	136	200	321	44 488	197	21.8	4.6	39.1
Webster	137	1 145	446	108	173	D	D	34	29 773	70	28.6	0.0	44.3
Wetzel	358	4 353	728	D	944	D	129	172	39 443	249	13.7	2.0	44.6
Wirt	63	409	D	D	79	D	D	9	21 711	217	19.4	6.0	37.3
Wood	2 052	33 351	7 021	2 843	6 189	962	1 003	1 105	33 129	816	30.3	1.3	34.1
Wyoming	286	3 590	764	D	654	75	56	156	43 559	27	33.3	3.7	33.3
WISCONSIN	137 983	2 401 032	387 964	434 460	298 106	137 769	100 940	102 083	42 516	69 754	32.2	8.8	49.8
Adams	329	3 157	438	416	437	D	61	88	27 920	313	19.8	16.6	55.3
Ashland	520	6 499	1 534	1 105	915	205	165	243	37 332	187	23.5	13.4	35.3
Barron	1 279	15 523	2 590	4 772	2 922	489	289	542	34 888	1 322	25.3	11.0	54.5
Bayfield	426	2 106	D	176	383	93	D	56	26 687	352	27.3	9.9	51.4
Brown	6 321	136 465	18 767	24 726	14 777	D	5 059	5 821	42 652	1 111	52.7	6.0	54.3
Buffalo	316	2 922	247	422	304	145	73	102	34 781	1 061	20.3	14.8	49.8
Burnett	403	3 265	635	763	556	89	83	101	30 829	406	27.1	10.6	42.9
Calumet	893	12 912	1 164	3 429	1 677	674	233	463	35 893	719	36.7	9.2	53.3
Chippewa	1 553	20 673	3 290	5 358	3 742	441	474	721	34 870	1 757	29.5	9.6	47.2
Clark	741	8 071	941	3 037	908	D	176	264	32 733	2 317	23.3	7.1	64.7
Columbia	1 378	19 020	2 498	4 462	3 028	406	410	639	33 577	1 564	39.5	9.6	52.9
Crawford	404	6 203	1 088	1 516	1 030	D	324	185	29 851	1 105	24.1	6.9	43.5
Dane	13 388	259 423	44 113	23 223	29 752	23 932	19 908	12 667	48 827	2 749	43.0	7.8	47.3

STATE County	Agriculture, 2012 (cont.): Land in farms: Acreage (1,000)	Land in farms: Percent change, 2007–2012	Land in farms: Acres: Average size of farm	Land in farms: Acres: Total irrigated (1,000)	Land in farms: Acres: Total cropland (1,000)	Value of land and buildings (dollars): Average per farm	Value of land and buildings (dollars): Average per acre	Value of machinery and equipment, average per farm (dollars)	Value of products sold: Total (mil dol)	Value of products sold: Average per farm (dollars)	Value of products sold: Percent from: Crops	Value of products sold: Percent from: Livestock and poultry products	Percent of farms with sales of: $10,000 or more	Percent of farms with sales of: $100,000 or more	Government payments: Total ($1,000)	Government payments: Percent of farms
	117	118	119	120	121	122	123	124	125	126	127	128	129	130	131	132
WEST VIRGINIA—Cont'd																
Brooke	15	-4.5	153	D	4.3	298 448	1 948	68 323	1.4	14 406	20.4	79.5	30.2	3.1	D	3.1
Cabell	42	-10.9	111	0.0	6.3	332 266	2 998	42 608	2.0	5 198	50.3	49.7	9.4	0.5	60	16.2
Calhoun	49	-11.7	218	0.0	7.4	331 432	1 521	38 423	2.1	9 326	17.9	82.1	17.2	2.6	40	6.6
Clay	20	0.6	176	D	2.2	329 789	1 873	34 000	0.5	4 570	30.3	69.7	10.5	0.0	37	6.1
Doddridge	65	-19.6	186	D	10.0	349 517	1 882	41 406	2.3	6 452	33.7	66.3	15.3	0.3	50	4.3
Fayette	23	-13.2	100	0.0	6.1	245 427	2 458	43 509	1.7	7 478	41.5	58.5	18.1	0.9	66	7.3
Gilmer	70	9.9	300	0.0	11.7	440 783	1 472	55 600	8.8	37 634	4.4	95.6	25.1	3.0	139	10.2
Grant	112	3.2	231	0.0	21.3	549 519	2 377	44 138	51.3	105 498	2.4	97.6	37.2	11.7	253	19.1
Greenbrier	190	7.4	232	0.0	35.7	658 885	2 837	71 835	76.8	93 722	2.8	97.2	37.6	8.5	461	15.4
Hampshire	142	10.0	178	0.1	34.8	641 143	3 601	51 271	39.2	49 102	19.3	80.7	26.2	5.5	227	16.9
Hancock	9	-7.9	93	D	3.1	271 469	2 932	59 625	0.6	6 750	53.1	46.9	13.5	1.0	2	5.2
Hardy	155	15.6	314	0.0	29.2	891 816	2 837	87 621	189.0	382 530	2.7	97.3	46.6	27.7	336	15.4
Harrison	117	4.8	150	0.0	25.7	318 695	2 119	45 731	9.5	12 264	25.2	74.8	20.3	2.1	71	3.3
Jackson	105	-19.1	143	0.0	25.8	315 790	2 207	42 680	7.4	10 067	28.8	71.2	20.8	1.2	256	8.9
Jefferson	67	-7.1	134	0.3	41.4	918 731	6 874	74 527	35.5	70 920	45.0	55.0	36.7	9.6	852	24.8
Kanawha	26	9.5	124	0.0	4.1	268 152	2 165	31 386	1.3	6 310	33.3	66.7	18.6	0.5	25	8.1
Lewis	82	-10.5	173	D	16.2	341 069	1 969	42 935	7.0	14 735	14.0	86.0	35.1	1.5	73	3.6
Lincoln	26	-20.8	172	0.0	3.3	348 013	2 021	38 450	0.9	6 087	37.6	62.4	12.8	1.3	63	24.8
Logan	1	-40.3	76	D	0.0	147 273	1 949	34 455	0.1	5 364	89.8	10.2	18.2	0.0	0	0.0
McDowell	1	-29.7	95	0.0	0.2	227 091	2 400	47 091	D	D	D	D	9.1	9.1	0	0.0
Marion	53	-8.0	96	0.0	12.7	206 381	2 155	42 246	2.4	4 370	39.1	60.9	11.8	0.0	49	3.6
Marshall	86	-10.3	126	0.0	22.8	277 150	2 199	46 801	3.3	4 890	40.9	59.1	11.9	0.0	121	7.6
Mason	139	5.0	159	0.3	39.7	335 312	2 114	52 757	34.1	38 965	74.1	25.9	24.1	4.6	465	17.5
Mercer	52	-4.0	129	0.0	9.7	287 660	2 222	45 280	3.9	9 790	33.2	66.8	19.8	1.8	34	2.8
Mineral	76	-2.3	178	0.1	16.7	533 772	3 006	49 399	22.2	51 849	6.9	93.1	22.6	5.6	257	11.7
Mingo	2	-49.2	102	0.0	0.1	143 850	1 417	23 300	0.1	5 300	D	D	10.0	0.0	0	0.0
Monongalia	58	-2.1	127	0.0	14.9	391 255	3 090	48 055	4.0	8 784	27.8	72.2	21.8	0.9	165	6.1
Monroe	145	8.9	182	0.0	29.2	414 754	2 283	52 758	31.4	39 447	9.5	90.5	36.8	7.5	426	15.8
Morgan	18	-18.1	94	0.1	7.8	419 311	4 470	39 770	3.0	15 408	77.2	22.8	19.4	3.1	86	6.6
Nicholas	58	13.2	148	0.0	13.6	377 216	2 552	42 771	4.6	11 649	16.8	83.2	22.9	2.0	37	8.7
Ohio	30	-2.4	153	D	11.9	353 061	2 312	80 888	3.5	17 660	20.5	79.5	28.4	5.6	64	24.4
Pendleton	170	0.1	306	D	24.4	711 710	2 326	68 344	118.8	213 608	2.4	97.6	58.6	21.0	207	17.1
Pleasants	21	-16.6	143	D	4.1	277 013	1 933	55 173	D	D	D	D	14.7	2.7	D	1.3
Pocahontas	118	-2.8	305	0.0	18.7	670 208	2 201	61 131	9.3	23 779	11.3	88.7	40.1	4.4	174	21.9
Preston	161	5.5	148	0.1	44.9	365 799	2 467	55 455	18.2	16 749	28.1	71.9	31.5	2.8	222	8.4
Putnam	60	-9.7	110	0.1	12.2	281 868	2 556	39 509	10.1	18 603	83.1	16.9	14.3	1.1	85	9.6
Raleigh	37	-15.1	111	0.0	8.1	276 123	2 487	47 337	3.0	9 036	24.6	75.4	17.2	0.9	47	6.0
Randolph	94	-9.9	232	D	19.8	422 042	1 815	54 812	9.4	23 173	21.8	78.2	35.1	3.2	147	9.9
Ritchie	89	-2.3	207	0.0	17.6	331 741	1 599	54 668	7.6	17 776	15.1	84.9	21.7	1.2	57	4.0
Roane	111	-5.7	193	D	21.6	330 957	1 716	42 193	5.6	9 781	26.2	73.8	23.1	0.7	209	9.6
Summers	58	-2.8	168	0.0	10.9	369 194	2 198	42 614	5.0	14 365	25.7	74.3	25.2	3.5	45	6.7
Taylor	49	-8.7	122	0.0	10.4	301 597	2 481	50 545	3.7	9 228	19.2	80.8	18.1	1.5	131	4.2
Tucker	34	-2.7	210	D	6.7	641 191	3 059	47 975	2.2	13 580	22.6	77.4	29.0	1.9	37	9.9
Tyler	48	1.4	169	0.0	11.5	309 413	1 836	41 035	2.2	7 829	35.1	64.9	26.2	0.3	34	7.0
Upshur	68	-3.4	150	0.0	15.0	348 270	2 320	46 175	6.8	14 925	18.8	81.3	24.6	2.6	48	3.9
Wayne	30	-24.2	153	0.0	3.7	288 345	1 880	36 102	1.0	5 183	40.7	59.2	12.2	1.0	24	4.1
Webster	8	-31.2	113	0.0	1.8	248 500	2 194	25 086	0.3	4 743	62.7	37.3	15.7	0.0	D	2.9
Wetzel	38	-26.5	153	D	7.6	279 361	1 826	34 867	1.2	4 727	43.9	56.1	6.8	0.4	45	4.4
Wirt	38	-7.8	175	D	7.7	287 650	1 642	42 065	2.2	10 286	28.8	71.2	20.3	1.4	55	8.8
Wood	88	-1.3	108	0.0	21.8	251 165	2 333	34 237	6.1	7 496	30.9	69.1	14.0	0.2	102	3.4
Wyoming	3	-26.5	110	D	0.5	227 889	2 072	42 407	0.1	2 556	15.9	84.1	3.7	0.0	0	0.0
WISCONSIN	14 569	-4.1	209	421.7	9 911.0	819 551	3 924	129 561	11 744.5	168 370	39.2	60.8	52.3	24.6	237 304	55.8
Adams	118	2.6	378	44.3	87.5	1 467 256	3 879	173 677	105.7	337 601	88.5	11.5	52.4	23.0	882	54.3
Ashland	46	-17.3	245	0.0	21.2	450 973	1 841	83 807	12.0	64 364	20.9	79.1	42.2	8.0	214	18.2
Barron	310	-4.5	234	11.7	202.9	655 775	2 799	148 573	343.1	259 503	29.1	70.9	58.5	29.0	4 643	59.5
Bayfield	72	-19.6	204	0.1	36.3	414 466	2 031	70 830	13.9	39 528	35.3	64.7	34.9	10.8	267	19.6
Brown	181	-3.2	163	0.5	151.3	884 833	5 425	149 589	307.5	276 792	17.4	82.6	52.8	27.2	3 585	48.7
Buffalo	305	-0.6	288	4.6	162.7	968 225	3 365	147 399	225.8	212 814	32.1	67.9	58.9	30.3	4 876	68.7
Burnett	84	-13.1	206	0.2	44.4	506 421	2 459	84 613	37.2	91 626	38.8	61.2	39.7	13.5	661	42.4
Calumet	142	-6.1	198	0.0	120.9	1 092 981	5 520	172 268	213.2	296 527	25.5	74.5	64.4	33.1	3 196	64.0
Chippewa	385	8.8	219	5.7	249.9	597 028	2 727	114 201	253.2	144 107	38.1	61.9	51.5	24.6	5 088	54.5
Clark	458	4.1	198	0.6	310.9	618 184	3 126	119 200	401.9	173 441	22.9	77.1	64.2	38.2	5 774	38.1
Columbia	308	-2.6	197	1.6	234.1	993 045	5 043	129 485	214.3	137 021	55.7	44.3	51.0	20.5	5 783	51.3
Crawford	217	-9.1	196	0.2	98.4	530 437	2 706	78 187	74.9	67 783	50.3	49.7	48.1	15.3	2 373	61.3
Dane	504	-5.8	183	4.6	396.3	1 111 346	6 057	145 729	471.6	171 553	39.1	60.9	50.5	23.2	12 023	62.2

STATE County	Water use, 2010		Wholesale trade,[1] 2007				Retail trade,[2] 2007				Real estate and rental and leasing,[2] 2007			
	Total water withdrawn (mil gal/day)	Gallons withdrawn per person per day	Number of establish-ments	Number of employees	Sales (mil dol)	Annual payroll (mil dol)	Number of establish-ments	Number of employees	Sales (mil dol)	Annual payroll (mil dol)	Number of establish-ments	Number of employees	Receipts (mil dol)	Annual payroll (mil dol)
	133	134	135	136	137	138	139	140	141	142	143	144	145	146
WEST VIRGINIA—Cont'd														
Brooke	12.5	518	11	D	D	D	63	651	158.1	14.4	6	21	4.8	0.5
Cabell	29.3	304	112	1 698	778.9	66.7	486	7 531	1 496.1	142.7	113	413	68.4	10.8
Calhoun	0.8	106	1	D	D	D	25	147	34.1	2.2	5	11	0.6	0.2
Clay	1.1	121	NA	NA	NA	NA	24	148	41.3	2.5	1	D	D	D
Doddridge	1.1	135	2	D	D	D	16	105	19.3	1.2	2	D	D	D
Fayette	7.8	169	27	D	D	D	165	1 860	345.7	34.4	24	58	7.5	0.8
Gilmer	2.9	331	3	D	D	D	24	153	34.3	2.9	3	4	0.3	0.0
Grant	1 120.9	93 903	2	D	D	D	44	394	118.3	7.8	8	18	1.4	0.1
Greenbrier	8.9	250	30	256	59.1	7.3	198	2 133	490.2	43.1	43	150	21.4	3.5
Hampshire	2.6	110	7	D	D	D	57	442	112.2	8.3	14	D	D	D
Hancock	78.7	2 565	10	157	118.0	4.7	109	1 247	238.5	22.6	29	93	10.0	1.9
Hardy	16.4	1 172	3	31	7.2	0.9	54	660	132.1	12.5	8	23	2.2	0.5
Harrison	55.4	802	72	858	322.8	30.5	334	4 909	1 148.5	96.0	61	337	107.7	8.5
Jackson	4.1	139	15	171	77.4	5.5	110	1 467	325.2	28.2	16	43	5.3	1.0
Jefferson	9.9	184	20	D	D	D	138	2 356	455.7	49.9	52	172	23.3	4.1
Kanawha	590.8	3 060	270	3 829	1 727.0	163.6	853	13 517	2 947.3	259.8	277	1 799	367.7	54.8
Lewis	2.5	151	15	93	54.8	3.4	78	843	212.9	14.5	12	33	4.6	0.8
Lincoln	1.9	88	3	D	D	D	47	359	73.4	5.9	7	D	D	D
Logan	9.4	256	36	354	155.7	15.7	151	2 006	494.7	41.2	30	109	13.0	3.1
McDowell	3.6	162	6	20	20.0	0.6	66	711	129.4	11.7	10	35	4.3	0.9
Marion	16.4	291	43	D	D	D	189	2 277	614.9	48.1	43	197	25.3	4.0
Marshall	433.9	13 105	14	D	D	D	96	1 341	272.4	25.4	12	41	3.2	0.9
Mason	643.1	23 536	5	D	D	D	62	675	135.4	11.2	18	58	5.7	1.0
Mercer	10.2	163	48	D	D	D	281	3 612	765.6	74.5	45	183	58.1	4.6
Mineral	4.3	153	13	D	D	D	87	1 009	223.6	18.5	12	D	D	D
Mingo	6.6	246	13	165	50.5	6.0	68	481	108.2	10.1	17	45	12.1	0.8
Monongalia	115.4	1 199	47	413	370.3	16.8	383	6 453	1 289.7	112.7	130	589	78.5	14.7
Monroe	3.1	230	7	29	3.7	0.5	35	190	31.6	3.2	5	10	0.5	0.1
Morgan	4.4	249	5	26	5.7	0.6	48	458	94.8	8.8	15	45	2.9	0.7
Nicholas	4.8	185	20	173	136.7	6.1	111	1 460	345.9	28.6	19	42	5.8	1.1
Ohio	10.5	236	74	1 578	3 117.0	54.3	213	3 045	649.9	62.4	66	368	37.0	8.2
Pendleton	9.7	1 257	4	12	4.2	0.1	28	215	39.4	3.5	2	D	D	D
Pleasants	67.7	8 899	2	D	D	D	18	152	40.4	3.0	3	D	D	D
Pocahontas	5.7	649	2	D	D	D	39	332	60.2	5.2	7	49	9.8	0.7
Preston	7.9	236	16	D	D	D	104	912	221.1	15.3	21	36	4.2	0.8
Putnam	47.7	859	67	904	541.7	41.2	185	2 366	589.8	42.8	48	225	42.0	6.6
Raleigh	12.3	156	94	D	D	D	376	5 507	1 260.8	114.0	76	328	43.8	8.5
Randolph	13.6	461	24	309	366.9	10.5	135	1 513	319.2	28.2	24	81	12.7	1.8
Ritchie	1.6	154	6	54	23.3	1.6	35	259	60.4	4.0	5	12	1.1	0.2
Roane	2.3	151	9	57	40.7	1.8	56	613	142.0	11.7	10	21	2.0	0.4
Summers	5.7	406	6	D	D	D	28	274	53.7	5.1	4	6	0.6	0.2
Taylor	2.3	134	5	D	D	D	30	435	91.7	8.7	2	D	D	D
Tucker	1.5	210	2	D	D	D	32	239	53.4	4.3	11	78	4.3	1.0
Tyler	13.5	1 468	1	D	D	D	29	248	45.5	3.5	1	D	D	D
Upshur	5.0	205	12	216	179.3	7.4	90	1 202	297.1	24.4	21	104	6.4	1.4
Wayne	13.0	305	18	288	77.4	10.1	123	1 112	232.8	19.1	21	83	5.7	1.0
Webster	3.5	387	3	D	D	D	31	176	40.1	3.5	5	D	D	D
Wetzel	4.0	242	8	43	14.4	1.2	80	967	206.4	19.6	15	76	9.1	1.4
Wirt	0.5	93	1	D	D	D	15	76	14.4	0.9	2	D	D	D
Wood	63.3	728	84	760	330.7	26.1	422	6 796	1 712.2	131.8	85	D	D	D
Wyoming	2.9	124	5	31	5.9	0.6	91	671	147.0	12.3	9	41	5.7	0.8
WISCONSIN	6 157.6	1 083	6 215	99 773	59 996.2	4 639.0	21 205	320 140	72 283.3	6 778.3	5 119	27 226	4 043.5	788.9
Adams	50.9	2 436	6	27	12.6	0.8	50	440	130.4	9.0	13	38	3.9	0.9
Ashland	35.1	2 169	13	105	30.2	3.6	90	846	193.6	19.4	20	74	7.6	1.4
Barron	11.6	253	51	433	126.6	14.8	256	3 268	670.8	65.2	41	100	15.8	2.1
Bayfield	10.7	713	9	62	29.6	1.7	78	520	107.6	9.0	12	38	2.9	0.5
Brown	312.8	1 261	349	5 907	3 388.3	270.8	984	15 914	3 538.4	327.1	236	1 594	229.9	45.4
Buffalo	344.1	25 322	7	75	24.2	2.7	51	311	74.0	5.5	7	19	0.9	0.1
Burnett	2.7	177	9	24	5.5	0.7	78	622	118.7	10.8	19	38	3.6	0.7
Calumet	5.9	119	33	401	149.0	14.6	116	1 801	390.1	36.6	23	89	8.7	1.2
Chippewa	19.3	310	43	464	206.0	16.7	246	3 712	1 059.6	83.8	28	107	13.9	2.9
Clark	6.1	174	34	252	107.2	9.7	119	1 014	263.9	20.3	10	24	1.3	0.2
Columbia	29.0	510	45	435	203.4	17.9	217	2 819	631.3	54.9	48	D	D	D
Crawford	3.4	204	15	368	101.0	8.4	88	1 159	218.3	22.7	12	23	2.5	0.3
Dane	72.2	148	600	11 205	6 043.0	529.6	1 788	32 582	7 132.4	715.1	683	4 691	638.1	144.2

1. Merchant wholesalers, except manufacturers' sales branches and offices. 2. Employer establishments.

STATE County	Professional, scientific, and technical services,[1] 2007				Manufacturing, 2007				Accommodation and food services, 2007			
	Number of establish-ments	Number of employees	Receipts (mil dol)	Annual payroll (mil dol)	Number of establish-ments	Number of employees	Receipts (mil dol)	Annual payroll (mil dol)	Number of establish-ments	Number of employees	Sales (mil dol)	Annual payroll (mil dol)
	147	148	149	150	151	152	153	154	155	156	157	158
WEST VIRGINIA—Cont'd												
Brooke	17	D	D	D	24	3 217	2 645.1	181.0	58	711	31.3	8.0
Cabell	195	D	D	D	97	5 623	D	D	279	5 340	205.2	57.9
Calhoun	6	D	D	D	NA	NA	NA	NA	7	42	1.3	0.4
Clay	1	D	D	D	NA	NA	NA	NA	7	39	1.3	0.3
Doddridge	3	D	D	D	NA	NA	NA	NA	2	D	D	D
Fayette	57	D	D	D	31	694	D	30.0	69	803	35.7	9.3
Gilmer	9	43	4.7	0.9	NA	NA	NA	NA	13	190	5.2	1.3
Grant	14	66	4.5	1.4	NA	NA	NA	NA	20	176	6.1	1.5
Greenbrier	65	D	D	D	33	886	148.3	31.9	85	2 595	139.5	47.9
Hampshire	24	D	D	D	NA	NA	NA	NA	41	373	17.4	4.6
Hancock	54	D	D	D	22	2 278	D	79.4	93	851	34.0	8.1
Hardy	17	40	4.5	0.8	13	D	D	D	27	447	10.8	3.7
Harrison	115	D	D	D	58	D	D	D	162	2 911	117.6	32.3
Jackson	33	135	12.0	3.6	21	2 211	1 296.6	124.8	49	815	31.8	8.3
Jefferson	81	D	D	D	22	D	D	D	112	1 463	71.9	20.7
Kanawha	587	D	D	D	133	3 450	D	193.4	480	9 058	414.9	115.0
Lewis	19	D	D	D	NA	NA	NA	NA	34	559	27.3	9.3
Lincoln	18	104	8.4	3.0	NA	NA	NA	NA	13	84	2.8	0.7
Logan	35	D	D	D	38	706	124.9	26.4	67	1 134	39.6	10.3
McDowell	16	D	D	D	NA	NA	NA	NA	19	166	6.9	1.7
Marion	112	D	D	D	53	1 285	546.4	49.3	111	1 692	67.2	17.2
Marshall	27	D	D	D	NA	NA	NA	NA	57	793	26.3	7.0
Mason	23	67	6.0	1.6	21	707	D	D	29	319	12.1	3.6
Mercer	80	D	D	D	63	1 741	252.5	D	108	2 299	88.4	24.1
Mineral	32	D	D	D	14	1 620	D	86.7	53	538	21.4	5.3
Mingo	55	D	D	D	NA	NA	NA	NA	38	281	10.0	2.9
Monongalia	195	D	D	D	66	3 099	D	151.7	229	5 085	192.8	53.3
Monroe	11	31	2.2	0.6	NA	NA	NA	NA	14	87	2.8	0.8
Morgan	16	D	D	D	NA	NA	NA	NA	25	309	11.5	4.1
Nicholas	42	D	D	D	32	800	192.6	27.8	51	756	30.5	8.2
Ohio	141	D	D	D	59	1 329	D	D	131	2 403	98.3	27.5
Pendleton	8	D	D	D	NA	NA	NA	NA	12	83	3.1	0.7
Pleasants	7	D	D	D	10	D	D	D	11	191	6.6	1.8
Pocahontas	10	D	D	D	NA	NA	NA	NA	23	1 760	60.4	22.2
Preston	36	D	D	D	32	819	D	22.1	37	316	12.2	3.0
Putnam	92	652	67.2	24.8	37	2 156	D	119.9	87	1 441	61.6	15.2
Raleigh	125	D	D	D	65	1 284	D	49.9	151	3 402	144.3	40.8
Randolph	42	D	D	D	29	1 873	321.5	55.4	61	965	30.7	8.6
Ritchie	10	40	2.4	0.8	17	1 116	D	33.5	17	94	3.6	0.7
Roane	15	52	4.5	1.3	NA	NA	NA	NA	9	201	7.3	1.7
Summers	11	94	13.5	5.3	NA	NA	NA	NA	20	243	9.1	2.5
Taylor	8	D	D	D	NA	NA	NA	NA	18	D	D	D
Tucker	9	25	1.3	0.4	NA	NA	NA	NA	30	358	12.1	3.0
Tyler	5	D	D	D	7	D	218.6	35.3	8	39	1.8	0.3
Upshur	37	162	9.5	3.4	23	1 314	264.8	55.7	50	609	24.5	6.1
Wayne	23	D	D	D	29	791	D	D	50	457	18.4	5.0
Webster	7	28	1.6	0.5	NA	NA	NA	NA	12	74	2.0	0.6
Wetzel	20	95	5.0	1.7	16	1 394	D	92.1	46	522	21.0	5.4
Wirt	5	D	D	D	NA	NA	NA	NA	5	34	0.9	0.3
Wood	138	D	D	D	69	D	D	D	228	4 173	157.9	47.7
Wyoming	17	79	3.8	1.4	NA	NA	NA	NA	27	286	9.9	2.8
WISCONSIN	11 255	97 445	12 797.3	4 999.0	9 659	487 573	163 563.2	21 850.3	14 439	227 475	9 247.3	2 535.2
Adams	19	71	5.0	2.2	NA	NA	NA	NA	60	928	42.0	12.3
Ashland	26	155	11.7	5.0	35	1 411	222.4	50.6	78	730	29.5	8.2
Barron	71	316	38.3	11.9	95	5 176	1 207.4	182.5	139	1 425	50.4	13.8
Bayfield	16	42	2.7	1.0	NA	NA	NA	NA	111	700	34.2	9.0
Brown	511	D	D	D	446	25 490	9 321.9	1 099.3	613	12 801	464.6	135.1
Buffalo	22	76	4.5	1.4	NA	NA	NA	NA	44	D	D	D
Burnett	25	85	9.2	2.7	28	856	227.0	34.0	69	D	D	D
Calumet	55	210	16.4	7.1	66	3 946	1 355.2	169.0	86	1 515	40.1	11.1
Chippewa	86	555	71.1	30.9	131	5 184	1 575.0	202.3	158	1 512	56.3	13.6
Clark	32	150	22.2	5.8	75	3 001	1 475.2	106.3	64	D	D	D
Columbia	83	D	D	D	100	4 853	1 744.1	D	194	4 000	164.2	45.8
Crawford	19	75	5.9	2.3	24	2 048	820.8	69.8	49	629	22.6	6.1
Dane	1 584	D	D	D	590	27 640	6 968.1	1 295.0	1 204	23 413	916.7	268.9

1. Establishment subject to federal tax.

STATE County	Health care and social assistance, 2007				Other services, 2007				Nonemployer businesses, 2013		Value of residential construction authorized by building permits, 2014	
	Number of establish-ments	Number of employees	Receipts (mil dol)	Annual payroll (mil dol)	Number of establish-ments	Number of employees	Receipts (mil dol)	Annual payroll (mil dol)	Number	Receipts (mil dol)	New Construction ($1,000)	Number of housing units
	159	160	161	162	163	164	165	166	167	168	169	170
WEST VIRGINIA—Cont'd												
Brooke	62	1 774	153.3	62.5	36	155	8.8	2.4	981	40.8	687	4
Cabell	370	D	D	D	193	1 104	96.4	23.8	4 681	172.8	12 445	138
Calhoun	9	D	D	D	8	D	D	D	521	12.8	NA	NA
Clay	20	344	14.4	7.0	5	D	D	D	367	11.3	568	9
Doddridge	10	D	D	D	4	D	D	D	233	9.7	NA	NA
Fayette	93	1 811	135.4	49.3	59	288	34.7	6.9	1 690	53.1	4 850	34
Gilmer	16	209	9.9	4.4	7	19	1.1	0.3	370	10.6	120	6
Grant	24	627	36.1	15.3	19	64	5.3	1.3	654	27.1	4 169	66
Greenbrier	141	2 482	208.1	80.7	68	212	18.9	3.8	2 127	75.7	19 863	53
Hampshire	40	789	37.7	17.1	26	87	6.9	1.7	1 376	53.0	7 663	66
Hancock	83	1 193	60.1	23.8	52	234	15.2	3.8	1 313	40.4	3 272	16
Hardy	35	420	19.4	7.8	19	61	4.7	1.0	838	26.1	4 632	34
Harrison	222	D	D	D	136	643	57.4	12.2	3 884	157.3	20 629	105
Jackson	60	946	60.2	23.7	33	139	12.8	3.1	1 509	55.5	81	2
Jefferson	73	1 041	87.0	34.9	71	411	47.8	10.2	3 454	133.7	50 625	200
Kanawha	739	16 612	1 720.2	627.3	419	3 169	299.7	77.6	9 314	379.9	29 942	296
Lewis	32	1 112	86.2	33.9	37	117	8.8	1.8	893	33.0	209	1
Lincoln	26	461	20.9	9.5	17	D	D	D	769	24.3	1 419	11
Logan	90	1 753	151.6	48.5	58	458	77.8	16.3	1 224	49.3	146	1
McDowell	41	812	55.8	19.7	22	106	12.3	5.1	478	12.1	558	7
Marion	158	2 944	233.3	89.6	107	747	51.5	19.4	2 545	86.3	1 072	13
Marshall	69	1 475	89.7	36.2	45	216	14.3	4.0	1 201	36.2	222	1
Mason	35	1 052	91.3	38.3	33	98	5.9	1.4	968	26.2	290	1
Mercer	225	4 790	399.6	147.9	102	805	71.5	22.0	2 968	116.2	665	5
Mineral	62	1 083	54.1	22.5	42	221	13.4	3.3	1 385	42.1	5 993	32
Mingo	46	727	65.4	23.8	25	D	D	D	891	26.8	174	5
Monongalia	221	D	D	D	143	990	163.0	23.8	5 203	243.0	8 273	100
Monroe	18	D	D	D	13	38	2.5	0.6	797	27.0	0	0
Morgan	16	D	D	D	30	178	19.5	7.2	1 096	39.9	7 577	48
Nicholas	53	1 339	86.8	35.8	41	189	18.0	4.9	1 191	44.1	0	0
Ohio	236	6 249	553.5	210.2	131	923	75.3	20.8	2 448	103.5	6 189	55
Pendleton	17	271	13.7	5.6	13	61	6.5	1.5	489	15.1	1 942	18
Pleasants	15	D	D	D	11	D	D	D	295	10.3	1 066	5
Pocahontas	23	369	21.0	8.6	25	171	7.2	2.1	575	19.6	180	3
Preston	51	D	D	D	43	200	14.2	3.5	1 602	57.9	90	1
Putnam	125	1 624	138.6	45.7	61	380	37.6	10.8	2 876	111.3	29 132	166
Raleigh	274	6 168	560.5	224.8	138	820	70.6	19.7	3 463	130.0	19 237	91
Randolph	110	2 418	164.4	65.5	43	156	15.5	3.4	1 456	43.9	872	10
Ritchie	16	179	8.7	3.8	12	42	3.8	0.7	723	27.3	179	1
Roane	29	671	37.2	17.8	12	D	D	D	914	27.7	2 333	35
Summers	26	485	30.1	12.2	17	49	2.7	0.8	474	15.8	2 265	16
Taylor	28	D	D	D	20	D	D	D	692	19.4	509	3
Tucker	12	259	11.7	5.3	15	123	12.7	3.0	393	11.2	363	3
Tyler	14	467	21.0	10.3	11	30	2.4	0.5	392	10.1	1 176	7
Upshur	75	1 593	75.8	35.8	32	134	9.7	3.3	1 244	50.7	10 840	100
Wayne	61	D	D	D	46	187	18.6	5.6	1 548	50.3	1 652	16
Webster	12	401	20.3	8.7	9	D	D	D	327	10.0	0	0
Wetzel	42	609	46.3	17.4	41	121	7.0	1.8	639	15.9	967	20
Wirt	4	D	D	D	4	D	D	D	294	8.1	1 284	19
Wood	286	D	D	D	170	943	81.1	17.2	4 206	177.3	19 197	105
Wyoming	31	793	34.2	16.1	17	69	5.6	1.5	743	20.7	277	2
WISCONSIN	14 417	369 289	33 841.3	14 082.9	10 724	66 392	6 359.6	1 678.7	335 177	15 055.2	2 599 187	14 622
Adams	29	519	35.1	14.0	25	124	11.0	3.2	1 064	41.5	10 963	61
Ashland	66	1 484	112.1	52.3	36	D	D	D	1 133	43.2	1 734	8
Barron	128	2 608	234.9	96.3	101	345	25.7	7.1	3 092	126.5	14 190	127
Bayfield	17	207	9.2	4.7	25	57	6.4	1.7	1 500	54.9	7 695	51
Brown	586	19 287	2 001.9	777.2	480	3 089	233.0	66.2	12 969	650.6	139 160	867
Buffalo	26	401	17.1	8.2	22	D	D	D	1 032	45.0	5 656	33
Burnett	31	587	30.1	15.3	22	75	6.6	1.6	1 157	44.2	11 911	62
Calumet	66	920	62.5	26.3	70	250	15.8	4.0	2 399	96.7	28 815	209
Chippewa	126	3 053	236.3	97.9	102	566	56.6	15.8	3 848	185.2	35 214	220
Clark	60	1 295	53.3	27.1	63	179	14.3	3.3	2 216	124.0	6 083	37
Columbia	113	2 602	189.6	80.0	99	395	35.9	8.9	3 730	156.0	25 589	186
Crawford	51	1 212	69.5	31.9	31	109	7.3	1.8	1 095	43.6	5 268	27
Dane	1 188	39 141	4 098.2	1 670.0	1 054	8 466	1 352.9	263.8	35 012	1 726.0	588 538	3 543

STATE County	Government employment and payroll, 2012									Local government finances, 2012				
			March payroll (percent of total)							General revenue				
												Taxes		
													Per capita[1] (dollars)	
	Full-time equivalent employees	March payroll (dollars)	Adminis-tration, judicial, and legal	Police and Corrections	Fire Protection	Highways and transpor-tation	Health and Welfare	Natural resources and utilities	Education and libraries	Total (mil dol)	Inter-govern-mental (mil dol)	Total (mil dol)	Total	Property
	171	172	173	174	175	176	177	178	179	180	181	182	183	184
WEST VIRGINIA—Cont'd														
Brooke	700	2 209 915	5.0	5.9	0.0	2.9	3.5	5.7	73.7	55.0	24.1	20.4	854	747
Cabell	2 866	9 646 891	2.5	7.4	3.4	4.5	2.0	4.8	70.4	298.6	122.6	110.8	1 142	895
Calhoun	235	856 049	5.0	1.6	0.0	0.1	2.0	2.3	88.7	15.2	10.3	3.4	451	395
Clay	380	1 124 468	6.3	1.8	0.0	0.0	5.2	2.2	84.1	27.4	19.9	4.1	442	430
Doddridge	298	898 174	6.8	2.9	0.0	0.0	5.3	2.4	82.0	22.4	10.1	9.7	1 188	1 164
Fayette	1 528	4 553 455	4.1	5.0	0.3	1.5	1.0	5.1	80.2	107.2	57.1	37.1	808	664
Gilmer	243	631 014	10.3	2.7	0.0	0.5	1.7	3.3	80.9	15.5	7.0	5.8	665	612
Grant	680	2 034 759	3.4	1.7	0.0	3.5	45.2	3.2	40.6	59.3	13.0	10.1	852	816
Greenbrier	1 170	3 506 733	7.6	5.7	0.3	0.6	1.5	5.0	78.7	105.9	52.9	33.6	939	809
Hampshire	737	2 045 370	7.4	3.3	0.0	0.4	2.4	3.6	80.9	45.1	25.8	14.3	602	574
Hancock	1 042	3 202 337	5.3	8.5	2.6	2.7	1.3	6.7	66.6	87.7	34.1	29.9	986	818
Hardy	415	1 314 488	8.0	4.5	0.0	1.3	3.9	3.7	78.2	29.6	15.9	10.0	724	691
Harrison	2 683	9 099 926	6.8	6.1	3.8	3.1	1.3	6.8	71.1	209.4	84.1	90.4	1 308	979
Jackson	990	3 308 041	4.4	4.8	0.0	0.8	4.8	4.0	80.4	73.7	39.2	26.2	895	804
Jefferson	1 638	5 678 847	10.1	5.7	0.0	0.8	0.7	3.3	76.3	146.5	52.8	59.7	1 096	978
Kanawha	6 718	23 530 157	5.6	7.2	4.5	3.9	6.5	3.5	65.5	605.2	237.9	258.2	1 344	860
Lewis	544	1 762 505	8.2	4.5	0.7	0.9	5.8	2.3	77.1	39.7	21.5	16.2	990	848
Lincoln	667	2 364 650	4.5	2.3	0.0	1.6	1.0	3.2	85.7	53.6	38.2	11.4	526	507
Logan	1 162	3 939 889	5.9	3.5	0.7	0.2	1.5	5.1	81.4	91.3	48.4	36.2	1 001	949
McDowell	898	2 888 117	9.6	3.1	0.0	0.2	2.7	2.7	81.5	73.1	34.6	20.5	959	873
Marion	1 717	5 814 952	5.2	6.4	2.4	3.4	0.7	6.1	74.1	167.3	77.9	56.2	991	827
Marshall	1 141	3 323 871	5.8	8.5	0.5	1.2	2.2	5.2	75.5	112.7	45.9	46.4	1 420	1 271
Mason	808	2 759 625	5.8	3.8	1.1	0.5	1.8	4.4	81.7	67.3	31.9	24.3	894	820
Mercer	2 791	9 567 647	3.0	2.7	1.1	1.6	34.9	3.3	53.2	241.4	83.0	39.7	634	442
Mineral	785	2 765 305	6.5	4.1	0.0	1.4	1.0	5.1	80.1	68.4	36.1	19.1	682	591
Mingo	985	3 045 535	7.8	3.4	0.6	0.0	0.8	5.9	81.3	90.1	46.0	25.0	959	895
Monongalia	2 739	8 098 611	6.5	7.5	2.5	4.8	3.8	8.2	63.2	216.0	81.0	90.9	906	711
Monroe	414	1 100 622	5.2	1.8	0.0	0.0	1.4	2.7	86.0	27.7	19.5	5.8	431	417
Morgan	518	1 614 401	8.1	3.1	0.0	0.2	3.5	2.2	81.4	35.9	14.8	15.4	884	845
Nicholas	1 289	3 992 571	5.3	3.7	0.0	1.2	46.4	3.6	39.7	111.9	37.5	19.6	748	569
Ohio	2 026	6 205 898	4.8	7.0	5.8	5.4	1.5	21.6	51.3	195.9	55.2	71.7	1 626	865
Pendleton	226	700 064	8.4	1.3	0.0	0.8	2.2	3.9	80.7	15.5	10.2	4.1	537	478
Pleasants	324	1 102 661	10.6	2.5	0.0	0.4	3.5	3.5	79.3	32.6	11.4	12.9	1 701	1 664
Pocahontas	405	1 184 054	6.2	3.0	0.0	0.0	30.8	3.2	53.8	31.5	10.0	9.0	1 038	857
Preston	940	2 685 410	7.1	3.2	0.9	1.2	1.0	4.1	82.2	66.4	36.1	18.3	541	504
Putnam	1 860	6 184 199	4.2	3.8	0.1	0.5	2.8	5.9	81.7	150.7	66.0	58.4	1 035	970
Raleigh	2 440	7 917 866	5.4	5.4	1.7	1.5	2.8	5.6	75.8	223.2	112.9	76.2	964	750
Randolph	999	2 905 572	3.8	2.3	0.5	0.9	3.4	6.7	80.2	72.1	40.5	17.4	593	462
Ritchie	297	909 321	8.7	3.8	0.0	1.0	0.1	2.4	84.1	24.5	12.7	8.6	838	761
Roane	376	1 154 052	6.1	3.9	0.0	1.0	2.1	6.9	79.1	31.0	21.0	6.6	447	384
Summers	287	926 192	9.8	3.8	1.5	1.2	2.4	1.1	80.2	23.4	14.8	6.1	443	343
Taylor	364	895 244	5.7	4.2	1.5	2.1	4.6	11.1	66.9	51.2	18.8	11.0	648	459
Tucker	275	825 484	9.3	1.5	0.0	1.3	7.1	3.8	69.5	25.7	10.2	7.0	1 003	837
Tyler	484	1 507 476	5.2	4.0	0.0	1.0	29.5	1.8	58.1	30.4	11.4	7.0	778	752
Upshur	769	2 460 649	3.9	3.4	0.6	1.2	4.6	5.0	78.3	57.1	29.8	16.0	654	566
Wayne	1 363	3 245 672	6.1	5.2	0.0	0.5	1.6	4.5	81.4	101.8	63.8	27.0	648	573
Webster	358	989 930	7.5	2.5	2.2	1.0	1.1	6.1	78.1	23.4	16.4	3.8	420	365
Wetzel	861	2 789 337	4.5	3.5	0.0	0.7	30.1	6.0	54.4	69.9	21.7	17.0	1 038	859
Wirt	221	579 537	5.0	1.0	0.0	0.0	0.0	1.9	92.1	12.0	8.3	2.5	428	408
Wood	2 923	9 783 040	4.6	5.6	2.1	2.8	2.7	6.6	73.9	223.4	105.4	75.1	866	645
Wyoming	818	2 431 168	7.1	3.1	0.0	0.1	2.6	2.9	82.3	59.6	32.3	21.1	906	862
WISCONSIN	X	X	X	X	X	X	X	X	X	X	X	X	X	X
Adams	752	2 398 694	11.0	12.5	0.7	11.1	19.9	3.2	40.0	75.0	26.6	36.5	1 766	1 664
Ashland	751	2 545 721	7.6	8.1	4.1	10.6	10.7	7.0	49.8	79.8	47.9	22.4	1 398	1 298
Barron	1 838	6 618 589	8.0	8.4	1.3	6.3	10.3	4.0	60.6	190.4	84.2	79.1	1 729	1 625
Bayfield	707	2 315 340	13.5	8.9	0.8	14.7	14.5	4.4	42.0	70.7	26.8	33.0	2 186	2 071
Brown	9 417	41 301 919	3.9	9.3	3.3	3.0	7.6	3.8	67.8	1 182.5	506.0	459.7	1 817	1 685
Buffalo	479	1 597 741	7.7	7.1	0.2	11.0	7.2	3.7	62.0	50.4	28.0	18.4	1 378	1 318
Burnett	687	2 258 798	11.7	9.6	0.3	13.5	8.5	4.2	51.0	63.0	23.4	33.2	2 157	2 077
Calumet	1 110	4 057 590	8.1	8.8	0.2	5.3	10.0	4.7	61.8	111.1	46.0	47.5	956	941
Chippewa	1 941	7 086 033	6.6	8.6	2.6	10.3	6.3	4.1	60.8	196.6	102.1	74.2	1 179	1 086
Clark	1 398	4 771 022	6.3	8.0	0.1	9.4	23.0	4.1	48.3	140.3	73.6	38.4	1 115	1 055
Columbia	2 325	8 247 107	8.1	9.2	0.4	3.5	8.2	3.5	65.9	255.2	98.3	121.8	2 154	2 025
Crawford	593	1 975 908	11.0	8.6	0.2	10.4	5.2	3.1	60.2	77.0	46.6	24.3	1 469	1 348
Dane	19 136	83 118 268	5.7	10.6	3.0	6.3	5.9	6.9	59.9	2 389.4	787.6	1 194.7	2 373	2 225

1. Based on the resident population estimated as of July 1 of the year shown.

STATE County	Local government finances, 2012 (cont.) — Direct general expenditure: Total (mil dol)	Per capita[1] (dollars)	Percent of total for: Educa-tion	Health and hospitals	Police protec-tion	Public welfare	High-ways	Debt outstanding: Total (mil dol)	Per capita[1] (dollars)	Government employment, 2013: Federal civilian	Federal military	State and local	Presidential election,[2] 2012 — Percent of vote cast: Demo-cratic	Republi-can	All other
	185	186	187	188	189	190	191	192	193	194	195	196	197	198	199
WEST VIRGINIA—Cont'd															
Brooke	57.1	2 394	62.3	1.0	9.7	0.1	2.8	99.9	4 186	30	114	922	47.9	50.3	1.8
Cabell	294.4	3 035	46.5	1.1	6.6	0.4	1.3	141.0	1 454	968	590	7 107	44.2	54.3	1.5
Calhoun	16.5	2 170	67.3	0.0	4.6	0.1	0.1	13.0	1 714	19	38	300	40.9	56.2	2.9
Clay	29.0	3 117	78.1	4.6	7.4	0.0	0.0	1.2	128	19	46	520	43.5	53.8	2.7
Doddridge	22.0	2 695	75.1	2.0	2.2	0.0	0.2	8.1	994	12	38	522	24.4	73.5	2.2
Fayette	113.9	2 482	68.7	0.5	5.7	0.0	1.6	47.9	1 045	291	223	3 108	47.7	50.4	1.9
Gilmer	17.4	1 988	61.7	1.3	6.6	0.0	0.4	4.5	516	333	32	650	39.8	57.3	2.9
Grant	59.2	5 007	30.0	52.8	2.8	0.0	0.1	13.9	1 177	42	58	898	23.6	75.1	1.3
Greenbrier	128.0	3 574	63.2	0.6	4.9	0.1	1.0	116.1	3 241	96	175	2 564	42.8	55.1	2.1
Hampshire	52.8	2 229	71.4	1.4	6.3	0.0	0.5	31.5	1 328	40	114	1 312	35.7	62.6	1.7
Hancock	95.4	3 148	57.0	1.9	5.9	0.4	3.5	88.0	2 903	55	150	1 380	41.6	56.9	1.5
Hardy	30.9	2 227	67.5	1.2	3.9	0.1	1.5	61.4	4 426	48	69	788	35.2	62.4	2.4
Harrison	213.8	3 092	57.6	0.7	4.7	0.0	3.1	154.5	2 234	4 144	342	3 910	42.6	55.9	1.5
Jackson	77.4	2 647	65.9	3.3	6.4	0.0	0.9	34.3	1 172	79	145	1 301	39.7	58.4	1.9
Jefferson	165.6	3 037	64.7	0.4	7.7	0.0	1.5	64.5	1 183	702	268	3 087	51.8	47.0	1.1
Kanawha	630.4	3 280	49.5	0.7	6.4	0.0	3.1	316.3	1 646	2 063	970	19 818	49.2	49.6	1.1
Lewis	44.9	2 740	61.9	2.9	2.7	0.3	0.8	5.9	361	56	81	1 433	31.9	65.6	2.5
Lincoln	56.1	2 593	81.6	0.7	1.6	0.1	0.0	11.6	535	30	107	865	44.3	53.2	2.5
Logan	90.2	2 493	72.3	0.9	1.5	0.0	1.1	10.2	281	111	176	2 091	43.6	54.4	2.0
McDowell	77.6	3 641	65.1	0.4	3.6	0.0	1.0	12.9	606	386	102	1 694	53.3	44.8	1.8
Marion	168.8	2 978	58.1	1.2	4.9	0.0	1.1	273.1	4 819	329	277	4 203	49.2	48.7	2.1
Marshall	98.2	3 004	56.7	2.0	5.2	0.2	2.1	187.9	5 751	48	159	1 751	42.8	55.4	1.8
Mason	71.4	2 625	63.5	7.2	3.0	0.1	1.4	29.8	1 097	104	132	1 496	42.3	55.2	2.5
Mercer	244.7	3 914	40.5	39.9	4.2	0.0	1.0	92.7	1 483	184	303	4 842	35.4	63.0	1.6
Mineral	67.8	2 426	67.5	0.9	6.0	0.1	1.0	39.5	1 413	73	135	1 520	32.5	66.0	1.6
Mingo	98.5	3 774	63.6	0.6	2.1	0.1	1.1	29.5	1 128	72	129	1 299	43.0	55.0	2.0
Monongalia	226.2	2 254	54.5	2.7	5.6	0.4	2.1	196.0	1 954	1 217	485	15 469	51.1	47.3	1.6
Monroe	25.2	1 875	79.9	0.7	5.6	0.1	0.8	11.1	828	210	67	514	36.1	60.9	2.9
Morgan	37.8	2 162	73.4	1.3	6.3	0.0	0.5	22.3	1 279	28	87	738	37.4	60.9	1.7
Nicholas	110.3	4 207	42.1	40.3	4.8	0.0	1.0	40.6	1 546	100	129	1 686	46.5	51.3	2.1
Ohio	204.2	4 634	34.0	0.9	7.3	0.2	3.3	309.3	7 017	406	205	3 855	44.0	54.7	1.3
Pendleton	16.3	2 160	74.5	2.0	1.0	0.0	0.2	4.2	549	114	191	347	38.6	59.9	1.5
Pleasants	31.1	4 098	51.5	1.1	2.8	1.2	0.9	168.6	22 201	10	35	623	38.4	59.6	2.1
Pocahontas	32.3	3 712	42.6	29.0	6.8	0.3	0.3	7.5	861	59	42	772	42.5	55.2	2.3
Preston	67.7	2 001	71.9	0.8	3.4	0.0	0.8	71.7	2 120	708	157	1 542	35.6	62.1	2.3
Putnam	187.6	3 324	75.3	0.9	5.2	0.0	0.4	178.8	3 168	174	282	2 068	37.7	61.2	1.1
Raleigh	227.9	2 884	60.0	0.6	7.4	0.1	1.6	109.6	1 387	1 802	397	3 723	36.2	62.1	1.7
Randolph	78.4	2 667	59.6	0.4	4.2	0.1	1.6	33.1	1 126	166	136	1 984	41.9	55.9	2.2
Ritchie	26.4	2 577	64.5	8.2	3.8	0.1	1.0	5.0	492	29	50	547	25.9	72.3	1.7
Roane	32.6	2 218	76.9	1.3	2.2	0.0	1.1	10.7	731	28	73	636	45.1	52.9	2.0
Summers	26.4	1 922	59.2	1.1	4.3	0.0	1.2	7.1	514	45	61	741	43.1	54.4	2.5
Taylor	50.1	2 947	47.3	30.5	3.2	0.0	2.7	25.2	1 485	46	82	1 070	39.7	58.1	2.2
Tucker	25.6	3 656	47.4	5.2	1.8	0.0	0.6	6.1	873	49	34	622	36.7	60.5	2.7
Tyler	31.5	3 490	53.3	28.3	3.8	0.0	0.6	14.5	1 606	17	45	550	33.2	64.6	2.3
Upshur	57.5	2 351	66.4	0.5	2.2	0.1	1.6	23.7	969	126	117	1 167	32.6	65.9	1.5
Wayne	99.1	2 380	75.7	1.2	4.2	0.1	0.6	56.7	1 362	1 372	211	1 879	39.8	58.0	2.2
Webster	23.6	2 613	67.1	0.1	6.5	0.0	0.6	2.3	257	13	44	558	50.8	45.3	3.9
Wetzel	76.4	4 650	43.1	35.0	3.3	0.0	1.3	24.0	1 459	36	80	1 118	45.6	51.8	2.6
Wirt	12.5	2 133	82.9	0.0	0.1	0.0	0.6	1.6	280	12	29	262	33.6	64.3	2.1
Wood	223.9	2 582	63.1	0.1	5.4	0.0	4.0	189.9	2 190	2 163	429	4 322	34.9	63.6	1.5
Wyoming	60.0	2 578	76.4	0.9	3.5	0.1	0.4	21.2	910	115	114	1 117	36.3	61.4	2.3
WISCONSIN	X	X	X	X	X	X	X	X	X	28 730	16 491	386 484	56.2	42.3	1.5
Adams	74.9	3 623	28.9	10.0	7.1	4.2	20.2	54.3	2 624	299	54	871	58.1	39.8	2.1
Ashland	80.3	5 021	41.4	3.1	6.4	7.4	11.1	35.5	2 221	159	43	1 923	67.9	30.7	1.4
Barron	194.8	4 259	48.2	0.6	5.4	8.5	14.2	109.9	2 402	132	127	4 003	52.8	45.7	1.5
Bayfield	74.2	4 916	33.4	7.0	4.7	0.1	19.4	43.1	2 852	113	59	1 327	63.1	35.5	1.4
Brown	1 202.2	4 751	49.8	5.5	6.3	4.1	6.6	1 130.3	4 467	1 051	730	17 299	53.9	44.8	1.3
Buffalo	53.1	3 982	48.0	1.8	3.5	5.5	22.8	23.0	1 723	160	37	678	56.4	41.8	1.8
Burnett	66.0	4 292	45.3	5.0	4.3	3.4	18.5	34.6	2 248	25	42	1 768	49.9	48.3	1.7
Calumet	110.0	2 217	42.6	3.7	6.9	6.6	12.0	109.5	2 206	117	138	1 289	50.2	48.1	1.7
Chippewa	206.5	3 282	53.4	4.8	4.8	2.5	14.8	127.7	2 030	200	170	3 323	53.7	44.6	1.7
Clark	143.7	4 173	42.9	4.9	4.0	14.6	11.4	69.7	2 024	116	95	1 962	52.5	45.0	2.5
Columbia	257.0	4 546	51.3	1.4	5.7	6.8	11.3	215.7	3 815	173	159	3 515	56.9	41.7	1.4
Crawford	74.8	4 519	39.3	3.0	5.3	4.1	18.5	47.8	2 889	62	44	991	62.5	35.5	2.1
Dane	2 429.4	4 825	46.4	1.9	6.1	8.3	5.9	2 890.1	5 740	5 133	1 482	72 455	72.8	25.8	1.4

1. Based on the resident population estimated as of July 1 of the year shown. 2.

STATE/ County code	CBSA code[1]	County type[2]	STATE County	Land area,[3] (sq km) 2010	Population, 2014: Total persons 2014	Population, 2014: Rank	Population, 2014: Per square kilometer	Population and population characteristics, 2013: Race alone or in combination, not Hispanic or Latino (percent): White	Black	American Indian, Alaska Native	Asian and Pacific Islander	Percent Hispanic or Latino[4]	Age (percent): Under 5 years	5 to 17 years	18 to 24 years	25 to 34 years	35 to 44 years	45 to 54 years
				1	2	3	4	5	6	7	8	9	10	11	12	13	14	15
			WISCONSIN—Cont'd															
55 027	13180	4	Dodge	2 268	88 574	646	39.1	91.6	3.3	0.7	0.8	4.4	4.9	16.0	7.8	12.7	12.8	16.2
55 029	...	6	Door	1 248	27 766	1 505	22.2	95.5	1.0	1.0	0.7	2.8	4.1	13.1	6.1	8.8	9.8	14.3
55 031	20260	2	Douglas	3 378	43 698	1 097	12.9	94.7	2.0	3.4	1.4	1.3	5.7	15.4	9.2	12.9	11.8	14.6
55 033	32860	6	Dunn	2 202	44 305	1 085	20.1	94.5	1.0	0.8	3.2	1.7	5.1	15.0	19.0	11.5	10.8	12.5
55 035	20740	3	Eau Claire	1 652	101 564	588	61.5	92.8	1.6	0.9	4.1	2.1	5.7	14.8	17.3	13.8	10.7	12.1
55 037	27020	9	Florence	1 264	4 481	2 867	3.5	97.5	0.8	1.2	0.8	0.9	3.7	12.2	5.7	8.1	9.5	18.0
55 039	22540	3	Fond du Lac	1 864	101 759	583	54.6	92.2	1.9	0.8	1.5	4.8	5.7	16.2	8.9	12.1	11.8	15.1
55 041	...	9	Forest	2 626	9 127	2 503	3.5	83.2	1.5	15.2	0.7	1.9	5.5	15.2	8.8	9.6	10.2	13.9
55 043	38420	6	Grant	2 970	51 829	961	17.5	96.4	1.5	0.5	1.0	1.4	5.4	15.3	17.1	10.7	9.9	12.6
55 045	31540	6	Green	1 512	37 063	1 248	24.5	95.7	1.0	0.4	0.9	2.9	5.7	17.6	7.0	10.7	12.7	15.5
55 047	...	6	Green Lake	905	18 836	1 878	20.8	93.9	0.8	0.6	0.8	4.6	5.5	17.3	6.5	10.0	10.3	14.6
55 049	31540	2	Iowa	1 975	23 825	1 648	12.1	97.1	0.8	0.5	0.8	1.7	6.2	17.5	6.8	10.9	11.6	15.8
55 051	...	9	Iron	1 964	5 917	2 764	3.0	97.9	0.5	1.4	0.6	0.8	3.8	12.1	5.4	7.6	9.7	15.5
55 053	...	6	Jackson	2 558	20 652	1 794	8.1	88.1	2.5	7.0	0.8	3.1	6.2	16.4	7.6	12.0	11.9	14.8
55 055	48020	4	Jefferson	1 441	84 395	668	58.6	91.2	1.2	0.6	1.1	6.9	5.5	17.2	9.8	12.0	12.8	14.9
55 057	...	7	Juneau	1 986	26 395	1 549	13.3	92.9	2.6	1.8	0.8	2.9	5.4	15.0	6.9	11.4	11.9	16.2
55 059	16980	1	Kenosha	704	168 068	378	238.7	79.0	7.8	0.8	2.2	12.4	6.1	18.4	9.9	12.6	13.0	15.5
55 061	24580	2	Kewaunee	887	20 444	1 809	23.0	96.4	0.6	0.9	0.6	2.3	5.4	17.0	6.9	10.4	12.0	15.6
55 063	29100	3	La Crosse	1 170	118 011	520	100.9	92.1	2.1	0.8	4.9	1.7	5.7	15.0	15.6	13.1	11.0	12.8
55 065	...	8	Lafayette	1 641	16 853	1 991	10.3	95.3	0.5	0.5	0.6	3.7	6.4	18.3	8.0	10.8	10.6	14.9
55 067	...	6	Langlade	2 255	19 410	1 861	8.6	96.1	1.1	1.6	0.6	1.9	5.0	15.2	6.9	9.3	10.3	15.5
55 069	32980	6	Lincoln	2 277	28 493	1 471	12.5	96.8	1.1	0.8	0.8	1.4	4.6	15.5	7.2	9.7	11.6	16.4
55 071	31820	4	Manitowoc	1 526	80 160	692	52.5	92.7	1.0	0.9	3.0	3.5	5.2	16.2	7.6	10.6	11.4	15.7
55 073	48140	3	Marathon	4 001	135 780	464	33.9	90.7	1.2	0.8	6.0	2.5	6.2	17.5	8.0	12.1	12.2	15.1
55 075	31940	6	Marinette	3 624	41 298	1 143	11.4	96.9	0.7	1.1	0.9	1.5	4.6	14.9	7.8	10.0	10.2	15.3
55 077	...	8	Marquette	1 180	15 050	2 098	12.8	95.3	0.9	0.9	0.8	3.0	5.0	14.8	6.0	9.1	10.2	15.9
55 078	43020	8	Menominee	926	4 522	2 862	4.9	13.4	1.4	81.1	0.9	5.1	10.5	22.5	9.6	11.3	9.6	13.4
55 079	33340	1	Milwaukee	625	956 406	49	1 530.2	55.2	27.6	1.2	4.2	14.0	7.2	17.3	10.5	16.2	12.5	12.7
55 081	...	6	Monroe	2 333	45 379	1 063	19.5	92.7	1.9	1.5	1.2	3.9	6.9	18.8	7.3	12.2	11.5	14.7
55 083	24580	2	Oconto	2 585	37 417	1 239	14.5	96.5	0.5	1.8	0.5	1.7	5.0	15.9	6.8	9.6	11.9	17.2
55 085	...	7	Oneida	2 883	35 563	1 284	12.3	96.7	0.8	1.6	0.8	1.4	4.6	12.9	6.7	9.3	9.8	15.8
55 087	11540	3	Outagamie	1 651	182 006	353	110.2	90.1	1.7	2.0	3.7	3.9	6.4	17.9	8.9	13.4	12.8	15.5
55 089	33340	1	Ozaukee	604	87 470	657	144.8	93.7	1.8	0.5	2.5	2.6	5.1	17.2	8.4	9.6	11.5	16.1
55 091	...	8	Pepin	601	7 335	2 648	12.2	97.5	0.6	0.6	0.5	1.5	5.3	17.1	7.0	9.4	10.5	14.7
55 093	33460	1	Pierce	1 486	40 958	1 154	27.6	96.3	1.1	0.8	1.3	1.8	5.5	16.0	16.9	11.2	11.3	14.2
55 095	...	6	Polk	2 367	43 437	1 103	18.4	96.5	0.7	1.4	0.8	1.7	5.3	16.8	6.9	10.1	11.9	15.8
55 097	44620	4	Portage	2 074	70 482	761	34.0	93.2	1.2	0.7	3.2	2.9	5.1	14.8	17.0	11.9	10.5	13.6
55 099	...	9	Price	3 249	13 675	2 195	4.2	96.5	0.7	1.0	1.3	1.6	3.9	14.0	6.1	7.8	10.4	16.4
55 101	39540	3	Racine	861	195 163	333	226.7	75.1	12.2	0.8	1.5	12.3	6.3	17.8	8.3	12.1	12.3	15.4
55 103	...	6	Richland	1 518	17 662	1 937	11.6	96.2	1.0	0.6	0.9	2.2	5.6	16.9	7.7	9.9	11.1	13.6
55 105	27500	3	Rock	1 860	161 188	395	86.7	85.7	6.0	0.7	1.5	8.0	6.0	17.9	8.8	12.5	12.7	14.4
55 107	...	6	Rusk	2 366	14 333	2 144	6.1	97.0	0.9	1.0	0.6	1.6	5.4	15.9	6.6	8.6	10.2	15.1
55 109	33460	1	St. Croix	1 871	86 759	661	46.4	95.8	1.1	0.7	1.5	2.1	6.4	19.9	6.9	12.5	14.4	15.6
55 111	12660	4	Sauk	2 152	63 379	826	29.5	92.7	1.1	1.6	1.0	4.8	6.2	17.1	7.5	12.4	12.2	14.5
55 113	...	9	Sawyer	3 256	16 437	2 011	5.0	80.6	1.0	18.9	0.6	2.1	5.5	14.7	6.6	8.8	10.0	14.3
55 115	43020	6	Shawano	2 313	41 579	1 137	18.0	89.1	0.7	8.9	0.8	2.5	5.5	16.4	7.2	10.3	11.5	15.5
55 117	43100	3	Sheboygan	1 324	115 290	531	87.1	87.3	2.1	0.7	5.2	5.8	5.7	17.2	8.0	11.6	12.1	15.3
55 119	...	6	Taylor	2 525	20 540	1 800	8.1	97.3	0.6	0.5	0.6	1.7	6.0	17.8	6.9	10.0	11.5	15.6
55 121	...	8	Trempealeau	1 898	29 509	1 439	15.5	92.3	0.6	0.5	0.7	6.5	6.7	17.7	7.3	11.3	11.9	14.8
55 123	...	6	Vernon	2 050	30 362	1 421	14.8	97.4	0.8	0.5	0.6	1.6	7.1	18.8	6.9	9.7	10.4	14.1
55 125	...	9	Vilas	2 219	21 398	1 757	9.6	87.2	0.6	11.3	0.6	1.6	4.0	13.0	5.8	7.4	9.0	14.9
55 127	48580	4	Walworth	1 438	103 527	573	72.0	86.9	1.4	0.6	1.3	10.9	5.3	17.0	12.5	10.9	11.6	14.4
55 129	...	6	Washburn	2 065	15 694	2 061	7.6	96.3	0.8	2.1	0.7	1.5	5.1	14.6	6.0	9.0	10.1	14.8
55 131	33340	1	Washington	1 116	133 251	473	119.4	94.6	1.4	0.6	1.5	2.9	5.5	17.8	7.1	10.8	12.7	17.0
55 133	33340	1	Waukesha	1 423	395 118	173	277.7	90.8	1.8	0.5	3.6	4.5	5.2	17.5	7.5	10.5	12.2	16.4
55 135	...	6	Waupaca	1 937	52 066	958	26.9	95.9	0.6	0.9	0.6	2.8	5.3	16.3	7.1	10.4	11.5	15.7
55 137	...	8	Waushara	1 622	24 178	1 638	14.9	90.7	2.3	0.9	0.6	6.3	4.8	14.3	6.5	9.8	11.1	15.8
55 139	36780	3	Winnebago	1 125	169 511	374	150.7	91.1	2.5	0.9	3.1	3.8	5.7	15.4	12.5	13.1	12.0	14.4
55 141	49220	4	Wood	2 054	73 608	742	35.8	94.1	1.1	1.0	2.1	2.6	5.8	16.2	7.5	11.2	11.2	15.5
56 000	...	X	WYOMING	251 470	584 153	X	2.3	85.6	2.0	2.9	1.5	9.7	6.6	17.0	10.1	14.0	11.9	13.1
56 001	29660	4	Albany	11 069	37 811	1 229	3.4	85.2	2.2	1.3	3.9	9.3	5.3	11.0	28.4	16.2	9.5	9.4
56 003	...	9	Big Horn	8 125	11 930	2 301	1.5	88.5	1.5	1.5	0.7	8.8	6.3	19.0	7.9	10.4	10.6	12.9
56 005	23940	5	Campbell	12 439	48 320	1 009	3.9	89.2	1.3	1.9	1.1	8.2	8.2	19.8	9.3	16.8	13.1	13.7
56 007	...	7	Carbon	20 455	15 854	2 053	0.8	79.3	1.8	1.7	1.2	17.2	6.2	16.9	8.3	14.5	12.1	13.4
56 009	...	6	Converse	11 020	14 097	2 160	1.3	89.9	1.3	1.6	0.8	7.6	6.9	18.2	8.0	12.3	12.5	14.4

1. CBSA = Core Based Statistical Area. See Appendix A for explanation. See Appendix B for list of metropolitan areas with component counties. 2. County type code from the Economic Research Service of USDA Rural-Urban Continuum Codes. See Appendix A for definition. 3. Dry land or land partially or temporarily covered by water. 4. May be of any race.

STATE County	Population, 2013 (cont.)				Population change and components of change, 2000–2014							Households, 2009–2013				
	Age (percent) (cont.)				Total persons		Percent change		Components of change, 2010–2014					Percent		
	55 to 64 years	65 to 74 years	75 years and over	Percent female	2000	2010	2000–2010	2010–2014	Births	Deaths	Net migration	Number	Persons per house-hold	Family house-holds	Female family house-holder[1]	One per-son
	16	17	18	19	20	21	22	23	24	25	26	27	28	29	30	31
WISCONSIN—Cont'd																
Dodge	13.6	8.2	7.8	47.2	85 897	88 759	3.3	-0.2	3 574	3 644	-175	33 173	2.51	67.0	8.0	28.6
Door	18.3	14.5	11.0	50.8	27 961	27 785	-0.6	-0.1	874	1 389	436	13 459	2.04	63.0	5.2	29.8
Douglas	14.9	8.8	6.8	49.9	43 287	44 159	2.0	-1.0	1 897	1 772	-539	18 933	2.25	61.5	10.2	31.8
Dunn	12.1	7.8	6.1	49.6	39 858	43 857	10.0	1.0	1 932	1 266	-319	16 222	2.50	64.7	7.8	25.2
Eau Claire	11.9	7.4	6.1	50.7	93 142	98 736	6.0	2.7	4 970	3 114	849	39 754	2.39	59.0	8.1	29.9
Florence	18.1	14.4	10.4	48.5	5 088	4 423	-13.1	1.3	113	209	103	1 767	2.50	74.3	7.5	22.0
Fond du Lac	14.0	8.5	7.6	50.8	97 296	101 633	4.5	0.1	4 653	3 833	-597	41 267	2.38	67.0	9.0	27.8
Forest	15.1	11.9	9.8	49.0	10 024	9 304	-7.2	-1.9	463	470	-148	3 739	2.39	67.6	10.5	28.1
Grant	12.7	8.2	8.2	48.0	49 597	51 208	3.2	1.2	2 255	1 992	391	19 420	2.43	62.4	7.3	27.2
Green	14.5	8.9	7.6	50.4	33 647	36 842	9.5	0.6	1 692	1 453	-71	14 640	2.49	69.2	7.9	24.7
Green Lake	15.5	11.0	9.3	49.7	19 105	19 051	-0.3	-1.1	867	936	-119	8 001	2.35	66.7	7.2	28.9
Iowa	15.1	9.0	7.1	50.0	22 780	23 687	4.0	0.6	1 173	834	-272	9 610	2.44	68.7	6.2	25.2
Iron	17.8	14.8	13.2	50.2	6 861	5 916	-13.8	0.0	158	348	180	2 953	1.97	62.9	8.2	31.5
Jackson	14.0	9.6	7.5	46.7	19 100	20 449	7.1	1.0	1 036	768	-43	8 112	2.35	64.8	9.6	28.6
Jefferson	13.4	8.3	6.1	50.2	74 021	83 686	13.1	0.9	3 832	2 641	-348	32 137	2.51	67.3	9.2	26.5
Juneau	14.5	10.6	8.0	47.0	24 316	26 664	9.7	-1.0	1 173	1 099	-321	10 194	2.50	66.7	9.5	28.6
Kenosha	12.3	6.7	5.4	50.5	149 577	166 426	11.3	1.0	8 361	5 532	-1 138	62 560	2.60	67.0	13.8	26.5
Kewaunee	14.5	9.5	8.7	49.2	20 187	20 574	1.9	-0.6	863	777	-240	8 145	2.50	68.1	5.4	27.6
La Crosse	12.5	7.5	6.8	51.0	107 120	114 638	7.0	2.9	5 370	4 073	2 071	45 949	2.40	60.6	8.6	29.4
Lafayette	14.5	8.4	8.0	49.0	16 137	16 836	4.3	0.1	884	553	-335	6 605	2.53	69.7	7.3	25.4
Langlade	15.9	11.6	10.3	49.8	20 740	19 977	-3.7	-2.8	836	982	-461	8 758	2.23	64.5	8.2	29.0
Lincoln	15.4	10.4	9.1	49.4	29 641	28 743	-3.0	-0.9	1 136	1 289	-51	12 513	2.23	66.7	6.3	27.7
Manitowoc	15.2	9.5	8.6	50.1	82 887	81 442	-1.7	-1.6	3 526	3 390	-1 403	34 067	2.35	64.5	7.0	30.1
Marathon	13.5	8.3	7.2	49.8	125 834	134 063	6.5	1.3	6 856	4 742	-522	53 079	2.50	68.0	7.9	25.9
Marinette	16.0	11.6	9.5	50.0	43 384	41 749	-3.8	-1.1	1 666	2 073	45	18 573	2.18	61.8	7.1	32.7
Marquette	16.8	12.8	9.4	49.2	15 832	15 404	-2.7	-2.3	647	700	-309	6 453	2.34	68.4	6.7	26.3
Menominee	10.7	8.3	4.2	50.9	4 562	4 232	-7.2	6.9	404	195	66	1 220	3.47	72.4	19.4	21.6
Milwaukee	11.6	6.2	5.8	51.7	940 164	947 735	0.8	0.9	59 849	34 389	-15 647	379 637	2.45	57.0	16.8	34.9
Monroe	13.6	8.6	6.5	49.4	40 899	44 673	9.2	1.6	2 622	1 729	-194	17 543	2.52	67.7	9.4	27.2
Oconto	15.8	10.5	7.5	49.0	35 634	37 660	5.7	-0.6	1 469	1 459	-225	15 701	2.37	69.6	6.5	24.7
Oneida	17.5	12.9	10.4	50.1	36 776	35 998	-2.1	-1.2	1 318	1 875	122	15 797	2.22	64.5	5.9	31.0
Outagamie	12.4	7.0	5.7	50.2	160 971	176 695	9.8	3.0	9 612	5 213	985	69 572	2.51	67.4	8.5	26.3
Ozaukee	15.3	9.2	7.7	50.9	82 317	86 395	5.0	1.2	3 391	3 068	698	34 108	2.51	71.2	7.6	24.6
Pepin	15.8	10.6	9.5	49.5	7 213	7 469	3.5	-1.8	319	301	-173	3 085	2.36	65.6	5.1	29.1
Pierce	12.9	6.9	5.1	50.6	36 804	41 019	11.5	-0.1	1 713	1 044	-743	15 069	2.53	67.0	7.2	22.7
Polk	15.3	10.1	7.8	49.6	41 319	44 205	7.0	-1.7	1 785	1 743	-803	18 266	2.38	69.1	8.7	25.8
Portage	12.9	7.8	6.3	49.8	67 182	70 019	4.2	0.7	2 962	2 118	-363	27 975	2.38	62.7	7.3	27.4
Price	18.3	12.6	10.6	49.2	15 822	14 159	-10.5	-3.4	454	698	-248	6 776	2.04	64.5	6.3	30.9
Racine	13.6	7.9	6.4	50.4	188 831	195 408	3.5	-0.1	10 253	7 014	-3 356	75 087	2.53	65.6	11.7	29.0
Richland	15.9	9.8	9.4	49.8	17 924	18 021	0.5	-2.0	760	730	-391	7 343	2.39	68.0	7.9	28.1
Rock	13.0	8.0	6.7	50.9	152 307	160 331	5.3	0.5	8 149	5 916	-1 302	63 309	2.48	67.3	12.5	26.3
Rusk	16.4	11.6	10.3	50.0	15 347	14 755	-3.9	-2.9	606	714	-323	6 430	2.23	65.4	8.8	28.7
St. Croix	12.5	7.0	4.7	50.0	63 155	84 345	33.6	2.9	4 446	2 346	267	32 114	2.62	72.7	9.6	21.9
Sauk	13.7	9.0	7.4	50.3	55 225	61 976	12.2	2.3	3 218	2 444	502	25 206	2.44	66.7	8.7	27.1
Sawyer	17.3	13.7	9.0	49.4	16 196	16 557	2.2	-0.7	713	806	19	7 663	2.11	66.7	12.4	26.8
Shawano	14.1	10.7	8.9	50.0	40 664	41 949	3.2	-0.9	1 865	1 802	-433	17 245	2.38	68.2	8.8	26.0
Sheboygan	14.1	8.4	7.4	49.8	112 646	115 507	2.5	-0.2	5 426	4 461	-1 256	46 312	2.42	66.2	8.3	27.9
Taylor	14.4	8.9	8.9	49.1	19 680	20 689	5.1	-0.7	926	774	-392	8 761	2.33	65.3	7.0	28.5
Trempealeau	13.6	8.8	7.9	49.4	27 010	28 816	6.7	2.4	1 681	1 156	156	11 745	2.43	67.5	8.6	27.7
Vernon	14.7	9.7	8.5	50.0	28 056	29 773	6.1	2.0	1 770	1 264	31	11 790	2.51	67.5	7.9	27.5
Vilas	17.8	16.0	12.1	49.4	21 033	21 430	1.9	-0.1	770	1 216	429	10 636	1.99	61.8	7.7	31.7
Walworth	13.4	8.4	6.5	50.0	93 759	102 228	9.0	1.3	4 388	3 664	515	39 929	2.50	66.7	9.6	25.2
Washburn	17.1	13.6	9.7	50.5	16 036	15 911	-0.8	-1.4	664	861	-34	7 348	2.12	64.1	7.8	31.0
Washington	14.0	8.3	6.8	50.3	117 493	131 887	12.3	1.0	5 583	4 363	105	52 053	2.52	72.4	8.9	23.4
Waukesha	14.7	8.6	7.3	50.9	360 767	389 891	8.1	1.3	16 167	13 303	2 215	153 422	2.52	70.5	7.0	24.5
Waupaca	14.7	9.8	9.2	49.6	51 731	52 410	1.3	-0.7	2 216	3 024	462	21 388	2.37	67.3	8.1	27.0
Waushara	16.1	12.1	9.6	47.5	23 154	24 496	5.8	-1.3	957	1 075	-154	9 902	2.34	67.2	6.6	28.0
Winnebago	12.7	7.5	6.8	49.7	156 763	166 994	6.5	1.5	8 013	6 027	527	68 140	2.33	60.3	8.6	30.8
Wood	14.5	9.3	8.8	50.7	75 555	74 749	-1.1	-1.5	3 584	3 077	-1 531	32 037	2.29	64.4	8.2	30.4
WYOMING	13.8	7.9	5.6	49.0	493 782	563 626	14.1	3.6	31 985	19 028	7 195	222 846	2.50	66.0	8.7	27.5
Albany	10.7	5.7	3.8	47.8	32 014	36 299	13.4	4.2	1 777	779	479	15 257	2.25	48.9	5.6	32.5
Big Horn	14.1	10.6	8.1	49.5	11 461	11 668	1.8	2.2	605	565	223	4 462	2.59	69.0	6.3	28.2
Campbell	12.3	4.4	2.3	48.0	33 698	46 133	36.9	4.7	3 192	1 069	36	17 108	2.71	71.0	8.7	21.0
Carbon	15.0	8.4	5.4	45.3	15 639	15 885	1.6	-0.2	832	500	-370	6 077	2.42	65.9	9.3	28.5
Converse	14.2	7.8	5.7	49.1	12 052	13 833	14.8	1.9	771	516	-6	5 746	2.41	68.5	8.4	27.9

1. No spouse present.

Table B. States and Counties — **Population, Vital Statistics, Medicare, and Crime**

STATE County	Persons in group quarters, 2014	Daytime population, 2009–2013: Number	Daytime population, 2009–2013: Employment/residence ratio	Births, 2014: Total	Births, 2014: Rate[1]	Deaths, 2014: Number	Deaths, 2014: Rate[1]	Persons under 65 with no health insurance, 2013: Number	Persons under 65 with no health insurance, 2013: Percent	Medicare, 2014: Eligible for Medicare	Medicare, 2014: Enrolled in Medicare Advantage	Medicare, 2014: Enrolled in a Medicare prescription drug plan	Serious crimes known to police,[2] 2013: Total: Number	Serious crimes known to police,[2] 2013: Total: Rate[3]
	32	33	34	35	36	37	38	39	40	41	42	43	44	45
WISCONSIN—Cont'd														
Dodge	6 306	82 040	0.84	826	9.3	865	9.8	6 199	9.0	15 766	4 858	6 911	1 515	1 714
Door	343	27 191	0.95	197	7.1	350	12.6	2 293	11.1	8 305	2 013	3 922	306	1 098
Douglas	1 343	40 525	0.84	406	9.3	397	9.1	3 719	10.3	8 989	3 414	3 709	2 105	4 819
Dunn	3 253	40 483	0.84	442	10.0	298	6.7	3 565	10.2	8 317	2 274	4 408	747	1 692
Eau Claire	4 865	106 588	1.13	1 208	11.9	718	7.1	8 554	10.3	17 540	4 713	8 469	2 043	2 016
Florence	54	3 734	0.60	23	5.1	47	10.5	473	14.0	1 279	328	520	95	2 105
Fond du Lac	3 516	96 952	0.91	1 089	10.7	870	8.5	7 717	9.4	19 337	8 812	6 296	1 854	1 818
Forest	353	8 961	0.92	111	12.2	102	11.2	1 103	15.6	2 460	734	903	174	1 895
Grant	4 795	46 883	0.83	533	10.3	472	9.1	4 568	11.6	9 725	3 527	5 987	832	1 628
Green	380	34 158	0.86	399	10.8	348	9.4	2 907	9.5	7 050	1 088	3 474	588	1 591
Green Lake	165	17 769	0.86	200	10.6	221	11.7	1 668	11.2	4 527	2 268	1 369	302	1 585
Iowa	220	22 757	0.92	269	11.3	177	7.4	1 965	9.9	4 508	1 385	2 447	250	1 047
Iron	86	5 478	0.82	35	5.9	86	14.5	564	13.4	1 869	733	684	NA	NA
Jackson	1 297	19 692	0.91	240	11.6	163	7.9	2 225	14.0	4 089	1 536	1 482	283	1 380
Jefferson	3 398	74 593	0.78	879	10.4	650	7.7	6 950	10.0	14 770	3 905	7 413	1 401	1 652
Juneau	1 647	25 010	0.86	284	10.8	247	9.4	2 654	13.0	5 969	1 090	2 613	485	1 821
Kenosha	4 508	146 865	0.74	1 939	11.5	1 267	7.5	16 607	11.6	25 671	5 839	13 977	3 763	2 233
Kewaunee	177	18 650	0.81	190	9.3	191	9.3	1 638	9.8	4 082	1 838	1 245	257	1 244
La Crosse	5 820	123 661	1.14	1 229	10.4	944	8.0	8 899	9.3	20 072	8 642	7 280	2 574	2 199
Lafayette	95	13 963	0.66	214	12.7	133	7.9	2 099	15.1	3 163	899	1 701	170	1 007
Langlade	256	19 412	0.95	193	9.9	235	12.1	1 845	12.2	5 078	1 969	1 838	623	3 185
Lincoln	941	25 701	0.78	267	9.4	295	10.4	2 242	10.0	6 768	2 556	2 287	500	1 767
Manitowoc	1 048	76 991	0.90	826	10.3	803	10.0	5 804	8.8	17 495	7 106	5 937	1 428	1 773
Marathon	1 623	136 783	1.03	1 586	11.7	1 065	7.8	11 438	10.1	24 359	10 581	7 911	2 168	1 629
Marinette	841	42 805	1.06	401	9.7	459	11.1	3 358	10.5	10 846	3 673	4 143	808	1 945
Marquette	152	12 946	0.65	139	9.2	157	10.4	1 483	12.7	4 130	1 179	1 653	193	1 274
Menominee	59	5 173	1.68	93	20.6	63	13.9	646	17.0	773	188	319	38	869
Milwaukee	23 760	987 527	1.09	13 963	14.6	8 071	8.4	113 152	13.8	144 850	50 562	62 016	48 230	5 034
Monroe	812	46 887	1.09	617	13.6	411	9.1	4 392	11.6	8 058	2 551	2 523	765	1 708
Oconto	284	28 944	0.54	338	9.0	363	9.7	3 384	11.1	8 243	4 007	2 277	161	431
Oneida	501	36 833	1.06	308	8.7	441	12.4	3 003	11.1	10 360	3 166	4 180	589	1 652
Outagamie	3 032	182 760	1.05	2 250	12.4	1 213	6.7	15 279	9.9	28 611	16 361	7 143	2 897	1 613
Ozaukee	1 896	81 587	0.88	799	9.1	740	8.5	4 257	6.0	17 078	5 735	6 881	928	1 066
Pepin	134	6 495	0.75	74	10.1	86	11.7	649	11.2	1 954	353	990	71	963
Pierce	2 517	29 603	0.49	390	9.5	260	6.3	2 918	8.7	6 306	2 441	2 694	649	1 593
Polk	431	39 442	0.79	406	9.3	424	9.8	4 102	11.6	9 403	3 533	3 993	583	1 342
Portage	3 602	70 327	1.01	679	9.6	483	6.9	5 610	9.8	12 043	4 606	4 345	1 194	1 691
Price	201	14 265	1.04	106	7.8	149	10.9	1 149	10.9	3 918	1 394	1 447	201	1 457
Racine	4 849	182 488	0.86	2 369	12.1	1 567	8.0	18 092	11.1	35 901	12 389	13 919	5 156	2 648
Richland	345	16 586	0.84	175	9.9	174	9.9	1 693	12.0	3 667	576	1 741	115	647
Rock	2 721	148 817	0.84	1 901	11.8	1 371	8.5	16 988	12.6	29 696	9 144	17 862	4 354	2 711
Rusk	178	14 334	0.96	139	9.7	161	11.2	1 442	12.9	3 645	1 397	1 223	196	1 381
St. Croix	815	73 489	0.74	991	11.4	559	6.4	5 273	7.0	12 091	4 770	5 292	1 136	1 370
Sauk	725	64 951	1.08	740	11.7	583	9.2	6 249	12.0	12 347	4 337	6 242	1 761	2 802
Sawyer	304	17 044	1.07	172	10.5	192	11.7	1 835	14.6	4 794	1 361	1 992	294	1 772
Shawano	711	37 034	0.76	430	10.3	387	9.3	4 331	13.1	9 159	4 853	2 335	690	1 662
Sheboygan	2 846	115 821	1.01	1 260	10.9	1 048	9.1	9 429	10.0	21 720	8 623	6 809	2 225	1 936
Taylor	216	20 010	0.94	202	9.8	189	9.2	2 119	12.6	3 844	1 660	1 182	268	1 310
Trempealeau	531	28 700	0.97	411	13.9	269	9.1	2 723	11.2	5 632	2 149	1 959	238	808
Vernon	363	27 371	0.80	428	14.1	311	10.2	3 396	13.8	6 386	3 029	1 934	292	1 050
Vilas	184	21 266	0.99	191	8.9	290	13.6	2 643	17.3	7 693	2 133	3 325	243	1 140
Walworth	3 183	96 480	0.88	1 019	9.8	877	8.5	9 887	11.6	17 952	3 335	9 015	1 752	1 699
Washburn	204	15 613	0.97	150	9.6	198	12.6	1 455	12.2	4 734	1 591	1 930	363	2 297
Washington	1 134	115 234	0.76	1 300	9.8	1 045	7.8	7 614	6.8	23 448	8 121	9 151	2 177	1 637
Waukesha	5 539	417 498	1.13	3 820	9.7	3 203	8.1	20 246	6.2	73 829	25 366	29 443	4 995	1 413
Waupaca	1 585	49 537	0.89	531	10.2	702	13.5	4 521	10.8	11 808	5 997	3 477	987	1 895
Waushara	1 232	21 487	0.71	221	9.1	231	9.6	2 411	13.5	6 119	2 840	1 875	390	1 594
Winnebago	8 029	177 813	1.12	1 883	11.1	1 406	8.3	12 421	9.0	29 049	15 171	8 786	3 187	1 880
Wood	815	78 983	1.13	810	11.0	704	9.6	5 700	9.5	16 032	8 011	4 699	1 344	1 807
WYOMING	14 257	577 270	1.02	7 626	13.1	4 511	7.7	77 868	15.8	93 149	73	54 271	14 004	2 403
Albany	2 280	36 155	0.97	409	10.8	176	4.7	5 149	16.3	4 247	236	2 478	901	2 390
Big Horn	183	11 492	0.95	151	12.7	117	9.8	1 913	19.9	2 430	25	1 522	57	601
Campbell	422	51 309	1.17	754	15.6	288	6.0	5 752	12.9	4 227	14	2 604	1 302	2 678
Carbon	798	15 601	0.97	198	12.5	128	8.1	2 375	18.5	2 513	102	1 535	375	2 461
Converse	103	13 427	0.93	183	13.0	122	8.7	1 649	13.4	2 231	16	1 481	316	2 238

1. Per 1,000 estimated resident population. 2. Data for serious crimes have not been adjusted for underreporting; this may affect comparability between geographic areas and over time.
3. Per 100,000 population estimated by the FBI.

STATE County	Serious crimes known to police, 2013 (cont.)[1]		Education						Money income, 2009–2013				Income and poverty, 2013			
	Rate[2]		School enrollment and attainment, 2009–2013				Local government expenditures,[5] 2012–2013			Households				Percent below poverty level		
			Enrollment[3]		Attainment[4] (percent)											
	Violent	Property	Total	Percent private	High school graduate or less	Bachelor's degree or more	Total current spending (mil dol)	Current spending per student (dollars)	Per capita income[6] (dollars)	Median income (dollars)	Mean income (dollars)	Percent with income of $200,000 or more	Median household income (dollars)	All persons	Children under 18 years	Children 5 to 17 years in families
	46	47	48	49	50	51	52	53	54	55	56	57	58	59	60	61
WISCONSIN—Cont'd																
Dodge	84	1 630	19 565	18.1	52.4	15.8	119.2	10 975	24 573	53 075	62 604	1.4	51 623	9.4	12.0	10.3
Door	86	1 012	4 786	8.6	40.6	29.0	44.8	12 537	30 657	50 438	64 854	2.8	51 761	10.1	16.4	14.8
Douglas	236	4 583	10 858	8.0	39.7	21.7	70.0	10 800	25 129	45 418	57 810	1.5	43 417	17.3	22.0	20.4
Dunn	122	1 569	14 882	6.6	43.5	24.7	63.0	10 296	22 499	48 893	58 208	1.0	50 425	14.9	16.8	14.3
Eau Claire	142	1 874	30 862	10.9	35.0	31.0	156.7	11 008	25 287	48 090	62 168	2.2	49 345	13.7	16.3	14.6
Florence	199	1 906	907	5.3	52.1	14.5	6.6	15 656	22 434	47 960	54 518	1.4	44 139	13.5	20.4	18.3
Fond du Lac	196	1 622	24 496	20.7	48.7	20.0	146.4	10 908	26 368	53 820	64 409	1.9	54 649	9.1	12.2	10.9
Forest	283	1 612	1 966	6.5	55.9	12.2	20.5	12 692	20 462	39 963	48 798	0.6	40 153	18.1	24.2	22.6
Grant	153	1 476	15 024	10.9	50.4	19.1	82.7	11 739	21 705	46 963	55 584	1.3	45 854	17.2	18.9	16.3
Green	108	1 483	8 788	7.4	47.9	20.6	65.2	11 238	27 060	55 584	67 331	2.2	55 732	10.7	14.2	11.4
Green Lake	52	1 532	4 083	16.5	54.7	16.6	34.1	10 708	25 275	46 994	60 183	1.9	44 184	13.9	22.0	19.5
Iowa	71	976	5 479	11.6	44.0	21.7	43.2	12 240	26 625	55 659	65 588	2.1	53 186	11.0	13.9	12.7
Iron	NA	NA	987	3.1	44.4	20.8	10.4	13 610	23 324	39 051	47 810	0.8	37 412	15.3	23.9	22.5
Jackson	137	1 243	4 176	8.2	56.1	14.8	34.4	10 839	21 849	44 149	54 278	1.5	46 442	16.0	22.5	20.8
Jefferson	169	1 483	22 894	17.9	45.8	23.0	149.9	10 954	25 625	53 454	65 414	2.1	52 399	10.6	13.0	12.0
Juneau	218	1 603	5 788	12.7	56.5	12.4	43.8	11 691	23 343	45 297	57 546	1.6	45 167	14.8	24.1	21.9
Kenosha	196	2 037	47 166	13.6	44.9	23.2	326.7	11 024	26 514	54 930	69 060	3.2	51 929	15.8	20.7	18.9
Kewaunee	29	1 215	4 740	14.9	55.3	13.5	37.8	10 727	25 282	53 588	62 206	1.5	52 954	10.0	11.9	10.9
La Crosse	126	2 073	35 153	14.9	35.4	29.9	191.4	11 985	26 271	51 339	64 676	2.5	51 324	14.8	15.0	13.8
Lafayette	47	959	3 816	11.1	54.3	16.5	33.1	11 752	23 483	49 107	59 386	1.8	46 422	11.7	20.2	18.5
Langlade	82	3 103	4 195	20.5	56.3	13.2	36.3	11 658	22 974	42 389	52 012	1.2	42 025	16.1	23.4	20.3
Lincoln	148	1 619	6 353	14.7	51.7	14.5	48.6	10 453	24 669	49 021	56 926	1.2	47 721	12.4	17.9	15.6
Manitowoc	140	1 633	18 810	20.1	50.6	18.7	117.0	10 719	25 825	48 881	60 533	1.7	47 835	10.7	14.5	12.2
Marathon	93	1 536	33 977	13.5	47.7	22.2	219.9	11 071	27 607	53 363	69 186	2.6	51 830	11.1	15.3	14.2
Marinette	60	1 885	9 225	12.5	53.4	13.6	67.6	10 841	23 555	40 490	52 335	1.3	41 446	14.3	20.1	17.6
Marquette	26	1 247	2 916	11.9	57.1	12.9	20.5	11 278	23 490	46 077	55 362	0.8	47 760	11.5	20.6	18.0
Menominee	114	755	1 184	7.1	49.5	15.8	15.9	20 015	14 710	33 333	46 144	0.3	32 769	38.8	58.5	56.0
Milwaukee	919	4 115	272 387	25.4	43.3	28.1	1 637.9	12 389	24 295	43 193	58 861	2.3	42 058	22.4	33.2	32.0
Monroe	145	1 563	10 547	15.5	51.5	17.4	76.3	10 830	23 456	49 774	59 149	1.3	51 411	14.2	22.2	19.9
Oconto	27	404	8 298	8.4	53.3	14.9	48.7	11 212	25 941	51 615	61 854	1.2	52 800	9.7	13.9	12.2
Oneida	185	1 467	6 933	12.5	42.1	23.6	58.7	13 477	27 041	45 759	59 843	2.4	46 773	11.6	18.0	16.8
Outagamie	131	1 482	46 641	16.6	41.8	26.4	346.6	10 210	28 186	58 318	70 780	2.6	57 124	8.6	10.9	9.7
Ozaukee	32	1 034	23 377	26.4	26.4	44.9	139.3	10 833	42 041	75 457	105 314	9.9	74 392	6.0	5.9	5.2
Pepin	68	895	1 616	19.5	52.2	17.1	15.4	13 112	24 367	47 701	57 758	1.9	50 728	12.7	19.9	18.2
Pierce	150	1 443	13 059	9.8	39.0	25.7	78.6	10 516	27 462	59 226	73 090	2.4	60 824	10.6	10.3	9.4
Polk	260	1 082	10 196	8.6	47.5	19.3	84.7	11 227	25 751	48 538	61 415	1.9	49 138	10.5	15.0	13.5
Portage	112	1 579	22 029	7.8	42.9	27.5	95.1	10 026	24 972	50 996	61 850	2.0	51 587	13.8	12.9	10.6
Price	181	1 275	2 600	12.3	53.8	15.3	24.0	11 693	23 723	42 644	50 100	1.1	43 004	15.5	19.6	16.8
Racine	182	2 466	50 036	18.5	45.0	23.0	330.7	11 143	27 141	54 090	68 672	2.8	54 403	13.3	20.3	17.3
Richland	11	636	4 081	20.1	52.9	15.0	19.7	11 420	22 778	45 271	55 133	1.2	43 635	15.7	24.2	21.5
Rock	229	2 482	40 861	13.2	49.2	19.4	306.9	11 026	24 094	49 435	60 186	1.7	49 157	14.3	20.9	19.1
Rusk	141	1 240	2 909	11.5	57.9	14.3	25.9	12 938	21 004	38 658	48 426	0.7	37 350	18.5	29.6	27.2
St. Croix	71	1 299	23 046	13.6	32.7	33.0	141.5	9 883	32 220	68 426	83 941	4.6	69 641	6.3	7.2	6.4
Sauk	124	2 678	14 249	11.9	47.8	21.0	130.1	10 900	25 988	52 140	63 007	1.9	50 923	12.0	16.9	15.2
Sawyer	175	1 597	3 218	10.8	44.3	22.0	27.0	11 945	23 809	39 904	52 525	1.8	40 608	17.6	31.5	29.2
Shawano	67	1 594	9 263	11.7	56.3	15.3	60.6	10 808	23 500	46 559	57 060	1.6	45 953	14.2	20.1	17.2
Sheboygan	142	1 794	29 120	17.9	46.7	22.4	210.0	10 803	26 126	52 920	64 358	1.9	52 106	11.0	15.8	13.5
Taylor	196	1 115	4 832	12.0	59.4	13.6	33.4	10 986	23 032	44 869	54 538	1.4	45 985	13.8	21.2	18.9
Trempealeau	54	753	6 466	8.9	52.8	17.5	64.1	10 972	25 017	49 143	61 182	1.7	50 953	9.9	14.9	14.4
Vernon	72	978	6 851	25.6	50.3	19.5	40.2	11 352	22 680	45 488	57 215	1.4	47 063	13.9	25.7	24.8
Vilas	75	1 065	3 974	10.5	41.9	24.1	41.5	15 314	26 252	40 833	54 316	1.8	40 454	14.4	25.1	22.9
Walworth	79	1 619	28 692	10.6	42.3	26.2	183.3	11 299	27 130	54 020	68 685	2.8	52 610	12.9	15.7	13.7
Washburn	177	2 120	3 003	9.9	47.9	20.3	32.2	12 310	24 850	41 924	54 114	1.4	43 588	13.6	23.9	21.4
Washington	65	1 572	32 770	20.7	38.9	27.6	207.6	10 359	32 020	66 159	80 106	4.0	67 276	7.0	8.2	7.4
Waukesha	72	1 340	101 375	23.2	29.5	40.2	678.3	10 747	37 577	75 850	94 756	7.6	75 652	5.8	6.3	5.6
Waupaca	92	1 803	11 617	13.4	53.9	16.6	98.3	10 976	25 956	50 822	61 887	1.7	48 056	12.3	17.8	14.4
Waushara	82	1 512	4 944	14.1	55.1	14.3	31.3	11 459	22 888	43 070	55 252	1.3	43 175	13.1	21.6	19.8
Winnebago	159	1 721	44 256	11.9	43.8	25.5	232.2	10 204	26 955	51 010	65 606	2.4	50 469	12.6	15.7	14.6
Wood	38	1 770	16 698	13.1	48.7	18.8	144.8	11 516	25 961	47 685	59 667	2.1	48 723	11.7	16.3	14.8
WYOMING	205	2 198	147 363	9.6	37.6	24.7	1 445.3	15 700	28 902	57 406	71 081	2.9	58 424	10.9	13.5	12.0
Albany	117	2 273	16 426	8.9	20.1	48.0	61.1	16 376	24 758	42 774	58 263	2.5	42 443	20.2	14.2	13.6
Big Horn	137	464	2 900	6.0	41.2	21.2	41.8	17 148	25 119	52 589	62 929	1.3	49 052	11.2	15.4	13.3
Campbell	152	2 526	11 931	9.0	45.7	18.8	129.9	14 923	33 850	79 488	90 425	4.4	81 652	7.5	9.2	8.2
Carbon	276	2 185	3 438	10.0	47.0	17.7	44.1	17 597	25 947	55 347	64 704	1.2	54 210	14.2	14.1	11.7
Converse	184	2 054	3 169	13.4	44.7	18.8	39.0	16 117	30 941	63 918	74 086	3.0	62 438	9.4	11.9	10.6

1. Data for serious crimes have not been adjusted for underreporting; this may affect comparability between geographic areas and over time. 2. Per 100,000 population estimated by the FBI.
3. All persons 3 years old and over enrolled in nursery school through college. 4. Persons 25 years old and over. 5. Elementary and secondary education expenditures.
6. Based on population estimated by the American Community Survey, 2009–2013.

STATE County	Personal income, 2013										Earnings, 2013		
			Per capita[1]			Supplements to wages and salaries; employer contributions (mil dol)						Contributions for government social insurance (mil dol)	
	Total (mil dol)	Percent change, 2012–2013	Dollars	Rank	Wages and salaries (mil dol)	Pension and insurance	Government social insurance	Proprietors' income (mil dol)	Dividends, interest, and rent (mil dol)	Personal transfer receipts (mil dol)	Total (mil dol)	From employee and self-employed	From employer
	62	63	64	65	66	67	68	69	70	71	72	73	74
WISCONSIN—Cont'd													
Dodge	3 462	1.7	39 189	1 264	1 464	310	122	405	539	588	2 301	135	122
Door	1 319	2.5	47 300	529	447	104	41	114	373	269	706	45	41
Douglas	1 508	1.4	34 363	2 021	696	165	61	64	255	400	987	63	61
Dunn	1 603	2.0	36 332	1 686	674	176	55	115	252	315	1 020	59	55
Eau Claire	4 151	1.6	40 925	1 062	2 325	498	184	370	778	706	3 377	198	184
Florence	177	1.4	39 186	1 267	26	9	2	3	40	45	40	3	2
Fond du Lac	4 161	2.2	40 873	1 071	1 955	396	165	302	716	739	2 818	169	165
Forest	331	2.6	36 299	1 695	107	37	8	33	60	95	185	12	8
Grant	1 959	4.8	38 351	1 393	681	203	54	255	355	372	1 192	66	54
Green	1 563	4.1	42 136	926	582	136	48	202	271	249	968	54	48
Green Lake	833	2.3	43 915	764	258	61	21	94	216	158	435	26	21
Iowa	1 027	3.0	43 238	821	407	81	35	110	176	153	634	36	35
Iron	258	2.3	43 750	780	52	14	5	54	57	70	125	9	5
Jackson	798	1.4	38 669	1 342	339	88	27	99	122	156	553	31	27
Jefferson	3 207	2.0	37 950	1 439	1 307	296	107	268	516	564	1 978	117	107
Juneau	910	1.2	34 288	2 035	344	91	28	67	158	224	530	32	28
Kenosha	6 439	2.2	38 382	1 391	2 327	507	188	397	906	1 178	3 419	209	188
Kewaunee	825	0.6	40 220	1 147	342	79	23	47	133	141	492	28	23
La Crosse	4 865	2.2	41 681	976	2 906	617	237	273	916	821	4 033	238	237
Lafayette	687	12.7	41 000	1 050	138	39	11	155	129	112	342	15	11
Langlade	771	2.0	39 397	1 242	264	63	22	108	135	193	457	28	22
Lincoln	1 049	3.3	36 564	1 653	419	98	35	66	172	257	618	40	35
Manitowoc	3 334	0.9	41 336	1 012	1 428	306	118	209	615	639	2 061	125	118
Marathon	5 478	2.1	40 454	1 116	2 884	583	236	449	895	905	4 151	245	236
Marinette	1 630	2.4	39 178	1 268	762	175	64	125	281	412	1 125	70	64
Marquette	513	3.9	33 836	2 114	123	33	10	34	91	140	200	14	10
Menominee	132	1.3	30 567	2 615	72	37	5	1	18	44	115	6	5
Milwaukee	39 213	1.3	41 017	1 047	25 041	4 626	1 961	3 242	6 449	8 495	34 869	2 053	1 961
Monroe	1 643	1.9	36 269	1 697	787	198	67	117	307	318	1 170	66	67
Oconto	1 515	2.0	40 603	1 099	298	82	26	119	226	294	525	34	26
Oneida	1 518	1.7	42 524	887	613	132	51	140	341	378	935	61	51
Outagamie	7 372	2.4	40 877	1 069	4 690	870	385	527	1 187	1 046	6 473	379	385
Ozaukee	5 760	0.7	66 164	64	1 830	348	144	292	1 413	569	2 614	159	144
Pepin	296	-0.5	40 279	1 142	81	20	6	28	56	69	136	8	6
Pierce	1 507	0.7	36 788	1 625	373	126	29	102	267	237	629	36	29
Polk	1 653	2.3	38 021	1 429	576	143	48	83	283	370	850	54	48
Portage	2 827	2.7	40 167	1 153	1 408	309	114	197	462	484	2 029	116	114
Price	528	1.7	38 287	1 402	206	51	17	27	114	144	300	20	17
Racine	8 086	1.0	41 458	999	3 481	715	272	307	1 555	1 511	4 775	294	272
Richland	655	5.0	36 998	1 586	227	64	18	62	109	147	372	21	18
Rock	6 117	5.5	38 054	1 425	2 923	570	225	308	1 028	1 228	4 027	250	225
Rusk	457	2.6	31 733	2 443	169	49	15	34	81	140	267	17	15
St. Croix	3 691	1.0	42 950	846	1 240	270	103	184	541	459	1 797	106	103
Sauk	2 560	2.8	40 524	1 109	1 368	281	116	244	439	437	2 009	118	116
Sawyer	655	2.5	39 673	1 208	238	65	20	48	144	184	371	24	20
Shawano	1 513	2.7	36 325	1 689	437	113	36	152	238	335	738	45	36
Sheboygan	5 345	2.0	46 508	587	2 613	497	212	669	1 056	784	3 991	235	212
Taylor	653	1.2	31 678	2 453	292	66	25	70	100	144	454	26	25
Trempealeau	1 143	2.2	38 649	1 346	552	121	45	80	184	228	799	46	45
Vernon	1 010	3.7	33 317	2 201	312	80	25	107	167	224	524	31	25
Vilas	879	2.7	41 147	1 035	234	65	20	67	266	246	387	29	20
Walworth	3 970	2.3	38 566	1 363	1 539	372	129	259	779	687	2 299	136	129
Washburn	614	2.2	39 134	1 275	198	55	16	33	133	186	302	21	16
Washington	6 496	2.6	48 935	421	2 318	444	189	278	1 158	825	3 229	198	189
Waukesha	23 386	1.2	59 379	117	12 387	2 034	982	1 271	4 568	2 557	16 674	999	982
Waupaca	2 119	1.9	40 523	1 110	748	181	62	95	356	472	1 086	68	62
Waushara	883	3.8	36 301	1 694	216	59	17	70	179	209	361	23	17
Winnebago	6 953	1.6	41 008	1 048	4 480	848	351	323	1 307	1 091	6 002	358	351
Wood	3 125	1.0	42 252	914	2 053	391	156	111	511	612	2 711	164	156
WYOMING	30 779	1.7	52 826	X	13 703	2 299	1 355	3 365	8 772	3 778	20 722	1 140	1 355
Albany	1 557	1.4	41 611	982	631	142	61	57	547	202	892	49	61
Big Horn	450	2.1	37 502	1 505	186	37	19	47	110	85	289	16	19
Campbell	2 455	0.1	50 969	332	1 667	233	155	197	488	199	2 253	125	155
Carbon	762	4.5	48 399	458	349	76	36	47	227	100	508	28	36
Converse	733	3.4	51 204	328	319	55	31	60	161	93	465	26	31

1. Based on the resident population estimated as of July 1 of the year shown.

Table B. States and Counties — **Earnings, Social Security, and Housing**

STATE County	Earnings, 2013 (cont.) — Percent by selected industries: Farm	Mining	Construction	Manu-facturing	Infor-mation: professional, scientific, technical services	Retail trade	Finance, insur-ance, real estate and leasing	Health care and social assistance	Govern-ment	Social Security beneficiaries, December 2013: Number	Rate[1]	Supple-mental Security Income recipients, December 2013	Housing units, 2014: Total	Percent change, 2010–2014
	75	76	77	78	79	80	81	82	83	84	85	86	87	88
WISCONSIN—Cont'd														
Dodge	4.3	D	12.9	26.8	2.8	5.3	2.1	10.0	14.8	17 490	198	873	37 370	1.0
Door	3.8	D	7.5	18.7	D	9.7	5.0	12.2	16.4	8 890	319	277	24 351	1.6
Douglas	0.3	D	10.8	10.9	2.9	6.4	2.7	7.4	21.3	9 305	212	1 199	22 892	0.3
Dunn	6.0	0.5	4.7	18.9	3.9	5.6	3.2	D	26.1	9 090	206	744	18 077	0.6
Eau Claire	0.7	D	6.2	9.5	5.9	7.4	7.1	20.0	17.1	19 225	189	1 974	43 043	2.1
Florence	0.8	0.0	5.4	21.6	D	3.9	5.0	6.2	36.4	1 480	328	111	4 809	0.6
Fond du Lac	3.4	0.6	7.3	26.7	4.1	6.4	4.2	12.8	13.6	20 820	205	1 377	44 489	1.3
Forest	0.7	D	3.7	7.5	D	4.7	2.3	D	53.0	2 735	300	234	9 059	1.0
Grant	11.7	D	4.9	12.4	D	6.4	4.4	8.2	27.8	10 845	212	761	21 782	0.9
Green	8.7	D	3.6	23.6	6.5	12.1	2.6	12.8	13.5	7 630	206	425	15 853	0.0
Green Lake	7.3	1.1	8.1	19.5	D	5.7	5.0	14.0	15.4	4 970	262	297	10 632	0.2
Iowa	10.4	D	5.4	9.3	2.3	30.5	2.6	D	13.5	4 900	206	336	10 757	0.4
Iron	1.0	D	8.7	28.1	D	8.1	3.8	8.6	19.0	2 100	357	146	6 011	0.2
Jackson	7.7	D	14.7	10.5	1.2	4.4	2.4	9.7	25.3	4 545	221	431	9 774	0.5
Jefferson	3.4	D	6.1	31.1	4.3	6.3	3.7	9.1	13.2	16 265	192	994	35 293	0.4
Juneau	4.5	0.0	4.2	24.3	1.3	5.7	2.6	D	28.6	6 705	253	616	14 808	0.9
Kenosha	0.7	D	4.1	14.8	5.0	7.4	3.0	13.4	19.7	29 195	174	3 738	69 587	0.4
Kewaunee	10.9	D	4.5	21.1	2.2	3.4	2.5	D	14.9	4 515	221	208	9 337	0.4
La Crosse	0.4	D	4.9	13.0	5.0	6.4	6.3	21.5	16.2	21 625	184	2 144	49 302	1.9
Lafayette	35.0	D	4.4	14.1	D	3.3	2.3	D	17.9	3 530	211	243	7 220	-0.1
Langlade	8.8	D	5.7	17.9	2.2	13.0	3.9	D	15.1	5 685	290	448	12 370	0.1
Lincoln	1.4	D	6.0	26.1	1.7	6.8	11.7	7.0	18.4	7 570	264	443	16 868	0.5
Manitowoc	4.6	0.2	5.3	30.8	2.9	5.2	2.7	11.3	13.5	19 390	241	1 388	37 181	0.0
Marathon	2.1	0.1	5.3	22.5	5.9	7.5	9.8	12.2	12.7	26 915	199	2 160	58 362	1.1
Marinette	3.1	D	4.4	37.4	2.2	6.9	2.9	D	12.2	12 200	294	815	30 403	0.1
Marquette	11.2	0.0	2.9	31.6	2.3	5.0	3.5	D	22.5	4 535	299	260	9 858	-0.4
Menominee	0.0	0.0	0.3	D	D	0.4	D	0.3	96.4	920	210	262	2 256	0.1
Milwaukee	0.0	D	2.6	13.5	10.2	4.6	10.4	14.7	13.8	160 135	167	42 664	417 082	-0.2
Monroe	3.9	1.4	5.8	17.4	2.4	5.4	2.6	7.0	30.8	8 855	196	844	19 528	1.7
Oconto	10.2	0.1	6.1	20.4	D	6.9	2.5	D	21.7	9 255	248	599	23 717	0.8
Oneida	0.7	0.0	8.2	10.4	4.8	14.0	5.3	17.2	16.9	11 560	324	619	30 442	1.1
Outagamie	1.2	0.1	8.2	21.4	7.1	6.3	8.0	11.4	12.4	32 090	178	2 249	75 140	2.7
Ozaukee	0.6	D	4.2	25.5	9.9	5.9	8.9	12.8	10.3	17 785	204	530	36 722	1.3
Pepin	15.8	0.0	8.2	D	D	7.2	3.8	10.4	19.2	2 140	290	105	3 612	0.9
Pierce	6.3	D	4.9	12.3	3.1	4.5	3.8	4.6	39.0	6 825	168	318	16 276	0.9
Polk	3.3	D	4.5	22.7	D	6.5	3.5	16.7	19.8	10 625	245	630	24 279	0.1
Portage	4.9	D	3.0	12.0	4.2	6.9	18.8	9.0	18.3	13 295	188	927	30 363	1.0
Price	2.0	D	1.9	41.2	5.7	5.6	2.7	8.7	17.3	4 315	313	300	11 179	0.5
Racine	0.8	0.1	4.5	34.7	4.5	5.6	4.4	12.0	14.5	39 915	205	5 181	82 265	0.1
Richland	7.2	D	5.1	26.0	D	7.4	2.7	11.5	22.2	4 125	232	414	8 881	0.1
Rock	2.1	0.3	5.7	15.8	4.4	6.5	3.0	16.0	15.6	33 680	210	3 826	68 301	-0.2
Rusk	6.4	D	2.6	26.5	D	5.9	2.5	D	25.2	4 195	292	393	8 994	1.2
St. Croix	2.7	0.1	6.4	21.9	6.4	7.6	5.0	12.9	15.8	13 255	154	680	34 691	2.1
Sauk	3.1	D	10.0	18.0	4.2	8.1	5.4	10.4	16.3	13 385	212	884	29 869	0.5
Sawyer	1.6	D	6.1	10.0	4.1	9.2	4.6	D	31.7	5 315	322	377	16 225	1.6
Shawano	10.4	0.0	5.0	17.6	D	6.9	3.2	9.7	20.4	10 105	243	664	20 714	0.0
Sheboygan	1.3	D	4.5	42.8	2.8	5.5	5.5	11.0	9.9	24 045	209	1 819	50 595	-0.3
Taylor	7.8	D	4.9	22.1	3.4	6.2	3.3	D	13.0	4 300	209	271	10 602	0.2
Trempealeau	7.3	D	2.9	41.9	2.0	4.1	2.6	D	17.0	6 300	213	421	12 770	1.2
Vernon	13.3	0.0	4.6	7.4	D	6.6	4.6	D	19.7	7 055	233	599	13 785	0.5
Vilas	1.1	D	8.7	3.8	2.5	8.4	3.5	6.1	32.4	8 250	386	369	25 443	1.3
Walworth	2.4	D	4.5	24.1	3.5	6.6	3.9	7.5	22.8	19 830	192	1 180	51 696	0.3
Washburn	2.9	0.0	2.6	18.4	D	9.3	2.6	D	27.3	5 185	331	377	13 048	0.5
Washington	1.1	0.2	5.1	29.2	4.5	7.1	7.0	10.6	11.6	25 730	194	903	55 516	1.5
Waukesha	0.1	0.2	7.0	21.2	11.0	6.0	9.1	9.9	7.8	78 270	199	2 828	162 596	1.1
Waupaca	4.5	D	3.9	35.3	3.6	6.2	3.0	9.8	19.5	13 070	250	779	25 456	0.2
Waushara	15.2	D	6.0	13.6	D	6.0	2.4	D	23.8	6 845	281	444	14 895	0.3
Winnebago	0.6	D	5.7	30.7	6.7	4.6	5.0	9.7	13.0	32 275	191	2 562	74 185	1.2
Wood	1.8	D	3.7	14.8	4.0	4.8	2.4	37.8	12.4	17 695	239	1 375	34 405	0.9
WYOMING	1.7	18.1	8.9	3.7	5.4	5.7	5.4	7.0	22.9	99 134	170	6 888	268 222	2.4
Albany	0.7	0.6	4.8	2.1	8.2	6.2	5.2	8.9	49.1	4 265	114	298	18 726	4.4
Big Horn	8.9	16.1	7.3	5.8	D	4.2	2.8	2.1	29.3	2 555	213	149	5 366	-0.2
Campbell	0.4	40.7	7.3	2.1	3.4	4.2	2.4	2.8	14.7	4 715	98	291	19 620	3.5
Carbon	2.7	5.9	11.5	D	4.0	5.8	2.8	D	25.0	2 610	165	160	8 575	0.0
Converse	1.9	30.0	8.3	2.2	3.0	3.7	2.8	D	21.2	2 400	168	150	6 509	1.7

1. Per 1,000 resident population estimated as of July 1 of the year shown.

STATE County	Housing units, 2009–2013: Occupied units: Total	Owner-occupied: Percent	Owner-occupied: Median value[1]	Owner-occupied: Median owner cost as a percent of income: With a mortgage	Owner-occupied: Median owner cost as a percent of income: Without a mortgage[2]	Renter-occupied: Median rent[3]	Renter-occupied: Median rent as a percent of income[2]	Substandard units[4] (percent)	Civilian labor force, 2014: Total	Civilian labor force, 2014: Percent change, 2013–2014	Unemployment: Total	Unemployment: Rate[5]	Civilian employment,[6] 2009–2013: Total	Percent: Management, business, science and arts	Percent: Construction, production, and maintenance occupations
	89	90	91	92	93	94	95	96	97	98	99	100	101	102	103
WISCONSIN—Cont'd															
Dodge	33 173	74.1	154 000	25.1	14.6	743	26.1	1.3	47 254	-0.5	2 646	5.6	42 873	27.0	35.4
Door	13 459	78.2	192 200	24.9	14.7	696	27.3	2.1	15 556	-1.2	1 273	8.2	13 882	30.1	24.6
Douglas	18 933	67.8	130 600	22.8	12.9	672	29.9	2.2	23 672	0.2	1 361	5.7	21 676	30.4	23.5
Dunn	16 222	68.1	156 200	24.3	13.4	703	28.7	1.9	23 614	0.1	1 254	5.3	21 949	30.0	27.7
Eau Claire	39 754	63.5	150 000	22.4	12.8	699	31.3	2.2	58 324	0.5	2 671	4.6	53 538	33.4	20.0
Florence	1 767	87.5	131 100	25.6	14.0	635	24.2	1.9	2 226	1.4	166	7.5	1 912	26.5	34.7
Fond du Lac	41 267	70.7	145 800	23.0	13.3	683	26.7	2.9	57 371	0.3	2 891	5.0	52 808	28.1	33.7
Forest	3 739	76.2	122 400	24.6	13.9	456	22.5	3.0	4 009	-1.7	351	8.8	3 702	26.1	31.8
Grant	19 420	71.8	124 800	22.4	13.0	642	27.4	1.5	27 616	-0.3	1 326	4.8	25 743	29.0	31.0
Green	14 640	75.2	158 300	24.0	15.1	674	27.8	2.3	21 112	1.0	964	4.6	19 513	30.8	29.9
Green Lake	8 001	75.9	140 500	24.2	13.0	575	24.9	1.6	10 150	-0.8	664	6.5	9 216	24.4	35.8
Iowa	9 610	77.3	160 500	24.7	14.8	695	26.1	4.2	13 675	0.8	709	5.2	12 593	31.6	27.8
Iron	2 953	80.1	108 300	23.2	14.4	486	28.1	4.0	2 726	-0.3	263	9.6	2 577	28.6	28.2
Jackson	8 112	73.8	124 000	24.6	14.7	610	27.6	1.5	10 116	-0.6	617	6.1	9 065	28.1	30.2
Jefferson	32 137	70.9	176 900	25.0	14.8	746	28.2	2.7	45 981	-0.1	2 385	5.2	43 453	29.8	29.4
Juneau	10 194	76.0	116 000	25.2	14.3	668	28.3	2.2	13 373	-1.1	895	6.7	11 890	23.9	31.0
Kenosha	62 560	67.5	169 600	25.2	14.8	829	31.8	1.6	87 594	0.2	5 369	6.1	78 420	33.1	25.0
Kewaunee	8 145	81.0	149 000	23.9	13.9	619	26.5	1.8	10 983	0.2	560	5.1	10 194	27.0	38.6
La Crosse	45 949	65.0	154 700	22.0	13.0	726	29.3	2.3	66 659	-0.4	2 933	4.4	61 532	34.9	21.9
Lafayette	6 605	78.1	121 800	24.9	14.4	606	25.0	4.7	9 368	0.0	406	4.3	8 725	29.0	34.7
Langlade	8 758	76.2	108 000	22.3	13.2	600	34.1	2.1	9 722	-1.0	733	7.5	9 252	25.2	32.6
Lincoln	12 513	77.1	129 100	22.2	13.2	600	28.4	1.5	15 075	-1.0	978	6.5	13 982	24.9	35.1
Manitowoc	34 067	76.5	125 200	22.3	13.2	588	25.7	2.3	42 493	-0.7	2 642	6.2	40 731	25.4	36.2
Marathon	53 079	74.0	142 300	22.1	12.5	692	27.9	1.9	73 096	1.1	3 762	5.1	69 232	32.4	29.0
Marinette	18 573	77.5	108 200	23.0	14.3	582	28.2	1.8	21 371	-0.6	1 465	6.9	18 551	23.5	37.7
Marquette	6 453	79.9	142 000	25.7	15.4	723	26.0	7.1	7 513	-0.1	538	7.2	6 876	22.8	36.1
Menominee	1 220	71.2	88 500	19.3	12.4	503	21.6	3.1	1 540	-2.3	202	13.1	1 325	24.6	23.1
Milwaukee	379 637	51.3	158 400	25.1	15.7	792	32.6	4.0	480 920	0.2	33 647	7.0	436 143	34.5	21.1
Monroe	17 543	68.2	135 300	23.1	12.6	743	25.9	1.4	22 584	-0.9	1 235	5.5	21 124	28.2	32.6
Oconto	15 701	83.1	147 700	24.0	14.1	590	28.4	0.6	20 504	0.1	1 281	6.2	18 813	27.2	36.0
Oneida	15 797	81.4	165 200	24.9	14.4	714	31.9	1.8	18 418	-1.2	1 301	7.1	16 679	28.7	26.2
Outagamie	69 572	72.3	155 700	22.4	13.0	723	25.4	0.5	101 302	0.6	4 931	4.9	94 110	32.5	27.5
Ozaukee	34 108	77.8	250 200	22.8	12.6	812	27.2	2.6	47 942	0.7	2 072	4.3	44 704	45.4	17.0
Pepin	3 085	77.4	134 800	24.6	14.9	589	27.4	1.7	4 042	0.1	197	4.9	3 689	30.3	31.8
Pierce	15 069	73.7	191 300	24.6	13.9	758	29.2	1.8	24 371	1.4	1 095	4.5	22 641	30.2	29.7
Polk	18 266	78.2	159 100	27.1	14.8	708	29.1	1.7	24 296	-0.3	1 438	5.9	21 131	28.7	33.4
Portage	27 975	68.6	145 600	21.7	12.0	669	29.6	3.0	38 892	-0.3	2 211	5.7	35 857	30.4	25.0
Price	6 776	78.5	114 100	23.9	14.3	573	28.1	1.8	6 795	-1.0	368	5.4	6 727	27.5	38.3
Racine	75 087	69.5	170 100	24.1	14.6	759	31.3	3.8	100 103	0.1	6 760	6.8	89 785	32.6	27.2
Richland	7 343	75.1	124 000	24.6	13.7	617	28.8	1.9	9 325	-0.4	480	5.1	8 624	26.2	36.5
Rock	63 309	71.1	133 000	24.1	13.3	743	31.4	3.1	83 165	1.0	5 177	6.2	74 771	29.3	29.8
Rusk	6 430	76.7	106 800	24.7	14.2	622	28.1	2.0	6 675	-1.1	472	7.1	6 473	24.4	38.9
St. Croix	32 114	77.8	206 900	23.7	13.0	860	29.0	1.9	48 527	1.3	2 192	4.5	44 635	37.7	23.8
Sauk	25 206	70.1	168 800	23.7	14.0	742	29.0	4.0	35 321	-0.4	1 786	5.1	32 634	27.8	28.1
Sawyer	7 663	75.3	162 500	25.6	14.0	614	30.3	1.9	8 061	-1.6	721	8.9	7 281	29.8	24.6
Shawano	17 245	75.6	129 900	23.6	14.6	617	25.7	1.4	21 346	-0.7	1 290	6.0	19 959	27.3	31.7
Sheboygan	46 312	71.8	152 300	22.4	14.0	658	26.7	3.0	61 603	1.2	2 844	4.6	58 459	29.1	31.8
Taylor	8 761	76.9	126 100	24.9	13.9	558	28.8	2.5	10 949	-0.7	591	5.4	10 057	27.4	42.0
Trempealeau	11 745	74.4	135 200	23.5	14.3	618	24.8	6.0	16 387	-0.4	772	4.7	14 790	30.0	36.7
Vernon	11 790	78.7	138 200	24.2	13.7	615	26.1	1.3	15 083	-0.5	746	4.9	13 372	31.3	32.1
Vilas	10 636	77.0	186 000	27.6	15.2	677	29.0	3.0	10 062	-1.3	867	8.6	9 166	31.4	21.5
Walworth	39 929	68.7	194 900	25.9	14.2	816	30.6	2.6	56 765	-0.2	3 218	5.7	51 863	30.8	26.7
Washburn	7 348	79.8	146 000	25.6	14.5	631	30.2	1.0	7 966	-0.6	513	6.4	6 849	30.0	29.0
Washington	52 053	77.4	222 900	23.8	13.9	820	26.5	1.1	75 840	0.6	3 516	4.6	70 631	35.0	26.5
Waukesha	153 422	76.9	253 800	23.0	13.4	908	27.8	1.8	220 918	0.6	9 995	4.5	205 338	43.1	17.4
Waupaca	21 388	76.1	136 300	23.3	14.2	657	25.4	2.5	27 225	-0.6	1 586	5.8	25 363	25.2	37.7
Waushara	9 902	81.1	136 800	25.3	14.4	644	29.1	1.4	11 745	-0.8	841	7.2	10 532	24.0	36.0
Winnebago	68 140	66.3	141 300	22.2	13.4	659	27.0	1.5	91 977	0.2	4 880	5.3	84 082	30.2	26.6
Wood	32 037	74.5	119 300	21.5	12.2	582	28.4	1.5	38 800	-0.7	2 356	6.1	36 283	29.3	29.8
WYOMING	222 846	70.1	185 900	21.5	10.0	764	25.8	2.5	306 928	0.1	13 239	4.3	289 823	32.4	28.3
Albany	15 257	51.3	201 500	22.0	10.0	726	38.1	3.0	20 558	-0.7	733	3.6	20 051	45.3	16.4
Big Horn	4 462	75.7	131 000	21.1	10.0	601	19.9	3.0	5 646	1.1	263	4.7	5 223	33.3	33.6
Campbell	17 108	74.9	201 900	19.7	10.0	912	24.0	2.9	26 328	2.4	916	3.5	26 045	24.7	41.1
Carbon	6 077	73.7	143 500	20.0	10.0	777	21.8	2.3	8 426	0.5	350	4.2	7 807	27.3	34.7
Converse	5 746	76.2	180 900	20.4	10.0	660	22.5	2.2	8 348	2.9	265	3.2	7 455	26.3	41.6

1. Specified owner-occupied units. 2. A value of 10.0 represents 10 percent or less; a value of 50.0 represents 50 percent or more. 3. Specified renter-occupied units.
4. Overcrowded or lacking complete plumbing facilities. 5. Percent of civilian labor force. 6. Persons 16 years old and over.

STATE County	Private nonfarm establishments, employment and payroll, 2013									Agriculture, 2012			
		Employment						Annual payroll		Farms			
											Percent with:		
	Number of establish-ments	Total	Health care and social assistance	Manufac-turing	Retail trade	Finance and insurance	Professional, scientific, and technical services	Total (mil dol)	Average per employee (dollars)	Number	Fewer than 50 acres	500 acres or more	Farm operators whose principal occu-pation is farming (percent)
	104	105	106	107	108	109	110	111	112	113	114	115	116
WISCONSIN—Cont'd													
Dodge	1 738	30 589	4 469	9 842	3 210	704	488	1 516	49 565	2 012	36.9	9.7	47.5
Door	1 305	10 366	1 639	2 198	1 684	320	239	353	34 022	803	40.6	6.2	45.0
Douglas	1 026	13 173	1 760	1 456	2 083	D	418	489	37 113	364	29.4	5.8	42.0
Dunn	888	13 346	2 673	2 556	1 752	D	389	475	35 561	1 404	24.0	12.0	45.4
Eau Claire	2 673	48 223	10 995	4 725	6 918	2 885	1 900	1 729	35 849	1 313	31.7	4.0	42.3
Florence	103	583	D	D	D	D	D	14	23 772	90	31.1	0.0	38.9
Fond du Lac	2 365	40 881	6 337	8 625	5 553	1 611	1 467	1 481	36 223	1 399	31.9	10.7	59.0
Forest	254	1 658	256	257	287	D	D	47	28 059	127	21.3	9.4	54.3
Grant	1 218	13 511	2 276	2 348	2 439	651	480	428	31 652	2 436	25.6	10.7	53.8
Green	915	13 021	2 009	3 570	1 541	345	282	457	35 101	1 545	42.0	7.4	45.8
Green Lake	491	5 703	1 080	1 319	938	279	83	203	35 656	608	26.8	13.2	48.4
Iowa	554	8 287	1 018	978	D	179	123	313	37 721	1 588	25.8	9.9	47.2
Iron	216	1 467	318	193	230	28	30	35	23 690	61	34.4	8.2	32.8
Jackson	429	5 965	D	741	772	193	D	244	40 837	864	23.0	11.5	49.4
Jefferson	1 906	29 052	4 189	8 778	3 824	661	626	1 018	35 034	1 225	39.7	6.9	46.1
Juneau	550	6 349	1 062	2 150	958	D	D	221	34 828	827	29.7	8.1	39.4
Kenosha	3 025	48 460	8 585	6 099	8 913	949	1 198	1 727	35 635	359	51.5	11.1	46.8
Kewaunee	452	5 199	459	1 889	544	D	154	234	45 034	734	27.9	9.4	49.7
La Crosse	3 011	59 715	11 701	7 107	8 720	2 087	1 837	2 134	35 741	748	23.7	10.0	46.9
Lafayette	362	2 859	237	675	408	150	D	82	28 607	1 252	28.9	13.1	57.1
Langlade	553	6 275	1 033	1 498	1 303	244	110	213	33 915	396	24.2	14.6	56.3
Lincoln	664	8 520	1 037	2 353	1 252	D	120	303	35 594	449	28.1	6.2	48.8
Manitowoc	1 756	29 609	4 497	10 020	3 530	723	628	1 142	38 579	1 224	39.1	7.9	47.7
Marathon	3 281	60 858	9 475	14 885	9 861	3 879	1 960	2 279	37 456	2 266	23.2	7.5	55.0
Marinette	1 080	16 236	2 762	6 217	2 065	458	244	575	35 395	535	31.2	11.8	51.6
Marquette	290	3 618	362	1 283	300	D	D	108	29 923	478	28.0	9.2	52.1
Menominee	26	D	D	NA	NA	NA	D	D	D	5	60.0	0.0	0.0
Milwaukee	19 389	443 721	88 160	48 204	42 661	35 808	22 447	21 672	48 843	82	76.8	2.4	59.8
Monroe	959	14 838	D	3 408	1 852	421	478	548	36 963	1 926	25.7	6.1	44.3
Oconto	757	6 815	1 553	2 041	886	D	170	209	30 720	929	35.1	9.1	48.1
Oneida	1 338	13 433	3 036	1 290	3 408	333	D	462	34 366	150	43.3	9.3	28.0
Outagamie	4 899	95 420	11 865	17 089	12 709	5 479	3 180	3 948	41 378	1 170	38.7	10.7	56.0
Ozaukee	2 732	36 758	5 480	8 517	4 667	1 835	2 291	1 531	41 656	416	38.5	7.0	53.4
Pepin	219	1 656	278	116	245	78	44	59	35 911	459	22.9	10.0	47.3
Pierce	788	6 442	965	1 057	957	295	201	202	31 315	1 259	31.6	7.8	52.2
Polk	1 110	11 464	2 506	3 311	1 820	263	349	373	32 565	1 313	30.1	8.1	47.8
Portage	1 615	28 001	3 765	3 570	3 815	4 181	948	1 058	37 796	969	27.1	11.8	51.2
Price	428	4 605	923	1 826	584	D	85	159	34 563	472	26.1	7.8	47.2
Racine	3 976	67 537	11 283	15 846	8 576	2 052	1 970	2 953	43 731	575	51.0	8.2	45.6
Richland	366	4 845	D	1 621	845	156	60	146	30 188	1 260	27.9	6.7	44.4
Rock	3 202	54 042	9 832	9 029	8 511	1 713	1 106	2 083	38 549	1 509	44.1	10.3	50.0
Rusk	318	4 253	828	1 588	602	101	D	131	30 689	529	16.8	10.0	62.9
St. Croix	2 133	27 935	3 948	6 081	4 225	866	1 325	988	35 364	1 417	39.0	8.0	41.6
Sauk	1 781	29 550	3 776	5 276	3 922	866	977	1 024	34 650	1 665	29.1	8.2	51.2
Sawyer	660	4 920	767	622	911	193	144	162	32 830	172	26.7	11.0	47.1
Shawano	898	10 047	1 524	2 175	1 493	290	205	312	31 073	1 278	26.7	8.1	54.4
Sheboygan	2 655	49 417	6 330	15 979	5 928	1 913	1 228	1 961	39 687	986	42.4	10.1	52.7
Taylor	484	7 048	1 014	2 409	D	284	112	225	31 966	967	25.9	8.8	52.7
Trempealeau	648	11 920	1 236	6 124	1 016	306	216	430	36 070	1 436	26.5	9.5	48.7
Vernon	610	6 925	1 823	D	1 151	D	170	207	29 938	2 228	31.7	4.2	49.2
Vilas	924	5 247	519	281	1 027	203	85	147	27 925	47	59.6	6.4	40.4
Walworth	2 589	33 511	4 201	8 335	4 439	784	1 008	1 114	33 245	870	45.3	11.1	51.8
Washburn	519	4 383	1 004	1 021	713	123	191	118	26 826	405	27.4	7.4	39.8
Washington	3 173	49 387	5 945	13 847	6 949	2 010	1 792	1 941	39 299	712	43.3	8.6	51.4
Waukesha	12 424	222 812	26 275	43 358	24 447	13 658	12 994	10 863	48 755	557	54.0	7.7	51.2
Waupaca	1 209	15 799	2 562	5 631	2 350	541	277	543	34 340	1 145	30.0	7.9	49.8
Waushara	480	4 807	836	989	674	122	172	135	27 995	592	27.2	9.6	44.6
Winnebago	3 489	83 823	13 058	21 891	8 171	3 182	2 532	4 003	47 754	1 117	48.5	6.0	39.2
Wood	1 762	34 380	9 655	5 934	4 239	1 274	549	1 476	42 927	1 067	27.8	9.3	56.7
WYOMING	20 620	212 636	32 229	9 986	30 004	6 652	9 301	9 773	45 962	11 736	28.8	36.3	49.8
Albany	1 024	9 773	2 101	348	1 740	463	746	307	31 439	448	26.8	45.5	40.4
Big Horn	301	2 664	D	D	384	85	D	102	38 310	627	32.1	26.6	54.4
Campbell	1 470	22 950	1 830	573	2 493	D	631	1 323	57 640	744	30.4	44.9	36.4
Carbon	530	4 012	565	D	688	D	109	167	41 515	319	16.3	59.9	60.2
Converse	475	4 712	633	D	420	D	111	234	49 742	410	18.3	51.7	57.8

STATE County	Agriculture, 2012 (cont.) — Land in farms: Acreage (1,000)	Land in farms: Percent change, 2007–2012	Land in farms — Acres: Average size of farm	Acres: Total irrigated (1,000)	Acres: Total cropland (1,000)	Value of land and buildings (dollars): Average per farm	Value of land and buildings (dollars): Average per acre	Value of machinery and equipment, average per farm (dollars)	Value of products sold: Total (mil dol)	Value of products sold: Average per farm (dollars)	Value of products sold — Percent from: Crops	Percent from: Livestock and poultry products	Percent of farms with sales of: $10,000 or more	Percent of farms with sales of: $100,000 or more	Government payments: Total ($1,000)	Government payments: Percent of farms
	117	118	119	120	121	122	123	124	125	126	127	128	129	130	131	132
WISCONSIN—Cont'd																
Dodge	402	-2.6	200	0.8	332.6	1 069 970	5 355	169 021	373.5	185 612	45.8	54.2	57.6	30.2	7 872	58.2
Door	132	-1.9	164	0.9	94.3	668 813	4 070	99 567	82.6	102 905	46.1	53.9	45.0	16.4	1 826	50.7
Douglas	71	-2.9	194	0.1	29.1	336 918	1 738	55 228	7.8	21 434	52.1	48.0	25.0	5.5	74	4.9
Dunn	372	-2.7	265	36.3	252.5	879 304	3 316	141 909	263.2	187 452	48.9	51.1	52.4	23.5	4 915	59.5
Eau Claire	204	-0.8	155	3.1	128.8	465 939	3 003	79 664	113.3	86 287	49.6	50.4	43.0	15.2	3 239	52.9
Florence	13	-33.9	149	0.0	4.9	463 544	3 115	43 489	1.0	11 067	D	D	24.4	1.1	28	26.7
Fond du Lac	316	-6.0	226	2.1	262.1	1 128 100	5 001	182 828	412.3	294 743	26.9	73.1	62.2	37.8	7 648	74.2
Forest	30	-10.5	238	D	10.3	490 488	2 059	82 496	2.9	22 449	62.0	38.0	28.3	3.1	33	15.7
Grant	588	-3.8	241	1.3	361.3	1 004 051	4 163	147 729	404.8	166 171	31.9	68.1	58.2	31.1	11 713	70.4
Green	302	-1.5	196	3.4	238.6	855 977	4 375	130 524	200.3	129 669	36.3	63.7	47.4	25.6	6 293	61.5
Green Lake	155	8.3	254	4.6	119.9	1 155 334	4 544	166 630	102.5	168 615	59.6	40.4	58.7	26.5	1 945	55.6
Iowa	351	-3.9	221	4.6	198.2	881 751	3 991	116 704	195.3	123 008	29.9	70.1	47.4	22.0	7 074	74.4
Iron	10	1.0	167	0.2	4.9	386 016	2 307	91 934	5.6	91 967	D	D	24.6	8.2	63	13.1
Jackson	240	0.4	278	7.2	139.3	859 022	3 093	155 612	169.6	196 263	53.2	46.8	54.5	27.0	3 186	60.1
Jefferson	228	-6.7	186	9.5	181.8	964 365	5 184	134 604	256.1	209 024	42.4	57.6	53.2	22.7	4 367	68.7
Juneau	180	-0.6	218	7.4	108.8	670 272	3 079	129 543	124.8	150 871	62.5	37.5	45.2	17.0	2 210	56.5
Kenosha	77	-9.1	213	0.2	68.1	1 075 507	5 038	145 295	68.9	191 827	70.1	29.9	51.3	28.4	1 592	46.8
Kewaunee	177	0.7	241	0.2	144.7	1 047 736	4 351	177 185	276.6	376 865	21.3	78.7	59.3	34.3	4 137	72.6
La Crosse	159	-4.0	212	1.0	86.9	709 759	3 345	118 472	86.5	115 671	44.7	55.3	53.5	21.4	2 565	62.7
Lafayette	369	7.6	294	0.2	276.1	1 440 604	4 895	191 424	287.3	229 493	34.4	65.6	62.1	35.8	8 268	73.6
Langlade	114	-7.3	288	19.7	73.1	796 227	2 769	178 447	103.9	262 381	58.4	41.6	51.8	28.0	1 114	48.0
Lincoln	77	-11.4	171	0.2	38.2	422 924	2 471	75 920	29.9	66 588	33.6	66.3	41.0	10.9	415	26.9
Manitowoc	231	-7.1	189	1.1	186.9	995 194	5 279	142 426	343.8	280 845	21.8	78.2	52.9	29.5	5 698	64.4
Marathon	479	-2.4	211	6.2	320.1	616 429	2 916	136 874	391.1	172 605	24.8	75.2	61.9	32.7	6 615	48.5
Marinette	132	-8.5	247	2.8	84.7	749 350	3 035	124 665	101.4	189 608	28.7	71.3	44.5	22.2	1 557	41.7
Marquette	120	-11.6	251	8.5	84.2	862 079	3 429	127 736	69.7	145 774	54.9	45.1	43.1	15.7	1 410	45.6
Menominee	1	76.4	112	0.0	0.4	144 200	1 285	29 200	0.0	4 200	0.0	100.0	0.0	0.0	D	20.0
Milwaukee	5	-16.4	56	0.1	3.5	526 354	9 459	56 915	7.6	92 878	99.6	0.4	57.3	19.5	64	19.5
Monroe	338	-3.8	175	4.3	173.2	562 429	3 206	98 238	202.0	104 903	45.4	54.6	50.4	17.2	4 423	50.9
Oconto	189	-8.0	204	1.2	141.0	667 081	3 272	114 002	165.9	178 589	39.2	60.8	48.2	26.5	2 856	54.6
Oneida	35	-10.8	233	3.0	12.1	975 653	4 190	86 700	20.2	134 973	84.8	15.2	30.7	12.7	D	12.0
Outagamie	251	1.3	214	0.4	210.1	1 129 579	5 271	174 059	302.2	258 319	34.9	65.1	60.2	37.2	5 994	65.0
Ozaukee	65	-8.1	156	0.3	51.7	876 038	5 608	110 024	64.7	155 505	37.4	62.6	55.5	25.7	1 218	51.0
Pepin	104	-4.4	226	3.6	63.0	741 634	3 286	130 987	71.7	156 288	38.8	61.2	58.4	27.5	1 966	69.7
Pierce	246	-9.3	195	0.5	166.3	773 024	3 957	130 292	178.7	141 902	52.8	47.2	50.8	25.3	4 639	62.0
Polk	256	-11.4	195	1.5	159.9	555 723	2 851	93 011	167.0	127 214	40.5	59.5	42.3	18.3	3 252	51.0
Portage	279	-1.0	288	92.5	201.4	946 737	3 292	203 829	295.1	304 528	71.8	28.2	53.3	23.3	2 782	52.0
Price	92	-9.9	196	D	39.4	371 648	1 901	65 871	31.6	66 892	22.8	77.2	38.3	10.6	537	25.0
Racine	110	-8.7	191	1.9	92.6	1 042 289	5 450	127 732	94.8	164 887	77.6	22.4	50.3	21.7	1 972	50.6
Richland	228	-10.2	181	1.7	111.8	544 504	3 011	83 011	115.5	91 628	28.2	71.8	41.9	14.6	2 969	63.1
Rock	354	2.7	234	16.2	303.7	1 294 782	5 523	154 109	274.4	181 858	60.4	39.6	49.8	23.5	7 892	68.2
Rusk	134	-16.8	253	0.1	70.1	514 170	2 036	104 786	64.2	121 367	28.4	71.6	58.6	24.8	1 236	47.6
St. Croix	268	-13.2	189	8.3	196.1	793 838	4 202	115 975	214.3	151 251	50.1	49.9	49.4	20.5	4 492	59.6
Sauk	333	-7.3	200	19.7	209.8	775 477	3 881	132 189	207.1	124 356	34.4	65.6	49.4	22.3	5 597	57.4
Sawyer	44	-7.5	253	1.0	21.9	580 750	2 293	124 134	25.3	147 145	40.0	60.0	48.3	20.3	552	32.0
Shawano	261	-3.9	204	0.3	183.5	734 011	3 592	133 984	254.1	198 858	26.0	74.0	61.4	33.6	4 470	61.8
Sheboygan	190	-0.8	193	0.2	155.9	1 011 178	5 243	162 747	242.1	245 507	27.1	72.9	59.2	29.8	3 790	51.4
Taylor	217	-10.7	224	0.1	120.0	491 262	2 189	102 087	136.5	141 155	24.7	75.3	51.3	26.1	2 265	43.2
Trempealeau	323	-5.3	225	7.9	197.8	719 451	3 197	124 753	268.9	187 243	32.6	67.4	52.3	24.4	4 772	67.7
Vernon	346	-3.1	155	0.5	181.5	512 496	3 301	76 915	221.4	99 359	32.2	67.8	52.4	16.3	3 703	46.0
Vilas	7	-30.8	146	1.0	2.8	783 574	5 352	94 830	10.2	216 894	95.6	4.4	40.4	17.0	42	21.3
Walworth	188	-13.7	216	2.8	163.9	1 323 506	6 134	154 289	168.6	193 830	46.9	53.1	53.8	23.8	4 539	60.2
Washburn	87	-14.2	216	0.8	38.2	535 677	2 483	81 933	32.5	80 294	48.1	51.9	36.0	12.3	494	33.6
Washington	133	2.8	187	0.5	107.3	1 093 001	5 832	165 548	122.7	172 313	39.9	60.1	55.3	25.8	2 609	48.0
Waukesha	92	6.5	166	1.3	75.6	1 080 562	6 527	104 210	55.1	98 860	75.9	24.1	40.6	16.9	1 587	33.9
Waupaca	215	-8.1	188	7.0	141.5	722 332	3 841	120 088	160.0	139 767	31.6	68.4	50.8	22.7	4 066	53.5
Waushara	145	-2.5	245	39.9	108.7	848 429	3 459	129 704	134.1	226 603	77.6	22.4	50.7	19.4	1 156	40.4
Winnebago	156	-5.2	139	0.4	126.2	585 332	4 204	97 747	126.6	113 315	41.3	58.7	41.5	20.1	3 245	54.3
Wood	223	0.3	209	6.2	132.9	656 817	3 147	127 231	160.3	150 256	53.2	46.8	59.0	26.1	2 887	48.2
WYOMING	30 364	0.6	2 587	1 435.7	2 418.9	1 759 200	680	114 212	1 689.4	143 952	26.0	74.0	48.8	23.5	28 146	23.9
Albany	1 964	5.8	4 385	94.4	120.4	2 466 013	562	99 815	93.4	208 509	8.6	91.4	48.0	23.2	473	8.5
Big Horn	303	-30.9	483	108.7	99.2	736 719	1 527	116 603	88.8	141 684	59.7	40.3	48.5	23.0	900	32.7
Campbell	2 878	22.7	3 868	1.8	140.7	2 239 153	579	94 640	67.2	90 269	5.3	94.7	41.4	18.7	2 305	20.6
Carbon	2 374	9.3	7 442	165.5	126.4	4 187 091	563	144 317	78.6	246 326	14.3	85.7	56.4	37.0	362	6.0
Converse	2 447	3.4	5 969	31.9	60.9	2 256 332	378	125 300	48.6	118 507	12.7	87.3	57.1	27.3	1 303	15.9

STATE County	Water use, 2010		Wholesale trade,[1] 2007				Retail trade,[2] 2007				Real estate and rental and leasing,[2] 2007			
	Total water withdrawn (mil gal/day)	Gallons withdrawn per person per day	Number of establish-ments	Number of employees	Sales (mil dol)	Annual payroll (mil dol)	Number of establish-ments	Number of employees	Sales (mil dol)	Annual payroll (mil dol)	Number of establish-ments	Number of employees	Receipts (mil dol)	Annual payroll (mil dol)
	133	134	135	136	137	138	139	140	141	142	143	144	145	146
WISCONSIN—Cont'd														
Dodge	12.3	138	68	1 064	557.8	35.5	238	3 387	735.7	68.5	50	136	14.0	2.6
Door	5.1	183	27	112	40.5	4.5	284	1 771	406.3	38.7	53	201	19.2	3.9
Douglas	7.0	159	48	D	D	D	163	2 174	504.5	48.9	34	96	10.8	1.8
Dunn	19.2	437	39	D	D	D	125	1 640	381.8	33.0	25	75	6.6	1.3
Eau Claire	13.9	141	104	1 899	909.8	72.6	442	7 608	1 512.5	144.2	109	683	76.8	14.4
Florence	0.2	43	6	D	D	D	17	77	21.4	1.3	2	D	D	D
Fond du Lac	14.4	142	104	1 330	993.6	59.5	407	5 999	1 277.7	118.3	77	305	34.3	5.3
Forest	0.8	89	7	40	10.4	1.3	35	301	56.6	4.5	6	29	3.4	0.3
Grant	136.9	2 673	62	481	210.6	16.3	204	2 190	480.1	41.5	50	148	9.6	2.3
Green	7.5	203	48	D	D	D	155	2 338	766.6	72.2	18	63	7.2	1.3
Green Lake	11.8	620	16	95	30.6	2.8	91	1 180	252.9	23.0	13	51	4.7	0.6
Iowa	7.8	330	28	252	150.6	12.5	108	4 385	1 707.9	164.1	13	D	D	D
Iron	2.1	357	7	90	16.3	1.9	34	318	74.6	6.5	9	26	3.8	0.4
Jackson	18.0	882	12	133	31.2	3.5	74	966	251.0	17.4	16	30	5.7	0.5
Jefferson	17.3	207	74	D	D	D	296	4 179	857.2	76.4	74	292	33.2	5.8
Juneau	19.1	718	21	154	51.9	3.8	95	983	284.5	19.9	15	66	3.8	0.8
Kenosha	30.2	181	108	1 805	1 547.8	89.0	526	7 504	1 800.6	165.7	148	629	87.3	12.9
Kewaunee	550.9	26 778	10	73	15.1	2.0	80	640	152.9	12.1	7	9	0.6	0.1
La Crosse	34.9	304	129	D	D	D	449	8 676	1 799.7	166.7	125	604	82.5	14.9
Lafayette	3.4	201	16	209	88.8	7.9	51	452	96.8	8.8	7	11	0.8	0.1
Langlade	22.3	1 115	28	310	438.8	14.0	109	1 350	309.2	30.6	18	56	6.6	1.6
Lincoln	14.1	491	19	D	D	D	133	1 395	289.5	25.9	19	73	7.1	2.4
Manitowoc	787.1	9 664	65	D	D	D	302	3 808	815.5	74.5	49	346	21.6	5.4
Marathon	126.8	946	184	2 965	1 146.4	122.1	505	10 000	2 139.1	196.5	99	473	75.4	11.9
Marinette	15.5	370	32	D	D	D	214	2 616	526.9	47.4	19	44	8.9	0.7
Marquette	6.4	414	9	47	12.2	1.3	45	352	79.7	6.4	13	27	2.2	0.3
Menominee	0.5	121	NA	NA	NA	NA	3	33	5.2	0.4	1	D	D	D
Milwaukee	1 753.0	1 850	904	17 503	10 955.3	871.9	2 889	46 927	10 207.3	1 006.5	808	5 418	1 080.4	205.4
Monroe	44.0	984	38	432	306.1	18.2	161	1 985	502.2	41.5	29	141	16.9	2.8
Oconto	6.4	170	25	98	28.4	2.6	123	969	257.5	18.8	30	94	7.6	1.6
Oneida	17.2	479	34	465	186.7	20.5	254	3 527	921.2	81.3	56	256	45.9	5.2
Outagamie	67.2	380	272	4 467	3 528.1	222.3	794	13 406	2 903.0	272.2	147	793	152.3	24.0
Ozaukee	473.9	5 485	160	1 751	707.5	84.4	331	4 584	976.5	99.3	111	362	57.4	9.1
Pepin	3.2	432	9	250	134.7	7.8	40	320	90.0	6.9	4	4	1.3	0.2
Pierce	5.7	139	21	D	D	D	99	959	208.5	18.2	35	51	5.1	1.3
Polk	9.6	218	26	355	134.3	12.9	197	2 069	423.2	39.7	40	82	7.7	1.1
Portage	79.6	1 137	71	D	D	D	257	4 518	937.9	86.4	56	268	31.6	6.9
Price	15.4	1 085	16	100	31.0	3.8	86	622	121.1	12.8	10	43	3.2	0.6
Racine	28.6	146	186	D	D	D	654	10 082	2 230.0	198.7	140	596	64.5	13.4
Richland	3.8	213	12	55	73.6	1.5	80	1 037	223.3	22.0	11	36	3.1	0.6
Rock	28.3	176	132	3 075	2 700.1	151.1	579	9 269	2 439.8	216.8	126	432	92.6	10.3
Rusk	3.6	241	7	108	12.5	2.6	59	889	198.4	15.5	11	33	1.4	0.3
St. Croix	17.3	205	83	919	1 987.0	44.7	258	3 919	933.4	87.8	87	244	27.2	4.5
Sauk	16.4	264	61	D	D	D	343	4 506	1 050.9	95.8	68	429	80.5	16.1
Sawyer	4.3	258	16	155	50.2	7.2	117	1 040	224.1	21.7	37	108	9.7	1.9
Shawano	12.2	291	40	467	256.4	18.1	144	1 636	414.0	34.6	19	83	6.3	1.6
Sheboygan	328.5	2 844	88	1 206	503.5	58.1	427	6 386	1 398.7	131.5	80	372	73.8	12.1
Taylor	2.5	123	12	83	26.0	2.7	82	827	189.1	14.7	11	31	2.2	0.4
Trempealeau	7.6	262	31	237	114.7	9.0	106	1 025	251.8	21.6	8	23	2.4	0.4
Vernon	101.9	3 421	21	273	153.8	15.3	111	1 194	250.5	24.2	17	34	3.1	0.7
Vilas	6.5	305	13	102	29.4	3.2	198	1 381	312.2	28.5	39	79	15.9	3.1
Walworth	13.0	127	104	1 678	1 124.6	86.8	396	4 746	1 091.2	103.5	104	405	50.8	8.5
Washburn	4.4	277	13	146	27.9	3.6	98	762	178.1	15.5	21	65	10.7	1.8
Washington	13.3	101	156	2 852	2 800.5	144.1	389	7 320	1 760.0	151.4	90	323	56.1	8.5
Waukesha	40.1	103	913	14 527	6 882.1	788.2	1 403	27 197	5 955.0	596.1	465	3 554	480.0	114.7
Waupaca	11.1	211	33	289	86.2	10.9	221	2 371	516.6	49.2	33	111	12.3	1.9
Waushara	40.3	1 643	16	150	49.8	5.9	86	768	203.0	15.2	15	36	3.1	0.7
Winnebago	35.3	211	160	2 536	1 109.2	102.8	540	8 027	1 796.5	162.1	125	756	97.5	19.6
Wood	174.4	2 333	57	1 591	893.2	90.5	337	4 542	1 002.9	95.7	65	238	39.5	5.3
WYOMING	4 701.5	8 342	705	6 347	6 352.9	306.6	2 951	32 033	8 957.6	758.1	1 121	4 651	991.6	159.7
Albany	189.3	5 215	21	149	113.5	4.7	170	1 927	468.8	38.6	56	158	23.8	3.4
Big Horn	392.8	33 664	7	D	D	D	53	377	71.0	6.3	13	27	2.0	0.3
Campbell	121.4	2 632	93	1 219	917.3	68.7	191	2 490	775.1	63.3	71	375	90.1	11.7
Carbon	375.7	23 651	9	47	51.5	1.5	96	819	295.3	18.5	28	92	28.2	1.6
Converse	156.1	11 284	10	D	D	D	65	511	134.3	10.0	22	53	5.0	0.8

1. Merchant wholesalers, except manufacturers' sales branches and offices. 2. Employer establishments.

STATE County	Professional, scientific, and technical services,[1] 2007				Manufacturing, 2007				Accommodation and food services, 2007			
	Number of establish-ments	Number of employees	Receipts (mil dol)	Annual payroll (mil dol)	Number of establish-ments	Number of employees	Receipts (mil dol)	Annual payroll (mil dol)	Number of establish-ments	Number of employees	Sales (mil dol)	Annual payroll (mil dol)
	147	148	149	150	151	152	153	154	155	156	157	158
WISCONSIN—Cont'd												
Dodge	79	558	63.1	25.1	155	9 924	3 094.4	429.8	179	2 148	66.1	18.1
Door	78	324	30.5	12.0	59	2 204	432.8	85.8	250	2 120	130.1	35.4
Douglas	65	D	D	D	49	1 246	1 311.6	57.9	167	2 126	76.6	20.5
Dunn	56	349	32.7	13.4	56	2 768	1 613.5	117.1	98	1 425	42.6	11.9
Eau Claire	179	1 205	124.3	54.4	97	5 578	1 534.0	221.9	260	4 893	170.3	49.5
Florence	7	D	D	D	NA	NA	NA	NA	27	165	4.6	1.1
Fond du Lac	157	1 320	101.9	65.4	151	9 745	2 903.2	392.3	242	4 001	131.5	37.5
Forest	9	81	8.9	2.8	NA	NA	NA	NA	39	D	D	D
Grant	75	458	43.5	18.2	73	2 390	D	82.0	139	1 297	40.9	10.3
Green	64	D	D	D	80	2 722	925.8	95.9	89	956	33.5	8.8
Green Lake	29	112	9.1	3.1	41	1 636	321.5	58.2	58	655	22.4	7.3
Iowa	48	D	D	D	37	874	395.5	D	61	609	25.9	7.1
Iron	9	D	D	D	NA	NA	NA	NA	57	D	D	D
Jackson	28	119	8.0	3.4	27	947	229.1	28.6	59	659	23.2	6.1
Jefferson	123	645	82.7	23.7	154	9 430	3 674.3	387.6	204	2 475	86.4	22.8
Juneau	21	85	6.5	3.3	46	1 720	374.9	63.7	81	666	28.3	7.5
Kenosha	208	D	D	D	197	7 716	3 093.7	353.0	362	5 419	214.0	59.3
Kewaunee	27	D	D	D	44	1 923	408.1	79.1	51	513	14.4	3.9
La Crosse	225	D	D	D	166	7 109	D	254.6	313	6 067	214.4	63.0
Lafayette	15	52	5.5	1.5	21	525	209.7	17.4	37	D	D	D
Langlade	21	126	7.4	3.8	54	1 684	372.3	60.5	69	625	25.3	6.5
Lincoln	29	124	9.1	3.8	53	3 135	D	121.1	97	780	27.2	6.9
Manitowoc	98	596	66.4	21.4	197	11 319	3 018.8	459.1	177	2 699	82.4	23.4
Marathon	235	D	D	D	250	18 678	D	765.6	321	4 813	173.7	48.8
Marinette	49	217	19.3	8.2	90	6 520	1 784.2	276.9	153	1 466	54.4	14.4
Marquette	16	50	4.3	1.3	25	1 260	254.8	49.1	48	D	D	D
Menominee	2	D	D	D	NA	NA	NA	NA	1	D	D	D
Milwaukee	2 024	24 421	3 245.0	1 426.3	1 164	60 678	19 065.4	3 148.4	1 913	35 759	1 570.6	442.9
Monroe	53	278	23.4	8.8	65	3 644	1 055.8	124.8	116	1 791	71.4	20.3
Oconto	50	D	D	D	62	2 069	400.5	66.5	105	793	28.2	7.5
Oneida	89	351	33.5	12.9	55	1 439	494.2	64.9	200	1 796	84.1	21.3
Outagamie	357	4 411	478.4	188.3	349	18 954	6 802.6	875.2	438	8 070	296.1	82.4
Ozaukee	357	D	D	D	222	10 712	3 161.9	540.1	203	3 558	124.9	38.4
Pepin	11	38	2.9	1.1	NA	NA	NA	NA	29	D	D	D
Pierce	71	D	D	D	54	1 217	529.0	53.4	92	972	32.9	8.4
Polk	73	D	D	D	116	4 143	958.5	149.4	129	1 158	41.8	11.2
Portage	107	D	D	D	86	4 636	1 449.5	185.3	187	2 908	97.0	27.1
Price	26	101	7.9	2.9	49	2 317	529.4	82.5	45	D	D	D
Racine	346	D	D	D	345	17 183	7 863.3	890.8	388	6 239	242.7	66.1
Richland	23	66	4.9	1.6	32	1 827	613.1	73.6	38	D	D	D
Rock	199	D	D	D	236	13 527	12 381.6	720.3	383	5 673	211.7	58.6
Rusk	14	48	3.2	1.0	24	1 735	301.2	54.2	26	D	D	D
St. Croix	206	D	D	D	169	5 973	1 347.3	245.7	198	3 239	110.9	32.4
Sauk	123	D	D	D	92	5 942	1 638.3	224.0	258	7 494	462.1	122.5
Sawyer	37	148	13.6	5.3	46	621	180.9	28.6	128	1 222	74.7	20.6
Shawano	37	236	15.5	6.0	74	2 252	582.0	87.3	120	1 290	42.7	11.0
Sheboygan	176	1 743	209.1	70.5	246	18 774	6 126.1	816.0	271	4 869	193.0	54.8
Taylor	16	89	8.9	3.6	44	3 142	630.7	106.0	44	D	D	D
Trempealeau	37	199	13.8	5.9	66	6 224	1 438.9	234.4	80	D	D	D
Vernon	44	161	12.4	4.1	36	778	178.4	28.0	60	D	D	D
Vilas	44	138	18.0	5.7	NA	NA	NA	NA	231	2 691	161.6	47.3
Walworth	187	924	85.4	34.9	212	8 944	2 247.4	381.9	293	5 925	267.2	76.4
Washburn	34	157	14.5	5.6	33	1 005	D	40.1	88	681	25.3	6.7
Washington	225	D	D	D	331	14 138	3 393.4	615.3	259	4 495	152.9	42.5
Waukesha	1 361	D	D	D	1 023	45 147	15 663.5	2 286.8	819	15 832	616.6	177.5
Waupaca	61	337	25.5	9.6	97	6 303	2 133.6	275.0	145	1 645	55.6	14.9
Waushara	19	103	6.1	2.6	35	772	111.3	25.3	75	787	25.1	7.3
Winnebago	250	D	D	D	319	23 777	9 198.9	1 149.8	377	6 071	212.1	58.4
Wood	97	D	D	D	126	6 990	2 562.6	311.7	193	2 373	84.3	24.2
WYOMING	1 890	8 711	1 079.3	387.5	596	11 904	8 834.8	573.7	1 768	26 992	1 469.0	411.9
Albany	114	D	D	D	NA	NA	NA	NA	105	1 608	65.8	18.1
Big Horn	20	83	4.5	1.9	NA	NA	NA	NA	28	202	5.6	1.5
Campbell	116	711	70.9	28.9	36	716	262.5	36.6	79	1 713	89.2	23.3
Carbon	34	92	10.9	4.3	NA	NA	NA	NA	80	791	42.9	11.2
Converse	23	74	10.8	2.1	NA	NA	NA	NA	36	490	20.9	5.2

1. Establishment subject to federal tax.

STATE County	Health care and social assistance, 2007				Other services, 2007				Nonemployer businesses, 2013		Value of residential construction authorized by building permits, 2014	
	Number of establish-ments	Number of employees	Receipts (mil dol)	Annual payroll (mil dol)	Number of establish-ments	Number of employees	Receipts (mil dol)	Annual payroll (mil dol)	Number	Receipts (mil dol)	New Construction ($1,000)	Number of housing units
	159	160	161	162	163	164	165	166	167	168	169	170
WISCONSIN—Cont'd												
Dodge	207	4 080	318.3	138.0	146	1 209	39.1	32.6	4 475	192.7	26 537	129
Door	68	1 360	99.9	44.0	91	736	42.9	11.1	2 776	114.4	32 485	134
Douglas	114	2 153	143.6	57.9	81	518	28.1	8.8	2 128	81.2	10 214	72
Dunn	93	2 327	143.8	64.6	72	330	19.7	7.7	2 561	105.8	11 686	68
Eau Claire	315	9 957	981.7	441.6	211	1 181	94.2	27.0	5 758	275.9	41 056	243
Florence	3	D	D	D	5	D	D	D	335	13.9	4 030	27
Fond du Lac	266	6 180	607.2	223.9	193	1 206	88.4	24.4	4 862	218.7	35 031	240
Forest	18	310	10.6	5.7	14	45	3.4	0.7	726	38.6	3 900	41
Grant	103	2 299	130.7	58.4	117	409	38.7	7.7	3 278	131.9	14 902	82
Green	70	1 988	166.1	71.1	78	D	D	D	2 483	99.6	8 651	36
Green Lake	50	1 086	84.4	36.9	39	147	9.0	2.7	1 336	58.3	7 852	25
Iowa	56	1 043	67.5	27.5	36	130	9.6	2.5	1 889	75.6	7 864	40
Iron	12	279	10.9	6.7	13	D	D	D	490	22.1	5 625	29
Jackson	37	918	61.4	28.4	29	127	7.3	2.0	1 148	48.9	6 044	36
Jefferson	208	3 809	268.8	118.9	145	774	45.7	13.8	4 860	210.3	27 821	109
Juneau	48	1 115	86.5	37.3	48	199	18.8	4.7	1 429	64.5	14 362	69
Kenosha	401	8 243	692.6	291.2	252	1 578	92.5	29.7	8 284	348.0	54 278	267
Kewaunee	37	486	18.0	8.7	33	65	7.5	1.5	1 227	43.5	6 396	30
La Crosse	271	D	D	D	233	D	D	D	6 189	264.2	49 766	254
Lafayette	21	283	18.4	5.7	22	146	15.7	4.1	1 311	68.9	2 444	16
Langlade	53	943	95.3	34.4	55	216	12.2	3.6	1 246	51.5	10 955	98
Lincoln	64	D	D	D	54	D	D	D	1 735	68.0	10 911	77
Manitowoc	191	4 811	358.8	171.3	140	621	46.6	12.5	3 892	157.3	20 649	120
Marathon	345	9 438	926.4	379.0	253	1 591	139.1	36.2	7 687	362.1	54 273	383
Marinette	115	2 700	208.5	93.3	82	D	D	D	2 266	92.1	10 945	76
Marquette	29	311	13.3	6.4	32	384	32.9	11.3	1 021	39.5	5 425	28
Menominee	NA	NA	NA	NA	2	D	D	D	109	3.6	2 875	14
Milwaukee	3 129	84 815	8 090.0	3 381.2	1 613	12 259	1 464.3	359.9	47 132	1 881.5	90 206	795
Monroe	77	2 387	181.4	95.4	66	371	25.7	7.5	2 511	113.0	15 257	96
Oconto	72	1 279	84.6	35.5	41	114	10.4	2.2	2 208	98.5	16 276	107
Oneida	118	2 972	298.8	119.9	99	388	31.2	8.8	2 972	112.4	28 840	132
Outagamie	467	11 774	1 169.2	491.3	358	2 530	217.6	59.7	9 474	460.2	118 598	721
Ozaukee	278	4 369	395.2	165.7	202	1 285	78.0	25.1	6 620	356.7	77 929	264
Pepin	16	230	19.8	7.5	16	D	D	D	552	26.6	3 730	18
Pierce	64	738	41.6	18.6	66	D	D	D	2 672	111.1	21 132	105
Polk	102	2 090	163.3	69.8	77	261	20.4	4.7	3 299	126.2	15 544	83
Portage	151	3 874	299.9	126.6	131	817	63.1	17.5	3 647	222.4	26 885	122
Price	46	978	47.3	22.8	34	94	6.6	1.8	1 128	39.5	7 534	52
Racine	417	11 897	946.4	478.0	343	2 167	162.7	49.1	9 433	371.2	45 776	207
Richland	43	810	61.3	24.3	26	113	7.8	2.0	1 184	50.9	4 472	24
Rock	330	9 276	878.5	337.0	285	1 578	108.7	30.6	8 085	315.1	27 005	143
Rusk	28	899	66.8	24.5	20	D	D	D	995	39.7	10 702	52
St. Croix	157	3 042	282.0	108.2	145	D	D	D	6 209	261.0	61 298	292
Sauk	143	3 776	286.8	124.6	144	492	42.9	13.4	4 322	198.9	24 702	113
Sawyer	38	642	50.0	21.8	46	190	12.9	3.6	1 586	60.1	16 081	82
Shawano	79	1 482	115.5	42.6	71	247	16.3	4.8	2 461	108.6	6 713	44
Sheboygan	292	6 709	501.4	242.7	217	1 093	76.8	20.2	5 542	218.6	23 524	111
Taylor	40	1 005	64.3	28.6	36	122	9.4	2.2	1 396	72.6	3 750	28
Trempealeau	53	1 344	80.2	33.5	42	133	12.0	3.1	1 946	90.9	17 796	134
Vernon	58	1 540	106.9	44.4	47	113	7.7	1.7	2 414	92.7	9 352	62
Vilas	45	685	40.7	16.0	64	329	26.5	13.8	2 401	99.9	32 716	141
Walworth	216	4 082	284.3	120.9	209	1 025	68.6	20.2	6 778	295.3	47 552	203
Washburn	40	862	45.8	20.5	32	122	9.2	2.7	1 418	54.7	11 294	71
Washington	253	5 876	470.4	203.1	263	1 421	102.1	31.4	8 088	369.9	78 018	337
Waukesha	1 219	23 720	2 271.3	960.5	848	6 424	610.5	199.0	26 370	1 501.6	261 576	1 020
Waupaca	112	2 526	151.6	67.5	102	339	28.3	7.0	3 075	119.1	14 944	88
Waushara	40	803	42.3	18.0	39	93	7.6	1.7	1 518	71.6	10 382	54
Winnebago	430	12 589	1 344.9	476.6	290	2 355	199.8	61.9	8 117	362.0	76 395	511
Wood	182	9 246	1 105.4	432.7	146	731	84.9	16.6	3 876	164.1	25 414	236
WYOMING	1 710	29 242	2 576.3	1 072.8	1 385	6 526	766.2	179.3	46 297	2 158.3	502 643	1 901
Albany	112	1 936	157.5	64.9	89	453	93.0	9.9	2 453	80.9	17 677	99
Big Horn	21	305	18.6	8.7	22	45	3.4	0.7	868	30.9	1 965	13
Campbell	85	1 583	154.8	71.9	135	873	118.0	32.7	3 252	146.7	66 417	163
Carbon	56	619	55.0	19.5	39	143	15.3	3.6	1 066	44.3	4 693	31
Converse	25	538	45.3	18.7	33	102	9.0	2.1	1 054	51.6	7 880	43

STATE County	Government employment and payroll, 2012: Full-time equivalent employees	Government employment and payroll, 2012: March payroll (dollars)	March payroll (percent of total): Administration, judicial, and legal	March payroll (percent of total): Police and Corrections	March payroll (percent of total): Fire Protection	March payroll (percent of total): Highways and transportation	March payroll (percent of total): Health and Welfare	March payroll (percent of total): Natural resources and utilities	March payroll (percent of total): Education and libraries	Local government finances, 2012, General revenue: Total (mil dol)	General revenue: Intergovernmental (mil dol)	Taxes: Total (mil dol)	Taxes: Per capita[1] (dollars): Total	Taxes: Per capita[1] (dollars): Property
	171	172	173	174	175	176	177	178	179	180	181	182	183	184
WISCONSIN—Cont'd														
Dodge	2 529	9 541 340	7.2	13.4	1.1	6.9	16.7	4.2	48.9	269.1	119.0	102.8	1 162	1 082
Door	1 091	4 311 224	10.3	10.3	2.4	7.1	11.5	5.3	51.6	140.6	38.4	81.9	2 946	2 757
Douglas	2 164	7 766 579	6.6	9.7	2.6	4.7	3.9	4.3	66.9	239.4	102.3	103.0	2 352	2 221
Dunn	1 509	5 639 405	7.9	8.3	2.6	8.0	16.0	4.0	50.9	163.0	74.1	60.7	1 377	1 302
Eau Claire	3 593	14 808 173	5.9	7.8	3.1	4.5	5.6	4.3	67.1	406.0	166.9	179.3	1 781	1 647
Florence	185	612 638	17.1	13.9	0.2	11.3	10.7	4.5	42.3	20.9	8.4	9.9	2 211	2 114
Fond du Lac	3 703	15 389 801	4.9	9.2	2.4	4.4	10.7	3.5	63.8	424.7	174.4	182.3	1 790	1 688
Forest	493	1 528 680	11.1	10.4	0.1	9.6	6.8	1.9	59.2	43.8	19.4	21.0	2 284	2 224
Grant	2 070	7 484 129	5.4	5.9	0.1	7.1	11.1	4.5	64.9	195.5	97.7	59.2	1 159	1 089
Green	1 522	5 434 245	4.8	8.5	0.3	10.0	14.6	4.1	57.2	147.1	64.1	57.3	1 551	1 465
Green Lake	764	2 599 596	7.3	12.4	0.1	5.7	12.4	4.5	56.6	82.2	28.8	43.6	2 290	2 188
Iowa	1 004	3 519 446	8.0	6.3	0.3	11.9	9.5	4.0	59.0	96.3	43.2	39.1	1 641	1 551
Iron	343	1 294 139	9.8	10.2	0.3	17.8	25.1	5.0	30.4	30.8	12.7	13.2	2 218	2 077
Jackson	903	2 811 059	8.8	7.7	0.2	16.9	6.6	2.7	55.8	82.1	42.1	26.7	1 304	1 221
Jefferson	2 850	11 172 911	7.2	10.2	3.2	5.1	9.1	5.9	58.7	312.5	124.7	137.1	1 622	1 528
Juneau	1 087	3 617 443	10.2	11.0	0.2	10.0	8.0	7.6	51.7	107.4	51.9	43.2	1 624	1 536
Kenosha	6 796	30 615 896	4.1	10.1	3.6	2.9	5.4	4.3	68.6	855.8	363.2	367.3	2 187	2 088
Kewaunee	848	3 565 289	8.2	10.2	0.1	10.8	12.1	3.4	53.7	87.1	41.2	29.7	1 440	1 419
La Crosse	4 828	18 746 528	5.8	8.4	2.7	4.3	18.1	4.4	55.5	639.3	314.3	218.1	1 873	1 730
Lafayette	850	2 868 337	5.6	5.1	0.3	8.3	23.6	4.4	52.0	87.8	38.3	24.8	1 472	1 414
Langlade	760	2 800 264	10.3	8.9	3.8	7.9	3.0	5.0	60.4	84.0	40.2	32.5	1 656	1 556
Lincoln	1 136	4 470 314	7.0	8.8	2.5	7.1	16.7	4.1	52.4	126.6	51.7	46.2	1 628	1 550
Manitowoc	2 832	11 154 230	5.9	8.4	4.1	9.0	10.6	8.0	52.8	283.3	138.4	103.3	1 281	1 252
Marathon	5 721	22 517 091	4.6	6.0	1.9	5.6	19.3	2.6	59.4	701.3	346.1	232.0	1 722	1 622
Marinette	1 554	5 323 156	6.8	9.6	2.0	8.0	9.0	6.7	56.8	164.4	77.1	65.5	1 576	1 476
Marquette	499	1 734 369	8.4	12.2	0.1	8.1	10.6	1.6	56.1	50.8	18.7	27.4	1 805	1 741
Menominee	308	1 058 752	4.7	7.1	0.5	4.3	17.3	0.5	64.4	30.1	23.2	5.7	1 306	1 299
Milwaukee	34 086	166 779 941	5.4	14.8	5.3	4.3	9.0	4.7	53.9	5 067.2	2 122.5	1 803.2	1 888	1 733
Monroe	1 770	5 806 833	5.3	7.6	0.2	6.8	15.8	3.7	59.6	171.3	88.6	56.7	1 258	1 152
Oconto	1 242	4 597 591	8.0	8.3	1.4	7.3	18.7	4.2	50.7	129.3	64.1	50.5	1 349	1 293
Oneida	1 507	5 601 172	7.6	9.0	2.1	9.2	4.7	4.2	61.9	177.2	45.0	110.8	3 102	2 972
Outagamie	6 670	30 535 826	4.5	7.0	2.4	3.0	7.4	3.1	70.7	783.6	353.3	271.9	1 521	1 483
Ozaukee	2 849	10 891 062	5.8	12.2	1.1	5.8	11.9	5.0	57.3	314.5	88.3	173.0	1 993	1 870
Pepin	383	1 190 672	6.0	7.9	0.0	9.8	16.0	3.3	54.8	32.7	15.7	13.8	1 862	1 799
Pierce	1 550	5 604 968	7.8	8.1	0.6	7.2	7.5	3.9	64.3	161.3	69.8	71.2	1 743	1 678
Polk	1 872	6 676 347	6.7	6.6	0.1	8.1	13.3	2.7	61.5	182.9	73.8	81.7	1 873	1 795
Portage	2 267	8 603 550	8.0	9.1	2.6	7.5	10.8	4.0	57.1	239.8	105.3	94.6	1 343	1 237
Price	681	1 985 878	8.8	8.8	0.2	14.3	8.2	2.4	55.9	60.2	26.4	26.8	1 934	1 859
Racine	6 208	25 453 020	4.3	13.6	5.6	3.5	5.9	4.0	61.9	757.1	345.7	302.7	1 554	1 513
Richland	693	2 209 583	6.2	8.6	0.0	9.2	22.4	9.3	43.6	68.8	31.9	17.8	999	928
Rock	6 252	25 471 665	5.9	9.6	3.9	4.4	7.9	4.5	62.6	723.4	387.9	249.8	1 557	1 471
Rusk	655	2 410 554	18.7	7.8	0.0	7.6	8.7	4.6	51.6	86.0	34.2	18.5	1 293	1 209
St. Croix	2 777	10 535 818	8.9	8.5	0.6	5.0	10.3	3.3	61.9	287.9	124.7	126.4	1 483	1 393
Sauk	2 740	9 073 443	5.8	14.7	0.2	6.1	14.5	4.3	52.3	342.6	171.4	136.3	2 178	1 826
Sawyer	647	2 033 247	11.4	10.0	0.3	11.0	9.7	2.2	53.1	68.2	23.3	37.0	2 229	2 110
Shawano	1 508	5 334 917	7.7	11.2	0.3	6.9	9.6	4.4	58.3	146.4	73.0	52.6	1 264	1 190
Sheboygan	4 469	19 622 392	8.8	8.8	2.1	5.2	8.0	3.0	63.5	489.1	213.6	207.1	1 801	1 746
Taylor	791	2 632 338	8.6	8.5	0.1	7.8	13.4	3.7	56.2	77.9	42.6	26.0	1 270	1 206
Trempealeau	1 609	5 095 842	6.3	7.1	0.0	5.3	19.8	4.5	56.5	151.2	71.4	42.1	1 437	1 369
Vernon	1 200	3 885 090	13.0	10.1	0.0	9.9	7.7	3.8	53.3	116.3	57.2	38.4	1 270	1 203
Vilas	838	2 943 859	11.7	11.7	1.3	12.5	6.2	4.2	50.1	90.0	23.9	58.7	2 751	2 602
Walworth	3 935	15 369 324	8.6	14.6	5.1	5.4	7.1	4.6	53.9	432.3	127.0	247.7	2 409	2 279
Washburn	809	2 970 221	6.5	8.7	0.0	6.2	26.7	4.1	45.5	75.6	23.6	43.2	2 729	2 639
Washington	3 924	16 777 954	5.5	11.3	2.0	3.5	11.1	4.9	60.4	533.8	224.7	238.1	1 795	1 685
Waukesha	12 148	56 004 430	5.2	10.5	3.1	3.9	3.5	4.4	68.1	1 501.6	376.8	897.3	2 287	2 229
Waupaca	2 041	7 209 482	6.6	9.8	1.0	6.0	8.5	3.2	64.1	213.4	94.7	87.0	1 668	1 589
Waushara	768	2 669 797	12.8	9.7	0.0	7.3	14.0	2.2	51.2	79.8	31.6	38.3	1 565	1 495
Winnebago	5 300	21 156 305	4.4	11.7	4.6	5.5	11.2	7.1	54.5	697.9	338.4	249.0	1 475	1 436
Wood	3 170	12 767 826	6.1	9.1	3.2	5.9	6.1	3.5	65.8	337.6	146.1	136.7	1 837	1 741
WYOMING	X	X	X	X	X	X	X	X	X	X	X	X	X	X
Albany	2 004	7 113 079	5.9	6.8	3.8	1.8	26.8	5.7	48.8	203.8	74.7	35.3	948	550
Big Horn	940	3 298 694	4.9	6.2	0.2	2.2	30.5	4.5	51.0	99.0	52.6	18.8	1 595	1 308
Campbell	3 518	15 943 966	6.3	7.1	1.0	2.6	31.3	5.6	43.0	513.4	102.2	227.8	4 757	4 113
Carbon	1 195	4 095 546	7.4	9.7	1.4	3.4	23.3	5.9	44.5	136.5	41.4	57.8	3 691	2 846
Converse	1 098	4 194 426	4.6	6.9	0.0	1.8	33.4	4.4	47.4	123.9	29.5	48.7	3 477	2 778

1. Based on the resident population estimated as of July 1 of the year shown.

STATE County	Local government finances, 2012 (cont.): Direct general expenditure: Total (mil dol)	Per capita[1] (dollars)	Percent of total for: Education	Health and hospitals	Police protection	Public welfare	Highways	Debt outstanding: Total (mil dol)	Per capita[1] (dollars)	Government employment, 2013: Federal civilian	Federal military	State and local	Presidential election,[2] 2012: Percent of vote cast: Democratic	Republican	All other
	185	186	187	188	189	190	191	192	193	194	195	196	197	198	199
WISCONSIN—Cont'd															
Dodge	312.6	3 536	31.9	3.5	7.1	19.1	11.6	247.2	2 795	183	230	5 016	44.8	53.7	1.5
Door	143.6	5 161	33.0	8.5	5.0	3.5	16.6	112.6	4 047	78	153	1 784	58.0	40.7	1.3
Douglas	245.2	5 600	52.1	1.4	5.6	3.7	10.6	236.8	5 408	159	121	3 157	65.8	32.6	1.7
Dunn	163.3	3 704	41.6	2.5	5.7	12.3	12.7	105.8	2 402	86	114	4 452	56.6	41.6	1.8
Eau Claire	470.2	4 671	54.2	3.8	7.3	3.4	9.5	361.0	3 586	351	270	8 365	60.3	38.1	1.6
Florence	21.2	4 727	37.2	8.9	7.2	0.6	19.4	5.9	1 314	17	12	252	42.2	56.3	1.5
Fond du Lac	449.6	4 415	51.8	7.3	5.2	3.9	9.0	580.9	5 704	203	276	5 421	44.8	53.8	1.3
Forest	45.1	4 904	47.2	2.3	5.4	5.0	13.7	7.9	854	95	25	1 646	57.1	41.9	1.0
Grant	214.5	4 199	52.3	3.3	4.2	7.2	12.4	147.8	2 894	142	132	5 595	61.2	37.3	1.6
Green	151.7	4 109	48.0	2.6	6.1	10.5	13.8	103.5	2 805	81	103	2 057	62.1	36.3	1.6
Green Lake	81.9	4 301	48.2	3.2	6.9	5.3	9.5	68.9	3 620	53	52	1 107	41.9	56.6	1.5
Iowa	95.1	3 993	48.5	1.0	5.7	8.7	15.3	45.1	1 896	79	66	1 309	66.7	32.0	1.3
Iron	31.8	5 354	32.4	7.4	7.7	0.5	21.4	22.9	3 853	16	16	345	55.8	42.7	1.6
Jackson	85.1	4 152	52.3	2.5	4.5	6.0	13.4	40.6	1 983	48	54	2 477	60.2	38.4	1.4
Jefferson	322.8	3 820	49.7	5.1	6.2	5.7	8.1	312.0	3 693	178	226	3 896	49.7	48.9	1.4
Juneau	108.2	4 063	46.9	4.1	5.3	3.2	12.3	117.9	4 426	247	79	1 982	53.7	44.6	1.7
Kenosha	850.4	5 064	53.7	3.4	6.5	6.9	5.1	759.4	4 522	249	486	9 180	58.2	40.1	1.7
Kewaunee	102.8	4 983	40.7	9.0	4.0	5.5	16.5	50.3	2 438	67	58	1 150	54.7	43.7	1.6
La Crosse	639.1	5 488	42.3	2.8	3.9	23.8	4.9	409.7	3 518	458	316	9 727	60.9	37.5	1.6
Lafayette	90.2	5 355	43.0	14.6	2.7	11.4	12.9	33.1	1 965	55	47	1 012	60.4	38.1	1.5
Langlade	87.8	4 467	47.1	4.3	4.7	3.7	13.7	55.1	2 802	42	54	1 064	49.8	48.8	1.3
Lincoln	128.6	4 529	40.0	5.5	5.8	12.3	13.4	69.0	2 431	62	79	1 701	55.2	42.7	2.1
Manitowoc	296.5	3 675	42.9	1.3	6.2	6.4	9.3	337.8	4 187	188	249	3 862	52.9	45.3	1.8
Marathon	710.6	5 274	41.9	10.2	3.9	18.8	7.9	440.9	3 273	467	376	7 441	53.5	44.7	1.8
Marinette	165.7	3 988	44.3	5.4	5.8	7.1	14.3	116.0	2 790	127	116	2 121	52.7	45.8	1.6
Marquette	54.9	3 612	43.4	5.5	7.6	3.4	17.9	23.8	1 566	52	42	707	51.8	46.6	1.6
Menominee	30.7	7 067	60.2	0.0	5.9	18.3	5.8	5.7	1 309	0	12	2 131	86.8	12.8	0.4
Milwaukee	5 034.7	5 271	40.9	10.3	8.2	1.9	4.9	6 485.7	6 790	9 359	2 958	52 203	67.3	31.4	1.2
Monroe	165.6	3 672	50.0	1.1	5.0	10.2	11.3	105.8	2 346	2 486	242	2 472	53.2	45.2	1.5
Oconto	134.4	3 590	40.5	9.2	4.7	5.0	18.4	80.7	2 154	95	104	1 820	52.3	46.2	1.5
Oneida	201.2	5 634	52.6	2.8	6.1	3.2	10.2	98.0	2 743	185	98	2 059	54.3	43.9	1.8
Outagamie	855.9	4 786	56.0	2.4	5.0	4.7	8.6	649.4	3 632	564	528	10 445	54.9	43.3	1.7
Ozaukee	321.3	3 701	46.5	2.6	7.4	7.0	10.8	290.2	3 342	146	239	3 570	38.6	60.3	1.2
Pepin	34.1	4 609	48.2	4.5	4.1	3.3	20.4	10.3	1 392	25	20	480	55.7	42.9	1.4
Pierce	163.8	4 014	51.4	3.3	5.2	3.2	16.2	140.8	3 451	92	108	4 138	53.4	44.4	2.2
Polk	186.0	4 265	50.3	5.5	4.6	6.5	13.2	178.6	4 095	135	120	2 638	48.0	49.8	2.1
Portage	238.8	3 391	43.8	5.1	6.1	6.5	12.7	142.9	2 029	174	192	5 955	63.0	35.0	2.0
Price	60.0	4 326	45.1	2.0	5.7	8.2	16.4	25.8	1 862	78	38	856	55.6	42.2	2.1
Racine	764.1	3 923	45.5	3.8	9.7	5.3	7.3	710.7	3 648	332	533	8 471	53.1	45.7	1.3
Richland	68.5	3 844	34.6	2.0	4.7	20.1	12.9	25.0	1 405	59	49	1 335	59.7	39.0	1.3
Rock	729.2	4 546	49.6	7.4	6.2	7.1	5.3	614.8	3 833	286	442	8 642	63.8	34.6	1.6
Rusk	90.1	6 292	32.1	22.9	3.9	8.8	12.1	51.6	3 603	42	40	1 093	53.0	44.7	2.3
St. Croix	287.7	3 375	50.6	2.2	5.7	8.2	13.4	288.4	3 383	153	238	4 353	47.2	51.0	1.8
Sauk	331.0	5 288	35.3	5.0	4.8	22.8	8.1	211.8	3 384	148	175	5 509	60.8	37.8	1.5
Sawyer	72.4	4 365	38.2	6.1	5.3	7.8	21.4	22.8	1 377	79	45	2 027	52.4	46.2	1.3
Shawano	157.1	3 776	42.7	6.0	5.5	4.6	17.3	107.1	2 575	111	114	2 718	51.1	47.5	1.5
Sheboygan	492.9	4 286	55.2	3.6	5.7	6.1	8.2	375.9	3 269	202	332	5 576	48.9	49.6	1.5
Taylor	77.2	3 770	44.9	3.6	5.2	8.1	16.4	38.0	1 857	59	57	926	48.8	49.1	2.1
Trempealeau	154.8	5 283	44.9	1.8	4.6	18.1	10.5	112.0	3 824	117	81	2 174	62.5	36.1	1.4
Vernon	117.6	3 887	43.6	1.7	3.8	13.5	14.5	68.6	2 265	113	84	1 757	60.1	38.1	1.7
Vilas	84.7	3 971	43.9	2.5	7.8	5.4	13.1	52.1	2 443	65	59	2 136	47.2	51.3	1.5
Walworth	423.9	4 121	48.5	3.3	9.0	4.8	9.2	448.4	4 360	188	280	7 943	47.9	50.5	1.5
Washburn	75.7	4 781	45.6	1.7	4.0	5.9	18.7	56.9	3 597	89	43	1 261	51.5	47.2	1.3
Washington	537.2	4 049	42.6	2.9	6.1	19.2	7.1	398.2	3 001	249	369	5 239	34.6	64.1	1.3
Waukesha	1 525.8	3 890	54.5	2.7	7.1	2.3	6.8	1 282.0	3 268	770	1 088	17 060	36.6	62.3	1.0
Waupaca	217.6	4 174	48.6	2.1	6.1	7.4	12.8	224.2	4 301	128	142	3 392	50.8	47.9	1.3
Waushara	86.2	3 523	39.0	3.9	8.2	9.2	13.7	34.2	1 400	44	65	1 325	49.5	48.7	1.8
Winnebago	708.5	4 197	35.6	2.5	5.6	20.8	8.3	688.0	4 076	432	458	11 555	54.9	43.3	1.8
Wood	353.7	4 752	52.5	6.5	5.5	4.9	9.8	274.0	3 681	196	206	4 995	55.6	42.5	1.9
WYOMING	X	X	X	X	X	X	X	X	X	7 430	6 233	62 074	32.5	64.8	2.7
Albany	193.6	5 194	32.5	30.5	5.1	0.3	6.1	57.2	1 535	159	201	7 891	50.5	46.4	3.1
Big Horn	99.3	8 416	44.8	21.5	3.8	0.1	2.7	33.3	2 823	107	64	1 416	20.9	76.2	3.0
Campbell	532.9	11 131	37.0	22.6	3.1	1.5	5.4	188.2	3 931	86	260	4 708	18.3	79.7	2.0
Carbon	136.8	8 731	40.1	19.3	4.0	0.4	2.9	63.8	4 069	207	81	1 867	34.1	63.2	2.7
Converse	125.0	8 921	39.9	31.1	4.0	0.2	6.5	11.6	826	70	77	1 477	21.4	76.3	2.3

1. Based on the resident population estimated as of July 1 of the year shown. 2.

STATE/ County code	CBSA code[1]	County type[2]	STATE County	Land area,[3] (sq km) 2010	Population, 2014: Total persons 2014	Population, 2014: Rank	Population, 2014: Per square kilometer	Population and population characteristics, 2013: Race alone or in combination, not Hispanic or Latino (percent): White	Black	American Indian, Alaska Native	Asian and Pacific Islander	Percent Hispanic or Latino[4]	Age (percent): Under 5 years	5 to 17 years	18 to 24 years	25 to 34 years	35 to 44 years	45 to 54 years
				1	2	3	4	5	6	7	8	9	10	11	12	13	14	15
			WYOMING—Cont'd															
56 011	...	9	Crook	7 393	7 248	2 655	1.0	95.1	1.4	1.6	0.4	2.8	6.6	17.0	6.7	11.0	10.2	14.3
56 013	40180	7	Fremont	23 786	40 703	1 161	1.7	72.8	1.1	21.0	0.9	6.5	7.5	17.8	8.4	12.7	10.7	12.8
56 015	...	7	Goshen	5 764	13 514	2 205	2.3	87.4	1.2	1.2	0.8	10.3	5.6	14.4	10.6	11.2	10.5	13.3
56 017	...	7	Hot Springs	5 191	4 816	2 849	0.9	93.4	1.2	2.4	0.8	3.6	4.6	15.8	6.0	10.6	9.1	13.2
56 019	...	7	Johnson	10 759	8 573	2 553	0.8	92.8	1.3	1.8	1.0	4.4	6.0	16.0	6.5	11.1	11.0	12.6
56 021	16940	3	Laramie	6 956	96 389	609	13.9	80.7	4.0	1.4	2.0	14.1	6.6	17.0	10.1	14.1	12.0	13.4
56 023	...	7	Lincoln	10 557	18 567	1 889	1.8	93.4	1.1	1.2	1.0	4.5	6.7	20.4	6.4	11.1	12.6	13.3
56 025	16220	3	Natrona	13 831	81 624	682	5.9	88.4	2.4	1.6	1.4	8.0	6.6	17.1	9.8	15.2	12.2	13.2
56 027	...	9	Niobrara	6 801	2 463	3 009	0.4	94.6	1.6	1.9	0.8	2.9	4.7	13.1	6.9	14.1	12.1	11.9
56 029	...	7	Park	17 980	28 989	1 456	1.6	91.4	1.7	1.3	1.2	5.8	5.5	15.1	9.0	11.5	10.3	13.4
56 031	...	7	Platte	5 398	8 799	2 530	1.6	90.3	1.2	0.9	1.0	7.8	4.9	15.3	7.1	9.5	9.9	14.8
56 033	43260	7	Sheridan	6 537	30 032	1 428	4.6	92.5	1.3	1.8	1.3	4.3	5.6	15.7	8.3	11.7	11.7	13.4
56 035	...	9	Sublette	12 656	10 057	2 433	0.8	89.1	1.6	1.4	1.3	7.7	6.2	17.6	7.2	13.3	14.1	15.0
56 037	40540	5	Sweetwater	27 005	45 010	1 068	1.7	81.0	1.9	1.4	1.3	15.9	7.6	19.6	9.2	16.1	12.8	12.8
56 039	27220	7	Teton	10 348	22 930	1 691	2.2	81.8	1.6	0.9	1.9	15.0	5.9	13.2	6.5	19.2	15.9	13.6
56 041	21740	7	Uinta	5 390	20 904	1 781	3.9	88.9	1.1	1.4	1.1	9.1	7.6	21.9	8.1	13.2	12.3	13.0
56 043	...	7	Washakie	5 798	8 322	2 573	1.4	83.8	1.1	1.3	0.9	14.2	5.8	18.6	6.8	11.0	10.8	13.4
56 045	...	7	Weston	6 211	7 201	2 660	1.2	94.0	0.9	2.5	0.7	3.8	6.3	15.3	7.5	12.3	11.4	13.9

1. CBSA = Core Based Statistical Area. See Appendix A for explanation. See Appendix B for list of metropolitan areas with component counties. 2. County type code from the Economic Research Service of USDA Rural-Urban Continuum Codes. See Appendix A for definition. 3. Dry land or land partially or temporarily covered by water. 4. May be of any race.

STATE County	Population, 2013 (cont.)				Population change and components of change, 2000–2014							Households, 2009–2013				
	Age (percent) (cont.)				Total persons		Percent change		Components of change, 2010–2014					Percent		
	55 to 64 years	65 to 74 years	75 years and over	Percent female	2000	2010	2000–2010	2010–2014	Births	Deaths	Net migration	Number	Persons per household	Family households	Female family householder[1]	One person
	16	17	18	19	20	21	22	23	24	25	26	27	28	29	30	31
WYOMING—Cont'd																
Crook	16.9	10.7	6.7	48.9	5 887	7 083	20.3	2.3	398	263	56	3 010	2.34	70.8	8.1	26.2
Fremont	14.3	9.1	6.6	50.0	35 804	40 123	12.1	1.4	2 554	1 861	-122	15 425	2.58	67.0	10.4	27.2
Goshen	14.8	11.0	8.7	47.7	12 538	13 249	5.7	2.0	588	559	236	5 255	2.40	65.1	7.1	32.1
Hot Springs	17.8	12.4	10.7	50.5	4 882	4 812	-1.4	0.1	215	276	74	2 238	2.10	58.9	5.0	35.2
Johnson	16.6	11.6	8.6	49.0	7 075	8 569	21.1	0.0	398	334	-67	3 679	2.31	64.7	3.1	31.4
Laramie	13.1	7.8	5.9	49.7	81 607	91 738	12.4	4.9	5 336	3 216	2 384	36 859	2.48	66.8	10.5	27.7
Lincoln	15.0	9.0	5.3	49.3	14 573	18 106	24.2	2.5	1 039	500	-81	6 245	2.88	76.1	6.2	21.6
Natrona	13.3	6.8	5.8	49.5	66 533	75 450	13.4	8.2	4 652	2 908	4 408	31 116	2.44	66.4	11.3	26.5
Niobrara	16.9	10.4	9.9	54.0	2 407	2 484	3.2	-0.8	94	89	-22	1 045	2.18	57.4	5.7	34.1
Park	16.1	11.0	8.2	50.4	25 786	28 205	9.4	2.8	1 344	1 105	535	11 801	2.35	65.2	7.6	29.2
Platte	16.5	12.7	9.2	49.6	8 807	8 667	-1.6	1.5	366	404	192	3 642	2.36	62.2	9.1	35.4
Sheridan	16.2	10.1	7.3	50.0	26 560	29 116	9.6	3.1	1 421	1 255	678	12 381	2.29	63.1	6.9	32.0
Sublette	14.3	7.9	4.4	46.3	5 920	10 247	73.1	-1.9	549	182	-600	3 502	2.84	76.4	5.5	21.2
Sweetwater	12.9	5.6	3.4	47.9	37 613	43 806	16.5	2.7	2 684	1 118	-341	16 682	2.62	70.6	8.8	23.5
Teton	13.8	7.6	4.2	48.0	18 251	21 294	16.7	7.7	1 071	308	846	7 583	2.76	59.8	5.9	27.5
Uinta	13.4	6.7	3.8	49.3	19 742	21 118	7.0	-1.0	1 343	565	-1 016	7 290	2.85	73.0	12.3	23.5
Washakie	14.5	10.5	8.7	49.7	8 289	8 533	2.9	-2.5	402	371	-247	3 468	2.40	63.4	7.1	33.2
Weston	16.0	9.4	8.0	47.6	6 644	7 208	8.5	-0.1	354	285	-80	2 975	2.29	64.1	5.3	33.0

1. No spouse present.

STATE County	Persons in group quarters, 2014	Daytime population, 2009–2013: Number	Daytime population, 2009–2013: Employment/residence ratio	Births, 2014: Total	Births, 2014: Rate[1]	Deaths, 2014: Number	Deaths, 2014: Rate[1]	Persons under 65 with no health insurance, 2013: Number	Persons under 65 with no health insurance, 2013: Percent	Medicare, 2014: Eligible for Medicare	Medicare, 2014: Enrolled in Medicare Advantage	Medicare, 2014: Enrolled in a Medicare prescription drug plan	Serious crimes known to police,[2] 2013: Total: Number	Serious crimes known to police,[2] 2013: Total: Rate[3]
	32	33	34	35	36	37	38	39	40	41	42	43	44	45
WYOMING—Cont'd														
Crook	34	6 296	0.77	94	13.0	61	8.4	933	15.8	1 388	66	759	86	1 195
Fremont	881	40 346	0.99	583	14.3	454	11.2	7 121	21.0	7 567	569	4 320	1 124	2 705
Goshen	1 172	13 083	0.94	147	10.9	132	9.8	1 726	17.6	2 928	20	1 868	218	1 584
Hot Springs	86	4 775	0.98	53	11.0	74	15.4	759	20.5	1 321	NA	849	103	2 126
Johnson	71	8 021	0.87	93	10.8	79	9.2	1 215	17.8	1 860	17	1 131	171	1 974
Laramie	1 884	95 431	1.05	1 266	13.1	762	7.9	11 463	14.2	16 232	535	8 727	2 824	2 953
Lincoln	71	16 751	0.84	244	13.1	110	5.9	2 399	15.4	3 044	60	1 708	188	1 111
Natrona	1 781	77 821	1.01	1 183	14.5	713	8.7	10 513	15.1	12 305	488	7 701	2 536	3 170
Niobrara	246	2 498	1.00	25	10.2	16	6.5	344	19.3	576	NA	358	12	490
Park	861	28 704	1.01	328	11.3	243	8.4	3 886	17.0	6 598	70	4 078	510	1 761
Platte	100	8 911	1.05	91	10.3	83	9.4	1 103	16.3	2 164	31	1 344	167	1 895
Sheridan	1 018	28 597	0.95	329	11.0	306	10.2	3 684	15.4	6 212	275	3 250	471	1 578
Sublette	550	11 451	1.24	129	12.8	44	4.4	1 327	15.1	1 279	16	708	133	1 272
Sweetwater	731	46 411	1.09	612	13.6	248	5.5	5 839	14.4	5 211	194	2 869	1 092	2 374
Teton	268	24 807	1.24	255	11.1	72	3.1	3 875	19.9	2 889	129	1 668	NA	NA
Uinta	255	20 377	0.93	319	15.3	137	6.6	2 735	14.7	2 692	258	1 401	471	2 481
Washakie	140	8 666	1.05	90	10.8	81	9.7	1 245	18.5	1 791	NA	1 091	58	685
Weston	322	6 340	0.76	90	12.5	65	9.0	861	15.3	1 444	73	821	106	1 767

1. Per 1,000 estimated resident population. 2. Data for serious crimes have not been adjusted for underreporting; this may affect comparability between geographic areas and over time.
3. Per 100,000 population estimated by the FBI.

STATE County	Serious crimes known to police, 2013 (cont.)[1] Rate[2]		Education School enrollment and attainment, 2009–2013 Enrollment[3]		Attainment[4] (percent)		Local government expenditures,[5] 2012–2013		Money income, 2009–2013	Households			Income and poverty, 2013	Percent below poverty level		
	Violent	Property	Total	Percent private	High school graduate or less	Bachelor's degree or more	Total current spending (mil dol)	Current spending per student (dollars)	Per capita income[6] (dollars)	Median income (dollars)	Mean income (dollars)	Percent with income of $200,000 or more	Median household income (dollars)	All persons	Children under 18 years	Children 5 to 17 years in families
	46	47	48	49	50	51	52	53	54	55	56	57	58	59	60	61
WYOMING—Cont'd																
Crook	42	1 154	1 552	12.8	43.3	20.9	20.4	18 935	28 212	53 237	64 388	2.7	59 490	7.8	10.7	10.2
Fremont	180	2 524	9 717	8.2	38.8	21.2	128.5	19 033	24 037	50 418	61 029	1.9	51 920	15.3	21.0	18.5
Goshen	218	1 366	3 313	13.7	44.0	20.5	31.0	18 009	23 475	43 257	56 612	1.0	43 311	16.3	20.0	17.2
Hot Springs	83	2 044	928	8.7	44.4	17.9	12.0	18 464	26 544	42 019	56 141	2.1	42 694	12.5	16.1	14.0
Johnson	242	1 732	1 909	11.9	37.6	26.6	22.0	17 080	28 072	57 004	64 572	1.9	51 521	8.7	11.0	10.1
Laramie	207	2 746	24 022	9.2	34.1	25.1	218.6	15 257	28 505	55 864	69 621	2.5	59 712	10.2	14.1	12.8
Lincoln	65	1 046	4 621	5.4	39.0	21.0	50.7	16 048	25 834	64 205	70 898	2.0	67 256	8.9	11.7	10.2
Natrona	211	2 959	19 652	10.6	36.7	22.3	180.8	13 823	29 877	57 791	72 600	4.0	57 701	10.1	13.3	11.7
Niobrara	122	367	458	8.5	39.8	18.5	11.4	11 668	26 797	38 438	61 331	2.8	43 994	15.0	19.2	16.8
Park	269	1 492	6 486	5.5	35.6	27.8	61.8	15 542	27 824	53 951	65 352	1.9	50 967	10.0	15.2	13.7
Platte	170	1 725	1 810	15.0	35.7	23.2	23.9	19 318	26 335	45 512	58 729	1.0	48 621	10.9	16.3	14.2
Sheridan	80	1 497	6 855	13.5	34.6	27.4	67.0	15 684	27 948	52 008	64 326	2.7	51 628	10.1	13.0	11.6
Sublette	134	1 138	2 324	7.8	33.6	23.3	32.9	19 991	35 944	77 900	92 432	3.9	74 951	6.3	7.5	6.8
Sweetwater	320	2 054	11 800	10.2	44.7	18.1	115.2	14 100	30 517	71 525	79 517	2.8	72 899	8.7	11.3	10.0
Teton	NA	NA	4 395	14.9	25.6	48.7	43.8	17 596	43 444	68 078	107 054	9.2	70 201	7.7	10.5	9.7
Uinta	37	2 444	5 939	6.1	45.6	18.9	64.6	14 776	25 513	58 515	70 089	2.9	60 953	12.0	13.5	11.8
Washakie	94	590	2 061	10.0	39.0	23.6	25.8	17 104	28 308	47 104	65 450	3.2	50 740	11.3	14.5	12.8
Weston	167	1 600	1 657	9.3	45.4	17.2	19.2	18 420	28 764	55 461	65 573	1.8	59 314	9.9	12.2	11.2

1. Data for serious crimes have not been adjusted for underreporting; this may affect comparability between geographic areas and over time. 2. Per 100,000 population estimated by the FBI.
3. All persons 3 years old and over enrolled in nursery school through college. 4. Persons 25 years old and over. 5. Elementary and secondary education expenditures.
6. Based on population estimated by the American Community Survey, 2009–2013.

Table B. States and Counties — **Personal Income**

STATE County	Personal income, 2013										Earnings, 2013		
			Per capita[1]			Supplements to wages and salaries; employer contributions (mil dol)						Contributions for government social insurance (mil dol)	
	Total (mil dol)	Percent change, 2012–2013	Dollars	Rank	Wages and salaries (mil dol)	Pension and insurance	Government social insurance	Proprietors' income (mil dol)	Dividends, interest, and rent (mil dol)	Personal transfer receipts (mil dol)	Total (mil dol)	From employee and self-employed	From employer
	62	63	64	65	66	67	68	69	70	71	72	73	74
WYOMING—Cont'd													
Crook	341	1.8	47 493	511	97	19	10	37	89	45	163	9	10
Fremont	1 795	1.4	43 781	778	725	131	71	102	531	335	1 028	61	71
Goshen	544	1.3	39 984	1 173	173	35	17	47	158	107	272	16	17
Hot Springs	232	3.3	47 871	491	84	16	8	22	63	51	129	8	8
Johnson	396	3.7	45 903	625	135	25	14	42	135	60	217	13	14
Laramie	4 970	2.2	51 870	302	2 289	457	238	339	1 388	711	3 323	181	238
Lincoln	757	2.1	41 249	1 021	261	53	25	66	243	109	405	23	25
Natrona	4 776	2.1	58 983	120	2 174	289	212	760	1 228	519	3 435	188	212
Niobrara	130	5.8	51 148	329	40	9	4	21	37	21	74	4	4
Park	1 532	1.1	52 426	290	571	103	57	143	552	228	874	50	57
Platte	421	5.8	48 073	476	165	34	18	56	105	77	272	15	18
Sheridan	1 561	1.4	52 325	293	554	101	59	127	544	221	840	49	59
Sublette	608	-3.7	60 572	99	320	46	29	79	151	44	474	25	29
Sweetwater	2 627	1.0	58 077	131	1 482	219	136	589	396	229	2 425	126	136
Teton	2 356	2.3	105 821	4	796	96	91	301	1 241	104	1 284	67	91
Uinta	983	1.6	46 640	573	429	70	42	56	194	126	598	34	42
Washakie	380	0.4	44 923	694	161	30	16	37	104	63	244	14	16
Weston	412	3.5	57 517	148	94	23	9	133	81	50	259	12	9

1. Based on the resident population estimated as of July 1 of the year shown.

Table B. States and Counties — **Earnings, Social Security, and Housing**

STATE County	Earnings, 2013 (cont.) Percent by selected industries: Farm	Mining	Construction	Manufacturing	Information: professional, scientific, technical services	Retail trade	Finance, insurance, real estate and leasing	Health care and social assistance	Government	Social Security beneficiaries, December 2013: Number	Rate[1]	Supplemental Security Income recipients, December 2013	Housing units, 2014: Total	Percent change, 2010–2014
	75	76	77	78	79	80	81	82	83	84	85	86	87	88
WYOMING—Cont'd														
Crook	5.7	15.9	10.2	8.3	D	5.8	2.9	D	24.4	1 465	205	46	3 575	-0.6
Fremont	2.8	11.2	6.7	1.2	5.0	7.3	4.8	D	33.9	8 405	205	874	17 716	-0.4
Goshen	10.2	0.4	4.9	5.2	4.5	5.2	4.4	14.7	31.5	3 050	225	229	5 952	-0.3
Hot Springs	3.2	D	D	2.5	3.2	D	2.7	10.2	24.2	1 450	299	83	2 550	-1.2
Johnson	2.4	10.1	19.4	0.8	5.2	5.0	6.5	D	29.4	1 990	231	48	4 530	-0.5
Laramie	2.1	1.0	8.0	3.4	6.9	6.6	5.9	8.0	38.8	16 755	175	1 579	41 653	2.9
Lincoln	2.7	18.6	11.4	1.9	D	6.1	4.4	3.3	26.9	3 330	182	144	9 014	0.8
Natrona	0.2	20.1	9.9	4.1	5.2	5.9	6.3	12.0	11.8	13 445	166	1 202	35 825	6.0
Niobrara	18.9	8.4	D	D	D	D	3.8	D	34.6	600	235	34	1 337	-0.1
Park	3.2	10.0	9.9	3.4	5.5	7.6	4.7	10.1	25.7	7 020	241	279	13 913	2.6
Platte	12.2	D	10.7	1.0	2.4	6.1	3.5	D	19.0	2 260	259	106	4 704	0.8
Sheridan	0.5	3.7	10.1	2.7	7.5	7.6	6.5	9.4	28.5	6 395	214	294	14 362	3.0
Sublette	2.6	37.8	14.9	0.5	D	3.9	3.7	D	15.8	1 355	134	49	5 866	1.7
Sweetwater	0.3	47.2	5.5	6.7	2.5	3.8	3.4	2.4	12.1	5 830	129	373	19 077	1.8
Teton	0.5	0.5	11.0	0.8	11.2	7.0	16.2	4.7	13.0	2 750	123	54	13 269	3.6
Uinta	0.8	11.6	19.1	3.6	7.3	6.3	3.7	D	20.3	3 015	143	278	8 773	0.7
Washakie	7.9	7.3	7.9	10.8	4.7	5.7	4.4	D	21.2	1 940	230	108	3 810	-0.6
Weston	1.9	25.0	13.9	D	3.5	6.2	7.6	D	18.1	1 535	215	61	3 500	-0.9

1. Per 1,000 resident population estimated as of July 1 of the year shown.

STATE County	Housing units, 2009–2013: Occupied units: Total	Owner-occupied: Percent	Owner-occupied: Median value[1]	Median owner cost as a percent of income: With a mortgage	Median owner cost as a percent of income: Without a mortgage[2]	Renter-occupied: Median rent[3]	Renter-occupied: Median rent as a percent of income[2]	Substandard units[4] (percent)	Civilian labor force, 2014: Total	Civilian labor force, 2014: Percent change, 2013–2014	Unemployment: Total	Unemployment: Rate[5]	Civilian employment,[6] 2009–2013: Total	Percent: Management, business, science and arts	Percent: Construction, production, and maintenance occupations
	89	90	91	92	93	94	95	96	97	98	99	100	101	102	103
WYOMING—Cont'd															
Crook	3 010	77.4	172 200	20.8	10.0	720	18.0	4.8	3 714	0.6	150	4.0	3 679	34.2	34.9
Fremont	15 425	72.0	181 000	21.6	10.1	663	25.3	1.7	20 620	-2.1	1 070	5.2	18 783	32.7	23.7
Goshen	5 255	75.7	139 700	22.8	10.0	611	27.1	1.5	7 224	-1.5	270	3.7	6 349	33.5	29.8
Hot Springs	2 238	70.4	143 900	22.9	10.0	566	22.5	1.9	2 492	-2.6	108	4.3	2 241	32.5	25.0
Johnson	3 679	74.1	228 800	21.6	10.5	746	25.9	1.4	4 482	0.1	210	4.7	4 433	39.0	26.9
Laramie	36 859	68.2	181 700	22.1	10.0	760	26.8	3.5	48 899	0.6	2 193	4.5	44 909	35.3	22.3
Lincoln	6 245	82.8	190 900	21.9	10.0	804	26.9	1.9	8 210	0.4	441	5.4	8 331	30.5	31.4
Natrona	31 116	69.7	178 300	21.0	10.0	804	26.0	0.0	43 305	0.4	1 819	4.2	40 615	30.1	26.6
Niobrara	1 045	62.2	147 700	24.4	10.5	559	24.6	2.0	1 368	-0.9	48	3.5	1 151	41.5	24.0
Park	11 801	72.1	212 100	23.3	11.9	666	20.6	1.2	15 795	-0.5	739	4.7	15 014	29.8	26.4
Platte	3 642	78.3	147 100	22.0	10.2	606	27.1	2.6	4 782	-0.5	193	4.0	4 169	33.9	25.5
Sheridan	12 381	69.3	220 400	23.6	10.7	748	26.9	3.5	15 960	1.0	766	4.8	14 310	35.6	26.2
Sublette	3 502	74.4	282 800	23.1	10.0	1 157	23.5	3.4	4 874	-4.1	218	4.5	5 380	40.5	36.6
Sweetwater	16 682	71.5	177 300	19.4	10.0	907	22.7	4.1	23 353	-2.3	972	4.2	22 890	24.8	38.3
Teton	7 583	59.1	660 100	24.6	11.9	1 099	29.2	2.5	14 387	1.9	690	4.8	13 571	39.3	15.6
Uinta	7 290	72.7	181 700	19.8	10.0	661	26.4	2.1	9 891	-0.7	498	5.0	9 965	31.0	32.9
Washakie	3 468	71.7	162 600	24.4	11.1	482	19.6	4.5	4 300	-1.5	194	4.5	3 990	30.7	31.3
Weston	2 975	76.1	136 000	20.8	10.0	719	18.4	0.0	3 970	0.3	136	3.4	3 462	29.2	39.3

1. Specified owner-occupied units. 2. A value of 10.0 represents 10 percent or less; a value of 50.0 represents 50 percent or more. 3. Specified renter-occupied units.
4. Overcrowded or lacking complete plumbing facilities. 5. Percent of civilian labor force. 6. Persons 16 years old and over.

STATE County	Private nonfarm establishments, employment and payroll, 2013									Agriculture, 2012			
		Employment						Annual payroll		Farms			
											Percent with:		
	Number of establish-ments	Total	Health care and social assistance	Manufac-turing	Retail trade	Finance and insurance	Professional, scientific, and technical services	Total (mil dol)	Average per employee (dollars)	Number	Fewer than 50 acres	500 acres or more	Farm operators whose principal occu-pation is farming (percent)
	104	105	106	107	108	109	110	111	112	113	114	115	116
WYOMING—Cont'd													
Crook	228	1 504	208	D	177	55	30	62	41 547	482	10.4	58.5	61.8
Fremont	1 367	11 732	2 121	249	2 076	294	487	439	37 449	1 363	37.0	20.4	55.0
Goshen	347	3 235	793	D	421	116	162	87	26 863	790	15.4	43.0	59.6
Hot Springs	187	1 668	429	D	155	D	48	60	35 966	178	32.6	31.5	42.7
Johnson	418	2 402	D	69	360	128	155	83	34 669	358	19.0	53.4	51.7
Laramie	2 909	33 066	6 732	1 172	5 645	1 725	1 891	1 311	39 648	1 116	33.5	31.2	37.3
Lincoln	625	4 021	708	275	625	119	109	185	46 028	608	41.0	20.1	46.4
Natrona	2 944	35 672	5 495	2 005	5 001	1 124	1 761	1 727	48 404	397	31.5	33.5	49.4
Niobrara	93	457	69	D	121	D	D	13	28 079	234	6.0	82.5	80.8
Park	1 204	9 394	D	500	1 528	309	365	372	39 625	860	37.4	18.8	47.4
Platte	269	2 113	342	D	385	68	D	85	40 205	505	18.2	46.9	59.4
Sheridan	1 142	9 474	2 272	405	1 598	D	640	334	35 229	702	36.3	31.8	45.9
Sublette	460	3 416	188	D	314	D	132	224	65 512	398	32.4	41.5	51.5
Sweetwater	1 347	17 053	1 369	1 787	2 414	306	495	980	57 447	255	27.8	36.9	30.6
Teton	1 952	15 357	1 155	131	1 687	387	807	629	40 957	154	50.6	12.3	41.6
Uinta	595	7 712	1 384	207	1 124	D	265	403	52 291	315	28.9	33.3	44.1
Washakie	378	2 986	831	355	367	102	114	105	35 054	209	39.2	35.4	52.6
Weston	220	1 668	364	D	281	D	35	61	36 592	264	7.2	50.4	51.1

STATE County	Agriculture, 2012 (cont.)															
	Land in farms					Value of land and buildings (dollars)			Value of products sold				Percent of farms with sales of:		Government payments	
			Acres								Percent from:					
	Acreage (1,000)	Percent change, 2007–2012	Average size of farm	Total irrigated (1,000)	Total cropland (1,000)	Average per farm	Average per acre	Value of machinery and equipment, average per farm (dollars)	Total (mil dol)	Average per farm (dollars)	Crops	Live-stock and poultry products	$10,000 or more	$100,000 or more	Total ($1,000)	Percent of farms
	117	118	119	120	121	122	123	124	125	126	127	128	129	130	131	132
WYOMING—Cont'd																
Crook	1 587	1.1	3 292	7.8	151.3	2 920 595	887	130 118	67.1	139 137	8.6	91.4	57.3	26.8	1 205	43.2
Fremont	1 710	-5.0	1 255	157.1	168.0	1 091 768	870	103 492	102.5	75 189	49.8	50.2	45.3	21.4	2 052	17.2
Goshen	1 370	0.1	1 735	109.2	241.5	1 346 967	777	141 356	246.6	312 103	26.8	73.2	58.1	33.3	4 662	55.6
Hot Springs	517	-5.4	2 906	12.6	28.1	2 030 427	699	84 197	16.4	92 388	12.7	87.3	49.4	17.4	361	10.7
Johnson	2 036	4.6	5 686	40.0	59.8	3 452 782	607	119 444	51.7	144 441	8.9	91.1	57.8	32.4	750	14.5
Laramie	1 676	-0.9	1 502	59.3	338.1	1 079 159	719	110 585	190.7	170 918	24.4	75.6	37.0	17.6	4 938	32.7
Lincoln	344	0.3	565	72.7	98.5	1 017 597	1 800	87 056	40.8	67 153	30.7	69.3	45.6	19.9	732	27.8
Natrona	1 691	-22.5	4 259	28.9	43.3	2 656 418	624	133 912	42.9	108 118	16.5	83.5	49.6	23.7	634	11.3
Niobrara	1 359	-6.2	5 807	14.6	75.4	3 112 043	536	122 726	45.3	193 684	18.0	82.0	78.6	49.6	1 331	39.7
Park	813	-7.8	946	110.3	109.9	1 324 298	1 401	105 421	100.3	116 611	63.4	36.6	42.8	18.3	1 271	27.1
Platte	1 224	-6.4	2 424	72.2	147.9	1 743 954	719	178 135	130.4	258 151	23.3	76.7	61.0	32.3	2 397	40.0
Sheridan	1 305	6.6	1 859	49.8	74.6	1 532 138	824	87 229	59.8	85 190	16.5	83.5	46.0	17.1	537	10.5
Sublette	778	29.7	1 954	143.1	122.6	2 626 852	1 345	104 369	54.2	136 116	14.5	85.5	43.5	24.6	373	5.5
Sweetwater	1 665	12.0	6 531	28.4	36.0	1 321 392	202	106 012	21.1	82 894	35.2	64.8	49.8	14.9	250	16.5
Teton	40	-24.1	261	14.7	10.5	829 494	3 181	69 526	9.0	58 675	24.2	75.8	34.4	7.1	16	1.9
Uinta	650	-12.5	2 064	70.1	68.7	1 518 038	735	99 092	29.9	94 816	10.2	89.8	53.7	21.6	88	3.8
Washakie	341	-27.3	1 633	38.4	39.9	1 450 273	888	172 411	51.9	248 153	51.2	48.8	57.9	29.7	451	20.6
Weston	1 290	-2.9	4 888	4.2	57.0	2 282 818	467	132 371	52.2	197 833	4.3	95.7	45.5	26.9	757	27.3

Table B. States and Counties — **Water Use, Wholesale Trade, Retail Trade, and Real Estate**

STATE County	Water use, 2010		Wholesale trade,[1] 2007				Retail trade,[2] 2007				Real estate and rental and leasing,[2] 2007			
	Total water withdrawn (mil gal/day)	Gallons withdrawn per person per day	Number of establish-ments	Number of employees	Sales (mil dol)	Annual payroll (mil dol)	Number of establish-ments	Number of employees	Sales (mil dol)	Annual payroll (mil dol)	Number of establish-ments	Number of employees	Receipts (mil dol)	Annual payroll (mil dol)
	133	134	135	136	137	138	139	140	141	142	143	144	145	146
WYOMING—Cont'd														
Crook	50.5	7 124	6	29	14.1	1.4	29	177	56.4	3.6	5	6	0.6	0.2
Fremont	510.0	12 711	36	254	76.2	8.0	203	2 145	558.4	53.8	78	439	116.1	19.0
Goshen	395.2	29 829	20	131	52.4	4.7	61	517	116.1	9.1	22	35	4.4	0.7
Hot Springs	78.3	16 268	3	D	D	D	34	228	38.3	3.4	7	9	0.9	0.1
Johnson	118.4	13 814	5	D	D	D	55	407	71.8	7.3	27	56	9.4	2.1
Laramie	236.4	2 577	98	800	628.1	35.2	360	5 603	1 720.5	133.4	134	519	94.2	14.3
Lincoln	204.3	11 282	9	103	26.8	2.7	92	699	221.7	14.7	24	62	4.5	0.8
Natrona	172.3	2 283	158	1 765	2 889.4	90.0	406	5 138	1 377.0	130.4	164	1 076	263.3	45.7
Niobrara	68.9	27 738	3	D	D	D	12	86	19.6	1.5	5	5	1.2	0.0
Park	305.0	10 813	37	200	155.5	8.5	213	1 588	388.4	37.4	67	161	19.0	2.7
Platte	350.2	40 404	5	63	34.1	2.1	47	413	93.4	7.9	15	32	3.8	0.6
Sheridan	198.2	6 808	40	D	D	D	176	1 769	478.2	43.7	66	234	32.3	6.2
Sublette	167.1	16 311	7	D	D	D	43	364	82.8	8.9	32	143	23.0	3.5
Sweetwater	169.0	3 859	62	573	437.5	32.0	202	2 753	898.2	69.7	74	426	105.3	18.8
Teton	31.2	1 466	32	D	D	D	261	2 043	515.6	57.9	150	528	138.7	22.1
Uinta	217.9	10 316	28	225	159.4	12.3	101	1 262	414.0	25.7	33	138	14.2	3.1
Washakie	165.5	19 393	10	69	12.1	2.0	51	476	98.3	8.9	19	68	10.1	1.7
Weston	27.9	3 869	6	51	11.5	2.1	30	241	64.3	4.3	9	9	1.5	0.2

1. Merchant wholesalers, except manufacturers' sales branches and offices. 2. Employer establishments.

STATE County	Professional, scientific, and technical services,[1] 2007				Manufacturing, 2007				Accommodation and food services, 2007			
	Number of establish-ments	Number of employees	Receipts (mil dol)	Annual payroll (mil dol)	Number of establish-ments	Number of employees	Receipts (mil dol)	Annual payroll (mil dol)	Number of establish-ments	Number of employees	Sales (mil dol)	Annual payroll (mil dol)
	147	148	149	150	151	152	153	154	155	156	157	158
WYOMING—Cont'd												
Crook	12	22	3.2	0.8	NA	NA	NA	NA	31	147	6.1	1.5
Fremont	118	406	55.5	14.8	NA	NA	NA	NA	133	1 495	67.0	18.4
Goshen	20	D	D	D	19	500	147.9	14.2	31	362	11.8	2.7
Hot Springs	18	46	3.3	1.3	NA	NA	NA	NA	24	309	10.4	3.0
Johnson	45	147	15.2	5.3	NA	NA	NA	NA	43	400	20.7	5.8
Laramie	312	1 402	182.0	65.2	61	1 710	2 420.2	80.9	185	3 938	173.7	52.1
Lincoln	46	124	11.6	4.1	22	539	D	29.4	61	435	21.1	4.3
Natrona	271	D	D	D	94	2 525	1 230.6	114.9	185	3 853	168.0	50.0
Niobrara	4	D	D	D	NA	NA	NA	NA	13	69	3.1	0.7
Park	93	374	40.3	15.5	54	541	62.7	20.0	157	1 363	133.0	32.8
Platte	22	56	5.2	1.2	NA	NA	NA	NA	34	347	12.1	3.2
Sheridan	119	D	D	D	NA	NA	NA	NA	96	1 398	66.8	19.0
Sublette	54	125	14.3	4.6	NA	NA	NA	NA	46	225	19.7	3.9
Sweetwater	104	447	64.5	22.2	34	2 122	D	145.8	108	2 040	150.4	30.1
Teton	253	D	D	D	NA	NA	NA	NA	180	4 525	327.4	112.2
Uinta	51	D	D	D	NA	NA	NA	NA	51	773	35.5	8.1
Washakie	28	115	10.8	3.5	NA	NA	NA	NA	33	299	10.2	2.8
Weston	13	D	D	D	NA	NA	NA	NA	29	210	7.5	1.8

1. Establishment subject to federal tax.

Table B. States and Counties — **Health Care and Social Assistance, Other Services, Nonemployer Businesses, and Residential Construction**

STATE County	Health care and social assistance, 2007				Other services, 2007				Nonemployer businesses, 2013		Value of residential construction authorized by building permits, 2014	
	Number of establish-ments	Number of employees	Receipts (mil dol)	Annual payroll (mil dol)	Number of establish-ments	Number of employees	Receipts (mil dol)	Annual payroll (mil dol)	Number	Receipts (mil dol)	New Construction ($1,000)	Number of housing units
	159	160	161	162	163	164	165	166	167	168	169	170
WYOMING—Cont'd												
Crook	16	D	D	D	12	D	D	D	651	25.7	598	5
Fremont	129	1 842	148.8	58.2	85	340	32.4	8.8	3 030	110.9	3 034	18
Goshen	24	763	39.2	19.3	26	86	6.8	1.6	918	34.2	240	1
Hot Springs	16	358	26.5	10.9	16	63	4.0	1.0	430	14.1	0	0
Johnson	24	428	30.0	13.1	23	84	6.9	2.2	1 030	45.9	2 058	12
Laramie	281	6 040	563.1	232.9	180	947	83.0	25.0	7 085	391.6	63 198	403
Lincoln	52	635	44.9	18.2	37	94	11.4	2.0	1 818	70.1	17 232	68
Natrona	283	4 819	482.2	203.0	202	1 200	141.1	34.1	5 545	299.8	72 398	330
Niobrara	6	D	D	D	8	D	D	D	256	11.5	37	1
Park	108	1 569	144.9	58.6	81	296	23.6	5.3	3 057	132.0	26 973	131
Platte	23	403	25.7	10.9	19	58	5.0	0.8	758	26.9	4 187	22
Sheridan	106	2 320	219.6	100.3	72	346	39.4	7.4	2 676	107.2	26 940	117
Sublette	20	192	13.2	5.7	29	150	25.8	6.6	969	45.7	6 890	27
Sweetwater	98	1 091	115.3	36.8	94	448	54.2	14.5	2 165	100.2	38 630	227
Teton	114	D	D	D	94	461	67.4	14.5	4 609	282.7	131 298	145
Uinta	69	1 403	97.1	39.5	47	143	13.3	2.9	1 366	62.0	9 359	40
Washakie	25	675	47.6	19.9	30	112	6.9	1.9	665	22.6	768	4
Weston	17	382	20.2	8.4	12	41	3.7	0.8	576	21.1	170	1

Table B. States and Counties — Government Employment and Payroll, and Local Government Finances

STATE County	Government employment and payroll, 2012									Local government finances, 2012				
			March payroll (percent of total)							General revenue				
												Taxes		
													Per capita[1] (dollars)	
	Full-time equivalent employees	March payroll (dollars)	Adminis-tration, judicial, and legal	Police and Corrections	Fire Protection	Highways and transpor-tation	Health and Welfare	Natural resources and utilities	Education and libraries	Total (mil dol)	Inter-govern-mental (mil dol)	Total (mil dol)	Total	Property
	171	172	173	174	175	176	177	178	179	180	181	182	183	184
WYOMING—Cont'd														
Crook	486	1 567 725	9.6	7.3	0.1	2.9	16.3	2.3	60.3	47.3	23.8	13.5	1 893	1 459
Fremont	2 549	9 152 411	3.7	7.9	0.4	2.1	3.0	9.4	71.6	264.6	168.1	62.0	1 509	1 270
Goshen	800	2 841 581	5.6	7.0	0.0	2.4	1.3	5.3	77.7	86.6	58.5	10.5	773	552
Hot Springs	363	1 248 475	7.7	7.2	0.0	3.0	30.6	3.5	46.8	44.5	12.8	14.8	3 062	2 366
Johnson	670	2 461 238	5.8	13.9	1.0	2.9	30.1	3.1	42.7	83.0	14.4	44.9	5 208	4 585
Laramie	6 173	27 578 286	2.8	4.6	1.9	1.8	39.8	1.5	46.1	796.0	292.8	103.3	1 094	589
Lincoln	1 211	4 847 475	5.1	5.7	0.0	2.9	30.1	3.4	50.4	146.8	60.4	43.1	2 402	2 075
Natrona	3 954	15 321 295	4.4	7.8	3.5	2.3	2.0	5.1	72.5	442.5	254.7	108.8	1 384	938
Niobrara	300	1 035 735	7.3	4.9	0.0	2.2	34.2	5.3	43.5	21.1	9.3	5.8	2 352	1 687
Park	2 084	8 399 901	4.2	4.7	0.4	2.6	27.2	5.2	52.8	238.1	92.8	47.9	1 668	1 494
Platte	543	2 168 168	5.1	7.9	0.2	2.2	1.5	6.3	74.9	46.5	26.6	13.3	1 519	995
Sheridan	2 207	8 719 701	3.2	4.7	1.0	2.3	30.0	3.0	54.6	234.1	106.6	40.1	1 354	946
Sublette	677	2 840 346	8.1	15.4	0.0	10.5	11.9	4.2	49.3	142.2	33.5	91.3	8 805	8 657
Sweetwater	2 985	12 809 450	6.0	8.4	2.4	2.6	20.2	5.8	52.6	382.6	116.8	165.8	3 662	2 797
Teton	1 475	6 340 874	5.4	7.3	1.5	7.9	37.5	5.7	32.3	225.0	41.2	80.1	3 695	2 344
Uinta	1 240	4 518 508	5.8	7.1	0.8	2.5	1.9	5.2	73.2	117.5	70.3	38.1	1 811	1 505
Washakie	459	1 506 233	5.8	5.8	0.7	2.9	2.6	6.0	75.1	45.2	28.7	12.2	1 442	998
Weston	521	1 865 375	4.5	8.0	0.4	2.9	23.8	5.3	54.7	44.2	22.9	9.7	1 375	1 062

1. Based on the resident population estimated as of July 1 of the year shown.

STATE County	Local government finances, 2012 (cont.) — Direct general expenditure — Total (mil dol)	Per capita[1] (dollars)	Percent of total for: Education	Health and hospitals	Police protection	Public welfare	Highways	Debt outstanding — Total (mil dol)	Per capita[1] (dollars)	Government employment, 2013 — Federal civilian	Federal military	State and local	Presidential election,[2] 2012 — Percent of vote cast: Democratic	Republican	All other
	185	186	187	188	189	190	191	192	193	194	195	196	197	198	199
WYOMING—Cont'd															
Crook	47.5	6 641	47.4	16.7	4.3	0.1	7.7	3.6	504	85	39	633	16.6	80.6	2.8
Fremont	258.8	6 295	73.2	1.1	4.0	0.4	3.3	31.2	759	479	218	5 488	34.2	63.0	2.8
Goshen	86.2	6 325	66.3	1.5	3.7	0.9	7.3	10.3	756	81	67	1 420	31.0	66.7	2.3
Hot Springs	44.9	9 306	33.3	31.7	3.7	0.0	5.2	4.5	931	12	26	551	24.3	72.0	3.7
Johnson	95.5	11 080	33.0	26.7	3.3	0.5	6.3	14.7	1 711	129	46	873	20.9	76.6	2.6
Laramie	781.4	8 270	37.0	40.5	2.5	0.2	3.1	132.4	1 401	2 589	3 647	11 412	38.6	59.0	2.4
Lincoln	144.3	8 033	47.9	26.3	3.6	0.1	4.8	60.9	3 388	115	99	1 636	21.3	75.7	3.0
Natrona	436.0	5 546	59.1	0.4	4.8	0.7	4.1	147.1	1 871	658	431	5 118	31.5	65.8	2.7
Niobrara	27.9	11 371	45.7	24.9	4.4	0.1	4.6	111.4	45 347	14	13	435	18.9	78.7	2.5
Park	277.9	9 682	41.4	36.2	2.5	0.0	2.9	79.0	2 754	783	154	2 846	25.1	72.3	2.6
Platte	48.9	5 582	54.4	2.9	7.4	0.1	4.1	8.7	993	111	47	849	30.9	65.8	3.3
Sheridan	252.8	8 543	49.0	26.5	2.5	0.0	5.2	33.2	1 121	738	156	2 679	29.8	67.9	2.3
Sublette	154.1	14 868	43.1	8.2	4.0	1.8	11.0	9.5	919	127	51	934	21.5	76.1	2.4
Sweetwater	389.7	8 609	48.2	17.5	5.5	0.3	4.3	69.5	1 536	231	242	4 368	34.5	62.0	3.5
Teton	218.0	10 059	24.1	34.3	3.8	0.0	2.4	92.9	4 287	406	119	1 890	60.7	37.1	2.3
Uinta	121.7	5 787	64.9	0.8	5.8	0.9	4.8	14.0	665	71	113	2 069	27.6	68.7	3.6
Washakie	52.1	6 153	68.3	0.8	4.1	0.4	3.0	12.8	1 512	120	45	739	25.5	72.3	2.2
Weston	48.0	6 780	47.5	21.6	4.2	0.6	10.3	2.0	286	52	37	775	19.4	77.2	3.4

1. Based on the resident population estimated as of July 1 of the year shown. 2.

PART C.

Metropolitan Areas

(For explanation of symbols, see page viii)

Page

Metropolitan Area Highlights and Rankings

Figure C-1. Top Ten Fastest Growing Metropolitan Areas Among the 75 Largest, 2010–2014

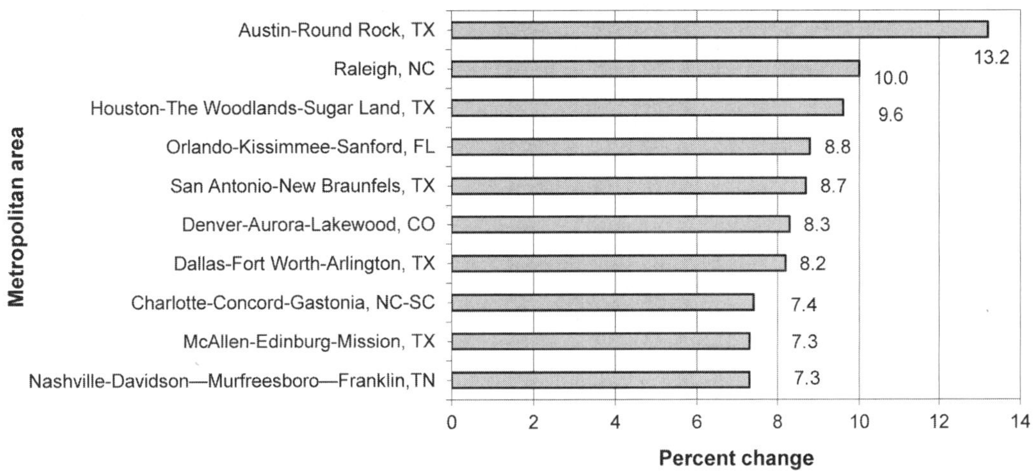

In 2014, 85.5 percent of Americans lived in metropolitan areas, but these metropolitan areas made up a mere 28 percent of the nation's land area. After nearly a decade of research and development, the Office of Management and Budget (OMB) first established new rules for defining metropolitan areas and issued a completely new list after the 2000 census. This scheme defines a variety of areas called "Core Based Statistical Areas" (CBSAs). Along with the new definition of metropolitan areas, OMB defined a new type of area—called a micropolitan area—that defines the many American communities with population clusters that are too small to meet the 50,000 minimum that defines a metropolitan area. Appendix C lists these micropolitan areas as of February 2013, but, because of size constraints, *County and City Extra* continues to include only metropolitan area data in Table C. In 2013, the Census Bureau released data for new metropolitan and micropolitan areas based on the 2010 census. This edition of *County and City Extra* uses these metropolitan area delineations. Most of the data producers are now releasing data for the new metropolitan areas. For a few data sources, the counties have been aggregated to the new areas.

With over 20 million people, the New York metropolitan area was the largest, followed by Los Angeles with a population of over 13 million. Chicago ranked third with 9.5 million people. Another 11 metropolitan areas had more than 4 million residents (Dallas, Houston, Philadelphia, Washington, Miami, Atlanta, Boston, San Francisco, Phoenix, Riverside, and Detroit), while 39 other metropolitan areas had between 1 million and 4 million people. Nearly 56 percent of the U.S. population lived in these 53 metropolitan areas with one million or more residents.

Eighty-four metropolitan areas grew by 5 percent or more between 2010 and 2014. The Villages, FL had the highest growth rate, increasing by 22.4 percent to a 2014 population of 114,350 residents. Among the 75 largest metropolitan areas, Austin-Round Rock-San Marcos, TX had the largest increase at 13.2 percent followed by Raleigh, NC at 10.0 percent. Two of the most populous metropolitan areas lost population since 2010—New Haven-Milford, CT and Cleveland-Elyria, OH.

Among metropolitan areas, New York and Los Angeles shared the top spots for density as well as for total population. With 1,056 persons per square kilometer, Los Angeles-Long Beach-Anaheim, CA was the most densely populated metropolitan area in the country. At the other extreme, three of the largest metropolitan areas had fewer than 50 persons per square kilometer. All three of these had large land areas and were located in western states (Albuquerque, NM; Bakersfield, CA; and Tucson, AZ).

In 2014, 13 metropolitan areas had an unemployment rate at 10 percent or higher. In contrast, 131 metropolitan areas had an unemployment rate at 10 percent or higher in 2010. Topping the list are El Centro, CA and Yuma, AZ, two metropolitan areas with large agricultural workforces and unemployment rates over 23 percent. Eight of the 10 metropolitan areas with the highest unemployment were in California. Two of the 75 most populous metropolitan areas had unemployment rates higher than 10 percent, topped by Fresno, CA with an unemployment rate of 11.6 percent. Eighty-five metropolitan areas had unemployment rates below 5 percent in 2014. Many of them were relatively small areas. Fargo, ND-MN had the lowest unemployment rate among all metropolitan areas at 2.7 percent followed by Sioux Falls, SD and Bismark, ND at 2.8 percent.

75 Largest Metropolitan Areas by 2014 Population
Selected Rankings

Population, 2014			Total land area, 2010			
Population rank	Metropolitan area	Population [col 2]	Population rank	Land area rank	Metropolitan area	Land area (square kilometers) [col 1]
1	New York-Newark-Jersey City, NY-NJ-PA	20 092 883	13	1	Riverside-San Bernardino-Ontario, CA	70 612
2	Los Angeles-Long Beach-Anaheim, CA	13 262 220	12	2	Phoenix-Mesa-Scottsdale, AZ	37 725
3	Chicago-Naperville-Elgin, IL-IN-WI	9 554 598	59	3	Albuquerque, NM	24 042
4	Dallas-Fort Worth-Arlington, TX	6 954 330	4	4	Dallas-Fort Worth-Arlington, TX	24 029
5	Houston-The Woodlands-Sugar Land, TX	6 490 180	53	5	Tucson, AZ	23 794
6	Philadelphia-Camden-Wilmington, PA-NJ-DE-MD	6 051 170	9	6	Atlanta-Sandy Springs-Roswell, GA	22 498
7	Washington-Arlington-Alexandria, DC-VA-MD-WV	6 033 737	21	7	Denver-Aurora-Lakewood, CO	21 616
8	Miami-Fort Lauderdale-West Palm Beach, FL	5 929 819	1	8	New York-Newark-Jersey City, NY-NJ-PA	21 480
9	Atlanta-Sandy Springs-Roswell, GA	5 614 323	5	9	Houston-The Woodlands-Sugar Land, TX	21 388
10	Boston-Cambridge-Newton, MA-NH	4 732 161	62	10	Bakersfield, CA	21 062
11	San Francisco-Oakland-Hayward, CA	4 594 060	30	11	Las Vegas-Henderson-Paradise, NV	20 439
12	Phoenix-Mesa-Scottsdale, AZ	4 489 109	19	12	St. Louis, MO-IL	20 366
13	Riverside-San Bernardino-Ontario, CA	4 441 890	48	13	Salt Lake City, UT	19 901
14	Detroit-Warren-Dearborn, MI	4 296 611	16	14	Minneapolis-St. Paul-Bloomington, MN	19 779
15	Seattle-Tacoma-Bellevue, WA	3 671 478	25	15	San Antonio-New Braunfels, TX	18 941
16	Minneapolis-St. Paul-Bloomington, MN	3 495 176	29	16	Kansas City, MO-KS	18 793
17	San Diego-Carlsbad, CA	3 263 431	3	17	Chicago-Naperville-Elgin, IL-IN-WI	18 639
18	Tampa-St. Petersburg-Clearwater, FL	2 915 582	24	18	Portland-Vancouver-Hillsboro, OR-WA	17 311
19	St. Louis, MO-IL	2 806 207	36	19	Nashville-Davidson—Murfreesboro—Franklin, TN	16 320
20	Baltimore-Columbia-Towson, MD	2 785 874	55	20	Tulsa, OK	16 237
21	Denver-Aurora-Lakewood, CO	2 754 258	7	21	Washington-Arlington-Alexandria, DC-VA-MD-WV	16 172
22	Charlotte-Concord-Gastonia, NC-SC	2 380 314	56	22	Fresno, CA	15 431
23	Pittsburgh, PA	2 355 968	15	23	Seattle-Tacoma-Bellevue, WA	15 209
24	Portland-Vancouver-Hillsboro, OR-WA	2 348 247	67	24	El Paso, TX	14 462
25	San Antonio-New Braunfels, TX	2 328 652	42	25	Oklahoma City, OK	14 274
26	Orlando-Kissimmee-Sanford, FL	2 321 418	23	26	Pittsburgh, PA	13 679
27	Sacramento—Roseville—Arden-Arcade, CA	2 244 397	49	27	Birmingham-Hoover, AL	13 673
28	Cincinnati, OH-KY-IN	2 149 449	27	28	Sacramento—Roseville—Arden-Arcade, CA	13 193
29	Kansas City, MO-KS	2 071 133	8	29	Miami-Fort Lauderdale-West Palm Beach, FL	13 150
30	Las Vegas-Henderson-Paradise, NV	2 069 681	22	30	Charlotte-Concord-Gastonia, NC-SC	13 123
31	Cleveland-Elyria, OH	2 063 598	41	31	Memphis, TN-MS-AR	12 909
32	Columbus, OH	1 994 536	2	32	Los Angeles-Long Beach-Anaheim, CA	12 558
33	Indianapolis-Carmel-Anderson, IN	1 971 274	32	33	Columbus, OH	12 423
34	San Jose-Sunnyvale-Santa Clara, CA	1 952 872	6	34	Philadelphia-Camden-Wilmington, PA-NJ-DE-MD	11 919
35	Austin-Round Rock, TX	1 943 299	44	35	Richmond, VA	11 852
36	Nashville-Davidson—Murfreesboro—Franklin, TN	1 792 649	60	36	Omaha-Council Bluffs, NE-IA	11 266
37	Virginia Beach-Norfolk-Newport News, VA-NC	1 716 624	33	37	Indianapolis-Carmel-Anderson, IN	11 153
38	Providence-Warwick, RI-MA	1 609 367	35	38	Austin-Round Rock, TX	10 929
39	Milwaukee-Waukesha-West Allis, WI	1 572 245	17	39	San Diego-Carlsbad, CA	10 895
40	Jacksonville, FL	1 419 127	28	40	Cincinnati, OH-KY-IN	10 797
41	Memphis, TN-MS-AR	1 343 230	75	41	Little Rock-North Little Rock-Conway, AR	10 580
42	Oklahoma City, OK	1 336 767	70	42	Baton Rouge, LA	10 429
43	Louisville/Jefferson County, KY-IN	1 269 702	14	43	Detroit-Warren-Dearborn, MI	10 070
44	Richmond, VA	1 260 029	72	44	Columbia, SC	9 590
45	New Orleans-Metairie, LA	1 251 849	43	45	Louisville/Jefferson County, KY-IN	9 267
46	Raleigh, NC	1 242 974	65	46	Knoxville, TN	9 066
47	Hartford-West Hartford-East Hartford, CT	1 214 295	10	47	Boston-Cambridge-Newton, MA-NH	9 033
48	Salt Lake City, UT	1 153 340	26	48	Orlando-Kissimmee-Sanford, FL	9 009
49	Birmingham-Hoover, AL	1 143 772	51	49	Rochester, NY	8 459
50	Buffalo-Cheektowaga-Niagara Falls, NY	1 136 360	45	50	New Orleans-Metairie, LA	8 294
51	Rochester, NY	1 083 393	40	51	Jacksonville, FL	8 291
52	Grand Rapids-Wyoming, MI	1 027 703	61	52	Albany-Schenectady-Troy, NY	7 283
53	Tucson, AZ	1 004 516	63	53	Greenville-Anderson-Mauldin, SC	7 021
54	Urban Honolulu, HI	991 788	37	54	Virginia Beach-Norfolk-Newport News, VA-NC	6 969
55	Tulsa, OK	969 224	34	55	San Jose-Sunnyvale-Santa Clara, CA	6 938
56	Fresno, CA	965 974	52	56	Grand Rapids-Wyoming, MI	6 913
57	Bridgeport-Stamford-Norwalk, CT	945 438	20	57	Baltimore-Columbia-Towson, MD	6 738
58	Worcester, MA-CT	930 473	18	58	Tampa-St. Petersburg-Clearwater, FL	6 509
59	Albuquerque, NM	904 587	11	59	San Francisco-Oakland-Hayward, CA	6 398
60	Omaha-Council Bluffs, NE-IA	904 421	46	60	Raleigh, NC	5 485
61	Albany-Schenectady-Troy, NY	880 167	58	61	Worcester, MA-CT	5 241
62	Bakersfield, CA	874 589	31	62	Cleveland-Elyria, OH	5 172
63	Greenville-Anderson-Mauldin, SC	862 463	74	63	Greensboro-High Point, NC	5 164
64	New Haven-Milford, CT	861 277	66	64	Oxnard-Thousand Oaks-Ventura, CA	4 774
65	Knoxville, TN	857 585	38	65	Providence-Warwick, RI-MA	4 111
66	Oxnard-Thousand Oaks-Ventura, CA	846 178	68	66	McAllen-Edinburg-Mission, TX	4 069
67	El Paso, TX	836 698	50	67	Buffalo-Cheektowaga-Niagara Falls, NY	4 054
68	McAllen-Edinburg-Mission, TX	831 073	47	68	Hartford-West Hartford-East Hartford, CT	3 922
69	Allentown-Bethlehem-Easton, PA-NJ	829 835	39	69	Milwaukee-Waukesha-West Allis, WI	3 768
70	Baton Rouge, LA	825 478	69	70	Allentown-Bethlehem-Easton, PA-NJ	3 763
71	Dayton, OH	800 836	73	71	North Port-Sarasota-Bradenton, FL	3 364
72	Columbia, SC	800 495	71	72	Dayton, OH	3 320
73	North Port-Sarasota-Bradenton, FL	748 708	57	73	Bridgeport-Stamford-Norwalk, CT	1 618
74	Greensboro-High Point, NC	746 593	64	74	New Haven-Milford, CT	1 566
75	Little Rock-North Little Rock-Conway, AR	729 135	54	75	Urban Honolulu, HI	1 556

75 Largest Metropolitan Areas by 2014 Population

Selected Rankings

Population density, 2014				Percent population change, 2010–2014			
Population rank	Density rank	Metropolitan area	Density (per square kilometer) [col 4]	Population rank	Percent change rank	Metropolitan area	Percent change [col 23]
2	1	Los Angeles-Long Beach-Anaheim, CA	1 056	35	1	Austin-Round Rock, TX	13.2
1	2	New York-Newark-Jersey City, NY-NJ-PA	935	46	2	Raleigh, NC	10.0
11	3	San Francisco-Oakland-Hayward, CA	718	5	3	Houston-The Woodlands-Sugar Land, TX	9.6
54	4	Urban Honolulu, HI	637	26	4	Orlando-Kissimmee-Sanford, FL	8.8
57	5	Bridgeport-Stamford-Norwalk, CT	584	25	5	San Antonio-New Braunfels, TX	8.7
64	6	New Haven-Milford, CT	550	21	6	Denver-Aurora-Lakewood, CO	8.3
10	7	Boston-Cambridge-Newton, MA-NH	524	4	7	Dallas-Fort Worth-Arlington, TX	8.2
3	8	Chicago-Naperville-Elgin, IL-IN-WI	513	22	8	Charlotte-Concord-Gastonia, NC-SC	7.4
6	9	Philadelphia-Camden-Wilmington, PA-NJ-DE-MD	508	36	9	Nashville-Davidson—Murfreesboro—Franklin, TN	7.3
8	10	Miami-Fort Lauderdale-West Palm Beach, FL	451	68	9	McAllen-Edinburg-Mission, TX	7.3
18	11	Tampa-St. Petersburg-Clearwater, FL	448	12	11	Phoenix-Mesa-Scottsdale, AZ	7.1
14	12	Detroit-Warren-Dearborn, MI	427	7	12	Washington-Arlington-Alexandria, DC-VA-MD-WV	7.0
39	13	Milwaukee-Waukesha-West Allis, WI	417	15	13	Seattle-Tacoma-Bellevue, WA	6.7
20	14	Baltimore-Columbia-Towson, MD	414	42	13	Oklahoma City, OK	6.7
31	15	Cleveland-Elyria, OH	399	73	15	North Port-Sarasota-Bradenton, FL	6.6
38	16	Providence-Warwick, RI-MA	392	8	16	Miami-Fort Lauderdale-West Palm Beach, FL	6.5
7	17	Washington-Arlington-Alexandria, DC-VA-MD-WV	373	34	17	San Jose-Sunnyvale-Santa Clara, CA	6.3
47	18	Hartford-West Hartford-East Hartford, CT	310	9	18	Atlanta-Sandy Springs-Roswell, GA	6.2
5	19	Houston-The Woodlands-Sugar Land, TX	303	30	19	Las Vegas-Henderson-Paradise, NV	6.1
17	20	San Diego-Carlsbad, CA	300	11	20	San Francisco-Oakland-Hayward, CA	6.0
4	21	Dallas-Fort Worth-Arlington, TX	289	48	20	Salt Lake City, UT	6.0
34	22	San Jose-Sunnyvale-Santa Clara, CA	282	24	22	Portland-Vancouver-Hillsboro, OR-WA	5.5
50	23	Buffalo-Cheektowaga-Niagara Falls, NY	280	40	22	Jacksonville, FL	5.5
26	24	Orlando-Kissimmee-Sanford, FL	258	17	24	San Diego-Carlsbad, CA	5.4
9	25	Atlanta-Sandy Springs-Roswell, GA	250	45	25	New Orleans-Metairie, LA	5.2
37	26	Virginia Beach-Norfolk-Newport News, VA-NC	246	13	26	Riverside-San Bernardino-Ontario, CA	5.1
15	27	Seattle-Tacoma-Bellevue, WA	241	32	27	Columbus, OH	4.9
71	28	Dayton, OH	241	18	28	Tampa-St. Petersburg-Clearwater, FL	4.7
46	29	Raleigh, NC	227	63	28	Greenville-Anderson-Mauldin, SC	4.7
73	30	North Port-Sarasota-Bradenton, FL	223	60	30	Omaha-Council Bluffs, NE-IA	4.5
69	31	Allentown-Bethlehem-Easton, PA-NJ	221	16	31	Minneapolis-St. Paul-Bloomington, MN	4.4
68	32	McAllen-Edinburg-Mission, TX	204	27	31	Sacramento—Roseville—Arden-Arcade, CA	4.4
28	33	Cincinnati, OH-KY-IN	199	33	31	Indianapolis-Carmel-Anderson, IN	4.4
22	34	Charlotte-Concord-Gastonia, NC-SC	181	44	34	Richmond, VA	4.3
35	35	Austin-Round Rock, TX	178	72	34	Columbia, SC	4.3
58	36	Worcester, MA-CT	178	62	36	Bakersfield, CA	4.2
66	37	Oxnard-Thousand Oaks-Ventura, CA	177	75	36	Little Rock-North Little Rock-Conway, AR	4.2
16	38	Minneapolis-St. Paul-Bloomington, MN	177	67	38	El Paso, TX	4.1
33	38	Indianapolis-Carmel-Anderson, IN	177	54	39	Urban Honolulu, HI	4.0
23	40	Pittsburgh, PA	172	10	40	Boston-Cambridge-Newton, MA-NH	3.9
40	41	Jacksonville, FL	171	52	40	Grand Rapids-Wyoming, MI	3.9
27	42	Sacramento—Roseville—Arden-Arcade, CA	170	56	42	Fresno, CA	3.8
32	43	Columbus, OH	161	2	43	Los Angeles-Long Beach-Anaheim, CA	3.4
45	44	New Orleans-Metairie, LA	151	55	43	Tulsa, OK	3.4
52	45	Grand Rapids-Wyoming, MI	149	29	45	Kansas City, MO-KS	3.1
74	46	Greensboro-High Point, NC	145	57	45	Bridgeport-Stamford-Norwalk, CT	3.1
19	47	St. Louis, MO-IL	138	74	45	Greensboro-High Point, NC	3.1
43	48	Louisville/Jefferson County, KY-IN	137	70	48	Baton Rouge, LA	2.9
24	49	Portland-Vancouver-Hillsboro, OR-WA	136	20	49	Baltimore-Columbia-Towson, MD	2.8
51	50	Rochester, NY	128	43	49	Louisville/Jefferson County, KY-IN	2.8
21	51	Denver-Aurora-Lakewood, CO	127	66	49	Oxnard-Thousand Oaks-Ventura, CA	2.8
25	52	San Antonio-New Braunfels, TX	123	1	52	New York-Newark-Jersey City, NY-NJ-PA	2.7
63	53	Greenville-Anderson-Mauldin, SC	123	53	53	Tucson, AZ	2.5
61	54	Albany-Schenectady-Troy, NY	121	37	54	Virginia Beach-Norfolk-Newport News, VA-NC	2.4
12	55	Phoenix-Mesa-Scottsdale, AZ	119	65	54	Knoxville, TN	2.4
29	56	Kansas City, MO-KS	110	59	56	Albuquerque, NM	2.0
36	57	Nashville-Davidson—Murfreesboro—Franklin, TN	110	28	57	Cincinnati, OH-KY-IN	1.6
44	58	Richmond, VA	106	58	58	Worcester, MA-CT	1.5
41	59	Memphis, TN-MS-AR	104	6	59	Philadelphia-Camden-Wilmington, PA-NJ-DE-MD	1.4
30	60	Las Vegas-Henderson-Paradise, NV	101	41	59	Memphis, TN-MS-AR	1.4
65	61	Knoxville, TN	95	49	59	Birmingham-Hoover, AL	1.4
42	62	Oklahoma City, OK	81	61	62	Albany-Schenectady-Troy, NY	1.1
49	63	Birmingham-Hoover, AL	84	3	63	Chicago-Naperville-Elgin, IL-IN-WI	1.0
72	64	Columbia, SC	84	39	63	Milwaukee-Waukesha-West Allis, WI	1.0
60	65	Omaha-Council Bluffs, NE-IA	80	69	63	Allentown-Bethlehem-Easton, PA-NJ	1.0
70	66	Baton Rouge, LA	79	19	66	St. Louis, MO-IL	0.7
75	67	Little Rock-North Little Rock-Conway, AR	69	38	67	Providence-Warwick, RI-MA	0.5
13	68	Riverside-San Bernardino-Ontario, CA	63	51	68	Rochester, NY	0.3
56	69	Fresno, CA	63	47	69	Hartford-West Hartford-East Hartford, CT	0.2
55	70	Tulsa, OK	60	71	69	Dayton, OH	0.2
48	71	Salt Lake City, UT	58	50	71	Buffalo-Cheektowaga-Niagara Falls, NY	0.1
67	72	El Paso, TX	58	14	72	Detroit-Warren-Dearborn, MI	0.0
53	73	Tucson, AZ	42	23	72	Pittsburgh, PA	0.0
62	74	Bakersfield, CA	42	64	74	New Haven-Milford, CT	-0.1
59	75	Albuquerque, NM	38	31	75	Cleveland-Elyria, OH	-0.7

75 Largest Metropolitan Areas by 2014 Population

Selected Rankings

Percent White, not Hispanic or Latino, alone or in combination, 2013

Population rank	White rank	Metropolitan area	Percent White [col 5]
65	1	Knoxville, TN	89.1
23	2	Pittsburgh, PA	87.9
61	3	Albany-Schenectady-Troy, NY	83.6
28	4	Cincinnati, OH-KY-IN	82.5
52	5	Grand Rapids-Wyoming, MI	81.9
58	6	Worcester, MA-CT	81.7
38	7	Providence-Warwick, RI-MA	80.4
50	8	Buffalo-Cheektowaga-Niagara Falls, NY	80.2
16	9	Minneapolis-St. Paul-Bloomington, MN	79.9
73	10	North Port-Sarasota-Bradenton, FL	79.8
60	11	Omaha-Council Bluffs, NE-IA	79.7
71	12	Dayton, OH	79.6
43	13	Louisville/Jefferson County, KY-IN	79.5
51	14	Rochester, NY	79.3
24	15	Portland-Vancouver-Hillsboro, OR-WA	78.4
69	16	Allentown-Bethlehem-Easton, PA-NJ	77.8
32	17	Columbus, OH	77.7
19	18	St. Louis, MO-IL	76.1
33	18	Indianapolis-Carmel-Anderson, IN	76.1
29	20	Kansas City, MO-KS	75.7
48	21	Salt Lake City, UT	75.5
10	22	Boston-Cambridge-Newton, MA-NH	75.2
36	22	Nashville-Davidson—Murfreesboro—Franklin, TN	75.2
63	24	Greenville-Anderson-Mauldin, SC	75.0
31	25	Cleveland-Elyria, OH	72.6
55	26	Tulsa, OK	72.3
47	27	Hartford-West Hartford-East Hartford, CT	71.2
15	28	Seattle-Tacoma-Bellevue, WA	70.5
42	29	Oklahoma City, OK	70.2
75	29	Little Rock-North Little Rock-Conway, AR	70.2
39	31	Milwaukee-Waukesha-West Allis, WI	69.6
14	32	Detroit-Warren-Dearborn, MI	69.2
18	33	Tampa-St. Petersburg-Clearwater, FL	67.5
21	34	Denver-Aurora-Lakewood, CO	67.3
64	35	New Haven-Milford, CT	67.1
40	36	Jacksonville, FL	66.8
57	37	Bridgeport-Stamford-Norwalk, CT	65.7
49	38	Birmingham-Hoover, AL	65.3
6	39	Philadelphia-Camden-Wilmington, PA-NJ-DE-MD	65.2
22	40	Charlotte-Concord-Gastonia, NC-SC	64.7
46	41	Raleigh, NC	64.1
74	42	Greensboro-High Point, NC	62.1
20	43	Baltimore-Columbia-Towson, MD	60.6
44	44	Richmond, VA	60.3
12	45	Phoenix-Mesa-Scottsdale, AZ	59.4
37	46	Virginia Beach-Norfolk-Newport News, VA-NC	59.1
72	47	Columbia, SC	58.9
70	48	Baton Rouge, LA	58.3
27	49	Sacramento—Roseville—Arden-Arcade, CA	57.9
53	50	Tucson, AZ	55.5
3	51	Chicago-Naperville-Elgin, IL-IN-WI	55.4
35	51	Austin-Round Rock, TX	55.4
45	53	New Orleans-Metairie, LA	53.8
26	54	Orlando-Kissimmee-Sanford, FL	52.5
9	55	Atlanta-Sandy Springs-Roswell, GA	51.1
4	56	Dallas-Fort Worth-Arlington, TX	50.4
17	57	San Diego-Carlsbad, CA	49.9
7	58	Washington-Arlington-Alexandria, DC-VA-MD-WV	49.8
1	59	New York-Newark-Jersey City, NY-NJ-PA	49.4
66	60	Oxnard-Thousand Oaks-Ventura, CA	49.3
30	61	Las Vegas-Henderson-Paradise, NV	48.8
41	62	Memphis, TN-MS-AR	46.3
11	63	San Francisco-Oakland-Hayward, CA	44.6
59	64	Albuquerque, NM	42.6
5	65	Houston-The Woodlands-Sugar Land, TX	39.5
62	66	Bakersfield, CA	38.6
13	67	Riverside-San Bernardino-Ontario, CA	36.7
34	68	San Jose-Sunnyvale-Santa Clara, CA	36.6
25	69	San Antonio-New Braunfels, TX	36.5
8	70	Miami-Fort Lauderdale-West Palm Beach, FL	34.2
56	71	Fresno, CA	33.0
54	72	Urban Honolulu, HI	32.9
2	73	Los Angeles-Long Beach-Anaheim, CA	32.6
67	74	El Paso, TX	14.2
68	75	McAllen-Edinburg-Mission, TX	7.4

Percent Black, not Hispanic or Latino, alone or in combination, 2013

Population rank	Black rank	Metropolitan area	Percent Black [col 6]
41	1	Memphis, TN-MS-AR	46.8
70	2	Baton Rouge, LA	36.2
45	3	New Orleans-Metairie, LA	35.2
72	4	Columbia, SC	34.2
9	5	Atlanta-Sandy Springs-Roswell, GA	33.6
37	6	Virginia Beach-Norfolk-Newport News, VA-NC	31.9
44	7	Richmond, VA	31.0
20	8	Baltimore-Columbia-Towson, MD	29.8
49	9	Birmingham-Hoover, AL	29.1
74	10	Greensboro-High Point, NC	27.1
7	11	Washington-Arlington-Alexandria, DC-VA-MD-WV	26.3
14	12	Detroit-Warren-Dearborn, MI	23.4
75	12	Little Rock-North Little Rock-Conway, AR	23.4
22	14	Charlotte-Concord-Gastonia, NC-SC	23.0
40	15	Jacksonville, FL	22.3
6	16	Philadelphia-Camden-Wilmington, PA-NJ-DE-MD	21.4
46	17	Raleigh, NC	21.0
8	18	Miami-Fort Lauderdale-West Palm Beach, FL	20.9
31	19	Cleveland-Elyria, OH	20.8
19	20	St. Louis, MO-IL	19.3
39	21	Milwaukee-Waukesha-West Allis, WI	17.5
63	21	Greenville-Anderson-Mauldin, SC	17.5
3	23	Chicago-Naperville-Elgin, IL-IN-WI	17.4
5	23	Houston-The Woodlands-Sugar Land, TX	17.4
71	25	Dayton, OH	16.9
1	26	New York-Newark-Jersey City, NY-NJ-PA	16.7
26	27	Orlando-Kissimmee-Sanford, FL	16.3
32	28	Columbus, OH	16.1
36	28	Nashville-Davidson—Murfreesboro—Franklin, TN	16.1
33	30	Indianapolis-Carmel-Anderson, IN	15.9
4	31	Dallas-Fort Worth-Arlington, TX	15.8
43	32	Louisville/Jefferson County, KY-IN	15.3
29	33	Kansas City, MO-KS	13.6
28	34	Cincinnati, OH-KY-IN	13.2
64	35	New Haven-Milford, CT	13.1
50	36	Buffalo-Cheektowaga-Niagara Falls, NY	12.9
18	37	Tampa-St. Petersburg-Clearwater, FL	12.4
51	38	Rochester, NY	12.0
42	39	Oklahoma City, OK	11.8
30	40	Las Vegas-Henderson-Paradise, NV	11.7
47	41	Hartford-West Hartford-East Hartford, CT	11.3
57	42	Bridgeport-Stamford-Norwalk, CT	11.2
55	43	Tulsa, OK	9.6
23	44	Pittsburgh, PA	9.3
11	45	San Francisco-Oakland-Hayward, CA	8.8
16	45	Minneapolis-St. Paul-Bloomington, MN	8.8
60	45	Omaha-Council Bluffs, NE-IA	8.8
61	48	Albany-Schenectady-Troy, NY	8.7
27	49	Sacramento—Roseville—Arden-Arcade, CA	8.4
10	50	Boston-Cambridge-Newton, MA-NH	8.0
13	50	Riverside-San Bernardino-Ontario, CA	8.0
35	52	Austin-Round Rock, TX	7.7
52	53	Grand Rapids-Wyoming, MI	7.5
2	54	Los Angeles-Long Beach-Anaheim, CA	7.2
73	54	North Port-Sarasota-Bradenton, FL	7.2
15	56	Seattle-Tacoma-Bellevue, WA	7.1
25	57	San Antonio-New Braunfels, TX	6.9
65	58	Knoxville, TN	6.6
21	59	Denver-Aurora-Lakewood, CO	6.2
38	60	Providence-Warwick, RI-MA	5.9
62	60	Bakersfield, CA	5.9
12	62	Phoenix-Mesa-Scottsdale, AZ	5.7
17	62	San Diego-Carlsbad, CA	5.7
69	64	Allentown-Bethlehem-Easton, PA-NJ	5.5
56	65	Fresno, CA	5.3
58	66	Worcester, MA-CT	4.6
53	67	Tucson, AZ	4.0
54	68	Urban Honolulu, HI	3.8
24	69	Portland-Vancouver-Hillsboro, OR-WA	3.7
67	70	El Paso, TX	3.4
34	71	San Jose-Sunnyvale-Santa Clara, CA	2.9
59	71	Albuquerque, NM	2.9
66	73	Oxnard-Thousand Oaks-Ventura, CA	2.2
48	74	Salt Lake City, UT	2.0
68	75	McAllen-Edinburg-Mission, TX	0.5

75 Largest Metropolitan Areas by 2014 Population

Selected Rankings

Percent American Indian, Alaska Native, alone or in combination, 2013

Population rank	American Indian Alaska native rank	Metropolitan area	Percent American Indian, Alaska Native [col 7]
55	1	Tulsa, OK	12.8
42	2	Oklahoma City, OK	6.7
59	3	Albuquerque, NM	5.8
53	4	Tucson, AZ	3.1
12	5	Phoenix-Mesa-Scottsdale, AZ	2.4
15	6	Seattle-Tacoma-Bellevue, WA	2.0
24	7	Portland-Vancouver-Hillsboro, OR-WA	1.7
27	8	Sacramento—Roseville—Arden-Arcade, CA	1.5
54	8	Urban Honolulu, HI	1.5
16	10	Minneapolis-St. Paul-Bloomington, MN	1.3
62	10	Bakersfield, CA	1.3
29	12	Kansas City, MO-KS	1.2
56	12	Fresno, CA	1.2
21	14	Denver-Aurora-Lakewood, CO	1.1
37	14	Virginia Beach-Norfolk-Newport News, VA-NC	1.1
48	14	Salt Lake City, UT	1.1
75	14	Little Rock-North Little Rock-Conway, AR	1.1
13	18	Riverside-San Bernardino-Ontario, CA	1.0
17	18	San Diego-Carlsbad, CA	1.0
30	18	Las Vegas-Henderson-Paradise, NV	1.0
50	18	Buffalo-Cheektowaga-Niagara Falls, NY	1.0
60	18	Omaha-Council Bluffs, NE-IA	1.0
74	18	Greensboro-High Point, NC	1.0
4	24	Dallas-Fort Worth-Arlington, TX	0.9
11	24	San Francisco-Oakland-Hayward, CA	0.9
14	24	Detroit-Warren-Dearborn, MI	0.9
22	24	Charlotte-Concord-Gastonia, NC-SC	0.9
38	24	Providence-Warwick, RI-MA	0.9
39	24	Milwaukee-Waukesha-West Allis, WI	0.9
44	24	Richmond, VA	0.9
52	24	Grand Rapids-Wyoming, MI	0.9
7	32	Washington-Arlington-Alexandria, DC-VA-MD-WV	0.8
20	32	Baltimore-Columbia-Towson, MD	0.8
32	32	Columbus, OH	0.8
35	32	Austin-Round Rock, TX	0.8
40	32	Jacksonville, FL	0.8
45	32	New Orleans-Metairie, LA	0.8
46	32	Raleigh, NC	0.8
65	32	Knoxville, TN	0.8
66	32	Oxnard-Thousand Oaks-Ventura, CA	0.8
71	32	Dayton, OH	0.8
72	32	Columbia, SC	0.8
9	43	Atlanta-Sandy Springs-Roswell, GA	0.7
18	43	Tampa-St. Petersburg-Clearwater, FL	0.7
19	43	St. Louis, MO-IL	0.7
34	43	San Jose-Sunnyvale-Santa Clara, CA	0.7
36	43	Nashville-Davidson—Murfreesboro—Franklin, TN	0.7
43	43	Louisville/Jefferson County, KY-IN	0.7
49	43	Birmingham-Hoover, AL	0.7
2	50	Los Angeles-Long Beach-Anaheim, CA	0.6
5	50	Houston-The Woodlands-Sugar Land, TX	0.6
6	50	Philadelphia-Camden-Wilmington, PA-NJ-DE-MD	0.6
25	50	San Antonio-New Braunfels, TX	0.6
26	50	Orlando-Kissimmee-Sanford, FL	0.6
28	50	Cincinnati, OH-KY-IN	0.6
31	50	Cleveland-Elyria, OH	0.6
33	50	Indianapolis-Carmel-Anderson, IN	0.6
41	50	Memphis, TN-MS-AR	0.6
47	50	Hartford-West Hartford-East Hartford, CT	0.6
51	50	Rochester, NY	0.6
58	50	Worcester, MA-CT	0.6
61	50	Albany-Schenectady-Troy, NY	0.6
63	50	Greenville-Anderson-Mauldin, SC	0.6
64	50	New Haven-Milford, CT	0.6
70	50	Baton Rouge, LA	0.6
1	66	New York-Newark-Jersey City, NY-NJ-PA	0.5
3	66	Chicago-Naperville-Elgin, IL-IN-WI	0.5
10	66	Boston-Cambridge-Newton, MA-NH	0.5
23	66	Pittsburgh, PA	0.5
67	66	El Paso, TX	0.5
73	66	North Port-Sarasota-Bradenton, FL	0.5
8	72	Miami-Fort Lauderdale-West Palm Beach, FL	0.4
57	72	Bridgeport-Stamford-Norwalk, CT	0.4
69	72	Allentown-Bethlehem-Easton, PA-NJ	0.4
68	75	McAllen-Edinburg-Mission, TX	0.1

Percent Asian and Pacific Islander, alone or in combination, 2013

Population rank	Asian and Pacific Islander rank	Metropolitan area	Percent Asian and Pacific Islander [col 8]
54	1	Urban Honolulu, HI	77.3
34	2	San Jose-Sunnyvale-Santa Clara, CA	35.2
11	3	San Francisco-Oakland-Hayward, CA	27.8
2	4	Los Angeles-Long Beach-Anaheim, CA	16.8
15	5	Seattle-Tacoma-Bellevue, WA	15.9
27	6	Sacramento—Roseville—Arden-Arcade, CA	15.7
17	7	San Diego-Carlsbad, CA	13.9
30	8	Las Vegas-Henderson-Paradise, NV	12.1
1	9	New York-Newark-Jersey City, NY-NJ-PA	11.4
7	10	Washington-Arlington-Alexandria, DC-VA-MD-WV	11.2
56	11	Fresno, CA	10.8
66	12	Oxnard-Thousand Oaks-Ventura, CA	8.6
24	13	Portland-Vancouver-Hillsboro, OR-WA	8.5
10	14	Boston-Cambridge-Newton, MA-NH	8.0
13	15	Riverside-San Bernardino-Ontario, CA	7.8
5	16	Houston-The Woodlands-Sugar Land, TX	7.7
16	17	Minneapolis-St. Paul-Bloomington, MN	7.0
3	18	Chicago-Naperville-Elgin, IL-IN-WI	6.8
4	19	Dallas-Fort Worth-Arlington, TX	6.6
6	20	Philadelphia-Camden-Wilmington, PA-NJ-DE-MD	6.1
48	20	Salt Lake City, UT	6.1
9	22	Atlanta-Sandy Springs-Roswell, GA	6.0
20	22	Baltimore-Columbia-Towson, MD	6.0
35	22	Austin-Round Rock, TX	6.0
57	25	Bridgeport-Stamford-Norwalk, CT	5.9
46	26	Raleigh, NC	5.7
62	27	Bakersfield, CA	5.3
26	28	Orlando-Kissimmee-Sanford, FL	5.1
37	28	Virginia Beach-Norfolk-Newport News, VA-NC	5.1
21	30	Denver-Aurora-Lakewood, CO	4.9
47	30	Hartford-West Hartford-East Hartford, CT	4.9
12	32	Phoenix-Mesa-Scottsdale, AZ	4.7
40	32	Jacksonville, FL	4.7
58	34	Worcester, MA-CT	4.6
61	35	Albany-Schenectady-Troy, NY	4.5
14	36	Detroit-Warren-Dearborn, MI	4.4
44	36	Richmond, VA	4.4
64	36	New Haven-Milford, CT	4.4
18	39	Tampa-St. Petersburg-Clearwater, FL	4.0
32	39	Columbus, OH	4.0
42	41	Oklahoma City, OK	3.8
74	41	Greensboro-High Point, NC	3.8
39	43	Milwaukee-Waukesha-West Allis, WI	3.7
53	43	Tucson, AZ	3.7
22	45	Charlotte-Concord-Gastonia, NC-SC	3.6
38	46	Providence-Warwick, RI-MA	3.5
29	47	Kansas City, MO-KS	3.4
45	48	New Orleans-Metairie, LA	3.3
51	48	Rochester, NY	3.3
69	48	Allentown-Bethlehem-Easton, PA-NJ	3.3
50	51	Buffalo-Cheektowaga-Niagara Falls, NY	3.1
60	51	Omaha-Council Bluffs, NE-IA	3.1
8	53	Miami-Fort Lauderdale-West Palm Beach, FL	3.0
33	53	Indianapolis-Carmel-Anderson, IN	3.0
36	53	Nashville-Davidson—Murfreesboro—Franklin, TN	3.0
19	56	St. Louis, MO-IL	2.9
25	56	San Antonio-New Braunfels, TX	2.9
59	56	Albuquerque, NM	2.9
52	59	Grand Rapids-Wyoming, MI	2.8
28	60	Cincinnati, OH-KY-IN	2.7
71	60	Dayton, OH	2.7
31	62	Cleveland-Elyria, OH	2.6
55	62	Tulsa, OK	2.6
72	64	Columbia, SC	2.5
23	65	Pittsburgh, PA	2.4
41	65	Memphis, TN-MS-AR	2.4
70	65	Baton Rouge, LA	2.4
43	68	Louisville/Jefferson County, KY-IN	2.3
63	69	Greenville-Anderson-Mauldin, SC	2.1
73	69	North Port-Sarasota-Bradenton, FL	2.1
75	69	Little Rock-North Little Rock-Conway, AR	2.1
65	72	Knoxville, TN	1.8
49	73	Birmingham-Hoover, AL	1.7
67	74	El Paso, TX	1.6
68	75	McAllen-Edinburg-Mission, TX	1.1

75 Largest Metropolitan Areas by 2014 Population

Selected Rankings

Percent Hispanic or Latino,[1] 2013

Population rank	Hispanic or Latino rank	Metropolitan area	Percent Hispanic or Latino [col 9]
68	1	McAllen-Edinburg-Mission, TX	90.7
67	2	El Paso, TX	80.7
25	3	San Antonio-New Braunfels, TX	54.4
56	4	Fresno, CA	51.5
62	5	Bakersfield, CA	50.8
13	6	Riverside-San Bernardino-Ontario, CA	48.8
59	7	Albuquerque, NM	47.7
2	8	Los Angeles-Long Beach-Anaheim, CA	44.8
8	9	Miami-Fort Lauderdale-West Palm Beach, FL	42.5
66	10	Oxnard-Thousand Oaks-Ventura, CA	41.5
5	11	Houston-The Woodlands-Sugar Land, TX	36.0
53	12	Tucson, AZ	35.6
17	13	San Diego-Carlsbad, CA	32.8
35	14	Austin-Round Rock, TX	31.9
30	15	Las Vegas-Henderson-Paradise, NV	30.0
12	16	Phoenix-Mesa-Scottsdale, AZ	29.9
4	17	Dallas-Fort Worth-Arlington, TX	28.0
34	18	San Jose-Sunnyvale-Santa Clara, CA	27.6
26	19	Orlando-Kissimmee-Sanford, FL	27.3
1	20	New York-Newark-Jersey City, NY-NJ-PA	23.4
21	21	Denver-Aurora-Lakewood, CO	22.7
11	22	San Francisco-Oakland-Hayward, CA	21.8
3	23	Chicago-Naperville-Elgin, IL-IN-WI	21.4
27	24	Sacramento—Roseville—Arden-Arcade, CA	20.8
57	25	Bridgeport-Stamford-Norwalk, CT	18.2
18	26	Tampa-St. Petersburg-Clearwater, FL	17.3
48	26	Salt Lake City, UT	17.3
64	28	New Haven-Milford, CT	16.4
7	29	Washington-Arlington-Alexandria, DC-VA-MD-WV	14.7
69	30	Allentown-Bethlehem-Easton, PA-NJ	14.5
47	31	Hartford-West Hartford-East Hartford, CT	13.6
42	32	Oklahoma City, OK	12.1
73	33	North Port-Sarasota-Bradenton, FL	11.7
24	34	Portland-Vancouver-Hillsboro, OR-WA	11.3
38	35	Providence-Warwick, RI-MA	11.2
9	36	Atlanta-Sandy Springs-Roswell, GA	10.5
46	37	Raleigh, NC	10.3
58	38	Worcester, MA-CT	10.2
39	39	Milwaukee-Waukesha-West Allis, WI	10.1
10	40	Boston-Cambridge-Newton, MA-NH	9.9
22	41	Charlotte-Concord-Gastonia, NC-SC	9.6
15	42	Seattle-Tacoma-Bellevue, WA	9.5
60	42	Omaha-Council Bluffs, NE-IA	9.5
54	44	Urban Honolulu, HI	9.2
52	45	Grand Rapids-Wyoming, MI	9.0
55	46	Tulsa, OK	8.9
29	47	Kansas City, MO-KS	8.6
6	48	Philadelphia-Camden-Wilmington, PA-NJ-DE-MD	8.5
45	49	New Orleans-Metairie, LA	8.3
74	50	Greensboro-High Point, NC	7.9
40	51	Jacksonville, FL	7.6
36	52	Nashville-Davidson—Murfreesboro—Franklin, TN	6.8
51	53	Rochester, NY	6.6
63	54	Greenville-Anderson-Mauldin, SC	6.4
33	55	Indianapolis-Carmel-Anderson, IN	6.3
37	56	Virginia Beach-Norfolk-Newport News, VA-NC	6.1
16	57	Minneapolis-St. Paul-Bloomington, MN	5.6
44	57	Richmond, VA	5.6
72	59	Columbia, SC	5.3
41	60	Memphis, TN-MS-AR	5.2
20	61	Baltimore-Columbia-Towson, MD	5.1
31	61	Cleveland-Elyria, OH	5.1
75	63	Little Rock-North Little Rock-Conway, AR	5.0
61	64	Albany-Schenectady-Troy, NY	4.7
50	65	Buffalo-Cheektowaga-Niagara Falls, NY	4.5
49	66	Birmingham-Hoover, AL	4.4
43	67	Louisville/Jefferson County, KY-IN	4.3
14	68	Detroit-Warren-Dearborn, MI	4.1
32	69	Columbus, OH	3.8
70	70	Baton Rouge, LA	3.7
65	71	Knoxville, TN	3.4
19	72	St. Louis, MO-IL	2.8
28	72	Cincinnati, OH-KY-IN	2.8
71	74	Dayton, OH	2.4
23	75	Pittsburgh, PA	1.5

Percent under 18 years old, 2013

Population rank	Under 18 years old rank	Metropolitan area	Percent Under 18 years old [cols 10 and 11]
68	1	McAllen-Edinburg-Mission, TX	34.0
62	2	Bakersfield, CA	29.6
56	3	Fresno, CA	29.2
67	4	El Paso, TX	28.9
48	5	Salt Lake City, UT	28.8
5	6	Houston-The Woodlands-Sugar Land, TX	27.3
13	7	Riverside-San Bernardino-Ontario, CA	27.2
4	8	Dallas-Fort Worth-Arlington, TX	27.1
25	9	San Antonio-New Braunfels, TX	26.0
60	9	Omaha-Council Bluffs, NE-IA	26.0
9	11	Atlanta-Sandy Springs-Roswell, GA	25.7
41	11	Memphis, TN-MS-AR	25.7
33	13	Indianapolis-Carmel-Anderson, IN	25.4
46	13	Raleigh, NC	25.4
12	15	Phoenix-Mesa-Scottsdale, AZ	25.3
55	16	Tulsa, OK	25.2
29	17	Kansas City, MO-KS	25.1
52	18	Grand Rapids-Wyoming, MI	25.1
42	19	Oklahoma City, OK	24.9
22	20	Charlotte-Concord-Gastonia, NC-SC	24.8
35	21	Austin-Round Rock, TX	24.6
66	22	Oxnard-Thousand Oaks-Ventura, CA	24.5
28	23	Cincinnati, OH-KY-IN	24.3
16	24	Minneapolis-St. Paul-Bloomington, MN	24.3
30	25	Las Vegas-Henderson-Paradise, NV	24.2
32	26	Columbus, OH	24.2
75	26	Little Rock-North Little Rock-Conway, AR	24.2
3	28	Chicago-Naperville-Elgin, IL-IN-WI	24.1
21	28	Denver-Aurora-Lakewood, CO	24.1
70	30	Baton Rouge, LA	24.0
27	31	Sacramento—Roseville—Arden-Arcade, CA	23.9
57	31	Bridgeport-Stamford-Norwalk, CT	23.9
39	33	Milwaukee-Waukesha-West Allis, WI	23.9
36	34	Nashville-Davidson—Murfreesboro—Franklin, TN	23.8
59	35	Albuquerque, NM	23.7
34	36	San Jose-Sunnyvale-Santa Clara, CA	23.5
7	37	Washington-Arlington-Alexandria, DC-VA-MD-WV	23.4
49	37	Birmingham-Hoover, AL	23.4
14	39	Detroit-Warren-Dearborn, MI	23.2
2	40	Los Angeles-Long Beach-Anaheim, CA	23.2
43	40	Louisville/Jefferson County, KY-IN	23.2
19	42	St. Louis, MO-IL	23.0
40	42	Jacksonville, FL	23.0
63	42	Greenville-Anderson-Mauldin, SC	23.0
24	45	Portland-Vancouver-Hillsboro, OR-WA	22.8
72	45	Columbia, SC	22.8
74	45	Greensboro-High Point, NC	22.8
26	48	Orlando-Kissimmee-Sanford, FL	22.7
45	48	New Orleans-Metairie, LA	22.7
17	50	San Diego-Carlsbad, CA	22.6
37	50	Virginia Beach-Norfolk-Newport News, VA-NC	22.6
6	52	Philadelphia-Camden-Wilmington, PA-NJ-DE-MD	22.5
44	53	Richmond, VA	22.4
15	54	Seattle-Tacoma-Bellevue, WA	22.3
20	55	Baltimore-Columbia-Towson, MD	22.3
31	56	Cleveland-Elyria, OH	22.2
71	56	Dayton, OH	22.2
1	58	New York-Newark-Jersey City, NY-NJ-PA	22.2
53	59	Tucson, AZ	22.1
58	60	Worcester, MA-CT	22.0
69	61	Allentown-Bethlehem-Easton, PA-NJ	21.8
54	62	Urban Honolulu, HI	21.7
51	63	Rochester, NY	21.5
47	64	Hartford-West Hartford-East Hartford, CT	21.3
64	64	New Haven-Milford, CT	21.3
65	66	Knoxville, TN	21.2
8	67	Miami-Fort Lauderdale-West Palm Beach, FL	20.9
10	68	Boston-Cambridge-Newton, MA-NH	20.8
18	69	Tampa-St. Petersburg-Clearwater, FL	20.7
38	69	Providence-Warwick, RI-MA	20.7
50	69	Buffalo-Cheektowaga-Niagara Falls, NY	20.7
11	72	San Francisco-Oakland-Hayward, CA	20.6
61	73	Albany-Schenectady-Troy, NY	20.4
23	74	Pittsburgh, PA	19.5
73	75	North Port-Sarasota-Bradenton, FL	17.5

75 Largest Metropolitan Areas by 2014 Population

Selected Rankings

Percent 65 years old and over, 2013

Population rank	65 years old and over rank	Metropolitan area	Percent 65 years old and over [cols 17 + 18]
73	1	North Port-Sarasota-Bradenton, FL	29.5
18	2	Tampa-St. Petersburg-Clearwater, FL	18.3
23	3	Pittsburgh, PA	18.0
53	4	Tucson, AZ	17.2
8	5	Miami-Fort Lauderdale-West Palm Beach, FL	16.7
50	6	Buffalo-Cheektowaga-Niagara Falls, NY	16.5
65	7	Knoxville, TN	16.4
69	7	Allentown-Bethlehem-Easton, PA-NJ	16.4
31	9	Cleveland-Elyria, OH	16.3
71	10	Dayton, OH	16.1
38	11	Providence-Warwick, RI-MA	15.5
51	11	Rochester, NY	15.5
54	11	Urban Honolulu, HI	15.5
47	14	Hartford-West Hartford-East Hartford, CT	15.4
64	15	New Haven-Milford, CT	15.3
61	16	Albany-Schenectady-Troy, NY	15.2
63	17	Greenville-Anderson-Mauldin, SC	14.8
74	18	Greensboro-High Point, NC	14.5
19	19	St. Louis, MO-IL	14.4
14	20	Detroit-Warren-Dearborn, MI	14.3
6	21	Philadelphia-Camden-Wilmington, PA-NJ-DE-MD	14.2
57	21	Bridgeport-Stamford-Norwalk, CT	14.2
10	23	Boston-Cambridge-Newton, MA-NH	14.1
49	23	Birmingham-Hoover, AL	14.1
1	25	New York-Newark-Jersey City, NY-NJ-PA	13.9
43	25	Louisville/Jefferson County, KY-IN	13.9
55	25	Tulsa, OK	13.9
12	28	Phoenix-Mesa-Scottsdale, AZ	13.8
58	28	Worcester, MA-CT	13.8
59	28	Albuquerque, NM	13.8
20	31	Baltimore-Columbia-Towson, MD	13.7
11	32	San Francisco-Oakland-Hayward, CA	13.6
40	32	Jacksonville, FL	13.6
27	34	Sacramento—Roseville—Arden-Arcade, CA	13.5
26	35	Orlando-Kissimmee-Sanford, FL	13.4
39	35	Milwaukee-Waukesha-West Allis, WI	13.4
75	35	Little Rock-North Little Rock-Conway, AR	13.4
28	38	Cincinnati, OH-KY-IN	13.3
44	38	Richmond, VA	13.3
45	40	New Orleans-Metairie, LA	13.2
66	40	Oxnard-Thousand Oaks-Ventura, CA	13.2
29	42	Kansas City, MO-KS	13.0
24	43	Portland-Vancouver-Hillsboro, OR-WA	12.8
30	43	Las Vegas-Henderson-Paradise, NV	12.8
72	43	Columbia, SC	12.8
37	46	Virginia Beach-Norfolk-Newport News, VA-NC	12.7
52	46	Grand Rapids-Wyoming, MI	12.7
42	48	Oklahoma City, OK	12.5
3	49	Chicago-Naperville-Elgin, IL-IN-WI	12.4
17	49	San Diego-Carlsbad, CA	12.4
2	51	Los Angeles-Long Beach-Anaheim, CA	12.1
22	51	Charlotte-Concord-Gastonia, NC-SC	12.1
16	53	Minneapolis-St. Paul-Bloomington, MN	12.0
33	53	Indianapolis-Carmel-Anderson, IN	12.0
15	55	Seattle-Tacoma-Bellevue, WA	11.9
25	55	San Antonio-New Braunfels, TX	11.9
34	55	San Jose-Sunnyvale-Santa Clara, CA	11.9
36	55	Nashville-Davidson—Murfreesboro—Franklin, TN	11.9
60	55	Omaha-Council Bluffs, NE-IA	11.9
70	55	Baton Rouge, LA	11.9
32	61	Columbus, OH	11.7
41	61	Memphis, TN-MS-AR	11.7
13	63	Riverside-San Bernardino-Ontario, CA	11.5
21	64	Denver-Aurora-Lakewood, CO	11.3
7	65	Washington-Arlington-Alexandria, DC-VA-MD-WV	11.0
56	66	Fresno, CA	10.9
67	66	El Paso, TX	10.9
9	68	Atlanta-Sandy Springs-Roswell, GA	10.4
46	69	Raleigh, NC	10.3
68	70	McAllen-Edinburg-Mission, TX	10.1
4	71	Dallas-Fort Worth-Arlington, TX	9.9
5	72	Houston-The Woodlands-Sugar Land, TX	9.6
62	72	Bakersfield, CA	9.6
35	74	Austin-Round Rock, TX	9.2
48	74	Salt Lake City, UT	9.2

Percent female-headed family households, 2013

Population rank	Female households rank	Metropolitan area	Percent female households [col 30]
68	1	McAllen-Edinburg-Mission, TX	20.3
67	2	El Paso, TX	20.1
41	3	Memphis, TN-MS-AR	19.5
56	4	Fresno, CA	18.3
45	5	New Orleans-Metairie, LA	17.6
70	6	Baton Rouge, LA	17.1
62	7	Bakersfield, CA	16.9
37	8	Virginia Beach-Norfolk-Newport News, VA-NC	16.0
8	9	Miami-Fort Lauderdale-West Palm Beach, FL	15.8
49	9	Birmingham-Hoover, AL	15.8
44	11	Richmond, VA	15.6
25	12	San Antonio-New Braunfels, TX	15.4
1	13	New York-Newark-Jersey City, NY-NJ-PA	15.3
72	13	Columbia, SC	15.3
13	15	Riverside-San Bernardino-Ontario, CA	15.2
20	15	Baltimore-Columbia-Towson, MD	15.2
14	17	Detroit-Warren-Dearborn, MI	14.8
2	18	Los Angeles-Long Beach-Anaheim, CA	14.7
5	18	Houston-The Woodlands-Sugar Land, TX	14.7
9	18	Atlanta-Sandy Springs-Roswell, GA	14.7
31	21	Cleveland-Elyria, OH	14.6
64	21	New Haven-Milford, CT	14.6
74	23	Greensboro-High Point, NC	14.5
71	24	Dayton, OH	14.4
6	25	Philadelphia-Camden-Wilmington, PA-NJ-DE-MD	14.2
59	25	Albuquerque, NM	14.2
22	27	Charlotte-Concord-Gastonia, NC-SC	14.1
38	27	Providence-Warwick, RI-MA	14.1
40	29	Jacksonville, FL	13.9
19	30	St. Louis, MO-IL	13.8
26	30	Orlando-Kissimmee-Sanford, FL	13.8
4	32	Dallas-Fort Worth-Arlington, TX	13.7
30	33	Las Vegas-Henderson-Paradise, NV	13.6
33	33	Indianapolis-Carmel-Anderson, IN	13.6
47	33	Hartford-West Hartford-East Hartford, CT	13.6
43	36	Louisville/Jefferson County, KY-IN	13.5
75	37	Little Rock-North Little Rock-Conway, AR	13.4
3	38	Chicago-Naperville-Elgin, IL-IN-WI	13.3
28	38	Cincinnati, OH-KY-IN	13.3
39	40	Milwaukee-Waukesha-West Allis, WI	13.2
51	40	Rochester, NY	13.2
63	40	Greenville-Anderson-Mauldin, SC	13.2
27	43	Sacramento—Roseville—Arden-Arcade, CA	13.0
53	43	Tucson, AZ	13.0
29	45	Kansas City, MO-KS	12.9
58	45	Worcester, MA-CT	12.9
12	47	Phoenix-Mesa-Scottsdale, AZ	12.8
55	47	Tulsa, OK	12.8
7	49	Washington-Arlington-Alexandria, DC-VA-MD-WV	12.7
50	50	Buffalo-Cheektowaga-Niagara Falls, NY	12.6
32	51	Columbus, OH	12.5
17	52	San Diego-Carlsbad, CA	12.4
18	52	Tampa-St. Petersburg-Clearwater, FL	12.4
42	52	Oklahoma City, OK	12.4
46	52	Raleigh, NC	12.4
36	56	Nashville-Davidson—Murfreesboro—Franklin, TN	12.3
69	56	Allentown-Bethlehem-Easton, PA-NJ	12.3
10	58	Boston-Cambridge-Newton, MA-NH	12.1
66	58	Oxnard-Thousand Oaks-Ventura, CA	12.1
57	60	Bridgeport-Stamford-Norwalk, CT	12.0
54	61	Urban Honolulu, HI	11.9
60	62	Omaha-Council Bluffs, NE-IA	11.8
23	63	Pittsburgh, PA	11.2
35	63	Austin-Round Rock, TX	11.2
11	65	San Francisco-Oakland-Hayward, CA	11.0
65	66	Knoxville, TN	10.8
21	67	Denver-Aurora-Lakewood, CO	10.6
34	67	San Jose-Sunnyvale-Santa Clara, CA	10.6
24	69	Portland-Vancouver-Hillsboro, OR-WA	10.5
48	69	Salt Lake City, UT	10.5
16	71	Minneapolis-St. Paul-Bloomington, MN	10.4
52	71	Grand Rapids-Wyoming, MI	10.4
61	73	Albany-Schenectady-Troy, NY	10.2
15	74	Seattle-Tacoma-Bellevue, WA	9.8
73	75	North Port-Sarasota-Bradenton, FL	9.5

75 Largest Metropolitan Areas by 2014 Population

Selected Rankings

Birth rate, 2014				Percent under 65 who have no health insurance, 2013			
Population rank	Birth rate rank	Metropolitan area	Births (per 1,000 population) [col 36]	Population rank	No health insurance rank	Metropolitan area	Percent with no health insurance [col 40]
68	1	McAllen-Edinburg-Mission, TX	19.4	68	1	McAllen-Edinburg-Mission, TX	38.2
62	2	Bakersfield, CA	16.9	67	2	El Paso, TX	30.7
48	3	Salt Lake City, UT	16.5	8	3	Miami-Fort Lauderdale-West Palm Beach, FL	29.1
56	3	Fresno, CA	16.5	5	4	Houston-The Woodlands-Sugar Land, TX	25.2
67	5	El Paso, TX	16.2	73	5	North Port-Sarasota-Bradenton, FL	23.9
5	6	Houston-The Woodlands-Sugar Land, TX	14.6	4	6	Dallas-Fort Worth-Arlington, TX	23.8
60	6	Omaha-Council Bluffs, NE-IA	14.6	30	6	Las Vegas-Henderson-Paradise, NV	23.8
42	8	Oklahoma City, OK	14.2	26	8	Orlando-Kissimmee-Sanford, FL	23.2
4	9	Dallas-Fort Worth-Arlington, TX	14.0	2	9	Los Angeles-Long Beach-Anaheim, CA	22.5
41	9	Memphis, TN-MS-AR	14.0	25	10	San Antonio-New Braunfels, TX	22.2
25	11	San Antonio-New Braunfels, TX	13.9	13	11	Riverside-San Bernardino-Ontario, CA	21.2
54	11	Urban Honolulu, HI	13.9	9	12	Atlanta-Sandy Springs-Roswell, GA	21.1
13	13	Riverside-San Bernardino-Ontario, CA	13.8	18	12	Tampa-St. Petersburg-Clearwater, FL	21.1
17	14	San Diego-Carlsbad, CA	13.7	62	14	Bakersfield, CA	20.4
55	14	Tulsa, OK	13.7	35	15	Austin-Round Rock, TX	20.3
32	16	Columbus, OH	13.6	56	15	Fresno, CA	20.3
7	17	Washington-Arlington-Alexandria, DC-VA-MD-WV	13.5	59	17	Albuquerque, NM	19.9
33	17	Indianapolis-Carmel-Anderson, IN	13.5	12	18	Phoenix-Mesa-Scottsdale, AZ	19.8
29	19	Kansas City, MO-KS	13.4	42	19	Oklahoma City, OK	19.7
52	19	Grand Rapids-Wyoming, MI	13.4	45	19	New Orleans-Metairie, LA	19.7
75	19	Little Rock-North Little Rock-Conway, AR	13.4	55	21	Tulsa, OK	19.6
12	22	Phoenix-Mesa-Scottsdale, AZ	13.3	53	22	Tucson, AZ	18.8
35	22	Austin-Round Rock, TX	13.3	74	23	Greensboro-High Point, NC	18.7
37	22	Virginia Beach-Norfolk-Newport News, VA-NC	13.3	63	24	Greenville-Anderson-Mauldin, SC	18.6
70	22	Baton Rouge, LA	13.3	40	25	Jacksonville, FL	18.3
16	26	Minneapolis-St. Paul-Bloomington, MN	13.1	66	26	Oxnard-Thousand Oaks-Ventura, CA	18.1
2	27	Los Angeles-Long Beach-Anaheim, CA	12.8	17	27	San Diego-Carlsbad, CA	17.9
9	27	Atlanta-Sandy Springs-Roswell, GA	12.8	22	28	Charlotte-Concord-Gastonia, NC-SC	17.8
21	27	Denver-Aurora-Lakewood, CO	12.8	41	29	Memphis, TN-MS-AR	17.3
28	27	Cincinnati, OH-KY-IN	12.8	70	30	Baton Rouge, LA	17.2
34	27	San Jose-Sunnyvale-Santa Clara, CA	12.8	72	31	Columbia, SC	16.7
36	27	Nashville-Davidson—Murfreesboro—Franklin, TN	12.8	48	32	Salt Lake City, UT	16.5
49	33	Birmingham-Hoover, AL	12.7	75	32	Little Rock-North Little Rock-Conway, AR	16.5
15	34	Seattle-Tacoma-Bellevue, WA	12.6	27	34	Sacramento—Roseville—Arden-Arcade, CA	15.9
30	34	Las Vegas-Henderson-Paradise, NV	12.6	3	35	Chicago-Naperville-Elgin, IL-IN-WI	15.8
39	34	Milwaukee-Waukesha-West Allis, WI	12.6	21	35	Denver-Aurora-Lakewood, CO	15.8
1	37	New York-Newark-Jersey City, NY-NJ-PA	12.5	24	37	Portland-Vancouver-Hillsboro, OR-WA	15.7
3	37	Chicago-Naperville-Elgin, IL-IN-WI	12.5	36	37	Nashville-Davidson—Murfreesboro—Franklin, TN	15.7
22	37	Charlotte-Concord-Gastonia, NC-SC	12.5	33	39	Indianapolis-Carmel-Anderson, IN	15.6
45	37	New Orleans-Metairie, LA	12.5	43	40	Louisville/Jefferson County, KY-IN	15.5
66	37	Oxnard-Thousand Oaks-Ventura, CA	12.5	46	41	Raleigh, NC	15.3
40	42	Jacksonville, FL	12.4	65	42	Knoxville, TN	14.7
46	42	Raleigh, NC	12.4	49	43	Birmingham-Hoover, AL	14.6
43	44	Louisville/Jefferson County, KY-IN	12.3	44	44	Richmond, VA	14.4
27	45	Sacramento—Roseville—Arden-Arcade, CA	12.2	1	45	New York-Newark-Jersey City, NY-NJ-PA	14.2
20	46	Baltimore-Columbia-Towson, MD	12.1	15	46	Seattle-Tacoma-Bellevue, WA	14.1
19	47	St. Louis, MO-IL	12.0	29	46	Kansas City, MO-KS	14.1
63	47	Greenville-Anderson-Mauldin, SC	12.0	37	48	Virginia Beach-Norfolk-Newport News, VA-NC	13.8
71	47	Dayton, OH	12.0	11	49	San Francisco-Oakland-Hayward, CA	13.4
6	50	Philadelphia-Camden-Wilmington, PA-NJ-DE-MD	11.9	57	50	Bridgeport-Stamford-Norwalk, CT	13.3
26	50	Orlando-Kissimmee-Sanford, FL	11.9	14	51	Detroit-Warren-Dearborn, MI	13.2
44	50	Richmond, VA	11.9	32	51	Columbus, OH	13.2
53	50	Tucson, AZ	11.9	71	53	Dayton, OH	13.1
59	50	Albuquerque, NM	11.9	34	54	San Jose-Sunnyvale-Santa Clara, CA	12.8
24	55	Portland-Vancouver-Hillsboro, OR-WA	11.8	31	55	Cleveland-Elyria, OH	12.7
72	55	Columbia, SC	11.8	28	56	Cincinnati, OH-KY-IN	12.5
74	57	Greensboro-High Point, NC	11.7	19	57	St. Louis, MO-IL	12.4
14	58	Detroit-Warren-Dearborn, MI	11.6	7	58	Washington-Arlington-Alexandria, DC-VA-MD-WV	12.3
11	59	San Francisco-Oakland-Hayward, CA	11.5	69	58	Allentown-Bethlehem-Easton, PA-NJ	12.3
31	60	Cleveland-Elyria, OH	11.2	52	60	Grand Rapids-Wyoming, MI	12.0
8	61	Miami-Fort Lauderdale-West Palm Beach, FL	11.1	6	61	Philadelphia-Camden-Wilmington, PA-NJ-DE-MD	11.7
10	61	Boston-Cambridge-Newton, MA-NH	11.1	60	61	Omaha-Council Bluffs, NE-IA	11.7
65	61	Knoxville, TN	11.1	39	63	Milwaukee-Waukesha-West Allis, WI	10.9
18	64	Tampa-St. Petersburg-Clearwater, FL	10.7	38	64	Providence-Warwick, RI-MA	10.7
50	64	Buffalo-Cheektowaga-Niagara Falls, NY	10.7	64	64	New Haven-Milford, CT	10.7
51	64	Rochester, NY	10.7	20	66	Baltimore-Columbia-Towson, MD	10.2
57	64	Bridgeport-Stamford-Norwalk, CT	10.7	23	67	Pittsburgh, PA	9.8
58	64	Worcester, MA-CT	10.7	47	68	Hartford-West Hartford-East Hartford, CT	9.7
61	69	Albany-Schenectady-Troy, NY	10.4	51	69	Rochester, NY	9.5
64	69	New Haven-Milford, CT	10.4	16	70	Minneapolis-St. Paul-Bloomington, MN	9.2
69	69	Allentown-Bethlehem-Easton, PA-NJ	10.4	50	71	Buffalo-Cheektowaga-Niagara Falls, NY	8.8
38	72	Providence-Warwick, RI-MA	10.3	61	72	Albany-Schenectady-Troy, NY	8.6
23	73	Pittsburgh, PA	10.1	54	73	Urban Honolulu, HI	6.7
47	74	Hartford-West Hartford-East Hartford, CT	9.9	58	74	Worcester, MA-CT	5.1
73	75	North Port-Sarasota-Bradenton, FL	8.5	10	75	Boston-Cambridge-Newton, MA-NH	4.9

75 Largest Metropolitan Areas by 2014 Population

Selected Rankings

Percent college graduates (bachelor's degree or more), 2013

Population rank	Percent college graduates rank	Metropolitan area	Percent college graduates [col 51]
7	1	Washington-Arlington-Alexandria, DC-VA-MD-WV	48.7
34	2	San Jose-Sunnyvale-Santa Clara, CA	46.7
57	3	Bridgeport-Stamford-Norwalk, CT	45.5
11	4	San Francisco-Oakland-Hayward, CA	45.2
10	5	Boston-Cambridge-Newton, MA-NH	44.8
46	6	Raleigh, NC	43.7
35	7	Austin-Round Rock, TX	41.5
21	8	Denver-Aurora-Lakewood, CO	40.3
15	9	Seattle-Tacoma-Bellevue, WA	39.4
16	10	Minneapolis-St. Paul-Bloomington, MN	39.3
1	11	New York-Newark-Jersey City, NY-NJ-PA	37.4
20	12	Baltimore-Columbia-Towson, MD	36.8
47	13	Hartford-West Hartford-East Hartford, CT	36.5
9	14	Atlanta-Sandy Springs-Roswell, GA	35.2
3	15	Chicago-Naperville-Elgin, IL-IN-WI	35.1
24	15	Portland-Vancouver-Hillsboro, OR-WA	35.1
6	17	Philadelphia-Camden-Wilmington, PA-NJ-DE-MD	34.6
17	17	San Diego-Carlsbad, CA	34.6
61	19	Albany-Schenectady-Troy, NY	34.3
29	20	Kansas City, MO-KS	33.7
32	20	Columbus, OH	33.7
64	22	New Haven-Milford, CT	33.5
54	23	Urban Honolulu, HI	33.4
60	23	Omaha-Council Bluffs, NE-IA	33.4
39	25	Milwaukee-Waukesha-West Allis, WI	33.2
58	26	Worcester, MA-CT	32.9
4	27	Dallas-Fort Worth-Arlington, TX	32.6
51	27	Rochester, NY	32.6
19	29	St. Louis, MO-IL	32.5
44	29	Richmond, VA	32.5
36	31	Nashville-Davidson—Murfreesboro—Franklin, TN	32.3
23	32	Pittsburgh, PA	32.2
22	33	Charlotte-Concord-Gastonia, NC-SC	32.0
2	34	Los Angeles-Long Beach-Anaheim, CA	31.7
28	35	Cincinnati, OH-KY-IN	31.2
48	35	Salt Lake City, UT	31.2
66	35	Oxnard-Thousand Oaks-Ventura, CA	31.2
5	38	Houston-The Woodlands-Sugar Land, TX	30.9
27	39	Sacramento—Roseville—Arden-Arcade, CA	30.8
33	39	Indianapolis-Carmel-Anderson, IN	30.8
59	41	Albuquerque, NM	30.7
72	41	Columbia, SC	30.7
52	43	Grand Rapids-Wyoming, MI	30.6
73	43	North Port-Sarasota-Bradenton, FL	30.6
50	45	Buffalo-Cheektowaga-Niagara Falls, NY	30.1
53	45	Tucson, AZ	30.1
31	47	Cleveland-Elyria, OH	29.8
37	48	Virginia Beach-Norfolk-Newport News, VA-NC	29.6
38	48	Providence-Warwick, RI-MA	29.6
26	50	Orlando-Kissimmee-Sanford, FL	29.5
8	51	Miami-Fort Lauderdale-West Palm Beach, FL	29.3
12	52	Phoenix-Mesa-Scottsdale, AZ	29.2
14	53	Detroit-Warren-Dearborn, MI	29.0
49	54	Birmingham-Hoover, AL	28.6
40	55	Jacksonville, FL	28.3
42	56	Oklahoma City, OK	27.9
18	57	Tampa-St. Petersburg-Clearwater, FL	27.6
69	57	Allentown-Bethlehem-Easton, PA-NJ	27.6
74	59	Greensboro-High Point, NC	27.5
45	60	New Orleans-Metairie, LA	27.4
75	60	Little Rock-North Little Rock-Conway, AR	27.4
70	62	Baton Rouge, LA	27.3
65	63	Knoxville, TN	27.1
43	64	Louisville/Jefferson County, KY-IN	27.0
63	65	Greenville-Anderson-Mauldin, SC	26.8
25	66	San Antonio-New Braunfels, TX	26.7
71	67	Dayton, OH	26.6
41	68	Memphis, TN-MS-AR	26.4
55	69	Tulsa, OK	26.0
30	70	Las Vegas-Henderson-Paradise, NV	22.1
67	71	El Paso, TX	20.8
13	72	Riverside-San Bernardino-Ontario, CA	20.1
56	73	Fresno, CA	19.8
68	74	McAllen-Edinburg-Mission, TX	16.2
62	75	Bakersfield, CA	14.4

Median household income, 2013

Population rank	Median income rank	Metropolitan area	Median income (dollars) [col 55]
57	1	Bridgeport-Stamford-Norwalk, CT	136 019
34	2	San Jose-Sunnyvale-Santa Clara, CA	123 386
7	3	Washington-Arlington-Alexandria, DC-VA-MD-WV	116 153
11	4	San Francisco-Oakland-Hayward, CA	112 911
66	5	Oxnard-Thousand Oaks-Ventura, CA	101 302
10	6	Boston-Cambridge-Newton, MA-NH	100 687
1	7	New York-Newark-Jersey City, NY-NJ-PA	96 934
54	8	Urban Honolulu, HI	92 931
20	9	Baltimore-Columbia-Towson, MD	90 854
15	10	Seattle-Tacoma-Bellevue, WA	89 940
47	11	Hartford-West Hartford-East Hartford, CT	89 700
16	12	Minneapolis-St. Paul-Bloomington, MN	86 712
17	13	San Diego-Carlsbad, CA	85 967
2	14	Los Angeles-Long Beach-Anaheim, CA	85 536
21	15	Denver-Aurora-Lakewood, CO	84 810
6	16	Philadelphia-Camden-Wilmington, PA-NJ-DE-MD	84 501
3	17	Chicago-Naperville-Elgin, IL-IN-WI	83 898
35	18	Austin-Round Rock, TX	83 593
46	19	Raleigh, NC	82 896
5	20	Houston-The Woodlands-Sugar Land, TX	82 660
4	21	Dallas-Fort Worth-Arlington, TX	81 531
64	22	New Haven-Milford, CT	81 252
48	23	Salt Lake City, UT	80 117
58	24	Worcester, MA-CT	78 909
24	25	Portland-Vancouver-Hillsboro, OR-WA	77 510
9	26	Atlanta-Sandy Springs-Roswell, GA	77 327
27	27	Sacramento—Roseville—Arden-Arcade, CA	76 775
61	28	Albany-Schenectady-Troy, NY	76 670
44	29	Richmond, VA	75 966
38	30	Providence-Warwick, RI-MA	74 920
29	31	Kansas City, MO-KS	74 518
69	32	Allentown-Bethlehem-Easton, PA-NJ	74 355
28	33	Cincinnati, OH-KY-IN	73 584
19	34	St. Louis, MO-IL	73 426
32	35	Columbus, OH	73 084
22	36	Charlotte-Concord-Gastonia, NC-SC	72 972
37	37	Virginia Beach-Norfolk-Newport News, VA-NC	72 966
60	38	Omaha-Council Bluffs, NE-IA	72 701
39	39	Milwaukee-Waukesha-West Allis, WI	71 659
40	40	Jacksonville, FL	71 515
36	41	Nashville-Davidson—Murfreesboro—Franklin, TN	71 471
70	42	Baton Rouge, LA	71 432
8	43	Miami-Fort Lauderdale-West Palm Beach, FL	71 172
12	44	Phoenix-Mesa-Scottsdale, AZ	71 150
14	45	Detroit-Warren-Dearborn, MI	70 882
33	46	Indianapolis-Carmel-Anderson, IN	70 631
13	47	Riverside-San Bernardino-Ontario, CA	70 282
23	48	Pittsburgh, PA	69 814
43	49	Louisville/Jefferson County, KY-IN	69 070
73	50	North Port-Sarasota-Bradenton, FL	68 970
25	51	San Antonio-New Braunfels, TX	68 688
52	52	Grand Rapids-Wyoming, MI	68 510
51	53	Rochester, NY	68 486
31	54	Cleveland-Elyria, OH	68 423
49	55	Birmingham-Hoover, AL	67 640
42	56	Oklahoma City, OK	67 369
45	57	New Orleans-Metairie, LA	67 164
30	58	Las Vegas-Henderson-Paradise, NV	67 150
41	59	Memphis, TN-MS-AR	66 046
55	60	Tulsa, OK	65 987
50	61	Buffalo-Cheektowaga-Niagara Falls, NY	65 471
75	62	Little Rock-North Little Rock-Conway, AR	65 319
59	63	Albuquerque, NM	64 625
18	64	Tampa-St. Petersburg-Clearwater, FL	64 234
26	65	Orlando-Kissimmee-Sanford, FL	63 634
62	66	Bakersfield, CA	63 385
72	67	Columbia, SC	63 201
65	68	Knoxville, TN	62 864
71	69	Dayton, OH	62 821
74	70	Greensboro-High Point, NC	61 828
53	71	Tucson, AZ	61 719
56	72	Fresno, CA	61 208
63	73	Greenville-Anderson-Mauldin, SC	60 265
67	74	El Paso, TX	54 728
68	75	McAllen-Edinburg-Mission, TX	49 432

75 Largest Metropolitan Areas by 2014 Population

Selected Rankings

Percent of population below the poverty level, 2013

Population rank	Poverty rate rank	Metropolitan area	Poverty rate [col 59]
68	1	McAllen-Edinburg-Mission, TX	34.3
56	2	Fresno, CA	28.8
62	3	Bakersfield, CA	22.8
67	4	El Paso, TX	22.6
74	5	Greensboro-High Point, NC	19.9
41	6	Memphis, TN-MS-AR	19.8
53	7	Tucson, AZ	19.5
59	8	Albuquerque, NM	19.4
45	9	New Orleans-Metairie, LA	19.3
70	10	Baton Rouge, LA	18.7
13	11	Riverside-San Bernardino-Ontario, CA	18.2
8	12	Miami-Fort Lauderdale-West Palm Beach, FL	17.7
2	13	Los Angeles-Long Beach-Anaheim, CA	17.6
12	13	Phoenix-Mesa-Scottsdale, AZ	17.6
65	15	Knoxville, TN	17.5
63	16	Greenville-Anderson-Mauldin, SC	17.4
26	17	Orlando-Kissimmee-Sanford, FL	17.1
14	18	Detroit-Warren-Dearborn, MI	16.9
49	18	Birmingham-Hoover, AL	16.9
27	20	Sacramento—Roseville—Arden-Arcade, CA	16.6
72	20	Columbia, SC	16.6
5	22	Houston-The Woodlands-Sugar Land, TX	16.4
71	22	Dayton, OH	16.4
25	24	San Antonio-New Braunfels, TX	16.3
30	25	Las Vegas-Henderson-Paradise, NV	16.1
9	26	Atlanta-Sandy Springs-Roswell, GA	15.9
39	26	Milwaukee-Waukesha-West Allis, WI	15.9
31	28	Cleveland-Elyria, OH	15.6
18	29	Tampa-St. Petersburg-Clearwater, FL	15.4
17	30	San Diego-Carlsbad, CA	15.2
33	30	Indianapolis-Carmel-Anderson, IN	15.2
75	30	Little Rock-North Little Rock-Conway, AR	15.2
4	33	Dallas-Fort Worth-Arlington, TX	15.0
42	34	Oklahoma City, OK	14.9
50	34	Buffalo-Cheektowaga-Niagara Falls, NY	14.9
22	36	Charlotte-Concord-Gastonia, NC-SC	14.8
32	36	Columbus, OH	14.8
40	36	Jacksonville, FL	14.8
55	36	Tulsa, OK	14.8
51	40	Rochester, NY	14.7
1	41	New York-Newark-Jersey City, NY-NJ-PA	14.6
28	42	Cincinnati, OH-KY-IN	14.5
3	43	Chicago-Naperville-Elgin, IL-IN-WI	14.4
73	43	North Port-Sarasota-Bradenton, FL	14.4
35	45	Austin-Round Rock, TX	14.3
38	45	Providence-Warwick, RI-MA	14.3
52	47	Grand Rapids-Wyoming, MI	14.0
44	48	Richmond, VA	13.9
43	49	Louisville/Jefferson County, KY-IN	13.8
36	50	Nashville-Davidson—Murfreesboro—Franklin, TN	13.7
6	51	Philadelphia-Camden-Wilmington, PA-NJ-DE-MD	13.5
24	51	Portland-Vancouver-Hillsboro, OR-WA	13.5
58	53	Worcester, MA-CT	13.3
37	54	Virginia Beach-Norfolk-Newport News, VA-NC	13.0
19	55	St. Louis, MO-IL	12.9
64	55	New Haven-Milford, CT	12.9
23	57	Pittsburgh, PA	12.8
60	58	Omaha-Council Bluffs, NE-IA	12.7
15	59	Seattle-Tacoma-Bellevue, WA	12.6
29	59	Kansas City, MO-KS	12.6
61	61	Albany-Schenectady-Troy, NY	12.5
48	62	Salt Lake City, UT	12.4
69	62	Allentown-Bethlehem-Easton, PA-NJ	12.4
21	64	Denver-Aurora-Lakewood, CO	12.1
46	65	Raleigh, NC	12.0
66	66	Oxnard-Thousand Oaks-Ventura, CA	11.9
11	67	San Francisco-Oakland-Hayward, CA	11.5
20	68	Baltimore-Columbia-Towson, MD	11.2
47	69	Hartford-West Hartford-East Hartford, CT	10.8
34	70	San Jose-Sunnyvale-Santa Clara, CA	10.5
10	71	Boston-Cambridge-Newton, MA-NH	10.4
16	72	Minneapolis-St. Paul-Bloomington, MN	10.3
57	73	Bridgeport-Stamford-Norwalk, CT	9.6
54	74	Urban Honolulu, HI	9.4
7	75	Washington-Arlington-Alexandria, DC-VA-MD-WV	8.5

Percent of children under 18 years old below the poverty level, 2013

Population rank	Poverty rate rank	Metropolitan area	Poverty rate [col 60]
68	1	McAllen-Edinburg-Mission, TX	44.9
56	2	Fresno, CA	42.8
62	3	Bakersfield, CA	30.9
67	4	El Paso, TX	30.8
41	5	Memphis, TN-MS-AR	30.6
74	6	Greensboro-High Point, NC	29.1
59	7	Albuquerque, NM	28.7
45	8	New Orleans-Metairie, LA	28.6
53	9	Tucson, AZ	26.7
63	10	Greenville-Anderson-Mauldin, SC	25.9
12	11	Phoenix-Mesa-Scottsdale, AZ	25.4
13	11	Riverside-San Bernardino-Ontario, CA	25.4
26	11	Orlando-Kissimmee-Sanford, FL	25.4
49	11	Birmingham-Hoover, AL	25.4
2	15	Los Angeles-Long Beach-Anaheim, CA	25.3
65	16	Knoxville, TN	25.0
71	17	Dayton, OH	24.9
14	18	Detroit-Warren-Dearborn, MI	24.7
73	19	North Port-Sarasota-Bradenton, FL	24.5
70	20	Baton Rouge, LA	24.4
39	21	Milwaukee-Waukesha-West Allis, WI	23.9
5	22	Houston-The Woodlands-Sugar Land, TX	23.7
8	22	Miami-Fort Lauderdale-West Palm Beach, FL	23.7
30	24	Las Vegas-Henderson-Paradise, NV	23.5
25	25	San Antonio-New Braunfels, TX	22.9
50	26	Buffalo-Cheektowaga-Niagara Falls, NY	22.8
18	27	Tampa-St. Petersburg-Clearwater, FL	22.7
31	27	Cleveland-Elyria, OH	22.7
9	29	Atlanta-Sandy Springs-Roswell, GA	22.6
72	30	Columbia, SC	22.2
75	31	Little Rock-North Little Rock-Conway, AR	22.0
27	32	Sacramento—Roseville—Arden-Arcade, CA	21.9
51	32	Rochester, NY	21.9
55	32	Tulsa, OK	21.9
4	35	Dallas-Fort Worth-Arlington, TX	21.6
42	35	Oklahoma City, OK	21.6
40	37	Jacksonville, FL	21.3
33	38	Indianapolis-Carmel-Anderson, IN	21.1
32	39	Columbus, OH	20.8
38	39	Providence-Warwick, RI-MA	20.8
1	41	New York-Newark-Jersey City, NY-NJ-PA	20.6
3	41	Chicago-Naperville-Elgin, IL-IN-WI	20.6
36	43	Nashville-Davidson—Murfreesboro—Franklin, TN	20.5
28	44	Cincinnati, OH-KY-IN	20.3
22	45	Charlotte-Concord-Gastonia, NC-SC	19.8
44	45	Richmond, VA	19.8
17	47	San Diego-Carlsbad, CA	19.4
58	48	Worcester, MA-CT	19.3
37	49	Virginia Beach-Norfolk-Newport News, VA-NC	19.2
43	49	Louisville/Jefferson County, KY-IN	19.2
69	49	Allentown-Bethlehem-Easton, PA-NJ	19.2
6	52	Philadelphia-Camden-Wilmington, PA-NJ-DE-MD	18.7
19	52	St. Louis, MO-IL	18.7
66	54	Oxnard-Thousand Oaks-Ventura, CA	18.3
35	55	Austin-Round Rock, TX	17.8
23	56	Pittsburgh, PA	17.7
64	56	New Haven-Milford, CT	17.7
29	58	Kansas City, MO-KS	17.6
52	58	Grand Rapids-Wyoming, MI	17.6
61	60	Albany-Schenectady-Troy, NY	17.2
15	61	Seattle-Tacoma-Bellevue, WA	16.9
21	61	Denver-Aurora-Lakewood, CO	16.9
24	61	Portland-Vancouver-Hillsboro, OR-WA	16.9
60	64	Omaha-Council Bluffs, NE-IA	16.7
46	65	Raleigh, NC	16.2
48	66	Salt Lake City, UT	16.0
47	67	Hartford-West Hartford-East Hartford, CT	15.2
20	68	Baltimore-Columbia-Towson, MD	14.9
34	69	San Jose-Sunnyvale-Santa Clara, CA	13.4
10	70	Boston-Cambridge-Newton, MA-NH	13.3
16	70	Minneapolis-St. Paul-Bloomington, MN	13.3
11	72	San Francisco-Oakland-Hayward, CA	13.0
54	73	Urban Honolulu, HI	12.0
57	74	Bridgeport-Stamford-Norwalk, CT	11.9
7	75	Washington-Arlington-Alexandria, DC-VA-MD-WV	11.1

75 Largest Metropolitan Areas by 2014 Population

Selected Rankings

Median value of owner-occupied housing units, 2013

Population rank	Median value rank	Metropolitan area	Median value (dollars) [col 91]
34	1	San Jose-Sunnyvale-Santa Clara, CA	672 900
11	2	San Francisco-Oakland-Hayward, CA	602 800
54	3	Urban Honolulu, HI	573 800
2	4	Los Angeles-Long Beach-Anaheim, CA	453 500
66	5	Oxnard-Thousand Oaks-Ventura, CA	443 700
57	6	Bridgeport-Stamford-Norwalk, CT	420 600
17	7	San Diego-Carlsbad, CA	411 000
1	8	New York-Newark-Jersey City, NY-NJ-PA	392 700
7	9	Washington-Arlington-Alexandria, DC-VA-MD-WV	373 500
10	10	Boston-Cambridge-Newton, MA-NH	363 200
15	11	Seattle-Tacoma-Bellevue, WA	307 900
27	12	Sacramento—Roseville—Arden-Arcade, CA	278 500
20	13	Baltimore-Columbia-Towson, MD	270 000
24	14	Portland-Vancouver-Hillsboro, OR-WA	264 000
21	15	Denver-Aurora-Lakewood, CO	257 000
38	16	Providence-Warwick, RI-MA	246 100
64	17	New Haven-Milford, CT	242 000
58	18	Worcester, MA-CT	241 400
47	19	Hartford-West Hartford-East Hartford, CT	241 100
13	20	Riverside-San Bernardino-Ontario, CA	234 000
6	21	Philadelphia-Camden-Wilmington, PA-NJ-DE-MD	233 600
37	22	Virginia Beach-Norfolk-Newport News, VA-NC	229 700
48	23	Salt Lake City, UT	225 100
3	24	Chicago-Naperville-Elgin, IL-IN-WI	206 300
16	25	Minneapolis-St. Paul-Bloomington, MN	206 100
35	26	Austin-Round Rock, TX	205 000
44	27	Richmond, VA	204 800
46	28	Raleigh, NC	202 900
69	29	Allentown-Bethlehem-Easton, PA-NJ	197 300
61	30	Albany-Schenectady-Troy, NY	195 600
8	31	Miami-Fort Lauderdale-West Palm Beach, FL	188 800
39	32	Milwaukee-Waukesha-West Allis, WI	188 100
56	33	Fresno, CA	185 200
12	34	Phoenix-Mesa-Scottsdale, AZ	177 900
59	35	Albuquerque, NM	176 900
45	36	New Orleans-Metairie, LA	173 100
36	37	Nashville-Davidson—Murfreesboro—Franklin, TN	172 400
73	38	North Port-Sarasota-Bradenton, FL	167 700
22	39	Charlotte-Concord-Gastonia, NC-SC	164 000
30	40	Las Vegas-Henderson-Paradise, NV	162 300
62	41	Bakersfield, CA	161 000
9	42	Atlanta-Sandy Springs-Roswell, GA	160 800
70	43	Baton Rouge, LA	158 300
29	44	Kansas City, MO-KS	157 400
53	45	Tucson, AZ	155 300
32	46	Columbus, OH	154 800
19	47	St. Louis, MO-IL	153 000
4	48	Dallas-Fort Worth-Arlington, TX	152 700
40	49	Jacksonville, FL	152 200
28	50	Cincinnati, OH-KY-IN	152 000
26	51	Orlando-Kissimmee-Sanford, FL	151 700
43	52	Louisville/Jefferson County, KY-IN	148 700
65	53	Knoxville, TN	148 400
60	54	Omaha-Council Bluffs, NE-IA	146 500
5	55	Houston-The Woodlands-Sugar Land, TX	144 400
49	56	Birmingham-Hoover, AL	144 100
74	57	Greensboro-High Point, NC	141 700
63	58	Greenville-Anderson-Mauldin, SC	141 000
33	59	Indianapolis-Carmel-Anderson, IN	139 600
72	60	Columbia, SC	138 900
75	61	Little Rock-North Little Rock-Conway, AR	137 300
42	62	Oklahoma City, OK	137 100
52	63	Grand Rapids-Wyoming, MI	136 400
31	64	Cleveland-Elyria, OH	136 100
51	65	Rochester, NY	135 700
18	66	Tampa-St. Petersburg-Clearwater, FL	135 400
25	67	San Antonio-New Braunfels, TX	134 000
23	68	Pittsburgh, PA	130 700
41	69	Memphis, TN-MS-AR	128 600
55	70	Tulsa, OK	128 100
50	71	Buffalo-Cheektowaga-Niagara Falls, NY	123 400
71	72	Dayton, OH	120 600
14	73	Detroit-Warren-Dearborn, MI	120 500
67	74	El Paso, TX	110 900
68	75	McAllen-Edinburg-Mission, TX	79 400

Mean gross rent of renter-occupied housing units, 2013

Population rank	Median gross rent	Metropolitan area	Mean rent (dollars) [col 94]
34	1	San Jose-Sunnyvale-Santa Clara, CA	$1 640
54	2	Urban Honolulu, HI	$1 535
66	3	Oxnard-Thousand Oaks-Ventura, CA	$1 518
7	4	Washington-Arlington-Alexandria, DC-VA-MD-WV	$1 481
11	5	San Francisco-Oakland-Hayward, CA	$1 435
57	6	Bridgeport-Stamford-Norwalk, CT	$1 330
17	7	San Diego-Carlsbad, CA	$1 289
2	8	Los Angeles-Long Beach-Anaheim, CA	$1 265
1	9	New York-Newark-Jersey City, NY-NJ-PA	$1 237
10	10	Boston-Cambridge-Newton, MA-NH	$1 207
15	11	Seattle-Tacoma-Bellevue, WA	$1 135
20	12	Baltimore-Columbia-Towson, MD	$1 132
13	13	Riverside-San Bernardino-Ontario, CA	$1 125
8	14	Miami-Fort Lauderdale-West Palm Beach, FL	$1 120
27	15	Sacramento—Roseville—Arden-Arcade, CA	$1 060
37	16	Virginia Beach-Norfolk-Newport News, VA-NC	$1 052
64	17	New Haven-Milford, CT	$1 026
35	18	Austin-Round Rock, TX	$1 000
21	19	Denver-Aurora-Lakewood, CO	$998
6	20	Philadelphia-Camden-Wilmington, PA-NJ-DE-MD	$997
26	21	Orlando-Kissimmee-Sanford, FL	$991
30	22	Las Vegas-Henderson-Paradise, NV	$979
47	23	Hartford-West Hartford-East Hartford, CT	$978
24	24	Portland-Vancouver-Hillsboro, OR-WA	$969
3	25	Chicago-Naperville-Elgin, IL-IN-WI	$959
44	25	Richmond, VA	$959
73	27	North Port-Sarasota-Bradenton, FL	$958
40	28	Jacksonville, FL	$949
9	29	Atlanta-Sandy Springs-Roswell, GA	$947
12	30	Phoenix-Mesa-Scottsdale, AZ	$936
48	31	Salt Lake City, UT	$935
18	32	Tampa-St. Petersburg-Clearwater, FL	$925
69	33	Allentown-Bethlehem-Easton, PA-NJ	$918
58	34	Worcester, MA-CT	$914
16	35	Minneapolis-St. Paul-Bloomington, MN	$911
4	36	Dallas-Fort Worth-Arlington, TX	$908
45	36	New Orleans-Metairie, LA	$908
46	36	Raleigh, NC	$908
62	39	Bakersfield, CA	$894
61	40	Albany-Schenectady-Troy, NY	$889
5	41	Houston-The Woodlands-Sugar Land, TX	$886
38	42	Providence-Warwick, RI-MA	$885
56	43	Fresno, CA	$859
25	44	San Antonio-New Braunfels, TX	$857
36	45	Nashville-Davidson—Murfreesboro—Franklin, TN	$849
22	46	Charlotte-Concord-Gastonia, NC-SC	$835
29	47	Kansas City, MO-KS	$834
14	48	Detroit-Warren-Dearborn, MI	$829
72	49	Columbia, SC	$828
41	50	Memphis, TN-MS-AR	$825
59	51	Albuquerque, NM	$818
19	52	St. Louis, MO-IL	$814
39	53	Milwaukee-Waukesha-West Allis, WI	$807
32	54	Columbus, OH	$804
53	55	Tucson, AZ	$798
51	56	Rochester, NY	$790
33	57	Indianapolis-Carmel-Anderson, IN	$789
49	58	Birmingham-Hoover, AL	$787
60	59	Omaha-Council Bluffs, NE-IA	$783
70	60	Baton Rouge, LA	$777
42	61	Oklahoma City, OK	$762
52	62	Grand Rapids-Wyoming, MI	$761
75	63	Little Rock-North Little Rock-Conway, AR	$754
67	64	El Paso, TX	$749
43	65	Louisville/Jefferson County, KY-IN	$740
55	65	Tulsa, OK	$740
65	67	Knoxville, TN	$737
31	68	Cleveland-Elyria, OH	$734
71	69	Dayton, OH	$733
28	70	Cincinnati, OH-KY-IN	$729
50	71	Buffalo-Cheektowaga-Niagara Falls, NY	$718
63	72	Greenville-Anderson-Mauldin, SC	$715
23	73	Pittsburgh, PA	$712
74	74	Greensboro-High Point, NC	$711
68	75	McAllen-Edinburg-Mission, TX	$655

75 Largest Metropolitan Areas by 2014 Population

Selected Rankings

Unemployment rate, 2014

Population rank	Unemployment rate rank	Metropolitan area	Unemployment rate [col 100]
56	1	Fresno, CA	11.6
62	2	Bakersfield, CA	10.4
68	3	McAllen-Edinburg-Mission, TX	8.7
14	4	Detroit-Warren-Dearborn, MI	8.5
13	5	Riverside-San Bernardino-Ontario, CA	8.2
30	6	Las Vegas-Henderson-Paradise, NV	7.8
2	7	Los Angeles-Long Beach-Anaheim, CA	7.6
38	7	Providence-Warwick, RI-MA	7.6
41	7	Memphis, TN-MS-AR	7.6
27	10	Sacramento—Roseville—Arden-Arcade, CA	7.2
64	10	New Haven-Milford, CT	7.2
3	12	Chicago-Naperville-Elgin, IL-IN-WI	7.0
9	13	Atlanta-Sandy Springs-Roswell, GA	6.8
66	14	Oxnard-Thousand Oaks-Ventura, CA	6.7
47	15	Hartford-West Hartford-East Hartford, CT	6.5
67	15	El Paso, TX	6.5
74	15	Greensboro-High Point, NC	6.5
1	18	New York-Newark-Jersey City, NY-NJ-PA	6.4
17	18	San Diego-Carlsbad, CA	6.4
24	18	Portland-Vancouver-Hillsboro, OR-WA	6.4
45	18	New Orleans-Metairie, LA	6.4
59	18	Albuquerque, NM	6.4
8	23	Miami-Fort Lauderdale-West Palm Beach, FL	6.3
19	23	St. Louis, MO-IL	6.3
58	23	Worcester, MA-CT	6.3
31	26	Cleveland-Elyria, OH	6.2
40	26	Jacksonville, FL	6.2
50	26	Buffalo-Cheektowaga-Niagara Falls, NY	6.2
53	26	Tucson, AZ	6.2
57	26	Bridgeport-Stamford-Norwalk, CT	6.2
65	26	Knoxville, TN	6.2
6	32	Philadelphia-Camden-Wilmington, PA-NJ-DE-MD	6.1
18	32	Tampa-St. Petersburg-Clearwater, FL	6.1
20	32	Baltimore-Columbia-Towson, MD	6.1
69	32	Allentown-Bethlehem-Easton, PA-NJ	6.1
12	36	Phoenix-Mesa-Scottsdale, AZ	6.0
22	36	Charlotte-Concord-Gastonia, NC-SC	6.0
39	36	Milwaukee-Waukesha-West Allis, WI	6.0
49	36	Birmingham-Hoover, AL	6.0
26	40	Orlando-Kissimmee-Sanford, FL	5.9
43	40	Louisville/Jefferson County, KY-IN	5.9
51	42	Rochester, NY	5.8
70	42	Baton Rouge, LA	5.8
71	42	Dayton, OH	5.8
72	42	Columbia, SC	5.8
73	42	North Port-Sarasota-Bradenton, FL	5.8
33	47	Indianapolis-Carmel-Anderson, IN	5.7
37	47	Virginia Beach-Norfolk-Newport News, VA-NC	5.7
63	47	Greenville-Anderson-Mauldin, SC	5.7
23	50	Pittsburgh, PA	5.6
29	50	Kansas City, MO-KS	5.6
44	52	Richmond, VA	5.5
75	52	Little Rock-North Little Rock-Conway, AR	5.5
28	54	Cincinnati, OH-KY-IN	5.4
34	55	San Jose-Sunnyvale-Santa Clara, CA	5.3
10	56	Boston-Cambridge-Newton, MA-NH	5.2
11	56	San Francisco-Oakland-Hayward, CA	5.2
15	56	Seattle-Tacoma-Bellevue, WA	5.2
36	56	Nashville-Davidson—Murfreesboro—Franklin, TN	5.2
61	60	Albany-Schenectady-Troy, NY	5.1
4	61	Dallas-Fort Worth-Arlington, TX	5.0
7	61	Washington-Arlington-Alexandria, DC-VA-MD-WV	5.0
52	61	Grand Rapids-Wyoming, MI	5.0
5	64	Houston-The Woodlands-Sugar Land, TX	4.9
46	64	Raleigh, NC	4.9
21	66	Denver-Aurora-Lakewood, CO	4.8
32	66	Columbus, OH	4.8
25	68	San Antonio-New Braunfels, TX	4.6
55	69	Tulsa, OK	4.5
35	70	Austin-Round Rock, TX	4.2
54	71	Urban Honolulu, HI	4.1
42	72	Oklahoma City, OK	4.0
16	73	Minneapolis-St. Paul-Bloomington, MN	3.9
48	74	Salt Lake City, UT	3.7
60	74	Omaha-Council Bluffs, NE-IA	3.7

Percent of Votes for Barack Obama, 2012

Population Rank	Vote for Obama rank	Metropolitan area	Percent of votes for Obama [col 197]
11	1	San Francisco-Oakland-Hayward, CA	75.4
68	2	McAllen-Edinburg-Mission, TX	70.4
34	3	San Jose-Sunnyvale-Santa Clara, CA	69.8
54	4	Urban Honolulu, HI	68.9
7	5	Washington-Arlington-Alexandria, DC-VA-MD-WV	67.3
67	6	El Paso, TX	65.4
1	7	New York-Newark-Jersey City, NY-NJ-PA	64.8
6	8	Philadelphia-Camden-Wilmington, PA-NJ-DE-MD	64.0
3	9	Chicago-Naperville-Elgin, IL-IN-WI	63.8
15	10	Seattle-Tacoma-Bellevue, WA	63.6
2	11	Los Angeles-Long Beach-Anaheim, CA	63.4
8	12	Miami-Fort Lauderdale-West Palm Beach, FL	62.6
31	13	Cleveland-Elyria, OH	61.5
38	13	Providence-Warwick, RI-MA	61.5
47	15	Hartford-West Hartford-East Hartford, CT	60.7
64	15	New Haven-Milford, CT	60.7
10	17	Boston-Cambridge-Newton, MA-NH	60.1
24	18	Portland-Vancouver-Hillsboro, OR-WA	60.0
14	19	Detroit-Warren-Dearborn, MI	59.5
20	20	Baltimore-Columbia-Towson, MD	57.8
61	21	Albany-Schenectady-Troy, NY	57.0
30	22	Las Vegas-Henderson-Paradise, NV	56.4
50	23	Buffalo-Cheektowaga-Niagara Falls, NY	55.9
41	24	Memphis, TN-MS-AR	55.7
21	25	Denver-Aurora-Lakewood, CO	55.5
57	26	Bridgeport-Stamford-Norwalk, CT	54.9
37	27	Virginia Beach-Norfolk-Newport News, VA-NC	54.8
16	28	Minneapolis-St. Paul-Bloomington, MN	54.7
51	29	Rochester, NY	54.4
59	30	Albuquerque, NM	54.0
58	31	Worcester, MA-CT	53.9
26	32	Orlando-Kissimmee-Sanford, FL	53.4
27	33	Sacramento—Roseville—Arden-Arcade, CA	53.1
32	34	Columbus, OH	52.7
17	35	San Diego-Carlsbad, CA	52.6
19	35	St. Louis, MO-IL	52.6
53	35	Tucson, AZ	52.6
66	38	Oxnard-Thousand Oaks-Ventura, CA	52.3
39	39	Milwaukee-Waukesha-West Allis, WI	52.1
46	39	Raleigh, NC	52.1
44	41	Richmond, VA	52.0
35	42	Austin-Round Rock, TX	51.9
13	43	Riverside-San Bernardino-Ontario, CA	51.0
18	43	Tampa-St. Petersburg-Clearwater, FL	51.0
69	45	Allentown-Bethlehem-Easton, PA-NJ	50.6
72	46	Columbia, SC	50.2
56	47	Fresno, CA	49.9
74	48	Greensboro-High Point, NC	49.8
9	49	Atlanta-Sandy Springs-Roswell, GA	49.6
45	50	New Orleans-Metairie, LA	49.2
23	51	Pittsburgh, PA	48.8
43	52	Louisville/Jefferson County, KY-IN	48.1
29	53	Kansas City, MO-KS	47.9
22	54	Charlotte-Concord-Gastonia, NC-SC	47.2
71	55	Dayton, OH	46.2
25	56	San Antonio-New Braunfels, TX	45.3
33	57	Indianapolis-Carmel-Anderson, IN	45.2
73	58	North Port-Sarasota-Bradenton, FL	44.8
60	59	Omaha-Council Bluffs, NE-IA	44.0
5	60	Houston-The Woodlands-Sugar Land, TX	43.6
12	61	Phoenix-Mesa-Scottsdale, AZ	43.5
75	62	Little Rock-North Little Rock-Conway, AR	43.2
70	63	Baton Rouge, LA	43.0
4	64	Dallas-Fort Worth-Arlington, TX	41.9
52	65	Grand Rapids-Wyoming, MI	41.5
28	66	Cincinnati, OH-KY-IN	41.4
36	67	Nashville-Davidson—Murfreesboro—Franklin, TN	41.0
62	68	Bakersfield, CA	40.4
40	69	Jacksonville, FL	40.0
49	70	Birmingham-Hoover, AL	39.3
48	71	Salt Lake City, UT	37.6
42	72	Oklahoma City, OK	36.5
55	73	Tulsa, OK	33.9
63	74	Greenville-Anderson-Mauldin, SC	33.3
65	75	Knoxville, TN	31.2

75 Largest Metropolitan Areas by 2014 Population

Selected Rankings

Employment in manufacturing as a percent of total nonfarm employment, 2013

Population rank	Manufacturing rank	Metropolitan area	Percent employed in manufacturing [col 107/ col 105]
52	1	Grand Rapids-Wyoming, MI	21.6
74	2	Greensboro-High Point, NC	16.8
63	3	Greenville-Anderson-Mauldin, SC	15.8
39	4	Milwaukee-Waukesha-West Allis, WI	15.1
55	5	Tulsa, OK	13.5
31	6	Cleveland-Elyria, OH	13.3
71	7	Dayton, OH	13.2
14	8	Detroit-Warren-Dearborn, MI	12.8
51	8	Rochester, NY	12.8
43	10	Louisville/Jefferson County, KY-IN	12.3
58	10	Worcester, MA-CT	12.3
47	12	Hartford-West Hartford-East Hartford, CT	11.4
50	13	Buffalo-Cheektowaga-Niagara Falls, NY	11.1
65	14	Knoxville, TN	11.0
24	15	Portland-Vancouver-Hillsboro, OR-WA	10.7
69	16	Allentown-Bethlehem-Easton, PA-NJ	10.6
28	17	Cincinnati, OH-KY-IN	10.5
38	17	Providence-Warwick, RI-MA	10.5
16	19	Minneapolis-St. Paul-Bloomington, MN	10.3
15	20	Seattle-Tacoma-Bellevue, WA	10.1
2	21	Los Angeles-Long Beach-Anaheim, CA	9.8
3	22	Chicago-Naperville-Elgin, IL-IN-WI	9.7
22	22	Charlotte-Concord-Gastonia, NC-SC	9.7
34	22	San Jose-Sunnyvale-Santa Clara, CA	9.7
56	22	Fresno, CA	9.7
64	26	New Haven-Milford, CT	9.6
72	26	Columbia, SC	9.6
37	28	Virginia Beach-Norfolk-Newport News, VA-NC	9.5
66	29	Oxnard-Thousand Oaks-Ventura, CA	9.3
5	30	Houston-The Woodlands-Sugar Land, TX	9.1
48	31	Salt Lake City, UT	9.0
13	32	Riverside-San Bernardino-Ontario, CA	8.8
33	32	Indianapolis-Carmel-Anderson, IN	8.8
17	34	San Diego-Carlsbad, CA	8.5
29	34	Kansas City, MO-KS	8.5
49	34	Birmingham-Hoover, AL	8.5
4	37	Dallas-Fort Worth-Arlington, TX	8.4
19	37	St. Louis, MO-IL	8.4
23	37	Pittsburgh, PA	8.4
36	37	Nashville-Davidson—Murfreesboro—Franklin, TN	8.4
57	41	Bridgeport-Stamford-Norwalk, CT	8.3
75	42	Little Rock-North Little Rock-Conway, AR	8.1
53	43	Tucson, AZ	8.0
60	44	Omaha-Council Bluffs, NE-IA	7.6
32	45	Columbus, OH	7.4
70	46	Baton Rouge, LA	7.1
41	47	Memphis, TN-MS-AR	6.8
6	48	Philadelphia-Camden-Wilmington, PA-NJ-DE-MD	6.7
62	49	Bakersfield, CA	6.6
10	50	Boston-Cambridge-Newton, MA-NH	6.5
73	50	North Port-Sarasota-Bradenton, FL	6.5
61	52	Albany-Schenectady-Troy, NY	6.4
67	52	El Paso, TX	6.4
9	54	Atlanta-Sandy Springs-Roswell, GA	6.3
12	54	Phoenix-Mesa-Scottsdale, AZ	6.3
42	56	Oklahoma City, OK	6.2
44	57	Richmond, VA	6.0
35	58	Austin-Round Rock, TX	5.9
45	59	New Orleans-Metairie, LA	5.7
59	59	Albuquerque, NM	5.7
11	61	San Francisco-Oakland-Hayward, CA	5.6
25	62	San Antonio-New Braunfels, TX	5.4
18	63	Tampa-St. Petersburg-Clearwater, FL	5.2
21	64	Denver-Aurora-Lakewood, CO	5.1
27	65	Sacramento—Roseville—Arden-Arcade, CA	4.9
20	66	Baltimore-Columbia-Towson, MD	4.8
46	66	Raleigh, NC	4.8
40	68	Jacksonville, FL	4.4
1	69	New York-Newark-Jersey City, NY-NJ-PA	4.3
68	70	McAllen-Edinburg-Mission, TX	3.9
26	71	Orlando-Kissimmee-Sanford, FL	3.7
8	72	Miami-Fort Lauderdale-West Palm Beach, FL	3.4
54	73	Urban Honolulu, HI	2.7
30	74	Las Vegas-Henderson-Paradise, NV	2.4
7	75	Washington-Arlington-Alexandria, DC-VA-MD-WV	1.9

Employment in professional, scientific, and technical services as a percent of total nonfarm employment, 2013

Population rank	Professional services rank	Metropolitan area	Percent employed in services [col 110/ col 105]
7	1	Washington-Arlington-Alexandria, DC-VA-MD-WV	20.9
34	2	San Jose-Sunnyvale-Santa Clara, CA	14.2
11	3	San Francisco-Oakland-Hayward, CA	11.6
20	4	Baltimore-Columbia-Towson, MD	11.4
17	5	San Diego-Carlsbad, CA	11.2
46	6	Raleigh, NC	10.5
35	7	Austin-Round Rock, TX	10.4
14	8	Detroit-Warren-Dearborn, MI	9.9
10	9	Boston-Cambridge-Newton, MA-NH	9.8
21	10	Denver-Aurora-Lakewood, CO	9.7
66	11	Oxnard-Thousand Oaks-Ventura, CA	9.0
1	12	New York-Newark-Jersey City, NY-NJ-PA	8.9
18	13	Tampa-St. Petersburg-Clearwater, FL	8.8
57	13	Bridgeport-Stamford-Norwalk, CT	8.8
5	15	Houston-The Woodlands-Sugar Land, TX	8.6
9	15	Atlanta-Sandy Springs-Roswell, GA	8.6
2	17	Los Angeles-Long Beach-Anaheim, CA	8.5
37	18	Virginia Beach-Norfolk-Newport News, VA-NC	8.2
3	19	Chicago-Naperville-Elgin, IL-IN-WI	8.1
6	19	Philadelphia-Camden-Wilmington, PA-NJ-DE-MD	8.1
48	19	Salt Lake City, UT	8.1
29	22	Kansas City, MO-KS	8.0
4	23	Dallas-Fort Worth-Arlington, TX	7.9
61	23	Albany-Schenectady-Troy, NY	7.9
15	25	Seattle-Tacoma-Bellevue, WA	7.8
27	26	Sacramento—Roseville—Arden-Arcade, CA	7.7
19	27	St. Louis, MO-IL	7.6
8	28	Miami-Fort Lauderdale-West Palm Beach, FL	7.4
24	28	Portland-Vancouver-Hillsboro, OR-WA	7.4
44	30	Richmond, VA	7.3
71	30	Dayton, OH	7.3
23	32	Pittsburgh, PA	7.2
47	33	Hartford-West Hartford-East Hartford, CT	7.1
59	34	Albuquerque, NM	7.0
45	35	New Orleans-Metairie, LA	6.8
16	36	Minneapolis-St. Paul-Bloomington, MN	6.7
33	37	Indianapolis-Carmel-Anderson, IN	6.6
62	37	Bakersfield, CA	6.6
65	37	Knoxville, TN	6.6
50	40	Buffalo-Cheektowaga-Niagara Falls, NY	6.5
28	41	Cincinnati, OH-KY-IN	6.3
70	41	Baton Rouge, LA	6.3
12	43	Phoenix-Mesa-Scottsdale, AZ	6.2
22	43	Charlotte-Concord-Gastonia, NC-SC	6.2
26	43	Orlando-Kissimmee-Sanford, FL	6.2
40	43	Jacksonville, FL	6.2
42	43	Oklahoma City, OK	6.2
32	48	Columbus, OH	6.0
60	49	Omaha-Council Bluffs, NE-IA	5.9
73	49	North Port-Sarasota-Bradenton, FL	5.9
25	51	San Antonio-New Braunfels, TX	5.8
63	51	Greenville-Anderson-Mauldin, SC	5.8
51	53	Rochester, NY	5.7
55	53	Tulsa, OK	5.7
31	55	Cleveland-Elyria, OH	5.5
53	55	Tucson, AZ	5.5
58	55	Worcester, MA-CT	5.5
72	55	Columbia, SC	5.5
36	59	Nashville-Davidson—Murfreesboro—Franklin, TN	5.3
09	50	Milwaukoo-Waukesha-West Allis, WI	5.3
54	59	Urban Honolulu, HI	5.3
30	62	Las Vegas-Henderson-Paradise, NV	5.2
43	63	Louisville/Jefferson County, KY-IN	4.9
49	63	Birmingham-Hoover, AL	4.9
38	65	Providence-Warwick, RI-MA	4.6
56	65	Fresno, CA	4.6
75	65	Little Rock-North Little Rock-Conway, AR	4.6
64	68	New Haven-Milford, CT	4.5
67	69	El Paso, TX	4.3
52	70	Grand Rapids-Wyoming, MI	3.9
74	70	Greensboro-High Point, NC	3.9
69	72	Allentown-Bethlehem-Easton, PA-NJ	3.8
13	73	Riverside-San Bernardino-Ontario, CA	3.3
41	73	Memphis, TN-MS-AR	3.3
68	75	McAllen-Edinburg-Mission, TX	2.9

75 Largest Metropolitan Areas by 2014 Population

Selected Rankings

Per capita local government taxes, 2012

Population rank	Local taxes rank	Metropolitan area	Local per capita taxes (dollars) [col 183]
1	1	New York-Newark-Jersey City, NY-NJ-PA	4 280
57	2	Bridgeport-Stamford-Norwalk, CT	3 419
7	3	Washington-Arlington-Alexandria, DC-VA-MD-WV	3 255
3	4	Chicago-Naperville-Elgin, IL-IN-WI	2 701
11	5	San Francisco-Oakland-Hayward, CA	2 658
61	6	Albany-Schenectady-Troy, NY	2 620
34	7	San Jose-Sunnyvale-Santa Clara, CA	2 585
47	8	Hartford-West Hartford-East Hartford, CT	2 512
51	9	Rochester, NY	2 381
31	10	Cleveland-Elyria, OH	2 378
10	11	Boston-Cambridge-Newton, MA-NH	2 362
64	12	New Haven-Milford, CT	2 358
6	13	Philadelphia-Camden-Wilmington, PA-NJ-DE-MD	2 356
50	14	Buffalo-Cheektowaga-Niagara Falls, NY	2 326
32	15	Columbus, OH	2 274
35	16	Austin-Round Rock, TX	2 267
21	17	Denver-Aurora-Lakewood, CO	2 240
20	18	Baltimore-Columbia-Towson, MD	2 145
4	19	Dallas-Fort Worth-Arlington, TX	2 139
8	20	Miami-Fort Lauderdale-West Palm Beach, FL	2 106
69	20	Allentown-Bethlehem-Easton, PA-NJ	2 106
15	22	Seattle-Tacoma-Bellevue, WA	2 088
5	23	Houston-The Woodlands-Sugar Land, TX	2 087
29	24	Kansas City, MO-KS	2 040
60	25	Omaha-Council Bluffs, NE-IA	2 037
38	26	Providence-Warwick, RI-MA	2 018
45	27	New Orleans-Metairie, LA	1 991
39	28	Milwaukee-Waukesha-West Allis, WI	1 986
2	29	Los Angeles-Long Beach-Anaheim, CA	1 870
71	30	Dayton, OH	1 861
19	31	St. Louis, MO-IL	1 841
17	32	San Diego-Carlsbad, CA	1 791
28	33	Cincinnati, OH-KY-IN	1 786
23	34	Pittsburgh, PA	1 785
24	35	Portland-Vancouver-Hillsboro, OR-WA	1 774
70	36	Baton Rouge, LA	1 760
9	37	Atlanta-Sandy Springs-Roswell, GA	1 744
37	38	Virginia Beach-Norfolk-Newport News, VA-NC	1 733
73	39	North Port-Sarasota-Bradenton, FL	1 684
25	40	San Antonio-New Braunfels, TX	1 669
66	41	Oxnard-Thousand Oaks-Ventura, CA	1 650
58	42	Worcester, MA-CT	1 628
26	43	Orlando-Kissimmee-Sanford, FL	1 583
16	44	Minneapolis-St. Paul-Bloomington, MN	1 558
41	45	Memphis, TN-MS-AR	1 555
44	46	Richmond, VA	1 521
27	47	Sacramento—Roseville—Arden-Arcade, CA	1 504
22	48	Charlotte-Concord-Gastonia, NC-SC	1 487
49	49	Birmingham-Hoover, AL	1 483
12	50	Phoenix-Mesa-Scottsdale, AZ	1 447
36	51	Nashville-Davidson—Murfreesboro—Franklin, TN	1 445
40	51	Jacksonville, FL	1 445
53	53	Tucson, AZ	1 438
33	54	Indianapolis-Carmel-Anderson, IN	1 402
48	55	Salt Lake City, UT	1 399
72	56	Columbia, SC	1 385
18	57	Tampa-St. Petersburg-Clearwater, FL	1 381
14	58	Detroit-Warren-Dearborn, MI	1 374
30	59	Las Vegas-Henderson-Paradise, NV	1 367
62	60	Bakersfield, CA	1 365
54	61	Urban Honolulu, HI	1 348
46	62	Raleigh, NC	1 332
42	63	Oklahoma City, OK	1 331
13	64	Riverside-San Bernardino-Ontario, CA	1 326
67	65	El Paso, TX	1 321
55	66	Tulsa, OK	1 319
43	67	Louisville/Jefferson County, KY-IN	1 265
74	68	Greensboro-High Point, NC	1 262
59	69	Albuquerque, NM	1 208
65	70	Knoxville, TN	1 191
52	71	Grand Rapids-Wyoming, MI	1 159
56	72	Fresno, CA	1 131
68	73	McAllen-Edinburg-Mission, TX	1 071
63	74	Greenville-Anderson-Mauldin, SC	978
75	75	Little Rock-North Little Rock-Conway, AR	838

Violent crime rate, 2013 (violent crimes known to police)

Population rank	Crime rate rank	Metropolitan area	Crime rate (per 100,000 population) [col 46]
41	1	Memphis, TN-MS-AR	1 035
75	2	Little Rock-North Little Rock-Conway, AR	711
30	3	Las Vegas-Henderson-Paradise, NV	678
59	4	Albuquerque, NM	668
33	5	Indianapolis-Carmel-Anderson, IN	662
20	6	Baltimore-Columbia-Towson, MD	612
39	7	Milwaukee-Waukesha-West Allis, WI	599
36	8	Nashville-Davidson—Murfreesboro—Franklin, TN	596
62	9	Bakersfield, CA	576
72	9	Columbia, SC	576
14	11	Detroit-Warren-Dearborn, MI	571
63	12	Greenville-Anderson-Mauldin, SC	561
5	13	Houston-The Woodlands-Sugar Land, TX	559
11	13	San Francisco-Oakland-Hayward, CA	559
26	15	Orlando-Kissimmee-Sanford, FL	540
8	16	Miami-Fort Lauderdale-West Palm Beach, FL	538
55	17	Tulsa, OK	521
56	18	Fresno, CA	510
70	18	Baton Rouge, LA	510
49	20	Birmingham-Hoover, AL	507
42	21	Oklahoma City, OK	503
6	22	Philadelphia-Camden-Wilmington, PA-NJ-DE-MD	499
40	23	Jacksonville, FL	496
45	24	New Orleans-Metairie, LA	474
29	25	Kansas City, MO-KS	469
25	26	San Antonio-New Braunfels, TX	460
19	27	St. Louis, MO-IL	440
31	28	Cleveland-Elyria, OH	431
53	28	Tucson, AZ	431
50	30	Buffalo-Cheektowaga-Niagara Falls, NY	430
58	31	Worcester, MA-CT	422
73	31	North Port-Sarasota-Bradenton, FL	422
27	33	Sacramento—Roseville—Arden-Arcade, CA	416
22	34	Charlotte-Concord-Gastonia, NC-SC	404
3	35	Chicago-Naperville-Elgin, IL-IN-WI	403
43	36	Louisville/Jefferson County, KY-IN	397
18	37	Tampa-St. Petersburg-Clearwater, FL	396
9	38	Atlanta-Sandy Springs-Roswell, GA	393
64	39	New Haven-Milford, CT	392
1	40	New York-Newark-Jersey City, NY-NJ-PA	391
60	41	Omaha-Council Bluffs, NE-IA	388
12	42	Phoenix-Mesa-Scottsdale, AZ	386
48	43	Salt Lake City, UT	359
10	44	Boston-Cambridge-Newton, MA-NH	355
2	45	Los Angeles-Long Beach-Anaheim, CA	353
65	46	Knoxville, TN	352
17	47	San Diego-Carlsbad, CA	348
74	48	Greensboro-High Point, NC	340
38	49	Providence-Warwick, RI-MA	339
67	49	El Paso, TX	339
4	51	Dallas-Fort Worth-Arlington, TX	333
13	51	Riverside-San Bernardino-Ontario, CA	333
7	53	Washington-Arlington-Alexandria, DC-VA-MD-WV	332
21	54	Denver-Aurora-Lakewood, CO	328
15	55	Seattle-Tacoma-Bellevue, WA	319
37	56	Virginia Beach-Norfolk-Newport News, VA-NC	304
52	56	Grand Rapids-Wyoming, MI	304
32	58	Columbus, OH	298
28	59	Cincinnati, OH-KY-IN	295
23	60	Pittsburgh, PA	291
68	61	McAllen-Edinburg-Mission, TX	286
51	62	Rochester, NY	284
16	63	Minneapolis-St. Paul-Bloomington, MN	274
35	64	Austin-Round Rock, TX	271
71	64	Dayton, OH	271
61	66	Albany-Schenectady-Troy, NY	266
47	67	Hartford-West Hartford-East Hartford, CT	265
24	68	Portland-Vancouver-Hillsboro, OR-WA	251
34	69	San Jose-Sunnyvale-Santa Clara, CA	250
57	70	Bridgeport-Stamford-Norwalk, CT	245
44	71	Richmond, VA	242
46	72	Raleigh, NC	218
66	73	Oxnard-Thousand Oaks-Ventura, CA	194
69	74	Allentown-Bethlehem-Easton, PA-NJ	187
54	75	Urban Honolulu, HI	115

All Metropolitan Areas

Selected Rankings

Nonemployer businesses, 2013

Population rank	Nonemployer business	Metropolitan area	Nonemployer business [col 167]
1	1	New York-Newark-Jersey City, NY-NJ-PA	1 772 736
2	2	Los Angeles-Long Beach-Anaheim, CA	1 224 211
8	3	Miami-Fort Lauderdale-West Palm Beach, FL	784 044
3	4	Chicago-Naperville-Elgin, IL-IN-WI	738 009
4	5	Dallas-Fort Worth-Arlington, TX	566 067
5	6	Houston-The Woodlands-Sugar Land, TX	522 568
9	7	Atlanta-Sandy Springs-Roswell, GA	521 102
7	8	Washington-Arlington-Alexandria, DC-VA-MD-WV	488 647
11	9	San Francisco-Oakland-Hayward, CA	395 627
6	10	Philadelphia-Camden-Wilmington, PA-NJ-DE-MD	386 271
10	11	Boston-Cambridge-Newton, MA-NH	353 419
14	12	Detroit-Warren-Dearborn, MI	325 593
12	13	Phoenix-Mesa-Scottsdale, AZ	290 916
13	14	Riverside-San Bernardino-Ontario, CA	288 256
16	15	Minneapolis-St. Paul-Bloomington, MN	256 066
17	16	San Diego-Carlsbad, CA	246 649
15	17	Seattle-Tacoma-Bellevue, WA	231 707
21	18	Denver-Aurora-Lakewood, CO	228 988
18	19	Tampa-St. Petersburg-Clearwater, FL	224 508
20	20	Baltimore-Columbia-Towson, MD	199 635
26	21	Orlando-Kissimmee-Sanford, FL	196 646
19	22	St. Louis, MO-IL	179 278
22	23	Charlotte-Concord-Gastonia, NC-SC	172 530
24	24	Portland-Vancouver-Hillsboro, OR-WA	159 188
35	25	Austin-Round Rock, TX	158 665
25	26	San Antonio-New Braunfels, TX	157 377
27	27	Sacramento—Roseville—Arden-Arcade, CA	152 625
36	28	Nashville-Davidson—Murfreesboro—Franklin, TN	147 628
31	29	Cleveland-Elyria, OH	143 629
30	30	Las Vegas-Henderson-Paradise, NV	141 658
32	31	Columbus, OH	141 139
29	32	Kansas City, MO-KS	137 259
23	33	Pittsburgh, PA	137 016
28	34	Cincinnati, OH-KY-IN	135 514
34	35	San Jose-Sunnyvale-Santa Clara, CA	132 037
33	36	Indianapolis-Carmel-Anderson, IN	129 587
45	37	New Orleans-Metairie, LA	111 106
41	38	Memphis, TN-MS-AR	105 730
38	39	Providence-Warwick, RI-MA	104 664
42	40	Oklahoma City, OK	99 772
40	41	Jacksonville, FL	98 407
37	42	Virginia Beach-Norfolk-Newport News, VA-NC	93 106
46	43	Raleigh, NC	91 107
57	44	Bridgeport-Stamford-Norwalk, CT	88 363
39	45	Milwaukee-Waukesha-West Allis, WI	88 210
43	46	Louisville/Jefferson County, KY-IN	82 071
48	47	Salt Lake City, UT	79 125
47	48	Hartford-West Hartford-East Hartford, CT	78 617
44	49	Richmond, VA	77 910
49	50	Birmingham-Hoover, AL	76 710
52	51	Grand Rapids-Wyoming, MI	69 082
55	52	Tulsa, OK	69 046
68	53	McAllen-Edinburg-Mission, TX	66 167
73	54	North Port-Sarasota-Bradenton, FL	64 761
66	55	Oxnard-Thousand Oaks-Ventura, CA	64 224
51	56	Rochester, NY	62 646
70	57	Baton Rouge, LA	61 017
53	58	Tucson, AZ	60 686
54	59	Urban Honolulu, HI	60 220
65	60	Knoxville, TN	58 708
64	61	New Haven-Milford, CT	57 091
58	62	Worcester, MA-CT	56 393
60	63	Omaha-Council Bluffs, NE-IA	56 347
63	64	Greenville-Anderson-Mauldin, SC	55 891
50	65	Buffalo-Cheektowaga-Niagara Falls, NY	55 078
67	66	El Paso, TX	54 021
74	67	Greensboro-High Point, NC	52 274
61	68	Albany-Schenectady-Troy, NY	51 538
72	69	Columbia, SC	50 616
59	70	Albuquerque, NM	50 356
56	71	Fresno, CA	49 304
69	72	Allentown-Bethlehem-Easton, PA-NJ	48 406
75	73	Little Rock-North Little Rock-Conway, AR	48 320
71	74	Dayton, OH	47 778
62	75	Bakersfield, CA	43 515

Value of residential construction authorized by building permits, 2014

Population rank	New Construction rank	Metropolitan area	New Construction [col 169]
5	1	Houston-The Woodlands-Sugar Land, TX	9 250 783
4	2	Dallas-Fort Worth-Arlington, TX	7 773 054
1	3	New York-Newark-Jersey City, NY-NJ-PA	6 998 012
2	4	Los Angeles-Long Beach-Anaheim, CA	5 982 336
15	5	Seattle-Tacoma-Bellevue, WA	4 469 256
9	6	Atlanta-Sandy Springs-Roswell, GA	4 391 656
12	7	Phoenix-Mesa-Scottsdale, AZ	4 309 793
7	8	Washington-Arlington-Alexandria, DC-VA-MD-WV	3 898 607
26	9	Orlando-Kissimmee-Sanford, FL	3 566 667
8	10	Miami-Fort Lauderdale-West Palm Beach, FL	3 482 242
3	11	Chicago-Naperville-Elgin, IL-IN-WI	3 385 179
22	12	Charlotte-Concord-Gastonia, NC-SC	3 237 476
35	13	Austin-Round Rock, TX	3 235 961
21	14	Denver-Aurora-Lakewood, CO	2 934 436
18	15	Tampa-St. Petersburg-Clearwater, FL	2 845 319
11	16	San Francisco-Oakland-Hayward, CA	2 793 204
16	17	Minneapolis-St. Paul-Bloomington, MN	2 726 636
36	18	Nashville-Davidson—Murfreesboro—Franklin, TN	2 681 399
10	19	Boston-Cambridge-Newton, MA-NH	2 643 771
24	20	Portland-Vancouver-Hillsboro, OR-WA	2 353 394
6	21	Philadelphia-Camden-Wilmington, PA-NJ-DE-MD	2 141 915
13	22	Riverside-San Bernardino-Ontario, CA	2 099 037
46	23	Raleigh, NC	1 953 945
34	24	San Jose-Sunnyvale-Santa Clara, CA	1 894 413
25	25	San Antonio-New Braunfels, TX	1 722 123
40	26	Jacksonville, FL	1 674 047
17	27	San Diego-Carlsbad, CA	1 504 007
33	28	Indianapolis-Carmel-Anderson, IN	1 498 510
42	29	Oklahoma City, OK	1 456 882
29	30	Kansas City, MO-KS	1 426 821
19	31	St. Louis, MO-IL	1 424 810
14	32	Detroit-Warren-Dearborn, MI	1 412 223
73	33	North Port-Sarasota-Bradenton, FL	1 296 644
32	34	Columbus, OH	1 254 408
20	35	Baltimore-Columbia-Towson, MD	1 173 415
27	36	Sacramento—Roseville—Arden-Arcade, CA	1 172 225
30	37	Las Vegas-Henderson-Paradise, NV	1 132 984
48	38	Salt Lake City, UT	936 040
28	39	Cincinnati, OH-KY-IN	906 061
23	40	Pittsburgh, PA	901 168
63	41	Greenville-Anderson-Mauldin, SC	869 758
37	42	Virginia Beach-Norfolk-Newport News, VA-NC	849 773
55	43	Tulsa, OK	741 914
70	44	Baton Rouge, LA	712 426
53	45	Tucson, AZ	697 362
44	46	Richmond, VA	690 026
72	47	Columbia, SC	676 849
60	48	Omaha-Council Bluffs, NE-IA	661 078
31	49	Cleveland-Elyria, OH	647 535
45	50	New Orleans-Metairie, LA	634 641
49	51	Birmingham-Hoover, AL	614 997
57	52	Bridgeport-Stamford-Norwalk, CT	614 242
43	53	Louisville/Jefferson County, KY-IN	604 712
52	54	Grand Rapids-Wyoming, MI	588 788
41	55	Memphis, TN-MS-AR	524 520
74	56	Greensboro-High Point, NC	518 982
39	57	Milwaukee-Waukesha-West Allis, WI	494 068
65	58	Knoxville, TN	483 253
56	59	Fresno, CA	445 222
67	60	El Paso, TX	439 382
59	61	Albuquerque, NM	436 320
62	62	Bakersfield, CA	409 140
61	63	Albany-Schenectady-Troy, NY	406 696
54	64	Urban Honolulu, HI	376 974
68	65	McAllen-Edinburg-Mission, TX	372 002
51	66	Rochester, NY	346 696
50	67	Buffalo-Cheektowaga-Niagara Falls, NY	343 116
75	68	Little Rock-North Little Rock-Conway, AR	333 495
38	69	Providence-Warwick, RI-MA	331 881
66	70	Oxnard-Thousand Oaks-Ventura, CA	279 531
58	71	Worcester, MA-CT	268 077
69	72	Allentown-Bethlehem-Easton, PA-NJ	261 907
47	73	Hartford-West Hartford-East Hartford, CT	221 598
71	74	Dayton, OH	218 850
64	75	New Haven-Milford, CT	150 265

75 Metropolitan Areas with Highest Agricultural Sales
Selected rankings

Value of sales rank	Metropolitan area	Value of sales (millions of dollars) [col 125]	Value of sales rank	Number of farms rank	Metropolitan area	Number of farms [col 113]
	Value of agricultural products sold, 2012				Number of farms, 2012	
1	Fresno, CA	4 973.0	56	1	Dallas-Fort Worth-Arlington, TX	29 659
2	Visalia-Porterville, CA	4 017.1	9	2	Minneapolis-St. Paul-Bloomington, MN	13 251
3	Bakersfield, CA	3 999.0	51	3	Kansas City, MO-KS	12 757
4	Salinas, CA	2 979.7	26	4	St. Louis, MO-IL	11 270
5	Merced, CA	2 967.5	35	5	Portland-Vancouver-Hillsboro, OR-WA	10 838
6	Stockton-Lodi, CA	2 250.2	28	6	Columbus, OH	8 198
7	Modesto, CA	2 228.1	32	7	Madison, WI	7 446
8	Chicago-Naperville-Elgin, IL-IN-WI	2 187.2	8	8	Chicago-Naperville-Elgin, IL-IN-WI	6 841
9	Minneapolis-St. Paul-Bloomington, MN	2 169.8	24	9	Fayetteville-Springdale-Rogers, AR-M	6 835
10	Phoenix-Mesa-Scottsdale, AZ	1 931.2	25	10	Philadelphia-Camden-Wilmington, PA-N	6 543
11	El Centro, CA	1 888.6	36	11	Indianapolis-Carmel-Anderson, IN	6 205
12	Greeley, CO	1 860.7	16	12	Omaha-Council Bluffs, NE-IA	6 055
13	Hanford-Corcoran, CA	1 829.2	58	13	San Diego-Carlsbad, CA	5 732
14	Kennewick-Richland, WA	1 663.2	1	14	Fresno, CA	5 683
15	Miami-Fort Lauderdale-West Palm Beac	1 650.7	21	15	Lancaster, PA	5 657
16	Omaha-Council Bluffs, NE-IA	1 649.3	49	16	Wichita, KS	5 345
17	Yakima, WA	1 645.5	33	17	Boise City, ID	5 077
18	Riverside-San Bernardino-Ontario, CA	1 621.2	42	18	Sacramento—Roseville—Arden-Arcade,	5 076
19	Madera, CA	1 602.8	15	19	Miami-Fort Lauderdale-West Palm Beac	4 978
20	Salisbury, MD-DE	1 575.7	2	20	Visalia-Porterville, CA	4 931
21	Lancaster, PA	1 475.0	48	21	Des Moines-West Des Moines, IA	4 898
22	Sioux City, IA-NE-SD	1 460.1	30	22	Grand Rapids-Wyoming, MI	4 680
23	Oxnard-Thousand Oaks-Ventura, CA	1 440.1	38	23	St. Cloud, MN	4 459
24	Fayetteville-Springdale-Rogers, AR-M	1 356.1	44	24	Rochester, NY	4 268
25	Philadelphia-Camden-Wilmington, PA-N	1 264.9	31	25	Rochester, MN	4 233
26	St. Louis, MO-IL	1 235.6	18	26	Riverside-San Bernardino-Ontario, CA	4 198
27	Grand Island, NE	1 227.8	64	27	Jackson, MS	4 186
28	Columbus, OH	1 180.0	7	28	Modesto, CA	4 143
29	Santa Maria-Santa Barbara, CA	1 177.9	61	29	Memphis, TN-MS-AR	3 934
30	Grand Rapids-Wyoming, MI	1 120.3	57	30	Salem, OR	3 710
31	Rochester, MN	1 111.6	46	31	Cedar Rapids, IA	3 678
32	Madison, WI	1 081.6	22	32	Sioux City, IA-NE-SD	3 644
33	Boise City, ID	1 071.7	43	33	Peoria, IL	3 605
34	Grand Forks, ND-MN	1 023.3	6	34	Stockton-Lodi, CA	3 580
35	Portland-Vancouver-Hillsboro, OR-WA	1 008.7	39	35	Santa Rosa, CA	3 579
36	Indianapolis-Carmel-Anderson, IN	985.1	12	36	Greeley, CO	3 525
37	Yuma, AZ	985.0	41	37	Davenport-Moline-Rock Island, IA-IL	3 513
38	St. Cloud, MN	976.0	53	38	Sioux Falls, SD	3 418
39	Santa Rosa, CA	974.4	10	39	Phoenix-Mesa-Scottsdale, AZ	3 417
40	Fargo, ND-MN	965.2	17	40	Yakima, WA	3 143
41	Davenport-Moline-Rock Island, IA-IL	964.4	73	41	Orlando-Kissimmee-Sanford, FL	3 123
42	Sacramento—Roseville—Arden-Arcade,	961.8	66	42	Columbia, SC	3 085
43	Peoria, IL	960.8	55	43	Green Bay, WI	2 774
44	Rochester, NY	930.7	60	44	San Luis Obispo-Paso Robles-Arroyo G	2 666
45	Waterloo-Cedar Falls, IA	921.7	45	45	Waterloo-Cedar Falls, IA	2 643
46	Cedar Rapids, IA	918.4	5	46	Merced, CA	2 486
47	Mankato-North Mankato, MN	892.1	52	47	Iowa City, IA	2 481
48	Des Moines-West Des Moines, IA	891.6	14	48	Kennewick-Richland, WA	2 392
49	Wichita, KS	864.4	20	49	Salisbury, MD-DE	2 384
50	Champaign-Urbana, IL	802.9	69	50	Bismarck, ND	2 367
51	Kansas City, MO-KS	785.7	27	51	Grand Island, NE	2 339
52	Iowa City, IA	785.1	34	52	Grand Forks, ND-MN	2 292
53	Sioux Falls, SD	781.7	50	53	Champaign-Urbana, IL	2 284
54	Amarillo, TX	776.4	59	54	Yuba City, CA	2 153
55	Green Bay, WI	750.0	23	55	Oxnard-Thousand Oaks-Ventura, CA	2 150
56	Dallas-Fort Worth-Arlington, TX	743.8	71	56	Chico, CA	2 056
57	Salem, OR	742.7	75	57	Reading, PA	2 039
58	San Diego-Carlsbad, CA	726.0	63	58	Bloomington, IL	2 000
59	Yuba City, CA	701.6	54	59	Amarillo, TX	1 976
60	San Luis Obispo-Paso Robles-Arroyo G	665.0	3	60	Bakersfield, CA	1 938
61	Memphis, TN-MS-AR	661.4	62	61	Harrisonburg, VA	1 902
62	Harrisonburg, VA	659.0	47	62	Mankato-North Mankato, MN	1 834
63	Bloomington, IL	655.9	40	63	Fargo, ND-MN	1 772
64	Jackson, MS	633.0	74	64	Napa, CA	1 685
65	Lafayette-West Lafayette, IN	583.0	29	65	Santa Maria-Santa Barbara, CA	1 597
66	Columbia, SC	578.6	65	66	Lafayette-West Lafayette, IN	1 574
67	Goldsboro, NC	577.2	19	67	Madera, CA	1 507
68	Santa Cruz-Watsonville, CA	565.8	4	68	Salinas, CA	1 179
69	Bismarck, ND	553.1	13	69	Hanford-Corcoran, CA	1 056
70	Jonesboro, AR	549.0	72	70	Pine Bluff, AR	1 032
71	Chico, CA	541.3	70	71	Jonesboro, AR	980
72	Pine Bluff, AR	540.5	68	72	Santa Cruz-Watsonville, CA	667
73	Orlando-Kissimmee-Sanford, FL	539.8	67	73	Goldsboro, NC	563
74	Napa, CA	536.1	37	74	Yuma, AZ	562
75	Reading, PA	528.7	11	75	El Centro, CA	421

75 Metropolitan Areas with Highest Agricultural Sales

Selected rankings

Land in farms, 2012				Average value of agricultural land and buildings per acre, 2012			
Value of sales rank	Land in farms rank	Metropolitan area	Land in farms (1,000 acres) [col 117]	Value of sales rank	Value per Acre rank	Metropolitan area	Value per acre (1,000 acres) [col 123]
1	56	Dallas-Fort Worth-Arlington, TX	4 075	74	1	Napa, CA	21 801
2	69	Bismarck, ND	3 139	58	2	San Diego-Carlsbad, CA	17 964
3	51	Kansas City, MO-KS	3 124	23	3	Oxnard-Thousand Oaks-Ventura, CA	15 621
4	26	St. Louis, MO-IL	2 912	39	4	Santa Rosa, CA	14 620
5	54	Amarillo, TX	2 889	21	5	Lancaster, PA	12 529
6	49	Wichita, KS	2 856	68	6	Santa Cruz-Watsonville, CA	12 390
7	9	Minneapolis-St. Paul-Bloomington, MN	2 598	18	7	Riverside-San Bernardino-Ontario, CA	10 807
8	16	Omaha-Council Bluffs, NE-IA	2 373	25	8	Philadelphia-Camden-Wilmington, PA-N	10 682
9	3	Bakersfield, CA	2 330	35	9	Portland-Vancouver-Hillsboro, OR-WA	10 520
10	8	Chicago-Naperville-Elgin, IL-IN-WI	2 232	6	10	Stockton-Lodi, CA	10 090
11	12	Greeley, CO	1 956	15	11	Miami-Fort Lauderdale-West Palm Beac	9 911
12	34	Grand Forks, ND-MN	1 911	7	12	Modesto, CA	9 636
13	17	Yakima, WA	1 780	75	13	Reading, PA	8 859
14	28	Columbus, OH	1 746	1	14	Fresno, CA	8 286
15	22	Sioux City, IA-NE-SD	1 733	50	15	Champaign-Urbana, IL	8 014
16	1	Fresno, CA	1 721	63	16	Bloomington, IL	7 961
17	40	Fargo, ND-MN	1 718	45	17	Waterloo-Cedar Falls, IA	7 913
18	36	Indianapolis-Carmel-Anderson, IN	1 689	5	18	Merced, CA	7 737
19	10	Phoenix-Mesa-Scottsdale, AZ	1 651	19	19	Madera, CA	7 614
20	61	Memphis, TN-MS-AR	1 573	71	20	Chico, CA	7 599
21	53	Sioux Falls, SD	1 521	2	21	Visalia-Porterville, CA	7 535
22	32	Madison, WI	1 466	29	22	Santa Maria-Santa Barbara, CA	7 365
23	33	Boise City, ID	1 376	57	23	Salem, OR	7 337
24	48	Des Moines-West Des Moines, IA	1 371	43	24	Peoria, IL	7 332
25	60	San Luis Obispo-Paso Robles-Arroyo G	1 339	8	25	Chicago-Naperville-Elgin, IL-IN-WI	7 285
26	14	Kennewick-Richland, WA	1 329	37	26	Yuma, AZ	7 220
27	43	Peoria, IL	1 288	62	27	Harrisonburg, VA	7 055
28	4	Salinas, CA	1 268	11	28	El Centro, CA	7 002
29	2	Visalia-Porterville, CA	1 239	20	29	Salisbury, MD-DE	6 943
30	50	Champaign-Urbana, IL	1 184	46	30	Cedar Rapids, IA	6 910
31	27	Grand Island, NE	1 181	42	31	Sacramento—Roseville—Arden-Arcade,	6 892
32	31	Rochester, MN	1 158	41	32	Davenport-Moline-Rock Island, IA-IL	6 834
33	64	Jackson, MS	1 156	65	33	Lafayette-West Lafayette, IN	6 657
34	41	Davenport-Moline-Rock Island, IA-IL	1 101	52	34	Iowa City, IA	6 496
35	46	Cedar Rapids, IA	1 075	47	35	Mankato-North Mankato, MN	6 445
36	24	Fayetteville-Springdale-Rogers, AR-M	1 073	59	36	Yuba City, CA	6 343
37	5	Merced, CA	979	16	37	Omaha-Council Bluffs, NE-IA	6 064
38	38	St. Cloud, MN	946	13	38	Hanford-Corcoran, CA	6 031
39	42	Sacramento—Roseville—Arden-Arcade,	927	48	39	Des Moines-West Des Moines, IA	5 875
39	44	Rochester, NY	927	22	40	Sioux City, IA-NE-SD	5 823
41	63	Bloomington, IL	888	36	41	Indianapolis-Carmel-Anderson, IN	5 724
42	45	Waterloo-Cedar Falls, IA	886	73	42	Orlando-Kissimmee-Sanford, FL	5 374
43	73	Orlando-Kissimmee-Sanford, FL	853	26	43	St. Louis, MO-IL	5 260
44	6	Stockton-Lodi, CA	787	9	44	Minneapolis-St. Paul-Bloomington, MN	5 180
45	7	Modesto, CA	768	31	45	Rochester, MN	5 117
46	30	Grand Rapids-Wyoming, MI	746	32	46	Madison, WI	5 002
47	70	Jonesboro, AR	723	28	47	Columbus, OH	4 928
48	29	Santa Maria-Santa Barbara, CA	701	4	48	Salinas, CA	4 893
49	65	Lafayette-West Lafayette, IN	679	53	49	Sioux Falls, SD	4 792
50	13	Hanford-Corcoran, CA	674	30	50	Grand Rapids-Wyoming, MI	4 790
51	19	Madera, CA	654	27	51	Grand Island, NE	4 451
52	25	Philadelphia-Camden-Wilmington, PA-N	653	3	52	Bakersfield, CA	4 435
53	47	Mankato-North Mankato, MN	651	55	53	Green Bay, WI	4 333
54	35	Portland-Vancouver-Hillsboro, OR-WA	644	56	54	Dallas-Fort Worth-Arlington, TX	4 260
55	52	Iowa City, IA	643	60	55	San Luis Obispo-Paso Robles-Arroyo G	4 212
56	15	Miami-Fort Lauderdale-West Palm Beac	610	67	56	Goldsboro, NC	4 124
57	39	Santa Rosa, CA	590	38	57	St. Cloud, MN	3 808
58	59	Yuba City, CA	563	24	58	Fayetteville-Springdale-Rogers, AR-M	3 541
59	55	Green Bay, WI	547	10	59	Phoenix-Mesa-Scottsdale, AZ	3 326
60	66	Columbia, SC	522	66	60	Columbia, SC	3 177
61	20	Salisbury, MD-DE	520	70	61	Jonesboro, AR	3 134
62	72	Pine Bluff, AR	519	40	62	Fargo, ND-MN	3 097
63	11	El Centro, CA	516	51	63	Kansas City, MO-KS	3 062
64	21	Lancaster, PA	439	44	64	Rochester, NY	3 055
65	57	Salem, OR	431	72	65	Pine Bluff, AR	2 912
66	18	Riverside-San Bernardino-Ontario, CA	421	14	66	Kennewick-Richland, WA	2 827
67	71	Chico, CA	381	33	67	Boise City, ID	2 809
68	23	Oxnard-Thousand Oaks-Ventura, CA	281	61	68	Memphis, TN-MS-AR	2 682
69	74	Napa, CA	253	34	69	Grand Forks, ND-MN	2 559
70	75	Reading, PA	234	64	70	Jackson, MS	2 409
71	58	San Diego-Carlsbad, CA	222	12	71	Greeley, CO	1 979
71	62	Harrisonburg, VA	222	49	72	Wichita, KS	1 907
73	37	Yuma, AZ	215	17	73	Yakima, WA	1 803
74	67	Goldsboro, NC	191	69	74	Bismarck, ND	1 116
75	68	Santa Cruz-Watsonville, CA	100	54	75	Amarillo, TX	788

Table C. Metropolitan Areas — **Land Area and Population**

CBSA/ DIV code[1]	Area name		Population 2014			Population characteristics, 2013										
						Race alone or in combination, not Hispanic or Latino (percent)					Age (percent)					
		Land area,[2] 2010 (sq km)	Total persons	Rank	Per square kilometer	White	Black	American Indian, Alaska Native	Asian and Pacific Islander	Percent Hispanic or Latino[3]	Under 5 years	5 to 17 years	18 to 24 years	25 to 34 years	35 to 44 years	45 to 54 years
		1	2	3	4	5	6	7	8	9	10	11	12	13	14	15

1. CBSA = Core Based Statistical Area. DIV = Metropolitan Division. See Appendix A for explanation. See Appendix B for list of metropolitan areas identified by type. 2. Dry land or land partially or temporarily covered by water. 3. May be of any race.

Table C. Metropolitan Areas — **Population and Households**

Area name	Population, 2013 (cont.)				Population change and components of change, 2000–2014							Households, 2013				
	Age (percent) (cont.)				Total persons		Percent change		Components of change, 2010–2014					Percent		
	55 to 64 years	65 to 74 years	75 years and over	Percent female	2000	2010	2000–2010	2010–2014	Births	Deaths	Net migration	Number	Persons per household	Family households	Female family householder[1]	One person
	16	17	18	19	20	21	22	23	24	25	26	27	28	29	30	31

1. No spouse present.

Table C. Metropolitan Areas — **Population, Vital Statistics, Medicare, and Crime**

Area name		Daytime population, 2013		Births, 2014		Deaths, 2014		Persons under 65 with no health insurance 2013		Medicare, 2014			Serious crimes known to police,[2] 2013	
													Total	
	Persons in group quarters, 2014	Number	Employment/ residence ratio	Total	Rate[1]	Number	Rate[1]	Number	Percent	Eligible for Medicare	Enrolled in Medicare Advantage	Enrolled in a Medicare prescription drug plan	Number	Rate[3]
	32	33	34	35	36	37	38	39	40	41	42	43	44	45

1. Per 1,000 estimated resident population. 2. Data for serious crimes have not been adjusted for underreporting; this may affect comparability between geographic areas and over time. 3. Per 100,000 population estimated by the FBI.

Table C. Metropolitan Areas — **Crime, Education, Money Income, and Poverty**

Area name	Serious crimes known to police, 2013 (cont.)[1]		Education						Income and Poverty, 2013							
	Rate[2]		School enrollment and attainment, 2013				Local government expenditures,[5] 2012–2013							Percent below poverty level		
			Enrollment[3]		Attainment[4] (percent)											
	Violent	Property	Total	Percent private	High school graduate or less	Bachelor's degree or more	Total current expenditures (mil dol)	Current expenditures per student (dollars)	Per capita income[6] (dollars)	Mean household income (dollars)	Median household income	Percent of households with income of less than $25,000	Percent of households with income of $200,000 or more	All persons	Children under 18 years	Age 65 years and older
	46	47	48	49	50	51	52	53	54	55	56	57	58	59	60	61

1. Data for serious crimes have not been adjusted for underreporting; this may affect comparability between geographic areas and over time. 2. Per 100,000 population estimated by the FBI. 3. All persons 3 years old and over enrolled in nursery school through college. 4. Persons 25 years old and over. 5. Elementary and secondary education expenditures. 6. Based on resident population estimated in the 2008-2012 American Community Survey.

Table C. Metropolitan Areas — **Personal Income**

Area name	Personal income, 2013										Earnings, 2013		
			Per capita[1]			Supplements to wages and salaries; employer contributions (mil dol)						Contributions for government social insurance (mil dol)	
	Total (mil dol)	Percent change 2012–2013	Dollars	Rank	Wages and salaries (mil dol)	Pension and insurance	Government social insurance	Proprietors' income (mil dol)	Dividends, interest, and rent (mil dol)	Personal transfer receipts (mil dol)	Total (mil dol)	From employee and self-employed	From employer
	62	63	64	65	66	67	68	69	70	71	72	73	74

1. Based on the resident population estimated as of July 1 of the year shown.

Table C. Metropolitan Areas — **Earnings, Social Security, and Housing**

Area name	Earnings, 2013 (cont.)									Social Security beneficiaries, December 2013			Housing units, 2014	
	Percent by selected industries													
	Farm	Mining	Construction	Manufacturing	Information, professional, scientific, technical services	Retail trade	Finance, insurance, real estate, rental and leasing	Health care and social assistance	Government	Number	Rate[1]	Supplemental Security Income recipients, December 2013	Total	Percent change, 2000–2014
	75	76	77	78	79	80	81	82	83	84	85	86	87	88

1. Per 1,000 resident population estimated as of July 1, 2011 of the year shown.

Table C. Metropolitan Areas — **Housing, Labor Force, and Employment**

Area name	Housing units, 2013								Civilian labor force, 2014				Civilian employment[6], 2013		
	Occupied units										Unemployment			Percent	
		Owner-occupied				Renter-occupied									
				Median owner cost as a percent of income											
	Total	Percent	Median value[1]	With a mortgage	Without a mortgage[2]	Median rent[3]	Median rent as a percent of income	Substandard units[4] (percent)	Total	Percent change, 2013–2014	Total	Rate[5]	Total employed	Management, professional, and related occupations	Construction, production, and related occupations
	89	90	91	92	93	94	95	96	97	98	99	100	101	102	103

1. Specified owner-occupied units. 2. A value of 10.0 represents 10 percent or less. 3. Specified renter-occupied units. 4. Overcrowded or lacking complete plumbing facilities.
5. Percent of civilian labor force. 6. Persons 16 years old and over.

Table C. Metropolitan Areas — **Nonfarm Employment and Agriculture**

Area name	Private nonfarm establishments, employment and payroll, 2013									Agriculture, 2012			
		Employment						Annual payroll		Farms			
											Percent with:		
	Number of establishments	Total	Health care and social assistance	Manufacturing	Retail trade	Finance and insurance	Professional, scientific, and technical services	Total (mil dol)	Average per employee (dollars)	Number	Fewer than 50 acres	500 acres or more	Farm operators whose principal occupation is farming (percent)
	104	105	106	107	108	109	110	111	112	113	114	115	116

Table C. Metropolitan Areas — **Agriculture**

Area name	Agriculture, 2012 (cont.)															
	Land in farms					Value of land and buildings (dollars)		Value of machinery and equipment, average per farm (dollars)	Value of products sold				Percent of farms with sales of:		Government payments	
	Acreage (1,000)	Percent change, 2007–2012	Acres: Average size of farm	Acres: Total irrigated (1,000)	Acres: Total cropland (1,000)	Average per farm	Average per acre		Total (mil dol)	Average per farm (dollars)	Percent from: Crops	Percent from: Livestock and poultry products	$10,000 or more	$100,000 or more	Total ($1,000)	Percent of farms
	117	118	119	120	121	122	123	124	125	126	127	128	129	130	131	132

Table C. Metropolitan Areas — **Water Use, Wholesale Trade, Retail Trade, and Real Estate**

Area name	Water use, 2010		Wholesale trade,[1] 2007				Retail trade, 2007				Real estate and rental and leasing, 2007			
	Total water withdrawn (mil gal/day)	Gallons withdrawn per person per day	Number of establish-ments	Number of employees	Sales (mil dol)	Annual payroll (mil dol)	Number of establish-ments	Number of employees	Sales (mil dol)	Annual payroll (mil dol)	Number of establish-ments	Number of employees	Receipts (mil dol)	Annual payroll (mil dol)
	133	134	135	136	137	138	139	140	141	142	143	144	145	146

1. Merchant wholesalers, except manufacturers' sales branches and offices.

Table C. Metropolitan Areas — **Professional Services, Manufacturing, and Accommodation and Food Services**

Area name	Professional, scientific, and technical services,[1] 2007				Manufacturing, 2007				Accommodation and food services, 2007			
	Number of establish-ments	Number of employees	Sales (mil dol)	Annual payroll (mil dol)	Number of establish-ments	Number of employees	Sales (mil dol)	Annual payroll (mil dol)	Number of establish-ments	Number of employees	Sales (mil dol)	Annual payroll (mil dol)
	147	148	149	150	151	152	153	154	155	156	157	158

1. Establishments subject to federal tax.

Table C. Metropolitan Areas — **Health Care and Social Assistance, Other Services, Nonemployer Business and Residential Construction**

Area name	Health care and social assistance,[1] 2007				Other services,[1] 2007				Nonemployer business, 2013		Value of residential construction authorized by building permits, 2014	
	Number of establish-ments	Number of employees	Receipts (mil dol)	Annual payroll (mil dol)	Number of establish-ments	Number of employees	Receipts (mil dol)	Annual payroll (mil dol)	Number	Receipts (mil dol)	New construc-tion ($1,000)	Number of housing units
	159	160	161	162	163	164	165	166	167	168	169	170

1. Establishments subject to federal tax.

Table C. Metropolitan Areas — **Government Employment and Payroll and Local Government Finances**

Area name	Government employment and payroll, 2012									Local government finances, 2012				
			March payroll (percent of total)							General revenue				
												Taxes		
													Per capita[1] (dollars)	
	Full-time equivalent employees	March Payroll (dollars)	Adminis-tration, judicial, and legal	Police and corrections	Fire protection	Highways and transporta-tion	Health and welfare	Natural resources and utilities	Education and libraries	Total (mil dol)	Inter-govern-mental (mil dol)	Total (mil dol)	Total	Property
	171	172	173	174	175	176	177	178	179	180	181	182	183	184

1. Based on the resident population estimated as of July 1 of the year shown.

Table C. Metropolitan Areas — **Local Government Finances, Government Employment, and Voting**

Area name	Local government finances, 2012 (cont.)									Government employment, 2013			Presidential election,[2] 2012		
	Direct general expenditure							Debt outstanding					Percent of vote cast:		
			Percent of total for:												
	Total (mil dol)	Per capita[1] (dollars)	Educa-tion	Health and hospitals	Police protec-tion	Public welfare	High-ways	Total (mil dol)	Per capita[1] (dollars)	Federal civilian	Federal military	State and local	Demo-cratic	Republi-can	All other
	185	186	187	188	189	190	191	192	193	194	195	196	197	198	199

1. Based on the resident population estimated as of July 1 of the year shown. 2.

CBSA/ DIV code[1]	Area name	Land area,[2] 2010 (sq km)	Population 2014			Population characteristics, 2013										
						Race alone or in combination, not Hispanic or Latino (percent)					Age (percent)					
			Total persons	Rank	Per square kilometer	White	Black	American Indian, Alaska Native	Asian and Pacific Islander	Percent Hispanic or Latino[3]	Under 5 years	5 to 17 years	18 to 24 years	25 to 34 years	35 to 44 years	45 to 54 years
		1	2	3	4	5	6	7	8	9	10	11	12	13	14	15
10180	Abilene, TX	7 105	168 592	244	23.7	68.5	7.9	0.9	2.1	22.4	6.9	16.6	13.9	14.1	11.0	12.1
10420	Akron, OH	2 331	703 825	78	301.9	83.4	13.4	0.7	2.9	1.8	5.4	15.9	11.1	12.1	11.8	14.4
10500	Albany, GA	5 005	154 925	261	31.0	43.6	53.1	0.6	1.5	2.5	7.1	18.0	11.0	13.0	12.1	13.0
10540	Albany, OR	5 931	119 356	323	20.1	88.9	0.9	2.6	2.1	8.2	6.3	17.2	8.3	12.6	11.9	13.0
10580	Albany-Schenectady-Troy, NY	7 283	880 167	61	120.9	83.6	8.7	0.6	4.5	4.7	5.2	15.2	11.3	12.6	12.1	14.8
10740	Albuquerque, NM	24 042	904 587	59	37.6	42.6	2.9	5.8	2.9	47.7	6.3	17.4	9.5	14.2	12.4	13.4
10780	Alexandria, LA	5 079	154 872	262	30.5	65.3	30.2	1.5	1.6	3.0	6.7	18.2	9.0	13.6	12.1	13.6
10900	Allentown-Bethlehem-Easton, PA-NJ	3 763	829 835	69	220.5	77.8	5.5	0.4	3.3	14.5	5.4	16.4	9.2	11.7	12.3	15.1
11020	Altoona, PA	1 362	125 955	313	92.5	96.3	2.5	0.4	0.9	1.1	5.5	15.1	9.2	11.2	11.8	13.8
11100	Amarillo, TX	13 338	259 885	182	19.5	63.7	6.6	1.0	3.2	26.8	7.4	18.6	9.9	14.8	12.4	12.6
11180	Ames, IA	1 484	94 073	364	63.4	87.5	3.1	0.5	7.1	3.2	5.0	12.5	30.3	13.3	9.2	9.4
11260	Anchorage, AK	68 149	398 892	134	5.9	71.3	6.3	11.1	11.1	7.6	7.4	18.3	11.3	16.1	12.7	13.5
11460	Ann Arbor, MI	1 828	356 874	147	195.2	74.2	14.1	1.0	9.6	4.4	5.3	14.7	18.1	13.9	11.9	12.8
11500	Anniston-Oxford-Jacksonville, AL	1 569	115 916	330	73.9	74.5	21.4	1.0	1.3	3.5	5.8	16.4	10.4	12.6	12.1	13.6
11540	Appleton, WI	2 475	231 497	193	93.5	90.7	1.5	1.8	3.5	3.9	6.4	18.2	8.5	12.9	13.0	15.7
11700	Asheville, NC	5 265	442 316	117	84.0	87.2	5.4	1.0	1.4	6.7	5.1	14.5	7.9	12.0	12.6	13.6
12020	Athens-Clarke County, GA	2 654	199 016	219	75.0	68.2	20.5	0.5	4.1	8.2	5.7	14.5	20.8	14.3	11.7	11.2
12060	Atlanta-Sandy Springs-Roswell, GA	22 498	5 614 323	9	249.5	51.1	33.6	0.7	6.0	10.5	6.8	18.9	9.4	14.0	14.9	14.6
12100	Atlantic City-Hammonton, NJ	1 439	275 209	170	191.3	58.6	15.7	0.6	8.8	18.1	6.1	16.3	9.6	11.8	12.1	15.2
12220	Auburn-Opelika, AL	1 574	154 255	264	98.0	69.5	23.8	0.7	3.6	3.8	5.7	16.1	19.8	14.6	12.2	11.7
12260	Augusta-Richmond County, GA-SC	9 015	583 632	92	64.7	57.5	36.2	0.9	2.7	4.9	6.5	17.4	10.0	13.7	12.1	13.7
12420	Austin-Round Rock, TX	10 929	1 943 299	35	177.8	55.4	7.7	0.8	6.0	31.9	6.9	17.7	10.4	17.2	15.4	12.9
12540	Bakersfield, CA	21 062	874 589	62	41.5	38.6	5.9	1.3	5.3	50.8	8.4	21.2	11.2	14.9	12.5	12.2
12580	Baltimore-Columbia-Towson, MD	6 738	2 785 874	20	413.5	60.6	29.8	0.8	6.0	5.1	6.1	16.2	9.6	14.2	12.6	14.9
12620	Bangor, ME	8 799	153 414	266	17.4	95.8	1.2	2.0	1.4	1.2	4.8	14.0	11.8	12.6	11.5	14.9
12700	Barnstable Town, MA	1 020	214 914	203	210.7	93.1	3.0	1.1	1.9	2.6	4.0	12.2	7.1	8.6	9.3	14.7
12940	Baton Rouge, LA	10 429	825 478	70	79.2	58.3	36.2	0.6	2.4	3.7	6.6	17.4	12.0	14.6	12.5	13.1
12980	Battle Creek, MI	1 829	134 878	298	73.7	82.0	12.6	1.4	2.4	4.7	6.0	17.3	9.5	11.8	11.8	14.0
13020	Bay City, MI	1 146	106 179	343	92.7	92.4	2.5	1.1	0.9	4.9	5.3	16.0	8.4	11.7	11.6	14.5
13140	Beaumont-Port Arthur, TX	7 859	405 427	130	51.6	59.0	24.7	0.8	3.0	13.7	6.6	17.4	9.8	13.7	12.3	13.7
13220	Beckley, WV	3 281	123 373	317	37.6	91.0	7.6	0.8	0.9	1.3	6.1	14.9	7.8	12.0	13.1	13.1
13380	Bellingham, WA	5 457	208 351	210	38.2	83.3	1.8	3.8	6.0	8.6	5.6	14.7	15.0	12.7	11.6	12.4
13460	Bend-Redmond, OR	7 817	170 388	239	21.8	90.0	0.8	1.7	2.0	7.7	5.4	16.4	7.1	12.3	13.1	13.4
13740	Billings, MT	15 170	166 885	246	11.0	90.1	1.3	4.9	1.2	5.0	6.3	16.9	8.5	13.4	12.0	13.5
13780	Binghamton, NY	3 171	247 219	188	78.0	89.1	5.1	0.6	3.9	3.3	5.1	15.1	12.6	11.2	10.5	14.4
13820	Birmingham-Hoover, AL	13 673	1 143 772	49	83.7	65.3	29.1	0.7	1.7	4.4	6.4	17.0	8.9	13.6	13.2	13.7
13900	Bismarck, ND	13 923	126 597	312	9.1	90.1	1.3	7.4	0.9	1.9	6.8	16.5	9.8	14.6	11.9	13.3
13980	Blacksburg-Christiansburg-Radford, VA	3 762	181 605	228	48.3	89.5	5.0	0.6	4.2	2.4	4.6	12.4	22.7	12.3	11.1	11.6
14010	Bloomington, IL	4 095	190 345	225	46.5	83.6	8.0	0.5	5.4	4.5	6.0	16.2	17.2	13.1	12.2	12.7
14020	Bloomington, IN	2 020	164 308	251	81.3	88.5	3.8	0.7	6.2	2.9	4.6	12.3	25.5	14.0	10.2	10.9
14100	Bloomsburg-Berwick, PA	1 588	85 763	368	54.0	94.3	2.1	0.4	1.6	2.4	4.9	13.8	14.5	10.8	10.9	13.7
14260	Boise City, ID	30 473	664 422	81	21.8	83.3	1.4	1.3	3.2	13.0	6.9	20.0	8.9	13.9	13.5	12.9
14460	Boston-Cambridge-Newton, MA-NH	9 033	4 732 161	10	523.9	75.2	8.0	0.5	8.0	9.9	5.5	15.3	10.2	14.5	12.9	14.9
14460	Boston, MA Div 14454	2 884	1 966 530	X	681.9	69.4	13.3	0.6	7.9	10.5	5.5	14.8	11.0	15.7	12.8	14.3
14460	Cambridge-Newton-Framingham, MA Div 15764	3 394	2 339 406	X	689.3	76.6	4.8	0.4	9.0	10.8	5.7	15.6	9.5	14.0	13.1	15.1
14460	Rockingham County-Strafford County, NH 40484	2 755	426 225	X	154.7	94.4	1.3	0.6	2.8	2.4	4.8	15.9	10.2	11.1	12.4	16.9
14500	Boulder, CO	1 881	313 333	160	166.6	80.6	1.4	0.9	5.6	13.7	5.1	15.4	15.3	13.0	13.2	13.7
14540	Bowling Green, KY	4 183	165 732	248	39.6	86.4	7.8	0.7	2.7	4.2	6.1	16.4	14.3	13.0	12.2	12.9
14740	Bremerton-Silverdale, WA	1 023	254 183	185	248.5	82.5	4.0	2.9	9.1	7.0	5.7	15.5	10.6	13.3	11.3	13.9
14860	Bridgeport-Stamford-Norwalk, CT	1 618	945 438	57	584.3	65.7	11.2	0.4	5.9	18.2	5.8	18.1	8.6	11.7	13.2	15.9
15180	Brownsville-Harlingen, TX	2 307	420 392	125	182.2	10.3	0.4	0.2	0.8	88.3	8.8	23.3	10.7	12.2	12.7	11.0
15260	Brunswick, GA	3 332	114 806	333	34.5	69.8	24.3	0.8	1.6	5.2	6.2	16.9	8.4	11.7	12.0	14.1
15380	Buffalo-Cheektowaga-Niagara Falls, NY	4 054	1 136 360	50	280.3	80.2	12.9	1.0	3.1	4.5	5.3	15.4	10.1	12.8	11.3	14.6
15500	Burlington, NC	1 098	155 792	259	141.9	67.5	19.7	0.8	1.8	11.8	5.8	17.1	10.3	11.6	12.9	14.3
15540	Burlington-South Burlington, VT	3 243	216 167	202	66.7	93.4	2.4	1.2	3.2	1.9	5.1	14.8	13.8	13.1	12.2	14.6
15680	California-Lexington Park, MD	925	110 382	339	119.3	78.2	15.6	0.9	3.8	4.5	6.7	18.4	9.8	13.7	12.7	15.7
15940	Canton-Massillon, OH	2 512	403 923	133	160.8	90.0	8.6	0.8	1.1	1.8	5.5	16.6	8.9	11.3	11.7	14.2
15980	Cape Coral-Fort Myers, FL	2 032	679 513	80	334.4	70.9	8.7	0.5	2.0	19.1	4.9	14.0	7.4	10.6	10.8	12.6
16020	Cape Girardeau, MO-IL	3 708	97 929	357	26.4	87.7	9.7	0.8	1.4	2.0	6.0	15.9	13.2	12.1	11.2	13.1
16060	Carbondale-Marion, IL	2 601	126 685	311	48.7	85.2	10.0	0.8	2.8	3.2	5.4	14.6	15.8	13.6	11.3	12.2
16180	Carson City, NV	375	54 522	381	145.4	70.9	2.4	2.8	3.2	22.7	5.3	15.5	8.5	12.0	11.6	14.3
16220	Casper, WY	13 831	81 624	376	5.9	88.4	2.4	1.6	1.4	8.0	6.6	17.1	9.8	15.2	12.2	13.2

1. CBSA = Core Based Statistical Area. DIV = Metropolitan Division. See Appendix A for explanation. See Appendix B for list of metropolitan areas identified by type. 2. Dry land or land partially or temporarily covered by water. 3. May be of any race.

Area name	Population, 2013 (cont.): Age (percent) (cont.): 55 to 64 years	65 to 74 years	75 years and over	Percent female	Population change and components of change, 2000–2014: Total persons: 2000	2010	Percent change: 2000–2010	2010–2014	Components of change, 2010–2014: Births	Deaths	Net migration	Households, 2013: Number	Persons per household	Percent: Family households	Female family householder[1]	One person
	16	17	18	19	20	21	22	23	24	25	26	27	28	29	30	31
Abilene, TX	11.1	7.6	6.7	49.5	160 245	165 252	3.1	2.0	9 934	6 774	132	60 588	2.56	65.2	10.6	29.0
Akron, OH	13.9	8.4	7.0	51.5	694 960	703 200	1.2	0.1	32 228	29 040	-1 891	281 324	2.45	62.1	12.2	31.5
Albany, GA	12.7	7.7	5.5	52.6	157 833	157 308	-0.3	-1.6	9 314	5 948	-5 996	56 505	2.65	66.1	22.1	29.7
Albany, OR	13.9	9.7	7.1	50.5	103 069	116 672	13.2	2.3	6 101	4 819	1 351	43 911	2.68	67.4	13.8	25.8
Albany-Schenectady-Troy, NY	13.6	8.4	6.8	51.1	825 875	870 716	5.4	1.1	38 851	32 357	3 497	347 942	2.43	60.5	10.2	31.5
Albuquerque, NM	12.8	8.1	5.7	50.8	729 649	887 077	21.6	2.0	46 560	29 043	-49	336 614	2.64	64.1	14.2	29.3
Alexandria, LA	12.3	8.2	6.2	50.6	145 035	153 922	6.1	0.6	8 610	6 646	-882	55 320	2.66	63.1	15.1	32.8
Allentown-Bethlehem-Easton, PA-NJ	13.5	8.7	7.7	51.1	740 395	821 173	10.9	1.0	36 523	32 800	4 981	313 226	2.57	67.9	12.3	26.1
Altoona, PA	14.6	9.8	9.1	51.3	129 144	127 089	-1.6	-0.9	5 714	6 751	-197	51 284	2.40	64.8	10.8	30.3
Amarillo, TX	11.7	7.0	5.5	49.8	228 707	251 933	10.2	3.2	16 101	9 416	1 225	96 382	2.59	67.1	13.3	25.5
Ames, IA	9.7	5.6	5.0	48.2	79 981	89 542	12.0	5.1	4 018	1 960	2 552	36 340	2.31	50.7	5.8	28.5
Anchorage, AK	12.0	5.7	2.9	48.5	319 605	380 821	19.2	4.7	25 538	8 887	1 392	133 717	2.89	69.5	9.9	22.8
Ann Arbor, MI	11.8	6.8	4.7	50.7	322 895	344 791	6.8	3.4	15 903	8 870	4 926	137 728	2.44	56.9	10.0	31.7
Anniston-Oxford-Jacksonville, AL	13.5	8.9	6.6	51.7	112 249	118 572	5.6	-2.3	5 682	5 818	-2 391	43 851	2.60	65.2	19.3	30.8
Appleton, WI	12.5	7.1	5.7	50.1	201 602	225 666	11.9	2.6	12 026	6 531	356	89 376	2.53	67.6	9.0	25.9
Asheville, NC	14.3	11.2	8.8	51.8	369 171	424 858	15.1	4.1	18 743	19 517	17 510	182 426	2.34	62.0	10.4	31.6
Athens-Clarke County, GA	10.4	6.7	4.6	51.7	166 079	192 541	15.9	3.4	9 527	5 485	2 246	71 847	2.60	56.2	11.6	30.5
Atlanta-Sandy Springs-Roswell, GA	11.1	6.5	3.9	51.4	4 263 438	5 286 728	24.0	6.2	308 508	140 347	155 218	1 954 348	2.78	67.3	14.7	26.9
Atlantic City-Hammonton, NJ	13.5	8.7	6.7	51.4	252 552	274 549	8.7	0.2	14 331	10 755	-2 692	101 721	2.65	68.6	16.4	26.4
Auburn-Opelika, AL	9.9	6.1	3.9	50.5	115 092	140 247	21.9	9.9	7 368	3 969	10 314	56 840	2.55	64.0	15.4	25.1
Augusta-Richmond County, GA-SC	12.9	8.2	5.5	51.2	508 032	564 873	11.2	3.3	31 360	21 462	8 429	204 221	2.77	67.1	17.1	29.2
Austin-Round Rock, TX	10.3	5.6	3.6	49.9	1 249 763	1 716 289	37.3	13.2	107 591	36 873	152 058	688 938	2.68	62.1	11.2	27.1
Bakersfield, CA	9.8	5.7	3.9	48.7	661 645	839 631	26.9	4.2	61 710	23 511	-2 517	257 183	3.24	74.5	16.9	20.0
Baltimore-Columbia-Towson, MD	12.8	7.8	5.9	51.7	2 552 994	2 710 489	6.2	2.8	143 546	99 291	32 315	1 037 921	2.60	64.6	15.2	28.9
Bangor, ME	14.4	8.8	7.2	50.6	144 919	153 923	6.2	-0.3	6 205	6 326	-427	62 039	2.36	62.3	10.2	27.5
Barnstable Town, MA	16.9	14.5	12.6	52.5	222 230	215 888	-2.9	-0.5	6 791	11 891	4 107	94 479	2.25	62.7	9.6	32.4
Baton Rouge, LA	11.9	7.1	4.8	50.9	705 973	802 484	13.7	2.9	46 640	27 191	3 622	301 385	2.65	66.7	17.1	27.2
Battle Creek, MI	13.7	8.6	7.3	51.2	137 985	136 146	-1.3	-0.9	7 045	6 195	-2 118	52 980	2.47	64.6	15.9	29.2
Bay City, MI	14.7	9.8	8.0	50.8	110 157	107 771	-2.2	-1.5	4 625	4 898	-1 262	44 918	2.34	65.5	14.2	28.3
Beaumont-Port Arthur, TX	12.6	7.6	6.2	49.4	400 162	403 190	0.8	0.6	22 793	16 780	-3 564	150 700	2.57	66.1	15.0	30.1
Beckley, WV	15.3	9.9	7.8	49.8	126 799	124 898	-1.5	-1.2	6 460	7 081	-861	47 633	2.49	67.6	15.8	28.7
Bellingham, WA	13.0	8.8	6.1	50.4	166 814	201 140	20.6	3.6	9 620	6 361	3 992	78 330	2.56	61.4	10.0	27.0
Bend-Redmond, OR	14.8	10.8	6.7	50.7	115 367	157 733	36.7	8.0	7 188	5 548	10 860	65 065	2.53	62.9	9.8	28.1
Billings, MT	13.8	8.5	6.9	50.9	139 946	158 934	13.6	5.0	8 878	6 235	5 206	66 597	2.43	62.7	10.1	30.2
Binghamton, NY	13.7	9.0	8.4	50.9	252 320	251 725	-0.2	-1.8	10 882	10 653	-4 503	96 729	2.44	63.4	11.5	29.0
Birmingham-Hoover, AL	13.0	8.1	6.0	51.8	1 052 238	1 128 047	7.2	1.4	62 255	47 802	1 807	431 462	2.59	66.9	15.8	29.1
Bismarck, ND	12.9	7.5	6.6	50.2	100 828	114 778	13.8	10.3	7 315	4 182	8 422	50 980	2.37	62.2	7.8	30.0
Blacksburg-Christiansburg-Radford, VA	11.5	8.1	5.7	49.3	165 146	178 237	7.9	1.9	7 218	6 161	2 434	69 246	2.41	58.8	9.9	27.2
Bloomington, IL	11.2	6.3	5.2	51.1	167 231	186 133	11.3	2.3	9 897	5 506	-151	72 165	2.56	62.2	8.9	29.1
Bloomington, IN	10.7	6.7	5.1	50.2	142 349	159 549	12.1	3.0	6 417	4 596	2 964	61 647	2.41	52.5	10.5	35.1
Bloomsburg-Berwick, PA	13.8	9.3	8.3	51.9	82 387	85 562	3.9	0.2	3 615	3 744	342	33 976	2.38	62.6	9.9	26.8
Boise City, ID	11.5	7.5	5.0	50.2	464 840	616 561	32.6	7.8	36 542	17 400	28 046	233 789	2.73	68.6	9.6	24.6
Boston-Cambridge-Newton, MA-NH	12.7	7.7	6.4	51.5	4 391 344	4 552 402	3.7	3.9	220 495	146 972	110 476	1 763 437	2.56	63.6	12.1	28.1
Boston, MA Div 14454	12.1	7.5	6.2	51.7	1 812 937	1 887 792	4.1	4.2	93 338	61 035	47 952	726 986	2.57	61.1	14.0	29.7
Cambridge-Newton-Framingham, MA Div 15764	12.8	7.7	6.6	51.4	2 188 815	2 246 244	2.6	4.1	110 975	72 923	57 707	871 033	2.57	64.9	11.1	27.5
Rockingham County-Strafford County, NH 40484	14.3	8.3	6.0	50.8	389 592	418 366	7.4	1.9	16 182	13 014	4 817	165 418	2.50	68.2	9.6	24.0
Boulder, CO	12.6	7.0	4.7	49.8	269 814	294 567	NA	6.4	12 720	6 847	12 836	123 498	2.43	57.8	7.3	28.6
Bowling Green, KY	11.8	7.8	5.4	50.8	134 976	158 599	17.5	4.5	8 408	5 726	4 522	62 741	2.49	68.0	11.4	25.0
Bremerton-Silverdale, WA	14.3	9.4	5.9	49.1	231 969	251 133	8.3	1.2	12 439	8 519	-1 158	97 854	2.52	66.9	9.6	26.2
Bridgeport-Stamford-Norwalk, CT	12.5	7.6	6.6	51.3	882 567	916 829	3.9	3.1	43 273	27 599	13 990	328 062	2.81	70.0	12.0	24.1
Brownsville-Harlingen, TX	9.4	6.7	5.0	51.7	335 227	406 220	21.2	3.5	31 690	10 285	-7 350	118 546	3.49	78.5	19.6	19.5
Brunswick, GA	13.9	10.4	6.5	52.2	93 044	112 370	20.8	2.2	5 823	4 579	1 092	42 749	2.02	60.3	15.5	28.2
Buffalo-Cheektowaga-Niagara Falls, NY	13.9	8.6	7.9	51.6	1 170 111	1 135 509	-3.0	0.1	51 216	50 289	1 931	469 897	2.35	60.6	12.6	32.9
Burlington, NC	12.4	8.6	7.1	52.2	130 800	151 131	15.5	3.0	7 452	6 442	3 445	59 200	2.53	68.3	13.3	27.7
Burlington-South Burlington, VT	13.3	7.5	5.5	50.9	198 889	211 261	6.2	2.3	9 369	6 002	1 646	84 400	2.43	62.3	8.9	27.3
California-Lexington Park, MD	11.5	6.9	4.6	50.1	86 211	105 151	22.0	5.0	6 003	3 114	2 195	36 083	2.95	69.8	9.0	25.1
Canton-Massillon, OH	14.4	9.4	8.0	51.4	406 934	404 422	-0.6	-0.1	18 490	18 104	-313	160 166	2.46	65.8	11.5	29.0
Cape Coral-Fort Myers, FL	14.0	14.6	11.1	50.9	440 888	618 754	40.3	9.8	27 063	26 381	57 918	241 238	2.69	66.8	10.2	27.3
Cape Girardeau, MO-IL	12.9	8.4	7.2	51.3	90 312	96 275	6.6	1.7	4 904	3 957	661	36 158	2.52	63.9	10.4	29.9
Carbondale-Marion, IL	12.0	8.5	6.6	50.0	120 908	126 575	4.7	0.1	6 112	5 028	-861	50 870	2.37	59.8	11.9	32.8
Carson City, NV	14.2	10.3	8.2	48.8	52 457	55 274	5.4	-1.4	2 436	2 753	-520	21 076	2.47	57.1	14.2	35.1
Casper, WY	13.3	6.8	5.8	49.5	66 533	75 450	13.4	8.2	4 652	2 908	4 408	32 665	2.43	64.6	9.6	27.3

1. No spouse present.

Table C. Metropolitan Areas — **Population, Vital Statistics, Medicare, and Crime**

Area name	Persons in group quarters, 2014	Daytime population, 2013: Number	Daytime population, 2013: Employment/residence ratio	Births, 2014: Total	Births, 2014: Rate[1]	Deaths, 2014: Number	Deaths, 2014: Rate[1]	Persons under 65 with no health insurance 2013: Number	Persons under 65 with no health insurance 2013: Percent	Medicare, 2014: Eligible for Medicare	Medicare, 2014: Enrolled in Medicare Advantage	Medicare, 2014: Enrolled in a Medicare prescription drug plan	Serious crimes known to police,[2] 2013: Total: Number	Serious crimes known to police,[2] 2013: Total: Rate[3]
	32	33	34	35	36	37	38	39	40	41	42	43	44	45
Abilene, TX	10 483	170 171	1.03	2 351	13.9	1 655	9.8	30 616	22.8	28 437	5 388	15 396	6 082	3 618
Akron, OH	18 211	788 448	1.32	7 604	10.8	6 924	9.8	72 206	12.5	129 377	61 813	56 771	21 042	3 252
Albany, GA	5 688	163 965	1.15	2 093	13.5	1 421	9.2	26 048	19.9	26 798	7 052	11 320	7 843	5 190
Albany, OR	1 196	129 817	1.33	1 412	11.8	1 186	9.9	15 655	15.9	25 010	12 455	7 469	4 116	3 454
Albany-Schenectady-Troy, NY	33 311	923 191	1.11	9 186	10.4	7 735	8.8	61 449	8.6	161 728	65 519	60 456	22 446	2 560
Albuquerque, NM	14 860	911 072	1.02	10 774	11.9	7 214	8.0	151 977	19.9	151 239	73 051	37 706	44 323	4 910
Alexandria, LA	7 452	161 626	1.13	2 014	13.0	1 557	10.1	23 016	18.2	30 108	4 109	15 936	8 235	5 633
Allentown-Bethlehem-Easton, PA-NJ	22 391	874 616	1.16	8 630	10.4	7 679	9.3	82 785	12.3	162 482	41 438	82 452	19 709	2 378
Altoona, PA	3 727	139 344	1.26	1 327	10.5	1 627	12.9	10 999	10.9	29 303	14 496	10 529	2 435	1 916
Amarillo, TX	9 488	263 042	1.03	3 793	14.6	2 212	8.5	48 048	22.1	38 447	7 000	21 559	10 379	3 987
Ames, IA	10 372	104 166	1.29	938	10.0	492	5.2	6 421	8.7	11 515	1 221	7 298	1 968	2 311
Anchorage, AK	11 059	400 080	1.02	6 040	15.1	2 207	5.5	67 175	18.9	42 838	200	17 018	NA	NA
Ann Arbor, MI	17 791	426 514	1.54	3 690	10.3	2 139	6.0	30 716	10.4	50 709	13 584	26 381	8 518	2 412
Anniston-Oxford-Jacksonville, AL	2 809	126 101	1.28	1 292	11.1	1 401	12.1	15 348	16.0	25 849	3 733	12 278	4 987	4 266
Appleton, WI	3 214	260 939	1.38	2 808	12.1	1 551	6.7	18 510	9.4	35 649	20 674	8 665	3 474	1 514
Asheville, NC	11 048	451 540	1.08	4 486	10.1	4 721	10.7	68 017	19.8	103 999	25 890	49 066	12 829	2 965
Athens-Clarke County, GA	10 846	213 519	1.22	2 242	11.3	1 291	6.5	35 992	22.0	28 535	7 180	13 887	6 563	3 343
Atlanta-Sandy Springs-Roswell, GA	86 089	5 624 436	1.04	71 724	12.8	35 043	6.2	1 024 130	21.1	704 269	226 996	276 681	206 329	3 749
Atlantic City-Hammonton, NJ	6 216	306 822	1.31	3 315	12.0	2 637	9.6	40 449	17.6	50 989	4 740	31 488	9 354	3 388
Auburn-Opelika, AL	4 552	162 350	1.25	1 837	11.9	1 006	6.5	21 142	16.1	19 919	2 706	10 190	NA	NA
Augusta-Richmond County, GA-SC	17 654	594 387	1.06	7 390	12.7	5 169	8.9	84 712	17.5	100 266	27 538	39 289	22 452	3 947
Austin-Round Rock, TX	42 280	1 924 147	1.04	25 782	13.3	9 207	4.7	339 704	20.3	210 324	52 079	100 024	64 731	3 451
Bakersfield, CA	31 798	884 481	1.07	14 763	16.9	5 763	6.6	153 624	20.4	103 910	36 598	42 487	38 350	4 448
Baltimore-Columbia-Towson, MD	69 369	2 930 589	1.13	33 812	12.1	24 520	8.8	238 847	10.2	444 950	39 635	238 270	97 081	3 503
Bangor, ME	7 330	163 942	1.17	1 455	9.5	1 497	9.8	17 547	14.3	33 398	6 927	16 913	4 479	2 917
Barnstable Town, MA	3 992	225 564	1.13	1 572	7.3	2 817	13.1	7 313	4.7	68 461	7 160	35 584	6 147	2 848
Baton Rouge, LA	25 617	851 045	1.09	11 012	13.3	6 662	8.1	119 808	17.2	122 816	54 012	39 742	34 813	4 305
Battle Creek, MI	4 015	152 239	1.37	1 683	12.5	1 373	10.2	14 469	13.0	28 814	5 374	16 312	5 019	3 766
Bay City, MI	1 438	116 282	1.34	1 043	9.8	1 140	10.7	10 945	12.5	24 392	6 502	16 271	2 578	2 414
Beaumont-Port Arthur, TX	17 833	418 111	1.09	5 381	13.3	4 067	10.0	72 855	21.9	69 770	22 859	32 420	15 823	3 897
Beckley, WV	5 490	130 529	1.17	1 479	12.0	1 711	13.9	17 173	17.6	29 611	7 031	14 004	3 962	3 301
Bellingham, WA	5 939	211 581	1.06	2 257	10.8	1 518	7.3	31 984	18.7	38 009	13 088	13 352	6 841	3 302
Bend-Redmond, OR	1 214	171 114	1.07	1 707	10.0	1 304	7.7	25 407	18.7	35 503	10 493	15 493	4 678	2 849
Billings, MT	3 836	170 195	1.06	2 130	12.8	1 459	8.7	24 925	18.2	29 637	5 993	14 001	7 119	4 319
Binghamton, NY	11 255	259 273	1.12	2 576	10.4	2 514	10.2	19 176	9.8	53 054	18 532	26 069	7 327	2 956
Birmingham-Hoover, AL	24 534	1 171 704	1.07	14 471	12.7	11 422	10.0	139 330	14.6	211 873	84 731	77 041	44 682	4 014
Bismarck, ND	4 039	127 854	1.05	1 836	14.5	988	7.8	11 326	10.9	20 464	4 271	13 504	2 943	2 369
Blacksburg-Christiansburg-Radford, VA	14 006	191 042	1.16	1 754	9.7	1 435	7.9	22 113	15.5	31 314	6 031	16 827	3 753	2 091
Bloomington, IL	10 937	207 560	1.17	2 356	12.4	1 334	7.0	15 018	9.5	26 320	7 253	12 388	4 492	2 397
Bloomington, IN	15 342	177 519	1.21	1 500	9.1	1 070	6.5	20 861	16.1	23 316	3 956	12 574	4 542	3 194
Bloomsburg-Berwick, PA	5 202	100 427	1.50	858	10.0	894	10.4	7 065	10.7	17 709	7 391	7 941	1 669	1 962
Boise City, ID	13 798	653 346	1.01	8 721	13.1	4 198	6.3	94 950	17.1	100 370	46 617	26 174	12 481	1 928
Boston-Cambridge-Newton, MA-NH	164 880	4 995 383	1.14	52 482	11.1	35 657	7.5	189 046	4.9	782 087	141 805	369 878	103 706	2 244
Boston, MA Div 14454	79 216	NA	NA	22 213	11.3	14 974	7.6	67 519	4.2	315 606	56 339	150 450	49 297	2 598
Cambridge-Newton-Framingham, MA Div 15764	74 518	NA	NA	26 453	11.3	17 570	7.5	81 698	4.2	388 943	80 339	179 826	45 497	1 967
Rockingham County-Strafford County, NH 40484	11 146	NA	NA	3 816	9.0	3 113	7.3	39 829	11.3	77 538	5 127	39 602	8 912	2 176
Boulder, CO	10 468	370 988	1.47	3 028	9.7	1 725	5.5	36 902	13.9	42 139	15 392	15 397	6 763	2 742
Bowling Green, KY	7 066	171 412	1.12	2 004	12.1	1 367	8.2	26 117	19.3	27 878	6 111	16 254	4 057	2 482
Bremerton-Silverdale, WA	8 764	265 461	1.12	2 895	11.4	2 094	8.2	28 297	13.6	46 689	9 216	14 767	8 131	3 165
Bridgeport-Stamford-Norwalk, CT	19 745	1 056 267	1.33	10 087	10.7	6 579	7.0	105 291	13.3	144 985	31 114	72 687	17 212	1 869
Brownsville-Harlingen, TX	3 881	426 016	1.07	7 277	17.3	2 505	6.0	127 645	35.2	55 008	19 740	25 583	15 746	3 750
Brunswick, GA	1 321	118 138	1.14	1 321	11.5	1 102	9.6	20 419	21.8	22 234	5 368	9 683	4 878	4 359
Buffalo-Cheektowaga-Niagara Falls, NY	32 824	1 154 735	1.04	12 215	10.7	11 907	10.5	80 822	8.8	231 757	128 550	58 021	35 858	3 159
Burlington, NC	4 293	170 081	1.33	1 759	11.3	1 524	9.8	24 672	19.5	29 366	14 904	9 620	5 562	3 583
Burlington-South Burlington, VT	10 336	228 070	1.12	2 236	10.3	1 406	6.5	13 858	7.8	35 762	2 852	21 300	5 239	2 441
California-Lexington Park, MD	2 861	119 219	1.23	1 389	12.6	774	7.0	8 163	8.7	14 178	169	5 981	2 731	2 476
Canton-Massillon, OH	9 503	433 001	1.21	4 370	10.8	4 191	10.4	41 808	12.8	84 610	41 214	32 531	11 734	2 936
Cape Coral-Fort Myers, FL	8 482	676 470	1.07	6 516	9.6	6 568	9.7	131 059	27.1	159 250	48 298	70 988	16 584	2 527
Cape Girardeau, MO-IL	4 535	103 461	1.22	1 150	11.7	908	9.3	10 938	13.9	18 722	1 580	11 375	3 459	3 547
Carbondale-Marion, IL	5 964	138 802	1.26	1 432	11.3	1 178	9.3	13 670	13.3	23 023	3 991	12 024	3 412	2 840
Carson City, NV	2 854	82 207	NA	580	10.6	625	11.5	9 145	22.0	12 005	960	6 275	1 057	1 924
Casper, WY	1 781	83 683	1.07	1 183	14.5	713	8.7	10 513	15.1	12 305	488	7 701	2 536	3 170

1. Per 1,000 estimated resident population. 2. Data for serious crimes have not been adjusted for underreporting; this may affect comparability between geographic areas and over time.
3. Per 100,000 population estimated by the FBI.

Area name	Serious crimes known to police, 2013 (cont.)[1] — Rate[2] — Violent	Serious crimes known to police, 2013 (cont.)[1] — Rate[2] — Property	Education — School enrollment and attainment, 2013 — Enrollment[3] — Total	Education — Enrollment[3] — Percent private	Education — Attainment[4] (percent) — High school graduate or less	Education — Attainment[4] (percent) — Bachelor's degree or more	Education — Local government expenditures,[5] 2012–2013 — Total current expenditures (mil dol)	Education — Local government expenditures,[5] 2012–2013 — Current expenditures per student (dollars)	Income and Poverty, 2013 — Per capita income[6] (dollars)	Income and Poverty, 2013 — Mean household income (dollars)	Income and Poverty, 2013 — Median household income	Income and Poverty, 2013 — Percent of households with income of less than $25,000	Income and Poverty, 2013 — Percent of households with income of $200,000 or more	Percent below poverty level — All persons	Percent below poverty level — Children under 18 years	Percent below poverty level — Age 65 years and older
	46	47	48	49	50	51	52	53	54	55	56	57	58	59	60	61
Abilene, TX	333	3 285	45 274	20.7	47.4	22.1	247.0	8 732	21 653	57 937	44 149	28.8	2.7	16.8	23.9	14.2
Akron, OH	311	2 940	186 828	12.3	43.5	29.7	1 111.2	11 692	27 828	67 507	49 984	24.9	3.9	15.4	20.4	7.9
Albany, GA	680	4 510	51 060	9.6	50.4	16.4	246.8	9 020	18 796	49 937	34 756	35.6	1.8	24.9	32.1	15.7
Albany, OR	81	3 373	29 451	7.6	40.8	18.3	197.8	8 945	20 594	53 222	45 130	26.7	0.8	20.5	30.7	5.9
Albany-Schenectady-Troy, NY	266	2 294	222 793	24.3	35.9	34.3	2 025.5	17 228	31 226	76 670	59 626	20.2	4.3	12.5	17.2	7.8
Albuquerque, NM	668	4 243	244 512	14.2	37.5	30.7	1 129.2	8 561	25 407	64 625	48 355	26.9	3.2	19.4	28.7	10.5
Alexandria, LA	813	4 820	39 085	16.0	53.2	17.7	249.2	9 109	21 952	57 562	39 960	30.9	2.8	18.7	27.2	10.3
Allentown-Bethlehem-Easton, PA-NJ	187	2 192	199 183	23.3	46.3	27.6	1 756.2	14 927	29 152	74 355	56 543	20.7	4.5	12.4	19.2	6.2
Altoona, PA	209	1 707	26 603	10.9	58.0	19.7	229.4	13 023	23 872	56 985	42 164	28.0	2.6	16.5	27.0	6.2
Amarillo, TX	530	3 457	71 284	7.6	41.5	23.4	425.9	8 634	26 319	68 852	49 207	24.7	2.3	16.0	23.1	7.0
Ames, IA	156	2 155	41 541	3.1	24.1	48.2	105.8	9 640	25 162	63 311	50 279	27.3	2.1	23.5	9.2	7.4
Anchorage, AK	NA	NA	111 069	13.4	33.9	30.0	1 031.2	15 481	34 511	96 026	76 831	11.4	7.2	7.1	7.6	5.2
Ann Arbor, MI	309	2 102	122 406	9.7	20.8	53.5	462.8	12 094	33 801	83 022	59 660	22.2	7.5	16.7	15.5	6.3
Anniston-Oxford-Jacksonville, AL	531	3 735	29 527	10.1	53.1	15.0	164.3	9 010	19 800	48 969	36 205	33.5	1.4	21.8	28.3	6.8
Appleton, WI	125	1 389	61 047	17.3	40.4	27.6	385.9	10 197	27 709	70 408	58 410	18.0	2.2	8.1	10.0	7.6
Asheville, NC	223	2 742	96 059	14.3	38.2	32.7	467.5	8 686	25 365	58 571	43 916	27.8	2.6	15.9	20.4	9.7
Athens-Clarke County, GA	272	3 071	69 430	8.5	40.7	31.6	278.4	10 555	21 587	56 594	38 227	34.8	2.6	28.6	32.0	10.4
Atlanta-Sandy Springs-Roswell, GA	393	3 356	1 578 138	16.8	36.6	35.2	8 619.3	9 135	28 450	77 327	55 733	21.0	5.4	15.9	22.6	9.0
Atlantic City-Hammonton, NJ	443	2 945	67 261	13.0	49.9	23.5	833.0	18 329	26 567	69 941	52 127	24.4	4.2	18.0	27.4	11.6
Auburn-Opelika, AL	NA	NA	51 908	8.3	33.9	37.9	193.4	8 989	25 024	64 697	46 068	30.6	3.0	20.7	22.1	9.2
Augusta-Richmond County, GA-SC	287	3 660	151 926	12.7	45.2	24.5	842.2	8 905	23 888	62 461	44 187	30.0	2.7	19.8	31.3	10.6
Austin-Round Rock, TX	271	3 179	531 706	12.5	30.7	41.5	2 621.6	8 599	31 791	83 593	61 750	18.1	6.7	14.3	17.8	6.6
Bakersfield, CA	576	3 872	262 141	8.9	53.9	14.4	1 708.5	9 682	19 590	63 385	46 879	26.5	3.2	22.8	30.9	10.9
Baltimore-Columbia-Towson, MD	612	2 891	731 808	20.6	36.6	36.8	5 404.6	13 724	35 174	90 854	68 455	17.7	7.9	11.2	14.9	8.4
Bangor, ME	91	2 826	39 505	13.0	45.9	23.6	262.5	11 775	24 909	59 874	43 598	28.2	2.6	16.1	20.2	8.9
Barnstable Town, MA	437	2 411	40 396	14.9	32.1	37.1	400.2	16 305	36 160	80 103	61 026	20.3	5.0	9.1	14.9	6.2
Baton Rouge, LA	510	3 795	226 234	19.3	45.2	27.3	1 235.7	10 553	27 380	71 432	51 134	25.7	4.0	18.7	24.4	11.6
Battle Creek, MI	554	3 212	34 674	12.0	42.1	20.8	239.7	12 695	23 468	58 496	44 520	26.3	1.6	18.6	29.6	7.7
Bay City, MI	302	2 113	25 125	11.5	46.2	19.2	155.3	11 226	23 157	54 804	41 281	29.2	1.1	17.4	23.4	10.0
Beaumont-Port Arthur, TX	536	3 361	98 854	7.4	50.1	17.4	616.2	8 953	24 626	63 015	45 019	29.2	3.6	18.6	27.0	13.9
Beckley, WV	351	2 950	23 830	8.6	59.7	15.9	215.9	11 104	20 123	49 915	36 781	35.9	1.4	21.8	31.1	11.0
Bellingham, WA	203	3 100	57 548	9.7	31.9	32.2	253.3	9 366	25 624	64 236	50 186	26.0	2.6	17.0	17.4	9.4
Bend-Redmond, OR	222	2 628	41 463	8.8	30.1	33.8	235.4	9 490	27 093	65 182	46 791	28.3	3.6	16.0	19.7	11.7
Billings, MT	311	4 008	37 815	13.0	39.3	26.8	231.7	9 529	29 044	71 220	52 583	24.0	3.9	12.9	15.8	10.4
Binghamton, NY	216	2 740	64 850	7.9	44.9	26.4	600.3	17 025	25 588	63 774	46 836	27.9	3.2	16.4	23.2	7.0
Birmingham-Hoover, AL	507	3 507	284 308	15.5	41.0	28.6	1 634.1	9 209	26 662	67 640	48 328	25.9	3.9	16.9	25.4	8.7
Bismarck, ND	243	2 126	29 116	17.8	30.8	30.5	187.1	11 032	31 678	78 128	64 626	16.0	4.6	8.3	10.7	5.3
Blacksburg-Christiansburg-Radford, VA	174	1 917	59 474	8.9	42.3	29.3	196.6	9 676	23 170	58 595	42 242	30.9	3.6	22.7	19.3	6.9
Bloomington, IL	316	2 081	61 828	11.6	31.5	41.8	305.0	10 901	29 996	77 606	61 401	21.2	4.7	15.0	13.4	6.9
Bloomington, IN	286	2 907	63 603	6.5	33.7	40.6	157.0	9 691	24 688	61 347	42 085	32.4	3.6	22.7	15.9	5.7
Bloomsburg-Berwick, PA	217	1 744	22 842	9.2	54.5	23.0	111.9	12 914	25 533	64 246	48 007	27.6	3.0	16.5	19.9	10.9
Boise City, ID	218	1 710	181 799	11.8	34.5	30.7	708.8	6 488	24 163	65 462	49 583	23.1	3.3	16.9	20.9	10.3
Boston-Cambridge-Newton, MA-NH	355	1 889	1 240 283	30.2	32.8	44.8	9 990.1	15 660	39 061	100 687	72 907	18.0	10.0	10.4	13.3	8.2
Boston, MA Div 14454	506	2 092	523 378	34.9	34.6	43.3	4 123.3	16 112	37 921	97 416	69 535	19.7	9.6	12.2	15.1	9.8
Cambridge-Newton-Framingham, MA Div 15764	265	1 702	608 766	28.1	31.4	47.3	5 033.5	15 764	40 592	105 448	76 746	17.1	11.1	9.6	13.0	7.5
Rockingham County-Strafford County, NH 40484	169	2 007	108 139	19.6	31.8	37.8	833.2	13 285	35 931	89 988	70 107	15.0	6.2	6.3	6.7	5.0
Boulder, CO	219	2 523	93 735	12.0	19.2	58.5	521.1	8 769	38 538	94 913	71 604	18.1	9.2	13.9	13.6	6.6
Bowling Green, KY	147	2 335	44 945	7.3	49.4	25.3	212.0	8 283	23 274	59 425	46 586	26.8	3.2	19.7	25.3	6.8
Bremerton-Silverdale, WA	271	2 894	59 358	13.6	27.8	30.9	356.6	9 822	31 987	79 656	62 672	17.4	4.2	11.3	15.9	6.1
Bridgeport-Stamford-Norwalk, CT	245	1 623	254 053	24.0	32.8	45.5	2 503.2	17 442	49 129	136 019	82 084	16.6	18.2	9.6	11.9	7.7
Brownsville-Harlingen, TX	239	3 510	132 393	4.6	58.8	17.1	912.1	9 142	15 268	50 443	34 374	38.2	2.0	32.5	45.2	25.8
Brunswick, GA	472	3 887	26 408	4.7	46.7	23.4	164.6	9 150	22 637	56 917	39 967	32.6	3.2	19.8	26.4	12.0
Buffalo-Cheektowaga-Niagara Falls, NY	430	2 729	278 252	17.0	38.8	30.1	2 597.1	17 446	27 715	65 471	50 548	25.4	3.0	14.9	22.8	9.2
Burlington, NC	382	3 201	40 171	22.8	45.9	22.0	181.0	7 914	22 006	55 539	42 512	32.1	1.4	20.7	29.7	12.1
Burlington-South Burlington, VT	125	2 316	56 234	16.9	31.5	43.3	496.0	16 221	33 033	82 011	62 022	21.4	5.4	10.5	11.4	8.8
California-Lexington Park, MD	219	2 257	29 652	11.9	42.4	29.5	217.6	12 469	33 592	91 175	78 233	15.6	7.9	6.4	7.8	6.5
Canton-Massillon, OH	268	2 667	103 986	16.3	49.5	21.4	606.1	10 096	25 187	61 862	45 168	27.8	2.4	15.7	23.9	7.9
Cape Coral-Fort Myers, FL	333	2 194	133 430	10.8	44.9	26.2	756.4	8 819	26 598	66 957	46 383	25.4	4.0	16.5	27.8	6.6
Cape Girardeau, MO-IL	490	3 057	26 801	13.4	47.5	24.9	112.4	8 659	21 883	53 960	41 491	31.0	1.5	18.0	28.2	9.0
Carbondale-Marion, IL	293	2 547	36 858	6.2	36.8	27.5	194.0	10 928	22 713	54 254	38 903	34.7	1.8	22.8	29.1	4.5
Carson City, NV	242	1 682	14 516	5.2	41.5	18.8	82.4	10 502	26 216	63 183	46 616	29.1	2.5	15.1	20.7	9.6
Casper, WY	211	2 959	19 862	9.0	33.9	23.5	180.8	13 823	31 145	74 571	58 635	18.2	6.0	9.4	11.9	8.1

1. Data for serious crimes have not been adjusted for underreporting; this may affect comparability between geographic areas and over time. 2. Per 100,000 population estimated by the FBI. 3. All persons 3 years old and over enrolled in nursery school through college. 4. Persons 25 years old and over. 5. Elementary and secondary education expenditures. 6. Based on resident population estimated in the 2008-2012 American Community Survey.

Area name	Personal income, 2013: Total (mil dol)	Personal income, 2013: Percent change 2012–2013	Per capita[1]: Dollars	Per capita[1]: Rank	Wages and salaries (mil dol)	Supplements to wages and salaries; employer contributions (mil dol): Pension and insurance	Supplements to wages and salaries; employer contributions (mil dol): Government social insurance	Proprietors' income (mil dol)	Dividends, interest, and rent (mil dol)	Personal transfer receipts (mil dol)	Earnings, 2013: Total (mil dol)	Contributions for government social insurance (mil dol): From employee and self-employed	Contributions for government social insurance (mil dol): From employer
	62	63	64	65	66	67	68	69	70	71	72	73	74
Abilene, TX	6 743	3.0	40 259	170	2 831	507	207	831	1 417	1 347	4 375	222	207
Akron, OH	30 154	1.8	42 729	116	14 874	2 801	1 096	2 065	4 599	5 611	20 836	1 158	1 096
Albany, GA	5 318	0.7	34 154	321	2 445	501	175	421	950	1 323	3 543	196	175
Albany, OR	3 739	1.7	31 483	366	1 650	280	156	174	661	1 140	2 261	151	156
Albany-Schenectady-Troy, NY	43 626	2.1	49 693	35	22 213	5 609	1 793	2 888	8 354	7 328	32 503	1 688	1 793
Albuquerque, NM	32 759	-0.1	36 287	273	16 780	2 903	1 346	1 793	6 132	6 522	22 822	1 430	1 346
Alexandria, LA	5 963	1.3	38 530	207	2 539	492	168	533	1 032	1 577	3 731	201	168
Allentown-Bethlehem-Easton, PA-NJ	36 239	1.7	43 817	97	16 299	3 054	1 305	2 255	6 374	6 921	22 913	1 385	1 305
Altoona, PA	4 821	1.3	38 169	214	2 313	515	201	275	861	1 271	3 304	206	201
Amarillo, TX	10 327	2.0	39 998	173	4 949	773	345	1 505	1 758	1 727	7 572	383	345
Ames, IA	3 821	0.5	41 349	149	1 939	448	145	449	793	444	2 981	162	145
Anchorage, AK	20 875	1.5	52 696	20	10 774	2 451	906	2 297	3 652	2 678	16 428	863	906
Ann Arbor, MI	15 561	2.0	43 927	93	9 975	2 066	738	850	3 214	2 110	13 629	771	738
Anniston-Oxford-Jacksonville, AL	3 786	-1.1	32 432	356	1 721	357	134	219	694	1 067	2 431	157	134
Appleton, WI	9 721	2.0	42 273	129	5 166	970	425	719	1 482	1 294	7 281	427	425
Asheville, NC	16 206	1.5	37 029	251	6 877	1 137	544	1 278	3 697	3 908	9 835	648	544
Athens-Clarke County, GA	6 682	2.4	33 762	330	3 373	778	226	431	1 366	1 201	4 809	257	226
Atlanta-Sandy Springs-Roswell, GA	228 135	2.7	41 307	150	133 546	19 416	9 278	20 710	35 861	31 059	182 950	10 407	9 278
Atlantic City-Hammonton, NJ	11 704	0.5	42 425	124	6 026	1 058	507	1 165	2 170	2 508	8 756	519	507
Auburn-Opelika, AL	4 603	2.7	30 499	372	1 927	390	145	347	858	830	2 810	168	145
Augusta-Richmond County, GA-SC	20 672	1.0	35 625	292	10 078	2 034	763	1 138	3 611	4 615	14 014	808	763
Austin-Round Rock, TX	84 286	3.2	44 760	81	47 044	6 304	3 117	9 007	17 509	8 958	65 473	3 276	3 117
Bakersfield, CA	30 976	3.0	35 847	288	14 653	3 218	1 053	4 566	4 424	5 724	23 490	1 204	1 053
Baltimore-Columbia-Towson, MD	150 886	1.2	54 457	17	77 599	12 998	5 893	10 736	27 531	21 800	107 226	6 163	5 893
Bangor, ME	5 630	2.7	36 713	262	2 766	536	208	398	816	1 460	3 908	245	208
Barnstable Town, MA	13 370	1.9	62 187	6	4 106	806	316	1 037	4 208	2 408	6 266	362	316
Baton Rouge, LA	34 263	3.1	41 776	136	18 681	3 162	1 174	2 992	5 374	5 719	26 009	1 341	1 174
Battle Creek, MI	4 924	2.5	36 468	268	2 753	472	215	190	796	1 253	3 630	227	215
Bay City, MI	3 770	0.5	35 293	297	1 513	259	118	184	646	1 059	2 073	140	118
Beaumont-Port Arthur, TX	16 074	-0.1	39 702	177	7 892	1 370	556	1 218	2 911	3 573	11 037	599	556
Beckley, WV	4 463	-0.8	35 867	287	1 848	370	146	388	595	1 347	2 752	181	146
Bellingham, WA	8 476	2.7	41 076	155	3 699	664	345	668	2 062	1 529	5 375	317	345
Bend-Redmond, OR	6 548	4.1	39 456	184	2 595	420	246	723	1 679	1 382	3 984	258	246
Billings, MT	7 014	1.5	42 417	126	3 566	546	328	574	1 521	1 128	5 015	325	328
Binghamton, NY	9 787	0.2	39 498	183	4 221	1 154	348	574	1 932	2 249	6 298	351	348
Birmingham-Hoover, AL	48 542	1.5	42 570	119	24 432	3 636	1 799	5 885	8 176	8 882	35 752	2 198	1 799
Bismarck, ND	5 802	2.4	46 884	53	3 251	453	256	410	1 117	816	4 370	268	256
Blacksburg-Christiansburg-Radford, VA	5 803	1.6	32 174	361	2 807	594	210	258	1 207	1 218	3 868	241	210
Bloomington, IL	8 663	4.3	45 342	72	5 162	916	343	871	1 445	1 023	7 292	367	343
Bloomington, IN	5 372	0.8	32 937	347	2 746	627	204	283	1 040	967	3 859	225	204
Bloomsburg-Berwick, PA	3 149	1.6	36 900	258	2 003	447	146	327	552	716	2 923	170	146
Boise City, ID	23 917	4.7	36 780	261	11 707	1 848	1 046	2 737	4 600	4 043	17 339	1 051	1 046
Boston-Cambridge-Newton, MA-NH	289 276	1.7	61 754	7	171 886	25 169	11 814	27 462	55 807	36 396	236 331	12 682	11 814
Boston, MA Div 14454	120 097	1.7	61 740	NA	80 871	12 050	5 431	14 183	21 949	16 639	112 535	5 892	5 431
Cambridge-Newton-Framingham, MA Div 15764	146 360	1.7	63 213	NA	81 432	11 555	5 690	11 171	29 748	17 007	109 847	5 953	5 690
Rockingham County-Strafford County, NH 40484	22 819	2.0	53 853	NA	9 583	1 565	693	2 108	4 110	2 750	13 948	837	693
Boulder, CO	17 043	2.4	54 968	16	10 261	1 347	707	1 441	4 452	1 517	13 756	743	707
Bowling Green, KY	5 376	2.0	32 874	348	2 583	505	201	486	811	1 217	3 775	226	201
Bremerton-Silverdale, WA	11 564	1.1	45 533	69	4 471	1 066	422	471	3 102	1 914	6 430	359	422
Bridgeport-Stamford-Norwalk, CT	77 080	1.0	82 009	2	36 272	4 499	2 199	10 591	19 037	7 024	53 561	2 902	2 199
Brownsville-Harlingen, TX	10 349	2.1	24 802	380	4 285	880	308	836	1 368	3 271	6 308	339	308
Brunswick, GA	3 955	1.8	34 747	309	1 626	333	117	181	938	892	2 257	136	117
Buffalo-Cheektowaga-Niagara Falls, NY	50 242	1.1	44 301	89	23 653	5 549	1 955	3 292	9 272	10 424	34 449	1 880	1 955
Burlington, NC	5 224	0.8	33 840	328	2 298	350	183	443	896	1 212	3 275	214	183
Burlington-South Burlington, VT	10 332	2.5	48 102	42	5 835	1 022	480	845	1 874	1 597	8 182	502	480
California-Lexington Park, MD	5 227	0.8	47 677	47	2 998	612	237	257	1 038	661	4 104	224	237
Canton-Massillon, OH	15 522	3.0	38 449	210	6 821	1 283	540	1 328	2 414	3 487	9 972	585	540
Cape Coral-Fort Myers, FL	28 292	3.5	42 795	113	9 342	1 530	682	1 747	10 492	5 801	13 301	892	682
Cape Girardeau, MO-IL	3 659	1.9	37 556	234	1 754	336	129	391	686	789	2 610	152	129
Carbondale-Marion, IL	4 677	1.8	36 901	257	2 223	573	152	286	903	993	3 233	163	152
Carson City, NV	2 369	0.4	43 798	98	1 269	360	76	243	609	436	1 948	85	76
Casper, WY	4 776	2.1	58 983	10	2 174	289	212	760	1 228	519	3 435	188	212

1. Based on the resident population estimated as of July 1 of the year shown.

Area name	Earnings, 2013 (cont.) — Percent by selected industries: Farm	Mining	Construction	Manufacturing	Information, professional, scientific, technical services	Retail trade	Finance, insurance, real estate, rental and leasing	Health care and social assistance	Government	Social Security beneficiaries, December 2013: Number	Rate[1]	Supplemental Security Income recipients, December 2013	Housing units, 2014: Total	Percent change, 2000–2014
	75	76	77	78	79	80	81	82	83	84	85	86	87	88
Abilene, TX	0.7	10.3	7.0	3.3	5.7	6.8	6.8	13.1	23.6	30 695	183	4 575	70 704	1.4
Akron, OH	0.1	0.3	4.7	13.7	8.3	6.6	6.2	13.9	15.1	134 565	191	16 685	313 201	0.2
Albany, GA	6.5	D	D	D	D	6.4	D	15.6	25.2	30 200	194	7 195	66 380	0.4
Albany, OR	2.4	D	6.2	23.3	3.2	7.1	2.9	11.0	16.6	27 440	231	3 253	49 300	1.0
Albany-Schenectady-Troy, NY	0.1	0.3	6.1	7.1	12.4	5.8	7.3	11.1	29.4	175 190	199	21 658	397 231	1.0
Albuquerque, NM	0.3	D	6.2	6.1	D	6.8	5.6	D	26.4	161 325	179	23 400	380 816	1.7
Alexandria, LA	1.2	D	9.0	7.7	D	7.8	D	D	24.3	31 955	206	7 873	66 118	2.4
Allentown-Bethlehem-Easton, PA-NJ	0.2	D	D	11.8	8.3	6.4	5.4	16.3	13.1	176 975	214	19 547	344 187	0.6
Altoona, PA	0.7	D	4.9	12.8	6.3	8.4	3.1	19.9	16.7	29 860	236	4 916	56 064	-0.4
Amarillo, TX	2.1	D	6.6	12.1	D	7.5	5.9	12.6	15.7	40 175	155	4 605	107 060	3.6
Ames, IA	2.3	D	5.2	17.5	6.5	4.7	3.0	6.9	39.1	11 925	128	678	38 103	3.6
Anchorage, AK	0.0	4.6	8.4	1.1	12.4	5.7	5.7	12.4	27.2	45 010	113	7 359	155 645	0.8
Ann Arbor, MI	0.2	0.0	2.2	9.1	15.5	4.4	4.7	11.0	36.2	53 530	151	5 392	148 470	0.6
Anniston-Oxford-Jacksonville, AL	0.4	D	2.9	14.4	5.3	8.1	3.2	10.2	32.2	29 475	253	4 731	53 289	0.0
Appleton, WI	1.8	D	8.1	22.0	D	6.4	7.8	D	12.2	40 035	174	2 671	95 125	2.5
Asheville, NC	0.7	0.1	5.4	12.6	D	8.3	8.0	D	16.6	111 585	255	10 193	216 929	1.5
Athens-Clarke County, GA	2.2	0.2	3.7	10.1	D	6.3	6.6	15.4	33.0	31 380	159	4 859	83 147	1.7
Atlanta-Sandy Springs-Roswell, GA	0.1	0.1	5.1	7.0	18.1	5.9	D	9.0	12.0	761 975	138	109 458	2 215 709	2.0
Atlantic City-Hammonton, NJ	1.0	D	6.4	1.7	6.2	7.0	4.0	14.4	23.2	55 330	200	6 818	127 375	0.6
Auburn-Opelika, AL	0.2	0.1	5.6	11.9	5.1	7.3	4.9	6.6	35.8	22 660	149	3 440	65 566	5.1
Augusta-Richmond County, GA-SC	0.7	D	6.4	D	D	6.0	4.4	10.8	28.6	112 440	194	17 073	248 956	3.0
Austin-Round Rock, TX	0.1	1.9	6.6	8.9	18.1	6.1	8.7	8.7	16.9	215 355	114	27 198	764 763	8.2
Bakersfield, CA	10.7	8.8	6.3	4.6	5.4	5.6	3.9	7.6	21.8	113 340	131	34 210	291 454	2.5
Baltimore-Columbia-Towson, MD	0.1	0.1	6.5	5.0	15.6	5.1	8.2	12.3	23.2	458 470	165	67 791	1 150 339	1.6
Bangor, ME	0.1	D	5.3	5.9	5.4	9.9	4.3	22.5	20.4	35 670	232	5 507	74 282	0.6
Barnstable Town, MA	0.1	D	10.0	2.3	9.5	9.5	6.6	17.1	20.1	68 700	320	3 261	161 718	0.9
Baton Rouge, LA	0.6	0.6	D	11.1	9.6	6.0	D	10.2	17.8	132 000	161	26 256	341 949	3.7
Battle Creek, MI	1.3	D	3.4	23.7	D	5.4	1.9	13.0	21.5	32 025	238	4 996	60 677	-0.6
Bay City, MI	2.0	0.1	3.7	12.8	13.8	8.2	4.0	17.8	18.4	28 105	263	3 299	48 016	-0.4
Beaumont-Port Arthur, TX	0.2	1.8	12.6	22.7	D	7.2	D	10.3	13.8	77 810	192	13 647	173 951	2.6
Beckley, WV	-0.1	17.2	4.6	4.2	5.6	8.6	3.0	D	20.2	33 840	272	6 256	57 535	0.0
Bellingham, WA	2.8	0.2	8.5	13.6	9.7	8.4	4.8	11.6	19.3	39 250	190	4 369	92 466	2.0
Bend-Redmond, OR	-0.4	0.1	9.3	6.3	11.7	9.4	7.4	18.2	14.4	37 930	229	2 213	82 414	2.8
Billings, MT	0.2	D	D	D	D	D	D	D	12.8	31 550	191	2 622	74 004	4.4
Binghamton, NY	0.3	0.2	5.7	16.2	D	6.8	4.1	14.8	25.7	58 870	237	8 511	112 011	-0.7
Birmingham-Hoover, AL	0.2	0.9	8.5	7.7	D	6.0	11.3	12.8	14.3	240 000	211	37 736	507 076	1.4
Bismarck, ND	0.9	D	8.6	3.3	8.7	D	D	16.8	20.8	21 565	174	1 427	56 125	12.1
Blacksburg-Christiansburg-Radford, VA	0.0	0.1	4.7	20.5	D	6.3	3.7	8.8	33.1	34 135	189	3 347	79 287	1.2
Bloomington, IL	6.0	D	3.5	4.6	D	4.6	21.2	D	14.4	27 945	146	2 002	78 919	2.3
Bloomington, IN	0.6	0.4	4.6	14.8	D	5.6	3.9	D	31.4	25 205	154	2 233	70 094	1.3
Bloomsburg-Berwick, PA	0.5	D	4.9	11.0	5.1	5.2	2.6	D	14.4	19 555	228	1 952	37 629	0.4
Boise City, ID	2.3	0.4	7.0	12.2	D	8.2	D	D	15.2	109 040	168	11 998	255 749	3.9
Boston-Cambridge-Newton, MA-NH	0.0	D	D	D	20.9	4.3	13.8	12.4	11.3	776 220	165	108 820	1 901 233	1.0
Boston, MA Div 14454	0.0	D	4.3	D	17.7	3.9	21.1	14.9	12.2	311 750	160	55 702	793 690	1.0
Cambridge-Newton-Framingham, MA Div 15764	0.1	0.1	4.9	12.5	25.3	4.1	6.7	10.2	10.2	382 015	165	48 628	926 696	0.9
Rockingham County-Strafford County, NH 40484	0.0	D	D	10.8	12.1	9.1	10.2	10.2	12.7	82 455	195	4 490	180 847	1.4
Boulder, CO	0.0	0.4	3.8	12.3	31.0	4.9	5.4	9.4	14.9	40 405	130	2 526	130 938	3.0
Bowling Green, KY	2.1	D	D	D	D	9.0	D	12.4	17.5	30 910	189	5 455	71 412	3.7
Bremerton-Silverdale, WA	0.0	0.1	4.9	1.9	7.2	6.1	3.1	11.0	52.8	47 255	187	5 227	109 327	1.8
Bridgeport-Stamford-Norwalk, CT	0.0	0.2	4.3	9.4	14.1	5.3	26.3	8.4	7.6	147 460	157	12 134	364 954	1.0
Brownsville-Harlingen, TX	0.9	0.1	4.2	5.2	3.9	9.1	4.4	20.6	28.3	60 040	144	23 153	146 182	3.0
Brunswick, GA	0.3	0.1	6.8	7.0	5.0	7.6	4.3	8.2	32.6	24 335	213	2 904	58 948	1.6
Buffalo-Cheektowaga-Niagara Falls, NY	0.3	D	4.4	11.0	8.7	6.2	7.5	12.7	22.1	254 790	224	36 611	520 302	0.2
Burlington, NC	0.4	0.1	5.6	15.8	4.3	7.6	7.9	20.7	11.1	32 425	210	3 233	68 102	2.2
Burlington-South Burlington, VT	0.8	D	6.5	13.5	D	7.0	6.4	D	19.4	37 895	176	4 392	94 365	2.2
California-Lexington Park, MD	0.2	D	3.9	1.0	25.9	3.8	1.5	6.2	45.4	14 620	134	1 540	43 252	4.8
Canton-Massillon, OH	0.4	2.7	7.0	19.6	D	7.1	6.3	16.2	12.6	90 110	223	9 940	179 147	0.1
Cape Coral-Fort Myers, FL	0.2	0.3	7.7	2.7	10.2	10.0	6.5	12.2	20.3	166 040	251	12 198	375 682	1.2
Cape Girardeau, MO-IL	1.5	0.3	5.8	11.9	D	8.0	4.2	D	15.2	20 735	212	2 563	42 803	0.7
Carbondale-Marion, IL	1.4	3.1	4.8	5.5	4.2	6.8	5.3	16.4	36.5	24 130	190	3 184	59 416	0.8
Carson City, NV	0.0	D	3.2	8.8	5.6	6.6	6.1	13.8	38.8	12 220	226	918	23 464	-0.3
Casper, WY	0.2	20.1	9.9	4.1	5.2	5.9	6.3	12.0	11.8	13 445	166	1 202	35 825	6.0

1. Per 1,000 resident population estimated as of July 1, 2011 of the year shown.

Area name	Housing units, 2013: Occupied units: Owner-occupied: Total	Housing units, 2013: Occupied units: Owner-occupied: Percent	Housing units, 2013: Occupied units: Owner-occupied: Median value[1]	Median owner cost as a percent of income: With a mortgage	Median owner cost as a percent of income: Without a mortgage[2]	Renter-occupied: Median rent[3]	Renter-occupied: Median rent as a percent of income	Sub-standard units[4] (percent)	Civilian labor force, 2014: Total	Civilian labor force, 2014: Percent change, 2013–2014	Unemployment: Total	Unemployment: Rate[5]	Civilian employment[6], 2013: Total employed	Percent: Management, professional, and related occupations	Percent: Construction, production, and related occupations
	89	90	91	92	93	94	95	96	97	98	99	100	101	102	103
Abilene, TX	60 588	64.5	86 800	18.3	12.2	716	27.3	NA	77 016	0.4	3 320	4.3	73 159	28.7	22.0
Akron, OH	281 324	65.9	136 600	21.2	11.7	736	31.4	1.3	359 367	0.0	20 826	5.8	342 020	34.6	21.7
Albany, GA	56 505	54.7	104 300	22.1	12.7	658	32.7	NA	66 572	-2.2	5 625	8.4	58 828	31.3	25.9
Albany, OR	43 911	64.3	173 800	23.9	13.4	821	34.2	NA	54 020	1.0	4 520	8.4	48 787	26.4	28.2
Albany-Schenectady-Troy, NY	347 942	64.7	195 600	21.7	13.2	889	30.0	1.1	445 520	-1.9	22 523	5.1	432 169	41.2	16.4
Albuquerque, NM	336 614	65.8	176 900	23.3	10.0	818	32.5	3.7	412 507	-0.6	26 441	6.4	402 003	38.2	18.6
Alexandria, LA	55 320	65.4	119 500	20.3	10.0	732	31.9	NA	66 998	2.2	4 499	6.7	60 156	31.2	22.3
Allentown-Bethlehem-Easton, PA-NJ	313 226	69.5	197 300	24.0	14.5	918	32.1	2.5	425 576	-0.8	25 838	6.1	390 667	35.0	22.9
Altoona, PA	51 284	71.5	115 200	19.2	11.8	600	29.4	NA	60 764	-1.2	3 420	5.6	58 622	31.5	25.1
Amarillo, TX	96 382	64.0	122 900	20.2	10.0	747	27.9	4.7	131 847	0.1	4 825	3.7	124 882	30.3	23.7
Ames, IA	36 340	51.6	158 100	19.0	10.0	758	32.8	NA	56 826	3.8	1 669	2.9	50 725	44.1	17.3
Anchorage, AK	133 717	63.1	275 100	21.9	10.2	1 150	27.5	5.9	204 138	0.8	11 762	5.8	193 843	37.7	20.0
Ann Arbor, MI	137 728	59.4	207 500	21.2	12.0	930	32.6	NA	186 775	1.1	8 970	4.8	174 723	50.9	14.0
Anniston-Oxford-Jacksonville, AL	43 851	67.1	92 900	21.5	10.5	589	31.6	NA	46 924	-2.6	3 716	7.9	43 982	25.3	29.9
Appleton, WI	89 376	72.6	159 000	21.2	12.5	714	25.0	NA	128 754	0.6	6 098	4.7	122 542	32.6	28.8
Asheville, NC	182 426	66.9	183 100	23.2	11.0	797	29.5	2.8	212 715	-0.4	10 232	4.8	199 053	37.2	20.9
Athens-Clarke County, GA	71 847	51.5	154 500	20.7	11.5	746	35.9	NA	94 409	-0.1	6 119	6.5	88 489	37.9	21.6
Atlanta-Sandy Springs-Roswell, GA	1 954 348	63.3	160 800	21.9	10.0	947	31.0	2.4	2 807 690	0.6	192 045	6.8	2 578 904	39.0	18.9
Atlantic City-Hammonton, NJ	101 721	66.5	218 600	29.4	19.7	1 023	34.7	4.7	133 130	-3.0	13 817	10.4	125 609	28.8	15.8
Auburn-Opelika, AL	56 840	57.8	138 100	19.0	10.0	782	32.9	NA	70 960	0.8	3 969	5.6	69 899	42.3	20.1
Augusta-Richmond County, GA-SC	204 221	67.1	123 100	20.9	10.4	774	32.6	2.0	256 053	-0.4	18 798	7.3	231 774	34.3	23.0
Austin-Round Rock, TX	688 938	58.2	205 000	22.2	11.2	1 000	30.4	4.4	1 050 972	2.7	43 619	4.2	974 838	44.1	15.9
Bakersfield, CA	257 183	53.5	161 000	23.5	10.8	894	33.1	8.3	394 849	0.2	41 204	10.4	323 328	24.8	35.2
Baltimore-Columbia-Towson, MD	1 037 921	65.9	270 000	22.9	11.2	1 132	31.3	1.8	1 455 463	-0.4	89 256	6.1	1 378 453	45.5	14.7
Bangor, ME	62 039	65.4	133 000	21.1	12.5	738	33.0	NA	79 253	-1.4	4 928	6.2	71 564	31.9	20.6
Barnstable Town, MA	94 479	77.6	361 300	26.9	16.6	1 072	32.8	NA	111 763	1.2	7 833	7.0	101 935	34.9	20.0
Baton Rouge, LA	301 385	67.9	158 300	19.1	10.0	777	29.8	2.3	415 388	3.3	24 245	5.8	376 073	35.5	22.0
Battle Creek, MI	52 980	69.0	95 300	20.1	13.1	686	28.2	NA	64 096	1.6	4 013	6.3	59 384	28.0	27.0
Bay City, MI	44 918	76.5	88 400	22.4	12.9	634	33.1	NA	53 296	0.0	3 808	7.1	45 958	30.3	24.5
Beaumont-Port Arthur, TX	150 700	68.2	98 000	19.7	10.0	716	29.1	4.5	180 768	0.1	14 262	7.9	166 187	30.4	28.1
Beckley, WV	47 633	74.5	87 200	19.8	10.0	607	29.6	NA	47 855	-2.0	3 583	7.5	45 289	26.8	24.9
Bellingham, WA	78 330	62.5	278 600	23.2	11.8	894	34.6	NA	101 872	0.1	6 769	6.6	97 288	32.4	22.8
Bend-Redmond, OR	65 065	64.0	240 000	24.4	13.4	900	33.1	NA	80 907	3.5	6 384	7.9	74 338	34.3	17.3
Billings, MT	66 597	66.0	193 200	21.0	10.0	735	30.0	NA	85 887	0.4	3 230	3.8	82 464	32.6	22.5
Binghamton, NY	96 729	69.8	107 600	20.8	12.4	638	33.8	NA	112 353	-3.5	7 292	6.5	110 051	36.0	19.7
Birmingham-Hoover, AL	431 462	68.9	144 100	20.9	10.7	787	30.8	1.3	534 471	-0.9	32 009	6.0	500 280	37.8	20.3
Bismarck, ND	50 980	72.8	191 300	18.9	10.0	715	25.5	NA	66 218	0.9	1 862	2.8	70 183	36.4	24.1
Blacksburg-Christiansburg-Radford, VA	69 246	61.0	151 300	20.8	10.0	782	31.6	NA	92 237	0.6	4 989	5.4	81 089	36.0	21.0
Bloomington, IL	72 165	68.4	154 800	19.1	10.3	741	27.8	NA	98 906	-1.7	5 559	5.6	100 571	42.5	17.0
Bloomington, IN	61 647	55.4	149 600	19.3	10.0	817	36.7	1.7	76 884	0.6	4 683	6.1	80 168	38.5	19.6
Bloomsburg-Berwick, PA	33 976	70.3	139 100	18.9	14.1	740	33.0	NA	43 407	-3.2	2 481	5.7	40 424	32.6	25.9
Boise City, ID	233 789	68.1	162 800	21.8	10.0	799	29.7	2.8	314 429	1.5	14 594	4.6	293 708	37.6	20.0
Boston-Cambridge-Newton, MA-NH	1 763 437	60.7	363 200	23.8	14.6	1 207	29.6	2.2	2 546 640	1.4	131 158	5.2	2 458 317	46.6	14.2
Boston, MA Div 14454	726 986	56.9	366 800	24.2	14.6	1 242	30.2	2.2	1 045 780	1.6	56 496	5.4	1 017 914	45.4	13.3
Cambridge-Newton-Framingham, MA Div 15764	871 033	61.7	383 600	23.3	14.1	1 206	29.1	2.3	1 254 841	1.5	63 657	5.1	1 206 652	48.9	13.9
Rockingham County-Strafford County, NH 40484	165 418	72.2	257 800	24.7	17.3	1 074	29.0	1.6	246 019	0.1	11 005	4.5	233 751	39.9	19.9
Boulder, CO	123 498	63.3	349 100	20.8	10.0	1 168	34.0	2.0	177 744	1.2	7 276	4.1	167 744	52.7	12.2
Bowling Green, KY	62 741	65.5	125 200	19.9	10.0	676	27.5	NA	78 144	-2.3	4 601	5.9	76 370	31.2	24.2
Bremerton-Silverdale, WA	97 854	68.7	255 000	24.9	10.2	1 020	32.8	NA	113 148	-0.1	7 123	6.3	113 865	38.5	20.6
Bridgeport-Stamford-Norwalk, CT	328 062	67.8	420 600	24.8	18.5	1 330	31.5	3.5	475 888	1.1	29 360	6.2	463 442	42.3	15.2
Brownsville-Harlingen, TX	118 546	68.7	82 300	22.5	12.5	612	31.4	13.2	167 645	0.0	13 870	8.3	142 179	31.8	20.5
Brunswick, GA	42 749	64.1	122 800	24.1	10.8	746	29.9	NA	50 195	-1.7	3 950	7.9	45 593	31.1	23.5
Buffalo-Cheektowaga-Niagara Falls, NY	469 897	66.0	123 400	19.8	13.1	718	29.3	1.5	550 311	-2.3	34 374	6.2	537 478	37.0	18.2
Burlington, NC	59 200	65.6	139 800	21.8	12.3	736	28.9	NA	76 272	-1.2	4 273	5.6	69 053	32.6	27.3
Burlington-South Burlington, VT	84 400	67.2	251 800	23.2	14.6	996	33.5	NA	126 235	-0.4	4 283	3.4	117 333	43.6	17.7
California-Lexington Park, MD	36 083	74.5	290 400	22.2	12.1	1 063	28.3	NA	53 908	-0.5	2 913	5.4	52 299	42.9	19.4
Canton-Massillon, OH	160 166	69.7	119 800	19.9	11.3	655	29.0	NA	202 264	-0.5	11 568	5.7	182 465	30.8	26.5
Cape Coral-Fort Myers, FL	241 238	69.3	154 800	24.6	13.5	937	31.8	2.9	311 695	4.0	18 617	6.0	263 579	30.5	18.8
Cape Girardeau, MO-IL	36 158	65.0	124 800	20.8	10.0	642	30.0	NA	49 184	-0.2	2 885	5.9	43 853	28.2	23.6
Carbondale-Marion, IL	50 870	63.9	106 400	18.7	13.3	617	34.8	NA	58 347	-1.2	4 069	7.0	55 674	32.2	20.4
Carson City, NV	21 076	54.7	163 100	25.5	11.6	806	28.3	NA	25 068	-1.5	2 128	8.5	NA	NA	NA
Casper, WY	32 665	67.9	187 800	19.9	10.0	804	24.5	NA	43 305	0.4	1 819	4.2	41 279	33.7	25.7

1. Specified owner-occupied units. 2. A value of 10.0 represents 10 percent or less. 3. Specified renter-occupied units. 4. Overcrowded or lacking complete plumbing facilities. 5. Percent of civilian labor force. 6. Persons 16 years old and over.

Area name	Private nonfarm establishments, employment and payroll, 2013									Agriculture, 2012			
		Employment						Annual payroll		Farms			
											Percent with:		
	Number of establish-ments	Total	Health care and social assistance	Manufac-turing	Retail trade	Finance and insurance	Professional, scientific, and technical services	Total (mil dol)	Average per employee (dollars)	Number	Fewer than 50 acres	500 acres or more	Farm operators whose principal occu-pation is farming (percent)
	104	105	106	107	108	109	110	111	112	113	114	115	116
Abilene, TX	3 865	57 895	12 334	2 664	8 860	2 922	2 027	1 914	33 058	3 155	27.5	20.3	39.8
Akron, OH	16 357	285 016	49 854	38 801	38 144	10 648	16 522	12 100	42 453	1 151	60.7	2.6	42.5
Albany, GA	3 174	46 584	9 308	3 997	7 775	1 520	2 542	1 597	34 289	1 198	26.8	25.6	51.3
Albany, OR	2 437	32 742	4 765	6 643	4 611	886	853	1 217	37 169	2 083	64.8	6.7	48.7
Albany-Schenectady-Troy, NY	21 149	335 490	65 818	21 618	46 643	20 917	26 418	14 528	43 304	2 273	36.8	5.7	55.3
Albuquerque, NM	18 578	286 958	53 539	16 470	39 804	10 896	20 103	11 037	38 462	4 231	70.2	11.9	45.3
Alexandria, LA	3 318	49 569	14 000	3 899	8 130	1 616	2 233	1 736	35 028	1 091	50.4	9.6	45.6
Allentown-Bethlehem-Easton, PA-NJ	18 266	305 723	58 582	32 381	42 719	11 629	11 750	13 460	44 027	1 963	61.2	4.5	50.2
Altoona, PA	3 212	52 021	12 007	6 725	8 913	1 710	1 703	1 812	34 827	525	35.8	5.9	58.5
Amarillo, TX	6 215	94 450	17 076	7 966	14 560	5 501	2 821	3 567	37 766	1 976	22.8	38.7	41.6
Ames, IA	2 006	30 774	5 106	4 967	5 012	733	1 220	1 106	35 952	966	42.8	20.9	49.1
Anchorage, AK	10 679	169 184	28 721	2 043	18 539	5 384	15 263	9 803	57 941	291	56.7	5.8	56.4
Ann Arbor, MI	7 971	143 487	D	14 255	16 639	4 369	13 136	7 175	50 004	1 236	55.3	6.9	48.8
Anniston-Oxford-Jacksonville, AL	2 311	34 871	6 102	5 643	6 032	890	1 024	1 105	31 681	592	45.4	3.5	46.1
Appleton, WI	5 792	108 332	13 029	20 518	14 386	6 153	3 413	4 412	40 724	1 889	38.0	10.1	54.9
Asheville, NC	11 595	148 093	29 835	18 946	25 212	3 881	5 721	5 255	35 487	2 844	60.2	1.6	46.2
Athens-Clarke County, GA	4 435	57 165	11 590	6 196	9 348	1 562	2 621	1 957	34 226	1 616	44.1	3.8	45.4
Atlanta-Sandy Springs-Roswell, GA	131 783	2 119 397	237 948	133 107	251 210	107 971	181 918	107 494	50 719	7 760	52.7	3.4	47.1
Atlantic City-Hammonton, NJ	6 495	114 051	17 643	1 549	17 239	2 922	4 889	4 042	35 436	402	69.4	2.2	61.4
Auburn-Opelika, AL	2 500	38 782	5 625	6 177	6 458	1 021	1 410	1 172	30 226	315	32.7	7.6	37.1
Augusta-Richmond County, GA-SC	10 259	174 922	35 412	20 957	24 916	4 627	9 703	6 962	39 799	2 510	43.7	8.4	37.1
Austin-Round Rock, TX	45 223	714 948	86 380	41 963	94 928	34 019	74 214	36 038	50 407	8 819	46.4	7.9	42.5
Bakersfield, CA	12 344	195 927	29 499	12 864	28 943	6 076	12 859	8 449	43 122	1 938	40.6	26.6	63.2
Baltimore-Columbia-Towson, MD	65 680	1 111 131	196 704	53 748	141 359	52 033	126 938	55 983	50 384	3 518	57.8	6.3	45.2
Bangor, ME	4 104	57 343	13 919	3 472	11 147	2 027	1 805	2 012	35 079	677	36.9	7.7	51.7
Barnstable Town, MA	8 323	71 779	16 710	1 951	13 904	2 202	4 774	3 003	41 843	333	91.9	0.0	58.0
Baton Rouge, LA	17 833	336 853	46 480	23 885	42 658	14 704	21 204	15 412	45 754	2 686	48.6	11.1	41.9
Battle Creek, MI	2 630	50 801	9 284	12 096	6 077	988	2 018	2 257	44 424	1 023	35.1	10.8	45.7
Bay City, MI	2 245	30 719	7 112	3 376	5 442	1 031	1 385	1 148	37 368	766	36.9	14.6	54.4
Beaumont-Port Arthur, TX	7 920	130 426	19 228	20 258	19 565	3 360	5 609	6 019	46 148	2 545	62.5	8.0	39.3
Beckley, WV	2 603	38 644	9 460	1 632	6 889	746	1 044	1 486	38 446	564	42.7	2.0	46.8
Bellingham, WA	6 218	69 793	9 524	9 765	11 343	2 264	3 346	2 803	40 169	1 702	74.7	2.5	45.4
Bend-Redmond, OR	6 078	53 397	9 692	3 949	9 670	1 774	2 651	1 965	36 804	1 283	78.9	3.0	44.0
Billings, MT	5 949	70 949	13 904	3 403	10 772	3 765	3 480	2 790	39 330	2 213	37.5	28.2	51.1
Binghamton, NY	5 120	83 356	16 433	9 238	12 635	2 486	7 082	3 183	38 181	1 099	28.7	5.8	51.4
Birmingham-Hoover, AL	25 231	443 609	69 522	37 742	56 502	33 541	21 546	19 789	44 609	3 790	43.5	4.7	44.9
Bismarck, ND	3 850	57 567	13 258	1 871	8 404	2 546	3 606	2 493	43 305	2 367	19.9	43.7	50.3
Blacksburg-Christiansburg-Radford, VA	3 446	50 281	6 261	12 683	8 168	1 354	2 866	1 776	35 315	2 289	33.6	7.4	43.5
Bloomington, IL	4 127	82 017	9 063	4 486	10 074	22 669	3 038	4 090	49 867	2 000	33.3	27.9	55.6
Bloomington, IN	3 191	52 192	8 966	7 936	7 558	1 404	1 967	1 818	34 825	1 011	43.5	5.5	39.1
Bloomsburg-Berwick, PA	1 831	37 309	11 259	5 694	4 116	D	1 414	1 723	46 178	1 403	39.2	3.6	41.6
Boise City, ID	16 512	224 662	37 629	24 742	29 170	10 331	14 087	8 956	39 866	5 077	68.9	8.0	48.3
Boston-Cambridge-Newton, MA-NH	124 704	2 349 632	421 292	152 822	253 324	176 611	229 197	147 720	62 869	3 363	72.9	1.0	51.7
Boston, MA Div 14454	X	X	X	X	X	X	X	X	X	1 090	75.3	1.7	51.9
Cambridge-Newton-Framingham, MA Div 15764	X	X	X	X	X	X	X	X	X	1 261	76.8	0.5	54.0
Rockingham County-Strafford County, NH 40484	X	X	X	X	X	X	X	X	X	1 012	65.6	0.9	48.7
Boulder, CO	11 696	139 136	19 197	14 133	16 688	3 395	23 750	7 965	57 247	855	72.0	4.3	44.9
Bowling Green, KY	3 456	54 897	8 976	9 054	8 003	1 790	1 980	1 956	35 638	4 063	37.3	5.2	37.4
Bremerton-Silverdale, WA	5 598	55 664	11 749	1 847	10 646	2 003	4 739	2 047	36 769	706	94.9	0.1	44.6
Bridgeport-Stamford-Norwalk, CT	26 972	403 375	64 409	33 541	49 718	38 384	35 648	30 707	76 125	439	82.2	1.6	57.9
Brownsville-Harlingen, TX	6 306	99 190	30 767	4 935	17 561	3 433	2 447	2 570	25 912	1 305	66.3	11.5	45.4
Brunswick, GA	2 798	31 866	5 091	2 434	5 376	828	882	1 032	32 371	324	50.2	0.7	47.8
Buffalo-Cheektowaga-Niagara Falls, NY	26 986	472 334	82 707	52 244	64 946	30 436	30 793	18 902	40 017	1 804	46.1	5.9	55.5
Burlington, NC	3 162	50 672	8 407	8 912	8 797	1 571	1 384	1 732	34 179	732	42.5	4.6	41.7
Burlington-South Burlington, VT	6 723	102 110	18 154	12 100	14 675	3 451	10 793	4 413	43 215	1 444	38.6	8.4	53.3
California-Lexington Park, MD	1 928	28 844	4 078	219	4 595	476	8 541	1 454	50 404	632	48.3	3.3	53.6
Canton-Massillon, OH	8 759	144 618	29 428	26 586	20 973	6 518	4 221	5 041	34 855	1 901	47.2	4.1	44.3
Cape Coral-Fort Myers, FL	16 403	184 629	31 751	4 527	36 112	5 342	9 980	6 545	35 450	844	79.5	4.5	48.1
Cape Girardeau, MO-IL	2 677	42 111	12 008	4 114	6 476	1 050	1 236	1 381	32 806	2 071	24.4	11.8	46.4
Carbondale-Marion, IL	2 905	39 832	9 944	3 089	7 441	2 058	1 312	1 324	33 244	1 485	39.5	8.6	40.9
Carson City, NV	1 935	20 226	3 635	2 901	3 137	953	1 053	845	41 796	21	81.0	4.8	47.6
Casper, WY	2 944	35 672	5 495	2 005	5 001	1 124	1 761	1 727	48 404	397	31.5	33.5	49.4

Area name	Agriculture, 2012 (cont.)															
	Land in farms					Value of land and buildings (dollars)		Value of machinery and equipment, average per farm (dollars)	Value of products sold				Percent of farms with sales of:		Government payments	
	Acreage (1,000)	Percent change, 2007–2012	Acres: Average size of farm	Acres: Total irrigated (1,000)	Acres: Total cropland (1,000)	Average per farm	Average per acre		Total (mil dol)	Average per farm (dollars)	Percent from: Crops	Percent from: Livestock and poultry products	$10,000 or more	$100,000 or more	Total ($1,000)	Percent of farms
	117	118	119	120	121	122	123	124	125	126	127	128	129	130	131	132
Abilene, TX	1 705	1.2	540	5.4	548.0	675 529	1 250	64 184	110.8	35 122	41.5	58.5	27.1	5.7	11 170	39.2
Akron, OH	100	2.0	87	0.6	68.4	497 519	5 734	73 795	55.0	47 754	76.4	23.6	32.8	7.7	730	15.8
Albany, GA	667	-1.6	557	133.4	343.6	1 500 641	2 694	179 389	412.2	344 040	D	D	40.2	26.3	14 085	67.6
Albany, OR	331	-12.0	159	28.7	227.5	769 891	4 840	89 696	241.2	115 812	77.1	22.9	31.3	11.7	882	6.8
Albany-Schenectady-Troy, NY	349	3.8	154	2.1	195.0	515 614	3 356	92 574	222.7	97 955	43.5	56.5	44.1	12.2	2 936	21.7
Albuquerque, NM	3 835	22.5	906	62.8	101.5	520 688	574	45 045	143.0	33 799	34.8	65.2	16.8	3.0	4 887	10.8
Alexandria, LA	259	13.1	237	21.5	149.1	585 570	2 467	92 173	140.1	128 375	87.5	12.5	39.2	14.7	4 367	22.2
Allentown-Bethlehem-Easton, PA-NJ	235	-5.0	120	3.0	178.6	1 046 204	8 721	96 891	234.9	119 650	69.2	30.8	41.4	13.2	2 510	23.3
Altoona, PA	90	3.1	172	0.3	63.3	783 611	4 565	106 916	107.7	205 145	16.2	83.8	54.1	29.0	1 416	32.6
Amarillo, TX	2 889	-6.3	1 462	76.3	812.6	1 152 791	788	110 223	776.4	392 933	10.2	89.8	35.3	15.3	17 080	54.4
Ames, IA	306	-13.1	317	0.4	279.4	2 482 983	7 838	205 934	292.8	303 082	79.6	20.4	60.0	37.3	6 566	73.5
Anchorage, AK	36	-5.2	125	1.3	17.1	879 979	7 039	92 491	30.0	103 158	47.3	52.7	46.0	14.8	354	17.5
Ann Arbor, MI	170	2.0	138	3.6	133.5	701 358	5 095	92 338	87.8	71 004	77.0	23.0	42.5	14.6	3 466	31.7
Anniston-Oxford-Jacksonville, AL	81	6.6	137	0.9	21.4	418 128	3 046	61 630	92.4	156 052	11.8	88.2	30.1	7.3	406	17.4
Appleton, WI	393	-1.5	208	0.5	330.9	1 115 648	5 361	173 377	515.4	272 862	31.0	69.0	61.8	35.6	9 190	64.6
Asheville, NC	212	-8.8	75	4.9	54.9	530 540	7 101	45 581	136.0	47 831	76.2	23.8	23.8	5.0	4 540	21.5
Athens-Clarke County, GA	206	-7.3	128	3.1	51.5	642 869	5 039	60 082	508.8	314 880	D	D	40.8	20.5	1 712	22.3
Atlanta-Sandy Springs-Roswell, GA	856	-11.2	110	D	215.3	543 881	4 933	53 993	D	D	D	89.5	28.3	9.1	4 842	13.1
Atlantic City-Hammonton, NJ	29	-2.9	73	11.3	18.9	903 438	12 320	135 682	125.4	312 040	98.2	1.8	51.7	25.4	247	8.2
Auburn-Opelika, AL	59	-6.6	187	0.9	12.2	707 330	3 775	71 403	D	D	D	D	32.4	4.8	692	19.0
Augusta-Richmond County, GA-SC	486	-7.1	194	35.2	183.2	584 162	3 018	74 457	284.3	113 255	D	D	27.8	8.0	5 008	22.2
Austin-Round Rock, TX	1 754	0.4	199	7.7	419.3	808 944	4 067	50 217	284.5	32 265	49.0	51.0	22.8	4.2	8 012	15.2
Bakersfield, CA	2 330	-1.3	1 202	730.0	899.4	5 332 548	4 435	332 960	3 999.0	2 063 462	80.8	19.2	62.0	43.8	5 306	15.5
Baltimore-Columbia-Towson, MD	491	-2.0	140	18.6	347.9	1 191 135	8 534	104 999	452.4	128 582	71.1	28.9	36.1	15.2	9 885	34.4
Bangor, ME	113	-1.4	167	2.3	35.6	336 186	2 015	63 316	50.2	74 084	32.3	67.7	33.4	9.0	1 044	13.3
Barnstable Town, MA	5	-10.6	14	1.2	1.5	500 691	35 657	50 009	19.1	57 438	50.8	49.2	40.5	11.4	358	7.5
Baton Rouge, LA	778	11.7	290	9.9	343.2	876 897	3 026	117 136	323.6	120 465	81.1	18.9	34.9	8.5	4 656	17.8
Battle Creek, MI	225	-1.4	220	10.7	175.6	807 980	3 676	117 543	133.0	130 044	64.6	35.4	43.4	17.5	3 618	47.7
Bay City, MI	194	4.0	253	6.3	174.5	1 015 918	4 017	198 977	165.3	215 789	95.1	4.9	58.6	31.9	2 628	68.0
Beaumont-Port Arthur, TX	534	-2.4	210	24.5	151.1	428 972	2 044	65 018	D	D	61.3	D	20.2	3.9	D	7.7
Beckley, WV	60	-14.3	106	0.1	14.3	263 496	2 476	45 762	4.7	8 395	30.8	69.2	17.6	0.9	113	6.6
Bellingham, WA	116	12.9	68	35.5	78.7	786 343	11 554	80 437	357.3	209 937	33.5	66.5	31.2	15.5	3 425	17.6
Bend-Redmond, OR	131	1.3	102	34.0	28.9	716 430	7 015	52 158	20.6	16 033	54.1	45.9	22.1	2.4	241	3.4
Billings, MT	3 168	2.8	1 431	153.0	623.2	1 177 360	822	103 667	315.1	142 371	29.9	70.1	43.6	18.2	7 886	34.5
Binghamton, NY	188	-3.0	171	0.8	88.8	383 313	2 246	75 197	67.5	61 384	27.2	72.8	38.1	10.1	1 882	27.6
Birmingham-Hoover, AL	513	-2.6	135	2.7	128.0	458 537	3 386	57 174	D	D	D	85.7	31.0	7.8	2 312	11.9
Bismarck, ND	3 139	-0.4	1 326	D	1 364.8	1 479 235	1 116	191 431	553.1	233 661	65.8	34.2	59.5	31.8	14 391	59.9
Blacksburg-Christiansburg-Radford, VA	414	15.3	181	0.6	112.1	662 932	3 664	64 339	94.6	41 344	26.5	73.5	38.9	5.9	931	8.9
Bloomington, IL	888	1.5	444	1.7	836.5	3 533 991	7 961	280 254	655.9	327 951	88.7	11.3	65.4	44.9	16 405	79.7
Bloomington, IN	148	4.9	147	0.2	90.1	573 007	3 907	66 578	36.5	36 101	77.0	23.0	28.7	6.9	2 291	40.3
Bloomsburg-Berwick, PA	166	-3.8	118	0.8	114.7	580 503	4 899	80 597	121.8	86 797	63.4	36.6	41.8	15.0	2 766	44.8
Boise City, ID	1 376	9.6	271	450.6	446.8	761 085	2 809	98 357	1 071.7	211 086	40.0	60.0	38.2	14.9	5 503	19.9
Boston-Cambridge-Newton, MA-NH	191	4.6	57	D	D	712 383	12 555	55 708	253.6	75 420	84.7	15.3	34.7	10.3	D	8.9
Boston, MA Div 14454	74	19.8	67	D	D	891 116	13 214	60 695	120.7	110 755	90.5	9.5	43.8	17.3	D	10.9
Cambridge-Newton-Framingham, MA Div 15764	51	-18.0	40	2.3	19.9	798 193	19 881	52 883	101.7	80 665	85.3	14.7	33.8	9.3	689	7.1
Rockingham County-Strafford County, NH 40484	67	12.4	66	0.6	16.6	412 952	6 267	53 856	31.2	30 825	59.9	40.1	26.1	4.1	647	8.9
Boulder, CO	133	-3.4	155	30.1	39.2	888 591	5 715	49 384	33.9	39 629	D	D	22.8	5.8	474	12.0
Bowling Green, KY	630	-10.3	155	0.9	296.1	450 659	2 907	60 060	230.6	56 745	43.0	57.0	32.9	7.2	12 288	43.1
Bremerton-Silverdale, WA	10	-34.2	14	0.5	2.5	377 215	26 446	27 010	5.3	7 513	70.0	30.0	14.3	1.4	30	2.5
Bridgeport-Stamford-Norwalk, CT	54	36.4	123	0.3	5.0	1 492 513	12 145	68 132	34.8	79 317	60.1	39.9	35.3	7.5	160	5.5
Brownsville-Harlingen, TX	310	-11.4	237	112.3	209.2	697 056	2 937	84 762	160.4	122 916	91.9	8.1	32.1	13.3	4 851	45.4
Brunswick, GA	44	9.4	136	1.1	8.7	388 679	2 857	67 997	11.6	35 846	55.8	44.2	34.9	5.6	164	18.2
Buffalo-Cheektowaga-Niagara Falls, NY	285	-2.2	158	4.8	212.4	415 481	2 625	122 739	255.8	141 808	53.9	46.1	43.5	15.7	3 547	25.3
Burlington, NC	84	-4.9	114	0.9	31.8	538 171	4 715	60 452	32.9	44 986	46.8	53.2	30.3	9.2	470	17.5
Burlington-South Burlington, VT	279	-0.6	193	1.2	119.8	630 386	3 264	113 641	245.7	170 130	23.2	76.8	49.6	23.2	4 004	28.6
California-Lexington Park, MD	67	-2.3	106	0.7	41.2	700 921	6 603	80 758	21.8	34 494	87.4	12.6	42.6	6.6	783	30.1
Canton-Massillon, OH	242	-5.1	127	0.9	163.8	601 600	4 726	95 972	169.9	89 370	50.8	49.2	43.9	14.1	2 682	27.0
Cape Coral-Fort Myers, FL	87	1.6	103	13.6	22.8	979 161	9 485	53 895	105.9	125 478	95.8	4.2	32.8	7.3	61	1.7
Cape Girardeau, MO-IL	516	-7.6	249	23.3	288.5	677 065	2 720	76 665	135.0	65 193	69.5	30.5	45.0	10.6	5 488	50.7
Carbondale-Marion, IL	318	-0.3	214	1.5	245.1	874 978	4 091	111 110	89.9	60 533	84.5	15.5	29.9	10.2	4 275	53.7
Carson City, NV	D	D	D	D	D	665 048	D	108 429	5.8	275 476	D	D	23.8	19.0	0	0.0
Casper, WY	1 691	-22.5	4 259	28.9	43.3	2 656 418	624	133 912	42.9	108 118	16.5	83.5	49.6	23.7	634	11.3

Area name	Water use, 2010		Wholesale trade,[1] 2007				Retail trade, 2007				Real estate and rental and leasing, 2007			
	Total water withdrawn (mil gal/day)	Gallons withdrawn per person per day	Number of establish-ments	Number of employees	Sales (mil dol)	Annual payroll (mil dol)	Number of establish-ments	Number of employees	Sales (mil dol)	Annual payroll (mil dol)	Number of establish-ments	Number of employees	Receipts (mil dol)	Annual payroll (mil dol)
	133	134	135	136	137	138	139	140	141	142	143	144	145	146
Abilene, TX	21.8	132	170	1 712	1 479.2	63.5	669	9 119	2 345.5	198.2	179	691	138.1	20.3
Akron, OH	74.8	106	1 002	16 992	8 939.0	847.9	2 352	37 531	9 041.6	837.9	631	3 366	550.4	99.0
Albany, GA	207.0	1 316	197	D	D	D	713	8 401	1 873.5	169.0	191	D	D	D
Albany, OR	122.6	1 051	126	1 577	956.9	59.9	355	4 708	1 159.0	108.4	114	470	55.0	9.7
Albany-Schenectady-Troy, NY	321.9	370	823	11 526	7 907.3	571.2	3 171	49 200	13 228.4	1 093.7	837	5 299	996.6	172.8
Albuquerque, NM	433.7	489	906	12 553	6 313.4	520.1	2 639	43 054	11 242.3	1 044.5	1 142	5 807	964.0	165.4
Alexandria, LA	553.2	3 594	146	D	D	D	632	8 233	1 984.9	175.9	142	D	D	D
Allentown-Bethlehem-Easton, PA-NJ	369.3	450	800	D	D	D	2 820	42 384	10 520.7	957.2	609	D	D	D
Altoona, PA	22.8	179	123	2 160	1 511.2	87.6	619	9 366	2 038.7	179.6	82	393	66.7	10.3
Amarillo, TX	123.5	490	262	D	D	D	961	13 937	4 024.4	309.8	D	D	D	D
Ames, IA	12.5	140	80	599	432.0	24.7	320	4 611	968.3	91.7	96	371	38.1	10.1
Anchorage, AK	80.0	210	375	5 866	3 051.0	275.9	1 156	19 042	5 336.6	528.7	450	2 688	490.9	100.8
Ann Arbor, MI	34.8	101	291	3 705	3 631.0	194.4	1 148	16 403	3 681.1	355.3	368	2 595	712.4	98.3
Anniston-Oxford-Jacksonville, AL	29.3	247	104	D	D	D	552	6 854	1 543.0	139.1	93	459	66.3	10.2
Appleton, WI	73.0	324	305	4 868	3 677.1	236.9	910	15 207	3 293.1	308.8	170	882	161.0	25.2
Asheville, NC	424.0	998	428	4 392	2 073.7	170.4	1 972	24 609	5 974.9	545.7	650	2 118	361.0	65.9
Athens-Clarke County, GA	27.9	145	158	2 461	1 921.7	101.2	750	10 066	2 184.3	208.0	299	D	D	D
Atlanta-Sandy Springs-Roswell, GA	727.7	138	7 541	D	D	D	18 065	271 220	69 108.9	6 452.3	8 215	D	D	D
Atlantic City-Hammonton, NJ	60.1	219	196	2 916	1 342.2	127.1	1 291	17 258	4 429.4	428.6	287	1 867	378.7	56.9
Auburn-Opelika, AL	18.2	130	68	D	D	D	472	6 391	1 451.6	125.3	122	636	79.4	15.0
Augusta-Richmond County, GA-SC	436.2	772	390	D	D	D	2 020	25 727	6 199.0	548.8	512	2 521	402.0	64.6
Austin-Round Rock, TX	622.0	362	1 597	23 816	16 174.2	1 564.2	5 347	85 862	26 735.2	2 106.9	2 431	15 328	2 945.7	588.8
Bakersfield, CA	2 159.9	2 572	559	7 850	5 730.5	377.0	1 993	30 123	7 876.0	725.6	627	3 414	565.5	112.8
Baltimore-Columbia-Towson, MD	1 090.7	402	2 761	47 016	27 186.0	2 466.6	9 536	141 052	36 584.1	3 462.3	3 126	D	D	D
Bangor, ME	58.4	379	158	D	D	D	777	10 842	2 983.9	241.6	172	782	124.9	21.8
Barnstable Town, MA	60.8	282	189	D	D	D	1 628	16 213	3 973.2	427.7	385	1 632	270.6	50.3
Baton Rouge, LA	1 239.1	1 544	839	D	D	D	2 955	42 265	10 269.4	925.3	790	D	D	D
Battle Creek, MI	28.1	206	103	D	D	D	531	7 074	1 571.3	136.0	95	475	62.7	11.7
Bay City, MI	608.3	5 644	95	D	D	D	430	5 580	1 301.0	115.5	77	316	39.9	6.0
Beaumont-Port Arthur, TX	666.7	1 654	329	4 543	3 012.8	213.2	1 490	20 315	5 488.4	456.3	375	D	D	D
Beckley, WV	20.1	161	121	D	D	D	541	7 367	1 606.5	148.4	100	386	51.3	9.3
Bellingham, WA	85.5	425	306	3 294	1 373.6	144.5	851	11 100	2 556.0	263.5	352	1 254	240.2	33.3
Bend-Redmond, OR	157.5	998	234	2 089	1 222.6	93.9	867	10 952	2 809.1	271.9	452	1 782	229.7	48.2
Billings, MT	877.3	5 520	310	D	D	D	817	D	D	D	283	938	147.3	27.2
Binghamton, NY	53.6	213	217	D	D	D	904	13 259	2 875.2	264.9	169	1 138	195.2	31.6
Birmingham-Hoover, AL	1 815.0	1 609	1 568	D	D	D	4 676	62 472	15 876.0	1 402.7	1 167	9 929	1 714.4	357.8
Bismarck, ND	501.2	4 367	172	D	D	D	490	7 915	1 766.3	163.4	143	440	67.4	9.9
Blacksburg-Christiansburg-Radford, VA	192.7	1 081	89	627	211.6	23.9	646	8 365	1 774.4	172.9	158	707	110.2	18.3
Bloomington, IL	781.5	4 199	199	2 963	5 558.2	161.5	672	10 400	2 419.6	211.5	162	979	145.6	25.5
Bloomington, IN	20.8	130	94	D	D	D	552	7 906	1 637.1	155.5	198	1 152	146.6	29.7
Bloomsburg-Berwick, PA	29.3	342	53	592	287.2	21.8	343	4 382	983.1	85.6	66	235	35.0	6.2
Boise City, ID	2 865.1	4 647	764	9 402	7 048.0	456.5	2 086	31 707	8 214.6	755.8	1 166	4 330	626.0	134.3
Boston-Cambridge-Newton, MA-NH	2 405.3	528	5 623	97 123	78 042.2	6 461.2	17 098	252 997	62 993.3	6 370.9	5 163	38 734	12 365.6	1 975.4
Boston, MA Div 14454	663.8	352	2 194	37 942	26 567.3	2 330.3	6 996	101 159	25 422.3	2 592.9	2 351	21 098	7 628.9	1 225.5
Cambridge-Newton-Framingham, MA Div 15764	851.4	379	2 828	51 515	45 279.0	3 654.3	7 996	119 287	29 483.2	2 998.6	2 337	15 666	4 386.8	681.1
Rockingham County-Strafford County, NH 40484	890.2	2 128	601	7 666	6 195.9	476.6	2 106	32 551	8 087.8	779.4	475	1 970	349.9	68.8
Boulder, CO	231.6	786	397	5 129	2 782.1	427.1	1 244	17 620	4 039.3	444.5	669	2 365	441.7	83.2
Bowling Green, KY	26.0	164	152	D	D	D	665	8 523	1 893.8	166.6	151	1 223	121.4	30.7
Bremerton-Silverdale, WA	32.1	128	150	1 011	553.1	41.7	840	11 918	2 936.2	301.3	392	1 332	224.2	37.3
Bridgeport-Stamford-Norwalk, CT	494.3	539	1 220	17 035	78 881.6	1 391.9	3 770	53 738	15 702.2	1 648.8	1 174	7 465	2 283.4	450.7
Brownsville-Harlingen, TX	281.5	693	341	3 704	1 516.6	96.3	1 230	17 667	3 911.7	340.0	341	1 593	169.4	30.0
Brunswick, GA	67.9	604	99	D	D	D	613	5 777	1 528.2	131.1	210	746	98.2	20.8
Buffalo-Cheektowaga-Niagara Falls, NY	850.2	749	1 270	22 985	20 475.4	1 069.8	4 106	63 093	13 292.2	1 288.6	962	6 639	1 001.2	187.1
Burlington, NC	23.9	158	153	1 839	655.8	73.3	631	8 251	1 968.8	168.1	135	523	83.0	14.7
Burlington-South Burlington, VT	29.4	139	308	4 494	2 814.9	216.3	1 161	14 844	3 325.7	338.5	280	1 674	268.5	48.8
California-Lexington Park, MD	7.9	75	30	D	D	D	314	4 531	1 193.0	97.9	92	466	66.1	15.0
Canton-Massillon, OH	48.2	119	391	5 697	2 734.8	239.1	1 463	22 719	5 127.3	489.6	336	1 611	212.8	37.4
Cape Coral-Fort Myers, FL	746.6	1 207	589	5 590	2 271.6	225.7	2 624	38 417	9 193.1	923.2	1 307	5 643	1 000.1	171.3
Cape Girardeau, MO-IL	52.7	548	145	D	D	D	502	6 629	1 435.5	130.8	123	D	D	D
Carbondale-Marion, IL	287.2	2 269	84	D	D	D	552	7 659	1 671.6	151.6	137	623	82.3	16.1
Carson City, NV	17.0	307	92	D	D	D	262	3 698	991.5	99.5	147	569	73.4	16.0
Casper, WY	172.3	2 283	158	1 765	2 889.4	90.0	406	5 138	1 377.0	130.4	164	1 076	263.3	45.7

1. Merchant wholesalers, except manufacturers' sales branches and offices.

Table C. Metropolitan Areas — **Professional Services, Manufacturing, and Accommodation and Food Services**

Area name	Professional, scientific, and technical services,[1] 2007				Manufacturing, 2007				Accommodation and food services, 2007			
	Number of establish-ments	Number of employees	Sales (mil dol)	Annual payroll (mil dol)	Number of establish-ments	Number of employees	Sales (mil dol)	Annual payroll (mil dol)	Number of establish-ments	Number of employees	Sales (mil dol)	Annual payroll (mil dol)
	147	148	149	150	151	152	153	154	155	156	157	158
Abilene, TX	299	D	D	D	D	D	D	D	317	6 881	258.4	72.4
Akron, OH	1 871	D	D	D	1 188	43 853	12 245.1	1 954.4	1 528	27 058	1 072.7	304.9
Albany, GA	257	D	D	D	D	D	D	D	261	D	D	D
Albany, OR	170	D	D	D	198	7 814	2 737.6	393.7	200	2 746	125.4	33.1
Albany-Schenectady-Troy, NY	2 360	D	D	D	D	D	D	D	2 110	29 445	1 417.6	403.9
Albuquerque, NM	2 517	D	D	D	D	D	D	D	1 584	35 110	1 617.4	473.9
Alexandria, LA	289	1 767	208.0	69.4	D	D	D	D	228	D	D	D
Allentown-Bethlehem-Easton, PA-NJ	1 687	D	D	D	951	38 581	13 681.2	1 779.0	1 763	24 480	1 153.8	305.4
Altoona, PA	228	D	D	D	139	7 282	1 931.2	285.6	274	4 841	178.9	52.0
Amarillo, TX	487	D	D	D	D	D	D	D	538	10 391	463.2	122.6
Ames, IA	193	D	D	D	75	4 668	1 970.8	213.4	224	4 388	151.0	43.4
Anchorage, AK	1 224	D	D	D	D	D	D	D	905	15 805	1 047.0	314.1
Ann Arbor, MI	1 215	14 248	1 788.8	1 017.4	324	15 543	5 331.8	881.4	679	13 734	613.5	180.4
Anniston-Oxford-Jacksonville, AL	171	D	D	D	141	6 961	2 680.0	279.3	224	5 129	186.5	51.5
Appleton, WI	412	4 621	494.8	195.4	415	22 900	8 157.8	1 044.2	524	9 585	336.2	93.5
Asheville, NC	1 181	D	D	D	D	D	D	D	1 042	20 002	966.0	282.4
Athens-Clarke County, GA	476	D	D	D	D	D	D	D	421	8 235	341.3	92.1
Atlanta-Sandy Springs-Roswell, GA	20 488	D	D	D	D	D	D	D	10 567	208 370	10 730.1	2 972.4
Atlantic City-Hammonton, NJ	648	D	D	D	140	2 974	D	113.8	862	56 370	6 093.0	1 505.4
Auburn-Opelika, AL	189	D	D	D	123	D	D	D	271	5 515	201.2	55.8
Augusta-Richmond County, GA-SC	948	D	D	D	D	D	D	D	932	18 843	735.2	198.2
Austin-Round Rock, TX	6 052	D	D	D	1 254	47 630	31 352.5	2 345.8	3 350	73 490	3 795.9	1 061.4
Bakersfield, CA	1 123	D	D	D	390	12 789	9 456.2	583.7	1 203	19 344	940.3	252.2
Baltimore-Columbia-Towson, MD	9 266	D	D	D	1 923	70 099	24 306.5	3 737.9	5 326	97 405	5 371.3	1 450.2
Bangor, ME	333	D	D	D	155	4 795	1 088.5	171.9	320	5 179	224.2	68.1
Barnstable Town, MA	753	D	D	D	210	2 461	533.3	110.3	1 100	12 721	891.0	261.6
Baton Rouge, LA	2 098	D	D	D	D	D	D	D	1 330	29 936	1 290.4	354.2
Battle Creek, MI	209	D	D	D	179	11 532	4 954.0	537.5	284	4 558	182.0	54.1
Bay City, MI	174	D	D	D	126	3 532	1 107.2	191.2	238	3 973	134.7	41.3
Beaumont-Port Arthur, TX	673	D	D	D	D	D	D	D	616	12 266	511.9	142.4
Beckley, WV	182	D	D	D	96	1 978	D	79.9	220	4 205	180.0	50.1
Bellingham, WA	670	3 562	419.2	163.4	334	10 165	11 809.7	467.2	505	8 461	407.9	116.2
Bend-Redmond, OR	650	D	D	D	299	5 359	897.4	201.7	504	8 078	416.4	121.1
Billings, MT	598	D	D	D	D	D	D	D	422	8 256	380.6	103.0
Binghamton, NY	386	D	D	D	248	12 807	3 061.2	D	590	8 663	359.1	102.8
Birmingham-Hoover, AL	2 807	D	D	D	D	D	D	D	1 941	37 945	1 780.1	490.7
Bismarck, ND	315	D	D	D	D	D	D	D	231	D	D	D
Blacksburg-Christiansburg-Radford, VA	340	D	D	D	D	D	D	D	343	6 375	244.3	69.3
Bloomington, IL	367	D	D	D	D	D	D	D	413	9 041	350.0	101.5
Bloomington, IN	304	D	D	D	141	8 429	D	D	358	7 587	298.2	82.1
Bloomsburg-Berwick, PA	124	1 287	82.5	53.6	108	7 519	D	301.0	194	2 986	118.1	32.6
Boise City, ID	1 896	D	D	D	D	D	D	D	1 214	22 484	956.0	263.5
Boston-Cambridge-Newton, MA-NH	17 498	D	D	D	5 111	195 861	61 691.3	11 207.1	10 883	185 188	11 243.7	3 263.1
Boston, MA Div 14454	7 059	D	D	D	1 634	52 290	16 621.4	2 675.9	4 715	90 155	5 884.5	1 711.7
Cambridge-Newton-Framingham, MA Div 15764	9 104	D	D	D	2 850	120 751	39 971.3	7 486.6	5 080	78 271	4 551.7	1 310.0
Rockingham County-Strafford County, NH 40484	1 335	D	D	D	627	22 820	5 098.6	1 044.6	1 088	16 762	807.5	241.4
Boulder, CO	2 447	23 459	5 054.5	1 781.8	534	16 791	3 855.9	896.9	815	14 563	668.9	208.4
Bowling Green, KY	231	D	D	D	D	D	D	D	260	5 975	251.1	68.7
Bremerton-Silverdale, WA	716	D	D	D	163	2 154	D	78.3	505	7 483	392.8	117.4
Bridgeport-Stamford-Norwalk, CT	3 778	38 942	7 103.5	3 058.3	1 029	42 123	20 028.4	2 455.4	2 094	27 883	1 861.9	523.1
Brownsville-Harlingen, TX	474	D	D	D	221	D	D	D	643	12 287	503.1	131.4
Brunswick, GA	288	D	D	D	D	D	D	D	301	8 019	422.4	169.0
Buffalo-Cheektowaga-Niagara Falls, NY	2 438	D	D	D	1 381	58 267	19 306.9	2 971.6	2 602	45 852	2 125.2	585.3
Burlington, NC	233	D	D	D	236	11 733	3 163.1	445.0	281	5 080	219.4	62.8
Burlington-South Burlington, VT	796	6 254	963.7	364.3	D	D	D	D	548	8 285	406.9	118.1
California-Lexington Park, MD	274	D	D	D	35	D	D	D	162	3 011	132.3	34.1
Canton-Massillon, OH	766	D	D	D	591	28 877	10 732.0	1 239.0	827	14 271	536.9	159.5
Cape Coral-Fort Myers, FL	1 848	10 115	1 305.2	511.3	403	5 988	1 181.8	222.6	1 095	23 070	1 192.0	344.2
Cape Girardeau, MO-IL	173	D	D	D	D	D	D	D	210	D	D	D
Carbondale-Marion, IL	247	D	D	D	81	2 579	858.8	D	300	5 726	226.9	62.2
Carson City, NV	381	D	D	D	143	3 528	621.6	141.7	167	2 664	127.7	37.8
Casper, WY	271	D	D	D	94	2 525	1 230.6	114.9	185	3 853	168.0	50.0

1. Establishments subject to federal tax.

Area name	Health care and social assistance,[1] 2007				Other services,[1] 2007				Nonemployer business, 2013		Value of residential construction authorized by building permits, 2014	
	Number of establish-ments	Number of employees	Receipts (mil dol)	Annual payroll (mil dol)	Number of establish-ments	Number of employees	Receipts (mil dol)	Annual payroll (mil dol)	Number	Receipts (mil dol)	New construc-tion ($1,000)	Number of housing units
	159	160	161	162	163	164	165	166	167	168	169	170
Abilene, TX	414	12 311	867.5	349.6	282	1 664	155.5	33.1	11 822	556.1	58 424	284
Akron, OH	1 747	45 542	4 061.6	1 663.6	1 385	9 299	848.2	233.6	47 087	1 972.8	181 440	763
Albany, GA	381	D	D	D	261	D	D	D	10 845	331.3	30 971	271
Albany, OR	214	3 654	320.4	126.2	149	1 075	112.6	34.9	5 715	227.9	77 351	393
Albany-Schenectady-Troy, NY	2 387	59 709	5 105.9	2 166.3	1 562	11 148	1 149.0	327.4	51 538	2 285.9	406 696	2 231
Albuquerque, NM	1 980	47 563	4 218.4	1 840.5	1 252	8 778	735.3	228.7	50 356	1 936.5	436 320	2 543
Alexandria, LA	504	D	D	D	234	1 217	103.1	28.2	8 660	378.4	57 600	323
Allentown-Bethlehem-Easton, PA-NJ	2 303	52 271	5 144.5	2 080.4	1 597	9 216	808.4	228.4	48 406	2 190.1	261 907	1 801
Altoona, PA	403	10 162	909.5	373.1	299	1 686	115.7	33.5	6 055	284.4	17 545	100
Amarillo, TX	698	D	D	D	433	D	D	D	18 590	912.4	173 848	918
Ames, IA	172	5 026	415.3	172.4	148	1 096	212.9	28.7	5 377	216.0	88 154	539
Anchorage, AK	1 265	23 414	2 932.2	1 066.8	693	4 558	498.1	139.1	25 603	1 293.1	229 454	887
Ann Arbor, MI	958	34 745	3 715.8	1 627.0	557	3 917	443.2	122.6	27 876	1 190.6	117 826	570
Anniston-Oxford-Jacksonville, AL	283	6 307	545.7	206.7	186	944	81.3	22.1	6 352	223.1	14 522	114
Appleton, WI	533	12 694	1 231.7	517.6	428	2 780	233.4	63.7	11 873	557.0	147 412	930
Asheville, NC	1 187	30 282	2 822.7	1 140.4	736	4 230	346.8	97.5	38 760	1 501.4	410 058	1 832
Athens-Clarke County, GA	502	D	D	D	288	D	D	D	14 411	545.6	145 365	930
Atlanta-Sandy Springs-Roswell, GA	11 670	D	D	D	8 742	D	D	D	521 102	20 539.7	4 391 656	26 683
Atlantic City-Hammonton, NJ	821	16 172	1 780.0	702.6	547	3 496	270.1	81.7	15 850	764.3	125 566	722
Auburn-Opelika, AL	221	6 157	469.5	191.8	152	748	49.7	14.2	9 361	387.5	237 588	943
Augusta-Richmond County, GA-SC	1 208	30 382	3 179.0	1 186.9	728	4 383	408.2	98.5	35 732	1 255.8	454 009	2 847
Austin-Round Rock, TX	3 713	65 629	7 015.7	2 738.5	2 745	23 514	2 463.9	746.5	158 665	8 056.1	3 235 961	19 949
Bakersfield, CA	1 456	25 119	2 746.4	1 042.9	857	5 637	569.1	145.0	43 515	2 079.8	409 140	2 297
Baltimore-Columbia-Towson, MD	7 208	173 557	19 053.4	7 171.1	4 997	36 876	4 149.1	1 100.6	199 635	8 616.7	1 173 415	7 100
Bangor, ME	563	14 538	1 318.9	561.5	276	1 350	139.8	33.6	9 215	340.3	34 740	231
Barnstable Town, MA	807	15 247	1 466.2	620.7	601	3 279	334.9	88.2	24 948	1 269.6	185 209	640
Baton Rouge, LA	1 846	D	D	D	1 286	D	D	D	61 017	2 517.9	712 426	3 568
Battle Creek, MI	341	8 967	898.1	372.5	225	1 249	503.8	42.5	6 582	217.9	8 374	56
Bay City, MI	315	5 902	513.3	209.5	196	1 068	75.9	21.8	5 549	199.4	10 990	62
Beaumont-Port Arthur, TX	1 077	21 233	1 838.7	673.0	551	D	D	D	23 797	976.2	183 873	1 606
Beckley, WV	367	7 979	695.9	274.1	197	1 108	105.3	26.6	5 153	183.1	24 087	125
Bellingham, WA	636	9 730	862.9	348.7	390	2 155	207.5	59.0	14 229	670.8	178 949	1 007
Bend-Redmond, OR	543	8 144	974.3	351.5	322	1 761	169.5	46.5	15 397	737.8	325 824	1 330
Billings, MT	532	D	D	D	396	2 015	200.8	49.3	12 265	583.2	132 349	651
Binghamton, NY	509	14 884	1 302.9	525.9	393	2 253	180.7	49.2	12 833	508.7	14 124	85
Birmingham-Hoover, AL	2 532	67 157	7 562.0	2 840.9	1 808	D	D	D	76 710	3 354.5	614 997	3 364
Bismarck, ND	281	D	D	D	312	D	D	D	9 425	485.9	254 334	1 771
Blacksburg-Christiansburg-Radford, VA	370	D	D	D	282	D	D	D	9 021	338.7	71 046	353
Bloomington, IL	359	9 166	905.9	366.8	284	2 490	195.6	61.9	10 187	398.9	48 455	271
Bloomington, IN	327	7 955	709.5	307.0	242	D	D	D	10 175	384.6	83 091	539
Bloomsburg-Berwick, PA	228	D	D	D	148	853	68.5	19.2	4 228	175.5	22 319	113
Boise City, ID	1 697	31 482	2 897.6	1 212.9	1 042	D	D	D	47 240	2 004.3	959 697	5 183
Boston-Cambridge-Newton, MA-NH	12 525	363 736	38 593.3	16 468.7	9 748	68 801	7 926.9	2 151.0	353 419	19 688.6	2 643 771	12 024
Boston, MA Div 14454	4 996	196 332	22 166.2	9 425.4	4 172	31 341	3 772.0	965.7	NA	NA	X	X
Cambridge-Newton-Framingham, MA Div 15764	6 416	146 639	14 464.8	6 235.7	4 672	32 388	3 673.9	1 044.4	NA	NA	X	X
Rockingham County-Strafford County, NH 40484	1 113	20 765	1 962.3	807.6	904	5 072	481.0	140.9	NA	NA	X	X
Boulder, CO	1 158	17 109	1 712.5	716.4	711	4 509	794.5	161.0	35 710	1 846.2	288 246	1 371
Bowling Green, KY	372	D	D	D	197	1 288	91.9	27.0	11 506	577.5	102 506	603
Bremerton-Silverdale, WA	659	12 424	1 169.6	482.9	392	2 004	157.5	48.0	13 526	579.1	138 312	598
Bridgeport-Stamford-Norwalk, CT	2 739	60 497	6 923.5	2 604.2	2 056	13 357	1 722.7	431.1	88 363	6 108.6	614 242	1 889
Brownsville-Harlingen, TX	925	27 384	1 711.7	686.6	424	2 214	140.9	36.3	29 992	1 122.6	138 336	1 417
Brunswick, GA	288	D	D	D	180	984	79.4	22.5	8 075	336.5	119 169	462
Buffalo-Cheektowaga-Niagara Falls, NY	3 234	83 751	7 057.8	2 815.2	2 120	14 710	1 200.4	353.0	55 078	2 388.5	343 116	1 878
Burlington, NC	335	6 483	549.1	227.9	201	1 165	93.5	27.7	9 280	335.1	85 140	606
Burlington-South Burlington, VT	683	15 754	1 488.9	590.1	485	2 339	195.7	60.5	18 050	846.3	122 135	706
California-Lexington Park, MD	159	3 563	311.3	126.3	146	877	83.7	27.4	6 594	239.0	102 481	457
Canton-Massillon, OH	1 035	27 536	2 171.5	939.1	772	5 203	433.9	121.3	25 256	1 018.6	107 354	551
Cape Coral-Fort Myers, FL	1 389	25 867	3 068.2	1 115.8	1 206	6 552	589.9	162.5	57 794	2 755.3	934 206	4 095
Cape Girardeau, MO-IL	307	D	D	D	184	D	D	D	6 341	247.6	33 624	187
Carbondale-Marion, IL	371	9 160	909.4	324.9	198	908	86.7	18.1	7 435	254.3	33 255	245
Carson City, NV	220	3 407	453.3	164.1	149	948	83.3	25.4	4 878	405.4	11 679	35
Casper, WY	283	4 819	482.2	203.0	202	1 200	141.1	34.1	5 545	299.8	72 398	330

1. Establishments subject to federal tax.

Table C. Metropolitan Areas — Government Employment and Payroll and Local Government Finances

Area name	Government employment and payroll, 2012: Full-time equivalent employees	March Payroll (dollars)	March payroll (percent of total): Adminis-tration, judicial, and legal	Police and corrections	Fire protection	Highways and transporta-tion	Health and welfare	Natural resources and utilities	Education and libraries	Local government finances, 2012: General revenue: Total (mil dol)	Inter-govern-mental (mil dol)	Taxes: Total (mil dol)	Per capita[1] (dollars): Total	Property
	171	172	173	174	175	176	177	178	179	180	181	182	183	184
Abilene, TX	6 849	21 021 831	5.9	11.8	4.6	1.9	9.1	4.7	60.5	518.5	218.5	216.8	1 298	958
Akron, OH	26 841	107 374 120	7.1	9.8	5.3	5.1	11.5	6.3	53.1	3 076.7	1 096.1	1 324.2	1 886	1 236
Albany, GA	7 162	21 657 598	7.9	10.7	4.5	3.1	5.4	7.1	58.2	562.0	254.3	209.6	1 331	844
Albany, OR	3 984	16 207 525	6.1	11.2	5.6	4.0	5.1	4.9	61.9	447.9	223.4	146.4	1 237	1 133
Albany-Schenectady-Troy, NY	36 516	166 624 101	5.4	11.1	2.5	4.0	8.5	3.7	63.1	4 760.1	1 679.6	2 291.7	2 620	1 927
Albuquerque, NM	30 074	112 231 236	6.2	14.9	5.8	5.5	4.5	5.9	55.8	3 116.0	1 545.5	1 089.1	1 208	691
Alexandria, LA	6 219	18 920 106	10.2	14.7	7.3	3.5	1.6	5.7	54.5	537.9	262.7	207.5	1 343	529
Allentown-Bethlehem-Easton, PA-NJ	28 544	125 365 734	7.1	11.0	1.6	3.5	8.4	4.3	62.3	3 830.4	1 426.8	1 741.8	2 106	1 770
Altoona, PA	4 030	13 533 958	4.8	8.4	2.3	5.0	8.5	7.0	62.6	402.4	214.5	126.2	993	707
Amarillo, TX	11 385	38 289 774	6.0	11.5	5.0	2.8	5.4	3.4	64.4	911.4	355.4	389.8	1 513	1 141
Ames, IA	2 892	10 932 541	7.4	7.6	2.9	7.7	10.1	9.9	52.8	476.0	102.3	138.3	1 518	1 219
Anchorage, AK	12 850	64 974 760	5.2	7.0	5.6	4.8	2.6	8.4	65.2	1 699.8	812.1	683.6	1 741	1 513
Ann Arbor, MI	9 997	45 620 706	8.5	10.1	3.0	4.2	5.2	5.4	62.0	1 472.6	631.4	577.8	1 646	1 596
Anniston-Oxford-Jacksonville, AL	5 708	17 129 463	3.6	6.8	2.8	2.8	32.2	7.0	43.2	507.7	169.3	112.4	958	366
Appleton, WI	7 780	34 593 416	4.9	7.3	2.2	3.3	7.7	3.3	69.6	894.7	399.3	319.4	1 398	1 365
Asheville, NC	17 505	58 826 655	4.2	7.0	2.1	1.1	24.6	5.0	53.1	1 741.6	575.9	513.1	1 187	868
Athens-Clarke County, GA	7 394	23 449 444	6.9	10.8	3.3	3.2	5.2	6.6	61.6	987.4	199.2	256.9	1 308	933
Atlanta-Sandy Springs-Roswell, GA	203 403	731 570 783	7.2	9.5	4.1	4.5	5.7	5.0	62.5	20 074.6	5 922.8	9 520.7	1 744	1 190
Atlantic City-Hammonton, NJ	14 001	71 971 044	5.3	13.7	4.7	1.7	5.3	3.8	63.4	1 749.6	507.4	1 016.6	3 691	3 639
Auburn-Opelika, AL	6 506	23 295 526	2.9	5.8	2.5	1.6	40.7	4.1	41.4	640.1	158.1	164.2	1 115	594
Augusta-Richmond County, GA-SC	20 099	65 183 308	7.2	9.6	2.7	2.9	4.2	5.7	66.1	1 739.1	746.8	669.1	1 162	761
Austin-Round Rock, TX	73 039	288 365 719	6.7	12.6	4.5	3.0	4.9	13.3	53.3	7 348.5	1 653.0	4 159.1	2 267	1 895
Bakersfield, CA	32 191	158 787 344	5.1	10.1	4.5	2.2	16.0	4.2	56.8	6 098.2	2 797.6	1 169.0	1 365	1 151
Baltimore-Columbia-Towson, MD	99 896	465 911 722	4.8	11.2	4.8	2.5	4.4	5.4	65.0	11 911.4	4 396.6	5 905.6	2 145	1 222
Bangor, ME	5 352	18 128 721	5.6	7.8	5.2	7.6	1.3	6.1	64.9	466.9	185.2	205.7	1 338	1 324
Barnstable Town, MA	7 548	35 968 725	7.2	11.5	10.0	4.2	3.5	6.4	53.6	1 003.5	207.7	645.0	2 994	2 809
Baton Rouge, LA	30 360	102 896 811	8.5	10.0	4.5	3.6	6.5	7.1	57.0	3 050.2	1 092.8	1 434.7	1 760	767
Battle Creek, MI	4 008	16 572 500	10.0	11.0	3.1	3.3	5.9	4.4	61.4	671.0	371.6	175.1	1 296	1 142
Bay City, MI	4 027	15 471 429	6.7	5.7	2.4	4.8	13.5	5.1	61.1	536.8	284.0	123.7	1 157	1 137
Beaumont-Port Arthur, TX	17 005	59 961 656	6.9	13.5	4.6	3.6	4.5	7.9	57.9	1 621.0	485.7	770.1	1 905	1 584
Beckley, WV	3 968	12 471 321	4.9	5.2	1.2	1.5	2.1	5.4	77.4	330.4	170.0	113.2	907	718
Bellingham, WA	5 120	25 193 563	10.0	10.9	7.5	8.7	1.8	7.1	50.4	696.1	261.3	292.4	1 424	871
Bend-Redmond, OR	4 773	21 188 503	8.1	12.1	5.4	2.6	5.0	7.0	55.3	649.0	217.1	283.8	1 749	1 579
Billings, MT	5 275	20 966 552	5.5	8.5	4.5	5.0	8.4	5.9	55.7	507.5	191.1	179.3	1 101	1 025
Binghamton, NY	11 995	45 564 792	4.9	8.0	2.3	4.3	9.9	2.6	66.0	1 446.5	620.9	619.4	2 492	1 689
Birmingham-Hoover, AL	41 677	145 061 797	5.5	12.3	6.2	3.5	6.2	8.1	54.6	3 941.4	1 461.0	1 685.8	1 483	659
Bismarck, ND	3 791	13 709 939	4.6	8.1	3.4	4.7	6.7	8.1	61.8	473.7	232.8	141.1	1 176	966
Blacksburg-Christiansburg-Radford, VA	5 444	17 603 156	8.2	10.4	0.7	3.0	3.2	6.1	64.4	493.5	224.5	187.6	1 048	749
Bloomington, IL	7 152	27 482 356	6.5	10.1	4.3	4.2	7.4	5.2	60.3	732.2	198.8	386.9	2 050	1 720
Bloomington, IN	4 067	13 951 012	10.1	10.5	4.9	5.1	2.9	7.9	58.1	391.1	166.8	163.4	1 006	789
Bloomsburg-Berwick, PA	2 432	8 805 660	6.5	10.1	0.0	3.5	1.8	3.7	73.5	290.1	113.0	109.7	1 287	914
Boise City, ID	19 235	61 842 070	8.7	13.8	5.3	3.5	3.2	5.5	58.0	1 734.2	757.9	596.2	935	874
Boston-Cambridge-Newton, MA-NH	153 708	758 103 739	4.2	10.4	7.6	2.3	4.2	5.6	63.4	20 238.4	6 374.7	10 961.5	2 362	2 272
Boston, MA Div 14454	62 159	318 038 206	3.6	12.1	8.7	2.3	3.8	6.0	61.6	8 478.9	2 834.2	4 659.2	2 419	2 297
Cambridge-Newton-Framingham, MA Div 15764	76 602	380 709 237	4.6	9.0	6.9	2.4	4.4	5.7	64.4	10 119.6	3 073.3	5 273.3	2 300	2 225
Rockingham County-Strafford County, NH 40484	14 947	59 356 296	4.6	10.5	5.5	2.5	4.3	3.2	67.3	1 639.9	467.1	1 028.9	2 439	2 409
Boulder, CO	11 666	48 102 144	8.2	10.8	5.0	2.7	5.3	10.3	53.3	1 374.3	334.5	816.3	2 674	1 840
Bowling Green, KY	5 785	16 747 663	3.0	7.9	3.3	1.9	4.2	9.0	67.7	397.4	175.4	150.8	930	466
Bremerton-Silverdale, WA	6 732	32 797 634	7.2	7.7	9.1	6.6	1.0	9.5	56.8	1 053.2	532.7	344.8	1 352	960
Bridgeport-Stamford-Norwalk, CT	32 029	179 963 079	3.5	9.1	5.1	3.1	3.2	3.7	70.6	4 597.7	963.2	3 193.1	3 419	3 370
Brownsville-Harlingen, TX	21 552	67 816 703	3.9	8.4	2.8	2.4	1.6	5.2	74.0	1 662.8	982.8	420.5	1 012	795
Brunswick, GA	6 136	22 282 830	5.0	6.9	2.5	1.3	40.1	3.5	40.2	600.6	116.0	196.4	1 731	1 127
Buffalo-Cheektowaga-Niagara Falls, NY	44 201	202 514 083	3.8	12.1	3.3	3.0	5.4	4.9	65.5	6 495.4	2 759.6	2 637.8	2 326	1 539
Burlington, NC	1 005 835	17 822 770	4.1	10.8	2.8	1.7	7.8	5.8	64.0	420.3	210.4	147.7	960	694
Burlington-South Burlington, VT	8 073	32 538 734	4.7	5.9	2.3	6.1	0.9	7.3	71.2	830.6	537.1	145.5	681	585
California-Lexington Park, MD	3 187	14 069 480	5.9	10.5	0.0	2.3	1.5	4.3	73.2	356.5	125.4	191.8	1 760	923
Canton-Massillon, OH	12 345	44 734 873	4.8	6.7	4.6	4.4	2.5	5.9	70.3	1 381.0	667.7	493.7	1 224	920
Cape Coral-Fort Myers, FL	29 739	118 190 826	4.0	7.9	5.4	3.4	39.4	4.7	33.6	3 672.5	586.2	1 065.4	1 651	1 448
Cape Girardeau, MO-IL	3 276	8 670 805	6.6	8.7	4.7	6.8	1.2	9.4	60.9	259.7	107.2	113.5	1 169	651
Carbondale-Marion, IL	4 224	14 371 667	6.4	9.2	3.2	3.8	4.1	6.6	65.5	411.6	200.9	146.7	1 158	929
Carson City, NV	1 396	6 652 347	9.5	13.4	7.3	4.2	3.5	6.4	53.3	189.1	96.1	54.9	1 001	717
Casper, WY	3 954	15 321 295	4.4	7.8	3.5	2.3	2.0	5.1	72.5	442.5	254.7	108.8	1 384	938

1. Based on the resident population estimated as of July 1 of the year shown.

Table C. Metropolitan Areas — **Local Government Finances, Government Employment, and Voting**

Area name	Local government finances, 2012 (cont.) — Direct general expenditure — Total (mil dol)	Per capita[1] (dollars)	Percent of total for: Education	Health and hospitals	Police protection	Public welfare	Highways	Debt outstanding — Total (mil dol)	Per capita[1] (dollars)	Government employment, 2013 — Federal civilian	Federal military	State and local	Presidential election,[2] 2012 — Percent of vote cast: Democratic	Republican	All other
	185	186	187	188	189	190	191	192	193	194	195	196	197	198	199
Abilene, TX	488.6	2 927	54.4	6.6	7.0	0.5	3.1	339.1	2 031	1 202	4 703	11 369	21.7	76.9	1.4
Akron, OH	2 952.8	4 205	42.5	10.2	5.2	4.1	3.5	4 519.2	6 435	2 255	1 807	45 218	56.0	42.5	1.5
Albany, GA	576.8	3 665	46.3	10.0	6.0	0.1	3.2	314.8	2 000	3 079	784	10 405	53.6	45.9	0.6
Albany, OR	449.1	3 794	51.6	3.6	6.2	0.4	4.4	449.9	3 801	307	327	5 845	39.6	56.3	4.1
Albany-Schenectady-Troy, NY	4 877.2	5 576	47.3	3.9	3.9	11.4	4.6	4 658.9	5 327	6 517	3 350	93 213	57.0	41.0	2.0
Albuquerque, NM	2 976.7	3 301	50.0	1.6	8.3	1.5	5.0	4 360.6	4 836	14 638	6 074	66 351	54.0	41.0	5.0
Alexandria, LA	559.7	3 624	51.4	0.1	8.2	0.1	5.0	528.4	3 421	2 994	720	10 777	32.2	66.4	1.4
Allentown-Bethlehem-Easton, PA-NJ	4 050.8	4 897	50.0	3.0	3.6	9.9	3.0	7 000.9	8 464	2 228	2 121	38 526	50.6	48.1	1.4
Altoona, PA	409.0	3 217	49.0	3.1	3.0	8.6	3.9	474.2	3 730	961	329	7 719	32.4	66.3	1.3
Amarillo, TX	915.3	3 553	53.8	4.6	5.9	0.0	2.6	933.7	3 625	2 105	684	17 970	18.8	79.8	1.4
Ames, IA	440.2	4 830	30.3	42.8	3.2	0.5	3.7	391.5	4 295	1 023	367	18 601	55.6	41.7	2.7
Anchorage, AK	1 661.6	4 233	54.5	2.2	8.1	0.0	6.1	2 262.7	5 764	8 948	15 212	24 976	NA	NA	NA
Ann Arbor, MI	1 495.8	4 262	46.0	12.6	6.5	0.9	4.9	2 033.3	5 794	3 870	633	69 462	67.3	31.4	1.3
Anniston-Oxford-Jacksonville, AL	517.7	4 414	32.7	36.2	5.9	0.0	3.9	358.0	3 052	3 968	587	8 252	33.5	65.3	1.2
Appleton, WI	965.9	4 228	54.4	2.6	5.2	4.9	9.0	758.9	3 322	681	666	11 734	47.2	51.2	1.6
Asheville, NC	1 591.2	3 680	36.5	20.8	7.4	7.0	1.7	929.8	2 150	3 584	1 129	23 387	48.4	49.8	1.8
Athens-Clarke County, GA	1 058.7	5 390	28.8	41.0	3.3	0.2	2.0	748.8	3 812	1 312	617	26 524	45.5	52.6	2.0
Atlanta-Sandy Springs-Roswell, GA	19 663.2	3 603	49.2	7.0	6.1	0.9	3.6	35 894.1	6 577	45 231	16 587	270 567	49.6	49.2	1.2
Atlantic City-Hammonton, NJ	1 718.6	6 240	52.7	0.6	6.1	2.1	1.7	1 314.6	4 773	2 642	963	21 168	58.0	41.1	0.9
Auburn-Opelika, AL	638.8	4 338	33.9	39.7	4.1	0.0	2.6	782.4	5 313	296	720	17 037	39.2	59.1	1.7
Augusta-Richmond County, GA-SC	1 747.7	3 035	52.5	4.4	5.9	0.3	3.6	1 584.4	2 751	8 890	12 115	37 955	45.3	53.7	1.1
Austin-Round Rock, TX	7 452.3	4 063	43.6	5.9	6.4	0.6	7.0	22 572.2	12 306	11 927	4 166	156 474	51.9	44.8	3.3
Bakersfield, CA	5 683.5	6 638	55.4	8.5	3.6	6.7	3.0	3 571.0	4 171	10 091	3 983	46 676	40.4	57.2	2.4
Baltimore-Columbia-Towson, MD	12 715.1	4 618	49.6	1.9	6.8	0.5	4.0	11 152.6	4 051	80 939	26 052	169 686	57.8	39.8	2.4
Bangor, ME	527.2	3 429	48.1	1.1	3.8	0.2	4.2	409.3	2 662	1 222	491	13 096	50.2	47.3	2.5
Barnstable Town, MA	1 041.6	4 835	45.9	1.1	5.3	0.2	3.5	892.5	4 143	1 703	1 241	13 169	53.2	45.4	1.4
Baton Rouge, LA	3 383.6	4 150	44.3	5.0	6.4	0.2	4.9	3 940.9	4 834	2 834	4 018	68 254	43.0	55.4	1.6
Battle Creek, MI	680.5	5 037	45.5	17.6	4.3	2.6	5.4	473.1	3 502	2 955	285	7 824	50.2	48.6	1.2
Bay City, MI	521.5	4 877	44.7	20.6	3.3	4.5	4.2	246.5	2 305	243	242	5 682	52.2	46.7	1.1
Beaumont-Port Arthur, TX	1 598.1	3 954	44.3	3.2	7.1	0.5	5.0	5 940.9	14 699	2 132	1 078	23 103	38.6	60.5	0.9
Beckley, WV	341.8	2 737	62.9	0.6	6.8	0.1	1.6	157.5	1 261	2 093	620	6 831	30.7	67.5	1.8
Bellingham, WA	644.4	3 139	42.5	4.3	6.1	0.0	5.7	595.5	2 901	1 369	625	14 043	55.4	41.4	3.1
Bend-Redmond, OR	663.5	4 089	49.1	3.5	7.4	0.4	5.0	1 093.2	6 736	867	457	7 482	45.1	51.8	3.0
Billings, MT	545.0	3 346	48.4	6.7	5.9	0.2	6.4	248.2	1 524	1 798	844	7 678	38.1	59.1	2.8
Binghamton, NY	1 497.1	6 024	49.5	3.4	2.7	11.2	4.5	1 460.3	5 875	683	397	21 370	49.5	48.4	2.2
Birmingham-Hoover, AL	3 959.1	3 483	45.9	4.8	7.2	0.1	4.3	8 903.8	7 833	8 634	5 578	69 384	39.3	59.6	1.1
Bismarck, ND	438.5	3 652	44.7	1.5	5.4	1.8	11.0	308.2	2 567	1 408	829	13 285	33.4	63.5	3.1
Blacksburg-Christiansburg-Radford, VA	489.3	2 734	47.9	0.6	7.5	5.4	3.8	652.1	3 644	475	600	20 815	43.8	53.5	2.8
Bloomington, IL	735.9	3 900	45.5	3.6	4.9	1.2	5.6	815.8	4 323	574	369	15 891	42.7	55.2	2.1
Bloomington, IN	330.0	2 032	47.5	1.0	4.6	0.4	4.3	424.9	2 617	318	517	22 177	55.5	42.2	2.3
Bloomsburg-Berwick, PA	287.0	3 367	58.3	0.0	2.7	3.0	4.5	1 108.2	13 001	181	215	6 571	41.8	56.5	1.7
Boise City, ID	1 619.0	2 538	42.6	1.3	9.7	0.9	6.7	1 042.0	1 633	6 009	2 463	37 531	38.6	58.3	3.1
Boston-Cambridge-Newton, MA-NH	19 978.0	4 305	50.4	5.7	5.4	0.8	2.6	12 543.9	2 703	35 850	14 907	263 651	60.1	38.2	1.7
Boston, MA Div 14454	8 442.8	4 384	47.1	3.7	6.6	0.7	2.2	5 428.2	2 818	19 009	6 101	126 288	61.9	36.5	1.6
Cambridge-Newton-Framingham, MA Div 15764	9 961.0	4 344	52.0	8.3	4.3	0.2	2.7	6 297.2	2 746	15 535	7 137	112 686	60.9	37.3	1.8
Rockingham County-Strafford County, NH 40484	1 574.2	3 731	58.3	0.3	6.2	4.9	4.0	818.5	1 940	1 306	1 669	24 677	49.6	48.9	1.5
Boulder, CO	1 414.6	4 633	43.6	2.5	8.2	2.3	4.6	1 940.0	6 354	1 990	887	30 192	69.7	27.8	2.5
Bowling Green, KY	401.0	2 472	50.4	4.6	5.8	0.1	3.9	1 131.7	6 976	675	519	11 858	35.0	63.4	1.5
Bremerton-Silverdale, WA	1 054.5	4 135	42.3	4.6	3.5	0.0	3.5	748.5	2 935	16 522	10 765	12 643	54.5	42.8	2.6
Bridgeport-Stamford-Norwalk, CT	4 616.9	4 944	50.9	1.2	6.6	1.0	3.1	4 013.1	4 297	2 820	1 900	43 889	54.9	44.2	0.9
Brownsville-Harlingen, TX	1 613.4	3 883	61.9	0.8	4.4	0.5	3.7	1 801.3	4 335	3 164	991	27 261	65.0	33.9	1.1
Brunswick, GA	608.7	5 365	32.5	39.7	4.6	0.1	2.6	370.2	3 264	1 710	[illegible]	8 385	31.6	64.4	1.0
Buffalo-Cheektowaga-Niagara Falls, NY	6 848.3	6 038	44.7	9.1	3.7	9.2	3.7	6 125.0	5 400	9 471	2 131	79 168	55.9	42.3	1.7
Burlington, NC	427.7	2 779	50.9	3.4	8.3	5.8	1.6	182.0	1 183	215	377	6 826	42.3	56.7	1.1
Burlington-South Burlington, VT	830.6	3 887	64.1	0.3	4.8	0.1	6.2	632.9	2 962	3 739	1 535	17 868	67.5	30.1	2.4
California-Lexington Park, MD	331.8	3 045	62.8	2.2	6.2	0.9	2.7	197.3	1 810	8 999	2 456	4 631	41.2	56.0	2.8
Canton-Massillon, OH	1 338.5	3 318	54.8	4.8	5.6	5.1	5.6	461.4	1 144	1 026	1 047	19 017	48.8	49.2	2.0
Cape Coral-Fort Myers, FL	3 730.8	5 782	25.4	32.3	4.8	0.5	3.9	5 119.6	7 934	2 407	1 324	35 542	41.4	57.9	0.7
Cape Girardeau, MO-IL	263.0	2 710	55.0	0.5	5.3	0.1	9.3	203.7	2 098	437	342	6 956	28.9	69.3	1.8
Carbondale-Marion, IL	466.0	3 677	59.1	1.7	5.1	2.0	4.7	325.9	2 572	1 854	253	16 349	45.1	52.2	2.7
Carson City, NV	205.0	3 738	48.3	2.1	8.1	1.2	5.3	391.1	7 131	543	143	8 892	44.1	53.1	2.7
Casper, WY	436.0	5 546	59.1	0.4	4.8	0.7	4.1	147.1	1 871	658	431	5 118	27.7	68.4	4.0

1. Based on the resident population estimated as of July 1 of the year shown. 2.

CBSA/ DIV code[1]	Area name	Land area,[2] 2010 (sq km)	Population 2014: Total persons	Population 2014: Rank	Population 2014: Per square kilometer	Race alone or in combination, not Hispanic or Latino (percent): White	Black	American Indian, Alaska Native	Asian and Pacific Islander	Percent Hispanic or Latino[3]	Age (percent): Under 5 years	5 to 17 years	18 to 24 years	25 to 34 years	35 to 44 years	45 to 54 years
		1	2	3	4	5	6	7	8	9	10	11	12	13	14	15
16300	Cedar Rapids, IA	5 203	263 885	179	50.7	91.6	4.8	0.6	2.3	2.6	6.2	17.5	9.3	13.1	12.7	14.1
16540	Chambersburg-Waynesboro, PA	2 000	152 892	268	76.4	90.8	4.2	0.5	1.4	4.8	6.2	17.0	7.9	11.7	12.5	13.9
16580	Champaign-Urbana, IL	4 976	237 252	191	47.7	75.3	11.9	0.5	9.5	5.1	5.5	14.1	21.3	14.4	10.8	11.1
16620	Charleston, WV	4 520	222 878	198	49.3	91.4	7.6	0.8	1.3	1.0	5.6	15.2	7.9	12.0	12.5	13.9
16700	Charleston-North Charleston, SC	6 704	727 689	76	108.5	65.4	27.7	0.9	2.6	5.3	6.5	16.1	10.2	15.7	12.8	13.6
16740	Charlotte-Concord-Gastonia, NC-SC	13 123	2 380 314	22	181.4	64.7	23.0	0.9	3.6	9.6	6.5	18.3	9.0	13.5	14.7	14.4
16820	Charlottesville, VA	5 761	226 968	196	39.4	77.2	15.0	0.7	4.6	4.7	5.5	14.5	12.4	14.1	11.9	13.4
16860	Chattanooga, TN-GA	5 411	544 559	99	100.6	80.3	14.4	0.8	2.0	4.0	5.8	16.0	9.4	12.7	12.9	13.8
16940	Cheyenne, WY	6 956	96 389	359	13.9	80.7	4.0	1.4	2.0	14.1	6.6	17.0	10.1	14.1	12.0	13.4
16980	Chicago-Naperville-Elgin, IL-IN-WI	18 639	9 554 598	3	512.6	55.4	17.4	0.5	6.8	21.4	6.4	17.7	9.5	14.4	13.6	14.1
16980	Chicago-Naperville-Arlington Heights, IL Div 16974	8 939	7 343 641	X	821.5	52.3	19.4	0.4	7.5	21.8	6.4	17.3	9.4	15.1	13.7	13.9
16980	Elgin, IL Div 20994	2 982	632 768	X	212.2	62.9	6.2	0.4	4.0	27.8	6.7	20.0	10.8	12.6	13.6	13.9
16980	Gary, IN Div 23844	4 865	704 935	X	144.9	65.5	18.6	0.6	1.7	14.9	6.1	18.2	9.1	12.3	12.6	14.0
16980	Lake County-Kenosha County, IL-WI Div 29404	1 853	873 254	X	471.3	68.0	7.5	0.5	6.6	19.0	6.0	19.5	9.9	11.4	13.2	15.6
17020	Chico, CA	4 238	224 241	197	52.9	77.1	2.4	3.0	5.9	15.1	5.4	14.9	15.9	11.8	10.3	11.8
17140	Cincinnati, OH-KY-IN	10 797	2 149 449	28	199.1	82.5	13.2	0.6	2.7	2.8	6.5	17.8	9.5	13.1	12.6	14.4
17300	Clarksville, TN-KY	4 397	278 353	168	63.3	70.2	20.4	1.2	3.4	8.3	8.7	18.4	12.5	17.7	12.5	11.2
17420	Cleveland, TN	1 977	119 705	322	60.5	89.9	4.6	0.9	1.2	4.9	5.6	16.7	9.9	12.1	13.1	14.2
17460	Cleveland-Elyria, OH	5 172	2 063 598	31	399.0	72.6	20.8	0.6	2.6	5.1	5.6	16.6	8.7	12.0	12.0	14.7
17660	Coeur d'Alene, ID	3 222	147 326	282	45.7	93.3	0.7	2.2	1.7	4.2	6.1	17.7	8.5	12.2	12.1	13.4
17780	College Station-Bryan, TX	5 439	242 905	189	44.7	59.6	12.0	0.7	5.3	23.6	6.3	14.7	25.9	14.7	10.2	9.9
17820	Colorado Springs, CO	6 951	686 908	79	98.8	74.6	7.4	1.5	4.7	15.6	6.9	18.2	11.2	14.8	12.4	13.5
17860	Columbia, MO	1 775	172 717	235	97.3	82.9	10.7	1.0	5.0	3.2	6.0	14.6	20.9	15.3	11.3	11.3
17900	Columbia, SC	9 590	800 495	72	83.5	58.9	34.2	0.8	2.5	5.3	6.1	16.7	12.3	13.6	12.7	13.5
17980	Columbus, GA-AL	5 014	314 005	158	62.6	50.8	41.1	1.0	2.8	6.7	7.3	17.2	11.4	15.6	12.4	12.8
18020	Columbus, IN	1 054	80 217	377	76.1	86.2	2.8	0.6	5.4	6.4	6.5	17.8	8.4	13.4	13.3	13.5
18140	Columbus, OH	12 423	1 994 536	32	160.6	77.7	16.1	0.8	4.0	3.8	6.7	17.5	9.7	15.1	13.7	13.8
18580	Corpus Christi, TX	4 621	448 108	113	97.0	35.7	3.5	0.6	2.1	58.9	6.7	18.6	10.0	13.9	12.0	12.9
18700	Corvallis, OR	1 751	86 316	367	49.3	85.4	1.6	1.6	7.9	7.0	4.2	12.7	23.4	12.3	10.0	10.8
18880	Crestview-Fort Walton Beach-Destin, FL	5 096	258 042	183	50.6	80.1	9.7	1.4	4.2	7.8	6.4	15.4	9.6	14.8	11.6	14.0
19060	Cumberland, MD-WV	1 948	100 530	351	51.6	90.9	7.7	0.5	1.0	1.4	4.8	13.4	11.9	11.9	11.9	13.7
19100	Dallas-Fort Worth-Arlington, TX	24 029	6 954 330	4	289.4	50.4	15.8	0.9	6.6	28.0	7.3	19.8	9.4	14.7	14.5	13.9
19100	Dallas-Plano-Irving, TX Div 19124	13 661	4 604 097	X	337.0	47.2	16.9	0.8	7.4	29.2	7.3	19.8	9.4	14.9	14.9	13.9
19100	Fort Worth-Arlington, TX Div 23104	10 368	2 350 233	X	226.7	56.7	13.6	0.9	5.0	25.5	7.2	19.7	9.4	14.2	13.7	13.9
19140	Dalton, GA	1 644	142 952	287	87.0	68.0	3.5	0.6	1.4	27.6	7.0	19.8	9.5	13.0	13.5	13.8
19180	Danville, IL	2 327	79 728	378	34.3	81.3	14.3	0.6	1.1	4.7	6.5	17.4	8.6	11.7	11.7	13.5
19300	Daphne-Fairhope-Foley, AL	4 118	200 111	218	48.6	84.4	9.9	1.3	1.3	4.6	5.7	16.7	7.8	11.5	12.5	13.9
19340	Davenport-Moline-Rock Island, IA-IL	5 880	383 030	137	65.1	82.7	8.2	0.7	2.4	8.2	6.3	16.9	8.7	12.7	12.0	13.7
19380	Dayton, OH	3 320	800 836	71	241.2	79.6	16.9	0.8	2.7	2.4	5.9	16.3	10.3	12.8	11.6	13.8
19460	Decatur, AL	3 289	153 084	267	46.5	79.0	12.7	3.3	0.9	6.5	6.0	16.9	8.6	12.0	12.8	14.9
19500	Decatur, IL	1 504	108 350	340	72.0	79.6	18.6	0.6	1.6	2.1	6.0	16.2	9.6	11.7	11.5	13.3
19660	Deltona-Daytona Beach-Ormond Beach, FL	4 109	609 939	90	148.4	75.9	11.1	0.7	2.3	11.5	4.7	13.6	8.4	10.4	10.6	13.7
19740	Denver-Aurora-Lakewood, CO	21 616	2 754 258	21	127.4	67.3	6.2	1.1	4.9	22.7	6.6	17.5	8.5	15.8	14.6	13.8
19780	Des Moines-West Des Moines, IA	7 469	611 549	89	81.9	84.2	5.9	0.6	4.0	7.0	7.2	18.5	8.6	15.1	13.7	13.6
19820	Detroit-Warren-Dearborn, MI	10 070	4 296 611	14	426.7	69.2	23.4	0.9	4.4	4.1	5.9	17.3	9.0	12.1	12.9	15.0
19820	Detroit-Dearborn-Livonia, MI Div 19804	1 585	1 764 804	X	1 113.4	51.8	40.3	1.0	3.6	5.6	6.5	17.7	10.0	12.4	12.7	14.1
19820	Warren-Troy-Farmington Hills, MI Div 47664	8 485	2 531 807	X	298.4	81.4	11.5	0.9	5.0	3.2	5.4	17.0	8.3	11.8	13.0	15.6
20020	Dothan, AL	4 445	148 095	280	33.3	72.1	24.1	1.0	1.1	3.2	6.2	17.2	8.1	12.3	12.6	13.7
20100	Dover, DE	1 518	171 987	237	113.3	66.2	26.0	1.4	3.1	6.6	6.6	17.2	11.0	13.0	11.7	13.6
20220	Dubuque, IA	1 576	96 370	360	61.1	93.4	3.4	0.5	1.9	2.1	6.1	16.9	10.2	12.8	11.0	13.9
20260	Duluth, MN-WI	21 790	280 218	164	12.9	93.6	2.2	3.8	1.4	1.4	5.3	14.7	11.5	12.0	11.0	13.8
20500	Durham-Chapel Hill, NC	4 555	542 710	100	119.1	56.4	27.8	1.0	5.4	11.4	6.2	15.3	12.2	15.0	13.4	13.1
20700	East Stroudsburg, PA	1 575	166 314	247	105.6	70.4	13.7	0.8	2.8	14.2	4.6	17.1	11.0	9.9	11.7	16.8
20740	Eau Claire, WI	4 264	165 024	249	38.7	93.7	1.7	0.9	3.2	1.8	5.8	15.6	13.5	13.4	11.4	13.2
20940	El Centro, CA	10 817	179 091	231	16.6	13.3	2.7	1.0	1.7	81.4	8.3	20.5	11.2	14.0	12.2	12.1
21060	Elizabethtown-Fort Knox, KY	3 082	151 585	270	49.2	82.8	11.2	1.1	2.9	5.0	6.7	18.4	9.9	13.5	13.0	14.4
21140	Elkhart-Goshen, IN	1 200	201 971	216	168.3	78.1	6.9	0.7	1.4	14.9	7.5	20.5	8.9	12.7	12.7	13.0
21300	Elmira, NY	1 055	87 770	366	83.2	89.2	8.0	0.7	1.8	2.8	5.9	15.9	9.3	12.2	11.7	14.4
21340	El Paso, TX	14 462	836 698	67	57.9	14.2	3.4	0.5	1.6	80.7	8.2	20.7	11.8	14.1	12.7	12.0
21500	Erie, PA	2 070	278 443	167	134.5	87.7	8.3	0.5	1.7	3.7	5.8	16.1	11.2	12.6	11.4	13.7
21660	Eugene, OR	11 793	358 337	146	30.4	87.0	1.7	2.7	4.4	8.0	4.9	14.2	13.4	12.4	11.5	12.4
21780	Evansville, IN-KY	3 794	315 162	156	83.1	89.6	8.0	0.5	1.6	2.1	6.2	16.6	9.5	13.0	11.9	13.9

1. CBSA = Core Based Statistical Area. DIV = Metropolitan Division. See Appendix A for explanation. See Appendix B for list of metropolitan areas identified by type. 2. Dry land or land partially or temporarily covered by water. 3. May be of any race.

Area name	Population, 2013 (cont.): Age (percent) (cont.): 55 to 64 years	65 to 74 years	75 years and over	Percent female	Population change and components of change, 2000–2014: Total persons: 2000	2010	Percent change: 2000–2010	2010–2014	Components of change, 2010–2014: Births	Deaths	Net migration	Households, 2013: Number	Persons per household	Percent: Family households	Female family householder[1]	One person
	16	17	18	19	20	21	22	23	24	25	26	27	28	29	30	31
Cedar Rapids, IA	12.5	7.8	6.8	50.4	237 230	257 940	8.7	2.3	13 548	8 645	1 242	105 035	2.43	63.0	9.7	30.0
Chambersburg-Waynesboro, PA	13.0	9.6	8.2	51.1	129 313	149 618	15.7	2.2	7 870	6 044	1 352	59 145	2.53	64.5	9.0	29.7
Champaign-Urbana, IL	11.0	6.3	5.5	50.1	210 275	231 891	10.3	2.3	11 334	6 682	767	90 474	2.40	55.8	10.6	32.5
Charleston, WV	15.4	9.7	7.8	51.6	235 938	227 078	-3.8	-1.8	10 992	12 015	-2 863	95 251	2.32	63.6	13.4	31.8
Charleston-North Charleston, SC	12.2	7.9	4.9	51.1	549 033	664 607	21.1	9.5	39 133	21 330	43 165	268 003	2.60	62.8	13.7	28.6
Charlotte-Concord-Gastonia, NC-SC	11.5	7.3	4.8	51.4	1 717 372	2 217 012	29.1	7.4	125 143	71 315	106 419	859 709	2.68	67.2	14.1	26.8
Charlottesville, VA	13.0	8.7	6.6	51.6	189 644	218 705	15.3	3.8	10 291	7 137	4 820	84 595	2.49	62.4	10.1	29.0
Chattanooga, TN-GA	13.5	9.1	6.8	51.5	476 531	528 143	10.8	3.1	26 457	22 047	12 071	209 304	2.51	69.0	13.1	26.2
Cheyenne, WY	13.1	7.8	5.9	49.7	81 607	91 738	12.4	4.9	5 336	3 216	2 384	35 785	2.62	69.1	10.0	25.2
Chicago-Naperville-Elgin, IL-IN-WI	12.0	7.0	5.4	51.1	9 098 316	9 461 105	4.0	1.0	516 295	289 440	-129 346	3 450 331	2.72	65.7	13.3	28.6
Chicago-Naperville-Arlington Heights, IL Div 16974	11.9	7.0	5.5	51.2	7 135 324	7 262 718	1.8	1.1	403 706	222 783	-95 461	2 667 460	2.71	64.3	13.7	29.7
Elgin, IL Div 20994	11.2	6.5	4.6	50.2	493 088	620 429	25.8	2.0	34 410	15 601	-7 387	209 499	2.95	70.9	10.1	23.2
Gary, IN Div 23844	13.5	8.0	6.3	51.3	675 971	708 070	4.7	-0.4	35 546	27 528	-10 556	265 555	2.61	68.7	15.5	26.8
Lake County-Kenosha County, IL-WI Div 29404	12.5	6.8	5.1	50.2	793 933	869 888	9.6	0.4	42 633	23 528	-15 942	307 817	2.76	71.7	10.9	24.0
Chico, CA	13.3	9.1	7.6	50.4	203 171	220 000	8.3	1.9	10 200	9 512	3 513	85 158	2.55	58.7	12.2	29.2
Cincinnati, OH-KY-IN	12.8	7.5	5.8	51.0	1 994 830	2 114 580	6.0	1.6	117 072	77 345	-3 767	822 005	2.54	66.2	13.3	27.8
Clarksville, TN-KY	9.2	5.8	4.0	49.5	219 630	260 625	18.7	6.8	21 503	7 963	3 781	96 258	2.73	72.0	14.3	22.6
Cleveland, TN	12.6	9.5	6.4	51.2	104 015	115 788	11.3	3.4	5 552	4 863	3 148	46 157	2.54	70.4	13.9	25.2
Cleveland-Elyria, OH	14.1	8.7	7.6	51.8	2 148 143	2 077 240	-3.3	-0.7	98 504	88 446	-22 414	844 428	2.39	61.5	14.6	33.0
Coeur d'Alene, ID	13.7	9.8	6.6	50.7	108 685	138 494	27.4	6.4	7 300	5 151	6 431	55 836	2.55	72.4	11.6	22.0
College Station-Bryan, TX	8.7	5.3	4.2	49.5	184 885	228 660	23.7	6.2	12 792	5 354	6 672	85 573	2.62	58.1	12.2	27.4
Colorado Springs, CO	11.7	6.8	4.5	49.6	537 484	645 613	20.1	6.4	39 850	17 177	18 317	250 601	2.64	68.6	11.2	24.5
Columbia, MO	10.5	5.7	4.4	51.6	135 454	162 642	20.1	6.2	9 015	4 264	5 242	67 680	2.38	54.9	10.9	28.6
Columbia, SC	12.3	7.7	5.1	51.3	647 158	767 598	18.6	4.3	40 206	26 542	18 958	296 310	2.55	64.0	15.3	28.8
Columbus, GA-AL	11.3	6.9	5.1	50.2	281 768	294 865	4.6	6.3	20 028	11 372	9 470	110 901	2.70	65.0	20.2	29.9
Columbus, IN	12.4	8.4	6.3	50.2	71 435	76 794	7.5	4.5	4 469	2 963	1 973	30 359	2.59	65.8	8.1	27.9
Columbus, OH	11.8	6.8	4.9	50.8	1 675 013	1 901 974	13.5	4.9	113 392	62 011	41 657	750 394	2.56	63.1	12.5	28.6
Corpus Christi, TX	12.2	7.8	5.8	50.7	403 280	428 185	6.2	4.7	25 379	15 567	10 055	160 549	2.72	69.7	15.1	23.2
Corvallis, OR	12.8	7.8	5.8	49.8	78 153	85 579	9.5	0.9	3 100	2 267	-118	33 609	2.40	54.0	5.6	29.8
Crestview-Fort Walton Beach-Destin, FL	12.7	8.9	6.6	49.2	211 099	235 865	11.7	9.4	14 122	8 933	16 550	98 219	2.51	67.5	13.9	27.3
Cumberland, MD-WV	13.3	10.5	8.5	48.6	102 008	103 299	1.3	-2.7	4 155	5 196	-1 633	37 773	2.45	57.4	9.9	38.8
Dallas-Fort Worth-Arlington, TX	10.6	6.0	3.9	50.7	5 204 126	6 426 214	23.5	8.2	409 580	166 100	282 419	2 406 092	2.80	69.4	13.7	24.9
Dallas-Plano-Irving, TX Div 19124	10.4	5.8	3.7	50.6	3 445 899	4 230 520	22.8	8.8	271 899	103 551	204 511	1 590 389	2.80	69.2	14.0	24.9
Fort Worth-Arlington, TX Div 23104	11.1	6.5	4.3	50.8	1 758 227	2 195 694	24.9	7.0	137 681	62 549	77 908	815 703	2.80	69.9	13.1	24.9
Dalton, GA	10.9	7.5	4.9	50.2	120 031	142 227	18.5	0.5	8 112	4 740	-2 653	48 318	2.91	72.9	13.1	22.0
Danville, IL	13.6	9.3	7.8	50.3	83 919	81 625	-2.7	-2.3	4 567	3 951	-2 417	31 482	2.47	65.2	13.0	31.0
Daphne-Fairhope-Foley, AL	13.7	10.8	7.3	51.2	140 415	182 265	29.8	9.8	9 159	8 099	16 080	70 259	2.75	66.8	9.4	29.4
Davenport-Moline-Rock Island, IA-IL	13.6	8.8	7.3	50.8	376 019	379 690	1.0	0.9	19 667	15 265	-699	153 566	2.44	64.7	11.6	30.5
Dayton, OH	13.3	8.8	7.3	51.5	805 816	799 232	-0.8	0.2	40 683	33 636	-4 673	323 890	2.40	62.9	14.4	31.6
Decatur, AL	13.2	9.3	6.4	51.0	145 867	153 829	5.5	-0.5	7 525	6 800	-1 353	60 129	2.51	70.0	14.0	27.6
Decatur, IL	14.3	9.2	8.2	52.0	114 706	110 768	-3.4	-2.2	5 767	4 936	-3 174	44 965	2.35	62.4	11.9	32.5
Deltona-Daytona Beach-Ormond Beach, FL	14.9	12.9	10.7	51.4	493 175	590 289	19.7	3.3	23 257	31 390	26 849	235 616	2.50	62.6	11.1	30.6
Denver-Aurora-Lakewood, CO	12.0	6.7	4.6	50.2	2 179 240	2 543 482	D	8.3	147 484	68 341	128 381	1 035 096	2.57	62.4	10.6	29.4
Des Moines-West Des Moines, IA	11.5	6.7	5.2	50.8	481 394	569 633	18.3	7.4	36 423	17 602	22 718	233 644	2.52	66.7	10.6	26.4
Detroit-Warren-Dearborn, MI	13.6	8.0	6.3	51.5	4 452 557	4 296 250	-3.5	0.0	212 571	166 387	-45 035	1 658 085	2.56	64.9	14.8	29.8
Detroit-Dearborn-Livonia, MI Div 19804	13.1	7.4	6.1	51.9	2 061 162	1 820 584	-11.7	-3.1	99 655	74 536	-80 977	664 415	2.64	62.6	19.7	32.5
Warren-Troy-Farmington Hills, MI Div 47664	13.9	8.4	6.5	51.2	2 391 395	2 475 666	3.5	2.3	112 916	91 851	35 942	993 670	2.51	[illegible]	11.0	20.0
Dothan, AL	13.3	9.6	7.1	51.8	130 861	145 639	11.3	1.7	7 556	6 737	1 632	57 990	2.52	66.7	16.6	29.9
Dover, DE	11.8	8.9	6.2	51.8	126 697	162 310	28.1	5.9	9 320	6 172	6 319	62 053	2.64	70.8	17.2	23.3
Dubuque, IA	13.3	8.1	7.7	50.6	89 143	93 653	5.1	2.9	4 992	3 649	1 411	36 801	2.48	64.7	10.1	28.4
Duluth, MN-WI	15.0	8.9	7.7	49.6	275 486	279 771	1.6	0.2	12 313	12 047	472	115 589	2.31	59.1	10.1	33.3
Durham-Chapel Hill, NC	12.2	7.4	5.3	52.0	426 493	504 357	18.3	7.1	27 873	15 133	21 881	209 290	2.44	61.0	12.3	31.0
East Stroudsburg, PA	14.4	8.7	5.8	50.6	138 687	169 842	22.5	-2.1	6 069	5 732	-3 752	58 496	2.82	73.7	12.7	19.4
Eau Claire, WI	12.6	7.9	6.5	49.8	148 337	161 151	8.6	2.3	8 079	5 269	880	64 494	2.44	61.7	6.7	29.3
El Centro, CA	10.2	6.2	5.3	48.8	142 361	174 528	22.6	2.6	12 966	3 967	-4 593	47 430	3.52	78.2	19.4	17.2
Elizabethtown-Fort Knox, KY	11.9	7.2	5.1	50.1	133 896	148 338	10.8	2.2	8 524	5 230	-154	56 888	2.60	68.7	11.2	25.7
Elkhart-Goshen, IN	11.6	7.1	5.9	50.5	182 791	197 559	8.1	2.2	12 815	6 556	-1 749	71 056	2.77	73.6	14.3	21.2
Elmira, NY	13.9	8.8	7.8	50.2	91 070	88 830	-2.5	-1.2	4 370	3 965	-1 413	35 838	2.33	60.7	12.7	30.8
El Paso, TX	9.8	6.0	4.9	50.9	682 966	804 123	17.7	4.1	58 399	20 493	-5 259	259 580	3.14	74.2	20.1	23.1
Erie, PA	13.8	8.2	7.1	50.7	280 843	280 566	-0.1	-0.8	13 450	11 673	-3 533	110 733	2.42	63.4	13.7	30.7
Eugene, OR	14.4	9.7	7.1	50.9	322 959	351 715	8.9	1.9	14 759	13 838	5 692	144 166	2.42	58.8	10.8	30.4
Evansville, IN-KY	13.7	8.3	6.8	51.3	296 195	311 552	5.2	1.2	16 203	13 136	840	124 343	2.46	65.6	11.7	29.1

1. No spouse present.

Area name	Persons in group quarters, 2014	Daytime population, 2013: Number	Daytime population, 2013: Employment/residence ratio	Births, 2014: Total	Births, 2014: Rate[1]	Deaths, 2014: Number	Deaths, 2014: Rate[1]	Persons under 65 with no health insurance 2013: Number	Persons under 65 with no health insurance 2013: Percent	Medicare, 2014: Eligible for Medicare	Medicare, 2014: Enrolled in Medicare Advantage	Medicare, 2014: Enrolled in a Medicare prescription drug plan	Serious crimes known to police,[2] 2013: Total: Number	Serious crimes known to police,[2] 2013: Total: Rate[3]
	32	33	34	35	36	37	38	39	40	41	42	43	44	45
Cedar Rapids, IA	6 676	277 635	1.13	3 154	12.0	2 064	7.8	16 937	7.7	45 120	11 103	24 179	6 478	2 666
Chambersburg-Waynesboro, PA	2 569	163 988	1.24	1 824	11.9	1 500	9.8	16 646	13.5	32 386	7 353	15 833	3 192	2 105
Champaign-Urbana, IL	16 586	247 256	1.13	2 662	11.2	1 610	6.8	23 610	12.3	31 986	13 301	9 343	6 920	2 997
Charleston, WV	3 383	253 940	1.34	2 542	11.4	2 851	12.8	28 147	15.4	52 142	15 977	23 149	6 789	3 324
Charleston-North Charleston, SC	16 143	722 933	1.03	9 336	12.8	5 290	7.3	111 194	18.4	114 342	21 079	46 870	24 937	3 526
Charlotte-Concord-Gastonia, NC-SC	36 247	2 406 680	1.07	29 696	12.5	17 446	7.3	358 901	17.8	350 158	99 285	161 274	77 650	3 359
Charlottesville, VA	12 224	242 544	1.19	2 450	10.8	1 705	7.5	27 067	15.1	39 168	4 920	21 287	97 016	3 529
Chattanooga, TN-GA	13 464	566 173	1.12	6 299	11.6	5 375	9.9	73 214	16.5	105 232	33 076	46 669	24 169	4 466
Cheyenne, WY	1 884	100 995	1.11	1 266	13.1	762	7.9	11 463	14.2	16 232	535	8 727	2 824	2 953
Chicago-Naperville-Elgin, IL-IN-WI	161 010	9 656 678	1.03	119 405	12.5	70 059	7.3	1 297 037	15.8	1 384 346	238 790	714 051	260 507	2 771
Chicago-Naperville-Arlington Heights, IL Div 16974	113 448	NA	NA	93 482	12.7	53 967	7.3	1 027 323	16.2	1 059 629	190 851	537 894	210 855	2 914
Elgin, IL Div 20994	13 474	NA	NA	7 878	12.5	3 798	6.0	83 868	15.4	79 957	14 718	39 745	10 366	1 661
Gary, IN Div 23844	10 926	NA	NA	8 156	11.6	6 688	9.5	92 352	15.6	122 551	17 141	69 463	22 528	3 330
Lake County-Kenosha County, IL-WI Div 29404	23 162	NA	NA	9 889	11.3	5 606	6.4	93 494	12.5	122 209	16 080	66 949	16 758	1 934
Chico, CA	5 327	229 271	1.09	2 409	10.7	2 287	10.2	31 203	17.1	46 647	650	31 480	6 857	3 084
Cincinnati, OH-KY-IN	47 663	2 187 977	1.06	27 504	12.8	18 739	8.7	227 216	12.5	351 899	134 274	157 041	71 104	3 490
Clarksville, TN-KY	8 878	285 826	1.13	5 154	18.5	1 922	6.9	36 304	15.3	34 887	7 307	14 237	8 099	2 912
Cleveland, TN	2 991	130 820	1.29	1 333	11.1	1 157	9.7	17 124	17.6	24 842	8 465	10 156	4 284	3 614
Cleveland-Elyria, OH	43 217	2 177 498	1.13	23 033	11.2	20 585	10.0	214 765	12.7	395 657	150 808	193 225	52 161	2 974
Coeur d'Alene, ID	1 488	149 837	1.12	1 745	11.8	1 242	8.4	22 209	18.6	30 308	8 921	11 256	4 479	3 106
College Station-Bryan, TX	14 217	245 543	1.07	3 028	12.5	1 308	5.4	45 466	22.6	26 714	4 899	11 359	6 740	2 842
Colorado Springs, CO	18 696	691 563	1.04	9 476	13.8	4 323	6.3	78 295	13.4	94 174	27 577	28 143	24 574	3 642
Columbia, MO	9 008	182 876	1.15	2 187	12.7	1 030	6.0	19 037	13.1	22 421	3 040	12 527	6 182	3 621
Columbia, SC	33 569	823 394	1.09	9 445	11.8	6 478	8.1	109 684	16.7	126 319	24 543	62 319	33 180	4 199
Columbus, GA-AL	12 251	341 854	1.23	4 783	15.2	2 798	8.9	50 676	18.9	49 795	13 256	17 797	16 801	5 348
Columbus, IN	1 147	94 878	1.48	1 089	13.6	674	8.4	9 971	14.9	14 258	2 445	8 821	2 822	3 523
Columbus, OH	50 425	2 029 121	1.07	27 042	13.6	15 131	7.6	223 321	13.2	286 392	122 851	140 057	72 237	3 746
Corpus Christi, TX	7 057	458 979	1.07	6 149	13.7	3 673	8.2	88 164	23.4	72 245	32 824	22 378	21 146	4 784
Corvallis, OR	4 472	95 082	1.30	729	8.4	526	6.1	9 451	13.5	13 617	6 077	4 986	2 326	2 675
Crestview-Fort Walton Beach-Destin, FL	6 899	270 179	1.15	3 447	13.4	2 208	8.6	42 176	20.3	46 845	6 474	15 610	6 973	2 760
Cumberland, MD-WV	8 353	105 982	1.14	973	9.7	1 250	12.4	9 504	12.7	22 875	1 575	15 269	3 132	3 127
Dallas-Fort Worth-Arlington, TX	82 720	6 895 426	1.03	97 026	14.0	41 151	5.9	1 442 718	23.8	813 175	245 130	348 573	229 309	3 369
Dallas-Plano-Irving, TX Div 19124	54 099	NA	NA	64 252	14.0	25 769	5.6	972 928	24.2	514 303	136 289	236 626	144 606	3 213
Fort Worth-Arlington, TX Div 23104	28 621	NA	NA	32 774	13.9	15 382	6.5	469 790	23.1	298 872	108 841	111 947	84 703	3 673
Dalton, GA	1 223	156 517	1.27	1 855	13.0	1 141	8.0	32 679	26.4	22 679	3 365	13 234	4 224	3 007
Danville, IL	2 903	85 060	1.17	1 080	13.5	919	11.5	7 843	12.2	17 102	6 321	6 355	3 628	4 586
Daphne-Fairhope-Foley, AL	2 296	203 674	1.13	2 169	10.8	1 947	9.7	27 538	17.5	43 284	13 751	16 521	5 249	2 715
Davenport-Moline-Rock Island, IA-IL	8 727	399 893	1.10	4 764	12.4	3 540	9.2	34 694	11.0	72 668	14 776	35 402	10 786	2 860
Dayton, OH	24 632	864 085	1.19	9 571	12.0	7 948	9.9	85 461	13.1	152 587	65 949	60 275	28 294	3 594
Decatur, AL	2 349	167 571	1.32	1 729	11.3	1 581	10.3	22 295	17.5	31 477	3 685	19 553	4 091	2 662
Decatur, IL	4 062	120 087	1.25	1 351	12.5	1 138	10.5	9 296	10.6	23 008	4 284	12 517	3 186	2 900
Deltona-Daytona Beach-Ormond Beach, FL	13 858	612 248	1.06	5 480	9.0	7 493	12.3	106 441	23.7	157 503	67 580	51 415	20 905	3 500
Denver-Aurora-Lakewood, CO	34 114	2 767 361	1.05	35 245	12.8	16 921	6.1	372 752	15.8	357 409	170 676	95 983	82 659	3 070
Des Moines-West Des Moines, IA	12 131	627 366	1.09	8 814	14.4	4 286	7.0	45 838	8.8	87 931	15 274	48 883	18 113	3 037
Detroit-Warren-Dearborn, MI	47 806	4 408 686	1.06	49 732	11.6	39 427	9.2	479 568	13.2	769 512	235 472	451 910	134 813	3 144
Detroit-Dearborn-Livonia, MI Div 19804	22 714	NA	NA	22 936	13.0	17 419	9.9	240 458	15.8	311 713	96 379	184 952	86 619	4 874
Warren-Troy-Farmington Hills, MI Div 47664	25 092	NA	NA	26 796	10.6	22 008	8.7	239 110	11.3	457 799	139 093	266 958	48 194	1 920
Dothan, AL	1 846	157 082	1.19	1 727	11.7	1 615	10.9	20 217	16.6	32 479	4 397	17 525	4 719	3 196
Dover, DE	4 578	181 395	1.22	2 219	12.9	1 542	9.0	14 497	10.4	31 124	2 107	18 980	5 826	3 433
Dubuque, IA	4 256	106 855	1.24	1 194	12.4	872	9.0	6 092	7.9	18 105	7 477	13 943	2 043	2 134
Duluth, MN-WI	12 623	288 240	1.07	2 857	10.2	2 777	9.9	21 831	9.7	58 178	26 987	27 078	10 086	3 600
Durham-Chapel Hill, NC	23 396	636 673	1.50	6 597	12.2	3 686	6.8	76 567	17.2	80 425	24 670	34 367	18 681	3 523
East Stroudsburg, PA	3 816	183 798	1.36	1 413	8.5	1 443	8.7	19 406	14.0	29 592	5 095	15 738	4 744	2 819
Eau Claire, WI	7 479	174 695	1.14	1 933	11.7	1 255	7.6	13 862	10.3	29 603	8 248	13 589	2 981	1 813
El Centro, CA	8 800	235 265	NA	3 028	16.9	935	5.2	31 736	21.5	27 061	2 946	17 110	6 215	3 658
Elizabethtown-Fort Knox, KY	3 780	160 188	1.15	1 943	12.8	1 239	8.2	20 296	15.8	24 784	3 895	10 942	2 374	1 575
Elkhart-Goshen, IN	3 760	236 999	1.46	3 042	15.1	1 542	7.6	37 492	21.8	31 389	8 351	15 093	4 811	2 395
Elmira, NY	4 853	99 230	1.36	1 019	11.6	939	10.7	5 948	8.6	18 882	5 944	8 201	2 199	2 470
El Paso, TX	16 004	848 160	1.05	13 532	16.2	4 932	5.9	222 284	30.7	113 603	53 491	33 285	21 122	2 508
Erie, PA	12 891	290 166	1.08	3 108	11.2	2 730	9.8	24 756	10.9	54 287	24 149	20 663	7 361	2 625
Eugene, OR	7 827	363 973	1.05	3 488	9.7	3 304	9.2	53 281	18.3	73 232	35 956	22 355	13 192	3 736
Evansville, IN-KY	9 553	330 108	1.12	3 829	12.1	3 135	9.9	36 382	14.0	59 761	15 083	29 055	9 883	3 342

1. Per 1,000 estimated resident population. 2. Data for serious crimes have not been adjusted for underreporting; this may affect comparability between geographic areas and over time.
3. Per 100,000 population estimated by the FBI.

Area name	Serious crimes known to police, 2013 (cont.)[1] Rate[2] Violent	Rate[2] Property	Education: School enrollment and attainment, 2013: Enrollment[3] Total	Enrollment[3] Percent private	Attainment[4] (percent) High school graduate or less	Attainment[4] (percent) Bachelor's degree or more	Local government expenditures,[5] 2012–2013: Total current expenditures (mil dol)	Current expenditures per student (dollars)	Income and Poverty, 2013: Per capita income[6] (dollars)	Mean household income (dollars)	Median household income	Percent of households with income of less than $25,000	Percent of households with income of $200,000 or more	Percent below poverty level: All persons	Children under 18 years	Age 65 years and older
	46	47	48	49	50	51	52	53	54	55	56	57	58	59	60	61
Cedar Rapids, IA	204	2 463	69 098	19.3	35.9	27.6	481.2	11 096	29 150	70 978	56 397	18.5	2.9	9.2	10.5	7.0
Chambersburg-Waynesboro, PA	152	1 953	34 722	15.9	56.6	19.1	250.5	10 985	27 133	67 211	54 303	19.5	2.1	12.9	20.9	6.3
Champaign-Urbana, IL	480	2 517	87 929	7.4	31.2	39.4	356.9	11 705	26 030	64 570	47 258	29.5	4.0	20.4	19.6	5.8
Charleston, WV	426	2 898	45 606	9.7	50.7	22.8	400.8	11 408	26 955	61 816	45 251	26.8	3.5	16.3	25.2	7.2
Charleston-North Charleston, SC	362	3 165	184 580	16.3	35.2	33.0	1 007.6	9 928	27 827	71 044	51 771	23.8	4.2	16.2	23.8	8.8
Charlotte-Concord-Gastonia, NC-SC	404	2 955	620 255	15.4	38.1	32.0	3 032.1	8 196	28 003	72 972	51 251	22.5	4.9	14.8	19.8	9.5
Charlottesville, VA	343	3 186	67 054	14.2	36.4	42.2	333.8	11 758	30 465	79 178	58 375	19.3	6.0	16.0	18.9	6.0
Chattanooga, TN-GA	529	3 937	127 691	19.5	44.8	23.7	644.3	8 671	25 095	63 458	47 702	26.5	3.1	16.1	23.9	8.1
Cheyenne, WY	207	2 746	24 525	9.3	28.8	28.2	218.6	15 257	28 761	72 830	61 661	14.7	2.3	9.5	12.1	4.1
Chicago-Naperville-Elgin, IL-IN-WI	403	2 368	2 579 797	19.8	37.7	35.1	20 132.2	12 876	31 302	83 898	60 564	20.9	6.7	14.4	20.6	9.6
Chicago-Naperville-Arlington Heights, IL Div 16974	456	2 458	1 962 633	21.3	37.0	36.4	15 188.1	13 270	31 429	83 544	60 046	21.5	6.8	14.8	21.1	10.3
Elgin, IL Div 20994	173	1 487	189 822	13.2	40.4	31.1	1 569.6	11 244	29 884	87 184	66 835	16.6	6.1	12.5	17.5	7.1
Gary, IN Div 23844	345	2 985	182 605	16.9	47.5	20.6	1 084.2	9 612	25 776	66 765	51 508	24.0	2.6	16.0	25.0	7.6
Lake County-Kenosha County, IL-WI Div 29404	166	1 768	244 737	14.8	33.6	38.8	2 290.3	13 749	35 733	99 513	68 645	16.7	10.4	10.7	15.5	6.4
Chico, CA	285	2 799	61 616	6.2	34.6	26.6	306.8	9 812	23 744	59 522	42 752	30.3	2.9	21.5	22.3	7.9
Cincinnati, OH-KY-IN	295	3 195	558 184	19.6	40.9	31.2	3 354.1	10 996	29 014	73 584	53 378	22.9	5.0	14.5	20.3	8.4
Clarksville, TN-KY	381	2 531	78 522	9.0	40.6	23.2	347.3	8 231	22 854	62 454	48 938	23.3	2.2	16.4	22.9	10.1
Cleveland, TN	435	3 178	28 307	19.6	51.9	17.6	141.0	7 617	22 521	55 583	42 107	30.4	1.7	19.8	33.8	16.5
Cleveland-Elyria, OH	431	2 543	517 412	25.0	40.3	29.8	3 529.6	13 202	28 686	68 423	49 358	26.0	4.0	15.6	22.7	9.9
Coeur d'Alene, ID	321	2 785	33 610	14.5	37.3	23.0	136.4	6 501	26 150	66 107	54 919	20.3	3.7	12.0	16.8	2.8
College Station-Bryan, TX	369	2 473	94 667	4.8	40.6	34.2	286.9	8 728	22 081	59 322	39 657	33.7	3.0	28.4	32.6	10.9
Colorado Springs, CO	361	3 281	197 030	13.3	26.5	35.3	934.9	8 160	29 238	76 055	57 484	17.9	4.0	10.8	12.4	6.3
Columbia, MO	333	3 288	60 660	11.4	27.3	45.3	220.1	9 502	26 622	66 572	48 953	27.8	4.1	21.2	17.5	8.5
Columbia, SC	576	3 623	219 626	13.2	39.0	30.7	1 323.5	10 816	24 839	63 201	48 672	24.2	2.7	16.6	22.2	8.8
Columbus, GA-AL	413	4 935	89 182	8.6	44.8	21.1	476.1	9 526	21 520	55 878	40 388	31.8	2.1	21.6	30.1	14.7
Columbus, IN	185	3 338	19 136	14.6	45.2	27.0	112.6	9 142	27 383	68 995	52 505	18.9	2.6	12.1	17.4	6.4
Columbus, OH	298	3 448	525 707	16.4	39.3	33.7	3 458.3	12 150	28 601	73 084	54 079	21.7	4.2	14.8	20.8	7.8
Corpus Christi, TX	524	4 261	112 238	8.6	48.9	17.5	676.6	8 522	23 890	64 041	48 688	25.7	2.3	17.3	24.2	12.6
Corvallis, OR	120	2 555	33 582	6.2	19.7	52.2	81.2	9 368	26 293	64 811	47 808	29.2	4.0	23.1	11.4	9.9
Crestview-Fort Walton Beach-Destin, FL	413	2 347	59 174	10.9	40.2	25.6	324.9	8 642	27 419	68 460	53 000	23.3	3.7	15.7	23.6	6.9
Cumberland, MD-WV	309	2 819	24 268	7.4	56.1	16.5	176.8	13 420	19 242	47 952	35 211	38.2	0.9	17.6	23.7	10.9
Dallas-Fort Worth-Arlington, TX	333	3 035	1 909 247	12.7	38.0	32.6	9 993.2	8 068	29 738	81 531	57 398	19.8	6.2	15.0	21.6	8.8
Dallas-Plano-Irving, TX Div 19124	318	2 894	1 268 634	12.7	37.4	34.5	6 682.2	8 094	30 458	83 559	57 585	19.6	6.7	15.0	21.9	9.1
Fort Worth-Arlington, TX Div 23104	362	3 311	640 613	12.7	39.3	29.0	3 311.0	8 018	28 335	77 578	57 109	20.1	5.3	14.8	21.1	8.4
Dalton, GA	238	2 769	36 325	8.1	61.7	12.2	245.8	8 644	17 830	49 143	37 659	31.0	1.5	21.8	31.1	10.7
Danville, IL	662	3 924	17 555	8.0	56.3	13.9	146.8	10 877	22 301	55 410	45 089	27.7	1.8	19.3	29.7	8.6
Daphne-Fairhope-Foley, AL	219	2 496	42 227	12.1	38.7	29.0	243.6	8 279	25 389	65 071	44 874	26.5	3.9	14.5	19.8	6.0
Davenport-Moline-Rock Island, IA-IL	364	2 496	94 571	18.4	41.9	26.5	656.4	10 565	27 639	67 877	51 288	23.6	3.1	14.5	22.9	7.6
Dayton, OH	271	3 323	218 761	19.2	39.9	26.6	1 251.5	11 800	26 164	62 821	47 063	26.5	2.8	16.4	24.9	8.0
Decatur, AL	183	2 478	32 344	6.0	51.5	18.9	228.6	9 376	22 515	56 042	42 598	29.6	1.2	17.5	24.4	11.8
Decatur, IL	354	2 546	27 597	20.4	46.9	21.3	211.2	12 747	26 148	62 101	45 957	28.1	2.5	18.3	25.6	10.6
Deltona-Daytona Beach-Ormond Beach, FL	393	3 107	128 949	15.5	44.0	21.3	594.0	8 029	23 656	56 507	41 554	27.5	2.1	16.2	24.4	6.9
Denver-Aurora-Lakewood, CO	328	2 743	704 517	14.1	30.3	40.3	3 911.3	8 857	33 636	84 810	62 760	17.9	6.6	12.1	16.9	7.0
Des Moines-West Des Moines, IA	268	2 769	157 194	17.3	33.5	35.4	1 068.5	10 248	31 873	80 656	61 194	17.3	5.3	11.0	14.1	9.3
Detroit-Warren-Dearborn, MI	571	2 573	1 109 472	13.1	38.8	29.0	6 622.4	11 295	28 080	70 882	51 857	24.9	4.2	16.9	24.7	9.2
Detroit-Dearborn-Livonia, MI Div 19804	1 052	3 821	478 742	12.5	45.2	22.1	2 525.1	11 693	22 538	57 325	40 487	33.0	2.5	24.9	36.6	13.2
Warren-Troy-Farmington Hills, MI Div 47664	231	1 689	630 730	13.6	34.4	33.6	4 097.4	11 063	31 985	79 946	60 454	19.5	5.4	11.2	15.6	6.7
Dothan, AL	389	2 808	34 888	9.7	49.1	18.3	186.6	8 342	22 492	54 981	40 186	32.2	2.3	18.0	31.1	11.3
Dover, DE	456	2 977	46 791	15.8	45.5	23.9	306.6	13 046	25 192	66 594	54 794	20.2	2.5	12.4	17.1	7.1
Dubuque, IA	160	1 974	26 182	35.3	45.8	26.6	144.7	9 945	26 640	66 198	51 735	21.2	3.6	13.7	17.7	9.2
Duluth, MN-WI	231	3 369	73 068	11.2	38.7	25.2	401.1	11 162	25 425	59 302	46 385	27.7	2.1	17.0	20.0	8.4
Durham-Chapel Hill, NC	375	3 148	153 175	20.3	31.0	45.5	674.5	10 163	31 656	79 146	53 492	22.8	7.0	16.9	18.9	7.4
East Stroudsburg, PA	367	2 451	43 201	12.3	49.4	22.6	435.0	15 532	25 199	69 895	55 536	18.9	2.7	10.8	13.6	3.7
Eau Claire, WI	125	1 688	43 810	10.3	38.8	25.0	251.4	10 899	24 573	61 697	49 046	23.5	2.1	12.0	10.0	8.3
El Centro, CA	304	3 354	53 355	7.7	54.4	12.7	354.7	9 692	16 107	57 230	43 310	29.1	1.9	22.1	29.1	17.7
Elizabethtown-Fort Knox, KY	82	1 494	41 751	12.6	47.7	21.6	212.3	8 617	22 678	58 528	46 680	24.1	1.6	15.8	22.4	9.3
Elkhart-Goshen, IN	287	2 108	50 580	13.6	56.0	17.8	347.2	9 626	20 321	55 697	45 387	24.7	1.7	16.2	20.6	7.8
Elmira, NY	170	2 300	19 237	15.4	48.3	23.9	180.4	14 937	25 674	63 093	45 237	29.5	2.6	17.1	25.9	8.0
El Paso, TX	339	2 168	262 259	6.4	48.8	20.8	1 529.6	8 572	18 302	54 728	39 873	32.3	2.0	22.6	30.8	19.7
Erie, PA	246	2 378	67 618	24.0	50.4	26.6	502.3	13 085	24 248	59 282	44 292	27.8	2.3	18.3	28.4	8.8
Eugene, OR	171	3 565	92 602	10.3	32.3	29.2	443.9	9 761	25 154	60 051	43 459	30.3	2.4	21.5	25.1	9.5
Evansville, IN-KY	274	3 068	79 287	20.0	43.6	24.5	428.0	9 695	24 765	60 899	45 332	26.2	2.2	16.1	24.2	7.6

1. Data for serious crimes have not been adjusted for underreporting; this may affect comparability between geographic areas and over time. 2. Per 100,000 population estimated by the FBI. 3. All persons 3 years old and over enrolled in nursery school through college. 4. Persons 25 years old and over. 5. Elementary and secondary education expenditures. 6. Based on resident population estimated in the 2008-2012 American Community Survey.

Area name	Personal income, 2013										Earnings, 2013		
			Per capita[1]			Supplements to wages and salaries; employer contributions (mil dol)						Contributions for government social insurance (mil dol)	
	Total (mil dol)	Percent change 2012–2013	Dollars	Rank	Wages and salaries (mil dol)	Pension and insurance	Government social insurance	Proprietors' income (mil dol)	Dividends, interest, and rent (mil dol)	Personal transfer receipts (mil dol)	Total (mil dol)	From employee and self-employed	From employer
	62	63	64	65	66	67	68	69	70	71	72	73	74
Cedar Rapids, IA	11 851	1.8	45 159	76	6 636	1 000	518	1 070	2 158	1 770	9 223	550	518
Chambersburg-Waynesboro, PA	5 684	1.6	37 377	240	2 286	493	196	345	1 114	1 190	3 319	202	196
Champaign-Urbana, IL	9 797	4.9	41 662	140	4 732	1 173	305	903	2 165	1 259	7 112	311	305
Charleston, WV	9 530	0.4	42 402	127	5 323	1 010	406	1 127	1 317	2 381	7 866	477	406
Charleston-North Charleston, SC	29 167	2.6	40 953	160	14 483	2 524	1 131	3 349	5 355	4 776	21 487	1 259	1 131
Charlotte-Concord-Gastonia, NC-SC	97 256	2.3	41 645	141	55 881	7 579	4 220	10 966	14 043	15 256	78 646	4 718	4 220
Charlottesville, VA	10 765	1.9	48 045	43	5 117	960	368	1 035	2 819	1 411	7 480	439	368
Chattanooga, TN-GA	20 659	1.7	38 134	218	10 193	1 836	744	2 147	3 126	4 412	14 921	884	744
Cheyenne, WY	4 970	2.2	51 870	25	2 289	457	238	339	1 388	711	3 323	181	238
Chicago-Naperville-Elgin, IL-IN-WI	468 001	1.5	49 071	36	260 863	41 197	18 605	38 430	83 817	66 581	359 095	19 704	18 605
Chicago-Naperville-Arlington Heights, IL Div 16974	365 651	1.6	49 866	NA	210 754	32 676	15 051	32 459	64 449	52 476	290 940	15 885	15 051
Elgin, IL Div 20994	24 683	2.1	39 280	NA	11 231	2 193	829	1 403	4 379	3 353	15 657	820	829
Gary, IN Div 23844	28 447	0.8	40 323	NA	12 527	2 012	944	1 904	3 688	5 664	17 388	1 081	944
Lake County-Kenosha County, IL-WI Div 29404	49 220	1.1	56 524	NA	26 352	4 315	1 780	2 664	11 302	5 088	35 110	1 917	1 780
Chico, CA	8 251	3.4	37 150	247	2 984	704	219	710	1 793	2 159	4 616	289	219
Cincinnati, OH-KY-IN	93 882	1.6	43 923	94	51 362	8 452	3 813	7 566	15 291	15 478	71 193	4 046	3 813
Clarksville, TN-KY	10 792	0.2	39 591	179	5 042	1 286	454	869	2 018	1 827	7 651	363	454
Cleveland, TN	4 123	2.3	34 783	306	1 656	321	126	660	512	1 002	2 762	166	126
Cleveland-Elyria, OH	94 455	1.8	45 747	64	51 660	8 945	3 882	8 884	15 363	17 486	73 371	4 089	3 882
Coeur d'Alene, ID	5 263	3.0	36 478	267	1 960	350	188	338	1 172	1 069	2 836	188	188
College Station-Bryan, TX	7 930	3.2	33 484	336	3 937	758	249	624	1 692	1 218	5 567	262	249
Colorado Springs, CO	27 981	1.6	41 250	151	14 224	2 560	1 133	1 270	6 163	4 484	19 187	999	1 133
Columbia, MO	7 006	2.9	41 028	156	3 859	920	263	436	1 370	1 010	5 478	283	263
Columbia, SC	29 934	2.7	37 711	230	15 972	2 942	1 240	2 019	4 671	5 665	22 173	1 308	1 240
Columbus, GA-AL	12 349	1.4	39 012	194	6 300	1 387	499	622	2 541	2 465	8 808	467	499
Columbus, IN	3 496	0.6	43 923	94	2 423	365	179	270	581	568	3 237	194	179
Columbus, OH	86 289	3.1	43 867	96	49 456	9 114	3 514	7 557	12 024	13 412	69 641	3 607	3 514
Corpus Christi, TX	18 736	3.1	42 331	128	8 724	1 462	628	2 687	3 080	3 606	13 501	682	628
Corvallis, OR	3 507	1.3	40 502	165	1 700	335	145	235	886	495	2 416	144	145
Crestview-Fort Walton Beach-Destin, FL	11 046	2.9	43 556	102	5 355	1 111	444	529	3 347	1 931	7 438	404	444
Cumberland, MD-WV	3 574	2.0	35 311	295	1 512	324	126	172	627	1 071	2 134	141	126
Dallas-Fort Worth-Arlington, TX	320 035	2.9	46 989	52	177 663	22 537	12 245	49 781	49 543	36 909	262 225	13 134	12 245
Dallas-Plano-Irving, TX Div 19124	218 696	2.9	48 591	NA	130 185	15 737	8 869	36 101	33 905	23 497	190 891	9 518	8 869
Fort Worth-Arlington, TX Div 23104	101 339	2.8	43 867	NA	47 478	6 800	3 376	13 680	15 638	13 412	71 334	3 617	3 376
Dalton, GA	4 186	2.1	29 431	374	2 579	450	193	369	616	954	3 591	210	193
Danville, IL	2 883	4.5	35 892	286	1 184	268	90	311	498	729	1 853	101	90
Daphne-Fairhope-Foley, AL	7 646	3.2	39 100	192	2 242	348	173	542	1 557	1 540	3 306	227	173
Davenport-Moline-Rock Island, IA-IL	17 043	1.5	44 420	86	8 674	1 498	651	1 605	3 133	3 033	12 427	707	651
Dayton, OH	32 383	1.4	40 353	169	17 068	3 344	1 316	2 154	5 743	6 714	23 882	1 322	1 316
Decatur, AL	5 172	1.4	33 721	333	2 239	388	170	376	781	1 249	3 174	206	170
Decatur, IL	4 730	1.8	43 280	106	2 458	450	188	428	907	976	3 524	198	188
Deltona-Daytona Beach-Ormond Beach, FL	20 966	1.9	34 900	305	6 718	1 142	505	579	5 800	5 816	8 944	658	505
Denver-Aurora-Lakewood, CO	140 123	2.9	51 946	23	77 541	10 134	5 464	16 831	26 443	15 276	109 970	5 994	5 464
Des Moines-West Des Moines, IA	28 557	2.3	47 612	48	16 850	2 348	1 294	3 357	4 558	3 619	23 849	1 404	1 294
Detroit-Warren-Dearborn, MI	184 199	0.9	42 887	111	100 132	13 993	7 815	14 634	28 265	37 091	136 573	8 536	7 815
Detroit-Dearborn-Livonia, MI Div 19804	63 947	-0.1	36 021	NA	39 375	5 774	3 026	4 309	8 775	18 025	52 483	3 294	3 026
Warren-Troy-Farmington Hills, MI Div 47664	120 251	1.4	47 724	NA	60 757	8 219	4 789	10 325	19 490	19 066	84 090	5 242	4 789
Dothan, AL	5 304	1.5	35 913	285	2 151	376	164	461	907	1 296	3 151	201	164
Dover, DE	6 252	2.4	36 905	256	2 825	705	223	580	1 027	1 472	4 333	230	223
Dubuque, IA	3 945	0.9	41 229	152	2 341	351	192	344	782	682	3 228	201	192
Duluth, MN-WI	11 025	2.8	39 391	187	5 382	933	450	725	1 925	2 655	7 490	475	450
Durham-Chapel Hill, NC	24 066	1.5	45 018	78	17 319	2 570	1 244	2 432	4 725	3 454	23 565	1 377	1 244
East Stroudsburg, PA	5 671	1.0	33 930	327	2 275	549	191	277	889	1 241	3 292	199	191
Eau Claire, WI	6 566	1.6	39 899	176	3 220	705	258	642	1 172	1 190	4 825	284	258
El Centro, CA	5 690	3.6	32 225	360	2 312	690	165	699	761	1 436	3 866	188	165
Elizabethtown-Fort Knox, KY	5 995	0.8	39 582	180	2 683	670	233	440	1 108	1 134	4 026	211	233
Elkhart-Goshen, IN	7 266	3.3	36 229	274	5 028	827	408	623	1 120	1 333	6 885	409	408
Elmira, NY	3 460	0.4	39 096	193	1 644	410	136	177	600	835	2 367	132	136
El Paso, TX	25 891	1.2	31 156	368	12 236	2 615	938	2 690	4 313	5 754	18 480	909	938
Erie, PA	10 575	0.8	37 729	229	5 172	1 135	426	544	1 825	2 579	7 277	438	426
Eugene, OR	13 048	2.1	36 630	263	5 785	1 027	534	876	2 798	3 031	8 221	533	534
Evansville, IN-KY	13 106	1.4	41 701	138	6 449	1 088	493	1 351	2 378	2 498	9 381	568	493

1. Based on the resident population estimated as of July 1 of the year shown.

Area name	Earnings, 2013 (cont.): Percent by selected industries: Farm	Mining	Construction	Manufacturing	Information, professional, scientific, technical services	Retail trade	Finance, insurance, real estate, rental and leasing	Health care and social assistance	Government	Social Security beneficiaries, December 2013: Number	Rate[1]	Supplemental Security Income recipients, December 2013	Housing units, 2014: Total	Percent change, 2000–2014
	75	76	77	78	79	80	81	82	83	84	85	86	87	88
Cedar Rapids, IA	3.2	0.1	6.4	21.4	8.5	7.0	10.1	D	11.0	48 910	186	4 065	114 649	2.1
Chambersburg-Waynesboro, PA	2.3	0.1	4.7	18.9	4.9	7.1	3.2	15.1	18.6	34 515	227	2 729	64 125	1.4
Champaign-Urbana, IL	7.4	D	3.9	6.9	D	4.9	4.0	D	36.4	32 515	138	3 339	102 872	1.7
Charleston, WV	0.0	D	5.8	4.5	D	5.8	D	16.8	18.0	58 595	261	9 649	108 024	-0.2
Charleston-North Charleston, SC	0.1	0.1	5.8	9.8	11.6	6.9	10.9	9.0	23.3	123 110	173	13 533	313 010	4.8
Charlotte-Concord-Gastonia, NC-SC	0.4	0.1	5.6	9.3	D	6.3	16.8	7.2	12.3	385 490	165	41 745	973 046	3.9
Charlottesville, VA	-0.1	D	5.1	D	12.9	5.2	7.8	9.6	33.2	40 345	179	3 229	100 192	4.0
Chattanooga, TN-GA	0.1	0.1	D	14.2	D	7.4	D	D	17.1	115 615	213	13 941	238 229	1.6
Cheyenne, WY	2.1	1.0	8.0	3.4	6.9	6.6	5.9	8.0	38.8	16 755	175	1 579	41 653	2.9
Chicago-Naperville-Elgin, IL-IN-WI	0.3	0.1	4.9	10.6	D	5.1	10.8	9.7	13.0	1 430 680	150	209 676	3 803 716	0.2
Chicago-Naperville-Arlington Heights, IL Div 16974	0.1	0.1	4.6	8.4	16.9	4.6	12.0	9.6	12.5	1 081 675	147	176 785	2 950 948	0.0
Elgin, IL Div 20994	1.5	D	6.9	16.2	8.1	6.3	5.1	11.4	20.0	83 160	132	5 840	225 017	0.8
Gary, IN Div 23844	1.6	0.1	11.1	22.1	4.5	7.1	3.4	13.9	11.0	137 705	195	15 588	296 798	0.9
Lake County-Kenosha County, IL-WI Div 29404	0.1	0.0	3.4	21.1	9.6	7.5	7.0	7.5	14.4	128 140	147	11 463	330 953	0.4
Chico, CA	4.6	0.1	5.6	5.1	7.0	8.9	5.1	19.7	22.4	49 185	221	11 679	97 486	1.7
Cincinnati, OH-KY-IN	0.1	0.2	5.2	12.4	D	5.5	9.5	12.2	12.0	374 945	175	48 224	918 672	0.8
Clarksville, TN-KY	2.1	0.3	4.8	7.9	D	5.0	3.2	6.6	52.0	40 005	146	6 205	114 569	6.7
Cleveland, TN	-0.1	0.1	5.5	21.2	D	6.7	3.9	D	11.5	27 995	236	3 255	50 784	2.8
Cleveland-Elyria, OH	0.1	D	4.5	13.6	10.9	5.3	9.8	14.0	13.7	409 570	198	63 377	956 592	0.1
Coeur d'Alene, ID	0.1	0.9	7.6	9.2	6.9	11.0	6.8	12.4	21.6	32 900	228	2 625	66 130	4.7
College Station-Bryan, TX	0.5	6.8	6.4	5.4	D	7.5	4.4	D	34.7	27 885	117	4 673	100 945	6.2
Colorado Springs, CO	0.0	D	5.0	D	16.2	6.4	6.1	8.9	34.1	99 075	146	8 700	274 896	3.5
Columbia, MO	0.3	0.2	5.0	4.3	7.9	7.3	7.2	11.0	37.4	23 965	140	2 676	73 174	5.2
Columbia, SC	0.5	0.1	5.0	8.8	D	6.4	9.5	9.5	26.3	139 595	176	16 328	341 837	3.1
Columbus, GA-AL	0.3	D	3.9	D	D	5.1	D	10.0	38.6	56 365	178	10 396	131 775	2.8
Columbus, IN	1.5	D	3.5	46.4	4.5	5.3	3.6	6.7	9.9	16 025	201	1 250	33 548	1.4
Columbus, OH	0.5	0.4	4.8	7.9	11.9	6.0	11.1	10.3	18.6	295 970	150	44 921	839 991	2.3
Corpus Christi, TX	1.1	D	12.2	7.7	5.9	5.9	4.2	D	17.6	78 560	177	16 404	188 363	3.0
Corvallis, OR	0.9	0.1	3.1	12.1	11.5	5.3	3.0	14.9	30.4	14 175	165	961	37 107	2.4
Crestview-Fort Walton Beach-Destin, FL	0.3	0.1	4.6	3.8	10.6	6.9	5.7	7.7	40.7	50 225	198	4 179	142 862	3.9
Cumberland, MD-WV	0.1	D	4.9	13.7	D	7.3	4.1	D	26.4	24 060	238	3 016	46 323	-0.1
Dallas-Fort Worth-Arlington, TX	0.0	D	6.4	9.7	D	5.6	D	D	10.3	846 730	124	128 430	2 645 540	4.6
Dallas-Plano-Irving, TX Div 19124	0.0	4.5	6.2	8.7	16.4	5.4	12.4	9.2	9.7	533 055	118	86 150	1 746 201	5.4
Fort Worth-Arlington, TX Div 23104	0.0	7.7	7.0	12.3	8.0	6.3	7.9	0.0	12.0	313 675	136	42 280	899 339	3.3
Dalton, GA	0.3	D	2.2	36.8	D	7.0	2.2	D	11.1	25 810	181	3 642	55 419	-0.8
Danville, IL	9.8	D	2.5	18.8	2.1	6.1	5.5	8.7	21.0	18 815	234	2 825	36 008	-0.9
Daphne-Fairhope-Foley, AL	0.9	0.2	8.4	6.6	5.2	13.5	8.4	11.9	15.1	47 355	242	3 494	107 374	3.2
Davenport-Moline-Rock Island, IA-IL	3.7	D	5.5	15.1	7.0	6.6	5.5	10.5	15.4	77 415	202	7 555	168 289	0.7
Dayton, OH	0.4	0.0	4.1	11.7	D	5.6	6.4	14.9	23.1	159 360	199	20 250	367 824	0.2
Decatur, AL	2.7	D	7.6	30.7	D	6.9	4.0	D	15.3	36 205	236	4 918	66 667	0.4
Decatur, IL	4.2	0.1	6.6	27.5	5.0	5.3	3.5	12.5	11.1	24 670	225	3 253	50 353	-0.2
Deltona-Daytona Beach-Ormond Beach, FL	0.5	D	5.4	7.5	7.2	10.2	5.6	18.5	17.1	170 440	284	13 332	305 655	0.9
Denver-Aurora-Lakewood, CO	0.0	5.0	5.7	5.2	D	4.9	D	8.3	12.7	358 605	133	36 263	1 114 330	3.3
Des Moines-West Des Moines, IA	1.3	0.1	7.9	5.7	9.4	5.4	23.9	9.9	12.5	93 790	156	8 867	254 459	5.9
Detroit-Warren-Dearborn, MI	0.1	D	4.5	15.4	D	5.7	7.4	12.2	10.7	855 560	199	133 065	1 890 911	0.2
Detroit-Dearborn-Livonia, MI Div 19804	0.0	0.2	3.8	14.2	13.9	4.6	5.7	13.9	13.2	355 320	200	84 449	814 399	-0.9
Warren-Troy-Farmington Hills, MI Div 47664	0.1	0.1	4.9	16.2	17.2	6.4	8.5	11.2	9.1	500 240	199	48 616	1 076 512	1.1
Dothan, AL	3.8	D	0.7	7.8	D	9.9	4.4	D	18.6	36 475	247	6 062	68 049	1.7
Dover, DE	1.8	D	4.8	D	4.8	7.3	7.1	12.0	38.9	34 155	201	3 732	67 874	3.9
Dubuque, IA	3.0	D	5.7	19.4	9.0	6.8	8.6	13.9	8.2	19 835	207	1 523	40 369	3.6
Duluth, MN-WI	0.1	7.1	6.6	7.0	5.7	6.9	4.7	20.1	19.7	62 515	223	7 065	141 912	0.3
Durham-Chapel Hill, NC	0.2	0.0	2.5	16.9	13.6	3.6	9.5	13.5	19.9	84 400	158	9 714	233 454	4.8
East Stroudsburg, PA	0.0	0.1	4.3	14.6	4.4	8.5	3.3	11.9	28.3	33 830	202	3 019	80 685	0.4
Eau Claire, WI	1.7	D	6.8	13.9	5.1	8.2	5.7	17.0	16.7	32 690	198	3 121	70 716	2.0
El Centro, CA	14.5	D	3.0	3.4	2.4	6.9	2.6	5.4	38.8	29 090	164	10 735	56 972	1.6
Elizabethtown-Fort Knox, KY	1.5	0.2	3.7	11.4	D	5.5	3.6	D	47.9	27 985	185	4 292	64 168	4.9
Elkhart-Goshen, IN	1.2	0.0	3.3	47.9	2.8	4.6	2.7	8.5	6.7	34 540	172	3 247	77 933	0.2
Elmira, NY	0.1	2.6	5.2	15.9	3.6	7.2	5.1	15.5	24.3	21 180	239	3 604	38 382	0.0
El Paso, TX	0.1	D	D	D	D	7.4	D	10.0	37.1	119 595	143	30 232	288 188	6.0
Erie, PA	0.4	0.2	4.1	22.0	4.9	6.9	7.5	17.1	16.6	60 935	218	11 500	119 816	0.6
Eugene, OR	0.3	0.2	5.5	10.6	8.7	9.0	5.6	16.3	20.0	77 830	219	8 769	157 899	1.1
Evansville, IN-KY	2.3	3.2	8.5	19.7	6.0	6.4	3.6	D	9.7	66 325	211	7 375	140 130	1.0

1. Per 1,000 resident population estimated as of July 1, 2011 of the year shown.

Area name	Housing units, 2013: Occupied units: Total	Owner-occupied: Percent	Owner-occupied: Median value[1]	Median owner cost as a percent of income: With a mortgage	Median owner cost as a percent of income: Without a mortgage[2]	Renter-occupied: Median rent[3]	Renter-occupied: Median rent as a percent of income	Substandard units[4] (percent)	Civilian labor force, 2014: Total	Percent change, 2013–2014	Unemployment: Total	Unemployment: Rate[5]	Civilian employment[6], 2013: Total employed	Percent: Management, professional, and related occupations	Percent: Construction, production, and related occupations
	89	90	91	92	93	94	95	96	97	98	99	100	101	102	103
Cedar Rapids, IA	105 035	73.9	144 500	19.3	12.9	672	27.3	NA	145 142	0.7	6 747	4.6	136 236	36.6	22.5
Chambersburg-Waynesboro, PA	59 145	74.1	176 900	22.3	10.7	791	29.3	NA	76 085	-0.6	4 023	5.3	71 325	31.6	28.7
Champaign-Urbana, IL	90 474	59.5	141 900	19.7	11.0	776	33.9	NA	118 105	0.1	7 129	6.0	115 991	42.6	16.1
Charleston, WV	95 251	70.7	102 600	19.1	10.0	644	26.8	NA	100 183	-1.5	6 311	6.3	97 088	35.5	19.9
Charleston-North Charleston, SC	268 003	63.5	187 700	22.6	11.8	952	32.4	1.8	348 755	1.6	19 111	5.5	338 548	37.2	19.1
Charlotte-Concord-Gastonia, NC-SC	859 709	65.0	164 000	20.7	10.6	835	29.3	2.6	1 191 694	0.8	71 849	6.0	1 108 897	36.9	20.6
Charlottesville, VA	84 595	66.8	261 500	22.5	10.6	1 059	29.4	NA	115 503	2.5	5 204	4.5	102 542	49.5	14.7
Chattanooga, TN-GA	209 304	67.4	142 600	20.6	10.0	722	29.4	2.7	249 173	-3.0	16 223	6.5	246 403	36.3	23.1
Cheyenne, WY	35 785	68.4	197 800	20.9	10.0	788	31.0	NA	48 899	0.6	2 193	4.5	47 460	34.1	22.4
Chicago-Naperville-Elgin, IL-IN-WI	3 450 331	64.1	206 300	24.5	14.1	959	30.3	3.6	4 904 192	-0.2	345 576	7.0	4 551 636	37.7	20.1
Chicago-Naperville-Arlington Heights, IL Div 16974	2 667 460	62.1	216 400	24.9	14.6	973	30.3	3.8	3 793 550	-0.3	268 846	7.1	3 510 636	38.5	19.3
Elgin, IL Div 20994	209 499	70.9	194 000	24.5	13.3	939	31.0	4.4	318 695	-0.1	21 964	6.9	307 695	32.8	23.5
Gary, IN Div 23844	265 555	70.6	144 400	20.6	11.6	813	30.2	2.3	338 206	0.5	25 539	7.6	315 771	30.2	28.3
Lake County-Kenosha County, IL-WI Div 29404	307 817	71.5	213 100	23.9	13.5	962	30.7	2.5	453 741	0.2	29 227	6.4	417 534	40.7	18.9
Chico, CA	85 158	57.5	217 600	24.7	11.9	864	36.0	3.7	101 924	0.0	8 820	8.7	91 352	33.9	18.4
Cincinnati, OH-KY-IN	822 005	65.5	152 000	20.8	11.6	729	28.2	1.7	1 077 786	-0.3	58 202	5.4	1 013 976	38.1	19.4
Clarksville, TN-KY	96 258	59.5	139 900	21.9	10.0	847	27.5	NA	107 943	-2.2	7 495	6.9	103 333	33.9	26.2
Cleveland, TN	46 157	69.1	139 500	20.5	10.3	671	30.6	NA	55 318	-3.1	3 562	6.4	50 919	27.7	26.1
Cleveland-Elyria, OH	844 428	64.8	136 100	21.0	12.6	734	30.6	1.3	1 046 490	0.4	64 491	6.2	970 595	38.0	19.8
Coeur d'Alene, ID	55 836	74.4	170 800	22.4	10.4	798	29.5	NA	70 488	1.8	3 982	5.6	62 483	29.4	21.6
College Station-Bryan, TX	85 573	48.6	137 400	20.0	10.1	831	39.0	NA	119 710	1.3	4 838	4.0	112 510	36.8	20.4
Colorado Springs, CO	250 601	63.4	211 100	22.2	10.0	976	30.8	2.8	319 744	-0.1	19 291	6.0	298 994	41.1	17.2
Columbia, MO	67 680	53.2	172 900	19.6	10.0	781	33.7	NA	98 362	1.0	4 058	4.1	95 032	44.1	14.4
Columbia, SC	296 310	67.5	138 900	21.3	10.3	828	29.7	2.2	383 675	1.0	22 291	5.8	364 033	36.2	20.2
Columbus, GA-AL	110 901	53.7	132 600	23.7	12.3	788	30.4	NA	127 600	-1.7	10 050	7.9	115 278	29.8	21.9
Columbus, IN	30 359	69.5	129 800	19.4	10.5	743	25.3	NA	42 798	2.8	1 906	4.5	37 170	42.2	25.9
Columbus, OH	750 394	61.8	154 800	21.3	12.2	804	28.3	2.4	1 027 198	0.9	49 505	4.8	972 725	40.2	19.0
Corpus Christi, TX	160 549	59.8	106 700	21.2	10.9	842	28.1	5.2	212 176	1.1	11 067	5.2	206 600	26.0	25.6
Corvallis, OR	33 609	57.3	276 300	22.5	10.0	839	37.5	NA	44 024	1.2	2 341	5.3	38 879	47.8	15.5
Crestview-Fort Walton Beach-Destin, FL	98 219	65.2	181 100	24.9	10.0	966	29.2	NA	120 345	0.9	6 204	5.2	107 475	30.2	18.5
Cumberland, MD-WV	37 773	67.3	117 100	21.0	12.3	486	27.1	NA	44 917	-0.8	3 274	7.3	39 118	28.9	23.4
Dallas-Fort Worth-Arlington, TX	2 406 092	59.5	152 700	21.5	11.7	908	28.6	5.0	3 559 553	2.1	177 101	5.0	3 327 474	37.6	20.9
Dallas-Plano-Irving, TX Div 19124	1 590 389	57.8	161 500	21.8	11.7	925	28.6	5.1	2 368 870	2.5	118 146	5.0	2 222 696	38.6	19.8
Fort Worth-Arlington, TX Div 23104	815 703	62.8	137 700	21.0	11.5	876	28.6	4.7	1 190 683	1.4	58 955	5.0	1 104 778	35.6	23.2
Dalton, GA	48 318	62.7	107 900	22.2	10.0	654	31.1	NA	60 832	0.4	5 074	8.3	61 049	21.4	38.5
Danville, IL	31 482	72.0	72 000	17.9	11.4	587	29.8	NA	35 643	-1.1	3 059	8.6	33 313	26.0	31.3
Daphne-Fairhope-Foley, AL	70 259	69.5	167 500	22.0	10.7	809	32.9	NA	85 815	0.8	5 195	6.1	85 191	32.3	24.5
Davenport-Moline-Rock Island, IA-IL	153 566	69.2	126 200	19.1	11.1	667	27.4	NA	195 158	0.0	12 258	6.3	183 299	32.2	25.9
Dayton, OH	323 890	63.6	120 600	21.4	12.2	733	28.6	1.7	381 617	-0.4	21 987	5.8	362 098	37.8	21.2
Decatur, AL	60 129	73.5	113 600	21.6	10.0	589	25.2	NA	69 787	-1.8	4 847	6.9	62 823	26.5	33.2
Decatur, IL	44 965	71.3	96 100	18.9	11.5	648	30.2	NA	50 806	-3.2	4 406	8.7	49 327	29.8	25.5
Deltona-Daytona Beach-Ormond Beach, FL	235 616	70.8	131 500	25.3	12.4	918	34.7	2.8	282 340	0.9	19 225	6.8	232 730	29.1	20.6
Denver-Aurora-Lakewood, CO	1 035 096	63.5	257 000	22.2	10.0	998	30.6	2.9	1 495 013	1.7	72 222	4.8	1 383 946	41.6	17.1
Des Moines-West Des Moines, IA	233 644	69.1	159 100	19.3	11.1	795	27.0	3.0	339 767	2.6	14 388	4.2	321 187	39.6	18.0
Detroit-Warren-Dearborn, MI	1 658 085	68.6	120 500	21.2	13.4	829	31.8	2.3	2 021 137	-0.2	171 439	8.5	1 907 552	36.7	20.8
Detroit-Dearborn-Livonia, MI Div 19804	664 415	62.7	78 100	21.9	14.5	783	35.7	3.1	766 626	-0.7	76 863	10.0	696 644	31.3	23.7
Warren-Troy-Farmington Hills, MI Div 47664	993 670	72.6	150 400	20.9	12.6	874	29.2	1.8	1 254 511	0.2	94 576	7.5	1 210 908	39.8	19.1
Dothan, AL	57 990	68.3	107 600	21.2	10.0	650	28.3	1.4	62 416	-1.8	4 286	6.9	62 025	28.6	28.4
Dover, DE	62 053	71.9	192 800	23.4	11.6	955	28.8	NA	75 239	2.0	4 780	6.4	76 286	32.3	25.1
Dubuque, IA	36 801	70.8	146 100	20.7	10.0	681	29.0	NA	55 858	1.5	2 387	4.3	50 300	33.2	25.0
Duluth, MN-WI	115 589	71.2	138 800	21.4	11.0	657	31.3	1.7	142 959	-0.5	7 386	5.2	135 333	31.8	21.8
Durham-Chapel Hill, NC	209 290	59.2	197 900	20.3	10.3	870	29.2	2.9	273 850	0.5	13 614	5.0	259 448	47.3	14.0
East Stroudsburg, PA	58 496	77.2	176 600	26.5	17.7	1 031	33.9	NA	79 673	-2.4	5 919	7.4	77 282	30.5	22.8
Eau Claire, WI	64 494	67.7	149 600	20.8	11.6	709	28.7	NA	91 450	0.4	4 490	4.9	85 256	32.4	22.8
El Centro, CA	47 430	54.1	148 400	24.6	10.4	759	30.7	11.3	80 266	1.9	18 957	23.6	59 931	22.0	29.8
Elizabethtown-Fort Knox, KY	56 888	63.5	136 500	20.3	10.0	698	26.6	NA	64 423	-2.8	4 138	6.4	63 948	32.6	28.0
Elkhart-Goshen, IN	71 056	69.3	119 300	19.5	10.2	696	30.2	NA	102 117	3.0	5 305	5.2	92 067	22.7	39.5
Elmira, NY	35 838	67.4	96 500	19.4	12.5	677	34.5	NA	38 420	-3.0	2 407	6.3	38 468	36.4	21.4
El Paso, TX	259 580	60.9	110 900	23.4	11.3	749	29.8	6.3	349 194	-0.3	22 724	6.5	328 688	29.9	22.9
Erie, PA	110 733	68.1	116 100	20.6	12.8	697	32.1	NA	134 343	-1.2	8 231	6.1	128 869	32.4	24.1
Eugene, OR	144 166	60.0	206 700	24.1	12.2	863	38.8	3.0	169 465	1.2	11 980	7.1	160 005	35.7	19.9
Evansville, IN-KY	124 343	70.2	120 900	19.8	11.1	674	30.4	NA	158 139	0.8	8 573	5.4	143 628	33.0	24.3

1. Specified owner-occupied units. 2. A value of 10.0 represents 10 percent or less. 3. Specified renter-occupied units. 4. Overcrowded or lacking complete plumbing facilities.
5. Percent of civilian labor force. 6. Persons 16 years old and over.

Area name	Private nonfarm establishments, employment and payroll, 2013: Number of establish-ments	Employment: Total	Employment: Health care and social assistance	Employment: Manufac-turing	Employment: Retail trade	Employment: Finance and insurance	Employment: Professional, scientific, and technical services	Annual payroll: Total (mil dol)	Annual payroll: Average per employee (dollars)	Agriculture, 2012: Farms: Number	Farms: Percent with: Fewer than 50 acres	Farms: Percent with: 500 acres or more	Farm operators whose principal occu-pation is farming (percent)
	104	105	106	107	108	109	110	111	112	113	114	115	116
Cedar Rapids, IA	6 484	124 987	17 529	18 463	16 379	9 565	5 921	5 469	43 760	3 678	32.5	19.9	55.6
Chambersburg-Waynesboro, PA	3 022	47 802	7 710	8 448	7 317	1 143	1 768	1 709	35 749	1 596	35.9	6.3	60.8
Champaign-Urbana, IL	4 842	73 439	D	7 827	11 308	3 236	3 061	2 684	36 551	2 284	28.5	32.7	56.8
Charleston, WV	5 574	95 494	20 222	3 084	12 536	5 016	6 192	3 944	41 296	343	29.2	1.7	40.5
Charleston-North Charleston, SC	16 973	246 959	34 584	23 481	36 393	7 582	19 074	9 918	40 161	1 143	56.3	7.0	45.2
Charlotte-Concord-Gastonia, NC-SC	55 460	938 684	123 577	90 924	110 754	76 905	57 992	45 577	48 554	7 328	50.8	4.6	44.6
Charlottesville, VA	5 920	78 200	16 741	3 936	11 137	4 093	5 954	3 538	45 244	2 311	33.3	8.0	43.4
Chattanooga, TN-GA	11 118	209 546	30 355	33 517	25 792	13 516	8 337	8 009	38 218	2 018	44.2	5.0	43.8
Cheyenne, WY	2 909	33 066	6 732	1 172	5 645	1 725	1 891	1 311	39 648	1 116	33.5	31.2	37.3
Chicago-Naperville-Elgin, IL-IN-WI	239 691	4 004 396	586 050	386 575	437 570	224 582	324 703	215 199	53 741	6 841	47.6	18.3	56.1
Chicago-Naperville-Arlington Heights, IL Div 16974	X	X	X	X	X	X	X	X	X	2 789	48.8	16.7	58.6
Elgin, IL Div 20994	X	X	X	X	X	X	X	X	X	1 470	40.2	22.6	63.2
Gary, IN Div 23844	X	X	X	X	X	X	X	X	X	1 874	45.0	21.5	48.8
Lake County-Kenosha County, IL-WI Div 29404	X	X	X	X	X	X	X	X	X	708	65.4	7.8	51.4
Chico, CA	4 637	56 166	13 454	4 102	10 494	2 126	2 507	1 962	34 940	2 056	66.8	7.0	59.4
Cincinnati, OH-KY-IN	45 330	878 601	138 343	92 484	103 051	54 400	55 135	40 800	46 438	9 242	46.3	4.5	40.7
Clarksville, TN-KY	4 203	66 501	11 323	11 327	11 652	2 117	2 509	2 161	32 493	2 359	31.5	9.6	41.3
Cleveland, TN	2 091	39 190	5 216	7 890	5 042	1 641	850	1 419	36 214	1 062	49.4	4.8	44.9
Cleveland-Elyria, OH	51 352	915 152	177 257	121 442	100 391	53 403	50 171	42 518	46 460	2 975	59.3	3.6	49.1
Coeur d'Alene, ID	4 345	44 971	8 639	4 268	8 164	2 035	2 881	1 564	34 779	824	58.4	6.7	48.1
College Station-Bryan, TX	4 597	63 234	8 746	5 167	11 310	1 836	2 947	2 150	34 003	4 361	35.0	10.1	44.6
Colorado Springs, CO	16 681	227 349	32 839	10 625	30 759	9 809	20 957	9 631	42 362	1 329	45.4	17.6	48.5
Columbia, MO	4 447	71 502	16 923	3 848	11 278	6 890	3 682	2 595	36 289	1 171	39.5	8.6	38.3
Columbia, SC	16 688	274 169	43 142	26 267	37 291	21 474	15 170	10 570	38 551	3 085	44.1	7.2	42.0
Columbus, GA-AL	5 594	93 312	16 471	10 046	13 577	D	2 886	3 405	36 496	770	32.2	13.1	42.2
Columbus, IN	1 827	43 638	4 750	11 686	4 655	926	3 362	1 954	44 780	623	44.1	14.4	44.8
Columbus, OH	40 433	821 998	132 371	60 750	96 690	78 036	49 138	37 229	45 291	8 198	47.4	9.9	43.1
Corpus Christi, TX	9 419	153 064	28 716	11 613	21 422	4 535	6 214	6 200	40 506	1 555	45.8	20.6	38.6
Corvallis, OR	2 081	25 350	5 478	3 002	3 530	592	2 069	1 096	43 217	886	71.4	5.6	46.3
Crestview-Fort Walton Beach-Destin, FL	6 904	75 730	11 250	2 627	15 592	2 663	6 619	2 577	34 032	1 147	46.7	5.8	41.9
Cumberland, MD-WV	2 062	30 602	7 072	4 401	4 827	984	1 196	1 003	32 775	720	32.9	5.3	37.2
Dallas-Fort Worth-Arlington, TX	148 959	2 767 535	336 974	231 789	319 127	194 739	217 297	141 881	51 266	29 659	61.7	4.8	35.8
Dallas-Plano-Irving, TX Div 19124	X	X	X	X	X	X	X	X	X	16 257	61.9	4.6	35.6
Fort Worth-Arlington, TX Div 23104	X	X	X	X	X	X	X	X	X	13 402	61.5	4.9	36.1
Dalton, GA	2 570	53 437	4 830	19 335	5 587	864	1 671	1 954	36 566	698	46.7	3.2	44.6
Danville, IL	1 460	23 526	5 001	5 043	3 518	1 417	407	887	37 693	956	36.6	29.5	54.5
Daphne-Fairhope-Foley, AL	4 871	54 988	6 843	3 939	12 940	1 611	1 979	1 669	30 351	989	52.6	8.1	45.8
Davenport-Moline-Rock Island, IA-IL	9 028	160 913	24 296	24 954	21 777	6 136	6 240	6 751	41 957	3 513	34.0	19.0	55.7
Dayton, OH	16 610	309 248	62 385	40 941	39 545	12 615	22 592	12 710	41 100	2 638	59.4	8.7	41.3
Decatur, AL	2 996	46 801	6 665	12 339	6 384	1 514	1 470	1 846	39 441	2 788	42.7	4.1	42.7
Decatur, IL	2 456	46 406	7 968	7 758	5 775	1 415	1 239	1 876	40 430	674	35.9	29.5	59.1
Deltona-Daytona Beach-Ormond Beach, FL	13 835	147 846	28 734	8 651	27 561	5 080	6 864	4 767	32 245	1 481	78.8	3.4	55.0
Denver-Aurora-Lakewood, CO	76 185	1 122 319	135 110	57 029	128 695	66 008	108 445	59 070	52 632	4 856	52.4	14.4	43.8
Des Moines-West Des Moines, IA	15 082	291 244	39 703	19 410	37 035	48 261	16 089	13 409	46 042	4 898	41.1	16.0	44.2
Detroit-Warren-Dearborn, MI	97 343	1 621 981	258 338	207 036	196 998	76 560	159 919	80 846	49 844	4 242	56.9	5.8	54.0
Detroit-Dearborn-Livonia, MI Div 19804	X	X	X	X	X	X	X	X	X	287	77.7	1.4	59.9
Warren-Troy-Farmington Hills, MI Div 47664	X	X	X	X	X	X	X	X	X	3 955	55.3	0.1	50.5
Dothan, AL	3 395	49 684	10 401	4 920	8 824	1 428	1 400	1 786	35 944	2 331	31.5	12.2	43.5
Dover, DE	3 166	48 071	9 638	4 450	9 019	1 242	2 111	1 712	35 624	863	54.5	9.0	56.8
Dubuque, IA	2 772	53 122	7 764	9 030	7 207	3 283	2 700	1 982	37 306	1 462	28.3	10.3	52.5
Duluth, MN-WI	7 025	106 699	27 603	7 003	15 873	4 201	3 863	4 131	38 718	1 550	25.4	6.1	41.0
Durham-Chapel Hill, NC	11 860	224 978	41 004	15 455	24 157	7 637	31 277	11 886	52 830	2 410	48.6	4.0	46.7
East Stroudsburg, PA	3 360	44 388	6 627	D	8 954	988	1 276	1 546	34 822	283	53.0	2.5	55.1
Eau Claire, WI	4 226	68 896	14 285	10 083	10 660	3 326	2 374	2 450	35 556	3 070	30.4	7.2	45.1
El Centro, CA	2 419	31 319	4 634	3 670	7 589	D	775	979	31 268	421	29.7	40.6	69.4
Elizabethtown-Fort Knox, KY	2 894	41 409	8 124	6 360	6 571	1 731	1 705	1 328	32 065	2 831	44.0	5.5	44.5
Elkhart-Goshen, IN	4 853	112 276	10 183	57 400	8 753	1 962	1 865	4 523	40 288	1 724	62.8	3.9	38.3
Elmira, NY	1 816	31 960	6 705	5 677	5 285	997	735	1 193	37 341	372	27.2	4.3	53.8
El Paso, TX	13 847	221 514	39 531	14 179	37 307	6 619	9 467	6 716	30 317	824	67.7	17.0	43.9
Erie, PA	6 229	113 617	24 201	21 565	16 143	D	3 649	4 096	36 047	1 422	41.2	4.1	48.7
Eugene, OR	9 538	117 026	21 572	12 753	18 846	5 316	5 247	4 215	36 016	2 660	73.9	2.9	44.5
Evansville, IN-KY	7 596	147 729	25 091	20 946	17 039	4 774	5 242	5 545	37 534	1 527	41.5	19.9	48.6

Area name	Agriculture, 2012 (cont.)															
	Land in farms					Value of land and buildings (dollars)		Value of machinery and equipment, average per farm (dollars)	Value of products sold				Percent of farms with sales of:		Government payments	
	Acreage (1,000)	Percent change, 2007–2012	Acres: Average size of farm	Acres: Total irrigated (1,000)	Acres: Total cropland (1,000)	Average per farm	Average per acre		Total (mil dol)	Average per farm (dollars)	Percent from: Crops	Percent from: Livestock and poultry products	$10,000 or more	$100,000 or more	Total ($1,000)	Percent of farms
	117	118	119	120	121	122	123	124	125	126	127	128	129	130	131	132
Cedar Rapids, IA	1 075	1.4	292	0.4	930.0	2 020 529	6 910	203 111	918.4	249 694	69.5	30.5	63.3	38.3	28 988	76.7
Chambersburg-Waynesboro, PA	265	9.0	166	2.8	201.8	1 101 504	6 646	133 634	413.8	259 277	21.6	78.4	66.3	40.4	4 302	34.1
Champaign-Urbana, IL	1 184	8.8	518	19.6	1 140.6	4 153 230	8 014	311 067	802.9	351 514	92.5	7.5	73.2	50.6	21 102	84.3
Charleston, WV	48	5.0	141	D	6.4	285 079	2 024	31 985	1.9	5 522	32.7	67.3	15.2	0.3	D	7.6
Charleston-North Charleston, SC	185	16.1	162	4.0	62.8	651 877	4 027	59 942	D	D	D	52.2	27.9	7.1	1 317	18.1
Charlotte-Concord-Gastonia, NC-SC	939	2.4	128	5.0	437.2	717 330	5 599	71 406	D	D	D	D	31.1	10.8	D	13.6
Charlottesville, VA	407	4.8	176	2.5	114.7	1 095 125	6 216	61 828	101.3	43 836	40.3	59.7	35.3	5.0	871	13.3
Chattanooga, TN-GA	267	2.2	132	D	94.7	532 958	4 035	67 110	213.6	105 852	10.7	89.3	31.1	9.0	1 684	11.3
Cheyenne, WY	1 676	-0.9	1 502	59.3	338.1	1 079 159	719	110 585	190.7	170 918	24.4	75.6	37.0	17.6	4 938	32.7
Chicago-Naperville-Elgin, IL-IN-WI	2 232	-2.6	326	D	2 069.2	2 377 211	7 285	210 709	2 187.2	319 717	75.5	24.5	57.9	36.1	44 738	55.3
Chicago-Naperville-Arlington Heights, IL Div 16974	831	-0.5	298	D	776.8	2 382 011	7 995	200 859	604.2	216 622	89.5	10.5	58.1	33.3	14 208	51.8
Elgin, IL Div 20994	566	0.6	385	5.1	537.8	3 142 503	8 157	253 384	671.1	456 510	74.7	25.3	66.4	48.0	16 157	63.7
Gary, IN Div 23844	728	-5.9	389	45.5	664.5	2 295 203	5 904	227 225	807.7	430 977	66.3	33.7	55.1	36.6	12 509	64.2
Lake County-Kenosha County, IL-WI Div 29404	107	-10.3	151	0.7	90.1	986 410	6 547	117 194	104.3	147 323	70.9	29.1	47.2	21.6	1 864	28.2
Chico, CA	381	1.9	185	199.7	227.3	1 408 199	7 599	135 591	541.3	263 266	97.3	2.7	59.7	26.2	9 386	13.7
Cincinnati, OH-KY-IN	1 216	-5.6	132	D	698.5	582 601	4 427	73 512	418.6	45 298	82.2	17.8	31.2	7.8	14 347	34.1
Clarksville, TN-KY	637	0.5	270	5.5	401.2	958 646	3 552	104 747	280.3	118 814	80.1	19.9	43.1	15.8	9 847	46.5
Cleveland, TN	122	-4.6	115	0.2	44.8	593 111	5 157	61 272	153.7	144 771	6.4	93.6	31.5	12.4	397	9.4
Cleveland-Elyria, OH	304	3.1	102	4.4	217.0	614 628	6 011	86 924	375.3	126 146	83.2	16.8	42.2	13.4	3 173	19.7
Coeur d'Alene, ID	124	-5.1	151	13.8	64.3	624 138	4 139	57 726	23.7	28 750	83.8	16.2	19.5	4.1	1 075	20.1
College Station-Bryan, TX	1 102	0.9	253	46.6	231.0	736 281	2 914	63 936	321.5	73 722	24.9	75.1	32.1	5.4	5 786	11.1
Colorado Springs, CO	720	4.4	542	8.3	57.0	696 877	1 287	43 971	45.2	33 977	46.2	53.8	23.9	4.8	1 334	10.2
Columbia, MO	241	-7.0	206	5.3	144.4	749 119	3 644	69 631	52.2	44 565	66.0	34.0	34.9	8.1	1 837	31.0
Columbia, SC	522	3.0	169	D	198.1	537 771	3 177	78 787	578.6	187 568	26.8	73.2	29.9	11.0	4 185	19.8
Columbus, GA-AL	206	-3.8	267	5.7	51.8	724 603	2 715	63 508	58.6	76 142	D	D	25.8	6.0	1 166	26.8
Columbus, IN	172	3.2	275	13.5	153.4	1 619 191	5 878	151 406	95.6	153 387	89.5	10.5	54.9	27.1	4 647	63.7
Columbus, OH	1 746	5.0	213	2.9	1 448.9	1 049 293	4 928	131 542	1 180.0	143 942	76.3	23.7	42.8	18.9	28 755	43.7
Corpus Christi, TX	938	0.9	603	6.0	612.9	949 925	1 575	166 062	172.2	110 713	85.3	14.8	31.6	12.9	9 227	35.0
Corvallis, OR	124	8.2	140	11.3	68.2	830 059	5 932	68 867	103.3	116 597	78.2	21.8	28.6	10.4	486	6.4
Crestview-Fort Walton Beach-Destin, FL	209	8.7	183	1.5	49.3	565 418	3 097	49 066	38.8	33 870	49.0	51.0	22.1	5.3	1 802	27.6
Cumberland, MD-WV	112	-1.9	156	0.1	28.5	493 965	3 163	50 556	25.4	35 232	13.4	86.6	25.8	3.8	510	19.7
Dallas-Fort Worth-Arlington, TX	4 075	10.8	137	29.3	1 275.6	585 215	4 260	50 241	743.8	25 077	46.4	53.6	19.6	2.8	10 166	7.2
Dallas-Plano-Irving, TX Div 19124	2 203	9.1	136	18.2	853.9	558 320	4 120	49 299	483.1	29 718	53.6	46.4	19.4	2.9	7 646	9.0
Fort Worth-Arlington, TX Div 23104	1 872	12.9	140	11.1	421.7	617 838	4 424	51 384	260.7	19 449	33.3	66.7	19.9	2.7	2 520	4.9
Dalton, GA	86	4.1	123	0.6	29.3	560 004	4 542	73 451	222.9	319 338	5.8	94.2	37.8	17.3	358	11.6
Danville, IL	434	-5.0	454	0.2	409.5	3 200 276	7 043	259 283	283.6	296 653	95.7	4.3	60.4	41.8	7 122	76.2
Daphne-Fairhope-Foley, AL	192	1.3	194	7.7	100.9	773 980	3 980	107 905	135.6	137 070	85.3	14.7	35.2	11.7	2 649	26.7
Davenport-Moline-Rock Island, IA-IL	1 101	-10.0	313	21.3	970.1	2 141 963	6 834	206 181	964.4	274 514	77.8	22.2	59.6	39.0	28 824	74.8
Dayton, OH	454	-3.5	172	4.2	394.2	1 006 136	5 845	111 095	282.7	107 154	89.5	10.5	44.1	17.8	6 976	51.1
Decatur, AL	396	3.2	142	5.0	167.3	471 748	3 318	68 907	301.3	108 081	23.3	76.7	32.3	11.8	6 226	31.2
Decatur, IL	337	15.8	499	0.0	321.7	3 911 432	7 833	294 921	211.3	313 540	95.7	4.3	66.0	42.7	5 762	80.1
Deltona-Daytona Beach-Ormond Beach, FL	150	5.6	101	12.9	28.8	564 216	5 584	45 579	128.4	86 726	90.0	10.0	35.0	9.6	D	7.6
Denver-Aurora-Lakewood, CO	2 490	-8.7	513	D	923.4	890 955	1 737	67 853	D	D	D	D	24.4	6.5	D	17.4
Des Moines-West Des Moines, IA	1 371	-3.9	280	D	1 079.5	1 644 653	5 875	143 481	891.6	182 028	70.5	29.5	49.3	22.9	32 090	65.6
Detroit-Warren-Dearborn, MI	557	2.2	131	7.3	437.7	626 459	4 770	106 037	399.2	94 113	83.9	16.1	41.1	14.6	6 302	21.4
Detroit-Dearborn-Livonia, MI Div 19804	16	-9.6	55	0.3	10.9	408 840	7 442	80 902	26.5	92 456	98.2	1.8	36.9	8.4	102	9.4
Warren-Troy-Farmington Hills, MI Div 47664	541	2.6	137	7.0	426.9	642 251	4 692	107 860	372.7	94 233	82.9	17.1	41.4	15.1	6 200	22.3
Dothan, AL	587	-0.7	252	20.0	263.4	586 922	2 332	93 694	342.7	147 028	44.1	55.9	34.8	15.3	13 121	60.3
Dover, DE	172	-0.9	200	31.8	147.4	1 596 656	7 999	121 074	277.7	321 816	D	D	53.3	29.8	2 550	37.2
Dubuque, IA	291	-6.2	199	0.0	224.3	1 214 544	6 093	172 274	387.8	265 260	31.0	69.0	67.5	39.7	11 080	81.2
Duluth, MN-WI	290	-9.1	187	D	131.9	345 245	1 843	52 513	35.8	23 111	54.9	45.1	34.8	3.6	D	7.3
Durham-Chapel Hill, NC	285	-1.5	118	5.1	104.5	611 832	5 181	58 915	245.0	101 639	28.0	72.0	35.7	9.9	2 245	21.0
East Stroudsburg, PA	26	-9.2	94	0.1	13.0	735 583	7 861	71 198	11.0	38 777	66.8	33.2	35.7	8.5	174	15.5
Eau Claire, WI	588	5.3	192	8.7	378.7	540 963	2 823	99 430	366.5	119 378	41.7	58.3	47.9	20.6	8 327	53.8
El Centro, CA	516	20.7	1 225	455.0	487.9	8 577 865	7 002	745 304	1 888.6	4 486 078	69.4	30.6	84.3	66.7	2 788	29.5
Elizabethtown-Fort Knox, KY	434	-7.4	153	0.9	245.1	523 605	3 412	77 721	136.4	48 180	66.5	33.5	36.8	7.3	4 749	44.3
Elkhart-Goshen, IN	173	5.8	100	25.5	140.2	808 782	8 067	83 012	296.8	172 178	28.0	72.0	51.8	27.4	2 785	20.1
Elmira, NY	58	-10.8	156	0.2	28.1	376 065	2 407	75 599	16.0	43 143	41.2	58.8	28.5	8.6	482	22.8
El Paso, TX	2 461	1.4	2 986	43.0	101.6	2 030 155	680	101 518	80.0	97 103	80.4	19.6	33.7	12.0	2 091	14.7
Erie, PA	169	-2.6	119	0.9	96.2	407 705	3 438	75 158	91.7	64 469	76.5	23.5	41.5	12.8	1 693	20.5
Eugene, OR	220	-10.6	83	19.3	100.0	563 427	6 824	49 734	142.5	53 574	74.6	25.4	23.5	5.6	575	5.1
Evansville, IN-KY	581	-0.1	380	D	524.8	1 668 276	4 386	228 634	294.2	192 650	90.1	9.9	51.7	27.9	10 066	67.8

Table C. Metropolitan Areas — **Water Use, Wholesale Trade, Retail Trade, and Real Estate**

Area name	Water use, 2010: Total water withdrawn (mil gal/day)	Water use, 2010: Gallons withdrawn per person per day	Wholesale trade,[1] 2007: Number of establish-ments	Wholesale trade,[1] 2007: Number of employees	Wholesale trade,[1] 2007: Sales (mil dol)	Wholesale trade,[1] 2007: Annual payroll (mil dol)	Retail trade, 2007: Number of establish-ments	Retail trade, 2007: Number of employees	Retail trade, 2007: Sales (mil dol)	Retail trade, 2007: Annual payroll (mil dol)	Real estate and rental and leasing, 2007: Number of establish-ments	Real estate and rental and leasing, 2007: Number of employees	Real estate and rental and leasing, 2007: Receipts (mil dol)	Real estate and rental and leasing, 2007: Annual payroll (mil dol)
	133	134	135	136	137	138	139	140	141	142	143	144	145	146
Cedar Rapids, IA	153.4	595	363	4 901	2 864.0	223.9	971	16 000	4 026.9	346.5	264	1 765	363.3	93.1
Chambersburg-Waynesboro, PA	19.1	127	120	D	D	D	503	7 526	1 750.0	160.6	92	485	71.2	13.7
Champaign-Urbana, IL	42.0	181	227	3 715	3 163.0	139.6	773	12 055	2 578.2	232.9	246	1 707	352.2	51.7
Charleston, WV	595.0	2 620	280	D	D	D	958	14 624	3 179.2	278.6	286	D	D	D
Charleston-North Charleston, SC	658.6	991	649	8 849	5 204.1	411.8	2 799	37 845	8 752.8	841.3	1 044	5 212	935.9	169.8
Charlotte-Concord-Gastonia, NC-SC	4 214.7	1 901	3 180	D	D	D	7 819	110 312	28 005.2	2 521.9	3 034	D	D	D
Charlottesville, VA	148.2	678	161	2 025	797.2	97.5	900	11 702	2 708.4	274.7	316	1 710	239.9	52.9
Chattanooga, TN-GA	1 991.2	3 770	608	D	D	D	2 094	27 398	6 586.2	607.2	501	D	D	D
Cheyenne, WY	236.4	2 577	98	800	628.1	35.2	360	5 603	1 720.5	133.4	134	519	94.2	14.3
Chicago-Naperville-Elgin, IL-IN-WI	7 722.8	816	12 995	211 156	191 268.1	12 409.8	30 234	475 144	129 112.0	11 514.4	11 251	75 220	19 819.6	3 665.8
Chicago-Naperville-Arlington Heights, IL Div 16974	4 602.2	634	10 326	163 439	148 730.8	9 253.4	22 837	357 638	90 635.7	8 545.0	9 044	64 016	17 705.8	3 253.6
Elgin, IL Div 20994	76.2	123	847	11 478	9 839.3	642.5	1 944	29 953	6 778.5	638.3	568	3 327	487.5	100.2
Gary, IN Div 23844	2 357.1	3 329	593	7 564	5 096.9	370.2	2 397	35 715	9 560.9	758.3	645	3 292	456.8	86.1
Lake County-Kenosha County, IL-WI Div 29404	687.4	790	1 229	28 675	27 601.1	2 143.7	3 056	51 838	22 136.9	1 572.8	994	4 585	1 169.5	225.9
Chico, CA	715.3	3 252	165	1 824	796.4	71.6	798	11 316	2 400.7	256.8	264	1 462	158.8	32.6
Cincinnati, OH-KY-IN	1 580.1	747	2 423	D	D	D	6 925	109 675	25 702.2	2 387.1	2 138	D	D	D
Clarksville, TN-KY	46.0	176	144	D	D	D	832	11 643	2 884.6	256.9	226	916	145.5	22.1
Cleveland, TN	23.6	204	63	D	D	D	444	4 970	1 232.3	113.4	90	478	89.7	12.8
Cleveland-Elyria, OH	1 768.5	851	3 085	44 049	24 312.9	2 237.4	7 396	106 023	24 195.4	2 304.5	2 258	18 202	6 344.0	782.1
Coeur d'Alene, ID	56.5	408	142	1 550	843.3	64.0	609	7 398	2 175.2	187.5	249	876	155.3	27.4
College Station-Bryan, TX	531.0	2 322	130	D	D	D	748	10 070	2 418.1	209.7	241	1 240	208.2	34.5
Colorado Springs, CO	123.7	192	471	5 478	2 836.9	266.3	2 158	31 970	8 119.2	787.7	1 183	4 028	603.3	117.2
Columbia, MO	18.7	115	125	1 422	610.4	56.7	646	11 317	3 012.3	239.7	243	D	D	D
Columbia, SC	1 216.5	1 585	710	D	D	D	2 790	39 139	8 967.9	819.2	786	5 179	1 090.3	172.0
Columbus, GA-AL	95.8	325	204	D	D	D	1 097	15 393	3 468.2	313.0	321	D	D	D
Columbus, IN	18.2	237	80	1 012	747.3	50.5	375	5 133	1 075.2	106.7	74	319	50.1	8.9
Columbus, OH	294.4	155	1 796	D	D	D	5 880	102 984	27 247.3	2 412.6	2 135	13 006	2 524.5	470.7
Corpus Christi, TX	247.1	577	441	4 712	3 127.2	216.8	1 449	20 267	5 177.6	440.6	541	3 012	461.3	86.6
Corvallis, OR	38.8	454	48	537	387.1	21.2	275	3 559	685.2	73.0	119	543	58.1	11.3
Crestview-Fort Walton Beach-Destin, FL	40.1	170	157	1 285	442.0	44.7	1 284	15 744	3 736.0	344.6	574	2 722	405.8	90.0
Cumberland, MD-WV	46.5	450	55	D	D	D	391	5 051	1 088.8	91.2	70	D	D	D
Dallas-Fort Worth-Arlington, TX	3 374.1	525	7 665	D	D	D	19 306	304 158	86 410.1	7 577.2	7 411	D	D	D
Dallas-Plano-Irving, TX Div 19124	902.2	213	5 419	D	D	D	12 690	200 636	57 340.8	5 048.2	5 269	45 626	10 405.6	2 340.6
Fort Worth-Arlington, TX Div 23104	2 471.9	1 126	2 246	34 949	27 390.6	1 683.6	6 616	103 522	29 069.3	2 529.0	2 142	D	D	D
Dalton, GA	26.4	186	264	3 886	1 441.3	148.4	605	6 525	1 659.1	146.9	100	412	61.5	12.0
Danville, IL	14.0	171	77	D	D	D	281	3 443	757.9	68.5	59	254	34.3	6.6
Daphne-Fairhope-Foley, AL	64.4	353	183	D	D	D	1 019	12 920	2 966.5	282.6	358	1 987	266.7	59.5
Davenport-Moline-Rock Island, IA-IL	1 271.5	3 349	504	D	D	D	1 492	22 567	5 127.3	480.3	357	2 521	378.9	62.4
Dayton, OH	173.3	217	755	11 096	9 211.1	514.0	2 672	41 791	9 954.4	882.6	804	4 745	706.5	150.9
Decatur, AL	196.5	1 277	174	2 080	1 237.7	87.5	631	6 676	1 804.6	144.0	109	448	63.0	11.4
Decatur, IL	39.4	356	113	D	D	D	432	6 231	1 450.6	132.5	91	454	64.6	12.6
Deltona-Daytona Beach-Ormond Beach, FL	251.7	426	496	D	D	D	2 178	29 104	6 784.0	642.2	1 037	4 486	598.7	115.3
Denver-Aurora-Lakewood, CO	748.1	294	3 383	D	D	D	8 476	129 655	34 016.2	3 309.8	4 608	25 955	5 102.4	1 132.6
Des Moines-West Des Moines, IA	71.5	126	791	D	D	D	2 118	35 904	8 120.4	790.3	655	3 810	754.5	137.3
Detroit-Warren-Dearborn, MI	3 379.8	787	5 003	68 178	63 875.4	3 723.8	15 985	204 938	49 928.4	4 590.6	4 085	29 503	9 253.8	1 012.8
Detroit-Dearborn-Livonia, MI Div 19804	1 797.3	987	1 649	26 806	26 102.9	1 405.1	6 361	68 272	17 275.8	1 451.0	1 276	7 929	5 528.0	241.0
Warren-Troy-Farmington Hills, MI Div 47664	1 502.5	630	3 354	41 372	37 772.5	2 318.7	9 624	136 666	32 652.6	3 139.6	2 809	21 574	3 725.8	771.8
Dothan, AL	132.0	906	194	D	D	D	780	9 231	2 172.2	202.3	143	601	85.1	17.9
Dover, DE	43.3	267	100	D	D	D	632	9 614	2 589.2	224.6	127	604	91.0	22.0
Dubuque, IA	40.5	432	154	2 388	1 847.7	91.6	467	7 056	1 433.5	135.0	103	446	73.6	16.6
Duluth, MN-WI	376.0	1 344	269	D	D	D	1 313	16 792	3 622.4	344.6	266	1 146	180.8	25.5
Durham-Chapel Hill, NC	1 319.2	2 616	366	10 587	8 559.8	928.1	1 658	24 387	5 274.2	536.1	536	2 686	514.3	98.2
East Stroudsburg, PA	33.1	195	98	D	D	D	688	9 091	2 014.9	190.0	166	583	84.7	14.8
Eau Claire, WI	33.3	206	147	2 363	1 115.8	89.3	688	11 320	2 572.1	228.0	137	790	90.7	17.3
El Centro, CA	1 169.2	6 699	212	D	D	D	534	8 052	1 727.3	170.2	134	555	73.4	12.5
Elizabethtown-Fort Knox, KY	27.6	186	76	590	341.7	19.0	530	6 902	1 669.4	147.9	124	D	D	D
Elkhart-Goshen, IN	33.0	167	371	6 096	3 231.4	255.2	727	9 710	2 416.9	219.0	180	813	109.4	20.4
Elmira, NY	9.8	111	86	1 077	357.9	43.2	388	5 580	1 207.2	111.0	79	410	65.6	10.7
El Paso, TX	397.4	494	912	D	D	D	2 347	34 001	8 473.4	683.6	674	D	D	D
Erie, PA	49.4	176	279	3 118	1 157.2	124.0	1 051	15 831	3 428.4	314.5	187	1 115	135.3	25.9
Eugene, OR	224.2	637	444	5 530	2 889.2	242.0	1 403	20 408	4 452.2	456.9	569	2 554	380.1	59.6
Evansville, IN-KY	826.3	2 652	379	6 905	4 211.8	338.5	1 246	18 604	4 287.4	399.1	303	1 851	271.0	48.0

1. Merchant wholesalers, except manufacturers' sales branches and offices.

Area name	Professional, scientific, and technical services,[1] 2007				Manufacturing, 2007				Accommodation and food services, 2007			
	Number of establish-ments	Number of employees	Sales (mil dol)	Annual payroll (mil dol)	Number of establish-ments	Number of employees	Sales (mil dol)	Annual payroll (mil dol)	Number of establish-ments	Number of employees	Sales (mil dol)	Annual payroll (mil dol)
	147	148	149	150	151	152	153	154	155	156	157	158
Cedar Rapids, IA	568	4 799	591.8	251.2	297	19 479	8 586.8	1 183.3	564	10 050	373.0	108.6
Chambersburg-Waynesboro, PA	227	D	D	D	222	10 149	3 244.4	412.7	278	3 837	164.5	45.5
Champaign-Urbana, IL	513	3 125	317.2	134.5	D	D	D	D	569	10 437	395.9	110.3
Charleston, WV	607	D	D	D	D	D	D	D	511	9 446	429.4	119.1
Charleston-North Charleston, SC	1 821	D	D	D	493	22 043	13 226.8	1 041.8	1 406	31 250	1 647.9	448.6
Charlotte-Concord-Gastonia, NC-SC	5 860	D	D	D	2 611	108 670	D	4 506.4	4 248	D	D	D
Charlottesville, VA	694	D	D	D	D	D	D	D	471	D	D	D
Chattanooga, TN-GA	947	D	D	D	653	37 654	D	1 484.3	1 014	19 768	823.1	238.9
Cheyenne, WY	312	1 402	182.0	65.2	61	1 710	2 420.2	80.9	185	3 938	173.7	52.1
Chicago-Naperville-Elgin, IL-IN-WI	32 985	D	D	D	12 022	482 380	177 305.4	D	19 142	351 200	20 892.1	5 611.5
Chicago-Naperville-Arlington Heights, IL Div 16974	26 741	D	D	D	9 250	347 540	116 482.9	D	14 779	275 924	17 247.3	4 617.1
Elgin, IL Div 20994	1 680	D	D	D	1 025	38 683	11 315.4	1 743.3	1 118	18 706	809.1	233.9
Gary, IN Div 23844	1 335	D	D	D	628	39 027	30 031.9	2 198.6	1 391	26 183	1 322.4	335.4
Lake County-Kenosha County, IL-WI Div 29404	3 229	D	D	D	1 119	57 130	19 475.2	4 070.8	1 854	30 387	1 513.3	425.1
Chico, CA	426	D	D	D	224	4 404	987.4	150.6	429	7 708	355.8	96.7
Cincinnati, OH-KY-IN	4 928	D	D	D	D	D	D	D	4 206	D	D	D
Clarksville, TN-KY	260	D	D	D	160	12 378	D	D	434	8 550	336.6	90.0
Cleveland, TN	162	D	D	D	D	D	D	D	187	3 386	139.3	38.1
Cleveland-Elyria, OH	6 163	D	D	D	3 774	141 166	42 181.1	6 876.6	4 714	79 741	3 496.8	963.9
Coeur d'Alene, ID	438	D	D	D	246	4 401	992.2	163.3	363	6 773	303.7	96.0
College Station-Bryan, TX	418	D	D	D	D	D	D	D	427	9 138	368.3	98.0
Colorado Springs, CO	2 423	D	D	D	D	D	D	D	1 316	25 914	1 281.8	388.6
Columbia, MO	382	D	D	D	96	4 601	D	D	422	8 458	315.1	93.0
Columbia, SC	1 897	D	D	D	D	D	D	D	1 411	29 213	1 237.6	352.0
Columbus, GA-AL	453	D	D	D	D	D	D	D	551	12 099	529.9	150.0
Columbus, IN	157	D	D	D	143	11 711	4 843.9	502.9	160	3 416	139.7	39.9
Columbus, OH	4 758	D	D	D	1 571	71 738	D	D	3 901	79 936	3 502.0	1 008.3
Corpus Christi, TX	907	D	D	D	D	D	D	D	1 030	18 298	788.4	218.7
Corvallis, OR	282	D	D	D	92	4 322	590.5	209.8	206	3 197	134.0	37.2
Crestview-Fort Walton Beach-Destin, FL	828	D	D	D	D	D	D	D	596	15 001	804.6	242.1
Cumberland, MD-WV	140	D	D	D	74	4 299	D	195.6	227	3 386	146.1	39.7
Dallas-Fort Worth-Arlington, TX	17 812	D	D	D	D	D	D	D	11 215	D	D	D
Dallas-Plano-Irving, TX Div 19124	13 179	D	D	D	3 928	D	59 178.0	D	7 518	D	D	D
Fort Worth-Arlington, TX Div 23104	4 633	D	D	D	D	D	D	D	3 697	82 015	4 144.6	1 139.5
Dalton, GA	187	D	D	D	399	27 729	9 130.6	863.7	232	4 001	169.4	45.4
Danville, IL	93	396	44.7	12.9	100	5 458	2 576.4	239.7	156	2 370	85.0	24.6
Daphne-Fairhope-Foley, AL	458	D	D	D	162	4 795	1 410.3	169.3	414	8 368	437.0	122.4
Davenport-Moline-Rock Island, IA-IL	766	D	D	D	D	D	D	D	902	16 365	695.7	189.8
Dayton, OH	1 803	D	D	D	1 158	48 798	17 780.6	2 204.6	1 612	32 736	1 293.6	382.9
Decatur, AL	262	1 563	124.3	50.5	223	13 563	D	D	249	4 299	177.4	47.4
Decatur, IL	181	1 185	125.8	51.1	112	8 762	9 590.8	409.4	219	4 733	170.9	52.0
Deltona-Daytona Beach-Ormond Beach, FL	1 550	D	D	D	421	10 522	2 184.3	396.1	1 137	21 760	1 014.0	277.4
Denver-Aurora-Lakewood, CO	12 019	D	D	D	D	D	D	D	5 380	108 481	5 759.0	1 667.2
Des Moines-West Des Moines, IA	1 616	13 296	1 965.3	705.0	D	D	D	D	1 307	23 794	976.6	285.1
Detroit-Warren-Dearborn, MI	11 820	D	D	D	5 987	234 520	112 084.5	13 174.2	8 135	146 138	6 950.0	1 976.1
Detroit-Dearborn-Livonia, MI Div 19804	2 880	D	D	D	1 729	87 991	55 896.9	5 545.3	3 215	57 836	3 112.4	857.5
Warren-Troy-Farmington Hills, MI Div 47664	8 940	D	D	D	4 258	146 529	56 187.6	7 628.9	4 920	88 302	3 837.6	1 118.6
Dothan, AL	292	D	D	D	170	7 348	1 889.8	253.6	282	5 007	195.0	53.1
Dover, DE	248	D	D	D	87	5 253	2 361.8	213.8	236	5 352	447.9	76.2
Dubuque, IA	168	D	D	D	150	9 378	4 711.2	380.3	253	4 502	145.7	42.5
Duluth, MN-WI	529	D	D	D	310	8 551	D	D	812	12 944	607.8	148.9
Durham-Chapel Hill, NC	1 655	D	D	D	373	21 560	D	1 044.8	1 045	20 891	1 081.9	304.5
East Stroudsburg, PA	340	1 671	198.0	53.9	131	5 322	2 656.5	317.4	386	7 491	394.4	113.0
Eau Claire, WI	265	1 760	195.4	85.3	228	10 762	3 109.0	424.2	418	6 405	226.6	63.1
El Centro, CA	153	D	D	D	58	2 846	1 207.9	96.9	261	3 719	167.8	46.2
Elizabethtown-Fort Knox, KY	175	D	D	D	104	D	D	D	221	D	D	D
Elkhart-Goshen, IN	338	D	D	D	852	64 309	15 779.8	2 508.4	385	7 395	272.4	76.0
Elmira, NY	115	D	D	D	93	6 348	1 280.8	285.8	198	3 151	123.1	35.2
El Paso, TX	1 152	D	D	D	D	D	D	D	1 274	24 597	1 033.3	268.9
Erie, PA	416	D	D	D	505	24 441	6 890.8	1 190.2	646	10 728	428.1	114.6
Eugene, OR	988	5 097	554.6	217.5	606	20 273	6 219.9	853.6	920	13 385	607.7	171.5
Evansville, IN-KY	675	D	D	D	423	26 205	D	D	658	14 216	625.5	178.1

1. Establishments subject to federal tax.

Area name	Health care and social assistance,[1] 2007				Other services,[1] 2007				Nonemployer business, 2013		Value of residential construction authorized by building permits, 2014	
	Number of establish-ments	Number of employees	Receipts (mil dol)	Annual payroll (mil dol)	Number of establish-ments	Number of employees	Receipts (mil dol)	Annual payroll (mil dol)	Number	Receipts (mil dol)	New construc-tion ($1,000)	Number of housing units
	159	160	161	162	163	164	165	166	167	168	169	170
Cedar Rapids, IA	636	14 920	1 253.3	527.7	494	2 818	266.2	68.4	16 086	669.7	102 281	881
Chambersburg-Waynesboro, PA	307	7 302	640.1	267.8	297	1 653	121.0	33.1	8 745	362.0	56 283	356
Champaign-Urbana, IL	425	D	D	D	334	2 303	437.6	58.4	13 596	491.6	244 202	1 489
Charleston, WV	800	17 649	1 770.0	648.8	446	D	D	D	10 416	411.9	32 171	321
Charleston-North Charleston, SC	1 558	31 530	3 817.2	1 308.4	1 159	7 555	652.8	196.1	53 025	2 492.5	1 213 233	6 155
Charlotte-Concord-Gastonia, NC-SC	4 619	D	D	D	3 409	22 563	2 938.3	606.1	172 530	7 158.3	3 237 476	18 537
Charlottesville, VA	518	D	D	D	396	D	D	D	17 225	792.2	194 788	873
Chattanooga, TN-GA	1 272	D	D	D	789	D	D	D	35 506	1 612.4	313 794	2 346
Cheyenne, WY	281	6 040	563.1	232.9	180	947	83.0	25.0	7 085	391.6	63 198	403
Chicago-Naperville-Elgin, IL-IN-WI	23 636	518 516	54 052.8	21 616.2	17 377	133 283	17 238.9	4 354.1	738 009	32 413.2	3 385 179	15 679
Chicago-Naperville-Arlington Heights, IL Div 16974	18 493	413 766	43 671.1	17 451.5	13 622	107 794	14 989.5	3 707.7	NA	NA	X	X
Elgin, IL Div 20994	1 270	25 024	2 475.8	1 005.3	997	6 591	643.2	181.8	NA	NA	X	X
Gary, IN Div 23844	1 654	40 530	3 833.0	1 495.6	1 260	8 871	726.0	216.3	NA	NA	X	X
Lake County-Kenosha County, IL-WI Div 29404	2 219	39 196	4 072.9	1 663.8	1 498	10 027	880.2	248.3	NA	NA	X	X
Chico, CA	737	12 120	1 179.3	427.5	321	2 168	173.6	49.9	13 031	603.4	92 522	550
Cincinnati, OH-KY-IN	4 787	D	D	D	3 399	D	D	D	135 514	5 917.4	906 061	5 206
Clarksville, TN-KY	466	D	D	D	308	1 893	133.1	38.8	13 128	570.2	180 071	1 507
Cleveland, TN	249	4 750	393.6	151.3	121	D	D	D	7 734	372.8	82 123	689
Cleveland-Elyria, OH	5 520	159 804	14 974.6	6 459.7	4 195	28 804	2 837.6	766.6	143 629	6 323.6	647 535	2 900
Coeur d'Alene, ID	458	7 004	573.4	238.0	240	1 242	82.8	24.6	10 934	468.0	208 068	1 047
College Station-Bryan, TX	430	7 750	909.3	302.9	311	2 033	374.0	45.6	14 370	649.5	256 777	1 803
Colorado Springs, CO	1 796	27 724	2 934.4	1 110.7	1 127	8 222	1 328.2	259.3	47 420	1 868.0	1 212 896	3 673
Columbia, MO	562	15 933	1 695.8	615.7	323	D	D	D	10 871	534.1	262 282	1 414
Columbia, SC	1 596	D	D	D	1 327	8 711	803.3	233.4	50 616	2 088.8	676 849	4 067
Columbus, GA-AL	665	D	D	D	452	D	D	D	20 239	624.3	129 998	955
Columbus, IN	228	5 095	439.1	178.5	120	857	82.8	19.5	4 130	161.4	62 387	254
Columbus, OH	4 265	109 240	10 303.2	4 309.8	3 130	24 928	3 018.0	776.5	141 139	6 189.7	1 254 408	7 044
Corpus Christi, TX	1 152	26 350	2 242.0	859.6	698	4 703	492.0	130.7	29 507	1 334.1	375 101	2 864
Corvallis, OR	229	4 356	504.0	201.1	128	855	158.3	22.7	5 510	221.7	86 020	451
Crestview-Fort Walton Beach-Destin, FL	599	9 891	979.2	364.0	470	2 454	208.4	56.5	20 666	1 111.4	605 860	1 666
Cumberland, MD-WV	318	6 931	612.8	232.2	201	1 079	76.8	20.7	4 472	161.5	8 985	57
Dallas-Fort Worth-Arlington, TX	14 643	D	D	D	8 519	D	D	D	566 067	28 828.5	7 773 054	41 418
Dallas-Plano-Irving, TX Div 19124	10 042	181 135	21 411.2	8 165.7	5 635	D	D	D	NA	NA	X	X
Fort Worth-Arlington, TX Div 23104	4 601	D	D	D	2 884	22 706	1 979.5	567.9	NA	NA	X	X
Dalton, GA	228	4 281	480.5	183.3	166	839	77.6	24.0	7 494	340.4	19 350	121
Danville, IL	149	4 729	437.7	203.4	138	780	54.8	14.5	4 382	137.8	922	6
Daphne-Fairhope-Foley, AL	388	6 647	624.0	230.6	274	1 202	169.0	32.1	16 508	774.3	264 926	1 384
Davenport-Moline-Rock Island, IA-IL	967	21 784	1 824.2	791.6	724	4 533	376.3	104.8	20 437	787.2	132 169	655
Dayton, OH	2 016	D	D	D	1 352	9 206	910.1	252.0	47 778	1 844.3	218 850	779
Decatur, AL	384	6 863	547.9	220.1	212	1 159	99.7	28.5	9 496	350.3	22 527	136
Decatur, IL	282	7 449	750.1	281.3	197	1 526	222.4	33.5	5 900	180.0	9 541	53
Deltona-Daytona Beach-Ormond Beach, FL	1 395	25 978	2 689.0	1 019.7	1 154	5 893	534.8	128.8	46 075	1 928.7	556 937	1 921
Denver-Aurora-Lakewood, CO	6 481	D	D	D	5 126	D	D	D	228 988	10 998.7	2 934 436	15 767
Des Moines-West Des Moines, IA	1 302	36 966	3 416.4	1 483.0	1 157	D	D	D	41 964	1 945.6	897 523	4 436
Detroit-Warren-Dearborn, MI	12 227	241 649	24 485.4	10 037.0	7 434	46 504	5 094.0	1 259.1	325 593	13 735.5	1 412 223	6 295
Detroit-Dearborn-Livonia, MI Div 19804	4 200	99 597	10 640.0	4 241.8	2 859	18 419	2 068.3	511.0	NA	NA	X	X
Warren-Troy-Farmington Hills, MI Div 47644	8 027	142 052	13 845.4	5 795.2	4 575	28 085	3 025.7	748.1	NA	NA	X	X
Dothan, AL	390	D	D	D	238	D	D	D	9 437	391.3	63 683	336
Dover, DE	354	7 773	672.8	269.3	249	1 460	100.8	32.3	9 126	499.0	134 398	998
Dubuque, IA	242	7 056	592.0	264.0	208	1 505	102.2	27.4	6 130	268.6	48 756	276
Duluth, MN-WI	887	26 320	2 359.8	1 086.9	574	3 348	266.5	68.8	15 523	587.9	107 307	598
Durham-Chapel Hill, NC	1 263	39 491	4 277.7	1 577.9	769	5 961	1 025.2	213.3	40 411	1 532.9	521 970	2 587
East Stroudsburg, PA	367	6 064	537.3	221.1	308	1 590	119.9	36.2	9 813	444.6	38 574	153
Eau Claire, WI	441	13 010	1 218.0	539.5	313	1 747	150.8	42.8	9 606	461.1	76 271	463
El Centro, CA	265	4 257	394.1	142.6	163	1 046	83.2	25.1	9 691	317.4	43 915	246
Elizabethtown-Fort Knox, KY	359	D	D	D	193	D	D	D	7 940	301.2	56 806	492
Elkhart-Goshen, IN	347	9 746	1 024.6	358.1	374	2 298	195.7	60.1	12 323	511.3	57 187	270
Elmira, NY	221	6 722	587.1	247.0	129	786	59.9	15.7	3 832	138.5	21 995	61
El Paso, TX	1 346	D	D	D	918	D	D	D	54 021	2 226.3	439 382	3 043
Erie, PA	893	21 880	1 847.7	783.0	563	3 529	242.4	70.2	13 801	567.3	43 914	321
Eugene, OR	993	18 660	1 947.8	735.6	684	3 684	516.8	95.3	22 051	927.6	240 004	1 316
Evansville, IN-KY	865	D	D	D	566	D	D	D	16 866	681.1	114 463	727

1. Establishments subject to federal tax.

Table C. Metropolitan Areas — **Government Employment and Payroll and Local Government Finances**

Area name	Government employment and payroll, 2012									Local government finances, 2012				
			March payroll (percent of total)							General revenue				
												Taxes		
													Per capita[1] (dollars)	
	Full-time equivalent employees	March Payroll (dollars)	Adminis-tration, judicial, and legal	Police and corrections	Fire protection	Highways and transporta-tion	Health and welfare	Natural resources and utilities	Education and libraries	Total (mil dol)	Inter-govern-mental (mil dol)	Total (mil dol)	Total	Property
	171	172	173	174	175	176	177	178	179	180	181	182	183	184
Cedar Rapids, IA	10 705	42 251 213	4.0	6.0	2.5	6.3	2.3	4.9	72.2	1 343.4	584.3	503.5	1 924	1 486
Chambersburg-Waynesboro, PA	3 820	13 644 359	7.7	8.8	1.7	2.3	9.1	6.1	63.5	415.1	130.8	191.4	1 265	978
Champaign-Urbana, IL	8 553	32 026 460	5.7	8.9	3.4	7.5	6.1	5.5	61.1	891.5	342.7	404.0	1 728	1 506
Charleston, WV	8 227	28 589 774	5.5	6.5	3.8	3.3	7.9	3.1	66.9	735.0	295.9	299.7	1 326	910
Charleston-North Charleston, SC	22 813	76 849 945	8.2	12.8	6.2	2.8	3.9	8.3	55.3	2 449.1	759.7	1 206.4	1 730	1 171
Charlotte-Concord-Gastonia, NC-SC	106 366	436 927 670	3.6	7.0	2.3	1.5	39.9	4.1	40.2	12 067.6	3 110.9	3 416.0	1 487	1 141
Charlottesville, VA	7 679	26 539 813	8.0	9.0	2.3	2.5	3.9	4.9	64.7	782.8	292.5	365.6	1 641	1 221
Chattanooga, TN-GA	19 778	70 912 137	6.7	7.6	2.9	3.3	31.0	10.3	37.0	2 452.8	620.7	669.9	1 245	910
Cheyenne, WY	6 173	27 578 286	2.8	4.6	1.9	1.8	39.8	1.5	46.1	796.0	292.8	103.3	1 094	589
Chicago-Naperville-Elgin, IL-IN-WI	358 119	1 755 095 339	5.6	15.8	4.2	6.1	4.0	6.3	56.6	49 995.8	16 211.6	25 716.1	2 701	2 261
Chicago-Naperville-Arlington Heights, IL Div 16974	272 297	1 388 594 555	5.4	17.5	4.2	7.0	4.3	6.3	54.0	39 231.9	12 680.6	19 977.9	2 730	2 208
Elgin, IL Div 20994	25 482	114 832 272	5.3	10.3	5.2	2.2	1.5	6.6	67.5	3 172.7	934.1	1 826.9	2 913	2 670
Gary, IN Div 23844	25 614	86 646 440	8.5	10.0	3.9	4.2	3.6	7.3	60.8	3 048.3	1 320.8	1 243.6	1 759	1 670
Lake County-Kenosha County, IL-WI Div 29404	34 726	165 022 072	5.5	8.7	3.9	2.4	4.0	6.2	68.5	4 542.9	1 276.0	2 667.7	3 066	2 896
Chico, CA	8 734	37 694 370	6.4	9.6	2.6	2.0	12.6	5.9	58.9	1 079.1	643.7	243.0	1 097	878
Cincinnati, OH-KY-IN	72 643	287 857 130	6.6	10.8	6.5	4.5	6.9	6.8	56.1	8 861.6	3 178.0	3 802.3	1 786	1 197
Clarksville, TN-KY	8 620	27 138 883	4.3	10.6	3.8	3.1	6.5	6.8	62.4	701.2	298.6	267.5	975	569
Cleveland, TN	4 049	11 684 208	5.5	10.1	5.8	3.7	9.5	2.4	62.1	282.7	134.8	92.6	786	497
Cleveland-Elyria, OH	92 435	406 449 865	6.4	10.2	4.7	5.9	15.2	7.7	48.3	11 282.4	3 960.2	4 907.0	2 378	1 483
Coeur d'Alene, ID	6 580	25 436 541	6.0	8.3	3.6	2.4	37.6	3.3	38.1	678.7	158.8	148.1	1 040	972
College Station-Bryan, TX	8 862	27 409 320	8.4	12.4	4.3	4.5	3.2	11.0	51.4	682.0	173.0	393.1	1 676	1 379
Colorado Springs, CO	25 178	98 225 856	5.3	9.9	3.8	2.2	15.3	15.2	45.7	2 631.8	836.0	850.3	1 272	745
Columbia, MO	6 008	20 052 275	7.9	5.3	3.3	2.8	2.7	11.3	63.5	497.3	161.0	228.2	1 354	805
Columbia, SC	33 084	120 753 751	4.2	6.5	2.3	1.0	25.0	4.6	54.7	3 250.3	958.1	1 087.0	1 385	1 204
Columbus, GA-AL	13 084	41 360 235	6.9	10.8	4.0	2.6	6.1	6.8	60.6	1 009.9	422.9	376.5	1 213	848
Columbus, IN	4 371	15 688 309	3.2	6.6	2.9	1.3	44.5	3.1	37.7	469.7	111.3	106.7	1 348	1 076
Columbus, OH	70 274	306 173 279	9.4	10.4	7.0	4.4	8.1	5.2	53.9	9 594.0	3 610.3	4 421.2	2 274	1 428
Corpus Christi, TX	19 396	62 362 670	4.9	10.1	3.6	4.7	4.1	5.7	63.6	1 651.1	548.8	775.1	1 773	1 396
Corvallis, OR	1 834	7 923 562	9.3	13.4	6.2	3.8	7.4	9.4	45.7	259.6	93.0	115.4	1 335	1 185
Crestview-Fort Walton Beach-Destin, FL	8 719	30 209 052	6.5	11.1	6.5	3.5	2.3	6.1	60.8	813.5	261.8	380.6	1 537	1 209
Cumberland, MD-WV	3 611	14 623 810	4.0	5.7	1.6	3.1	0.5	6.1	76.2	340.7	169.2	105.4	1 034	723
Dallas-Fort Worth-Arlington, TX	263 325	1 034 080 549	5.5	11.1	4.7	4.3	9.8	4.8	58.2	28 591.5	7 248.4	14 334.2	2 139	1 724
Dallas-Plano-Irving, TX Div 19124	172 608	694 884 179	5.0	10.6	4.8	5.5	10.3	4.8	57.3	19 625.6	4 888.2	9 734.9	2 199	1 766
Fort Worth-Arlington, TX Div 23104	90 717	339 196 370	6.6	12.1	4.4	1.7	8.6	4.7	60.2	8 965.9	2 360.2	4 599.3	2 022	1 644
Dalton, GA	5 343	18 100 335	4.0	6.7	3.7	3.2	5.9	9.7	65.2	440.0	199.5	149.2	1 045	674
Danville, IL	3 642	12 242 579	7.0	7.8	2.7	3.5	3.6	4.2	67.9	289.5	151.8	91.4	1 132	940
Daphne-Fairhope-Foley, AL	7 374	22 581 577	7.4	8.0	2.9	4.3	20.7	5.6	47.7	640.7	189.9	231.1	1 211	537
Davenport-Moline-Rock Island, IA-IL	14 533	58 873 005	5.4	9.2	3.4	4.7	5.9	5.6	64.3	1 610.6	616.3	675.0	1 764	1 489
Dayton, OH	31 140	126 902 617	7.8	9.6	4.5	5.3	8.1	7.6	55.4	3 577.2	1 408.5	1 490.6	1 861	1 242
Decatur, AL	6 083	20 609 391	3.2	7.4	2.8	2.6	21.3	8.4	53.1	589.6	255.2	134.1	870	438
Decatur, IL	4 204	17 133 160	5.9	11.8	4.5	3.0	2.0	8.2	63.3	407.1	180.7	163.9	1 488	1 260
Deltona-Daytona Beach-Ormond Beach, FL	23 653	83 363 572	6.3	11.3	4.7	2.1	21.7	6.5	45.3	2 404.0	575.9	895.2	1 504	1 170
Denver-Aurora-Lakewood, CO	95 098	432 423 959	6.6	12.7	5.6	6.2	10.7	9.5	46.7	13 355.6	3 846.7	5 924.4	2 240	1 358
Des Moines-West Des Moines, IA	22 853	93 893 961	5.5	8.0	3.0	4.3	8.9	5.3	63.7	2 778.1	968.6	1 212.2	2 058	1 784
Detroit-Warren-Dearborn, MI	115 282	533 695 857	7.4	12.9	5.0	4.6	2.5	4.5	60.8	18 679.3	8 819.4	5 896.0	1 374	1 225
Detroit-Dearborn-Livonia, MI Div 19804	52 078	243 918 311	7.3	16.2	6.7	6.5	2.2	6.4	52.0	9 260.6	4 384.4	2 686.6	1 499	1 195
Warren-Troy-Farmington Hills, MI Div 47664	63 204	289 777 546	7.4	10.1	3.5	3.0	2.7	2.9	68.2	9 418.7	4 435.0	3 209.5	1 284	1 246
Dothan, AL	7 365	24 527 281	3.9	6.4	3.0	2.7	40.1	5.5	36.7	730.7	179.2	156.0	1 057	387
Dover, DE	4 210	17 226 252	4.7	6.0	0.1	0.6	1.6	5.6	79.4	494.8	323.1	88.0	525	459
Dubuque, IA	3 261	12 486 456	6.7	9.6	3.9	7.2	5.0	6.0	60.6	400.9	169.8	165.8	1 743	1 320
Duluth, MN-WI	11 586	52 151 960	6.8	9.8	2.9	6.5	13.3	7.0	48.7	1 488.3	728.3	373.6	1 337	1 215
Durham-Chapel Hill, NC	18 475	63 324 374	5.8	6.4	1.4	2.2	10.3	6.8	63.0	1 793.6	701.9	824.7	1 577	1 277
East Stroudsburg, PA	5 957	25 067 544	5.7	4.3	0.0	5.4	1.6	1.5	80.9	719.0	225.3	441.5	2 616	2 404
Eau Claire, WI	5 534	21 894 206	6.1	8.1	3.0	6.4	5.8	4.3	65.0	602.6	268.9	253.5	1 549	1 431
El Centro, CA	10 122	49 143 599	4.2	6.0	1.7	1.1	19.5	16.2	45.5	1 293.3	740.8	180.2	1 019	733
Elizabethtown-Fort Knox, KY	6 654	21 761 001	1.7	4.2	1.5	1.3	37.6	3.5	49.3	547.6	189.2	112.2	746	448
Elkhart-Goshen, IN	6 985	24 411 992	5.4	8.4	4.1	2.5	1.6	3.6	73.6	630.5	315.1	218.4	1 094	907
Elmira, NY	3 853	14 858 297	5.0	9.7	2.9	4.0	13.2	3.8	59.7	476.3	219.3	175.3	1 971	1 236
El Paso, TX	38 548	140 371 856	4.5	10.4	3.7	3.1	8.1	3.1	65.5	3 358.7	1 620.5	1 097.5	1 321	1 022
Erie, PA	8 523	32 472 819	5.3	9.7	2.6	5.6	3.9	6.0	65.7	1 197.6	616.5	364.0	1 297	1 046
Eugene, OR	11 647	50 155 119	7.2	10.9	5.2	6.9	4.1	11.4	48.1	1 390.4	585.1	463.2	1 306	1 120
Evansville, IN-KY	10 347	34 710 256	6.8	10.9	4.5	3.9	1.7	8.5	62.2	995.2	463.1	341.3	1 089	857

1. Based on the resident population estimated as of July 1 of the year shown.

Area name	Local government finances, 2012 (cont.): Direct general expenditure: Total (mil dol)	Per capita[1] (dollars)	Percent of total for: Educa- tion	Health and hospitals	Police protec- tion	Public welfare	High- ways	Debt outstanding: Total (mil dol)	Per capita[1] (dollars)	Government employment, 2013: Federal civilian	Federal military	State and local	Presidential election,[2] 2012: Percent of vote cast: Demo- cratic	Republi- can	All other
	185	186	187	188	189	190	191	192	193	194	195	196	197	198	199
Cedar Rapids, IA	1 498.7	5 725	47.4	3.1	3.7	1.0	5.5	1 735.1	6 629	1 177	1 061	15 669	56.7	41.5	1.9
Chambersburg-Waynesboro, PA	452.7	2 992	54.1	4.1	1.9	5.5	4.8	619.1	4 092	2 453	406	6 193	30.1	68.6	1.3
Champaign-Urbana, IL	941.0	4 025	49.1	2.4	5.0	2.5	6.1	728.3	3 115	1 319	478	36 869	49.0	48.3	2.7
Charleston, WV	776.4	3 436	50.7	3.1	6.2	0.1	2.6	329.2	1 457	2 153	1 136	21 979	41.8	56.3	1.8
Charleston-North Charleston, SC	2 212.6	3 173	45.5	1.1	9.5	0.2	4.7	5 523.5	7 920	10 288	12 985	50 528	46.5	51.8	1.6
Charlotte-Concord-Gastonia, NC-SC	11 496.9	5 006	29.1	35.1	5.3	2.9	2.0	12 295.6	5 354	9 536	6 454	136 569	47.2	51.6	1.2
Charlottesville, VA	798.6	3 583	47.8	6.8	5.5	6.6	2.1	859.4	3 856	1 375	1 141	31 832	56.0	42.3	1.7
Chattanooga, TN-GA	2 273.9	4 228	31.4	31.0	4.8	0.8	2.7	1 828.1	3 399	6 399	1 736	30 225	36.6	61.6	1.7
Cheyenne, WY	781.4	8 270	37.0	40.5	2.5	0.2	3.1	132.4	1 401	2 589	3 647	11 412	36.2	60.5	3.3
Chicago-Naperville-Elgin, IL-IN-WI	48 512.9	5 095	44.9	3.1	7.1	1.3	4.3	81 674.3	8 577	54 456	32 490	509 832	63.8	34.8	1.5
Chicago-Naperville-Arlington Heights, IL Div 16974	38 566.5	5 270	42.7	3.4	7.4	1.3	4.3	70 331.4	9 610	44 917	15 081	387 011	66.5	32.0	1.5
Elgin, IL Div 20994	3 112.0	4 962	53.7	0.6	6.3	0.5	5.5	4 822.0	7 688	1 790	1 248	42 357	50.1	48.2	1.8
Gary, IN Div 23844	2 464.8	3 487	47.7	2.5	4.8	0.9	2.2	2 682.0	3 795	1 897	2 248	34 325	59.7	38.9	1.4
Lake County-Kenosha County, IL-WI Div 29404	4 369.5	5 022	56.1	2.3	6.1	1.8	4.4	3 838.9	4 412	5 852	13 913	46 139	53.9	44.7	1.4
Chico, CA	1 098.2	4 957	46.2	6.8	4.4	11.8	3.6	480.5	2 169	561	348	14 319	47.0	49.0	4.0
Cincinnati, OH-KY-IN	9 065.0	4 259	41.6	5.6	6.4	3.8	4.1	13 076.8	6 143	16 004	5 936	110 562	41.4	57.1	1.6
Clarksville, TN-KY	654.4	2 385	56.0	3.0	7.0	0.1	4.1	4 800.5	17 498	6 024	31 357	13 314	41.4	57.2	1.4
Cleveland, TN	268.7	2 281	54.1	7.7	7.1	0.1	5.2	242.0	2 054	266	375	5 443	23.5	75.0	1.4
Cleveland-Elyria, OH	11 203.3	5 429	41.3	12.0	5.9	3.4	4.1	14 162.1	6 863	17 910	5 750	113 420	61.5	37.2	1.2
Coeur d'Alene, ID	637.0	4 475	29.8	40.2	5.8	0.4	3.9	121.1	851	551	536	9 629	31.5	65.8	2.7
College Station-Bryan, TX	708.6	3 022	50.7	1.9	5.8	0.4	5.6	1 389.0	5 923	844	542	34 915	31.5	66.4	2.0
Colorado Springs, CO	2 586.9	3 871	37.1	21.4	6.1	2.0	8.1	4 453.6	6 663	13 117	39 118	36 799	38.3	59.2	2.6
Columbia, MO	580.4	3 444	44.8	3.1	4.3	0.2	6.2	2 592.5	15 382	2 492	601	28 391	50.2	47.1	2.7
Columbia, SC	3 328.6	4 242	44.0	20.7	4.0	0.1	1.1	7 155.9	9 119	10 080	13 242	69 204	50.2	48.5	1.4
Columbus, GA-AL	1 107.4	3 566	50.3	6.1	5.6	1.9	4.1	1 051.1	3 385	6 962	24 098	17 972	54.1	45.1	0.7
Columbus, IN	465.6	5 883	32.7	40.9	1.8	0.5	0.9	364.3	4 603	158	255	6 081	36.2	61.7	2.1
Columbus, OH	9 248.5	4 757	41.8	5.3	5.8	5.4	4.5	10 699.7	5 504	14 059	5 464	152 057	52.7	45.7	1.6
Corpus Christi, TX	1 702.5	3 895	49.7	4.7	6.4	0.2	3.7	3 153.1	7 214	6 605	4 613	26 252	44.8	53.9	1.3
Corvallis, OR	259.2	2 999	46.3	7.4	9.6	0.0	4.2	233.8	2 705	529	264	10 653	62.0	33.5	4.5
Crestview-Fort Walton Beach-Destin, FL	907.3	3 663	47.7	3.2	7.3	0.3	4.4	501.5	2 025	8 369	17 382	10 906	24.4	74.3	1.2
Cumberland, MD-WV	335.7	3 292	62.0	0.8	3.9	0.5	4.1	213.3	2 092	611	346	7 715	31.0	66.3	2.6
Dallas-Fort Worth-Arlington, TX	28 447.6	4 245	42.1	11.3	5.7	0.4	4.3	75 576.3	11 278	45 235	16 531	347 915	41.9	56.7	1.4
Dallas-Plano-Irving, TX Div 19124	19 555.5	4 418	41.1	11.5	5.2	0.5	4.4	53 566.2	12 101	29 622	10 566	236 242	44.5	54.2	1.4
Fort Worth-Arlington, TX Div 23104	8 892.1	3 910	44.2	11.0	6.7	0.1	4.1	22 010.2	9 677	15 613	5 965	111 673	37.0	61.6	1.4
Dalton, GA	487.6	3 416	54.9	8.7	3.9	0.4	4.8	143.3	1 004	240	411	6 674	25.6	72.9	1.5
Danville, IL	308.3	3 819	56.4	0.7	6.4	3.5	6.3	102.1	1 265	1 535	156	4 360	42.5	55.7	1.8
Daphne-Fairhope-Foley, AL	700.0	3 669	34.5	19.2	6.1	0.1	7.7	911.0	4 775	330	898	8 598	21.6	77.2	1.2
Davenport-Moline-Rock Island, IA-IL	1 675.1	4 378	48.5	5.0	5.5	1.5	4.6	1 215.2	3 176	6 086	1 539	20 415	56.7	41.8	1.5
Dayton, OH	3 712.9	4 635	47.4	3.3	6.4	7.2	5.2	3 143.4	3 924	18 273	7 548	43 039	46.2	52.1	1.7
Decatur, AL	670.1	4 345	54.9	16.9	4.4	0.3	3.3	924.8	5 996	407	704	8 311	29.1	69.6	1.3
Decatur, IL	452.8	4 112	52.8	2.0	7.8	0.1	8.1	462.5	4 200	324	224	5 565	46.6	51.8	1.7
Deltona-Daytona Beach-Ormond Beach, FL	2 484.9	4 174	30.8	22.3	7.3	0.4	3.9	3 027.1	5 085	1 266	1 189	22 022	48.4	50.7	1.0
Denver-Aurora-Lakewood, CO	12 432.0	4 700	33.7	6.3	6.2	4.2	4.8	24 877.2	9 405	28 072	9 829	163 441	55.5	42.2	2.2
Des Moines-West Des Moines, IA	3 004.6	5 101	48.5	8.3	4.2	1.2	5.5	3 647.7	6 193	6 101	2 583	36 711	53.3	44.9	1.8
Detroit-Warren-Dearborn, MI	19 021.2	4 432	43.4	5.7	6.5	3.0	3.8	31 478.0	7 334	28 131	8 344	165 000	59.5	39.5	0.9
Detroit-Dearborn-Livonia, MI Div 19804	9 500.3	5 300	36.3	3.3	7.0	5.2	2.9	21 084.6	11 764	14 181	3 495	76 006	73.0	26.2	0.8
Warren-Troy-Farmington Hills, MI Div 47664	9 520.9	3 809	50.5	8.0	6.0	0.9	4.7	10 393.4	4 158	13 950	4 849	88 994	50.9	48.1	1.0
Dothan, AL	704.8	4 774	29.3	42.3	4.1	0.1	4.1	485.5	3 289	413	709	10 135	28.2	71.0	0.8
Dover, DE	527.3	3 145	73.4	1.1	4.4	0.0	1.5	478.7	2 856	1 801	4 542	17 489	51.7	46.8	1.5
Dubuque, IA	405.9	4 268	37.6	4.5	4.7	2.0	7.0	372.4	3 916	247	397	4 424	56.5	41.8	1.7
Duluth, MN-WI	1 639.0	5 865	37.0	6.4	5.3	6.4	9.4	1 391.0	4 977	1 658	1 079	23 318	63.5	34.0	2.5
Durham-Chapel Hill, NC	1 919.0	3 670	40.5	5.6	8.2	5.6	2.1	1 899.7	3 633	6 190	1 495	58 017	69.0	29.7	1.3
East Stroudsburg, PA	739.9	4 384	67.9	0.1	3.0	3.9	2.5	1 201.0	7 115	3 756	467	8 521	56.0	42.7	1.3
Eau Claire, WI	676.7	4 137	54.0	4.1	6.5	3.1	11.1	488.8	2 988	551	440	11 688	53.5	45.0	1.5
El Centro, CA	1 172.3	6 625	40.7	23.6	4.1	7.5	2.9	1 408.8	7 962	2 445	480	15 020	65.2	33.1	1.7
Elizabethtown-Fort Knox, KY	515.1	3 425	39.9	37.7	2.7	0.0	2.2	447.0	2 972	6 453	9 253	8 902	37.7	60.6	1.7
Elkhart-Goshen, IN	609.8	3 055	58.2	1.0	3.9	0.2	3.5	758.8	3 801	253	638	8 359	36.0	62.5	1.6
Elmira, NY	467.0	5 252	42.9	3.0	3.0	18.1	8.9	490.6	5 518	214	138	6 170	48.1	50.4	1.5
El Paso, TX	3 277.0	3 945	52.3	15.5	5.0	0.4	1.0	4 036.3	4 859	13 191	28 922	54 859	65.4	33.3	1.3
Erie, PA	1 203.4	4 288	44.0	5.6	2.7	14.2	3.5	1 705.3	6 076	1 509	765	16 029	57.4	41.3	1.3
Eugene, OR	1 390.2	3 921	44.2	5.1	6.9	2.2	4.3	1 580.1	4 457	1 598	1 054	23 620	59.7	36.4	3.9
Evansville, IN-KY	984.8	3 142	43.4	0.7	5.9	0.3	3.2	1 444.5	4 609	1 159	997	15 356	41.6	56.7	1.8

1. Based on the resident population estimated as of July 1 of the year shown. 2.

Table C. Metropolitan Areas — **Land Area and Population**

CBSA/ DIV code[1]	Area name	Land area,[2] 2010 (sq km)	Population 2014: Total persons	Population 2014: Rank	Population 2014: Per square kilometer	Population characteristics, 2013: Race alone or in combination, not Hispanic or Latino (percent): White	Black	American Indian, Alaska Native	Asian and Pacific Islander	Percent Hispanic or Latino[3]	Age (percent): Under 5 years	5 to 17 years	18 to 24 years	25 to 34 years	35 to 44 years	45 to 54 years
		1	2	3	4	5	6	7	8	9	10	11	12	13	14	15
21820	Fairbanks, AK	19 006	99 357	352	5.2	77.0	6.3	10.2	5.1	7.7	7.9	16.8	14.8	18.1	12.0	11.7
22020	Fargo, ND-MN	7 278	228 291	195	31.4	91.1	3.3	1.9	2.7	2.8	6.8	15.4	16.5	16.1	11.9	11.5
22140	Farmington, NM	14 279	123 785	315	8.7	42.4	1.1	38.2	0.9	19.3	7.5	20.3	9.5	14.0	11.7	12.6
22180	Fayetteville, NC	2 701	377 939	139	139.9	48.1	37.6	3.5	3.9	10.9	8.4	18.0	12.2	17.0	12.1	12.1
22220	Fayetteville-Springdale-Rogers, AR-MO	8 193	501 653	105	61.2	76.9	2.8	2.6	4.6	15.5	7.3	18.9	11.1	14.7	13.4	12.4
22380	Flagstaff, AZ	48 223	137 682	292	2.9	56.9	1.9	27.0	2.7	13.8	6.2	16.1	19.6	13.3	10.9	11.8
22420	Flint, MI	1 650	412 895	129	250.2	74.6	21.9	1.3	1.4	3.2	6.0	17.7	9.2	11.6	12.3	14.4
22500	Florence, SC	3 525	207 030	211	58.7	54.8	42.1	0.7	1.3	2.3	6.4	17.6	9.6	11.9	12.6	13.6
22520	Florence-Muscle Shoals, AL	3 264	147 639	281	45.2	84.0	13.0	1.0	0.9	2.4	5.4	15.6	10.6	11.2	11.8	13.6
22540	Fond du Lac, WI	1 864	101 759	349	54.6	92.2	1.9	0.8	1.5	4.8	5.7	16.2	8.9	12.1	11.8	15.1
22660	Fort Collins, CO	6 724	324 122	152	48.2	85.5	1.4	1.1	3.0	10.9	5.5	15.1	14.6	13.9	12.0	12.4
22900	Fort Smith, AR-OK	8 774	279 592	165	31.9	77.8	4.7	9.6	3.0	9.2	6.4	18.3	9.0	12.5	12.4	13.9
23060	Fort Wayne, IN	3 524	427 183	123	121.2	80.5	11.6	0.8	3.2	6.2	7.1	18.9	9.2	13.0	12.6	13.4
23420	Fresno, CA	15 431	965 974	56	62.6	33.0	5.3	1.2	10.8	51.5	8.4	20.8	11.3	14.7	12.1	11.9
23460	Gadsden, AL	1 386	103 531	346	74.7	79.8	16.0	1.0	1.0	3.6	5.8	16.5	8.9	11.6	12.9	13.7
23540	Gainesville, FL	3 172	273 377	173	86.2	66.6	20.0	0.7	6.3	8.7	5.6	12.6	22.0	14.7	10.3	10.9
23580	Gainesville, GA	1 017	190 761	224	187.6	63.3	7.9	0.6	2.2	27.2	7.1	19.9	9.3	12.9	13.5	13.3
23900	Gettysburg, PA	1 343	101 714	350	75.7	91.0	2.1	0.5	1.0	6.5	5.2	15.8	9.9	10.3	11.8	15.1
24020	Glens Falls, NY	4 398	127 345	308	29.0	94.8	2.5	0.7	1.0	2.3	4.9	14.8	8.3	11.2	12.0	15.7
24140	Goldsboro, NC	1 432	124 456	314	86.9	56.3	32.3	0.8	1.9	10.7	6.8	17.4	10.6	13.1	12.1	13.4
24220	Grand Forks, ND-MN	8 825	101 842	348	11.5	89.3	2.9	3.1	2.4	4.3	6.5	14.7	18.8	14.0	10.0	11.6
24260	Grand Island, NE	5 552	84 755	369	15.3	77.8	1.9	0.7	1.4	19.2	7.2	19.0	8.4	12.2	12.1	13.3
24300	Grand Junction, CO	8 622	148 255	278	17.2	83.9	1.2	1.4	1.5	13.8	6.4	16.3	10.1	13.3	11.2	12.7
24340	Grand Rapids-Wyoming, MI	6 913	1 027 703	52	148.7	81.9	7.5	0.9	2.8	9.0	6.7	18.4	10.7	13.6	12.2	13.7
24420	Grants Pass, OR	4 247	83 599	370	19.7	90.4	0.8	2.9	1.9	6.8	4.9	14.8	7.1	9.7	10.1	12.8
24500	Great Falls, MT	6 988	82 344	374	11.8	89.2	2.3	6.1	1.9	3.9	6.8	15.9	10.3	13.7	10.6	13.0
24540	Greeley, CO	10 327	277 670	169	26.9	68.6	1.3	1.1	1.9	28.3	7.3	19.7	10.3	14.1	13.5	12.9
24580	Green Bay, WI	4 844	314 531	157	64.9	86.6	2.7	2.8	2.9	6.7	6.5	17.4	9.0	13.1	12.4	15.0
24660	Greensboro-High Point, NC	5 164	746 593	74	144.6	62.1	27.1	1.0	3.8	7.9	5.9	16.9	10.2	12.6	13.1	14.2
24780	Greenville, NC	1 689	175 354	234	103.8	58.0	35.1	0.7	2.3	5.8	6.2	15.8	18.8	13.6	12.0	11.7
24860	Greenville-Anderson-Mauldin, SC	7 021	862 463	63	122.8	75.0	17.5	0.6	2.1	6.4	6.2	16.8	10.6	12.5	12.8	13.8
25060	Gulfport-Biloxi-Pascagoula, MS	4 586	386 144	136	84.2	70.9	21.9	1.0	3.2	5.2	6.6	17.6	9.7	13.6	12.5	13.8
25180	Hagerstown-Martinsburg, MD-WV	2 018	260 070	181	128.9	85.4	10.6	0.7	1.9	3.9	6.0	17.2	8.2	13.1	13.5	15.0
25220	Hammond, LA	2 049	127 049	309	62.0	65.1	30.6	0.8	1.0	3.8	7.1	17.8	11.7	14.3	11.8	12.6
25260	Hanford-Corcoran, CA	3 599	150 269	273	41.8	36.0	7.0	1.4	5.1	52.7	8.2	19.5	11.5	16.6	13.8	12.6
25420	Harrisburg-Carlisle, PA	4 201	560 849	95	133.5	81.2	11.1	0.6	3.8	5.4	5.7	15.8	9.2	13.0	12.3	14.4
25500	Harrisonburg, VA	2 244	130 649	302	58.2	83.2	4.5	0.5	2.5	10.8	5.4	14.6	20.0	12.6	10.9	11.8
25540	Hartford-West Hartford-East Hartford, CT	3 922	1 214 295	47	309.6	71.2	11.3	0.6	4.9	13.6	5.2	16.1	10.1	12.4	12.2	15.3
25620	Hattiesburg, MS	4 171	148 656	277	35.6	67.1	29.4	0.6	1.3	2.8	7.0	17.4	13.2	15.0	12.4	12.2
25860	Hickory-Lenoir-Morganton, NC	4 240	362 896	145	85.6	83.3	7.7	0.6	3.1	6.7	5.4	16.5	8.7	10.8	13.1	15.1
25940	Hilton Head Island-Bluffton-Beaufort, NC	3 190	203 022	215	63.6	64.5	22.9	0.6	1.7	11.9	6.0	14.4	9.8	12.2	10.9	11.4
25980	Hinesville, GA	2 306	82 311	375	35.7	48.9	38.4	1.2	3.6	11.6	10.6	18.4	13.8	18.6	11.6	10.9
26140	Homosassa Springs, FL	1 507	139 377	289	92.5	90.2	3.4	0.9	2.0	4.9	3.8	11.4	5.7	7.4	8.3	12.6
26300	Hot Springs, AR	1 755	97 322	358	55.5	85.0	9.2	1.5	1.2	5.2	5.6	15.1	7.9	11.2	11.1	13.2
26380	Houma-Thibodaux, LA	5 957	211 348	208	35.5	73.9	17.2	5.1	1.3	4.4	6.8	18.0	9.8	14.2	11.9	14.5
26420	Houston-The Woodlands-Sugar Land, TX	21 388	6 490 180	5	303.4	39.5	17.4	0.6	7.7	36.0	7.6	19.7	9.6	15.1	14.3	13.3
26580	Huntington-Ashland, WV-KY-OH	6 545	363 325	144	55.5	95.6	3.1	0.7	0.9	1.1	5.6	16.0	9.0	11.9	12.8	13.8
26620	Huntsville, AL	3 526	441 086	118	125.1	70.0	22.8	1.5	3.0	4.9	6.0	16.9	9.5	13.6	12.8	15.6
26820	Idaho Falls, ID	13 445	138 266	290	10.3	86.1	0.9	1.2	1.5	11.9	8.9	22.9	8.4	13.9	11.8	11.6
26900	Indianapolis-Carmel-Anderson, IN	11 153	1 971 274	33	176.7	76.1	15.9	0.6	3.0	6.3	6.9	18.5	8.9	14.2	13.5	14.1
26980	Iowa City, IA	3 063	164 357	250	53.7	84.9	5.6	0.6	5.6	5.4	6.2	14.6	19.2	15.9	11.5	11.1
27060	Ithaca, NY	1 229	104 691	345	85.2	81.3	5.0	0.8	11.2	4.6	4.2	11.4	27.2	13.2	9.9	10.9
27100	Jackson, MI	1 817	159 741	256	87.9	87.4	9.6	1.0	1.1	3.2	5.6	16.8	9.4	11.7	12.4	14.7
27140	Jackson, MS	12 041	577 564	93	48.0	47.9	48.9	0.4	1.4	2.3	6.8	18.5	10.0	14.2	12.9	13.3
27180	Jackson, TN	2 871	130 225	303	45.4	64.2	31.5	0.6	1.2	4.0	6.3	16.9	11.4	12.2	11.9	13.6
27260	Jacksonville, FL	8 291	1 419 127	40	171.2	66.8	22.3	0.8	4.7	7.6	6.2	16.8	9.3	14.0	12.9	14.4
27340	Jacksonville, NC	1 975	187 589	226	95.0	70.3	16.6	1.4	3.7	11.8	10.0	15.6	21.7	18.6	9.9	8.7
27500	Janesville-Beloit, WI	1 860	161 188	255	86.7	85.7	6.0	0.7	1.5	8.0	6.0	17.9	8.8	12.5	12.7	14.4
27620	Jefferson City, MO	5 822	150 866	272	25.9	88.7	8.4	0.9	1.2	2.5	6.0	16.9	9.7	13.2	12.7	14.5
27740	Johnson City, TN	2 212	201 091	217	90.9	93.0	3.7	0.7	1.2	2.8	5.1	14.6	10.9	11.8	12.6	13.9
27780	Johnstown, PA	1 783	137 732	291	77.2	94.0	4.5	0.3	0.8	1.6	4.9	14.3	9.5	10.6	11.5	14.0
27860	Jonesboro, AR	3 796	126 764	310	33.4	81.7	13.5	0.8	1.2	4.2	6.9	17.8	11.2	14.4	12.5	12.4

1. CBSA = Core Based Statistical Area. DIV = Metropolitan Division. See Appendix A for explanation. See Appendix B for list of metropolitan areas identified by type. 2. Dry land or land partially or temporarily covered by water. 3. May be of any race.

Area name	Population, 2013 (cont.): Age (percent) (cont.): 55 to 64 years	65 to 74 years	75 years and over	Percent female	Population change and components of change, 2000–2014: Total persons: 2000	2010	Percent change: 2000–2010	2010–2014	Components of change, 2010–2014: Births	Deaths	Net migration	Households, 2013: Number	Persons per household	Percent: Family households	Female family householder[1]	One person
	16	17	18	19	20	21	22	23	24	25	26	27	28	29	30	31
Fairbanks, AK	11.2	5.1	2.4	46.2	82 840	97 581	17.8	1.8	6 996	1 907	-3 422	34 056	2.84	54.2	5.4	36.5
Fargo, ND-MN	10.7	5.7	5.4	49.7	174 367	208 777	19.7	9.3	13 405	5 741	11 578	90 959	2.35	58.5	8.6	30.4
Farmington, NM	12.1	7.0	5.4	50.4	113 801	130 044	14.3	-4.8	7 913	3 960	-10 339	37 847	3.31	70.3	17.9	25.1
Fayetteville, NC	10.1	6.0	4.1	51.0	336 609	366 383	8.8	3.2	28 531	11 141	-6 128	142 827	2.56	66.1	17.7	28.1
Fayetteville-Springdale-Rogers, AR-MO	10.3	6.9	5.0	50.2	347 045	463 204	33.5	8.3	30 037	14 050	22 031	178 227	2.70	69.5	10.7	22.7
Flagstaff, AZ	11.8	6.6	3.7	50.6	116 320	134 421	15.6	2.4	7 353	3 135	-1 134	49 002	2.58	63.5	14.0	24.0
Flint, MI	13.6	8.4	6.8	51.8	436 141	425 790	-2.4	-3.0	21 208	18 186	-15 968	163 740	2.50	63.7	16.5	30.3
Florence, SC	13.5	9.0	5.9	52.9	193 155	205 566	6.4	0.7	11 043	9 496	162	77 550	2.59	68.5	19.6	27.9
Florence-Muscle Shoals, AL	13.8	10.2	7.8	52.0	142 950	147 137	2.9	0.3	6 509	7 387	1 492	61 383	2.36	65.8	13.2	30.3
Fond du Lac, WI	14.0	8.5	7.6	50.8	97 296	101 633	4.5	0.1	4 653	3 833	-597	41 202	2.39	67.4	7.7	27.1
Fort Collins, CO	13.0	8.0	5.5	50.3	251 494	299 630	19.1	8.2	14 376	8 162	17 677	123 877	2.48	61.0	8.1	25.8
Fort Smith, AR-OK	12.6	8.8	6.2	50.7	255 399	280 467	9.8	-0.3	14 801	12 115	-3 507	107 030	2.58	68.7	12.9	26.9
Fort Wayne, IN	12.5	7.3	5.9	51.1	390 156	416 257	6.7	2.6	25 439	14 515	378	166 620	2.51	65.3	12.8	29.5
Fresno, CA	10.0	6.1	4.8	50.0	799 407	930 450	16.4	3.8	68 262	27 223	-5 425	293 517	3.19	73.3	18.3	21.3
Gadsden, AL	13.8	9.9	7.0	51.5	103 459	104 430	0.9	-0.9	5 020	5 834	12	40 135	2.56	70.0	13.3	26.5
Gainesville, FL	11.5	7.1	5.3	51.4	232 392	264 275	13.7	3.4	13 072	8 184	4 088	104 294	2.46	51.4	9.6	34.1
Gainesville, GA	10.7	7.8	5.3	50.0	139 277	179 684	29.0	6.2	10 789	5 343	5 294	60 937	3.04	71.1	14.6	23.3
Gettysburg, PA	14.2	9.8	7.8	50.8	91 292	101 407	11.1	0.3	4 265	3 967	-195	37 242	2.62	73.7	9.6	20.7
Glens Falls, NY	14.8	10.2	8.0	49.8	124 345	128 923	3.7	-1.2	5 159	5 384	-1 243	51 414	2.42	65.1	13.4	28.7
Goldsboro, NC	12.5	8.1	6.0	50.8	113 329	122 623	8.2	1.5	7 328	4 815	-597	46 834	2.60	70.8	19.1	24.1
Grand Forks, ND-MN	11.6	6.7	6.1	48.9	97 478	98 461	1.0	3.4	5 849	3 442	948	40 982	2.30	59.3	7.7	30.7
Grand Island, NE	12.5	8.0	7.3	49.8	77 708	81 850	5.3	3.5	5 000	3 101	1 037	31 723	2.61	67.0	9.3	26.5
Grand Junction, CO	13.7	9.0	7.3	50.3	116 255	146 723	26.2	1.0	7 884	5 718	-710	58 466	2.46	67.7	13.8	23.7
Grand Rapids-Wyoming, MI	12.1	7.0	5.7	50.6	930 670	988 938	6.3	3.9	57 551	30 324	11 604	370 818	2.68	68.0	10.4	25.1
Grants Pass, OR	16.2	13.8	10.5	51.3	75 726	82 713	9.2	1.1	3 404	4 875	2 357	34 517	2.38	62.5	12.0	30.5
Great Falls, MT	13.3	8.8	7.6	49.7	80 357	81 327	1.2	1.3	5 011	3 382	-545	34 492	2.31	65.9	11.0	28.6
Greeley, CO	11.3	6.6	4.3	49.7	180 926	252 825	NA	9.8	16 389	6 371	14 339	92 426	2.85	72.9	12.1	21.6
Green Bay, WI	12.9	7.6	6.1	50.1	282 599	306 241	8.4	2.7	16 825	9 637	1 308	122 600	2.49	65.2	9.8	27.8
Greensboro-High Point, NC	12.6	8.3	6.2	52.0	643 430	723 801	12.5	3.1	36 800	26 911	12 967	289 205	2.50	65.7	14.5	27.8
Greenville, NC	10.9	6.4	4.5	52.8	133 798	168 148	25.7	4.3	9 100	4 938	3 000	67 573	2.49	59.3	16.0	31.3
Greenville-Anderson-Mauldin, SC	12.5	8.7	6.1	51.3	725 680	824 112	13.6	4.7	43 859	32 409	26 089	320 628	2.58	68.1	13.2	27.1
Gulfport-Biloxi-Pascagoula, MS	12.4	8.1	5.5	50.5	363 988	370 702	1.8	4.1	20 495	14 635	9 295	143 330	2.62	66.5	17.3	27.4
Hagerstown-Martinsburg, MD-WV	12.7	8.3	6.1	49.6	207 828	251 599	21.1	3.4	13 229	10 029	5 173	97 681	2.54	67.8	11.7	26.9
Hammond, LA	12.3	7.6	4.8	51.5	100 588	121 097	20.4	4.9	8 079	4 810	2 639	46 039	2.64	64.8	14.4	27.5
Hanford-Corcoran, CA	9.0	5.1	3.7	44.3	129 461	152 982	18.2	-1.8	10 344	3 385	-9 845	41 813	3.20	76.8	20.2	17.2
Harrisburg-Carlisle, PA	13.8	8.6	7.1	51.0	509 074	549 475	7.9	2.1	27 681	21 238	5 463	224 798	2.39	62.9	10.3	30.4
Harrisonburg, VA	11.0	7.2	6.4	51.6	108 193	125 228	15.7	4.3	5 930	3 919	3 037	45 285	2.65	65.4	11.3	24.7
Hartford-West Hartford-East Hartford, CT	13.4	8.3	7.1	51.3	1 148 618	1 212 381	5.6	0.2	51 568	43 436	-4 864	464 315	2.51	65.5	13.6	28.7
Hattiesburg, MS	10.6	7.1	5.1	52.0	123 812	142 842	15.4	4.1	8 697	5 103	2 022	53 052	2.72	65.7	17.5	25.2
Hickory-Lenoir-Morganton, NC	13.6	10.0	6.8	50.5	341 851	365 497	6.9	-0.7	16 200	15 964	-2 927	136 858	2.60	67.1	12.9	28.1
Hilton Head Island-Bluffton-Beaufort, NC	13.2	13.7	8.4	50.4	141 615	187 010	32.1	8.6	10 182	6 651	11 952	74 931	2.57	67.2	11.8	26.1
Hinesville, GA	8.8	4.8	2.5	49.4	71 914	77 917	8.3	5.6	7 070	1 663	-1 335	28 505	2.79	73.3	17.3	21.9
Homosassa Springs, FL	16.3	18.9	15.6	51.6	118 085	141 236	19.6	-1.3	4 421	10 004	3 553	62 131	2.21	66.6	9.3	28.9
Hot Springs, AR	14.5	11.9	9.4	51.7	88 068	96 024	9.0	1.4	4 814	5 675	2 421	41 865	2.27	66.2	16.4	25.5
Houma-Thibodaux, LA	11.9	7.6	5.3	50.7	194 477	208 178	7.0	1.5	11 869	7 686	-878	73 418	2.81	71.9	14.7	22.5
Houston-The Woodlands-Sugar Land, TX	11.0	5.9	3.7	50.2	4 693 161	5 920 416	26.1	9.6	395 388	148 318	321 525	2 158 139	2.89	70.8	14.7	24.0
Huntington-Ashland, WV-KY-OH	14.0	9.7	7.3	51.0	362 346	364 908	0.7	-0.4	17 587	17 453	-1 420	145 100	2.46	66.8	12.1	27.8
Huntsville, AL	12.3	7.7	5.6	50.8	342 376	417 593	22.0	5.6	21 624	14 378	15 745	169 951	2.50	66.5	13.3	29.7
Idaho Falls, ID	10.7	6.7	5.0	50.1	104 576	133 265	27.4	3.7	10 527	3 864	-1 786	45 964	2.95	73.7	11.1	21.8
Indianapolis-Carmel-Anderson, IN	11.8	6.9	5.1	51.1	1 658 462	1 887 877	13.8	4.4	113 127	64 207	34 367	739 503	2.59	65.4	13.6	28.7
Iowa City, IA	10.7	6.0	4.8	50.2	131 676	152 586	15.9	7.7	8 793	3 698	6 597	64 564	2.36	54.3	6.7	29.9
Ithaca, NY	11.3	6.8	5.1	50.7	96 501	101 564	5.2	3.0	3 883	2 683	1 913	37 524	2.39	52.9	9.8	33.0
Jackson, MI	13.8	8.6	6.9	48.8	158 422	160 248	1.2	-0.3	7 604	6 699	-1 293	61 235	2.47	67.5	13.8	27.4
Jackson, MS	12.1	7.1	5.2	52.0	525 346	567 122	8.0	1.7	32 498	20 903	-1 847	207 205	2.09	60.7	20.3	27.3
Jackson, TN	12.7	8.5	6.5	52.5	121 909	130 011	6.6	0.2	6 988	5 264	-1 427	47 027	2.66	64.8	15.6	30.3
Jacksonville, FL	12.8	8.1	5.5	51.3	1 122 750	1 345 596	19.8	5.5	74 607	48 931	46 565	516 144	2.65	65.0	13.9	28.8
Jacksonville, NC	7.3	4.8	3.3	45.5	150 355	177 772	18.2	5.5	18 455	3 817	-5 177	60 764	2.82	72.3	13.6	21.2
Janesville-Beloit, WI	13.0	8.0	6.7	50.9	152 307	160 331	5.3	0.5	8 149	5 916	-1 302	64 088	2.46	67.4	12.8	26.4
Jefferson City, MO	13.0	8.0	6.0	48.9	140 052	149 807	7.0	0.7	7 625	5 228	-1 196	53 981	2.56	63.1	11.1	31.2
Johnson City, TN	13.6	10.3	7.3	51.1	181 607	198 716	9.4	1.2	8 758	9 199	2 792	83 446	2.32	64.0	11.1	32.0
Johnstown, PA	15.5	10.0	9.7	50.4	152 598	143 679	-5.8	-4.1	5 715	7 676	-3 851	57 407	2.29	63.0	11.2	31.3
Jonesboro, AR	11.2	7.8	5.7	51.3	107 762	121 026	12.3	4.7	7 325	5 047	3 418	47 799	2.55	69.0	14.9	23.5

1. No spouse present.

Area name	Persons in group quarters, 2014	Daytime population, 2013: Number	Daytime population, 2013: Employment/residence ratio	Births, 2014: Total	Births, 2014: Rate[1]	Deaths, 2014: Number	Deaths, 2014: Rate[1]	Persons under 65 with no health insurance 2013: Number	Persons under 65 with no health insurance 2013: Percent	Medicare, 2014: Eligible for Medicare	Medicare, 2014: Enrolled in Medicare Advantage	Medicare, 2014: Enrolled in a Medicare prescription drug plan	Serious crimes known to police,[2] 2013: Total: Number	Serious crimes known to police,[2] 2013: Total: Rate[3]
	32	33	34	35	36	37	38	39	40	41	42	43	44	45
Fairbanks, AK	5 084	149 646	NA	1 611	16.2	445	4.5	16 771	18.8	9 216	40	3 176	NA	NA
Fargo, ND-MN	9 242	231 472	1.07	3 311	14.5	1 407	6.2	19 965	10.5	29 498	7 907	16 355	5 665	2 550
Farmington, NM	1 735	129 361	1.06	1 781	14.4	985	8.0	27 529	24.9	18 057	693	10 473	3 380	2 650
Fayetteville, NC	9 177	414 297	1.25	6 560	17.4	2 667	7.1	54 194	16.4	51 264	11 846	17 366	20 267	5 361
Fayetteville-Springdale-Rogers, AR-MO	10 168	503 334	1.05	7 178	14.3	3 292	6.6	83 318	19.7	73 457	19 590	31 524	13 016	2 699
Flagstaff, AZ	10 628	141 006	1.08	1 697	12.3	772	5.6	24 148	21.1	16 970	1 939	8 394	4 620	3 372
Flint, MI	5 978	443 007	1.23	4 904	11.9	4 371	10.6	39 719	11.4	83 583	28 110	59 739	15 134	3 636
Florence, SC	4 731	220 700	1.20	2 585	12.5	2 254	10.9	28 234	16.4	40 531	5 425	24 124	10 325	5 014
Florence-Muscle Shoals, AL	2 516	155 869	1.17	1 527	10.3	1 739	11.8	17 577	14.8	33 648	3 935	19 689	4 497	3 062
Fond du Lac, WI	3 516	112 750	1.30	1 089	10.7	870	8.5	7 717	9.4	19 337	8 812	6 296	1 854	1 818
Fort Collins, CO	8 637	338 383	1.17	3 447	10.6	1 965	6.1	37 675	14.1	50 304	13 470	23 275	7 452	2 359
Fort Smith, AR-OK	5 022	288 075	1.08	3 627	13.0	2 938	10.5	52 644	22.4	55 913	14 240	25 013	9 891	3 521
Fort Wayne, IN	7 009	448 403	1.14	6 003	14.1	3 485	8.2	60 821	16.8	70 350	29 865	29 961	13 268	3 307
Fresno, CA	17 319	985 722	1.09	15 977	16.5	6 721	7.0	170 295	20.3	124 126	35 776	59 029	41 566	4 356
Gadsden, AL	2 083	109 015	1.18	1 144	11.0	1 431	13.8	13 664	16.1	24 273	5 887	12 884	4 725	4 859
Gainesville, FL	14 405	294 628	1.19	3 060	11.2	2 021	7.4	43 379	19.4	40 954	6 766	17 240	9 475	3 502
Gainesville, GA	2 812	212 861	1.43	2 494	13.1	1 367	7.2	39 337	24.5	30 016	7 909	14 082	4 499	2 402
Gettysburg, PA	4 019	110 103	1.32	974	9.6	931	9.2	9 962	12.4	21 301	6 261	9 014	1 372	1 352
Glens Falls, NY	3 861	140 024	1.25	1 169	9.2	1 303	10.2	10 647	10.4	28 423	10 550	10 462	2 172	1 691
Goldsboro, NC	2 996	133 715	1.23	1 749	14.1	1 217	9.8	18 981	18.2	22 111	3 923	10 788	4 578	3 744
Grand Forks, ND-MN	5 508	105 029	1.08	1 418	13.9	797	7.8	9 564	11.5	15 373	4 194	8 898	2 374	2 362
Grand Island, NE	1 497	88 237	1.10	1 195	14.1	712	8.4	10 969	15.6	14 628	NA	9 201	2 944	3 785
Grand Junction, CO	4 494	149 793	1.04	1 825	12.3	1 356	9.1	21 117	17.5	28 383	10 319	10 965	4 294	2 891
Grand Rapids-Wyoming, MI	23 159	1 082 102	1.15	13 817	13.4	7 274	7.1	103 918	12.0	163 510	79 439	63 246	22 717	2 258
Grants Pass, OR	1 544	86 825	1.16	826	9.9	1 119	13.4	10 724	17.1	23 843	9 057	8 168	3 514	4 225
Great Falls, MT	2 546	83 908	1.04	1 169	14.2	763	9.3	12 026	17.9	16 359	3 727	6 174	3 172	3 859
Greeley, CO	5 778	296 918	1.37	3 980	14.3	1 546	5.6	40 203	17.1	34 980	10 501	15 392	5 913	2 255
Green Bay, WI	6 997	337 154	1.17	3 945	12.5	2 238	7.1	28 038	10.6	52 409	25 160	15 312	5 969	1 908
Greensboro-High Point, NC	18 274	807 806	1.24	8 750	11.7	6 631	8.9	115 748	18.7	133 226	65 670	42 152	27 373	3 695
Greenville, NC	6 745	187 429	1.19	2 136	12.2	1 227	7.0	26 379	17.7	25 195	3 591	13 869	6 626	3 855
Greenville-Anderson-Mauldin, SC	23 607	897 555	1.14	10 342	12.0	7 795	9.0	130 786	18.6	162 650	48 611	74 961	39 018	4 584
Gulfport-Biloxi-Pascagoula, MS	7 294	404 537	1.14	4 741	12.3	3 413	8.8	67 881	21.0	67 085	12 700	27 841	14 004	3 726
Hagerstown-Martinsburg, MD-WV	9 326	279 408	1.27	3 164	12.2	2 425	9.3	28 301	13.3	46 152	5 932	24 139	6 246	2 423
Hammond, LA	3 645	136 713	1.33	1 937	15.2	1 211	9.5	22 179	20.8	20 144	5 704	9 506	8 026	6 462
Hanford-Corcoran, CA	17 030	164 570	1.32	2 345	15.6	818	5.4	22 593	18.8	15 486	1 821	8 836	4 448	2 941
Harrisburg-Carlisle, PA	20 217	632 420	1.30	6 537	11.7	4 993	8.9	50 455	11.1	105 737	45 196	43 170	12 384	2 239
Harrisonburg, VA	9 044	142 143	1.24	1 411	10.8	921	7.0	18 990	18.4	20 584	2 958	11 958	2 211	1 705
Hartford-West Hartford-East Hartford, CT	48 326	1 313 153	1.19	12 059	9.9	10 289	8.5	96 239	9.7	216 667	58 937	99 327	25 287	2 470
Hattiesburg, MS	3 971	161 134	1.23	2 044	13.7	1 176	7.9	25 376	20.2	23 364	3 951	12 380	NA	NA
Hickory-Lenoir-Morganton, NC	7 721	379 757	1.13	3 796	10.5	3 748	10.3	56 022	18.8	76 703	23 227	36 817	10 889	3 005
Hilton Head Island-Bluffton-Beaufort, NC	6 460	204 869	1.08	2 386	11.8	1 622	8.0	33 463	22.7	46 519	7 746	24 369	6 406	3 255
Hinesville, GA	2 803	90 104	1.31	1 672	20.3	391	4.8	13 678	19.0	7 121	1 638	2 094	2 405	2 899
Homosassa Springs, FL	2 249	176 108	NA	1 009	7.2	2 410	17.3	19 393	21.5	51 527	15 547	21 384	3 177	2 333
Hot Springs, AR	2 172	103 002	1.19	1 141	11.7	1 288	13.2	16 109	21.4	26 223	5 363	12 577	5 637	5 802
Houma-Thibodaux, LA	3 105	225 875	1.20	2 755	13.0	1 862	8.8	36 948	20.5	35 067	6 323	18 442	7 366	3 519
Houston-The Woodlands-Sugar Land, TX	79 648	6 392 482	1.03	94 872	14.6	37 096	5.7	1 417 057	25.2	713 356	249 583	277 352	253 852	4 042
Huntington-Ashland, WV-KY-OH	7 916	383 656	1.17	4 127	11.4	4 154	11.4	47 572	16.1	81 784	21 473	39 594	8 103	2 407
Huntsville, AL	10 567	466 070	1.16	5 033	11.4	3 495	7.9	51 820	14.2	72 350	10 933	32 631	16 678	3 838
Idaho Falls, ID	1 371	146 446	1.18	2 467	17.8	915	6.6	22 061	18.4	19 703	NA	8 923	2 748	1 998
Indianapolis-Carmel-Anderson, IN	39 382	2 010 593	1.06	26 630	13.5	15 200	7.7	261 194	15.6	294 788	73 011	150 641	73 347	4 138
Iowa City, IA	8 297	178 797	1.23	2 121	12.9	896	5.5	13 242	9.7	20 813	2 553	10 832	3 730	2 326
Ithaca, NY	13 269	119 989	1.36	948	9.1	599	5.7	9 151	11.6	14 605	2 994	6 042	NA	NA
Jackson, MI	9 481	172 545	1.26	1 756	11.0	1 592	10.0	15 291	12.1	31 584	7 461	18 061	4 226	2 718
Jackson, MS	21 549	596 977	1.08	7 413	12.8	5 069	8.8	87 120	18.0	94 138	18 890	47 188	16 256	3 341
Jackson, TN	5 908	150 279	1.42	1 658	12.7	1 230	9.4	16 366	15.4	25 060	4 231	14 036	5 926	4 534
Jacksonville, FL	27 544	1 419 163	1.04	17 664	12.4	12 192	8.6	215 943	18.3	236 148	61 505	91 699	51 878	3 724
Jacksonville, NC	15 499	197 204	1.15	4 327	23.1	937	5.0	24 742	15.9	19 972	2 352	8 115	1 555	840
Janesville-Beloit, WI	2 721	171 140	1.20	1 901	11.8	1 371	8.5	16 988	12.6	29 696	9 144	17 862	4 354	2 711
Jefferson City, MO	10 540	161 272	1.21	1 804	12.0	1 259	8.3	16 470	13.8	26 306	3 111	15 993	3 669	2 437
Johnson City, TN	6 283	214 861	1.20	2 056	10.2	2 159	10.7	26 017	16.2	45 338	19 682	13 905	5 815	2 887
Johnstown, PA	6 492	151 532	1.25	1 300	9.4	1 771	12.9	11 055	10.4	34 474	20 943	10 114	2 799	1 987
Jonesboro, AR	4 129	133 002	1.16	1 752	13.8	1 218	9.6	19 758	18.8	22 670	3 536	12 930	4 810	3 847

1. Per 1,000 estimated resident population. 2. Data for serious crimes have not been adjusted for underreporting; this may affect comparability between geographic areas and over time.
3. Per 100,000 population estimated by the FBI.

Area name	Serious crimes known to police, 2013 (cont.)[1] Rate[2] Violent	Rate[2] Property	Education: School enrollment and attainment, 2013 — Enrollment[3] Total	Enrollment[3] Percent private	Attainment[4] (percent) High school graduate or less	Attainment[4] (percent) Bachelor's degree or more	Local government expenditures,[5] 2012–2013 Total current expenditures (mil dol)	Current expenditures per student (dollars)	Income and Poverty, 2013 — Per capita income[6] (dollars)	Mean household income (dollars)	Median household income	Percent of households with income of less than $25,000	Percent of households with income of $200,000 or more	Percent below poverty level All persons	Children under 18 years	Age 65 years and older
	46	47	48	49	50	51	52	53	54	55	56	57	58	59	60	61
Fairbanks, AK	NA	NA	31 143	12.6	31.2	32.6	275.6	17 384	30 872	82 347	69 113	17.6	5.2	7.7	9.4	1.7
Fargo, ND-MN	253	2 296	65 601	14.7	28.4	35.3	330.6	10 720	28 374	69 174	51 961	22.1	3.9	13.9	13.6	5.3
Farmington, NM	490	2 160	34 483	4.7	50.2	12.9	211.3	8 814	20 179	59 018	43 787	30.0	1.7	22.7	26.3	16.5
Fayetteville, NC	487	4 873	109 309	15.5	37.9	22.3	500.3	8 157	21 736	55 317	42 968	28.0	1.7	18.8	27.5	10.8
Fayetteville-Springdale-Rogers, AR-MO	333	2 366	138 303	10.5	46.1	28.2	760.1	9 067	24 557	66 435	47 905	23.5	4.0	16.8	22.3	8.4
Flagstaff, AZ	329	3 043	46 613	6.5	31.4	34.3	134.3	7 962	25 178	68 635	50 637	25.8	2.2	24.1	30.3	9.9
Flint, MI	727	2 909	108 868	8.8	43.1	19.3	699.6	10 792	22 445	55 459	41 249	29.7	1.9	21.6	33.2	7.2
Florence, SC	475	4 539	56 928	12.0	51.8	20.5	308.5	9 206	20 939	53 523	38 577	32.5	2.4	22.9	31.1	18.1
Florence-Muscle Shoals, AL	327	2 735	35 544	8.8	50.3	17.0	199.4	9 342	22 809	53 672	42 898	30.2	1.5	15.9	21.0	7.1
Fond du Lac, WI	196	1 622	23 786	24.5	45.3	22.6	146.4	10 908	26 907	65 161	54 198	20.6	2.0	8.1	8.1	8.1
Fort Collins, CO	203	2 156	92 852	9.8	24.5	43.3	379.0	8 405	31 546	78 307	59 052	19.6	5.1	14.3	12.7	4.8
Fort Smith, AR-OK	402	3 119	69 665	6.6	55.0	16.7	431.1	8 610	20 736	52 882	37 633	33.8	2.6	23.8	35.1	16.6
Fort Wayne, IN	279	3 028	116 284	19.6	42.2	24.3	577.7	9 191	24 374	61 453	46 005	23.8	2.1	16.0	24.5	6.4
Fresno, CA	510	3 846	287 306	7.2	48.2	19.8	1 841.6	9 403	19 682	61 208	43 925	29.4	2.9	28.8	42.8	12.6
Gadsden, AL	591	4 268	24 256	5.3	49.4	16.2	132.2	8 058	20 018	50 005	39 459	33.8	1.0	18.9	23.5	14.0
Gainesville, FL	542	2 961	98 782	9.1	30.5	37.5	267.6	8 803	22 722	57 097	38 658	32.8	3.5	26.8	29.1	10.5
Gainesville, GA	156	2 246	49 526	9.3	51.7	21.7	290.9	8 521	22 373	63 948	44 998	24.8	3.7	21.9	34.0	11.9
Gettysburg, PA	98	1 255	24 645	28.2	53.6	23.6	276.2	20 032	27 356	73 000	59 029	15.9	3.2	8.9	15.4	5.3
Glens Falls, NY	97	1 594	26 300	9.6	47.1	23.6	320.5	17 446	28 191	68 128	53 562	22.0	3.3	12.7	19.7	9.3
Goldsboro, NC	366	3 379	32 606	8.3	45.1	17.4	153.4	7 765	21 007	54 320	42 193	29.2	1.5	21.4	35.7	7.0
Grand Forks, ND-MN	219	2 143	31 409	5.1	34.4	27.4	156.4	11 387	27 549	66 469	50 891	26.1	3.4	15.4	9.5	12.7
Grand Island, NE	192	3 593	20 022	13.4	47.9	18.2	178.1	11 522	23 970	61 009	50 567	21.1	1.7	15.1	25.2	6.4
Grand Junction, CO	312	2 578	36 304	6.6	39.6	27.6	174.7	7 802	25 981	64 523	46 723	26.3	3.0	16.7	22.1	8.9
Grand Rapids-Wyoming, MI	304	1 954	282 220	19.6	37.3	30.6	1 677.8	10 931	25 598	68 510	52 485	20.8	3.1	14.0	17.6	6.5
Grants Pass, OR	164	4 062	16 065	8.0	46.8	18.3	99.3	9 292	23 866	58 375	38 298	33.9	2.7	17.0	20.9	9.5
Great Falls, MT	255	3 604	17 550	11.3	38.3	29.4	109.4	9 502	25 654	60 627	43 947	28.4	3.0	16.0	25.3	6.7
Greeley, CO	299	1 956	77 005	10.2	39.1	27.4	325.5	8 426	25 855	72 246	58 611	19.2	2.9	13.4	17.5	6.2
Green Bay, WI	200	1 708	78 044	14.6	42.1	27.0	538.6	10 524	27 343	68 087	51 148	21.5	3.6	12.0	16.7	9.6
Greensboro-High Point, NC	340	3 355	192 658	13.7	42.7	27.5	972.4	8 739	24 780	61 828	43 791	28.9	2.9	19.9	29.1	9.5
Greenville, NC	461	3 395	63 514	8.6	37.3	28.4	197.0	8 282	24 087	59 751	40 639	33.6	3.1	25.6	32.5	9.4
Greenville-Anderson-Mauldin, SC	561	4 023	218 970	18.8	43.0	26.8	1 095.7	8 387	23 636	60 265	44 853	28.3	2.6	17.4	25.9	8.8
Gulfport-Biloxi-Pascagoula, MS	267	3 459	91 038	13.3	44.8	19.3	517.5	8 485	21 204	53 942	44 951	28.9	1.1	19.3	30.0	10.3
Hagerstown-Martinsburg, MD-WV	231	2 192	63 712	12.0	51.0	21.3	473.0	11 659	26 054	68 024	56 424	20.2	2.5	12.4	16.6	7.8
Hammond, LA	873	5 589	33 935	10.8	55.5	19.3	176.4	8 892	21 307	56 206	44 166	31.9	2.3	21.7	28.5	17.3
Hanford-Corcoran, CA	479	2 461	42 961	5.3	52.7	12.9	255.8	8 888	17 948	60 976	45 774	25.1	2.6	21.4	29.6	8.9
Harrisburg-Carlisle, PA	256	1 983	128 377	18.3	45.6	29.4	913.7	13 575	29 983	73 459	56 484	18.8	3.9	11.4	15.9	5.0
Harrisonburg, VA	130	1 575	44 688	11.0	51.5	25.6	180.3	10 607	23 147	63 123	46 710	21.2	2.2	16.9	14.3	5.4
Hartford-West Hartford-East Hartford, CT	265	2 205	321 797	15.7	37.9	36.5	3 002.5	16 972	35 330	89 700	66 356	19.1	7.4	10.8	15.2	7.5
Hattiesburg, MS	NA	NA	49 675	9.6	38.5	32.6	201.2	8 544	20 723	55 320	40 364	31.3	2.5	23.7	28.9	11.6
Hickory-Lenoir-Morganton, NC	206	2 799	83 767	11.8	52.3	17.5	462.7	8 286	20 776	52 770	38 039	31.4	1.7	17.3	26.2	8.7
Hilton Head Island-Bluffton-Beaufort, NC	483	2 773	41 953	13.2	31.5	36.7	266.0	11 393	30 659	74 154	52 269	21.6	5.1	16.1	25.3	5.1
Hinesville, GA	275	2 624	21 261	8.5	42.5	20.9	120.4	9 206	19 720	51 984	40 559	28.7	1.5	20.4	25.8	14.7
Homosassa Springs, FL	388	1 945	22 461	17.2	48.3	18.9	136.2	8 895	22 817	50 370	40 015	32.9	1.3	16.8	24.4	9.6
Hot Springs, AR	472	5 329	21 252	8.4	41.5	21.1	141.5	9 550	23 499	53 570	39 589	35.5	1.5	24.0	41.3	9.6
Houma-Thibodaux, LA	299	3 220	49 318	16.2	66.1	13.2	306.4	9 210	24 794	66 607	54 070	24.2	3.3	13.6	17.3	12.8
Houston-The Woodlands-Sugar Land, TX	559	3 483	1 790 150	11.6	41.8	30.9	9 374.1	7 944	29 212	82 660	57 366	21.3	7.2	16.4	23.7	10.0
Huntington-Ashland, WV-KY-OH	168	2 238	84 198	8.2	50.9	18.8	623.1	10 817	24 786	61 246	43 543	31.3	2.8	20.2	29.1	10.8
Huntsville, AL	483	3 355	113 426	15.4	33.9	36.5	594.7	9 188	30 197	75 740	55 857	21.5	4.3	15.0	21.1	8.6
Idaho Falls, ID	158	1 839	38 503	10.6	39.4	24.5	164.5	5 917	20 813	61 391	50 439	19.5	1.5	11.2	13.9	5.4
Indianapolis-Carmel-Anderson, IN	662	3 476	509 547	17.8	40.1	30.8	2 946.3	9 676	27 657	70 631	51 087	23.5	4.0	15.2	21.1	7.9
Iowa City, IA	305	2 021	57 440	9.6	23.2	48.6	202.3	9 947	29 430	72 991	52 220	22.3	5.2	15.6	11.0	4.2
Ithaca, NY	NA	NA	41 308	34.2	27.4	50.9	209.0	19 154	26 677	71 076	48 516	24.7	5.0	20.3	20.5	3.5
Jackson, MI	409	2 309	39 176	11.6	44.4	19.1	257.0	11 350	22 339	56 509	43 668	29.9	1.7	19.3	31.6	7.4
Jackson, MS	395	2 946	168 910	19.0	38.7	29.3	749.9	8 053	23 230	61 545	43 611	30.6	3.6	22.0	30.3	15.2
Jackson, TN	660	3 665	34 520	27.4	47.0	23.8	155.7	8 092	23 525	57 967	38 663	32.8	3.1	20.9	29.0	12.7
Jacksonville, FL	496	3 229	357 444	19.7	37.6	28.3	1 724.7	8 235	27 958	71 515	51 495	22.5	4.5	14.8	21.3	8.2
Jacksonville, NC	66	774	43 311	14.8	40.4	17.8	198.2	7 762	20 687	54 335	44 673	24.6	1.2	17.0	23.6	12.7
Janesville-Beloit, WI	229	2 482	41 695	12.1	50.0	19.7	306.9	11 026	23 843	59 182	47 118	23.3	1.6	14.6	22.0	9.2
Jefferson City, MO	283	2 154	37 396	16.6	49.3	24.0	176.4	8 646	22 693	59 917	47 586	23.6	2.0	13.3	18.4	7.1
Johnson City, TN	315	2 572	51 951	13.3	49.4	24.8	222.0	8 031	23 509	54 439	37 423	35.4	1.9	19.3	27.1	11.0
Johnstown, PA	190	1 797	30 601	22.2	56.6	18.7	228.6	12 404	22 262	53 223	41 423	30.8	0.9	16.4	25.7	7.3
Jonesboro, AR	359	3 488	35 051	7.8	50.3	23.1	190.3	8 684	21 141	54 345	39 552	31.8	0.7	21.4	33.7	8.3

1. Data for serious crimes have not been adjusted for underreporting; this may affect comparability between geographic areas and over time. 2. Per 100,000 population estimated by the FBI. 3. All persons 3 years old and over enrolled in nursery school through college. 4. Persons 25 years old and over. 5. Elementary and secondary education expenditures. 6. Based on resident population estimated in the 2008-2012 American Community Survey.

Area name	Personal income, 2013										Earnings, 2013		
	Total (mil dol)	Percent change 2012–2013	Per capita[1]		Wages and salaries (mil dol)	Supplements to wages and salaries; employer contributions (mil dol)		Proprietors' income (mil dol)	Dividends, interest, and rent (mil dol)	Personal transfer receipts (mil dol)	Total (mil dol)	Contributions for government social insurance (mil dol)	
			Dollars	Rank		Pension and insurance	Government social insurance					From employee and self-employed	From employer
	62	63	64	65	66	67	68	69	70	71	72	73	74
Fairbanks, AK	4 551	-1.3	45 313	73	2 499	699	213	285	983	651	3 696	177	213
Fargo, ND-MN	10 509	1.1	47 023	51	5 792	783	450	1 346	2 021	1 284	8 370	497	450
Farmington, NM	4 211	-0.2	33 289	341	2 349	408	176	270	591	863	3 203	197	176
Fayetteville, NC	16 479	-0.3	43 689	101	8 689	2 186	795	746	3 213	3 056	12 415	604	795
Fayetteville-Springdale-Rogers, AR-MO	18 628	4.3	37 863	225	10 365	1 440	754	1 412	3 723	2 893	13 971	861	754
Flagstaff, AZ	4 906	3.4	35 933	283	2 462	525	184	314	896	929	3 485	198	184
Flint, MI	13 709	1.0	33 003	345	5 761	984	466	816	1 921	4 237	8 028	548	466
Florence, SC	7 146	2.4	34 646	311	3 611	627	278	456	998	1 892	4 971	316	278
Florence-Muscle Shoals, AL	4 971	1.9	33 742	332	1 995	356	156	417	874	1 293	2 924	192	156
Fond du Lac, WI	4 161	2.2	40 873	162	1 955	396	165	302	716	739	2 818	169	165
Fort Collins, CO	13 545	3.9	42 866	112	6 500	1 005	454	848	3 105	1 805	8 808	475	454
Fort Smith, AR-OK	9 718	0.0	34 711	310	4 221	672	344	835	2 101	2 383	6 072	393	344
Fort Wayne, IN	15 920	0.7	37 537	235	8 711	1 406	672	1 366	2 677	3 048	12 155	746	672
Fresno, CA	34 041	4.0	35 635	291	14 589	3 336	1 087	3 858	5 753	7 928	22 871	1 235	1 087
Gadsden, AL	3 447	1.2	33 162	342	1 254	211	99	279	531	1 022	1 843	129	99
Gainesville, FL	10 255	2.3	37 929	224	5 574	1 215	401	447	2 218	1 828	7 637	426	401
Gainesville, GA	6 373	4.0	33 945	326	3 318	570	223	509	1 139	1 216	4 620	271	223
Gettysburg, PA	3 699	1.5	36 428	270	1 307	276	111	260	685	772	1 954	121	111
Glens Falls, NY	5 289	1.0	41 182	153	2 162	557	183	279	1 077	1 143	3 180	178	183
Goldsboro, NC	4 213	0.1	33 815	329	1 858	385	153	238	732	1 045	2 633	153	153
Grand Forks, ND-MN	4 362	-0.9	43 299	105	2 212	377	180	424	912	693	3 193	178	180
Grand Island, NE	3 632	2.4	43 238	107	1 615	294	120	615	705	574	2 644	140	120
Grand Junction, CO	5 492	1.0	37 222	244	2 551	384	193	395	1 222	1 048	3 524	209	193
Grand Rapids-Wyoming, MI	38 950	2.4	38 314	212	21 997	3 438	1 752	3 126	6 524	6 747	30 314	1 844	1 752
Grants Pass, OR	2 655	1.9	31 869	364	799	144	78	186	587	946	1 207	94	78
Great Falls, MT	3 358	0.5	40 759	164	1 493	291	142	290	789	647	2 216	138	142
Greeley, CO	9 009	5.0	33 393	338	4 284	626	313	937	1 560	1 456	6 161	330	313
Green Bay, WI	13 331	1.9	42 671	117	7 707	1 498	603	1 099	2 366	2 002	10 907	636	603
Greensboro-High Point, NC	27 488	0.9	37 092	249	15 460	2 315	1 210	1 921	4 740	5 663	20 906	1 303	1 210
Greenville, NC	6 300	0.7	36 153	279	3 172	631	240	384	982	1 278	4 427	259	240
Greenville-Anderson-Mauldin, SC	31 081	2.8	36 525	265	16 242	2 549	1 274	2 194	4 579	6 590	22 260	1 414	1 274
Gulfport-Biloxi-Pascagoula, MS	13 606	1.3	35 570	293	7 174	1 315	569	853	2 502	2 942	9 911	601	569
Hagerstown-Martinsburg, MD-WV	9 341	0.6	36 164	278	4 160	803	334	468	1 523	1 917	5 766	354	334
Hammond, LA	4 118	1.2	32 836	350	1 612	327	96	278	535	1 147	2 312	122	96
Hanford-Corcoran, CA	4 927	1.9	32 635	351	2 009	570	152	753	792	961	3 484	150	152
Harrisburg-Carlisle, PA	25 440	2.2	45 615	67	15 851	3 326	1 252	1 645	4 543	4 468	22 074	1 251	1 252
Harrisonburg, VA	4 412	2.4	34 166	320	2 421	432	179	384	939	747	3 415	200	179
Hartford-West Hartford-East Hartford, CT	67 269	0.8	55 355	13	38 131	6 023	2 752	5 760	13 478	10 126	52 665	2 855	2 752
Hattiesburg, MS	4 824	1.1	32 595	352	2 268	374	170	480	813	1 109	3 291	205	170
Hickory-Lenoir-Morganton, NC	12 047	0.8	33 136	343	5 440	935	445	1 034	1 961	3 088	7 854	511	445
Hilton Head Island-Bluffton-Beaufort, NC	8 269	2.2	41 663	139	3 109	591	259	566	2 675	1 636	4 525	280	259
Hinesville, GA	2 318	1.6	28 705	376	1 856	565	175	50	647	452	2 646	108	175
Homosassa Springs, FL	4 788	1.3	34 380	318	1 253	227	93	168	1 332	1 741	1 740	153	93
Hot Springs, AR	3 744	0.3	38 526	208	1 294	195	105	246	1 131	999	1 840	134	105
Houma-Thibodaux, LA	10 021	5.4	47 745	44	5 456	802	343	1 316	1 388	1 510	7 918	422	343
Houston-The Woodlands-Sugar Land, TX	327 841	3.4	51 930	24	179 940	22 142	11 710	61 276	46 476	34 755	275 067	13 449	11 710
Huntington-Ashland, WV-KY-OH	12 856	0.5	35 308	296	5 759	1 128	461	681	1 680	3 491	8 029	521	461
Huntsville, AL	18 257	2.1	41 899	134	11 550	1 915	886	1 141	3 441	2 888	15 492	912	886
Idaho Falls, ID	5 093	3.2	37 152	246	2 421	353	218	926	894	841	3 917	223	218
Indianapolis-Carmel-Anderson, IN	83 125	2.1	42 542	121	47 384	7 254	3 533	7 752	12 088	13 458	65 923	3 930	3 533
Iowa City, IA	7 361	2.5	45 673	66	4 031	931	310	636	1 491	804	5 908	315	310
Ithaca, NY	4 102	0.5	39 592	178	2 424	474	209	236	991	609	3 343	172	209
Jackson, MI	5 506	4.2	34 331	319	2 542	486	202	277	870	1 377	3 507	223	202
Jackson, MS	23 023	1.4	39 945	175	11 475	1 748	846	3 151	3 448	4 493	17 219	1 043	846
Jackson, TN	4 944	2.0	37 842	226	2 502	513	183	639	695	1 170	3 836	216	183
Jacksonville, FL	60 176	1.8	43 149	108	30 521	4 693	2 282	3 152	13 937	10 349	40 648	2 414	2 282
Jacksonville, NC	8 343	-0.9	45 041	77	4 289	1 220	418	248	1 826	1 123	6 175	265	418
Janesville-Beloit, WI	6 117	5.5	38 054	220	2 923	570	225	308	1 028	1 228	4 027	250	225
Jefferson City, MO	5 805	2.9	38 573	206	3 015	743	208	405	1 114	1 048	4 371	231	208
Johnson City, TN	7 042	0.8	35 039	302	2 921	613	215	493	1 085	1 872	4 241	268	215
Johnstown, PA	5 082	-0.1	36 173	277	2 078	477	173	301	826	1 517	3 029	199	173
Jonesboro, AR	4 399	0.7	35 014	303	1 946	305	157	524	782	1 042	2 932	180	157

1. Based on the resident population estimated as of July 1 of the year shown.

Area name	Earnings, 2013 (cont.): Percent by selected industries: Farm	Mining	Construction	Manufacturing	Information, professional, scientific, technical services	Retail trade	Finance, insurance, real estate, rental and leasing	Health care and social assistance	Government	Social Security beneficiaries, December 2013: Number	Rate[1]	Supplemental Security Income recipients, December 2013	Housing units, 2014: Total	Percent change, 2000–2014
	75	76	77	78	79	80	81	82	83	84	85	86	87	88
Fairbanks, AK	0.2	4.6	8.2	1.4	4.6	5.7	3.5	9.3	46.4	9 760	97	1 143	41 684	-0.2
Fargo, ND-MN	3.1	D	7.9	7.6	9.6	7.1	11.7	12.7	13.5	31 025	139	2 833	100 074	8.9
Farmington, NM	0.4	22.8	7.9	2.4	2.5	7.2	3.3	11.1	21.2	20 465	162	4 197	49 618	0.6
Fayetteville, NC	0.5	D	3.5	4.9	D	4.6	3.0	5.0	61.6	58 865	156	11 351	163 885	6.6
Fayetteville-Springdale-Rogers, AR-MO	1.3	0.2	4.6	9.5	D	6.2	5.2	8.9	12.5	82 245	167	8 990	204 627	3.2
Flagstaff, AZ	0.0	D	3.7	10.6	3.4	6.9	3.7	16.1	33.5	18 115	133	2 746	64 217	1.4
Flint, MI	0.2	0.0	4.4	12.2	9.2	8.5	6.4	18.1	17.8	97 015	233	17 016	190 901	-0.7
Florence, SC	0.7	D	3.7	15.6	6.1	7.6	11.7	12.3	18.1	45 905	222	8 714	89 302	0.4
Florence-Muscle Shoals, AL	3.9	D	7.4	17.4	3.4	10.0	4.6	11.7	21.0	38 295	260	4 972	70 545	1.4
Fond du Lac, WI	3.4	0.6	7.3	26.7	4.1	6.4	4.2	12.8	13.6	20 820	205	1 377	44 489	1.3
Fort Collins, CO	0.3	0.6	8.3	13.1	13.0	6.7	4.7	9.1	23.3	50 315	159	2 625	138 534	4.4
Fort Smith, AR-OK	1.2	5.0	5.3	16.1	6.1	7.0	4.7	13.5	15.8	64 305	230	10 594	123 026	1.8
Fort Wayne, IN	1.3	D	5.7	20.1	6.8	6.1	7.5	16.3	10.1	78 470	185	8 342	180 637	1.4
Fresno, CA	8.1	0.2	4.7	6.2	6.0	6.5	6.6	13.2	22.0	127 580	133	43 157	324 126	2.7
Gadsden, AL	0.3	0.2	4.9	15.4	3.7	8.4	5.0	21.5	15.8	28 310	272	4 789	47 505	0.1
Gainesville, FL	0.6	D	3.5	4.6	D	5.8	5.6	D	39.5	43 980	163	6 455	121 289	1.0
Gainesville, GA	0.7	D	5.2	20.4	4.1	6.8	5.8	15.2	12.5	32 980	176	3 083	69 492	1.0
Gettysburg, PA	2.0	D	7.8	19.4	5.3	7.2	3.8	D	16.2	22 915	226	1 177	41 281	1.1
Glens Falls, NY	0.8	0.4	7.2	14.4	D	8.0	4.2	13.2	23.9	31 840	249	3 473	68 011	0.7
Goldsboro, NC	4.0	D	5.8	11.6	3.3	6.8	4.5	11.7	33.4	24 865	200	4 691	53 213	0.5
Grand Forks, ND-MN	7.2	0.5	6.8	6.2	4.8	8.1	4.2	D	27.3	16 240	161	1 359	46 039	4.7
Grand Island, NE	13.9	D	5.8	16.7	D	7.3	4.7	9.7	15.0	15 620	186	1 204	34 979	2.4
Grand Junction, CO	0.3	9.1	7.7	4.4	6.7	8.0	5.8	15.5	16.7	29 385	199	2 412	63 779	1.8
Grand Rapids-Wyoming, MI	1.0	D	5.0	23.5	D	6.4	6.8	D	10.6	182 125	179	20 617	408 247	0.9
Grants Pass, OR	-0.4	D	6.0	10.5	4.5	12.0	5.6	19.7	15.6	26 110	314	2 623	38 022	0.1
Great Falls, MT	0.9	D	6.3	2.9	6.7	8.6	6.5	16.2	28.3	17 560	213	1 884	37 565	0.8
Greeley, CO	4.6	10.8	12.4	10.8	4.1	6.0	5.2	7.7	13.1	36 935	137	3 440	100 070	3.9
Green Bay, WI	1.9	D	5.3	17.5	D	5.6	8.4	12.4	13.0	58 305	187	5 422	140 359	2.3
Greensboro-High Point, NC	0.3	D	4.9	17.3	D	6.5	8.8	11.8	12.7	147 065	198	17 602	328 015	1.6
Greenville, NC	1.1	D	3.9	9.9	4.5	6.7	6.4	11.9	37.2	28 185	162	5 849	76 619	2.2
Greenville-Anderson-Mauldin, SC	0.0	0.1	5.3	17.0	9.9	6.9	7.2	D	15.5	181 285	213	17 795	369 018	1.9
Gulfport-Biloxi-Pascagoula, MS	0.0	D	8.4	16.5	6.0	6.1	4.0	D	28.8	75 670	198	10 789	174 468	4.4
Hagerstown-Martinsburg, MD-WV	0.7	D	5.7	9.5	6.9	9.0	9.2	14.5	22.5	50 420	195	5 587	107 411	1.7
Hammond, LA	0.2	0.5	5.7	5.7	4.2	10.1	9.9	11.7	27.0	22 190	177	5 322	52 548	4.9
Hanford-Corcoran, CA	19.8	0.0	2.1	8.3	2.2	4.6	2.0	8.5	39.5	16 800	111	4 698	44 864	2.3
Harrisburg-Carlisle, PA	0.5	D	4.4	7.1	9.0	4.9	9.2	13.8	22.2	112 600	202	11 041	245 206	1.8
Harrisonburg, VA	4.2	D	6.2	18.0	7.3	6.8	4.1	11.7	17.7	21 895	169	1 706	52 605	2.9
Hartford-West Hartford-East Hartford, CT	0.1	D	4.9	12.7	11.0	5.2	17.5	12.1	15.9	226 035	186	23 312	508 498	0.3
Hattiesburg, MS	1.1	1.0	5.4	7.2	D	9.5	D	17.4	24.5	26 855	182	4 700	62 384	0.8
Hickory-Lenoir-Morganton, NC	0.8	0.0	3.8	25.5	3.9	7.2	5.7	D	16.2	86 420	238	7 607	162 178	-0.3
Hilton Head Island-Bluffton-Beaufort, NC	0.8	0.1	7.0	1.3	D	9.0	8.2	9.1	32.8	47 795	241	2 748	105 177	1.8
Hinesville, GA	0.2	D	1.4	D	D	2.3	D	1.5	78.4	8 160	101	1 422	33 403	1.9
Homosassa Springs, FL	0.1	0.3	7.3	1.0	6.2	11.4	4.0	23.6	14.9	55 645	400	3 122	77 717	-0.4
Hot Springs, AR	0.4	0.7	6.9	7.4	5.9	11.1	7.9	22.1	14.6	29 025	299	3 873	50 542	0.0
Houma-Thibodaux, LA	0.7	11.9	6.9	11.5	4.4	5.0	5.2	6.7	9.9	39 410	188	8 137	84 232	2.1
Houston-The Woodlands-Sugar Land, TX	0.0	13.8	8.3	10.4	D	4.5	6.4	D	9.1	740 405	117	139 184	2 441 161	6.4
Huntington-Ashland, WV-KY-OH	0.0	3.1	8.7	11.5	D	7.2	4.4	D	16.8	87 935	241	17 620	164 637	0.1
Huntsville, AL	0.9	D	4.0	11.6	23.5	5.5	3.3	6.7	29.8	77 385	177	8 965	189 897	4.7
Idaho Falls, ID	7.5	D	5.5	5.2	D	7.6	D	11.7	10.2	22 065	161	2 484	50 947	2.3
Indianapolis-Carmel-Anderson, IN	1.0	0.1	6.5	12.8	D	5.9	8.8	12.9	12.7	327 230	168	36 301	835 958	2.4
Iowa City, IA	3.1	0.2	5.0	7.7	6.4	5.5	3.9	7.0	42.4	21 565	133	1 957	68 323	4.3
Ithaca, NY	0.7	1.2	2.3	7.9	7.4	5.3	3.4	D	14.9	15 195	146	1 723	42 080	0.9
Jackson, MI	0.9	0.2	3.5	18.5	4.9	6.6	3.3	14.0	15.1	36 055	225	4 610	69 077	-0.5
Jackson, MS	1.1	D	5.5	6.8	D	6.7	9.8	12.4	20.9	105 650	183	20 848	237 550	2.1
Jackson, TN	2.0	D	D	16.8	D	8.0	4.5	12.3	21.8	28 040	215	4 272	56 106	1.5
Jacksonville, FL	0.2	D	4.8	5.5	11.5	6.8	13.1	D	16.2	252 650	181	31 098	615 772	2.9
Jacksonville, NC	0.4	D	3.0	0.8	2.0	4.0	2.5	2.9	75.4	22 510	121	2 909	76 054	11.5
Janesville-Beloit, WI	2.1	0.3	5.7	15.8	4.4	6.5	3.0	16.0	15.6	33 680	210	3 826	68 301	-0.2
Jefferson City, MO	1.9	D	6.3	7.6	7.3	6.1	4.8	9.0	34.1	30 285	201	3 052	63 992	0.7
Johnson City, TN	-0.1	0.1	5.8	11.0	D	8.3	5.8	D	22.7	50 135	249	6 053	95 570	1.9
Johnstown, PA	0.8	1.4	4.2	7.8	8.1	7.8	5.8	22.0	18.1	37 975	273	5 171	65 240	-0.6
Jonesboro, AR	6.4	D	6.0	12.3	4.1	7.6	5.0	19.4	15.9	26 125	208	5 610	54 248	5.5

1. Per 1,000 resident population estimated as of July 1, 2011 of the year shown.

Area name	Housing units, 2013: Total	Occupied units: Owner-occupied: Percent	Owner-occupied: Median value[1]	Median owner cost as a percent of income: With a mortgage	Median owner cost as a percent of income: Without a mortgage[2]	Renter-occupied: Median rent[3]	Renter-occupied: Median rent as a percent of income	Substandard units[4] (percent)	Civilian labor force, 2014: Total	Percent change, 2013–2014	Unemployment: Total	Unemployment: Rate[5]	Civilian employment[6], 2013: Total employed	Percent: Management, professional, and related occupations	Percent: Construction, production, and related occupations
	89	90	91	92	93	94	95	96	97	98	99	100	101	102	103
Fairbanks, AK	34 056	61.1	218 200	22.1	11.0	1 141	33.2	NA	47 119	-0.5	2 708	5.7	46 321	39.2	21.8
Fargo, ND-MN	90 959	55.3	166 900	20.8	10.0	705	27.8	NA	129 129	1.9	3 510	2.7	126 392	37.0	21.0
Farmington, NM	37 847	74.5	130 500	19.3	10.0	722	30.8	8.5	55 116	1.0	3 463	6.3	50 415	25.1	31.5
Fayetteville, NC	142 827	52.4	132 200	22.8	12.0	826	30.4	2.1	145 568	-3.0	11 347	7.8	130 719	31.4	21.4
Fayetteville-Springdale-Rogers, AR-MO	178 227	62.2	141 000	19.3	10.0	733	27.2	4.0	238 937	2.6	10 983	4.6	226 056	34.6	25.4
Flagstaff, AZ	49 002	57.0	204 800	23.3	10.0	1 059	31.6	10.9	71 901	1.2	5 146	7.2	64 735	36.9	19.7
Flint, MI	163 740	70.5	82 800	22.4	13.3	705	33.4	NA	184 458	-0.2	14 299	7.8	162 987	30.8	24.2
Florence, SC	77 550	63.8	112 600	20.7	10.4	632	29.8	NA	93 333	-1.3	6 978	7.5	82 040	32.7	23.6
Florence-Muscle Shoals, AL	61 383	68.7	111 000	20.1	11.2	566	23.6	NA	67 383	0.8	5 085	7.5	62 017	27.8	28.9
Fond du Lac, WI	41 202	71.2	142 600	20.6	12.8	695	27.9	NA	57 371	0.3	2 891	5.0	52 889	29.2	34.6
Fort Collins, CO	123 877	64.6	260 100	21.8	10.0	986	34.1	NA	177 264	1.3	7 578	4.3	163 279	41.2	16.4
Fort Smith, AR-OK	107 030	66.7	105 800	21.9	11.0	604	27.3	2.8	118 965	-1.7	7 376	6.2	111 295	29.1	29.3
Fort Wayne, IN	166 620	69.9	113 000	19.1	10.0	664	29.0	2.9	206 276	0.7	11 722	5.7	198 753	31.8	27.6
Fresno, CA	293 517	52.0	185 200	25.7	10.7	859	35.0	11.6	441 022	0.3	51 217	11.6	371 604	28.4	29.0
Gadsden, AL	40 135	72.0	101 900	20.5	12.0	601	30.6	NA	43 578	-0.3	3 063	7.0	39 960	30.4	31.3
Gainesville, FL	104 294	53.2	151 200	23.2	11.3	831	34.9	NA	137 602	1.0	7 224	5.2	121 129	43.5	12.5
Gainesville, GA	60 937	62.8	160 900	22.4	11.4	831	32.1	NA	90 087	0.6	5 338	5.9	86 179	27.1	32.4
Gettysburg, PA	37 242	78.0	192 900	22.5	13.5	821	30.0	NA	54 997	-0.6	2 472	4.5	50 325	29.0	33.2
Glens Falls, NY	51 414	70.2	165 400	22.4	13.9	826	30.5	NA	60 949	-2.1	3 832	6.3	61 961	33.1	23.2
Goldsboro, NC	46 834	56.3	117 700	20.6	10.4	753	35.5	NA	53 587	-1.9	3 363	6.3	50 689	31.1	33.3
Grand Forks, ND-MN	40 982	57.2	155 100	18.7	10.3	718	34.8	NA	54 581	0.0	1 839	3.4	53 690	32.3	23.3
Grand Island, NE	31 723	67.4	111 600	19.1	11.0	655	25.9	NA	45 230	0.0	1 681	3.7	42 849	24.7	37.9
Grand Junction, CO	58 466	67.8	204 800	23.9	10.0	821	33.0	NA	73 608	-0.2	4 540	6.2	67 000	33.2	21.7
Grand Rapids-Wyoming, MI	370 818	72.1	136 400	20.3	11.8	761	29.2	1.9	542 586	2.2	27 126	5.0	486 146	34.3	25.4
Grants Pass, OR	34 517	66.0	205 800	25.6	12.9	840	39.3	NA	32 925	2.2	3 175	9.6	26 918	32.3	25.9
Great Falls, MT	34 492	64.1	160 800	21.6	10.0	639	27.0	NA	38 560	-0.1	1 679	4.4	37 619	34.2	20.9
Greeley, CO	92 426	69.8	195 200	21.9	10.0	833	29.6	4.4	146 103	4.5	6 584	4.5	126 735	33.4	24.9
Green Bay, WI	122 600	67.6	158 700	20.8	13.1	706	27.3	NA	170 327	0.3	8 683	5.1	157 352	32.4	25.8
Greensboro-High Point, NC	289 205	61.6	141 700	20.8	10.4	711	30.5	2.8	357 833	-1.8	23 175	6.5	333 361	33.4	24.0
Greenville, NC	67 573	52.8	134 200	20.8	11.2	697	33.5	NA	86 461	-1.1	5 432	6.3	79 763	38.6	15.6
Greenville-Anderson-Mauldin, SC	320 628	67.9	141 000	20.2	10.0	715	29.8	1.9	402 323	0.9	22 832	5.7	377 859	34.5	24.0
Gulfport-Biloxi-Pascagoula, MS	143 330	61.6	126 100	23.0	10.8	813	29.1	NA	161 064	-3.4	12 083	7.5	162 509	26.9	24.7
Hagerstown-Martinsburg, MD-WV	97 681	66.4	172 000	22.4	10.7	879	27.6	NA	128 368	-1.1	7 731	6.0	117 745	31.8	25.2
Hammond, LA	46 039	68.6	136 300	18.8	10.5	734	36.5	NA	54 165	2.1	4 061	7.5	53 197	29.2	26.2
Hanford-Corcoran, CA	41 813	50.4	169 200	23.7	10.0	825	30.1	NA	57 393	-1.2	6 920	12.1	52 551	26.5	35.8
Harrisburg-Carlisle, PA	224 798	67.3	170 600	21.0	11.1	846	27.2	2.1	288 582	-0.7	14 179	4.9	275 412	38.0	19.1
Harrisonburg, VA	45 285	63.1	199 000	22.9	10.0	821	30.7	NA	64 921	0.2	3 344	5.2	63 355	29.2	23.6
Hartford-West Hartford-East Hartford, CT	464 315	66.7	241 100	23.4	15.1	978	30.3	1.7	647 549	0.9	42 291	6.5	599 081	41.8	16.7
Hattiesburg, MS	53 052	57.8	131 000	20.6	10.9	746	32.4	NA	63 696	-1.8	4 219	6.6	64 861	36.4	20.4
Hickory-Lenoir-Morganton, NC	136 858	69.7	125 900	20.9	10.5	629	30.4	2.6	166 339	-1.9	10 571	6.4	151 393	29.9	31.5
Hilton Head Island-Bluffton-Beaufort, NC	74 931	69.6	247 100	27.2	11.9	976	29.4	NA	79 809	2.2	4 521	5.7	86 012	29.3	21.1
Hinesville, GA	28 505	47.8	117 700	24.0	11.5	903	30.6	NA	32 429	-1.5	2 511	7.7	28 750	28.7	26.9
Homosassa Springs, FL	62 131	80.4	107 500	22.8	12.0	747	34.6	NA	48 578	-1.7	4 108	8.5	43 395	24.0	21.9
Hot Springs, AR	41 865	66.0	121 500	19.1	10.0	675	35.1	NA	40 044	-0.8	2 564	6.4	37 860	36.8	23.5
Houma-Thibodaux, LA	73 418	77.5	135 700	17.9	10.0	768	24.7	3.6	103 595	3.4	5 004	4.8	91 236	23.8	36.5
Houston-The Woodlands-Sugar Land, TX	2 158 139	60.1	144 400	21.1	10.9	886	29.0	5.9	3 258 325	2.0	159 403	4.9	2 995 320	37.2	23.2
Huntington-Ashland, WV-KY-OH	145 100	71.5	100 700	19.3	10.0	618	31.7	1.9	150 211	-1.6	9 791	6.5	141 910	32.5	22.0
Huntsville, AL	169 951	68.2	156 700	18.5	10.0	725	27.5	NA	208 672	-0.8	12 834	6.2	202 947	43.9	19.9
Idaho Falls, ID	45 964	74.3	151 400	23.2	10.0	696	27.8	NA	63 140	1.2	2 649	4.2	57 104	32.8	26.2
Indianapolis-Carmel-Anderson, IN	739 503	64.6	139 600	19.8	10.7	789	30.5	2.1	993 216	1.6	56 869	5.7	932 534	36.8	22.3
Iowa City, IA	64 564	58.9	187 300	19.0	10.0	799	31.4	NA	96 817	1.9	3 132	3.2	90 805	47.2	14.5
Ithaca, NY	37 524	56.8	173 100	21.2	13.7	904	33.1	NA	54 643	-2.0	2 362	4.3	50 177	51.6	13.5
Jackson, MI	61 235	69.6	111 000	20.1	12.9	705	35.5	NA	72 918	0.5	4 834	6.6	65 590	29.1	25.9
Jackson, MS	207 205	65.5	121 200	20.9	10.7	776	32.3	3.5	257 679	-2.3	16 533	6.4	251 179	36.7	20.5
Jackson, TN	47 027	65.1	115 800	22.8	11.1	672	33.8	NA	61 050	-3.2	4 286	7.0	55 719	32.1	21.9
Jacksonville, FL	516 144	65.3	152 200	23.4	10.4	949	31.6	2.1	719 458	1.2	44 681	6.2	629 682	36.7	18.2
Jacksonville, NC	60 764	50.2	157 000	23.1	11.9	915	31.2	NA	63 739	-0.3	3 769	5.9	61 780	26.4	24.2
Janesville-Beloit, WI	64 088	69.8	125 400	22.9	12.2	712	29.1	NA	83 165	1.0	5 177	6.2	75 405	29.1	31.4
Jefferson City, MO	53 981	69.5	126 600	19.8	10.0	617	24.0	NA	76 359	0.8	3 990	5.2	65 456	33.3	21.7
Johnson City, TN	83 446	67.3	128 500	20.0	10.1	596	30.6	NA	88 119	-3.5	6 089	6.9	90 199	33.9	22.1
Johnstown, PA	57 407	74.7	85 300	19.7	13.2	554	28.7	NA	62 959	-2.6	4 363	6.9	59 720	33.8	24.3
Jonesboro, AR	47 799	57.8	112 700	18.4	10.0	613	28.7	NA	59 215	0.7	3 398	5.7	54 309	33.3	27.4

1. Specified owner-occupied units. 2. A value of 10.0 represents 10 percent or less. 3. Specified renter-occupied units. 4. Overcrowded or lacking complete plumbing facilities. 5. Percent of civilian labor force. 6. Persons 16 years old and over.

Table C. Metropolitan Areas — **Nonfarm Employment and Agriculture**

Area name	Private nonfarm establishments, employment and payroll, 2013										Agriculture, 2012			
		Employment						Annual payroll		Farms			
											Percent with:		
	Number of establish-ments	Total	Health care and social assistance	Manufac-turing	Retail trade	Finance and insurance	Professional, scientific, and technical services	Total (mil dol)	Average per employee (dollars)	Number	Fewer than 50 acres	500 acres or more	Farm operators whose principal occu-pation is farming (percent)
	104	105	106	107	108	109	110	111	112	113	114	115	116
Fairbanks, AK	2 471	27 466	5 945	622	4 891	765	1 632	1 376	50 111	217	39.2	20.7	47.9
Fargo, ND-MN	6 426	114 699	20 820	9 537	15 469	8 080	5 424	4 616	40 245	1 772	20.8	42.4	60.1
Farmington, NM	2 806	39 476	6 624	2 057	6 351	962	1 222	1 764	44 698	2 628	61.7	20.8	54.2
Fayetteville, NC	6 061	99 329	19 675	8 926	17 049	2 539	6 125	3 296	33 186	591	43.3	11.7	48.6
Fayetteville-Springdale-Rogers, AR-MO	10 883	186 030	22 127	25 327	23 976	5 302	9 915	8 636	46 422	6 835	37.1	5.7	46.8
Flagstaff, AZ	3 518	44 834	7 671	D	7 486	827	1 522	1 657	36 962	2 239	92.0	3.8	72.5
Flint, MI	7 745	114 923	26 465	11 288	19 736	4 349	3 400	4 287	37 300	835	58.6	6.2	50.1
Florence, SC	4 152	73 861	15 689	8 666	10 775	5 280	2 523	2 777	37 600	1 017	34.7	14.5	45.0
Florence-Muscle Shoals, AL	3 193	45 659	7 030	8 942	8 243	1 636	1 072	1 437	31 482	2 153	43.9	6.4	42.2
Fond du Lac, WI	2 365	40 881	6 337	8 625	5 553	1 611	1 467	1 481	36 223	1 399	31.9	10.7	59.0
Fort Collins, CO	9 723	112 150	18 490	9 922	17 565	3 624	8 790	4 556	40 626	1 625	60.7	8.5	46.5
Fort Smith, AR-OK	5 921	96 441	17 890	17 677	12 563	2 840	2 193	3 275	33 955	4 703	36.8	6.9	45.2
Fort Wayne, IN	10 335	181 446	33 003	32 067	22 456	9 505	5 975	7 173	39 533	3 071	52.7	9.9	42.5
Fresno, CA	15 973	239 776	41 485	23 176	35 099	9 301	10 967	9 121	38 041	5 683	59.7	11.2	59.6
Gadsden, AL	2 008	29 796	7 277	5 068	4 355	1 015	1 185	923	30 980	853	51.1	2.9	40.3
Gainesville, FL	6 064	85 849	22 612	3 290	13 542	4 170	4 882	3 166	36 878	2 243	68.8	5.0	42.9
Gainesville, GA	3 953	64 743	10 804	17 461	7 754	2 010	1 624	2 612	40 339	622	59.0	2.3	51.3
Gettysburg, PA	1 902	27 938	4 428	5 798	3 280	532	533	930	33 277	1 188	48.2	6.3	50.9
Glens Falls, NY	3 404	40 862	8 259	6 967	7 553	1 407	1 071	1 540	37 683	968	34.7	10.2	55.5
Goldsboro, NC	2 135	33 406	7 132	5 787	5 786	1 126	787	1 093	32 719	563	40.1	18.1	60.9
Grand Forks, ND-MN	2 677	41 891	9 227	3 495	7 275	1 265	1 792	1 450	34 617	2 292	11.9	36.6	58.9
Grand Island, NE	2 498	35 512	5 402	7 729	5 726	1 514	814	1 162	32 732	2 339	26.5	34.1	62.0
Grand Junction, CO	4 431	49 355	9 740	2 389	8 259	1 749	2 477	1 980	40 116	2 264	75.4	5.4	48.6
Grand Rapids-Wyoming, MI	23 262	440 762	61 270	95 045	46 105	16 292	17 037	18 070	40 997	4 680	49.2	6.5	49.6
Grants Pass, OR	1 899	20 079	4 585	2 340	4 120	594	568	612	30 483	617	76.3	0.6	55.8
Great Falls, MT	2 429	28 891	6 657	798	5 072	1 754	1 121	927	32 090	1 105	36.0	29.3	47.8
Greeley, CO	5 376	71 783	8 029	11 023	8 979	3 718	2 195	3 131	43 619	3 525	35.5	19.6	49.8
Green Bay, WI	7 530	148 479	20 779	28 656	16 207	D	5 383	6 264	42 188	2 774	40.3	8.0	51.0
Greensboro-High Point, NC	17 401	313 104	45 369	52 638	35 149	14 979	12 103	12 495	39 906	3 350	49.0	3.5	46.6
Greenville, NC	3 526	57 690	15 790	4 657	8 383	2 019	1 913	2 035	35 275	391	34.8	21.5	59.3
Greenville-Anderson-Mauldin, SC	18 843	310 158	38 156	49 075	39 961	10 292	17 975	11 764	37 928	4 152	55.1	2.7	36.6
Gulfport-Biloxi-Pascagoula, MS	7 041	125 157	20 288	D	17 575	3 900	6 413	5 052	40 366	988	59.6	2.0	39.9
Hagerstown-Martinsburg, MD-WV	5 000	81 777	15 392	8 065	13 882	7 339	2 680	2 923	35 748	1 536	51.2	4.6	43.0
Hammond, LA	2 280	34 973	8 780	2 387	6 320	2 542	1 010	1 106	31 621	1 070	52.1	3.0	44.1
Hanford-Corcoran, CA	1 575	23 441	4 955	3 932	4 143	495	456	820	34 973	1 056	51.2	18.6	66.0
Harrisburg-Carlisle, PA	13 238	262 683	49 659	15 181	32 653	19 366	14 376	11 378	43 315	3 115	43.4	3.7	50.2
Harrisonburg, VA	2 988	50 542	7 414	9 527	7 311	1 281	1 392	1 777	35 157	1 902	43.2	2.8	54.6
Hartford-West Hartford-East Hartford, CT	29 158	537 579	100 492	61 346	63 355	58 517	38 354	29 412	54 712	1 995	71.1	1.6	44.9
Hattiesburg, MS	3 283	49 945	11 458	4 712	9 551	1 686	1 741	1 691	33 865	1 093	43.8	4.0	39.5
Hickory-Lenoir-Morganton, NC	7 392	122 347	19 232	37 318	16 012	2 355	2 564	4 311	35 237	2 198	56.5	2.6	47.5
Hilton Head Island-Bluffton-Beaufort, NC	5 360	55 771	8 251	735	10 757	2 023	3 226	1 800	32 274	252	49.6	19.4	51.2
Hinesville, GA	883	12 632	2 068	1 937	1 993	396	881	454	35 910	113	39.8	7.1	41.6
Homosassa Springs, FL	2 665	26 477	8 268	221	5 352	694	811	854	32 241	559	73.9	3.4	49.7
Hot Springs, AR	2 696	32 235	7 425	2 354	5 869	972	1 596	959	29 740	361	49.3	2.5	55.4
Houma-Thibodaux, LA	4 850	79 958	10 946	8 907	11 050	2 119	3 300	3 876	48 476	596	44.5	12.1	43.6
Houston-The Woodlands-Sugar Land, TX	129 490	2 449 510	302 885	223 777	276 145	95 571	210 426	146 412	59 772	15 026	56.9	7.3	38.6
Huntington-Ashland, WV-KY-OH	7 146	111 234	27 585	10 990	17 135	3 063	4 373	4 271	38 395	2 683	28.7	2.6	39.7
Huntsville, AL	9 403	168 609	25 209	19 404	21 868	D	33 347	7 714	45 749	2 263	44.1	7.4	47.9
Idaho Falls, ID	3 733	48 741	8 211	3 425	7 634	1 295	D	1 879	38 545	1 883	49.7	19.3	44.7
Indianapolis-Carmel-Anderson, IN	44 904	832 592	132 041	73 326	94 603	41 829	54 787	37 898	45 518	6 205	54.5	14.8	46.0
Iowa City, IA	3 891	66 294	17 229	6 158	10 089	2 192	2 285	2 558	38 588	2 481	33.2	15.9	51.9
Ithaca, NY	2 346	46 909	5 670	2 677	5 126	864	2 279	1 675	35 712	558	43.9	6.8	50.5
Jackson, MI	2 954	49 019	9 570	8 770	7 213	1 303	2 933	2 060	42 016	1 073	48.7	7.7	45.4
Jackson, MS	13 049	210 091	47 327	16 757	28 745	11 072	10 207	8 250	39 308	4 186	30.1	12.6	43.3
Jackson, TN	2 988	55 225	12 702	9 103	7 547	1 410	1 324	1 922	34 803	1 352	32.8	10.4	40.5
Jacksonville, FL	34 744	509 307	78 391	22 483	68 718	48 913	31 467	22 404	43 988	1 768	74.4	3.8	46.2
Jacksonville, NC	2 743	34 624	5 440	1 055	7 823	1 036	1 796	926	26 748	347	48.4	7.2	54.2
Janesville-Beloit, WI	3 202	54 042	9 832	9 029	8 511	1 713	1 106	2 083	38 549	1 509	44.1	10.3	50.0
Jefferson City, MO	3 606	50 039	9 065	5 814	7 524	2 465	2 038	1 827	36 519	4 676	23.1	9.0	39.7
Johnson City, TN	3 717	63 428	16 654	7 009	10 755	2 948	3 006	2 176	34 302	1 898	54.8	1.9	45.2
Johnstown, PA	3 337	48 133	12 313	4 595	7 165	2 143	2 532	1 607	33 394	551	33.4	5.6	37.4
Jonesboro, AR	2 841	41 659	8 842	6 471	7 435	1 141	990	1 404	33 701	980	31.9	39.2	57.8

Area name	Agriculture, 2012 (cont.) — Land in farms — Acreage (1,000)	Land in farms — Percent change, 2007–2012	Land in farms — Acres — Average size of farm	Land in farms — Acres — Total irrigated (1,000)	Land in farms — Acres — Total cropland (1,000)	Value of land and buildings (dollars) — Average per farm	Value of land and buildings (dollars) — Average per acre	Value of machinery and equipment, average per farm (dollars)	Value of products sold — Total (mil dol)	Value of products sold — Average per farm (dollars)	Value of products sold — Percent from: Crops	Value of products sold — Percent from: Livestock and poultry products	Percent of farms with sales of: $10,000 or more	Percent of farms with sales of: $100,000 or more	Government payments — Total ($1,000)	Government payments — Percent of farms
	117	118	119	120	121	122	123	124	125	126	127	128	129	130	131	132
Fairbanks, AK	100	-10.1	459	1.0	61.4	580 382	1 264	94 359	9.1	42 120	84.8	15.2	42.4	10.6	1 354	30.9
Fargo, ND-MN	1 718	4.0	970	19.2	1 599.8	3 003 294	3 097	390 421	965.2	544 686	94.1	5.9	65.4	48.4	22 932	77.1
Farmington, NM	2 580	58.2	982	85.9	115.6	341 496	348	41 084	71.3	27 135	88.9	11.1	13.3	1.2	1 023	14.0
Fayetteville, NC	141	-5.2	238	4.1	85.1	752 283	3 155	117 093	201.6	341 140	33.5	66.5	41.5	19.6	1 876	40.4
Fayetteville-Springdale-Rogers, AR-MO	1 073	3.0	157	2.0	278.5	555 647	3 541	64 923	1 356.1	198 410	1.4	98.6	44.7	13.9	6 743	15.3
Flagstaff, AZ	5 816	-4.7	2 597	1.9	8.3	543 406	209	23 731	25.8	11 528	9.1	90.9	9.6	1.4	987	23.0
Flint, MI	123	-4.6	148	1.5	102.6	570 910	3 867	107 984	91.3	109 389	88.7	11.3	38.4	12.9	2 131	32.2
Florence, SC	333	0.5	327	9.1	208.0	768 491	2 348	125 798	183.2	180 155	70.2	29.8	39.1	17.2	5 109	48.9
Florence-Muscle Shoals, AL	364	2.2	169	4.0	165.6	491 966	2 907	64 124	139.4	64 748	55.0	45.0	31.2	7.4	4 969	33.6
Fond du Lac, WI	316	-6.0	226	2.1	262.1	1 128 100	5 001	182 828	412.3	294 743	26.9	73.1	62.2	37.8	7 648	74.2
Fort Collins, CO	450	-8.0	277	52.5	106.4	854 599	3 083	72 401	128.6	79 167	44.6	55.4	28.8	7.6	1 061	11.2
Fort Smith, AR-OK	854	-7.3	182	13.9	251.1	405 541	2 233	56 091	507.6	107 930	11.2	88.8	35.2	9.0	4 858	15.0
Fort Wayne, IN	611	4.3	199	2.7	550.8	1 191 722	5 987	120 572	498.0	162 173	73.6	26.4	52.0	24.7	12 089	58.8
Fresno, CA	1 721	5.2	303	968.7	1 153.4	2 509 484	8 286	161 509	4 973.0	875 073	74.4	25.6	71.9	41.9	10 149	9.0
Gadsden, AL	86	-8.6	101	0.1	19.5	359 368	3 559	51 635	83.7	98 161	6.5	93.5	27.8	8.2	450	11.8
Gainesville, FL	272	11.5	121	23.3	102.5	575 798	4 750	53 346	189.9	84 661	51.3	48.7	30.4	6.6	1 400	7.7
Gainesville, GA	52	-9.3	84	0.1	12.3	686 416	8 212	68 188	166.3	267 434	2.1	97.9	34.9	19.8	115	8.2
Gettysburg, PA	171	-1.9	144	2.2	125.6	898 623	6 232	113 572	201.7	169 817	56.5	43.5	48.6	19.2	1 818	28.5
Glens Falls, NY	199	-5.9	205	0.7	103.4	514 006	2 501	104 877	D	D	D	D	50.3	19.8	D	25.2
Goldsboro, NC	191	9.1	340	4.8	146.8	1 400 607	4 124	199 504	577.2	1 025 265	27.4	72.6	61.5	44.8	2 943	56.5
Grand Forks, ND-MN	1 911	-0.7	834	28.3	1 740.6	2 134 497	2 559	375 743	1 023.3	446 464	95.7	4.3	55.9	39.2	28 960	87.6
Grand Island, NE	1 181	0.6	505	726.0	901.2	2 248 299	4 451	272 145	1 227.8	524 935	63.4	36.6	71.4	50.1	18 245	71.1
Grand Junction, CO	387	3.9	171	75.3	71.4	575 360	3 367	51 431	84.6	37 360	48.1	51.9	25.7	6.1	821	7.1
Grand Rapids-Wyoming, MI	746	-0.7	159	88.2	559.1	763 593	4 790	120 642	1 120.3	239 375	60.9	39.1	44.8	18.7	10 536	31.0
Grants Pass, OR	28	-25.1	46	9.0	8.4	460 319	10 052	35 806	18.8	30 481	D	D	25.0	4.7	129	2.9
Great Falls, MT	1 255	-9.1	1 136	33.4	427.7	1 197 706	1 055	96 719	111.1	100 568	48.2	51.8	40.9	16.2	5 952	51.5
Greeley, CO	1 956	-6.3	555	299.9	850.2	1 098 289	1 979	146 652	1 860.7	527 863	20.1	79.9	42.8	20.2	15 649	39.7
Green Bay, WI	547	-3.7	197	1.9	437.0	855 013	4 333	144 973	750.0	270 384	23.7	76.3	53.0	28.8	10 578	57.0
Greensboro-High Point, NC	360	-0.3	107	6.0	135.9	527 298	4 910	60 005	327.4	97 730	24.8	75.2	30.5	10.7	2 649	17.5
Greenville, NC	172	0.2	439	3.6	131.7	1 397 719	3 181	233 246	215.9	552 194	51.5	48.5	60.1	38.9	3 877	57.3
Greenville-Anderson-Mauldin, SC	400	-6.4	96	3.7	115.1	441 917	4 592	45 588	128.7	30 999	D	D	20.6	3.1	2 211	9.5
Gulfport-Biloxi-Pascagoula, MS	87	-17.2	88	0.3	24.7	396 775	4 504	47 253	20.6	20 805	D	D	22.6	2.4	515	9.5
Hagerstown-Martinsburg, MD-WV	200	5.6	130	1.0	118.5	767 295	5 902	89 473	138.2	89 995	50.2	49.8	38.0	15.6	1 452	21.0
Hammond, LA	107	-13.8	100	0.7	36.3	410 570	4 117	54 967	45.7	42 694	40.2	59.8	29.1	7.2	790	17.3
Hanford-Corcoran, CA	674	-1.0	638	407.4	501.5	3 847 243	6 031	340 454	1 829.2	1 732 231	46.7	53.3	68.3	45.1	7 901	36.4
Harrisburg-Carlisle, PA	419	7.2	135	2.6	260.9	795 107	5 906	98 039	458.3	147 142	25.3	74.7	52.9	24.6	4 537	30.3
Harrisonburg, VA	222	-4.7	117	5.6	100.5	823 606	7 055	88 252	659.0	346 475	7.2	92.8	58.4	35.0	2 741	15.9
Hartford-West Hartford-East Hartford, CT	126	15.0	63	6.0	52.0	750 128	11 887	66 721	222.4	111 456	87.0	13.0	31.4	8.9	1 294	7.6
Hattiesburg, MS	150	-5.8	138	1.5	35.1	458 851	3 335	65 786	67.7	61 954	19.7	80.3	32.2	6.5	1 676	24.4
Hickory-Lenoir-Morganton, NC	192	2.0	87	3.5	75.0	487 357	5 573	57 925	318.1	144 744	16.2	83.8	34.3	14.5	839	9.2
Hilton Head Island-Bluffton-Beaufort, NC	111	9.1	440	D	15.2	1 305 794	2 970	85 413	D	D	D	14.2	29.4	6.0	111	13.9
Hinesville, GA	16	-26.8	146	D	3.4	339 894	2 330	48 301	11.8	104 841	7.2	92.8	32.7	7.1	143	31.0
Homosassa Springs, FL	41	1.3	73	0.7	7.3	480 195	6 621	29 451	14.1	25 190	54.9	45.1	17.7	3.4	146	3.6
Hot Springs, AR	36	-9.6	99	0.3	8.4	364 504	3 688	43 119	24.1	66 756	18.6	81.4	24.7	5.3	93	8.9
Houma-Thibodaux, LA	251	-11.8	421	1.0	73.9	919 569	2 183	127 193	95.1	159 572	61.9	38.1	39.8	8.7	146	4.5
Houston-The Woodlands-Sugar Land, TX	2 677	2.4	178	73.1	765.7	699 599	3 927	58 371	D	D	67.9	D	24.8	4.1	18 927	11.1
Huntington-Ashland, WV-KY-OH	323	-13.2	121	0.4	64.8	274 665	2 279	44 660	25.8	9 618	63.1	36.9	14.9	0.9	931	18.0
Huntsville, AL	456	4.5	202	18.2	271.4	787 164	3 906	96 602	206.9	91 443	72.1	27.9	33.9	9.6	6 761	34.3
Idaho Falls, ID	857	-4.7	455	367.6	538.5	1 055 110	2 318	147 762	500.6	265 869	65.4	34.6	48.1	23.4	8 915	45.0
Indianapolis-Carmel-Anderson, IN	1 689	7.5	272	13.4	1 525.2	1 558 263	5 724	150 794	985.1	158 753	D	D	44.8	22.9	28 897	50.0
Iowa City, IA	643	-0.6	259	0.4	549.7	1 683 794	6 496	164 372	785.1	316 447	43.6	56.4	59.0	36.6	21 083	71.5
Ithaca, NY	91	-16.5	163	0.3	54.4	448 507	2 757	113 717	67.4	120 772	33.7	66.3	43.7	16.1	900	25.8
Jackson, MI	183	0.4	171	3.9	136.0	652 247	3 822	85 794	78.2	72 866	69.2	30.8	36.4	12.0	4 210	32.1
Jackson, MS	1 156	-5.8	276	46.8	400.9	665 400	2 409	73 821	633.0	151 223	33.9	66.1	29.3	10.4	17 513	39.4
Jackson, TN	357	-10.2	264	12.6	258.1	669 964	2 534	100 337	138.2	102 192	93.9	6.1	33.9	12.1	5 638	60.1
Jacksonville, FL	186	16.2	105	13.8	38.5	565 515	5 383	56 509	117.4	66 417	77.0	23.0	20.4	3.5	D	3.5
Jacksonville, NC	58	4.4	166	1.5	38.4	634 349	3 819	115 625	187.7	540 928	15.6	84.4	46.4	30.5	1 001	38.3
Janesville-Beloit, WI	354	2.7	234	16.2	303.7	1 294 782	5 523	154 109	274.4	181 858	60.4	39.6	49.8	23.5	7 892	68.2
Jefferson City, MO	1 011	-3.2	216	8.8	410.6	590 339	2 731	71 559	375.4	80 288	19.9	80.1	49.5	9.2	6 757	35.2
Johnson City, TN	157	-3.3	83	D	63.6	504 477	6 084	61 423	D	D	31.1	D	26.3	4.5	483	19.3
Johnstown, PA	77	-12.6	140	0.1	45.4	457 327	3 277	82 508	32.6	59 240	55.5	44.5	42.3	8.5	775	31.9
Jonesboro, AR	723	6.7	738	581.6	684.0	2 311 689	3 134	359 641	549.0	560 225	99.4	0.6	60.0	44.9	25 872	68.1

Table C. Metropolitan Areas — **Water Use, Wholesale Trade, Retail Trade, and Real Estate**

Area name	Water use, 2010: Total water withdrawn (mil gal/day)	Water use, 2010: Gallons withdrawn per person per day	Wholesale trade,[1] 2007: Number of establish-ments	Wholesale trade,[1] 2007: Number of employees	Wholesale trade,[1] 2007: Sales (mil dol)	Wholesale trade,[1] 2007: Annual payroll (mil dol)	Retail trade, 2007: Number of establish-ments	Retail trade, 2007: Number of employees	Retail trade, 2007: Sales (mil dol)	Retail trade, 2007: Annual payroll (mil dol)	Real estate and rental and leasing, 2007: Number of establish-ments	Real estate and rental and leasing, 2007: Number of employees	Real estate and rental and leasing, 2007: Receipts (mil dol)	Real estate and rental and leasing, 2007: Annual payroll (mil dol)
	133	134	135	136	137	138	139	140	141	142	143	144	145	146
Fairbanks, AK	53.6	549	72	D	D	D	339	5 236	1 574.3	146.7	136	745	152.5	29.9
Fargo, ND-MN	23.8	114	404	D	D	D	843	14 809	3 515.9	311.1	308	1 809	243.8	49.0
Farmington, NM	343.7	2 643	146	1 454	866.4	70.4	482	6 671	1 742.0	155.5	120	879	211.5	45.2
Fayetteville, NC	71.9	196	171	1 800	953.1	72.5	1 140	16 425	4 019.1	351.4	350	1 723	256.5	49.4
Fayetteville-Springdale-Rogers, AR-MO	414.0	894	468	D	D	D	1 658	22 909	5 451.9	497.6	609	3 481	362.7	93.6
Flagstaff, AZ	52.2	388	98	1 149	475.6	40.2	674	7 861	1 691.7	169.3	237	754	187.5	24.2
Flint, MI	13.4	31	296	5 871	3 554.9	382.9	1 614	21 531	4 836.7	440.5	339	1 813	270.2	47.7
Florence, SC	259.6	1 263	221	3 071	1 584.8	118.3	1 027	11 963	2 765.4	233.1	170	815	182.6	21.2
Florence-Muscle Shoals, AL	1 361.8	9 255	162	2 134	866.0	64.2	683	8 102	1 952.9	167.1	124	556	68.2	12.5
Fond du Lac, WI	14.4	142	104	1 330	993.6	59.5	407	5 999	1 277.7	118.3	77	305	34.3	5.3
Fort Collins, CO	412.9	1 378	290	3 156	1 265.2	146.8	1 306	17 510	3 922.9	402.7	562	2 181	327.1	63.6
Fort Smith, AR-OK	72.5	258	282	D	D	D	1 017	12 784	3 016.7	259.4	261	1 307	210.9	40.3
Fort Wayne, IN	60.2	145	611	D	D	D	1 569	24 077	5 339.0	493.9	466	2 102	343.3	58.9
Fresno, CA	2 813.2	3 024	814	12 843	7 846.8	582.0	2 579	38 046	9 808.3	905.0	755	4 478	695.2	132.1
Gadsden, AL	146.3	1 401	96	1 064	518.4	36.1	453	4 786	1 114.8	92.7	79	428	68.7	12.1
Gainesville, FL	62.9	238	191	D	D	D	1 010	14 849	3 204.7	304.8	405	2 086	316.2	60.0
Gainesville, GA	100.2	558	252	3 732	4 914.5	170.8	630	8 134	2 220.7	206.5	229	558	125.5	18.4
Gettysburg, PA	20.2	199	62	D	D	D	376	3 798	832.4	79.9	52	230	42.8	5.9
Glens Falls, NY	86.8	673	102	1 004	427.1	41.0	658	7 833	1 867.8	182.4	106	435	72.7	11.5
Goldsboro, NC	34.3	280	102	1 843	1 094.5	71.2	501	5 759	1 388.0	113.7	70	288	35.3	6.6
Grand Forks, ND-MN	30.6	311	136	1 628	1 071.2	65.4	458	7 262	1 536.0	141.6	75	511	62.7	10.6
Grand Island, NE	555.2	6 783	138	1 725	1 330.5	70.4	444	5 876	1 282.8	111.6	82	D	D	D
Grand Junction, CO	754.7	5 144	219	2 463	1 179.3	103.2	693	8 856	2 389.5	223.8	323	1 101	246.9	40.1
Grand Rapids-Wyoming, MI	1 010.0	1 021	1 326	25 520	15 338.5	1 306.5	3 436	47 800	11 265.1	1 009.9	892	5 085	725.2	137.3
Grants Pass, OR	30.2	365	60	D	D	D	347	4 549	1 024.3	107.4	110	450	47.1	9.5
Great Falls, MT	166.9	2 052	118	1 077	672.0	42.5	388	5 507	1 302.3	121.0	137	378	56.3	8.3
Greeley, CO	462.1	1 828	248	D	D	D	650	8 735	2 246.1	212.9	227	838	115.6	23.7
Green Bay, WI	870.1	2 841	384	6 078	3 431.8	275.4	1 187	17 523	3 948.8	358.0	273	1 697	238.1	47.1
Greensboro-High Point, NC	222.8	308	1 233	17 398	12 653.3	813.2	2 782	38 394	9 248.9	890.9	824	5 046	1 517.8	158.0
Greenville, NC	28.8	171	137	1 700	898.9	70.5	668	8 846	2 176.0	188.8	201	D	D	D
Greenville-Anderson-Mauldin, SC	364.5	442	1 020	D	D	D	3 141	40 362	9 564.9	868.5	875	4 182	919.1	146.6
Gulfport-Biloxi-Pascagoula, MS	686.9	1 853	228	D	D	D	1 390	17 838	4 591.4	403.1	389	1 407	236.9	40.2
Hagerstown-Martinsburg, MD-WV	87.6	348	186	2 856	1 838.8	124.5	951	13 762	3 349.7	293.7	224	971	177.2	24.7
Hammond, LA	20.1	166	89	1 782	953.7	77.1	452	6 607	1 742.4	140.8	90	417	44.6	9.0
Hanford-Corcoran, CA	1 298.9	8 490	60	D	D	D	326	4 267	1 035.9	93.9	95	343	55.4	7.2
Harrisburg-Carlisle, PA	137.3	250	525	13 121	10 199.5	633.7	2 125	33 703	7 947.8	725.1	462	3 430	807.8	123.9
Harrisonburg, VA	38.5	307	116	2 023	918.4	84.3	601	8 250	1 920.8	200.1	127	1 285	172.6	37.5
Hartford-West Hartford-East Hartford, CT	350.3	289	1 254	22 232	16 799.6	1 158.9	4 578	66 748	17 156.2	1 646.8	1 188	7 661	1 500.4	298.6
Hattiesburg, MS	53.0	371	115	D	D	D	739	9 647	3 173.8	199.2	166	D	D	D
Hickory-Lenoir-Morganton, NC	1 139.5	3 118	414	8 015	4 663.4	320.3	1 441	16 856	4 209.7	367.0	320	1 098	190.5	29.5
Hilton Head Island-Bluffton-Beaufort, NC	53.6	287	143	949	443.3	44.1	935	11 265	2 655.9	257.3	481	3 975	466.1	150.1
Hinesville, GA	18.8	241	9	D	D	D	204	2 004	556.7	42.0	55	238	29.4	5.9
Homosassa Springs, FL	1 201.2	8 505	84	D	D	D	516	5 836	1 405.6	131.1	202	605	59.4	12.3
Hot Springs, AR	17.6	183	91	D	D	D	523	5 898	1 443.4	126.9	158	614	88.0	14.6
Houma-Thibodaux, LA	49.5	238	265	3 201	1 787.4	135.2	796	11 724	2 832.9	259.9	256	2 290	488.0	102.9
Houston-The Woodlands-Sugar Land, TX	2 798.0	473	7 537	D	D	D	16 907	250 858	69 929.7	6 070.0	6 447	47 072	11 093.2	2 018.1
Huntington-Ashland, WV-KY-OH	159.4	437	289	D	D	D	1 411	19 127	4 191.2	355.7	288	D	D	D
Huntsville, AL	2 823.4	6 761	393	4 926	3 218.7	230.2	1 594	21 451	5 161.9	479.9	487	2 247	369.3	69.3
Idaho Falls, ID	2 282.8	17 130	185	D	D	D	583	7 947	1 982.0	168.9	162	574	92.6	12.5
Indianapolis-Carmel-Anderson, IN	611.0	324	2 210	36 897	23 766.6	1 778.8	6 386	99 948	24 143.0	2 290.9	2 266	15 267	2 793.9	567.0
Iowa City, IA	42.5	279	121	1 498	753.3	59.0	639	9 417	1 848.1	185.7	157	D	D	D
Ithaca, NY	232.7	2 291	54	426	189.6	15.5	372	5 068	1 018.3	106.1	95	748	116.2	19.8
Jackson, MI	20.3	127	146	D	D	D	582	7 462	1 690.9	153.6	118	608	64.9	12.5
Jackson, MS	156.4	276	681	D	D	D	2 217	29 470	7 073.4	646.3	615	3 203	706.6	107.6
Jackson, TN	22.8	175	177	2 232	1 296.9	91.6	612	7 769	1 879.2	167.1	118	793	100.7	10.7
Jacksonville, FL	880.8	655	1 479	D	D	D	5 190	74 132	18 173.6	1 692.4	2 141	D	D	D
Jacksonville, NC	32.3	182	40	259	96.9	10.7	550	7 276	1 913.9	154.2	185	757	108.4	17.2
Janesville-Beloit, WI	28.3	176	132	3 075	2 700.1	151.1	579	9 269	2 439.8	216.8	126	432	92.6	10.3
Jefferson City, MO	104.5	697	118	2 987	909.9	89.6	606	7 808	1 827.3	158.6	116	D	D	D
Johnson City, TN	49.6	250	156	D	D	D	749	10 577	2 449.9	216.8	162	1 079	128.8	20.4
Johnstown, PA	27.1	189	123	1 362	582.5	44.2	588	7 207	1 626.5	137.9	99	584	65.8	16.7
Jonesboro, AR	1 360.0	11 237	150	D	D	D	587	7 419	1 634.0	139.8	115	545	79.7	13.2

1. Merchant wholesalers, except manufacturers' sales branches and offices.

Table C. Metropolitan Areas — **Professional Services, Manufacturing, and Accommodation and Food Services**

Area name	Professional, scientific, and technical services,[1] 2007				Manufacturing, 2007				Accommodation and food services, 2007			
	Number of establish-ments	Number of employees	Sales (mil dol)	Annual payroll (mil dol)	Number of establish-ments	Number of employees	Sales (mil dol)	Annual payroll (mil dol)	Number of establish-ments	Number of employees	Sales (mil dol)	Annual payroll (mil dol)
	147	148	149	150	151	152	153	154	155	156	157	158
Fairbanks, AK	228	1 329	174.9	64.7	78	745	D	37.3	220	3 430	221.6	60.9
Fargo, ND-MN	483	D	D	D	249	9 191	2 797.2	346.6	452	10 382	399.7	117.5
Farmington, NM	239	D	D	D	91	1 649	668.7	64.3	192	4 108	173.2	45.8
Fayetteville, NC	528	D	D	D	126	10 561	D	450.1	609	D	D	D
Fayetteville-Springdale-Rogers, AR-MO	1 134	D	D	D	457	30 601	D	1 007.3	858	17 438	664.6	191.6
Flagstaff, AZ	322	D	D	D	109	4 219	1 526.8	240.5	531	11 181	717.7	181.9
Flint, MI	694	D	D	D	309	14 878	12 579.5	1 099.6	762	13 583	528.7	151.9
Florence, SC	287	D	D	D	182	11 892	5 318.8	546.3	374	7 173	303.9	81.7
Florence-Muscle Shoals, AL	270	D	D	D	203	7 312	3 166.9	301.3	249	5 128	198.5	56.3
Fond du Lac, WI	157	1 320	101.9	65.4	151	9 745	2 903.2	392.3	242	4 001	131.5	37.5
Fort Collins, CO	1 327	7 876	867.5	387.3	420	11 764	3 226.8	664.5	807	14 244	604.4	181.9
Fort Smith, AR-OK	483	D	D	D	318	24 586	6 944.3	D	456	7 960	321.7	87.8
Fort Wayne, IN	978	7 253	753.3	346.6	694	38 250	22 548.5	1 837.4	803	16 997	598.1	182.2
Fresno, CA	1 564	D	D	D	646	26 898	7 827.3	1 018.0	1 460	25 553	1 147.2	320.9
Gadsden, AL	156	876	76.6	26.8	118	5 430	1 253.0	203.7	177	3 381	138.0	38.1
Gainesville, FL	810	5 326	629.8	265.2	D	D	D	D	543	11 333	502.1	135.7
Gainesville, GA	419	D	D	D	265	17 296	6 069.0	602.5	272	4 930	224.1	62.5
Gettysburg, PA	135	D	D	D	126	8 038	2 498.3	297.9	206	4 098	160.1	46.1
Glens Falls, NY	250	1 196	113.7	43.8	176	7 263	1 962.7	302.8	529	5 579	325.0	97.8
Goldsboro, NC	143	825	65.7	22.8	84	6 147	1 474.8	221.7	197	3 485	132.1	36.2
Grand Forks, ND-MN	157	D	D	D	94	4 495	1 519.4	153.0	247	5 190	177.8	51.3
Grand Island, NE	136	D	D	D	D	D	D	D	177	2 950	108.7	31.2
Grand Junction, CO	547	D	D	D	177	2 691	539.6	104.9	301	6 307	268.8	77.6
Grand Rapids-Wyoming, MI	2 287	D	D	D	1 872	98 360	26 315.6	4 630.9	1 699	34 147	1 280.5	387.4
Grants Pass, OR	134	D	D	D	127	3 127	471.3	105.0	205	2 493	108.9	33.0
Great Falls, MT	199	D	D	D	81	1 094	670.9	44.8	247	3 997	174.3	48.6
Greeley, CO	462	D	D	D	284	10 186	4 193.7	451.8	379	6 099	217.2	63.8
Green Bay, WI	588	D	D	D	552	29 482	10 130.5	1 244.9	769	14 107	507.2	146.5
Greensboro-High Point, NC	1 814	D	D	D	1 194	63 505	31 456.5	2 461.4	1 432	27 982	1 260.4	353.2
Greenville, NC	310	1 750	198.5	77.0	98	6 930	D	265.8	306	7 187	293.5	79.2
Greenville-Anderson-Mauldin, SC	1 899	D	D	D	1 047	53 935	18 730.0	2 167.3	1 654	30 864	1 250.2	346.9
Gulfport-Biloxi-Pascagoula, MS	689	D	D	D	224	D	D	D	658	23 736	1 930.9	516.1
Hagerstown-Martinsburg, MD-WV	366	D	D	D	194	D	D	D	469	7 813	386.1	101.0
Hammond, LA	189	D	D	D	92	2 773	D	81.3	225	4 169	164.6	41.3
Hanford-Corcoran, CA	101	535	52.9	16.9	73	4 291	2 107.7	148.7	171	4 209	360.1	77.5
Harrisburg-Carlisle, PA	1 390	D	D	D	450	20 726	D	876.1	1 264	22 498	1 101.2	315.8
Harrisonburg, VA	233	D	D	D	134	10 112	6 183.8	399.9	257	6 326	230.7	73.7
Hartford-West Hartford-East Hartford, CT	2 900	D	D	D	1 813	77 946	19 374.0	4 299.5	2 577	41 547	2 104.5	622.3
Hattiesburg, MS	292	D	D	D	110	D	D	198.1	281	6 813	263.5	73.4
Hickory-Lenoir-Morganton, NC	584	D	D	D	845	50 686	10 725.5	1 618.2	645	11 611	466.1	127.0
Hilton Head Island-Bluffton-Beaufort, NC	589	D	D	D	113	1 607	299.8	52.0	514	10 365	562.9	182.3
Hinesville, GA	57	D	D	D	D	D	D	D	101	1 767	64.7	16.5
Homosassa Springs, FL	274	D	D	D	D	D	D	D	188	2 931	109.7	32.4
Hot Springs, AR	218	D	D	D	119	2 786	661.7	99.9	265	5 080	203.3	62.2
Houma-Thibodaux, LA	441	D	D	D	185	8 372	1 729.9	360.8	397	7 226	339.7	95.2
Houston-The Woodlands-Sugar Land, TX	15 645	D	D	D	5 475	D	D	D	9 607	197 224	10 221.2	2 739.3
Huntington-Ashland, WV-KY-OH	510	D	D	D	D	D	D	D	637	11 712	450.7	123.3
Huntsville, AL	1 374	32 363	5 761.5	2 244.1	391	27 771	9 598.0	1 303.6	739	15 537	664.4	184.8
Idaho Falls, ID	428	D	D	D	D	D	D	D	232	D	D	D
Indianapolis-Carmel-Anderson, IN	5 109	D	D	D	D	D	D	D	3 844	79 427	3 568.7	1 047.6
Iowa City, IA	293	D	D	D	122	6 712	D	263.8	370	8 130	373.5	97.0
Ithaca, NY	273	D	D	D	92	3 152	742.8	137.3	308	3 742	177.7	51.9
Jackson, MI	235	D	D	D	284	9 250	2 783.0	403.6	300	4 999	185.4	53.5
Jackson, MS	1 424	D	D	D	D	D	D	D	1 015	20 082	830.9	221.7
Jackson, TN	216	D	D	D	D	D	D	D	245	5 902	223.5	59.7
Jacksonville, FL	4 453	D	D	D	D	D	D	D	2 713	53 981	2 747.6	786.4
Jacksonville, NC	210	D	D	D	43	1 016	253.0	31.8	310	6 265	287.9	71.5
Janesville-Beloit, WI	199	D	D	D	236	13 527	12 381.6	720.3	383	5 673	211.7	58.6
Jefferson City, MO	303	1 653	192.5	69.1	160	5 992	D	239.2	267	4 426	173.1	50.1
Johnson City, TN	285	D	D	D	212	10 146	2 223.0	D	348	7 873	302.0	90.3
Johnstown, PA	221	D	D	D	146	5 409	1 439.8	199.6	307	4 135	156.0	40.9
Jonesboro, AR	194	D	D	D	139	7 289	2 002.3	259.0	215	4 324	158.3	44.2

1. Establishments subject to federal tax.

Table C. Metropolitan Areas — **Health Care and Social Assistance, Other Services, Nonemployer Business and Residential Construction**

Area name	Health care and social assistance,[1] 2007				Other services,[1] 2007				Nonemployer business, 2013		Value of residential construction authorized by building permits, 2014	
	Number of establish-ments	Number of employees	Receipts (mil dol)	Annual payroll (mil dol)	Number of establish-ments	Number of employees	Receipts (mil dol)	Annual payroll (mil dol)	Number	Receipts (mil dol)	New construc-tion ($1,000)	Number of housing units
	159	160	161	162	163	164	165	166	167	168	169	170
Fairbanks, AK	267	4 867	570.5	223.9	195	1 081	106.8	31.3	5 249	223.1	9 925	54
Fargo, ND-MN	575	16 573	1 463.9	604.3	481	D	D	D	15 046	795.6	454 461	3 766
Farmington, NM	265	6 274	534.2	226.2	192	1 363	170.4	37.1	5 381	230.7	35 978	173
Fayetteville, NC	813	20 659	1 652.0	682.7	434	2 787	182.8	57.2	18 818	687.9	179 595	1 089
Fayetteville-Springdale-Rogers, AR-MO	945	D	D	D	617	D	D	D	32 693	1 417.7	658 641	3 353
Flagstaff, AZ	389	6 628	878.6	305.9	247	1 493	100.8	32.2	8 342	335.1	105 408	560
Flint, MI	1 261	25 790	2 505.1	1 005.4	648	3 695	418.1	103.4	28 250	923.3	65 470	343
Florence, SC	437	14 058	1 532.9	574.6	291	1 792	155.3	40.6	12 367	441.1	56 874	379
Florence-Muscle Shoals, AL	405	7 284	660.9	251.0	219	1 393	120.9	31.9	10 206	408.3	24 728	197
Fond du Lac, WI	266	6 180	607.2	223.9	193	1 206	88.4	24.4	4 862	218.7	35 031	240
Fort Collins, CO	908	15 177	1 400.5	610.6	612	3 123	286.8	77.2	28 499	1 234.1	524 427	2 498
Fort Smith, AR-OK	655	16 762	1 317.3	555.9	348	1 697	139.4	38.6	17 457	813.9	77 258	604
Fort Wayne, IN	1 114	31 151	2 944.2	1 142.2	825	5 686	457.1	140.8	26 266	1 038.5	226 061	1 245
Fresno, CA	2 099	36 707	4 150.8	1 713.0	1 069	7 309	704.7	191.7	49 304	2 326.6	445 222	1 892
Gadsden, AL	302	6 515	626.7	229.8	121	691	54.0	15.8	6 988	303.1	10 935	79
Gainesville, FL	729	D	D	D	390	2 806	658.1	88.3	17 449	651.0	111 632	799
Gainesville, GA	398	8 599	1 046.7	384.6	272	1 384	136.1	36.5	13 987	599.8	120 068	722
Gettysburg, PA	185	3 887	313.4	130.3	165	1 004	81.8	20.2	6 356	268.5	60 304	272
Glens Falls, NY	365	7 916	610.8	283.2	220	1 029	97.8	27.8	8 361	355.6	47 163	368
Goldsboro, NC	294	7 587	573.0	248.6	159	949	70.0	20.5	5 815	222.2	40 390	257
Grand Forks, ND-MN	244	8 510	646.3	281.6	215	D	D	D	6 103	266.5	142 713	999
Grand Island, NE	213	D	D	D	220	1 152	85.0	20.6	5 586	231.3	51 910	304
Grand Junction, CO	425	8 480	847.4	336.2	317	1 599	160.1	42.3	11 002	495.1	114 227	504
Grand Rapids-Wyoming, MI	2 178	53 864	5 010.9	1 983.4	1 719	11 123	1 026.7	281.8	69 082	3 246.7	588 788	3 171
Grants Pass, OR	251	4 055	356.7	128.0	131	605	40.6	12.5	5 578	236.4	34 689	149
Great Falls, MT	269	6 050	517.8	206.6	166	845	65.4	18.8	4 611	185.7	71 028	463
Greeley, CO	429	8 538	763.1	292.3	340	1 513	161.2	40.0	19 020	875.3	540 224	2 708
Green Bay, WI	695	21 052	2 104.5	821.4	554	3 268	250.9	69.9	16 404	792.6	161 832	1 004
Greensboro-High Point, NC	1 655	38 752	3 478.3	1 436.8	1 186	6 684	843.5	177.2	52 274	2 137.4	518 982	2 632
Greenville, NC	439	D	D	D	185	1 084	108.0	21.6	10 067	378.2	113 145	905
Greenville-Anderson-Mauldin, SC	1 660	36 852	3 674.8	1 463.9	1 196	8 529	757.8	231.5	55 891	2 366.4	869 758	4 479
Gulfport-Biloxi-Pascagoula, MS	784	D	D	D	487	2 713	262.7	70.1	25 825	981.2	266 674	1 954
Hagerstown-Martinsburg, MD-WV	601	D	D	D	401	2 481	210.3	58.4	13 636	560.4	156 419	975
Hammond, LA	269	7 321	568.5	226.1	150	919	86.4	21.7	9 305	344.5	78 352	592
Hanford-Corcoran, CA	204	4 106	433.8	153.1	105	582	47.0	13.4	4 180	170.1	56 757	434
Harrisburg-Carlisle, PA	1 485	43 317	3 960.3	1 674.8	1 290	9 051	1 003.4	273.6	32 770	1 498.3	274 735	1 602
Harrisonburg, VA	245	6 349	549.2	229.3	237	1 233	118.5	30.3	7 877	322.9	66 550	404
Hartford-West Hartford-East Hartford, CT	3 459	91 507	8 632.4	3 847.9	2 515	18 825	1 935.8	541.0	78 617	4 210.4	221 598	1 393
Hattiesburg, MS	329	10 401	1 074.6	453.7	167	1 033	73.2	20.9	10 037	436.6	21 236	166
Hickory-Lenoir-Morganton, NC	761	17 609	1 598.0	630.0	483	2 583	257.5	67.2	22 420	888.3	118 208	594
Hilton Head Island-Bluffton-Beaufort, NC	426	7 044	700.3	253.1	344	3 207	248.6	87.7	15 518	796.7	515 106	1 426
Hinesville, GA	70	D	D	D	72	D	D	D	3 337	94.9	50 602	242
Homosassa Springs, FL	340	6 762	661.8	239.8	221	857	52.8	16.3	8 790	337.9	6 838	233
Hot Springs, AR	276	6 590	613.4	244.4	179	1 309	80.6	26.6	7 724	304.3	12 298	43
Houma-Thibodaux, LA	440	9 563	954.3	373.8	288	2 161	280.2	78.5	14 519	719.6	158 127	664
Houston-The Woodlands-Sugar Land, TX	12 465	255 389	27 865.0	10 590.6	7 939	67 484	7 689.3	2 122.9	522 568	26 335.5	9 250 783	63 741
Huntington-Ashland, WV-KY-OH	1 019	D	D	D	525	D	D	D	17 093	611.1	49 469	358
Huntsville, AL	1 001	20 402	2 020.2	828.1	569	4 019	619.5	103.1	28 098	1 077.1	349 496	2 817
Idaho Falls, ID	505	D	D	D	186	996	88.2	23.3	9 983	427.3	70 976	482
Indianapolis-Carmel-Anderson, IN	4 477	113 500	11 734.4	4 532.8	3 336	25 796	3 676.2	737.2	129 587	5 439.4	1 498 510	8 006
Iowa City, IA	423	16 714	1 562.5	607.2	263	1 529	193.2	38.7	10 623	491.0	194 027	1 104
Ithaca, NY	250	4 919	388.7	152.9	149	945	129.2	21.6	7 170	257.9	43 102	301
Jackson, MI	379	8 717	810.5	346.6	241	1 528	147.0	41.2	8 876	311.5	16 728	89
Jackson, MS	1 328	38 870	3 816.0	1 425.4	904	5 631	548.2	153.4	46 594	2 032.1	399 377	1 962
Jackson, TN	356	11 495	1 083.5	460.1	177	1 030	79.2	27.5	8 422	380.5	40 900	205
Jacksonville, FL	3 270	69 014	7 365.6	2 800.4	2 485	D	D	D	98 407	3 995.7	1 674 047	7 781
Jacksonville, NC	246	5 465	433.8	163.4	213	1 136	68.0	21.4	8 433	301.6	126 275	1 081
Janesville-Beloit, WI	330	9 276	878.5	337.0	285	1 578	108.7	30.6	8 085	315.1	27 005	143
Jefferson City, MO	374	9 056	781.8	308.9	341	1 987	199.8	56.8	8 865	355.5	25 909	240
Johnson City, TN	429	13 218	1 334.9	525.0	267	D	D	D	11 684	493.0	88 990	706
Johnstown, PA	545	11 825	872.0	383.6	320	1 590	114.3	28.9	6 190	237.1	11 445	61
Jonesboro, AR	346	8 212	792.6	294.5	161	887	71.6	18.0	8 537	369.2	67 624	680

1. Establishments subject to federal tax.

Area name	Government employment and payroll, 2012: Full-time equivalent employees	March Payroll (dollars)	March payroll (percent of total): Adminis-tration, judicial, and legal	Police and corrections	Fire protection	Highways and transporta-tion	Health and welfare	Natural resources and utilities	Education and libraries	Local government finances, 2012: General revenue: Total (mil dol)	Inter-govern-mental (mil dol)	Taxes: Total (mil dol)	Per capita[1] (dollars): Total	Property
	171	172	173	174	175	176	177	178	179	180	181	182	183	184
Fairbanks, AK	2 949	14 833 210	7.9	3.4	2.6	2.4	1.8	5.3	75.9	380.0	201.2	148.5	1 481	1 335
Fargo, ND-MN	6 888	27 847 634	5.1	9.5	2.7	4.4	9.5	7.5	60.2	969.4	445.6	298.8	1 381	1 058
Farmington, NM	5 857	21 149 302	4.2	11.0	2.6	2.0	1.9	8.4	68.4	491.8	290.9	126.9	987	702
Fayetteville, NC	20 611	71 938 105	1.4	6.0	1.8	0.8	38.1	3.6	42.6	1 147.7	620.9	372.5	995	717
Fayetteville-Springdale-Rogers, AR-MO	15 951	51 196 846	5.5	9.4	4.3	3.2	1.0	5.4	70.1	1 400.1	793.7	404.4	839	367
Flagstaff, AZ	4 575	17 536 070	11.8	13.5	9.2	3.5	4.5	6.4	48.1	469.7	159.1	223.4	1 643	979
Flint, MI	15 234	64 330 939	5.5	5.9	1.4	3.5	24.1	3.5	55.1	2 005.4	1 056.8	353.2	844	786
Florence, SC	6 966	21 627 471	5.6	9.2	1.9	2.7	6.2	5.3	67.5	538.5	250.7	178.7	867	649
Florence-Muscle Shoals, AL	5 882	19 596 410	3.1	6.8	3.3	3.2	20.6	13.8	47.1	488.1	192.2	137.3	934	418
Fond du Lac, WI	3 703	15 389 801	4.9	9.2	2.4	4.4	10.7	3.5	63.8	424.7	174.4	182.3	1 790	1 688
Fort Collins, CO	10 782	47 317 101	8.8	11.5	1.1	2.8	7.5	18.4	46.2	1 178.8	292.6	577.8	1 861	1 211
Fort Smith, AR-OK	9 950	33 824 806	6.1	6.9	2.1	3.1	5.0	11.1	65.4	795.9	453.2	202.5	722	305
Fort Wayne, IN	12 482	46 187 211	6.4	12.8	3.8	4.6	1.3	5.6	63.8	1 286.9	601.6	479.3	1 137	913
Fresno, CA	34 954	165 436 346	4.1	10.3	2.1	3.3	9.7	4.5	65.0	5 127.4	3 047.2	1 071.6	1 131	789
Gadsden, AL	3 980	11 900 349	4.3	10.5	6.2	3.7	6.9	8.4	56.6	284.1	137.1	99.7	955	293
Gainesville, FL	10 035	36 051 916	10.0	15.5	4.4	4.8	3.2	11.5	46.9	897.9	290.9	376.2	1 402	1 085
Gainesville, GA	6 523	22 620 107	6.4	9.1	7.3	1.6	4.4	4.9	65.4	563.5	217.3	266.2	1 436	890
Gettysburg, PA	2 548	9 790 732	7.8	9.5	0.9	2.6	2.1	3.4	73.2	374.0	165.8	167.3	1 648	1 256
Glens Falls, NY	6 698	24 733 643	6.0	8.2	0.4	6.9	8.7	2.7	65.0	745.4	272.2	360.1	2 803	2 155
Goldsboro, NC	5 237	14 176 474	3.0	6.2	2.1	1.3	9.2	6.0	66.2	346.7	199.6	101.5	817	585
Grand Forks, ND-MN	4 147	14 917 010	5.7	8.3	2.6	5.2	15.5	10.4	50.1	471.6	218.9	130.8	1 323	1 063
Grand Island, NE	4 036	14 835 732	5.6	6.7	2.9	4.0	6.4	15.9	57.5	355.7	117.9	148.0	1 773	1 410
Grand Junction, CO	5 197	18 735 519	8.2	13.3	5.0	4.1	7.0	9.6	48.8	498.4	180.8	228.0	1 542	966
Grand Rapids-Wyoming, MI	26 602	112 436 599	7.9	9.0	2.5	4.3	3.1	4.9	66.6	3 718.2	1 877.6	1 165.3	1 159	1 055
Grants Pass, OR	2 192	8 995 230	6.6	12.9	2.5	3.4	1.3	3.1	68.4	243.6	119.9	70.8	854	781
Great Falls, MT	2 704	9 771 107	6.8	13.0	3.8	5.6	3.7	6.9	59.0	238.3	103.2	77.2	944	913
Greeley, CO	8 663	35 763 495	8.2	17.4	4.0	5.2	6.6	11.0	45.5	919.9	308.8	411.9	1 562	1 194
Green Bay, WI	11 507	49 464 799	4.6	9.3	2.9	4.0	8.9	3.8	65.2	1 398.9	611.3	539.9	1 735	1 620
Greensboro-High Point, NC	26 780	99 652 358	4.7	9.7	3.6	2.0	7.2	5.5	64.4	2 394.5	1 098.1	928.6	1 262	995
Greenville, NC	6 107	20 619 861	3.8	8.9	3.2	2.0	4.2	10.9	60.2	555.7	265.7	167.7	972	677
Greenville-Anderson-Mauldin, SC	32 635	116 071 503	4.0	6.4	3.0	1.4	33.6	5.1	45.4	3 592.7	858.8	824.2	978	830
Gulfport-Biloxi-Pascagoula, MS	18 635	68 245 147	4.0	7.4	3.9	3.0	36.0	3.0	41.5	2 388.7	948.4	466.4	1 229	1 099
Hagerstown-Martinsburg, MD-WV	8 853	33 633 765	4.2	5.9	2.5	1.9	0.9	6.7	76.6	810.6	360.1	325.5	1 270	912
Hammond, LA	6 393	23 444 209	4.2	6.0	1.2	1.7	46.4	1.8	37.5	621.2	213.8	128.9	1 044	366
Hanford-Corcoran, CA	4 882	22 137 016	6.6	11.1	2.5	1.2	11.7	3.6	60.7	623.0	383.4	130.2	860	727
Harrisburg-Carlisle, PA	18 305	73 828 976	7.2	11.2	0.6	3.9	3.7	5.0	66.8	2 496.2	893.1	1 022.1	1 845	1 338
Harrisonburg, VA	4 180	13 504 909	5.9	8.1	4.4	2.7	4.3	7.2	63.8	389.9	157.1	146.9	1 145	791
Hartford-West Hartford-East Hartford, CT	41 889	212 590 921	3.4	7.9	3.6	2.6	3.3	4.5	73.1	5 466.8	1 915.2	3 050.0	2 512	2 484
Hattiesburg, MS	9 029	27 151 166	3.5	4.9	2.0	2.5	47.7	1.9	36.9	819.4	196.1	154.2	1 050	973
Hickory-Lenoir-Morganton, NC	15 251	50 474 252	3.6	5.9	2.0	1.2	24.3	3.5	56.8	1 280.9	597.8	326.4	898	671
Hilton Head Island-Bluffton-Beaufort, NC	6 425	25 024 387	7.0	9.7	6.6	1.7	25.2	3.9	43.8	837.8	157.8	429.0	2 213	1 771
Hinesville, GA	3 104	9 754 876	5.6	9.3	1.5	1.2	15.4	1.8	61.7	272.2	113.4	80.9	993	612
Homosassa Springs, FL	3 890	11 674 757	8.6	11.3	0.1	3.6	5.4	3.4	65.1	322.4	98.7	162.1	1 163	1 064
Hot Springs, AR	2 929	9 379 603	4.7	8.8	4.0	3.5	3.4	5.5	68.3	270.5	155.0	62.1	640	262
Houma-Thibodaux, LA	10 111	34 879 997	4.6	9.7	0.6	2.6	31.8	4.0	45.8	1 130.5	411.7	323.8	1 550	688
Houston-The Woodlands-Sugar Land, TX	234 372	897 703 915	4.7	10.8	3.1	4.2	7.4	3.2	64.5	25 851.7	7 434.4	12 890.3	2 087	1 738
Huntington-Ashland, WV-KY-OH	12 579	40 423 670	4.4	6.3	2.0	2.6	4.4	5.0	73.1	1 054.7	525.7	330.6	907	701
Huntsville, AL	20 024	74 872 202	3.7	6.3	3.0	2.8	37.7	7.5	35.8	2 192.6	900.1	428.1	994	510
Idaho Falls, ID	4 554	14 040 874	6.5	10.1	4.5	3.7	7.6	7.0	58.6	341.3	174.7	100.7	740	715
Indianapolis-Carmel-Anderson, IN	70 652	276 197 106	4.2	7.9	5.6	1.8	17.0	11.3	51.5	8 491.1	3 269.0	2 704.9	1 402	1 025
Iowa City, IA	3 919	16 365 120	7.2	7.7	1.2	4.7	10.4	5.1	60.1	620.3	195.2	302.5	1 912	1 555
Ithaca, NY	4 530	19 870 493	5.0	6.2	2.8	4.4	7.3	3.5	68.0	531.9	184.0	252.8	2 465	1 857
Jackson, MI	4 304	17 626 740	7.6	8.1	2.4	4.2	3.5	3.4	69.5	585.1	325.3	139.2	868	809
Jackson, MS	21 103	60 140 323	6.0	10.4	4.8	2.9	1.9	4.3	69.2	1 733.1	846.9	586.9	1 017	965
Jackson, TN	8 999	31 890 237	2.6	6.7	2.4	1.5	58.7	4.5	23.0	995.9	160.4	156.2	1 197	685
Jacksonville, FL	42 905	156 841 760	5.8	13.6	6.1	2.2	1.4	6.6	57.0	4 877.5	1 516.3	1 990.7	1 445	1 051
Jacksonville, NC	5 873	18 455 158	3.9	7.0	1.9	1.2	10.7	4.8	66.2	585.4	209.5	152.5	832	536
Janesville-Beloit, WI	6 252	25 471 665	5.9	9.6	3.9	4.4	7.9	4.5	62.6	723.4	387.9	249.8	1 557	1 471
Jefferson City, MO	4 566	13 402 962	7.4	8.2	3.3	4.3	4.8	6.3	65.4	359.6	122.3	173.3	1 154	721
Johnson City, TN	6 906	20 205 200	5.5	9.0	2.8	6.4	4.7	12.5	56.6	469.5	191.0	177.3	884	595
Johnstown, PA	4 484	15 273 184	8.2	8.3	1.4	5.9	5.7	6.0	63.9	555.1	293.7	143.3	1 012	781
Jonesboro, AR	4 524	13 523 979	4.9	9.6	2.5	3.7	1.1	9.1	68.6	354.5	215.8	87.8	708	311

1. Based on the resident population estimated as of July 1 of the year shown.

Area name	Local government finances, 2012 (cont.)									Government employment, 2013			Presidential election,[2] 2012		
	Direct general expenditure							Debt outstanding					Percent of vote cast:		
			Percent of total for:												
	Total (mil dol)	Per capita[1] (dollars)	Education	Health and hospitals	Police protection	Public welfare	Highways	Total (mil dol)	Per capita[1] (dollars)	Federal civilian	Federal military	State and local	Democratic	Republican	All other
	185	186	187	188	189	190	191	192	193	194	195	196	197	198	199
Fairbanks, AK	342.4	3 415	63.0	1.6	2.3	0.0	6.2	170.2	1 698	3 037	8 775	8 202	NA	NA	NA
Fargo, ND-MN	990.1	4 577	37.7	0.6	5.3	4.1	12.4	1 641.6	7 589	2 358	1 321	16 106	48.6	48.4	3.0
Farmington, NM	551.0	4 287	55.6	3.3	6.3	1.2	4.3	2 140.3	16 652	1 546	348	9 900	34.3	62.4	3.3
Fayetteville, NC	1 203.8	3 214	51.4	3.6	7.6	6.4	1.2	604.8	1 615	14 746	50 327	25 447	59.3	39.7	1.0
Fayetteville-Springdale-Rogers, AR-MO	1 387.0	2 876	60.9	0.3	5.5	0.0	4.9	2 146.7	4 452	2 490	2 187	28 189	33.4	63.6	3.0
Flagstaff, AZ	457.2	3 361	35.9	3.4	6.5	1.6	7.6	377.9	2 779	2 810	289	15 449	56.6	41.0	2.4
Flint, MI	2 064.7	4 935	41.9	28.1	3.5	1.1	3.3	995.9	2 380	1 067	711	20 538	63.6	35.4	1.1
Florence, SC	530.6	2 575	60.9	4.4	6.7	0.2	1.8	374.1	1 815	749	868	15 187	49.9	49.2	0.9
Florence-Muscle Shoals, AL	484.2	3 294	44.6	19.9	4.8	0.1	5.0	444.4	3 023	1 175	675	9 003	35.8	62.6	1.6
Fond du Lac, WI	449.6	4 415	51.8	7.3	5.2	3.9	9.0	580.9	5 704	203	276	5 421	41.9	56.8	1.3
Fort Collins, CO	1 080.2	3 479	37.9	4.5	6.4	3.0	9.0	1 388.6	4 472	2 460	845	31 720	51.5	45.7	2.8
Fort Smith, AR-OK	802.3	2 860	58.0	2.8	5.0	0.2	6.3	1 030.6	3 674	1 401	1 249	16 551	28.7	69.5	1.8
Fort Wayne, IN	1 126.6	2 673	51.6	0.6	6.1	0.3	3.5	1 205.7	2 861	1 996	1 378	19 538	38.8	59.5	1.6
Fresno, CA	5 031.5	5 308	44.7	7.0	5.6	10.3	3.4	3 847.5	4 059	10 051	1 581	54 713	49.9	48.1	2.0
Gadsden, AL	278.9	2 672	46.7	1.9	11.2	0.2	4.8	218.9	2 097	327	472	5 211	30.0	68.3	1.6
Gainesville, FL	944.7	3 522	39.3	3.8	8.2	1.7	4.8	1 953.5	7 283	4 443	584	38 399	55.8	42.6	1.6
Gainesville, GA	566.0	3 053	55.8	6.1	4.5	0.8	2.5	1 522.9	8 213	449	539	9 688	21.2	77.4	1.4
Gettysburg, PA	458.0	4 513	68.9	3.6	1.4	3.2	2.7	405.6	3 997	739	261	3 454	35.5	63.0	1.4
Glens Falls, NY	755.6	5 881	49.4	4.6	2.6	10.7	7.9	575.7	4 481	312	205	9 563	50.1	47.9	1.9
Goldsboro, NC	344.7	2 774	55.1	4.8	6.3	6.3	1.4	151.3	1 217	1 241	4 818	8 264	45.4	53.8	0.8
Grand Forks, ND-MN	433.5	4 384	39.7	1.2	4.5	5.2	9.0	875.4	8 852	1 189	2 163	12 260	46.5	50.7	2.8
Grand Island, NE	357.6	4 284	52.8	8.0	4.1	0.3	5.6	317.1	3 799	745	313	6 018	32.3	65.6	2.2
Grand Junction, CO	517.8	3 502	35.4	1.7	13.1	5.6	9.4	476.5	3 223	1 474	395	8 127	32.7	65.1	2.2
Grand Rapids-Wyoming, MI	3 715.2	3 694	53.0	6.3	4.2	1.7	4.7	5 263.1	5 234	3 359	1 849	43 377	41.5	57.3	1.2
Grants Pass, OR	253.3	3 055	59.6	2.9	7.1	0.1	5.0	145.0	1 748	249	227	2 742	37.2	58.8	4.0
Great Falls, MT	242.5	2 968	53.0	1.0	9.7	1.4	5.2	90.0	1 101	1 675	3 660	4 104	44.1	53.1	2.9
Greeley, CO	839.9	3 185	42.6	1.2	7.3	4.0	6.6	868.6	3 294	579	707	15 375	42.3	55.0	2.6
Green Bay, WI	1 439.4	4 627	48.3	6.1	6.0	4.3	8.4	1 261.2	4 054	1 213	892	20 269	47.9	50.9	1.2
Greensboro-High Point, NC	2 532.1	3 440	46.9	4.0	7.4	4.8	2.6	2 453.8	3 334	4 260	1 868	40 618	49.8	49.1	1.1
Greenville, NC	557.6	3 232	46.8	1.8	9.9	5.2	2.1	400.7	2 322	454	461	24 379	53.1	45.9	1.0
Greenville-Anderson-Mauldin, SC	3 672.8	4 358	32.8	39.0	3.5	0.2	1.5	5 469.6	6 489	2 397	3 540	52 822	33.3	65.0	1.7
Gulfport-Biloxi-Pascagoula, MS	2 433.4	6 411	24.7	32.2	3.8	0.1	4.4	1 537.8	4 051	8 972	10 890	23 773	33.0	65.7	1.2
Hagerstown-Martinsburg, MD-WV	838.7	3 272	65.4	0.7	4.2	0.3	3.3	710.6	2 773	4 490	1 058	13 369	39.3	58.3	2.4
Hammond, LA	692.4	5 610	29.5	47.0	3.7	0.0	2.7	361.5	2 929	310	585	10 019	35.4	63.1	1.6
Hanford-Corcoran, CA	602.9	3 983	45.9	6.6	4.9	9.6	2.9	261.9	1 730	1 146	5 069	11 566	41.3	56.2	2.4
Harrisburg-Carlisle, PA	2 716.3	4 903	51.9	3.9	3.3	8.1	2.6	3 833.1	6 919	7 250	2 252	54 357	45.3	53.3	1.4
Harrisonburg, VA	400.5	3 120	46.7	1.9	4.0	7.4	5.5	729.3	5 681	338	390	10 591	37.1	60.9	2.0
Hartford-West Hartford-East Hartford, CT	5 447.0	4 485	58.0	0.9	5.6	0.7	4.2	3 350.1	2 759	5 977	2 454	93 044	60.7	38.1	1.2
Hattiesburg, MS	821.7	5 598	26.1	51.6	3.1	0.0	4.2	543.5	3 703	797	1 249	13 846	33.4	65.4	1.2
Hickory-Lenoir-Morganton, NC	1 270.8	3 495	44.3	23.2	5.0	6.0	1.2	476.3	1 310	674	893	23 159	33.7	64.7	1.6
Hilton Head Island-Bluffton-Beaufort, NC	819.4	4 226	33.8	18.0	6.2	1.1	2.3	1 530.6	7 895	2 433	10 547	8 833	42.7	56.2	1.0
Hinesville, GA	286.7	3 516	55.3	16.9	4.8	0.2	3.0	89.3	1 095	4 139	17 937	4 099	59.6	39.4	1.0
Homosassa Springs, FL	362.7	2 602	47.4	5.5	9.1	2.5	6.6	493.5	3 541	216	288	4 259	38.5	60.4	1.1
Hot Springs, AR	268.9	2 775	57.5	0.3	5.6	0.0	3.6	344.1	3 551	505	433	4 251	33.9	63.9	2.2
Houma-Thibodaux, LA	1 104.3	5 286	31.2	30.4	4.8	0.4	2.8	502.1	2 403	398	1 056	12 153	26.6	71.4	2.0
Houston-The Woodlands-Sugar Land, TX	25 345.7	4 103	45.4	8.8	5.5	0.2	5.0	71 316.9	11 545	27 770	14 680	334 877	43.6	55.2	1.3
Huntington-Ashland, WV-KY-OH	1 087.6	2 982	60.9	2.7	4.7	1.1	2.2	804.6	2 206	3 157	1 620	19 711	38.4	59.6	1.9
Huntsville, AL	2 106.9	4 891	33.3	37.0	3.8	0.1	2.7	2 214.6	5 141	20 576	2 774	29 536	37.6	60.8	1.5
Idaho Falls, ID	346.6	2 547	46.8	2.7	7.1	0.3	4.8	344.6	2 532	876	530	6 472	20.5	77.3	2.2
Indianapolis-Carmel-Anderson, IN	8 480.2	4 396	36.1	22.7	4.0	0.2	1.7	17 097.1	8 863	16 529	6 703	113 219	45.2	52.9	1.9
Iowa City, IA	652.2	4 122	35.8	7.3	3.9	0.8	6.6	863.6	5 458	1 869	675	34 742	64.1	33.6	2.2
Ithaca, NY	541.1	5 276	48.3	4.4	2.7	8.0	5.5	696.7	6 794	293	164	6 156	68.7	28.0	3.2
Jackson, MI	586.0	3 666	54.4	10.1	2.6	3.6	6.4	539.6	3 366	326	262	7 580	46.5	52.3	1.2
Jackson, MS	1 812.3	3 142	55.0	1.6	6.1	0.3	7.0	2 027.9	3 516	6 512	3 418	54 002	50.7	40.5	0.8
Jackson, TN	966.4	7 408	17.5	58.3	3.3	0.1	2.4	1 066.4	8 174	495	406	13 469	41.2	57.9	0.9
Jacksonville, FL	4 951.5	3 594	40.9	2.0	9.1	1.2	4.9	13 946.9	10 122	17 125	15 303	57 409	40.0	59.1	0.9
Jacksonville, NC	563.2	3 073	38.6	24.7	6.7	6.5	1.0	439.4	2 398	7 156	47 603	8 016	35.9	62.7	1.4
Janesville-Beloit, WI	729.2	4 546	49.6	7.4	6.2	7.1	5.3	614.8	3 833	286	442	8 642	61.0	37.8	1.2
Jefferson City, MO	363.3	2 419	52.7	3.5	8.9	0.0	8.7	294.3	1 960	812	523	24 976	30.8	67.4	1.8
Johnson City, TN	497.7	2 480	48.2	7.3	6.4	0.4	5.3	765.4	3 814	2 717	669	12 930	27.8	70.4	1.8
Johnstown, PA	571.5	4 037	49.2	3.2	5.7	14.0	3.6	641.5	4 531	969	384	7 385	40.1	58.1	1.8
Jonesboro, AR	344.4	2 776	59.5	0.3	5.9	0.1	5.2	518.7	4 182	385	559	8 953	32.9	64.5	2.6

1. Based on the resident population estimated as of July 1 of the year shown. 2.

CBSA/ DIV code[1]	Area name	Land area,[2] 2010 (sq km)	Population 2014: Total persons	Population 2014: Rank	Population 2014: Per square kilometer	Population characteristics, 2013: Race alone or in combination, not Hispanic or Latino (percent): White	Black	American Indian, Alaska Native	Asian and Pacific Islander	Percent Hispanic or Latino[3]	Age (percent): Under 5 years	5 to 17 years	18 to 24 years	25 to 34 years	35 to 44 years	45 to 54 years
		1	2	3	4	5	6	7	8	9	10	11	12	13	14	15
27900	Joplin, MO	3 272	176 141	233	53.8	88.5	2.5	3.2	2.0	6.5	6.9	18.2	9.5	13.0	12.2	13.1
27980	Kahului-Wailuku-Lahaina, HI	3 039	163 108	252	53.7	45.0	1.5	1.8	66.8	10.6	6.2	16.3	7.6	13.4	13.2	14.4
28020	Kalamazoo-Portage, MI	3 028	334 017	151	110.3	82.1	10.9	1.3	2.7	5.9	6.0	16.7	14.3	12.5	11.5	12.7
28100	Kankakee, IL	1 752	111 375	338	63.6	74.2	16.0	0.5	1.4	9.5	6.1	18.3	10.5	12.1	12.2	13.7
28140	Kansas City, MO-KS	18 793	2 071 133	29	110.2	75.7	13.6	1.2	3.4	8.6	6.8	18.3	8.3	14.1	13.2	14.0
28420	Kennewick-Richland, WA	7 621	274 295	171	36.0	65.1	2.2	1.4	3.5	30.0	8.3	20.8	9.2	14.4	12.4	12.3
28660	Killeen-Temple, TX	7 293	424 858	124	58.3	54.9	20.8	1.2	4.7	21.9	8.4	18.8	12.3	17.5	12.8	11.5
28700	Kingsport-Bristol-Bristol, TN-VA	5 206	308 079	161	59.2	95.5	2.6	0.7	0.8	1.5	5.0	15.1	7.9	10.6	12.5	14.7
28740	Kingston, NY	2 912	180 445	229	62.0	82.5	6.9	0.8	2.6	9.5	4.6	14.3	10.0	11.4	12.2	15.9
28940	Knoxville, TN	9 066	857 585	65	94.6	89.1	6.6	0.8	1.8	3.4	5.5	15.7	10.2	12.1	12.6	14.0
29020	Kokomo, IN	759	82 982	373	109.3	88.6	8.5	0.9	1.5	2.9	6.0	17.0	8.2	11.3	12.0	14.2
29100	La Crosse-Onalaska, WI-MN	2 600	136 749	294	52.6	92.9	2.0	0.7	4.4	1.5	5.6	15.3	14.4	12.7	11.0	13.1
29180	Lafayette, LA	8 829	484 974	108	54.9	69.5	25.6	0.7	1.9	3.5	6.9	18.3	10.1	14.6	12.2	13.7
29200	Lafayette-West Lafayette, IN	3 311	211 697	206	63.9	82.5	4.7	0.6	6.5	7.4	6.1	15.0	21.9	13.8	10.9	11.0
29340	Lake Charles, LA	6 083	203 883	212	33.5	71.0	25.1	1.0	1.6	2.9	6.8	18.1	9.9	13.8	11.8	13.4
29420	Lake Havasu City-Kingman, AZ	34 476	203 361	213	5.9	79.9	1.5	2.9	1.9	15.5	4.8	14.3	6.9	9.7	9.6	12.9
29460	Lakeland-Winter Haven, FL	4 656	634 638	85	136.3	64.2	15.4	0.7	2.2	19.0	6.0	17.0	8.8	12.1	11.8	12.8
29540	Lancaster, PA	2 444	533 320	102	218.2	84.9	4.2	0.4	2.4	9.5	6.6	17.6	9.6	12.4	11.6	13.6
29620	Lansing-East Lansing, MI	4 397	470 458	110	107.0	80.1	10.3	1.2	4.7	6.5	5.6	15.7	15.8	12.9	11.3	12.9
29700	Laredo, TX	8 706	266 673	176	30.6	3.8	0.3	0.1	0.6	94.8	9.9	24.5	11.5	13.5	13.4	11.0
29740	Las Cruces, NM	9 861	213 676	204	21.7	30.0	1.7	1.2	1.5	66.5	7.4	18.5	14.8	12.7	10.7	11.5
29820	Las Vegas-Henderson-Paradise, NV	20 439	2 069 681	30	101.3	48.8	11.7	1.0	12.1	30.0	6.6	17.6	9.2	14.7	14.3	13.5
29940	Lawrence, KS	1 181	116 585	327	98.7	83.5	5.6	3.6	5.3	5.5	5.2	13.8	24.1	15.4	11.1	10.3
30020	Lawton, OK	4 408	131 183	301	29.8	63.2	18.3	7.8	4.4	12.2	7.4	17.1	13.1	16.4	12.2	12.3
30140	Lebanon, PA	937	136 359	296	145.5	85.9	2.4	0.4	1.5	10.8	6.3	16.6	8.5	11.4	11.9	14.0
30300	Lewiston, ID-WA	3 845	62 196	380	16.2	91.1	0.9	5.2	1.6	3.4	5.7	15.6	8.9	12.1	11.1	13.2
30340	Lewiston-Auburn, ME	1 212	107 440	342	88.6	93.4	4.6	1.1	1.3	1.7	6.2	16.0	8.9	12.3	12.3	15.1
30460	Lexington-Fayette, KY	3 804	494 189	107	129.9	80.3	12.1	0.6	3.1	5.9	6.3	16.0	12.5	14.3	13.5	13.4
30620	Lima, OH	1 042	105 040	344	100.8	84.1	14.0	0.6	1.2	2.7	6.1	17.3	10.8	11.8	11.5	13.4
30700	Lincoln, NE	3 649	318 945	155	87.4	86.1	4.6	1.1	4.3	6.1	6.8	16.4	15.0	14.4	12.0	11.9
30780	Little Rock-North Little Rock-Conway, AR	10 580	729 135	75	68.9	70.2	23.4	1.1	2.1	5.0	6.7	17.5	9.8	14.5	13.0	13.2
30860	Logan, UT-ID	4 736	131 364	300	27.7	86.7	0.8	0.9	3.2	9.8	9.3	22.2	17.8	14.2	11.0	8.8
30980	Longview, TX	4 611	217 481	201	47.2	66.2	17.9	1.0	1.2	15.2	7.1	17.7	9.7	13.2	12.0	13.2
31020	Longview, WA	2 953	102 133	347	34.6	87.8	1.3	3.0	2.8	8.2	5.9	17.2	8.2	11.1	11.8	13.6
31080	Los Angeles-Long Beach-Anaheim, CA	12 558	13 262 220	2	1 056.1	32.6	7.2	0.6	16.8	44.8	6.3	16.9	10.6	15.1	14.0	13.9
31080	Anaheim-Santa Ana-Irvine, CA Div 11244	2 048	3 145 515	X	1 535.9	44.8	2.0	0.6	20.9	34.1	6.1	17.2	10.2	14.0	13.8	14.6
31080	Los Angeles-Long Beach-Glendale, CA Div 31084	10 510	10 116 705	X	962.6	28.8	8.9	0.6	15.6	48.1	6.4	16.8	10.7	15.4	14.1	13.7
31140	Louisville/Jefferson County, KY-IN	9 267	1 269 702	43	137.0	79.5	15.3	0.7	2.3	4.3	6.2	17.0	8.6	13.4	13.1	14.4
31180	Lubbock, TX	6 962	305 644	162	43.9	56.3	7.4	0.7	2.6	34.0	6.9	17.4	16.9	14.3	10.9	11.3
31340	Lynchburg, VA	5 491	257 835	184	47.0	78.3	18.4	0.8	1.9	2.4	5.3	15.1	13.3	11.2	11.1	13.7
31420	Macon, GA	4 461	230 450	194	51.7	51.6	44.4	0.6	1.8	2.8	6.7	17.7	10.0	12.5	12.0	13.8
31460	Madera, CA	5 535	154 548	263	27.9	37.8	3.5	1.9	2.7	55.8	7.8	20.4	10.3	13.6	12.3	12.2
31540	Madison, WI	8 571	633 787	86	73.9	85.4	5.3	0.7	5.1	5.5	6.0	15.6	12.3	15.0	12.8	13.6
31700	Manchester-Nashua, NH	2 269	405 184	131	178.6	88.2	2.8	0.6	4.2	5.8	5.6	16.6	8.8	12.6	13.1	16.5
31740	Manhattan, KS	3 757	98 091	356	26.1	83.1	6.4	1.3	4.7	7.2	7.2	13.3	27.1	17.8	9.3	8.3
31860	Mankato-North Mankato, MN	3 099	98 478	354	31.8	91.5	3.4	0.6	2.6	3.4	5.9	14.6	19.1	14.2	10.4	11.5
31900	Mansfield, OH	1 283	121 942	318	95.0	88.3	10.2	0.7	1.0	1.7	5.6	16.3	8.6	11.7	12.0	14.0
32580	McAllen-Edinburg-Mission, TX	4 069	831 073	68	204.2	7.4	0.5	0.1	1.1	90.7	9.7	24.3	11.1	13.3	13.1	10.4
32780	Medford, OR	7 209	210 287	209	29.2	85.0	1.2	2.4	2.5	11.7	5.8	15.5	8.4	11.8	11.2	12.8
32820	Memphis, TN-MS-AR	12 909	1 343 230	41	104.1	46.3	46.8	0.6	2.4	5.2	7.0	18.7	10.0	13.6	13.1	13.6
32900	Merced, CA	5 012	266 353	177	53.1	31.7	3.8	1.0	8.7	56.7	8.2	22.2	11.9	14.0	12.2	11.8
33100	Miami-Fort Lauderdale-West Palm Beach, FL	13 150	5 929 819	8	450.9	34.2	20.9	0.4	3.0	42.5	5.7	15.2	8.9	13.2	13.5	14.8
33100	Fort Lauderdale-Pompano Beach-Deerfield Beach, FL Div 22744	3 133	1 869 235	X	596.6	41.9	28.0	0.5	4.4	26.8	5.9	15.9	8.6	13.3	13.5	15.2
33100	Miami-Miami Beach-Kendall, FL Div 33124	4 915	2 662 874	X	541.8	15.7	17.2	0.2	2.0	65.0	5.9	14.9	9.6	14.0	14.3	14.9
33100	West Palm Beach-Boca Raton-Delray Beach, FL Div 48424	5 102	1 397 710	X	274.0	59.2	18.3	0.4	3.2	20.2	5.2	14.6	8.1	11.4	11.8	13.9
33140	Michigan City-La Porte, IN	1 550	111 444	337	71.9	82.3	12.1	0.7	0.9	5.9	6.0	16.2	8.6	13.1	12.6	14.3
33220	Midland, MI	1 337	83 427	371	62.4	93.5	1.8	0.9	2.7	2.4	5.4	17.0	9.3	11.6	11.8	15.5
33260	Midland, TX	4 702	161 290	254	34.3	51.0	6.4	0.8	1.7	41.1	8.3	19.3	10.2	16.3	11.9	12.3
33340	Milwaukee-Waukesha-West Allis, WI	3 768	1 572 245	39	417.3	69.6	17.5	0.9	3.7	10.1	6.5	17.4	9.4	14.0	12.4	14.2
33460	Minneapolis-St. Paul-Bloomington, MN	19 779	3 495 176	16	176.7	79.9	8.8	1.3	7.0	5.6	6.6	17.7	8.8	14.8	13.2	14.7
33540	Missoula, MT	6 717	112 684	336	16.8	92.5	1.0	4.0	2.2	2.9	5.4	14.0	15.6	15.3	11.8	11.9
33660	Mobile, AL	3 184	415 123	127	130.4	59.3	35.7	1.5	2.3	2.6	6.7	17.5	9.9	13.4	12.1	13.5

1. CBSA = Core Based Statistical Area. DIV = Metropolitan Division. See Appendix A for explanation. See Appendix B for list of metropolitan areas identified by type. 2. Dry land or land partially or temporarily covered by water. 3. May be of any race.

Area name	Population, 2013 (cont.)				Population change and components of change, 2000–2014							Households, 2013				
	Age (percent) (cont.)				Total persons		Percent change		Components of change, 2010–2014					Percent		
	55 to 64 years	65 to 74 years	75 years and over	Percent female	2000	2010	2000–2010	2010–2014	Births	Deaths	Net migration	Number	Persons per house-hold	Family house-holds	Female family house-holder[1]	One person
	16	17	18	19	20	21	22	23	24	25	26	27	28	29	30	31
Joplin, MO	12.2	8.4	6.5	50.8	157 322	175 518	11.6	0.4	10 490	7 333	-2 662	67 701	2.54	67.2	9.2	27.3
Kahului-Wailuku-Lahaina, HI	14.2	8.9	5.8	49.6	128 241	154 924	20.8	5.3	8 619	4 804	4 434	54 005	2.92	65.1	11.6	26.5
Kalamazoo-Portage, MI	12.6	7.7	6.0	50.9	314 866	326 589	3.7	2.3	17 239	11 487	1 834	130 076	2.47	61.6	11.4	29.2
Kankakee, IL	12.6	7.9	6.6	50.9	103 833	113 449	9.3	-1.8	5 744	4 514	-3 292	41 822	2.55	68.6	15.0	27.7
Kansas City, MO-KS	12.3	7.3	5.7	50.9	1 811 254	2 009 342	10.9	3.1	117 872	68 102	12 621	798 618	2.53	65.2	12.9	28.6
Kennewick-Richland, WA	11.4	6.7	4.6	49.2	191 822	253 340	32.1	8.3	17 964	6 883	9 527	92 768	2.88	73.1	14.3	21.6
Killeen-Temple, TX	9.0	5.7	4.0	50.1	330 714	405 300	22.6	4.8	31 824	10 540	-2 036	132 578	3.02	71.2	13.8	25.9
Kingsport-Bristol-Bristol, TN-VA	14.5	11.4	8.3	51.3	298 484	309 544	3.7	-0.5	12 900	15 839	1 689	126 215	2.40	66.7	12.2	29.6
Kingston, NY	14.8	9.5	7.3	50.3	177 749	182 493	2.7	-1.1	6 885	6 779	-2 030	68 650	2.47	62.8	10.8	30.4
Knoxville, TN	13.4	9.6	6.8	51.1	748 259	837 571	11.9	2.4	39 851	36 283	16 502	340 089	2.45	64.9	10.8	28.2
Kokomo, IN	13.7	10.0	7.7	51.8	84 964	82 752	-2.6	0.3	4 309	3 746	-316	34 435	2.37	62.5	10.2	32.1
La Crosse-Onalaska, WI-MN	12.9	7.9	7.2	50.9	126 838	133 665	5.4	2.3	6 146	4 797	1 708	53 723	2.42	63.0	10.8	26.6
Lafayette, LA	12.1	6.9	5.2	51.1	425 020	466 750	9.8	3.9	28 206	16 867	6 958	178 778	2.64	67.2	16.0	27.1
Lafayette-West Lafayette, IN	10.2	6.2	4.8	49.1	178 541	201 789	13.0	4.9	10 991	5 705	4 766	79 375	2.45	60.8	9.5	27.4
Lake Charles, LA	12.6	7.8	5.7	51.2	193 568	199 607	3.1	2.1	11 813	8 166	843	79 392	2.50	66.2	16.1	29.2
Lake Havasu City-Kingman, AZ	15.8	15.4	10.5	49.7	155 032	200 186	29.1	1.6	8 005	10 954	5 464	81 257	2.41	61.4	9.5	30.3
Lakeland-Winter Haven, FL	12.3	10.9	8.3	51.0	483 924	602 095	24.4	5.4	30 903	25 499	26 568	214 500	2.84	67.6	13.3	26.7
Lancaster, PA	12.6	8.3	7.7	51.1	470 658	519 445	10.4	2.7	29 773	19 622	3 521	194 493	2.65	70.3	8.8	24.0
Lansing-East Lansing, MI	12.7	7.6	5.5	51.3	447 728	464 036	3.6	1.4	22 095	14 894	-900	183 135	2.44	60.5	11.6	30.7
Laredo, TX	7.9	4.9	3.5	51.0	193 117	250 304	29.6	6.5	23 165	5 185	-1 504	68 696	3.78	83.8	22.4	14.3
Las Cruces, NM	10.8	7.7	5.9	50.7	174 682	209 233	19.8	2.1	13 060	6 284	-2 428	74 898	2.79	66.7	16.0	24.7
Las Vegas-Henderson-Paradise, NV	11.4	8.0	4.8	49.8	1 375 765	1 951 269	41.8	6.1	111 857	60 256	64 729	713 577	2.81	64.4	13.6	28.2
Lawrence, KS	10.0	5.7	4.3	50.0	99 962	110 826	10.9	5.2	5 352	2 576	2 995	42 470	2.48	54.4	9.1	32.7
Lawton, OK	10.4	6.3	4.8	48.1	121 610	130 291	7.1	0.7	8 835	4 437	-3 567	45 871	2.66	63.5	16.3	29.9
Lebanon, PA	13.4	9.5	8.6	51.1	120 327	133 568	11.0	2.1	7 029	5 977	1 744	51 901	2.55	69.5	11.3	26.3
Lewiston, ID-WA	14.2	10.3	9.0	51.0	57 961	60 888	5.0	2.1	3 048	3 025	1 328	24 527	2.48	67.6	11.2	27.3
Lewiston-Auburn, ME	13.7	8.6	6.8	50.9	103 793	107 702	3.8	-0.2	5 572	4 322	-1 526	43 736	2.39	59.4	12.0	31.4
Lexington-Fayette, KY	11.9	7.0	5.1	51.0	408 326	472 099	15.6	4.7	26 354	15 089	10 882	193 193	2.45	63.5	12.4	27.4
Lima, OH	13.5	8.3	7.3	49.7	108 473	106 331	-2.0	-1.2	5 438	4 524	-2 185	40 359	2.50	65.8	14.6	29.0
Lincoln, NE	11.6	6.6	5.4	49.9	266 787	302 157	13.3	5.6	18 008	8 720	7 417	123 469	2.45	61.2	8.3	29.1
Little Rock-North Little Rock-Conway, AR	12.1	7.9	5.5	51.5	610 518	699 757	14.6	4.2	41 827	26 209	13 905	267 748	2.66	64.6	13.4	29.8
Logan, UT-ID	7.9	4.9	4.0	50.1	102 720	125 442	22.1	4.7	11 057	2 431	-2 798	39 593	3.18	75.8	7.6	17.6
Longview, TX	12.4	8.1	6.6	50.0	194 042	214 369	10.5	1.4	12 972	9 267	-608	76 957	2.69	69.2	14.8	26.5
Longview, WA	14.4	10.4	7.2	50.4	92 948	102 410	10.2	-0.3	5 007	4 418	-848	38 483	2.62	66.3	9.9	26.7
Los Angeles-Long Beach-Anaheim, CA	11.2	6.7	5.4	50.6	12 365 627	12 828 837	3.7	3.4	721 209	332 090	55 805	4 251 495	3.04	68.0	14.7	24.7
Anaheim-Santa Ana-Irvine, CA Div 11244	11.5	7.1	5.7	50.5	2 846 289	3 010 232	5.8	4.5	162 288	77 737	52 028	1 003 790	3.06	72.1	12.1	21.0
Los Angeles-Long Beach-Glendale, CA Div 31084	11.1	6.6	5.3	50.7	9 519 338	9 818 605	3.1	3.0	558 921	254 353	3 777	3 247 705	3.03	66.8	15.5	25.8
Louisville/Jefferson County, KY-IN	13.2	8.0	5.9	51.2	1 121 109	1 235 708	10.2	2.8	66 549	48 698	17 212	494 276	2.50	64.8	13.5	29.1
Lubbock, TX	10.4	6.5	5.3	50.5	256 250	290 805	13.5	5.1	17 578	10 031	7 140	110 295	2.65	63.4	13.3	27.0
Lynchburg, VA	13.4	9.7	7.3	51.8	228 616	252 634	10.5	2.0	11 672	10 655	4 140	102 320	2.42	67.8	13.4	28.0
Macon, GA	13.1	8.3	5.9	52.1	222 368	232 293	4.5	-0.8	13 060	10 047	-4 994	80 190	2.76	66.6	18.5	29.1
Madera, CA	10.9	7.4	5.2	51.3	123 109	150 865	22.5	2.4	9 823	4 266	-1 705	44 549	3.25	75.4	16.7	19.4
Madison, WI	12.4	7.0	5.3	50.3	535 421	605 435	13.1	4.7	31 280	17 069	13 607	258 127	2.37	58.3	8.7	30.9
Manchester-Nashua, NH	13.5	7.7	5.8	50.4	380 841	400 721	5.2	1.1	18 483	12 510	-1 338	155 036	2.55	68.0	11.8	24.1
Manhattan, KS	8.3	4.7	4.1	47.5	81 052	92 719	14.4	5.8	6 443	2 043	850	35 044	2.53	58.8	8.6	26.2
Mankato-North Mankato, MN	11.5	6.7	6.1	49.7	85 712	96 740	12.9	1.8	4 774	2 830	-217	37 358	2.46	61.8	7.1	27.1
Mansfield, OH	14.0	9.5	8.2	49.5	128 852	124 475	-3.4	-2.0	5 970	5 610	-2 815	47 847	2.40	61.7	12.1	33.1
McAllen-Edinburg-Mission, TX	8.0	5.6	4.5	51.0	569 463	774 769	36.1	7.3	68 625	16 186	3 373	223 367	3.61	81.2	20.3	15.9
Medford, OR	15.0	11.0	8.5	51.3	181 269	203 206	12.1	3.5	9 870	9 291	6 211	82 983	2.47	64.9	12.8	29.2
Memphis, TN-MS-AR	12.2	6.9	4.8	52.0	1 213 230	1 324 829	9.2	1.4	80 551	47 084	-14 697	492 311	2.68	66.5	19.5	28.5
Merced, CA	9.5	5.8	4.4	49.4	210 554	255 793	21.5	4.1	18 116	6 717	-679	77 651	3.30	75.0	19.4	19.9
Miami-Fort Lauderdale-West Palm Beach, FL	12.0	8.6	8.1	51.4	5 007 564	5 564 635	11.1	6.5	280 951	199 669	279 218	2 032 438	2.83	65.1	15.8	28.7
Fort Lauderdale-Pompano Beach-Deerfield Beach, FL Div 22744	12.5	8.0	7.0	51.4	1 623 018	1 748 066	7.7	6.9	90 351	62 161	92 844	662 488	2.75	63.9	16.5	29.5
Miami-Miami Beach-Kendall, FL Div 33124	11.4	7.9	7.0	51.4	2 253 362	2 496 435	10.8	6.6	131 349	80 077	112 470	839 491	3.06	68.0	17.8	26.3
West Palm Beach-Boca Raton-Delray Beach, FL Div 48424	12.5	10.7	11.8	51.6	1 131 184	1 320 134	16.7	5.9	59 251	57 431	73 904	530 459	2.55	62.0	11.8	31.6
Michigan City-La Porte, IN	13.9	8.9	6.4	48.2	110 106	111 467	1.2	0.0	5 505	4 829	-633	42 746	2.39	64.3	12.1	29.1
Midland, MI	13.7	8.3	7.5	50.9	82 874	83 629	0.9	-0.2	3 617	2 944	-844	33 858	2.44	64.8	9.5	29.0
Midland, TX	11.2	5.4	5.0	50.1	120 755	141 671	17.3	13.8	10 939	4 490	12 895	54 082	2.84	66.7	12.9	24.3
Milwaukee-Waukesha-West Allis, WI	12.8	7.1	6.3	51.3	1 500 741	1 555 908	3.7	1.0	84 990	55 123	-12 629	622 962	2.47	62.3	13.2	30.5
Minneapolis-St. Paul-Bloomington, MN	12.3	6.8	5.2	50.6	3 031 918	3 348 859	10.5	4.4	192 866	90 773	45 394	1 332 110	2.55	64.5	10.4	27.8
Missoula, MT	12.9	7.9	5.2	49.8	95 802	109 299	14.1	3.1	5 163	3 359	1 597	45 820	2.37	55.5	10.3	33.7
Mobile, AL	12.8	8.3	5.8	52.1	399 843	412 992	3.3	0.5	23 716	17 784	-3 698	148 025	2.73	68.7	18.8	27.3

1. No spouse present.

Area name	Persons in group quarters, 2014	Daytime population, 2013: Number	Daytime population, 2013: Employment/residence ratio	Births, 2014: Total	Births, 2014: Rate[1]	Deaths, 2014: Number	Deaths, 2014: Rate[1]	Persons under 65 with no health insurance 2013: Number	Persons under 65 with no health insurance 2013: Percent	Medicare, 2014: Eligible for Medicare	Medicare, 2014: Enrolled in Medicare Advantage	Medicare, 2014: Enrolled in a Medicare prescription drug plan	Serious crimes known to police,[2] 2013: Total: Number	Serious crimes known to police,[2] 2013: Total: Rate[3]
	32	33	34	35	36	37	38	39	40	41	42	43	44	45
Joplin, MO	3 358	186 347	1.15	2 451	13.9	1 687	9.6	26 942	18.3	32 680	6 950	16 319	8 116	4 659
Kahului-Wailuku-Lahaina, HI	2 756	240 556	NA	2 046	12.5	1 253	7.7	12 719	9.2	24 978	NA	NA	6 154	3 855
Kalamazoo-Portage, MI	9 411	354 781	1.18	4 094	12.3	2 811	8.4	37 982	13.6	58 542	18 221	29 145	10 247	3 119
Kankakee, IL	5 113	119 054	1.19	1 305	11.7	1 091	9.8	11 349	12.3	20 325	3 202	11 289	3 193	2 850
Kansas City, MO-KS	31 541	2 092 737	1.04	27 732	13.4	16 321	7.9	247 602	14.1	324 502	91 379	138 195	75 903	3 709
Kennewick-Richland, WA	4 281	277 398	1.06	4 196	15.3	1 680	6.1	43 775	18.5	37 863	4 736	20 283	6 863	2 509
Killeen-Temple, TX	19 973	437 262	1.08	7 393	17.4	2 544	6.0	70 730	19.4	53 012	14 570	14 876	12 979	3 061
Kingsport-Bristol-Bristol, TN-VA	5 649	332 978	1.24	3 077	10.0	3 617	11.7	36 793	15.1	79 405	39 182	24 622	9 213	2 979
Kingston, NY	11 769	192 003	1.20	1 562	8.7	1 637	9.1	18 032	12.5	36 801	8 223	18 380	3 574	1 966
Knoxville, TN	19 705	883 722	1.09	9 487	11.1	8 582	10.0	101 860	14.7	175 427	70 353	59 528	29 077	3 411
Kokomo, IN	1 280	93 515	1.36	1 031	12.4	903	10.9	9 708	14.4	18 386	2 234	13 737	2 686	3 232
La Crosse-Onalaska, WI-MN	6 077	147 164	1.18	1 420	10.4	1 128	8.2	10 206	9.2	24 171	10 455	9 268	2 681	1 973
Lafayette, LA	8 387	499 862	1.10	6 776	14.0	4 138	8.5	79 730	19.3	75 134	7 624	42 524	18 070	3 874
Lafayette-West Lafayette, IN	14 690	228 299	1.21	2 667	12.6	1 343	6.3	29 603	17.2	27 730	4 700	14 735	5 683	3 113
Lake Charles, LA	3 816	212 375	1.12	2 821	13.8	1 951	9.6	32 201	18.8	35 279	5 007	18 258	10 942	5 424
Lake Havasu City-Kingman, AZ	4 809	206 046	1.06	1 857	9.1	2 799	13.8	32 388	22.2	56 259	14 887	23 070	7 152	3 571
Lakeland-Winter Haven, FL	12 575	650 948	1.15	7 268	11.5	6 215	9.8	117 135	23.8	132 554	59 478	42 013	20 402	3 276
Lancaster, PA	12 933	556 538	1.13	7 067	13.3	4 774	9.0	60 893	14.0	99 193	35 036	44 437	10 750	2 033
Lansing-East Lansing, MI	20 710	505 041	1.19	5 200	11.1	3 635	7.7	43 622	11.3	76 549	20 193	48 453	11 619	2 624
Laredo, TX	3 529	266 050	1.04	5 457	20.5	1 211	4.5	82 557	34.9	28 464	5 160	16 034	12 012	4 568
Las Cruces, NM	4 583	223 277	1.13	2 950	13.8	1 506	7.0	45 396	25.2	34 279	10 315	13 757	6 904	3 264
Las Vegas-Henderson-Paradise, NV	22 796	2 049 030	1.02	26 178	12.6	14 963	7.2	416 594	23.8	291 050	108 464	89 248	74 792	3 692
Lawrence, KS	8 794	123 101	1.19	1 269	10.9	605	5.2	13 787	14.6	14 378	1 677	8 264	4 560	4 022
Lawton, OK	10 360	137 072	1.10	1 946	14.8	1 102	8.4	19 935	18.7	18 194	781	7 573	6 412	4 805
Lebanon, PA	3 675	150 167	1.39	1 630	12.0	1 424	10.4	13 650	12.6	28 585	10 763	11 015	2 718	2 003
Lewiston, ID-WA	1 135	64 184	1.08	752	12.1	700	11.3	7 545	15.2	14 624	2 957	7 196	2 169	3 509
Lewiston-Auburn, ME	2 765	121 049	1.36	1 273	11.8	992	9.2	11 034	12.5	22 914	5 658	11 389	3 087	2 872
Lexington-Fayette, KY	16 890	531 905	1.19	6 247	12.6	3 570	7.2	69 021	16.7	74 560	22 272	34 784	19 590	4 003
Lima, OH	6 082	120 488	1.38	1 288	12.3	1 063	10.1	10 741	12.8	20 515	5 394	13 280	3 897	3 711
Lincoln, NE	15 861	333 928	1.11	4 243	13.3	2 028	6.4	32 022	12.2	45 275	3 908	27 519	11 062	3 528
Little Rock-North Little Rock-Conway, AR	15 247	754 534	1.10	9 788	13.4	6 215	8.5	101 450	16.5	127 266	20 079	60 535	38 707	5 849
Logan, UT-ID	3 692	131 974	1.04	2 573	19.6	574	4.4	16 930	14.8	13 496	5 012	4 494	1 609	1 239
Longview, TX	10 318	238 798	1.29	3 022	13.9	2 190	10.1	42 800	24.3	38 735	8 681	20 638	8 122	3 741
Longview, WA	1 207	107 506	1.18	1 135	11.1	1 051	10.3	14 186	17.0	23 089	10 434	6 967	4 430	4 336
Los Angeles-Long Beach-Anaheim, CA	220 832	13 562 640	1.07	169 963	12.8	82 136	6.2	2 571 019	22.5	1 776 397	830 914	595 493	336 495	2 561
Anaheim-Santa Ana-Irvine, CA Div 11244	42 968	NA	NA	38 295	12.2	19 073	6.1	506 359	18.8	439 930	205 160	147 499	67 692	2 170
Los Angeles-Long Beach-Glendale, CA Div 31084	177 864	NA	NA	131 668	13.0	63 063	6.2	2 064 660	23.7	1 336 467	625 754	447 994	268 803	2 682
Louisville/Jefferson County, KY-IN	25 693	1 296 927	1.06	15 635	12.3	11 440	9.0	164 831	15.5	226 304	59 368	117 791	46 830	3 919
Lubbock, TX	11 562	313 498	1.06	4 169	13.6	2 440	8.0	58 497	22.9	42 900	12 703	22 013	14 744	4 902
Lynchburg, VA	13 041	269 756	1.09	2 737	10.6	2 509	9.7	30 575	15.1	54 599	8 411	32 032	4 633	1 804
Macon, GA	7 825	253 470	1.32	2 946	12.8	2 465	10.7	38 607	20.2	43 649	13 667	17 643	12 050	5 179
Madera, CA	8 151	163 596	1.39	2 224	14.4	960	6.2	29 028	22.8	21 951	6 942	9 608	4 951	3 241
Madison, WI	14 888	670 166	1.13	7 438	11.7	4 030	6.4	47 962	8.9	94 274	20 972	52 668	15 501	2 481
Manchester-Nashua, NH	7 937	458 248	1.38	4 241	10.5	3 036	7.5	42 957	12.5	69 424	5 545	37 136	10 223	2 676
Manhattan, KS	9 447	102 870	1.12	1 521	15.5	499	5.1	9 421	11.7	10 209	691	5 648	1 940	1 967
Mankato-North Mankato, MN	6 898	108 864	1.22	1 092	11.1	678	6.9	6 962	8.7	15 051	7 310	8 929	2 807	2 842
Mansfield, OH	7 234	133 651	1.31	1 413	11.6	1 313	10.8	13 008	13.8	26 356	6 747	15 959	5 895	4 852
McAllen-Edinburg-Mission, TX	7 268	825 229	1.03	16 120	19.4	4 060	4.9	276 623	38.2	89 877	29 108	47 640	32 558	3 974
Medford, OR	3 554	214 154	1.07	2 316	11.0	2 172	10.3	32 868	19.8	48 833	15 399	19 138	8 966	4 312
Memphis, TN-MS-AR	24 339	1 373 035	1.05	18 801	14.0	11 601	8.6	200 354	17.3	202 056	45 011	94 732	67 641	5 334
Merced, CA	6 452	274 215	1.17	4 267	16.0	1 625	6.1	48 769	21.0	32 325	2 505	19 951	9 651	3 649
Miami-Fort Lauderdale-West Palm Beach, FL	78 620	5 883 034	1.02	65 943	11.1	49 224	8.3	1 389 924	29.1	986 488	509 401	308 693	246 392	4 214
Fort Lauderdale-Pompano Beach-Deerfield Beach, FL Div 22744	16 161	NA	NA	21 354	11.4	15 069	8.1	398 540	25.8	282 197	149 012	77 864	71 058	3 855
Miami-Miami Beach-Kendall, FL Div 33124	41 775	NA	NA	30 445	11.4	19 975	7.5	725 898	33.1	418 177	255 829	113 430	126 865	4 823
West Palm Beach-Boca Raton-Delray Beach, FL Div 48424	20 684	NA	NA	14 144	10.1	14 180	10.1	265 486	25.4	286 114	104 560	117 399	48 469	3 531
Michigan City-La Porte, IN	6 819	122 147	1.34	1 280	11.5	1 172	10.5	13 541	15.4	21 183	2 348	12 157	3 138	2 905
Midland, MI	1 289	96 329	1.48	831	10.0	694	8.3	7 240	10.4	16 287	4 899	8 916	961	1 144
Midland, TX	1 737	179 937	1.36	2 807	17.4	1 080	6.7	30 404	21.9	18 251	3 034	10 357	4 547	2 919
Milwaukee-Waukesha-West Allis, WI	32 329	1 638 708	1.10	19 882	12.6	13 059	8.3	145 269	10.9	259 205	89 784	107 491	56 330	3 678
Minneapolis-St. Paul-Bloomington, MN	65 348	3 531 995	1.04	45 934	13.1	21 854	6.3	275 925	9.2	496 049	271 962	185 901	99 074	2 870
Missoula, MT	3 638	169 922	NA	1 219	10.8	794	7.0	17 993	19.1	18 636	2 874	8 867	3 782	3 375
Mobile, AL	7 274	436 780	1.15	5 501	13.3	4 290	10.3	58 018	16.6	76 799	31 601	26 499	20 988	5 069

1. Per 1,000 estimated resident population. 2. Data for serious crimes have not been adjusted for underreporting; this may affect comparability between geographic areas and over time.
3. Per 100,000 population estimated by the FBI.

Area name	Serious crimes known to police, 2013 (cont.)[1]		Education						Income and Poverty, 2013							
	Rate[2]		School enrollment and attainment, 2013				Local government expenditures,[5] 2012–2013							Percent below poverty level		
			Enrollment[3]		Attainment[4] (percent)											
	Violent	Property	Total	Percent private	High school graduate or less	Bachelor's degree or more	Total current expenditures (mil dol)	Current expenditures per student (dollars)	Per capita income[6] (dollars)	Mean household income (dollars)	Median household income	Percent of households with income of less than $25,000	Percent of households with income of $200,000 or more	All persons	Children under 18 years	Age 65 years and older
	46	47	48	49	50	51	52	53	54	55	56	57	58	59	60	61
Joplin, MO	300	4 359	44 020	17.6	49.0	19.9	239.2	7 965	22 295	56 818	40 852	28.2	2.3	17.1	23.0	13.4
Kahului-Wailuku-Lahaina, HI	282	3 573	37 344	20.8	38.4	27.4	NA	NA	29 903	83 896	65 541	17.1	6.3	9.5	7.9	6.3
Kalamazoo-Portage, MI	447	2 672	99 746	9.8	35.1	31.0	549.5	11 189	24 688	61 422	45 699	26.8	2.8	17.8	20.9	7.8
Kankakee, IL	302	2 548	30 994	20.9	46.5	16.6	204.9	10 598	23 838	62 730	49 761	22.0	1.0	17.1	22.6	10.5
Kansas City, MO-KS	469	3 240	535 316	16.4	35.3	33.7	3 206.7	9 668	29 688	74 518	56 248	20.3	4.1	12.6	17.6	6.9
Kennewick-Richland, WA	222	2 287	73 347	9.8	42.8	24.8	471.6	9 051	25 323	72 796	58 542	20.0	3.9	14.6	20.4	10.1
Killeen-Temple, TX	314	2 747	124 123	11.2	38.8	21.6	653.4	7 999	21 785	62 332	50 447	22.1	2.1	14.2	18.8	9.8
Kingsport-Bristol-Bristol, TN-VA	305	2 674	67 321	15.1	53.8	18.6	390.1	8 888	22 330	52 695	39 128	32.4	1.6	18.1	30.7	10.1
Kingston, NY	162	1 804	43 201	11.5	40.8	29.8	527.3	21 935	29 821	75 070	58 429	19.5	4.6	11.3	11.3	7.8
Knoxville, TN	352	3 060	196 496	16.1	44.7	27.1	987.4	8 042	25 592	62 864	45 051	27.8	3.3	17.5	25.0	8.5
Kokomo, IN	265	2 967	20 081	10.9	48.8	19.5	128.0	9 608	23 841	55 634	44 265	27.4	2.0	15.5	21.2	5.7
La Crosse-Onalaska, WI-MN	123	1 850	40 691	13.4	34.5	29.5	237.4	11 378	26 080	63 986	51 024	24.1	3.0	15.8	18.8	7.4
Lafayette, LA	444	3 430	119 394	20.5	52.5	21.6	690.4	9 543	25 934	66 453	48 105	28.5	4.0	16.4	22.3	14.0
Lafayette-West Lafayette, IN	267	2 845	76 279	9.3	39.5	32.5	243.3	9 325	23 460	61 507	48 372	28.2	2.0	19.3	17.0	5.6
Lake Charles, LA	603	4 821	52 318	12.0	49.2	20.3	349.4	10 417	25 445	62 881	43 479	29.0	3.5	15.6	20.4	8.0
Lake Havasu City-Kingman, AZ	211	3 360	38 209	16.5	54.3	11.3	131.8	6 291	20 940	50 777	39 058	29.0	1.0	21.2	31.0	6.7
Lakeland-Winter Haven, FL	367	2 908	144 630	15.4	51.5	18.4	888.4	9 165	20 507	55 506	42 435	27.8	1.9	19.4	29.4	11.1
Lancaster, PA	171	1 862	125 071	26.8	53.8	26.1	949.3	13 988	26 645	71 281	56 922	17.8	3.6	10.4	14.1	8.0
Lansing-East Lansing, MI	413	2 210	149 207	9.7	31.9	32.4	732.3	11 283	26 213	65 179	49 383	24.4	3.0	18.1	20.7	6.3
Laredo, TX	431	4 138	88 324	3.8	59.7	16.8	557.4	8 189	14 625	53 207	39 991	34.2	1.9	31.1	41.3	23.3
Las Cruces, NM	316	2 948	67 131	3.6	43.8	27.9	353.6	8 696	19 393	52 617	36 343	36.5	2.1	27.8	39.3	12.9
Las Vegas-Henderson-Paradise, NV	678	3 014	496 463	10.7	44.6	22.1	2 555.2	8 066	25 161	67 150	51 057	22.1	3.0	16.1	23.5	9.2
Lawrence, KS	337	3 685	41 837	7.5	21.4	50.4	137.2	9 243	27 745	69 922	52 150	24.9	3.4	17.1	15.7	4.5
Lawton, OK	712	4 093	32 141	8.3	44.7	20.5	181.9	7 643	21 839	56 698	41 813	29.5	1.6	20.4	31.2	9.2
Lebanon, PA	178	1 825	29 631	25.5	57.8	20.1	221.1	11 553	26 667	68 552	55 973	18.4	3.1	10.9	13.6	7.1
Lewiston, ID-WA	184	3 324	14 799	8.8	38.7	22.1	81.6	9 258	23 281	56 742	45 417	22.7	1.9	13.4	19.8	9.6
Lewiston-Auburn, ME	148	2 725	26 090	14.6	49.8	18.3	196.7	11 599	23 682	55 709	44 127	28.0	1.8	17.1	23.0	10.7
Lexington-Fayette, KY	258	3 745	141 729	16.5	35.7	35.7	686.8	9 887	27 667	68 529	50 279	25.0	4.0	17.1	21.0	7.8
Lima, OH	379	3 332	26 563	15.4	49.6	17.1	161.7	11 172	21 962	56 070	43 030	27.4	2.1	15.0	18.9	9.1
Lincoln, NE	330	3 198	96 244	17.5	30.1	36.3	472.8	10 623	27 009	68 463	52 300	21.3	3.3	15.5	18.3	6.3
Little Rock-North Little Rock-Conway, AR	711	5 138	188 168	16.7	41.8	27.4	1 037.1	9 669	25 497	65 319	48 304	24.3	2.9	15.2	22.0	6.6
Logan, UT-ID	56	1 183	48 949	6.7	30.6	35.9	156.1	6 152	19 243	60 016	47 377	22.6	1.5	14.6	14.7	6.3
Longview, TX	416	3 325	51 997	9.9	49.3	16.1	345.1	8 798	23 201	61 076	45 175	28.2	1.8	18.9	26.8	8.5
Longview, WA	355	3 981	22 392	10.7	41.7	15.6	156.7	9 254	23 743	60 777	48 417	25.7	1.9	14.5	18.5	5.0
Los Angeles-Long Beach-Anaheim, CA	353	2 207	3 613 235	15.3	41.2	31.7	20 050.7	9 722	28 994	85 536	58 869	22.2	7.7	17.6	25.3	12.6
Anaheim-Santa Ana-Irvine, CA Div 11244	194	1 977	864 391	14.6	33.8	37.1	4 361.7	8 692	33 839	101 242	74 163	16.1	10.5	13.5	18.8	9.2
Los Angeles-Long Beach-Glendale, CA Div 31084	403	2 279	2 748 844	15.5	43.5	30.1	15 689.0	10 053	27 488	80 682	54 529	24.1	6.8	18.9	27.3	13.7
Louisville/Jefferson County, KY-IN	397	3 522	311 633	21.1	42.9	27.0	1 864.8	10 216	27 739	69 070	50 905	23.5	3.8	13.8	19.2	7.6
Lubbock, TX	659	4 243	100 135	8.9	40.9	26.9	440.5	8 785	24 421	65 462	47 172	25.7	4.1	17.6	24.3	7.4
Lynchburg, VA	193	1 611	72 562	35.2	45.4	24.6	321.7	9 403	24 173	60 112	47 821	26.4	2.2	15.5	21.6	7.4
Macon, GA	388	4 791	58 588	17.9	54.2	20.4	354.2	9 602	21 102	56 618	39 484	34.4	2.2	25.1	39.9	10.7
Madera, CA	666	2 575	40 701	7.0	52.5	13.0	269.6	8 845	17 046	56 655	39 758	26.2	2.0	23.6	31.0	18.3
Madison, WI	218	2 264	180 336	11.3	28.4	42.4	1 054.6	11 386	32 505	77 574	59 466	18.7	4.6	13.4	15.1	6.4
Manchester-Nashua, NH	293	2 383	98 579	24.2	37.1	34.5	721.9	12 670	33 966	85 775	67 574	15.9	5.9	9.6	12.0	5.7
Manhattan, KS	198	1 769	36 925	8.9	24.3	37.8	112.6	9 878	25 185	67 828	46 375	23.0	3.1	20.3	15.1	6.8
Mankato-North Mankato, MN	181	2 661	31 436	18.6	36.8	28.8	139.9	11 111	27 089	70 049	53 047	24.2	3.2	16.7	9.6	8.3
Mansfield, OH	197	4 655	28 023	18.1	54.6	15.3	200.6	13 157	21 181	51 740	39 455	29.4	1.9	17.6	25.5	8.4
McAllen-Edinburg-Mission, TX	286	3 688	263 829	5.8	61.6	16.2	1 868.5	9 112	14 305	49 432	35 098	38.2	1.4	34.3	44.9	26.1
Medford, OR	339	3 973	45 967	12.1	38.2	26.0	279.8	9 729	23 867	57 279	43 363	27.6	1.5	18.9	27.6	8.1
Memphis, TN-MS-AR	1 035	4 300	366 998	18.0	43.2	26.4	1 995.9	8 816	25 093	66 046	46 962	27.2	3.7	19.8	30.6	10.8
Merced, CA	588	3 061	87 373	7.6	56.1	13.5	540.7	9 596	17 223	55 311	40 687	28.8	1.8	25.2	35.2	14.1
Miami-Fort Lauderdale-West Palm Beach, FL	538	3 677	1 433 981	21.3	43.0	29.3	7 059.4	8 891	26 722	71 172	46 946	27.0	5.1	17.7	23.7	15.9
Fort Lauderdale-Pompano Beach-Deerfield Beach, FL Div 22744	405	3 420	470 869	21.4	38.7	30.5	2 183.4	8 390	27 804	72 233	50 446	24.3	4.8	15.1	18.9	14.1
Miami-Miami Beach-Kendall, FL Div 33124	655	4 168	647 903	21.8	48.5	26.8	3 183.4	8 986	22 832	64 339	41 913	31.5	4.3	21.0	27.7	22.5
West Palm Beach-Boca Raton-Delray Beach, FL Div 48424	450	3 080	315 209	20.2	38.5	32.5	1 692.7	9 429	32 690	80 662	51 804	23.2	6.6	14.9	22.5	9.1
Michigan City-La Porte, IN	163	2 742	24 587	13.7	55.4	17.4	178.6	10 209	22 654	59 212	46 506	28.5	1.9	17.4	32.1	7.2
Midland, MI	121	1 023	22 107	13.8	36.5	33.2	126.4	10 591	28 588	70 375	49 913	23.4	5.1	16.6	19.6	9.8
Midland, TX	281	2 638	39 949	12.9	41.6	27.3	224.5	8 544	37 335	102 205	71 442	15.3	9.0	9.3	13.1	10.0
Milwaukee-Waukesha-West Allis, WI	599	3 078	423 866	25.1	37.2	33.2	2 663.0	11 669	29 069	71 659	51 957	23.6	4.0	15.9	23.9	9.0
Minneapolis-St. Paul-Bloomington, MN	274	2 595	920 645	17.7	29.8	39.3	6 126.2	11 758	34 029	86 712	67 194	16.7	6.1	10.3	13.3	6.8
Missoula, MT	310	3 066	30 957	6.5	27.6	39.8	136.0	10 192	26 009	61 207	48 077	28.3	2.9	17.9	17.2	6.2
Mobile, AL	582	4 486	105 126	20.0	46.3	22.3	563.8	8 881	21 283	55 932	42 944	32.0	2.0	20.0	30.4	13.5

1. Data for serious crimes have not been adjusted for underreporting; this may affect comparability between geographic areas and over time. 2. Per 100,000 population estimated by the FBI. 3. All persons 3 years old and over enrolled in nursery school through college. 4. Persons 25 years old and over. 5. Elementary and secondary education expenditures. 6. Based on resident population estimated in the 2008-2012 American Community Survey.

Area name	Personal income, 2013: Total (mil dol)	Personal income, 2013: Percent change 2012–2013	Per capita[1]: Dollars	Per capita[1]: Rank	Wages and salaries (mil dol)	Supplements to wages and salaries; employer contributions (mil dol): Pension and insurance	Supplements to wages and salaries; employer contributions (mil dol): Government social insurance	Proprietors' income (mil dol)	Dividends, interest, and rent (mil dol)	Personal transfer receipts (mil dol)	Earnings, 2013: Total (mil dol)	Contributions for government social insurance (mil dol): From employee and self-employed	Contributions for government social insurance (mil dol): From employer
	62	63	64	65	66	67	68	69	70	71	72	73	74
Joplin, MO	6 092	1.4	34 762	307	3 042	586	225	427	1 128	1 410	4 280	257	225
Kahului-Wailuku-Lahaina, HI	6 206	3.3	38 714	200	2 983	507	263	617	1 344	1 040	4 370	261	263
Kalamazoo-Portage, MI	12 548	1.7	37 775	228	6 275	1 097	492	662	2 400	2 509	8 526	523	492
Kankakee, IL	4 136	4.0	36 892	259	1 746	363	132	259	633	935	2 500	136	132
Kansas City, MO-KS	93 597	2.0	45 558	68	51 613	7 980	3 884	9 646	15 843	13 752	73 123	4 266	3 884
Kennewick-Richland, WA	10 347	1.4	38 163	216	5 322	848	498	968	1 823	1 839	7 635	415	498
Killeen-Temple, TX	16 727	-0.5	39 520	182	7 968	1 862	668	941	3 399	2 917	11 438	521	668
Kingsport-Bristol-Bristol, TN-VA	10 871	0.2	35 264	298	4 974	944	361	792	1 765	3 036	7 070	470	361
Kingston, NY	8 059	0.7	44 527	84	2 425	715	202	370	1 781	1 664	3 712	208	202
Knoxville, TN	32 834	1.9	38 506	209	16 425	2 773	1 190	3 646	4 980	7 028	24 034	1 440	1 190
Kokomo, IN	2 854	1.9	34 488	314	1 805	280	141	163	444	784	2 388	154	141
La Crosse-Onalaska, WI-MN	5 694	1.8	42 022	132	3 066	650	251	333	1 083	972	4 300	256	251
Lafayette, LA	21 272	2.6	44 399	87	10 772	1 520	692	3 273	3 542	3 399	16 257	855	692
Lafayette-West Lafayette, IN	7 105	2.0	33 989	325	3 906	765	292	659	1 236	1 162	5 621	317	292
Lake Charles, LA	7 815	2.0	38 682	202	4 156	775	266	636	1 325	1 561	5 833	313	266
Lake Havasu City-Kingman, AZ	5 679	2.4	27 971	377	1 697	298	131	316	1 016	1 910	2 442	194	131
Lakeland-Winter Haven, FL	21 427	3.4	34 393	317	8 323	1 406	611	1 080	4 513	5 303	11 420	757	611
Lancaster, PA	21 775	1.9	41 116	154	9 658	1 806	791	2 206	4 273	3 942	14 462	844	791
Lansing-East Lansing, MI	16 972	1.7	36 317	271	9 209	1 742	708	1 026	2 831	3 347	12 685	764	708
Laredo, TX	7 114	2.1	27 102	379	3 346	650	236	899	901	1 686	5 131	254	236
Las Cruces, NM	6 750	0.9	31 620	365	2 721	584	216	524	1 169	1 661	4 045	245	216
Las Vegas-Henderson-Paradise, NV	75 957	1.4	37 457	238	39 842	6 202	2 853	5 875	15 542	11 984	54 772	2 957	2 853
Lawrence, KS	4 220	2.6	36 911	255	1 814	360	141	226	914	596	2 542	150	141
Lawton, OK	4 991	1.1	38 074	219	2 428	573	219	246	978	965	3 466	172	219
Lebanon, PA	5 690	1.4	41 994	133	1 968	459	163	341	989	1 113	2 931	178	163
Lewiston, ID-WA	2 367	2.8	38 162	217	1 016	180	92	192	515	568	1 481	97	92
Lewiston-Auburn, ME	4 054	2.2	37 680	231	1 938	327	152	267	528	1 071	2 684	176	152
Lexington-Fayette, KY	19 769	1.7	40 391	168	11 395	2 060	869	1 823	3 398	3 228	16 148	916	869
Lima, OH	3 625	2.5	34 428	316	2 154	429	169	312	604	909	3 064	171	169
Lincoln, NE	13 427	2.3	42 743	115	7 347	1 350	550	1 022	2 776	1 848	10 270	598	550
Little Rock-North Little Rock-Conway, AR	30 970	0.4	42 753	114	15 667	2 411	1 235	2 356	6 896	5 683	21 669	1 328	1 235
Logan, UT-ID	4 046	3.7	31 183	367	1 847	426	149	325	863	596	2 747	152	149
Longview, TX	9 319	2.6	43 036	109	4 673	635	334	1 381	1 480	1 835	7 023	371	334
Longview, WA	3 667	3.1	36 002	281	1 665	270	163	256	652	1 020	2 353	154	163
Los Angeles-Long Beach-Anaheim, CA	635 892	2.2	48 425	41	331 444	56 342	23 372	71 299	127 677	99 603	482 457	27 936	23 372
Anaheim-Santa Ana-Irvine, CA Div 11244	169 793	1.9	54 519	NA	87 037	13 783	6 247	18 511	34 435	18 870	125 578	7 291	6 247
Los Angeles-Long Beach-Glendale, CA Div 31084	466 099	2.3	46 530	NA	244 407	42 559	17 125	52 789	93 241	80 733	356 879	20 645	17 125
Louisville/Jefferson County, KY-IN	52 355	1.0	41 477	145	27 842	4 391	2 156	4 360	9 002	9 679	38 749	2 363	2 156
Lubbock, TX	11 649	4.1	38 695	201	5 310	896	356	1 478	2 308	2 110	8 040	392	356
Lynchburg, VA	9 279	1.8	36 183	276	4 203	670	315	467	1 791	2 244	5 655	377	315
Macon, GA	8 582	1.6	37 110	248	4 038	735	289	550	1 473	2 050	5 612	337	289
Madera, CA	4 920	3.1	32 287	358	1 888	457	135	838	779	1 071	3 318	161	135
Madison, WI	31 319	3.9	49 917	32	17 796	3 847	1 378	2 297	5 983	3 679	25 318	1 419	1 378
Manchester-Nashua, NH	21 213	1.9	52 509	21	11 137	1 707	798	1 791	3 572	2 704	15 433	919	798
Manhattan, KS	4 173	-0.9	42 545	120	1 481	308	113	185	916	434	2 087	119	113
Mankato-North Mankato, MN	3 951	-1.3	40 091	172	2 044	345	167	418	771	658	2 973	169	167
Mansfield, OH	4 016	1.5	32 979	346	1 918	410	151	180	622	1 084	2 659	155	151
McAllen-Edinburg-Mission, TX	18 828	2.6	23 073	381	7 782	1 535	543	2 405	2 185	5 613	12 265	624	543
Medford, OR	7 687	3.1	36 861	260	3 107	537	293	648	1 759	1 928	4 585	305	293
Memphis, TN-MS-AR	54 994	1.0	40 987	158	29 668	4 598	2 082	6 571	7 359	10 096	42 918	2 448	2 082
Merced, CA	8 406	4.6	31 935	363	2 847	748	204	1 155	1 293	2 126	4 954	244	204
Miami-Fort Lauderdale-West Palm Beach, FL	264 464	2.4	45 377	71	120 123	17 222	8 551	20 867	71 428	45 267	166 763	10 186	8 551
Fort Lauderdale-Pompano Beach-Deerfield Beach, FL Div 22744	80 526	2.8	43 792	NA	37 092	5 304	2 674	5 162	18 058	12 598	50 231	3 046	2 674
Miami-Miami Beach-Kendall, FL Div 33124	104 373	2.0	39 880	NA	54 535	8 072	3 893	10 440	22 057	21 177	76 941	4 667	3 893
West Palm Beach-Boca Raton-Delray Beach, FL Div 48424	79 565	2.5	57 985	NA	28 495	3 846	1 985	5 266	31 314	11 492	39 591	2 474	1 985
Michigan City-La Porte, IN	3 716	0.4	33 397	337	1 672	289	131	252	560	883	2 344	148	131
Midland, MI	3 879	0.2	46 228	58	1 983	330	146	172	789	644	2 631	160	146
Midland, TX	13 573	5.2	86 574	1	5 643	678	368	5 075	1 812	846	11 765	504	368
Milwaukee-Waukesha-West Allis, WI	74 854	1.3	47 688	46	41 575	7 452	3 277	5 082	13 587	12 446	57 386	3 409	3 277
Minneapolis-St. Paul-Bloomington, MN	177 051	1.8	51 183	28	103 933	13 959	7 989	14 357	31 059	23 369	140 237	8 305	7 989
Missoula, MT	4 181	1.7	37 397	239	2 156	376	204	343	953	719	3 078	196	204
Mobile, AL	13 599	0.8	32 843	349	7 689	1 222	583	1 201	2 111	3 411	10 694	675	583

1. Based on the resident population estimated as of July 1 of the year shown.

Table C. Metropolitan Areas — **Earnings, Social Security, and Housing**

Area name	Earnings, 2013 (cont.): Percent by selected industries: Farm	Mining	Construction	Manufacturing	Information, professional, scientific, technical services	Retail trade	Finance, insurance, real estate, rental and leasing	Health care and social assistance	Government	Social Security beneficiaries, December 2013: Number	Rate[1]	Supplemental Security Income recipients, December 2013	Housing units, 2014: Total	Percent change, 2000–2014
	75	76	77	78	79	80	81	82	83	84	85	86	87	88
Joplin, MO	1.7	D	5.1	17.4	4.0	8.4	3.9	15.4	12.3	36 880	210	4 614	75 640	0.9
Kahului-Wailuku-Lahaina, HI	2.9	D	8.1	1.4	4.3	8.4	6.5	7.1	17.3	27 050	168	2 027	71 580	1.5
Kalamazoo-Portage, MI	1.3	D	4.7	20.4	6.3	6.0	7.7	14.6	16.2	65 610	197	8 551	146 955	0.1
Kankakee, IL	6.3	D	3.9	17.6	D	7.2	4.8	17.1	16.3	21 910	195	2 765	45 154	-0.2
Kansas City, MO-KS	0.5	0.2	5.9	8.7	D	5.6	D	10.6	14.6	347 110	169	34 096	884 640	1.5
Kennewick-Richland, WA	7.9	0.0	6.6	6.2	14.8	6.1	3.1	9.3	18.5	40 115	148	5 413	98 749	6.1
Killeen-Temple, TX	0.1	D	6.0	3.6	4.6	5.5	2.9	11.2	52.1	58 645	139	9 059	168 819	5.9
Kingsport-Bristol-Bristol, TN-VA	-0.3	D	D	24.9	D	7.3	D	D	13.2	89 700	291	10 702	147 367	0.3
Kingston, NY	0.7	0.2	4.8	5.7	5.6	9.3	4.3	12.7	34.3	39 925	221	4 673	83 710	0.1
Knoxville, TN	-0.1	D	D	10.6	13.2	7.4	D	13.3	15.4	192 035	225	23 495	386 534	1.4
Kokomo, IN	2.0	D	2.9	44.5	3.3	6.2	3.4	12.1	10.6	21 140	255	2 201	38 688	0.0
La Crosse-Onalaska, WI-MN	0.8	D	5.2	12.8	D	6.4	6.1	20.9	16.6	26 045	191	2 343	57 936	1.6
Lafayette, LA	1.5	17.5	7.5	9.1	D	6.2	7.7	D	10.0	81 920	171	15 675	201 853	3.0
Lafayette-West Lafayette, IN	4.2	D	3.9	D	D	5.4	D	12.6	26.5	30 710	146	2 428	87 256	3.3
Lake Charles, LA	0.0	1.6	14.3	17.9	D	D	D	11.7	14.7	38 890	192	6 397	89 557	4.6
Lake Havasu City-Kingman, AZ	0.4	1.6	5.0	6.1	4.6	12.7	5.6	20.8	19.6	61 605	304	4 529	112 313	1.3
Lakeland-Winter Haven, FL	1.0	0.7	5.2	8.9	5.6	8.6	7.8	14.1	14.8	144 565	232	19 954	282 730	0.5
Lancaster, PA	2.2	0.2	10.4	16.5	7.3	7.2	6.2	13.8	10.2	105 865	200	10 166	206 404	1.7
Lansing-East Lansing, MI	0.9	0.3	4.4	12.1	7.7	5.4	9.0	12.3	27.2	85 730	183	10 192	199 985	0.5
Laredo, TX	0.1	8.2	3.1	0.6	4.1	8.3	4.2	10.6	27.3	30 765	117	12 604	78 048	6.2
Las Cruces, NM	4.8	0.1	5.5	3.9	8.8	6.1	3.5	14.1	33.8	36 755	172	7 772	84 221	3.3
Las Vegas-Henderson-Paradise, NV	0.0	0.1	6.4	2.7	8.9	7.4	6.3	8.7	16.3	308 355	152	37 209	863 010	2.7
Lawrence, KS	0.4	0.5	5.5	9.8	9.6	6.9	4.5	7.1	34.8	15 235	133	1 366	48 278	3.3
Lawton, OK	0.3	D	4.0	D	D	5.7	3.8	5.3	55.0	20 665	158	3 309	54 661	1.7
Lebanon, PA	2.4	0.0	4.9	17.9	5.4	7.5	2.9	13.3	20.8	30 850	227	2 490	56 209	1.1
Lewiston, ID-WA	2.0	D	5.4	17.1	4.5	8.8	7.1	D	19.0	16 150	260	1 776	27 260	-0.2
Lewiston-Auburn, ME	0.5	D	7.7	11.2	7.0	8.1	8.1	20.9	11.3	25 085	234	4 011	49 142	0.1
Lexington-Fayette, KY	1.2	1.2	5.8	14.7	9.8	6.5	5.3	9.9	21.0	79 550	163	11 564	214 914	2.8
Lima, OH	1.7	D	4.7	23.0	3.8	7.0	3.4	19.2	13.3	22 325	212	3 104	44 840	-0.4
Lincoln, NE	1.8	D	5.5	8.8	9.0	6.0	9.8	D	21.9	46 435	148	4 854	131 814	3.2
Little Rock-North Little Rock-Conway, AR	0.7	1.1	6.5	6.1	D	7.2	D	12.1	23.4	140 675	194	25 283	318 311	3.7
Logan, UT-ID	2.8	D	5.3	22.9	D	7.0	4.3	D	22.6	14 515	112	996	44 018	5.9
Longview, TX	0.1	16.7	11.1	9.9	D	7.0	4.3	D	8.6	42 445	196	6 680	89 529	2.5
Longview, WA	-0.1	1.0	12.4	23.0	3.5	6.7	2.9	13.0	15.2	25 650	252	3 732	43 510	0.1
Los Angeles-Long Beach-Anaheim, CA	0.0	0.5	4.0	9.2	18.6	5.7	10.6	9.6	13.9	1 658 830	126	497 642	4 554 527	1.3
Anaheim-Santa Ana-Irvine, CA Div 11244	0.0	0.2	6.2	11.5	14.3	5.9	14.5	8.6	10.8	413 340	132	74 566	1 072 011	2.2
Los Angeles-Long Beach-Glendale, CA Div 31084	0.0	0.6	3.3	8.4	20.1	5.6	9.3	10.0	15.0	1 245 490	124	423 076	3 482 516	1.1
Louisville/Jefferson County, KY-IN	0.4	D	D	13.8	8.9	5.6	D	13.8	13.4	247 325	196	35 561	548 209	1.4
Lubbock, TX	3.9	2.0	D	D	D	8.8	D	D	22.6	45 880	152	6 967	126 683	5.0
Lynchburg, VA	-0.5	D	D	18.4	D	6.9	6.2	13.5	13.2	59 970	234	6 488	114 586	1.8
Macon, GA	0.4	0.8	D	D	7.1	7.8	0.0	19.7	15.2	48 105	208	9 611	102 267	0.7
Madera, CA	20.8	D	3.4	9.0	2.8	5.1	2.0	14.0	22.2	23 915	157	4 751	49 891	1.5
Madison, WI	1.6	0.1	5.4	9.7	13.6	6.0	9.7	D	23.1	100 565	160	8 764	275 143	2.4
Manchester-Nashua, NH	0.0	0.0	5.8	14.9	15.0	8.3	11.2	11.3	10.7	74 820	185	6 876	167 418	0.8
Manhattan, KS	1.6	D	7.1	7.5	5.5	7.5	5.3	D	34.8	10 770	109	730	38 755	5.2
Mankato-North Mankato, MN	6.2	D	5.2	16.0	D	6.8	4.5	D	17.0	16 025	164	1 349	40 325	3.2
Mansfield, OH	0.4	0.0	5.5	22.0	4.8	8.1	4.3	14.5	18.8	28 340	232	3 368	54 275	-0.6
McAllen-Edinburg-Mission, TX	0.8	2.4	5.4	2.7	4.2	10.5	4.4	19.4	25.4	98 885	121	42 920	261 184	5.2
Medford, OR	0.2	0.1	7.6	9.2	6.7	10.8	5.0	18.4	15.6	52 270	251	4 590	91 919	1.1
Memphis, TN-MS-AR	0.8	0.1	5.3	9.5	5.6	D	D	12.0	14.5	224 745	168	47 028	563 811	1.6
Merced, CA	17.3	D	3.7	10.8	2.5	6.2	2.8	9.2	25.5	35 005	133	11 291	84 167	0.6
Miami-Fort Lauderdale-West Palm Beach, FL	0.4	0.1	4.7	3.3	13.5	7.8	10.8	11.7	14.2	995 340	170	221 788	2 496 492	1.3
Fort Lauderdale-Pompano Beach-Deerfield Beach, FL Div 22744	0.0	0.1	5.4	3.8	13.9	8.6	9.9	10.2	15.0	296 985	161	43 214	817 277	0.9
Miami-Miami Beach-Kendall, FL Div 33124	0.3	0.1	4.1	3.0	13.2	7.5	10.7	11.8	14.8	400 300	152	155 746	1 004 371	1.5
West Palm Beach-Boca Raton-Delray Beach, FL Div 48424	1.1	0.2	4.9	3.5	13.5	7.4	12.3	13.4	12.1	298 055	217	22 828	674 844	1.5
Michigan City-La Porte, IN	2.9	D	8.1	20.8	2.9	6.9	3.5	14.2	15.8	23 820	214	2 250	48 769	0.7
Midland, MI	0.6	D	6.2	25.7	4.9	4.6	3.1	11.3	8.7	18 500	221	1 672	36 274	0.9
Midland, TX	0.3	D	D	D	D	3.3	D	D	5.0	19 405	123	2 380	59 862	6.5
Milwaukee-Waukesha-West Allis, WI	0.1	D	4.1	17.2	10.1	5.2	9.7	13.0	11.7	281 920	180	46 925	671 916	0.3
Minneapolis-St. Paul-Bloomington, MN	0.3	0.1	4.8	12.1	D	5.0	12.9	10.2	12.1	517 650	150	59 978	1 416 931	2.2
Missoula, MT	-0.1	0.2	6.1	3.3	9.3	8.9	6.8	18.1	20.4	19 380	173	2 143	51 411	2.6
Mobile, AL	0.2	0.8	6.6	14.1	9.0	6.8	7.1	11.4	16.0	87 650	211	15 409	181 611	1.9

1. Per 1,000 resident population estimated as of July 1, 2011 of the year shown.

Area name	Housing units, 2013: Total	Occupied units: Owner-occupied: Percent	Owner-occupied: Median value[1]	Median owner cost as a percent of income: With a mortgage	Median owner cost as a percent of income: Without a mortgage[2]	Renter-occupied: Median rent[3]	Renter-occupied: Median rent as a percent of income	Substandard units[4] (percent)	Civilian labor force, 2014: Total	Percent change, 2013–2014	Unemployment: Total	Unemployment: Rate[5]	Civilian employment[6], 2013: Total employed	Percent: Management, professional, and related occupations	Percent: Construction, production, and related occupations
	89	90	91	92	93	94	95	96	97	98	99	100	101	102	103
Joplin, MO	67 701	66.6	108 900	20.4	11.5	662	29.1	NA	86 788	0.0	4 589	5.3	80 218	27.6	30.1
Kahului-Wailuku-Lahaina, HI	54 005	59.1	471 800	29.8	10.0	1 292	28.5	10.7	82 639	3.5	3 732	4.5	83 035	26.6	21.9
Kalamazoo-Portage, MI	130 076	66.7	123 700	21.9	12.8	698	30.0	1.8	162 964	1.4	9 869	6.1	154 311	36.0	20.9
Kankakee, IL	41 822	67.5	135 100	22.6	14.0	794	27.1	NA	55 367	-0.6	4 484	8.1	49 917	29.5	27.9
Kansas City, MO-KS	798 618	64.5	157 400	20.7	11.9	834	28.4	2.0	1 101 036	2.0	61 658	5.6	1 019 894	38.7	19.0
Kennewick-Richland, WA	92 768	68.0	172 600	19.7	10.0	833	28.3	7.5	128 228	-0.1	10 129	7.9	118 212	32.7	28.4
Killeen-Temple, TX	132 578	57.5	127 100	21.0	10.5	820	27.1	NA	170 253	0.0	9 918	5.8	158 444	29.9	23.4
Kingsport-Bristol-Bristol, TN-VA	126 215	74.6	120 800	20.9	10.4	587	29.6	1.5	139 115	-2.3	9 067	6.5	127 191	29.2	26.1
Kingston, NY	68 650	70.5	218 500	27.4	15.6	1 001	35.4	NA	88 232	-2.1	5 096	5.8	86 254	41.6	19.5
Knoxville, TN	340 089	67.2	148 400	21.2	10.0	737	29.9	2.2	398 587	-2.1	24 548	6.2	375 182	34.2	21.5
Kokomo, IN	34 435	68.2	98 000	17.7	10.0	591	30.4	NA	37 099	1.7	2 360	6.4	37 109	27.9	28.0
La Crosse-Onalaska, WI-MN	53 723	66.4	156 800	21.2	12.0	693	28.5	NA	77 117	-0.4	3 389	4.4	72 767	34.9	21.4
Lafayette, LA	178 778	71.1	125 200	18.9	10.0	697	26.6	4.0	233 101	1.9	12 512	5.4	221 981	31.9	25.5
Lafayette-West Lafayette, IN	79 375	55.8	124 300	18.5	10.0	791	30.9	NA	105 714	1.5	5 432	5.1	100 318	37.1	22.5
Lake Charles, LA	79 392	68.3	114 800	18.1	10.0	749	32.0	NA	98 111	5.5	5 767	5.9	89 945	28.2	27.8
Lake Havasu City-Kingman, AZ	81 257	66.8	123 900	23.8	11.0	763	27.9	5.0	78 247	1.3	6 905	8.8	66 666	25.2	20.9
Lakeland-Winter Haven, FL	214 500	68.6	101 800	23.5	11.8	850	29.4	3.5	281 330	0.7	19 982	7.1	246 894	28.0	23.4
Lancaster, PA	194 493	68.6	186 500	22.9	11.8	896	31.6	2.4	270 239	0.1	12 349	4.6	256 995	33.6	26.6
Lansing-East Lansing, MI	183 135	63.1	130 400	21.0	12.8	789	31.6	NA	241 154	0.6	13 910	5.8	220 823	37.6	18.9
Laredo, TX	68 696	65.6	107 800	24.4	13.9	711	29.3	16.5	111 815	0.9	5 674	5.1	93 877	22.9	24.9
Las Cruces, NM	74 898	64.3	134 600	23.3	10.0	650	32.4	5.1	93 212	-0.7	6 687	7.2	89 853	31.2	21.9
Las Vegas-Henderson-Paradise, NV	713 577	51.9	162 300	24.3	10.0	979	30.0	5.0	1 019 653	1.3	79 647	7.8	920 124	26.7	17.4
Lawrence, KS	42 470	53.4	186 400	21.3	11.4	836	29.4	NA	64 754	1.9	2 626	4.1	61 654	48.2	12.0
Lawton, OK	45 871	53.3	110 100	20.0	10.3	769	29.6	NA	51 567	-2.8	2 452	4.8	50 434	30.7	22.5
Lebanon, PA	51 901	69.0	162 300	21.4	12.2	772	24.8	NA	70 020	-1.0	3 421	4.9	63 725	31.1	27.8
Lewiston, ID-WA	24 527	73.9	166 500	24.7	11.1	639	27.9	NA	30 147	0.3	1 411	4.7	28 349	30.4	25.2
Lewiston-Auburn, ME	43 736	57.1	145 900	23.1	13.0	690	30.3	NA	56 165	-0.7	3 070	5.5	52 010	29.7	26.2
Lexington-Fayette, KY	193 193	57.4	164 400	19.6	10.0	771	29.3	2.6	258 522	-1.0	12 896	5.0	243 094	39.5	20.8
Lima, OH	40 359	64.6	111 200	19.9	10.9	651	29.0	NA	48 461	-2.3	2 773	5.7	48 626	25.8	29.5
Lincoln, NE	123 469	61.3	153 600	19.8	11.3	719	30.1	2.6	179 303	0.4	5 257	2.9	170 921	38.1	20.4
Little Rock-North Little Rock-Conway, AR	267 748	65.9	137 300	20.2	10.0	754	27.8	2.3	339 162	-0.9	18 635	5.5	337 030	36.1	20.3
Logan, UT-ID	39 593	67.9	179 800	23.5	10.0	693	28.7	NA	65 280	1.7	2 111	3.2	59 601	36.8	24.9
Longview, TX	76 957	64.5	117 700	18.9	10.6	718	31.5	4.4	105 163	0.4	5 128	4.9	92 270	25.4	33.2
Longview, WA	38 483	67.5	179 300	22.8	11.0	763	34.3	NA	44 048	1.7	3 697	8.4	41 470	26.3	33.6
Los Angeles-Long Beach-Anaheim, CA	4 251 495	48.3	453 500	28.3	10.8	1 265	35.1	11.7	6 601 489	0.8	501 530	7.6	6 123 960	36.3	19.7
Anaheim-Santa Ana-Irvine, CA Div 11244	1 003 790	57.5	539 000	26.8	10.0	1 499	34.6	8.9	1 575 606	0.6	86 442	5.5	1 509 266	39.9	16.9
Los Angeles-Long Beach-Glendale, CA Div 31084	3 247 705	45.5	420 200	28.9	11.2	1 205	35.2	12.5	5 025 883	0.9	415 088	8.3	4 614 694	35.1	20.6
Louisville/Jefferson County, KY-IN	494 276	67.7	148 700	20.2	10.2	740	27.9	1.6	630 397	-1.0	36 948	5.9	601 263	34.4	24.5
Lubbock, TX	110 295	58.8	104 800	20.0	10.9	799	32.9	3.5	154 374	0.5	6 059	3.9	145 630	34.7	20.4
Lynchburg, VA	102 320	70.2	164 400	21.4	10.1	739	33.2	NA	124 640	0.4	6 946	5.6	116 703	32.8	25.1
Macon, GA	80 190	59.6	118 700	24.3	12.1	742	32.8	NA	104 555	-0.5	8 101	7.7	85 617	33.0	20.6
Madera, CA	44 549	57.4	174 700	27.3	11.5	968	31.7	NA	63 184	0.8	6 981	11.0	51 909	24.8	39.2
Madison, WI	258 127	60.6	217 100	22.7	13.1	875	29.2	2.1	372 259	1.3	14 823	4.0	348 366	45.1	17.1
Manchester-Nashua, NH	155 036	65.6	240 800	23.7	15.3	1 061	29.2	2.6	228 666	0.1	10 321	4.5	208 924	41.4	19.9
Manhattan, KS	35 044	51.6	168 400	20.1	12.0	908	32.5	NA	48 907	0.8	1 829	3.7	44 814	39.4	17.6
Mankato-North Mankato, MN	37 358	67.7	165 400	21.0	10.0	692	29.5	NA	58 565	0.1	1 910	3.3	55 026	31.7	22.5
Mansfield, OH	47 847	66.7	101 400	20.9	10.5	567	28.6	NA	54 719	-0.6	3 503	6.4	48 935	26.4	29.5
McAllen-Edinburg-Mission, TX	223 367	67.4	79 400	24.7	12.7	655	30.6	14.0	334 457	0.6	29 029	8.7	297 399	25.1	25.8
Medford, OR	82 983	62.8	199 800	27.0	13.5	887	36.1	NA	97 104	1.2	8 356	8.6	87 779	31.9	20.2
Memphis, TN-MS-AR	492 311	60.3	128 600	22.3	11.2	825	31.7	3.2	606 639	-2.9	46 126	7.6	606 545	33.6	23.8
Merced, CA	77 651	52.3	147 200	24.5	11.1	864	32.5	10.3	115 386	0.4	14 771	12.8	90 765	22.5	37.0
Miami-Fort Lauderdale-West Palm Beach, FL	2 032 438	60.7	188 800	28.3	14.9	1 120	38.1	4.8	3 002 772	2.1	188 475	6.3	2 682 612	33.1	17.6
Fort Lauderdale-Pompano Beach-Deerfield Beach, FL Div 22744	662 488	63.1	181 000	28.2	15.2	1 162	36.8	3.9	994 081	2.0	58 071	5.8	872 375	35.1	16.0
Miami-Miami Beach-Kendall, FL Div 33124	839 491	53.2	192 500	29.6	14.9	1 086	39.8	6.5	1 320 447	2.2	89 806	6.8	1 190 891	31.1	19.3
West Palm Beach-Boca Raton-Delray Beach, FL Div 48424	530 459	69.5	193 000	26.8	14.8	1 132	36.0	3.2	688 244	2.1	40 598	5.9	619 346	34.0	16.7
Michigan City-La Porte, IN	42 746	70.8	125 200	19.3	12.7	693	30.7	NA	48 934	-0.2	3 779	7.7	47 527	27.3	30.1
Midland, MI	33 858	75.7	125 700	19.5	12.1	702	29.9	NA	41 494	1.2	2 501	6.0	36 551	40.1	21.0
Midland, TX	54 082	63.2	161 200	19.3	10.0	1 088	25.8	NA	94 291	6.0	2 692	2.9	79 127	32.5	28.6
Milwaukee-Waukesha-West Allis, WI	622 962	60.5	188 100	22.9	13.9	807	30.3	2.3	825 620	0.4	49 230	6.0	768 188	37.2	20.6
Minneapolis-St. Paul-Bloomington, MN	1 332 110	69.5	206 100	21.6	11.1	911	28.8	2.4	1 917 300	0.6	74 366	3.9	1 845 218	42.0	18.0
Missoula, MT	45 820	57.0	242 300	23.0	11.9	777	32.9	NA	60 284	0.9	2 702	4.5	57 639	38.3	14.7
Mobile, AL	148 025	66.3	121 200	21.9	10.9	761	33.3	2.7	184 133	-1.2	14 186	7.7	168 057	31.7	22.9

1. Specified owner-occupied units. 2. A value of 10.0 represents 10 percent or less. 3. Specified renter-occupied units. 4. Overcrowded or lacking complete plumbing facilities.
5. Percent of civilian labor force. 6. Persons 16 years old and over.

Area name	Private nonfarm establishments, employment and payroll, 2013: Number of establish-ments	Employment: Total	Employment: Health care and social assistance	Employment: Manufac-turing	Employment: Retail trade	Employment: Finance and insurance	Employment: Professional, scientific, and technical services	Annual payroll: Total (mil dol)	Annual payroll: Average per employee (dollars)	Agriculture, 2012: Farms: Number	Farms: Percent with: Fewer than 50 acres	Farms: Percent with: 500 acres or more	Farm operators whose principal occu-pation is farming (percent)
	104	105	106	107	108	109	110	111	112	113	114	115	116
Joplin, MO	4 160	69 836	14 997	11 605	9 813	1 757	1 489	2 453	35 123	2 877	35.9	6.1	39.6
Kahului-Wailuku-Lahaina, HI	4 410	60 723	6 209	1 057	9 392	1 002	1 475	2 162	35 608	1 128	89.0	3.5	54.0
Kalamazoo-Portage, MI	6 777	118 501	21 263	18 206	15 320	6 309	5 382	5 144	43 409	1 847	52.1	6.2	51.4
Kankakee, IL	2 369	37 103	7 539	5 345	5 639	2 019	736	1 309	35 268	818	33.7	24.4	56.8
Kansas City, MO-KS	50 197	881 954	132 039	74 560	106 050	59 704	70 982	41 470	47 020	12 757	35.5	10.8	42.8
Kennewick-Richland, WA	5 419	79 001	12 069	6 898	12 114	2 055	8 607	3 593	45 485	2 392	61.8	14.9	51.4
Killeen-Temple, TX	5 970	99 103	24 263	6 648	16 064	3 564	4 645	3 563	35 956	4 858	42.7	11.4	38.9
Kingsport-Bristol-Bristol, TN-VA	5 983	106 121	17 963	25 397	15 563	3 087	3 056	4 206	39 636	5 405	45.3	2.7	40.6
Kingston, NY	4 682	44 305	8 774	3 554	8 825	2 262	1 488	1 481	33 431	486	48.4	5.1	67.3
Knoxville, TN	17 531	317 675	51 409	34 885	44 991	14 337	21 116	12 645	39 804	5 613	46.9	1.8	42.6
Kokomo, IN	1 753	30 882	5 488	9 015	4 845	684	685	1 346	43 585	476	40.8	15.5	57.4
La Crosse-Onalaska, WI-MN	3 449	63 730	12 711	7 552	9 331	2 203	1 925	2 241	35 162	1 668	18.8	10.7	47.8
Lafayette, LA	13 166	195 945	34 199	15 860	26 333	5 516	10 618	8 729	44 547	3 276	53.8	10.9	47.0
Lafayette-West Lafayette, IN	3 937	70 350	11 208	16 894	9 443	2 917	2 629	2 630	37 388	1 574	42.7	22.9	48.7
Lake Charles, LA	4 497	71 941	12 660	8 681	10 724	2 091	4 446	2 920	40 592	1 244	44.3	12.4	35.4
Lake Havasu City-Kingman, AZ	3 603	39 476	8 263	2 809	8 946	1 219	909	1 275	32 297	335	59.1	23.9	51.3
Lakeland-Winter Haven, FL	10 922	166 924	27 427	13 997	23 914	10 647	6 305	6 176	36 996	2 415	64.4	7.2	45.3
Lancaster, PA	12 266	213 446	35 200	33 732	30 036	7 022	9 925	8 334	39 047	5 657	44.1	1.3	72.2
Lansing-East Lansing, MI	9 469	156 760	27 720	17 203	21 543	12 249	7 383	6 349	40 499	3 235	46.2	9.9	49.0
Laredo, TX	5 091	71 445	14 226	622	13 352	2 633	1 894	2 005	28 063	696	15.1	48.6	48.6
Las Cruces, NM	3 554	49 387	12 912	2 502	8 049	1 744	3 739	1 424	28 832	2 184	85.6	4.5	37.7
Las Vegas-Henderson-Paradise, NV	40 969	767 816	75 656	18 061	99 696	26 063	39 545	29 628	38 588	252	78.6	2.0	46.8
Lawrence, KS	2 635	36 252	5 965	3 240	6 061	1 011	1 698	1 103	30 413	945	38.5	9.7	35.8
Lawton, OK	2 255	32 638	6 276	3 320	5 565	1 661	806	1 058	32 402	1 607	19.1	27.8	46.2
Lebanon, PA	2 634	43 681	8 241	8 163	6 889	873	1 112	1 520	34 800	1 219	48.2	2.3	58.9
Lewiston, ID-WA	1 541	20 993	4 084	3 660	3 387	1 403	689	743	35 391	615	39.5	33.0	54.6
Lewiston-Auburn, ME	2 678	43 936	9 327	5 218	6 072	3 206	2 006	1 604	36 508	463	51.6	5.0	56.4
Lexington-Fayette, KY	12 017	214 267	36 585	25 715	28 094	6 818	15 572	8 620	40 232	4 727	44.1	7.6	46.4
Lima, OH	2 463	46 512	12 431	7 051	6 062	1 193	961	1 724	37 074	904	38.8	11.8	42.9
Lincoln, NE	8 488	133 324	23 725	13 082	18 307	10 643	8 939	5 070	38 029	2 828	46.0	17.8	38.7
Little Rock-North Little Rock-Conway, AR	17 669	272 562	53 141	22 139	37 538	14 953	12 449	10 871	39 886	3 534	40.0	9.0	42.9
Logan, UT-ID	3 322	40 710	5 454	11 670	6 025	1 198	2 861	1 279	31 413	2 051	46.9	14.0	41.4
Longview, TX	5 395	84 095	12 596	11 448	11 495	2 700	3 768	3 446	40 978	3 671	42.6	5.3	35.3
Longview, WA	2 159	29 580	5 303	6 155	4 670	883	723	1 286	43 461	492	72.4	2.8	46.7
Los Angeles-Long Beach-Anaheim, CA	342 723	5 180 979	655 717	508 526	549 229	244 410	440 624	267 461	51 624	1 606	88.2	3.3	60.2
Anaheim-Santa Ana-Irvine, CA Div 11244	X	X	X	X	X	X	X	X	X	312	85.3	4.8	58.7
Los Angeles-Long Beach-Glendale, CA Div 31084	X	X	X	X	X	X	X	X	X	1 294	88.9	2.9	60.6
Louisville/Jefferson County, KY-IN	28 564	533 347	86 534	65 394	59 924	32 561	26 274	22 259	41 734	7 555	48.0	4.9	43.3
Lubbock, TX	7 101	108 601	21 978	5 217	17 458	5 466	4 033	3 588	33 038	2 002	23.9	35.5	50.1
Lynchburg, VA	5 894	93 760	14 356	15 756	14 262	3 927	5 358	3 600	38 397	2 966	29.9	7.5	40.9
Macon, GA	5 058	82 348	17 116	5 183	11 325	8 948	2 874	2 939	35 695	734	38.4	6.7	44.0
Madera, CA	1 883	25 438	5 879	3 483	3 437	475	512	954	37 507	1 507	44.8	14.3	57.9
Madison, WI	16 235	299 751	49 638	32 233	38 165	24 862	20 723	14 075	46 956	7 446	38.4	8.5	48.1
Manchester-Nashua, NH	10 764	173 304	28 199	28 142	27 944	5 679	11 439	8 534	49 243	688	64.0	1.5	50.0
Manhattan, KS	2 129	28 333	4 762	1 816	6 092	1 050	1 205	853	30 119	1 383	23.1	23.4	43.5
Mankato-North Mankato, MN	2 561	46 687	10 419	7 313	7 031	1 253	1 541	1 640	35 131	1 834	25.5	21.8	57.4
Mansfield, OH	2 639	42 940	7 748	8 033	6 394	1 126	933	1 370	31 906	1 010	37.2	5.0	52.0
McAllen-Edinburg-Mission, TX	11 678	178 553	55 082	6 909	35 943	6 490	5 127	4 734	26 515	2 161	57.9	14.7	51.4
Medford, OR	5 861	66 354	13 098	5 980	11 692	2 450	2 415	2 303	34 709	1 722	72.1	2.4	56.2
Memphis, TN-MS-AR	25 188	523 688	81 127	35 867	63 785	19 111	17 238	23 277	44 448	3 934	32.7	15.3	44.0
Merced, CA	2 852	41 183	6 643	8 757	7 899	946	821	1 447	35 131	2 486	56.7	12.8	64.5
Miami-Fort Lauderdale-West Palm Beach, FL	180 470	1 979 425	295 498	66 454	303 236	100 187	145 850	87 200	44 053	4 978	92.1	1.9	55.8
Fort Lauderdale-Pompano Beach-Deerfield Beach, FL Div 22744	X	X	X	X	X	X	X	X	X	615	93.7	1.3	50.1
Miami-Miami Beach-Kendall, FL Div 33124	X	X	X	X	X	X	X	X	X	2 954	92.8	1.2	56.5
West Palm Beach-Boca Raton-Delray Beach, FL Div 48424	X	X	X	X	X	X	X	X	X	1 409	90.0	3.5	56.7
Michigan City-La Porte, IN	2 299	35 042	5 660	7 682	5 713	832	966	1 224	34 928	731	43.8	17.1	51.4
Midland, MI	1 747	36 377	5 847	6 339	4 123	D	844	2 110	58 002	555	47.9	7.0	46.7
Midland, TX	5 076	80 859	7 007	3 137	8 994	2 080	4 554	4 839	59 846	954	32.8	29.6	38.5
Milwaukee-Waukesha-West Allis, WI	37 718	752 678	125 860	113 926	78 724	53 311	39 524	36 008	47 839	1 767	47.1	7.6	52.2
Minneapolis-St. Paul-Bloomington, MN	92 724	1 721 040	264 259	176 604	181 973	126 133	115 435	91 153	52 964	13 251	40.4	9.2	49.4
Missoula, MT	4 177	46 400	9 127	1 494	7 678	1 976	3 140	1 502	32 363	637	58.4	10.0	38.3
Mobile, AL	8 567	147 574	20 148	17 209	19 298	5 836	9 030	5 784	39 195	698	60.9	4.4	48.6

Area name	Agriculture, 2012 (cont.): Land in farms: Acreage (1,000)	Land in farms: Percent change, 2007–2012	Land in farms: Acres: Average size of farm	Land in farms: Acres: Total irrigated (1,000)	Land in farms: Acres: Total cropland (1,000)	Value of land and buildings (dollars): Average per farm	Value of land and buildings (dollars): Average per acre	Value of machinery and equipment, average per farm (dollars)	Value of products sold: Total (mil dol)	Value of products sold: Average per farm (dollars)	Value of products sold: Percent from: Crops	Value of products sold: Percent from: Livestock and poultry products	Percent of farms with sales of: $10,000 or more	Percent of farms with sales of: $100,000 or more	Government payments: Total ($1,000)	Government payments: Percent of farms
	117	118	119	120	121	122	123	124	125	126	127	128	129	130	131	132
Joplin, MO	494	-2.0	172	3.8	221.1	422 288	2 457	61 142	352.0	122 343	13.5	86.5	43.1	9.2	3 356	26.2
Kahului-Wailuku-Lahaina, HI	229	1.6	203	41.5	49.6	1 998 207	9 836	53 229	188.1	166 755	96.5	3.5	37.1	7.1	558	10.5
Kalamazoo-Portage, MI	319	-3.5	173	73.1	237.9	782 997	4 538	138 933	438.6	237 484	81.1	18.9	47.4	18.5	4 898	23.6
Kankakee, IL	343	-11.2	419	14.6	327.9	2 769 373	6 612	264 800	287.5	351 460	90.2	9.8	71.8	48.5	5 827	76.5
Kansas City, MO-KS	3 124	-5.1	245	D	1 916.0	749 999	3 062	83 462	785.7	61 589	68.9	31.1	41.2	10.1	34 070	44.7
Kennewick-Richland, WA	1 329	7.0	555	404.5	971.3	1 569 965	2 827	192 328	1 663.2	695 308	D	D	44.1	26.5	14 367	21.2
Killeen-Temple, TX	1 329	-0.5	274	3.7	306.5	727 280	2 658	57 979	169.6	34 905	45.8	54.2	25.2	4.0	3 614	15.2
Kingsport-Bristol-Bristol, TN-VA	569	-2.9	105	0.5	161.6	374 389	3 558	48 349	126.4	23 393	15.2	84.8	26.1	3.5	6 226	30.7
Kingston, NY	71	-5.3	147	4.2	26.1	738 835	5 042	103 237	55.9	115 019	83.0	17.0	43.0	12.6	328	10.1
Knoxville, TN	538	-6.7	96	1.6	194.1	495 626	5 174	57 244	158.2	28 176	56.8	43.2	22.7	2.2	1 294	13.0
Kokomo, IN	144	-11.1	303	D	134.5	1 924 391	6 353	182 880	140.4	294 874	81.1	18.9	68.1	37.2	2 993	67.0
La Crosse-Onalaska, WI-MN	388	-5.3	233	1.1	216.2	792 875	3 409	126 932	232.8	139 555	48.7	51.3	56.6	25.2	7 429	71.6
Lafayette, LA	761	-3.1	232	152.3	537.5	627 401	2 702	115 382	440.9	134 575	84.1	15.9	32.9	11.7	14 740	39.4
Lafayette-West Lafayette, IN	679	-0.4	431	D	638.6	2 869 720	6 657	239 864	583.0	370 363	75.3	24.7	57.4	39.8	12 438	64.2
Lake Charles, LA	573	-1.8	461	27.4	141.2	1 029 838	2 235	77 753	52.3	42 007	60.6	39.4	27.3	6.2	3 549	22.7
Lake Havasu City-Kingman, AZ	1 244	45.0	3 714	20.8	29.1	1 792 487	483	75 743	30.2	90 102	68.9	31.1	33.7	11.9	1 242	11.3
Lakeland-Winter Haven, FL	521	-5.1	216	79.9	125.1	1 052 028	5 480	64 954	350.3	145 042	90.2	9.8	48.1	18.3	419	1.4
Lancaster, PA	439	3.3	78	6.1	332.0	973 388	12 529	101 987	1 475.0	260 731	17.7	82.3	74.2	48.4	5 843	18.4
Lansing-East Lansing, MI	668	-1.8	206	7.4	549.2	837 223	4 057	126 959	513.0	158 584	63.2	36.8	46.4	19.6	9 730	43.6
Laredo, TX	2 098	13.1	3 015	2.6	25.2	3 265 045	1 083	57 487	30.3	43 476	2.8	97.2	31.2	7.0	1 169	14.1
Las Cruces, NM	660	12.0	302	76.3	93.8	540 877	1 790	75 238	351.0	160 729	47.5	52.5	23.9	8.1	1 453	9.5
Las Vegas-Henderson-Paradise, NV	16	-82.3	62	3.7	4.4	347 790	5 611	66 325	6.8	27 083	48.2	51.8	33.7	4.4	34	3.6
Lawrence, KS	211	-4.5	223	3.3	127.3	636 186	2 854	82 519	43.9	46 436	66.2	33.8	37.7	8.4	2 332	46.9
Lawton, OK	863	-0.2	537	0.8	322.6	678 021	1 263	80 981	111.8	69 573	41.7	58.3	46.7	14.1	8 694	54.8
Lebanon, PA	121	7.0	100	1.5	97.4	1 052 028	10 562	122 164	348.9	286 245	13.1	86.9	64.1	37.6	2 250	26.6
Lewiston, ID-WA	585	-6.7	952	1.3	265.7	1 245 914	1 309	136 184	101.7	165 337	87.2	12.8	44.4	26.0	7 534	54.0
Lewiston-Auburn, ME	59	16.9	128	0.8	22.0	329 181	2 564	72 955	53.8	116 266	22.1	77.9	32.8	8.0	445	15.6
Lexington-Fayette, KY	759	-6.0	161	3.1	281.9	895 506	5 577	77 863	459.8	97 273	19.6	80.4	42.7	11.0	7 009	31.4
Lima, OH	183	-2.2	203	D	163.0	1 070 715	5 284	144 872	144.1	159 393	76.2	23.8	61.7	30.3	3 593	74.4
Lincoln, NE	844	11.9	298	151.4	696.9	1 423 260	4 770	156 127	486.3	171 957	68.0	32.0	48.6	23.8	15 528	63.6
Little Rock-North Little Rock-Conway, AR	788	-2.6	223	233.1	424.9	654 503	2 936	91 716	348.0	98 485	68.6	31.4	33.2	7.8	16 332	22.1
Logan, UT-ID	531	11.5	259	137.5	278.0	718 986	2 776	105 031	249.0	121 400	24.9	75.1	44.4	16.3	5 876	39.8
Longview, TX	525	-3.6	143	1.2	98.9	371 975	2 602	49 545	139.5	37 992	18.1	81.9	22.0	2.9	634	2.3
Longview, WA	39	27.1	79	7.6	18.6	689 236	8 693	67 535	28.8	58 482	D	D	19.5	6.9	44	1.6
Los Angeles-Long Beach-Anaheim, CA	152	-22.3	95	47.7	74.7	1 534 556	16 194	50 774	351.6	218 935	94.1	5.9	35.6	12.9	290	3.4
Anaheim-Santa Ana-Irvine, CA Div 11244	60	-30.8	194	8.1	15.2	4 237 538	21 854	70 968	158.5	508 055	99.0	1.0	41.3	18.3	43	4.8
Los Angeles-Long Beach-Glendale, CA Div 31084	92	-15.5	71	39.7	59.6	882 832	12 459	45 905	193.1	149 225	90.1	9.9	34.2	11.6	247	3.1
Louisville/Jefferson County, KY-IN	1 068	-8.0	141	D	607.7	573 173	4 054	69 317	410.6	54 342	60.1	39.9	33.6	7.7	13 211	37.0
Lubbock, TX	1 533	-1.9	766	338.8	1 130.1	915 687	1 196	206 678	314.0	156 835	72.9	27.1	45.8	27.4	28 253	73.9
Lynchburg, VA	552	6.9	186	D	151.2	674 238	3 620	60 278	74.4	25 088	28.4	71.6	35.9	4.1	2 334	18.5
Macon, GA	145	-14.1	197	10.1	46.0	599 775	3 039	77 030	120.5	164 170	31.4	68.6	28.5	10.6	1 459	19.1
Madera, CA	654	-3.8	434	292.3	304.2	3 302 033	7 614	182 022	1 602.8	1 063 547	77.4	22.6	70.2	46.8	2 400	11.4
Madison, WI	1 466	-3.8	197	14.2	1 067.2	984 545	5 002	132 972	1 081.6	145 256	40.2	59.8	49.3	22.9	31 173	62.4
Manchester-Nashua, NH	48	-5.0	69	0.7	11.1	450 385	6 495	52 282	22.5	32 759	69.8	30.2	22.8	7.0	261	6.8
Manhattan, KS	628	-5.0	454	26.0	264.3	853 839	1 881	103 492	171.4	123 929	51.7	48.3	54.2	19.6	4 125	59.9
Mankato-North Mankato, MN	651	-5.6	355	1.7	588.8	2 286 660	6 445	257 171	892.1	486 398	49.3	50.7	71.0	49.7	13 782	82.1
Mansfield, OH	161	9.6	159	0.1	120.3	789 172	4 962	110 557	128.7	127 408	51.7	48.3	55.0	29.5	1 806	32.5
McAllen-Edinburg-Mission, TX	795	10.0	368	183.6	465.6	1 117 900	3 038	115 296	452.8	209 517	91.7	8.3	33.2	14.2	9 106	20.0
Medford, OR	214	-12.3	124	36.5	32.8	582 023	4 682	40 415	64.1	37 240	57.6	42.4	25.7	3.4	252	3.8
Memphis, TN-MS-AR	1 573	-0.6	400	D	1 086.1	1 072 560	2 682	131 704	661.4	168 123	D	D	32.2	13.4	26 335	44.6
Merced, CA	979	-6.0	394	468.2	522.6	3 045 778	7 737	236 454	2 967.5	1 193 694	42.9	57.1	76.0	45.7	9 528	20.2
Miami-Fort Lauderdale-West Palm Beach, FL	610	1.4	122	409.8	509.9	1 213 970	9 911	83 861	1 650.7	331 597	98.0	2.0	52.0	15.2	8 726	7.1
Fort Lauderdale-Pompano Beach-Deerfield Beach, FL Div 22744	14	65.9	24	1.8	4.3	540 185	22 916	31 886	47.4	77 099	91.2	8.8	41.0	8.6	246	2.9
Miami-Miami Beach-Kendall, FL Div 33124	81	21.3	28	45.2	64.9	699 727	25 423	47 644	604.2	204 549	98.0	2.0	58.5	16.0	6 944	8.5
West Palm Beach-Boca Raton-Delray Beach, FL Div 48424	514	-2.2	365	362.7	440.7	2 586 187	7 090	182 476	999.0	709 041	98.3	1.7	43.2	16.2	1 536	6.0
Michigan City-La Porte, IN	228	-11.0	312	54.4	209.3	1 896 432	6 084	188 253	223.1	305 215	80.5	19.5	55.7	33.8	4 036	58.4
Midland, MI	90	-1.2	161	1.0	69.5	580 838	3 600	98 339	70.1	126 285	67.9	32.1	39.1	14.1	2 310	44.3
Midland, TX	858	-6.2	899	27.9	342.0	1 097 884	1 221	116 852	37.5	39 285	78.2	21.8	21.3	8.8	7 024	48.4
Milwaukee-Waukesha-West Allis, WI	295	0.9	167	2.2	238.1	1 011 705	6 056	128 100	250.1	141 516	49.0	51.0	50.8	22.7	5 478	43.0
Minneapolis-St. Paul-Bloomington, MN	2 598	-1.6	196	105.7	2 044.9	1 015 662	5 180	136 564	2 169.8	163 748	66.3	33.7	52.7	22.9	43 747	54.6
Missoula, MT	247	-12.3	388	16.8	19.9	1 074 215	2 769	40 830	13.6	21 355	29.8	70.2	22.1	4.6	395	9.4
Mobile, AL	89	-21.9	127	2.8	36.6	516 701	4 062	78 354	84.7	121 289	90.7	9.3	33.2	8.5	796	12.2

Area name	Water use, 2010		Wholesale trade,[1] 2007				Retail trade, 2007				Real estate and rental and leasing, 2007			
	Total water withdrawn (mil gal/day)	Gallons withdrawn per person per day	Number of establishments	Number of employees	Sales (mil dol)	Annual payroll (mil dol)	Number of establishments	Number of employees	Sales (mil dol)	Annual payroll (mil dol)	Number of establishments	Number of employees	Receipts (mil dol)	Annual payroll (mil dol)
	133	134	135	136	137	138	139	140	141	142	143	144	145	146
Joplin, MO	40.5	231	182	2 761	1 285.2	92.6	799	10 096	2 573.1	208.2	182	835	95.1	19.2
Kahului-Wailuku-Lahaina, HI	278.1	1 795	139	1 286	575.9	55.5	853	9 861	2 474.8	262.0	319	2 776	594.1	96.8
Kalamazoo-Portage, MI	218.7	670	305	D	D	D	1 180	16 579	3 365.5	327.6	271	2 701	239.2	72.1
Kankakee, IL	26.8	236	116	D	D	D	389	5 737	1 258.5	118.1	105	342	63.5	9.5
Kansas City, MO-KS	1 626.1	809	2 587	40 250	40 482.2	2 100.6	6 744	109 788	26 981.4	2 499.1	2 703	D	D	D
Kennewick-Richland, WA	894.8	3 532	203	2 353	1 783.4	93.8	762	11 477	2 910.5	280.3	270	1 276	244.7	37.2
Killeen-Temple, TX	80.7	199	147	3 038	4 248.5	129.7	1 125	14 902	3 999.7	334.1	377	1 704	232.0	45.0
Kingsport-Bristol-Bristol, TN-VA	929.6	3 003	282	D	D	D	1 238	15 165	3 555.5	316.1	242	D	D	D
Kingston, NY	458.2	2 511	150	1 607	946.5	86.5	794	9 242	2 241.1	216.3	209	676	125.2	18.4
Knoxville, TN	699.1	835	922	D	D	D	3 154	49 104	12 100.6	1 146.6	804	D	D	D
Kokomo, IN	17.5	212	62	510	319.5	24.1	374	5 240	1 194.7	105.6	83	320	47.7	7.5
La Crosse-Onalaska, WI-MN	37.3	279	149	D	D	D	526	9 273	1 952.2	178.2	131	614	84.0	15.1
Lafayette, LA	436.2	935	654	D	D	D	1 858	25 117	6 176.4	548.8	663	6 952	1 712.3	395.8
Lafayette-West Lafayette, IN	39.9	198	136	D	D	D	668	10 651	2 232.6	205.4	213	1 099	190.2	35.7
Lake Charles, LA	250.2	1 254	198	2 227	1 405.7	95.2	853	11 942	2 812.8	249.5	215	1 053	231.5	35.6
Lake Havasu City-Kingman, AZ	121.2	605	117	976	423.8	33.0	730	10 672	2 837.7	248.0	280	876	133.3	22.7
Lakeland-Winter Haven, FL	298.7	496	580	8 024	13 241.7	337.4	1 876	25 321	6 420.1	586.4	741	3 423	517.8	95.9
Lancaster, PA	78.2	151	604	10 635	6 333.6	435.7	2 000	30 083	6 542.3	644.4	348	2 223	420.1	74.3
Lansing-East Lansing, MI	239.1	515	358	5 424	5 900.1	239.1	1 590	23 293	5 115.1	468.2	456	3 348	399.8	88.9
Laredo, TX	43.5	174	351	2 519	1 472.1	79.2	819	12 864	2 913.5	235.4	205	724	119.6	18.9
Las Cruces, NM	397.2	1 899	120	1 076	448.2	34.1	536	7 881	1 925.6	159.5	229	1 009	143.2	22.2
Las Vegas-Henderson-Paradise, NV	486.6	249	1 698	23 067	11 493.1	1 114.8	5 744	99 817	26 676.6	2 656.9	3 356	25 654	5 235.4	925.5
Lawrence, KS	19.1	172	81	D	D	D	407	6 121	1 202.2	110.5	170	711	93.4	17.5
Lawton, OK	32.1	247	57	D	D	D	450	5 666	1 240.3	109.6	136	D	D	D
Lebanon, PA	14.6	109	104	3 250	2 802.6	122.3	451	6 611	1 488.6	144.1	68	271	43.5	7.3
Lewiston, ID-WA	133.2	2 188	57	D	D	D	273	3 586	911.9	90.6	64	241	29.7	5.9
Lewiston-Auburn, ME	15.3	142	104	1 277	444.6	51.3	489	6 386	1 704.3	145.2	119	509	82.0	13.4
Lexington-Fayette, KY	183.8	389	494	D	D	D	1 831	29 937	6 901.1	679.3	647	2 907	484.6	85.3
Lima, OH	34.6	325	135	D	D	D	464	6 950	1 577.5	133.6	105	481	67.1	12.2
Lincoln, NE	73.2	242	297	4 005	2 857.0	174.3	1 108	17 746	3 772.5	356.2	376	1 575	252.8	43.3
Little Rock-North Little Rock-Conway, AR	619.6	885	901	15 321	14 161.9	664.0	2 709	37 562	9 186.1	813.7	904	4 417	768.4	131.5
Logan, UT-ID	513.5	4 094	129	942	411.1	33.8	440	5 855	1 208.6	106.2	202	D	D	D
Longview, TX	1 708.9	7 972	272	3 514	1 559.7	140.8	942	11 426	2 976.2	264.8	217	1 437	302.8	58.4
Longview, WA	146.6	1 431	78	1 136	1 415.8	51.8	360	5 018	1 219.7	117.1	117	442	54.3	9.7
Los Angeles-Long Beach-Anaheim, CA	3 829.4	298	28 236	354 769	296 399.4	17 905.4	40 170	577 963	164 134.3	15 153.5	19 651	134 213	37 478.6	6 290.8
Anaheim-Santa Ana-Irvine, CA Div 11244	765.4	254	6 559	94 938	97 963.6	5 642.5	9 991	159 810	45 022.5	4 304.3	5 566	43 366	10 688.2	2 161.6
Los Angeles-Long Beach-Glendale, CA Div 31084	3 064.0	312	21 677	259 831	198 435.8	12 262.9	30 179	418 153	119 111.8	10 849.2	14 085	90 847	26 790.4	4 129.2
Louisville/Jefferson County, KY-IN	1 008.9	816	1 385	D	D	D	4 279	63 198	14 979.5	1 391.9	1 369	8 447	2 210.2	297.7
Lubbock, TX	260.9	897	393	D	D	D	1 078	17 007	3 968.4	350.2	387	D	D	D
Lynchburg, VA	47.7	189	196	2 563	1 367.5	95.3	1 039	13 775	3 187.3	286.2	288	908	128.4	25.9
Macon, GA	131.1	565	247	D	D	D	1 011	12 921	2 769.7	271.2	259	D	D	D
Madera, CA	748.7	4 963	79	678	353.1	28.8	368	3 883	1 010.2	89.3	100	409	36.7	9.4
Madison, WI	116.5	192	721	D	D	D	2 268	42 124	10 238.2	1 006.3	762	D	D	D
Manchester-Nashua, NH	55.1	137	515	6 535	3 873.1	386.1	1 657	27 793	7 647.3	678.7	443	2 664	554.7	96.4
Manhattan, KS	46.0	496	55	844	254.2	29.0	368	5 491	1 012.5	96.8	126	540	58.1	11.4
Mankato-North Mankato, MN	41.1	425	121	1 740	1 470.2	74.6	441	7 099	1 376.4	126.4	105	766	84.9	16.1
Mansfield, OH	17.0	137	127	2 113	1 010.6	76.7	497	7 387	1 489.5	145.8	108	571	59.2	12.3
McAllen-Edinburg-Mission, TX	470.2	607	670	7 808	4 301.1	257.5	2 132	32 803	7 898.8	635.3	491	2 289	366.9	53.2
Medford, OR	392.4	1 931	230	2 304	1 047.1	90.9	991	12 243	3 422.4	290.1	360	1 563	205.4	36.5
Memphis, TN-MS-AR	1 088.0	821	1 507	29 955	32 527.8	1 513.4	4 494	64 603	15 843.6	1 493.3	1 286	D	D	D
Merced, CA	1 494.7	5 843	97	D	D	D	578	8 005	2 001.3	179.9	153	641	85.6	15.1
Miami-Fort Lauderdale-West Palm Beach, FL	2 446.7	440	13 772	121 182	104 189.2	5 538.0	23 239	304 024	84 738.5	7 682.7	11 250	55 949	11 006.7	2 137.1
Fort Lauderdale-Pompano Beach-Deerfield Beach, FL Div 22744	1 279.1	732	3 946	37 891	31 411.6	1 819.5	7 382	104 336	30 886.3	2 710.6	3 624	18 044	3 555.6	648.1
Miami-Miami Beach-Kendall, FL Div 33124	461.0	185	7 819	65 657	60 760.1	2 818.0	10 293	123 559	34 530.5	3 055.6	4 935	25 546	5 367.9	985.2
West Palm Beach-Boca Raton-Delray Beach, FL Div 48424	706.5	535	2 007	17 634	12 017.5	900.5	5 564	76 129	19 321.7	1 916.5	2 691	12 359	2 083.2	503.8
Michigan City-La Porte, IN	44.0	395	123	1 446	856.2	54.1	495	6 054	1 363.6	114.9	102	438	60.4	11.1
Midland, MI	10.6	127	49	D	D	D	323	4 382	869.3	79.5	82	D	D	D
Midland, TX	73.9	521	263	3 362	2 436.1	163.4	569	7 879	2 322.1	186.8	227	1 418	270.7	56.8
Milwaukee-Waukesha-West Allis, WI	2 280.3	1 466	2 133	36 633	21 345.4	1 888.6	5 012	86 028	18 898.8	1 853.3	1 474	9 657	1 673.9	337.7
Minneapolis-St. Paul-Bloomington, MN	1 762.8	526	4 652	D	D	D	11 217	190 781	46 818.0	4 439.0	5 085	D	D	D
Missoula, MT	85.6	783	169	1 825	860.1	69.5	587	8 668	2 179.4	194.6	227	952	126.3	21.6
Mobile, AL	1 096.7	2 656	546	6 904	3 268.7	296.1	1 644	22 271	5 225.5	483.4	448	2 460	417.2	77.8

1. Merchant wholesalers, except manufacturers' sales branches and offices.

Table C. Metropolitan Areas — **Professional Services, Manufacturing, and Accommodation and Food Services**

Area name	Professional, scientific, and technical services,[1] 2007				Manufacturing, 2007				Accommodation and food services, 2007			
	Number of establishments	Number of employees	Sales (mil dol)	Annual payroll (mil dol)	Number of establishments	Number of employees	Sales (mil dol)	Annual payroll (mil dol)	Number of establishments	Number of employees	Sales (mil dol)	Annual payroll (mil dol)
	147	148	149	150	151	152	153	154	155	156	157	158
Joplin, MO	269	D	D	D	269	13 785	3 983.3	490.7	352	6 754	251.9	73.2
Kahului-Wailuku-Lahaina, HI	368	D	D	D	D	D	D	D	526	21 927	2 452.2	630.1
Kalamazoo-Portage, MI	647	D	D	D	434	21 099	8 458.8	1 065.0	675	13 767	495.1	153.7
Kankakee, IL	169	D	D	D	115	5 633	3 418.9	280.8	229	D	D	D
Kansas City, MO-KS	6 114	D	D	D	D	D	D	D	3 826	83 515	4 340.6	1 177.1
Kennewick-Richland, WA	470	D	D	D	190	5 975	D	241.7	447	6 634	305.7	89.1
Killeen-Temple, TX	427	D	D	D	D	D	D	D	610	10 940	462.9	120.2
Kingsport-Bristol-Bristol, TN-VA	463	2 941	300.8	109.1	320	27 089	9 083.1	1 150.4	568	11 315	434.2	122.2
Kingston, NY	455	D	D	D	202	D	D	165.3	533	6 542	321.4	103.9
Knoxville, TN	1 844	D	D	D	D	D	D	D	1 449	33 060	1 401.8	414.7
Kokomo, IN	131	D	D	D	76	11 980	2 923.2	877.5	186	3 921	150.5	44.5
La Crosse-Onalaska, WI-MN	253	D	D	D	189	7 756	D	273.9	355	6 275	222.4	64.8
Lafayette, LA	1 572	D	D	D	567	18 475	D	733.8	813	17 601	795.1	206.0
Lafayette-West Lafayette, IN	334	D	D	D	D	D	D	D	432	8 989	337.0	98.1
Lake Charles, LA	455	D	D	D	D	D	D	D	332	10 366	880.0	181.8
Lake Havasu City-Kingman, AZ	251	D	D	D	164	3 814	1 350.0	139.6	381	6 380	274.3	77.3
Lakeland-Winter Haven, FL	1 093	6 654	781.8	310.5	438	16 160	7 178.0	697.4	765	16 084	699.6	199.4
Lancaster, PA	939	D	D	D	920	40 077	13 269.9	1 735.9	935	17 060	763.9	221.2
Lansing-East Lansing, MI	1 087	7 810	928.7	375.1	385	20 365	D	1 187.2	901	17 436	652.2	194.7
Laredo, TX	309	D	D	D	89	914	242.4	30.7	360	7 489	317.3	86.5
Las Cruces, NM	315	D	D	D	141	2 349	931.9	84.2	298	5 955	238.7	64.9
Las Vegas-Henderson-Paradise, NV	5 282	43 063	6 982.5	2 498.8	1 096	26 478	7 180.7	1 086.3	3 797	266 845	24 857.8	7 431.8
Lawrence, KS	285	D	D	D	88	3 848	976.5	143.0	299	5 937	213.7	60.1
Lawton, OK	182	D	D	D	D	D	D	D	212	D	D	D
Lebanon, PA	193	D	D	D	213	9 655	2 393.6	363.3	241	3 075	125.3	35.3
Lewiston, ID-WA	109	D	D	D	D	D	D	D	134	2 278	87.5	27.6
Lewiston-Auburn, ME	182	D	D	D	158	6 945	2 186.2	300.2	226	3 422	149.7	44.0
Lexington-Fayette, KY	1 347	D	D	D	459	30 392	D	D	960	22 013	985.7	286.1
Lima, OH	170	D	D	D	136	8 661	10 009.0	475.9	219	4 469	173.2	47.4
Lincoln, NE	804	8 361	1 112.3	386.2	272	14 390	D	577.4	685	12 466	486.0	136.3
Little Rock-North Little Rock-Conway, AR	2 013	D	D	D	D	D	D	D	1 238	25 036	1 087.4	307.0
Logan, UT-ID	363	D	D	D	D	D	D	D	155	2 921	101.0	31.2
Longview, TX	436	D	D	D	250	12 506	D	522.3	380	7 316	296.6	86.3
Longview, WA	150	D	D	D	128	7 001	2 914.7	356.7	215	2 782	124.0	36.2
Los Angeles-Long Beach-Anaheim, CA	44 767	D	D	D	20 509	628 771	202 475.6	29 161.5	26 330	481 517	28 485.9	7 936.8
Anaheim-Santa Ana-Irvine, CA Div 11244	14 013	D	D	D	5 351	177 115	49 131.9	8 641.4	6 854	141 702	8 247.8	2 366.7
Los Angeles-Long Beach-Glendale, CA Div 31084	30 754	D	D	D	15 158	451 656	153 343.7	20 520.1	19 476	339 815	20 238.1	5 570.1
Louisville/Jefferson County, KY-IN	3 099	D	D	D	D	D	D	D	2 242	D	D	D
Lubbock, TX	591	3 427	375.4	129.0	D	D	D	D	592	D	D	D
Lynchburg, VA	518	D	D	D	302	18 731	D	898.1	431	7 932	297.1	89.1
Macon, GA	486	D	D	D	D	D	D	D	470	8 618	346.2	92.6
Madera, CA	124	D	D	D	116	4 143	1 452.9	170.3	192	2 265	125.1	33.1
Madison, WI	1 779	D	D	D	807	36 089	10 033.5	D	1 548	28 978	1 140.3	330.6
Manchester-Nashua, NH	1 347	D	D	D	633	31 243	7 707.6	1 944.4	875	15 987	732.3	224.9
Manhattan, KS	198	D	D	D	61	2 421	D	89.6	190	3 848	137.2	36.5
Mankato-North Mankato, MN	169	D	D	D	140	8 903	3 601.0	308.9	214	4 840	164.6	48.6
Mansfield, OH	194	1 044	110.4	41.0	192	11 080	3 563.7	555.3	277	4 802	178.9	52.5
McAllen-Edinburg-Mission, TX	793	D	D	D	276	6 007	1 503.2	183.5	896	17 219	758.0	186.5
Medford, OR	491	D	D	D	324	6 115	2 037.5	228.8	590	7 946	372.9	108.9
Memphis, TN-MS-AR	2 275	D	D	D	D	D	D	D	2 257	62 998	3 489.7	954.9
Merced, CA	170	D	D	D	122	9 208	3 954.2	348.6	302	5 130	219.4	55.2
Miami-Fort Lauderdale-West Palm Beach, FL	27 747	141 555	22 331.1	8 589.7	5 041	83 698	20 748.6	3 370.1	10 669	218 145	13 303.6	3 718.9
Fort Lauderdale-Pompano Beach-Deerfield Beach, FL Div 22744	9 509	46 243	6 635.1	2 550.4	1 734	29 333	7 160.8	1 185.5	3 693	70 373	4 209.1	1 140.1
Miami-Miami Beach-Kendall, FL Div 33124	11 294	60 310	9 603.2	3 755.1	2 312	40 446	9 347.1	1 556.0	4 358	91 230	6 005.9	1 659.8
West Palm Beach-Boca Raton-Delray Beach, FL Div 48424	6 944	35 002	6 092.8	2 284.2	995	13 919	4 240.7	628.6	2 618	56 542	3 088.6	919.0
Michigan City-La Porte, IN	169	D	D	D	184	8 808	2 364.0	363.9	259	5 254	389.7	80.1
Midland, MI	164	D	D	D	55	5 103	2 821.3	363.1	129	2 545	108.0	30.6
Midland, TX	442	D	D	D	D	D	D	D	257	D	D	D
Milwaukee-Waukesha-West Allis, WI	3 967	D	D	D	2 740	130 675	41 284.2	6 590.6	3 194	59 644	2 465.0	701.3
Minneapolis-St. Paul-Bloomington, MN	13 381	D	D	D	5 117	204 972	64 545.7	10 579.6	6 473	D	D	D
Missoula, MT	458	D	D	D	112	2 159	674.9	93.8	332	6 209	269.1	70.0
Mobile, AL	901	D	D	D	385	16 776	12 407.2	840.9	652	13 252	562.4	155.0

1. Establishments subject to federal tax.

Table C. Metropolitan Areas — **Health Care and Social Assistance, Other Services, Nonemployer Business and Residential Construction**

Area name	Health care and social assistance,[1] 2007: Number of establishments	Health care and social assistance,[1] 2007: Number of employees	Health care and social assistance,[1] 2007: Receipts (mil dol)	Health care and social assistance,[1] 2007: Annual payroll (mil dol)	Other services,[1] 2007: Number of establishments	Other services,[1] 2007: Number of employees	Other services,[1] 2007: Receipts (mil dol)	Other services,[1] 2007: Annual payroll (mil dol)	Nonemployer business, 2013: Number	Nonemployer business, 2013: Receipts (mil dol)	Value of residential construction authorized by building permits, 2014: New construction ($1,000)	Value of residential construction authorized by building permits, 2014: Number of housing units
	159	160	161	162	163	164	165	166	167	168	169	170
Joplin, MO	507	12 259	1 089.4	435.8	344	1 675	117.2	34.6	10 190	410.4	41 903	408
Kahului-Wailuku-Lahaina, HI	387	5 899	619.8	282.0	389	2 352	227.1	60.6	15 150	735.9	85 196	338
Kalamazoo-Portage, MI	754	20 517	1 978.8	776.8	523	3 982	511.6	103.0	20 432	804.4	138 100	561
Kankakee, IL	290	6 260	618.8	228.6	193	1 080	105.7	26.6	6 232	207.4	23 395	127
Kansas City, MO-KS	4 814	115 685	11 521.0	4 700.0	3 609	D	D	D	137 259	6 052.5	1 426 821	8 201
Kennewick-Richland, WA	613	9 790	952.5	374.5	325	1 808	151.3	44.5	11 430	496.5	327 522	1 264
Killeen-Temple, TX	558	D	D	D	504	3 083	239.7	67.0	19 248	811.0	352 465	2 371
Kingsport-Bristol-Bristol, TN-VA	726	D	D	D	433	D	D	D	17 674	667.2	65 401	340
Kingston, NY	520	D	D	D	316	1 559	117.0	30.2	15 868	640.6	68 499	289
Knoxville, TN	1 877	D	D	D	1 248	D	D	D	58 708	2 713.6	483 253	3 109
Kokomo, IN	223	5 618	513.4	195.6	131	711	53.2	14.1	4 233	137.9	19 488	140
La Crosse-Onalaska, WI-MN	315	D	D	D	275	D	D	D	7 599	328.0	58 066	298
Lafayette, LA	1 463	28 033	2 475.8	907.8	757	5 348	551.1	143.6	40 500	1 985.0	498 908	2 362
Lafayette-West Lafayette, IN	364	9 594	935.1	353.2	299	1 980	249.4	49.5	10 553	423.6	163 616	1 081
Lake Charles, LA	520	11 058	1 037.5	352.6	284	D	D	D	13 204	588.8	171 339	1 302
Lake Havasu City-Kingman, AZ	456	7 612	911.1	284.4	315	1 895	129.4	38.0	10 217	431.6	105 884	535
Lakeland-Winter Haven, FL	971	24 347	2 613.7	926.8	727	3 850	323.5	94.6	38 465	1 453.7	502 521	2 559
Lancaster, PA	1 062	32 573	2 878.0	1 163.1	1 042	6 812	587.2	157.1	39 855	2 035.5	196 564	1 109
Lansing-East Lansing, MI	1 182	24 945	2 329.6	970.1	864	6 760	748.3	209.1	30 611	1 256.6	168 697	755
Laredo, TX	441	12 142	723.4	284.3	257	1 465	124.3	28.6	22 688	1 027.2	186 840	1 719
Las Cruces, NM	474	10 748	798.2	323.2	230	1 237	94.1	27.7	12 098	441.3	133 152	617
Las Vegas-Henderson-Paradise, NV	3 978	67 163	8 517.4	3 017.6	2 313	18 791	1 602.5	473.7	141 658	6 992.8	1 132 984	10 036
Lawrence, KS	283	5 331	375.5	163.3	190	1 429	277.4	33.7	7 712	298.3	56 590	347
Lawton, OK	287	6 335	585.1	226.3	177	905	65.4	15.7	4 929	197.9	19 843	114
Lebanon, PA	266	7 662	626.6	286.9	233	1 059	93.0	25.2	7 968	360.9	52 952	348
Lewiston, ID-WA	190	3 784	356.0	121.9	119	607	39.9	11.6	3 213	121.3	16 601	90
Lewiston-Auburn, ME	421	9 495	872.4	355.7	203	945	69.8	21.2	5 969	269.9	17 348	91
Lexington-Fayette, KY	1 323	D	D	D	844	6 104	586.4	171.1	33 861	1 534.3	254 346	1 888
Lima, OH	330	11 408	999.0	417.5	213	1 448	93.3	27.9	5 373	210.0	10 975	61
Lincoln, NE	874	22 175	1 978.1	811.0	700	4 372	561.1	121.1	20 923	787.2	297 189	1 994
Little Rock-North Little Rock-Conway, AR	2 041	48 896	5 101.2	1 964.1	1 188	D	D	D	48 320	2 125.4	333 495	2 082
Logan, UT-ID	326	D	D	D	181	D	D	D	8 892	318.9	117 058	784
Longview, TX	534	11 452	1 080.5	387.2	338	2 189	221.1	60.5	14 715	736.7	42 184	290
Longview, WA	249	5 122	487.3	198.6	146	894	75.9	22.8	4 100	174.9	36 202	178
Los Angeles-Long Beach-Anaheim, CA	37 695	577 980	69 501.3	25 483.8	21 200	152 375	18 866.4	4 337.0	1 224 211	64 677.9	5 982 336	26 950
Anaheim-Santa Ana-Irvine, CA Div 11244	9 967	133 174	16 300.4	5 915.0	5 111	34 627	3 636.0	967.4	NA	NA	X	X
Los Angeles-Long Beach-Glendale, CA Div 31084	27 728	444 806	53 200.9	19 568.8	16 089	117 748	15 230.4	3 369.6	NA	NA	X	X
Louisville/Jefferson County, KY-IN	3 201	D	D	D	2 079	D	D	D	82 071	3 563.4	604 712	4 011
Lubbock, TX	831	D	D	D	485	D	D	D	20 333	1 023.3	292 665	2 136
Lynchburg, VA	532	D	D	D	458	2 354	175.4	53.1	13 924	485.4	141 738	921
Macon, GA	637	D	D	D	371	2 066	213.6	57.3	17 539	584.8	43 443	218
Madera, CA	221	5 836	554.7	255.8	119	609	48.9	12.9	6 970	312.2	56 883	214
Madison, WI	1 427	44 774	4 521.4	1 848.6	1 267	D	D	D	43 114	2 057.2	630 642	3 805
Manchester-Nashua, NH	1 020	26 771	2 503.8	1 065.3	828	5 317	501.5	155.6	27 576	1 548.7	141 651	968
Manhattan, KS	216	4 875	314.2	127.9	181	1 689	289.8	51.9	4 833	210.2	105 672	514
Mankato-North Mankato, MN	270	9 523	694.8	321.8	220	1 326	205.1	28.4	6 229	248.6	65 888	430
Mansfield, OH	354	7 670	663.5	263.1	238	1 533	109.3	29.3	6 815	264.6	12 430	61
McAllen-Edinburg-Mission, TX	1 655	44 931	2 877.2	1 137.1	573	3 257	238.5	61.9	66 167	2 411.8	372 002	3 473
Medford, OR	627	11 160	1 173.9	434.7	357	2 107	182.0	56.9	16 219	712.7	166 991	747
Memphis, TN-MS-AR	2 711	D	D	D	1 733	D	D	D	105 730	3 865.2	524 520	3 154
Merced, CA	443	6 048	592.2	235.3	209	899	73.9	19.3	10 521	492.7	42 954	169
Miami-Fort Lauderdale-West Palm Beach, FL	18 858	276 188	34 308.4	11 820.3	12 419	68 297	7 169.8	1 706.1	784 044	33 058.7	3 482 242	15 259
Fort Lauderdale-Pompano Beach-Deerfield Beach, FL Div 22744	5 732	88 155	10 883.5	3 647.7	4 174	22 705	2 171.8	586.7	NA	NA	X	X
Miami-Miami Beach-Kendall, FL Div 33124	8 311	120 152	15 042.3	5 194.3	5 065	27 878	3 185.8	659.3	NA	NA	X	X
West Palm Beach-Boca Raton-Delray Beach, FL Div 48424	4 815	67 881	8 382.6	2 978.3	3 180	17 714	1 812.2	460.1	NA	NA	X	X
Michigan City-La Porte, IN	236	4 900	521.2	188.2	207	1 172	74.6	22.2	5 747	202.7	24 548	125
Midland, MI	242	5 442	539.3	192.0	144	947	147.4	22.3	4 875	184.0	24 643	262
Midland, TX	369	6 167	706.7	246.5	262	2 486	289.0	65.9	15 330	1 157.5	235 993	1 556
Milwaukee-Waukesha-West Allis, WI	4 879	118 780	11 226.9	4 710.5	2 926	21 389	2 254.9	615.4	88 210	4 109.7	494 068	2 355
Minneapolis-St. Paul-Bloomington, MN	8 552	230 542	22 448.7	9 723.6	6 730	D	D	D	256 066	11 704.1	2 726 636	11 425
Missoula, MT	451	8 022	754.8	278.6	288	1 618	150.7	37.8	9 374	418.3	49 236	578
Mobile, AL	741	23 845	2 160.0	894.7	666	4 681	412.6	116.5	29 500	1 070.8	124 217	746

1. Establishments subject to federal tax.

Area name	Government employment and payroll, 2012: Full-time equivalent employees	Government employment and payroll, 2012: March Payroll (dollars)	March payroll (percent of total): Administration, judicial, and legal	March payroll (percent of total): Police and corrections	March payroll (percent of total): Fire protection	March payroll (percent of total): Highways and transportation	March payroll (percent of total): Health and welfare	March payroll (percent of total): Natural resources and utilities	March payroll (percent of total): Education and libraries	Local government finances, 2012, General revenue: Total (mil dol)	General revenue: Intergovernmental (mil dol)	Taxes: Total (mil dol)	Taxes: Per capita[1] (dollars): Total	Taxes: Per capita[1] (dollars): Property
	171	172	173	174	175	176	177	178	179	180	181	182	183	184
Joplin, MO	6 292	18 337 340	4.7	8.3	3.6	3.0	2.0	3.3	74.4	510.9	199.2	185.7	1 065	527
Kahului-Wailuku-Lahaina, HI	2 328	11 762 934	19.0	23.7	16.4	6.9	6.2	25.4	0.0	252.6	23.1	224.7	1 419	1 316
Kalamazoo-Portage, MI	9 976	43 436 306	7.0	10.5	12.8	2.9	6.0	3.3	56.6	1 340.8	705.4	408.5	1 238	1 210
Kankakee, IL	4 413	16 356 166	7.8	13.5	3.6	3.7	1.5	3.4	65.4	441.9	208.0	169.2	1 496	1 433
Kansas City, MO-KS	86 196	339 122 341	5.7	9.8	5.2	3.5	13.8	6.1	54.6	9 183.3	2 533.9	4 159.3	2 040	1 219
Kennewick-Richland, WA	10 152	53 295 192	5.2	7.0	3.2	4.4	10.2	28.7	40.3	1 194.4	543.2	325.4	1 213	704
Killeen-Temple, TX	19 513	61 961 488	4.6	8.5	3.2	1.8	4.0	4.2	72.6	1 379.2	598.6	457.1	1 087	854
Kingsport-Bristol-Bristol, TN-VA	11 566	36 313 120	5.1	10.8	2.2	3.5	5.1	5.7	66.0	805.9	377.3	312.3	1 011	695
Kingston, NY	8 282	38 442 668	5.7	7.7	1.3	4.8	8.8	1.7	68.0	1 095.2	330.4	630.3	3 467	2 848
Knoxville, TN	29 145	97 687 242	5.6	9.5	2.6	3.1	10.2	13.4	54.2	2 517.0	845.0	1 010.5	1 191	718
Kokomo, IN	4 091	15 459 399	5.0	6.2	3.5	2.0	35.8	3.0	42.2	435.8	136.7	118.7	1 433	1 170
La Crosse-Onalaska, WI-MN	5 559	21 504 753	6.0	8.2	2.4	4.3	16.8	4.2	57.0	720.4	365.8	237.4	1 755	1 630
Lafayette, LA	17 787	55 296 831	6.7	12.0	3.2	3.4	8.4	8.0	57.3	1 668.5	663.9	685.1	1 444	587
Lafayette-West Lafayette, IN	5 636	18 225 886	7.4	11.9	4.8	5.8	2.8	5.4	60.9	552.8	259.3	207.6	1 006	798
Lake Charles, LA	9 670	30 588 485	5.1	13.5	3.3	5.8	7.9	5.3	57.2	1 055.7	360.2	475.0	2 361	1 046
Lake Havasu City-Kingman, AZ	5 613	20 393 845	13.0	13.4	11.7	4.5	2.0	5.6	47.4	538.5	183.2	229.9	1 131	849
Lakeland-Winter Haven, FL	22 910	75 047 946	7.9	12.5	4.2	2.1	2.6	10.6	56.6	1 844.2	710.5	644.8	1 047	726
Lancaster, PA	12 622	54 624 168	5.9	11.7	0.8	2.8	3.4	3.5	70.9	1 833.2	668.6	843.7	1 601	1 327
Lansing-East Lansing, MI	15 249	64 035 635	8.2	8.0	3.0	4.4	9.2	6.8	56.5	1 895.2	923.3	587.0	1 260	1 174
Laredo, TX	14 741	48 977 584	5.1	9.2	5.1	3.0	3.0	3.7	70.4	1 245.0	614.2	391.8	1 512	1 216
Las Cruces, NM	7 916	26 726 295	5.8	10.4	2.7	2.6	2.1	5.9	66.7	732.8	425.3	209.7	978	447
Las Vegas-Henderson-Paradise, NV	51 796	300 546 553	8.1	16.4	5.9	3.4	8.6	10.1	45.3	8 606.7	3 678.4	2 735.1	1 367	869
Lawrence, KS	4 535	18 551 008	5.6	11.2	5.0	2.9	33.2	7.9	33.4	537.2	114.0	188.6	1 671	1 239
Lawton, OK	6 503	22 717 032	3.8	5.7	3.0	2.2	36.2	3.3	45.2	523.3	171.6	106.3	802	354
Lebanon, PA	4 116	14 939 586	6.1	9.0	1.7	2.8	9.0	5.5	65.4	485.8	160.6	191.5	1 416	1 136
Lewiston, ID-WA	2 076	7 939 079	7.0	11.4	5.6	6.0	7.0	7.6	51.8	188.3	89.3	64.0	1 042	932
Lewiston-Auburn, ME	3 959	13 779 680	4.1	8.3	4.8	4.2	2.0	5.1	70.2	355.6	153.6	163.3	1 517	1 507
Lexington-Fayette, KY	16 579	58 038 313	4.2	11.6	6.9	2.1	7.1	4.3	61.5	1 418.6	398.6	746.8	1 540	758
Lima, OH	4 029	14 917 726	8.3	9.1	4.8	3.4	9.8	5.8	55.9	394.8	197.5	125.6	1 195	774
Lincoln, NE	11 413	48 128 898	5.2	7.7	3.8	4.5	4.1	11.5	61.4	1 034.8	326.0	505.1	1 628	1 186
Little Rock-North Little Rock-Conway, AR	24 915	82 533 612	5.8	10.8	5.3	3.7	2.5	8.9	61.2	2 303.6	1 228.7	601.7	838	423
Logan, UT-ID	3 888	12 693 319	7.2	7.0	2.3	3.6	11.8	5.5	59.8	338.7	155.8	113.9	888	560
Longview, TX	9 132	29 631 047	5.5	10.9	3.9	2.0	4.4	4.8	66.6	721.4	245.0	370.6	1 710	1 319
Longview, WA	3 301	15 112 407	7.8	11.6	3.0	7.2	3.7	14.2	51.3	420.9	170.2	127.1	1 246	848
Los Angeles-Long Beach-Anaheim, CA	471 707	2 757 691 350	8.8	12.1	4.7	5.2	12.5	8.6	45.7	77 422.5	34 902.2	24 415.1	1 870	1 275
Anaheim-Santa Ana-Irvine, CA Div 11244	85 251	527 595 855	5.4	11.0	4.8	3.1	7.4	5.7	58.4	14 543.9	5 867.6	5 580.4	1 806	1 406
Los Angeles-Long Beach-Glendale, CA Div 31084	386 456	2 230 095 495	9.6	12.3	4.7	5.7	13.7	9.3	42.7	62 878.6	29 034.6	18 834.7	1 891	1 234
Louisville/Jefferson County, KY-IN	45 148	162 939 795	3.7	9.1	3.7	3.4	14.2	6.3	58.2	4 084.7	1 333.6	1 583.1	1 265	787
Lubbock, TX	13 751	49 840 306	4.7	10.3	4.2	1.2	27.8	5.7	45.1	1 319.2	362.2	422.7	1 420	1 113
Lynchburg, VA	9 196	26 684 206	6.4	11.2	3.2	1.3	7.0	5.1	63.4	712.1	348.1	270.1	1 058	752
Macon, GA	9 317	31 505 415	6.5	10.3	4.0	2.8	5.6	5.3	64.2	803.6	331.4	347.0	1 491	1 002
Madera, CA	4 578	20 019 402	8.1	8.1	0.2	2.2	10.1	5.2	64.4	627.3	366.3	154.2	1 013	706
Madison, WI	23 987	100 319 066	5.9	10.2	2.5	6.5	6.7	6.3	60.2	2 887.9	993.2	1 412.8	2 276	2 136
Manchester-Nashua, NH	13 991	56 054 764	4.1	10.8	6.0	4.5	3.9	3.8	65.8	1 458.9	470.6	808.2	2 006	1 981
Manhattan, KS	3 088	9 783 062	8.5	11.2	3.9	5.6	3.6	7.1	58.8	275.9	79.3	146.5	1 497	1 108
Mankato-North Mankato, MN	3 049	12 248 005	8.1	9.4	1.0	5.0	10.7	5.9	57.5	419.6	200.3	109.1	1 113	999
Mansfield, OH	5 091	18 513 991	8.5	9.4	5.0	4.1	11.2	8.3	52.0	473.0	237.7	163.9	1 336	864
McAllen-Edinburg-Mission, TX	39 042	129 583 687	3.7	6.7	1.7	1.6	2.9	3.9	78.6	3 159.2	1 926.2	864.1	1 071	868
Medford, OR	4 931	20 369 335	9.1	14.6	6.5	6.1	5.2	6.8	50.0	668.0	291.3	260.8	1 263	1 068
Memphis, TN-MS-AR	53 881	181 275 652	6.8	14.3	6.6	4.1	9.1	12.2	45.2	5 455.9	2 056.3	2 087.0	1 555	1 086
Merced, CA	10 959	49 202 192	6.5	7.6	1.6	1.1	10.0	6.7	63.4	1 305.5	840.8	219.3	836	680
Miami-Fort Lauderdale-West Palm Beach, FL	222 370	1 025 593 818	5.5	14.7	6.9	4.6	20.6	7.6	34.5	30 329.9	7 063.4	12 134.4	2 106	1 662
Fort Lauderdale-Pompano Beach-Deerfield Beach, FL Div 22744	73 864	331 154 408	5.1	13.2	6.2	3.7	29.6	6.0	33.6	9 918.0	2 186.8	3 161.3	1 742	1 392
Miami-Miami Beach-Kendall, FL Div 33124	102 308	498 941 928	4.9	14.9	6.0	5.9	20.8	6.6	32.3	14 058.6	3 695.7	5 524.1	2 132	1 564
West Palm Beach-Boca Raton-Delray Beach, FL Div 48424	46 198	195 497 482	7.6	16.4	10.2	2.6	5.1	13.1	41.6	6 353.4	1 180.9	3 449.0	2 542	2 211
Michigan City-La Porte, IN	4 264	12 639 630	5.9	11.9	4.3	3.5	3.5	6.6	63.1	369.8	180.5	137.0	1 231	1 055
Midland, MI	2 175	9 622 686	11.4	7.8	3.3	4.0	3.3	5.7	62.5	271.7	113.5	103.5	1 235	1 220
Midland, TX	7 075	27 853 270	5.2	7.7	3.9	1.9	29.9	1.6	47.9	800.8	131.1	362.9	2 393	1 787
Milwaukee-Waukesha-West Allis, WI	53 007	250 453 387	5.4	13.5	4.4	4.2	8.1	4.6	57.7	7 417.1	2 812.4	3 111.6	1 986	1 860
Minneapolis-St. Paul-Bloomington, MN	104 532	577 809 573	7.1	9.9	1.7	3.7	7.6	5.5	63.0	15 990.0	6 976.7	5 332.5	1 558	1 450
Missoula, MT	3 035	11 623 602	8.8	11.6	6.2	6.3	5.7	3.6	55.2	333.0	140.7	131.9	1 189	1 156
Mobile, AL	15 334	47 151 677	5.5	11.5	5.1	4.9	9.2	7.3	53.7	1 405.0	626.1	561.4	1 356	491

1. Based on the resident population estimated as of July 1 of the year shown.

Area name	Local government finances, 2012 (cont.)									Government employment, 2013			Presidential election,[2] 2012		
	Direct general expenditure							Debt outstanding					Percent of vote cast:		
			Percent of total for:												
	Total (mil dol)	Per capita[1] (dollars)	Education	Health and hospitals	Police protection	Public welfare	Highways	Total (mil dol)	Per capita[1] (dollars)	Federal civilian	Federal military	State and local	Democratic	Republican	All other
	185	186	187	188	189	190	191	192	193	194	195	196	197	198	199
Joplin, MO	524.5	3 009	58.0	8.8	4.8	0.2	5.1	349.6	2 005	439	637	9 445	27.4	70.5	2.2
Kahului-Wailuku-Lahaina, HI	264.1	1 668	0.0	0.0	15.8	6.0	2.7	281.6	1 779	855	1 151	8 919	74.1	23.8	2.1
Kalamazoo-Portage, MI	1 323.6	4 011	48.7	15.6	6.2	1.0	5.0	1 469.4	4 452	884	563	19 128	54.7	44.1	1.2
Kankakee, IL	442.3	3 912	52.1	0.7	6.1	0.1	5.9	327.2	2 894	229	217	6 182	47.5	50.8	1.7
Kansas City, MO-KS	8 722.0	4 278	43.2	9.9	7.0	0.6	5.4	16 793.0	8 237	26 727	11 758	123 705	47.9	50.2	1.9
Kennewick-Richland, WA	1 130.0	4 213	43.9	21.1	4.0	0.0	3.7	7 044.2	26 261	1 242	757	17 225	35.8	61.8	2.4
Killeen-Temple, TX	1 411.2	3 357	57.9	3.8	4.8	0.5	5.9	2 196.8	5 226	10 811	42 180	26 567	38.3	60.4	1.3
Kingsport-Bristol-Bristol, TN-VA	860.9	2 786	50.0	3.8	6.6	1.8	4.1	782.5	2 532	949	983	15 890	26.4	72.0	1.6
Kingston, NY	1 119.8	6 160	51.1	2.0	2.8	12.1	5.4	695.1	3 823	442	299	13 143	60.3	37.4	2.3
Knoxville, TN	2 428.1	2 862	44.3	9.6	6.5	0.1	3.1	4 983.9	5 875	5 593	2 807	52 458	31.2	67.0	1.8
Kokomo, IN	406.5	4 907	32.7	36.7	3.9	0.3	1.8	200.3	2 417	234	265	5 031	41.7	56.0	2.3
La Crosse-Onalaska, WI-MN	720.8	5 328	43.6	2.8	4.0	21.7	5.6	467.2	3 453	528	384	10 836	56.8	41.5	1.7
Lafayette, LA	1 702.8	3 589	44.6	7.6	6.9	0.4	5.4	2 036.0	4 292	1 354	2 307	24 687	31.3	67.1	1.6
Lafayette-West Lafayette, IN	486.9	2 359	51.4	0.5	5.8	0.7	6.1	413.5	2 003	573	677	24 748	44.6	52.8	2.5
Lake Charles, LA	995.9	4 950	38.4	7.2	6.5	0.4	6.8	2 332.0	11 591	551	1 053	14 151	33.7	64.5	1.9
Lake Havasu City-Kingman, AZ	555.1	2 730	33.9	2.7	6.9	0.1	8.7	627.7	3 087	488	437	7 431	27.9	70.2	1.9
Lakeland-Winter Haven, FL	1 992.7	3 234	48.6	3.2	8.2	1.6	5.5	2 776.3	4 506	1 068	1 238	26 981	46.1	52.9	1.0
Lancaster, PA	2 018.4	3 831	55.1	5.4	4.3	5.1	3.3	3 447.0	6 543	1 209	1 383	19 281	39.8	58.7	1.5
Lansing-East Lansing, MI	1 885.3	4 048	47.2	10.6	4.5	3.4	4.3	2 304.1	4 947	2 009	934	46 297	57.2	41.5	1.3
Laredo, TX	1 204.4	4 647	58.3	1.3	6.0	0.4	1.5	1 569.6	6 056	3 385	549	18 217	76.6	22.6	0.9
Las Cruces, NM	719.6	3 356	57.5	1.3	6.7	1.9	4.1	440.1	2 052	3 757	591	16 868	55.9	41.1	3.0
Las Vegas-Henderson-Paradise, NV	9 171.7	4 584	29.1	8.3	9.6	2.7	7.2	21 727.8	10 860	12 515	15 775	81 774	56.4	41.8	1.8
Lawrence, KS	474.7	4 206	28.6	35.1	4.9	0.0	3.3	544.9	4 828	460	488	14 827	61.0	36.3	2.8
Lawton, OK	533.8	4 027	37.6	38.9	4.3	0.0	3.4	253.8	1 915	4 347	12 317	10 763	40.4	59.6	0.0
Lebanon, PA	507.4	3 752	47.7	2.2	2.9	15.0	5.1	705.4	5 215	2 829	354	5 424	35.2	63.4	1.4
Lewiston, ID-WA	188.3	3 065	43.4	3.1	7.2	0.1	7.4	47.1	767	244	208	4 990	39.1	58.4	2.5
Lewiston-Auburn, ME	348.5	3 239	53.0	0.2	4.0	0.4	5.6	353.5	3 285	265	346	5 019	54.8	42.1	3.1
Lexington-Fayette, KY	1 363.2	2 811	49.9	3.2	5.3	0.7	2.2	2 544.8	5 247	4 455	1 603	45 987	43.8	54.0	2.2
Lima, OH	385.4	3 665	49.5	5.4	6.9	4.3	6.7	180.7	1 719	324	258	5 860	37.1	61.2	1.7
Lincoln, NE	1 130.3	3 642	53.2	1.9	4.3	0.9	6.9	2 872.1	9 255	3 059	1 172	30 849	47.7	50.0	2.3
Little Rock-North Little Rock-Conway, AR	2 292.8	3 195	53.1	2.7	6.0	0.0	4.2	3 061.0	4 265	9 557	8 758	61 870	43.2	54.5	2.3
Logan, UT-ID	308.4	2 404	52.6	4.4	6.1	0.3	5.4	194.5	1 516	376	546	11 551	13.7	84.0	2.3
Longview, TX	736.4	3 399	58.8	4.2	5.0	0.0	4.6	1 187.1	5 479	445	438	11 102	26.4	72.7	0.9
Longview, WA	424.6	4 163	38.6	3.9	5.4	0.0	4.9	609.4	5 974	225	281	5 400	50.9	46.5	2.6
Los Angeles-Long Beach-Anaheim, CA	74 228.5	5 687	36.2	9.6	7.8	8.4	3.3	106 636.6	8 170	58 662	23 690	637 188	63.4	34.1	2.5
Anaheim-Santa Ana-Irvine, CA Div 11244	13 915.7	4 503	41.4	2.9	7.7	7.3	4.5	22 316.3	7 222	11 036	5 519	134 370	45.6	51.9	2.5
Los Angeles-Long Beach-Glendale, CA Div 31084	60 312.8	6 054	35.0	11.1	7.8	8.7	3.1	84 320.3	8 464	47 626	18 171	502 818	69.7	27.8	2.5
Louisville/Jefferson County, KY-IN	4 180.4	3 341	44.5	11.9	4.0	0.3	2.5	7 079.6	5 658	9 098	4 301	68 444	48.1	50.3	1.6
Lubbock, TX	1 388.9	4 666	35.4	31.5	4.7	0.1	2.3	2 311.9	7 767	1 328	671	26 839	28.9	69.6	1.6
Lynchburg, VA	701.3	2 747	47.7	1.7	5.7	7.2	1.9	641.2	2 511	575	821	13 476	34.6	63.8	1.6
Macon, GA	816.9	3 510	46.8	7.0	6.4	0.3	2.9	577.8	2 483	1 168	739	13 611	51.4	47.8	0.8
Madera, CA	649.2	4 265	45.6	3.7	3.9	8.8	6.2	475.5	3 124	311	233	9 482	40.2	57.3	2.5
Madison, WI	2 933.1	4 725	47.0	1.8	6.0	8.3	7.1	3 254.4	5 243	5 466	1 810	79 336	68.9	29.7	1.4
Manchester-Nashua, NH	1 496.1	3 713	52.0	0.6	6.1	3.8	4.7	1 157.0	2 872	3 900	1 376	18 007	49.7	48.6	1.6
Manhattan, KS	320.7	3 279	52.2	2.1	6.0	0.0	6.6	601.2	6 146	526	414	12 359	37.0	60.0	3.0
Mankato-North Mankato, MN	409.8	4 181	36.2	5.3	4.8	5.7	13.5	455.8	4 650	303	385	8 039	52.9	43.9	3.2
Mansfield, OH	480.9	3 920	52.3	8.7	5.0	4.8	5.5	209.0	1 703	554	298	7 241	39.3	58.7	2.0
McAllen-Edinburg-Mission, TX	3 161.8	3 920	67.1	2.0	3.8	0.5	2.9	3 738.4	4 635	3 777	1 814	50 344	70.4	28.6	1.0
Medford, OR	678.0	3 285	42.6	5.3	8.6	0.0	6.1	887.0	4 297	1 686	570	8 760	45.8	50.5	3.7
Memphis, TN-MS-AR	5 764.4	4 296	46.3	6.7	8.6	0.9	2.8	6 748.2	5 030	14 773	5 918	72 375	55.7	43.5	0.9
Merced, CA	1 403.1	5 349	48.6	3.6	4.1	10.0	2.7	901.0	3 435	746	412	16 241	53.2	44.4	2.4
Miami-Fort Lauderdale-West Palm Beach, FL	31 257.3	5 424	25.8	15.2	8.8	2.5	2.0	39 629.0	6 877	33 756	14 143	267 177	62.6	36.9	0.5
Fort Lauderdale-Pompano Beach-Deerfield Beach, FL Div 22744	10 214.0	5 627	24.6	26.3	10.2	1.2	1.4	8 639.5	4 760	7 192	3 954	92 921	67.2	32.3	0.5
Miami-Miami Beach-Kendall, FL Div 33124	14 468.1	5 584	25.8	12.2	7.5	3.5	2.2	23 549.3	9 089	20 053	7 437	119 756	61.6	37.9	0.4
West Palm Beach-Boca Raton-Delray Beach, FL Div 48424	6 575.2	4 847	27.6	4.7	9.3	2.5	2.5	7 440.3	5 485	6 511	2 752	54 500	58.2	41.2	0.6
Michigan City-La Porte, IN	330.9	2 974	53.0	1.0	4.1	0.3	2.3	311.4	2 799	172	360	6 755	55.2	42.6	2.2
Midland, MI	272.5	3 250	51.0	2.8	4.1	2.1	7.6	318.6	3 800	136	143	3 323	41.8	57.3	0.9
Midland, TX	864.5	5 700	32.3	45.1	3.2	0.0	1.2	654.6	4 316	524	328	8 368	18.5	80.2	1.4
Milwaukee-Waukesha-West Allis, WI	7 419.0	4 735	44.0	7.8	7.8	3.4	5.7	8 456.0	5 396	10 524	4 654	78 072	52.1	46.9	1.0
Minneapolis-St. Paul-Bloomington, MN	16 677.1	4 873	39.7	6.9	5.5	5.4	7.0	24 523.9	7 166	20 410	12 948	222 669	54.7	43.0	2.3
Missoula, MT	338.7	3 052	44.0	5.5	7.0	0.8	5.2	188.8	1 701	1 338	547	9 196	57.4	39.6	3.0
Mobile, AL	1 433.8	3 464	41.2	6.0	6.8	0.5	8.3	1 386.2	3 349	2 634	2 829	23 568	45.0	54.2	0.8

1. Based on the resident population estimated as of July 1 of the year shown. 2.

CBSA/ DIV code[1]	Area name	Land area,[2] 2010 (sq km)	Population 2014: Total persons	Population 2014: Rank	Population 2014: Per square kilometer	Population characteristics, 2013: Race alone or in combination, not Hispanic or Latino (percent): White	Black	American Indian, Alaska Native	Asian and Pacific Islander	Percent Hispanic or Latino[3]	Age (percent): Under 5 years	5 to 17 years	18 to 24 years	25 to 34 years	35 to 44 years	45 to 54 years
		1	2	3	4	5	6	7	8	9	10	11	12	13	14	15
33700	Modesto, CA	3 872	531 997	103	137.4	47.3	3.2	1.3	7.5	43.4	7.4	20.2	10.4	13.9	12.6	12.9
33740	Monroe, LA	3 852	178 864	232	46.4	60.8	36.1	0.6	1.2	2.4	7.0	18.3	10.5	13.7	12.0	12.7
33780	Monroe, MI	1 423	149 824	274	105.3	93.5	3.0	0.9	0.9	3.3	5.5	17.4	8.4	10.9	12.3	15.6
33860	Montgomery, AL	7 027	373 141	141	53.1	51.4	43.9	0.7	2.2	3.1	6.5	17.6	10.4	13.8	13.0	13.5
34060	Morgantown, WV	2 613	137 251	293	52.5	92.6	3.9	0.5	2.9	1.7	5.0	11.8	20.0	16.0	11.5	11.8
34100	Morristown, TN	1 127	115 713	331	102.7	88.2	3.9	0.7	1.0	7.6	5.8	16.6	8.7	11.2	12.7	14.3
34580	Mount Vernon-Anacortes, WA	4 484	120 365	320	26.8	77.8	1.1	2.8	3.0	17.6	6.2	16.4	8.4	12.1	11.4	13.0
34620	Muncie, IN	1 016	117 074	326	115.2	89.5	8.1	0.7	1.7	2.0	5.2	14.0	20.1	10.9	10.5	12.0
34740	Muskegon, MI	1 293	172 344	236	133.3	79.3	15.4	1.6	1.0	5.1	6.3	17.8	9.2	12.3	11.9	14.1
34820	Myrtle Beach-Conway-North Myrtle Beach, NC-SC	5 131	417 668	126	81.4	79.9	13.6	1.0	1.5	5.7	5.1	13.9	8.0	11.5	11.6	13.0
34900	Napa, CA	1 938	141 667	288	73.1	56.5	2.4	1.1	9.0	33.3	5.7	16.6	9.1	12.3	12.6	13.8
34940	Naples-Immokalee-Marco Island, FL	5 176	348 777	148	67.4	65.5	7.0	0.4	1.7	26.2	4.9	13.6	6.9	10.0	10.3	12.4
34980	Nashville-Davidson—Murfreesboro—Franklin, TN	16 320	1 792 649	36	109.8	75.2	16.1	0.7	3.0	6.8	6.5	17.3	9.7	14.7	13.9	14.0
35100	New Bern, NC	3 927	127 534	305	32.5	68.8	23.1	1.0	2.9	6.4	6.7	15.2	12.2	12.8	10.5	11.9
35300	New Haven-Milford, CT	1 566	861 277	64	550.0	67.1	13.1	0.6	4.4	16.4	5.3	16.0	10.0	13.1	12.3	14.9
35380	New Orleans-Metairie, LA	8 294	1 251 849	45	150.9	53.8	35.2	0.8	3.3	8.3	6.3	16.4	9.2	15.1	12.5	14.1
35620	New York-Newark-Jersey City, NY-NJ-PA	21 480	20 092 883	1	935.4	49.4	16.7	0.5	11.4	23.4	6.2	16.0	9.3	14.5	13.5	14.5
35620	Dutchess County-Putnam County, NY Div 20524	2 658	396 066	X	149.0	76.8	8.7	0.5	4.1	11.6	4.7	16.2	10.6	10.7	12.3	16.9
35620	Nassau County-Suffolk County, NY Div 35004	3 099	2 861 595	X	923.4	67.9	9.6	0.4	6.7	16.7	5.4	17.1	9.1	11.2	12.6	16.0
35620	Newark, NJ-PA Div 35084	6 430	2 508 124	X	390.1	54.9	19.8	0.4	7.8	18.5	5.9	17.6	8.6	11.9	13.6	16.1
35620	New York-Jersey City-White Plains, NY-NJ Div 35614	9 293	14 327 098	X	1 541.7	44.0	17.8	0.5	13.1	26.0	6.4	15.6	9.5	15.7	13.6	13.9
35660	Niles-Benton Harbor, MI	1 470	155 233	260	105.6	77.5	16.2	1.2	2.4	5.0	6.2	16.6	8.6	11.1	11.5	14.3
35840	North Port-Sarasota-Bradenton, FL	3 364	748 708	73	222.6	79.8	7.2	0.5	2.1	11.7	4.5	13.0	6.6	9.1	9.9	12.9
35980	Norwich-New London, CT	1 722	273 676	172	158.9	79.2	7.2	1.8	5.3	9.6	5.2	15.5	10.4	12.6	11.8	15.3
36100	Ocala, FL	4 104	339 167	150	82.6	73.9	13.1	0.8	2.0	11.7	5.0	13.9	7.3	10.0	10.0	12.6
36140	Ocean City, NJ	651	95 344	362	146.5	87.4	5.1	0.5	1.5	7.0	4.9	13.1	8.3	10.1	9.6	14.5
36220	Odessa, TX	2 325	153 904	265	66.2	38.1	4.5	0.8	1.1	56.4	8.9	20.7	11.2	15.8	12.0	11.7
36260	Ogden-Clearfield, UT	18 725	632 293	87	33.8	84.3	1.6	0.9	3.2	12.0	8.8	23.1	9.6	14.8	13.0	11.1
36420	Oklahoma City, OK	14 274	1 336 767	42	93.7	70.2	11.8	6.7	3.8	12.1	7.1	17.8	10.6	15.0	12.6	12.7
36500	Olympia-Tumwater, WA	1 870	265 851	178	142.2	81.2	4.4	2.7	8.7	8.1	6.1	16.2	9.0	14.2	12.9	13.3
36540	Omaha-Council Bluffs, NE-IA	11 266	904 421	60	80.3	79.7	8.8	1.0	3.1	9.5	7.4	18.6	9.0	15.0	12.9	13.5
36740	Orlando-Kissimmee-Sanford, FL	9 009	2 321 418	26	257.7	52.5	16.3	0.6	5.1	27.3	6.0	16.7	10.5	14.6	13.5	13.9
36780	Oshkosh-Neenah, WI	1 125	169 511	242	150.7	91.1	2.5	0.9	3.1	3.8	5.7	15.4	12.5	13.1	12.0	14.4
36980	Owensboro, KY	2 327	116 506	329	50.1	92.4	5.4	0.4	1.0	2.5	6.6	17.8	8.4	12.1	12.2	14.0
37100	Oxnard-Thousand Oaks-Ventura, CA	4 774	846 178	66	177.2	49.3	2.2	0.8	8.6	41.5	6.4	18.1	10.1	12.9	12.8	14.3
37340	Palm Bay-Melbourne-Titusville, FL	2 631	556 885	97	211.7	78.2	11.0	0.9	3.2	9.0	4.7	14.2	7.9	10.5	10.5	15.2
37460	Panama City, FL	3 425	194 929	222	56.9	80.2	12.6	1.5	3.2	5.3	6.0	15.0	9.1	13.8	12.3	14.7
37620	Parkersburg-Vienna, WV	1 551	92 082	365	59.4	97.0	1.9	0.7	0.9	0.9	5.6	15.8	7.7	11.3	12.3	14.7
37860	Pensacola-Ferry Pass-Brent, FL	4 320	474 081	109	109.7	74.2	17.9	1.7	4.0	5.2	6.0	15.7	11.5	13.5	11.6	14.0
37900	Peoria, IL	6 400	380 040	138	59.4	85.0	10.4	0.6	2.6	3.2	6.4	17.1	8.9	12.9	12.3	13.3
37980	Philadelphia-Camden-Wilmington, PA-NJ-DE-MD	11 919	6 051 170	6	507.7	65.2	21.4	0.6	6.1	8.5	6.1	16.4	9.7	13.7	12.5	14.6
37980	Camden, NJ Div 15804	3 475	1 251 711	X	360.2	69.0	16.8	0.6	5.4	10.2	5.9	17.1	8.9	12.6	12.8	15.4
37980	Montgomery County-Bucks County-Chester County, PA Div 33874	4 760	1 956 326	X	411.0	82.5	7.2	0.4	6.1	5.3	5.5	17.0	8.2	11.6	12.6	15.7
37980	Philadelphia, PA Div 37964	823	2 123 257	X	2 579.9	46.5	37.1	0.7	7.0	10.6	6.7	15.6	11.5	16.3	12.1	12.9
37980	Wilmington, DE-MD-NJ Div 48864	2 861	719 876	X	251.6	67.0	21.4	0.7	4.6	8.3	6.1	16.5	10.2	13.3	12.6	14.8
38060	Phoenix-Mesa-Scottsdale, AZ	37 725	4 489 109	12	119.0	59.4	5.7	2.4	4.7	29.9	6.7	18.6	9.6	14.1	13.4	12.8
38220	Pine Bluff, AR	5 257	94 716	363	18.0	49.1	48.3	0.8	1.0	2.1	5.9	16.8	10.4	13.0	11.9	13.9
38300	Pittsburgh, PA	13 679	2 355 968	23	172.2	87.9	9.3	0.5	2.4	1.5	5.1	14.4	8.9	12.7	11.6	14.6
38340	Pittsfield, MA	2 400	128 715	304	53.6	91.7	3.8	0.6	2.0	3.8	4.5	13.8	9.7	10.3	10.7	15.1
38540	Pocatello, ID	2 880	83 347	372	28.9	87.4	1.1	3.5	2.3	7.6	7.5	19.4	10.9	15.5	11.6	11.1
38860	Portland-South Portland, ME	5 386	523 552	104	97.2	94.5	2.3	0.9	2.2	1.7	4.9	15.1	8.4	11.9	12.4	15.8
38900	Portland-Vancouver-Hillsboro, OR-WA	17 311	2 348 247	24	135.7	78.4	3.7	1.7	8.5	11.3	6.1	16.7	8.5	14.9	14.6	13.6
38940	Port St. Lucie, FL	2 889	444 420	115	153.8	67.8	15.2	0.6	2.1	15.7	4.9	14.9	7.4	10.1	10.9	13.7
39140	Prescott, AZ	21 040	218 844	199	10.4	82.8	1.1	2.3	1.6	13.9	4.2	13.5	6.8	8.9	9.0	12.6
39300	Providence-Warwick, RI-MA	4 111	1 609 367	38	391.5	80.4	5.9	0.9	3.5	11.2	5.2	15.5	10.7	12.6	12.3	15.0
39340	Provo-Orem, UT	13 975	571 460	94	40.9	85.7	0.9	0.9	3.8	10.9	10.3	24.7	16.5	14.7	11.9	8.3
39380	Pueblo, CO	6 180	161 875	253	26.2	54.3	2.2	1.3	1.2	42.3	6.1	17.4	9.7	12.3	11.7	12.9
39460	Punta Gorda, FL	1 762	168 474	245	95.6	86.1	6.2	0.7	1.8	6.5	3.2	10.2	5.6	7.2	8.0	12.2
39540	Racine, WI	861	195 163	220	226.7	75.1	12.2	0.8	1.5	12.3	6.3	17.8	8.3	12.1	12.3	15.4
39580	Raleigh, NC	5 485	1 242 974	46	226.6	64.1	21.0	0.8	5.7	10.3	6.6	18.8	9.2	14.1	15.6	14.6
39660	Rapid City, SD	20 214	143 638	285	7.1	85.2	2.3	9.4	1.8	4.4	6.7	16.9	9.3	13.8	11.2	13.0
39740	Reading, PA	2 218	413 691	128	186.5	76.1	5.0	0.4	1.8	18.1	5.9	17.1	10.1	11.6	12.1	14.8

1. CBSA = Core Based Statistical Area. DIV = Metropolitan Division. See Appendix A for explanation. See Appendix B for list of metropolitan areas identified by type. 2. Dry land or land partially or temporarily covered by water. 3. May be of any race.

Area name	Population, 2013 (cont.): Age (percent) (cont.): 55 to 64 years	65 to 74 years	75 years and over	Percent female	Population change and components of change, 2000–2014: Total persons: 2000	2010	Percent change: 2000–2010	2010–2014	Components of change, 2010–2014: Births	Deaths	Net migration	Households, 2013: Number	Persons per household	Percent: Family households	Female family householder[1]	One person
	16	17	18	19	20	21	22	23	24	25	26	27	28	29	30	31
Modesto, CA	10.8	6.6	5.1	50.5	446 997	514 453	15.1	3.4	32 444	15 917	938	167 411	3.11	73.7	17.1	20.8
Monroe, LA	12.1	7.6	6.0	51.9	170 053	176 441	3.8	1.3	10 782	7 277	-1 117	65 989	2.56	67.2	19.6	29.9
Monroe, MI	14.7	8.7	6.5	50.7	145 945	152 021	4.2	-1.4	6 446	5 844	-2 849	58 479	2.55	65.8	11.2	28.3
Montgomery, AL	12.0	7.7	5.6	52.1	346 528	374 536	8.1	-0.4	20 492	14 379	-7 694	141 137	2.57	65.4	18.3	31.1
Morgantown, WV	11.7	7.0	5.2	48.5	111 200	129 709	16.6	5.8	5 848	4 121	5 744	50 295	2.52	57.5	9.1	32.9
Morristown, TN	12.9	10.8	7.0	51.0	102 422	113 951	11.3	1.4	5 615	5 350	1 256	42 874	2.63	69.4	12.4	27.0
Mount Vernon-Anacortes, WA	14.3	10.5	7.6	50.4	102 979	116 901	13.5	3.0	6 156	4 695	1 856	45 234	2.59	67.7	11.1	25.4
Muncie, IN	11.6	8.6	7.1	51.8	118 769	117 671	-0.9	-0.5	5 271	4 978	-726	46 431	2.37	58.6	12.4	28.8
Muskegon, MI	13.7	8.3	6.5	50.6	170 200	172 188	1.2	0.1	9 018	7 006	-1 850	65 559	2.51	67.6	14.9	25.7
Myrtle Beach-Conway-North Myrtle Beach, NC-SC	15.5	13.9	7.4	51.4	269 772	376 722	39.6	10.9	17 442	16 830	38 740	162 547	2.47	67.8	12.3	26.7
Napa, CA	13.4	9.1	7.4	50.2	124 279	136 484	9.8	3.8	6 314	5 106	3 924	47 482	2.87	68.3	9.7	25.3
Naples-Immokalee-Marco Island, FL	13.0	15.2	13.6	50.7	251 377	321 520	27.9	8.5	13 602	12 684	25 365	130 614	2.57	65.7	9.9	29.3
Nashville-Davidson—Murfreesboro—Franklin, TN	12.0	7.1	4.8	51.2	1 381 287	1 670 890	21.0	7.3	96 440	55 846	79 681	662 187	2.60	65.0	12.3	28.7
New Bern, NC	12.9	10.1	7.7	49.4	114 751	126 802	10.5	0.6	7 629	5 265	-1 861	48 962	2.54	71.2	13.3	23.6
New Haven-Milford, CT	13.1	8.2	7.1	51.7	824 008	862 477	4.7	-0.1	38 580	32 109	-6 836	321 048	2.59	63.7	14.6	30.9
New Orleans-Metairie, LA	13.2	7.7	5.5	51.5	1 337 726	1 189 866	-11.1	5.2	65 920	44 816	39 817	479 366	2.55	62.1	17.6	31.9
New York-Newark-Jersey City, NY-NJ-PA	12.1	7.6	6.3	51.6	18 944 519	19 567 410	3.3	2.7	1 071 626	601 421	71 119	7 080 691	2.76	66.1	15.3	28.1
Dutchess County-Putnam County, NY Div 20524	13.8	8.4	6.5	50.3	375 895	397 198	5.7	-0.3	15 197	12 972	-3 266	140 003	2.68	70.1	12.0	24.5
Nassau County-Suffolk County, NY Div 35004	13.1	8.3	7.2	51.1	2 753 913	2 832 882	2.9	1.0	127 598	96 119	361	935 546	2.99	74.7	12.3	21.5
Newark, NJ-PA Div 35084	12.8	7.5	6.0	51.3	2 396 333	2 471 171	3.1	1.6	120 414	77 399	-3 737	876 304	2.79	70.4	14.0	25.1
New York-Jersey City-White Plains, NY-NJ Div 35614	11.8	7.4	6.2	51.8	13 418 378	13 866 159	3.3	3.3	808 417	414 931	77 761	5 128 838	2.71	63.7	16.1	29.9
Niles-Benton Harbor, MI	14.3	9.5	7.9	51.2	162 453	156 813	-3.5	-1.0	7 791	6 971	-2 430	59 239	2.54	65.4	13.3	30.2
North Port-Sarasota-Bradenton, FL	14.6	15.3	14.2	52.0	589 959	702 281	19.0	6.6	26 719	36 475	53 878	302 518	2.39	61.4	9.5	32.4
Norwich-New London, CT	13.7	8.7	6.9	50.0	259 088	274 055	5.8	-0.1	11 799	9 737	-2 139	106 886	2.45	66.5	12.9	26.4
Ocala, FL	13.9	15.3	12.0	52.0	258 916	331 298	28.0	2.4	14 131	19 089	12 313	133 098	2.47	66.7	13.2	28.3
Ocean City, NJ	16.3	13.0	10.4	51.2	102 326	97 265	-4.9	-2.0	3 914	5 352	-264	38 210	2.44	64.0	7.6	32.1
Odessa, TX	10.0	5.5	4.2	49.8	121 123	137 130	13.2	12.2	11 401	4 890	10 226	51 962	2.84	73.3	19.9	21.1
Ogden-Clearfield, UT	9.6	5.6	4.4	49.7	485 401	597 159	23.0	5.9	45 783	14 485	3 828	195 180	3.16	78.1	9.5	18.3
Oklahoma City, OK	11.7	7.2	5.3	50.7	1 095 421	1 252 987	14.4	6.7	80 111	46 181	48 743	493 315	2.61	64.7	12.4	29.3
Olympia-Tumwater, WA	13.7	8.7	5.9	51.0	207 355	252 264	21.7	5.4	13 167	8 353	8 739	99 815	2.59	65.6	9.0	27.0
Omaha-Council Bluffs, NE-IA	11.8	6.7	5.2	50.5	767 041	865 350	12.8	4.5	55 860	26 829	10 766	343 054	2.56	64.8	11.8	29.0
Orlando-Kissimmee-Sanford, FL	11.4	7.7	5.7	51.0	1 644 561	2 134 411	29.8	8.8	114 387	65 679	135 950	780 174	2.85	65.9	13.8	26.5
Oshkosh-Neenah, WI	12.7	7.5	6.8	49.7	156 763	166 994	6.5	1.5	8 013	6 027	527	68 985	2.33	60.3	9.3	31.7
Owensboro, KY	13.0	8.9	7.0	51.1	109 875	114 752	4.4	1.5	6 589	4 989	181	45 776	2.49	68.7	10.9	27.8
Oxnard-Thousand Oaks-Ventura, CA	12.2	7.4	5.8	50.4	753 197	823 318	9.3	2.8	45 529	22 396	-544	265 788	3.11	73.7	12.1	20.2
Palm Bay-Melbourne-Titusville, FL	14.9	11.7	10.3	51.2	476 230	543 376	14.1	2.5	21 451	26 811	17 928	218 325	2.50	63.8	12.7	30.3
Panama City, FL	13.0	9.1	6.9	49.5	161 549	184 715	14.3	5.5	10 054	7 835	7 684	69 032	2.71	67.1	12.8	26.4
Parkersburg-Vienna, WV	14.5	10.4	7.7	51.5	93 859	92 673	-1.3	-0.6	4 154	4 616	-30	38 799	2.36	62.7	10.2	33.0
Pensacola-Ferry Pass-Brent, FL	12.8	8.7	6.3	49.8	412 153	448 991	8.9	5.6	24 147	18 689	19 143	172 663	2.56	63.6	11.9	29.4
Peoria, IL	13.2	8.4	7.3	51.0	366 899	379 186	3.3	0.2	20 810	15 783	-3 881	152 051	2.46	65.0	10.9	30.2
Philadelphia-Camden-Wilmington, PA-NJ-DE-MD	12.8	7.7	6.5	51.7	5 687 147	5 965 343	4.9	1.4	309 611	224 752	5 004	2 218 312	2.65	64.0	14.2	30.1
Camden, NJ Div 15804	13.0	7.9	6.4	51.3	1 186 999	1 250 679	5.4	0.1	59 352	45 140	-12 462	451 883	2.72	69.7	14.4	25.3
Montgomery County-Bucks County-Chester County, PA Div 33874	13.8	8.4	7.2	51.1	1 781 233	1 924 009	8.0	1.7	86 616	69 879	15 757	724 010	2.63	69.5	9.6	25.4
Philadelphia, PA Div 37964	11.8	6.9	6.1	52.6	2 068 414	2 084 985	0.8	1.8	127 246	84 675	-1 729	782 213	2.61	54.8	18.3	37.9
Wilmington, DE-MD-NJ Div 48864	12.8	7.8	5.9	51.4	650 501	705 670	8.5	2.0	36 397	25 058	3 438	260 206	2.68	66.3	14.3	27.9
Phoenix-Mesa-Scottsdale, AZ	11.0	8.0	5.8	50.3	3 251 876	4 192 887	28.9	7.1	252 055	124 226	161 289	1 553 429	2.79	66.3	12.8	26.7
Pine Bluff, AR	13.2	8.4	6.4	49.3	107 341	100 258	-6.6	-5.5	4 923	4 462	-5 965	35 484	2.41	64.9	18.1	30.3
Pittsburgh, PA	14.8	9.3	8.7	51.5	2 431 087	2 356 285	-3.1	0.0	100 888	114 531	16 940	988 106	2.33	61.0	11.2	32.9
Pittsfield, MA	15.7	10.7	9.6	51.7	134 953	131 219	-2.8	-1.9	4 856	6 018	-1 183	54 963	2.23	60.2	12.5	32.8
Pocatello, ID	11.8	7.1	5.3	50.2	75 565	82 839	9.6	0.6	5 606	2 720	-2 323	30 265	2.68	66.0	11.7	26.3
Portland-South Portland, ME	14.9	9.4	7.3	51.4	487 568	514 098	5.4	1.8	20 970	19 261	7 367	213 413	2.38	62.0	9.3	29.4
Portland-Vancouver-Hillsboro, OR-WA	12.8	7.6	5.2	50.6	1 927 881	2 226 009	15.5	5.5	117 482	67 820	70 835	881 822	2.58	63.6	10.5	27.7
Port St. Lucie, FL	13.7	12.7	11.6	51.0	319 426	424 107	32.8	4.8	17 655	19 572	21 092	165 882	2.60	66.7	13.4	28.0
Prescott, AZ	17.6	16.1	11.3	51.2	167 517	211 033	26.0	3.7	7 763	11 180	10 862	91 064	2.32	60.7	8.5	33.3
Providence-Warwick, RI-MA	13.2	8.3	7.2	51.5	1 582 997	1 600 852	1.1	0.5	70 850	61 604	-155	618 975	2.50	64.4	14.1	29.5
Provo-Orem, UT	6.5	4.1	3.0	49.6	376 774	526 810	39.8	8.5	51 501	8 991	2 163	149 549	3.66	81.6	8.8	12.8
Pueblo, CO	13.4	9.1	7.5	50.8	141 472	159 063	12.4	1.8	8 081	6 902	1 664	62 604	2.50	65.6	15.3	30.0
Punta Gorda, FL	16.7	19.9	17.2	51.4	141 627	159 978	13.0	5.3	4 312	9 854	13 557	69 035	2.33	64.5	7.0	28.0
Racine, WI	13.6	7.9	6.4	50.4	188 831	195 408	3.5	-0.1	10 253	7 014	-3 356	72 057	2.64	64.5	11.4	30.1
Raleigh, NC	10.8	6.3	4.0	51.2	797 071	1 130 490	41.8	10.0	65 387	27 302	72 742	449 589	2.64	66.6	12.4	25.7
Rapid City, SD	14.0	8.4	6.7	49.6	120 093	134 598	12.1	6.7	8 232	4 441	5 120	55 969	2.45	65.7	11.1	27.2
Reading, PA	12.9	8.3	7.3	50.8	373 638	411 442	10.1	0.5	20 544	15 526	-2 363	153 271	2.61	68.1	10.9	24.7

1. No spouse present.

Area name	Persons in group quarters, 2014	Daytime population, 2013		Births, 2014		Deaths, 2014		Persons under 65 with no health insurance 2013		Medicare, 2014			Serious crimes known to police,[2] 2013	
		Number	Employ-ment/ residence ratio	Total	Rate[1]	Number	Rate[1]	Number	Percent	Eligible for Medicare	Enrolled in Medicare Advantage	Enrolled in a Medicare prescription drug plan	Total Number	Total Rate[3]
	32	33	34	35	36	37	38	39	40	41	42	43	44	45
Modesto, CA	6 310	550 826	1.16	7 550	14.2	3 747	7.0	95 255	20.7	77 509	32 428	30 493	23 254	4 433
Monroe, LA	6 022	189 158	1.16	2 521	14.1	1 791	10.0	28 286	19.0	30 962	5 853	16 504	9 572	5 526
Monroe, MI	1 462	160 276	1.32	1 453	9.7	1 361	9.1	13 291	10.5	28 478	8 438	17 853	3 788	2 577
Montgomery, AL	15 010	391 147	1.10	4 705	12.6	3 455	9.3	44 575	14.4	66 711	18 927	25 832	13 850	3 693
Morgantown, WV	9 662	148 833	1.22	1 391	10.1	989	7.2	18 678	17.0	19 488	5 415	8 879	2 324	1 854
Morristown, TN	2 645	126 303	1.31	1 296	11.2	1 273	11.0	17 296	18.6	26 299	10 496	9 874	3 858	3 345
Mount Vernon-Anacortes, WA	1 627	129 844	1.28	1 458	12.1	1 116	9.3	18 026	18.6	25 859	7 784	9 573	5 390	4 529
Muncie, IN	9 139	128 204	1.26	1 226	10.5	1 159	9.9	14 921	16.4	22 784	3 564	13 713	4 023	3 422
Muskegon, MI	6 496	183 547	1.25	2 100	12.2	1 666	9.7	17 395	12.2	35 550	13 615	15 802	6 794	4 002
Myrtle Beach-Conway-North Myrtle Beach, NC-SC	3 823	422 132	1.12	4 105	9.8	4 178	10.0	72 654	23.1	106 222	17 225	55 071	19 418	4 872
Napa, CA	5 028	161 236	1.39	1 446	10.2	1 241	8.8	20 081	17.6	26 532	9 908	9 789	2 991	2 137
Naples-Immokalee-Marco Island, FL	4 548	364 642	1.20	3 187	9.1	3 156	9.0	71 254	29.9	82 582	16 186	44 026	6 021	1 787
Nashville-Davidson—Murfreesboro—Franklin, TN	39 541	1 813 309	1.07	22 977	12.8	13 580	7.6	237 607	15.7	262 014	98 674	97 224	58 200	3 334
New Bern, NC	5 893	139 156	1.24	1 700	13.3	1 237	9.7	17 454	17.5	26 751	2 462	14 003	3 979	3 329
New Haven-Milford, CT	29 800	945 308	1.27	8 974	10.4	7 625	8.9	75 876	10.7	152 836	41 574	66 286	26 013	3 216
New Orleans-Metairie, LA	19 820	1 290 454	1.09	15 639	12.5	10 968	8.8	208 544	19.7	204 553	101 719	57 487	44 935	3 626
New York-Newark-Jersey City, NY-NJ-PA	420 229	20 283 270	1.04	251 368	12.5	146 346	7.3	2 406 507	14.2	3 118 973	842 082	1 525 102	397 860	2 001
Dutchess County-Putnam County, NY Div 20524	22 130	NA	NA	3 528	8.9	3 156	8.0	29 747	9.3	70 372	12 552	38 297	5 719	1 464
Nassau County-Suffolk County, NY Div 35004	50 513	NA	NA	29 634	10.4	23 117	8.1	249 955	10.5	510 253	113 080	268 229	44 642	1 564
Newark, NJ-PA Div 35084	48 838	NA	NA	27 913	11.1	18 535	7.4	309 648	14.6	382 837	55 146	215 505	50 970	2 041
New York-Jersey City-White Plains, NY-NJ Div 35614	298 748	NA	NA	190 293	13.3	101 538	7.1	1 817 157	15.0	2 155 511	661 304	1 003 071	296 529	2 097
Niles-Benton Harbor, MI	3 532	167 942	1.23	1 823	11.7	1 610	10.4	18 760	14.9	33 395	7 897	18 758	4 712	3 063
North Port-Sarasota-Bradenton, FL	10 443	753 686	1.08	6 364	8.5	8 928	11.9	121 625	23.9	204 514	56 062	93 663	23 690	3 252
Norwich-New London, CT	12 755	300 899	1.24	2 761	10.1	2 361	8.6	20 276	9.2	50 329	8 718	24 463	NA	NA
Ocala, FL	9 223	348 529	1.12	3 268	9.6	4 566	13.5	57 134	24.1	100 422	37 689	36 988	8 413	2 492
Ocean City, NJ	2 642	104 491	1.29	903	9.5	1 284	13.5	10 416	14.4	25 492	2 655	16 619	4 168	4 336
Odessa, TX	2 280	165 881	1.31	2 911	18.9	1 177	7.6	33 718	25.4	17 806	3 198	9 816	7 496	5 084
Ogden-Clearfield, UT	5 957	639 611	1.08	10 795	17.1	3 373	5.3	69 997	12.6	74 485	24 800	17 923	16 100	2 607
Oklahoma City, OK	31 768	1 351 350	1.05	18 985	14.2	10 887	8.1	222 852	19.7	199 674	40 589	90 050	58 748	4 466
Olympia-Tumwater, WA	4 051	281 859	1.24	3 157	11.9	2 010	7.6	30 695	13.9	48 168	15 882	12 768	7 538	2 889
Omaha-Council Bluffs, NE-IA	17 961	917 853	1.05	13 193	14.6	6 312	7.0	90 199	11.7	131 349	26 356	64 912	32 279	3 627
Orlando-Kissimmee-Sanford, FL	45 408	2 366 753	1.10	27 574	11.9	16 439	7.1	448 209	23.2	357 868	142 828	116 292	89 179	3 960
Oshkosh-Neenah, WI	8 029	203 220	1.55	1 883	11.1	1 406	8.3	12 421	9.0	29 049	15 171	8 786	3 187	1 880
Owensboro, KY	2 678	125 200	1.18	1 557	13.4	1 177	10.1	13 699	14.3	24 405	4 733	13 868	2 773	2 380
Oxnard-Thousand Oaks-Ventura, CA	10 452	884 088	1.14	10 602	12.5	5 597	6.6	129 926	18.1	128 467	38 105	53 515	18 029	2 145
Palm Bay-Melbourne-Titusville, FL	6 726	560 425	1.05	5 043	9.1	6 512	11.7	84 893	20.0	135 515	47 077	42 429	18 282	3 321
Panama City, FL	7 533	196 746	1.06	2 424	12.4	1 951	10.0	30 087	19.5	37 478	6 367	15 555	8 283	4 378
Parkersburg-Vienna, WV	1 000	100 962	1.28	941	10.2	1 081	11.7	11 903	15.9	22 336	4 531	12 205	2 475	2 766
Pensacola-Ferry Pass-Brent, FL	27 028	475 719	1.05	5 750	12.1	4 605	9.7	69 002	18.5	90 484	23 545	29 090	18 215	3 905
Peoria, IL	9 196	399 283	1.10	4 922	13.0	3 730	9.8	32 364	10.3	70 436	19 178	27 136	9 645	2 685
Philadelphia-Camden-Wilmington, PA-NJ-DE-MD	169 310	6 198 884	1.06	72 217	11.9	54 179	9.0	588 666	11.7	1 028 025	275 571	504 979	180 028	2 983
Camden, NJ Div 15804	24 485	NA	NA	13 701	10.9	10 936	8.7	124 218	11.8	217 432	38 009	122 694	33 149	2 636
Montgomery County-Bucks County-Chester County, PA Div 33874	43 688	NA	NA	20 258	10.4	16 945	8.7	136 363	8.5	348 799	95 930	169 360	35 667	1 834
Philadelphia, PA Div 37964	80 332	NA	NA	29 814	14.0	20 269	9.5	266 475	15.0	343 006	130 748	136 528	85 950	4 065
Wilmington, DE-MD-NJ Div 48864	20 805	NA	NA	8 444	11.7	6 029	8.4	61 610	10.3	118 788	10 884	76 397	25 262	3 518
Phoenix-Mesa-Scottsdale, AZ	84 746	4 420 038	1.01	59 914	13.3	30 617	6.8	734 803	19.8	646 226	268 406	208 416	156 430	3 568
Pine Bluff, AR	8 581	102 570	1.21	1 109	11.7	1 065	11.2	11 845	16.1	19 135	3 842	9 458	4 416	4 570
Pittsburgh, PA	63 032	2 415 629	1.05	23 838	10.1	27 282	11.6	184 836	9.8	505 176	313 204	111 453	50 376	2 140
Pittsfield, MA	6 035	136 697	1.13	1 108	8.6	1 426	11.1	4 162	4.2	31 804	1 356	20 386	3 310	2 772
Pocatello, ID	1 980	85 149	1.06	1 261	15.1	629	7.5	11 377	16.0	13 016	4 297	5 633	2 752	3 257
Portland-South Portland, ME	12 618	545 626	1.11	4 983	9.5	4 693	9.0	50 152	11.9	108 590	25 009	48 698	12 539	2 416
Portland-Vancouver-Hillsboro, OR-WA	39 376	2 355 670	1.04	27 739	11.8	16 578	7.1	311 828	15.7	356 067	196 911	83 240	74 758	3 243
Port St. Lucie, FL	7 228	450 873	1.09	4 110	9.2	4 899	11.0	80 743	24.8	106 397	32 533	44 834	11 205	2 565
Prescott, AZ	3 750	217 529	1.03	1 821	8.3	2 647	12.1	33 933	22.0	66 641	17 547	26 768	4 700	2 194
Providence-Warwick, RI-MA	57 827	1 664 105	1.10	16 585	10.3	14 642	9.1	140 225	10.7	310 936	85 838	142 429	43 325	2 700
Provo-Orem, UT	12 209	580 061	1.09	12 144	21.3	2 132	3.7	70 354	13.8	47 363	17 775	14 943	11 018	1 962
Pueblo, CO	4 556	166 024	1.08	1 908	11.8	1 638	10.1	20 197	15.4	33 645	11 294	14 136	9 903	6 102
Punta Gorda, FL	3 221	173 793	1.26	1 037	6.2	2 420	14.4	23 743	23.4	57 516	17 229	25 473	3 799	2 317
Racine, WI	4 849	215 206	1.36	2 369	12.1	1 567	8.0	18 092	11.1	35 901	12 389	13 919	5 156	2 648
Raleigh, NC	24 083	1 291 146	1.16	15 437	12.4	6 832	5.5	162 996	15.3	154 180	43 997	67 042	29 701	2 469
Rapid City, SD	3 617	145 668	1.06	1 963	13.7	1 048	7.3	15 910	13.5	27 817	4 741	13 041	3 978	2 823
Reading, PA	11 817	443 118	1.20	4 838	11.7	3 692	8.9	41 629	12.3	77 202	26 183	35 593	8 929	2 177

1. Per 1,000 estimated resident population. 2. Data for serious crimes have not been adjusted for underreporting; this may affect comparability between geographic areas and over time.
3. Per 100,000 population estimated by the FBI.

Area name	Serious crimes known to police, 2013 (cont.)[1]		Education						Income and Poverty, 2013							
	Rate[2]		School enrollment and attainment, 2013				Local government expenditures,[5] 2012–2013							Percent below poverty level		
			Enrollment[3]		Attainment[4] (percent)											
	Violent	Property	Total	Percent private	High school graduate or less	Bachelor's degree or more	Total current expenditures (mil dol)	Current expenditures per student (dollars)	Per capita income[6] (dollars)	Mean household income (dollars)	Median household income	Percent of households with income of less than $25,000	Percent of households with income of $200,000 or more	All persons	Children under 18 years	Age 65 years and older
	46	47	48	49	50	51	52	53	54	55	56	57	58	59	60	61
Modesto, CA	518	3 915	150 499	8.5	51.6	16.0	996.5	9 467	22 556	67 565	47 962	25.8	3.2	22.1	32.6	9.7
Monroe, LA	580	4 946	43 146	8.7	49.6	21.7	310.0	9 987	20 819	54 931	37 536	37.3	3.6	25.3	36.8	10.6
Monroe, MI	263	2 314	37 083	11.6	44.3	19.4	245.8	10 550	26 825	67 005	53 561	22.3	2.8	12.9	17.3	3.5
Montgomery, AL	344	3 349	103 729	23.9	45.2	25.9	464.8	8 296	24 046	62 057	45 859	27.4	2.4	19.1	29.1	9.2
Morgantown, WV	275	1 579	44 937	7.4	44.3	32.5	168.6	10 804	24 952	62 160	47 051	31.4	3.2	19.2	17.9	5.8
Morristown, TN	313	3 032	25 914	10.8	60.2	14.4	131.6	7 390	20 454	52 772	40 957	31.7	1.2	17.7	24.7	10.2
Mount Vernon-Anacortes, WA	213	4 317	25 803	8.0	38.6	23.7	197.5	10 426	26 906	68 632	52 448	21.8	3.2	17.8	24.5	9.2
Muncie, IN	275	3 147	37 537	6.6	45.4	24.1	148.2	9 741	20 365	50 407	36 402	37.7	1.4	22.6	26.0	8.1
Muskegon, MI	469	3 533	41 591	9.1	46.4	17.3	294.0	10 921	20 246	52 010	41 630	29.8	1.2	20.6	28.2	12.7
Myrtle Beach-Conway-North Myrtle Beach, NC-SC	487	4 384	80 469	7.7	42.7	22.7	524.5	10 003	23 937	57 058	43 540	27.1	2.3	18.3	30.1	6.6
Napa, CA	298	1 839	35 154	14.0	34.0	32.2	216.5	10 447	33 881	93 591	70 914	17.3	8.9	9.0	11.5	8.3
Naples-Immokalee-Marco Island, FL	233	1 554	64 171	17.5	40.7	32.4	445.8	10 182	36 746	89 719	54 406	19.8	9.2	12.8	21.4	7.8
Nashville-Davidson—Murfreesboro—Franklin, TN	596	2 738	454 031	20.9	40.5	32.3	2 233.5	8 311	28 013	71 471	51 996	21.5	4.4	13.7	20.5	8.0
New Bern, NC	275	3 054	32 103	10.9	43.1	18.9	150.0	8 529	23 235	57 200	44 560	26.0	1.3	16.0	27.4	7.6
New Haven-Milford, CT	392	2 824	225 699	23.4	41.0	33.5	2 073.6	16 895	31 896	81 252	58 571	21.6	6.0	12.9	17.7	8.5
New Orleans-Metairie, LA	474	3 152	311 452	29.0	44.3	27.4	1 650.8	12 304	27 281	67 164	45 981	29.0	4.6	19.3	28.6	11.8
New York-Newark-Jersey City, NY-NJ-PA	391	1 610	5 074 650	23.3	40.3	37.4	57 989.5	21 284	35 780	96 934	65 786	21.1	10.0	14.6	20.6	11.8
Dutchess County-Putnam County, NY Div 20524	159	1 305	106 151	27.2	36.4	33.8	1 190.0	20 431	35 374	95 449	77 305	14.8	7.9	7.9	10.6	3.9
Nassau County-Suffolk County, NY Div 35004	140	1 424	732 150	20.8	36.8	38.1	10 471.1	23 199	39 268	115 669	89 894	12.7	13.6	6.7	9.1	5.3
Newark, NJ-PA Div 35084	340	1 701	658 041	17.9	37.6	39.7	7 719.1	19 848	39 662	109 399	75 249	17.4	13.0	10.4	13.7	8.0
New York-Jersey City-White Plains, NY-NJ Div 35614	457	1 640	3 578 308	24.8	41.6	37.0	38 609.4	21 144	34 409	91 427	60 414	23.5	8.9	17.1	24.6	14.1
Niles-Benton Harbor, MI	441	2 622	39 476	22.3	42.7	24.9	262.7	11 019	24 005	60 408	44 747	26.8	2.0	16.3	22.5	9.5
North Port-Sarasota-Bradenton, FL	422	2 830	135 930	14.4	40.3	30.6	819.9	9 396	29 878	68 970	48 283	24.4	4.5	14.4	24.5	6.8
Norwich-New London, CT	NA	NA	66 722	18.6	39.5	32.0	618.5	17 545	32 991	82 557	62 883	15.7	5.2	9.0	12.9	4.9
Ocala, FL	430	2 061	68 297	15.0	51.4	19.0	350.4	8 344	21 430	51 039	38 695	33.3	1.5	19.5	28.2	10.3
Ocean City, NJ	258	4 078	19 226	12.0	42.5	33.7	257.1	19 903	31 995	76 676	60 560	18.8	4.7	9.4	10.3	7.9
Odessa, TX	806	4 277	40 230	10.9	55.4	13.8	219.9	7 418	26 923	76 085	55 710	18.1	5.0	14.6	21.6	8.3
Ogden-Clearfield, UT	171	2 435	192 654	9.6	32.2	29.0	831.7	6 520	24 046	74 632	62 785	15.9	3.3	10.4	13.3	7.0
Oklahoma City, OK	503	3 962	358 756	11.8	40.8	27.9	1 614.8	7 286	26 191	67 369	50 136	22.6	3.5	14.9	21.6	8.0
Olympia-Tumwater, WA	200	2 689	63 531	14.2	31.7	32.0	385.2	9 472	28 429	71 766	59 785	19.1	3.2	12.8	16.8	5.7
Omaha-Council Bluffs, NE-IA	388	3 239	259 322	18.4	33.8	33.4	1 615.2	10 835	28 469	72 701	55 382	20.5	4.3	12.7	16.7	8.4
Orlando-Kissimmee-Sanford, FL	540	3 420	608 429	16.0	40.2	29.5	2 794.8	8 091	23 608	63 634	46 962	24.2	3.3	17.1	25.4	9.9
Oshkosh-Neenah, WI	159	1 721	43 226	10.0	45.2	26.4	232.2	10 204	26 499	63 327	49 776	24.1	2.4	12.9	17.6	8.7
Owensboro, KY	138	2 241	30 147	17.0	51.3	17.4	181.2	9 236	23 848	59 180	46 268	26.2	2.6	16.2	23.5	8.7
Oxnard-Thousand Oaks-Ventura, CA	194	1 951	230 770	15.4	36.7	31.2	1 248.7	8 813	33 481	101 302	77 363	14.6	10.6	11.9	18.3	6.4
Palm Bay-Melbourne-Titusville, FL	525	2 796	117 560	18.0	37.5	26.5	568.2	7 977	25 615	60 739	46 472	25.4	2.5	15.0	21.5	8.5
Panama City, FL	516	3 862	43 344	11.9	47.3	18.8	227.8	7 975	22 960	60 267	45 620	25.3	2.7	17.7	28.7	7.8
Parkersburg-Vienna, WV	296	2 470	20 340	9.2	51.4	16.9	161.1	11 204	23 348	53 425	40 945	31.8	1.1	19.1	31.7	12.1
Pensacola-Ferry Pass-Brent, FL	510	3 395	112 481	16.1	37.4	25.4	543.5	8 166	23 697	60 483	47 336	25.0	2.1	16.1	24.4	7.9
Peoria, IL	347	2 338	96 280	22.0	39.6	27.4	644.9	10 725	28 217	69 625	52 614	21.3	3.1	12.8	19.1	6.2
Philadelphia-Camden-Wilmington, PA-NJ-DE-MD	499	2 484	1 544 585	25.8	41.2	34.6	13 258.8	17 304	32 400	84 501	60 482	21.4	6.9	13.5	18.7	9.2
Camden, NJ Div 15804	319	2 317	318 441	15.2	41.6	31.2	3 522.0	17 773	32 407	86 572	68 590	17.4	6.0	10.5	16.1	6.7
Montgomery County-Bucks County-Chester County, PA Div 33874	139	1 694	484 093	26.5	33.2	44.2	4 319.7	16 555	40 178	105 686	77 773	13.8	11.0	6.6	8.4	5.8
Philadelphia, PA Div 37964	938	3 127	559 329	32.8	48.9	28.0	4 038.1	18 940	25 342	63 791	41 778	31.8	3.8	22.2	30.2	15.3
Wilmington, DE-MD-NJ Div 48864	493	3 025	182 722	21.1	40.5	32.5	1 379.1	14 681	32 072	84 212	63 409	17.9	6.3	11.8	17.9	7.2
Phoenix-Mesa-Scottsdale, AZ	386	3 182	1 177 873	11.4	37.6	29.2	4 660.5	7 210	26 403	71 150	51 847	22.7	4.2	17.6	25.4	8.2
Pine Bluff, AR	672	3 899	24 593	9.8	58.0	13.8	152.1	10 021	18 035	47 807	34 665	36.9	1.0	24.4	30.0	10.2
Pittsburgh, PA	291	1 850	535 795	20.9	42.2	32.2	4 241.6	14 342	29 985	69 814	51 291	24.7	4.0	12.8	17.7	8.6
Pittsfield, MA	288	2 484	29 655	26.0	40.7	32.4	275.5	16 468	30 917	71 181	52 514	23.6	4.0	12.3	15.6	10.5
Pocatello, ID	283	2 975	25 745	9.9	32.6	28.4	89.6	6 374	21 777	58 017	42 174	28.3	1.5	17.1	19.5	12.3
Portland-South Portland, ME	145	2 271	119 829	18.7	33.9	35.8	918.2	12 837	30 901	73 210	54 766	22.3	4.7	11.4	13.8	8.4
Portland-Vancouver-Hillsboro, OR-WA	251	2 991	576 765	16.9	31.0	35.1	3 279.9	9 632	30 450	77 510	59 168	19.5	5.0	13.5	16.9	8.1
Port St. Lucie, FL	337	2 228	98 503	13.6	44.4	23.1	495.0	8 487	27 037	67 428	45 322	27.2	4.2	17.2	25.4	9.3
Prescott, AZ	240	1 953	42 747	16.1	36.4	24.3	139.2	6 708	23 259	51 801	39 895	30.6	1.4	16.1	19.7	9.3
Providence-Warwick, RI-MA	339	2 361	403 180	23.0	43.3	29.6	3 214.2	15 008	29 866	74 920	55 055	24.0	4.6	14.3	20.8	9.5
Provo-Orem, UT	72	1 891	224 078	23.0	22.8	37.7	715.0	5 919	20 886	74 889	60 051	17.5	3.5	13.7	12.3	7.1
Pueblo, CO	651	5 451	43 325	6.4	41.7	21.3	210.6	7 852	20 987	52 754	41 218	31.5	1.0	20.1	27.3	12.3
Punta Gorda, FL	238	2 079	24 120	18.1	48.3	21.0	146.4	8 952	25 459	57 263	43 698	25.4	1.6	14.1	22.4	6.7
Racine, WI	182	2 466	49 226	19.6	44.5	23.4	330.7	11 143	27 391	70 215	54 209	21.0	2.7	12.8	19.4	8.5
Raleigh, NC	218	2 250	350 593	16.1	28.9	43.7	1 519.4	7 858	31 525	82 896	61 710	17.3	6.3	12.0	16.2	6.8
Rapid City, SD	382	2 441	36 096	12.9	37.5	24.5	175.5	8 239	25 976	63 509	48 641	21.2	3.4	14.5	23.3	8.4
Reading, PA	298	1 879	103 728	16.8	53.2	22.5	944.1	13 729	27 288	71 525	56 043	22.5	3.8	14.4	22.8	6.8

1. Data for serious crimes have not been adjusted for underreporting; this may affect comparability between geographic areas and over time. 2. Per 100,000 population estimated by the FBI. 3. All persons 3 years old and over enrolled in nursery school through college. 4. Persons 25 years old and over. 5. Elementary and secondary education expenditures. 6. Based on resident population estimated in the 2008-2012 American Community Survey.

Table C. Metropolitan Areas — **Personal Income**

Area name	Personal income, 2013: Total (mil dol)	Percent change 2012–2013	Per capita[1]: Dollars	Per capita[1]: Rank	Wages and salaries (mil dol)	Supplements to wages and salaries; employer contributions (mil dol): Pension and insurance	Supplements: Government social insurance	Proprietors' income (mil dol)	Dividends, interest, and rent (mil dol)	Personal transfer receipts (mil dol)	Earnings, 2013: Total (mil dol)	Contributions for government social insurance (mil dol): From employee and self-employed	Contributions: From employer
	62	63	64	65	66	67	68	69	70	71	72	73	74
Modesto, CA	18 528	3.2	35 259	299	7 462	1 595	557	1 811	2 963	4 112	11 424	652	557
Monroe, LA	6 481	2.2	36 293	272	2 988	526	192	693	1 035	1 554	4 399	236	192
Monroe, MI	5 944	4.4	39 525	181	1 920	329	148	278	797	1 173	2 675	178	148
Montgomery, AL	14 350	1.3	38 419	211	7 214	1 332	554	1 272	2 508	2 992	10 372	617	554
Morgantown, WV	5 076	2.8	37 290	243	2 889	611	219	414	760	941	4 134	237	219
Morristown, TN	3 574	1.4	31 027	369	1 591	307	118	254	517	1 051	2 271	148	118
Mount Vernon-Anacortes, WA	5 101	3.0	42 927	110	2 052	402	198	293	1 307	1 057	2 946	176	198
Muncie, IN	3 789	0.9	32 255	359	1 772	344	137	280	625	1 028	2 534	160	137
Muskegon, MI	5 541	1.5	32 405	357	2 462	437	200	271	839	1 556	3 371	223	200
Myrtle Beach-Conway-North Myrtle Beach, NC-SC	12 996	3.3	32 094	362	5 034	828	415	948	2 600	3 760	7 225	508	415
Napa, CA	7 947	3.8	56 634	12	3 589	748	265	720	1 829	1 050	5 322	295	265
Naples-Immokalee-Marco Island, FL	22 033	1.9	64 872	5	5 979	781	416	1 245	11 993	2 823	8 421	544	416
Nashville-Davidson—Murfreesboro—Franklin, TN	80 440	3.0	45 759	63	41 685	6 320	2 937	15 167	10 731	11 644	66 109	3 645	2 937
New Bern, NC	5 007	-0.6	39 226	189	2 287	541	197	350	1 097	1 138	3 375	187	197
New Haven-Milford, CT	44 568	0.9	51 685	26	19 824	3 191	1 540	3 339	8 678	7 916	27 894	1 555	1 540
New Orleans-Metairie, LA	55 529	1.6	44 746	83	27 897	4 458	1 808	6 890	10 398	9 206	41 052	2 176	1 808
New York-Newark-Jersey City, NY-NJ-PA	1 181 931	1.1	59 246	9	622 666	98 792	43 830	117 632	225 901	180 278	882 920	47 638	43 830
Dutchess County-Putnam County, NY Div 20524	20 610	0.3	51 971	NA	6 979	1 598	561	882	3 803	3 123	10 020	546	561
Nassau County-Suffolk County, NY Div 35004	183 492	0.4	64 341	NA	70 202	14 067	5 552	14 095	39 851	24 492	103 915	5 461	5 552
Newark, NJ-PA Div 35084	155 578	1.2	62 315	NA	80 534	11 954	5 825	14 673	29 235	18 789	112 985	6 474	5 825
New York-Jersey City-White Plains, NY-NJ Div 35614	822 252	1.3	57 887	NA	464 952	71 173	31 892	87 982	153 012	133 874	656 000	35 157	31 892
Niles-Benton Harbor, MI	5 991	2.6	38 589	204	2 764	532	213	360	1 044	1 434	3 869	243	213
North Port-Sarasota-Bradenton, FL	36 526	2.4	49 863	34	11 100	1 641	811	2 218	13 484	7 038	15 770	1 076	811
Norwich-New London, CT	13 796	0.2	50 322	30	6 763	1 370	501	781	3 402	2 260	9 415	492	501
Ocala, FL	11 618	1.9	34 437	315	3 572	647	267	389	2 785	3 658	4 875	378	267
Ocean City, NJ	5 172	1.1	53 932	19	1 545	321	141	453	1 372	1 111	2 459	161	141
Odessa, TX	6 598	4.2	44 168	91	4 175	490	278	680	807	892	5 623	294	278
Ogden-Clearfield, UT	22 949	3.5	36 920	254	9 494	1 954	789	1 540	3 993	3 051	13 776	784	789
Oklahoma City, OK	58 435	2.7	44 280	90	29 003	4 609	2 279	9 140	9 894	8 823	45 031	2 373	2 279
Olympia-Tumwater, WA	11 671	2.1	44 481	85	4 745	965	426	602	2 460	2 035	6 736	394	426
Omaha-Council Bluffs, NE-IA	42 731	2.7	47 736	45	22 543	3 565	1 724	5 432	7 690	5 672	33 264	1 931	1 724
Orlando-Kissimmee-Sanford, FL	83 892	2.9	36 992	253	48 038	6 760	3 471	4 732	15 737	15 507	63 002	3 784	3 471
Oshkosh-Neenah, WI	6 953	1.6	41 008	157	4 480	848	351	323	1 307	1 091	6 002	358	351
Owensboro, KY	4 528	3.6	38 898	196	2 049	398	156	463	815	1 020	3 065	179	156
Oxnard-Thousand Oaks-Ventura, CA	42 406	1.7	50 507	29	17 253	3 183	1 227	3 056	8 867	5 384	24 720	1 420	1 227
Palm Bay-Melbourne-Titusville, FL	21 714	1.2	39 420	186	9 398	1 493	694	868	5 201	5 136	12 453	813	694
Panama City, FL	7 063	1.9	37 014	252	3 193	605	251	350	1 630	1 621	4 400	265	251
Parkersburg-Vienna, WV	3 192	1.7	34 521	313	1 536	333	124	178	532	915	2 171	141	124
Pensacola-Ferry Pass-Brent, FL	17 820	1.9	38 165	215	7 367	1 452	585	600	4 061	3 826	10 004	591	585
Peoria, IL	17 529	-1.3	45 875	62	9 396	1 539	696	1 288	3 486	2 816	12 920	707	696
Philadelphia-Camden-Wilmington, PA-NJ-DE-MD	316 838	1.4	52 503	22	159 831	26 066	12 271	32 298	54 067	52 038	230 467	13 172	12 271
Camden, NJ Div 15804	59 748	0.9	47 648	NA	26 223	4 513	2 173	4 044	9 839	10 288	36 953	2 224	2 173
Montgomery County-Bucks County-Chester County, PA Div 33874	126 949	1.1	65 141	NA	61 261	9 324	4 612	13 354	24 574	14 449	88 551	5 006	4 612
Philadelphia, PA Div 37964	95 801	1.9	45 293	NA	52 558	9 136	4 056	11 769	14 098	21 587	77 519	4 400	4 056
Wilmington, DE-MD-NJ Div 48864	34 341	2.5	47 911	NA	19 790	3 094	1 429	3 131	5 557	5 714	27 444	1 542	1 429
Phoenix-Mesa-Scottsdale, AZ	170 431	2.3	38 745	199	91 470	12 796	6 633	15 176	29 349	29 382	126 074	7 572	6 633
Pine Bluff, AR	3 209	-1.2	33 494	335	1 395	257	114	241	528	882	2 007	125	114
Pittsburgh, PA	115 799	1.6	49 049	37	58 768	10 270	4 588	10 581	19 657	22 029	84 207	5 010	4 588
Pittsfield, MA	6 310	1.4	48 695	40	2 641	518	200	452	1 462	1 441	3 810	215	200
Pocatello, ID	2 575	1.7	30 926	371	1 158	231	111	160	438	628	1 660	105	111
Portland-South Portland, ME	24 155	2.4	46 461	56	12 196	2 034	931	1 784	4 422	4 288	16 945	1 059	931
Portland-Vancouver-Hillsboro, OR-WA	101 210	2.4	43 728	99	56 299	8 104	4 902	7 039	19 201	15 333	76 343	4 641	4 902
Port St. Lucie, FL	17 143	1.7	39 131	190	5 162	871	382	751	6 148	3 982	7 166	501	382
Prescott, AZ	6 993	2.8	32 503	355	2 126	373	160	295	1 971	2 141	2 955	233	160
Providence-Warwick, RI-MA	74 351	1.6	46 345	57	33 445	6 026	2 684	5 164	12 664	14 896	47 319	2 979	2 684
Provo-Orem, UT	16 251	5.0	28 904	375	8 276	1 403	665	1 760	2 489	2 328	12 104	687	665
Pueblo, CO	5 427	1.7	33 616	334	2 366	390	179	317	987	1 492	3 253	195	179
Punta Gorda, FL	6 192	3.2	37 588	233	1 637	269	123	269	2 055	1 934	2 298	189	123
Racine, WI	8 086	1.0	41 458	147	3 481	715	272	307	1 555	1 511	4 775	294	272
Raleigh, NC	53 374	2.8	43 947	92	28 547	3 938	2 146	5 252	8 221	6 476	39 882	2 355	2 146
Rapid City, SD	6 001	1.1	42 428	123	2 635	485	204	568	1 543	1 018	3 892	236	204
Reading, PA	17 121	1.1	41 403	148	7 694	1 592	622	1 171	2 935	3 495	11 079	655	622

1. Based on the resident population estimated as of July 1 of the year shown.

Area name	Earnings, 2013 (cont.) — Percent by selected industries: Farm	Mining	Construction	Manufacturing	Information, professional, scientific, technical services	Retail trade	Finance, insurance, real estate, rental and leasing	Health care and social assistance	Government	Social Security beneficiaries, December 2013: Number	Rate[1]	Supplemental Security Income recipients, December 2013	Housing units, 2014: Total	Percent change, 2000–2014
	75	76	77	78	79	80	81	82	83	84	85	86	87	88
Modesto, CA	8.2	0.0	4.8	13.2	4.0	7.7	5.0	16.0	18.1	82 435	157	22 290	180 278	0.4
Monroe, LA	1.1	D	5.4	D	9.8	8.4	8.8	16.6	16.8	33 250	186	7 767	77 723	2.5
Monroe, MI	1.8	D	7.3	17.0	D	7.2	2.8	9.7	13.4	32 520	217	2 649	63 502	0.8
Montgomery, AL	1.1	0.1	6.4	11.7	D	6.4	D	10.3	28.3	75 110	201	14 974	164 600	1.9
Morgantown, WV	-0.2	2.7	7.6	9.5	7.6	5.4	3.6	D	27.5	21 300	157	2 932	59 538	2.1
Morristown, TN	0.1	D	D	26.2	D	8.2	3.4	D	14.6	29 825	259	3 402	50 659	0.4
Mount Vernon-Anacortes, WA	3.5	0.1	8.6	15.5	5.0	9.3	5.0	8.1	24.9	27 140	229	2 460	51 870	0.8
Muncie, IN	1.9	D	3.9	10.3	7.3	7.9	5.8	19.4	22.8	25 740	219	2 998	52 512	0.3
Muskegon, MI	0.7	D	4.9	26.5	4.0	10.0	3.6	17.0	15.2	40 880	237	6 426	73 310	-0.3
Myrtle Beach-Conway-North Myrtle Beach, NC-SC	0.2	D	7.8	3.6	6.7	11.0	11.8	10.4	17.1	114 250	282	8 131	274 506	4.2
Napa, CA	2.9	D	6.0	18.7	6.3	5.4	6.1	10.5	16.4	26 200	186	2 738	55 317	1.0
Naples-Immokalee-Marco Island, FL	2.3	0.4	9.1	2.4	8.8	9.2	10.1	14.5	11.0	83 055	244	3 793	203 070	2.9
Nashville-Davidson—Murfreesboro—Franklin, TN	0.1	0.2	6.0	8.2	11.8	6.1	D	20.4	10.7	286 830	163	32 650	730 589	3.9
New Bern, NC	2.2	D	3.7	6.5	D	5.3	D	8.9	49.6	28 875	226	3 115	58 374	1.7
New Haven-Milford, CT	0.1	0.1	5.8	10.6	10.2	6.2	6.2	15.9	15.2	159 190	184	19 439	362 262	0.1
New Orleans-Metairie, LA	0.1	4.6	7.8	8.0	D	5.9	7.1	9.1	15.3	218 370	176	44 994	553 627	1.3
New York-Newark-Jersey City, NY-NJ-PA	0.0	D	4.4	D	18.0	5.0	18.5	10.5	14.3	3 169 125	158	632 527	7 880 495	1.2
Dutchess County-Putnam County, NY Div 20524	0.1	0.2	6.2	13.5	6.9	6.4	4.2	15.4	25.2	75 865	191	6 898	157 439	0.4
Nassau County-Suffolk County, NY Div 35004	0.1	0.1	6.6	5.8	12.6	7.2	9.4	14.6	19.8	537 270	188	41 786	1 037 346	-0.1
Newark, NJ-PA Div 35084	0.0	0.1	4.7	9.2	18.1	5.3	10.1	9.3	14.1	396 635	159	50 404	984 030	0.9
New York-Jersey City-White Plains, NY-NJ Div 35614	0.0	0.1	3.9	2.8	19.1	4.6	21.6	10.0	13.2	2 159 355	152	533 439	5 701 680	1.6
Niles-Benton Harbor, MI	1.8	0.2	3.9	30.2	4.1	5.6	4.1	11.6	14.2	37 375	241	4 979	76 768	-0.2
North Port-Sarasota-Bradenton, FL	1.5	0.1	7.4	6.2	10.9	9.6	8.8	16.4	11.7	211 730	289	10 425	410 022	2.2
Norwich-New London, CT	0.5	0.1	4.8	17.7	8.2	5.8	2.8	11.5	29.7	53 050	194	3 927	121 248	0.2
Ocala, FL	-0.3	0.1	5.9	8.8	6.0	11.0	5.4	16.4	21.1	108 585	323	9 121	163 542	-0.3
Ocean City, NJ	0.3	D	10.1	1.4	4.9	10.3	6.8	11.9	28.2	27 640	288	1 806	98 922	0.6
Odessa, TX	0.1	22.5	11.8	7.9	4.0	6.1	4.7	5.3	10.2	19 540	131	3 680	56 500	6.5
Ogden-Clearfield, UT	0.5	D	8.2	14.8	D	7.1	5.5	D	26.0	77 140	124	6 610	212 880	4.3
Oklahoma City, OK	0.2	D	5.6	6.5	D	6.4	7.1	10.6	19.3	216 275	164	27 681	557 380	3.4
Olympia-Tumwater, WA	0.4	0.0	4.8	3.5	6.0	6.7	4.1	12.6	40.4	51 880	198	5 286	111 807	3.4
Omaha-Council Bluffs, NE-IA	2.0	0.3	8.2	7.4	D	5.6	10.5	10.9	14.4	137 490	154	14 293	374 329	3.3
Orlando-Kissimmee-Sanford, FL	0.2	0.1	5.3	4.6	13.1	7.5	9.6	11.5	12.2	388 460	171	56 920	974 601	3.4
Oshkosh-Neenah, WI	0.6	D	5.7	30.7	6.7	4.6	5.0	9.7	13.0	32 275	191	2 562	74 185	1.2
Owensboro, KY	5.8	D	6.3	20.8	D	6.7	D	7.9	19.7	27 615	237	4 279	50 515	2.1
Oxnard-Thousand Oaks-Ventura, CA	3.7	1.9	4.4	15.5	9.6	6.8	9.3	9.0	17.1	127 775	152	16 662	284 504	1.0
Palm Bay-Melbourne-Titusville, FL	0.1	0.0	4.4	15.5	11.2	7.2	4.3	14.3	17.9	146 240	265	11 302	272 297	0.9
Panama City, FL	0.0	0.1	5.7	5.5	8.2	8.9	6.1	D	27.3	41 105	215	5 214	109 503	0.7
Parkersburg-Vienna, WV	-0.2	D	D	D	D	10.0	D	16.2	20.7	24 955	270	4 126	43 473	0.1
Pensacola-Ferry Pass-Brent, FL	0.6	0.2	5.1	4.3	8.5	7.3	6.3	14.9	31.2	99 225	212	12 703	206 240	2.4
Peoria, IL	4.5	D	5.3	24.3	D	4.8	D	14.2	10.9	76 675	201	7 200	165 539	0.8
Philadelphia-Camden-Wilmington, PA-NJ-DE-MD	0.2	D	D	D	18.0	5.2	11.3	13.2	13.1	1 083 390	179	184 663	2 448 852	0.6
Camden, NJ Div 15804	0.3	0.0	6.4	8.4	10.3	7.7	8.0	13.9	19.3	235 410	188	26 739	496 537	1.3
Montgomery County-Bucks County-Chester County, PA Div 33874	0.2	0.2	7.3	9.5	19.4	5.7	12.3	11.5	8.1	361 075	185	19 887	769 937	0.8
Philadelphia, PA Div 37964	0.0	D	2.8	4.4	20.7	3.6	9.5	15.2	15.5	358 975	169	124 687	892 322	-0.1
Wilmington, DE-MD-NJ Div 48864	0.3	D	4.6	D	16.3	4.9	17.6	11.8	14.2	127 930	179	13 350	290 056	1.4
Phoenix-Mesa-Scottsdale, AZ	0.4	0.5	6.1	8.2	10.8	7.4	12.2	11.7	13.3	692 965	157	66 267	1 845 778	2.6
Pine Bluff, AR	7.3	D	3.7	16.4	D	6.1	D	D	28.1	21 025	220	5 410	42 148	0.5
Pittsburgh, PA	0.0	2.9	6.1	8.7	12.6	5.7	8.7	13.6	11.3	547 830	232	70 461	1 105 877	0.3
Pittsfield, MA	0.0	0.1	6.9	9.9	8.7	7.9	7.6	19.0	15.1	33 380	258	3 940	68 354	-0.2
Pocatello, ID	1.3	D	5.0	7.4	D	8.2	6.6	15.9	25.5	13 690	164	1 850	33 380	0.6
Portland-South Portland, ME	0.1	D	5.9	D	10.5	7.2	10.8	14.8	15.9	112 375	216	9 946	265 973	1.2
Portland-Vancouver-Hillsboro, OR-WA	0.4	0.2	6.2	13.9	D	5.9	7.2	D	13.9	371 830	161	43 160	947 031	2.4
Port St. Lucie, FL	0.9	D	5.8	5.0	8.3	10.1	5.9	16.8	17.1	113 775	260	8 227	216 287	0.5
Prescott, AZ	0.3	3.2	6.2	6.4	4.7	10.2	5.0	16.1	22.3	70 725	328	3 687	112 523	1.9
Providence-Warwick, RI-MA	0.1	D	5.5	D	9.6	6.4	8.3	15.3	17.2	330 685	206	51 938	693 911	0.0
Provo-Orem, UT	0.6	0.2	8.7	10.2	D	7.7	5.9	D	13.1	52 175	93	4 524	161 012	6.0
Pueblo, CO	0.4	0.3	7.4	11.6	5.1	8.0	3.2	19.9	21.8	34 195	212	6 265	70 054	0.8
Punta Gorda, FL	1.1	0.2	6.2	1.5	7.2	12.8	5.7	24.6	16.7	60 510	367	2 615	101 365	0.7
Racine, WI	0.8	0.1	4.5	34.7	4.5	5.6	4.4	12.0	14.5	39 915	205	5 181	82 265	0.1
Raleigh, NC	0.3	D	6.2	8.3	17.8	5.7	11.8	8.7	15.1	164 100	135	17 855	499 008	7.1
Rapid City, SD	0.8	D	7.7	3.9	6.4	8.0	8.4	D	24.6	29 620	210	2 441	63 172	4.3
Reading, PA	0.8	0.1	6.0	19.5	7.4	7.6	4.9	13.5	14.4	83 670	202	10 609	164 822	0.0

1. Per 1,000 resident population estimated as of July 1, 2011 of the year shown.

Area name	Housing units, 2013: Occupied units: Total	Owner-occupied: Percent	Owner-occupied: Median value[1]	Median owner cost as a percent of income: With a mortgage	Median owner cost as a percent of income: Without a mortgage[2]	Renter-occupied: Median rent[3]	Renter-occupied: Median rent as a percent of income	Substandard units[4] (percent)	Civilian labor force, 2014: Total	Percent change, 2013–2014	Unemployment: Total	Unemployment: Rate[5]	Civilian employment[6], 2013: Total employed	Percent: Management, professional, and related occupations	Percent: Construction, production, and related occupations
	89	90	91	92	93	94	95	96	97	98	99	100	101	102	103
Modesto, CA	167 411	56.6	175 000	24.3	11.8	967	35.2	NA	241 446	-0.1	27 085	11.2	210 456	26.1	30.2
Monroe, LA	65 989	63.2	122 800	21.1	10.0	670	33.3	NA	81 812	1.8	5 740	7.0	72 425	33.7	22.4
Monroe, MI	58 479	78.7	132 100	21.3	11.1	754	27.8	NA	75 701	1.2	4 630	6.1	65 527	28.2	31.5
Montgomery, AL	141 137	64.1	122 400	20.1	10.0	796	30.8	NA	170 554	-1.2	11 346	6.7	160 090	33.3	22.3
Morgantown, WV	50 295	64.7	149 600	18.8	10.0	706	32.5	NA	64 650	-0.2	3 038	4.7	66 750	35.7	21.3
Morristown, TN	42 874	68.6	130 100	22.3	10.0	622	29.1	NA	49 079	-2.7	3 630	7.4	49 213	25.5	35.5
Mount Vernon-Anacortes, WA	45 234	67.9	246 600	24.9	13.5	984	35.0	NA	56 596	0.1	4 164	7.4	51 605	31.7	25.4
Muncie, IN	46 431	62.1	85 700	18.7	10.6	723	39.3	NA	53 717	-1.0	3 821	7.1	53 328	30.0	20.2
Muskegon, MI	65 559	74.2	96 200	20.9	12.1	657	39.0	NA	76 809	0.5	5 686	7.4	71 099	26.9	29.8
Myrtle Beach-Conway-North Myrtle Beach, NC-SC	162 547	70.9	160 300	24.8	12.5	811	30.9	1.5	180 306	0.3	13 234	7.3	172 921	27.5	19.7
Napa, CA	47 482	62.3	443 000	27.1	11.1	1 299	32.0	NA	74 041	1.6	4 129	5.6	69 758	34.0	20.6
Naples-Immokalee-Marco Island, FL	130 614	71.0	260 400	26.6	14.0	993	33.5	NA	161 233	3.4	9 506	5.9	138 998	30.0	18.6
Nashville-Davidson—Murfreesboro—Franklin, TN	662 187	65.7	172 400	21.8	10.5	849	29.2	2.4	903 786	-0.7	47 401	5.2	866 111	37.4	21.0
New Bern, NC	48 962	65.0	147 500	22.9	11.8	867	32.6	NA	50 682	-1.0	3 417	6.7	48 812	30.2	26.7
New Haven-Milford, CT	321 048	61.8	242 000	25.1	16.8	1 026	34.8	2.4	455 537	0.7	32 912	7.2	415 518	38.8	17.6
New Orleans-Metairie, LA	479 366	60.8	173 100	23.7	10.7	908	33.9	2.0	598 722	2.6	38 070	6.4	570 431	34.6	22.4
New York-Newark-Jersey City, NY-NJ-PA	7 080 691	51.6	392 700	27.6	16.8	1 237	32.4	6.1	9 938 939	0.1	637 864	6.4	9 474 555	40.5	15.9
Dutchess County-Putnam County, NY Div 20524	140 003	72.7	292 000	26.6	17.3	1 129	34.0	NA	192 256	-2.0	10 021	5.2	200 002	40.1	16.2
Nassau County-Suffolk County, NY Div 35004	935 546	79.4	396 400	28.5	19.1	1 504	35.8	2.5	1 451 572	-1.4	73 443	5.1	1 395 652	40.1	16.6
Newark, NJ-PA Div 35084	876 304	63.4	359 000	26.2	16.8	1 137	31.5	3.1	1 263 221	-0.2	80 401	6.4	1 216 409	41.8	17.2
New York-Jersey City-White Plains, NY-NJ Div 35614	5 128 838	44.0	407 000	27.7	16.0	1 236	32.3	7.3	7 031 890	0.5	473 999	6.7	6 662 492	40.3	15.5
Niles-Benton Harbor, MI	59 239	70.3	123 100	19.9	12.0	653	29.7	NA	73 339	0.7	4 926	6.7	67 887	34.2	25.0
North Port-Sarasota-Bradenton, FL	302 518	72.8	167 700	24.9	12.9	958	32.5	NA	337 017	3.1	19 490	5.8	285 690	31.3	18.2
Norwich-New London, CT	106 886	66.2	241 100	24.6	15.8	1 015	28.5	NA	137 254	-0.3	9 254	6.7	136 491	39.0	17.5
Ocala, FL	133 098	74.2	107 100	23.5	12.4	787	34.1	2.4	132 815	1.2	9 669	7.3	116 277	28.1	20.0
Ocean City, NJ	38 210	79.3	308 200	25.8	17.5	999	36.1	NA	48 961	0.0	5 893	12.0	43 124	36.4	18.2
Odessa, TX	51 962	64.8	91 600	17.7	10.0	925	22.9	8.1	83 057	5.1	2 817	3.4	70 962	21.7	35.6
Ogden-Clearfield, UT	195 180	74.5	199 600	21.8	10.0	840	27.3	3.2	299 681	1.4	11 629	3.9	282 608	36.7	22.5
Oklahoma City, OK	493 315	63.4	137 100	20.5	10.5	762	28.2	3.2	645 550	-0.7	25 818	4.0	626 437	34.9	22.0
Olympia-Tumwater, WA	99 815	63.6	237 000	24.8	10.5	1 032	30.3	NA	123 119	0.6	8 184	6.6	113 047	37.3	18.6
Omaha-Council Bluffs, NE-IA	343 054	64.8	146 500	21.0	12.1	783	28.4	2.9	480 044	0.8	17 528	3.7	462 196	38.5	19.8
Orlando-Kissimmee-Sanford, FL	780 174	60.7	151 700	24.6	11.7	991	33.8	2.8	1 212 107	2.5	71 941	5.9	1 060 772	34.3	16.8
Oshkosh-Neenah, WI	68 985	63.7	143 400	21.3	13.1	661	27.8	NA	91 977	0.2	4 880	5.3	86 547	28.3	29.5
Owensboro, KY	45 776	71.2	109 900	18.8	10.0	627	23.9	NA	54 275	-3.5	3 136	5.8	51 675	26.8	31.2
Oxnard-Thousand Oaks-Ventura, CA	265 788	63.3	443 700	26.4	10.0	1 518	34.0	7.0	431 547	-0.6	28 827	6.7	403 569	37.0	21.5
Palm Bay-Melbourne-Titusville, FL	218 325	71.6	135 900	23.6	11.5	876	33.3	NA	260 004	0.2	17 991	6.9	227 309	35.6	19.1
Panama City, FL	69 032	61.2	142 700	24.6	10.0	877	31.2	NA	94 086	1.5	5 874	6.2	83 857	30.9	20.4
Parkersburg-Vienna, WV	38 799	71.6	103 900	19.8	10.0	605	28.7	NA	40 223	-1.5	2 446	6.1	38 919	29.8	26.3
Pensacola-Ferry Pass-Brent, FL	172 663	64.8	132 400	21.9	10.8	897	31.6	NA	215 182	1.0	12 981	6.0	192 257	33.3	19.0
Peoria, IL	152 051	69.7	128 400	18.9	11.6	689	26.8	NA	187 666	-1.9	13 447	7.2	175 900	37.2	20.5
Philadelphia-Camden-Wilmington, PA-NJ-DE-MD	2 218 312	66.9	233 600	23.7	14.5	997	32.4	1.8	3 024 278	-0.5	185 989	6.1	2 852 562	41.7	16.3
Camden, NJ Div 15804	451 883	73.2	213 500	24.8	17.2	1 038	32.5	1.8	636 420	-1.0	44 421	7.0	601 127	40.2	17.5
Montgomery County-Bucks County-Chester County, PA Div 33874	724 010	73.8	300 900	23.1	13.7	1 120	30.1	1.2	1 042 327	-0.4	48 768	4.7	995 967	46.1	15.6
Philadelphia, PA Div 37964	782 213	55.6	161 700	24.1	14.9	925	33.9	2.4	979 231	-1.0	71 102	7.3	907 573	37.9	16.2
Wilmington, DE-MD-NJ Div 48864	260 206	70.4	237 500	22.1	11.3	1 013	31.4	1.8	366 300	1.7	21 698	5.9	347 895	41.4	16.8
Phoenix-Mesa-Scottsdale, AZ	1 553 429	61.0	177 900	22.1	10.6	936	29.5	4.6	2 107 929	2.2	125 885	6.0	1 928 178	36.3	17.9
Pine Bluff, AR	35 484	66.4	76 500	19.5	11.5	640	32.0	NA	36 776	-4.6	3 145	8.6	34 956	24.7	34.3
Pittsburgh, PA	988 106	69.8	130 700	19.2	12.2	712	28.1	1.2	1 209 609	-1.0	67 803	5.6	1 142 816	38.6	19.4
Pittsfield, MA	54 963	67.9	199 700	21.4	13.2	747	29.6	NA	66 116	0.2	4 290	6.5	62 392	41.3	16.4
Pocatello, ID	30 265	65.9	145 300	19.6	10.0	591	29.5	NA	41 703	0.7	1 911	4.6	37 925	33.6	20.2
Portland-South Portland, ME	213 413	69.6	232 300	23.8	14.8	902	31.7	1.6	288 663	-1.1	13 760	4.8	268 445	39.3	19.6
Portland-Vancouver-Hillsboro, OR-WA	881 822	60.3	264 000	24.0	12.2	969	30.4	3.2	1 201 500	1.6	76 922	6.4	1 116 546	40.3	19.1
Port St. Lucie, FL	165 882	70.3	144 700	24.8	13.4	947	35.3	NA	200 315	1.6	14 699	7.3	172 893	31.4	19.1
Prescott, AZ	91 064	66.3	173 500	28.8	12.7	868	32.9	NA	95 402	2.9	6 049	6.3	84 363	29.7	21.4
Providence-Warwick, RI-MA	618 975	60.6	246 100	24.4	14.6	885	31.1	1.8	842 252	-0.1	63 637	7.6	776 297	35.6	20.2
Provo-Orem, UT	149 549	66.3	220 700	23.0	10.0	890	30.0	4.4	260 388	2.5	9 097	3.5	239 174	39.4	17.5
Pueblo, CO	62 604	63.6	141 000	24.2	12.3	755	32.3	NA	73 037	-0.8	5 358	7.3	63 453	28.4	24.3
Punta Gorda, FL	69 035	78.6	138 000	28.7	12.0	888	34.8	NA	67 003	1.2	4 510	6.7	53 051	28.2	19.3
Racine, WI	72 057	70.9	160 600	22.3	14.5	771	31.6	NA	100 103	0.1	6 760	6.8	89 125	34.1	27.6
Raleigh, NC	449 589	64.9	202 900	20.1	10.0	908	28.6	3.6	630 600	1.3	31 020	4.9	604 940	47.2	14.8
Rapid City, SD	55 969	68.1	157 500	22.6	11.6	747	30.3	NA	71 366	0.6	2 440	3.4	69 703	30.0	22.8
Reading, PA	153 271	73.6	166 900	22.8	14.8	826	32.1	NA	210 590	-0.4	11 525	5.5	198 055	31.1	27.7

1. Specified owner-occupied units. 2. A value of 10.0 represents 10 percent or less. 3. Specified renter-occupied units. 4. Overcrowded or lacking complete plumbing facilities.
5. Percent of civilian labor force. 6. Persons 16 years old and over.

Area name	Private nonfarm establishments, employment and payroll, 2013: Number of establishments	Employment: Total	Employment: Health care and social assistance	Employment: Manufacturing	Employment: Retail trade	Employment: Finance and insurance	Employment: Professional, scientific, and technical services	Annual payroll: Total (mil dol)	Annual payroll: Average per employee (dollars)	Agriculture, 2012: Farms: Number	Farms: Percent with: Fewer than 50 acres	Farms: Percent with: 500 acres or more	Farm operators whose principal occupation is farming (percent)
	104	105	106	107	108	109	110	111	112	113	114	115	116
Modesto, CA	8 516	128 728	23 373	18 837	22 227	3 337	5 057	5 390	41 874	4 143	68.8	5.9	59.1
Monroe, LA	4 507	67 222	15 216	6 202	9 933	4 804	2 850	2 291	34 082	863	40.0	6.7	44.5
Monroe, MI	2 303	35 969	5 829	6 670	5 015	880	800	1 472	40 922	1 144	53.0	10.9	46.3
Montgomery, AL	7 583	127 528	19 740	17 613	17 760	4 772	6 680	4 884	38 297	1 985	33.0	15.7	47.5
Morgantown, WV	2 782	48 734	15 276	4 235	7 172	931	2 424	1 829	37 532	1 542	26.3	3.3	42.6
Morristown, TN	1 942	36 573	5 144	10 448	5 563	802	464	1 234	33 746	1 550	47.2	1.6	45.5
Mount Vernon-Anacortes, WA	3 351	38 170	7 241	5 278	6 865	1 549	1 561	1 585	41 534	1 074	73.0	4.4	48.0
Muncie, IN	2 321	37 892	9 184	4 288	6 152	2 617	1 463	1 281	33 814	610	49.5	13.3	54.8
Muskegon, MI	3 134	50 724	10 768	12 053	7 705	1 025	1 301	1 889	37 233	514	56.6	4.9	48.4
Myrtle Beach-Conway-North Myrtle Beach, NC-SC	10 513	121 678	14 430	4 267	25 647	4 179	3 889	3 524	28 960	1 192	46.0	9.2	48.9
Napa, CA	4 043	58 272	10 351	10 409	6 843	1 402	1 760	2 801	48 063	1 685	71.9	5.3	34.9
Naples-Immokalee-Marco Island, FL	10 622	108 607	16 923	2 705	19 578	3 722	4 885	4 313	39 711	319	74.0	10.3	43.9
Nashville-Davidson—Murfreesboro—Franklin, TN	39 849	738 050	120 723	62 293	87 202	40 809	39 422	34 221	46 366	13 301	39.9	4.5	41.6
New Bern, NC	2 551	30 223	7 244	2 875	4 923	917	1 836	1 063	35 156	506	41.3	17.2	61.3
New Haven-Milford, CT	19 431	331 081	72 961	31 847	42 507	12 359	15 043	16 252	49 088	695	77.3	1.2	43.0
New Orleans-Metairie, LA	29 794	475 098	71 024	27 262	59 528	19 168	32 447	21 675	45 621	1 027	65.4	7.4	45.2
New York-Newark-Jersey City, NY-NJ-PA	564 394	7 870 219	1 423 121	338 127	915 394	567 465	699 804	517 669	65 776	6 758	68.3	2.9	50.9
Dutchess County-Putnam County, NY Div 20524	X	X	X	X	X	X	X	X	X	750	47.2	6.9	53.9
Nassau County-Suffolk County, NY Div 35004	X	X	X	X	X	X	X	X	X	659	72.1	1.5	67.4
Newark, NJ-PA Div 35084	X	X	X	X	X	X	X	X	X	3 169	71.7	2.1	43.4
New York-Jersey City-White Plains, NY-NJ Div 35614	X	X	X	X	X	X	X	X	X	2 180	69.6	3.0	55.9
Niles-Benton Harbor, MI	3 610	51 314	8 909	8 387	6 792	1 273	2 006	2 200	42 871	1 063	57.9	7.0	51.0
North Port-Sarasota-Bradenton, FL	20 830	212 702	41 598	13 843	38 446	7 943	12 552	7 771	36 533	972	65.3	8.8	43.7
Norwich-New London, CT	5 698	103 244	17 133	D	14 424	2 095	7 714	5 107	49 467	949	64.0	1.3	48.6
Ocala, FL	6 787	74 910	15 911	5 482	14 864	2 338	3 741	2 516	33 591	3 870	76.7	2.2	49.5
Ocean City, NJ	3 806	24 732	4 757	458	5 622	1 111	1 021	962	38 906	152	75.7	1.3	48.0
Odessa, TX	3 582	62 316	6 992	4 552	8 348	1 426	1 610	3 184	51 088	264	70.5	14.4	28.8
Ogden-Clearfield, UT	12 723	168 923	21 829	28 301	25 848	6 540	14 794	6 085	36 025	3 150	64.5	11.0	37.7
Oklahoma City, OK	34 197	491 330	77 563	30 706	64 061	23 043	30 655	20 940	42 618	9 797	35.7	12.4	43.2
Olympia-Tumwater, WA	5 840	64 870	13 091	2 559	12 085	2 516	4 980	2 428	37 435	1 336	79.3	2.0	30.7
Omaha-Council Bluffs, NE-IA	22 660	400 970	58 237	30 514	52 675	38 256	23 657	17 704	44 154	6 055	35.4	26.4	56.8
Orlando-Kissimmee-Sanford, FL	57 572	928 943	112 280	33 929	131 952	38 444	57 710	36 476	39 266	3 123	76.1	4.8	47.9
Oshkosh-Neenah, WI	3 489	83 823	13 058	21 891	8 171	3 182	2 532	4 003	47 754	1 117	48.5	6.0	39.2
Owensboro, KY	2 557	46 018	8 541	8 048	6 185	3 201	1 878	1 683	36 581	1 600	41.6	11.8	46.0
Oxnard-Thousand Oaks-Ventura, CA	20 089	247 116	33 429	23 031	38 595	13 531	22 247	12 013	48 614	2 150	78.0	5.2	48.7
Palm Bay-Melbourne-Titusville, FL	13 084	161 218	29 730	18 801	25 978	4 479	12 336	6 604	40 962	513	80.3	5.1	38.8
Panama City, FL	4 655	58 862	10 201	4 551	10 930	1 980	3 431	1 979	33 618	149	64.4	3.4	45.0
Parkersburg-Vienna, WV	2 115	33 760	7 099	2 969	6 268	979	1 013	1 114	32 990	1 033	28.0	2.3	34.8
Pensacola-Ferry Pass-Brent, FL	9 050	120 422	24 483	4 460	19 948	6 222	7 986	4 332	35 970	1 395	64.1	5.7	42.3
Peoria, IL	8 522	166 599	28 720	19 671	19 196	6 040	7 334	8 090	48 559	3 605	32.5	22.3	52.8
Philadelphia-Camden-Wilmington, PA-NJ-DE-MD	145 040	2 511 505	457 281	168 032	301 008	171 574	204 677	133 440	53 131	6 543	65.1	3.9	54.8
Camden, NJ Div 15804	X	X	X	X	X	X	X	X	X	1 597	72.5	3.7	51.6
Montgomery County-Bucks County-Chester County, PA Div 33874	X	X	X	X	X	X	X	X	X	3 153	64.2	2.3	57.2
Philadelphia, PA Div 37964	X	X	X	X	X	X	X	X	X	98	68.4	0.0	48.0
Wilmington, DE-MD-NJ Div 48864	X	X	X	X	X	X	X	X	X	1 695	59.6	7.4	53.7
Phoenix-Mesa-Scottsdale, AZ	89 356	1 538 013	218 445	96 817	199 250	109 545	94 833	69 257	45 030	3 417	76.9	10.4	54.2
Pine Bluff, AR	1 607	23 463	4 934	5 645	3 644	D	477	793	33 805	1 032	32.0	19.6	54.9
Pittsburgh, PA	59 503	1 080 243	198 360	90 481	128 407	56 592	77 255	50 403	46 659	7 048	37.1	3.0	45.3
Pittsfield, MA	3 928	53 041	11 214	4 921	8 794	2 219	D	2 135	40 260	525	49.9	4.4	51.0
Pocatello, ID	1 953	23 611	4 795	1 752	4 446	1 892	1 223	714	30 228	819	46.6	16.1	42.6
Portland-South Portland, ME	17 245	222 290	44 072	20 874	32 936	14 781	12 908	9 406	42 315	1 726	56.6	2.8	50.2
Portland-Vancouver-Hillsboro, OR-WA	63 998	907 979	128 708	97 067	107 658	42 461	67 372	44 853	49 398	10 838	79.1	1.9	42.3
Port St. Lucie, FL	10 203	103 383	19 308	4 933	21 720	3 056	5 473	3 613	34 948	993	64.7	13.1	54.0
Prescott, AZ	5 548	53 338	11 973	2 984	9 940	1 311	1 653	1 774	33 261	940	69.9	13.1	64.1
Providence-Warwick, RI-MA	40 556	599 016	126 717	62 777	81 494	28 914	27 603	25 537	42 632	1 960	72.3	0.8	49.5
Provo-Orem, UT	11 562	172 407	21 988	16 993	23 303	5 048	13 384	6 500	37 703	2 815	73.2	6.1	30.3
Pueblo, CO	3 036	46 754	12 228	4 248	8 013	1 150	1 715	1 684	36 026	894	38.9	21.3	52.3
Punta Gorda, FL	3 692	35 239	9 018	396	8 520	1 103	1 361	1 094	31 055	284	61.3	12.0	51.1
Racine, WI	3 976	67 537	11 283	15 846	8 576	2 052	1 970	2 953	43 731	575	51.0	8.2	45.6
Raleigh, NC	30 006	457 181	60 580	22 109	61 573	21 991	48 082	21 117	46 191	2 500	50.5	6.7	45.9
Rapid City, SD	4 631	52 534	10 713	2 682	9 343	3 443	2 189	1 873	35 652	1 936	24.9	42.6	54.8
Reading, PA	8 246	148 933	25 075	29 883	20 780	5 993	6 703	6 331	42 508	2 039	47.8	3.5	61.4

Area name	Agriculture, 2012 (cont.) — Land in farms: Acreage (1,000)	Land in farms: Percent change, 2007–2012	Land in farms — Acres: Average size of farm	Acres: Total irrigated (1,000)	Acres: Total cropland (1,000)	Value of land and buildings (dollars): Average per farm	Value of land and buildings (dollars): Average per acre	Value of machinery and equipment, average per farm (dollars)	Value of products sold: Total (mil dol)	Value of products sold: Average per farm (dollars)	Value of products sold — Percent from: Crops	Percent from: Livestock and poultry products	Percent of farms with sales of: $10,000 or more	Percent of farms with sales of: $100,000 or more	Government payments: Total ($1,000)	Government payments: Percent of farms
	117	118	119	120	121	122	123	124	125	126	127	128	129	130	131	132
Modesto, CA	768	-2.7	185	320.8	340.9	1 786 289	9 636	117 810	2 228.1	537 807	47.7	52.3	66.5	33.9	7 049	10.7
Monroe, LA	156	2.0	180	12.2	64.3	525 813	2 913	73 651	142.0	164 531	20.0	80.0	34.8	12.4	2 099	17.8
Monroe, MI	215	3.2	188	9.8	196.2	853 688	4 553	135 682	173.9	152 008	95.5	4.5	54.6	20.3	3 653	50.8
Montgomery, AL	640	2.6	322	10.1	172.7	753 146	2 337	72 061	200.1	100 782	D	D	36.2	8.4	4 011	25.6
Morgantown, WV	219	3.4	142	0.1	59.8	373 360	2 633	53 257	22.2	14 383	28.0	72.0	28.7	2.2	387	7.7
Morristown, TN	154	-9.7	100	D	65.1	510 717	5 127	57 306	59.8	38 562	26.4	73.6	27.5	3.4	754	15.3
Mount Vernon-Anacortes, WA	107	-1.8	99	19.2	66.8	752 365	7 585	118 998	272.3	253 515	73.8	26.2	29.1	12.2	1 442	11.1
Muncie, IN	175	13.5	287	0.0	160.4	1 522 762	5 300	152 951	125.6	205 836	93.2	6.8	52.1	26.9	3 980	67.4
Muskegon, MI	74	-6.8	144	9.5	49.0	741 080	5 130	95 333	76.0	147 860	61.6	38.4	38.9	15.6	658	21.8
Myrtle Beach-Conway-North Myrtle Beach, NC-SC	223	7.4	187	6.8	135.5	613 356	3 278	93 415	159.5	133 816	67.5	32.5	32.0	13.7	2 576	41.3
Napa, CA	253	13.5	150	54.6	63.0	3 278 130	21 801	85 134	536.1	318 188	97.8	2.2	74.5	34.1	85	1.1
Naples-Immokalee-Marco Island, FL	124	12.4	387	26.4	66.9	1 736 727	4 482	151 806	202.8	635 583	98.1	1.9	36.4	14.7	207	2.8
Nashville-Davidson—Murfreesboro—Franklin, TN	1 868	-3.1	140	6.1	733.8	592 188	4 217	60 620	D	D	D	D	28.9	4.6	7 865	17.8
New Bern, NC	177	-5.0	349	4.4	136.2	1 010 889	2 893	192 399	276.9	547 283	D	D	49.4	31.8	4 482	57.7
New Haven-Milford, CT	42	-7.4	61	1.3	14.1	764 679	12 561	56 881	84.6	121 755	91.7	8.3	31.9	10.1	383	7.3
New Orleans-Metairie, LA	230	-15.3	224	D	68.4	635 817	2 843	75 303	77.8	75 785	71.4	28.6	33.7	7.6	D	6.3
New York-Newark-Jersey City, NY-NJ-PA	D	D	D	D	D	D	D	D	D	D	D	D	39.5	13.2	D	9.8
Dutchess County-Putnam County, NY Div 20524	118	9.6	158	D	47.2	820 965	5 201	92 353	52.3	69 704	55.5	44.5	47.2	16.4	451	10.0
Nassau County-Suffolk County, NY Div 35004	39	8.3	59	11.9	23.5	713 168	12 158	131 416	246.1	373 389	84.3	15.7	62.4	31.1	790	6.5
Newark, NJ-PA Div 35084	235	-3.4	74	2.8	117.1	1 055 516	14 250	59 764	144.7	45 663	D	D	27.8	6.2	D	8.4
New York-Jersey City-White Plains, NY-NJ Div 35614	D	D	D	10.2	D	D	D	D	D	D	D	D	46.8	16.9	D	12.8
Niles-Benton Harbor, MI	156	-7.5	147	18.1	126.1	822 736	5 591	123 913	161.5	151 968	90.3	9.7	51.6	20.6	3 303	29.4
North Port-Sarasota-Bradenton, FL	267	-6.9	274	52.1	75.1	1 468 749	5 356	94 934	323.5	332 798	89.0	11.0	38.4	12.4	395	1.3
Norwich-New London, CT	65	2.8	69	0.8	22.8	709 299	10 330	47 891	118.3	124 690	43.2	56.8	26.9	6.7	537	9.2
Ocala, FL	321	20.6	83	13.2	69.8	776 909	9 353	37 481	188.2	48 624	23.3	76.7	27.8	8.2	483	2.1
Ocean City, NJ	7	-7.8	48	2.2	4.3	557 868	11 534	51 809	8.0	52 809	93.4	6.6	40.1	10.5	D	2.0
Odessa, TX	429	1.2	1 624	0.8	3.6	786 019	484	48 008	2.2	8 296	28.9	71.1	16.3	1.5	211	5.3
Ogden-Clearfield, UT	1 572	-11.5	499	163.5	390.3	891 628	1 787	88 691	266.5	84 616	48.0	52.0	35.1	12.3	8 138	20.8
Oklahoma City, OK	2 466	-7.5	252	31.6	839.6	492 117	1 955	64 720	451.1	46 043	32.4	67.6	32.8	6.8	13 028	25.7
Olympia-Tumwater, WA	77	-4.9	57	5.3	23.1	498 439	8 689	40 468	122.4	91 634	39.9	60.1	19.5	5.2	267	2.4
Omaha-Council Bluffs, NE-IA	2 373	9.9	392	D	2 092.0	2 376 608	6 064	217 610	1 649.3	272 378	74.2	25.8	60.6	39.0	40 234	69.0
Orlando-Kissimmee-Sanford, FL	853	-9.2	273	55.0	81.9	1 468 380	5 374	45 570	539.8	172 845	88.9	11.1	37.6	14.1	632	1.6
Oshkosh-Neenah, WI	156	-5.2	139	0.4	126.2	585 332	4 204	97 747	126.6	113 315	41.3	58.7	41.5	20.1	3 245	54.3
Owensboro, KY	414	-10.9	259	11.3	310.1	959 871	3 711	135 426	370.2	231 353	49.6	50.4	43.7	18.8	6 252	57.9
Oxnard-Thousand Oaks-Ventura, CA	281	8.5	131	87.1	101.1	2 041 990	15 621	94 136	1 440.1	669 829	99.3	0.7	65.1	24.7	154	2.0
Palm Bay-Melbourne-Titusville, FL	146	-12.3	286	13.4	19.3	1 545 698	5 414	45 433	46.0	89 651	77.2	22.8	36.8	6.6	142	2.1
Panama City, FL	15	-12.4	101	D	3.2	494 671	4 886	36 826	3.6	24 436	63.6	36.4	18.8	2.0	D	7.4
Parkersburg-Vienna, WV	126	-3.3	122	D	29.5	258 830	2 124	35 881	8.3	8 082	30.4	69.6	15.3	0.5	157	4.5
Pensacola-Ferry Pass-Brent, FL	172	13.2	123	7.1	109.7	508 622	4 120	72 795	105.3	75 502	92.7	7.3	24.9	9.5	3 971	27.7
Peoria, IL	1 288	2.9	357	D	1 149.9	2 619 353	7 332	215 209	960.8	266 524	87.7	12.3	62.8	41.4	25 748	76.4
Philadelphia-Camden-Wilmington, PA-NJ-DE-MD	653	-3.8	100	51.0	456.1	1 066 581	10 682	100 412	1 264.9	193 316	D	D	43.9	18.2	D	16.8
Camden, NJ Div 15804	146	3.6	92	24.7	89.0	960 535	10 485	93 126	204.6	128 112	95.0	5.0	39.6	14.6	2 659	12.4
Montgomery County-Bucks County-Chester County, PA Div 33874	259	-8.9	82	2.9	173.7	1 068 407	12 992	94 153	748.8	237 474	80.2	19.8	47.1	20.3	2 503	14.3
Philadelphia, PA Div 37964	5	8.4	51	0.1	1.3	797 133	15 593	51 439	10.5	107 643	98.7	1.3	36.7	7.1	D	2.0
Wilmington, DE-MD-NJ Div 48864	243	-2.4	143	23.3	192.1	1 178 678	8 232	121 753	301.0	177 561	D	D	42.4	18.3	4 693	26.5
Phoenix-Mesa-Scottsdale, AZ	1 651	7.7	483	416.5	525.1	1 606 626	3 326	134 243	1 931.2	565 178	39.5	60.5	37.0	18.4	14 937	14.7
Pine Bluff, AR	519	-0.3	503	D	421.0	1 463 373	2 912	248 855	540.5	523 758	58.2	41.8	49.1	33.6	18 108	53.1
Pittsburgh, PA	818	-6.7	116	2.4	409.7	491 395	4 235	76 477	231.1	32 792	59.1	40.9	34.4	6.1	5 514	18.6
Pittsfield, MA	62	-7.1	117	0.2	18.4	824 924	7 024	51 476	22.5	42 796	45.1	54.9	29.5	6.7	268	9.3
Pocatello, ID	295	-8.3	360	52.6	164.1	651 077	1 807	83 179	54.3	66 267	66.6	33.4	29.4	9.2	3 067	37.0
Portland-South Portland, ME	147	13.6	85	2.1	44.1	404 259	4 737	57 375	D	D	D	D	32.4	6.8	994	7.0
Portland-Vancouver-Hillsboro, OR-WA	644	-2.7	59	75.1	340.4	624 772	10 520	59 443	1 008.7	93 072	D	D	27.6	7.6	5 384	7.7
Port St. Lucie, FL	334	18.2	337	94.1	110.4	1 858 422	5 518	72 106	333.5	335 878	77.8	22.2	42.8	17.1	1 270	5.5
Prescott, AZ	825	29.0	877	7.6	10.7	1 382 518	1 576	51 250	41.6	44 285	25.5	74.5	32.2	12.0	141	3.2
Providence-Warwick, RI-MA	D	D	D	5.6	34.5	757 972	D	54 363	97.3	49 648	81.1	18.9	35.9	8.7	D	14.3
Provo-Orem, UT	586	-3.3	208	95.6	157.4	753 272	3 619	70 725	251.0	89 161	43.7	56.3	31.4	6.9	2 120	11.0
Pueblo, CO	895	-1.7	1 001	18.6	88.5	735 098	734	62 169	51.1	57 149	35.4	64.6	27.2	8.1	2 223	20.6
Punta Gorda, FL	217	30.8	765	13.7	18.4	3 875 556	5 067	65 965	103.4	364 088	91.8	8.2	38.0	13.0	92	1.8
Racine, WI	110	-8.7	191	1.9	92.6	1 042 289	5 450	127 732	94.8	164 887	77.6	22.4	50.3	21.7	1 972	50.6
Raleigh, NC	396	1.0	158	10.6	237.5	902 766	5 700	94 320	411.9	164 756	65.9	34.1	35.6	14.4	6 265	34.1
Rapid City, SD	3 730	-6.6	1 927	12.9	619.5	1 464 509	760	105 970	208.2	107 542	27.8	72.2	56.0	24.1	9 162	33.6
Reading, PA	234	5.2	115	1.6	182.3	1 015 554	8 859	120 253	528.7	259 299	42.6	57.4	58.5	30.2	3 646	28.3

Table C. Metropolitan Areas — **Water Use, Wholesale Trade, Retail Trade, and Real Estate**

Area name	Water use, 2010		Wholesale trade,[1] 2007				Retail trade, 2007				Real estate and rental and leasing, 2007			
	Total water withdrawn (mil gal/day)	Gallons withdrawn per person per day	Number of establish-ments	Number of employees	Sales (mil dol)	Annual payroll (mil dol)	Number of establish-ments	Number of employees	Sales (mil dol)	Annual payroll (mil dol)	Number of establish-ments	Number of employees	Receipts (mil dol)	Annual payroll (mil dol)
	133	134	135	136	137	138	139	140	141	142	143	144	145	146
Modesto, CA	1 642.7	3 193	397	5 460	3 759.1	248.8	1 500	23 394	5 661.9	561.1	500	2 988	472.6	90.3
Monroe, LA	72.2	409	190	D	D	D	809	10 259	2 369.7	208.0	198	874	151.1	27.7
Monroe, MI	1 830.0	12 038	91	D	D	D	427	5 637	1 465.3	120.3	95	373	48.8	7.5
Montgomery, AL	113.7	303	350	D	D	D	1 448	19 572	4 558.3	428.7	389	D	D	D
Morgantown, WV	123.3	950	63	D	D	D	487	7 365	1 510.8	128.0	151	625	82.7	15.5
Morristown, TN	18.2	160	76	1 471	627.0	60.9	452	5 849	1 609.3	127.4	91	374	52.8	7.8
Mount Vernon-Anacortes, WA	45.3	388	124	1 557	698.0	61.2	616	7 788	2 134.8	200.4	181	653	105.5	18.3
Muncie, IN	15.6	132	97	984	424.1	31.6	484	6 563	1 516.8	130.8	113	575	89.0	17.2
Muskegon, MI	271.7	1 578	119	D	D	D	608	7 878	1 656.7	154.5	112	484	67.0	12.0
Myrtle Beach-Conway-North Myrtle Beach, NC-SC	1 525.6	4 050	330	2 815	1 114.3	102.7	2 202	25 336	5 971.4	549.5	922	6 528	943.1	209.9
Napa, CA	96.9	710	143	D	D	D	537	6 463	1 665.0	180.7	206	893	153.0	31.1
Naples-Immokalee-Marco Island, FL	256.9	799	331	2 678	1 649.0	137.9	1 500	20 122	5 186.5	535.5	958	2 874	552.3	118.0
Nashville-Davidson—Murfreesboro—Franklin, TN	891.7	534	1 857	D	D	D	6 202	88 491	21 986.3	2 078.8	1 935	D	D	D
New Bern, NC	44.8	353	85	920	889.6	32.8	498	5 029	1 212.4	110.0	134	D	D	D
New Haven-Milford, CT	113.5	132	980	14 619	9 890.7	814.1	3 172	46 058	11 785.3	1 112.5	780	5 470	1 611.1	192.9
New Orleans-Metairie, LA	4 541.9	3 817	1 499	D	D	D	4 361	61 789	15 717.6	1 507.3	1 275	9 087	1 701.0	318.3
New York-Newark-Jersey City, NY-NJ-PA	7 105.0	363	36 669	D	D	D	78 300	893 275	246 883.0	24 184.3	34 292	D	D	D
Dutchess County-Putnam County, NY Div 20524	84.5	213	347	2 997	1 487.0	152.4	1 437	17 803	4 521.5	441.0	497	2 144	345.9	74.2
Nassau County-Suffolk County, NY Div 35004	1 136.2	401	6 117	D	D	D	13 106	168 238	47 632.5	4 491.6	4 314	D	D	D
Newark, NJ-PA Div 35084	410.6	166	3 853	D	D	D	9 491	121 393	33 885.1	3 204.0	2 781	D	D	D
New York-Jersey City-White Plains, NY-NJ Div 35614	5 473.7	395	26 352	D	D	D	54 266	585 841	160 843.9	16 047.7	26 700	149 516	47 697.0	7 500.4
Niles-Benton Harbor, MI	2 019.0	12 875	143	1 836	689.1	65.2	609	7 360	1 622.8	153.9	189	796	105.6	19.3
North Port-Sarasota-Bradenton, FL	157.8	225	780	6 756	3 285.8	295.9	2 927	39 824	9 474.3	943.1	1 479	5 402	930.0	169.3
Norwich-New London, CT	2 249.8	8 209	147	D	D	D	1 123	15 660	3 883.0	390.4	232	D	D	D
Ocala, FL	65.4	197	318	3 812	1 639.5	149.7	1 208	16 639	4 218.8	379.2	466	1 598	217.9	39.9
Ocean City, NJ	79.6	818	65	561	276.1	25.3	746	6 103	1 584.9	164.8	258	836	177.1	27.0
Odessa, TX	60.2	439	286	4 048	2 004.3	219.0	476	6 660	2 090.6	167.6	157	1 383	338.4	74.3
Ogden-Clearfield, UT	795.6	1 332	449	D	D	D	1 652	26 789	6 518.4	572.1	800	D	D	D
Oklahoma City, OK	263.1	210	1 464	D	D	D	4 391	61 143	15 683.6	1 371.5	1 650	D	D	D
Olympia-Tumwater, WA	52.3	207	177	1 766	1 003.4	78.8	822	12 136	3 103.0	313.2	323	1 234	238.8	31.6
Omaha-Council Bluffs, NE-IA	1 570.7	1 815	1 111	15 509	11 953.9	712.1	2 857	51 994	13 052.9	1 153.3	1 018	6 713	1 146.9	215.0
Orlando-Kissimmee-Sanford, FL	509.9	239	2 656	33 772	23 703.9	1 594.1	8 295	126 325	32 378.3	2 870.4	4 241	36 652	7 857.9	1 398.3
Oshkosh-Neenah, WI	35.3	211	160	2 536	1 109.2	102.8	540	8 027	1 796.5	162.1	125	756	97.5	19.6
Owensboro, KY	577.6	5 034	106	1 279	860.0	48.9	488	6 298	1 359.0	129.8	85	D	D	D
Oxnard-Thousand Oaks-Ventura, CA	719.5	874	1 024	D	D	D	2 766	40 773	11 083.6	1 074.8	1 051	5 064	1 006.1	196.0
Palm Bay-Melbourne-Titusville, FL	251.4	463	493	3 683	1 852.7	155.1	2 073	28 911	6 594.0	630.4	777	2 795	401.1	74.8
Panama City, FL	303.6	1 644	177	D	D	D	864	10 557	2 548.3	234.4	336	1 240	176.3	35.2
Parkersburg-Vienna, WV	63.8	689	85	D	D	D	437	6 872	1 726.6	132.7	87	D	D	D
Pensacola-Ferry Pass-Brent, FL	337.9	753	350	3 437	1 987.8	135.5	1 596	21 249	5 163.7	470.9	591	2 008	333.3	55.7
Peoria, IL	648.5	1 710	435	D	D	D	1 404	20 008	4 598.1	430.9	352	D	D	D
Philadelphia-Camden-Wilmington, PA-NJ-DE-MD	5 352.0	897	7 116	D	D	D	20 970	316 013	84 725.1	7 790.7	5 693	D	D	D
Camden, NJ Div 15804	239.2	191	1 531	D	D	D	4 494	69 542	17 216.9	1 694.7	1 046	D	D	D
Montgomery County-Bucks County-Chester County, PA Div 33874	488.6	254	3 303	44 811	30 443.4	2 824.0	7 619	130 538	39 579.5	3 387.3	2 149	D	D	D
Philadelphia, PA Div 37964	1 157.1	555	1 615	25 359	15 786.1	1 426.7	6 281	76 687	17 526.2	1 775.3	1 537	14 824	3 125.0	629.9
Wilmington, DE-MD-NJ Div 48864	3 467.2	4 913	667	D	D	D	2 576	39 246	10 402.5	933.4	961	D	D	D
Phoenix-Mesa-Scottsdale, AZ	3 083.7	735	4 286	67 713	50 210.7	3 493.1	11 992	226 298	60 721.4	5 507.8	6 325	38 676	7 904.0	1 582.1
Pine Bluff, AR	576.3	5 748	77	D	D	D	363	4 353	937.2	84.7	83	D	D	D
Pittsburgh, PA	1 712.7	727	2 661	D	D	D	8 858	132 058	32 663.5	2 755.1	2 016	13 928	2 677.4	508.1
Pittsfield, MA	24.3	185	113	D	D	D	766	8 942	1 901.8	208.8	128	770	123.3	22.9
Pocatello, ID	168.1	2 029	78	636	386.6	24.1	350	4 972	1 099.2	97.7	96	323	52.2	6.9
Portland-South Portland, ME	114.0	222	663	8 223	4 246.0	350.8	2 637	34 309	7 984.1	803.4	900	3 763	622.4	126.8
Portland-Vancouver-Hillsboro, OR-WA	733.4	329	3 193	48 471	43 092.1	2 542.2	7 404	113 736	29 223.2	2 847.2	3 702	20 226	3 772.3	729.0
Port St. Lucie, FL	1 302.5	3 071	439	3 292	1 435.2	137.8	1 514	24 047	6 168.1	578.4	653	2 609	377.2	72.5
Prescott, AZ	92.3	437	175	1 652	831.4	61.1	920	11 795	2 695.4	266.6	469	1 776	293.9	55.4
Providence-Warwick, RI-MA	1 257.6	786	1 825	28 352	16 902.6	1 429.6	6 499	87 944	20 934.1	2 061.9	1 705	8 944	1 844.9	297.8
Provo-Orem, UT	422.2	801	411	6 076	2 444.3	276.9	1 391	24 306	5 884.4	523.1	755	D	D	D
Pueblo, CO	288.9	1 816	85	850	431.0	37.8	548	8 064	1 864.6	192.4	165	667	94.9	18.3
Punta Gorda, FL	58.8	367	94	592	211.7	22.0	582	8 761	1 898.1	187.9	289	877	120.7	22.1
Racine, WI	28.6	146	186	D	D	D	654	10 082	2 230.0	198.7	140	596	64.5	13.4
Raleigh, NC	153.6	136	1 207	17 014	12 333.2	983.1	3 899	58 236	14 941.6	1 340.3	1 502	7 839	1 990.0	337.6
Rapid City, SD	74.5	554	180	D	D	D	716	8 832	2 213.6	199.1	196	788	131.1	18.3
Reading, PA	57.1	139	375	6 306	4 417.6	306.7	1 327	20 433	4 953.2	466.8	273	1 384	210.2	39.4

1. Merchant wholesalers, except manufacturers' sales branches and offices.

Area name	Professional, scientific, and technical services,[1] 2007				Manufacturing, 2007				Accommodation and food services, 2007			
	Number of establish-ments	Number of employees	Sales (mil dol)	Annual payroll (mil dol)	Number of establish-ments	Number of employees	Sales (mil dol)	Annual payroll (mil dol)	Number of establish-ments	Number of employees	Sales (mil dol)	Annual payroll (mil dol)
	147	148	149	150	151	152	153	154	155	156	157	158
Modesto, CA	701	D	D	D	443	24 127	9 476.0	1 032.9	842	13 881	615.1	171.7
Monroe, LA	462	D	D	D	146	D	D	D	302	6 798	260.5	70.3
Monroe, MI	147	944	84.3	39.6	143	8 555	3 503.0	440.6	274	4 682	171.5	47.8
Montgomery, AL	817	7 278	1 020.9	377.6	318	18 749	D	D	653	13 159	539.6	150.2
Morgantown, WV	231	D	D	D	98	3 918	D	173.8	266	5 401	205.0	56.3
Morristown, TN	120	D	D	D	165	15 605	4 076.9	537.8	179	3 671	139.6	39.9
Mount Vernon-Anacortes, WA	305	D	D	D	205	6 387	8 918.2	294.5	347	4 734	251.0	74.1
Muncie, IN	169	D	D	D	150	5 268	1 280.6	232.7	216	4 981	160.8	48.3
Muskegon, MI	239	D	D	D	290	13 271	3 675.8	609.1	344	5 763	221.0	64.6
Myrtle Beach-Conway-North Myrtle Beach, NC-SC	872	D	D	D	243	6 111	D	246.9	1 416	29 216	1 634.4	438.7
Napa, CA	419	D	D	D	436	13 165	4 529.3	632.4	363	8 904	620.4	195.4
Naples-Immokalee-Marco Island, FL	1 271	D	D	D	228	3 035	606.7	109.5	704	17 421	1 037.2	308.3
Nashville-Davidson—Murfreesboro—Franklin, TN	3 761	D	D	D	D	D	D	D	3 240	72 509	3 561.2	1 015.5
New Bern, NC	244	D	D	D	D	D	D	D	209	4 210	167.1	44.8
New Haven-Milford, CT	2 015	D	D	D	1 289	40 188	10 493.0	1 976.9	1 920	24 768	1 345.9	371.7
New Orleans-Metairie, LA	3 726	D	D	D	792	37 663	D	2 123.1	2 853	60 740	3 688.9	1 046.7
New York-Newark-Jersey City, NY-NJ-PA	69 625	D	D	D	D	D	D	D	42 601	555 917	40 812.4	11 049.8
Dutchess County-Putnam County, NY Div 20524	1 117	D	D	D	309	17 978	D	1 366.5	910	9 876	519.1	141.7
Nassau County-Suffolk County, NY Div 35004	12 596	D	D	D	3 577	D	D	4 056.0	6 466	79 474	4 815.8	1 331.5
Newark, NJ-PA Div 35084	9 718	D	D	D	D	D	D	D	5 307	69 136	4 293.7	1 162.4
New York-Jersey City-White Plains, NY-NJ Div 35614	46 194	D	D	D	12 261	D	D	11 662.5	29 918	397 431	31 183.8	8 414.2
Niles-Benton Harbor, MI	287	D	D	D	332	10 831	2 298.3	474.7	413	5 519	219.5	64.1
North Port-Sarasota-Bradenton, FL	2 687	D	D	D	630	17 798	4 351.8	763.1	1 335	26 200	1 288.2	381.4
Norwich-New London, CT	555	D	D	D	201	D	D	848.8	690	30 404	3 444.7	856.8
Ocala, FL	698	3 459	361.6	132.0	221	8 904	1 841.5	320.9	443	7 784	353.1	100.0
Ocean City, NJ	250	D	D	D	81	662	D	18.9	832	5 615	517.0	144.9
Odessa, TX	224	D	D	D	240	4 814	2 049.7	222.0	245	5 213	228.6	59.4
Ogden-Clearfield, UT	1 341	D	D	D	D	D	D	D	807	15 845	578.0	161.0
Oklahoma City, OK	3 836	D	D	D	D	D	D	D	2 428	52 115	2 111.6	588.3
Olympia-Tumwater, WA	598	D	D	D	189	3 118	870.1	120.7	497	7 612	346.7	102.7
Omaha-Council Bluffs, NE-IA	2 196	D	D	D	D	D	D	D	1 826	37 671	1 782.4	479.4
Orlando-Kissimmee-Sanford, FL	7 667	D	D	D	1 473	43 017	14 026.9	2 060.1	4 190	126 780	8 735.7	2 143.5
Oshkosh-Neenah, WI	250	D	D	D	319	23 777	9 198.9	1 149.8	377	6 071	212.1	58.4
Owensboro, KY	182	D	D	D	D	D	D	D	196	4 171	152.7	45.8
Oxnard-Thousand Oaks-Ventura, CA	2 597	16 457	6 370.8	1 032.7	954	33 602	8 769.0	1 643.4	1 602	29 832	1 478.2	422.9
Palm Bay-Melbourne-Titusville, FL	1 683	19 711	3 364.7	1 589.6	473	22 772	6 767.6	1 172.5	1 019	19 057	855.5	240.1
Panama City, FL	437	D	D	D	D	D	D	D	467	9 452	499.2	139.2
Parkersburg-Vienna, WV	143	D	D	D	D	D	D	D	233	4 207	158.8	48.0
Pensacola-Ferry Pass-Brent, FL	1 042	D	D	D	246	5 710	2 191.9	271.0	718	14 399	629.0	173.6
Peoria, IL	679	D	D	D	D	D	D	D	920	15 634	733.6	193.4
Philadelphia-Camden-Wilmington, PA-NJ-DE-MD	18 282	D	D	D	5 881	224 483	122 510.0	12 018.5	12 139	185 139	9 992.4	2 727.4
Camden, NJ Div 15804	3 525	D	D	D	1 180	48 041	25 901.8	2 543.1	2 398	35 317	1 715.2	470.0
Montgomery County-Bucks County-Chester County, PA Div 33874	8 382	D	D	D	2 811	101 973	36 468.1	5 318.7	3 983	62 876	3 231.4	888.8
Philadelphia, PA Div 37964	4 306	D	D	D	1 371	48 794	37 129.8	2 555.0	4 424	63 600	3 830.9	1 044.1
Wilmington, DE-MD-NJ Div 48864	2 069	D	D	D	519	25 675	23 010.3	1 601.7	1 334	23 346	1 214.9	324.5
Phoenix-Mesa-Scottsdale, AZ	11 954	D	D	D	3 520	124 958	42 332.0	6 195.2	7 078	162 741	8 750.8	2 534.6
Pine Bluff, AR	99	D	D	D	D	D	D	D	156	D	D	D
Pittsburgh, PA	5 990	D	D	D	2 755	101 747	38 078.2	4 809.7	5 348	93 669	3 940.5	1 134.6
Pittsfield, MA	366	D	D	D	173	6 204	1 425.5	317.1	516	7 600	401.9	125.6
Pocatello, ID	164	D	D	D	58	D	D	D	180	3 056	117.8	31.9
Portland-South Portland, ME	1 868	D	D	D	715	D	D	D	1 733	23 504	1 285.5	383.3
Portland-Vancouver-Hillsboro, OR-WA	7 698	D	D	D	D	D	D	D	5 340	83 103	4 170.3	1 226.8
Port St. Lucie, FL	1 178	D	D	D	295	6 106	1 772.6	231.8	665	13 151	547.3	161.6
Prescott, AZ	584	D	D	D	233	3 618	764.0	143.6	578	8 737	456.5	126.2
Providence-Warwick, RI-MA	4 206	D	D	D	2 628	88 819	20 939.7	4 034.3	4 132	65 292	3 033.8	883.8
Provo-Orem, UT	1 442	16 746	1 354.1	509.1	D	D	D	D	564	11 935	458.9	130.2
Pueblo, CO	251	D	D	D	106	3 838	1 705.8	180.3	344	5 602	220.9	61.8
Punta Gorda, FL	366	D	D	D	D	D	D	D	240	4 322	178.0	53.2
Racine, WI	346	D	D	D	345	17 183	7 863.3	890.8	388	6 239	242.7	66.1
Raleigh, NC	4 380	36 371	5 527.1	2 271.0	810	27 491	17 544.1	1 263.7	2 087	41 492	1 945.2	537.1
Rapid City, SD	341	D	D	D	D	D	D	D	470	6 819	347.7	96.1
Reading, PA	735	6 289	1 449.0	389.4	550	32 597	8 461.8	1 487.9	715	11 030	446.0	124.4

1. Establishments subject to federal tax.

Table C. Metropolitan Areas — **Health Care and Social Assistance, Other Services, Nonemployer Business and Residential Construction**

Area name	Health care and social assistance,[1] 2007				Other services,[1] 2007				Nonemployer business, 2013		Value of residential construction authorized by building permits, 2014	
	Number of establish-ments	Number of employees	Receipts (mil dol)	Annual payroll (mil dol)	Number of establish-ments	Number of employees	Receipts (mil dol)	Annual payroll (mil dol)	Number	Receipts (mil dol)	New construc-tion ($1,000)	Number of housing units
	159	160	161	162	163	164	165	166	167	168	169	170
Modesto, CA	1 108	21 628	2 662.6	967.7	650	4 205	380.9	119.5	25 939	1 252.0	97 036	454
Monroe, LA	616	13 311	1 180.9	416.2	245	1 573	138.5	38.0	13 733	556.9	116 195	726
Monroe, MI	284	4 733	381.3	158.7	195	1 172	93.7	30.3	8 193	340.8	44 179	239
Montgomery, AL	917	19 608	1 977.5	741.6	654	D	D	D	23 611	960.6	160 895	1 129
Morgantown, WV	272	D	D	D	186	1 190	177.2	27.3	6 805	301.0	8 364	101
Morristown, TN	233	D	D	D	132	579	41.6	11.8	6 615	264.1	36 276	151
Mount Vernon-Anacortes, WA	342	6 346	614.5	241.6	237	1 158	94.1	27.6	7 287	345.2	55 927	274
Muncie, IN	316	10 078	836.1	335.6	203	1 206	119.8	26.7	5 564	205.1	15 776	98
Muskegon, MI	398	9 463	864.8	374.1	283	1 440	116.0	27.8	9 498	339.5	38 511	181
Myrtle Beach-Conway-North Myrtle Beach, NC-SC	800	11 913	1 189.6	446.7	615	3 652	307.3	75.8	31 412	1 349.9	956 646	5 446
Napa, CA	425	10 004	1 150.0	502.2	219	1 172	142.5	38.4	11 274	677.7	44 721	147
Naples-Immokalee-Marco Island, FL	914	14 861	1 796.1	703.8	828	4 364	393.3	113.0	34 947	1 935.6	1 111 395	3 610
Nashville-Davidson—Murfreesboro—Franklin, TN	4 025	D	D	D	2 634	D	D	D	147 628	7 432.1	2 681 399	14 944
New Bern, NC	307	7 788	689.5	281.9	180	902	72.8	18.5	7 256	262.3	37 338	264
New Haven-Milford, CT	2 371	68 663	6 467.8	2 792.6	1 772	10 629	948.2	288.9	57 091	2 961.1	150 265	1 140
New Orleans-Metairie, LA	3 056	D	D	D	1 948	D	D	D	111 106	5 088.2	634 641	2 991
New York-Newark-Jersey City, NY-NJ-PA	57 144	D	D	D	46 231	262 485	41 955.5	8 774.4	1 772 736	94 015.1	6 998 012	47 984
Dutchess County-Putnam County, NY Div 20524	1 177	22 708	2 114.7	881.6	858	3 658	387.2	104.0	NA	NA	X	X
Nassau County-Suffolk County, NY Div 35004	10 014	179 244	19 852.0	8 240.8	7 604	37 690	3 737.4	1 042.6	NA	NA	X	X
Newark, NJ-PA Div 35084	7 585	D	D	D	5 639	32 424	3 702.8	968.3	NA	NA	X	X
New York-Jersey City-White Plains, NY-NJ Div 35614	38 368	940 077	96 837.4	40 481.6	32 130	188 713	34 128.1	6 659.5	NA	NA	X	X
Niles-Benton Harbor, MI	394	8 821	701.7	282.8	281	1 468	112.2	35.1	9 735	366.3	69 136	184
North Port-Sarasota-Bradenton, FL	2 244	35 836	3 772.8	1 384.5	1 431	7 361	577.7	160.1	64 761	3 146.1	1 296 644	5 658
Norwich-New London, CT	703	16 048	1 467.8	617.5	479	2 549	234.3	59.3	15 978	754.8	99 303	646
Ocala, FL	817	14 493	1 590.4	566.1	467	2 408	201.6	51.4	22 900	927.4	154 203	754
Ocean City, NJ	268	D	D	D	288	1 124	91.2	29.5	7 862	444.4	206 176	638
Odessa, TX	300	6 988	644.3	248.5	246	2 115	283.6	64.3	10 328	628.6	108 454	556
Ogden-Clearfield, UT	1 263	19 521	1 690.2	651.9	774	D	D	D	37 649	1 524.1	544 730	2 678
Oklahoma City, OK	3 832	73 078	8 033.7	2 723.7	2 034	12 913	1 348.9	318.9	99 772	4 865.3	1 456 882	7 870
Olympia-Tumwater, WA	710	11 596	1 238.4	447.6	464	2 812	273.7	88.2	13 931	572.3	242 844	1 003
Omaha-Council Bluffs, NE-IA	2 141	53 429	5 209.5	2 133.1	1 591	D	D	D	56 347	2 454.6	661 078	4 192
Orlando-Kissimmee-Sanford, FL	4 863	92 989	9 853.4	3 908.8	3 611	24 032	2 345.8	664.8	196 646	7 568.6	3 566 667	16 115
Oshkosh-Neenah, WI	430	12 589	1 344.9	476.6	290	2 355	199.8	61.9	8 117	362.0	76 395	511
Owensboro, KY	324	D	D	D	178	D	D	D	6 350	262.7	27 328	323
Oxnard-Thousand Oaks-Ventura, CA	2 317	29 522	3 140.0	1 200.9	1 196	7 303	839.6	195.9	64 224	3 413.3	279 531	1 314
Palm Bay-Melbourne-Titusville, FL	1 417	26 415	2 796.8	1 085.6	1 039	4 868	395.3	121.0	39 045	1 549.9	424 956	1 286
Panama City, FL	518	9 888	1 003.4	362.5	333	1 860	126.6	39.2	13 526	660.8	151 354	693
Parkersburg-Vienna, WV	290	D	D	D	174	D	D	D	4 500	185.5	20 481	124
Pensacola-Ferry Pass-Brent, FL	983	23 199	2 412.9	894.2	649	3 468	283.3	86.2	29 581	1 194.8	262 534	1 825
Peoria, IL	845	D	D	D	669	D	D	D	19 140	689.1	214 487	890
Philadelphia-Camden-Wilmington, PA-NJ-DE-MD	16 323	415 348	42 566.0	17 480.7	11 395	74 963	9 790.8	2 169.8	386 271	20 265.5	2 141 915	13 631
Camden, NJ Div 15804	3 328	68 999	7 081.2	2 808.5	2 319	14 328	1 135.9	363.5	NA	NA	X	X
Montgomery County-Bucks County-Chester County, PA Div 33874	6 014	129 580	12 648.9	5 131.6	4 305	27 864	3 805.4	812.3	NA	NA	X	X
Philadelphia, PA Div 37964	5 145	170 431	18 071.5	7 410.6	3 521	24 715	4 083.7	772.5	NA	NA	X	X
Wilmington, DE-MD-NJ Div 48864	1 836	46 338	4 764.4	2 130.0	1 250	8 056	765.8	221.5	NA	NA	X	X
Phoenix-Mesa-Scottsdale, AZ	10 008	180 870	20 217.2	7 822.3	5 750	47 116	4 481.5	1 223.9	290 916	14 026.1	4 309 793	20 341
Pine Bluff, AR	289	D	D	D	116	D	D	D	4 781	162.8	5 064	55
Pittsburgh, PA	7 734	184 576	17 470.6	6 919.7	5 279	31 880	3 755.3	782.6	137 016	6 296.3	901 168	4 190
Pittsfield, MA	450	10 869	981.1	429.8	309	1 742	142.3	38.5	10 054	437.5	53 836	177
Pocatello, ID	291	D	D	D	132	669	59.4	14.2	5 073	186.7	19 128	162
Portland-South Portland, ME	2 031	40 747	3 487.0	1 505.2	1 188	6 117	543.8	147.9	45 476	2 136.3	341 520	1 696
Portland-Vancouver-Hillsboro, OR-WA	6 374	D	D	D	4 041	24 286	2 985.0	726.9	159 188	7 706.4	2 353 394	12 356
Port St. Lucie, FL	1 087	17 254	1 857.4	671.3	734	3 709	288.0	85.8	35 932	1 531.8	351 471	1 394
Prescott, AZ	737	10 268	930.0	370.7	386	1 822	141.9	41.0	17 762	697.2	226 052	968
Providence-Warwick, RI-MA	4 642	118 319	10 073.2	4 455.7	3 434	20 277	1 914.7	504.5	104 664	4 790.7	331 881	1 775
Provo-Orem, UT	1 035	D	D	D	547	D	D	D	40 971	1 696.0	963 879	5 295
Pueblo, CO	410	11 085	872.7	388.5	237	1 160	92.3	25.4	7 860	297.9	28 074	157
Punta Gorda, FL	474	7 731	897.1	308.2	275	1 186	90.0	24.7	11 764	523.6	140 869	610
Racine, WI	417	11 897	946.4	478.0	343	2 167	162.7	49.1	9 433	371.2	45 775	207
Raleigh, NC	2 601	D	D	D	1 869	13 363	1 516.1	408.2	91 107	4 045.1	1 953 945	11 647
Rapid City, SD	380	D	D	D	317	1 749	151.2	39.4	10 869	483.9	107 416	671
Reading, PA	799	21 887	2 014.4	848.1	781	4 670	398.8	108.0	23 771	1 094.0	71 145	458

1. Establishments subject to federal tax.

Area name	Government employment and payroll, 2012									Local government finances, 2012				
			March payroll (percent of total)							General revenue				
												Taxes		
													Per capita[1] (dollars)	
	Full-time equivalent employees	March Payroll (dollars)	Adminis-tration, judicial, and legal	Police and corrections	Fire protection	Highways and transporta-tion	Health and welfare	Natural resources and utilities	Education and libraries	Total (mil dol)	Inter-govern-mental (mil dol)	Total (mil dol)	Total	Property
	171	172	173	174	175	176	177	178	179	180	181	182	183	184
Modesto, CA	19 446	94 702 481	5.9	8.3	2.5	1.6	11.8	9.4	58.2	2 696.4	1 547.9	554.1	1 062	825
Monroe, LA	8 044	23 625 209	7.1	11.1	3.2	2.1	4.4	5.4	65.9	699.4	335.0	289.5	1 628	585
Monroe, MI	3 882	16 268 085	7.1	8.4	1.4	3.3	1.1	4.8	72.4	475.7	225.8	166.5	1 102	1 074
Montgomery, AL	12 833	40 413 140	4.7	13.6	5.4	3.2	3.3	7.9	56.9	1 415.6	468.2	359.9	954	325
Morgantown, WV	3 679	10 784 021	6.6	6.4	2.1	3.9	3.1	7.2	67.9	282.4	117.1	109.2	814	659
Morristown, TN	3 406	10 523 184	5.5	8.9	3.2	3.2	3.1	11.3	62.6	288.5	121.7	106.7	928	541
Mount Vernon-Anacortes, WA	5 963	27 675 332	5.4	5.4	2.0	4.5	41.5	4.7	33.8	852.8	275.6	199.6	1 688	1 157
Muncie, IN	3 335	10 832 587	6.2	9.0	3.6	4.7	3.7	4.2	64.9	345.4	171.1	109.1	930	778
Muskegon, MI	5 428	21 789 876	7.5	7.4	2.5	3.3	9.1	3.1	65.4	721.5	413.6	168.4	989	913
Myrtle Beach-Conway-North Myrtle Beach, NC-SC	13 720	47 691 925	8.0	11.3	4.0	2.9	7.2	7.6	55.9	1 554.9	373.0	787.2	1 995	1 260
Napa, CA	5 012	27 819 123	11.8	13.2	3.0	2.1	9.4	6.0	49.6	811.6	274.6	367.8	2 645	2 138
Naples-Immokalee-Marco Island, FL	9 918	41 162 175	6.9	15.7	6.7	3.5	4.2	9.1	52.0	1 300.6	231.7	737.4	2 218	2 006
Nashville-Davidson—Murfreesboro—Franklin, TN	62 367	213 611 379	6.4	10.6	4.9	2.3	11.3	9.7	53.1	5 944.5	1 864.0	2 495.0	1 445	925
New Bern, NC	6 791	24 592 380	3.3	4.8	1.6	1.2	45.2	4.1	38.0	754.9	290.2	112.7	880	654
New Haven-Milford, CT	28 448	140 929 161	3.5	10.1	6.3	2.6	2.7	5.4	68.7	3 790.8	1 443.5	2 034.2	2 358	2 333
New Orleans-Metairie, LA	43 957	168 084 037	8.4	14.9	3.0	2.9	22.4	8.9	37.2	7 012.5	2 504.9	2 443.4	1 991	986
New York-Newark-Jersey City, NY-NJ-PA	859 136	4 981 795 701	4.0	15.9	3.9	8.2	12.0	4.2	49.2	158 755.3	48 519.4	84 882.7	4 280	2 827
Dutchess County-Putnam County, NY Div 20524	15 834	82 439 707	5.8	9.6	2.2	4.0	5.7	1.6	70.0	2 303.5	678.0	1 388.4	3 498	2 873
Nassau County-Suffolk County, NY Div 35004	123 812	732 874 581	4.1	11.7	0.9	2.5	7.4	3.2	68.6	20 978.5	5 325.7	13 527.4	4 749	3 856
Newark, NJ-PA Div 35084	95 852	533 906 989	5.6	13.8	3.9	2.5	4.8	4.3	63.1	13 124.9	3 533.4	8 066.3	3 241	3 160
New York-Jersey City-White Plains, NY-NJ Div 35614	623 638	3 632 574 424	3.8	17.2	4.5	10.3	14.2	4.4	42.7	122 348.4	38 982.3	61 900.6	4 391	2 559
Niles-Benton Harbor, MI	4 813	18 604 576	9.6	10.9	2.0	2.9	2.9	4.5	64.6	601.1	301.4	200.9	1 288	1 264
North Port-Sarasota-Bradenton, FL	26 901	101 649 100	7.7	11.2	6.0	3.4	20.0	5.4	43.7	3 172.2	626.1	1 212.8	1 684	1 368
Norwich-New London, CT	8 967	42 369 410	4.4	7.7	3.8	3.8	2.3	8.0	68.3	1 101.6	386.5	598.5	2 183	2 159
Ocala, FL	10 760	33 096 942	6.2	11.8	9.0	0.5	2.5	5.9	63.0	875.9	312.2	296.0	883	746
Ocean City, NJ	5 885	27 086 618	8.8	13.8	3.3	3.6	9.4	7.3	49.4	701.1	152.6	449.5	4 667	4 561
Odessa, TX	6 915	26 339 816	4.0	7.3	3.2	1.3	27.3	2.1	53.3	690.5	140.4	269.5	1 867	1 389
Ogden-Clearfield, UT	19 885	69 703 618	6.0	9.0	3.0	1.6	5.2	6.0	67.8	1 758.6	707.7	680.0	1 110	794
Oklahoma City, OK	43 376	150 970 463	5.1	11.2	7.5	3.0	11.2	5.1	56.1	4 132.3	1 264.1	1 725.9	1 331	666
Olympia-Tumwater, WA	7 290	36 403 899	10.9	9.6	5.9	9.3	2.0	8.9	51.8	946.4	372.7	391.6	1 516	997
Omaha-Council Bluffs, NE-IA	36 524	145 002 288	4.4	9.9	3.3	3.6	4.1	18.6	55.0	3 737.9	1 239.7	1 804.1	2 037	1 532
Orlando-Kissimmee-Sanford, FL	79 591	284 688 968	6.3	14.2	7.2	4.2	4.2	8.8	52.4	8 588.1	2 537.2	3 519.5	1 583	1 131
Oshkosh-Neenah, WI	5 300	21 156 305	4.4	11.7	4.6	5.5	11.2	7.1	54.5	697.9	338.4	249.0	1 475	1 436
Owensboro, KY	5 043	15 494 560	4.3	6.6	2.9	2.8	6.8	13.2	62.0	421.7	154.4	115.6	996	570
Oxnard-Thousand Oaks-Ventura, CA	27 714	159 457 912	10.1	10.8	4.6	3.0	13.0	7.6	49.2	4 630.9	2 005.3	1 379.1	1 650	1 378
Palm Bay-Melbourne-Titusville, FL	19 755	66 076 682	7.5	12.3	7.0	4.4	7.8	7.9	52.0	1 764.4	557.0	634.8	1 160	923
Panama City, FL	8 675	32 038 863	3.7	6.7	2.4	3.9	34.3	5.0	42.7	881.5	209.8	288.2	1 536	1 098
Parkersburg-Vienna, WV	3 144	10 362 577	4.7	5.3	2.0	2.6	2.6	6.3	74.9	235.4	113.7	77.6	838	630
Pensacola-Ferry Pass-Brent, FL	14 772	47 095 540	7.2	13.2	2.2	2.6	3.7	6.5	62.2	1 288.3	501.5	467.6	1 014	750
Peoria, IL	13 803	52 130 853	6.3	10.3	3.9	4.6	3.2	6.6	63.1	1 517.9	612.5	635.6	1 671	1 435
Philadelphia-Camden-Wilmington, PA-NJ-DE-MD	205 195	1 004 418 815	6.6	13.0	2.3	7.2	5.0	5.0	59.4	31 396.9	12 075.3	14 182.1	2 356	1 683
Camden, NJ Div 15804	50 866	263 407 426	3.8	10.2	2.3	2.9	4.8	3.0	70.8	6 825.7	2 374.5	3 161.2	2 520	2 481
Montgomery County-Bucks County-Chester County, PA Div 33874	55 254	262 211 582	6.4	11.3	0.4	2.9	4.5	3.7	69.4	8 269.3	2 143.8	4 825.6	2 485	2 076
Philadelphia, PA Div 37964	78 984	387 798 667	9.0	16.8	3.9	13.9	6.0	7.3	42.1	13 846.4	6 463.2	5 279.8	2 504	1 061
Wilmington, DE-MD-NJ Div 48864	20 091	91 001 140	5.5	9.7	1.2	2.8	2.8	4.4	71.6	2 455.5	1 093.8	915.5	1 283	1 049
Phoenix-Mesa-Scottsdale, AZ	139 712	587 672 336	8.5	13.3	5.3	2.9	6.2	12.0	50.6	15 082.4	5 190.2	6 265.2	1 447	928
Pine Bluff, AR	3 495	9 830 121	6.5	12.0	3.9	3.6	1.5	2.1	68.3	261.9	169.1	57.9	594	257
Pittsburgh, PA	76 232	322 348 429	6.5	11.1	1.8	8.6	5.9	6.4	58.3	10 916.6	4 733.0	4 213.3	1 785	1 286
Pittsfield, MA	4 790	19 230 480	4.3	8.5	3.3	5.5	1.3	4.1	71.5	506.3	218.2	246.7	1 897	1 828
Pocatello, ID	2 618	8 746 568	9.9	14.1	5.7	4.5	6.0	6.6	51.4	238.0	114.9	73.0	871	828
Portland-South Portland, ME	19 117	71 307 958	5.3	8.8	5.0	4.0	3.6	6.3	65.4	1 897.9	500.0	1 074.0	2 073	2 046
Portland-Vancouver-Hillsboro, OR-WA	70 641	332 827 613	7.2	11.0	5.2	8.1	4.4	8.5	51.7	10 118.9	3 858.3	4 062.9	1 774	1 375
Port St. Lucie, FL	15 221	57 466 642	7.0	15.0	8.7	2.3	1.8	6.2	55.9	1 562.3	448.2	714.5	1 651	1 400
Prescott, AZ	6 155	23 081 009	10.4	13.4	9.4	4.0	2.1	5.5	45.2	648.3	201.2	335.8	1 579	1 029
Providence-Warwick, RI-MA	47 209	226 744 364	3.5	10.7	8.1	2.2	1.2	5.2	67.9	6 092.6	2 097.6	3 232.0	2 018	1 964
Provo-Orem, UT	14 474	53 579 798	6.4	8.0	2.5	1.5	4.8	8.4	66.6	1 615.5	670.1	586.2	1 064	722
Pueblo, CO	5 698	21 434 409	5.8	12.3	11.0	3.0	6.6	9.0	49.7	552.8	247.0	223.3	1 388	895
Punta Gorda, FL	4 654	16 650 878	13.2	15.5	8.9	5.6	2.0	7.8	45.5	559.2	101.1	264.1	1 626	1 290
Racine, WI	6 208	25 453 020	4.3	13.6	5.6	3.5	5.9	4.0	61.9	757.1	345.7	302.7	1 554	1 513
Raleigh, NC	40 839	150 997 987	3.4	8.5	3.1	3.1	10.3	5.9	61.8	4 020.3	1 569.5	1 583.3	1 332	1 007
Rapid City, SD	5 051	15 769 374	6.1	10.9	1.5	3.1	2.5	4.6	66.3	484.3	139.9	245.9	1 773	1 269
Reading, PA	14 566	69 528 665	6.1	16.3	5.1	2.6	4.7	5.3	58.7	2 039.3	792.5	835.6	2 021	1 642

1. Based on the resident population estimated as of July 1 of the year shown.

Area name	Local government finances, 2012 (cont.) — Direct general expenditure: Total (mil dol)	Per capita[1] (dollars)	Percent of total for: Education	Health and hospitals	Police protection	Public welfare	Highways	Debt outstanding: Total (mil dol)	Per capita[1] (dollars)	Government employment, 2013: Federal civilian	Federal military	State and local	Presidential election,[2] 2012 — Percent of vote cast: Democratic	Republican	All other
	185	186	187	188	189	190	191	192	193	194	195	196	197	198	199
Modesto, CA	2 792.3	5 352	50.1	6.9	4.9	10.2	3.4	4 496.8	8 619	849	834	25 239	50.0	47.3	2.7
Monroe, LA	748.1	4 208	53.1	2.8	5.8	0.1	2.9	495.7	2 788	524	828	11 583	37.5	61.2	1.3
Monroe, MI	515.6	3 414	53.6	6.7	3.7	0.2	9.1	557.6	3 691	221	258	5 421	49.8	48.9	1.3
Montgomery, AL	1 403.7	3 722	34.2	33.5	5.6	0.3	2.9	1 403.6	3 722	6 540	4 354	32 978	49.8	49.5	0.7
Morgantown, WV	293.9	2 191	58.5	2.3	5.1	0.3	1.8	267.7	1 996	1 925	642	17 011	39.3	58.0	2.7
Morristown, TN	294.2	2 560	53.3	1.8	5.5	4.4	4.6	336.9	2 932	288	368	5 846	25.2	73.3	1.5
Mount Vernon-Anacortes, WA	797.6	6 747	26.4	43.2	2.9	0.1	3.4	556.4	4 706	373	326	10 816	51.9	45.4	2.7
Muncie, IN	323.3	2 755	48.4	0.8	3.9	0.5	2.7	191.9	1 635	290	355	10 569	50.4	47.3	2.4
Muskegon, MI	746.4	4 386	51.2	13.2	3.2	3.6	4.5	688.6	4 046	333	312	7 478	58.3	40.5	1.1
Myrtle Beach-Conway-North Myrtle Beach, NC-SC	1 496.4	3 793	37.4	11.8	6.6	1.4	4.4	2 146.9	5 441	1 007	1 547	19 579	35.9	63.0	1.2
Napa, CA	821.7	5 909	37.5	5.9	7.5	4.2	4.0	746.0	5 365	223	216	9 638	63.0	34.3	2.8
Naples-Immokalee-Marco Island, FL	1 313.8	3 952	37.5	3.0	12.1	0.6	6.0	2 257.5	6 791	637	645	12 042	34.7	64.7	0.6
Nashville-Davidson—Murfreesboro—Franklin, TN	5 917.9	3 427	40.3	11.8	6.7	0.7	3.2	9 772.4	5 660	12 299	6 046	93 578	41.0	57.4	1.5
New Bern, NC	730.7	5 704	24.7	49.9	4.0	4.0	0.8	197.3	1 540	5 436	9 467	8 463	40.9	58.1	1.0
New Haven-Milford, CT	4 427.8	5 132	58.4	0.6	4.3	0.3	2.5	3 649.0	4 229	5 377	1 935	44 161	60.7	38.3	1.0
New Orleans-Metairie, LA	6 862.8	5 593	28.3	16.1	5.5	1.0	4.4	9 273.5	7 557	12 027	9 027	72 284	49.2	48.9	2.0
New York-Newark-Jersey City, NY-NJ-PA	155 295.2	7 831	37.1	7.8	6.1	10.2	2.3	228 317.6	11 513	112 976	43 403	1 161 811	64.8	34.2	1.0
Dutchess County-Putnam County, NY Div 20524	2 273.0	5 726	57.0	3.2	3.6	6.6	4.3	1 817.8	4 580	1 334	614	23 679	50.6	47.8	1.6
Nassau County-Suffolk County, NY Div 35004	22 106.9	7 761	50.8	5.4	7.0	5.6	3.2	19 089.0	6 701	16 802	5 222	166 488	52.2	46.7	1.1
Newark, NJ-PA Div 35084	13 275.6	5 334	50.9	2.5	6.4	2.0	2.6	11 054.8	4 442	18 514	5 229	159 259	58.9	40.1	1.0
New York-Jersey City-White Plains, NY-NJ Div 35614	117 639.8	8 345	32.6	8.9	6.0	12.1	2.1	196 356.0	13 928	76 326	32 338	812 385	69.7	29.3	1.0
Niles-Benton Harbor, MI	618.7	3 965	53.9	7.1	5.5	1.4	5.2	398.2	2 551	307	286	9 106	46.2	52.7	1.1
North Port-Sarasota-Bradenton, FL	3 246.3	4 509	31.7	19.9	6.6	0.3	4.4	3 286.5	4 564	1 764	1 474	24 324	44.8	54.3	0.9
Norwich-New London, CT	1 142.0	4 165	60.1	0.7	5.5	0.6	6.1	911.5	3 324	2 545	7 723	30 905	58.3	40.1	1.6
Ocala, FL	879.1	2 623	48.9	2.0	7.6	0.7	6.3	732.6	2 186	689	634	16 034	41.4	57.7	0.9
Ocean City, NJ	808.9	8 400	33.8	1.5	5.3	4.4	4.9	673.4	6 992	437	929	8 339	45.2	53.8	1.0
Odessa, TX	691.3	4 790	36.3	40.0	3.5	0.0	2.4	385.4	2 670	149	311	9 109	25.0	73.8	1.2
Ogden-Clearfield, UT	1 761.7	2 877	51.2	2.7	6.1	1.8	3.1	1 655.4	2 703	18 823	6 289	30 740	20.0	78.0	2.1
Oklahoma City, OK	3 850.3	2 970	45.9	9.2	8.1	0.1	5.6	3 940.9	3 039	27 626	11 573	93 537	36.5	63.5	0.0
Olympia-Tumwater, WA	952.8	3 688	42.4	5.4	4.0	0.0	7.1	917.5	3 552	872	775	34 556	58.3	38.8	2.9
Omaha-Council Bluffs, NE-IA	3 646.7	4 118	52.0	2.7	5.1	0.7	4.4	7 717.4	8 714	9 404	9 247	53 101	44.0	54.0	2.0
Orlando-Kissimmee-Sanford, FL	8 694.5	3 910	39.3	3.5	7.5	0.8	5.5	14 655.7	6 591	12 396	4 621	101 201	53.4	45.7	0.9
Oshkosh-Neenah, WI	708.5	4 197	35.6	2.5	5.6	20.8	8.3	688.0	4 076	432	458	11 555	51.0	47.2	1.8
Owensboro, KY	454.5	3 917	36.1	5.3	3.4	0.1	3.3	1 881.3	16 214	291	394	9 716	38.6	59.5	1.9
Oxnard-Thousand Oaks-Ventura, CA	4 471.8	5 349	38.6	13.1	7.5	4.6	3.5	3 011.8	3 603	7 082	5 110	35 491	52.3	45.3	2.5
Palm Bay-Melbourne-Titusville, FL	1 830.9	3 345	36.4	11.6	7.9	0.4	4.3	1 872.2	3 421	6 251	2 879	22 525	43.1	55.8	1.1
Panama City, FL	987.2	5 261	32.4	23.6	6.5	0.0	4.6	937.7	4 998	3 685	3 785	9 741	27.7	71.1	1.2
Parkersburg-Vienna, WV	236.3	2 554	64.2	0.1	5.1	0.0	3.8	191.5	2 070	2 175	458	4 584	33.0	65.3	1.7
Pensacola-Ferry Pass-Brent, FL	1 512.8	3 280	44.3	2.8	7.1	0.2	4.4	3 484.8	7 556	6 676	15 151	20 873	33.7	65.2	1.1
Peoria, IL	1 492.8	3 924	48.0	1.3	5.9	1.7	6.8	1 259.9	3 312	2 252	827	19 499	44.2	53.9	1.9
Philadelphia-Camden-Wilmington, PA-NJ-DE-MD	30 309.1	5 036	49.1	6.0	5.4	5.2	2.6	44 541.2	7 400	52 170	23 542	292 550	64.0	34.9	1.1
Camden, NJ Div 15804	6 604.3	5 265	56.5	2.6	4.4	2.8	3.3	7 416.2	5 912	8 124	7 829	73 150	61.4	37.5	1.1
Montgomery County-Bucks County-Chester County, PA Div 33874	8 574.7	4 415	57.3	2.4	4.9	5.8	3.8	11 320.4	5 829	6 344	5 287	79 174	52.6	46.3	1.1
Philadelphia, PA Div 37964	12 546.9	5 950	37.7	11.3	5.9	7.0	1.3	23 338.7	11 068	32 646	6 666	97 286	77.9	21.2	0.8
Wilmington, DE-MD-NJ Div 48864	2 583.2	3 020	50.6	1.0	6.6	0.5	3.1	2 465.8	3 456	5 056	3 760	42 940	61.2	37.2	1.6
Phoenix-Mesa-Scottsdale, AZ	15 046.5	3 475	42.0	5.1	8.3	1.5	4.0	29 018.4	6 702	21 626	13 637	208 399	43.5	54.7	1.8
Pine Bluff, AR	262.8	2 696	61.5	0.1	6.9	0.1	4.7	246.8	2 533	1 679	425	8 772	57.4	40.8	1.8
Pittsburgh, PA	10 894.8	4 615	46.7	6.2	3.8	6.8	3.4	20 628.3	8 738	17 450	6 660	103 201	48.8	50.0	1.2
Pittsfield, MA	629.4	4 841	60.3	0.5	3.2	0.3	5.9	274.5	2 111	365	323	8 343	75.7	22.1	2.2
Pocatello, ID	221.0	2 637	41.2	2.7	8.1	1.0	5.5	54.8	654	537	306	7 576	37.5	59.6	2.9
Portland-South Portland, ME	1 867.4	3 604	49.3	0.7	4.6	1.6	5.8	1 662.8	3 209	7 925	4 244	28 402	59.9	37.6	2.4
Portland-Vancouver-Hillsboro, OR-WA	9 964.4	4 352	40.1	4.1	5.7	2.0	5.7	15 721.1	6 866	17 885	6 827	117 898	60.0	36.6	3.3
Port St. Lucie, FL	1 660.8	3 838	40.0	3.2	8.5	1.4	5.4	2 747.3	6 349	1 032	904	17 468	47.5	51.7	0.7
Prescott, AZ	653.7	3 074	36.5	2.1	7.2	1.8	9.0	725.7	3 413	1 372	475	9 106	33.8	64.3	1.9
Providence-Warwick, RI-MA	5 907.2	3 689	56.8	0.5	6.6	0.5	2.8	4 257.8	2 659	11 269	8 972	81 462	61.5	36.5	2.0
Provo-Orem, UT	1 466.7	2 663	52.0	4.0	6.1	0.1	5.2	2 448.4	4 445	948	2 408	28 565	9.8	88.3	2.0
Pueblo, CO	566.4	3 521	40.3	1.5	6.6	5.3	3.7	456.3	2 837	1 014	436	11 541	55.8	41.9	2.3
Punta Gorda, FL	563.6	3 470	33.1	3.8	11.0	1.5	11.1	628.4	3 868	312	313	5 335	42.4	56.7	0.9
Racine, WI	764.1	3 923	45.5	3.8	9.7	5.3	7.3	710.7	3 648	332	533	8 471	51.3	47.7	1.0
Raleigh, NC	4 137.2	3 481	42.6	8.6	6.0	3.5	1.9	9 884.5	8 316	5 417	3 538	87 704	52.1	46.4	1.5
Rapid City, SD	516.0	3 719	46.0	1.5	5.8	0.4	9.0	476.3	3 433	3 055	4 139	8 014	32.4	65.0	2.6
Reading, PA	2 024.3	4 896	54.5	3.4	4.1	7.2	2.8	3 478.7	8 413	934	1 077	21 670	48.7	49.7	1.5

1. Based on the resident population estimated as of July 1 of the year shown. 2.

Table C. Metropolitan Areas — **Land Area and Population**

CBSA/ DIV code[1]	Area name	Land area,[2] 2010 (sq km)	Population 2014: Total persons	Population 2014: Rank	Population 2014: Per square kilometer	Population characteristics, 2013: Race alone or in combination, not Hispanic or Latino (percent): White	Black	American Indian, Alaska Native	Asian and Pacific Islander	Percent Hispanic or Latino[3]	Age (percent): Under 5 years	5 to 17 years	18 to 24 years	25 to 34 years	35 to 44 years	45 to 54 years
		1	2	3	4	5	6	7	8	9	10	11	12	13	14	15
39820	Redding, CA	9 778	179 804	230	18.4	84.7	1.7	4.1	4.1	9.1	5.7	16.0	8.7	12.1	10.6	13.5
39900	Reno, NV	17 004	443 990	116	26.1	67.2	3.0	2.0	7.4	23.1	6.1	16.6	10.0	14.0	12.3	13.7
40060	Richmond, VA	11 852	1 260 029	44	106.3	60.3	31.0	0.9	4.4	5.6	5.9	16.5	9.7	13.8	13.0	14.6
40140	Riverside-San Bernardino-Ontario, CA	70 612	4 441 890	13	62.9	36.7	8.0	1.0	7.8	48.8	7.1	20.1	11.0	13.8	12.9	13.1
40220	Roanoke, VA	4 839	313 388	159	64.8	81.4	14.0	0.6	2.3	3.5	5.5	15.4	8.7	11.6	12.1	14.5
40340	Rochester, MN	6 416	212 778	205	33.2	87.5	4.6	0.5	5.0	4.0	7.0	17.9	7.6	13.8	12.3	14.1
40380	Rochester, NY	8 459	1 083 393	51	128.1	79.3	12.0	0.6	3.3	6.6	5.5	16.0	10.8	12.5	11.5	14.7
40420	Rockford, IL	2 057	342 411	149	166.5	73.7	11.8	0.6	2.8	13.1	6.2	18.3	8.8	11.9	12.6	14.2
40580	Rocky Mount, NC	2 709	149 290	275	55.1	47.6	46.2	1.0	0.9	5.7	6.0	17.1	9.1	11.2	12.1	14.3
40660	Rome, GA	1 321	96 063	361	72.7	73.8	15.3	0.6	1.7	10.1	6.3	17.5	10.5	12.2	12.5	13.3
40900	Sacramento—Roseville—Arden-Arcade, CA	13 193	2 244 397	27	170.1	57.9	8.4	1.5	15.7	20.8	6.3	17.6	10.2	13.8	12.7	13.7
40980	Saginaw, MI	2 072	195 012	221	94.1	71.8	19.6	0.8	1.5	8.0	5.7	16.5	10.5	11.4	11.3	13.8
41060	St. Cloud, MN	4 536	192 418	223	42.4	91.7	3.9	0.7	2.4	2.8	6.3	16.8	14.3	13.4	11.2	13.3
41100	St. George, UT	6 284	151 948	269	24.2	86.9	0.9	1.6	2.5	9.9	7.6	21.2	8.9	12.6	10.7	9.5
41140	St. Joseph, MO-KS	4 288	127 431	307	29.7	88.3	6.4	1.1	1.3	4.7	6.3	16.1	10.0	13.6	12.3	14.0
41180	St. Louis, MO-IL	20 366	2 806 207	19	137.8	76.1	19.3	0.7	2.9	2.8	6.1	16.9	9.1	13.5	12.4	14.5
41420	Salem, OR	4 981	404 026	132	81.1	72.2	1.6	2.3	3.8	23.0	6.8	18.5	10.6	13.0	12.2	12.3
41500	Salinas, CA	8 497	431 344	121	50.8	33.5	3.3	0.9	8.0	56.8	7.8	18.7	10.9	15.0	13.0	12.2
41540	Salisbury, MD-DE	5 435	389 922	135	71.7	73.2	18.9	0.9	2.0	7.0	5.5	14.3	10.2	10.9	10.5	13.5
41620	Salt Lake City, UT	19 901	1 153 340	48	58.0	75.5	2.0	1.1	6.1	17.3	8.2	20.6	9.9	16.7	13.9	11.4
41660	San Angelo, TX	6 666	118 182	325	17.7	57.3	4.5	0.8	1.8	37.1	6.8	16.7	13.0	15.0	10.5	11.9
41700	San Antonio-New Braunfels, TX	18 941	2 328 652	25	122.9	36.5	6.9	0.6	2.9	54.4	7.0	19.0	10.4	14.6	13.1	13.0
41740	San Diego-Carlsbad, CA	10 895	3 263 431	17	299.5	49.9	5.7	1.0	13.9	32.8	6.5	16.1	11.4	15.9	13.2	13.2
41860	San Francisco-Oakland-Hayward, CA	6 398	4 594 060	11	718.0	44.6	8.8	0.9	27.8	21.8	5.7	14.9	8.5	15.4	14.7	14.5
41860	Oakland-Hayward-Berkeley, CA Div 36084	3 768	2 722 260	X	722.5	41.8	11.7	0.9	26.2	23.5	6.0	16.5	9.1	14.3	14.3	14.5
41860	San Francisco-Redwood City-South San Francisco, CA Div 41884	1 282	1 611 050	X	1 256.7	44.2	4.8	0.7	33.8	20.0	5.3	12.0	7.8	18.4	15.5	14.2
41860	San Rafael, CA Div 42034	1 348	260 750	X	193.4	75.4	3.2	0.8	8.0	15.7	5.0	15.6	6.3	9.1	13.3	16.1
41940	San Jose-Sunnyvale-Santa Clara, CA	6 938	1 952 872	34	281.5	36.6	2.9	0.7	35.2	27.6	6.5	17.0	8.8	15.0	15.1	14.5
42020	San Luis Obispo-Paso Robles-Arroyo Grande, CA	8 543	279 083	166	32.7	72.2	2.4	1.3	5.0	21.7	4.9	13.5	15.6	11.5	10.7	12.7
42100	Santa Cruz-Watsonville, CA	1 153	271 804	175	235.7	61.2	1.6	1.2	6.1	32.9	5.7	14.8	15.4	12.0	12.0	13.4
42140	Santa Fe, NM	4 945	148 164	279	30.0	44.5	1.0	3.0	1.6	51.1	5.0	14.9	7.6	11.3	12.0	14.1
42200	Santa Maria-Santa Barbara, CA	7 084	440 668	120	62.2	48.4	2.3	1.0	6.5	44.1	6.5	16.1	16.1	13.2	11.4	12.0
42220	Santa Rosa, CA	4 081	500 292	106	122.6	67.6	2.2	1.6	5.7	25.8	5.4	15.5	9.2	12.9	12.1	14.1
42340	Savannah, GA	3 470	372 708	142	107.4	58.2	34.4	0.7	3.1	5.6	6.9	16.7	11.4	15.6	12.6	12.7
42540	Scranton—Wilkes-Barre—Hazleton, PA	4 524	559 679	96	123.7	88.3	3.5	0.4	1.7	7.2	5.1	14.7	9.6	11.8	11.8	14.4
42660	Seattle-Tacoma-Bellevue, WA	15 209	3 671 478	15	241.4	70.5	7.1	2.0	15.9	9.5	6.4	15.9	9.1	15.7	14.3	14.3
42660	Seattle-Bellevue-Everett, WA Div 42644	10 885	2 839 550	X	260.9	69.4	6.6	1.8	17.4	9.4	6.2	15.5	8.8	16.0	14.7	14.5
42660	Tacoma-Lakewood, WA Div 45104	4 324	831 928	X	192.4	74.1	9.1	2.6	10.8	9.9	6.9	17.3	9.9	14.8	12.9	13.8
42680	Sebastian-Vero Beach, FL	1 302	144 755	284	111.2	77.7	9.5	0.6	1.8	11.7	4.5	13.5	6.8	9.0	9.4	12.8
42700	Sebring, FL	2 633	98 236	355	37.3	70.3	10.1	0.9	1.8	18.1	4.7	13.2	6.5	8.9	8.7	11.0
43100	Sheboygan, WI	1 324	115 290	332	87.1	87.3	2.1	0.7	5.2	5.8	5.7	17.2	8.0	11.6	12.1	15.3
43300	Sherman-Denison, TX	2 416	123 534	316	51.1	79.3	6.7	2.3	1.6	12.2	6.2	17.6	9.0	11.7	11.6	13.8
43340	Shreveport-Bossier City, LA	8 255	445 142	114	53.9	56.0	39.2	1.0	1.8	3.6	7.1	17.4	9.5	14.2	12.1	12.9
43420	Sierra Vista-Douglas, AZ	15 969	127 448	306	8.0	58.9	4.8	1.6	3.5	33.8	6.4	16.1	9.5	12.7	10.7	12.2
43580	Sioux City, IA-NE-SD	7 606	168 806	243	22.2	79.5	3.1	2.0	2.7	14.7	7.1	19.1	9.4	12.3	11.9	13.2
43620	Sioux Falls, SD	6 671	248 351	186	37.2	88.9	4.4	2.7	2.0	3.9	7.8	18.1	8.9	15.6	12.8	13.2
43780	South Bend-Mishawaka, IN-MI	2 455	319 226	154	130.0	79.0	12.9	1.1	2.5	7.2	6.2	17.4	10.6	12.4	11.9	13.3
43900	Spartanburg, SC	3 425	321 418	153	93.8	70.3	22.4	0.6	2.4	5.8	6.3	17.4	9.8	12.0	12.7	14.1
44060	Spokane-Spokane Valley, WA	14 611	540 953	101	37.0	89.2	2.7	3.1	3.8	4.9	6.0	16.5	10.3	13.5	11.8	13.3
44100	Springfield, IL	3 063	211 567	207	69.1	84.5	12.8	0.6	2.3	2.1	6.1	17.0	8.5	12.8	12.2	14.4
44140	Springfield, MA	2 964	629 100	88	212.2	72.2	7.3	0.6	3.4	18.1	5.3	15.6	14.0	11.9	11.3	14.0
44180	Springfield, MO	7 788	452 297	112	58.1	92.7	3.1	1.5	1.9	3.0	6.3	16.6	12.0	13.4	12.0	12.9
44220	Springfield, OH	1 029	136 554	295	132.7	87.2	10.5	0.9	1.1	3.0	5.9	17.1	8.5	11.4	11.6	13.9
44300	State College, PA	2 875	158 742	257	55.2	88.6	3.7	0.4	6.1	2.6	4.1	11.4	26.8	13.0	10.3	11.5
44420	Staunton-Waynesboro, VA	2 596	119 766	321	46.1	88.8	8.0	0.7	1.1	3.2	5.2	15.3	8.5	11.8	11.9	14.5
44700	Stockton-Lodi, CA	3 604	715 597	77	198.6	37.3	7.9	1.2	17.0	40.1	7.5	20.7	10.5	13.4	12.8	13.0
44940	Sumter, SC	1 723	107 919	341	62.6	47.9	47.4	0.8	1.9	3.7	7.1	17.6	11.3	13.2	11.4	13.2
45060	Syracuse, NY	6 177	661 478	82	107.1	84.9	9.1	1.2	3.2	3.8	5.6	16.2	11.2	12.4	11.4	14.9
45220	Tallahassee, FL	6 184	375 751	140	60.8	58.1	33.5	0.8	3.1	6.3	5.5	14.3	19.6	13.7	11.3	12.0
45300	Tampa-St. Petersburg-Clearwater, FL	6 509	2 915 582	18	447.9	67.5	12.4	0.7	4.0	17.3	5.5	15.2	8.4	12.5	12.5	14.3
45460	Terre Haute, IN	3 794	171 480	238	45.2	91.1	6.1	0.7	1.7	2.1	5.8	15.6	12.6	12.6	12.2	13.2
45500	Texarkana, TX-AR	5 291	149 235	276	28.2	69.0	24.7	1.4	1.1	5.6	6.5	17.5	8.9	13.2	12.8	13.5

1. CBSA = Core Based Statistical Area. DIV = Metropolitan Division. See Appendix A for explanation. See Appendix B for list of metropolitan areas identified by type. 2. Dry land or land partially or temporarily covered by water. 3. May be of any race.

Area name	Population, 2013 (cont.) Age (percent) (cont.) 55 to 64 years	65 to 74 years	75 years and over	Percent female	Population change and components of change, 2000–2014 Total persons 2000	2010	Percent change 2000–2010	2010–2014	Components of change, 2010–2014 Births	Deaths	Net migration	Households, 2013 Number	Persons per household	Percent Family households	Female family householder[1]	One person
	16	17	18	19	20	21	22	23	24	25	26	27	28	29	30	31
Redding, CA	14.7	10.9	7.9	50.9	163 256	177 223	8.6	1.5	8 866	8 700	2 201	69 729	2.52	62.7	13.2	30.5
Reno, NV	13.2	8.9	5.3	49.6	342 885	425 417	24.1	4.4	22 701	14 787	10 299	166 432	2.60	60.7	10.9	30.1
Richmond, VA	13.0	7.8	5.5	51.7	1 055 683	1 208 101	14.4	4.3	62 824	41 861	30 559	467 399	2.59	64.3	15.6	28.8
Riverside-San Bernardino-Ontario, CA	10.5	6.6	4.9	50.2	3 254 821	4 224 851	29.8	5.1	260 601	117 679	71 960	1 297 675	3.31	74.4	15.2	20.6
Roanoke, VA	14.5	10.0	7.7	51.7	288 309	308 707	7.1	1.5	14 386	14 138	4 315	128 318	2.36	64.3	12.3	30.1
Rochester, MN	12.7	7.7	6.9	50.8	184 740	206 877	12.0	2.9	12 130	6 187	-143	82 956	2.51	66.5	9.4	27.4
Rochester, NY	13.4	8.5	7.0	51.3	1 062 452	1 079 671	1.6	0.3	49 633	40 266	-5 276	425 603	2.45	62.7	13.2	30.1
Rockford, IL	12.9	8.4	6.6	51.0	320 204	349 431	9.1	-2.0	17 870	12 786	-12 081	131 292	2.59	68.7	14.2	27.0
Rocky Mount, NC	14.2	9.3	6.7	52.4	143 026	152 392	6.5	-2.0	7 564	6 620	-4 084	58 462	2.52	64.5	19.5	30.7
Rome, GA	12.3	8.6	6.7	51.5	90 565	96 317	6.4	-0.3	5 024	4 277	-971	33 099	2.77	65.6	15.6	29.5
Sacramento—Roseville—Arden-Arcade, CA	12.2	7.6	5.9	51.0	1 796 857	2 149 127	19.6	4.4	116 893	67 943	45 093	792 639	2.75	66.2	13.0	26.0
Saginaw, MI	14.0	9.1	7.6	51.5	210 039	200 169	-4.7	-2.6	9 696	8 592	-6 132	77 518	2.45	63.4	15.6	31.8
St. Cloud, MN	11.5	6.9	6.2	49.6	167 392	189 093	13.0	1.8	10 375	5 259	-1 725	72 873	2.50	64.1	10.1	26.8
St. George, UT	10.7	10.3	8.6	50.6	90 354	138 115	52.9	10.0	9 484	4 623	8 510	49 394	2.95	76.4	9.2	17.4
St. Joseph, MO-KS	12.7	8.1	6.9	48.5	122 336	127 329	4.1	0.1	6 711	5 467	-1 126	46 237	2.61	66.2	13.5	27.3
St. Louis, MO-IL	13.2	7.9	6.5	51.6	2 675 343	2 787 701	4.2	0.7	145 080	105 428	-20 234	1 105 652	2.48	65.7	13.8	29.0
Salem, OR	12.2	8.1	6.3	50.4	347 214	390 738	12.5	3.4	22 265	13 737	4 599	142 174	2.72	67.7	13.0	25.4
Salinas, CA	10.8	6.4	5.2	48.6	401 762	415 057	3.3	3.9	28 447	10 023	-1 696	125 553	3.27	72.0	13.1	21.8
Salisbury, MD-DE	14.5	12.2	8.3	51.2	312 572	373 802	19.6	4.3	17 866	16 772	14 616	143 465	2.59	67.7	13.6	25.5
Salt Lake City, UT	9.9	5.4	3.8	49.7	939 122	1 087 873	15.8	6.0	80 678	26 355	11 999	366 765	3.08	71.6	10.5	21.9
San Angelo, TX	11.7	7.8	6.7	50.5	105 781	111 823	5.7	5.7	6 568	4 240	4 084	44 059	2.51	62.7	10.1	29.5
San Antonio-New Braunfels, TX	11.0	6.9	5.0	50.7	1 711 703	2 142 508	25.2	8.7	133 807	65 317	114 872	778 939	2.87	68.5	15.4	26.1
San Diego-Carlsbad, CA	11.3	6.8	5.6	49.7	2 813 833	3 095 313	10.0	5.4	188 675	86 169	65 485	1 093 386	2.86	66.7	12.4	24.5
San Francisco-Oakland-Hayward, CA	12.6	7.6	6.0	50.6	4 123 740	4 335 391	5.1	6.0	221 365	123 927	163 956	1 654 554	2.68	62.5	11.0	27.9
Oakland-Hayward-Berkeley, CA Div 36084	12.3	7.3	5.5	51.0	2 392 557	2 559 296	7.0	6.4	134 407	71 469	101 120	938 265	2.80	67.5	12.6	25.0
San Francisco-Redwood City-South San Francisco, CA Div 41884	12.5	7.6	6.7	49.9	1 483 894	1 523 686	2.7	5.7	77 127	44 600	56 138	613 442	2.53	54.9	8.9	31.9
San Rafael, CA Div 42034	15.6	11.0	7.9	51.1	247 289	252 409	2.1	3.3	9 831	7 858	6 698	102 847	2.44	62.4	8.9	31.0
San Jose-Sunnyvale-Santa Clara, CA	11.2	6.6	5.3	49.7	1 735 819	1 836 911	5.8	6.3	105 447	41 927	54 559	636 628	2.96	71.6	10.6	21.4
San Luis Obispo-Paso Robles-Arroyo Grande, CA	14.2	9.4	7.4	49.0	246 681	269 637	9.3	3.5	11 123	9 431	7 564	104 669	2.49	63.1	9.0	26.4
Santa Cruz-Watsonville, CA	14.0	7.7	5.1	50.3	255 602	262 382	2.7	3.6	13 337	7 379	3 463	93 982	2.74	60.9	9.7	27.5
Santa Fe, NM	16.6	11.7	6.7	51.2	129 292	144 170	11.5	2.8	5 928	4 418	2 416	60 405	2.39	59.0	11.8	35.4
Santa Maria-Santa Barbara, CA	11.1	7.1	6.6	49.7	399 347	423 895	6.1	3.9	24 146	12 491	5 121	140 665	2.96	64.9	10.6	25.4
Santa Rosa, CA	14.7	9.3	6.7	50.9	458 614	483 878	5.5	3.4	22 052	16 792	10 856	189 087	2.57	60.8	10.8	28.7
Savannah, GA	11.5	7.4	5.1	51.4	293 000	347 611	18.6	7.2	21 834	11 902	14 777	132 260	2.67	65.9	15.5	28.0
Scranton—Wilkes-Barre—Hazleton, PA	14.0	9.7	8.9	51.1	560 625	563 631	0.5	-0.7	23 680	29 173	2 376	223 354	2.42	62.9	12.6	31.9
Seattle-Tacoma-Bellevue, WA	12.3	6.9	5.0	50.1	3 043 878	3 439 809	13.0	6.7	192 611	98 037	137 018	1 392 337	2.55	62.9	9.8	28.5
Seattle-Bellevue-Everett, WA Div 42644	12.4	6.9	5.0	50.0	2 343 058	2 644 584	12.9	7.4	145 115	72 731	122 946	1 090 050	2.52	61.7	9.3	29.0
Tacoma-Lakewood, WA Div 45104	12.1	7.2	5.1	50.3	700 820	795 225	13.5	4.6	47 496	25 306	14 072	302 287	2.65	67.1	11.7	26.5
Sebastian-Vero Beach, FL	14.7	14.6	14.6	52.0	112 947	138 028	22.2	4.9	5 362	7 600	8 312	57 435	2.44	64.9	9.2	28.5
Sebring, FL	13.2	16.9	16.7	51.3	87 366	98 786	13.1	-0.6	3 848	6 168	1 709	40 368	2.38	62.3	9.5	32.0
Sheboygan, WI	14.1	8.4	7.4	49.8	112 646	115 507	2.5	-0.2	5 426	4 461	-1 256	47 295	2.36	66.5	9.5	29.1
Sherman-Denison, TX	13.3	9.6	7.1	51.2	110 595	120 877	9.3	2.2	6 372	5 605	1 901	46 311	2.59	67.6	13.2	26.9
Shreveport-Bossier City, LA	12.6	7.9	6.3	51.8	417 796	439 811	5.3	1.2	27 592	18 660	-3 384	169 481	2.58	63.2	17.9	33.3
Sierra Vista-Douglas, AZ	13.3	11.2	7.9	48.9	117 755	131 346	11.5	-3.0	7 194	5 154	-5 955	48 368	2.40	67.8	11.9	26.6
Sioux City, IA-NE-SD	12.7	7.7	6.6	50.3	167 902	168 563	0.4	0.1	10 290	6 210	-3 674	63 754	2.59	67.5	12.1	27.8
Sioux Falls, SD	11.7	6.5	5.4	50.0	187 093	228 261	22.0	8.8	16 041	7 045	10 813	94 244	2.52	65.4	8.7	27.6
South Bend-Mishawaka, IN-MI	13.3	8.0	6.8	51.3	316 663	319 224	0.8	0.0	16 782	12 519	-3 965	123 138	2.49	62.0	13.6	31.8
Spartanburg, SC	12.8	8.9	6.1	51.6	283 672	313 268	10.4	2.6	16 525	13 385	5 068	119 827	2.59	68.6	18.0	28.1
Spokane-Spokane Valley, WA	13.6	8.7	6.3	50.4	469 737	527 753	12.4	2.5	27 660	20 011	5 476	208 513	2.49	62.2	10.9	29.5
Springfield, IL	14.0	8.4	6.8	52.0	201 437	210 170	4.3	0.7	10 578	8 682	-448	87 918	2.36	63.4	13.1	30.5
Springfield, MA	13.1	8.0	6.8	52.1	608 479	621 570	2.2	1.2	27 878	23 232	3 449	234 947	2.51	65.7	15.6	27.3
Springfield, MO	11.9	8.3	6.6	51.0	368 374	436 712	18.6	3.6	23 947	16 640	8 116	179 138	2.43	63.9	10.5	28.1
Springfield, OH	14.1	9.7	7.8	51.4	144 742	138 333	-4.4	-1.3	6 796	6 974	-1 543	54 372	2.45	66.0	13.5	27.6
State College, PA	10.6	6.7	5.6	47.9	135 758	153 990	13.4	3.1	5 505	4 027	3 329	56 729	2.45	60.3	7.3	25.9
Staunton-Waynesboro, VA	14.1	10.6	8.1	51.2	108 988	118 502	8.7	1.1	5 280	5 296	1 032	46 086	2.43	64.8	9.4	31.0
Stockton-Lodi, CA	10.7	6.5	4.9	50.2	563 598	685 306	21.6	4.4	43 512	20 912	7 325	216 309	3.18	75.3	16.5	19.7
Sumter, SC	12.0	8.0	6.1	51.6	104 646	107 456	2.7	0.4	6 500	4 233	-1 786	39 739	2.66	67.6	19.8	27.5
Syracuse, NY	13.4	8.0	6.8	51.3	650 154	662 577	1.9	-0.2	31 455	24 254	-7 866	256 161	2.48	62.4	13.0	31.0
Tallahassee, FL	11.8	7.1	4.7	51.3	320 304	367 413	14.7	1.9	17 160	10 871	516	143 291	2.45	58.7	14.3	29.8
Tampa-St. Petersburg-Clearwater, FL	13.2	9.9	8.4	51.6	2 395 997	2 783 243	16.2	4.7	132 427	124 034	120 478	1 139 923	2.48	60.9	12.4	32.3
Terre Haute, IN	12.9	8.4	6.7	49.3	170 943	172 425	0.9	-0.5	8 460	7 858	-1 541	63 793	2.44	63.2	10.0	29.9
Texarkana, TX-AR	12.4	8.8	6.4	50.1	143 377	149 198	4.1	0.0	8 336	6 701	-1 434	54 354	2.63	69.8	16.9	26.0

1. No spouse present.

Area name	Persons in group quarters, 2014	Daytime population, 2013		Births, 2014		Deaths, 2014		Persons under 65 with no health insurance 2013		Medicare, 2014			Serious crimes known to police,[2] 2013	
													Total	
		Number	Employ-ment/ residence ratio	Total	Rate[1]	Number	Rate[1]	Number	Percent	Eligible for Medicare	Enrolled in Medicare Advantage	Enrolled in a Medicare prescription drug plan	Number	Rate[3]
	32	33	34	35	36	37	38	39	40	41	42	43	44	45
Redding, CA	2 745	183 924	1.08	2 107	11.7	2 058	11.4	25 986	18.0	44 177	2 299	27 741	7 044	3 930
Reno, NV	5 299	453 173	1.07	5 354	12.1	3 540	8.0	80 156	21.6	74 704	21 448	26 734	12 758	2 910
Richmond, VA	36 567	1 284 511	1.06	14 932	11.9	10 076	8.0	151 127	14.4	203 449	45 565	92 745	31 957	2 572
Riverside-San Bernardino-Ontario, CA	74 159	4 498 464	1.09	61 427	13.8	29 192	6.6	808 922	21.2	574 005	321 427	137 706	137 369	3 128
Roanoke, VA	8 084	334 153	1.17	3 409	10.9	3 330	10.6	37 151	14.8	69 209	15 645	34 671	8 350	2 682
Rochester, MN	3 514	225 718	1.14	2 812	13.2	1 479	7.0	14 817	8.3	35 547	14 839	15 343	3 784	1 792
Rochester, NY	41 073	1 110 598	1.06	11 602	10.7	9 405	8.7	84 189	9.5	210 595	128 596	47 501	29 116	2 695
Rockford, IL	4 997	365 640	1.16	4 084	11.9	3 001	8.8	38 783	13.4	63 054	16 498	30 605	13 214	3 873
Rocky Mount, NC	3 087	163 437	1.27	1 741	11.7	1 584	10.6	21 661	17.5	30 462	5 198	17 981	5 895	3 956
Rome, GA	3 922	108 135	1.38	1 125	11.7	1 032	10.7	17 517	22.5	18 861	4 230	9 567	4 208	4 378
Sacramento—Roseville—Arden-Arcade, CA	34 489	2 281 429	1.08	27 409	12.2	16 596	7.4	302 139	15.9	360 033	155 501	123 273	70 448	3 183
Saginaw, MI	7 125	223 166	1.42	2 259	11.6	2 018	10.3	18 984	12.0	42 489	12 649	28 367	5 824	2 941
St. Cloud, MN	8 883	212 793	1.24	2 384	12.4	1 185	6.2	14 536	9.1	29 981	15 816	14 496	4 989	2 605
St. George, UT	1 923	150 211	1.04	2 188	14.4	1 094	7.2	22 756	19.4	29 271	8 495	11 035	3 132	2 161
St. Joseph, MO-KS	8 617	138 330	1.19	1 537	12.1	1 208	9.5	15 299	15.1	23 041	1 655	13 884	5 558	4 328
St. Louis, MO-IL	55 366	2 839 678	1.03	33 623	12.0	25 458	9.1	292 074	12.4	492 936	160 704	213 178	87 601	3 171
Salem, OR	12 588	421 681	1.15	5 181	12.8	3 312	8.2	61 612	18.6	70 473	40 242	17 995	13 827	3 466
Salinas, CA	17 598	449 392	1.13	6 613	15.3	2 450	5.7	88 415	24.4	57 067	988	34 202	12 734	2 955
Salisbury, MD-DE	13 794	397 957	1.09	4 222	10.8	4 215	10.8	42 385	14.3	91 507	3 508	58 178	14 261	3 702
Salt Lake City, UT	14 703	1 240 547	1.19	19 072	16.5	6 310	5.5	168 224	16.5	128 354	50 281	39 025	55 340	4 849
San Angelo, TX	5 277	121 498	1.09	1 550	13.1	1 017	8.6	21 765	22.9	19 913	3 571	11 108	4 362	3 753
San Antonio-New Braunfels, TX	49 235	2 308 640	1.03	32 280	13.9	16 050	6.9	435 175	22.2	336 563	123 648	97 204	110 614	4 873
San Diego-Carlsbad, CA	104 750	3 284 458	1.05	44 860	13.7	21 128	6.5	490 023	17.9	460 117	209 452	122 473	81 449	2 540
San Francisco-Oakland-Hayward, CA	88 862	4 786 697	1.14	52 901	11.5	30 528	6.6	517 101	13.4	696 253	295 573	245 767	185 816	4 130
Oakland-Hayward-Berkeley, CA Div 36084	47 674	NA	NA	32 210	11.8	17 771	6.5	327 853	14.2	391 131	173 903	130 680	107 184	4 028
San Francisco-Redwood City-South San Francisco, CA Div 41884	32 855	NA	NA	18 435	11.4	10 924	6.8	165 185	12.3	252 313	102 730	94 152	73 129	4 626
San Rafael, CA Div 42034	8 333	NA	NA	2 256	8.7	1 833	7.0	24 063	11.9	52 809	18 940	20 935	5 503	2 137
San Jose-Sunnyvale-Santa Clara, CA	31 359	2 152 880	1.29	25 083	12.8	10 543	5.4	214 006	12.8	251 514	91 463	102 453	50 050	2 614
San Luis Obispo-Paso Robles-Arroyo Grande, CA	16 619	289 049	1.11	2 610	9.4	2 199	7.9	33 835	15.8	54 090	5 973	31 782	7 277	2 629
Santa Cruz-Watsonville, CA	12 910	288 734	1.20	3 105	11.4	1 804	6.6	41 619	18.5	41 915	3 503	25 734	9 142	3 408
Santa Fe, NM	2 629	162 094	1.27	1 356	9.2	1 041	7.0	27 769	23.5	31 326	9 087	12 395	2 155	1 471
Santa Maria-Santa Barbara, CA	19 070	461 399	1.14	5 636	12.8	3 013	6.8	75 743	21.1	69 035	9 576	38 386	11 240	2 589
Santa Rosa, CA	10 750	515 106	1.10	5 196	10.4	4 115	8.2	70 240	17.2	92 253	36 517	33 484	10 000	2 021
Savannah, GA	14 683	383 568	1.12	5 246	14.1	2 924	7.8	62 701	20.4	55 375	17 018	20 624	12 334	3 365
Scranton—Wilkes-Barre—Hazleton, PA	20 766	590 124	1.12	5 486	9.8	6 891	12.3	52 626	11.9	125 690	31 439	66 692	13 721	2 436
Seattle-Tacoma-Bellevue, WA	65 257	3 697 117	1.05	46 315	12.6	24 262	6.6	442 026	14.1	515 896	178 236	168 320	153 772	4 273
Seattle-Bellevue-Everett, WA Div 42644	48 585	NA	NA	35 024	12.3	17 880	6.3	337 185	13.9	387 071	141 547	127 711	116 544	4 194
Tacoma-Lakewood, WA Div 45104	16 672	NA	NA	11 291	13.6	6 382	7.7	104 841	14.8	128 825	36 689	40 609	37 228	4 541
Sebastian-Vero Beach, FL	1 320	149 728	1.18	1 256	8.7	1 887	13.0	26 288	26.5	42 657	9 149	20 639	3 402	2 398
Sebring, FL	1 733	100 786	1.13	881	9.0	1 442	14.7	17 847	27.8	29 986	8 058	13 789	3 309	3 696
Sheboygan, WI	2 846	124 907	1.21	1 260	10.9	1 048	9.1	9 429	10.0	21 720	8 623	6 809	2 225	1 936
Sherman-Denison, TX	2 213	132 126	1.25	1 497	12.1	1 290	10.4	23 205	23.1	24 902	4 577	12 647	3 387	2 783
Shreveport-Bossier City, LA	10 341	459 718	1.07	6 426	14.4	4 450	10.0	69 272	18.5	78 968	13 221	35 643	18 154	4 074
Sierra Vista-Douglas, AZ	5 017	133 022	1.08	1 622	12.7	1 205	9.5	17 527	17.7	27 654	8 289	7 897	NA	NA
Sioux City, IA-NE-SD	3 364	173 611	1.07	2 388	14.1	1 383	8.2	18 279	12.9	28 813	5 960	16 105	5 059	3 034
Sioux Falls, SD	7 021	251 900	1.07	3 870	15.6	1 634	6.6	22 720	10.8	38 188	7 777	22 235	6 473	2 679
South Bend-Mishawaka, IN-MI	11 691	344 045	1.24	3 969	12.4	2 930	9.2	42 833	16.4	56 547	16 114	25 821	10 570	3 380
Spartanburg, SC	8 662	350 510	1.30	3 883	12.1	3 209	10.0	51 234	19.4	64 651	22 229	28 193	11 607	3 638
Spokane-Spokane Valley, WA	15 066	550 124	1.07	6 615	12.2	4 861	9.0	74 504	16.7	102 751	31 924	34 959	32 520	6 077
Springfield, IL	4 121	229 393	1.19	2 420	11.4	2 157	10.2	17 764	10.0	39 222	13 504	13 796	9 551	4 733
Springfield, MA	37 930	656 959	1.12	6 554	10.4	5 510	8.8	24 282	4.8	121 924	31 740	49 268	21 336	3 440
Springfield, MO	14 431	465 471	1.08	5 642	12.5	3 996	8.8	64 235	17.4	84 572	35 016	29 973	22 639	5 053
Springfield, OH	2 829	146 957	1.27	1 567	11.5	1 631	11.9	15 102	13.6	28 802	13 585	14 141	6 465	4 724
State College, PA	19 455	170 211	1.23	1 325	8.3	979	6.2	13 841	11.6	21 666	9 978	8 498	2 291	1 474
Staunton-Waynesboro, VA	4 156	123 924	1.16	1 241	10.4	1 222	10.2	13 871	14.7	26 770	3 657	15 673	2 221	1 865
Stockton-Lodi, CA	14 176	748 819	1.23	10 078	14.1	5 074	7.1	118 403	19.2	98 033	33 935	41 704	33 583	4 739
Sumter, SC	2 784	115 702	1.20	1 529	14.2	1 006	9.3	15 777	17.5	19 542	3 191	9 325	4 662	4 289
Syracuse, NY	26 662	687 805	1.09	7 394	11.2	5 693	8.6	55 594	10.3	123 153	40 825	46 766	17 781	2 690
Tallahassee, FL	23 542	384 154	1.06	3 908	10.4	2 615	7.0	55 454	18.0	53 987	23 516	13 305	15 040	3 976
Tampa-St. Petersburg-Clearwater, FL	49 542	2 914 960	1.04	31 260	10.7	30 593	10.5	486 804	21.1	583 616	273 253	173 975	89 859	3 129
Terre Haute, IN	12 350	178 959	1.18	1 959	11.4	1 799	10.5	21 353	15.8	32 891	3 769	18 917	5 246	3 548
Texarkana, TX-AR	7 799	154 799	1.09	1 970	13.2	1 559	10.4	22 774	19.0	29 136	5 183	14 104	6 656	4 431

1. Per 1,000 estimated resident population. 2. Data for serious crimes have not been adjusted for underreporting; this may affect comparability between geographic areas and over time.
3. Per 100,000 population estimated by the FBI.

Table C. Metropolitan Areas — **Crime, Education, Money Income, and Poverty**

Area name	Serious crimes known to police, 2013 (cont.)[1] Rate[2] Violent	Rate[2] Property	Education: School enrollment and attainment, 2013 — Enrollment[3] Total	Enrollment[3] Percent private	Attainment[4] (percent) High school graduate or less	Attainment[4] (percent) Bachelor's degree or more	Local government expenditures,[5] 2012–2013 Total current expenditures (mil dol)	Current expenditures per student (dollars)	Income and Poverty, 2013 Per capita income[6] (dollars)	Mean household income (dollars)	Median household income	Percent of households with income of less than $25,000	Percent of households with income of $200,000 or more	Percent below poverty level All persons	Children under 18 years	Age 65 years and older
	46	47	48	49	50	51	52	53	54	55	56	57	58	59	60	61
Redding, CA	642	3 288	45 243	16.3	38.2	17.3	276.2	10 161	22 558	54 920	40 332	30.4	2.1	20.1	29.4	7.6
Reno, NV	374	2 536	110 595	7.9	36.1	28.4	552.9	8 453	29 096	72 995	53 948	24.4	4.6	15.0	19.0	7.4
Richmond, VA	242	2 331	326 971	15.5	39.1	32.5	1 888.9	9 737	29 527	75 966	57 286	20.5	5.1	13.9	19.8	7.6
Riverside-San Bernardino-Ontario, CA	333	2 794	1 286 381	11.1	46.3	20.1	7 170.7	8 564	22 048	70 282	53 220	22.5	3.8	18.2	25.4	10.3
Roanoke, VA	240	2 442	71 267	15.0	42.9	27.1	458.3	10 249	27 252	64 933	47 890	25.2	2.8	14.4	22.9	7.0
Rochester, MN	143	1 650	54 409	17.2	32.1	35.3	335.1	10 050	33 248	83 308	62 645	15.9	5.8	7.9	8.5	5.5
Rochester, NY	284	2 411	275 015	22.9	37.7	32.6	2 776.0	17 900	27 923	68 486	51 857	23.7	3.6	14.7	21.9	6.8
Rockford, IL	730	3 143	92 110	24.4	46.1	21.0	645.1	11 345	24 870	63 922	48 027	24.7	2.8	15.5	25.0	7.4
Rocky Mount, NC	535	3 421	37 993	10.4	50.3	16.3	215.2	9 107	20 653	51 804	36 949	32.0	2.4	18.9	28.2	14.8
Rome, GA	375	4 003	26 201	17.7	50.8	18.2	163.8	10 091	18 648	49 345	37 296	34.4	0.9	22.3	29.2	14.4
Sacramento—Roseville—Arden-Arcade, CA	416	2 767	624 544	11.7	34.1	30.8	3 138.7	8 787	28 276	76 775	57 027	21.9	5.2	16.6	21.9	9.6
Saginaw, MI	757	2 184	52 780	10.8	45.3	20.7	299.4	11 025	23 077	56 990	41 548	29.8	2.5	17.8	27.9	8.2
St. Cloud, MN	168	2 437	57 927	16.5	38.8	24.0	306.5	10 309	27 225	69 156	55 513	21.1	2.8	13.6	14.1	7.0
St. George, UT	144	2 017	45 556	10.7	30.8	32.0	182.0	6 673	23 122	66 145	51 063	21.4	3.1	15.9	21.4	6.7
St. Joseph, MO-KS	359	3 969	30 641	9.0	53.7	18.3	171.6	9 434	21 077	55 805	45 024	27.3	1.4	15.5	23.4	7.0
St. Louis, MO-IL	440	2 731	731 718	22.9	35.6	32.5	4 505.0	11 103	29 675	73 426	54 449	21.9	4.6	12.9	18.7	7.5
Salem, OR	235	3 231	106 182	14.8	41.3	23.6	645.5	9 787	21 582	58 848	47 232	24.5	1.4	19.4	29.6	8.0
Salinas, CA	416	2 539	121 131	9.7	49.7	22.2	734.8	9 999	24 145	78 296	57 052	19.5	5.4	17.9	25.3	12.4
Salisbury, MD-DE	443	3 259	83 631	9.7	51.0	22.5	733.9	14 014	25 654	65 421	50 009	24.3	3.0	15.4	23.5	7.9
Salt Lake City, UT	359	4 490	345 483	11.9	33.2	31.2	1 382.4	6 874	26 819	80 117	61 520	17.0	5.3	12.4	16.0	7.7
San Angelo, TX	263	3 490	29 815	7.3	46.7	22.2	156.9	8 639	24 799	62 893	46 010	22.8	2.6	12.2	15.3	8.4
San Antonio-New Braunfels, TX	460	4 414	651 391	12.8	42.7	26.7	3 379.2	8 226	24 597	68 688	51 716	23.6	3.8	16.3	22.9	10.3
San Diego-Carlsbad, CA	348	2 192	861 153	14.3	34.1	34.6	4 493.3	9 033	30 844	85 967	61 426	19.5	7.2	15.2	19.4	9.3
San Francisco-Oakland-Hayward, CA	559	3 571	1 128 717	19.5	28.7	45.2	5 594.7	9 771	42 695	112 911	79 624	16.6	14.3	11.5	13.0	8.9
Oakland-Hayward-Berkeley, CA Div 36084	590	3 438	707 475	15.3	31.1	41.1	3 538.8	9 083	37 117	102 484	75 269	17.1	11.9	12.1	14.5	7.7
San Francisco-Redwood City-South San Francisco, CA Div 41884	566	4 061	357 771	26.6	26.8	49.9	1 678.4	11 104	49 169	122 798	83 479	16.5	16.9	11.0	10.5	11.5
San Rafael, CA Div 42034	191	1 947	63 471	26.4	18.3	55.1	377.6	11 849	60 689	149 066	96 580	13.2	20.4	8.4	9.9	5.4
San Jose-Sunnyvale-Santa Clara, CA	250	2 364	520 278	19.1	28.9	46.7	2 695.2	9 476	42 212	123 386	91 533	13.5	17.3	10.5	13.4	8.6
San Luis Obispo-Paso Robles-Arroyo Grande, CA	386	2 243	79 172	10.2	29.8	31.5	324.7	9 366	29 819	76 395	58 158	20.2	4.9	15.3	14.5	5.5
Santa Cruz-Watsonville, CA	374	3 034	79 778	13.9	27.2	38.9	399.3	9 881	31 521	87 206	68 438	19.8	7.4	14.9	18.4	6.6
Santa Fe, NM	144	1 327	34 961	14.6	34.0	41.7	146.9	9 052	30 920	71 652	51 833	26.6	5.1	19.4	31.1	8.1
Santa Maria-Santa Barbara, CA	326	2 263	131 625	9.3	37.5	32.2	640.6	9 585	31 357	92 050	62 421	19.4	7.9	16.3	20.6	7.6
Santa Rosa, CA	360	1 661	123 622	11.9	32.7	31.7	674.3	9 575	33 357	84 692	61 029	18.5	6.2	12.4	16.8	5.5
Savannah, GA	315	3 050	103 935	24.7	37.8	31.3	497.8	8 869	25 301	66 772	48 958	26.7	4.2	17.3	24.2	8.7
Scranton—Wilkes-Barre—Hazleton, PA	230	2 206	126 853	26.1	49.1	23.6	957.2	12 664	24 549	59 403	45 333	28.8	2.5	15.5	25.8	9.9
Seattle-Tacoma-Bellevue, WA	319	3 954	880 493	16.9	28.7	39.4	4 976.7	9 813	35 779	89 940	67 479	17.3	7.5	12.6	16.9	8.9
Seattle-Bellevue-Everett, WA Div 42644	282	3 912	675 276	17.6	26.2	43.4	3 724.3	9 808	38 074	94 658	70 725	16.5	8.5	12.1	16.0	9.2
Tacoma-Lakewood, WA Div 45104	445	4 096	205 217	14.9	37.5	25.4	1 252.4	9 826	27 968	72 924	57 660	20.0	3.7	14.0	19.5	7.6
Sebastian-Vero Beach, FL	295	2 102	28 420	14.3	42.7	26.2	144.9	8 047	28 355	66 564	42 401	27.0	5.4	13.4	21.3	5.3
Sebring, FL	390	3 307	16 351	8.9	53.3	15.1	103.3	8 558	21 482	48 403	33 811	34.2	1.3	18.8	27.6	10.6
Sheboygan, WI	142	1 794	27 807	16.9	45.9	21.1	210.0	10 803	25 317	61 297	50 678	20.5	1.1	11.5	20.1	6.8
Sherman-Denison, TX	267	2 516	30 731	10.3	44.5	18.6	184.2	8 670	23 758	60 658	44 378	26.2	2.9	16.7	18.3	10.3
Shreveport-Bossier City, LA	530	3 544	107 199	13.1	46.5	24.2	791.0	10 599	24 443	60 661	41 583	30.5	2.9	20.4	28.9	12.9
Sierra Vista-Douglas, AZ	NA	NA	33 770	9.8	34.4	24.5	125.5	7 181	24 093	62 559	46 647	26.7	3.3	19.1	27.0	13.0
Sioux City, IA-NE-SD	255	2 779	44 787	13.7	49.6	20.8	333.7	10 921	23 335	60 445	47 270	23.6	1.8	14.8	21.1	9.2
Sioux Falls, SD	296	2 382	62 840	19.8	34.4	32.3	309.5	7 745	28 379	71 949	55 952	16.4	4.5	9.0	11.1	7.2
South Bend-Mishawaka, IN-MI	312	3 068	87 759	28.7	45.5	24.4	456.1	10 173	22 723	56 673	40 784	28.8	2.1	20.1	30.2	9.4
Spartanburg, SC	469	3 169	81 882	15.6	46.3	22.6	492.5	9 653	21 470	54 484	41 062	30.8	1.8	18.8	27.8	13.3
Spokane-Spokane Valley, WA	346	5 730	137 823	17.7	36.2	25.9	807.7	9 957	24 559	60 832	47 485	26.3	1.9	16.8	19.9	6.9
Springfield, IL	798	3 935	52 613	18.1	35.6	34.0	378.6	11 696	30 857	72 481	55 366	22.6	4.1	15.6	23.0	6.4
Springfield, MA	524	2 916	176 275	16.9	43.6	29.2	1 365.9	15 500	27 162	70 360	52 397	26.7	3.2	16.8	26.0	8.6
Springfield, MO	533	4 520	119 296	15.5	42.6	25.8	553.0	8 205	22 988	56 737	41 034	28.9	2.1	18.7	24.4	9.0
Springfield, OH	348	4 376	33 000	17.4	49.9	18.9	217.1	10 699	24 059	59 914	43 742	30.1	1.9	18.6	28.8	9.1
State College, PA	95	1 380	60 178	9.3	40.4	41.7	193.1	14 954	25 875	69 025	53 207	23.0	4.2	19.8	14.0	9.5
Staunton-Waynesboro, VA	161	1 704	23 013	21.9	51.8	22.4	162.5	9 730	29 773	73 025	49 767	22.2	3.6	11.4	14.0	7.2
Stockton-Lodi, CA	703	4 036	206 219	12.9	47.7	17.2	1 189.0	8 545	21 397	66 389	51 432	24.8	2.7	19.9	26.8	11.4
Sumter, SC	673	3 615	29 004	22.1	45.3	23.3	143.8	8 563	20 217	52 558	39 780	32.0	1.3	19.9	33.2	10.5
Syracuse, NY	257	2 433	178 811	22.3	39.9	29.9	1 710.3	16 863	27 560	68 595	51 496	23.7	3.7	16.0	23.8	8.2
Tallahassee, FL	582	3 394	127 561	9.6	33.5	36.6	403.4	8 852	24 145	61 497	44 420	28.7	3.3	21.5	24.9	8.3
Tampa-St. Petersburg-Clearwater, FL	396	2 732	662 248	16.9	41.7	27.6	3 377.9	8 586	26 821	64 234	45 880	26.6	3.7	15.4	22.7	9.4
Terre Haute, IN	177	3 372	41 531	11.6	49.2	19.4	240.2	9 434	21 681	51 455	40 629	35.1	1.8	22.3	29.9	11.0
Texarkana, TX-AR	555	3 876	32 904	9.0	51.8	16.8	236.1	8 845	23 051	59 202	40 382	32.8	2.7	21.4	32.6	10.8

1. Data for serious crimes have not been adjusted for underreporting; this may affect comparability between geographic areas and over time. 2. Per 100,000 population estimated by the FBI. 3. All persons 3 years old and over enrolled in nursery school through college. 4. Persons 25 years old and over. 5. Elementary and secondary education expenditures. 6. Based on resident population estimated in the 2008-2012 American Community Survey.

Area name	Personal income, 2013: Total (mil dol)	Personal income, 2013: Percent change 2012–2013	Per capita[1]: Dollars	Per capita[1]: Rank	Wages and salaries (mil dol)	Supplements to wages and salaries; employer contributions (mil dol): Pension and insurance	Supplements to wages and salaries; employer contributions (mil dol): Government social insurance	Proprietors' income (mil dol)	Dividends, interest, and rent (mil dol)	Personal transfer receipts (mil dol)	Earnings, 2013: Total (mil dol)	Contributions for government social insurance (mil dol): From employee and self-employed	Contributions for government social insurance (mil dol): From employer
	62	63	64	65	66	67	68	69	70	71	72	73	74
Redding, CA	6 941	2.6	38 780	198	2 470	581	184	531	1 482	2 050	3 766	251	184
Reno, NV	19 769	1.3	45 168	75	8 881	1 586	642	1 293	6 018	2 685	12 402	659	642
Richmond, VA	57 452	1.9	46 118	60	31 760	5 043	2 337	3 576	11 832	8 621	42 717	2 527	2 337
Riverside-San Bernardino-Ontario, CA	144 677	3.1	33 025	344	55 803	12 517	4 143	9 752	24 388	29 257	82 215	4 946	4 143
Roanoke, VA	13 111	1.7	42 044	131	6 816	1 125	530	764	2 846	2 659	9 234	586	530
Rochester, MN	9 582	-0.1	45 231	74	5 760	776	438	591	1 752	1 431	7 565	451	438
Rochester, NY	49 497	1.2	45 692	65	23 199	5 145	1 902	3 993	9 969	9 535	34 239	1 836	1 902
Rockford, IL	12 925	1.7	37 505	237	6 535	1 203	512	775	2 309	2 644	9 026	516	512
Rocky Mount, NC	5 085	-0.5	33 749	331	2 256	414	178	397	768	1 444	3 245	204	178
Rome, GA	3 319	1.4	34 641	312	1 567	289	114	205	534	854	2 176	133	114
Sacramento—Roseville—Arden-Arcade, CA	103 030	3.2	46 499	55	50 237	11 970	3 331	8 319	19 468	17 658	73 858	3 928	3 331
Saginaw, MI	6 561	0.1	33 383	339	3 509	601	282	369	1 029	1 915	4 761	309	282
St. Cloud, MN	7 315	0.4	38 236	213	4 098	653	347	620	1 359	1 357	5 718	336	347
St. George, UT	4 423	4.5	29 928	373	1 756	330	149	332	1 123	1 037	2 567	167	149
St. Joseph, MO-KS	4 767	2.9	37 310	242	2 273	443	167	461	722	1 042	3 344	191	167
St. Louis, MO-IL	128 826	1.6	45 992	61	67 253	11 055	4 888	9 355	25 990	21 286	92 551	5 407	4 888
Salem, OR	14 051	2.7	35 092	301	6 281	1 205	562	986	2 470	3 291	9 035	553	562
Salinas, CA	19 233	4.0	44 851	80	8 299	1 796	632	2 101	4 635	2 782	12 828	656	632
Salisbury, MD-DE	15 170	3.0	39 357	188	5 610	1 081	446	1 236	3 381	3 887	8 374	514	446
Salt Lake City, UT	47 384	3.5	41 547	143	31 391	5 335	2 482	4 574	8 321	5 784	43 783	2 483	2 482
San Angelo, TX	4 839	2.8	41 515	144	2 011	361	145	509	1 188	895	3 027	155	145
San Antonio-New Braunfels, TX	90 990	2.9	39 951	174	43 308	6 998	3 106	10 213	17 495	15 748	63 624	3 235	3 106
San Diego-Carlsbad, CA	165 008	2.5	51 384	27	83 427	15 768	6 089	13 362	36 859	22 163	118 647	6 631	6 089
San Francisco-Oakland-Hayward, CA	312 195	3.0	69 127	4	171 626	25 086	10 668	28 298	67 485	31 784	235 678	13 453	10 668
Oakland-Hayward-Berkeley, CA Div 36084	156 749	2.9	58 639	NA	69 138	11 869	4 799	11 015	30 710	19 262	96 821	5 602	4 799
San Francisco-Redwood City-South San Francisco, CA Div 41884	130 353	3.4	82 251	NA	95 403	12 089	5 384	14 675	29 128	10 659	127 551	7 183	5 384
San Rafael, CA Div 42034	25 093	1.7	97 124	NA	7 085	1 129	485	2 608	7 647	1 864	11 306	668	485
San Jose-Sunnyvale-Santa Clara, CA	132 849	4.6	69 205	3	99 127	10 729	5 652	8 078	27 236	11 531	123 585	7 174	5 652
San Luis Obispo-Paso Robles-Arroyo Grande, CA	12 547	3.1	45 388	70	4 761	1 127	339	1 233	3 555	1 898	7 461	436	339
Santa Cruz-Watsonville, CA	14 810	3.9	54 970	15	4 716	964	325	1 320	3 479	1 795	7 325	417	325
Santa Fe, NM	6 532	0.6	44 309	88	2 788	507	209	457	1 810	1 080	3 960	250	209
Santa Maria-Santa Barbara, CA	21 726	2.0	49 864	33	9 656	1 940	690	2 054	6 652	2 743	14 341	797	690
Santa Rosa, CA	24 906	3.8	50 312	31	9 158	1 778	676	2 241	6 348	3 588	13 852	843	676
Savannah, GA	14 986	2.3	40 940	161	7 251	1 331	537	852	2 871	2 610	9 971	563	537
Scranton—Wilkes-Barre—Hazleton, PA	22 609	0.9	40 227	171	10 002	2 107	849	1 366	4 072	5 511	14 324	885	849
Seattle-Tacoma-Bellevue, WA	199 243	2.7	55 190	14	116 324	16 340	9 931	16 264	39 400	23 324	158 859	9 135	9 931
Seattle-Bellevue-Everett, WA Div 42644	163 189	3.0	58 483	NA	101 048	13 367	8 449	14 094	32 711	17 072	136 958	7 912	8 449
Tacoma-Lakewood, WA Div 45104	36 054	1.7	43 982	NA	15 277	2 972	1 482	2 170	6 688	6 251	21 901	1 224	1 482
Sebastian-Vero Beach, FL	7 731	0.9	54 448	18	1 960	295	146	320	3 878	1 455	2 721	192	146
Sebring, FL	3 022	1.6	30 962	370	925	170	70	118	781	1 106	1 283	100	70
Sheboygan, WI	5 345	2.0	46 508	54	2 613	497	212	669	1 056	784	3 991	235	212
Sherman-Denison, TX	4 417	3.4	36 098	280	1 852	277	128	276	762	1 105	2 533	148	128
Shreveport-Bossier City, LA	18 513	-0.2	41 465	146	8 115	1 505	547	2 265	3 770	3 743	12 432	641	547
Sierra Vista-Douglas, AZ	4 740	-1.3	36 612	264	1 886	443	156	195	983	1 361	2 679	157	156
Sioux City, IA-NE-SD	7 333	5.5	43 465	103	3 377	562	264	1 316	1 273	1 148	5 518	300	264
Sioux Falls, SD	11 909	3.5	48 906	38	6 129	880	448	2 123	2 232	1 368	9 580	555	448
South Bend-Mishawaka, IN-MI	12 038	0.5	37 781	227	5 452	896	423	1 190	2 036	2 452	7 961	494	423
Spartanburg, SC	10 859	2.2	34 040	322	5 845	953	457	1 000	1 706	2 576	8 255	527	457
Spokane-Spokane Valley, WA	20 351	2.4	37 987	221	9 947	1 713	939	1 062	4 436	4 576	13 661	837	939
Springfield, IL	9 170	2.9	43 307	104	4 630	961	322	890	1 949	1 525	6 802	338	322
Springfield, MA	27 405	1.7	43 715	100	12 188	2 639	876	1 353	4 668	6 674	17 056	895	876
Springfield, MO	15 757	2.0	35 115	300	7 583	1 409	564	1 556	2 814	3 376	11 112	674	564
Springfield, OH	5 087	1.4	37 361	241	1 915	380	149	296	737	1 296	2 740	165	149
State College, PA	6 510	2.3	41 894	135	3 313	1 276	253	474	1 238	896	5 315	266	253
Staunton-Waynesboro, VA	4 502	2.4	37 664	232	1 862	337	139	356	985	958	2 694	175	139
Stockton-Lodi, CA	24 481	3.4	34 755	308	9 503	2 074	713	2 326	4 033	5 924	14 616	839	713
Sumter, SC	3 602	1.9	33 310	340	1 775	396	153	184	693	939	2 508	143	153
Syracuse, NY	28 082	0.7	42 425	124	13 757	3 281	1 126	1 824	4 958	5 691	19 988	1 061	1 126
Tallahassee, FL	13 509	1.2	36 193	275	6 905	1 511	491	675	2 825	2 350	9 583	542	491
Tampa-St. Petersburg-Clearwater, FL	116 042	2.2	40 425	167	57 262	8 681	4 162	6 883	26 388	24 444	76 989	4 796	4 162
Terre Haute, IN	5 861	1.8	34 040	322	2 704	513	210	525	943	1 475	3 952	241	210
Texarkana, TX-AR	5 235	-1.1	34 990	304	2 294	416	171	434	1 027	1 273	3 316	193	171

1. Based on the resident population estimated as of July 1 of the year shown.

Area name	Earnings, 2013 (cont.)									Social Security beneficiaries, December 2013		Supplemental Security Income recipients, December 2013	Housing units, 2014	
	Percent by selected industries													
	Farm	Mining	Construction	Manufacturing	Information, professional, scientific, technical services	Retail trade	Finance, insurance, real estate, rental and leasing	Health care and social assistance	Government	Number	Rate[1]		Total	Percent change, 2000–2014
	75	76	77	78	79	80	81	82	83	84	85	86	87	88
Redding, CA	0.3	D	6.6	3.7	6.4	10.1	5.5	19.4	24.5	47 510	265	10 006	77 915	0.8
Reno, NV	0.1	D	6.4	6.9	D	6.7	D	D	18.1	77 935	178	6 680	189 127	1.2
Richmond, VA	0.1	D	D	6.1	12.2	D	11.7	11.4	19.9	218 815	175	26 655	519 067	2.3
Riverside-San Bernardino-Ontario, CA	0.4	0.3	7.2	7.3	5.4	8.6	5.6	11.7	25.1	606 660	138	134 793	1 528 233	1.9
Roanoke, VA	0.0	D	5.4	D	D	D	7.0	17.5	14.8	72 315	231	7 943	145 861	0.6
Rochester, MN	1.7	0.1	4.8	12.7	4.0	5.1	3.1	D	9.7	37 455	177	2 768	89 685	1.7
Rochester, NY	1.0	D	6.1	13.8	11.1	5.8	5.6	12.0	18.3	230 395	213	34 248	473 684	1.0
Rockford, IL	1.4	0.0	4.7	26.6	4.5	6.8	5.1	15.6	12.6	69 275	201	7 658	145 509	-0.3
Rocky Mount, NC	3.7	0.1	5.1	20.7	D	7.4	5.9	D	18.1	34 220	228	6 415	67 067	-0.1
Rome, GA	0.4	D	2.4	16.8	D	6.8	4.2	24.8	15.1	21 405	223	3 336	40 428	-0.3
Sacramento—Roseville—Arden-Arcade, CA	0.6	0.1	5.4	4.5	11.5	5.8	8.3	11.2	33.2	360 175	162	81 396	884 874	1.5
Saginaw, MI	1.2	0.3	3.8	19.6	6.5	7.6	5.6	18.5	15.2	48 655	247	8 669	86 783	-0.1
St. Cloud, MN	3.1	0.1	8.2	14.7	D	7.5	5.8	D	14.7	32 235	168	2 870	79 383	1.6
St. George, UT	-0.1	0.4	10.3	5.0	6.6	10.3	6.7	17.0	16.1	30 960	210	1 244	62 434	8.1
St. Joseph, MO-KS	4.4	0.1	5.7	22.9	D	6.8	5.1	D	15.6	25 150	197	2 966	53 584	-0.1
St. Louis, MO-IL	0.6	D	D	10.7	12.2	5.5	D	12.6	13.2	532 720	190	60 339	1 236 676	0.9
Salem, OR	3.1	D	6.1	6.5	D	6.9	4.9	15.8	30.5	75 970	190	9 201	153 056	1.2
Salinas, CA	9.6	0.3	3.5	2.9	5.8	5.7	4.7	7.7	26.3	58 140	135	9 293	140 144	0.8
Salisbury, MD-DE	3.1	0.0	7.0	9.0	5.3	10.5	6.5	15.6	18.5	97 550	253	7 177	238 523	3.2
Salt Lake City, UT	0.0	1.2	6.2	9.4	D	7.7	11.0	8.0	15.8	135 630	119	14 072	396 825	3.5
San Angelo, TX	1.0	8.4	D	D	D	D	D	D	23.6	21 500	184	2 981	48 554	2.4
San Antonio-New Braunfels, TX	0.1	D	7.5	5.1	9.9	7.1	10.5	10.5	22.0	360 020	158	63 942	863 046	3.0
San Diego-Carlsbad, CA	0.3	0.1	4.8	8.1	17.5	5.3	8.9	8.4	24.3	452 445	140	84 827	1 187 625	2.0
San Francisco-Oakland-Hayward, CA	0.1	D	4.7	6.7	26.2	4.7	11.4	8.4	13.5	649 200	143	141 306	1 771 525	1.7
Oakland-Hayward-Berkeley, CA Div 36084	0.1	0.7	6.5	9.6	16.5	5.7	7.3	12.1	15.8	372 655	139	80 033	999 127	1.7
San Francisco-Redwood City-South San Francisco, CA Div 41884	0.0	D	3.3	4.9	34.0	3.8	14.2	5.4	11.9	227 165	143	57 534	660 103	1.9
San Rafael, CA Div 42034	0.2	0.7	5.6	1.7	20.8	7.0	14.9	10.9	13.5	49 380	191	3 739	112 295	1.0
San Jose-Sunnyvale-Santa Clara, CA	0.1	D	3.1	22.8	D	4.4	5.3	6.8	7.3	230 110	119	49 314	669 269	3.0
San Luis Obispo-Paso Robles-Arroyo Grande, CA	2.2	0.2	8.4	6.2	8.0	8.2	6.8	10.9	22.8	54 445	197	5 142	119 143	1.6
Santa Cruz-Watsonville, CA	4.7	D	8.2	7.8	7.7	6.8	5.1	12.9	20.3	41 770	155	5 792	105 275	0.8
Santa Fe, NM	0.1	1.3	5.2	1.3	9.3	9.1	9.4	13.4	30.2	32 270	219	2 948	71 749	0.7
Santa Maria-Santa Barbara, CA	3.5	1.9	4.7	7.7	13.6	6.2	6.7	10.3	21.8	69 435	159	9 438	154 401	1.0
Santa Rosa, CA	1.4	0.2	7.8	12.6	9.5	7.7	7.2	13.9	15.3	91 640	185	9 551	207 232	1.3
Savannah, GA	0.1	D	4.1	16.3	D	6.7	5.0	D	20.1	59 975	164	8 109	156 057	3.3
Scranton—Wilkes-Barre—Hazleton, PA	0.0	0.7	5.1	11.9	D	7.9	6.4	D	15.3	138 680	247	17 650	258 197	-0.2
Seattle-Tacoma-Bellevue, WA	0.0	0.0	5.6	12.4	20.8	6.5	6.7	9.1	15.8	519 485	144	70 041	1 510 908	3.3
Seattle-Bellevue-Everett, WA Div 42644	0.0	0.0	5.4	13.4	23.4	6.5	7.0	8.2	12.8	383 560	137	50 527	1 178 196	3.5
Tacoma-Lakewood, WA Div 45104	0.1	0.1	6.9	6.2	4.6	6.1	5.0	14.8	34.9	135 925	166	19 514	332 712	2.3
Sebastian-Vero Beach, FL	1.6	0.2	6.0	4.3	9.4	10.6	8.1	18.4	12.4	44 485	313	2 255	77 340	1.3
Sebring, FL	6.2	0.0	3.2	2.4	4.0	10.8	3.8	23.4	18.4	32 190	329	2 662	54 894	-0.9
Sheboygan, WI	1.3	D	4.5	42.8	2.8	5.5	5.5	11.0	9.9	24 045	209	1 819	50 595	-0.3
Sherman-Denison, TX	0.5	0.9	9.3	18.3	4.3	8.1	6.4	17.5	13.4	26 605	217	2 986	54 399	1.3
Shreveport-Bossier City, LA	0.2	9.1	6.2	6.8	5.2	7.5	5.7	13.8	22.7	84 570	189	19 776	198 571	2.9
Sierra Vista-Douglas, AZ	2.2	0.2	2.9	1.0	9.4	6.2	2.8	7.3	52.1	29 815	230	2 990	60 504	2.5
Sioux City, IA-NE-SD	11.8	D	7.0	D	D	6.0	5.4	10.9	11.5	31 260	185	2 629	69 283	0.9
Sioux Falls, SD	4.3	D	5.8	D	D	7.0	D	D	8.9	40 285	165	3 175	101 661	6.0
South Bend-Mishawaka, IN-MI	0.9	0.0	4.7	15.8	8.9	6.2	5.4	D	10.9	62 750	197	6 876	141 480	0.5
Spartanburg, SC	0.4	D	5.4	24.7	D	6.3	6.8	D	16.4	72 920	229	8 418	138 520	1.3
Spokane-Spokane Valley, WA	0.0	0.2	5.9	8.2	D	7.7	7.6	D	20.9	108 150	202	15 700	235 268	2.1
Springfield, IL	5.6	D	4.4	3.0	D	5.8	8.7	D	25.0	42 975	203	4 893	96 196	0.7
Springfield, MA	0.0	0.1	5.4	9.5	6.2	6.4	8.2	17.7	23.1	127 000	202	32 969	254 672	0.0
Springfield, MO	0.2	D	D	9.6	8.5	8.3	6.9	17.3	14.6	92 765	207	10 016	197 166	2.5
Springfield, OH	1.8	0.2	4.0	15.8	D	7.0	8.2	14.3	15.9	30 440	223	3 993	61 192	-0.4
State College, PA	0.0	0.9	4.4	5.5	8.3	5.4	3.8	9.6	50.3	22 880	145	1 514	65 107	2.9
Staunton-Waynesboro, VA	1.5	D	D	17.8	7.2	7.1	3.6	D	17.5	29 395	246	2 092	53 581	1.8
Stockton-Lodi, CA	6.3	0.1	5.4	8.3	4.0	7.3	6.0	12.3	20.6	101 855	144	29 545	237 542	1.6
Sumter, SC	0.9	0.0	6.2	13.9	3.9	5.5	3.0	11.2	39.1	22 390	207	4 195	47 029	2.2
Syracuse, NY	0.6	D	5.3	9.6	9.8	6.4	6.8	12.5	22.2	136 320	206	19 904	289 904	0.8
Tallahassee, FL	0.4	D	3.8	2.1	D	6.2	5.7	11.7	39.7	58 170	156	9 801	165 583	1.5
Tampa-St. Petersburg-Clearwater, FL	0.3	0.1	4.6	5.7	14.7	7.7	11.1	13.8	14.2	630 825	219	75 420	1 375 715	1.7
Terre Haute, IN	4.5	2.7	6.1	19.7	3.4	6.7	D	14.9	17.3	36 920	214	4 544	74 477	0.5
Texarkana, TX-AR	1.5	D	5.4	11.3	3.8	7.9	6.3	D	24.3	31 930	213	6 672	64 998	1.2

1. Per 1,000 resident population estimated as of July 1, 2011 of the year shown.

Area name	Housing units, 2013: Occupied units: Total	Owner-occupied: Percent	Owner-occupied: Median value[1]	Median owner cost as a percent of income: With a mortgage	Median owner cost as a percent of income: Without a mortgage[2]	Renter-occupied: Median rent[3]	Renter-occupied: Median rent as a percent of income	Substandard units[4] (percent)	Civilian labor force, 2014: Total	Percent change, 2013–2014	Unemployment: Total	Unemployment: Rate[5]	Civilian employment[6], 2013: Total employed	Percent: Management, professional, and related occupations	Percent: Construction, production, and related occupations
	89	90	91	92	93	94	95	96	97	98	99	100	101	102	103
Redding, CA	69 729	61.2	209 700	26.9	13.6	893	36.4	4.0	75 458	0.0	7 293	9.7	66 686	29.8	20.4
Reno, NV	166 432	56.3	200 700	23.1	10.0	870	29.5	4.5	224 503	0.3	16 724	7.4	209 801	34.2	18.0
Richmond, VA	467 399	64.1	204 800	22.2	10.2	959	30.9	1.8	656 435	1.2	35 868	5.5	603 417	39.5	17.5
Riverside-San Bernardino-Ontario, CA	1 297 675	61.9	234 000	27.2	12.0	1 125	35.5	7.8	1 919 894	1.2	156 569	8.2	1 743 257	29.2	25.2
Roanoke, VA	128 318	69.4	164 600	21.9	10.2	748	28.4	NA	161 480	0.7	8 372	5.2	147 572	35.9	20.0
Rochester, MN	82 956	76.5	166 500	19.9	10.5	763	27.5	2.4	117 140	-0.7	4 211	3.6	112 817	42.6	19.2
Rochester, NY	425 603	67.3	135 700	21.3	13.6	790	33.2	1.7	524 825	-2.3	30 521	5.8	512 671	40.4	18.4
Rockford, IL	131 292	68.7	120 000	22.9	12.4	727	28.2	2.9	168 661	-0.5	13 952	8.3	155 145	31.1	28.2
Rocky Mount, NC	58 462	62.6	96 000	22.6	12.8	658	32.6	NA	66 838	-3.2	5 779	8.6	64 206	26.1	31.0
Rome, GA	33 099	56.1	115 500	21.5	13.3	626	26.5	NA	43 404	-0.9	3 441	7.9	38 546	25.2	32.7
Sacramento—Roseville—Arden-Arcade, CA	792 639	57.8	278 500	25.4	10.7	1 060	32.9	4.4	1 049 244	0.2	75 058	7.2	951 238	38.6	17.1
Saginaw, MI	77 518	71.2	95 100	21.2	12.9	670	31.9	NA	89 280	0.0	6 562	7.3	81 993	27.9	23.7
St. Cloud, MN	72 873	69.2	162 200	20.9	10.6	700	28.0	NA	109 225	0.8	4 584	4.2	106 467	30.5	26.1
St. George, UT	49 394	71.2	204 300	27.6	10.0	912	28.4	NA	61 496	3.3	2 654	4.3	58 552	31.6	19.3
St. Joseph, MO-KS	46 237	64.3	111 200	19.5	10.8	703	28.3	NA	66 211	0.7	3 610	5.5	57 457	27.9	30.9
St. Louis, MO-IL	1 105 652	69.6	153 000	20.7	11.7	814	29.2	1.5	1 455 416	0.9	91 672	6.3	1 353 117	38.5	18.6
Salem, OR	142 174	59.5	182 200	24.7	11.8	739	29.9	4.7	184 807	1.6	13 648	7.4	173 995	29.5	25.9
Salinas, CA	125 553	49.3	363 800	28.0	10.2	1 217	34.1	11.4	219 814	1.4	19 920	9.1	172 574	29.0	29.9
Salisbury, MD-DE	143 465	72.1	204 200	24.2	12.7	937	29.7	2.4	178 717	0.7	12 983	7.3	166 905	31.1	22.4
Salt Lake City, UT	366 765	66.5	225 100	22.5	10.0	935	28.9	4.3	606 482	1.1	22 544	3.7	559 528	38.2	20.2
San Angelo, TX	44 059	63.7	111 400	20.1	11.0	746	27.6	NA	55 619	0.6	2 243	4.0	52 150	31.4	27.3
San Antonio-New Braunfels, TX	778 939	61.4	134 000	21.1	11.2	857	29.0	5.0	1 095 172	1.7	50 422	4.6	1 035 860	34.0	19.7
San Diego-Carlsbad, CA	1 093 386	52.8	411 000	27.0	11.2	1 289	33.5	6.6	1 546 363	0.0	99 216	6.4	1 431 442	39.9	16.3
San Francisco-Oakland-Hayward, CA	1 654 554	53.6	602 800	25.8	10.7	1 435	30.2	6.2	2 458 842	1.4	128 596	5.2	2 272 152	46.6	14.0
Oakland-Hayward-Berkeley, CA Div 36084	938 265	57.1	477 600	25.4	10.3	1 352	31.8	5.7	1 355 368	0.6	81 192	6.0	1 277 037	44.1	16.1
San Francisco-Redwood City-South San Francisco, CA Div 41884	613 442	46.2	763 100	26.3	10.8	1 560	28.5	7.5	963 423	2.5	41 424	4.3	867 624	49.3	11.4
San Rafael, CA Div 42034	102 847	65.7	784 200	27.0	13.4	1 632	31.0	NA	140 051	0.8	5 980	4.3	127 491	53.1	10.7
San Jose-Sunnyvale-Santa Clara, CA	636 628	56.0	672 900	25.4	10.0	1 640	29.5	8.2	1 024 498	2.1	54 467	5.3	936 729	49.7	15.5
San Luis Obispo-Paso Robles-Arroyo Grande, CA	104 669	56.8	436 000	26.3	11.3	1 203	34.5	NA	139 865	1.4	7 838	5.6	128 815	36.8	19.2
Santa Cruz-Watsonville, CA	93 982	60.0	535 500	28.4	11.2	1 350	38.3	7.0	142 626	0.3	12 469	8.7	129 221	39.1	19.9
Santa Fe, NM	60 405	70.9	263 900	24.8	10.0	921	27.9	2.6	71 510	-1.6	3 843	5.4	66 840	44.3	16.5
Santa Maria-Santa Barbara, CA	140 665	52.0	437 300	25.8	11.9	1 336	33.7	9.8	218 721	0.7	13 300	6.1	206 144	34.5	22.6
Santa Rosa, CA	189 087	58.5	406 900	26.7	11.6	1 285	33.6	5.3	257 295	1.8	14 351	5.6	238 568	36.4	20.1
Savannah, GA	132 260	58.5	169 300	23.5	11.0	903	32.0	NA	173 493	0.4	12 231	7.0	159 706	34.9	23.7
Scranton—Wilkes-Barre—Hazleton, PA	223 354	68.0	135 200	21.9	14.2	679	29.6	1.2	279 452	-1.2	19 448	7.0	255 447	31.2	23.3
Seattle-Tacoma-Bellevue, WA	1 392 337	59.1	307 900	24.4	12.3	1 135	29.8	3.3	1 937 442	1.5	101 298	5.2	1 797 681	43.4	17.7
Seattle-Bellevue-Everett, WA Div 42644	1 090 050	58.8	342 000	24.2	12.3	1 169	29.3	3.3	1 553 537	1.8	73 626	4.7	1 437 538	45.8	16.3
Tacoma-Lakewood, WA Div 45104	302 287	60.5	223 300	24.9	12.2	993	32.1	3.6	383 905	0.2	27 672	7.2	360 143	33.9	23.1
Sebastian-Vero Beach, FL	57 435	71.8	151 100	24.5	12.4	858	36.1	NA	62 028	0.7	4 852	7.8	54 927	29.4	18.2
Sebring, FL	40 368	75.9	80 500	23.0	10.7	670	29.6	NA	36 531	1.1	2 984	8.2	30 036	28.5	25.0
Sheboygan, WI	47 295	71.0	146 500	21.3	13.4	644	25.2	NA	61 603	1.2	2 844	4.6	58 181	26.9	34.5
Sherman-Denison, TX	46 311	63.8	99 300	22.1	10.9	767	27.7	NA	60 948	0.3	2 943	4.8	52 811	30.9	21.7
Shreveport-Bossier City, LA	169 481	64.1	121 100	20.7	10.0	726	30.1	2.6	196 679	0.8	13 892	7.1	192 045	32.6	23.3
Sierra Vista-Douglas, AZ	48 368	70.4	150 000	20.3	10.0	802	30.9	4.5	50 978	-0.6	4 301	8.4	44 066	35.0	18.9
Sioux City, IA-NE-SD	63 754	71.0	110 200	19.1	11.7	649	24.4	NA	93 753	1.7	4 098	4.4	84 092	28.5	30.4
Sioux Falls, SD	94 244	68.0	157 200	20.7	10.0	685	25.3	NA	141 678	1.8	4 037	2.8	134 302	35.9	20.4
South Bend-Mishawaka, IN-MI	123 138	68.9	105 300	20.5	10.9	687	29.5	NA	152 888	1.3	10 230	6.7	142 862	31.6	25.1
Spartanburg, SC	119 827	67.9	118 700	19.6	10.0	680	30.6	2.3	146 388	-0.1	9 502	6.5	139 385	30.6	27.8
Spokane-Spokane Valley, WA	208 513	63.3	177 600	22.7	11.2	769	31.8	2.1	247 216	-0.7	18 215	7.4	229 096	34.4	20.2
Springfield, IL	87 918	70.0	130 100	19.1	10.2	741	29.0	NA	110 651	0.0	6 628	6.0	102 253	39.0	15.9
Springfield, MA	234 947	62.7	210 900	22.9	14.0	850	33.3	2.8	308 836	1.1	21 743	7.0	293 143	35.9	19.3
Springfield, MO	179 138	62.2	124 800	19.8	10.0	683	31.8	1.8	227 771	2.6	11 610	5.1	208 477	35.0	20.2
Springfield, OH	54 372	68.1	102 300	19.6	11.5	649	32.8	NA	65 345	-1.1	3 644	5.6	60 077	28.6	27.9
State College, PA	56 729	61.9	198 700	21.1	10.7	869	34.2	NA	77 752	-0.3	3 219	4.1	73 669	41.9	16.6
Staunton-Waynesboro, VA	46 086	69.6	187 800	22.3	10.0	720	30.6	NA	59 146	0.2	2 894	4.9	54 810	32.0	23.6
Stockton-Lodi, CA	216 309	55.3	208 900	25.8	10.9	995	35.6	7.1	311 061	-0.1	33 094	10.6	277 997	26.5	30.0
Sumter, SC	39 739	64.9	117 700	19.3	10.0	764	29.7	NA	43 964	0.0	3 223	7.3	42 756	30.8	28.9
Syracuse, NY	256 161	67.2	124 300	20.4	12.7	736	29.9	2.0	313 314	-2.8	19 082	6.1	309 771	38.2	19.1
Tallahassee, FL	143 291	55.3	159 700	22.9	10.3	845	33.6	NA	189 820	1.5	10 963	5.8	175 232	40.9	13.1
Tampa-St. Petersburg-Clearwater, FL	1 139 923	63.4	135 400	23.8	12.1	925	31.9	2.5	1 442 589	1.3	87 314	6.1	1 277 506	37.0	16.8
Terre Haute, IN	63 793	64.8	89 700	19.5	11.5	670	33.5	NA	77 752	-0.7	5 978	7.7	70 391	31.4	26.8
Texarkana, TX-AR	54 354	64.7	104 700	18.8	10.8	673	31.9	NA	64 507	-1.8	4 024	6.2	60 570	26.9	29.8

1. Specified owner-occupied units. 2. A value of 10.0 represents 10 percent or less. 3. Specified renter-occupied units. 4. Overcrowded or lacking complete plumbing facilities.
5. Percent of civilian labor force. 6. Persons 16 years old and over.

Area name	Private nonfarm establishments, employment and payroll, 2013: Number of establishments	Employment: Total	Employment: Health care and social assistance	Employment: Manufacturing	Employment: Retail trade	Employment: Finance and insurance	Employment: Professional, scientific, and technical services	Annual payroll: Total (mil dol)	Annual payroll: Average per employee (dollars)	Agriculture, 2012: Farms: Number	Farms: Percent with: Fewer than 50 acres	Farms: Percent with: 500 acres or more	Farm operators whose principal occupation is farming (percent)
	104	105	106	107	108	109	110	111	112	113	114	115	116
Redding, CA	4 126	47 159	10 049	2 031	9 284	1 970	2 033	1 690	35 842	1 544	72.9	6.1	44.9
Reno, NV	11 558	167 692	22 151	13 702	22 142	5 934	10 174	7 169	42 748	485	69.7	7.0	43.5
Richmond, VA	30 366	508 268	78 277	30 658	64 423	48 839	36 950	23 632	46 496	3 131	43.1	8.6	48.2
Riverside-San Bernardino-Ontario, CA	67 199	1 031 643	151 642	91 039	166 617	24 794	34 155	38 693	37 507	4 198	86.0	3.0	51.5
Roanoke, VA	8 107	136 116	25 113	15 462	18 406	8 946	5 683	5 354	39 336	2 094	34.0	6.6	46.1
Rochester, MN	5 095	93 232	35 417	11 657	12 522	2 376	2 212	4 149	44 500	4 233	29.7	14.5	53.4
Rochester, NY	24 471	434 699	77 836	55 560	58 761	14 697	24 792	17 981	41 364	4 268	38.0	9.1	61.0
Rockford, IL	7 328	132 375	21 340	34 006	15 991	3 835	5 103	5 321	40 198	1 286	47.4	13.6	47.5
Rocky Mount, NC	2 802	46 374	8 100	9 447	6 591	1 589	1 005	1 665	35 914	702	37.9	16.7	54.8
Rome, GA	1 950	32 861	7 668	5 800	4 282	D	768	1 166	35 476	559	44.4	3.6	36.5
Sacramento—Roseville—Arden-Arcade, CA	45 392	659 498	107 527	32 010	93 579	39 650	50 463	31 374	47 573	5 076	71.7	6.4	50.7
Saginaw, MI	4 358	78 238	18 000	10 708	12 977	2 728	2 301	2 815	35 983	1 318	41.0	12.1	48.9
St. Cloud, MN	5 244	92 695	18 842	15 224	13 042	3 878	2 612	3 561	38 418	4 459	24.5	8.3	54.6
St. George, UT	4 195	40 096	7 143	2 406	7 666	1 465	1 770	1 259	31 397	579	63.0	13.1	43.5
St. Joseph, MO-KS	2 954	49 806	8 607	13 391	6 399	2 369	1 219	1 775	35 633	2 838	26.1	14.6	44.1
St. Louis, MO-IL	71 358	1 185 778	183 330	99 282	142 431	65 379	90 187	54 820	46 231	11 270	35.8	13.6	43.9
Salem, OR	9 021	107 816	20 815	10 536	17 035	3 720	4 321	3 674	34 080	3 710	70.5	5.4	48.7
Salinas, CA	8 408	101 020	15 086	5 614	16 469	3 260	7 823	4 218	41 755	1 179	42.0	26.4	61.7
Salisbury, MD-DE	10 348	118 900	22 380	13 250	23 150	3 624	3 745	4 164	35 025	2 384	51.8	10.4	63.4
Salt Lake City, UT	30 644	535 321	62 004	48 104	59 261	38 384	43 164	24 796	46 319	1 106	77.0	8.0	30.1
San Angelo, TX	2 796	39 957	7 643	3 287	6 359	1 513	1 494	1 402	35 088	1 358	41.6	23.9	40.5
San Antonio-New Braunfels, TX	42 361	780 690	121 407	42 265	102 523	62 255	44 970	32 305	41 380	14 598	41.6	10.4	40.4
San Diego-Carlsbad, CA	78 379	1 181 133	152 207	100 475	145 051	51 448	132 252	59 966	50 770	5 732	91.6	0.9	47.6
San Francisco-Oakland-Hayward, CA	121 802	1 893 104	243 240	105 958	200 986	115 214	219 546	144 005	76 068	1 717	61.4	13.6	53.2
Oakland-Hayward-Berkeley, CA Div 36084	X	X	X	X	X	X	X	X	X	1 054	67.6	9.8	50.6
San Francisco-Redwood City-South San Francisco, CA Div 41884	X	X	X	X	X	X	X	X	X	340	62.4	6.2	56.5
San Rafael, CA Div 42034	X	X	X	X	X	X	X	X	X	323	39.9	34.1	58.5
San Jose-Sunnyvale-Santa Clara, CA	47 139	936 927	100 283	90 839	83 196	24 412	133 121	89 138	95 139	1 631	66.8	12.4	56.9
San Luis Obispo-Paso Robles-Arroyo Grande, CA	7 873	86 125	15 276	5 943	14 346	2 431	4 792	3 288	38 176	2 666	55.8	12.2	47.0
Santa Cruz-Watsonville, CA	6 779	70 493	12 437	4 516	11 769	2 030	3 977	2 955	41 914	667	73.8	4.6	62.1
Santa Fe, NM	4 714	44 633	7 812	754	9 349	1 860	2 425	1 748	39 164	715	67.0	13.4	43.6
Santa Maria-Santa Barbara, CA	11 211	137 623	20 275	13 333	19 242	4 385	9 753	6 353	46 162	1 597	63.9	11.3	51.7
Santa Rosa, CA	13 370	152 105	23 442	18 224	23 924	5 782	9 228	6 984	45 916	3 579	71.3	6.0	51.3
Savannah, GA	8 499	133 518	20 615	16 167	18 696	3 236	4 672	5 262	39 412	281	50.9	9.3	43.1
Scranton—Wilkes-Barre—Hazleton, PA	13 223	236 479	47 344	28 191	33 204	10 533	11 781	8 587	36 312	1 367	32.8	2.9	44.0
Seattle-Tacoma-Bellevue, WA	97 968	1 507 055	209 389	152 339	168 039	62 203	118 228	91 677	60 832	4 753	86.4	0.6	42.5
Seattle-Bellevue-Everett, WA Div 42644	X	X	X	X	X	X	X	X	X	3 275	86.9	0.7	40.5
Tacoma-Lakewood, WA Div 45104	X	X	X	X	X	X	X	X	X	1 478	85.3	0.3	47.0
Sebastian-Vero Beach, FL	3 976	39 372	8 099	1 668	7 980	1 316	1 630	1 373	34 882	461	73.1	7.2	49.0
Sebring, FL	1 862	18 901	5 286	626	4 309	544	639	564	29 815	969	64.3	11.0	49.3
Sheboygan, WI	2 655	49 417	6 330	15 979	5 928	1 913	1 228	1 961	39 687	986	42.4	10.1	52.7
Sherman-Denison, TX	2 513	39 572	8 535	6 508	6 012	2 391	883	1 337	33 792	2 562	50.8	5.6	44.1
Shreveport-Bossier City, LA	9 957	159 902	34 074	9 509	23 853	4 909	6 138	5 815	36 364	2 202	45.9	7.6	49.0
Sierra Vista-Douglas, AZ	2 245	26 387	4 895	328	5 270	646	3 654	905	34 297	1 093	43.8	22.4	56.1
Sioux City, IA-NE-SD	4 425	75 336	11 832	14 711	9 871	3 242	1 447	2 713	36 016	3 644	26.2	30.3	61.9
Sioux Falls, SD	7 252	129 746	D	13 798	16 865	14 815	4 602	5 237	40 367	3 418	32.9	28.4	53.1
South Bend-Mishawaka, IN-MI	6 519	119 328	19 060	15 835	15 493	4 094	4 069	4 441	37 217	1 489	48.6	10.8	47.1
Spartanburg, SC	6 590	124 316	15 060	27 456	14 833	2 325	5 099	4 960	39 898	1 602	53.6	2.4	42.1
Spokane-Spokane Valley, WA	13 293	180 753	35 477	15 472	26 753	10 864	9 246	7 290	40 334	3 937	54.2	9.4	42.8
Springfield, IL	5 290	83 244	21 056	2 752	12 562	7 209	4 405	3 279	39 392	1 461	40.4	21.7	52.1
Springfield, MA	13 223	225 407	56 950	23 513	30 927	11 949	8 669	8 898	39 477	1 381	62.6	1.2	46.8
Springfield, MO	11 322	165 386	32 753	14 779	24 215	8 662	8 181	5 849	35 367	7 459	37.1	6.4	45.1
Springfield, OH	2 364	43 251	9 816	5 750	5 570	2 679	1 250	1 487	34 376	785	53.2	11.3	49.6
State College, PA	3 252	44 783	8 227	3 990	8 120	1 312	3 128	1 556	34 737	1 192	40.1	4.8	57.4
Staunton-Waynesboro, VA	2 776	39 302	8 053	6 363	6 067	1 035	1 026	1 333	33 909	1 706	42.3	6.2	48.8
Stockton-Lodi, CA	10 668	166 252	27 516	18 531	25 203	6 167	4 460	6 522	39 229	3 580	63.5	8.3	59.0
Sumter, SC	1 777	29 965	5 641	5 614	4 499	820	719	968	32 319	515	44.3	14.2	45.8
Syracuse, NY	15 294	256 061	46 261	23 834	36 349	12 748	16 557	10 448	40 803	2 176	34.1	8.5	56.1
Tallahassee, FL	8 688	107 724	19 658	3 088	17 785	4 524	12 695	4 042	37 520	1 474	59.2	5.7	39.4
Tampa-St. Petersburg-Clearwater, FL	71 821	1 017 850	166 827	52 829	141 420	73 283	89 174	43 087	42 331	4 448	78.6	3.0	51.6
Terre Haute, IN	3 560	59 060	10 767	12 180	8 764	1 553	1 376	2 132	36 106	1 732	43.6	18.7	46.1
Texarkana, TX-AR	3 058	45 235	8 202	5 743	8 142	1 679	1 080	1 556	34 394	2 592	38.7	9.6	42.6

Area name	Agriculture, 2012 (cont.)															
	Land in farms					Value of land and buildings (dollars)			Value of products sold				Percent of farms with sales of:		Government payments	
				Acres							Percent from:					
	Acreage (1,000)	Percent change, 2007–2012	Average size of farm	Total irrigated (1,000)	Total cropland (1,000)	Average per farm	Average per acre	Value of machinery and equipment, average per farm (dollars)	Total (mil dol)	Average per farm (dollars)	Crops	Livestock and poultry products	$10,000 or more	$100,000 or more	Total ($1,000)	Percent of farms
	117	118	119	120	121	122	123	124	125	126	127	128	129	130	131	132
Redding, CA	376	-3.7	244	38.2	36.9	682 565	2 801	36 550	65.6	42 501	36.6	63.4	26.2	4.8	420	4.6
Reno, NV	443	-8.9	913	D	D	749 691	821	52 786	D	D	D	D	27.4	6.6	75	3.9
Richmond, VA	649	-1.9	207	D	325.5	853 057	4 118	85 962	338.0	107 947	D	D	32.0	10.1	12 201	26.8
Riverside-San Bernardino-Ontario, CA	421	-51.5	100	167.7	257.1	1 084 366	10 807	78 134	1 621.2	386 179	50.1	49.9	47.9	14.7	3 038	4.5
Roanoke, VA	332	2.0	159	1.1	102.0	599 779	3 783	70 357	93.2	44 495	D	D	33.2	6.5	1 600	16.1
Rochester, MN	1 158	-7.6	274	D	906.6	1 399 848	5 117	185 604	1 111.6	262 609	59.8	40.2	63.1	35.0	23 694	71.1
Rochester, NY	927	-6.2	217	9.2	701.3	663 751	3 055	158 475	930.7	218 057	61.4	38.6	56.4	29.8	11 479	29.3
Rockford, IL	318	-1.0	247	1.4	286.5	1 617 918	6 550	156 317	205.4	159 703	83.9	16.1	48.3	27.9	8 500	57.8
Rocky Mount, NC	267	-8.9	381	11.9	181.9	1 238 600	3 253	197 288	340.4	484 865	61.8	38.2	49.1	32.2	4 184	58.5
Rome, GA	70	-17.1	126	0.8	19.6	489 283	3 898	54 420	77.0	137 828	6.9	93.1	29.3	8.6	616	19.7
Sacramento—Roseville—Arden-Arcade, CA	927	-11.5	183	343.4	457.4	1 259 225	6 892	84 057	961.8	189 475	D	D	39.7	14.6	10 256	9.9
Saginaw, MI	310	-4.5	235	2.3	274.5	896 656	3 816	144 832	243.6	184 855	91.7	8.3	55.8	27.6	6 093	71.6
St. Cloud, MN	946	5.8	212	63.5	722.7	808 127	3 808	165 913	976.0	218 883	34.3	65.7	66.3	35.3	19 180	71.8
St. George, UT	148	-15.0	256	14.8	20.2	934 487	3 656	50 485	12.6	21 843	51.1	48.9	29.2	5.5	210	7.8
St. Joseph, MO-KS	810	-14.3	285	D	576.3	947 085	3 320	103 711	265.9	93 709	82.2	17.8	51.1	17.0	14 038	67.9
St. Louis, MO-IL	2 912	-0.9	258	14.1	2 232.2	1 359 070	5 260	137 402	1 235.6	109 636	73.4	26.6	46.7	19.4	42 877	56.7
Salem, OR	431	-9.1	116	105.3	314.8	852 208	7 337	116 718	742.7	200 189	80.7	19.3	38.6	16.2	2 495	11.7
Salinas, CA	1 268	-4.5	1 076	263.8	358.3	5 263 068	4 893	396 806	2 979.7	2 527 341	98.5	1.5	59.6	35.4	635	7.0
Salisbury, MD-DE	520	-2.4	218	105.7	399.5	1 515 910	6 943	176 840	1 575.7	660 933	24.2	75.8	66.0	48.9	11 071	48.2
Salt Lake City, UT	425	18.0	384	29.8	53.7	709 106	1 845	65 829	61.9	55 974	41.1	58.9	26.7	7.1	250	4.3
San Angelo, TX	1 453	-6.1	1 070	31.8	179.0	1 146 386	1 071	85 947	138.9	102 282	24.0	76.0	29.2	9.4	6 065	25.5
San Antonio-New Braunfels, TX	3 642	3.0	249	102.6	629.7	791 780	3 174	49 698	D	D	D	55.8	22.7	3.3	11 155	13.4
San Diego-Carlsbad, CA	222	-27.1	39	45.2	68.2	694 313	17 964	34 672	726.0	126 657	89.3	10.7	42.9	9.1	451	1.7
San Francisco-Oakland-Hayward, CA	525	-3.2	305	42.7	89.8	2 135 551	6 991	67 439	D	D	D	D	48.0	16.4	1 746	6.8
Oakland-Hayward-Berkeley, CA Div 36084	305	-13.1	290	36.2	66.9	1 951 273	6 733	66 327	146.9	139 355	83.9	16.1	43.0	11.7	281	4.7
San Francisco-Redwood City-South San Francisco, CA Div 41884	48	-15.6	142	2.8	8.5	1 604 941	11 328	69 188	D	D	D	D	48.2	14.4	182	4.1
San Rafael, CA Div 42034	171	28.2	529	3.7	14.4	3 295 415	6 229	69 226	91.8	284 238	9.3	90.7	64.1	34.1	1 283	16.4
San Jose-Sunnyvale-Santa Clara, CA	834	-5.2	511	37.0	76.9	2 000 239	3 911	78 560	407.9	250 068	88.1	11.9	47.1	15.1	194	3.6
San Luis Obispo-Paso Robles-Arroyo Grande, CA	1 339	-2.2	502	81.6	255.4	2 115 410	4 212	92 222	665.0	249 431	92.9	7.1	52.2	19.1	3 488	9.0
Santa Cruz-Watsonville, CA	100	110.5	150	28.9	41.1	1 857 240	12 390	113 943	565.8	848 328	96.9	3.1	59.2	28.0	D	0.1
Santa Fe, NM	718	26.0	1 004	8.9	13.1	848 969	846	39 010	12.8	17 869	75.1	24.9	15.0	2.7	394	5.7
Santa Maria-Santa Barbara, CA	701	-3.6	439	96.7	132.3	3 233 061	7 365	125 663	1 177.9	737 581	95.8	4.2	58.8	29.4	554	1.5
Santa Rosa, CA	590	11.1	165	75.0	130.6	2 409 158	14 620	78 965	974.4	272 253	62.2	37.8	60.3	24.3	2 615	4.1
Savannah, GA	59	-8.5	212	D	23.3	629 249	2 972	99 313	D	D	105.4	D	32.0	9.6	D	25.6
Scranton—Wilkes-Barre—Hazleton, PA	162	-11.9	119	0.5	82.9	519 072	4 369	72 280	48.8	35 732	71.8	28.2	32.1	8.2	1 730	32.5
Seattle-Tacoma-Bellevue, WA	167	-3.9	35	12.3	60.3	598 066	17 015	38 276	351.2	73 883	37.3	62.7	20.9	4.7	1 507	3.5
Seattle-Bellevue-Everett, WA Div 42644	118	-6.8	36	9.5	48.7	653 085	18 191	39 507	260.2	79 461	41.2	58.8	22.3	5.4	1 411	4.4
Tacoma-Lakewood, WA Div 45104	49	3.8	33	2.8	11.5	476 152	14 222	35 548	90.9	61 524	26.3	73.7	17.9	3.0	96	1.3
Sebastian-Vero Beach, FL	162	3.3	352	57.6	54.8	1 359 020	3 856	54 672	144.9	314 419	92.2	7.8	49.7	18.4	809	4.1
Sebring, FL	490	2.9	506	61.8	84.0	1 484 852	2 937	82 911	273.4	282 121	72.6	27.4	41.4	21.4	609	2.2
Sheboygan, WI	190	-0.8	193	0.2	155.9	1 011 178	5 243	162 747	242.1	245 507	27.1	72.9	59.2	29.8	3 790	51.4
Sherman-Denison, TX	431	7.7	168	3.5	176.4	632 363	3 757	58 110	91.9	35 889	72.7	27.3	24.6	4.3	1 948	14.2
Shreveport-Bossier City, LA	438	-7.2	199	D	127.3	581 894	2 927	75 391	96.1	43 622	61.7	38.3	27.8	5.2	4 003	11.5
Sierra Vista-Douglas, AZ	917	11.2	839	65.5	123.3	1 175 308	1 401	81 234	150.0	137 235	D	D	37.6	13.3	2 594	16.9
Sioux City, IA-NE-SD	1 733	4.6	476	102.0	1 485.9	2 768 921	5 823	252 868	1 460.1	400 692	50.7	49.3	70.1	45.3	32 806	77.9
Sioux Falls, SD	1 521	2.1	445	D	1 281.2	2 132 173	4 792	221 113	781.7	228 689	59.5	40.5	61.6	35.5	22 368	70.5
South Bend-Mishawaka, IN-MI	341	-7.7	229	85.2	284.3	1 128 461	4 932	144 874	310.7	208 639	74.9	25.1	45.5	22.1	5 134	51.0
Spartanburg, SC	149	-4.0	93	2.0	46.7	380 610	4 088	39 334	49.9	31 150	43.0	57.0	20.0	2.2	1 136	9.2
Spokane-Spokane Valley, WA	1 108	-8.6	281	17.9	473.7	632 566	2 247	63 943	190.1	48 275	80.3	19.7	26.8	8.2	8 308	19.6
Springfield, IL	672	-2.2	460	5.3	615.7	3 274 998	7 122	262 928	442.9	303 152	94.0	6.0	51.0	34.3	12 337	73.8
Springfield, MA	93	3.4	67	1.7	32.6	521 085	7 767	50 067	72.8	52 742	74.9	25.1	28.8	8.6	1 162	10.7
Springfield, MO	1 216	-3.9	163	2.2	367.2	435 524	2 671	46 051	274.8	36 841	11.5	88.5	41.9	6.8	3 665	10.0
Springfield, OH	174	-1.7	222	1.6	149.8	1 141 031	5 138	147 288	145.1	184 896	80.4	19.6	45.1	23.8	2 754	47.6
State College, PA	162	9.1	136	1.1	84.9	736 207	5 416	86 739	91.6	76 830	34.3	65.7	47.2	20.0	1 985	30.3
Staunton-Waynesboro, VA	260	-9.1	152	3.3	89.6	953 997	6 256	79 365	232.1	136 059	11.9	88.1	49.1	15.1	1 677	18.2
Stockton-Lodi, CA	787	6.7	220	485.4	517.9	2 218 140	10 090	145 302	2 250.2	628 536	73.7	26.3	73.5	39.3	5 508	9.4
Sumter, SC	176	14.7	342	8.9	69.5	792 967	2 320	105 033	130.5	253 379	36.9	63.1	27.2	10.9	1 870	57.3
Syracuse, NY	432	-1.6	199	2.7	258.2	481 316	2 425	122 464	317.4	145 856	32.1	67.9	47.7	19.0	4 474	26.8
Tallahassee, FL	293	-6.7	198	7.2	46.2	899 716	4 533	43 945	108.8	73 841	D	D	25.0	4.1	761	14.9
Tampa-St. Petersburg-Clearwater, FL	449	5.2	101	35.5	116.5	824 501	8 159	47 987	482.9	108 574	75.8	24.2	31.0	8.7	1 670	2.4
Terre Haute, IN	569	-3.3	329	D	489.0	1 408 309	4 286	168 128	261.3	150 886	84.3	15.7	46.0	24.4	9 160	68.2
Texarkana, TX-AR	609	0.4	235	21.4	223.1	475 867	2 027	61 443	188.1	72 558	30.0	70.0	34.1	7.9	3 271	16.9

Area name	Water use, 2010		Wholesale trade,[1] 2007				Retail trade, 2007				Real estate and rental and leasing, 2007			
	Total water withdrawn (mil gal/day)	Gallons withdrawn per person per day	Number of establish-ments	Number of employees	Sales (mil dol)	Annual payroll (mil dol)	Number of establish-ments	Number of employees	Sales (mil dol)	Annual payroll (mil dol)	Number of establish-ments	Number of employees	Receipts (mil dol)	Annual payroll (mil dol)
	133	134	135	136	137	138	139	140	141	142	143	144	145	146
Redding, CA	239.0	1 349	179	1 748	829.0	69.4	722	10 287	2 526.4	260.1	225	1 201	128.2	26.1
Reno, NV	134.9	317	602	10 370	6 317.7	461.6	1 577	25 079	6 674.2	672.1	765	D	D	D
Richmond, VA	1 231.6	1 019	1 387	D	D	D	4 509	68 673	17 672.4	1 573.6	1 442	9 186	1 903.1	365.0
Riverside-San Bernardino-Ontario, CA	1 758.7	416	3 885	55 515	44 492.2	2 414.3	10 338	173 855	45 863.8	4 276.1	3 960	21 722	4 366.9	731.4
Roanoke, VA	44.4	144	439	D	D	D	1 338	18 897	4 121.4	413.9	411	D	D	D
Rochester, MN	48.4	234	178	1 949	1 231.0	84.6	881	12 588	2 661.5	268.3	191	882	122.6	22.6
Rochester, NY	714.6	662	1 075	16 371	7 855.5	837.8	3 652	56 761	12 235.0	1 200.4	1 047	7 286	1 167.9	215.8
Rockford, IL	41.5	119	398	5 154	2 770.9	220.7	1 154	17 650	4 306.9	383.0	270	1 653	219.2	47.5
Rocky Mount, NC	35.9	235	131	D	D	D	636	7 312	1 595.9	144.6	123	533	96.1	13.9
Rome, GA	474.7	4 928	94	1 274	636.2	46.9	431	4 718	1 039.8	94.0	82	353	58.0	10.1
Sacramento—Roseville—Arden-Arcade, CA	1 708.2	795	1 847	28 997	26 473.9	1 353.0	6 166	99 917	25 165.5	2 583.3	2 808	17 197	2 790.3	601.2
Saginaw, MI	22.3	111	184	2 319	1 070.8	92.0	973	12 584	2 534.3	243.3	149	751	101.8	17.4
St. Cloud, MN	58.0	307	225	5 318	2 326.6	228.0	842	13 555	2 918.8	265.8	206	1 126	121.4	27.4
St. George, UT	122.2	885	146	1 260	510.8	48.3	593	8 035	2 087.8	185.9	367	856	122.0	20.0
St. Joseph, MO-KS	99.5	781	129	D	D	D	486	7 006	1 671.9	147.8	144	D	D	D
St. Louis, MO-IL	3 444.4	1 236	3 471	D	D	D	9 936	148 390	35 613.8	3 651.6	3 261	D	D	D
Salem, OR	324.1	829	345	4 012	3 532.0	168.6	1 259	18 547	4 391.7	438.2	556	2 924	359.1	69.8
Salinas, CA	545.5	1 314	392	D	D	D	1 497	18 392	4 541.1	487.8	487	2 423	500.6	86.6
Salisbury, MD-DE	311.4	833	343	D	D	D	2 146	24 677	5 740.5	569.5	656	2 739	413.6	84.8
Salt Lake City, UT	596.8	549	1 663	28 110	17 030.0	1 355.4	3 524	61 906	17 262.3	1 547.6	2 120	11 561	2 035.7	385.9
San Angelo, TX	59.6	533	120	D	D	D	452	D	D	D	135	631	76.0	15.8
San Antonio-New Braunfels, TX	1 571.4	733	1 725	25 957	14 609.8	1 184.5	5 913	95 964	27 169.2	2 233.8	2 164	13 556	2 433.8	464.0
San Diego-Carlsbad, CA	2 818.2	910	4 002	55 934	33 704.9	4 120.7	9 948	151 425	38 710.6	3 889.2	5 810	33 067	7 190.2	1 345.2
San Francisco-Oakland-Hayward, CA	787.0	182	5 984	83 067	67 861.1	5 177.7	14 412	210 050	56 861.0	6 077.9	7 206	45 485	12 223.7	2 307.7
Oakland-Hayward-Berkeley, CA Div 36084	557.6	218	3 332	52 480	42 318.0	3 196.2	7 325	113 400	29 672.9	3 125.0	3 484	19 990	4 688.7	820.5
San Francisco-Redwood City-South San Francisco, CA Div 41884	186.6	122	2 271	26 956	23 170.0	1 763.0	5 926	81 218	22 598.8	2 480.1	3 089	22 373	6 386.8	1 349.4
San Rafael, CA Div 42034	42.9	170	381	3 631	2 373.1	218.5	1 161	15 432	4 589.3	472.8	633	3 122	1 148.2	137.8
San Jose-Sunnyvale-Santa Clara, CA	383.7	209	2 523	63 480	60 963.7	6 218.6	5 421	87 932	26 844.4	2 947.1	2 664	14 946	5 189.1	752.0
San Luis Obispo-Paso Robles-Arroyo Grande, CA	2 579.1	9 565	277	2 329	955.0	104.1	1 262	14 652	3 548.4	353.6	475	2 050	293.4	56.7
Santa Cruz-Watsonville, CA	66.4	253	273	D	D	D	981	12 454	3 725.4	316.0	380	1 793	311.1	58.6
Santa Fe, NM	49.8	345	134	D	D	D	887	9 949	2 426.3	261.6	311	1 092	206.0	40.8
Santa Maria-Santa Barbara, CA	264.3	623	438	5 713	4 023.6	350.4	1 605	20 281	4 983.4	524.4	681	3 452	620.7	119.5
Santa Rosa, CA	259.5	536	585	7 631	3 953.6	454.3	1 925	26 177	6 427.2	718.5	718	3 237	604.1	114.2
Savannah, GA	404.3	1 163	359	4 631	3 997.5	233.8	1 491	18 989	4 551.8	422.7	487	2 223	387.6	68.7
Scranton—Wilkes-Barre—Hazleton, PA	150.5	267	583	9 784	5 397.5	384.1	2 383	34 129	8 691.1	694.7	393	2 628	385.5	72.2
Seattle-Tacoma-Bellevue, WA	658.8	192	4 931	72 509	53 841.6	3 960.8	11 549	176 728	55 952.6	4 867.7	6 187	33 954	7 698.5	1 344.9
Seattle-Bellevue-Everett, WA Div 42644	461.6	175	4 227	61 161	47 751.1	3 492.3	9 243	140 913	46 211.0	3 915.4	5 093	28 259	6 727.9	1 183.7
Tacoma-Lakewood, WA Div 45104	197.2	248	704	11 348	6 090.5	468.5	2 306	35 815	9 741.6	952.3	1 094	5 695	970.6	161.2
Sebastian-Vero Beach, FL	154.5	1 119	132	D	D	D	699	9 096	1 851.7	203.3	260	945	146.5	24.1
Sebring, FL	107.8	1 091	83	D	D	D	364	4 513	1 089.6	99.0	112	337	52.6	8.1
Sheboygan, WI	328.5	2 844	88	1 206	503.5	58.1	427	6 386	1 398.7	131.5	80	372	73.8	12.1
Sherman-Denison, TX	22.3	185	103	1 004	651.7	33.1	497	6 333	1 594.7	140.4	114	456	69.9	11.1
Shreveport-Bossier City, LA	206.3	469	440	D	D	D	1 718	23 683	6 118.0	523.2	446	2 648	383.4	71.3
Sierra Vista-Douglas, AZ	238.4	1 815	54	359	102.3	10.4	455	6 305	1 313.7	129.1	139	504	65.1	12.4
Sioux City, IA-NE-SD	1 055.6	6 263	249	D	D	D	719	10 324	2 323.3	196.4	154	D	D	D
Sioux Falls, SD	45.5	200	396	5 331	3 569.3	244.3	1 035	16 679	4 364.1	370.7	245	D	D	D
South Bend-Mishawaka, IN-MI	68.2	214	389	D	D	D	1 072	17 506	3 866.8	367.3	267	1 498	225.2	44.4
Spartanburg, SC	40.7	149	455	D	D	D	1 196	14 822	3 830.6	325.9	293	1 316	224.5	45.8
Spokane-Spokane Valley, WA	219.0	415	685	9 552	5 403.2	400.6	1 887	28 379	7 089.4	730.9	711	D	D	D
Springfield, IL	325.6	1 549	206	2 876	1 970.0	113.5	842	12 798	2 931.5	255.7	235	1 069	163.0	25.1
Springfield, MA	176.6	284	499	8 456	7 013.6	389.1	2 270	31 757	7 214.8	718.1	537	2 690	444.9	83.6
Springfield, MO	249.7	572	566	8 547	5 415.1	348.9	1 781	25 165	6 142.1	548.1	589	3 103	379.3	74.0
Springfield, OH	25.8	187	95	D	D	D	460	6 625	1 398.7	131.7	101	485	64.0	10.9
State College, PA	45.4	295	92	1 091	572.3	70.9	548	8 014	1 604.3	151.0	129	922	184.7	26.2
Staunton-Waynesboro, VA	46.4	391	82	1 464	487.8	56.0	497	6 178	1 470.4	134.1	139	511	62.2	14.4
Stockton-Lodi, CA	1 753.4	2 559	558	9 517	9 001.3	437.3	1 756	27 329	7 109.7	653.0	634	3 363	577.5	104.4
Sumter, SC	23.5	219	73	D	D	D	417	4 919	1 021.5	91.8	87	308	36.7	6.8
Syracuse, NY	1 098.7	1 658	755	12 997	17 441.8	597.7	2 368	35 712	8 023.1	762.2	763	3 899	714.7	134.1
Tallahassee, FL	68.0	185	284	3 063	1 225.9	115.3	1 298	19 641	4 230.5	396.3	505	2 565	381.3	71.6
Tampa-St. Petersburg-Clearwater, FL	4 151.3	1 492	3 436	44 630	31 116.6	1 950.9	10 024	148 740	40 337.5	3 561.3	4 391	22 538	3 987.3	813.4
Terre Haute, IN	1 382.6	8 019	150	D	D	D	705	10 036	2 312.1	199.5	129	720	88.0	19.4
Texarkana, TX-AR	136.7	917	154	D	D	D	674	8 256	2 031.3	179.1	128	561	78.6	13.1

1. Merchant wholesalers, except manufacturers' sales branches and offices.

Table C. Metropolitan Areas — **Professional Services, Manufacturing, and Accommodation and Food Services**

Area name	Professional, scientific, and technical services,[1] 2007				Manufacturing, 2007				Accommodation and food services, 2007			
	Number of establishments	Number of employees	Sales (mil dol)	Annual payroll (mil dol)	Number of establishments	Number of employees	Sales (mil dol)	Annual payroll (mil dol)	Number of establishments	Number of employees	Sales (mil dol)	Annual payroll (mil dol)
	147	148	149	150	151	152	153	154	155	156	157	158
Redding, CA	400	D	D	D	167	2 794	662.9	117.1	403	5 862	281.0	74.9
Reno, NV	1 696	10 101	1 444.3	549.0	D	D	D	D	1 003	35 540	2 404.2	730.7
Richmond, VA	3 336	D	D	D	D	D	D	D	2 290	D	D	D
Riverside-San Bernardino-Ontario, CA	5 662	D	D	D	3 668	122 090	32 530.8	4 855.1	6 404	128 663	7 590.0	2 021.0
Roanoke, VA	744	D	D	D	D	D	D	D	628	D	D	D
Rochester, MN	369	D	D	D	208	13 327	D	743.4	457	8 701	370.2	105.1
Rochester, NY	2 466	D	D	D	1 365	67 801	D	3 067.4	2 225	33 565	1 436.4	416.2
Rockford, IL	727	D	D	D	756	33 901	13 467.1	1 742.1	662	11 409	492.4	135.5
Rocky Mount, NC	222	1 232	133.0	48.2	145	12 735	4 183.1	500.7	266	5 058	200.2	55.2
Rome, GA	174	703	80.1	24.8	109	7 726	3 346.1	312.7	198	3 423	144.3	38.1
Sacramento—Roseville—Arden-Arcade, CA	5 856	D	D	D	1 598	44 504	12 821.7	1 859.4	4 304	77 056	4 168.5	1 100.3
Saginaw, MI	355	3 009	429.9	121.3	219	11 437	4 604.8	659.0	383	8 620	337.3	102.2
St. Cloud, MN	351	D	D	D	330	17 503	4 584.6	694.0	452	8 241	293.3	83.5
St. George, UT	432	D	D	D	154	3 225	609.6	117.4	279	5 631	254.5	74.5
St. Joseph, MO-KS	209	D	D	D	D	D	D	D	232	4 492	165.7	48.5
St. Louis, MO-IL	7 316	D	D	D	D	D	D	D	5 818	120 828	5 541.5	1 581.7
Salem, OR	826	4 270	445.6	172.5	448	12 783	3 262.1	438.0	773	D	D	D
Salinas, CA	818	D	D	D	301	7 333	2 227.6	268.4	983	18 026	1 197.1	345.4
Salisbury, MD-DE	740	D	D	D	D	D	D	D	1 194	18 501	1 165.2	320.2
Salt Lake City, UT	3 818	D	D	D	1 522	D	D	D	1 881	41 143	1 909.8	565.4
San Angelo, TX	188	D	D	D	D	D	D	D	210	D	D	D
San Antonio-New Braunfels, TX	4 284	D	D	D	D	D	D	D	3 944	86 014	4 291.7	1 200.1
San Diego-Carlsbad, CA	11 972	117 497	18 834.7	7 694.0	3 182	102 168	27 541.1	5 244.6	6 599	144 287	9 551.5	2 567.2
San Francisco-Oakland-Hayward, CA	18 729	D	D	D	4 462	143 318	77 651.2	8 277.0	11 166	184 046	12 143.1	3 499.3
Oakland-Hayward-Berkeley, CA Div 36084	8 416	D	D	D	2 703	99 553	57 258.3	5 791.5	5 162	75 932	4 370.1	1 203.1
San Francisco-Redwood City-South San Francisco, CA Div 41884	8 516	D	D	D	1 530	41 560	19 995.7	2 397.5	5 310	97 201	7 146.4	2 110.3
San Rafael, CA Div 42034	1 797	D	D	D	229	2 205	397.2	88.0	694	10 913	626.6	185.9
San Jose-Sunnyvale-Santa Clara, CA	7 885	123 833	21 593.3	13 561.4	2 683	145 580	45 719.1	10 397.9	4 190	69 623	4 197.8	1 173.9
San Luis Obispo-Paso Robles-Arroyo Grande, CA	930	5 709	593.8	222.6	377	6 517	2 548.2	260.4	850	14 903	767.9	219.7
Santa Cruz-Watsonville, CA	914	D	D	D	329	6 689	1 502.4	301.6	657	9 774	513.8	148.8
Santa Fe, NM	693	D	D	D	153	980	D	34.5	398	9 203	540.4	166.3
Santa Maria-Santa Barbara, CA	1 359	D	D	D	505	13 149	3 174.1	676.8	1 029	21 380	1 361.5	360.1
Santa Rosa, CA	1 538	D	D	D	885	24 077	5 841.9	1 201.2	1 173	17 739	1 005.4	283.8
Savannah, GA	816	D	D	D	D	D	D	D	921	18 424	933.8	252.8
Scranton—Wilkes-Barre—Hazleton, PA	1 107	D	D	D	649	32 526	D	1 238.4	1 369	19 758	825.7	225.5
Seattle-Tacoma-Bellevue, WA	11 939	D	D	D	4 024	165 676	64 901.7	8 809.4	8 615	134 167	7 701.2	2 239.5
Seattle-Bellevue-Everett, WA Div 42644	10 553	D	D	D	3 356	145 350	59 943.1	7 915.2	7 037	110 091	6 528.7	1 906.8
Tacoma-Lakewood, WA Div 45104	1 386	D	D	D	668	20 326	4 958.6	894.2	1 578	24 076	1 172.5	332.7
Sebastian-Vero Beach, FL	473	2 076	235.3	97.2	99	2 179	413.0	87.7	232	4 557	190.5	56.2
Sebring, FL	152	D	D	D	56	927	306.1	33.1	133	2 408	100.8	28.0
Sheboygan, WI	176	1 743	209.1	70.5	246	18 774	6 126.1	816.0	271	4 869	193.0	54.8
Sherman-Denison, TX	220	1 086	92.5	34.5	132	6 148	2 542.8	293.7	226	4 001	167.7	48.6
Shreveport-Bossier City, LA	840	5 486	609.8	211.5	336	14 756	D	D	756	23 173	1 426.1	359.1
Sierra Vista-Douglas, AZ	208	D	D	D	56	576	181.3	20.6	277	4 100	171.4	47.8
Sioux City, IA-NE-SD	285	D	D	D	196	D	D	D	411	6 674	221.2	63.9
Sioux Falls, SD	556	D	D	D	D	D	D	D	510	10 672	423.1	127.5
South Bend-Mishawaka, IN-MI	616	D	D	D	512	20 781	8 722.3	975.8	618	11 918	466.8	134.1
Spartanburg, SC	492	D	D	D	493	28 170	12 220.2	1 277.3	560	10 556	430.0	118.5
Spokane-Spokane Valley, WA	1 304	8 883	1 180.9	441.3	649	19 392	D	D	1 114	17 927	817.1	242.3
Springfield, IL	594	4 726	567.6	230.3	D	D	D	D	543	9 450	373.7	112.2
Springfield, MA	1 246	D	D	D	830	28 316	7 099.9	1 304.2	1 345	20 103	887.2	259.4
Springfield, MO	1 033	D	D	D	538	18 405	D	664.6	881	18 123	691.9	202.4
Springfield, OH	163	D	D	D	182	7 164	2 494.3	299.2	241	4 574	173.1	49.6
State College, PA	376	D	D	D	150	4 341	1 216.5	181.0	301	5 961	240.1	68.8
Staunton-Waynesboro, VA	174	D	D	D	130	7 419	2 443.9	302.2	229	4 125	171.5	48.7
Stockton-Lodi, CA	801	D	D	D	585	23 442	8 272.5	938.6	1 079	15 195	745.8	199.3
Sumter, SC	139	D	D	D	82	7 707	1 922.0	253.3	149	3 173	109.4	29.8
Syracuse, NY	1 462	D	D	D	633	29 539	10 634.2	1 467.2	1 527	22 740	990.0	286.7
Tallahassee, FL	1 488	D	D	D	D	D	D	D	684	14 779	597.6	161.8
Tampa-St. Petersburg-Clearwater, FL	10 175	D	D	D	2 323	65 945	18 564.6	2 763.1	4 995	99 165	5 143.5	1 423.1
Terre Haute, IN	279	D	D	D	D	D	D	D	372	6 181	244.5	67.0
Texarkana, TX-AR	221	D	D	D	110	6 164	D	316.8	246	5 022	216.3	63.6

1. Establishments subject to federal tax.

Table C. Metropolitan Areas — **Health Care and Social Assistance, Other Services, Nonemployer Business and Residential Construction**

Area name	Health care and social assistance,[1] 2007				Other services,[1] 2007				Nonemployer business, 2013		Value of residential construction authorized by building permits, 2014	
	Number of establish-ments	Number of employees	Receipts (mil dol)	Annual payroll (mil dol)	Number of establish-ments	Number of employees	Receipts (mil dol)	Annual payroll (mil dol)	Number	Receipts (mil dol)	New construc-tion ($1,000)	Number of housing units
	159	160	161	162	163	164	165	166	167	168	169	170
Redding, CA	661	10 015	1 124.5	420.3	320	1 697	168.2	43.3	11 542	521.8	50 129	242
Reno, NV	1 113	D	D	D	765	D	D	D	29 888	1 624.2	470 889	2 216
Richmond, VA	2 895	D	D	D	2 437	16 360	1 995.2	475.6	77 910	3 226.5	690 026	4 312
Riverside-San Bernardino-Ontario, CA	7 225	129 700	14 971.6	5 514.6	4 810	32 342	2 927.7	850.7	288 256	12 000.6	2 099 037	10 166
Roanoke, VA	763	D	D	D	685	D	D	D	18 372	736.7	93 054	511
Rochester, MN	471	D	D	D	391	D	D	D	13 982	605.6	166 853	832
Rochester, NY	2 509	D	D	D	1 731	10 067	978.9	255.5	62 646	2 727.5	346 696	1 791
Rockford, IL	734	20 112	1 949.4	814.4	617	4 043	332.5	97.7	21 240	746.3	18 376	150
Rocky Mount, NC	343	9 283	711.5	306.8	213	1 198	197.7	29.8	8 068	272.8	34 761	216
Rome, GA	259	7 910	785.1	310.9	108	D	D	D	6 748	237.1	14 421	75
Sacramento—Roseville—Arden-Arcade, CA	5 027	96 068	12 292.3	4 739.2	3 314	28 694	4 276.1	1 121.0	152 625	7 238.4	1 172 225	4 159
Saginaw, MI	584	16 811	1 512.5	605.3	369	2 191	178.2	46.5	11 242	383.9	29 450	214
St. Cloud, MN	487	15 066	1 357.4	637.4	450	D	D	D	12 857	607.6	103 208	577
St. George, UT	393	6 648	628.5	250.2	198	1 116	95.0	27.4	12 017	549.6	309 142	1 628
St. Joseph, MO-KS	352	D	D	D	235	D	D	D	6 487	252.4	18 534	104
St. Louis, MO-IL	7 489	D	D	D	5 170	35 548	3 388.7	1 002.6	179 278	7 628.4	1 424 810	6 992
Salem, OR	1 047	17 339	1 580.1	655.6	596	2 876	235.9	70.2	19 700	873.0	205 833	944
Salinas, CA	970	13 789	1 876.6	723.7	556	3 651	425.9	104.6	23 865	1 293.0	72 040	361
Salisbury, MD-DE	1 024	20 002	1 855.0	783.3	713	3 926	310.8	91.4	27 073	1 277.1	399 584	2 796
Salt Lake City, UT	2 736	D	D	D	1 964	13 491	1 282.8	361.0	79 125	3 801.2	936 040	5 318
San Angelo, TX	260	D	D	D	214	D	D	D	8 100	351.4	69 568	629
San Antonio-New Braunfels, TX	4 849	109 941	10 646.6	3 893.0	3 063	21 362	1 732.3	509.8	157 377	7 263.4	1 722 123	10 332
San Diego-Carlsbad, CA	7 924	133 893	15 954.7	5 872.9	5 176	37 084	3 732.5	1 015.3	246 649	12 284.5	1 504 007	6 875
San Francisco-Oakland-Hayward, CA	13 103	221 320	28 727.3	11 570.1	8 537	59 689	12 556.4	2 072.7	395 627	22 673.7	2 793 204	10 001
Oakland-Hayward-Berkeley, CA Div 36084	6 975	118 515	15 333.8	6 289.8	4 270	28 823	3 413.7	946.9	NA	NA	X	X
San Francisco-Redwood City-South San Francisco, CA Div 41884	5 062	88 847	11 798.3	4 631.2	3 650	26 617	8 512.3	958.6	NA	NA	X	X
San Rafael, CA Div 42034	1 066	13 958	1 595.2	649.1	617	4 249	630.4	167.2	NA	NA	X	X
San Jose-Sunnyvale-Santa Clara, CA	5 161	D	D	D	2 970	19 637	2 838.4	664.1	132 037	7 610.1	1 894 413	10 037
San Luis Obispo-Paso Robles-Arroyo Grande, CA	864	14 341	1 341.2	546.4	464	2 808	222.0	60.3	23 558	1 179.3	271 870	983
Santa Cruz-Watsonville, CA	863	11 416	1 441.4	505.0	452	2 702	258.2	72.1	23 649	1 176.8	52 651	291
Santa Fe, NM	518	8 465	809.4	318.0	341	1 849	231.0	54.1	15 652	732.8	37 092	161
Santa Maria-Santa Barbara, CA	1 322	19 124	2 076.4	784.0	767	5 005	816.9	141.4	32 058	1 820.0	172 341	755
Santa Rosa, CA	1 516	23 219	2 623.9	1 065.9	873	4 877	508.1	138.8	43 454	2 224.5	130 618	663
Savannah, GA	767	D	D	D	538	3 467	306.4	91.1	24 587	1 030.4	401 723	2 211
Scranton—Wilkes-Barre—Hazleton, PA	1 761	43 009	3 621.4	1 482.6	1 034	5 467	429.8	114.7	29 885	1 453.7	461 949	2 301
Seattle-Tacoma-Bellevue, WA	10 071	189 085	21 143.3	8 376.0	6 953	43 575	6 464.1	1 357.4	231 707	12 055.2	4 469 256	21 953
Seattle-Bellevue-Everett, WA Div 42644	8 191	147 038	16 748.1	6 594.7	5 652	35 082	5 661.0	1 106.2	NA	NA	X	X
Tacoma-Lakewood, WA Div 45104	1 880	42 047	4 395.2	1 781.3	1 301	8 493	803.1	251.2	NA	NA	X	X
Sebastian-Vero Beach, FL	446	7 230	836.4	300.9	264	1 169	97.0	26.7	12 372	651.4	271 374	707
Sebring, FL	300	4 876	483.4	180.7	142	540	40.7	10.4	5 719	221.6	21 357	92
Sheboygan, WI	292	6 709	501.4	242.7	217	1 093	76.8	20.2	5 542	218.6	23 524	111
Sherman-Denison, TX	382	8 254	706.2	279.6	165	820	59.1	16.6	8 927	396.8	32 590	271
Shreveport-Bossier City, LA	1 125	D	D	D	642	4 399	336.4	95.0	31 945	1 372.8	258 550	1 719
Sierra Vista-Douglas, AZ	273	4 773	380.3	152.0	162	718	44.2	12.3	6 369	185.9	35 149	261
Sioux City, IA-NE-SD	478	D	D	D	325	D	D	D	10 135	454.1	80 453	408
Sioux Falls, SD	599	22 420	2 079.8	952.1	456	D	D	D	18 034	917.7	306 830	2 330
South Bend-Mishawaka, IN-MI	728	D	D	D	581	4 088	431.2	102.9	18 405	704.9	93 891	512
Spartanburg, SC	548	14 192	1 054.0	548.1	469	3 050	290.9	72.2	18 637	780.7	177 532	1 104
Spokane-Spokane Valley, WA	1 530	D	D	D	937	5 646	498.1	136.9	30 882	1 295.9	382 175	1 960
Springfield, IL	477	D	D	D	501	3 555	387.4	109.6	13 062	478.6	88 151	455
Springfield, MA	1 581	45 330	4 007.3	1 733.1	1 131	7 003	578.7	172.1	36 146	1 670.0	106 622	506
Springfield, MO	981	D	D	D	851	5 346	465.0	133.8	32 949	1 400.5	273 582	2 105
Springfield, OH	319	8 186	619.8	258.2	237	1 402	188.1	38.4	6 735	230.7	11 313	53
State College, PA	332	6 543	549.7	238.6	228	1 270	100.7	27.6	9 288	444.9	101 610	511
Staunton-Waynesboro, VA	252	6 586	578.3	225.5	213	1 263	105.0	32.5	6 863	310.1	73 386	603
Stockton-Lodi, CA	1 351	26 658	3 045.8	1 141.3	879	5 576	462.8	144.6	34 735	1 719.2	329 446	1 265
Sumter, SC	180	4 812	469.3	172.7	152	1 141	69.7	21.7	6 023	200.9	36 844	289
Syracuse, NY	1 658	42 157	4 003.5	1 689.3	1 158	7 158	629.1	177.8	36 568	1 582.8	167 518	1 163
Tallahassee, FL	783	D	D	D	721	4 825	727.3	168.0	24 838	932.6	180 726	1 260
Tampa-St. Petersburg-Clearwater, FL	7 869	147 093	16 779.5	6 160.9	5 037	31 222	2 816.8	781.2	224 508	9 550.8	2 845 319	12 386
Terre Haute, IN	477	D	D	D	284	1 811	133.1	36.2	7 913	280.3	34 914	338
Texarkana, TX-AR	390	8 539	756.0	300.8	206	D	D	D	7 990	344.5	14 229	133

1. Establishments subject to federal tax.

Table C. Metropolitan Areas — Government Employment and Payroll and Local Government Finances

Area name	Government employment and payroll, 2012									Local government finances, 2012				
			March payroll (percent of total)							General revenue				
												Taxes		
													Per capita[1] (dollars)	
	Full-time equivalent employees	March Payroll (dollars)	Adminis-tration, judicial, and legal	Police and corrections	Fire protection	Highways and transporta-tion	Health and welfare	Natural resources and utilities	Education and libraries	Total (mil dol)	Inter-govern-mental (mil dol)	Total (mil dol)	Total	Property
	171	172	173	174	175	176	177	178	179	180	181	182	183	184
Redding, CA	6 528	30 533 939	6.7	8.7	2.8	3.4	15.6	9.0	52.2	922.9	498.8	217.9	1 220	1 000
Reno, NV	13 611	57 292 494	10.4	14.1	5.7	4.2	4.2	8.4	50.4	1 736.5	755.1	608.1	1 402	1 025
Richmond, VA	47 868	168 064 481	7.1	13.2	5.2	1.8	6.2	5.1	57.6	4 453.2	1 860.0	1 873.9	1 521	1 127
Riverside-San Bernardino-Ontario, CA	137 986	750 815 862	7.1	10.8	3.0	2.2	12.9	6.4	55.7	22 872.7	12 544.1	5 769.7	1 326	1 022
Roanoke, VA	11 938	41 210 661	8.0	9.5	5.8	2.0	5.0	6.0	62.2	1 089.3	447.6	480.6	1 550	1 087
Rochester, MN	6 278	37 136 188	6.6	8.4	1.8	3.7	9.6	6.9	60.3	935.5	426.1	273.1	1 303	1 205
Rochester, NY	48 625	209 834 432	4.8	9.5	2.6	3.2	6.4	4.2	67.9	6 041.6	2 624.6	2 577.1	2 381	1 781
Rockford, IL	11 902	48 299 662	5.1	11.8	5.6	3.5	3.6	7.1	62.7	1 352.3	558.1	615.0	1 777	1 610
Rocky Mount, NC	8 741	30 617 673	3.2	6.0	2.3	1.7	32.7	6.1	46.8	725.6	291.0	136.9	903	699
Rome, GA	3 631	12 476 709	5.7	9.3	4.2	4.2	1.7	5.5	67.7	620.3	284.0	151.4	1 574	957
Sacramento—Roseville—Arden-Arcade, CA	74 788	405 371 174	6.2	12.5	5.4	3.7	8.2	11.7	48.6	11 604.0	5 395.4	3 303.5	1 504	1 115
Saginaw, MI	5 686	21 466 345	8.3	8.5	2.2	2.7	9.8	4.8	61.7	786.5	475.8	154.2	777	684
St. Cloud, MN	5 890	30 573 727	7.4	9.3	1.2	4.2	13.3	3.7	58.2	806.5	393.2	236.4	1 241	1 100
St. George, UT	4 130	14 492 173	7.3	10.1	1.7	2.6	6.5	13.4	56.5	453.7	154.1	197.8	1 366	972
St. Joseph, MO-KS	4 475	13 492 001	5.7	7.9	3.9	3.6	2.8	5.1	69.9	408.2	157.7	172.1	1 346	855
St. Louis, MO-IL	99 216	391 779 336	5.2	10.7	5.1	5.6	2.8	5.2	63.6	10 918.1	3 849.2	5 146.2	1 841	1 249
Salem, OR	13 276	58 238 836	5.8	9.3	3.5	3.1	4.0	3.9	68.1	1 449.9	756.3	442.2	1 116	1 009
Salinas, CA	16 674	95 953 296	5.6	9.2	2.7	3.8	28.8	5.1	41.4	3 062.0	1 376.2	682.3	1 599	1 199
Salisbury, MD-DE	12 705	51 865 541	5.6	9.0	1.0	1.9	3.6	5.9	70.9	1 432.6	624.3	557.2	1 459	1 077
Salt Lake City, UT	36 279	131 818 213	7.3	10.3	5.1	9.5	5.0	8.7	51.6	3 934.4	1 398.7	1 572.5	1 399	1 008
San Angelo, TX	4 541	12 163 357	8.9	16.3	6.6	1.5	3.5	6.2	55.4	335.7	127.3	150.0	1 306	1 006
San Antonio-New Braunfels, TX	94 742	356 044 474	4.4	8.7	3.2	3.7	9.8	10.5	58.5	8 697.5	3 005.2	3 729.5	1 669	1 358
San Diego-Carlsbad, CA	97 178	529 647 292	9.3	10.8	3.9	3.4	11.1	7.0	52.0	16 495.7	6 780.5	5 691.2	1 791	1 381
San Francisco-Oakland-Hayward, CA	155 343	998 941 828	7.6	12.2	5.4	11.0	17.4	9.2	35.0	32 009.2	10 425.4	11 842.8	2 658	1 820
Oakland-Hayward-Berkeley, CA Div 36084	87 214	540 452 372	5.4	11.4	5.0	8.5	17.1	9.7	40.0	17 465.2	6 071.1	5 674.3	2 154	1 538
San Francisco-Redwood City-South San Francisco, CA Div 41884	59 585	406 735 774	10.1	13.4	5.7	15.2	18.9	8.4	27.1	13 022.2	4 026.7	5 343.5	3 414	2 179
San Rafael, CA Div 42034	8 544	51 753 682	10.8	11.2	8.5	4.2	8.9	10.4	44.3	1 521.9	327.6	825.0	3 222	2 533
San Jose-Sunnyvale-Santa Clara, CA	61 998	413 816 866	7.6	10.1	4.9	4.9	20.6	6.4	42.8	13 018.5	4 094.2	4 897.7	2 585	1 941
San Luis Obispo-Paso Robles-Arroyo Grande, CA	8 194	48 094 004	7.2	11.4	2.8	2.5	6.9	6.4	57.6	1 189.7	435.4	547.8	1 994	1 615
Santa Cruz-Watsonville, CA	9 292	50 504 116	8.1	10.1	3.9	7.3	13.5	7.9	47.1	1 432.9	632.4	483.8	1 813	1 441
Santa Fe, NM	4 848	18 022 225	9.3	12.0	6.4	3.8	4.1	9.6	48.1	527.4	253.9	199.3	1 361	807
Santa Maria-Santa Barbara, CA	15 712	89 085 924	7.3	11.4	5.3	3.7	14.4	7.2	48.4	2 761.9	960.5	877.6	2 035	1 531
Santa Rosa, CA	16 072	90 178 192	9.5	12.6	3.9	2.6	12.9	7.2	47.9	2 545.8	918.8	972.6	1 978	1 555
Savannah, GA	13 962	46 151 027	10.0	13.9	3.6	3.3	6.0	6.9	53.1	1 947.0	409.1	744.0	2 056	1 229
Scranton—Wilkes-Barre—Hazleton, PA	16 712	64 672 766	7.6	11.9	3.2	3.8	5.2	5.6	61.4	1 935.2	804.6	806.0	1 430	1 072
Seattle-Tacoma-Bellevue, WA	109 144	628 710 550	8.0	10.0	6.7	11.2	9.8	13.4	38.7	18 576.7	5 896.1	7 417.8	2 088	1 239
Seattle-Bellevue-Everett, WA Div 42644	85 210	497 008 852	7.8	10.1	6.0	12.0	11.7	13.8	36.5	15 276.4	4 566.4	6 183.2	2 256	1 287
Tacoma-Lakewood, WA Div 45104	23 934	131 701 698	8.7	9.5	9.2	8.4	2.7	12.1	47.1	3 300.2	1 329.7	1 234.7	1 521	1 076
Sebastian-Vero Beach, FL	4 188	14 858 891	4.7	16.3	4.8	5.0	5.1	12.6	48.7	445.1	88.8	266.5	1 896	1 553
Sebring, FL	3 358	10 445 615	8.2	12.8	2.4	5.5	3.7	6.4	56.9	264.2	111.3	100.2	1 021	799
Sheboygan, WI	4 469	19 622 392	8.8	8.8	2.1	5.2	8.0	3.0	63.5	489.1	213.6	207.1	1 801	1 746
Sherman-Denison, TX	5 248	18 290 717	5.6	9.2	3.5	2.7	4.2	4.8	69.0	414.8	144.6	188.3	1 544	1 271
Shreveport-Bossier City, LA	18 558	60 559 700	6.4	15.5	6.0	2.9	2.1	5.0	60.8	1 909.4	657.9	985.4	2 204	997
Sierra Vista-Douglas, AZ	4 879	16 984 358	11.7	10.2	5.2	2.9	3.0	3.3	61.1	397.9	175.5	144.2	1 092	821
Sioux City, IA-NE-SD	7 016	27 062 681	5.1	8.4	2.6	4.9	5.3	5.2	67.0	775.3	326.0	295.7	1 751	1 347
Sioux Falls, SD	7 176	25 345 869	6.6	9.8	3.7	4.0	2.2	5.5	66.9	751.2	210.8	404.9	1 707	1 166
South Bend-Mishawaka, IN-MI	10 955	36 623 695	5.5	11.4	6.3	4.0	1.2	6.4	63.3	1 211.4	523.3	434.1	1 362	1 022
Spartanburg, SC	15 589	60 744 767	3.4	5.1	1.5	0.6	46.5	4.0	38.2	1 645.4	411.5	361.9	1 142	1 015
Spokane-Spokane Valley, WA	15 408	75 996 689	9.2	11.0	6.8	7.0	5.4	7.5	51.4	2 043.9	939.8	680.9	1 279	830
Springfield, IL	9 009	38 285 598	5.0	9.2	3.6	4.6	2.0	19.1	56.1	823.8	336.6	347.9	1 641	1 427
Springfield, MA	24 505	106 805 892	3.3	9.5	6.2	2.5	1.8	7.6	67.7	2 499.8	1 290.8	947.8	1 515	1 471
Springfield, MO	15 530	53 052 304	4.5	7.1	2.8	3.8	8.8	10.0	56.5	1 328.3	481.9	530.1	1 192	662
Springfield, OH	5 386	19 627 638	7.6	10.0	4.2	2.3	8.2	4.4	57.6	501.3	270.1	168.3	1 227	774
State College, PA	3 965	14 048 206	7.5	8.6	0.0	7.9	9.9	5.8	58.3	455.2	154.4	216.4	1 394	1 018
Staunton-Waynesboro, VA	4 314	12 615 495	6.6	13.2	3.6	1.7	3.9	3.8	64.6	321.2	157.8	126.3	1 064	712
Stockton-Lodi, CA	23 911	123 453 125	6.5	12.7	3.3	2.6	14.7	5.0	53.3	3 894.7	2 276.8	855.2	1 217	851
Sumter, SC	6 341	17 021 292	4.2	6.1	1.7	1.8	1.6	3.3	80.4	271.8	124.5	114.5	1 060	719
Syracuse, NY	30 026	133 886 154	3.8	8.2	2.5	4.2	6.3	4.1	69.2	3 812.8	1 691.2	1 541.0	2 332	1 687
Tallahassee, FL	14 377	48 690 908	8.9	11.4	3.1	5.3	3.7	13.3	50.6	1 358.3	476.8	458.3	1 221	865
Tampa-St. Petersburg-Clearwater, FL	98 152	350 589 348	7.0	15.7	5.6	4.0	2.8	8.5	53.8	9 943.4	3 586.7	3 926.4	1 381	1 060
Terre Haute, IN	5 719	18 131 023	7.8	8.7	4.1	4.4	5.0	5.4	63.3	562.1	284.5	168.7	978	782
Texarkana, TX-AR	6 292	19 132 215	5.6	9.2	3.4	2.8	3.9	5.8	68.2	458.1	217.9	156.0	1 042	715

1. Based on the resident population estimated as of July 1 of the year shown.

Area name	Local government finances, 2012 (cont.)									Government employment, 2013			Presidential election,[2] 2012		
	Direct general expenditure							Debt outstanding					Percent of vote cast:		
			Percent of total for:												
	Total (mil dol)	Per capita[1] (dollars)	Education	Health and hospitals	Police protection	Public welfare	Highways	Total (mil dol)	Per capita[1] (dollars)	Federal civilian	Federal military	State and local	Democratic	Republican	All other
	185	186	187	188	189	190	191	192	193	194	195	196	197	198	199
Redding, CA	906.1	5 074	43.3	8.1	5.8	10.6	4.0	544.3	3 048	1 306	324	11 153	33.8	63.0	3.2
Reno, NV	1 700.3	3 919	35.7	1.0	6.7	4.2	3.4	4 528.8	10 439	3 523	1 247	23 897	50.7	47.2	2.1
Richmond, VA	4 393.3	3 566	45.4	3.2	6.9	3.5	2.9	4 997.3	4 056	16 689	13 396	94 983	52.0	46.6	1.4
Riverside-San Bernardino-Ontario, CA	23 480.7	5 398	39.0	11.9	6.3	7.3	4.9	24 738.9	5 687	20 494	24 098	210 975	51.0	46.7	2.3
Roanoke, VA	1 134.6	3 659	44.3	2.7	5.5	7.8	1.9	1 358.0	4 379	4 004	1 005	17 687	41.6	56.1	2.3
Rochester, MN	953.0	4 547	35.9	2.2	5.0	7.4	11.0	3 142.1	14 990	1 008	770	10 726	49.4	47.9	2.7
Rochester, NY	6 147.1	5 680	50.8	4.1	3.8	11.1	4.2	4 984.9	4 606	4 546	1 824	71 134	54.4	43.7	1.8
Rockford, IL	1 291.0	3 731	51.6	1.6	7.8	2.7	5.4	877.0	2 534	923	710	15 702	51.0	47.2	1.8
Rocky Mount, NC	764.0	5 037	34.6	34.0	5.2	5.1	1.5	144.7	954	393	370	10 412	56.5	42.9	0.6
Rome, GA	658.4	6 846	27.4	47.2	2.2	0.1	2.6	238.0	2 474	211	270	5 773	29.4	69.2	1.4
Sacramento—Roseville—Arden-Arcade, CA	11 753.9	5 351	35.4	5.1	5.1	7.8	5.9	20 700.4	9 424	13 623	4 281	231 254	53.1	44.2	2.7
Saginaw, MI	801.9	4 043	42.8	14.5	5.8	0.7	5.8	494.0	2 490	1 453	339	9 583	55.5	43.6	1.0
St. Cloud, MN	798.0	4 189	41.0	7.6	5.1	5.3	11.0	1 171.2	6 149	2 192	678	11 457	42.5	54.9	2.6
St. George, UT	401.3	2 771	50.1	0.8	7.7	0.0	6.0	585.2	4 041	564	636	7 148	15.4	82.8	1.8
St. Joseph, MO-KS	361.2	2 824	56.2	2.3	8.0	0.6	5.5	644.5	5 038	583	446	9 386	39.8	57.8	2.4
St. Louis, MO-IL	11 016.7	3 940	50.5	2.4	7.4	0.6	5.2	13 307.4	4 760	28 600	14 031	140 113	52.6	45.7	1.7
Salem, OR	1 466.0	3 699	55.7	4.1	5.3	0.2	4.7	2 202.9	5 558	1 372	1 082	36 563	46.7	50.1	3.2
Salinas, CA	2 904.3	6 806	36.5	22.7	4.6	5.4	2.6	1 444.4	3 385	5 553	6 527	24 805	67.1	30.3	2.6
Salisbury, MD-DE	1 397.6	3 660	55.9	1.9	6.1	1.0	2.5	1 055.9	2 765	1 044	1 897	22 064	43.8	54.7	1.5
Salt Lake City, UT	3 773.6	3 358	42.9	1.2	5.6	2.1	5.3	7 423.5	6 606	11 645	5 271	90 852	37.6	59.4	3.1
San Angelo, TX	359.0	3 125	52.5	3.3	5.7	0.2	2.7	590.0	5 137	1 272	3 326	7 540	25.1	73.4	1.5
San Antonio-New Braunfels, TX	8 877.6	3 974	45.3	13.6	5.3	1.8	3.0	21 467.3	9 609	35 360	35 796	125 381	45.3	53.3	1.4
San Diego-Carlsbad, CA	16 846.0	5 302	37.0	9.8	5.3	6.9	2.9	27 732.0	8 729	46 943	101 931	180 024	52.6	45.0	2.4
San Francisco-Oakland-Hayward, CA	31 954.0	7 172	25.5	16.6	5.8	5.5	3.3	56 702.8	12 726	32 382	9 553	266 585	75.4	21.8	2.8
Oakland-Hayward-Berkeley, CA Div 36084	18 716.4	7 105	26.5	15.3	5.6	5.5	3.2	31 762.2	12 057	13 902	5 939	138 375	73.6	23.7	2.8
San Francisco-Redwood City-South San Francisco, CA Div 41884	11 668.6	7 455	22.7	19.9	6.1	5.8	3.5	22 636.4	14 463	17 724	2 991	113 794	78.5	18.5	3.0
San Rafael, CA Div 42034	1 569.1	6 127	34.5	6.9	6.2	4.1	3.1	2 304.2	8 998	756	623	14 416	74.1	23.1	2.8
San Jose-Sunnyvale-Santa Clara, CA	12 193.4	6 437	32.5	22.1	5.1	5.2	2.2	18 023.9	9 514	10 042	3 364	78 043	69.8	27.5	2.7
San Luis Obispo-Paso Robles-Arroyo Grande, CA	1 206.8	4 391	38.5	5.9	6.2	8.2	3.9	850.7	3 096	610	567	19 818	48.8	47.7	3.5
Santa Cruz-Watsonville, CA	1 415.2	5 305	36.6	6.6	6.3	8.5	2.3	1 074.8	4 029	525	412	17 693	75.6	20.0	4.4
Santa Fe, NM	578.2	3 950	45.8	1.3	6.0	2.2	3.5	916.2	6 259	962	408	16 202	73.5	22.4	4.1
Santa Maria-Santa Barbara, CA	2 786.6	6 462	32.4	18.7	5.7	6.7	3.0	1 346.9	3 123	3 799	3 394	30 596	57.6	39.6	2.8
Santa Rosa, CA	2 601.9	5 290	35.4	10.3	6.3	6.4	5.0	2 547.1	5 179	1 423	1 349	24 840	71.1	25.3	3.6
Savannah, GA	1 874.0	5 178	31.0	28.9	9.3	0.3	2.3	889.2	2 457	2 972	6 170	20 132	48.3	50.7	1.1
Scranton—Wilkes-Barre—Hazleton, PA	2 105.8	3 736	51.8	0.4	3.4	5.0	4.2	2 409.6	4 275	4 065	1 482	25 763	56.0	42.7	1.3
Seattle-Tacoma-Bellevue, WA	17 216.0	4 847	33.8	9.8	5.1	1.0	5.3	30 708.3	8 645	34 962	51 739	228 912	63.6	34.0	2.4
Seattle-Bellevue-Everett, WA Div 42644	13 942.5	5 088	31.5	11.7	5.0	1.1	5.2	26 143.1	9 540	22 599	13 334	184 546	66.0	31.5	2.4
Tacoma-Lakewood, WA Div 45104	3 273.5	4 033	43.7	2.1	5.8	0.6	5.6	4 565.2	5 624	12 363	38 405	44 366	54.4	43.3	2.3
Sebastian-Vero Beach, FL	470.0	3 343	38.2	4.8	9.4	0.8	8.2	436.2	3 103	349	271	4 708	38.5	60.8	0.7
Sebring, FL	276.6	2 818	46.6	3.7	7.8	0.6	6.0	143.0	1 457	238	186	3 784	38.0	61.1	0.9
Sheboygan, WI	492.9	4 286	55.2	3.6	5.7	6.1	8.2	375.9	3 269	202	332	5 576	44.6	54.4	1.1
Sherman-Denison, TX	423.3	3 471	54.8	3.3	5.1	0.0	6.0	717.6	5 885	319	255	6 114	25.2	73.2	1.6
Shreveport-Bossier City, LA	1 871.4	4 185	49.7	1.4	7.4	0.2	3.7	1 823.7	4 078	4 990	7 639	29 776	43.5	55.4	1.2
Sierra Vista-Douglas, AZ	407.1	3 082	44.0	3.5	12.3	4.9	7.3	161.6	1 223	5 560	4 984	6 484	37.8	60.2	2.0
Sioux City, IA-NE-SD	799.7	4 734	53.5	7.0	4.5	1.1	5.7	754.0	4 464	930	706	10 067	44.4	53.7	1.8
Sioux Falls, SD	772.0	3 254	47.6	1.5	5.3	0.5	10.0	951.0	4 008	2 559	1 494	10 327	42.7	55.4	2.0
South Bend-Mishawaka, IN-MI	1 028.2	3 227	51.4	1.7	4.7	1.1	3.4	1 041.8	3 270	1 009	990	14 783	49.6	49.0	1.4
Spartanburg, SC	1 655.8	5 223	33.7	46.8	3.0	0.4	1.0	1 083.5	3 418	538	1 302	21 261	38.6	60.1	1.3
Spokane-Spokane Valley, WA	2 096.5	3 939	45.9	6.2	5.2	0.2	4.3	1 764.2	3 315	4 902	4 403	34 387	44.6	52.6	2.8
Springfield, IL	869.8	4 103	52.8	1.5	7.5	0.9	4.5	2 540.3	11 983	1 865	465	19 520	44.0	53.9	2.1
Springfield, MA	2 618.5	4 185	57.6	0.6	4.8	0.6	3.1	1 821.1	2 910	5 221	1 742	47 612	64.2	33.6	2.2
Springfield, MO	1 305.4	2 936	50.3	8.6	6.8	0.8	6.6	1 931.0	4 343	2 363	1 558	25 414	33.1	64.8	2.1
Springfield, OH	474.6	3 459	49.3	5.8	5.9	6.2	3.3	206.0	1 502	545	348	6 544	48.8	49.6	1.6
State College, PA	453.5	2 923	51.0	2.2	3.5	7.9	6.1	486.7	3 136	442	447	46 951	49.1	48.8	2.1
Staunton-Waynesboro, VA	339.0	2 856	51.3	2.7	4.7	6.7	3.4	294.4	2 480	256	376	8 494	35.4	62.8	1.8
Stockton-Lodi, CA	3 717.2	5 291	40.5	9.2	5.9	8.8	3.5	3 309.2	4 710	3 524	1 178	31 880	55.8	42.0	2.2
Sumter, SC	256.2	2 371	55.2	1.2	7.1	0.3	2.5	245.3	2 270	1 491	5 933	5 569	58.3	40.7	0.9
Syracuse, NY	4 111.0	6 220	49.2	3.2	3.0	9.8	5.1	4 285.9	6 485	4 741	1 188	50 497	57.6	40.6	1.8
Tallahassee, FL	1 372.1	3 655	40.1	1.3	7.9	0.1	7.2	4 333.3	11 544	1 963	768	58 551	59.9	39.1	1.0
Tampa-St. Petersburg-Clearwater, FL	10 477.2	3 685	38.4	3.3	8.7	2.4	4.2	11 252.6	3 958	22 177	12 513	123 991	51.0	47.9	1.1
Terre Haute, IN	504.6	2 925	50.6	6.3	3.2	0.5	3.2	559.6	3 244	1 289	539	11 223	44.8	53.1	2.1
Texarkana, TX-AR	437.3	2 921	59.2	2.4	5.9	1.0	4.9	430.1	2 873	4 352	448	9 247	29.2	69.7	1.2

1. Based on the resident population estimated as of July 1 of the year shown. 2.

Table C. Metropolitan Areas — **Land Area and Population**

CBSA/ DIV code[1]	Area name	Land area,[2] 2010 (sq km)	Population 2014: Total persons	Population 2014: Rank	Population 2014: Per square kilometer	Race alone or in combination, not Hispanic or Latino (percent): White	Black	American Indian, Alaska Native	Asian and Pacific Islander	Percent Hispanic or Latino[3]	Age (percent): Under 5 years	5 to 17 years	18 to 24 years	25 to 34 years	35 to 44 years	45 to 54 years
		1	2	3	4	5	6	7	8	9	10	11	12	13	14	15
45540	The Villages, FL	1 417	114 350	335	80.7	84.8	8.6	0.6	1.0	5.6	2.1	5.7	3.5	6.1	6.9	7.8
45780	Toledo, OH	3 532	607 456	91	172.0	77.6	15.5	0.7	2.0	6.4	6.1	16.7	11.8	12.8	11.9	13.4
45820	Topeka, KS	8 372	233 758	192	27.9	81.5	7.9	2.5	1.6	9.5	6.5	18.0	8.2	12.3	11.5	13.7
45940	Trenton, NJ	582	371 537	143	638.4	53.9	20.3	0.5	10.9	16.2	5.8	16.2	11.2	12.7	13.4	14.8
46060	Tucson, AZ	23 794	1 004 516	53	42.2	55.5	4.0	3.1	3.7	35.6	6.0	16.1	12.1	12.3	11.4	12.2
46140	Tulsa, OK	16 237	969 224	55	59.7	72.3	9.6	12.8	2.6	8.9	6.9	18.3	9.1	13.5	12.6	13.3
46220	Tuscaloosa, AL	7 374	237 761	190	32.2	62.4	33.6	0.6	1.6	3.0	6.0	15.3	18.0	13.3	11.5	11.9
46340	Tyler, TX	2 387	218 842	200	91.7	62.5	18.1	0.8	1.7	18.3	7.0	18.1	10.3	13.3	11.8	12.4
46520	Urban Honolulu, HI	1 556	991 788	54	637.4	32.9	3.8	1.5	77.3	9.2	6.5	15.2	10.5	15.4	12.6	12.5
46540	Utica-Rome, NY	6 796	296 615	163	43.6	87.5	5.9	0.6	3.2	4.5	5.6	15.7	9.9	11.7	11.4	14.7
46660	Valdosta, GA	4 117	143 317	286	34.8	57.9	35.0	0.8	2.1	6.0	7.4	17.2	16.6	14.1	11.4	11.7
46700	Vallejo-Fairfield, CA	2 128	431 131	122	202.6	44.1	15.9	1.4	19.0	25.2	6.2	17.1	10.0	13.9	12.4	14.3
47020	Victoria, TX	4 492	98 630	353	22.0	48.4	6.4	0.6	1.3	44.2	7.0	18.7	9.3	13.3	11.5	12.9
47220	Vineland-Bridgeton, NJ	1 253	157 389	258	125.6	50.1	20.1	1.4	1.8	28.7	6.9	16.9	9.2	14.6	13.6	13.8
47260	Virginia Beach-Norfolk-Newport News, VA-NC	6 969	1 716 624	37	246.3	59.1	31.9	1.1	5.1	6.1	6.4	16.2	11.8	15.2	12.1	13.8
47300	Visalia-Porterville, CA	12 495	458 198	111	36.7	32.2	1.7	1.2	4.1	62.2	9.0	22.9	10.9	14.1	12.2	11.5
47380	Waco, TX	4 669	260 430	180	55.8	58.6	15.6	0.7	1.9	24.6	7.0	17.6	14.5	13.0	11.1	12.2
47460	Walla Walla, WA	5 540	63 829	379	11.5	75.7	2.1	1.6	2.6	19.9	5.7	16.1	13.3	12.1	11.0	12.2
47580	Warner Robins, GA	2 007	187 516	227	93.4	59.0	32.8	0.8	3.3	6.4	6.8	18.3	10.6	14.2	12.5	14.2
47900	Washington-Arlington-Alexandria, DC-VA-MD-WV	16 172	6 033 737	7	373.1	49.8	26.3	0.8	11.2	14.7	6.7	16.7	9.1	15.6	14.5	14.7
47900	Silver Spring-Frederick-Rockville, MD Div 43524	2 982	1 274 122	X	427.3	54.8	16.8	0.6	14.1	16.3	6.4	17.3	7.9	13.4	13.9	15.2
47900	Washington-Arlington-Alexandria, DC-VA-MD-WV Div 47894	13 190	4 759 615	X	360.9	48.5	28.8	0.8	10.5	14.3	6.8	16.5	9.4	16.2	14.7	14.6
47940	Waterloo-Cedar Falls, IA	3 893	169 993	240	43.7	87.8	8.1	0.5	2.1	3.4	6.0	15.6	14.9	12.6	10.8	11.9
48060	Watertown-Fort Drum, NY	3 286	119 103	324	36.2	84.8	6.9	1.1	2.7	7.0	8.6	16.3	13.1	16.9	11.6	11.8
48140	Wausau, WI	4 001	135 780	297	33.9	90.7	1.2	0.8	6.0	2.5	6.2	17.5	8.0	12.1	12.2	15.1
48260	Weirton-Steubenville, WV-OH	1 503	121 336	319	80.7	94.3	4.9	0.6	0.7	1.2	4.7	14.7	9.1	10.0	11.6	14.2
48300	Wenatchee, WA	12 276	114 392	334	9.3	69.5	0.8	1.6	1.6	28.1	7.0	18.2	8.7	12.0	11.3	13.0
48540	Wheeling, WV-OH	2 443	145 205	283	59.4	95.2	4.0	0.6	0.8	0.9	5.0	14.3	9.0	11.5	11.7	14.0
48620	Wichita, KS	12 982	641 076	84	49.4	75.8	8.8	2.0	4.2	12.1	7.3	19.1	9.5	13.7	11.9	13.1
48660	Wichita Falls, TX	6 785	151 536	271	22.3	71.7	9.7	1.4	2.6	16.4	6.4	16.4	12.9	14.2	11.2	12.7
48700	Williamsport, PA	3 182	116 508	328	36.6	92.9	5.7	0.5	1.0	1.6	5.5	14.9	10.4	12.4	11.3	14.2
48900	Wilmington, NC	2 749	272 548	174	99.1	77.7	15.6	1.0	1.9	5.6	5.4	14.8	12.0	13.3	12.9	13.2
49020	Winchester, VA-WV	2 753	133 403	299	48.5	85.3	6.1	0.6	1.9	7.9	5.8	17.2	8.7	12.2	12.8	15.0
49180	Winston-Salem, NC	5 202	655 015	83	125.9	70.9	18.2	0.8	1.9	9.8	5.9	17.2	9.1	11.7	13.0	14.7
49340	Worcester, MA-CT	5 241	930 473	58	177.5	81.7	4.6	0.6	4.6	10.2	5.5	16.5	10.0	12.1	12.8	15.9
49420	Yakima, WA	11 125	247 687	187	22.3	47.2	1.2	4.6	1.8	47.0	8.5	21.4	10.2	13.0	11.9	11.7
49620	York-Hanover, PA	2 342	440 755	119	188.2	86.7	6.4	0.5	1.8	6.3	5.8	16.8	8.5	11.9	12.8	15.2
49660	Youngstown-Warren-Boardman, OH-PA	4 409	553 263	98	125.5	85.4	11.7	0.6	1.0	3.0	5.1	15.8	8.8	10.8	11.5	14.1
49700	Yuba City, CA	3 196	169 813	241	53.1	55.6	3.5	2.6	13.8	28.4	7.6	19.8	10.1	14.1	12.0	12.6
49740	Yuma, AZ	14 281	203 247	214	14.2	34.5	2.3	1.5	1.8	60.9	7.5	19.2	11.9	13.0	10.9	11.1

1. CBSA = Core Based Statistical Area. DIV = Metropolitan Division. See Appendix A for explanation. See Appendix B for list of metropolitan areas identified by type. 2. Dry land or land partially or temporarily covered by water. 3. May be of any race.

Area name	Population, 2013 (cont.)				Population change and components of change, 2000–2014							Households, 2013				
	Age (percent) (cont.)				Total persons		Percent change		Components of change, 2010–2014					Percent		
	55 to 64 years	65 to 74 years	75 years and over	Percent female	2000	2010	2000–2010	2010–2014	Births	Deaths	Net migration	Number	Persons per household	Family households	Female family householder[1]	One person
	16	17	18	19	20	21	22	23	24	25	26	27	28	29	30	31
The Villages, FL	16.4	33.0	18.6	48.9	53 345	93 420	75.1	22.4	1 939	5 575	23 294	49 672	1.97	72.4	5.6	23.3
Toledo, OH	13.2	7.8	6.4	51.4	618 203	610 001	-1.3	-0.4	32 024	24 226	-10 366	242 975	2.43	59.4	13.9	33.7
Topeka, KS	13.9	8.7	7.2	51.1	224 551	233 870	4.2	0.0	12 931	9 523	-3 400	92 747	2.47	64.3	11.1	30.0
Trenton, NJ	12.5	7.3	6.2	51.0	350 761	366 513	4.5	1.1	18 427	12 052	-2 219	131 623	2.67	68.1	14.2	25.8
Tucson, AZ	12.6	9.6	7.6	50.8	843 746	980 263	16.2	2.5	51 183	37 412	9 905	391 975	2.48	61.1	13.0	31.4
Tulsa, OK	12.4	8.0	5.9	50.9	859 532	937 478	9.1	3.4	56 426	37 901	13 158	369 747	2.56	66.5	12.8	28.6
Tuscaloosa, AL	11.7	7.1	5.3	51.7	203 009	230 162	13.4	3.3	12 107	8 708	4 218	81 401	2.75	66.8	17.1	28.1
Tyler, TX	11.9	8.4	6.8	51.7	174 706	209 714	20.0	4.4	12 721	8 222	4 534	79 043	2.67	67.8	14.4	27.4
Urban Honolulu, HI	11.7	8.2	7.3	49.3	876 156	953 207	8.8	4.0	58 047	31 518	13 102	308 800	3.06	70.3	11.9	23.3
Utica-Rome, NY	13.7	9.1	8.3	50.3	299 896	299 397	-0.2	-0.9	13 915	13 324	-3 097	116 113	2.43	60.3	12.9	33.2
Valdosta, GA	10.1	6.8	4.7	50.8	119 560	139 588	16.8	2.6	8 813	4 750	-693	51 631	2.70	61.1	15.8	27.7
Vallejo-Fairfield, CA	13.1	7.7	5.3	50.1	394 542	413 344	4.8	4.3	21 742	12 699	8 558	142 577	2.90	70.0	14.9	23.4
Victoria, TX	12.6	8.2	6.5	50.8	91 016	94 003	3.3	4.9	5 751	3 486	2 392	35 115	2.70	75.1	16.0	20.7
Vineland-Bridgeton, NJ	11.6	7.5	5.9	48.5	146 438	156 898	7.1	0.3	9 195	6 089	-2 388	50 066	2.89	70.0	19.1	23.7
Virginia Beach-Norfolk-Newport News, VA-NC	11.8	7.3	5.4	50.8	1 580 057	1 676 822	6.1	2.4	96 734	55 425	-1 282	625 540	2.62	66.8	16.0	27.0
Visalia-Porterville, CA	9.5	5.8	4.3	49.8	368 021	442 179	20.2	3.6	34 179	11 918	-5 743	133 409	3.36	78.2	18.3	18.2
Waco, TX	11.3	7.2	6.2	51.3	232 093	252 772	8.9	3.0	15 468	9 183	1 525	93 195	2.64	63.5	15.3	29.5
Walla Walla, WA	12.9	8.7	8.0	49.2	59 244	62 859	6.1	1.5	3 048	2 491	360	23 390	2.47	60.7	11.5	33.3
Warner Robins, GA	11.4	7.0	5.0	51.6	144 021	179 605	24.7	4.4	10 504	5 802	2 943	66 537	2.71	67.3	13.7	27.8
Washington-Arlington-Alexandria, DC-VA-MD-WV	11.6	6.6	4.4	51.2	4 837 428	5 636 232	16.5	7.0	342 557	137 346	191 956	2 133 062	2.74	66.4	12.7	26.5
Silver Spring-Frederick-Rockville, MD Div 43524	12.7	7.3	5.8	51.5	1 068 618	1 205 162	12.8	5.7	67 560	31 474	33 279	453 274	2.75	70.7	11.4	23.8
Washington-Arlington-Alexandria, DC-VA-MD-WV Div 47894	11.4	6.4	4.1	51.0	3 768 810	4 431 070	17.6	7.4	274 997	105 872	158 677	1 679 788	2.74	65.2	13.0	27.3
Waterloo-Cedar Falls, IA	12.7	8.0	7.4	51.0	163 706	167 819	2.5	1.3	8 743	6 386	-12	66 602	2.43	61.3	9.4	30.5
Watertown-Fort Drum, NY	10.0	6.7	5.2	47.8	111 738	116 229	4.0	2.5	9 288	3 810	-2 798	42 466	2.67	69.4	11.3	24.8
Wausau, WI	13.5	8.3	7.2	49.8	125 834	134 063	6.5	1.3	6 856	4 742	-522	54 422	2.46	67.1	8.9	28.4
Weirton-Steubenville, WV-OH	16.0	10.4	9.2	51.6	132 008	124 454	-5.7	-2.5	4 750	7 211	-544	50 523	2.39	63.5	13.0	30.3
Wenatchee, WA	13.5	9.2	7.2	49.9	99 219	110 884	11.8	3.2	6 172	4 017	1 323	41 368	2.70	69.7	9.0	25.8
Wheeling, WV-OH	15.7	10.0	8.8	50.4	153 172	147 950	-3.4	-1.9	6 393	7 989	-858	60 546	2.29	63.7	11.0	31.7
Wichita, KS	12.3	7.1	6.0	50.4	579 839	630 919	8.8	1.6	40 276	23 025	-7 142	242 612	2.58	65.8	11.8	29.7
Wichita Falls, TX	12.0	7.6	6.7	48.6	151 524	151 306	-0.1	0.0	8 232	6 270	-1 883	57 532	2.38	65.9	15.8	29.3
Williamsport, PA	14.1	9.0	8.2	50.8	120 044	116 111	-3.3	0.3	5 424	5 331	431	44 961	2.47	64.5	11.0	28.9
Wilmington, NC	12.9	9.2	6.3	51.4	201 389	254 884	26.6	6.9	12 136	9 147	14 319	106 814	2.44	58.9	11.6	32.5
Winchester, VA-WV	12.9	9.1	6.3	50.2	102 997	128 472	24.7	3.8	6 554	4 647	3 066	49 477	2.52	64.6	8.9	31.6
Winston-Salem, NC	13.1	8.9	6.6	51.8	569 207	640 595	12.5	2.3	31 876	25 268	7 691	255 660	2.49	64.8	13.4	30.3
Worcester, MA-CT	13.2	7.6	6.2	50.6	860 054	916 980	6.6	1.5	42 144	32 177	4 264	345 518	2.59	67.4	12.9	26.1
Yakima, WA	10.7	7.0	5.4	49.8	222 581	243 231	9.3	1.8	17 587	7 943	-5 114	79 742	3.05	71.2	15.1	23.5
York-Hanover, PA	13.5	8.7	6.8	50.6	381 751	434 972	13.9	1.3	20 979	15 895	991	164 937	2.61	68.9	10.9	25.5
Youngstown-Warren-Boardman, OH-PA	15.1	9.8	9.1	51.3	602 964	565 773	-6.2	-2.2	23 686	29 196	-6 259	229 074	2.34	63.0	13.2	32.5
Yuba City, CA	11.1	7.3	5.4	49.8	139 149	166 892	19.9	1.8	10 733	5 321	-2 461	56 806	2.93	73.0	15.0	21.9
Yuma, AZ	9.6	9.1	7.7	48.9	160 026	195 751	22.3	3.8	13 509	5 796	-840	69 744	2.78	75.2	11.4	21.2

1. No spouse present.

Table C. Metropolitan Areas — **Population, Vital Statistics, Medicare, and Crime**

Area name	Persons in group quarters, 2014	Daytime population, 2013: Number	Daytime population, 2013: Employment/residence ratio	Births, 2014: Total	Births, 2014: Rate[1]	Deaths, 2014: Number	Deaths, 2014: Rate[1]	Persons under 65 with no health insurance 2013: Number	Persons under 65 with no health insurance 2013: Percent	Medicare, 2014: Eligible for Medicare	Medicare, 2014: Enrolled in Medicare Advantage	Medicare, 2014: Enrolled in a Medicare prescription drug plan	Serious crimes known to police,[2] 2013: Total: Number	Serious crimes known to police,[2] 2013: Total: Rate[3]
	32	33	34	35	36	37	38	39	40	41	42	43	44	45
The Villages, FL	8 302	132 455	NA	479	4.2	1 439	12.6	7 898	18.2	58 076	17 543	25 788	1 157	1 125
Toledo, OH	17 674	650 189	1.17	7 569	12.5	5 787	9.5	68 717	13.5	107 427	41 139	59 120	16 246	2 870
Topeka, KS	5 051	247 520	1.14	3 005	12.9	2 231	9.5	26 334	13.6	46 912	3 908	28 459	8 962	3 876
Trenton, NJ	19 387	474 717	1.87	4 278	11.5	2 862	7.7	44 180	14.6	62 062	9 070	40 143	8 877	2 404
Tucson, AZ	25 764	1 009 157	1.03	11 980	11.9	9 087	9.0	151 382	18.8	186 122	85 371	52 860	52 482	5 250
Tulsa, OK	15 539	983 060	1.05	13 245	13.7	9 183	9.5	160 175	19.6	163 291	45 188	72 140	36 697	3 822
Tuscaloosa, AL	12 293	247 297	1.15	2 885	12.1	2 095	8.8	30 229	15.4	41 601	4 518	23 614	8 542	3 692
Tyler, TX	4 272	237 206	1.26	3 005	13.7	1 951	8.9	45 409	25.3	39 578	8 388	21 320	7 015	3 258
Urban Honolulu, HI	36 546	988 489	1.01	13 743	13.9	7 869	7.9	54 264	6.7	164 800	78 921	38 197	16 890	1 715
Utica-Rome, NY	14 365	306 745	1.08	3 219	10.9	3 112	10.5	24 141	10.3	63 825	21 247	25 800	7 127	2 429
Valdosta, GA	6 703	150 927	1.13	1 982	13.8	1 165	8.1	25 508	21.2	21 024	4 643	9 660	4 269	2 938
Vallejo-Fairfield, CA	11 255	458 032	1.31	5 151	11.9	3 175	7.4	52 961	14.7	67 117	30 163	15 069	15 534	3 667
Victoria, TX	1 834	103 457	1.19	1 393	14.1	834	8.5	18 757	22.9	17 269	3 665	9 691	3 652	3 730
Vineland-Bridgeton, NJ	12 423	174 258	1.40	2 063	13.1	1 437	9.1	22 837	18.0	26 762	4 076	17 275	7 673	4 848
Virginia Beach-Norfolk-Newport News, VA-NC	70 407	1 741 273	1.04	22 826	13.3	13 559	7.9	196 852	13.8	262 066	47 548	96 138	55 827	3 286
Visalia-Porterville, CA	5 066	470 527	1.12	8 019	17.5	2 862	6.2	85 820	21.2	56 263	6 787	35 745	16 387	3 597
Waco, TX	11 487	267 972	1.10	3 644	14.0	2 203	8.5	50 086	23.4	41 994	11 602	19 484	9 368	3 707
Walla Walla, WA	4 641	68 597	1.23	723	11.3	611	9.6	8 955	18.3	12 677	1 335	6 285	2 364	3 709
Warner Robins, GA	4 183	200 261	1.24	2 467	13.2	1 475	7.9	30 150	18.9	28 332	5 204	8 539	7 670	4 223
Washington-Arlington-Alexandria, DC-VA-MD-WV	106 974	6 254 624	1.10	81 330	13.5	34 180	5.7	638 242	12.3	732 271	82 753	268 461	148 636	2 503
Silver Spring-Frederick-Rockville, MD Div 43524	13 336	NA	NA	15 936	12.5	7 499	5.9	128 213	11.9	176 648	15 896	70 254	22 779	1 810
Washington-Arlington-Alexandria, DC-VA-MD-WV Div 47894	93 638	NA	NA	65 394	13.7	26 681	5.6	510 029	12.4	555 623	66 857	198 207	125 857	2 689
Waterloo-Cedar Falls, IA	7 439	181 835	1.16	2 072	12.2	1 510	8.9	12 723	9.3	31 223	3 818	21 400	3 792	2 238
Watertown-Fort Drum, NY	6 216	128 043	1.17	2 184	18.3	916	7.7	10 236	10.3	18 603	4 415	7 475	2 370	2 008
Wausau, WI	1 623	149 159	1.23	1 586	11.7	1 065	7.8	11 438	10.1	24 359	10 581	7 911	2 168	1 629
Weirton-Steubenville, WV-OH	3 459	132 787	1.23	1 122	9.2	1 667	13.7	13 401	14.1	29 250	9 294	14 874	NA	NA
Wenatchee, WA	1 118	115 716	1.05	1 429	12.5	948	8.3	20 398	21.7	21 872	4 135	9 829	2 722	2 388
Wheeling, WV-OH	6 923	157 168	1.21	1 553	10.7	1 806	12.4	16 465	14.6	32 741	14 298	14 528	2 518	1 814
Wichita, KS	11 515	648 201	1.04	9 451	14.7	5 466	8.5	80 686	14.8	101 875	17 076	55 516	30 062	4 733
Wichita Falls, TX	12 391	154 908	1.06	1 929	12.7	1 484	9.8	26 464	22.3	26 495	3 393	14 566	5 860	3 919
Williamsport, PA	5 456	125 490	1.19	1 288	11.1	1 297	11.1	10 435	11.3	24 473	7 699	13 520	2 744	2 337
Wilmington, NC	7 716	288 471	1.18	2 874	10.5	2 240	8.2	41 683	19.0	49 611	7 818	26 635	10 410	3 937
Winchester, VA-WV	2 436	142 412	1.35	1 526	11.4	1 089	8.2	18 331	16.7	23 959	2 902	12 150	2 873	2 184
Winston-Salem, NC	12 942	687 425	1.17	7 458	11.4	5 983	9.1	94 773	17.6	122 469	65 759	36 329	25 030	3 866
Worcester, MA-CT	33 015	998 266	1.23	9 938	10.7	7 745	8.3	39 187	5.1	160 475	53 913	65 075	20 417	2 418
Yakima, WA	3 481	251 769	1.05	4 052	16.4	1 938	7.8	57 774	27.0	38 454	7 406	18 715	9 112	3 664
York-Hanover, PA	8 740	468 765	1.20	4 906	11.1	3 787	8.6	39 785	10.9	82 699	27 902	33 497	8 921	2 035
Youngstown-Warren-Boardman, OH-PA	18 674	584 145	1.14	5 579	10.1	6 804	12.3	57 334	13.1	127 605	59 563	56 011	16 967	3 085
Yuba City, CA	1 979	177 529	1.21	2 477	14.6	1 211	7.1	29 074	19.9	26 944	977	16 730	5 597	3 323
Yuma, AZ	8 468	203 299	1.03	3 137	15.4	1 415	7.0	38 185	24.0	29 797	6 177	12 127	6 172	3 102

1. Per 1,000 estimated resident population. 2. Data for serious crimes have not been adjusted for underreporting; this may affect comparability between geographic areas and over time.
3. Per 100,000 population estimated by the FBI.

Area name	Serious crimes known to police, 2013 (cont.)[1]		Education						Income and Poverty, 2013							
	Rate[2]		School enrollment and attainment, 2013				Local government expenditures,[5] 2012–2013							Percent below poverty level		
			Enrollment[3]		Attainment[4] (percent)											
	Violent	Property	Total	Percent private	High school graduate or less	Bachelor's degree or more	Total current expenditures (mil dol)	Current expenditures per student (dollars)	Per capita income[6] (dollars)	Mean household income (dollars)	Median household income	Percent of households with income of less than $25,000	Percent of households with income of $200,000 or more	All persons	Children under 18 years	Age 65 years and older
	46	47	48	49	50	51	52	53	54	55	56	57	58	59	60	61
The Villages, FL	170	955	9 099	9.2	36.8	31.3	68.5	8 569	31 539	65 569	52 891	20.4	4.0	10.5	30.0	6.4
Toledo, OH	560	2 310	168 336	15.0	43.2	24.8	1 015.6	13 299	24 368	59 370	42 792	31.1	2.6	19.5	25.8	9.3
Topeka, KS	352	3 525	60 076	13.7	42.6	26.3	390.7	10 206	25 045	61 897	50 369	24.6	1.6	15.4	20.3	8.5
Trenton, NJ	408	1 995	100 877	25.6	38.6	40.4	1 078.0	18 652	36 160	99 334	70 857	18.9	10.6	11.8	15.7	7.5
Tucson, AZ	431	4 819	257 652	9.8	36.1	30.1	1 033.5	8 133	25 014	61 719	43 824	28.8	2.8	19.5	26.7	8.3
Tulsa, OK	521	3 302	246 415	15.3	42.0	26.0	1 243.0	7 628	26 227	65 987	48 327	24.9	3.2	14.8	21.9	9.0
Tuscaloosa, AL	378	3 314	68 166	9.1	45.8	24.7	299.3	8 935	21 427	57 677	44 895	29.3	2.1	17.3	23.4	9.2
Tyler, TX	279	2 978	57 989	9.2	39.9	25.3	272.8	8 242	24 752	65 102	47 745	24.8	2.7	17.0	25.6	6.8
Urban Honolulu, HI	115	1 600	242 271	25.9	35.2	33.4	2 199.3	11 903	30 895	92 931	73 388	14.4	7.6	9.4	12.0	6.7
Utica-Rome, NY	224	2 205	70 721	15.2	47.0	21.9	703.6	16 179	23 163	56 058	43 396	28.2	1.8	17.5	26.8	9.2
Valdosta, GA	224	2 713	48 631	9.8	46.4	20.1	201.1	8 676	17 441	46 505	35 104	36.2	0.8	26.9	29.5	14.8
Vallejo-Fairfield, CA	472	3 195	110 943	13.5	35.8	24.5	544.6	8 255	28 388	80 551	63 520	17.6	4.8	13.0	18.8	6.7
Victoria, TX	497	3 233	22 882	14.1	53.0	15.7	143.7	8 506	25 741	69 188	52 111	23.1	3.5	15.2	22.0	8.8
Vineland-Bridgeton, NJ	537	4 311	37 159	5.6	62.8	13.7	504.4	18 695	21 129	59 490	45 978	29.7	2.4	20.6	30.1	10.2
Virginia Beach-Norfolk-Newport News, VA-NC	304	2 982	467 434	14.8	35.1	29.6	2 771.7	10 325	28 240	72 966	56 161	19.2	3.9	13.0	19.2	7.5
Visalia-Porterville, CA	460	3 137	135 873	6.3	59.2	13.3	974.8	9 752	16 595	54 293	39 422	32.6	2.4	30.1	40.8	11.7
Waco, TX	345	3 362	80 703	18.1	46.2	19.7	404.8	9 020	21 836	57 593	40 170	30.4	2.7	21.3	27.6	9.2
Walla Walla, WA	188	3 521	16 770	29.2	35.8	28.1	95.4	10 032	22 282	57 666	43 870	31.0	2.7	18.4	24.8	9.4
Warner Robins, GA	380	3 842	54 459	8.9	45.6	20.1	309.7	9 443	22 795	60 990	48 553	22.7	2.0	15.9	22.2	8.2
Washington-Arlington-Alexandria, DC-VA-MD-WV	332	2 171	1 593 029	20.3	28.6	48.7	11 908.0	13 655	42 897	116 153	90 149	11.6	13.8	8.5	11.1	7.7
Silver Spring-Frederick-Rockville, MD Div 43524	189	1 621	335 407	20.9	25.4	53.6	2 755.2	14 560	46 590	127 013	95 442	9.7	15.5	6.9	9.3	7.2
Washington-Arlington-Alexandria, DC-VA-MD-WV Div 47894	370	2 319	1 257 622	20.1	29.4	47.3	9 152.8	13 404	41 906	113 222	88 401	12.1	13.4	8.9	11.5	7.8
Waterloo-Cedar Falls, IA	442	1 796	47 463	11.1	44.9	25.0	306.7	11 585	26 209	64 448	49 050	24.2	2.6	15.0	19.7	4.2
Watertown-Fort Drum, NY	116	1 892	30 524	14.1	46.1	18.9	276.6	14 686	22 784	59 121	46 683	23.9	1.6	15.9	23.2	6.4
Wausau, WI	93	1 536	34 336	14.6	45.9	22.2	219.9	11 071	27 093	66 143	51 635	23.6	2.2	11.0	15.2	9.0
Weirton-Steubenville, WV-OH	NA	NA	29 740	17.7	53.5	15.7	184.4	10 999	22 121	52 277	39 277	30.2	1.8	16.2	24.5	8.7
Wenatchee, WA	137	2 251	26 376	6.6	50.1	20.2	206.7	9 935	23 884	62 203	51 177	27.4	1.6	14.8	20.4	11.8
Wheeling, WV-OH	254	1 560	31 082	15.5	52.3	20.0	209.1	11 158	24 273	56 665	40 289	30.2	2.6	15.5	23.7	10.2
Wichita, KS	571	4 163	183 553	14.6	36.9	29.0	1 063.0	9 623	25 470	64 734	49 476	24.4	3.0	14.9	21.6	8.0
Wichita Falls, TX	340	3 579	37 844	8.0	46.3	20.5	208.3	8 405	22 743	58 439	44 702	28.8	2.4	18.9	27.1	10.5
Williamsport, PA	165	2 171	25 979	17.0	51.9	19.0	222.2	13 719	24 319	60 388	47 373	26.2	2.5	13.5	18.8	8.8
Wilmington, NC	363	3 574	69 059	9.7	34.0	34.6	292.5	8 456	27 574	66 863	47 594	25.1	3.6	19.8	26.5	8.5
Winchester, VA-WV	189	1 996	26 884	20.2	48.0	24.2	221.9	10 622	27 665	69 105	55 045	20.1	3.9	6.8	8.9	4.4
Winston-Salem, NC	369	3 498	161 541	16.3	45.4	25.7	820.7	8 263	24 749	61 314	42 563	28.9	3.3	20.0	30.4	9.7
Worcester, MA-CT	422	1 996	242 863	18.0	40.1	32.9	2 059.4	14 419	30 262	78 909	61 789	21.5	5.3	13.3	19.3	8.6
Yakima, WA	293	3 371	65 457	9.4	54.7	15.5	509.4	9 783	18 387	53 764	41 917	26.6	1.6	20.8	28.8	9.3
York-Hanover, PA	224	1 811	102 387	21.2	52.4	21.9	849.3	13 141	28 015	71 587	57 065	19.1	3.4	11.0	18.9	6.1
Youngstown-Warren-Boardman, OH-PA	262	2 824	124 213	14.5	52.7	20.3	967.1	12 831	23 160	54 720	41 992	29.4	2.0	17.4	28.7	7.2
Yuba City, CA	306	3 017	47 776	8.7	45.4	17.0	303.5	8 686	21 064	60 686	46 773	24.7	1.8	18.7	26.0	4.4
Yuma, AZ	409	2 694	53 560	5.2	55.1	13.9	207.3	5 941	19 531	55 512	41 666	26.9	2.1	17.8	26.7	13.4

1. Data for serious crimes have not been adjusted for underreporting; this may affect comparability between geographic areas and over time. 2. Per 100,000 population estimated by the FBI. 3. All persons 3 years old and over enrolled in nursery school through college. 4. Persons 25 years old and over. 5. Elementary and secondary education expenditures. 6. Based on resident population estimated in the 2008-2012 American Community Survey.

Area name	Personal income, 2013: Total (mil dol)	Percent change 2012–2013	Per capita[1]: Dollars	Per capita[1]: Rank	Wages and salaries (mil dol)	Supplements to wages and salaries; employer contributions (mil dol): Pension and insurance	Supplements to wages and salaries; employer contributions (mil dol): Government social insurance	Proprietors' income (mil dol)	Dividends, interest, and rent (mil dol)	Personal transfer receipts (mil dol)	Earnings, 2013: Total (mil dol)	Contributions for government social insurance (mil dol): From employee and self-employed	Contributions for government social insurance (mil dol): From employer
	62	63	64	65	66	67	68	69	70	71	72	73	74
The Villages, FL	3 983	6.0	37 206	245	1 026	188	75	86	1 313	1 709	1 375	138	75
Toledo, OH	23 477	1.8	38 604	203	12 927	2 478	989	2 248	3 418	5 115	18 641	1 010	989
Topeka, KS	9 546	1.8	40 760	163	4 815	826	375	551	1 805	1 943	6 567	409	375
Trenton, NJ	21 079	2.2	56 906	11	14 773	2 290	1 097	1 593	4 207	2 983	19 752	1 127	1 097
Tucson, AZ	36 935	1.4	37 063	250	16 428	2 962	1 225	2 044	8 313	8 359	22 659	1 411	1 225
Tulsa, OK	45 479	2.2	47 297	50	20 604	2 985	1 669	8 948	7 939	6 980	34 206	1 789	1 669
Tuscaloosa, AL	8 324	2.0	35 329	294	4 106	738	306	666	1 411	1 806	5 816	355	306
Tyler, TX	9 199	2.2	42 573	118	4 137	610	290	1 533	1 900	1 726	6 571	339	290
Urban Honolulu, HI	47 990	2.0	48 798	39	24 625	5 291	2 205	3 420	10 031	6 645	35 541	1 998	2 205
Utica-Rome, NY	11 744	0.9	39 439	185	4 919	1 405	406	694	2 204	2 880	7 424	411	406
Valdosta, GA	4 645	2.4	32 504	354	2 099	491	160	375	879	1 033	3 124	163	160
Vallejo-Fairfield, CA	18 057	4.5	42 509	122	7 271	1 577	520	809	3 186	3 114	10 177	600	520
Victoria, TX	4 504	4.9	46 197	59	1 944	284	132	698	763	784	3 057	156	132
Vineland-Bridgeton, NJ	5 636	0.6	35 825	289	2 652	559	226	457	866	1 471	3 895	235	226
Virginia Beach-Norfolk-Newport News, VA-NC	76 414	1.0	44 756	82	38 604	7 777	3 094	4 114	16 926	11 926	53 588	2 966	3 094
Visalia-Porterville, CA	14 782	3.1	32 550	353	5 511	1 416	403	2 094	2 290	3 635	9 423	469	403
Waco, TX	9 303	1.8	35 922	284	4 535	745	319	748	1 652	2 008	6 347	343	319
Walla Walla, WA	2 478	1.5	38 990	195	1 128	216	102	231	559	531	1 677	90	102
Warner Robins, GA	6 703	1.2	35 995	282	3 294	837	255	317	1 309	1 301	4 704	249	255
Washington-Arlington-Alexandria, DC-VA-MD-WV	365 955	0.8	61 507	8	222 003	35 473	16 148	31 722	70 873	31 839	305 346	16 708	16 148
Silver Spring-Frederick-Rockville, MD Div 43524	85 695	0.6	68 116	NA	38 355	5 953	2 826	9 722	18 121	6 829	56 856	3 162	2 826
Washington-Arlington-Alexandria, DC-VA-MD-WV Div 47894	280 260	0.9	59 734	NA	183 649	29 520	13 322	21 999	52 753	25 011	248 490	13 546	13 322
Waterloo-Cedar Falls, IA	7 079	1.4	41 769	137	3 848	623	302	657	1 273	1 273	5 430	323	302
Watertown-Fort Drum, NY	5 374	-0.8	44 968	79	2 669	829	253	242	1 093	865	3 993	178	253
Wausau, WI	5 478	2.1	40 454	166	2 884	583	236	449	895	905	4 151	245	236
Weirton-Steubenville, WV-OH	4 152	1.8	34 037	324	1 548	338	126	230	591	1 242	2 242	147	126
Wenatchee, WA	4 439	2.1	39 128	191	1 893	330	184	294	1 067	932	2 701	153	184
Wheeling, WV-OH	5 624	4.2	38 587	205	2 683	525	203	509	936	1 403	3 920	240	203
Wichita, KS	26 809	1.9	42 060	130	13 452	2 246	1 065	3 626	4 617	4 289	20 389	1 191	1 065
Wichita Falls, TX	6 292	1.4	41 615	142	2 434	469	182	1 045	1 336	1 228	4 129	201	182
Williamsport, PA	4 534	0.5	38 832	197	2 260	495	184	249	826	994	3 189	194	184
Wilmington, NC	10 076	2.2	37 514	236	4 727	771	368	1 190	2 106	2 061	7 055	432	368
Winchester, VA-WV	5 012	2.8	37 979	222	2 487	410	189	330	974	852	3 416	210	189
Winston-Salem, NC	24 694	0.9	37 943	223	11 342	1 670	884	2 451	4 286	5 075	16 348	1 040	884
Worcester, MA-CT	43 983	1.3	47 462	49	18 548	3 548	1 342	2 380	6 874	7 577	25 819	1 386	1 342
Yakima, WA	9 016	1.5	36 497	266	3 793	649	372	924	1 760	2 159	5 738	299	372
York-Hanover, PA	17 989	1.5	40 979	159	7 807	1 555	642	906	3 225	3 352	10 911	656	642
Youngstown-Warren-Boardman, OH-PA	20 243	1.0	36 440	269	8 582	1 726	685	1 582	3 370	5 496	12 575	767	685
Yuba City, CA	6 011	3.8	35 636	290	2 114	566	162	673	1 061	1 515	3 515	189	162
Yuma, AZ	5 530	1.9	27 483	378	2 544	524	211	406	890	1 379	3 685	204	211

1. Based on the resident population estimated as of July 1 of the year shown.

Area name	Earnings, 2013 (cont.) — Percent by selected industries: Farm	Mining	Construction	Manufacturing	Information, professional, scientific, technical services	Retail trade	Finance, insurance, real estate, rental and leasing	Health care and social assistance	Government	Social Security beneficiaries, December 2013: Number	Rate[1]	Supplemental Security Income recipients, December 2013	Housing units, 2014: Total	Percent change, 2000–2014
	75	76	77	78	79	80	81	82	83	84	85	86	87	88
The Villages, FL	0.9	0.7	12.1	5.8	D	8.5	4.6	14.1	23.4	57 715	532	1 537	64 510	21.7
Toledo, OH	0.8	D	5.8	18.7	D	6.5	5.4	15.3	16.2	113 010	186	19 792	273 312	0.0
Topeka, KS	1.3	0.7	D	6.9	D	5.2	D	14.7	24.0	49 810	213	5 753	104 211	0.4
Trenton, NJ	0.0	0.0	2.9	5.7	20.9	4.0	11.2	9.6	19.7	65 775	177	9 992	144 991	1.3
Tucson, AZ	0.1	1.4	4.5	10.4	9.8	6.8	5.9	14.7	25.8	197 965	198	20 132	448 843	1.8
Tulsa, OK	0.2	D	7.5	12.6	8.4	5.7	6.7	10.1	8.9	180 480	188	22 020	421 148	2.8
Tuscaloosa, AL	1.4	D	5.1	17.4	5.5	6.2	D	9.3	27.1	47 945	204	9 272	104 875	2.8
Tyler, TX	0.2	14.5	4.7	6.3	8.0	8.5	5.5	21.3	11.6	42 045	194	5 406	88 440	1.3
Urban Honolulu, HI	0.3	0.1	6.9	1.9	8.1	5.5	7.3	9.8	33.8	165 805	168	16 925	343 017	1.8
Utica-Rome, NY	0.8	0.1	3.8	9.5	6.0	7.7	7.0	14.8	32.6	70 485	236	10 762	137 313	-0.2
Valdosta, GA	4.4	D	5.7	7.3	5.1	D	4.6	D	35.2	23 815	167	4 773	59 156	3.0
Vallejo-Fairfield, CA	1.1	0.3	8.2	14.1	3.9	6.9	5.4	15.7	26.0	68 670	161	12 621	154 981	1.5
Victoria, TX	0.1	16.9	7.2	7.9	D	11.4	5.9	D	12.1	18 625	191	2 889	39 746	1.6
Vineland-Bridgeton, NJ	2.2	0.3	5.5	13.8	3.4	7.0	2.9	14.1	28.5	29 890	190	5 570	56 348	0.9
Virginia Beach-Norfolk-Newport News, VA-NC	0.1	D	D	7.9	D	5.3	D	9.7	35.2	278 630	163	33 122	706 782	2.7
Visalia-Porterville, CA	15.4	0.1	3.8	8.1	3.3	7.1	3.5	6.7	24.6	60 930	134	19 316	145 503	2.7
Waco, TX	0.5	D	7.2	17.8	D	6.4	8.3	11.3	17.0	45 560	176	8 005	105 003	2.1
Walla Walla, WA	12.0	D	3.7	14.2	4.0	5.5	3.8	D	24.6	13 150	207	1 536	26 018	1.7
Warner Robins, GA	1.4	D	D	D	7.7	6.0	0.0	D	52.1	30 130	162	4 877	76 964	3.3
Washington-Arlington-Alexandria, DC-VA-MD-WV	0.0	D	D	1.6	D	3.7	6.4	6.6	27.8	681 411	114	86 660	2 302 967	3.0
Silver Spring-Frederick-Rockville, MD Div 43524	0.1	0.0	7.2	3.3	25.5	4.7	10.0	8.9	21.5	160 430	127	16 083	479 293	2.8
Washington-Arlington-Alexandria, DC-VA-MD-WV Div 47894	0.0	0.1	D	1.2	28.2	3.5	5.6	6.1	29.3	520 981	111	70 577	1 823 674	3.1
Waterloo-Cedar Falls, IA	4.9	0.1	5.3	24.8	4.3	6.1	7.1	11.3	15.1	33 865	200	3 472	72 575	1.7
Watertown-Fort Drum, NY	1.4	0.1	4.4	3.7	2.6	5.8	2.0	8.7	60.3	21 200	177	2 984	58 769	1.4
Wausau, WI	2.1	0.1	5.3	22.5	5.9	7.5	9.8	12.2	12.7	26 915	199	2 160	58 362	1.1
Weirton-Steubenville, WV-OH	0.1	1.0	D	19.4	3.8	7.0	3.4	17.4	13.5	32 595	267	4 111	57 860	-0.8
Wenatchee, WA	9.1	0.1	5.8	6.1	5.0	8.0	3.6	15.5	22.9	23 385	206	2 087	52 469	1.9
Wheeling, WV-OH	-0.1	D	D	9.3	D	8.0	5.8	14.8	13.4	35 920	246	4 581	69 059	-0.7
Wichita, KS	1.8	4.1	5.5	24.1	D	6.0	4.5	11.6	12.9	111 300	174	12 730	270 066	1.2
Wichita Falls, TX	0.4	16.7	3.9	9.4	4.7	6.7	D	D	23.8	28 805	190	4 305	65 319	0.8
Williamsport, PA	0.4	6.8	6.0	16.5	5.1	6.6	4.5	13.8	18.6	26 940	231	3 407	52 598	0.2
Wilmington, NC	0.7	D	6.9	9.0	D	9.0	10.1	11.6	19.6	53 490	199	5 513	132 756	3.6
Winchester, VA-WV	-0.1	D	D	14.1	D	9.3	5.4	D	18.4	25 705	194	2 286	58 090	2.1
Winston-Salem, NC	0.7	0.0	4.5	12.4	D	7.0	D	15.0	11.0	135 935	209	13 653	290 881	1.3
Worcester, MA-CT	0.1	D	D	13.7	9.5	6.3	6.6	16.2	17.9	167 960	181	24 471	378 253	0.6
Yakima, WA	14.5	0.1	4.4	8.2	3.1	6.9	3.2	14.1	19.0	42 050	170	7 521	86 374	1.1
York-Hanover, PA	0.4	0.3	8.0	19.6	7.8	6.5	4.1	13.3	14.6	90 015	205	8 673	180 653	1.1
Youngstown-Warren-Boardman, OH-PA	0.3	0.9	5.6	17.5	D	8.1	6.9	15.8	15.3	139 330	251	19 232	258 427	-0.5
Yuba City, CA	8.9	0.6	4.2	4.1	3.8	6.8	3.5	11.9	35.8	28 710	170	8 118	62 111	1.0
Yuma, AZ	7.0	0.1	4.0	3.0	5.5	7.3	3.5	11.4	34.6	32 905	163	4 230	89 918	2.4

1. Per 1,000 resident population estimated as of July 1, 2011 of the year shown.

Area name	Housing units, 2013								Civilian labor force, 2014				Civilian employment[6], 2013		
	Occupied units										Unemployment			Percent	
		Owner-occupied				Renter-occupied									
				Median owner cost as a percent of income											
	Total	Percent	Median value[1]	With a mortgage	Without a mortgage[2]	Median rent[3]	Median rent as a percent of income	Substandard units[4] (percent)	Total	Percent change, 2013–2014	Total	Rate[5]	Total employed	Management, professional, and related occupations	Construction, production, and related occupations
	89	90	91	92	93	94	95	96	97	98	99	100	101	102	103
The Villages, FL	49 672	87.0	218 800	21.5	10.4	844	28.8	NA	28 306	2.9	2 186	7.7	20 719	33.5	16.7
Toledo, OH	242 975	62.0	110 900	21.3	12.2	651	31.4	1.2	300 336	-0.9	18 098	6.0	275 656	32.0	24.8
Topeka, KS	92 747	66.5	117 500	19.1	12.5	696	29.6	NA	122 481	0.7	5 834	4.8	107 357	36.4	21.0
Trenton, NJ	131 623	64.0	275 200	24.9	16.4	1 096	30.9	3.1	194 539	0.4	11 126	5.7	179 313	42.5	15.7
Tucson, AZ	391 975	60.5	155 300	23.5	10.3	798	31.6	4.0	461 806	0.7	28 485	6.2	421 925	35.4	17.7
Tulsa, OK	369 747	65.0	128 100	20.2	10.6	740	27.6	3.1	463 145	-0.9	20 733	4.5	446 593	33.9	23.7
Tuscaloosa, AL	81 401	64.3	139 200	20.7	11.0	722	30.0	NA	110 482	1.3	6 984	6.3	99 280	34.5	27.1
Tyler, TX	79 043	66.4	127 700	21.8	11.0	843	29.6	NA	102 952	0.9	5 330	5.2	97 364	33.0	26.2
Urban Honolulu, HI	308 800	53.2	573 800	26.8	10.0	1 535	33.3	9.4	463 568	2.7	18 890	4.1	444 852	36.2	17.9
Utica-Rome, NY	116 113	65.4	109 000	21.0	13.7	669	29.7	NA	132 720	-3.0	8 283	6.2	131 957	34.1	23.4
Valdosta, GA	51 631	53.3	117 100	23.4	11.5	701	33.9	NA	63 257	-0.2	4 605	7.3	57 102	25.1	21.1
Vallejo-Fairfield, CA	142 577	59.1	259 800	25.1	10.0	1 257	35.2	NA	203 706	-0.3	15 186	7.5	183 698	33.8	22.2
Victoria, TX	35 115	68.4	117 200	20.7	10.0	810	29.0	NA	50 149	1.2	2 075	4.1	44 171	26.5	30.1
Vineland-Bridgeton, NJ	50 066	63.0	158 800	25.7	16.7	961	42.3	NA	67 165	-2.9	6 629	9.9	58 343	24.7	28.0
Virginia Beach-Norfolk-Newport News, VA-NC	625 540	61.1	229 700	24.7	11.8	1 052	32.0	2.2	844 219	0.0	47 712	5.7	778 465	36.8	19.9
Visalia-Porterville, CA	133 409	53.1	160 400	26.4	11.5	811	34.3	9.5	198 631	-1.1	26 272	13.2	165 958	24.4	36.9
Waco, TX	93 195	55.6	109 000	21.7	11.3	725	31.7	NA	119 389	0.0	6 104	5.1	117 578	31.7	22.4
Walla Walla, WA	23 390	60.6	171 100	22.7	11.5	659	31.4	NA	30 061	-0.4	1 980	6.6	25 760	32.3	23.3
Warner Robins, GA	66 537	63.0	124 300	19.4	10.0	805	31.9	NA	81 845	-2.0	5 996	7.3	76 836	34.0	24.9
Washington-Arlington-Alexandria, DC-VA-MD-WV	2 133 062	62.7	373 500	22.6	10.0	1 481	29.3	3.0	3 262 248	0.1	163 634	5.0	3 140 416	50.5	12.3
Silver Spring-Frederick-Rockville, MD Div 43524	453 274	67.6	404 100	22.4	10.0	1 504	30.0	2.6	667 764	-0.4	30 206	4.5	671 931	53.2	11.2
Washington-Arlington-Alexandria, DC-VA-MD-WV Div 47894	1 679 788	61.4	364 500	22.6	10.0	1 474	29.1	3.1	2 594 484	0.3	133 428	5.1	2 468 485	49.8	12.7
Waterloo-Cedar Falls, IA	66 602	69.7	131 400	19.2	10.2	685	31.1	NA	93 429	1.2	4 536	4.9	84 885	31.2	25.6
Watertown-Fort Drum, NY	42 466	54.3	143 800	20.1	13.8	943	26.8	NA	46 699	-3.0	3 569	7.6	44 171	32.1	20.6
Wausau, WI	54 422	72.3	141 900	21.7	12.5	678	29.2	NA	73 096	1.1	3 762	5.1	70 400	31.6	27.9
Weirton-Steubenville, WV-OH	50 523	70.8	84 800	17.6	11.9	573	27.6	NA	53 320	-2.1	4 174	7.8	52 385	28.4	27.2
Wenatchee, WA	41 368	63.3	222 900	23.4	11.3	784	27.9	NA	60 238	1.9	3 991	6.6	52 681	24.4	33.3
Wheeling, WV-OH	60 546	73.5	93 500	18.8	10.6	559	28.1	NA	67 245	-0.7	4 353	6.5	64 656	28.4	27.7
Wichita, KS	242 612	65.0	121 700	20.6	10.4	705	28.0	2.4	311 768	0.5	16 313	5.2	299 582	35.9	24.9
Wichita Falls, TX	57 532	64.0	88 700	21.1	12.3	724	27.9	NA	66 417	-0.8	3 204	4.8	65 107	35.6	21.9
Williamsport, PA	44 961	72.2	133 600	22.1	14.7	717	29.0	NA	61 303	-0.9	3 721	6.1	52 348	29.3	26.6
Wilmington, NC	106 814	59.5	190 700	23.9	12.4	888	31.6	NA	134 497	0.2	8 065	6.0	129 032	37.6	18.0
Winchester, VA-WV	49 477	64.5	196 000	23.0	10.0	890	27.8	NA	68 746	0.8	3 378	4.9	62 292	33.0	26.3
Winston-Salem, NC	255 660	67.9	144 000	21.1	11.1	689	30.4	3.3	311 949	-1.2	18 379	5.9	286 748	35.0	24.5
Worcester, MA-CT	345 518	64.7	241 400	24.2	14.1	914	30.2	1.9	488 362	1.4	30 939	6.3	457 998	40.4	19.0
Yakima, WA	79 742	61.7	159 800	24.4	11.9	772	33.5	8.9	119 318	0.6	10 648	8.9	101 428	24.3	37.0
York-Hanover, PA	164 937	73.1	165 300	22.8	13.8	834	29.6	NA	229 957	-1.0	12 268	5.3	218 782	32.0	27.4
Youngstown-Warren-Boardman, OH-PA	229 074	69.3	97 400	21.2	11.9	620	30.3	1.4	253 909	-1.6	16 789	6.6	237 271	29.8	26.4
Yuba City, CA	56 806	58.1	174 200	26.3	11.0	942	36.0	NA	72 620	-0.8	8 811	12.1	61 363	30.5	24.5
Yuma, AZ	69 744	69.7	108 800	22.7	11.4	818	29.3	7.0	92 838	-2.5	21 640	23.3	72 884	24.8	29.9

1. Specified owner-occupied units. 2. A value of 10.0 represents 10 percent or less. 3. Specified renter-occupied units. 4. Overcrowded or lacking complete plumbing facilities.
5. Percent of civilian labor force. 6. Persons 16 years old and over.

Table C. Metropolitan Areas — **Nonfarm Employment and Agriculture**

Area name	Private nonfarm establishments, employment and payroll, 2013									Agriculture, 2012			
		Employment						Annual payroll		Farms			
											Percent with:		
	Number of establish-ments	Total	Health care and social assistance	Manufac-turing	Retail trade	Finance and insurance	Professional, scientific, and technical services	Total (mil dol)	Average per employee (dollars)	Number	Fewer than 50 acres	500 acres or more	Farm operators whose principal occu-pation is farming (percent)
	104	105	106	107	108	109	110	111	112	113	114	115	116
The Villages, FL	1 319	17 523	3 438	1 006	2 917	591	583	645	36 781	1 367	70.1	4.0	34.7
Toledo, OH	13 260	261 565	46 124	35 880	31 334	7 039	11 301	10 290	39 340	2 246	43.9	13.4	45.9
Topeka, KS	5 217	84 054	20 200	6 558	10 702	5 596	4 537	3 379	40 198	4 507	27.3	16.6	39.9
Trenton, NJ	9 701	185 388	30 948	7 074	19 466	14 509	22 025	11 360	61 277	272	71.0	2.9	46.0
Tucson, AZ	19 962	305 393	56 519	24 549	45 124	11 666	16 943	11 618	38 043	855	79.4	9.4	49.0
Tulsa, OK	24 113	389 893	59 454	52 693	46 163	17 281	22 217	17 708	45 417	9 103	39.4	11.1	37.6
Tuscaloosa, AL	4 470	77 590	12 910	14 032	10 765	1 913	2 348	2 937	37 858	1 386	33.4	11.8	44.3
Tyler, TX	5 668	89 369	21 520	7 284	12 210	4 973	4 261	3 505	39 222	2 961	54.8	3.0	45.3
Urban Honolulu, HI	21 173	347 954	50 413	9 555	47 539	16 589	18 269	14 466	41 573	999	90.6	2.1	66.3
Utica-Rome, NY	5 984	98 408	21 490	12 250	13 779	7 020	3 697	3 527	35 844	1 753	23.8	8.1	57.8
Valdosta, GA	2 954	41 536	8 048	3 422	6 780	1 159	1 251	1 229	29 585	901	43.4	13.7	47.7
Vallejo-Fairfield, CA	6 677	103 470	22 106	9 571	18 725	4 338	3 634	4 697	45 398	860	62.9	11.7	53.7
Victoria, TX	2 488	35 207	6 547	2 237	5 984	1 162	1 025	1 505	42 746	2 708	35.7	14.3	42.8
Vineland-Bridgeton, NJ	2 898	43 640	9 748	7 456	7 237	1 231	984	1 616	37 040	583	61.7	5.3	55.2
Virginia Beach-Norfolk-Newport News, VA-NC	36 903	593 365	88 382	56 126	87 062	27 184	48 691	23 491	39 589	1 546	57.2	11.5	48.3
Visalia-Porterville, CA	6 142	88 795	15 293	12 212	15 419	3 095	2 576	3 131	35 263	4 931	61.2	8.4	58.3
Waco, TX	5 245	98 522	17 632	14 576	11 898	4 654	2 628	3 374	34 248	4 541	47.3	7.9	42.8
Walla Walla, WA	1 478	19 617	4 010	D	2 375	768	471	678	34 562	1 251	45.6	27.3	46.9
Warner Robins, GA	2 947	43 860	7 784	5 825	7 991	1 248	4 229	1 438	32 782	592	50.2	13.3	42.4
Washington-Arlington-Alexandria, DC-VA-MD-WV	145 526	2 514 470	292 714	48 828	267 783	99 340	524 387	153 362	60 992	9 020	55.6	5.5	44.4
Silver Spring-Frederick-Rockville, MD Div 43524	X	X	X	X	X	X	X	X	X	1 848	54.5	5.7	46.0
Washington-Arlington-Alexandria, DC-VA-MD-WV Div 47894	X	X	X	X	X	X	X	X	X	7 172	55.9	5.4	43.9
Waterloo-Cedar Falls, IA	4 118	81 407	16 717	16 688	10 719	3 961	4 065	3 013	37 017	2 643	33.6	21.2	53.4
Watertown-Fort Drum, NY	2 453	30 639	6 565	2 277	6 834	750	1 000	1 029	33 599	876	20.5	17.2	57.4
Wausau, WI	3 281	60 858	9 475	14 885	9 861	3 879	1 960	2 279	37 456	2 266	23.2	7.5	55.0
Weirton-Steubenville, WV-OH	2 265	36 229	7 944	6 052	4 945	836	859	1 197	33 030	685	29.5	4.2	39.0
Wenatchee, WA	3 107	32 519	6 328	2 139	5 724	1 056	1 111	1 217	37 425	1 739	58.0	14.1	55.8
Wheeling, WV-OH	3 415	56 472	13 145	2 674	8 534	2 192	2 615	1 930	34 178	1 579	25.4	3.5	42.2
Wichita, KS	14 548	254 430	40 711	51 060	32 513	10 792	10 365	10 698	42 047	5 345	27.9	25.2	45.7
Wichita Falls, TX	3 471	47 514	11 281	4 829	7 865	1 959	1 332	1 614	33 979	2 031	24.1	25.8	42.8
Williamsport, PA	2 850	46 696	8 560	7 834	7 502	1 432	1 630	1 684	36 053	1 207	32.4	3.7	44.0
Wilmington, NC	7 756	92 253	17 064	5 413	15 567	2 737	5 966	3 666	39 736	385	54.3	7.0	50.1
Winchester, VA-WV	3 084	48 294	9 298	6 549	8 101	1 854	1 792	1 866	38 641	1 479	42.7	7.4	40.4
Winston-Salem, NC	12 963	222 329	41 302	28 127	28 365	11 378	8 222	9 121	41 027	4 242	53.3	2.0	47.5
Worcester, MA-CT	19 727	310 917	68 109	38 333	43 645	14 921	17 252	13 972	44 938	2 252	63.7	1.6	45.8
Yakima, WA	4 606	62 573	13 210	7 960	9 526	1 567	1 882	2 270	36 275	3 143	73.9	5.5	51.9
York-Hanover, PA	8 578	159 069	22 976	31 332	22 130	3 675	5 342	6 263	39 374	2 171	56.6	4.4	48.9
Youngstown-Warren-Boardman, OH-PA	12 513	199 892	42 213	31 481	29 572	5 451	5 915	7 156	35 798	2 651	38.1	4.1	46.4
Yuba City, CA	2 516	29 092	5 663	2 065	5 819	855	1 309	1 048	36 010	2 153	55.4	12.7	56.9
Yuma, AZ	2 851	39 710	6 064	3 025	7 822	1 230	1 304	1 221	30 739	562	64.4	14.4	54.8

Area name	Agriculture, 2012 (cont.) — Land in farms: Acreage (1,000)	Land in farms: Percent change, 2007–2012	Land in farms — Acres: Average size of farm	Acres: Total irrigated (1,000)	Acres: Total cropland (1,000)	Value of land and buildings (dollars): Average per farm	Value of land and buildings (dollars): Average per acre	Value of machinery and equipment, average per farm (dollars)	Value of products sold: Total (mil dol)	Value of products sold: Average per farm (dollars)	Value of products sold — Percent from: Crops	Percent from: Livestock and poultry products	Percent of farms with sales of: $10,000 or more	Percent of farms with sales of: $100,000 or more	Government payments: Total ($1,000)	Government payments: Percent of farms
	117	118	119	120	121	122	123	124	125	126	127	128	129	130	131	132
The Villages, FL	183	14.7	134	3.1	20.7	717 143	5 350	45 931	42.1	30 773	58.9	41.1	19.3	5.3	164	2.9
Toledo, OH	526	0.8	234	2.9	491.5	1 339 764	5 717	160 193	469.6	209 092	80.6	19.4	61.5	34.6	10 688	72.1
Topeka, KS	1 606	-4.5	356	30.4	746.2	645 650	1 812	88 309	290.6	64 475	54.1	45.9	44.2	12.8	13 372	51.5
Trenton, NJ	20	-9.1	73	1.1	12.4	1 474 301	20 310	59 195	19.7	72 533	83.1	16.9	43.0	11.0	310	14.3
Tucson, AZ	D	D	D	32.4	36.7	1 651 870	D	64 622	97.3	113 786	76.8	23.2	31.2	10.3	1 085	5.3
Tulsa, OK	2 757	-8.9	303	12.2	525.7	487 549	1 610	48 596	320.1	35 165	20.5	79.5	31.0	5.0	10 260	18.1
Tuscaloosa, AL	349	-15.0	252	D	79.8	579 205	2 299	70 007	203.4	146 773	D	D	35.1	12.3	1 801	22.9
Tyler, TX	302	0.0	102	2.5	77.1	386 589	3 786	43 300	76.8	25 934	77.5	22.5	18.6	2.6	189	1.8
Urban Honolulu, HI	69	14.5	69	10.8	22.2	1 396 597	20 171	56 908	161.5	161 650	90.0	10.0	54.6	12.7	283	6.1
Utica-Rome, NY	345	4.0	197	0.3	195.1	387 175	1 965	102 671	183.6	104 752	32.6	67.4	52.0	21.4	3 569	31.7
Valdosta, GA	268	-17.4	298	37.0	127.0	994 700	3 343	118 135	172.8	191 747	73.9	26.1	35.2	14.1	4 463	47.7
Vallejo-Fairfield, CA	407	13.6	473	130.9	169.6	2 631 010	5 558	146 770	307.4	357 463	79.0	21.0	53.1	22.7	1 911	15.7
Victoria, TX	933	-3.2	344	4.1	113.1	748 694	2 174	54 903	67.0	24 741	47.2	52.8	28.4	4.1	3 202	14.4
Vineland-Bridgeton, NJ	65	-7.1	111	19.3	49.7	889 362	8 035	130 184	170.4	292 216	97.2	2.8	50.9	22.1	520	14.9
Virginia Beach-Norfolk-Newport News, VA-NC	348	-3.4	225	5.6	D	954 757	4 240	128 940	D	D	D	D	39.2	17.0	7 172	37.0
Visalia-Porterville, CA	1 239	6.0	251	557.4	677.5	1 893 271	7 535	144 666	4 017.1	814 657	41.6	58.4	70.2	36.6	12 174	13.5
Waco, TX	936	-4.0	206	8.6	418.3	479 933	2 328	62 287	318.4	70 112	40.8	59.2	26.8	6.6	8 368	20.6
Walla Walla, WA	943	-5.3	753	95.2	750.3	1 331 341	1 767	176 191	495.1	395 756	D	D	41.5	23.7	17 645	52.1
Warner Robins, GA	145	1.2	245	33.2	89.1	763 294	3 110	139 532	129.7	219 166	72.7	27.3	30.7	14.9	2 575	34.1
Washington-Arlington-Alexandria, DC-VA-MD-WV	1 192	-2.8	132	D	D	1 082 771	8 191	74 808	479.4	53 150	D	D	31.3	7.8	9 447	15.6
Silver Spring-Frederick-Rockville, MD Div 43524	245	-9.2	133	2.4	172.7	1 095 421	8 262	106 409	198.8	107 576	58.6	41.4	37.6	15.7	3 896	28.8
Washington-Arlington-Alexandria, DC-VA-MD-WV Div 47894	947	-1.0	132	D	D	1 079 511	8 173	66 666	280.6	39 126	D	D	29.7	5.7	5 551	12.2
Waterloo-Cedar Falls, IA	886	5.4	335	0.8	817.5	2 653 546	7 913	260 785	921.7	348 721	69.2	30.8	66.5	46.6	23 091	81.8
Watertown-Fort Drum, NY	291	10.9	332	0.3	173.5	544 535	1 640	133 429	183.6	209 551	24.7	75.3	51.6	24.1	2 974	31.5
Wausau, WI	479	-2.4	211	6.2	320.1	616 429	2 916	136 874	391.1	172 605	24.8	75.2	61.9	32.7	6 615	48.5
Weirton-Steubenville, WV-OH	92	-2.7	134	D	33.3	354 781	2 643	67 448	9.9	14 394	44.8	55.2	27.9	3.1	D	15.5
Wenatchee, WA	890	-8.9	512	41.1	577.0	858 859	1 678	96 734	405.5	233 192	98.3	1.7	60.6	34.7	13 598	27.3
Wheeling, WV-OH	229	-10.3	145	D	69.6	403 551	2 779	56 892	26.9	17 067	24.1	75.9	25.3	2.5	798	10.6
Wichita, KS	2 856	-1.3	534	147.5	1 911.4	1 018 921	1 907	140 007	864.4	161 729	63.3	36.7	54.3	23.6	25 429	62.2
Wichita Falls, TX	1 541	2.7	759	4.8	332.0	968 725	1 277	78 397	194.6	95 797	23.0	77.0	45.3	14.2	6 647	35.8
Williamsport, PA	158	-1.2	131	0.6	79.7	559 934	4 265	73 065	72.2	59 819	53.8	46.2	41.6	13.2	2 246	39.1
Wilmington, NC	59	-11.1	152	1.8	31.7	719 145	4 720	86 745	178.9	464 691	21.8	78.2	41.3	24.4	1 612	31.2
Winchester, VA-WV	243	6.7	164	0.3	74.5	747 885	4 556	53 968	73.5	49 694	44.1	55.9	30.0	5.5	625	11.7
Winston-Salem, NC	379	-5.4	89	2.1	174.8	500 191	5 592	54 495	252.2	59 444	37.1	62.9	26.1	6.9	3 083	19.6
Worcester, MA-CT	160	-3.9	71	1.8	52.3	619 520	8 716	50 890	101.7	45 155	56.7	43.3	27.4	7.0	1 949	9.0
Yakima, WA	1 780	8.0	566	224.4	306.9	1 021 212	1 803	118 874	1 645.5	523 548	65.0	35.0	45.7	22.4	5 804	11.5
York-Hanover, PA	262	-10.4	121	0.8	195.0	910 957	7 547	87 005	234.1	107 814	62.9	37.1	45.3	16.5	2 746	22.2
Youngstown-Warren-Boardman, OH-PA	352	-2.5	133	1.2	229.7	523 104	3 940	102 994	214.6	80 935	58.1	41.9	46.8	15.9	3 340	30.7
Yuba City, CA	563	8.1	261	326.8	365.6	1 658 114	6 343	168 077	701.6	325 882	93.5	6.5	66.0	35.1	14 667	22.8
Yuma, AZ	215	2.0	382	181.4	200.1	2 758 098	7 220	372 064	985.0	1 752 685	D	D	61.7	28.5	1 815	17.1

Area name	Water use, 2010		Wholesale trade,[1] 2007				Retail trade, 2007				Real estate and rental and leasing, 2007			
	Total water withdrawn (mil gal/day)	Gallons withdrawn per person per day	Number of establish-ments	Number of employees	Sales (mil dol)	Annual payroll (mil dol)	Number of establish-ments	Number of employees	Sales (mil dol)	Annual payroll (mil dol)	Number of establish-ments	Number of employees	Receipts (mil dol)	Annual payroll (mil dol)
	133	134	135	136	137	138	139	140	141	142	143	144	145	146
The Villages, FL	32.0	342	42	D	D	D	178	2 696	672.1	52.1	90	153	19.7	3.7
Toledo, OH	701.5	1 150	735	10 622	6 687.5	461.2	2 251	33 638	7 758.4	710.2	596	3 605	1 104.5	126.7
Topeka, KS	47.9	205	207	2 212	992.2	88.3	926	11 716	2 569.8	237.6	269	D	D	D
Trenton, NJ	477.6	1 303	359	9 737	8 421.0	816.7	1 412	20 683	5 089.1	505.0	357	D	D	D
Tucson, AZ	305.4	312	744	8 132	3 056.8	324.6	2 982	51 830	11 928.5	1 208.9	1 449	8 133	1 211.7	251.8
Tulsa, OK	387.7	414	1 249	D	D	D	3 152	45 953	11 623.3	996.4	1 169	D	D	D
Tuscaloosa, AL	65.7	285	160	D	D	D	896	11 436	2 645.8	239.7	209	D	D	D
Tyler, TX	30.8	147	242	2 216	922.1	97.5	855	12 347	3 110.1	287.8	229	1 447	204.5	41.3
Urban Honolulu, HI	799.2	838	1 244	14 049	7 377.1	565.1	3 058	46 613	11 518.3	1 144.1	1 294	9 867	2 660.2	399.9
Utica-Rome, NY	48.2	161	213	2 675	1 126.2	102.8	1 091	14 414	3 254.1	309.8	250	1 014	172.0	22.4
Valdosta, GA	41.3	296	145	D	D	D	632	D	D	D	144	D	D	D
Vallejo-Fairfield, CA	452.8	1 095	249	D	D	D	1 167	19 117	4 828.0	482.7	404	1 913	347.9	58.5
Victoria, TX	456.6	4 858	107	D	D	D	427	6 100	1 471.6	131.4	128	D	D	D
Vineland-Bridgeton, NJ	58.9	375	160	D	D	D	564	7 602	1 952.7	185.4	125	540	88.3	16.2
Virginia Beach-Norfolk-Newport News, VA-NC	1 494.4	891	1 308	D	D	D	6 293	95 026	20 980.0	2 052.3	2 235	D	D	D
Visalia-Porterville, CA	2 600.3	5 881	337	D	D	D	1 140	16 005	3 900.9	367.4	294	1 260	189.1	32.3
Waco, TX	84.6	335	256	3 276	4 659.3	125.6	916	12 033	3 014.2	254.7	223	1 440	287.0	54.8
Walla Walla, WA	168.5	2 681	75	603	288.3	20.2	235	2 687	563.0	62.0	69	220	27.1	5.4
Warner Robins, GA	62.6	348	76	D	D	D	617	7 936	1 926.2	173.5	170	593	86.5	14.9
Washington-Arlington-Alexandria, DC-VA-MD-WV	6 238.9	1 107	3 738	D	D	D	17 159	273 951	70 454.8	7 128.5	7 201	D	D	D
Silver Spring-Frederick-Rockville, MD Div 43524	778.5	646	943	11 649	8 678.7	700.5	3 742	60 739	16 322.1	1 654.7	1 732	16 740	4 566.7	922.2
Washington-Arlington-Alexandria, DC-VA-MD-WV Div 47894	5 460.4	1 232	2 795	D	D	D	13 417	213 212	54 132.7	5 473.8	5 469	D	D	D
Waterloo-Cedar Falls, IA	43.2	257	189	2 866	1 654.0	111.1	683	10 226	2 307.2	208.9	177	D	D	D
Watertown-Fort Drum, NY	24.2	208	71	D	D	D	506	7 188	1 867.7	163.4	122	543	98.9	14.3
Wausau, WI	126.8	946	184	2 965	1 146.4	122.1	505	10 000	2 139.1	196.5	99	473	75.4	11.9
Weirton-Steubenville, WV-OH	1 825.2	14 665	76	D	D	D	443	5 421	1 118.1	105.3	82	351	42.1	7.4
Wenatchee, WA	103.7	935	137	2 494	915.7	85.0	505	5 984	1 435.6	145.4	146	628	86.4	15.6
Wheeling, WV-OH	623.9	4 217	131	D	D	D	640	8 930	1 811.1	171.2	126	681	70.0	14.6
Wichita, KS	185.4	294	717	8 996	12 929.5	409.2	2 191	31 209	7 591.0	674.2	716	3 676	534.0	98.7
Wichita Falls, TX	83.4	551	176	1 474	596.8	55.2	589	7 894	1 832.9	164.9	189	D	D	D
Williamsport, PA	16.0	138	116	1 933	701.9	62.0	519	6 968	1 458.4	130.8	94	444	80.7	11.4
Wilmington, NC	55.0	216	329	3 902	1 994.0	167.8	1 265	16 421	4 157.3	381.4	489	2 140	347.7	69.5
Winchester, VA-WV	18.9	147	122	D	D	D	557	8 428	2 231.6	192.4	143	D	D	D
Winston-Salem, NC	1 381.9	2 157	650	D	D	D	2 317	29 708	7 340.0	659.3	608	D	D	D
Worcester, MA-CT	316.8	346	902	13 008	7 460.4	663.7	3 114	45 376	11 237.8	1 093.0	746	D	D	D
Yakima, WA	608.4	2 501	251	D	D	D	780	9 900	2 425.6	239.5	255	977	151.6	23.7
York-Hanover, PA	2 641.2	6 072	371	6 539	3 822.9	299.4	1 344	21 762	4 942.7	455.6	285	2 158	294.5	75.5
Youngstown-Warren-Boardman, OH-PA	214.8	380	548	D	D	D	2 352	31 815	6 785.7	625.9	447	2 936	398.2	78.5
Yuba City, CA	983.7	5 894	93	D	D	D	430	6 136	1 489.0	147.0	136	723	80.9	15.5
Yuma, AZ	1 161.4	5 933	133	D	D	D	540	8 905	2 004.6	180.2	190	734	119.2	17.5

1. Merchant wholesalers, except manufacturers' sales branches and offices.

Area name	Professional, scientific, and technical services,[1] 2007				Manufacturing, 2007				Accommodation and food services, 2007			
	Number of establish-ments	Number of employees	Sales (mil dol)	Annual payroll (mil dol)	Number of establish-ments	Number of employees	Sales (mil dol)	Annual payroll (mil dol)	Number of establish-ments	Number of employees	Sales (mil dol)	Annual payroll (mil dol)
	147	148	149	150	151	152	153	154	155	156	157	158
The Villages, FL	99	D	D	D	29	889	367.9	33.5	95	2 367	79.9	22.5
Toledo, OH	1 198	D	D	D	875	47 005	27 822.3	2 430.8	1 394	26 527	954.4	278.2
Topeka, KS	534	D	D	D	D	D	D	D	442	D	D	D
Trenton, NJ	1 646	30 900	5 790.4	2 345.3	293	9 352	D	420.1	834	12 103	695.8	197.7
Tucson, AZ	2 692	16 250	1 886.4	777.8	760	30 567	10 365.2	1 877.0	1 758	42 002	2 135.2	601.8
Tulsa, OK	2 815	18 151	2 527.6	937.0	D	D	D	D	1 809	34 896	1 421.1	399.4
Tuscaloosa, AL	382	D	D	D	187	14 666	D	D	405	8 469	336.8	89.9
Tyler, TX	548	D	D	D	224	10 737	5 423.5	474.5	339	7 563	337.3	93.6
Urban Honolulu, HI	2 433	18 508	2 686.9	1 056.8	684	10 996	8 201.9	398.9	2 347	57 064	4 123.8	1 126.5
Utica-Rome, NY	462	D	D	D	329	13 713	3 798.2	547.0	662	7 136	314.7	89.3
Valdosta, GA	230	D	D	D	D	D	D	D	272	D	D	D
Vallejo-Fairfield, CA	598	D	D	D	296	10 357	8 377.3	578.9	731	12 523	573.3	153.4
Victoria, TX	167	D	D	D	D	D	D	D	182	3 263	134.7	36.5
Vineland-Bridgeton, NJ	231	D	D	D	175	9 037	2 591.4	341.6	262	3 263	155.1	40.0
Virginia Beach-Norfolk-Newport News, VA-NC	3 962	D	D	D	D	D	D	D	3 635	D	D	D
Visalia-Porterville, CA	446	D	D	D	278	12 443	5 016.0	458.3	558	8 282	379.4	102.8
Waco, TX	360	D	D	D	D	D	D	D	488	D	D	D
Walla Walla, WA	113	D	D	D	D	D	D	D	133	1 790	78.5	23.4
Warner Robins, GA	325	D	D	D	D	D	D	D	318	6 439	248.5	65.1
Washington-Arlington-Alexandria, DC-VA-MD-WV	28 078	D	D	D	D	D	D	D	11 222	221 027	14 595.4	4 037.1
Silver Spring-Frederick-Rockville, MD Div 43524	6 399	D	D	D	640	17 874	6 267.8	982.8	2 145	37 600	2 229.3	614.1
Washington-Arlington-Alexandria, DC-VA-MD-WV Div 47894	21 679	D	D	D	D	D	D	D	9 077	183 427	12 366.1	3 423.0
Waterloo-Cedar Falls, IA	295	D	D	D	215	15 137	6 723.8	652.4	355	6 885	215.6	65.2
Watertown-Fort Drum, NY	123	899	103.8	37.4	73	2 624	839.9	108.5	320	3 748	172.0	49.7
Wausau, WI	235	D	D	D	250	18 678	D	765.6	321	4 813	173.7	48.8
Weirton-Steubenville, WV-OH	161	D	D	D	83	8 433	D	428.3	308	3 446	131.6	34.2
Wenatchee, WA	226	D	D	D	D	D	D	D	327	4 080	201.6	60.4
Wheeling, WV-OH	271	D	D	D	D	D	D	D	316	5 713	215.8	61.3
Wichita, KS	1 300	D	D	D	D	D	D	D	1 279	24 450	955.0	276.3
Wichita Falls, TX	252	D	D	D	D	D	D	D	306	6 775	258.8	81.0
Williamsport, PA	183	1 367	102.9	39.6	183	10 240	3 358.2	408.7	277	3 721	147.9	40.0
Wilmington, NC	906	D	D	D	237	7 159	D	361.8	685	13 434	561.0	161.6
Winchester, VA-WV	274	D	D	D	D	D	D	D	267	4 790	208.7	59.1
Winston-Salem, NC	1 330	D	D	D	761	36 800	D	1 509.1	1 101	20 335	869.9	244.4
Worcester, MA-CT	2 011	D	D	D	1 286	45 469	12 482.6	2 208.6	1 927	26 997	1 287.0	369.5
Yakima, WA	320	D	D	D	255	8 696	2 686.1	304.4	427	5 287	245.6	70.8
York-Hanover, PA	726	5 437	620.4	240.9	600	38 016	11 957.4	1 669.8	736	13 112	527.9	146.4
Youngstown-Warren-Boardman, OH-PA	937	D	D	D	840	37 611	14 779.7	1 879.9	1 249	20 511	752.7	213.9
Yuba City, CA	199	D	D	D	116	2 470	664.9	94.6	238	3 553	153.1	42.1
Yuma, AZ	208	D	D	D	82	2 856	891.6	88.0	316	5 942	271.9	69.6

1. Establishments subject to federal tax.

Table C. Metropolitan Areas — **Health Care and Social Assistance, Other Services, Nonemployer Business and Residential Construction**

Area name	Health care and social assistance,[1] 2007				Other services,[1] 2007				Nonemployer business, 2013		Value of residential construction authorized by building permits, 2014	
	Number of establishments	Number of employees	Receipts (mil dol)	Annual payroll (mil dol)	Number of establishments	Number of employees	Receipts (mil dol)	Annual payroll (mil dol)	Number	Receipts (mil dol)	New construction ($1,000)	Number of housing units
	159	160	161	162	163	164	165	166	167	168	169	170
The Villages, FL	83	1 335	136.0	51.0	59	245	17.9	4.5	5 521	218.7	733 957	2 570
Toledo, OH	1 617	47 110	4 155.6	1 785.1	1 088	7 387	657.7	173.6	34 425	1 443.7	157 091	1 075
Topeka, KS	593	18 560	1 465.1	651.6	489	D	D	D	13 175	569.4	56 509	315
Trenton, NJ	1 147	26 724	2 609.3	1 180.7	860	6 084	828.6	214.7	23 100	1 240.6	60 726	368
Tucson, AZ	2 672	51 151	5 459.8	2 073.5	1 494	12 045	1 020.6	289.4	60 686	2 442.0	697 362	3 250
Tulsa, OK	2 622	D	D	D	1 502	8 672	926.6	228.3	69 046	3 285.2	741 914	4 533
Tuscaloosa, AL	439	D	D	D	266	D	D	D	12 942	548.6	202 775	1 386
Tyler, TX	636	19 044	2 002.7	784.8	334	2 556	192.7	71.9	17 017	857.9	112 257	389
Urban Honolulu, HI	2 473	47 727	5 055.4	2 047.9	2 083	15 228	1 462.7	388.7	60 220	2 873.7	376 974	1 578
Utica-Rome, NY	727	22 040	1 606.9	753.9	513	3 534	223.8	66.3	15 012	590.4	76 244	236
Valdosta, GA	359	D	D	D	190	D	D	D	8 153	396.7	60 323	410
Vallejo-Fairfield, CA	861	18 135	2 136.5	895.9	541	3 240	324.0	92.5	21 658	868.0	167 513	646
Victoria, TX	334	6 395	593.2	236.1	174	1 225	114.0	33.4	6 551	309.7	85 492	835
Vineland-Bridgeton, NJ	399	8 351	820.8	333.3	273	1 439	103.0	31.1	6 032	267.8	24 627	212
Virginia Beach-Norfolk-Newport News, VA-NC	3 392	D	D	D	3 008	D	D	D	93 106	3 745.5	849 773	5 715
Visalia-Porterville, CA	806	13 734	1 295.3	493.8	384	2 298	208.1	62.9	19 668	900.7	200 612	1 092
Waco, TX	549	15 994	1 250.4	516.6	412	2 663	247.5	65.0	14 753	653.9	199 237	1 471
Walla Walla, WA	176	4 122	399.2	165.6	93	510	41.7	9.9	3 297	131.3	40 554	214
Warner Robins, GA	320	D	D	D	207	D	D	D	11 470	345.0	134 817	780
Washington-Arlington-Alexandria, DC-VA-MD-WV	14 249	D	D	D	12 574	133 335	30 150.3	6 675.2	488 647	22 003.9	3 898 607	24 804
Silver Spring-Frederick-Rockville, MD Div 43524	3 907	64 067	7 490.2	2 943.7	2 339	19 995	3 645.4	832.2	NA	NA	X	X
Washington-Arlington-Alexandria, DC-VA-MD-WV Div 47894	10 342	D	D	D	10 235	113 340	26 504.9	5 843.0	NA	NA	X	X
Waterloo-Cedar Falls, IA	423	12 317	963.0	414.8	294	D	D	D	9 616	430.7	85 764	407
Watertown-Fort Drum, NY	234	5 780	429.1	201.9	195	898	78.3	18.3	5 087	192.2	52 239	519
Wausau, WI	345	9 438	926.4	379.0	253	1 591	139.1	36.2	7 687	362.1	54 273	383
Weirton-Steubenville, WV-OH	306	7 421	547.3	226.0	207	1 016	61.2	16.7	5 296	177.2	5 793	41
Wenatchee, WA	261	D	D	D	204	806	69.8	16.6	6 101	257.1	90 408	460
Wheeling, WV-OH	485	11 961	937.5	371.9	310	1 787	124.7	34.2	6 892	263.3	6 919	61
Wichita, KS	1 632	D	D	D	1 060	6 796	605.6	181.0	39 004	1 719.1	260 991	1 514
Wichita Falls, TX	399	D	D	D	284	1 544	144.7	35.7	9 371	458.4	24 135	157
Williamsport, PA	285	8 065	675.8	272.5	244	1 521	150.1	33.0	6 204	268.6	36 448	214
Wilmington, NC	761	19 175	1 892.3	795.0	523	3 130	251.8	70.7	22 299	1 024.8	365 673	2 208
Winchester, VA-WV	352	7 680	775.7	341.1	202	1 181	104.3	31.5	8 512	377.5	102 286	525
Winston-Salem, NC	1 170	36 988	3 377.3	1 334.1	939	5 531	503.5	126.0	43 473	1 620.1	301 055	2 085
Worcester, MA-CT	2 219	62 602	6 052.5	2 428.7	1 525	8 427	834.7	241.7	56 393	2 655.5	268 077	1 384
Yakima, WA	537	11 636	1 119.8	441.2	297	1 767	132.9	33.9	9 131	411.2	89 790	442
York-Hanover, PA	925	20 265	1 931.3	790.7	746	5 098	582.7	115.6	24 995	1 139.8	138 969	816
Youngstown-Warren-Boardman, OH-PA	1 768	38 812	3 155.1	1 254.3	1 030	6 263	474.0	130.4	34 243	1 402.2	62 913	313
Yuba City, CA	347	5 793	722.3	228.5	186	991	95.8	26.5	8 334	427.0	51 926	280
Yuma, AZ	329	6 463	654.6	235.7	208	1 217	85.2	26.0	8 290	317.1	91 377	594

1. Establishments subject to federal tax.

Table C. Metropolitan Areas — **Government Employment and Payroll and Local Government Finances**

Area name	Government employment and payroll, 2012									Local government finances, 2012				
			March payroll (percent of total)							General revenue				
												Taxes		
													Per capita[1] (dollars)	
	Full-time equivalent employees	March Payroll (dollars)	Adminis-tration, judicial, and legal	Police and corrections	Fire protection	Highways and transporta-tion	Health and welfare	Natural resources and utilities	Education and libraries	Total (mil dol)	Inter-govern-mental (mil dol)	Total (mil dol)	Total	Property
	171	172	173	174	175	176	177	178	179	180	181	182	183	184
The Villages, FL	1 509	4 669 736	4.3	3.1	1.1	6.4	1.4	4.3	72.3	251.5	43.7	105.9	1 042	834
Toledo, OH	20 923	85 663 164	9.0	10.9	7.2	4.7	9.5	5.3	52.3	2 794.2	1 171.7	1 080.1	1 774	1 098
Topeka, KS	10 897	35 463 350	4.3	10.3	3.4	3.2	2.7	5.2	70.1	954.7	354.8	369.2	1 574	1 171
Trenton, NJ	15 352	84 285 619	4.4	12.4	3.3	2.0	4.4	4.9	64.8	2 164.5	711.0	1 168.1	3 172	3 117
Tucson, AZ	31 634	115 785 276	10.5	14.5	6.6	3.5	2.2	7.1	52.9	3 257.1	1 214.5	1 427.3	1 438	1 057
Tulsa, OK	33 451	106 348 173	5.8	9.5	5.7	4.2	2.6	6.1	63.2	2 858.0	992.1	1 256.0	1 319	714
Tuscaloosa, AL	11 519	40 376 521	3.7	7.3	3.3	3.6	45.3	3.8	32.1	1 108.1	293.7	229.4	983	397
Tyler, TX	8 764	29 028 100	7.6	10.8	2.8	1.5	6.8	3.6	65.8	648.3	207.0	325.4	1 515	1 170
Urban Honolulu, HI	9 304	47 881 176	14.1	35.4	14.0	2.6	6.8	20.8	0.0	2 232.4	331.8	1 316.4	1 348	833
Utica-Rome, NY	13 622	60 609 793	5.4	11.3	5.5	6.7	5.6	4.7	59.5	1 597.5	779.4	603.1	2 024	1 388
Valdosta, GA	7 094	22 829 566	3.5	7.5	1.9	1.7	36.8	2.6	44.7	654.5	164.9	169.0	1 171	661
Vallejo-Fairfield, CA	14 386	72 410 858	7.6	13.9	3.4	2.8	9.9	7.1	53.4	1 896.3	937.5	594.6	1 413	1 051
Victoria, TX	5 691	19 191 140	4.0	10.2	2.9	1.9	29.7	3.0	47.2	483.0	112.9	173.9	1 800	1 367
Vineland-Bridgeton, NJ	7 697	36 180 326	5.2	9.1	0.8	1.2	4.3	5.3	72.5	886.9	544.0	234.1	1 483	1 435
Virginia Beach-Norfolk-Newport News, VA-NC	78 042	285 080 100	5.2	9.8	4.7	2.6	8.9	7.9	57.4	7 361.3	2 849.8	2 945.6	1 733	1 190
Visalia-Porterville, CA	21 502	97 324 423	4.7	7.2	1.7	1.1	30.4	3.5	50.1	3 132.9	1 499.7	450.9	998	665
Waco, TX	11 156	37 341 296	5.7	11.3	3.0	2.0	4.2	8.5	64.1	1 218.5	462.8	380.3	1 484	1 179
Walla Walla, WA	2 119	9 087 256	8.5	10.7	5.3	6.5	9.7	4.4	51.5	269.2	118.5	82.8	1 307	907
Warner Robins, GA	6 945	22 535 113	5.6	9.7	2.9	2.1	4.2	3.2	70.2	591.5	229.4	253.3	1 365	800
Washington-Arlington-Alexandria, DC-VA-MD-WV	238 082	1 225 240 040	6.3	10.4	4.1	8.1	7.2	5.9	54.7	35 371.1	10 257.7	19 074.9	3 255	1 833
Silver Spring-Frederick-Rockville, MD Div 43524	49 143	284 578 074	3.5	7.4	4.0	2.8	6.0	9.5	65.7	6 273.9	1 440.7	3 712.4	2 984	1 415
Washington-Arlington-Alexandria, DC-VA-MD-WV Div 47894	188 939	940 661 966	7.1	11.3	4.2	9.7	7.5	4.8	51.4	29 097.2	8 817.0	15 362.6	3 328	1 946
Waterloo-Cedar Falls, IA	5 986	22 105 854	5.2	9.3	3.5	4.9	8.6	9.6	56.3	779.9	309.2	283.0	1 677	1 331
Watertown-Fort Drum, NY	5 239	20 682 670	6.0	6.1	2.2	6.7	6.7	3.0	66.9	631.5	312.9	217.3	1 807	1 154
Wausau, WI	5 721	22 517 091	4.6	6.0	1.9	5.6	19.3	2.6	59.4	701.3	346.1	232.0	1 722	1 622
Weirton-Steubenville, WV-OH	4 496	13 800 652	7.0	10.6	2.3	5.5	8.0	7.2	56.9	422.2	201.3	126.9	1 036	755
Wenatchee, WA	4 724	22 972 485	4.8	6.6	2.1	5.8	6.9	31.1	41.1	513.2	239.9	153.9	1 361	918
Wheeling, WV-OH	5 774	18 658 082	6.6	9.0	3.0	7.2	6.7	13.1	53.0	499.7	202.4	181.6	1 241	837
Wichita, KS	24 964	87 029 872	6.0	10.7	4.3	3.5	5.1	4.4	64.0	2 420.1	936.4	884.7	1 391	1 088
Wichita Falls, TX	6 724	21 253 583	6.4	13.3	6.1	3.0	9.1	5.3	54.1	453.8	154.7	207.0	1 372	1 062
Williamsport, PA	3 615	14 906 594	7.7	7.9	1.8	4.3	2.7	6.0	68.7	451.3	198.0	155.7	1 329	953
Wilmington, NC	13 583	50 754 541	2.9	7.0	2.4	1.1	45.2	4.5	33.4	1 618.1	350.1	385.0	1 461	1 059
Winchester, VA-WV	5 411	16 715 382	6.8	13.2	4.1	1.2	2.9	3.6	66.6	418.3	170.3	190.4	1 454	1 027
Winston-Salem, NC	1 023 990	75 606 649	4.5	8.8	4.0	1.2	8.6	5.0	65.1	1 918.0	964.0	681.2	1 052	828
Worcester, MA-CT	32 279	147 826 569	3.6	7.7	4.7	3.3	1.4	4.3	74.0	3 495.3	1 632.4	1 503.7	1 628	1 589
Yakima, WA	8 019	34 900 911	7.0	10.7	3.2	2.8	3.3	5.9	66.0	970.4	601.4	232.4	941	607
York-Hanover, PA	12 293	50 416 660	6.7	12.2	1.5	2.7	6.3	3.6	64.5	1 771.5	572.5	787.5	1 799	1 467
Youngstown-Warren-Boardman, OH-PA	20 254	71 750 350	7.4	10.2	3.8	3.6	7.7	6.8	59.4	1 994.8	1 016.8	698.5	1 251	866
Yuba City, CA	6 669	32 864 622	7.3	8.3	2.0	2.2	10.3	3.3	64.0	941.7	532.4	189.6	1 129	918
Yuma, AZ	7 924	25 609 990	12.0	12.1	3.1	2.2	2.4	7.3	59.9	638.9	314.0	221.6	1 108	716

1. Based on the resident population estimated as of July 1 of the year shown.

Area name	Local government finances, 2012 (cont.)									Government employment, 2013			Presidential election,[2] 2012		
	Direct general expenditure							Debt outstanding					Percent of vote cast:		
			Percent of total for:												
	Total (mil dol)	Per capita[1] (dollars)	Educa-tion	Health and hospitals	Police protec-tion	Public welfare	High-ways	Total (mil dol)	Per capita[1] (dollars)	Federal civilian	Federal military	State and local	Demo-cratic	Republi-can	All other
	185	186	187	188	189	190	191	192	193	194	195	196	197	198	199
The Villages, FL	263.4	2 592	27.3	1.6	6.0	0.5	7.8	594.1	5 846	1 598	189	2 982	32.3	67.2	0.5
Toledo, OH	2 631.6	4 323	42.5	7.5	6.3	6.1	4.2	2 796.0	4 593	2 260	1 642	42 070	60.4	37.7	1.9
Topeka, KS	921.3	3 928	54.3	2.2	6.2	0.2	4.0	1 441.3	6 144	3 656	1 241	23 710	44.9	52.7	2.4
Trenton, NJ	2 145.5	5 825	52.3	0.9	5.3	4.3	1.4	1 928.9	5 237	2 371	741	39 979	68.0	30.8	1.2
Tucson, AZ	3 531.8	3 559	37.0	3.1	9.1	2.7	5.3	5 788.9	5 833	12 621	8 564	67 100	52.6	45.7	1.6
Tulsa, OK	2 829.0	2 972	48.0	4.0	5.9	0.6	8.2	3 865.4	4 061	4 551	3 741	49 205	33.9	66.1	0.0
Tuscaloosa, AL	1 116.2	4 783	30.5	41.4	4.7	0.0	5.1	682.1	2 923	1 662	1 054	23 520	43.2	55.7	1.1
Tyler, TX	645.1	3 003	55.0	5.1	5.6	0.2	3.4	1 145.0	5 330	726	481	12 677	27.0	72.0	1.0
Urban Honolulu, HI	1 596.7	1 635	0.0	1.5	15.2	0.0	7.8	5 300.0	5 428	31 103	54 254	67 083	68.9	29.8	1.3
Utica-Rome, NY	1 653.0	5 546	53.3	2.7	2.8	10.6	6.2	1 633.5	5 480	2 373	515	28 290	46.4	51.8	1.8
Valdosta, GA	724.2	5 017	28.8	47.7	4.1	0.7	2.5	413.2	2 862	1 178	5 000	11 945	43.8	55.3	0.8
Vallejo-Fairfield, CA	1 873.8	4 454	35.1	6.1	9.3	7.8	4.2	1 624.0	3 860	3 799	7 412	19 731	63.5	34.2	2.3
Victoria, TX	470.7	4 872	36.4	29.6	5.8	0.0	7.0	443.6	4 591	214	210	6 677	30.7	68.0	1.2
Vineland-Bridgeton, NJ	880.4	5 580	60.1	2.7	3.8	3.4	2.5	354.4	2 246	638	299	13 173	61.6	37.4	1.0
Virginia Beach-Norfolk-Newport News, VA-NC	7 765.7	4 568	42.7	6.6	4.8	4.0	3.4	9 372.3	5 513	50 780	86 504	108 455	54.8	43.7	1.4
Visalia-Porterville, CA	3 186.6	7 050	39.0	24.4	3.2	8.0	4.7	1 380.8	3 055	1 123	719	29 814	41.3	56.3	2.4
Waco, TX	1 187.0	4 631	42.3	2.5	5.0	0.6	1.8	11 603.4	45 270	3 208	620	15 345	34.7	64.1	1.2
Walla Walla, WA	257.4	4 061	43.0	9.4	5.8	0.0	7.2	267.1	4 213	1 253	166	4 740	38.0	59.3	2.7
Warner Robins, GA	571.7	3 082	54.7	6.0	6.4	0.1	5.0	263.3	1 419	15 693	4 205	11 956	41.1	57.9	1.0
Washington-Arlington-Alexandria, DC-VA-MD-WV	35 473.9	6 053	40.6	3.4	5.3	10.4	3.3	44 210.4	7 544	389 596	66 531	314 560	67.3	31.1	1.6
Silver Spring-Frederick-Rockville, MD Div 43524	6 498.3	5 222	51.5	1.7	5.2	3.2	3.5	7 084.9	5 694	50 763	10 033	54 045	66.1	31.8	2.2
Washington-Arlington-Alexandria, DC-VA-MD-WV Div 47894	28 975.7	6 277	38.1	3.8	5.3	12.0	3.3	37 125.5	8 043	338 833	56 498	260 515	67.6	30.9	1.5
Waterloo-Cedar Falls, IA	855.9	5 072	49.6	11.0	4.2	0.3	7.5	561.2	3 325	612	692	14 128	56.3	42.1	1.6
Watertown-Fort Drum, NY	631.0	5 247	49.6	3.4	2.6	9.2	6.9	554.7	4 612	3 279	17 670	8 295	47.9	50.8	1.4
Wausau, WI	710.6	5 274	41.9	10.2	3.9	18.8	7.9	440.9	3 273	467	376	7 441	46.3	52.4	1.3
Weirton-Steubenville, WV-OH	426.7	3 482	52.1	4.9	6.0	2.5	5.9	341.9	2 790	256	435	5 463	44.1	53.8	2.1
Wenatchee, WA	488.0	4 317	47.1	12.8	4.5	0.0	5.8	1 944.4	17 202	851	312	7 736	38.7	59.0	2.3
Wheeling, WV-OH	488.4	3 335	43.9	3.2	5.0	2.6	4.4	552.7	3 775	612	535	9 411	40.8	57.2	2.1
Wichita, KS	2 506.2	3 940	49.5	4.3	5.3	0.1	5.5	6 729.7	10 580	5 301	5 564	35 982	37.4	60.2	2.4
Wichita Falls, TX	440.1	2 918	47.9	5.2	7.0	0.7	4.4	688.7	4 566	1 996	5 440	9 817	23.5	75.0	1.5
Williamsport, PA	560.5	4 783	43.8	0.0	2.2	3.1	4.4	997.6	8 514	365	299	8 913	32.7	65.9	1.4
Wilmington, NC	1 610.9	6 115	23.7	45.2	4.9	2.9	1.0	1 660.3	6 303	986	885	20 985	45.5	53.1	1.4
Winchester, VA-WV	404.5	3 090	60.9	0.7	5.4	3.3	1.5	564.7	4 314	1 881	473	7 303	36.7	61.0	2.3
Winston-Salem, NC	2 021.7	3 121	49.9	5.3	7.8	4.7	1.7	1 785.1	2 756	1 948	1 634	30 414	42.3	56.4	1.2
Worcester, MA-CT	3 721.4	4 029	62.3	0.4	3.9	0.2	3.5	2 671.4	2 892	3 350	2 265	57 484	53.9	44.1	2.0
Yakima, WA	1 052.2	4 260	60.9	3.2	4.2	0.8	4.9	606.3	2 455	1 230	799	15 760	43.2	54.9	2.0
York-Hanover, PA	1 790.5	4 089	47.4	3.5	3.3	9.2	2.6	2 454.1	5 605	4 225	1 330	16 445	38.7	59.9	1.4
Youngstown-Warren-Boardman, OH-PA	2 023.9	3 626	53.2	5.1	6.2	4.2	4.0	1 224.6	2 194	1 973	1 458	27 739	59.5	39.0	1.5
Yuba City, CA	962.8	5 733	49.2	5.2	4.2	8.2	2.8	640.8	3 816	1 476	4 953	9 797	39.2	58.0	2.8
Yuma, AZ	616.3	3 081	47.8	2.1	6.0	2.5	4.6	668.5	3 342	3 705	4 178	11 066	43.0	55.7	1.3

1. Based on the resident population estimated as of July 1 of the year shown. 2.

PART D.

Cities of 25,000 or More

(For explanation of symbols, see page viii)

Page

City Highlights and Rankings

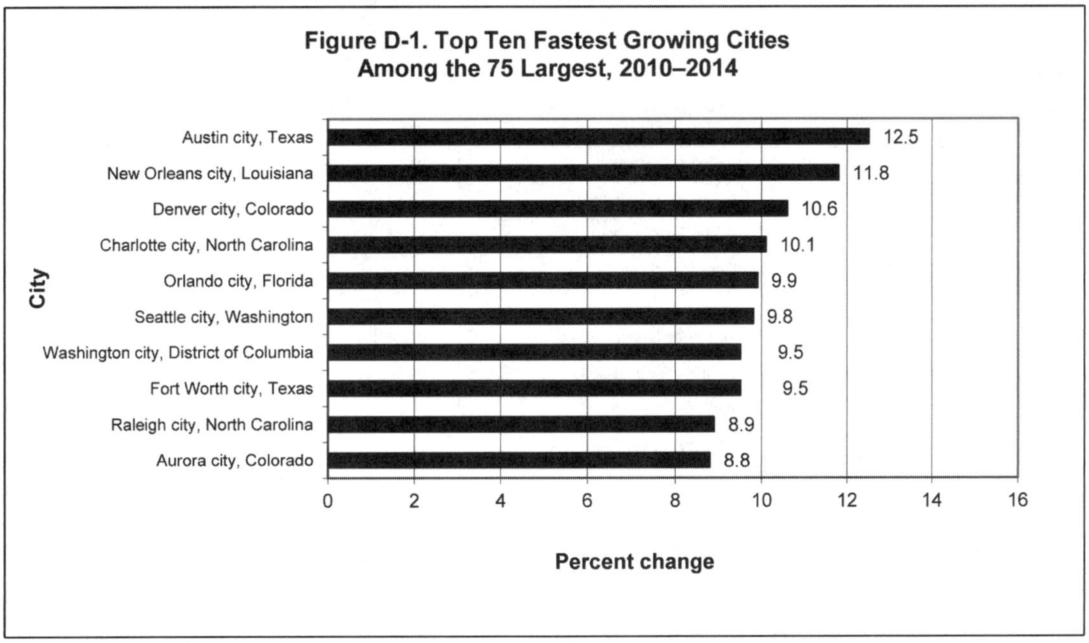

In 2014, 10 cities had more than 1 million residents, led by New York City with over 8.4 million people, Los Angeles with 3.9 million people, and Chicago with 2.7 million people. California had 14 cities among the nation's 75 most populous, as well as four among the top 15 (Los Angeles, San Diego, San Jose, and San Francisco). Texas had nine cities in the top 75, and also had four among the top 15 (Houston, San Antonio, Dallas, and Austin).

Among the largest cities, 41 had growth rates equaling 5 percent or higher from 2010 to 2014, and four had growth rates exceeding 10 percent. Many of these cities were in the south. Austin, TX had the highest growth rate at 12.5 percent. Texas had two cities in the top ten (Austin and Fort Worth), as did North Carolina (Charlotte, Raleigh) and Colorado (Denver, Aurora). Fifty-two of the largest cities equaled or exceeded the U.S. growth rate of 3.3 percent.

Among the 75 largest cities, five lost population between 2010 and 2014. Detroit, Cleveland, and Toledo each lost more than 1 percent of their populations. Though New Orleans lost 29.1 percent of its population between 2000 and 2010, it actually grew by nearly two-thirds between 2006 and 2010, after losing more than half of its population after Hurricane Katrina in 2005. It was the second fastest growing city from 2010 to 2014, but its 2014 population is still more than 70,000 short of its pre-Katrina total.

Among all cities of 25,000 or more, 88 cities had unemployment rates of 10 percent or more, significantly lower than four years earlier, when 555 cities had an unemployment rate of 10 percent or more. Twelve of the twenty-five cities with the highest unemployment rates were located in California, six were in Michigan, two each were in Arizona, Illinois, and New Jersey, and one was in Misssissippi. Among the largest cities, Detroit, MI had the highest unemployment rate at 16.7 percent followed by Fresno, CA at 12.6 percent, while Lincoln and Omaha, NE had the lowest unemployment rates at 2.9 percent and 3.6 percent respectively. Among all cities, 172 had unemployment rates of 4 percent or lower. Five of the ten cities with the lowest unemployment rates were in North Dakota.

While the 2010 census provides updated counts of the population and basic demographic characteristics, updated information on social and economic characteristics is now obtained through the ongoing American Community Survey (ACS). For states, counties, and metropolitan areas, the official intercensal estimates are provided by age, sex, race, and Hispanic origin through the Population Estimates Program. Estimates of these demographic characteristics are not included for cities through the Population Estimates Program, but are available through the ACS. This book includes ACS 3-year estimates for 2011–2013, including data on education, income, housing characteristics, and more.

Between the 2000 census and the late-decade information from the ACS, housing values increased dramatically in many cities, while the median household income increased less markedly. Among the largest cities, four out of the five cities topped the rankings for median household income in 2000 and 2011–2013: Plano, San Jose, Anchorage, and San Francisco. Washington, DC ranked in the top five in 2011–2013, replacing Henderson, NV. San Francisco retains its spot at the top with an estimated median housing value of $740,700, up from $396,400 in 2000. Cleveland and Detroit had the lowest median housing values among the large cities.

In the 2011–2013 time period, there were 19 of the largest cities where 10 percent or more of the residents had moved there during the previous year. This may result from population growth: Denver, CO had one of the highest growth rates in recent years as well as one of the highest proportion of people who had moved there in the past year. Other cities have large shifts because of student or military population groups: Pittsburgh, PA lost 8.6 percent of its population from 2000 to 2010, but 11.5 percent of its population were new residents in the 2011–2013 time period, reflecting the 17.4 percent of residents who were between the ages of 18 and 24, well above the 10.0 percent national average.

75 Largest Cities by 2014 Population

Selected Rankings

Population, 2014			Land area, 2010				Population density, 2014			
Population rank	City	Population [col 2]	Population rank	Land area rank	City	Land area (square kilometers) [col 1]	Population rank	Density rank	City	Density (per square kilometer) [col 4]
1	New York city, New York	8 491 079	64	1	Anchorage municipality, Alaska	4 415.1	1	1	New York city, New York	10 833
2	Los Angeles city, California	3 928 864	12	2	Jacksonville city, Florida	1 934.7	13	2	San Francisco city, California	7 022
3	Chicago city, Illinois	2 722 389	27	3	Oklahoma City city, Oklahoma	1 570.6	74	3	Jersey City city, New Jersey	6 845
4	Houston city, Texas	2 239 558	4	4	Houston city, Texas	1 552.9	24	4	Boston city, Massachusetts	5 247
5	Philadelphia city, Pennsylvania	1 560 297	6	5	Phoenix city, Arizona	1 338.3	57	5	Santa Ana city, California	4 744
6	Phoenix city, Arizona	1 537 058	25	6	Nashville-Davidson metro gov, Tennessee	1 230.6	44	6	Miami city, Florida	4 632
7	San Antonio city, Texas	1 436 697	2	7	Los Angeles city, California	1 213.9	3	7	Chicago city, Illinois	4 617
8	San Diego city, California	1 381 069	7	8	San Antonio city, Texas	1 193.8	5	8	Philadelphia city, Pennsylvania	4 493
9	Dallas city, Texas	1 281 047	14	9	Indianapolis city, Indiana	949.1	69	9	Newark city, New Jersey	4 482
10	San Jose city, California	1 015 785	9	10	Dallas city, Texas	881.9	22	10	Washington city, District of Columbia	4 168
11	Austin city, Texas	912 791	16	11	Fort Worth city, Texas	880.1	36	11	Long Beach city, California	3 635
12	Jacksonville city, Florida	853 382	30	12	Louisville/Jefferson metro gov, Kentucky	842.4	2	12	Los Angeles city, California	3 237
13	San Francisco city, California	852 469	8	13	San Diego city, California	842.2	20	13	Seattle city, Washington	3 074
14	Indianapolis city, Indiana	848 788	23	14	Memphis city, Tennessee	816.0	26	14	Baltimore city, Maryland	2 971
15	Columbus city, Ohio	835 957	37	15	Kansas City city, Missouri	815.7	46	15	Minneapolis city, Minnesota	2 913
16	Fort Worth city, Texas	812 238	1	16	New York city, New York	783.8	45	16	Oakland city, California	2 864
17	Charlotte city, North Carolina	809 958	11	17	Austin city, Texas	771.6	56	17	Anaheim city, California	2 688
18	Detroit city, Michigan	680 250	17	18	Charlotte city, North Carolina	771.0	31	18	Milwaukee city, Wisconsin	2 408
19	El Paso city, Texas	679 036	61	19	Lexington-Fayette urban county, Kentucky	734.7	55	19	Urban Honolulu CDP, Hawaii	2 235
20	Seattle city, Washington	668 342	19	20	El Paso city, Texas	661.1	10	20	San Jose city, California	2 222
21	Denver city, Colorado	663 862	40	21	Virginia Beach city, Virginia	645.0	66	21	St. Paul city, Minnesota	2 211
22	Washington city, District of Columbia	658 893	3	22	Chicago city, Illinois	589.6	62	22	Pittsburgh city, Pennsylvania	2 130
23	Memphis city, Tennessee	656 861	33	23	Tucson city, Arizona	587.2	75	23	Chula Vista city, California	2 031
24	Boston city, Massachusetts	655 884	15	24	Columbus city, Ohio	562.5	60	24	St. Louis city, Missouri	1 980
25	Nashville-Davidson metro gov, Tennessee	644 014	47	25	Tulsa city, Oklahoma	509.6	48	25	Cleveland city, Ohio	1 936
26	Baltimore city, Maryland	622 793	42	26	Colorado Springs city, Colorado	503.9	35	26	Sacramento city, California	1 913
27	Oklahoma City city, Oklahoma	620 602	32	27	Albuquerque city, New Mexico	486.2	63	27	Stockton city, California	1 894
28	Portland city, Oregon	619 360	10	28	San Jose city, California	457.2	18	28	Detroit city, Michigan	1 893
29	Las Vegas city, Nevada	613 599	50	29	New Orleans city, Louisiana	438.8	28	29	Portland city, Oregon	1 792
30	Louisville/Jefferson metro gov, Kentucky	612 780	58	30	Corpus Christi city, Texas	416.0	34	30	Fresno city, California	1 779
31	Milwaukee city, Wisconsin	599 642	49	31	Wichita city, Kansas	412.6	29	31	Las Vegas city, Nevada	1 744
32	Albuquerque city, New Mexico	557 169	54	32	Aurora city, Colorado	400.8	21	32	Denver city, Colorado	1 675
33	Tucson city, Arizona	527 972	21	33	Denver city, Colorado	396.3	8	33	San Diego city, California	1 640
34	Fresno city, California	515 986	43	34	Raleigh city, North Carolina	370.1	51	34	Arlington city, Texas	1 543
35	Sacramento city, California	485 199	52	35	Bakersfield city, California	368.2	59	35	Riverside city, California	1 520
36	Long Beach city, California	473 577	18	36	Detroit city, Michigan	359.4	70	36	Plano city, Texas	1 502
37	Kansas City city, Missouri	470 800	38	37	Mesa city, Arizona	353.4	15	37	Columbus city, Ohio	1 486
38	Mesa city, Arizona	464 704	29	38	Las Vegas city, Nevada	351.8	65	38	Cincinnati city, Ohio	1 477
39	Atlanta city, Georgia	456 002	5	39	Philadelphia city, Pennsylvania	347.3	9	39	Dallas city, Texas	1 453
40	Virginia Beach city, Virginia	450 980	28	40	Portland city, Oregon	345.6	4	40	Houston city, Texas	1 442
41	Omaha city, Nebraska	446 599	39	41	Atlanta city, Georgia	344.9	41	41	Omaha city, Nebraska	1 357
42	Colorado Springs city, Colorado	445 830	41	42	Omaha city, Nebraska	329.2	68	42	Toledo city, Ohio	1 345
43	Raleigh city, North Carolina	439 896	67	43	Greensboro city, North Carolina	327.7	39	43	Atlanta city, Georgia	1 322
44	Miami city, Florida	430 332	53	44	Tampa city, Florida	293.7	38	44	Mesa city, Arizona	1 315
45	Oakland city, California	413 775	34	45	Fresno city, California	290.0	53	45	Tampa city, Florida	1 221
46	Minneapolis city, Minnesota	407 207	71	46	Henderson city, Nevada	279.0	7	46	San Antonio city, Texas	1 204
47	Tulsa city, Oklahoma	399 682	73	47	Orlando city, Florida	265.2	43	47	Raleigh city, North Carolina	1 189
48	Cleveland city, Ohio	389 521	35	48	Sacramento city, California	253.6	11	48	Austin city, Texas	1 183
49	Wichita city, Kansas	388 413	31	49	Milwaukee city, Wisconsin	249.0	72	48	Lincoln city, Nebraska	1 183
50	New Orleans city, Louisiana	384 320	51	50	Arlington city, Texas	248.3	6	50	Phoenix city, Arizona	1 149
51	Arlington city, Texas	383 204	72	51	Lincoln city, Nebraska	230.8	32	51	Albuquerque city, New Mexico	1 146
52	Bakersfield city, California	368 759	20	52	Seattle city, Washington	217.4	17	52	Charlotte city, North Carolina	1 051
53	Tampa city, Florida	358 699	59	53	Riverside city, California	210.2	19	53	El Paso city, Texas	1 027
54	Aurora city, Colorado	353 108	26	54	Baltimore city, Maryland	209.6	52	54	Bakersfield city, California	1 002
55	Urban Honolulu CDP, Hawaii	350 399	68	55	Toledo city, Ohio	209.0	71	55	Henderson city, Nevada	994
56	Anaheim city, California	346 997	65	56	Cincinnati city, Ohio	201.9	73	56	Orlando city, Florida	989
57	Santa Ana city, California	334 909	48	57	Cleveland city, Ohio	201.2	49	57	Wichita city, Kansas	941
58	Corpus Christi city, Texas	320 434	70	58	Plano city, Texas	185.4	16	58	Fort Worth city, Texas	923
59	Riverside city, California	319 504	60	59	St. Louis city, Missouri	160.3	14	59	Indianapolis city, Indiana	907
60	St. Louis city, Missouri	317 419	63	60	Stockton city, California	159.7	33	60	Tucson city, Arizona	899
61	Lexington-Fayette urban county, Kentucky	310 797	22	61	Washington city, District of Columbia	158.1	42	61	Colorado Springs city, Colorado	885
62	Pittsburgh city, Pennsylvania	305 412	55	62	Urban Honolulu CDP, Hawaii	156.8	54	62	Aurora city, Colorado	881
63	Stockton city, California	302 389	45	63	Oakland city, California	144.5	50	63	New Orleans city, Louisiana	876
64	Anchorage municipality, Alaska	301 010	62	64	Pittsburgh city, Pennsylvania	143.4	67	64	Greensboro city, North Carolina	862
65	Cincinnati city, Ohio	298 165	46	65	Minneapolis city, Minnesota	139.8	23	65	Memphis city, Tennessee	805
66	St. Paul city, Minnesota	297 640	66	66	St. Paul city, Minnesota	134.6	47	66	Tulsa city, Oklahoma	784
67	Greensboro city, North Carolina	282 586	36	67	Long Beach city, California	130.3	58	67	Corpus Christi city, Texas	770
68	Toledo city, Ohio	281 031	56	68	Anaheim city, California	129.1	30	68	Louisville/Jefferson metro gov, Kentucky	727
69	Newark city, New Jersey	280 579	75	69	Chula Vista city, California	128.5	40	69	Virginia Beach city, Virginia	699
70	Plano city, Texas	278 480	24	70	Boston city, Massachusetts	125.0	37	70	Kansas City city, Missouri	577
71	Henderson city, Nevada	277 440	13	71	San Francisco city, California	121.4	25	71	Nashville-Davidson metro gov, Tennessee	523
72	Lincoln city, Nebraska	272 996	44	72	Miami city, Florida	92.9	12	72	Jacksonville city, Florida	441
73	Orlando city, Florida	262 372	57	73	Santa Ana city, California	70.6	61	73	Lexington-Fayette urban county, Kentucky	423
74	Jersey City city, New Jersey	262 146	69	74	Newark city, New Jersey	62.6	27	74	Oklahoma City city, Oklahoma	395
75	Chula Vista city, California	260 988	74	75	Jersey City city, New Jersey	38.3	64	75	Anchorage municipality, Alaska	68

75 Largest Cities by 2014 Population

Selected Rankings

Population rank	Percent change rank	Percent population change, 2010–2014: City	Percent change [col 26]
11	1	Austin city, Texas	12.5
50	2	New Orleans city, Louisiana	11.8
21	3	Denver city, Colorado	10.6
17	4	Charlotte city, North Carolina	10.1
73	5	Orlando city, Florida	9.9
20	6	Seattle city, Washington	9.8
16	7	Fort Worth city, Texas	9.5
22	7	Washington city, District of Columbia	9.5
43	9	Raleigh city, North Carolina	8.9
54	10	Aurora city, Colorado	8.8
39	11	Atlanta city, Georgia	8.5
7	12	San Antonio city, Texas	8.2
71	13	Henderson city, Nevada	7.8
44	14	Miami city, Florida	7.7
70	15	Plano city, Texas	7.2
9	16	Dallas city, Texas	7.0
27	16	Oklahoma City city, Oklahoma	7.0
75	16	Chula Vista city, California	7.0
4	19	Houston city, Texas	6.8
42	19	Colorado Springs city, Colorado	6.8
53	19	Tampa city, Florida	6.8
25	22	Nashville-Davidson metro gov, Tennessee	6.7
10	23	San Jose city, California	6.6
46	24	Minneapolis city, Minnesota	6.4
6	25	Phoenix city, Arizona	6.2
24	25	Boston city, Massachusetts	6.2
8	27	San Diego city, California	6.1
28	27	Portland city, Oregon	6.1
52	27	Bakersfield city, California	6.1
15	30	Columbus city, Ohio	6.0
13	31	San Francisco city, California	5.9
45	31	Oakland city, California	5.9
74	31	Jersey City city, New Jersey	5.9
38	34	Mesa city, Arizona	5.6
72	34	Lincoln city, Nebraska	5.6
41	36	Omaha city, Nebraska	5.5
59	37	Riverside city, California	5.1
61	37	Lexington-Fayette urban county, Kentucky	5.1
67	37	Greensboro city, North Carolina	5.1
29	40	Las Vegas city, Nevada	5.0
58	40	Corpus Christi city, Texas	5.0
51	42	Arlington city, Texas	4.9
19	43	El Paso city, Texas	4.6
66	44	St. Paul city, Minnesota	4.4
34	45	Fresno city, California	4.0
35	45	Sacramento city, California	4.0
1	47	New York city, New York	3.9
55	47	Urban Honolulu CDP, Hawaii	3.9
12	49	Jacksonville city, Florida	3.8
63	50	Stockton city, California	3.7
2	51	Los Angeles city, California	3.6
14	52	Indianapolis city, Indiana	3.5
56	53	Anaheim city, California	3.1
57	53	Santa Ana city, California	3.1
64	53	Anchorage municipality, Alaska	3.1
40	56	Virginia Beach city, Virginia	3.0
30	57	Louisville/Jefferson metro gov, Kentucky	2.6
36	58	Long Beach city, California	2.4
37	58	Kansas City city, Missouri	2.4
5	60	Philadelphia city, Pennsylvania	2.2
32	61	Albuquerque city, New Mexico	2.0
47	61	Tulsa city, Oklahoma	2.0
49	63	Wichita city, Kansas	1.6
33	64	Tucson city, Arizona	1.4
69	65	Newark city, New Jersey	1.2
3	66	Chicago city, Illinois	1.0
23	67	Memphis city, Tennessee	0.8
31	67	Milwaukee city, Wisconsin	0.8
65	69	Cincinnati city, Ohio	0.4
26	70	Baltimore city, Maryland	0.3
62	71	Pittsburgh city, Pennsylvania	-0.1
60	72	St. Louis city, Missouri	-0.6
48	73	Cleveland city, Ohio	-1.8
68	74	Toledo city, Ohio	-2.2
18	75	Detroit city, Michigan	-4.7

Population rank	White rank	Percent White, alone or in combination, 2011–2013: City	Percent White [col 5]
72	1	Lincoln city, Nebraska	89.6
58	2	Corpus Christi city, Texas	85.9
38	3	Mesa city, Arizona	85.7
19	4	El Paso city, Texas	85.1
42	5	Colorado Springs city, Colorado	84.3
71	6	Henderson city, Nevada	81.7
28	7	Portland city, Oregon	81.6
49	8	Wichita city, Kansas	79.8
6	9	Phoenix city, Arizona	78.9
41	10	Omaha city, Nebraska	78.6
7	11	San Antonio city, Texas	78.5
61	12	Lexington-Fayette urban county, Kentucky	78.3
21	13	Denver city, Colorado	77.9
11	14	Austin city, Texas	77.6
33	15	Tucson city, Arizona	77.2
44	16	Miami city, Florida	76.3
32	17	Albuquerque city, New Mexico	75.2
20	18	Seattle city, Washington	74.9
64	19	Anchorage municipality, Alaska	73.7
30	20	Louisville/Jefferson metro gov, Kentucky	73.6
27	21	Oklahoma City city, Oklahoma	73.5
75	22	Chula Vista city, California	72.8
47	23	Tulsa city, Oklahoma	72.5
70	24	Plano city, Texas	72.0
40	25	Virginia Beach city, Virginia	71.8
59	26	Riverside city, California	70.6
52	27	Bakersfield city, California	70.4
46	28	Minneapolis city, Minnesota	70.2
56	28	Anaheim city, California	70.2
51	30	Arlington city, Texas	69.3
54	30	Aurora city, Colorado	69.3
62	32	Pittsburgh city, Pennsylvania	69.0
29	33	Las Vegas city, Nevada	68.8
16	34	Fort Worth city, Texas	68.7
68	35	Toledo city, Ohio	68.4
8	36	San Diego city, California	68.1
53	37	Tampa city, Florida	66.1
15	38	Columbus city, Ohio	64.7
14	39	Indianapolis city, Indiana	64.0
66	40	St. Paul city, Minnesota	63.9
12	41	Jacksonville city, Florida	63.2
25	42	Nashville-Davidson metro gov, Tennessee	63.0
37	43	Kansas City city, Missouri	62.6
43	44	Raleigh city, North Carolina	62.1
73	45	Orlando city, Florida	61.5
9	46	Dallas city, Texas	60.2
4	47	Houston city, Texas	59.7
36	48	Long Beach city, California	58.4
24	49	Boston city, Massachusetts	57.1
2	50	Los Angeles city, California	55.2
35	51	Sacramento city, California	55.0
17	52	Charlotte city, North Carolina	54.2
34	53	Fresno city, California	54.1
65	54	Cincinnati city, Ohio	53.5
13	55	San Francisco city, California	53.1
67	56	Greensboro city, North Carolina	50.8
57	57	Santa Ana city, California	50.3
3	58	Chicago city, Illinois	50.2
31	59	Milwaukee city, Wisconsin	50.0
10	60	San Jose city, California	49.0
63	61	Stockton city, California	48.7
60	62	St. Louis city, Missouri	47.6
1	63	New York city, New York	45.8
45	64	Oakland city, California	45.6
5	65	Philadelphia city, Pennsylvania	43.4
48	65	Cleveland city, Ohio	43.4
22	67	Washington city, District of Columbia	42.2
39	68	Atlanta city, Georgia	41.8
74	69	Jersey City city, New Jersey	37.3
50	70	New Orleans city, Louisiana	35.3
26	71	Baltimore city, Maryland	31.7
23	72	Memphis city, Tennessee	31.3
55	73	Urban Honolulu CDP, Hawaii	30.4
69	74	Newark city, New Jersey	27.5
18	75	Detroit city, Michigan	14.0

Population rank	Black rank	Percent Black, alone or in combination, 2011–2013: City	Percent Black [col 6]
18	1	Detroit city, Michigan	82.4
26	2	Baltimore city, Maryland	64.6
23	3	Memphis city, Tennessee	64.1
50	4	New Orleans city, Louisiana	60.5
39	5	Atlanta city, Georgia	53.7
48	5	Cleveland city, Ohio	53.7
69	5	Newark city, New Jersey	53.7
22	8	Washington city, District of Columbia	50.7
60	9	St. Louis city, Missouri	49.6
65	10	Cincinnati city, Ohio	45.1
5	11	Philadelphia city, Pennsylvania	44.6
67	12	Greensboro city, North Carolina	43.3
31	13	Milwaukee city, Wisconsin	41.7
17	14	Charlotte city, North Carolina	36.7
3	15	Chicago city, Illinois	32.7
12	16	Jacksonville city, Florida	32.1
43	17	Raleigh city, North Carolina	30.6
37	18	Kansas City city, Missouri	30.5
15	19	Columbus city, Ohio	30.3
68	20	Toledo city, Ohio	29.7
14	21	Indianapolis city, Indiana	29.5
25	21	Nashville-Davidson metro gov, Tennessee	29.5
45	23	Oakland city, California	28.9
73	24	Orlando city, Florida	28.7
24	25	Boston city, Massachusetts	28.3
53	26	Tampa city, Florida	27.5
62	27	Pittsburgh city, Pennsylvania	26.9
74	28	Jersey City city, New Jersey	26.5
1	29	New York city, New York	26.2
9	30	Dallas city, Texas	25.6
30	31	Louisville/Jefferson metro gov, Kentucky	24.7
4	32	Houston city, Texas	23.8
40	33	Virginia Beach city, Virginia	21.7
46	34	Minneapolis city, Minnesota	20.6
44	35	Miami city, Florida	20.3
51	36	Arlington city, Texas	20.1
16	37	Fort Worth city, Texas	19.9
54	38	Aurora city, Colorado	18.6
66	39	St. Paul city, Minnesota	18.0
47	40	Tulsa city, Oklahoma	17.9
35	41	Sacramento city, California	16.8
27	42	Oklahoma City city, Oklahoma	16.7
61	43	Lexington-Fayette urban county, Kentucky	16.2
36	44	Long Beach city, California	15.7
41	45	Omaha city, Nebraska	14.6
63	46	Stockton city, California	14.1
49	47	Wichita city, Kansas	13.3
29	48	Las Vegas city, Nevada	13.2
21	49	Denver city, Colorado	11.1
2	50	Los Angeles city, California	10.1
52	51	Bakersfield city, California	9.8
34	52	Fresno city, California	9.5
20	53	Seattle city, Washington	9.4
11	54	Austin city, Texas	9.0
64	55	Anchorage municipality, Alaska	8.7
70	56	Plano city, Texas	8.4
42	57	Colorado Springs city, Colorado	8.1
7	58	San Antonio city, Texas	7.9
8	58	San Diego city, California	7.9
6	60	Phoenix city, Arizona	7.8
28	61	Portland city, Oregon	7.4
59	61	Riverside city, California	7.4
71	63	Henderson city, Nevada	7.2
13	64	San Francisco city, California	6.8
33	65	Tucson city, Arizona	6.5
75	66	Chula Vista city, California	5.9
72	67	Lincoln city, Nebraska	5.5
58	68	Corpus Christi city, Texas	5.1
38	69	Mesa city, Arizona	4.9
32	70	Albuquerque city, New Mexico	4.5
19	71	El Paso city, Texas	4.2
10	72	San Jose city, California	3.9
56	73	Anaheim city, California	3.2
55	74	Urban Honolulu CDP, Hawaii	3.1
57	75	Santa Ana city, California	1.4

75 Largest Cities by 2014 Population

Selected Rankings

Percent American Indian, Alaska Native, 2011–2013

Population rank	American Indian, Alaska Native rank	City	Percent American Indian, Alaska Native [col 7]
64	1	Anchorage municipality, Alaska	12.4
47	2	Tulsa city, Oklahoma	9.6
27	3	Oklahoma City city, Oklahoma	7.6
32	4	Albuquerque city, New Mexico	5.7
36	5	Long Beach city, California	3.9
33	6	Tucson city, Arizona	3.6
38	7	Mesa city, Arizona	3.1
46	7	Minneapolis city, Minnesota	3.1
63	7	Stockton city, California	3.1
49	10	Wichita city, Kansas	2.8
6	11	Phoenix city, Arizona	2.7
59	12	Riverside city, California	2.5
66	12	St. Paul city, Minnesota	2.5
35	14	Sacramento city, California	2.4
52	14	Bakersfield city, California	2.4
20	16	Seattle city, Washington	2.3
28	16	Portland city, Oregon	2.3
34	16	Fresno city, California	2.3
54	16	Aurora city, Colorado	2.3
21	20	Denver city, Colorado	2.2
45	21	Oakland city, California	2.1
42	22	Colorado Springs city, Colorado	2
31	23	Milwaukee city, Wisconsin	1.9
8	24	San Diego city, California	1.7
16	24	Fort Worth city, Texas	1.7
41	24	Omaha city, Nebraska	1.7
55	24	Urban Honolulu CDP, Hawaii	1.7
72	28	Lincoln city, Nebraska	1.6
10	29	San Jose city, California	1.5
7	30	San Antonio city, Texas	1.4
17	30	Charlotte city, North Carolina	1.4
29	30	Las Vegas city, Nevada	1.4
37	30	Kansas City city, Missouri	1.4
68	30	Toledo city, Ohio	1.4
2	35	Los Angeles city, California	1.3
11	35	Austin city, Texas	1.3
15	35	Columbus city, Ohio	1.3
40	38	Virginia Beach city, Virginia	1.2
60	38	St. Louis city, Missouri	1.2
62	38	Pittsburgh city, Pennsylvania	1.2
71	38	Henderson city, Nevada	1.2
75	38	Chula Vista city, California	1.2
9	43	Dallas city, Texas	1.1
13	43	San Francisco city, California	1.1
48	43	Cleveland city, Ohio	1.1
58	43	Corpus Christi city, Texas	1.1
18	47	Detroit city, Michigan	1
26	47	Baltimore city, Maryland	1
51	47	Arlington city, Texas	1
56	47	Anaheim city, California	1
67	47	Greensboro city, North Carolina	1
70	47	Plano city, Texas	1
74	47	Jersey City city, New Jersey	1
1	54	New York city, New York	0.9
4	54	Houston city, Texas	0.9
5	54	Philadelphia city, Pennsylvania	0.9
12	54	Jacksonville city, Florida	0.9
19	54	El Paso city, Texas	0.9
22	54	Washington city, District of Columbia	0.9
24	54	Boston city, Massachusetts	0.9
53	54	Tampa city, Florida	0.9
14	62	Indianapolis city, Indiana	0.8
23	62	Memphis city, Tennessee	0.8
30	62	Louisville/Jefferson metro gov, Kentucky	0.8
39	62	Atlanta city, Georgia	0.8
50	62	New Orleans city, Louisiana	0.8
61	62	Lexington-Fayette urban county, Kentucky	0.8
65	62	Cincinnati city, Ohio	0.8
69	62	Newark city, New Jersey	0.8
3	70	Chicago city, Illinois	0.7
25	70	Nashville-Davidson metro gov, Tennessee	0.7
43	70	Raleigh city, North Carolina	0.7
57	70	Santa Ana city, California	0.7
73	74	Orlando city, Florida	0.6
44	75	Miami city, Florida	0.3

Percent Asian and Pacific Islander, 2011–2013

Population rank	Asian and Pacific Islander rank	City	Percent Asian and Pacific Islander [col 8]
55	1	Urban Honolulu CDP, Hawaii	67.4
13	2	San Francisco city, California	36.1
10	3	San Jose city, California	35.4
74	4	Jersey City city, New Jersey	26.2
63	5	Stockton city, California	24.8
35	6	Sacramento city, California	21.5
70	7	Plano city, Texas	19.9
8	8	San Diego city, California	19.1
45	9	Oakland city, California	19.0
66	10	St. Paul city, Minnesota	17.1
75	10	Chula Vista city, California	17.1
20	12	Seattle city, Washington	16.9
56	13	Anaheim city, California	16.8
34	14	Fresno city, California	14.6
1	15	New York city, New York	14.2
36	15	Long Beach city, California	14.2
2	17	Los Angeles city, California	12.9
57	18	Santa Ana city, California	11.2
64	19	Anchorage municipality, Alaska	10.9
71	20	Henderson city, Nevada	10.1
24	21	Boston city, Massachusetts	9.9
28	22	Portland city, Oregon	9.3
29	23	Las Vegas city, Nevada	8.6
59	24	Riverside city, California	8.3
40	25	Virginia Beach city, Virginia	8.0
11	26	Austin city, Texas	7.9
52	26	Bakersfield city, California	7.9
51	28	Arlington city, Texas	7.8
5	29	Philadelphia city, Pennsylvania	7.2
4	30	Houston city, Texas	6.9
46	30	Minneapolis city, Minnesota	6.9
3	32	Chicago city, Illinois	6.6
17	33	Charlotte city, North Carolina	6.0
54	34	Aurora city, Colorado	5.9
49	35	Wichita city, Kansas	5.6
62	35	Pittsburgh city, Pennsylvania	5.6
12	37	Jacksonville city, Florida	5.5
15	38	Columbus city, Ohio	5.1
43	38	Raleigh city, North Carolina	5.1
53	40	Tampa city, Florida	5.0
27	41	Oklahoma City city, Oklahoma	4.8
72	42	Lincoln city, Nebraska	4.7
21	43	Denver city, Colorado	4.6
22	43	Washington city, District of Columbia	4.6
42	45	Colorado Springs city, Colorado	4.5
16	46	Fort Worth city, Texas	4.4
67	46	Greensboro city, North Carolina	4.4
73	46	Orlando city, Florida	4.4
39	49	Atlanta city, Georgia	4.3
6	50	Phoenix city, Arizona	4.1
33	50	Tucson city, Arizona	4.1
61	50	Lexington-Fayette urban county, Kentucky	4.1
31	53	Milwaukee city, Wisconsin	4.0
25	54	Nashville-Davidson metro gov, Tennessee	3.9
32	55	Albuquerque city, New Mexico	3.6
60	55	St. Louis city, Missouri	3.6
41	57	Omaha city, Nebraska	3.4
9	58	Dallas city, Texas	3.3
37	58	Kansas City city, Missouri	3.3
50	58	New Orleans city, Louisiana	3.3
7	61	San Antonio city, Texas	3.1
47	61	Tulsa city, Oklahoma	3.1
26	63	Baltimore city, Maryland	3.0
30	64	Louisville/Jefferson metro gov, Kentucky	2.9
14	65	Indianapolis city, Indiana	2.8
38	66	Mesa city, Arizona	2.5
65	67	Cincinnati city, Ohio	2.4
58	68	Corpus Christi city, Texas	2.3
48	69	Cleveland city, Ohio	2.2
23	70	Memphis city, Tennessee	2.1
19	71	El Paso city, Texas	1.8
69	71	Newark city, New Jersey	1.8
68	73	Toledo city, Ohio	1.7
18	74	Detroit city, Michigan	1.6
44	75	Miami city, Florida	1.1

Percent Hispanic or Latino,[1] 2011–2013

Population rank	Hispanic or Latino rank	City	Percent Hispanic or Latino [col 10]
19	1	El Paso city, Texas	79.7
57	2	Santa Ana city, California	78.6
44	3	Miami city, Florida	70.3
7	4	San Antonio city, Texas	63.0
58	5	Corpus Christi city, Texas	60.7
75	6	Chula Vista city, California	58.5
56	7	Anaheim city, California	52.6
59	8	Riverside city, California	52.2
2	9	Los Angeles city, California	48.6
34	10	Fresno city, California	48.0
32	11	Albuquerque city, New Mexico	46.9
52	11	Bakersfield city, California	46.9
4	13	Houston city, Texas	43.8
33	14	Tucson city, Arizona	42.6
63	15	Stockton city, California	42.1
9	16	Dallas city, Texas	41.8
36	17	Long Beach city, California	41.6
6	18	Phoenix city, Arizona	40.6
69	19	Newark city, New Jersey	34.7
16	20	Fort Worth city, Texas	34.5
11	21	Austin city, Texas	33.9
10	22	San Jose city, California	33.4
29	23	Las Vegas city, Nevada	31.7
21	24	Denver city, Colorado	31.2
8	25	San Diego city, California	29.9
3	26	Chicago city, Illinois	29.1
54	27	Aurora city, Colorado	28.9
1	28	New York city, New York	28.8
51	29	Arlington city, Texas	28.3
73	30	Orlando city, Florida	27.7
35	31	Sacramento city, California	27.5
74	32	Jersey City city, New Jersey	27.3
38	33	Mesa city, Arizona	26.4
45	34	Oakland city, California	25.9
53	35	Tampa city, Florida	22.6
24	36	Boston city, Massachusetts	18.5
27	37	Oklahoma City city, Oklahoma	18.3
31	38	Milwaukee city, Wisconsin	17.6
42	39	Colorado Springs city, Colorado	17.1
49	40	Wichita city, Kansas	15.9
13	41	San Francisco city, California	15.3
47	42	Tulsa city, Oklahoma	14.6
70	43	Plano city, Texas	14.2
71	44	Henderson city, Nevada	14.1
17	45	Charlotte city, North Carolina	13.4
41	46	Omaha city, Nebraska	13.3
5	47	Philadelphia city, Pennsylvania	13.0
43	48	Raleigh city, North Carolina	11.3
48	49	Cleveland city, Ohio	10.5
25	50	Nashville-Davidson metro gov, Tennessee	10.1
46	50	Minneapolis city, Minnesota	10.1
37	52	Kansas City city, Missouri	10.0
22	53	Washington city, District of Columbia	9.9
14	54	Indianapolis city, Indiana	9.7
28	55	Portland city, Oregon	9.6
66	55	St. Paul city, Minnesota	9.6
64	57	Anchorage municipality, Alaska	8.3
12	58	Jacksonville city, Florida	8.2
68	59	Toledo city, Ohio	7.8
18	60	Detroit city, Michigan	7.5
67	61	Greensboro city, North Carolina	7.4
40	62	Virginia Beach city, Virginia	7.2
61	63	Lexington-Fayette urban county, Kentucky	6.9
20	64	Seattle city, Washington	6.8
23	65	Memphis city, Tennessee	6.7
72	65	Lincoln city, Nebraska	6.7
55	67	Urban Honolulu CDP, Hawaii	6.0
15	68	Columbus city, Ohio	5.8
50	69	New Orleans city, Louisiana	5.4
39	70	Atlanta city, Georgia	5.3
30	71	Louisville/Jefferson metro gov, Kentucky	4.8
26	72	Baltimore city, Maryland	4.5
60	73	St. Louis city, Missouri	3.7
65	74	Cincinnati city, Ohio	2.9
62	75	Pittsburgh city, Pennsylvania	2.5

75 Largest Cities by 2014 Population

Selected Rankings

Percent under 18 years old, 2011–2013				Percent 65 years old and over, 2011–2013				Percent high school graduate or less, 2011–2013			
Population rank	Under 18 years old rank	City	Percent under 18 years old [col 12 and 13]	Population rank	65 years old and over rank	City	Percent 65 years old and over [col 19 and 20]	Population rank	Percent high school graduate or less rank	City	Percent high school graduate or less [col 40]
52	1	Bakersfield city, California	30.6	55	1	Urban Honolulu CDP, Hawaii	17.9	57	1	Santa Ana city, California	68.7
63	2	Stockton city, California	29.9	71	2	Henderson city, Nevada	16.4	69	2	Newark city, New Jersey	64.0
34	3	Fresno city, California	29.6	44	3	Miami city, Florida	15.9	44	3	Miami city, Florida	57.9
57	4	Santa Ana city, California	29.3	38	4	Mesa city, Arizona	15.2	48	4	Cleveland city, Ohio	55.6
16	5	Fort Worth city, Texas	29.0	13	5	San Francisco city, California	13.9	18	5	Detroit city, Michigan	54.7
19	6	El Paso city, Texas	28.1	62	5	Pittsburgh city, Pennsylvania	13.9	5	6	Philadelphia city, Pennsylvania	52.7
6	7	Phoenix city, Arizona	27.1	29	7	Las Vegas city, Nevada	13.2	68	7	Toledo city, Ohio	49.6
51	8	Arlington city, Texas	27.0	30	7	Louisville/Jefferson metro gov, Kentucky	13.2	63	8	Stockton city, California	49.3
54	9	Aurora city, Colorado	26.8	32	9	Albuquerque city, New Mexico	12.9	56	9	Anaheim city, California	48.7
31	10	Milwaukee city, Wisconsin	26.7	47	10	Tulsa city, Oklahoma	12.8	31	10	Milwaukee city, Wisconsin	48.6
75	11	Chula Vista city, California	26.6	68	11	Toledo city, Ohio	12.7	26	11	Baltimore city, Maryland	48.4
49	12	Wichita city, Kansas	26.3	1	12	New York city, New York	12.5	34	12	Fresno city, California	48.2
7	13	San Antonio city, Texas	26.2	33	12	Tucson city, Arizona	12.5	9	13	Dallas city, Texas	47.7
56	14	Anaheim city, California	26.1	48	14	Cleveland city, Ohio	12.4	58	14	Corpus Christi city, Texas	46.5
59	14	Riverside city, California	26.1	5	15	Philadelphia city, Pennsylvania	12.3	4	15	Houston city, Texas	46.4
9	16	Dallas city, Texas	25.8	58	15	Corpus Christi city, Texas	12.3	29	16	Las Vegas city, Nevada	46.3
27	17	Oklahoma City city, Oklahoma	25.7	18	17	Detroit city, Michigan	12.2	23	17	Memphis city, Tennessee	46.2
69	18	Newark city, New Jersey	25.6	67	18	Greensboro city, North Carolina	12.0	19	18	El Paso city, Texas	46.1
18	19	Detroit city, Michigan	25.5	26	19	Baltimore city, Maryland	11.9	59	19	Riverside city, California	45.9
58	19	Corpus Christi city, Texas	25.5	49	19	Wichita city, Kansas	11.9	52	20	Bakersfield city, California	45.8
4	21	Houston city, Texas	25.4	12	21	Jacksonville city, Florida	11.7	2	21	Los Angeles city, California	44.8
64	22	Anchorage municipality, Alaska	25.3	41	21	Omaha city, Nebraska	11.7	16	22	Fort Worth city, Texas	44.7
70	22	Plano city, Texas	25.3	37	23	Kansas City city, Missouri	11.6	1	23	New York city, New York	44.5
23	24	Memphis city, Tennessee	25.2	45	23	Oakland city, California	11.6	7	23	San Antonio city, Texas	44.5
66	24	St. Paul city, Minnesota	25.2	19	25	El Paso city, Texas	11.5	14	25	Indianapolis city, Indiana	44.4
17	26	Charlotte city, North Carolina	25.0	35	26	Sacramento city, California	11.4	6	26	Phoenix city, Arizona	43.1
38	27	Mesa city, Arizona	24.9	40	26	Virginia Beach city, Virginia	11.4	30	27	Louisville/Jefferson metro gov, Kentucky	43.0
41	27	Omaha city, Nebraska	24.9	50	26	New Orleans city, Louisiana	11.4	65	28	Cincinnati city, Ohio	42.4
14	29	Indianapolis city, Indiana	24.8	8	29	San Diego city, California	11.3	3	29	Chicago city, Illinois	41.9
29	30	Las Vegas city, Nevada	24.6	20	29	Seattle city, Washington	11.3	12	30	Jacksonville city, Florida	41.5
36	31	Long Beach city, California	24.5	22	29	Washington city, District of Columbia	11.3	27	31	Oklahoma City city, Oklahoma	40.8
42	31	Colorado Springs city, Colorado	24.5	42	29	Colorado Springs city, Colorado	11.3	60	31	St. Louis city, Missouri	40.8
47	31	Tulsa city, Oklahoma	24.5	53	29	Tampa city, Florida	11.3	53	33	Tampa city, Florida	40.1
10	34	San Jose city, California	24.0	72	29	Lincoln city, Nebraska	11.3	33	34	Tucson city, Arizona	39.9
35	34	Sacramento city, California	24.0	27	35	Oklahoma City city, Oklahoma	11.2	75	35	Chula Vista city, California	39.6
37	36	Kansas City city, Missouri	23.6	65	35	Cincinnati city, Ohio	11.2	36	36	Long Beach city, California	39.3
32	37	Albuquerque city, New Mexico	23.5	7	37	San Antonio city, Texas	11.0	49	37	Wichita city, Kansas	39.2
12	38	Jacksonville city, Florida	23.4	28	37	Portland city, Oregon	11.0	54	37	Aurora city, Colorado	39.2
30	38	Louisville/Jefferson metro gov, Kentucky	23.4	60	37	St. Louis city, Missouri	11.0	38	39	Mesa city, Arizona	39.0
40	38	Virginia Beach city, Virginia	23.4	61	37	Lexington-Fayette urban county, Kentucky	11.0	50	39	New Orleans city, Louisiana	39.0
68	41	Toledo city, Ohio	23.3	2	41	Los Angeles city, California	10.9	51	41	Arlington city, Texas	38.5
15	42	Columbus city, Ohio	23.1	10	41	San Jose city, California	10.9	47	42	Tulsa city, Oklahoma	38.4
48	42	Cleveland city, Ohio	23.1	14	43	Indianapolis city, Indiana	10.8	15	43	Columbus city, Ohio	38.2
43	44	Raleigh city, North Carolina	22.9	3	44	Chicago city, Illinois	10.7	74	43	Jersey City city, New Jersey	38.2
72	45	Lincoln city, Nebraska	22.7	63	44	Stockton city, California	10.7	62	45	Pittsburgh city, Pennsylvania	38.1
3	46	Chicago city, Illinois	22.4	21	46	Denver city, Colorado	10.6	35	46	Sacramento city, California	38.0
5	47	Philadelphia city, Pennsylvania	22.3	23	46	Memphis city, Tennessee	10.6	37	46	Kansas City city, Missouri	38.0
2	48	Los Angeles city, California	22.2	75	46	Chula Vista city, California	10.6	25	48	Nashville-Davidson metro gov, Tennessee	37.9
67	48	Greensboro city, North Carolina	22.2	24	49	Boston city, Massachusetts	10.5	24	49	Boston city, Massachusetts	37.4
73	48	Orlando city, Florida	22.2	25	50	Nashville-Davidson metro gov, Tennessee	10.4	55	50	Urban Honolulu CDP, Hawaii	36.7
33	51	Tucson city, Arizona	22.1	70	51	Plano city, Texas	10.3	73	51	Orlando city, Florida	36.2
65	51	Cincinnati city, Ohio	22.1	56	52	Anaheim city, California	10.1	45	52	Oakland city, California	36.0
71	51	Henderson city, Nevada	22.1	39	53	Atlanta city, Georgia	10.0	10	53	San Jose city, California	35.8
11	54	Austin city, Texas	21.7	36	54	Long Beach city, California	9.9	41	54	Omaha city, Nebraska	35.6
25	54	Nashville-Davidson metro gov, Tennessee	21.7	74	55	Jersey City city, New Jersey	9.8	66	55	St. Paul city, Minnesota	35.0
53	56	Tampa city, Florida	21.6	34	56	Fresno city, California	9.7	67	56	Greensboro city, North Carolina	34.4
8	57	San Diego city, California	21.5	54	56	Aurora city, Colorado	9.7	71	56	Henderson city, Nevada	34.4
1	58	New York city, New York	21.4	73	56	Orlando city, Florida	9.7	32	58	Albuquerque city, New Mexico	34.1
21	59	Denver city, Colorado	21.1	59	59	Riverside city, California	9.6	21	59	Denver city, Colorado	32.1
26	59	Baltimore city, Maryland	21.1	4	60	Houston city, Texas	9.5	64	60	Anchorage municipality, Alaska	31.9
61	59	Lexington-Fayette urban county, Kentucky	21.1	31	61	Milwaukee city, Wisconsin	9.3	61	61	Lexington-Fayette urban county, Kentucky	31.5
45	62	Oakland city, California	21.0	9	62	Dallas city, Texas	9.1	17	62	Charlotte city, North Carolina	31.2
50	63	New Orleans city, Louisiana	20.8	66	62	St. Paul city, Minnesota	9.1	39	63	Atlanta city, Georgia	30.5
60	64	St. Louis city, Missouri	20.6	6	64	Phoenix city, Arizona	9.0	22	64	Washington city, District of Columbia	29.6
74	65	Jersey City city, New Jersey	20.5	15	65	Columbus city, Ohio	8.9	8	65	San Diego city, California	29.3
46	66	Minneapolis city, Minnesota	20.3	17	65	Charlotte city, North Carolina	8.9	11	65	Austin city, Texas	29.3
44	67	Miami city, Florida	18.7	43	67	Raleigh city, North Carolina	8.8	72	67	Lincoln city, Nebraska	29.1
28	68	Portland city, Oregon	18.6	51	67	Arlington city, Texas	8.8	40	68	Virginia Beach city, Virginia	28.9
39	69	Atlanta city, Georgia	18.5	52	67	Bakersfield city, California	8.8	46	69	Minneapolis city, Minnesota	28.2
55	70	Urban Honolulu CDP, Hawaii	17.8	16	70	Fort Worth city, Texas	8.5	42	70	Colorado Springs city, Colorado	27.7
22	71	Washington city, District of Columbia	17.0	69	70	Newark city, New Jersey	8.5	43	71	Raleigh city, North Carolina	26.8
24	72	Boston city, Massachusetts	16.7	46	72	Minneapolis city, Minnesota	8.4	13	72	San Francisco city, California	26.6
62	73	Pittsburgh city, Pennsylvania	16.1	64	73	Anchorage municipality, Alaska	8.2	28	73	Portland city, Oregon	26.3
20	74	Seattle city, Washington	15.8	11	74	Austin city, Texas	7.3	70	74	Plano city, Texas	19.6
13	75	San Francisco city, California	13.4	57	75	Santa Ana city, California	7.2	20	75	Seattle city, Washington	18.4

75 Largest Cities by 2014 Population

Selected Rankings

Percent college graduates (bachelor's degree or more), 2011–2013

Population rank	Percent college graduate rank	City	Percent college graduates [col 41]
20	1	Seattle city, Washington	57.8
70	2	Plano city, Texas	53.7
22	3	Washington city, District of Columbia	53.5
13	4	San Francisco city, California	52.9
39	5	Atlanta city, Georgia	48.2
43	6	Raleigh city, North Carolina	47.0
46	6	Minneapolis city, Minnesota	47.0
11	8	Austin city, Texas	45.8
28	9	Portland city, Oregon	44.4
21	10	Denver city, Colorado	44.1
24	11	Boston city, Massachusetts	43.8
74	12	Jersey City city, New Jersey	42.3
8	13	San Diego city, California	41.9
61	14	Lexington-Fayette urban county, Kentucky	40.7
17	15	Charlotte city, North Carolina	40.6
45	16	Oakland city, California	39.1
66	17	St. Paul city, Minnesota	38.9
10	18	San Jose city, California	37.6
62	19	Pittsburgh city, Pennsylvania	37.3
67	20	Greensboro city, North Carolina	36.7
72	20	Lincoln city, Nebraska	36.7
42	22	Colorado Springs city, Colorado	36.6
25	23	Nashville-Davidson metro gov, Tennessee	35.7
55	24	Urban Honolulu CDP, Hawaii	35.0
1	25	New York city, New York	34.9
3	26	Chicago city, Illinois	34.4
50	27	New Orleans city, Louisiana	34.2
53	28	Tampa city, Florida	33.9
40	29	Virginia Beach city, Virginia	33.7
73	29	Orlando city, Florida	33.7
32	31	Albuquerque city, New Mexico	33.6
41	32	Omaha city, Nebraska	33.3
15	33	Columbus city, Ohio	33.0
64	34	Anchorage municipality, Alaska	32.4
37	35	Kansas City city, Missouri	31.9
65	36	Cincinnati city, Ohio	31.4
2	37	Los Angeles city, California	31.3
47	38	Tulsa city, Oklahoma	30.4
71	38	Henderson city, Nevada	30.4
60	40	St. Louis city, Missouri	30.3
4	41	Houston city, Texas	30.0
9	42	Dallas city, Texas	29.6
35	43	Sacramento city, California	29.2
51	43	Arlington city, Texas	29.2
36	45	Long Beach city, California	28.8
27	46	Oklahoma City city, Oklahoma	28.3
49	46	Wichita city, Kansas	28.3
26	48	Baltimore city, Maryland	27.5
14	49	Indianapolis city, Indiana	27.3
30	50	Louisville/Jefferson metro gov, Kentucky	27.0
54	51	Aurora city, Colorado	26.9
16	52	Fort Worth city, Texas	26.6
75	52	Chula Vista city, California	26.6
6	54	Phoenix city, Arizona	26.5
12	55	Jacksonville city, Florida	25.7
7	56	San Antonio city, Texas	25.1
38	57	Mesa city, Arizona	24.7
23	58	Memphis city, Tennessee	24.5
33	58	Tucson city, Arizona	24.5
5	60	Philadelphia city, Pennsylvania	24.4
56	61	Anaheim city, California	24.3
44	62	Miami city, Florida	23.3
19	63	El Paso city, Texas	23.0
31	64	Milwaukee city, Wisconsin	22.5
59	65	Riverside city, California	22.3
29	66	Las Vegas city, Nevada	21.7
58	67	Corpus Christi city, Texas	20.6
52	68	Bakersfield city, California	20.2
34	69	Fresno city, California	19.6
63	70	Stockton city, California	17.1
68	71	Toledo city, Ohio	16.9
48	72	Cleveland city, Ohio	15.5
18	73	Detroit city, Michigan	13.0
69	73	Newark city, New Jersey	13.0
57	75	Santa Ana city, California	10.9

Percent female-headed family households, 2011–2013

Population rank	Female households rank	City	Percent female households [col 29]
18	1	Detroit city, Michigan	29.3
69	2	Newark city, New Jersey	28.7
23	3	Memphis city, Tennessee	23.9
48	4	Cleveland city, Ohio	23.4
26	5	Baltimore city, Maryland	22.3
31	6	Milwaukee city, Wisconsin	22.2
63	7	Stockton city, California	21.3
5	8	Philadelphia city, Pennsylvania	20.3
34	9	Fresno city, California	19.9
19	10	El Paso city, Texas	19.8
50	11	New Orleans city, Louisiana	19.6
65	12	Cincinnati city, Ohio	19.5
68	13	Toledo city, Ohio	19.2
1	14	New York city, New York	18.3
57	15	Santa Ana city, California	18.2
60	16	St. Louis city, Missouri	18.0
44	17	Miami city, Florida	17.9
7	18	San Antonio city, Texas	17.8
58	19	Corpus Christi city, Texas	17.5
73	19	Orlando city, Florida	17.5
74	21	Jersey City city, New Jersey	17.4
24	22	Boston city, Massachusetts	17.3
52	23	Bakersfield city, California	17.1
3	24	Chicago city, Illinois	17.0
67	24	Greensboro city, North Carolina	17.0
36	26	Long Beach city, California	16.8
14	27	Indianapolis city, Indiana	16.7
4	28	Houston city, Texas	16.3
30	28	Louisville/Jefferson metro gov, Kentucky	16.3
16	30	Fort Worth city, Texas	16.2
12	31	Jacksonville city, Florida	16.1
22	31	Washington city, District of Columbia	16.1
9	33	Dallas city, Texas	16.0
17	34	Charlotte city, North Carolina	15.9
15	35	Columbus city, Ohio	15.8
37	35	Kansas City city, Missouri	15.8
56	35	Anaheim city, California	15.8
59	35	Riverside city, California	15.8
75	35	Chula Vista city, California	15.8
51	40	Arlington city, Texas	15.7
6	41	Phoenix city, Arizona	15.6
35	41	Sacramento city, California	15.6
47	41	Tulsa city, Oklahoma	15.6
54	41	Aurora city, Colorado	15.6
33	45	Tucson city, Arizona	15.5
53	45	Tampa city, Florida	15.5
2	47	Los Angeles city, California	15.3
29	47	Las Vegas city, Nevada	15.3
45	49	Oakland city, California	15.1
39	50	Atlanta city, Georgia	14.8
40	51	Virginia Beach city, Virginia	14.7
32	52	Albuquerque city, New Mexico	14.5
43	52	Raleigh city, North Carolina	14.5
62	52	Pittsburgh city, Pennsylvania	14.5
66	55	St. Paul city, Minnesota	14.3
25	56	Nashville-Davidson metro gov, Tennessee	14.1
41	57	Omaha city, Nebraska	13.7
38	58	Mesa city, Arizona	13.3
49	58	Wichita city, Kansas	13.3
27	60	Oklahoma City city, Oklahoma	13.2
10	61	San Jose city, California	12.6
61	62	Lexington-Fayette urban county, Kentucky	12.2
8	63	San Diego city, California	11.9
64	63	Anchorage municipality, Alaska	11.9
11	65	Austin city, Texas	11.8
55	65	Urban Honolulu CDP, Hawaii	11.8
71	65	Henderson city, Nevada	11.8
42	68	Colorado Springs city, Colorado	11.6
46	69	Minneapolis city, Minnesota	11.5
21	70	Denver city, Colorado	10.5
70	71	Plano city, Texas	10.1
72	72	Lincoln city, Nebraska	9.9
28	73	Portland city, Oregon	9.6
13	74	San Francisco city, California	8.6
20	75	Seattle city, Washington	7.2

Percent of households composed of one person, 2011–2013

Population rank	One-person household rank	City	Percent one-person households [col 30]
39	1	Atlanta city, Georgia	46.6
22	2	Washington city, District of Columbia	44.7
60	3	St. Louis city, Missouri	44.1
65	4	Cincinnati city, Ohio	44.0
48	5	Cleveland city, Ohio	42.2
20	6	Seattle city, Washington	41.3
62	6	Pittsburgh city, Pennsylvania	41.3
26	8	Baltimore city, Maryland	40.8
21	9	Denver city, Colorado	40.6
50	9	New Orleans city, Louisiana	40.6
5	11	Philadelphia city, Pennsylvania	40.0
46	11	Minneapolis city, Minnesota	40.0
13	13	San Francisco city, California	38.4
18	14	Detroit city, Michigan	38.2
24	15	Boston city, Massachusetts	37.7
73	15	Orlando city, Florida	37.7
53	17	Tampa city, Florida	37.4
25	18	Nashville-Davidson metro gov, Tennessee	36.8
3	19	Chicago city, Illinois	36.7
15	19	Columbus city, Ohio	36.7
68	19	Toledo city, Ohio	36.7
44	22	Miami city, Florida	36.5
37	23	Kansas City city, Missouri	36.3
23	24	Memphis city, Tennessee	35.8
33	25	Tucson city, Arizona	35.6
66	26	St. Paul city, Minnesota	35.5
31	27	Milwaukee city, Wisconsin	35.3
28	28	Portland city, Oregon	35.1
45	28	Oakland city, California	35.1
47	30	Tulsa city, Oklahoma	34.8
9	31	Dallas city, Texas	34.6
14	32	Indianapolis city, Indiana	34.1
41	33	Omaha city, Nebraska	33.9
55	33	Urban Honolulu CDP, Hawaii	33.9
67	33	Greensboro city, North Carolina	33.9
11	36	Austin city, Texas	33.8
1	37	New York city, New York	33.1
43	37	Raleigh city, North Carolina	33.1
35	39	Sacramento city, California	33.0
30	40	Louisville/Jefferson metro gov, Kentucky	32.8
61	40	Lexington-Fayette urban county, Kentucky	32.8
49	42	Wichita city, Kansas	32.5
32	43	Albuquerque city, New Mexico	32.4
4	44	Houston city, Texas	32.2
17	45	Charlotte city, North Carolina	31.5
12	46	Jacksonville city, Florida	31.2
27	47	Oklahoma City city, Oklahoma	31.1
72	47	Lincoln city, Nebraska	31.1
36	49	Long Beach city, California	30.6
2	50	Los Angeles city, California	30.3
69	50	Newark city, New Jersey	30.3
74	52	Jersey City city, New Jersey	30.1
42	53	Colorado Springs city, Colorado	29.1
8	54	San Diego city, California	29.0
6	55	Phoenix city, Arizona	28.8
29	56	Las Vegas city, Nevada	28.7
7	57	San Antonio city, Texas	28.5
54	57	Aurora city, Colorado	28.5
38	59	Mesa city, Arizona	27.6
16	60	Fort Worth city, Texas	27.1
71	61	Henderson city, Nevada	26.6
64	62	Anchorage municipality, Alaska	26.3
51	63	Arlington city, Texas	25.9
58	64	Corpus Christi city, Texas	25.2
40	65	Virginia Beach city, Virginia	24.2
70	66	Plano city, Texas	23.7
19	67	El Paso city, Texas	23.2
34	68	Fresno city, California	23.1
63	69	Stockton city, California	22.2
59	70	Riverside city, California	21.8
10	71	San Jose city, California	19.7
52	72	Bakersfield city, California	19.5
75	73	Chula Vista city, California	19.3
56	74	Anaheim city, California	18.1
57	75	Santa Ana city, California	13.3

75 Largest Cities by 2014 Population

Selected Rankings

Median household income, 2011–2013				Median value of owner-occupied housing units, 2011–2013				Median gross rent of renter-occupied housing units, 2011–2013			
Population rank	Median income rank	City	Median income (dollars) [col 43]	Population rank	Median value rank	City	Median value (dollars) [col 52]	Population rank	Median rent rank	City	Median rent (dollars) [col 56]
70	1	Plano city, Texas	$81 800	13	1	San Francisco city, California	$740 700	13	1	San Francisco city, California	1 487
10	2	San Jose city, California	$80 609	55	2	Urban Honolulu CDP, Hawaii	$563 300	10	2	San Jose city, California	1 470
64	3	Anchorage municipality, Alaska	$76 159	10	3	San Jose city, California	$561 600	56	3	Anaheim city, California	1 350
13	4	San Francisco city, California	$74 559	1	4	New York city, New York	$485 700	8	4	San Diego city, California	1 320
22	5	Washington city, District of Columbia	$66 950	22	5	Washington city, District of Columbia	$451 800	57	5	Santa Ana city, California	1 274
20	6	Seattle city, Washington	$65 454	2	6	Los Angeles city, California	$437 700	22	6	Washington city, District of Columbia	1 264
40	7	Virginia Beach city, Virginia	$64 771	8	7	San Diego city, California	$435 400	24	7	Boston city, Massachusetts	1 261
8	8	San Diego city, California	$63 258	45	8	Oakland city, California	$426 500	55	8	Urban Honolulu CDP, Hawaii	1 247
75	9	Chula Vista city, California	$62 284	20	9	Seattle city, Washington	$426 300	75	9	Chula Vista city, California	1 225
71	10	Henderson city, Nevada	$61 538	36	10	Long Beach city, California	$409 300	40	10	Virginia Beach city, Virginia	1 221
55	11	Urban Honolulu CDP, Hawaii	$59 490	56	11	Anaheim city, California	$396 300	1	11	New York city, New York	1 210
56	12	Anaheim city, California	$57 938	24	12	Boston city, Massachusetts	$372 400	2	12	Los Angeles city, California	1 172
74	13	Jersey City city, New Jersey	$57 076	75	13	Chula Vista city, California	$346 500	74	13	Jersey City city, New Jersey	1 166
52	14	Bakersfield city, California	$54 675	57	14	Santa Ana city, California	$338 700	64	14	Anchorage municipality, Alaska	1 150
11	15	Austin city, Texas	$54 331	74	15	Jersey City city, New Jersey	$313 100	71	15	Henderson city, Nevada	1 137
43	16	Raleigh city, North Carolina	$54 088	64	16	Anchorage municipality, Alaska	$287 500	59	16	Riverside city, California	1 112
59	17	Riverside city, California	$53 639	28	17	Portland city, Oregon	$278 500	20	17	Seattle city, Washington	1 104
42	18	Colorado Springs city, Colorado	$53 619	40	18	Virginia Beach city, Virginia	$261 000	70	17	Plano city, Texas	1 104
24	19	Boston city, Massachusetts	$52 465	21	19	Denver city, Colorado	$254 700	45	19	Oakland city, California	1 095
28	20	Portland city, Oregon	$52 421	59	20	Riverside city, California	$232 400	36	20	Long Beach city, California	1 094
51	21	Arlington city, Texas	$52 407	11	21	Austin city, Texas	$225 500	35	21	Sacramento city, California	986
45	22	Oakland city, California	$51 851	69	22	Newark city, New Jersey	$222 600	11	22	Austin city, Texas	984
1	23	New York city, New York	$51 526	70	23	Plano city, Texas	$218 600	52	23	Bakersfield city, California	977
36	24	Long Beach city, California	$51 358	3	24	Chicago city, Illinois	$217 700	73	24	Orlando city, Florida	976
17	25	Charlotte city, North Carolina	$51 271	35	25	Sacramento city, California	$215 500	29	25	Las Vegas city, Nevada	959
57	26	Santa Ana city, California	$51 221	42	26	Colorado Springs city, Colorado	$208 000	54	25	Aurora city, Colorado	959
16	27	Fort Worth city, Texas	$51 168	43	27	Raleigh city, North Carolina	$201 800	39	27	Atlanta city, Georgia	953
21	28	Denver city, Colorado	$50 728	44	28	Miami city, Florida	$198 500	69	28	Newark city, New Jersey	951
54	29	Aurora city, Colorado	$50 247	39	29	Atlanta city, Georgia	$198 200	3	29	Chicago city, Illinois	938
46	30	Minneapolis city, Minnesota	$49 777	46	30	Minneapolis city, Minnesota	$197 800	44	30	Miami city, Florida	936
58	31	Corpus Christi city, Texas	$49 036	71	31	Henderson city, Nevada	$194 400	63	31	Stockton city, California	931
35	32	Sacramento city, California	$48 807	32	32	Albuquerque city, New Mexico	$183 600	28	32	Portland city, Oregon	929
29	33	Las Vegas city, Nevada	$48 676	50	33	New Orleans city, Louisiana	$183 100	53	32	Tampa city, Florida	929
72	34	Lincoln city, Nebraska	$48 329	54	34	Aurora city, Colorado	$175 000	12	34	Jacksonville city, Florida	915
61	35	Lexington-Fayette urban county, Kentucky	$47 977	52	35	Bakersfield city, California	$174 000	50	35	New Orleans city, Louisiana	910
2	36	Los Angeles city, California	$47 812	66	36	St. Paul city, Minnesota	$170 000	26	36	Baltimore city, Maryland	906
41	37	Omaha city, Nebraska	$47 275	34	37	Fresno city, California	$168 200	5	37	Philadelphia city, Pennsylvania	894
38	38	Mesa city, Arizona	$47 121	61	38	Lexington-Fayette urban county, Kentucky	$166 800	43	38	Raleigh city, North Carolina	890
66	39	St. Paul city, Minnesota	$47 083	17	39	Charlotte city, North Carolina	$166 700	21	39	Denver city, Colorado	889
39	40	Atlanta city, Georgia	$46 783	25	40	Nashville-Davidson metro gov, Tennessee	$163 100	17	40	Charlotte city, North Carolina	882
32	41	Albuquerque city, New Mexico	$46 668	63	41	Stockton city, California	$158 900	42	41	Colorado Springs city, Colorado	881
3	42	Chicago city, Illinois	$46 014	29	42	Las Vegas city, Nevada	$152 300	34	42	Fresno city, California	879
12	43	Jacksonville city, Florida	$45 978	26	43	Baltimore city, Maryland	$151 700	6	43	Phoenix city, Arizona	861
6	44	Phoenix city, Arizona	$45 775	73	44	Orlando city, Florida	$149 900	38	44	Mesa city, Arizona	857
25	45	Nashville-Davidson metro gov, Tennessee	$45 542	53	45	Tampa city, Florida	$149 000	16	45	Fort Worth city, Texas	851
7	46	San Antonio city, Texas	$45 253	67	46	Greensboro city, North Carolina	$148 000	58	45	Corpus Christi city, Texas	851
27	47	Oklahoma City city, Oklahoma	$45 073	6	47	Phoenix city, Arizona	$147 600	4	47	Houston city, Texas	837
37	48	Kansas City city, Missouri	$44 613	72	48	Lincoln city, Nebraska	$144 800	25	48	Nashville-Davidson metro gov, Tennessee	833
49	49	Wichita city, Kansas	$44 532	38	49	Mesa city, Arizona	$140 800	46	49	Minneapolis city, Minnesota	830
4	50	Houston city, Texas	$44 451	5	50	Philadelphia city, Pennsylvania	$140 200	9	50	Dallas city, Texas	828
30	51	Louisville/Jefferson metro gov, Kentucky	$43 963	30	51	Louisville/Jefferson metro gov, Kentucky	$139 500	51	51	Arlington city, Texas	820
63	52	Stockton city, California	$43 786	27	52	Oklahoma City city, Oklahoma	$134 300	66	52	St. Paul city, Minnesota	818
15	53	Columbus city, Ohio	$43 441	41	53	Omaha city, Nebraska	$132 600	7	53	San Antonio city, Texas	817
9	54	Dallas city, Texas	$42 026	12	54	Jacksonville city, Florida	$132 400	23	54	Memphis city, Tennessee	807
73	54	Orlando city, Florida	$42 026	37	55	Kansas City city, Missouri	$130 800	15	55	Columbus city, Ohio	805
53	56	Tampa city, Florida	$41 927	33	56	Tucson city, Arizona	$129 400	37	56	Kansas City city, Missouri	789
19	57	El Paso city, Texas	$41 657	51	57	Arlington city, Texas	$128 600	32	57	Albuquerque city, New Mexico	786
47	58	Tulsa city, Oklahoma	$41 162	9	58	Dallas city, Texas	$127 700	41	58	Omaha city, Nebraska	771
14	59	Indianapolis city, Indiana	$41 154	15	59	Columbus city, Ohio	$126 000	62	59	Pittsburgh city, Pennsylvania	770
20	60	Baltimore city, Maryland	$40 708	4	60	Houston city, Texas	$121 200	14	60	Indianapolis city, Indiana	769
34	61	Fresno city, California	$40 439	31	61	Milwaukee city, Wisconsin	$121 700	31	61	Milwaukee city, Wisconsin	766
67	62	Greensboro city, North Carolina	$40 415	47	62	Tulsa city, Oklahoma	$121 300	27	62	Oklahoma City city, Oklahoma	756
62	63	Pittsburgh city, Pennsylvania	$39 527	65	63	Cincinnati city, Ohio	$120 900	61	63	Lexington-Fayette urban county, Kentucky	755
5	64	Philadelphia city, Pennsylvania	$36 222	16	64	Fort Worth city, Texas	$118 400	19	64	El Paso city, Texas	742
33	65	Tucson city, Arizona	$35 837	19	65	El Paso city, Texas	$118 200	18	65	Detroit city, Michigan	741
50	65	New Orleans city, Louisiana	$35 837	49	66	Wichita city, Kansas	$118 100	67	66	Greensboro city, North Carolina	737
23	67	Memphis city, Tennessee	$35 455	14	67	Indianapolis city, Indiana	$116 900	33	67	Tucson city, Arizona	733
31	68	Milwaukee city, Wisconsin	$34 664	60	68	St. Louis city, Missouri	$116 300	60	68	St. Louis city, Missouri	725
60	69	St. Louis city, Missouri	$33 770	7	69	San Antonio city, Texas	$113 700	47	69	Tulsa city, Oklahoma	720
69	70	Newark city, New Jersey	$32 338	58	70	Corpus Christi city, Texas	$111 700	30	70	Louisville/Jefferson metro gov, Kentucky	704
65	71	Cincinnati city, Ohio	$32 316	23	71	Memphis city, Tennessee	$92 700	72	70	Lincoln city, Nebraska	704
68	72	Toledo city, Ohio	$32 263	62	72	Pittsburgh city, Pennsylvania	$90 900	49	72	Wichita city, Kansas	691
44	73	Miami city, Florida	$30 126	68	73	Toledo city, Ohio	$78 400	48	73	Cleveland city, Ohio	651
48	74	Cleveland city, Ohio	$25 696	48	74	Cleveland city, Ohio	$71 600	65	74	Cincinnati city, Ohio	631
18	75	Detroit city, Michigan	$24 970	18	75	Detroit city, Michigan	$42 300	68	75	Toledo city, Ohio	623

75 Largest Cities by 2014 Population

Selected Rankings

Percent of population below the poverty level, 2011–2013

Population rank	Poverty rate rank	City	Poverty rate [col 46]
18	1	Detroit city, Michigan	36.2
48	2	Cleveland city, Ohio	30.7
69	3	Newark city, New Jersey	27.1
44	4	Miami city, Florida	26.0
65	4	Cincinnati city, Ohio	26.0
34	6	Fresno city, California	25.6
31	7	Milwaukee city, Wisconsin	25.4
68	8	Toledo city, Ohio	24.0
23	9	Memphis city, Tennessee	23.2
50	9	New Orleans city, Louisiana	23.2
60	11	St. Louis city, Missouri	22.6
63	12	Stockton city, California	21.8
5	13	Philadelphia city, Pennsylvania	21.6
9	14	Dallas city, Texas	21.1
4	15	Houston city, Texas	19.9
26	16	Baltimore city, Maryland	19.8
39	17	Atlanta city, Georgia	19.7
57	18	Santa Ana city, California	19.6
3	19	Chicago city, Illinois	19.5
33	20	Tucson city, Arizona	19.3
35	21	Sacramento city, California	19.0
6	22	Phoenix city, Arizona	18.7
2	23	Los Angeles city, California	18.6
19	23	El Paso city, Texas	18.6
1	25	New York city, New York	17.9
24	26	Boston city, Massachusetts	17.6
36	27	Long Beach city, California	17.5
52	27	Bakersfield city, California	17.5
53	29	Tampa city, Florida	17.4
14	30	Indianapolis city, Indiana	17.3
15	31	Columbus city, Ohio	17.1
66	31	St. Paul city, Minnesota	17.1
73	33	Orlando city, Florida	16.9
45	34	Oakland city, California	16.8
7	35	San Antonio city, Texas	16.6
47	36	Tulsa city, Oklahoma	16.2
74	36	Jersey City city, New Jersey	16.2
62	38	Pittsburgh city, Pennsylvania	16.1
16	39	Fort Worth city, Texas	16.0
46	40	Minneapolis city, Minnesota	15.8
67	41	Greensboro city, North Carolina	15.7
37	42	Kansas City city, Missouri	15.6
22	43	Washington city, District of Columbia	15.3
59	44	Riverside city, California	15.0
32	45	Albuquerque city, New Mexico	14.8
27	46	Oklahoma City city, Oklahoma	14.6
56	47	Anaheim city, California	14.5
12	48	Jacksonville city, Florida	14.1
30	48	Louisville/Jefferson metro gov, Kentucky	14.1
51	48	Arlington city, Texas	14.1
17	51	Charlotte city, North Carolina	14.0
21	51	Denver city, Colorado	14.0
25	51	Nashville-Davidson metro gov, Tennessee	14.0
29	54	Las Vegas city, Nevada	13.8
49	54	Wichita city, Kansas	13.8
58	56	Corpus Christi city, Texas	13.6
11	57	Austin city, Texas	13.3
38	58	Mesa city, Arizona	13.0
41	59	Omaha city, Nebraska	12.7
54	60	Aurora city, Colorado	12.5
28	61	Portland city, Oregon	12.2
43	62	Raleigh city, North Carolina	11.5
61	63	Lexington-Fayette urban county, Kentucky	11.3
75	64	Chula Vista city, California	11.0
8	65	San Diego city, California	10.9
72	66	Lincoln city, Nebraska	10.4
42	67	Colorado Springs city, Colorado	9.7
10	68	San Jose city, California	8.9
13	69	San Francisco city, California	8.6
55	70	Urban Honolulu CDP, Hawaii	8.4
20	71	Seattle city, Washington	8.0
71	72	Henderson city, Nevada	7.6
40	73	Virginia Beach city, Virginia	6.9
70	74	Plano city, Texas	5.5
64	75	Anchorage municipality, Alaska	5.0

Unemployment rate, 2014

Population rank	Unemployment rate rank	City	Unemployment rate [col 64]
18	1	Detroit city, Michigan	16.7
34	2	Fresno city, California	12.6
63	3	Stockton city, California	11.5
69	4	Newark city, New Jersey	10.2
52	5	Bakersfield city, California	9.3
36	6	Long Beach city, California	9.0
2	7	Los Angeles city, California	8.7
23	7	Memphis city, Tennessee	8.7
26	7	Baltimore city, Maryland	8.7
31	10	Milwaukee city, Wisconsin	8.1
5	11	Philadelphia city, Pennsylvania	8.0
29	11	Las Vegas city, Nevada	8.0
48	11	Cleveland city, Ohio	8.0
75	11	Chula Vista city, California	8.0
59	15	Riverside city, California	7.9
22	16	Washington city, District of Columbia	7.8
39	16	Atlanta city, Georgia	7.8
71	16	Henderson city, Nevada	7.8
3	19	Chicago city, Illinois	7.7
35	19	Sacramento city, California	7.7
60	19	St. Louis city, Missouri	7.7
45	22	Oakland city, California	7.3
1	23	New York city, New York	7.2
44	24	Miami city, Florida	7.0
50	24	New Orleans city, Louisiana	7.0
56	26	Anaheim city, California	6.9
68	26	Toledo city, Ohio	6.9
37	28	Kansas City city, Missouri	6.7
74	29	Jersey City city, New Jersey	6.6
12	30	Jacksonville city, Florida	6.5
14	30	Indianapolis city, Indiana	6.5
33	30	Tucson city, Arizona	6.5
57	33	Santa Ana city, California	6.3
6	34	Phoenix city, Arizona	6.2
8	35	San Diego city, California	6.1
30	35	Louisville/Jefferson metro gov, Kentucky	6.1
19	37	El Paso city, Texas	6.0
28	38	Portland city, Oregon	5.9
32	38	Albuquerque city, New Mexico	5.9
38	38	Mesa city, Arizona	5.9
42	38	Colorado Springs city, Colorado	5.9
53	38	Tampa city, Florida	5.9
65	38	Cincinnati city, Ohio	5.9
67	38	Greensboro city, North Carolina	5.9
10	45	San Jose city, California	5.8
49	46	Wichita city, Kansas	5.6
54	46	Aurora city, Colorado	5.6
62	46	Pittsburgh city, Pennsylvania	5.6
73	49	Orlando city, Florida	5.5
24	50	Boston city, Massachusetts	5.3
9	51	Dallas city, Texas	5.2
17	52	Charlotte city, North Carolina	5.1
25	52	Nashville-Davidson metro gov, Tennessee	5.1
64	52	Anchorage municipality, Alaska	5.1
51	55	Arlington city, Texas	5.0
16	56	Fort Worth city, Texas	4.9
21	56	Denver city, Colorado	4.9
40	56	Virginia Beach city, Virginia	4.9
58	56	Corpus Christi city, Texas	4.9
15	60	Columbus city, Ohio	4.8
61	60	Lexington-Fayette urban county, Kentucky	4.8
4	62	Houston city, Texas	4.7
7	63	San Antonio city, Texas	4.5
43	63	Raleigh city, North Carolina	4.5
70	63	Plano city, Texas	4.5
13	66	San Francisco city, California	4.4
47	67	Tulsa city, Oklahoma	4.2
20	68	Seattle city, Washington	4.1
66	68	St. Paul city, Minnesota	4.1
27	70	Oklahoma City city, Oklahoma	3.9
46	71	Minneapolis city, Minnesota	3.8
11	72	Austin city, Texas	3.7
41	73	Omaha city, Nebraska	3.6
72	74	Lincoln city, Nebraska	2.9
55		Urban Honolulu CDP, Hawaii	NA

Percent change in civilian labor force, 2013–2014

Population rank	Percent change rank	City	Percent change [col 62]
11	1	Austin city, Texas	2.8
73	2	Orlando city, Florida	2.6
13	3	San Francisco city, California	2.5
44	3	Miami city, Florida	2.5
50	3	New Orleans city, Louisiana	2.5
70	3	Plano city, Texas	2.5
9	7	Dallas city, Texas	2.4
6	8	Phoenix city, Arizona	2.2
38	8	Mesa city, Arizona	2.2
28	10	Portland city, Oregon	2.1
4	11	Houston city, Texas	2.0
37	11	Kansas City city, Missouri	2.0
10	13	San Jose city, California	1.9
20	13	Seattle city, Washington	1.9
7	15	San Antonio city, Texas	1.7
21	16	Denver city, Colorado	1.6
24	16	Boston city, Massachusetts	1.6
54	16	Aurora city, Colorado	1.6
43	19	Raleigh city, North Carolina	1.5
71	19	Henderson city, Nevada	1.5
16	21	Fort Worth city, Texas	1.4
51	21	Arlington city, Texas	1.4
59	23	Riverside city, California	1.3
1	24	New York city, New York	1.2
12	24	Jacksonville city, Florida	1.2
14	24	Indianapolis city, Indiana	1.2
58	24	Corpus Christi city, Texas	1.2
17	28	Charlotte city, North Carolina	1.1
22	28	Washington city, District of Columbia	1.1
29	28	Las Vegas city, Nevada	1.1
53	28	Tampa city, Florida	1.1
60	32	St. Louis city, Missouri	1.0
2	33	Los Angeles city, California	0.8
15	33	Columbus city, Ohio	0.8
64	33	Anchorage municipality, Alaska	0.8
36	36	Long Beach city, California	0.7
33	37	Tucson city, Arizona	0.6
46	37	Minneapolis city, Minnesota	0.6
41	39	Omaha city, Nebraska	0.5
49	39	Wichita city, Kansas	0.5
72	39	Lincoln city, Nebraska	0.5
39	42	Atlanta city, Georgia	0.4
57	42	Santa Ana city, California	0.4
66	42	St. Paul city, Minnesota	0.4
45	45	Oakland city, California	0.3
52	45	Bakersfield city, California	0.3
56	45	Anaheim city, California	0.3
8	48	San Diego city, California	0.1
34	48	Fresno city, California	0.1
35	48	Sacramento city, California	0.1
40	48	Virginia Beach city, Virginia	0.1
48	48	Cleveland city, Ohio	0.1
65	48	Cincinnati city, Ohio	0.1
42	54	Colorado Springs city, Colorado	0.0
63	55	Stockton city, California	-0.2
19	56	El Paso city, Texas	-0.3
75	57	Chula Vista city, California	-0.4
3	58	Chicago city, Illinois	-0.5
31	58	Milwaukee city, Wisconsin	-0.5
32	58	Albuquerque city, New Mexico	-0.5
74	58	Jersey City city, New Jersey	-0.5
25	62	Nashville-Davidson metro gov, Tennessee	-0.6
26	63	Baltimore city, Maryland	-0.8
27	63	Oklahoma City city, Oklahoma	-0.8
47	63	Tulsa city, Oklahoma	-0.8
61	66	Lexington-Fayette urban county, Kentucky	-1.0
62	66	Pittsburgh city, Pennsylvania	-1.0
69	66	Newark city, New Jersey	-1.0
68	69	Toledo city, Ohio	-1.2
5	70	Philadelphia city, Pennsylvania	-1.3
67	71	Greensboro city, North Carolina	-1.5
18	72	Detroit city, Michigan	-1.9
30	73	Louisville/Jefferson metro gov, Kentucky	-2.0
23	74	Memphis city, Tennessee	-3.3
55		Urban Honolulu CDP, Hawaii	NA

75 Largest Cities by 2014 Population

Selected Rankings

Per capita local government taxes, 2007				Per capita city government debt outstanding, 2012				Violent crime rate, 2013 (violent crimes known to police)			
Population rank	Local taxes rank	City	Local per capita taxes (dollars) [col 121]	Population rank	Debt rank	City	Debt per capita (dollars) [col 138]	Population rank	Violent crime rate rank	City	Violent crimes (per 100,000) population) [col 37]
22	1	Washington city, District of Columbia	9 344	22	1	Washington city, District of Columbia	17 761	18	1	Detroit city, Michigan	2 072
1	2	New York city, New York	5 077	39	2	Atlanta city, Georgia	16 770	45	2	Oakland city, California	1 977
13	3	San Francisco city, California	3 430	13	3	San Francisco city, California	15 759	23	3	Memphis city, Tennessee	1 656
24	4	Boston city, Massachusetts	2 844	1	4	New York city, New York	15 714	60	4	St. Louis city, Missouri	1 594
5	5	Philadelphia city, Pennsylvania	2 089	12	5	Jacksonville city, Florida	12 465	48	5	Cleveland city, Ohio	1 486
26	6	Baltimore city, Maryland	1 989	18	6	Detroit city, Michigan	11 720	26	6	Baltimore city, Maryland	1 401
25	7	Nashville-Davidson metro gov, Tennessee	1 952	21	7	Denver city, Colorado	11 106	31	7	Milwaukee city, Wisconsin	1 364
64	8	Anchorage municipality, Alaska	1 830	49	8	Wichita city, Kansas	9 003	69	8	Newark city, New Jersey	1 264
40	9	Virginia Beach city, Virginia	1 817	46	9	Minneapolis city, Minnesota	8 754	37	9	Kansas City city, Missouri	1 262
21	10	Denver city, Colorado	1 748	25	10	Nashville-Davidson metro gov, Tennessee	7 828	14	10	Indianapolis city, Indiana	1 233
60	11	St. Louis city, Missouri	1 706	3	11	Chicago city, Illinois	7 811	39	11	Atlanta city, Georgia	1 223
37	12	Kansas City city, Missouri	1 599	14	12	Indianapolis city, Indiana	7 191	22	12	Washington city, District of Columbia	1 219
20	13	Seattle city, Washington	1 438	20	13	Seattle city, Washington	6 556	63	13	Stockton city, California	1 208
45	14	Oakland city, California	1 420	48	14	Cleveland city, Ohio	6 465	44	14	Miami city, Florida	1 182
65	15	Cincinnati city, Ohio	1 400	4	15	Houston city, Texas	6 459	5	15	Philadelphia city, Pennsylvania	1 099
50	16	New Orleans city, Louisiana	1 349	11	16	Austin city, Texas	6 438	25	16	Nashville-Davidson metro gov, Tennessee	1 049
39	17	Atlanta city, Georgia	1 173	9	17	Dallas city, Texas	6 389	68	17	Toledo city, Ohio	1 025
46	18	Minneapolis city, Minnesota	1 170	7	18	San Antonio city, Texas	6 374	46	18	Minneapolis city, Minnesota	1 019
62	19	Pittsburgh city, Pennsylvania	1 166	37	19	Kansas City city, Missouri	6 347	47	19	Tulsa city, Oklahoma	970
12	20	Jacksonville city, Florida	1 104	42	20	Colorado Springs city, Colorado	6 097	65	20	Cincinnati city, Ohio	964
69	21	Newark city, New Jersey	1 099	59	21	Riverside city, California	6 092	4	21	Houston city, Texas	963
18	22	Detroit city, Michigan	1 078	10	22	San Jose city, California	6 013	3	22	Chicago city, Illinois	944
48	23	Cleveland city, Ohio	1 071	64	23	Anchorage municipality, Alaska	5 991	73	23	Orlando city, Florida	915
14	24	Indianapolis city, Indiana	1 064	2	24	Los Angeles city, California	5 983	13	24	San Francisco city, California	847
61	25	Lexington-Fayette urban county, Kentucky	1 045	60	25	St. Louis city, Missouri	5 832	27	25	Oklahoma City city, Oklahoma	826
28	26	Portland city, Oregon	1 016	51	26	Arlington city, Texas	5 724	64	26	Anchorage municipality, Alaska	813
27	27	Oklahoma City city, Oklahoma	1 003	45	27	Oakland city, California	5 709	49	27	Wichita city, Kansas	794
2	28	Los Angeles city, California	997	28	28	Portland city, Oregon	5 608	50	28	New Orleans city, Louisiana	786
44	29	Miami city, Florida	976	6	29	Phoenix city, Arizona	5 557	24	29	Boston city, Massachusetts	782
15	30	Columbus city, Ohio	958	50	30	New Orleans city, Louisiana	5 454	32	30	Albuquerque city, New Mexico	775
3	31	Chicago city, Illinois	930	56	31	Anaheim city, California	5 304	29	31	Las Vegas city, Nevada	758
74	32	Jersey City city, New Jersey	918	36	32	Long Beach city, California	5 095	66	32	St. Paul city, Minnesota	747
70	33	Plano city, Texas	907	5	33	Philadelphia city, Pennsylvania	4 985	62	33	Pittsburgh city, Pennsylvania	734
41	34	Omaha city, Nebraska	903	72	34	Lincoln city, Nebraska	4 876	9	34	Dallas city, Texas	664
73	35	Orlando city, Florida	895	73	35	Orlando city, Florida	4 219	35	35	Sacramento city, California	656
4	36	Houston city, Texas	888	26	36	Baltimore city, Maryland	4 208	74	36	Jersey City city, New Jersey	644
36	37	Long Beach city, California	877	17	37	Charlotte city, North Carolina	4 165	33	37	Tucson city, Arizona	641
10	38	San Jose city, California	876	53	38	Tampa city, Florida	3 945	6	38	Phoenix city, Arizona	632
9	39	Dallas city, Texas	872	40	39	Virginia Beach city, Virginia	3 811	7	39	San Antonio city, Texas	631
47	40	Tulsa city, Oklahoma	862	23	40	Memphis city, Tennessee	3 791	21	39	Denver city, Colorado	631
8	41	San Diego city, California	838	32	41	Albuquerque city, New Mexico	3 769	1	41	New York city, New York	624
17	42	Charlotte city, North Carolina	803	58	42	Corpus Christi city, Texas	3 689	12	42	Jacksonville city, Florida	620
23	43	Memphis city, Tennessee	789	54	43	Aurora city, Colorado	3 582	58	43	Corpus Christi city, Texas	616
16	44	Fort Worth city, Texas	783	38	44	Mesa city, Arizona	3 305	17	44	Charlotte city, North Carolina	608
56	45	Anaheim city, California	779	74	45	Jersey City city, New Jersey	3 300	53	45	Tampa city, Florida	597
53	46	Tampa city, Florida	774	61	46	Lexington-Fayette urban county, Kentucky	3 277	20	46	Seattle city, Washington	585
35	47	Sacramento city, California	771	47	47	Tulsa city, Oklahoma	3 179	41	47	Omaha city, Nebraska	576
30	48	Louisville/Jefferson metro gov, Kentucky	753	15	48	Columbus city, Ohio	3 153	16	48	Fort Worth city, Texas	563
67	49	Greensboro city, North Carolina	711	65	49	Cincinnati city, Ohio	3 091	15	49	Columbus city, Ohio	545
11	50	Austin city, Texas	709	16	50	Fort Worth city, Texas	3 084	30	50	Louisville/Jefferson metro gov, Kentucky	543
43	51	Raleigh city, North Carolina	679	66	51	St. Paul city, Minnesota	2 646	67	51	Greensboro city, North Carolina	519
6	52	Phoenix city, Arizona	663	30	52	Louisville/Jefferson metro gov, Kentucky	2 633	52	52	Bakersfield city, California	513
32	52	Albuquerque city, New Mexico	663	8	53	San Diego city, California	2 563	34	53	Fresno city, California	501
51	54	Arlington city, Texas	644	24	54	Boston city, Massachusetts	2 454	36	54	Long Beach city, California	500
54	55	Aurora city, Colorado	638	41	55	Omaha city, Nebraska	2 411	51	55	Arlington city, Texas	485
59	56	Riverside city, California	631	43	56	Raleigh city, North Carolina	2 373	28	56	Portland city, Oregon	483
57	57	Santa Ana city, California	621	69	57	Newark city, New Jersey	2 366	42	57	Colorado Springs city, Colorado	429
68	58	Toledo city, Ohio	618	62	58	Pittsburgh city, Pennsylvania	2 300	2	58	Los Angeles city, California	426
58	60	Corpus Christi city, Texas	614	35	59	Sacramento city, California	2 286	59	59	Riverside city, California	420
66	60	St. Paul city, Minnesota	602	19	60	El Paso city, Texas	2 270	54	60	Aurora city, Colorado	416
19	61	El Paso city, Texas	572	33	61	Tucson city, Arizona	2 236	38	61	Mesa city, Arizona	396
63	62	Stockton city, California	544	27	62	Oklahoma City city, Oklahoma	2 199	8	62	San Diego city, California	393
7	63	San Antonio city, Texas	534	31	63	Milwaukee city, Wisconsin	2 181	43	63	Raleigh city, North Carolina	392
33	63	Tucson city, Arizona	534	34	64	Fresno city, California	2 099	19	64	El Paso city, Texas	371
34	65	Fresno city, California	529	44	65	Miami city, Florida	2 095	72	65	Lincoln city, Nebraska	370
72	66	Lincoln city, Nebraska	516	75	66	Chula Vista city, California	2 027	11	66	Austin city, Texas	363
31	67	Milwaukee city, Wisconsin	505	63	67	Stockton city, California	1 926	57	67	Santa Ana city, California	337
75	68	Chula Vista city, California	501	67	68	Greensboro city, North Carolina	1 603	56	68	Anaheim city, California	327
42	69	Colorado Springs city, Colorado	494	70	69	Plano city, Texas	1 293	10	69	San Jose city, California	324
71	70	Henderson city, Nevada	487	68	70	Toledo city, Ohio	1 260	61	70	Lexington-Fayette urban county, Kentucky	306
49	71	Wichita city, Kansas	435	71	71	Henderson city, Nevada	1 165	75	71	Chula Vista city, California	233
52	72	Bakersfield city, California	417	57	72	Santa Ana city, California	1 080	40	72	Virginia Beach city, Virginia	164
38	73	Mesa city, Arizona	346	29	73	Las Vegas city, Nevada	1 069	70	73	Plano city, Texas	148
29	74	Las Vegas city, Nevada	336	52	74	Bakersfield city, California	966	71	74	Henderson city, Nevada	137
55		Urban Honolulu CDP, Hawaii	NA	55		Urban Honolulu CDP, Hawaii	NA	55		Urban Honolulu CDP, Hawaii	NA

75 Largest Cities by 2014 Population

Selected Rankings

Property crime rate, 2010

Population rank	Property crime rate rank	City	Property crimes (per 100,000) population) [col 38]
60	1	St. Louis city, Missouri	6 619
33	2	Tucson city, Arizona	6 582
73	3	Orlando city, Florida	6 511
45	4	Oakland city, California	6 233
39	5	Atlanta city, Georgia	6 103
23	6	Memphis city, Tennessee	6 063
48	7	Cleveland city, Ohio	5 978
65	8	Cincinnati city, Ohio	5 836
13	9	San Francisco city, California	5 795
18	9	Detroit city, Michigan	5 795
7	11	San Antonio city, Texas	5 715
20	12	Seattle city, Washington	5 595
32	13	Albuquerque city, New Mexico	5 470
49	14	Wichita city, Kansas	5 397
27	15	Oklahoma City city, Oklahoma	5 368
47	16	Tulsa city, Oklahoma	5 318
37	17	Kansas City city, Missouri	5 296
14	18	Indianapolis city, Indiana	5 246
4	19	Houston city, Texas	5 087
63	20	Stockton city, California	5 030
44	21	Miami city, Florida	5 002
15	22	Columbus city, Ohio	4 970
26	23	Baltimore city, Maryland	4 945
46	24	Minneapolis city, Minnesota	4 886
28	25	Portland city, Oregon	4 865
11	26	Austin city, Texas	4 850
52	27	Bakersfield city, California	4 647
58	28	Corpus Christi city, Texas	4 642
22	29	Washington city, District of Columbia	4 574
31	30	Milwaukee city, Wisconsin	4 496
41	31	Omaha city, Nebraska	4 495
34	32	Fresno city, California	4 438
16	33	Fort Worth city, Texas	4 355
30	34	Louisville/Jefferson metro gov, Kentucky	4 288
42	35	Colorado Springs city, Colorado	4 167
9	36	Dallas city, Texas	4 165
67	37	Greensboro city, North Carolina	4 130
61	38	Lexington-Fayette urban county, Kentucky	4 057
64	39	Anchorage municipality, Alaska	4 018
6	40	Phoenix city, Arizona	4 000
51	41	Arlington city, Texas	3 960
12	42	Jacksonville city, Florida	3 903
25	43	Nashville-Davidson metro gov, Tennessee	3 871
50	44	New Orleans city, Louisiana	3 853
35	45	Sacramento city, California	3 760
66	46	St. Paul city, Minnesota	3 724
21	47	Denver city, Colorado	3 660
17	48	Charlotte city, North Carolina	3 649
3	49	Chicago city, Illinois	3 583
72	50	Lincoln city, Nebraska	3 496
5	51	Philadelphia city, Pennsylvania	3 442
59	52	Riverside city, California	3 352
62	53	Pittsburgh city, Pennsylvania	3 266
69	54	Newark city, New Jersey	3 222
29	55	Las Vegas city, Nevada	3 197
54	56	Aurora city, Colorado	3 138
43	57	Raleigh city, North Carolina	3 063
38	58	Mesa city, Arizona	2 831
56	59	Anaheim city, California	2 783
24	60	Boston city, Massachusetts	2 773
36	61	Long Beach city, California	2 768
10	62	San Jose city, California	2 571
68	63	Toledo city, Ohio	2 532
53	64	Tampa city, Florida	2 511
40	65	Virginia Beach city, Virginia	2 500
8	66	San Diego city, California	2 351
19	67	El Paso city, Texas	2 289
2	68	Los Angeles city, California	2 213
70	69	Plano city, Texas	2 173
75	70	Chula Vista city, California	2 072
71	71	Henderson city, Nevada	1 997
57	72	Santa Ana city, California	1 930
74	73	Jersey City city, New Jersey	1 883
1	74	New York city, New York	1 691
55		Urban Honolulu CDP, Hawaii	NA

Full time equivalent local government employees

Population rank	Government employees rank	City	Government employees [col 108]
1	1	New York city, New York	404 260
2	2	Los Angeles city, California	47 505
22	3	Washington city, District of Columbia	34 002
5	4	Philadelphia city, Pennsylvania	29 409
13	5	San Francisco city, California	28 349
26	6	Baltimore city, Maryland	26 392
3	7	Chicago city, Illinois	25 630
23	8	Memphis city, Tennessee	24 196
25	9	Nashville-Davidson metro gov, Tennessee	21 697
4	10	Houston city, Texas	21 007
24	11	Boston city, Massachusetts	19 230
40	12	Virginia Beach city, Virginia	18 286
7	13	San Antonio city, Texas	15 382
9	14	Dallas city, Texas	14 235
6	15	Phoenix city, Arizona	13 392
11	16	Austin city, Texas	12 580
18	17	Detroit city, Michigan	12 364
14	18	Indianapolis city, Indiana	12 328
21	19	Denver city, Colorado	11 914
20	20	Seattle city, Washington	10 193
12	21	Jacksonville city, Florida	10 137
64	22	Anchorage municipality, Alaska	9 819
8	23	San Diego city, California	9 425
30	24	Louisville/Jefferson metro gov, Kentucky	8 264
39	25	Atlanta city, Georgia	8 214
15	26	Columbus city, Ohio	8 035
17	27	Charlotte city, North Carolina	7 449
48	28	Cleveland city, Ohio	7 389
42	29	Colorado Springs city, Colorado	6 835
50	30	New Orleans city, Louisiana	6 570
16	31	Fort Worth city, Texas	6 536
37	32	Kansas City city, Missouri	6 482
31	33	Milwaukee city, Wisconsin	6 455
32	34	Albuquerque city, New Mexico	6 438
60	35	St. Louis city, Missouri	6 234
19	36	El Paso city, Texas	5 996
36	37	Long Beach city, California	5 861
28	38	Portland city, Oregon	5 804
65	39	Cincinnati city, Ohio	5 222
10	40	San Jose city, California	5 214
46	41	Minneapolis city, Minnesota	5 068
33	42	Tucson city, Arizona	4 691
35	43	Sacramento city, California	4 483
27	44	Oklahoma City city, Oklahoma	4 418
53	45	Tampa city, Florida	4 247
62	46	Pittsburgh city, Pennsylvania	4 176
45	47	Oakland city, California	3 940
43	48	Raleigh city, North Carolina	3 936
47	49	Tulsa city, Oklahoma	3 932
61	50	Lexington-Fayette urban county, Kentucky	3 926
69	51	Newark city, New Jersey	3 857
44	52	Miami city, Florida	3 807
38	53	Mesa city, Arizona	3 616
34	54	Fresno city, California	3 214
67	55	Greensboro city, North Carolina	3 098
66	56	St. Paul city, Minnesota	3 092
74	57	Jersey City city, New Jersey	2 936
49	58	Wichita city, Kansas	2 864
41	59	Omaha city, Nebraska	2 835
73	60	Orlando city, Florida	2 773
58	61	Corpus Christi city, Texas	2 747
57	62	Santa Ana city, California	2 711
72	63	Lincoln city, Nebraska	2 609
29	64	Las Vegas city, Nevada	2 582
54	65	Aurora city, Colorado	2 579
51	66	Arlington city, Texas	2 551
59	67	Riverside city, California	2 260
71	68	Henderson city, Nevada	2 239
56	69	Anaheim city, California	2 214
68	70	Toledo city, Ohio	2 146
70	71	Plano city, Texas	2 089
63	72	Stockton city, California	2 010
52	73	Bakersfield city, California	1 424
75	74	Chula Vista city, California	1 114
55		Urban Honolulu CDP, Hawaii	NA

Local government employee payroll for March 2012

Population rank	Government employee payroll rank	City	Government payroll (thousands of dollars) [col 109]
1	1	New York city, New York	2 380 283 176
2	2	Los Angeles city, California	361 983 103
13	3	San Francisco city, California	217 722 943
22	4	Washington city, District of Columbia	194 813 463
3	5	Chicago city, Illinois	175 627 618
5	6	Philadelphia city, Pennsylvania	148 399 324
26	7	Baltimore city, Maryland	122 552 640
24	8	Boston city, Massachusetts	112 444 857
4	9	Houston city, Texas	99 616 057
25	10	Nashville-Davidson metro gov, Tennessee	83 700 973
23	11	Memphis city, Tennessee	79 305 378
20	12	Seattle city, Washington	71 586 796
7	13	San Antonio city, Texas	70 371 976
6	14	Phoenix city, Arizona	69 633 897
9	15	Dallas city, Texas	67 511 933
11	16	Austin city, Texas	64 599 610
40	17	Virginia Beach city, Virginia	64 539 702
21	18	Denver city, Colorado	62 559 560
8	19	San Diego city, California	62 476 850
18	20	Detroit city, Michigan	57 433 160
64	21	Anchorage municipality, Alaska	51 971 256
14	22	Indianapolis city, Indiana	49 785 804
12	23	Jacksonville city, Florida	46 960 164
15	24	Columbus city, Ohio	42 573 757
10	25	San Jose city, California	38 715 963
42	26	Colorado Springs city, Colorado	37 084 390
36	27	Long Beach city, California	36 050 392
28	28	Portland city, Oregon	35 656 383
17	29	Charlotte city, North Carolina	34 348 745
32	30	Albuquerque city, New Mexico	33 331 138
48	31	Cleveland city, Ohio	33 318 506
30	32	Louisville/Jefferson metro gov, Kentucky	32 734 538
31	33	Milwaukee city, Wisconsin	32 385 292
16	34	Fort Worth city, Texas	32 292 472
39	35	Atlanta city, Georgia	31 551 612
45	36	Oakland city, California	30 153 764
35	37	Sacramento city, California	29 508 935
65	38	Cincinnati city, Ohio	26 843 252
46	39	Minneapolis city, Minnesota	26 103 507
50	40	New Orleans city, Louisiana	26 033 023
69	41	Newark city, New Jersey	25 580 741
60	42	St. Louis city, Missouri	25 364 525
27	43	Oklahoma City city, Oklahoma	24 268 820
19	44	El Paso city, Texas	23 812 936
53	45	Tampa city, Florida	22 517 912
33	46	Tucson city, Arizona	21 780 237
37	47	Kansas City city, Missouri	21 087 489
38	48	Mesa city, Arizona	20 622 110
74	49	Jersey City city, New Jersey	18 762 329
44	50	Miami city, Florida	18 642 774
34	51	Fresno city, California	18 551 770
66	52	St. Paul city, Minnesota	18 028 194
29	53	Las Vegas city, Nevada	17 371 881
47	54	Tulsa city, Oklahoma	16 951 552
62	55	Pittsburgh city, Pennsylvania	16 527 485
61	56	Lexington-Fayette urban county, Kentucky	16 180 537
43	57	Raleigh city, North Carolina	15 850 858
56	58	Anaheim city, California	15 281 363
41	59	Omaha city, Nebraska	15 258 712
59	60	Riverside city, California	15 114 251
73	61	Orlando city, Florida	14 180 368
71	62	Henderson city, Nevada	13 759 509
54	63	Aurora city, Colorado	13 742 359
72	64	Lincoln city, Nebraska	13 359 820
57	65	Santa Ana city, California	12 719 386
63	66	Stockton city, California	12 427 436
49	67	Wichita city, Kansas	12 396 633
51	68	Arlington city, Texas	12 130 944
67	69	Greensboro city, North Carolina	11 503 988
58	70	Corpus Christi city, Texas	10 789 288
70	71	Plano city, Texas	10 395 648
68	72	Toledo city, Ohio	10 282 276
52	73	Bakersfield city, California	8 316 644
75	74	Chula Vista city, California	7 346 424
55		Urban Honolulu CDP, Hawaii	NA

Table D. Cities — Land Area and Population

STATE Place code	City	Land area,[1] 2010 (sq km)	Population, 2014			Race alone or in combination (percent), 2011-2013					Percent Hispanic or Latino[2], 2011-2013	Percent foreign born 2011–2013
			Total persons	Rank	Per square kilometer	White	Black	American Indian, Alaska Native	Asian	Hawaiian Pacific Islander		
		1	2	3	4	5	6	7	8	9	10	11

1. Dry land or land partially or temporarily covered by water. 2. May be of any race.

Table D. Cities — Population

City	Age of population (percent), 2011-2013									Median age 2011-2013	Percent female 2011-2013	Population			
												Census counts		Percent change	
	Under 5 years	5 to 17 years	18 to 24 years	25 to 34 years	35 to 44 years	45 to 54 years	55 to 64 years	65 to 74 years	75 years and over			2000	2010	2000–2010	2010–2014
	12	13	14	15	16	17	18	19	20	21	22	23	24	25	26

Table D. Cities — Households, Group Quarters, Crime, and Education

City	Households, 2011-2013				Persons in group quarters, 2010				Serious crimes known to police,[2] 2013				Educational attainment, 2011–2013		
			Percent			Institutional			Total		Rate[3]			Attainment[4] (percent)	
	Number	Persons per household	Female family householder[1]	One-person	Total	Total	Persons in nursing facilities	Non-institutional	Number	Rate[3]	Violent	Property	Population age 25 and older	High school graduate or less	Bachelor's degree or more
	27	28	29	30	31	32	33	34	35	36	37	38	39	40	41

1. No spouse present. 2. Data for serious crimes have not been adjusted for underreporting. This may affect comparability between geographic areas and over time. 3. Per 100,000 population estimated by the FBI. 4. Persons 25 years old and over.

Table D. Cities — Income, Poverty, and Housing

City	Money income, 2011–2013					Housing units, 2010			Occupied housing units 2011–2013				
		Households								Owner-occupied		Median owner costs as a percent of income	
	Per capita income[1] (dollars)	Median income	Percent with income of $200,000 or more	Percent with income of less than $25,000	Families with income below poverty (percent)	Total	Percent change, 2000–2010	Vacant units for sale or rent[2]	Total	Percent	Median value[3] (dollars)	With a mortgage[4]	Without a mortgage[5]
	42	43	44	45	46	47	48	49	50	51	52	53	54

1. Based on population estimated by the American Community Survey. 2. Includes units rented or sold but not occupied. 3. Specified owner-occupied units; $1,000,000 represents $1,000,000 or more 4. 50.0 represents 50 percent or more. 5. 10.0 represents 10 percent or less.

Table D. Cities — Housing, Labor Force, and Employment

City	Occupied housing units, 2011–2013 (cont.)				Migration, 2011–2013		Civilian labor force, 2014				Civilian employment[4], 2011–2013			
									Unemployment			Percent		
	Percent renter occupied	Median gross rent[1]	Median rent as a percent of income[2]	Percent with no vehicle available	Percent who lived in the same house one year ago	Percent who lived outside current city one year ago	Total	Percent change, 2013–2014	Total	Rate[3]	Population age 16 and older	In labor force	Civilian full-year full-time workers	Households with no workers (percent)
	55	56	57	58	59	60	61	62	63	64	65	66	67	68

1. $2,000 represents $2,000 or more. 2. 50.0 represents 50 percent or more. 3. Percent of civilian labor force. 4. Persons 16 years old and over.

Table D. Cities — Construction, Wholesale Trade, and Retail Trade

City	Value of residential construction authorized by building permits, 2014			Wholesale trade,[1] 2007				Retail trade,[2] 2007			
	New construction ($1,000)	Number of housing units	Percent single family	Number of establishments	Number of employees	Sales (mil dol)	Annual payroll (mil dol)	Number of establishments	Number of employees	Sales (mil dol)	Annual payroll (mil dol)
	69	70	71	72	73	74	75	76	77	78	79

1. Merchant wholesalers except manufacturers' sales branches and offices. 2. Establishments with payroll.

Table D. Cities — Real Estate, Professional Services, and Manufacturing

City	Real estate and rental and leasing, 2007				Professional, scientific, and technical services,[1] 2007				Manufacturing, 2007			
	Number of establishments	Number of employees	Receipts (mil dol)	Annual payroll (mil dol)	Number of establishments	Number of employees	Receipts (mil dol)	Annual payroll (mil dol)	Number of establishments	Number of employees	Receipts (mil dol)	Annual payroll (mil dol)
	80	81	82	83	84	85	86	87	88	89	90	91

1. Establishments subject to federal tax.

Table D. Cities — Accommodation and Food Services, Arts, Entertainment, and Recreation, and Health Care and Social Assistance

City	Accommodation and food services, 2007				Arts, entertainment, and recreation,[1] 2007				Health care and social assistance,[1] 2007			
	Number of establishments	Number of employees	Sales (mil dol)	Annual payroll (mil dol)	Number of establishments	Number of employees	Receipts (mil dol)	Annual payroll (mil dol)	Number of establishments	Number of employees	Receipts (mil dol)	Annual payroll (mil dol)
	92	93	94	95	96	97	98	99	100	101	102	103

1. Establishments subject to federal tax.

Table D. Cities — Other Services and Government Employment and Payroll

City	Other services[1], 2007				Government employment and payroll, 2012								
						March payroll							
							Percent of total for:						
	Number of establish-ments	Number of employees	Receipts (mil dol)	Annual payroll (mil dol)	Full-time equivalent employees	Total (dollars)	Adminis-tration, judicial, and legal	Police and Corrections	Fire Protection	Highways and trans-portation	Health and welfare	Natural resources and utilities	Education and libraries
	104	105	106	107	108	109	110	111	112	113	114	115	116

1. Establishments subject to federal tax.

Table D. Cities — City Government Finances

City	City government finances, 2007									
	General revenue							General expenditure		
		Intergovernmental		Taxes					Per capita[1] (dollars)	
					Per capita[1] (dollars)					
	Total (mil dol)	Total (mil dol)	Percent from state government	Total (mil dol)	Total	Property	Sales and gross receipts	Total (mil dol)	Total	Capital outlays
	117	118	119	120	121	122	123	124	125	126

1. Based on population estimated as of July 1 of the year shown.

Table D. Cities — City Government Finances

City	City government finances, 2012 (cont.)									
	General expenditure (cont.)									
	Percent of total for:									
	Public welfare	Highways	Parking facilities	Education	Health and hospitals	Police protection	Sewerage and sanitation	Parks and recreation	Housing and community development	Interest on debt
	127	128	129	130	131	132	133	134	135	136

Table D. Cities — City Government Finances, City Government Employment, and Climate

City	City government finances, 2012 (cont.)			Climate[2]						
	Debt outstanding			Average daily temperature (degrees Fahrenheit)						
				Mean		Limits				
	Total (mil dol)	Per capita[1] (dollars)	Debt issued during year	January	July	January[3]	July[4]	Annual precipitation (inches)	Heating degree days	Cooling degree days
	137	138	139	140	141	142	143	144	145	146

1. Based on the population estimated as of July 1 of the year shown. 2. Represents normal values based on the 30-year period, 1971–2000. 3. Average daily minimum.
4. Average daily maximum.

Table D. Cities — **Land Area and Population**

STATE Place code	City	Land area,[1] 2010 (sq km)	Population, 2014: Total persons	Population, 2014: Rank	Population, 2014: Per square kilometer	Race alone or in combination (percent), 2011-2013: White	Race: Black	Race: American Indian, Alaska Native	Race: Asian	Race: Hawaiian Pacific Islander	Percent Hispanic or Latino[2], 2011-2013	Percent foreign born 2011–2013
		1	2	3	4	5	6	7	8	9	10	11
00 00000	United States	9 147 592.7	318 857 056	X	34.9	76.3	13.7	1.7	5.9	0.4	16.9	13.0
01 00000	ALABAMA	131 170.8	4 849 377	X	37.0	70.5	27.1	1.2	1.5	0.1	4.0	3.4
01 00820	Alabaster	64.9	31 545	1 180	486.1	78.0	14.6	0.8	0.4	NA	11.1	8.1
01 03076	Auburn	150.4	60 258	598	400.7	73.7	18.2	0.5	7.2	NA	3.3	8.6
01 05980	Bessemer	103.2	26 949	1 362	261.1	24.8	73.2	NA	NA	NA	2.5	1.3
01 07000	Birmingham	378.3	212 247	101	561.1	24.0	73.7	0.6	1.3	0.0	3.3	3.6
01 20104	Decatur	139.0	55 532	662	399.5	73.6	22.6	2.3	1.2	NA	12.8	6.8
01 21184	Dothan	231.5	68 409	504	295.5	64.2	34.2	0.8	1.6	0.1	2.9	2.5
01 24184	Enterprise	80.9	27 772	1 316	343.3	75.7	22.0	1.3	2.5	NA	8.6	5.9
01 26896	Florence	67.3	40 215	922	597.5	77.3	21.0	0.8	1.3	NA	2.5	2.7
01 28696	Gadsden	96.3	36 295	1 026	376.9	60.4	37.3	1.6	0.9	NA	5.2	3.3
01 35800	Homewood	21.7	25 802	1 402	1 189.0	79.2	17.0	NA	3.0	NA	7.2	9.7
01 35896	Hoover	122.2	84 353	382	690.3	76.4	14.2	1.1	5.1	NA	6.7	7.6
01 37000	Huntsville	541.5	188 226	125	347.6	64.6	32.3	1.3	3.1	0.3	5.8	6.3
01 45784	Madison	76.7	46 450	808	605.6	78.4	13.7	1.6	8.1	NA	3.3	8.4
01 50000	Mobile	360.3	194 675	122	540.3	46.3	52.2	0.7	1.5	0.0	2.5	3.2
01 51000	Montgomery	413.3	200 481	114	485.1	37.5	59.0	0.5	2.7	NA	3.7	4.5
01 57048	Opelika	154.3	29 171	1 263	189.1	52.6	40.5	1.3	1.1	NA	6.6	7.1
01 59472	Phenix City	71.9	37 540	985	522.1	50.0	48.2	1.1	1.6	NA	5.7	2.5
01 62328	Prattville	85.1	35 317	1 056	415.0	76.7	20.0	1.0	2.3	NA	4.1	2.3
01 77256	Tuscaloosa	156.0	96 122	311	616.2	53.3	43.7	0.4	2.6	0.2	3.7	5.0
01 78552	Vestavia Hills	50.3	34 124	1 092	678.4	90.1	4.2	0.4	5.3	NA	2.0	5.0
02 00000	ALASKA	1 477 953.2	736 732	X	0.5	73.5	5.1	19.4	7.4	1.6	6.3	7.1
02 03000	Anchorage	4 415.1	301 010	64	68.2	73.7	8.7	12.4	10.9	2.8	8.3	9.4
02 24230	Fairbanks	82.1	32 469	1 145	395.5	73.8	10.7	15.2	6.8	1.1	11.5	8.3
02 36400	Juneau	6 998.0	32 406	1 149	4.6	77.0	1.9	19.1	8.2	1.4	5.9	6.9
04 00000	ARIZONA	294 207.3	6 731 484	X	22.9	81.6	5.1	5.4	3.8	0.4	30.1	13.4
04 02830	Apache Junction	90.6	38 131	972	420.9	94.4	1.6	2.9	1.7	NA	14.3	6.9
04 04720	Avondale	118.1	79 646	412	674.4	79.2	10.7	2.4	4.2	0.3	52.5	15.3
04 07940	Buckeye	971.9	59 470	609	61.2	79.4	8.5	2.9	1.7	0.4	37.6	8.8
04 08220	Bullhead City	153.8	39 364	943	255.9	91.9	2.0	3.7	3.0	0.5	21.9	9.6
04 10530	Casa Grande	284.0	51 478	725	181.3	83.2	5.7	2.4	3.8	NA	34.9	11.9
04 12000	Chandler	166.8	254 276	78	1 524.4	82.0	6.5	2.3	10.1	0.6	22.3	14.0
04 22220	El Mirage	26.0	33 532	1 110	1 289.7	81.5	6.8	2.5	3.2	0.5	49.8	19.6
04 23620	Flagstaff	165.4	68 785	499	415.9	76.5	2.9	13.1	3.2	1.5	18.9	7.2
04 23760	Florence	135.9	26 912	1 365	198.0	83.7	5.7	3.8	1.1	0.6	40.4	22.2
04 27400	Gilbert	176.0	239 277	86	1 359.5	87.4	4.3	1.2	7.9	0.3	16.9	9.5
04 27820	Glendale	155.3	237 517	88	1 529.4	80.2	7.6	2.3	4.9	0.4	37.2	17.5
04 28380	Goodyear	495.9	75 664	444	152.6	81.0	9.2	2.0	7.5	0.6	27.1	11.1
04 37620	Kingman	90.2	28 549	1 286	316.5	93.9	1.3	5.0	2.5	1.9	15.9	3.1
04 39370	Lake Havasu City	115.1	53 103	697	461.4	95.3	1.7	1.1	1.2	0.3	12.7	5.2
04 44270	Marana	314.6	39 888	931	126.8	84.9	5.9	1.7	5.2	NA	21.0	7.3
04 44410	Maricopa	123.0	47 442	792	385.7	76.9	13.5	1.7	4.8	NA	23.0	10.8
04 46000	Mesa	353.4	464 704	38	1 315.0	85.7	4.9	3.1	2.5	0.7	26.4	12.3
04 51600	Oro Valley	92.0	42 018	879	456.7	92.1	1.5	1.4	4.1	NA	10.3	6.8
04 54050	Peoria	451.7	166 934	148	369.6	90.4	4.5	1.6	4.7	0.4	17.8	8.9
04 55000	Phoenix	1 338.3	1 537 058	6	1 148.5	78.9	7.8	2.7	4.1	0.4	40.6	20.1
04 57380	Prescott	107.1	40 958	902	382.4	94.9	1.5	3.1	1.9	NA	6.7	7.2
04 57450	Prescott Valley	100.1	41 075	899	410.3	94.8	0.9	1.8	1.9	NA	17.6	6.0
04 58150	Queen Creek	72.6	32 236	1 160	444.0	89.8	2.2	2.3	2.0	NA	19.3	3.9
04 62140	Sahuarita	80.4	27 547	1 333	342.6	89.8	3.6	NA	4.9	NA	33.8	10.5
04 63470	San Luis	83.0	31 091	1 189	374.6	96.1	0.9	1.3	NA	NA	95.7	45.4
04 65000	Scottsdale	476.4	230 512	95	483.9	91.1	2.4	1.6	4.8	0.1	10.6	10.5
04 66820	Sierra Vista	394.4	43 806	847	111.1	79.3	10.8	1.5	6.4	NA	24.1	10.3
04 71510	Surprise	273.9	126 275	215	461.0	90.0	6.5	1.0	2.4	0.3	18.0	9.7
04 73000	Tempe	103.4	172 816	142	1 671.3	77.3	6.3	2.8	8.7	0.8	22.0	12.9
04 77000	Tucson	587.2	527 972	33	899.1	77.2	6.5	3.6	4.1	0.5	42.6	15.2
04 85540	Yuma	311.5	93 400	326	299.8	72.2	4.2	1.5	2.6	NA	56.7	20.5
05 00000	ARKANSAS	134 771.3	2 966 369	X	22.0	80.0	16.2	1.7	1.6	0.3	6.7	4.6
05 04840	Bella Vista	114.6	27 688	1 321	241.6	96.2	1.6	1.3	1.9	NA	4.7	4.3
05 05290	Benton	57.6	33 625	1 107	583.8	89.8	9.9	0.7	0.5	NA	4.7	2.3
05 05320	Bentonville	81.0	41 613	889	513.7	85.7	1.8	2.0	9.9	NA	8.8	13.0
05 15190	Conway	117.4	64 490	547	549.3	79.7	16.7	0.8	2.8	0.1	5.1	4.2
05 23290	Fayetteville	139.5	80 621	406	577.9	84.8	6.6	2.5	4.5	NA	7.4	7.6
05 24550	Fort Smith	160.5	87 351	359	544.2	82.5	10.6	3.6	6.3	NA	17.2	12.6
05 33400	Hot Springs	90.7	35 673	1 047	393.3	73.0	20.3	1.6	0.7	NA	8.5	4.0

1. Dry land or land partially or temporarily covered by water. 2. May be of any race.

City	Age of population (percent), 2011-2013: Under 5 years	5 to 17 years	18 to 24 years	25 to 34 years	35 to 44 years	45 to 54 years	55 to 64 years	65 to 74 years	75 years and over	Median age 2011-2013	Percent female 2011-2013	Population: Census counts: 2000	2010	Percent change: 2000–2010	2010–2014
	12	13	14	15	16	17	18	19	20	21	22	23	24	25	26
United States	6.4	17.1	10.0	13.5	12.9	14.1	12.3	7.6	6.1	37.4	50.8	281 421 906	308 745 538	9.7	3.3
ALABAMA	6.2	17.0	10.1	12.7	12.7	14.0	12.8	8.3	6.2	38.3	51.6	4 447 100	4 779 736	7.5	1.4
Alabaster	5.9	21.2	8.8	12.9	16.3	15.1	9.3	6.3	4.2	35.8	51.4	22 619	30 352	34.2	3.9
Auburn	4.8	13.5	36.6	14.3	9.6	8.2	6.1	4.2	2.6	23.5	49.1	42 987	53 380	24.2	12.9
Bessemer	7.1	18.8	7.9	12.9	11.0	13.4	13.1	7.4	8.4	38.6	52.5	29 672	27 456	-7.5	-1.9
Birmingham	7.0	13.9	12.2	15.5	12.0	13.8	13.0	6.6	6.1	36.0	53.4	242 820	212 237	-12.6	0.0
Decatur	6.1	17.1	9.6	12.5	13.6	13.9	12.4	8.3	6.5	37.9	51.7	53 929	55 683	3.3	-0.3
Dothan	6.8	16.9	8.8	13.8	12.6	13.6	12.6	8.2	6.7	38.1	52.3	57 737	65 496	13.4	3.8
Enterprise	7.3	19.2	8.5	14.4	15.1	12.4	10.1	6.8	6.2	35.3	50.5	21 178	26 562	25.4	4.3
Florence	5.4	13.2	16.0	12.3	10.0	11.5	13.5	9.4	8.7	37.7	55.1	36 264	39 319	8.4	2.2
Gadsden	7.4	14.8	9.5	13.4	11.4	13.7	13.1	8.9	7.6	39.4	52.9	38 978	36 856	-5.4	-1.6
Homewood	7.9	16.0	17.3	19.7	12.8	8.6	8.7	4.2	4.8	29.2	49.1	25 043	25 167	0.5	2.5
Hoover	6.5	19.2	6.0	14.9	14.6	12.9	12.8	7.7	5.4	37.2	52.6	62 742	81 619	30.1	4.1
Huntsville	6.2	15.2	11.4	14.7	12.0	14.7	11.7	7.7	6.3	36.7	51.1	158 216	180 105	13.8	4.4
Madison	6.1	20.4	8.9	12.9	12.6	18.5	11.7	5.4	3.4	36.7	49.5	29 329	42 938	46.4	8.2
Mobile	6.7	16.4	11.4	14.0	12.0	12.8	12.4	7.7	6.5	36.1	52.2	198 915	195 111	-1.9	-0.3
Montgomery	7.2	17.8	11.8	14.5	12.3	12.5	11.5	7.0	5.4	34.2	53.2	201 568	205 764	2.1	-2.5
Opelika	6.6	17.1	9.9	14.1	11.8	13.7	12.9	7.6	6.4	37.2	53.1	23 498	26 477	12.7	10.4
Phenix City	8.4	19.6	10.7	16.2	12.5	12.2	9.5	5.7	5.2	31.9	52.8	28 265	32 822	16.1	14.2
Prattville	6.5	19.4	9.8	12.8	14.1	15.1	9.4	7.6	5.2	36.2	52.9	24 303	33 960	39.7	4.0
Tuscaloosa	5.1	12.9	27.9	13.4	10.4	10.2	9.8	5.1	5.1	27.3	52.4	77 906	90 468	16.1	6.2
Vestavia Hills	6.7	19.1	5.1	12.0	13.3	14.9	13.1	6.9	8.8	41.2	52.3	24 476	34 033	39.0	0.2
ALASKA	7.5	18.3	11.0	15.2	12.6	14.3	12.6	5.6	3.0	33.5	47.8	626 932	710 231	13.3	3.7
Anchorage	7.5	17.8	11.6	16.4	12.9	14.0	11.7	5.2	3.0	32.7	49.1	260 283	291 826	12.1	3.1
Fairbanks	9.8	18.0	16.2	21.3	9.7	8.2	9.1	4.3	3.6	27.4	45.8	30 224	31 535	4.3	3.0
Juneau	6.2	16.8	8.8	14.2	13.6	16.5	14.9	5.8	3.1	37.4	48.1	30 711	31 275	1.8	3.6
ARIZONA	6.7	18.0	10.0	13.3	12.6	12.8	11.7	8.5	6.3	36.6	50.3	5 130 632	6 392 017	24.6	5.3
Apache Junction	4.8	16.0	5.5	8.3	10.8	11.7	13.8	16.2	12.9	49.2	51.7	31 814	35 840	12.7	6.4
Avondale	9.0	22.3	11.5	16.1	15.0	11.8	8.0	4.5	1.8	29.3	52.1	35 883	76 238	112.5	4.6
Buckeye	7.8	21.9	9.2	16.6	14.4	11.7	9.9	6.1	2.3	32.2	47.0	6 537	50 876	678.3	16.9
Bullhead City	5.9	14.2	7.1	6.8	9.7	14.0	15.0	17.0	10.2	49.7	50.4	33 769	39 540	17.1	-0.4
Casa Grande	7.5	19.4	7.4	11.2	12.6	11.8	12.1	10.4	7.6	38.7	49.5	25 224	48 571	92.6	6.0
Chandler	7.4	19.6	9.2	14.8	15.5	14.6	10.2	5.3	3.4	34.3	50.4	176 581	236 123	33.7	7.7
El Mirage	9.4	21.9	10.3	17.2	14.1	10.8	7.4	5.6	3.3	30.8	49.3	7 609	31 797	317.9	5.5
Flagstaff	6.3	13.5	28.4	15.3	10.8	9.5	9.5	4.8	2.1	25.9	50.0	52 894	65 870	24.5	4.1
Florence	1.5	8.0	8.7	19.3	16.7	15.1	10.1	14.9	5.7	42.2	28.7	17 054	25 536	49.7	5.4
Gilbert	8.2	24.5	7.1	14.1	17.5	13.3	8.3	4.8	2.3	32.4	50.4	109 697	208 453	90.0	14.8
Glendale	7.1	19.3	11.6	14.0	13.3	13.8	11.1	5.8	4.1	33.5	50.2	218 812	226 721	3.6	4.9
Goodyear	6.1	20.3	7.2	15.2	15.5	12.6	10.7	8.7	3.8	36.0	52.9	18 911	65 275	245.2	16.0
Kingman	6.2	15.4	6.7	13.8	9.4	16.4	11.7	11.0	9.4	43.6	51.1	20 069	28 068	39.9	1.7
Lake Havasu City	3.5	13.6	6.2	8.7	7.9	13.4	16.1	17.4	13.2	52.9	52.6	41 938	52 527	25.2	1.1
Marana	7.4	17.5	6.7	12.1	14.5	10.9	13.8	9.8	7.2	39.4	50.3	13 556	34 961	157.9	15.4
Maricopa	10.0	19.8	6.4	17.5	17.3	10.5	11.9	4.8	1.9	33.6	50.7	1 040	43 482	4 081.0	9.1
Mesa	7.1	17.8	9.9	14.4	11.9	12.7	11.0	7.9	7.3	35.5	50.9	396 375	439 041	10.8	5.6
Oro Valley	3.9	14.6	7.8	7.6	8.9	13.9	15.4	16.7	11.3	50.3	53.1	29 700	41 011	38.1	2.5
Peoria	5.8	19.5	7.9	12.1	13.2	14.1	12.1	8.2	7.0	39.0	51.9	108 364	154 065	42.2	8.3
Phoenix	7.7	19.4	10.5	15.4	14.2	13.5	10.2	5.3	3.7	33.0	50.0	1 321 045	1 445 632	9.4	6.2
Prescott	1.9	9.2	9.5	8.6	7.1	11.8	17.7	16.5	17.7	55.7	51.5	33 938	39 843	17.4	2.8
Prescott Valley	7.0	17.0	8.6	13.5	9.2	10.6	13.7	11.3	9.2	40.6	52.2	23 535	38 822	65.0	5.8
Queen Creek	9.2	30.3	5.3	10.3	18.3	11.7	8.3	4.9	1.8	30.5	51.7	4 316	26 361	510.8	22.3
Sahuarita	10.9	20.2	4.9	13.2	14.2	9.7	10.5	10.4	6.0	35.5	49.9	3 242	25 259	679.1	9.1
San Luis	8.2	23.9	13.0	14.9	12.5	14.1	7.0	4.1	2.5	27.3	46.5	15 322	25 505	66.5	11.4
Scottsdale	4.7	13.2	7.0	13.0	12.5	14.4	14.5	11.9	8.9	44.7	51.7	202 705	217 385	7.2	6.0
Sierra Vista	6.5	18.1	13.9	14.4	10.7	10.6	10.3	8.4	7.2	33.0	51.8	37 775	43 888	16.2	-3.0
Surprise	7.3	21.5	5.3	11.7	13.8	9.9	9.5	13.1	7.8	38.3	52.0	30 848	117 517	281.0	7.5
Tempe	5.2	11.4	24.4	19.1	11.1	10.2	10.2	5.0	3.4	28.5	48.2	158 625	161 719	2.0	6.8
Tucson	6.3	15.8	15.8	14.3	12.0	12.2	11.2	6.7	5.8	33.3	50.3	486 699	520 116	6.9	1.4
Yuma	7.6	20.4	13.8	14.5	11.6	10.5	8.4	7.1	6.1	30.2	48.1	77 515	93 064	20.1	3.0
ARKANSAS	6.6	17.5	9.8	13.0	12.4	13.4	12.4	8.5	6.5	37.6	50.9	2 673 400	2 915 918	9.1	1.7
Bella Vista	5.2	12.2	4.0	8.6	12.0	11.3	13.0	17.6	16.1	52.3	52.0	16 582	26 461	59.6	4.6
Benton	7.4	19.1	8.3	14.8	13.0	13.6	10.3	7.4	6.1	35.3	52.0	21 906	30 681	40.1	9.6
Bentonville	7.5	19.8	8.4	16.8	16.9	14.1	9.3	3.9	3.3	33.3	48.7	19 730	35 301	78.9	17.9
Conway	6.2	16.9	21.0	16.9	11.9	9.3	9.1	4.5	4.2	27.9	50.3	43 167	58 908	36.5	9.5
Fayetteville	5.0	12.7	26.3	18.5	11.3	9.3	8.7	4.2	4.1	27.7	50.1	58 047	73 580	26.8	9.6
Fort Smith	7.6	17.3	10.0	15.0	11.8	13.6	12.0	6.6	6.0	35.0	50.3	80 268	86 209	7.4	1.3
Hot Springs	6.2	15.5	9.7	12.8	10.1	12.5	13.0	9.5	10.7	40.8	52.1	35 750	35 193	-1.6	1.4

Table D. Cities — Households, Group Quarters, Crime, and Education

City	Households, 2011-2013				Persons in group quarters, 2010				Serious crimes known to police,[2] 2013				Educational attainment, 2011–2013		
			Percent			Institutional			Total		Rate[3]			Attainment[4] (percent)	
	Number	Persons per house-hold	Female family house-holder[1]	One-person	Total	Total	Persons in nursing facilities	Non-institu-tional	Number	Rate[3]	Violent	Property	Population age 25 and older	High school graduate or less	Bachelor's degree or more
	27	28	29	30	31	32	33	34	35	36	37	38	39	40	41
United States	115 731 304	2.64	13.1	27.7	7 987 323	3 993 659	1 502 264	3 993 664	9 824 500	3 108	377	2 731	208 797 616	41.8	29.1
ALABAMA	1 837 292	2.56	15.3	28.6	115 816	67 004	22 995	48 812	182 819	3 782	431	3 351	3 213 252	47.2	23.0
Alabaster	10 495	2.93	11.3	21.2	300	297	293	3	684	2 194	141	2 053	19 889	33.3	33.8
Auburn	21 528	2.45	10.1	31.4	3 827	130	130	3 697	2 045	3 528	198	3 329	25 651	18.6	61.3
Bessemer	10 243	2.57	27.2	35.0	871	519	472	352	3 726	13 678	1 935	11 744	18 010	54.8	12.3
Birmingham	88 251	2.30	23.4	40.7	9 035	3 300	1 559	5 735	17 009	8 023	1 345	6 678	141 523	43.3	24.0
Decatur	22 329	2.46	13.3	34.3	966	767	246	199	2 702	4 817	266	4 552	37 503	46.2	25.5
Dothan	26 140	2.54	17.4	30.1	1 369	1 171	484	198	2 836	4 182	493	3 690	45 521	44.2	24.8
Enterprise	10 097	2.72	16.4	27.1	279	245	245	34	886	3 148	398	2 750	18 019	39.4	29.5
Florence	17 717	2.15	13.2	36.5	1 701	524	370	1 177	2 014	5 101	524	4 577	26 008	43.9	26.8
Gadsden	14 716	2.41	22.0	33.6	1 752	1 189	380	563	3 358	9 172	1 158	8 014	25 034	53.5	14.1
Homewood	9 143	2.57	10.1	31.9	1 864	18	0	1 846	1 111	4 391	257	4 135	14 930	20.7	59.7
Hoover	31 941	2.59	10.6	26.7	408	393	361	15	2 669	3 172	88	3 084	56 802	16.7	55.5
Huntsville	76 624	2.31	14.6	37.1	6 786	1 924	874	4 862	10 723	5 804	816	4 989	123 318	30.4	38.9
Madison	16 667	2.75	8.7	21.0	270	270	225	0	1 333	2 927	292	2 635	29 803	16.2	56.9
Mobile	75 966	2.45	21.4	34.4	5 598	2 632	1 196	2 966	14 552	5 808	615	5 193	127 551	42.2	26.1
Montgomery	79 316	2.50	21.6	32.7	6 879	2 967	1 005	3 912	9 095	4 435	406	4 029	129 248	39.8	31.0
Opelika	11 042	2.44	21.4	30.0	572	481	141	91	1 674	5 915	583	5 332	18 605	45.6	27.3
Phenix City	14 238	2.58	23.1	31.2	557	494	203	63	2 615	7 017	566	6 451	22 935	43.9	23.4
Prattville	12 374	2.78	12.3	26.4	398	362	181	36	1 370	3 897	245	3 653	22 332	41.2	26.8
Tuscaloosa	31 633	2.66	17.8	32.2	9 659	942	144	8 717	4 946	5 255	461	4 794	50 683	39.7	33.4
Vestavia Hills	13 825	2.45	8.1	29.4	141	138	138	3	561	1 645	50	1 595	23 546	12.0	66.5
ALASKA	250 875	2.80	11.3	26.0	26 352	6 458	1 626	19 894	25 918	3 526	640	2 885	461 441	36.3	27.4
Anchorage	104 980	2.77	11.9	26.3	8 450	2 828	1 137	5 622	14 467	4 831	813	4 018	188 313	31.9	32.4
Fairbanks	11 236	2.68	13.0	31.3	2 518	427	81	2 091	1 482	4 559	655	3 904	18 031	38.0	21.9
Juneau	12 044	2.63	12.3	23.7	887	408	57	479	1 197	3 633	407	3 226	22 095	25.7	38.7
ARIZONA	2 381 501	2.69	12.9	27.4	139 384	84 788	13 819	54 596	252 842	3 816	416	3 399	4 274 066	38.7	27.2
Apache Junction	15 439	2.36	12.0	30.1	283	120	120	163	1 285	3 508	298	3 211	26 986	51.3	11.1
Avondale	22 800	3.42	22.9	16.3	160	146	132	14	3 607	4 571	270	4 301	44 636	46.4	20.3
Buckeye	15 093	3.25	13.2	18.2	5 094	5 084	0	10	1 377	2 472	88	2 384	33 377	46.1	16.3
Bullhead City	16 695	2.36	14.1	27.8	166	96	93	70	1 792	4 528	192	4 336	28 743	49.5	12.7
Casa Grande	17 471	2.84	11.9	23.4	282	47	3	235	2 204	4 403	457	3 945	32 756	43.4	18.3
Chandler	86 150	2.83	11.1	23.0	546	136	94	410	6 475	2 603	231	2 372	156 266	26.2	40.0
El Mirage	9 801	3.32	19.1	19.5	13	0	0	13	1 259	3 834	262	3 572	19 032	54.4	11.8
Flagstaff	23 579	2.50	12.7	25.3	8 076	668	114	7 408	3 115	4 583	362	4 221	34 955	26.0	43.0
Florence	5 926	2.28	6.9	33.2	17 700	17 700	0	0	222	832	90	742	21 489	55.7	10.3
Gilbert	70 877	3.12	10.7	16.7	304	4	0	300	3 701	1 643	88	1 555	133 440	21.2	40.1
Glendale	78 920	2.89	17.7	26.0	3 257	1 000	836	2 257	14 531	6 210	387	5 823	143 760	44.6	21.4
Goodyear	22 926	2.88	9.3	17.5	3 828	3 670	164	158	1 810	2 548	132	2 415	46 433	32.5	27.7
Kingman	10 898	2.50	13.3	28.9	699	541	132	158	1 749	6 158	451	5 708	20 281	50.5	12.6
Lake Havasu City	23 120	2.28	10.4	28.0	201	151	142	50	1 339	2 532	164	2 367	40 552	47.7	14.3
Marana	13 840	2.67	7.4	19.1	520	499	0	21	1 093	2 917	99	2 818	25 271	22.9	40.5
Maricopa	14 325	3.13	11.1	15.4	0	0	0	0	881	1 963	138	1 825	28 624	33.6	26.7
Mesa	165 911	2.70	13.3	27.6	3 538	1 344	928	2 194	14 723	3 228	396	2 831	293 941	39.0	24.7
Oro Valley	17 112	2.42	7.9	22.9	68	63	42	5	678	1 634	60	1 574	30 572	16.0	52.6
Peoria	58 519	2.71	11.8	24.7	1 227	868	826	359	4 084	2 527	157	2 369	106 504	33.4	28.3
Phoenix	519 395	2.83	15.6	28.8	21 738	13 589	2 696	8 149	69 577	4 632	632	4 000	929 076	43.1	26.5
Prescott	19 314	1.99	10.6	37.7	2 008	675	474	1 333	1 209	2 967	304	2 662	32 021	24.3	36.7
Prescott Valley	15 403	2.53	12.2	26.6	209	158	118	51	833	2 125	209	1 915	26 452	41.1	19.4
Queen Creek	8 352	3.36	11.4	13.4	16	0	0	16	NA	NA	NA	NA	15 498	21.2	40.1
Sahuarita	9 090	2.88	7.4	16.6	63	44	44	19	366	1 379	64	1 315	16 852	26.4	33.0
San Luis	8 343	3.41	19.8	8.5	524	502	0	22	576	2 040	131	1 909	16 814	68.2	8.4
Scottsdale	100 324	2.21	7.7	33.6	1 159	686	622	473	6 103	2 706	149	2 557	167 832	17.9	53.2
Sierra Vista	17 529	2.41	13.8	27.1	3 037	233	217	2 804	NA	NA	NA	NA	28 192	27.1	32.7
Surprise	44 079	2.75	11.2	22.3	274	89	80	185	2 269	1 852	122	1 731	79 978	33.4	28.6
Tempe	63 400	2.46	11.3	34.0	10 188	298	280	9 890	8 707	5 167	493	4 674	97 943	26.2	41.5
Tucson	203 741	2.47	15.5	35.6	20 706	9 920	1 798	10 786	37 955	7 223	641	6 582	326 001	39.9	24.5
Yuma	32 624	2.69	13.9	21.3	5 128	3 291	308	1 837	5 394	3 464	489	2 975	54 176	49.3	16.5
ARKANSAS	1 130 417	2.54	13.4	28.2	78 931	47 287	18 532	31 644	120 234	4 063	460	3 603	1 951 058	51.1	20.7
Bella Vista	11 693	2.33	4.2	20.9	133	133	133	0	161	583	94	489	21 516	35.2	34.9
Benton	11 703	2.72	13.0	26.2	493	462	289	31	1 477	4 538	329	4 209	21 061	41.9	29.2
Bentonville	14 148	2.67	8.7	22.0	258	179	160	79	747	1 909	156	1 753	24 760	31.6	44.3
Conway	23 296	2.50	10.3	28.7	4 038	1 118	372	2 920	3 055	4 769	378	4 391	35 155	30.8	37.4
Fayetteville	32 510	2.17	8.2	37.6	6 818	1 124	405	5 694	3 520	4 519	436	4 082	43 262	27.9	44.8
Fort Smith	34 617	2.49	13.9	32.5	1 930	1 083	592	847	5 227	5 952	690	5 262	56 897	49.2	20.2
Hot Springs	15 036	2.26	16.6	39.2	1 692	1 127	578	565	3 321	9 342	394	8 948	24 366	44.4	20.8

1. No spouse present. 2. Data for serious crimes have not been adjusted for underreporting. This may affect comparability between geographic areas and over time. 3. Per 100,000 population estimated by the FBI. 4. Persons 25 years old and over.

City	Money income, 2011–2013					Housing units, 2010			Occupied housing units 2011–2013				
		Households								Owner-occupied		Median owner costs as a percent of income	
	Per capita income[1] (dollars)	Median income	Percent with income of $200,000 or more	Percent with income of less than $25,000	Families with income below poverty (percent)	Total	Percent change, 2000–2010	Vacant units for sale or rent[2]	Total	Percent	Median value[3] (dollars)	With a mortgage[4]	Without a mortgage[5]
	42	43	44	45	46	47	48	49	50	51	52	53	54
United States	27 884	52 176	4.8	23.9	11.7	131 704 730	13.6	14 988 438	115 731 304	64.0	173 200	23.7	12.3
ALABAMA	23 386	42 757	2.5	30.4	14.6	2 171 853	10.6	288 062	1 837 292	69.0	122 800	21.5	11.3
Alabaster	26 963	68 222	2.6	16.0	8.2	11 295	28.3	667	10 495	84.5	162 500	21.1	10.0
Auburn	24 126	39 378	3.6	38.2	12.0	24 646	22.7	2 535	21 528	44.8	202 500	22.0	10.0
Bessemer	15 939	28 991	0.4	45.6	28.5	12 369	-3.2	1 658	10 243	56.5	88 800	25.6	13.5
Birmingham	19 389	30 665	1.4	42.6	26.2	108 981	-2.9	19 599	88 251	47.9	86 000	25.7	14.0
Decatur	24 647	41 051	2.2	31.7	17.5	24 538	2.2	1 962	22 329	61.4	120 300	21.3	10.0
Dothan	25 425	42 140	3.7	30.3	14.9	29 274	12.6	2 429	26 140	59.2	138 700	20.2	10.0
Enterprise	25 349	52 906	1.7	26.1	14.0	11 616	20.2	1 103	10 097	59.7	168 000	20.0	10.0
Florence	23 776	36 688	2.2	37.0	17.6	19 299	9.1	2 032	17 717	56.8	132 300	22.0	10.0
Gadsden	17 233	27 368	1.7	46.2	24.6	17 672	-5.9	2 501	14 716	59.5	69 700	23.0	14.0
Homewood	32 363	61 144	7.1	16.8	6.2	11 385	0.5	1 293	9 143	54.0	261 000	20.1	10.0
Hoover	38 825	77 304	8.8	11.2	4.0	35 474	31.2	2 996	31 941	67.4	262 400	20.5	10.0
Huntsville	29 649	47 575	4.4	27.4	13.1	84 949	15.4	7 916	76 624	58.8	158 100	19.7	10.0
Madison	39 409	93 954	8.7	7.8	4.9	17 203	43.1	1 092	16 667	72.4	227 300	17.5	10.0
Mobile	22 648	37 913	2.8	35.1	21.0	89 127	3.5	10 168	75 966	56.7	121 400	23.9	11.7
Montgomery	23 876	42 834	3.0	31.4	19.9	92 115	6.1	10 629	79 316	57.4	115 500	22.1	10.6
Opelika	23 028	43 046	2.0	30.2	18.7	11 751	14.4	1 228	11 042	62.0	152 000	19.5	10.6
Phenix City	20 254	36 584	0.5	32.7	20.6	15 198	15.0	1 955	14 238	50.6	120 500	23.3	12.0
Prattville	24 717	53 997	3.2	21.5	9.4	13 541	40.7	830	12 374	66.9	147 100	19.1	10.0
Tuscaloosa	20 414	37 901	2.9	36.2	16.7	40 842	16.8	4 657	31 633	49.2	162 300	24.0	12.3
Vestavia Hills	52 974	76 446	16.2	14.3	4.5	14 952	40.8	965	13 825	73.2	348 000	20.5	10.5
ALASKA	32 438	70 477	5.6	15.1	6.8	306 967	17.6	48 909	250 875	63.0	245 300	22.9	11.0
Anchorage	35 769	76 159	7.4	11.7	5.0	113 032	12.6	5 700	104 980	59.1	287 500	23.0	11.2
Fairbanks	26 143	53 299	1.3	22.9	9.0	13 056	5.2	1 522	11 236	36.7	195 400	28.6	16.3
Juneau	37 784	84 415	6.4	8.4	3.7	13 055	6.3	868	12 044	65.2	321 800	23.7	10.1
ARIZONA	24 961	48 546	3.4	25.0	13.7	2 844 526	29.9	463 536	2 381 501	62.9	157 100	23.9	10.9
Apache Junction	20 048	34 043	1.2	35.8	19.7	22 564	-1.0	6 990	15 439	73.2	84 000	27.9	11.7
Avondale	19 877	53 590	2.1	17.5	15.4	27 001	136.6	3 615	22 800	57.6	125 400	23.2	10.4
Buckeye	19 453	57 715	2.2	19.0	14.0	18 207	NA	3 783	15 093	65.1	135 600	21.8	10.0
Bullhead City	21 452	36 405	2.2	32.9	16.0	23 464	27.5	6 703	16 695	59.7	101 800	24.2	12.4
Casa Grande	21 663	43 847	1.7	22.5	9.7	22 400	104.8	4 749	17 471	68.5	107 600	24.5	13.3
Chandler	31 624	71 399	5.3	14.0	7.1	94 404	41.7	7 480	86 150	62.7	208 800	21.8	10.0
El Mirage	17 374	41 776	0.7	21.6	18.5	11 326	NA	1 910	9 801	58.3	90 400	25.6	12.2
Flagstaff	24 822	47 232	3.2	26.6	15.6	26 254	22.5	3 418	23 579	43.9	257 300	22.4	10.0
Florence	14 454	43 485	0.8	28.4	7.9	5 224	60.5	1 894	5 926	69.1	96 300	19.5	10.0
Gilbert	30 849	79 327	6.0	9.9	5.2	74 907	102.2	5 535	70 877	71.1	216 200	21.7	10.0
Glendale	21 517	45 375	2.2	26.7	17.8	90 505	13.6	11 391	78 920	56.3	129 500	23.0	11.7
Goodyear	27 297	67 188	3.7	10.9	6.8	25 027	275.6	3 536	22 926	68.4	180 000	22.0	10.0
Kingman	22 695	41 781	1.9	30.4	17.4	12 724	48.6	1 507	10 898	62.0	101 800	21.5	11.3
Lake Havasu City	23 909	41 533	1.3	26.4	10.6	32 327	40.6	9 159	23 120	67.2	187 900	25.9	12.2
Marana	32 302	72 788	4.7	12.5	2.8	14 726	160.3	1 653	13 840	72.9	204 600	23.0	10.0
Maricopa	25 711	64 705	2.6	10.1	3.2	17 240	NA	2 881	14 325	79.4	123 900	23.2	11.8
Mesa	23 816	47 121	2.2	24.9	13.0	201 173	14.5	35 799	165 911	59.7	140 800	23.2	10.6
Oro Valley	39 426	75 368	6.5	12.5	4.6	20 340	45.2	2 536	17 112	74.8	276 200	22.2	10.0
Peoria	28 896	62 545	3.6	17.7	7.8	64 818	51.9	7 361	58 519	69.6	168 800	23.1	10.1
Phoenix	23 367	45 775	3.4	27.0	18.7	590 149	19.0	75 343	519 395	53.8	147 600	24.2	11.8
Prescott	28 111	42 181	2.4	28.2	10.0	22 159	27.1	3 548	19 314	63.4	255 500	26.1	12.7
Prescott Valley	20 432	39 959	1.2	30.6	15.6	17 494	84.5	2 130	15 403	57.5	157 600	26.5	10.3
Queen Creek	32 542	81 846	9.2	8.5	7.0	8 557	NA	837	8 352	79.2	227 700	25.9	10.0
Sahuarita	25 934	63 795	1.7	11.9	4.0	10 615	NA	1 595	9 090	81.4	179 100	24.3	10.3
San Luis	9 908	30 036	NA	41.2	28.7	6 525	95.8	572	8 343	77.8	110 100	30.2	14.3
Scottsdale	49 648	70 078	12.4	16.5	6.5	124 001	18.2	22 728	100 324	65.5	359 700	24.3	11.8
Sierra Vista	27 450	58 040	3.4	21.0	10.0	18 742	20.0	1 683	17 529	53.8	183 900	19.3	10.0
Surprise	24 154	56 741	1.0	15.5	8.1	52 586	222.5	9 314	44 079	73.2	169 200	24.2	11.2
Tempe	26 120	47 148	3.3	27.0	12.3	73 462	9.6	7 462	63 400	43.5	187 800	23.2	10.0
Tucson	20 015	35 837	1.2	36.1	19.3	229 762	9.5	24 372	203 741	48.6	129 400	24.5	12.2
Yuma	20 299	43 465	2.6	26.9	14.0	38 626	10.2	7 912	32 624	59.0	118 400	24.2	12.6
ARKANSAS	21 909	40 457	2.1	31.8	14.6	1 316 299	12.2	169 215	1 130 417	66.2	108 000	20.4	10.6
Bella Vista	31 174	60 735	4.4	15.7	2.3	13 241	49.2	1 512	11 693	85.7	146 800	20.5	10.0
Benton	25 165	51 423	2.3	21.2	7.4	12 902	38.9	1 068	11 703	67.1	137 600	21.6	11.5
Bentonville	34 852	68 470	7.7	15.7	3.4	14 693	84.9	1 440	14 148	56.7	163 700	17.6	10.0
Conway	23 681	47 776	2.6	27.8	9.9	24 402	41.2	2 003	23 296	50.1	159 000	20.2	10.0
Fayetteville	24 993	36 619	3.6	37.2	11.6	36 188	42.9	5 462	32 510	40.2	177 700	19.4	10.0
Fort Smith	22 079	35 566	2.7	35.3	20.3	37 899	7.2	3 547	34 617	51.8	112 000	20.5	10.4
Hot Springs	20 373	29 853	1.7	45.7	23.2	18 947	1.2	3 372	15 036	52.2	116 600	24.6	10.4

1. Based on population estimated by the American Community Survey. 2. Includes units rented or sold but not occupied. 3. Specified owner-occupied units; $1,000,000 represents $1,000,000 or more 4. 50.0 represents 50 percent or more. 5. 10.0 represents 10 percent or less.

Table D. Cities — **Housing, Labor Force, and Employment**

City	Occupied housing units, 2011–2013 (cont.)				Migration, 2011–2013		Civilian labor force, 2014				Civilian employment[4], 2011–2013			
									Unemployment			Percent		
	Percent renter occupied	Median gross rent[1]	Median rent as a percent of income[2]	Percent with no vehicle available	Percent who lived in the same house one year ago	Percent who lived outside current city one year ago	Total	Percent change, 2013–2014	Total	Rate[3]	Population age 16 and older	In labor force	Civilian full-year full-time workers	Households with no workers (percent)
	55	56	57	58	59	60	61	62	63	64	65	66	67	68
United States	36.0	900	31.3	9.2	84.9	10.1	156 219 626	0.4	9 636 189	6.2	248 553 975	63.8	39.5	27.2
ALABAMA	31.0	701	30.6	6.5	85.0	10.5	2 150 118	-0.9	146 208	6.8	3 826 543	58.7	37.3	32.4
Alabaster	15.5	1 031	32.2	1.2	88.6	9.7	16 687	-0.6	723	4.3	23 606	69.0	47.3	18.0
Auburn	55.2	791	41.6	3.7	64.7	18.2	27 686	0.8	1 566	5.7	47 887	58.8	30.4	26.5
Bessemer	43.5	663	34.3	15.8	84.4	9.2	10 059	-1.2	912	9.1	20 941	48.1	28.4	46.3
Birmingham	52.1	710	34.5	15.1	79.3	9.2	93 017	-1.0	7 307	7.9	171 712	58.7	33.8	35.6
Decatur	38.6	574	26.1	6.8	84.7	7.9	26 702	-1.5	1 809	6.8	44 254	64.5	39.6	31.3
Dothan	40.8	682	29.6	6.9	85.7	6.4	29 316	-1.4	1 990	6.8	53 263	61.2	40.8	30.4
Enterprise	40.3	779	26.6	5.3	77.9	17.8	10 536	-1.2	667	6.3	21 341	63.4	35.2	26.5
Florence	43.2	556	29.8	7.0	82.2	8.8	18 672	0.8	1 325	7.1	33 321	55.8	31.4	36.4
Gadsden	40.5	572	34.0	11.3	82.7	9.3	14 000	-0.3	1 194	8.5	29 202	51.1	29.8	42.3
Homewood	46.0	905	25.7	4.1	77.2	18.2	14 000	-0.9	583	4.2	20 006	69.5	46.5	18.6
Hoover	32.6	951	27.7	3.1	83.6	11.4	43 762	-0.6	1 880	4.3	63 924	69.2	47.3	20.8
Huntsville	41.2	715	29.6	6.9	81.0	8.9	90 332	-0.9	5 570	6.2	148 871	64.7	40.2	27.8
Madison	27.6	876	23.6	1.7	85.1	12.6	23 112	-0.7	1 136	4.9	35 321	70.0	48.3	15.4
Mobile	43.3	747	34.4	10.0	82.6	7.1	86 350	-1.1	6 920	8.0	155 022	59.1	36.5	32.6
Montgomery	42.6	787	32.8	8.5	77.0	9.2	92 288	-1.1	6 381	6.9	158 554	61.2	38.9	29.1
Opelika	38.0	675	31.7	8.7	81.9	10.0	13 584	0.6	788	5.8	22 321	60.6	38.4	28.7
Phenix City	49.4	713	29.6	10.4	78.2	13.8	15 616	-1.0	903	5.8	27 912	62.5	38.4	28.5
Prattville	33.1	894	33.0	4.2	80.3	14.9	16 521	-1.2	847	5.1	26 702	65.0	41.9	25.3
Tuscaloosa	50.8	755	35.7	10.4	72.3	15.4	43 738	1.5	2 869	6.6	79 005	54.3	31.5	31.1
Vestavia Hills	26.8	1 048	35.9	4.9	88.1	9.9	17 264	-0.5	652	3.8	26 263	63.3	45.7	24.3
ALASKA	37.0	1 113	27.9	9.6	80.7	11.1	367 166	0.4	24 956	6.8	561 408	70.8	40.2	20.3
Anchorage	40.9	1 150	28.3	5.8	80.2	7.5	159 955	0.8	8 224	5.1	230 929	74.2	45.3	15.6
Fairbanks	63.3	1 224	33.7	13.0	66.5	24.9	12 760	-0.5	864	6.8	23 798	72.9	33.3	23.6
Juneau	34.8	1 169	24.6	6.4	82.5	5.4	17 457	-0.9	883	5.1	25 869	72.1	50.7	16.9
ARIZONA	37.1	889	30.5	7.0	80.7	11.2	3 090 628	1.6	212 985	6.9	5 112 715	60.0	36.8	30.2
Apache Junction	26.8	807	35.1	10.6	82.9	7.4	13 327	1.2	1 193	9.0	29 975	43.4	22.3	57.2
Avondale	42.4	1 033	26.9	5.0	80.4	14.3	39 601	2.2	2 551	6.4	56 406	69.4	45.6	14.3
Buckeye	34.9	1 142	30.8	3.3	80.2	14.9	22 491	1.8	1 661	7.4	40 433	51.4	33.7	24.7
Bullhead City	40.3	754	31.3	7.5	72.1	13.8	15 566	1.8	1 370	8.8	32 624	49.3	29.1	47.1
Casa Grande	31.5	871	29.3	6.0	83.3	8.5	21 380	1.4	1 605	7.5	37 975	54.7	35.8	36.6
Chandler	37.3	1 097	26.0	3.3	81.3	12.8	138 101	2.5	7 047	5.1	185 071	72.8	49.6	15.8
El Mirage	41.7	1 054	31.1	4.6	87.3	10.0	14 966	2.2	1 037	6.9	23 453	63.8	39.5	20.9
Flagstaff	56.1	1 033	35.4	7.4	67.6	16.8	39 380	1.5	2 023	5.1	55 850	70.0	34.8	17.9
Florence	30.9	741	31.4	5.0	66.4	29.8	3 170	1.6	262	8.3	24 002	16.5	NA	57.0
Gilbert	28.9	1 255	26.6	2.1	81.6	12.2	123 028	2.6	5 821	4.7	156 675	73.0	49.5	14.5
Glendale	43.7	831	32.7	9.1	82.9	12.6	112 319	2.1	7 092	6.3	178 121	65.3	41.3	23.2
Goodyear	31.6	1 188	28.5	3.1	83.0	12.8	33 824	2.0	2 037	6.0	53 181	59.5	41.9	23.6
Kingman	38.0	816	27.4	7.2	71.5	14.2	12 066	0.6	972	8.1	22 767	50.2	30.9	43.8
Lake Havasu City	32.8	859	32.6	4.7	82.8	9.0	22 535	1.7	2 007	8.9	45 136	48.2	25.1	47.7
Marana	27.1	1 278	28.4	3.5	79.4	14.2	19 253	1.1	949	4.9	28 640	62.1	42.7	28.7
Maricopa	20.6	1 295	27.3	1.2	82.9	9.0	22 273	1.6	1 439	6.5	32 615	66.8	48.0	16.2
Mesa	40.3	857	31.9	7.4	79.0	11.6	219 555	2.2	12 938	5.9	350 728	62.1	38.6	29.9
Oro Valley	25.2	1 034	26.6	3.9	84.1	11.4	17 962	0.9	988	5.5	35 044	52.4	30.1	41.0
Peoria	30.4	1 066	31.1	6.0	85.2	10.0	81 672	2.3	4 478	5.5	124 338	64.0	42.4	27.2
Phoenix	46.2	861	30.8	9.1	79.9	7.6	738 605	2.2	45 452	6.2	1 128 410	65.8	42.4	22.4
Prescott	36.6	772	33.6	10.3	76.0	16.3	16 770	3.1	1 159	6.9	36 327	45.0	21.5	50.7
Prescott Valley	42.5	854	34.8	5.8	78.7	14.8	18 971	2.8	1 116	5.9	30 752	57.5	28.7	37.6
Queen Creek	20.8	1 367	24.0	0.5	74.9	17.0	14 282	2.8	647	4.5	17 988	70.7	51.7	14.7
Sahuarita	18.6	1 162	27.3	0.9	85.0	7.9	11 315	0.8	636	5.6	18 348	58.4	39.3	28.8
San Luis	22.2	547	38.5	8.7	89.8	9.0	19 040	-5.3	9 323	49.0	22 459	52.3	24.5	35.2
Scottsdale	34.5	1 115	27.0	4.3	80.7	11.5	124 135	2.3	5 865	4.7	188 534	64.2	42.6	27.5
Sierra Vista	46.2	921	28.6	6.3	72.7	20.8	18 900	-0.6	1 340	7.1	35 598	63.8	31.5	30.3
Surprise	26.8	1 143	29.7	3.1	84.7	9.8	50 305	2.1	3 245	6.5	89 989	55.0	36.0	35.0
Tempe	56.5	923	30.4	10.1	66.8	22.3	97 623	2.3	5 326	5.5	141 777	68.5	39.1	21.9
Tucson	51.4	733	33.9	12.7	74.8	9.4	249 870	0.6	16 297	6.5	421 613	61.9	33.6	29.7
Yuma	41.0	891	31.5	6.1	74.4	12.0	41 263	-1.7	6 349	15.4	69 583	60.9	33.7	29.4
ARKANSAS	33.8	658	30.0	6.4	84.1	10.3	1 300 608	-0.5	79 733	6.1	2 315 039	59.0	38.4	31.6
Bella Vista	14.3	934	31.1	2.2	84.6	10.1	11 171	2.4	581	5.2	22 920	50.4	34.8	42.3
Benton	32.9	771	25.2	8.0	84.5	8.7	15 435	-0.8	763	4.9	24 762	63.8	44.9	26.0
Bentonville	43.3	773	21.0	3.5	75.8	19.2	20 096	2.7	852	4.2	28 927	67.6	52.9	14.3
Conway	49.9	713	30.0	6.2	80.0	10.3	31 777	-0.9	1 750	5.5	49 506	68.4	43.5	20.8
Fayetteville	59.8	703	33.2	7.7	64.4	19.2	41 542	2.6	1 910	4.6	65 083	64.2	35.0	24.4
Fort Smith	48.2	614	30.2	9.2	82.1	6.7	39 422	-1.4	2 315	5.9	68 273	60.1	40.1	28.7
Hot Springs	47.8	670	34.8	16.0	77.5	10.1	14 064	-0.8	1 014	7.2	29 007	55.2	29.7	38.9

1. $2,000 represents $2,000 or more. 2. 50.0 represents 50 percent or more. 3. Percent of civilian labor force. 4. Persons 16 years old and over.

City	Value of residential construction authorized by building permits, 2014: New construction ($1,000)	Number of housing units	Percent single family	Wholesale trade,[1] 2007: Number of establish-ments	Number of employees	Sales (mil dol)	Annual payroll (mil dol)	Retail trade,[2] 2007: Number of establish-ments	Number of employees	Sales (mil dol)	Annual payroll (mil dol)
	69	70	71	72	73	74	75	76	77	78	79
United States	193 243 022	1 046 363	60.6	369 387	5 098 545	4 174 286.5	260 532.1	1 128 112	15 515 396	3 917 663.5	362 818.7
ALABAMA	2 204 675	13 369	71.1	4 824	70 469	52 252.8	3 032.2	19 722	238 922	57 344.9	5 112.0
Alabaster	18 578	214	100.0	38	330	306.5	14.6	98	1 700	388.7	42.6
Auburn	155 035	615	69.4	22	200	88.3	6.8	207	3 148	672.4	62.5
Bessemer	311	1	100.0	70	1 208	769.1	60.9	211	2 550	633.2	60.2
Birmingham	105 012	1 005	7.6	537	11 374	6 667.8	523.1	1 137	15 093	4 690.4	358.1
Decatur	7 793	37	100.0	82	1 163	793.0	51.6	355	4 319	1 159.6	97.5
Dothan	57 161	289	60.9	140	D	D	D	551	7 329	1 790.2	167.1
Enterprise	9 539	54	100.0	10	58	15.3	1.7	177	2 196	570.2	49.3
Florence	5 905	45	100.0	50	443	143.3	13.0	307	4 425	951.7	87.0
Gadsden	651	11	100.0	38	331	168.7	11.6	276	3 364	722.6	63.6
Homewood	7 867	19	100.0	78	864	670.5	43.7	257	3 891	662.8	82.8
Hoover	109 394	413	100.0	81	1 092	1 045.4	90.8	418	8 411	2 117.6	197.0
Huntsville	116 562	1 874	47.9	238	3 505	2 425.2	166.1	1 016	15 593	3 675.8	351.6
Madison	130 024	338	100.0	48	634	382.7	33.7	133	2 066	530.8	48.2
Mobile	22 235	109	100.0	350	4 591	2 311.0	208.0	1 004	15 513	3 557.8	341.6
Montgomery	73 538	571	52.0	263	4 995	3 039.3	211.3	952	13 945	3 132.0	304.9
Opelika	29 672	135	100.0	30	671	659.2	26.9	207	2 792	675.1	54.1
Phenix City	21 553	113	100.0	13	205	74.1	8.9	114	1 077	233.2	21.2
Prattville	34 660	131	100.0	21	123	39.5	4.2	169	2 312	598.2	58.4
Tuscaloosa	166 832	1 232	23.2	85	1 051	473.6	45.0	504	7 545	1 693.2	159.4
Vestavia Hills	43 841	109	100.0	37	686	443.4	46.9	146	1 689	388.4	38.3
ALASKA	353 712	1 518	74.1	658	8 262	4 563.6	391.6	2 641	34 977	9 303.4	936.8
Anchorage	211 518	770	74.3	339	5 498	2 914.0	261.0	923	15 842	4 482.7	441.8
Fairbanks	0	0	0.0	51	714	355.1	33.4	244	4 031	1 185.6	113.4
Juneau	NA	NA	NA	33	D	D	D	172	1 933	465.3	52.0
ARIZONA	5 666 004	26 997	62.4	5 874	84 029	57 573.5	4 116.4	19 384	337 529	86 758.8	8 010.8
Apache Junction	5 259	41	92.7	17	66	24.7	1.8	96	2 181	447.5	45.4
Avondale	12 222	42	100.0	14	181	73.4	11.3	126	4 287	1 601.3	126.1
Buckeye	194 595	749	100.0	9	D	D	D	48	449	215.2	14.2
Bullhead City	14 497	61	100.0	9	70	26.1	2.5	146	2 668	570.7	58.1
Casa Grande	23 901	106	100.0	23	374	139.4	12.8	195	2 981	676.7	64.4
Chandler	339 919	1 683	38.8	220	4 198	4 585.9	291.8	694	15 714	3 608.3	353.3
El Mirage	13 185	69	100.0	5	43	17.9	1.7	25	487	89.1	10.0
Flagstaff	67 761	383	40.5	66	856	405.9	29.8	362	5 566	1 174.4	119.0
Florence	47 676	146	100.0	NA	NA	NA	NA	17	104	30.0	2.8
Gilbert	277 937	1 484	96.7	147	1 450	649.3	59.7	441	8 466	2 079.1	207.2
Glendale	8 641	21	100.0	135	2 079	1 013.5	70.0	714	15 566	3 627.8	332.3
Goodyear	227 127	842	94.1	17	D	D	D	109	2 955	631.7	61.4
Kingman	26 920	149	100.0	19	240	136.9	9.5	154	3 085	993.6	72.5
Lake Havasu City	44 837	246	94.3	58	361	97.5	10.8	272	3 279	862.8	82.4
Marana	172 027	639	100.0	21	255	98.8	12.1	98	3 098	748.7	72.1
Maricopa	61 825	284	100.0	7	D	D	D	30	524	149.6	11.2
Mesa	333 102	1 010	99.6	301	3 372	2 037.3	174.1	1 507	28 855	6 294.5	653.9
Oro Valley	60 908	134	100.0	11	38	11.8	1.3	79	1 999	395.9	37.0
Peoria	260 674	1 039	99.4	56	368	251.2	14.8	353	8 143	2 340.4	216.9
Phoenix	935 003	5 138	31.3	1 946	34 585	23 670.5	1 650.7	4 266	77 534	21 859.5	1 913.7
Prescott	58 066	204	100.0	64	509	276.5	22.0	318	5 205	1 227.5	121.5
Prescott Valley	74 912	337	97.6	29	611	393.1	22.4	109	1 274	281.2	28.8
Queen Creek	269 930	693	100.0	15	94	42.8	2.6	36	1 033	241.1	21.9
Sahuarita	43 126	183	100.0	3	22	3.5	1.0	19	766	168.0	19.1
San Luis	20 336	136	100.0	5	25	7.0	0.8	34	383	77.2	6.3
Scottsdale	488 017	2 517	19.8	538	5 811	3 445.5	314.3	1 378	22 923	6 645.4	664.9
Sierra Vista	14 678	87	88.5	13	120	28.4	3.5	163	3 284	726.4	73.8
Surprise	100 955	320	100.0	23	97	20.4	3.5	147	4 064	888.2	85.7
Tempe	252 172	2 120	2.6	511	11 117	7 286.1	722.2	847	16 389	6 172.5	447.5
Tucson	208 900	1 471	35.1	473	5 730	2 124.6	224.0	2 080	37 716	8 647.0	887.8
Yuma	54 410	300	100.0	79	1 318	817.9	51.8	391	7 294	1 683.6	153.0
ARKANSAS	1 250 185	7 666	68.6	2 977	38 988	29 659.8	1 536.3	11 906	140 018	32 974.3	2 889.2
Bella Vista	14 564	51	100.0	6	18	2.9	0.4	30	415	66.9	8.6
Benton	33 913	204	99.0	17	106	75.4	3.6	146	1 839	488.4	38.7
Bentonville	185 952	1 089	41.2	63	1 624	447.3	52.9	134	2 038	703.3	55.6
Conway	31 097	213	55.9	47	438	229.7	17.6	301	4 595	1 077.3	91.8
Fayetteville	137 137	649	84.6	60	798	440.2	30.6	430	7 281	1 646.9	147.5
Fort Smith	47 650	372	44.6	172	2 275	1 216.1	90.0	545	7 273	1 667.4	152.7
Hot Springs	12 298	43	100.0	48	325	120.6	10.3	386	4 741	1 184.0	104.4

1. Merchant wholesalers except manufacturers' sales branches and offices. 2. Establishments with payroll.

City	Real estate and rental and leasing, 2007				Professional, scientific, and technical services,[1] 2007				Manufacturing, 2007			
	Number of establish-ments	Number of employees	Receipts (mil dol)	Annual payroll (mil dol)	Number of establish-ments	Number of employees	Receipts (mil dol)	Annual payroll (mil dol)	Number of establish-ments	Number of employees	Receipts (mil dol)	Annual payroll (mil dol)
	80	81	82	83	84	85	86	87	88	89	90	91
United States	384 297	2 188 479	485 058.6	84 764.9	842 607	7 678 304	1 220 434.1	489 965.4	332 536	13 395 670	5 319 456.3	613 768.6
ALABAMA	4 554	27 100	4 073.2	823.4	9 437	92 759	13 623.2	4 996.4	4 928	271 986	112 858.8	11 351.6
Alabaster	11	53	8.5	1.4	60	600	268.2	31.4	25	1 094	287.6	45.8
Auburn	62	357	44.4	8.8	105	D	D	D	55	3 672	869.0	135.3
Bessemer	35	131	17.5	4.1	75	D	D	D	51	1 780	373.1	70.3
Birmingham	339	3 706	526.1	145.8	901	D	D	D	305	15 835	4 724.8	749.4
Decatur	74	290	39.9	6.7	159	970	80.9	31.8	90	4 463	2 650.1	204.3
Dothan	115	D	D	D	222	D	D	D	102	5 180	1 153.6	183.0
Enterprise	49	223	24.7	5.6	57	346	41.8	10.4	18	856	318.4	24.8
Florence	62	255	40.5	7.2	154	D	D	D	64	2 700	987.2	100.3
Gadsden	46	226	41.0	5.6	118	626	51.3	19.9	58	4 239	977.8	167.6
Homewood	65	438	76.0	16.7	183	1 545	241.3	79.7	27	1 297	594.3	57.6
Hoover	97	720	247.7	25.5	280	2 269	460.3	136.1	NA	NA	NA	NA
Huntsville	330	1 720	277.8	54.7	997	28 335	5 091.5	1 988.4	195	21 059	8 209.6	1 028.7
Madison	59	253	48.2	7.9	130	D	D	D	33	1 205	D	50.1
Mobile	324	1 729	282.3	51.3	739	D	D	D	156	7 341	2 338.8	362.5
Montgomery	292	2 333	288.1	71.5	633	6 216	876.2	335.8	176	11 155	6 943.7	499.7
Opelika	38	175	21.3	3.6	69	D	D	D	47	2 801	D	112.5
Phenix City	38	136	18.5	2.7	42	205	13.8	4.6	29	1 659	D	93.5
Prattville	32	124	19.3	3.4	57	D	D	D	21	1 335	D	D
Tuscaloosa	142	925	142.0	26.0	262	1 978	180.0	66.7	64	5 390	2 115.6	216.1
Vestavia Hills	67	D	D	D	147	D	D	D	NA	NA	NA	NA
ALASKA	852	4 370	840.6	160.2	1 799	12 509	2 006.8	745.4	544	13 298	8 204.0	489.5
Anchorage	378	2 416	453.5	94.0	1 092	D	D	D	194	2 305	D	D
Fairbanks	91	518	116.9	22.9	140	D	D	D	NA	NA	NA	NA
Juneau	58	241	41.1	5.9	95	D	D	D	NA	NA	NA	NA
ARIZONA	9 441	52 627	10 077.6	1 994.3	16 563	128 188	17 617.1	7 239.5	5 074	172 438	57 977.8	8 774.3
Apache Junction	42	123	23.5	3.8	30	122	9.7	2.7	NA	NA	NA	NA
Avondale	54	228	32.6	8.6	44	200	20.6	6.2	NA	NA	NA	NA
Buckeye	15	58	46.9	2.3	22	149	22.1	7.1	NA	NA	NA	NA
Bullhead City	65	231	33.9	6.0	51	D	D	D	NA	NA	NA	NA
Casa Grande	61	244	40.4	7.3	49	D	D	D	28	1 624	1 040.0	73.6
Chandler	301	1 171	228.0	37.7	610	7 138	373.9	490.9	162	8 577	3 956.0	502.4
El Mirage	7	15	3.2	0.4	6	D	D	D	NA	NA	NA	NA
Flagstaff	156	533	105.5	17.1	255	D	D	D	72	3 429	1 314.2	213.1
Florence	4	11	0.7	0.2	7	D	D	D	NA	NA	NA	NA
Gilbert	307	1 003	185.2	34.7	462	D	D	D	115	2 941	415.9	94.5
Glendale	250	1 208	202.9	30.9	302	D	D	D	159	3 904	913.0	193.7
Goodyear	61	166	33.7	5.6	67	355	36.6	15.1	20	760	185.5	30.2
Kingman	53	181	26.5	5.7	65	D	D	D	NA	NA	NA	NA
Lake Havasu City	108	307	55.8	8.0	100	350	45.3	14.5	78	1 399	238.6	49.8
Marana	40	107	14.6	3.2	53	205	20.4	7.0	28	783	243.7	39.1
Maricopa	14	33	3.2	0.6	29	83	5.5	3.7	NA	NA	NA	NA
Mesa	594	2 834	524.9	80.1	1 081	7 105	708.1	301.8	257	8 764	3 072.5	585.6
Oro Valley	72	D	D	D	125	481	49.4	24.4	13	D	D	D
Peoria	152	710	114.5	25.1	218	D	D	D	54	1 341	267.8	45.3
Phoenix	2 227	17 353	3 261.0	746.4	5 038	46 488	7 094.6	2 922.4	1 626	57 398	16 926.9	2 733.3
Prescott	188	444	81.9	11.5	237	D	D	D	71	1 536	267.6	61.2
Prescott Valley	54	187	39.0	6.2	50	200	12.2	4.4	42	856	214.5	31.9
Queen Creek	31	46	4.2	0.8	50	117	11.2	3.2	NA	NA	NA	NA
Sahuarita	5	17	1.4	0.3	11	27	2.3	0.8	NA	NA	NA	NA
San Luis	10	22	3.4	0.4	5	D	D	D	NA	NA	NA	NA
Scottsdale	1 102	5 637	1 992.0	335.8	1 970	D	D	D	252	8 620	4 806.6	611.1
Sierra Vista	62	337	44.3	9.1	102	D	D	D	NA	NA	NA	NA
Surprise	55	445	48.1	6.8	83	437	27.5	11.1	NA	NA	NA	NA
Tempe	451	3 423	768.9	138.5	1 005	10 930	1 321.4	606.0	453	17 621	5 877.6	835.4
Tucson	865	5 832	834.2	176.8	1 759	12 057	1 416.0	567.6	459	10 964	3 446.1	489.9
Yuma	143	572	90.3	13.2	169	D	D	D	53	2 662	830.4	82.6
ARKANSAS	3 162	14 115	1 968.1	374.9	5 588	D	D	D	3 088	184 568	60 735.6	6 518.4
Bella Vista	36	73	7.9	1.7	35	69	6.5	2.0	NA	NA	NA	NA
Benton	33	106	14.5	2.0	62	210	15.8	5.7	29	571	124.3	D
Bentonville	66	223	32.1	5.2	186	2 300	191.4	135.6	25	1 074	293.8	57.6
Conway	98	336	48.7	8.8	159	614	62.3	19.0	56	5 036	1 540.8	207.2
Fayetteville	160	1 797	126.9	48.4	354	D	D	D	59	5 223	1 309.7	178.0
Fort Smith	150	675	128.8	20.2	265	D	D	D	160	18 247	5 080.4	589.3
Hot Springs	97	491	68.5	11.7	150	D	D	D	47	D	D	D

1. Establishments subject to federal tax.

Table D. Cities — Accommodation and Food Services, Arts, Entertainment, and Recreation, and Health Care and Social Assistance

City	Accommodation and food services, 2007				Arts, entertainment, and recreation,[1] 2007				Health care and social assistance,[1] 2007			
	Number of establish-ments	Number of employees	Sales (mil dol)	Annual payroll (mil dol)	Number of establish-ments	Number of employees	Receipts (mil dol)	Annual payroll (mil dol)	Number of establish-ments	Number of employees	Receipts (mil dol)	Annual payroll (mil dol)
	92	93	94	95	96	97	98	99	100	101	102	103
United States	634 361	11 600 751	613 795.7	170 826.8	100 656	1 496 869	151 958.0	45 916.0	647 120	8 322 326	818 394.6	330 887.7
ALABAMA	8 093	150 791	6 426.3	1 751.4	843	11 475	950.1	188.1	8 502	134 925	12 637.2	5 167.2
Alabaster	44	737	38.4	10.0	5	D	D	D	83	D	D	D
Auburn	168	3 419	123.1	32.7	14	D	D	D	79	D	D	D
Bessemer	75	1 427	62.3	16.5	11	128	12.8	3.2	87	D	D	D
Birmingham	549	11 539	587.7	165.0	45	749	61.4	13.4	738	13 898	1 705.5	701.3
Decatur	144	3 009	122.4	33.1	10	D	D	D	219	2 770	259.0	97.8
Dothan	208	4 333	174.0	47.8	17	D	D	D	255	D	D	D
Enterprise	74	1 401	47.5	12.4	8	D	D	D	73	D	D	D
Florence	113	3 145	118.7	36.0	14	D	D	D	190	D	D	D
Gadsden	105	2 299	94.6	27.3	7	D	D	D	185	4 572	514.5	182.6
Homewood	121	2 962	142.5	38.8	5	D	D	D	177	D	D	D
Hoover	176	4 257	224.0	64.5	20	292	18.5	4.3	196	D	D	D
Huntsville	480	10 921	471.9	133.4	48	D	D	D	593	D	D	D
Madison	89	1 580	72.7	19.3	9	102	3.1	1.0	85	1 270	93.5	36.5
Mobile	461	10 113	427.5	122.1	42	485	23.4	6.5	470	10 484	983.1	458.6
Montgomery	456	9 565	395.9	110.4	31	D	D	D	572	8 657	931.2	356.1
Opelika	75	1 893	71.4	21.3	3	D	D	D	83	D	D	D
Phenix City	65	1 156	45.9	11.8	5	D	D	D	49	D	D	D
Prattville	87	2 054	83.3	23.7	6	D	D	D	61	D	D	D
Tuscaloosa	276	6 318	260.7	68.7	17	266	11.8	4.4	219	2 808	282.4	122.7
Vestavia Hills	66	1 218	50.4	13.5	14	257	14.0	5.6	88	D	D	D
ALASKA	1 996	25 638	1 851.3	529.8	392	3 738	291.8	55.1	1 603	15 416	1 820.6	714.2
Anchorage	720	14 031	933.3	283.9	109	D	D	D	851	9 685	1 181.7	451.7
Fairbanks	139	2 569	155.7	43.1	26	765	25.6	5.0	131	D	D	D
Juneau	97	1 228	86.9	21.6	24	D	D	D	87	648	65.7	25.4
ARIZONA	11 610	250 716	13 268.5	3 766.3	1 510	39 112	3 816.4	1 171.2	13 643	154 061	16 655.7	6 572.3
Apache Junction	58	915	36.3	8.5	8	161	6.2	1.5	39	D	D	D
Avondale	97	2 113	94.6	26.1	11	D	D	D	85	D	D	D
Buckeye	25	271	17.2	4.1	5	D	D	D	9	D	D	D
Bullhead City	80	1 240	54.6	15.3	7	231	5.9	3.3	106	D	D	D
Casa Grande	80	1 758	75.2	20.4	7	94	4.9	1.5	107	1 424	127.8	52.1
Chandler	456	10 153	500.9	153.6	48	2 316	314.3	66.6	557	5 196	540.8	186.1
El Mirage	7	47	2.4	0.7	1	D	D	D	4	D	D	D
Flagstaff	269	5 546	294.5	77.3	30	630	23.8	9.3	292	2 407	259.8	107.0
Florence	18	379	28.7	5.5	4	D	D	D	11	D	D	D
Gilbert	248	4 450	191.2	54.5	35	D	D	D	421	D	D	D
Glendale	394	7 516	340.7	97.5	37	1 444	97.7	69.9	514	6 077	747.4	291.7
Goodyear	76	2 167	105.1	32.5	10	D	D	D	101	D	D	D
Kingman	93	1 716	75.6	21.0	9	D	D	D	104	D	D	D
Lake Havasu City	136	2 574	104.7	30.3	14	255	12.2	3.0	161	D	D	D
Marana	88	1 903	76.6	20.9	12	D	D	D	38	D	D	D
Maricopa	30	457	18.3	5.0	2	D	D	D	22	D	D	D
Mesa	788	16 920	753.2	210.0	79	1 677	80.5	22.6	1 096	12 584	1 403.7	543.9
Oro Valley	52	1 630	81.8	23.1	9	221	6.7	3.7	93	1 323	142.7	53.6
Peoria	217	6 006	258.5	78.5	30	623	30.9	11.3	293	3 900	350.9	152.0
Phoenix	2 600	61 385	3 644.4	1 027.3	333	7 211	729.6	285.8	3 232	39 166	4 469.4	1 897.0
Prescott	164	2 528	111.2	32.8	14	109	3.9	1.3	294	2 682	241.5	92.7
Prescott Valley	72	993	40.6	12.0	8	258	10.8	3.0	90	783	53.9	19.6
Queen Creek	34	527	25.6	6.8	7	D	D	D	55	508	31.7	15.5
Sahuarita	14	217	7.8	2.0	3	D	D	D	10	D	D	D
San Luis	14	234	11.0	2.4	1	D	D	D	7	D	D	D
Scottsdale	705	22 206	1 314.3	403.3	160	4 435	306.6	102.6	1 272	10 821	1 295.3	516.9
Sierra Vista	99	1 854	86.8	24.2	5	D	D	D	124	1 347	122.3	52.1
Surprise	112	2 720	115.1	34.8	11	D	D	D	111	D	D	D
Tempe	566	11 197	606.8	163.2	61	1 420	292.7	159.2	495	7 572	960.3	306.7
Tucson	1 210	27 059	1 214.9	347.5	137	1 582	74.6	22.6	1 476	18 451	1 869.0	784.8
Yuma	232	5 084	230.0	60.3	13	D	D	D	259	3 240	305.6	116.7
ARKANSAS	5 112	89 933	3 559.8	994.1	607	6 136	346.2	92.6	5 718	77 215	7 150.8	2 895.5
Bella Vista	19	178	8.6	2.3	2	D	D	D	22	298	18.7	8.7
Benton	55	856	33.3	9.5	9	55	2.8	0.8	79	D	D	D
Bentonville	123	2 275	88.5	26.5	11	182	7.6	2.5	97	1 531	173.6	63.5
Conway	135	3 325	122.3	33.0	15	D	D	D	194	2 488	202.1	81.4
Fayetteville	281	5 943	231.9	66.1	23	284	11.2	4.5	245	3 139	355.4	136.7
Fort Smith	233	4 785	197.0	54.0	16	D	D	D	294	5 620	516.1	248.4
Hot Springs	188	4 262	168.9	52.6	34	D	D	D	186	3 079	342.2	140.0

1. Establishments subject to federal tax.

Table D. Cities — **Other Services and Government Employment and Payroll**

City	Other services[1], 2007				Government employment and payroll, 2012								
						March payroll							
							Percent of total for:						
	Number of establish-ments	Number of employees	Receipts (mil dol)	Annual payroll (mil dol)	Full-time equivalent employees	Total (dollars)	Adminis-tration, judicial, and legal	Police and Corrections	Fire Protection	Highways and trans-portation	Health and welfare	Natural resources and utilities	Education and libraries
	104	105	106	107	108	109	110	111	112	113	114	115	116
United States	432 302	2 598 622	219 837.5	66 828.9	X	X	X	X	X	X	X	X	X
ALABAMA	5 606	33 791	3 102.5	851.5	X	X	X	X	X	X	X	X	X
Alabaster	37	D	D	D	226	902 906	9.2	32.9	29.4	6.0	0.0	14.0	4.0
Auburn	62	367	20.2	6.6	541	1 872 172	15.3	25.8	16.5	9.6	0.9	24.2	4.1
Bessemer	54	492	62.3	15.5	570	2 109 401	7.5	25.2	23.3	0.5	0.9	32.7	1.8
Birmingham	409	3 825	367.7	123.2	4 784	19 867 336	9.5	27.6	17.4	3.5	0.9	29.6	4.1
Decatur	96	D	D	D	695	2 762 157	6.2	20.0	17.7	5.1	1.4	45.8	0.0
Dothan	153	D	D	D	980	3 540 917	11.7	22.1	20.0	3.1	0.8	33.9	0.0
Enterprise	48	D	D	D	572	1 406 470	3.3	16.3	8.9	3.8	48.7	17.5	0.8
Florence	87	D	D	D	814	2 966 594	5.4	16.5	13.1	6.3	0.6	51.8	0.0
Gadsden	56	D	D	D	813	2 569 152	8.3	19.3	20.9	8.8	0.9	30.2	2.8
Homewood	65	440	38.9	12.7	357	1 440 394	4.5	33.6	23.3	6.7	0.0	16.2	7.0
Hoover	91	570	54.3	17.8	663	3 382 691	10.6	31.1	26.9	5.3	0.7	8.2	7.7
Huntsville	289	2 629	502.4	71.1	2 636	11 833 638	8.9	19.0	14.5	7.2	2.2	32.4	0.0
Madison	38	206	12.6	3.9	374	1 553 149	16.6	30.8	22.6	2.6	0.0	24.9	0.0
Mobile	345	2 892	177.2	65.0	2 894	9 605 291	10.7	26.2	21.6	4.7	1.5	25.1	3.9
Montgomery	311	D	D	D	2 884	10 068 707	8.1	26.1	17.3	7.2	0.4	29.4	2.1
Opelika	43	175	14.6	3.9	355	1 405 862	10.4	27.1	19.6	3.6	0.5	35.2	2.4
Phenix City	50	D	D	D	795	2 466 225	53.9	13.6	9.1	2.5	0.4	18.3	0.5
Prattville	43	D	D	D	328	1 108 761	10.0	29.2	32.0	3.9	0.0	16.8	0.0
Tuscaloosa	118	1 122	76.9	25.5	1 302	4 845 351	13.7	29.6	21.7	13.7	0.3	17.3	0.0
Vestavia Hills	60	422	25.1	9.8	264	1 136 169	7.5	27.3	44.1	1.9	0.0	6.9	5.2
ALASKA	871	4 874	477.0	145.2	X	X	X	X	X	X	X	X	X
Anchorage	394	2 642	241.2	78.2	9 819	51 971 256	4.5	7.8	6.6	5.5	1.4	9.1	63.8
Fairbanks	88	648	60.5	19.8	207	1 185 064	19.9	35.9	23.3	6.8	8.7	5.4	0.0
Juneau	47	228	18.1	5.1	1 960	10 163 476	5.6	5.4	3.1	7.4	27.2	8.1	43.2
ARIZONA	7 444	52 045	3 940.2	1 230.9	X	X	X	X	X	X	X	X	X
Apache Junction	43	143	10.2	3.0	234	1 013 473	20.4	42.8	0.0	10.1	7.9	13.1	5.7
Avondale	43	322	19.7	6.8	512	2 677 540	26.3	33.3	15.4	3.4	3.4	12.3	1.8
Buckeye	7	D	D	D	391	1 821 664	27.3	19.8	28.2	3.6	1.6	9.5	2.0
Bullhead City	40	223	16.9	4.8	298	1 290 523	21.2	44.5	0.0	12.9	1.8	11.0	0.0
Casa Grande	58	426	23.6	7.5	385	1 771 597	18.0	31.5	19.5	7.8	0.7	17.0	3.4
Chandler	237	2 032	136.7	53.4	1 623	9 363 010	16.5	33.2	15.8	6.3	4.4	16.4	3.0
El Mirage	18	79	5.8	1.7	144	789 368	14.2	35.0	17.6	4.7	0.0	9.4	0.0
Flagstaff	132	890	58.7	18.8	767	3 403 748	18.4	24.3	12.4	4.2	3.2	21.7	4.8
Florence	4	D	D	D	163	645 551	22.7	26.9	19.9	12.8	1.7	13.7	2.3
Gilbert	198	1 083	68.4	19.9	1 117	5 590 864	15.8	33.0	20.5	2.9	0.1	18.9	0.0
Glendale	297	1 597	127.0	40.4	1 775	9 436 681	12.7	32.7	19.8	5.2	1.8	16.0	2.7
Goodyear	35	181	9.2	3.3	482	2 715 439	27.9	20.6	25.2	2.4	0.0	14.0	0.0
Kingman	51	438	32.0	10.0	335	1 383 755	16.2	24.7	22.1	11.4	0.0	22.8	0.0
Lake Havasu City	122	689	47.7	14.3	484	2 122 419	13.0	26.9	20.4	8.0	0.0	20.7	0.0
Marana	57	D	D	D	306	1 328 433	22.4	36.4	0.0	14.2	1.2	11.8	0.0
Maricopa	12	D	D	D	204	1 087 610	13.2	32.5	35.7	1.6	0.0	5.6	2.4
Mesa	596	5 247	320.5	103.4	3 616	20 622 110	15.1	36.5	16.1	6.6	1.6	17.7	1.6
Oro Valley	47	D	D	D	311	1 409 218	13.9	47.7	0.0	6.6	0.8	15.0	4.3
Peoria	185	1 009	80.0	22.2	1 162	6 255 922	23.5	26.8	16.6	7.4	0.0	20.3	2.2
Phoenix	1 829	15 911	1 318.6	380.6	13 392	69 633 897	11.5	35.6	16.7	9.5	5.0	18.7	1.5
Prescott	115	552	41.8	12.6	538	2 411 836	19.0	24.9	16.7	6.7	0.0	14.5	3.4
Prescott Valley	54	207	15.9	5.2	189	851 635	20.9	38.1	0.0	4.8	7.5	7.0	8.5
Queen Creek	26	114	9.2	3.0	217	1 060 750	23.5	0.0	16.7	8.1	23.4	23.1	0.0
Sahuarita	6	D	D	D	131	644 309	29.4	41.1	0.0	11.3	0.0	7.5	0.0
San Luis	4	D	D	D	233	639 318	48.6	5.8	13.3	7.7	0.0	21.5	0.0
Scottsdale	531	3 388	257.0	85.0	2 454	13 029 893	23.6	31.2	13.0	3.8	2.1	18.0	3.7
Sierra Vista	41	252	14.5	4.7	380	1 580 863	16.3	28.2	17.1	6.7	1.2	17.2	2.1
Surprise	76	425	48.0	17.1	738	4 192 160	14.5	25.4	22.6	5.1	6.0	22.1	0.0
Tempe	286	2 437	202.4	69.8	1 762	9 492 774	16.0	31.6	13.1	6.2	9.5	18.8	1.5
Tucson	810	5 535	417.7	133.5	4 691	21 780 237	12.6	30.8	18.8	10.4	3.2	19.2	0.0
Yuma	125	728	52.3	16.8	946	3 797 070	16.5	30.3	16.4	7.6	3.3	23.1	0.0
ARKANSAS	3 325	18 421	1 407.7	426.5	X	X	X	X	X	X	X	X	X
Bella Vista	7	D	D	D	93	498 217	10.0	35.9	53.0	1.1	0.0	0.0	0.0
Benton	50	237	20.4	5.9	270	875 166	13.5	25.7	22.5	4.2	2.4	27.6	0.0
Bentonville	54	638	28.3	20.8	435	1 712 143	20.1	20.9	18.7	4.1	0.0	33.1	3.1
Conway	79	D	D	D	474	1 540 085	12.3	31.7	27.5	7.8	0.0	17.9	0.0
Fayetteville	118	765	43.4	14.6	692	2 378 996	14.3	27.3	16.7	11.7	2.3	20.9	0.0
Fort Smith	140	D	D	D	880	3 505 049	10.2	26.1	17.9	14.1	2.6	29.1	0.0
Hot Springs	84	411	25.3	8.5	597	2 082 915	9.8	24.7	17.9	10.7	1.2	28.2	0.0

1. Establishments subject to federal tax.

City	City government finances, 2007									
	General revenue							General expenditure		
		Intergovernmental		Taxes					Per capita[1] (dollars)	
					Per capita[1] (dollars)					
	Total (mil dol)	Total (mil dol)	Percent from state government	Total (mil dol)	Total	Property	Sales and gross receipts	Total (mil dol)	Total	Capital outlays
	117	118	119	120	121	122	123	124	125	126
United States	X	X	X	X	X	X	X	X	X	X
ALABAMA	X	X	X	X	X	X	X	X	X	X
Alabaster	27.6	0.0	0.0	19.2	619	107	511	23.9	773	0
Auburn	94.7	3.9	77.7	64.8	1 135	368	766	67.3	1 180	135
Bessemer	51.9	5.8	81.8	34.8	1 279	240	1 039	52.4	1 924	4
Birmingham	436.4	42.3	52.9	334.4	1 583	243	985	466.4	2 207	235
Decatur	174.2	68.7	100.0	61.6	1 103	209	877	202.0	3 616	209
Dothan	93.4	4.5	88.0	70.5	1 046	66	980	98.8	1 467	83
Enterprise	30.6	1.8	95.9	23.0	826	157	670	32.1	1 155	209
Florence	64.7	4.1	76.8	43.9	1 107	284	821	58.6	1 477	59
Gadsden	64.3	6.9	28.4	44.2	1 206	66	731	60.4	1 647	45
Homewood	54.6	1.8	36.5	50.5	1 996	632	1 363	51.4	2 034	100
Hoover	104.2	6.8	51.4	83.0	998	121	853	95.0	1 143	78
Huntsville	329.0	28.2	93.3	217.9	1 186	320	866	337.4	1 836	440
Madison	51.4	5.9	79.3	34.9	777	291	451	50.2	1 117	123
Mobile	353.3	20.4	65.4	248.6	1 275	83	1 192	344.5	1 767	296
Montgomery	280.1	36.3	46.1	169.8	830	151	679	218.0	1 065	80
Opelika	54.6	2.4	35.3	39.9	1 425	328	810	51.4	1 834	224
Phenix City	33.7	1.9	100.0	26.0	717	165	552	36.4	1 007	213
Prattville	35.5	1.0	99.2	26.5	765	71	695	28.2	814	6
Tuscaloosa	163.4	34.6	20.3	77.7	834	145	637	163.0	1 750	124
Vestavia Hills	34.2	1.8	33.1	29.1	857	387	470	34.6	1 017	160
ALASKA	X	X	X	X	X	X	X	X	X	X
Anchorage	1 296.8	572.1	91.3	546.6	1 830	1 623	208	1 251.1	4 190	417
Fairbanks	42.7	11.6	100.0	21.4	659	432	227	39.7	1 220	110
Juneau	316.5	94.8	75.9	83.0	2 561	1 130	1 431	302.2	9 325	1 605
ARIZONA	X	X	X	X	X	X	X	X	X	X
Apache Junction	26.7	11.0	100.0	11.6	316	0	316	29.2	793	0
Avondale	84.4	25.7	100.0	40.9	523	67	456	73.8	945	93
Buckeye	61.1	12.9	69.2	27.9	512	172	339	48.2	882	7
Bullhead City	48.4	17.4	91.6	11.3	286	0	285	42.5	1 075	35
Casa Grande	70.3	17.3	83.1	29.4	586	128	458	77.3	1 541	234
Chandler	333.6	72.6	90.2	151.1	617	130	487	266.6	1 089	179
El Mirage	30.1	8.5	100.0	9.5	290	94	196	33.0	1 011	114
Flagstaff	130.0	35.8	90.1	54.3	801	176	624	120.0	1 768	130
Florence	23.1	8.7	80.8	6.8	254	38	210	20.6	772	122
Gilbert	261.7	63.3	83.0	136.2	614	108	503	189.6	854	154
Glendale	324.3	103.3	81.2	145.1	625	87	538	226.0	974	13
Goodyear	108.3	19.5	99.3	60.0	864	237	627	78.8	1 135	56
Kingman	39.6	14.2	100.0	12.5	439	0	439	31.4	1 108	1
Lake Havasu City	80.6	21.3	85.8	26.9	509	186	322	98.9	1 874	405
Marana	50.4	18.1	58.5	27.9	760	14	742	43.7	1 189	179
Maricopa	36.8	14.6	100.0	19.2	428	242	187	33.5	747	45
Mesa	511.1	172.3	70.6	156.6	346	32	309	601.2	1 330	186
Oro Valley	29.7	10.8	100.0	15.4	373	0	373	29.9	723	49
Peoria	190.2	41.3	95.5	90.5	566	140	418	239.6	1 498	187
Phoenix	2 902.9	848.4	63.4	987.1	663	152	507	2 651.7	1 780	445
Prescott	74.7	16.1	77.8	30.5	761	71	684	77.2	1 928	429
Prescott Valley	38.2	14.1	87.4	14.0	357	47	310	41.2	1 051	74
Queen Creek	50.6	8.0	99.8	20.6	739	223	477	52.0	1 861	347
Sahuarita	26.6	12.6	63.4	10.0	379	11	368	22.4	852	221
San Luis	21.1	8.0	87.4	6.9	228	0	228	26.1	861	37
Scottsdale	477.7	126.1	80.7	238.4	1 068	291	776	562.4	2 518	823
Sierra Vista	48.4	13.6	97.0	18.9	407	9	398	48.8	1 052	142
Surprise	112.2	31.8	91.0	40.3	332	56	276	106.8	880	55
Tempe	344.4	69.4	71.3	183.5	1 097	215	883	286.8	1 715	177
Tucson	736.3	277.0	50.0	280.3	534	76	458	608.5	1 159	174
Yuma	125.5	30.9	90.5	51.1	545	108	435	125.6	1 341	167
ARKANSAS	X	X	X	X	X	X	X	X	X	X
Bella Vista	12.2	6.0	28.9	3.3	122	28	94	12.1	440	15
Benton	23.3	4.6	40.9	12.8	398	73	324	22.8	712	138
Bentonville	57.6	8.2	48.3	30.3	790	159	630	57.0	1 486	389
Conway	95.8	7.8	55.2	33.5	532	61	471	88.6	1 408	244
Fayetteville	107.6	24.4	45.2	48.2	626	53	572	96.7	1 256	246
Fort Smith	133.9	29.8	38.6	61.3	700	146	554	126.0	1 439	456
Hot Springs	69.7	12.2	60.6	26.7	752	1	751	69.2	1 951	328

1. Based on population estimated as of July 1 of the year shown.

City	City government finances, 2012 (cont.)									
	General expenditure (cont.)									
	Percent of total for:									
	Public welfare	Highways	Parking facilities	Education	Health and hospitals	Police protection	Sewerage and sanitation	Parks and recreation	Housing and community development	Interest on debt
	127	128	129	130	131	132	133	134	135	136
United States	X	X	X	X	X	X	X	X	X	X
ALABAMA	X	X	X	X	X	X	X	X	X	X
Alabaster	0.0	6.5	0.0	0.0	0.0	25.9	23.2	8.6	0.0	0.0
Auburn	0.0	5.6	0.0	0.0	2.5	16.6	14.8	7.9	1.4	12.2
Bessemer	0.0	6.1	0.0	0.0	0.0	21.1	6.2	3.2	0.0	6.0
Birmingham	0.0	12.7	1.3	0.0	0.0	16.8	0.0	4.0	1.4	4.9
Decatur	0.3	5.0	0.0	53.7	2.3	6.1	12.6	3.4	0.9	1.1
Dothan	0.0	10.4	0.0	4.0	2.8	16.8	17.1	8.5	0.5	3.4
Enterprise	0.0	8.4	0.0	16.6	0.7	13.2	23.7	7.3	0.0	8.6
Florence	0.0	9.8	0.0	14.4	0.0	15.5	16.1	11.6	0.3	2.8
Gadsden	0.0	6.2	0.0	0.0	0.0	16.2	16.8	9.0	2.3	4.3
Homewood	0.1	5.6	0.0	28.6	0.0	16.9	4.9	6.2	0.0	4.2
Hoover	0.0	9.1	0.0	2.1	0.3	21.8	8.8	8.6	0.0	4.5
Huntsville	0.2	6.6	0.5	5.6	1.2	12.4	8.8	9.0	2.3	8.1
Madison	0.0	14.5	0.0	0.0	0.0	14.0	12.2	7.0	0.0	6.1
Mobile	0.0	7.7	2.7	0.0	0.4	12.3	20.0	8.1	0.1	4.3
Montgomery	0.0	5.6	1.7	0.0	0.0	20.0	7.3	12.6	1.3	6.6
Opelika	0.0	8.4	0.0	14.7	0.6	16.6	11.9	9.8	0.5	6.3
Phenix City	0.0	1.8	0.0	5.6	0.3	16.9	14.0	10.2	0.0	3.9
Prattville	0.0	0.0	0.0	0.0	0.0	22.0	13.5	6.2	0.0	8.8
Tuscaloosa	0.1	14.2	0.3	7.9	0.1	17.4	9.0	8.0	1.4	2.3
Vestavia Hills	0.0	4.8	0.0	0.7	0.5	12.9	7.4	16.4	0.0	5.5
ALASKA	X	X	X	X	X	X	X	X	X	X
Anchorage	0.0	5.9	0.4	53.2	2.1	9.9	5.0	1.7	0.0	2.8
Fairbanks	0.0	33.1	0.6	0.0	0.0	15.6	0.0	0.0	0.0	0.5
Juneau	0.0	4.5	0.0	28.1	32.3	5.7	3.6	4.3	1.4	3.0
ARIZONA	X	X	X	X	X	X	X	X	X	X
Apache Junction	0.0	24.4	0.0	0.0	0.0	30.0	0.0	11.6	6.9	0.0
Avondale	3.8	15.7	0.0	0.0	0.0	31.7	20.3	3.4	4.4	6.6
Buckeye	0.0	4.5	0.0	0.0	0.0	19.8	24.3	3.3	0.4	17.7
Bullhead City	0.0	20.8	0.0	0.0	4.2	23.1	21.7	7.4	1.4	6.7
Casa Grande	0.0	8.0	0.0	0.0	0.0	17.5	17.4	8.7	0.9	6.8
Chandler	0.0	7.7	0.0	0.0	0.0	21.8	19.2	0.9	13.7	4.7
El Mirage	0.0	8.4	0.0	0.0	1.4	31.0	25.8	3.8	0.3	1.9
Flagstaff	0.0	14.0	0.0	0.0	0.0	13.5	14.1	0.0	12.3	3.7
Florence	0.0	8.9	3.0	0.0	0.0	25.5	11.9	4.9	4.2	6.6
Gilbert	0.0	20.7	0.0	0.0	0.0	19.1	13.1	5.3	0.8	8.4
Glendale	0.0	3.3	0.2	0.0	0.0	22.4	12.4	4.5	6.7	18.5
Goodyear	0.0	2.1	0.0	0.0	0.0	16.8	9.8	9.8	5.8	13.2
Kingman	0.0	5.6	0.0	0.0	0.0	23.3	22.2	11.9	2.1	2.3
Lake Havasu City	0.0	6.5	0.0	0.0	0.0	11.7	38.4	6.7	0.4	10.7
Marana	0.0	15.9	0.0	0.0	0.0	23.0	2.8	3.8	0.9	10.8
Maricopa	0.0	3.8	0.0	0.0	0.0	20.8	0.0	6.7	29.9	3.2
Mesa	0.6	10.4	0.0	0.0	0.0	26.2	11.2	7.4	3.3	6.1
Oro Valley	0.0	14.5	0.0	0.0	0.0	40.4	0.0	9.9	0.0	0.0
Peoria	0.0	9.6	0.0	0.2	0.0	12.3	12.7	11.6	0.7	5.5
Phoenix	0.0	6.6	0.0	0.9	0.0	17.8	11.1	7.4	7.3	10.4
Prescott	0.0	26.8	0.1	0.0	0.0	16.5	17.0	7.8	0.3	3.3
Prescott Valley	0.0	10.3	0.0	0.0	0.0	20.4	14.9	3.7	0.0	11.3
Queen Creek	0.0	6.0	0.0	0.0	0.0	3.2	8.0	12.7	1.3	8.9
Sahuarita	0.0	27.9	0.0	0.0	0.0	23.8	7.8	5.8	0.0	11.5
San Luis	0.5	5.6	0.0	0.0	0.0	14.5	18.2	0.0	0.6	24.2
Scottsdale	0.0	5.4	0.0	0.0	0.0	14.2	16.1	6.3	1.5	9.3
Sierra Vista	0.0	26.3	0.0	0.0	0.0	32.3	13.8	9.6	2.6	2.4
Surprise	0.0	14.1	0.0	0.0	0.0	19.0	11.3	12.5	5.8	4.6
Tempe	0.0	10.3	0.0	0.0	0.0	21.8	10.9	1.8	14.8	5.2
Tucson	0.0	5.0	0.0	0.0	0.0	21.9	6.7	8.0	12.2	6.0
Yuma	0.0	11.8	0.0	0.0	0.6	17.9	15.0	9.1	1.2	11.1
ARKANSAS	X	X	X	X	X	X	X	X	X	X
Bella Vista	0.0	26.0	0.0	0.0	0.0	19.9	13.8	0.0	0.0	0.0
Benton	0.0	22.3	0.0	0.0	1.5	20.7	12.3	6.4	0.0	7.0
Bentonville	0.0	16.9	0.0	0.0	0.0	12.6	25.2	11.3	0.2	5.6
Conway	0.0	14.7	0.0	0.0	0.4	11.7	15.7	4.1	0.0	15.9
Fayetteville	0.0	11.2	1.0	0.0	1.0	16.4	26.2	5.7	0.5	5.3
Fort Smith	0.0	13.8	0.2	0.0	0.1	12.5	25.6	2.5	1.0	8.9
Hot Springs	0.0	6.7	0.2	0.0	0.9	15.8	27.9	2.4	0.4	2.1

City	City government finances, 2012 (cont.) — Debt outstanding — Total (mil dol)	City government finances, 2012 (cont.) — Debt outstanding — Per capita[1] (dollars)	City government finances, 2012 (cont.) — Debt issued during year	Climate[2] — Average daily temperature (degrees Fahrenheit) — Mean — January	Climate[2] — Average daily temperature — Mean — July	Climate[2] — Average daily temperature — Limits — January[3]	Climate[2] — Average daily temperature — Limits — July[4]	Climate[2] — Annual precipitation (inches)	Climate[2] — Heating degree days	Climate[2] — Cooling degree days
	137	138	139	140	141	142	143	144	145	146
United States	X	X	X	X	X	X	X	X	X	X
ALABAMA	X	X	X	X	X	X	X	X	X	X
Alabaster	101.5	3 276	0.0	NA	NA	NA	NA	NA	NA	NA
Auburn	229.8	4 028	11.0	44.7	79.9	34.2	89.7	52.63	2 507	1 932
Bessemer	103.0	3 783	12.0	42.9	81.0	30.8	93.6	59.38	2 766	1 943
Birmingham	573.7	2 715	109.7	42.6	80.2	32.3	90.6	53.99	2 823	1 881
Decatur	508.8	9 106	6.5	38.9	79.2	29.1	90.3	55.31	3 469	1 609
Dothan	84.7	1 257	3.4	47.7	81.3	36.2	93.3	56.61	2 058	2 264
Enterprise	79.9	2 876	8.3	NA	NA	NA	NA	NA	NA	NA
Florence	116.3	2 932	59.9	39.9	80.2	30.7	90.6	55.80	3 236	1 789
Gadsden	75.3	2 052	5.0	40.3	79.8	29.9	90.5	56.10	3 220	1 716
Homewood	49.2	1 946	0.3	42.6	80.2	32.3	90.6	53.99	2 823	1 881
Hoover	108.5	1 306	58.5	42.9	81.0	30.8	93.6	59.38	2 766	1 943
Huntsville	774.8	4 216	13.8	39.8	79.5	30.7	89.4	57.51	3 262	1 671
Madison	75.1	1 672	13.3	46.6	81.8	35.5	92.7	54.77	2 194	2 252
Mobile	547.6	2 809	13.3	50.1	81.5	39.5	91.2	66.29	1 681	2 539
Montgomery	275.9	1 348	38.8	46.6	81.8	35.5	92.7	54.77	2 194	2 252
Opelika	162.2	5 790	70.3	NA	NA	NA	NA	NA	NA	NA
Phenix City	139.4	3 853	52.5	46.8	82.0	36.6	91.7	48.57	2 154	2 296
Prattville	61.2	1 766	5.6	NA	NA	NA	NA	NA	NA	NA
Tuscaloosa	198.6	2 132	1.3	42.9	80.4	32.5	90.8	54.99	2 787	1 893
Vestavia Hills	41.6	1 224	0.0	NA	NA	NA	NA	NA	NA	NA
ALASKA	X	X	X	X	X	X	X	X	X	X
Anchorage	1 789.0	5 991	62.0	15.8	58.4	9.3	65.3	16.08	10 470	3
Fairbanks	2.3	71	0.0	-9.7	62.4	-19.0	73.0	10.34	13 980	74
Juneau	193.0	5 956	14.8	25.7	56.8	20.7	64.3	58.33	8 574	0
ARIZONA	X	X	X	X	X	X	X	X	X	X
Apache Junction	10.8	294	0.0	52.7	89.5	40.0	104.3	12.29	1 542	3 443
Avondale	93.9	1 202	0.0	54.7	93.5	41.3	107.6	9.03	1 173	4 166
Buckeye	160.3	2 937	1.5	NA	NA	NA	NA	NA	NA	NA
Bullhead City	73.4	1 858	0.0	54.4	95.6	43.3	111.7	5.84	1 164	4 508
Casa Grande	119.9	2 388	14.4	52.4	90.4	37.3	105.1	9.22	1 572	3 554
Chandler	579.4	2 367	0.0	54.3	91.3	41.5	105.7	9.23	1 271	3 798
El Mirage	27.3	836	0.0	NA	NA	NA	NA	NA	NA	NA
Flagstaff	118.5	1 746	34.4	29.7	66.1	16.5	82.2	22.91	6 999	126
Florence	18.6	697	0.0	NA	NA	NA	NA	NA	NA	NA
Gilbert	479.5	2 159	37.9	54.3	91.3	41.5	105.7	9.23	1 271	3 798
Glendale	1 053.0	4 536	86.3	52.5	90.6	39.2	104.2	7.78	1 535	3 488
Goodyear	426.4	6 140	38.6	NA	NA	NA	NA	NA	NA	NA
Kingman	55.1	1 944	11.1	NA	NA	NA	NA	NA	NA	NA
Lake Havasu City	321.9	6 096	8.4	53.9	95.2	42.9	107.5	6.25	1 230	4 523
Marana	94.8	2 584	0.1	NA	NA	NA	NA	NA	NA	NA
Maricopa	19.3	430	0.0	NA	NA	NA	NA	NA	NA	NA
Mesa	1 494.6	3 305	352.1	54.3	91.3	41.5	105.7	9.23	1 271	3 798
Oro Valley	64.1	1 547	21.8	50.6	86.3	34.6	100.7	12.40	1 831	2 810
Peoria	511.6	3 199	51.7	54.7	93.5	41.3	107.6	9.03	1 173	4 166
Phoenix	8 278.0	5 557	760.6	54.2	92.8	43.4	104.2	8.29	1 125	4 189
Prescott	73.2	1 829	3.5	37.1	73.4	23.3	88.3	19.19	4 849	742
Prescott Valley	104.9	2 678	33.8	NA	NA	NA	NA	NA	NA	NA
Queen Creek	165.6	5 930	0.1	NA	NA	NA	NA	NA	NA	NA
Sahuarita	56.9	2 161	0.4	NA	NA	NA	NA	NA	NA	NA
San Luis	169.5	5 602	0.0	NA	NA	NA	NA	NA	NA	NA
Scottsdale	1 200.6	5 375	53.3	54.2	92.8	43.4	104.2	8.29	1 125	4 189
Sierra Vista	37.2	803	9.3	47.7	79.1	33.7	92.6	14.02	2 369	1 739
Surprise	37.0	305	0.0	54.7	93.5	41.3	107.6	9.03	1 173	4 166
Tempe	740.2	4 427	68.6	54.1	89.9	40.1	103.6	9.36	1 390	3 655
Tucson	1 174.4	2 236	152.8	54.0	88.5	41.9	100.5	12.00	1 333	3 501
Yuma	302.8	3 234	0.0	58.1	94.1	46.2	107.3	3.01	782	4 540
ARKANSAS	X	X	X	X	X	X	X	X	X	X
Bella Vista	0.0	0	0.0	NA	NA	NA	NA	NA	NA	NA
Benton	44.1	1 373	0.0	NA	NA	NA	NA	NA	NA	NA
Bentonville	97.5	2 541	0.0	NA	NA	NA	NA	NA	NA	NA
Conway	383.2	6 092	0.0	38.3	82.1	28.1	92.4	48.67	3 320	1 961
Fayetteville	139.6	1 813	0.0	34.3	78.9	24.2	89.1	46.02	4 166	1 439
Fort Smith	454.0	5 184	22.1	38.0	82.2	27.8	92.9	43.87	3 437	1 929
Hot Springs	68.3	1 925	1.0	40.2	82.2	29.6	94.3	57.69	3 133	1 993

1. Based on the population estimated as of July 1 of the year shown. 2. Represents normal values based on the 30-year period, 1971–2000. 3. Average daily minimum. 4. Average daily maximum.

STATE Place code	City	Land area,[1] 2010 (sq km)	Population, 2014: Total persons	Population, 2014: Rank	Population, 2014: Per square kilometer	Race alone or in combination (percent), 2011-2013: White	Black	American Indian, Alaska Native	Asian	Hawaiian Pacific Islander	Percent Hispanic or Latino[2], 2011-2013	Percent foreign born 2011–2013
		1	2	3	4	5	6	7	8	9	10	11
	ARKANSAS—Cont'd											
05 34750	Jacksonville	72.8	28 808	1 278	395.7	61.5	37.1	1.5	2.8	NA	8.0	5.6
05 35710	Jonesboro	206.9	72 210	473	349.0	77.4	19.5	1.1	1.8	0.2	5.3	5.1
05 41000	Little Rock	308.7	197 706	119	640.4	53.1	43.0	0.8	3.6	0.1	5.9	6.3
05 50450	North Little Rock	133.4	66 810	521	500.8	58.0	41.6	1.2	1.1	NA	8.3	4.5
05 53390	Paragould	80.8	27 465	1 337	339.9	98.4	0.8	1.7	NA	NA	3.1	1.3
05 55310	Pine Bluff	115.5	45 332	820	392.5	22.0	76.4	0.5	1.2	NA	1.3	1.6
05 60410	Rogers	98.3	61 464	579	625.3	88.4	2.3	1.7	3.5	NA	29.9	17.5
05 61670	Russellville	73.2	28 993	1 271	396.1	90.0	8.9	1.6	2.4	NA	13.2	5.7
05 63800	Sherwood	53.4	30 407	1 218	569.4	77.5	19.5	1.1	1.4	NA	5.6	3.8
05 66080	Springdale	108.3	76 565	437	707.0	64.8	3.0	2.4	2.1	7.1	34.6	23.6
05 68810	Texarkana	107.9	30 014	1 232	278.2	65.1	34.2	2.1	NA	NA	3.3	1.0
05 74540	West Memphis	73.7	25 423	1 410	345.0	33.6	65.3	NA	1.5	NA	0.5	1.7
06 00000	CALIFORNIA	403 466.3	38 802 500	X	96.2	65.9	7.1	1.8	15.3	0.8	38.2	27.0
06 00296	Adelanto	145.1	32 728	1 131	225.6	61.8	23.9	1.0	2.0	NA	56.7	19.5
06 00562	Alameda	27.5	77 660	431	2 824.0	53.5	9.7	1.3	35.2	2.0	12.5	27.3
06 00884	Alhambra	19.8	85 569	376	4 321.7	27.4	2.0	0.6	52.0	0.4	36.2	49.8
06 00947	Aliso Viejo	19.4	50 231	743	2 589.2	74.6	3.4	1.1	20.5	0.8	16.1	21.1
06 02000	Anaheim	129.1	346 997	56	2 687.8	70.2	3.2	1.0	16.8	0.7	52.6	36.9
06 02252	Antioch	73.4	108 930	261	1 484.1	57.2	20.5	2.4	14.5	2.0	32.9	20.7
06 02364	Apple Valley	189.6	71 595	478	377.6	84.0	8.9	2.4	3.8	0.2	29.8	7.8
06 02462	Arcadia	28.3	58 232	631	2 057.7	32.2	1.2	0.4	61.8	0.7	11.3	49.8
06 03064	Atascadero	66.4	29 134	1 265	438.8	90.8	1.8	1.3	3.4	NA	17.3	7.5
06 03162	Atwater	15.8	29 022	1 270	1 836.8	68.0	5.1	2.6	6.3	1.1	51.9	21.0
06 03386	Azusa	25.0	48 799	771	1 952.0	45.3	3.7	1.1	10.4	0.3	65.2	32.0
06 03526	Bakersfield	368.2	368 759	52	1 001.5	70.4	9.8	2.4	7.9	0.4	46.9	19.3
06 03666	Baldwin Park	17.2	77 119	434	4 483.7	38.1	1.1	1.3	16.5	0.2	78.1	45.9
06 03820	Banning	59.8	30 769	1 201	514.5	75.8	8.9	2.1	4.5	NA	38.8	16.9
06 04758	Beaumont	80.1	42 277	870	527.8	71.6	9.3	2.5	8.5	NA	37.7	15.7
06 04870	Bell	6.5	36 217	1 029	5 571.8	67.0	1.6	0.6	0.7	NA	92.7	42.3
06 04982	Bellflower	15.8	78 236	425	4 951.6	46.5	15.5	1.2	12.4	0.7	53.3	27.8
06 04996	Bell Gardens	6.4	43 146	858	6 741.6	73.8	1.3	0.5	0.4	NA	96.5	42.7
06 05108	Belmont	12.0	27 073	1 354	2 256.1	71.0	2.4	0.6	26.9	0.5	14.2	29.6
06 05290	Benicia	33.5	27 930	1 311	833.7	79.4	6.2	1.8	16.7	0.9	16.0	12.0
06 06000	Berkeley	27.1	118 853	227	4 385.7	67.1	10.0	1.8	22.8	0.5	11.6	21.2
06 06308	Beverly Hills	14.8	34 871	1 068	2 356.1	87.6	2.2	1.2	10.2	0.4	6.1	37.7
06 08100	Brea	31.3	41 508	891	1 326.1	76.5	1.2	0.9	21.4	1.0	27.9	22.2
06 08142	Brentwood	38.3	57 019	645	1 488.7	79.8	6.3	1.0	13.3	1.1	28.5	17.3
06 08786	Buena Park	27.3	83 105	391	3 044.1	62.8	4.9	0.7	28.5	1.1	38.7	37.6
06 08954	Burbank	44.9	105 368	276	2 346.7	78.4	3.3	0.8	14.0	0.4	26.7	34.5
06 09066	Burlingame	11.4	30 298	1 223	2 657.7	73.3	2.7	1.7	24.6	0.9	12.4	23.2
06 09710	Calexico	21.7	39 799	935	1 834.1	77.0	NA	NA	1.8	NA	96.9	49.2
06 10046	Camarillo	50.6	66 923	519	1 322.6	79.9	2.9	1.1	13.2	0.9	27.1	14.8
06 10345	Campbell	15.0	41 119	897	2 741.3	75.0	2.9	1.2	21.2	0.5	18.2	24.2
06 11194	Carlsbad	97.7	112 299	245	1 149.4	86.8	2.8	1.2	9.6	0.8	14.4	13.9
06 11530	Carson	48.5	93 271	329	1 923.1	42.6	25.4	8.9	27.8	3.0	41.1	34.5
06 12048	Cathedral City	55.7	53 437	694	959.4	73.1	4.2	1.9	6.4	0.2	59.5	33.9
06 12524	Ceres	20.8	47 343	793	2 276.1	71.9	2.0	4.0	8.2	1.5	57.3	26.5
06 12552	Cerritos	22.6	50 004	746	2 212.6	26.8	8.8	0.6	62.5	NA	11.8	45.6
06 13014	Chico	85.3	89 180	348	1 045.5	90.0	3.8	3.6	4.9	0.5	16.2	7.2
06 13210	Chino	76.8	84 723	379	1 103.2	65.2	6.6	3.7	14.3	0.5	51.6	22.1
06 13214	Chino Hills	115.7	77 005	435	665.6	59.5	4.4	1.1	32.6	0.3	30.2	27.7
06 13392	Chula Vista	128.5	260 988	75	2 031.0	72.8	5.9	1.2	17.1	0.9	58.5	31.1
06 13588	Citrus Heights	36.9	86 145	371	2 334.6	83.8	4.2	3.0	5.3	1.4	18.5	15.0
06 13756	Claremont	34.6	36 054	1 037	1 042.0	72.8	5.2	1.9	18.1	0.6	21.9	18.6
06 14218	Clovis	60.3	102 189	291	1 694.7	75.7	3.0	2.2	12.4	0.3	25.9	10.8
06 14260	Coachella	75.0	44 132	836	588.4	32.4	1.5	0.9	NA	NA	97.0	42.3
06 14890	Colton	39.7	54 053	687	1 361.5	57.6	8.4	2.6	4.6	0.8	74.0	25.2
06 15044	Compton	25.9	98 597	303	3 806.8	32.9	32.5	1.0	0.9	NA	66.0	29.8
06 16000	Concord	79.1	127 522	212	1 612.2	74.7	5.8	1.6	13.3	1.3	30.5	25.5
06 16350	Corona	100.6	161 486	153	1 605.2	74.3	6.3	1.0	12.9	1.1	42.2	25.8
06 16532	Costa Mesa	40.5	112 784	243	2 784.8	69.4	1.6	0.7	11.0	0.8	35.4	24.7
06 16742	Covina	18.2	49 002	766	2 692.4	58.4	4.6	1.5	14.0	NA	57.0	23.0
06 17568	Culver City	13.2	39 691	937	3 006.9	68.4	10.8	1.2	17.2	0.3	23.6	22.5
06 17610	Cupertino	29.2	60 668	588	2 077.7	33.5	0.2	0.8	67.0	0.3	5.0	50.1
06 17750	Cypress	17.0	49 240	760	2 896.5	61.3	4.1	1.4	35.2	0.7	18.3	29.6
06 17918	Daly City	19.9	106 094	274	5 331.4	25.7	3.7	0.9	60.3	0.6	23.6	51.7
06 17946	Dana Point	16.8	34 116	1 094	2 030.7	87.2	1.4	0.9	5.2	0.5	14.1	12.4
06 17988	Danville	46.7	43 909	843	940.2	86.2	1.1	0.8	13.7	NA	5.3	11.4
06 18100	Davis	25.6	66 742	523	2 607.1	69.7	3.6	1.5	25.6	0.7	14.0	20.0

1. Dry land or land partially or temporarily covered by water. 2. May be of any race.

Table D. Cities — **Population**

City	Age of population (percent), 2011-2013									Median age 2011-2013	Percent female 2011-2013	Population			
												Census counts		Percent change	
	Under 5 years	5 to 17 years	18 to 24 years	25 to 34 years	35 to 44 years	45 to 54 years	55 to 64 years	65 to 74 years	75 years and over			2000	2010	2000–2010	2010–2014
	12	13	14	15	16	17	18	19	20	21	22	23	24	25	26
ARKANSAS—Cont'd															
Jacksonville	7.4	21.4	13.2	15.3	11.3	10.8	9.2	6.9	4.6	30.3	49.0	29 916	28 364	-5.2	1.5
Jonesboro	7.6	17.1	14.5	15.6	12.2	11.1	10.2	5.8	5.9	31.2	51.7	55 515	67 263	21.2	7.2
Little Rock	6.8	16.3	9.5	15.7	13.6	13.1	12.4	7.0	5.6	36.5	52.2	183 133	193 524	5.7	2.2
North Little Rock	8.4	18.2	9.2	16.6	11.5	11.5	12.8	5.9	5.9	33.7	52.0	60 433	62 304	3.1	7.1
Paragould	6.3	18.8	9.6	13.8	13.2	11.2	12.8	7.8	6.5	36.3	51.3	22 017	26 113	18.6	5.2
Pine Bluff	6.6	17.9	12.3	13.0	10.8	12.8	13.2	6.8	6.6	35.2	53.0	55 085	49 083	-10.9	-7.6
Rogers	9.3	21.7	9.8	16.7	13.4	11.6	8.4	4.9	4.0	30.6	51.0	38 829	55 964	44.1	9.8
Russellville	6.9	16.7	21.7	10.5	13.2	9.6	8.9	6.7	5.8	29.2	52.0	23 682	27 920	17.9	3.9
Sherwood	7.6	14.9	10.3	13.3	14.9	15.3	11.4	7.7	4.6	37.2	52.2	21 511	29 523	37.2	2.4
Springdale	10.6	23.4	8.8	15.9	14.8	10.0	7.8	4.6	4.1	29.9	48.9	45 798	69 797	52.4	8.2
Texarkana	7.6	16.5	8.3	14.8	12.3	13.5	12.4	7.7	6.8	37.2	50.0	26 448	29 919	13.1	0.3
West Memphis	8.6	18.7	9.8	13.5	10.9	13.0	12.3	7.8	5.5	34.7	53.2	27 666	26 245	-5.1	-3.1
CALIFORNIA	6.6	17.6	10.5	14.5	13.6	13.8	11.3	6.7	5.4	35.6	50.3	33 871 648	37 253 956	10.0	4.2
Adelanto	12.9	24.9	13.8	15.0	11.9	11.2	4.5	3.5	2.3	23.9	49.8	18 130	31 765	75.2	3.0
Alameda	5.4	15.0	6.8	14.3	14.9	16.4	13.8	7.6	5.8	40.9	50.9	72 259	73 812	2.1	5.2
Alhambra	5.1	13.2	9.6	15.8	12.8	15.7	13.3	7.3	7.1	40.7	51.7	85 804	83 089	-3.2	3.0
Aliso Viejo	8.8	18.3	6.7	14.2	19.7	17.5	7.8	4.8	2.2	36.1	51.6	40 166	47 823	19.1	4.5
Anaheim	7.5	18.6	10.8	16.0	13.8	13.4	9.8	5.5	4.6	32.9	50.1	328 014	336 265	2.5	3.1
Antioch	5.7	21.0	11.1	12.6	12.0	14.5	13.7	5.9	3.5	34.6	51.6	90 532	102 372	13.1	6.4
Apple Valley	6.5	19.4	10.3	11.4	9.9	13.1	13.4	9.0	7.0	37.8	51.2	54 239	69 135	27.5	3.6
Arcadia	3.9	17.1	7.8	10.2	13.3	18.5	12.6	8.2	8.4	43.7	52.9	53 054	56 364	6.2	3.3
Atascadero	5.5	15.7	8.7	12.5	10.9	15.7	15.6	8.0	7.4	42.6	47.8	26 411	28 310	7.2	2.9
Atwater	7.9	23.9	10.3	13.9	13.4	11.3	9.6	5.6	4.2	30.7	51.9	23 113	28 168	21.9	3.0
Azusa	5.8	17.4	21.2	15.1	12.5	11.7	8.7	4.9	2.7	28.2	50.5	44 712	46 361	3.7	5.3
Bakersfield	9.1	21.5	11.5	15.1	12.8	12.1	9.3	5.0	3.8	30.1	50.3	247 057	347 483	40.6	6.1
Baldwin Park	6.4	20.1	12.8	14.0	14.4	13.1	9.7	5.7	3.8	32.5	49.6	75 837	75 390	-0.6	2.3
Banning	5.8	12.8	9.1	13.5	9.1	11.1	10.2	12.4	16.0	44.5	52.4	23 562	29 603	25.6	3.9
Beaumont	10.1	20.4	8.0	14.2	14.7	11.8	9.7	7.7	3.2	33.6	50.9	11 384	36 877	223.9	14.6
Bell	8.6	20.5	13.4	14.0	14.7	12.3	8.7	4.4	3.4	30.0	48.3	36 664	35 477	-3.2	2.1
Bellflower	7.8	21.0	10.9	15.0	13.6	12.5	10.1	5.1	3.9	31.5	52.1	72 878	76 616	5.1	2.1
Bell Gardens	10.3	25.0	10.7	16.9	14.3	9.8	7.5	3.4	2.1	27.1	50.2	44 054	42 072	-4.5	2.6
Belmont	6.3	15.1	6.6	10.9	16.8	15.7	13.3	7.5	7.8	41.3	50.1	25 123	25 835	2.8	4.8
Benicia	5.1	18.7	6.8	11.7	10.6	17.0	16.7	9.3	4.2	42.2	52.3	26 865	26 997	0.5	3.5
Berkeley	3.8	8.7	24.5	17.3	11.5	10.2	10.7	8.0	5.3	31.8	50.9	102 743	112 580	9.6	5.7
Beverly Hills	4.9	15.2	7.5	13.4	11.5	15.7	11.2	11.1	9.5	43.1	54.8	33 784	34 109	1.0	2.2
Brea	5.9	17.4	10.7	12.4	14.9	13.9	12.2	7.0	5.7	38.4	50.3	35 410	39 282	10.9	5.9
Brentwood	6.6	23.5	7.7	9.0	17.9	14.8	8.7	6.9	4.7	36.2	48.7	23 302	51 481	120.9	10.5
Buena Park	6.2	17.6	10.7	13.6	14.0	14.7	11.4	6.9	5.0	36.2	50.9	78 282	80 530	2.9	3.1
Burbank	5.3	14.6	7.2	16.8	15.9	15.2	11.0	7.2	6.9	38.9	52.6	100 316	103 340	3.0	2.0
Burlingame	6.8	14.6	5.7	12.4	19.1	15.6	12.6	6.6	6.6	40.5	51.0	28 158	28 806	2.3	5.2
Calexico	7.4	22.5	11.2	10.6	13.0	10.6	12.4	6.1	6.2	33.4	53.1	27 109	38 572	42.3	3.2
Camarillo	6.3	17.0	8.1	12.7	13.0	14.8	11.7	7.7	8.6	39.4	51.4	57 077	65 201	14.2	2.6
Campbell	5.4	14.6	9.4	16.7	15.7	16.0	10.9	5.9	5.4	37.8	49.9	38 138	39 349	3.2	4.5
Carlsbad	5.6	17.1	6.2	11.4	14.6	16.1	13.4	7.6	8.0	41.9	49.7	78 247	105 328	34.6	6.5
Carson	6.0	15.9	11.2	13.7	12.3	14.7	11.4	8.4	6.5	37.6	51.7	89 730	91 714	2.2	1.7
Cathedral City	7.5	20.7	9.1	12.6	13.7	13.2	9.6	7.7	5.9	35.1	48.2	42 647	51 200	20.1	4.4
Ceres	8.1	21.1	12.5	15.0	13.7	11.0	9.4	4.6	4.6	30.5	50.1	34 609	45 417	31.2	3.2
Cerritos	3.6	16.4	8.4	9.2	13.5	14.7	15.1	10.5	8.5	44.3	53.3	51 488	49 041	-4.8	2.0
Chico	6.0	13.9	23.2	14.3	11.4	10.3	9.9	5.5	5.5	29.5	52.3	59 954	86 187	43.8	3.5
Chino	6.6	16.9	10.8	16.4	14.4	15.2	10.6	5.9	3.4	34.7	47.2	67 168	77 983	16.1	8.7
Chino Hills	5.3	20.6	11.5	10.1	14.2	18.6	12.0	4.7	2.9	37.1	49.8	66 787	74 799	12.0	2.9
Chula Vista	6.8	19.8	10.4	14.9	13.4	14.0	10.1	5.7	4.9	33.8	51.1	173 556	243 916	40.5	7.0
Citrus Heights	6.1	15.4	10.4	15.5	12.2	14.4	12.2	8.1	5.8	36.9	52.1	85 071	83 301	-2.1	3.5
Claremont	3.1	17.4	16.3	9.2	10.6	12.3	13.6	9.0	8.5	40.1	51.5	33 998	34 926	2.7	3.2
Clovis	6.6	21.8	10.3	12.6	13.2	14.0	10.5	6.1	4.9	34.0	52.3	68 468	95 631	39.7	6.9
Coachella	10.1	27.4	10.8	18.1	13.2	9.2	6.1	3.3	1.7	25.8	49.5	22 724	40 704	79.1	8.4
Colton	9.6	23.5	13.9	14.9	12.0	11.6	7.9	4.0	2.6	27.2	50.1	47 662	52 154	9.4	3.6
Compton	9.3	23.2	12.4	14.6	12.8	11.7	8.0	4.5	3.4	28.1	51.8	93 493	96 455	3.2	2.3
Concord	7.8	15.6	8.2	16.3	13.6	14.3	11.7	7.0	5.6	36.4	49.7	121 780	122 067	0.2	4.3
Corona	7.2	21.0	10.7	14.0	15.1	14.6	9.5	4.7	3.2	32.9	49.8	124 966	152 374	21.9	6.0
Costa Mesa	6.8	14.8	10.1	20.0	15.1	14.1	10.2	5.0	3.9	33.7	49.1	108 724	109 960	1.1	2.6
Covina	7.3	18.7	10.0	14.4	11.8	14.7	11.2	5.9	6.0	34.6	51.6	46 837	47 796	2.0	2.5
Culver City	5.8	13.9	6.4	15.8	16.5	13.0	12.6	9.2	6.9	39.9	52.1	38 816	38 883	0.2	2.1
Cupertino	6.0	21.8	4.9	8.2	18.7	17.2	10.7	6.7	5.9	40.2	51.5	50 546	58 302	15.3	3.6
Cypress	5.3	17.5	10.9	10.6	12.7	17.6	12.5	6.9	6.2	40.3	52.1	46 229	47 802	3.4	2.9
Daly City	5.8	13.5	10.2	15.9	15.0	12.6	13.3	7.7	6.1	38.3	50.1	103 621	101 123	-2.4	4.9
Dana Point	5.4	11.6	5.6	13.7	12.1	15.2	18.0	10.4	8.1	46.7	50.1	35 110	33 351	-5.0	2.5
Danville	5.8	20.9	5.4	5.9	11.0	17.3	16.7	8.7	8.4	45.6	52.4	41 715	42 039	0.8	4.9
Davis	4.3	12.8	31.6	12.8	9.8	10.8	8.9	5.0	4.0	25.7	51.4	60 308	65 622	8.8	1.7

City	Households, 2011-2013				Persons in group quarters, 2010				Serious crimes known to police,[2] 2013				Educational attainment, 2011–2013		
			Percent			Institutional			Total		Rate[3]			Attainment[4] (percent)	
	Number	Persons per house-hold	Female family house-holder[1]	One-person	Total	Total	Persons in nursing facilities	Non-institu-tional	Number	Rate[3]	Violent	Property	Population age 25 and older	High school graduate or less	Bachelor's degree or more
	27	28	29	30	31	32	33	34	35	36	37	38	39	40	41
ARKANSAS—Cont'd															
Jacksonville	9 846	2.83	18.6	27.5	847	100	98	747	1 681	5 849	762	5 087	16 684	47.6	18.9
Jonesboro	26 721	2.51	16.5	26.1	3 412	1 238	800	2 174	3 350	4 711	450	4 261	42 721	41.7	29.8
Little Rock	79 191	2.44	16.1	38.1	4 543	2 781	1 074	1 762	18 387	9 315	1 413	7 901	132 470	34.6	38.4
North Little Rock	24 928	2.57	17.4	36.3	870	638	583	232	4 362	6 670	705	5 965	41 593	40.1	27.1
Paragould	10 676	2.47	11.6	31.3	550	391	226	159	1 819	6 664	465	6 199	17 583	60.0	15.8
Pine Bluff	18 142	2.38	23.2	37.9	3 999	2 512	429	1 487	3 432	7 397	1 220	6 177	29 746	52.2	19.1
Rogers	19 893	2.94	11.6	24.9	450	312	312	138	1 917	3 206	348	2 858	34 883	49.4	28.4
Russellville	9 675	2.60	16.8	32.7	3 251	448	277	2 803	1 244	4 325	327	3 999	15 591	45.8	26.6
Sherwood	11 685	2.55	13.0	31.1	85	85	85	0	1 420	4 749	435	4 314	20 102	37.4	31.6
Springdale	25 021	2.99	16.4	22.9	830	678	577	152	3 005	4 064	479	3 585	43 370	57.7	18.5
Texarkana	12 049	2.40	17.7	36.7	1 468	1 251	300	217	2 009	6 680	1 014	5 666	20 325	51.1	16.0
West Memphis	9 666	2.60	31.0	31.2	608	505	206	103	2 066	8 102	1 553	6 549	16 203	61.1	12.5
CALIFORNIA	12 581 722	2.96	13.7	24.4	819 816	397 142	111 884	422 674	1 173 036	3 060	402	2 658	24 793 022	39.3	30.8
Adelanto	7 625	3.93	29.0	11.8	1 753	1 723	0	30	1 084	3 478	635	2 843	15 225	63.2	6.1
Alameda	30 194	2.47	11.6	30.0	1 496	639	639	857	2 060	2 703	207	2 496	55 030	22.3	48.7
Alhambra	29 636	2.82	14.8	26.1	614	482	455	132	1 937	2 287	192	2 094	60 607	40.8	33.5
Aliso Viejo	18 910	2.60	10.3	26.2	469	19	19	450	340	680	50	630	32 812	14.0	59.4
Anaheim	98 662	3.43	15.8	18.1	3 557	1 537	1 376	2 020	10 741	3 110	327	2 783	216 209	48.7	24.3
Antioch	32 688	3.20	18.7	18.6	664	260	229	404	5 386	5 060	889	4 171	65 543	42.2	19.6
Apple Valley	23 595	2.97	15.6	21.2	461	300	104	161	1 779	2 500	260	2 240	44 976	45.3	15.9
Arcadia	19 692	2.89	10.9	20.5	862	223	220	639	1 595	2 757	133	2 624	40 696	23.5	51.9
Atascadero	11 056	2.54	10.8	21.8	1 324	1 100	91	224	641	2 215	335	1 880	20 210	30.4	27.4
Atwater	8 881	3.21	20.0	19.6	102	71	63	31	1 505	5 207	630	4 577	16 591	56.4	12.8
Azusa	11 804	3.58	21.9	17.1	2 802	111	97	2 691	1 344	2 814	515	2 299	26 249	54.8	18.7
Bakersfield	110 057	3.22	17.1	19.5	3 395	1 301	749	2 094	18 671	5 160	513	4 647	207 606	45.8	20.2
Baldwin Park	17 169	4.42	21.4	9.2	406	318	276	88	1 590	2 072	287	1 785	46 305	70.9	10.7
Banning	11 530	2.51	13.8	31.6	1 365	1 111	177	254	937	3 072	423	2 649	21 876	54.5	14.9
Beaumont	12 778	3.07	13.1	20.2	474	211	137	263	1 383	3 440	211	3 228	24 249	37.2	23.6
Bell	9 135	3.82	23.3	15.1	579	89	89	490	743	2 068	579	1 489	20 590	72.1	7.5
Bellflower	23 265	3.29	22.3	21.4	739	340	329	399	2 161	2 785	360	2 425	46 592	51.4	15.8
Bell Gardens	9 507	4.44	25.3	9.3	424	299	299	125	883	2 054	279	1 775	23 038	79.5	5.8
Belmont	10 266	2.53	6.1	29.6	514	120	120	394	464	1 738	101	1 637	19 061	17.6	55.1
Benicia	10 734	2.55	12.5	26.3	26	0	0	26	413	1 499	109	1 390	19 012	19.9	42.8
Berkeley	45 931	2.26	8.2	36.9	12 849	419	237	12 430	5 939	5 110	484	4 627	72 651	12.8	69.2
Beverly Hills	14 255	2.42	7.2	36.6	121	0	0	121	1 256	3 611	221	3 390	24 955	19.3	58.6
Brea	13 727	2.93	12.3	22.4	69	0	0	69	1 274	3 138	158	2 980	26 627	24.2	42.2
Brentwood	16 311	3.29	10.3	12.9	146	5	5	141	1 303	2 400	164	2 236	33 381	31.7	29.4
Buena Park	23 413	3.48	15.3	12.9	814	261	242	553	2 386	2 888	267	2 620	53 854	41.9	28.8
Burbank	40 875	2.54	11.9	31.6	573	282	268	291	2 601	2 484	163	2 320	76 112	29.7	37.9
Burlingame	12 561	2.31	9.7	36.2	449	294	294	155	702	2 345	124	2 221	21 556	16.7	58.3
Calexico	9 344	4.18	26.6	11.9	100	0	0	100	1 566	3 962	233	3 729	23 092	61.9	11.7
Camarillo	22 990	2.84	9.9	22.8	496	341	227	155	1 203	1 818	110	1 708	45 175	26.2	38.0
Campbell	15 934	2.51	10.9	26.5	201	122	114	79	1 669	4 116	261	3 855	28 403	23.8	46.6
Carlsbad	42 938	2.53	9.2	26.4	915	456	451	459	2 306	2 087	200	1 887	77 694	16.0	50.8
Carson	24 975	3.66	19.2	16.0	1 303	133	49	1 170	2 651	2 838	428	2 410	61 788	42.2	24.7
Cathedral City	17 007	3.07	14.0	24.4	295	32	32	263	1 267	2 388	281	2 107	32 907	52.7	15.6
Ceres	13 113	3.48	17.9	14.5	353	60	38	293	1 853	4 039	290	3 749	27 069	62.0	9.4
Cerritos	15 085	3.27	10.9	12.3	104	18	18	86	1 884	3 782	165	3 617	35 460	23.1	48.6
Chico	34 013	2.47	12.3	31.5	3 178	587	577	2 591	2 871	3 254	339	2 915	49 729	25.1	34.7
Chino	21 280	3.36	12.5	18.1	7 064	6 900	3	164	2 302	2 852	320	2 533	52 757	46.0	21.7
Chino Hills	23 327	3.26	12.2	15.8	155	147	0	8	1 080	1 404	82	1 322	47 630	24.6	43.7
Chula Vista	77 434	3.24	15.8	19.3	1 736	1 080	538	656	5 879	2 305	233	2 072	159 194	39.6	26.6
Citrus Heights	32 523	2.58	13.2	28.2	486	182	131	304	2 973	3 484	375	3 109	57 639	37.8	18.9
Claremont	11 735	2.64	8.3	26.7	5 124	198	192	4 926	931	2 613	104	2 510	22 429	16.0	57.4
Clovis	33 631	2.92	14.4	22.4	388	258	221	130	3 585	3 604	182	3 422	60 329	32.3	29.8
Coachella	9 646	4.41	23.3	6.4	58	0	0	58	1 490	3 439	272	3 166	21 958	77.8	4.5
Colton	14 408	3.65	23.6	19.3	330	245	243	85	2 097	3 927	301	3 625	28 104	58.3	11.7
Compton	23 251	4.16	28.4	15.6	755	112	84	643	3 780	3 861	1 269	2 592	53 751	66.4	6.9
Concord	44 995	2.74	12.6	23.2	1 047	535	469	512	4 764	3 797	324	3 473	85 292	36.2	29.9
Corona	45 344	3.46	12.2	15.6	511	282	268	229	3 601	2 248	101	2 147	96 180	40.2	26.7
Costa Mesa	40 906	2.68	11.6	28.4	2 970	738	581	2 232	3 808	3 384	224	3 160	76 159	32.2	36.4
Covina	15 056	3.18	17.7	20.2	435	367	341	68	1 482	3 054	284	2 770	30 917	38.4	24.4
Culver City	16 374	2.37	10.9	36.0	311	227	227	84	1 777	4 504	408	4 096	29 012	19.7	51.9
Cupertino	20 463	2.90	8.2	18.2	337	276	258	61	853	1 411	68	1 343	40 174	8.8	76.7
Cypress	15 539	3.11	14.2	16.2	502	0	0	502	984	2 005	102	1 904	32 339	27.7	41.3
Daly City	30 866	3.33	13.0	20.7	681	408	397	273	2 056	1 967	213	1 753	73 159	36.3	31.7
Dana Point	14 985	2.25	6.4	32.8	241	81	77	160	656	1 915	204	1 710	26 220	16.9	47.5
Danville	15 571	2.74	5.9	20.7	243	187	183	56	430	991	39	951	29 094	11.1	63.7
Davis	23 981	2.66	7.3	25.1	2 100	277	203	1 823	1 880	2 843	156	2 687	33 770	12.7	70.2

1. No spouse present. 2. Data for serious crimes have not been adjusted for underreporting. This may affect comparability between geographic areas and over time. 3. Per 100,000 population estimated by the FBI. 4. Persons 25 years old and over.

Table D. Cities — **Income, Poverty, and Housing**

City	Money income, 2011–2013: Per capita income[1] (dollars)	Money income, 2011–2013: Households: Median income	Money income, 2011–2013: Households: Percent with income of $200,000 or more	Money income, 2011–2013: Households: Percent with income of less than $25,000	Money income, 2011–2013: Families with income below poverty (percent)	Housing units, 2010: Total	Housing units, 2010: Percent change, 2000–2010	Housing units, 2010: Vacant units for sale or rent[2]	Occupied housing units 2011–2013: Total	Occupied housing units 2011–2013: Owner-occupied: Percent	Occupied housing units 2011–2013: Owner-occupied: Median value[3] (dollars)	Occupied housing units 2011–2013: Median owner costs as a percent of income: With a mortgage[4]	Occupied housing units 2011–2013: Median owner costs as a percent of income: Without a mortgage[5]
	42	43	44	45	46	47	48	49	50	51	52	53	54
ARKANSAS—Cont'd													
Jacksonville	18 462	40 504	0.5	25.2	14.7	12 412	4.8	1 476	9 846	54.2	110 700	22.4	10.0
Jonesboro	23 366	41 886	2.8	32.4	18.2	28 321	16.5	2 210	26 721	53.5	139 900	19.2	10.0
Little Rock	28 976	44 911	4.8	30.2	12.8	91 288	7.5	9 270	79 191	57.2	153 700	22.0	11.2
North Little Rock	21 802	40 584	2.1	32.2	16.8	29 437	6.8	2 907	24 928	56.9	117 900	20.7	11.8
Paragould	19 250	35 775	0.5	35.6	11.7	11 070	12.9	782	10 676	54.7	109 600	20.6	11.8
Pine Bluff	17 341	30 820	1.4	41.9	24.0	20 923	-6.2	2 852	18 142	55.1	77 400	21.4	12.8
Rogers	25 697	52 330	5.4	20.3	13.6	22 022	47.9	2 347	19 893	58.1	140 900	19.6	10.0
Russellville	18 217	35 229	1.9	38.9	21.2	11 124	8.9	806	9 675	52.8	121 900	22.1	10.0
Sherwood	27 932	57 399	2.1	20.7	9.5	12 924	40.5	717	11 685	70.0	146 100	20.0	10.1
Springdale	18 710	40 527	1.7	26.9	20.1	25 614	50.4	2 809	25 021	52.9	129 200	19.7	10.6
Texarkana	21 232	38 961	1.1	33.6	16.7	13 375	13.5	1 343	12 049	57.6	107 200	19.8	10.9
West Memphis	17 562	30 773	2.1	42.5	25.5	10 966	-0.5	1 131	9 666	45.9	85 400	20.9	13.9
CALIFORNIA	29 103	59 645	7.2	21.3	12.7	13 680 081	12.0	1 102 583	12 581 722	54.2	359 400	28.3	11.5
Adelanto	9 233	32 603	0.2	44.3	41.6	9 086	62.6	1 277	7 625	55.5	94 500	33.4	14.8
Alameda	42 485	74 424	11.1	15.7	7.0	32 351	2.2	2 228	30 194	47.4	603 400	25.0	10.8
Alhambra	25 565	54 038	3.8	24.1	12.2	30 915	2.8	1 698	29 636	39.7	474 200	28.0	11.8
Aliso Viejo	45 823	99 775	13.8	7.5	5.5	18 867	13.6	663	18 910	61.3	448 800	27.2	10.0
Anaheim	23 230	57 938	4.7	20.5	14.5	104 237	4.7	5 943	98 662	46.4	396 300	28.7	10.0
Antioch	24 157	63 483	4.0	20.1	12.1	34 849	15.5	2 597	32 688	60.3	224 700	28.9	11.2
Apple Valley	21 856	45 104	3.0	30.5	19.7	26 117	29.5	2 519	23 595	66.8	161 200	25.9	14.5
Arcadia	39 546	78 439	13.3	17.8	9.2	20 686	3.5	1 094	19 692	60.9	817 500	29.5	12.4
Atascadero	29 362	61 017	2.4	18.5	9.0	11 505	16.8	768	11 056	61.5	360 000	28.7	12.1
Atwater	17 055	39 330	1.8	29.5	22.5	9 771	20.8	933	8 881	46.9	125 700	24.4	11.4
Azusa	18 450	54 798	2.6	23.1	15.9	13 386	3.6	670	11 804	51.8	300 800	27.8	10.0
Bakersfield	22 699	54 675	3.9	23.9	17.5	120 725	36.9	9 593	110 057	55.1	174 000	24.9	10.9
Baldwin Park	15 079	51 465	1.4	19.3	15.7	17 736	1.8	547	17 169	59.3	285 500	32.8	10.0
Banning	20 112	39 690	1.1	31.0	14.7	12 144	24.7	1 306	11 530	67.1	152 500	25.2	15.5
Beaumont	25 514	65 091	3.7	19.1	10.2	12 908	203.1	1 107	12 778	74.0	197 900	28.5	12.8
Bell	11 860	35 141	NA	34.6	24.9	9 217	0.0	347	9 135	26.6	258 700	36.7	10.0
Bellflower	19 903	47 174	2.9	25.0	15.5	24 897	2.9	1 246	23 265	38.4	332 900	29.8	10.0
Bell Gardens	11 294	36 359	0.7	28.9	25.8	9 986	2.0	331	9 507	23.3	277 200	29.7	12.8
Belmont	53 785	104 711	22.9	11.6	4.8	11 028	3.8	453	10 266	58.5	893 800	25.5	10.0
Benicia	41 714	83 856	10.9	11.1	3.8	11 306	7.1	620	10 734	68.4	405 500	23.6	10.7
Berkeley	41 478	62 761	12.2	27.9	7.7	49 454	5.5	3 425	45 931	42.3	687 000	26.1	10.9
Beverly Hills	82 155	89 225	22.4	15.8	4.6	16 394	3.4	1 525	14 255	42.4	1 000 000	34.1	16.0
Brea	34 579	79 222	8.6	12.8	5.3	14 785	11.4	519	13 727	61.1	510 000	26.9	10.0
Brentwood	32 682	92 480	7.3	8.8	4.0	17 523	125.6	1 029	16 311	72.3	345 100	27.3	17.6
Buena Park	23 935	69 268	4.6	16.6	9.6	24 623	3.1	937	23 413	57.4	385 000	26.6	11.7
Burbank	32 831	64 842	5.7	19.6	6.8	44 309	3.4	2 369	40 875	41.4	549 600	30.7	10.0
Burlingame	58 910	85 194	22.4	14.0	5.1	13 027	1.3	666	12 561	46.9	1 000 000	28.3	10.7
Calexico	12 057	33 327	0.9	37.8	27.0	10 651	52.5	535	9 344	50.8	146 400	29.3	11.5
Camarillo	38 421	87 035	9.7	10.9	3.7	25 702	17.2	1 198	22 990	70.6	443 600	26.1	10.0
Campbell	43 643	85 366	13.0	13.6	4.8	16 950	3.7	787	15 934	51.6	672 200	27.6	11.2
Carlsbad	42 301	78 884	13.3	18.6	11.0	44 673	32.5	3 328	42 938	60.8	607 400	27.1	11.4
Carson	23 736	71 097	3.4	15.8	7.3	26 226	3.6	794	24 975	76.7	329 300	28.5	10.0
Cathedral City	18 598	39 773	2.2	29.7	19.0	20 995	17.9	3 948	17 007	60.4	171 700	34.2	17.6
Ceres	19 453	45 285	1.9	25.4	16.7	13 673	26.6	981	13 113	60.0	148 000	28.7	12.0
Cerritos	34 160	89 806	10.3	8.4	2.5	15 859	1.6	333	15 085	80.3	592 400	27.1	10.0
Chico	23 066	39 582	1.9	31.0	14.2	37 050	52.1	2 245	34 013	42.8	256 300	25.6	11.4
Chino	23 502	68 020	3.9	16.4	9.4	21 797	21.0	1 025	21 280	70.4	326 600	31.1	10.0
Chino Hills	34 328	90 944	10.5	10.0	6.0	23 617	15.8	676	23 327	78.4	475 000	28.7	10.9
Chula Vista	24 665	62 284	3.7	20.3	11.0	79 416	33.4	3 901	77 434	58.6	346 500	31.0	10.0
Citrus Heights	23 933	49 196	1.2	21.5	11.7	35 075	0.4	2 389	32 523	53.4	180 400	27.1	10.0
Claremont	37 006	87 275	13.2	13.0	4.6	12 156	5.0	548	11 735	66.3	511 500	25.5	10.0
Clovis	27 866	62 670	5.4	18.9	11.5	35 306	40.4	1 887	33 631	61.0	235 600	26.1	12.4
Coachella	11 563	39 088	0.3	29.0	29.0	9 903	98.8	905	9 646	64.2	135 200	33.3	15.3
Colton	14 967	40 436	1.1	30.0	22.8	16 350	3.6	1 379	14 408	53.0	153 000	31.6	12.1
Compton	13 190	40 876	0.7	32.1	26.1	24 523	3.1	1 461	23 251	53.2	229 700	34.2	12.4
Concord	30 738	64 737	4.6	18.4	10.3	47 125	4.8	2 847	44 995	60.0	350 100	27.2	12.1
Corona	26 305	75 157	5.5	14.5	9.6	47 174	20.2	2 224	45 344	66.3	324 300	28.0	12.1
Costa Mesa	32 715	63 377	6.7	17.0	10.3	42 120	4.3	2 174	40 906	37.0	573 500	28.6	10.0
Covina	25 328	63 070	3.7	15.6	10.1	16 570	0.9	721	15 066	60.1	361 100	28.4	10.0
Culver City	45 114	80 590	11.3	15.3	6.0	17 491	2.1	712	16 374	54.0	616 600	27.6	10.4
Cupertino	55 851	134 129	29.0	8.4	2.7	21 027	12.4	846	20 463	64.1	1 000 000	26.0	10.0
Cypress	31 320	75 897	7.1	9.8	5.3	16 068	0.3	414	15 539	66.7	482 000	27.8	10.2
Daly City	27 904	69 619	6.6	15.0	5.2	32 588	4.3	1 498	30 866	55.8	550 400	30.4	10.9
Dana Point	51 778	81 584	14.9	13.0	5.6	15 938	1.8	1 756	14 985	59.3	697 800	26.6	10.1
Danville	60 833	130 946	27.6	7.2	3.1	15 934	3.9	514	15 571	85.0	823 900	25.8	12.1
Davis	32 694	57 458	8.7	27.5	7.2	25 869	9.6	996	23 981	43.7	520 000	23.0	10.0

1. Based on population estimated by the American Community Survey. 2. Includes units rented or sold but not occupied. 3. Specified owner-occupied units; $1,000,000 represents $1,000,000 or more 4. 50.0 represents 50 percent or more. 5. 10.0 represents 10 percent or less.

City	Occupied housing units, 2011–2013 (cont.): Percent renter occupied	Occupied housing units, 2011–2013 (cont.): Median gross rent[1]	Occupied housing units, 2011–2013 (cont.): Median rent as a percent of income[2]	Occupied housing units, 2011–2013 (cont.): Percent with no vehicle available	Migration, 2011–2013: Percent who lived in the same house one year ago	Migration, 2011–2013: Percent who lived outside current city one year ago	Civilian labor force, 2014: Total	Civilian labor force, 2014: Percent change, 2013–2014	Civilian labor force, 2014: Unemployment: Total	Civilian labor force, 2014: Unemployment: Rate[3]	Civilian employment[4], 2011–2013: Population age 16 and older	Civilian employment[4], 2011–2013: Percent: In labor force	Civilian employment[4], 2011–2013: Percent: Civilian full-year full-time workers	Civilian employment[4], 2011–2013: Households with no workers (percent)
	55	56	57	58	59	60	61	62	63	64	65	66	67	68
ARKANSAS—Cont'd														
Jacksonville	45.8	748	28.5	6.7	77.9	12.6	11 553	-1.3	786	6.8	21 411	62.0	37.5	24.4
Jonesboro	46.5	656	32.5	7.3	71.9	11.9	34 404	0.7	1 904	5.5	54 863	62.5	39.0	30.2
Little Rock	42.8	761	30.2	8.4	85.8	5.6	94 121	-1.0	5 203	5.5	156 268	65.2	42.7	28.0
North Little Rock	43.1	743	32.9	11.2	80.7	12.6	29 078	-1.0	1 748	6.0	48 886	63.7	41.8	30.7
Paragould	45.3	659	29.7	4.3	76.7	9.1	12 112	0.9	821	6.8	20 926	54.5	36.3	39.4
Pine Bluff	44.9	652	35.5	8.7	86.6	4.4	17 732	-4.9	1 788	10.1	36 683	55.5	31.7	33.4
Rogers	41.9	803	25.4	3.5	78.6	11.0	30 295	2.9	1 470	4.9	42 950	67.4	49.1	16.9
Russellville	47.2	646	32.9	9.7	78.1	15.2	13 483	-0.5	825	6.1	22 436	61.6	33.1	24.6
Sherwood	30.0	797	26.7	3.3	81.7	13.8	14 889	-0.6	688	4.6	23 862	70.2	50.0	20.0
Springdale	47.1	652	30.2	5.7	78.7	11.8	34 821	2.5	1 522	4.4	51 609	68.5	47.7	18.6
Texarkana	42.4	684	32.6	9.9	77.2	13.0	13 235	-1.5	860	6.5	23 509	60.3	40.4	32.2
West Memphis	54.1	670	36.6	14.4	80.9	6.3	10 580	-0.6	879	8.3	19 384	59.0	39.9	32.2
CALIFORNIA	45.8	1 216	34.0	7.9	84.5	9.5	18 811 395	0.7	1 414 276	7.5	29 868 822	63.8	37.0	25.1
Adelanto	44.5	992	50.0	7.0	69.5	26.8	8 861	0.0	1 181	13.3	20 883	41.4	NA	41.8
Alameda	52.6	1 342	29.4	8.4	83.1	11.7	40 695	0.8	2 064	5.1	62 043	69.0	42.2	22.7
Alhambra	60.3	1 188	32.3	8.7	86.2	10.6	45 001	1.5	2 432	5.4	70 565	63.4	41.3	21.8
Aliso Viejo	38.7	1 811	28.7	4.2	83.7	13.1	29 113	0.8	1 251	4.3	37 440	76.7	52.1	11.3
Anaheim	53.6	1 350	37.0	7.7	83.8	9.4	169 611	0.3	11 779	6.9	262 660	67.8	40.9	19.2
Antioch	39.7	1 327	37.2	7.3	82.0	8.8	50 491	0.2	4 292	8.5	81 279	63.4	35.3	25.4
Apple Valley	33.2	956	39.5	5.3	82.3	10.8	27 523	1.1	2 362	8.6	54 906	49.1	26.4	38.0
Arcadia	39.1	1 402	31.1	4.3	87.9	9.0	28 444	1.6	1 365	4.8	47 115	60.6	39.9	24.1
Atascadero	38.5	1 137	32.5	3.5	87.0	9.9	14 985	1.6	696	4.6	23 313	58.4	36.9	27.6
Atwater	53.1	878	36.3	9.9	81.5	10.0	12 429	0.2	1 750	14.1	20 824	58.8	34.2	32.1
Azusa	48.2	1 184	36.3	7.0	83.9	12.3	23 560	1.3	1 472	6.2	37 533	63.4	37.2	19.1
Bakersfield	44.9	977	33.0	7.3	80.8	7.0	180 268	0.3	16 803	9.3	261 652	64.3	37.6	23.4
Baldwin Park	40.7	1 178	34.9	6.7	89.8	7.5	35 692	0.4	3 884	10.9	58 990	63.1	34.4	15.0
Banning	32.9	931	34.0	7.4	82.4	14.3	10 547	1.4	769	7.3	25 265	42.3	25.6	54.2
Beaumont	26.0	1 080	33.3	3.6	87.2	7.8	18 032	2.0	886	4.9	28 394	63.2	38.7	24.7
Bell	73.4	973	38.4	10.6	88.5	9.2	15 600	0.3	1 738	11.1	26 483	62.9	33.7	15.7
Bellflower	61.6	1 161	36.7	7.8	89.1	7.9	36 097	1.0	2 833	7.8	57 711	63.5	39.3	22.4
Bell Gardens	76.7	1 126	39.5	9.6	85.5	9.8	18 459	0.6	1 754	9.5	29 298	64.7	36.4	15.8
Belmont	41.5	1 590	32.3	5.1	85.9	11.3	15 948	2.6	589	3.7	21 269	69.6	47.0	20.8
Benicia	31.6	1 319	35.5	2.6	81.9	10.9	14 572	0.3	680	4.7	21 717	67.3	41.9	23.1
Berkeley	57.7	1 305	33.1	21.3	71.4	20.0	60 518	0.9	2 867	4.7	102 883	60.7	30.8	29.8
Beverly Hills	57.6	1 955	30.6	7.9	84.1	11.6	18 514	1.0	1 454	7.9	28 666	65.3	41.5	23.5
Brea	38.9	1 566	30.6	3.3	83.7	13.2	21 646	0.6	1 140	5.3	32 139	67.9	42.4	18.7
Brentwood	27.7	1 836	32.5	1.9	85.4	8.6	25 581	0.9	1 330	5.2	39 787	66.4	41.8	18.4
Buena Park	42.6	1 349	34.4	5.6	86.3	11.3	39 871	0.7	1 876	4.7	65 379	62.1	39.4	19.0
Burbank	58.6	1 340	32.7	7.7	86.2	9.2	58 060	1.2	3 936	6.8	85 961	68.7	43.2	22.7
Burlingame	53.1	1 519	29.0	7.1	82.2	13.8	17 370	2.8	571	3.3	23 784	69.6	46.3	20.5
Calexico	49.2	749	39.8	8.9	89.3	3.9	18 568	1.6	5 069	27.3	28 644	55.6	24.7	30.0
Camarillo	29.4	1 635	33.5	4.2	85.8	7.9	33 699	-0.4	1 892	5.6	51 817	67.3	42.1	25.8
Campbell	48.4	1 481	29.6	4.6	86.0	11.8	24 849	2.5	936	3.8	33 156	72.1	50.2	17.5
Carlsbad	39.2	1 629	33.0	3.5	85.7	11.1	53 523	0.1	3 109	5.8	87 034	61.1	36.6	31.2
Carson	23.3	1 282	32.7	4.8	88.9	7.5	47 189	0.4	4 991	10.6	74 747	65.3	37.2	22.3
Cathedral City	39.6	1 106	37.9	6.4	81.9	8.4	24 576	1.5	1 651	6.7	39 335	61.6	35.1	30.6
Ceres	40.0	998	38.0	6.2	83.0	12.7	21 402	-0.2	2 568	12.0	34 335	64.3	32.2	23.1
Cerritos	19.7	1 991	32.9	3.5	94.6	4.1	24 502	1.3	1 506	6.1	40 953	59.2	40.3	22.1
Chico	57.2	893	36.9	7.8	69.0	13.4	46 976	0.3	3 401	7.2	72 032	63.4	29.9	31.1
Chino	29.6	1 295	35.7	4.1	79.5	17.1	37 128	1.6	2 302	6.2	64 121	58.9	35.1	16.9
Chino Hills	21.6	1 788	32.9	2.8	89.7	6.9	40 550	1.7	2 405	5.9	59 307	69.4	40.7	14.6
Chula Vista	41.4	1 225	37.0	5.7	89.2	6.4	120 007	-0.4	9 656	8.0	193 736	64.8	37.5	22.5
Citrus Heights	46.6	997	32.1	5.9	79.1	15.5	43 033	0.1	3 316	7.7	68 386	66.0	34.1	28.3
Claremont	33.7	1 248	31.0	7.2	84.9	12.4	16 818	1.0	1 321	7.9	29 262	57.8	31.4	30.3
Clovis	39.0	1 025	32.3	6.1	85.6	9.4	50 030	0.7	4 519	9.0	74 135	64.3	38.8	26.0
Coachella	35.8	868	41.4	4.3	83.5	9.4	18 211	0.3	2 297	12.6	28 160	71.3	35.6	15.3
Colton	47.0	971	38.7	7.3	79.4	14.3	23 460	1.2	1 892	8.1	37 550	66.0	34.7	22.4
Compton	46.8	1 059	41.5	9.0	88.2	7.3	40 729	0.0	5 164	12.7	69 207	60.2	32.0	28.2
Concord	40.0	1 271	35.2	6.4	85.1	8.7	65 733	0.6	4 384	6.7	98 133	66.3	37.8	22.5
Corona	33.7	1 317	35.0	3.9	90.2	6.8	77 670	1.6	5 010	6.5	118 428	66.8	43.1	14.5
Costa Mesa	63.0	1 510	32.9	5.4	83.9	10.9	65 078	0.5	3 618	5.6	89 998	74.4	45.7	17.5
Covina	40.9	1 220	34.1	4.0	83.7	14.8	24 490	0.6	2 400	9.8	37 385	67.1	39.5	20.9
Culver City	46.0	1 618	28.8	8.1	85.3	12.0	22 548	1.3	1 375	6.1	32 014	70.4	43.7	25.3
Cupertino	35.9	2 000	22.5	4.0	85.0	11.6	29 011	2.3	1 219	4.2	45 168	62.7	46.2	18.4
Cypress	33.3	1 571	32.0	2.1	86.6	11.3	24 557	0.9	920	3.7	38 940	63.3	38.2	18.2
Daly City	44.2	1 525	34.1	8.3	88.6	8.8	62 559	2.3	3 219	5.1	85 769	70.2	43.2	19.1
Dana Point	40.7	1 741	34.2	2.6	81.5	11.8	18 845	0.6	969	5.1	28 716	67.2	40.9	27.8
Danville	15.0	2 000	34.4	3.4	88.0	8.2	20 345	1.0	997	4.9	32 736	61.9	39.3	24.6
Davis	56.3	1 240	43.9	10.7	67.3	18.0	34 339	0.7	2 031	5.9	56 101	60.0	29.1	25.9

1. $2,000 represents $2,000 or more. 2. 50.0 represents 50 percent or more. 3. Percent of civilian labor force. 4. Persons 16 years old and over.

City	Value of residential construction authorized by building permits, 2014			Wholesale trade,[1] 2007				Retail trade,[2] 2007			
	New construction ($1,000)	Number of housing units	Percent single family	Number of establish-ments	Number of employees	Sales (mil dol)	Annual payroll (mil dol)	Number of establish-ments	Number of employees	Sales (mil dol)	Annual payroll (mil dol)
	69	70	71	72	73	74	75	76	77	78	79
ARKANSAS—Cont'd											
Jacksonville	7 337	46	69.6	15	163	49.7	6.1	101	1 594	347.2	37.9
Jonesboro	61 384	598	54.7	104	1 204	495.5	50.2	440	6 193	1 335.6	119.1
Little Rock	130 768	779	43.4	387	7 632	3 999.3	339.0	1 008	14 560	3 359.2	330.4
North Little Rock	12 482	71	97.2	192	3 792	7 809.5	175.7	422	6 705	1 509.5	132.7
Paragould	16 670	178	57.9	31	269	82.1	7.8	161	1 554	336.8	31.3
Pine Bluff	2 041	27	40.7	52	394	211.9	13.7	280	3 646	798.7	74.2
Rogers	77 071	543	60.4	55	1 124	314.2	42.1	308	4 921	995.1	104.2
Russellville	3 917	40	57.5	50	331	204.6	13.3	251	3 290	852.8	68.1
Sherwood	23 251	147	100.0	30	173	78.8	7.4	92	1 480	579.7	39.2
Springdale	63 025	224	100.0	148	1 706	865.2	73.6	259	3 536	875.2	87.6
Texarkana	5 654	37	94.6	41	D	D	D	133	1 438	397.2	30.2
West Memphis	2 590	18	77.8	32	383	668.7	17.8	122	1 805	586.5	36.5
CALIFORNIA	18 742 105	83 645	46.9	53 963	745 785	598 456.5	42 334.5	114 438	1 683 023	455 032.3	44 328.9
Adelanto	9 503	34	100.0	5	48	25.2	2.3	13	205	52.2	5.0
Alameda	7 795	57	8.8	62	1 405	2 014.7	146.9	180	2 258	517.3	58.6
Alhambra	3 400	17	64.7	261	1 088	561.3	36.6	249	4 014	1 491.5	113.4
Aliso Viejo	0	0	0.0	65	1 903	1 273.0	136.9	69	1 078	662.8	28.8
Anaheim	206 092	1 241	4.1	797	12 461	7 962.1	580.1	866	14 042	3 679.3	367.0
Antioch	25 338	83	100.0	27	261	162.8	17.6	253	4 315	957.1	104.2
Apple Valley	17 099	129	96.9	15	32	12.6	1.6	106	2 213	493.0	49.0
Arcadia	39 146	215	27.4	293	1 233	619.7	45.8	330	4 965	900.1	98.0
Atascadero	33 060	185	76.2	24	121	32.3	4.8	126	1 556	356.3	36.8
Atwater	673	4	100.0	2	D	D	D	54	632	151.9	15.1
Azusa	101 432	297	100.0	73	890	404.0	41.7	96	1 162	427.0	31.2
Bakersfield	316 961	1 659	77.0	274	4 127	3 299.9	193.0	1 062	19 677	5 104.1	487.2
Baldwin Park	4 159	17	100.0	145	1 044	546.8	41.1	134	2 451	643.9	59.8
Banning	0	0	0.0	13	452	95.9	13.1	63	771	233.2	20.8
Beaumont	74 958	454	100.0	4	6	1.2	0.2	53	1 109	298.1	27.8
Bell	0	0	0.0	51	747	639.5	40.5	62	664	212.4	21.0
Bellflower	16 090	73	100.0	39	244	76.3	8.7	189	1 676	438.2	45.2
Bell Gardens	3 087	12	83.3	37	534	155.8	18.7	72	854	186.6	21.5
Belmont	6 945	17	41.2	19	D	D	D	56	916	363.8	36.2
Benicia	1 380	5	100.0	79	1 468	859.1	78.5	74	868	175.5	29.9
Berkeley	39 795	364	5.5	118	1 394	620.3	66.8	506	5 975	1 274.6	168.3
Beverly Hills	63 406	30	100.0	137	741	725.7	63.6	443	6 018	2 512.0	269.8
Brea	42 827	172	74.4	262	5 315	4 709.8	258.2	329	6 144	1 079.6	123.2
Brentwood	83 020	476	100.0	18	63	24.4	3.5	128	1 969	463.2	48.6
Buena Park	9 231	71	1.4	175	2 543	1 770.0	120.4	230	4 538	1 649.8	136.1
Burbank	8 945	27	81.5	213	3 581	6 364.4	219.5	426	8 247	2 276.9	195.5
Burlingame	14 269	25	76.0	153	1 040	935.4	61.1	201	2 425	819.4	94.5
Calexico	9 210	56	1.8	73	414	346.7	9.8	195	2 591	545.2	50.6
Camarillo	54 987	295	30.8	132	1 651	647.2	87.2	299	4 855	1 276.2	134.9
Campbell	11 472	38	100.0	82	906	470.0	57.2	174	3 008	691.4	79.6
Carlsbad	97 105	283	100.0	247	3 622	2 305.2	225.1	513	8 049	2 270.1	236.3
Carson	11 858	28	100.0	369	6 927	4 918.7	335.5	237	4 830	1 703.9	180.3
Cathedral City	6 566	32	100.0	22	108	44.2	5.0	160	2 478	962.7	83.7
Ceres	11 021	52	100.0	19	289	205.6	11.0	88	1 633	402.9	38.0
Cerritos	0	0	0.0	257	4 835	5 247.7	288.1	266	8 177	2 681.5	232.4
Chico	58 752	396	50.8	86	983	434.1	38.3	464	8 018	1 642.3	174.1
Chino	120 592	431	68.9	390	4 599	2 468.8	197.2	236	4 455	952.0	95.7
Chino Hills	43 650	326	12.3	72	159	79.2	5.6	124	2 311	597.7	53.7
Chula Vista	191 131	1 086	19.8	297	2 045	1 156.6	83.7	651	11 801	2 754.1	271.1
Citrus Heights	4 236	18	100.0	21	31	12.0	1.5	309	5 362	1 151.8	113.7
Claremont	25 710	104	100.0	35	116	84.1	6.1	89	1 021	442.8	37.0
Clovis	158 671	604	100.0	41	175	87.6	7.3	286	5 804	1 569.5	137.9
Coachella	10 914	62	80.6	18	352	178.2	19.4	57	695	197.7	15.2
Colton	10 929	119	15.1	42	647	420.2	29.7	111	2 120	645.5	66.5
Compton	186	1	100.0	122	3 251	2 195.2	176.3	158	1 124	267.9	30.0
Concord	2 278	7	100.0	135	1 302	553.7	69.4	505	8 856	2 578.5	256.5
Corona	72 458	654	4.6	299	5 283	6 720.2	200.7	405	8 050	2 418.0	220.8
Costa Mesa	40 563	196	90.8	336	4 639	4 176.2	303.2	740	14 696	3 875.8	401.4
Covina	640	2	100.0	82	524	250.8	20.3	193	3 013	765.3	81.6
Culver City	5 913	16	100.0	150	3 233	1 965.9	206.2	334	5 847	1 605.6	163.6
Cupertino	16 345	43	95.3	66	1 194	1 139.3	96.5	157	3 266	3 703.0	77.2
Cypress	7 194	41	100.0	110	3 530	7 669.6	262.6	104	2 011	597.4	51.5
Daly City	3 111	9	100.0	25	D	D	D	217	4 005	943.2	90.9
Dana Point	51 252	39	100.0	44	150	188.7	10.1	123	1 115	351.7	32.0
Danville	23 277	45	64.4	42	156	105.6	7.8	131	1 324	316.8	35.1
Davis	2 508	11	81.8	15	170	171.6	10.3	146	2 061	480.5	50.8

1. Merchant wholesalers except manufacturers' sales branches and offices. 2. Establishments with payroll.

City	Real estate and rental and leasing, 2007				Professional, scientific, and technical services,[1] 2007				Manufacturing, 2007			
	Number of establish-ments	Number of employees	Receipts (mil dol)	Annual payroll (mil dol)	Number of establish-ments	Number of employees	Receipts (mil dol)	Annual payroll (mil dol)	Number of establish-ments	Number of employees	Receipts (mil dol)	Annual payroll (mil dol)
	80	81	82	83	84	85	86	87	88	89	90	91
ARKANSAS—Cont'd												
Jacksonville	43	157	15.5	3.1	33	D	D	D	30	1 192	378.6	48.5
Jonesboro	99	468	73.2	11.7	157	D	D	D	101	6 186	1 703.7	221.2
Little Rock	414	2 643	455.0	87.8	1 173	D	D	D	188	8 669	3 918.1	402.2
North Little Rock	89	434	142.9	11.6	193	1 544	122.6	47.6	80	2 500	767.0	106.4
Paragould	27	D	D	D	51	355	19.7	7.9	36	3 648	D	D
Pine Bluff	60	182	35.5	5.1	73	D	D	D	44	D	1 151.5	119.0
Rogers	98	529	69.3	17.7	179	1 816	220.4	82.8	68	5 922	1 607.5	207.5
Russellville	66	213	42.0	5.4	100	D	D	D	52	4 024	1 318.0	D
Sherwood	29	105	17.7	3.1	55	431	45.9	16.5	NA	NA	NA	NA
Springdale	94	397	56.6	9.9	150	947	89.5	39.7	107	9 022	2 131.7	289.8
Texarkana	21	66	10.5	1.5	37	D	D	D	26	D	D	D
West Memphis	27	136	17.8	4.4	41	D	D	D	31	D	D	38.1
CALIFORNIA	51 597	312 488	76 805.0	13 446.7	111 954	1 231 372	194 406.3	80 738.1	44 296	1 448 485	491 372.1	71 247.3
Adelanto	10	21	2.0	0.3	5	46	4.7	1.6	43	1 829	385.8	71.9
Alameda	113	D	D	D	247	2 254	642.6	202.3	59	2 567	1 219.3	186.1
Alhambra	116	597	66.1	17.8	245	D	D	D	98	1 944	393.7	69.4
Aliso Viejo	69	1 013	135.4	58.0	234	D	D	D	35	1 437	558.2	78.1
Anaheim	377	3 858	677.4	168.9	717	D	D	D	818	30 787	7 648.1	1 479.1
Antioch	64	311	46.4	9.3	106	777	65.6	27.0	NA	NA	NA	NA
Apple Valley	55	268	41.7	7.1	63	267	25.3	9.3	NA	NA	NA	NA
Arcadia	150	540	135.8	17.3	282	1 726	388.6	92.9	67	1 044	192.5	43.4
Atascadero	37	123	21.4	2.8	84	D	D	D	NA	NA	NA	NA
Atwater	16	66	7.6	1.2	12	D	D	D	11	519	158.6	17.5
Azusa	36	189	30.9	6.9	22	127	7.0	2.9	123	4 986	1 444.6	247.7
Bakersfield	358	1 956	309.4	63.4	752	D	D	D	152	2 514	820.8	102.6
Baldwin Park	29	124	20.9	3.5	28	129	9.1	2.8	119	2 207	383.0	79.0
Banning	30	202	18.6	5.0	12	61	4.4	1.8	22	890	176.6	21.9
Beaumont	19	67	11.8	1.8	21	53	5.6	2.1	18	543	131.7	18.7
Bell	19	D	D	D	9	D	D	D	23	1 004	396.6	43.9
Bellflower	82	367	37.4	10.9	74	420	28.1	12.2	NA	NA	NA	NA
Bell Gardens	9	54	3.8	0.9	9	53	4.7	1.4	57	1 020	237.6	38.8
Belmont	52	482	49.1	18.4	95	309	60.9	22.4	NA	NA	NA	NA
Benicia	51	273	58.6	10.9	103	640	93.4	35.6	84	2 520	D	193.3
Berkeley	181	766	185.4	25.5	589	3 864	750.5	256.3	155	4 733	D	262.9
Beverly Hills	498	2 568	851.9	146.9	1 017	D	D	D	NA	NA	NA	NA
Brea	107	520	134.1	30.3	257	2 326	360.5	131.6	172	6 822	1 690.6	299.4
Brentwood	54	223	36.9	6.4	74	356	33.1	14.9	NA	NA	NA	NA
Buena Park	65	239	52.0	7.3	129	1 124	161.8	51.2	106	4 906	1 671.4	226.0
Burbank	239	2 543	810.8	127.0	527	144 144	6 976.0	3 869.3	220	5 429	1 028.5	249.5
Burlingame	149	1 025	219.0	34.9	264	D	D	D	60	1 678	364.3	83.6
Calexico	26	137	11.4	2.7	32	119	8.9	3.3	NA	NA	NA	NA
Camarillo	103	714	125.9	28.1	268	D	D	D	145	6 110	1 530.4	316.3
Campbell	108	592	121.2	23.5	296	D	D	D	111	1 977	371.5	109.9
Carlsbad	342	1 883	328.5	71.5	760	D	D	D	178	11 834	3 775.2	733.4
Carson	68	4 455	1 141.3	210.4	117	1 859	356.6	121.8	263	12 324	12 083.3	621.0
Cathedral City	54	308	53.0	7.8	45	142	13.0	4.6	NA	NA	NA	NA
Ceres	38	144	20.9	3.3	20	171	12.4	4.8	30	613	122.0	21.2
Cerritos	97	411	115.7	12.7	178	3 990	304.0	113.1	155	3 548	852.2	145.3
Chico	147	947	107.5	20.9	297	D	D	D	84	2 009	504.6	70.8
Chino	76	381	71.6	13.0	128	912	103.2	34.0	244	9 023	1 902.9	332.3
Chino Hills	52	125	33.0	3.6	144	371	39.3	13.7	NA	NA	NA	NA
Chula Vista	307	1 156	215.9	31.9	331	D	D	D	160	4 237	1 233.2	274.0
Citrus Heights	88	441	64.2	10.6	135	1 196	102.9	40.1	NA	NA	NA	NA
Claremont	60	D	D	D	147	D	D	D	27	803	118.3	26.8
Clovis	81	292	59.4	7.2	168	1 084	117.6	41.7	51	3 547	719.2	151.1
Coachella	13	56	6.5	0.9	5	D	D	D	15	551	108.3	25.4
Colton	29	187	29.2	5.3	50	505	57.4	21.6	57	4 043	1 157.0	128.9
Compton	19	180	98.4	3.4	21	D	D	D	133	4 940	1 083.7	176.9
Concord	166	1 014	242.2	42.4	323	D	D	D	120	2 705	528.6	122.9
Corona	200	909	184.9	38.2	315	2 105	211.0	115.0	372	16 971	4 279.7	708.0
Costa Mesa	294	2 676	686.1	128.6	764	D	D	D	258	7 604	1 962.7	386.2
Covina	102	542	75.7	20.5	159	682	79.5	27.8	103	1 833	393.7	72.8
Culver City	129	1 305	161.9	53.7	384	D	D	D	82	2 384	566.7	118.5
Cupertino	91	D	D	D	394	2 692	609.6	283.6	46	1 786	669.8	148.0
Cypress	68	255	40.7	8.3	131	1 949	649.1	150.4	44	1 683	431.2	97.9
Daly City	63	290	96.3	10.2	81	262	25.0	8.3	NA	NA	NA	NA
Dana Point	79	233	70.0	10.0	185	699	108.8	43.7	NA	NA	NA	NA
Danville	108	399	110.9	20.8	201	854	159.2	59.5	NA	NA	NA	NA
Davis	112	640	69.0	18.2	197	D	D	D	NA	NA	NA	NA

1. Establishments subject to federal tax.

Table D. Cities — Accommodation and Food Services, Arts, Entertainment, and Recreation, and Health Care and Social Assistance

City	Accommodation and food services, 2007				Arts, entertainment, and recreation,[1] 2007				Health care and social assistance,[1] 2007			
	Number of establish-ments	Number of employees	Sales (mil dol)	Annual payroll (mil dol)	Number of establish-ments	Number of employees	Receipts (mil dol)	Annual payroll (mil dol)	Number of establish-ments	Number of employees	Receipts (mil dol)	Annual payroll (mil dol)
	92	93	94	95	96	97	98	99	100	101	102	103
ARKANSAS—Cont'd												
Jacksonville	49	1 016	39.8	11.0	6	D	D	D	55	D	D	D
Jonesboro	171	3 866	144.0	40.7	12	D	D	D	246	D	D	D
Little Rock	522	11 312	532.7	154.3	60	872	55.2	15.2	846	10 964	1 447.6	595.8
North Little Rock	201	4 206	184.5	51.3	24	D	D	D	222	D	D	D
Paragould	57	967	37.5	10.4	3	D	D	D	66	D	D	D
Pine Bluff	115	1 912	77.6	20.3	5	D	D	D	191	D	D	D
Rogers	120	3 283	142.1	42.5	13	D	D	D	126	D	D	D
Russellville	98	2 144	74.6	19.9	7	D	D	D	110	D	D	D
Sherwood	32	477	19.8	5.4	2	D	D	D	56	D	D	D
Springdale	130	2 893	105.9	30.8	15	123	4.2	1.6	135	D	D	D
Texarkana	58	1 113	42.1	12.2	4	D	D	D	52	D	D	D
West Memphis	64	1 304	51.9	14.6	8	D	D	D	68	790	64.5	25.8
CALIFORNIA	75 989	1 366 926	80 852.8	22 374.8	18 025	243 993	31 778.7	10 364.4	84 335	883 552	102 703.1	38 944.0
Adelanto	16	143	8.9	2.2	4	D	D	D	3	D	D	D
Alameda	191	1 983	107.6	30.4	30	D	D	D	176	1 562	178.8	68.7
Alhambra	204	3 116	143.1	41.0	11	D	D	D	255	2 512	270.4	84.3
Aliso Viejo	63	964	53.5	15.7	12	D	D	D	105	D	D	D
Anaheim	686	22 020	1 405.3	438.7	74	D	D	D	781	9 799	1 159.6	435.0
Antioch	152	2 528	121.3	33.8	15	D	D	D	200	2 204	343.5	102.3
Apple Valley	67	1 035	49.5	13.4	6	D	D	D	172	D	D	D
Arcadia	189	3 531	180.3	48.8	72	1 913	208.8	54.4	371	D	D	D
Atascadero	60	850	36.6	10.6	7	D	D	D	78	D	D	D
Atwater	38	583	27.9	6.7	4	D	D	D	24	D	D	D
Azusa	84	936	44.6	11.6	4	D	D	D	43	D	D	D
Bakersfield	631	12 254	593.1	163.4	61	1 638	57.0	19.3	871	10 618	1 240.1	440.9
Baldwin Park	81	1 198	66.5	15.9	2	D	D	D	67	D	D	D
Banning	50	821	39.2	10.8	2	D	D	D	49	738	76.2	21.9
Beaumont	36	448	25.0	7.8	4	162	6.6	3.0	32	D	D	D
Bell	52	794	41.8	10.7	1	D	D	D	23	D	D	D
Bellflower	109	1 262	61.8	16.9	11	108	5.8	1.8	144	D	D	D
Bell Gardens	61	774	48.5	10.6	2	D	D	D	27	489	35.6	15.2
Belmont	53	722	45.8	12.4	8	D	D	D	49	407	33.4	12.8
Benicia	61	908	35.4	9.7	11	142	3.7	1.0	56	305	41.4	10.5
Berkeley	424	5 666	323.8	96.2	63	970	131.3	28.9	401	2 931	392.5	160.7
Beverly Hills	214	7 899	648.9	196.1	846	5 001	2 182.7	890.5	980	5 865	1 104.5	350.9
Brea	155	4 055	211.1	61.8	14	D	D	D	135	D	D	D
Brentwood	86	1 194	58.6	15.4	9	308	12.3	4.6	70	443	37.9	15.1
Buena Park	189	3 086	173.2	45.5	15	D	D	D	142	1 327	162.9	42.7
Burbank	289	6 989	427.3	113.2	276	D	D	D	411	D	D	D
Burlingame	144	3 984	286.5	85.2	20	246	21.1	4.1	149	D	D	D
Calexico	65	955	44.8	11.8	4	D	D	D	26	106	8.6	3.2
Camarillo	165	3 002	146.2	39.4	26	D	D	D	207	1 806	158.3	59.9
Campbell	126	2 267	130.9	36.7	13	D	D	D	134	D	D	D
Carlsbad	220	6 891	551.8	148.8	56	1 133	88.2	30.8	214	2 106	244.2	81.3
Carson	145	2 422	124.0	32.9	21	D	D	D	131	977	78.4	27.3
Cathedral City	90	1 441	69.5	21.2	12	336	19.1	5.5	58	583	38.4	18.2
Ceres	67	1 061	50.0	13.5	2	D	D	D	44	D	D	D
Cerritos	148	2 850	145.8	42.8	10	158	11.3	2.3	162	1 948	196.8	76.6
Chico	268	5 112	207.8	57.9	24	780	21.7	7.1	371	3 703	333.5	116.6
Chino	131	2 579	115.8	32.4	18	D	D	D	145	1 724	208.7	65.6
Chino Hills	110	1 681	81.2	20.9	16	D	D	D	104	D	D	D
Chula Vista	383	6 389	333.5	93.3	34	799	65.8	13.5	464	3 697	383.6	139.9
Citrus Heights	129	2 660	120.5	33.5	11	D	D	D	154	1 834	144.0	58.7
Claremont	79	1 238	64.4	18.6	13	D	D	D	120	1 035	80.3	32.7
Clovis	182	3 223	132.4	36.9	15	141	8.4	1.9	166	D	D	D
Coachella	42	538	27.8	6.8	2	D	D	D	10	55	2.9	1.3
Colton	94	1 311	60.3	16.9	5	D	D	D	82	D	D	D
Compton	77	1 270	86.5	21.5	4	0	0.4	0.1	61	461	35.6	13.7
Concord	272	4 480	241.0	66.2	26	716	41.5	11.7	345	3 376	349.0	144.8
Corona	300	5 785	247.7	69.3	38	D	D	D	293	2 858	287.7	98.5
Costa Mesa	402	8 460	512.1	142.0	46	544	47.8	11.6	310	3 058	274.3	103.9
Covina	117	1 886	91.8	23.3	10	D	D	D	185	2 824	236.0	104.6
Culver City	173	2 837	189.5	51.2	139	897	185.1	89.6	164	3 302	257.0	105.5
Cupertino	141	2 774	163.1	47.9	14	238	13.5	5.3	170	1 499	145.4	54.4
Cypress	109	2 044	105.4	27.9	22	D	D	D	105	D	D	D
Daly City	137	2 424	142.2	39.1	9	D	D	D	225	D	D	D
Dana Point	107	3 837	290.5	84.6	27	D	D	D	73	D	D	D
Danville	88	1 370	69.8	20.9	16	445	36.2	11.5	116	880	96.5	35.9
Davis	164	D	D	D	17	D	D	D	119	1 072	165.6	42.3

1. Establishments subject to federal tax.

City	Other services[1], 2007				Government employment and payroll, 2012								
						March payroll							
							Percent of total for:						
	Number of establish-ments	Number of employees	Receipts (mil dol)	Annual payroll (mil dol)	Full-time equivalent employees	Total (dollars)	Adminis-tration, judicial, and legal	Police and Corrections	Fire Protection	Highways and trans-portation	Health and welfare	Natural resources and utilities	Education and libraries
	104	105	106	107	108	109	110	111	112	113	114	115	116
ARKANSAS—Cont'd													
Jacksonville	33	D	D	D	351	1 152 915	9.7	28.8	19.4	4.2	5.3	27.7	0.0
Jonesboro	100	D	D	D	689	2 345 837	8.5	24.7	13.3	9.8	1.2	42.4	0.0
Little Rock	322	2 405	179.6	53.0	2 851	11 721 278	7.5	27.1	19.0	8.2	12.4	20.1	0.0
North Little Rock	133	762	57.5	17.0	971	3 614 112	10.1	25.8	20.1	6.7	0.9	29.4	2.5
Paragould	40	D	D	D	282	995 938	7.4	13.5	10.1	7.0	0.0	34.9	0.0
Pine Bluff	67	D	D	D	430	1 262 555	9.4	40.1	30.3	11.6	2.7	0.0	0.0
Rogers	84	518	26.4	9.0	478	1 723 247	11.6	29.5	25.6	5.5	1.0	18.2	4.6
Russellville	68	344	22.9	7.6	247	826 281	6.7	26.5	27.2	7.8	0.0	20.1	0.0
Sherwood	43	193	16.7	4.8	260	794 982	19.0	40.7	0.0	5.0	4.1	26.7	0.1
Springdale	102	824	54.2	21.6	584	1 997 062	10.3	28.7	23.9	6.6	1.7	21.9	3.3
Texarkana	27	D	D	D	237	974 321	9.2	47.4	27.7	4.9	2.8	2.3	0.0
West Memphis	46	D	D	D	383	1 214 605	9.2	23.7	21.2	5.8	0.8	25.0	1.3
CALIFORNIA	47 780	308 788	30 937.3	8 721.2	X	X	X	X	X	X	X	X	X
Adelanto	6	D	D	D	122	519 045	17.9	63.0	0.0	6.8	0.0	11.6	0.0
Alameda	98	386	33.9	11.1	658	4 669 134	6.4	25.2	22.5	8.7	5.7	19.2	3.1
Alhambra	105	453	45.7	10.9	423	2 729 610	8.0	33.5	27.5	3.8	4.0	18.8	4.5
Aliso Viejo	43	D	D	D	20	114 486	83.1	0.0	0.0	0.0	0.0	16.9	0.0
Anaheim	376	2 850	270.6	85.3	2 214	15 281 363	10.2	31.2	18.4	2.6	1.6	22.9	1.9
Antioch	98	716	62.0	18.9	306	1 931 728	10.7	57.2	0.0	6.0	2.1	20.9	0.0
Apple Valley	32	174	10.5	4.5	115	584 392	38.7	9.0	0.0	3.2	20.4	28.7	0.0
Arcadia	99	432	36.6	9.9	327	2 164 149	7.3	33.8	24.4	10.7	0.9	4.2	5.7
Atascadero	37	165	13.9	4.2	131	738 888	19.1	30.8	22.5	9.0	0.0	14.3	0.0
Atwater	20	D	D	D	124	673 870	13.1	42.2	13.9	5.5	4.6	18.3	0.0
Azusa	70	292	27.0	7.9	312	2 003 992	16.2	36.1	0.0	4.3	3.4	34.3	3.5
Bakersfield	351	2 690	231.1	65.2	1 424	8 316 644	6.2	38.5	18.9	8.6	0.9	17.6	0.0
Baldwin Park	48	D	D	D	227	1 307 981	10.1	58.7	0.0	11.0	9.8	10.4	0.0
Banning	30	148	9.6	3.3	195	1 176 594	19.1	35.3	0.3	9.9	1.7	30.2	0.0
Beaumont	31	D	D	D	168	910 677	6.3	58.6	0.8	7.4	3.3	11.9	0.0
Bell	27	D	D	D	208	970 721	15.5	65.9	0.0	1.2	2.2	15.3	0.0
Bellflower	135	606	61.7	18.6	135	560 170	32.9	10.6	0.0	29.1	9.0	18.3	0.0
Bell Gardens	35	177	18.1	4.5	195	974 379	15.1	53.7	0.0	4.2	3.0	14.3	0.0
Belmont	48	261	23.7	7.1	110	851 441	1.4	33.4	0.0	4.3	7.0	30.3	0.0
Benicia	50	558	86.6	23.1	293	1 695 705	13.1	23.5	18.0	3.4	0.0	29.9	7.0
Berkeley	194	1 512	103.3	57.1	1 669	13 806 771	10.8	38.3	13.0	4.5	13.4	11.2	4.6
Beverly Hills	266	1 963	218.2	56.2	680	6 033 141	8.8	32.8	21.5	1.8	6.2	14.5	3.8
Brea	109	1 028	93.4	31.6	435	2 822 410	14.6	42.7	17.3	2.4	1.3	14.0	0.0
Brentwood	58	373	35.3	10.4	277	2 032 978	16.0	33.4	0.0	3.6	6.7	27.5	0.0
Buena Park	76	D	D	D	314	1 712 183	10.2	51.5	0.0	9.3	10.0	14.8	0.0
Burbank	250	2 210	195.8	78.5	1 339	10 789 444	10.5	20.6	13.7	5.7	4.5	35.6	3.0
Burlingame	114	671	54.9	17.9	257	2 033 098	7.4	25.4	24.0	8.9	0.0	20.2	9.2
Calexico	20	D	D	D	180	959 584	5.6	39.4	18.0	0.4	3.6	18.6	2.2
Camarillo	104	832	88.8	26.1	150	1 175 192	38.2	4.5	0.0	28.2	1.2	24.7	0.0
Campbell	171	999	91.2	29.2	194	1 441 718	19.7	44.4	0.0	5.3	0.4	13.4	0.0
Carlsbad	133	1 245	109.3	30.4	776	4 824 420	15.7	25.6	15.4	11.2	1.9	15.0	9.2
Carson	110	1 136	138.1	34.1	510	2 517 774	28.5	6.7	0.0	15.0	7.7	26.1	0.0
Cathedral City	89	612	49.5	15.2	175	1 230 278	13.0	52.3	30.1	4.1	0.0	0.6	0.0
Ceres	50	D	D	D	182	1 207 924	11.0	48.7	18.9	7.5	0.0	8.8	0.0
Cerritos	63	630	69.5	18.5	300	1 151 269	17.9	4.7	0.0	2.1	2.0	12.8	8.8
Chico	155	779	68.6	19.2	388	2 759 409	11.9	39.0	24.3	7.0	1.6	8.0	0.0
Chino	118	1 486	114.1	49.7	425	2 145 199	12.8	49.4	0.0	3.6	12.3	20.9	0.0
Chino Hills	62	334	15.5	5.1	182	1 001 156	45.8	0.0	0.0	13.9	0.0	34.0	0.0
Chula Vista	216	1 585	135.5	38.4	1 114	7 346 424	14.6	37.1	17.1	15.8	1.2	10.8	2.8
Citrus Heights	83	673	80.3	17.9	204	1 278 252	11.3	69.4	0.0	6.6	1.3	2.7	0.0
Claremont	31	139	9.2	3.2	169	958 849	29.8	43.5	0.0	0.0	0.0	26.7	0.0
Clovis	120	657	52.3	15.5	505	2 897 575	9.7	32.5	16.7	12.7	3.2	20.0	0.0
Coachella	11	D	D	D	79	428 436	23.4	3.0	0.0	9.0	11.1	39.1	0.0
Colton	52	671	55.9	15.1	360	2 494 835	14.1	29.0	19.7	3.6	3.4	18.7	1.8
Compton	62	392	23.2	7.7	329	1 870 002	18.8	5.9	37.1	8.5	3.7	15.6	0.0
Concord	221	1 246	141.4	42.7	443	2 858 330	14.9	60.6	0.0	9.1	1.2	10.7	0.0
Corona	221	1 312	129.4	36.3	692	4 620 304	10.2	34.8	23.7	7.6	2.3	16.8	2.3
Costa Mesa	332	2 166	222.6	67.8	499	4 282 210	13.5	43.0	28.9	5.5	1.1	5.7	0.0
Covina	117	711	71.0	20.0	187	1 234 035	14.5	55.3	0.0	3.8	3.1	11.5	0.0
Culver City	136	2 856	115.9	49.9	409	1 848 474	11.4	41.4	12.9	4.7	9.6	15.5	0.0
Cupertino	58	398	23.9	8.8	154	1 132 814	34.4	0.0	0.0	21.5	0.0	26.3	0.0
Cypress	77	472	58.4	14.7	171	1 179 800	19.6	48.1	0.0	5.4	0.7	14.5	0.0
Daly City	84	505	40.1	12.4	560	4 065 527	12.0	29.6	20.8	3.3	3.1	19.2	3.3
Dana Point	50	347	53.3	8.7	66	459 856	20.0	0.0	0.0	25.3	33.8	14.3	0.0
Danville	63	297	22.9	6.6	101	575 902	34.0	3.2	0.0	27.3	0.0	27.4	0.0
Davis	51	248	22.8	7.3	423	2 817 726	14.4	26.2	16.3	3.9	5.3	24.3	0.0

1. Establishments subject to federal tax.

City	City government finances, 2007									
	General revenue							General expenditure		
		Intergovernmental		Taxes					Per capita[1] (dollars)	
					Per capita[1] (dollars)					
	Total (mil dol)	Total (mil dol)	Percent from state government	Total (mil dol)	Total	Property	Sales and gross receipts	Total (mil dol)	Total	Capital outlays
	117	118	119	120	121	122	123	124	125	126
ARKANSAS—Cont'd										
Jacksonville	66.7	10.5	44.6	9.9	344	27	317	75.1	2 619	339
Jonesboro	78.3	23.6	30.3	30.7	435	65	371	71.4	1 014	147
Little Rock	376.0	98.2	37.1	121.4	617	247	370	369.8	1 881	297
North Little Rock	90.5	26.5	30.0	39.2	606	159	447	97.5	1 506	165
Paragould	29.1	6.0	40.6	7.3	270	31	239	27.7	1 027	152
Pine Bluff	45.8	15.6	31.1	17.4	370	78	293	42.9	915	56
Rogers	66.9	18.0	35.4	33.4	565	89	476	49.1	832	178
Russellville	28.8	7.4	31.7	14.0	492	24	468	23.4	820	49
Sherwood	26.4	11.3	17.7	7.8	261	19	243	26.0	868	128
Springdale	72.7	20.3	30.2	29.9	406	72	333	53.9	732	67
Texarkana	31.4	6.9	34.8	13.5	449	104	344	26.4	879	33
West Memphis	33.0	8.5	26.7	13.1	507	50	458	32.5	1 262	139
CALIFORNIA	X	X	X	X	X	X	X	X	X	X
Adelanto	12.0	0.9	64.5	6.2	197	83	105	18.3	586	65
Alameda	117.1	11.9	69.1	72.8	961	544	346	118.5	1 564	250
Alhambra	94.9	11.0	57.2	48.2	570	309	260	85.5	1 012	77
Aliso Viejo	19.0	1.4	100.0	14.0	283	134	120	22.2	448	112
Anaheim	697.7	119.6	21.0	267.6	779	340	436	658.5	1 917	451
Antioch	69.2	16.1	79.1	35.4	336	194	139	57.9	550	87
Apple Valley	55.7	5.3	91.3	27.5	389	258	118	55.8	790	105
Arcadia	68.8	2.9	73.3	48.5	848	441	400	64.5	1 130	99
Atascadero	31.8	7.6	92.3	15.9	555	349	188	28.1	978	301
Atwater	26.6	3.9	48.1	8.3	291	192	93	49.2	1 714	675
Azusa	58.3	7.2	30.8	36.3	767	353	363	55.0	1 161	37
Bakersfield	360.1	84.2	69.9	149.4	417	223	192	382.6	1 069	301
Baldwin Park	50.2	15.9	46.5	25.1	328	172	153	43.8	572	46
Banning	33.1	4.9	90.4	13.0	427	251	175	30.4	1 003	237
Beaumont	83.3	0.7	100.0	14.4	366	160	203	79.5	2 017	1 172
Bell	29.7	1.8	72.8	16.9	471	317	154	30.0	835	223
Bellflower	32.9	3.7	60.2	25.4	328	163	163	34.3	442	71
Bell Gardens	36.8	3.6	71.1	22.7	531	201	329	31.1	726	78
Belmont	43.6	2.2	83.1	25.6	965	712	247	44.8	1 687	160
Benicia	43.3	1.4	100.0	29.1	1 061	603	453	46.0	1 679	414
Berkeley	293.3	31.1	90.2	147.9	1 281	526	494	300.7	2 605	242
Beverly Hills	261.2	5.5	72.9	142.7	4 124	1 370	2 727	226.1	6 532	1 003
Brea	90.0	3.5	86.5	56.2	1 395	893	497	87.6	2 176	593
Brentwood	78.8	1.8	100.0	33.7	628	397	152	88.6	1 654	238
Buena Park	87.0	7.0	64.8	64.8	788	449	336	105.8	1 285	278
Burbank	265.6	36.3	55.0	147.7	1 412	849	560	282.4	2 701	443
Burlingame	72.1	2.7	100.0	42.6	1 436	445	977	70.0	2 356	686
Calexico	34.0	6.5	59.4	15.9	405	203	194	33.5	852	103
Camarillo	73.4	5.0	40.6	40.7	617	335	278	73.6	1 117	261
Campbell	46.2	3.4	53.9	33.2	823	390	428	49.3	1 222	160
Carlsbad	179.5	13.2	50.3	112.9	1 033	528	496	160.2	1 465	200
Carson	105.5	19.8	56.9	74.0	799	340	456	135.1	1 459	403
Cathedral City	70.1	6.3	64.9	52.7	1 002	695	304	69.7	1 324	144
Ceres	34.3	3.7	83.6	18.9	406	213	188	38.7	834	89
Cerritos	96.9	2.0	89.7	65.5	1 320	774	541	96.8	1 950	141
Chico	99.3	7.9	55.7	69.9	799	467	330	91.9	1 050	275
Chino	102.9	7.3	90.6	54.2	677	425	248	109.3	1 365	144
Chino Hills	60.2	3.8	89.2	21.6	283	154	126	65.7	861	137
Chula Vista	240.2	25.5	80.3	126.8	501	240	258	247.0	976	73
Citrus Heights	52.7	10.0	85.5	32.4	382	164	216	48.9	578	136
Claremont	35.2	1.7	82.5	23.2	653	293	356	34.7	978	122
Clovis	110.7	10.2	67.2	46.4	470	218	249	105.9	1 074	201
Coachella	37.8	11.0	71.9	18.0	421	228	167	49.1	1 150	551
Colton	50.0	6.2	92.7	27.9	524	332	190	44.1	829	84
Compton	98.6	17.9	28.9	54.6	558	319	236	114.4	1 170	108
Concord	120.0	9.6	80.8	70.7	566	241	321	128.3	1 026	86
Corona	225.6	16.4	78.9	106.2	672	397	245	219.2	1 388	272
Costa Mesa	117.6	9.7	76.3	92.1	823	381	439	111.9	1 001	113
Covina	49.3	4.1	69.9	32.6	672	369	300	49.1	1 013	132
Culver City	173.5	27.4	43.4	99.6	2 528	1 144	1 336	143.8	3 651	482
Cupertino	60.4	2.0	89.4	42.9	716	306	399	59.2	989	78
Cypress	43.8	2.7	66.2	33.4	683	409	270	44.8	917	226
Daly City	103.9	12.0	48.5	57.4	551	324	225	112.7	1 082	108
Dana Point	29.3	1.6	100.0	25.1	740	287	445	31.5	929	121
Danville	35.0	6.4	100.0	21.8	508	306	190	34.7	809	181
Davis	96.8	18.9	87.5	47.1	714	397	221	90.4	1 372	150

1. Based on population estimated as of July 1 of the year shown.

City	Public welfare	Highways	Parking facilities	Education	Health and hospitals	Police protection	Sewerage and sanitation	Parks and recreation	Housing and community development	Interest on debt
	City government finances, 2012 (cont.)									
	General expenditure (cont.)									
	Percent of total for:									
	127	128	129	130	131	132	133	134	135	136
ARKANSAS—Cont'd										
Jacksonville	0.0	4.8	0.0	0.0	51.2	10.2	15.6	3.1	0.4	2.2
Jonesboro	0.0	12.4	0.0	0.0	1.1	17.0	17.2	3.4	0.5	15.4
Little Rock	0.0	4.7	0.2	0.0	5.8	15.0	12.9	10.2	2.6	6.0
North Little Rock	0.0	6.2	0.0	0.0	0.4	18.6	16.6	6.3	3.6	5.9
Paragould	0.2	9.6	0.0	0.0	0.5	10.6	23.1	6.0	0.0	2.5
Pine Bluff	0.5	10.5	0.0	0.0	0.1	24.5	18.2	6.0	4.3	1.9
Rogers	0.0	9.9	0.0	0.0	0.8	17.6	15.7	9.0	0.0	5.8
Russellville	0.0	20.6	0.0	0.0	1.1	18.7	18.5	6.1	0.0	0.0
Sherwood	0.0	20.6	0.0	0.0	1.0	23.1	14.0	13.5	0.0	1.2
Springdale	0.0	8.2	0.0	0.0	1.0	20.7	17.2	4.4	1.2	9.5
Texarkana	0.0	5.7	0.0	0.0	1.2	28.6	21.0	1.4	0.8	3.8
West Memphis	0.0	13.7	0.0	0.0	0.5	20.8	16.6	4.2	2.0	3.0
CALIFORNIA	X	X	X	X	X	X	X	X	X	X
Adelanto	0.0	9.8	0.0	0.0	1.4	25.8	0.0	4.3	9.3	0.0
Alameda	0.0	8.5	0.8	0.0	14.8	22.2	8.2	11.0	6.1	3.5
Alhambra	0.0	9.2	2.7	0.0	0.1	28.1	12.5	7.4	4.9	4.2
Aliso Viejo	0.0	15.3	0.0	0.0	1.0	28.2	0.0	7.9	0.5	9.0
Anaheim	0.0	8.5	0.0	0.0	0.1	16.5	8.2	12.1	18.0	10.6
Antioch	0.0	16.1	0.0	0.0	2.4	43.6	4.2	9.6	8.8	3.6
Apple Valley	0.0	8.4	0.0	0.0	2.9	19.9	23.3	8.7	11.7	5.3
Arcadia	0.0	9.9	0.0	0.0	6.9	25.6	2.2	4.2	3.1	1.5
Atascadero	0.0	7.5	0.0	0.0	0.0	21.1	6.6	9.2	20.1	4.0
Atwater	0.0	2.7	0.0	0.0	0.0	14.1	51.3	3.5	5.4	8.0
Azusa	0.0	3.3	0.0	0.0	1.2	30.7	8.1	6.3	8.1	11.6
Bakersfield	0.0	10.0	0.0	0.0	0.0	17.9	17.4	6.8	2.6	3.6
Baldwin Park	0.0	15.9	0.0	0.0	0.0	41.3	0.6	8.7	17.9	3.9
Banning	0.0	11.9	0.0	0.0	0.3	24.5	18.5	2.1	18.5	4.9
Beaumont	0.0	3.8	0.0	0.0	0.6	12.7	7.1	4.6	0.6	0.5
Bell	0.0	6.8	0.0	0.0	0.0	22.5	4.9	3.5	21.8	9.1
Bellflower	0.0	31.2	0.0	0.0	0.0	30.7	0.0	6.3	6.8	6.6
Bell Gardens	0.0	13.1	0.0	0.0	0.0	42.3	7.6	15.9	3.0	3.7
Belmont	0.0	9.5	0.0	0.0	0.0	21.4	17.5	8.4	8.9	2.3
Benicia	0.0	7.0	0.0	0.0	0.0	19.3	14.2	10.6	0.2	3.1
Berkeley	0.0	7.4	2.4	0.0	11.4	18.1	14.2	5.9	6.0	1.9
Beverly Hills	0.0	5.7	21.3	0.0	4.9	17.9	10.5	9.5	0.1	1.7
Brea	0.0	14.6	0.0	0.0	4.1	30.3	6.4	10.8	11.8	1.2
Brentwood	0.0	14.0	0.0	0.0	0.0	18.8	17.9	12.0	9.8	9.7
Buena Park	0.0	12.0	0.0	0.0	0.3	20.3	3.1	4.7	23.0	5.3
Burbank	0.0	7.2	0.3	0.0	4.6	15.9	9.3	5.7	14.2	5.8
Burlingame	0.0	24.2	2.0	0.0	0.0	13.4	14.4	8.0	0.0	2.4
Calexico	0.0	6.0	0.0	0.0	0.9	30.5	16.3	3.8	10.3	0.4
Camarillo	0.0	24.2	0.0	0.0	0.3	20.3	17.6	0.9	6.1	5.0
Campbell	0.0	13.9	0.0	0.0	0.0	26.2	0.0	12.0	10.3	3.4
Carlsbad	0.0	8.7	0.0	0.0	8.2	17.9	8.5	13.4	4.7	1.6
Carson	0.0	13.8	1.0	0.0	0.1	16.4	0.1	13.3	26.3	7.1
Cathedral City	0.0	9.7	0.0	0.0	4.2	22.1	0.6	1.4	22.4	15.6
Ceres	0.0	8.7	0.0	0.0	1.2	28.2	19.7	5.0	9.7	5.6
Cerritos	0.0	10.6	0.0	0.0	0.3	14.0	3.4	14.7	6.5	8.1
Chico	0.0	17.5	1.9	0.0	0.3	23.6	6.6	3.2	11.8	6.1
Chino	0.0	13.4	0.0	0.0	0.0	25.6	18.7	5.2	15.2	6.1
Chino Hills	0.0	20.8	0.0	0.0	0.0	17.3	14.6	6.5	0.4	6.1
Chula Vista	0.0	10.6	0.1	0.0	0.9	20.6	17.6	9.9	2.7	7.6
Citrus Heights	0.0	22.4	0.0	0.0	1.3	38.7	1.2	0.1	14.3	2.1
Claremont	0.0	12.7	0.0	0.0	0.8	28.4	15.5	9.0	4.2	2.9
Clovis	0.0	10.8	0.0	0.0	0.7	21.2	28.1	5.4	3.1	2.4
Coachella	0.0	33.0	0.0	0.0	0.4	12.4	16.2	10.2	4.8	5.7
Colton	0.0	6.2	0.0	0.0	1.3	23.1	11.2	3.9	8.2	9.8
Compton	0.0	8.3	0.0	0.0	0.0	15.0	9.0	2.9	15.0	1.3
Concord	0.0	12.7	0.0	0.0	0.0	33.4	16.2	6.9	3.5	2.3
Corona	0.0	4.4	0.1	0.0	0.5	18.5	23.8	3.9	7.9	9.2
Costa Mesa	0.0	8.7	0.0	0.0	1.0	33.4	0.0	6.1	2.3	2.0
Covina	0.0	5.4	0.2	0.0	0.7	30.8	3.6	5.8	13.9	6.1
Culver City	0.0	5.6	0.2	0.0	3.7	19.6	11.6	4.8	13.5	6.5
Cupertino	0.0	11.9	0.0	0.0	0.3	28.1	2.6	25.6	1.8	3.2
Cypress	0.0	21.7	0.0	0.0	0.5	31.3	3.4	13.1	11.8	1.7
Daly City	0.0	10.1	0.0	0.0	0.5	24.9	20.5	8.8	1.7	0.4
Dana Point	0.0	24.9	0.0	0.0	1.0	30.4	0.0	14.2	0.0	1.4
Danville	0.0	21.8	0.0	0.0	1.0	21.0	0.0	21.4	0.4	1.5
Davis	0.0	8.9	0.0	0.0	0.0	16.4	20.0	26.2	3.7	2.4

City	City government finances, 2012 (cont.)			Climate[2]						
	Debt outstanding			Average daily temperature (degrees Fahrenheit)						
				Mean		Limits				
	Total (mil dol)	Per capita[1] (dollars)	Debt issued during year	January	July	January[3]	July[4]	Annual precipitation (inches)	Heating degree days	Cooling degree days
	137	138	139	140	141	142	143	144	145	146
ARKANSAS—Cont'd										
Jacksonville	28.9	1 008	1.9	38.2	79.9	27.4	91.1	50.56	3 470	1 699
Jonesboro	298.0	4 230	2.9	35.6	81.6	25.8	92.3	46.18	3 737	1 858
Little Rock	511.4	2 601	23.9	40.1	82.4	30.8	92.8	50.93	3 084	2 086
North Little Rock	204.0	3 152	19.6	40.1	82.4	30.8	92.8	50.93	3 084	2 086
Paragould	25.8	953	7.4	NA	NA	NA	NA	NA	NA	NA
Pine Bluff	29.1	619	9.6	40.8	82.4	31.5	92.4	52.48	2 935	2 099
Rogers	160.5	2 718	85.8	32.9	77.5	22.0	88.8	46.92	4 483	1 269
Russellville	0.0	0	0.0	NA	NA	NA	NA	NA	NA	NA
Sherwood	8.3	277	0.0	NA	NA	NA	NA	NA	NA	NA
Springdale	110.5	1 501	0.0	34.3	78.9	24.2	89.1	46.02	4 166	1 439
Texarkana	34.1	1 136	0.0	44.3	82.7	35.6	92.7	47.38	2 421	2 280
West Memphis	31.2	1 214	0.0	37.5	81.5	28.5	90.9	52.80	3 417	1 903
CALIFORNIA	X	X	X	X	X	X	X	X	X	X
Adelanto	0.0	0	0.0	NA	NA	NA	NA	NA	NA	NA
Alameda	152.6	2 014	3.6	50.9	64.9	44.7	72.7	22.94	2 400	377
Alhambra	70.5	834	0.0	56.3	75.6	42.6	89.0	18.56	1 295	1 575
Aliso Viejo	34.0	686	0.0	56.7	72.4	47.2	82.3	14.03	1 465	1 183
Anaheim	1 822.5	5 304	0.0	56.9	73.2	45.2	84.0	11.23	1 286	1 294
Antioch	41.8	397	0.0	45.7	74.4	37.8	90.7	13.33	2 714	1 179
Apple Valley	63.0	893	0.0	45.5	80.0	31.4	99.1	6.20	2 929	1 735
Arcadia	40.4	707	0.0	56.3	75.6	42.6	89.0	18.56	1 295	1 575
Atascadero	27.6	962	0.0	47.3	71.6	33.1	91.3	14.71	2 932	785
Atwater	93.3	3 253	0.0	NA	NA	NA	NA	NA	NA	NA
Azusa	235.4	4 970	0.0	54.6	73.8	41.5	88.7	16.96	1 727	1 191
Bakersfield	345.9	966	49.8	47.8	83.1	39.3	96.9	6.49	2 120	2 286
Baldwin Park	66.8	873	0.0	56.3	75.6	42.6	89.0	18.56	1 295	1 575
Banning	48.2	1 591	0.0	NA	NA	NA	NA	NA	NA	NA
Beaumont	9.6	244	0.4	NA	NA	NA	NA	NA	NA	NA
Bell	55.7	1 550	0.0	58.8	76.6	47.9	88.9	14.44	949	1 837
Bellflower	31.8	410	0.0	57.0	73.8	46.0	82.9	12.94	1 211	1 186
Bell Gardens	36.7	856	0.0	58.8	76.6	47.9	88.9	14.44	949	1 837
Belmont	38.8	1 460	0.0	48.1	69.7	36.4	88.2	28.71	2 769	569
Benicia	55.1	2 008	4.3	46.3	71.2	38.8	87.4	19.58	2 757	786
Berkeley	188.8	1 635	0.0	50.0	62.8	43.6	70.4	25.40	2 857	142
Beverly Hills	142.3	4 111	0.0	57.9	69.5	49.4	76.9	18.68	1 379	893
Brea	39.1	971	0.0	56.9	73.2	45.2	84.0	11.23	1 286	1 294
Brentwood	194.1	3 622	22.4	NA	NA	NA	NA	NA	NA	NA
Buena Park	115.5	1 403	0.0	57.0	73.8	46.0	82.9	12.94	1 211	1 186
Burbank	463.3	4 430	9.8	54.8	75.5	42.0	88.9	17.49	1 575	1 455
Burlingame	33.1	1 114	0.0	50.0	62.7	42.9	70.5	23.35	2 720	184
Calexico	2.8	71	0.0	55.8	91.4	41.3	107.0	2.96	1 080	3 952
Camarillo	90.1	1 367	7.6	55.7	66.0	45.3	74.0	13.61	1 961	389
Campbell	28.0	694	0.1	48.7	70.3	38.8	85.4	22.64	2 641	613
Carlsbad	65.0	594	0.2	54.7	67.6	45.4	72.1	11.13	2 009	505
Carson	217.3	2 347	0.0	56.3	69.4	46.2	77.6	14.79	1 526	742
Cathedral City	271.4	5 160	0.3	57.3	92.1	44.2	108.2	5.23	951	4 224
Ceres	50.3	1 083	0.0	47.2	77.7	40.1	93.6	13.12	2 358	1 570
Cerritos	153.8	3 099	0.0	57.0	73.8	46.0	82.9	12.94	1 211	1 186
Chico	163.2	1 865	0.8	44.5	76.9	35.2	93.0	26.23	2 945	1 334
Chino	211.8	2 645	12.9	54.6	73.8	41.5	88.7	16.96	1 727	1 191
Chino Hills	127.2	1 667	0.0	56.9	73.2	45.2	84.0	11.23	1 286	1 294
Chula Vista	512.8	2 027	4.0	57.3	70.1	46.1	76.1	9.95	1 321	862
Citrus Heights	28.5	337	0.0	46.9	77.7	39.2	94.8	24.61	2 532	1 528
Claremont	26.2	739	0.0	54.6	73.8	41.5	88.7	16.96	1 727	1 191
Clovis	232.4	2 358	0.0	46.0	81.4	38.4	96.6	11.23	2 447	1 963
Coachella	94.7	2 219	2.4	NA	NA	NA	NA	NA	NA	NA
Colton	96.4	1 813	0.0	54.4	79.6	41.8	96.0	16.43	1 599	1 937
Compton	73.6	752	0.0	57.0	73.8	46.0	82.9	12.94	1 211	1 186
Concord	63.7	510	0.0	46.3	71.2	38.8	87.4	19.58	2 757	786
Corona	346.1	2 191	25.3	54.7	75.9	41.5	92.0	12.00	1 599	1 534
Costa Mesa	38.8	347	0.0	55.9	67.3	48.2	71.4	11.65	1 719	543
Covina	86.2	1 779	2.3	54.6	73.8	41.5	88.7	16.96	1 727	1 191
Culver City	206.5	5 244	0.0	56.7	70.8	46.1	80.0	13.32	1 344	959
Cupertino	43.9	734	43.9	48.7	70.3	38.8	85.4	22.64	2 641	613
Cypress	8.8	181	0.0	57.0	73.8	46.0	82.9	12.94	1 211	1 186
Daly City	45.3	435	0.0	50.6	57.3	44.6	61.1	19.77	3 665	17
Dana Point	8.2	241	0.0	55.4	68.7	43.9	77.3	13.56	1 756	666
Danville	12.9	300	0.0	47.5	72.4	39.3	85.2	23.96	3 267	983
Davis	55.0	835	0.0	45.2	74.3	37.1	92.7	19.05	2 853	1 127

1. Based on the population estimated as of July 1 of the year shown. 2. Represents normal values based on the 30-year period, 1971–2000. 3. Average daily minimum.
4. Average daily maximum.

STATE Place code	City	Land area,[1] 2010 (sq km)	Population, 2014: Total persons	Population, 2014: Rank	Population, 2014: Per square kilometer	Race alone or in combination (percent), 2011-2013: White	Black	American Indian, Alaska Native	Asian	Hawaiian Pacific Islander	Percent Hispanic or Latino[2], 2011-2013	Percent foreign born 2011–2013
		1	2	3	4	5	6	7	8	9	10	11
	CALIFORNIA—Cont'd											
06 18394	Delano	37.0	52 651	703	1 423.0	67.6	6.0	1.0	14.8	0.4	74.5	38.5
06 18996	Desert Hot Springs	61.2	28 164	1 299	460.2	58.6	7.1	2.8	4.5	1.4	56.8	25.1
06 19192	Diamond Bar	38.5	56 784	647	1 474.9	32.9	4.7	1.0	55.2	NA	19.8	42.3
06 19766	Downey	32.1	114 172	240	3 556.8	70.1	4.9	0.6	7.5	0.2	71.3	33.7
06 20018	Dublin	38.6	54 695	676	1 417.0	55.1	9.2	1.2	34.8	1.0	12.8	28.5
06 20956	East Palo Alto	6.5	29 530	1 246	4 543.1	59.5	16.0	1.0	4.3	7.8	63.0	40.2
06 21712	El Cajon	37.4	103 091	285	2 756.4	80.0	7.6	1.8	5.6	2.4	28.5	29.7
06 21782	El Centro	28.7	43 763	849	1 524.8	73.1	3.1	1.9	3.1	NA	83.6	32.9
06 22020	Elk Grove	109.3	163 553	151	1 496.4	52.2	13.6	1.4	31.6	2.5	18.7	22.5
06 22230	El Monte	24.8	116 631	234	4 702.9	54.2	1.0	0.8	29.2	0.2	65.9	49.3
06 22300	El Paso de Robles (Paso Robles)	49.5	31 287	1 185	632.1	80.0	3.6	2.7	3.3	NA	39.4	20.2
06 22678	Encinitas	48.7	62 254	568	1 278.3	89.8	0.7	0.5	7.8	0.5	13.2	12.1
06 22804	Escondido	95.3	150 243	167	1 576.5	83.7	3.0	1.1	7.2	0.5	47.0	27.9
06 23042	Eureka	24.3	26 925	1 364	1 108.0	87.0	3.3	7.0	6.6	1.1	7.7	6.0
06 23182	Fairfield	96.8	111 125	250	1 148.0	52.4	17.1	1.9	19.3	1.9	28.1	21.9
06 24638	Folsom	56.8	75 361	447	1 326.8	75.7	6.2	1.0	16.9	0.8	12.2	15.7
06 24680	Fontana	109.9	204 950	108	1 864.9	59.3	11.8	1.5	8.1	0.9	66.6	30.0
06 25338	Foster City	9.7	32 754	1 130	3 376.7	50.0	4.0	NA	49.3	0.9	6.5	41.7
06 25380	Fountain Valley	23.4	57 010	646	2 436.3	55.4	1.7	0.5	35.9	0.6	16.8	31.7
06 26000	Fremont	200.6	228 758	97	1 140.4	34.0	4.8	1.1	56.6	1.0	14.4	44.1
06 27000	Fresno	290.0	515 986	34	1 779.3	54.1	9.5	2.3	14.6	0.6	48.0	21.0
06 28000	Fullerton	57.9	139 677	186	2 412.4	60.0	3.0	1.8	25.3	0.7	35.9	30.8
06 28168	Gardena	15.1	60 395	592	3 999.7	26.0	25.8	1.3	29.4	0.5	35.6	34.1
06 29000	Garden Grove	46.5	175 078	136	3 765.1	46.4	1.9	0.8	39.7	1.0	35.8	43.7
06 29504	Gilroy	41.8	52 533	705	1 256.8	69.5	2.6	1.0	7.3	NA	60.1	27.0
06 30000	Glendale	78.9	200 167	116	2 537.0	76.5	2.0	0.9	18.7	0.2	17.3	55.2
06 30014	Glendora	50.2	51 442	726	1 024.7	78.1	4.3	1.2	9.7	NA	32.0	16.7
06 30378	Goleta	20.5	30 797	1 199	1 502.3	72.6	1.4	3.0	11.8	0.7	37.8	21.9
06 31960	Hanford	43.0	55 065	669	1 280.6	81.0	5.6	1.5	5.6	NA	49.8	15.9
06 32548	Hawthorne	15.8	87 583	358	5 543.2	53.0	27.8	3.8	7.8	1.7	54.7	33.6
06 33000	Hayward	117.4	154 612	161	1 317.0	43.4	12.9	1.8	26.6	3.8	40.3	39.3
06 33182	Hemet	72.1	83 032	393	1 151.6	73.8	9.9	2.1	4.1	0.2	37.3	15.5
06 33434	Hesperia	189.3	92 749	333	490.0	76.6	7.9	2.5	2.1	0.5	48.6	14.4
06 33588	Highland	48.6	54 651	677	1 124.5	62.0	12.6	2.3	8.8	0.3	51.2	20.5
06 34120	Hollister	18.9	37 086	1 002	1 962.2	86.6	1.9	1.8	4.7	0.5	67.7	24.2
06 36000	Huntington Beach	69.3	200 809	112	2 897.7	81.3	1.6	1.1	13.0	1.0	18.4	16.5
06 36056	Huntington Park	7.8	59 362	611	7 610.5	70.9	0.8	0.9	0.7	NA	97.6	50.5
06 36294	Imperial Beach	10.8	27 149	1 351	2 513.8	76.5	5.7	1.7	11.5	1.5	49.5	19.6
06 36448	Indio	75.6	85 633	375	1 132.7	55.3	3.0	1.7	3.0	0.4	68.5	26.9
06 36546	Inglewood	23.5	111 905	248	4 761.9	30.6	45.4	1.0	1.9	0.6	50.0	26.6
06 36770	Irvine	171.2	248 531	82	1 451.7	55.3	2.9	0.8	42.3	0.5	9.6	36.7
06 39220	Laguna Hills	17.3	30 972	1 196	1 790.3	72.3	2.9	1.7	16.3	1.1	18.4	25.6
06 39248	Laguna Niguel	38.4	65 448	539	1 704.4	83.2	2.0	1.1	11.6	NA	16.2	19.7
06 39290	La Habra	19.1	62 066	574	3 249.5	64.3	2.3	1.3	9.6	0.2	60.9	27.2
06 39486	Lake Elsinore	93.8	60 029	602	640.0	60.5	6.7	0.6	6.7	1.6	50.9	20.9
06 39496	Lake Forest	46.1	80 148	409	1 738.6	68.6	2.2	0.9	17.6	0.9	24.8	24.3
06 39892	Lakewood	24.4	81 653	401	3 346.4	59.6	8.9	2.0	19.0	2.4	32.0	21.5
06 40004	La Mesa	23.5	59 177	616	2 518.2	78.5	10.9	2.3	9.0	0.8	22.5	14.0
06 40032	La Mirada	20.3	49 459	756	2 436.4	61.0	3.2	1.3	20.7	0.3	41.3	25.8
06 40130	Lancaster	244.2	161 043	154	659.5	67.7	21.9	1.8	5.9	0.6	39.9	15.0
06 40340	La Puente	9.0	40 735	910	4 526.1	59.5	1.8	1.0	12.0	NA	84.0	41.9
06 40354	La Quinta	91.0	39 964	929	439.2	85.2	2.7	1.0	5.0	NA	31.3	13.7
06 40830	La Verne	21.8	32 288	1 153	1 481.1	80.4	4.2	2.2	9.3	NA	29.8	15.2
06 40886	Lawndale	5.1	33 442	1 112	6 557.3	59.8	13.7	4.7	11.6	NA	63.5	38.8
06 41124	Lemon Grove	10.1	26 511	1 380	2 624.9	62.7	13.0	2.8	8.1	2.4	42.6	17.1
06 41474	Lincoln	52.1	45 902	815	881.0	89.0	1.2	2.5	8.2	1.2	18.4	12.1
06 41992	Livermore	65.2	86 870	364	1 332.4	84.4	2.4	1.1	12.9	0.6	19.6	16.9
06 42202	Lodi	35.3	63 950	550	1 811.6	85.7	1.2	7.6	9.3	0.3	35.2	19.0
06 42524	Lompoc	30.0	44 013	838	1 467.1	68.4	6.3	3.1	5.9	1.3	55.1	20.7
06 43000	Long Beach	130.3	473 577	36	3 634.5	58.4	15.7	3.9	14.2	1.3	41.6	25.3
06 43280	Los Altos	16.8	30 288	1 225	1 802.9	73.5	NA	NA	30.3	NA	3.5	22.4
06 44000	Los Angeles	1 213.9	3 928 864	2	3 236.6	55.2	10.1	1.3	12.9	0.4	48.6	38.6
06 44028	Los Banos	25.9	37 126	999	1 433.4	81.3	5.8	2.6	3.3	NA	69.5	26.3
06 44112	Los Gatos	28.7	30 735	1 203	1 070.9	82.5	0.8	2.0	16.6	NA	5.4	19.5
06 44574	Lynwood	12.5	71 839	474	5 747.1	41.2	9.0	1.2	1.3	NA	88.9	38.6
06 45022	Madera	40.9	63 605	554	1 555.1	82.6	3.6	2.2	4.2	0.2	78.5	32.6
06 45400	Manhattan Beach	10.2	35 881	1 043	3 517.7	85.8	1.9	0.9	13.2	NA	9.1	11.8
06 45484	Manteca	45.9	73 494	462	1 601.2	73.3	4.4	1.6	10.2	1.4	39.1	14.9
06 46114	Martinez	31.4	37 567	984	1 196.4	84.3	3.7	2.1	11.3	0.9	15.1	10.9
06 46492	Maywood	3.1	27 937	1 310	9 011.9	83.7	0.8	NA	0.4	NA	97.6	45.3
06 46842	Menifee	120.4	85 182	378	707.5	79.2	6.4	1.5	8.1	0.7	33.6	14.4

1. Dry land or land partially or temporarily covered by water. 2. May be of any race.

Table D. Cities — **Population**

City	Age of population (percent), 2011-2013									Median age 2011-2013	Percent female 2011-2013	Population			
												Census counts		Percent change	
	Under 5 years	5 to 17 years	18 to 24 years	25 to 34 years	35 to 44 years	45 to 54 years	55 to 64 years	65 to 74 years	75 years and over			2000	2010	2000–2010	2010–2014
	12	13	14	15	16	17	18	19	20	21	22	23	24	25	26
CALIFORNIA—Cont'd															
Delano	8.6	20.6	13.4	17.4	15.0	10.7	7.7	3.7	2.9	28.5	42.2	38 824	53 041	36.6	-0.7
Desert Hot Springs	8.0	22.7	10.2	13.8	14.3	12.4	8.5	6.2	3.8	32.5	48.0	16 582	25 938	56.4	4.1
Diamond Bar	4.0	17.2	9.3	13.4	13.1	16.1	14.5	7.9	4.6	41.0	52.4	56 287	55 544	-1.3	2.2
Downey	7.5	18.0	11.7	15.2	14.6	12.1	10.2	5.9	4.7	33.4	51.0	107 323	111 772	4.1	2.1
Dublin	7.6	16.4	7.3	16.6	18.8	16.3	8.8	5.9	2.3	36.3	50.4	29 973	46 036	53.6	18.8
East Palo Alto	9.1	21.8	11.6	19.7	12.3	11.0	8.6	3.6	2.3	29.2	52.6	29 506	28 155	-4.6	4.9
El Cajon	7.7	18.4	11.9	15.9	11.5	13.3	10.1	5.7	5.4	32.5	50.9	94 869	99 478	4.9	3.6
El Centro	8.9	21.2	12.2	14.8	11.8	10.7	11.0	5.4	3.9	29.8	51.4	37 835	42 598	12.6	2.7
Elk Grove	6.1	23.8	8.6	12.1	14.7	14.7	10.4	5.5	4.1	34.6	50.7	59 984	153 015	155.1	6.9
El Monte	7.1	17.9	9.7	15.8	14.2	13.0	10.6	6.6	5.2	34.7	50.4	115 965	113 475	-2.1	2.8
El Paso de Robles (Paso Robles)	7.6	18.2	8.4	14.9	13.8	12.9	11.5	5.8	7.0	35.5	51.7	24 297	29 793	22.6	5.0
Encinitas	6.8	14.4	6.5	13.8	14.1	14.9	15.0	8.1	6.5	41.3	50.7	58 014	59 518	2.6	4.6
Escondido	8.3	18.2	11.3	15.8	13.5	12.7	9.9	4.9	5.3	32.9	50.8	133 559	143 911	7.8	4.4
Eureka	5.7	13.4	13.1	16.8	9.6	14.0	13.6	7.1	6.7	35.7	49.1	26 128	27 191	4.1	-1.0
Fairfield	7.0	18.0	12.0	15.1	12.7	14.0	10.1	5.8	5.3	33.5	51.0	96 178	105 321	9.5	5.5
Folsom	6.6	18.4	7.7	12.6	17.3	15.9	11.5	5.3	4.6	37.7	45.7	51 884	72 203	39.2	4.4
Fontana	7.8	23.2	11.8	15.4	14.6	12.4	8.3	3.9	2.5	29.5	50.2	128 929	196 069	52.1	4.5
Foster City	6.1	15.5	4.9	13.3	18.0	12.5	13.8	9.2	6.7	40.8	51.1	28 803	30 567	6.1	7.2
Fountain Valley	4.5	14.7	8.9	11.6	12.7	16.3	12.9	10.2	8.2	43.3	50.2	54 978	55 313	0.6	3.0
Fremont	6.8	17.5	7.2	14.8	16.8	14.8	11.3	6.1	4.7	37.0	50.7	203 413	214 089	5.2	6.9
Fresno	9.0	20.6	12.1	15.9	11.8	11.5	9.5	5.4	4.3	29.8	50.7	427 652	494 665	15.7	4.0
Fullerton	6.6	16.8	12.2	16.2	12.8	13.5	9.9	5.9	6.1	33.8	51.4	126 003	135 161	7.3	3.3
Gardena	6.3	15.2	8.7	14.5	12.2	15.3	12.1	7.2	8.4	39.4	51.5	57 746	58 829	1.9	2.7
Garden Grove	5.8	18.8	10.6	13.0	14.4	14.5	11.4	6.5	5.1	36.3	49.5	165 196	170 883	3.4	2.4
Gilroy	8.3	21.3	9.5	13.7	15.5	13.1	9.6	5.5	3.4	33.1	50.2	41 464	48 821	17.7	7.6
Glendale	5.5	13.5	8.3	14.2	14.8	14.0	13.5	7.9	8.2	40.8	52.3	194 973	191 719	-1.7	4.4
Glendora	3.7	18.5	10.2	11.0	11.9	16.2	14.0	7.4	7.1	40.3	50.6	49 415	50 073	1.3	2.7
Goleta	5.2	15.6	16.8	13.0	11.1	13.0	10.9	6.9	7.5	34.6	50.8	55 204	29 888	-45.9	3.0
Hanford	7.6	23.5	9.4	14.9	12.7	11.3	10.3	5.7	4.8	30.9	51.3	41 686	53 967	29.5	1.8
Hawthorne	7.2	20.2	11.5	18.2	14.1	12.3	9.1	4.9	2.5	30.8	51.7	84 112	84 293	0.2	3.9
Hayward	6.7	16.3	10.8	16.5	13.6	13.8	11.2	5.9	5.2	34.8	51.4	140 030	144 186	3.0	7.1
Hemet	6.1	18.9	8.7	11.8	10.0	11.3	10.5	11.1	11.7	39.5	51.8	58 812	78 657	33.7	5.6
Hesperia	7.3	23.0	9.8	14.2	12.2	13.8	9.8	6.2	3.8	32.0	49.0	62 582	90 173	44.1	2.9
Highland	7.4	24.5	11.6	13.0	13.1	13.8	9.4	4.4	2.7	29.3	51.0	44 605	53 104	19.1	2.9
Hollister	8.1	21.8	9.9	15.3	13.5	13.3	10.3	4.4	3.4	31.8	50.5	34 413	34 928	1.5	6.3
Huntington Beach	4.9	14.8	8.8	13.7	13.6	16.1	12.6	8.9	6.6	41.1	50.9	189 594	189 992	0.2	5.1
Huntington Park	9.1	20.7	12.9	16.1	14.3	10.8	9.4	3.9	2.7	29.6	50.7	61 348	58 114	-5.3	2.1
Imperial Beach	8.0	18.6	13.6	17.7	10.6	12.9	9.7	3.7	5.4	30.0	49.4	26 992	26 324	-2.5	3.1
Indio	8.0	21.5	8.7	13.8	13.4	10.7	10.3	8.5	5.3	33.7	50.5	49 116	76 036	54.8	8.2
Inglewood	7.4	18.9	9.3	16.2	13.4	13.4	11.3	6.2	3.9	33.8	52.7	112 580	109 673	-2.6	2.0
Irvine	5.3	16.6	13.6	15.8	15.5	13.6	9.9	5.6	3.9	34.2	50.8	143 072	212 375	48.4	17.3
Laguna Hills	4.4	15.0	9.3	13.0	13.0	14.2	16.3	7.8	6.8	41.7	51.7	31 178	30 344	-2.7	2.4
Laguna Niguel	5.9	15.8	8.4	10.4	12.9	16.7	16.7	8.2	5.0	42.8	51.8	61 891	62 979	1.8	3.9
La Habra	7.4	18.3	10.2	16.7	12.7	13.6	10.3	5.1	5.8	33.4	51.2	58 974	60 239	2.1	3.0
Lake Elsinore	8.2	24.7	10.4	14.1	14.9	11.9	9.6	4.0	2.3	29.1	50.4	28 928	51 821	79.1	13.6
Lake Forest	5.5	17.7	8.4	13.1	15.0	17.3	12.3	6.5	4.1	38.5	50.7	58 707	77 264	31.6	3.5
Lakewood	6.4	17.7	9.2	12.0	14.4	15.3	13.5	5.6	5.8	38.6	52.2	79 345	80 048	0.9	2.0
La Mesa	7.0	13.7	10.4	17.1	12.8	12.7	12.0	6.2	8.2	36.5	52.4	54 749	57 065	4.2	3.7
La Mirada	5.3	15.7	14.2	12.2	10.7	13.5	12.1	8.6	7.6	38.2	50.7	46 783	48 527	3.7	1.9
Lancaster	8.3	20.8	11.0	13.6	13.7	13.1	10.6	5.2	3.6	32.2	49.1	118 718	156 633	31.9	2.8
La Puente	8.0	18.8	11.1	15.7	13.8	13.8	9.4	5.4	4.1	32.9	51.4	41 063	39 816	-3.0	2.3
La Quinta	5.4	17.0	6.4	9.0	10.3	12.9	15.2	16.3	7.5	46.2	51.8	23 694	37 467	58.1	6.7
La Verne	4.8	16.1	10.8	10.6	10.5	14.8	13.5	10.3	8.5	43.0	51.4	31 638	31 063	-1.8	3.9
Lawndale	8.1	20.4	10.2	16.5	14.9	13.5	8.2	4.5	3.7	32.1	50.0	31 711	32 769	3.3	2.1
Lemon Grove	5.3	19.4	11.0	12.2	12.4	14.7	13.9	6.1	5.1	36.8	50.3	24 918	25 320	1.6	4.7
Lincoln	6.5	16.3	5.2	10.9	14.3	10.1	10.5	15.0	11.2	42.1	52.6	11 205	42 819	282.1	7.3
Livermore	6.9	17.4	8.1	13.3	13.8	17.1	12.0	6.3	5.1	38.1	49.7	73 345	80 968	10.4	7.1
Lodi	7.0	20.8	10.3	12.0	12.6	13.3	10.6	6.9	6.8	35.0	51.1	56 999	62 134	9.0	2.9
Lompoc	9.3	19.0	10.9	14.7	13.5	12.4	10.5	5.5	4.2	31.8	47.8	41 103	42 434	3.2	3.7
Long Beach	7.0	17.5	11.6	15.3	14.5	13.5	10.7	5.6	4.3	34.0	50.7	461 522	462 257	0.2	2.4
Los Altos	5.7	20.6	3.5	5.2	13.8	16.7	14.3	9.8	10.4	45.8	50.8	27 693	28 976	4.6	4.4
Los Angeles	6.6	15.7	11.3	17.1	14.8	13.3	10.5	6.0	5.0	34.6	50.0	3 694 820	3 792 621	2.6	3.0
Los Banos	8.7	24.0	11.1	12.8	13.1	11.6	8.7	6.4	3.8	30.3	51.1	25 869	35 972	39.1	3.2
Los Gatos	4.1	18.8	5.5	7.6	13.0	18.8	14.1	9.7	8.4	45.4	51.4	28 592	29 413	2.9	4.4
Lynwood	9.1	24.9	12.1	14.0	15.7	10.5	7.1	3.7	2.9	27.7	51.4	69 845	69 772	-0.1	3.0
Madera	10.0	24.3	11.7	14.7	13.4	10.7	7.2	4.7	3.4	27.2	48.8	43 207	61 416	42.1	3.6
Manhattan Beach	5.2	19.1	4.4	11.1	15.5	17.8	13.0	7.3	6.8	41.5	51.7	33 852	35 135	3.8	2.1
Manteca	8.0	20.9	9.5	13.6	13.2	12.7	11.4	6.2	4.6	33.5	51.4	49 258	67 096	36.2	9.2
Martinez	4.4	14.3	7.8	12.3	12.8	17.2	16.8	9.2	5.2	44.1	51.5	35 866	35 824	-0.1	4.2
Maywood	9.5	24.0	13.4	14.0	14.7	10.9	7.4	3.8	2.4	27.2	50.3	28 083	27 395	-2.4	2.0
Menifee	6.7	17.6	8.8	13.6	11.7	11.5	10.6	10.3	9.1	37.5	51.0	NA	77 519	NA	9.9

City	Households, 2011-2013				Persons in group quarters, 2010				Serious crimes known to police,[2] 2013				Educational attainment, 2011–2013		
			Percent			Institutional			Total		Rate[3]			Attainment[4] (percent)	
	Number	Persons per household	Female family householder[1]	One-person	Total	Total	Persons in nursing facilities	Non-institutional	Number	Rate[3]	Violent	Property	Population age 25 and older	High school graduate or less	Bachelor's degree or more
	27	28	29	30	31	32	33	34	35	36	37	38	39	40	41
CALIFORNIA—Cont'd															
Delano	10 511	4.23	20.4	10.1	10 897	10 719	189	178	2 258	4 325	592	3 733	30 312	73.6	7.6
Desert Hot Springs	9 171	3.00	15.7	26.1	118	0	0	118	1 380	4 940	992	3 948	16 343	61.7	10.3
Diamond Bar	17 652	3.17	13.7	12.7	129	27	22	102	948	1 674	110	1 565	39 076	22.7	50.4
Downey	32 529	3.44	19.3	17.0	683	561	534	122	3 618	3 195	288	2 908	70 724	48.6	21.0
Dublin	15 992	2.84	8.4	23.2	5 774	5 682	0	92	809	1 625	141	1 484	33 850	22.5	51.3
East Palo Alto	6 945	4.14	15.8	18.0	154	4	0	150	944	3 246	1 193	2 053	16 626	59.9	16.7
El Cajon	32 751	3.01	18.3	23.7	2 482	1 350	1 339	1 132	3 116	3 055	378	2 676	62 884	50.7	18.3
El Centro	12 308	3.43	22.5	18.6	816	520	98	296	2 183	5 048	333	4 715	24 866	50.8	17.7
Elk Grove	47 621	3.31	13.8	15.5	669	209	133	460	3 432	2 133	291	1 841	97 396	29.8	35.1
El Monte	30 355	3.75	19.2	14.1	1 080	763	618	317	2 522	2 182	294	1 888	75 215	69.4	11.6
El Paso de Robles (Paso Robles)	11 232	2.70	12.5	17.8	169	5	0	164	951	3 088	334	2 754	20 068	38.6	21.8
Encinitas	22 931	2.64	7.5	24.4	528	405	405	123	1 208	1 966	207	1 760	44 034	18.8	56.1
Escondido	44 428	3.27	13.2	19.4	2 119	786	657	1 333	4 561	3 068	401	2 667	91 632	48.0	20.5
Eureka	10 692	2.39	13.4	35.5	1 883	449	8	1 434	2 279	8 478	714	7 764	18 290	38.4	25.3
Fairfield	34 488	3.06	12.2	19.4	2 489	1 268	332	1 221	4 032	3 719	459	3 259	67 800	38.8	23.4
Folsom	25 310	2.63	6.6	25.7	6 960	6 772	96	188	1 434	1 944	133	1 811	49 101	23.0	46.3
Fontana	48 355	4.15	18.1	10.9	444	228	194	216	4 813	2 366	356	2 010	115 092	53.9	15.6
Foster City	12 040	2.63	7.3	23.7	109	57	57	52	320	980	46	934	23 393	14.9	63.6
Fountain Valley	18 672	2.99	11.9	18.6	437	180	160	257	1 262	2 222	162	2 060	40 500	28.3	38.2
Fremont	71 486	3.07	10.4	16.7	1 651	682	662	969	4 370	1 947	122	1 825	151 659	27.5	51.5
Fresno	160 355	3.10	19.9	23.1	8 867	4 552	1 825	4 315	25 136	4 940	501	4 438	294 741	48.2	19.6
Fullerton	43 963	3.06	12.9	19.7	3 077	759	629	2 318	4 231	3 029	266	2 763	88 945	32.9	37.3
Gardena	21 173	2.78	18.2	29.4	794	672	631	122	1 576	2 640	410	2 229	41 597	45.7	24.1
Garden Grove	46 358	3.71	16.0	15.1	1 941	707	624	1 234	3 852	2 195	259	1 936	112 823	51.1	18.6
Gilroy	14 500	3.45	15.9	14.8	806	164	128	642	1 920	3 747	351	3 396	30 806	45.1	24.2
Glendale	70 310	2.74	13.2	26.3	1 429	1 206	1 181	223	3 379	1 730	93	1 637	141 384	35.5	37.3
Glendora	16 593	3.00	12.8	19.1	765	573	519	192	1 405	2 761	128	2 633	34 327	29.3	31.2
Goleta	10 288	2.76	12.0	27.7	201	178	170	23	494	1 625	141	1 484	18 893	28.6	42.2
Hanford	17 368	3.09	17.7	19.6	899	616	296	283	2 238	4 112	549	3 563	32 430	45.3	19.1
Hawthorne	28 405	2.99	21.0	27.1	539	331	311	208	2 822	3 276	673	2 603	52 284	51.0	18.2
Hayward	46 111	3.18	16.6	20.9	2 724	770	723	1 954	5 433	3 599	390	3 209	98 814	46.0	24.3
Hemet	30 326	2.65	15.1	31.3	614	459	421	155	4 410	5 398	547	4 851	53 799	52.5	11.5
Hesperia	26 335	3.48	15.5	16.9	28	6	6	22	2 701	2 916	401	2 516	54 952	55.5	9.2
Highland	14 642	3.68	19.5	14.5	172	96	96	76	1 553	2 852	351	2 501	30 495	51.3	19.3
Hollister	10 062	3.57	16.1	15.4	115	106	102	9	765	2 101	536	1 565	21 713	52.9	15.0
Huntington Beach	74 146	2.62	10.7	24.4	890	403	391	487	5 296	2 704	185	2 519	139 546	23.6	41.0
Huntington Park	14 717	3.97	25.5	12.0	255	7	0	248	2 171	3 689	610	3 079	33 564	77.0	5.9
Imperial Beach	8 784	2.98	16.5	27.3	619	0	0	619	587	2 174	493	1 682	16 072	43.4	18.0
Indio	24 951	3.27	15.2	18.3	949	584	135	365	3 167	3 947	583	3 364	50 936	52.5	16.4
Inglewood	37 178	2.94	23.0	28.8	1 502	515	405	987	3 457	3 096	662	2 434	71 554	48.2	18.1
Irvine	83 228	2.66	9.9	24.6	6 556	588	55	5 968	3 398	1 441	48	1 393	147 562	12.4	64.3
Laguna Hills	10 527	2.90	7.6	19.5	369	136	136	233	561	1 802	170	1 632	21 881	23.7	46.1
Laguna Niguel	24 139	2.65	7.9	24.1	248	0	0	248	681	1 049	88	962	44 910	15.6	54.4
La Habra	18 983	3.21	13.9	21.1	340	171	167	169	1 243	2 013	143	1 871	39 327	45.4	22.3
Lake Elsinore	14 790	3.78	14.6	13.5	432	208	0	224	1 597	2 840	183	2 657	31 761	48.7	15.3
Lake Forest	26 690	2.93	10.1	20.9	515	216	216	299	918	1 157	132	1 025	53 886	24.3	43.5
Lakewood	26 383	3.06	16.2	20.1	109	0	0	109	2 287	2 820	277	2 543	53 852	36.0	26.7
La Mesa	23 575	2.44	13.4	33.1	657	533	512	124	2 149	3 675	309	3 365	40 137	26.5	36.9
La Mirada	14 017	3.29	11.7	19.2	2 857	271	271	2 586	913	1 858	146	1 711	31 688	35.9	28.4
Lancaster	48 092	3.14	17.9	22.9	8 259	6 775	486	1 484	4 327	2 708	521	2 187	94 945	49.1	15.2
La Puente	9 142	4.40	19.9	11.2	43	0	0	43	636	1 574	354	1 220	25 011	68.7	9.6
La Quinta	15 315	2.52	9.1	23.3	57	7	7	50	1 562	3 990	174	3 816	27 527	28.8	35.2
La Verne	10 881	2.83	12.8	22.8	676	175	104	501	790	2 513	118	2 395	21 513	26.8	37.0
Lawndale	9 780	3.37	17.0	20.0	175	17	0	158	581	1 748	487	1 261	20 277	55.8	16.2
Lemon Grove	8 274	3.08	15.8	25.3	346	146	129	200	654	2 500	554	1 946	16 674	49.7	13.9
Lincoln	17 256	2.57	8.6	23.6	115	85	85	30	578	1 289	56	1 234	32 030	25.0	32.6
Livermore	29 305	2.84	11.2	20.0	510	121	121	389	2 100	2 490	320	2 170	56 552	27.4	39.5
Lodi	22 011	2.84	11.7	26.4	677	490	470	187	2 588	4 067	451	3 616	39 140	46.4	20.4
Lompoc	13 265	2.99	17.9	24.8	3 656	3 557	163	99	1 239	2 843	431	2 412	26 103	55.9	13.5
Long Beach	163 332	2.81	16.8	30.6	8 277	2 956	2 370	5 321	15 345	3 267	500	2 768	298 919	39.3	28.8
Los Altos	10 908	2.70	5.1	20.5	227	193	193	34	381	1 261	76	1 184	20 841	6.3	79.2
Los Angeles	1 325 553	2.84	15.3	30.3	84 601	26 415	13 845	58 186	102 368	2 639	426	2 213	2 563 571	44.8	31.3
Los Banos	10 341	3.53	19.4	16.1	181	78	78	103	1 169	3 162	295	2 868	20 620	63.0	8.9
Los Gatos	12 086	2.46	6.4	27.1	350	258	238	92	576	1 898	82	1 815	21 571	9.5	69.1
Lynwood	14 708	4.62	26.6	9.7	2 652	2 203	370	449	1 964	2 763	613	2 150	38 054	73.4	6.3
Madera	16 313	3.81	24.0	16.8	591	173	173	418	2 423	3 848	902	2 946	33 834	64.0	8.5
Manhattan Beach	13 707	2.59	6.5	28.0	28	0	0	28	917	2 552	178	2 374	25 316	8.9	73.1
Manteca	22 326	3.14	14.9	18.6	495	345	341	150	2 911	4 028	293	3 735	43 581	49.7	15.6
Martinez	14 441	2.51	11.9	27.4	1 296	1 061	268	235	877	2 376	144	2 232	27 115	26.1	36.9
Maywood	6 330	4.35	25.3	11.4	119	119	119	0	432	1 557	404	1 153	14 697	81.1	4.7
Menifee	26 826	3.03	9.2	24.3	188	107	106	81	1 779	2 153	120	2 033	54 540	42.7	16.2

1. No spouse present. 2. Data for serious crimes have not been adjusted for underreporting. This may affect comparability between geographic areas and over time. 3. Per 100,000 population estimated by the FBI. 4. Persons 25 years old and over.

City	Money income, 2011–2013: Per capita income[1] (dollars)	Money income, 2011–2013: Households: Median income	Households: Percent with income of $200,000 or more	Households: Percent with income of less than $25,000	Families with income below poverty (percent)	Housing units, 2010: Total	Housing units, 2010: Percent change, 2000–2010	Housing units, 2010: Vacant units for sale or rent[2]	Occupied housing units 2011–2013: Total	Owner-occupied: Percent	Owner-occupied: Median value[3] (dollars)	Median owner costs as a percent of income: With a mortgage[4]	Median owner costs as a percent of income: Without a mortgage[5]
	42	43	44	45	46	47	48	49	50	51	52	53	54
CALIFORNIA—Cont'd													
Delano	10 345	35 582	0.5	30.4	28.5	10 713	21.0	453	10 511	51.5	131 600	29.2	12.3
Desert Hot Springs	13 528	31 377	0.5	39.1	32.7	10 902	55.2	2 252	9 171	42.1	121 700	31.2	11.4
Diamond Bar	35 241	90 000	11.0	11.0	5.0	18 455	2.8	575	17 652	78.1	527 700	27.9	12.2
Downey	22 515	60 041	4.6	17.2	10.0	35 601	2.4	1 665	32 529	49.9	393 100	31.3	10.0
Dublin	42 551	113 936	16.5	7.8	2.1	15 782	59.6	869	15 992	62.1	560 300	27.4	10.0
East Palo Alto	18 116	46 685	3.1	22.3	17.9	7 819	10.8	879	6 945	37.3	374 200	29.8	13.7
El Cajon	19 762	41 610	2.4	31.1	22.4	35 850	1.9	1 716	32 751	37.9	318 800	27.9	11.5
El Centro	17 467	39 798	2.5	34.2	23.3	14 476	17.8	1 368	12 308	50.5	139 500	23.6	10.8
Elk Grove	28 823	75 275	6.7	12.0	7.7	50 634	167.9	2 707	47 621	71.1	254 100	26.2	10.9
El Monte	14 871	36 064	1.4	33.5	24.0	29 069	4.8	1 255	30 355	40.3	339 900	34.2	11.7
El Paso de Robles (Paso Robles)	27 687	58 071	5.0	18.0	12.7	11 426	30.1	593	11 232	51.1	341 600	27.3	11.9
Encinitas	46 358	91 844	15.3	14.6	5.7	25 740	7.8	1 658	22 931	66.4	707 700	27.1	10.0
Escondido	20 900	47 462	3.5	25.2	16.5	48 044	6.8	2 560	44 428	48.9	328 500	29.7	12.8
Eureka	21 196	37 683	1.1	33.0	14.0	11 891	2.6	741	10 692	44.7	229 200	27.9	10.0
Fairfield	26 219	62 455	4.6	18.3	10.7	37 184	16.7	2 700	34 488	55.4	251 200	28.8	10.0
Folsom	37 213	97 241	8.5	10.0	1.7	26 109	45.5	1 158	25 310	67.2	369 000	24.3	12.5
Fontana	19 191	63 702	3.0	16.0	13.0	51 857	44.5	2 741	48 355	66.5	242 100	28.4	10.8
Foster City	54 045	113 454	21.2	7.0	2.0	12 458	3.7	442	12 040	58.6	841 600	25.6	12.3
Fountain Valley	33 823	83 011	7.3	15.3	5.8	19 164	3.7	516	18 672	71.1	597 700	27.0	10.0
Fremont	40 315	100 946	15.9	9.6	4.2	73 989	6.5	2 985	71 486	62.5	599 200	24.6	10.0
Fresno	18 801	40 439	2.6	32.5	25.6	171 288	15.0	12 939	160 355	46.7	168 200	26.9	11.4
Fullerton	29 102	64 234	7.5	19.4	12.3	47 869	7.0	2 478	43 963	53.2	474 900	28.5	10.0
Gardena	23 104	46 420	2.1	25.6	11.3	21 472	2.1	914	21 173	50.6	336 400	33.3	12.5
Garden Grove	20 922	58 003	4.1	20.4	14.2	47 755	2.0	1 718	46 358	55.1	393 000	28.9	10.0
Gilroy	28 510	76 276	7.0	16.5	11.8	14 854	22.1	679	14 500	57.5	422 900	27.9	11.6
Glendale	28 317	50 801	6.2	27.3	11.3	76 269	3.5	4 000	70 310	35.9	587 200	31.0	11.4
Glendora	31 083	72 549	7.1	13.9	7.2	17 778	3.5	637	16 593	69.6	442 300	28.9	12.0
Goleta	33 245	78 948	6.9	13.3	2.9	11 473	-43.6	570	10 288	53.4	598 800	29.5	10.0
Hanford	21 780	51 014	2.7	23.0	17.6	18 493	25.4	1 001	17 368	55.3	165 900	24.7	10.0
Hawthorne	19 594	43 097	1.9	27.2	18.3	29 869	1.0	1 383	28 405	27.7	379 900	31.8	10.9
Hayward	25 044	60 318	5.8	20.6	12.0	48 296	5.1	2 931	46 111	52.5	319 700	28.9	11.0
Hemet	17 043	31 782	0.9	40.2	21.9	35 305	19.8	5 213	30 326	57.2	108 100	29.3	16.0
Hesperia	15 690	41 437	1.0	28.9	21.5	29 004	36.2	2 573	26 335	60.9	134 500	28.3	11.6
Highland	19 810	52 476	3.8	21.9	18.0	16 578	10.9	1 107	14 642	62.9	239 500	27.0	12.2
Hollister	22 250	64 985	2.8	18.0	8.0	10 401	4.5	541	10 062	57.6	280 600	29.4	11.2
Huntington Beach	42 315	80 925	10.8	12.6	6.8	78 003	2.9	3 718	74 146	58.2	622 600	27.5	10.0
Huntington Park	11 905	34 395	0.5	36.2	28.1	15 151	-1.2	554	14 717	25.1	272 400	35.8	10.0
Imperial Beach	19 318	47 810	0.6	24.0	11.0	9 882	1.5	770	8 784	32.6	332 400	31.8	10.0
Indio	20 505	47 862	2.5	26.7	16.2	28 971	71.4	5 593	24 951	62.5	189 800	28.9	13.5
Inglewood	20 049	41 204	1.6	29.2	18.5	38 429	-0.5	2 040	37 178	35.2	320 100	34.4	11.7
Irvine	41 485	90 126	14.1	14.5	6.2	83 899	56.2	4 921	83 228	48.4	647 300	26.7	10.0
Laguna Hills	44 067	92 294	14.5	10.4	4.1	11 046	-2.5	577	10 527	69.3	571 000	26.5	10.0
Laguna Niguel	51 986	100 625	20.5	10.4	4.0	25 312	5.9	1 080	24 139	71.6	662 000	27.2	10.0
La Habra	24 988	58 412	4.7	19.0	13.3	19 924	2.0	947	18 983	53.9	369 800	27.5	10.0
Lake Elsinore	19 445	57 199	1.1	18.7	12.9	16 253	70.6	1 465	14 790	63.8	203 600	28.7	13.4
Lake Forest	37 957	89 001	10.3	9.8	4.9	27 088	31.6	864	26 690	70.0	482 900	25.7	10.4
Lakewood	28 265	74 374	3.6	12.6	5.3	27 470	0.7	927	26 383	68.9	391 000	28.3	10.0
La Mesa	30 351	54 025	3.1	19.9	8.4	26 167	5.1	1 655	23 575	46.1	360 200	27.1	11.4
La Mirada	27 889	78 604	5.4	16.1	4.6	15 092	1.9	411	14 017	75.9	394 100	27.9	10.0
Lancaster	18 918	46 743	2.3	27.1	19.1	51 835	24.4	4 843	48 092	57.4	151 100	28.3	14.5
La Puente	15 767	54 510	0.6	17.0	11.3	9 761	1.0	310	9 142	55.8	286 500	31.8	10.0
La Quinta	38 757	65 272	10.1	19.1	4.6	23 489	99.7	8 669	15 315	70.0	337 200	28.7	17.9
La Verne	33 787	72 892	8.2	18.4	6.3	11 686	3.5	425	10 881	73.5	444 300	26.0	13.6
Lawndale	17 364	44 724	0.7	23.9	13.5	10 151	2.8	470	9 780	32.3	348 800	30.1	12.6
Lemon Grove	21 111	51 135	1.0	22.1	12.9	8 868	1.2	434	8 274	54.5	282 600	32.4	11.6
Lincoln	32 079	71 519	2.6	16.6	6.3	17 457	322.6	978	17 256	77.2	320 300	30.6	12.3
Livermore	41 629	97 205	13.6	10.3	4.5	30 342	14.3	1 208	29 305	69.0	474 200	26.7	10.0
Lodi	23 980	48 607	3.6	24.5	13.6	23 792	11.2	1 695	22 011	54.7	218 200	27.2	12.7
Lompoc	19 099	42 186	2.3	27.0	20.4	14 416	5.8	1 061	13 265	43.0	219 000	26.9	10.0
Long Beach	26 050	51 358	4.6	25.9	17.5	176 032	2.5	12 501	163 332	40.2	409 300	29.1	10.3
Los Altos	87 397	167 610	43.3	7.3	0.8	11 204	4.4	459	10 908	84.7	1 000 000	24.4	10.0
Los Angeles	27 345	47 812	6.3	28.2	18.6	1 413 995	5.7	95 827	1 325 553	36.4	437 700	32.8	13.3
Los Banos	15 762	42 307	1.5	27.9	23.8	11 375	40.9	1 116	10 341	52.6	138 900	27.7	15.6
Los Gatos	67 999	121 776	28.0	8.9	3.6	13 050	5.2	695	12 086	63.7	1 000 000	26.6	10.0
Lynwood	12 297	41 343	0.6	27.9	24.3	15 277	1.8	597	14 708	46.1	266 000	34.7	12.1
Madera	14 144	40 975	0.4	29.5	23.3	17 049	34.7	1 111	16 313	46.8	140 500	30.3	10.0
Manhattan Beach	83 163	144 522	36.1	7.5	3.1	14 929	-1.1	891	13 707	67.8	1 000 000	24.5	10.0
Manteca	23 013	57 478	1.9	18.7	10.0	23 132	36.9	1 514	22 326	58.4	208 800	28.9	11.7
Martinez	38 652	83 072	8.9	12.5	5.2	14 976	2.3	689	14 441	65.4	403 600	25.5	10.7
Maywood	11 451	34 920	0.1	36.0	33.2	6 766	1.0	207	6 330	25.8	281 900	32.1	10.5
Menifee	22 761	54 427	2.1	18.9	6.8	30 269	NA	2 808	26 826	74.5	191 700	29.3	13.7

1. Based on population estimated by the American Community Survey. 2. Includes units rented or sold but not occupied. 3. Specified owner-occupied units; $1,000,000 represents $1,000,000 or more 4. 50.0 represents 50 percent or more. 5. 10.0 represents 10 percent or less.

City	Occupied housing units, 2011–2013 (cont.)				Migration, 2011–2013		Civilian labor force, 2014				Civilian employment[4], 2011–2013			
									Unemployment			Percent		
	Percent renter occupied	Median gross rent[1]	Median rent as a percent of income[2]	Percent with no vehicle available	Percent who lived in the same house one year ago	Percent who lived outside current city one year ago	Total	Percent change, 2013–2014	Total	Rate[3]	Population age 16 and older	In labor force	Civilian full-year full-time workers	Households with no workers (percent)
	55	56	57	58	59	60	61	62	63	64	65	66	67	68
CALIFORNIA—Cont'd														
Delano	48.5	762	33.3	4.5	80.4	13.0	19 619	-0.1	2 449	12.5	39 300	50.3	24.3	19.3
Desert Hot Springs	57.9	902	45.4	8.4	75.1	13.7	11 033	0.9	1 078	9.8	19 836	56.7	29.1	32.8
Diamond Bar	21.9	1 782	32.8	2.4	88.4	9.5	29 603	1.5	1 568	5.3	46 475	64.8	42.7	17.4
Downey	50.1	1 207	34.1	4.6	88.9	6.6	57 087	1.1	4 188	7.3	87 228	65.4	41.6	18.5
Dublin	37.9	1 784	27.6	3.7	79.1	17.9	26 600	1.2	975	3.7	38 805	66.0	43.9	14.5
East Palo Alto	62.7	1 238	39.7	8.1	82.4	14.2	14 719	1.9	980	6.7	21 086	69.7	35.0	18.4
El Cajon	62.1	1 079	40.5	8.7	80.8	12.6	46 355	-0.6	4 246	9.2	78 380	63.0	31.7	28.0
El Centro	49.5	727	36.3	8.6	80.3	7.1	21 730	2.0	4 783	22.0	31 539	60.2	30.7	26.7
Elk Grove	28.9	1 445	30.2	2.9	83.8	8.8	77 179	0.6	4 363	5.7	117 815	66.0	41.5	19.3
El Monte	59.7	1 050	44.9	10.0	92.6	4.8	52 619	0.5	5 354	10.2	90 063	59.0	35.2	20.4
El Paso de Robles (Paso Robles)	48.9	1 136	31.5	4.2	80.5	10.0	16 101	1.2	1 011	6.3	23 519	68.5	39.8	21.3
Encinitas	33.6	1 689	31.4	3.4	87.9	8.7	32 814	0.3	1 708	5.2	49 539	67.3	41.1	21.9
Escondido	51.1	1 165	38.5	6.2	86.1	6.7	68 916	0.0	4 431	6.4	112 676	61.3	35.8	25.7
Eureka	55.3	804	34.3	12.1	76.0	13.3	12 865	-0.6	853	6.6	22 464	61.5	33.9	29.1
Fairfield	44.6	1 294	34.6	6.0	80.4	10.0	50 987	-0.1	3 426	6.7	83 959	65.2	35.6	24.6
Folsom	32.8	1 419	23.7	3.7	85.9	9.4	34 508	0.8	1 646	4.8	56 556	64.0	41.2	19.8
Fontana	33.5	1 074	36.8	4.3	86.9	7.9	93 411	1.0	8 158	8.7	146 182	66.5	37.2	15.4
Foster City	41.4	2 000	25.7	1.8	84.4	11.4	18 434	2.6	714	3.9	25 652	68.1	45.5	19.0
Fountain Valley	28.9	1 493	32.9	6.4	89.3	7.6	28 595	0.6	1 540	5.4	46 994	62.3	38.7	26.9
Fremont	37.5	1 621	26.7	4.0	86.5	8.1	114 739	0.9	5 285	4.6	173 394	66.3	45.2	31.4
Fresno	53.3	879	36.8	11.4	80.2	6.4	236 266	0.1	29 735	12.6	372 453	61.6	32.3	29.1
Fullerton	46.8	1 298	36.3	5.4	80.7	14.2	70 146	0.4	4 362	6.2	109 530	66.2	37.6	21.3
Gardena	49.4	1 106	35.3	7.4	88.0	9.1	30 187	0.9	2 487	8.2	48 091	64.2	40.3	24.2
Garden Grove	44.9	1 313	34.7	5.7	88.8	7.8	83 404	0.3	5 677	6.8	137 044	63.9	38.6	19.3
Gilroy	42.5	1 359	32.1	6.7	85.1	8.1	26 710	1.6	1 816	6.8	37 051	70.8	41.3	18.1
Glendale	64.1	1 266	39.8	13.8	86.9	8.2	100 241	0.9	8 021	8.0	162 331	61.2	36.0	26.8
Glendora	30.4	1 417	31.5	4.4	87.8	9.9	25 275	1.1	1 781	7.0	41 350	63.3	36.7	25.4
Goleta	46.6	1 587	29.1	5.6	79.8	17.7	17 281	1.2	626	3.6	24 845	68.4	42.9	23.3
Hanford	44.7	924	30.9	7.5	80.6	7.6	24 009	-1.0	2 621	10.9	39 270	64.7	38.5	26.6
Hawthorne	72.3	992	35.7	9.6	82.8	11.1	43 679	1.0	3 235	7.4	65 063	68.0	40.2	19.0
Hayward	47.5	1 283	35.0	7.4	84.3	10.2	76 779	0.0	6 283	8.2	118 860	67.2	38.2	22.2
Hemet	42.8	907	42.5	12.0	77.1	13.9	28 390	0.5	3 219	11.3	63 014	47.9	22.4	51.4
Hesperia	39.1	1 019	40.0	6.5	82.7	11.2	34 650	0.5	3 780	10.9	67 433	53.5	28.1	30.4
Highland	37.1	942	35.0	5.0	82.8	11.4	23 444	1.4	1 650	7.0	38 682	62.2	36.4	23.0
Hollister	42.4	1 282	32.7	2.7	81.1	6.7	18 291	1.4	1 729	9.5	26 434	70.8	36.6	18.9
Huntington Beach	41.8	1 551	32.2	4.2	87.6	7.2	106 571	0.6	5 640	5.3	161 207	67.2	40.4	23.5
Huntington Park	74.9	931	38.5	15.6	88.5	7.4	27 460	0.4	2 969	10.8	42 843	67.0	37.4	16.1
Imperial Beach	67.4	1 188	32.9	9.7	76.6	18.5	12 349	-0.8	1 216	9.8	20 523	65.9	34.6	24.6
Indio	37.5	959	34.1	6.6	79.3	9.6	36 723	1.1	3 271	8.9	60 268	63.5	33.5	29.6
Inglewood	64.8	1 062	37.5	9.5	87.6	8.9	54 408	0.4	5 880	10.8	85 378	66.3	37.4	27.2
Irvine	51.6	1 843	29.9	3.7	78.1	14.3	121 801	0.8	5 007	4.1	184 777	65.6	41.6	18.3
Laguna Hills	30.7	1 759	31.7	4.2	86.3	11.8	16 858	0.7	845	5.0	25 680	69.3	44.4	17.8
Laguna Niguel	28.4	1 808	34.9	2.9	87.2	10.6	34 464	0.7	1 731	5.0	52 013	68.6	44.0	19.4
La Habra	46.1	1 273	35.0	5.4	85.7	8.4	30 781	0.4	1 916	6.2	47 417	67.2	41.0	19.1
Lake Elsinore	36.2	1 164	34.6	4.5	83.5	10.8	25 638	1.1	2 250	8.8	39 774	66.6	37.9	16.8
Lake Forest	30.0	1 652	31.6	2.6	88.3	8.9	44 766	0.9	1 751	3.9	63 006	72.6	48.1	15.4
Lakewood	31.1	1 466	32.5	4.2	86.6	10.2	42 473	1.2	2 713	6.4	63 739	66.6	43.9	20.1
La Mesa	53.9	1 222	34.1	10.2	77.0	16.7	30 501	0.0	1 981	6.5	47 257	65.7	40.4	28.3
La Mirada	24.1	1 587	32.5	4.2	90.8	7.4	23 782	1.4	1 387	5.8	39 967	59.0	36.5	26.0
Lancaster	42.6	1 040	35.8	7.4	87.8	7.7	64 131	0.7	5 913	9.2	118 316	53.4	35.8	29.1
La Puente	44.2	1 172	31.8	6.0	87.6	9.1	18 960	1.1	1 382	7.3	30 500	63.9	41.7	15.8
La Quinta	30.0	1 301	33.0	3.8	88.9	7.5	17 208	1.9	900	5.2	31 351	54.1	27.3	39.1
La Verne	26.5	1 304	31.2	5.9	87.2	10.0	15 514	1.3	982	6.3	25 733	59.6	35.2	31.3
Lawndale	67.7	1 312	35.3	4.5	88.1	8.8	16 738	0.9	1 321	7.9	24 561	67.9	41.6	16.5
Lemon Grove	45.5	1 134	35.6	9.1	91.5	6.7	12 437	-0.4	1 045	8.4	20 376	64.1	36.4	26.6
Lincoln	22.8	1 532	32.5	2.3	90.2	7.2	18 297	0.2	1 250	6.8	35 035	53.7	32.3	43.5
Livermore	31.0	1 473	28.8	3.7	86.6	8.2	45 707	1.1	1 830	4.0	65 459	69.9	45.3	19.4
Lodi	45.3	957	33.6	7.6	82.4	7.1	28 648	0.0	2 866	10.0	47 966	64.2	32.4	27.0
Lompoc	57.0	961	35.9	9.9	76.0	10.8	18 232	0.4	1 446	7.9	32 347	57.2	32.3	27.6
Long Beach	59.8	1 094	33.6	10.8	82.1	8.6	240 156	0.7	21 672	9.0	367 071	66.1	37.8	24.0
Los Altos	15.3	2 000	24.3	2.0	90.1	9.0	14 082	2.6	477	3.4	22 946	58.9	39.7	26.4
Los Angeles	63.6	1 172	36.8	13.5	85.2	5.6	2 015 679	0.8	176 133	8.7	3 099 659	66.2	38.3	23.7
Los Banos	47.4	1 055	36.7	4.7	82.0	7.9	15 953	0.3	2 087	13.1	25 695	59.1	27.3	27.8
Los Gatos	36.3	1 711	26.8	2.6	87.9	8.7	15 482	2.5	544	3.5	24 005	62.9	41.9	21.3
Lynwood	53.9	1 014	41.0	7.5	88.9	8.2	29 055	0.5	2 950	10.2	49 787	58.9	35.3	17.7
Madera	53.2	870	30.7	10.9	90.4	4.2	27 477	1.1	2 623	9.5	43 370	58.2	28.4	42.7
Manhattan Beach	32.2	1 981	24.7	2.0	88.0	8.7	19 005	1.9	648	3.4	27 846	67.3	48.1	19.7
Manteca	41.6	1 170	32.4	5.2	81.9	11.6	34 310	-0.1	3 675	10.7	52 365	65.2	36.7	24.0
Martinez	34.6	1 410	32.2	3.3	87.1	9.1	20 269	0.8	1 123	5.5	30 818	68.4	40.3	22.8
Maywood	74.2	980	42.9	12.8	NA	NA	12 579	0.8	1 080	8.6	19 288	65.1	41.1	14.4
Menifee	25.5	1 370	38.6	4.4	84.2	10.2	35 479	0.9	3 413	9.6	63 785	58.0	32.4	34.0

1. $2,000 represents $2,000 or more. 2. 50.0 represents 50 percent or more. 3. Percent of civilian labor force. 4. Persons 16 years old and over.

City	Value of residential construction authorized by building permits, 2014			Wholesale trade,[1] 2007				Retail trade,[2] 2007			
	New construction ($1,000)	Number of housing units	Percent single family	Number of establish-ments	Number of employees	Sales (mil dol)	Annual payroll (mil dol)	Number of establish-ments	Number of employees	Sales (mil dol)	Annual payroll (mil dol)
	69	70	71	72	73	74	75	76	77	78	79
CALIFORNIA—Cont'd											
Delano	383	4	100.0	16	247	208.8	11.4	81	1 072	258.9	23.8
Desert Hot Springs	0	0	0.0	NA	NA	NA	NA	38	639	120.9	13.9
Diamond Bar	13 270	44	100.0	203	698	463.5	31.6	125	1 576	391.9	34.2
Downey	10 440	42	100.0	96	947	376.1	37.7	320	5 367	1 216.2	132.1
Dublin	383 156	1 095	74.5	57	503	251.8	25.5	185	3 939	1 249.9	114.8
East Palo Alto	188	2	100.0	5	D	D	D	22	819	220.2	19.4
El Cajon	6 603	28	100.0	129	1 243	459.1	47.3	508	7 503	1 968.4	193.6
El Centro	7 998	43	100.0	48	363	202.2	13.6	213	3 848	756.0	81.7
Elk Grove	126 048	571	100.0	54	D	D	D	274	6 684	1 950.0	177.9
El Monte	9 395	43	100.0	339	1 976	858.9	66.1	300	4 461	2 140.4	153.6
El Paso de Robles (Paso Robles)	18 277	61	100.0	38	317	166.6	16.0	172	2 401	634.7	59.1
Encinitas	46 676	157	100.0	91	423	155.1	18.1	302	4 309	1 082.8	105.9
Escondido	13 260	139	12.2	160	1 328	642.0	64.8	593	10 151	2 698.3	267.6
Eureka	1 583	11	36.4	48	469	159.3	18.5	274	3 689	968.6	87.4
Fairfield	85 588	316	100.0	62	1 616	681.9	68.9	344	5 687	1 346.3	135.0
Folsom	80 474	300	100.0	33	405	824.8	31.4	288	6 074	1 766.7	157.2
Fontana	97 280	396	84.8	138	3 302	2 405.0	148.0	336	6 599	1 852.5	167.8
Foster City	48 667	232	0.0	42	D	D	D	37	885	279.6	25.2
Fountain Valley	1 828	7	100.0	124	1 925	6 251.7	138.8	250	3 805	1 283.1	99.9
Fremont	89 403	274	94.2	500	10 709	11 312.2	801.9	456	8 160	2 721.8	254.5
Fresno	195 072	918	69.8	533	8 235	4 831.4	362.0	1 658	25 728	6 358.8	611.1
Fullerton	60 487	446	33.0	235	3 219	2 275.7	143.4	401	6 034	1 608.6	152.9
Gardena	4 311	28	78.6	185	1 875	1 049.5	84.3	182	2 702	757.4	78.7
Garden Grove	4 320	22	100.0	246	2 541	1 379.0	113.2	418	4 760	1 410.7	119.5
Gilroy	75 501	243	100.0	53	649	274.0	31.3	330	4 907	1 141.0	112.9
Glendale	43 555	373	4.6	244	2 112	894.2	97.0	734	11 451	3 224.0	298.7
Glendora	33 705	284	1.4	43	471	145.0	25.6	141	2 500	727.6	66.6
Goleta	583	4	100.0	63	1 662	1 166.2	124.9	125	2 346	668.3	62.1
Hanford	26 241	194	62.9	27	376	164.6	16.4	201	3 186	733.0	68.4
Hawthorne	52 693	331	39.0	75	1 423	549.2	57.6	176	3 460	1 039.2	88.4
Hayward	128 125	586	37.9	493	7 787	4 967.5	403.8	443	6 868	1 785.7	188.8
Hemet	31 856	138	100.0	28	149	30.6	4.5	243	4 614	876.4	115.1
Hesperia	15 478	75	100.0	43	324	274.5	12.1	186	1 977	508.7	48.0
Highland	1 609	7	100.0	12	186	38.3	4.7	60	677	160.5	15.6
Hollister	19 757	76	100.0	22	547	128.8	25.4	102	1 393	315.0	37.3
Huntington Beach	59 297	503	10.3	457	6 703	4 698.0	426.4	596	9 070	2 364.8	230.3
Huntington Park	366	2	100.0	60	1 113	463.0	44.3	219	2 514	652.2	63.7
Imperial Beach	5 265	29	65.5	4	13	2.6	0.3	39	271	68.1	6.0
Indio	100 696	517	100.0	45	567	237.5	26.6	171	2 797	789.3	80.3
Inglewood	551	3	33.3	91	1 825	958.0	69.2	263	3 849	1 099.6	88.5
Irvine	646 474	3 248	48.2	902	18 358	33 740.7	1 324.0	636	13 736	4 566.8	438.6
Laguna Hills	39 273	289	0.0	85	548	252.3	30.3	226	3 124	571.1	62.9
Laguna Niguel	39 699	157	9.6	94	374	161.5	19.2	174	3 853	1 304.3	117.1
La Habra	5 157	31	61.3	69	560	235.4	24.7	183	3 446	971.7	85.4
Lake Elsinore	90 540	491	100.0	42	290	69.0	9.7	171	2 938	773.2	71.4
Lake Forest	138 429	833	31.0	218	3 761	2 875.0	244.4	241	3 826	1 225.8	103.0
Lakewood	0	0	0.0	36	174	46.5	4.6	241	5 437	1 056.0	109.0
La Mesa	38 938	309	13.6	25	124	37.6	4.6	264	4 631	1 236.3	117.5
La Mirada	8 793	35	100.0	123	3 364	5 047.9	187.2	104	1 554	424.5	42.6
Lancaster	25 862	93	100.0	65	905	928.6	40.1	343	6 023	1 754.4	156.5
La Puente	1 516	8	100.0	33	230	97.5	6.4	113	1 205	227.3	27.3
La Quinta	59 233	182	95.6	21	57	20.1	2.1	108	3 127	784.7	72.6
La Verne	17 742	78	53.8	92	1 036	472.0	48.2	94	1 380	288.3	31.0
Lawndale	674	4	100.0	17	150	43.2	5.1	93	871	253.5	22.5
Lemon Grove	6 106	22	100.0	15	123	31.9	4.3	76	1 266	402.1	36.0
Lincoln	81 253	286	100.0	17	244	115.7	11.0	52	848	193.5	20.5
Livermore	21 299	86	82.6	159	3 337	2 130.0	206.4	240	4 278	1 315.2	138.0
Lodi	4 361	16	100.0	49	331	436.0	13.8	236	3 617	853.9	91.7
Lompoc	4 000	22	100.0	7	47	8.3	1.6	128	1 725	385.3	39.2
Long Beach	59 121	323	7.7	331	4 884	7 337.1	286.7	1 012	13 851	4 320.9	[illegible]
Los Altos	73 195	217	16.1	24	50	36.8	2.3	113	1 163	265.0	35.1
Los Angeles	2 325 891	11 264	14.8	8 693	84 842	49 819.9	3 788.8	11 880	140 076	36 672.8	3 602.7
Los Banos	7 025	36	88.9	9	81	62.2	3.2	94	1 487	350.9	33.3
Los Gatos	42 013	39	100.0	44	540	321.5	42.8	187	2 387	721.0	68.4
Lynwood	3 890	23	100.0	41	709	334.4	32.8	132	1 345	274.1	27.1
Madera	40 536	156	100.0	28	271	169.0	11.8	175	2 363	518.9	52.2
Manhattan Beach	62 231	98	98.0	38	D	D	D	182	3 187	721.9	71.8
Manteca	80 748	427	100.0	27	285	163.7	13.0	174	2 826	679.6	72.1
Martinez	12 018	83	45.8	23	143	38.1	5.1	72	1 256	312.0	35.6
Maywood	0	0	0.0	23	409	171.1	15.3	50	563	104.2	13.0
Menifee	167 929	570	86.0	NA	NA	NA	NA	NA	NA	NA	NA

1. Merchant wholesalers except manufacturers' sales branches and offices. 2. Establishments with payroll.

City	Real estate and rental and leasing, 2007				Professional, scientific, and technical services,[1] 2007				Manufacturing, 2007			
	Number of establish-ments	Number of employees	Receipts (mil dol)	Annual payroll (mil dol)	Number of establish-ments	Number of employees	Receipts (mil dol)	Annual payroll (mil dol)	Number of establish-ments	Number of employees	Receipts (mil dol)	Annual payroll (mil dol)
	80	81	82	83	84	85	86	87	88	89	90	91
CALIFORNIA—Cont'd												
Delano	21	58	9.0	1.2	20	D	D	D	NA	NA	NA	NA
Desert Hot Springs	14	155	14.7	4.7	11	292	5.9	3.6	NA	NA	NA	NA
Diamond Bar	100	322	53.7	9.1	245	1 342	198.1	64.2	24	968	319.5	43.8
Downey	197	1 217	154.0	31.0	142	D	D	D	95	2 738	1 141.7	109.9
Dublin	52	319	75.6	13.5	150	1 184	190.8	81.2	23	1 430	D	92.8
East Palo Alto	15	44	24.3	1.7	16	D	D	D	NA	NA	NA	NA
El Cajon	175	843	150.8	24.0	208	1 303	125.5	47.8	183	5 660	999.1	233.7
El Centro	58	221	31.6	4.9	84	D	D	D	NA	NA	NA	NA
Elk Grove	103	368	67.1	10.6	177	835	88.8	35.9	39	1 155	281.5	48.0
El Monte	73	499	46.6	13.8	122	D	D	D	182	4 537	806.7	180.9
El Paso de Robles (Paso Robles)	55	164	30.4	5.0	95	392	59.7	16.9	85	2 418	489.5	98.4
Encinitas	217	473	114.6	18.8	474	D	D	D	NA	NA	NA	NA
Escondido	197	948	482.9	42.2	386	D	D	D	197	3 321	572.2	126.4
Eureka	68	297	53.6	9.3	111	D	D	D	34	557	117.4	19.6
Fairfield	97	401	85.5	12.9	162	1 148	111.2	50.0	62	2 642	1 358.5	139.8
Folsom	120	494	100.5	17.6	276	D	D	D	33	502	110.7	24.9
Fontana	88	598	115.6	21.7	78	D	D	D	127	6 095	1 839.3	231.3
Foster City	48	609	161.2	47.4	182	D	D	D	20	D	D	D
Fountain Valley	102	412	77.4	15.6	289	2 186	455.1	136.3	99	2 926	3 201.1	154.1
Fremont	281	1 441	407.7	56.8	948	D	D	D	343	22 496	8 724.6	1 577.6
Fresno	487	3 393	507.9	104.2	1 154	D	D	D	366	13 192	3 965.6	495.9
Fullerton	183	1 097	221.8	37.8	394	D	D	D	226	6 982	2 128.2	287.8
Gardena	50	392	35.0	8.4	68	375	43.2	13.2	276	5 692	1 426.1	220.4
Garden Grove	133	743	109.4	24.5	277	D	D	D	333	8 131	1 705.1	324.1
Gilroy	52	D	D	D	75	D	D	D	59	1 846	566.1	81.6
Glendale	309	2 441	1 049.5	150.9	806	7 801	1 854.0	543.7	240	5 156	606.6	206.8
Glendora	80	252	49.2	7.9	130	1 107	89.7	39.6	35	965	388.8	36.1
Goleta	56	348	44.6	10.3	155	D	D	D	123	5 686	1 658.8	376.2
Hanford	49	215	30.6	4.7	58	337	31.3	10.4	28	962	343.5	38.9
Hawthorne	69	340	42.3	8.5	69	869	149.5	44.9	81	2 976	516.3	116.4
Hayward	167	1 207	241.9	46.1	256	D	D	D	340	12 570	3 295.8	580.8
Hemet	74	399	55.8	9.0	93	525	49.8	16.9	28	970	185.3	33.5
Hesperia	51	220	39.4	6.6	67	543	34.6	11.5	73	718	112.3	28.1
Highland	22	75	12.4	1.5	29	93	9.9	3.3	NA	NA	NA	NA
Hollister	39	91	11.5	2.5	41	151	17.4	4.9	38	1 639	355.5	53.6
Huntington Beach	341	1 692	337.7	57.9	797	D	D	D	380	13 155	4 423.5	849.2
Huntington Park	24	123	17.4	2.8	35	244	21.4	5.6	127	3 412	561.9	106.0
Imperial Beach	26	96	13.7	2.4	16	73	4.8	1.7	NA	NA	NA	NA
Indio	56	365	57.0	9.7	67	D	D	D	41	774	124.5	29.3
Inglewood	77	650	108.3	19.0	58	D	D	D	69	2 184	438.0	102.0
Irvine	622	8 462	1 739.3	462.0	2 428	D	D	D	433	29 937	8 761.5	1 704.0
Laguna Hills	92	843	127.8	37.4	364	1 726	250.2	94.4	72	583	D	26.7
Laguna Niguel	150	571	115.5	20.0	315	1 410	292.8	79.1	NA	NA	NA	NA
La Habra	57	262	44.4	6.8	84	468	39.8	17.3	70	1 250	215.0	46.7
Lake Elsinore	44	162	60.6	4.9	49	307	29.0	9.1	62	892	121.0	31.7
Lake Forest	124	1 203	200.1	52.9	399	3 383	452.7	208.1	111	4 953	1 238.8	238.2
Lakewood	52	296	73.2	7.8	64	236	20.3	8.3	NA	NA	NA	NA
La Mesa	161	985	117.1	29.4	256	1 343	140.5	55.2	NA	NA	NA	NA
La Mirada	40	341	83.0	16.8	62	646	75.8	33.0	58	2 726	859.9	118.6
Lancaster	116	654	114.8	17.8	144	D	D	D	56	1 192	258.6	50.2
La Puente	21	72	11.6	1.9	17	D	D	D	NA	NA	NA	NA
La Quinta	81	204	42.5	7.5	92	419	60.2	20.6	NA	NA	NA	NA
La Verne	30	145	20.8	4.0	68	281	30.9	10.0	54	1 398	294.6	54.6
Lawndale	24	324	62.5	9.6	35	D	D	D	NA	NA	NA	NA
Lemon Grove	22	99	19.5	1.8	25	118	8.1	3.2	NA	NA	NA	NA
Lincoln	27	82	15.9	2.0	46	D	D	D	24	868	214.2	40.7
Livermore	109	593	179.4	27.5	192	D	D	D	150	5 221	1 803.8	299.9
Lodi	91	928	67.0	22.0	114	670	63.6	24.5	92	3 433	687.1	114.1
Lompoc	35	151	22.3	4.7	37	D	D	D	NA	NA	NA	NA
Long Beach	504	3 206	1 099.2	134.4	1 005	D	D	D	273	12 425	6 198.3	856.7
Los Altos	88	371	127.7	19.8	270	D	D	D	NA	NA	NA	NA
Los Angeles	5 912	38 870	13 742.3	1 904.9	14 157	178 164	27 271.5	10 738.3	6 118	129 537	41 805.6	5 391.5
Los Banos	23	57	10.4	1.1	23	130	12.7	4.9	11	604	412.9	25.9
Los Gatos	106	726	822.5	80.5	288	1 360	251.1	102.4	31	620	112.6	32.6
Lynwood	15	63	10.0	2.9	16	D	D	D	57	1 630	374.1	58.6
Madera	37	120	16.0	3.5	33	D	D	D	41	D	394.6	58.2
Manhattan Beach	134	556	81.0	23.8	281	1 119	194.8	92.1	NA	NA	NA	NA
Manteca	65	236	37.9	6.2	49	239	19.4	6.6	32	941	293.7	41.3
Martinez	48	176	29.1	6.0	92	D	D	D	26	949	D	D
Maywood	3	D	D	D	5	D	D	D	NA	NA	NA	NA
Menifee	NA	NA	NA	NA	NA	NA	NA	NA	NA	NA	NA	NA

1. Establishments subject to federal tax.

Table D. Cities — Accommodation and Food Services, Arts, Entertainment, and Recreation, and Health Care and Social Assistance

City	Accommodation and food services, 2007				Arts, entertainment, and recreation,[1] 2007				Health care and social assistance,[1] 2007			
	Number of establish-ments	Number of employees	Sales (mil dol)	Annual payroll (mil dol)	Number of establish-ments	Number of employees	Receipts (mil dol)	Annual payroll (mil dol)	Number of establish-ments	Number of employees	Receipts (mil dol)	Annual payroll (mil dol)
	92	93	94	95	96	97	98	99	100	101	102	103
CALIFORNIA—Cont'd												
Delano	43	495	25.9	5.8	2	D	D	D	69	807	64.8	25.3
Desert Hot Springs	33	353	18.2	4.4	1	D	D	D	13	D	D	D
Diamond Bar	116	1 377	64.7	17.4	10	D	D	D	161	1 223	108.4	36.2
Downey	202	3 424	181.5	50.4	13	197	14.7	3.6	293	4 008	455.3	174.0
Dublin	123	2 287	135.8	36.5	12	D	D	D	79	653	59.1	23.4
East Palo Alto	13	668	41.9	17.8	2	D	D	D	14	133	21.1	11.3
El Cajon	244	3 526	171.3	45.9	17	D	D	D	232	3 318	265.9	109.4
El Centro	107	1 857	81.9	23.3	3	D	D	D	119	741	81.9	32.4
Elk Grove	208	4 110	169.6	47.7	18	D	D	D	225	2 184	294.2	72.5
El Monte	161	1 526	84.0	19.9	5	D	D	D	146	1 865	146.7	55.5
El Paso de Robles (Paso Robles)	113	2 193	98.0	29.4	14	D	D	D	62	521	32.8	11.7
Encinitas	193	3 638	180.1	50.6	44	D	D	D	318	2 422	296.9	101.7
Escondido	276	4 149	211.6	57.8	30	564	28.3	8.1	305	3 511	332.5	140.6
Eureka	133	1 928	91.8	25.5	11	D	D	D	109	1 086	91.9	34.4
Fairfield	193	3 467	162.3	42.3	18	D	D	D	218	2 200	295.1	93.8
Folsom	200	3 442	159.1	48.0	23	505	24.1	6.1	197	D	D	D
Fontana	202	3 325	158.0	42.1	13	245	15.2	4.0	132	D	D	D
Foster City	60	1 236	78.6	22.8	10	D	D	D	63	537	66.6	25.2
Fountain Valley	146	2 093	115.3	30.1	18	D	D	D	357	D	D	D
Fremont	384	5 456	296.6	80.7	37	719	41.9	12.6	552	6 413	787.1	303.6
Fresno	944	17 909	813.6	229.4	92	2 061	116.1	32.3	1 326	15 864	1 749.4	729.6
Fullerton	293	5 125	253.5	69.2	22	384	33.1	7.4	339	D	D	D
Gardena	180	1 842	102.2	24.9	10	D	D	D	153	1 940	225.3	74.4
Garden Grove	359	5 564	344.2	89.8	20	D	D	D	447	4 441	450.7	157.0
Gilroy	120	2 070	103.3	28.0	11	D	D	D	124	1 231	151.3	45.8
Glendale	376	5 760	324.0	86.6	131	658	94.5	30.5	842	6 977	780.0	281.9
Glendora	94	1 298	68.3	18.9	21	D	D	D	189	D	D	D
Goleta	91	1 862	93.0	24.4	9	140	9.4	2.9	109	812	85.8	35.4
Hanford	97	D	D	D	8	D	D	D	120	1 197	106.9	44.7
Hawthorne	129	1 840	103.2	24.1	11	D	D	D	114	1 812	165.8	62.3
Hayward	306	3 593	210.5	51.6	17	D	D	D	234	4 312	575.6	254.5
Hemet	139	2 340	113.2	32.3	14	D	D	D	208	D	D	D
Hesperia	107	1 653	86.2	21.9	8	D	D	D	68	470	39.0	13.9
Highland	35	490	24.3	6.0	3	D	D	D	46	D	D	D
Hollister	63	783	36.4	10.3	11	D	D	D	68	D	D	D
Huntington Beach	416	7 878	445.0	125.1	51	645	43.6	9.2	567	4 484	495.4	191.9
Huntington Park	100	1 634	86.2	21.3	3	D	D	D	113	D	D	D
Imperial Beach	39	380	20.1	4.7	3	D	D	D	19	149	12.1	3.7
Indio	104	D	D	D	12	D	D	D	105	1 484	182.1	70.4
Inglewood	159	2 285	129.6	33.2	39	D	D	D	276	2 691	358.4	113.6
Irvine	534	12 383	755.8	204.4	68	2 360	160.2	39.2	752	7 108	1 063.8	393.9
Laguna Hills	110	2 363	115.5	36.1	7	D	D	D	298	D	D	D
Laguna Niguel	119	1 814	98.1	27.1	21	D	D	D	202	1 077	117.8	39.4
La Habra	131	2 001	99.6	27.2	6	D	D	D	99	D	D	D
Lake Elsinore	104	1 622	73.1	21.0	11	234	12.1	4.7	47	D	D	D
Lake Forest	186	3 615	172.7	49.2	25	D	D	D	158	D	D	D
Lakewood	156	3 150	155.5	41.3	10	263	14.8	3.5	139	1 708	223.7	80.5
La Mesa	146	3 359	155.6	51.9	13	D	D	D	293	D	D	D
La Mirada	92	1 443	77.7	19.3	10	D	D	D	111	1 301	123.1	45.4
Lancaster	222	3 733	178.1	45.9	19	D	D	D	367	5 511	701.4	213.3
La Puente	81	685	36.6	9.2	2	D	D	D	52	D	D	D
La Quinta	74	3 505	219.2	70.3	21	D	D	D	58	269	30.7	10.3
La Verne	78	1 239	58.1	17.0	8	169	10.4	2.6	45	321	32.1	11.3
Lawndale	47	599	34.4	8.8	5	13	2.7	0.7	55	236	22.0	6.1
Lemon Grove	51	D	D	D	4	45	1.3	0.4	38	592	35.2	15.8
Lincoln	55	637	28.7	8.3	8	D	D	D	52	487	93.1	25.7
Livermore	159	2 296	132.0	36.2	16	D	D	D	141	1 241	151.1	50.6
Lodi	148	2 020	90.6	24.3	10	D	D	D	180	D	D	D
Lompoc	85	1 275	59.1	14.9	5	23	0.8	0.2	64	D	D	D
Long Beach	852	17 187	924.8	266.0	77	1 597	106.8	25.8	1 007	12 146	1 257.0	485.9
Los Altos	56	959	67.1	17.2	14	120	6.9	4.4	137	1 012	114.6	46.7
Los Angeles	7 609	130 390	8 271.8	2 279.2	6 627	31 958	8 263.6	3 056.4	9 129	98 549	11 732.8	4 226.3
Los Banos	53	957	42.7	10.8	7	D	D	D	39	245	23.3	9.4
Los Gatos	121	2 281	125.9	41.6	17	D	D	D	289	D	D	D
Lynwood	72	1 036	59.4	13.4	1	D	D	D	105	D	D	D
Madera	74	890	46.9	11.2	8	D	D	D	110	D	D	D
Manhattan Beach	141	3 357	206.9	57.6	57	322	50.5	19.2	158	D	D	D
Manteca	116	1 654	86.5	22.9	11	316	12.0	3.6	100	2 172	333.3	123.2
Martinez	73	777	43.2	10.5	6	51	5.9	0.9	37	D	D	D
Maywood	34	393	21.1	5.2	1	D	D	D	30	D	D	D
Menifee	NA	NA	NA	NA	NA	NA	NA	NA	NA	NA	NA	NA

1. Establishments subject to federal tax.

City	Other services[1], 2007				Government employment and payroll, 2012								
						March payroll							
							Percent of total for:						
	Number of establish-ments	Number of employees	Receipts (mil dol)	Annual payroll (mil dol)	Full-time equivalent employees	Total (dollars)	Adminis-tration, judicial, and legal	Police and Corrections	Fire Protection	Highways and trans-portation	Health and welfare	Natural resources and utilities	Education and libraries
	104	105	106	107	108	109	110	111	112	113	114	115	116
CALIFORNIA—Cont'd													
Delano	18	103	10.3	4.7	220	881 307	8.4	41.4	0.0	13.6	3.9	30.6	0.0
Desert Hot Springs	15	28	6.2	0.6	73	440 127	17.0	60.5	0.0	11.0	10.1	1.4	0.0
Diamond Bar	75	247	17.4	5.0	72	380 697	40.0	0.0	0.0	16.5	10.9	32.6	0.0
Downey	140	818	73.1	18.9	505	3 402 608	8.6	42.0	25.6	4.8	1.5	12.4	2.5
Dublin	80	511	52.9	16.6	106	716 632	36.7	5.5	0.8	23.0	3.5	24.9	0.0
East Palo Alto	8	D	D	D	112	1 036 706	21.8	57.6	0.0	11.0	9.5	0.0	0.0
El Cajon	162	974	90.4	23.7	443	2 609 521	7.2	42.2	14.7	6.2	11.0	13.4	0.0
El Centro	59	D	D	D	964	4 003 786	4.7	10.9	5.9	2.3	69.2	5.8	0.5
Elk Grove	112	610	52.1	15.4	280	1 987 037	15.1	76.6	0.0	2.4	1.4	1.1	0.0
El Monte	134	704	58.4	16.1	336	2 338 846	6.8	63.2	0.0	15.0	2.5	12.4	0.0
El Paso de Robles (Paso Robles)	43	249	23.4	6.7	164	981 684	11.7	27.8	19.1	3.0	4.3	20.5	2.9
Encinitas	127	785	64.2	20.8	242	1 673 551	30.3	0.0	25.3	14.3	0.8	20.7	0.0
Escondido	240	1 349	137.9	39.1	1 133	10 074 411	16.4	29.3	13.9	7.9	0.9	24.7	3.3
Eureka	85	497	41.9	12.5	282	1 300 511	8.5	31.6	18.8	2.4	4.7	21.0	0.0
Fairfield	123	699	60.2	18.2	645	3 404 101	10.9	36.3	15.3	11.5	3.2	11.0	0.0
Folsom	77	505	41.5	12.8	483	3 244 300	14.2	23.2	21.7	8.2	0.0	28.9	1.6
Fontana	165	1 149	92.5	29.4	767	4 073 819	10.2	49.0	0.0	8.3	6.6	23.2	0.0
Foster City	21	123	7.9	2.7	192	1 556 154	16.6	27.7	24.1	6.3	0.0	25.3	0.0
Fountain Valley	102	610	61.1	18.0	232	1 801 733	11.7	37.6	26.9	4.9	0.9	10.1	0.0
Fremont	265	2 159	168.7	61.8	881	7 171 062	20.6	30.1	20.1	9.2	7.6	8.2	0.0
Fresno	578	4 197	371.4	107.5	3 214	18 551 770	10.2	39.0	13.4	20.0	0.0	15.9	0.0
Fullerton	183	732	73.0	19.1	676	4 122 933	7.6	39.6	18.4	6.3	5.0	12.8	3.4
Gardena	124	778	65.2	21.1	419	2 062 110	7.9	42.6	0.0	28.2	6.3	8.7	0.0
Garden Grove	243	1 117	89.5	24.3	657	4 420 328	10.0	44.2	22.5	0.7	7.8	7.6	0.0
Gilroy	68	431	41.1	12.9	258	1 936 702	13.1	41.6	20.3	4.9	2.7	13.4	0.0
Glendale	308	2 041	156.6	58.0	1 864	13 741 087	17.0	23.8	18.6	3.2	4.9	27.1	3.1
Glendora	97	D	D	D	321	1 582 591	10.6	43.7	0.0	11.9	6.9	19.8	7.2
Goleta	62	D	D	D	47	334 846	63.8	0.0	0.0	23.1	5.9	7.2	0.0
Hanford	48	D	D	D	259	1 321 734	9.8	38.2	13.4	8.8	0.0	24.1	0.0
Hawthorne	103	405	39.8	9.7	283	1 907 186	16.2	40.8	0.0	5.5	2.8	5.5	0.0
Hayward	209	1 653	158.1	44.1	761	6 582 512	8.9	39.0	24.1	6.2	3.7	9.7	2.7
Hemet	89	446	29.7	7.8	409	2 543 919	11.5	33.8	20.3	7.4	2.2	11.7	3.6
Hesperia	85	449	41.3	11.6	127	669 050	29.0	0.1	0.0	16.7	15.9	0.0	0.0
Highland	33	191	11.4	3.8	38	273 354	31.6	0.0	0.0	15.6	10.8	4.6	0.0
Hollister	48	D	D	D	131	912 911	12.2	25.2	24.4	4.8	4.9	18.9	0.0
Huntington Beach	342	1 994	153.9	46.6	1 071	7 579 599	14.4	34.3	23.5	5.3	1.3	14.6	2.6
Huntington Park	47	D	D	D	208	1 200 684	11.4	67.5	0.0	5.5	5.1	6.0	0.0
Imperial Beach	18	75	4.7	1.4	82	452 081	44.4	0.0	17.6	4.4	3.2	9.8	0.0
Indio	61	366	37.7	9.9	253	1 534 809	8.8	49.5	0.0	12.9	5.9	15.1	0.0
Inglewood	143	993	78.1	22.3	724	3 812 741	19.1	49.5	0.0	10.8	5.9	11.8	2.9
Irvine	278	2 176	188.5	62.3	977	6 075 973	20.0	39.1	0.0	10.5	2.9	13.8	0.0
Laguna Hills	71	470	34.4	10.7	40	246 065	39.8	0.0	0.0	13.2	20.3	26.7	0.0
Laguna Niguel	86	538	45.0	14.6	79	590 935	24.7	1.6	0.0	17.2	21.8	28.0	0.0
La Habra	123	653	61.8	16.5	325	1 702 615	11.2	45.6	0.0	0.0	0.0	0.0	0.0
Lake Elsinore	51	341	21.9	6.9	66	784 724	0.4	0.0	0.0	8.2	0.0	11.8	0.0
Lake Forest	112	768	84.2	22.2	79	477 565	58.7	1.2	0.0	5.1	13.9	21.1	0.0
Lakewood	70	D	D	D	255	1 549 892	26.5	6.5	0.0	16.3	2.1	41.0	0.0
La Mesa	118	697	44.3	13.7	283	1 642 547	12.9	41.7	20.9	5.6	2.7	10.2	0.0
La Mirada	33	309	14.2	6.4	142	702 597	25.1	9.5	0.0	0.0	9.3	25.7	0.0
Lancaster	150	917	74.2	21.2	338	1 643 288	21.1	3.3	0.0	28.3	10.6	32.5	0.0
La Puente	41	147	8.8	2.4	44	173 692	49.1	0.0	0.0	14.7	2.7	17.6	0.0
La Quinta	29	217	9.3	3.6	94	580 882	30.3	0.0	0.0	26.7	22.0	0.0	0.0
La Verne	42	D	D	D	200	1 245 972	16.1	41.5	26.1	2.8	0.0	10.1	0.0
Lawndale	64	D	D	D	72	370 627	35.6	0.0	0.0	27.9	0.0	17.4	0.0
Lemon Grove	52	223	21.5	5.6	50	320 723	14.9	0.0	50.2	14.0	7.5	6.0	0.0
Lincoln	29	D	D	D	204	1 072 286	18.7	28.4	11.2	10.5	9.3	10.6	1.8
Livermore	117	630	63.7	22.8	431	3 325 675	14.6	36.7	0.0	16.4	4.9	18.3	6.5
Lodi	112	637	54.5	17.5	481	2 698 469	10.3	27.2	16.3	7.0	1.8	29.2	2.7
Lompoc	44	223	20.9	5.5	391	1 833 592	11.8	26.5	9.3	5.4	0.4	32.9	2.7
Long Beach	538	4 265	470.4	114.9	5 861	36 050 392	7.5	28.9	14.8	19.5	6.1	12.6	1.4
Los Altos	44	189	13.2	4.8	127	885 014	8.2	40.0	0.0	11.6	3.4	17.8	0.0
Los Angeles	5 424	36 122	3 211.8	885.5	47 505	361 983 103	11.8	27.5	11.6	12.8	4.2	30.5	1.2
Los Banos	22	D	D	D	285	749 390	11.4	40.2	15.6	5.1	2.2	19.0	0.0
Los Gatos	97	515	40.0	11.5	148	1 210 153	16.6	44.9	0.0	10.6	7.2	6.5	7.5
Lynwood	46	190	20.6	4.4	230	916 329	42.8	2.5	0.0	20.8	5.6	28.3	0.0
Madera	51	278	25.0	6.2	274	1 196 996	16.2	35.6	0.0	9.9	12.2	22.5	0.0
Manhattan Beach	76	474	31.4	9.1	381	1 720 027	11.4	41.4	12.9	4.7	9.6	15.5	0.0
Manteca	80	333	25.5	7.4	345	2 165 170	13.0	35.1	16.6	6.2	1.2	25.5	0.0
Martinez	47	232	23.6	7.7	52	324 363	4.1	88.0	0.0	0.0	4.6	1.4	0.0
Maywood	22	D	D	D	18	66 828	51.7	0.0	0.0	0.0	5.9	31.7	0.0
Menifee	NA	NA	NA	NA	23	165 702	68.9	0.0	0.0	10.5	13.6	0.0	0.0

1. Establishments subject to federal tax.

City	City government finances, 2007 — General revenue — Total (mil dol)	General revenue — Intergovernmental — Total (mil dol)	General revenue — Intergovernmental — Percent from state government	General revenue — Taxes — Total (mil dol)	General revenue — Taxes — Per capita[1] (dollars) — Total	General revenue — Taxes — Per capita[1] (dollars) — Property	General revenue — Taxes — Per capita[1] (dollars) — Sales and gross receipts	General expenditure — Total (mil dol)	General expenditure — Per capita[1] (dollars) — Total	General expenditure — Per capita[1] (dollars) — Capital outlays
	117	118	119	120	121	122	123	124	125	126
CALIFORNIA—Cont'd										
Delano	32.5	6.6	92.1	16.4	313	163	105	31.3	597	53
Desert Hot Springs	20.2	3.1	33.2	12.4	446	214	213	27.4	988	219
Diamond Bar	24.3	2.3	77.9	16.9	300	165	128	31.6	561	189
Downey	89.0	11.9	58.4	53.0	468	227	239	98.0	866	54
Dublin	67.1	3.0	97.7	50.4	1 032	529	415	63.3	1 298	122
East Palo Alto	36.0	3.8	90.2	24.9	858	568	285	31.6	1 090	142
El Cajon	103.0	8.1	84.7	70.6	695	308	385	103.4	1 017	157
El Centro	182.9	11.7	52.8	25.2	582	256	318	173.8	4 019	507
Elk Grove	117.6	21.2	77.7	55.8	352	138	210	116.8	737	118
El Monte	92.1	16.0	67.9	64.7	561	290	268	92.7	803	118
El Paso de Robles (Paso Robles)	46.5	6.6	62.1	30.0	983	513	466	43.1	1 414	272
Encinitas	74.3	4.1	60.5	49.4	809	584	217	77.2	1 265	265
Escondido	143.3	14.3	60.1	78.5	531	315	209	135.9	919	78
Eureka	46.5	7.0	68.0	27.9	1 036	386	648	49.7	1 845	324
Fairfield	135.2	23.7	86.3	87.3	811	437	371	120.8	1 122	219
Folsom	106.2	4.7	81.7	61.5	840	482	272	106.9	1 459	214
Fontana	243.1	25.3	66.9	150.7	748	563	182	241.4	1 198	265
Foster City	51.6	1.9	100.0	38.7	1 203	920	277	53.2	1 654	65
Fountain Valley	51.8	4.2	91.1	35.6	630	394	227	53.9	954	197
Fremont	214.4	29.7	64.9	141.4	637	367	230	244.1	1 100	468
Fresno	632.4	127.3	42.9	267.5	529	240	287	528.7	1 045	197
Fullerton	151.4	23.8	80.4	79.9	576	371	202	188.8	1 362	506
Gardena	78.5	10.8	48.9	56.0	938	205	564	63.5	1 065	158
Garden Grove	143.3	12.1	44.0	78.1	448	263	183	176.5	1 012	138
Gilroy	73.7	6.7	42.5	38.7	762	281	360	72.6	1 432	389
Glendale	315.9	29.1	55.9	145.8	748	379	366	334.4	1 717	239
Glendora	41.0	5.3	97.4	28.1	553	361	190	34.8	685	69
Goleta	31.1	4.4	87.8	22.0	727	257	426	33.8	1 118	384
Hanford	41.5	3.7	86.5	19.3	355	224	123	40.0	736	127
Hawthorne	103.1	37.8	12.8	48.4	564	260	302	99.8	1 163	96
Hayward	216.5	39.7	29.1	108.3	724	336	353	190.5	1 273	255
Hemet	71.2	3.5	72.5	44.9	552	243	299	68.8	846	126
Hesperia	73.7	15.0	93.8	44.5	483	317	165	101.5	1 103	350
Highland	29.3	5.5	73.6	17.0	315	231	64	34.1	631	199
Hollister	49.1	1.4	100.0	27.1	753	551	186	40.2	1 115	356
Huntington Beach	237.1	14.8	87.5	142.7	732	378	348	245.0	1 257	137
Huntington Park	53.9	9.0	53.2	35.6	605	397	207	47.0	799	63
Imperial Beach	31.4	1.9	89.6	17.2	640	488	150	27.2	1 012	70
Indio	79.4	8.3	78.1	47.6	577	315	258	80.9	980	123
Inglewood	168.9	42.5	51.9	97.4	874	422	400	161.6	1 451	100
Irvine	221.8	16.6	67.8	150.8	656	245	405	296.0	1 289	255
Laguna Hills	26.8	8.5	93.2	16.2	524	301	209	23.6	764	235
Laguna Niguel	38.2	3.2	97.6	31.8	495	300	189	40.3	626	203
La Habra	54.3	8.3	81.6	32.0	521	283	239	52.1	847	84
Lake Elsinore	62.9	4.4	97.8	38.1	682	451	180	70.3	1 261	194
Lake Forest	48.6	4.3	66.7	38.8	491	253	234	69.4	879	338
Lakewood	58.5	5.6	92.9	38.4	474	248	223	55.1	680	68
La Mesa	60.0	3.3	82.3	42.5	729	333	392	58.2	999	181
La Mirada	53.4	5.0	48.8	36.5	744	494	247	62.4	1 271	395
Lancaster	155.7	14.4	70.0	98.7	621	395	225	158.8	999	170
La Puente	17.0	3.2	83.5	10.1	251	139	110	16.8	417	64
La Quinta	92.3	4.4	99.5	69.5	1 801	1 413	377	79.1	2 049	214
La Verne	36.0	1.3	97.5	23.8	756	457	290	35.3	1 123	55
Lawndale	21.9	4.6	43.6	15.6	470	264	205	22.6	682	195
Lemon Grove	23.6	3.5	40.3	12.9	495	317	176	23.1	888	142
Lincoln	39.4	1.9	82.7	16.0	363	218	137	39.2	887	142
Livermore	144.6	12.8	81.4	70.9	848	452	391	146.1	1 746	314
Lodi	74.4	14.8	61.1	37.4	591	232	358	65.7	1 040	203
Lompoc	49.0	7.6	70.8	20.7	479	244	198	57.4	1 329	168
Long Beach	1 850.9	195.5	44.1	411.1	877	540	331	1 760.6	3 753	846
Los Altos	38.7	1.3	98.4	24.5	820	464	333	41.7	1 397	179
Los Angeles	9 274.5	847.5	41.5	3 849.3	997	441	528	8 678.1	2 247	524
Los Banos	30.8	1.2	94.3	16.0	437	268	87	30.9	844	146
Los Gatos	39.5	1.7	100.0	30.5	1 010	550	425	44.6	1 477	382
Lynwood	48.4	7.5	65.9	33.0	465	265	191	48.6	685	116
Madera	61.9	6.4	52.4	35.7	571	205	290	58.8	939	220
Manhattan Beach	64.9	2.0	100.0	40.2	1 132	649	468	68.9	1 939	189
Manteca	96.8	11.6	80.0	40.6	571	382	177	94.8	1 335	419
Martinez	24.4	2.4	100.0	18.2	493	310	179	24.1	653	42
Maywood	11.1	1.5	55.8	8.9	321	203	117	10.0	361	22
Menifee	33.2	8.6	100.0	19.8	243	138	102	27.8	341	43

1. Based on population estimated as of July 1 of the year shown.

City	Public welfare	Highways	Parking facilities	Education	Health and hospitals	Police protection	Sewerage and sanitation	Parks and recreation	Housing and community development	Interest on debt
	City government finances, 2012 (cont.)									
	General expenditure (cont.)									
	Percent of total for:									
	127	128	129	130	131	132	133	134	135	136
CALIFORNIA—Cont'd										
Delano	0.0	7.9	0.1	0.0	0.7	35.9	16.1	5.8	6.3	4.8
Desert Hot Springs	0.0	19.3	0.0	0.0	1.2	32.8	0.0	2.7	15.7	5.8
Diamond Bar	0.0	11.3	0.0	0.0	0.4	17.3	1.0	17.5	2.2	2.7
Downey	0.0	10.4	0.0	0.0	3.3	29.8	2.0	12.8	8.4	2.2
Dublin	0.0	9.9	0.0	0.0	0.9	23.6	5.1	13.7	4.2	0.4
East Palo Alto	0.0	15.7	0.0	0.0	0.0	32.7	8.2	3.9	9.5	7.2
El Cajon	0.0	7.2	0.0	0.0	4.9	29.0	15.2	4.3	14.7	2.9
El Centro	0.0	3.7	0.0	0.0	71.3	5.1	5.8	1.4	1.4	2.7
Elk Grove	0.0	20.1	0.0	0.0	0.7	26.4	11.1	0.6	15.2	3.0
El Monte	0.0	8.9	0.1	0.0	0.1	24.2	0.0	3.9	14.8	4.7
El Paso de Robles (Paso Robles)	0.0	14.0	0.0	0.0	0.0	18.5	11.1	8.4	4.2	5.6
Encinitas	0.0	11.1	0.0	0.0	1.4	14.8	5.7	11.7	3.2	0.4
Escondido	0.0	9.0	0.0	0.0	1.1	26.8	15.4	5.9	4.7	6.9
Eureka	0.0	7.4	0.3	0.0	0.2	21.6	17.7	5.2	11.4	6.1
Fairfield	0.0	22.4	0.0	0.0	0.9	26.9	0.0	8.9	8.3	6.3
Folsom	0.0	7.4	0.0	0.0	0.6	18.0	10.0	10.4	7.7	6.6
Fontana	0.0	16.0	0.0	0.0	0.0	21.8	4.9	5.1	16.6	14.1
Foster City	0.0	4.8	0.0	0.0	0.0	17.3	12.1	18.0	5.0	0.0
Fountain Valley	0.0	16.9	0.0	0.0	5.8	26.6	8.8	7.4	11.0	1.2
Fremont	0.1	18.2	0.0	0.0	4.6	27.3	2.1	6.1	8.7	3.7
Fresno	0.0	9.2	0.9	0.0	1.8	27.9	21.5	4.8	2.7	8.1
Fullerton	0.0	19.9	0.0	0.0	3.1	19.1	8.1	6.3	16.0	3.9
Gardena	0.0	12.4	0.0	0.0	3.2	33.0	1.6	5.6	7.1	2.4
Garden Grove	0.0	9.7	0.0	0.0	3.7	26.6	4.0	4.9	25.2	3.8
Gilroy	0.0	3.9	0.0	0.0	0.1	23.5	11.0	1.2	31.3	2.7
Glendale	0.0	6.5	1.9	0.0	0.2	20.8	9.9	5.1	16.0	1.2
Glendora	0.0	7.3	0.0	0.0	0.3	38.7	0.0	9.5	14.0	4.6
Goleta	0.0	35.2	0.0	0.0	1.4	19.9	0.0	7.5	6.3	2.1
Hanford	0.0	14.3	0.0	0.0	1.1	20.5	28.6	8.9	2.1	3.4
Hawthorne	0.0	13.4	0.0	0.0	0.0	30.2	0.7	1.5	12.0	4.8
Hayward	0.0	22.7	0.0	0.0	1.1	29.9	8.1	0.9	3.9	2.6
Hemet	0.0	13.6	0.0	0.0	0.3	23.8	21.6	1.1	10.9	0.9
Hesperia	0.0	18.2	0.0	0.0	1.8	12.4	0.0	0.0	33.4	8.9
Highland	0.0	33.6	0.0	0.0	3.7	20.5	0.0	3.0	9.1	8.3
Hollister	0.0	9.2	0.0	0.0	1.5	15.8	30.4	3.1	12.4	4.5
Huntington Beach	0.0	12.4	1.3	0.0	1.9	28.9	8.3	6.7	4.8	2.2
Huntington Park	0.0	8.1	1.2	0.0	5.3	33.4	0.8	4.2	12.8	4.9
Imperial Beach	0.0	9.3	0.0	0.0	0.7	26.9	16.9	5.6	13.1	5.9
Indio	0.0	11.9	0.0	0.0	5.2	25.3	0.2	5.0	15.5	8.5
Inglewood	0.0	9.8	0.2	0.0	1.6	19.3	8.5	5.2	14.3	7.4
Irvine	0.0	25.6	0.0	0.0	1.6	18.7	0.0	21.6	1.9	12.6
Laguna Hills	0.0	25.2	0.0	0.0	0.3	27.3	0.0	23.3	0.3	2.6
Laguna Niguel	0.0	23.9	0.0	0.0	0.8	23.4	0.0	17.7	0.2	0.0
La Habra	0.0	8.8	0.0	0.0	1.8	30.7	10.8	10.5	12.4	2.9
Lake Elsinore	0.0	5.0	0.0	0.0	0.7	12.7	0.0	16.1	15.7	24.3
Lake Forest	0.0	38.6	0.0	0.0	0.2	18.1	0.0	16.3	6.7	0.7
Lakewood	0.0	18.5	0.0	0.0	0.5	20.7	12.1	21.5	3.7	3.9
La Mesa	0.0	19.6	0.3	0.0	0.9	25.3	16.9	6.5	1.6	2.5
La Mirada	0.0	37.1	0.0	0.0	0.1	12.1	0.0	18.7	14.6	3.8
Lancaster	0.0	12.1	0.0	0.0	0.4	17.3	0.0	6.5	26.8	11.9
La Puente	0.0	11.0	0.0	0.0	1.7	27.8	3.9	17.2	8.0	4.3
La Quinta	0.0	10.7	0.0	0.0	0.5	15.3	0.0	8.3	24.6	17.5
La Verne	0.0	8.7	0.0	0.0	5.5	33.7	3.3	6.8	15.6	2.9
Lawndale	0.0	12.3	0.0	0.0	0.6	20.2	0.2	10.8	29.6	4.8
Lemon Grove	0.0	4.3	0.0	0.0	0.7	19.3	17.8	3.7	15.4	4.9
Lincoln	0.0	14.1	0.0	0.0	0.0	13.0	24.9	4.2	2.1	3.8
Livermore	0.0	17.3	0.0	0.0	0.4	17.7	12.7	1.7	2.3	2.6
Lodi	0.0	12.3	0.0	0.0	0.6	24.8	16.8	7.4	2.4	0.1
Lompoc	0.0	9.5	0.0	0.0	0.6	34.0	20.4	5.7	8.5	1.8
Long Beach	0.0	3.4	0.0	0.0	3.0	11.4	5.2	7.6	7.6	4.6
Los Altos	0.0	14.1	0.0	0.0	0.8	22.9	12.7	6.1	2.6	0.2
Los Angeles	0.0	8.1	0.4	0.0	2.6	19.6	8.6	4.5	4.2	6.1
Los Banos	0.0	9.9	0.0	0.0	0.3	24.6	26.0	13.3	5.1	2.8
Los Gatos	0.0	12.1	0.0	0.0	0.3	26.6	0.3	7.1	9.0	2.5
Lynwood	0.0	22.5	0.0	0.0	1.0	16.7	1.5	5.8	13.5	1.6
Madera	0.0	25.5	0.1	0.0	1.7	16.8	19.2	6.0	4.6	5.3
Manhattan Beach	0.0	10.0	4.3	0.0	4.5	30.5	9.0	13.7	0.0	1.3
Manteca	0.0	16.3	0.0	0.0	0.3	15.0	25.2	6.9	13.6	4.5
Martinez	0.0	10.7	1.3	0.0	0.0	41.2	0.0	13.9	0.1	3.6
Maywood	0.0	11.2	0.0	0.0	0.0	39.4	0.0	6.2	4.2	10.1
Menifee	0.0	9.1	0.0	0.0	1.3	31.9	0.0	0.0	6.7	0.3

City	City government finances, 2012 (cont.)			Climate[2]						
	Debt outstanding			Average daily temperature (degrees Fahrenheit)						
				Mean		Limits				
	Total (mil dol)	Per capita[1] (dollars)	Debt issued during year	January	July	January[3]	July[4]	Annual precipitation (inches)	Heating degree days	Cooling degree days
	137	138	139	140	141	142	143	144	145	146
CALIFORNIA—Cont'd										
Delano	62.8	1 196	0.0	46.6	81.1	36.5	99.0	7.34	2 434	1 990
Desert Hot Springs	12.2	440	6.2	NA	NA	NA	NA	NA	NA	NA
Diamond Bar	0.0	0	12.0	54.6	73.8	41.5	88.7	16.96	1 727	1 191
Downey	63.1	558	1.5	57.0	73.8	46.0	82.9	12.94	1 211	1 186
Dublin	6.2	127	0.0	47.2	72.0	37.4	89.1	14.82	2 755	858
East Palo Alto	47.6	1 643	0.0	49.0	68.0	40.4	78.8	15.71	2 584	452
El Cajon	68.2	671	0.1	54.9	74.7	41.6	87.0	11.96	1 560	1 371
El Centro	100.3	2 320	0.0	55.8	91.4	41.3	107.0	2.96	1 080	3 852
Elk Grove	95.6	603	0.0	46.3	75.4	38.8	92.4	17.93	2 666	1 248
El Monte	168.9	1 465	13.3	56.3	75.6	42.6	89.0	18.56	1 295	1 575
El Paso de Robles (Paso Robles)	54.4	1 784	6.4	NA	NA	NA	NA	NA	NA	NA
Encinitas	40.7	667	0.0	55.5	75.1	42.5	88.6	15.10	1 464	1 436
Escondido	191.9	1 298	11.4	55.5	75.1	42.5	88.6	15.10	1 464	1 436
Eureka	109.2	4 052	9.4	47.9	58.1	40.8	63.3	38.10	4 430	7
Fairfield	271.5	2 523	10.5	46.1	72.6	37.5	88.8	23.46	2 649	975
Folsom	237.5	3 241	15.0	46.9	77.7	39.2	94.8	24.61	2 532	1 528
Fontana	677.9	3 364	0.8	56.6	78.3	45.3	95.0	14.77	1 364	1 901
Foster City	0.0	0	0.0	48.4	68.0	39.1	80.8	20.16	2 764	422
Fountain Valley	9.7	171	0.0	58.0	72.9	46.6	87.7	13.84	1 153	1 299
Fremont	313.6	1 414	53.3	49.8	68.0	42.0	78.3	14.85	2 367	530
Fresno	1 062.2	2 099	0.0	46.0	81.4	38.4	96.6	11.23	2 447	1 963
Fullerton	195.2	1 408	0.0	56.9	73.2	45.2	84.0	11.23	1 286	1 294
Gardena	24.8	415	0.0	56.3	69.4	46.2	77.6	14.79	1 526	742
Garden Grove	179.2	1 028	6.7	58.0	72.9	46.6	87.7	13.84	1 153	1 299
Gilroy	54.9	1 083	0.0	49.7	72.0	39.4	88.3	20.60	2 278	913
Glendale	322.6	1 656	38.3	54.8	75.5	42.0	88.9	17.49	1 575	1 455
Glendora	46.8	921	0.0	54.6	73.8	41.5	88.7	16.96	1 727	1 191
Goleta	15.7	518	0.0	53.1	67.0	40.8	76.7	16.93	2 121	482
Hanford	43.0	792	0.0	44.7	79.6	35.7	95.9	8.58	2 749	1 724
Hawthorne	104.9	1 223	0.0	57.1	69.3	48.6	75.3	13.15	1 274	679
Hayward	196.8	1 315	0.0	49.7	64.6	41.7	75.2	26.30	2 810	261
Hemet	13.7	168	0.0	52.4	79.9	38.4	97.8	12.55	1 914	1 903
Hesperia	168.7	1 834	0.0	45.5	80.0	31.4	99.1	6.20	2 929	1 735
Highland	73.8	1 364	0.0	54.4	79.6	41.8	96.0	16.43	1 599	1 937
Hollister	43.7	1 213	0.0	49.5	66.6	37.8	80.9	13.61	2 724	405
Huntington Beach	257.9	1 323	36.3	55.9	67.3	48.2	71.4	11.65	1 719	543
Huntington Park	42.4	720	0.0	58.3	74.2	48.5	83.8	15.14	928	1 506
Imperial Beach	40.1	1 493	0.0	57.3	70.1	46.1	76.1	9.95	1 321	862
Indio	184.2	2 232	0.0	56.8	92.8	42.0	107.1	3.15	903	4 388
Inglewood	277.3	2 489	30.8	57.1	69.3	48.6	75.3	13.15	1 274	679
Irvine	1 400.1	6 096	270.1	54.5	72.1	41.4	83.8	13.87	1 794	1 102
Laguna Hills	15.6	507	0.0	56.7	72.4	47.2	82.3	14.03	1 465	1 183
Laguna Niguel	0.0	0	0.0	55.4	68.7	43.9	77.3	13.56	1 756	666
La Habra	55.8	908	0.0	56.9	73.2	45.2	84.0	11.23	1 286	1 294
Lake Elsinore	410.2	7 355	1.5	52.2	79.6	38.3	98.1	12.09	1 924	1 874
Lake Forest	18.8	238	11.0	56.7	72.4	47.2	82.3	14.03	1 465	1 183
Lakewood	42.5	525	0.0	57.0	73.8	46.0	82.9	12.94	1 211	1 186
La Mesa	46.3	795	0.9	57.1	73.0	45.7	83.6	13.75	1 313	1 261
La Mirada	92.9	1 893	1.9	58.8	76.6	47.9	88.9	14.44	949	1 837
Lancaster	431.7	2 716	0.0	43.9	80.8	31.0	95.5	7.40	3 241	1 733
La Puente	9.5	236	0.0	58.8	76.6	47.9	88.9	14.44	949	1 837
La Quinta	324.4	8 401	0.0	NA	NA	NA	NA	NA	NA	NA
La Verne	19.4	618	0.0	54.6	73.8	41.5	88.7	16.96	1 727	1 191
Lawndale	21.1	635	0.0	57.1	69.3	48.6	75.3	13.15	1 274	679
Lemon Grove	26.5	1 021	0.0	NA	NA	NA	NA	NA	NA	NA
Lincoln	35.5	801	0.0	NA	NA	NA	NA	NA	NA	NA
Livermore	175.1	2 093	0.0	47.2	72.0	37.4	89.1	14.82	2 755	858
Lodi	0.2	4	0.0	46.1	73.8	37.5	91.1	18.22	2 710	1 057
Lompoc	54.1	1 253	0.0	53.7	64.5	41.4	75.4	15.85	2 250	322
Long Beach	2 390.0	5 095	112.4	57.0	73.8	46.0	82.9	12.94	1 211	1 186
Los Altos	1.9	62	0.0	49.0	68.0	40.4	78.8	15.71	2 584	452
Los Angeles	23 104.2	5 983	2 268.6	58.3	74.2	48.5	83.8	15.14	920	1 506
Los Banos	28.4	774	0.0	45.9	78.1	36.8	94.6	9.95	2 570	1 547
Los Gatos	23.8	789	0.0	48.7	70.3	38.8	85.4	22.64	2 641	613
Lynwood	30.0	423	0.0	58.3	74.2	48.5	83.8	15.14	928	1 506
Madera	114.1	1 823	0.0	45.7	79.6	37.2	96.5	11.94	2 670	1 706
Manhattan Beach	37.6	1 058	0.0	57.1	69.3	48.6	75.3	13.15	1 274	679
Manteca	214.3	3 017	1.7	46.0	77.3	38.1	93.8	13.84	2 563	1 456
Martinez	29.2	790	18.7	46.3	71.2	38.8	87.4	19.58	2 757	786
Maywood	0.0	0	0.0	58.3	74.2	48.5	83.8	15.14	928	1 506
Menifee	20.0	246	20.0	NA	NA	NA	NA	NA	NA	NA

1. Based on the population estimated as of July 1 of the year shown. 2. Represents normal values based on the 30-year period, 1971–2000. 3. Average daily minimum. 4. Average daily maximum.

STATE Place code	City	Land area,[1] 2010 (sq km)	Population, 2014			Race alone or in combination (percent), 2011-2013					Percent Hispanic or Latino[2], 2011-2013	Percent foreign born 2011–2013
			Total persons	Rank	Per square kilometer	White	Black	American Indian, Alaska Native	Asian	Hawaiian Pacific Islander		
		1	2	3	4	5	6	7	8	9	10	11
	CALIFORNIA—Cont'd											
06 46870	Menlo Park	25.4	33 309	1 119	1 311.4	77.4	4.8	NA	13.0	2.3	17.7	22.7
06 46898	Merced	60.4	81 743	400	1 353.4	58.9	6.5	1.8	14.2	NA	50.5	22.6
06 47766	Milpitas	35.2	73 672	460	2 093.0	22.7	3.2	1.5	66.9	1.3	16.0	51.5
06 48256	Mission Viejo	45.9	97 209	308	2 117.8	85.6	2.5	0.8	11.5	0.7	17.0	19.9
06 48354	Modesto	95.5	209 286	104	2 191.5	75.9	5.7	2.8	8.8	1.3	37.7	17.6
06 48648	Monrovia	35.2	37 415	989	1 062.9	60.6	6.4	1.1	15.0	0.2	39.6	26.7
06 48788	Montclair	14.3	38 465	965	2 689.9	41.3	4.0	0.8	9.2	NA	71.4	31.9
06 48816	Montebello	21.6	63 929	551	2 959.7	74.3	1.6	1.7	12.7	0.1	75.4	37.3
06 48872	Monterey	21.9	28 276	1 296	1 291.1	83.3	3.4	1.1	12.2	NA	17.2	19.6
06 48914	Monterey Park	19.9	61 458	580	3 088.3	19.6	0.8	0.7	62.9	0.8	32.6	52.6
06 49138	Moorpark	32.6	35 550	1 049	1 090.5	80.2	1.8	0.9	9.2	NA	30.6	18.6
06 49270	Moreno Valley	132.8	202 976	110	1 528.4	58.9	19.2	1.5	6.5	0.7	56.6	25.1
06 49278	Morgan Hill	33.4	42 068	877	1 259.5	70.9	4.0	0.8	12.5	1.4	32.2	18.8
06 49670	Mountain View	31.1	79 378	414	2 552.3	66.0	3.0	1.0	30.1	0.8	21.4	37.9
06 50076	Murrieta	87.0	108 368	268	1 245.6	72.2	10.1	2.2	10.5	1.2	27.7	12.9
06 50258	Napa	46.2	80 011	411	1 731.8	83.8	1.5	2.0	3.4	0.5	37.8	24.2
06 50398	National City	18.9	60 343	595	3 192.8	56.6	5.6	1.0	19.7	0.5	65.7	41.1
06 50916	Newark	35.9	44 723	826	1 245.8	43.8	4.8	1.5	31.9	1.2	34.1	33.8
06 51182	Newport Beach	61.7	87 266	361	1 414.4	88.1	0.9	1.1	8.9	0.5	8.8	14.8
06 51560	Norco	36.2	26 959	1 361	744.7	79.7	6.8	2.9	5.4	0.7	30.6	15.0
06 52526	Norwalk	25.1	107 096	270	4 266.8	57.0	5.6	1.8	12.3	NA	71.6	34.1
06 52582	Novato	71.1	55 005	670	773.6	82.6	3.2	1.2	7.2	0.2	20.4	18.6
06 53000	Oakland	144.5	413 775	45	2 863.5	45.6	28.9	2.1	19.0	0.9	25.9	26.1
06 53070	Oakley	41.1	39 224	947	954.4	73.2	8.3	3.1	10.9	0.9	36.7	16.3
06 53322	Oceanside	106.8	174 558	137	1 634.4	69.9	7.0	1.8	9.6	2.0	37.0	20.4
06 53896	Ontario	129.4	169 089	146	1 306.7	60.2	6.6	2.2	6.3	0.6	70.2	30.0
06 53980	Orange	64.2	139 812	185	2 177.8	68.4	1.8	1.2	13.8	0.6	38.2	25.7
06 54652	Oxnard	69.7	205 437	106	2 947.4	77.1	3.4	2.0	9.6	0.6	73.8	36.2
06 54806	Pacifica	32.8	39 088	951	1 191.7	69.4	5.1	1.1	26.1	1.4	17.3	20.7
06 55156	Palmdale	274.4	158 279	156	576.8	45.9	15.0	1.8	5.5	0.1	56.5	26.1
06 55184	Palm Desert	69.4	51 202	733	737.8	86.2	1.8	0.7	7.2	1.5	24.9	16.8
06 55254	Palm Springs	243.8	46 854	801	192.2	81.2	5.7	1.8	6.5	0.9	22.5	20.9
06 55282	Palo Alto	61.9	66 955	517	1 081.7	68.2	2.5	0.6	31.8	NA	7.2	30.9
06 55520	Paradise	47.4	26 449	1 382	558.0	96.4	1.4	3.6	2.9	1.0	6.4	3.4
06 55618	Paramount	12.3	55 406	666	4 504.6	42.3	11.5	1.4	3.6	NA	78.9	37.4
06 56000	Pasadena	59.5	140 881	184	2 367.7	66.6	12.1	0.9	17.6	0.2	31.9	30.4
06 56700	Perris	81.3	73 756	458	907.2	46.9	12.7	1.3	4.0	NA	71.8	27.4
06 56784	Petaluma	37.3	59 953	605	1 607.3	82.9	1.9	1.4	5.7	0.1	23.2	18.0
06 56924	Pico Rivera	21.5	64 235	548	2 987.7	49.4	1.4	1.1	3.7	0.2	90.0	33.7
06 57456	Pittsburg	44.6	68 140	508	1 527.8	38.6	20.8	2.1	18.6	3.7	40.6	30.3
06 57526	Placentia	17.0	52 397	708	3 082.2	78.8	2.5	0.9	17.1	0.6	38.2	28.2
06 57764	Pleasant Hill	18.3	34 497	1 076	1 885.1	83.8	1.7	1.3	16.5	1.1	12.0	18.0
06 57792	Pleasanton	62.5	77 682	430	1 242.9	70.0	3.1	0.5	28.4	0.3	10.5	24.1
06 58072	Pomona	59.4	153 350	165	2 581.6	67.6	7.6	1.5	10.6	0.5	68.8	34.7
06 58240	Porterville	45.6	55 466	664	1 216.4	82.9	1.8	3.8	6.5	0.1	63.3	19.2
06 58520	Poway	101.2	49 848	749	492.6	84.2	2.0	2.9	14.5	0.2	16.4	15.7
06 59444	Rancho Cordova	86.8	69 740	493	803.5	68.5	13.9	2.4	13.1	2.4	19.1	24.1
06 59451	Rancho Cucamonga	103.2	174 305	138	1 689.0	71.2	10.6	1.4	15.3	1.0	35.8	20.2
06 59514	Rancho Palos Verdes	34.9	42 726	865	1 224.2	67.0	3.5	0.8	30.0	0.7	8.4	27.3
06 59587	Rancho Santa Margarita	33.6	49 359	758	1 469.0	84.2	1.8	0.5	12.4	0.4	18.1	17.0
06 59920	Redding	154.5	91 593	339	592.8	88.4	2.6	4.2	5.2	0.3	8.7	5.7
06 59962	Redlands	93.6	70 622	487	754.5	76.5	6.9	1.3	10.0	0.7	29.1	13.1
06 60018	Redondo Beach	16.1	68 149	507	4 232.9	78.0	4.7	1.2	15.6	0.4	17.3	18.4
06 60102	Redwood City	50.3	82 881	395	1 647.7	74.8	3.5	0.9	14.6	0.8	39.0	30.4
06 60466	Rialto	57.9	102 741	288	1 774.5	64.2	15.6	1.3	3.3	NA	70.8	26.9
06 60620	Richmond	77.9	108 565	265	1 393.6	49.3	24.8	1.9	16.5	1.3	40.0	32.4
06 60704	Ridgecrest	53.8	28 726	1 280	533.9	81.0	6.7	2.8	6.5	2.2	19.8	11.1
06 62000	Riverside	210.2	319 504	59	1 520.0	70.6	7.4	2.5	8.3	0.5	52.2	22.0
06 62364	Rocklin	50.6	60 344	594	1 192.6	85.7	3.4	2.3	11.4	1.0	14.6	10.0
06 62546	Rohnert Park	18.1	42 262	871	2 334.9	80.4	3.2	2.2	8.3	1.4	24.7	16.5
06 62896	Rosemead	13.4	54 947	674	4 100.5	27.6	0.3	0.7	63.0	0.8	31.9	56.3
06 62938	Roseville	93.8	128 615	205	1 371.2	84.0	2.4	1.7	11.5	0.7	13.7	12.7
06 64000	Sacramento	253.6	485 199	35	1 913.2	55.0	16.8	2.4	21.5	2.5	27.5	22.5
06 64224	Salinas	60.0	156 677	158	2 611.3	74.7	2.0	1.4	8.1	0.3	75.0	37.4
06 65000	San Bernardino	153.3	215 213	100	1 403.9	58.8	17.0	2.6	5.5	0.6	60.6	22.5
06 65028	San Bruno	14.2	43 009	860	3 028.8	54.6	3.0	1.2	29.2	5.5	29.5	35.9
06 65042	San Buenaventura (Ventura)	56.1	109 484	258	1 951.6	86.7	2.8	1.8	5.4	0.4	31.5	14.7
06 65070	San Carlos	14.3	29 803	1 243	2 084.1	83.6	2.2	NA	13.6	0.6	11.7	17.8
06 65084	San Clemente	48.5	65 326	540	1 346.9	88.0	0.6	1.7	4.9	0.2	18.9	10.4
06 66000	San Diego	842.2	1 381 069	8	1 639.8	68.1	7.9	1.7	19.1	0.8	29.9	26.3
06 66070	San Dimas	39.0	34 637	1 072	888.1	74.8	4.6	1.5	17.4	1.1	29.9	19.5

1. Dry land or land partially or temporarily covered by water. 2. May be of any race.

City	Age of population (percent), 2011-2013									Median age 2011-2013	Percent female 2011-2013	Population			
												Census counts		Percent change	
	Under 5 years	5 to 17 years	18 to 24 years	25 to 34 years	35 to 44 years	45 to 54 years	55 to 64 years	65 to 74 years	75 years and over			2000	2010	2000–2010	2010–2014
	12	13	14	15	16	17	18	19	20	21	22	23	24	25	26
CALIFORNIA—Cont'd															
Menlo Park	6.8	18.0	6.2	14.3	15.3	14.5	11.4	7.5	6.0	38.3	52.5	30 785	32 026	4.0	4.0
Merced	9.5	21.9	12.5	14.8	12.3	10.5	9.2	5.4	3.9	28.7	51.0	63 893	78 958	23.6	3.5
Milpitas	6.3	14.8	8.4	16.6	15.7	16.1	11.6	6.4	4.1	37.0	49.1	62 698	66 790	6.5	10.3
Mission Viejo	5.0	16.2	9.3	9.3	12.2	17.1	14.9	8.4	7.5	43.7	51.0	93 102	93 305	0.2	4.4
Modesto	7.4	18.6	11.2	14.1	11.8	13.8	11.2	6.5	5.4	33.9	51.6	188 856	201 165	6.5	3.0
Monrovia	8.6	14.4	7.8	16.3	13.5	15.5	12.1	7.2	4.6	37.3	50.9	36 929	36 590	-0.9	2.3
Montclair	6.9	19.8	13.1	13.2	13.7	14.6	9.5	5.4	3.9	32.3	48.3	33 049	36 664	10.9	4.9
Montebello	7.0	15.6	10.3	14.7	13.1	12.4	11.7	7.7	7.5	36.9	50.9	62 150	62 500	0.6	2.3
Monterey	5.6	11.7	9.7	19.1	12.9	11.3	11.9	8.5	9.3	37.8	49.5	29 674	27 810	-6.3	3.8
Monterey Park	4.9	12.8	9.4	13.4	12.7	15.1	13.3	8.3	10.1	42.5	51.0	60 051	60 269	0.4	2.0
Moorpark	5.8	20.6	9.6	11.6	13.5	18.2	11.7	5.9	3.0	37.5	50.9	31 415	34 421	9.6	3.3
Moreno Valley	7.6	22.3	12.5	14.8	13.3	12.1	10.1	4.4	2.9	29.4	51.5	142 381	193 365	35.8	5.0
Morgan Hill	6.9	18.9	8.5	11.2	14.8	17.0	12.3	6.2	4.3	38.4	52.9	33 556	37 882	12.9	11.1
Mountain View	6.7	14.1	7.0	20.4	17.0	13.5	10.5	6.0	4.8	35.8	48.1	70 708	74 066	4.7	7.2
Murrieta	7.0	22.0	9.5	13.1	14.0	13.8	10.0	5.6	5.0	33.6	52.3	44 282	103 466	133.7	4.8
Napa	6.8	17.3	8.8	14.9	12.1	13.7	12.5	7.3	6.5	36.8	50.6	72 585	76 915	6.0	3.9
National City	6.1	17.9	15.4	14.5	14.0	11.8	9.6	5.3	5.5	32.0	49.7	54 260	58 582	8.0	3.0
Newark	5.4	16.4	7.9	14.3	15.8	17.6	11.0	5.8	5.7	39.0	50.1	42 471	42 573	0.2	5.1
Newport Beach	4.0	14.2	7.9	12.7	13.2	14.8	14.3	10.2	8.8	43.9	49.6	70 032	85 186	21.6	2.4
Norco	4.3	16.5	10.3	13.6	13.8	18.1	11.5	6.1	5.7	39.3	43.6	24 157	27 063	12.0	-0.4
Norwalk	7.0	19.4	12.4	13.9	14.2	13.5	9.1	6.1	4.5	32.9	50.5	103 298	105 549	2.2	1.5
Novato	5.8	16.5	5.5	9.5	13.7	17.0	15.6	9.0	7.4	44.1	51.4	47 630	51 904	9.0	6.0
Oakland	6.5	14.5	9.1	17.7	15.5	13.0	12.1	6.5	5.1	36.4	51.4	399 484	390 724	-2.2	5.9
Oakley	6.8	22.0	9.3	13.3	15.1	15.0	10.3	5.0	3.1	34.0	50.1	25 619	35 432	38.3	10.7
Oceanside	6.4	16.1	10.9	14.7	13.7	13.4	11.7	6.9	6.1	36.1	48.8	161 029	167 086	3.8	4.5
Ontario	7.5	20.3	11.8	15.8	14.4	13.2	9.2	4.3	3.6	31.8	51.9	158 007	163 924	3.7	3.2
Orange	6.0	15.4	12.9	14.5	14.8	14.7	10.2	6.4	5.0	35.7	49.9	128 821	136 416	5.9	2.5
Oxnard	8.6	19.7	12.1	16.2	13.5	11.8	9.4	5.0	3.8	30.5	49.1	170 358	197 899	16.2	3.8
Pacifica	4.6	15.5	8.4	11.8	14.5	16.3	15.7	8.0	5.2	41.7	52.4	38 390	37 234	-3.0	4.8
Palmdale	9.1	23.3	11.7	12.4	13.1	14.2	8.6	4.4	3.2	29.0	50.6	116 670	152 750	30.9	3.6
Palm Desert	4.4	12.2	7.7	9.7	9.0	11.2	13.9	14.9	17.0	50.8	53.9	41 155	48 445	17.7	5.7
Palm Springs	3.4	9.7	5.6	9.2	9.9	17.3	18.2	14.0	12.8	52.3	43.3	42 807	44 552	4.1	5.2
Palo Alto	4.8	18.0	6.0	13.1	12.9	15.8	11.8	8.7	9.0	41.6	50.9	58 598	64 403	9.9	4.0
Paradise	3.5	12.0	10.6	8.1	10.1	13.3	17.9	11.3	13.1	49.7	49.6	26 408	26 218	-0.7	0.9
Paramount	7.4	24.2	12.0	13.9	16.2	12.1	7.5	4.7	2.0	29.6	50.5	55 266	54 098	-2.1	2.4
Pasadena	5.4	12.8	10.0	18.6	14.5	13.1	11.3	7.1	7.2	36.8	50.6	133 936	137 122	2.4	2.7
Perris	8.3	27.6	11.9	14.4	13.6	12.0	7.2	3.2	1.9	26.5	51.7	36 189	68 386	89.0	7.9
Petaluma	6.7	18.0	6.4	12.9	12.6	15.7	14.1	8.1	5.6	40.6	52.5	54 548	57 941	6.2	3.5
Pico Rivera	6.6	17.8	10.6	14.1	13.5	13.5	10.7	6.8	6.4	35.9	51.0	63 428	62 942	-0.8	2.1
Pittsburg	7.5	18.3	11.5	15.8	13.8	13.0	10.4	5.5	4.2	33.0	51.7	56 769	63 264	11.4	7.7
Placentia	6.5	17.8	9.7	13.4	14.0	14.1	11.2	7.7	5.6	36.8	50.3	46 488	50 533	8.7	3.0
Pleasant Hill	4.8	13.3	9.9	12.6	13.9	16.3	14.2	7.6	7.3	42.6	53.6	32 837	33 152	1.0	4.2
Pleasanton	5.0	21.1	7.1	8.8	14.5	18.8	12.0	7.7	5.1	41.3	50.1	63 654	70 285	10.4	10.5
Pomona	7.5	19.7	14.2	14.9	13.2	12.5	9.5	4.7	3.8	30.4	50.4	149 473	149 058	-0.3	2.9
Porterville	10.2	22.8	10.7	14.0	12.2	11.1	8.1	6.1	4.8	29.3	50.3	39 615	54 165	36.7	2.4
Poway	6.4	16.6	9.9	10.7	13.4	16.0	13.6	8.1	5.4	40.2	51.0	48 044	47 811	-0.5	4.3
Rancho Cordova	8.5	16.5	8.9	16.4	13.9	13.0	11.2	6.3	5.4	34.9	51.5	55 060	64 776	17.6	7.6
Rancho Cucamonga	6.1	18.5	10.5	14.3	15.4	14.6	11.1	5.5	4.0	35.3	49.9	127 743	165 269	29.4	5.4
Rancho Palos Verdes	3.6	19.0	4.6	6.2	10.4	17.3	14.4	11.5	12.9	49.2	52.0	41 145	41 643	1.2	2.6
Rancho Santa Margarita	5.9	21.0	8.6	12.3	14.7	20.2	10.7	3.8	2.8	36.5	50.1	47 214	47 853	1.4	3.1
Redding	5.9	16.6	11.0	13.3	10.7	12.9	12.4	8.8	8.4	38.0	50.4	80 865	89 861	11.1	1.9
Redlands	6.4	18.1	10.9	12.2	11.7	13.5	13.2	7.5	6.5	36.8	51.9	63 591	68 747	8.1	2.8
Redondo Beach	6.8	14.3	5.0	14.7	18.8	17.9	11.2	6.4	4.7	40.5	52.1	63 261	66 748	5.5	2.1
Redwood City	7.1	16.9	6.6	16.7	15.3	15.0	10.5	7.0	4.9	37.1	49.7	75 402	76 815	1.9	7.9
Rialto	8.9	23.0	12.8	13.4	12.9	12.7	8.5	4.5	3.2	28.4	49.9	91 873	99 171	7.9	3.6
Richmond	7.6	16.7	9.7	16.3	14.5	12.7	11.7	6.6	4.2	34.8	51.2	99 216	103 701	4.5	4.7
Ridgecrest	6.3	22.2	9.1	13.4	11.4	13.0	11.2	7.1	6.2	34.3	49.8	24 927	27 616	10.8	4.0
Riverside	7.0	19.1	15.6	14.0	12.7	13.1	9.0	5.1	4.5	30.8	50.3	255 166	303 871	19.1	5.1
Rocklin	5.8	21.6	8.4	12.7	14.8	14.9	10.9	5.6	5.3	35.9	51.5	36 330	56 974	56.8	5.8
Rohnert Park	5.9	12.2	18.3	15.3	11.9	15.0	11.7	5.0	4.8	33.7	53.8	42 236	40 971	-3.0	3.5
Rosemead	4.9	16.5	8.5	12.5	14.4	16.0	12.9	8.0	6.2	39.9	51.1	53 505	53 764	0.5	2.2
Roseville	6.6	18.9	8.4	13.3	13.6	14.4	11.3	6.9	6.6	37.5	52.8	79 921	118 788	48.6	8.4
Sacramento	7.1	16.9	11.0	16.5	13.1	12.6	11.3	6.1	5.3	34.0	51.4	407 018	466 488	14.6	4.0
Salinas	9.4	21.9	11.2	16.8	14.0	11.1	8.2	4.1	3.3	29.4	48.9	151 060	150 441	-0.4	4.1
San Bernardino	8.3	22.3	12.9	15.1	11.6	12.1	9.5	4.8	3.3	29.1	50.4	185 401	209 924	13.2	2.5
San Bruno	6.4	14.0	8.0	18.3	12.6	16.5	12.0	6.1	6.1	37.0	49.8	40 165	41 114	2.4	4.8
San Buenaventura (Ventura)	5.7	15.2	9.3	13.1	13.4	15.2	13.3	7.5	7.3	40.3	50.6	100 916	106 433	5.5	2.1
San Carlos	6.2	17.3	4.8	9.5	15.6	17.8	13.7	7.8	7.3	43.1	51.6	27 718	28 406	2.5	4.9
San Clemente	6.5	19.3	6.9	10.0	15.1	14.8	13.0	8.6	5.7	40.1	50.9	49 936	63 522	27.2	2.9
San Diego	6.4	15.1	12.6	17.9	13.5	13.0	10.3	6.2	5.1	33.6	49.6	1 223 400	1 307 402	6.9	6.1
San Dimas	4.7	15.0	10.7	12.4	11.3	16.0	14.3	8.7	6.9	41.3	51.9	34 980	33 371	-4.6	3.8

City	Households, 2011-2013: Number	Households, 2011-2013: Persons per household	Households, 2011-2013: Percent: Female family householder[1]	Households, 2011-2013: Percent: One-person	Persons in group quarters, 2010: Total	Persons in group quarters, 2010: Institutional: Total	Persons in group quarters, 2010: Institutional: Persons in nursing facilities	Persons in group quarters, 2010: Noninstitutional	Serious crimes known to police,[2] 2013: Total: Number	Serious crimes known to police,[2] 2013: Total: Rate[3]	Serious crimes known to police,[2] 2013: Rate[3]: Violent	Serious crimes known to police,[2] 2013: Rate[3]: Property	Educational attainment, 2011–2013: Population age 25 and older	Educational attainment, 2011–2013: Attainment[4] (percent): High school graduate or less	Educational attainment, 2011–2013: Attainment[4] (percent): Bachelor's degree or more
	27	28	29	30	31	32	33	34	35	36	37	38	39	40	41
CALIFORNIA—Cont'd															
Menlo Park	12 068	2.63	7.1	28.5	845	246	236	599	697	2 103	160	1 943	22 607	15.5	70.6
Merced	25 027	3.17	21.6	22.9	1 080	588	343	492	3 203	3 938	684	3 255	45 117	49.2	16.2
Milpitas	19 889	3.34	11.8	16.2	2 698	2 594	34	104	2 160	3 107	134	2 973	48 311	32.0	42.1
Mission Viejo	33 571	2.79	7.4	19.2	942	83	66	859	1 060	1 105	65	1 041	66 128	21.0	46.1
Modesto	68 961	2.91	17.3	24.6	2 955	1 766	1 169	1 189	11 693	5 725	834	4 891	127 905	47.2	18.1
Monrovia	12 910	2.85	11.1	25.8	156	95	76	61	863	2 328	154	2 174	25 575	32.5	37.9
Montclair	10 457	3.56	20.1	20.8	396	181	181	215	1 810	4 790	495	4 295	22 670	61.2	10.6
Montebello	19 691	3.19	22.8	22.8	400	361	350	39	1 939	3 050	288	2 762	42 416	58.2	18.2
Monterey	12 708	2.16	6.5	40.8	2 503	293	293	2 210	1 228	4 186	409	3 777	20 567	19.0	49.6
Monterey Park	18 389	3.29	19.8	16.3	230	189	186	41	1 266	2 070	170	1 900	44 412	47.7	28.4
Moorpark	10 442	3.35	8.1	12.9	0	0	0	0	446	1 265	105	1 160	22 389	27.2	37.5
Moreno Valley	51 116	3.88	23.1	12.4	554	83	27	471	6 510	3 234	317	2 917	114 438	52.0	15.2
Morgan Hill	13 012	3.01	13.5	16.1	386	222	144	164	739	1 852	158	1 694	26 075	30.6	36.3
Mountain View	32 295	2.36	7.5	32.9	265	120	107	145	1 863	2 407	203	2 204	55 152	19.3	64.2
Murrieta	32 886	3.22	9.0	18.6	429	138	56	291	1 710	1 587	65	1 522	65 484	30.7	28.6
Napa	28 186	2.74	12.5	26.1	1 237	669	343	568	1 664	2 113	324	1 789	52 583	40.7	28.3
National City	15 043	3.65	22.8	18.4	5 752	411	411	5 341	2 204	3 696	527	3 169	36 087	57.1	11.4
Newark	13 333	3.25	11.6	17.3	145	0	0	145	1 185	2 696	280	2 416	30 608	43.7	26.2
Newport Beach	37 920	2.28	8.1	32.3	402	251	221	151	2 231	2 546	83	2 462	64 069	10.9	64.5
Norco	7 017	3.38	9.5	17.4	4 397	4 322	0	75	636	2 313	153	2 160	18 742	50.5	16.3
Norwalk	26 907	3.89	20.1	13.6	1 615	1 300	474	315	2 653	2 491	382	2 109	65 125	53.7	13.9
Novato	21 080	2.50	8.7	28.4	626	177	175	449	943	1 755	199	1 556	38 537	22.8	44.4
Oakland	157 168	2.51	15.1	35.1	8 138	2 463	1 349	5 675	33 160	8 210	1 977	6 233	280 769	36.0	39.1
Oakley	11 070	3.37	14.2	14.9	103	28	6	75	567	1 499	185	1 314	23 130	45.4	15.2
Oceanside	59 590	2.86	11.2	25.8	936	134	91	802	5 128	2 972	367	2 605	113 919	38.5	24.5
Ontario	46 229	3.59	18.6	20.8	758	347	347	411	4 960	2 950	269	2 680	100 769	57.2	13.0
Orange	42 852	3.09	13.0	19.8	6 253	3 666	299	2 587	2 565	1 828	105	1 723	91 392	36.0	32.8
Oxnard	50 877	3.93	18.2	14.7	1 434	502	465	932	5 725	2 826	321	2 505	120 069	55.9	15.9
Pacifica	14 138	2.69	11.9	25.9	182	118	115	64	612	1 590	171	1 418	27 365	23.4	40.6
Palmdale	42 163	3.68	21.0	14.5	199	41	0	158	4 103	2 621	485	2 136	86 891	51.2	15.7
Palm Desert	24 055	2.06	9.6	39.5	308	210	210	98	2 325	4 608	218	4 390	37 766	28.3	34.9
Palm Springs	22 932	1.98	7.1	45.8	539	196	190	343	2 605	5 629	551	5 078	37 236	31.0	35.8
Palo Alto	26 382	2.48	7.3	28.9	583	378	323	205	1 537	2 295	81	2 215	47 057	7.1	79.9
Paradise	11 104	2.32	9.0	37.9	408	269	246	139	598	2 281	259	2 021	19 347	34.2	25.4
Paramount	13 575	4.01	21.1	15.0	310	283	283	27	1 855	3 381	405	2 976	30 860	70.7	7.4
Pasadena	55 153	2.44	11.0	34.9	3 493	1 021	890	2 472	4 213	3 031	312	2 719	99 509	25.3	51.0
Perris	16 327	4.35	24.7	9.7	240	100	71	140	2 279	3 158	334	2 824	37 199	64.1	8.4
Petaluma	21 341	2.73	10.8	25.9	724	363	363	361	1 192	2 013	302	1 710	40 608	30.4	36.4
Pico Rivera	16 794	3.75	18.0	16.2	454	415	415	39	1 728	2 712	325	2 387	41 289	62.0	11.7
Pittsburg	20 231	3.23	18.9	19.3	291	138	123	153	2 207	3 324	279	3 046	41 108	46.2	18.1
Placentia	15 718	3.27	13.1	16.2	337	84	73	253	850	1 635	127	1 508	34 258	35.3	33.0
Pleasant Hill	13 990	2.38	8.3	33.0	463	312	291	151	1 524	4 477	162	4 315	24 323	19.2	48.4
Pleasanton	25 421	2.84	8.6	17.5	456	136	129	320	1 341	1 838	82	1 755	48 449	17.0	58.4
Pomona	38 699	3.76	18.4	17.0	4 138	1 356	1 166	2 782	5 203	3 437	534	2 903	88 291	58.1	16.7
Porterville	16 431	3.26	18.2	20.1	1 147	940	931	207	1 700	3 076	351	2 725	30 925	56.4	11.0
Poway	16 352	2.96	10.4	17.3	550	266	260	284	665	1 345	182	1 163	32 955	24.1	45.3
Rancho Cordova	23 992	2.77	16.7	24.4	325	155	143	170	2 554	3 776	520	3 256	44 292	36.4	26.1
Rancho Cucamonga	54 294	3.07	13.5	20.8	3 124	2 988	73	136	4 155	2 412	192	2 220	110 097	29.0	32.5
Rancho Palos Verdes	15 641	2.68	8.2	21.8	340	27	27	313	610	1 434	71	1 363	30 711	13.0	64.9
Rancho Santa Margarita	16 944	2.88	10.5	18.7	2	0	0	2	307	624	35	590	31 449	20.7	47.4
Redding	34 996	2.53	13.3	29.1	2 020	882	543	1 138	4 359	4 788	643	4 146	60 317	36.5	21.2
Redlands	24 962	2.69	10.1	29.6	2 368	512	485	1 856	3 235	4 603	306	4 297	44 999	28.3	39.5
Redondo Beach	28 267	2.38	8.4	30.9	431	64	64	367	1 748	2 571	235	2 336	49 799	15.2	57.1
Redwood City	28 520	2.73	11.3	27.7	1 547	1 139	53	408	2 061	2 586	238	2 347	55 029	34.0	41.4
Rialto	25 221	4.00	20.3	14.4	447	193	153	254	3 151	3 074	423	2 650	56 116	60.6	9.0
Richmond	36 689	2.86	19.7	28.5	1 583	913	172	670	5 938	5 532	1 036	4 496	70 288	44.2	25.6
Ridgecrest	10 942	2.57	7.6	32.2	196	87	87	109	724	2 537	540	1 997	17 633	33.5	28.2
Riverside	90 709	3.33	15.8	21.8	11 549	2 624	1 153	8 925	11 938	3 773	420	3 352	182 659	45.9	22.3
Rocklin	21 307	2.74	14.8	20.3	637	181	176	456	1 073	1 800	104	1 696	37 829	20.5	39.2
Rohnert Park	15 704	2.61	12.6	29.1	397	6	6	391	867	2 098	436	1 662	26 192	36.3	23.5
Rosemead	14 547	3.70	15.9	12.8	413	278	208	135	1 216	2 228	273	1 955	38 073	62.2	15.7
Roseville	45 655	2.71	11.4	24.2	847	369	361	478	3 604	2 855	207	2 648	82 487	24.8	36.1
Sacramento	176 504	2.65	15.6	33.0	8 314	4 046	1 367	4 268	21 117	4 416	656	3 760	308 726	38.0	29.2
Salinas	40 757	3.72	17.8	16.9	2 465	1 807	531	658	6 357	4 082	643	3 439	88 685	62.2	12.0
San Bernardino	56 996	3.58	25.4	20.0	7 325	4 247	878	3 078	11 338	5 290	909	4 381	120 250	59.3	11.0
San Bruno	14 566	2.85	10.6	26.1	398	82	72	316	1 104	2 598	240	2 358	30 103	30.9	34.1
San Buenaventura (Ventura)	41 616	2.56	13.1	29.7	2 493	1 738	293	755	4 289	3 964	242	3 722	75 590	29.5	33.5
San Carlos	11 613	2.49	8.5	28.4	91	12	12	79	NA	NA	NA	NA	20 854	13.1	61.5
San Clemente	24 368	2.64	8.9	25.0	273	28	0	245	900	1 378	86	1 293	43 474	17.6	46.7
San Diego	476 083	2.73	11.9	29.0	51 956	7 050	2 902	44 906	37 031	2 744	393	2 351	882 468	29.3	41.9
San Dimas	11 655	2.84	12.9	22.3	540	220	128	320	771	2 277	192	2 085	23 493	26.9	36.5

1. No spouse present. 2. Data for serious crimes have not been adjusted for underreporting. This may affect comparability between geographic areas and over time. 3. Per 100,000 population estimated by the FBI. 4. Persons 25 years old and over.

Table D. Cities — **Income, Poverty, and Housing**

City	Money income, 2011–2013					Housing units, 2010			Occupied housing units 2011–2013				
		Households								Owner-occupied		Median owner costs as a percent of income	
	Per capita income[1] (dollars)	Median income	Percent with income of $200,000 or more	Percent with income of less than $25,000	Families with income below poverty (percent)	Total	Percent change, 2000–2010	Vacant units for sale or rent[2]	Total	Percent	Median value[3] (dollars)	With a mortgage[4]	Without a mortgage[5]
	42	43	44	45	46	47	48	49	50	51	52	53	54
CALIFORNIA—Cont'd													
Menlo Park	66 328	112 476	29.2	7.5	4.0	13 085	2.7	738	12 068	56.9	1 000 000	26.4	10.0
Merced	16 912	36 585	1.2	34.4	25.5	27 446	27.4	2 547	25 027	42.7	140 100	24.3	11.3
Milpitas	34 083	94 977	12.4	13.1	7.1	19 806	14.0	622	19 889	64.1	508 900	26.9	10.0
Mission Viejo	39 983	94 376	11.9	10.4	3.7	34 228	4.0	1 020	33 571	77.5	541 900	27.7	10.0
Modesto	21 848	45 206	2.6	27.0	17.9	75 044	11.5	5 937	68 961	52.3	158 500	26.7	11.7
Monrovia	32 037	71 940	7.1	19.7	9.1	14 473	3.9	711	12 910	51.3	531 500	29.2	10.9
Montclair	17 413	48 501	1.0	23.0	12.1	9 911	8.0	388	10 457	62.5	251 000	28.2	12.0
Montebello	20 681	44 485	2.7	26.2	10.9	19 768	1.8	756	19 691	46.3	385 500	30.9	11.5
Monterey	36 467	61 416	5.8	19.8	3.2	13 584	1.2	1 400	12 708	30.9	593 700	28.7	10.0
Monterey Park	24 447	56 180	5.2	24.6	12.1	20 850	3.3	887	18 389	51.1	481 700	29.2	10.0
Moorpark	35 353	100 477	13.1	7.5	4.9	10 738	18.1	254	10 442	73.3	521 400	27.2	11.7
Moreno Valley	17 737	53 392	2.1	20.1	17.2	55 559	34.0	3 967	51 116	60.0	180 600	28.9	10.0
Morgan Hill	40 219	94 238	16.5	13.3	6.8	12 859	15.7	533	13 012	70.6	569 600	27.1	12.5
Mountain View	56 409	97 994	20.5	13.3	7.9	33 881	4.5	1 924	32 295	41.2	795 700	22.1	10.8
Murrieta	27 773	71 554	5.3	12.0	6.4	35 294	136.5	2 545	32 886	66.4	273 600	29.1	12.9
Napa	29 667	62 500	5.1	17.9	7.2	30 149	8.6	1 983	28 186	53.0	391 700	28.2	12.1
National City	16 416	36 963	0.8	35.9	24.8	16 762	8.0	1 260	15 043	30.2	264 900	30.3	10.0
Newark	30 587	84 090	6.8	12.3	6.6	13 414	2.0	442	13 333	68.0	429 100	27.5	10.5
Newport Beach	77 297	107 257	26.1	13.6	5.7	44 193	18.4	5 442	37 920	54.1	1 000 000	29.7	11.1
Norco	26 286	84 756	8.4	12.5	6.0	7 322	17.7	299	7 017	78.5	367 400	29.5	11.8
Norwalk	18 621	59 017	1.3	16.8	10.9	28 083	1.9	953	26 907	63.5	309 500	29.7	10.0
Novato	45 216	75 988	12.4	14.0	3.5	21 158	11.5	879	21 080	66.2	533 500	30.6	11.4
Oakland	32 425	51 851	7.4	27.2	16.8	169 710	7.7	15 919	157 168	39.8	426 500	28.2	12.7
Oakley	27 162	77 457	3.7	15.7	7.8	11 484	44.0	757	11 070	75.6	239 300	27.6	11.5
Oceanside	25 794	54 902	3.7	20.2	10.4	64 435	8.3	5 197	59 590	56.2	334 800	29.2	11.9
Ontario	18 141	52 735	1.5	21.0	15.6	47 449	5.2	2 518	46 229	54.8	242 500	31.7	10.4
Orange	30 739	76 174	9.4	14.7	9.4	45 111	8.0	1 744	42 852	58.7	490 500	26.9	10.0
Oxnard	20 438	59 465	3.5	18.0	14.0	52 772	16.8	2 975	50 877	54.8	320 700	29.1	11.3
Pacifica	44 370	94 370	14.3	10.8	4.3	14 523	1.9	556	14 138	68.0	598 900	27.9	10.8
Palmdale	18 468	51 403	2.5	24.9	19.8	46 544	25.3	3 592	42 163	60.7	167 300	28.6	12.4
Palm Desert	38 507	51 280	5.2	20.3	6.7	37 073	32.1	13 956	24 055	61.8	298 400	31.0	16.0
Palm Springs	35 529	43 378	4.5	30.6	14.0	34 794	12.3	12 048	22 932	56.5	260 300	29.5	17.2
Palo Alto	73 431	122 366	31.8	11.6	4.4	28 216	7.9	1 723	26 382	54.8	1 000 000	25.1	10.0
Paradise	24 241	37 811	1.5	32.7	11.2	12 981	5.4	1 088	11 104	70.0	192 700	29.0	14.9
Paramount	14 614	45 612	0.8	25.4	22.7	14 571	-0.4	690	13 575	39.2	253 300	32.6	10.4
Pasadena	41 874	70 341	11.3	19.8	8.2	59 551	10.0	4 281	55 153	43.5	597 800	27.7	12.0
Perris	12 680	46 401	0.5	25.4	22.9	17 906	70.5	1 541	16 327	61.6	151 500	33.9	10.0
Petaluma	33 607	77 507	6.2	16.6	6.3	22 736	11.8	999	21 341	65.9	415 200	26.4	12.9
Pico Rivera	18 716	54 255	1.2	19.1	11.3	17 109	1.8	543	16 794	68.8	321 500	30.7	10.4
Pittsburg	23 110	56 467	2.8	23.9	15.3	21 126	14.9	1 599	20 231	53.2	212 200	28.5	12.1
Placentia	29 066	78 763	7.3	14.6	8.5	16 872	9.4	507	15 718	64.0	486 300	29.0	11.8
Pleasant Hill	42 313	72 289	9.3	16.5	3.5	14 321	2.0	613	13 990	56.1	480 500	26.1	10.0
Pleasanton	50 394	120 845	22.0	9.3	3.9	26 053	8.6	808	25 421	69.6	711 800	25.7	10.0
Pomona	16 977	48 209	1.8	25.5	17.9	40 685	2.7	2 208	38 699	52.9	251 200	31.3	12.4
Porterville	16 621	39 666	1.5	30.7	23.2	16 734	31.4	1 090	16 431	56.4	135 900	26.7	12.7
Poway	40 558	90 074	12.4	11.3	3.6	16 715	5.6	587	16 352	75.5	484 600	24.9	12.7
Rancho Cordova	23 164	49 014	2.2	21.6	13.0	25 479	18.5	2 031	23 992	55.7	178 500	27.0	11.1
Rancho Cucamonga	30 657	77 619	6.7	14.1	6.5	56 618	34.1	2 235	54 294	64.2	355 900	27.3	12.6
Rancho Palos Verdes	55 359	115 878	24.1	7.6	3.5	16 179	3.3	618	15 641	81.2	931 100	25.6	10.0
Rancho Santa Margarita	42 972	102 637	12.7	9.0	3.1	17 260	3.7	595	16 944	71.8	499 100	27.1	12.2
Redding	22 966	41 579	2.6	29.5	13.0	38 679	14.5	2 549	34 996	52.3	209 400	25.8	14.3
Redlands	32 549	64 781	7.9	18.6	9.1	26 634	7.1	1 870	24 962	59.4	285 800	25.1	10.0
Redondo Beach	53 396	102 062	16.3	11.4	3.1	30 609	3.6	1 598	28 267	52.2	711 900	27.9	10.0
Redwood City	41 196	78 650	15.2	12.2	5.9	29 167	0.8	1 210	28 520	50.3	769 100	28.1	11.7
Rialto	15 844	48 426	1.0	22.6	17.7	27 203	5.4	2 001	25 221	63.0	174 800	29.4	13.3
Richmond	25 567	54 316	4.4	22.6	14.8	39 328	8.8	3 235	36 689	50.9	250 500	28.6	10.0
Ridgecrest	26 234	57 708	1.3	20.0	10.0	11 915	4.8	1 134	10 942	57.8	174 700	20.4	10.0
Riverside	21 621	53 639	4.0	23.5	15.0	98 444	14.4	6 512	90 709	55.0	232 400	27.3	10.0
Rocklin	33 178	72 253	6.7	15.6	8.0	22 010	52.4	1 210	21 307	64.0	316 700	26.0	12.9
Rohnert Park	26 888	56 347	1.7	22.5	7.1	16 551	4.6	743	15 704	50.7	307 100	28.6	13.4
Rosemead	16 351	41 702	1.6	29.3	19.0	14 805	3.4	558	14 547	46.5	413 900	34.5	10.0
Roseville	33 657	74 446	6.3	15.1	5.6	47 757	49.3	2 698	45 655	62.5	304 500	24.3	13.4
Sacramento	24 952	48 807	3.2	27.3	19.0	190 911	16.5	16 287	176 504	47.4	215 500	26.6	10.0
Salinas	17 212	47 705	1.3	22.9	17.8	42 651	7.7	2 264	40 757	41.9	245 600	29.4	10.0
San Bernardino	14 253	36 482	1.1	34.9	28.6	65 401	3.1	6 118	56 996	47.4	145 900	28.5	11.8
San Bruno	34 460	80 040	7.6	10.1	5.1	15 356	2.7	655	14 566	54.5	582 200	28.9	10.3
San Buenaventura (Ventura)	32 082	63 095	5.6	19.6	7.3	42 827	7.5	2 389	41 616	52.7	406 600	26.6	10.6
San Carlos	61 166	116 052	23.9	8.5	2.0	12 018	3.6	494	11 613	69.3	923 100	26.1	12.6
San Clemente	47 158	92 294	16.1	12.2	5.8	25 966	25.7	2 060	24 368	63.9	707 600	29.8	10.0
San Diego	32 658	63 258	7.3	19.7	10.9	516 033	9.9	32 941	476 083	46.9	435 400	27.6	10.1
San Dimas	35 493	79 797	9.3	13.3	3.1	12 506	-0.6	476	11 655	75.2	417 100	27.0	11.9

1. Based on population estimated by the American Community Survey. 2. Includes units rented or sold but not occupied. 3. Specified owner-occupied units; $1,000,000 represents $1,000,000 or more 4. 50.0 represents 50 percent or more. 5. 10.0 represents 10 percent or less.

City	Occupied housing units, 2011–2013 (cont.): Percent renter occupied	Occupied housing units, 2011–2013 (cont.): Median gross rent[1]	Occupied housing units, 2011–2013 (cont.): Median rent as a percent of income[2]	Occupied housing units, 2011–2013 (cont.): Percent with no vehicle available	Migration, 2011–2013: Percent who lived in the same house one year ago	Migration, 2011–2013: Percent who lived outside current city one year ago	Civilian labor force, 2014: Total	Civilian labor force, 2014: Percent change, 2013–2014	Civilian labor force, 2014: Unemployment: Total	Civilian labor force, 2014: Unemployment: Rate[3]	Civilian employment[4], 2011–2013: Population age 16 and older	Civilian employment[4], 2011–2013: Percent: In labor force	Civilian employment[4], 2011–2013: Percent: Civilian full-year full-time workers	Civilian employment[4], 2011–2013: Households with no workers (percent)
	55	56	57	58	59	60	61	62	63	64	65	66	67	68
CALIFORNIA—Cont'd														
Menlo Park	43.1	1 757	26.2	4.1	85.9	11.6	18 410	2.7	612	3.3	25 373	66.0	43.2	21.8
Merced	57.3	821	35.1	11.1	77.8	9.4	34 859	0.5	4 216	12.1	57 428	61.1	30.3	30.6
Milpitas	35.9	1 737	28.0	4.8	84.7	10.6	36 642	2.2	1 790	4.9	55 639	66.3	42.8	19.2
Mission Viejo	22.5	1 848	34.2	3.9	87.5	9.5	49 920	0.6	2 562	5.1	77 689	65.5	41.6	22.3
Modesto	47.7	979	37.0	8.6	80.1	8.8	94 390	0.0	10 373	11.0	156 871	61.4	32.0	29.8
Monrovia	48.7	1 268	29.9	3.6	85.2	12.2	20 736	1.3	1 318	6.4	29 028	71.5	43.9	19.3
Montclair	37.5	1 100	35.5	8.3	89.2	9.8	18 057	1.5	1 234	6.8	28 770	62.6	41.5	18.7
Montebello	53.7	1 120	37.7	10.4	92.1	6.4	28 693	1.1	2 030	7.1	50 566	55.8	39.0	29.1
Monterey	69.1	1 381	31.3	6.2	73.1	21.8	15 633	1.8	1 017	6.5	23 832	65.2	36.6	29.2
Monterey Park	48.9	1 208	34.1	9.8	91.7	6.6	29 407	1.1	2 162	7.4	51 266	59.2	36.6	25.4
Moorpark	26.7	1 751	36.1	2.2	89.2	8.5	19 255	-0.3	1 001	5.2	26 670	72.2	44.8	12.0
Moreno Valley	40.0	1 229	38.3	4.8	81.3	9.1	90 203	1.1	7 924	8.8	146 659	63.0	35.0	20.7
Morgan Hill	29.4	1 637	34.2	2.9	86.1	9.2	21 758	1.9	1 250	5.7	30 845	68.0	39.4	17.5
Mountain View	58.8	1 656	25.5	6.6	81.6	15.0	48 298	2.4	1 919	4.0	61 837	74.2	51.3	16.5
Murrieta	33.6	1 604	34.4	2.7	78.5	14.8	50 868	1.6	3 370	6.6	79 171	66.2	39.6	22.2
Napa	47.0	1 321	33.3	6.3	85.9	5.5	42 020	1.5	2 481	5.9	61 662	69.4	39.1	25.5
National City	69.8	938	35.7	12.2	89.7	6.7	24 695	-0.4	2 004	8.1	47 425	62.9	29.1	25.7
Newark	32.0	1 546	29.4	4.0	91.6	6.0	23 281	0.8	1 170	5.0	34 844	67.8	45.2	37.0
Newport Beach	45.9	1 940	29.5	3.6	80.7	12.6	45 567	0.8	2 064	4.5	72 799	63.1	38.7	27.5
Norco	21.5	1 633	32.2	5.3	89.3	9.0	11 480	1.6	760	6.6	22 380	54.4	31.0	23.0
Norwalk	36.5	1 289	35.3	5.7	91.6	5.5	50 875	0.8	4 297	8.4	81 602	62.8	39.8	18.0
Novato	33.8	1 616	32.9	4.3	83.6	10.5	29 054	0.9	1 221	4.2	43 024	66.1	36.7	26.1
Oakland	60.2	1 095	33.0	17.3	82.7	8.9	208 597	0.3	15 136	7.3	326 150	66.8	36.6	27.6
Oakley	24.4	1 430	35.5	4.5	91.5	7.3	18 600	0.3	1 426	7.7	27 907	68.5	40.8	16.6
Oceanside	43.8	1 358	37.6	5.5	84.1	10.2	81 918	0.0	5 398	6.6	137 060	62.0	34.7	28.9
Ontario	45.2	1 196	36.4	4.6	86.7	8.5	80 649	1.2	6 519	8.1	125 668	66.0	37.7	19.9
Orange	41.3	1 491	35.0	4.4	84.1	11.2	72 014	0.6	3 727	5.2	112 865	65.3	40.6	17.4
Oxnard	45.2	1 314	36.3	4.9	88.4	4.8	100 380	-0.7	7 294	7.3	151 081	69.0	39.5	19.5
Pacifica	32.0	1 815	27.8	3.4	90.5	7.3	23 402	2.6	911	3.9	31 533	70.1	45.9	18.7
Palmdale	39.3	1 137	40.4	6.1	83.2	8.7	65 050	0.3	7 157	11.0	111 128	58.8	34.1	21.8
Palm Desert	38.2	1 066	30.4	5.9	83.0	13.9	22 552	1.7	1 328	5.9	42 543	53.8	29.0	43.2
Palm Springs	43.5	954	36.4	8.7	79.4	13.5	21 310	1.5	1 443	6.8	40 602	53.6	29.1	44.6
Palo Alto	45.2	2 000	27.9	6.8	82.1	13.8	34 802	2.5	1 244	3.6	52 912	62.8	42.3	27.0
Paradise	30.0	884	35.9	6.5	84.1	9.0	11 247	0.2	846	7.5	22 634	49.0	24.4	49.7
Paramount	60.8	1 181	35.7	5.9	88.4	9.0	25 041	0.6	2 415	9.6	39 828	64.0	39.3	17.9
Pasadena	56.5	1 322	30.1	10.4	81.7	12.8	77 371	1.1	5 689	7.4	116 103	68.6	42.9	23.9
Perris	38.4	1 241	39.0	3.6	87.5	7.4	28 766	0.4	3 420	11.9	48 788	61.0	30.6	20.7
Petaluma	34.1	1 422	30.1	4.5	87.4	6.1	32 448	2.2	1 402	4.3	45 719	70.5	41.0	20.7
Pico Rivera	31.2	1 196	34.7	6.9	89.5	7.7	30 264	1.0	2 304	7.6	50 142	62.8	39.9	22.0
Pittsburg	46.8	1 271	36.0	6.9	80.8	11.5	32 463	0.4	2 390	7.4	50 390	65.7	34.8	23.2
Placentia	36.0	1 481	33.1	4.8	85.6	10.9	26 178	0.4	1 618	6.2	40 696	68.0	40.5	18.9
Pleasant Hill	43.9	1 483	32.7	8.4	85.1	13.1	17 916	0.9	921	5.1	28 201	63.2	38.9	27.2
Pleasanton	30.4	1 718	27.1	2.6	90.5	6.5	37 230	1.0	1 697	4.6	56 153	65.3	42.9	19.4
Pomona	47.1	1 115	38.0	7.9	84.8	9.6	67 631	0.7	6 229	9.2	114 437	60.5	33.4	21.9
Porterville	43.6	773	32.2	5.9	85.5	5.3	23 128	-1.2	3 170	13.7	38 489	58.6	32.6	29.2
Poway	24.5	1 440	33.3	5.7	89.2	7.7	25 387	0.5	1 052	4.1	39 921	65.1	41.4	20.1
Rancho Cordova	44.3	927	33.0	6.9	77.9	12.8	32 756	0.0	2 652	8.1	51 847	66.2	37.9	25.6
Rancho Cucamonga	35.8	1 443	33.5	4.0	83.3	10.6	89 976	1.7	5 400	6.0	134 505	67.9	40.1	18.6
Rancho Palos Verdes	18.8	2 000	31.7	2.2	91.2	6.9	19 061	1.7	764	4.0	34 315	55.9	35.6	30.5
Rancho Santa Margarita	28.2	1 705	32.6	3.3	87.7	9.2	27 555	1.0	880	3.2	37 408	76.5	52.2	11.5
Redding	47.7	952	37.1	8.0	77.7	10.7	40 115	0.2	3 565	8.9	72 763	56.7	29.1	37.5
Redlands	40.6	1 122	31.5	4.9	84.1	11.6	33 250	2.0	1 557	4.7	54 819	59.2	37.6	27.4
Redondo Beach	47.8	1 676	27.9	4.3	85.4	10.8	40 342	1.5	2 062	5.1	54 425	74.1	48.7	19.1
Redwood City	49.7	1 521	32.0	5.2	88.4	7.9	46 523	2.6	1 787	3.8	62 106	72.2	45.8	19.0
Rialto	37.0	1 043	35.2	6.0	83.8	9.3	43 645	0.9	4 172	9.6	72 822	64.6	35.0	21.4
Richmond	49.1	1 162	34.1	9.3	82.6	11.9	52 967	0.5	3 755	7.1	83 334	65.5	37.1	25.3
Ridgecrest	42.2	858	27.1	7.8	81.2	6.8	14 510	0.6	1 019	7.0	21 306	63.2	38.8	27.9
Riverside	45.0	1 112	36.7	6.3	82.4	9.2	145 762	1.3	11 498	7.9	241 521	62.4	34.4	23.8
Rocklin	36.0	1 344	33.4	3.7	83.8	10.3	29 977	0.3	1 899	6.3	44 448	68.3	39.0	23.1
Rohnert Park	49.3	1 207	36.3	5.3	82.0	13.0	22 741	1.8	1 315	5.8	34 707	67.4	34.9	24.8
Rosemead	53.5	1 159	46.7	7.8	92.4	6.3	25 603	0.6	2 431	9.5	44 497	58.8	34.5	22.0
Roseville	37.5	1 284	31.2	4.1	82.3	10.9	63 515	0.4	3 756	5.9	96 921	65.5	40.4	24.6
Sacramento	52.6	986	33.5	11.1	78.5	10.2	226 625	0.1	17 545	7.7	373 218	63.7	36.0	29.5
Salinas	58.1	1 141	34.7	5.6	86.7	4.0	79 622	1.3	7 602	9.5	111 214	64.5	34.2	22.1
San Bernardino	52.6	914	39.1	12.4	80.3	11.0	82 952	0.7	8 464	10.2	155 717	55.6	28.2	31.3
San Bruno	45.5	1 706	30.8	5.3	89.2	8.0	25 804	2.5	1 053	4.1	34 520	72.2	45.4	17.0
San Buenaventura (Ventura)	47.3	1 338	33.5	6.9	87.3	6.4	57 247	-0.6	3 872	6.8	88 039	65.5	38.9	27.7
San Carlos	30.7	1 666	28.5	4.1	90.4	6.8	16 742	2.5	697	4.2	22 788	71.6	44.7	19.0
San Clemente	36.1	1 659	38.4	3.3	83.2	8.9	31 544	0.7	1 435	4.5	49 609	65.8	38.6	22.9
San Diego	53.1	1 320	32.2	7.6	82.1	8.2	692 657	0.1	42 281	6.1	1 082 397	67.7	40.0	21.9
San Dimas	24.8	1 518	35.2	5.4	85.4	13.2	17 497	1.2	1 143	6.5	28 213	61.8	37.8	24.8

1. $2,000 represents $2,000 or more. 2. 50.0 represents 50 percent or more. 3. Percent of civilian labor force. 4. Persons 16 years old and over.

Table D. Cities — **Construction, Wholesale Trade, and Retail Trade**

City	Value of residential construction authorized by building permits, 2014: New construction ($1,000)	Number of housing units	Percent single family	Wholesale trade,[1] 2007: Number of establish-ments	Number of employees	Sales (mil dol)	Annual payroll (mil dol)	Retail trade,[2] 2007: Number of establish-ments	Number of employees	Sales (mil dol)	Annual payroll (mil dol)
	69	70	71	72	73	74	75	76	77	78	79
CALIFORNIA—Cont'd											
Menlo Park	32 340	49	100.0	45	640	411.0	50.2	115	1 483	354.3	48.2
Merced	11 678	46	100.0	32	818	1 204.2	35.7	270	4 509	1 057.5	103.5
Milpitas	270 416	1 200	10.6	146	5 498	4 231.2	512.4	312	5 088	993.9	103.3
Mission Viejo	850	2	100.0	117	1 385	598.4	89.7	372	7 291	1 727.6	181.8
Modesto	9 726	62	19.4	108	1 147	1 311.9	52.7	737	12 116	2 599.3	268.2
Monrovia	7 190	34	100.0	82	931	475.8	43.6	135	2 753	907.2	81.3
Montclair	5 196	28	35.7	77	699	257.8	24.1	260	5 046	1 136.0	123.1
Montebello	1 618	11	100.0	106	1 635	759.0	64.7	212	3 782	820.0	80.0
Monterey	799	2	100.0	45	1 701	2 172.2	94.1	227	2 684	512.9	70.4
Monterey Park	9 170	31	87.1	228	1 354	653.7	47.5	222	1 937	477.2	41.1
Moorpark	67 704	178	100.0	54	731	401.8	34.6	60	1 013	192.8	20.3
Moreno Valley	12 681	46	100.0	30	147	62.1	5.5	310	5 564	1 853.2	129.5
Morgan Hill	88 145	342	90.9	63	2 221	1 332.4	144.7	112	1 584	418.3	40.2
Mountain View	128 665	669	15.8	125	3 295	2 750.6	373.0	262	4 609	1 290.1	131.9
Murrieta	35 975	280	5.7	79	409	238.2	19.1	229	4 293	1 073.7	98.0
Napa	13 167	80	31.3	67	557	302.7	28.3	324	4 411	1 129.0	116.3
National City	26 312	128	11.7	96	940	946.4	43.8	322	5 688	1 483.3	150.3
Newark	9 292	26	100.0	57	1 734	755.4	79.0	195	3 705	781.8	76.5
Newport Beach	84 339	127	66.1	224	2 091	2 564.4	174.1	467	7 369	2 614.3	250.3
Norco	394	1	100.0	28	244	123.5	8.6	98	1 659	521.0	51.1
Norwalk	264	1	100.0	85	769	385.1	31.9	163	3 410	1 160.4	98.5
Novato	44 221	258	34.9	87	1 259	596.3	90.1	188	2 919	969.4	90.4
Oakland	49 131	257	31.5	424	5 473	3 541.5	277.3	1 099	11 176	2 987.1	314.0
Oakley	23 863	73	100.0	8	D	D	D	49	499	141.3	12.0
Oceanside	28 163	86	100.0	144	1 516	502.5	54.4	400	6 645	1 688.3	159.2
Ontario	45 594	438	30.1	596	12 375	13 263.9	539.7	583	10 441	3 160.6	268.2
Orange	29 261	349	2.0	349	4 806	6 253.9	253.2	608	7 997	2 101.9	211.0
Oxnard	70 849	502	14.1	193	4 187	2 837.6	207.0	458	7 877	2 348.6	212.2
Pacifica	1 155	4	100.0	8	D	D	D	65	663	177.5	15.9
Palmdale	7 899	42	100.0	34	259	51.3	8.1	314	7 319	1 670.4	163.2
Palm Desert	89 997	304	68.4	76	559	195.2	23.0	472	6 874	1 538.1	163.9
Palm Springs	58 846	203	95.6	50	249	106.3	10.8	222	2 753	643.7	71.4
Palo Alto	53 294	91	95.6	70	941	1 584.9	64.0	340	5 719	1 535.7	182.6
Paradise	5 065	22	100.0	6	17	6.1	0.6	83	878	168.5	19.7
Paramount	1 147	5	100.0	239	1 965	1 163.4	79.6	120	1 710	423.9	42.3
Pasadena	125 479	684	2.2	150	D	D	D	652	10 857	2 707.8	280.7
Perris	19 398	200	59.5	15	234	78.2	9.6	79	2 638	537.3	61.0
Petaluma	19 005	159	9.4	100	1 460	795.8	110.7	289	3 803	947.3	104.1
Pico Rivera	941	4	100.0	108	2 268	1 218.7	90.6	116	2 611	927.7	55.6
Pittsburg	48 231	217	100.0	33	398	217.9	21.3	123	2 535	650.0	69.6
Placentia	10 203	47	78.7	128	1 105	480.1	55.3	104	1 354	384.5	38.6
Pleasant Hill	741	2	100.0	26	146	113.8	9.1	140	2 472	510.8	54.8
Pleasanton	80 572	333	23.4	138	2 228	3 957.5	172.4	355	6 810	1 605.1	179.6
Pomona	7 658	39	89.7	302	3 199	1 629.7	139.6	291	4 139	1 102.6	100.4
Porterville	26 052	280	11.4	23	140	44.6	5.5	158	2 448	540.1	56.2
Poway	9 623	19	100.0	106	2 104	1 444.6	146.8	147	3 097	1 002.8	90.6
Rancho Cordova	55 807	222	74.8	102	1 053	453.8	56.8	191	2 828	543.9	68.7
Rancho Cucamonga	67 384	261	97.7	292	3 728	3 078.3	170.4	444	8 301	1 803.6	175.4
Rancho Palos Verdes	3 210	8	100.0	33	119	123.8	6.1	56	481	112.6	11.0
Rancho Santa Marga-rita	0	0	0.0	68	622	345.4	32.1	86	2 005	608.4	54.1
Redding	24 102	112	100.0	129	1 429	724.2	58.5	500	7 820	1 953.9	199.2
Redlands	15 598	67	86.6	49	650	174.7	25.1	253	5 303	1 581.1	133.4
Redondo Beach	34 381	102	100.0	63	295	102.2	12.6	303	4 570	815.7	101.6
Redwood City	168 414	781	1.3	73	1 243	1 189.7	114.5	245	4 925	1 613.7	175.2
Rialto	5 903	28	85.7	47	698	766.6	38.3	130	2 420	524.4	52.7
Richmond	1 749	8	100.0	94	1 871	1 127.9	94.9	261	4 139	1 024.6	103.5
Ridgecrest	954	8	100.0	6	33	12.0	1.6	96	1 442	298.2	32.1
Riverside	70 655	315	73.0	312	5 066	2 854.9	229.3	922	16 855	4 757.5	439.1
Rocklin	110 269	408	72.8	71	1 433	855.4	88.0	142	1 927	545.9	60.0
Rohnert Park	2 464	32	0.0	31	476	225.3	24.0	114	2 220	610.8	57.4
Rosemead	1 120	4	100.0	113	447	220.5	11.1	172	2 201	453.9	42.0
Roseville	171 031	809	79.7	107	2 175	2 233.8	109.0	549	13 868	3 923.2	372.1
Sacramento	60 400	281	91.1	488	9 008	8 940.1	402.1	1 282	20 067	4 307.5	486.9
Salinas	10 784	66	45.5	159	2 031	1 588.9	111.7	507	7 654	1 933.2	194.9
San Bernardino	31 845	115	82.6	142	2 655	2 265.4	96.8	592	10 661	2 845.1	268.5
San Bruno	0	0	0.0	23	224	340.5	9.9	133	2 403	512.7	53.7
San Buenaventura (Ven-tura)	11 532	96	32.3	179	1 885	747.8	91.9	568	7 907	1 980.7	201.9
San Carlos	1 420	2	100.0	101	933	455.6	55.6	148	1 669	494.5	51.8
San Clemente	43 713	103	62.1	162	2 010	914.9	107.7	197	2 185	580.7	56.7
San Diego	524 088	2 743	26.0	1 902	33 209	21 927.7	3 017.4	4 368	65 695	16 525.8	1 687.8
San Dimas	642	2	100.0	81	570	371.3	25.4	116	2 583	542.0	53.3

1. Merchant wholesalers except manufacturers' sales branches and offices. 2. Establishments with payroll.

City	Real estate and rental and leasing, 2007: Number of establishments	Number of employees	Receipts (mil dol)	Annual payroll (mil dol)	Professional, scientific, and technical services,[1] 2007: Number of establishments	Number of employees	Receipts (mil dol)	Annual payroll (mil dol)	Manufacturing, 2007: Number of establishments	Number of employees	Receipts (mil dol)	Annual payroll (mil dol)
	80	81	82	83	84	85	86	87	88	89	90	91
CALIFORNIA—Cont'd												
Menlo Park	95	454	126.4	21.7	307	D	D	D	60	3 102	1 095.0	191.9
Merced	69	374	50.3	9.8	103	D	D	D	35	1 979	605.7	81.5
Milpitas	88	520	167.2	13.8	220	D	D	D	179	16 051	4 831.9	1 432.6
Mission Viejo	186	884	233.6	43.4	408	1 545	232.4	84.2	61	1 038	548.0	66.0
Modesto	235	1 251	245.9	39.0	445	D	D	D	97	6 161	2 924.1	326.1
Monrovia	51	522	106.1	36.3	142	1 940	373.2	132.3	112	2 832	501.9	119.4
Montclair	41	191	38.1	6.3	34	214	17.8	6.7	83	999	177.7	36.4
Montebello	74	524	133.6	20.7	70	983	75.6	18.0	102	6 193	955.2	244.4
Monterey	98	592	79.0	17.6	260	D	D	D	49	836	152.3	38.4
Monterey Park	82	747	59.0	16.7	174	D	D	D	47	895	165.8	35.9
Moorpark	23	102	22.5	4.4	94	318	59.1	17.1	58	3 026	661.5	128.9
Moreno Valley	80	334	73.9	9.5	79	590	37.4	15.2	21	1 255	248.5	45.0
Morgan Hill	82	215	59.0	9.7	145	3 503	132.1	56.7	93	3 607	922.0	216.8
Mountain View	137	738	159.6	27.2	541	15 440	3 164.0	1 548.6	148	6 514	1 751.4	430.6
Murrieta	128	373	72.4	13.9	185	700	92.0	34.9	69	914	124.9	32.5
Napa	99	419	69.7	13.8	247	D	D	D	112	3 299	D	177.9
National City	59	339	76.2	11.0	62	546	42.4	16.1	93	2 215	332.1	78.7
Newark	42	D	D	D	111	1 979	496.8	184.0	78	3 754	954.3	196.3
Newport Beach	702	6 702	3 369.6	519.1	1 294	D	D	D	92	3 369	495.2	167.2
Norco	34	154	25.2	5.3	59	1 004	97.8	35.7	34	630	81.0	28.8
Norwalk	62	364	58.3	10.6	68	D	D	D	60	990	188.2	33.9
Novato	113	721	95.0	23.1	266	D	D	D	57	515	99.6	24.4
Oakland	475	2 942	763.2	112.0	1 442	14 607	2 039.2	1 104.7	407	8 970	1 797.7	387.0
Oakley	20	62	14.0	2.8	24	110	10.7	3.3	NA	NA	NA	NA
Oceanside	163	823	142.3	21.8	297	1 217	134.4	44.5	171	3 973	698.2	138.2
Ontario	194	1 535	680.8	72.8	246	D	D	D	443	17 492	4 945.1	655.4
Orange	299	2 198	485.8	100.3	741	D	D	D	294	8 054	1 721.4	334.9
Oxnard	148	672	128.8	24.9	224	D	D	D	185	11 928	3 490.0	567.8
Pacifica	31	80	14.0	2.1	64	218	30.7	10.3	NA	NA	NA	NA
Palmdale	119	591	66.0	10.5	109	1 048	171.5	53.7	44	5 026	1 277.9	342.5
Palm Desert	180	780	159.4	33.1	312	D	D	D	NA	NA	NA	NA
Palm Springs	151	850	167.7	22.9	186	767	125.7	38.9	32	737	D	D
Palo Alto	193	1 215	917.6	104.4	775	12 475	3 061.8	1 523.5	72	6 530	2 767.7	496.3
Paradise	35	224	16.6	4.5	34	118	10.0	2.7	NA	NA	NA	NA
Paramount	31	231	28.4	6.2	37	251	23.7	8.6	228	4 847	1 554.7	226.4
Pasadena	322	1 812	421.8	93.7	1 182	D	D	D	104	1 467	327.1	71.2
Perris	30	189	34.3	5.7	24	97	14.9	4.4	40	2 894	462.4	104.2
Petaluma	93	463	83.4	17.5	214	D	D	D	115	4 248	1 213.7	206.5
Pico Rivera	45	244	40.6	7.3	34	219	23.7	6.4	77	1 631	434.7	62.4
Pittsburg	39	308	43.7	11.9	46	297	29.6	10.7	45	2 112	1 526.5	138.0
Placentia	59	285	58.0	9.7	115	534	63.6	23.0	134	2 644	478.8	103.9
Pleasant Hill	63	265	78.6	14.8	149	723	109.2	41.5	NA	NA	NA	NA
Pleasanton	189	1 017	360.2	45.0	528	5 335	958.7	409.3	89	2 608	590.2	159.2
Pomona	87	640	125.3	21.7	125	D	D	D	244	7 424	1 829.3	264.4
Porterville	37	124	22.6	3.0	50	229	18.5	5.2	24	1 117	243.3	34.7
Poway	93	490	69.6	19.0	253	1 756	253.1	106.7	103	5 111	1 317.6	256.8
Rancho Cordova	86	470	71.5	16.5	207	D	D	D	93	5 233	1 016.2	296.5
Rancho Cucamonga	235	1 170	244.9	43.5	371	D	D	D	266	9 878	3 182.4	409.2
Rancho Palos Verdes	66	D	D	D	140	1 012	98.3	47.0	NA	NA	NA	NA
Rancho Santa Margarita	72	368	52.3	15.4	197	D	D	D	48	1 846	544.8	100.0
Redding	155	795	90.3	18.3	310	D	D	D	84	929	172.1	34.4
Redlands	99	460	87.2	14.0	214	D	D	D	53	1 234	194.3	42.5
Redondo Beach	117	340	66.6	12.0	298	D	D	D	37	D	D	D
Redwood City	121	915	184.8	37.6	412	D	D	D	79	3 813	985.3	214.3
Rialto	47	190	33.9	5.1	36	225	16.4	7.0	75	2 720	596.0	98.3
Richmond	84	431	85.6	13.3	122	D	D	D	121	4 313	D	250.1
Ridgecrest	22	118	14.9	2.9	56	826	96.7	40.9	NA	NA	NA	NA
Riverside	334	1 953	402.7	66.4	636	D	D	D	303	9 480	2 569.9	380.9
Rocklin	77	D	D	D	156	1 485	242.8	86.0	38	710	143.4	27.8
Rohnert Park	52	320	52.9	14.3	66	403	40.0	18.5	44	968	194.9	45.1
Rosemead	32	99	13.5	2.5	68	278	26.2	7.7	59	1 038	191.4	30.1
Roseville	235	2 824	473.3	103.0	467	4 209	671.5	243.5	69	4 969	2 114.7	176.5
Sacramento	591	4 017	687.3	181.3	1 766	D	D	D	388	11 961	3 985.5	442.8
Salinas	132	613	152.1	18.8	221	D	D	D	102	3 523	1 232.1	124.9
San Bernardino	143	704	112.9	20.1	264	D	D	D	131	3 008	837.0	115.1
San Bruno	33	284	35.7	8.3	69	509	93.1	46.5	NA	NA	NA	NA
San Buenaventura (Ventura)	196	1 134	168.1	32.7	493	D	D	D	162	2 579	457.1	108.9
San Carlos	74	271	74.3	14.4	216	D	D	D	121	2 443	846.7	134.7
San Clemente	122	486	449.9	34.6	372	1 843	270.9	112.3	97	1 844	431.5	86.3
San Diego	2 902	20 071	4 600.7	905.2	7 038	90 341	15 331.3	6 345.2	1 213	45 502	12 989.0	2 520.1
San Dimas	67	560	70.5	14.1	144	1 959	343.6	94.5	85	1 805	1 850.9	74.6

1. Establishments subject to federal tax.

Table D. Cities — **Accommodation and Food Services, Arts, Entertainment, and Recreation, and Health Care and Social Assistance**

City	Accommodation and food services, 2007				Arts, entertainment, and recreation,[1] 2007				Health care and social assistance,[1] 2007			
	Number of establish-ments	Number of employees	Sales (mil dol)	Annual payroll (mil dol)	Number of establish-ments	Number of employees	Receipts (mil dol)	Annual payroll (mil dol)	Number of establish-ments	Number of employees	Receipts (mil dol)	Annual payroll (mil dol)
	92	93	94	95	96	97	98	99	100	101	102	103
CALIFORNIA—Cont'd												
Menlo Park	96	1 375	92.0	28.9	21	112	10.0	3.4	111	910	94.0	43.0
Merced	139	2 582	104.9	26.4	9	D	D	D	241	2 195	218.1	80.2
Milpitas	259	4 520	278.8	76.6	23	D	D	D	173	1 390	227.8	62.0
Mission Viejo	187	2 980	148.4	42.3	25	D	D	D	397	D	D	D
Modesto	416	7 813	338.5	95.4	30	585	27.3	7.9	616	10 051	1 245.5	477.3
Monrovia	92	1 770	91.1	25.6	19	D	D	D	75	1 045	155.8	77.7
Montclair	89	1 881	84.3	23.9	5	D	D	D	81	1 379	131.1	52.6
Montebello	124	1 796	97.0	25.0	7	D	D	D	172	D	D	D
Monterey	216	5 359	374.3	113.1	23	D	D	D	277	D	D	D
Monterey Park	162	2 162	109.3	30.2	6	D	D	D	250	3 310	428.0	144.2
Moorpark	51	951	47.0	13.8	11	154	8.9	3.4	25	D	D	D
Moreno Valley	200	3 684	176.0	48.0	9	D	D	D	203	1 559	154.2	54.7
Morgan Hill	103	1 292	70.2	20.0	11	D	D	D	78	D	D	D
Mountain View	278	3 796	275.1	71.6	25	278	30.8	6.1	290	D	D	D
Murrieta	142	2 097	96.1	27.1	28	D	D	D	189	D	D	D
Napa	176	3 429	213.4	63.2	19	265	12.2	3.6	241	2 343	295.7	117.4
National City	175	2 429	132.9	32.8	6	96	8.7	1.9	136	1 301	117.5	38.0
Newark	139	1 956	113.3	30.4	4	D	D	D	65	351	40.5	13.4
Newport Beach	354	10 889	695.8	219.1	99	1 175	123.8	38.7	777	D	D	D
Norco	75	1 125	57.5	14.8	6	D	D	D	32	272	26.0	9.8
Norwalk	137	1 805	89.4	22.3	7	327	11.0	3.8	125	D	D	D
Novato	115	1 834	93.0	26.6	21	D	D	D	146	1 267	174.3	65.0
Oakland	826	11 240	749.5	200.1	77	1 953	350.4	203.5	892	11 401	1 454.0	755.9
Oakley	24	295	15.4	3.5	6	D	D	D	18	D	D	D
Oceanside	294	4 866	243.4	66.3	36	862	57.4	16.3	249	2 099	232.3	78.5
Ontario	309	7 496	417.5	112.7	29	547	45.5	11.0	181	2 562	232.1	86.0
Orange	364	7 252	390.7	102.7	47	D	D	D	603	7 938	945.9	402.6
Oxnard	266	4 962	225.8	58.4	28	542	38.4	11.1	391	3 732	404.5	151.1
Pacifica	70	667	37.1	9.5	11	121	4.6	1.4	40	D	D	D
Palmdale	177	3 649	181.9	50.5	14	D	D	D	158	1 293	128.1	45.3
Palm Desert	196	5 865	321.5	98.0	34	1 171	88.1	27.9	193	1 730	186.4	66.9
Palm Springs	252	4 927	298.3	88.8	31	1 398	221.0	36.7	244	4 290	633.4	200.8
Palo Alto	271	5 585	348.6	107.0	24	458	18.4	6.6	333	D	D	D
Paradise	44	546	21.4	6.7	7	D	D	D	99	D	D	D
Paramount	80	706	41.8	9.6	3	29	2.1	0.5	83	D	D	D
Pasadena	449	10 635	623.8	182.1	137	1 009	107.9	40.3	720	9 243	1 140.8	431.9
Perris	62	906	52.7	11.4	5	D	D	D	40	256	35.6	14.1
Petaluma	169	2 351	132.5	36.0	31	D	D	D	174	1 602	195.5	63.8
Pico Rivera	105	1 467	81.5	20.7	3	D	D	D	73	867	68.2	25.9
Pittsburg	82	1 331	69.9	18.6	3	D	D	D	65	576	48.0	22.1
Placentia	106	1 359	74.3	18.0	9	D	D	D	99	1 365	130.9	51.6
Pleasant Hill	80	1 507	89.3	23.0	15	184	11.5	4.3	109	1 173	88.0	34.7
Pleasanton	230	4 001	242.3	67.8	35	827	59.3	22.5	257	2 449	436.5	135.5
Pomona	202	3 080	165.7	43.7	15	D	D	D	261	3 419	318.8	119.2
Porterville	77	1 176	48.8	13.6	6	D	D	D	132	1 451	113.3	41.5
Poway	109	1 692	81.7	21.8	30	D	D	D	139	D	D	D
Rancho Cordova	136	1 756	95.5	23.6	11	164	9.2	2.1	84	D	D	D
Rancho Cucamonga	315	6 865	341.0	94.7	32	D	D	D	285	3 533	296.7	109.6
Rancho Palos Verdes	53	D	D	D	12	D	D	D	99	D	D	D
Rancho Santa Margarita	90	1 795	86.1	25.3	23	D	D	D	94	D	D	D
Redding	256	4 780	220.6	59.6	24	D	D	D	467	4 993	487.2	188.5
Redlands	173	3 330	160.5	45.8	22	D	D	D	242	2 509	353.7	106.8
Redondo Beach	188	3 470	196.2	57.0	39	D	D	D	184	1 080	187.4	53.8
Redwood City	226	3 120	214.5	58.0	24	550	33.7	10.5	249	2 861	454.6	206.5
Rialto	96	1 424	68.7	18.1	6	D	D	D	100	967	65.3	24.6
Richmond	128	1 199	64.5	16.6	24	D	D	D	137	2 358	292.7	133.4
Ridgecrest	55	897	45.5	12.1	4	D	D	D	51	D	D	D
Riverside	531	9 412	456.5	129.8	61	830	46.3	12.1	693	11 292	1 314.8	526.5
Rocklin	104	1 631	71.4	21.0	15	D	D	D	119	D	D	D
Rohnert Park	97	1 862	94.9	26.5	13	D	D	D	77	708	81.4	23.3
Rosemead	130	1 733	87.6	24.2	5	130	17.5	2.8	109	D	D	D
Roseville	333	7 021	344.2	97.8	31	839	38.5	11.7	377	5 257	807.8	302.2
Sacramento	1 055	19 705	1 021.4	294.9	90	2 939	327.9	106.1	1 025	13 515	1 875.7	756.7
Salinas	268	3 602	190.0	49.7	12	160	16.9	3.2	289	2 817	332.7	125.4
San Bernardino	343	6 514	330.5	87.1	27	D	D	D	356	4 923	421.0	165.9
San Bruno	104	1 427	83.3	23.0	7	D	D	D	66	648	112.5	26.5
San Buenaventura (Ventura)	333	5 799	309.8	87.1	50	764	41.5	11.6	442	3 917	406.7	162.4
San Carlos	87	919	57.2	16.5	8	10	1.6	0.4	90	523	46.9	17.7
San Clemente	158	2 374	122.4	31.1	28	D	D	D	185	981	111.1	37.6
San Diego	3 345	77 459	5 154.5	1 402.6	422	9 206	988.9	403.7	3 258	34 412	4 510.9	1 730.2
San Dimas	69	1 208	64.7	15.1	12	261	31.8	6.6	100	D	D	D

1. Establishments subject to federal tax.

City	Other services[1], 2007				Government employment and payroll, 2012								
						March payroll							
							Percent of total for:						
	Number of establishments	Number of employees	Receipts (mil dol)	Annual payroll (mil dol)	Full-time equivalent employees	Total (dollars)	Administration, judicial, and legal	Police and Corrections	Fire Protection	Highways and transportation	Health and welfare	Natural resources and utilities	Education and libraries
	104	105	106	107	108	109	110	111	112	113	114	115	116
CALIFORNIA—Cont'd													
Menlo Park	60	D	D	D	265	1 760 354	14.1	39.6	0.0	11.5	2.4	17.6	6.2
Merced	67	343	28.9	8.7	442	2 547 548	11.6	31.0	16.4	3.0	2.2	22.9	0.0
Milpitas	99	1 017	172.5	35.0	391	3 312 573	25.8	33.3	22.1	4.4	1.1	10.0	0.0
Mission Viejo	156	972	89.8	24.5	180	959 036	31.7	0.0	0.0	15.3	6.3	22.8	18.2
Modesto	258	1 621	130.7	38.0	1 217	6 592 366	14.4	32.0	18.1	7.5	1.5	23.8	0.0
Monrovia	70	465	71.3	11.1	256	1 668 764	17.2	33.0	27.7	1.5	3.1	13.2	3.5
Montclair	76	D	D	D	251	1 296 597	25.0	33.8	17.4	1.8	13.1	5.5	0.0
Montebello	90	694	48.6	16.3	486	2 561 705	6.5	30.7	19.8	32.0	1.1	6.0	0.0
Monterey	60	484	31.3	11.5	506	3 399 804	0.1	18.1	19.6	2.7	1.3	10.8	4.3
Monterey Park	72	D	D	D	327	1 888 775	11.2	36.1	23.6	5.9	0.0	17.1	5.2
Moorpark	16	110	8.9	2.8	67	465 036	35.0	0.0	0.0	14.4	20.2	30.4	0.0
Moreno Valley	120	619	43.7	12.6	743	3 360 444	15.3	2.0	2.4	17.1	12.4	15.5	1.9
Morgan Hill	66	341	35.2	10.8	182	1 516 788	12.8	39.9	0.0	2.3	1.1	25.1	0.0
Mountain View	154	944	113.8	32.0	600	5 229 873	11.3	28.6	21.6	9.3	5.2	17.2	4.4
Murrieta	143	862	78.0	21.9	339	2 066 931	19.5	46.2	23.2	0.5	0.0	6.5	3.4
Napa	127	681	64.3	22.7	431	3 308 340	12.4	30.1	19.6	7.4	8.5	18.7	0.0
National City	119	698	60.9	20.3	361	2 077 359	8.6	42.0	20.4	3.0	4.5	9.8	7.3
Newark	61	D	D	D	169	764 266	14.7	51.1	0.0	5.4	1.7	15.4	0.0
Newport Beach	197	1 320	115.4	33.3	797	6 997 470	14.3	26.3	21.3	6.9	1.1	16.5	4.6
Norco	54	309	38.1	8.2	81	317 544	33.7	2.4	2.2	9.4	11.1	25.1	0.0
Norwalk	67	338	30.9	7.9	339	1 671 145	18.7	10.3	0.0	35.5	8.6	18.6	0.0
Novato	91	671	86.1	28.5	190	1 241 125	11.4	43.9	0.0	18.8	2.5	18.0	0.0
Oakland	600	3 665	318.9	93.0	3 940	30 153 764	10.1	31.4	20.4	17.1	7.7	5.5	3.1
Oakley	22	D	D	D	26	121 823	56.5	10.1	0.0	3.7	0.0	20.3	0.0
Oceanside	184	1 195	100.1	30.5	950	5 925 758	16.2	36.9	16.2	3.6	4.4	18.2	2.3
Ontario	212	2 110	192.3	62.0	1 078	8 143 877	8.3	39.1	22.6	0.5	2.8	14.8	2.5
Orange	289	1 813	158.1	43.5	662	5 240 608	10.8	40.5	25.9	5.9	1.0	10.0	3.4
Oxnard	179	947	91.2	24.9	1 267	7 972 661	9.1	36.5	12.3	4.2	8.3	23.4	2.6
Pacifica	36	127	10.8	3.2	186	1 351 528	12.4	28.8	17.8	10.7	2.1	16.8	0.0
Palmdale	109	615	48.4	12.0	315	1 381 568	13.7	8.9	0.0	20.8	15.6	20.9	2.9
Palm Desert	118	796	54.3	17.7	122	957 854	30.8	0.0	0.0	28.3	24.5	7.0	0.0
Palm Springs	76	372	29.7	9.6	513	3 307 054	15.7	33.0	17.9	11.3	2.5	5.4	3.1
Palo Alto	102	974	86.7	30.2	921	7 610 093	16.4	17.4	16.0	3.9	0.9	38.7	3.0
Paradise	37	121	13.5	3.0	88	528 134	9.9	38.1	34.1	5.6	8.4	2.9	0.0
Paramount	65	684	80.6	26.6	210	830 396	17.7	15.7	0.0	19.4	8.9	20.4	0.0
Pasadena	305	2 180	374.8	77.3	1 821	13 044 662	12.2	21.1	13.6	1.9	4.8	27.1	0.2
Perris	29	D	D	D	76	396 603	36.6	0.0	0.0	22.9	32.0	8.5	0.0
Petaluma	104	543	48.1	15.2	301	2 362 449	10.3	35.7	22.9	9.0	1.1	20.1	0.0
Pico Rivera	69	685	56.6	17.2	288	1 134 401	19.4	0.0	0.0	28.7	11.6	40.3	0.0
Pittsburg	61	347	31.0	9.1	267	1 784 475	10.5	44.3	0.0	7.0	2.9	12.6	0.0
Placentia	69	419	32.3	9.7	175	1 008 861	10.4	58.5	0.0	7.4	1.7	17.6	0.0
Pleasant Hill	43	281	20.5	5.9	125	907 055	21.9	52.8	0.0	22.8	2.3	0.0	0.0
Pleasanton	133	834	91.4	29.9	509	4 073 003	13.7	23.1	30.7	5.5	2.2	14.7	4.4
Pomona	148	923	85.0	25.4	630	2 988 643	8.4	51.9	0.0	5.9	6.3	15.1	2.8
Porterville	38	230	17.0	10.4	323	1 445 053	12.8	29.5	14.5	7.6	0.7	28.3	2.8
Poway	91	562	43.2	13.0	291	1 821 500	20.9	0.0	28.9	10.0	4.0	27.1	0.0
Rancho Cordova	79	394	34.9	11.2	67	438 835	46.2	0.0	0.0	25.2	6.1	0.0	0.0
Rancho Cucamonga	209	1 245	150.7	37.9	639	3 536 504	13.7	0.0	32.8	6.4	4.3	31.3	5.3
Rancho Palos Verdes	31	221	31.6	9.1	69	423 058	29.0	0.0	0.0	13.7	0.0	30.2	0.0
Rancho Santa Margarita	47	408	27.7	8.1	27	142 356	100.0	0.0	0.0	0.0	0.0	0.0	0.0
Redding	195	1 095	90.5	27.9	747	5 047 088	9.6	20.1	14.2	8.9	1.6	42.2	0.0
Redlands	102	606	42.2	12.8	429	2 798 020	10.0	32.4	23.6	5.8	1.1	19.2	3.1
Redondo Beach	124	846	145.3	28.7	980	23 723 684	11.5	36.3	24.3	11.4	4.1	9.3	3.2
Redwood City	123	1 049	247.6	43.6	543	4 492 820	13.2	30.5	20.6	0.0	1.1	19.6	6.0
Rialto	73	331	41.5	9.9	357	2 259 378	9.8	38.9	27.3	6.1	4.1	10.2	0.0
Richmond	86	406	45.6	13.2	843	5 538 248	8.5	38.6	12.2	3.0	6.2	8.4	4.2
Ridgecrest	30	150	11.8	3.3	106	565 833	18.2	47.9	0.0	13.3	4.0	14.5	0.0
Riverside	396	2 521	214.2	67.0	2 260	15 114 251	6.2	28.2	15.6	5.5	4.5	29.8	1.6
Rocklin	72	D	D	D	287	1 697 873	10.7	35.7	20.8	8.4	6.6	17.7	0.0
Rohnert Park	50	299	26.6	7.9	176	1 106 615	17.8	57.7	0.0	0.0	1.6	22.9	0.0
Rosemead	92	374	30.7	6.8	102	521 909	25.8	14.7	0.0	10.3	10.6	24.2	0.0
Roseville	172	D	D	D	1 160	7 733 037	12.9	18.3	15.7	2.8	2.2	35.9	2.0
Sacramento	627	4 186	392.7	116.6	4 483	29 508 935	6.7	46.8	16.2	10.8	3.9	15.6	0.0
Salinas	157	1 027	103.9	28.1	553	3 536 035	7.9	43.0	21.0	11.8	4.5	3.6	5.1
San Bernardino	209	1 287	113.9	31.6	1 527	9 251 817	6.8	36.8	22.6	1.2	6.6	19.6	1.2
San Bruno	56	259	31.4	9.4	262	1 918 097	12.9	28.0	20.2	5.7	0.5	17.9	6.2
San Buenaventura (Ventura)	194	1 086	104.6	29.4	659	4 241 287	13.8	29.9	21.1	8.7	1.1	23.0	0.0
San Carlos	95	778	71.7	26.6	99	739 930	23.5	0.0	27.1	4.5	4.5	27.8	0.0
San Clemente	86	454	34.0	9.5	220	909 552	22.8	0.0	0.0	23.9	7.3	44.4	0.0
San Diego	1 982	13 678	1 183.4	360.3	9 425	62 476 850	19.9	28.7	13.9	2.4	0.3	25.5	2.3
San Dimas	55	D	D	D	106	558 552	25.6	0.0	0.0	20.9	21.8	31.7	0.0

1. Establishments subject to federal tax.

City	City government finances, 2007									
	General revenue							General expenditure		
		Intergovernmental		Taxes					Per capita[1] (dollars)	
					Per capita[1] (dollars)					
	Total (mil dol)	Total (mil dol)	Percent from state government	Total (mil dol)	Total	Property	Sales and gross receipts	Total (mil dol)	Total	Capital outlays
	117	118	119	120	121	122	123	124	125	126
CALIFORNIA—Cont'd										
Menlo Park	57.5	3.5	90.3	37.8	1 149	690	444	61.2	1 859	334
Merced	96.3	17.9	51.3	32.3	401	192	205	102.4	1 271	255
Milpitas	117.5	7.2	69.9	80.2	1 162	727	430	122.5	1 776	418
Mission Viejo	74.4	7.3	60.1	55.9	588	365	219	78.4	825	168
Modesto	229.0	48.3	51.3	90.4	440	167	270	226.5	1 101	147
Monrovia	51.2	2.2	84.3	38.6	1 042	714	321	56.5	1 525	198
Montclair	47.1	5.3	94.7	33.5	892	526	363	50.6	1 346	152
Montebello	97.7	20.3	71.7	57.3	904	479	394	66.8	1 053	70
Monterey	96.6	3.5	87.7	44.7	1 575	505	1 065	99.9	3 520	328
Monterey Park	60.2	3.6	69.4	41.1	674	471	200	56.7	929	44
Moorpark	30.0	1.5	80.3	17.5	500	296	187	35.7	1 021	81
Moreno Valley	147.5	17.1	68.1	88.6	446	252	192	166.7	838	157
Morgan Hill	67.3	2.7	96.6	37.9	960	628	229	61.1	1 548	436
Mountain View	174.0	5.3	63.1	102.5	1 337	778	411	183.3	2 392	549
Murrieta	80.7	26.1	46.3	39.0	366	220	142	83.1	780	255
Napa	110.6	18.2	18.2	57.4	732	363	365	117.8	1 502	144
National City	79.9	19.2	23.1	47.7	801	407	387	70.4	1 183	258
Newark	41.0	2.5	91.0	33.4	766	334	424	40.3	924	81
Newport Beach	200.4	9.9	61.5	127.8	1 472	878	579	233.0	2 684	829
Norco	33.0	2.3	44.5	21.6	787	582	187	36.0	1 314	451
Norwalk	85.6	27.5	48.8	49.4	464	166	296	67.8	637	38
Novato	49.0	2.3	100.0	35.6	669	475	189	48.6	913	211
Oakland	1 343.3	204.3	54.6	570.6	1 420	810	448	1 312.4	3 266	765
Oakley	29.3	2.8	84.6	16.7	447	271	122	25.9	696	242
Oceanside	233.9	38.0	49.7	106.3	620	416	200	212.9	1 241	113
Ontario	317.2	21.8	84.9	172.3	1 031	570	459	290.2	1 736	274
Orange	142.3	16.7	75.8	101.3	726	444	279	160.6	1 151	284
Oxnard	312.9	40.3	93.9	115.8	575	339	234	320.7	1 592	328
Pacifica	41.0	2.7	100.0	20.9	544	352	188	44.4	1 157	119
Palmdale	135.7	21.8	54.2	85.7	550	380	156	117.3	753	85
Palm Desert	168.1	3.9	64.2	125.5	2 515	1 931	574	156.3	3 132	538
Palm Springs	141.9	13.2	18.3	76.2	1 662	780	860	157.5	3 436	660
Palo Alto	217.5	3.5	57.6	84.1	1 269	530	666	250.9	3 789	623
Paradise	16.8	4.1	95.7	11.0	420	262	156	14.4	551	19
Paramount	37.4	3.7	65.3	29.9	546	300	244	36.2	660	87
Pasadena	411.2	38.8	79.2	194.6	1 402	638	686	403.1	2 905	429
Perris	49.1	3.7	86.4	26.8	376	223	151	54.9	770	150
Petaluma	90.6	5.2	59.0	46.6	792	514	263	83.8	1 424	233
Pico Rivera	61.1	23.1	28.9	26.9	422	222	200	71.3	1 118	307
Pittsburg	89.1	17.2	34.3	46.4	708	555	146	101.3	1 544	207
Placentia	41.3	4.4	89.2	26.6	512	274	225	39.0	750	113
Pleasant Hill	28.8	3.6	100.0	22.5	664	309	316	29.7	877	199
Pleasanton	134.8	6.1	84.2	81.3	1 125	737	334	130.6	1 807	174
Pomona	196.5	41.6	62.7	104.5	692	386	299	201.6	1 334	134
Porterville	49.1	8.8	73.5	21.3	387	135	246	51.3	933	177
Poway	88.7	1.8	88.7	67.5	1 375	1 096	258	85.0	1 731	191
Rancho Cordova	68.7	14.0	40.7	44.1	660	234	422	65.9	985	308
Rancho Cucamonga	230.6	19.5	59.9	162.0	950	784	163	207.7	1 218	193
Rancho Palos Verdes	29.2	1.6	88.9	24.4	577	282	294	28.5	673	66
Rancho Santa Margarita	16.9	2.4	90.6	13.9	285	143	138	17.3	354	60
Redding	182.1	39.5	29.9	57.9	638	314	302	162.8	1 795	572
Redlands	93.8	3.7	75.1	56.2	805	451	352	85.8	1 228	162
Redondo Beach	117.9	8.1	72.6	58.6	867	423	419	113.6	1 680	108
Redwood City	145.3	7.3	85.5	81.5	1 028	589	431	149.2	1 881	250
Rialto	107.1	8.8	38.5	65.0	639	365	273	111.4	1 095	208
Richmond	254.5	35.4	49.7	151.0	1 416	681	645	274.3	2 573	398
Ridgecrest	21.9	1.1	90.4	15.8	556	343	211	20.8	736	131
Riverside	410.7	63.1	60.7	197.7	631	327	295	486.0	1 551	356
Rocklin	52.5	5.7	74.5	32.4	549	319	184	53.8	911	89
Rohnert Park	59.0	3.3	100.0	32.1	700	488	289	57.7	1 402	280
Rosemead	34.4	2.8	59.2	25.5	469	313	155	32.2	592	173
Roseville	251.3	19.4	55.2	91.7	738	331	402	243.4	1 960	236
Sacramento	884.8	128.8	66.1	366.7	771	418	342	806.3	1 695	296
Salinas	117.7	16.6	57.5	82.1	532	198	333	122.6	794	103
San Bernardino	250.9	21.3	61.3	132.6	621	311	305	230.8	1 081	128
San Bruno	58.6	3.4	100.0	29.7	704	334	342	51.8	1 228	135
San Buenaventura (Ventura)	132.2	9.8	64.9	71.9	662	319	341	135.5	1 247	155
San Carlos	46.8	1.0	100.0	27.3	933	565	359	38.4	1 315	156
San Clemente	74.5	6.4	93.0	44.4	685	501	177	82.7	1 276	289
San Diego	2 616.7	370.0	40.2	1 122.2	838	439	397	2 361.5	1 763	396
San Dimas	30.5	1.5	86.2	23.3	690	367	317	33.2	982	105

1. Based on population estimated as of July 1 of the year shown.

City	City government finances, 2012 (cont.)									
	General expenditure (cont.)									
	Percent of total for:									
	Public welfare	Highways	Parking facilities	Education	Health and hospitals	Police protection	Sewerage and sanitation	Parks and recreation	Housing and community development	Interest on debt
	127	128	129	130	131	132	133	134	135	136
CALIFORNIA—Cont'd										
Menlo Park	0.0	9.7	2.0	0.0	0.0	23.7	0.7	24.5	5.2	7.1
Merced	0.0	14.7	0.0	0.0	0.2	17.9	21.6	4.9	8.8	3.6
Milpitas	0.0	8.7	0.0	0.0	10.6	17.8	7.2	5.0	24.5	5.9
Mission Viejo	0.0	22.7	0.0	0.0	2.2	20.0	0.0	20.2	7.8	1.5
Modesto	0.0	11.8	0.5	0.3	0.4	20.9	16.0	9.7	4.4	2.0
Monrovia	0.0	4.3	0.0	0.0	3.4	33.5	2.0	4.6	10.1	7.2
Montclair	0.0	8.2	0.0	0.0	8.2	20.5	7.9	8.1	24.7	6.2
Montebello	0.0	6.7	0.0	0.0	0.3	27.9	5.1	15.8	5.7	8.2
Monterey	0.0	11.5	6.8	0.0	0.0	12.8	1.9	15.4	6.0	0.7
Monterey Park	0.0	6.8	0.0	0.0	1.2	26.8	11.0	5.8	9.8	4.7
Moorpark	0.0	11.6	0.0	0.0	1.1	18.2	0.9	12.0	18.3	2.7
Moreno Valley	0.0	19.1	0.0	0.0	1.3	26.1	0.0	9.0	14.2	3.7
Morgan Hill	0.0	10.4	0.0	0.0	0.0	18.6	10.0	10.1	21.8	3.2
Mountain View	0.0	4.2	0.1	0.0	0.0	16.0	15.2	21.1	2.5	1.5
Murrieta	0.0	30.4	0.0	0.0	0.0	29.4	0.0	11.0	5.8	4.3
Napa	0.0	15.7	0.4	0.0	2.6	16.9	17.1	6.9	13.2	1.1
National City	0.0	3.6	0.0	0.0	1.7	30.9	9.9	3.5	23.8	4.2
Newark	0.0	12.0	0.0	0.0	0.6	32.5	0.4	11.1	0.5	1.2
Newport Beach	0.0	13.8	0.0	0.0	2.6	17.7	1.5	10.0	0.0	3.5
Norco	0.0	9.4	0.0	0.0	5.5	12.6	18.0	6.1	16.3	12.3
Norwalk	0.0	12.1	0.7	0.0	7.3	19.7	0.0	10.0	18.0	8.9
Novato	0.0	12.8	0.0	0.0	1.2	25.4	0.0	19.0	6.7	9.6
Oakland	0.0	3.5	0.7	0.0	5.4	14.9	3.4	3.6	9.4	7.2
Oakley	0.0	20.6	0.0	0.0	0.7	28.9	0.0	14.6	12.4	5.7
Oceanside	0.0	7.9	0.8	0.0	0.1	22.7	19.9	6.2	10.5	3.6
Ontario	0.0	7.4	0.0	0.0	0.4	24.6	11.6	5.0	10.1	4.7
Orange	0.0	11.8	0.0	0.0	6.7	23.1	3.8	11.6	10.8	2.7
Oxnard	0.0	12.2	0.3	0.0	0.0	21.3	22.0	10.3	4.4	7.3
Pacifica	0.0	14.4	0.0	0.0	1.7	20.3	20.0	8.3	0.5	4.7
Palmdale	0.0	15.6	0.0	0.0	0.7	16.8	2.5	12.1	20.8	10.5
Palm Desert	0.0	10.2	0.0	0.0	2.6	10.4	0.0	10.7	38.1	11.7
Palm Springs	0.0	15.8	0.3	0.0	0.8	12.8	3.7	14.0	5.4	3.7
Palo Alto	0.0	4.4	0.1	2.9	0.3	13.8	24.8	13.4	0.2	1.9
Paradise	0.0	15.3	0.0	0.0	1.1	27.0	4.7	0.2	1.9	7.0
Paramount	0.0	18.4	0.0	0.0	0.0	29.4	0.0	12.7	10.6	4.9
Pasadena	0.0	6.9	2.7	0.0	4.4	15.8	4.9	10.1	6.4	3.9
Perris	0.0	14.3	0.0	0.0	0.8	20.1	3.8	3.3	23.1	17.7
Petaluma	0.0	9.4	0.0	0.0	1.0	18.2	19.3	5.4	15.3	10.8
Pico Rivera	0.0	35.5	0.0	0.0	0.0	14.1	0.0	10.4	18.0	0.0
Pittsburg	0.0	7.8	0.0	0.0	0.4	18.5	2.0	3.9	33.7	17.9
Placentia	0.0	16.3	0.0	0.0	0.3	28.1	8.9	5.7	6.5	3.6
Pleasant Hill	0.0	29.3	0.0	0.0	0.6	35.4	0.8	0.0	9.2	2.4
Pleasanton	0.0	10.4	0.0	0.0	0.2	18.3	10.1	17.9	1.6	2.7
Pomona	0.0	15.1	0.0	0.0	0.0	20.1	6.5	1.6	23.4	13.4
Porterville	0.0	8.0	0.1	0.0	0.2	15.8	24.2	9.3	3.5	6.2
Poway	0.0	11.2	0.0	0.0	0.4	12.3	9.1	7.3	12.9	15.2
Rancho Cordova	0.0	34.1	0.0	0.0	0.7	24.0	0.0	1.0	7.5	1.7
Rancho Cucamonga	0.0	11.8	0.0	1.1	1.4	12.6	1.6	3.3	19.8	13.7
Rancho Palos Verdes	0.0	21.5	0.0	0.0	0.7	14.0	1.6	11.5	1.2	3.6
Rancho Santa Margarita	0.0	22.7	0.0	0.0	2.1	43.6	0.0	5.7	0.0	3.1
Redding	0.0	8.9	0.0	0.0	0.4	15.2	34.2	5.3	9.1	2.7
Redlands	0.0	5.8	0.0	0.0	5.2	24.9	19.0	6.7	5.8	3.4
Redondo Beach	0.0	6.3	0.0	0.0	4.0	24.5	5.8	5.0	14.1	1.4
Redwood City	0.0	12.8	1.2	0.0	0.5	20.3	14.1	6.2	5.9	3.2
Rialto	0.0	8.0	0.0	0.4	4.0	23.1	8.6	5.0	18.0	8.2
Richmond	0.0	11.3	0.0	0.0	0.5	23.5	3.7	1.7	15.8	7.2
Ridgecrest	0.0	9.8	0.0	0.0	0.0	30.5	5.8	8.8	15.7	7.3
Riverside	0.0	11.4	1.0	0.0	0.1	18.0	8.8	5.0	13.1	6.9
Rocklin	0.0	10.2	0.0	0.0	0.0	21.7	0.0	12.6	9.7	4.8
Rohnert Park	0.0	4.3	0.0	0.0	1.7	17.8	25.1	6.1	17.1	5.0
Rosemead	0.0	5.7	0.0	0.0	0.9	20.7	0.0	7.6	18.2	4.3
Roseville	0.0	11.4	0.0	0.0	0.0	12.0	14.3	9.5	4.3	15.7
Sacramento	0.0	18.4	1.9	0.0	2.2	16.9	15.2	7.8	3.6	5.8
Salinas	0.0	8.9	1.2	0.0	3.6	33.3	3.9	3.8	3.4	1.3
San Bernardino	0.0	5.3	0.0	0.0	1.1	29.7	15.7	3.3	9.8	1.9
San Bruno	0.0	6.9	0.0	0.0	0.0	23.1	16.6	12.8	1.6	0.9
San Buenaventura (Ventura)	0.0	11.6	0.5	0.0	0.2	22.4	15.1	9.0	2.0	3.7
San Carlos	0.0	9.3	0.2	0.0	0.0	18.2	15.9	9.3	3.0	2.2
San Clemente	0.0	8.3	0.0	0.0	3.0	14.5	11.0	25.3	3.1	1.1
San Diego	0.0	9.7	0.1	0.0	0.6	12.7	12.6	9.9	19.7	6.2
San Dimas	0.0	13.5	0.1	0.0	0.4	15.5	0.1	11.6	10.1	3.7

City	City government finances, 2012 (cont.)			Climate[2]						
	Debt outstanding			Average daily temperature (degrees Fahrenheit)						
				Mean		Limits				
	Total (mil dol)	Per capita[1] (dollars)	Debt issued during year	January	July	January[3]	July[4]	Annual precipitation (inches)	Heating degree days	Cooling degree days
	137	138	139	140	141	142	143	144	145	146
CALIFORNIA—Cont'd										
Menlo Park	89.8	2 729	9.8	49.0	68.0	40.4	78.8	15.71	2 584	452
Merced	93.3	1 159	0.0	46.3	78.6	37.5	96.5	12.50	2 602	1 578
Milpitas	171.2	2 482	0.0	50.5	70.9	41.7	84.3	15.08	2 171	811
Mission Viejo	47.5	500	0.0	56.7	72.4	47.2	82.3	14.03	1 465	1 183
Modesto	441.0	2 144	52.8	47.2	77.7	40.1	93.6	13.12	2 358	1 570
Monrovia	103.5	2 796	0.0	56.1	75.3	44.3	89.4	21.09	1 398	1 558
Montclair	77.9	2 073	0.0	54.6	73.8	41.5	88.7	16.96	1 727	1 191
Montebello	88.0	1 388	0.0	58.8	76.6	47.9	88.9	14.44	949	1 837
Monterey	14.8	521	0.0	51.6	60.2	43.4	68.1	20.35	3 092	74
Monterey Park	83.1	1 363	0.0	56.3	75.6	42.6	89.0	18.56	1 295	1 575
Moorpark	27.6	788	0.0	54.7	68.3	41.2	80.7	18.41	1 911	602
Moreno Valley	91.6	461	0.0	54.2	77.4	42.0	93.5	10.67	1 674	1 697
Morgan Hill	124.6	3 156	0.0	43.5	70.7	37.5	78.2	23.73	4 566	747
Mountain View	83.5	1 090	39.4	49.0	68.0	40.4	78.8	15.71	2 584	452
Murrieta	90.8	852	0.0	52.2	79.6	38.3	98.1	12.09	1 924	1 874
Napa	95.7	1 221	0.0	47.9	68.6	39.2	82.6	26.46	2 689	529
National City	84.5	1 419	0.0	57.3	70.1	46.1	76.1	9.95	1 321	862
Newark	11.4	261	9.7	49.8	68.0	42.0	78.3	14.85	2 367	530
Newport Beach	270.0	3 110	2.6	55.9	67.3	48.2	71.4	11.65	1 719	543
Norco	136.8	4 999	0.0	NA	NA	NA	NA	NA	NA	NA
Norwalk	142.9	1 342	2.1	57.0	73.8	46.0	82.9	12.94	1 211	1 186
Novato	141.1	2 647	0.0	48.8	67.7	41.3	80.9	34.29	2 621	451
Oakland	2 294.4	5 709	429.5	50.9	64.9	44.7	72.7	22.94	2 400	377
Oakley	39.5	1 060	0.0	45.7	74.4	37.8	90.7	13.33	2 714	1 179
Oceanside	200.5	1 168	7.7	54.7	67.6	45.4	72.1	11.13	2 009	505
Ontario	212.5	1 271	0.9	54.6	73.8	41.5	88.7	16.96	1 727	1 191
Orange	107.1	768	3.0	58.0	72.9	46.6	82.7	13.84	1 153	1 299
Oxnard	484.3	2 404	9.3	55.6	65.9	45.5	72.7	15.62	1 936	403
Pacifica	52.3	1 363	0.0	49.4	62.8	42.9	71.1	20.11	2 862	142
Palmdale	251.2	1 614	2.2	46.6	81.7	34.3	97.5	7.36	2 704	1 998
Palm Desert	450.5	9 024	1.0	56.8	92.8	42.0	107.1	3.15	903	4 388
Palm Springs	165.5	3 611	68.9	57.3	92.1	44.2	108.2	5.23	951	4 224
Palo Alto	142.0	2 144	17.2	49.0	68.0	40.4	78.8	15.71	2 584	452
Paradise	14.9	568	0.0	45.7	77.8	37.7	91.7	56.20	3 145	1 464
Paramount	69.2	1 262	0.0	57.0	73.8	46.0	82.9	12.94	1 211	1 186
Pasadena	766.2	5 522	88.3	56.1	75.3	44.3	89.4	21.09	1 398	1 558
Perris	262.8	3 686	0.0	51.2	78.3	36.1	97.8	11.40	2 123	1 710
Petaluma	244.3	4 153	12.9	48.4	67.3	38.9	82.7	25.85	2 741	385
Pico Rivera	49.9	784	0.0	58.3	74.2	48.5	83.8	15.14	928	1 506
Pittsburg	474.6	7 230	0.0	45.7	74.4	37.8	90.7	13.33	2 714	1 179
Placentia	28.8	554	0.0	58.0	72.9	46.6	82.7	13.84	1 153	1 299
Pleasant Hill	21.7	641	0.0	46.3	71.2	38.8	87.4	19.58	2 757	786
Pleasanton	82.6	1 143	0.0	47.2	72.0	37.4	89.1	14.82	2 755	858
Pomona	411.1	2 721	0.0	54.6	73.8	41.5	88.7	16.96	1 727	1 191
Porterville	72.6	1 321	0.1	48.7	82.8	39.4	98.1	11.49	2 053	2 246
Poway	246.1	5 010	0.2	55.3	70.9	43.5	80.8	11.97	1 808	979
Rancho Cordova	23.3	349	0.0	48.2	77.4	41.3	93.8	19.87	2 226	1 597
Rancho Cucamonga	503.8	2 954	0.4	56.6	78.3	45.3	95.0	14.77	1 364	1 901
Rancho Palos Verdes	24.4	575	0.3	56.3	69.4	46.2	77.6	14.79	1 526	742
Rancho Santa Margarita	11.4	233	0.0	56.7	72.4	47.2	82.3	14.03	1 465	1 183
Redding	140.7	1 552	25.2	45.5	81.3	35.5	98.5	33.52	2 961	1 741
Redlands	63.1	903	0.0	52.9	78.0	40.4	94.4	13.62	1 904	1 714
Redondo Beach	53.3	789	0.0	57.1	69.3	48.6	75.3	13.15	1 274	679
Redwood City	164.1	2 069	10.0	48.4	68.0	39.1	80.8	20.16	2 764	422
Rialto	226.0	2 222	0.0	54.4	79.6	41.8	96.0	16.43	1 599	1 937
Richmond	657.3	6 165	25.9	50.0	62.7	42.9	70.5	23.35	2 720	184
Ridgecrest	40.5	1 430	0.0	NA	NA	NA	NA	NA	NA	NA
Riverside	1 908.6	6 092	61.7	55.3	78.7	42.7	94.1	10.22	1 475	1 863
Rocklin	85.0	1 439	11.8	46.9	77.7	39.2	94.8	24.61	2 532	1 528
Rohnert Park	71.7	1 743	0.0	48.7	67.6	39.5	82.2	31.01	2 694	526
Rosemead	43.5	799	0.0	56.3	75.6	42.6	89.0	18.56	1 295	1 575
Roseville	1 069.1	8 607	0.0	46.9	77.7	39.2	94.8	24.61	2 532	1 528
Sacramento	1 087.3	2 286	1.8	46.3	75.4	38.8	92.4	17.93	2 666	1 248
Salinas	42.6	276	18.0	51.2	63.2	41.3	71.3	12.91	2 770	210
San Bernardino	121.7	570	0.0	54.4	79.6	41.8	96.0	16.43	1 599	1 937
San Bruno	11.6	274	0.0	49.4	62.8	42.9	71.1	20.11	2 862	142
San Buenaventura (Ventura)	122.9	1 132	23.5	55.6	65.9	45.5	72.7	15.62	1 936	403
San Carlos	24.3	832	0.0	48.4	68.0	39.1	80.8	20.16	2 764	422
San Clemente	18.2	280	5.0	55.4	68.7	43.9	77.3	13.56	1 756	666
San Diego	3 433.7	2 563	465.2	57.8	70.9	49.7	75.8	10.77	1 063	866
San Dimas	19.7	582	0.0	54.6	73.8	41.5	88.7	16.96	1 727	1 191

1. Based on the population estimated as of July 1 of the year shown. 2. Represents normal values based on the 30-year period, 1971–2000. 3. Average daily minimum. 4. Average daily maximum.

Table D. Cities — **Land Area and Population**

STATE Place code	City	Land area,[1] 2010 (sq km)	Population, 2014			Race alone or in combination (percent), 2011-2013					Percent Hispanic or Latino[2], 2011-2013	Percent foreign born 2011–2013
			Total persons	Rank	Per square kilometer	White	Black	American Indian, Alaska Native	Asian	Hawaiian Pacific Islander		
		1	2	3	4	5	6	7	8	9	10	11
	CALIFORNIA—Cont'd											
06 67000	San Francisco	121.4	852 469	13	7 022.0	53.1	6.8	1.1	36.1	0.8	15.3	35.8
06 67042	San Gabriel	10.7	40 519	913	3 786.8	23.3	1.1	0.6	64.1	NA	24.4	56.8
06 67112	San Jacinto	66.6	46 490	807	698.0	67.9	9.0	4.0	6.3	0.9	51.7	21.8
06 68000	San Jose	457.2	1 015 785	10	2 221.8	49.6	3.9	1.5	35.4	1.0	33.4	38.7
06 68028	San Juan Capistrano	36.6	36 282	1 027	991.3	66.8	0.3	1.1	4.3	NA	39.1	28.4
06 68084	San Leandro	34.6	89 351	347	2 582.4	47.7	13.9	1.9	34.5	1.5	25.8	35.5
06 68154	San Luis Obispo	33.1	46 730	804	1 411.8	87.4	3.1	1.7	7.5	0.3	15.5	8.8
06 68196	San Marcos	63.1	92 929	331	1 472.7	80.2	2.6	0.9	10.9	0.8	35.1	24.9
06 68252	San Mateo	31.4	102 893	286	3 276.8	68.1	3.6	1.0	21.3	2.7	27.2	34.4
06 68294	San Pablo	6.8	30 050	1 231	4 419.1	56.3	19.1	2.9	16.0	0.6	53.3	40.1
06 68364	San Rafael	42.7	59 237	614	1 387.3	71.6	4.0	1.0	8.1	0.4	29.2	28.1
06 68378	San Ramon	46.8	75 332	448	1 609.7	54.8	3.3	0.8	44.5	0.6	8.9	31.6
06 69000	Santa Ana	70.6	334 909	57	4 743.8	50.3	1.4	0.7	11.2	0.4	78.6	47.6
06 69070	Santa Barbara	50.4	91 196	343	1 809.4	77.9	2.8	1.1	4.5	0.3	40.6	26.3
06 69084	Santa Clara	47.7	122 192	219	2 561.7	49.7	4.6	0.8	41.7	0.8	19.3	41.3
06 69088	Santa Clarita	136.5	181 557	133	1 330.1	79.2	4.4	2.4	11.6	0.7	31.2	20.2
06 69112	Santa Cruz	33.0	63 364	556	1 920.1	82.4	3.5	1.7	11.8	0.5	20.2	14.5
06 69196	Santa Maria	58.9	103 410	284	1 755.7	65.1	1.8	1.4	6.3	0.5	71.1	34.6
06 70000	Santa Monica	21.8	92 987	330	4 265.5	84.5	5.4	2.1	11.2	0.4	14.1	22.1
06 70042	Santa Paula	11.9	30 441	1 213	2 558.1	74.7	0.3	1.7	1.9	NA	78.3	31.1
06 70098	Santa Rosa	107.0	174 170	139	1 627.8	78.5	3.7	3.0	6.5	1.1	30.2	18.8
06 70224	Santee	42.1	57 052	642	1 355.2	89.6	3.1	2.4	7.1	1.8	16.6	7.7
06 70280	Saratoga	32.1	31 001	1 194	965.8	53.8	0.5	0.2	47.0	NA	3.0	35.1
06 70742	Seaside	23.9	34 182	1 085	1 430.2	57.9	10.9	3.2	11.6	2.9	40.9	31.4
06 72016	Simi Valley	107.4	126 871	214	1 181.3	82.5	2.2	1.9	10.9	0.6	23.3	18.2
06 72520	Soledad	11.4	25 336	1 417	2 222.5	74.7	13.9	4.4	3.7	0.2	70.2	31.6
06 73080	South Gate	18.7	96 312	310	5 150.4	52.8	1.3	0.8	0.8	0.1	95.9	42.4
06 73220	South Pasadena	8.8	26 156	1 394	2 972.3	58.6	5.0	1.2	33.4	1.2	21.9	26.5
06 73262	South San Francisco	23.7	67 009	516	2 827.4	40.0	3.0	1.8	40.7	4.0	34.6	39.7
06 73962	Stanton	8.2	38 719	958	4 721.8	52.6	2.8	1.7	26.0	0.4	51.6	45.0
06 75000	Stockton	159.7	302 389	63	1 893.5	48.7	14.1	3.1	24.8	1.3	42.1	26.1
06 75630	Suisun City	10.6	29 256	1 257	2 760.0	42.2	25.9	2.0	22.1	2.6	26.1	20.4
06 77000	Sunnyvale	57.0	149 980	168	2 631.2	51.2	3.1	0.9	44.5	0.6	17.9	44.5
06 78120	Temecula	78.1	109 428	259	1 401.1	78.6	5.3	3.4	12.2	1.2	25.6	15.2
06 78148	Temple City	10.4	36 334	1 023	3 493.7	29.8	0.9	0.3	59.4	NA	17.6	48.1
06 78582	Thousand Oaks	142.5	129 342	201	907.7	82.0	1.9	0.8	11.2	0.4	18.8	19.0
06 80000	Torrance	53.0	148 495	172	2 801.8	55.8	4.0	1.2	38.5	0.8	16.9	29.3
06 80238	Tracy	57.0	85 841	373	1 506.0	67.7	9.1	3.4	17.8	3.2	38.0	24.7
06 80644	Tulare	54.2	61 867	575	1 141.5	84.5	5.1	2.2	3.3	0.5	59.9	19.8
06 80812	Turlock	43.8	71 245	482	1 626.6	85.4	2.2	1.4	7.9	1.3	37.7	23.8
06 80854	Tustin	28.7	80 621	406	2 809.1	54.1	2.9	1.1	24.3	0.9	39.3	35.3
06 80994	Twentynine Palms	153.2	25 902	1 399	169.1	79.0	9.9	2.2	7.0	2.6	22.5	5.7
06 81204	Union City	50.4	73 621	461	1 460.7	27.3	6.4	2.0	55.3	3.5	23.4	46.8
06 81344	Upland	40.5	76 043	440	1 877.6	64.4	7.1	1.8	10.6	0.2	39.6	18.6
06 81554	Vacaville	73.5	95 856	313	1 304.2	72.7	11.1	1.9	9.7	1.4	22.2	12.6
06 81666	Vallejo	79.4	120 228	224	1 514.2	46.4	24.0	1.8	28.3	1.9	24.1	28.7
06 82590	Victorville	189.5	121 901	220	643.3	61.3	18.8	2.0	6.7	0.4	51.5	18.5
06 82954	Visalia	93.9	129 281	202	1 376.8	83.7	3.3	2.7	7.0	0.9	45.5	14.1
06 82996	Vista	48.4	98 079	307	2 026.4	86.2	4.3	1.2	5.7	0.8	48.3	25.5
06 83332	Walnut	23.3	30 214	1 229	1 296.7	26.8	3.6	0.5	66.5	0.6	18.0	48.9
06 83346	Walnut Creek	51.2	67 673	512	1 321.7	81.9	3.1	0.8	15.8	0.4	8.7	23.3
06 83542	Wasco	24.4	26 303	1 386	1 078.0	79.4	7.4	0.9	0.8	NA	78.3	30.1
06 83668	Watsonville	17.3	53 111	696	3 070.0	75.3	0.4	1.9	4.6	0.4	81.3	38.2
06 84200	West Covina	41.6	108 455	266	2 607.1	41.3	5.3	1.0	28.4	0.6	54.6	34.6
06 84410	West Hollywood	4.9	35 883	1 042	7 323.1	84.1	4.9	1.0	8.3	0.5	12.3	26.7
06 84550	Westminster	26.0	92 068	335	3 541.1	40.5	1.5	1.1	49.4	1.1	23.5	45.2
06 84816	West Sacramento	55.5	51 847	718	934.2	70.1	7.1	4.1	13.4	2.5	30.7	23.8
06 85292	Whittier	37.9	87 318	360	2 303.9	59.8	1.6	1.4	6.3	0.5	66.2	17.7
06 85446	Wildomar	61.4	35 377	1 054	576.2	75.9	4.2	1.3	3.2	1.6	37.0	16.5
06 85922	Windsor	18.8	27 414	1 341	1 458.2	79.8	1.0	4.6	6.7	NA	28.6	14.2
06 86328	Woodland	39.6	57 432	638	1 450.3	75.5	2.0	2.4	8.0	0.5	48.2	22.5
06 86832	Yorba Linda	50.5	67 826	510	1 343.1	78.7	1.2	1.7	20.4	NA	17.7	19.0
06 86972	Yuba City	37.8	65 773	537	1 740.0	70.5	4.5	2.7	21.9	0.8	27.9	24.7
06 87042	Yucaipa	72.2	53 096	698	735.4	81.8	2.8	1.7	1.9	2.3	31.5	10.0
08 00000	COLORADO	268 431.3	5 355 866	X	20.0	87.2	5.1	2.1	3.8	0.3	20.9	9.7
08 03455	Arvada	91.0	113 574	242	1 248.1	93.3	1.2	1.6	2.8	0.1	14.4	4.8
08 04000	Aurora	400.8	353 108	54	881.0	69.3	18.6	2.3	5.9	0.5	28.9	20.1
08 07850	Boulder	63.9	105 112	278	1 644.9	92.1	1.3	1.1	6.1	0.4	8.3	9.7
08 08675	Brighton	51.8	36 765	1 009	709.7	90.8	2.9	1.4	1.6	NA	42.8	14.7
08 09280	Broomfield	85.6	62 138	572	725.9	90.8	2.0	1.4	7.2	NA	12.3	9.6

1. Dry land or land partially or temporarily covered by water. 2. May be of any race.

City	Age of population (percent), 2011-2013									Median age 2011-2013	Percent female 2011-2013	Population			
												Census counts		Percent change	
	Under 5 years	5 to 17 years	18 to 24 years	25 to 34 years	35 to 44 years	45 to 54 years	55 to 64 years	65 to 74 years	75 years and over			2000	2010	2000–2010	2010–2014
	12	13	14	15	16	17	18	19	20	21	22	23	24	25	26
CALIFORNIA—Cont'd															
San Francisco	4.5	8.9	8.4	21.9	16.4	13.7	12.2	7.1	6.8	38.6	49.1	776 733	805 235	3.7	5.9
San Gabriel	3.7	14.2	8.0	12.8	15.2	16.7	13.6	8.0	7.7	42.4	51.7	39 804	39 718	-0.2	2.0
San Jacinto	9.0	21.8	11.0	12.7	14.5	11.6	8.7	5.7	5.0	31.3	50.8	23 779	44 199	85.9	5.2
San Jose	6.8	17.2	9.3	15.2	15.4	14.3	10.8	6.0	4.9	35.8	49.7	894 943	945 942	5.7	6.6
San Juan Capistrano	6.0	18.0	8.5	8.9	11.6	13.5	16.5	8.0	8.9	42.5	50.6	33 826	34 593	2.3	4.5
San Leandro	5.0	16.0	8.3	12.6	14.6	16.1	13.9	6.8	6.7	40.7	49.8	79 452	84 950	6.9	5.2
San Luis Obispo	3.3	8.6	36.9	13.5	8.0	9.0	8.9	5.2	6.5	25.5	47.0	44 174	45 119	2.1	3.5
San Marcos	6.2	19.2	9.7	13.9	17.4	13.0	9.3	5.7	5.5	35.6	52.5	54 977	83 781	52.4	11.1
San Mateo	6.7	13.6	7.5	15.2	16.7	13.8	11.5	7.1	7.9	39.1	50.9	92 482	97 207	5.1	5.8
San Pablo	6.9	18.8	12.8	14.8	13.0	14.3	9.1	4.9	5.4	32.2	50.9	30 215	29 139	-3.6	3.1
San Rafael	6.8	14.0	8.2	13.1	13.8	14.2	12.8	8.4	8.7	40.8	50.7	56 063	57 713	2.9	2.6
San Ramon	6.2	24.0	5.3	9.7	19.9	17.6	9.8	4.4	3.1	37.4	51.3	44 722	72 148	61.3	4.3
Santa Ana	8.3	21.0	12.6	16.1	15.0	12.2	7.5	4.2	3.0	29.5	49.8	337 977	324 528	-4.0	3.1
Santa Barbara	6.4	12.8	13.6	16.7	12.0	12.3	12.1	6.9	7.2	35.4	50.3	92 325	88 410	-4.2	3.2
Santa Clara	8.1	14.3	10.1	18.8	17.2	12.8	9.0	5.3	4.4	34.4	49.8	102 361	116 468	13.8	4.9
Santa Clarita	6.1	19.5	9.8	12.6	13.6	15.7	12.3	6.4	4.1	36.8	50.2	151 088	176 320	16.7	3.0
Santa Cruz	4.3	10.4	30.1	12.7	11.4	11.1	11.0	5.2	4.0	29.0	50.4	54 593	59 946	9.8	5.7
Santa Maria	8.5	22.4	12.3	15.6	12.2	11.8	7.5	4.7	5.0	29.3	49.0	77 423	99 553	28.6	3.8
Santa Monica	4.6	9.5	8.6	19.3	15.9	14.9	11.8	7.9	7.6	40.1	51.8	84 084	89 736	6.7	3.6
Santa Paula	7.8	22.0	12.1	11.9	14.7	12.2	8.4	5.5	5.4	32.3	47.7	28 598	29 321	2.5	3.8
Santa Rosa	6.1	17.3	9.1	13.9	13.1	14.1	12.7	7.0	6.7	37.8	50.2	147 595	167 815	13.7	3.8
Santee	6.5	18.1	9.5	14.1	14.1	16.6	10.6	6.1	4.4	36.1	53.0	52 975	53 413	0.8	6.8
Saratoga	2.9	21.4	4.6	4.7	12.2	19.4	15.0	10.2	9.6	47.3	51.3	29 843	29 926	0.3	3.4
Seaside	9.1	17.7	11.7	16.7	15.5	10.8	10.0	4.6	4.1	31.8	53.1	31 696	33 025	4.2	3.5
Simi Valley	6.2	17.9	8.6	12.0	13.8	16.4	12.7	7.6	4.7	38.9	51.4	111 351	124 237	11.6	2.1
Soledad	6.4	13.7	10.0	16.7	20.3	18.0	9.5	3.2	2.0	36.6	29.5	11 263	25 738	128.5	-1.6
South Gate	7.7	20.7	12.2	16.0	13.8	12.1	9.2	4.9	3.3	30.5	49.8	96 375	94 396	-2.1	2.0
South Pasadena	5.5	18.1	7.0	14.3	14.5	15.6	12.8	7.2	5.1	39.1	52.0	24 292	25 619	5.5	2.1
South San Francisco	6.8	15.7	8.4	14.3	12.9	15.4	12.3	7.6	6.6	38.2	50.3	60 552	63 632	5.1	5.3
Stanton	6.9	19.7	10.1	15.0	13.9	13.4	10.6	5.0	5.2	33.7	51.2	37 403	38 186	2.1	2.4
Stockton	8.3	21.6	11.7	14.1	12.3	11.4	10.0	6.1	4.6	30.7	51.3	243 771	291 707	19.7	3.7
Suisun City	6.9	23.2	8.3	15.1	13.1	14.1	11.0	5.5	2.8	32.6	49.5	26 118	28 111	7.6	4.1
Sunnyvale	8.3	14.0	6.9	20.4	15.6	13.6	9.8	6.1	5.2	35.2	48.8	131 760	140 081	6.3	7.1
Temecula	6.2	24.0	10.0	10.3	15.0	16.1	10.1	4.9	3.4	34.2	51.6	57 716	100 097	73.4	9.3
Temple City	5.0	17.3	6.9	10.2	15.0	15.7	14.0	7.8	7.9	41.9	53.0	33 377	35 558	6.5	2.2
Thousand Oaks	4.4	19.2	8.4	10.1	12.4	16.2	13.5	8.5	7.2	42.0	51.3	117 005	126 683	8.3	2.2
Torrance	5.4	15.7	8.0	11.6	14.2	17.5	11.7	7.9	8.0	41.8	52.4	137 946	145 438	5.4	2.1
Tracy	7.7	22.3	9.4	12.4	15.4	15.5	9.5	5.1	2.8	33.9	48.2	56 929	82 922	45.7	3.3
Tulare	9.3	22.2	11.7	14.4	12.4	11.3	9.6	5.0	4.2	30.1	51.6	43 994	59 278	34.7	4.3
Turlock	7.1	20.2	10.6	14.7	13.5	10.7	11.2	6.4	5.7	33.0	50.3	55 810	68 549	22.8	3.9
Tustin	7.8	18.4	10.1	16.7	15.4	13.5	9.3	4.6	4.2	33.4	51.2	67 504	75 540	11.9	7.0
Twentynine Palms	13.7	11.6	27.4	19.3	9.2	6.2	6.9	3.5	2.3	24.2	48.4	14 764	25 048	69.7	3.4
Union City	7.2	16.3	9.3	14.7	14.7	13.3	11.9	7.1	5.4	36.3	50.8	66 869	69 516	4.0	5.9
Upland	6.4	17.7	10.0	13.7	13.0	14.5	11.2	7.8	5.6	36.4	53.3	68 393	73 732	7.8	3.1
Vacaville	5.8	16.9	10.2	14.1	13.4	16.2	11.7	6.9	4.9	38.0	46.8	88 625	92 428	4.3	3.7
Vallejo	6.4	14.9	10.0	13.5	12.0	14.6	15.7	7.1	5.8	39.1	51.7	116 760	115 942	-0.7	3.7
Victorville	8.7	24.5	10.9	14.8	14.0	11.2	8.1	4.8	3.0	29.2	51.5	64 029	115 903	81.0	5.2
Visalia	8.7	20.7	9.7	15.4	12.7	12.9	9.3	6.3	4.4	31.8	51.2	91 565	124 442	35.9	3.9
Vista	6.5	15.7	11.1	17.9	15.4	13.5	9.6	5.0	5.3	34.5	50.1	89 857	93 834	4.4	4.5
Walnut	3.3	16.6	10.5	10.5	11.5	17.0	17.1	8.8	4.7	43.0	50.7	30 004	29 172	-2.8	3.6
Walnut Creek	4.4	12.9	6.2	11.1	12.3	14.7	11.9	12.1	14.5	46.9	53.9	64 296	64 173	-0.2	5.5
Wasco	8.9	18.4	13.6	19.6	14.9	11.5	7.7	2.4	3.0	29.3	37.3	21 263	25 545	20.1	2.9
Watsonville	9.6	21.7	12.9	13.4	13.7	11.6	8.4	4.3	4.4	28.9	50.4	44 265	51 199	15.7	3.7
West Covina	5.9	17.5	10.7	14.6	12.7	13.5	12.1	6.5	6.4	35.9	51.5	105 080	106 098	1.0	2.2
West Hollywood	1.2	2.1	5.5	30.6	17.4	18.0	10.2	7.4	7.6	40.9	43.3	35 716	34 399	-3.7	4.3
Westminster	5.5	16.8	9.6	12.6	13.5	14.8	11.9	8.0	7.3	39.6	51.1	88 207	89 701	1.7	2.7
West Sacramento	7.0	18.9	10.6	16.5	13.9	12.9	8.5	6.6	5.0	33.4	50.5	31 615	48 744	54.2	6.4
Whittier	7.0	18.0	11.4	13.8	13.4	14.3	10.0	5.2	6.8	34.9	51.5	83 680	85 331	2.0	2.3
Wildomar	7.0	20.6	9.7	12.7	13.5	12.6	13.5	5.7	4.8	35.1	48.2	14 064	32 176	128.8	9.8
Windsor	6.2	20.2	9.4	10.0	12.9	16.3	11.4	7.0	6.5	37.9	50.3	22 744	26 801	17.8	2.3
Woodland	7.2	18.9	10.1	13.4	13.5	13.1	11.5	6.5	5.8	35.3	50.8	49 151	55 468	12.9	3.5
Yorba Linda	5.5	17.7	8.6	9.4	12.0	18.4	14.5	7.9	6.0	42.8	50.9	58 918	64 234	9.0	5.7
Yuba City	7.0	19.4	11.3	13.3	12.5	12.8	10.1	7.0	6.2	34.0	50.0	36 758	64 925	76.6	1.3
Yucaipa	6.2	19.6	9.7	11.6	12.8	13.1	12.6	8.1	6.3	37.5	51.0	41 207	51 367	24.7	3.4
COLORADO	6.5	17.3	9.8	14.7	13.7	13.9	12.4	6.9	4.9	36.2	49.8	4 301 261	5 029 196	16.9	6.5
Arvada	5.6	17.0	8.1	12.4	12.9	15.3	14.2	8.0	6.4	40.2	51.5	102 153	106 433	4.2	6.7
Aurora	8.0	18.8	9.8	15.9	14.2	12.7	11.0	5.8	3.9	33.4	51.0	276 393	325 078	17.6	8.8
Boulder	3.9	10.5	30.3	15.0	10.7	10.5	9.4	5.4	4.3	27.8	49.9	94 673	97 385	2.9	7.8
Brighton	7.4	23.2	9.1	15.0	15.4	11.8	10.0	4.8	3.3	32.5	50.9	20 905	33 352	59.5	8.8
Broomfield	6.5	19.0	8.1	16.0	15.3	13.6	10.3	6.5	4.6	35.3	50.7	38 272	55 889	46.0	11.2

City	Households, 2011-2013: Number	Households, 2011-2013: Persons per house-hold	Households, 2011-2013: Percent: Female family house-holder[1]	Households, 2011-2013: Percent: One-person	Persons in group quarters, 2010: Total	Persons in group quarters, 2010: Institutional: Total	Persons in group quarters, 2010: Institutional: Persons in nursing facilities	Persons in group quarters, 2010: Non-institu-tional	Serious crimes known to police,[2] 2013: Total: Number	Serious crimes known to police,[2] 2013: Total: Rate[3]	Serious crimes known to police,[2] 2013: Rate[3]: Violent	Serious crimes known to police,[2] 2013: Rate[3]: Property	Educational attainment, 2011-2013: Population age 25 and older	Educational attainment, 2011-2013: Attainment[4] (percent): High school graduate or less	Educational attainment, 2011-2013: Attainment[4] (percent): Bachelor's degree or more
	27	28	29	30	31	32	33	34	35	36	37	38	39	40	41
CALIFORNIA—Cont'd															
San Francisco	348 751	2.31	8.6	38.4	24 264	5 362	2 942	18 902	55 388	6 642	847	5 795	646 279	26.6	52.9
San Gabriel	12 862	3.09	14.2	22.4	452	418	395	34	827	2 053	256	1 797	29 742	48.0	29.6
San Jacinto	13 117	3.44	16.5	19.5	228	59	43	169	1 929	4 220	271	3 948	26 463	55.6	11.9
San Jose	310 975	3.12	12.6	19.7	13 322	3 780	2 190	9 542	28 725	2 895	324	2 571	655 601	35.8	37.6
San Juan Capistrano	11 692	3.03	10.9	22.3	87	0	0	87	496	1 394	160	1 234	23 960	37.0	32.4
San Leandro	31 060	2.78	12.2	27.6	650	368	364	282	4 354	4 977	450	4 526	61 448	44.0	28.0
San Luis Obispo	17 840	2.50	7.4	31.5	1 182	215	206	967	1 936	4 200	349	3 851	23 449	19.8	49.6
San Marcos	28 649	3.01	13.0	22.8	844	108	108	736	1 614	1 840	244	1 596	56 597	38.4	27.7
San Mateo	37 439	2.62	9.6	29.6	1 316	341	306	975	2 304	2 294	238	2 056	72 038	28.6	43.5
San Pablo	8 863	3.27	20.3	18.3	441	373	373	68	1 370	4 583	669	3 914	18 105	60.9	14.0
San Rafael	22 148	2.55	12.8	29.2	2 119	805	497	1 314	2 018	3 436	351	3 086	41 544	28.1	45.5
San Ramon	25 293	2.91	7.7	18.0	75	23	0	52	787	1 057	36	1 021	47 607	11.8	66.2
Santa Ana	73 463	4.45	18.2	13.3	4 658	3 243	895	1 415	7 546	2 267	337	1 930	192 299	68.7	10.9
Santa Barbara	34 037	2.58	9.5	31.7	1 627	455	375	1 172	3 032	3 369	402	2 966	60 196	29.6	43.1
Santa Clara	42 830	2.70	9.4	26.2	3 196	336	318	2 860	3 195	2 659	143	2 516	80 384	23.5	53.0
Santa Clarita	58 934	3.00	12.4	19.1	1 410	129	111	1 281	2 989	1 458	135	1 324	115 527	30.0	32.8
Santa Cruz	21 154	2.52	7.2	32.8	8 289	379	2	7 910	3 570	5 710	651	5 059	34 301	21.4	51.1
Santa Maria	27 560	3.64	16.8	21.1	1 007	419	263	588	3 424	3 355	480	2 875	57 570	59.0	12.7
Santa Monica	46 476	1.93	6.8	49.6	2 126	827	783	1 299	3 868	4 182	350	3 832	70 728	13.0	65.5
Santa Paula	8 382	3.56	14.2	18.1	133	89	89	44	644	2 135	358	1 777	17 414	58.2	14.5
Santa Rosa	62 833	2.67	12.0	28.9	3 410	1 713	830	1 697	4 047	2 359	315	2 044	115 179	34.9	29.9
Santee	19 141	2.83	15.7	20.7	966	889	274	77	1 321	2 362	279	2 083	36 474	32.0	25.2
Saratoga	10 792	2.82	5.3	16.2	199	165	161	34	236	764	45	719	21 777	6.8	78.1
Seaside	10 122	3.22	16.0	20.3	1 127	0	0	1 127	711	2 082	351	1 731	20 800	47.6	23.0
Simi Valley	42 134	2.96	11.6	18.1	660	178	123	482	1 841	1 459	105	1 354	84 468	30.6	32.2
Soledad	3 651	4.19	15.4	8.0	10 103	10 103	55	0	325	1 220	274	946	18 334	71.4	3.7
South Gate	23 414	4.07	21.4	12.4	88	72	72	16	3 194	3 341	519	2 822	56 575	74.2	6.3
South Pasadena	10 017	2.57	13.1	29.8	163	155	151	8	597	2 302	112	2 190	17 966	13.5	60.9
South San Francisco	21 003	3.08	11.0	22.0	579	51	18	528	1 306	1 974	178	1 796	45 235	40.0	28.8
Stanton	11 788	3.25	17.2	21.4	350	258	240	92	814	2 080	286	1 794	24 329	52.5	20.0
Stockton	90 239	3.22	21.3	22.2	5 734	1 838	1 558	3 896	18 702	6 238	1 208	5 030	173 398	49.3	17.1
Suisun City	8 463	3.36	20.6	14.4	44	17	5	27	694	2 409	222	2 187	17 618	37.2	18.6
Sunnyvale	55 066	2.63	7.1	25.8	849	469	457	380	2 578	1 740	97	1 643	103 303	20.9	59.8
Temecula	31 767	3.29	11.7	14.5	129	8	0	121	2 939	2 755	85	2 670	62 658	29.9	29.2
Temple City	11 349	3.12	12.4	19.4	422	393	388	29	524	1 445	132	1 312	25 419	36.0	34.3
Thousand Oaks	45 693	2.76	8.1	22.7	1 742	352	348	1 390	1 743	1 352	108	1 245	87 045	21.9	49.0
Torrance	55 824	2.61	12.2	25.8	1 146	640	578	506	2 973	2 015	127	1 888	104 156	24.8	43.4
Tracy	24 129	3.48	10.1	13.1	316	247	245	69	2 388	2 804	178	2 625	51 204	43.2	21.1
Tulare	18 139	3.33	16.6	16.9	278	216	216	62	3 043	4 954	700	4 254	34 427	60.2	10.9
Turlock	23 621	2.92	16.5	21.2	1 207	520	445	687	2 940	4 196	442	3 753	43 351	47.3	22.6
Tustin	25 021	3.07	15.6	20.8	520	180	150	340	1 573	1 995	127	1 868	49 319	33.2	39.5
Twentynine Palms	8 341	2.68	15.5	24.9	3 347	0	0	3 347	427	1 648	286	1 362	12 136	39.6	21.7
Union City	20 187	3.51	13.3	15.6	518	96	75	422	1 852	2 555	301	2 254	48 122	40.1	35.1
Upland	26 708	2.78	16.0	25.9	682	377	359	305	2 397	3 169	215	2 953	49 435	33.7	30.2
Vacaville	31 382	2.75	13.8	24.7	8 022	7 989	171	33	2 297	2 435	213	2 222	62 930	36.5	22.5
Vallejo	40 562	2.87	18.9	26.3	1 663	533	483	1 130	6 753	5 707	861	4 846	80 977	38.3	23.8
Victorville	30 817	3.73	20.2	15.4	5 103	4 762	294	341	4 816	3 957	535	3 422	66 929	53.1	9.2
Visalia	41 647	3.01	16.8	21.4	1 326	720	408	606	5 353	4 188	391	3 797	77 240	41.3	22.8
Vista	31 297	3.01	12.5	21.2	2 045	1 384	588	661	2 490	2 575	460	2 115	64 037	50.3	16.6
Walnut	8 528	3.49	10.2	8.5	34	12	10	22	500	1 651	122	1 529	20 757	19.5	52.3
Walnut Creek	29 377	2.20	6.4	36.1	1 002	826	826	176	2 239	3 385	118	3 267	50 378	13.1	61.6
Wasco	5 191	3.79	19.4	13.6	5 720	5 710	0	10	NA	NA	NA	NA	15 228	77.0	4.5
Watsonville	14 110	3.65	18.2	19.2	528	206	201	322	1 545	2 967	455	2 512	29 004	65.0	9.9
West Covina	30 872	3.45	18.6	16.3	674	323	299	351	3 601	3 338	214	3 124	70 764	40.4	26.1
West Hollywood	21 777	1.60	3.3	61.8	109	0	0	109	1 651	4 730	619	4 112	31 825	14.6	60.9
Westminster	27 318	3.32	14.3	17.8	670	289	197	381	2 759	3 003	308	2 695	62 258	48.8	21.8
West Sacramento	17 446	2.82	13.7	24.6	338	92	82	246	1 688	3 393	412	2 981	31 426	43.1	21.0
Whittier	27 218	3.10	16.4	21.6	1 635	552	434	1 083	2 606	3 014	258	2 757	54 851	40.6	24.8
Wildomar	10 262	3.24	13.5	16.7	42	4	4	38	576	1 722	120	1 602	20 880	39.2	16.0
Windsor	9 183	2.94	8.9	21.3	51	0	0	51	374	1 373	385	987	17 365	33.2	31.0
Woodland	19 747	2.79	14.6	26.8	985	829	323	156	2 214	3 917	481	3 436	35 819	45.1	24.0
Yorba Linda	22 102	2.99	7.9	15.6	190	93	93	97	730	1 082	44	1 037	45 306	16.9	49.9
Yuba City	21 339	3.02	16.0	21.0	580	455	247	125	2 154	3 307	267	3 040	40 514	45.2	16.3
Yucaipa	17 856	2.89	12.8	22.4	554	327	242	227	1 033	1 967	204	1 763	33 735	39.4	19.1
COLORADO	1 989 371	2.55	10.3	28.2	115 878	61 591	18 079	54 287	156 283	2 966	308	2 658	3 449 352	31.5	37.3
Arvada	43 581	2.50	11.3	26.3	506	343	314	163	2 832	2 556	146	2 410	75 927	30.6	36.7
Aurora	122 667	2.75	15.6	28.5	2 556	1 850	1 145	706	12 208	3 554	416	3 138	215 372	39.2	26.9
Boulder	41 319	2.26	5.8	33.1	8 105	1 080	531	7 025	3 167	3 080	212	2 868	56 321	10.7	73.6
Brighton	10 095	3.26	16.4	19.1	1 546	1 518	197	28	1 169	3 338	240	3 098	20 832	50.2	17.6
Broomfield	22 464	2.58	8.6	26.5	282	279	207	3	1 241	2 088	56	2 033	38 669	19.4	48.8

1. No spouse present. 2. Data for serious crimes have not been adjusted for underreporting. This may affect comparability between geographic areas and over time. 3. Per 100,000 population estimated by the FBI. 4. Persons 25 years old and over.

Table D. Cities — **Income, Poverty, and Housing**

City	Money income, 2011–2013: Per capita income[1] (dollars)	Money income, 2011–2013: Households: Median income	Money income, 2011–2013: Households: Percent with income of $200,000 or more	Money income, 2011–2013: Households: Percent with income of less than $25,000	Money income, 2011–2013: Families with income below poverty (percent)	Housing units, 2010: Total	Housing units, 2010: Percent change, 2000–2010	Housing units, 2010: Vacant units for sale or rent[2]	Occupied housing units 2011–2013: Total	Occupied housing units 2011–2013: Owner-occupied: Percent	Occupied housing units 2011–2013: Owner-occupied: Median value[3] (dollars)	Occupied housing units 2011–2013: Median owner costs as a percent of income: With a mortgage[4]	Occupied housing units 2011–2013: Median owner costs as a percent of income: Without a mortgage[5]
	42	43	44	45	46	47	48	49	50	51	52	53	54
CALIFORNIA—Cont'd													
San Francisco	48 861	74 559	14.5	21.4	8.6	376 942	8.8	31 131	348 751	36.0	740 700	28.4	11.2
San Gabriel	22 925	50 059	3.0	20.4	11.5	13 237	3.0	695	12 862	47.3	565 600	33.2	12.0
San Jacinto	16 779	46 449	0.6	27.7	15.3	14 977	58.7	1 825	13 117	65.1	137 700	28.9	13.2
San Jose	34 059	80 609	12.3	15.4	8.9	314 038	11.5	12 672	310 975	56.4	561 600	27.2	10.3
San Juan Capistrano	36 159	69 364	12.2	19.0	12.3	11 940	5.3	546	11 692	71.9	485 600	30.0	13.1
San Leandro	29 442	63 719	5.0	16.2	7.3	32 419	3.6	1 702	31 060	55.8	359 800	28.1	10.0
San Luis Obispo	26 790	45 530	4.2	31.8	9.8	20 553	6.3	1 360	17 840	36.7	522 700	27.1	10.0
San Marcos	23 580	53 299	3.9	24.4	14.1	28 641	51.5	1 439	28 649	59.3	354 800	32.9	13.6
San Mateo	42 899	81 915	12.9	10.7	4.3	40 014	4.7	1 781	37 439	51.6	710 000	28.6	10.9
San Pablo	16 741	42 708	0.6	26.8	18.1	9 571	2.5	810	8 863	42.2	163 700	29.6	12.2
San Rafael	44 187	71 898	14.0	19.1	9.1	24 011	4.6	1 247	22 148	52.6	683 500	27.4	11.2
San Ramon	51 518	126 677	25.9	6.0	3.1	26 222	50.5	938	25 293	68.3	690 900	26.4	10.9
Santa Ana	15 781	51 221	2.3	20.9	19.6	76 896	3.3	3 722	73 463	44.6	338 700	31.5	10.0
Santa Barbara	35 548	64 782	8.6	18.9	8.1	37 820	1.7	2 371	34 037	39.5	800 100	29.9	11.6
Santa Clara	41 097	93 655	12.8	12.5	5.7	45 147	14.0	2 126	42 830	45.7	615 100	26.0	10.0
Santa Clarita	34 101	82 336	9.1	12.4	7.1	62 055	18.3	2 548	58 934	68.4	372 500	27.8	12.2
Santa Cruz	29 521	62 580	8.6	24.4	7.7	23 316	8.6	1 659	21 154	42.2	632 600	28.4	10.0
Santa Maria	17 729	47 112	1.8	23.8	17.4	28 294	24.0	1 386	27 560	49.7	241 000	28.5	12.3
Santa Monica	56 163	70 879	13.5	21.1	5.8	50 912	6.4	3 995	46 476	26.4	1 000 000	27.9	13.0
Santa Paula	19 177	52 179	2.1	26.4	16.3	8 749	4.5	402	8 382	60.5	292 300	29.3	11.1
Santa Rosa	29 133	58 908	4.7	18.4	9.3	67 396	17.2	3 806	62 833	52.7	351 500	27.7	11.8
Santee	29 824	71 908	3.6	12.5	6.8	20 048	6.6	742	19 141	68.8	327 000	27.2	12.3
Saratoga	80 390	170 373	44.6	7.3	1.9	11 123	4.3	389	10 792	85.0	1 000 000	24.3	10.0
Seaside	20 790	51 287	2.0	20.9	14.7	10 872	-1.2	779	10 122	36.6	320 500	28.0	10.0
Simi Valley	36 499	86 963	10.1	10.5	4.3	42 506	13.9	1 269	42 134	74.1	421 000	26.8	10.6
Soledad	9 508	51 847	3.4	23.1	23.3	3 876	52.4	212	3 651	53.0	191 900	26.8	10.0
South Gate	14 156	42 125	1.0	25.9	19.2	24 160	-0.5	882	23 414	47.5	289 200	35.1	12.1
South Pasadena	44 875	81 398	13.1	11.4	3.9	11 118	2.5	651	10 017	44.9	838 200	28.0	10.0
South San Francisco	30 000	73 034	7.5	15.7	5.5	21 814	8.2	876	21 003	59.1	575 800	30.2	10.0
Stanton	18 528	45 163	1.0	23.9	17.9	11 283	3.1	458	11 788	49.8	272 500	31.6	15.8
Stockton	18 908	43 786	2.5	30.4	21.8	99 637	21.3	9 032	90 239	49.3	158 900	26.8	11.0
Suisun City	24 552	64 760	3.9	15.7	10.9	9 454	16.0	536	8 463	62.2	202 000	26.6	10.0
Sunnyvale	46 759	100 850	16.8	11.4	5.0	55 791	3.8	2 407	55 066	45.8	735 000	23.9	10.1
Temecula	27 222	78 493	4.3	12.8	6.9	34 004	78.8	2 223	31 767	63.8	299 000	27.6	13.5
Temple City	26 824	67 969	5.6	19.9	6.5	12 117	3.5	511	11 349	65.7	571 100	31.7	10.1
Thousand Oaks	45 054	97 152	16.3	11.8	5.2	47 497	10.6	1 661	45 693	71.8	583 100	27.5	12.1
Torrance	35 713	76 367	7.3	15.7	5.1	58 377	4.3	2 376	55 824	55.8	606 000	28.9	10.3
Tracy	25 805	73 559	4.6	11.1	5.6	25 963	43.9	1 632	24 129	65.0	254 800	27.2	11.4
Tulare	17 755	43 644	1.6	30.2	19.4	18 863	32.6	1 143	18 139	60.4	147 800	25.4	13.2
Turlock	22 883	50 084	3.2	23.5	13.2	24 627	29.3	1 855	23 621	52.5	188 200	26.8	11.9
Tustin	30 484	68 503	8.4	14.2	8.8	26 476	3.9	1 273	25 021	50.5	472 500	30.1	10.0
Twentynine Palms	20 962	41 727	1.2	22.6	12.3	9 431	38.9	1 336	8 341	30.1	124 500	24.7	10.0
Union City	28 659	78 139	9.1	14.9	5.8	21 258	12.7	825	20 187	63.9	466 800	27.5	11.5
Upland	28 111	56 721	4.8	20.3	12.3	27 355	7.4	1 532	26 708	54.9	398 300	28.1	10.0
Vacaville	30 063	73 092	5.9	14.3	9.1	32 814	14.4	1 722	31 382	60.6	264 400	25.8	10.0
Vallejo	25 491	55 459	3.7	24.5	14.2	44 433	7.9	3 874	40 562	56.9	206 300	27.8	10.3
Victorville	15 146	45 892	0.4	29.9	22.6	36 655	61.8	4 097	30 817	59.7	130 900	25.9	14.5
Visalia	22 272	51 099	3.1	23.1	17.7	44 205	34.8	2 856	41 647	57.1	166 500	26.5	11.3
Vista	20 142	43 367	1.8	25.3	14.6	30 986	3.5	1 669	31 297	47.9	335 200	33.3	14.2
Walnut	35 067	98 311	12.4	9.2	5.1	8 753	4.3	220	8 528	86.2	628 600	28.9	11.3
Walnut Creek	50 186	80 192	14.5	14.3	3.2	32 681	3.8	2 238	29 377	65.0	573 400	26.1	16.3
Wasco	10 411	37 773	0.3	36.5	31.3	5 477	28.2	346	5 191	45.3	127 600	24.2	12.5
Watsonville	16 746	43 734	2.1	27.7	19.5	14 089	19.7	561	14 110	40.3	314 000	30.2	12.4
West Covina	23 796	65 027	3.1	16.5	7.8	32 705	2.2	1 109	30 872	64.5	376 300	31.2	10.0
West Hollywood	55 699	52 829	8.1	26.3	6.4	24 588	2.0	2 077	21 777	20.4	579 400	26.8	13.5
Westminster	22 992	52 185	4.6	22.9	14.5	27 650	2.7	1 486	27 318	54.3	443 000	30.3	11.4
West Sacramento	23 375	48 607	2.5	27.3	15.2	18 681	54.1	1 260	17 446	53.3	223 100	26.3	10.1
Whittier	27 371	64 401	5.0	19.1	10.9	29 591	1.9	1 318	27 218	57.4	418 000	27.8	10.0
Wildomar	23 357	59 236	1.9	18.4	10.5	10 806	128.0	814	10 262	74.0	220 400	29.1	10.4
Windsor	32 479	84 182	6.0	12.8	2.3	9 549	23.4	579	9 183	77.7	373 300	28.5	14.8
Woodland	25 115	51 623	3.2	22.4	9.7	19 806	15.8	1 085	19 747	54.3	238 300	26.9	11.2
Yorba Linda	46 627	113 845	19.3	8.6	2.3	22 305	14.2	729	22 102	83.6	679 800	27.8	11.1
Yuba City	22 064	47 440	2.4	25.3	16.5	23 174	66.6	1 624	21 339	57.3	171 100	26.6	11.9
Yucaipa	24 859	55 406	4.0	21.7	10.2	19 042	21.0	1 411	17 856	72.3	199 500	29.3	13.8
COLORADO	30 982	57 892	5.3	20.2	9.1	2 212 898	22.4	240 030	1 989 371	64.4	236 100	23.4	10.2
Arvada	33 593	67 521	5.4	15.7	6.8	44 427	12.1	1 726	43 581	74.0	242 500	22.9	10.0
Aurora	23 865	50 247	2.3	20.7	12.5	131 040	20.1	9 139	122 667	56.3	175 000	24.7	10.4
Boulder	37 315	57 012	9.7	25.8	5.6	43 479	6.6	2 177	41 319	48.8	487 400	22.6	10.0
Brighton	22 265	58 963	1.2	16.1	8.3	11 387	63.0	599	10 095	69.4	192 500	24.0	10.6
Broomfield	38 002	78 745	7.6	15.3	6.5	22 646	57.8	1 232	22 464	66.1	281 800	21.4	10.3

1. Based on population estimated by the American Community Survey. 2. Includes units rented or sold but not occupied. 3. Specified owner-occupied units; $1,000,000 represents $1,000,000 or more 4. 50.0 represents 50 percent or more. 5. 10.0 represents 10 percent or less.

City	Occupied housing units, 2011–2013 (cont.)				Migration, 2011–2013		Civilian labor force, 2014				Civilian employment[4], 2011–2013			
									Unemployment			Percent		
	Percent renter occupied	Median gross rent[1]	Median rent as a percent of income[2]	Percent with no vehicle available	Percent who lived in the same house one year ago	Percent who lived outside current city one year ago	Total	Percent change, 2013–2014	Total	Rate[3]	Population age 16 and older	In labor force	Civilian full-year full-time workers	Households with no workers (percent)
	55	56	57	58	59	60	61	62	63	64	65	66	67	68
CALIFORNIA—Cont'd														
San Francisco	64.0	1 487	28.3	30.4	84.1	8.2	532 645	2.5	23 307	4.4	727 362	69.0	43.5	24.6
San Gabriel	52.7	1 233	37.1	7.2	89.1	8.0	20 801	1.5	1 054	5.1	33 938	60.7	37.7	20.0
San Jacinto	34.9	983	37.9	7.8	82.7	14.0	18 074	0.3	2 208	12.2	32 884	59.1	27.2	33.2
San Jose	43.6	1 470	31.9	5.5	86.1	6.3	531 920	1.9	30 891	5.8	771 170	67.6	41.8	18.3
San Juan Capistrano	28.1	1 737	50.0	6.0	85.9	10.9	17 245	0.5	1 046	6.1	28 158	63.1	33.9	28.1
San Leandro	44.2	1 231	29.1	7.3	86.6	7.6	46 424	0.5	2 940	6.3	70 679	66.9	41.0	23.3
San Luis Obispo	63.3	1 225	44.8	7.6	63.3	18.5	25 559	1.3	1 514	5.9	40 927	61.2	28.4	28.1
San Marcos	40.7	1 244	34.1	2.8	90.3	6.6	39 343	0.3	1 982	5.0	67 634	58.6	34.9	30.3
San Mateo	48.4	1 651	30.1	6.3	83.7	10.6	60 838	2.5	2 472	4.1	81 281	70.6	43.7	22.3
San Pablo	57.8	1 062	37.6	11.9	84.9	11.3	13 941	-0.1	1 316	9.4	22 746	62.9	30.6	24.6
San Rafael	47.4	1 389	35.6	10.5	85.1	9.1	32 938	0.8	1 466	4.5	47 288	67.0	39.0	26.5
San Ramon	31.7	1 752	28.0	3.2	86.4	10.8	39 097	1.2	1 616	4.1	54 387	72.8	50.1	11.5
Santa Ana	55.4	1 274	37.1	6.9	87.5	5.4	159 182	0.4	10 032	6.3	245 752	67.2	40.3	13.2
Santa Barbara	60.5	1 487	33.5	10.2	81.9	11.1	51 505	0.9	2 500	4.9	73 959	70.1	40.7	24.9
Santa Clara	54.3	1 640	27.2	4.7	82.1	14.3	65 361	2.2	3 061	4.7	94 462	68.3	44.7	19.3
Santa Clarita	31.6	1 486	32.2	4.5	83.5	9.7	95 617	1.0	7 231	7.6	138 931	69.5	41.0	18.8
Santa Cruz	57.8	1 511	39.3	9.2	70.2	19.9	33 176	0.5	2 589	7.8	54 091	61.9	29.7	25.2
Santa Maria	50.3	1 136	35.4	8.0	80.7	6.1	48 129	0.5	3 545	7.4	72 997	66.4	38.5	23.2
Santa Monica	73.6	1 534	30.7	10.4	79.9	15.2	56 088	1.1	3 939	7.0	79 989	71.9	42.4	26.7
Santa Paula	39.5	1 107	39.5	9.6	86.7	5.4	14 108	-1.0	1 222	8.7	21 883	65.7	36.5	24.2
Santa Rosa	47.3	1 254	33.6	6.4	83.5	6.6	88 223	1.7	5 478	6.2	135 433	66.0	35.9	26.4
Santee	31.2	1 321	33.0	3.6	85.1	11.8	28 727	0.0	1 806	6.3	43 755	68.0	41.7	21.8
Saratoga	15.0	2 000	26.7	2.7	90.9	8.1	14 537	2.5	537	3.7	24 088	58.4	39.3	26.1
Seaside	63.4	1 449	38.7	5.3	80.6	13.5	18 374	1.3	1 709	9.3	25 521	68.9	36.0	17.8
Simi Valley	25.9	1 660	34.3	4.1	88.9	5.6	69 793	-0.5	4 107	5.9	99 300	70.1	42.8	20.9
Soledad	47.0	1 024	38.1	3.7	77.3	15.1	8 126	0.8	1 018	12.5	21 350	32.2	19.3	23.6
South Gate	52.5	978	39.7	7.5	87.5	8.0	44 020	0.4	4 727	10.7	71 697	63.3	36.1	17.5
South Pasadena	55.1	1 394	27.1	3.7	84.1	11.9	14 749	1.4	864	5.9	20 456	70.5	43.4	17.4
South San Francisco	40.9	1 519	32.0	8.6	89.3	8.4	37 666	2.4	1 687	4.5	52 301	68.7	41.9	22.8
Stanton	50.2	1 230	38.1	9.2	86.7	10.6	18 896	0.2	1 365	7.2	29 497	66.2	38.7	20.6
Stockton	50.7	931	38.1	10.2	79.7	6.8	127 082	-0.2	14 580	11.5	217 812	59.8	30.7	31.7
Suisun City	37.8	1 492	38.5	5.8	79.2	15.4	14 168	-0.1	921	6.5	20 819	69.3	38.2	19.9
Sunnyvale	54.2	1 665	23.7	4.6	81.6	14.2	83 243	2.2	3 884	4.7	116 126	70.1	47.2	17.2
Temecula	36.2	1 551	34.6	3.5	81.7	13.4	49 809	1.7	2 970	6.0	77 729	64.5	37.7	19.3
Temple City	34.3	1 353	34.2	4.9	92.1	6.1	17 793	1.5	962	5.4	29 445	60.2	39.4	21.3
Thousand Oaks	28.2	1 809	33.7	4.6	85.2	9.4	67 808	-0.6	4 411	6.5	101 413	66.6	39.3	25.2
Torrance	44.2	1 407	29.8	5.0	87.6	7.9	77 577	1.4	4 485	5.8	119 310	65.0	41.2	24.5
Tracy	35.0	1 377	29.6	3.2	84.9	8.0	41 161	0.2	3 705	9.0	62 086	69.6	39.6	13.8
Tulare	39.6	883	34.6	5.8	85.3	4.1	26 922	-0.9	3 022	11.2	43 222	62.1	37.7	25.4
Turlock	47.5	952	34.0	8.9	79.2	8.5	33 687	0.1	3 388	10.1	53 054	64.3	33.4	27.2
Tustin	49.5	1 480	35.0	4.2	79.8	15.3	41 626	0.6	2 131	5.1	59 365	71.9	45.2	13.8
Twentynine Palms	69.9	933	30.6	7.2	56.1	30.3	6 777	0.7	702	10.4	19 436	71.3	21.0	21.8
Union City	36.1	1 492	33.1	7.6	91.1	6.6	36 289	0.8	1 926	5.3	56 696	64.2	40.6	33.1
Upland	45.1	1 159	37.3	5.3	84.2	11.9	37 374	1.7	2 225	6.0	59 580	62.5	40.2	23.6
Vacaville	39.4	1 335	30.9	5.3	82.2	9.7	43 913	0.0	2 618	6.0	74 967	62.5	35.7	21.9
Vallejo	43.1	1 183	36.3	8.4	82.4	8.6	58 000	-0.9	5 840	10.1	95 715	63.1	33.9	28.9
Victorville	40.3	1 076	42.0	5.4	80.3	11.9	44 090	1.1	3 802	8.6	84 201	52.9	30.6	26.7
Visalia	42.9	941	32.9	7.8	80.4	8.2	59 992	-0.9	6 429	10.7	93 921	64.8	37.5	25.1
Vista	52.1	1 176	37.2	3.3	91.3	6.0	43 267	0.2	2 473	5.7	76 595	56.5	32.8	29.2
Walnut	13.8	1 942	31.3	2.1	91.8	6.5	15 732	1.3	932	5.9	24 936	63.4	40.8	17.2
Walnut Creek	35.0	1 428	29.1	8.0	84.1	13.2	33 084	1.1	1 401	4.2	55 808	59.1	36.2	35.1
Wasco	54.7	661	28.6	13.0	70.9	21.2	8 571	-0.3	1 182	13.8	19 270	44.4	21.9	24.5
Watsonville	59.7	1 185	36.9	10.9	91.0	4.0	25 238	-0.2	2 830	11.2	37 632	66.2	32.7	21.6
West Covina	35.5	1 380	34.9	5.0	85.3	11.1	54 260	0.5	5 462	10.1	85 688	65.0	37.0	22.6
West Hollywood	79.6	1 351	32.5	12.9	78.5	18.4	25 397	1.2	1 742	6.9	33 778	77.7	46.4	25.3
Westminster	45.7	1 362	38.7	6.2	86.5	10.0	42 839	0.2	3 230	7.5	73 735	61.2	35.9	24.1
West Sacramento	46.7	884	36.0	10.0	79.7	10.6	24 434	0.1	2 174	8.9	38 058	63.8	37.5	28.6
Whittier	42.6	1 149	33.5	6.0	89.8	6.6	43 061	1.2	2 809	6.5	67 327	64.3	40.9	22.3
Wildomar	26.0	1 400	38.4	2.2	84.9	12.2	NA	NA	NA	NA	25 108	64.6	33.3	24.0
Windsor	22.3	1 724	30.3	4.3	88.5	6.7	13 940	2.0	670	4.8	20 720	66.0	39.1	26.6
Woodland	45.7	888	31.0	8.9	85.2	6.7	28 737	0.3	2 339	8.1	43 590	64.8	38.0	28.3
Yorba Linda	16.4	1 618	40.2	4.7	89.7	7.9	34 282	0.7	1 650	4.8	52 918	67.2	42.6	20.4
Yuba City	42.7	899	34.6	7.8	83.3	7.0	30 833	-1.1	4 187	13.6	49 940	61.3	31.9	30.7
Yucaipa	27.7	1 063	29.8	3.9	85.9	7.9	24 349	1.2	1 996	8.2	40 635	62.5	34.2	28.2
COLORADO	35.6	950	30.9	5.7	80.4	13.1	2 817 334	1.4	141 387	5.0	4 088 424	68.6	42.1	22.8
Arvada	26.0	983	30.8	3.8	85.2	10.6	62 516	1.6	2 862	4.6	87 599	70.5	46.8	23.8
Aurora	43.7	959	33.6	6.9	76.4	13.2	180 871	1.6	10 117	5.6	257 494	71.1	42.9	20.4
Boulder	51.2	1 173	40.4	9.0	61.2	21.3	60 252	1.3	2 456	4.1	88 976	67.8	33.5	22.1
Brighton	30.6	964	28.9	5.0	87.4	10.4	17 569	1.0	992	5.6	25 052	67.1	43.3	17.4
Broomfield	33.9	1 259	27.2	4.5	79.5	17.2	33 583	2.0	1 436	4.3	44 667	72.0	48.9	20.9

1. $2,000 represents $2,000 or more. 2. 50.0 represents 50 percent or more. 3. Percent of civilian labor force. 4. Persons 16 years old and over.

Table D. Cities — **Construction, Wholesale Trade, and Retail Trade**

City	Value of residential construction authorized by building permits, 2014			Wholesale trade,[1] 2007				Retail trade,[2] 2007			
	New construction ($1,000)	Number of housing units	Percent single family	Number of establish-ments	Number of employees	Sales (mil dol)	Annual payroll (mil dol)	Number of establish-ments	Number of employees	Sales (mil dol)	Annual payroll (mil dol)
	69	70	71	72	73	74	75	76	77	78	79
CALIFORNIA—Cont'd											
San Francisco	768 892	2 711	1.3	1 195	11 786	10 562.2	668.1	3 710	45 079	12 400.0	1 395.9
San Gabriel	7 554	24	100.0	146	726	220.1	21.5	221	1 651	440.4	35.5
San Jacinto	9 141	56	100.0	13	167	60.0	5.9	54	744	195.6	19.5
San Jose	595 056	4 445	8.6	1 098	21 549	30 166.7	1 922.0	2 397	41 343	11 482.4	1 666.4
San Juan Capistrano	26 097	59	100.0	62	414	318.7	21.9	150	1 883	535.9	53.9
San Leandro	22 960	116	0.9	263	5 151	2 428.6	271.5	320	5 597	1 557.9	151.9
San Luis Obispo	44 060	200	69.5	74	855	312.9	38.2	382	5 357	1 283.3	125.4
San Marcos	41 025	101	94.1	155	1 757	800.0	72.7	263	4 611	1 224.6	129.9
San Mateo	23 644	96	100.0	101	887	438.3	69.3	408	7 320	1 652.2	203.4
San Pablo	7 751	31	100.0	8	D	D	D	82	956	222.8	23.1
San Rafael	113	1	100.0	138	1 523	1 049.6	82.9	373	5 583	1 657.5	178.3
San Ramon	6 076	48	0.0	90	956	2 534.8	75.7	136	2 546	679.1	70.4
Santa Ana	19 782	95	100.0	560	7 262	2 881.5	372.9	920	13 893	3 346.1	372.8
Santa Barbara	25 749	119	5.9	111	1 330	558.9	51.8	617	7 579	1 729.6	205.3
Santa Clara	305 287	1 687	3.3	399	12 368	7 464.8	1 298.6	403	5 602	1 806.7	192.1
Santa Clarita	90 637	322	94.1	194	3 053	6 452.9	169.3	531	10 207	2 903.2	251.6
Santa Cruz	16 675	50	100.0	48	927	622.4	62.2	287	3 601	830.5	95.0
Santa Maria	52 179	344	37.8	108	1 218	673.7	52.3	349	5 531	1 448.8	139.3
Santa Monica	65 012	228	18.0	171	3 840	3 259.4	191.9	750	10 025	4 944.7	340.1
Santa Paula	604	2	100.0	14	D	D	D	64	724	168.6	17.7
Santa Rosa	44 969	248	74.2	157	2 514	1 522.5	155.8	729	11 971	2 977.2	334.8
Santee	19 963	176	2.3	51	447	152.8	15.8	131	2 835	672.9	64.2
Saratoga	14 667	19	100.0	24	145	75.9	7.5	51	542	108.8	13.1
Seaside	0	0	0.0	13	62	33.6	2.0	96	1 871	563.3	53.1
Simi Valley	2 286	3	100.0	140	2 137	852.5	100.5	468	6 857	1 689.6	159.3
Soledad	0	0	0.0	5	D	D	D	31	290	72.7	6.3
South Gate	35 943	224	1.3	64	915	717.4	41.2	185	2 518	787.0	61.8
South Pasadena	1 921	5	100.0	27	122	163.5	8.6	66	837	192.3	21.8
South San Francisco	731	5	100.0	332	5 350	3 150.1	339.0	193	2 676	791.9	83.3
Stanton	9 574	52	100.0	34	331	100.0	13.4	117	1 293	347.5	34.1
Stockton	21 907	96	79.2	248	4 783	3 701.8	199.4	759	13 076	3 340.1	301.2
Suisun City	0	0	0.0	4	D	D	D	33	520	172.5	13.9
Sunnyvale	133 544	821	23.9	228	12 043	10 557.8	1 587.1	316	5 524	1 863.1	159.2
Temecula	79 397	662	35.3	166	2 804	2 112.1	104.6	480	8 447	2 371.3	206.5
Temple City	37 086	104	100.0	80	327	112.2	7.6	110	964	180.6	18.5
Thousand Oaks	13 270	48	33.3	184	2 385	1 462.0	170.5	594	9 292	2 853.8	273.1
Torrance	7 377	27	100.0	586	6 226	13 175.4	321.5	762	14 145	4 877.8	371.1
Tracy	44 538	135	100.0	59	981	1 101.0	57.9	269	4 306	1 106.0	101.3
Tulare	32 642	203	100.0	41	541	182.3	21.7	185	2 838	662.4	65.4
Turlock	19 356	95	100.0	53	667	265.9	27.9	238	4 092	987.2	96.9
Tustin	920	3	100.0	195	2 709	1 343.4	160.8	286	4 961	1 849.9	147.2
Twentynine Palms	909	8	100.0	4	15	4.1	0.4	31	326	93.8	7.4
Union City	66	1	100.0	140	3 814	2 905.4	235.0	120	2 716	665.3	84.4
Upland	14 193	54	100.0	103	665	188.4	25.7	280	4 124	918.8	94.8
Vacaville	41 786	138	100.0	35	D	D	D	348	6 010	1 430.5	135.5
Vallejo	4 366	17	100.0	29	599	398.7	30.0	269	4 432	1 192.8	123.9
Victorville	13 341	46	100.0	39	217	169.9	11.0	372	7 457	1 939.5	173.1
Visalia	108 591	435	98.2	134	1 334	1 566.1	60.2	468	7 658	1 943.0	177.9
Vista	108 020	753	7.2	196	3 485	1 694.8	169.6	294	4 914	1 246.6	135.0
Walnut	6 129	14	100.0	265	988	611.5	36.0	106	1 082	209.7	21.2
Walnut Creek	73 610	325	4.3	74	484	583.0	31.0	356	7 089	1 918.4	231.7
Wasco	2 400	24	100.0	3	28	12.7	1.0	39	432	82.4	8.3
Watsonville	6 357	71	43.7	71	1 494	1 081.9	78.0	166	2 627	1 540.4	69.6
West Covina	8 078	18	100.0	72	182	100.2	5.0	284	6 118	1 563.9	144.7
West Hollywood	67 415	292	3.8	121	771	369.9	44.2	348	4 397	1 285.7	130.6
Westminster	5 784	21	85.7	103	487	229.8	16.1	442	6 101	1 625.6	147.8
West Sacramento	17 338	61	100.0	143	4 622	5 685.7	203.3	127	2 296	523.6	57.7
Whittier	15 342	71	1.4	74	414	157.1	15.2	228	3 661	815.0	80.5
Wildomar	470	3	100.0	5	D	D	D	31	367	126.7	10.3
Windsor	3 585	8	100.0	23	322	80.1	17.0	52	1 120	278.9	29.6
Woodland	39 854	128	100.0	74	1 020	528.8	43.6	178	2 748	586.0	60.0
Yorba Linda	32 609	94	100.0	112	1 614	1 021.1	120.1	119	1 878	578.0	49.5
Yuba City	16 724	57	82.5	45	527	199.3	21.4	262	4 323	983.7	100.0
Yucaipa	902	4	100.0	19	96	33.7	3.4	86	973	229.5	23.4
COLORADO	6 479 529	28 686	59.6	5 850	81 144	53 599.0	4 191.0	19 428	261 962	65 896.8	6 537.5
Arvada	157 518	597	100.0	83	661	532.6	33.6	279	4 037	958.8	97.7
Aurora	220 809	1 024	81.3	237	6 062	5 839.6	295.2	909	16 098	3 664.5	366.7
Boulder	114 852	608	17.1	194	2 414	1 131.8	212.2	614	8 421	1 919.5	224.0
Brighton	18 993	98	100.0	28	465	378.0	19.6	87	1 757	476.5	45.7
Broomfield	190 713	820	53.5	68	D	D	D	279	5 355	1 139.8	111.3

1. Merchant wholesalers except manufacturers' sales branches and offices. 2. Establishments with payroll.

City	Real estate and rental and leasing, 2007				Professional, scientific, and technical services,[1] 2007				Manufacturing, 2007			
	Number of establish-ments	Number of employees	Receipts (mil dol)	Annual payroll (mil dol)	Number of establish-ments	Number of employees	Receipts (mil dol)	Annual payroll (mil dol)	Number of establish-ments	Number of employees	Receipts (mil dol)	Annual payroll (mil dol)
	80	81	82	83	84	85	86	87	88	89	90	91
CALIFORNIA—Cont'd												
San Francisco	1 843	14 332	4 309.7	984.3	5 600	D	D	D	788	11 339	2 077.5	422.5
San Gabriel	92	510	75.2	10.6	119	349	40.1	12.1	NA	NA	NA	NA
San Jacinto	23	104	15.6	2.5	23	180	16.0	6.1	34	640	83.7	20.0
San Jose	1 124	6 677	1 637.4	278.1	2 771	44 768	5 497.4	5 265.1	960	43 662	17 377.9	2 967.7
San Juan Capistrano	88	399	78.5	21.9	211	897	145.9	46.3	30	1 086	229.5	49.9
San Leandro	130	2 372	426.1	89.7	127	1 010	141.5	58.7	211	6 620	2 061.6	285.8
San Luis Obispo	137	802	106.9	23.6	330	D	D	D	64	979	166.6	39.3
San Marcos	106	500	100.0	19.2	221	D	D	D	188	4 916	1 141.6	220.2
San Mateo	205	1 065	462.8	76.1	526	D	D	D	57	579	D	27.1
San Pablo	25	78	16.0	2.2	11	D	D	D	NA	NA	NA	NA
San Rafael	167	1 019	535.4	46.9	518	D	D	D	88	832	154.4	32.8
San Ramon	125	897	192.4	41.4	439	5 264	996.0	429.9	NA	NA	NA	NA
Santa Ana	347	2 868	443.7	125.3	1 012	10 987	1 650.8	664.6	875	23 728	5 339.9	954.4
Santa Barbara	269	1 408	293.0	53.3	684	4 647	897.8	307.6	117	1 326	233.3	58.4
Santa Clara	193	1 411	364.6	77.7	850	D	D	D	542	18 177	5 296.3	1 306.0
Santa Clarita	225	1 012	186.3	31.6	501	D	D	D	246	9 292	1 860.4	463.1
Santa Cruz	89	415	87.5	11.7	306	D	D	D	100	1 600	310.9	69.0
Santa Maria	93	523	84.5	17.7	159	1 195	133.3	59.3	100	3 020	666.8	110.3
Santa Monica	438	3 095	1 205.9	194.7	1 192	D	D	D	100	1 201	256.0	46.2
Santa Paula	26	138	26.8	5.2	25	146	17.2	6.4	23	563	123.8	23.4
Santa Rosa	274	1 267	267.8	44.1	606	D	D	D	182	7 583	1 124.2	481.8
Santee	73	252	41.4	7.7	88	D	D	D	88	1 401	232.1	54.0
Saratoga	82	226	90.5	10.9	159	504	77.1	29.6	NA	NA	NA	NA
Seaside	15	97	12.4	2.7	18	D	D	D	NA	NA	NA	NA
Simi Valley	127	501	75.8	14.1	360	2 001	422.4	124.7	158	4 012	831.6	181.1
Soledad	7	25	2.5	0.4	4	28	1.5	0.6	NA	NA	NA	NA
South Gate	52	251	172.4	8.3	36	310	34.2	12.1	146	6 065	2 260.3	245.7
South Pasadena	46	163	26.9	5.3	158	D	D	D	NA	NA	NA	NA
South San Francisco	94	979	164.4	36.3	178	D	D	D	130	13 709	D	975.8
Stanton	27	157	27.3	3.2	30	176	12.9	5.0	76	978	131.3	37.8
Stockton	280	1 569	250.5	54.3	403	D	D	D	204	7 622	2 506.6	303.1
Suisun City	15	50	8.8	1.1	20	168	46.6	8.6	NA	NA	NA	NA
Sunnyvale	147	1 184	298.2	56.2	741	17 893	3 543.1	1 623.4	276	40 837	10 241.2	3 029.2
Temecula	196	747	132.9	32.2	377	D	D	D	129	7 716	1 929.2	377.3
Temple City	52	170	24.6	5.3	69	232	20.2	6.6	NA	NA	NA	NA
Thousand Oaks	290	1 294	359.1	67.4	787	5 177	4 358.1	359.6	132	3 373	1 113.9	234.1
Torrance	352	2 184	420.2	72.2	897	D	D	D	280	14 673	5 621.3	816.0
Tracy	77	235	139.0	7.7	112	514	45.8	16.2	53	2 512	1 063.0	111.1
Tulare	45	166	37.8	4.5	48	258	38.9	16.0	32	1 786	1 165.2	76.4
Turlock	62	334	37.0	8.1	71	515	46.9	16.5	77	3 762	1 605.0	137.5
Tustin	206	1 196	179.1	42.3	560	D	D	D	131	4 401	1 654.1	215.4
Twentynine Palms	16	113	9.5	1.5	11	92	11.3	2.5	NA	NA	NA	NA
Union City	48	395	116.3	19.7	106	433	70.0	23.9	90	4 149	1 088.0	218.8
Upland	106	965	366.5	57.1	220	1 498	182.5	73.1	116	1 078	210.7	44.4
Vacaville	90	565	95.9	17.0	121	639	77.3	25.9	54	3 414	1 054.7	172.3
Vallejo	92	413	59.8	10.2	123	D	D	D	NA	NA	NA	NA
Victorville	93	711	92.8	19.9	104	D	D	D	31	1 272	501.8	60.3
Visalia	131	695	104.6	20.8	259	D	D	D	81	2 657	617.4	99.6
Vista	142	599	105.7	20.1	252	D	D	D	197	8 746	2 730.7	347.4
Walnut	41	118	30.7	6.3	108	337	47.9	12.8	NA	NA	NA	NA
Walnut Creek	243	1 439	313.9	73.7	747	6 760	1 399.6	566.2	39	1 144	531.9	57.3
Wasco	10	41	4.8	0.9	5	22	2.1	0.4	NA	NA	NA	NA
Watsonville	59	253	46.3	9.1	79	D	D	D	74	1 982	459.4	80.2
West Covina	84	703	78.6	16.4	149	1 355	101.9	42.6	NA	NA	NA	NA
West Hollywood	137	982	434.5	42.1	372	D	D	D	NA	NA	NA	NA
Westminster	91	425	83.1	12.3	161	667	111.9	21.7	105	1 104	195.3	34.8
West Sacramento	69	565	120.6	24.9	88	D	D	D	59	1 962	588.0	84.2
Whittier	101	372	49.3	10.1	178	1 074	102.4	41.9	61	1 287	214.3	48.3
Wildomar	12	112	7.9	2.6	23	68	4.4	1.6	NA	NA	NA	NA
Windsor	27	214	42.1	7.3	54	290	36.4	8.2	26	814	136.5	33.2
Woodland	60	273	47.9	8.3	77	D	D	D	68	2 896	841.2	108.0
Yorba Linda	130	449	119.5	18.0	219	1 135	143.0	46.8	64	1 638	713.1	113.6
Yuba City	89	589	58.4	12.7	112	D	D	D	55	1 245	421.8	D
Yucaipa	47	196	27.9	5.4	66	270	35.6	8.9	NA	NA	NA	NA
COLORADO	10 011	47 568	8 460.9	1 793.0	22 522	156 859	28 932.6	10 515.7	5 288	137 880	46 332.0	6 789.7
Arvada	131	415	47.3	10.8	371	1 675	191.6	79.8	105	2 239	508.7	106.5
Aurora	335	1 555	325.3	58.5	620	D	D	D	132	3 144	767.2	137.4
Boulder	321	1 336	270.6	50.7	1 196	D	D	D	216	7 933	2 193.3	442.8
Brighton	34	127	14.7	3.2	52	D	D	D	NA	NA	NA	NA
Broomfield	91	525	105.3	15.3	271	D	D	D	85	3 939	2 255.5	192.9

1. Establishments subject to federal tax.

City	Accommodation and food services, 2007				Arts, entertainment, and recreation,[1] 2007				Health care and social assistance,[1] 2007			
	Number of establish-ments	Number of employees	Sales (mil dol)	Annual payroll (mil dol)	Number of establish-ments	Number of employees	Receipts (mil dol)	Annual payroll (mil dol)	Number of establish-ments	Number of employees	Receipts (mil dol)	Annual payroll (mil dol)
	92	93	94	95	96	97	98	99	100	101	102	103
CALIFORNIA—Cont'd												
San Francisco	3 525	66 365	5 039.2	1 496.8	325	6 697	871.5	300.1	2 252	15 376	2 123.6	823.6
San Gabriel	167	1 318	71.6	18.5	5	D	D	D	178	D	D	D
San Jacinto	34	396	21.0	5.5	1	D	D	D	18	147	11.1	3.5
San Jose	1 793	30 188	1 714.6	474.1	134	4 474	403.1	160.8	2 010	22 791	2 620.3	1 078.0
San Juan Capistrano	71	1 287	68.5	20.5	18	D	D	D	117	2 632	275.7	125.0
San Leandro	173	2 162	118.5	32.1	15	D	D	D	225	2 637	291.7	110.7
San Luis Obispo	196	4 507	223.9	63.6	18	182	7.8	2.6	276	3 411	416.4	160.2
San Marcos	158	2 632	122.5	36.1	15	D	D	D	113	1 113	109.6	43.8
San Mateo	277	4 506	306.4	87.0	37	726	85.5	18.6	382	2 552	303.3	110.0
San Pablo	53	516	29.8	7.4	3	D	D	D	31	752	61.7	29.4
San Rafael	197	2 335	136.4	38.8	62	466	66.6	14.5	220	2 573	303.2	162.2
San Ramon	127	2 434	161.8	44.6	15	405	30.1	7.8	248	2 948	377.5	136.7
Santa Ana	518	7 690	447.4	119.2	29	333	28.7	6.2	745	8 689	960.6	384.0
Santa Barbara	400	7 984	447.1	124.4	59	843	43.6	17.8	457	3 945	519.1	194.7
Santa Clara	369	6 250	455.3	121.2	33	1 811	296.7	168.3	200	D	D	D
Santa Clarita	328	6 417	301.5	84.6	108	893	67.2	21.2	391	3 664	445.3	132.8
Santa Cruz	230	3 745	193.0	55.4	23	962	55.8	19.7	166	1 544	191.5	72.0
Santa Maria	168	2 993	150.5	41.7	14	249	9.0	2.7	262	2 144	212.7	78.0
Santa Monica	401	10 715	791.3	221.9	719	2 419	684.4	272.9	821	6 413	941.3	308.2
Santa Paula	45	522	22.0	5.6	3	D	D	D	39	298	29.4	10.3
Santa Rosa	394	5 911	300.2	84.4	50	756	35.2	12.0	609	7 234	941.9	398.9
Santee	89	1 522	68.4	20.6	10	186	9.7	3.1	57	486	38.7	14.8
Saratoga	51	561	38.5	11.4	6	84	5.4	2.4	86	561	50.2	19.5
Seaside	62	950	56.6	16.4	4	D	D	D	15	110	7.8	2.6
Simi Valley	252	4 191	204.9	59.3	53	D	D	D	270	2 059	216.9	79.9
Soledad	21	222	12.8	2.8	1	D	D	D	7	D	D	D
South Gate	113	1 137	62.2	15.0	5	D	D	D	74	744	74.1	24.9
South Pasadena	48	787	39.7	11.5	30	D	D	D	90	D	D	D
South San Francisco	203	3 466	289.6	73.7	16	131	11.4	2.9	160	2 413	272.2	141.7
Stanton	85	918	51.9	12.5	7	D	D	D	27	D	D	D
Stockton	471	6 765	343.5	89.5	37	687	40.0	14.5	602	8 582	972.7	367.3
Suisun City	29	411	17.5	4.5	4	D	D	D	26	85	6.1	2.2
Sunnyvale	327	4 318	276.7	75.2	25	D	D	D	302	3 741	375.3	188.1
Temecula	287	6 255	304.0	87.2	30	D	D	D	270	1 763	187.3	62.1
Temple City	65	845	40.0	11.2	11	20	1.0	0.3	93	968	69.1	23.5
Thousand Oaks	308	6 796	347.9	102.6	99	832	57.7	18.8	549	5 540	680.5	250.1
Torrance	432	8 920	503.2	140.5	59	D	D	D	936	8 131	1 136.1	353.8
Tracy	152	2 127	101.5	28.6	17	D	D	D	144	D	D	D
Tulare	95	1 184	59.7	16.0	8	D	D	D	88	D	D	D
Turlock	141	2 382	105.5	28.9	11	D	D	D	155	D	D	D
Tustin	201	3 407	176.4	55.2	20	D	D	D	343	2 771	292.5	109.9
Twentynine Palms	33	402	23.8	5.5	5	D	D	D	7	D	D	D
Union City	115	1 770	90.6	25.6	6	D	D	D	115	936	72.0	32.8
Upland	158	2 259	107.2	30.3	26	D	D	D	315	D	D	D
Vacaville	160	3 544	154.3	42.4	15	D	D	D	149	1 864	237.0	80.2
Vallejo	201	2 874	145.6	38.1	22	D	D	D	231	4 519	435.2	283.4
Victorville	199	3 777	182.0	49.9	13	D	D	D	171	3 260	325.6	113.8
Visalia	221	4 420	187.1	53.2	15	D	D	D	322	3 294	336.7	132.3
Vista	182	2 368	103.0	28.2	20	D	D	D	215	2 532	241.3	97.0
Walnut	67	641	32.8	8.2	4	D	D	D	70	722	43.8	19.6
Walnut Creek	202	4 666	258.8	76.6	35	524	30.4	9.6	412	D	D	D
Wasco	21	D	D	D	1	D	D	D	12	D	D	D
Watsonville	99	1 238	69.4	18.1	6	D	D	D	119	1 349	180.9	74.5
West Covina	200	3 635	177.5	49.0	15	D	D	D	281	D	D	D
West Hollywood	205	6 211	423.7	124.8	473	D	D	D	214	1 009	128.8	44.6
Westminster	232	2 780	139.3	39.2	17	D	D	D	275	2 164	229.7	75.3
West Sacramento	91	D	D	D	9	D	D	D	47	D	D	D
Whittier	100	2 070	144.0	41.9	11	D	D	D	309	D	D	D
Wildomar	20	245	13.0	3.3	8	155	4.9	1.3	45	D	D	D
Windsor	46	632	32.4	9.2	4	90	4.9	1.7	40	213	18.4	6.5
Woodland	109	D	D	D	10	D	D	D	90	1 126	108.6	54.9
Yorba Linda	87	1 706	78.6	24.6	22	D	D	D	153	1 228	139.0	44.4
Yuba City	126	2 274	90.7	25.6	13	D	D	D	202	D	D	D
Yucaipa	57	820	35.0	9.6	10	D	D	D	82	1 165	77.1	31.2
COLORADO	12 075	231 721	11 440.4	3 408.2	1 957	41 153	3 253.2	1 051.0	11 557	127 029	12 599.1	5 234.2
Arvada	169	2 963	128.1	35.4	19	D	D	D	187	1 382	121.1	46.1
Aurora	529	9 480	444.8	128.3	40	568	31.4	9.1	545	8 884	875.7	339.9
Boulder	402	8 121	390.5	120.6	90	944	59.9	15.1	510	3 719	352.1	158.3
Brighton	69	1 279	52.9	15.5	7	D	D	D	53	D	D	D
Broomfield	137	3 370	163.4	53.3	25	D	D	D	101	866	71.7	30.1

1. Establishments subject to federal tax.

Table D. Cities — **Other Services and Government Employment and Payroll**

City	Other services[1], 2007: Number of establish-ments	Other services[1], 2007: Number of employees	Other services[1], 2007: Receipts (mil dol)	Other services[1], 2007: Annual payroll (mil dol)	Government employment and payroll, 2012: Full-time equivalent employees	March payroll: Total (dollars)	Percent of total for: Adminis-tration, judicial, and legal	Police and Corrections	Fire Protection	Highways and trans-portation	Health and welfare	Natural resources and utilities	Education and libraries
	104	105	106	107	108	109	110	111	112	113	114	115	116
CALIFORNIA—Cont'd													
San Francisco	1 489	9 487	843.1	247.3	28 349	217 722 943	13.9	17.4	7.3	22.7	24.7	11.1	2.1
San Gabriel	79	448	40.7	13.3	191	1 327 334	11.3	38.5	24.6	6.9	3.8	11.2	0.0
San Jacinto	27	80	7.9	1.9	65	267 518	30.0	0.0	0.0	10.8	18.2	28.6	0.0
San Jose	1 100	7 036	896.0	232.2	5 214	38 715 963	8.8	33.1	18.0	9.9	1.0	14.9	3.3
San Juan Capistrano	46	295	21.0	6.7	115	698 016	51.1	0.6	0.0	8.3	1.4	33.4	0.0
San Leandro	158	1 201	182.8	46.2	375	2 465 492	13.1	40.7	0.0	11.7	4.5	15.4	7.2
San Luis Obispo	112	648	55.4	14.9	406	3 104 703	10.0	27.1	17.3	3.8	5.5	22.1	0.0
San Marcos	132	776	72.6	22.9	279	1 870 622	14.4	0.0	37.4	21.7	5.6	15.9	0.0
San Mateo	213	1 052	104.9	30.2	610	5 077 524	8.5	28.2	20.6	5.7	5.0	23.9	4.0
San Pablo	35	D	D	D	74	394 492	49.3	1.6	0.0	13.4	12.2	22.1	0.0
San Rafael	192	1 222	154.4	52.2	864	2 915 776	12.5	26.3	32.7	4.3	0.0	17.6	4.1
San Ramon	107	706	67.5	22.2	279	2 017 589	12.1	37.5	0.0	31.3	1.9	13.4	0.0
Santa Ana	415	2 658	254.6	69.5	2 711	12 719 386	0.7	3.5	1.9	0.5	0.5	0.5	0.1
Santa Barbara	201	1 315	101.0	29.0	1 156	7 284 111	11.3	26.7	14.2	12.8	3.2	19.5	2.7
Santa Clara	227	1 477	162.3	48.2	961	8 545 138	10.4	22.6	18.9	6.8	0.6	30.5	3.6
Santa Clarita	244	1 784	171.0	45.8	434	2 697 699	16.1	0.0	0.0	6.2	6.5	35.1	0.0
Santa Cruz	103	618	56.7	17.0	774	4 763 881	12.0	20.2	14.4	4.6	2.0	33.9	8.6
Santa Maria	122	776	76.5	20.6	497	2 980 086	10.3	35.8	13.6	5.8	5.2	22.7	3.8
Santa Monica	328	2 365	196.0	53.0	2 163	15 220 898	14.3	23.8	11.2	20.8	3.2	14.6	3.3
Santa Paula	26	D	D	D	110	646 323	13.8	38.3	18.1	4.2	7.2	16.1	0.0
Santa Rosa	264	1 588	154.1	47.2	1 213	8 220 156	11.3	23.5	16.6	10.0	2.3	23.5	0.0
Santee	91	562	68.3	18.5	148	1 012 079	28.3	0.6	51.2	9.9	1.2	8.9	0.0
Saratoga	32	D	D	D	58	435 826	25.2	0.0	0.0	22.5	22.1	14.1	0.0
Seaside	49	202	23.9	6.4	158	994 460	9.5	41.0	20.0	8.9	0.9	6.0	0.0
Simi Valley	179	D	D	D	592	3 356 138	14.7	32.1	0.0	21.1	15.4	16.6	0.0
Soledad	4	D	D	D	45	264 288	21.2	60.5	0.0	1.9	0.0	16.4	0.0
South Gate	74	316	28.4	8.4	318	1 634 468	11.2	44.3	0.0	17.0	9.3	18.2	0.0
South Pasadena	32	D	D	D	168	950 670	11.5	35.7	20.9	5.1	8.3	7.4	9.4
South San Francisco	117	1 419	136.2	46.5	497	3 574 682	9.0	29.5	25.0	5.7	0.7	17.9	6.9
Stanton	58	266	27.1	7.1	38	219 326	37.8	0.0	0.0	18.7	21.0	22.5	0.0
Stockton	322	2 500	194.9	65.0	2 010	12 427 436	7.5	55.8	14.5	0.7	2.3	9.7	2.3
Suisun City	20	D	D	D	85	454 879	15.9	38.0	4.6	17.0	8.7	8.9	0.0
Sunnyvale	154	874	120.6	33.0	870	7 456 793	9.7	27.3	18.0	7.5	4.3	20.3	3.7
Temecula	185	997	80.7	22.7	200	1 117 348	29.5	0.5	0.7	25.3	14.8	29.0	0.0
Temple City	53	239	15.7	3.5	75	319 507	42.5	0.0	0.0	0.0	0.0	25.4	0.0
Thousand Oaks	217	1 172	105.8	29.1	440	2 648 993	26.5	1.5	0.0	28.8	2.2	20.8	12.0
Torrance	257	1 669	166.5	55.5	1 361	10 031 057	10.8	31.2	18.3	15.1	4.3	10.6	3.4
Tracy	96	434	37.9	10.0	420	2 906 444	11.9	31.9	22.5	6.6	1.4	20.4	0.0
Tulare	58	338	35.7	9.3	347	1 781 358	7.7	33.8	16.3	2.3	3.5	23.6	2.6
Turlock	84	716	50.8	16.7	394	2 010 112	13.5	34.3	14.7	8.6	2.6	22.0	0.0
Tustin	113	893	95.6	28.2	338	2 566 292	15.4	48.7	0.0	14.6	2.0	11.4	0.0
Twentynine Palms	13	D	D	D	26	143 616	18.5	18.8	0.0	23.3	0.0	39.5	0.0
Union City	61	542	88.2	19.1	252	1 774 885	14.0	49.2	0.0	3.0	5.2	19.0	0.0
Upland	152	769	63.9	18.5	892	4 437 479	3.7	19.6	11.3	3.4	2.6	5.7	1.6
Vacaville	94	515	41.7	11.8	584	4 121 808	12.2	30.0	19.8	13.3	4.5	20.2	0.0
Vallejo	119	615	50.8	15.9	573	3 266 338	8.6	32.1	16.0	8.2	5.4	28.1	0.0
Victorville	108	753	95.8	19.1	340	1 783 174	43.6	0.0	0.0	23.9	2.4	30.1	0.0
Visalia	159	1 096	94.8	26.2	612	3 335 649	7.1	37.8	15.7	9.2	6.0	23.1	0.0
Vista	127	759	75.1	22.4	290	1 741 746	25.7	0.0	39.6	9.1	5.0	16.8	0.0
Walnut	69	D	D	D	52	276 966	49.6	0.0	0.0	21.7	8.9	19.8	0.0
Walnut Creek	161	1 121	101.5	31.4	389	2 700 536	16.3	37.1	0.0	5.7	0.7	23.8	0.0
Wasco	11	33	3.5	0.7	60	270 885	30.6	0.0	0.0	10.8	0.0	46.4	0.0
Watsonville	68	234	23.8	6.0	373	2 335 983	9.1	27.3	13.3	4.5	1.8	31.8	5.7
West Covina	98	518	35.9	9.7	445	2 840 481	9.7	46.0	25.6	12.3	2.3	4.1	0.0
West Hollywood	165	1 107	82.2	21.3	216	1 683 338	37.7	0.0	0.0	20.8	29.7	11.7	0.0
Westminster	139	614	61.5	15.8	290	1 903 418	13.5	58.3	0.0	6.1	4.4	8.3	0.0
West Sacramento	78	576	68.6	20.1	402	3 250 336	14.1	25.4	25.1	1.9	6.5	14.5	0.0
Whittier	125	D	D	D	478	2 572 894	10.2	44.2	0.0	4.8	6.2	21.3	5.7
Wildomar	13	D	D	D	12	48 677	78.0	0.0	0.0	0.0	0.0	0.0	0.0
Windsor	29	142	12.8	4.1	98	584 900	39.6	0.0	0.0	13.3	0.0	47.2	0.0
Woodland	86	535	41.5	11.9	304	1 839 421	7.6	32.0	20.0	4.8	13.1	16.1	2.4
Yorba Linda	83	484	48.7	13.4	130	661 872	25.1	0.0	0.0	10.0	1.5	30.7	18.9
Yuba City	94	D	D	D	299	1 719 010	11.1	33.5	26.1	7.0	0.0	20.2	0.0
Yucaipa	43	192	15.0	3.7	44	165 657	7.8	0.0	0.0	38.1	0.0	54.1	0.0
COLORADO	7 904	45 358	3 811.5	1 178.5	X	X	X	X	X	X	X	X	X
Arvada	167	856	56.6	17.6	661	3 647 076	20.5	35.5	0.0	9.8	4.4	22.2	0.0
Aurora	379	2 366	197.5	58.5	2 579	13 742 359	13.6	38.9	14.9	4.2	2.6	20.7	1.4
Boulder	220	1 480	127.3	44.8	1 108	6 200 124	15.9	23.9	11.2	6.6	1.6	26.0	4.7
Brighton	56	292	28.0	8.3	297	2 531 155	9.4	15.0	0.0	3.0	57.8	11.9	0.0
Broomfield	76	577	92.6	37.8	687	3 465 198	16.4	35.0	0.0	2.4	18.0	19.6	3.9

1. Establishments subject to federal tax.

City	City government finances, 2007									
	General revenue							General expenditure		
		Intergovernmental		Taxes					Per capita[1] (dollars)	
					Per capita[1] (dollars)					
	Total (mil dol)	Total (mil dol)	Percent from state government	Total (mil dol)	Total	Property	Sales and gross receipts	Total (mil dol)	Total	Capital outlays
	117	118	119	120	121	122	123	124	125	126
CALIFORNIA—Cont'd										
San Francisco	7 274.1	2 355.9	68.6	2 846.2	3 430	1 747	885	5 704.0	6 875	846
San Gabriel	37.1	3.0	81.2	25.2	626	356	258	40.2	999	177
San Jacinto	28.1	1.5	100.0	14.5	318	213	92	31.0	681	34
San Jose	1 721.1	116.7	56.0	863.4	876	456	363	1 428.0	1 449	178
San Juan Capistrano	47.2	4.4	76.8	30.4	856	577	270	40.6	1 144	265
San Leandro	123.0	8.3	72.0	88.5	1 016	465	517	121.7	1 398	127
San Luis Obispo	81.4	6.3	56.0	48.1	1 049	330	716	76.5	1 668	350
San Marcos	121.3	7.6	84.2	76.6	879	491	384	132.6	1 523	283
San Mateo	145.7	11.0	62.3	86.7	867	454	370	148.4	1 483	264
San Pablo	44.1	1.8	97.0	39.1	1 326	549	776	38.0	1 291	386
San Rafael	85.9	4.1	86.9	52.8	903	369	506	87.5	1 496	47
San Ramon	74.2	3.7	100.0	41.1	557	343	208	75.1	1 017	190
Santa Ana	440.5	127.5	23.8	205.9	621	334	285	391.8	1 181	145
Santa Barbara	246.8	36.0	63.6	102.8	1 149	512	631	228.4	2 550	530
Santa Clara	280.5	11.7	71.5	124.3	1 039	577	456	212.3	1 776	110
Santa Clarita	152.4	24.6	54.9	80.2	448	205	233	145.6	814	191
Santa Cruz	132.1	4.8	59.8	60.6	977	437	528	145.4	2 345	279
Santa Maria	117.0	16.8	78.0	58.2	574	182	391	112.6	1 111	201
Santa Monica	560.2	57.7	51.4	332.1	3 618	1 337	2 095	538.6	5 867	1 727
Santa Paula	29.3	4.2	87.4	12.9	428	275	94	23.2	771	142
Santa Rosa	262.1	24.5	59.6	119.5	702	255	435	250.3	1 470	305
Santee	44.7	2.6	60.7	34.2	616	379	155	49.1	885	180
Saratoga	20.9	1.1	97.2	15.0	490	306	160	22.6	736	169
Seaside	27.0	2.8	39.4	22.4	662	372	288	30.5	899	206
Simi Valley	96.1	10.2	52.4	62.4	497	300	194	92.5	736	103
Soledad	15.7	1.0	97.1	6.1	229	125	103	14.9	563	43
South Gate	80.6	17.7	38.8	36.7	383	216	166	67.6	707	121
South Pasadena	28.7	3.5	84.1	19.0	731	429	296	28.2	1 089	148
South San Francisco	128.4	5.4	89.0	77.6	1 179	732	371	122.6	1 863	259
Stanton	32.9	2.6	78.3	26.3	682	496	169	38.1	989	253
Stockton	381.7	98.9	79.6	161.7	544	215	325	384.7	1 293	244
Suisun City	27.1	4.4	39.6	13.1	458	385	71	30.3	1 061	113
Sunnyvale	274.8	32.4	34.0	112.9	770	377	386	274.4	1 871	145
Temecula	113.3	14.0	33.6	69.7	665	351	310	129.7	1 238	371
Temple City	15.4	1.3	81.7	11.0	305	164	133	14.2	393	12
Thousand Oaks	143.2	11.9	64.9	84.5	660	350	305	145.4	1 135	190
Torrance	261.0	41.4	39.9	155.5	1 056	365	677	234.0	1 589	118
Tracy	114.6	11.3	53.2	47.1	556	256	297	128.6	1 519	332
Tulare	97.1	4.2	71.5	38.5	632	245	375	90.8	1 492	464
Turlock	69.6	5.8	56.0	34.6	496	222	216	83.2	1 193	431
Tustin	77.0	3.6	66.8	51.5	661	437	220	77.9	1 001	98
Twentynine Palms	11.2	1.2	85.8	9.5	370	226	143	12.3	477	86
Union City	85.1	5.7	83.5	61.0	850	562	282	92.0	1 283	294
Upland	71.1	4.5	65.1	37.7	502	337	159	74.2	987	59
Vacaville	153.8	33.0	26.6	79.6	848	575	270	156.0	1 662	571
Vallejo	195.2	49.6	22.5	64.7	549	229	308	152.7	1 295	112
Victorville	115.4	9.5	68.3	53.9	448	251	195	130.1	1 082	123
Visalia	157.6	23.1	61.9	68.5	540	218	320	143.8	1 134	282
Vista	132.0	9.1	80.1	57.8	601	345	252	117.1	1 217	321
Walnut	21.5	1.3	82.0	13.1	436	322	106	20.0	668	25
Walnut Creek	70.1	2.6	97.1	45.9	699	317	354	80.4	1 224	103
Wasco	13.5	2.6	29.2	5.5	217	145	72	13.2	517	75
Watsonville	67.3	6.4	30.2	31.1	599	394	194	72.0	1 387	113
West Covina	102.2	8.7	74.3	63.9	594	395	196	91.9	854	133
West Hollywood	88.9	5.0	44.0	55.8	1 601	602	980	93.6	2 685	485
Westminster	91.7	10.4	70.7	68.6	750	538	210	114.0	1 245	487
West Sacramento	140.9	23.6	64.6	66.7	1 344	812	401	129.2	2 601	822
Whittier	79.8	8.9	72.4	41.7	483	250	231	82.4	954	94
Wildomar	9.4	3.2	100.0	5.9	177	97	62	9.3	280	7
Windsor	23.5	2.8	29.7	16.3	603	373	188	23.2	859	267
Woodland	72.5	12.3	93.9	44.7	793	310	482	78.0	1 385	376
Yorba Linda	62.1	4.6	47.2	35.0	526	382	138	79.9	1 201	263
Yuba City	54.9	5.2	89.4	33.0	508	270	193	59.0	910	163
Yucaipa	28.1	0.9	94.5	20.9	398	293	82	29.1	554	111
COLORADO	X	X	X	X	X	X	X	X	X	X
Arvada	132.6	21.2	32.5	67.8	619	84	534	119.2	1 086	160
Aurora	380.8	48.7	50.2	216.5	638	102	536	400.3	1 180	162
Boulder	219.5	16.4	84.1	150.1	1 471	286	1 185	210.4	2 063	39
Brighton	32.9	3.4	84.3	21.9	624	53	567	24.3	691	69
Broomfield	149.9	15.4	40.7	113.5	1 924	654	1 161	109.7	1 860	53

1. Based on population estimated as of July 1 of the year shown.

City	City government finances, 2012 (cont.)									
	General expenditure (cont.)									
	Percent of total for:									
	Public welfare	Highways	Parking facilities	Education	Health and hospitals	Police protection	Sewerage and sanitation	Parks and recreation	Housing and community development	Interest on debt
	127	128	129	130	131	132	133	134	135	136
CALIFORNIA—Cont'd										
San Francisco	8.5	4.4	2.4	0.0	30.2	6.6	4.7	4.3	4.2	7.1
San Gabriel	0.0	12.3	0.0	0.0	0.0	30.1	0.2	11.5	3.0	0.2
San Jacinto	0.0	13.6	0.0	0.0	0.0	28.1	10.6	3.1	13.0	4.6
San Jose	0.0	6.0	0.5	0.0	0.1	17.6	18.1	6.3	3.6	18.3
San Juan Capistrano	0.0	12.0	0.0	0.0	1.3	17.5	6.8	9.2	9.6	7.7
San Leandro	0.0	9.1	0.2	0.0	1.1	22.2	6.5	5.1	9.9	2.9
San Luis Obispo	0.0	16.3	3.7	0.0	0.0	20.2	13.2	9.3	2.1	2.5
San Marcos	0.0	12.9	0.0	0.0	3.2	11.1	0.0	7.4	24.5	11.5
San Mateo	0.0	10.7	1.3	0.0	1.3	19.6	17.8	9.7	2.9	4.2
San Pablo	0.0	22.7	0.0	0.0	0.4	36.6	0.0	6.8	8.3	9.8
San Rafael	0.0	8.4	3.3	0.0	6.9	21.6	0.0	11.4	2.3	2.2
San Ramon	0.0	11.3	0.0	0.0	0.0	21.4	0.0	20.7	7.9	7.1
Santa Ana	0.0	9.8	1.0	0.0	2.9	30.3	5.4	5.0	15.2	5.2
Santa Barbara	0.0	12.0	2.9	0.0	0.2	15.2	15.9	8.4	3.7	1.3
Santa Clara	0.0	9.0	0.6	0.0	2.0	19.7	16.4	8.4	2.4	4.7
Santa Clarita	0.0	30.6	0.0	0.0	0.1	13.0	0.3	12.7	3.7	3.5
Santa Cruz	0.0	6.8	2.2	0.0	1.0	27.5	18.8	8.9	8.5	2.8
Santa Maria	0.0	11.1	0.0	0.0	0.0	18.5	25.1	6.9	0.4	3.7
Santa Monica	0.0	6.8	0.2	0.0	3.3	13.7	7.2	9.9	25.8	2.8
Santa Paula	0.0	10.9	0.0	0.0	0.8	23.3	14.7	14.4	4.7	6.1
Santa Rosa	0.0	11.5	1.9	0.0	0.9	17.4	23.0	7.1	3.3	7.1
Santee	0.0	15.5	0.0	0.0	6.2	21.7	0.0	3.5	17.3	4.1
Saratoga	0.0	23.5	0.0	0.0	3.2	18.0	0.0	18.8	0.4	2.4
Seaside	0.0	9.8	0.0	0.0	0.6	36.9	0.0	8.6	10.5	5.0
Simi Valley	0.0	9.2	0.0	0.0	1.4	30.9	17.3	1.0	10.4	3.5
Soledad	0.0	13.2	0.0	0.0	1.3	25.1	31.6	3.9	2.2	2.7
South Gate	0.0	24.1	0.0	0.0	0.1	28.3	7.2	6.6	3.6	9.8
South Pasadena	0.0	13.6	0.1	0.0	1.0	25.7	4.3	10.7	1.7	0.0
South San Francisco	0.0	19.1	0.7	0.0	6.2	17.3	14.3	8.2	4.4	5.1
Stanton	0.0	6.3	0.0	0.0	0.2	22.4	1.8	5.3	35.3	8.9
Stockton	0.0	9.4	0.6	0.0	0.6	24.6	11.6	5.1	6.1	5.1
Suisun City	0.0	7.8	0.0	0.0	0.0	16.2	0.0	6.2	22.0	8.1
Sunnyvale	0.0	8.6	0.5	0.3	0.5	11.3	28.1	8.2	2.4	1.5
Temecula	0.0	19.9	0.0	0.0	0.2	17.4	4.7	15.3	10.4	3.5
Temple City	0.0	9.2	1.0	0.0	1.7	23.9	0.2	13.7	6.8	1.8
Thousand Oaks	0.0	22.4	0.0	0.0	0.5	17.9	13.0	6.9	8.4	2.8
Torrance	0.0	12.5	0.0	0.0	4.5	28.2	6.5	8.3	2.8	3.0
Tracy	0.0	6.2	0.0	0.0	0.4	16.6	24.2	12.4	3.8	5.1
Tulare	0.0	20.9	0.0	0.0	1.3	13.0	23.7	3.4	6.2	11.6
Turlock	0.0	9.9	0.0	0.0	0.5	33.2	16.6	4.4	11.0	1.6
Tustin	0.0	13.4	0.0	0.0	0.0	29.4	0.0	4.0	8.8	9.1
Twentynine Palms	0.0	17.8	0.0	0.0	5.0	25.2	0.0	13.8	5.5	4.2
Union City	0.0	8.6	0.0	0.0	0.6	22.1	0.8	13.1	17.7	7.7
Upland	0.0	9.8	0.0	0.0	1.4	22.4	19.7	2.8	10.4	2.3
Vacaville	0.0	6.6	0.0	0.0	4.4	17.0	29.3	4.9	18.9	3.8
Vallejo	0.0	10.3	0.0	0.0	0.4	22.0	15.1	0.9	18.2	3.0
Victorville	0.0	6.3	0.0	0.0	0.4	13.7	19.3	5.0	2.1	11.3
Visalia	0.0	12.5	0.0	0.0	0.0	19.7	23.2	7.4	2.8	1.1
Vista	0.0	9.8	0.0	0.0	3.8	15.0	17.2	7.4	9.0	7.5
Walnut	0.0	20.0	0.0	0.0	0.6	30.8	0.0	17.0	5.4	5.1
Walnut Creek	0.0	11.1	4.4	0.0	0.0	23.7	0.0	30.1	1.5	0.3
Wasco	0.0	17.2	0.0	0.0	1.0	28.0	26.1	0.0	8.4	1.4
Watsonville	0.0	7.2	0.0	0.0	1.0	19.7	25.5	4.2	6.2	0.5
West Covina	0.0	14.3	0.4	0.0	2.6	31.7	0.0	5.3	5.0	7.9
West Hollywood	0.0	10.7	3.8	0.0	7.0	16.4	2.5	5.8	5.8	3.5
Westminster	0.0	7.6	0.0	0.0	0.9	22.8	0.0	3.0	44.5	5.1
West Sacramento	0.0	18.1	0.0	0.0	0.3	13.0	10.0	6.8	11.0	8.6
Whittier	0.0	9.9	0.0	0.0	0.0	33.8	13.2	11.2	4.0	4.8
Wildomar	0.0	21.2	0.0	0.0	2.4	22.8	0.0	0.9	0.0	0.0
Windsor	0.0	20.4	0.0	0.0	1.0	24.7	0.0	3.9	13.1	4.1
Woodland	0.0	17.7	0.0	0.0	0.0	19.0	12.1	6.1	4.4	3.6
Yorba Linda	0.0	25.6	0.0	0.0	0.0	14.8	6.4	14.1	10.6	6.2
Yuba City	0.0	6.1	0.0	0.0	0.8	23.5	22.2	5.7	6.5	1.7
Yucaipa	0.0	24.1	0.0	0.0	4.3	22.0	0.0	13.1	11.5	2.4
COLORADO	X	X	X	X	X	X	X	X	X	X
Arvada	0.0	15.3	0.0	0.0	0.0	19.8	10.3	18.6	8.4	1.3
Aurora	0.0	13.0	0.0	0.0	0.0	21.5	14.3	11.3	2.9	2.2
Boulder	0.0	17.2	3.0	0.0	0.0	21.6	5.5	19.0	9.4	2.5
Brighton	0.0	11.9	0.0	0.0	0.0	22.3	16.7	14.5	0.0	7.4
Broomfield	10.4	8.0	0.0	0.0	1.6	14.4	5.1	12.8	0.0	12.6

City	City government finances, 2012 (cont.)			Climate[2]						
	Debt outstanding			Average daily temperature (degrees Fahrenheit)						
				Mean		Limits				
	Total (mil dol)	Per capita[1] (dollars)	Debt issued during year	January	July	January[3]	July[4]	Annual precipitation (inches)	Heating degree days	Cooling degree days
	137	138	139	140	141	142	143	144	145	146
CALIFORNIA—Cont'd										
San Francisco	13 075.2	15 759	3 426.5	52.3	61.3	46.4	68.2	22.28	2 597	163
San Gabriel	3.0	74	3.3	56.3	75.6	42.6	89.0	18.56	1 295	1 575
San Jacinto	24.5	538	0.0	NA	NA	NA	NA	NA	NA	NA
San Jose	5 924.6	6 013	690.9	50.5	70.9	41.7	84.3	15.08	2 171	811
San Juan Capistrano	68.5	1 928	0.0	55.4	68.7	43.9	77.3	13.56	1 756	666
San Leandro	78.3	899	0.0	50.0	62.8	43.6	70.4	25.40	2 857	142
San Luis Obispo	65.5	1 429	0.0	53.3	66.5	41.9	80.3	24.36	2 138	476
San Marcos	501.2	5 755	0.0	56.4	71.6	45.1	82.2	13.69	1 514	1 047
San Mateo	159.9	1 599	0.0	48.4	68.0	39.1	80.8	20.16	2 764	422
San Pablo	81.2	2 754	0.2	48.8	67.7	41.3	80.9	34.29	2 621	451
San Rafael	46.5	794	0.1	48.8	67.7	41.3	80.9	34.29	2 621	451
San Ramon	108.0	1 464	11.6	47.2	72.0	37.4	89.1	14.82	2 755	858
Santa Ana	358.1	1 080	0.0	58.0	72.9	46.6	87.7	13.84	1 153	1 299
Santa Barbara	112.5	1 257	1.5	53.1	67.0	40.8	76.7	16.93	2 121	482
Santa Clara	388.8	3 251	0.0	50.5	70.9	41.7	84.3	15.08	2 171	811
Santa Clarita	94.2	526	0.0	50.3	74.1	36.1	94.2	13.96	2 502	1 139
Santa Cruz	79.2	1 278	0.0	50.6	63.7	40.2	74.8	30.67	2 836	162
Santa Maria	66.7	658	51.7	51.6	63.5	39.3	73.5	14.01	2 783	121
Santa Monica	353.1	3 846	20.3	57.0	65.5	50.2	68.8	13.27	1 810	429
Santa Paula	69.0	2 299	0.0	54.7	68.3	41.2	80.7	18.41	1 911	602
Santa Rosa	483.1	2 836	59.1	48.7	67.6	39.5	82.2	31.01	2 694	526
Santee	52.7	950	3.0	57.1	73.0	45.7	83.6	13.75	1 313	1 261
Saratoga	12.0	391	12.0	50.5	70.9	41.7	84.3	15.08	2 171	811
Seaside	39.4	1 164	0.0	51.6	60.2	43.4	68.1	20.35	3 092	74
Simi Valley	147.8	1 177	0.0	53.7	76.0	39.5	95.0	17.79	1 822	1 485
Soledad	45.3	1 710	0.0	NA	NA	NA	NA	NA	NA	NA
South Gate	167.3	1 750	0.0	58.3	74.2	48.5	83.8	15.14	928	1 506
South Pasadena	7.3	280	0.0	NA	NA	NA	NA	NA	NA	NA
South San Francisco	146.4	2 225	0.0	49.4	62.8	42.9	71.1	20.11	2 862	142
Stanton	76.1	1 975	0.0	58.0	72.9	46.6	87.7	13.84	1 153	1 299
Stockton	572.9	1 926	0.1	46.0	77.3	38.1	93.8	13.84	2 563	1 456
Suisun City	69.5	2 431	0.5	46.1	72.6	37.5	88.8	23.46	2 649	975
Sunnyvale	125.4	855	0.0	50.5	70.9	41.7	84.3	15.08	2 171	811
Temecula	96.6	922	0.0	51.2	78.3	36.1	97.8	11.40	2 123	1 710
Temple City	6.3	174	0.0	56.3	75.6	42.6	89.0	18.56	1 295	1 575
Thousand Oaks	133.2	1 040	0.0	53.7	76.0	39.5	95.0	17.79	1 822	1 485
Torrance	148.8	1 010	0.0	56.3	69.4	46.2	77.6	14.79	1 526	742
Tracy	222.9	2 633	0.0	47.1	76.4	38.5	92.5	12.51	2 421	1 470
Tulare	200.3	3 290	0.0	45.8	79.3	37.4	93.8	11.03	2 588	1 685
Turlock	69.6	997	0.0	46.4	77.6	39.0	93.3	12.43	2 519	1 506
Tustin	193.5	2 486	8.9	54.5	72.1	41.4	83.8	13.87	1 794	1 102
Twentynine Palms	11.0	429	0.0	50.0	88.4	36.1	105.8	4.57	1 910	3 064
Union City	178.1	2 483	0.0	49.8	68.0	42.0	78.3	14.85	2 367	530
Upland	41.7	555	0.0	54.6	73.8	41.5	88.7	16.96	1 727	1 191
Vacaville	190.4	2 028	31.2	47.2	77.3	38.8	95.8	24.55	2 410	1 498
Vallejo	192.2	1 630	0.0	46.3	71.2	38.8	87.4	19.58	2 757	786
Victorville	370.9	3 084	0.0	45.5	80.0	31.4	99.1	6.20	2 929	1 735
Visalia	31.2	246	0.0	45.8	79.3	37.4	93.8	11.03	2 588	1 685
Vista	245.6	2 552	0.0	56.4	71.6	45.1	82.2	13.69	1 514	1 047
Walnut	28.7	956	0.0	54.6	73.8	41.5	88.7	16.96	1 727	1 191
Walnut Creek	4.9	74	0.2	47.5	72.4	39.3	85.2	23.96	3 267	983
Wasco	4.4	173	0.0	NA	NA	NA	NA	NA	NA	NA
Watsonville	36.2	698	0.0	49.7	62.4	38.7	72.0	23.25	3 080	123
West Covina	181.9	1 691	8.9	56.3	75.6	42.6	89.0	18.56	1 295	1 575
West Hollywood	100.2	2 875	0.0	58.3	74.2	48.5	83.8	15.14	928	1 506
Westminster	142.2	1 553	0.0	58.0	72.9	46.6	82.7	13.84	1 153	1 299
West Sacramento	368.8	7 425	94.7	46.3	75.4	38.8	92.4	17.93	2 666	1 248
Whittier	98.6	1 142	7.7	56.3	75.6	42.6	89.0	18.56	1 295	1 575
Wildomar	0.0	0	0.0	NA	NA	NA	NA	NA	NA	NA
Windsor	27.1	1 000	12.5	NA	NA	NA	NA	NA	NA	NA
Woodland	111.4	1 977	5.9	45.7	76.4	37.6	94.0	20.78	2 683	1 417
Yorba Linda	117.7	1 760	2.7	58.9	73.2	45.2	84.0	11.23	1 286	1 294
Yuba City	63.6	980	0.0	46.3	78.9	37.8	96.3	22.07	2 488	1 687
Yucaipa	35.9	684	0.0	52.9	78.0	40.4	94.4	13.62	1 904	1 714
COLORADO	X	X	X	X	X	X	X	X	X	X
Arvada	120.5	1 098	0.0	31.2	71.5	15.6	88.3	18.17	5 988	496
Aurora	1 215.3	3 582	2.6	29.2	73.4	15.2	88.0	15.81	6 128	696
Boulder	155.7	1 527	18.5	32.5	71.6	19.2	87.2	19.93	5 687	552
Brighton	76.1	2 167	0.0	NA	NA	NA	NA	NA	NA	NA
Broomfield	293.0	4 968	0.0	32.5	71.6	19.2	87.2	19.93	5 687	552

1. Based on the population estimated as of July 1 of the year shown. 2. Represents normal values based on the 30-year period, 1971–2000. 3. Average daily minimum. 4. Average daily maximum.

STATE Place code	City	Land area,[1] 2010 (sq km)	Population, 2014: Total persons	Population, 2014: Rank	Population, 2014: Per square kilometer	Race alone or in combination (percent), 2011-2013: White	Black	Amer-ican Indian, Alaska Native	Asian	Hawaiian Pacific Islander	Percent Hispanic or Latino[2], 2011-2013	Percent foreign born 2011–2013
		1	2	3	4	5	6	7	8	9	10	11
	COLORADO—Cont'd											
08 12415	Castle Rock	87.5	55 747	659	637.1	95.3	1.4	1.4	3.2	NA	11.6	6.9
08 12815	Centennial	74.4	107 201	269	1 440.9	89.5	3.3	1.3	5.2	0.2	7.5	8.4
08 16000	Colorado Springs	503.9	445 830	42	884.8	84.3	8.1	2.0	4.5	0.6	17.1	8.2
08 16495	Commerce City	88.8	51 762	722	582.9	86.8	4.0	3.5	3.6	NA	46.4	15.1
08 20000	Denver	396.3	663 862	21	1 675.2	77.9	11.1	2.2	4.6	0.3	31.2	15.8
08 24785	Englewood	17.0	32 480	1 144	1 910.6	88.3	3.6	1.8	2.8	0.2	16.1	9.1
08 27425	Fort Collins	140.6	156 480	159	1 112.9	92.7	2.2	1.8	4.3	0.2	10.6	6.1
08 27865	Fountain	62.1	27 631	1 326	444.9	79.5	14.8	2.2	6.7	1.2	14.9	6.7
08 31660	Grand Junction	99.0	60 210	599	608.2	92.4	2.2	2.6	1.8	0.5	16.1	4.7
08 32155	Greeley	120.6	98 596	304	817.5	79.1	2.6	2.2	1.8	0.2	36.3	10.7
08 43000	Lakewood	111.1	149 643	169	1 346.9	92.0	2.3	2.4	3.9	0.4	22.4	8.4
08 45255	Littleton	33.6	44 669	827	1 329.4	93.9	1.5	1.2	3.5	0.1	11.4	7.2
08 45970	Longmont	67.8	90 237	345	1 330.9	87.7	2.2	1.9	4.1	0.2	26.1	14.1
08 46465	Loveland	87.0	72 651	469	835.1	93.1	1.4	1.6	2.6	NA	10.5	4.6
08 54330	Northglenn	19.2	38 596	961	2 010.2	90.7	3.0	3.5	3.8	NA	29.6	10.0
08 57630	Parker	53.0	49 857	748	940.7	95.2	2.1	1.3	4.0	NA	8.7	4.4
08 62000	Pueblo	138.9	108 423	267	780.6	77.6	4.1	5.0	1.2	NA	51.1	4.4
08 77290	Thornton	90.2	130 307	197	1 444.6	87.4	2.1	1.6	6.1	0.2	32.1	11.3
08 83835	Westminster	81.7	112 090	247	1 372.0	88.5	2.3	2.6	7.4	NA	20.9	10.3
08 84440	Wheat Ridge	24.1	31 034	1 192	1 287.7	93.8	0.9	2.8	2.6	NA	23.2	7.1
09 00000	CONNECTICUT	12 541.6	3 596 677	X	286.8	79.9	11.7	0.9	4.7	0.1	14.3	13.7
09 08000	Bridgeport	41.4	147 612	175	3 565.5	43.1	38.3	1.1	4.0	0.2	39.8	28.5
09 08420	Bristol	68.4	60 570	590	885.5	91.6	6.2	1.3	1.8	NA	9.7	9.3
09 18430	Danbury	108.5	83 784	387	772.2	67.5	9.4	1.0	6.7	0.1	28.0	32.8
09 37000	Hartford	45.0	124 705	218	2 771.2	40.9	41.5	1.0	2.7	0.2	44.9	22.5
09 46450	Meriden	61.6	60 293	596	978.8	78.7	12.2	1.2	1.8	NA	27.9	9.2
09 47290	Middletown	106.2	47 043	797	443.0	79.9	17.0	1.0	4.5	NA	9.0	10.6
09 47500	Milford	56.7	51 857	717	914.6	91.7	3.0	0.7	4.9	0.0	7.0	9.5
09 49880	Naugatuck	42.2	31 659	1 174	750.2	88.4	8.0	NA	2.8	NA	10.4	12.8
09 50370	New Britain	34.7	72 878	468	2 100.2	68.4	13.8	0.8	3.3	0.2	38.9	18.9
09 52000	New Haven	48.4	130 282	198	2 691.8	45.2	35.5	0.8	5.4	0.1	28.0	16.2
09 52280	New London	14.5	27 374	1 345	1 887.9	63.8	22.0	1.7	4.5	NA	29.9	14.7
09 55990	Norwalk	59.2	88 145	354	1 488.9	75.8	16.4	0.5	5.0	NA	23.3	25.2
09 56200	Norwich	72.7	40 178	925	552.7	75.0	15.9	5.2	9.4	1.0	12.7	12.2
09 68100	Shelton	79.3	41 295	894	520.7	94.2	1.1	0.4	4.8	NA	4.5	12.0
09 73000	Stamford	97.5	128 278	208	1 315.7	62.0	15.2	0.2	9.2	0.0	25.9	33.3
09 76500	Torrington	103.0	35 190	1 061	341.7	93.4	3.3	1.0	3.5	NA	8.8	10.0
09 80000	Waterbury	73.9	109 307	260	1 479.1	66.6	21.5	1.2	2.4	0.1	35.0	15.0
09 82800	West Haven	27.8	54 905	675	1 975.0	66.2	25.2	1.3	5.0	NA	16.1	14.5
10 00000	DELAWARE	5 046.7	935 614	X	185.4	71.8	23.3	1.0	4.0	0.1	8.6	8.5
10 21200	Dover	60.0	37 355	992	622.6	50.9	45.8	2.8	3.4	NA	8.7	7.6
10 50670	Newark	23.8	33 008	1 125	1 386.9	83.9	9.8	0.3	7.0	NA	5.4	9.5
10 77580	Wilmington	28.2	71 817	475	2 546.7	37.3	58.9	0.4	1.4	NA	13.1	6.8
11 00000	DISTRICT OF COLUMBIA	158.1	658 893	X	4 167.6	42.2	50.7	0.9	4.6	0.1	9.9	14.2
11 50000	Washington	158.1	658 893	22	4 167.6	42.2	50.7	0.9	4.6	0.1	9.9	14.2
12 00000	FLORIDA	138 887.5	19 893 297	X	143.2	78.1	17.2	0.8	3.2	0.2	23.3	19.5
12 00950	Altamonte Springs	23.3	42 225	872	1 812.2	81.5	14.7	0.4	3.2	NA	23.8	13.8
12 01700	Apopka	80.9	47 084	796	582.0	65.1	24.0	1.0	5.2	0.6	25.6	20.3
12 02681	Aventura	6.9	37 451	988	5 427.7	93.2	4.9	NA	1.4	NA	33.1	47.1
12 07300	Boca Raton	76.0	91 332	341	1 201.7	89.2	5.7	0.6	3.4	NA	12.6	19.1
12 07525	Bonita Springs	100.0	49 299	759	493.0	90.0	1.3	1.8	3.2	NA	27.8	25.3
12 07875	Boynton Beach	41.9	73 124	466	1 745.2	62.9	31.6	0.3	4.1	NA	11.2	23.0
12 07950	Bradenton	36.7	52 769	702	1 437.8	77.5	19.1	0.5	1.0	NA	18.2	13.5
12 10275	Cape Coral	273.7	169 854	144	620.6	92.2	4.0	0.7	2.1	NA	19.1	14.3
12 11050	Casselberry	18.1	26 707	1 372	1 475.5	87.7	8.7	0.8	2.3	NA	23.3	9.3
12 12875	Clearwater	66.2	110 703	253	1 672.3	85.0	11.6	0.9	3.2	0.3	12.9	13.7
12 12925	Clermont	35.3	30 600	1 207	866.9	71.6	16.2	NA	6.3	NA	19.8	14.1
12 13275	Coconut Creek	30.7	58 536	625	1 906.7	76.9	14.6	0.1	5.6	NA	25.1	26.5
12 14125	Cooper City	20.8	34 923	1 067	1 679.0	84.2	9.0	NA	7.1	NA	30.0	22.6
12 14250	Coral Gables	33.5	51 227	732	1 529.2	93.3	4.5	NA	2.6	NA	53.5	36.5
12 14400	Coral Springs	61.6	127 952	211	2 077.1	71.5	21.1	0.6	5.1	NA	24.0	27.3
12 15968	Cutler Bay	25.5	44 321	833	1 738.1	80.6	15.6	0.1	1.9	NA	49.8	36.2
12 16335	Dania Beach	21.0	31 117	1 188	1 481.8	70.8	24.6	0.2	2.4	0.4	24.7	27.3
12 16475	Davie	90.4	98 895	302	1 094.0	80.9	9.7	0.3	5.6	0.2	32.8	25.9
12 16525	Daytona Beach	151.3	63 011	562	416.5	61.3	34.2	1.1	2.8	NA	8.6	7.7

1. Dry land or land partially or temporarily covered by water. 2. May be of any race.

City	Age of population (percent), 2011-2013: Under 5 years	5 to 17 years	18 to 24 years	25 to 34 years	35 to 44 years	45 to 54 years	55 to 64 years	65 to 74 years	75 years and over	Median age 2011-2013	Percent female 2011-2013	Population: Census counts 2000	Census counts 2010	Percent change 2000–2010	Percent change 2010–2014
	12	13	14	15	16	17	18	19	20	21	22	23	24	25	26
COLORADO—Cont'd															
Castle Rock	8.7	21.9	6.6	12.4	18.3	14.2	10.2	5.1	2.5	35.2	50.4	20 224	48 231	138.5	15.5
Centennial	5.6	18.4	6.8	11.8	13.3	16.3	14.3	8.3	5.2	40.8	50.7	NA	100 377	NA	6.6
Colorado Springs	7.1	17.4	11.2	15.3	12.4	13.8	11.3	6.4	4.9	34.0	50.4	360 890	416 427	15.4	6.8
Commerce City	10.3	22.8	6.5	16.9	16.1	10.7	10.2	4.0	2.5	31.7	50.5	20 991	45 913	118.7	12.7
Denver	7.0	14.1	9.3	21.5	15.3	11.7	10.5	5.8	4.8	34.0	50.0	554 636	600 158	8.2	10.6
Englewood	6.0	12.1	9.3	18.7	13.9	15.2	12.5	5.9	6.4	37.6	48.9	31 727	30 255	-4.6	7.4
Fort Collins	5.5	13.9	22.3	16.4	11.5	11.7	9.8	5.0	4.0	29.7	50.5	118 652	143 986	21.4	8.6
Fountain	9.3	23.6	7.6	17.7	14.5	13.4	7.1	4.3	2.5	29.5	52.2	15 197	25 846	70.1	6.7
Grand Junction	6.6	15.5	13.0	14.5	11.4	11.3	12.1	7.4	8.1	35.3	50.6	41 986	58 566	39.5	2.0
Greeley	6.8	17.8	17.0	14.3	12.8	10.2	10.0	5.8	5.2	30.5	50.4	76 930	92 889	20.7	6.2
Lakewood	6.0	13.9	9.3	15.2	13.2	13.3	13.9	8.2	6.9	38.8	49.8	144 126	142 980	-0.8	4.6
Littleton	6.0	15.5	8.3	12.9	13.1	14.5	13.8	8.3	7.5	40.8	51.9	40 340	41 737	3.5	7.0
Longmont	7.1	18.1	9.1	13.9	13.9	14.2	11.9	6.8	5.0	36.4	49.1	71 093	86 270	21.3	4.6
Loveland	6.6	17.3	7.6	14.5	12.8	13.2	12.6	8.1	7.3	38.0	51.2	50 608	66 859	32.1	8.7
Northglenn	6.3	16.9	11.2	18.7	12.8	11.6	10.3	6.4	5.8	32.7	48.8	31 575	35 789	13.3	7.9
Parker	6.7	24.5	7.5	12.3	19.2	15.8	8.1	4.2	1.8	34.2	49.6	23 558	45 297	92.3	10.1
Pueblo	6.6	16.8	10.2	13.3	12.1	12.6	13.0	7.4	8.1	37.8	50.9	102 121	106 595	4.4	1.8
Thornton	8.3	21.4	9.2	15.5	15.3	13.6	8.9	4.7	3.1	32.2	49.7	82 384	118 772	44.2	9.7
Westminster	6.7	16.9	8.5	17.0	14.3	14.7	11.7	5.9	4.3	35.6	50.4	100 940	106 114	5.1	5.6
Wheat Ridge	5.5	13.9	8.0	14.1	13.7	14.1	13.6	8.1	9.1	42.3	53.0	32 913	30 166	-8.3	2.8
CONNECTICUT	5.4	16.7	9.5	12.1	12.7	15.7	13.1	7.8	7.0	40.3	51.3	3 405 565	3 574 097	4.9	0.6
Bridgeport	7.0	18.4	11.8	17.1	13.5	12.8	9.7	5.1	4.6	32.2	51.7	139 529	144 229	3.4	2.3
Bristol	4.9	15.7	7.8	12.5	13.2	16.0	13.3	7.9	8.6	42.4	50.3	60 062	60 477	0.7	0.2
Danbury	5.9	13.9	10.7	16.3	15.8	13.9	11.3	6.7	5.6	36.6	51.0	74 848	80 893	8.1	3.6
Hartford	6.8	18.6	16.2	16.5	11.5	11.7	9.3	5.3	4.1	29.8	51.1	121 578	124 775	2.6	-0.1
Meriden	6.7	14.2	8.0	15.0	13.7	13.9	14.2	7.7	6.6	39.1	50.6	58 244	60 868	4.5	-0.9
Middletown	4.2	13.6	14.4	15.0	12.2	14.4	12.2	7.3	6.6	37.2	52.8	43 167	47 648	10.4	-1.3
Milford	4.8	14.5	6.7	11.2	13.7	18.8	13.4	8.9	8.1	44.4	51.3	52 305	51 271	1.3	1.1
Naugatuck	5.8	16.1	10.5	14.1	11.6	16.2	13.2	6.6	5.9	38.2	48.9	30 989	31 862	2.8	-0.7
New Britain	6.1	17.2	13.2	15.0	11.3	13.4	11.1	6.2	6.5	34.0	53.9	71 538	73 206	2.3	-0.4
New Haven	6.1	16.0	15.7	20.3	12.0	10.6	8.5	5.5	5.2	30.4	52.8	123 626	129 779	5.0	0.3
New London	5.2	14.3	21.2	15.0	12.0	13.5	8.7	5.7	4.5	30.9	53.6	25 671	27 620	7.6	-0.9
Norwalk	6.3	12.3	7.8	15.5	14.9	15.0	14.0	7.4	6.7	41.1	50.5	82 951	85 603	3.2	2.9
Norwich	7.1	15.8	9.5	16.1	11.6	15.0	11.4	6.4	6.9	35.9	50.9	36 117	40 493	12.1	-0.8
Shelton	3.9	15.3	8.5	10.3	11.5	18.6	13.1	10.0	8.9	45.3	53.1	38 101	39 559	3.8	4.4
Stamford	7.1	14.8	8.3	17.2	14.6	14.0	10.9	6.6	6.3	36.6	50.7	117 083	122 643	4.7	4.6
Torrington	5.5	13.6	7.2	11.2	11.5	18.2	14.9	9.6	8.5	45.8	51.2	35 202	36 383	3.4	-3.3
Waterbury	7.7	17.4	10.4	14.5	13.5	13.5	11.0	6.3	5.6	35.0	51.8	107 271	110 366	2.9	-0.9
West Haven	6.4	15.6	13.5	12.3	13.3	13.7	13.0	6.9	5.3	36.8	52.8	52 360	55 564	6.1	-1.2
DELAWARE	6.1	16.2	10.1	12.7	12.2	14.5	12.9	8.8	6.5	39.1	51.6	783 600	897 934	14.6	4.2
Dover	6.3	14.4	20.5	14.9	10.7	11.2	8.7	6.4	6.9	29.8	52.8	32 135	36 047	12.2	4.0
Newark	2.8	8.3	44.2	11.2	7.0	7.6	8.5	5.0	5.4	22.5	54.1	28 547	31 454	10.2	4.7
Wilmington	7.5	16.6	9.8	17.2	13.2	13.6	10.4	6.6	5.1	34.1	53.5	72 664	70 851	-2.5	1.4
DISTRICT OF COLUMBIA	6.1	10.9	13.0	22.2	13.7	12.0	10.7	6.2	5.1	33.7	52.7	572 059	601 723	5.2	9.5
Washington	6.1	10.9	13.0	22.2	13.7	12.0	10.7	6.2	5.1	33.7	52.7	572 059	601 723	5.2	9.5
FLORIDA	5.6	15.2	9.2	12.4	12.5	14.2	12.8	9.8	8.4	41.2	51.1	15 982 378	18 801 310	17.6	5.8
Altamonte Springs	5.8	13.1	7.5	17.7	14.2	14.4	12.3	9.3	5.6	39.3	54.1	41 200	41 496	0.7	1.7
Apopka	7.3	19.4	9.3	12.1	16.4	12.8	12.3	5.8	4.6	36.7	50.4	26 642	41 542	55.9	13.0
Aventura	5.9	13.4	2.0	11.5	15.4	12.7	10.7	14.0	14.3	46.0	53.2	25 267	35 762	41.5	4.7
Boca Raton	3.7	14.0	11.1	9.6	10.8	15.0	14.0	10.6	11.2	45.7	50.3	74 764	84 392	12.9	8.2
Bonita Springs	3.5	10.7	6.4	12.2	9.6	11.0	14.4	17.8	14.2	52.0	51.5	32 797	43 914	33.9	12.5
Boynton Beach	5.3	13.6	7.9	13.9	12.5	13.6	11.8	8.3	13.0	42.8	53.2	60 389	68 217	13.0	7.2
Bradenton	6.0	14.5	7.8	13.3	12.1	10.7	12.3	10.2	13.0	42.0	52.3	49 504	49 546	0.1	7.1
Cape Coral	5.7	17.6	6.7	10.3	12.3	14.5	14.1	10.9	7.8	43.0	51.1	102 286	154 305	50.9	10.1
Casselberry	6.1	12.1	9.6	16.2	13.6	17.3	11.4	8.2	5.5	40.2	51.3	22 629	26 241	16.0	1.7
Clearwater	6.0	13.4	7.6	12.5	11.6	15.1	10.1	9.5	11.3	44.0	52.2	108 787	107 685	-1.0	2.2
Clermont	6.2	20.4	6.9	8.3	15.4	10.8	11.5	12.3	8.2	40.6	50.5	9 333	28 742	208.0	6.5
Coconut Creek	6.2	16.0	8.1	13.1	15.0	13.2	10.2	7.3	11.0	39.5	51.7	43 566	52 909	21.4	10.6
Cooper City	5.2	19.6	8.6	12.8	11.5	16.8	14.8	6.3	4.4	38.5	50.8	27 939	28 547	2.2	22.3
Coral Gables	4.8	11.7	15.4	11.2	13.4	14.2	12.5	10.1	6.7	41.4	51.0	42 249	46 780	10.7	9.5
Coral Springs	7.0	19.5	10.5	11.4	15.3	15.9	11.5	5.6	3.3	36.2	51.6	117 549	121 096	3.0	5.7
Cutler Bay	6.4	17.9	8.7	16.9	13.1	17.0	9.0	6.2	4.9	35.1	48.5	NA	40 286	NA	10.0
Dania Beach	6.5	14.2	9.5	13.9	12.4	14.7	14.4	9.2	5.1	39.7	51.8	20 061	29 639	47.7	5.0
Davie	5.7	16.8	11.5	13.0	12.8	16.7	11.5	7.2	4.8	36.9	52.0	75 720	91 992	21.5	7.5
Daytona Beach	5.4	9.9	16.3	14.2	9.9	12.9	13.2	9.2	9.0	39.9	50.8	64 112	61 005	-4.8	3.3

City	Households, 2011-2013				Persons in group quarters, 2010				Serious crimes known to police,[2] 2013				Educational attainment, 2011–2013		
			Percent			Institutional			Total		Rate[3]			Attainment[4] (percent)	
	Number	Persons per house-hold	Female family house-holder[1]	One-person	Total	Total	Persons in nursing facilities	Non-institu-tional	Number	Rate[3]	Violent	Property	Population age 25 and older	High school graduate or less	Bachelor's degree or more
	27	28	29	30	31	32	33	34	35	36	37	38	39	40	41
COLORADO—Cont'd															
Castle Rock	17 924	2.85	10.3	17.7	460	390	108	70	601	1 149	86	1 063	32 294	21.1	45.6
Centennial	38 146	2.71	9.9	21.1	1 701	1 559	307	142	1 335	1 274	135	1 140	72 083	17.6	52.1
Colorado Springs	168 914	2.53	11.6	29.1	7 629	3 467	1 657	4 162	20 044	4 596	429	4 167	278 506	27.7	36.6
Commerce City	14 833	3.25	12.9	19.4	351	191	191	160	1 702	3 459	315	3 144	29 396	48.8	20.6
Denver	269 868	2.30	10.5	40.6	15 981	6 518	2 333	9 463	27 848	4 291	631	3 660	441 738	32.1	44.1
Englewood	14 020	2.20	11.6	40.7	291	238	238	53	1 679	5 338	172	5 166	22 639	35.8	32.8
Fort Collins	57 572	2.46	8.4	26.2	7 085	1 437	514	5 648	4 162	2 773	238	2 536	86 920	18.8	51.7
Fountain	9 123	2.95	13.3	16.4	0	0	0	0	694	2 555	276	2 279	16 015	32.2	21.3
Grand Junction	24 208	2.34	11.2	30.7	2 884	1 077	395	1 807	2 814	4 677	435	4 242	38 746	36.5	28.4
Greeley	33 045	2.72	12.9	25.9	4 853	1 627	627	3 226	3 721	3 872	510	3 362	55 614	42.1	25.5
Lakewood	61 329	2.31	11.8	33.5	2 171	1 552	1 064	619	7 511	5 134	427	4 708	103 039	32.6	35.4
Littleton	18 927	2.32	9.2	35.3	491	448	313	43	1 325	2 986	99	2 887	31 129	23.6	45.1
Longmont	34 011	2.59	11.6	26.4	639	498	482	141	2 242	2 507	256	2 251	58 233	33.6	37.3
Loveland	29 203	2.39	8.9	28.3	510	416	414	94	1 820	2 552	208	2 344	48 127	31.6	31.3
Northglenn	13 902	2.65	10.8	32.3	129	129	129	0	1 198	3 218	255	2 963	24 248	44.8	17.8
Parker	16 428	2.88	7.8	18.8	28	0	0	28	572	1 198	113	1 085	29 043	15.6	51.9
Pueblo	42 518	2.43	15.1	35.1	4 045	3 050	1 444	995	8 614	7 971	929	7 042	71 655	44.7	19.8
Thornton	41 840	2.96	11.9	21.5	462	430	430	32	3 652	2 904	251	2 652	76 129	40.6	25.8
Westminster	42 004	2.59	11.6	26.7	467	448	348	19	3 228	2 932	196	2 736	74 243	31.1	35.1
Wheat Ridge	13 635	2.21	10.0	37.9	554	434	381	120	1 232	3 989	334	3 656	22 282	37.6	30.6
CONNECTICUT	1 348 275	2.58	13.1	27.9	118 152	49 370	26 371	68 782	80 430	2 237	263	1 974	2 456 170	38.0	36.9
Bridgeport	49 672	2.86	26.0	29.4	4 838	1 960	759	2 878	5 861	3 985	950	3 035	92 039	56.9	16.6
Bristol	25 063	2.39	11.7	31.9	849	637	611	212	1 481	2 442	135	2 307	43 331	47.9	22.4
Danbury	29 177	2.72	11.4	27.9	3 953	1 904	538	2 049	1 365	1 637	130	1 508	57 582	47.1	30.0
Hartford	45 038	2.60	31.4	35.1	8 951	2 194	777	6 757	6 509	5 210	1 179	4 031	73 168	59.8	15.8
Meriden	23 729	2.51	17.3	28.7	955	688	660	267	1 678	2 771	289	2 482	43 114	53.4	17.8
Middletown	19 167	2.24	13.4	36.4	3 731	998	552	2 733	887	1 878	127	1 751	32 190	38.2	34.9
Milford	20 828	2.46	8.7	31.4	472	355	344	117	1 597	3 011	79	2 932	38 209	35.5	39.6
Naugatuck	12 154	2.59	12.1	26.5	267	236	236	31	806	2 539	123	2 416	21 446	44.6	22.7
New Britain	27 338	2.56	22.2	32.6	3 194	790	557	2 404	2 525	3 453	361	3 092	46 461	56.7	18.2
New Haven	49 922	2.42	23.0	37.4	11 220	1 774	768	9 446	7 866	6 001	1 295	4 707	81 416	47.7	32.3
New London	10 903	2.15	15.4	40.2	3 713	225	225	3 488	1 091	3 933	1 078	2 855	16 373	49.7	22.3
Norwalk	35 480	2.43	11.8	34.5	797	461	405	336	1 966	2 245	272	1 973	64 109	35.1	41.4
Norwich	16 287	2.45	16.6	32.7	514	219	205	295	1 132	2 796	321	2 475	27 295	51.4	18.0
Shelton	14 770	2.70	9.3	24.2	502	446	442	56	465	1 149	44	1 104	29 210	33.7	39.2
Stamford	46 190	2.68	12.4	29.1	1 280	662	653	618	2 284	1 814	268	1 547	87 301	33.7	45.2
Torrington	15 057	2.32	10.7	35.3	838	611	559	227	920	2 582	166	2 416	26 410	50.4	21.1
Waterbury	40 617	2.66	23.7	31.0	1 938	1 149	886	789	5 046	4 597	374	4 224	70 864	56.3	15.5
West Haven	20 372	2.56	17.7	31.6	2 857	458	362	2 399	1 806	3 263	524	2 739	35 603	47.9	22.0
DELAWARE	337 245	2.64	14.0	26.4	24 413	11 673	4 591	12 740	32 928	3 557	491	3 066	620 032	43.6	29.3
Dover	13 002	2.52	19.6	35.3	3 745	569	340	3 176	2 357	6 302	706	5 596	21 814	42.1	28.3
Newark	9 569	2.62	7.6	29.2	7 128	0	0	7 128	950	2 908	358	2 549	14 431	21.3	57.1
Wilmington	28 801	2.38	25.8	37.9	3 226	2 324	531	902	4 897	6 853	1 630	5 223	47 106	52.2	25.1
DISTRICT OF COLUMBIA	268 015	2.21	16.1	44.7	40 021	7 339	3 064	32 682	39 489	6 109	1 300	4 808	442 952	29.6	53.5
Washington	268 015	2.21	16.1	44.7	40 021	7 339	3 064	32 682	37 449	5 793	1 219	4 574	442 952	29.6	53.5
FLORIDA	7 168 502	2.64	13.3	29.4	421 709	254 506	73 372	167 203	699 158	3 576	470	3 105	13 523 012	43.5	26.6
Altamonte Springs	16 199	2.56	14.4	39.0	448	444	444	4	1 714	4 077	357	3 720	30 870	32.9	33.1
Apopka	14 336	3.08	16.9	15.7	178	118	118	60	1 705	3 756	392	3 364	28 476	41.6	25.5
Aventura	18 392	2.01	6.7	42.7	96	96	96	0	2 085	5 581	150	5 431	29 090	24.9	48.8
Boca Raton	35 965	2.35	8.3	33.4	3 444	430	415	3 014	2 467	2 780	186	2 594	62 581	22.2	51.2
Bonita Springs	18 381	2.51	7.1	29.7	157	12	0	145	NA	NA	NA	NA	36 661	43.6	28.0
Boynton Beach	28 837	2.40	12.6	38.0	1 000	649	630	351	3 373	4 771	519	4 252	51 272	42.8	26.0
Bradenton	20 813	2.37	12.2	38.2	1 757	1 074	966	683	2 355	4 616	688	3 928	36 374	49.6	20.6
Cape Coral	56 264	2.87	10.9	22.0	445	350	307	95	3 572	2 185	121	2 065	113 175	47.9	20.6
Casselberry	9 856	2.67	14.7	37.5	51	12	5	39	1 289	4 861	569	4 291	19 099	40.3	22.7
Clearwater	46 819	2.27	13.6	39.3	3 584	1 011	1 000	2 573	4 934	4 530	567	3 963	79 581	42.1	26.9
Clermont	10 972	2.67	10.1	21.3	199	177	177	22	963	3 251	284	2 968	19 666	36.4	29.1
Coconut Creek	21 845	2.52	11.3	34.0	146	138	65	8	1 558	2 799	144	2 655	38 559	38.8	31.6
Cooper City	10 362	3.10	14.4	13.7	40	0	0	40	608	1 804	148	1 655	21 420	26.3	40.7
Coral Gables	17 704	2.51	6.9	31.6	4 540	1	0	4 539	2 298	4 573	167	4 406	33 350	16.6	60.5
Coral Springs	40 353	3.09	19.7	18.3	359	227	222	132	2 802	2 213	187	2 026	78 875	30.4	35.1
Cutler Bay	12 779	3.30	15.0	20.5	338	245	199	93	1 829	4 270	315	3 955	28 460	37.9	28.0
Dania Beach	11 947	2.53	19.0	35.1	329	294	87	35	1 578	5 112	612	4 499	21 239	46.3	23.9
Davie	32 669	2.88	14.3	23.2	1 355	86	50	1 269	3 699	3 830	317	3 513	62 928	36.2	34.0
Daytona Beach	25 923	2.24	13.5	43.2	5 048	1 094	1 059	3 954	4 823	7 732	1 281	6 451	42 217	48.3	17.5

1. No spouse present. 2. Data for serious crimes have not been adjusted for underreporting. This may affect comparability between geographic areas and over time. 3. Per 100,000 population estimated by the FBI. 4. Persons 25 years old and over.

City	Money income, 2011–2013: Per capita income[1] (dollars)	Households: Median income	Households: Percent with income of $200,000 or more	Households: Percent with income of less than $25,000	Families with income below poverty (percent)	Housing units, 2010: Total	Housing units, 2010: Percent change, 2000–2010	Housing units, 2010: Vacant units for sale or rent[2]	Occupied housing units 2011–2013: Total	Owner-occupied: Percent	Owner-occupied: Median value[3] (dollars)	Median owner costs as a percent of income: With a mortgage[4]	Median owner costs as a percent of income: Without a mortgage[5]
	42	43	44	45	46	47	48	49	50	51	52	53	54
COLORADO—Cont'd													
Castle Rock	35 294	83 963	8.8	11.9	5.3	17 626	135.5	938	17 924	75.7	274 400	23.1	12.3
Centennial	40 019	88 023	9.8	9.7	4.2	38 779	NA	1 330	38 146	81.0	290 400	22.1	10.0
Colorado Springs	28 854	53 619	3.7	21.7	9.7	179 607	20.7	11 819	168 914	58.0	208 000	23.1	10.0
Commerce City	22 960	63 776	2.3	15.9	11.7	15 452	123.7	973	14 833	73.5	183 300	25.2	11.0
Denver	33 654	50 728	6.0	25.1	14.0	285 797	13.7	22 690	269 868	49.2	254 700	22.7	10.5
Englewood	27 521	46 746	2.2	26.1	12.3	15 478	4.0	1 103	14 020	47.6	212 300	24.2	11.0
Fort Collins	28 766	53 435	4.0	25.0	7.5	60 503	26.7	2 674	57 572	55.1	249 100	22.8	10.0
Fountain	22 997	54 170	0.9	15.2	6.9	9 371	80.1	647	9 123	66.3	169 700	22.6	10.0
Grand Junction	25 330	44 409	2.2	26.7	14.1	26 170	38.7	1 859	24 208	59.3	207 100	23.6	10.0
Greeley	21 985	46 209	1.8	27.7	15.4	36 323	25.9	2 896	33 045	54.8	164 900	22.0	10.0
Lakewood	30 652	55 417	3.4	21.7	9.9	65 758	5.3	3 772	61 329	57.7	241 400	23.1	10.1
Littleton	35 035	61 154	6.3	21.8	7.3	19 434	7.1	1 122	18 927	61.4	268 400	22.9	10.0
Longmont	29 497	60 941	4.1	20.1	11.1	35 008	27.6	1 756	34 011	61.7	237 900	21.2	10.0
Loveland	27 627	51 890	2.2	21.7	6.7	28 557	40.5	1 404	29 203	61.7	212 600	22.6	10.0
Northglenn	23 404	51 911	1.2	21.3	10.8	14 274	17.5	782	13 902	57.2	180 400	24.5	11.7
Parker	37 153	96 429	9.1	7.9	3.3	16 533	97.8	616	16 428	78.1	283 000	21.8	10.0
Pueblo	19 581	34 152	1.1	36.2	18.2	47 593	10.4	4 303	42 518	56.3	114 000	24.6	13.1
Thornton	25 875	62 928	3.2	13.7	7.2	43 230	46.6	1 871	41 840	69.8	206 500	24.3	11.2
Westminster	30 677	64 135	4.4	14.1	6.7	43 968	11.4	1 927	42 004	63.3	226 000	22.8	10.0
Wheat Ridge	28 279	46 671	2.6	25.4	10.8	14 868	-0.7	892	13 635	52.1	235 500	23.5	11.5
CONNECTICUT	37 468	68 130	9.0	18.6	7.8	1 487 891	7.4	116 804	1 348 275	67.0	271 500	25.3	16.6
Bridgeport	19 754	40 133	2.1	34.4	20.6	57 012	4.9	5 757	49 672	40.6	172 000	32.5	24.2
Bristol	29 989	57 727	2.5	20.0	8.5	27 011	3.4	1 691	25 063	66.7	195 900	24.9	17.2
Danbury	30 786	63 972	5.5	19.6	8.3	31 154	9.2	2 247	29 177	59.7	290 300	27.5	17.7
Hartford	16 182	28 592	1.1	45.5	33.5	51 822	2.3	6 698	45 038	23.0	161 900	31.9	17.2
Meriden	25 929	51 210	1.5	22.8	12.9	25 892	5.1	1 915	23 729	59.5	178 000	26.8	16.1
Middletown	33 491	61 548	4.9	17.3	7.9	21 223	7.7	1 360	19 167	53.7	232 000	23.9	14.6
Milford	39 544	77 103	9.1	17.8	4.4	23 074	5.1	1 366	20 828	77.9	297 900	25.6	20.7
Naugatuck	28 522	58 268	2.3	20.6	7.8	13 061	5.8	722	12 154	63.4	189 600	25.1	19.8
New Britain	20 202	38 570	1.2	33.9	19.0	31 226	0.2	3 068	27 338	39.3	161 200	27.5	17.5
New Haven	22 655	36 423	3.1	35.8	22.7	54 967	3.8	6 090	49 922	29.7	193 800	29.2	18.4
New London	21 512	37 580	1.5	37.5	23.4	11 840	2.4	1 467	10 903	37.0	183 000	29.1	15.8
Norwalk	42 553	72 202	10.5	17.3	6.5	35 415	4.9	2 198	35 480	62.0	405 400	30.3	19.9
Norwich	25 927	45 876	2.2	24.0	13.9	18 659	12.4	2 060	16 287	52.3	183 200	25.9	18.7
Shelton	42 325	88 956	10.3	11.1	4.1	16 146	9.8	821	14 770	82.6	338 900	24.9	16.7
Stamford	44 926	75 764	16.3	16.4	7.3	50 573	6.9	3 216	46 190	55.8	502 500	28.4	18.4
Torrington	29 021	53 264	1.8	24.0	5.7	16 761	3.8	1 518	15 057	68.1	173 200	27.1	20.1
Waterbury	20 386	40 285	1.3	34.2	21.1	47 991	2.5	5 230	40 617	46.2	140 900	28.7	19.6
West Haven	25 378	50 265	2.4	23.4	12.3	22 446	0.5	1 334	20 372	56.0	203 600	29.1	23.8
DELAWARE	29 547	59 399	4.7	19.0	8.1	405 885	18.3	63 588	337 245	71.4	230 000	23.4	11.0
Dover	20 992	44 135	1.1	28.3	16.5	15 024	12.5	1 253	13 002	50.5	177 400	25.5	11.5
Newark	23 308	52 710	5.5	28.6	5.4	10 475	12.5	641	9 569	54.9	269 400	21.7	10.0
Wilmington	24 742	39 343	3.1	33.0	22.1	32 820	2.1	4 205	28 801	45.3	163 400	23.6	12.7
DISTRICT OF COLUMBIA	45 851	66 950	12.1	22.6	15.3	296 719	8.0	30 012	268 015	41.1	451 800	23.2	10.4
Washington	45 851	66 950	12.1	22.6	15.3	296 719	8.0	30 012	268 015	41.1	451 800	23.2	10.4
FLORIDA	25 821	45 872	3.7	26.6	12.4	8 989 580	23.1	1 568 778	7 168 502	65.8	150 900	26.9	13.3
Altamonte Springs	25 107	45 510	1.7	23.3	9.8	22 088	9.5	2 962	16 199	47.7	126 800	28.4	13.3
Apopka	25 093	59 917	3.8	19.7	13.1	15 707	55.9	1 347	14 336	77.9	145 400	27.0	11.4
Aventura	44 430	59 128	8.2	24.4	10.7	26 120	30.5	8 228	18 392	63.5	303 100	36.5	24.5
Boca Raton	47 033	68 986	13.2	16.1	6.1	44 539	18.3	7 761	35 965	69.0	348 400	28.4	14.9
Bonita Springs	37 142	51 009	7.9	22.3	13.0	31 716	35.2	11 699	18 381	73.0	225 000	27.4	13.8
Boynton Beach	26 635	45 129	2.5	28.0	13.7	36 289	18.6	7 185	28 837	64.8	128 300	27.6	16.4
Bradenton	22 221	40 348	1.8	29.3	14.2	26 767	7.3	5 362	20 813	52.0	118 600	26.3	14.6
Cape Coral	22 251	48 095	1.4	23.0	11.2	78 948	72.7	18 181	56 264	68.5	137 500	28.0	14.8
Casselberry	22 546	41 990	1.3	28.0	8.8	12 708	22.5	1 278	9 856	60.6	101 500	28.8	13.8
Clearwater	27 874	42 077	3.5	30.2	12.3	59 156	4.3	11 518	46 819	58.0	148 900	27.8	15.1
Clermont	23 332	49 667	1.3	22.9	11.1	12 730	NA	1 514	10 072	67.9	168 900	24.6	12.9
Coconut Creek	27 268	52 519	1.8	21.2	7.0	25 926	17.1	3 172	21 845	65.9	121 200	25.1	21.2
Cooper City	36 475	84 294	11.0	8.9	3.9	9 912	7.4	284	10 362	86.7	275 200	28.5	13.3
Coral Gables	55 658	91 019	21.7	15.3	2.9	20 266	13.9	2 320	17 704	64.7	604 100	25.0	15.0
Coral Springs	28 886	62 907	6.1	15.5	8.9	45 433	10.0	3 619	40 353	62.7	261 800	28.5	13.6
Cutler Bay	23 454	60 237	4.8	18.4	8.0	14 620	NA	1 282	12 779	79.1	170 200	29.9	15.2
Dania Beach	23 521	39 482	2.4	32.5	21.0	15 671	44.1	2 794	11 947	50.6	148 100	27.9	15.1
Davie	30 627	58 106	7.4	21.2	7.6	37 306	19.6	2 991	32 669	72.1	197 900	27.3	15.6
Daytona Beach	18 020	27 172	0.6	45.5	22.9	33 920	1.6	6 606	25 923	44.9	110 600	29.7	14.6

1. Based on population estimated by the American Community Survey. 2. Includes units rented or sold but not occupied. 3. Specified owner-occupied units; $1,000,000 represents $1,000,000 or more 4. 50.0 represents 50 percent or more. 5. 10.0 represents 10 percent or less.

City	Occupied housing units, 2011–2013 (cont.): Percent renter occupied	Occupied housing units, 2011–2013 (cont.): Median gross rent[1]	Occupied housing units, 2011–2013 (cont.): Median rent as a percent of income[2]	Occupied housing units, 2011–2013 (cont.): Percent with no vehicle available	Migration, 2011–2013: Percent who lived in the same house one year ago	Migration, 2011–2013: Percent who lived outside current city one year ago	Civilian labor force, 2014: Total	Civilian labor force, 2014: Percent change, 2013–2014	Civilian labor force, 2014: Unemployment: Total	Civilian labor force, 2014: Unemployment: Rate[3]	Civilian employment[4], 2011–2013: Population age 16 and older	Civilian employment[4], 2011–2013: Percent: In labor force	Civilian employment[4], 2011–2013: Percent: Civilian full-year full-time workers	Civilian employment[4], 2011–2013: Households with no workers (percent)
	55	56	57	58	59	60	61	62	63	64	65	66	67	68
COLORADO—Cont'd														
Castle Rock	24.3	1 184	33.3	2.1	82.4	10.4	28 344	2.2	1 183	4.2	36 993	75.1	47.5	14.1
Centennial	19.0	1 346	28.7	2.4	86.8	11.4	60 313	1.9	2 818	4.7	82 456	70.5	46.2	17.8
Colorado Springs	42.0	881	30.2	5.6	74.8	12.1	216 680	0.0	12 837	5.9	337 859	67.7	39.1	23.5
Commerce City	26.5	924	29.2	4.8	83.9	12.1	25 087	0.9	1 468	5.9	33 798	70.5	48.1	16.3
Denver	50.8	889	29.7	11.7	77.4	12.3	370 487	1.6	18 060	4.9	512 527	70.9	45.6	23.2
Englewood	52.4	862	28.9	9.7	78.1	18.2	18 888	1.7	911	4.8	25 913	72.8	43.4	25.4
Fort Collins	44.9	1 014	35.6	5.4	70.8	15.3	88 466	1.4	3 642	4.1	123 358	69.8	37.0	20.2
Fountain	33.7	1 176	34.4	1.9	76.9	20.7	11 496	-0.9	785	6.8	18 771	68.4	43.3	20.3
Grand Junction	40.7	817	32.2	9.3	71.5	15.6	29 766	-0.7	2 105	7.1	47 422	63.1	36.4	33.0
Greeley	45.2	740	32.0	7.7	73.2	15.0	49 298	4.4	2 442	5.0	74 242	64.0	35.7	25.6
Lakewood	42.3	947	31.9	7.4	81.1	13.1	80 672	1.6	4 064	5.0	119 444	67.3	42.7	26.5
Littleton	38.6	899	31.1	7.5	79.7	16.1	23 857	1.7	1 082	4.5	35 926	66.8	43.2	26.3
Longmont	38.3	978	31.2	5.8	79.2	10.6	48 518	0.9	2 270	4.7	68 891	69.8	41.2	22.5
Loveland	38.3	932	32.1	4.9	84.0	9.8	38 385	1.1	1 823	4.7	55 222	68.2	42.1	24.7
Northglenn	42.8	964	33.1	8.7	82.4	16.1	20 248	1.2	1 191	5.9	29 297	70.2	43.2	25.0
Parker	21.9	1 140	26.4	1.1	82.3	11.4	27 706	2.2	1 157	4.2	33 751	79.5	56.4	11.9
Pueblo	43.7	718	34.3	12.0	79.3	7.1	47 213	-0.9	3 828	8.1	85 274	56.0	31.6	36.7
Thornton	30.2	1 071	30.7	3.6	85.3	10.0	69 599	1.3	3 727	5.4	91 053	74.0	48.5	15.5
Westminster	36.7	1 053	29.5	3.9	81.7	13.5	63 090	1.2	3 142	5.0	86 108	73.4	48.2	19.2
Wheat Ridge	47.9	817	31.9	8.6	80.8	16.4	16 549	1.4	925	5.6	25 330	65.7	42.0	29.9
CONNECTICUT	33.0	1 042	32.0	9.3	87.9	8.6	1 885 126	0.9	124 705	6.6	2 895 096	67.7	40.5	25.5
Bridgeport	59.4	1 063	37.7	21.2	80.7	7.2	71 518	0.2	7 281	10.2	112 920	69.4	35.6	29.0
Bristol	33.3	878	29.2	7.0	91.1	4.8	32 747	0.8	2 380	7.3	49 398	66.9	41.0	30.5
Danbury	40.3	1 188	31.5	9.3	85.4	8.9	46 468	1.7	2 430	5.2	68 522	73.7	42.5	21.0
Hartford	77.0	861	36.0	35.7	78.2	9.7	54 544	-0.4	6 649	12.2	97 497	61.6	29.1	35.3
Meriden	40.5	937	34.5	11.4	87.2	6.2	32 352	0.6	2 740	8.5	49 415	65.5	40.6	29.1
Middletown	46.3	983	27.6	9.7	82.3	10.5	26 172	1.0	1 713	6.5	40 313	66.1	40.6	26.4
Milford	22.1	1 307	34.0	6.1	89.6	6.3	29 616	1.2	1 691	5.7	42 732	69.1	43.8	28.0
Naugatuck	36.6	978	27.5	7.7	92.1	4.5	17 372	0.4	1 323	7.6	25 532	72.5	40.9	27.6
New Britain	60.7	878	31.8	17.7	82.5	8.1	36 708	0.2	3 486	9.5	57 858	64.9	35.3	31.2
New Haven	70.3	1 074	36.8	29.2	80.8	10.1	64 702	0.1	5 831	9.0	104 843	63.1	33.3	32.6
New London	63.0	863	33.7	17.4	77.8	15.1	12 258	-1.5	1 192	9.7	22 953	66.0	33.4	30.6
Norwalk	38.0	1 333	30.4	9.4	89.0	7.1	49 901	1.3	2 788	5.6	72 844	73.9	45.5	21.6
Norwich	47.7	913	32.1	14.3	86.6	9.6	20 566	-0.6	1 697	8.3	32 116	68.9	37.6	27.4
Shelton	17.4	1 133	26.3	3.9	89.9	6.9	21 951	1.1	1 371	6.2	33 719	66.2	41.8	25.1
Stamford	44.2	1 513	32.4	11.8	87.3	7.0	68 186	1.2	3 746	5.5	100 073	73.7	44.8	20.4
Torrington	31.9	840	32.3	10.9	90.2	4.5	19 830	0.4	1 429	7.2	29 863	67.1	40.3	30.4
Waterbury	53.8	877	35.2	18.2	85.7	6.1	51 573	0.0	5 522	10.7	85 097	62.1	35.0	33.2
West Haven	44.0	1 069	37.8	11.9	87.8	7.6	30 118	0.5	2 414	8.0	44 344	69.0	40.5	24.6
DELAWARE	28.6	989	30.3	6.5	86.4	11.7	451 767	2.1	25 854	5.7	734 994	64.0	40.3	26.8
Dover	49.5	920	32.6	12.2	77.2	16.8	15 639	1.7	1 218	7.8	30 159	61.2	33.6	27.6
Newark	45.1	976	42.8	5.9	62.9	26.9	15 324	2.3	852	5.6	29 063	51.2	23.8	25.8
Wilmington	54.7	912	33.3	24.4	79.8	11.2	33 060	1.7	2 552	7.7	55 727	63.3	37.7	32.8
DISTRICT OF COLUMBIA	58.9	1 264	29.6	37.9	80.0	9.4	377 448	1.1	29 399	7.8	535 963	68.4	45.6	25.1
Washington	58.9	1 264	29.6	37.9	80.0	9.4	377 448	1.1	29 399	7.8	535 963	68.4	45.6	25.1
FLORIDA	34.2	973	34.8	7.3	83.7	12.3	9 637 536	1.7	603 296	6.3	15 780 095	59.5	36.2	32.8
Altamonte Springs	52.3	945	29.6	4.7	81.1	14.3	24 925	2.7	1 370	5.5	35 014	67.9	43.9	22.8
Apopka	22.1	1 020	32.3	4.3	89.4	8.6	24 485	2.7	1 277	5.2	34 335	66.3	42.5	21.3
Aventura	36.5	1 513	36.3	9.2	79.9	16.0	16 759	2.4	900	5.4	30 603	53.9	36.8	41.1
Boca Raton	31.0	1 388	34.9	4.8	80.6	13.2	48 269	2.6	2 240	4.6	74 549	61.9	34.9	31.6
Bonita Springs	27.0	1 070	33.6	3.2	82.4	12.2	21 533	4.4	1 169	5.4	40 208	48.9	28.0	49.3
Boynton Beach	35.2	1 186	37.0	7.3	85.7	10.4	36 147	1.9	2 057	5.7	58 226	62.1	37.1	34.8
Bradenton	48.0	906	34.3	8.7	77.5	14.8	24 456	3.1	1 443	5.9	41 584	56.3	34.8	39.7
Cape Coral	31.5	1 046	33.2	3.9	80.9	11.3	82 084	4.0	4 955	6.0	128 141	59.5	33.7	33.6
Casselberry	39.4	943	31.8	5.1	84.6	10.1	14 724	2.4	845	5.7	22 222	65.1	41.7	27.8
Clearwater	42.0	899	34.6	12.9	83.8	11.6	55 983	1.3	3 076	5.5	89 620	58.9	38.2	36.3
Clermont	32.1	1 080	47.0	5.2	85.7	9.2	14 116	3.0	808	5.7	22 834	56.5	33.4	35.1
Coconut Creek	34.1	1 312	33.6	6.4	83.7	12.7	31 106	2.0	1 592	5.1	44 575	67.8	41.5	30.7
Cooper City	13.3	1 710	28.7	1.0	89.4	9.5	19 589	2.1	899	4.6	25 234	72.5	45.0	14.4
Coral Gables	35.3	1 312	34.5	5.1	79.4	16.5	25 779	2.6	1 254	4.9	42 228	61.4	41.9	21.8
Coral Springs	37.3	1 254	34.4	5.3	83.9	10.1	71 300	1.8	3 855	5.4	96 445	73.4	44.8	14.2
Cutler Bay	20.9	1 208	32.6	5.0	90.8	8.0	22 815	1.7	1 344	5.9	33 757	65.0	47.3	18.2
Dania Beach	49.4	1 120	39.9	8.1	79.2	16.6	16 092	2.2	869	5.4	24 593	66.8	36.7	26.7
Davie	27.9	1 172	37.3	5.5	83.6	13.0	54 794	2.1	2 643	4.8	76 603	67.8	42.0	21.1
Daytona Beach	55.1	734	36.8	17.8	79.3	14.8	29 201	1.3	2 203	7.5	53 853	51.4	26.6	43.3

1. $2,000 represents $2,000 or more. 2. 50.0 represents 50 percent or more. 3. Percent of civilian labor force. 4. Persons 16 years old and over.

City	Value of residential construction authorized by building permits, 2014: New construction ($1,000)	Number of housing units	Percent single family	Wholesale trade,[1] 2007: Number of establish-ments	Number of employees	Sales (mil dol)	Annual payroll (mil dol)	Retail trade,[2] 2007: Number of establish-ments	Number of employees	Sales (mil dol)	Annual payroll (mil dol)
	69	70	71	72	73	74	75	76	77	78	79
COLORADO—Cont'd											
Castle Rock	211 220	821	100.0	26	163	48.3	7.6	210	2 869	636.9	69.8
Centennial	13 891	92	81.5	190	2 740	1 970.0	181.8	264	3 983	1 942.9	128.6
Colorado Springs	NA	NA	NA	358	4 471	2 482.4	225.2	1 741	27 411	7 027.3	678.4
Commerce City	60 022	354	97.7	129	2 820	2 015.9	154.2	101	1 496	458.6	40.5
Denver	811 547	5 958	28.7	1 174	21 245	14 920.9	1 064.5	2 271	27 979	6 835.4	752.6
Englewood	4 112	19	89.5	106	1 845	667.0	97.4	226	2 968	1 598.1	80.7
Fort Collins	230 800	1 152	64.4	101	933	371.7	50.1	595	9 642	2 152.3	222.3
Fountain	NA	NA	NA	3	D	D	D	42	1 070	242.8	24.6
Grand Junction	NA	NA	NA	160	1 856	921.5	79.3	535	7 495	2 002.3	191.5
Greeley	98 826	789	45.8	92	1 115	606.1	53.0	341	5 563	1 222.6	122.4
Lakewood	181 727	1 195	14.9	129	877	475.8	46.9	695	10 817	2 671.8	271.3
Littleton	51 415	447	4.3	67	961	288.2	43.2	255	4 575	1 688.6	150.0
Longmont	82 850	411	50.9	66	736	669.5	57.5	309	4 761	1 054.5	106.4
Loveland	145 897	772	40.3	62	900	387.1	39.3	350	5 218	1 211.7	117.8
Northglenn	0	0	0.0	17	280	65.2	8.9	91	1 559	366.2	41.0
Parker	154 622	654	53.2	33	396	127.9	9.8	135	2 460	629.4	57.2
Pueblo	NA	NA	NA	57	525	244.0	23.3	441	6 907	1 563.9	163.8
Thornton	92 742	376	98.4	28	207	118.2	16.7	194	5 057	1 267.0	131.7
Westminster	10 370	34	88.2	64	1 011	452.4	71.0	358	6 595	1 421.5	140.0
Wheat Ridge	15 063	49	91.8	61	570	178.5	29.3	186	2 402	637.7	69.8
CONNECTICUT	1 148 276	5 329	51.8	3 848	58 291	107 917.0	3 587.9	13 807	196 133	52 165.5	5 160.4
Bridgeport	10 037	134	11.2	125	1 732	794.3	94.8	313	3 555	1 122.2	112.3
Bristol	5 055	61	24.6	37	600	253.4	27.9	178	3 046	803.3	74.9
Danbury	68 156	317	63.4	99	1 041	1 037.3	65.0	473	8 219	2 176.7	217.6
Hartford	1 068	10	70.0	130	2 759	1 413.4	128.1	381	3 620	1 299.1	110.2
Meriden	770	5	100.0	36	451	169.2	22.6	257	3 907	828.6	78.9
Middletown	7 883	61	60.7	40	761	262.0	34.4	139	1 868	526.7	52.8
Milford	NA	NA	NA	113	1 763	840.5	94.4	332	5 958	1 546.1	138.4
Naugatuck	2 442	19	100.0	27	429	240.6	25.8	71	1 066	275.4	24.0
New Britain	9 704	102	20.6	43	613	407.4	26.7	164	2 079	589.8	55.9
New Haven	36 053	412	5.8	78	1 042	1 077.9	51.7	345	3 366	907.2	88.0
New London	6 786	41	100.0	13	254	266.3	12.4	124	1 542	505.4	50.1
Norwalk	34 031	236	14.8	139	2 437	2 929.7	143.4	389	6 949	2 164.2	230.5
Norwich	4 298	42	50.0	18	450	248.3	27.0	151	2 134	517.6	51.4
Shelton	4 998	47	70.2	57	1 235	977.3	91.3	109	1 984	648.5	64.0
Stamford	44 578	391	11.5	222	4 587	64 886.5	568.9	492	6 157	1 596.1	186.7
Torrington	1 177	7	100.0	37	294	197.4	15.2	175	2 621	725.5	65.8
Waterbury	3 890	44	29.5	[illegible]	1 000	622.0	52.7	442	6 706	1 526.4	152.7
West Haven	1 289	11	100.0	62	1 148	486.8	58.0	129	1 487	443.1	40.9
DELAWARE	615 472	5 194	79.8	819	9 065	5 727.4	416.9	3 907	55 432	14 202.1	1 322.8
Dover	16 365	116	37.9	38	730	216.4	27.0	300	4 944	1 291.4	103.9
Newark	29 025	361	21.1	37	355	349.5	22.5	161	2 956	894.9	79.9
Wilmington	3 315	133	21.1	100	1 016	700.0	46.7	331	4 128	1 105.7	109.5
DISTRICT OF COLUMBIA	374 396	4 189	6.9	316	3 680	2 118.0	216.4	1 827	19 117	3 843.7	485.9
Washington	374 397	4 189	6.9	316	3 680	2 118.0	216.4	1 827	19 117	3 843.7	485.9
FLORIDA	19 548 769	84 075	66.9	27 442	279 300	221 641.5	12 566.1	73 794	1 016 290	262 341.1	24 049.7
Altamonte Springs	22 126	265	1.1	83	1 081	328.1	37.1	372	6 966	1 503.8	152.0
Apopka	95 306	292	100.0	55	464	128.6	14.4	144	2 082	567.7	48.8
Aventura	0	0	0.0	106	429	929.8	22.1	327	6 995	1 390.1	145.2
Boca Raton	123 609	469	14.1	421	4 906	5 249.8	314.8	746	10 183	2 348.5	272.7
Bonita Springs	255 257	902	67.1	38	410	188.3	15.0	228	2 762	663.1	73.7
Boynton Beach	5 197	29	100.0	119	963	457.4	42.8	356	6 019	1 191.8	118.8
Bradenton	60 241	511	24.1	42	574	322.4	27.0	216	2 930	718.4	71.5
Cape Coral	160 093	663	100.0	98	422	115.5	13.4	391	5 407	1 228.0	122.7
Casselberry	9 395	48	100.0	35	118	36.1	4.1	153	2 618	578.9	56.6
Clearwater	36 942	495	7.5	184	1 773	902.4	90.8	675	11 269	2 938.8	260.9
Clermont	64 619	551	47.7	18	120	34.7	4.4	131	2 935	703.2	63.6
Coconut Creek	4 902	41	100.0	80	394	327.5	20.1	131	3 121	1 437.4	110.3
Cooper City	2 315	10	100.0	50	169	81.3	7.2	86	1 556	278.8	29.7
Coral Gables	46 614	60	93.3	169	1 124	7 011.7	93.3	316	4 545	1 436.4	151.2
Coral Springs	949	2	100.0	208	2 019	1 009.5	63.4	508	8 734	1 900.2	184.9
Cutler Bay	4 210	115	2.6	NA	NA	NA	NA	NA	NA	NA	NA
Dania Beach	1 615	7	71.4	134	1 054	581.3	52.2	193	2 053	564.1	55.5
Davie	23 578	378	12.2	253	1 589	633.3	76.0	412	6 288	2 010.5	170.0
Daytona Beach	48 701	302	43.0	96	1 054	447.8	40.5	500	7 644	1 810.6	168.7

1. Merchant wholesalers except manufacturers' sales branches and offices. 2. Establishments with payroll.

City	Real estate and rental and leasing, 2007				Professional, scientific, and technical services,[1] 2007				Manufacturing, 2007			
	Number of establish-ments	Number of employees	Receipts (mil dol)	Annual payroll (mil dol)	Number of establish-ments	Number of employees	Receipts (mil dol)	Annual payroll (mil dol)	Number of establish-ments	Number of employees	Receipts (mil dol)	Annual payroll (mil dol)
	80	81	82	83	84	85	86	87	88	89	90	91
COLORADO—Cont'd												
Castle Rock	93	237	36.3	6.4	158	422	54.4	19.6	NA	NA	NA	NA
Centennial	246	1 688	336.3	67.2	719	4 300	772.7	283.7	76	1 451	436.5	75.6
Colorado Springs	942	3 364	521.5	99.7	1 871	D	D	D	379	11 518	3 819.9	577.9
Commerce City	48	380	111.1	18.6	35	189	20.8	7.2	78	2 424	4 019.7	125.9
Denver	1 451	11 600	2 536.4	623.7	3 856	D	D	D	840	19 480	5 189.9	826.0
Englewood	79	414	57.5	15.6	172	D	D	D	147	4 032	988.4	183.5
Fort Collins	289	1 274	185.2	34.0	768	D	D	D	126	5 852	2 179.3	367.0
Fountain	15	61	6.4	1.0	18	62	4.5	1.0	11	563	296.2	16.6
Grand Junction	232	830	203.1	32.2	373	D	D	D	106	2 082	D	83.0
Greeley	133	586	80.7	17.2	198	D	D	D	69	3 814	1 821.0	135.7
Lakewood	264	1 089	177.1	36.2	816	D	D	D	111	2 598	744.5	118.9
Littleton	113	466	58.7	12.6	351	D	D	D	34	D	D	D
Longmont	137	479	84.2	13.6	350	2 353	410.7	168.9	119	3 102	587.8	125.0
Loveland	112	462	60.1	13.4	210	1 108	125.1	41.4	92	2 885	563.6	181.6
Northglenn	44	257	19.8	5.4	51	179	14.9	6.0	36	804	128.4	29.5
Parker	66	176	26.2	4.1	186	580	80.1	28.7	NA	NA	NA	NA
Pueblo	121	581	85.1	16.5	202	D	D	D	59	2 046	D	104.6
Thornton	77	276	49.7	7.0	160	983	152.9	53.3	NA	NA	NA	NA
Westminster	158	584	87.6	17.1	335	D	D	D	52	813	271.7	41.2
Wheat Ridge	52	175	24.0	4.0	180	913	127.0	56.4	49	1 101	248.3	56.1
CONNECTICUT	3 609	22 455	5 686.6	994.0	9 828	101 384	15 771.7	7 988.8	4 924	190 790	58 404.9	10 345.1
Bridgeport	96	507	156.6	17.3	200	D	D	D	199	4 736	946.8	211.8
Bristol	40	138	30.1	4.1	74	416	38.5	17.2	148	3 675	719.2	160.1
Danbury	84	1 956	287.6	107.9	238	3 976	398.7	219.9	100	5 096	1 736.9	311.6
Hartford	174	1 562	257.6	77.4	404	7 844	1 666.5	639.6	80	1 314	242.9	51.5
Meriden	49	404	63.4	10.7	78	781	82.0	37.4	73	2 974	652.6	160.9
Middletown	49	404	140.7	21.6	113	D	D	D	64	3 390	1 668.0	199.8
Milford	60	910	863.6	43.0	187	2 126	224.6	95.9	167	3 477	1 102.4	190.5
Naugatuck	15	48	9.2	1.1	39	151	15.3	6.4	52	1 488	355.7	72.1
New Britain	45	153	30.0	4.7	94	D	D	D	103	3 382	713.2	157.6
New Haven	137	956	159.9	34.4	390	D	D	D	79	2 999	584.0	125.1
New London	27	166	21.2	6.3	106	D	D	D	NA	NA	NA	NA
Norwalk	100	386	92.2	18.1	374	D	D	D	131	3 220	991.2	207.6
Norwich	41	159	22.0	3.9	64	453	40.9	16.6	34	981	176.7	46.1
Shelton	44	263	93.5	19.3	152	D	D	D	74	4 316	1 195.7	301.0
Stamford	232	1 856	569.9	126.1	701	D	D	D	125	4 371	2 200.5	224.2
Torrington	28	123	15.9	4.1	65	254	30.4	8.9	63	1 998	415.4	90.4
Waterbury	89	352	87.1	12.0	159	D	D	D	177	4 187	1 009.4	186.5
West Haven	44	179	36.3	5.5	64	D	D	D	50	1 549	377.9	72.7
DELAWARE	1 248	5 807	11 057.2	222.4	2 383	D	D	D	673	34 866	25 679.9	1 759.7
Dover	60	388	60.5	15.5	143	D	D	D	26	D	1 413.5	D
Newark	66	D	D	D	117	D	D	D	36	4 372	3 070.0	311.7
Wilmington	244	861	2 285.7	39.0	567	D	D	D	77	1 578	397.2	76.2
DISTRICT OF COLUMBIA	1 140	9 663	2 747.8	624.8	4 373	82 107	24 177.7	8 660.6	137	2 015	332.8	80.8
Washington	1 140	9 663	2 747.8	624.8	4 373	82 107	24 177.7	8 660.6	137	2 015	332.8	80.8
FLORIDA	33 653	170 859	32 235.4	6 094.2	69 083	427 536	61 599.8	24 264.5	14 324	355 386	104 832.9	15 227.2
Altamonte Springs	142	783	137.5	28.1	332	2 172	264.2	98.0	NA	NA	NA	NA
Apopka	44	162	23.2	3.9	103	360	36.8	12.0	35	878	173.2	38.2
Aventura	174	828	217.1	32.1	261	864	145.1	55.0	NA	NA	NA	NA
Boca Raton	516	3 740	555.0	179.9	1 544	D	D	D	150	1 997	385.2	95.3
Bonita Springs	124	475	112.6	22.1	199	976	168.4	52.0	NA	NA	NA	NA
Boynton Beach	115	462	96.6	13.6	271	906	101.8	35.7	73	777	108.1	27.8
Bradenton	97	355	55.7	10.4	248	D	D	D	26	618	100.0	19.1
Cape Coral	295	637	82.1	15.5	347	1 318	136.9	48.8	85	745	101.2	27.9
Casselberry	59	295	49.1	9.0	108	411	50.5	15.3	NA	NA	NA	NA
Clearwater	286	1 151	198.5	39.5	772	D	D	D	112	1 301	219.6	49.6
Clermont	80	235	33.8	5.9	103	408	37.0	14.6	NA	NA	NA	NA
Coconut Creek	42	D	D	D	145	368	38.8	12.7	NA	NA	NA	NA
Cooper City	44	99	23.2	3.0	136	376	43.9	13.3	NA	NA	NA	NA
Coral Gables	385	2 418	403.9	89.7	1 424	D	D	D	45	512	D	27.7
Coral Springs	241	905	209.2	38.2	801	2 940	341.6	111.9	84	903	166.0	36.4
Cutler Bay	NA	NA	NA	NA	NA	NA	NA	NA	NA	NA	NA	NA
Dania Beach	69	204	52.4	7.2	154	638	85.1	29.9	59	792	131.8	29.5
Davie	219	875	213.1	35.0	503	D	D	D	99	2 449	331.4	113.3
Daytona Beach	158	1 515	209.2	41.9	333	D	D	D	62	1 382	316.3	58.7

1. Establishments subject to federal tax.

City	Accommodation and food services, 2007				Arts, entertainment, and recreation,[1] 2007				Health care and social assistance,[1] 2007			
	Number of establish-ments	Number of employees	Sales (mil dol)	Annual payroll (mil dol)	Number of establish-ments	Number of employees	Receipts (mil dol)	Annual payroll (mil dol)	Number of establish-ments	Number of employees	Receipts (mil dol)	Annual payroll (mil dol)
	92	93	94	95	96	97	98	99	100	101	102	103
COLORADO—Cont'd												
Castle Rock	93	1 680	67.3	21.3	14	D	D	D	92	818	55.7	25.0
Centennial	168	2 680	125.4	36.1	33	D	D	D	305	2 419	230.1	98.7
Colorado Springs	1 008	20 874	1 011.9	309.4	146	1 492	81.9	22.5	1 354	14 224	1 406.1	583.1
Commerce City	52	814	37.1	11.3	4	D	D	D	14	262	17.1	7.7
Denver	1 778	38 701	2 279.0	656.3	204	4 981	626.2	320.9	1 595	22 442	2 562.4	1 047.8
Englewood	104	1 469	65.7	19.6	13	D	D	D	218	4 579	651.1	259.0
Fort Collins	392	8 324	328.0	99.9	52	813	35.1	9.8	486	5 257	531.3	223.6
Fountain	37	528	25.4	6.7	3	53	2.1	0.8	11	121	12.0	4.3
Grand Junction	210	4 746	211.3	61.0	34	733	18.4	6.8	313	D	D	D
Greeley	187	3 828	134.5	40.7	20	197	7.0	1.8	228	3 326	273.9	116.4
Lakewood	350	7 742	347.4	108.1	44	727	30.9	10.1	440	5 841	504.5	226.8
Littleton	127	2 229	94.6	29.3	19	160	7.5	2.6	203	2 238	244.2	114.8
Longmont	183	3 285	144.5	45.6	27	226	6.4	1.9	226	2 350	201.4	91.1
Loveland	181	3 274	128.6	37.4	26	D	D	D	180	1 842	177.5	68.7
Northglenn	56	1 516	69.3	20.6	8	D	D	D	42	495	38.7	16.4
Parker	98	2 117	87.9	26.0	12	D	D	D	107	D	D	D
Pueblo	282	4 840	194.1	55.0	24	D	D	D	318	D	D	D
Thornton	143	3 048	135.5	38.8	17	D	D	D	162	2 845	316.5	120.2
Westminster	234	5 207	259.6	82.5	26	D	D	D	206	2 579	232.4	108.6
Wheat Ridge	99	1 553	67.1	18.8	16	100	5.0	1.3	167	1 666	189.4	91.7
CONNECTICUT	7 941	132 001	9 138.4	2 483.1	1 206	14 325	1 834.8	457.0	7 687	122 425	11 534.8	5 062.3
Bridgeport	193	D	D	D	17	315	30.7	6.9	214	3 925	364.7	161.7
Bristol	101	1 251	62.1	16.9	12	169	30.8	7.7	108	D	D	D
Danbury	208	3 248	200.3	54.3	16	D	D	D	195	D	D	D
Hartford	350	5 163	294.9	84.8	15	746	123.7	57.6	248	4 850	714.9	346.3
Meriden	120	1 402	72.5	19.9	3	D	D	D	95	1 616	145.8	62.3
Middletown	117	1 238	83.4	21.3	8	84	3.8	0.8	118	2 491	245.4	114.5
Milford	184	2 470	129.0	35.9	20	229	19.1	6.2	134	2 416	231.6	101.7
Naugatuck	51	398	20.1	5.1	4	D	D	D	39	1 081	50.8	23.7
New Britain	81	1 091	49.1	14.8	8	D	D	D	104	1 366	193.4	84.7
New Haven	331	3 739	266.0	66.2	17	340	80.9	7.8	277	4 295	431.1	209.7
New London	94	D	D	D	13	113	11.6	4.8	85	D	D	D
Norwalk	238	2 777	207.0	54.0	53	720	101.8	30.9	196	2 901	283.3	124.4
Norwich	89	D	D	D	9	D	D	D	120	1 890	195.3	74.7
Shelton	95	1 683	99.2	30.4	10	D	D	D	92	1 923	223.7	72.7
Stamford	349	4 437	353.1	106.8	57	D	D	D	340	3 368	424.1	169.5
Torrington	90	1 114	56.6	15.6	7	D	D	D	102	1 834	170.1	70.4
Waterbury	215	2 848	138.7	40.8	16	161	8.6	2.1	242	6 276	552.2	252.4
West Haven	118	1 358	74.5	20.9	6	D	D	D	61	D	D	D
DELAWARE	1 850	32 194	1 910.8	468.8	291	3 722	349.3	82.6	1 877	25 319	2 620.7	1 155.8
Dover	123	3 732	378.6	57.0	16	D	D	D	165	2 272	205.7	90.6
Newark	124	2 513	138.6	32.2	12	135	7.1	2.4	161	2 563	334.4	151.5
Wilmington	212	3 315	198.1	56.4	27	380	31.7	10.0	253	3 791	521.9	218.2
DISTRICT OF COLUMBIA	2 148	52 998	4 278.2	1 238.4	198	4 721	612.3	240.4	1 419	19 710	2 098.8	944.4
Washington	2 148	52 998	4 278.2	1 238.4	198	4 721	612.3	240.4	1 419	19 710	2 098.8	944.4
FLORIDA	35 012	746 214	41 922.1	11 470.0	6 629	133 359	13 402.7	3 497.8	46 687	538 050	61 636.7	22 586.4
Altamonte Springs	161	4 366	219.1	65.5	19	D	D	D	220	D	D	D
Apopka	67	1 112	51.9	14.0	11	D	D	D	71	537	59.9	29.4
Aventura	86	3 455	237.0	69.0	24	120	12.7	2.7	219	2 603	439.8	131.2
Boca Raton	398	10 638	682.8	202.2	92	661	78.8	14.1	700	7 297	935.2	341.9
Bonita Springs	107	1 978	104.5	29.3	36	1 146	72.5	27.6	112	813	114.8	32.5
Boynton Beach	150	3 081	138.0	43.5	24	D	D	D	283	D	D	D
Bradenton	123	2 196	103.0	27.6	24	220	10.9	4.0	262	5 984	765.1	241.2
Cape Coral	178	2 822	125.9	36.0	40	246	18.9	3.9	232	2 145	263.6	85.2
Casselberry	76	1 251	49.8	14.8	13	225	10.4	2.5	56	612	45.1	20.2
Clearwater	358	6 966	361.3	102.3	57	771	43.8	12.5	474	5 699	634.8	264.1
Clermont	85	1 862	80.7	23.8	15	D	D	D	101	D	D	D
Coconut Creek	51	537	27.9	7.8	20	D	D	D	82	D	D	D
Cooper City	49	875	33.0	10.0	32	174	15.5	5.6	97	D	D	D
Coral Gables	210	4 645	292.2	93.0	42	237	25.3	10.0	454	D	D	D
Coral Springs	275	4 595	246.9	64.7	67	623	35.6	10.3	497	D	D	D
Cutler Bay	NA	NA	NA	NA	NA	NA	NA	NA	NA	NA	NA	NA
Dania Beach	80	1 646	106.4	26.9	25	D	D	D	37	D	D	D
Davie	217	3 335	175.4	46.0	62	D	D	D	190	1 187	140.7	36.3
Daytona Beach	267	6 442	337.1	85.5	34	D	D	D	229	3 544	356.4	160.1

1. Establishments subject to federal tax.

City	Other services[1], 2007				Government employment and payroll, 2012								
						March payroll							
							Percent of total for:						
	Number of establish-ments	Number of employees	Receipts (mil dol)	Annual payroll (mil dol)	Full-time equivalent employees	Total (dollars)	Adminis-tration, judicial, and legal	Police and Corrections	Fire Protection	Highways and trans-portation	Health and welfare	Natural resources and utilities	Education and libraries
	104	105	106	107	108	109	110	111	112	113	114	115	116
COLORADO—Cont'd													
Castle Rock	79	405	29.4	9.8	454	2 257 316	12.3	18.0	21.0	7.0	3.2	27.7	0.0
Centennial	167	872	94.6	27.4	56	312 389	97.1	0.0	0.0	0.0	0.0	0.0	0.0
Colorado Springs	690	4 198	324.7	101.7	6 835	37 084 390	4.0	14.0	7.5	3.0	35.7	34.0	0.0
Commerce City	81	684	79.1	20.8	331	1 840 907	22.9	42.5	0.0	11.7	8.4	14.5	0.0
Denver	1 131	8 938	732.5	229.9	11 914	62 559 560	13.5	28.4	10.9	11.0	11.2	19.1	2.3
Englewood	142	874	89.8	29.5	496	2 612 051	12.2	19.8	16.5	5.4	2.5	32.9	2.4
Fort Collins	221	1 252	84.2	28.3	1 475	7 276 841	19.4	25.1	0.0	10.9	0.5	39.9	0.0
Fountain	13	D	D	D	195	852 760	16.1	9.5	14.2	2.6	3.5	38.5	0.0
Grand Junction	198	1 227	116.9	31.8	684	3 402 863	13.8	30.4	21.4	6.4	0.5	21.7	0.0
Greeley	123	633	48.7	14.5	980	4 950 974	9.9	28.6	15.1	7.5	1.4	32.8	0.0
Lakewood	271	1 301	99.1	33.3	1 014	5 146 071	18.0	47.7	0.0	3.7	1.4	18.8	0.0
Littleton	101	497	42.2	12.9	427	2 523 624	11.4	21.4	46.3	4.8	4.3	5.3	4.2
Longmont	149	794	53.8	17.9	895	4 775 325	12.8	26.4	13.8	4.3	4.2	29.7	3.4
Loveland	127	733	53.6	18.1	677	3 104 613	23.9	23.9	13.3	6.0	0.0	25.8	3.5
Northglenn	54	D	D	D	323	4 495 142	20.4	39.8	0.0	2.3	0.0	30.8	0.0
Parker	100	489	35.6	11.4	295	1 383 773	22.2	35.4	0.0	13.3	0.0	22.5	0.0
Pueblo	141	724	56.4	15.6	859	4 316 626	8.8	33.4	18.2	8.7	0.5	28.3	0.0
Thornton	83	699	48.3	19.7	842	4 836 932	20.0	27.9	10.2	10.4	4.4	24.7	0.0
Westminster	123	783	46.8	15.8	992	5 125 430	12.9	29.5	16.6	4.2	3.5	24.3	3.3
Wheat Ridge	108	512	48.1	14.7	198	835 164	27.5	56.8	0.0	15.6	0.0	0.0	0.0
CONNECTICUT	5 911	36 724	3 068.8	980.2	X	X	X	X	X	X	X	X	X
Bridgeport	159	760	72.3	19.3	4 248	23 926 290	4.5	12.4	5.7	0.9	3.3	1.9	70.6
Bristol	97	427	33.7	9.7	1 756	9 163 919	3.3	10.9	5.8	2.6	1.2	5.4	69.3
Danbury	160	1 023	90.8	28.0	1 817	10 016 152	3.5	11.0	8.0	3.2	1.8	2.8	68.2
Hartford	208	2 359	139.9	47.3	5 207	24 306 797	2.8	9.1	6.3	1.0	3.8	0.9	76.1
Meriden	78	385	28.6	10.0	1 673	9 260 984	3.4	12.3	8.7	1.1	3.7	5.2	65.5
Middletown	77	380	51.2	11.6	1 621	8 623 913	3.5	13.7	9.7	2.6	6.4	5.0	55.8
Milford	133	782	61.5	19.8	2 207	11 763 788	2.2	6.1	6.4	1.6	1.9	2.6	77.1
Naugatuck	38	192	14.1	4.4	976	4 533 881	3.1	10.0	5.6	1.8	1.8	2.7	73.9
New Britain	81	335	29.7	9.5	2 064	11 112 239	2.6	10.0	9.5	2.3	1.6	6.1	66.2
New Haven	174	967	76.8	24.4	4 808	23 846 140	3.9	13.4	10.0	1.1	2.8	3.0	65.4
New London	48	314	23.1	7.7	789	3 869 245	5.6	17.4	11.4	1.4	2.1	4.5	54.9
Norwalk	186	1 017	99.2	29.4	2 837	13 813 488	4.1	12.3	8.1	3.0	1.2	1.8	68.2
Norwich	72	515	32.3	10.9	984	5 092 687	3.2	11.7	7.1	3.7	4.1	20.9	47.0
Shelton	59	351	22.4	7.3	952	5 269 099	4.2	8.4	0.5	4.0	2.3	3.1	77.5
Stamford	221	1 431	125.4	39.5	3 375	22 400 736	3.9	13.4	9.4	1.1	5.3	3.3	60.5
Torrington	73	542	30.5	21.9	923	4 776 132	2.9	12.2	7.3	3.8	3.3	2.6	66.3
Waterbury	152	1 092	72.9	25.4	3 875	18 570 027	3.9	12.3	7.5	1.2	2.6	5.2	67.1
West Haven	81	368	37.3	11.0	1 404	6 641 617	4.9	17.7	4.6	4.7	2.6	0.6	64.8
DELAWARE	1 256	7 893	569.1	195.3	X	X	X	X	X	X	X	X	X
Dover	65	626	34.4	12.0	348	1 666 145	16.3	43.4	1.4	2.0	1.1	25.4	3.3
Newark	64	430	20.4	7.9	258	1 304 591	12.9	41.6	0.4	3.6	4.4	29.6	0.0
Wilmington	148	1 043	76.4	27.8	1 254	5 779 211	16.3	41.1	15.0	4.0	5.1	11.7	0.0
DISTRICT OF COLUMBIA	969	7 011	566.2	170.4	X	X	X	X	X	X	X	X	X
Washington	969	7 011	566.2	170.4	34 002	194 813 463	15.0	19.3	5.8	2.2	15.5	8.1	25.7
FLORIDA	28 522	149 369	11 718.0	3 529.5	X	X	X	X	X	X	X	X	X
Altamonte Springs	109	640	41.0	13.5	387	1 562 231	12.2	35.2	0.0	2.6	0.0	35.5	1.2
Apopka	59	293	20.8	6.2	391	1 780 824	13.9	31.5	26.1	2.1	0.0	17.9	0.0
Aventura	65	411	23.1	7.5	366	1 349 401	17.9	28.7	27.3	9.0	0.5	15.5	0.0
Boca Raton	347	1 954	142.7	47.5	1 418	6 984 386	9.9	26.8	24.4	3.6	0.1	27.8	2.2
Bonita Springs	68	318	18.8	6.6	55	213 459	44.7	0.0	0.0	0.0	0.0	11.7	0.0
Boynton Beach	133	772	52.7	15.5	747	4 117 701	10.9	32.9	22.3	0.2	0.5	25.1	2.4
Bradenton	95	393	28.6	8.9	434	1 525 511	8.1	37.6	20.9	3.9	0.5	24.1	0.0
Cape Coral	203	831	65.3	18.4	1 360	5 329 766	17.8	25.1	19.0	5.1	0.4	27.7	0.0
Casselberry	63	299	22.9	6.8	217	833 769	18.9	28.6	21.7	6.1	0.0	23.7	0.0
Clearwater	240	1 253	100.1	30.8	1 653	6 760 407	11.2	29.1	14.6	5.7	0.6	28.3	3.3
Clermont	45	211	13.6	4.1	262	960 550	4.5	26.8	25.5	20.2	0.0	23.0	0.0
Coconut Creek	65	276	37.0	8.5	330	1 913 611	28.0	41.4	1.7	4.0	0.0	17.4	0.0
Cooper City	43	D	D	D	138	525 375	17.6	0.0	0.0	0.0	0.0	48.0	0.0
Coral Gables	132	653	48.9	15.4	793	4 845 710	17.3	32.6	27.2	4.5	0.5	12.9	0.0
Coral Springs	242	1 001	76.5	20.8	845	4 451 797	13.6	41.1	25.3	2.0	0.0	11.7	0.0
Cutler Bay	NA	NA	NA	NA	47	173 292	50.2	1.3	0.0	11.8	0.0	32.6	0.0
Dania Beach	102	583	57.8	16.3	113	516 841	46.4	0.0	0.0	4.7	3.0	37.2	0.0
Davie	216	1 096	105.3	29.2	617	4 513 053	8.3	40.2	31.1	7.0	1.3	8.4	0.0
Daytona Beach	132	853	51.7	15.1	1 046	4 375 710	11.9	39.3	11.4	5.1	1.4	26.4	0.0

1. Establishments subject to federal tax.

City	City government finances, 2007									
	General revenue							General expenditure		
		Intergovernmental		Taxes					Per capita[1] (dollars)	
					Per capita[1] (dollars)					
	Total (mil dol)	Total (mil dol)	Percent from state government	Total (mil dol)	Total	Property	Sales and gross receipts	Total (mil dol)	Total	Capital outlays
	117	118	119	120	121	122	123	124	125	126
COLORADO—Cont'd										
Castle Rock	72.3	4.3	100.0	39.3	764	86	677	61.6	1 198	135
Centennial	67.4	9.9	66.5	52.6	505	129	376	66.6	640	152
Colorado Springs	1 020.1	65.7	31.6	214.4	494	52	442	968.4	2 233	239
Commerce City	59.2	2.8	60.8	47.8	984	138	846	61.0	1 256	0
Denver	2 940.6	477.1	60.5	1 107.9	1 748	610	1 138	2 623.4	4 139	261
Englewood	60.4	3.3	42.3	31.3	1 002	139	864	53.0	1 698	1
Fort Collins	238.1	30.8	16.5	125.6	843	119	724	233.7	1 569	354
Fountain	12.7	1.1	60.7	10.1	374	74	300	26.4	981	22
Grand Junction	114.1	18.2	45.4	60.4	1 009	214	795	130.2	2 176	564
Greeley	114.2	13.2	62.0	60.1	630	105	514	99.4	1 042	109
Lakewood	155.5	22.9	36.1	96.4	663	105	514	144.6	994	114
Littleton	70.6	17.6	14.5	32.8	749	95	655	75.6	1 725	102
Longmont	98.1	6.6	75.4	57.7	650	161	388	98.8	1 114	42
Loveland	115.2	11.2	96.5	59.5	847	268	579	109.1	1 554	315
Northglenn	32.1	4.4	67.4	19.9	539	82	457	33.8	914	210
Parker	53.8	8.3	22.1	33.0	699	35	636	55.5	1 175	321
Pueblo	152.7	29.0	69.9	79.2	734	146	589	141.8	1 315	332
Thornton	147.1	14.0	41.5	89.2	717	95	617	134.0	1 078	204
Westminster	153.4	13.5	40.6	99.8	914	126	788	145.3	1 330	246
Wheat Ridge	30.8	2.8	58.9	23.1	752	27	726	32.0	1 043	219
CONNECTICUT	X	X	X	X	X	X	X	X	X	X
Bridgeport	693.1	370.2	98.3	277.5	1 888	1 865	23	743.6	5 058	849
Bristol	263.8	119.3	95.5	120.4	1 987	1 939	38	318.7	5 258	1 671
Danbury	280.7	82.5	95.8	171.7	2 074	2 030	44	248.5	3 001	199
Hartford	809.1	477.2	84.9	283.3	2 262	2 204	49	793.7	6 336	712
Meriden	212.7	85.0	99.7	110.3	1 819	1 801	2	226.8	3 739	412
Middletown	189.7	68.5	99.3	101.5	2 142	2 129	12	158.3	3 339	308
Milford	203.4	27.7	97.5	162.8	3 160	3 130	13	206.1	4 000	448
Naugatuck	113.1	38.6	96.7	67.3	2 115	2 091	21	123.1	3 870	120
New Britain	264.0	124.4	97.4	111.2	1 521	1 505	16	274.7	3 758	394
New Haven	723.5	431.0	93.9	232.5	1 776	1 722	46	1 130.4	8 633	3 741
New London	123.5	69.0	97.3	39.7	1 438	1 415	23	112.6	4 081	298
Norwalk	353.8	52.6	97.8	263.8	3 023	2 994	29	360.1	4 125	476
Norwich	159.1	79.8	97.7	64.1	1 584	1 562	13	163.0	4 029	489
Shelton	121.4	15.0	88.2	99.0	2 457	2 415	42	115.7	2 872	166
Stamford	535.4	50.2	94.1	426.4	3 408	3 340	47	551.6	4 408	402
Torrington	128.3	39.4	97.2	77.2	2 158	2 136	0	121.9	3 409	87
Waterbury	498.5	253.0	94.0	220.5	2 006	1 989	11	626.2	5 696	845
West Haven	172.1	67.7	99.0	89.3	1 617	1 606	11	169.2	3 062	287
DELAWARE	X	X	X	X	X	X	X	X	X	X
Dover	42.7	9.6	91.3	15.8	426	298	91	55.8	1 506	400
Newark	23.4	3.3	100.0	8.4	258	155	72	32.7	1 010	108
Wilmington	193.4	38.2	53.3	110.5	1 550	547	108	166.5	2 334	116
DISTRICT OF COLUMBIA	X	X	X	X	X	X	X	X	X	X
Washington	10 710.4	3 077.7	0.0	5 933.8	9 344	2 957	2 601	11 199.3	17 636	2 228
FLORIDA	X	X	X	X	X	X	X	X	X	X
Altamonte Springs	42.8	3.7	94.1	21.6	515	214	300	30.6	731	144
Apopka	48.2	9.5	80.2	19.4	437	163	273	45.1	1 012	64
Aventura	42.7	11.2	85.4	25.0	671	315	355	38.3	1 028	79
Boca Raton	195.4	30.0	30.6	109.3	1 242	718	524	210.8	2 397	278
Bonita Springs	18.8	4.9	87.3	11.2	243	125	118	17.6	382	76
Boynton Beach	116.4	15.6	61.0	50.6	721	474	247	120.3	1 714	146
Bradenton	58.2	10.3	29.0	24.6	488	329	158	58.4	1 157	9
Cape Coral	245.7	47.7	00.0	92.3	572	430	143	240.6	1 492	184
Casselberry	34.0	7.5	31.2	12.8	484	228	256	41.1	1 552	195
Clearwater	200.9	27.4	47.6	81.7	751	363	387	194.0	1 782	189
Clermont	32.1	6.1	87.7	12.5	423	203	221	30.7	1 043	125
Coconut Creek	61.2	5.4	70.6	29.6	537	289	249	52.9	959	77
Cooper City	35.4	2.6	92.2	17.7	547	292	255	32.2	994	12
Coral Gables	158.0	11.2	62.7	97.1	1 954	1 350	604	127.4	2 564	171
Coral Springs	123.2	15.5	67.5	65.4	521	261	253	133.1	1 060	84
Cutler Bay	23.2	9.8	41.7	11.1	260	99	161	26.0	611	269
Dania Beach	52.7	10.5	66.3	24.3	793	518	275	52.7	1 718	156
Davie	104.7	13.7	53.9	70.6	738	407	331	98.2	1 027	73
Daytona Beach	124.9	15.8	46.5	44.7	724	392	332	118.4	1 915	146

1. Based on population estimated as of July 1 of the year shown.

City	Public welfare	Highways	Parking facilities	Education	Health and hospitals	Police protection	Sewerage and sanitation	Parks and recreation	Housing and community development	Interest on debt
	City government finances, 2012 (cont.)									
	General expenditure (cont.)									
	Percent of total for:									
	127	128	129	130	131	132	133	134	135	136
COLORADO—Cont'd										
Castle Rock	0.0	16.9	0.0	0.0	0.0	12.1	16.6	16.7	0.0	4.0
Centennial	0.0	26.3	0.0	0.0	0.0	29.9	0.0	9.5	5.1	0.2
Colorado Springs	0.0	8.7	0.2	0.0	53.3	9.2	3.9	2.2	0.5	2.8
Commerce City	0.0	7.9	0.0	0.0	0.0	23.6	3.0	10.5	3.7	7.1
Denver	6.4	5.9	0.0	0.0	2.0	8.6	3.3	7.4	4.4	11.0
Englewood	0.0	6.9	0.0	0.0	0.0	19.6	18.4	14.4	2.6	5.1
Fort Collins	0.0	22.5	0.0	0.0	0.0	13.6	7.0	20.8	0.0	1.9
Fountain	0.0	4.7	0.0	0.0	0.8	19.5	0.0	3.1	0.3	0.0
Grand Junction	0.0	12.8	0.3	0.0	0.0	27.0	12.8	14.2	1.8	5.2
Greeley	0.0	6.4	0.3	0.0	0.0	27.1	11.9	13.9	4.4	3.0
Lakewood	0.0	10.8	0.0	0.0	0.9	27.9	2.2	12.3	1.2	1.7
Littleton	0.4	8.2	0.0	0.0	0.0	14.2	10.6	3.0	0.1	2.6
Longmont	0.0	1.0	0.2	0.0	0.0	22.5	18.0	19.4	5.9	2.3
Loveland	0.0	11.3	0.0	0.0	0.0	15.0	10.4	11.8	13.3	0.5
Northglenn	1.3	36.3	0.0	0.0	0.0	21.1	7.6	18.5	0.7	0.0
Parker	0.0	15.6	0.0	0.0	0.0	16.9	2.2	37.3	2.0	5.8
Pueblo	0.0	5.5	0.8	0.0	0.0	18.6	20.0	6.8	11.0	1.6
Thornton	0.0	19.8	0.0	0.0	0.0	19.1	12.4	16.7	1.5	2.1
Westminster	0.0	5.0	0.0	0.0	0.0	13.9	6.9	14.9	9.1	4.9
Wheat Ridge	0.0	14.0	0.0	0.0	0.0	32.8	6.3	20.9	0.0	0.3
CONNECTICUT	X	X	X	X	X	X	X	X	X	X
Bridgeport	0.4	1.9	0.3	44.8	0.5	12.4	5.2	0.8	1.2	5.5
Bristol	0.0	5.0	0.0	63.2	2.8	4.2	3.8	1.2	0.3	0.8
Danbury	0.2	4.2	0.5	53.7	1.2	6.5	3.4	2.5	0.2	2.4
Hartford	1.6	3.6	0.1	58.0	1.8	8.2	0.4	0.2	8.4	1.9
Meriden	0.6	1.9	0.1	57.5	1.4	5.2	4.0	0.9	0.4	1.6
Middletown	0.1	2.3	0.3	50.9	0.6	8.1	3.9	1.7	0.3	1.8
Milford	0.5	1.5	0.0	54.6	1.2	4.9	13.6	0.5	0.4	1.1
Naugatuck	0.2	2.0	0.0	56.2	0.8	4.8	6.3	1.1	0.0	3.5
New Britain	0.1	4.1	0.0	51.5	0.6	12.7	4.6	3.5	1.1	5.1
New Haven	0.0	1.2	1.6	66.9	0.3	3.3	1.0	0.5	1.0	1.6
New London	0.0	9.3	0.5	48.4	0.2	11.0	4.0	8.9	1.6	1.9
Norwalk	0.0	4.6	1.3	50.9	0.6	5.2	5.7	3.8	0.4	3.4
Norwich	1.6	10.4	0.2	52.7	0.0	7.4	10.4	1.5	1.0	0.7
Shelton	0.0	2.6	0.0	60.5	2.6	4.5	4.5	1.7	0.1	2.3
Stamford	2.7	1.6	0.6	47.9	4.0	10.2	4.2	0.6	0.6	3.4
Torrington	0.0	4.5	0.0	56.8	5.0	6.7	4.0	1.2	0.2	1.8
Waterbury	0.6	1.7	0.0	58.3	0.5	4.8	4.0	0.7	1.1	4.5
West Haven	0.2	3.3	0.0	53.9	0.9	7.6	10.9	1.1	0.5	4.1
DELAWARE	X	X	X	X	X	X	X	X	X	X
Dover	0.0	4.4	0.0	0.0	0.1	25.4	18.7	1.5	0.7	0.2
Newark	0.0	8.2	2.2	0.0	0.0	30.5	22.1	7.9	1.1	0.3
Wilmington	0.0	5.8	4.3	0.0	0.0	30.6	10.4	4.8	6.2	3.2
DISTRICT OF COLUMBIA	X	X	X	X	X	X	X	X	X	X
Washington	25.6	4.7	0.2	21.2	6.0	5.0	5.3	1.8	4.9	4.5
FLORIDA	X	X	X	X	X	X	X	X	X	X
Altamonte Springs	0.0	19.8	0.0	0.0	0.0	30.9	9.3	11.4	0.0	0.1
Apopka	0.0	5.4	0.0	0.0	8.7	26.1	18.4	5.7	0.0	1.3
Aventura	0.0	8.4	0.0	17.8	0.0	41.5	0.0	7.7	0.0	3.2
Boca Raton	0.0	5.0	0.0	0.0	0.0	17.6	14.0	17.3	0.2	1.6
Bonita Springs	0.0	31.5	0.0	0.0	1.0	9.5	0.0	12.6	1.6	7.3
Boynton Beach	0.0	1.9	0.0	0.0	0.0	21.9	20.0	8.6	0.3	2.3
Bradenton	0.0	3.5	1.4	0.0	0.0	22.9	24.5	5.3	9.3	1.9
Cape Coral	0.0	10.9	0.0	10.4	0.0	15.1	5.4	7.0	3.0	4.8
Casselberry	0.0	6.3	0.0	0.0	0.1	13.0	22.3	3.0	0.0	1.2
Clearwater	0.1	6.4	2.0	0.0	3.0	19.9	21.2	14.6	0.6	1.4
Clermont	0.0	3.8	0.0	0.0	0.0	20.7	33.3	12.1	0.0	0.5
Coconut Creek	0.0	3.4	0.0	0.0	0.0	29.3	2.2	9.1	1.0	1.9
Cooper City	0.0	2.4	0.1	0.0	0.0	31.4	17.8	9.4	0.0	0.4
Coral Gables	0.0	4.8	3.5	0.0	0.0	29.1	12.4	6.3	0.5	1.9
Coral Springs	0.0	4.5	0.0	0.0	6.2	37.8	6.6	11.4	0.0	1.5
Cutler Bay	0.0	2.3	0.0	0.0	0.0	30.8	0.0	32.3	0.0	3.8
Dania Beach	0.0	4.0	2.3	0.0	0.0	19.8	10.2	6.8	0.0	1.4
Davie	0.0	8.0	0.0	0.0	0.0	36.2	0.0	7.4	2.6	3.2
Daytona Beach	0.0	11.2	0.0	0.0	0.0	29.4	13.1	11.5	1.8	3.5

City	City government finances, 2012 (cont.)			Climate[2]						
	Debt outstanding			Average daily temperature (degrees Fahrenheit)						
				Mean		Limits				
	Total (mil dol)	Per capita[1] (dollars)	Debt issued during year	January	July	January[3]	July[4]	Annual precipitation (inches)	Heating degree days	Cooling degree days
	137	138	139	140	141	142	143	144	145	146
COLORADO—Cont'd										
Castle Rock	110.8	2 154	0.0	NA	NA	NA	NA	NA	NA	NA
Centennial	2.8	27	0.0	NA	NA	NA	NA	NA	NA	NA
Colorado Springs	2 643.8	6 097	167.5	28.1	69.6	14.5	84.4	17.40	6 480	404
Commerce City	182.6	3 760	0.1	NA	NA	NA	NA	NA	NA	NA
Denver	7 039.4	11 106	660.3	31.2	71.5	15.6	88.3	18.17	5 988	496
Englewood	89.9	2 879	0.3	28.2	70.2	12.7	85.8	17.06	6 773	435
Fort Collins	216.4	1 453	11.2	28.2	71.5	14.5	86.2	13.98	6 256	524
Fountain	29.0	1 078	9.0	NA	NA	NA	NA	NA	NA	NA
Grand Junction	74.2	1 241	0.0	27.4	77.5	16.8	91.9	9.06	5 489	1 098
Greeley	155.4	1 629	0.0	27.8	74.0	15.6	88.7	14.22	5 980	759
Lakewood	74.1	509	0.0	28.2	70.2	12.7	85.8	17.06	6 773	435
Littleton	52.5	1 198	2.4	28.2	70.2	12.7	85.8	17.06	6 773	435
Longmont	86.1	971	2.5	27.1	72.2	12.0	88.9	14.15	6 415	587
Loveland	5.0	71	0.0	28.2	71.5	14.5	86.2	13.98	6 256	524
Northglenn	9.0	244	0.0	30.0	72.0	16.2	87.9	13.25	6 074	590
Parker	55.9	1 184	0.0	NA	NA	NA	NA	NA	NA	NA
Pueblo	144.1	1 337	15.5	30.8	77.0	14.7	93.8	12.60	5 346	997
Thornton	191.4	1 539	0.0	30.0	72.0	16.2	87.9	13.25	6 074	590
Westminster	297.6	2 724	5.2	29.2	73.4	15.2	88.0	15.81	6 128	696
Wheat Ridge	2.7	86	0.0	31.2	71.5	15.6	88.3	18.17	5 988	496
CONNECTICUT	X	X	X	X	X	X	X	X	X	X
Bridgeport	742.4	5 050	77.6	29.9	74.0	22.9	81.9	44.15	5 466	789
Bristol	95.9	1 582	23.9	23.4	70.5	12.6	83.3	51.03	6 825	395
Danbury	169.5	2 047	37.8	26.5	72.5	17.6	83.9	51.77	6 159	597
Hartford	413.5	3 301	78.1	25.9	73.6	16.3	83.8	44.29	6 121	654
Meriden	121.0	1 994	1.8	28.3	73.4	20.3	84.2	52.35	5 791	669
Middletown	145.6	3 071	0.0	29.9	74.0	22.9	81.9	44.15	5 466	789
Milford	167.9	3 259	24.1	29.9	74.0	22.9	81.9	44.15	5 466	789
Naugatuck	75.9	2 387	0.0	29.9	74.0	22.9	81.9	44.15	5 466	789
New Britain	280.1	3 831	34.0	28.3	73.4	20.3	84.2	52.35	5 791	669
New Haven	585.6	4 473	50.6	25.9	72.5	16.9	82.8	52.73	6 271	558
New London	63.6	2 305	6.8	28.9	71.8	20.0	80.7	48.72	5 799	511
Norwalk	269.9	3 093	45.1	27.8	73.4	18.8	84.2	48.38	5 854	652
Norwich	48.2	1 190	17.7	27.6	73.2	17.3	83.8	52.78	5 916	627
Shelton	84.7	2 103	22.7	29.9	74.0	22.9	81.9	44.15	5 466	789
Stamford	448.3	3 582	64.9	28.7	73.5	19.2	85.4	52.79	5 582	692
Torrington	36.3	1 015	0.0	23.6	69.5	13.9	80.7	54.59	6 839	323
Waterbury	472.8	4 301	67.1	25.9	72.5	16.9	82.8	52.73	6 271	558
West Haven	122.2	2 213	51.1	25.9	72.5	16.9	82.8	52.73	6 271	558
DELAWARE	X	X	X	X	X	X	X	X	X	X
Dover	41.3	1 115	4.1	35.3	77.8	26.9	87.4	46.28	4 212	1 262
Newark	13.6	418	12.7	32.5	76.4	23.5	87.6	45.35	4 746	1 047
Wilmington	353.0	4 950	53.2	31.5	76.6	23.7	86.0	42.81	4 888	1 125
DISTRICT OF COLUMBIA	X	X	X	X	X	X	X	X	X	X
Washington	11 278.8	17 761	1 642.8	34.9	79.2	27.3	88.3	39.35	4 055	1 531
FLORIDA	X	X	X	X	X	X	X	X	X	X
Altamonte Springs	0.0	0	0.0	58.7	81.5	47.0	91.9	51.31	799	3 017
Apopka	33.4	751	0.0	58.7	81.5	47.0	91.9	51.31	799	3 017
Aventura	32.5	872	6.8	67.9	82.7	62.6	87.0	46.60	141	4 090
Boca Raton	139.0	1 580	0.0	67.2	83.3	57.8	91.8	57.27	219	4 241
Bonita Springs	24.3	526	0.0	64.3	82.0	53.4	91.2	51.90	316	3 646
Boynton Beach	126.0	1 795	0.0	66.2	82.5	57.3	90.1	61.39	246	3 999
Bradenton	34.5	683	0.0	61.6	81.9	50.9	91.3	54.12	538	3 327
Cape Coral	907.6	5 629	196.0	62.7	81.3	50.3	91.3	50.07	427	3 287
Casselberry	20.3	766	9.1	NA	NA	NA	NA	NA	NA	NA
Clearwater	247.9	2 276	47.0	61.3	82.5	52.4	89.7	44.77	591	3 482
Clermont	19.7	668	0.0	NA	NA	NA	NA	NA	NA	NA
Coconut Creek	22.8	413	0.0	67.2	83.3	57.8	91.8	57.27	219	4 241
Cooper City	6.1	189	1.5	67.5	82.6	59.2	89.8	64.19	167	4 120
Coral Gables	79.3	1 596	50.7	67.9	82.7	62.6	87.0	46.60	141	4 090
Coral Springs	71.6	570	8.8	67.2	83.3	57.8	91.8	57.27	219	4 241
Cutler Bay	18.6	437	3.6	NA	NA	NA	NA	NA	NA	NA
Dania Beach	30.3	988	3.6	NA	NA	NA	NA	NA	NA	NA
Davie	144.9	1 515	20.0	66.2	82.5	57.3	90.1	61.39	246	3 999
Daytona Beach	154.8	2 505	36.2	57.1	81.2	44.5	91.2	57.03	954	2 819

1. Based on the population estimated as of July 1 of the year shown. 2. Represents normal values based on the 30-year period, 1971–2000. 3. Average daily minimum.
4. Average daily maximum.

STATE Place code	City	Land area,[1] 2010 (sq km)	Population, 2014: Total persons	Population, 2014: Rank	Population, 2014: Per square kilometer	Race alone or in combination (percent), 2011-2013: White	Race alone or in combination (percent), 2011-2013: Black	Race alone or in combination (percent), 2011-2013: American Indian, Alaska Native	Race alone or in combination (percent), 2011-2013: Asian	Race alone or in combination (percent), 2011-2013: Hawaiian Pacific Islander	Percent Hispanic or Latino[2], 2011-2013	Percent foreign born 2011–2013
		1	2	3	4	5	6	7	8	9	10	11
	FLORIDA—Cont'd											
12 16725	Deerfield Beach	39.1	78 881	418	2 017.4	69.9	27.3	0.4	2.3	NA	15.6	30.1
12 16875	DeLand	45.6	29 194	1 261	640.2	72.3	18.0	0.3	5.6	NA	11.1	7.6
12 17100	Delray Beach	40.9	65 055	545	1 590.6	66.6	29.6	0.3	3.1	NA	9.4	23.4
12 17200	Deltona	97.2	86 890	363	893.9	78.4	11.9	1.9	1.5	NA	32.1	9.7
12 17935	Doral	35.9	54 116	686	1 507.4	91.8	2.7	0.5	5.5	NA	76.2	62.2
12 18575	Dunedin	26.8	35 819	1 045	1 336.5	95.1	2.8	NA	2.7	NA	4.8	8.6
12 24000	Fort Lauderdale	90.0	176 013	135	1 955.7	63.9	32.5	0.6	2.1	0.4	15.8	22.6
12 24125	Fort Myers	103.5	70 918	483	685.2	62.2	31.8	0.7	1.8	NA	19.5	14.7
12 24300	Fort Pierce	53.3	43 601	852	818.0	57.1	38.5	0.6	0.3	NA	20.4	18.2
12 25175	Gainesville	158.8	128 460	206	808.9	68.4	24.7	0.8	8.0	0.2	10.1	12.5
12 27322	Greenacres	15.0	39 157	949	2 610.5	76.8	23.4	0.7	2.4	NA	42.0	34.1
12 28452	Hallandale Beach	10.9	39 051	953	3 582.7	77.1	18.2	1.0	3.0	NA	30.7	49.0
12 30000	Hialeah	55.6	235 563	90	4 236.7	95.2	2.6	0.2	0.6	NA	94.7	72.1
12 32000	Hollywood	70.9	148 047	173	2 088.1	75.4	18.8	0.5	3.4	0.2	31.9	32.1
12 32275	Homestead	39.2	65 524	538	1 671.5	74.2	22.2	NA	2.9	NA	59.9	39.0
12 35000	Jacksonville	1 934.7	853 382	12	441.1	63.2	32.1	0.9	5.5	0.2	8.2	9.6
12 35875	Jupiter	55.6	60 681	587	1 091.4	95.3	0.8	0.9	2.7	NA	13.4	12.6
12 36950	Kissimmee	54.9	66 722	524	1 215.3	74.6	14.9	0.6	3.9	0.3	63.1	27.1
12 38250	Lakeland	169.1	102 346	290	605.2	75.5	22.8	0.6	2.0	NA	13.8	8.9
12 39075	Lake Worth	15.2	37 097	1 001	2 440.6	72.0	26.1	1.6	1.2	NA	40.5	37.7
12 39425	Largo	45.6	79 019	416	1 732.9	88.8	10.0	0.9	3.4	0.2	11.2	11.6
12 39525	Lauderdale Lakes	9.5	34 410	1 079	3 622.1	13.9	84.6	1.0	1.8	NA	5.9	48.3
12 39550	Lauderhill	22.1	70 626	486	3 195.7	17.8	80.5	0.5	2.1	NA	7.1	34.3
12 43125	Margate	22.9	56 061	656	2 448.1	64.2	27.8	0.5	5.7	0.3	22.9	32.9
12 43975	Melbourne	87.7	78 490	423	895.0	86.2	11.4	1.2	3.7	NA	8.3	10.3
12 45000	Miami	92.9	430 332	44	4 632.2	76.3	20.3	0.3	1.1	0.1	70.3	57.0
12 45025	Miami Beach	19.8	91 732	337	4 632.9	76.8	5.9	1.2	2.1	NA	52.6	51.9
12 45060	Miami Gardens	47.2	112 265	246	2 378.5	23.4	74.9	0.3	1.0	NA	25.0	30.1
12 45100	Miami Lakes	14.6	30 791	1 200	2 109.0	93.9	3.7	NA	2.5	NA	82.1	52.7
12 45975	Miramar	76.5	134 989	192	1 764.6	42.7	50.0	0.2	5.0	0.1	36.1	43.0
12 49425	North Lauderdale	11.9	43 214	855	3 631.4	37.8	57.1	NA	3.0	0.4	25.9	42.0
12 49450	North Miami	21.8	61 420	581	2 817.4	34.3	60.0	0.2	2.7	NA	26.6	49.5
12 49475	North Miami Beach	12.5	43 664	851	3 493.1	53.6	41.7	NA	3.7	NA	35.4	49.9
12 49675	North Port	257.9	60 380	593	234.1	89.3	10.8	0.5	NA	NA	6.8	11.1
12 50575	Oakland Park	19.3	43 800	848	2 269.4	65.7	29.4	0.4	3.8	NA	26.6	31.4
12 50750	Ocala	116.1	57 586	634	496.0	72.2	23.6	1.7	3.6	NA	11.6	5.9
12 51075	Ocoee	38.1	41 073	900	1 078.0	62.3	21.8	NA	7.1	NA	20.1	19.3
12 53000	Orlando	265.2	262 372	73	989.3	61.5	28.7	0.6	4.4	0.1	27.7	18.4
12 53150	Ormond Beach	82.7	39 075	952	472.5	90.8	6.5	0.5	3.7	NA	3.1	8.1
12 53575	Oviedo	39.4	38 020	973	965.0	83.9	8.2	1.1	7.3	NA	15.4	11.3
12 54000	Palm Bay	170.2	105 838	275	621.8	78.0	19.9	1.0	2.1	NA	13.6	11.8
12 54075	Palm Beach Gardens	142.7	51 919	716	363.8	89.8	4.7	NA	5.1	NA	10.2	13.1
12 54200	Palm Coast	232.8	80 600	408	346.2	80.6	14.2	0.3	3.0	NA	10.5	14.7
12 54700	Panama City	75.8	37 681	981	497.1	75.8	21.9	2.3	4.8	NA	8.1	5.9
12 55775	Pembroke Pines	85.8	164 626	150	1 918.7	70.0	19.4	1.0	6.8	NA	44.7	35.7
12 55925	Pensacola	58.4	53 068	699	908.7	72.2	27.9	0.8	2.8	NA	3.9	4.8
12 56975	Pinellas Park	40.2	50 946	736	1 267.3	85.1	5.9	0.4	7.9	NA	11.4	14.6
12 57425	Plantation	56.3	91 457	340	1 624.5	71.6	21.6	0.4	5.7	0.2	21.8	27.1
12 57550	Plant City	70.4	36 627	1 015	520.3	80.1	13.5	0.4	1.7	NA	27.7	14.6
12 58050	Pompano Beach	62.2	106 105	273	1 705.9	64.6	32.8	0.4	1.3	0.5	18.4	25.8
12 58575	Port Orange	69.1	58 742	622	850.1	93.4	4.2	1.2	1.7	NA	5.1	6.6
12 58715	Port St. Lucie	295.1	174 110	140	590.0	76.3	19.2	0.7	2.8	0.2	19.8	16.8
12 60975	Riviera Beach	22.1	33 649	1 105	1 522.6	27.5	70.5	0.7	2.3	NA	6.1	16.3
12 62100	Royal Palm Beach	29.0	37 015	1 005	1 276.4	70.9	23.8	NA	3.8	NA	19.8	20.1
12 62625	St. Cloud	46.0	43 005	861	934.9	91.8	6.3	NA	3.7	NA	32.2	10.1
12 63000	St. Petersburg	159.9	253 693	79	1 586.6	71.1	25.6	0.7	3.7	0.4	7.4	10.5
12 63650	Sanford	59.5	57 525	636	966.8	66.9	28.4	0.9	4.4	NA	20.7	11.0
12 64175	Sarasota	38.0	54 214	684	1 426.7	82.3	15.6	0.9	2.2	0.2	18.0	17.5
12 69700	Sunrise	46.9	91 256	342	1 945.8	59.6	33.8	0.5	5.1	0.1	27.6	37.3
12 70600	Tallahassee	259.6	188 107	126	724.6	58.2	37.2	0.9	4.5	0.1	6.6	7.9
12 70675	Tamarac	30.1	63 793	552	2 119.4	66.0	30.9	0.4	2.1	0.2	24.8	33.9
12 71000	Tampa	293.7	358 699	53	1 221.3	66.1	27.5	0.9	5.0	0.2	22.6	15.2
12 71900	Titusville	76.1	44 557	829	585.5	80.4	16.2	1.2	2.9	NA	6.7	5.5
12 75812	Wellington	116.3	61 485	578	528.7	81.8	13.0	0.3	4.5	NA	18.9	19.6
12 76582	Weston	65.2	69 100	496	1 059.8	88.5	5.9	0.3	5.4	NA	47.6	38.8
12 76600	West Palm Beach	143.2	104 031	281	726.5	62.8	32.3	0.5	2.4	NA	23.2	26.2
12 78250	Winter Garden	39.9	38 746	956	971.1	66.1	19.4	NA	5.2	NA	24.1	15.4
12 78275	Winter Haven	81.1	36 371	1 021	448.5	69.5	27.7	0.5	2.1	NA	12.4	10.8
12 78300	Winter Park	22.5	29 442	1 251	1 308.5	87.0	9.0	0.8	3.5	NA	8.4	8.7
12 78325	Winter Springs	38.0	34 169	1 087	899.2	91.3	6.4	0.6	3.4	NA	17.1	9.7

1. Dry land or land partially or temporarily covered by water. 2. May be of any race.

City	Age of population (percent), 2011-2013: Under 5 years	5 to 17 years	18 to 24 years	25 to 34 years	35 to 44 years	45 to 54 years	55 to 64 years	65 to 74 years	75 years and over	Median age 2011-2013	Percent female 2011-2013	Population: Census counts: 2000	Census counts: 2010	Percent change: 2000–2010	Percent change: 2010–2014
	12	13	14	15	16	17	18	19	20	21	22	23	24	25	26
FLORIDA—Cont'd															
Deerfield Beach	5.4	14.1	6.5	13.7	12.4	13.4	11.6	10.5	12.3	42.9	52.0	64 583	75 018	16.2	5.1
DeLand	4.8	17.3	13.8	8.6	14.0	11.1	10.1	10.1	10.2	38.7	51.8	20 904	27 031	29.3	8.3
Delray Beach	4.4	10.7	7.1	13.5	10.9	14.2	14.8	11.2	13.2	47.4	53.3	60 020	60 522	0.8	7.3
Deltona	6.1	17.9	9.4	12.5	12.3	14.5	13.1	7.8	6.5	38.6	50.6	69 543	85 182	22.5	2.0
Doral	9.4	20.3	7.7	15.9	18.7	14.4	7.5	4.1	2.1	33.2	52.9	20 438	45 704	123.6	18.4
Dunedin	5.5	11.7	4.7	12.0	8.1	12.9	16.3	14.3	14.5	51.9	55.4	35 691	35 321	-1.0	1.3
Fort Lauderdale	4.9	12.7	7.5	15.4	12.9	16.4	14.5	8.9	6.8	42.5	47.4	152 397	165 521	8.6	6.3
Fort Myers	5.5	14.8	8.7	13.5	13.8	12.8	12.6	10.4	7.9	40.3	48.9	48 208	62 298	29.2	14.0
Fort Pierce	9.0	15.6	11.0	13.6	10.2	10.8	13.3	8.8	7.7	35.6	51.7	37 516	41 590	10.9	4.2
Gainesville	4.5	8.2	36.9	16.4	8.4	8.0	9.1	4.2	4.2	25.1	52.0	95 447	124 354	30.3	3.2
Greenacres	6.5	18.5	9.3	14.3	16.1	12.3	8.9	7.6	6.5	35.8	51.8	27 569	37 573	36.3	4.2
Hallandale Beach	5.1	9.5	5.0	13.5	14.0	12.9	14.4	12.7	12.9	46.9	52.8	34 282	37 113	8.3	5.2
Hialeah	5.2	13.5	9.8	11.4	14.7	15.8	10.1	9.8	9.7	42.0	52.4	226 419	224 669	-0.8	4.8
Hollywood	5.7	15.2	7.8	12.6	13.9	16.0	13.1	8.3	7.3	41.8	50.8	139 357	140 768	1.0	5.2
Homestead	7.9	21.1	9.4	18.1	15.0	12.8	7.7	5.5	2.5	32.0	49.0	31 909	60 512	89.6	8.3
Jacksonville	7.0	16.4	10.3	15.4	13.1	14.1	12.0	6.8	4.9	35.7	51.5	735 617	821 784	11.7	3.8
Jupiter	4.9	14.6	4.6	12.4	11.6	15.5	14.5	11.2	10.7	46.0	51.3	39 328	55 156	40.2	9.8
Kissimmee	7.4	18.9	11.3	14.8	13.2	15.3	8.5	6.5	4.0	32.7	50.7	47 814	59 682	24.8	11.9
Lakeland	6.2	15.3	11.5	12.2	11.0	11.7	12.0	10.5	9.7	39.9	52.6	78 452	97 422	24.2	5.0
Lake Worth	7.1	15.8	8.9	17.4	12.6	15.2	10.1	6.7	6.2	35.5	46.7	35 133	34 910	-0.6	6.3
Largo	3.5	11.7	7.5	11.7	12.1	14.7	13.5	12.6	12.7	47.8	51.5	69 371	77 648	11.9	1.1
Lauderdale Lakes	7.6	17.1	9.7	13.2	10.4	13.0	12.8	9.0	7.2	38.5	56.6	31 705	32 593	2.8	5.4
Lauderhill	7.3	17.2	11.3	13.4	12.3	14.8	11.1	7.4	5.2	35.5	54.2	57 585	66 887	16.2	5.5
Margate	5.1	13.8	8.2	12.1	13.7	14.5	13.2	10.8	8.7	43.3	52.0	53 909	53 284	-1.2	5.2
Melbourne	4.7	11.9	9.8	13.0	9.9	15.9	13.4	10.3	11.2	45.6	51.6	71 382	76 068	6.6	3.0
Miami	6.3	12.4	8.6	16.7	14.8	14.2	11.2	7.9	8.0	39.0	50.0	362 470	399 457	10.2	7.7
Miami Beach	6.6	10.1	6.7	18.2	17.9	14.5	10.4	7.5	8.0	39.5	47.6	87 933	87 779	-0.2	4.5
Miami Gardens	6.3	17.7	11.9	14.5	12.9	13.3	11.8	6.6	5.0	34.7	53.3	NA	107 167	NA	4.8
Miami Lakes	6.5	16.0	8.5	13.2	14.1	16.2	10.9	7.8	6.8	38.9	53.1	22 676	29 361	29.5	4.9
Miramar	5.9	20.4	9.8	14.2	15.9	15.4	10.6	3.9	4.0	34.9	51.9	72 739	122 041	67.8	10.6
North Lauderdale	10.0	20.0	12.4	16.3	13.7	13.0	8.7	3.9	2.0	29.5	51.3	32 264	41 023	27.1	5.3
North Miami	5.7	16.8	12.7	13.1	15.7	14.3	11.2	6.1	4.3	36.2	50.9	59 880	58 786	-1.8	4.3
North Miami Beach	4.8	17.1	10.1	15.8	14.2	12.8	12.2	7.2	5.7	36.8	50.5	40 786	41 523	1.8	5.2
North Port	5.2	18.3	7.8	8.9	12.0	12.9	14.2	13.1	7.6	43.2	51.0	22 797	57 357	151.6	5.3
Oakland Park	8.6	13.1	8.2	15.2	14.2	15.8	13.8	7.1	4.1	38.7	47.4	30 966	41 363	33.6	5.8
Ocala	7.4	16.2	10.0	14.2	12.2	12.1	11.0	8.5	8.5	36.1	51.7	45 943	56 315	22.6	2.2
Ocoee	6.9	20.6	10.4	12.2	18.4	14.6	7.1	5.4	4.3	34.8	51.2	24 391	35 579	45.9	14.9
Orlando	7.3	14.9	11.4	19.5	14.9	12.8	9.4	5.4	4.3	32.9	51.8	185 951	238 300	28.2	9.9
Ormond Beach	3.8	12.4	7.2	9.0	11.3	12.5	14.9	13.4	15.4	50.1	52.3	36 301	38 137	5.1	2.4
Oviedo	5.7	21.7	8.7	13.8	14.1	17.5	11.0	4.5	3.0	35.0	51.1	26 316	33 342	26.7	13.6
Palm Bay	5.9	16.9	8.2	11.4	11.1	16.3	13.6	9.3	7.3	41.8	54.2	79 413	103 190	29.9	2.6
Palm Beach Gardens	4.1	12.0	5.0	11.0	12.4	14.5	13.6	14.2	13.1	48.7	53.4	35 058	48 452	38.2	6.9
Palm Coast	4.7	15.4	7.4	8.6	12.1	11.5	14.7	15.3	10.4	46.9	52.9	32 732	75 180	129.7	7.2
Panama City	6.7	16.6	10.0	12.9	11.9	14.4	10.6	8.1	8.6	38.1	52.4	36 417	36 484	0.2	6.1
Pembroke Pines	5.3	16.6	8.6	13.0	13.5	15.9	11.7	7.1	8.3	40.0	52.5	137 427	154 750	12.6	6.9
Pensacola	5.4	13.6	9.8	14.0	11.5	14.8	13.1	9.5	8.2	41.2	51.5	56 255	51 923	-7.7	2.1
Pinellas Park	5.0	12.5	7.1	12.8	12.5	15.1	15.1	11.7	8.3	45.1	49.0	45 658	49 079	7.5	3.6
Plantation	5.4	15.5	7.3	14.6	13.9	16.3	13.3	7.6	6.1	40.9	51.6	82 934	84 955	2.4	7.8
Plant City	7.4	19.7	7.7	14.1	13.7	14.7	11.1	7.1	4.5	35.9	51.6	29 915	34 721	16.1	5.6
Pompano Beach	6.3	12.3	8.9	14.5	13.0	14.6	12.4	7.8	10.1	41.2	48.6	78 191	99 845	27.7	6.3
Port Orange	4.4	13.5	7.4	9.1	10.2	15.8	14.6	13.2	11.9	49.1	52.6	45 823	56 048	22.3	3.8
Port St. Lucie	5.8	19.1	7.8	11.4	13.3	14.4	11.8	9.0	7.4	39.9	50.8	88 769	164 603	85.4	5.7
Riviera Beach	7.6	15.4	10.4	12.5	14.2	13.8	12.6	7.1	6.4	38.8	52.3	29 884	32 488	8.7	3.6
Royal Palm Beach	5.1	21.3	8.8	10.3	13.4	15.9	13.1	7.2	4.8	37.5	52.4	21 523	34 140	58.6	8.4
St. Cloud	8.9	17.1	8.3	14.5	13.7	13.9	11.0	8.1	4.6	36.0	51.3	20 074	35 183	75.3	18.4
St. Petersburg	5.1	13.9	9.0	13.0	12.7	15.6	14.3	8.6	7.7	41.9	52.1	248 232	244 769	-1.4	3.5
Sanford	7.5	19.6	10.1	15.9	14.7	12.8	9.4	6.2	3.9	32.9	52.1	38 291	53 570	39.9	7.1
Sarasota	4.9	10.8	9.0	12.5	12.0	14.4	12.9	11.2	12.2	45.6	51.2	52 715	51 917	-1.5	4.1
Sunrise	6.6	14.3	8.8	14.2	13.4	14.8	12.1	7.1	8.6	39.3	55.0	85 779	84 439	-1.6	8.1
Tallahassee	5.1	11.8	30.5	16.4	9.9	9.2	8.6	4.5	4.1	26.1	52.1	150 624	181 376	20.4	3.7
Tamarac	4.0	14.0	5.6	11.7	14.5	13.1	11.9	11.6	13.6	45.2	55.5	55 588	60 427	8.7	5.4
Tampa	6.1	15.5	12.3	15.9	13.6	14.3	11.0	6.0	5.3	35.2	51.1	303 447	335 709	10.6	6.8
Titusville	5.0	13.0	9.2	10.2	13.5	13.2	12.9	10.5	11.6	43.8	52.5	40 670	43 761	7.6	1.8
Wellington	5.2	21.6	8.6	8.2	14.2	17.1	12.5	8.0	4.7	40.4	52.4	38 216	56 508	47.9	8.4
Weston	4.8	25.3	7.8	7.5	15.0	19.6	11.3	5.3	3.4	38.6	50.8	49 286	65 333	32.6	5.8
West Palm Beach	5.8	12.6	10.7	15.4	12.3	13.3	12.3	8.8	8.7	39.5	50.9	82 103	99 919	21.7	3.7
Winter Garden	7.3	20.3	8.0	14.5	15.5	16.8	8.6	4.8	4.2	34.6	52.3	14 351	34 568	140.9	11.8
Winter Haven	5.5	14.2	7.4	10.0	12.4	13.5	12.1	13.0	12.0	45.9	54.2	26 487	33 874	27.9	7.4
Winter Park	5.4	14.0	13.7	11.3	8.8	13.2	14.9	9.0	9.8	42.1	51.2	24 090	27 852	15.6	5.7
Winter Springs	4.2	16.9	9.3	12.9	12.6	14.5	14.5	8.7	6.4	39.2	50.6	31 666	33 282	5.1	2.7

City	Households, 2011-2013: Number	Households, 2011-2013: Persons per house-hold	Households, 2011-2013: Percent: Female family house-holder[1]	Households, 2011-2013: Percent: One-person	Persons in group quarters, 2010: Total	Persons in group quarters, 2010: Institutional: Total	Persons in group quarters, 2010: Institutional: Persons in nursing facilities	Persons in group quarters, 2010: Non-institu-tional	Serious crimes known to police,[2] 2013: Total: Number	Serious crimes known to police,[2] 2013: Total: Rate[3]	Serious crimes known to police,[2] 2013: Rate[3]: Violent	Serious crimes known to police,[2] 2013: Rate[3]: Property	Educational attainment, 2011–2013: Population age 25 and older	Educational attainment, 2011–2013: Attainment[4] (percent): High school graduate or less	Educational attainment, 2011–2013: Attainment[4] (percent): Bachelor's degree or more
	27	28	29	30	31	32	33	34	35	36	37	38	39	40	41
FLORIDA—Cont'd															
Deerfield Beach	31 554	2.42	13.8	38.3	1 046	863	229	183	2 691	3 441	390	3 051	57 174	49.6	21.9
DeLand	9 900	2.56	13.8	34.1	2 377	595	587	1 782	1 500	5 440	540	4 899	17 769	44.0	21.7
Delray Beach	26 825	2.30	10.4	40.8	1 114	584	539	530	3 594	5 715	774	4 941	48 716	37.2	34.6
Deltona	28 321	3.02	12.2	21.7	166	127	127	39	NA	NA	NA	NA	57 114	52.3	14.6
Doral	14 640	3.32	15.7	14.7	6	0	0	6	2 386	4 880	162	4 718	30 467	24.0	55.8
Dunedin	16 331	2.15	10.6	40.4	385	344	338	41	863	2 431	259	2 172	27 728	37.7	27.6
Fort Lauderdale	72 270	2.32	11.3	42.2	3 418	1 861	324	1 557	11 106	6 442	845	5 598	127 791	39.7	33.9
Fort Myers	23 333	2.63	17.4	36.4	3 236	2 520	598	716	3 031	4 535	1 125	3 410	46 823	49.4	23.6
Fort Pierce	16 817	2.50	19.3	36.9	577	455	314	122	2 886	6 733	1 372	5 361	27 495	58.1	13.8
Gainesville	47 924	2.35	11.6	37.7	12 493	1 796	748	10 697	5 792	4 575	637	3 939	63 728	28.9	42.5
Greenacres	12 758	3.00	19.6	26.3	51	5	5	46	1 552	4 007	475	3 532	25 179	52.7	18.3
Hallandale Beach	18 352	2.08	12.1	44.3	101	0	0	101	2 143	5 536	721	4 815	30 745	40.8	29.3
Hialeah	69 369	3.32	20.3	20.6	1 493	727	700	766	7 324	3 127	331	2 797	166 100	67.0	13.6
Hollywood	54 698	2.63	14.6	33.0	1 203	608	476	595	7 270	4 958	491	4 467	103 417	43.9	26.9
Homestead	19 455	3.23	17.4	24.8	450	227	223	223	4 191	6 546	1 432	5 114	38 935	58.7	15.7
Jacksonville	312 257	2.62	16.1	31.2	19 747	8 158	3 155	11 589	38 253	4 523	620	3 903	554 634	41.5	25.7
Jupiter	23 568	2.41	7.8	30.1	393	131	131	262	1 221	2 112	220	1 892	43 428	28.3	44.4
Kissimmee	20 148	3.12	24.1	22.5	595	317	54	278	3 505	5 424	839	4 585	39 483	50.7	14.6
Lakeland	39 030	2.45	15.1	33.7	4 126	1 140	1 094	2 986	5 870	5 828	457	5 371	66 886	47.7	23.9
Lake Worth	11 998	2.92	18.2	31.9	618	518	409	100	2 521	6 992	1 273	5 719	24 320	58.4	19.0
Largo	35 428	2.15	11.4	40.7	1 026	941	836	85	3 276	4 205	452	3 753	60 288	50.5	19.5
Lauderdale Lakes	11 326	2.94	27.7	29.2	392	387	363	5	2 046	5 996	985	5 011	22 092	58.9	13.6
Lauderhill	23 591	2.90	28.0	31.3	592	225	225	367	3 183	4 560	658	3 903	44 313	49.3	19.7
Margate	21 506	2.54	15.2	35.7	169	6	6	163	1 283	2 309	221	2 087	40 039	48.5	21.7
Melbourne	32 611	2.29	12.8	38.6	2 125	746	713	1 379	4 034	5 220	850	4 370	56 688	42.1	24.1
Miami	152 200	2.66	17.9	36.5	8 161	5 133	1 526	3 028	25 873	6 184	1 182	5 002	301 264	57.9	23.3
Miami Beach	42 791	2.09	8.9	47.4	1 026	534	473	492	10 670	11 670	1 005	10 665	69 380	34.2	43.3
Miami Gardens	31 327	3.49	29.9	22.7	1 367	64	11	1 303	5 581	4 989	823	4 166	71 047	58.0	13.7
Miami Lakes	9 305	3.26	13.0	20.2	28	0	0	28	671	2 185	98	2 087	20 982	37.7	31.1
Miramar	38 901	3.29	22.5	19.1	87	24	11	63	3 640	2 780	364	2 417	81 886	35.2	29.7
North Lauderdale	11 273	3.75	27.3	14.6	31	0	0	31	1 378	3 217	488	2 729	24 383	62.4	12.9
North Miami	17 493	3.37	22.8	27.7	1 640	539	539	1 101	3 278	5 363	884	4 480	39 279	54.2	18.4
North Miami Beach	14 079	3.03	17.3	29.3	236	151	148	85	1 999	4 604	742	3 863	29 172	47.2	20.2
North Port	22 289	2.62	9.8	25.7	119	100	100	19	1 072	1 826	184	1 642	40 159	46.9	16.4
Oakland Park	17 683	2.41	14.6	39.0	205	19	0	186	2 426	5 604	684	4 921	29 996	43.2	21.9
Ocala	22 206	2.43	18.0	35.1	3 281	2 856	922	425	3 221	5 637	581	5 056	37 942	44.4	21.8
Ocoee	11 919	3.19	15.5	19.9	287	225	225	62	1 382	3 525	413	3 112	23 712	40.3	28.9
Orlando	101 436	2.41	17.5	37.7	3 294	1 227	1 009	2 067	18 805	7 426	915	6 511	165 771	36.2	33.7
Ormond Beach	15 265	2.49	9.8	30.4	458	434	434	24	1 518	3 949	343	3 605	29 408	34.5	30.1
Oviedo	10 459	3.38	11.1	14.0	103	94	94	9	536	1 493	159	1 335	22 640	23.8	44.8
Palm Bay	37 506	2.76	15.7	26.4	430	331	320	99	2 409	2 308	432	1 876	71 921	46.0	17.9
Palm Beach Gardens	22 501	2.20	7.5	35.7	235	205	154	30	1 586	3 151	139	3 012	39 418	24.0	46.1
Palm Coast	27 250	2.84	8.5	23.6	319	282	144	37	NA	NA	NA	NA	56 303	44.8	21.0
Panama City	14 389	2.45	16.2	34.2	2 782	2 453	553	329	2 621	7 209	886	6 323	24 176	44.1	21.7
Pembroke Pines	56 685	2.80	15.0	27.8	1 397	1 187	125	210	4 298	2 652	170	2 482	110 963	33.1	32.9
Pensacola	21 797	2.37	13.5	37.4	727	284	224	443	3 002	5 723	742	4 982	37 301	33.0	33.6
Pinellas Park	20 465	2.38	10.8	35.9	1 165	510	337	655	2 936	5 886	505	5 380	37 499	51.6	16.3
Plantation	32 800	2.68	14.1	27.8	363	307	304	56	3 427	3 854	350	3 504	63 456	28.6	39.5
Plant City	12 523	2.85	15.7	27.1	185	118	118	67	1 759	4 849	510	4 339	23 407	53.7	18.5
Pompano Beach	40 395	2.46	14.9	38.8	4 267	3 680	415	587	5 948	5 721	788	4 933	74 745	50.6	22.9
Port Orange	23 928	2.37	9.9	32.0	167	118	102	49	1 611	2 834	90	2 744	42 453	42.5	24.9
Port St. Lucie	57 605	2.92	13.3	20.5	711	330	322	381	2 764	1 627	178	1 449	113 795	45.7	20.9
Riviera Beach	11 796	2.78	22.6	32.0	323	134	134	189	1 314	3 943	1 020	2 923	22 031	46.1	21.6
Royal Palm Beach	11 349	3.09	15.0	18.5	236	229	119	7	1 103	3 109	327	2 782	22 889	40.0	25.6
St. Cloud	13 141	2.97	19.6	22.1	448	375	349	73	1 099	2 733	346	2 387	25 929	48.5	17.1
St. Petersburg	104 590	2.31	13.5	39.3	6 607	2 719	2 364	3 888	15 560	6 297	963	5 335	178 214	39.6	29.1
Sanford	18 011	2.96	20.7	32.1	1 531	996	180	535	3 879	7 056	813	6 243	34 509	42.0	22.1
Sarasota	22 814	2.18	11.5	38.9	3 582	1 632	738	1 950	3 155	5 948	779	5 169	39 807	40.9	31.8
Sunrise	31 683	2.77	17.7	28.8	578	506	496	72	3 554	3 937	294	3 643	62 103	44.7	24.2
Tallahassee	73 597	2.34	13.7	32.7	14 623	3 231	718	11 392	9 514	5 041	741	4 301	97 691	24.1	47.5
Tamarac	26 282	2.37	17.5	37.2	261	234	234	27	1 447	2 289	316	1 973	47 735	42.6	25.2
Tampa	140 717	2.40	15.5	37.4	12 282	2 138	876	10 144	10 920	3 108	597	2 511	231 075	40.1	33.9
Titusville	18 034	2.41	13.5	31.8	473	344	344	129	1 932	4 392	746	3 646	31 610	40.8	21.9
Wellington	19 780	2.97	10.8	17.6	2	0	0	2	1 385	2 336	212	2 123	37 982	25.8	43.6
Weston	20 969	3.22	9.7	13.6	0	0	0	0	536	784	69	715	41 965	14.7	58.3
West Palm Beach	40 953	2.41	15.4	38.4	2 943	1 196	1 093	1 747	5 564	5 428	684	4 744	72 079	41.2	31.7
Winter Garden	12 283	2.98	11.5	21.9	497	483	483	14	1 590	4 204	471	3 734	23 710	32.0	35.3
Winter Haven	14 178	2.43	13.2	32.4	598	491	490	107	1 792	5 073	609	4 464	25 563	51.4	15.6
Winter Park	11 340	2.39	7.6	34.6	1 609	338	338	1 271	1 166	3 985	342	3 643	19 316	19.0	55.9
Winter Springs	11 677	2.87	13.8	26.4	31	31	0	0	420	1 249	152	1 097	23 394	30.7	38.6

1. No spouse present. 2. Data for serious crimes have not been adjusted for underreporting. This may affect comparability between geographic areas and over time. 3. Per 100,000 population estimated by the FBI. 4. Persons 25 years old and over.

City	Money income, 2011–2013					Housing units, 2010			Occupied housing units 2011–2013				
		Households								Owner-occupied		Median owner costs as a percent of income	
	Per capita income[1] (dollars)	Median income	Percent with income of $200,000 or more	Percent with income of less than $25,000	Families with income below poverty (percent)	Total	Percent change, 2000–2010	Vacant units for sale or rent[2]	Total	Percent	Median value[3] (dollars)	With a mortgage[4]	Without a mortgage[5]
	42	43	44	45	46	47	48	49	50	51	52	53	54
FLORIDA—Cont'd													
Deerfield Beach	22 938	38 629	1.5	32.4	15.3	42 671	14.3	9 301	31 554	63.9	99 600	32.6	19.3
DeLand	20 061	38 829	1.7	29.9	15.9	12 610	35.6	1 864	9 900	53.1	144 600	24.2	13.5
Delray Beach	35 019	49 486	7.0	25.9	12.1	34 156	7.9	6 963	26 825	64.5	165 700	29.7	16.5
Deltona	18 448	43 620	0.4	26.3	12.1	34 089	28.4	3 866	28 321	79.3	101 100	27.5	13.5
Doral	27 317	68 326	5.8	15.2	10.6	17 785	89.4	2 541	14 640	52.7	283 900	29.4	14.6
Dunedin	29 947	45 926	3.2	26.7	5.1	21 113	5.0	3 495	16 331	64.0	141 200	26.6	15.0
Fort Lauderdale	35 670	50 446	6.2	26.7	15.5	93 159	15.3	18 373	72 270	52.4	239 500	28.9	14.8
Fort Myers	23 271	36 250	4.6	35.0	20.0	35 138	60.9	10 170	23 333	47.7	114 400	24.8	13.4
Fort Pierce	16 194	25 275	1.0	49.4	32.4	21 357	24.1	5 507	16 817	43.2	75 400	32.7	16.4
Gainesville	19 235	31 584	2.3	40.5	17.2	57 576	43.5	6 547	47 924	36.2	139 700	23.2	11.3
Greenacres	17 730	40 390	1.0	28.3	17.5	17 249	21.0	2 865	12 758	66.3	94 200	29.7	17.0
Hallandale Beach	25 137	31 328	2.5	41.1	18.5	27 057	7.8	8 756	18 352	56.1	131 500	30.7	23.2
Hialeah	13 486	28 246	0.4	44.5	24.0	74 067	2.6	2 862	69 369	47.1	145 000	35.1	17.0
Hollywood	25 270	45 123	3.5	27.0	12.7	71 070	3.9	12 632	54 698	60.0	169 900	31.2	15.6
Homestead	17 724	39 727	2.2	31.5	28.6	23 419	111.0	4 423	19 455	42.0	103 500	25.1	15.0
Jacksonville	24 870	45 978	3.0	26.9	14.1	366 273	18.6	43 167	312 257	60.8	132 400	24.9	12.3
Jupiter	44 196	68 068	10.4	15.3	5.8	29 825	41.7	5 905	23 568	71.3	276 700	27.0	13.6
Kissimmee	16 388	34 784	1.4	34.1	24.2	26 275	33.6	5 549	20 148	43.7	105 400	30.3	13.5
Lakeland	21 477	38 483	1.9	30.6	16.1	48 218	23.3	7 460	39 030	54.5	105 700	24.6	13.1
Lake Worth	18 589	34 712	1.9	38.2	28.5	16 473	3.6	3 515	11 998	47.5	115 600	29.6	16.5
Largo	27 110	38 867	1.9	30.5	10.8	46 859	16.4	8 837	35 428	56.6	88 400	24.6	14.3
Lauderdale Lakes	15 641	31 261	0.4	39.7	21.6	15 000	4.5	3 109	11 326	59.8	85 700	37.3	19.2
Lauderhill	18 167	35 194	0.6	32.7	17.1	29 519	15.0	4 693	23 591	54.7	97 200	31.0	19.6
Margate	21 614	40 610	1.6	29.6	12.5	24 863	0.5	3 380	21 506	77.3	103 800	31.2	17.8
Melbourne	23 245	37 311	1.7	32.6	12.4	38 955	15.7	4 915	32 611	58.9	109 900	25.3	14.0
Miami	21 416	30 126	3.5	43.3	26.0	183 994	23.9	25 677	152 200	31.8	198 500	35.7	16.7
Miami Beach	42 657	42 295	8.3	32.2	12.7	67 499	13.0	20 331	42 791	34.8	358 400	29.0	20.3
Miami Gardens	16 682	37 822	0.9	32.8	19.2	34 284	NA	2 065	31 327	67.6	119 800	35.9	13.7
Miami Lakes	25 629	63 559	6.3	16.7	11.2	10 698	18.8	445	9 305	66.5	279 200	30.6	12.8
Miramar	24 338	60 585	3.5	14.6	8.1	40 294	55.6	2 874	38 901	71.9	174 300	32.9	13.7
North Lauderdale	14 750	40 842	0.5	26.3	19.9	14 709	28.1	1 732	11 273	52.1	97 000	32.9	16.1
North Miami	17 870	36 482	2.5	35.8	25.2	22 110	-0.7	2 835	17 493	48.3	123 200	32.3	15.1
North Miami Beach	19 039	39 064	1.3	30.9	19.0	16 402	7.1	1 990	14 079	56.1	131 300	31.7	15.5
North Port	23 137	47 510	1.6	26.5	9.8	27 986	170.2	5 555	22 289	75.0	116 200	23.3	13.9
Oakland Park	24 373	42 793	1.4	27.0	17.7	20 076	38.1	2 577	17 683	54.1	142 800	29.6	13.8
Ocala	21 472	33 426	3.2	38.2	21.7	26 764	29.8	3 661	22 206	47.9	117 800	23.4	14.2
Ocoee	24 496	61 115	3.5	16.6	10.6	12 802	53.8	1 010	11 919	72.1	161 600	26.0	11.9
Orlando	25 083	42 026	3.0	29.6	16.9	121 254	36.8	18 733	101 436	37.2	149 900	26.7	14.4
Ormond Beach	29 771	48 096	4.5	24.0	8.2	19 576	12.8	2 514	15 265	76.9	161 200	26.9	12.3
Oviedo	29 298	82 143	6.0	10.3	5.4	11 720	28.9	595	10 459	79.4	205 600	22.8	10.0
Palm Bay	20 122	41 540	0.8	27.8	13.9	45 220	37.3	5 738	37 506	75.1	96 600	27.1	11.0
Palm Beach Gardens	49 012	64 241	11.2	17.4	5.5	27 663	52.6	4 859	22 501	72.5	285 800	28.3	14.8
Palm Coast	22 210	45 593	1.5	23.6	11.1	35 058	132.0	5 253	27 250	79.0	152 200	28.3	13.1
Panama City	21 849	36 818	2.3	34.1	15.2	17 438	5.5	2 646	14 389	48.5	124 500	23.2	13.4
Pembroke Pines	27 776	59 673	4.0	21.8	7.2	61 703	11.6	4 830	56 685	72.1	192 400	28.1	19.1
Pensacola	26 617	44 702	3.0	26.0	10.6	26 848	-0.3	3 256	21 797	59.0	144 000	23.0	12.5
Pinellas Park	23 267	42 182	1.0	28.0	11.4	23 458	7.5	2 835	20 465	66.0	104 200	25.7	14.4
Plantation	34 927	67 185	7.0	15.6	7.4	37 587	7.1	3 397	32 800	66.9	229 200	26.8	14.6
Plant City	22 559	43 846	3.1	27.6	15.3	13 732	16.5	1 493	12 523	57.6	124 100	23.1	11.3
Pompano Beach	23 965	39 101	2.8	32.9	20.3	55 885	25.9	13 703	40 395	53.6	149 000	29.7	15.3
Port Orange	25 775	42 388	2.9	25.2	6.2	27 972	34.2	3 131	23 928	75.4	130 900	27.6	13.5
Port St. Lucie	22 460	48 566	2.3	22.2	13.2	70 877	92.0	9 975	57 605	76.5	125 400	28.4	13.9
Riviera Beach	22 895	38 352	2.6	29.5	18.0	17 124	19.4	4 744	11 796	56.6	117 900	29.2	12.2
Royal Palm Beach	26 804	65 880	3.8	15.9	6.1	12 854	58.1	1 298	11 349	79.4	169 400	24.4	12.9
St. Cloud	20 106	47 765	1.7	25.1	14.4	14 544	68.6	1 979	13 141	67.9	109 200	25.9	13.7
St. Petersburg	27 841	43 756	3.4	27.9	12.1	129 401	3.9	20 586	104 590	57.7	135 400	26.7	13.6
Sanford	17 146	37 344	0.3	32.5	20.0	23 061	49.0	2 943	18 011	54.7	99 400	28.8	10.4
Sarasota	29 318	42 782	4.3	29.1	15.4	29 151	8.2	6 009	22 814	53.5	145 100	30.2	14.1
Sunrise	23 155	46 188	1.4	28.6	11.3	37 609	5.5	5 116	31 683	69.4	124 800	29.3	21.3
Tallahassee	23 752	39 868	3.1	34.5	14.6	84 248	23.2	9 433	73 597	40.3	177 000	23.1	10.7
Tamarac	23 865	42 545	0.9	26.1	10.9	32 794	10.3	4 379	26 282	71.8	111 400	28.9	17.9
Tampa	28 945	41 927	5.6	31.9	17.4	157 130	15.8	21 175	140 717	49.5	149 000	25.6	12.0
Titusville	23 624	40 485	1.3	27.5	13.4	22 729	18.2	3 712	18 034	67.8	87 500	23.7	10.8
Wellington	34 841	77 233	9.2	13.6	7.2	22 685	54.2	3 026	19 780	78.8	286 700	27.5	14.0
Weston	39 950	91 982	16.1	11.7	5.5	24 394	28.9	3 174	20 969	74.2	373 200	27.7	14.5
West Palm Beach	30 200	43 967	5.0	27.3	14.8	54 179	34.1	11 267	40 953	50.8	162 900	30.7	14.5
Winter Garden	26 261	56 602	6.0	17.6	6.8	13 260	128.8	1 385	12 283	69.6	194 400	28.7	12.1
Winter Haven	22 791	37 583	2.6	33.9	12.9	17 037	22.3	2 714	14 178	62.0	96 600	26.6	12.9
Winter Park	45 753	60 434	15.3	23.5	6.0	13 626	18.2	1 398	11 340	63.1	300 300	22.4	13.8
Winter Springs	31 240	60 010	5.9	15.9	7.7	14 052	14.3	951	11 677	79.1	189 000	24.4	11.4

1. Based on population estimated by the American Community Survey. 2. Includes units rented or sold but not occupied. 3. Specified owner-occupied units; $1,000,000 represents $1,000,000 or more 4. 50.0 represents 50 percent or more. 5. 10.0 represents 10 percent or less.

City	Occupied housing units, 2011–2013 (cont.)				Migration, 2011–2013		Civilian labor force, 2014				Civilian employment[4], 2011–2013			
									Unemployment			Percent		
	Percent renter occupied	Median gross rent[1]	Median rent as a percent of income[2]	Percent with no vehicle available	Percent who lived in the same house one year ago	Percent who lived outside current city one year ago	Total	Percent change, 2013–2014	Total	Rate[3]	Population age 16 and older	In labor force	Civilian full-year full-time workers	Households with no workers (percent)
	55	56	57	58	59	60	61	62	63	64	65	66	67	68
FLORIDA—Cont'd														
Deerfield Beach	36.1	1 120	32.5	10.8	80.7	15.8	39 815	1.9	2 119	5.3	63 714	60.4	37.4	36.7
DeLand	46.9	955	38.5	11.2	82.1	13.5	12 368	1.3	792	6.4	22 496	49.0	29.7	40.3
Delray Beach	35.5	1 243	34.2	7.3	86.0	10.4	34 089	2.5	1 937	5.7	54 417	61.3	35.0	36.0
Deltona	20.7	1 076	37.5	3.4	90.3	7.4	42 858	1.5	3 017	7.0	67 215	57.1	37.1	31.5
Doral	47.3	1 670	36.4	2.5	79.1	13.6	25 702	2.2	1 190	4.6	35 666	66.4	49.5	10.9
Dunedin	36.0	903	32.4	10.9	84.3	9.9	18 069	1.2	1 007	5.6	30 000	57.7	36.3	39.8
Fort Lauderdale	47.6	1 031	34.3	10.2	77.1	14.4	93 559	2.1	5 173	5.5	144 315	64.9	39.0	29.8
Fort Myers	52.3	787	35.9	12.6	74.2	16.4	30 098	4.0	1 835	6.1	54 336	52.8	28.8	39.3
Fort Pierce	56.8	777	45.7	18.7	85.0	9.4	18 296	1.4	2 106	11.5	33 375	53.9	NA	46.0
Gainesville	63.8	825	37.3	12.9	67.7	17.3	65 386	1.0	3 461	5.3	112 469	57.1	28.8	29.9
Greenacres	33.7	1 125	39.1	5.0	82.2	15.3	20 830	2.6	977	4.7	30 080	66.5	38.6	28.2
Hallandale Beach	43.9	1 043	40.1	12.2	77.1	16.0	18 317	2.5	1 304	7.1	33 328	56.7	33.8	40.9
Hialeah	52.9	987	45.5	12.7	93.3	3.4	112 312	1.1	7 823	7.0	194 434	58.7	36.1	30.0
Hollywood	40.0	996	37.8	8.6	83.7	10.5	78 643	1.9	4 735	6.0	118 093	65.8	39.4	27.3
Homestead	58.0	1 005	41.3	17.0	79.5	11.2	29 243	2.1	1 891	6.5	46 487	65.6	39.4	22.0
Jacksonville	39.2	915	33.2	8.3	81.4	6.2	437 016	1.2	28 521	6.5	661 210	66.0	40.4	26.5
Jupiter	28.7	1 420	34.3	4.3	87.9	8.8	31 164	2.4	1 344	4.3	47 064	62.6	39.6	32.8
Kissimmee	56.3	905	39.6	10.3	86.7	9.4	34 691	2.2	2 226	6.4	48 665	65.5	38.2	25.0
Lakeland	45.5	852	32.3	10.2	79.2	11.0	44 676	0.8	2 898	6.5	81 082	53.8	31.7	38.3
Lake Worth	52.5	930	39.8	13.3	78.8	13.2	18 644	2.1	1 047	5.6	28 292	70.1	37.4	29.7
Largo	43.4	880	33.0	11.9	78.4	17.1	38 991	1.2	2 116	5.4	67 254	58.6	34.7	41.4
Lauderdale Lakes	40.2	982	47.1	13.1	87.8	10.8	16 931	1.7	1 117	6.6	26 495	67.0	33.4	28.8
Lauderhill	45.3	974	42.5	14.4	80.5	13.0	35 316	1.8	2 207	6.2	53 912	67.3	37.1	28.3
Margate	22.7	1 120	37.8	9.3	85.2	12.3	29 519	1.9	1 794	6.1	45 640	64.6	35.7	31.8
Melbourne	41.1	798	33.7	7.6	84.0	11.0	37 224	0.5	2 507	6.7	65 912	56.8	33.1	38.6
Miami	68.2	936	39.5	21.5	83.3	8.2	209 158	2.5	14 690	7.0	344 289	61.9	38.4	30.8
Miami Beach	65.2	1 088	36.0	28.7	74.6	13.9	55 624	2.3	2 677	4.8	76 761	68.3	47.6	27.2
Miami Gardens	32.4	1 077	42.9	7.4	91.8	6.0	53 944	2.7	5 632	10.4	87 119	62.7	37.1	25.6
Miami Lakes	33.5	1 386	38.9	3.3	94.5	4.9	15 898	2.0	852	5.4	24 360	63.0	43.8	17.9
Miramar	28.1	1 423	40.2	2.9	87.9	8.6	72 720	2.4	4 305	5.9	98 972	73.0	47.4	12.4
North Lauderdale	47.9	1 170	42.5	7.7	78.2	17.2	23 277	2.1	1 376	5.9	30 976	73.5	38.7	15.6
North Miami	51.7	933	44.5	12.8	84.1	12.8	31 216	4.1	3 061	9.8	48 479	63.2	38.3	21.6
North Miami Beach	43.9	975	39.2	12.9	88.2	8.7	22 711	3.1	1 795	7.9	34 790	66.1	41.2	22.3
North Port	25.0	889	29.8	4.8	85.2	9.5	26 357	2.8	1 642	6.2	46 817	54.9	35.4	40.0
Oakland Park	45.9	1 036	37.3	9.5	82.0	14.4	25 463	2.2	1 262	5.0	34 356	72.2	41.1	23.9
Ocala	52.1	786	36.5	12.5	75.5	13.7	24 943	1.3	1 672	6.7	45 054	55.9	33.0	37.8
Ocoee	27.9	1 136	29.6	3.3	85.6	12.9	22 378	2.9	1 052	4.7	28 637	72.9	46.1	18.3
Orlando	62.8	976	34.3	8.5	72.2	16.0	151 995	2.6	8 309	5.5	199 246	72.7	45.4	21.0
Ormond Beach	23.1	942	34.2	5.5	88.7	9.2	18 109	1.9	1 061	5.9	33 114	47.3	28.0	44.6
Oviedo	20.6	1 313	31.2	1.3	89.4	8.9	20 108	2.9	958	4.8	26 812	71.3	47.0	14.5
Palm Bay	24.9	888	39.4	4.4	86.5	6.9	50 272	0.2	3 693	7.3	83 532	58.5	34.2	33.8
Palm Beach Gardens	27.5	1 365	32.4	5.0	84.3	12.1	26 624	2.7	1 145	4.3	42 924	57.6	38.4	36.4
Palm Coast	21.0	1 036	32.2	3.8	87.2	8.0	34 276	-2.1	2 526	7.4	63 904	48.6	29.7	44.8
Panama City	51.5	838	33.6	11.2	77.4	13.0	17 344	1.3	1 184	6.8	28 515	62.3	36.0	32.1
Pembroke Pines	27.9	1 392	37.7	7.7	86.5	9.0	88 186	2.0	4 731	5.4	128 671	66.9	42.9	24.8
Pensacola	41.0	829	29.3	8.7	83.0	10.6	27 521	1.1	1 456	5.3	43 608	63.7	38.5	31.9
Pinellas Park	34.0	913	32.4	8.3	89.3	8.7	25 191	1.7	1 260	5.0	42 384	59.1	39.5	32.9
Plantation	33.1	1 365	29.6	4.1	84.0	12.1	52 670	2.1	2 593	4.9	72 313	68.9	45.8	20.1
Plant City	42.4	841	34.5	5.5	82.4	8.2	18 694	1.4	1 072	5.7	27 312	66.1	43.7	26.7
Pompano Beach	46.4	1 046	41.1	13.4	78.8	14.8	50 249	1.9	2 912	5.8	85 898	58.9	35.5	35.7
Port Orange	24.6	974	31.7	4.3	87.9	9.0	29 008	2.1	1 632	5.6	48 045	52.8	32.2	40.2
Port St. Lucie	23.5	1 174	37.5	3.4	81.8	11.1	82 722	1.3	5 560	6.7	132 437	62.2	36.0	31.6
Riviera Beach	43.4	998	40.4	11.0	83.6	10.2	15 943	2.1	1 125	7.1	26 748	67.4	36.9	26.5
Royal Palm Beach	20.6	1 349	29.3	3.2	86.9	9.1	19 876	2.4	957	4.8	27 542	69.2	47.8	18.0
St. Cloud	32.1	1 044	31.6	6.6	83.9	12.2	20 103	2.6	1 056	5.3	30 282	64.7	39.5	28.0
St. Petersburg	42.3	902	33.0	10.3	82.2	8.6	135 390	1.2	7 597	5.6	206 035	64.3	40.4	30.8
Sanford	45.3	919	38.2	7.8	86.2	9.3	26 821	2.7	1 768	6.6	41 875	63.1	33.5	27.4
Sarasota	46.5	898	30.8	11.3	76.0	15.0	26 662	2.8	1 442	5.4	45 759	59.6	33.1	36.0
Sunrise	30.6	1 188	34.5	8.4	85.6	11.6	50 645	1.9	2 867	5.7	71 966	66.6	41.8	26.6
Tallahassee	59.7	906	40.0	7.8	64.2	15.5	99 081	1.7	5 685	5.7	157 429	67.5	35.0	23.6
Tamarac	28.2	1 123	34.0	8.2	82.7	14.0	33 619	2.0	2 048	6.1	52 900	62.6	37.2	34.0
Tampa	50.5	929	33.4	11.7	78.4	11.6	185 745	1.1	11 021	5.9	282 244	64.7	40.1	27.9
Titusville	32.2	817	32.1	7.5	83.2	9.2	20 193	-0.3	1 400	6.9	36 614	56.4	34.9	39.3
Wellington	21.2	1 397	38.0	2.8	87.1	10.2	32 310	2.5	1 543	4.8	45 572	66.4	42.9	20.2
Weston	25.8	1 840	32.1	2.3	85.8	10.0	35 639	2.1	1 683	4.7	49 468	69.6	43.3	13.1
West Palm Beach	49.2	1 038	33.5	11.5	79.5	11.8	55 335	2.0	2 979	5.4	84 758	64.3	39.7	29.5
Winter Garden	30.4	948	32.5	4.4	82.1	12.5	19 783	2.6	915	4.6	27 322	70.1	46.6	15.9
Winter Haven	38.0	751	33.9	10.9	82.1	11.5	15 324	1.2	1 030	6.7	28 832	53.2	30.2	41.3
Winter Park	36.9	1 030	33.5	10.3	81.9	14.6	14 291	2.8	721	5.0	23 960	55.8	36.8	33.0
Winter Springs	20.9	1 055	31.3	1.9	85.4	12.4	18 664	2.8	987	5.3	27 346	68.2	38.8	22.3

1. $2,000 represents $2,000 or more. 2. 50.0 represents 50 percent or more. 3. Percent of civilian labor force. 4. Persons 16 years old and over.

City	Value of residential construction authorized by building permits, 2014			Wholesale trade,[1] 2007				Retail trade,[2] 2007			
	New construction ($1,000)	Number of housing units	Percent single family	Number of establish-ments	Number of employees	Sales (mil dol)	Annual payroll (mil dol)	Number of establish-ments	Number of employees	Sales (mil dol)	Annual payroll (mil dol)
	69	70	71	72	73	74	75	76	77	78	79
FLORIDA—Cont'd											
Deerfield Beach	3 600	10	100.0	204	3 698	10 610.9	210.4	327	4 122	1 145.9	110.3
DeLand	116 130	335	100.0	34	258	99.5	10.8	177	2 821	674.8	66.9
Delray Beach	53 093	283	39.2	118	994	477.9	44.3	395	4 993	1 568.8	143.5
Deltona	21 644	61	100.0	14	47	7.6	1.2	95	1 461	294.3	27.0
Doral	97 010	605	67.8	1 277	13 811	17 259.1	597.7	571	8 569	2 282.9	212.7
Dunedin	518	2	100.0	29	197	81.4	9.3	126	1 218	225.0	24.9
Fort Lauderdale	50 627	362	21.8	612	6 433	3 213.9	288.4	1 216	13 480	4 715.7	406.5
Fort Myers	178 249	849	84.3	156	2 381	1 049.5	100.8	624	9 748	2 577.7	245.9
Fort Pierce	6 280	21	76.2	52	263	130.1	11.3	239	3 260	966.7	78.8
Gainesville	23 681	330	20.3	131	1 691	1 089.2	63.6	639	9 918	2 168.4	211.8
Greenacres	7 209	40	100.0	15	70	23.0	3.1	101	1 584	473.2	44.2
Hallandale Beach	2 691	4	100.0	78	348	208.4	15.1	132	1 537	360.9	36.2
Hialeah	27 120	127	84.3	512	3 463	1 438.1	116.2	1 055	11 206	2 449.7	244.0
Hollywood	5 804	22	36.4	309	1 940	1 278.6	98.4	594	6 753	1 781.7	162.8
Homestead	48 088	246	100.0	46	321	155.4	9.8	143	2 043	512.7	45.7
Jacksonville	543 925	3 302	63.8	1 116	19 604	17 104.0	953.9	3 169	49 068	12 749.7	1 165.2
Jupiter	159 676	706	51.6	89	769	401.6	42.4	291	3 544	828.5	85.0
Kissimmee	82 884	441	61.5	46	D	D	D	297	4 262	1 003.2	96.7
Lakeland	26 867	104	98.1	150	2 848	10 346.8	138.5	598	9 096	2 250.1	209.6
Lake Worth	4 499	17	100.0	61	698	364.4	37.2	172	1 290	312.1	33.4
Largo	28 420	197	22.3	83	D	D	D	354	5 197	1 308.0	128.2
Lauderdale Lakes	0	0	0.0	25	176	52.0	4.3	81	1 090	243.7	23.7
Lauderhill	6 647	62	100.0	32	161	104.6	4.8	200	1 800	355.9	39.9
Margate	6 584	240	0.0	59	345	163.9	12.5	194	3 041	1 071.4	88.3
Melbourne	42 644	146	100.0	125	1 276	675.7	61.0	479	7 029	1 695.4	162.2
Miami	950 530	3 786	1.9	1 438	9 237	11 188.2	420.8	2 362	20 112	5 622.5	498.8
Miami Beach	109 144	140	45.0	136	487	409.6	27.9	528	5 232	1 102.3	119.7
Miami Gardens	6 790	125	10.4	187	3 917	1 820.1	207.2	277	4 364	1 592.6	124.8
Miami Lakes	2 546	7	100.0	111	1 656	974.4	74.0	94	1 186	376.7	33.7
Miramar	35 597	177	100.0	154	2 920	2 158.9	169.3	184	4 052	1 881.9	123.9
North Lauderdale	0	0	0.0	21	65	10.2	1.3	71	1 012	226.1	22.1
North Miami	2 400	6	100.0	94	522	292.2	22.1	204	1 833	434.1	44.9
North Miami Beach	6 197	44	100.0	83	287	148.9	10.5	234	2 483	731.1	64.1
North Port	136 629	557	100.0	21	161	32.3	4.1	61	1 256	257.9	26.2
Oakland Park	1 879	13	61.5	158	880	430.4	43.7	270	2 444	594.3	59.9
Ocala	24 381	84	100.0	170	2 228	1 071.6	86.4	597	9 774	2 529.6	233.5
Ocoee	97 664	723	33.1	27	837	551.6	44.4	191	3 505	573.7	61.4
Orlando	525 686	2 849	32.1	589	9 294	5 439.6	450.3	1 552	23 831	7 481.2	580.2
Ormond Beach	37 277	104	100.0	49	931	393.7	32.2	188	2 433	525.7	50.7
Oviedo	10 984	42	100.0	40	180	107.6	10.8	147	1 979	310.3	34.4
Palm Bay	36 082	162	100.0	41	241	122.1	11.4	189	2 945	719.1	63.6
Palm Beach Gardens	86 742	237	79.3	52	230	185.8	11.8	342	6 687	1 380.2	151.5
Palm Coast	95 293	339	100.0	34	96	37.1	4.1	121	2 154	532.5	50.2
Panama City	NA	NA	NA	67	539	275.1	25.0	381	5 211	1 327.8	116.7
Pembroke Pines	398	2	100.0	163	563	320.5	24.5	597	11 008	3 020.6	265.1
Pensacola	10 802	46	100.0	73	957	472.3	39.0	437	5 921	1 160.4	115.9
Pinellas Park	13 628	66	100.0	180	2 550	1 030.5	93.9	304	6 201	2 770.0	185.3
Plantation	9 884	19	100.0	127	567	332.8	21.6	364	6 326	1 343.9	130.7
Plant City	20 222	142	100.0	89	1 508	860.6	52.9	155	2 615	711.7	68.4
Pompano Beach	27 939	281	29.5	515	7 335	4 374.9	332.9	654	9 001	3 788.0	274.4
Port Orange	40 432	131	100.0	41	346	383.8	15.6	166	2 603	519.0	51.3
Port St. Lucie	100 987	820	66.5	99	309	108.9	12.2	302	8 458	2 177.3	210.4
Riviera Beach	1 121	3	100.0	112	2 816	1 383.4	140.1	129	1 328	474.8	41.6
Royal Palm Beach	18 785	74	100.0	23	54	15.4	1.7	123	2 632	592.6	59.9
St. Cloud	82 879	554	100.0	14	D	D	D	103	1 727	411.6	37.9
St. Petersburg	98 686	538	32.9	205	1 976	806.3	83.4	970	13 597	3 261.7	298.0
Sanford	4 194	20	100.0	88	1 581	570.5	61.5	364	5 966	1 462.3	126.2
Sarasota	77 951	157	58.6	87	629	308.4	27.4	491	5 483	1 117.6	127.8
Sunrise	14 205	160	0.0	250	2 908	1 828.5	156.3	500	8 288	2 125.2	186.2
Tallahassee	112 530	903	30.0	162	1 641	533.7	65.3	890	14 333	2 927.8	286.2
Tamarac	5 990	76	40.3	71	1 015	955.1	45.2	149	2 977	546.6	88.7
Tampa	406 253	2 555	27.9	634	8 805	6 460.5	423.1	1 726	24 672	6 572.1	620.1
Titusville	19 351	77	97.4	25	320	108.6	11.3	164	2 698	613.1	59.9
Wellington	52 618	144	98.6	90	285	195.5	13.5	250	3 310	558.6	66.6
Weston	3 508	4	100.0	224	1 914	1 577.3	107.4	154	1 952	404.9	48.7
West Palm Beach	110 682	904	11.8	167	1 712	1 068.0	79.0	578	9 352	3 028.8	260.9
Winter Garden	100 326	456	100.0	37	434	303.3	17.1	119	1 005	298.0	28.5
Winter Haven	59 123	359	100.0	41	464	205.7	16.4	213	3 007	667.5	66.4
Winter Park	60 278	117	96.6	54	382	230.9	20.8	253	2 997	785.4	73.4
Winter Springs	21 427	115	68.7	23	105	30.8	3.7	51	323	84.2	7.6

1. Merchant wholesalers except manufacturers' sales branches and offices. 2. Establishments with payroll.

City	Real estate and rental and leasing, 2007				Professional, scientific, and technical services,[1] 2007				Manufacturing, 2007			
	Number of establish-ments	Number of employees	Receipts (mil dol)	Annual payroll (mil dol)	Number of establish-ments	Number of employees	Receipts (mil dol)	Annual payroll (mil dol)	Number of establish-ments	Number of employees	Receipts (mil dol)	Annual payroll (mil dol)
	80	81	82	83	84	85	86	87	88	89	90	91
FLORIDA—Cont'd												
Deerfield Beach	147	905	142.8	35.2	384	2 273	312.7	101.5	119	2 642	496.9	104.6
DeLand	77	342	36.3	7.3	132	726	69.6	27.0	52	2 269	403.1	90.8
Delray Beach	156	555	111.3	21.0	434	1 938	238.3	94.1	64	652	152.3	22.5
Deltona	44	98	11.0	2.6	78	237	19.4	6.4	NA	NA	NA	NA
Doral	206	686	249.7	30.1	503	D	D	D	131	3 187	632.3	130.3
Dunedin	49	140	26.2	3.0	176	3 115	98.2	49.1	NA	NA	NA	NA
Fort Lauderdale	729	3 653	742.5	147.6	2 323	D	D	D	324	4 977	1 068.8	208.2
Fort Myers	226	1 469	277.1	45.1	469	D	D	D	93	2 002	367.8	73.9
Fort Pierce	72	252	47.0	7.4	142	D	D	D	35	681	145.8	24.6
Gainesville	255	1 350	235.1	40.0	495	D	D	D	88	2 132	589.2	96.6
Greenacres	28	120	27.4	4.5	68	335	29.8	13.1	NA	NA	NA	NA
Hallandale Beach	94	188	36.5	5.9	146	429	63.1	19.8	NA	NA	NA	NA
Hialeah	271	768	188.7	20.3	364	1 289	127.6	37.1	468	6 542	917.0	205.4
Hollywood	334	1 128	201.7	35.7	885	D	D	D	121	2 181	401.3	76.8
Homestead	43	138	21.2	3.8	98	395	32.9	13.7	NA	NA	NA	NA
Jacksonville	1 257	7 869	1 955.8	347.0	2 820	D	D	D	624	25 890	11 145.3	1 233.1
Jupiter	159	697	90.0	25.0	390	D	D	D	57	1 127	515.7	62.5
Kissimmee	176	797	134.3	30.0	171	687	70.5	28.6	NA	NA	NA	NA
Lakeland	204	1 197	189.0	33.7	385	D	D	D	84	3 540	1 001.5	138.5
Lake Worth	59	143	26.0	3.8	149	D	D	D	58	547	146.2	20.9
Largo	139	1 562	236.0	80.6	252	D	D	D	92	3 512	640.9	144.3
Lauderdale Lakes	19	211	20.0	5.6	38	107	8.8	3.8	NA	NA	NA	NA
Lauderhill	57	493	76.8	15.7	99	375	35.8	11.9	NA	NA	NA	NA
Margate	84	392	66.4	11.3	147	656	68.9	23.4	NA	NA	NA	NA
Melbourne	183	929	146.7	26.4	396	3 372	590.4	196.8	114	6 354	2 784.6	339.8
Miami	1 115	4 189	1 317.6	197.2	3 235	23 525	4 436.8	1 906.4	396	4 176	1 079.4	139.1
Miami Beach	458	2 249	602.3	162.0	559	D	D	D	NA	NA	NA	NA
Miami Gardens	66	279	85.3	9.7	98	476	44.7	18.3	73	2 716	547.6	98.4
Miami Lakes	116	700	156.2	32.8	266	1 306	215.2	59.3	27	3 455	D	216.5
Miramar	83	224	69.6	7.8	229	1 191	175.7	69.4	41	1 157	203.9	64.3
North Lauderdale	24	111	19.0	2.6	56	D	D	D	NA	NA	NA	NA
North Miami	108	265	45.2	8.3	163	847	83.7	39.7	33	613	114.9	20.5
North Miami Beach	91	534	74.4	11.4	216	D	D	D	NA	NA	NA	NA
North Port	33	79	10.5	2.0	48	191	13.9	6.6	NA	NA	NA	NA
Oakland Park	119	555	73.3	17.3	263	D	D	D	131	1 338	246.7	49.6
Ocala	222	990	139.3	25.5	389	2 171	240.8	94.0	112	6 586	1 297.9	236.9
Ocoee	32	1 133	37.4	29.6	93	449	36.8	14.7	NA	NA	NA	NA
Orlando	779	8 239	2 231.9	363.2	1 835	D	D	D	281	12 806	5 742.1	707.5
Ormond Beach	97	453	62.4	11.6	176	989	98.3	34.8	48	951	152.8	35.3
Oviedo	75	171	48.8	5.4	154	D	D	D	NA	NA	NA	NA
Palm Bay	79	219	33.2	5.1	120	D	D	D	52	10 509	2 894.8	D
Palm Beach Gardens	131	591	117.9	30.4	458	D	D	D	20	605	135.5	39.8
Palm Coast	133	316	40.5	8.7	133	429	79.3	37.4	23	768	D	D
Panama City	107	426	66.9	12.2	206	D	D	D	45	1 622	862.4	72.1
Pembroke Pines	213	698	180.7	19.6	564	1 763	193.4	68.5	NA	NA	NA	NA
Pensacola	136	543	122.3	15.3	444	4 210	477.8	215.6	48	934	300.5	41.8
Pinellas Park	71	305	54.2	8.9	164	D	D	D	256	10 171	2 230.7	419.3
Plantation	229	1 417	210.3	56.8	676	D	D	D	39	1 023	D	61.8
Plant City	53	235	39.4	5.5	80	D	D	D	63	3 846	1 215.6	140.0
Pompano Beach	260	1 585	285.9	57.7	505	2 028	354.2	93.2	307	7 410	1 562.8	273.5
Port Orange	95	394	52.7	10.5	123	483	49.9	18.3	NA	NA	NA	NA
Port St. Lucie	169	500	80.6	13.7	260	1 248	115.6	45.3	44	854	408.4	40.9
Riviera Beach	47	219	60.6	8.6	68	369	47.7	16.7	90	1 499	1 199.7	61.2
Royal Palm Beach	32	94	12.1	2.2	85	314	37.9	11.2	NA	NA	NA	NA
St. Cloud	56	123	16.2	2.6	54	221	19.9	9.3	NA	NA	NA	NA
St. Petersburg	388	1 905	304.1	66.7	1 132	D	D	D	157	4 557	1 601.2	213.3
Sanford	89	557	148.5	16.6	134	D	D	D	72	2 405	701.6	86.5
Sarasota	271	932	206.0	31.7	656	D	D	D	60	672	93.6	31.4
Sunrise	120	532	249.6	19.7	367	2 420	297.8	115.6	65	787	211.0	35.3
Tallahassee	373	2 141	330.0	61.1	1 183	9 322	1 822.7	629.6	83	1 976	574.2	84.9
Tamarac	80	379	52.8	11.4	150	744	68.3	23.7	28	634	86.8	21.6
Tampa	845	5 600	1 167.2	254.0	2 497	23 091	3 950.6	1 662.3	371	9 239	2 836.5	380.4
Titusville	48	231	26.7	4.7	89	561	59.7	26.3	NA	NA	NA	NA
Wellington	128	549	76.1	25.2	277	823	109.9	40.6	NA	NA	NA	NA
Weston	187	346	84.2	11.1	461	1 342	196.5	94.3	20	534	55.6	18.5
West Palm Beach	288	1 547	284.8	64.8	1 013	7 964	1 374.6	608.4	114	2 482	473.6	123.1
Winter Garden	63	179	28.8	7.0	81	313	30.5	12.4	25	527	212.4	18.1
Winter Haven	81	383	62.3	12.2	130	584	58.4	25.4	27	567	279.2	25.5
Winter Park	181	586	82.5	23.5	482	3 471	560.2	239.7	NA	NA	NA	NA
Winter Springs	39	48	8.6	1.3	102	238	21.0	8.6	NA	NA	NA	NA

1. Establishments subject to federal tax.

Table D. Cities — Accommodation and Food Services, Arts, Entertainment, and Recreation, and Health Care and Social Assistance

City	Accommodation and food services, 2007				Arts, entertainment, and recreation,[1] 2007				Health care and social assistance,[1] 2007			
	Number of establish-ments	Number of employees	Sales (mil dol)	Annual payroll (mil dol)	Number of establish-ments	Number of employees	Receipts (mil dol)	Annual payroll (mil dol)	Number of establish-ments	Number of employees	Receipts (mil dol)	Annual payroll (mil dol)
	92	93	94	95	96	97	98	99	100	101	102	103
FLORIDA—Cont'd												
Deerfield Beach	162	3 235	184.3	48.3	28	299	50.5	6.6	186	D	D	D
DeLand	84	1 539	57.7	17.0	11	D	D	D	109	1 643	204.0	60.4
Delray Beach	204	3 683	218.4	59.5	45	308	23.5	7.2	335	3 854	570.6	185.0
Deltona	46	694	27.2	6.6	12	D	D	D	68	550	46.6	18.0
Doral	186	4 503	308.8	80.3	37	D	D	D	151	2 539	315.9	114.9
Dunedin	88	1 151	48.7	13.1	15	D	D	D	109	D	D	D
Fort Lauderdale	679	18 389	1 356.2	363.0	153	1 105	131.9	32.0	773	11 439	1 196.1	481.1
Fort Myers	257	4 685	260.1	66.8	33	988	52.3	19.6	340	4 660	591.5	230.9
Fort Pierce	118	2 217	97.7	28.0	9	152	14.4	3.0	178	2 792	353.2	115.8
Gainesville	359	7 338	315.0	84.8	36	751	32.4	10.2	397	6 146	697.1	259.7
Greenacres	58	987	41.6	11.5	7	19	0.8	0.2	70	662	56.6	20.1
Hallandale Beach	77	2 145	98.2	35.4	22	D	D	D	140	D	D	D
Hialeah	312	4 015	232.2	55.9	38	D	D	D	811	8 639	1 067.7	323.6
Hollywood	332	5 433	395.1	119.8	92	425	49.0	7.3	509	D	D	D
Homestead	74	1 428	65.6	17.6	11	139	37.6	3.6	132	989	101.9	33.9
Jacksonville	1 655	31 715	1 568.2	441.2	213	3 762	396.7	143.1	1 804	25 425	2 813.3	1 141.4
Jupiter	138	2 925	132.0	39.0	41	1 019	63.0	25.5	260	D	D	D
Kissimmee	124	3 419	291.5	77.6	26	D	D	D	232	3 496	499.7	169.4
Lakeland	234	6 154	261.1	76.1	33	512	24.9	8.2	308	5 434	665.2	208.7
Lake Worth	88	1 056	47.1	14.7	18	D	D	D	80	1 035	74.8	32.9
Largo	175	2 843	127.7	38.3	22	D	D	D	310	6 535	626.9	242.5
Lauderdale Lakes	36	411	22.9	5.8	2	D	D	D	99	D	D	D
Lauderhill	86	1 010	48.7	12.3	17	D	D	D	117	1 317	97.2	29.8
Margate	101	1 403	73.3	18.9	17	D	D	D	177	D	D	D
Melbourne	202	3 872	165.8	50.0	36	483	20.2	6.2	354	5 573	705.7	288.4
Miami	994	19 303	1 337.8	355.2	191	2 853	385.2	158.4	1 797	13 565	1 659.3	539.5
Miami Beach	549	16 909	1 345.6	386.9	112	1 411	140.1	39.2	370	2 520	297.6	113.2
Miami Gardens	90	1 372	76.5	18.6	18	D	D	D	119	1 121	86.6	29.2
Miami Lakes	60	1 556	84.7	25.4	17	D	D	D	145	D	D	D
Miramar	95	1 470	69.4	18.9	26	D	D	D	165	D	D	D
North Lauderdale	34	508	26.9	6.4	4	D	D	D	35	D	D	D
North Miami	94	1 550	78.8	20.1	17	D	D	D	126	1 110	95.8	32.0
North Miami Beach	104	1 592	90.3	22.7	18	264	13.6	2.8	232	2 466	274.8	89.3
North Port	29	524	20.2	6.1	4	54	2.0	1.0	47	581	39.0	15.7
Oakland Park	109	1 648	82.7	21.7	20	D	D	D	135	1 853	207.7	70.4
Ocala	242	5 391	245.6	70.9	28	D	D	D	497	7 844	969.9	337.6
Ocoee	74	1 081	54.9	14.7	21	D	D	D	99	1 135	130.9	50.6
Orlando	851	22 678	1 514.5	373.8	133	15 577	1 613.8	418.3	793	8 550	1 133.7	503.3
Ormond Beach	117	2 473	105.8	32.0	23	D	D	D	223	D	D	D
Oviedo	64	1 126	41.1	11.3	14	224	8.0	2.0	116	D	D	D
Palm Bay	99	1 701	70.4	19.4	9	D	D	D	126	1 605	123.6	56.4
Palm Beach Gardens	150	5 178	277.7	86.8	37	D	D	D	329	3 630	513.3	163.3
Palm Coast	76	1 776	88.4	24.8	15	213	12.2	4.2	104	D	D	D
Panama City	166	2 987	133.7	38.5	16	D	D	D	300	4 517	570.2	198.4
Pembroke Pines	284	5 793	271.3	76.0	54	D	D	D	501	D	D	D
Pensacola	187	4 497	208.6	59.4	22	D	D	D	338	6 369	827.5	329.5
Pinellas Park	119	1 878	128.8	34.9	14	144	6.9	2.3	126	1 592	140.5	56.1
Plantation	186	3 569	194.4	51.9	39	D	D	D	534	5 622	787.1	245.9
Plant City	80	1 597	77.5	19.1	5	D	D	D	98	D	D	D
Pompano Beach	266	3 739	197.7	50.2	62	D	D	D	269	2 650	282.6	93.3
Port Orange	88	1 785	70.6	20.1	20	D	D	D	117	D	D	D
Port St. Lucie	158	3 292	127.5	35.9	30	D	D	D	284	4 051	486.2	153.0
Riviera Beach	39	950	44.9	10.4	14	685	53.1	19.4	36	190	14.5	5.7
Royal Palm Beach	83	1 436	61.1	17.8	13	106	6.4	1.8	116	1 857	248.6	75.8
St. Cloud	63	1 340	57.3	16.0	8	D	D	D	43	D	D	D
St. Petersburg	465	8 782	451.1	126.6	56	1 412	200.1	90.3	774	9 186	1 214.4	427.9
Sanford	129	2 932	123.8	36.1	14	D	D	D	103	1 765	226.8	73.8
Sarasota	258	5 897	350.1	103.6	37	684	39.9	11.1	464	5 185	676.8	241.0
Sunrise	186	3 596	181.7	48.8	36	D	D	D	244	3 991	497.3	225.0
Tallahassee	538	12 939	514.5	142.2	52	998	112.0	15.7	504	8 075	801.3	353.6
Tamarac	86	1 310	64.5	15.1	15	D	D	D	203	2 744	305.0	106.8
Tampa	956	23 982	1 376.2	377.7	126	6 136	659.7	287.3	1 197	14 681	2 066.7	719.4
Titusville	97	1 986	89.2	23.1	11	113	5.6	1.6	137	D	D	D
Wellington	101	2 125	92.5	27.5	54	260	18.2	3.8	176	D	D	D
Weston	98	2 203	120.6	31.9	30	D	D	D	195	D	D	D
West Palm Beach	295	6 038	326.6	91.0	60	608	88.5	26.0	509	7 574	1 095.9	366.0
Winter Garden	48	547	25.7	6.7	8	D	D	D	43	515	41.7	18.2
Winter Haven	106	1 625	70.0	18.9	5	D	D	D	168	D	D	D
Winter Park	128	3 271	152.0	46.2	31	D	D	D	272	3 373	441.9	165.4
Winter Springs	26	257	9.6	2.5	14	D	D	D	29	D	D	D

1. Establishments subject to federal tax.

Table D. Cities — **Other Services and Government Employment and Payroll**

City	Other services[1], 2007: Number of establishments	Other services[1], 2007: Number of employees	Other services[1], 2007: Receipts (mil dol)	Other services[1], 2007: Annual payroll (mil dol)	Government employment and payroll, 2012: Full-time equivalent employees	March payroll: Total (dollars)	Percent of total for: Administration, judicial, and legal	Percent of total for: Police and Corrections	Percent of total for: Fire Protection	Percent of total for: Highways and transportation	Percent of total for: Health and welfare	Percent of total for: Natural resources and utilities	Percent of total for: Education and libraries
	104	105	106	107	108	109	110	111	112	113	114	115	116
FLORIDA—Cont'd													
Deerfield Beach	161	879	64.9	21.3	608	3 242 063	11.8	0.0	36.3	1.9	4.4	33.5	0.0
DeLand	71	371	24.4	8.4	339	1 192 527	21.8	28.4	14.3	9.1	0.0	23.5	0.0
Delray Beach	181	743	63.7	15.9	762	3 820 363	10.4	30.3	26.8	3.3	0.8	22.2	0.0
Deltona	44	165	7.4	2.4	304	1 105 426	18.7	0.0	34.0	5.8	0.9	31.1	0.0
Doral	130	1 131	134.6	30.2	269	1 347 474	13.6	55.1	0.0	6.7	0.0	8.2	0.0
Dunedin	79	260	29.3	5.7	343	1 392 549	13.9	0.0	21.1	7.5	1.6	43.2	5.9
Fort Lauderdale	559	3 246	314.4	91.4	2 346	13 506 065	10.3	32.6	25.0	0.5	4.6	19.2	0.0
Fort Myers	238	1 417	131.8	36.0	902	3 718 361	15.0	32.5	18.3	2.3	1.3	27.1	0.0
Fort Pierce	91	372	28.7	9.5	620	2 494 232	7.9	24.2	0.0	3.9	1.4	41.0	0.0
Gainesville	207	1 182	84.0	26.0	2 090	9 866 610	13.9	18.0	9.1	12.0	1.5	36.0	0.0
Greenacres	48	125	7.7	2.5	180	934 096	15.0	34.9	33.1	2.2	0.0	2.1	0.0
Hallandale Beach	88	471	34.9	11.6	437	2 597 020	14.5	36.5	23.5	4.3	3.1	15.3	0.0
Hialeah	478	1 814	146.7	38.5	1 644	7 468 317	8.8	33.3	26.1	4.7	2.0	17.7	4.4
Hollywood	264	1 888	138.5	45.5	1 340	7 260 474	10.2	35.7	23.9	4.1	2.7	17.3	0.0
Homestead	58	216	15.6	4.1	375	2 068 115	10.3	44.1	0.0	4.5	0.9	33.5	0.0
Jacksonville	1 368	D	D	D	10 137	46 960 164	11.8	32.9	13.5	4.4	2.3	13.0	2.0
Jupiter	143	665	46.7	15.8	368	1 870 904	18.7	37.5	0.0	8.8	0.2	23.5	0.0
Kissimmee	111	407	32.7	9.3	912	3 901 999	9.5	20.8	12.3	5.7	0.0	51.1	0.0
Lakeland	156	875	61.7	20.2	2 156	10 065 334	11.3	18.9	7.3	4.3	2.7	48.5	1.5
Lake Worth	98	347	24.7	7.8	267	1 224 227	13.4	0.0	0.0	3.3	7.0	68.8	1.3
Largo	160	676	50.2	16.1	823	3 637 673	0.0	25.8	22.2	6.2	1.2	25.5	3.2
Lauderdale Lakes	31	83	7.5	2.2	79	272 557	39.0	0.0	0.0	5.4	19.3	16.1	0.0
Lauderhill	83	341	24.1	6.7	410	2 557 908	13.6	36.5	29.7	0.9	1.2	14.4	0.0
Margate	107	399	35.5	8.0	486	2 719 607	9.8	35.2	29.2	0.0	0.8	18.8	0.0
Melbourne	167	802	54.4	18.7	870	3 653 445	13.0	26.1	21.7	11.7	0.9	24.0	0.0
Miami	879	4 795	360.0	97.3	3 807	18 642 774	9.5	38.6	27.3	0.0	1.0	10.5	0.0
Miami Beach	176	1 483	112.6	24.6	1 861	12 515 293	9.7	37.2	16.1	3.6	1.8	12.8	0.0
Miami Gardens	51	1 605	44.1	20.0	499	2 715 980	13.8	61.9	0.0	4.0	1.2	10.9	0.0
Miami Lakes	30	92	7.0	2.1	31	181 241	72.9	0.0	0.0	4.7	0.0	22.4	0.0
Miramar	92	395	33.4	10.4	758	4 183 683	11.9	34.2	25.2	4.0	4.9	19.8	0.0
North Lauderdale	45	221	23.8	7.1	153	612 914	14.4	0.0	35.9	6.8	9.5	24.3	0.0
North Miami	99	392	26.3	6.0	424	1 773 052	15.3	47.6	0.0	2.6	1.4	24.9	1.4
North Miami Beach	103	394	28.3	8.0	481	2 472 451	13.4	37.7	0.0	7.0	0.3	17.7	1.3
North Port	38	118	8.7	2.8	511	2 449 083	12.2	24.5	20.8	13.4	0.8	17.6	0.0
Oakland Park	185	584	51.7	14.1	238	1 116 830	16.6	0.0	36.2	5.5	0.7	31.5	2.1
Ocala	181	1 059	79.9	23.2	961	3 935 258	12.7	25.3	17.5	2.8	1.6	37.3	0.0
Ocoee	53	D	D	D	332	1 430 323	11.3	31.2	19.8	7.4	8.7	21.6	0.0
Orlando	501	4 728	334.7	100.1	2 773	14 180 368	10.1	36.7	27.1	2.9	0.6	17.8	0.0
Ormond Beach	74	308	18.3	5.6	333	1 242 053	17.4	24.9	18.0	7.1	0.0	25.6	0.0
Oviedo	58	300	19.0	5.7	281	1 140 501	10.0	30.2	24.7	5.4	5.6	24.1	0.0
Palm Bay	96	326	27.5	8.5	738	2 860 974	8.8	34.4	22.7	12.9	2.8	18.3	0.0
Palm Beach Gardens	95	498	38.8	13.8	497	2 744 921	6.6	31.5	34.9	3.9	0.0	13.0	0.0
Palm Coast	58	213	11.7	3.6	367	1 477 520	33.5	0.4	16.8	0.0	0.0	49.3	0.0
Panama City	92	624	40.1	12.3	560	1 720 128	8.5	23.2	16.5	21.6	2.5	23.8	0.0
Pembroke Pines	196	1 128	78.6	21.7	811	4 498 652	8.1	38.2	36.8	0.0	0.5	11.6	0.0
Pensacola	111	820	58.4	17.0	835	3 072 149	10.7	26.9	15.4	10.9	2.2	25.7	4.6
Pinellas Park	147	869	84.5	25.5	495	2 118 077	13.5	29.2	22.2	4.8	5.1	17.7	4.0
Plantation	154	858	52.5	24.3	805	3 820 829	9.6	44.3	2.6	5.4	9.5	17.4	1.1
Plant City	51	269	20.8	6.6	501	1 604 248	10.1	22.3	11.9	11.1	2.3	30.0	3.2
Pompano Beach	297	1 607	157.0	40.4	750	3 541 060	16.9	0.0	31.9	13.8	1.8	23.5	0.0
Port Orange	82	413	21.6	6.5	401	1 524 545	16.2	27.0	16.3	4.0	8.0	26.5	0.0
Port St. Lucie	125	424	31.4	9.4	947	4 712 445	20.9	40.2	0.0	10.1	2.4	19.5	0.0
Riviera Beach	67	355	48.2	12.4	471	2 072 288	16.7	31.0	21.2	5.6	2.0	15.3	1.1
Royal Palm Beach	57	275	19.2	5.6	102	467 299	20.4	0.0	0.0	30.5	0.0	29.3	0.0
St. Cloud	41	D	D	D	437	1 502 512	12.4	20.0	15.5	4.7	0.0	25.9	0.0
St. Petersburg	418	1 877	120.7	40.4	3 700	17 064 309	4.8	45.6	11.2	0.8	1.0	27.0	1.2
Sanford	113	647	54.1	18.0	571	2 356 239	8.5	26.8	18.3	14.9	0.6	25.6	0.0
Sarasota	164	1 171	72.1	23.3	650	3 097 398	13.3	41.0	0.0	3.7	1.8	26.4	0.0
Sunrise	127	521	41.1	11.9	946	5 498 554	12.5	33.9	21.2	2.4	0.9	25.6	0.0
Tallahassee	312	1 966	132.7	45.5	3 027	13 645 644	13.9	19.4	10.3	12.4	2.1	36.5	0.0
Tamarac	63	278	15.6	4.7	364	1 617 407	25.5	0.0	24.3	8.4	1.2	29.4	0.0
Tampa	769	7 266	431.8	130.5	4 247	22 517 912	11.0	35.8	17.2	4.0	2.4	25.2	0.0
Titusville	73	528	45.1	20.9	452	1 810 027	17.0	25.5	15.5	4.3	0.7	33.4	0.0
Wellington	94	527	38.8	13.1	322	1 314 469	22.1	0.0	0.0	3.5	0.0	40.8	0.0
Weston	84	496	30.4	11.1	10	117 886	74.7	0.0	0.0	0.0	0.0	25.3	0.0
West Palm Beach	203	1 198	85.8	28.0	1 355	7 409 659	10.2	30.9	19.4	4.7	1.3	25.2	2.2
Winter Garden	41	193	15.4	4.1	272	1 145 114	16.2	35.8	18.5	3.2	0.0	17.7	0.0
Winter Haven	60	228	18.9	5.7	460	1 697 693	17.7	25.5	18.1	2.2	0.0	25.4	2.8
Winter Park	107	506	35.4	11.8	506	2 395 109	10.5	24.5	19.9	4.4	0.8	35.0	0.0
Winter Springs	28	65	5.5	1.4	207	765 305	16.8	45.2	0.0	0.0	0.0	34.3	0.0

1. Establishments subject to federal tax.

City	City government finances, 2007									
	General revenue							General expenditure		
		Intergovernmental		Taxes					Per capita[1] (dollars)	
					Per capita[1] (dollars)					
	Total (mil dol)	Total (mil dol)	Percent from state government	Total (mil dol)	Total	Property	Sales and gross receipts	Total (mil dol)	Total	Capital outlays
	117	118	119	120	121	122	123	124	125	126
FLORIDA—Cont'd										
Deerfield Beach	110.6	11.2	65.6	51.7	667	441	223	119.1	1 535	67
DeLand	35.7	3.0	61.4	17.0	614	289	325	31.5	1 139	109
Delray Beach	122.1	11.8	68.8	77.5	1 240	937	301	117.6	1 882	71
Deltona	54.5	13.8	48.2	29.8	348	137	212	53.3	623	113
Doral	55.0	5.7	60.4	41.1	848	410	438	61.9	1 277	597
Dunedin	36.4	4.4	84.4	17.5	493	184	309	42.1	1 185	73
Fort Lauderdale	351.8	52.9	32.9	172.6	1 007	601	406	357.5	2 086	178
Fort Myers	148.2	15.3	59.3	61.9	943	526	416	154.4	2 352	195
Fort Pierce	68.9	10.3	85.1	26.0	609	360	249	79.2	1 855	305
Gainesville	206.3	24.2	47.3	64.4	510	212	298	208.2	1 648	273
Greenacres	21.6	4.0	80.4	13.4	347	173	174	20.5	533	30
Hallandale Beach	73.9	8.7	37.1	31.8	827	546	281	76.5	1 992	86
Hialeah	219.5	58.6	43.0	103.2	442	208	234	207.3	887	63
Hollywood	276.4	29.3	52.2	122.9	843	565	278	276.3	1 896	231
Homestead	81.0	20.4	49.7	25.1	395	226	168	68.8	1 081	164
Jacksonville	1 946.9	245.5	61.0	924.4	1 104	595	506	1 888.1	2 255	340
Jupiter	55.9	5.9	86.7	35.6	621	347	274	60.5	1 056	189
Kissimmee	69.7	20.4	62.5	27.9	438	199	239	82.5	1 296	259
Lakeland	186.5	38.4	30.2	50.0	502	262	240	203.7	2 048	303
Lake Worth	47.4	10.9	39.7	14.0	389	189	201	55.1	1 538	116
Largo	106.7	10.7	72.0	39.5	505	186	318	110.7	1 416	238
Lauderdale Lakes	26.2	4.3	77.6	11.9	352	170	182	26.8	792	44
Lauderhill	67.1	12.7	52.9	27.3	394	187	208	71.1	1 026	65
Margate	70.3	9.0	65.1	33.0	598	364	233	69.8	1 266	200
Melbourne	117.4	17.7	39.8	45.0	584	287	297	113.2	1 469	76
Miami	722.3	172.2	31.3	406.9	976	638	338	740.7	1 777	262
Miami Beach	529.5	21.7	43.5	328.2	3 597	1 276	2 320	497.2	5 448	572
Miami Gardens	83.2	27.7	43.3	41.1	368	176	192	85.3	765	86
Miami Lakes	18.1	3.9	79.9	12.9	422	185	237	19.4	635	118
Miramar	143.9	25.7	45.7	72.6	562	324	239	135.3	1 048	75
North Lauderdale	36.7	5.7	71.1	13.9	327	169	158	33.0	775	30
North Miami	74.3	14.3	45.8	30.1	493	287	206	78.4	1 282	99
North Miami Beach	69.4	10.5	84.8	22.9	528	290	238	79.6	1 838	147
North Port	74.1	8.3	65.2	22.7	389	138	251	78.1	1 339	244
Oakland Park	60.8	8.4	54.6	23.5	546	294	252	60.3	1 403	122
Ocala	118.1	16.3	79.4	40.2	707	380	327	106.1	1 865	168
Ocoee	39.5	8.6	94.4	16.4	428	253	175	40.9	1 066	54
Orlando	675.7	172.7	30.5	223.8	895	417	478	644.8	2 578	124
Ormond Beach	49.2	7.5	40.8	21.3	554	253	301	51.7	1 346	298
Oviedo	37.7	4.2	64.8	18.8	531	271	260	40.7	1 151	91
Palm Bay	95.5	22.5	37.8	43.8	421	236	184	96.4	925	142
Palm Beach Gardens	72.5	6.7	77.4	55.9	1 116	914	202	73.8	1 475	130
Palm Coast	61.9	7.9	63.6	23.7	306	196	111	75.5	974	151
Panama City	60.3	8.8	82.6	27.9	771	279	492	64.4	1 779	119
Pembroke Pines	252.5	67.1	81.6	92.9	581	321	260	310.7	1 942	78
Pensacola	126.4	46.1	16.9	42.4	804	266	538	157.0	2 977	968
Pinellas Park	65.8	7.8	64.1	31.4	631	274	357	68.5	1 377	108
Plantation	103.5	13.9	50.3	55.4	628	333	295	108.1	1 225	75
Plant City	47.9	7.5	73.4	20.0	554	231	323	40.6	1 128	97
Pompano Beach	157.1	12.7	50.4	84.6	819	496	323	202.4	1 959	236
Port Orange	65.3	6.6	74.6	25.0	440	215	225	62.8	1 105	37
Port St. Lucie	168.3	26.2	39.2	71.3	422	209	214	184.5	1 092	286
Riviera Beach	85.9	14.2	26.9	47.7	1 438	1 016	422	92.1	2 775	315
Royal Palm Beach	21.1	5.0	54.1	11.9	338	100	237	26.3	747	203
St. Cloud	51.0	4.2	78.7	15.3	386	160	226	64.8	1 632	228
St. Petersburg	377.4	80.5	33.2	139.7	565	303	262	403.2	1 630	142
Sanford	92.0	18.1	67.1	32.7	597	311	286	78.2	1 427	372
Sarasota	157.9	32.8	32.3	54.1	1 023	523	501	163.4	3 091	774
Sunrise	184.3	17.8	52.4	62.2	698	352	347	170.9	1 920	274
Tallahassee	339.4	52.0	38.9	105.7	565	184	381	370.9	1 983	425
Tamarac	73.4	11.6	50.2	31.8	507	261	245	68.8	1 097	20
Tampa	643.2	135.9	37.9	270.1	774	350	424	634.2	1 817	201
Titusville	55.0	7.1	79.7	25.9	589	263	326	44.4	1 010	129
Wellington	61.9	10.3	59.9	28.2	481	219	261	61.6	1 048	256
Weston	90.1	5.2	88.6	38.6	569	177	392	83.3	1 228	132
West Palm Beach	226.7	39.5	30.6	109.6	1 069	714	355	255.4	2 491	117
Winter Garden	39.8	5.5	93.8	20.7	560	226	334	40.6	1 096	279
Winter Haven	52.2	3.8	56.0	20.8	594	282	312	58.7	1 677	299
Winter Park	63.4	8.3	60.7	29.5	1 019	622	397	65.0	2 246	474
Winter Springs	27.7	4.0	89.0	13.1	389	125	264	26.4	786	144

1. Based on population estimated as of July 1 of the year shown.

City	Public welfare	Highways	Parking facilities	Education	Health and hospitals	Police protection	Sewerage and sanitation	Parks and recreation	Housing and community development	Interest on debt
	City government finances, 2012 (cont.)									
	General expenditure (cont.)									
	Percent of total for:									
	127	128	129	130	131	132	133	134	135	136
FLORIDA—Cont'd										
Deerfield Beach	2.1	2.3	1.5	0.0	0.0	18.0	25.4	5.7	0.3	1.7
DeLand	0.0	8.4	0.0	0.0	0.0	21.9	18.8	9.0	1.4	1.9
Delray Beach	0.0	3.6	0.7	0.0	0.0	25.3	3.7	15.4	1.8	2.5
Deltona	0.0	8.7	0.0	0.0	0.0	17.3	17.9	5.0	6.3	2.0
Doral	0.0	13.4	0.0	0.0	0.0	19.6	0.0	27.0	0.0	2.4
Dunedin	0.0	7.2	0.0	0.0	0.0	9.4	14.6	15.8	0.0	0.9
Fort Lauderdale	0.0	3.4	3.0	0.0	0.0	27.5	5.4	11.4	4.4	0.7
Fort Myers	0.0	10.3	0.7	0.0	0.0	19.9	24.4	9.3	1.3	3.9
Fort Pierce	0.0	4.7	0.0	0.0	0.0	14.8	34.2	10.9	6.0	5.4
Gainesville	0.7	8.6	0.2	0.0	0.1	18.0	17.1	7.9	3.6	7.8
Greenacres	0.0	8.7	0.0	0.0	0.0	35.2	5.1	6.4	0.0	0.9
Hallandale Beach	1.2	1.0	0.0	0.0	0.0	25.2	20.9	3.0	3.1	1.7
Hialeah	0.0	4.5	0.0	0.0	0.0	23.0	17.8	7.3	2.2	2.2
Hollywood	0.0	2.8	2.4	0.0	0.0	25.1	19.0	7.2	1.2	3.5
Homestead	1.6	5.0	0.0	0.0	0.0	28.2	30.0	12.4	6.6	0.8
Jacksonville	2.5	7.5	0.2	0.0	3.3	15.9	10.3	4.6	0.7	8.6
Jupiter	0.0	10.0	0.0	0.0	0.0	32.3	4.8	3.6	0.0	2.5
Kissimmee	0.0	15.8	0.0	0.0	0.0	21.3	9.0	13.5	1.1	1.6
Lakeland	0.0	11.1	0.4	0.0	0.0	17.3	14.6	14.0	3.0	1.7
Lake Worth	0.0	2.8	0.2	0.0	0.0	27.6	23.1	9.1	0.0	0.7
Largo	0.0	3.0	0.0	0.0	0.0	17.3	27.9	13.2	2.4	0.4
Lauderdale Lakes	0.0	1.7	0.0	0.0	9.4	27.5	7.2	4.2	0.0	4.7
Lauderhill	0.0	1.7	0.0	0.0	6.5	22.9	6.6	4.3	3.2	4.5
Margate	0.0	3.6	0.0	0.0	0.0	27.0	14.4	4.2	3.5	3.0
Melbourne	0.0	12.5	0.2	0.0	0.0	16.1	13.2	8.2	2.2	0.5
Miami	0.2	9.5	3.7	0.0	0.0	18.5	3.2	14.9	5.4	5.4
Miami Beach	0.4	3.6	6.2	0.0	3.2	17.9	10.5	14.6	4.3	2.3
Miami Gardens	0.0	6.2	0.0	0.0	0.0	36.6	0.0	14.2	6.2	5.6
Miami Lakes	0.0	8.4	0.0	0.0	0.0	33.7	0.0	12.1	0.0	1.3
Miramar	0.0	5.5	0.0	0.0	0.0	29.7	6.2	8.7	0.9	3.6
North Lauderdale	0.0	3.0	0.0	0.0	0.0	26.0	17.3	11.7	2.6	1.3
North Miami	0.0	9.0	0.0	0.0	0.0	28.7	22.0	7.0	7.1	2.4
North Miami Beach	0.0	1.7	0.0	0.0	0.0	31.6	17.5	6.7	2.7	2.4
North Port	0.6	22.2	0.0	0.0	0.0	16.2	17.0	6.4	0.0	0.6
Oakland Park	0.0	6.0	0.0	0.0	0.0	20.6	19.4	7.9	0.0	1.9
Ocala	0.3	12.3	0.0	0.0	0.0	20.5	21.8	6.8	1.2	1.9
Ocoee	0.0	8.8	0.0	0.0	0.0	20.3	13.9	5.3	0.0	3.7
Orlando	0.0	6.8	2.6	0.0	1.0	19.2	13.7	12.9	1.7	7.0
Ormond Beach	0.0	9.6	0.0	0.0	0.0	14.8	20.0	21.6	0.0	0.6
Oviedo	0.0	31.0	0.0	0.0	0.0	16.7	17.4	8.4	0.0	3.0
Palm Bay	0.0	10.3	0.0	0.0	0.0	21.3	19.2	3.6	3.9	4.7
Palm Beach Gardens	0.0	1.7	0.0	0.0	0.0	30.2	0.0	12.4	0.0	1.4
Palm Coast	0.0	16.0	0.0	0.0	0.0	3.5	36.5	6.2	0.0	1.3
Panama City	0.0	8.9	0.0	0.0	0.0	14.5	8.1	9.2	1.3	0.7
Pembroke Pines	0.5	1.7	0.0	0.0	0.0	15.3	12.6	5.8	3.4	5.5
Pensacola	0.0	3.8	0.3	0.0	0.0	13.4	4.1	25.3	10.0	4.8
Pinellas Park	0.0	6.9	0.0	0.0	4.5	20.1	24.8	8.4	0.0	0.7
Plantation	0.0	2.8	0.0	0.0	7.5	32.2	15.5	12.9	1.7	1.6
Plant City	0.0	8.8	0.0	0.0	0.0	19.8	27.0	8.6	1.2	1.3
Pompano Beach	0.0	2.1	0.0	0.0	7.0	18.5	11.1	7.3	1.9	0.6
Port Orange	0.0	8.8	0.0	0.0	0.0	18.5	37.4	7.4	0.7	2.5
Port St. Lucie	0.0	24.4	0.0	0.0	0.7	19.0	7.9	6.5	2.6	16.5
Riviera Beach	0.2	7.4	0.0	0.0	0.0	18.1	17.9	6.3	0.2	1.0
Royal Palm Beach	0.0	11.4	0.0	0.0	0.0	27.6	0.0	26.9	0.0	0.6
St. Cloud	0.0	25.8	0.0	0.0	3.0	12.6	26.0	4.3	0.2	6.7
St. Petersburg	0.0	9.3	1.1	0.0	3.1	22.0	21.3	14.7	2.3	1.5
Sanford	0.7	8.9	0.0	0.0	0.0	15.9	18.1	5.9	1.9	2.5
Sarasota	0.0	7.1	0.7	0.0	0.0	17.6	23.5	19.7	10.7	3.1
Sunrise	0.0	3.6	0.0	0.0	0.0	29.4	25.2	8.3	0.6	0.8
Tallahassee	0.0	15.1	0.0	0.0	0.0	13.2	31.4	5.6	1.8	2.3
Tamarac	0.0	6.9	0.0	0.0	0.0	17.5	11.9	5.4	1.8	1.9
Tampa	0.0	8.7	2.2	0.0	0.0	23.8	21.2	8.9	5.4	4.1
Titusville	0.0	4.6	0.0	0.0	0.0	24.8	18.5	2.8	7.4	1.2
Wellington	0.0	15.3	0.0	0.0	0.0	12.1	9.3	6.6	0.0	1.2
Weston	0.0	0.8	0.0	0.0	0.0	12.7	18.5	6.4	1.7	0.6
West Palm Beach	0.0	4.1	1.6	0.0	0.7	18.7	24.9	7.1	2.6	4.0
Winter Garden	0.1	13.7	0.2	0.0	0.0	17.5	15.8	18.6	0.0	2.5
Winter Haven	1.2	4.2	2.4	0.0	0.0	17.1	25.7	14.3	0.4	3.8
Winter Park	0.0	2.8	0.0	0.0	0.0	17.7	13.9	8.8	0.0	2.4
Winter Springs	0.0	10.9	0.0	0.0	0.0	28.7	22.0	7.4	0.0	2.2

Table D. Cities — **City Government Finances, City Government Employment, and Climate**

City	City government finances, 2012 (cont.)			Climate[2]						
	Debt outstanding			Average daily temperature (degrees Fahrenheit)						
				Mean		Limits				
	Total (mil dol)	Per capita[1] (dollars)	Debt issued during year	January	July	January[3]	July[4]	Annual precipitation (inches)	Heating degree days	Cooling degree days
	137	138	139	140	141	142	143	144	145	146
FLORIDA—Cont'd										
Deerfield Beach	72.1	929	0.0	67.2	83.3	57.8	91.8	57.27	219	4 241
DeLand	33.4	1 206	9.3	NA	NA	NA	NA	NA	NA	NA
Delray Beach	86.4	1 383	5.4	66.2	82.5	57.3	90.1	61.39	246	3 999
Deltona	97.2	1 137	0.3	57.1	81.2	44.5	91.2	57.03	954	2 819
Doral	26.4	544	0.0	NA	NA	NA	NA	NA	NA	NA
Dunedin	35.3	995	0.0	60.9	82.5	50.2	91.3	52.42	623	3 414
Fort Lauderdale	587.6	3 429	67.9	67.5	82.6	59.2	89.8	64.19	167	4 120
Fort Myers	377.2	5 747	15.1	64.9	83.0	54.5	91.7	54.19	302	3 957
Fort Pierce	216.8	5 076	1.1	62.6	81.7	50.7	91.5	53.50	477	3 430
Gainesville	1 189.9	9 418	161.7	54.4	81.1	41.8	92.4	49.56	1 249	2 608
Greenacres	4.0	105	0.0	66.2	82.5	57.3	90.1	61.39	246	3 999
Hallandale Beach	31.5	819	0.0	68.1	83.7	59.6	90.9	58.53	149	4 361
Hialeah	169.3	725	81.6	67.9	82.7	62.6	87.0	46.60	141	4 090
Hollywood	379.0	2 602	4.3	67.5	82.6	59.2	89.8	64.19	167	4 120
Homestead	18.5	291	0.0	67.0	81.8	56.2	90.6	55.55	238	3 923
Jacksonville	10 439.0	12 465	630.5	54.5	82.5	42.6	92.7	51.88	1 222	2 810
Jupiter	66.9	1 167	0.0	66.2	82.5	57.3	90.1	61.39	246	3 999
Kissimmee	457.1	7 175	151.7	59.7	81.8	47.7	91.6	48.01	694	3 111
Lakeland	951.3	9 565	203.4	62.5	84.0	51.1	94.6	49.13	487	3 886
Lake Worth	74.3	2 072	6.8	65.1	81.1	52.5	91.3	58.44	273	3 438
Largo	31.5	403	14.0	61.3	82.5	52.4	89.7	44.77	591	3 482
Lauderdale Lakes	28.4	838	0.0	67.2	83.3	57.8	91.8	57.27	219	4 241
Lauderhill	118.7	1 711	18.3	67.5	82.6	59.2	89.8	64.19	167	4 120
Margate	53.5	971	0.0	67.2	83.3	57.8	91.8	57.27	219	4 241
Melbourne	132.5	1 720	1.5	60.9	81.2	50.0	90.5	48.29	595	3 186
Miami	873.2	2 095	120.6	68.1	83.7	59.6	90.9	58.53	149	4 361
Miami Beach	465.1	5 097	56.6	68.1	83.7	59.6	90.9	58.53	149	4 361
Miami Gardens	111.4	999	55.0	NA	NA	NA	NA	NA	NA	NA
Miami Lakes	7.5	246	7.3	NA	NA	NA	NA	NA	NA	NA
Miramar	182.5	1 414	0.0	68.1	83.7	59.6	90.9	58.53	149	4 361
North Lauderdale	8.6	203	0.0	67.5	82.6	59.2	89.8	64.19	167	4 120
North Miami	21.9	359	0.0	68.1	83.7	59.6	90.9	58.53	149	4 361
North Miami Beach	111.2	2 568	18.3	68.1	83.7	59.6	90.9	58.53	149	4 361
North Port	54.0	925	17.5	NA	NA	NA	NA	NA	NA	NA
Oakland Park	38.9	904	18.2	67.5	82.6	59.2	89.8	64.19	167	4 120
Ocala	201.6	3 544	13.9	58.1	81.7	45.7	92.2	49.68	902	2 971
Ocoee	54.8	1 428	2.1	NA	NA	NA	NA	NA	NA	NA
Orlando	1 055.4	4 219	67.0	60.9	82.4	49.9	92.2	48.35	580	3 428
Ormond Beach	54.1	1 408	5.6	60.9	82.4	49.9	92.2	48.35	580	3 428
Oviedo	79.7	2 256	1.3	58.7	81.5	47.0	91.9	51.31	799	3 017
Palm Bay	157.8	1 514	5.5	60.9	81.2	50.0	90.5	48.29	595	3 186
Palm Beach Gardens	25.8	515	4.4	66.2	82.5	57.3	90.1	61.39	246	3 999
Palm Coast	176.4	2 276	2.2	57.4	82.8	46.4	92.0	49.79	909	3 193
Panama City	35.5	980	0.0	50.3	80.0	38.7	89.0	64.76	1 810	2 174
Pembroke Pines	388.8	2 430	12.3	67.5	82.6	59.2	89.8	64.19	167	4 120
Pensacola	213.6	4 050	0.0	52.0	82.6	42.7	90.7	64.28	1 498	2 650
Pinellas Park	31.8	640	0.0	61.7	83.4	54.0	90.2	49.58	548	3 718
Plantation	39.9	452	2.8	67.5	82.6	59.2	89.8	64.19	167	4 120
Plant City	68.0	1 886	0.0	61.1	81.5	49.8	90.8	51.17	625	3 261
Pompano Beach	88.3	855	28.1	67.2	83.3	57.8	91.8	57.27	219	4 241
Port Orange	156.3	2 751	13.3	57.1	81.2	44.5	91.2	57.03	954	2 819
Port St. Lucie	1 015.1	6 008	42.9	64.5	81.8	54.7	89.5	59.53	315	3 600
Riviera Beach	67.2	2 025	26.5	66.2	82.5	57.3	90.1	61.39	246	3 999
Royal Palm Beach	20.5	582	20.5	NA	NA	NA	NA	NA	NA	NA
St. Cloud	123.7	3 114	57.6	NA	NA	NA	NA	NA	NA	NA
St. Petersburg	562.7	2 275	53.9	61.7	83.4	54.0	90.2	49.58	548	3 718
Sanford	79.7	1 455	6.1	58.7	81.5	47.0	91.9	51.31	799	3 017
Sarasota	156.6	2 962	30.9	61.7	83.4	54.0	90.2	49.58	548	3 718
Sunrise	298.7	3 356	9.6	67.5	82.6	59.2	89.8	64.19	167	4 120
Tallahassee	1 263.4	6 754	173.5	51.8	82.4	39.7	92.0	63.21	1 604	2 551
Tamarac	60.4	063	23.3	67.2	83.3	57.8	91.8	57.27	219	4 241
Tampa	1 377.0	3 945	202.8	61.3	82.5	52.4	89.7	44.77	591	3 482
Titusville	56.5	1 285	3.6	59.9	82.4	49.5	91.4	52.79	677	3 300
Wellington	22.8	388	0.0	66.2	82.5	57.3	90.1	61.39	246	3 999
Weston	12.6	186	0.0	67.5	82.6	59.2	89.8	64.19	167	4 120
West Palm Beach	437.5	4 267	0.0	66.2	82.5	57.3	90.1	61.39	246	3 999
Winter Garden	22.0	596	0.0	NA	NA	NA	NA	NA	NA	NA
Winter Haven	89.2	2 549	27.3	62.3	82.3	51.0	92.5	50.22	538	3 551
Winter Park	187.9	6 488	28.7	NA	NA	NA	NA	NA	NA	NA
Winter Springs	34.5	1 028	14.4	60.9	82.4	49.9	92.2	48.35	580	3 428

1. Based on the population estimated as of July 1 of the year shown. 2. Represents normal values based on the 30-year period, 1971–2000. 3. Average daily minimum. 4. Average daily maximum.

STATE Place code	City	Land area,[1] 2010 (sq km)	Population, 2014: Total persons	Population, 2014: Rank	Population, 2014: Per square kilometer	Race alone or in combination (percent), 2011-2013: White	Black	American Indian, Alaska Native	Asian	Hawaiian Pacific Islander	Percent Hispanic or Latino[2], 2011-2013	Percent foreign born 2011–2013
		1	2	3	4	5	6	7	8	9	10	11
13 00000	GEORGIA	148 959.2	10 097 343	X	67.8	62.2	32.0	0.8	4.0	0.1	9.1	9.6
13 01052	Albany	142.8	75 769	443	530.6	27.1	71.9	0.5	1.4	0.1	2.4	2.4
13 01696	Alpharetta	69.7	63 038	560	904.4	73.7	11.9	NA	16.4	NA	7.9	19.8
13 03436	Athens-Clarke County	301.4	119 648	225	397.0	67.2	27.5	0.6	5.1	0.1	10.6	9.9
13 04000	Atlanta	344.9	456 002	39	1 322.1	41.8	53.7	0.8	4.3	0.1	5.3	7.8
13 04200	Augusta-Richmond County	783.4	196 741	121	251.1	41.0	56.8	1.0	2.4	0.4	4.5	3.5
13 19000	Columbus	560.4	200 887	111	358.5	49.1	47.4	1.2	3.3	0.2	7.1	5.3
13 21380	Dalton	53.2	33 529	1 111	630.2	80.3	9.4	0.7	3.4	NA	48.6	28.7
13 23900	Douglasville	58.2	32 523	1 141	558.8	36.6	60.2	NA	1.8	NA	7.4	7.5
13 24600	Duluth	25.9	28 838	1 277	1 113.4	46.2	19.1	1.0	29.2	NA	10.1	29.4
13 24768	Dunwoody	33.5	48 000	781	1 432.8	71.0	13.3	1.0	14.1	NA	11.7	24.3
13 25720	East Point	38.0	35 488	1 050	933.9	16.5	75.4	2.3	0.5	NA	13.3	8.4
13 31908	Gainesville	82.7	36 306	1 024	439.0	65.2	19.4	0.5	3.8	NA	38.8	21.9
13 38964	Hinesville	52.8	34 815	1 069	659.4	47.4	45.8	0.7	4.2	1.1	12.7	6.6
13 42425	Johns Creek	79.6	83 102	392	1 044.0	64.4	12.0	0.7	23.7	NA	5.9	26.6
13 43192	Kennesaw	24.5	32 400	1 150	1 322.4	65.9	27.3	0.8	5.2	NA	12.0	14.4
13 44340	LaGrange	102.3	30 557	1 208	298.7	42.7	51.7	NA	3.0	NA	6.3	7.9
13 45488	Lawrenceville	34.7	30 212	1 230	870.7	40.7	42.8	1.6	5.3	NA	19.4	23.3
13 49000	Macon	645.6	153 691	164	238.1	29.6	69.3	0.6	1.4	NA	2.6	2.6
13 49756	Marietta	59.8	60 014	603	1 003.6	58.1	32.4	NA	4.2	NA	19.2	21.6
13 51670	Milton	99.8	36 662	1 014	367.4	75.1	11.9	NA	13.6	NA	6.7	18.2
13 55020	Newnan	47.4	36 203	1 030	763.8	64.3	32.8	NA	2.7	NA	11.1	9.5
13 59724	Peachtree City	63.6	35 063	1 064	551.3	86.2	6.6	0.7	7.8	NA	6.5	11.5
13 66668	Rome	80.1	35 997	1 039	449.4	60.3	26.1	1.5	1.9	NA	17.0	11.7
13 67284	Roswell	105.5	94 089	322	891.8	80.7	14.9	0.8	4.9	NA	13.5	18.6
13 68516	Sandy Springs	97.5	101 908	292	1 045.2	70.9	23.1	0.7	7.6	0.1	15.0	18.5
13 69000	Savannah	267.2	144 352	181	540.2	43.1	54.5	0.8	2.0	0.3	5.7	5.7
13 71492	Smyrna	39.8	54 958	671	1 380.9	56.0	32.3	NA	6.0	NA	15.0	16.2
13 73256	Statesboro	35.0	30 367	1 221	867.6	54.4	43.2	NA	3.3	NA	2.4	4.0
13 73704	Stockbridge	34.5	27 619	1 328	800.6	30.9	60.7	0.8	9.0	NA	6.1	13.8
13 78800	Valdosta	92.8	56 595	649	609.9	45.5	51.7	1.0	2.3	NA	5.7	4.3
13 80508	Warner Robins	90.8	73 271	464	806.9	53.2	39.7	0.4	4.5	NA	6.8	7.6
15 00000	HAWAII	16 634.5	1 419 561	X	85.3	42.6	3.3	2.2	56.3	25.9	9.6	17.9
15 06290	East Honolulu CDP	59.6	NA	NA	NA	41.9	1.0	2.0	67.2	13.3	5.4	15.2
15 14650	Hilo CDP	138.3	NA	NA	NA	45.3	1.2	2.5	62.9	39.3	10.0	6.4
15 22700	Kahului CDP	37.4	NA	NA	NA	29.5	1.2	4.0	68.5	32.2	12.2	30.9
15 23150	Kailua CDP (Honolulu County)	20.1	NA	NA	NA	66.2	2.2	2.2	40.3	20.2	6.5	8.6
15 28250	Kaneohe CDP	16.9	NA	NA	NA	46.7	1.8	2.8	63.0	30.5	7.5	7.2
15 51050	Mililani Town CDP	10.4	NA	NA	NA	42.5	5.6	2.3	68.9	22.4	9.1	9.4
15 62600	Pearl City CDP	23.6	NA	NA	NA	33.0	4.3	1.9	71.3	22.2	11.5	12.3
15 71550	Urban Honolulu CDP	156.8	350 399	55	2 234.7	30.4	3.1	1.7	67.4	18.6	6.0	27.8
15 79700	Waipahu CDP	7.2	NA	NA	NA	15.3	1.7	1.7	78.4	23.9	8.4	37.5
16 00000	IDAHO	214 044.7	1 634 464	X	7.6	94.2	1.1	2.3	2.0	0.3	11.6	5.9
16 08830	Boise City	205.6	216 282	99	1 052.0	92.5	2.0	2.1	5.0	0.4	7.6	7.4
16 12250	Caldwell	57.1	50 224	744	879.6	94.3	1.3	1.7	2.1	NA	32.9	9.3
16 16750	Coeur d'Alene	40.3	47 912	783	1 188.9	96.8	0.3	2.4	1.6	NA	5.8	2.2
16 39700	Idaho Falls	57.9	58 691	623	1 013.7	92.9	0.9	2.0	1.4	0.1	12.7	5.6
16 46540	Lewiston	44.6	32 482	1 143	728.3	97.1	0.8	3.0	1.1	NA	3.0	1.2
16 52120	Meridian	69.4	87 743	357	1 264.3	95.8	1.7	0.6	2.3	NA	7.7	5.2
16 56260	Nampa	80.8	88 211	353	1 091.7	92.4	1.1	1.6	1.3	0.5	23.6	7.7
16 64090	Pocatello	83.5	54 292	683	650.2	95.0	1.7	2.8	2.4	0.3	7.7	4.2
16 64810	Post Falls	36.5	29 896	1 239	819.1	96.6	1.4	2.3	2.0	NA	5.2	1.5
16 67420	Rexburg	25.3	27 094	1 353	1 070.9	96.5	1.1	0.7	2.0	0.7	4.2	5.0
16 82810	Twin Falls	46.9	46 528	806	992.1	92.6	1.0	2.6	2.9	0.4	14.9	9.7
17 00000	ILLINOIS	143 793.4	12 880 580	X	89.6	74.4	15.3	0.7	5.5	0.1	16.3	14.0
17 00243	Addison	25.3	37 297	994	1 474.2	85.4	4.6	0.3	7.0	NA	38.7	34.3
17 00685	Algonquin	31.7	30 410	1 216	959.3	90.5	3.0	NA	6.9	NA	7.4	10.7
17 01114	Alton	40.1	27 177	1 349	677.7	70.5	30.2	1.4	1.0	NA	2.0	0.9
17 02154	Arlington Heights	43.0	76 024	441	1 768.0	88.5	2.2	0.3	9.1	NA	6.0	18.4
17 03012	Aurora	116.4	200 456	115	1 722.1	59.1	10.3	1.1	8.2	0.1	41.7	25.9
17 04013	Bartlett	40.5	41 632	888	1 028.0	78.9	3.3	1.0	16.1	NA	8.2	19.4
17 04078	Batavia	25.0	26 424	1 383	1 057.0	93.0	3.9	1.4	1.8	NA	8.4	5.7
17 04845	Belleville	58.9	42 529	867	722.1	73.6	26.6	0.8	2.4	NA	2.2	1.9
17 05092	Belvidere	31.3	25 282	1 418	807.7	84.6	4.8	NA	1.3	NA	30.5	16.5
17 05573	Berwyn	10.1	56 693	648	5 613.2	73.4	8.1	0.8	2.2	NA	60.2	24.7
17 06613	Bloomington	70.5	78 730	419	1 116.7	79.4	12.8	0.6	8.5	NA	4.8	9.5
17 07133	Bolingbrook	62.3	74 180	455	1 190.7	58.1	22.3	1.0	11.1	NA	25.1	21.7
17 09447	Buffalo Grove	24.6	41 701	884	1 695.2	79.4	2.2	NA	17.9	NA	5.1	26.9

1. Dry land or land partially or temporarily covered by water. 2. May be of any race.

City	Age of population (percent), 2011-2013: Under 5 years	5 to 17 years	18 to 24 years	25 to 34 years	35 to 44 years	45 to 54 years	55 to 64 years	65 to 74 years	75 years and over	Median age 2011-2013	Percent female 2011-2013	Population: Census counts: 2000	2010	Percent change: 2000–2010	2010–2014
	12	13	14	15	16	17	18	19	20	21	22	23	24	25	26
GEORGIA	6.8	18.3	10.2	13.7	14.0	14.1	11.5	6.9	4.6	35.7	51.1	8 186 453	9 687 653	18.3	4.2
Albany	7.8	17.8	13.6	14.3	11.7	11.9	10.8	6.4	5.6	32.3	53.9	76 939	77 434	0.6	-2.2
Alpharetta	7.9	21.5	6.8	12.0	15.5	16.5	11.6	4.5	3.7	36.4	50.2	34 854	57 551	65.1	9.6
Athens-Clarke County	5.9	11.5	29.7	16.8	10.3	8.8	8.2	5.0	3.8	26.2	52.4	101 489	115 452	15.1	3.6
Atlanta	6.2	12.3	14.7	20.0	14.8	12.3	9.7	5.7	4.3	33.2	50.0	416 474	420 003	0.8	8.5
Augusta-Richmond County	7.2	17.0	12.0	15.9	11.4	12.8	11.8	6.9	5.0	33.2	51.6	199 775	195 844	0.3	0.5
Columbus	7.5	17.5	11.8	15.6	12.3	12.8	11.0	6.1	5.3	33.3	51.2	186 291	189 885	1.9	5.4
Dalton	8.4	19.7	10.8	14.1	13.1	12.3	9.5	6.1	6.1	32.5	53.2	27 912	33 128	18.7	1.3
Douglasville	8.3	21.9	9.6	14.4	15.8	13.7	8.3	5.0	2.9	32.0	55.2	20 065	30 961	54.3	5.1
Duluth	7.8	16.5	5.8	17.3	17.0	16.5	10.8	4.6	3.8	36.7	56.0	22 122	26 600	20.2	8.4
Dunwoody	6.9	17.0	5.8	18.1	17.4	12.3	10.1	7.4	5.1	36.4	50.5	32 808	46 267	41.0	3.7
East Point	8.6	17.3	10.9	13.3	14.8	12.3	13.3	6.0	3.5	35.0	52.4	39 595	33 712	-14.9	5.3
Gainesville	8.6	20.9	12.7	15.6	11.8	10.0	8.7	5.8	5.9	30.4	50.0	25 578	33 804	32.2	7.4
Hinesville	10.5	18.6	15.9	19.6	11.0	10.3	8.9	3.8	1.4	26.8	51.6	30 392	33 437	10.0	4.1
Johns Creek	6.4	23.2	7.1	7.6	17.5	18.1	11.7	5.6	2.7	39.2	50.9	NA	76 728	NA	8.3
Kennesaw	5.9	17.9	10.6	16.9	16.6	14.5	8.3	4.4	4.9	34.6	52.8	21 675	29 783	37.4	7.0
LaGrange	8.5	18.7	12.2	14.7	11.4	12.2	10.0	6.9	5.4	32.2	52.8	25 998	29 588	13.8	3.8
Lawrenceville	7.4	21.5	10.9	10.7	14.2	13.7	10.5	5.6	5.4	34.7	50.9	22 397	28 546	27.5	6.4
Macon	8.7	18.0	12.2	13.9	11.2	12.4	11.3	6.2	6.1	32.8	54.5	97 255	91 348	-6.1	NA
Marietta	6.9	15.3	12.4	18.1	16.9	12.0	8.2	6.0	4.3	33.2	51.5	58 748	56 579	-3.7	6.0
Milton	5.3	23.8	6.1	9.3	18.7	17.5	11.5	4.7	3.1	37.4	51.2	NA	32 661	NA	12.1
Newnan	8.2	21.0	7.2	13.7	17.4	12.4	9.6	6.6	3.7	34.9	54.8	16 242	33 039	103.4	9.1
Peachtree City	4.4	21.9	8.2	8.9	11.5	17.2	14.2	8.9	5.0	42.0	51.5	31 580	34 364	8.8	2.0
Rome	8.7	15.8	10.7	15.4	11.0	13.0	10.5	8.4	6.4	34.5	52.1	34 980	36 303	3.8	-0.9
Roswell	6.4	18.2	6.8	13.1	15.5	16.4	12.2	6.8	4.6	38.9	50.0	79 334	88 346	11.4	6.5
Sandy Springs	6.8	15.8	7.5	19.6	14.5	14.0	10.5	6.2	5.3	35.2	52.2	85 781	93 853	9.4	8.6
Savannah	6.8	15.4	15.5	16.5	11.0	11.6	10.7	6.7	5.8	31.9	52.6	131 510	136 286	3.6	5.9
Smyrna	8.5	13.7	7.6	22.0	18.3	13.5	8.3	4.9	3.2	34.3	52.7	40 999	51 271	25.1	7.2
Statesboro	4.0	9.2	49.8	11.8	5.4	7.1	5.1	3.6	3.9	22.1	52.9	22 698	28 422	25.2	6.9
Stockbridge	6.4	23.5	10.4	9.9	18.9	12.9	10.0	4.0	3.9	34.8	54.6	9 853	25 636	160.2	4.9
Valdosta	7.9	14.0	25.3	15.5	9.2	9.5	8.6	5.6	4.5	26.6	51.3	43 724	54 518	24.7	3.3
Warner Robins	8.7	19.4	10.2	18.2	12.5	12.7	8.8	5.1	4.3	31.1	51.9	48 804	66 588	36.4	6.8
HAWAII	6.5	15.5	9.8	14.3	12.5	13.3	12.9	8.1	7.0	38.2	49.7	1 211 537	1 360 301	12.3	4.4
East Honolulu CDP	3.9	14.7	6.4	8.6	13.4	14.5	14.4	13.5	10.8	47.2	51.7	NA	NA	NA	NA
Hilo CDP	4.5	15.3	10.5	13.1	9.8	12.8	15.3	9.3	9.4	41.3	50.5	40 759	43 263	6.1	NA
Kahului CDP	5.5	16.3	9.8	15.0	13.1	14.1	10.0	9.0	7.4	38.1	50.7	20 146	26 337	30.7	NA
Kailua CDP (Honolulu County)	4.5	16.2	7.4	13.3	11.9	14.4	16.1	8.6	7.5	42.0	51.3	36 513	38 635	5.8	NA
Kaneohe CDP	5.1	12.4	8.3	14.5	11.4	15.7	12.6	10.6	9.4	42.9	50.8	34 970	34 597	-1.1	NA
Mililani Town CDP	4.7	15.9	10.2	13.2	12.2	13.5	15.1	10.1	5.1	40.1	49.0	28 608	27 629	-3.4	NA
Pearl City CDP	6.9	15.2	9.2	13.4	11.4	12.0	11.9	10.1	9.8	40.5	47.0	30 976	47 698	54.0	NA
Urban Honolulu CDP	5.4	12.4	10.2	14.9	12.6	13.5	13.0	8.3	9.6	40.5	50.6	NA	337 256	NA	3.9
Waipahu CDP	6.5	15.6	10.3	14.6	11.7	13.4	11.6	8.0	8.3	37.7	50.6	33 108	38 216	15.4	NA
IDAHO	7.2	19.5	9.8	13.2	12.2	12.7	12.1	7.7	5.6	35.2	49.9	1 293 953	1 567 582	21.1	4.3
Boise City	5.9	16.0	11.2	15.4	13.3	13.9	12.6	6.5	5.2	36.0	50.5	185 787	205 671	10.7	4.9
Caldwell	10.1	20.2	11.3	16.7	12.5	9.8	8.8	6.2	4.4	29.8	50.3	25 967	46 237	78.1	8.5
Coeur d'Alene	7.5	16.4	11.7	14.4	11.2	12.1	12.5	7.6	6.8	35.1	50.0	34 514	44 137	27.9	8.6
Idaho Falls	9.1	19.7	9.0	15.3	11.6	11.2	11.8	6.4	6.0	33.1	51.3	50 730	56 813	12.0	3.2
Lewiston	5.9	15.3	10.8	12.6	11.0	13.5	12.5	9.1	9.2	39.6	50.9	30 904	31 894	3.2	1.8
Meridian	8.2	24.1	7.1	13.3	14.9	12.6	9.4	5.8	4.5	33.2	51.8	34 919	75 092	115.0	16.8
Nampa	8.0	24.6	9.8	13.8	12.9	11.3	8.1	7.1	4.3	30.4	51.0	51 867	81 557	57.2	7.9
Pocatello	7.4	18.3	13.7	16.8	10.3	11.6	11.1	5.7	4.9	31.2	50.3	51 466	54 255	5.4	0.1
Post Falls	8.6	19.9	6.5	16.8	14.4	10.8	11.5	6.2	5.3	33.6	53.7	17 247	27 574	59.9	8.4
Rexburg	9.1	13.5	43.0	16.6	5.6	4.3	3.4	2.5	2.0	22.6	52.1	17 257	25 484	47.7	6.4
Twin Falls	7.8	19.6	11.4	15.2	12.7	9.6	10.1	6.8	6.7	32.4	50.4	34 469	44 125	28.0	5.0
ILLINOIS	6.3	17.5	9.7	13.8	13.2	14.2	12.2	7.2	6.0	37.0	50.9	12 419 293	12 830 632	3.3	0.4
Addison	7.8	18.7	9.4	15.5	11.7	13.3	12.1	7.1	4.4	33.8	52.1	35 914	36 942	2.9	0.9
Algonquin	5.6	20.6	7.5	9.6	16.8	16.2	14.0	6.5	3.2	39.9	50.2	23 276	30 046	29.1	1.2
Alton	7.4	16.4	8.3	18.5	10.7	12.4	11.8	8.1	6.4	34.7	51.6	30 496	27 865	-8.6	-2.7
Arlington Heights	5.6	15.5	6.8	12.4	12.5	16.2	12.9	9.1	9.0	42.9	51.7	76 031	75 101	-1.2	1.2
Aurora	7.7	22.5	9.2	15.2	16.1	13.4	8.7	4.4	2.8	32.1	50.6	142 990	197 899	38.4	1.3
Bartlett	5.2	20.2	6.1	11.8	14.3	18.3	13.4	6.1	4.6	40.0	48.9	36 706	41 208	12.3	1.0
Batavia	5.8	21.3	6.9	9.6	13.8	17.7	14.3	5.7	4.9	39.9	53.1	23 866	26 045	9.1	1.0
Belleville	5.4	16.6	8.8	15.5	13.8	15.5	11.9	5.8	6.7	36.8	52.6	41 410	44 478	7.4	-3.5
Belvidere	5.7	23.8	10.7	10.2	16.2	13.1	9.0	6.0	5.2	34.7	51.8	20 820	25 585	22.9	-1.2
Berwyn	7.4	20.4	9.3	14.9	16.0	12.5	10.2	5.0	4.3	33.5	51.5	54 016	56 657	4.9	0.1
Bloomington	7.1	17.5	11.2	15.7	14.0	12.7	11.4	5.0	5.4	33.9	51.5	64 808	76 610	18.2	2.8
Bolingbrook	8.0	20.4	9.7	13.1	17.8	12.5	10.6	5.3	2.6	34.0	50.6	56 321	73 366	30.3	1.1
Buffalo Grove	5.2	18.3	6.0	10.5	15.0	16.8	15.8	7.1	5.4	42.3	51.8	42 909	41 496	-3.3	0.7

City	Households, 2011-2013				Persons in group quarters, 2010				Serious crimes known to police,[2] 2013				Educational attainment, 2011–2013		
			Percent			Institutional			Total		Rate[3]			Attainment[4] (percent)	
	Number	Persons per house-hold	Female family house-holder[1]	One-person	Total	Total	Persons in nursing facilities	Non-institu-tional	Number	Rate[3]	Violent	Property	Population age 25 and older	High school graduate or less	Bachelor's degree or more
	27	28	29	30	31	32	33	34	35	36	37	38	39	40	41
GEORGIA	3 522 934	2.74	15.3	26.9	253 199	144 545	34 738	108 654	370 940	3 712	366	3 347	6 403 956	43.7	28.1
Albany	28 980	2.52	25.8	34.1	4 288	1 421	400	2 867	5 410	6 993	968	6 025	46 772	50.0	16.9
Alpharetta	22 501	2.72	8.5	27.0	69	57	19	12	1 275	2 010	74	1 936	39 071	12.8	63.1
Athens-Clarke County	41 332	2.63	13.7	34.3	9 183	779	348	8 404	4 476	3 726	336	3 390	62 844	36.3	38.7
Atlanta	181 002	2.26	14.8	46.6	29 484	6 756	1 626	22 728	33 044	7 327	1 223	6 103	294 474	30.5	48.2
Augusta-Richmond County	69 773	2.69	21.9	34.7	10 508	3 907	1 137	6 601	11 484	5 788	391	5 397	125 392	47.5	20.9
Columbus	71 351	2.62	20.7	31.2	7 017	3 486	898	3 531	13 497	6 709	508	6 201	125 355	41.3	23.3
Dalton	11 403	2.84	15.9	29.9	904	754	340	150	1 384	4 134	194	3 940	20 429	59.6	17.8
Douglasville	11 124	2.74	28.4	26.7	937	826	0	111	2 213	7 060	683	6 377	18 919	39.7	28.4
Duluth	10 737	2.59	11.7	26.3	34	0	0	34	697	2 459	148	2 310	19 495	32.3	45.1
Dunwoody	19 314	2.43	4.0	37.2	154	0	0	154	1 895	3 987	120	3 867	33 162	18.3	64.0
East Point	12 846	2.71	24.3	38.0	420	44	27	376	4 325	11 957	1 161	10 796	22 279	44.0	26.2
Gainesville	11 090	2.99	20.8	29.0	1 713	649	434	1 064	1 620	4 614	328	4 286	20 198	57.4	21.8
Hinesville	12 882	2.65	17.1	22.0	310	263	0	47	1 542	4 367	340	4 027	18 976	38.0	20.7
Johns Creek	26 310	3.10	9.0	15.8	0	0	0	0	656	780	44	736	51 564	14.2	62.9
Kennesaw	12 474	2.47	13.2	34.1	244	244	99	0	537	1 716	109	1 608	20 499	27.6	36.7
LaGrange	11 078	2.59	28.4	32.4	1 242	627	381	615	1 844	6 002	319	5 683	18 297	53.9	20.4
Lawrenceville	9 981	2.92	23.6	23.1	268	238	238	30	936	3 139	218	2 921	17 686	49.5	22.8
Macon	32 589	2.63	27.4	35.3	4 292	2 026	680	2 266	NA	NA	NA	NA	55 586	58.1	16.2
Marietta	23 402	2.37	13.2	35.6	1 769	758	730	1 011	2 949	5 007	764	4 243	38 145	31.6	37.8
Milton	12 229	2.86	9.7	16.0	4	0	0	4	427	1 194	22	1 172	NA	NA	NA
Newnan	12 831	2.64	18.9	28.5	518	518	135	0	1 199	3 480	340	3 141	21 756	43.3	30.6
Peachtree City	12 230	2.83	8.3	20.8	118	118	118	0	462	1 331	66	1 265	22 776	19.8	54.3
Rome	13 537	2.57	16.8	35.2	1 606	1 409	447	197	2 425	6 718	684	6 034	23 435	51.0	20.8
Roswell	34 348	2.69	10.5	28.3	516	356	305	160	2 251	2 360	151	2 209	63 728	22.9	56.1
Sandy Springs	42 351	2.32	10.1	38.8	327	205	205	122	2 925	2 891	184	2 707	69 011	20.8	57.1
Savannah	52 618	2.54	19.4	35.4	10 014	4 499	584	5 515	9 309	3 958	362	3 596	88 324	43.5	27.4
Smyrna	23 311	2.25	12.7	37.2	279	269	112	10	1 925	3 627	345	3 282	37 022	24.4	51.1
Statesboro	10 081	2.45	18.6	25.5	4 290	266	266	4 024	1 449	4 798	291	4 506	11 006	39.4	27.1
Stockbridge	9 416	2.86	26.4	17.8	8	0	0	8	NA	NA	NA	NA	16 075	32.9	32.0
Valdosta	21 457	2.54	20.0	33.1	4 122	1 147	444	2 975	2 444	4 179	221	3 958	30 022	45.2	23.3
Warner Robins	26 883	2.65	17.4	34.8	338	223	208	115	4 577	6 391	508	5 883	44 232	43.3	20.3
HAWAII	449 296	3.00	12.3	24.0	42 880	11 306	5 198	31 574	46 408	3 305	252	3 054	948 912	37.3	30.3
East Honolulu CDP	16 724	2.85	9.2	17.5	235	160	160	75	NA	NA	NA	NA	36 004	21.0	53.2
Hilo CDP	15 133	2.84	15.0	26.6	1 648	605	575	1 043	NA	NA	NA	NA	30 863	40.4	28.0
Kahului CDP	6 641	3.72	19.8	18.7	1 740	1 296	564	444	NA	NA	NA	NA	18 121	53.7	16.4
Kailua CDP (Honolulu County)	12 691	3.15	13.1	17.7	119	30	8	89	NA	NA	NA	NA	28 968	24.7	43.6
Kaneohe CDP	10 564	3.07	14.5	16.1	643	411	411	232	NA	NA	NA	NA	24 561	38.3	34.0
Mililani Town CDP	9 128	3.09	10.7	16.0	0	0	0	0	NA	NA	NA	NA	19 525	28.2	32.8
Pearl City CDP	14 125	3.33	14.5	16.8	3 694	165	156	3 529	NA	NA	NA	NA	33 712	35.1	28.9
Urban Honolulu CDP	127 736	2.59	11.8	33.9	13 052	4 247	1 823	8 805	NA	NA	NA	NA	248 332	36.7	35.0
Waipahu CDP	8 050	4.65	19.4	12.7	910	390	369	520	NA	NA	NA	NA	26 465	50.3	16.0
IDAHO	583 452	2.69	9.8	24.3	28 951	17 076	4 820	11 875	33 553	2 081	217	1 864	1 014 097	38.3	25.6
Boise City	87 344	2.39	9.9	30.6	3 717	1 762	548	1 955	5 311	2 478	260	2 218	141 745	26.4	38.9
Caldwell	16 026	2.92	14.3	27.0	1 532	913	149	619	1 264	2 630	283	2 347	27 963	50.7	14.9
Coeur d'Alene	18 419	2.42	12.4	31.4	1 215	813	428	402	1 995	4 335	561	3 774	29 439	36.5	24.7
Idaho Falls	21 016	2.70	13.7	26.3	1 011	477	72	534	1 748	3 004	213	2 791	36 124	37.0	25.1
Lewiston	13 072	2.37	11.3	29.2	966	594	385	372	1 222	3 808	153	3 655	21 810	38.5	23.6
Meridian	27 420	2.93	8.9	19.4	307	126	103	181	1 143	1 393	129	1 264	48 864	28.5	33.8
Nampa	27 872	2.96	14.2	23.2	1 751	540	360	1 211	2 106	2 488	242	2 246	48 550	47.6	18.0
Pocatello	20 601	2.57	10.4	30.5	1 519	630	307	889	1 990	3 622	359	3 264	33 020	33.9	29.9
Post Falls	11 003	2.60	18.1	21.7	84	42	42	42	875	3 022	245	2 776	18 731	35.1	18.9
Rexburg	7 378	3.45	7.1	13.4	1 027	127	44	900	201	764	27	738	9 019	12.9	36.8
Twin Falls	16 312	2.72	12.6	24.4	897	592	314	305	1 441	3 176	262	2 913	27 710	42.7	18.4
ILLINOIS	4 763 457	2.64	12.7	28.9	301 773	159 989	81 516	141 784	341 957	2 655	380	2 274	8 556 788	39.6	31.7
Addison	11 997	3.08	15.4	19.8	112	46	0	66	680	1 819	107	1 712	23 738	52.3	20.0
Algonquin	10 456	2.86	6.9	18.4	0	0	0	0	537	1 791	60	1 731	19 836	23.1	45.8
Alton	11 996	2.24	17.7	35.1	518	356	202	162	1 425	5 224	429	4 795	18 621	41.7	18.2
Arlington Heights	30 142	2.48	6.2	28.7	723	545	538	178	842	1 108	55	1 053	54 511	22.9	53.7
Aurora	61 506	3.20	13.2	21.0	2 477	751	577	1 726	3 573	1 782	300	1 482	120 268	44.5	31.1
Bartlett	14 343	2.89	6.7	16.2	58	58	58	0	288	690	43	647	28 457	25.5	43.8
Batavia	9 340	2.77	7.5	22.4	157	148	148	9	371	1 405	76	1 329	17 164	20.0	50.8
Belleville	17 698	2.39	18.4	35.6	1 246	1 167	740	79	1 964	4 512	519	3 993	29 981	35.8	23.1
Belvidere	8 426	3.07	14.4	22.6	230	221	150	9	404	1 596	115	1 482	15 603	60.0	11.4
Berwyn	17 919	3.16	16.4	24.3	52	17	14	35	1 315	2 314	206	2 108	35 689	51.8	18.2
Bloomington	30 826	2.46	10.1	31.4	2 234	566	280	1 668	2 300	2 946	511	2 435	50 041	27.8	46.3
Bolingbrook	21 757	3.38	13.1	15.8	279	279	279	0	1 305	1 758	234	1 524	45 662	35.1	36.7
Buffalo Grove	16 117	2.59	6.6	24.7	118	112	112	6	341	816	19	797	29 574	15.2	62.7

1. No spouse present. 2. Data for serious crimes have not been adjusted for underreporting. This may affect comparability between geographic areas and over time. 3. Per 100,000 population estimated by the FBI. 4. Persons 25 years old and over.

City	Money income, 2011–2013: Per capita income[1] (dollars)	Money income, 2011–2013: Households: Median income	Money income, 2011–2013: Households: Percent with income of $200,000 or more	Money income, 2011–2013: Households: Percent with income of less than $25,000	Money income, 2011–2013: Families with income below poverty (percent)	Housing units, 2010: Total	Housing units, 2010: Percent change, 2000–2010	Housing units, 2010: Vacant units for sale or rent[2]	Occupied housing units 2011–2013: Total	Occupied housing units 2011–2013: Owner-occupied: Percent	Occupied housing units 2011–2013: Owner-occupied: Median value[3] (dollars)	Occupied housing units 2011–2013: Median owner costs as a percent of income: With a mortgage[4]	Occupied housing units 2011–2013: Median owner costs as a percent of income: Without a mortgage[5]
	42	43	44	45	46	47	48	49	50	51	52	53	54
GEORGIA	24 762	47 893	3.9	26.6	14.6	4 088 801	24.6	503 217	3 522 934	63.7	143 900	23.3	11.6
Albany	16 508	29 111	1.2	43.5	28.7	33 436	3.9	3 655	28 980	39.4	96 700	23.3	14.0
Alpharetta	41 331	84 222	13.0	13.4	5.7	23 029	57.2	1 287	22 501	64.3	312 200	21.8	11.0
Athens-Clarke County	18 885	31 884	2.8	41.8	23.6	51 068	21.2	5 654	41 332	42.1	152 600	22.6	11.6
Atlanta	36 091	46 783	8.5	31.3	19.7	224 573	20.1	39 431	181 002	44.2	198 200	23.9	13.6
Augusta-Richmond County	20 357	36 950	1.6	35.1	21.4	86 331	4.9	9 407	69 773	52.3	103 100	23.2	11.7
Columbus	22 576	41 170	2.6	31.2	15.5	82 690	8.5	8 609	71 351	50.5	131 000	23.0	11.0
Dalton	18 248	32 955	3.5	35.6	22.0	13 378	29.8	2 041	11 403	46.7	119 400	24.0	10.0
Douglasville	20 627	45 049	1.9	27.2	21.3	13 163	66.4	1 536	11 124	47.3	122 600	25.9	10.3
Duluth	29 380	58 931	3.2	21.8	16.4	11 313	23.6	758	10 737	51.7	169 400	21.3	10.0
Dunwoody	42 585	74 864	11.7	12.9	9.0	21 671	48.4	1 727	19 314	53.1	351 400	22.6	12.0
East Point	18 219	35 061	1.5	38.3	25.1	17 225	11.1	3 892	12 846	44.4	86 000	27.4	12.8
Gainesville	20 356	37 914	4.0	32.6	25.7	12 967	45.5	1 694	11 090	37.1	143 700	25.3	11.7
Hinesville	20 658	41 883	1.5	24.1	14.0	14 653	24.4	2 329	12 882	47.4	124 500	26.2	11.1
Johns Creek	42 322	101 829	18.6	7.6	4.6	27 744	NA	1 478	26 310	79.1	316 300	20.9	10.0
Kennesaw	28 878	57 662	1.7	15.4	5.4	12 328	40.7	915	12 474	61.8	142 800	23.8	10.0
LaGrange	18 461	30 732	2.3	43.5	29.0	12 846	16.7	1 603	11 078	38.9	104 000	26.5	12.5
Lawrenceville	18 440	38 785	0.5	33.5	19.4	11 187	45.8	1 214	9 981	50.8	114 500	22.9	13.3
Macon	15 193	25 063	1.4	49.9	33.9	42 794	-3.8	7 191	32 589	41.9	84 500	27.0	14.2
Marietta	24 462	40 345	2.7	28.9	18.2	26 918	6.0	3 853	23 402	41.9	197 200	23.0	11.0
Milton	57 345	112 905	26.7	6.6	2.2	12 328	NA	669	12 229	68.7	422 800	19.3	10.0
Newnan	24 660	48 664	3.2	27.8	19.1	13 860	108.6	1 421	12 831	54.9	174 300	22.9	10.0
Peachtree City	36 616	87 683	9.5	11.0	5.4	13 538	17.8	812	12 230	73.0	269 300	21.5	10.8
Rome	18 405	32 321	0.7	40.3	24.0	15 797	9.3	1 912	13 537	48.4	114 900	25.0	14.0
Roswell	40 903	77 266	13.0	13.2	6.5	36 344	15.8	2 399	34 348	66.6	283 000	20.8	10.0
Sandy Springs	50 436	60 777	14.1	19.5	8.7	46 955	9.9	4 621	42 351	45.0	416 600	20.5	10.0
Savannah	19 928	36 144	1.9	36.8	20.8	61 883	7.6	9 338	52 618	45.4	142 000	26.7	12.9
Smyrna	37 250	58 454	6.5	18.8	9.9	25 745	30.6	2 743	23 311	49.9	194 600	19.8	10.1
Statesboro	11 824	21 375	1.2	54.9	30.0	11 602	25.3	1 395	10 081	22.6	124 300	23.0	13.8
Stockbridge	21 487	51 992	1.2	19.1	13.3	10 312	NA	813	9 416	54.7	119 900	24.4	14.5
Valdosta	16 719	28 140	1.7	43.8	25.0	22 709	19.5	2 238	21 457	35.8	126 700	25.1	13.0
Warner Robins	20 463	43 683	0.8	29.1	20.3	29 084	33.2	2 948	26 883	56.2	111 600	20.8	10.7
HAWAII	28 825	66 308	5.8	17.2	8.0	519 508	12.8	64 170	449 296	56.5	495 400	28.9	10.0
East Honolulu CDP	46 592	106 926	17.9	8.4	3.3	18 774	NA	1 090	16 724	82.4	795 100	28.8	10.3
Hilo CDP	25 224	51 946	3.2	24.2	11.9	16 905	5.5	1 422	15 133	65.3	292 000	23.8	10.0
Kahului CDP	21 456	61 022	4.2	16.2	5.4	7 773	28.6	662	6 641	53.0	465 700	31.5	10.0
Kailua CDP (Honolulu County)	41 686	102 928	15.5	7.2	2.9	13 650	6.9	729	12 691	72.9	796 800	28.3	11.0
Kaneohe CDP	31 959	79 205	7.2	10.6	3.9	11 553	0.7	415	10 564	69.0	629 000	29.1	10.0
Mililani Town CDP	35 131	91 098	7.2	6.6	3.2	9 272	0.0	234	9 128	79.1	539 900	24.9	10.0
Pearl City CDP	29 957	82 748	6.0	12.0	5.0	14 622	60.5	354	14 125	71.1	576 400	25.0	10.0
Urban Honolulu CDP	30 378	59 490	5.4	20.1	8.4	143 173	NA	13 765	127 736	41.8	563 300	28.9	11.4
Waipahu CDP	20 586	69 882	6.1	18.4	9.7	8 850	10.2	467	8 050	55.4	517 900	26.1	10.0
IDAHO	22 332	46 011	2.2	25.1	11.3	667 796	26.5	88 388	583 452	68.7	157 700	23.5	10.0
Boise City	27 616	46 757	3.7	25.2	10.0	92 700	18.9	6 996	87 344	59.6	168 900	22.1	10.0
Caldwell	15 554	39 965	0.6	32.4	16.9	16 323	68.4	1 428	16 026	66.2	94 400	25.0	10.9
Coeur d'Alene	22 200	40 440	1.4	27.3	10.0	20 219	36.8	1 824	18 419	58.6	162 800	22.3	10.0
Idaho Falls	22 209	44 195	2.6	26.8	12.4	22 977	15.9	1 774	21 016	66.0	138 300	20.8	10.0
Lewiston	23 912	43 460	1.1	23.8	7.3	14 057	5.0	733	13 072	68.1	166 400	24.2	11.8
Meridian	25 848	62 007	2.8	15.1	7.2	26 674	117.1	1 372	27 420	73.2	181 500	22.0	10.0
Nampa	16 035	39 092	0.4	29.2	19.9	30 507	56.2	2 778	27 872	62.8	101 900	25.6	11.9
Pocatello	20 321	40 434	0.9	32.1	13.8	22 404	8.3	1 572	20 601	60.9	132 900	22.2	10.1
Post Falls	22 659	50 503	1.1	19.2	11.4	11 150	66.7	887	11 003	67.8	158 100	24.0	10.0
Rexburg	12 453	25 481	0.7	48.4	32.7	7 617	69.2	438	7 378	32.4	166 100	23.0	10.0
Twin Falls	19 110	41 028	1.6	26.3	14.0	18 033	27.4	1 289	16 312	57.4	141 900	24.6	10.0
ILLINOIS	29 338	55 799	5.3	22.5	10.9	5 296 715	8.4	459 743	4 763 457	66.7	172 600	24.3	13.5
Addison	23 539	52 587	2.9	23.1	14.9	12 581	7.3	641	11 997	66.5	219 800	27.6	17.7
Algonquin	38 392	94 162	10.6	10.1	3.3	10 727	33.4	480	10 456	88.3	231 000	22.9	15.9
Alton	20 000	35 608	0.6	34.5	16.6	13 266	-4.5	1 532	11 996	59.4	82 300	23.2	12.4
Arlington Heights	40 390	77 280	8.0	12.4	2.4	32 795	3.4	1 876	30 142	70.0	300 200	25.1	14.9
Aurora	26 445	61 657	5.6	15.9	11.2	67 273	37.5	4 709	61 506	68.2	168 300	26.0	13.4
Bartlett	37 864	97 590	7.3	9.8	2.1	14 509	17.4	436	14 343	91.1	248 300	26.6	14.4
Batavia	39 317	92 580	12.2	13.9	4.8	10 042	13.9	488	9 340	74.5	265 600	23.3	11.4
Belleville	23 715	44 221	1.2	28.5	15.4	21 099	9.4	2 304	17 698	63.4	101 500	22.5	12.4
Belvidere	19 570	46 148	2.2	27.2	14.3	9 565	20.5	762	8 426	75.6	104 900	25.6	13.6
Berwyn	21 361	54 715	1.0	22.6	11.7	20 719	0.1	1 809	17 919	59.6	169 200	29.1	18.2
Bloomington	32 793	61 836	6.2	20.4	7.8	34 339	20.4	2 676	30 826	62.2	161 300	19.8	12.0
Bolingbrook	27 593	76 598	5.0	12.2	8.4	23 141	29.2	929	21 757	82.5	198 100	25.9	13.4
Buffalo Grove	43 286	96 626	12.2	11.3	2.3	17 034	6.9	828	16 117	80.3	286 100	24.1	14.6

1. Based on population estimated by the American Community Survey. 2. Includes units rented or sold but not occupied. 3. Specified owner-occupied units; $1,000,000 represents $1,000,000 or more 4. 50.0 represents 50 percent or more. 5. 10.0 represents 10 percent or less.

City	Occupied housing units, 2011–2013 (cont.)				Migration, 2011–2013		Civilian labor force, 2014				Civilian employment[4], 2011–2013			
									Unemployment			Percent		
	Percent renter occupied	Median gross rent[1]	Median rent as a percent of income[2]	Percent with no vehicle available	Percent who lived in the same house one year ago	Percent who lived outside current city one year ago	Total	Percent change, 2013–2014	Total	Rate[3]	Population age 16 and older	In labor force	Civilian full-year full-time workers	Households with no workers (percent)
	55	56	57	58	59	60	61	62	63	64	65	66	67	68
GEORGIA	36.3	854	31.9	6.8	83.7	13.3	4 756 708	0.0	342 365	7.2	7 691 492	63.2	39.4	26.5
Albany	60.6	674	34.7	14.3	82.6	7.9	31 436	-2.5	3 002	9.5	59 558	58.2	31.5	38.3
Alpharetta	35.7	1 129	23.0	4.9	85.4	13.1	33 419	1.2	1 780	5.3	44 826	71.0	50.6	15.0
Athens-Clarke County	57.9	747	37.6	7.3	75.5	12.9	57 688	-0.2	3 985	6.9	99 793	58.8	28.6	29.5
Atlanta	55.8	953	31.5	16.9	76.6	12.0	231 228	0.4	17 950	7.8	366 651	65.0	39.8	28.1
Augusta-Richmond County	47.7	778	33.0	9.5	80.8	9.8	85 777	-1.1	7 436	8.7	153 643	59.1	33.1	32.4
Columbus	49.5	806	30.9	10.7	75.0	12.9	81 544	-1.9	6 965	8.5	154 621	62.0	34.1	31.1
Dalton	53.3	636	30.1	10.8	79.0	10.5	14 292	0.1	1 195	8.4	25 096	64.3	40.8	28.7
Douglasville	52.7	918	31.4	4.3	78.1	17.7	15 959	0.2	1 284	8.0	23 053	68.5	39.7	20.6
Duluth	48.3	979	28.6	2.8	87.0	11.5	15 183	0.4	1 007	6.6	21 857	66.9	44.9	24.3
Dunwoody	46.9	1 129	27.1	3.6	83.5	13.8	25 724	0.9	1 397	5.4	36 665	70.2	50.1	19.4
East Point	55.6	862	39.6	19.7	81.2	14.1	17 031	0.0	1 757	10.3	27 055	64.9	36.3	31.9
Gainesville	62.9	775	30.9	14.9	77.7	13.3	16 146	0.4	1 072	6.6	25 765	63.7	37.2	26.1
Hinesville	52.6	878	28.2	5.3	73.7	21.5	15 000	-1.5	1 130	7.5	25 193	70.8	35.7	16.9
Johns Creek	20.9	1 286	24.5	1.4	89.3	7.9	42 767	1.0	2 271	5.3	61 156	69.1	48.4	13.0
Kennesaw	38.2	1 060	28.6	5.1	80.1	16.7	18 482	0.8	1 262	6.8	25 009	76.3	46.9	15.2
LaGrange	61.1	745	35.4	15.7	71.9	14.1	15 134	-0.1	1 272	8.4	22 976	59.5	36.8	34.8
Lawrenceville	49.2	854	41.2	7.4	83.9	14.7	14 314	0.0	1 155	8.1	22 078	65.2	40.3	22.7
Macon	58.1	673	39.8	18.6	75.9	9.1	35 967	-0.9	3 503	9.7	69 153	54.3	27.6	40.6
Marietta	58.1	867	33.8	9.1	73.5	18.3	33 903	0.8	2 255	6.7	46 392	74.6	41.3	18.6
Milton	31.3	1 168	22.0	2.1	90.7	9.2	NA	NA	NA	NA	25 667	65.3	47.0	15.1
Newnan	45.1	921	29.1	6.3	80.0	16.0	15 805	0.6	1 107	7.0	25 008	64.9	42.5	28.4
Peachtree City	27.0	1 132	24.3	2.2	85.9	10.7	17 655	1.2	1 028	5.8	26 909	65.8	42.1	24.1
Rome	51.6	609	31.5	14.0	78.9	10.5	15 372	-1.0	1 393	9.1	28 188	56.7	32.3	37.6
Roswell	33.4	970	31.2	6.4	87.2	9.2	51 740	0.8	2 678	5.2	72 615	70.0	50.1	19.0
Sandy Springs	55.0	967	28.5	7.7	77.8	19.8	58 531	0.9	3 268	5.6	78 271	74.6	49.7	19.5
Savannah	54.6	884	35.8	12.1	79.0	11.8	64 915	0.3	5 268	8.1	113 567	61.2	35.3	30.4
Smyrna	50.1	900	28.4	4.0	75.2	20.1	32 331	0.9	1 943	6.0	41 601	77.7	55.8	16.5
Statesboro	77.4	719	45.4	9.4	65.5	26.2	13 391	0.4	1 268	9.5	26 263	49.5	20.3	30.5
Stockbridge	45.3	993	29.4	2.8	82.3	16.3	13 228	0.0	1 191	9.0	19 892	64.9	44.1	21.9
Valdosta	64.2	736	34.7	10.5	71.7	13.4	25 660	-0.6	1 952	7.6	45 466	63.3	30.3	32.3
Warner Robins	43.8	828	31.3	4.9	83.4	9.5	31 581	-2.2	2 329	7.4	53 495	66.8	41.4	25.0
HAWAII	43.5	1 387	33.2	8.8	84.9	11.4	668 177	2.6	29 153	4.4	1 116 841	65.1	39.5	23.0
East Honolulu CDP	17.6	2 000	29.7	4.3	92.1	5.4	NA	NA	NA	NA	40 215	62.7	42.9	26.6
Hilo CDP	34.7	859	34.2	5.8	90.2	5.1	NA	NA	NA	NA	36 785	57.0	35.2	31.2
Kahului CDP	47.0	1 098	28.7	9.8	79.2	12.1	NA	NA	NA	NA	21 623	66.4	38.0	21.6
Kailua CDP (Honolulu County)	27.1	2 000	31.4	2.3	89.1	8.0	NA	NA	NA	NA	33 191	66.8	42.2	19.6
Kaneohe CDP	31.0	1 862	35.2	4.0	88.4	9.0	NA	NA	NA	NA	28 101	65.5	41.1	20.8
Mililani Town CDP	20.9	1 902	37.3	2.5	90.3	7.7	NA	NA	NA	NA	22 997	67.6	42.0	19.6
Pearl City CDP	28.9	1 775	33.4	5.5	89.1	9.5	NA	NA	NA	NA	39 275	63.0	38.6	23.2
Urban Honolulu CDP	58.2	1 247	31.8	18.9	85.0	7.9	NA	NA	NA	NA	289 481	63.5	40.6	25.2
Waipahu CDP	44.6	1 163	30.9	11.0	89.4	7.7	NA	NA	NA	NA	31 633	62.9	38.4	21.3
IDAHO	31.3	718	29.8	4.7	82.7	11.6	777 238	0.8	37 404	4.8	1 214 167	63.2	37.3	27.3
Boise City	40.4	779	29.9	6.4	79.2	9.5	115 570	1.7	4 559	3.9	171 251	68.8	41.0	24.9
Caldwell	33.8	669	30.3	7.3	79.8	13.2	22 157	1.3	1 354	6.1	34 565	65.0	36.2	29.6
Coeur d'Alene	41.4	771	35.2	6.0	78.2	12.3	23 164	1.9	1 207	5.2	36 000	63.1	33.4	28.7
Idaho Falls	34.0	666	30.4	7.1	83.4	8.8	27 394	1.2	1 210	4.4	42 988	64.8	39.6	25.9
Lewiston	31.9	628	26.7	5.6	87.0	7.1	17 205	1.0	663	3.9	25 935	64.3	38.3	30.1
Meridian	26.8	974	29.6	3.4	85.4	9.3	40 045	2.1	1 637	4.1	56 213	68.8	48.4	21.3
Nampa	37.2	750	31.9	6.2	79.2	12.2	37 850	1.0	2 172	5.7	59 797	63.4	36.5	28.6
Pocatello	39.1	598	31.1	6.6	75.6	11.0	28 396	0.7	1 264	4.5	41 856	66.1	35.5	25.6
Post Falls	32.2	857	28.0	4.1	82.9	10.4	15 285	2.0	813	5.3	21 537	67.0	41.9	23.9
Rexburg	67.6	632	42.9	5.0	48.5	31.0	13 256	2.1	448	3.4	20 719	60.9	20.0	17.4
Twin Falls	42.6	684	28.0	4.7	74.1	12.8	22 117	-1.1	971	4.4	34 448	64.3	40.2	23.8
ILLINOIS	33.3	884	30.6	10.9	86.7	8.1	6 524 579	-0.5	460 363	7.1	10 167 657	66.1	40.6	26.0
Addison	33.5	901	31.3	4.5	85.3	7.3	19 687	0.0	1 334	6.8	28 023	70.4	41.8	22.6
Algonquin	11.7	1 326	24.6	2.1	91.7	7.2	16 992	0.0	985	5.8	22 943	74.5	51.5	15.8
Alton	40.6	722	31.7	10.4	87.2	7.6	11 738	-1.3	1 188	10.1	21 571	61.4	34.7	36.3
Arlington Heights	24.0	1 142	26.9	6.4	89.7	8.7	41 221	0.4	2 227	5.4	61 753	66.6	42.8	25.4
Aurora	31.8	1 017	31.4	5.4	84.8	7.8	101 726	-0.3	7 009	6.9	144 256	73.2	46.9	14.7
Bartlett	8.9	1 222	31.1	3.3	94.3	5.1	23 524	0.1	1 365	5.8	32 688	72.6	47.9	16.5
Batavia	25.5	1 005	28.2	4.7	93.0	5.2	13 714	0.5	842	6.1	19 914	71.9	46.8	22.2
Belleville	36.6	709	33.6	8.7	90.2	7.4	22 532	-0.9	1 796	8.0	35 254	64.2	41.1	27.6
Belvidere	24.4	662	29.2	7.5	86.0	5.4	11 744	-0.7	1 102	9.4	19 546	66.1	41.0	27.4
Berwyn	40.4	912	29.8	10.9	86.2	9.6	28 148	-0.8	2 198	7.8	42 559	67.2	42.6	23.3
Bloomington	37.8	745	25.1	8.9	81.7	9.8	41 172	-1.7	2 368	5.8	60 560	71.9	47.4	20.6
Bolingbrook	17.5	1 046	37.9	3.0	93.2	5.1	40 231	-0.2	2 771	6.9	55 036	72.5	47.7	11.9
Buffalo Grove	19.7	1 221	26.9	5.5	89.7	9.2	24 485	0.5	1 295	5.3	33 214	73.5	50.8	17.4

1. $2,000 represents $2,000 or more. 2. 50.0 represents 50 percent or more. 3. Percent of civilian labor force. 4. Persons 16 years old and over.

Table D. Cities — **Construction, Wholesale Trade, and Retail Trade**

City	Value of residential construction authorized by building permits, 2014: New construction ($1,000)	Number of housing units	Percent single family	Wholesale trade,[1] 2007: Number of establish-ments	Number of employees	Sales (mil dol)	Annual payroll (mil dol)	Retail trade,[2] 2007: Number of establish-ments	Number of employees	Sales (mil dol)	Annual payroll (mil dol)
	69	70	71	72	73	74	75	76	77	78	79
GEORGIA	6 541 383	39 423	69.8	11 545	166 619	141 962.4	8 246.5	36 218	475 344	117 516.9	10 760.2
Albany	7 154	80	55.0	137	1 857	1 108.6	73.6	495	6 561	1 428.5	129.1
Alpharetta	103 284	288	100.0	167	4 459	18 722.2	338.4	404	8 233	1 941.3	185.8
Athens-Clarke County	50 528	538	21.6	106	1 994	1 782.5	84.1	553	7 752	1 669.1	161.5
Atlanta	618 660	4 505	12.1	706	9 721	7 523.6	501.2	1 943	26 962	5 594.1	643.9
Augusta-Richmond County	NA	NA	NA	196	2 249	916.4	94.3	895	11 084	2 505.1	233.6
Columbus	53 634	585	56.9	173	1 906	1 173.6	81.2	845	12 642	2 889.2	260.7
Dalton	NA	NA	NA	132	2 689	977.8	103.3	312	3 304	828.4	73.2
Douglasville	14 879	44	100.0	25	175	57.5	8.4	270	5 181	1 034.5	100.4
Duluth	10 071	38	100.0	129	2 692	2 034.2	226.5	263	4 656	1 766.7	166.3
Dunwoody	18 011	40	100.0	57	D	D	D	286	6 132	1 016.3	126.8
East Point	5 071	40	100.0	32	591	437.9	29.6	103	1 325	271.2	26.4
Gainesville	43 507	259	97.7	107	1 554	3 411.9	65.1	341	4 748	1 138.6	115.1
Hinesville	37 183	171	74.3	2	D	D	D	137	1 585	379.8	33.6
Johns Creek	46 501	125	100.0	70	316	327.8	20.3	161	2 240	409.2	47.3
Kennesaw	33 658	289	12.8	97	1 790	971.6	91.6	169	2 587	665.6	64.7
LaGrange	8 995	38	100.0	30	577	365.5	23.9	212	2 831	670.2	60.6
Lawrenceville	9 152	48	91.7	116	1 348	1 083.1	63.6	381	4 681	1 074.3	112.8
Macon	NA	NA	NA	142	2 113	1 085.4	91.3	677	9 114	1 838.5	186.0
Marietta	36 810	145	92.4	300	4 304	2 585.3	213.1	463	7 449	2 465.7	223.1
Milton	72 956	344	100.0	17	81	76.8	11.2	30	351	61.4	7.7
Newnan	94 154	316	100.0	28	562	345.8	23.7	201	3 320	736.0	71.5
Peachtree City	12 022	39	100.0	91	985	620.1	50.1	159	2 667	533.2	53.9
Rome	NA	NA	NA	72	1 028	510.7	37.4	315	4 049	897.2	81.9
Roswell	71 098	172	100.0	191	1 892	1 568.3	135.3	386	5 589	1 761.7	162.0
Sandy Springs	103 725	1 743	14.7	150	3 211	6 167.9	285.4	270	3 899	1 176.9	121.0
Savannah	83 848	364	93.7	183	2 113	1 633.9	106.6	941	11 511	2 521.2	250.3
Smyrna	30 160	429	36.1	87	2 677	2 088.3	139.8	213	2 981	1 069.5	83.1
Statesboro	25 487	348	10.1	22	119	60.3	3.9	227	3 163	636.9	62.6
Stockbridge	NA	NA	NA	9	D	D	D	95	1 827	391.9	41.2
Valdosta	9 924	76	81.6	90	828	565.8	33.9	393	5 343	1 220.8	109.1
Warner Robins	36 837	195	96.9	23	222	59.9	8.3	295	4 669	1 080.6	104.3
HAWAII	1 011 786	3 066	71.7	1 629	17 707	8 894.7	699.1	5 012	70 661	17 611.9	1 766.4
East Honolulu CDP	NA	NA	NA	NA	NA	NA	NA	NA	NA	NA	NA
Hilo CDP	NA	NA	NA	77	950	428.4	30.2	258	4 178	1 156.3	108.9
Kahului CDP	NA	NA	NA	52	652	356.3	32.8	213	4 591	1 329.0	133.1
Kailua CDP (Honolulu County)	NA	NA	NA	23	74	21.8	3.5	103	1 578	350.9	38.2
Kaneohe CDP	NA	NA	NA	19	39	15.1	1.6	129	2 113	555.3	51.6
Mililani Town CDP	NA	NA	NA	7	10	2.2	0.3	36	1 106	248.1	26.0
Pearl City CDP	NA	NA	NA	32	378	228.8	15.2	50	1 666	474.2	39.1
Urban Honolulu CDP	NA	NA	NA	NA	NA	NA	NA	NA	NA	NA	NA
Waipahu CDP	NA	NA	NA	51	904	302.9	34.2	104	2 560	858.3	80.1
IDAHO	1 654 793	8 797	71.5	1 846	21 844	14 286.7	900.0	6 300	80 447	20 526.6	1 833.6
Boise City	195 635	1 260	37.1	354	5 159	4 925.8	259.2	1 002	16 168	3 893.1	366.1
Caldwell	55 613	415	99.0	35	240	83.4	9.5	132	2 148	611.8	54.1
Coeur d'Alene	64 628	458	53.1	46	713	379.1	28.0	333	4 317	1 234.6	110.5
Idaho Falls	9 971	106	100.0	96	1 192	1 151.1	47.5	389	5 750	1 453.1	121.4
Lewiston	9 573	55	47.3	41	490	434.9	19.6	202	2 700	680.5	67.0
Meridian	236 665	1 260	60.6	85	1 463	683.9	76.2	204	3 967	1 329.0	112.5
Nampa	52 956	389	78.7	94	1 148	709.7	54.2	311	5 342	1 483.9	134.9
Pocatello	7 408	65	100.0	65	579	383.1	20.8	250	3 246	762.6	67.8
Post Falls	32 476	161	96.3	21	318	181.8	16.8	108	1 598	519.9	41.4
Rexburg	50 697	355	14.9	27	342	139.5	8.5	102	1 586	386.3	35.3
Twin Falls	37 828	250	80.4	75	897	330.6	29.4	354	4 897	1 150.3	108.6
ILLINOIS	4 211 740	20 578	51.3	16 704	259 758	231 082.8	14 319.6	43 055	639 147	165 450.5	14 895.5
Addison	2 260	6	100.0	205	0 703	1 899.4	203.5	112	2 793	1 090.5	95.3
Algonquin	14 262	81	22.2	24	79	38.7	4.6	155	3 105	635.4	55.6
Alton	70	1	100.0	26	268	189.2	10.9	181	2 774	601.0	62.0
Arlington Heights	32 625	100	96.0	202	1 856	1 395.4	119.5	256	4 269	978.0	98.5
Aurora	26 275	101	100.0	138	2 866	7 694.2	151.8	597	10 131	2 148.1	204.5
Bartlett	3 280	16	100.0	51	548	318.2	26.1	49	744	150.8	16.2
Batavia	6 395	22	100.0	81	1 533	2 074.0	81.6	89	2 032	470.8	42.2
Belleville	4 147	28	100.0	38	424	207.0	18.4	203	2 498	616.4	66.2
Belvidere	790	5	100.0	11	119	78.2	5.8	79	1 366	365.2	30.9
Berwyn	282	1	100.0	10	54	7.0	1.2	127	1 378	328.8	36.9
Bloomington	20 013	108	94.4	75	1 344	3 984.1	73.8	382	5 581	1 298.3	118.7
Bolingbrook	20 448	124	100.0	86	5 309	4 024.5	250.8	204	4 916	1 046.4	102.9
Buffalo Grove	2 179	8	100.0	119	2 491	2 170.3	157.3	128	1 703	491.8	46.7

1. Merchant wholesalers except manufacturers' sales branches and offices. 2. Establishments with payroll.

City	Real estate and rental and leasing, 2007				Professional, scientific, and technical services,[1] 2007				Manufacturing, 2007			
	Number of establish-ments	Number of employees	Receipts (mil dol)	Annual payroll (mil dol)	Number of establish-ments	Number of employees	Receipts (mil dol)	Annual payroll (mil dol)	Number of establish-ments	Number of employees	Receipts (mil dol)	Annual payroll (mil dol)
	80	81	82	83	84	85	86	87	88	89	90	91
GEORGIA	12 620	65 875	14 021.9	2 903.2	27 668	213 419	34 966.0	12 689.5	8 699	411 158	144 280.8	16 128.1
Albany	129	564	78.6	14.9	192	D	D	D	70	4 975	3 263.0	246.5
Alpharetta	219	1 135	305.0	62.5	870	D	D	D	NA	NA	NA	NA
Athens-Clarke County	224	839	128.3	24.3	283	D	D	D	91	6 632	1 971.2	255.2
Atlanta	1 231	12 285	2 727.8	752.2	3 250	42 668	9 456.3	3 651.7	346	12 257	5 304.3	504.2
Augusta-Richmond County	233	1 449	220.1	38.5	437	3 181	397.2	144.3	129	9 055	5 256.3	452.0
Columbus	259	1 549	292.8	54.0	348	D	D	D	141	7 055	2 111.4	266.7
Dalton	66	281	41.4	7.7	117	D	D	D	191	16 869	6 207.2	531.4
Douglasville	60	225	33.0	6.7	130	587	51.9	21.6	NA	NA	NA	NA
Duluth	138	711	179.8	29.7	302	2 440	300.7	129.8	49	1 176	389.7	69.5
Dunwoody	147	1 016	551.9	122.8	505	5 866	921.7	381.2	16	D	D	D
East Point	36	620	92.7	14.1	71	D	D	D	31	854	295.9	36.5
Gainesville	97	300	76.0	10.5	201	D	D	D	111	8 629	2 533.2	308.6
Hinesville	42	182	26.8	4.6	34	194	16.1	4.6	NA	NA	NA	NA
Johns Creek	107	475	67.5	17.1	446	1 699	257.3	95.1	11	D	D	D
Kennesaw	65	268	46.7	8.1	166	645	73.7	27.6	58	1 380	326.3	58.5
LaGrange	50	406	34.8	8.0	62	325	29.8	13.6	47	4 325	1 613.2	184.0
Lawrenceville	89	438	73.4	16.0	251	D	D	D	74	2 976	933.7	133.5
Macon	147	838	163.1	23.3	311	D	D	D	91	2 482	644.5	113.5
Marietta	193	1 326	228.6	48.6	635	D	D	D	148	11 727	3 782.9	695.1
Milton	37	103	13.0	2.9	122	D	D	D	NA	NA	NA	NA
Newnan	66	233	40.8	7.4	87	420	54.3	19.5	34	1 378	344.6	47.7
Peachtree City	84	182	30.6	6.2	156	D	D	D	43	3 037	1 622.7	150.5
Rome	66	303	51.7	8.9	135	617	71.1	21.9	71	5 141	2 006.6	188.0
Roswell	214	839	193.5	37.1	792	7 311	811.2	307.9	57	694	107.3	27.5
Sandy Springs	368	D	D	D	976	10 482	2 097.8	754.7	NA	NA	NA	NA
Savannah	253	1 422	231.4	43.1	506	D	D	D	107	4 136	2 160.5	183.4
Smyrna	115	674	144.6	37.0	281	3 256	1 102.5	227.9	43	781	144.6	31.0
Statesboro	64	278	38.2	5.8	82	555	55.3	18.2	31	1 649	472.5	55.3
Stockbridge	36	100	18.4	2.8	77	487	60.2	20.4	NA	NA	NA	NA
Valdosta	94	675	64.1	16.7	168	D	D	D	71	3 570	1 918.8	124.4
Warner Robins	83	377	51.5	9.3	168	D	D	D	31	668	181.9	29.9
HAWAII	2 084	16 759	3 974.0	653.8	3 254	21 772	3 068.3	1 193.5	984	14 127	8 799.3	511.5
East Honolulu CDP	NA	NA	NA	NA	NA	NA	NA	NA	NA	NA	NA	NA
Hilo CDP	88	442	76.5	10.0	116	D	D	D	55	544	110.6	19.3
Kahului CDP	51	718	180.7	23.1	43	243	24.0	8.2	NA	NA	NA	NA
Kailua CDP (Honolulu County)	44	186	33.8	6.7	102	490	90.0	27.7	NA	NA	NA	NA
Kaneohe CDP	24	96	16.6	3.0	51	D	D	D	NA	NA	NA	NA
Mililani Town CDP	13	48	5.4	1.2	21	79	6.0	1.7	NA	NA	NA	NA
Pearl City CDP	12	53	6.1	1.3	16	90	8.5	4.0	NA	NA	NA	NA
Urban Honolulu CDP	NA	NA	NA	NA	NA	NA	NA	NA	NA	NA	NA	NA
Waipahu CDP	30	156	20.9	4.6	14	156	9.8	3.9	NA	NA	NA	NA
IDAHO	2 530	8 371	1 241.7	233.5	4 189	D	D	D	1 942	64 778	18 011.0	2 829.4
Boise City	545	2 533	396.3	88.0	1 173	D	D	D	223	18 120	4 442.3	1 138.1
Caldwell	51	220	20.1	4.4	50	D	D	D	69	2 147	D	66.6
Coeur d'Alene	122	580	117.6	20.1	250	D	D	D	67	1 211	388.1	45.5
Idaho Falls	119	451	74.6	10.4	308	D	D	D	76	1 302	376.8	48.0
Lewiston	37	D	D	D	74	D	D	D	29	D	D	45.2
Meridian	155	530	69.0	18.7	171	860	131.3	38.1	51	1 342	225.3	47.3
Nampa	121	323	39.7	6.5	137	762	68.0	27.7	97	4 996	1 412.6	184.2
Pocatello	81	263	43.4	5.8	136	D	D	D	45	D	634.8	D
Post Falls	44	123	15.0	2.9	52	668	61.3	25.8	47	1 266	217.0	45.4
Rexburg	47	145	19.6	2.6	52	873	34.0	9.7	18	D	D	D
Twin Falls	90	307	45.5	7.5	174	D	D	D	62	1 803	614.1	59.1
ILLINOIS	13 899	87 468	21 725.0	3 985.2	38 797	363 231	61 896.1	24 197.9	15 704	663 586	257 760.7	31 715.9
Addison	44	278	76.3	16.3	97	501	91.7	27.9	346	7 508	1 286.6	317.5
Algonquin	34	D	D	D	105	336	32.3	12.1	35	715	111.9	29.7
Alton	35	142	21.3	3.8	61	D	D	D	26	848	D	36.5
Arlington Heights	128	802	144.5	31.5	529	D	D	D	93	2 322	768.7	122.6
Aurora	132	818	127.6	20.2	413	2 269	297.6	115.6	157	9 917	4 331.0	506.8
Bartlett	27	75	13.4	2.6	125	285	48.5	14.8	26	1 102	274.2	49.6
Batavia	27	132	18.3	3.7	129	D	D	D	96	3 688	1 066.4	162.8
Belleville	64	239	32.7	6.3	171	1 118	132.1	64.3	49	1 856	435.7	73.7
Belvidere	18	57	6.9	1.1	41	D	D	D	35	5 701	5 359.5	348.1
Berwyn	45	127	18.0	2.6	77	312	27.7	11.1	14	503	D	D
Bloomington	103	565	90.9	14.4	224	D	D	D	60	2 753	821.0	129.9
Bolingbrook	45	172	31.3	4.5	149	932	99.8	37.7	52	3 218	1 362.4	131.7
Buffalo Grove	57	432	57.6	20.3	316	3 424	477.2	199.6	64	4 219	1 160.8	188.6

1. Establishments subject to federal tax.

Table D. Cities — **Accommodation and Food Services, Arts, Entertainment, and Recreation, and Health Care and Social Assistance**

City	Accommodation and food services, 2007: Number of establishments	Number of employees	Sales (mil dol)	Annual payroll (mil dol)	Arts, entertainment, and recreation,[1] 2007: Number of establishments	Number of employees	Receipts (mil dol)	Annual payroll (mil dol)	Health care and social assistance,[1] 2007: Number of establishments	Number of employees	Receipts (mil dol)	Annual payroll (mil dol)
	92	93	94	95	96	97	98	99	100	101	102	103
GEORGIA	18 640	355 423	16 976.2	4 704.4	2 319	31 121	2 527.7	836.4	18 379	229 101	23 274.0	9 144.8
Albany	208	4 015	165.6	41.3	18	D	D	D	237	D	D	D
Alpharetta	318	7 164	377.1	108.6	33	D	D	D	298	3 491	395.5	162.1
Athens-Clarke County	331	7 062	293.4	80.3	36	408	28.6	6.3	355	D	D	D
Atlanta	1 528	41 275	2 743.7	770.6	224	2 961	589.0	243.9	1 203	14 437	1 982.7	753.8
Augusta-Richmond County	431	9 726	395.4	108.6	32	D	D	D	548	7 955	964.8	347.7
Columbus	418	9 898	428.2	120.7	37	D	D	D	484	6 110	635.8	246.8
Dalton	143	2 775	117.2	31.6	8	D	D	D	132	D	D	D
Douglasville	137	3 446	145.2	40.0	9	210	10.0	2.4	108	D	D	D
Duluth	158	1 969	81.9	26.2	24	298	39.6	5.8	155	D	D	D
Dunwoody	119	3 326	198.3	59.0	13	D	D	D	180	2 292	259.8	98.3
East Point	74	1 889	119.7	34.9	13	31	11.6	2.8	82	D	D	D
Gainesville	156	2 562	116.4	30.6	16	D	D	D	245	D	D	D
Hinesville	70	1 294	50.2	12.0	1	D	D	D	42	461	28.2	11.9
Johns Creek	112	2 087	85.3	26.6	21	210	26.1	12.2	121	D	D	D
Kennesaw	100	1 760	76.1	21.7	19	D	D	D	74	D	D	D
LaGrange	92	1 878	71.7	19.3	6	D	D	D	86	D	D	D
Lawrenceville	137	2 044	106.7	27.6	20	D	D	D	231	D	D	D
Macon	261	4 791	184.4	49.9	14	D	D	D	393	D	D	D
Marietta	271	4 116	207.5	55.5	27	D	D	D	339	D	D	D
Milton	25	191	13.7	3.3	10	212	14.6	4.6	16	D	D	D
Newnan	104	2 566	104.0	30.4	7	D	D	D	72	D	D	D
Peachtree City	87	2 101	83.4	25.0	20	D	D	D	95	D	D	D
Rome	156	2 981	125.6	33.0	9	D	D	D	203	4 802	537.4	196.3
Roswell	239	3 862	181.7	52.9	44	441	30.7	9.2	340	5 303	459.1	183.0
Sandy Springs	264	4 087	250.2	65.2	44	574	38.7	12.4	598	7 763	1 218.0	497.0
Savannah	521	12 365	663.2	180.9	51	543	36.8	8.9	457	7 158	895.1	364.6
Smyrna	163	2 993	147.2	40.2	27	D	D	D	186	D	D	D
Statesboro	124	D	D	D	7	D	D	D	136	D	D	D
Stockbridge	68	957	39.7	9.4	11	D	D	D	131	D	D	D
Valdosta	171	4 114	159.6	41.9	9	76	4.3	1.1	244	D	D	D
Warner Robins	143	3 217	121.4	32.9	8	D	D	D	153	D	D	D
HAWAII	3 528	98 353	8 042.2	2 209.8	397	7 676	563.7	163.1	2 778	29 023	2 978.6	1 244.1
East Honolulu CDP	NA	NA	NA	NA	NA	NA	NA	NA	NA	NA	NA	NA
Hilo CDP	149	2 616	132.0	36.3	6	79	4.2	1.0	178	2 407	194.8	82.5
Kahului CDP	94	D	D	D	10	D	D	D	76	669	85.9	36.0
Kailua CDP (Honolulu County)	95	1 510	69.9	19.3	10	76	5.3	2.0	110	863	74.7	35.2
Kaneohe CDP	78	1 135	59.5	14.5	14	D	D	D	78	744	74.2	29.0
Mililani Town CDP	39	1 055	47.2	12.2	4	118	7.9	2.0	25	D	D	D
Pearl City CDP	43	716	36.8	9.7	1	D	D	D	32	409	45.1	19.3
Urban Honolulu CDP	NA	NA	NA	NA	NA	NA	NA	NA	NA	NA	NA	NA
Waipahu CDP	69	1 033	56.4	14.5	1	D	D	D	70	581	57.8	19.9
IDAHO	3 482	56 662	2 416.0	662.7	590	7 065	310.3	97.3	3 974	44 499	3 510.2	1 422.7
Boise City	606	13 055	593.2	163.9	67	1 514	56.5	16.7	832	9 567	901.7	402.3
Caldwell	63	971	36.8	10.3	6	D	D	D	90	1 327	118.2	44.3
Coeur d'Alene	192	3 801	180.7	50.1	29	D	D	D	246	D	D	D
Idaho Falls	166	3 070	124.0	33.5	21	D	D	D	382	4 361	379.9	147.3
Lewiston	91	1 664	63.9	20.0	10	D	D	D	125	D	D	D
Meridian	149	2 876	117.5	34.1	13	D	D	D	192	2 448	187.7	71.5
Nampa	145	2 698	97.0	25.9	15	426	7.3	2.5	175	D	D	D
Pocatello	130	2 350	92.7	25.1	14	D	D	D	225	D	D	D
Post Falls	62	1 034	39.1	12.1	8	D	D	D	80	D	D	D
Rexburg	46	1 028	29.5	8.3	7	111	4.2	1.0	74	D	D	D
Twin Falls	143	2 606	104.5	27.2	17	D	D	D	234	D	D	D
ILLINOIS	26 774	468 827	25 469.0	6 894.3	3 666	51 012	5 306.0	1 579.8	25 651	325 085	32 056.1	13 445.1
Addison	77	1 491	83.8	22.5	10	76	4.5	1.5	59	882	63.1	34.2
Algonquin	81	1 665	67.6	22.3	13	D	D	D	74	D	D	D
Alton	96	1 697	73.6	20.6	10	D	D	D	113	1 376	127.4	55.8
Arlington Heights	181	3 120	177.7	48.5	23	121	6.7	1.8	363	D	D	D
Aurora	267	4 486	211.9	57.6	31	1 781	475.8	43.6	277	4 139	491.5	190.6
Bartlett	50	615	33.3	7.7	8	139	4.0	1.5	54	D	D	D
Batavia	70	1 043	47.8	14.5	8	D	D	D	53	D	D	D
Belleville	145	1 964	87.4	23.0	14	D	D	D	203	3 418	332.9	166.7
Belvidere	51	754	35.3	9.3	6	49	2.3	0.5	39	D	D	D
Berwyn	94	1 184	61.5	15.4	9	76	5.3	1.7	138	3 191	343.6	156.5
Bloomington	233	5 530	221.2	65.5	24	355	11.8	3.7	184	2 680	306.2	138.0
Bolingbrook	139	2 787	143.5	41.2	14	257	10.1	4.7	100	907	72.3	33.0
Buffalo Grove	97	1 742	85.7	23.2	18	D	D	D	143	1 049	124.7	48.4

1. Establishments subject to federal tax.

Table D. Cities — **Other Services and Government Employment and Payroll**

City	Other services[1], 2007				Government employment and payroll, 2012								
						March payroll							
							Percent of total for:						
	Number of establish- ments	Number of employees	Receipts (mil dol)	Annual payroll (mil dol)	Full-time equivalent employees	Total (dollars)	Adminis- tration, judicial, and legal	Police and Corrections	Fire Protection	Highways and trans- portation	Health and welfare	Natural resources and utilities	Education and libraries
	104	105	106	107	108	109	110	111	112	113	114	115	116
GEORGIA	12 420	81 240	6 485.3	2 183.1	X	X	X	X	X	X	X	X	X
Albany	136	D	D	D	1 213	4 293 454	11.1	19.0	17.2	7.2	2.0	31.0	0.0
Alpharetta	150	D	D	D	443	2 007 691	5.5	32.0	22.6	9.9	0.0	9.9	0.0
Athens-Clarke County	160	D	D	D	1 759	6 225 567	17.5	31.3	12.0	9.2	0.6	19.8	3.4
Atlanta	904	8 419	671.6	204.2	8 214	31 551 612	15.9	34.2	13.9	16.0	0.2	18.5	0.0
Augusta-Richmond County	226	1 628	125.0	41.6	2 708	8 108 733	23.7	31.7	13.0	8.3	1.7	16.6	2.0
Columbus	277	1 862	122.7	42.3	3 147	10 081 635	11.8	34.7	14.0	7.5	4.7	18.9	2.8
Dalton	79	404	37.7	11.6	692	2 865 431	2.7	12.6	11.3	8.7	0.3	61.7	0.0
Douglasville	91	D	D	D	232	792 422	15.8	53.4	0.0	14.1	0.0	8.0	0.0
Duluth	163	1 111	93.4	41.0	140	565 431	33.5	44.9	0.0	10.3	0.0	10.1	0.0
Dunwoody	73	436	26.3	9.1	67	294 800	23.0	77.0	0.0	0.0	0.0	0.0	0.0
East Point	43	D	D	D	535	1 898 606	17.4	33.8	15.0	2.6	0.0	22.3	0.0
Gainesville	110	D	D	D	670	2 183 927	9.3	16.9	16.0	8.4	2.2	43.8	0.0
Hinesville	44	D	D	D	201	695 457	7.4	56.2	19.8	0.0	3.5	2.5	0.0
Johns Creek	91	D	D	D	8	41 438	87.5	12.5	0.0	0.0	0.0	0.0	0.0
Kennesaw	105	D	D	D	205	735 014	16.6	34.2	0.0	9.0	2.2	24.9	0.0
LaGrange	55	D	D	D	408	1 594 338	6.9	28.0	14.4	4.1	0.7	29.6	0.0
Lawrenceville	138	990	96.7	33.0	246	987 618	20.7	41.4	0.0	4.4	0.0	30.9	0.0
Macon	176	943	81.6	24.8	1 169	3 501 960	8.9	33.1	34.1	4.1	1.9	14.4	0.0
Marietta	232	1 399	153.9	46.5	734	3 368 637	23.6	11.1	12.3	4.3	11.8	24.4	0.0
Milton	19	D	D	D	121	520 911	22.5	27.5	44.2	3.3	0.0	2.5	0.0
Newnan	69	235	21.7	5.5	267	989 419	6.4	31.3	19.7	8.0	0.0	19.0	0.6
Peachtree City	79	D	D	D	270	1 079 307	11.4	29.0	29.7	14.7	0.0	5.3	3.6
Rome	67	D	D	D	589	1 937 155	8.3	18.6	26.8	11.5	0.6	25.2	0.0
Roswell	205	D	D	D	741	2 812 794	17.5	29.3	11.9	8.4	0.0	29.5	0.0
Sandy Springs	155	D	D	D	295	1 455 396	3.8	60.7	34.3	0.0	0.0	0.0	0.0
Savannah	227	1 505	124.1	38.6	2 548	9 836 488	9.9	34.9	11.9	8.9	2.7	25.8	0.0
Smyrna	99	434	41.8	12.0	391	1 523 989	10.9	37.3	23.1	6.6	3.6	14.0	2.3
Statesboro	60	298	21.9	5.6	279	845 101	12.3	28.4	12.3	12.1	0.0	32.0	0.0
Stockbridge	44	D	D	D	68	227 107	32.1	0.0	0.0	21.8	0.0	33.5	0.0
Valdosta	96	432	28.0	8.4	574	1 813 002	8.4	32.3	17.3	9.7	3.4	24.8	0.0
Warner Robins	84	D	D	D	536	1 642 600	10.8	31.9	21.3	10.1	3.3	20.5	0.0
HAWAII	1 615	11 669	908.6	279.4	X	X	X	X	X	X	X	X	X
East Honolulu CDP	NA	NA	NA	NA	NA	NA	NA	NA	NA	NA	NA	NA	NA
Hilo CDP	72	470	39.1	10.8	NA	NA	NA	NA	NA	NA	NA	NA	NA
Kahului CDP	60	577	46.3	13.9	NA	NA	NA	NA	NA	NA	NA	NA	NA
Kailua CDP (Honolulu County)	39	193	14.4	4.9	NA	NA	NA	NA	NA	NA	NA	NA	NA
Kaneohe CDP	43	363	22.0	7.9	NA	NA	NA	NA	NA	NA	NA	NA	NA
Mililani Town CDP	10	58	4.1	1.1	NA	NA	NA	NA	NA	NA	NA	NA	NA
Pearl City CDP	30	177	16.6	5.1	NA	NA	NA	NA	NA	NA	NA	NA	NA
Urban Honolulu CDP	NA	NA	NA	NA	NA	NA	NA	NA	NA	NA	NA	NA	NA
Waipahu CDP	52	258	22.0	6.5	NA	NA	NA	NA	NA	NA	NA	NA	NA
IDAHO	2 114	11 031	837.1	249.3	X	X	X	X	X	X	X	X	X
Boise City	368	2 413	175.6	62.7	1 617	7 522 788	17.0	29.2	23.6	4.2	0.9	17.7	4.2
Caldwell	46	307	24.9	7.8	228	861 823	8.7	36.4	24.0	12.2	0.0	13.3	3.2
Coeur d'Alene	91	579	37.6	11.4	318	1 619 497	16.8	30.1	21.9	7.8	0.2	19.0	3.2
Idaho Falls	92	D	D	D	659	2 848 455	10.4	20.7	20.0	4.4	0.0	33.4	2.9
Lewiston	68	D	D	D	314	1 377 725	8.6	24.1	24.4	12.2	3.9	16.1	2.7
Meridian	89	508	29.0	8.9	343	1 643 338	14.3	34.7	25.5	8.1	0.0	15.4	0.0
Nampa	105	598	42.2	12.1	565	2 435 649	5.6	35.1	21.4	3.5	2.1	14.7	2.4
Pocatello	81	D	D	D	561	2 333 293	10.6	25.9	18.5	10.3	1.9	26.0	2.6
Post Falls	47	294	19.0	5.5	169	673 051	14.6	40.3	0.0	12.1	1.2	22.8	0.0
Rexburg	21	D	D	D	115	440 960	21.3	29.6	8.0	11.5	0.8	17.1	0.0
Twin Falls	94	722	48.0	15.2	284	1 088 260	9.5	36.0	16.2	11.3	4.2	14.9	5.2
ILLINOIS	18 732	122 938	10 459.8	3 264.5	X	X	X	X	X	X	X	X	X
Addison	115	615	72.1	23.3	245	1 559 535	9.6	44.1	0.0	4.2	9.2	20.0	8.6
Algonquin	49	275	15.4	5.1	143	751 901	11.3	26.1	0.0	11.5	0.3	33.9	0.0
Alton	50	250	18.3	6.1	230	1 141 005	7.5	40.6	24.3	8.2	1.8	13.2	0.0
Arlington Heights	157	1 033	91.8	29.1	594	3 727 355	11.4	27.0	22.6	8.1	2.6	6.6	15.0
Aurora	184	1 136	102.6	25.8	1 402	8 465 715	9.4	32.8	18.5	7.5	8.1	14.5	5.4
Bartlett	46	D	D	D	166	992 280	14.8	48.1	0.0	13.2	11.3	12.4	0.0
Batavia	52	479	51.5	18.1	160	528 428	11.6	29.4	18.9	8.0	7.5	24.3	0.0
Belleville	112	661	47.6	17.4	345	1 469 633	6.3	35.6	25.0	5.2	0.0	14.8	4.1
Belvidere	33	D	D	D	125	645 335	6.9	38.7	26.4	8.1	0.0	13.1	4.0
Berwyn	61	195	19.3	4.7	402	2 004 230	7.2	46.5	25.8	5.7	1.5	5.4	6.1
Bloomington	120	956	66.5	22.1	723	3 168 188	7.2	25.0	19.2	14.3	0.0	27.5	5.8
Bolingbrook	80	444	44.2	13.7	391	2 517 306	8.3	44.4	26.4	8.1	0.0	9.5	0.0
Buffalo Grove	71	572	34.7	13.4	255	1 764 688	6.4	35.2	28.3	6.6	3.6	14.2	0.0

1. Establishments subject to federal tax.

Table D. Cities — **City Government Finances**

City	City government finances, 2007									
	General revenue							General expenditure		
		Intergovernmental		Taxes					Per capita[1] (dollars)	
					Per capita[1] (dollars)					
	Total (mil dol)	Total (mil dol)	Percent from state government	Total (mil dol)	Total	Property	Sales and gross receipts	Total (mil dol)	Total	Capital outlays
	117	118	119	120	121	122	123	124	125	126
GEORGIA	X	X	X	X	X	X	X	X	X	X
Albany	124.2	55.1	36.8	24.1	312	164	148	134.7	1 739	76
Alpharetta	73.1	15.6	8.8	42.0	678	393	285	72.3	1 166	291
Athens-Clarke County	206.5	69.1	26.0	71.2	598	405	191	249.4	2 095	484
Atlanta	1 789.4	282.2	8.0	521.0	1 173	704	465	1 567.5	3 530	1 093
Augusta-Richmond County	364.7	133.0	12.9	103.4	524	291	230	341.5	1 731	350
Columbus	354.1	116.0	29.3	135.0	675	498	175	364.1	1 820	349
Dalton	69.4	16.5	0.3	14.2	427	283	144	82.6	2 478	515
Douglasville	27.0	7.1	10.3	13.8	441	190	246	34.0	1 088	313
Duluth	24.7	9.0	7.9	11.7	419	226	192	21.2	761	234
Dunwoody	20.5	0.6	15.1	17.6	372	123	247	26.5	560	185
East Point	49.3	11.3	1.5	20.7	582	366	216	55.0	1 547	287
Gainesville	78.3	19.3	20.5	21.8	626	363	263	70.8	2 035	502
Hinesville	30.4	10.9	1.3	9.9	287	163	124	30.3	873	89
Johns Creek	48.5	16.3	1.2	29.0	352	203	148	41.5	504	64
Kennesaw	26.5	5.0	1.3	14.0	449	296	154	24.9	796	112
LaGrange	35.7	9.6	8.9	4.7	155	1	153	44.0	1 454	186
Lawrenceville	22.3	5.6	4.6	5.4	185	59	120	28.0	952	219
Macon	105.9	49.5	9.0	37.3	239	126	113	116.6	748	73
Marietta	82.2	22.8	7.9	30.6	524	231	293	98.4	1 683	284
Milton	21.7	4.6	14.9	15.2	433	294	139	20.2	577	192
Newnan	30.9	10.4	1.6	10.9	320	137	184	29.9	875	209
Peachtree City	37.7	9.3	2.0	19.4	559	360	199	41.6	1 200	340
Rome	65.6	22.8	6.9	19.0	526	247	230	61.5	1 706	503
Roswell	94.1	26.7	5.7	44.7	478	286	192	94.3	1 006	196
Sandy Springs	95.9	28.3	2.8	60.0	604	296	307	75.2	757	151
Savannah	345.6	126.6	7.8	105.1	739	418	308	307.5	2 161	358
Smyrna	56.3	11.1	0.4	27.0	513	327	184	52.4	994	224
Statesboro	31.5	5.9	3.1	9.5	316	131	185	31.3	1 045	125
Stockbridge	16.8	7.3	22.1	4.0	149	1	148	12.9	481	83
Valdosta	56.4	22.7	6.1	17.4	302	105	197	59.7	1 036	254
Warner Robins	55.2	4.5	3.8	28.0	390	229	159	54.2	755	88
HAWAII	X	X	X	X	X	X	X	X	X	X
East Honolulu CDP	NA	NA	NA	NA	NA	NA	NA	NA	NA	NA
Hilo CDP	NA	NA	NA	NA	NA	NA	NA	NA	NA	NA
Kahului CDP	NA	NA	NA	NA	NA	NA	NA	NA	NA	NA
Kailua CDP (Honolulu County)	NA	NA	NA	NA	NA	NA	NA	NA	NA	NA
Kaneohe CDP	NA	NA	NA	NA	NA	NA	NA	NA	NA	NA
Mililani Town CDP	NA	NA	NA	NA	NA	NA	NA	NA	NA	NA
Pearl City CDP	NA	NA	NA	NA	NA	NA	NA	NA	NA	NA
Urban Honolulu CDP	NA	NA	NA	NA	NA	NA	NA	NA	NA	NA
Waipahu CDP	NA	NA	NA	NA	NA	NA	NA	NA	NA	NA
IDAHO	X	X	X	X	X	X	X	X	X	X
Boise City	272.0	25.8	66.8	117.7	555	507	48	267.8	1 262	173
Caldwell	38.9	8.0	82.7	14.3	300	279	21	36.7	769	225
Coeur d'Alene	48.9	9.7	58.0	22.9	502	399	102	55.8	1 224	307
Idaho Falls	69.3	13.2	98.9	29.0	500	478	22	71.2	1 228	104
Lewiston	41.1	7.7	98.7	16.4	511	463	48	40.2	1 252	159
Meridian	53.9	9.9	100.0	23.3	290	242	48	42.4	528	89
Nampa	96.5	19.8	60.9	39.9	476	446	30	87.0	1 036	141
Pocatello	63.5	14.4	48.1	27.0	493	456	37	67.9	1 239	121
Post Falls	27.0	5.7	100.0	8.8	307	307	0	21.0	732	124
Rexburg	28.6	9.7	87.9	4.9	188	131	58	28.9	1 102	434
Twin Falls	39.5	5.6	70.4	19.5	433	398	35	33.6	747	116
ILLINOIS	X	X	X	X	X	X	X	X	X	X
Addison	44.6	12.7	100.0	22.1	594	338	250	39.8	1 067	5
Algonquin	27.6	11.4	100.0	12.4	415	200	215	21.1	704	36
Alton	40.8	15.1	100.0	14.7	535	282	253	34.8	1 267	124
Arlington Heights	98.7	20.5	94.8	68.0	897	574	324	81.7	1 078	28
Aurora	238.0	71.0	89.2	134.1	671	453	211	225.1	1 127	121
Bartlett	31.0	7.0	96.0	17.3	415	315	93	29.2	703	48
Batavia	30.0	8.1	95.0	13.2	500	278	223	38.7	1 468	511
Belleville	58.9	17.0	97.2	27.8	641	477	164	95.3	2 198	622
Belvidere	21.8	7.4	92.3	8.4	331	227	105	17.2	679	20
Berwyn	69.4	14.0	73.5	38.6	679	499	163	80.9	1 425	107
Bloomington	114.7	26.3	94.5	54.8	704	308	396	104.9	1 349	122
Bolingbrook	85.6	23.0	91.1	43.5	588	210	348	83.2	1 124	65
Buffalo Grove	47.2	12.4	82.1	22.3	535	338	184	50.5	1 215	102

1. Based on population estimated as of July 1 of the year shown.

City	City government finances, 2012 (cont.)									
	General expenditure (cont.)									
	Percent of total for:									
	Public welfare	Highways	Parking facilities	Education	Health and hospitals	Police protection	Sewerage and sanitation	Parks and recreation	Housing and community development	Interest on debt
	127	128	129	130	131	132	133	134	135	136
GEORGIA	X	X	X	X	X	X	X	X	X	X
Albany	0.0	4.9	0.0	0.0	0.0	11.4	15.9	5.6	5.6	1.4
Alpharetta	0.0	23.5	0.0	0.0	0.0	19.9	4.3	8.5	0.0	1.8
Athens-Clarke County	0.2	4.4	1.6	0.0	5.2	11.0	11.5	5.5	1.8	0.4
Atlanta	1.2	2.2	0.0	1.3	0.1	11.0	13.8	4.1	1.0	10.4
Augusta-Richmond County	0.2	6.6	0.1	0.0	6.2	11.7	18.1	4.9	6.5	1.3
Columbus	0.0	10.1	0.0	0.0	8.2	13.4	10.9	3.8	2.8	2.7
Dalton	0.8	5.6	0.0	0.0	0.0	10.7	27.0	11.8	0.1	2.3
Douglasville	0.0	4.7	0.0	0.0	0.0	25.3	15.3	31.6	0.8	3.5
Duluth	0.0	21.9	0.5	0.0	0.0	31.7	0.0	12.3	0.9	2.1
Dunwoody	0.0	22.3	0.0	0.0	0.0	22.3	2.5	23.3	8.6	0.3
East Point	0.0	6.9	0.0	0.0	0.0	25.4	20.7	2.7	3.3	3.1
Gainesville	4.3	4.3	0.0	0.0	0.0	12.4	22.0	12.2	0.9	2.6
Hinesville	0.0	11.7	0.0	0.0	0.0	23.7	19.6	1.5	4.0	1.6
Johns Creek	0.0	20.6	0.0	0.0	0.0	21.0	0.0	3.6	6.9	0.5
Kennesaw	0.0	17.6	0.0	0.0	0.0	21.1	7.9	9.3	2.7	4.0
LaGrange	0.0	12.7	0.0	0.0	0.5	20.4	32.2	2.5	1.6	0.5
Lawrenceville	0.0	16.5	0.0	0.0	0.0	37.1	18.1	0.0	1.5	0.0
Macon	0.0	2.6	0.1	0.0	0.4	20.4	8.6	5.0	5.9	1.3
Marietta	5.6	11.8	0.0	0.0	0.0	14.3	14.3	5.3	3.3	4.2
Milton	0.0	25.7	0.0	0.0	0.7	15.0	0.0	2.8	3.7	0.3
Newnan	0.0	11.4	0.0	0.0	0.2	21.1	23.1	3.7	1.2	0.0
Peachtree City	0.3	7.9	0.0	0.0	0.7	16.0	2.6	8.7	0.1	1.9
Rome	0.0	8.7	0.8	0.1	0.0	12.5	22.9	2.5	2.4	0.5
Roswell	0.0	12.1	0.0	0.0	0.0	17.7	10.8	11.8	2.1	1.2
Sandy Springs	0.0	27.3	0.0	0.0	0.0	23.0	1.9	6.3	1.1	0.3
Savannah	0.3	4.5	2.1	0.0	0.0	20.3	17.7	6.9	10.8	1.5
Smyrna	0.0	22.7	0.0	0.0	0.0	14.8	15.7	4.7	0.3	3.6
Statesboro	0.0	8.4	0.0	0.0	0.3	19.2	31.7	2.2	2.0	0.1
Stockbridge	0.0	17.1	0.0	0.0	0.0	8.4	17.0	3.3	1.1	5.7
Valdosta	0.0	12.1	0.0	0.0	0.0	21.5	25.4	2.4	1.0	0.2
Warner Robins	0.2	11.8	0.0	0.0	0.8	25.1	22.9	3.7	3.1	0.0
HAWAII	X	X	X	X	X	X	X	X	X	X
East Honolulu CDP	NA	NA	NA	NA	NA	NA	NA	NA	NA	NA
Hilo CDP	NA	NA	NA	NA	NA	NA	NA	NA	NA	NA
Kahului CDP	NA	NA	NA	NA	NA	NA	NA	NA	NA	NA
Kailua CDP (Honolulu County)	NA	NA	NA	NA	NA	NA	NA	NA	NA	NA
Kaneohe CDP	NA	NA	NA	NA	NA	NA	NA	NA	NA	NA
Mililani Town CDP	NA	NA	NA	NA	NA	NA	NA	NA	NA	NA
Pearl City CDP	NA	NA	NA	NA	NA	NA	NA	NA	NA	NA
Urban Honolulu CDP	NA	NA	NA	NA	NA	NA	NA	NA	NA	NA
Waipahu CDP	NA	NA	NA	NA	NA	NA	NA	NA	NA	NA
IDAHO	X	X	X	X	X	X	X	X	X	X
Boise City	0.0	0.9	0.0	0.0	0.0	16.9	19.6	7.6	2.4	0.6
Caldwell	0.0	10.3	0.0	0.0	0.0	19.7	16.9	5.7	0.0	1.3
Coeur d'Alene	0.0	10.0	0.3	0.0	0.0	18.0	32.7	5.5	0.2	1.6
Idaho Falls	0.0	6.6	0.0	0.0	4.4	14.1	16.6	12.8	0.0	0.1
Lewiston	0.0	13.4	0.0	0.0	0.0	15.9	27.8	7.7	3.2	0.7
Meridian	0.0	0.0	0.0	0.0	0.0	26.6	23.6	9.0	0.4	0.3
Nampa	0.0	7.3	0.1	0.0	0.6	21.3	17.3	14.0	0.9	3.1
Pocatello	0.0	9.8	0.0	0.0	4.3	16.7	12.7	5.2	1.4	1.8
Post Falls	0.0	12.2	0.0	0.0	0.0	22.6	27.3	8.3	0.0	3.4
Rexburg	0.0	9.2	0.0	0.0	0.7	6.6	16.2	20.9	2.6	1.0
Twin Falls	0.0	14.4	0.2	0.0	1.0	21.5	19.5	6.3	1.9	0.8
ILLINOIS	X	X	X	X	X	X	X	X	X	X
Addison	0.0	16.5	0.0	0.0	0.0	38.7	13.7	0.0	0.0	6.6
Algonquin	0.0	19.0	0.0	0.0	0.0	39.5	10.4	8.0	0.0	0.9
Alton	0.0	13.1	0.0	0.0	0.5	25.5	14.9	8.3	0.0	2.0
Arlington Heights	0.0	12.4	1.5	0.0	1.8	26.6	1.9	0.9	0.4	2.9
Aurora	0.0	10.8	0.6	0.0	0.4	28.0	2.2	3.8	2.0	11.6
Bartlett	0.0	16.3	0.7	0.0	0.0	37.2	10.5	8.1	0.0	7.2
Batavia	0.0	37.4	0.0	0.0	0.0	19.8	6.2	0.0	0.0	1.8
Belleville	0.0	8.5	0.0	0.0	0.0	9.1	31.1	1.7	0.0	4.9
Belvidere	0.0	14.5	0.0	0.0	0.1	33.8	11.9	1.0	0.0	2.3
Berwyn	0.3	11.0	0.1	0.0	0.0	26.6	8.8	2.9	4.0	5.8
Bloomington	0.0	5.5	0.9	0.0	0.0	14.8	15.4	16.9	0.6	2.8
Bolingbrook	0.0	14.2	0.0	0.0	0.0	22.2	9.2	11.1	0.3	10.3
Buffalo Grove	0.0	6.9	0.3	0.0	0.0	24.6	16.7	6.1	0.0	0.4

City	City government finances, 2012 (cont.)			Climate[2]						
	Debt outstanding			Average daily temperature (degrees Fahrenheit)						
				Mean		Limits				
	Total (mil dol)	Per capita[1] (dollars)	Debt issued during year	January	July	January[3]	July[4]	Annual precipitation (inches)	Heating degree days	Cooling degree days
	137	138	139	140	141	142	143	144	145	146
GEORGIA	X	X	X	X	X	X	X	X	X	X
Albany	71.8	926	16.6	47.5	81.4	35.1	92.5	53.40	2 106	2 264
Alpharetta	54.6	880	29.0	39.5	77.2	29.1	87.5	51.82	3 490	1 327
Athens-Clarke County	263.4	2 214	18.1	42.2	79.8	32.9	90.2	47.83	2 861	1 785
Atlanta	7 446.5	16 770	997.4	41.7	79.5	31.3	90.6	49.10	3 004	1 679
Augusta-Richmond County	619.6	3 141	0.0	44.8	80.8	33.1	92.0	44.58	2 525	1 986
Columbus	514.9	2 574	66.6	46.8	82.0	36.6	91.7	48.57	2 154	2 296
Dalton	51.3	1 540	0.5	39.4	78.0	28.8	89.8	53.64	3 534	1 393
Douglasville	43.7	1 399	13.4	NA	NA	NA	NA	NA	NA	NA
Duluth	10.1	363	0.0	NA	NA	NA	NA	NA	NA	NA
Dunwoody	7.3	154	5.2	NA	NA	NA	NA	NA	NA	NA
East Point	99.0	2 784	0.0	42.7	80.0	33.5	89.4	50.20	2 827	1 810
Gainesville	711.3	20 464	0.0	36.0	72.9	24.7	84.0	58.19	4 421	752
Hinesville	24.5	706	1.8	51.6	82.6	40.7	93.3	48.32	1 551	2 539
Johns Creek	3.2	39	0.2	NA	NA	NA	NA	NA	NA	NA
Kennesaw	25.6	819	0.0	NA	NA	NA	NA	NA	NA	NA
LaGrange	38.1	1 257	0.0	42.2	78.7	31.3	89.3	53.38	3 078	1 551
Lawrenceville	0.0	0	0.0	NA	NA	NA	NA	NA	NA	NA
Macon	46.4	298	19.4	45.5	81.1	34.5	91.8	45.00	2 364	2 115
Marietta	100.1	1 712	0.0	39.4	77.9	28.5	89.3	54.43	3 505	1 403
Milton	1.1	32	0.0	NA	NA	NA	NA	NA	NA	NA
Newnan	38.2	1 119	0.0	NA	NA	NA	NA	NA	NA	NA
Peachtree City	15.8	457	0.0	42.6	79.4	31.8	90.5	50.10	2 958	1 679
Rome	63.5	1 764	0.0	39.4	77.5	29.1	87.7	56.16	3 510	1 360
Roswell	12.2	130	1.7	39.5	77.2	29.1	87.5	51.82	3 490	1 327
Sandy Springs	2.8	29	0.0	NA	NA	NA	NA	NA	NA	NA
Savannah	184.3	1 296	0.0	49.2	82.1	38.0	92.3	49.58	1 799	2 454
Smyrna	50.4	956	0.0	42.7	80.0	33.5	89.4	50.20	2 827	1 810
Statesboro	18.7	623	0.1	NA	NA	NA	NA	NA	NA	NA
Stockbridge	17.6	656	0.4	NA	NA	NA	NA	NA	NA	NA
Valdosta	48.0	832	12.1	50.0	80.9	38.0	92.0	53.06	1 782	2 319
Warner Robins	39.6	552	31.7	45.5	81.1	34.5	91.8	45.00	2 364	2 115
HAWAII	X	X	X	X	X	X	X	X	X	X
East Honolulu CDP	NA	NA	NA	NA	NA	NA	NA	NA	NA	NA
Hilo CDP	NA	NA	NA	NA	NA	NA	NA	NA	NA	NA
Kahului CDP	NA	NA	NA	NA	NA	NA	NA	NA	NA	NA
Kailua CDP (Honolulu County)	NA	NA	NA	NA	NA	NA	NA	NA	NA	NA
Kaneohe CDP	NA	NA	NA	NA	NA	NA	NA	NA	NA	NA
Mililani Town CDP	NA	NA	NA	NA	NA	NA	NA	NA	NA	NA
Pearl City CDP	NA	NA	NA	NA	NA	NA	NA	NA	NA	NA
Urban Honolulu CDP	NA	NA	NA	NA	NA	NA	NA	NA	NA	NA
Waipahu CDP	NA	NA	NA	NA	NA	NA	NA	NA	NA	NA
IDAHO	X	X	X	X	X	X	X	X	X	X
Boise City	79.7	375	36.5	30.2	74.7	23.6	89.2	12.19	5 727	807
Caldwell	12.5	263	0.0	29.3	68.8	19.6	85.7	10.90	6 749	410
Coeur d'Alene	31.6	692	7.6	28.4	68.7	22.1	82.6	26.07	6 540	426
Idaho Falls	21.5	370	1.6	19.3	68.4	11.1	85.9	11.02	7 917	322
Lewiston	6.6	205	0.0	33.7	73.5	28.0	87.6	12.74	5 220	792
Meridian	1.3	17	1.3	29.4	71.8	22.1	89.2	9.94	5 752	579
Nampa	58.7	700	6.7	28.9	73.3	20.8	90.5	11.37	5 873	692
Pocatello	24.5	448	0.0	24.4	69.2	16.3	87.5	12.58	7 109	387
Post Falls	11.1	387	0.0	NA	NA	NA	NA	NA	NA	NA
Rexburg	14.4	549	10.0	NA	NA	NA	NA	NA	NA	NA
Twin Falls	43.5	967	0.0	28.2	72.2	19.7	87.9	9.42	6 300	587
ILLINOIS	X	X	X	X	X	X	X	X	X	X
Addison	59.7	1 602	6.8	22.0	73.3	14.3	83.5	36.27	6 498	830
Algonquin	13.6	453	0.1	NA	NA	NA	NA	NA	NA	NA
Alton	20.7	752	0.0	27.7	78.4	19.4	88.1	38.54	5 149	1 354
Arlington Heights	50.7	709	19.6	22.0	73.3	14.3	83.5	36.27	6 498	830
Aurora	553.2	2 769	9.1	20.0	72.4	10.5	84.2	38.39	6 859	661
Bartlett	54.9	1 320	13.6	19.3	72.6	10.9	83.0	37.22	6 975	679
Batavia	54.8	2 077	1.0	NA	NA	NA	NA	NA	NA	NA
Belleville	71.6	1 652	32.1	30.9	78.1	22.1	89.6	39.37	4 612	1 339
Belvidere	5.1	199	0.0	NA	NA	NA	NA	NA	NA	NA
Berwyn	97.3	1 712	7.4	25.8	75.3	17.3	86.2	40.96	5 555	1 027
Bloomington	96.3	1 238	12.7	22.4	75.2	13.7	85.6	37.45	6 190	998
Bolingbrook	272.1	3 679	5.0	23.1	74.8	14.2	86.8	37.94	6 053	942
Buffalo Grove	2.2	52	0.0	18.4	72.1	9.6	82.3	36.56	7 149	624

1. Based on the population estimated as of July 1 of the year shown. 2. Represents normal values based on the 30-year period, 1971–2000. 3. Average daily minimum. 4. Average daily maximum.

STATE Place code	City	Land area,[1] 2010 (sq km)	Population, 2014 Total persons	Rank	Per square kilometer	Race alone or in combination (percent), 2011-2013 White	Black	American Indian, Alaska Native	Asian	Hawaiian Pacific Islander	Percent Hispanic or Latino[2], 2011-2013	Percent foreign born 2011–2013
		1	2	3	4	5	6	7	8	9	10	11
	ILLINOIS—Cont'd											
17 09642	Burbank	10.8	29 218	1 258	2 705.4	85.6	1.4	0.7	4.3	NA	27.8	32.2
17 10487	Calumet City	18.6	37 213	997	2 000.7	23.6	72.9	NA	0.7	NA	15.1	8.4
17 11163	Carbondale	44.3	26 324	1 385	594.2	65.2	27.3	1.0	7.9	NA	7.5	11.8
17 11332	Carol Stream	23.6	40 349	920	1 709.7	75.6	5.1	0.4	18.2	NA	14.6	21.3
17 11358	Carpentersville	20.5	38 407	967	1 873.5	64.5	8.7	1.0	3.8	NA	51.2	30.5
17 12385	Champaign	58.1	84 513	380	1 454.6	70.4	17.9	0.3	13.0	NA	6.3	14.9
17 14000	Chicago	589.6	2 722 389	3	4 617.3	50.2	32.7	0.7	6.6	0.1	29.1	21.4
17 14026	Chicago Heights	26.1	30 436	1 214	1 166.1	45.6	40.3	0.5	NA	NA	35.1	10.9
17 14351	Cicero	15.2	84 354	381	5 549.6	47.9	3.6	1.2	0.5	NA	88.5	40.8
17 15599	Collinsville	38.0	24 883	1 424	654.8	88.2	11.6	0.9	0.5	NA	3.5	2.1
17 17887	Crystal Lake	47.5	40 493	914	852.5	91.4	4.0	NA	3.2	NA	11.7	11.8
17 18563	Danville	46.3	32 243	1 159	696.4	63.8	33.4	1.2	1.9	NA	6.7	3.6
17 18823	Decatur	109.4	74 010	456	676.5	74.8	25.9	1.2	1.6	0.1	2.2	2.3
17 19161	DeKalb	38.0	44 054	837	1 159.3	75.4	15.9	0.3	4.6	NA	13.5	8.4
17 19642	Des Plaines	37.0	58 947	620	1 593.2	76.8	2.0	0.6	14.0	NA	17.6	29.8
17 20591	Downers Grove	37.1	49 715	751	1 340.0	88.7	2.9	0.3	7.6	NA	4.9	10.6
17 22255	East St. Louis	36.2	26 672	1 374	736.8	2.5	96.7	0.6	0.3	NA	0.4	NA
17 23074	Elgin	96.3	111 117	251	1 153.9	65.3	7.7	0.9	6.7	NA	45.5	26.7
17 23256	Elk Grove Village	29.4	33 379	1 115	1 135.3	87.8	1.3	NA	7.0	NA	11.6	17.7
17 23620	Elmhurst	26.6	45 751	816	1 720.0	91.8	1.4	0.2	6.0	NA	6.5	9.6
17 24582	Evanston	20.2	75 658	445	3 745.4	69.7	19.8	1.0	11.2	0.1	10.4	20.0
17 27884	Freeport	30.5	24 851	1 425	814.8	81.4	19.9	1.1	2.6	NA	5.0	2.3
17 28326	Galesburg	46.0	31 659	1 174	688.2	83.1	13.9	0.6	1.5	NA	7.7	3.1
17 29730	Glendale Heights	13.9	34 530	1 075	2 484.2	64.8	8.5	0.6	24.2	NA	29.3	37.7
17 29756	Glen Ellyn	17.1	27 763	1 318	1 623.6	87.7	5.5	0.9	7.9	NA	6.6	12.3
17 29938	Glenview	36.1	46 767	803	1 295.5	85.9	1.2	0.4	13.1	NA	6.6	21.1
17 30926	Granite City	50.0	29 183	1 262	583.7	91.9	8.2	0.4	0.8	NA	4.1	1.8
17 32018	Gurnee	35.0	31 207	1 187	891.6	76.6	10.7	0.7	12.8	NA	13.0	17.9
17 32746	Hanover Park	16.4	38 476	964	2 346.1	55.3	9.3	0.5	17.1	NA	36.9	34.6
17 33383	Harvey	16.3	25 347	1 414	1 555.0	10.6	76.6	0.2	NA	NA	19.2	8.2
17 34722	Highland Park	31.6	29 871	1 240	945.3	94.2	3.7	NA	3.5	NA	9.2	13.2
17 35411	Hoffman Estates	53.9	52 347	710	971.2	64.6	4.0	0.9	24.1	NA	14.1	29.3
17 38570	Joliet	160.9	147 928	174	919.4	69.1	17.6	0.9	2.4	NA	28.3	15.2
17 38934	Kankakee	36.6	26 860	1 367	733.9	58.3	37.8	1.1	0.5	NA	20.6	10.7
17 41183	Lake in the Hills	26.9	28 893	1 276	1 074.1	90.2	2.7	NA	7.7	NA	12.8	11.1
17 42028	Lansing	17.6	28 522	1 289	1 620.6	62.6	31.9	NA	1.2	NA	15.0	8.1
17 44407	Lombard	26.6	43 893	845	1 650.1	84.2	5.4	1.6	10.3	NA	8.2	11.9
17 45694	McHenry	38.2	26 630	1 376	697.1	91.9	1.2	1.5	3.0	NA	10.8	7.5
17 48242	Melrose Park	11.0	25 511	1 408	2 319.2	51.8	7.2	0.7	1.6	NA	72.0	35.8
17 49867	Moline	42.6	42 685	866	1 002.0	86.4	6.6	1.1	3.2	0.2	17.0	9.4
17 51089	Mount Prospect	26.8	54 951	673	2 050.4	74.1	2.8	1.0	12.1	NA	16.6	31.7
17 51349	Mundelein	24.8	31 562	1 179	1 272.7	84.5	2.9	NA	10.4	NA	27.0	28.7
17 51622	Naperville	100.4	146 128	178	1 455.5	77.0	5.3	0.7	18.3	0.0	6.8	18.7
17 53000	Niles	15.1	30 000	1 234	1 986.8	78.4	1.5	1.1	19.2	NA	7.3	43.4
17 53234	Normal	47.5	54 594	679	1 149.3	87.6	8.3	0.7	4.0	NA	5.6	5.3
17 53481	Northbrook	34.2	33 655	1 104	984.1	85.9	1.0	NA	13.9	NA	2.9	19.2
17 53559	North Chicago	20.5	30 395	1 219	1 482.7	56.4	29.9	2.1	5.5	NA	29.7	17.9
17 54638	Oak Forest	15.4	28 174	1 298	1 829.5	86.3	6.8	3.1	3.6	NA	13.0	8.2
17 54820	Oak Lawn	22.3	57 034	644	2 557.6	87.9	6.8	0.4	2.0	NA	15.1	14.4
17 54885	Oak Park	12.2	52 008	713	4 263.0	69.9	24.3	0.6	6.9	NA	6.0	10.8
17 55249	O'Fallon	37.2	29 069	1 269	781.4	79.0	17.6	0.7	5.1	NA	3.7	4.9
17 56640	Orland Park	56.7	58 666	624	1 034.7	91.3	2.3	0.3	6.7	NA	6.2	14.8
17 56887	Oswego	40.2	33 099	1 124	823.4	88.6	8.6	NA	3.8	NA	10.0	5.4
17 57225	Palatine	35.3	69 387	495	1 965.6	74.6	4.0	0.4	13.2	NA	18.4	24.6
17 57875	Park Ridge	18.4	37 856	979	2 057.4	92.9	1.5	0.2	5.1	NA	6.8	14.1
17 58447	Pekin	37.7	33 824	1 098	897.2	97.3	2.9	0.6	NA	NA	2.6	1.2
17 59000	Peoria	124.3	115 828	236	931.8	65.5	29.7	1.0	5.8	0.2	5.4	8.0
17 60287	Plainfield	60.2	42 138	874	700.0	82.2	7.4	NA	8.9	NA	9.5	9.7
17 62367	Quincy	41.2	40 805	909	990.4	91.9	7.1	1.0	1.3	NA	1.4	1.8
17 65000	Rockford	158.2	149 123	171	942.6	71.1	23.5	0.8	2.9	0.1	17.0	10.4
17 65078	Rock Island	43.6	38 642	959	886.3	75.3	21.2	1.3	2.0	0.1	9.8	7.1
17 65442	Romeoville	47.8	39 679	938	830.1	69.6	15.0	1.1	8.3	NA	28.7	19.6
17 66040	Round Lake Beach	13.1	28 012	1 307	2 138.3	89.7	3.4	0.7	4.2	NA	50.3	30.4
17 66703	St. Charles	37.8	33 387	1 114	883.3	89.6	2.3	0.4	3.6	NA	9.2	10.0
17 68003	Schaumburg	49.8	74 896	452	1 503.9	70.7	4.6	0.4	21.6	NA	9.2	26.1
17 70122	Skokie	26.1	65 112	541	2 494.7	66.8	7.4	0.6	26.2	NA	9.6	41.6
17 72000	Springfield	154.1	116 809	233	758.0	77.2	20.8	0.6	2.8	NA	2.5	4.6
17 73157	Streamwood	20.2	40 345	921	1 997.3	60.7	5.9	NA	15.8	NA	30.4	30.4
17 75484	Tinley Park	41.5	57 280	639	1 380.2	88.0	3.4	NA	5.6	NA	8.7	10.4
17 77005	Urbana	30.2	42 044	878	1 392.2	64.7	18.3	0.6	18.8	NA	5.5	18.9
17 77694	Vernon Hills	20.0	25 911	1 397	1 295.6	78.2	1.8	NA	22.2	NA	10.4	31.0

1. Dry land or land partially or temporarily covered by water. 2. May be of any race.

Table D. Cities — **Population**

City	Age of population (percent), 2011-2013: Under 5 years	5 to 17 years	18 to 24 years	25 to 34 years	35 to 44 years	45 to 54 years	55 to 64 years	65 to 74 years	75 years and over	Median age 2011-2013	Percent female 2011-2013	Population: Census counts: 2000	Census counts: 2010	Percent change: 2000–2010	Percent change: 2010–2014
	12	13	14	15	16	17	18	19	20	21	22	23	24	25	26
ILLINOIS—Cont'd															
Burbank	5.6	18.4	10.7	13.0	12.0	15.3	11.6	7.2	6.2	37.0	51.1	27 902	28 925	3.7	1.0
Calumet City	5.6	22.8	8.5	13.3	14.2	13.2	10.6	7.1	4.7	34.9	53.5	39 071	37 042	-5.2	0.5
Carbondale	4.9	9.4	43.4	15.4	8.0	7.0	5.0	2.9	4.0	22.9	49.4	20 681	25 902	25.2	0.4
Carol Stream	4.5	17.8	10.8	14.2	12.8	17.7	12.5	5.1	4.6	37.4	51.2	40 438	39 711	-1.8	1.6
Carpentersville	8.6	25.8	10.3	15.5	14.3	14.5	6.6	3.0	1.4	29.1	49.9	30 586	37 691	23.2	1.9
Champaign	5.1	11.8	29.0	17.4	9.9	9.2	9.5	4.5	3.6	27.1	48.9	67 518	81 055	20.0	4.2
Chicago	6.8	15.6	10.9	19.2	14.2	12.4	10.3	5.9	4.8	33.5	51.4	2 896 016	2 695 598	-6.9	1.0
Chicago Heights	7.5	19.5	10.5	14.7	12.0	14.2	9.8	5.4	6.5	33.5	50.6	32 776	30 276	-7.6	0.4
Cicero	8.9	24.6	11.2	16.6	16.1	9.3	7.6	3.3	2.3	28.5	49.8	85 616	83 891	-2.0	0.1
Collinsville	6.9	14.7	10.4	13.4	14.7	15.3	11.3	8.1	5.2	38.3	52.5	24 707	25 579	3.5	-2.6
Crystal Lake	5.8	20.7	7.8	13.0	13.4	16.3	11.6	6.5	4.9	36.9	51.7	38 000	40 743	7.2	-0.6
Danville	6.8	18.4	10.6	12.2	12.0	12.0	12.2	8.4	7.4	37.1	50.8	33 904	33 027	-2.6	-2.4
Decatur	6.1	15.9	10.4	12.6	10.7	13.2	13.6	8.3	9.1	39.3	52.8	81 860	76 122	-7.0	-2.8
DeKalb	6.4	12.9	33.1	14.7	9.0	8.4	6.7	4.6	4.2	24.0	51.9	39 018	43 862	12.4	-0.1
Des Plaines	6.1	14.0	7.2	13.8	12.3	13.7	15.1	8.6	9.2	42.4	50.7	58 720	58 364	-0.6	1.0
Downers Grove	5.7	16.9	7.2	10.4	12.3	17.7	14.2	8.7	6.9	43.4	51.2	48 724	47 833	-1.8	1.7
East St. Louis	8.4	19.3	10.8	12.1	9.2	13.8	13.2	7.2	6.1	34.6	54.8	31 542	27 006	-14.4	-0.9
Elgin	9.2	20.0	9.6	15.6	14.3	12.4	9.8	5.3	3.8	32.4	50.0	94 487	108 188	14.5	2.7
Elk Grove Village	5.8	15.5	6.9	11.9	13.0	17.2	14.5	7.9	7.3	42.5	52.3	34 727	33 127	-4.6	0.8
Elmhurst	5.4	20.5	9.3	8.3	13.9	15.5	12.2	6.8	8.1	40.3	50.6	42 762	44 121	3.2	3.7
Evanston	6.5	14.1	16.4	13.9	13.1	11.9	11.5	6.4	6.2	34.2	52.2	74 239	74 486	0.3	1.6
Freeport	6.5	16.1	8.7	9.5	13.0	12.8	14.3	7.3	11.8	42.6	53.0	26 443	25 638	-3.0	-3.1
Galesburg	5.4	14.0	12.4	13.5	10.3	12.8	12.8	9.0	9.9	39.7	50.8	33 706	32 195	-4.5	-1.6
Glendale Heights	7.9	15.5	11.2	16.9	15.1	14.7	10.5	5.8	2.4	33.9	47.8	31 765	34 208	7.7	0.9
Glen Ellyn	6.4	19.9	6.5	9.6	14.9	15.5	14.3	5.7	7.3	40.8	52.5	26 999	27 450	1.7	1.4
Glenview	5.5	18.8	5.6	7.8	12.4	14.3	15.1	9.1	11.3	44.9	52.2	41 847	44 692	6.8	4.6
Granite City	4.8	17.6	10.0	12.8	11.0	14.1	13.7	7.9	8.1	39.3	49.2	31 301	29 849	-4.6	-2.2
Gurnee	4.6	21.9	8.1	8.7	16.5	19.3	11.3	5.4	4.3	38.6	51.9	28 834	31 295	8.5	-0.1
Hanover Park	6.7	22.1	8.9	15.6	14.7	15.1	10.2	4.5	2.2	33.0	50.1	38 278	37 973	-0.8	1.4
Harvey	7.6	18.0	11.3	12.3	12.5	14.4	10.8	8.1	5.1	35.8	52.7	30 000	25 282	-15.7	0.3
Highland Park	5.9	20.6	5.6	6.4	11.9	15.0	14.6	10.6	9.5	44.8	50.1	31 365	29 763	-5.1	0.5
Hoffman Estates	5.4	18.6	7.8	14.3	12.6	15.7	15.0	6.7	3.9	38.3	50.6	49 495	51 895	4.8	0.9
Joliet	8.3	21.4	9.3	14.9	15.9	13.1	8.5	4.5	4.1	32.4	50.8	106 221	147 433	38.8	0.3
Kankakee	8.9	21.1	7.9	13.5	13.4	12.0	9.7	7.2	6.4	34.0	48.5	27 491	27 537	0.2	-2.5
Lake in the Hills	7.0	22.4	7.4	14.0	17.8	16.2	8.3	3.8	3.1	34.6	48.8	23 152	28 965	25.1	-0.3
Lansing	5.1	18.1	8.4	12.2	10.8	15.3	13.4	8.9	7.8	41.0	51.8	28 332	28 331	0.0	0.5
Lombard	4.1	15.3	8.7	13.4	13.2	16.6	12.6	6.8	9.3	42.0	53.4	42 322	43 165	2.0	1.1
McHenry	6.4	18.5	8.8	13.6	11.8	17.8	10.9	6.2	6.0	38.2	50.0	21 501	26 992	25.5	-1.3
Melrose Park	9.3	21.0	11.0	14.8	14.8	10.1	9.8	5.3	4.1	31.0	49.5	23 171	25 411	9.7	0.4
Moline	5.9	16.7	7.9	13.9	12.4	12.6	14.5	7.9	8.3	39.4	50.6	43 768	43 483	-0.7	-1.8
Mount Prospect	5.8	17.3	6.9	14.5	14.0	15.9	11.4	7.2	7.0	39.3	50.8	56 265	54 167	-3.7	1.3
Mundelein	6.8	18.1	9.1	12.8	15.6	14.8	13.7	6.0	3.2	36.8	50.0	30 935	31 064	0.4	1.8
Naperville	5.4	21.9	9.0	9.9	14.0	17.2	12.0	6.3	4.3	38.1	50.9	128 358	141 853	10.5	2.8
Niles	5.0	11.7	5.5	13.5	9.6	14.0	15.0	10.7	14.9	49.1	54.9	30 068	29 803	-0.9	0.7
Normal	4.8	12.6	35.2	12.2	9.0	10.3	7.5	4.8	3.6	23.6	51.7	45 386	52 497	15.7	3.9
Northbrook	4.7	20.0	5.0	4.0	12.8	16.8	13.3	11.6	11.8	47.2	51.5	33 435	33 170	-0.8	1.5
North Chicago	7.6	13.2	34.4	18.2	9.2	6.7	5.7	2.9	2.0	23.7	41.6	35 918	32 574	-9.3	-6.7
Oak Forest	6.5	15.0	10.6	14.8	12.1	14.3	14.6	7.6	4.5	38.3	51.4	28 051	27 962	-0.3	0.8
Oak Lawn	6.0	15.4	8.0	14.4	10.2	16.0	12.5	7.1	10.5	41.1	52.3	55 245	56 690	2.6	0.6
Oak Park	6.2	18.1	5.8	13.7	15.9	16.1	13.4	6.6	4.3	39.1	53.9	52 524	51 878	-1.2	0.3
O'Fallon	5.9	22.3	8.9	10.7	16.6	14.9	10.3	6.3	4.0	36.5	51.5	21 910	28 281	29.1	1.4
Orland Park	4.5	14.7	8.5	8.9	11.2	17.1	13.9	11.2	10.1	46.1	53.2	51 077	56 767	11.1	3.5
Oswego	6.9	25.8	6.1	11.7	20.0	15.4	8.1	3.6	2.4	34.6	50.0	13 326	30 355	127.8	9.1
Palatine	7.6	17.5	7.1	15.4	14.1	14.8	12.4	7.0	4.1	36.9	51.3	65 479	68 557	4.7	1.2
Park Ridge	5.4	19.9	6.5	7.4	12.5	16.9	14.2	8.6	8.6	44.0	53.2	37 775	37 480	-0.8	1.0
Pekin	5.7	16.1	8.3	14.8	13.3	13.1	12.6	7.7	8.5	39.0	50.8	33 857	34 094	0.7	-0.8
Peoria	7.1	18.3	11.9	15.1	11.8	11.3	11.4	6.8	6.4	33.1	52.5	112 936	115 007	1.8	0.7
Plainfield	6.9	28.2	6.7	9.4	19.5	15.7	8.2	3.7	1.6	34.0	51.7	13 038	39 581	203.6	5.8
Quincy	7.0	15.9	9.1	13.9	11.3	12.0	12.6	8.3	9.8	38.1	52.6	40 366	40 633	0.7	0.4
Rockford	7.5	18.7	9.1	13.8	11.7	13.0	11.8	7.1	7.3	35.7	51.6	150 115	152 871	1.8	-2.6
Rock Island	6.9	16.7	13.1	12.8	9.8	13.1	12.0	7.7	8.0	35.4	52.8	39 684	39 018	-1.7	-0.9
Romeoville	6.0	24.1	11.9	14.0	15.8	13.0	7.3	4.9	3.1	31.7	52.0	21 153	39 680	87.6	0.2
Round Lake Beach	7.5	22.3	10.0	10.1	17.5	14.0	7.6	3.5	3.1	32.0	48.4	25 859	28 175	9.0	-0.3
St. Charles	3.8	18.6	5.8	11.7	13.8	15.5	15.1	7.5	8.2	42.5	50.7	27 896	32 974	18.2	1.3
Schaumburg	7.6	13.0	6.4	20.1	13.4	13.0	14.1	7.2	5.3	37.2	51.4	75 386	74 227	-1.5	0.9
Skokie	5.3	15.7	6.7	11.4	12.2	14.1	16.9	9.2	8.5	43.7	53.1	63 348	64 784	2.3	0.5
Springfield	6.3	15.9	9.8	13.5	11.6	14.1	13.7	7.6	7.5	38.9	51.9	111 454	116 250	4.3	0.4
Streamwood	6.0	21.0	8.0	16.7	13.8	15.5	9.5	6.0	3.5	33.8	49.3	36 407	39 858	9.5	1.2
Tinley Park	5.9	17.1	7.5	14.5	11.4	16.2	13.4	8.4	5.5	39.2	52.2	48 401	56 703	17.2	1.0
Urbana	4.4	7.4	42.2	16.2	7.3	6.5	8.0	3.1	4.8	23.8	51.1	36 395	41 250	13.3	1.4
Vernon Hills	6.2	19.5	7.2	11.3	16.6	18.0	10.9	5.1	5.1	37.7	50.1	20 120	25 113	24.8	3.5

Table D. Cities — **Households, Group Quarters, Crime, and Education**

City	Households, 2011-2013				Persons in group quarters, 2010				Serious crimes known to police,[2] 2013				Educational attainment, 2011–2013		
			Percent			Institutional			Total		Rate[3]			Attainment[4] (percent)	
	Number	Persons per household	Female family householder[1]	One-person	Total	Total	Persons in nursing facilities	Non-institutional	Number	Rate[3]	Violent	Property	Population age 25 and older	High school graduate or less	Bachelor's degree or more
	27	28	29	30	31	32	33	34	35	36	37	38	39	40	41
ILLINOIS—Cont'd															
Burbank	8 787	3.29	11.6	19.8	242	186	186	56	549	1 881	278	1 604	19 016	62.8	12.1
Calumet City	13 752	2.70	23.2	34.8	24	4	0	20	NA	NA	NA	NA	23 479	41.5	15.8
Carbondale	9 691	2.38	10.0	44.5	3 600	359	193	3 241	1 275	4 858	930	3 928	11 360	24.1	49.5
Carol Stream	14 529	2.73	8.3	27.5	44	44	44	0	483	1 196	72	1 124	26 609	32.5	37.3
Carpentersville	10 859	3.51	17.5	14.5	5	0	0	5	583	1 521	68	1 453	21 096	51.2	23.0
Champaign	32 471	2.29	9.9	36.7	8 514	392	341	8 122	2 929	3 530	788	2 742	44 721	22.3	51.2
Chicago	1 026 014	2.59	17.0	36.7	60 246	27 250	14 382	32 996	123 164	4 527	944	3 583	1 809 165	41.9	34.4
Chicago Heights	10 321	2.87	22.2	29.9	644	507	502	137	1 300	4 273	858	3 415	18 948	54.2	14.8
Cicero	21 465	3.90	19.1	15.5	196	173	173	23	2 177	2 585	411	2 174	46 483	74.5	6.4
Collinsville	10 898	2.31	16.4	30.3	65	59	59	6	813	3 235	131	3 103	17 150	38.4	26.8
Crystal Lake	14 084	2.83	11.4	22.6	267	163	163	104	831	2 058	116	1 941	26 361	28.4	40.4
Danville	12 635	2.44	20.0	35.7	2 422	2 243	159	179	2 484	7 636	1 217	6 418	20 958	53.2	16.1
Decatur	31 524	2.28	15.5	37.3	3 918	1 908	1 005	2 010	2 720	3 618	467	3 151	50 891	47.9	20.8
DeKalb	15 530	2.51	14.2	33.5	6 292	363	363	5 929	1 422	3 249	466	2 783	21 289	30.3	36.8
Des Plaines	22 733	2.56	9.1	31.4	888	822	702	66	840	1 424	95	1 329	42 809	38.2	35.4
Downers Grove	19 331	2.53	9.5	26.5	548	176	153	372	746	1 505	52	1 453	34 710	22.5	52.6
East St. Louis	10 387	2.54	35.6	38.5	433	109	90	324	2 952	11 091	4 918	6 173	16 409	52.7	8.3
Elgin	33 860	3.21	12.8	24.0	1 953	1 041	699	912	2 138	1 936	214	1 722	67 588	48.8	23.0
Elk Grove Village	13 414	2.47	9.1	32.5	132	96	96	36	649	1 942	75	1 867	23 934	31.9	36.4
Elmhurst	16 114	2.72	7.9	27.1	1 298	373	373	925	567	1 246	26	1 220	29 298	19.3	57.2
Evanston	28 929	2.36	10.1	37.7	7 024	1 297	1 150	5 727	2 032	2 684	244	2 440	47 495	16.3	67.2
Freeport	10 482	2.34	16.2	36.6	754	613	468	141	382	1 525	76	1 450	17 324	47.4	16.7
Galesburg	12 906	2.15	13.3	41.4	3 771	2 468	485	1 303	1 265	4 003	396	3 607	21 713	52.8	16.3
Glendale Heights	11 456	2.94	10.8	25.0	1	0	0	1	528	1 525	116	1 409	22 060	41.5	29.7
Glen Ellyn	10 342	2.65	9.6	27.4	5	0	0	5	317	1 143	36	1 107	18 468	17.6	59.1
Glenview	16 849	2.69	6.2	27.4	642	606	606	36	507	1 124	49	1 075	32 333	19.6	60.4
Granite City	12 230	2.40	16.7	31.3	256	158	158	98	1 028	3 491	591	2 900	20 018	54.0	14.5
Gurnee	11 338	2.75	10.5	23.9	89	61	61	28	1 492	4 774	122	4 652	20 457	25.0	48.3
Hanover Park	11 370	3.41	15.7	12.1	0	0	0	0	359	932	96	836	24 141	50.3	22.7
Harvey	9 479	2.68	27.7	40.9	252	192	192	60	1 829	7 199	1 602	5 597	16 238	64.7	9.3
Highland Park	11 297	2.62	6.0	24.4	255	183	173	72	348	1 162	80	1 082	20 301	15.1	69.0
Hoffman Estates	18 281	2.85	11.6	18.6	435	172	172	263	603	1 150	105	1 045	35 714	27.3	45.1
Joliet	46 546	3.12	15.0	22.0	2 945	2 185	1 189	760	3 774	2 542	375	2 167	90 119	45.9	24.6
Kankakee	9 533	2.66	21.8	34.4	1 810	921	305	889	1 259	4 614	718	3 896	16 891	57.9	10.0
Lake in the Hills	9 721	2.98	11.9	18.7	0	0	0	0	108	371	51	319	18 314	36.8	29.6
Lansing	11 078	2.58	16.6	33.4	91	83	83	8	1 279	4 485	382	4 102	19 577	44.5	17.2
Lombard	17 934	2.41	9.8	32.8	502	288	288	214	978	2 229	96	2 133	31 516	26.8	40.4
McHenry	9 704	2.74	9.3	23.9	194	186	186	8	471	1 760	138	1 622	17 787	43.7	23.3
Melrose Park	7 684	3.36	20.1	23.4	52	0	0	52	494	1 933	168	1 765	15 236	67.7	10.0
Moline	18 436	2.33	11.5	36.4	322	280	280	42	1 510	3 498	280	3 217	30 057	39.7	26.8
Mount Prospect	20 163	2.70	7.6	24.5	121	0	0	121	642	1 176	38	1 137	38 229	35.3	38.9
Mundelein	10 488	2.97	6.8	20.9	203	0	0	203	297	949	51	898	20 720	33.4	40.7
Naperville	48 758	2.90	8.0	18.7	2 489	1 188	1 108	1 301	1 974	1 369	73	1 296	91 717	15.6	65.0
Niles	10 986	2.58	12.3	29.6	1 118	1 100	1 100	18	755	2 516	117	2 399	22 954	47.9	27.6
Normal	18 716	2.60	9.0	29.5	8 332	391	377	7 941	1 409	2 598	212	2 386	25 833	25.8	51.1
Northbrook	12 218	2.68	4.4	21.7	678	611	611	67	487	1 451	24	1 427	23 487	13.2	69.3
North Chicago	7 069	2.93	24.1	26.8	12 741	196	0	12 545	822	2 856	507	2 349	13 619	46.9	19.2
Oak Forest	10 332	2.72	13.3	24.8	43	5	5	38	466	1 652	131	1 521	19 106	39.7	27.4
Oak Lawn	22 037	2.56	11.0	31.5	493	479	479	14	1 163	2 037	142	1 895	40 224	41.6	27.3
Oak Park	21 616	2.38	11.1	35.3	383	255	224	128	1 775	3 410	242	3 168	36 351	13.3	65.9
O'Fallon	10 750	2.73	11.5	24.2	0	0	0	0	580	1 974	116	1 858	18 432	19.6	48.7
Orland Park	21 556	2.65	9.0	23.7	464	451	451	13	1 349	2 343	30	2 313	41 604	32.2	39.4
Oswego	10 158	3.20	12.7	14.1	52	47	47	5	477	1 488	56	1 432	19 969	25.4	40.6
Palatine	25 820	2.67	11.0	28.2	168	134	134	34	697	1 006	48	958	46 891	28.9	48.7
Park Ridge	13 895	2.68	9.1	25.3	492	434	399	58	484	1 281	40	1 241	25 681	20.7	55.3
Pekin	13 992	2.31	13.4	32.0	2 042	1 933	281	109	996	2 922	326	2 596	23 630	49.4	15.9
Peoria	47 125	2.37	16.5	36.7	3 832	1 313	1 109	2 519	5 199	4 484	676	3 808	72 672	38.7	32.4
Plainfield	11 957	3.38	8.0	13.6	109	109	109	0	446	1 097	49	1 048	23 527	21.7	51.6
Quincy	16 637	2.38	12.8	35.7	2 087	1 378	1 015	709	1 496	3 663	460	3 203	27 760	43.7	23.1
Rockford	58 444	2.52	18.1	32.9	4 179	2 881	1 728	1 298	9 169	6 104	1 383	4 721	97 833	49.6	20.0
Rock Island	15 769	2.31	16.9	37.6	2 441	685	452	1 756	1 206	3 101	514	2 587	24 786	45.8	21.9
Romeoville	11 816	3.26	13.6	16.1	1 188	0	0	1 188	784	1 971	75	1 896	23 011	40.8	25.1
Round Lake Beach	8 050	3.46	11.7	17.3	139	139	139	0	666	2 371	132	2 239	16 625	58.4	15.6
St. Charles	13 148	2.52	8.5	26.3	1 211	1 121	161	90	582	1 741	57	1 684	24 135	26.9	47.3
Schaumburg	30 284	2.45	8.3	32.8	414	374	374	40	2 247	2 998	95	2 904	54 425	25.8	44.6
Skokie	22 821	2.82	12.1	24.9	706	494	475	212	1 732	2 658	241	2 417	47 021	30.4	45.8
Springfield	50 593	2.24	14.4	37.3	3 396	1 489	831	1 907	7 100	6 050	1 016	5 034	79 550	35.7	34.4
Streamwood	12 514	3.21	11.9	20.4	288	268	160	20	704	1 745	102	1 644	26 322	41.5	31.3
Tinley Park	20 836	2.73	9.7	23.9	45	0	0	45	945	1 650	80	1 570	39 492	33.3	35.1
Urbana	15 754	2.19	9.5	40.2	7 050	781	339	6 269	1 746	4 197	339	3 858	19 159	25.0	53.9
Vernon Hills	9 406	2.71	6.9	26.3	43	43	43	0	500	1 933	54	1 879	17 154	21.2	58.0

1. No spouse present. 2. Data for serious crimes have not been adjusted for underreporting. This may affect comparability between geographic areas and over time. 3. Per 100,000 population estimated by the FBI. 4. Persons 25 years old and over.

Table D. Cities — **Income, Poverty, and Housing**

City	Money income, 2011–2013					Housing units, 2010			Occupied housing units 2011–2013				
		Households								Owner-occupied		Median owner costs as a percent of income	
	Per capita income[1] (dollars)	Median income	Percent with income of $200,000 or more	Percent with income of less than $25,000	Families with income below poverty (percent)	Total	Percent change, 2000–2010	Vacant units for sale or rent[2]	Total	Percent	Median value[3] (dollars)	With a mortgage[4]	Without a mortgage[5]
	42	43	44	45	46	47	48	49	50	51	52	53	54
ILLINOIS—Cont'd													
Burbank	20 961	54 057	1.5	20.3	10.3	9 721	2.0	434	8 787	80.4	186 600	29.2	17.1
Calumet City	18 992	37 876	0.7	32.9	20.1	15 646	-1.8	1 668	13 752	58.7	98 400	32.6	15.2
Carbondale	13 725	17 236	0.9	60.0	31.1	12 419	12.7	1 384	9 691	25.2	122 100	19.6	11.5
Carol Stream	30 712	72 965	3.0	14.0	7.3	15 050	6.2	786	14 529	66.3	228 200	24.4	13.0
Carpentersville	21 312	57 462	4.1	18.2	14.8	11 583	29.6	731	10 859	70.2	153 500	25.2	14.2
Champaign	24 165	39 399	3.9	35.5	13.4	34 434	20.4	2 227	32 471	47.4	144 500	20.1	11.7
Chicago	27 979	46 014	5.2	29.6	19.5	1 194 337	3.6	148 777	1 026 014	43.9	217 700	27.7	15.5
Chicago Heights	19 218	42 016	1.7	34.9	24.4	11 060	-3.7	1 473	10 321	59.1	105 900	23.2	17.0
Cicero	14 143	39 690	1.0	25.4	20.2	24 329	-1.3	2 228	21 465	50.7	132 200	36.5	14.3
Collinsville	25 815	48 458	2.3	25.1	11.7	11 891	7.1	964	10 898	60.2	120 600	22.4	13.1
Crystal Lake	32 949	80 180	5.7	11.6	5.2	15 176	13.6	755	14 084	74.9	196 800	22.9	17.3
Danville	19 243	34 460	2.0	37.8	24.0	14 719	-1.0	1 876	12 635	61.6	65 200	19.2	12.5
Decatur	22 445	39 898	1.7	33.1	19.0	36 134	-3.0	3 790	31 524	61.1	79 600	18.7	12.3
DeKalb	18 979	37 004	1.2	36.7	22.5	16 436	21.4	1 050	15 530	41.9	153 800	23.6	13.0
Des Plaines	31 173	63 095	4.9	16.1	4.4	24 075	4.9	1 375	22 733	79.2	228 000	27.6	16.0
Downers Grove	42 316	83 545	12.6	15.1	4.0	20 478	4.9	1 291	19 331	76.7	314 100	23.4	13.1
East St. Louis	12 345	18 882	0.2	59.5	45.0	12 055	-6.6	1 936	10 387	46.0	58 900	35.4	15.0
Elgin	22 643	57 821	3.1	19.6	12.2	37 848	15.7	2 754	33 860	67.2	163 100	26.8	14.6
Elk Grove Village	32 330	64 199	3.5	15.9	4.7	13 905	3.3	598	13 414	72.1	256 600	27.3	14.9
Elmhurst	43 825	92 211	13.7	12.2	2.5	16 590	2.1	825	16 114	81.3	354 100	24.6	14.2
Evanston	40 042	67 610	12.2	20.4	5.8	33 181	7.7	3 134	28 929	55.6	344 100	25.0	16.4
Freeport	19 726	33 868	0.6	37.4	20.3	12 396	-0.7	1 364	10 482	63.7	77 900	21.5	13.3
Galesburg	18 952	31 794	0.9	39.0	20.1	14 280	1.2	1 272	12 906	59.8	70 700	19.9	12.9
Glendale Heights	23 888	57 692	1.7	15.4	10.4	11 864	7.3	607	11 456	67.6	169 600	30.1	15.6
Glen Ellyn	50 976	88 037	18.2	16.5	4.4	11 051	4.3	627	10 342	74.3	380 100	23.4	14.6
Glenview	49 663	87 494	20.2	11.2	2.7	17 746	12.2	963	16 849	80.7	454 500	24.3	15.8
Granite City	22 289	45 503	0.5	31.4	14.5	13 578	-3.9	1 364	12 230	66.9	81 500	18.1	11.0
Gurnee	36 836	86 033	8.6	11.9	4.7	12 031	11.2	495	11 338	73.3	248 800	24.0	13.6
Hanover Park	23 439	66 233	4.5	14.2	10.8	11 483	0.7	562	11 370	78.8	166 900	26.4	14.9
Harvey	12 750	19 531	0.1	58.4	33.7	9 805	-3.6	1 858	9 479	44.0	78 200	35.2	21.3
Highland Park	67 647	112 686	28.4	11.5	4.6	12 256	2.8	846	11 297	80.9	492 500	23.8	15.1
Hoffman Estates	35 649	82 554	9.0	10.0	3.1	18 970	8.5	838	18 281	74.4	250 000	24.9	11.8
Joliet	24 427	61 120	3.0	18.4	9.4	51 285	34.3	3 266	46 546	71.6	167 100	26.3	13.6
Kankakee	14 719	30 406	0.2	41.7	30.8	10 935	-0.1	1 289	9 533	50.2	97 100	29.3	16.3
Lake in the Hills	31 804	82 987	6.7	10.8	5.1	9 885	25.8	341	9 721	90.1	200 100	24.5	17.8
Lansing	23 770	49 505	2.3	22.8	9.9	11 741	0.1	784	11 078	75.3	125 300	28.4	17.5
Lombard	33 478	67 237	4.2	13.5	3.4	18 454	8.9	1 049	17 934	74.5	233 900	26.9	13.9
McHenry	28 717	64 180	2.5	18.1	6.5	10 741	32.1	666	9 704	77.0	167 900	25.0	14.6
Melrose Park	17 390	44 762	0.9	26.1	17.6	8 525	7.2	567	7 684	49.2	166 300	31.9	15.5
Moline	27 135	49 733	2.2	23.0	8.3	19 856	1.9	1 283	18 436	67.2	112 600	21.3	11.9
Mount Prospect	34 165	66 910	6.5	13.0	4.0	21 836	-1.1	1 272	20 163	71.4	281 700	26.5	17.1
Mundelein	32 213	74 857	7.4	11.4	5.1	10 992	8.3	485	10 488	76.1	209 700	25.2	15.9
Naperville	44 837	110 069	18.7	9.0	3.3	52 270	14.7	2 261	48 758	76.8	368 100	23.2	11.9
Niles	25 713	43 707	3.3	23.3	8.8	12 572	1.9	666	10 986	77.0	254 300	30.6	18.7
Normal	24 565	53 053	2.9	30.5	7.9	18 816	20.3	823	18 716	58.5	161 200	19.4	10.0
Northbrook	55 975	106 922	22.4	11.2	1.4	13 434	7.6	792	12 218	88.5	508 300	24.2	15.3
North Chicago	16 122	37 496	0.7	31.7	22.5	7 745	-7.3	1 125	7 069	38.7	117 400	36.4	17.5
Oak Forest	30 869	71 069	2.5	13.1	4.3	10 672	6.8	464	10 332	80.4	192 100	24.2	14.4
Oak Lawn	27 452	54 419	2.8	21.5	7.5	23 517	2.6	1 156	22 037	80.6	189 400	27.4	17.0
Oak Park	46 958	75 852	15.1	16.1	5.9	24 519	3.4	1 849	21 616	59.6	349 700	24.3	15.6
O'Fallon	36 861	73 000	7.3	18.3	9.6	11 414	32.7	667	10 750	70.6	198 300	19.4	13.0
Orland Park	39 141	77 582	8.6	11.5	4.6	22 443	17.6	804	21 556	89.5	269 900	25.8	15.7
Oswego	31 481	92 142	5.8	8.5	3.9	10 388	125.0	453	10 158	84.4	222 800	26.9	14.5
Palatine	35 089	70 862	7.5	15.8	8.0	28 621	9.2	1 745	25 820	66.3	264 000	25.7	15.7
Park Ridge	44 119	87 055	13.5	11.5	3.4	15 030	2.8	912	13 895	82.6	389 200	24.4	18.5
Pekin	23 607	45 904	0.6	24.3	9.5	14 714	5.1	894	13 992	66.9	97 000	19.6	10.9
Peoria	25 937	42 214	2.8	31.5	18.9	52 621	7.3	5 469	47 125	53.9	121 200	20.6	12.1
Plainfield	35 817	107 932	12.5	5.6	1.0	12 532	174.2	612	11 957	87.4	287 800	24.3	12.6
Quincy	21 578	38 805	1.2	31.8	15.5	18 655	3.7	1 504	16 637	62.6	98 700	20.8	10.4
Rockford	20 901	37 127	2.4	35.7	21.2	66 700	4.9	6 727	58 444	55.0	97 400	24.0	14.0
Rock Island	22 213	39 344	2.1	31.4	19.4	17 422	-0.5	1 492	15 769	63.6	98 200	20.0	13.7
Romeoville	22 165	66 034	0.6	7.6	5.2	12 623	71.3	636	11 816	82.3	163 700	28.6	12.3
Round Lake Beach	19 927	60 137	2.0	17.8	13.2	8 587	13.5	532	8 050	81.5	124 000	28.0	14.1
St. Charles	46 260	81 017	12.7	0.0	1.0	13 167	18.0	733	13 148	71.3	273 600	23.2	14.4
Schaumburg	35 156	72 574	4.7	12.3	4.3	33 610	1.6	2 071	30 284	63.8	236 300	26.7	14.5
Skokie	31 183	63 490	6.8	19.6	9.3	25 066	5.8	1 535	22 821	73.5	272 900	28.9	16.2
Springfield	28 023	47 571	3.1	27.4	14.2	55 729	3.4	5 015	50 593	62.7	117 600	19.4	11.3
Streamwood	27 717	73 123	4.4	11.2	3.7	13 629	10.0	595	12 514	88.4	177 200	26.8	14.0
Tinley Park	32 566	71 783	3.4	13.4	6.5	22 491	24.7	825	20 836	85.1	220 500	24.5	15.9
Urbana	19 123	28 085	2.3	45.9	15.5	19 090	25.2	2 129	15 754	35.0	150 300	22.6	11.2
Vernon Hills	42 159	92 146	13.7	9.8	1.5	9 956	25.2	439	9 406	72.1	311 900	24.5	14.2

1. Based on population estimated by the American Community Survey. 2. Includes units rented or sold but not occupied. 3. Specified owner-occupied units; $1,000,000 represents $1,000,000 or more 4. 50.0 represents 50 percent or more. 5. 10.0 represents 10 percent or less.

Table D. Cities — **Housing, Labor Force, and Employment**

City	Occupied housing units, 2011–2013 (cont.)				Migration, 2011–2013		Civilian labor force, 2014				Civilian employment[4], 2011–2013			
									Unemployment			Percent		
	Percent renter occupied	Median gross rent[1]	Median rent as a percent of income[2]	Percent with no vehicle available	Percent who lived in the same house one year ago	Percent who lived outside current city one year ago	Total	Percent change, 2013–2014	Total	Rate[3]	Population age 16 and older	In labor force	Civilian full-year full-time workers	Households with no workers (percent)
	55	56	57	58	59	60	61	62	63	64	65	66	67	68
ILLINOIS—Cont'd														
Burbank	19.6	1 040	27.4	7.0	91.7	7.8	14 459	-0.2	1 111	7.7	22 704	64.1	38.8	23.7
Calumet City	41.3	903	36.2	14.9	90.0	7.8	16 795	-1.0	1 854	11.0	27 805	67.5	34.9	33.2
Carbondale	74.8	683	50.0	19.8	66.5	18.1	11 481	-1.3	813	7.1	23 334	49.6	17.0	43.7
Carol Stream	33.7	984	31.9	6.2	90.1	7.7	24 001	-0.1	1 335	5.6	32 161	76.3	48.3	17.6
Carpentersville	29.8	997	38.0	3.8	85.7	8.0	19 061	-0.5	1 581	8.3	26 682	76.5	49.4	10.9
Champaign	52.6	833	38.5	13.6	67.1	19.2	42 092	0.1	2 563	6.1	70 116	63.5	33.1	25.4
Chicago	56.1	938	31.5	27.3	83.6	5.2	1 369 656	-0.5	105 422	7.7	2 170 608	66.4	40.1	26.4
Chicago Heights	40.9	804	39.7	13.5	91.7	6.3	13 323	-1.8	1 459	11.0	23 340	60.7	32.4	35.1
Cicero	49.3	847	31.7	10.4	88.7	4.5	37 408	-0.6	3 034	8.1	58 809	66.7	39.2	18.6
Collinsville	39.8	816	29.0	7.3	85.0	9.7	12 892	-0.4	945	7.3	20 373	67.1	39.1	29.3
Crystal Lake	25.1	1 134	26.6	4.6	87.6	7.3	22 630	-0.2	1 331	5.9	31 200	74.2	45.8	17.7
Danville	38.4	644	35.9	17.1	85.0	8.7	13 210	-1.9	1 228	9.3	25 377	54.3	31.7	38.2
Decatur	38.9	664	30.9	12.6	79.6	7.2	33 395	-3.6	3 243	9.7	60 377	61.0	34.0	34.3
DeKalb	58.1	816	41.7	11.6	67.0	17.9	22 609	0.3	1 536	6.8	36 833	67.5	29.3	26.6
Des Plaines	20.8	1 005	28.9	6.3	91.6	6.2	32 925	-0.1	2 076	6.3	48 357	66.9	43.4	26.1
Downers Grove	23.3	1 114	26.9	6.7	91.6	7.0	27 315	0.2	1 373	5.0	39 735	69.2	45.2	22.8
East St. Louis	54.0	544	35.5	28.7	93.9	3.4	9 097	-1.7	1 247	13.7	19 968	48.5	27.3	43.2
Elgin	32.8	939	33.4	6.4	86.0	6.2	56 663	-0.4	4 769	8.4	81 526	71.7	43.8	18.7
Elk Grove Village	27.9	1 018	31.1	4.8	89.1	9.5	19 365	-0.4	1 128	5.8	26 978	70.7	47.2	21.5
Elmhurst	18.7	1 365	28.6	5.0	91.0	7.2	23 089	0.1	1 230	5.3	34 769	65.9	41.3	22.7
Evanston	44.4	1 155	34.0	17.1	77.6	15.3	39 699	0.1	2 374	6.0	61 604	64.1	38.4	25.4
Freeport	36.3	590	33.3	13.3	83.3	5.4	10 959	-2.5	938	8.6	20 096	61.7	34.1	35.3
Galesburg	40.2	569	30.7	12.6	86.0	6.8	13 166	-0.8	982	7.5	26 216	51.3	29.6	40.5
Glendale Heights	32.4	1 038	30.8	5.1	81.1	13.4	19 532	0.1	1 278	6.5	26 521	76.4	46.2	13.0
Glen Ellyn	25.7	963	31.4	6.5	86.2	10.6	14 024	0.4	737	5.3	21 077	70.5	40.2	24.2
Glenview	19.3	1 719	37.3	6.7	91.6	6.6	22 068	0.1	1 122	5.1	36 251	60.8	42.0	29.2
Granite City	33.1	620	32.2	10.1	86.6	6.7	13 316	-0.8	1 147	8.6	23 946	58.9	36.8	32.9
Gurnee	26.7	1 153	29.4	3.4	88.9	9.3	17 243	0.4	994	5.8	24 411	71.8	45.7	14.8
Hanover Park	21.2	1 080	32.3	2.8	87.7	8.2	21 002	-0.5	1 537	7.3	28 926	73.6	48.5	15.1
Harvey	56.0	834	50.0	24.4	92.9	5.1	8 616	-2.2	1 215	14.1	20 075	52.0	22.9	50.0
Highland Park	19.1	1 409	29.5	3.6	90.6	6.6	15 023	0.7	756	5.0	22 897	63.6	41.0	25.7
Hoffman Estates	25.6	1 075	27.4	2.9	87.8	9.9	30 274	0.0	1 639	5.4	41 443	74.3	49.3	13.3
Joliet	28.4	877	31.6	7.6	87.6	6.2	75 507	-1.1	6 809	9.0	109 147	70.7	43.6	20.1
Kankakee	49.8	689	36.5	16.5	86.8	8.2	11 362	-1.9	1 227	10.8	19 905	57.1	30.3	38.3
Lake in the Hills	9.9	1 349	24.8	1.0	89.2	9.5	16 179	-0.2	992	6.1	21 285	77.9	52.5	12.1
Lansing	24.7	921	31.2	3.6	93.4	5.7	14 602	-1.1	1 172	8.0	22 904	66.9	38.5	30.5
Lombard	25.5	1 185	29.2	4.2	88.3	9.5	25 223	0.2	1 424	5.6	36 308	69.1	41.7	24.6
McHenry	23.0	1 050	33.5	5.7	91.6	6.6	14 155	0.0	933	6.6	20 936	72.8	44.1	22.8
Melrose Park	50.8	850	32.4	9.5	84.4	9.6	12 101	-1.6	888	7.3	18 799	68.5	40.9	20.8
Moline	32.8	701	26.2	7.7	88.9	8.0	22 323	-0.5	1 519	6.8	34 575	64.8	42.0	29.3
Mount Prospect	28.6	943	27.5	4.9	89.6	7.3	29 648	0.2	1 622	5.5	43 428	70.5	47.5	20.5
Mundelein	23.9	1 139	28.4	3.3	87.7	8.2	17 980	0.3	1 125	6.3	24 556	72.8	45.5	16.1
Naperville	23.2	1 274	25.3	3.6	87.0	8.6	76 941	0.3	4 200	5.5	110 635	70.1	45.8	14.9
Niles	23.0	973	44.9	12.3	89.8	8.3	14 032	0.1	893	6.4	25 221	53.8	32.4	34.2
Normal	41.5	794	41.0	6.5	69.0	18.5	28 870	-1.7	1 575	5.5	45 886	68.4	33.0	20.9
Northbrook	11.5	1 968	34.8	3.7	90.3	7.5	16 250	0.1	835	5.1	26 578	57.9	38.9	29.8
North Chicago	61.3	1 037	32.6	12.3	64.6	31.0	9 126	-0.2	846	9.3	24 453	78.4	21.4	25.3
Oak Forest	19.6	936	30.0	4.2	90.9	5.5	15 392	-0.3	1 101	7.2	23 210	70.6	44.4	19.8
Oak Lawn	19.4	1 038	38.7	7.8	92.2	5.6	29 066	0.0	2 048	7.0	46 376	63.4	38.5	31.3
Oak Park	40.4	1 020	28.9	13.3	86.9	10.4	29 520	-0.1	1 663	5.6	40 785	73.3	48.6	21.4
O'Fallon	29.4	1 028	30.4	2.7	82.0	16.0	13 618	-0.5	893	6.6	22 323	68.0	40.0	18.2
Orland Park	10.5	1 021	26.3	3.0	92.7	6.0	30 326	0.0	1 821	6.0	48 172	63.5	38.0	27.1
Oswego	15.6	1 832	23.1	1.0	90.2	6.1	17 593	0.0	1 043	5.9	23 175	78.6	53.8	10.9
Palatine	33.7	1 104	27.2	4.4	85.9	10.0	39 617	0.0	2 305	5.8	54 078	71.9	46.0	17.3
Park Ridge	17.4	1 118	26.8	4.7	93.4	5.0	19 659	0.5	1 094	5.6	29 146	65.0	42.2	23.8
Pekin	33.1	637	23.8	6.7	86.0	8.0	16 195	-2.4	1 279	7.9	27 150	60.2	40.7	31.3
Peoria	46.1	690	30.5	13.6	79.8	9.8	55 292	-2.1	4 367	7.9	89 356	63.5	37.5	29.0
Plainfield	12.6	1 390	26.2	4.1	91.5	7.9	21 857	0.1	1 409	6.4	27 844	76.2	53.3	9.7
Quincy	37.4	593	32.1	9.1	85.7	5.0	19 446	-1.1	1 114	5.7	32 324	63.6	39.3	32.3
Rockford	45.0	715	32.7	12.4	83.1	6.8	67 955	-0.8	6 626	9.8	115 650	62.2	33.4	34.6
Rock Island	36.4	661	34.3	12.2	81.6	9.1	18 596	-0.6	1 352	7.3	30 820	63.1	34.0	34.1
Romeoville	17.7	1 370	31.9	2.6	88.2	8.7	20 160	-0.7	1 708	8.5	29 499	68.3	44.5	18.1
Round Lake Beach	18.5	1 074	30.2	3.9	92.9	5.5	15 096	-0.3	1 372	9.1	20 774	73.8	42.0	14.7
St. Charles	28.7	1 033	27.5	6.5	86.2	8.5	18 581	0.2	1 027	5.5	27 341	68.1	46.7	21.1
Schaumburg	36.2	1 192	23.0	5.5	84.1	12.8	44 387	0.0	2 526	5.7	60 563	72.0	48.9	20.5
Skokie	26.5	1 108	36.8	8.5	93.4	4.9	33 214	0.0	1 968	5.9	53 357	63.3	38.3	24.8
Springfield	37.3	717	31.4	9.1	80.9	10.0	59 168	-0.1	3 798	6.4	93 765	64.7	39.5	30.6
Streamwood	11.6	1 392	29.8	1.9	89.5	8.9	23 689	0.0	1 602	6.8	30 683	75.0	48.6	15.5
Tinley Park	14.9	992	26.4	3.0	91.6	7.0	32 413	0.3	2 022	6.2	45 327	70.8	43.8	22.8
Urbana	65.0	761	39.3	22.5	57.9	30.7	21 025	0.0	1 374	6.5	37 342	59.8	21.4	28.1
Vernon Hills	27.9	1 201	32.7	7.5	84.6	11.2	14 435	0.6	745	5.2	19 661	74.4	49.0	16.1

1. $2,000 represents $2,000 or more. 2. 50.0 represents 50 percent or more. 3. Percent of civilian labor force. 4. Persons 16 years old and over.

City	Value of residential construction authorized by building permits, 2014			Wholesale trade,[1] 2007				Retail trade,[2] 2007			
	New construction ($1,000)	Number of housing units	Percent single family	Number of establish-ments	Number of employees	Sales (mil dol)	Annual payroll (mil dol)	Number of establish-ments	Number of employees	Sales (mil dol)	Annual payroll (mil dol)
	69	70	71	72	73	74	75	76	77	78	79
ILLINOIS—Cont'd											
Burbank	1 638	14	100.0	5	17	6.6	0.5	96	1 592	367.9	30.0
Calumet City	0	0	0.0	10	96	35.0	6.0	186	3 191	529.7	64.5
Carbondale	16 260	130	6.9	9	134	29.9	4.5	175	3 185	557.1	55.4
Carol Stream	4 648	36	100.0	117	3 082	6 930.4	180.9	93	1 557	385.2	35.6
Carpentersville	5 221	26	100.0	12	95	29.3	5.2	57	876	239.0	19.4
Champaign	142 414	914	10.1	61	1 644	922.4	61.0	405	7 172	1 354.4	126.8
Chicago	959 625	5 750	9.3	2 449	34 677	28 519.3	1 827.9	7 544	89 349	19 842.7	2 114.8
Chicago Heights	0	0	0.0	33	311	353.2	16.2	79	845	167.2	18.7
Cicero	0	0	0.0	46	635	479.6	29.8	135	1 996	536.7	43.1
Collinsville	2 548	18	100.0	33	334	208.9	16.5	103	1 581	473.0	39.8
Crystal Lake	2 949	18	100.0	82	712	485.2	37.7	223	4 188	1 077.4	101.0
Danville	760	5	100.0	44	D	D	D	168	2 405	512.3	48.6
Decatur	441	2	100.0	83	992	491.9	46.1	316	4 449	1 120.4	101.9
DeKalb	0	0	0.0	18	178	44.9	6.8	152	3 008	618.0	56.4
Des Plaines	2 312	4	100.0	138	3 148	2 063.7	200.8	197	2 520	740.9	65.1
Downers Grove	30 575	76	100.0	131	2 098	3 132.4	151.2	264	5 066	1 526.6	126.1
East St. Louis	24 904	207	2.4	17	239	351.1	8.5	65	516	80.6	10.4
Elgin	56 032	393	84.7	196	3 454	3 304.3	212.6	223	3 337	1 099.2	97.6
Elk Grove Village	0	0	0.0	499	7 758	4 987.2	429.0	124	2 844	815.0	88.0
Elmhurst	67 001	145	100.0	139	3 424	1 709.5	264.4	155	2 185	812.3	66.6
Evanston	7 818	24	79.2	53	552	395.3	26.9	250	4 311	1 010.6	108.0
Freeport	272	1	100.0	26	165	62.8	4.9	114	1 715	377.6	35.6
Galesburg	396	3	100.0	23	230	109.7	6.9	171	3 358	618.3	62.8
Glendale Heights	0	0	0.0	67	1 673	1 111.6	100.4	59	1 403	392.6	35.5
Glen Ellyn	22 236	52	100.0	34	280	276.9	14.7	111	1 443	359.8	33.6
Glenview	85 084	359	23.7	110	1 645	1 127.2	105.9	215	4 002	1 456.7	162.6
Granite City	4 324	26	23.1	29	360	363.2	19.0	86	1 270	297.8	29.6
Gurnee	1 353	4	100.0	73	1 072	777.1	68.7	273	5 486	1 116.7	102.0
Hanover Park	0	0	0.0	39	1 395	1 052.6	69.9	72	995	186.4	19.5
Harvey	0	0	0.0	26	297	108.6	14.2	67	531	175.7	15.2
Highland Park	20 218	28	100.0	67	198	591.3	18.2	204	3 007	1 003.3	86.1
Hoffman Estates	400	1	100.0	69	725	798.8	62.9	133	2 411	930.5	76.5
Joliet	26 480	122	100.0	98	1 099	511.8	51.9	420	8 658	1 985.3	185.5
Kankakee	562	6	100.0	22	207	134.5	10.4	89	1 057	246.3	23.5
Lake in the Hills	8 698	62	9.7	21	194	207.2	8.5	49	733	195.1	18.2
Lansing	0	0	0.0	25	301	109.2	18.7	122	2 282	479.0	48.4
Lombard	3 340	16	100.0	122	1 332	1 141.5	68.8	249	4 758	920.4	94.4
McHenry	4 254	41	17.1	46	2 056	789.1	118.8	148	2 636	607.7	57.3
Melrose Park	275	1	100.0	63	2 330	942.2	80.1	94	2 167	537.3	45.6
Moline	18 248	108	9.3	38	439	224.9	19.1	284	4 919	994.8	100.1
Mount Prospect	4 975	17	29.4	91	1 951	1 887.6	125.3	168	3 688	3 841.8	100.5
Mundelein	9 284	73	100.0	68	1 130	791.1	87.4	107	1 519	305.3	33.8
Naperville	121 012	460	81.5	217	4 725	3 000.6	391.0	495	9 752	3 362.0	262.2
Niles	1 883	3	100.0	89	1 459	610.0	80.3	276	6 189	1 618.3	147.0
Normal	8 273	87	93.1	23	711	372.6	39.8	134	2 868	636.4	56.4
Northbrook	26 682	46	100.0	212	2 524	2 692.6	169.5	257	4 273	1 038.9	117.9
North Chicago	0	0	0.0	16	451	333.7	29.7	34	207	71.4	5.1
Oak Forest	299	2	100.0	21	124	72.8	5.8	54	780	241.7	18.6
Oak Lawn	1 079	5	100.0	25	96	36.3	3.3	184	3 814	1 106.2	101.1
Oak Park	74 412	280	3.6	20	35	13.3	2.0	187	1 743	315.3	36.1
O'Fallon	32 543	126	100.0	17	74	23.5	3.2	109	2 493	812.5	64.8
Orland Park	19 540	81	100.0	50	345	100.6	13.0	398	8 924	1 900.6	187.3
Oswego	30 411	182	65.4	20	110	34.4	4.8	91	1 908	403.2	39.9
Palatine	21 170	89	38.2	89	486	450.0	26.7	191	3 270	831.7	74.4
Park Ridge	16 644	37	94.6	49	236	237.4	14.5	100	1 180	389.5	35.1
Pekin	4 687	28	100.0	16	210	128.5	6.9	151	2 363	561.9	53.1
Peoria	14 768	51	100.0	173	2 397	1 188.0	113.9	585	9 177	1 895.2	190.9
Plainfield	49 525	163	100.0	34	303	230.6	23.0	115	2 166	471.5	43.5
Quincy	11 695	83	83.1	68	1 276	563.7	45.8	281	4 382	838.5	81.4
Rockford	4 384	37	89.2	204	3 253	1 871.7	134.9	544	9 578	2 276.6	216.3
Rock Island	9 700	60	20.0	60	1 004	820.0	74.0	97	1 055	210.7	22.4
Romeoville	3 124	16	100.0	55	1 127	890.7	56.9	65	841	224.4	20.3
Round Lake Beach	0	0	0.0	5	9	2.9	0.5	65	1 537	313.6	29.8
St. Charles	7 326	23	100.0	113	1 209	1 240.5	64.2	210	4 171	996.5	97.4
Schaumburg	7 869	46	65.2	277	4 190	3 955.1	299.1	551	13 348	3 290.2	320.6
Skokie	3 719	8	100.0	147	D	D	D	367	6 024	1 224.5	134.4
Springfield	46 778	226	39.4	120	2 176	1 396.8	84.6	608	10 676	2 366.9	215.1
Streamwood	3 516	128	0.0	24	175	59.0	8.6	69	1 632	300.9	32.8
Tinley Park	5 781	34	100.0	59	702	429.5	37.3	167	3 799	1 134.9	94.2
Urbana	33 374	241	18.3	25	692	773.0	26.1	89	1 616	446.7	40.0
Vernon Hills	26 202	220	27.3	67	2 832	1 637.7	156.1	227	6 239	2 720.0	182.3

1. Merchant wholesalers except manufacturers' sales branches and offices. 2. Establishments with payroll.

Table D. Cities — **Real Estate, Professional Services, and Manufacturing**

City	Real estate and rental and leasing, 2007				Professional, scientific, and technical services,[1] 2007				Manufacturing, 2007			
	Number of establish-ments	Number of employees	Receipts (mil dol)	Annual payroll (mil dol)	Number of establish-ments	Number of employees	Receipts (mil dol)	Annual payroll (mil dol)	Number of establish-ments	Number of employees	Receipts (mil dol)	Annual payroll (mil dol)
	80	81	82	83	84	85	86	87	88	89	90	91
ILLINOIS—Cont'd												
Burbank	14	63	11.4	2.0	28	92	7.0	2.2	NA	NA	NA	NA
Calumet City	19	79	32.1	1.6	29	D	D	D	NA	NA	NA	NA
Carbondale	48	282	31.6	5.0	64	D	D	D	NA	NA	NA	NA
Carol Stream	49	284	44.9	9.8	97	D	D	D	101	5 322	1 527.9	259.4
Carpentersville	20	100	19.0	3.2	36	126	18.0	6.7	28	1 968	535.8	86.1
Champaign	116	1 040	242.6	32.3	263	D	D	D	56	1 898	897.7	74.7
Chicago	3 479	28 882	8 128.6	1 706.8	9 751	139 501	30 057.1	11 723.3	2 185	73 447	22 115.6	3 113.1
Chicago Heights	20	153	13.2	2.8	34	340	18.6	8.9	60	3 317	1 757.4	163.6
Cicero	24	101	17.0	2.9	38	293	13.3	4.3	93	3 371	1 051.5	157.2
Collinsville	27	170	26.6	5.7	68	471	54.5	19.7	NA	NA	NA	NA
Crystal Lake	59	373	61.6	13.6	214	863	160.2	40.1	90	3 406	751.9	164.9
Danville	41	183	25.1	3.8	62	307	37.5	10.5	52	4 183	1 805.3	185.3
Decatur	80	416	59.1	11.2	139	1 019	106.4	43.9	85	7 555	D	353.6
DeKalb	40	457	41.3	9.3	56	D	D	D	43	1 502	375.6	68.3
Des Plaines	94	1 405	1 224.9	68.6	259	D	D	D	125	9 476	2 294.5	446.1
Downers Grove	109	488	102.1	21.8	376	D	D	D	81	3 524	736.9	185.8
East St. Louis	15	65	7.9	1.7	14	D	D	D	NA	NA	NA	NA
Elgin	96	545	94.4	18.7	249	1 647	245.6	89.1	201	8 938	2 142.4	424.1
Elk Grove Village	66	531	134.4	28.0	172	2 318	373.0	107.1	477	18 094	4 638.5	821.2
Elmhurst	82	532	118.8	29.3	248	1 220	166.6	67.0	82	2 125	401.8	97.0
Evanston	109	629	86.4	19.5	438	D	D	D	61	1 347	315.9	69.6
Freeport	24	76	9.1	1.8	58	364	30.9	12.7	35	2 342	439.9	D
Galesburg	27	129	16.6	2.4	54	D	D	D	33	D	364.0	29.0
Glendale Heights	20	99	59.4	3.6	58	291	30.8	12.0	53	3 209	711.1	140.6
Glen Ellyn	44	165	33.5	7.8	196	821	122.8	48.9	NA	NA	NA	NA
Glenview	100	566	411.8	30.7	280	1 510	146.9	121.5	51	809	200.3	38.2
Granite City	29	213	24.2	5.2	51	D	D	D	33	4 851	2 388.4	276.4
Gurnee	49	276	61.7	12.6	133	367	70.8	19.9	76	2 157	664.5	101.1
Hanover Park	12	23	3.6	0.6	49	148	21.7	6.6	12	536	D	26.7
Harvey	10	75	27.3	3.6	7	46	2.7	1.2	32	1 939	697.4	88.0
Highland Park	68	203	87.2	11.0	245	547	109.4	39.6	28	898	234.8	30.5
Hoffman Estates	47	243	45.1	10.0	231	2 663	413.1	210.1	24	822	266.2	76.8
Joliet	101	478	77.1	14.7	233	D	D	D	84	3 672	1 596.7	201.9
Kankakee	27	93	14.2	2.5	58	D	D	D	31	1 912	969.7	106.2
Lake in the Hills	20	86	8.4	1.9	64	131	36.9	5.1	NA	NA	NA	NA
Lansing	33	121	28.6	3.8	75	281	26.4	11.0	33	1 565	289.0	65.4
Lombard	72	2 245	503.1	91.0	237	2 437	802.7	167.5	80	1 747	505.5	80.3
McHenry	37	249	24.2	6.3	81	505	60.1	28.9	66	1 940	336.9	76.2
Melrose Park	21	126	23.9	4.5	22	208	12.4	12.4	116	6 001	2 323.9	312.3
Moline	56	302	52.0	6.6	127	1 116	169.2	37.4	47	2 367	781.5	115.6
Mount Prospect	63	267	79.9	11.0	188	1 449	346.5	112.0	48	1 622	438.1	84.0
Mundelein	22	64	8.6	1.3	105	500	78.2	21.9	68	2 418	569.5	116.2
Naperville	227	842	253.1	34.5	1 002	D	D	D	99	2 472	579.3	119.8
Niles	54	410	81.4	14.6	94	467	69.3	20.6	81	3 541	1 048.1	171.4
Normal	37	337	44.2	9.5	71	D	D	D	28	2 342	D	125.3
Northbrook	137	614	143.1	38.0	610	19 892	1 308.5	715.2	89	3 140	696.9	151.4
North Chicago	10	68	12.5	6.3	11	D	D	D	19	1 365	355.9	D
Oak Forest	22	109	10.8	4.4	58	185	23.3	7.5	NA	NA	NA	NA
Oak Lawn	68	313	41.8	8.0	111	D	D	D	NA	NA	NA	NA
Oak Park	97	401	57.4	12.1	314	1 178	135.0	58.7	NA	NA	NA	NA
O'Fallon	48	D	D	D	81	D	D	D	NA	NA	NA	NA
Orland Park	92	311	80.9	7.6	241	1 078	124.8	48.0	41	1 477	496.7	90.9
Oswego	26	75	11.3	1.9	65	D	D	D	24	500	D	22.2
Palatine	90	308	52.1	9.9	330	1 481	206.3	75.6	41	1 786	670.0	81.0
Park Ridge	85	486	75.9	14.8	247	1 774	205.6	84.7	NA	NA	NA	NA
Pekin	25	89	11.8	2.5	50	294	22.2	9.5	30	1 224	D	55.7
Peoria	175	926	147.4	26.1	350	D	D	D	95	4 217	D	174.5
Plainfield	36	108	15.1	2.8	114	209	31.4	9.9	19	1 002	178.5	37.5
Quincy	53	249	28.4	6.0	121	749	61.6	22.3	55	D	D	D
Rockford	164	1 313	170.9	39.1	454	D	D	D	390	17 157	5 349.8	884.6
Rock Island	33	151	18.4	3.9	102	D	D	D	50	2 170	397.6	72.5
Romeoville	18	143	36.4	6.9	31	226	26.2	8.2	56	1 884	439.1	83.0
Round Lake Beach	12	46	7.3	1.0	22	D	D	D	NA	NA	NA	NA
St. Charles	92	339	99.9	15.4	265	1 700	249.5	111.1	105	5 588	1 559.1	259.1
Schaumburg	168	1 303	294.3	62.2	589	D	D	D	160	5 593	3 074.4	254.4
Skokie	115	1 199	188.0	42.7	398	2 529	552.1	197.9	154	6 021	1 355.1	289.8
Springfield	167	819	136.9	21.3	452	4 033	513.6	205.7	71	2 373	545.5	107.6
Streamwood	17	50	7.6	1.4	75	261	22.8	7.9	37	922	216.7	40.4
Tinley Park	52	175	27.0	4.3	148	1 273	156.8	45.6	43	1 421	358.8	65.8
Urbana	42	204	61.4	10.0	79	D	D	D	25	D	D	D
Vernon Hills	24	260	58.3	7.4	149	1 465	248.1	101.7	29	1 982	519.3	123.5

1. Establishments subject to federal tax.

Table D. Cities — Accommodation and Food Services, Arts, Entertainment, and Recreation, and Health Care and Social Assistance

City	Accommodation and food services, 2007				Arts, entertainment, and recreation,[1] 2007				Health care and social assistance,[1] 2007			
	Number of establish-ments	Number of employees	Sales (mil dol)	Annual payroll (mil dol)	Number of establish-ments	Number of employees	Receipts (mil dol)	Annual payroll (mil dol)	Number of establish-ments	Number of employees	Receipts (mil dol)	Annual payroll (mil dol)
	92	93	94	95	96	97	98	99	100	101	102	103
ILLINOIS—Cont'd												
Burbank	62	751	38.7	9.3	3	D	D	D	38	D	D	D
Calumet City	88	1 285	54.7	14.7	8	85	4.9	1.3	65	1 957	69.0	37.1
Carbondale	106	2 217	80.2	22.4	3	D	D	D	86	1 562	131.8	51.0
Carol Stream	66	992	55.2	12.6	9	206	4.4	1.3	59	563	49.5	22.5
Carpentersville	40	961	33.7	10.1	3	D	D	D	18	65	5.7	2.3
Champaign	288	6 348	241.5	68.8	21	283	9.2	3.5	151	2 550	293.0	111.9
Chicago	5 572	105 396	7 663.3	2 049.8	676	D	D	D	4 725	57 699	5 867.6	2 193.0
Chicago Heights	45	641	27.0	6.9	5	17	1.5	0.3	56	1 194	120.9	57.1
Cicero	84	978	57.6	13.8	12	D	D	D	52	677	49.2	19.3
Collinsville	80	1 597	64.9	18.7	10	D	D	D	50	374	25.9	10.3
Crystal Lake	107	2 373	99.0	29.9	21	216	7.1	1.7	182	1 890	185.2	85.4
Danville	99	1 764	64.0	19.4	9	D	D	D	82	D	D	D
Decatur	178	3 751	138.2	41.2	16	D	D	D	208	2 696	313.4	133.2
DeKalb	98	1 808	69.6	17.7	3	D	D	D	38	726	63.1	28.9
Des Plaines	166	2 446	134.6	34.1	13	D	D	D	185	2 611	264.7	96.0
Downers Grove	147	3 069	165.4	46.7	15	D	D	D	194	D	D	D
East St. Louis	37	D	D	D	1	D	D	D	31	471	25.0	12.5
Elgin	159	2 270	106.3	29.3	19	D	D	D	215	2 893	279.3	132.2
Elk Grove Village	85	1 384	85.5	21.7	16	D	D	D	118	D	D	D
Elmhurst	119	1 986	99.4	27.0	15	24	1.9	0.3	203	D	D	D
Evanston	212	3 654	210.3	56.0	44	322	29.1	9.3	269	3 216	501.8	268.6
Freeport	71	1 050	39.7	12.4	8	D	D	D	61	D	D	D
Galesburg	102	1 547	60.2	16.9	9	D	D	D	81	D	D	D
Glendale Heights	49	741	37.0	9.6	9	99	5.8	1.6	32	D	D	D
Glen Ellyn	60	866	42.6	11.3	8	211	6.7	2.5	80	972	99.4	42.1
Glenview	202	5 145	266.4	79.1	40	272	23.6	8.3	212	2 977	291.5	116.0
Granite City	63	1 176	42.9	12.9	10	D	D	D	61	1 567	156.0	60.6
Gurnee	121	2 985	141.0	40.8	13	D	D	D	146	1 163	152.7	60.8
Hanover Park	47	585	27.3	6.8	3	D	D	D	26	D	D	D
Harvey	43	411	22.2	5.1	1	D	D	D	48	D	D	D
Highland Park	73	1 294	68.1	20.9	25	228	10.6	4.4	164	D	D	D
Hoffman Estates	110	2 236	129.8	39.5	21	D	D	D	196	D	D	D
Joliet	229	6 100	564.3	107.9	24	520	72.5	11.0	285	3 936	475.4	210.1
Kankakee	62	756	28.4	6.9	6	D	D	D	72	D	D	D
Lake in the Hills	26	490	20.9	5.8	8	86	6.7	2.3	39	281	30.2	10.1
Lansing	60	1 220	53.4	15.5	8	D	D	D	48	364	24.4	9.6
Lombard	128	2 936	161.3	48.0	15	D	D	D	119	1 558	193.9	73.9
McHenry	78	1 301	59.4	15.6	9	69	5.8	1.4	86	D	D	D
Melrose Park	69	1 042	55.9	13.7	9	D	D	D	104	D	D	D
Moline	157	3 155	122.2	35.4	11	D	D	D	157	D	D	D
Mount Prospect	105	1 408	70.4	18.4	11	D	D	D	97	739	62.7	31.9
Mundelein	68	934	48.1	13.3	15	128	9.5	3.1	47	326	26.6	10.7
Naperville	311	6 770	335.2	100.8	48	600	28.6	9.5	508	D	D	D
Niles	128	1 851	102.2	26.5	3	D	D	D	140	2 499	189.7	72.5
Normal	93	2 468	91.4	27.4	5	D	D	D	61	D	D	D
Northbrook	103	2 029	158.2	50.3	30	D	D	D	254	2 408	242.9	103.9
North Chicago	39	595	27.5	7.1	1	D	D	D	9	D	D	D
Oak Forest	34	542	24.2	6.3	8	D	D	D	53	D	D	D
Oak Lawn	103	2 349	116.4	31.5	13	D	D	D	252	D	D	D
Oak Park	96	1 486	71.5	21.4	21	122	14.9	3.9	249	2 503	205.8	91.2
O'Fallon	69	1 460	54.1	15.9	11	D	D	D	49	809	65.3	21.7
Orland Park	156	4 138	176.5	53.1	31	D	D	D	262	D	D	D
Oswego	59	952	46.9	12.8	11	D	D	D	48	D	D	D
Palatine	126	1 841	85.9	23.4	21	D	D	D	123	985	78.8	34.1
Park Ridge	63	725	35.2	9.5	11	D	D	D	188	D	D	D
Pekin	89	1 342	53.1	15.0	9	D	D	D	75	902	64.4	30.7
Peoria	332	6 428	272.5	78.9	32	D	D	D	343	6 072	707.3	349.4
Plainfield	65	1 543	58.8	16.6	15	D	D	D	91	D	D	D
Quincy	122	2 280	79.4	22.7	15	D	D	D	103	1 682	244.7	80.3
Rockford	356	7 378	320.1	88.4	30	362	20.7	5.9	371	5 860	647.8	305.7
Rock Island	78	1 253	44.2	13.7	10	D	D	D	72	822	58.5	25.2
Romeoville	59	1 105	52.1	13.9	8	494	22.4	6.2	28	D	D	D
Round Lake Beach	39	706	43.1	8.5	5	D	D	D	26	D	D	D
St. Charles	139	3 102	156.4	48.6	15	212	14.9	4.2	148	1 483	165.1	72.4
Schaumburg	273	8 038	458.0	133.8	23	D	D	D	228	2 276	205.1	79.2
Skokie	150	3 055	172.3	47.6	24	362	26.8	7.1	332	3 530	339.9	141.3
Springfield	379	7 782	311.8	95.5	34	505	68.3	6.4	295	D	D	D
Streamwood	57	786	42.0	11.0	5	D	D	D	42	D	D	D
Tinley Park	111	2 632	124.2	32.4	19	D	D	D	145	1 754	157.1	51.8
Urbana	97	1 949	78.5	20.9	9	68	2.9	1.3	43	2 715	322.6	172.9
Vernon Hills	85	1 804	97.0	30.0	15	D	D	D	92	899	105.0	41.0

1. Establishments subject to federal tax.

Table D. Cities — **Other Services and Government Employment and Payroll**

City	Other services[1], 2007				Government employment and payroll, 2012								
						March payroll							
							Percent of total for:						
	Number of establish-ments	Number of employees	Receipts (mil dol)	Annual payroll (mil dol)	Full-time equivalent employees	Total (dollars)	Adminis-tration, judicial, and legal	Police and Corrections	Fire Protection	Highways and trans-portation	Health and welfare	Natural resources and utilities	Education and libraries
	104	105	106	107	108	109	110	111	112	113	114	115	116
ILLINOIS—Cont'd													
Burbank	30	D	D	D	134	786 445	7.6	47.7	28.5	12.5	0.0	0.0	0.0
Calumet City	41	179	14.4	4.5	270	1 459 484	9.0	47.4	26.2	6.4	3.6	3.2	4.2
Carbondale	44	D	D	D	243	1 024 650	20.3	36.8	14.6	7.4	0.7	17.5	0.0
Carol Stream	63	407	40.1	12.2	178	1 066 716	18.8	48.5	0.0	9.7	2.2	4.7	13.5
Carpentersville	24	107	5.5	1.6	197	1 212 358	9.8	38.1	25.5	7.4	4.7	10.2	0.0
Champaign	106	727	45.2	15.0	613	3 303 325	9.3	26.5	21.3	13.7	2.4	1.6	17.9
Chicago	3 320	23 822	2 101.5	609.9	25 630	175 627 618	2.8	74.4	7.6	3.4	2.3	5.3	1.0
Chicago Heights	44	313	19.6	6.4	294	1 453 188	3.9	43.8	28.2	5.0	0.3	9.0	5.7
Cicero	66	242	22.6	6.3	584	2 867 400	8.1	39.8	18.0	10.1	11.3	7.3	1.8
Collinsville	44	263	20.9	5.6	169	956 282	5.4	39.2	23.4	8.4	4.4	16.9	0.0
Crystal Lake	96	690	50.8	15.9	309	1 877 299	13.5	27.5	25.3	5.8	2.7	10.3	9.1
Danville	55	443	25.0	7.3	294	1 321 594	8.4	29.2	21.7	13.2	2.3	14.1	5.3
Decatur	114	D	D	D	554	2 990 379	8.4	39.2	24.9	9.4	4.8	6.5	5.6
DeKalb	47	275	17.3	5.1	198	1 271 653	11.8	36.9	32.8	11.6	1.9	5.0	0.0
Des Plaines	148	806	100.3	28.7	446	2 438 468	5.2	30.6	34.3	7.1	3.0	5.9	10.5
Downers Grove	115	1 075	154.0	49.0	390	2 164 897	16.2	30.8	26.2	1.6	2.8	10.9	8.4
East St. Louis	17	122	6.9	2.3	189	693 926	9.2	35.2	34.7	6.6	4.3	0.0	2.0
Elgin	145	1 449	136.5	47.6	718	4 472 423	10.3	39.1	24.6	3.4	0.0	18.7	0.0
Elk Grove Village	99	1 163	124.9	40.6	298	2 048 828	10.7	36.3	32.2	8.8	6.0	5.0	0.0
Elmhurst	98	810	72.7	27.1	587	3 047 235	10.6	25.1	12.8	8.0	0.0	13.7	21.9
Evanston	114	820	49.7	18.8	756	4 935 582	8.8	31.1	21.1	2.8	8.4	20.2	3.5
Freeport	51	D	D	D	191	868 424	5.9	37.1	28.7	6.7	0.0	12.7	3.3
Galesburg	49	D	D	D	284	1 182 039	9.7	30.8	19.6	8.9	4.7	17.2	4.2
Glendale Heights	34	D	D	D	240	1 253 066	11.8	42.0	0.0	9.8	5.4	20.6	0.0
Glen Ellyn	51	298	16.5	7.1	170	812 456	21.3	30.1	0.0	7.6	0.0	23.8	11.9
Glenview	109	699	54.4	19.6	368	2 419 770	8.4	26.3	34.2	5.3	3.0	8.4	10.8
Granite City	47	349	39.4	10.0	233	1 173 888	7.7	32.1	27.6	12.2	4.4	14.0	0.0
Gurnee	54	479	39.0	10.5	198	1 570 289	5.9	45.6	29.7	8.4	0.0	3.7	0.0
Hanover Park	36	D	D	D	207	1 331 356	9.4	44.7	23.0	7.5	3.0	8.6	0.0
Harvey	16	D	D	D	195	871 135	8.5	48.6	27.8	8.3	0.3	6.5	0.0
Highland Park	80	531	41.3	14.9	227	1 445 604	8.6	30.8	26.4	9.8	1.3	11.6	0.0
Hoffman Estates	50	371	21.2	11.6	347	2 420 731	11.8	35.1	29.9	4.6	1.4	10.1	0.0
Joliet	164	1 266	96.0	28.0	941	6 790 745	6.4	38.7	25.4	6.8	1.3	12.5	3.8
Kankakee	56	370	30.3	9.3	264	1 273 939	5.5	35.8	24.1	7.9	6.7	10.1	4.5
Lake in the Hills	30	D	D	D	131	726 848	15.2	43.1	0.0	11.6	4.1	15.1	0.0
Lansing	48	411	27.9	9.2	200	1 054 688	6.3	47.0	25.7	7.3	0.0	5.9	5.3
Lombard	106	826	63.6	22.8	289	1 794 844	9.3	33.8	26.1	6.4	0.8	8.5	8.0
McHenry	56	D	D	D	136	766 529	11.7	38.7	0.0	16.4	0.0	26.3	0.0
Melrose Park	43	D	D	D	274	1 377 728	3.3	43.1	26.6	6.0	1.7	8.5	5.6
Moline	84	600	43.9	13.8	392	2 247 548	10.9	28.1	19.6	8.6	0.7	17.4	6.2
Mount Prospect	83	515	40.6	12.0	445	2 620 859	6.5	27.8	21.6	6.5	3.5	10.4	15.1
Mundelein	56	D	D	D	167	523 415	11.5	34.6	14.6	10.6	0.0	10.8	0.0
Naperville	236	1 832	126.3	42.6	1 141	6 999 358	11.3	27.3	20.8	10.0	0.0	21.1	9.4
Niles	71	306	25.2	6.9	277	1 803 453	9.8	28.4	25.4	11.8	9.9	11.0	0.0
Normal	50	475	26.6	10.0	426	2 272 555	9.0	24.8	18.8	7.7	0.7	25.9	7.3
Northbrook	74	535	39.7	13.3	275	2 019 890	9.3	35.9	30.6	13.5	2.9	7.8	0.0
North Chicago	18	148	17.7	4.9	176	982 302	7.8	51.2	16.6	5.2	4.6	10.0	4.6
Oak Forest	38	164	18.2	4.8	137	814 381	8.2	43.6	26.4	10.5	0.1	10.0	0.0
Oak Lawn	99	734	52.7	17.0	421	2 260 980	6.9	39.4	25.9	7.3	0.7	8.8	7.3
Oak Park	87	536	33.3	11.4	450	2 566 842	9.0	37.0	19.6	5.0	4.3	3.8	10.5
O'Fallon	49	298	18.2	5.8	177	876 752	17.3	46.2	0.5	7.4	7.7	15.6	4.9
Orland Park	113	961	80.3	25.3	409	2 080 080	14.2	43.9	0.0	6.5	0.0	22.3	8.2
Oswego	51	362	24.7	7.8	107	609 946	20.4	64.0	0.0	0.0	0.0	15.5	0.0
Palatine	134	922	64.7	20.4	348	2 424 446	10.2	40.9	30.9	4.8	1.1	3.4	0.0
Park Ridge	59	303	20.0	7.1	255	1 549 856	7.5	29.7	26.8	7.3	4.0	6.5	14.1
Pekin	53	281	18.2	4.9	259	1 110 590	5.2	29.2	27.7	6.0	1.0	5.6	4.2
Peoria	178	2 909	254.2	120.5	831	4 963 632	9.9	36.9	26.3	5.9	1.3	5.1	5.3
Plainfield	54	D	D	D	131	858 893	12.3	62.1	0.0	9.7	0.0	13.1	0.0
Quincy	95	549	45.5	12.9	391	1 653 065	8.8	30.0	19.6	12.1	0.3	15.1	5.2
Rockford	247	2 058	164.3	51.5	1 085	6 113 597	5.6	33.3	36.5	5.3	7.4	4.8	4.2
Rock Island	50	402	34.7	11.2	372	1 377 794	14.6	16.8	10.5	8.7	9.2	29.1	7.6
Romeoville	38	480	60.2	16.5	297	1 580 154	8.8	38.4	18.0	2.8	3.6	17.7	0.0
Round Lake Beach	27	D	D	D	90	514 049	11.2	62.5	0.0	8.6	4.5	13.1	0.0
St. Charles	80	535	42.1	14.0	264	1 823 844	18.8	26.0	21.1	7.0	0.0	19.6	0.0
Schaumburg	204	1 621	135.5	45.7	536	3 458 405	11.4	32.6	25.6	5.7	7.4	8.7	0.0
Skokie	154	1 085	95.8	30.8	593	3 361 285	7.8	29.7	23.3	2.7	5.7	10.6	14.6
Springfield	190	1 536	104.6	35.6	1 621	10 142 573	6.4	16.0	12.6	5.8	1.5	56.2	1.6
Streamwood	47	307	19.0	6.6	179	1 160 444	8.6	42.2	27.2	3.9	3.6	10.8	0.0
Tinley Park	64	560	34.1	12.6	346	1 824 694	11.4	45.9	13.6	6.6	0.8	8.0	9.0
Urbana	44	D	D	D	302	1 464 071	11.1	26.0	23.5	13.2	5.3	4.2	11.9
Vernon Hills	34	406	25.6	9.1	101	697 505	10.9	66.3	0.0	16.7	0.0	0.0	0.0

1. Establishments subject to federal tax.

City	City government finances, 2007									
	General revenue							General expenditure		
		Intergovernmental		Taxes					Per capita[1] (dollars)	
					Per capita[1] (dollars)					
	Total (mil dol)	Total (mil dol)	Percent from state government	Total (mil dol)	Total	Property	Sales and gross receipts	Total (mil dol)	Total	Capital outlays
	117	118	119	120	121	122	123	124	125	126
ILLINOIS—Cont'd										
Burbank	19.3	6.5	97.7	12.0	410	185	219	17.0	584	9
Calumet City	50.9	11.6	90.1	34.2	919	681	229	45.9	1 232	103
Carbondale	32.4	10.9	88.9	14.1	533	69	464	31.8	1 202	47
Carol Stream	28.1	11.1	91.6	10.1	252	15	219	25.3	631	60
Carpentersville	32.2	12.8	86.2	12.7	332	234	98	36.5	955	239
Champaign	100.8	38.9	81.8	49.4	597	285	312	101.7	1 229	343
Chicago	6 690.6	1 758.6	65.4	2 526.4	930	327	547	7 439.1	2 740	425
Chicago Heights	44.6	13.6	76.8	22.9	750	593	155	45.7	1 500	202
Cicero	111.4	23.7	88.5	72.9	863	556	300	108.6	1 285	185
Collinsville	30.2	11.1	94.1	12.0	478	200	278	29.1	1 154	106
Crystal Lake	53.2	19.4	99.7	23.3	576	375	201	54.2	1 341	305
Danville	42.4	15.6	82.1	19.3	590	227	363	42.8	1 309	210
Decatur	75.9	32.1	85.6	34.5	458	179	279	89.1	1 182	206
DeKalb	53.3	19.6	68.3	26.9	614	331	283	45.2	1 031	260
Des Plaines	103.1	31.2	96.3	57.8	982	617	358	92.0	1 563	249
Downers Grove	65.8	18.9	98.8	39.1	793	447	346	58.7	1 190	157
East St. Louis	38.6	19.9	85.1	15.8	592	444	148	38.3	1 439	101
Elgin	136.9	44.5	93.0	66.3	605	479	126	125.2	1 141	155
Elk Grove Village	60.1	13.5	93.1	37.1	1 113	630	466	64.9	1 946	411
Elmhurst	70.4	17.9	99.2	36.4	806	479	320	65.4	1 450	192
Evanston	123.4	24.9	70.5	64.7	858	533	298	116.5	1 544	176
Freeport	29.6	13.3	99.7	8.0	317	186	130	28.8	1 144	64
Galesburg	39.9	19.3	93.4	14.5	455	218	236	38.4	1 207	64
Glendale Heights	35.6	10.2	99.2	15.9	460	241	210	43.0	1 246	422
Glen Ellyn	37.6	7.6	88.9	16.6	602	374	215	32.5	1 176	174
Glenview	101.0	27.2	76.5	62.0	1 377	1 042	336	95.5	2 120	282
Granite City	40.9	13.0	100.0	18.6	629	472	157	45.0	1 521	211
Gurnee	38.2	22.9	85.8	9.6	307	0	307	34.9	1 121	11
Hanover Park	38.2	10.2	89.4	21.6	563	376	180	53.4	1 392	426
Harvey	23.0	6.4	100.0	13.8	543	424	119	25.1	990	34
Highland Park	56.2	12.1	93.3	29.2	978	521	419	47.5	1 591	94
Hoffman Estates	82.1	13.5	91.6	51.3	982	736	239	64.6	1 237	110
Joliet	202.1	70.4	93.0	72.3	488	283	198	177.8	1 199	22
Kankakee	60.8	25.8	88.2	20.1	735	562	173	66.7	2 438	258
Lake in the Hills	20.2	7.5	78.9	9.1	314	217	97	18.0	620	82
Lansing	33.0	8.0	94.6	18.5	649	445	203	35.4	1 241	283
Lombard	90.1	27.3	90.2	20.3	464	194	270	97.6	2 231	83
McHenry	24.8	12.3	96.4	6.7	249	217	33	23.4	873	150
Melrose Park	43.6	13.9	98.6	23.4	918	732	185	48.9	1 914	285
Moline	72.2	20.2	84.2	35.3	819	413	405	74.2	1 720	148
Mount Prospect	70.6	19.0	93.5	43.9	805	533	265	70.0	1 283	142
Mundelein	36.2	9.6	91.1	18.0	577	372	205	32.6	1 046	94
Naperville	169.6	55.1	89.1	79.8	555	355	183	143.7	999	101
Niles	48.5	18.9	99.5	23.3	776	251	518	41.3	1 378	19
Normal	80.5	31.2	99.5	31.3	581	208	372	77.3	1 435	387
Northbrook	51.6	18.4	98.1	23.9	715	481	233	52.8	1 578	131
North Chicago	26.1	8.5	79.5	13.3	441	299	138	26.6	885	25
Oak Forest	21.4	5.3	98.7	12.5	444	315	129	20.9	744	55
Oak Lawn	62.1	19.1	99.2	28.3	496	394	96	68.1	1 194	211
Oak Park	89.0	14.1	80.8	58.0	1 115	815	268	90.4	1 737	226
O'Fallon	33.2	13.4	98.6	10.8	370	237	133	31.4	1 072	258
Orland Park	85.4	30.2	96.4	33.9	592	346	245	81.3	1 420	303
Oswego	21.0	9.6	98.5	6.3	198	46	152	17.5	553	6
Palatine	81.2	22.0	76.2	45.6	660	486	175	87.2	1 262	293
Park Ridge	46.1	10.0	100.0	30.9	818	523	283	47.4	1 255	36
Pekin	40.2	14.5	81.3	13.8	404	189	215	48.4	1 417	388
Peoria	185.6	76.4	95.2	81.2	702	306	396	173.5	1 500	288
Plainfield	34.8	10.0	90.4	14.1	348	155	193	27.5	680	54
Quincy	46.5	24.3	86.8	13.5	330	59	271	36.7	898	111
Rockford	205.7	107.8	70.0	75.0	407	306	100	178.2	1 180	127
Rock Island	69.8	23.7	74.6	23.3	601	427	175	75.1	1 934	393
Romeoville	58.3	11.7	84.0	28.8	726	381	336	58.2	1 465	267
Round Lake Beach	17.9	8.1	98.7	8.5	305	231	74	22.5	802	338
St. Charles	51.7	14.2	98.9	26.8	807	424	383	54.5	1 637	225
Schaumburg	155.0	40.4	92.8	70.0	937	341	596	138.1	1 847	106
Skokie	104.2	37.0	66.4	60.5	929	512	413	82.4	1 265	140
Springfield	137.9	49.3	90.7	68.8	587	235	353	135.8	1 159	63
Streamwood	29.9	8.7	93.2	15.7	390	250	135	26.2	650	57
Tinley Park	70.3	22.1	99.9	36.1	632	519	114	61.1	1 069	254
Urbana	47.8	17.7	62.5	22.2	531	252	279	48.4	1 159	285
Vernon Hills	21.2	13.2	99.1	5.7	222	0	222	18.9	740	29

1. Based on population estimated as of July 1 of the year shown.

City	City government finances, 2012 (cont.)									
	General expenditure (cont.)									
	Percent of total for:									
	Public welfare	Highways	Parking facilities	Education	Health and hospitals	Police protection	Sewerage and sanitation	Parks and recreation	Housing and community development	Interest on debt
	127	128	129	130	131	132	133	134	135	136
ILLINOIS—Cont'd										
Burbank	0.0	11.1	0.0	0.0	0.0	42.1	0.0	0.0	0.0	2.8
Calumet City	0.0	11.2	0.0	0.0	1.3	21.0	3.8	0.0	0.3	4.9
Carbondale	0.0	7.9	0.6	0.0	0.0	26.7	11.0	1.0	10.1	4.7
Carol Stream	0.0	12.8	0.0	0.0	0.0	46.9	11.5	0.0	0.0	1.4
Carpentersville	0.0	38.6	0.0	0.0	0.0	24.1	5.9	0.7	0.0	5.8
Champaign	0.3	8.8	2.1	0.0	0.0	19.0	14.5	0.0	0.8	3.1
Chicago	4.6	9.7	0.1	0.0	2.5	18.0	5.3	0.5	4.4	12.5
Chicago Heights	0.0	5.4	0.0	0.0	0.0	23.2	9.3	0.0	6.0	4.9
Cicero	0.3	10.4	0.0	0.0	1.4	22.1	4.8	0.3	1.6	5.0
Collinsville	0.0	8.9	0.0	0.0	0.6	27.3	16.9	0.0	0.0	5.9
Crystal Lake	0.0	25.3	0.0	0.0	0.2	19.8	6.0	1.9	0.0	2.7
Danville	0.0	17.2	0.0	0.0	0.0	16.9	12.9	5.0	1.7	1.3
Decatur	0.0	29.1	0.0	0.0	0.0	25.2	3.2	0.1	2.3	5.8
DeKalb	0.0	13.3	0.0	0.0	0.0	23.6	3.7	0.0	0.6	2.7
Des Plaines	0.0	20.8	0.2	0.0	0.0	21.7	6.9	0.0	0.3	2.6
Downers Grove	0.0	18.1	1.8	0.0	0.0	24.0	7.0	0.0	0.0	5.8
East St. Louis	0.0	6.6	0.0	0.0	0.0	18.9	0.4	0.0	6.8	5.2
Elgin	0.0	11.0	0.0	0.0	0.0	27.7	8.5	13.6	1.2	2.1
Elk Grove Village	0.0	19.6	0.0	0.0	0.0	23.4	3.9	0.0	0.0	5.1
Elmhurst	0.0	18.1	1.0	0.0	0.4	21.5	11.4	1.7	0.0	4.4
Evanston	1.7	7.6	6.0	0.0	2.3	18.5	5.9	10.8	6.7	7.0
Freeport	0.0	13.2	0.0	0.0	0.3	14.5	17.8	0.4	0.0	4.6
Galesburg	0.0	25.9	0.0	0.0	0.0	14.5	5.0	7.5	0.0	3.6
Glendale Heights	0.0	11.3	0.0	0.0	0.0	37.4	2.1	17.7	0.0	7.1
Glen Ellyn	0.0	21.1	0.6	0.0	0.0	22.1	17.3	8.7	0.0	1.6
Glenview	0.0	8.2	0.3	0.0	0.0	12.5	5.1	0.0	0.0	5.3
Granite City	0.0	20.6	0.0	0.0	0.0	20.0	15.5	0.0	0.0	3.9
Gurnee	0.0	13.7	0.0	0.0	0.0	33.2	3.7	0.6	0.0	1.0
Hanover Park	0.0	10.2	0.9	0.0	0.0	43.0	3.1	0.0	0.0	2.1
Harvey	0.0	17.0	0.7	0.0	0.0	22.3	4.4	0.3	0.0	8.0
Highland Park	0.0	10.3	2.4	0.0	0.0	27.0	7.1	5.1	0.0	3.1
Hoffman Estates	0.0	14.7	0.0	0.0	0.9	25.3	5.6	4.4	0.0	8.8
Joliet	0.0	9.3	0.7	0.0	0.0	20.1	10.8	4.0	1.9	1.3
Kankakee	0.0	10.0	0.0	0.0	0.0	14.5	21.2	0.0	1.5	5.0
Lake in the Hills	0.0	10.4	0.0	0.0	0.0	38.8	0.0	8.9	0.0	1.8
Lansing	0.0	15.2	0.0	0.0	0.0	25.7	5.9	0.0	0.0	2.9
Lombard	0.0	4.1	0.1	0.0	0.0	13.3	3.6	0.0	0.0	8.5
McHenry	0.0	14.9	0.0	0.0	0.0	39.0	22.4	8.5	0.0	2.9
Melrose Park	0.0	8.0	0.0	0.0	0.0	22.1	4.8	2.9	0.0	7.5
Moline	0.0	12.6	0.3	0.0	0.0	17.7	10.4	7.3	0.0	5.5
Mount Prospect	1.4	12.6	0.5	0.0	0.2	19.8	8.5	0.5	1.3	1.5
Mundelein	0.0	20.8	0.1	0.0	0.0	30.0	6.2	0.0	0.0	3.3
Naperville	0.0	19.4	0.7	0.0	0.0	24.1	7.8	5.9	0.0	3.5
Niles	0.0	16.1	0.0	0.0	0.0	31.3	5.8	3.8	0.0	1.7
Normal	0.0	7.7	0.0	0.0	0.0	14.0	6.7	12.9	0.2	5.5
Northbrook	0.0	16.7	0.3	0.0	0.0	24.8	2.5	0.0	0.0	5.0
North Chicago	0.0	8.1	0.0	0.0	0.0	30.4	1.8	0.0	1.3	5.2
Oak Forest	0.0	17.8	1.0	0.0	0.0	37.1	4.8	0.0	0.0	2.4
Oak Lawn	0.3	14.0	0.1	0.0	0.0	20.6	8.3	0.6	0.3	5.5
Oak Park	0.0	7.1	4.0	0.0	1.3	20.3	6.0	0.0	4.7	3.1
O'Fallon	0.1	13.1	0.0	0.0	0.0	15.5	10.4	15.1	0.0	9.0
Orland Park	0.0	27.8	0.4	0.0	0.0	21.1	12.3	10.6	0.0	3.0
Oswego	0.0	11.6	0.0	0.0	0.0	45.1	16.3	0.0	0.0	9.0
Palatine	0.0	7.7	0.6	0.0	0.0	41.7	6.7	0.0	0.2	6.5
Park Ridge	0.0	7.0	0.8	0.0	0.0	19.5	10.4	0.0	0.0	3.3
Pekin	0.0	9.3	0.0	0.0	0.0	17.4	28.2	0.0	1.1	3.9
Peoria	0.0	15.7	1.7	0.0	0.0	20.6	1.4	1.5	2.0	5.8
Plainfield	0.0	20.5	0.0	0.0	0.0	39.3	16.5	0.0	0.0	10.9
Quincy	0.0	11.6	0.0	0.0	0.3	22.6	10.1	1.7	2.9	2.4
Rockford	9.5	16.5	0.7	0.0	0.0	25.1	3.9	0.0	5.8	2.4
Rock Island	0.0	8.4	0.2	0.0	0.0	15.4	24.0	9.0	0.4	0.8
Romeoville	0.0	11.3	0.0	0.0	0.0	20.1	10.5	6.5	0.0	8.6
Round Lake Beach	0.0	7.7	0.0	0.0	0.0	28.5	0.0	0.6	0.0	4.2
St. Charles	0.0	20.9	0.0	0.0	1.2	19.4	13.9	0.0	0.0	9.3
Schaumburg	0.8	12.2	0.1	0.0	0.5	18.6	4.6	1.6	0.3	10.1
Skokie	0.0	10.7	0.1	0.0	1.7	19.6	5.0	2.4	1.0	3.2
Springfield	0.0	12.3	1.1	0.0	0.0	27.2	4.0	0.0	3.0	2.0
Streamwood	0.0	17.6	0.0	0.0	0.0	33.2	9.7	1.3	0.0	1.6
Tinley Park	0.0	17.1	0.9	0.0	0.0	26.6	4.6	0.0	0.0	3.6
Urbana	0.3	29.3	1.4	0.0	0.0	17.9	3.0	0.3	7.3	1.1
Vernon Hills	0.0	21.7	0.0	0.0	0.0	46.0	0.0	4.1	0.0	7.1

City	City government finances, 2012 (cont.)			Climate[2]						
	Debt outstanding			Average daily temperature (degrees Fahrenheit)						
				Mean		Limits				
	Total (mil dol)	Per capita[1] (dollars)	Debt issued during year	January	July	January[3]	July[4]	Annual precipitation (inches)	Heating degree days	Cooling degree days
	137	138	139	140	141	142	143	144	145	146
ILLINOIS—Cont'd										
Burbank	10.1	346	0.0	23.5	75.5	16.2	84.7	38.35	6 083	1 001
Calumet City	52.6	1 413	0.0	22.0	74.2	14.8	83.7	38.65	6 355	866
Carbondale	33.7	1 276	6.6	NA	NA	NA	NA	NA	NA	NA
Carol Stream	7.2	180	0.0	23.1	74.8	14.2	86.8	37.94	6 053	942
Carpentersville	49.4	1 295	0.0	19.3	72.6	10.9	83.0	37.22	6 975	679
Champaign	74.8	904	0.0	33.7	79.0	25.0	89.5	47.93	4 183	1 501
Chicago	21 209.6	7 811	2 295.0	25.3	75.4	18.3	84.4	38.01	5 787	994
Chicago Heights	67.7	2 223	46.7	22.0	74.2	14.8	83.7	38.65	6 355	866
Cicero	108.3	1 282	0.0	22.0	73.3	14.3	83.5	36.27	6 498	830
Collinsville	47.8	1 894	0.0	NA	NA	NA	NA	NA	NA	NA
Crystal Lake	42.4	1 049	0.0	28.6	76.3	19.0	87.2	46.96	5 168	1 112
Danville	12.0	367	4.4	25.8	75.3	17.3	86.2	40.96	5 555	1 027
Decatur	96.9	1 286	1.9	25.8	76.2	17.1	87.8	39.74	5 458	1 142
DeKalb	29.2	667	1.0	18.5	73.1	10.3	83.6	37.38	6 979	736
Des Plaines	71.7	1 218	4.0	22.0	73.3	14.3	83.5	36.27	6 498	830
Downers Grove	80.1	1 623	0.0	23.1	74.8	14.2	86.8	37.94	6 053	942
East St. Louis	25.4	954	0.0	29.1	78.6	20.0	88.7	40.33	4 826	1 378
Elgin	106.3	969	10.2	19.3	72.6	10.9	83.0	37.22	6 975	679
Elk Grove Village	52.6	1 579	0.3	22.0	73.3	14.3	83.5	36.27	6 498	830
Elmhurst	61.9	1 371	0.0	23.1	74.8	14.2	86.8	37.94	6 053	942
Evanston	237.9	3 154	19.4	22.0	72.9	13.7	83.2	36.80	6 630	702
Freeport	32.6	1 295	0.0	17.2	71.9	9.0	82.0	34.79	7 317	611
Galesburg	27.4	863	7.9	21.3	74.9	13.5	84.5	37.22	6 347	941
Glendale Heights	49.6	1 437	0.0	22.0	73.3	14.3	83.5	36.27	6 498	830
Glen Ellyn	13.3	482	0.0	21.7	74.4	12.2	85.7	38.58	6 359	888
Glenview	137.4	3 052	11.0	22.0	73.3	14.3	83.5	36.27	6 498	830
Granite City	30.0	1 015	2.2	27.7	78.4	19.4	88.1	38.54	5 149	1 354
Gurnee	16.1	518	10.0	19.9	72.2	12.1	82.2	35.50	6 955	634
Hanover Park	24.0	625	7.0	18.4	72.1	9.6	82.3	36.56	7 149	624
Harvey	50.8	2 004	0.0	22.0	74.2	14.8	83.7	38.65	6 355	866
Highland Park	44.8	1 503	4.6	22.0	72.9	13.7	83.2	36.80	6 630	702
Hoffman Estates	193.6	3 703	2.5	18.4	72.1	9.6	82.3	36.56	7 149	624
Joliet	61.9	417	12.6	21.7	73.7	13.5	84.6	36.96	6 464	809
Kankakee	78.1	2 856	8.7	21.7	74.4	12.2	85.7	38.58	6 359	888
Lake in the Hills	7.6	261	0.0	NA	NA	NA	NA	NA	NA	NA
Lansing	20.8	728	1.5	21.7	74.4	12.2	85.7	38.58	6 359	888
Lombard	219.0	5 007	0.0	23.1	74.8	14.2	86.8	37.94	6 053	942
McHenry	17.9	668	0.0	NA	NA	NA	NA	NA	NA	NA
Melrose Park	80.3	3 147	11.7	NA	NA	NA	NA	NA	NA	NA
Moline	79.9	1 853	18.2	21.8	76.4	13.3	85.1	35.10	6 179	1 100
Mount Prospect	40.7	745	9.3	22.0	73.3	14.3	83.5	36.27	6 498	830
Mundelein	21.6	693	0.0	18.4	72.1	9.6	82.3	36.56	7 149	624
Naperville	178.8	1 244	25.1	23.1	74.8	14.2	86.8	37.94	6 053	942
Niles	18.8	626	4.4	22.0	73.3	14.3	83.5	36.27	6 498	830
Normal	87.9	1 632	0.0	25.8	76.2	17.1	87.8	39.74	5 458	1 142
Northbrook	72.5	2 166	3.0	22.0	72.9	13.7	83.2	36.80	6 630	702
North Chicago	31.9	1 060	2.1	20.3	71.5	12.0	81.7	34.09	7 031	613
Oak Forest	30.0	1 067	0.0	22.0	74.2	14.8	83.7	38.65	6 355	866
Oak Lawn	87.5	1 535	9.2	23.5	75.5	16.2	84.7	38.35	6 083	1 001
Oak Park	104.7	2 013	11.4	22.0	73.3	14.3	83.5	36.27	6 498	830
O'Fallon	47.3	1 618	0.0	NA	NA	NA	NA	NA	NA	NA
Orland Park	81.7	1 427	10.0	23.5	75.5	16.2	84.7	38.35	6 083	1 001
Oswego	34.4	1 087	4.1	NA	NA	NA	NA	NA	NA	NA
Palatine	119.0	1 722	8.2	18.4	72.1	9.6	82.3	36.56	7 149	624
Park Ridge	45.7	1 210	7.5	22.0	73.3	14.3	83.5	36.27	6 498	830
Pekin	49.3	1 445	2.2	24.4	75.8	15.7	87.4	35.71	5 695	1 088
Peoria	222.0	1 920	9.4	22.5	75.1	14.3	85.7	36.03	6 097	998
Plainfield	63.7	1 575	8.4	NA	NA	NA	NA	NA	NA	NA
Quincy	20.2	494	0.0	24.9	76.8	16.0	88.0	35.63	5 707	1 117
Rockford	164.6	1 090	17.5	19.0	72.9	10.8	83.1	36.63	6 933	768
Rock Island	36.5	939	12.7	21.8	76.4	13.3	85.1	35.10	6 179	1 100
Romeoville	169.7	4 271	2.3	NA	NA	NA	NA	NA	NA	NA
Round Lake Beach	25.1	897	4.0	19.9	72.2	12.1	82.2	35.50	6 955	634
St. Charles	142.6	4 289	12.8	19.3	72.6	10.9	83.0	37.22	6 975	679
Schaumburg	302.1	4 043	23.0	18.4	72.1	9.6	82.3	36.56	7 149	624
Skokie	66.5	1 022	0.0	22.0	73.3	14.3	83.5	36.27	6 498	830
Springfield	703.4	6 000	0.3	25.1	76.3	17.1	86.5	35.56	5 596	1 165
Streamwood	10.0	249	0.0	19.3	72.6	10.9	83.0	37.22	6 975	679
Tinley Park	45.9	803	5.2	21.8	76.4	13.3	85.1	35.10	6 179	1 100
Urbana	11.4	273	0.0	20.7	73.2	12.4	83.7	34.47	6 606	774
Vernon Hills	24.7	969	9.5	NA	NA	NA	NA	NA	NA	NA

1. Based on the population estimated as of July 1 of the year shown. 2. Represents normal values based on the 30-year period, 1971–2000. 3. Average daily minimum. 4. Average daily maximum.

Table D. Cities — **Land Area and Population**

STATE Place code	City	Land area,[1] 2010 (sq km)	Population, 2014 Total persons	Rank	Per square kilometer	Race alone or in combination (percent), 2011-2013 White	Black	American Indian, Alaska Native	Asian	Hawaiian Pacific Islander	Percent Hispanic or Latino[2], 2011-2013	Percent foreign born 2011–2013
		1	2	3	4	5	6	7	8	9	10	11
	ILLINOIS—Cont'd											
17 79293	Waukegan	61.3	88 915	349	1 450.5	65.2	20.0	0.9	5.3	NA	54.2	30.0
17 80060	West Chicago	38.3	27 507	1 336	718.2	83.5	3.3	NA	6.9	NA	53.2	29.9
17 81048	Wheaton	29.1	53 644	691	1 843.4	87.5	4.9	0.6	8.4	NA	4.7	11.2
17 81087	Wheeling	22.5	38 010	974	1 689.3	69.3	2.2	NA	14.0	NA	32.7	41.9
17 82075	Wilmette	14.0	27 446	1 339	1 960.4	85.5	1.2	0.5	13.7	NA	4.6	17.8
17 83245	Woodridge	24.4	33 378	1 116	1 368.0	74.9	10.1	0.3	12.5	NA	13.4	19.8
18 00000	INDIANA	92 789.2	6 596 855	X	71.1	86.3	10.2	0.9	2.1	0.1	6.3	4.7
18 01468	Anderson	107.2	55 455	665	517.3	84.2	14.0	1.5	0.7	NA	5.6	2.8
18 05860	Bloomington	60.0	83 322	389	1 388.7	84.7	5.5	1.5	10.2	0.1	4.3	11.9
18 10342	Carmel	122.9	86 682	367	705.3	86.6	3.7	0.7	10.9	NA	2.7	12.4
18 14734	Columbus	71.2	46 124	812	647.8	86.7	4.4	0.7	7.9	NA	5.0	10.6
18 16138	Crown Point	45.9	28 623	1 284	623.6	89.2	6.6	0.5	2.5	NA	6.3	8.3
18 19486	East Chicago	36.5	28 990	1 272	794.2	31.9	38.9	1.1	0.4	NA	50.9	14.6
18 20728	Elkhart	60.7	51 421	727	847.1	75.0	15.7	1.7	1.4	NA	24.6	13.7
18 22000	Evansville	114.4	120 346	223	1 052.0	85.7	14.4	0.7	0.9	NA	3.0	2.3
18 23278	Fishers	87.0	86 325	368	992.2	87.8	6.8	0.4	6.5	NA	3.8	8.2
18 25000	Fort Wayne	286.5	258 522	77	902.3	77.1	18.2	1.1	4.0	0.2	8.3	7.8
18 27000	Gary	129.2	77 909	428	603.0	13.3	84.6	0.5	0.8	0.2	5.0	1.7
18 28386	Goshen	42.0	32 267	1 156	768.3	85.5	6.5	0.6	1.7	NA	26.3	17.3
18 29898	Greenwood	55.0	54 491	682	990.7	90.6	4.5	1.5	5.7	NA	4.4	7.1
18 31000	Hammond	59.0	78 384	424	1 328.5	52.1	23.6	2.0	1.6	NA	35.4	12.1
18 34114	Hobart	68.2	28 635	1 282	419.9	84.4	9.8	1.2	1.1	NA	15.3	5.7
18 36000	Indianapolis	949.1	848 788	14	906.7	64.0	29.5	0.8	2.8	0.1	9.7	8.3
18 38358	Jeffersonville	88.2	46 440	809	526.5	83.8	16.1	1.0	2.2	NA	4.7	3.9
18 40392	Kokomo	47.9	57 085	640	1 191.8	86.7	12.1	0.8	1.5	NA	3.4	2.8
18 40788	Lafayette	71.9	70 654	485	982.7	88.7	8.6	0.9	2.0	NA	12.8	7.3
18 42426	Lawrence	52.1	47 550	790	912.7	73.1	25.9	0.8	1.4	NA	11.9	7.1
18 46908	Marion	40.7	29 308	1 254	720.1	84.8	17.8	NA	1.2	NA	5.8	1.9
18 48528	Merrillville	86.0	35 450	1 052	412.2	48.0	47.2	1.6	1.9	NA	13.2	6.4
18 48798	Michigan City	50.7	31 487	1 181	621.0	69.6	30.4	0.7	1.5	NA	6.2	4.1
18 49932	Mishawaka	44.0	48 174	779	1 094.9	87.4	8.5	0.8	3.6	NA	5.5	5.9
18 51876	Muncie	70.4	70 211	490	997.3	88.5	9.6	4.2	2.1	0.2	2.6	2.6
18 52326	New Albany	38.7	36 589	1 017	945.5	89.6	9.4	0.8	0.7	NA	4.4	2.9
18 54180	Noblesville	81.3	57 584	635	708.3	92.4	5.2	0.3	1.9	NA	4.5	4.3
18 60246	Plainfield	57.7	30 409	1 217	527.0	85.9	7.4	0.8	5.7	NA	4.4	7.7
18 61092	Portage	66.4	36 760	1 010	553.6	89.2	9.2	NA	1.7	NA	18.6	5.5
18 64260	Richmond	61.9	36 159	1 033	584.2	89.3	10.0	1.0	1.4	0.1	4.1	3.6
18 68220	Schererville	38.1	28 926	1 274	759.2	87.8	5.0	NA	2.6	NA	12.6	9.6
18 71000	South Bend	107.4	101 190	295	942.2	66.4	30.0	1.3	1.3	0.1	13.8	7.5
18 75428	Terre Haute	89.5	60 956	585	681.1	86.7	12.7	1.1	2.1	NA	3.9	3.7
18 78326	Valparaiso	40.2	32 369	1 151	805.2	92.9	4.4	0.8	2.6	NA	7.0	4.4
18 82700	Westfield	69.5	35 297	1 058	507.9	93.1	3.5	NA	3.8	NA	4.8	4.4
18 82862	West Lafayette	19.7	32 109	1 162	1 629.9	75.5	5.0	0.2	21.1	NA	3.3	25.2
19 00000	IOWA	144 669.3	3 107 126	X	21.5	93.2	3.9	0.9	2.3	0.1	5.3	4.6
19 01855	Ames	62.7	63 266	558	1 009.0	86.6	4.3	0.6	10.2	NA	3.3	11.3
19 02305	Ankeny	76.0	53 801	690	707.9	96.7	1.8	1.1	2.5	NA	0.9	3.2
19 06355	Bettendorf	55.0	35 122	1 062	638.6	92.4	3.6	0.3	4.3	NA	2.6	4.5
19 09550	Burlington	37.5	25 539	1 407	681.0	91.9	9.2	0.9	0.6	NA	3.6	1.5
19 11755	Cedar Falls	74.5	40 859	907	548.4	95.0	2.1	0.4	3.1	NA	1.7	5.4
19 12000	Cedar Rapids	183.4	129 195	203	704.4	90.2	8.4	0.9	2.3	NA	3.7	3.3
19 14430	Clinton	91.1	26 246	1 390	288.1	92.0	7.1	0.9	1.4	NA	3.6	2.9
19 16860	Council Bluffs	106.1	62 245	571	586.7	96.2	3.1	0.9	0.7	0.1	8.7	3.5
19 19000	Davenport	163.0	102 448	289	628.5	84.4	13.6	1.2	2.8	NA	8.1	3.5
19 21000	Des Moines	209.5	209 220	105	998.7	80.5	12.7	1.0	5.4	0.1	12.4	11.5
19 22395	Dubuque	77.6	58 436	626	753.0	95.8	3.8	3.4	1.7	0.2	2.5	2.8
19 28515	Fort Dodge	41.6	24 594	1 429	591.2	90.7	7.6	0.8	1.4	NA	5.4	2.9
19 38595	Iowa City	64.8	73 415	463	1 132.9	83.6	6.9	0.7	8.1	NA	5.1	13.4
19 49485	Marion	41.6	36 774	1 008	884.0	94.0	2.2	NA	4.4	NA	1.0	4.0
19 49755	Marshalltown	49.9	27 727	1 320	555.7	80.6	2.8	0.9	3.8	NA	25.8	17.1
19 50160	Mason City	72.0	27 458	1 338	381.4	96.6	2.6	0.5	1.6	NA	3.6	1.7
19 60465	Ottumwa	41.1	24 682	1 428	600.5	92.1	2.6	0.9	1.5	NA	11.8	8.8
19 73335	Sioux City	148.5	82 517	396	555.7	84.9	4.7	3.5	3.4	NA	17.6	10.3
19 79950	Urbandale	56.8	43 150	857	759.7	93.3	3.6	0.4	4.5	NA	2.8	8.6
19 82425	Waterloo	159.0	68 364	506	430.0	81.2	17.7	0.7	2.0	NA	6.3	5.9
19 83910	West Des Moines	99.9	63 325	557	633.9	88.5	4.5	1.4	7.1	NA	5.7	10.9

1. Dry land or land partially or temporarily covered by water. 2. May be of any race.

City	Age of population (percent), 2011-2013									Median age 2011-2013	Percent female 2011-2013	Population			
												Census counts		Percent change	
	Under 5 years	5 to 17 years	18 to 24 years	25 to 34 years	35 to 44 years	45 to 54 years	55 to 64 years	65 to 74 years	75 years and over			2000	2010	2000–2010	2010–2014
	12	13	14	15	16	17	18	19	20	21	22	23	24	25	26
ILLINOIS—Cont'd															
Waukegan	7.8	20.7	11.8	15.7	12.4	13.3	10.1	4.2	3.9	31.0	49.9	87 901	89 078	1.3	-0.2
West Chicago	11.0	23.0	9.9	14.4	14.3	12.3	8.6	4.9	1.6	28.9	48.9	23 469	27 086	15.4	1.1
Wheaton	6.1	17.7	10.7	12.6	11.5	15.0	13.1	6.9	6.3	38.0	51.6	55 416	52 894	-4.6	1.3
Wheeling	7.2	14.1	7.2	17.4	14.3	13.0	13.1	6.7	7.0	38.1	53.5	34 496	37 648	9.1	1.0
Wilmette	6.0	24.8	5.3	4.3	13.4	15.3	13.4	10.0	7.5	42.8	49.9	27 651	27 087	-2.0	1.3
Woodridge	5.3	15.1	9.6	15.6	14.3	14.3	14.9	8.0	3.0	38.5	47.8	30 934	32 971	6.6	1.2
INDIANA	6.5	17.8	10.1	12.8	12.7	14.1	12.5	7.5	6.1	37.2	50.8	6 080 485	6 483 802	6.6	1.7
Anderson	5.8	17.0	11.5	13.3	11.7	12.7	11.9	8.1	8.1	37.0	52.4	59 734	56 129	-6.0	-1.3
Bloomington	4.3	7.2	44.4	14.5	8.8	6.5	6.0	4.2	4.2	23.3	49.9	69 291	80 405	16.0	3.8
Carmel	6.0	22.3	5.7	10.1	15.7	16.3	12.6	7.0	4.2	38.9	51.8	37 733	79 191	109.9	9.5
Columbus	6.3	18.6	8.1	14.8	14.3	12.9	10.1	7.4	7.5	36.2	51.0	39 059	44 061	12.8	4.6
Crown Point	4.0	15.8	7.0	13.8	14.1	14.9	13.4	8.3	8.7	41.2	50.7	19 806	27 317	37.9	2.8
East Chicago	9.2	22.3	10.7	13.2	10.7	11.7	10.8	6.0	5.3	30.5	53.6	32 414	29 698	-8.4	-2.4
Elkhart	8.4	19.5	10.3	14.6	12.9	13.0	10.1	5.1	6.0	33.1	52.0	51 874	50 949	-1.8	1.0
Evansville	6.8	15.2	10.9	15.4	10.7	13.9	12.1	7.4	7.6	36.6	52.8	121 582	117 429	-3.4	0.2
Fishers	8.1	24.2	6.0	14.0	18.1	16.0	7.6	3.6	2.4	33.7	51.2	37 835	76 794	103.0	12.3
Fort Wayne	7.5	18.4	10.3	13.8	12.5	13.0	11.8	6.6	6.1	35.0	51.8	205 727	253 691	23.3	1.9
Gary	7.3	20.2	9.2	11.4	10.7	12.7	13.3	8.1	7.2	36.8	55.2	102 746	80 294	-21.9	-3.0
Goshen	9.2	17.2	9.9	15.8	11.4	10.5	10.6	7.1	8.4	33.0	51.2	29 383	31 719	8.0	2.1
Greenwood	8.1	16.3	8.9	16.2	13.1	14.4	10.6	6.7	5.7	35.2	51.5	36 037	49 791	38.2	6.9
Hammond	7.9	19.9	10.5	14.5	12.0	15.2	10.2	5.1	4.8	32.9	51.0	83 048	80 830	-2.7	-3.0
Hobart	6.5	15.8	9.2	13.1	13.0	13.5	14.9	7.6	6.4	39.2	51.0	25 363	29 059	14.6	-2.4
Indianapolis	7.5	17.3	10.3	16.5	13.0	13.4	11.3	5.9	4.9	33.9	51.7	791 926	820 445	4.9	3.5
Jeffersonville	7.1	15.9	8.7	13.7	15.2	12.4	14.1	7.3	5.7	38.1	52.2	27 362	44 953	64.3	3.1
Kokomo	7.2	16.0	8.4	13.5	11.7	13.2	13.2	8.9	7.8	38.9	52.0	46 113	45 468	-1.4	0.4
Lafayette	7.9	16.2	13.6	18.3	11.8	11.2	10.2	5.4	5.6	31.1	52.1	56 397	67 140	19.0	2.6
Lawrence	7.9	20.6	7.0	15.8	11.8	15.6	11.1	5.3	4.7	33.7	51.1	38 915	46 001	18.2	3.4
Marion	6.2	13.1	17.7	11.5	10.6	13.0	11.2	7.7	9.0	37.0	55.5	31 320	29 948	-4.4	-2.0
Merrillville	6.2	19.0	7.5	14.4	14.4	12.2	13.5	6.7	6.1	37.2	49.9	30 560	35 246	15.3	1.4
Michigan City	7.0	15.4	10.7	13.3	12.5	14.9	12.0	8.0	6.3	37.9	49.8	32 900	31 479	-4.3	0.0
Mishawaka	7.5	15.8	12.8	15.6	12.8	12.5	10.1	6.0	6.8	33.4	52.7	46 557	48 252	3.6	-0.2
Muncie	4.7	11.6	29.2	11.9	8.6	10.2	10.1	7.3	6.4	27.9	53.2	67 430	70 085	3.9	0.0
New Albany	6.5	15.2	10.7	14.6	12.5	12.5	13.0	7.9	7.0	37.8	51.7	37 603	36 372	-3.3	0.7
Noblesville	8.3	20.3	6.4	15.9	16.1	12.2	10.2	5.9	4.6	34.4	50.6	28 590	51 969	81.8	10.5
Plainfield	5.8	16.8	8.5	14.9	14.8	13.5	12.1	6.8	6.7	38.0	49.9	18 396	27 631	50.2	10.0
Portage	5.9	18.3	10.0	14.2	12.4	13.7	12.7	7.9	4.9	36.6	51.9	33 496	36 828	9.9	-0.2
Richmond	6.9	14.3	11.9	12.6	11.4	13.6	12.5	8.8	8.0	38.6	51.7	39 124	36 812	-5.9	-1.7
Schererville	5.5	14.9	8.0	11.3	14.4	14.3	15.8	9.0	6.9	42.0	52.1	24 851	29 243	17.7	-1.1
South Bend	7.9	18.6	9.4	15.7	11.9	11.7	12.2	5.9	6.7	34.1	50.9	107 789	101 168	-6.1	0.1
Terre Haute	6.0	13.5	19.0	15.0	12.1	11.6	10.0	6.7	6.1	32.5	48.7	59 614	60 785	2.0	0.3
Valparaiso	5.0	16.4	14.3	15.8	12.9	11.2	10.7	5.4	8.3	33.6	50.2	27 428	31 730	15.7	2.0
Westfield	8.6	23.2	7.0	14.2	15.6	16.9	7.3	4.4	2.8	33.5	52.0	9 293	30 068	223.6	17.3
West Lafayette	3.2	8.9	47.9	11.5	6.9	7.0	5.9	3.0	5.7	22.9	45.2	28 778	29 596	2.8	8.5
IOWA	6.3	17.2	10.2	12.6	11.8	13.7	12.9	7.8	7.5	38.1	50.4	2 926 324	3 046 355	4.1	2.0
Ames	3.6	9.6	43.0	13.8	7.5	7.6	7.0	4.0	3.8	23.4	47.5	50 731	58 965	16.2	7.3
Ankeny	8.6	18.1	9.7	19.7	14.4	10.2	10.4	5.1	3.8	32.4	49.8	27 117	45 582	68.1	18.0
Bettendorf	6.3	17.3	6.0	10.9	13.8	16.1	13.5	8.6	7.5	41.6	51.5	31 275	33 217	6.2	5.7
Burlington	5.7	17.1	7.6	11.2	11.2	14.8	13.8	8.6	9.9	42.2	52.3	26 839	25 663	-4.4	-0.3
Cedar Falls	5.5	12.6	29.3	11.7	9.2	9.5	10.5	5.4	6.4	26.5	52.3	36 145	39 260	8.6	4.1
Cedar Rapids	6.9	16.2	12.2	14.2	12.4	12.8	12.1	6.6	6.6	35.4	51.1	120 758	126 326	4.6	2.3
Clinton	6.9	16.3	9.5	13.0	11.3	12.5	13.0	8.0	9.5	39.4	50.4	27 772	26 885	-3.2	-2.4
Council Bluffs	6.4	17.1	10.8	14.0	11.8	13.8	12.5	6.9	6.8	36.4	51.2	58 268	62 230	6.8	0.0
Davenport	7.2	17.0	10.3	15.6	12.2	12.8	12.4	6.5	6.1	35.0	50.9	98 359	99 685	1.3	2.8
Des Moines	8.0	17.1	10.5	17.0	12.8	12.8	10.9	6.0	5.0	33.2	50.7	198 682	203 433	2.4	2.5
Dubuque	5.6	14.8	13.0	13.3	10.5	13.3	12.6	7.5	9.3	38.2	52.0	57 686	57 637	-0.1	1.6
Fort Dodge	5.3	15.0	11.7	13.2	11.4	12.8	12.9	8.7	8.9	39.0	48.7	25 136	25 206	0.3	-2.4
Iowa City	4.9	10.7	32.7	16.3	8.7	9.2	8.7	4.7	4.2	25.6	49.9	62 220	67 862	9.1	8.1
Marion	6.4	20.2	6.4	14.9	14.1	14.2	10.1	7.4	6.2	36.7	50.6	26 294	34 768	32.2	5.8
Marshalltown	8.0	18.7	8.8	14.0	9.8	11.8	11.9	8.1	8.9	35.4	51.6	26 009	27 552	5.9	0.6
Mason City	4.5	16.3	9.4	10.6	12.2	15.0	13.6	8.6	9.8	43.4	50.7	29 172	28 079	-3.7	-2.2
Ottumwa	6.6	16.9	11.0	12.3	12.8	12.0	12.4	7.3	8.7	37.3	52.0	24 998	25 023	0.1	-1.4
Sioux City	7.8	18.0	11.1	13.7	11.8	12.6	11.9	6.9	6.0	34.4	50.7	85 013	82 684	-2.7	-0.2
Urbandale	6.2	19.9	6.5	12.1	15.3	15.7	12.3	6.9	5.0	38.8	52.4	29 072	39 463	35.7	9.4
Waterloo	7.0	16.1	11.3	14.6	10.9	12.1	12.5	7.7	7.7	35.7	50.8	68 747	68 406	-0.5	-0.1
West Des Moines	7.7	16.6	9.5	19.3	14.7	11.3	10.7	5.2	5.0	33.3	49.1	46 403	56 609	22.0	11.7

City	Households, 2011-2013				Persons in group quarters, 2010				Serious crimes known to police,[2] 2013				Educational attainment, 2011–2013		
			Percent			Institutional			Total		Rate[3]			Attainment[4] (percent)	
	Number	Persons per house-hold	Female family house-holder[1]	One-person	Total	Total	Persons in nursing facilities	Non-institu-tional	Number	Rate[3]	Violent	Property	Population age 25 and older	High school graduate or less	Bachelor's degree or more
	27	28	29	30	31	32	33	34	35	36	37	38	39	40	41
ILLINOIS—Cont'd															
Waukegan	28 899	3.01	19.7	24.9	2 077	1 586	842	491	2 914	3 283	456	2 827	53 089	57.1	17.1
West Chicago	7 327	3.68	11.6	13.2	333	325	325	8	418	1 511	119	1 392	15 320	51.7	24.8
Wheaton	19 066	2.65	7.1	26.2	3 379	1 395	578	1 984	487	908	60	849	34 988	16.6	60.5
Wheeling	14 428	2.59	10.5	29.3	465	461	461	4	503	1 323	105	1 218	27 111	38.6	35.4
Wilmette	9 479	2.87	8.4	20.9	126	69	69	57	379	1 385	26	1 360	17 488	6.1	82.8
Woodridge	12 747	2.55	8.9	27.9	88	86	0	2	447	1 338	72	1 266	22 813	23.5	47.2
INDIANA	2 482 558	2.56	12.4	27.9	186 923	95 336	41 158	91 587	211 023	3 211	357	2 854	4 287 171	47.5	23.5
Anderson	22 896	2.31	17.0	37.8	2 401	910	527	1 491	2 864	5 173	361	4 812	36 560	54.5	14.1
Bloomington	29 426	2.27	8.4	41.2	14 669	543	282	14 126	2 881	3 496	334	3 162	35 490	21.3	57.1
Carmel	30 700	2.72	7.3	19.8	600	579	470	21	764	900	24	877	55 315	11.4	69.0
Columbus	18 099	2.49	11.4	32.1	870	704	450	166	2 206	4 809	179	4 630	30 780	41.0	33.4
Crown Point	11 055	2.41	8.7	32.5	1 863	1 839	338	24	119	421	18	403	20 577	43.1	29.5
East Chicago	10 012	2.93	30.5	30.8	178	98	92	80	1 658	5 640	667	4 973	16 969	63.6	7.6
Elkhart	19 906	2.56	17.9	32.9	915	611	611	304	2 449	4 779	972	3 807	31 860	61.2	13.2
Evansville	50 843	2.27	16.3	37.1	4 727	2 103	1 194	2 624	6 423	5 340	469	4 871	80 675	50.1	18.4
Fishers	28 193	2.92	8.9	20.5	27	27	27	0	842	1 010	19	991	50 734	14.7	60.2
Fort Wayne	101 455	2.46	15.5	33.1	5 356	2 680	1 643	2 676	10 758	4 222	373	3 849	162 407	40.7	25.3
Gary	30 066	2.60	31.4	33.9	708	261	237	447	5 610	7 118	1 130	5 987	50 050	52.9	13.2
Goshen	11 549	2.61	17.7	26.0	1 467	808	411	659	1 128	3 504	93	3 410	20 230	57.8	21.7
Greenwood	20 782	2.52	11.2	29.2	481	456	405	25	2 108	3 962	376	3 586	35 195	42.4	26.6
Hammond	27 836	2.82	19.0	29.7	975	82	71	893	3 889	4 902	824	4 078	49 100	57.6	13.5
Hobart	11 609	2.48	9.2	32.0	144	1	0	143	1 598	5 581	213	5 368	19 834	53.1	16.4
Indianapolis	327 418	2.50	16.7	34.1	16 040	8 750	4 382	7 290	55 085	6 479	1 233	5 246	541 291	44.4	27.3
Jeffersonville	17 539	2.59	14.1	31.0	878	535	109	343	2 027	4 421	761	3 660	31 573	46.3	20.2
Kokomo	24 644	2.24	13.2	35.6	722	532	426	190	2 395	4 211	325	3 886	38 397	50.9	16.7
Lafayette	29 735	2.31	14.1	34.2	1 433	1 058	477	375	3 805	5 581	571	5 011	43 752	44.6	24.5
Lawrence	17 805	2.60	19.1	28.9	333	289	223	44	NA	NA	NA	NA	30 098	35.0	33.6
Marion	11 629	2.14	20.2	37.8	3 364	797	481	2 567	1 228	4 156	271	3 885	18 236	58.9	15.3
Merrillville	13 422	2.62	16.7	31.0	455	366	362	89	1 436	4 016	277	3 739	23 959	44.3	20.0
Michigan City	12 201	2.25	18.2	36.6	2 670	2 506	234	164	1 539	4 956	335	4 621	20 477	54.9	15.4
Mishawaka	20 938	2.28	14.7	37.2	1 013	212	83	801	2 840	5 921	284	5 637	31 162	47.7	22.6
Muncie	27 719	2.24	14.0	34.3	8 508	1 267	744	7 241	3 295	4 703	411	4 292	38 062	49.9	21.8
New Albany	15 033	2.37	17.7	34.4	1 008	724	429	284	2 089	5 725	238	5 486	24 716	52.5	16.1
Noblesville	21 716	2.60	9.0	27.0	661	632	316	29	119	213	18	195	37 214	24.1	46.6
Plainfield	9 811	2.64	11.9	23.2	2 615	2 595	145	20	936	3 157	169	2 989	19 392	40.7	26.9
Portage	13 584	2.70	17.9	24.3	255	233	233	22	936	2 539	190	2 349	24 323	54.1	15.4
Richmond	15 267	2.22	16.5	33.2	2 292	1 198	561	1 094	NA	NA	NA	NA	24 177	56.2	17.5
Schererville	11 623	2.49	9.9	26.7	120	63	0	57	694	2 474	71	2 403	20 866	37.3	34.0
South Bend	39 903	2.45	18.0	35.2	2 692	1 697	773	995	5 553	5 514	659	4 854	64 252	46.8	23.6
Terre Haute	21 276	2.44	14.1	36.8	8 875	4 173	589	4 702	3 438	5 616	289	5 327	37 337	48.2	20.5
Valparaiso	11 822	2.43	13.4	33.9	2 936	1 070	546	1 866	698	2 175	103	2 072	20 532	34.2	33.3
Westfield	11 555	2.78	10.4	21.0	139	99	99	40	509	1 557	64	1 492	19 775	19.6	56.8
West Lafayette	12 030	2.28	3.8	36.9	3 069	155	155	2 914	573	1 867	121	1 747	12 229	15.0	71.0
IOWA	1 227 201	2.43	9.5	29.0	98 112	43 282	26 871	54 830	76 188	2 465	271	2 194	2 038 371	41.4	26.1
Ames	23 425	2.26	4.1	31.1	7 767	294	181	7 473	1 536	2 510	154	2 356	26 703	14.8	62.4
Ankeny	19 252	2.53	7.8	23.6	663	174	146	489	743	1 480	86	1 395	31 351	19.2	45.7
Bettendorf	14 072	2.42	7.7	29.4	176	172	158	4	581	1 682	249	1 433	24 085	23.2	48.1
Burlington	10 933	2.30	16.6	31.6	495	367	235	128	906	3 528	569	2 960	17 821	44.9	19.8
Cedar Falls	14 034	2.51	5.1	28.4	4 574	354	354	4 220	550	1 368	129	1 238	21 019	28.1	45.2
Cedar Rapids	52 195	2.39	11.1	33.0	3 518	1 561	769	1 957	5 165	4 015	306	3 709	82 868	34.6	30.3
Clinton	11 102	2.33	14.0	31.5	713	379	347	334	1 228	4 621	670	3 952	17 958	46.7	18.7
Council Bluffs	24 524	2.45	16.0	31.1	1 908	964	440	944	5 210	8 400	943	7 457	40 825	48.7	17.7
Davenport	40 326	2.44	13.7	34.5	3 111	1 247	751	1 864	4 902	4 814	642	4 171	66 408	40.1	26.4
Des Moines	80 831	2.48	14.9	32.3	6 104	1 641	1 005	4 463	11 054	5 330	496	4 834	133 059	43.4	25.3
Dubuque	23 736	2.27	11.8	36.1	4 027	1 133	806	2 894	1 768	3 032	226	2 806	38 627	43.9	29.0
Fort Dodge	10 203	2.16	16.1	37.8	2 509	1 651	345	858	1 288	5 229	650	4 579	16 825	44.4	19.5
Iowa City	28 694	2.21	8.7	35.3	6 585	296	168	6 289	2 157	3 044	344	2 700	36 366	17.6	58.7
Marion	14 439	2.46	10.1	30.0	292	214	210	78	634	1 752	155	1 598	23 971	27.2	34.4
Marshalltown	9 857	2.71	12.1	26.5	1 190	1 040	985	150	909	3 279	620	2 659	17 947	48.8	20.2
Mason City	12 899	2.10	8.1	39.8	856	448	344	408	1 160	4 181	108	4 073	19 432	39.9	20.2
Ottumwa	10 204	2.36	14.2	33.3	826	371	248	455	1 262	5 101	299	4 802	16 279	52.8	15.7
Sioux City	31 146	2.56	14.4	30.8	2 565	743	437	1 822	4 000	4 838	400	4 438	52 062	51.3	18.6
Urbandale	16 215	2.53	7.9	24.1	234	230	222	4	737	1 776	161	1 614	27 801	22.7	49.9
Waterloo	28 562	2.36	13.5	36.4	1 165	687	515	478	2 596	3 803	844	2 959	44 794	51.8	19.2
West Des Moines	24 892	2.38	8.8	29.9	273	262	262	11	1 752	2 917	151	2 765	39 459	18.6	52.6

1. No spouse present. 2. Data for serious crimes have not been adjusted for underreporting. This may affect comparability between geographic areas and over time. 3. Per 100,000 population estimated by the FBI. 4. Persons 25 years old and over.

Table D. Cities — **Income, Poverty, and Housing**

City	Money income, 2011–2013: Per capita income[1] (dollars)	Money income, 2011–2013: Households: Median income	Money income, 2011–2013: Households: Percent with income of $200,000 or more	Money income, 2011–2013: Households: Percent with income of less than $25,000	Money income, 2011–2013: Families with income below poverty (percent)	Housing units, 2010: Total	Housing units, 2010: Percent change, 2000–2010	Housing units, 2010: Vacant units for sale or rent[2]	Occupied housing units 2011–2013: Total	Occupied housing units 2011–2013: Owner-occupied: Percent	Occupied housing units 2011–2013: Owner-occupied: Median value[3] (dollars)	Occupied housing units 2011–2013: Median owner costs as a percent of income: With a mortgage[4]	Occupied housing units 2011–2013: Median owner costs as a percent of income: Without a mortgage[5]
	42	43	44	45	46	47	48	49	50	51	52	53	54
ILLINOIS—Cont'd													
Waukegan	20 393	42 601	2.7	28.6	19.9	30 746	5.1	2 667	28 899	50.5	126 200	27.8	13.9
West Chicago	24 216	66 638	8.6	13.4	14.2	7 763	15.2	433	7 327	66.8	220 900	27.6	13.0
Wheaton	40 738	82 010	12.3	12.2	5.4	20 112	1.1	921	19 066	69.3	327 000	23.2	13.9
Wheeling	27 270	56 787	4.1	19.5	9.5	15 397	12.5	936	14 428	64.8	164 300	29.1	14.3
Wilmette	64 716	125 203	31.1	8.4	2.5	10 290	-0.4	548	9 479	86.5	603 400	26.4	14.9
Woodridge	40 300	74 821	8.5	8.0	3.3	13 392	14.6	746	12 747	66.3	252 900	24.5	14.1
INDIANA	24 514	47 839	2.6	25.1	11.6	2 795 541	10.4	293 387	2 482 558	69.2	122 300	20.2	10.8
Anderson	17 970	31 860	0.5	40.0	21.7	27 953	1.3	4 393	22 896	56.4	73 500	21.4	13.8
Bloomington	19 196	27 393	3.2	46.7	19.9	33 239	17.2	1 814	29 426	32.9	172 800	21.2	10.0
Carmel	52 683	107 580	19.1	7.6	2.7	30 738	117.0	1 741	30 700	77.9	300 400	18.1	10.0
Columbus	28 452	54 877	3.9	21.3	9.7	19 700	14.9	1 913	18 099	63.4	139 000	19.4	10.6
Crown Point	30 221	61 574	3.4	19.8	4.4	10 976	36.0	582	11 055	76.2	173 400	21.4	12.5
East Chicago	13 615	25 557	0.3	49.5	35.2	12 958	-2.3	2 234	10 012	43.8	78 300	23.7	13.3
Elkhart	16 354	33 547	0.4	35.1	26.4	22 699	4.9	3 438	19 906	50.9	83 100	22.1	12.4
Evansville	20 612	35 013	1.4	33.8	16.4	57 799	1.2	7 211	50 843	53.9	88 500	20.9	12.5
Fishers	38 534	93 203	8.9	6.7	1.9	28 511	82.0	1 293	28 193	85.1	207 800	19.6	10.0
Fort Wayne	22 911	42 309	1.8	28.2	16.4	113 541	24.9	11 956	101 455	62.8	98 700	19.4	10.0
Gary	15 548	25 969	0.7	48.5	36.3	39 531	-9.4	8 151	30 066	52.2	65 200	24.8	13.5
Goshen	18 511	40 746	0.8	30.0	17.9	12 631	12.2	1 287	11 549	58.2	112 900	22.7	12.2
Greenwood	25 203	50 964	0.8	21.1	13.4	21 339	33.6	1 724	20 782	60.7	129 400	19.5	10.1
Hammond	17 154	36 893	0.5	33.1	20.9	32 945	-3.5	2 996	27 836	61.6	88 700	22.7	13.1
Hobart	26 780	56 828	1.9	20.1	7.4	12 399	20.6	749	11 609	68.4	129 800	21.2	13.0
Indianapolis	23 722	41 154	2.4	30.2	17.3	384 414	7.6	48 228	327 418	53.9	116 900	21.0	11.7
Jeffersonville	24 857	50 375	1.8	24.1	10.0	19 991	60.9	1 411	17 539	71.4	125 900	20.6	11.9
Kokomo	21 371	35 555	1.1	33.8	16.1	23 010	3.0	3 162	24 644	62.4	80 100	19.6	10.5
Lafayette	20 960	40 153	0.9	29.8	15.9	31 260	22.4	2 715	29 735	48.3	101 300	19.4	10.2
Lawrence	24 188	49 672	1.6	23.2	14.4	19 515	19.9	1 651	17 805	67.2	122 100	21.0	15.7
Marion	17 627	31 700	1.0	38.5	25.0	13 715	-0.6	1 887	11 629	58.6	64 000	21.8	11.1
Merrillville	23 280	52 465	0.7	24.7	9.2	14 842	19.8	1 146	13 422	63.2	126 600	24.2	10.0
Michigan City	18 014	35 145	0.8	38.1	26.3	14 435	1.5	2 299	12 201	53.8	90 900	19.5	13.1
Mishawaka	20 104	36 157	0.7	31.1	18.0	24 088	11.4	2 745	20 938	47.9	92 200	21.6	12.1
Muncie	16 916	27 848	0.8	46.2	20.1	31 958	5.8	4 236	27 719	49.5	71 300	19.8	12.8
New Albany	21 887	40 452	1.2	34.8	20.9	17 315	1.5	1 740	15 033	56.1	113 600	22.6	11.3
Noblesville	31 204	65 530	4.9	14.3	6.1	21 121	86.3	2 041	21 716	71.9	171 400	21.4	11.1
Plainfield	25 437	60 778	1.8	15.5	4.3	10 386	38.3	639	9 811	77.0	147 300	19.8	12.8
Portage	23 310	57 089	0.6	23.7	13.1	14 807	11.1	815	13 584	72.3	135 200	19.8	11.9
Richmond	17 837	29 108	0.8	43.6	26.4	17 649	-0.4	2 551	15 267	58.4	77 900	22.5	12.3
Schererville	35 117	65 617	5.7	12.3	4.0	12 393	24.0	510	11 623	76.2	213 800	21.6	11.5
South Bend	19 052	33 820	1.5	36.9	23.7	46 324	0.2	6 564	39 903	60.0	82 100	21.2	11.4
Terre Haute	17 474	31 597	1.3	40.4	19.7	25 518	-0.3	2 873	21 276	54.5	77 200	19.6	11.8
Valparaiso	23 982	49 715	1.6	25.6	10.1	13 506	15.8	896	11 822	57.0	163 300	20.0	10.3
Westfield	36 763	79 326	8.2	11.6	5.1	11 209	NA	719	11 555	79.4	214 500	20.3	10.4
West Lafayette	21 166	29 901	3.9	44.3	8.1	12 591	16.5	646	12 030	31.7	174 100	16.7	10.0
IOWA	26 992	51 653	2.9	22.5	8.4	1 336 417	8.4	114 841	1 227 201	71.8	125 500	20.0	11.5
Ames	22 436	40 097	2.0	35.2	9.0	23 876	27.6	1 117	23 425	41.5	172 400	19.9	10.0
Ankeny	32 133	71 469	3.6	12.1	3.4	18 339	69.8	906	19 252	72.1	172 300	20.1	11.7
Bettendorf	39 589	75 020	9.0	15.5	4.7	14 437	10.6	756	14 072	76.5	180 000	18.7	10.4
Burlington	23 401	37 042	2.4	31.1	17.3	11 899	-1.0	961	10 933	68.2	86 200	21.7	13.9
Cedar Falls	25 066	51 921	2.8	24.4	7.6	15 477	16.4	869	14 034	64.1	167 500	18.7	10.0
Cedar Rapids	27 993	51 338	2.7	22.1	7.8	57 217	9.7	3 981	52 195	68.9	136 500	20.1	13.5
Clinton	24 225	42 549	2.2	29.1	15.2	12 202	-1.8	956	11 102	65.7	89 800	19.6	13.5
Council Bluffs	22 748	44 336	1.7	25.7	11.6	26 594	9.1	1 801	24 524	63.9	111 500	22.0	13.0
Davenport	23 740	45 323	1.4	27.2	12.8	44 087	6.6	3 467	40 326	60.3	120 600	20.4	12.5
Des Moines	23 359	44 830	1.8	26.6	15.6	88 729	4.3	7 360	80 831	62.4	117 300	21.7	13.2
Dubuque	24 626	44 415	2.2	26.4	10.8	25 029	5.1	1 523	23 736	63.1	130 800	20.7	12.8
Fort Dodge	21 914	35 618	1.8	36.5	16.0	11 215	0.1	940	10 203	61.4	80 800	19.4	10.6
Iowa City	25 400	40 996	4.2	34.4	11.1	29 270	12.4	1 613	28 694	46.8	183 400	21.5	10.1
Marion	30 435	64 582	3.6	18.1	2.8	15 064	37.2	956	14 439	76.4	144 200	19.8	11.6
Marshalltown	22 479	49 192	1.5	23.5	11.9	11 171	2.9	836	9 857	66.7	102 700	19.6	12.2
Mason City	25 434	40 851	2.0	31.5	10.3	13 352	2.3	986	12 899	66.7	101 100	20.6	13.6
Ottumwa	10 886	36 676	1.0	35.3	17.9	11 257	2.6	1 008	10 204	66.6	73 600	19.6	14.2
Sioux City	21 703	41 759	1.7	27.7	13.4	33 425	-1.1	1 854	31 146	64.7	94 400	20.4	12.1
Urbandale	40 311	75 700	8.5	10.3	4.2	16 319	37.7	723	16 215	83.0	189 200	19.7	10.0
Waterloo	21 518	40 466	1.1	28.5	14.3	30 723	4.2	2 116	28 562	64.3	101 100	20.7	12.1
West Des Moines	38 627	70 755	6.6	15.1	6.3	26 219	26.2	1 908	24 892	59.0	183 800	19.3	10.3

1. Based on population estimated by the American Community Survey. 2. Includes units rented or sold but not occupied. 3. Specified owner-occupied units; $1,000,000 represents $1,000,000 or more 4. 50.0 represents 50 percent or more. 5. 10.0 represents 10 percent or less.

City	Occupied housing units, 2011–2013 (cont.)				Migration, 2011–2013		Civilian labor force, 2014				Civilian employment[4], 2011–2013			
									Unemployment			Percent		
	Percent renter occupied	Median gross rent[1]	Median rent as a percent of income[2]	Percent with no vehicle available	Percent who lived in the same house one year ago	Percent who lived outside current city one year ago	Total	Percent change, 2013–2014	Total	Rate[3]	Population age 16 and older	In labor force	Civilian full-year full-time workers	Households with no workers (percent)
	55	56	57	58	59	60	61	62	63	64	65	66	67	68
ILLINOIS—Cont'd														
Waukegan	49.5	838	30.9	9.1	81.8	9.2	45 085	-0.2	3 954	8.8	66 612	69.8	40.2	23.2
West Chicago	33.2	922	36.1	3.4	88.2	5.1	14 505	-0.1	1 009	7.0	19 042	73.7	44.9	11.7
Wheaton	30.7	1 211	29.2	5.3	82.3	11.9	28 966	0.4	1 511	5.2	42 653	68.0	41.2	21.3
Wheeling	35.2	1 042	30.4	6.3	88.2	10.0	22 489	-0.1	1 317	5.9	30 537	73.1	50.9	18.8
Wilmette	13.5	1 642	24.0	3.3	91.3	6.1	12 855	0.7	665	5.2	19 913	60.6	40.4	22.5
Woodridge	33.7	1 090	25.2	3.0	89.9	9.6	20 198	0.5	1 143	5.7	26 788	76.2	52.6	15.8
INDIANA	30.8	727	30.1	7.0	85.0	9.5	3 230 540	1.2	194 959	6.0	5 129 665	64.0	39.6	27.4
Anderson	43.6	647	33.9	14.3	77.4	8.4	23 481	0.3	1 908	8.1	44 342	55.4	28.6	41.7
Bloomington	67.1	788	46.3	11.8	53.8	24.2	37 090	0.8	2 264	6.1	72 063	55.8	22.6	33.7
Carmel	22.1	1 108	21.9	2.9	86.8	9.1	45 332	2.4	1 796	4.0	62 940	71.6	49.6	16.8
Columbus	36.6	796	26.4	6.5	84.6	8.8	24 471	2.6	1 030	4.2	35 847	65.1	44.0	27.7
Crown Point	23.8	879	24.7	5.2	89.2	7.7	14 518	0.8	1 014	7.0	23 086	62.5	37.2	25.4
East Chicago	56.2	650	32.3	21.6	85.0	7.3	10 368	0.8	1 120	10.8	20 938	53.3	28.4	43.0
Elkhart	49.1	660	29.4	14.1	75.9	11.6	24 039	2.1	1 546	6.4	38 500	65.0	37.6	29.2
Evansville	46.1	693	31.0	11.7	81.9	7.0	59 056	1.0	3 504	5.9	96 335	62.0	39.4	30.3
Fishers	14.9	1 025	28.0	1.5	90.4	7.8	45 486	2.4	1 800	4.0	58 293	76.6	53.7	8.8
Fort Wayne	37.2	656	28.8	8.6	84.3	4.8	121 075	0.6	7 408	6.1	195 744	65.5	40.5	27.8
Gary	47.8	702	41.5	19.3	83.5	6.9	27 960	-1.0	3 226	11.5	59 670	50.6	25.8	45.1
Goshen	41.8	747	30.4	10.0	78.9	10.2	15 706	3.0	798	5.1	23 930	61.0	36.0	30.2
Greenwood	39.3	797	28.7	5.2	82.2	13.1	27 572	2.1	1 456	5.3	41 138	68.3	44.0	24.3
Hammond	38.4	785	33.3	8.9	85.7	8.0	35 281	0.1	2 904	8.2	59 854	61.6	33.8	30.0
Hobart	31.6	832	25.7	5.9	91.6	5.0	15 030	0.9	1 345	8.9	22 949	68.7	44.5	25.3
Indianapolis	46.1	769	32.3	9.9	83.1	5.9	429 511	1.2	27 881	6.5	648 367	67.5	40.6	26.5
Jeffersonville	28.6	717	29.0	6.6	89.6	6.2	23 533	2.2	1 110	4.7	36 547	65.3	43.1	28.5
Kokomo	37.6	614	34.4	11.4	80.5	8.0	24 847	1.7	1 546	6.2	44 585	60.0	34.1	35.7
Lafayette	51.7	744	29.9	9.0	75.9	11.7	37 420	1.0	1 950	5.2	54 821	70.5	43.5	23.7
Lawrence	32.8	798	27.8	6.9	83.3	13.5	25 264	1.4	1 484	5.9	34 445	75.3	46.2	19.9
Marion	41.4	567	27.6	16.0	80.4	8.2	13 066	0.4	1 091	8.3	23 926	52.3	27.8	42.9
Merrillville	36.8	910	31.1	7.9	82.7	14.1	17 171	0.5	1 392	8.1	27 677	66.8	39.6	26.9
Michigan City	46.2	692	33.9	11.5	79.0	11.2	12 977	-1.0	1 051	8.1	24 491	55.0	30.5	35.6
Mishawaka	52.1	702	27.6	7.9	77.7	15.3	24 545	1.1	1 617	6.6	38 495	66.4	37.8	27.0
Muncie	50.5	665	42.0	11.9	63.3	18.5	31 094	-1.0	2 304	7.4	60 037	55.9	24.4	37.4
New Albany	43.9	690	30.0	11.7	84.2	9.1	18 256	2.0	1 110	6.1	29 711	64.2	39.6	31.0
Noblesville	28.1	870	25.8	3.1	83.7	13.3	30 869	2.2	1 347	4.4	42 204	74.5	52.2	17.2
Plainfield	23.0	914	28.4	1.9	82.9	14.9	14 399	2.1	750	5.2	22 500	59.0	41.0	22.9
Portage	27.7	801	26.1	5.4	86.5	7.0	17 834	0.7	1 356	7.6	28 927	62.2	39.9	29.2
Richmond	41.6	602	31.6	15.5	78.5	10.1	15 182	1.5	1 112	7.3	29 405	52.7	28.3	37.0
Schererville	23.8	829	27.0	4.4	90.6	6.9	16 021	1.0	932	5.8	24 006	66.1	46.3	23.4
South Bend	40.0	685	32.9	13.1	80.9	9.1	45 970	0.8	3 523	7.7	76 257	65.0	34.8	31.1
Terre Haute	45.5	660	34.7	10.6	80.4	10.7	25 781	-0.9	2 147	8.3	50 181	54.7	27.2	33.3
Valparaiso	43.0	820	29.1	11.1	80.4	13.3	15 749	0.5	922	5.9	26 043	60.4	35.2	27.1
Westfield	20.6	884	25.7	6.1	88.9	8.7	17 931	2.5	674	3.8	23 304	72.8	52.7	11.0
West Lafayette	68.3	826	50.0	13.0	53.9	31.4	14 191	2.3	619	4.4	27 257	51.3	19.8	36.3
IOWA	28.2	673	27.9	5.7	84.9	9.2	1 704 575	1.9	75 249	4.4	2 433 609	67.6	44.0	25.7
Ames	58.5	747	38.3	7.1	57.5	22.5	38 435	3.9	1 039	2.7	53 759	66.8	31.2	22.1
Ankeny	27.9	790	24.7	3.4	80.7	12.8	30 333	2.7	868	2.9	37 157	77.8	56.4	15.2
Bettendorf	23.5	781	30.9	4.1	87.5	9.3	17 854	0.8	759	4.3	27 108	65.3	44.3	27.2
Burlington	31.8	655	30.1	10.4	86.0	5.4	13 005	2.1	702	5.4	20 465	61.9	37.4	32.0
Cedar Falls	35.9	739	34.8	5.9	77.4	13.0	23 081	1.0	803	3.5	33 488	68.0	33.5	25.5
Cedar Rapids	31.1	672	28.6	7.1	82.9	8.6	71 937	0.5	3 301	4.6	101 678	70.6	45.4	23.7
Clinton	34.3	610	30.4	9.4	83.6	4.9	12 958	-0.3	734	5.7	21 164	61.8	35.9	34.2
Council Bluffs	36.1	741	28.6	7.8	81.2	7.6	32 543	2.2	1 504	4.6	48 956	66.2	45.5	27.4
Davenport	39.7	687	29.9	8.5	84.5	6.8	51 714	0.5	3 017	5.8	79 340	64.7	41.0	28.1
Des Moines	37.6	734	31.3	8.8	78.6	8.9	112 507	2.4	5 817	5.2	159 324	70.4	44.8	24.8
Dubuque	36.9	690	30.6	8.5	81.2	9.6	33 490	1.4	1 388	4.1	47 366	66.4	41.0	27.4
Fort Dodge	38.6	539	31.6	7.7	78.1	14.1	12 685	0.8	672	5.3	20 368	58.2	33.3	34.6
Iowa City	53.2	831	39.6	10.8	62.7	18.2	42 829	1.9	1 332	3.1	60 583	67.5	34.1	22.0
Marion	23.6	642	24.9	4.9	84.4	10.7	19 666	0.8	757	3.8	27 125	72.5	49.3	22.0
Marshalltown	33.3	636	26.3	9.2	82.2	7.4	13 000	1.1	787	6.1	21 234	62.3	38.8	31.7
Mason City	33.3	598	29.8	10.8	88.1	6.2	14 778	0.1	702	4.8	22 908	67.0	40.3	29.1
Ottumwa	33.4	602	32.9	9.3	81.8	5.8	12 540	0.9	738	5.9	19 818	60.7	34.9	33.1
Sioux City	35.3	653	29.7	8.4	81.4	6.8	45 197	2.1	2 045	4.5	63 547	68.8	42.4	25.7
Urbandale	17.0	783	26.3	2.9	90.1	8.7	24 814	2.7	779	3.1	31 703	74.8	51.9	15.9
Waterloo	35.7	652	31.3	9.0	86.0	6.3	35 830	1.0	2 146	6.0	54 003	65.9	40.9	32.9
West Des Moines	41.0	884	24.3	3.8	78.6	16.7	37 550	2.9	1 196	3.2	46 668	76.2	53.5	17.6

1. $2,000 represents $2,000 or more. 2. 50.0 represents 50 percent or more. 3. Percent of civilian labor force. 4. Persons 16 years old and over.

City	Value of residential construction authorized by building permits, 2014			Wholesale trade,[1] 2007				Retail trade,[2] 2007			
	New construction ($1,000)	Number of housing units	Percent single family	Number of establish-ments	Number of employees	Sales (mil dol)	Annual payroll (mil dol)	Number of establish-ments	Number of employees	Sales (mil dol)	Annual payroll (mil dol)
	69	70	71	72	73	74	75	76	77	78	79
ILLINOIS—Cont'd											
Waukegan	6 299	41	65.9	67	1 398	1 285.6	76.0	236	4 515	1 112.9	139.7
West Chicago	1 617	6	100.0	80	1 592	946.9	84.1	93	1 241	372.0	35.8
Wheaton	21 987	61	100.0	58	253	168.7	17.4	191	3 068	603.8	61.6
Wheeling	9 450	96	0.0	137	2 218	1 125.9	127.3	108	1 271	334.2	35.6
Wilmette	26 485	44	100.0	28	75	102.3	4.2	129	1 398	297.8	38.1
Woodridge	8 010	29	100.0	55	1 904	1 509.1	115.2	92	1 702	428.3	40.9
INDIANA	3 222 176	17 816	68.1	6 756	97 219	67 634.9	4 295.6	23 692	333 172	78 745.6	7 123.1
Anderson	3 519	24	83.3	38	707	212.3	26.2	269	4 063	863.0	79.4
Bloomington	NA	NA	NA	49	628	450.6	27.5	394	6 324	1 267.8	122.0
Carmel	210 549	1 066	33.0	100	985	1 276.5	67.1	249	3 602	786.3	82.5
Columbus	NA	NA	NA	55	885	677.7	47.0	236	3 787	822.0	81.1
Crown Point	56 799	225	88.4	25	259	244.0	11.7	88	1 239	257.1	25.0
East Chicago	235	1	100.0	33	507	380.8	20.0	53	450	130.2	11.4
Elkhart	735	4	100.0	143	2 152	1 330.5	91.1	283	4 492	1 121.6	100.3
Evansville	14 057	92	95.7	194	4 327	2 395.3	230.9	728	11 399	2 450.3	245.5
Fishers	228 408	1 112	50.7	86	1 493	761.3	90.6	171	3 367	910.0	83.7
Fort Wayne	NA	NA	NA	422	6 310	4 927.4	242.8	1 157	19 477	4 392.0	402.2
Gary	1 315	7	100.0	55	1 323	802.3	75.6	198	1 522	548.1	29.8
Goshen	6 678	40	100.0	26	461	220.4	17.9	172	3 175	737.3	72.5
Greenwood	54 630	308	100.0	41	742	456.0	32.5	310	5 811	1 216.2	122.9
Hammond	862	4	100.0	64	1 067	512.8	53.8	236	3 116	1 031.8	70.3
Hobart	3 945	18	100.0	26	223	316.1	10.5	267	5 547	1 073.4	99.4
Indianapolis	167 626	1 126	50.8	1 264	24 462	15 103.1	1 201.6	3 036	49 297	12 140.2	1 192.8
Jeffersonville	26 076	250	47.2	41	761	629.0	33.3	106	1 435	330.7	32.8
Kokomo	14 766	108	70.4	46	388	237.2	18.0	328	4 829	1 078.4	97.3
Lafayette	16 209	166	50.6	74	859	285.3	37.8	431	7 594	1 596.7	150.1
Lawrence	10 139	69	100.0	37	281	205.1	12.9	123	2 004	408.3	43.3
Marion	3 284	36	41.7	27	249	95.0	9.7	203	2 684	607.0	55.3
Merrillville	5 009	39	64.1	30	323	195.8	15.2	199	3 869	1 071.2	90.4
Michigan City	1 600	40	40.0	38	559	332.9	22.3	262	3 721	730.1	68.0
Mishawaka	8 232	59	72.9	65	890	991.9	52.7	385	7 739	1 766.8	152.1
Muncie	7 151	62	29.0	63	801	320.7	25.3	379	5 143	1 044.6	99.6
New Albany	4 652	32	100.0	57	802	1 390.8	30.4	154	2 463	515.3	53.0
Noblesville	132 478	799	55.4	69	442	147.5	20.9	165	3 199	727.9	73.5
Plainfield	28 627	155	96.1	28	2 020	2 337.3	84.5	137	2 849	715.6	60.8
Portage	4 536	38	78.9	29	637	472.4	31.3	103	1 886	454.0	41.3
Richmond	7 381	71	11.3	43	427	248.2	16.5	220	3 612	902.5	76.6
Schererville	14 172	50	76.0	26	173	68.0	8.0	131	2 499	625.9	60.1
South Bend	NA	NA	NA	168	3 485	1 880.0	142.8	336	6 510	1 425.2	148.7
Terre Haute	17 050	186	5.9	83	1 001	432.7	36.2	362	5 627	1 174.3	112.5
Valparaiso	34 025	156	59.0	37	308	206.5	25.8	204	3 626	852.1	79.1
Westfield	142 575	647	64.1	29	433	180.9	20.2	100	2 268	492.6	47.0
West Lafayette	49 719	432	29.9	10	107	22.9	3.2	85	1 504	268.7	26.9
IOWA	1 907 579	10 256	68.1	4 361	55 874	41 068.3	2 276.7	13 203	177 156	39 234.6	3 561.1
Ames	66 548	441	20.6	42	270	150.6	12.0	224	3 950	836.1	80.0
Ankeny	243 075	1 180	82.5	56	1 262	1 118.3	54.9	122	2 988	755.5	65.2
Bettendorf	44 416	168	100.0	40	462	503.9	22.2	108	1 586	306.9	34.2
Burlington	4 387	29	100.0	24	308	331.5	10.2	121	1 633	261.0	29.8
Cedar Falls	44 807	181	83.4	42	776	416.1	29.4	161	2 767	611.0	57.3
Cedar Rapids	45 054	449	72.4	211	3 637	1 974.4	173.6	562	11 148	2 774.6	236.6
Clinton	8 294	61	27.9	25	177	66.2	5.7	142	2 145	470.9	42.5
Council Bluffs	14 891	73	100.0	59	1 115	1 984.8	50.9	253	5 378	1 294.8	106.1
Davenport	20 744	120	75.0	184	2 949	2 268.3	128.2	523	9 471	2 168.1	200.0
Des Moines	46 376	283	41.0	278	4 779	2 667.7	221.4	718	10 528	2 240.8	229.1
Dubuque	11 662	82	100.0	85	1 156	1 079.9	46.0	355	5 778	1 156.7	110.8
Fort Dodge	1 415	9	55.6	43	429	189.7	19.6	164	2 555	531.7	49.4
Iowa City	81 693	445	50.8	32	507	208.4	18.9	276	4 064	889.5	88.7
Marion	25 765	221	66.1	29	346	242.1	15.1	116	1 714	384.2	38.0
Marshalltown	411	4	0.0	23	289	186.7	13.5	145	1 984	373.0	39.1
Mason City	10 743	67	28.4	49	497	323.8	19.6	192	3 470	719.0	67.3
Ottumwa	316	4	50.0	21	223	123.4	7.8	140	2 323	458.8	43.3
Sioux City	17 741	88	86.4	137	2 298	1 492.6	97.6	418	7 017	1 425.6	136.0
Urbandale	63 123	246	63.4	103	1 440	817.5	72.1	164	2 938	961.1	93.5
Waterloo	10 786	93	84.9	82	1 411	641.8	51.6	320	5 346	1 134.5	108.0
West Des Moines	76 606	319	75.5	47	589	275.1	28.5	408	8 702	1 228.5	144.6

1. Merchant wholesalers except manufacturers' sales branches and offices. 2. Establishments with payroll.

City	Real estate and rental and leasing, 2007				Professional, scientific, and technical services,[1] 2007				Manufacturing, 2007			
	Number of establish-ments	Number of employees	Receipts (mil dol)	Annual payroll (mil dol)	Number of establish-ments	Number of employees	Receipts (mil dol)	Annual payroll (mil dol)	Number of establish-ments	Number of employees	Receipts (mil dol)	Annual payroll (mil dol)
	80	81	82	83	84	85	86	87	88	89	90	91
ILLINOIS—Cont'd												
Waukegan	55	304	53.8	8.6	158	D	D	D	86	5 521	1 601.4	287.8
West Chicago	32	226	52.2	10.4	82	D	D	D	107	5 323	2 130.7	224.2
Wheaton	67	306	46.2	11.3	401	D	D	D	NA	NA	NA	NA
Wheeling	34	119	60.0	4.7	126	966	125.9	58.8	166	9 448	2 714.0	421.2
Wilmette	64	297	72.9	11.8	182	415	74.5	27.4	NA	NA	NA	NA
Woodridge	33	273	36.6	9.1	89	875	211.6	68.0	32	1 682	365.4	71.9
INDIANA	6 389	34 272	5 448.1	1 061.6	12 959	95 701	12 128.9	4 785.9	9 015	536 907	221 877.8	24 474.7
Anderson	64	276	41.4	6.4	123	D	D	D	56	1 984	D	77.5
Bloomington	145	854	113.8	20.9	222	D	D	D	52	D	D	85.7
Carmel	141	2 014	385.4	102.8	442	3 251	501.2	197.6	51	783	459.4	31.5
Columbus	63	244	36.2	7.6	133	D	D	D	103	10 953	4 714.6	475.1
Crown Point	32	101	17.6	2.7	84	D	D	D	35	948	221.2	35.4
East Chicago	13	106	27.2	5.5	18	116	9.7	3.2	51	9 604	6 191.5	568.5
Elkhart	76	391	68.9	11.5	135	D	D	D	323	18 896	4 281.5	696.3
Evansville	171	1 105	153.9	28.0	358	D	D	D	184	10 577	5 534.5	454.6
Fishers	82	343	94.4	11.3	242	1 457	206.9	65.9	24	659	138.2	30.4
Fort Wayne	340	1 736	288.4	48.7	751	6 416	676.9	320.1	413	19 604	D	927.7
Gary	51	326	40.2	7.1	55	D	D	D	37	5 998	D	336.6
Goshen	42	166	20.4	4.3	74	D	D	D	116	13 960	3 666.5	587.1
Greenwood	84	370	69.6	9.6	129	791	66.6	23.8	45	D	D	D
Hammond	56	376	42.9	11.8	105	D	D	D	76	3 563	1 779.6	193.8
Hobart	28	131	24.8	3.6	48	D	D	D	22	546	87.3	17.8
Indianapolis	1 236	10 076	1 891.2	381.8	2 671	D	D	D	928	48 817	21 317.5	2 715.6
Jeffersonville	47	345	53.6	9.4	95	450	51.4	17.1	89	5 104	1 364.8	213.1
Kokomo	73	296	44.6	7.0	109	D	D	D	63	11 686	D	865.5
Lafayette	125	730	138.0	25.7	181	D	D	D	83	8 459	5 253.9	390.9
Lawrence	30	182	23.3	5.2	83	D	D	D	NA	NA	NA	NA
Marion	37	146	18.2	3.3	62	D	D	D	46	3 349	1 171.8	213.1
Merrillville	73	560	73.8	15.7	185	1 476	137.0	58.5	33	660	122.0	27.3
Michigan City	39	185	32.8	3.8	63	380	38.0	13.5	60	3 439	1 107.2	143.5
Mishawaka	67	465	79.9	13.7	106	873	73.7	29.3	106	3 665	1 542.7	156.5
Muncie	87	383	63.5	9.9	118	D	D	D	84	3 684	950.3	171.8
New Albany	52	254	27.3	5.3	115	D	D	D	89	D	D	227.0
Noblesville	59	190	28.4	4.7	151	D	D	D	55	2 173	568.1	85.0
Plainfield	27	105	14.8	2.2	42	648	60.3	25.3	24	580	125.1	D
Portage	37	221	31.4	5.8	47	331	43.2	13.0	23	1 874	D	113.2
Richmond	47	241	26.5	6.1	64	333	27.9	10.7	93	5 978	2 178.1	233.2
Schererville	40	167	35.4	4.0	85	D	D	D	20	729	201.3	37.2
South Bend	104	740	99.5	22.4	305	D	D	D	186	7 811	2 210.1	353.3
Terre Haute	78	498	60.1	14.5	171	1 067	99.1	33.5	85	6 902	D	309.9
Valparaiso	67	348	39.8	7.8	129	898	96.1	34.6	55	2 053	1 004.8	108.9
Westfield	26	81	12.7	2.1	67	D	D	D	28	1 547	267.5	59.6
West Lafayette	45	284	35.8	7.1	64	D	D	D	NA	NA	NA	NA
IOWA	2 969	14 667	2 556.0	473.0	6 181	42 118	5 015.6	1 883.8	3 802	223 049	97 592.1	9 525.7
Ames	71	290	29.5	7.5	127	744	65.5	31.6	40	2 586	1 418.7	140.2
Ankeny	60	174	36.4	5.3	81	472	46.2	21.1	28	2 392	1 178.1	135.0
Bettendorf	45	175	46.0	4.9	94	D	D	D	29	3 255	1 350.6	180.6
Burlington	28	593	94.2	22.8	41	266	23.9	11.2	36	D	920.8	D
Cedar Falls	48	199	51.5	6.5	93	1 446	107.7	90.3	41	1 254	D	47.5
Cedar Rapids	179	1 488	330.4	86.6	374	3 720	474.6	203.5	144	15 137	6 894.3	1 004.4
Clinton	34	104	16.2	3.0	50	318	26.9	11.9	28	3 097	3 532.8	149.0
Council Bluffs	79	384	62.7	9.7	114	D	D	D	46	4 342	D	156.9
Davenport	123	1 577	212.1	40.0	266	D	D	D	107	7 431	4 016.5	345.2
Des Moines	213	1 670	281.7	57.9	523	D	D	D	189	6 405	3 552.9	274.8
Dubuque	80	416	70.1	16.0	131	D	D	D	89	4 912	1 059.9	186.5
Fort Dodge	38	114	17.7	2.8	66	D	D	D	37	1 572	D	77.2
Iowa City	86	443	75.3	13.0	140	D	D	D	46	3 319	D	137.5
Marion	33	138	13.6	2.9	55	433	51.1	23.2	42	719	121.7	27.2
Marshalltown	35	344	43.2	10.1	46	329	48.9	11.8	39	D	D	D
Mason City	44	134	19.9	3.4	63	D	D	D	37	3 214	1 210.3	133.4
Ottumwa	25	78	12.8	2.0	43	D	D	D	21	D	D	D
Sioux City	90	554	83.7	14.1	165	D	D	D	82	4 396	2 288.0	177.8
Urbandale	52	197	32.7	5.6	176	1 444	182.6	80.2	31	1 411	556.9	60.1
Waterloo	92	481	61.4	12.2	124	D	D	D	92	8 328	4 506.4	396.9
West Des Moines	114	807	225.7	38.4	321	2 946	448.4	153.8	32	1 117	257.3	56.0

1. Establishments subject to federal tax.

Table D. Cities — Accommodation and Food Services, Arts, Entertainment, and Recreation, and Health Care and Social Assistance

City	Accommodation and food services, 2007				Arts, entertainment, and recreation,[1] 2007				Health care and social assistance,[1] 2007			
	Number of establish-ments	Number of employees	Sales (mil dol)	Annual payroll (mil dol)	Number of establish-ments	Number of employees	Receipts (mil dol)	Annual payroll (mil dol)	Number of establish-ments	Number of employees	Receipts (mil dol)	Annual payroll (mil dol)
	92	93	94	95	96	97	98	99	100	101	102	103
ILLINOIS—Cont'd												
Waukegan	148	2 162	110.9	28.4	10	126	8.3	1.9	105	2 413	282.4	103.8
West Chicago	58	736	31.5	8.7	6	73	5.5	1.8	21	361	23.6	10.1
Wheaton	106	1 973	89.0	26.4	17	336	14.6	5.3	168	1 721	152.2	74.7
Wheeling	68	1 920	110.9	36.2	7	D	D	D	62	D	D	D
Wilmette	45	D	D	D	21	D	D	D	102	675	57.9	25.7
Woodridge	39	800	37.4	10.7	6	D	D	D	79	461	44.9	16.4
INDIANA	12 932	254 293	11 669.8	3 175.2	1 687	25 762	2 558.3	769.6	11 919	181 493	17 014.6	6 813.4
Anderson	156	3 285	117.0	33.2	21	D	D	D	151	D	D	D
Bloomington	298	6 769	268.0	73.3	19	183	10.3	2.3	214	3 369	311.6	140.4
Carmel	140	2 845	134.9	40.3	36	368	17.0	6.3	276	5 761	657.7	235.8
Columbus	126	2 581	105.4	30.7	11	D	D	D	161	2 037	177.3	76.4
Crown Point	58	924	33.9	9.0	12	D	D	D	63	883	77.6	37.7
East Chicago	41	D	D	D	1	D	D	D	32	305	25.3	9.5
Elkhart	192	3 695	133.4	37.9	16	D	D	D	121	1 892	268.9	92.1
Evansville	366	9 033	426.8	118.6	35	D	D	D	388	D	D	D
Fishers	138	2 961	125.8	34.9	20	D	D	D	160	D	D	D
Fort Wayne	614	14 155	506.1	156.1	78	D	D	D	750	17 070	1 801.5	707.4
Gary	105	1 744	168.4	31.1	9	D	D	D	94	1 519	92.6	39.9
Goshen	91	2 019	71.4	19.4	6	D	D	D	71	935	84.5	35.7
Greenwood	148	3 414	134.2	41.0	19	317	11.7	4.0	111	D	D	D
Hammond	156	D	D	D	6	D	D	D	67	D	D	D
Hobart	92	D	D	D	8	135	3.7	1.2	53	D	D	D
Indianapolis	1 957	43 393	2 138.2	632.9	248	D	D	D	1 865	31 197	3 338.9	1 377.5
Jeffersonville	75	1 643	66.1	20.2	7	D	D	D	108	1 544	167.7	70.5
Kokomo	165	3 728	143.5	42.3	13	D	D	D	168	D	D	D
Lafayette	223	5 259	194.9	60.2	17	228	7.4	2.3	187	3 658	441.0	178.9
Lawrence	85	1 332	57.3	15.9	19	D	D	D	40	D	D	D
Marion	98	1 924	68.6	18.9	10	D	D	D	116	D	D	D
Merrillville	127	3 190	141.2	38.9	10	275	9.9	2.8	240	D	D	D
Michigan City	104	3 383	313.9	60.6	4	D	D	D	78	D	D	D
Mishawaka	181	4 692	179.5	53.3	20	D	D	D	130	D	D	D
Muncie	170	4 336	139.9	42.0	22	D	D	D	204	4 250	391.1	174.2
New Albany	73	1 358	57.0	15.9	10	D	D	D	140	2 025	161.4	66.7
Noblesville	96	1 830	75.5	21.6	20	D	D	D	120	D	D	D
Plainfield	77	1 933	82.7	23.3	6	D	D	D	40	D	D	D
Portage	72	1 310	53.5	14.6	7	D	D	D	55	915	76.5	29.2
Richmond	100	2 445	85.2	25.1	10	73	2.2	0.6	91	D	D	D
Schererville	88	D	D	D	6	114	3.3	1.1	76	D	D	D
South Bend	252	4 667	188.2	52.4	16	163	31.2	3.6	246	4 390	638.2	228.0
Terre Haute	206	4 053	171.6	47.9	15	151	26.1	3.0	229	D	D	D
Valparaiso	113	2 433	93.8	26.5	7	104	4.6	1.3	159	1 955	208.2	85.5
Westfield	58	1 441	58.4	17.6	13	D	D	D	40	D	D	D
West Lafayette	125	2 508	97.1	26.5	6	D	D	D	41	D	D	D
IOWA	7 014	116 838	4 737.7	1 276.0	978	13 748	1 216.6	259.1	5 399	70 263	5 853.9	2 731.9
Ames	182	3 872	136.2	39.4	13	189	6.6	2.3	88	1 719	174.9	79.5
Ankeny	95	1 926	70.2	20.8	18	D	D	D	71	761	54.4	22.8
Bettendorf	64	2 150	153.6	33.1	11	D	D	D	86	D	D	D
Burlington	83	1 811	63.4	19.0	9	D	D	D	64	563	35.0	13.4
Cedar Falls	99	2 785	81.2	25.1	7	25	1.1	0.3	58	D	D	D
Cedar Rapids	382	7 800	299.1	86.9	30	829	29.0	9.6	291	4 089	463.7	201.1
Clinton	79	1 173	45.5	12.3	7	D	D	D	79	1 069	84.5	33.0
Council Bluffs	153	5 312	431.9	92.4	14	D	D	D	132	1 692	148.2	68.6
Davenport	296	6 211	239.8	70.9	30	754	94.3	14.0	252	2 797	309.9	142.8
Des Moines	497	8 479	378.1	110.5	50	544	34.0	9.7	364	6 110	788.0	383.9
Dubuque	193	3 815	125.2	37.6	25	D	D	D	134	2 711	272.8	141.7
Fort Dodge	70	1 321	58.7	14.9	9	D	D	D	75	D	D	D
Iowa City	177	3 671	125.1	36.0	11	314	6.6	2.0	140	1 606	147.3	60.3
Marion	44	815	28.9	9.1	5	D	D	D	50	641	38.1	15.1
Marshalltown	75	1 143	39.3	10.9	8	D	D	D	41	D	D	D
Mason City	96	1 575	55.4	15.9	10	D	D	D	64	D	D	D
Ottumwa	69	1 085	40.9	11.2	6	D	D	D	70	D	D	D
Sioux City	225	4 384	149.4	44.6	21	715	66.5	13.4	198	2 175	246.1	102.2
Urbandale	81	1 752	71.9	20.1	15	D	D	D	63	727	50.5	20.9
Waterloo	159	3 077	101.8	31.8	22	D	D	D	140	1 818	188.6	95.2
West Des Moines	185	4 429	186.5	58.1	24	D	D	D	212	2 859	337.4	160.9

1. Establishments subject to federal tax.

City	Other services[1], 2007				Government employment and payroll, 2012								
						March payroll							
							Percent of total for:						
	Number of establish-ments	Number of employees	Receipts (mil dol)	Annual payroll (mil dol)	Full-time equivalent employees	Total (dollars)	Adminis-tration, judicial, and legal	Police and Corrections	Fire Protection	Highways and trans-portation	Health and welfare	Natural resources and utilities	Education and libraries
	104	105	106	107	108	109	110	111	112	113	114	115	116
ILLINOIS—Cont'd													
Waukegan	100	500	43.9	13.0	502	3 187 722	12.7	40.5	27.8	4.1	1.1	8.7	5.1
West Chicago	46	231	23.1	6.3	117	799 988	15.4	54.5	0.0	9.6	0.7	18.2	0.0
Wheaton	95	682	35.9	13.6	437	2 488 726	8.6	34.0	12.7	8.3	0.0	11.5	18.2
Wheeling	62	735	75.3	20.5	232	1 575 381	12.4	38.6	25.9	1.8	8.3	8.9	0.0
Wilmette	56	381	31.6	10.3	220	1 531 248	12.5	32.9	25.0	14.4	0.9	11.8	0.0
Woodridge	34	339	13.9	10.5	165	972 329	16.5	46.7	0.0	5.4	0.0	13.1	14.2
INDIANA	8 961	56 731	4 531.3	1 397.9	X	X	X	X	X	X	X	X	X
Anderson	94	664	44.1	14.7	638	2 851 826	7.5	21.3	15.8	10.2	3.5	35.9	0.0
Bloomington	109	D	D	D	814	3 124 701	11.6	21.8	16.1	13.9	5.2	29.9	0.0
Carmel	107	650	44.6	15.5	467	2 600 210	3.5	30.7	43.9	10.0	0.0	10.1	0.0
Columbus	80	652	48.4	15.6	432	1 650 956	6.5	22.9	26.7	7.3	1.6	34.1	0.0
Crown Point	65	514	45.0	11.4	201	804 519	8.2	32.5	18.8	9.5	0.4	23.3	0.0
East Chicago	25	155	15.5	3.9	698	2 567 542	8.3	26.6	16.1	7.5	4.7	36.8	0.0
Elkhart	129	931	77.9	26.3	536	2 197 116	9.6	30.1	28.2	10.0	0.6	18.8	0.0
Evansville	214	1 736	131.6	43.8	1 278	5 214 822	2.6	31.8	24.3	11.2	3.0	24.8	0.0
Fishers	83	666	29.6	12.4	389	1 761 025	11.8	31.1	35.0	5.2	0.0	6.0	0.0
Fort Wayne	469	3 671	264.3	93.8	2 016	8 885 678	3.7	33.2	19.0	14.2	5.3	20.6	0.0
Gary	71	500	41.4	12.8	1 123	2 786 750	11.6	16.2	20.1	6.3	10.1	27.4	0.0
Goshen	60	434	33.3	11.8	227	709 892	8.9	38.2	24.5	7.4	0.8	13.4	0.0
Greenwood	93	831	64.3	21.3	279	1 071 961	16.9	33.3	24.5	11.2	0.0	12.1	0.0
Hammond	120	880	88.1	27.6	849	3 866 970	4.7	34.3	24.6	4.0	3.3	25.4	0.0
Hobart	48	296	16.3	5.9	245	963 819	14.4	31.6	27.9	6.1	0.0	15.8	0.0
Indianapolis	1 133	9 402	830.9	258.2	12 328	49 785 804	10.1	20.7	10.8	4.3	40.3	12.3	0.0
Jeffersonville	61	542	40.9	13.8	348	1 320 589	10.0	25.0	25.4	9.1	2.7	26.2	0.0
Kokomo	89	D	D	D	458	1 913 705	2.4	27.7	28.3	8.2	3.0	16.6	0.0
Lafayette	145	D	D	D	727	2 921 411	4.8	26.6	23.4	22.4	1.3	19.2	0.0
Lawrence	64	307	24.7	7.0	310	1 228 922	6.9	27.5	42.0	4.8	1.5	16.4	0.0
Marion	46	237	12.9	4.1	258	851 770	12.9	39.0	29.5	14.0	1.8	2.1	0.0
Merrillville	69	458	37.2	12.1	123	450 414	14.0	61.3	1.8	18.1	0.0	2.7	0.0
Michigan City	53	265	17.7	5.7	429	1 619 412	5.6	25.8	23.0	10.4	1.1	32.5	0.0
Mishawaka	106	672	46.1	15.9	503	2 151 708	6.9	27.5	24.4	4.6	0.7	31.4	0.0
Muncie	123	804	57.3	17.8	505	1 776 621	4.8	23.6	21.0	18.0	2.0	19.4	0.0
New Albany	70	388	23.3	7.8	265	917 338	5.7	32.4	36.7	5.6	3.3	8.7	0.0
Noblesville	80	421	27.4	8.4	368	1 696 635	8.6	26.2	41.3	9.3	0.0	13.7	0.0
Plainfield	42	226	19.7	5.9	268	950 626	7.8	22.5	43.0	4.3	0.0	21.5	0.0
Portage	56	368	30.8	9.7	254	948 853	7.5	31.0	27.5	15.8	0.6	16.7	0.0
Richmond	58	250	20.6	6.4	513	1 860 795	5.6	18.1	16.9	7.3	0.0	51.7	0.0
Schererville	65	539	45.3	12.9	180	726 293	13.7	41.3	15.8	13.1	0.0	16.0	0.0
South Bend	197	1 845	164.8	49.8	1 318	5 351 987	3.8	29.1	24.4	12.9	2.3	21.5	0.0
Terre Haute	103	945	55.7	18.7	615	2 301 273	8.2	27.5	28.9	17.6	1.5	14.9	0.0
Valparaiso	89	681	48.7	17.7	288	1 148 922	5.9	21.1	26.3	6.8	0.0	39.9	0.0
Westfield	36	D	D	D	176	867 739	19.6	28.0	32.8	8.5	1.6	9.5	0.0
West Lafayette	29	D	D	D	229	856 416	6.6	32.8	21.3	4.1	5.3	24.8	0.0
IOWA	4 878	24 331	1 856.5	544.9	X	X	X	X	X	X	X	X	X
Ames	67	D	D	D	616	2 954 800	12.2	13.1	10.5	21.5	2.3	30.9	5.6
Ankeny	68	481	38.7	10.5	283	1 240 311	16.5	23.8	24.3	9.4	0.0	18.9	4.5
Bettendorf	59	D	D	D	243	1 226 060	11.1	23.4	12.3	14.0	5.9	13.4	10.5
Burlington	52	241	19.8	4.9	239	935 691	5.6	25.4	21.5	13.3	0.5	20.2	7.2
Cedar Falls	41	306	27.2	8.0	478	2 270 443	8.5	9.9	7.7	7.0	0.6	57.2	2.9
Cedar Rapids	230	1 605	108.0	36.4	1 296	6 423 374	10.4	21.6	12.8	16.4	1.8	24.1	3.3
Clinton	54	281	13.1	8.5	210	897 240	6.0	29.8	22.4	15.6	2.5	17.4	5.3
Council Bluffs	101	505	37.5	11.0	471	2 609 951	9.1	27.0	20.1	6.8	10.1	21.8	5.0
Davenport	180	1 258	87.2	29.3	906	4 276 351	9.9	26.0	20.2	14.2	1.5	17.2	5.2
Des Moines	297	2 100	146.3	48.2	1 956	10 193 831	8.0	24.9	16.0	11.6	5.0	26.6	3.2
Dubuque	126	1 038	63.9	19.6	645	3 046 153	13.2	22.4	16.1	21.5	5.8	14.0	4.4
Fort Dodge	48	D	D	D	118	524 670	9.2	38.3	26.4	3.8	0.0	16.1	6.2
Iowa City	102	646	42.5	14.6	20	1 762 642	14.5	13.9	9.2	13.9	4.6	17.2	6.5
Marion	45	198	15.9	5.1	184	916 685	6.3	31.1	21.9	10.4	6.4	17.3	6.7
Marshalltown	50	D	D	D	231	825 058	5.3	30.0	16.7	12.6	5.2	25.4	4.7
Mason City	64	348	23.5	7.7	326	1 435 146	5.2	16.5	11.1	10.8	8.2	18.1	25.1
Ottumwa	41	176	11.8	3.7	247	856 818	6.4	16.0	15.1	23.1	5.3	28.1	3.8
Sioux City	133	D	D	D	794	3 661 919	9.1	25.7	18.3	17.6	2.2	19.7	3.4
Urbandale	64	407	33.5	11.0	223	998 550	11.0	20.8	15.3	12.5	1.1	26.9	9.6
Waterloo	101	786	54.9	18.3	603	2 720 527	5.5	26.6	21.7	9.9	2.6	18.8	4.1
West Des Moines	82	487	28.2	12.1	435	2 294 576	8.6	23.7	13.4	9.2	16.6	19.7	4.4

1. Establishments subject to federal tax.

Table D. Cities — **City Government Finances**

City	City government finances, 2007									
	General revenue							General expenditure		
		Intergovernmental		Taxes					Per capita[1] (dollars)	
					Per capita[1] (dollars)					
	Total (mil dol)	Total (mil dol)	Percent from state government	Total (mil dol)	Total	Property	Sales and gross receipts	Total (mil dol)	Total	Capital outlays
	117	118	119	120	121	122	123	124	125	126
ILLINOIS—Cont'd										
Waukegan	87.3	16.1	90.5	46.7	525	307	218	72.7	819	47
West Chicago	29.0	8.4	99.1	8.9	324	172	153	28.0	1 022	227
Wheaton	56.0	12.7	96.7	32.9	616	438	167	46.6	872	33
Wheeling	45.9	10.7	93.0	29.0	765	553	212	45.1	1 188	197
Wilmette	38.5	7.6	85.0	22.4	821	509	287	38.9	1 425	199
Woodridge	30.1	9.8	82.4	14.4	434	225	199	26.2	789	18
INDIANA	X	X	X	X	X	X	X	X	X	X
Anderson	84.2	19.0	48.2	36.3	652	443	39	65.2	1 172	281
Bloomington	85.2	17.5	64.4	44.3	539	434	15	72.9	886	129
Carmel	111.9	17.9	66.3	72.8	871	597	53	93.8	1 122	60
Columbus	72.5	21.0	50.2	29.8	657	647	11	59.6	1 314	244
Crown Point	35.9	4.6	85.5	17.3	616	580	36	21.8	773	94
East Chicago	103.6	44.0	82.6	50.0	1 697	1 676	21	63.2	2 147	65
Elkhart	70.5	21.2	34.3	30.9	606	596	10	59.6	1 167	88
Evansville	183.6	54.1	55.1	68.3	568	460	15	192.0	1 598	442
Fishers	58.2	7.3	74.3	35.2	430	286	25	55.3	676	109
Fort Wayne	289.9	59.4	54.7	141.1	554	423	16	257.6	1 011	147
Gary	181.4	65.4	74.4	81.4	1 028	1 008	20	145.6	1 839	385
Goshen	35.1	9.7	53.7	14.5	454	447	7	47.8	1 498	416
Greenwood	47.0	10.2	33.2	19.8	376	365	12	34.0	645	24
Hammond	192.8	73.8	83.1	63.5	797	775	22	155.5	1 953	159
Hobart	40.0	5.7	88.9	23.0	794	772	22	36.0	1 242	112
Indianapolis	2 604.6	712.4	81.1	887.7	1 064	601	112	3 151.6	3 777	1 038
Jeffersonville	55.6	10.3	33.9	27.6	605	592	13	57.7	1 264	472
Kokomo	76.1	16.8	67.8	44.3	777	655	2	63.7	1 118	63
Lafayette	99.8	25.3	67.7	44.5	637	508	7	75.9	1 086	2
Lawrence	36.4	5.3	60.9	19.2	411	308	19	34.5	739	4
Marion	32.5	6.6	85.0	19.7	665	514	11	37.1	1 252	46
Merrillville	30.3	3.8	91.0	20.7	587	559	28	18.3	518	137
Michigan City	59.4	25.0	70.4	17.2	553	532	21	50.5	1 621	213
Mishawaka	83.6	10.9	75.5	54.8	1 142	914	13	78.3	1 630	554
Muncie	72.4	20.0	73.9	29.0	414	346	11	72.9	1 040	117
New Albany	59.3	15.9	55.8	20.6	564	548	16	50.5	1 385	371
Noblesville	84.0	18.9	89.5	45.5	823	556	66	67.7	1 226	347
Plainfield	48.8	11.2	29.1	24.9	854	718	136	35.1	1 203	268
Portage	42.2	5.4	93.6	22.3	604	531	19	46.8	1 270	181
Richmond	48.2	15.7	58.1	13.4	368	357	11	46.4	1 269	343
Schererville	33.2	3.7	90.7	21.3	734	702	32	19.4	667	73
South Bend	201.3	37.3	61.0	106.9	1 060	823	30	141.5	1 404	147
Terre Haute	82.6	28.3	35.8	31.8	519	512	8	64.3	1 051	189
Valparaiso	44.4	6.4	59.9	22.8	713	632	30	35.7	1 116	232
Westfield	33.7	3.8	75.3	18.3	572	359	56	25.9	808	40
West Lafayette	32.5	8.8	47.0	12.7	416	322	9	24.7	808	153
IOWA	X	X	X	X	X	X	X	X	X	X
Ames	250.4	24.1	59.9	29.1	475	382	93	219.0	3 578	476
Ankeny	57.6	6.0	79.4	32.3	658	584	74	69.7	1 421	618
Bettendorf	52.9	7.7	67.3	30.2	883	675	208	55.4	1 617	483
Burlington	34.5	5.6	56.2	17.9	700	447	253	35.7	1 395	364
Cedar Falls	77.7	19.4	43.0	31.2	783	598	185	81.6	2 049	977
Cedar Rapids	405.0	168.3	22.7	115.9	905	655	249	457.5	3 573	2 065
Clinton	48.5	10.4	28.4	20.3	761	562	198	67.1	2 521	1 417
Council Bluffs	118.7	29.8	38.3	61.1	983	702	281	111.9	1 801	467
Davenport	165.6	37.9	52.7	84.9	837	610	227	177.4	1 749	508
Des Moines	404.2	93.7	24.5	156.5	757	643	114	460.9	2 228	484
Dubuque	135.5	48.8	22.7	45.3	780	520	260	160.4	2 763	1 348
Fort Dodge	36.9	6.2	50.6	17.7	717	531	186	39.3	1 589	605
Iowa City	138.3	36.0	53.0	63.8	906	715	191	128.1	1 819	366
Marion	36.5	5.5	81.7	22.6	630	474	156	37.9	1 056	306
Marshalltown	34.2	10.2	31.7	16.6	595	411	184	35.1	1 262	431
Mason City	52.9	17.0	23.3	20.8	748	531	218	45.1	1 625	357
Ottumwa	40.4	7.9	63.1	16.8	679	503	177	37.3	1 505	459
Sioux City	139.6	32.9	58.3	63.3	766	553	213	143.7	1 737	477
Urbandale	41.8	4.8	80.6	29.6	721	645	76	40.8	995	315
Waterloo	115.1	25.8	46.6	59.1	865	644	221	119.5	1 749	524
West Des Moines	100.9	15.8	70.7	63.9	1 076	976	100	85.4	1 439	353

1. Based on population estimated as of July 1 of the year shown.

City	City government finances, 2012 (cont.)									
	General expenditure (cont.)									
	Percent of total for:									
	Public welfare	Highways	Parking facilities	Education	Health and hospitals	Police protection	Sewerage and sanitation	Parks and recreation	Housing and community development	Interest on debt
	127	128	129	130	131	132	133	134	135	136
ILLINOIS—Cont'd										
Waukegan	0.0	11.3	0.5	0.0	0.0	30.6	9.2	0.0	1.6	5.9
West Chicago	0.0	15.8	0.4	0.0	0.0	30.2	28.0	0.7	0.0	2.8
Wheaton	0.0	14.4	1.4	0.0	0.0	27.1	7.8	1.1	0.0	4.7
Wheeling	0.0	15.8	0.1	0.0	0.0	27.4	4.3	0.0	0.0	7.2
Wilmette	0.0	14.4	0.8	0.0	0.6	24.7	15.4	0.0	0.0	5.9
Woodridge	0.0	11.2	0.0	0.0	0.0	36.6	9.9	0.1	0.0	4.4
INDIANA	X	X	X	X	X	X	X	X	X	X
Anderson	0.0	5.6	0.1	0.0	0.3	14.5	38.2	1.7	3.5	2.5
Bloomington	0.0	7.2	2.0	0.0	1.5	13.2	15.3	10.4	1.4	3.6
Carmel	0.0	9.2	0.0	0.0	0.0	16.1	5.8	3.9	6.8	11.8
Columbus	0.0	3.5	0.0	0.0	0.5	9.2	28.6	6.4	0.8	4.1
Crown Point	0.0	12.6	0.0	0.0	0.3	15.8	28.1	3.3	0.0	1.9
East Chicago	0.0	1.5	0.0	0.0	4.1	14.6	18.5	4.4	3.2	0.9
Elkhart	0.0	9.1	0.0	0.0	0.0	15.2	19.4	5.4	1.3	2.0
Evansville	0.0	4.5	0.1	0.0	0.4	13.7	25.8	6.1	1.4	1.4
Fishers	0.0	15.5	0.0	0.0	0.0	12.7	15.0	1.2	0.0	7.5
Fort Wayne	0.0	6.4	0.2	0.0	0.9	19.3	29.0	5.5	5.1	2.8
Gary	0.0	2.5	0.0	0.0	2.6	8.6	23.7	5.0	3.3	1.1
Goshen	0.0	13.7	1.0	0.0	0.0	8.2	27.0	2.5	1.1	7.9
Greenwood	0.0	14.9	0.0	0.0	0.0	16.9	24.3	2.9	0.0	3.6
Hammond	0.0	2.9	0.0	0.0	0.0	16.8	11.7	12.4	3.7	2.7
Hobart	0.0	12.7	0.0	0.0	0.1	10.5	26.5	4.8	0.0	0.9
Indianapolis	0.0	1.2	0.4	0.0	35.8	6.6	8.7	11.7	4.3	10.4
Jeffersonville	0.0	1.9	0.0	0.0	0.6	13.1	50.7	3.9	2.0	4.1
Kokomo	0.0	6.8	0.0	0.0	0.0	19.6	18.4	4.5	3.7	1.9
Lafayette	0.0	6.9	0.0	0.0	0.0	16.5	15.5	7.3	3.9	5.6
Lawrence	0.0	3.7	0.0	0.0	2.8	16.4	18.9	3.1	0.0	1.4
Marion	0.0	5.7	0.0	0.0	0.0	20.7	14.4	2.8	0.0	1.5
Merrillville	0.0	6.0	0.0	0.0	0.0	21.1	8.9	0.9	0.0	4.6
Michigan City	0.0	3.1	0.0	0.0	0.5	13.7	18.8	10.2	2.7	3.3
Mishawaka	0.0	3.8	0.0	0.0	1.4	11.5	26.4	3.8	0.9	3.5
Muncie	0.0	3.7	0.1	0.0	0.3	11.3	46.5	1.9	1.2	2.0
New Albany	0.0	2.5	0.9	0.0	0.8	9.6	21.0	4.4	6.5	5.0
Noblesville	0.0	5.0	0.2	0.0	0.2	11.2	32.6	4.6	0.0	13.9
Plainfield	0.0	3.4	0.0	0.0	0.0	12.1	14.0	10.2	0.0	3.2
Portage	0.0	7.4	0.0	0.0	0.2	9.3	26.6	6.0	0.0	5.4
Richmond	0.0	3.5	0.1	0.0	1.1	13.2	43.5	6.3	0.0	2.2
Schererville	0.0	8.6	0.0	0.0	0.3	23.5	39.5	5.2	0.0	2.5
South Bend	0.0	5.8	0.5	0.0	0.3	16.8	22.7	12.5	1.8	5.0
Terre Haute	0.0	7.4	0.0	0.0	0.4	14.5	16.6	4.9	14.2	3.8
Valparaiso	0.0	12.1	0.1	0.0	0.0	9.7	21.3	7.1	0.0	3.4
Westfield	0.0	6.4	0.0	0.0	0.0	16.6	19.5	1.9	0.0	6.9
West Lafayette	0.0	12.3	0.0	0.0	0.0	16.7	38.4	6.0	2.0	4.7
IOWA	X	X	X	X	X	X	X	X	X	X
Ames	0.5	2.1	0.3	0.0	72.3	3.5	4.7	2.0	0.3	2.0
Ankeny	0.4	27.0	0.0	0.0	3.9	9.7	21.2	8.8	0.0	7.2
Bettendorf	0.0	12.9	0.0	0.0	0.0	11.1	12.3	17.3	0.9	8.1
Burlington	0.0	6.6	0.2	0.0	2.2	14.7	12.6	9.1	0.0	6.4
Cedar Falls	0.0	13.0	0.2	0.0	0.3	5.2	6.7	5.8	2.0	1.5
Cedar Rapids	0.0	7.6	0.9	0.0	0.2	7.2	13.4	2.0	1.6	3.1
Clinton	0.0	10.7	0.1	0.0	2.5	7.2	48.1	3.5	1.1	3.6
Council Bluffs	0.0	3.7	0.1	0.0	2.9	13.5	11.9	3.6	1.1	1.9
Davenport	0.0	4.9	0.6	0.0	0.0	13.1	17.7	6.8	6.3	6.4
Des Moines	2.3	11.4	1.8	0.0	0.0	12.6	19.8	4.9	6.4	5.1
Dubuque	0.3	10.6	1.2	0.0	1.4	7.8	26.9	4.5	3.9	3.8
Fort Dodge	0.8	9.9	0.4	0.0	0.1	9.5	14.8	11.3	1.5	5.7
Iowa City	0.0	8.1	3.7	0.0	0.5	8.4	16.3	4.9	8.7	4.8
Marion	0.0	7.5	0.0	0.0	0.1	13.8	13.7	4.6	1.9	5.3
Marshalltown	0.1	16.2	0.1	0.0	4.0	15.0	32.3	6.4	5.1	2.3
Mason City	1.7	6.4	0.2	0.0	4.0	12.0	17.3	4.5	0.0	4.0
Ottumwa	0.3	19.9	0.0	0.0	1.4	12.0	30.9	4.9	0.0	2.4
Sioux City	0.0	5.9	1.1	0.0	0.4	12.2	17.1	8.9	5.9	5.4
Urbandale	0.0	28.4	0.0	0.0	0.1	15.2	5.4	9.9	1.4	4.5
Waterloo	0.2	14.3	0.3	0.0	1.7	13.5	9.5	5.5	7.5	3.5
West Des Moines	1.3	14.3	0.0	0.0	5.2	10.7	16.9	5.3	0.9	4.8

City	City government finances, 2012 (cont.)			Climate[2]						
	Debt outstanding			Average daily temperature (degrees Fahrenheit)						
				Mean		Limits				
	Total (mil dol)	Per capita[1] (dollars)	Debt issued during year	January	July	January[3]	July[4]	Annual precipitation (inches)	Heating degree days	Cooling degree days
	137	138	139	140	141	142	143	144	145	146
ILLINOIS—Cont'd										
Waukegan	133.5	1 504	26.6	20.3	71.5	12.0	81.7	34.09	7 031	613
West Chicago	20.8	757	0.0	NA	NA	NA	NA	NA	NA	NA
Wheaton	45.4	849	0.0	23.1	74.8	14.2	86.8	37.94	6 053	942
Wheeling	84.5	2 228	8.5	18.4	72.1	9.6	82.3	36.56	7 149	624
Wilmette	76.2	2 790	14.3	22.0	73.3	14.3	83.5	36.27	6 498	830
Woodridge	24.8	746	3.3	23.1	74.8	14.2	86.8	37.94	6 053	942
INDIANA	X	X	X	X	X	X	X	X	X	X
Anderson	127.1	2 286	25.5	25.7	74.0	18.4	83.8	39.82	5 807	872
Bloomington	159.2	1 937	55.7	27.9	75.4	19.3	86.0	44.91	5 348	1 017
Carmel	367.8	4 400	0.0	25.3	74.2	17.0	84.5	42.85	5 901	873
Columbus	109.4	2 413	0.0	27.9	75.9	19.1	86.4	41.94	5 367	1 059
Crown Point	22.4	795	1.9	NA	NA	NA	NA	NA	NA	NA
East Chicago	42.0	1 427	0.0	23.7	74.0	15.3	84.8	38.13	6 055	887
Elkhart	28.7	562	0.0	22.8	72.1	14.3	83.3	38.56	6 487	663
Evansville	274.1	2 281	67.7	33.2	79.6	24.8	90.5	45.76	4 140	1 616
Fishers	131.1	1 603	33.0	25.3	74.2	17.0	84.5	42.85	5 901	873
Fort Wayne	435.4	1 708	0.0	23.6	73.4	16.1	84.3	36.55	6 205	830
Gary	85.2	1 076	21.7	22.2	73.5	13.9	83.9	38.02	6 497	776
Goshen	101.3	3 178	9.3	24.3	73.7	17.0	84.5	36.59	6 075	826
Greenwood	30.0	570	0.0	25.7	74.7	18.0	84.0	40.24	5 783	942
Hammond	112.1	1 407	0.0	22.2	73.5	13.9	83.9	38.02	6 497	776
Hobart	25.7	886	0.0	22.2	73.5	13.9	83.9	38.02	6 497	776
Indianapolis	6 001.3	7 191	2 503.6	26.5	75.4	18.5	85.6	40.95	5 521	1 042
Jeffersonville	54.0	1 182	0.0	31.3	75.8	21.4	88.5	45.47	4 829	1 079
Kokomo	32.5	570	0.0	22.8	73.0	15.0	84.1	41.54	6 368	771
Lafayette	133.7	1 913	0.0	23.0	73.5	14.3	84.5	36.90	6 206	842
Lawrence	27.5	589	0.0	25.7	74.7	18.0	84.0	40.24	5 783	942
Marion	11.4	385	0.0	24.2	73.8	16.3	84.5	39.01	6 143	819
Merrillville	22.7	644	0.2	21.1	72.7	12.1	83.6	40.04	6 642	734
Michigan City	54.0	1 733	7.8	23.4	73.0	15.7	83.1	39.70	6 294	812
Mishawaka	117.0	2 436	0.0	24.3	73.7	17.0	84.5	36.59	6 075	826
Muncie	33.5	478	0.0	24.4	72.5	15.9	83.9	41.23	6 215	717
New Albany	61.3	1 681	0.0	31.3	75.8	21.4	88.5	45.47	4 829	1 079
Noblesville	240.4	4 350	12.0	25.3	74.2	17.0	84.5	42.85	5 901	873
Plainfield	56.2	1 924	0.0	NA	NA	NA	NA	NA	NA	NA
Portage	59.2	1 607	0.0	22.9	73.0	15.5	83.1	40.06	6 270	745
Richmond	34.6	947	0.0	25.7	73.1	17.2	84.6	39.55	5 942	769
Schererville	18.2	626	0.0	NA	NA	NA	NA	NA	NA	NA
South Bend	230.5	2 286	60.5	23.4	73.0	15.7	83.1	39.70	6 294	812
Terre Haute	52.7	860	0.0	26.5	76.2	17.7	87.3	42.47	5 433	1 107
Valparaiso	56.6	1 769	9.8	22.9	73.0	15.5	83.1	40.06	6 270	745
Westfield	55.7	1 737	0.0	NA	NA	NA	NA	NA	NA	NA
West Lafayette	40.9	1 338	2.5	25.2	75.5	17.2	86.3	36.32	5 732	1 024
IOWA	X	X	X	X	X	X	X	X	X	X
Ames	127.9	2 091	71.7	18.5	73.8	9.6	84.3	34.07	6 791	830
Ankeny	178.3	3 634	21.3	18.2	74.8	8.7	85.8	33.38	6 961	881
Bettendorf	119.0	3 478	20.8	21.1	76.2	13.2	85.4	34.11	6 246	1 072
Burlington	62.6	2 447	19.5	22.8	76.3	15.1	85.4	37.94	5 948	1 095
Cedar Falls	86.6	2 177	4.4	16.1	73.6	6.3	85.0	33.15	7 348	758
Cedar Rapids	538.7	4 206	127.7	19.9	74.8	11.5	85.3	36.62	6 488	910
Clinton	83.3	3 130	29.0	20.4	74.7	12.5	85.0	35.68	6 416	915
Council Bluffs	125.8	2 024	15.1	21.1	76.2	10.4	87.7	33.25	6 323	1 057
Davenport	324.8	3 202	66.5	21.1	76.2	13.2	85.4	34.11	6 246	1 072
Des Moines	556.3	2 689	43.7	20.4	76.1	11.7	86.0	34.72	6 436	1 052
Dubuque	185.8	3 199	67.9	17.8	75.1	8.7	85.4	33.96	6 891	908
Fort Dodge	80.9	3 272	8.5	15.4	73.1	5.8	84.3	34.39	7 513	746
Iowa City	187.9	2 668	19.6	21.7	76.9	13.4	87.5	37.27	6 052	1 134
Marion	67.4	1 881	13.8	16.8	73.9	7.1	84.4	36.40	7 191	787
Marshalltown	31.2	1 121	12.4	16.8	73.0	7.1	84.4	36.40	7 191	787
Mason City	60.3	2 170	1.5	13.9	72.4	5.1	83.3	34.48	7 765	655
Ottumwa	37.1	1 498	13.2	NA	NA	NA	NA	NA	NA	NA
Sioux City	249.2	3 013	42.4	18.6	74.6	8.5	86.2	25.99	6 900	914
Urbandale	55.3	1 347	9.4	20.4	76.1	11.7	86.0	34.72	6 436	1 052
Waterloo	115.2	1 686	21.4	16.1	73.6	6.3	85.0	33.15	7 348	758
West Des Moines	136.6	2 302	44.3	20.4	76.1	11.7	86.0	34.72	6 436	1 052

1. Based on the population estimated as of July 1 of the year shown. 2. Represents normal values based on the 30-year period, 1971–2000. 3. Average daily minimum. 4. Average daily maximum.

STATE Place code	City	Land area,[1] 2010 (sq km)	Population, 2014			Race alone or in combination (percent), 2011-2013					Percent Hispanic or Latino[2], 2011-2013	Percent foreign born 2011–2013
			Total persons	Rank	Per square kilometer	White	Black	American Indian, Alaska Native	Asian	Hawaiian Pacific Islander		
		1	2	3	4	5	6	7	8	9	10	11
20 00000	KANSAS	211 754.1	2 904 021	X	13.7	88.4	7.2	2.1	3.1	0.2	11.0	6.8
20 18250	Dodge City	37.4	28 117	1 304	751.8	88.5	3.5	1.9	1.9	NA	59.2	30.6
20 25325	Garden City	22.8	27 004	1 359	1 184.4	81.1	4.3	1.7	4.7	NA	50.1	20.8
20 33625	Hutchinson	58.8	41 642	887	708.2	90.2	6.1	2.7	0.9	NA	11.2	3.5
20 36000	Kansas City	323.3	149 636	170	462.8	61.3	28.2	1.8	3.5	0.2	28.4	15.2
20 38900	Lawrence	86.9	92 763	332	1 067.5	87.3	6.4	4.1	6.2	NA	6.5	8.0
20 39000	Leavenworth	62.3	36 000	1 038	577.8	79.5	17.5	2.2	3.1	0.4	9.2	5.1
20 39075	Leawood	39.0	34 395	1 080	881.9	94.1	2.3	0.6	4.6	NA	1.8	4.5
20 39350	Lenexa	88.3	51 042	734	578.1	89.3	5.9	0.7	5.2	NA	7.4	8.9
20 44250	Manhattan	48.6	56 078	654	1 153.9	86.2	7.5	1.7	6.5	NA	6.8	7.7
20 52575	Olathe	154.5	133 062	194	861.2	88.6	6.1	0.8	5.6	0.2	10.6	10.8
20 53775	Overland Park	193.8	184 525	128	952.1	87.1	6.1	0.9	7.9	0.2	6.7	10.7
20 62700	Salina	65.0	47 867	785	736.4	90.1	5.6	1.0	2.9	NA	11.2	5.6
20 64500	Shawnee	108.4	64 599	546	595.9	92.7	6.0	2.2	2.5	NA	6.7	4.5
20 71000	Topeka	155.8	127 215	213	816.5	83.5	14.0	2.8	2.4	0.3	13.7	6.2
20 79000	Wichita	412.6	388 413	49	941.4	79.8	13.3	2.8	5.6	0.1	15.9	10.5
21 00000	KENTUCKY	102 269.1	4 413 457	X	43.2	89.6	9.1	0.7	1.6	0.1	3.2	3.3
21 08902	Bowling Green	97.9	62 479	567	638.2	76.6	15.5	0.3	4.7	0.3	6.8	11.4
21 17848	Covington	34.2	40 944	904	1 197.2	85.3	13.6	0.5	0.8	NA	3.8	1.8
21 24274	Elizabethtown	65.7	29 974	1 237	456.2	81.5	15.7	1.6	3.7	0.5	4.7	5.5
21 27982	Florence	26.7	31 888	1 167	1 194.3	89.8	7.1	0.6	3.9	NA	2.1	5.9
21 28900	Frankfort	37.1	27 557	1 332	742.8	78.0	21.7	NA	2.1	NA	4.9	3.9
21 30700	Georgetown	41.0	31 653	1 176	772.0	91.0	9.1	0.3	1.3	NA	3.7	2.6
21 35866	Henderson	39.6	28 900	1 275	729.8	85.9	14.0	0.3	0.7	NA	2.1	1.5
21 37918	Hopkinsville	79.4	32 634	1 136	411.0	69.9	30.2	1.3	2.1	NA	6.5	3.4
21 40222	Jeffersontown	25.7	26 949	1 362	1 048.6	86.0	13.2	0.8	2.2	NA	2.9	5.2
21 46027	Lexington-Fayette	734.7	310 797	61	423.0	78.3	16.2	0.8	4.1	0.1	6.9	9.0
21 48003	Louisville/Jefferson County	842.4	612 780	30	727.4	73.6	24.7	0.8	2.9	0.1	4.8	6.9
21 56136	Nicholasville	33.7	29 097	1 267	863.4	92.6	6.0	0.8	NA	NA	3.2	2.6
21 58620	Owensboro	49.5	58 374	629	1 179.3	90.2	9.5	0.5	1.2	NA	3.1	2.0
21 58836	Paducah	51.5	24 978	1 421	485.0	77.8	23.9	1.2	0.7	NA	1.4	1.2
21 65226	Richmond	59.1	33 556	1 108	567.8	88.3	10.2	1.3	2.7	NA	2.1	2.0
22 00000	LOUISIANA	111 897.6	4 649 676	X	41.6	64.4	33.0	1.3	1.9	0.1	4.6	3.9
22 00975	Alexandria	73.6	48 175	778	654.6	36.2	61.2	1.0	2.5	NA	1.2	2.8
22 05000	Baton Rouge	199.3	228 895	96	1 148.5	40.0	56.2	0.8	4.1	0.1	3.0	5.4
22 08920	Bossier City	109.7	67 472	513	615.1	68.4	28.4	0.9	3.5	NA	7.4	5.6
22 13960	Central	161.2	28 119	1 303	174.4	89.0	9.7	0.5	0.8	NA	2.3	2.3
22 36255	Houma	37.3	34 124	1 092	914.9	71.7	22.2	6.0	1.6	NA	5.3	5.2
22 39475	Kenner	38.5	67 064	515	1 741.9	68.1	24.4	0.4	3.8	NA	19.0	15.9
22 40735	Lafayette	127.5	126 066	216	988.8	65.9	31.8	0.9	2.4	NA	4.4	5.1
22 41155	Lake Charles	108.9	74 889	453	687.7	48.8	50.2	0.9	2.3	NA	3.3	3.0
22 51410	Monroe	75.7	49 601	753	655.2	33.0	66.2	NA	1.5	NA	0.9	2.0
22 54035	New Iberia	28.9	30 745	1 202	1 063.8	53.3	44.9	1.0	3.3	NA	4.4	3.7
22 55000	New Orleans	438.8	384 320	50	875.8	35.3	60.5	0.8	3.3	0.1	5.4	5.9
22 70000	Shreveport	272.9	198 242	117	726.4	41.9	56.0	0.8	1.6	0.1	2.8	2.5
22 70805	Slidell	38.4	27 622	1 327	719.3	80.6	18.8	1.6	0.7	NA	5.6	3.2
23 00000	MAINE	79 882.8	1 330 089	X	16.7	96.9	1.6	1.7	1.5	0.1	1.4	3.4
23 02795	Bangor	88.7	32 568	1 138	367.2	94.5	2.2	1.2	3.0	NA	1.9	3.8
23 38740	Lewiston	88.4	36 299	1 025	410.6	94.9	4.9	4.5	1.8	NA	3.2	4.5
23 60545	Portland	55.2	66 666	525	1 207.7	88.6	8.4	1.2	4.0	NA	2.8	11.9
23 71990	South Portland	31.0	25 424	1 409	820.1	91.4	3.5	0.8	6.8	NA	3.3	7.8
24 00000	MARYLAND	25 141.6	5 976 407	X	237.7	60.3	31.1	1.0	6.8	0.1	8.7	14.2
24 01600	Annapolis	18.6	38 856	955	2 089.0	63.4	24.6	0.2	2.4	NA	18.1	15.7
24 04000	Baltimore	209.6	622 793	26	2 971.3	31.7	64.6	1.0	3.0	0.2	4.5	7.5
24 08775	Bowie	47.7	57 646	633	1 208.5	45.0	50.8	0.9	4.9	NA	5.9	13.3
24 18750	College Park	14.6	32 256	1 158	2 209.3	63.5	18.1	0.6	15.1	0.2	10.0	19.5
24 30325	Frederick	57.0	68 400	505	1 200.0	70.0	20.0	1.6	6.3	0.4	16.0	17.7
24 31175	Gaithersburg	26.4	66 816	520	2 530.9	56.6	20.0	1.2	19.2	NA	21.7	38.6
24 36075	Hagerstown	30.5	40 364	919	1 323.4	77.9	23.6	2.3	2.1	NA	6.9	6.5
24 45900	Laurel	11.1	26 160	1 393	2 356.8	29.2	55.4	1.2	9.1	NA	15.0	24.5
24 67675	Rockville	35.0	65 937	532	1 883.9	65.4	9.6	0.8	23.0	0.5	14.3	34.2
24 69925	Salisbury	34.7	32 563	1 139	938.4	59.9	36.7	0.8	3.4	NA	8.2	12.8
25 00000	MASSACHUSETTS	20 202.1	6 745 408	X	333.9	82.4	8.6	0.7	6.5	0.1	10.2	15.2
25 00840	Agawam Town	60.4	28 772	1 279	476.4	93.9	1.4	0.4	3.8	NA	5.5	7.7
25 02690	Attleboro	69.4	43 970	840	633.6	89.1	6.0	0.7	4.0	NA	7.5	9.5
25 03690	Barnstable Town	154.9	44 529	830	287.5	92.1	4.7	1.2	1.3	NA	3.3	10.2

1. Dry land or land partially or temporarily covered by water. 2. May be of any race.

Table D. Cities — **Population**

City	Age of population (percent), 2011-2013: Under 5 years	5 to 17 years	18 to 24 years	25 to 34 years	35 to 44 years	45 to 54 years	55 to 64 years	65 to 74 years	75 years and over	Median age 2011-2013	Percent female 2011-2013	Population: Census counts: 2000	Census counts: 2010	Percent change: 2000–2010	Percent change: 2010–2014
	12	13	14	15	16	17	18	19	20	21	22	23	24	25	26
KANSAS	7.0	18.1	10.3	13.4	12.0	13.4	12.2	7.2	6.5	36.0	50.3	2 688 418	2 853 118	6.1	1.8
Dodge City	10.7	21.5	12.0	15.7	12.3	11.2	8.7	4.0	3.8	28.6	47.7	25 176	27 340	8.6	2.8
Garden City	10.1	21.1	10.6	15.3	11.5	11.5	9.9	5.3	4.6	30.3	48.7	28 451	26 658	-6.3	1.3
Hutchinson	7.0	15.9	9.6	13.1	11.9	12.9	13.1	8.0	8.5	38.3	50.7	40 787	42 080	3.2	-1.3
Kansas City	8.6	19.9	9.4	15.1	12.6	12.7	10.9	6.2	4.7	33.0	50.5	146 866	145 786	-0.7	2.6
Lawrence	5.2	12.2	28.7	17.2	10.1	9.5	8.7	4.4	4.1	27.0	50.3	80 098	87 643	9.4	5.8
Leavenworth	8.5	18.0	10.1	14.7	15.4	12.2	10.5	6.1	4.4	34.3	46.5	35 420	35 251	-0.5	2.1
Leawood	5.0	21.4	4.6	4.0	14.1	17.1	15.9	10.4	7.5	45.6	51.6	27 656	31 867	15.2	7.9
Lenexa	7.2	18.1	7.8	14.4	14.5	13.1	13.8	6.0	5.2	36.6	51.6	40 238	48 190	19.8	5.9
Manhattan	5.6	9.3	37.1	19.5	7.8	6.8	6.9	3.4	3.7	24.4	48.4	44 831	52 281	16.6	7.2
Olathe	8.0	21.3	7.9	14.3	16.1	14.0	10.4	4.9	3.1	34.2	50.2	92 962	125 872	35.4	5.7
Overland Park	6.3	17.6	7.5	15.6	12.4	14.7	12.6	6.8	6.3	37.3	51.6	149 080	173 372	16.3	6.5
Salina	7.4	17.6	10.5	13.0	12.0	13.2	11.4	7.9	6.9	36.1	50.7	45 679	47 707	4.4	0.3
Shawnee	6.4	20.8	7.9	13.0	14.9	15.9	10.5	5.8	4.7	36.5	51.5	47 996	62 209	29.6	3.8
Topeka	7.6	16.5	9.8	14.4	11.5	13.1	12.4	7.3	7.4	36.6	52.1	122 377	127 473	4.2	-0.2
Wichita	8.0	18.3	10.0	14.8	12.2	13.1	11.6	6.3	5.6	34.1	50.5	344 284	382 368	11.1	1.6
KENTUCKY	6.3	16.9	9.7	12.9	12.9	14.3	12.9	8.1	5.9	38.4	50.8	4 041 769	4 339 367	7.4	1.7
Bowling Green	6.8	14.1	24.3	14.5	10.9	10.4	8.3	5.4	5.3	27.5	51.9	49 296	58 067	17.8	6.1
Covington	7.4	15.7	10.5	14.7	13.8	15.5	11.4	5.7	5.3	35.8	51.5	43 370	40 640	-6.3	1.1
Elizabethtown	6.3	18.9	11.4	12.9	11.5	15.2	10.9	6.1	6.8	35.4	50.3	22 542	28 531	26.6	5.0
Florence	8.8	17.0	9.0	13.4	15.7	11.3	10.0	8.3	6.4	36.3	50.5	23 551	29 951	27.2	6.5
Frankfort	5.5	14.2	12.7	13.7	13.9	11.1	14.2	8.3	6.2	37.1	50.8	27 741	25 527	-8.0	1.1
Georgetown	7.7	19.3	11.4	16.4	15.3	12.3	9.2	4.8	3.5	32.0	51.6	18 080	29 098	60.9	8.7
Henderson	6.1	16.5	8.1	14.3	12.5	14.8	11.9	9.0	6.8	38.9	53.5	27 373	28 757	5.1	0.5
Hopkinsville	8.0	14.4	11.6	15.6	11.2	13.3	11.9	7.0	6.9	35.3	51.0	30 089	31 577	4.9	1.9
Jeffersontown	6.5	16.7	8.3	14.1	15.3	13.8	12.2	8.4	4.7	37.2	51.8	26 633	26 595	-0.1	1.3
Lexington-Fayette	6.3	14.8	14.4	16.1	13.3	12.9	11.3	6.2	4.8	34.0	50.9	260 512	295 803	13.5	5.1
Louisville/Jefferson County	6.7	16.7	9.4	14.3	12.8	14.2	12.8	7.0	6.2	37.4	51.7	693 604	597 337	7.9	2.6
Nicholasville	8.1	18.7	8.0	15.8	14.9	13.6	10.0	6.4	4.4	34.4	51.7	19 680	28 015	42.4	3.8
Owensboro	7.5	17.0	8.4	12.7	12.0	14.6	11.1	8.1	8.4	38.5	52.7	54 067	57 265	5.9	1.7
Paducah	7.1	12.9	8.0	14.8	9.8	14.4	13.6	9.4	10.0	42.6	54.7	26 307	25 024	-4.9	-0.2
Richmond	5.5	13.1	28.3	13.3	10.4	10.2	8.9	4.7	5.5	26.6	51.6	27 152	31 364	15.5	7.0
LOUISIANA	6.8	17.5	10.3	14.1	12.3	13.8	12.4	7.4	5.5	36.0	51.1	4 468 976	4 533 372	1.4	2.6
Alexandria	7.1	20.6	8.7	12.8	10.8	13.7	12.6	7.1	6.7	35.7	52.1	46 342	47 723	3.0	1.2
Baton Rouge	6.5	14.8	18.7	15.8	10.1	11.4	10.8	6.5	5.5	30.8	52.2	227 818	229 493	0.7	-0.2
Bossier City	7.8	17.3	11.6	16.2	12.7	11.6	10.3	6.1	6.4	32.6	52.9	56 461	61 315	8.6	9.5
Central	6.7	15.9	8.1	12.6	11.6	13.2	15.3	10.0	6.5	40.5	52.0	NA	26 864	NA	4.7
Houma	6.9	18.9	8.4	15.1	12.5	13.0	12.9	7.1	5.1	35.8	49.8	32 393	33 727	4.1	1.2
Kenner	6.2	14.8	9.2	15.7	10.8	15.0	13.1	9.1	6.1	38.6	52.7	70 517	66 702	-5.4	0.5
Lafayette	5.5	16.0	14.7	15.4	11.7	13.2	11.5	6.6	5.4	33.7	51.3	110 257	120 623	9.4	4.1
Lake Charles	6.9	16.3	12.8	13.6	10.4	13.5	12.8	7.2	6.6	35.7	51.7	71 757	71 993	0.3	4.0
Monroe	8.4	19.3	14.3	12.9	9.7	10.9	11.5	6.1	7.0	31.2	56.2	53 107	48 815	-8.1	0.9
New Iberia	8.2	20.5	8.4	13.1	9.9	13.6	11.9	8.5	6.0	34.9	54.3	32 623	30 617	-6.1	0.4
New Orleans	6.3	14.5	11.2	17.9	12.4	13.5	12.8	6.5	4.9	35.0	51.9	484 674	343 829	-29.1	11.8
Shreveport	7.4	17.7	10.3	15.3	11.3	12.9	12.2	6.7	6.3	34.6	52.9	200 145	199 311	-0.4	-1.1
Slidell	6.0	20.0	8.1	13.0	12.8	15.3	9.8	8.1	6.9	37.8	53.1	25 695	27 068	5.3	2.0
MAINE	4.9	15.0	8.7	11.1	12.2	15.8	15.2	9.4	7.6	43.6	51.0	1 274 923	1 328 361	4.2	0.1
Bangor	4.7	13.7	15.5	15.7	10.5	12.7	12.6	7.4	7.2	35.3	52.4	31 473	33 039	5.0	-1.4
Lewiston	5.8	13.5	12.9	13.1	10.5	13.9	13.1	8.9	8.3	40.6	51.7	35 690	36 592	2.5	-0.8
Portland	4.9	11.8	10.5	19.9	13.6	14.7	12.0	6.0	6.6	37.2	50.5	64 249	66 194	3.0	0.7
South Portland	5.2	14.7	10.0	12.8	14.8	14.5	13.1	8.5	6.4	40.4	55.1	23 324	25 002	7.2	1.7
MARYLAND	6.2	16.6	9.6	13.6	13.2	15.2	12.5	7.3	5.7	38.1	51.6	5 296 486	5 773 552	9.0	3.5
Annapolis	7.9	13.4	10.5	16.8	14.7	11.5	12.2	8.1	4.9	36.2	51.0	35 838	38 394	7.1	1.5
Baltimore	6.7	14.4	11.8	17.7	12.0	13.6	11.8	6.5	5.4	34.5	52.9	651 154	620 961	-4.6	0.3
Bowie	6.2	17.0	9.1	10.9	14.6	18.0	12.6	6.3	5.3	40.0	52.2	50 269	54 727	8.9	4.9
College Park	3.0	5.0	58.8	12.9	4.1	4.6	6.3	3.0	2.3	21.4	46.5	24 657	30 413	23.3	6.1
Frederick	7.1	15.8	9.9	17.0	14.0	13.6	11.3	6.2	5.1	35.2	51.8	52 767	65 239	23.6	4.8
Gaithersburg	8.1	17.7	6.5	18.5	14.6	13.2	11.1	5.6	4.7	34.7	51.8	52 613	59 933	13.9	11.6
Hagerstown	7.2	18.5	8.1	17.1	13.5	13.3	10.1	5.9	6.4	34.2	52.1	36 687	39 662	8.1	1.6
Laurel	9.8	14.7	6.9	19.1	18.0	14.2	9.8	5.2	2.1	34.6	53.7	19 960	25 115	25.8	4.2
Rockville	6.4	14.0	7.2	14.1	15.6	14.8	12.1	8.4	7.3	40.4	51.1	47 388	61 209	29.2	7.6
Salisbury	7.8	14.2	23.3	12.5	10.0	11.5	9.9	5.5	5.3	28.5	52.4	23 743	30 343	27.8	7.3
MASSACHUSETTS	5.5	15.6	10.4	13.4	12.8	15.1	12.8	7.6	6.8	39.3	51.6	6 349 097	6 547 629	3.1	3.0
Agawam Town	5.2	15.2	8.4	11.0	11.7	16.2	15.4	7.9	9.1	44.0	52.2	28 144	28 438	1.0	1.2
Attleboro	6.6	15.6	7.4	12.8	14.7	16.1	13.0	8.1	5.7	40.6	51.7	42 068	43 593	3.6	0.9
Barnstable Town	4.2	12.6	7.6	9.8	10.0	14.2	19.0	12.0	10.6	48.9	51.2	47 821	45 193	-5.5	-1.5

City	Households, 2011-2013				Persons in group quarters, 2010				Serious crimes known to police,[2] 2013				Educational attainment, 2011–2013		
			Percent			Institutional			Total		Rate[3]			Attainment[4] (percent)	
	Number	Persons per house-hold	Female family house-holder[1]	One-person	Total	Total	Persons in nursing facilities	Non-institu-tional	Number	Rate[3]	Violent	Property	Population age 25 and older	High school graduate or less	Bachelor's degree or more
	27	28	29	30	31	32	33	34	35	36	37	38	39	40	41
KANSAS	1 109 747	2.53	10.5	28.5	79 074	41 393	20 672	37 681	95 118	3 287	340	2 947	1 861 026	37.3	30.5
Dodge City	8 878	3.14	11.9	24.5	596	363	207	233	932	3 297	244	3 053	15 887	56.2	16.9
Garden City	9 354	2.82	13.2	24.7	548	231	96	317	825	3 050	455	2 595	15 663	52.4	18.1
Hutchinson	16 979	2.32	10.9	33.5	2 850	2 402	447	448	2 530	6 037	608	5 428	28 331	39.5	20.0
Kansas City	53 275	2.75	19.2	30.1	1 109	815	421	294	7 959	5 392	495	4 896	91 536	54.8	14.9
Lawrence	34 547	2.36	8.1	31.9	7 984	430	270	7 554	3 998	4 441	388	4 053	48 438	22.0	52.5
Leavenworth	12 089	2.67	15.1	27.2	4 031	3 352	72	679	1 328	3 692	648	3 045	22 642	39.6	29.3
Leawood	12 489	2.61	4.8	19.6	11	0	0	11	395	1 206	24	1 182	22 528	7.2	72.4
Lenexa	19 726	2.49	9.9	26.2	348	327	325	21	956	1 921	117	1 804	33 154	16.8	53.7
Manhattan	20 519	2.41	7.4	33.1	6 227	401	306	5 826	NA	NA	NA	NA	26 631	20.5	49.3
Olathe	45 809	2.80	9.1	20.8	1 418	789	661	629	2 458	1 871	141	1 731	81 756	23.9	45.5
Overland Park	73 829	2.40	10.9	30.0	1 343	1 215	1 040	128	3 814	2 112	157	1 955	122 516	16.2	57.6
Salina	19 325	2.41	14.4	30.0	1 435	545	377	890	2 125	4 416	333	4 084	31 051	45.0	22.8
Shawnee	23 656	2.67	8.5	24.8	406	384	384	22	1 178	1 839	136	1 703	41 299	26.6	42.7
Topeka	52 758	2.35	12.6	36.1	4 083	2 648	1 246	1 435	7 098	5 545	478	5 067	84 559	44.4	26.4
Wichita	149 595	2.53	13.3	32.5	6 420	3 555	1 666	2 865	23 929	6 191	794	5 397	245 239	39.2	28.3
KENTUCKY	1 693 399	2.51	13.0	28.0	125 870	70 779	26 044	55 091	113 079	2 573	210	2 363	2 937 179	50.2	21.8
Bowling Green	23 606	2.30	16.0	34.7	6 147	1 173	492	4 974	3 073	5 027	337	4 690	33 186	46.1	26.8
Covington	16 961	2.33	18.4	40.1	1 406	946	420	460	2 109	5 173	591	4 582	27 010	48.0	21.6
Elizabethtown	11 642	2.41	15.6	34.6	1 075	995	284	80	1 129	3 831	122	3 709	18 731	42.8	26.8
Florence	12 594	2.44	13.5	33.8	268	265	265	3	1 607	5 112	200	4 912	20 259	41.8	28.7
Frankfort	12 282	2.11	18.3	38.7	1 644	648	188	996	1 260	4 552	303	4 249	18 494	44.9	26.4
Georgetown	11 177	2.60	15.5	25.1	1 284	211	136	1 073	1 174	3 835	261	3 574	18 630	39.6	27.0
Henderson	12 273	2.25	18.3	34.4	1 162	806	262	356	1 085	3 748	228	3 520	20 011	50.7	17.7
Hopkinsville	13 061	2.35	18.9	33.7	1 425	1 204	348	221	1 381	4 153	322	3 831	21 460	48.1	17.3
Jeffersontown	10 730	2.47	9.9	28.3	351	351	351	0	739	2 735	137	2 598	18 438	31.0	37.1
Lexington-Fayette	123 413	2.37	12.2	32.8	12 804	3 996	1 092	8 808	13 470	4 363	306	4 057	196 723	31.5	40.7
Louisville/Jefferson County	243 396	2.43	16.3	32.8	14 153	8 529	4 831	5 624	32 424	4 831	543	4 288	407 259	43.0	27.0
Nicholasville	10 917	2.58	15.5	22.6	312	269	80	43	1 209	4 243	249	3 993	18 541	49.3	21.3
Owensboro	23 432	2.40	12.7	33.9	1 817	1 025	806	792	2 190	3 756	240	3 516	38 895	50.9	19.0
Paducah	11 105	2.16	14.8	42.3	1 090	1 024	510	66	1 276	5 091	287	4 804	18 061	43.9	19.8
Richmond	12 754	2.21	13.1	39.6	4 344	480	207	3 864	1 627	5 032	294	4 738	17 080	39.8	28.4
LOUISIANA	1 715 997	2.61	17.1	29.0	127 427	88 104	24 524	39 323	189 670	4 101	519	3 582	3 010 361	51.2	21.9
Alexandria	16 478	2.80	22.2	35.4	2 356	1 611	531	745	4 683	9 658	1 656	8 002	30 622	52.6	19.6
Baton Rouge	88 508	2.50	19.9	34.9	9 554	3 531	1 129	6 023	13 545	5 884	924	4 960	137 604	40.6	32.3
Bossier City	25 297	2.50	16.7	34.5	1 614	811	671	803	3 576	5 453	601	4 852	41 199	40.2	27.8
Central	10 058	2.72	12.0	16.7	59	0	0	59	NA	NA	NA	NA	19 007	44.8	20.4
Houma	12 422	2.70	15.2	29.8	212	134	114	78	1 778	5 273	605	4 668	22 252	57.8	16.6
Kenner	25 088	2.65	15.3	30.6	422	319	303	103	2 515	3 762	289	3 473	46 684	47.9	22.8
Lafayette	49 463	2.40	14.9	35.2	4 509	1 775	613	2 734	8 436	6 836	703	6 132	78 419	38.9	32.8
Lake Charles	29 596	2.38	20.3	34.7	3 149	2 018	596	1 131	4 082	5 524	740	4 784	47 080	45.9	22.7
Monroe	18 312	2.53	27.6	37.4	3 273	1 229	663	2 044	4 887	9 894	1 045	8 849	28 765	46.7	27.3
New Iberia	11 543	2.63	21.9	30.0	433	367	367	66	NA	NA	NA	NA	19 377	60.6	15.0
New Orleans	151 790	2.35	19.6	40.6	13 165	5 509	1 509	7 656	17 490	4 639	786	3 853	251 356	39.0	34.2
Shreveport	77 774	2.53	22.9	35.0	5 574	3 588	1 975	1 986	10 981	5 431	691	4 740	130 296	45.4	25.7
Slidell	9 741	2.78	17.1	21.6	315	286	286	29	1 644	5 989	350	5 639	18 059	42.0	23.9
MAINE	552 589	2.34	9.5	29.2	35 545	12 409	7 878	23 136	32 165	2 422	129	2 292	947 986	42.5	28.2
Bangor	14 333	2.12	10.7	38.1	2 690	854	561	1 836	1 914	5 845	214	5 632	21 691	39.5	28.6
Lewiston	16 064	2.13	15.3	34.7	2 117	365	344	1 752	1 314	3 608	255	3 352	24 720	53.5	15.1
Portland	29 992	2.14	10.2	39.5	2 613	1 065	592	1 548	2 789	4 209	267	3 942	48 202	30.2	44.4
South Portland	10 792	2.28	15.1	33.7	636	195	73	441	922	3 670	231	3 439	17 605	29.7	38.7
MARYLAND	2 149 424	2.67	14.7	27.4	138 375	66 838	28 001	71 537	186 002	3 137	474	2 663	3 970 798	36.8	37.1
Annapolis	16 055	2.37	12.9	36.4	603	143	143	460	1 225	3 170	437	2 732	26 286	31.7	44.9
Baltimore	242 243	2.47	22.3	40.8	25 199	9 951	3 793	15 248	39 514	6 346	1 401	4 945	416 965	48.4	27.5
Bowie	19 769	2.82	14.1	23.8	255	148	145	107	943	1 670	108	1 562	38 002	22.6	47.4
College Park	6 347	3.00	5.8	32.9	11 535	0	0	11 535	NA	NA	NA	NA	10 340	30.3	51.6
Frederick	26 277	2.47	15.2	30.9	1 785	803	803	982	2 120	3 178	492	2 686	44 684	34.4	37.3
Gaithersburg	22 911	2.75	14.7	25.5	547	372	366	175	NA	NA	NA	NA	42 866	26.3	51.4
Hagerstown	16 631	2.39	17.5	34.6	806	546	508	260	1 742	4 263	597	3 666	26 839	53.0	16.9
Laurel	9 942	2.56	18.4	36.8	183	0	0	183	970	3 778	573	3 205	17 549	34.8	40.8
Rockville	25 063	2.48	8.4	28.4	1 103	833	665	270	NA	NA	NA	NA	45 691	19.1	63.8
Salisbury	11 572	2.59	20.8	34.4	1 391	155	135	1 236	2 132	6 765	1 034	5 730	17 079	45.9	28.3
MASSACHUSETTS	2 528 592	2.53	12.7	28.9	238 882	74 667	43 833	164 215	164 952	2 465	413	2 051	4 556 615	36.3	39.6
Agawam Town	11 449	2.45	9.2	31.2	677	669	669	8	312	1 089	143	946	20 409	38.7	28.5
Attleboro	16 657	2.59	10.2	25.2	564	451	429	113	1 050	2 385	245	2 139	30 823	40.7	30.2
Barnstable Town	19 835	2.23	9.6	33.6	363	106	79	257	1 492	3 328	674	2 654	33 831	32.2	36.6

1. No spouse present. 2. Data for serious crimes have not been adjusted for underreporting. This may affect comparability between geographic areas and over time. 3. Per 100,000 population estimated by the FBI. 4. Persons 25 years old and over.

Table D. Cities — **Income, Poverty, and Housing**

City	Money income, 2011–2013: Per capita income[1] (dollars)	Money income, 2011–2013: Households: Median income	Money income, 2011–2013: Households: Percent with income of $200,000 or more	Money income, 2011–2013: Households: Percent with income of less than $25,000	Money income, 2011–2013: Families with income below poverty (percent)	Housing units, 2010: Total	Housing units, 2010: Percent change, 2000–2010	Housing units, 2010: Vacant units for sale or rent[2]	Occupied housing units 2011–2013: Total	Occupied housing units 2011–2013: Owner-occupied: Percent	Occupied housing units 2011–2013: Owner-occupied: Median value[3] (dollars)	Occupied housing units 2011–2013: Median owner costs as a percent of income: With a mortgage[4]	Occupied housing units 2011–2013: Median owner costs as a percent of income: Without a mortgage[5]
	42	43	44	45	46	47	48	49	50	51	52	53	54
KANSAS	26 752	50 808	3.3	22.8	9.4	1 233 215	9.0	121 119	1 109 747	66.7	129 500	20.9	11.9
Dodge City	17 522	46 957	1.9	23.8	14.8	9 378	4.3	601	8 878	52.8	89 900	20.9	11.4
Garden City	20 392	45 326	1.6	18.9	13.6	9 656	-1.7	585	9 354	57.9	113 500	24.1	12.7
Hutchinson	21 992	40 115	1.5	28.7	9.3	18 580	5.1	1 599	16 979	58.7	90 500	20.2	13.2
Kansas City	17 876	37 643	0.6	32.6	20.8	61 969	0.8	8 044	53 275	57.8	86 900	24.9	16.4
Lawrence	25 796	46 755	3.5	27.9	9.0	37 502	14.4	2 532	34 547	46.6	177 900	21.6	11.7
Leavenworth	22 157	51 606	1.1	22.1	11.7	13 670	5.9	1 414	12 089	47.0	111 800	22.1	11.8
Leawood	80 335	134 451	31.0	8.1	2.2	12 384	22.2	603	12 489	92.1	389 400	19.2	10.6
Lenexa	36 358	72 109	6.1	13.5	5.0	20 832	27.4	1 544	19 726	61.9	220 300	21.1	10.6
Manhattan	23 433	42 512	2.4	28.6	6.5	21 619	22.1	1 611	20 519	39.4	181 700	21.4	11.5
Olathe	31 557	76 426	4.4	12.2	4.6	46 851	40.6	2 344	45 809	73.6	193 900	21.1	10.0
Overland Park	38 668	69 354	7.8	13.2	3.8	76 280	21.7	4 837	73 829	63.8	222 800	21.2	10.0
Salina	24 596	43 458	1.9	27.9	13.5	20 803	6.1	1 412	19 325	62.7	114 900	22.3	12.2
Shawnee	32 861	72 039	6.4	12.8	4.4	24 954	30.6	1 303	23 656	70.9	195 100	20.3	11.7
Topeka	23 305	40 323	1.8	29.2	15.4	59 582	5.5	5 639	52 758	56.0	94 300	20.2	12.8
Wichita	24 236	44 532	2.7	27.0	13.8	167 310	10.0	15 492	149 595	59.7	118 100	21.4	11.8
KENTUCKY	23 285	42 576	2.5	30.5	14.6	1 927 164	10.1	207 199	1 693 399	67.7	120 700	21.0	10.7
Bowling Green	19 823	32 202	2.2	40.5	23.1	24 712	16.6	1 977	23 606	37.9	139 300	21.4	10.3
Covington	20 392	33 332	1.1	39.2	23.8	20 053	-1.9	3 020	16 961	49.7	98 200	22.4	13.2
Elizabethtown	24 295	40 874	2.0	28.4	14.7	12 664	26.3	953	11 642	48.6	149 700	19.9	10.0
Florence	26 135	51 591	1.8	25.3	6.4	13 447	31.2	954	12 594	50.0	133 300	20.3	10.0
Frankfort	24 154	40 172	1.4	28.6	19.0	12 938	-3.4	1 798	12 282	49.2	131 100	21.1	10.5
Georgetown	24 464	59 544	0.8	20.3	9.8	11 957	66.8	1 224	11 177	66.2	147 800	19.0	10.0
Henderson	19 539	34 050	1.2	37.1	20.4	13 171	4.0	1 080	12 273	54.6	89 000	22.7	11.7
Hopkinsville	20 769	32 977	2.2	37.7	21.1	14 318	7.8	1 464	13 061	50.0	110 300	21.4	10.0
Jeffersontown	29 431	60 621	2.8	15.1	5.7	11 800	5.5	735	10 730	67.6	163 100	18.8	10.0
Lexington-Fayette	29 203	47 977	4.7	26.7	11.3	135 160	16.3	12 117	123 413	54.9	166 800	20.1	10.0
Louisville/Jefferson County	26 043	43 963	3.5	29.2	14.1	337 616	NA	28 441	243 396	60.5	139 500	21.5	11.4
Nicholasville	20 291	42 496	1.1	30.0	18.6	11 405	47.0	913	10 917	56.8	135 400	21.8	12.9
Owensboro	21 991	39 415	2.1	33.2	16.5	26 072	7.0	1 857	23 432	59.3	104 700	20.3	10.6
Paducah	22 720	34 712	0.9	38.6	23.0	12 851	-2.5	1 389	11 105	50.1	85 600	19.9	10.3
Richmond	17 453	30 632	0.9	42.9	22.2	13 788	16.5	1 353	12 754	38.5	125 000	23.6	12.7
LOUISIANA	24 228	43 856	3.2	30.6	15.5	1 964 981	6.4	236 621	1 715 997	66.2	139 900	20.9	10.0
Alexandria	19 151	34 197	2.8	38.0	20.7	20 366	2.4	2 094	16 478	54.1	132 300	24.5	10.8
Baton Rouge	23 390	38 735	3.2	35.2	18.3	100 801	3.6	9 327	88 508	50.4	152 600	22.1	10.1
Bossier City	25 906	47 207	3.3	27.5	15.8	25 579	11.7	1 713	25 297	56.4	146 200	19.7	10.5
Central	31 820	71 890	5.8	13.4	6.0	10 574	NA	395	10 058	86.8	177 900	19.4	10.0
Houma	25 272	50 028	5.1	26.8	12.0	13 924	12.1	1 173	12 422	69.1	158 400	19.5	10.1
Kenner	25 212	45 149	3.5	25.0	11.8	28 076	2.5	3 232	25 088	59.8	169 200	24.0	10.0
Lafayette	28 454	45 317	4.7	30.9	13.6	53 356	13.9	3 912	49 463	56.7	170 400	21.3	10.4
Lake Charles	23 220	35 610	3.4	36.3	18.8	32 469	3.7	3 529	29 596	54.6	128 600	21.9	10.0
Monroe	20 383	26 630	4.5	47.4	30.0	20 570	-3.5	2 125	18 312	44.3	118 500	19.8	12.4
New Iberia	20 616	35 832	1.1	37.8	20.5	13 059	1.1	1 353	11 543	62.5	102 000	20.3	10.4
New Orleans	26 348	35 837	4.3	38.6	23.2	189 896	-11.7	47 738	151 790	46.2	183 100	26.4	13.8
Shreveport	24 095	38 213	3.3	33.1	18.9	88 253	1.5	7 602	77 774	55.7	124 700	21.3	10.2
Slidell	23 150	49 788	2.1	21.5	12.5	11 155	10.4	1 105	9 741	68.9	152 600	22.0	11.9
MAINE	26 691	47 405	2.8	26.0	9.5	721 830	10.7	164 611	552 589	70.8	172 300	23.7	14.0
Bangor	23 376	33 820	2.8	35.7	17.4	15 674	7.5	1 199	14 333	41.4	140 400	23.2	14.2
Lewiston	21 300	34 767	0.9	40.3	20.8	16 731	1.6	1 464	16 064	44.1	143 300	24.2	17.8
Portland	28 178	42 757	3.3	31.7	15.1	33 836	6.2	3 111	29 992	43.7	230 200	26.2	15.8
South Portland	29 860	51 938	2.7	21.5	11.0	11 484	11.0	607	10 792	55.8	221 500	24.2	14.9
MARYLAND	35 837	72 345	8.6	16.1	7.2	2 378 814	10.9	222 403	2 149 424	66.8	282 400	24.0	12.1
Annapolis	43 815	72 856	9.3	17.9	6.7	17 845	10.2	1 709	16 055	52.3	356 300	23.9	12.1
Baltimore	24 588	40 798	3.0	34.2	19.8	296 685	-1.3	46 782	242 243	47.1	151 700	25.3	14.9
Bowie	42 250	103 618	11.6	6.3	1.3	20 687	11.1	737	19 769	83.8	286 600	24.4	10.0
College Park	17 069	56 201	4.2	31.1	8.1	8 212	31.4	1 455	6 347	46.3	250 800	26.7	12.1
Frederick	31 896	62 874	4.2	15.6	7.7	27 559	25.0	2 207	26 277	52.4	231 500	24.4	12.8
Gaithersburg	40 283	76 283	11.4	12.9	9.0	23 337	13.5	1 337	22 911	57.2	361 800	23.7	10.5
Hagerstown	20 547	38 637	0.8	34.5	22.3	18 682	9.5	2 233	16 631	38.4	147 300	24.1	15.0
Laurel	33 197	66 737	4.3	13.3	8.9	11 397	19.4	899	9 942	47.8	234 100	28.4	10.0
Rockville	50 428	99 889	14.8	9.2	3.9	25 199	41.6	1 513	25 063	60.1	474 300	23.1	11.5
Salisbury	21 382	36 954	2.8	35.7	24.0	13 401	37.2	1 418	11 572	33.9	143 300	24.5	13.5
MASSACHUSETTS	35 518	66 135	8.0	20.5	8.4	2 808 254	7.1	261 179	2 528 592	62.0	325 800	24.6	14.9
Agawam Town	30 358	62 809	2.8	23.0	6.7	12 139	4.1	475	11 449	74.2	226 900	23.4	14.7
Attleboro	30 585	65 127	3.6	19.6	7.4	18 022	8.9	1 138	16 657	63.9	269 100	24.5	15.1
Barnstable Town	34 613	54 087	4.4	26.2	7.7	26 343	5.3	7 118	19 835	74.3	345 200	28.8	17.9

1. Based on population estimated by the American Community Survey. 2. Includes units rented or sold but not occupied. 3. Specified owner-occupied units; $1,000,000 represents $1,000,000 or more 4. 50.0 represents 50 percent or more. 5. 10.0 represents 10 percent or less.

City	Occupied housing units, 2011–2013 (cont.): Percent renter occupied	Occupied housing units, 2011–2013 (cont.): Median gross rent[1]	Occupied housing units, 2011–2013 (cont.): Median rent as a percent of income[2]	Occupied housing units, 2011–2013 (cont.): Percent with no vehicle available	Migration, 2011–2013: Percent who lived in the same house one year ago	Migration, 2011–2013: Percent who lived outside current city one year ago	Civilian labor force, 2014: Total	Civilian labor force, 2014: Percent change, 2013–2014	Civilian labor force, 2014: Unemployment: Total	Civilian labor force, 2014: Unemployment: Rate[3]	Civilian employment[4], 2011–2013: Population age 16 and older	Civilian employment[4], 2011–2013: Percent: In labor force	Civilian employment[4], 2011–2013: Percent: Civilian full-year full-time workers	Civilian employment[4], 2011–2013: Households with no workers (percent)
	55	56	57	58	59	60	61	62	63	64	65	66	67	68
KANSAS	33.3	734	28.2	5.4	83.4	9.6	1 500 353	0.9	67 994	4.5	2 235 776	67.4	43.5	24.2
Dodge City	47.2	572	22.9	6.2	83.1	7.4	14 770	-0.8	584	4.0	20 278	69.9	46.9	18.0
Garden City	42.1	695	23.1	5.7	85.1	5.6	14 856	1.7	527	3.5	19 358	72.8	49.6	14.9
Hutchinson	41.3	632	26.8	5.5	77.7	10.3	20 014	-0.5	934	4.7	33 255	60.2	40.9	31.0
Kansas City	42.2	743	31.5	10.5	82.5	7.4	69 693	1.6	4 882	7.0	109 679	66.2	39.0	28.2
Lawrence	53.4	854	33.3	5.4	68.2	13.1	51 712	1.8	2 081	4.0	75 571	70.7	38.1	18.8
Leavenworth	53.0	867	25.0	5.2	67.9	25.5	13 915	1.5	772	5.5	26 930	58.2	32.8	26.9
Leawood	7.9	1 240	29.6	2.9	91.7	7.1	16 618	2.3	561	3.4	24 792	64.0	43.9	23.1
Lenexa	38.1	954	26.6	4.5	81.6	15.9	29 377	2.1	1 091	3.7	38 462	74.4	50.4	16.4
Manhattan	60.6	848	32.5	6.6	72.9	16.8	30 606	0.9	1 039	3.4	47 996	64.8	30.7	19.8
Olathe	26.4	871	29.6	3.1	86.0	8.3	75 109	2.1	2 728	3.6	95 976	77.3	51.8	15.1
Overland Park	36.2	952	26.2	3.7	83.8	9.9	103 382	2.3	3 977	3.8	140 486	72.6	49.9	18.9
Salina	37.3	673	31.3	6.4	84.5	6.4	26 303	-0.5	1 144	4.3	37 198	70.7	46.0	22.9
Shawnee	29.1	794	27.0	2.8	86.6	10.2	35 683	2.1	1 412	4.0	48 013	72.4	49.3	16.8
Topeka	44.0	692	30.3	10.5	79.6	6.9	64 770	0.6	3 362	5.2	100 235	63.5	39.6	31.4
Wichita	40.3	691	29.0	7.1	82.3	5.6	188 735	0.5	10 568	5.6	293 693	67.2	42.3	25.0
KENTUCKY	32.3	653	29.4	7.9	84.8	10.6	2 005 252	-2.5	130 106	6.5	3 472 918	59.7	37.1	32.7
Bowling Green	62.1	649	33.1	10.7	65.9	18.6	30 096	-2.3	1 711	5.7	49 103	64.7	32.7	27.6
Covington	50.3	665	33.6	18.9	80.0	12.9	18 659	-2.4	1 172	6.3	32 067	63.3	36.1	33.5
Elizabethtown	51.4	694	28.3	9.9	73.6	17.2	13 413	-2.2	764	5.7	22 934	62.1	35.7	28.3
Florence	50.0	794	26.3	8.4	76.9	16.6	15 596	-2.1	812	5.2	23 336	68.2	45.3	25.7
Frankfort	50.8	669	31.5	8.4	73.3	14.0	13 757	-2.3	705	5.1	22 482	61.3	37.3	31.3
Georgetown	33.8	728	26.7	7.7	82.3	9.2	16 057	-0.9	751	4.7	22 748	72.1	49.5	20.9
Henderson	45.4	581	29.3	12.3	81.6	9.8	12 927	-2.3	779	6.0	23 079	57.2	34.2	38.6
Hopkinsville	50.0	583	30.9	9.9	80.7	10.2	12 685	-2.4	945	7.4	25 943	56.8	32.3	35.9
Jeffersontown	32.4	795	24.7	2.3	80.0	15.3	15 156	-1.4	772	5.1	21 284	73.1	47.6	19.4
Lexington-Fayette	45.1	755	30.5	8.9	76.6	9.4	166 862	-1.0	8 059	4.8	246 514	68.1	41.8	23.1
Louisville/Jefferson County	39.5	704	29.9	11.4	85.5	5.6	378 661	-2.0	23 045	6.1	479 343	65.2	40.2	29.7
Nicholasville	43.2	745	28.3	6.4	78.5	11.7	14 234	-1.6	736	5.2	21 475	67.8	43.3	24.6
Owensboro	40.7	634	28.8	7.6	81.7	7.4	26 155	-3.5	1 483	5.7	45 301	60.3	36.7	33.7
Paducah	49.9	569	26.5	15.0	82.6	9.9	10 421	-3.5	730	7.0	20 422	56.0	36.4	38.4
Richmond	61.5	619	31.5	8.9	71.7	15.7	17 233	-1.9	939	5.4	26 756	63.8	30.7	30.6
LOUISIANA	33.8	764	32.1	8.6	85.9	9.8	2 157 232	2.4	137 577	6.4	3 610 112	61.1	39.3	28.4
Alexandria	45.9	745	35.0	13.1	84.8	6.8	20 353	2.2	1 488	7.3	36 751	54.2	35.0	35.7
Baton Rouge	49.6	765	34.2	10.2	81.2	8.8	116 977	3.1	7 511	6.4	185 528	63.7	36.7	27.1
Bossier City	43.6	835	30.1	8.5	82.1	12.7	30 161	1.1	1 810	6.0	50 064	68.5	43.1	24.1
Central	13.2	856	30.6	1.9	92.9	5.1	15 087	3.6	779	5.2	22 141	66.3	43.0	24.1
Houma	30.9	756	24.9	9.0	83.9	10.2	16 807	3.3	833	5.0	26 191	62.4	44.6	26.4
Kenner	40.2	922	33.4	8.5	89.3	7.2	34 033	2.7	1 911	5.6	54 042	64.6	41.3	26.3
Lafayette	43.3	787	31.9	7.9	79.8	10.7	66 105	1.9	3 387	5.1	99 455	67.9	41.8	22.9
Lake Charles	45.4	723	32.7	11.2	77.4	10.8	36 118	5.7	2 268	6.3	58 353	62.7	33.7	30.3
Monroe	55.7	568	34.1	16.6	85.0	6.5	21 025	1.4	1 709	8.1	37 564	57.0	35.7	32.5
New Iberia	37.5	641	31.0	12.9	85.5	6.5	12 729	1.6	903	7.1	22 939	59.8	34.9	33.1
New Orleans	53.8	910	37.4	18.9	82.6	7.3	178 535	2.5	12 516	7.0	301 097	61.8	38.0	31.8
Shreveport	44.3	738	31.5	11.9	82.8	6.2	88 784	0.8	6 708	7.6	156 726	61.0	39.9	27.2
Slidell	31.1	979	33.6	7.0	83.3	9.3	12 717	2.8	902	7.1	21 201	64.6	39.7	26.9
MAINE	29.2	760	31.5	7.6	85.8	11.4	698 928	-1.2	39 876	5.7	1 095 764	63.9	38.2	30.8
Bangor	58.6	728	35.6	16.7	75.6	17.1	17 260	-1.2	917	5.3	27 609	62.0	35.8	32.0
Lewiston	55.9	668	29.9	17.2	78.8	10.8	17 600	-0.7	1 030	5.9	29 983	62.0	36.4	36.4
Portland	56.3	902	32.5	20.3	73.8	15.4	38 131	-1.5	1 658	4.3	56 262	69.0	39.5	28.9
South Portland	44.2	991	29.8	6.9	78.0	15.9	14 459	-1.3	641	4.4	20 695	71.5	45.3	22.9
MARYLAND	33.2	1 194	31.0	9.6	87.0	10.0	3 111 329	-0.4	181 352	5.8	4 695 115	68.8	45.4	22.1
Annapolis	47.7	1 355	27.3	8.9	84.4	11.4	21 615	-0.1	1 067	4.9	30 992	72.4	49.1	22.6
Baltimore	52.9	906	33.2	30.6	82.4	6.6	294 340	-0.8	25 516	8.7	503 706	62.3	37.7	32.9
Bowie	16.2	1 806	27.9	3.6	91.1	6.9	32 413	-0.1	1 580	4.9	44 908	74.9	51.7	17.4
College Park	53.7	1 428	50.0	12.0	64.7	29.6	14 221	-0.2	1 052	7.4	29 315	51.8	19.5	24.7
Frederick	47.6	1 222	30.3	10.1	79.9	12.0	35 885	-0.5	1 962	5.5	52 262	73.5	47.7	20.6
Gaithersburg	42.8	1 440	32.4	8.2	84.4	11.0	35 193	-0.4	1 564	4.4	48 450	72.3	49.5	15.3
Hagerstown	61.6	815	30.3	17.0	77.2	13.0	19 817	-1.6	1 601	8.1	31 056	66.1	41.5	32.2
Laurel	52.2	1 332	29.5	10.1	80.3	13.6	15 199	-0.4	789	5.2	19 674	79.8	58.0	13.2
Rockville	39.9	1 755	27.2	8.7	84.5	12.2	35 384	-0.4	1 414	4.0	51 584	73.2	50.8	17.7
Salisbury	66.1	994	36.7	13.2	70.3	16.5	14 714	-0.2	1 313	8.9	25 078	62.7	32.9	29.0
MASSACHUSETTS	38.0	1 063	30.2	12.6	86.9	9.0	3 557 472	1.4	204 809	5.8	5 420 428	67.5	40.7	26.0
Agawam Town	25.8	789	28.8	6.3	90.5	7.0	15 816	1.7	912	5.8	23 515	67.9	42.0	29.4
Attleboro	36.1	961	30.3	7.2	88.0	6.2	24 058	1.2	1 467	6.1	35 129	71.3	46.6	23.8
Barnstable Town	25.7	1 066	34.7	9.0	90.9	6.0	23 619	1.3	1 436	6.1	38 199	61.5	35.9	36.3

1. $2,000 represents $2,000 or more. 2. 50.0 represents 50 percent or more. 3. Percent of civilian labor force. 4. Persons 16 years old and over.

Table D. Cities — **Construction, Wholesale Trade, and Retail Trade**

City	Value of residential construction authorized by building permits, 2014			Wholesale trade,[1] 2007				Retail trade,[2] 2007			
	New construction ($1,000)	Number of housing units	Percent single family	Number of establish-ments	Number of employees	Sales (mil dol)	Annual payroll (mil dol)	Number of establish-ments	Number of employees	Sales (mil dol)	Annual payroll (mil dol)
	69	70	71	72	73	74	75	76	77	78	79
KANSAS	1 417 358	7 459	65.3	3 747	47 285	45 863.9	2 150.4	11 463	149 672	34 538.3	3 133.7
Dodge City	5 751	33	93.9	40	433	333.3	17.6	124	1 571	380.1	33.2
Garden City	2 253	14	71.4	14	132	132.4	5.3	152	2 248	461.2	43.5
Hutchinson	3 459	19	68.4	36	473	464.1	17.1	241	3 264	720.4	68.9
Kansas City	55 076	481	35.1	214	5 328	3 855.9	265.1	422	6 267	1 556.3	158.6
Lawrence	42 430	276	47.5	63	641	354.9	24.8	363	5 823	1 130.5	105.7
Leavenworth	2 206	10	100.0	7	19	5.4	0.7	121	1 529	353.2	32.0
Leawood	26 414	81	90.1	38	355	203.3	23.7	136	2 403	334.1	40.0
Lenexa	121 164	639	30.2	285	5 111	2 182.2	256.3	185	3 734	1 849.1	107.4
Manhattan	51 847	270	71.5	34	567	126.0	18.4	260	4 688	837.1	80.8
Olathe	145 127	502	98.4	136	2 873	1 426.9	140.5	408	7 408	2 090.1	176.5
Overland Park	210 187	936	41.0	272	2 390	9 823.7	196.8	772	15 086	2 809.9	324.8
Salina	8 613	56	96.4	66	909	505.5	35.8	267	4 131	1 047.1	84.6
Shawnee	51 330	201	76.6	49	829	632.8	42.7	194	3 595	726.3	78.9
Topeka	21 242	114	75.4	124	1 454	571.4	60.7	674	9 716	2 136.6	201.2
Wichita	105 584	732	75.1	519	7 491	11 827.5	349.6	1 518	23 854	5 765.6	519.7
KENTUCKY	1 304 713	9 536	63.7	3 794	59 854	74 680.8	2 869.5	16 404	214 782	50 405.9	4 502.2
Bowling Green	38 793	302	39.1	120	1 638	2 071.9	68.7	482	7 172	1 609.8	144.8
Covington	0	0	0.0	26	744	158.1	19.1	139	2 025	417.8	42.4
Elizabethtown	12 812	186	32.3	34	365	220.2	12.7	280	4 192	973.0	93.9
Florence	NA	NA	NA	40	697	814.2	37.1	325	6 780	1 579.0	140.1
Frankfort	5 863	52	30.8	14	215	205.3	9.2	140	1 998	402.8	40.0
Georgetown	NA	NA	NA	14	D	D	D	109	1 581	440.7	31.9
Henderson	2 915	23	52.2	26	351	419.3	16.8	168	2 315	581.3	48.7
Hopkinsville	3 748	32	71.9	50	856	776.5	31.8	197	2 427	584.7	54.4
Jeffersontown	3 347	18	100.0	155	2 419	1 186.1	122.6	150	3 074	866.8	74.2
Lexington-Fayette	134 483	1 225	56.1	375	8 540	4 442.4	568.5	1 249	22 335	4 778.5	510.4
Louisville/Jefferson County	289 055	2 413	40.0	1 026	16 413	13 000.6	763.2	2 775	43 687	10 002.4	978.5
Nicholasville	13 541	102	87.3	27	D	D	D	118	1 759	621.0	47.0
Owensboro	26 689	320	79.4	69	861	568.8	34.9	361	4 763	1 071.4	100.4
Paducah	13 060	92	17.4	72	1 503	3 423.6	61.2	373	5 842	1 408.6	121.2
Richmond	11 324	171	58.5	25	208	131.8	7.7	206	3 012	662.9	58.8
LOUISIANA	2 888 790	15 255	84.2	4 839	63 911	51 415.6	2 808.3	17 135	231 365	56 543.2	5 096.1
Alexandria	9 324	49	79.6	80	981	442.6	40.4	398	5 762	1 415.2	125.7
Baton Rouge	90 321	476	48.7	346	4 642	5 407.5	204.8	1 173	16 258	3 830.3	374.8
Bossier City	100 441	1 057	55.4	60	1 307	926.2	60.8	389	5 610	1 559.3	127.3
Central	31 411	134	100.0	NA	NA	NA	NA	NA	NA	NA	NA
Houma	NA	NA	NA	60	684	374.2	31.1	186	2 432	505.2	52.2
Kenner	6 259	19	100.0	124	1 009	518.1	42.9	369	6 512	1 875.1	164.1
Lafayette	NA	NA	NA	257	3 482	1 389.2	147.8	829	13 436	3 273.0	293.3
Lake Charles	81 511	826	17.6	75	937	411.1	34.1	505	6 847	1 507.5	142.2
Monroe	28 041	181	65.7	80	1 184	1 184.4	46.2	395	6 299	1 352.3	125.7
New Iberia	3 928	20	65.0	40	773	256.6	37.2	210	2 982	736.6	65.2
New Orleans	201 755	1 026	55.9	253	3 030	1 938.4	145.6	1 155	11 877	2 718.0	305.5
Shreveport	70 783	270	97.8	274	D	D	D	909	13 397	3 240.4	304.8
Slidell	9 393	94	20.2	36	328	253.1	12.3	288	5 190	1 143.6	109.3
MAINE	612 903	3 242	83.7	1 439	16 939	8 823.7	686.4	6 911	83 279	20 444.0	1 893.7
Bangor	3 752	17	76.5	71	1 272	854.1	50.6	332	6 123	1 824.0	136.5
Lewiston	2 166	10	100.0	46	689	252.8	28.5	169	2 029	561.0	45.2
Portland	16 024	100	36.0	172	2 475	1 124.5	105.2	416	5 116	1 321.8	131.0
South Portland	6 823	50	62.0	57	1 269	1 108.4	50.3	252	5 393	1 069.6	116.5
MARYLAND	2 889 171	16 331	64.5	5 020	79 868	51 276.8	4 158.4	19 601	294 806	75 664.2	7 290.8
Annapolis	52 833	372	41.9	58	495	812.5	30.2	311	3 368	973.6	95.9
Baltimore	94 235	821	29.4	534	9 046	4 843.4	468.9	1 950	16 682	4 348.8	401.5
Bowie	NA	NA	NA	12	47	16.6	2.1	167	4 136	854.4	85.5
College Park	NA	NA	NA	16	56	15.3	3.1	87	2 001	543.6	54.0
Frederick	72 247	672	20.6	70	1 101	487.0	59.8	356	5 491	1 398.0	141.1
Gaithersburg	27 241	247	60.3	73	858	499.1	55.4	371	7 650	2 068.4	202.1
Hagerstown	10 351	106	24.5	53	466	141.5	16.4	225	4 104	1 059.1	95.8
Laurel	0	0	0.0	12	139	33.9	7.0	154	2 280	460.1	47.8
Rockville	95 721	578	2.8	89	1 959	3 282.8	151.2	316	4 343	1 245.3	125.7
Salisbury	5 428	58	3.4	69	813	416.1	31.5	298	5 181	1 104.6	106.3
MASSACHUSETTS	3 300 622	14 486	50.6	7 284	123 267	95 275.7	7 644.3	25 469	360 218	88 083.0	8 916.5
Agawam Town	5 277	37	29.7	NA	NA	NA	NA	NA	NA	NA	NA
Attleboro	11 275	84	95.2	38	619	260.1	31.5	158	2 716	664.8	58.7
Barnstable Town	15 419	48	100.0	41	425	148.9	19.6	434	5 635	1 395.5	143.3

1. Merchant wholesalers except manufacturers' sales branches and offices. 2. Establishments with payroll.

City	Real estate and rental and leasing, 2007				Professional, scientific, and technical services,[1] 2007				Manufacturing, 2007			
	Number of establish-ments	Number of employees	Receipts (mil dol)	Annual payroll (mil dol)	Number of establish-ments	Number of employees	Receipts (mil dol)	Annual payroll (mil dol)	Number of establish-ments	Number of employees	Receipts (mil dol)	Annual payroll (mil dol)
	80	81	82	83	84	85	86	87	88	89	90	91
KANSAS	3 314	15 160	2 428.8	439.7	7 042	55 922	7 781.4	2 736.5	3 170	177 659	76 751.8	7 983.4
Dodge City	26	D	D	D	45	D	D	D	21	D	D	D
Garden City	29	100	13.8	2.4	53	D	D	D	NA	NA	NA	NA
Hutchinson	54	D	D	D	92	D	D	D	45	1 413	315.2	55.8
Kansas City	127	730	126.2	21.2	140	D	D	D	204	10 394	7 369.7	604.1
Lawrence	151	685	90.1	16.9	247	D	D	D	66	3 447	820.1	123.8
Leavenworth	32	175	20.7	4.4	68	D	D	D	14	535	D	19.0
Leawood	109	300	86.3	12.9	211	1 435	240.4	98.2	NA	NA	NA	NA
Lenexa	118	771	139.0	27.9	307	D	D	D	150	7 287	2 087.7	320.3
Manhattan	101	496	53.0	10.5	138	D	D	D	29	1 162	184.0	36.3
Olathe	148	577	108.3	18.5	358	D	D	D	110	5 447	3 245.9	279.9
Overland Park	397	2 043	438.2	80.8	1 155	D	D	D	97	1 358	238.1	57.3
Salina	69	277	44.9	6.3	115	D	D	D	58	3 765	1 026.9	145.9
Shawnee	74	313	58.8	6.9	191	1 372	144.1	47.0	48	1 759	758.1	106.0
Topeka	207	931	144.0	28.1	408	D	D	D	94	3 965	1 658.1	145.1
Wichita	520	3 170	467.8	87.1	983	D	D	D	478	33 140	14 213.2	1 655.3
KENTUCKY	3 898	20 146	3 894.3	593.4	8 075	61 428	7 872.2	2 831.6	4 165	247 096	119 105.4	10 773.2
Bowling Green	114	1 046	107.5	27.1	175	D	D	D	98	9 133	4 473.8	404.8
Covington	39	287	73.1	9.6	135	D	D	D	31	1 052	278.7	41.9
Elizabethtown	58	235	38.8	5.5	90	D	D	D	57	4 359	D	185.6
Florence	71	288	79.3	8.6	111	586	66.6	22.2	41	D	D	D
Frankfort	37	123	17.9	2.9	96	616	78.2	27.5	13	870	D	36.6
Georgetown	42	140	24.2	3.4	47	382	30.1	12.9	22	9 060	D	D
Henderson	35	203	15.8	4.4	73	385	32.4	10.6	59	4 336	D	152.0
Hopkinsville	51	179	22.0	3.2	61	346	30.1	11.4	54	D	D	197.5
Jeffersontown	75	713	194.4	22.9	156	D	D	D	101	4 718	865.7	173.1
Lexington-Fayette	476	2 268	391.2	68.2	1 053	D	D	D	255	9 602	3 061.2	401.7
Louisville/Jefferson County	991	6 888	1 995.1	263.3	2 266	15 049	2 652.2	793.2	797	45 142	25 695.4	2 233.8
Nicholasville	34	145	25.1	4.5	37	152	12.5	4.3	55	2 584	D	D
Owensboro	63	432	37.9	9.4	140	D	D	D	82	4 930	2 092.4	194.4
Paducah	69	336	53.6	8.8	139	D	D	D	32	1 274	345.2	D
Richmond	53	198	33.3	4.5	72	D	D	D	32	2 192	D	83.8
LOUISIANA	4 625	30 922	6 014.9	1 194.9	11 128	84 666	11 856.6	4 234.6	3 442	148 080	205 054.7	7 564.5
Alexandria	107	590	69.0	14.7	195	1 268	134.5	49.9	34	1 165	D	29.7
Baton Rouge	353	1 827	316.6	58.1	1 148	13 858	2 088.3	722.9	197	4 423	2 443.5	198.7
Bossier City	86	457	81.2	12.3	96	610	54.2	18.2	52	1 671	D	59.2
Central	NA	NA	NA	NA	NA	NA	NA	NA	NA	NA	NA	NA
Houma	79	602	110.2	25.4	168	D	D	D	37	812	138.2	36.3
Kenner	80	1 057	199.7	31.4	165	920	117.8	48.5	55	1 062	150.7	40.7
Lafayette	306	2 156	571.5	107.1	928	D	D	D	128	5 125	1 055.5	187.8
Lake Charles	121	440	77.4	12.8	304	D	D	D	40	2 358	D	184.8
Monroe	122	582	103.8	19.6	308	D	D	D	45	1 546	413.6	63.2
New Iberia	58	654	147.6	33.1	120	549	65.7	17.8	57	2 978	D	117.5
New Orleans	362	1 764	354.4	61.8	1 290	D	D	D	141	7 607	3 088.9	402.0
Shreveport	290	1 839	258.8	49.0	568	4 053	474.9	170.2	162	6 383	D	256.0
Slidell	40	171	31.4	4.1	138	D	D	D	NA	NA	NA	NA
MAINE	1 771	6 942	1 054.0	209.4	3 444	20 504	2 686.1	1 004.9	1 825	58 938	16 363.2	2 524.5
Bangor	96	482	92.3	15.1	163	D	D	D	45	1 022	225.3	41.7
Lewiston	46	285	34.0	6.5	71	D	D	D	70	2 240	537.5	90.2
Portland	248	1 376	261.2	48.8	570	D	D	D	105	3 198	886.7	124.6
South Portland	54	414	83.5	16.7	98	838	99.4	41.8	31	1 595	298.0	95.4
MARYLAND	6 768	49 766	12 391.9	2 262.6	19 345	D	D	D	3 680	127 780	41 456.1	6 453.7
Annapolis	104	618	106.3	25.6	387	D	D	D	47	618	127.6	26.6
Baltimore	647	4 677	837.5	214.9	1 506	D	D	D	479	16 253	5 730.9	726.5
Bowie	54	195	32.8	6.7	164	D	D	D	NA	NA	NA	NA
College Park	20	73	7.9	2.1	61	D	D	D	6	D	D	D
Frederick	105	765	120.1	27.2	368	D	D	D	55	2 317	1 614.3	121.4
Gaithersburg	117	756	207.7	44.4	425	D	D	D	40	1 996	559.5	137.1
Hagerstown	58	250	35.4	6.7	113	1 251	74.4	30.0	64	3 878	1 434.9	214.8
Laurel	36	593	62.3	19.7	91	D	D	D	NA	NA	NA	NA
Rockville	139	2 575	592.3	128.4	871	16 740	2 715.0	1 166.8	65	1 301	199.9	58.1
Salisbury	93	578	81.6	18.5	162	D	D	D	47	3 260	811.6	109.6
MASSACHUSETTS	7 053	48 576	14 029.8	2 287.6	21 773	243 374	49 085.7	20 652.0	7 737	289 256	86 429.0	15 712.0
Agawam Town	NA	NA	NA	NA	NA	NA	NA	NA	NA	NA	NA	NA
Attleboro	34	121	16.7	5.1	76	352	40.9	16.0	109	5 721	1 711.3	289.0
Barnstable Town	76	262	66.1	8.6	201	D	D	D	41	562	D	27.5

1. Establishments subject to federal tax.

Table D. Cities — Accommodation and Food Services, Arts, Entertainment, and Recreation, and Health Care and Social Assistance

City	Accommodation and food services, 2007				Arts, entertainment, and recreation,[1] 2007				Health care and social assistance,[1] 2007			
	Number of establish-ments	Number of employees	Sales (mil dol)	Annual payroll (mil dol)	Number of establish-ments	Number of employees	Receipts (mil dol)	Annual payroll (mil dol)	Number of establish-ments	Number of employees	Receipts (mil dol)	Annual payroll (mil dol)
	92	93	94	95	96	97	98	99	100	101	102	103
KANSAS	5 866	104 795	4 192.3	1 173.7	769	10 017	546.6	146.7	5 778	83 531	7 948.2	3 175.8
Dodge City	66	938	39.6	9.9	6	D	D	D	52	D	D	D
Garden City	65	1 107	48.4	12.3	4	D	D	D	64	D	D	D
Hutchinson	100	1 984	75.3	20.3	5	D	D	D	121	1 942	224.1	97.6
Kansas City	216	4 494	220.7	61.7	24	D	D	D	216	3 372	280.0	129.9
Lawrence	262	5 634	203.0	57.6	27	D	D	D	196	1 940	159.3	74.5
Leavenworth	56	933	35.0	9.7	4	D	D	D	57	519	39.3	18.5
Leawood	52	D	D	D	13	95	5.8	3.1	141	D	D	D
Lenexa	105	1 778	80.7	24.1	19	275	13.1	4.1	118	3 962	342.7	141.6
Manhattan	152	3 466	125.8	33.4	15	188	8.9	2.3	116	D	D	D
Olathe	225	5 329	203.2	61.8	27	603	21.6	6.9	225	2 689	272.7	110.4
Overland Park	438	10 877	525.9	158.3	75	1 669	79.3	25.0	561	10 621	1 331.7	510.3
Salina	120	2 509	94.0	26.2	13	D	D	D	136	1 767	189.1	73.0
Shawnee	108	1 966	82.2	23.1	15	D	D	D	105	D	D	D
Topeka	342	D	D	D	29	D	D	D	359	D	D	D
Wichita	937	18 895	758.6	222.1	86	1 813	81.0	23.8	905	17 563	2 125.6	749.3
KENTUCKY	7 309	151 551	6 300.9	1 787.4	1 021	12 434	893.9	260.1	8 686	115 673	10 089.6	4 218.4
Bowling Green	200	5 185	223.1	61.7	16	D	D	D	246	D	D	D
Covington	135	2 503	124.9	35.3	8	D	D	D	40	D	D	D
Elizabethtown	111	2 954	109.0	31.5	10	D	D	D	184	D	D	D
Florence	159	4 275	185.1	53.7	22	433	24.5	7.7	121	1 718	136.0	59.4
Frankfort	83	1 910	70.2	22.1	5	D	D	D	106	1 833	178.4	62.8
Georgetown	67	1 572	65.2	18.0	3	D	D	D	62	D	D	D
Henderson	81	1 298	52.9	14.6	8	D	D	D	108	D	D	D
Hopkinsville	79	1 568	56.8	15.1	7	D	D	D	140	1 482	125.5	43.4
Jeffersontown	108	2 904	131.1	40.9	15	D	D	D	89	2 394	201.8	69.6
Lexington-Fayette	704	17 027	785.7	230.3	102	1 609	114.8	40.9	821	11 213	1 149.2	526.2
Louisville/Jefferson County	1 561	35 897	1 629.2	480.6	243	3 741	291.3	95.9	1 909	27 997	2 708.5	1 159.0
Nicholasville	47	1 025	39.8	11.1	6	D	D	D	43	436	27.5	13.2
Owensboro	134	3 322	120.2	37.5	13	D	D	D	221	2 935	245.9	104.8
Paducah	169	4 156	158.9	46.4	9	D	D	D	184	D	D	D
Richmond	95	2 528	90.7	25.5	8	87	2.5	0.7	108	D	D	D
LOUISIANA	8 169	180 289	9 729.9	2 579.0	1 062	20 064	2 468.3	578.3	9 725	145 174	13 178.8	4 934.9
Alexandria	158	3 256	129.3	33.1	12	D	D	D	270	5 309	582.5	210.6
Baton Rouge	599	15 567	716.7	197.5	56	2 070	262.5	37.2	725	11 500	1 084.6	417.0
Bossier City	198	9 254	694.5	170.3	28	1 560	155.4	24.8	138	D	D	D
Central	NA	NA	NA	NA	NA	NA	NA	NA	NA	NA	NA	NA
Houma	105	1 662	90.6	26.2	15	122	6.4	2.2	147	D	D	D
Kenner	190	3 710	193.4	52.5	24	1 288	452.3	176.8	149	2 094	217.3	76.8
Lafayette	421	11 003	516.5	138.8	34	D	D	D	715	12 024	1 274.8	467.0
Lake Charles	189	6 553	563.8	116.2	29	D	D	D	317	4 658	482.8	168.7
Monroe	170	3 817	142.9	37.7	19	D	D	D	320	3 918	385.7	139.4
New Iberia	76	1 636	62.9	15.6	7	108	6.3	1.1	160	D	D	D
New Orleans	1 058	28 356	2 148.2	602.4	109	2 551	284.1	109.0	594	6 413	847.2	277.8
Shreveport	409	11 967	661.4	171.8	58	D	D	D	653	D	D	D
Slidell	172	3 029	133.0	36.1	13	D	D	D	197	2 356	283.8	108.1
MAINE	3 938	49 363	2 515.8	747.7	635	5 204	361.3	85.0	3 203	39 757	3 015.8	1 397.3
Bangor	140	2 886	136.1	40.7	12	D	D	D	220	3 696	310.0	151.0
Lewiston	83	1 250	52.0	14.8	14	114	5.7	2.0	127	1 589	132.3	58.4
Portland	287	5 067	246.0	78.4	40	354	29.1	6.1	312	4 231	397.4	186.2
South Portland	127	3 046	137.6	45.7	9	D	D	D	101	1 261	124.4	60.2
MARYLAND	10 802	192 619	10 758.4	2 915.9	1 735	26 548	2 140.5	743.0	12 542	143 677	15 363.7	6 218.0
Annapolis	170	4 132	230.4	70.9	32	560	40.1	11.3	136	D	D	D
Baltimore	1 481	21 456	1 434.7	372.1	104	2 595	312.5	164.3	1 065	13 768	1 480.1	622.9
Bowie	75	D	D	D	13	D	D	D	172	1 381	130.2	48.7
College Park	105	1 820	103.4	25.6	5	56	3.0	1.1	33	D	D	D
Frederick	197	3 508	168.4	50.9	23	238	11.9	3.3	300	3 880	422.6	181.0
Gaithersburg	238	4 085	265.9	69.0	21	D	D	D	160	1 968	174.0	73.2
Hagerstown	129	2 543	113.9	32.7	12	107	3.8	0.9	124	1 347	156.6	63.8
Laurel	83	1 956	106.8	32.0	19	D	D	D	95	1 256	133.1	57.9
Rockville	237	3 440	242.4	63.6	32	331	16.1	4.0	263	3 503	492.4	202.8
Salisbury	149	3 313	151.4	40.6	11	D	D	D	169	D	D	D
MASSACHUSETTS	16 039	257 302	14 917.2	4 339.7	2 261	34 183	3 137.0	1 122.2	12 828	202 678	21 341.6	9 279.6
Agawam Town	NA	NA	NA	NA	NA	NA	NA	NA	NA	NA	NA	NA
Attleboro	89	2 009	83.9	27.5	10	D	D	D	92	1 579	148.1	58.4
Barnstable Town	193	3 066	185.2	57.0	28	197	17.2	5.0	152	2 027	223.5	104.8

1. Establishments subject to federal tax.

City	Other services[1], 2007				Government employment and payroll, 2012								
						March payroll							
							Percent of total for:						
	Number of establish-ments	Number of employees	Receipts (mil dol)	Annual payroll (mil dol)	Full-time equivalent employees	Total (dollars)	Adminis-tration, judicial, and legal	Police and Corrections	Fire Protection	Highways and trans-portation	Health and welfare	Natural resources and utilities	Education and libraries
	104	105	106	107	108	109	110	111	112	113	114	115	116
KANSAS	4 281	24 265	1 825.9	572.9	X	X	X	X	X	X	X	X	X
Dodge City	39	D	D	D	249	803 190	14.8	27.3	12.1	6.2	2.3	27.5	6.6
Garden City	39	D	D	D	310	1 086 046	12.7	30.4	12.2	6.7	0.7	30.7	0.0
Hutchinson	73	D	D	D	392	1 720 937	8.7	26.7	25.6	7.2	2.1	25.6	0.0
Kansas City	177	D	D	D	2 707	14 492 572	12.6	24.6	15.1	5.6	5.3	29.9	0.0
Lawrence	118	731	45.0	14.3	1 978	10 089 159	4.2	10.8	8.9	2.8	58.2	13.8	0.0
Leavenworth	43	269	17.3	5.2	268	973 969	12.2	33.1	20.9	8.2	4.8	17.2	0.0
Leawood	42	588	49.8	11.7	262	1 218 472	17.8	32.5	22.4	11.6	1.7	11.1	0.0
Lenexa	84	660	65.7	21.6	414	1 898 039	18.6	33.0	22.5	12.1	0.0	11.7	0.0
Manhattan	81	D	D	D	362	1 385 412	18.7	0.0	25.9	14.5	5.9	32.8	0.0
Olathe	165	1 018	89.9	27.3	826	3 674 590	18.5	24.2	20.1	16.9	2.0	17.6	0.0
Overland Park	289	1 737	118.7	39.0	899	4 414 214	19.0	34.6	19.7	13.5	0.9	8.8	0.0
Salina	91	D	D	D	484	1 858 261	10.4	24.5	22.0	12.0	3.3	23.9	0.0
Shawnee	90	1 682	64.7	32.0	287	1 666 597	13.6	38.1	23.7	12.5	0.8	9.1	0.0
Topeka	217	1 409	102.5	31.7	1 062	3 978 506	7.7	32.8	28.1	11.7	1.6	15.4	0.0
Wichita	605	4 760	301.7	127.2	2 864	12 396 633	10.7	30.7	18.5	13.7	3.8	15.4	2.9
KENTUCKY	5 037	33 941	2 777.7	801.2	X	X	X	X	X	X	X	X	X
Bowling Green	114	911	64.5	18.8	699	2 772 912	7.1	20.2	19.5	5.5	2.9	30.0	0.0
Covington	68	481	32.8	10.9	421	1 788 490	6.5	36.3	30.5	3.6	11.9	5.7	0.0
Elizabethtown	69	542	38.4	12.1	289	996 440	11.3	24.1	21.7	8.8	0.0	27.7	0.0
Florence	76	592	33.2	11.3	198	919 937	6.2	36.7	28.5	4.6	0.0	11.5	0.0
Frankfort	51	226	14.7	4.5	530	2 153 521	5.6	15.6	18.6	4.9	2.2	22.3	0.0
Georgetown	36	D	D	D	179	621 131	11.9	34.9	35.4	6.1	0.0	6.7	0.0
Henderson	45	D	D	D	454	1 639 406	10.9	14.7	13.1	5.8	6.0	45.6	0.0
Hopkinsville	55	D	D	D	398	1 517 254	6.4	20.1	21.3	2.1	5.3	33.5	0.0
Jeffersontown	78	845	118.0	28.8	108	518 932	9.2	65.9	0.0	12.9	5.5	1.6	1.2
Lexington-Fayette	429	3 634	248.1	92.9	3 926	16 180 537	10.0	31.5	18.1	5.0	11.0	15.2	3.0
Louisville/Jefferson County	1 108	10 083	928.2	244.7	8 264	32 734 538	10.3	29.9	8.6	12.9	15.7	14.6	2.2
Nicholasville	50	D	D	D	214	748 387	13.4	32.1	20.0	4.1	0.0	17.4	0.0
Owensboro	101	755	50.5	17.2	840	3 418 017	7.9	17.9	10.1	5.1	3.1	53.8	0.0
Paducah	80	632	69.9	14.4	537	2 054 380	7.5	18.4	12.7	12.4	7.8	37.6	0.0
Richmond	48	241	14.1	4.2	264	708 015	11.1	30.0	21.4	6.8	9.1	12.4	0.0
LOUISIANA	5 446	35 039	3 464.7	965.6	X	X	X	X	X	X	X	X	X
Alexandria	100	662	52.2	14.4	858	3 139 622	13.3	29.0	18.9	9.8	0.4	22.4	0.0
Baton Rouge	423	3 042	248.2	81.5	7 745	28 842 476	18.7	20.3	13.5	8.8	15.7	11.6	4.2
Bossier City	99	765	47.4	13.8	738	2 695 669	13.1	32.2	30.2	2.8	1.1	15.5	0.0
Central	NA	NA	NA	NA	11	24 511	92.3	7.7	0.0	0.0	0.0	0.0	0.0
Houma	58	598	104.1	34.7	2 552	9 484 779	6.9	16.5	2.3	2.5	60.4	8.0	3.4
Kenner	129	851	97.4	24.9	633	2 227 138	15.0	42.0	19.4	6.5	3.2	7.8	0.0
Lafayette	261	1 993	151.3	47.3	3 047	10 656 600	18.8	30.9	10.4	8.4	1.8	24.1	2.4
Lake Charles	117	759	65.4	19.8	1 030	3 427 311	10.3	24.5	19.4	6.9	0.4	29.2	0.0
Monroe	74	628	47.6	14.8	1 137	2 092 527	21.1	3.5	2.5	12.5	15.1	42.2	0.0
New Iberia	72	D	D	D	222	646 974	12.2	1.2	36.3	13.5	4.6	27.2	0.0
New Orleans	408	2 514	196.4	55.7	6 570	26 033 023	13.9	33.2	9.9	2.7	8.0	23.7	1.6
Shreveport	308	D	D	D	2 841	10 287 795	8.1	28.1	26.4	6.9	2.4	18.7	7.2
Slidell	94	487	33.9	10.5	294	1 068 129	19.4	46.5	0.0	11.4	0.0	18.5	0.0
MAINE	2 124	9 136	812.9	218.9	X	X	X	X	X	X	X	X	X
Bangor	75	504	57.3	12.4	1 172	4 803 542	4.3	9.1	8.0	17.8	2.9	5.2	50.9
Lewiston	58	305	18.8	6.7	1 063	4 275 573	4.7	10.1	8.1	4.7	0.9	4.1	64.8
Portland	182	1 100	93.9	26.4	2 667	11 280 661	5.1	9.2	9.4	4.1	13.4	3.5	50.8
South Portland	69	526	31.2	9.6	774	2 806 318	7.4	11.7	11.2	5.1	0.2	9.9	54.4
MARYLAND	8 270	57 508	4 832.5	1 602.5	X	X	X	X	X	X	X	X	X
Annapolis	153	1 034	92.1	32.2	620	3 140 557	12.6	28.5	24.6	16.2	0.0	13.6	0.0
Baltimore	728	6 191	559.3	160.9	26 392	122 552 640	6.0	16.4	7.7	3.4	7.5	8.8	48.9
Bowie	53	377	25.4	7.6	332	1 491 481	15.5	19.2	0.0	6.4	9.8	36.4	0.0
College Park	43	D	D	D	308	540 180	25.6	19.0	0.0	6.4	12.3	21.9	0.0
Frederick	144	1 016	70.8	24.9	560	2 537 922	10.7	39.5	0.0	8.4	5.7	23.2	0.0
Gaithersburg	129	1 057	81.0	33.3	303	1 564 921	28.1	25.0	0.0	16.4	6.3	21.9	0.0
Hagerstown	79	445	37.1	10.0	445	2 038 054	10.3	26.5	16.9	6.9	0.7	32.9	0.0
Laurel	47	467	29.6	8.8	197	975 036	19.1	49.9	0.0	7.4	0.0	18.1	0.0
Rockville	182	1 047	106.8	33.2	652	3 046 807	18.3	18.4	0.0	9.1	8.6	45.6	0.0
Salisbury	89	790	60.0	20.7	375	1 345 111	6.4	35.5	18.2	7.5	4.4	26.4	0.0
MASSACHUSETTS	10 744	66 722	6 164.8	1 906.5	X	X	X	X	X	X	X	X	X
Agawam Town	NA	NA	NA	NA	958	3 825 533	4.3	9.2	8.3	3.0	2.5	2.9	64.5
Attleboro	60	267	21.3	5.8	1 376	5 707 365	4.1	9.4	7.8	1.4	1.4	7.2	68.0
Barnstable Town	127	747	60.4	21.5	1 040	5 101 618	12.3	17.0	0.0	7.1	2.3	6.5	50.4

1. Establishments subject to federal tax.

City	City government finances, 2007									
	General revenue							General expenditure		
		Intergovernmental		Taxes					Per capita[1] (dollars)	
					Per capita[1] (dollars)					
	Total (mil dol)	Total (mil dol)	Percent from state government	Total (mil dol)	Total	Property	Sales and gross receipts	Total (mil dol)	Total	Capital outlays
	117	118	119	120	121	122	123	124	125	126
KANSAS	X	X	X	X	X	X	X	X	X	X
Dodge City	42.1	4.4	73.2	19.0	676	272	403	61.8	2 199	497
Garden City	32.6	5.3	13.6	13.7	508	224	285	32.2	1 196	137
Hutchinson	47.8	10.1	16.6	24.0	572	287	285	36.3	867	15
Kansas City	345.7	20.8	59.0	197.9	1 342	609	724	304.9	2 068	35
Lawrence	300.0	35.4	66.1	51.1	569	251	318	265.3	2 952	315
Leavenworth	35.9	6.9	24.9	18.7	523	329	194	39.7	1 108	180
Leawood	52.4	9.2	26.4	36.5	1 121	518	604	38.2	1 173	233
Lenexa	84.1	15.1	53.5	48.4	979	537	442	101.5	2 056	664
Manhattan	75.3	14.5	19.2	38.3	675	346	329	70.4	1 243	66
Olathe	165.1	23.5	34.3	90.7	697	288	410	149.2	1 147	163
Overland Park	224.8	42.2	25.4	90.5	506	129	377	208.7	1 166	223
Salina	68.5	10.3	26.4	25.7	535	240	295	75.4	1 572	264
Shawnee	54.4	10.0	26.2	38.6	607	330	277	48.9	769	62
Topeka	206.4	27.9	31.8	106.8	835	320	515	153.6	1 201	139
Wichita	562.5	102.8	20.6	167.5	435	306	129	543.6	1 410	223
KENTUCKY	X	X	X	X	X	X	X	X	X	X
Bowling Green	98.4	10.3	24.6	55.7	916	177	90	76.0	1 251	71
Covington	71.2	13.5	27.4	40.2	989	171	183	54.8	1 350	183
Elizabethtown	45.8	8.2	36.9	25.3	863	132	268	37.6	1 280	347
Florence	43.3	5.6	79.1	28.8	928	238	141	28.8	926	346
Frankfort	67.6	2.6	55.3	25.5	937	148	150	57.0	2 091	104
Georgetown	46.6	3.3	36.0	15.8	523	64	100	38.6	1 277	68
Henderson	46.8	13.7	10.5	17.3	597	254	172	40.9	1 415	213
Hopkinsville	42.0	7.0	7.7	23.2	702	139	127	37.4	1 128	88
Jeffersontown	25.4	1.1	76.1	17.1	637	144	99	23.6	876	92
Lexington-Fayette	544.8	60.2	29.6	318.9	1 045	282	143	440.5	1 443	142
Louisville/Jefferson County	935.3	222.4	25.0	456.1	753	225	93	992.9	1 640	335
Nicholasville	20.8	2.5	72.9	13.4	473	139	110	18.1	638	35
Owensboro	98.3	27.0	14.9	35.0	602	166	123	105.2	1 812	630
Paducah	63.2	11.9	37.1	32.6	1 297	237	164	49.1	1 954	263
Richmond	34.6	1.4	35.9	20.5	631	93	132	25.5	785	137
LOUISIANA	X	X	X	X	X	X	X	X	X	X
Alexandria	82.5	13.7	28.9	53.7	1 121	153	967	92.8	1 936	198
Baton Rouge	959.1	199.4	55.2	458.1	1 992	692	1 300	1 203.6	5 233	1 750
Bossier City	108.4	8.2	55.5	71.3	1 090	181	909	129.1	1 975	823
Central	9.1	0.3	100.0	8.6	313	0	313	4.7	169	2
Houma	411.9	103.8	73.9	117.3	3 483	1 624	1 859	430.0	12 764	2 321
Kenner	77.5	40.2	21.3	22.2	332	125	207	70.3	1 050	164
Lafayette	402.4	70.2	47.1	201.1	1 631	828	803	443.4	3 597	882
Lake Charles	116.9	27.3	9.2	70.1	952	108	845	117.0	1 590	348
Monroe	129.3	28.8	34.5	77.5	1 564	218	1 346	140.8	2 843	755
New Iberia	32.2	4.6	29.3	21.4	693	131	562	42.4	1 376	297
New Orleans	1 505.1	535.6	44.1	499.4	1 349	692	647	1 604.4	4 334	1 371
Shreveport	369.6	59.6	35.0	209.5	1 037	312	725	315.2	1 560	169
Slidell	55.2	15.5	65.5	27.4	1 001	202	798	55.1	2 012	612
MAINE	X	X	X	X	X	X	X	X	X	X
Bangor	131.1	38.3	93.4	54.2	1 653	1 624	29	165.2	5 035	1 527
Lewiston	117.7	52.6	84.0	49.4	1 355	1 342	13	112.8	3 095	292
Portland	318.6	71.3	78.7	144.3	2 178	2 129	49	329.4	4 972	746
South Portland	82.8	11.7	92.5	61.0	2 430	2 411	20	82.1	3 270	347
MARYLAND	X	X	X	X	X	X	X	X	X	X
Annapolis	82.8	14.6	35.6	43.3	1 125	985	140	65.6	1 703	14
Baltimore	3 407.6	1 720.1	81.7	1 238.8	1 989	1 226	267	3 659.5	5 874	527
Bowie	46.8	10.8	16.7	27.6	491	444	47	42.1	748	0
College Park	15.3	2.1	19.1	9.8	315	239	76	14.1	451	4
Frederick	90.8	14.2	14.9	46.5	700	655	45	84.6	1 273	9
Gaithersburg	54.0	13.4	7.5	31.2	495	390	104	49.4	783	40
Hagerstown	57.3	7.1	21.8	26.1	645	527	114	50.2	1 239	16
Laurel	29.2	4.0	20.5	20.5	800	757	43	25.4	992	3
Rockville	92.8	17.8	12.0	40.8	644	553	86	94.1	1 486	5
Salisbury	51.7	5.3	32.3	22.5	725	675	49	39.7	1 279	49
MASSACHUSETTS	X	X	X	X	X	X	X	X	X	X
Agawam Town	84.8	27.5	99.5	50.0	1 745	1 720	26	102.8	3 589	65
Attleboro	126.9	47.0	97.8	61.9	1 412	1 380	32	113.5	2 593	116
Barnstable Town	177.7	41.0	87.9	109.9	2 458	2 319	139	175.2	3 917	633

1. Based on population estimated as of July 1 of the year shown.

City	City government finances, 2012 (cont.)									
	General expenditure (cont.)									
	Percent of total for:									
	Public welfare	Highways	Parking facilities	Education	Health and hospitals	Police protection	Sewerage and sanitation	Parks and recreation	Housing and community development	Interest on debt
	127	128	129	130	131	132	133	134	135	136
KANSAS	X	X	X	X	X	X	X	X	X	X
Dodge City	0.0	1.2	0.0	0.0	0.8	7.8	35.2	17.9	0.0	16.3
Garden City	0.0	11.0	0.0	0.0	0.0	19.9	11.8	14.6	0.0	1.0
Hutchinson	0.0	4.4	0.0	0.0	1.3	22.1	23.3	12.7	0.0	3.8
Kansas City	0.0	2.6	0.2	0.0	3.4	15.9	7.5	2.3	1.5	23.3
Lawrence	0.0	2.7	0.5	0.0	59.4	5.5	8.3	3.1	1.3	2.8
Leavenworth	0.0	10.0	0.0	0.0	0.0	17.1	12.8	5.5	9.0	2.9
Leawood	0.0	22.0	0.0	0.0	0.0	21.4	0.0	17.6	0.0	6.5
Lenexa	0.0	20.0	0.0	0.0	0.0	12.2	3.8	8.5	0.0	16.9
Manhattan	0.0	6.3	0.0	0.0	1.1	17.5	8.4	8.0	1.8	12.6
Olathe	0.0	15.8	0.0	0.0	0.2	13.0	15.5	3.6	0.0	9.4
Overland Park	0.0	21.1	0.0	0.0	0.0	14.4	2.5	5.2	0.0	25.8
Salina	0.0	9.2	0.0	0.0	1.6	11.2	10.5	9.0	5.0	11.5
Shawnee	0.0	12.9	0.0	0.0	0.0	24.3	6.3	9.2	0.0	18.0
Topeka	1.1	9.1	1.4	0.0	0.0	20.4	12.2	10.5	1.5	7.1
Wichita	0.0	13.4	0.0	0.0	0.7	13.7	8.7	4.9	0.0	31.2
KENTUCKY	X	X	X	X	X	X	X	X	X	X
Bowling Green	0.0	9.4	0.0	0.0	0.0	12.0	10.5	10.4	6.4	20.5
Covington	0.0	7.9	3.6	0.0	0.0	19.6	4.0	2.4	21.8	12.5
Elizabethtown	0.0	9.8	0.1	0.0	0.0	10.7	9.3	8.0	0.0	3.4
Florence	0.0	44.2	0.0	0.0	0.0	16.0	5.1	0.0	0.0	10.7
Frankfort	0.0	3.8	0.0	0.0	5.8	7.9	12.9	5.0	0.0	2.6
Georgetown	0.2	3.1	0.0	0.0	0.0	7.8	10.8	2.3	1.1	49.3
Henderson	0.0	5.4	0.0	0.0	0.0	9.2	27.0	2.5	13.3	1.8
Hopkinsville	0.7	5.7	0.0	0.0	0.0	20.8	13.6	1.2	13.7	14.5
Jeffersontown	0.0	9.1	0.0	0.0	0.0	23.5	4.4	2.6	2.8	37.7
Lexington-Fayette	2.0	2.5	0.3	0.0	3.6	10.8	15.8	4.0	1.1	4.1
Louisville/Jefferson County	1.2	6.8	7.9	5.7	3.3	10.2	1.5	5.7	6.5	9.9
Nicholasville	0.0	18.8	0.0	0.0	0.0	22.5	18.6	0.0	0.0	5.0
Owensboro	0.0	5.3	0.2	0.0	0.0	7.1	17.8	7.1	27.9	10.8
Paducah	0.0	8.5	0.0	3.6	0.0	12.3	6.2	4.9	18.9	2.5
Richmond	0.0	3.7	0.0	0.0	0.0	13.5	29.4	8.7	7.4	15.3
LOUISIANA	X	X	X	X	X	X	X	X	X	X
Alexandria	0.0	13.7	0.0	0.0	0.0	18.0	11.3	3.8	8.9	3.0
Baton Rouge	0.2	8.7	0.1	1.3	8.7	10.5	28.4	2.0	5.2	5.2
Bossier City	0.0	1.7	0.0	0.0	0.4	15.1	16.6	5.5	6.7	5.7
Central	0.0	4.9	0.0	0.0	2.1	3.8	0.0	0.0	0.0	0.0
Houma	0.4	4.2	0.0	0.0	41.2	6.3	5.5	2.3	1.7	1.6
Kenner	0.0	19.8	0.0	0.0	0.2	23.7	14.3	6.4	1.0	2.8
Lafayette	0.2	7.6	0.2	0.0	1.4	12.7	9.1	6.0	5.0	8.8
Lake Charles	0.7	13.5	0.0	0.0	0.5	14.4	17.5	8.9	13.5	3.4
Monroe	0.1	4.4	0.0	0.0	0.0	13.1	9.8	5.7	17.4	5.8
New Iberia	0.4	16.2	0.0	0.0	0.0	14.0	25.5	5.1	10.0	4.0
New Orleans	0.2	7.6	0.1	0.0	0.8	8.9	13.7	5.5	15.5	5.9
Shreveport	0.0	4.5	0.2	0.0	0.0	18.2	14.6	9.9	7.6	4.3
Slidell	0.0	11.7	0.0	0.0	0.7	14.9	13.3	2.9	10.4	1.7
MAINE	X	X	X	X	X	X	X	X	X	X
Bangor	0.0	0.0	0.4	26.4	2.3	4.8	3.0	22.8	0.9	2.0
Lewiston	0.9	3.4	0.0	49.5	0.0	5.9	6.7	0.6	1.5	5.2
Portland	7.7	5.4	0.6	30.3	1.3	4.1	8.1	2.0	1.0	5.2
South Portland	0.3	4.6	0.0	52.3	0.0	5.4	11.2	4.3	0.0	1.6
MARYLAND	X	X	X	X	X	X	X	X	X	X
Annapolis	0.0	7.2	2.3	0.0	0.0	25.6	12.0	5.3	0.0	5.0
Baltimore	0.0	5.7	0.8	38.4	3.3	10.2	6.6	1.6	2.1	1.4
Bowie	0.0	11.4	0.0	0.0	0.5	17.6	23.4	16.4	0.1	1.5
College Park	0.0	22.3	1.0	0.0	0.6	7.3	18.8	9.4	1.5	2.1
Frederick	0.0	10.8	3.8	0.0	0.0	30.2	13.3	9.7	0.6	5.8
Gaithersburg	0.0	8.4	0.0	0.0	1.2	15.6	4.7	20.3	1.6	11.6
Hagerstown	0.0	5.9	1.4	0.0	0.0	23.0	29.3	6.2	1.0	2.0
Laurel	0.0	4.9	0.0	0.0	0.0	34.6	4.6	9.1	0.2	1.9
Rockville	0.0	12.9	2.9	0.0	0.4	17.1	13.5	19.7	4.1	4.0
Salisbury	0.0	9.1	1.5	0.0	0.5	25.3	23.5	5.2	2.1	3.6
MASSACHUSETTS	X	X	X	X	X	X	X	X	X	X
Agawam Town	0.1	2.9	0.0	52.9	1.8	4.2	4.3	0.8	0.0	0.8
Attleboro	0.6	3.1	0.0	63.9	0.2	5.5	8.6	1.4	0.5	2.3
Barnstable Town	0.2	2.3	0.0	45.7	0.6	6.2	4.5	2.8	0.2	2.5

City	City government finances, 2012 (cont.)			Climate[2]						
	Debt outstanding			Average daily temperature (degrees Fahrenheit)						
				Mean		Limits				
	Total (mil dol)	Per capita[1] (dollars)	Debt issued during year	January	July	January[3]	July[4]	Annual precipitation (inches)	Heating degree days	Cooling degree days
	137	138	139	140	141	142	143	144	145	146
KANSAS	X	X	X	X	X	X	X	X	X	X
Dodge City	220.7	7 857	12.2	30.1	79.8	18.7	92.8	22.35	5 037	1 481
Garden City	42.2	1 564	3.5	28.6	77.8	14.7	92.1	18.77	5 423	1 191
Hutchinson	54.3	1 294	5.6	28.5	79.9	17.0	92.7	30.32	5 146	1 454
Kansas City	1 786.2	12 115	126.8	29.1	79.0	19.9	89.4	40.17	4 847	1 406
Lawrence	287.4	3 197	46.3	29.9	80.2	20.5	90.6	39.78	4 685	1 582
Leavenworth	32.8	917	10.5	26.6	79.1	16.4	89.8	40.94	5 331	1 356
Leawood	60.6	1 863	5.3	29.1	79.0	19.9	89.4	40.17	4 847	1 406
Lenexa	280.1	5 672	46.2	29.1	79.0	19.9	89.4	40.17	4 847	1 406
Manhattan	344.8	6 084	41.3	27.8	79.9	16.1	92.5	34.80	5 120	1 465
Olathe	1 141.4	8 779	55.5	29.1	79.0	19.9	89.4	40.17	4 847	1 406
Overland Park	1 428.3	7 983	15.2	29.1	79.0	19.9	89.4	40.17	4 847	1 406
Salina	168.5	3 513	22.8	29.0	81.3	18.8	93.3	32.19	4 952	1 600
Shawnee	215.7	3 390	22.2	29.1	79.0	19.9	89.4	40.17	4 847	1 406
Topeka	364.4	2 850	72.6	27.2	78.4	17.2	89.1	35.64	5 225	1 357
Wichita	3 471.3	9 003	335.8	30.2	81.0	20.3	92.9	30.38	4 765	1 658
KENTUCKY	X	X	X	X	X	X	X	X	X	X
Bowling Green	283.6	4 667	7.1	34.2	78.5	25.4	89.2	51.63	4 243	1 413
Covington	162.2	3 993	3.6	32.0	76.1	24.1	85.9	45.91	4 713	1 154
Elizabethtown	55.2	1 880	18.5	NA	NA	NA	NA	NA	NA	NA
Florence	69.3	2 230	3.1	NA	NA	NA	NA	NA	NA	NA
Frankfort	46.6	1 711	0.0	30.3	75.2	20.8	86.9	43.56	5 129	994
Georgetown	473.4	15 642	0.0	NA	NA	NA	NA	NA	NA	NA
Henderson	50.4	1 744	15.8	32.6	77.6	23.6	88.4	44.77	4 374	1 344
Hopkinsville	170.2	5 136	12.2	33.2	78.2	24.4	88.5	50.92	4 298	1 433
Jeffersontown	160.3	5 960	0.0	33.0	78.4	24.9	87.0	44.54	4 352	1 443
Lexington-Fayette	1 000.4	3 277	37.3	31.6	75.9	22.5	86.3	46.39	4 769	1 094
Louisville/Jefferson County	1 594.3	2 633	310.5	NA	NA	NA	NA	NA	NA	NA
Nicholasville	32.1	1 130	3.5	NA	NA	NA	NA	NA	NA	NA
Owensboro	399.8	6 888	55.2	33.5	79.2	24.4	90.7	46.53	4 159	1 565
Paducah	39.7	1 583	6.6	35.2	79.9	27.2	90.8	46.04	3 893	1 635
Richmond	104.2	3 208	2.7	34.7	75.8	25.6	87.0	47.33	4 231	1 150
LOUISIANA	X	X	X	X	X	X	X	X	X	X
Alexandria	94.9	1 980	2.6	48.1	83.3	38.0	92.8	61.44	1 908	2 602
Baton Rouge	1 639.8	7 130	219.4	50.1	81.7	40.2	90.7	63.08	1 689	2 628
Bossier City	360.5	5 513	5.7	48.3	81.0	37.4	91.0	61.06	1 981	2 220
Central	0.0	0	0.0	NA	NA	NA	NA	NA	NA	NA
Houma	213.1	6 326	64.3	53.1	82.5	43.4	90.7	63.67	1 346	2 804
Kenner	61.5	919	19.6	52.6	82.7	43.4	91.1	64.16	1 417	2 773
Lafayette	1 132.6	9 186	183.7	51.3	82.2	41.6	91.2	60.54	1 531	2 671
Lake Charles	92.3	1 253	3.7	50.9	82.6	41.2	91.0	57.19	1 546	2 705
Monroe	177.3	3 581	34.9	44.6	83.0	33.5	94.1	58.04	2 399	2 311
New Iberia	38.7	1 257	24.3	51.3	82.3	41.4	91.1	60.89	1 544	2 680
New Orleans	2 018.9	5 454	51.5	52.7	82.2	43.3	90.9	65.15	1 416	2 686
Shreveport	540.8	2 676	85.6	46.4	83.4	36.5	93.3	51.30	2 251	2 405
Slidell	25.1	916	0.0	50.7	82.1	40.2	91.1	62.66	1 652	2 548
MAINE	X	X	X	X	X	X	X	X	X	X
Bangor	109.4	3 335	32.1	18.0	69.2	8.3	79.6	39.57	7 676	313
Lewiston	152.4	4 182	7.6	20.5	71.4	11.5	81.5	45.79	7 107	465
Portland	423.0	6 384	38.7	21.7	68.7	12.5	78.8	45.83	7 318	347
South Portland	50.1	1 994	30.0	NA	NA	NA	NA	NA	NA	NA
MARYLAND	X	X	X	X	X	X	X	X	X	X
Annapolis	96.8	2 513	0.0	32.8	77.5	23.8	87.7	44.78	4 695	1 162
Baltimore	2 621.6	4 208	13.3	36.8	81.7	29.4	90.6	43.59	4 720	1 147
Bowie	18.0	320	0.1	31.8	75.2	21.2	87.1	44.66	4 970	917
College Park	8.4	269	0.0	NA	NA	NA	NA	NA	NA	NA
Frederick	224.2	3 375	31.4	33.3	77.9	25.1	88.9	40.64	4 430	1 272
Gaithersburg	142.6	2 261	0.0	31.8	75.3	23.8	85.4	43.08	4 990	983
Hagerstown	66.0	1 630	7.9	29.3	75.2	20.8	86.1	39.45	5 249	902
Laurel	10.1	396	0.1	NA	NA	NA	NA	NA	NA	NA
Rockville	135.9	2 144	40.7	31.8	75.3	23.8	85.4	43.08	4 990	983
Salisbury	70.9	2 286	15.2	NA	NA	NA	NA	NA	NA	NA
MASSACHUSETTS	X	X	X	X	X	X	X	X	X	X
Agawam Town	25.0	871	6.2	NA	NA	NA	NA	NA	NA	NA
Attleboro	72.7	1 660	1.5	27.4	72.2	17.8	83.0	48.34	6 012	558
Barnstable Town	131.5	2 941	18.5	29.2	70.5	21.2	77.8	43.03	6 026	413

1. Based on the population estimated as of July 1 of the year shown. 2. Represents normal values based on the 30-year period, 1971–2000. 3. Average daily minimum. 4. Average daily maximum.

STATE Place code	City	Land area,[1] 2010 (sq km)	Population, 2014: Total persons	Population, 2014: Rank	Population, 2014: Per square kilometer	Race alone or in combination (percent), 2011-2013: White	Race: Black	Race: American Indian, Alaska Native	Race: Asian	Race: Hawaiian Pacific Islander	Percent Hispanic or Latino[2], 2011-2013	Percent foreign born 2011–2013
		1	2	3	4	5	6	7	8	9	10	11
	MASSACHUSETTS—Cont'd											
25 05595	Beverly	39.1	40 952	903	1 047.4	95.2	2.1	0.7	2.9	NA	3.4	6.4
25 07000	Boston	125.0	655 884	24	5 247.1	57.1	28.3	0.9	9.9	0.2	18.5	26.9
25 07740	Braintree Town	35.6	37 362	991	1 049.5	86.2	5.5	NA	7.6	NA	3.1	13.7
25 09000	Brockton	55.2	94 779	318	1 717.0	48.8	42.0	0.9	2.6	0.3	8.9	25.4
25 11000	Cambridge	16.5	109 694	257	6 648.1	70.5	12.9	1.2	17.1	0.2	8.0	28.4
25 13205	Chelsea	5.7	38 861	954	6 817.7	78.5	33.4	0.5	3.4	NA	60.9	44.3
25 13660	Chicopee	59.1	55 795	658	944.1	87.5	4.5	0.9	1.5	NA	16.7	10.2
25 21990	Everett	8.9	44 231	834	4 969.8	71.8	21.1	0.9	4.6	NA	21.7	41.6
25 23000	Fall River	85.8	88 712	350	1 033.9	90.0	5.3	1.9	2.6	NA	7.5	18.5
25 23875	Fitchburg	72.1	40 445	915	561.0	79.6	7.0	0.3	5.8	NA	24.2	11.9
25 25172	Franklin Town	69.0	32 836	1 129	475.9	94.9	1.6	NA	3.7	NA	1.7	5.4
25 26150	Gloucester	67.9	29 626	1 245	436.3	97.4	1.8	0.8	0.9	NA	2.2	8.2
25 29405	Haverhill	85.4	62 488	565	731.7	86.7	3.1	0.6	1.3	NA	17.1	9.5
25 30840	Holyoke	55.1	40 124	927	728.2	84.8	4.9	1.0	1.5	NA	47.6	6.0
25 34550	Lawrence	17.9	78 197	426	4 368.5	41.3	10.1	0.5	2.8	0.1	75.7	38.1
25 35075	Leominster	74.6	41 150	896	551.6	84.8	7.1	1.6	3.8	NA	13.0	10.9
25 37000	Lowell	35.2	109 945	255	3 123.4	60.4	8.8	0.8	20.7	0.1	17.7	24.0
25 37490	Lynn	27.8	92 137	334	3 314.3	57.1	16.1	0.8	7.8	0.3	35.0	31.5
25 37875	Malden	13.1	60 859	586	4 645.7	59.0	15.1	1.4	26.6	NA	11.1	43.8
25 38715	Marlborough	54.0	39 612	940	733.6	90.2	13.9	1.3	5.7	NA	13.2	23.2
25 39835	Medford	21.0	57 437	637	2 735.1	84.3	9.3	0.6	8.3	NA	5.4	21.4
25 40115	Melrose	12.1	27 969	1 308	2 311.5	93.5	3.4	NA	3.7	NA	3.3	11.8
25 40710	Methuen Town	57.6	49 112	764	852.6	79.7	4.2	0.2	4.9	NA	19.5	16.9
25 45000	New Bedford	51.8	94 845	317	1 831.0	77.4	10.1	0.8	1.6	NA	18.1	21.4
25 45560	Newton	46.2	88 287	352	1 911.0	82.5	4.0	0.2	14.9	0.1	4.9	20.6
25 46330	Northampton	88.7	28 554	1 285	321.9	88.1	4.1	0.6	6.3	NA	8.7	9.8
25 52490	Peabody	42.0	52 376	709	1 247.0	86.8	4.5	0.3	4.0	NA	7.5	15.2
25 53960	Pittsfield	104.8	43 697	850	417.0	91.7	7.8	0.8	2.2	NA	4.6	5.8
25 55745	Quincy	42.9	93 397	327	2 177.1	68.9	6.2	0.8	24.7	0.1	3.4	28.5
25 56585	Revere	14.7	54 157	685	3 684.1	77.6	9.9	NA	6.6	NA	25.4	32.7
25 59105	Salem	21.4	42 824	863	2 001.1	84.4	7.8	1.3	3.0	NA	14.6	14.7
25 62535	Somerville	10.7	78 901	417	7 373.9	78.8	8.3	0.2	11.0	NA	10.8	23.8
25 67000	Springfield	82.5	153 991	162	1 866.6	55.9	24.5	1.3	2.4	0.1	40.9	10.7
25 69170	Taunton	121.0	56 544	650	467.3	91.0	6.1	0.7	1.6	0.2	6.3	11.7
25 72600	Waltham	33.0	63 014	561	1 909.5	78.8	7.1	0.5	12.7	NA	12.5	25.7
25 73440	Watertown Town	10.3	34 127	1 091	3 313.3	86.4	4.2	0.9	9.0	NA	7.2	23.3
25 76030	Westfield	120.0	41 608	890	346.7	91.6	1.9	0.6	3.0	NA	8.5	9.2
25 77890	West Springfield Town	43.3	28 627	1 283	661.1	87.3	5.5	0.5	5.0	NA	9.3	13.8
25 78972	Weymouth Town	43.5	55 643	661	1 279.1	89.1	4.3	0.5	7.0	NA	2.6	10.1
25 81035	Woburn	32.7	39 272	945	1 201.0	86.7	5.9	NA	7.6	NA	3.0	15.9
25 82000	Worcester	96.8	183 016	131	1 890.7	75.8	15.4	0.8	7.2	0.2	20.6	21.8
26 00000	MICHIGAN	146 435.1	9 909 877	X	67.7	81.6	15.3	1.5	3.1	0.1	4.6	6.2
26 01380	Allen Park	18.1	27 566	1 331	1 523.0	96.4	2.3	0.9	NA	NA	8.9	4.5
26 03000	Ann Arbor	72.1	117 770	229	1 633.4	77.0	8.8	0.9	16.4	NA	4.4	17.2
26 05920	Battle Creek	110.4	51 833	719	469.5	77.9	21.2	1.4	3.0	0.2	7.7	5.1
26 06020	Bay City	26.3	34 149	1 089	1 298.4	95.3	5.6	1.6	0.8	NA	8.7	1.3
26 12060	Burton	60.5	28 974	1 273	478.9	93.7	6.4	1.4	1.0	NA	3.2	1.5
26 21000	Dearborn	62.7	95 535	314	1 523.7	93.2	4.4	0.5	4.3	0.1	2.8	26.2
26 21020	Dearborn Heights	30.4	56 415	651	1 855.8	88.0	8.6	1.2	4.0	0.1	4.0	20.1
26 22000	Detroit	359.4	680 250	18	1 892.7	14.0	82.4	1.0	1.6	0.1	7.5	5.1
26 24120	East Lansing	35.2	48 648	775	1 382.0	78.8	11.0	1.2	12.4	NA	3.4	14.8
26 24290	Eastpointe	13.3	32 654	1 134	2 455.2	55.6	41.2	1.5	2.3	NA	3.6	3.5
26 27440	Farmington Hills	86.2	81 435	403	944.7	69.8	20.1	0.8	11.4	NA	2.7	18.3
26 29000	Flint	86.6	99 002	300	1 143.2	41.2	58.9	1.9	0.7	NA	4.0	1.1
26 31420	Garden City	15.2	27 052	1 355	1 779.7	95.1	3.9	1.1	0.9	NA	3.5	3.6
26 34000	Grand Rapids	115.0	193 792	123	1 685.1	73.3	23.8	1.6	2.9	0.1	15.0	9.6
26 38640	Holland	43.0	33 644	1 106	782.4	87.7	4.7	1.1	4.4	NA	25.9	13.3
26 40680	Inkster	16.2	24 786	1 426	1 530.0	19.1	80.6	1.8	0.8	NA	2.6	2.7
26 41420	Jackson	28.1	33 200	1 121	1 181.5	75.4	25.6	0.6	1.0	NA	6.3	2.1
26 42160	Kalamazoo	63.9	75 922	442	1 188.1	72.5	25.3	2.1	3.5	0.1	7.3	6.1
26 42820	Kentwood	54.1	50 764	740	938.3	73.5	19.5	2.0	8.3	NA	10.0	15.6
26 46000	Lansing	93.4	114 620	238	1 227.2	69.3	27.4	2.7	5.7	0.3	12.5	8.2
26 47800	Lincoln Park	15.3	37 231	995	2 433.4	86.6	7.3	0.6	0.4	NA	16.2	7.7
26 49000	Livonia	92.5	94 958	316	1 026.6	93.0	4.2	0.6	3.4	NA	2.6	6.8
26 50560	Madison Heights	18.4	30 267	1 227	1 644.9	86.8	7.8	2.2	5.1	NA	1.4	15.6
26 53780	Midland	87.3	41 957	880	480.6	91.6	2.5	1.0	4.6	NA	2.4	7.3
26 56020	Mount Pleasant	20.1	25 971	1 395	1 292.1	91.5	5.9	3.1	4.0	NA	2.7	5.4
26 56320	Muskegon	36.8	38 393	968	1 043.3	66.1	36.5	2.7	0.5	NA	6.4	1.5
26 59440	Novi	78.4	58 416	627	745.1	74.0	8.1	0.3	19.2	NA	2.4	19.6

1. Dry land or land partially or temporarily covered by water. 2. May be of any race.

City	Age of population (percent), 2011-2013: Under 5 years	5 to 17 years	18 to 24 years	25 to 34 years	35 to 44 years	45 to 54 years	55 to 64 years	65 to 74 years	75 years and over	Median age 2011-2013	Percent female 2011-2013	Population: Census counts: 2000	Census counts: 2010	Percent change: 2000–2010	Percent change: 2010–2014
	12	13	14	15	16	17	18	19	20	21	22	23	24	25	26
MASSACHUSETTS—Cont'd															
Beverly	5.3	13.8	13.3	11.7	12.9	14.2	14.1	7.9	6.7	39.4	53.4	39 862	39 502	-0.9	3.7
Boston	5.4	11.3	17.4	22.2	12.4	11.3	9.6	5.6	4.9	31.4	52.2	589 141	617 594	4.8	6.2
Braintree Town	5.0	16.4	9.4	12.5	12.3	14.9	13.7	6.5	9.2	41.1	51.6	33 698	35 744	6.1	4.5
Brockton	7.6	18.5	9.2	13.0	13.0	14.2	11.3	7.1	6.1	36.1	52.0	94 304	93 810	-0.5	1.0
Cambridge	4.0	7.3	21.0	27.9	11.8	8.9	8.7	5.9	4.6	30.4	51.8	101 355	105 162	3.8	4.3
Chelsea	9.5	15.8	9.7	20.9	14.9	13.6	6.8	4.9	4.0	31.7	49.4	35 080	35 177	0.3	10.5
Chicopee	5.5	14.0	9.2	15.3	11.5	14.3	12.9	9.2	8.1	40.3	50.9	54 653	55 298	1.2	0.9
Everett	5.0	15.3	9.7	16.2	15.8	15.6	9.6	5.7	7.1	37.3	50.8	38 037	41 667	9.5	6.2
Fall River	6.4	15.2	9.3	14.3	12.7	15.2	10.9	8.4	7.6	38.6	53.3	91 938	88 857	-3.4	-0.2
Fitchburg	6.5	15.2	13.7	14.0	11.4	14.1	11.3	7.1	6.8	35.7	49.5	39 102	40 318	3.1	0.3
Franklin Town	5.7	20.5	9.5	9.6	13.7	16.7	11.7	6.6	6.0	39.7	51.0	29 560	31 635	7.0	3.8
Gloucester	4.7	13.7	7.4	10.6	10.7	16.6	17.6	10.0	8.7	47.0	53.7	30 273	28 789	-4.9	2.9
Haverhill	7.2	15.2	8.8	13.4	13.9	16.3	12.8	6.1	6.5	39.5	52.4	58 969	60 879	3.2	2.6
Holyoke	7.3	17.6	10.1	14.0	12.3	14.4	10.3	5.6	8.3	35.7	52.3	39 838	39 880	0.1	0.6
Lawrence	8.6	19.4	13.1	15.1	12.6	11.9	10.4	4.6	4.5	30.5	52.5	72 043	76 377	6.0	2.4
Leominster	4.9	15.1	8.5	12.3	13.5	17.5	13.3	7.4	7.5	42.2	51.4	41 303	40 759	-1.3	1.0
Lowell	6.9	15.6	12.8	17.9	12.1	13.5	10.6	5.6	5.0	33.0	50.2	105 167	106 519	1.3	3.2
Lynn	8.0	18.2	9.8	16.7	12.3	13.6	10.4	6.2	4.8	33.5	51.6	89 050	90 329	1.4	2.0
Malden	5.9	13.3	11.2	19.0	14.5	14.2	11.3	5.4	5.2	35.4	51.8	56 340	59 450	5.5	2.3
Marlborough	7.9	14.4	7.5	15.4	15.2	14.9	13.0	5.6	6.2	38.9	49.4	36 255	38 499	6.2	2.9
Medford	5.6	9.7	12.7	19.4	13.0	12.7	12.0	7.0	7.8	36.5	52.7	55 765	56 173	0.7	2.1
Melrose	7.0	14.3	5.2	12.8	18.1	15.7	11.7	8.5	6.7	41.3	51.5	27 134	26 983	-0.6	3.7
Methuen Town	6.4	17.6	7.6	11.6	14.7	14.9	12.8	8.1	6.4	39.6	50.2	43 789	47 255	7.9	3.9
New Bedford	6.3	15.8	9.5	15.3	12.8	13.1	12.0	7.2	8.0	37.1	52.3	93 768	95 072	1.4	-0.2
Newton	5.7	16.1	12.4	9.3	13.5	13.7	13.1	8.6	7.5	40.1	52.8	83 829	85 146	1.6	3.7
Northampton	3.8	12.9	15.6	12.9	11.6	14.1	13.5	8.5	7.1	39.0	55.8	28 978	28 549	-1.5	0.0
Peabody	4.5	13.9	8.6	11.0	12.1	15.9	13.5	9.0	11.4	45.0	52.3	48 129	51 251	6.5	2.2
Pittsfield	5.6	13.7	8.6	12.5	11.4	14.1	15.2	9.8	9.1	43.7	52.4	45 793	44 737	-2.3	-2.3
Quincy	6.2	10.5	9.1	19.4	12.6	15.6	11.4	7.2	7.9	38.5	51.1	88 025	92 271	4.8	1.2
Revere	5.7	13.2	7.3	17.2	16.6	14.9	11.6	7.2	6.4	39.5	47.5	47 283	51 755	9.5	4.7
Salem	5.1	11.9	13.3	15.2	12.2	14.7	14.1	6.9	6.5	38.2	53.9	40 407	41 340	2.3	3.6
Somerville	5.2	8.2	13.8	31.2	14.7	10.1	7.1	5.1	4.6	31.5	50.9	77 478	75 754	-2.2	4.3
Springfield	7.1	19.5	13.3	13.8	11.8	12.5	10.8	6.2	5.1	32.5	52.2	152 082	153 060	0.6	0.5
Taunton	6.0	14.6	9.1	12.7	13.7	16.5	13.8	7.0	6.7	40.9	51.4	55 976	55 874	-0.2	1.2
Waltham	5.0	8.9	16.7	20.7	13.9	12.1	10.6	6.4	5.7	33.9	52.4	59 226	60 632	2.4	3.9
Watertown Town	6.0	9.5	5.3	22.7	15.1	15.2	10.3	9.6	6.3	38.3	51.2	32 986	31 915	-3.2	6.9
Westfield	6.4	14.5	16.7	10.7	11.0	13.9	13.2	7.6	6.1	37.0	51.0	40 072	41 094	2.6	1.3
West Springfield Town	5.7	16.0	10.5	14.2	11.7	13.7	13.2	7.6	7.4	38.0	51.7	27 899	28 391	1.8	0.8
Weymouth Town	4.5	16.0	6.9	10.5	14.6	16.7	14.7	8.6	7.5	43.3	52.6	53 988	53 743	-0.5	3.5
Woburn	6.7	13.1	6.2	19.1	12.7	14.2	13.6	7.0	7.5	39.0	49.9	37 258	38 120	2.3	3.0
Worcester	6.8	15.1	14.8	15.4	12.0	13.0	10.9	6.1	5.9	33.3	52.2	172 648	181 045	4.9	1.1
MICHIGAN	5.8	17.1	10.1	11.9	12.4	14.7	13.4	8.0	6.5	39.4	50.9	9 938 444	9 883 640	-0.6	0.3
Allen Park	5.4	15.7	8.8	10.7	13.1	15.9	13.8	7.4	9.2	42.4	52.8	29 376	28 210	-4.0	-2.3
Ann Arbor	4.2	10.0	30.0	17.4	9.5	9.2	9.5	5.5	4.7	27.7	49.9	114 024	113 934	-0.1	3.4
Battle Creek	7.7	18.2	9.6	13.6	12.4	13.1	11.5	7.2	6.8	35.5	52.3	53 364	52 347	-1.9	-1.0
Bay City	7.4	17.4	11.1	13.4	12.1	14.2	12.2	6.1	6.0	35.5	51.4	36 817	34 932	-5.1	-2.2
Burton	5.6	18.3	8.3	11.9	12.2	17.1	12.6	6.9	7.2	39.7	50.3	30 308	29 999	-1.0	-3.4
Dearborn	8.3	21.6	10.0	13.1	12.3	11.5	11.5	5.3	6.4	32.4	51.2	97 775	98 153	0.4	-2.7
Dearborn Heights	7.0	17.7	9.0	12.8	12.1	13.5	12.8	6.6	8.5	38.2	51.5	58 264	57 774	-0.8	-2.4
Detroit	7.1	18.4	12.1	12.3	12.4	13.2	12.3	6.7	5.5	35.1	52.5	951 270	713 777	-25.0	-4.7
East Lansing	2.3	5.8	60.5	10.2	5.0	4.0	5.6	3.1	3.4	21.4	48.8	46 525	48 579	4.4	0.2
Eastpointe	6.0	20.2	9.9	11.4	14.6	14.2	11.7	6.4	5.6	36.3	52.8	34 077	32 442	-4.8	0.7
Farmington Hills	4.8	15.0	7.6	12.1	13.2	14.2	15.4	8.7	9.0	42.9	52.8	82 111	79 740	-2.9	2.1
Flint	7.6	18.2	11.1	13.5	12.1	13.9	11.9	6.4	5.2	34.6	51.5	124 943	102 434	-18.0	-3.3
Garden City	6.6	14.7	8.1	13.4	12.4	17.3	13.4	7.1	6.9	40.8	50.2	30 047	27 692	-7.8	-2.3
Grand Rapids	7.9	16.4	14.2	17.5	11.8	10.9	10.0	5.2	6.2	31.1	51.3	197 800	188 040	-4.9	3.1
Holland	8.2	17.0	19.1	13.1	10.9	10.2	9.8	4.5	7.3	29.6	51.4	35 048	33 051	-5.7	1.8
Inkster	8.5	21.3	10.3	12.4	12.7	12.8	11.4	6.0	4.6	32.8	53.2	30 115	25 369	-15.8	-2.3
Jackson	9.2	20.7	9.8	16.1	11.8	11.3	11.0	5.9	4.2	31.0	54.2	36 316	33 534	-7.7	-1.0
Kalamazoo	5.5	14.8	28.3	13.6	10.9	8.8	8.8	4.2	5.4	25.7	49.7	77 145	74 262	-3.7	2.2
Kentwood	6.8	16.4	11.8	16.3	12.3	14.9	9.8	5.9	5.8	33.8	52.6	45 255	48 707	7.6	4.2
Lansing	7.7	15.7	13.5	16.9	12.4	12.2	11.5	5.7	4.5	32.0	52.5	119 128	114 297	-4.1	0.3
Lincoln Park	6.6	17.1	9.0	14.0	13.6	14.1	14.5	5.3	5.7	37.4	52.3	40 008	38 144	-4.7	-2.4
Livonia	4.6	15.3	7.5	11.3	11.7	16.7	15.2	8.8	9.1	44.7	50.9	100 545	96 942	-3.6	-2.0
Madison Heights	7.2	12.1	9.0	18.0	13.1	14.4	12.1	7.1	7.0	37.6	51.3	31 101	29 694	-4.5	1.9
Midland	5.8	16.9	10.3	13.1	11.6	14.3	12.3	6.7	9.1	37.9	51.9	41 685	41 863	0.4	0.2
Mount Pleasant	3.2	8.5	49.7	12.0	6.0	7.1	6.2	3.7	3.7	22.2	54.2	25 946	26 016	0.3	-0.2
Muskegon	6.9	14.9	12.5	15.0	11.8	14.9	12.1	5.7	6.4	35.7	47.9	40 105	38 401	-4.2	0.0
Novi	5.2	18.8	7.3	10.8	15.7	16.9	11.9	6.3	7.1	40.8	51.6	47 386	55 224	16.5	5.8

City	Households, 2011-2013: Number	Households, 2011-2013: Persons per house-hold	Households, 2011-2013: Percent: Female family house-holder[1]	Households, 2011-2013: Percent: One-person	Persons in group quarters, 2010: Total	Persons in group quarters, 2010: Institutional: Total	Persons in group quarters, 2010: Institutional: Persons in nursing facilities	Persons in group quarters, 2010: Non-institu-tional	Serious crimes known to police,[2] 2013: Total: Number	Serious crimes known to police,[2] 2013: Total: Rate[3]	Serious crimes known to police,[2] 2013: Rate[3]: Violent	Serious crimes known to police,[2] 2013: Rate[3]: Property	Educational attainment, 2011–2013: Population age 25 and older	Educational attainment, 2011–2013: Attainment[4] (percent): High school graduate or less	Educational attainment, 2011–2013: Attainment[4] (percent): Bachelor's degree or more
	27	28	29	30	31	32	33	34	35	36	37	38	39	40	41
MASSACHUSETTS—Cont'd															
Beverly	15 872	2.36	9.8	32.0	2 514	533	369	1 981	672	1 655	232	1 424	27 261	29.4	44.1
Boston	249 728	2.37	17.3	37.7	46 214	6 697	3 280	39 517	22 890	3 555	782	2 773	420 118	37.4	43.8
Braintree Town	13 097	2.73	12.4	23.5	545	524	514	21	863	2 365	227	2 137	25 135	36.4	36.9
Brockton	32 542	2.84	23.3	26.6	1 768	1 088	790	680	4 351	4 607	1 231	3 375	60 772	54.2	17.8
Cambridge	43 642	2.05	8.5	40.2	17 102	324	277	16 778	3 268	3 046	336	2 710	72 073	15.9	74.0
Chelsea	11 842	3.05	22.5	29.4	682	570	570	112	1 692	4 518	1 223	3 295	23 985	67.0	17.8
Chicopee	22 732	2.39	14.5	33.1	1 155	341	231	814	1 838	3 308	495	2 813	39 674	54.6	16.6
Everett	15 868	2.67	19.1	25.5	191	150	150	41	1 100	2 560	470	2 090	29 740	60.0	15.8
Fall River	38 395	2.27	19.1	35.3	1 735	1 071	994	664	3 308	3 708	1 059	2 649	61 272	60.1	14.4
Fitchburg	14 905	2.55	18.6	26.3	2 538	669	356	1 869	1 367	3 374	758	2 616	26 083	50.1	20.2
Franklin Town	10 885	2.88	7.9	19.5	875	79	72	796	179	549	25	524	20 816	25.4	51.8
Gloucester	12 196	2.36	10.1	29.4	450	230	216	220	405	1 378	75	1 303	21 643	42.3	32.1
Haverhill	23 816	2.54	15.7	29.8	1 300	671	618	629	2 036	3 271	670	2 601	42 526	41.8	27.6
Holyoke	15 296	2.55	28.7	28.7	1 385	1 086	934	299	3 082	7 664	1 042	6 622	26 084	52.8	21.5
Lawrence	25 857	2.95	34.0	23.7	902	542	310	360	3 049	3 918	997	2 921	45 551	64.8	10.9
Leominster	16 745	2.42	12.2	31.5	327	251	224	76	1 498	3 638	639	2 999	29 261	46.1	25.2
Lowell	39 094	2.65	18.8	30.5	4 346	1 112	1 101	3 234	4 013	3 667	572	3 095	70 109	54.1	21.3
Lynn	32 406	2.79	22.5	28.3	835	284	263	551	3 214	3 502	889	2 613	58 328	53.4	19.7
Malden	22 509	2.66	14.0	29.0	373	116	116	257	1 150	1 891	337	1 554	41 893	46.5	30.2
Marlborough	15 581	2.47	9.5	32.7	661	286	253	375	912	2 307	395	1 912	27 518	41.1	38.3
Medford	22 111	2.47	8.1	27.8	1 959	479	465	1 480	1 011	1 760	197	1 564	40 940	34.0	43.6
Melrose	11 453	2.37	8.2	31.2	267	229	223	38	283	1 024	76	948	20 167	22.6	51.9
Methuen Town	17 469	2.73	14.3	25.4	420	277	232	143	1 233	2 549	219	2 330	32 938	42.8	28.4
New Bedford	39 300	2.36	19.5	34.8	1 966	1 415	1 196	551	4 484	4 712	1 093	3 619	64 887	60.6	15.1
Newton	31 139	2.53	7.7	24.7	7 103	483	474	6 620	881	1 014	85	929	57 178	12.0	76.6
Northampton	11 667	2.14	10.6	37.5	3 156	846	527	2 310	932	3 261	455	2 806	19 346	24.7	55.6
Peabody	21 593	2.37	11.1	34.5	520	397	389	123	1 185	2 271	234	2 037	37 809	42.9	29.1
Pittsfield	19 497	2.21	14.8	36.7	1 184	894	501	290	1 462	3 323	252	3 071	31 907	44.2	25.4
Quincy	39 663	2.32	11.3	36.8	1 400	729	698	671	2 008	2 148	386	1 762	68 965	38.2	38.1
Revere	20 471	2.59	17.1	33.9	280	228	228	52	1 478	2 748	589	2 159	39 312	56.3	19.9
Salem	18 702	2.16	16.4	36.9	1 770	167	156	1 603	1 366	3 217	301	2 915	29 453	35.3	37.5
Somerville	32 186	2.33	12.3	31.7	2 269	37	22	2 232	1 716	2 207	246	1 961	56 586	31.9	53.8
Springfield	55 613	2.67	27.2	29.7	5 677	954	553	4 723	8 799	5 729	1 092	4 637	92 352	54.7	17.5
Taunton	21 655	2.55	15.3	29.3	784	574	406	210	1 171	2 081	371	1 710	39 357	54.6	17.6
Waltham	24 177	2.26	9.0	34.9	6 686	308	287	6 378	1 093	1 750	226	1 525	42 894	35.0	48.3
Watertown Town	14 240	2.27	6.7	33.2	234	104	0	130	518	1 558	162	1 395	25 857	23.1	59.6
Westfield	14 452	2.65	15.0	26.7	2 976	359	294	2 617	768	1 851	251	1 600	25 793	39.9	31.3
West Springfield Town	11 486	2.48	18.2	31.8	170	120	120	50	1 483	5 177	569	4 608	19 406	41.7	28.4
Weymouth Town	22 620	2.40	13.0	34.1	460	373	373	87	979	1 766	352	1 414	39 795	38.0	30.2
Woburn	14 584	2.64	11.3	27.5	323	238	238	85	664	1 690	211	1 479	28 767	40.5	34.2
Worcester	67 973	2.52	18.4	32.4	12 152	2 093	1 845	10 059	7 998	4 360	954	3 405	115 421	45.0	29.8
MICHIGAN	3 815 532	2.53	12.9	29.0	229 068	109 867	42 473	119 201	274 857	2 778	450	2 328	6 616 878	41.1	26.2
Allen Park	10 769	2.57	10.5	28.4	171	138	132	33	695	2 518	127	2 391	19 505	42.7	22.7
Ann Arbor	46 946	2.24	6.9	38.3	11 840	78	61	11 762	2 789	2 388	215	2 173	64 839	12.1	70.4
Battle Creek	20 353	2.49	18.3	33.7	1 399	862	228	537	2 966	4 860	764	4 096	33 523	42.6	22.7
Bay City	14 131	2.41	16.0	35.5	515	180	0	335	1 158	3 367	643	2 724	22 153	51.7	14.7
Burton	11 305	2.59	17.4	26.0	111	0	0	111	1 398	4 777	407	4 371	19 935	46.6	16.0
Dearborn	31 239	3.08	10.1	28.7	226	195	180	31	3 454	3 597	361	3 236	58 071	41.5	28.0
Dearborn Heights	20 738	2.72	13.7	29.7	602	504	344	98	1 551	2 741	375	2 366	37 762	49.3	19.7
Detroit	253 607	2.70	29.3	38.2	14 759	6 541	3 365	8 218	55 059	7 867	2 072	5 795	435 441	54.7	13.0
East Lansing	13 640	2.36	5.7	38.6	15 701	193	193	15 508	911	1 878	233	1 645	15 181	12.1	68.7
Eastpointe	12 113	2.67	25.7	31.6	21	0	0	21	1 457	4 497	910	3 586	20 741	50.3	13.0
Farmington Hills	34 166	2.33	9.1	33.2	693	319	251	374	1 195	1 474	91	1 383	58 611	22.8	52.6
Flint	40 558	2.41	25.1	37.8	3 193	988	85	2 205	6 226	6 230	1 955	4 275	63 332	53.0	10.9
Garden City	10 262	2.66	14.1	26.4	54	0	0	54	623	2 298	295	2 003	19 279	53.6	12.1
Grand Rapids	73 080	2.51	15.9	33.1	8 260	3 298	2 011	4 962	7 514	3 930	693	3 236	117 198	39.4	30.0
Holland	11 417	2.67	15.4	24.6	2 723	283	273	2 440	1 206	3 616	414	3 202	18 891	45.5	27.9
Inkster	8 995	2.76	32.1	33.4	230	18	3	212	1 431	5 759	1 594	4 165	14 992	50.5	11.1
Jackson	12 501	2.62	24.6	31.8	773	468	263	305	2 105	6 307	1 109	5 198	20 141	50.9	13.6
Kalamazoo	27 654	2.45	17.1	35.4	7 462	1 126	489	6 336	3 885	5 156	1 064	4 091	38 746	30.2	32.4
Kentwood	19 650	2.50	16.0	28.0	395	246	114	149	1 357	2 713	282	2 431	32 285	38.1	32.2
Lansing	47 819	2.36	17.4	36.7	1 181	273	120	908	5 177	4 545	1 056	3 489	71 747	39.7	24.2
Lincoln Park	14 223	2.64	15.5	30.2	64	13	0	51	1 575	4 223	622	3 601	25 279	57.4	8.6
Livonia	37 215	2.54	9.5	26.9	1 366	791	764	575	2 110	2 216	155	2 060	69 545	30.5	36.2
Madison Heights	13 070	2.29	11.5	37.8	156	149	149	7	947	3 148	266	2 882	21 555	46.7	22.0
Midland	17 589	2.33	9.5	32.0	1 159	489	352	670	473	1 124	83	1 041	28 227	28.3	42.9
Mount Pleasant	8 249	2.42	8.0	33.4	6 365	442	286	5 923	549	2 092	221	1 871	10 125	26.9	42.6
Muskegon	13 607	2.36	21.0	39.0	5 199	4 459	426	740	2 300	6 274	897	5 377	24 409	57.7	11.1
Novi	23 314	2.43	7.9	32.1	360	316	316	44	1 014	1 764	85	1 679	39 070	20.6	55.2

1. No spouse present. 2. Data for serious crimes have not been adjusted for underreporting. This may affect comparability between geographic areas and over time. 3. Per 100,000 population estimated by the FBI. 4. Persons 25 years old and over.

City	Money income, 2011–2013					Housing units, 2010			Occupied housing units 2011–2013				
		Households								Owner-occupied		Median owner costs as a percent of income	
	Per capita income[1] (dollars)	Median income	Percent with income of $200,000 or more	Percent with income of less than $25,000	Families with income below poverty (percent)	Total	Percent change, 2000–2010	Vacant units for sale or rent[2]	Total	Percent	Median value[3] (dollars)	With a mortgage[4]	Without a mortgage[5]
	42	43	44	45	46	47	48	49	50	51	52	53	54
MASSACHUSETTS—Cont'd													
Beverly	37 998	73 168	8.3	18.1	4.8	16 641	2.2	791	15 872	60.7	361 300	25.5	13.2
Boston	33 565	52 465	7.2	29.7	17.6	272 481	8.2	19 782	249 728	33.6	372 400	25.6	15.5
Braintree Town	35 123	81 537	7.3	14.0	4.9	14 302	10.7	566	13 097	68.2	364 500	24.8	14.3
Brockton	21 781	49 032	1.4	27.2	15.3	35 552	2.1	2 249	32 542	57.0	223 000	28.8	18.7
Cambridge	46 529	73 780	11.7	19.3	8.8	47 291	5.7	3 259	43 642	36.2	526 600	22.0	12.7
Chelsea	22 530	50 056	2.8	29.2	18.1	12 621	2.3	790	11 842	28.7	259 300	28.4	19.1
Chicopee	24 744	47 182	1.1	25.8	10.4	25 140	2.9	1 401	22 732	57.8	172 700	22.7	15.8
Everett	23 359	49 038	1.6	24.2	11.7	16 715	5.1	1 172	15 868	39.5	306 400	32.7	15.4
Fall River	21 233	33 416	1.2	39.2	19.8	42 750	2.1	4 293	38 395	36.1	233 000	26.9	15.7
Fitchburg	21 431	44 312	0.9	31.2	15.6	17 117	7.0	1 952	14 905	54.9	178 700	24.8	18.8
Franklin Town	42 061	100 847	16.2	12.4	3.7	11 394	10.3	399	10 885	77.3	377 500	21.6	13.3
Gloucester	36 572	58 919	6.7	21.8	6.2	14 557	4.3	2 071	12 196	61.4	348 100	27.6	14.8
Haverhill	29 426	57 474	3.2	22.0	10.3	25 657	8.1	1 507	23 816	61.0	249 500	25.3	14.7
Holyoke	20 889	33 030	2.1	40.7	28.3	16 384	1.1	1 023	15 296	41.1	183 900	24.5	15.1
Lawrence	16 333	32 293	1.2	40.3	27.6	27 137	6.0	1 956	25 857	27.0	204 500	31.0	14.0
Leominster	29 037	59 095	2.1	24.8	9.5	17 873	5.3	1 106	16 745	53.7	227 300	23.8	15.0
Lowell	22 332	46 652	1.8	29.4	16.6	41 431	5.0	2 961	39 094	43.0	227 500	27.0	13.8
Lynn	23 002	45 593	2.6	30.4	18.0	35 776	3.1	2 466	32 406	46.3	250 200	27.0	16.7
Malden	24 907	51 916	2.1	26.7	15.2	25 161	6.5	1 488	22 509	41.1	314 800	27.8	14.2
Marlborough	33 595	66 469	5.7	17.7	5.4	16 416	10.2	1 021	15 581	54.4	301 300	24.8	14.0
Medford	36 459	72 581	5.7	14.9	5.5	24 046	6.0	1 236	22 111	56.1	387 500	27.7	17.9
Melrose	43 083	81 421	9.8	12.4	1.4	11 751	4.5	538	11 453	67.6	420 300	25.0	15.1
Methuen Town	29 826	71 224	4.1	18.2	7.6	18 340	8.6	811	17 469	70.7	274 800	23.8	14.1
New Bedford	21 150	36 447	1.2	35.4	19.7	42 933	3.4	4 172	39 300	42.8	208 200	28.3	18.3
Newton	64 004	120 496	28.9	10.8	3.8	32 648	1.7	1 480	31 139	69.5	707 400	22.0	13.7
Northampton	34 986	57 908	5.0	24.2	7.8	12 728	2.6	728	11 667	57.3	287 400	25.4	14.1
Peabody	33 599	62 609	3.4	18.5	4.7	22 220	17.6	907	21 593	60.6	325 400	26.7	14.6
Pittsfield	26 098	42 460	2.3	30.6	15.4	21 487	0.6	1 834	19 497	61.5	172 600	23.9	15.3
Quincy	32 597	60 795	3.9	21.2	8.9	42 838	6.8	2 180	39 663	46.7	337 000	26.8	17.1
Revere	26 582	51 229	3.0	27.7	12.4	22 100	9.5	1 646	20 471	52.4	298 100	33.7	20.0
Salem	31 309	55 932	4.3	27.0	11.2	19 130	5.3	1 288	18 702	46.6	303 500	27.6	21.8
Somerville	35 245	65 110	5.6	20.0	12.1	33 720	3.8	1 615	32 186	34.9	435 600	27.4	16.7
Springfield	17 914	33 326	1.5	40.9	26.7	61 706	0.9	4 954	55 613	47.4	144 900	25.1	16.5
Taunton	25 997	50 790	2.6	25.6	10.4	23 896	4.3	1 564	21 655	61.9	231 800	27.1	15.2
Waltham	37 003	75 612	6.4	17.9	5.2	24 926	4.4	1 236	24 177	49.5	397 800	24.8	15.0
Watertown Town	45 746	89 414	9.5	13.4	4.2	15 584	3.8	875	14 240	52.8	434 000	25.5	14.1
Westfield	28 078	64 037	4.5	20.2	5.9	16 075	4.1	740	14 452	68.6	224 000	21.9	12.7
West Springfield Town	27 685	53 962	3.1	26.5	8.5	12 697	3.6	573	11 486	57.8	197 300	23.4	15.1
Weymouth Town	34 970	67 554	3.8	15.0	5.2	23 480	4.0	1 045	22 620	67.0	313 600	25.7	17.0
Woburn	34 671	77 170	5.4	16.5	5.2	16 309	6.0	785	14 584	58.3	361 600	23.2	15.3
Worcester	23 935	44 553	3.0	31.1	18.6	74 645	5.5	6 032	67 973	43.2	205 300	26.0	14.2
MICHIGAN	25 557	47 793	3.1	26.1	12.5	4 532 233	7.0	659 725	3 815 532	71.2	117 100	22.5	13.3
Allen Park	26 690	58 063	1.4	17.4	5.5	12 206	-0.4	626	10 769	84.8	89 600	20.5	14.0
Ann Arbor	34 905	53 458	6.9	25.9	6.9	49 789	5.5	2 729	46 946	45.2	227 800	22.0	11.2
Battle Creek	21 545	36 112	2.1	34.9	20.1	24 277	3.1	3 159	20 353	59.8	80 900	22.8	14.1
Bay City	18 607	33 067	0.3	35.6	16.4	15 923	-2.1	1 487	14 131	68.2	66 500	23.4	14.1
Burton	22 035	43 746	1.5	28.8	17.2	13 075	5.9	1 111	11 305	72.5	68 500	23.0	12.2
Dearborn	20 513	45 413	2.3	30.6	24.7	37 871	-2.8	3 529	31 239	67.6	96 300	24.0	14.8
Dearborn Heights	20 072	41 597	1.3	29.7	18.5	24 068	0.6	1 802	20 738	74.2	78 000	25.9	14.5
Detroit	14 464	24 970	0.7	50.0	36.2	349 170	-6.9	79 725	253 607	50.5	42 300	28.4	17.7
East Lansing	19 587	32 644	7.2	42.6	9.6	15 787	3.1	1 013	13 640	34.4	172 000	20.9	10.0
Eastpointe	18 079	40 808	0.1	33.1	22.6	13 796	-1.2	1 239	12 113	71.2	53 900	25.6	15.2
Farmington Hills	40 214	70 112	7.6	16.5	5.5	36 178	3.8	2 619	34 166	62.3	192 900	22.4	12.0
Flint	14 328	24 537	0.5	50.8	36.0	51 321	-7.5	10 849	40 558	57.0	34 200	26.3	16.2
Garden City	22 622	50 296	0.2	21.3	7.5	11 616	-0.9	722	10 262	78.4	75 600	22.2	14.0
Grand Rapids	20 358	39 308	1.3	32.1	19.6	80 619	3.4	8 493	73 080	54.7	104 300	21.9	12.5
Holland	21 343	43 532	1.8	26.6	13.8	13 212	5.2	1 191	11 417	64.3	111 300	22.1	13.7
Inkster	13 920	26 670	NA	46.8	31.1	11 647	-3.0	1 826	8 995	51.7	51 200	27.0	19.6
Jackson	14 834	27 181	0.7	46.1	32.8	15 457	1.4	2 163	12 501	49.5	62 700	22.0	14.1
Kalamazoo	18 602	32 361	1.7	40.3	22.2	32 433	2.0	3 292	27 654	45.0	96 100	23.1	13.3
Kentwood	24 510	48 428	2.2	25.3	11.3	21 584	10.7	1 843	19 650	59.9	125 200	22.6	14.6
Lansing	18 534	33 769	0.5	37.4	25.9	54 181	1.8	5 731	47 819	49.4	78 000	23.4	14.4
Lincoln Park	19 323	39 295	0.6	28.5	15.5	16 530	-1.7	1 606	14 223	70.9	57 700	21.9	14.8
Livonia	31 997	68 544	3.1	13.2	3.1	40 401	4.5	1 687	37 215	83.9	149 800	20.7	12.1
Madison Heights	21 813	39 455	0.8	31.1	16.9	13 685	0.5	973	13 070	62.4	77 200	23.0	12.8
Midland	30 490	50 723	5.3	25.7	10.9	18 578	4.7	1 072	17 589	64.0	140 400	19.0	12.0
Mount Pleasant	15 773	30 421	2.0	45.8	16.7	8 981	0.8	605	8 249	36.1	116 900	20.4	11.1
Muskegon	14 500	25 890	0.3	49.0	33.8	16 105	0.5	2 138	13 607	51.3	61 300	25.5	11.7
Novi	43 876	76 132	12.2	12.0	3.2	24 226	23.2	1 968	23 314	63.9	228 300	19.9	14.1

1. Based on population estimated by the American Community Survey. 2. Includes units rented or sold but not occupied. 3. Specified owner-occupied units; $1,000,000 represents $1,000,000 or more 4. 50.0 represents 50 percent or more. 5. 10.0 represents 10 percent or less.

City	Occupied housing units, 2011–2013 (cont.)				Migration, 2011–2013		Civilian labor force, 2014				Civilian employment[4], 2011–2013			
									Unemployment			Percent		
	Percent renter occupied	Median gross rent[1]	Median rent as a percent of income[2]	Percent with no vehicle available	Percent who lived in the same house one year ago	Percent who lived outside current city one year ago	Total	Percent change, 2013–2014	Total	Rate[3]	Population age 16 and older	In labor force	Civilian full-year full-time workers	Households with no workers (percent)
	55	56	57	58	59	60	61	62	63	64	65	66	67	68
MASSACHUSETTS—Cont'd														
Beverly	39.3	1 083	30.0	10.4	88.1	8.1	22 571	1.3	1 150	5.1	33 496	68.8	41.3	26.7
Boston	66.4	1 261	30.8	35.8	78.0	11.2	354 299	1.6	18 716	5.3	542 903	68.3	39.7	27.2
Braintree Town	31.8	1 266	32.6	7.7	90.9	5.9	19 958	1.9	1 052	5.3	29 603	68.8	43.0	23.7
Brockton	43.0	1 036	34.1	15.8	88.2	5.5	47 221	0.9	3 763	8.0	72 627	66.0	37.2	28.3
Cambridge	63.8	1 636	29.4	30.9	72.5	19.8	62 548	1.9	2 259	3.6	95 661	67.8	40.7	24.9
Chelsea	71.3	1 135	30.2	28.0	85.4	7.7	18 923	1.3	1 147	6.1	28 406	72.1	42.1	25.2
Chicopee	42.2	792	29.2	11.2	89.1	6.3	27 521	1.2	2 074	7.5	46 374	64.2	38.1	33.0
Everett	60.5	1 199	34.0	15.6	86.4	11.3	24 066	1.5	1 327	5.5	35 445	71.3	41.3	24.9
Fall River	63.9	715	32.0	19.9	83.7	6.7	40 052	0.2	4 086	10.2	71 661	59.4	32.7	39.7
Fitchburg	45.1	821	33.5	13.7	81.3	11.2	19 349	0.7	1 611	8.3	32 687	63.8	34.0	31.7
Franklin Town	22.7	1 065	24.5	7.5	92.2	6.5	17 363	1.6	826	4.8	25 029	71.7	43.8	20.3
Gloucester	38.6	953	27.7	9.4	89.7	5.9	15 454	1.0	1 173	7.6	24 492	66.3	35.1	30.1
Haverhill	39.0	988	32.3	10.0	86.6	7.5	33 578	1.3	2 078	6.2	49 479	69.4	42.7	24.2
Holyoke	58.9	643	31.2	25.3	85.3	7.2	16 330	0.7	1 539	9.4	31 353	57.2	28.3	41.4
Lawrence	73.0	988	34.9	26.0	84.1	6.4	35 300	-0.4	3 906	11.1	58 182	64.2	34.1	30.6
Leominster	46.3	883	28.5	10.2	88.0	7.8	21 770	1.2	1 518	7.0	33 474	68.4	39.8	28.7
Lowell	57.0	977	31.7	16.0	83.7	8.3	53 954	0.8	3 994	7.4	87 023	67.4	37.5	29.4
Lynn	53.7	961	33.5	20.9	82.6	7.3	46 586	1.4	3 036	6.5	69 646	68.2	42.7	28.3
Malden	58.9	1 219	32.5	21.6	82.9	12.1	33 064	1.4	1 748	5.3	50 200	70.6	41.7	24.8
Marlborough	45.6	1 082	28.3	7.6	86.7	8.6	23 232	1.8	1 124	4.8	31 297	74.0	48.1	18.9
Medford	43.9	1 452	28.1	10.5	83.8	12.8	33 166	1.9	1 574	4.7	49 118	70.6	45.9	20.9
Melrose	32.4	1 038	25.7	7.8	86.9	9.6	15 832	1.7	691	4.4	22 161	71.9	47.6	22.6
Methuen Town	29.3	979	30.6	8.5	91.5	5.1	26 016	1.0	1 666	6.4	37 959	69.3	43.6	26.1
New Bedford	57.2	763	30.4	19.7	86.2	4.4	47 095	0.2	4 798	10.2	76 099	62.4	33.2	35.8
Newton	30.5	1 638	27.9	6.5	84.9	11.2	46 087	1.8	1 908	4.1	70 206	66.8	42.7	22.3
Northampton	42.7	923	30.7	9.8	82.8	9.7	15 958	1.5	671	4.2	24 356	68.8	34.8	23.2
Peabody	39.4	1 259	30.6	9.4	90.7	6.5	28 568	1.1	1 518	5.3	43 359	65.9	40.2	30.8
Pittsfield	38.5	748	32.1	15.7	85.6	5.7	22 037	0.1	1 535	7.0	36 690	62.4	32.1	35.6
Quincy	53.3	1 202	29.3	16.2	83.2	11.7	52 855	1.6	2 921	5.5	79 205	69.8	44.1	24.5
Revere	47.6	1 137	34.2	20.2	87.4	8.5	28 399	1.4	1 665	5.9	44 193	69.7	42.5	26.8
Salem	53.4	1 064	30.2	16.9	82.5	12.6	23 663	1.1	1 391	5.9	36 023	67.0	40.6	31.1
Somerville	65.1	1 432	26.5	25.9	78.5	15.7	49 425	1.7	1 852	3.7	68 478	73.2	46.6	20.4
Springfield	52.6	817	38.6	22.3	83.4	6.3	64 038	0.1	6 935	10.8	117 413	58.4	30.2	37.7
Taunton	38.1	890	30.5	11.6	89.2	5.6	29 637	0.9	2 079	7.0	45 873	65.2	38.3	31.0
Waltham	50.5	1 352	26.8	10.4	82.8	13.2	36 388	1.8	1 595	4.4	53 945	70.0	43.7	22.3
Watertown Town	47.2	1 501	22.9	8.5	80.9	13.7	20 519	1.8	817	4.0	28 180	76.4	53.2	18.8
Westfield	31.4	828	30.8	7.1	85.2	9.3	20 934	1.5	1 383	6.6	33 814	65.9	36.8	26.6
West Springfield Town	42.2	819	26.3	10.0	84.7	11.6	14 575	1.2	928	6.4	23 341	66.4	40.1	28.6
Weymouth Town	33.0	1 116	30.0	9.3	91.3	5.5	30 116	1.5	1 743	5.8	45 308	69.1	42.6	28.0
Woburn	41.7	1 270	28.1	6.7	87.1	9.0	22 367	1.9	1 132	5.1	31 865	73.0	46.1	20.4
Worcester	56.8	901	31.9	16.6	84.9	7.4	90 753	1.2	6 389	7.0	147 158	63.5	37.2	30.6
MICHIGAN	28.8	764	32.3	8.0	85.2	11.3	4 750 279	0.5	347 972	7.3	7 891 768	61.3	34.9	32.3
Allen Park	15.2	890	28.1	4.3	92.4	5.7	13 582	-0.1	897	6.6	22 898	61.7	34.5	34.1
Ann Arbor	54.8	1 022	34.1	12.1	64.4	20.8	62 305	1.3	2 465	4.0	102 074	61.1	32.0	28.3
Battle Creek	40.2	675	32.7	12.5	79.9	9.9	23 506	1.3	1 728	7.4	40 108	60.5	34.1	36.0
Bay City	31.8	564	35.0	13.0	83.9	7.0	16 870	-0.6	1 547	9.2	26 961	61.2	31.0	36.8
Burton	27.5	769	34.2	9.1	87.4	8.7	13 545	-0.2	1 056	7.8	23 236	59.8	33.3	36.1
Dearborn	32.4	948	39.3	7.8	86.3	6.5	37 073	-0.1	2 460	6.6	70 669	53.9	30.2	31.7
Dearborn Heights	25.8	960	37.8	5.6	87.4	8.8	24 161	-0.3	1 798	7.4	44 385	56.8	31.4	35.6
Detroit	49.5	741	44.1	25.2	84.1	4.2	251 684	-1.9	41 992	16.7	541 204	52.7	23.6	46.6
East Lansing	65.6	850	50.0	11.1	44.9	37.8	23 500	0.9	1 005	4.3	44 889	52.9	16.1	30.6
Eastpointe	28.8	1 025	43.7	7.3	80.0	16.7	15 195	-0.6	1 785	11.7	25 195	62.8	33.1	35.4
Farmington Hills	37.7	992	28.5	6.6	82.4	14.6	42 236	0.7	1 860	4.4	66 607	65.4	41.4	25.4
Flint	43.0	658	46.4	18.5	78.3	8.4	35 476	-1.8	4 847	13.7	77 477	50.6	22.0	49.7
Garden City	21.6	930	31.2	5.5	87.4	10.1	14 218	-0.2	978	6.9	22 109	64.7	37.2	29.2
Grand Rapids	45.3	759	33.9	13.9	77.0	12.3	99 590	1.7	6 438	6.5	148 377	66.8	35.5	29.9
Holland	35.7	787	31.3	8.9	73.5	18.0	17 104	2.1	928	5.4	26 250	63.2	33.3	25.9
Inkster	48.3	721	38.9	17.2	78.1	15.8	8 883	-1.5	1 290	14.5	18 301	55.2	24.4	44.2
Jackson	50.5	642	34.8	15.9	72.5	12.8	14 105	-0.7	1 530	10.8	24 243	61.3	29.5	39.2
Kalamazoo	55.0	694	34.6	13.5	65.9	20.6	36 522	1.1	2 523	6.9	61 536	62.9	28.2	32.6
Kentwood	40.1	771	28.3	9.0	79.4	16.3	28 737	2.3	1 326	4.6	39 592	70.1	41.7	23.3
Lansing	50.6	720	34.6	12.8	77.5	11.9	57 960	-0.3	4 917	8.5	89 541	65.7	33.2	32.1
Lincoln Park	29.1	803	32.3	8.8	85.1	11.2	16 688	-0.3	1 292	7.7	29 542	59.2	34.2	32.5
Livonia	16.1	999	27.0	4.0	90.8	6.7	49 334	0.2	2 239	4.5	79 273	63.4	40.4	29.0
Madison Heights	37.6	719	32.1	12.2	85.1	10.0	15 259	-0.2	1 462	9.6	24 938	65.9	37.1	31.2
Midland	36.0	726	29.4	6.4	80.1	13.7	21 148	1.6	1 030	4.9	33 784	59.9	35.1	32.4
Mount Pleasant	63.9	687	42.4	12.3	51.7	29.0	13 163	1.1	779	5.9	23 634	59.8	19.9	29.6
Muskegon	48.7	613	41.2	19.9	76.5	14.5	14 021	-1.2	1 717	12.2	29 994	49.5	23.8	43.8
Novi	36.1	1 003	24.4	3.9	87.8	10.1	30 484	0.7	1 405	4.6	44 740	69.6	47.6	23.1

1. \$2,000 represents \$2,000 or more. 2. 50.0 represents 50 percent or more. 3. Percent of civilian labor force. 4. Persons 16 years old and over.

City	Value of residential construction authorized by building permits, 2014: New construction ($1,000)	Number of housing units	Percent single family	Wholesale trade,[1] 2007: Number of establish-ments	Number of employees	Sales (mil dol)	Annual payroll (mil dol)	Retail trade,[2] 2007: Number of establish-ments	Number of employees	Sales (mil dol)	Annual payroll (mil dol)
	69	70	71	72	73	74	75	76	77	78	79
MASSACHUSETTS—Cont'd											
Beverly	2 195	9	100.0	51	368	184.1	21.6	155	2 608	852.3	70.1
Boston	687 770	2 841	1.7	565	10 156	6 225.7	583.8	2 157	27 909	6 808.8	725.3
Braintree Town	7 178	55	7.3	NA	NA	NA	NA	NA	NA	NA	NA
Brockton	27 765	175	30.3	65	1 062	757.7	54.6	329	5 208	1 263.5	138.6
Cambridge	63 800	285	10.9	90	1 693	2 066.4	189.9	474	6 627	1 287.7	150.6
Chelsea	35 894	385	0.0	90	1 606	2 447.5	94.2	78	1 334	348.2	36.1
Chicopee	3 276	22	81.8	36	922	725.5	42.4	167	2 582	721.3	62.9
Everett	49 605	437	3.7	61	1 566	1 050.6	84.6	120	1 811	496.7	45.7
Fall River	3 895	38	100.0	76	1 642	727.8	63.9	298	3 488	931.2	91.4
Fitchburg	4 012	24	83.3	32	249	105.8	11.8	144	1 876	489.5	42.8
Franklin Town	10 969	47	44.7	NA	NA	NA	NA	NA	NA	NA	NA
Gloucester	16 825	65	63.1	56	417	491.5	21.3	117	1 146	253.7	29.2
Haverhill	12 536	101	36.6	51	722	266.2	39.3	143	2 230	648.0	60.2
Holyoke	650	4	50.0	29	421	125.3	16.3	261	4 373	712.6	77.6
Lawrence	4 151	33	18.2	66	1 204	538.2	58.1	173	1 579	429.6	45.9
Leominster	14 212	46	95.7	48	730	429.0	37.3	221	3 896	766.0	76.7
Lowell	17 531	101	64.4	65	964	523.4	51.0	224	2 331	573.9	54.1
Lynn	6 011	59	18.6	41	526	430.8	26.7	215	2 276	623.8	57.1
Malden	1 241	12	83.3	32	515	229.9	26.2	131	1 397	456.9	35.0
Marlborough	3 854	29	100.0	80	1 973	1 051.3	184.0	225	3 543	758.0	69.4
Medford	1 001	8	50.0	47	809	413.0	40.0	160	2 312	596.3	59.9
Melrose	612	3	100.0	11	73	24.6	4.2	61	768	173.1	19.1
Methuen Town	37 012	123	96.7	33	735	1 721.2	46.0	107	2 157	486.0	49.9
New Bedford	2 118	19	100.0	100	1 746	919.5	79.4	305	3 061	727.0	71.9
Newton	28 106	67	82.1	116	2 246	4 040.0	126.8	378	5 680	1 153.6	156.1
Northampton	9 554	39	69.2	28	217	65.1	7.6	185	2 140	468.9	50.7
Peabody	5 063	25	100.0	76	2 037	4 327.3	141.1	273	5 071	1 219.5	132.5
Pittsfield	2 926	13	100.0	43	561	217.9	22.5	209	3 205	747.8	77.3
Quincy	13 312	119	9.2	58	739	530.4	36.6	245	4 032	1 142.2	105.0
Revere	7 531	48	12.5	26	D	D	D	115	1 665	360.4	34.3
Salem	1 305	6	100.0	39	314	166.3	17.0	173	2 680	544.2	64.4
Somerville	0	0	0.0	46	560	291.2	33.4	172	2 962	761.5	69.1
Springfield	8 653	43	90.7	123	1 892	1 097.0	94.4	485	6 592	1 521.3	150.5
Taunton	10 461	87	58.6	57	1 932	1 393.0	105.4	242	4 868	1 085.1	107.3
Waltham	16 246	51	80.4	115	2 961	8 050.6	283.0	224	2 932	811.3	85.6
Watertown Town	2 609	13	15.4	39	506	193.4	26.5	171	3 392	889.4	97.8
Westfield	5 498	26	84.6	38	1 109	1 826.1	45.0	144	2 198	530.8	51.0
West Springfield Town	4 864	25	40.0	NA	NA	NA	NA	NA	NA	NA	NA
Weymouth Town	13 488	75	42.7	NA	NA	NA	NA	NA	NA	NA	NA
Woburn	16 246	67	67.2	224	3 716	2 178.4	215.0	192	3 601	1 010.7	111.9
Worcester	11 051	104	84.6	209	2 968	1 321.9	139.0	593	8 591	1 923.3	205.4
MICHIGAN	3 314 833	15 933	77.7	9 892	137 315	107 109.3	7 016.1	37 619	470 794	109 102.6	10 001.5
Allen Park	0	0	0.0	17	209	132.8	11.5	111	1 680	297.0	31.2
Ann Arbor	6 636	24	91.7	73	641	364.1	39.4	518	7 836	1 467.2	165.7
Battle Creek	1 927	10	100.0	39	490	344.6	21.9	261	3 920	757.6	72.7
Bay City	189	1	100.0	46	571	217.1	26.9	156	1 338	274.8	29.1
Burton	1 256	8	100.0	25	244	68.9	10.5	180	2 799	538.9	55.0
Dearborn	6 573	22	100.0	134	1 549	1 733.8	78.5	556	6 001	1 181.6	110.7
Dearborn Heights	3 668	12	100.0	42	152	69.4	6.3	193	1 781	377.8	35.0
Detroit	33 443	238	13.9	450	7 278	7 112.1	381.1	2 157	12 933	3 271.8	265.3
East Lansing	842	7	100.0	15	68	55.6	3.9	76	1 488	278.3	24.2
Eastpointe	60	1	100.0	19	56	13.3	2.0	137	1 404	342.7	37.7
Farmington Hills	14 452	43	100.0	212	2 920	2 236.2	188.5	267	4 095	1 151.2	103.6
Flint	786	6	100.0	71	1 557	757.6	95.5	432	4 597	876.5	89.6
Garden City	50	1	100.0	12	50	10.5	1.1	115	1 126	404.4	32.9
Grand Rapids	32 210	203	36.9	222	5 471	3 319.6	280.7	613	6 933	1 500.4	154.5
Holland	2 432	13	100.0	47	767	440.8	43.1	177	2 248	509.1	46.5
Inkster	75	0	0.0	9	152	76.7	11.9	51	278	72.3	5.5
Jackson	241	1	100.0	61	972	733.7	48.6	191	1 868	398.1	40.7
Kalamazoo	3 730	13	100.0	102	1 503	611.6	61.9	301	3 160	637.3	68.7
Kentwood	11 491	157	97.5	127	2 549	1 395.8	122.3	303	4 914	898.6	95.4
Lansing	4 509	14	100.0	125	1 949	1 657.6	88.9	451	6 709	1 552.2	149.7
Lincoln Park	0	0	0.0	14	165	75.4	7.1	140	1 637	347.3	32.9
Livonia	10 247	41	100.0	279	4 608	4 355.0	224.4	506	7 560	2 683.7	169.0
Madison Heights	988	11	100.0	111	1 943	965.8	102.6	175	3 589	891.5	84.4
Midland	11 801	199	22.1	32	D	D	D	244	3 910	746.7	71.1
Mount Pleasant	4 204	62	11.3	27	526	197.5	12.6	132	2 661	496.1	47.7
Muskegon	571	4	100.0	37	961	394.7	48.8	145	2 121	407.5	43.5
Novi	36 491	203	97.5	151	2 259	3 321.6	139.4	359	6 845	1 361.1	143.7

1. Merchant wholesalers except manufacturers' sales branches and offices. 2. Establishments with payroll.

City	Real estate and rental and leasing, 2007				Professional, scientific, and technical services,[1] 2007				Manufacturing, 2007			
	Number of establish-ments	Number of employees	Receipts (mil dol)	Annual payroll (mil dol)	Number of establish-ments	Number of employees	Receipts (mil dol)	Annual payroll (mil dol)	Number of establish-ments	Number of employees	Receipts (mil dol)	Annual payroll (mil dol)
	80	81	82	83	84	85	86	87	88	89	90	91
MASSACHUSETTS—Cont'd												
Beverly	43	193	31.8	6.8	164	D	D	D	57	3 090	722.2	208.3
Boston	1 022	11 955	5 544.2	846.9	2 971	52 195	13 235.0	5 456.7	319	9 922	3 193.3	580.7
Braintree Town	NA	NA	NA	NA	NA	NA	NA	NA	NA	NA	NA	NA
Brockton	56	317	49.2	10.0	150	D	D	D	91	2 702	443.3	104.2
Cambridge	160	937	332.5	44.6	824	D	D	D	75	2 906	800.2	184.4
Chelsea	25	137	15.4	4.3	37	385	45.1	20.2	43	2 102	367.8	73.0
Chicopee	44	161	31.2	4.9	48	220	21.0	8.4	85	4 401	1 118.3	192.7
Everett	18	92	17.0	4.2	36	145	12.1	4.2	49	811	145.8	37.5
Fall River	87	339	61.8	9.8	169	D	D	D	164	6 067	1 060.1	215.2
Fitchburg	35	142	18.3	3.5	63	314	28.3	10.6	74	2 271	464.4	102.7
Franklin Town	NA	NA	NA	NA	NA	NA	NA	NA	NA	NA	NA	NA
Gloucester	28	92	11.1	2.4	99	D	D	D	53	2 941	1 218.7	211.9
Haverhill	49	238	40.7	8.9	114	739	80.6	33.3	97	2 658	601.2	109.7
Holyoke	48	422	74.9	11.2	59	D	D	D	82	2 233	451.8	98.6
Lawrence	42	242	38.5	7.6	84	D	D	D	100	4 491	851.2	174.4
Leominster	44	295	46.7	12.8	99	D	D	D	97	3 225	1 024.3	142.3
Lowell	81	543	77.0	13.5	143	D	D	D	77	3 905	762.9	209.9
Lynn	54	275	53.5	8.1	86	D	D	D	43	4 887	D	D
Malden	62	318	111.3	13.5	77	528	37.2	14.7	48	1 694	372.3	71.0
Marlborough	51	242	70.3	8.9	176	D	D	D	73	6 934	2 661.5	638.8
Medford	37	189	43.3	7.0	115	D	D	D	39	506	79.9	23.5
Melrose	22	63	16.1	2.1	76	261	32.3	12.4	NA	NA	NA	NA
Methuen Town	39	136	22.5	4.5	85	369	47.4	19.4	42	1 641	543.5	90.4
New Bedford	81	400	53.6	12.4	181	D	D	D	129	7 611	1 995.0	292.4
Newton	166	1 677	1 370.8	83.8	599	D	D	D	48	787	284.9	43.4
Northampton	39	122	21.0	3.1	123	D	D	D	38	1 381	466.0	73.0
Peabody	46	318	76.0	10.4	112	854	113.1	43.4	74	2 784	708.4	165.4
Pittsfield	44	283	32.0	7.4	134	D	D	D	52	2 787	552.3	152.9
Quincy	96	706	106.2	27.8	294	D	D	D	47	613	246.1	35.3
Revere	23	332	31.2	7.5	44	237	17.8	7.4	16	D	D	D
Salem	39	205	40.2	7.4	171	D	D	D	49	789	157.9	39.4
Somerville	67	263	61.1	10.4	173	D	D	D	67	1 523	269.2	78.3
Springfield	117	772	119.9	27.9	354	D	D	D	123	4 822	1 158.3	226.4
Taunton	39	135	38.4	3.8	107	2 335	576.0	152.1	71	5 292	1 388.5	386.6
Waltham	97	906	196.2	40.6	404	D	D	D	117	4 172	1 017.4	231.3
Watertown Town	39	526	122.6	38.3	120	D	D	D	50	1 692	392.7	108.3
Westfield	37	162	25.0	4.1	62	499	75.0	28.1	97	3 323	783.4	153.3
West Springfield Town	NA	NA	NA	NA	NA	NA	NA	NA	NA	NA	NA	NA
Weymouth Town	NA	NA	NA	NA	NA	NA	NA	NA	NA	NA	NA	NA
Woburn	72	806	139.7	43.8	298	D	D	D	153	4 869	1 596.7	312.3
Worcester	169	1 526	295.0	51.7	451	D	D	D	212	8 673	2 116.0	454.6
MICHIGAN	8 862	54 874	12 858.6	1 685.7	22 552	249 864	29 536.8	15 304.5	13 675	581 739	234 455.8	29 910.3
Allen Park	27	D	D	D	57	1 813	113.7	80.5	NA	NA	NA	NA
Ann Arbor	175	1 685	405.9	58.0	602	7 037	799.1	455.3	64	1 400	D	62.0
Battle Creek	52	337	48.1	9.2	101	D	D	D	78	8 084	3 825.1	392.8
Bay City	31	136	13.1	2.5	97	754	56.3	33.0	52	2 103	613.3	127.0
Burton	19	107	16.2	4.7	40	220	20.8	6.1	NA	NA	NA	NA
Dearborn	102	D	D	D	284	D	D	D	96	10 493	D	759.2
Dearborn Heights	40	D	D	D	70	361	32.7	15.2	NA	NA	NA	NA
Detroit	321	D	D	D	685	13 636	2 451.1	929.0	472	22 962	20 216.1	1 486.3
East Lansing	58	687	61.7	20.5	126	D	D	D	NA	NA	NA	NA
Eastpointe	16	75	9.1	2.1	40	221	14.5	6.7	NA	NA	NA	NA
Farmington Hills	200	4 754	548.4	179.2	743	10 597	1 570.9	759.6	104	2 250	645.3	115.9
Flint	81	519	67.7	12.5	171	D	D	D	76	9 791	D	D
Garden City	13	D	D	D	17	75	7.4	3.1	NA	NA	NA	NA
Grand Rapids	188	1 136	145.9	27.9	615	D	D	D	315	19 627	5 497.9	1 068.9
Holland	39	204	35.3	5.9	98	D	D	D	99	8 901	2 669.1	367.1
Inkster	23	D	D	D	9	25	1.7	0.7	NA	NA	NA	NA
Jackson	45	201	26.3	4.0	102	D	D	D	101	2 578	660.6	107.7
Kalamazoo	98	807	83.3	18.3	236	D	D	D	116	4 462	1 347.5	210.5
Kentwood	56	417	82.1	10.5	132	1 418	173.3	68.9	130	8 624	1 838.1	357.2
Lansing	101	924	119.8	23.2	247	D	D	D	95	5 096	D	327.4
Lincoln Park	18	D	D	D	29	D	D	D	NA	NA	NA	NA
Livonia	139	1 077	150.9	28.1	394	D	D	D	280	11 265	3 195.9	604.9
Madison Heights	43	396	82.4	24.9	122	1 523	173.7	76.0	163	4 288	872.8	200.8
Midland	67	D	D	D	124	D	D	D	36	4 487	D	344.4
Mount Pleasant	33	D	D	D	81	1 141	48.8	26.7	26	D	D	D
Muskegon	19	100	12.4	2.6	86	D	D	D	79	3 806	991.6	173.4
Novi	78	497	94.0	19.0	274	4 007	589.0	259.7	80	2 211	D	109.7

1. Establishments subject to federal tax.

Table D. Cities — Accommodation and Food Services, Arts, Entertainment, and Recreation, and Health Care and Social Assistance

City	Accommodation and food services, 2007				Arts, entertainment, and recreation,[1] 2007				Health care and social assistance,[1] 2007			
	Number of establish-ments	Number of employees	Sales (mil dol)	Annual payroll (mil dol)	Number of establish-ments	Number of employees	Receipts (mil dol)	Annual payroll (mil dol)	Number of establish-ments	Number of employees	Receipts (mil dol)	Annual payroll (mil dol)
	92	93	94	95	96	97	98	99	100	101	102	103
MASSACHUSETTS—Cont'd												
Beverly	117	1 354	72.7	21.3	19	D	D	D	119	D	D	D
Boston	2 073	46 895	3 661.7	1 057.5	182	D	D	D	899	18 698	3 110.4	1 379.7
Braintree Town	NA	NA	NA	NA	NA	NA	NA	NA	NA	NA	NA	NA
Brockton	155	2 812	122.8	40.9	14	248	11.7	3.5	198	3 585	364.3	180.0
Cambridge	398	8 044	594.9	172.8	50	651	133.4	20.7	214	3 195	510.3	195.3
Chelsea	56	556	33.4	8.6	NA	NA	NA	NA	30	635	47.6	20.4
Chicopee	118	1 575	68.7	19.7	3	D	D	D	48	942	62.7	27.5
Everett	77	D	D	D	5	D	D	D	43	D	D	D
Fall River	181	2 574	105.5	29.9	13	D	D	D	200	3 976	351.5	167.6
Fitchburg	89	1 145	53.6	15.4	6	D	D	D	80	1 299	106.6	45.4
Franklin Town	NA	NA	NA	NA	NA	NA	NA	NA	NA	NA	NA	NA
Gloucester	119	1 031	61.1	17.9	15	111	11.5	3.8	55	488	49.8	22.7
Haverhill	124	1 695	84.0	23.3	24	D	D	D	98	2 404	254.5	98.1
Holyoke	96	D	D	D	9	81	5.5	1.5	82	1 262	107.0	52.4
Lawrence	91	858	42.1	11.1	5	39	2.3	0.4	67	1 017	136.9	56.1
Leominster	97	1 874	79.6	25.2	16	D	D	D	97	1 554	132.5	61.1
Lowell	183	2 207	107.9	28.8	17	388	14.1	5.0	145	2 819	252.6	125.8
Lynn	140	1 169	63.4	16.4	9	129	9.1	2.2	103	1 459	119.2	55.0
Malden	96	1 033	52.4	15.4	10	69	5.1	1.6	75	917	96.9	31.1
Marlborough	140	2 462	127.8	38.2	14	278	14.6	3.8	70	1 054	91.4	38.3
Medford	92	1 300	82.6	19.2	10	D	D	D	91	D	D	D
Melrose	36	377	20.4	5.9	2	D	D	D	67	D	D	D
Methuen Town	97	1 485	76.3	22.5	10	310	12.7	3.4	90	864	82.9	40.1
New Bedford	211	2 496	101.3	27.1	19	D	D	D	137	2 700	234.0	105.8
Newton	177	D	D	D	44	359	87.3	22.7	388	5 190	587.1	271.2
Northampton	101	1 874	81.7	25.5	18	113	7.6	2.0	108	1 603	153.7	78.0
Peabody	125	2 468	137.5	40.2	7	D	D	D	112	2 291	281.7	119.9
Pittsfield	131	2 142	92.6	28.1	18	214	10.9	3.2	146	1 679	182.7	86.8
Quincy	234	3 264	188.7	52.0	20	D	D	D	196	3 878	383.1	155.8
Revere	101	1 340	90.1	22.2	5	D	D	D	49	D	D	D
Salem	122	1 710	98.5	29.0	20	234	12.5	3.9	115	D	D	D
Somerville	181	D	D	D	16	D	D	D	59	1 026	117.1	44.7
Springfield	294	4 867	222.5	65.5	16	119	7.8	2.2	291	5 910	618.5	305.1
Taunton	111	2 130	90.8	27.4	6	D	D	D	86	1 045	125.8	50.7
Waltham	272	3 647	252.9	70.5	33	477	29.6	8.0	137	2 360	249.4	102.4
Watertown Town	90	1 117	64.0	17.4	10	303	16.7	5.0	88	1 340	170.9	62.4
Westfield	76	1 039	43.7	12.8	10	D	D	D	79	722	64.5	29.7
West Springfield Town	NA	NA	NA	NA	NA	NA	NA	NA	NA	NA	NA	NA
Weymouth Town	NA	NA	NA	NA	NA	NA	NA	NA	NA	NA	NA	NA
Woburn	100	1 855	115.7	31.1	15	D	D	D	107	1 936	279.3	96.5
Worcester	430	5 843	302.0	85.9	28	1 087	26.5	7.8	401	9 043	1 084.4	439.7
MICHIGAN	19 678	339 181	14 536.6	4 207.3	2 975	41 065	3 940.6	1 170.2	21 150	228 681	21 054.9	9 168.6
Allen Park	77	1 537	61.6	18.7	11	D	D	D	83	1 087	87.5	38.4
Ann Arbor	338	7 686	372.7	108.3	38	230	13.0	3.9	316	D	D	D
Battle Creek	145	2 830	110.2	33.6	14	252	8.4	3.7	159	2 051	192.8	77.3
Bay City	104	1 601	48.4	15.1	12	D	D	D	111	D	D	D
Burton	65	1 158	44.9	12.6	9	104	1.7	0.5	81	D	D	D
Dearborn	281	5 031	255.0	76.8	20	D	D	D	358	D	D	D
Dearborn Heights	99	1 718	64.6	18.5	9	D	D	D	91	926	80.7	34.3
Detroit	958	16 550	1 253.9	333.3	65	8 209	1 388.0	389.9	719	9 945	822.9	356.1
East Lansing	109	2 602	104.8	28.7	6	D	D	D	110	1 757	178.2	95.8
Eastpointe	51	749	28.0	8.5	5	D	D	D	94	D	D	D
Farmington Hills	172	2 758	131.9	37.5	32	D	D	D	417	4 287	432.5	191.1
Flint	183	2 152	87.2	22.5	5	D	D	D	182	1 638	224.9	77.5
Garden City	46	725	28.2	7.1	8	D	D	D	70	D	D	D
Grand Rapids	396	8 765	331.7	105.3	46	647	33.0	10.0	379	5 548	597.9	242.7
Holland	91	1 965	68.3	24.3	6	81	2.4	1.0	95	1 585	132.5	62.2
Inkster	23	187	10.5	2.6	1	D	D	D	17	118	6.3	2.3
Jackson	107	1 749	66.4	18.5	9	115	5.0	1.4	146	1 779	202.9	98.0
Kalamazoo	199	4 543	167.0	54.1	25	411	16.3	5.3	168	3 061	257.0	134.3
Kentwood	105	2 278	94.9	28.2	10	D	D	D	100	1 537	163.1	69.1
Lansing	227	3 774	152.7	44.4	19	398	63.1	8.9	233	D	D	D
Lincoln Park	66	944	39.7	9.5	5	D	D	D	64	638	57.1	26.0
Livonia	243	5 634	246.2	71.4	26	D	D	D	420	4 576	394.7	173.4
Madison Heights	104	1 861	79.7	22.3	10	116	8.8	2.4	99	D	D	D
Midland	102	2 267	97.1	27.8	10	D	D	D	155	D	D	D
Mount Pleasant	89	2 564	87.1	24.4	6	D	D	D	116	1 075	76.7	35.4
Muskegon	80	1 357	53.8	15.1	9	D	D	D	124	1 904	225.4	121.9
Novi	151	3 825	178.7	53.1	16	D	D	D	200	D	D	D

1. Establishments subject to federal tax.

Table D. Cities — **Other Services and Government Employment and Payroll**

City	Other services[1], 2007				Government employment and payroll, 2012								
						March payroll							
							Percent of total for:						
	Number of establish- ments	Number of employees	Receipts (mil dol)	Annual payroll (mil dol)	Full-time equivalent employees	Total (dollars)	Adminis- tration, judicial, and legal	Police and Corrections	Fire Protection	Highways and trans- portation	Health and welfare	Natural resources and utilities	Education and libraries
	104	105	106	107	108	109	110	111	112	113	114	115	116
MASSACHUSETTS—Cont'd													
Beverly	66	650	32.8	13.5	996	4 817 626	4.0	11.2	9.0	4.5	1.8	2.6	66.3
Boston	1 041	8 143	704.5	200.9	19 230	112 444 857	3.5	18.3	12.2	2.2	8.9	3.5	49.1
Braintree Town	NA	NA	NA	NA	1 198	6 476 545	2.5	10.2	9.4	2.2	1.8	15.8	58.0
Brockton	136	928	68.9	23.1	3 168	15 359 504	2.3	8.6	7.5	1.3	0.8	2.7	75.2
Cambridge	147	1 114	104.0	29.4	5 751	29 806 492	5.4	9.0	6.6	1.8	37.9	3.3	26.6
Chelsea	33	D	D	D	1 195	6 010 338	2.8	12.8	10.5	1.7	2.0	0.7	68.2
Chicopee	86	414	31.4	9.5	1 968	9 607 115	2.4	8.9	8.8	2.2	1.0	8.2	68.6
Everett	66	468	38.4	14.0	1 148	6 059 197	2.8	14.5	12.3	1.2	2.1	1.4	63.1
Fall River	148	745	52.9	15.5	2 306	10 353 050	2.4	15.4	12.8	3.5	0.6	2.2	61.8
Fitchburg	55	227	21.3	7.0	1 151	5 547 200	3.4	9.4	7.3	2.6	1.4	5.1	70.3
Franklin Town	NA	NA	NA	NA	966	4 884 796	3.9	7.4	6.9	0.9	1.2	3.4	75.4
Gloucester	56	239	17.5	5.6	1 097	5 414 614	3.5	6.3	6.5	1.4	2.1	2.0	78.1
Haverhill	80	D	D	D	1 832	8 913 896	3.7	7.9	7.8	2.3	3.5	5.7	67.6
Holyoke	50	238	16.9	4.9	1 884	8 334 885	2.7	13.7	8.2	1.9	1.5	16.1	55.4
Lawrence	82	519	43.1	14.7	537	3 239 260	9.3	38.4	19.3	2.8	4.3	18.5	2.0
Leominster	59	239	21.7	5.7	1 158	5 702 455	3.5	8.2	8.6	2.7	4.5	1.1	71.5
Lowell	142	695	56.9	18.6	2 860	17 379 993	21.6	7.8	6.2	1.2	1.9	2.6	57.2
Lynn	105	547	49.3	14.1	3 200	15 232 790	2.0	9.3	9.0	0.6	2.4	2.0	71.9
Malden	98	472	45.2	13.8	1 385	7 796 658	4.0	11.7	8.4	1.5	2.2	1.1	67.0
Marlborough	64	439	71.0	12.5	1 155	5 341 768	2.6	10.8	7.8	2.2	2.8	3.2	68.1
Medford	102	592	53.8	17.1	1 214	5 909 654	4.2	14.6	12.9	2.3	1.5	3.3	61.4
Melrose	34	177	19.0	5.8	763	3 328 642	4.7	9.6	9.5	2.3	3.8	3.1	64.8
Methuen Town	62	D	D	D	1 087	7 336 774	2.5	10.2	7.0	2.2	1.2	5.3	71.1
New Bedford	150	855	87.6	24.4	2 769	11 838 508	3.4	15.9	8.7	0.5	2.2	2.3	64.5
Newton	177	1 125	97.4	34.2	2 832	16 441 085	4.0	8.3	7.3	3.8	2.0	4.3	68.5
Northampton	69	335	22.6	7.7	1 315	6 640 659	6.9	16.3	15.0	3.3	4.8	8.4	45.1
Peabody	100	562	55.0	13.9	1 445	6 993 068	3.9	10.1	8.5	2.0	3.4	9.6	59.9
Pittsfield	83	483	34.3	12.3	1 418	6 191 800	2.1	11.1	7.7	3.1	2.0	2.3	70.3
Quincy	179	869	86.4	26.2	2 107	11 341 562	3.7	14.1	12.3	2.7	1.9	3.4	58.4
Revere	74	316	33.4	9.0	1 148	6 190 389	2.9	10.4	9.9	1.4	2.2	0.9	70.9
Salem	87	366	35.9	10.4	1 293	5 566 047	3.8	10.4	7.7	2.3	1.1	2.1	70.6
Somerville	99	1 295	99.2	35.3	1 637	10 044 072	4.6	10.5	15.6	1.3	3.6	1.4	56.7
Springfield	197	1 636	119.8	40.5	6 400	28 244 315	2.7	10.9	5.2	0.8	1.6	1.8	75.7
Taunton	78	352	26.6	8.2	1 574	7 371 663	2.8	12.1	9.6	1.1	6.5	4.4	62.0
Waltham	128	826	127.5	32.9	1 543	7 799 064	4.9	13.2	11.2	3.6	1.6	2.7	59.4
Watertown Town	65	842	90.1	43.2	718	3 483 060	6.4	20.3	14.0	1.6	1.6	4.8	50.1
Westfield	62	346	30.7	10.9	1 493	7 020 504	2.4	7.7	7.1	1.5	0.9	11.5	68.2
West Springfield Town	NA	NA	NA	NA	976	3 909 287	3.2	12.1	9.7	5.8	0.8	0.5	65.8
Weymouth Town	NA	NA	NA	NA	1 151	5 346 322	0.0	0.0	0.0	0.0	0.0	0.0	100.0
Woburn	95	D	D	D	1 052	4 899 436	3.8	10.6	8.5	4.3	1.8	2.5	67.9
Worcester	259	1 801	166.9	50.2	5 736	34 255 682	3.1	10.9	7.3	1.4	1.6	2.9	72.6
MICHIGAN	13 953	79 193	6 221.1	1 956.5	X	X	X	X	X	X	X	X	X
Allen Park	41	250	16.4	5.8	145	695 062	17.1	36.5	23.7	3.5	2.1	12.0	1.1
Ann Arbor	147	953	62.6	22.3	1 014	4 848 561	15.1	39.8	10.1	6.4	0.3	20.8	0.0
Battle Creek	87	D	D	D	520	2 297 856	15.9	27.9	16.4	20.0	2.1	17.3	0.0
Bay City	63	441	33.4	10.3	307	1 423 139	12.6	19.6	15.4	7.2	3.8	41.4	0.0
Burton	66	298	25.0	7.8	88	380 820	19.8	42.5	6.3	13.2	3.7	10.2	0.0
Dearborn	189	875	70.7	21.6	923	3 654 827	12.9	29.4	13.1	4.0	5.7	11.8	4.5
Dearborn Heights	93	434	32.5	10.0	306	1 426 569	13.6	40.6	19.1	3.5	0.6	11.8	3.5
Detroit	698	4 200	321.6	107.5	12 364	57 433 160	8.6	36.8	19.2	8.8	3.7	16.3	1.7
East Lansing	26	229	9.6	2.7	396	1 817 436	16.7	32.0	14.5	2.5	2.2	20.9	4.6
Eastpointe	57	230	21.3	6.6	180	830 736	14.8	39.6	19.5	6.0	0.0	11.0	3.5
Farmington Hills	149	943	82.9	25.9	445	2 178 404	16.2	39.5	19.9	10.2	0.0	13.4	0.0
Flint	129	923	54.4	30.7	3 484	16 192 746	3.4	5.1	4.1	1.1	80.7	4.6	0.0
Garden City	46	197	13.7	4.2	125	1 093 459	18.2	37.0	20.6	11.9	0.0	10.8	1.6
Grand Rapids	237	1 707	123.8	42.5	1 502	7 515 829	14.9	31.3	17.1	6.5	4.9	18.7	5.4
Holland	58	515	32.9	13.6	501	2 186 069	19.7	18.0	6.4	11.0	2.5	31.8	8.0
Inkster	19	D	D	D	210	862 765	16.2	39.6	11.9	3.5	10.7	10.1	0.0
Jackson	63	524	47.0	15.3	317	1 468 468	14.1	26.2	16.9	10.7	9.1	20.9	0.0
Kalamazoo	132	1 188	97.4	31.5	737	3 816 582	9.9	48.7	0.0	14.8	4.0	21.7	0.0
Kentwood	72	596	41.1	13.0	223	1 105 109	17.7	43.8	20.2	4.1	0.4	7.1	0.0
Lansing	150	1 314	86.5	28.7	1 615	8 042 053	9.4	18.0	12.0	4.6	2.5	31.5	0.0
Lincoln Park	68	336	25.6	8.0	136	745 448	11.3	45.2	24.4	3.7	3.5	7.7	0.1
Livonia	224	1 544	173.2	46.0	675	3 250 072	15.0	29.9	18.3	6.5	2.1	12.7	4.9
Madison Heights	76	761	79.8	25.4	168	954 270	18.4	39.5	19.8	4.4	6.9	6.2	3.1
Midland	76	616	47.5	13.4	384	1 817 246	18.5	13.7	13.1	13.3	3.3	24.4	7.5
Mount Pleasant	51	314	16.4	5.0	138	584 882	17.9	28.1	11.5	10.7	3.3	20.6	0.0
Muskegon	49	314	21.0	6.8	249	1 066 412	10.8	37.4	17.3	11.3	4.4	11.2	0.0
Novi	90	832	57.3	24.2	303	1 465 600	14.7	34.8	16.3	10.0	0.9	6.5	8.2

1. Establishments subject to federal tax.

City	City government finances, 2007									
	General revenue							General expenditure		
		Intergovernmental		Taxes					Per capita[1] (dollars)	
					Per capita[1] (dollars)					
	Total (mil dol)	Total (mil dol)	Percent from state government	Total (mil dol)	Total	Property	Sales and gross receipts	Total (mil dol)	Total	Capital outlays
	117	118	119	120	121	122	123	124	125	126
MASSACHUSETTS—Cont'd										
Beverly	134.3	32.2	93.2	84.0	2 083	2 032	50	122.1	3 027	262
Boston	3 134.7	946.2	90.8	1 822.2	2 844	2 612	231	3 160.4	4 932	468
Braintree Town	122.1	30.7	98.2	76.9	2 110	2 032	78	126.4	3 467	261
Brockton	341.1	188.9	94.9	118.0	1 255	1 218	36	341.2	3 628	290
Cambridge	1 412.6	295.2	74.5	338.8	3 195	2 843	352	1 310.4	12 357	887
Chelsea	149.1	80.2	94.0	48.9	1 320	1 254	66	146.8	3 958	166
Chicopee	183.1	93.0	88.2	72.3	1 298	1 255	43	183.1	3 289	279
Everett	159.8	65.9	97.2	88.8	2 084	2 072	12	163.2	3 832	25
Fall River	291.2	173.4	87.5	84.8	956	911	46	273.3	3 082	273
Fitchburg	133.3	69.5	95.2	44.8	1 108	1 068	40	123.9	3 067	250
Franklin Town	113.1	39.1	99.7	62.6	1 932	1 864	68	108.1	3 337	214
Gloucester	108.7	22.2	85.3	70.1	2 398	2 265	133	118.1	4 041	621
Haverhill	179.2	72.3	95.2	91.2	1 477	1 436	41	178.9	2 897	125
Holyoke	180.1	108.6	96.0	51.5	1 283	1 249	34	193.1	4 810	387
Lawrence	293.4	219.3	93.9	57.3	741	711	30	270.5	3 497	39
Leominster	137.6	72.2	98.2	57.3	1 401	1 379	22	130.9	3 200	778
Lowell	379.7	222.6	91.4	119.6	1 102	1 055	47	358.5	3 303	268
Lynn	304.3	187.6	95.4	107.6	1 179	1 155	24	313.0	3 429	13
Malden	196.5	94.6	92.6	74.5	1 234	1 215	19	199.3	3 301	386
Marlborough	132.1	30.2	96.1	91.0	2 319	2 265	54	126.8	3 229	96
Medford	142.6	31.8	91.0	94.1	1 650	1 604	46	142.2	2 492	58
Melrose	82.1	18.2	97.0	52.8	1 924	1 914	10	86.2	3 141	285
Methuen Town	133.7	50.8	97.6	70.6	1 469	1 434	35	135.9	2 829	221
New Bedford	342.6	197.7	87.3	103.4	1 091	1 041	50	319.6	3 371	394
Newton	352.9	45.9	82.2	268.4	3 076	2 977	99	348.0	3 989	200
Northampton	93.2	21.7	85.3	47.2	1 647	1 575	72	100.6	3 506	673
Peabody	155.1	38.9	89.5	98.2	1 894	1 799	95	155.3	2 995	158
Pittsfield	156.1	75.8	92.6	70.5	1 592	1 549	43	180.6	4 076	509
Quincy	303.7	68.6	83.6	184.2	1 983	1 919	64	317.7	3 420	279
Revere	167.2	86.7	75.9	74.7	1 396	1 343	53	159.6	2 981	128
Salem	150.4	51.6	89.1	76.8	1 818	1 779	39	149.1	3 528	208
Somerville	214.8	65.2	90.3	115.7	1 489	1 387	102	222.7	2 865	243
Springfield	710.6	501.8	92.6	183.4	1 192	1 136	56	702.0	4 562	459
Taunton	200.1	101.1	96.2	78.0	1 394	1 336	58	198.2	3 540	473
Waltham	215.4	26.2	94.8	161.6	2 606	2 487	119	206.3	3 326	185
Watertown Town	111.0	16.6	95.8	77.8	2 365	2 342	23	108.0	3 282	224
Westfield	141.0	61.2	91.3	63.5	1 541	1 514	27	132.3	3 207	439
West Springfield Town	111.8	41.7	97.5	63.7	2 226	2 135	90	122.2	4 273	802
Weymouth Town	149.6	43.6	97.1	86.4	1 571	1 532	40	133.5	2 426	127
Woburn	134.2	22.5	96.5	94.7	2 436	2 328	108	140.9	3 624	251
Worcester	673.9	351.9	90.1	250.3	1 373	1 328	45	681.7	3 738	461
MICHIGAN	X	X	X	X	X	X	X	X	X	X
Allen Park	38.0	4.5	94.9	19.7	707	622	85	43.2	1 545	192
Ann Arbor	205.6	39.3	54.4	89.8	775	705	70	199.0	1 717	426
Battle Creek	117.1	35.5	38.6	47.3	913	607	16	105.6	2 035	231
Bay City	52.3	16.3	64.9	12.8	371	359	12	52.6	1 522	200
Burton	18.2	5.5	93.6	4.3	148	132	16	18.3	623	116
Dearborn	175.2	29.5	56.1	86.0	888	866	22	163.2	1 685	219
Dearborn Heights	74.1	29.6	29.1	28.0	490	465	25	61.3	1 071	5
Detroit	2 146.1	681.0	63.6	750.8	1 078	381	362	2 248.4	3 227	289
East Lansing	62.4	13.1	74.3	22.1	455	428	27	63.0	1 296	67
Eastpointe	33.6	7.4	68.2	15.1	466	436	30	35.4	1 090	71
Farmington Hills	79.0	13.9	86.1	37.4	463	453	10	81.3	1 007	37
Flint	502.1	117.5	72.0	32.2	321	147	26	538.2	5 357	401
Garden City	29.5	6.1	87.6	10.9	398	370	28	24.0	874	14
Grand Rapids	321.9	89.0	37.4	121.3	637	264	15	325.6	1 709	174
Holland	45.8	12.0	77.2	16.8	504	489	15	51.4	1 542	413
Inkster	43.4	14.9	32.0	13.5	537	526	11	41.5	1 654	64
Jackson	52.5	18.8	34.8	18.5	555	325	11	61.6	1 847	294
Kalamazoo	130.6	43.5	46.0	43.7	580	555	25	121.7	1 617	207
Kentwood	37.6	7.9	86.2	20.9	420	392	28	37.4	753	60
Lansing	199.5	45.8	54.5	68.7	601	343	13	191.2	1 673	175
Lincoln Park	33.8	9.0	78.1	15.8	418	401	17	38.4	1 019	22
Livonia	124.8	25.5	60.0	56.3	586	566	21	115.2	1 199	38
Madison Heights	38.4	6.7	70.4	20.2	674	650	24	43.5	1 448	121
Midland	69.8	10.8	85.7	36.7	874	857	17	61.2	1 460	164
Mount Pleasant	19.8	5.1	79.3	8.1	309	295	14	19.6	748	41
Muskegon	40.9	9.9	74.7	17.3	468	235	33	46.3	1 248	68
Novi	64.1	7.6	98.2	31.7	557	530	26	58.8	1 034	128

1. Based on population estimated as of July 1 of the year shown.

City	City government finances, 2012 (cont.)									
	General expenditure (cont.)									
	Percent of total for:									
	Public welfare	Highways	Parking facilities	Education	Health and hospitals	Police protection	Sewerage and sanitation	Parks and recreation	Housing and community development	Interest on debt
	127	128	129	130	131	132	133	134	135	136
MASSACHUSETTS—Cont'd										
Beverly	0.3	3.4	0.0	51.9	0.4	5.3	7.8	1.4	0.2	2.4
Boston	1.5	1.6	0.1	34.9	9.0	10.0	7.1	2.1	3.3	1.8
Braintree Town	0.2	4.6	0.0	56.1	0.2	6.0	1.8	2.0	0.0	0.6
Brockton	0.3	2.4	0.1	69.7	0.2	5.1	4.9	0.4	0.7	2.6
Cambridge	0.1	0.8	0.1	15.3	59.9	2.3	2.5	1.4	0.1	0.8
Chelsea	0.4	1.5	0.0	55.8	0.0	5.6	1.8	0.1	1.3	0.9
Chicopee	0.5	2.5	0.0	55.4	0.2	5.1	10.9	1.4	1.6	1.4
Everett	0.3	4.8	0.3	53.5	0.9	5.4	1.6	0.1	0.5	1.6
Fall River	1.1	2.7	0.1	60.7	1.7	6.0	7.2	0.5	2.1	2.7
Fitchburg	0.4	3.8	0.1	55.3	0.5	5.0	7.7	0.4	1.1	1.6
Franklin Town	0.2	3.8	0.0	62.7	0.2	4.0	5.2	0.4	0.0	1.5
Gloucester	0.3	1.0	0.0	46.4	0.3	4.3	12.1	0.2	0.8	2.6
Haverhill	0.4	2.6	0.0	57.9	0.5	4.9	6.4	0.2	0.8	1.7
Holyoke	3.6	2.3	0.1	57.6	0.3	6.1	4.9	0.6	1.3	0.8
Lawrence	0.2	1.0	0.1	69.2	0.0	4.2	3.9	0.2	0.5	1.9
Leominster	0.3	5.4	0.0	62.2	0.3	4.8	12.4	0.5	0.4	0.5
Lowell	0.3	1.5	0.8	55.4	0.5	6.0	5.9	0.7	2.2	2.0
Lynn	0.3	2.2	0.3	60.6	0.0	5.4	1.5	0.1	1.5	1.0
Malden	0.1	1.8	0.0	51.9	0.3	4.9	1.7	0.4	2.1	1.9
Marlborough	0.1	6.3	0.0	59.3	0.3	5.4	5.3	0.2	0.3	0.9
Medford	0.2	2.1	0.0	42.8	0.3	7.6	4.1	0.4	1.6	0.9
Melrose	0.5	2.1	0.0	46.0	1.6	4.2	1.7	2.4	0.1	2.2
Methuen Town	0.4	4.2	0.0	68.1	0.5	6.5	5.7	0.1	0.7	1.2
New Bedford	1.1	1.1	0.2	57.4	1.0	6.6	5.2	0.4	1.7	2.7
Newton	0.1	2.9	0.0	59.6	0.6	4.5	3.4	1.2	1.0	2.4
Northampton	0.8	3.6	0.4	37.7	1.9	16.0	5.4	0.3	2.0	2.3
Peabody	0.1	2.7	0.0	56.3	0.7	5.9	2.5	1.9	2.2	0.9
Pittsfield	0.3	5.5	0.6	46.8	0.5	4.6	5.2	1.1	1.2	1.6
Quincy	0.5	2.3	0.0	39.4	0.6	6.9	3.3	0.7	2.0	1.2
Revere	0.7	1.0	0.1	51.2	0.2	5.2	7.3	0.3	0.7	1.4
Salem	0.2	3.0	0.5	53.2	0.3	5.4	2.7	1.9	0.9	1.3
Somerville	0.2	2.5	0.0	35.0	0.5	6.5	3.8	0.4	2.1	1.0
Springfield	0.4	1.8	0.0	65.3	0.2	5.5	1.3	1.2	0.9	1.9
Taunton	4.3	2.3	0.0	50.4	0.4	5.5	8.7	0.5	0.9	1.4
Waltham	0.2	3.7	0.1	36.6	0.4	6.4	4.4	0.7	0.6	1.4
Watertown Town	0.1	3.1	0.0	42.6	0.5	6.9	4.0	0.5	0.0	1.3
Westfield	0.5	3.3	0.0	62.6	1.6	4.9	3.8	1.5	0.2	1.7
West Springfield Town	0.5	8.0	0.0	57.3	1.3	5.5	3.0	0.4	0.7	0.9
Weymouth Town	0.4	2.0	0.0	50.6	0.4	6.9	5.0	0.4	0.7	1.5
Woburn	0.3	2.9	0.0	54.1	0.4	6.0	2.5	0.5	0.0	1.5
Worcester	0.0	3.3	0.2	50.4	0.0	6.0	6.2	0.7	1.5	4.3
MICHIGAN	X	X	X	X	X	X	X	X	X	X
Allen Park	0.0	6.4	0.0	0.0	0.0	14.5	38.3	2.2	0.9	7.5
Ann Arbor	0.0	12.0	16.4	0.0	0.0	13.0	19.6	7.4	7.6	4.1
Battle Creek	0.0	15.2	1.0	0.0	0.0	14.4	15.7	5.1	11.4	2.5
Bay City	0.0	12.0	0.0	0.0	0.0	11.7	20.5	1.6	9.1	4.9
Burton	0.0	14.3	0.0	0.0	2.0	21.7	30.0	0.2	0.0	1.5
Dearborn	0.0	11.9	0.7	0.0	0.0	20.4	25.1	8.8	1.7	3.2
Dearborn Heights	0.0	9.4	0.0	0.0	0.0	18.9	29.2	1.7	1.5	3.4
Detroit	0.3	4.1	0.2	2.6	3.2	16.5	19.9	1.5	2.3	14.4
East Lansing	0.0	8.7	6.6	0.0	0.1	13.6	17.4	9.9	5.3	4.2
Eastpointe	0.0	7.5	0.0	0.0	0.0	24.2	26.9	3.0	5.4	0.5
Farmington Hills	0.0	12.0	0.0	0.0	0.0	23.0	18.5	10.0	0.4	1.0
Flint	0.0	2.0	0.0	0.0	71.4	4.3	4.8	0.9	4.2	1.0
Garden City	0.0	11.4	0.0	0.0	0.2	16.2	27.1	1.4	0.6	2.6
Grand Rapids	0.0	8.3	1.9	0.0	0.0	14.7	16.6	1.9	16.1	6.7
Holland	0.2	23.5	0.0	0.0	0.6	14.8	25.5	11.0	1.1	2.2
Inkster	0.0	5.5	0.0	0.0	0.0	15.9	18.5	2.0	23.8	3.0
Jackson	0.0	33.1	0.4	0.0	0.0	12.4	10.4	5.3	12.6	2.4
Kalamazoo	0.0	11.0	0.0	0.0	0.0	27.5	24.5	3.5	2.8	2.5
Kentwood	0.0	17.7	0.0	0.0	0.0	26.5	9.2	5.2	0.1	2.3
Lansing	0.0	9.1	3.2	0.0	0.0	16.0	13.6	7.6	1.0	5.1
Lincoln Park	0.0	8.0	0.0	0.0	0.0	21.1	23.4	1.1	2.1	1.9
Livonia	0.0	11.9	0.0	0.0	0.0	19.1	24.0	8.3	8.3	1.5
Madison Heights	0.0	12.4	0.0	0.0	0.0	20.1	32.9	1.9	4.4	0.4
Midland	0.0	14.5	0.2	0.0	0.0	11.9	18.0	11.9	1.8	1.5
Mount Pleasant	0.0	13.1	1.1	0.0	0.0	24.5	10.3	7.8	4.3	1.3
Muskegon	0.0	13.1	0.0	0.0	0.0	19.8	27.3	2.8	7.1	1.1
Novi	0.0	18.7	0.0	0.0	0.0	19.2	17.0	6.8	0.0	4.0

Table D. Cities — **City Government Finances, City Government Employment, and Climate**

City	City government finances, 2012 (cont.)			Climate[2]						
	Debt outstanding			Average daily temperature (degrees Fahrenheit)						
				Mean		Limits				
	Total (mil dol)	Per capita[1] (dollars)	Debt issued during year	January	July	January[3]	July[4]	Annual precipitation (inches)	Heating degree days	Cooling degree days
	137	138	139	140	141	142	143	144	145	146
MASSACHUSETTS—Cont'd										
Beverly	89.1	2 208	0.0	28.8	72.6	20.4	82.1	45.51	5 704	582
Boston	1 572.5	2 454	245.5	29.3	73.9	22.1	82.2	42.53	5 630	777
Braintree Town	145.9	4 001	8.7	NA	NA	NA	NA	NA	NA	NA
Brockton	242.9	2 583	12.5	27.9	72.1	17.8	83.2	48.25	6 008	529
Cambridge	340.3	3 209	55.5	29.3	73.9	22.1	82.2	42.53	5 630	777
Chelsea	35.1	947	2.0	29.3	73.9	22.1	82.2	42.53	5 630	777
Chicopee	51.4	924	11.0	21.5	68.9	10.4	81.7	48.07	7 312	287
Everett	61.8	1 452	1.4	29.3	73.9	22.1	82.2	42.53	5 630	777
Fall River	271.7	3 064	39.8	28.5	74.2	20.0	83.1	50.77	5 734	740
Fitchburg	74.6	1 846	20.7	24.2	71.9	15.2	81.0	49.13	6 576	548
Franklin Town	55.4	1 710	16.4	NA	NA	NA	NA	NA	NA	NA
Gloucester	137.0	4 689	26.4	28.8	72.6	20.4	82.1	45.51	5 704	582
Haverhill	94.2	1 525	3.0	25.3	72.2	15.6	83.5	46.88	6 435	550
Holyoke	104.5	2 604	16.8	21.5	68.9	10.4	81.7	48.07	7 312	287
Lawrence	148.3	1 917	0.0	24.5	71.8	14.5	82.9	44.09	6 539	510
Leominster	58.1	1 421	13.9	24.2	71.9	15.2	81.0	49.13	6 576	548
Lowell	256.6	2 363	32.8	23.6	72.4	14.1	84.5	43.14	6 575	532
Lynn	67.5	740	0.0	29.3	73.9	22.1	82.2	42.53	5 630	777
Malden	106.3	1 761	5.1	29.3	73.9	22.1	82.2	42.53	5 630	777
Marlborough	60.4	1 537	31.1	25.9	73.4	16.2	84.0	45.87	6 060	651
Medford	45.4	795	34.5	29.3	73.9	22.1	82.2	42.53	5 630	777
Melrose	63.4	2 311	5.5	29.3	73.9	22.1	82.2	42.53	5 630	777
Methuen Town	66.0	1 374	0.5	24.5	71.8	14.5	82.9	44.09	6 539	510
New Bedford	257.5	2 716	19.6	28.5	74.2	20.0	83.1	50.77	5 734	740
Newton	217.6	2 495	9.9	25.9	73.4	16.2	84.0	45.87	6 060	651
Northampton	81.7	2 847	20.6	22.3	71.2	11.2	83.2	45.57	6 856	452
Peabody	45.3	874	10.0	28.8	72.6	20.4	82.1	45.51	5 704	582
Pittsfield	87.1	1 966	7.2	19.9	67.6	11.2	77.5	48.71	7 689	222
Quincy	211.7	2 279	14.8	26.0	71.6	18.1	81.2	51.19	6 371	558
Revere	59.8	1 117	0.2	29.3	73.9	22.1	82.2	42.53	5 630	777
Salem	62.2	1 472	6.0	28.8	72.6	20.4	82.1	45.51	5 704	582
Somerville	99.6	1 281	18.7	29.3	73.9	22.1	82.2	42.53	5 630	777
Springfield	260.5	1 693	0.0	25.7	73.7	17.2	84.9	46.16	6 104	759
Taunton	120.6	2 154	0.7	27.4	72.2	17.8	83.0	48.34	6 012	558
Waltham	106.4	1 717	23.1	25.4	71.5	15.7	82.7	46.95	6 370	485
Watertown Town	44.3	1 348	4.0	29.3	73.9	22.1	82.2	42.53	5 630	777
Westfield	98.9	2 398	0.0	21.5	68.9	10.4	81.7	48.07	7 312	287
West Springfield Town	43.5	1 522	0.0	NA	NA	NA	NA	NA	NA	NA
Weymouth Town	91.2	1 657	25.5	NA	NA	NA	NA	NA	NA	NA
Woburn	86.3	2 221	30.5	25.5	71.5	15.7	82.5	48.31	6 401	472
Worcester	657.7	3 607	57.8	23.6	70.1	15.8	79.3	49.05	6 831	371
MICHIGAN	X	X	X	X	X	X	X	X	X	X
Allen Park	85.9	3 076	3.7	24.5	73.5	17.8	83.4	32.89	6 422	736
Ann Arbor	244.9	2 113	25.9	23.4	72.6	16.6	83.0	35.35	6 503	691
Battle Creek	87.6	1 690	0.0	23.1	71.0	15.3	82.5	35.15	6 742	559
Bay City	72.6	2 101	3.7	21.0	71.5	13.8	81.5	31.25	7 106	545
Burton	12.1	411	3.5	21.3	70.6	13.3	82.0	31.61	7 005	555
Dearborn	274.1	2 831	7.6	24.7	73.7	16.1	85.7	33.58	6 224	788
Dearborn Heights	58.1	1 016	3.6	24.7	73.7	16.1	85.7	33.58	6 224	788
Detroit	8 166.1	11 720	1 166.2	24.7	73.7	16.1	85.7	33.58	6 224	788
East Lansing	60.8	1 250	0.0	21.6	70.3	13.9	82.1	31.53	7 098	558
Eastpointe	15.3	472	0.4	25.3	73.6	18.8	83.3	33.97	6 160	757
Farmington Hills	17.7	219	0.0	24.7	73.7	16.1	85.7	33.58	6 224	788
Flint	170.4	1 696	13.5	21.3	70.6	13.3	82.0	31.61	7 005	555
Garden City	50.5	1 842	12.9	24.7	73.7	16.1	85.7	33.58	6 224	788
Grand Rapids	552.9	2 902	23.4	22.4	71.4	15.6	82.3	37.13	6 896	613
Holland	47.8	1 433	12.8	24.4	71.4	17.6	82.5	36.25	6 589	611
Inkster	48.3	1 924	9.7	24.5	73.5	17.8	83.4	32.89	6 422	736
Jackson	42.3	1 268	13.0	22.2	71.3	14.7	82.7	30.67	6 070	570
Kalamazoo	453.2	6 023	117.6	24.3	73.2	17.0	84.2	37.41	6 235	773
Kentwood	20.1	405	0.0	22.4	71.4	15.6	82.3	37.13	6 896	613
Lansing	693.1	6 066	30.4	21.6	70.3	13.9	82.1	31.53	7 098	558
Lincoln Park	16.7	443	0.0	24.5	73.5	17.8	83.4	32.89	6 422	736
Livonia	52.7	549	0.0	24.7	73.7	16.1	85.7	33.58	6 224	788
Madison Heights	14.5	483	0.0	24.7	73.7	16.1	85.7	33.58	6 224	788
Midland	35.9	855	4.6	22.9	72.7	16.2	83.8	30.69	6 645	679
Mount Pleasant	13.0	496	1.5	20.7	70.6	13.5	82.2	31.57	7 329	492
Muskegon	30.6	826	6.5	23.5	69.9	17.1	80.0	32.88	6 943	487
Novi	48.0	844	0.0	22.1	71.0	14.3	81.7	29.28	6 989	550

1. Based on the population estimated as of July 1 of the year shown. 2. Represents normal values based on the 30-year period, 1971–2000. 3. Average daily minimum. 4. Average daily maximum.

STATE Place code	City	Land area,[1] 2010 (sq km)	Population, 2014			Race alone or in combination (percent), 2011-2013					Percent Hispanic or Latino[2], 2011-2013	Percent foreign born 2011–2013
			Total persons	Rank	Per square kilometer	White	Black	American Indian, Alaska Native	Asian	Hawaiian Pacific Islander		
		1	2	3	4	5	6	7	8	9	10	11
	MICHIGAN—Cont'd											
26 59920	Oak Park	13.4	29 834	1 242	2 226.4	38.4	62.1	2.7	1.6	NA	1.2	10.1
26 65440	Pontiac	51.7	59 808	607	1 156.8	42.3	56.1	2.4	3.1	NA	15.5	5.6
26 65560	Portage	83.5	47 837	787	572.9	89.1	7.9	1.1	4.3	NA	2.6	5.1
26 65820	Port Huron	20.9	29 168	1 264	1 395.6	89.2	10.8	2.5	1.7	NA	4.9	3.9
26 69035	Rochester Hills	85.0	73 125	465	860.3	84.9	5.4	1.2	10.4	NA	3.9	15.2
26 69800	Roseville	25.5	47 598	789	1 866.6	82.2	14.8	1.4	2.3	NA	2.7	3.8
26 70040	Royal Oak	30.5	59 069	619	1 936.7	93.5	3.5	0.2	3.9	NA	2.8	7.3
26 70520	Saginaw	44.9	49 844	750	1 110.1	51.2	47.8	1.3	0.7	NA	14.2	1.4
26 70760	St. Clair Shores	30.1	60 036	601	1 994.6	93.1	5.4	1.0	1.3	NA	2.0	5.1
26 74900	Southfield	68.1	73 002	467	1 072.0	26.6	72.4	1.7	2.6	NA	1.7	10.6
26 74960	Southgate	17.7	29 416	1 253	1 661.9	91.9	6.5	1.4	1.6	NA	5.7	5.1
26 76460	Sterling Heights	94.6	131 741	196	1 392.6	86.4	7.0	1.0	8.0	0.3	2.0	25.5
26 79000	Taylor	61.1	61 594	577	1 008.1	78.1	19.7	1.4	2.8	NA	5.2	4.7
26 80700	Troy	86.7	83 107	390	958.6	72.7	4.6	0.5	23.3	0.2	2.5	29.9
26 84000	Warren	89.1	135 099	191	1 516.3	78.6	15.8	1.1	6.7	NA	1.7	11.8
26 86000	Westland	52.9	82 314	398	1 556.0	77.3	18.5	1.6	4.7	NA	3.0	7.2
26 88900	Wyandotte	13.7	25 151	1 419	1 835.8	95.6	1.7	1.4	0.9	NA	4.7	2.5
26 88940	Wyoming	63.8	74 826	454	1 172.8	87.2	7.0	2.0	2.6	NA	20.7	11.0
27 00000	MINNESOTA	206 232.3	5 457 173	X	26.5	87.6	6.5	1.9	5.0	0.1	4.9	7.4
27 01486	Andover	87.7	31 996	1 164	364.8	96.0	1.3	1.1	3.2	NA	1.5	2.9
27 01900	Apple Valley	43.7	50 487	741	1 155.3	87.6	8.5	0.4	6.9	NA	3.6	9.7
27 06382	Blaine	87.7	61 190	583	697.7	85.4	4.9	1.5	8.3	NA	3.2	9.9
27 06616	Bloomington	89.8	86 314	369	961.2	81.9	9.7	1.2	6.5	0.3	7.2	10.9
27 07948	Brooklyn Center	20.6	30 729	1 204	1 491.7	50.7	33.8	1.6	15.8	NA	8.3	25.3
27 07966	Brooklyn Park	67.5	78 728	420	1 166.3	54.5	27.8	0.7	17.3	0.2	6.0	19.6
27 08794	Burnsville	64.5	61 630	576	955.5	79.1	13.3	1.2	6.1	NA	8.1	12.7
27 13114	Coon Rapids	58.6	62 112	573	1 059.9	88.6	8.5	1.6	3.9	NA	3.8	7.5
27 13456	Cottage Grove	87.1	35 630	1 048	409.1	90.0	4.2	0.7	6.7	NA	4.6	7.0
27 17000	Duluth	175.6	86 238	370	491.1	93.3	3.9	3.9	2.2	0.2	1.7	2.8
27 17288	Eagan	80.6	66 084	530	819.9	84.1	6.9	1.7	8.6	NA	4.7	10.5
27 18116	Eden Prairie	84.0	63 228	559	752.7	82.7	6.3	1.2	11.0	NA	3.3	14.0
27 18188	Edina	40.0	49 596	754	1 239.9	88.3	4.0	1.0	7.7	NA	3.5	9.9
27 22814	Fridley	26.3	27 670	1 323	1 052.1	77.6	14.3	2.3	5.9	NA	8.3	11.6
27 31076	Inver Grove Heights	71.9	34 709	1 071	482.7	89.3	5.9	1.0	3.6	NA	9.3	6.9
27 35180	Lakeville	93.4	59 866	606	641.0	91.4	2.9	NA	5.6	NA	4.5	7.4
27 39878	Mankato	46.4	40 411	917	870.9	92.7	5.1	0.8	3.7	NA	3.1	5.0
27 40166	Maple Grove	84.5	66 945	518	792.2	89.7	3.8	0.5	7.2	NA	2.6	9.3
27 40382	Maplewood	44.0	40 199	923	913.6	77.9	10.9	2.1	12.6	NA	7.2	11.2
27 43000	Minneapolis	139.8	407 207	46	2 912.8	70.2	20.6	3.1	6.9	0.3	10.1	15.0
27 43252	Minnetonka	69.7	51 486	724	738.7	91.0	6.2	0.4	4.2	NA	2.1	8.1
27 43864	Moorhead	51.3	39 857	933	776.9	94.3	2.7	2.5	3.0	NA	4.8	3.6
27 47680	Oakdale	28.4	28 033	1 306	987.1	82.4	10.1	0.6	8.5	NA	5.3	7.3
27 49300	Owatonna	37.6	25 625	1 404	681.5	92.2	4.6	0.4	1.5	NA	7.7	4.2
27 51730	Plymouth	84.7	75 057	451	886.2	86.4	6.0	1.0	9.0	NA	3.9	12.3
27 54214	Richfield	17.8	36 179	1 031	2 032.5	76.5	10.2	1.5	7.7	0.2	18.1	19.5
27 54880	Rochester	141.4	111 402	249	787.9	85.1	7.7	0.7	8.1	NA	5.5	12.6
27 55852	Roseville	33.7	35 319	1 055	1 048.0	83.2	6.3	1.4	10.5	NA	5.3	12.7
27 56896	St. Cloud	103.7	66 389	528	640.2	86.4	10.3	1.2	4.1	NA	2.2	7.3
27 57220	St. Louis Park	27.6	47 502	791	1 721.1	87.3	8.4	1.5	5.2	NA	4.3	9.7
27 58000	St. Paul	134.6	297 640	66	2 211.3	63.9	18.0	2.5	17.1	0.1	9.6	18.4
27 58738	Savage	40.5	29 208	1 259	721.2	86.4	5.7	0.6	9.7	NA	3.5	10.2
27 59350	Shakopee	72.5	39 677	939	547.3	81.5	4.9	3.0	11.2	NA	9.2	14.3
27 59998	Shoreview	27.9	26 194	1 391	938.9	88.8	2.4	0.4	9.4	NA	2.1	10.6
27 71032	Winona	48.8	27 384	1 344	561.1	95.2	2.7	0.9	1.6	NA	0.7	2.9
27 71428	Woodbury	90.0	66 807	522	742.3	84.1	7.3	0.9	10.3	0.2	3.5	10.7
28 00000	MISSISSIPPI	121 530.7	2 994 079	X	24.6	60.3	38.0	0.8	1.1	0.0	2.8	2.2
28 06220	Biloxi	99.0	44 984	825	454.4	70.4	22.4	1.5	6.5	0.3	7.1	7.4
28 14420	Clinton	108.3	25 411	1 411	234.6	58.0	35.7	NA	5.4	NA	2.9	5.7
28 29180	Greenville	69.7	32 704	1 132	469.2	21.3	78.0	0.6	1.0	NA	0.7	0.8
28 29700	Gulfport	144.0	71 750	476	498.3	61.7	37.4	0.9	1.9	NA	6.3	3.4
28 31020	Hattiesburg	138.3	47 016	798	340.0	42.3	54.3	0.5	2.1	NA	3.3	4.1
28 33700	Horn Lake	41.5	26 766	1 370	645.0	58.3	39.4	0.6	1.7	NA	6.6	3.7
28 36000	Jackson	287.6	171 155	143	595.1	18.1	81.2	0.3	0.4	NA	1.5	1.6
28 46640	Meridian	139.2	40 196	924	288.8	33.2	66.2	0.4	NA	NA	1.7	1.3
28 54040	Olive Branch	95.1	35 457	1 051	372.8	73.9	23.8	1.8	1.3	NA	4.8	5.0
28 55760	Pearl	61.1	26 388	1 384	431.9	78.1	20.9	NA	1.1	NA	4.2	2.4
28 69280	Southaven	106.8	51 824	720	485.2	72.7	25.5	0.1	2.2	NA	5.0	3.3
28 74840	Tupelo	132.5	35 688	1 046	269.3	61.3	39.5	NA	1.0	NA	3.5	2.9

1. Dry land or land partially or temporarily covered by water. 2. May be of any race.

City	Age of population (percent), 2011-2013									Median age 2011-2013	Percent female 2011-2013	Population			
												Census counts		Percent change	
	Under 5 years	5 to 17 years	18 to 24 years	25 to 34 years	35 to 44 years	45 to 54 years	55 to 64 years	65 to 74 years	75 years and over			2000	2010	2000–2010	2010–2014
	12	13	14	15	16	17	18	19	20	21	22	23	24	25	26
MICHIGAN—Cont'd															
Oak Park	6.2	18.2	12.3	11.4	14.9	12.8	11.4	6.1	6.6	36.5	53.9	29 793	29 319	-1.6	1.8
Pontiac	7.4	18.8	12.0	13.7	12.9	12.9	11.8	5.7	4.8	33.4	52.1	66 337	59 515	-10.3	0.5
Portage	8.0	16.3	10.3	13.6	13.1	13.6	11.7	7.8	5.6	36.6	52.4	44 897	46 292	3.1	3.3
Port Huron	6.0	18.2	10.6	13.3	11.7	13.6	12.0	8.6	6.0	36.7	50.7	32 338	30 184	-6.7	-3.3
Rochester Hills	5.8	16.9	7.2	11.9	13.0	15.5	15.3	7.8	6.6	42.1	50.9	68 825	70 995	3.2	3.0
Roseville	6.0	17.1	9.0	14.7	13.8	14.4	12.4	6.0	6.5	37.3	50.8	48 129	47 299	-1.7	0.6
Royal Oak	5.1	11.3	8.1	22.0	14.6	13.4	12.9	6.0	6.7	37.0	50.9	60 062	57 236	-4.7	3.2
Saginaw	7.1	20.3	12.2	11.2	12.3	13.4	12.0	5.6	5.9	34.2	52.0	61 799	51 508	-16.7	-3.2
St. Clair Shores	4.5	14.2	6.7	14.3	10.8	16.5	14.6	8.1	10.2	44.5	52.1	63 096	59 715	-5.4	0.5
Southfield	5.8	15.2	9.0	10.7	12.6	14.3	14.4	9.6	8.5	42.6	55.2	78 296	71 739	-8.4	1.8
Southgate	4.0	14.9	10.4	11.8	15.1	13.5	14.7	8.2	7.2	41.8	52.6	30 136	30 047	-0.3	-2.1
Sterling Heights	5.0	16.0	8.8	12.3	13.7	14.8	13.2	8.7	7.4	41.3	50.3	124 471	129 699	4.2	1.6
Taylor	6.3	17.4	9.6	12.5	12.8	15.6	11.3	7.9	6.5	38.4	52.1	65 868	63 131	-4.2	-2.4
Troy	5.2	17.8	7.4	11.0	13.8	15.9	14.0	9.0	6.0	41.6	51.5	80 959	80 980	0.0	2.6
Warren	6.2	16.0	9.8	12.3	12.8	14.4	12.7	7.4	8.4	39.7	51.6	138 247	134 056	-3.0	0.8
Westland	6.5	14.3	10.1	14.5	12.7	14.6	12.7	7.7	6.8	38.3	53.3	86 602	84 094	-2.9	-2.1
Wyandotte	5.3	14.4	8.7	14.4	14.0	16.9	12.5	7.5	6.5	40.9	50.9	28 006	25 883	-7.6	-2.8
Wyoming	7.7	16.9	10.8	17.8	12.8	13.2	11.8	5.4	3.6	33.1	49.0	69 368	72 125	4.0	3.7
MINNESOTA	6.5	17.3	9.4	13.7	12.4	14.6	12.6	7.3	6.3	37.6	50.3	4 919 479	5 303 925	7.8	2.9
Andover	4.4	24.3	9.0	9.3	14.7	18.4	12.3	5.6	2.0	37.6	49.6	26 588	30 598	15.1	4.6
Apple Valley	7.2	17.6	8.5	13.5	12.9	16.5	12.8	7.1	3.9	37.5	49.9	45 527	49 084	7.8	2.9
Blaine	8.4	19.3	6.9	14.7	15.4	14.1	12.2	5.5	3.6	35.4	50.3	44 942	57 186	27.2	7.0
Bloomington	5.6	13.8	6.8	14.1	12.1	14.2	13.9	9.5	9.9	43.0	51.6	85 172	82 893	-2.7	4.1
Brooklyn Center	8.1	18.0	8.4	17.2	14.6	12.8	9.8	5.2	6.0	33.3	53.2	29 172	30 104	3.2	2.0
Brooklyn Park	7.6	19.3	10.1	15.9	12.4	14.6	11.1	5.9	3.0	33.0	50.0	67 388	75 781	12.5	3.9
Burnsville	5.9	16.5	8.9	16.0	12.9	14.7	12.3	7.1	5.8	37.2	51.1	60 220	60 306	0.1	2.2
Coon Rapids	6.9	16.2	9.5	15.2	12.6	14.9	12.7	6.8	5.2	36.8	50.7	61 607	61 476	-0.2	1.0
Cottage Grove	6.8	21.9	7.2	13.3	14.3	16.8	10.0	5.2	4.4	35.4	50.5	30 582	34 589	13.1	3.0
Duluth	5.7	13.2	20.0	13.2	9.9	11.9	11.9	6.9	7.3	33.1	50.5	86 918	86 265	-0.8	0.0
Eagan	7.0	18.2	7.8	14.7	12.7	18.0	12.8	5.7	3.2	37.0	50.1	63 557	64 206	1.0	2.9
Eden Prairie	6.9	19.1	6.8	14.4	13.6	16.8	13.6	5.5	3.4	37.4	50.3	54 901	60 797	10.7	4.1
Edina	5.5	19.2	5.0	9.9	11.4	15.4	13.9	8.5	11.1	44.3	52.4	47 425	47 941	1.1	3.5
Fridley	7.7	14.2	9.8	16.0	11.9	14.8	11.6	7.7	6.4	37.4	50.5	27 449	27 208	-0.9	1.7
Inver Grove Heights	6.1	18.1	10.8	11.2	11.5	16.5	12.0	8.4	5.3	38.1	51.9	29 751	33 880	13.9	2.4
Lakeville	7.2	23.4	6.5	12.1	16.4	17.9	9.9	3.8	2.7	35.4	50.9	43 128	55 954	29.7	7.0
Mankato	5.7	10.2	32.2	15.1	9.1	8.5	8.4	4.9	5.9	25.9	50.4	32 427	39 309	21.2	2.7
Maple Grove	7.1	19.1	5.3	14.1	15.5	15.9	13.9	5.6	3.3	37.7	52.0	50 365	61 567	22.2	8.7
Maplewood	6.0	17.3	6.9	14.1	10.8	15.7	13.8	7.4	8.0	40.6	52.5	34 947	38 018	8.8	5.7
Minneapolis	6.9	13.4	14.1	21.4	13.3	11.9	10.4	4.8	3.6	31.8	49.5	382 618	382 578	0.0	6.4
Minnetonka	5.3	15.5	6.1	13.0	10.8	14.9	17.5	8.9	8.1	44.3	52.8	51 301	49 734	-3.1	3.5
Moorhead	7.0	13.3	23.2	14.8	9.9	10.6	10.1	4.8	6.3	29.2	51.3	32 177	38 065	18.3	4.7
Oakdale	5.4	17.8	11.3	12.2	10.6	17.9	12.1	7.6	5.1	38.1	51.7	26 653	27 378	2.7	2.4
Owatonna	7.7	18.6	7.8	12.6	13.3	13.8	11.2	7.9	7.1	38.5	50.7	22 434	25 599	14.1	0.1
Plymouth	6.0	16.9	6.0	15.3	13.5	15.7	13.7	7.2	5.7	40.1	51.5	65 894	70 576	7.1	6.4
Richfield	7.4	12.8	7.0	20.0	13.4	12.7	11.6	6.9	8.2	36.7	50.5	34 439	35 228	2.3	2.7
Rochester	7.4	17.1	8.5	16.5	12.5	13.4	11.3	6.9	6.6	35.4	51.5	85 806	106 769	24.4	4.4
Roseville	4.5	12.9	11.7	14.8	10.0	13.7	11.1	10.0	11.3	41.5	50.3	33 690	33 660	-0.1	4.9
St. Cloud	6.5	13.9	22.0	16.5	9.4	12.0	9.4	5.2	5.1	28.7	47.2	59 107	65 842	11.4	0.7
St. Louis Park	6.0	13.3	7.8	22.7	14.8	12.4	9.6	6.1	7.2	35.1	51.1	44 126	45 250	2.5	5.0
St. Paul	7.8	17.4	13.1	17.3	12.5	12.0	10.7	4.9	4.2	31.3	50.7	287 151	285 068	-0.7	4.4
Savage	7.0	23.6	6.7	13.0	15.9	18.9	8.5	3.9	2.6	34.8	49.8	21 115	26 911	27.4	8.5
Shakopee	8.5	20.7	7.6	17.5	19.2	12.1	7.6	3.9	2.9	32.8	49.8	20 568	37 076	80.3	7.0
Shoreview	5.4	16.2	5.9	11.5	12.1	15.2	17.7	9.8	6.3	44.1	53.4	25 924	25 043	-3.4	4.6
Winona	3.4	8.8	32.7	11.1	7.3	11.1	11.3	7.0	7.3	28.7	52.5	27 069	27 592	1.9	-0.8
Woodbury	7.4	20.8	6.5	13.1	15.2	16.1	11.4	5.9	3.6	36.2	52.6	46 463	61 961	33.4	7.8
MISSISSIPPI	6.8	18.1	10.5	12.8	12.6	13.5	12.2	7.7	5.7	36.4	51.4	2 844 658	2 967 297	4.3	0.9
Biloxi	6.6	15.0	14.8	14.6	12.1	13.4	11.3	5.5	6.8	34.4	47.7	50 644	44 054	-13.0	2.1
Clinton	5.9	17.6	11.5	13.5	11.8	14.7	10.4	7.8	6.8	36.0	52.3	23 347	25 216	8.0	0.8
Greenville	7.8	18.9	9.3	12.9	12.0	10.9	12.6	7.3	6.1	36.1	53.2	41 633	34 400	-17.4	-4.9
Gulfport	7.9	16.4	10.5	14.7	12.9	13.5	11.3	7.2	5.6	35.2	50.7	71 127	67 793	-4.7	5.8
Hattiesburg	6.6	12.6	23.4	17.6	10.9	9.4	8.6	5.5	5.5	28.2	52.5	44 779	45 989	2.7	2.7
Horn Lake	9.4	22.0	7.4	16.9	14.6	12.0	10.1	5.2	2.6	32.6	51.6	14 099	26 066	84.9	2.7
Jackson	7.5	19.2	12.4	15.3	11.7	12.2	11.1	5.8	4.6	31.6	53.8	184 256	173 514	-5.8	-1.4
Meridian	7.4	19.3	10.3	14.0	11.4	11.3	12.9	6.8	6.4	33.9	53.7	39 968	41 148	3.0	-2.3
Olive Branch	5.2	20.2	10.6	9.8	16.0	16.8	10.0	6.9	4.5	37.5	52.0	21 054	33 484	59.0	5.9
Pearl	7.4	17.7	11.7	14.8	13.1	13.1	9.1	8.2	4.9	34.4	53.5	21 961	25 092	14.3	2.7
Southaven	6.5	21.6	8.3	14.6	14.7	13.8	9.6	6.4	4.5	34.5	53.3	28 977	48 982	69.0	5.8
Tupelo	8.6	19.6	7.3	13.9	12.4	13.0	10.5	7.5	7.2	35.5	51.1	34 211	34 546	1.0	3.3

City	Households, 2011-2013				Persons in group quarters, 2010				Serious crimes known to police,[2] 2013				Educational attainment, 2011–2013		
			Percent			Institutional			Total		Rate[3]			Attainment[4] (percent)	
	Number	Persons per household	Female family householder[1]	One-person	Total	Total	Persons in nursing facilities	Non-institutional	Number	Rate[3]	Violent	Property	Population age 25 and older	High school graduate or less	Bachelor's degree or more
	27	28	29	30	31	32	33	34	35	36	37	38	39	40	41
MICHIGAN—Cont'd															
Oak Park	11 230	2.64	21.0	28.8	58	0	0	58	991	3 338	606	2 732	18 765	33.3	30.3
Pontiac	23 622	2.45	26.7	35.1	2 563	1 586	102	977	NA	NA	NA	NA	36 899	56.4	10.9
Portage	19 551	2.40	10.6	32.1	156	111	111	45	1 699	3 585	186	3 400	30 783	25.8	40.4
Port Huron	12 158	2.39	17.7	34.3	761	235	228	526	1 091	3 693	606	3 087	19 234	46.1	15.5
Rochester Hills	27 770	2.57	7.6	26.5	1 181	507	507	674	NA	NA	NA	NA	50 685	21.6	52.0
Roseville	19 581	2.40	19.3	33.7	245	148	148	97	2 197	4 642	463	4 179	32 138	54.0	9.9
Royal Oak	28 464	2.05	6.8	41.7	404	249	225	155	895	1 522	170	1 352	44 266	21.9	50.4
Saginaw	18 870	2.62	28.3	35.8	1 693	876	346	817	2 486	4 915	1 951	2 964	30 603	57.6	11.5
St. Clair Shores	26 917	2.21	11.9	37.5	277	248	248	29	973	1 628	213	1 416	44 638	38.8	23.6
Southfield	31 403	2.27	20.0	37.7	1 189	453	451	736	2 388	3 282	363	2 919	50 806	28.8	35.4
Southgate	12 149	2.43	13.3	30.6	117	88	88	29	1 140	3 870	292	3 578	20 976	47.0	15.5
Sterling Heights	49 207	2.63	9.5	26.6	772	566	554	206	2 727	2 088	187	1 901	91 542	43.0	25.7
Taylor	23 552	2.61	19.2	28.2	673	540	512	133	2 438	3 943	566	3 377	41 513	56.7	10.1
Troy	30 542	2.68	7.8	23.3	310	117	117	193	1 617	1 957	76	1 881	57 255	21.7	56.9
Warren	53 441	2.49	15.5	30.7	1 248	945	945	303	4 207	3 136	514	2 622	91 402	52.4	16.8
Westland	33 292	2.47	17.8	34.1	1 034	779	548	255	2 761	3 344	443	2 901	57 442	46.0	17.6
Wyandotte	10 524	2.41	10.8	36.2	88	0	0	88	627	2 471	221	2 250	18 203	49.1	17.9
Wyoming	27 431	2.66	10.8	27.2	358	149	149	209	1 961	2 658	423	2 235	47 394	48.1	19.9
MINNESOTA	2 109 924	2.49	9.7	28.3	135 395	56 308	32 989	79 087	143 900	2 655	234	2 420	3 596 719	34.2	33.1
Andover	9 999	3.12	7.5	11.9	39	0	0	39	NA	NA	NA	NA	19 457	30.1	30.6
Apple Valley	19 226	2.58	9.9	24.4	316	198	189	118	1 212	2 411	97	2 314	33 333	21.8	42.6
Blaine	21 750	2.72	11.2	22.3	147	71	31	76	1 766	2 939	82	2 857	38 818	32.5	29.7
Bloomington	36 829	2.29	9.1	33.9	991	489	481	502	3 411	3 918	147	3 771	62 994	28.1	40.7
Brooklyn Center	11 341	2.68	18.7	28.1	182	93	86	89	1 852	6 010	428	5 582	20 010	47.5	20.3
Brooklyn Park	26 786	2.89	16.3	23.6	209	17	8	192	2 704	3 451	317	3 135	48 929	35.6	28.9
Burnsville	25 119	2.41	10.3	30.9	443	294	287	149	1 967	3 205	155	3 050	41 918	29.0	35.8
Coon Rapids	23 641	2.60	12.2	26.3	359	205	201	154	1 860	2 997	151	2 846	41 679	36.4	25.4
Cottage Grove	12 052	2.91	10.4	16.8	64	13	7	51	708	2 003	71	1 933	22 543	32.4	32.0
Duluth	34 735	2.29	11.4	35.7	6 640	1 416	924	5 224	4 625	5 365	397	4 968	52 736	32.4	31.8
Eagan	25 586	2.53	9.7	24.8	197	61	61	136	1 324	2 035	57	1 978	43 518	19.0	50.6
Eden Prairie	24 396	2.54	7.9	25.6	208	127	112	81	933	1 488	62	1 426	41 814	14.5	59.2
Edina	20 806	2.35	6.3	32.7	190	112	100	78	953	1 929	32	1 897	34 453	12.4	68.1
Fridley	11 272	2.43	13.2	29.1	131	48	48	83	1 324	4 767	277	4 490	18 818	41.2	25.3
Inver Grove Heights	13 565	2.51	13.3	25.0	193	154	140	39	844	2 461	242	2 219	22 194	34.8	33.4
Lakeville	18 773	3.06	10.0	12.5	46	14	6	32	739	1 279	26	1 254	36 153	23.8	45.9
Mankato	15 197	2.37	5.9	34.0	4 347	324	239	4 023	1 860	4 609	265	4 343	20 791	31.9	33.7
Maple Grove	23 945	2.68	7.5	19.9	50	4	4	46	1 115	1 707	43	1 664	44 048	20.7	49.6
Maplewood	15 388	2.48	11.5	31.5	1 131	800	362	331	2 370	5 960	189	5 771	27 432	37.9	27.7
Minneapolis	165 785	2.27	11.5	40.0	18 066	3 896	2 814	14 170	23 396	5 905	1 019	4 886	258 140	28.2	47.0
Minnetonka	22 287	2.27	8.3	31.1	380	292	209	88	876	1 699	25	1 673	37 322	16.2	55.5
Moorhead	14 481	2.43	11.2	31.6	3 650	344	263	3 306	885	2 251	97	2 154	22 104	32.0	33.3
Oakdale	10 845	2.53	14.2	26.7	177	7	2	170	1 221	4 389	198	4 191	18 148	31.1	31.2
Owatonna	10 191	2.45	8.7	29.0	531	321	203	210	716	2 821	142	2 680	16 824	40.5	27.3
Plymouth	29 552	2.43	8.0	26.5	1 128	730	229	398	1 190	1 615	67	1 549	51 822	16.7	56.8
Richfield	15 088	2.36	10.2	34.7	347	112	110	235	1 063	2 923	242	2 681	26 180	35.4	35.1
Rochester	43 522	2.45	9.6	31.7	2 615	1 760	646	855	2 772	2 527	195	2 332	73 371	27.3	41.8
Roseville	14 876	2.22	5.9	37.4	1 426	342	292	1 084	1 533	4 381	149	4 233	24 514	26.7	45.1
St. Cloud	24 619	2.45	10.7	29.3	5 615	1 690	448	3 925	3 092	4 686	379	4 308	37 889	34.5	28.3
St. Louis Park	21 705	2.11	9.1	41.1	755	633	630	122	1 356	2 902	146	2 757	33 873	18.4	56.1
St. Paul	112 289	2.52	14.3	35.5	11 438	2 351	1 608	9 087	13 173	4 470	747	3 724	179 618	35.0	38.9
Savage	9 484	2.95	7.8	20.1	6	4	0	2	635	2 245	124	2 121	17 555	23.0	44.3
Shakopee	13 178	2.86	11.5	20.9	884	843	167	41	1 077	2 746	135	2 611	24 416	31.3	39.3
Shoreview	10 751	2.37	8.6	28.2	204	9	0	195	306	1 186	46	1 139	18 610	22.1	51.7
Winona	10 185	2.30	7.4	40.5	4 223	376	324	3 847	426	1 517	107	1 410	15 196	38.2	31.8
Woodbury	23 527	2.73	9.9	19.4	286	161	161	125	1 407	2 156	32	2 124	42 107	17.1	56.2
MISSISSIPPI	1 086 898	2.66	18.7	27.5	91 964	55 135	16 496	36 829	89 714	2 999	275	2 725	1 928 088	48.5	20.2
Biloxi	17 814	2.33	17.3	34.0	3 065	209	158	2 856	2 543	5 683	476	5 207	28 360	43.9	21.9
Clinton	8 999	2.79	13.7	24.7	397	265	265	132	NA	NA	NA	NA	16 598	26.1	41.5
Greenville	11 889	2.79	30.1	28.6	432	370	254	62	2 626	7 929	299	7 630	21 482	50.3	21.0
Gulfport	27 407	2.49	20.0	30.9	1 984	1 222	278	762	3 650	5 151	223	4 928	45 591	44.9	20.6
Hattiesburg	18 493	2.34	18.8	38.5	3 529	832	468	2 697	2 913	6 126	330	5 796	27 003	40.4	32.1
Horn Lake	9 084	2.91	24.2	23.6	56	56	56	0	613	2 298	131	2 167	16 227	50.8	11.5
Jackson	62 779	2.68	27.6	32.8	6 035	1 419	998	4 616	11 915	6 768	926	5 842	106 084	42.5	25.5
Meridian	15 860	2.49	29.0	32.5	1 678	1 161	268	517	2 648	6 498	572	5 927	25 788	43.4	20.9
Olive Branch	12 559	2.75	17.0	19.9	0	0	0	0	982	2 820	190	2 630	22 102	39.6	26.9
Pearl	10 465	2.49	21.8	25.9	70	57	57	13	651	2 476	95	2 381	16 513	43.5	17.8
Southaven	18 572	2.70	14.1	24.6	264	264	264	0	1 623	3 195	331	2 864	32 018	37.6	22.4
Tupelo	13 594	2.55	21.1	30.0	895	834	471	61	NA	NA	NA	NA	22 888	40.5	29.8

1. No spouse present. 2. Data for serious crimes have not been adjusted for underreporting. This may affect comparability between geographic areas and over time. 3. Per 100,000 population estimated by the FBI. 4. Persons 25 years old and over.

City	Money income, 2011–2013					Housing units, 2010			Occupied housing units 2011–2013				
		Households								Owner-occupied		Median owner costs as a percent of income	
	Per capita income[1] (dollars)	Median income	Percent with income of $200,000 or more	Percent with income of less than $25,000	Families with income below poverty (percent)	Total	Percent change, 2000–2010	Vacant units for sale or rent[2]	Total	Percent	Median value[3] (dollars)	With a mortgage[4]	Without a mortgage[5]
	42	43	44	45	46	47	48	49	50	51	52	53	54
MICHIGAN—Cont'd													
Oak Park	21 736	50 227	0.7	24.5	12.9	12 782	12.4	1 063	11 230	58.8	71 300	23.5	13.8
Pontiac	15 121	26 445	0.1	47.4	33.3	27 084	2.8	4 864	23 622	46.8	52 400	26.0	17.1
Portage	29 402	51 832	4.0	23.9	9.7	20 559	8.9	1 360	19 551	67.0	145 600	21.4	12.8
Port Huron	17 850	31 971	0.9	41.9	25.0	13 871	-0.9	1 694	12 158	53.8	70 300	23.8	14.1
Rochester Hills	39 720	79 379	10.4	12.4	3.4	29 494	8.1	1 916	27 770	75.5	213 500	20.7	12.3
Roseville	20 627	41 191	0.3	28.9	14.8	21 260	3.6	1 707	19 581	65.1	59 200	23.8	13.3
Royal Oak	38 936	62 377	3.7	17.2	3.4	30 207	0.9	2 144	28 464	66.2	155 300	19.9	13.9
Saginaw	13 905	27 188	0.4	46.9	32.8	23 574	-8.1	3 775	18 870	59.0	45 200	24.9	14.9
St. Clair Shores	28 697	52 055	1.2	22.8	8.7	28 467	0.9	1 882	26 917	77.7	87 300	21.0	13.6
Southfield	27 852	47 886	2.3	25.3	14.4	35 986	0.8	4 208	31 403	47.8	98 600	23.7	14.9
Southgate	26 152	49 699	0.7	21.4	7.9	13 933	4.3	871	12 149	67.3	80 400	19.8	13.2
Sterling Heights	26 471	57 038	2.4	20.7	11.2	52 190	9.8	2 739	49 207	72.5	137 200	22.2	12.7
Taylor	19 615	39 904	0.5	30.1	19.7	26 422	2.0	2 052	23 552	66.5	70 500	23.7	13.8
Troy	37 932	81 133	9.8	15.2	7.2	32 907	6.6	2 204	30 542	72.9	212 700	21.0	12.2
Warren	21 933	42 488	0.7	28.9	16.0	57 938	1.2	4 496	53 441	72.4	83 500	23.1	15.0
Westland	23 567	43 778	0.9	26.8	11.2	39 201	3.0	3 315	33 292	59.3	83 400	21.3	13.3
Wyandotte	25 793	50 244	1.1	27.5	9.2	12 081	-1.8	1 090	10 524	72.4	78 600	20.3	14.7
Wyoming	21 322	46 085	0.9	20.6	10.3	28 983	5.4	2 013	27 431	64.7	95 400	21.9	11.0
MINNESOTA	30 902	59 791	4.7	19.6	7.5	2 347 201	13.6	259 974	2 109 924	71.8	180 600	22.4	11.5
Andover	32 198	92 399	5.6	6.0	4.1	10 091	23.0	280	9 999	94.2	229 200	23.0	10.7
Apple Valley	35 416	75 048	6.2	10.8	4.8	19 600	18.5	725	19 226	76.5	206 700	21.7	10.0
Blaine	30 973	70 476	3.5	11.7	4.3	21 921	35.6	844	21 750	84.0	171 500	21.7	12.3
Bloomington	35 615	61 885	5.2	16.9	6.2	37 641	1.5	1 736	36 829	68.0	211 300	22.5	11.9
Brooklyn Center	19 799	43 287	0.5	25.0	17.6	11 640	0.4	884	11 341	61.3	130 300	24.3	14.0
Brooklyn Park	26 873	61 598	4.0	16.7	9.3	27 841	12.1	1 612	26 786	69.2	176 600	23.7	10.0
Burnsville	31 487	62 682	4.1	17.1	9.2	25 759	6.2	1 476	25 119	63.6	202 300	23.3	11.6
Coon Rapids	28 485	63 240	2.5	15.9	7.8	24 462	7.3	930	23 641	76.0	161 200	22.2	11.7
Cottage Grove	30 814	79 137	3.9	8.0	3.8	12 102	20.8	383	12 052	88.4	196 200	22.4	10.0
Duluth	24 737	42 759	3.1	31.8	12.7	38 208	3.3	2 503	34 735	60.5	147 500	22.3	11.8
Eagan	40 065	80 850	9.0	10.2	4.4	26 414	8.3	1 165	25 586	70.2	244 600	19.8	10.0
Eden Prairie	49 697	96 525	15.1	10.3	3.4	25 075	19.3	1 145	24 396	73.7	290 000	21.1	10.0
Edina	58 369	84 211	18.7	13.8	2.5	22 560	4.2	1 888	20 806	70.9	394 000	22.5	14.2
Fridley	27 129	53 897	1.7	17.5	11.0	11 760	2.2	650	11 272	64.2	166 500	23.2	13.1
Inver Grove Heights	32 701	63 162	5.3	15.8	6.0	14 062	22.8	586	13 565	69.8	197 000	22.7	10.9
Lakeville	35 465	93 334	9.3	8.9	5.0	19 456	41.0	773	18 773	89.0	236 300	22.2	10.0
Mankato	23 146	41 032	2.4	33.1	12.3	15 784	24.0	933	15 197	54.6	147 100	22.3	10.5
Maple Grove	43 397	92 452	12.5	8.6	5.3	23 626	33.2	759	23 945	84.8	239 400	21.0	10.0
Maplewood	29 390	60 582	2.3	15.8	4.4	15 561	11.1	679	15 388	74.0	173 700	23.6	11.6
Minneapolis	31 616	49 777	5.3	27.6	15.8	178 287	5.7	14 747	165 785	48.4	197 800	23.2	14.0
Minnetonka	46 453	74 503	11.6	12.4	3.7	23 294	4.8	1 393	22 287	71.1	284 800	22.8	13.0
Moorhead	22 909	47 442	1.8	26.1	8.6	15 274	25.5	970	14 481	62.3	154 500	21.2	11.5
Oakdale	31 035	67 048	3.0	13.0	5.8	11 388	9.5	440	10 845	76.5	183 600	21.6	10.0
Owatonna	27 330	52 155	2.9	21.9	9.4	10 724	20.0	656	10 191	71.7	148 800	20.7	11.6
Plymouth	45 584	82 806	12.0	12.0	4.9	29 982	18.7	1 319	29 552	70.9	282 800	20.4	10.6
Richfield	28 703	52 090	2.6	20.7	9.3	15 735	2.5	917	15 088	64.3	178 900	22.9	14.9
Rochester	32 709	62 105	5.2	18.0	5.5	45 683	29.7	2 658	43 522	69.7	162 000	20.5	10.0
Roseville	33 656	62 161	3.5	20.5	7.7	15 490	3.8	867	14 876	63.5	215 700	21.9	10.0
St. Cloud	22 244	44 715	2.1	31.0	14.0	27 338	17.8	1 899	24 619	52.8	142 700	21.5	10.9
St. Louis Park	39 493	66 895	5.5	14.7	5.8	23 285	10.2	1 542	21 705	56.7	226 300	21.5	12.6
St. Paul	25 819	47 083	3.4	27.6	17.1	120 795	4.4	9 794	112 289	49.1	170 000	23.1	11.6
Savage	36 751	91 146	9.2	7.7	4.1	9 429	34.5	313	9 484	88.0	243 400	21.6	10.0
Shakopee	32 623	78 540	5.4	10.1	5.0	13 339	71.2	567	13 178	78.6	197 100	21.6	10.0
Shoreview	40 699	75 230	9.6	12.1	3.5	10 826	5.2	424	10 751	82.5	223 600	21.5	12.5
Winona	21 871	38 198	2.1	33.6	6.6	10 989	3.1	540	10 185	62.0	139 100	24.4	10.0
Woodbury	41 592	96 796	12.2	8.0	1.5	23 568	34.4	974	23 527	77.3	259 400	20.6	10.0
MISSISSIPPI	20 369	38 087	2.0	34.4	18.2	1 274 719	9.7	158 951	1 086 898	68.5	99 400	22.6	11.8
Biloxi	21 794	35 869	2.0	38.8	22.9	21 278	-3.9	4 174	17 814	43.4	138 700	24.4	13.3
Clinton	27 046	55 850	4.5	20.2	8.9	10 359	16.2	593	8 999	67.2	155 700	19.7	10.0
Greenville	17 452	30 029	2.5	45.5	30.3	14 561	-10.5	1 883	11 889	53.4	77 000	20.9	13.3
Gulfport	20 824	36 777	1.7	34.6	21.1	31 602	6.8	5 295	27 407	52.6	118 700	26.2	11.9
Hattiesburg	19 431	25 991	2.2	48.4	29.3	21 381	11.5	2 000	18 403	36.8	103 100	23.3	12.1
Horn Lake	18 344	46 935	0.3	22.4	9.1	9 705	90.4	653	9 084	63.0	94 000	20.4	12.0
Jackson	17 987	30 770	2.1	42.1	27.5	74 537	-1.5	10 014	62 779	51.9	88 400	24.2	11.3
Meridian	19 831	28 846	1.9	45.8	31.8	18 591	3.6	2 082	15 860	50.4	85 400	23.9	10.0
Olive Branch	26 802	59 956	1.3	15.5	8.2	12 942	60.6	864	12 559	74.4	164 200	22.5	11.7
Pearl	22 334	46 474	1.0	23.4	8.6	10 396	14.6	604	10 465	62.1	112 200	20.4	10.0
Southaven	25 453	56 172	2.4	20.5	9.0	19 101	66.3	1 132	18 572	69.0	138 000	20.3	10.0
Tupelo	22 383	41 465	2.8	33.9	24.2	15 371	5.0	1 769	13 594	61.3	118 200	22.6	10.0

1. Based on population estimated by the American Community Survey. 2. Includes units rented or sold but not occupied. 3. Specified owner-occupied units; $1,000,000 represents $1,000,000 or more 4. 50.0 represents 50 percent or more. 5. 10.0 represents 10 percent or less.

City	Occupied housing units, 2011–2013 (cont.)				Migration, 2011–2013		Civilian labor force, 2014				Civilian employment[4], 2011–2013			
									Unemployment			Percent		
	Percent renter occupied	Median gross rent[1]	Median rent as a percent of income[2]	Percent with no vehicle available	Percent who lived in the same house one year ago	Percent who lived outside current city one year ago	Total	Percent change, 2013–2014	Total	Rate[3]	Population age 16 and older	In labor force	Civilian full-year full-time workers	Households with no workers (percent)
	55	56	57	58	59	60	61	62	63	64	65	66	67	68
MICHIGAN—Cont'd														
Oak Park	41.2	1 003	30.6	10.1	87.7	8.9	14 215	-0.5	1 585	11.2	23 516	63.8	34.5	27.0
Pontiac	53.2	716	38.2	18.7	77.2	9.3	25 331	-1.3	3 886	15.3	45 774	60.2	25.8	38.3
Portage	33.0	691	31.7	6.2	82.9	11.8	24 148	1.6	1 230	5.1	36 715	68.5	43.5	27.6
Port Huron	46.2	647	33.2	18.9	80.4	10.6	12 843	-1.0	1 694	13.2	23 122	58.6	28.7	41.5
Rochester Hills	24.5	1 036	26.3	4.2	86.9	10.1	37 224	0.5	2 107	5.7	57 580	66.8	42.8	25.2
Roseville	34.9	850	32.6	9.2	83.5	12.4	22 786	-0.4	2 367	10.4	37 572	65.3	38.7	33.0
Royal Oak	33.8	861	23.5	5.4	83.0	12.6	36 342	0.8	1 533	4.2	50 012	75.1	51.4	23.0
Saginaw	41.0	657	44.8	18.4	82.2	9.2	19 974	-1.4	2 531	12.7	38 422	55.6	24.7	44.0
St. Clair Shores	22.3	854	30.1	6.3	88.3	8.7	30 470	0.1	2 404	7.9	49 865	63.8	38.4	34.2
Southfield	52.2	946	34.1	11.0	80.8	13.2	34 035	-0.3	3 277	9.6	59 231	60.2	36.8	34.3
Southgate	32.7	786	26.3	5.9	85.1	12.2	14 947	0.0	900	6.0	25 233	61.3	35.3	32.4
Sterling Heights	27.5	855	30.3	5.3	86.5	9.7	64 296	0.1	5 003	7.8	107 029	63.3	37.6	27.7
Taylor	33.5	778	35.2	9.0	82.9	12.5	27 933	-0.7	2 785	10.0	49 044	61.0	33.1	35.3
Troy	27.1	1 008	24.5	4.2	87.1	9.9	41 157	0.5	2 314	5.6	66 014	64.3	40.7	22.9
Warren	27.6	811	36.0	9.8	85.6	10.2	62 018	-0.2	6 054	9.8	108 402	60.7	34.6	34.5
Westland	40.7	797	32.3	8.7	85.5	11.8	41 739	-0.2	2 966	7.1	67 567	64.2	37.5	32.0
Wyandotte	27.6	668	34.3	9.0	89.0	7.0	12 765	-0.2	885	6.9	21 044	66.4	36.7	32.2
Wyoming	35.3	705	26.9	7.4	83.6	12.2	42 653	2.1	2 275	5.3	56 947	73.8	45.0	21.1
MINNESOTA	28.2	821	29.5	7.2	85.5	10.3	2 974 102	0.3	121 626	4.1	4 245 984	70.1	43.5	24.1
Andover	5.8	1 019	39.9	2.7	92.6	6.6	18 160	0.5	639	3.5	23 665	77.9	50.8	11.8
Apple Valley	23.5	1 122	31.1	3.5	84.1	11.9	28 925	0.6	994	3.4	38 933	76.2	50.7	17.0
Blaine	16.0	983	27.5	3.6	90.9	6.4	34 417	0.4	1 271	3.7	44 505	77.4	50.5	15.3
Bloomington	32.0	918	29.3	7.0	85.9	9.2	46 736	0.5	1 801	3.9	70 740	67.7	42.1	27.7
Brooklyn Center	38.7	886	36.6	10.0	84.2	13.8	15 284	-0.1	714	4.7	23 443	66.5	41.5	25.8
Brooklyn Park	30.8	845	33.0	7.4	86.9	10.6	41 597	0.3	1 829	4.4	59 229	73.3	46.6	17.5
Burnsville	36.4	953	27.2	6.1	82.4	13.3	35 667	0.6	1 334	3.7	49 182	72.7	45.5	21.2
Coon Rapids	24.0	1 008	33.5	5.1	85.3	11.2	35 213	0.4	1 404	4.0	48 947	73.6	44.5	22.1
Cottage Grove	11.6	1 060	31.1	1.6	92.2	6.8	19 733	0.4	712	3.6	26 367	76.4	50.5	16.9
Duluth	39.5	691	34.4	13.0	77.0	10.5	45 691	-0.5	2 004	4.4	71 888	64.9	33.0	30.6
Eagan	29.8	975	25.7	3.9	85.3	10.9	39 194	0.8	1 307	3.3	50 720	77.3	52.6	16.1
Eden Prairie	26.3	1 169	23.5	2.5	88.1	9.1	35 489	0.6	1 117	3.1	47 691	74.9	51.3	16.4
Edina	29.1	1 134	26.0	7.3	87.0	11.8	24 563	0.7	758	3.1	38 520	63.5	41.3	29.9
Fridley	35.8	851	26.4	8.5	79.7	15.2	14 787	0.2	630	4.3	22 288	69.1	44.1	24.7
Inver Grove Heights	30.2	947	32.3	5.0	84.3	12.3	19 284	0.5	738	3.8	27 144	72.9	45.1	21.5
Lakeville	11.0	1 087	28.1	2.3	91.2	7.1	33 102	0.8	1 123	3.4	42 032	77.7	51.3	13.8
Mankato	45.4	677	35.6	9.4	74.6	16.7	24 675	0.1	887	3.6	34 204	71.5	34.8	24.5
Maple Grove	15.2	1 260	31.1	2.7	91.6	7.2	38 057	0.6	1 221	3.2	49 103	76.2	53.1	15.7
Maplewood	26.0	914	31.2	9.3	86.4	11.5	20 297	0.6	847	4.2	31 569	66.5	43.2	27.1
Minneapolis	51.6	830	29.8	18.1	75.7	12.7	228 247	0.6	8 589	3.8	320 867	73.2	42.6	23.0
Minnetonka	28.9	1 087	25.4	4.0	86.2	11.5	29 318	0.7	999	3.4	41 602	71.1	47.1	22.1
Moorhead	37.7	688	32.7	8.5	79.7	13.0	23 234	2.3	671	2.9	32 086	71.5	40.0	24.3
Oakdale	23.5	1 004	32.2	6.0	89.9	7.7	15 960	0.5	625	3.9	21 997	73.8	47.6	21.0
Owatonna	28.3	754	36.8	7.9	83.6	6.9	14 788	-1.3	565	3.8	19 719	68.6	44.8	27.9
Plymouth	29.1	1 114	27.1	3.3	83.7	13.0	41 843	0.6	1 380	3.3	58 035	71.4	48.5	20.2
Richfield	35.7	840	33.1	10.5	85.0	11.0	20 123	0.6	726	3.6	29 184	71.9	45.0	25.3
Rochester	30.3	782	29.7	7.4	84.2	8.1	60 973	-0.8	2 102	3.4	85 239	72.2	45.9	20.7
Roseville	36.5	875	28.5	9.7	84.5	13.3	18 729	0.6	648	3.5	28 985	64.5	39.8	32.4
St. Cloud	47.2	706	34.4	8.6	68.5	19.6	36 503	0.8	1 637	4.5	53 610	68.9	33.1	25.4
St. Louis Park	43.3	956	23.6	8.1	80.0	15.2	29 638	0.7	934	3.2	38 154	75.8	51.9	20.0
St. Paul	50.9	818	31.1	14.0	77.4	11.8	152 277	0.4	6 218	4.1	225 476	70.6	40.3	24.2
Savage	12.0	1 155	34.2	1.7	90.3	9.0	16 837	0.7	563	3.3	20 511	80.6	55.7	8.6
Shakopee	21.4	1 019	27.0	3.2	88.4	8.6	22 237	0.6	801	3.6	28 515	79.1	55.1	11.6
Shoreview	17.5	1 067	24.4	3.5	91.0	7.5	14 467	0.6	461	3.2	20 817	66.2	44.0	24.6
Winona	38.0	516	29.5	11.7	76.6	12.3	16 038	-0.9	639	4.0	24 716	69.3	30.9	27.7
Woodbury	22.7	1 315	24.4	2.2	87.6	10.6	36 885	0.7	1 075	2.9	48 178	75.3	52.7	15.0
MISSISSIPPI	31.5	697	32.0	7.0	85.8	10.5	1 236 310	-2.9	96 343	7.8	2 323 962	58.2	36.6	32.0
Biloxi	56.6	787	32.6	8.3	73.4	18.9	19 423	-3.5	1 436	7.4	36 016	67.6	34.0	28.1
Clinton	32.8	916	30.1	3.3	89.2	7.7	12 616	-2.0	620	4.9	20 226	63.5	40.6	22.6
Greenville	46.6	629	36.8	14.5	82.9	6.0	12 339	-4.9	1 630	13.2	25 591	59.2	32.6	36.2
Gulfport	47.4	828	34.4	6.4	74.1	14.7	29 367	-3.6	2 531	8.6	54 582	63.0	35.4	29.8
Hattiesburg	63.2	669	36.9	11.0	71.7	13.8	21 512	-2.5	1 902	8.8	38 889	65.7	30.3	29.4
Horn Lake	37.0	965	28.5	3.3	83.5	13.7	11 938	-2.1	691	5.8	19 089	70.1	48.2	17.7
Jackson	48.1	720	38.7	10.2	84.2	5.2	73 998	-2.7	5 827	7.9	132 762	62.2	37.9	29.7
Meridian	49.6	607	31.5	11.7	83.6	8.0	16 286	-7.0	1 635	10.0	31 165	59.7	38.2	32.2
Olive Branch	25.6	1 099	24.1	2.9	84.8	10.7	17 429	-2.5	836	4.8	26 961	73.6	52.2	15.5
Pearl	37.9	751	24.5	4.0	82.4	8.7	12 111	-2.5	558	4.6	20 082	68.6	48.9	25.6
Southaven	31.0	908	31.4	2.3	82.8	12.2	24 518	-2.3	1 188	4.8	37 712	71.0	49.1	19.7
Tupelo	38.7	661	32.9	7.3	84.1	10.4	15 732	-2.9	1 396	8.9	26 597	61.7	38.9	27.0

1. $2,000 represents $2,000 or more. 2. 50.0 represents 50 percent or more. 3. Percent of civilian labor force. 4. Persons 16 years old and over.

City	Value of residential construction authorized by building permits, 2014			Wholesale trade,[1] 2007				Retail trade,[2] 2007			
	New construction ($1,000)	Number of housing units	Percent single family	Number of establishments	Number of employees	Sales (mil dol)	Annual payroll (mil dol)	Number of establishments	Number of employees	Sales (mil dol)	Annual payroll (mil dol)
	69	70	71	72	73	74	75	76	77	78	79
MICHIGAN—Cont'd											
Oak Park	171	1	100.0	62	634	281.9	34.0	131	1 030	221.3	26.1
Pontiac	3 837	26	100.0	54	1 202	788.0	83.6	196	1 566	377.1	35.4
Portage	17 250	95	51.6	49	560	215.6	33.5	318	6 241	1 136.8	109.3
Port Huron	2 305	19	10.5	18	189	140.1	8.9	130	1 457	237.5	26.3
Rochester Hills	57 772	217	38.2	79	946	450.6	56.5	255	5 071	1 183.2	123.0
Roseville	145	2	100.0	64	747	380.2	36.0	264	5 045	1 178.8	106.9
Royal Oak	40 210	129	100.0	52	549	794.4	34.6	239	2 884	632.5	69.1
Saginaw	5 001	39	12.8	41	765	241.9	26.1	164	1 340	233.3	25.9
St. Clair Shores	4 126	27	100.0	48	214	95.2	8.2	189	2 125	518.0	52.0
Southfield	3 486	5	100.0	193	3 194	3 250.9	198.4	434	6 216	2 165.7	167.2
Southgate	2 349	9	100.0	10	47	8.9	1.4	136	2 547	791.5	58.1
Sterling Heights	22 695	108	63.9	149	1 781	774.7	88.5	494	8 239	1 628.0	170.5
Taylor	1 401	7	42.9	91	1 198	1 205.7	59.4	319	5 453	1 189.1	110.7
Troy	44 327	167	74.3	317	4 196	2 727.4	237.4	601	12 596	2 615.6	298.1
Warren	4 832	69	30.4	191	3 524	1 900.1	170.6	489	6 337	1 517.6	150.6
Westland	4 791	43	81.4	55	547	171.7	22.3	349	5 681	1 119.9	108.0
Wyandotte	1 156	6	100.0	13	50	18.5	1.3	83	532	141.1	12.8
Wyoming	8 542	58	100.0	173	6 179	3 358.9	346.0	278	4 402	978.3	101.0
MINNESOTA	3 680 420	16 990	62.9	6 913	110 487	82 878.1	6 417.8	20 777	307 034	71 384.1	6 685.6
Andover	14 817	52	100.0	11	D	D	D	41	704	145.8	13.0
Apple Valley	54 296	368	19.3	33	170	106.5	8.0	136	3 726	839.3	77.4
Blaine	96 213	343	100.0	68	934	563.0	48.2	261	4 357	766.7	85.3
Bloomington	2 449	11	100.0	243	5 523	4 442.9	409.7	547	13 463	2 847.6	375.0
Brooklyn Center	491	4	100.0	26	303	99.2	10.0	94	2 331	672.9	60.7
Brooklyn Park	25 595	114	100.0	94	1 505	1 101.7	84.7	161	3 018	851.6	77.4
Burnsville	8 118	34	100.0	155	2 140	775.6	109.0	354	6 030	1 357.5	138.6
Coon Rapids	3 415	12	100.0	29	295	152.1	19.0	207	5 303	1 133.2	117.9
Cottage Grove	22 751	77	100.0	11	D	D	D	59	1 168	226.3	22.7
Duluth	26 292	180	25.6	82	947	590.9	40.3	476	7 090	1 294.7	136.6
Eagan	43 450	173	90.2	155	3 978	1 729.2	234.8	176	3 625	906.9	82.0
Eden Prairie	21 136	61	100.0	207	3 428	7 152.9	218.9	232	6 651	2 684.2	203.7
Edina	87 438	231	52.8	123	1 032	707.8	67.9	317	5 655	984.1	121.5
Fridley	1 521	7	100.0	74	D	D	D	91	2 346	598.6	60.4
Inver Grove Heights	28 336	118	44.1	20	D	D	D	68	1 467	413.7	35.3
Lakeville	115 143	347	100.0	52	594	255.1	26.4	110	2 048	536.9	45.1
Mankato	25 259	222	34.7	49	837	970.1	38.5	281	5 875	1 128.1	103.4
Maple Grove	106 789	502	61.0	94	1 501	1 119.7	121.0	238	5 145	886.6	94.5
Maplewood	4 916	25	100.0	34	314	175.2	15.2	247	5 272	1 130.3	111.5
Minneapolis	365 662	1 959	7.0	518	7 683	5 518.6	391.2	1 164	14 740	3 867.0	386.8
Minnetonka	26 124	53	100.0	152	2 435	2 873.4	167.9	324	7 218	1 581.0	153.1
Moorhead	53 993	401	46.1	30	349	261.5	17.0	127	2 153	478.1	42.0
Oakdale	567	2	100.0	36	310	159.2	17.1	79	1 513	358.8	37.1
Owatonna	3 734	21	81.0	18	288	176.3	15.1	123	2 340	437.7	43.9
Plymouth	126 495	312	100.0	222	5 164	3 515.5	309.1	210	4 234	1 903.3	133.8
Richfield	1 610	6	100.0	17	307	78.9	17.5	126	2 400	1 768.0	70.7
Rochester	96 126	486	72.4	78	853	607.7	39.7	503	9 700	1 932.1	204.6
Roseville	4 479	12	100.0	83	1 436	823.4	68.4	314	7 056	1 335.0	137.9
St. Cloud	21 800	217	19.8	77	2 835	1 125.7	133.3	370	7 350	1 481.0	144.5
St. Louis Park	48 439	328	3.4	134	2 016	1 337.4	115.0	178	3 976	1 086.9	106.5
St. Paul	92 655	494	14.2	296	5 321	3 129.2	290.8	752	10 077	1 794.1	209.9
Savage	53 196	439	18.7	36	802	732.9	47.7	74	1 082	274.1	24.6
Shakopee	30 394	160	43.8	36	519	421.2	30.7	121	2 226	544.4	49.3
Shoreview	6 132	28	100.0	29	2 287	912.6	140.0	52	1 073	193.6	19.3
Winona	2 168	10	100.0	39	341	231.0	13.7	140	2 560	461.2	48.2
Woodbury	107 121	342	86.8	40	270	119.9	12.1	224	4 677	922.4	85.0
MISSISSIPPI	1 033 059	6 871	80.7	2 556	32 382	23 003.6	1 276.0	12 452	141 426	33 751.4	2 910.9
Biloxi	47 999	326	31.3	38	408	160.6	12.7	227	2 532	573.4	52.8
Clinton	16 507	74	100.0	15	97	27.1	4.7	93	906	194.5	17.1
Greenville	1 412	7	100.0	39	363	555.9	20.9	217	2 295	418.6	42.1
Gulfport	21 120	132	98.5	86	961	604.2	48.8	409	6 087	1 641.2	144.9
Hattiesburg	18 287	150	26.0	72	824	419.9	29.6	496	7 567	2 701.3	159.4
Horn Lake	10 969	65	100.0	11	57	17.8	1.9	69	1 164	288.2	24.7
Jackson	43 524	420	100.0	257	3 995	1 931.9	179.3	788	10 919	2 660.1	255.5
Meridian	4 123	10	100.0	61	1 261	889.7	50.9	381	4 875	1 100.4	103.8
Olive Branch	26 179	224	100.0	47	846	615.7	37.8	115	1 885	565.8	46.6
Pearl	7 189	42	81.0	61	1 173	743.3	62.1	118	1 818	423.1	39.4
Southaven	34 894	320	96.9	28	1 100	986.0	36.3	208	4 015	1 005.8	88.9
Tupelo	7 115	46	100.0	118	1 446	690.0	52.0	410	5 709	1 212.0	117.6

1. Merchant wholesalers except manufacturers' sales branches and offices. 2. Establishments with payroll.

Table D. Cities — **Real Estate, Professional Services, and Manufacturing**

City	Real estate and rental and leasing, 2007				Professional, scientific, and technical services,[1] 2007				Manufacturing, 2007			
	Number of establish-ments	Number of employees	Receipts (mil dol)	Annual payroll (mil dol)	Number of establish-ments	Number of employees	Receipts (mil dol)	Annual payroll (mil dol)	Number of establish-ments	Number of employees	Receipts (mil dol)	Annual payroll (mil dol)
	80	81	82	83	84	85	86	87	88	89	90	91
MICHIGAN—Cont'd												
Oak Park	36	485	26.9	14.7	40	203	25.5	9.6	61	1 099	189.1	45.8
Pontiac	36	137	21.0	4.1	57	D	D	D	52	4 423	D	416.6
Portage	52	1 232	79.8	35.8	133	D	D	D	64	7 052	4 511.5	439.1
Port Huron	31	134	16.1	3.3	75	D	D	D	62	4 210	1 619.5	184.4
Rochester Hills	47	217	33.4	5.6	253	3 209	553.3	188.2	104	3 147	868.3	167.7
Roseville	54	264	58.8	6.8	52	424	26.7	15.2	145	4 445	748.9	195.9
Royal Oak	69	440	48.5	14.0	255	1 957	184.9	123.2	73	1 982	394.6	59.3
Saginaw	28	100	13.3	2.3	95	1 114	92.1	43.0	62	3 783	1 543.3	232.1
St. Clair Shores	53	231	26.8	7.6	156	602	76.1	27.9	44	1 341	D	53.5
Southfield	252	3 264	661.7	129.5	818	D	D	D	89	3 013	1 041.3	161.4
Southgate	23	D	D	D	44	330	22.0	10.7	NA	NA	NA	NA
Sterling Heights	100	466	115.7	14.7	284	D	D	D	272	14 955	7 662.4	1 018.5
Taylor	48	D	D	D	86	D	D	D	91	4 058	1 251.1	171.4
Troy	147	1 390	263.6	51.5	925	16 536	2 697.5	1 115.9	270	8 351	1 590.5	356.0
Warren	93	655	127.0	21.3	203	D	D	D	381	16 381	7 570.1	873.5
Westland	63	D	D	D	66	432	35.5	12.1	71	1 546	335.1	70.0
Wyandotte	19	D	D	D	43	D	D	D	34	1 390	599.2	101.6
Wyoming	74	696	107.8	23.3	101	D	D	D	174	8 535	2 542.0	443.5
MINNESOTA	6 889	39 430	9 208.0	1 317.4	16 595	140 786	20 473.1	8 425.3	7 951	340 514	107 563.1	15 999.2
Andover	40	182	15.3	3.4	78	331	20.8	9.3	NA	NA	NA	NA
Apple Valley	65	278	43.5	6.0	155	D	D	D	16	551	D	27.6
Blaine	68	251	63.0	6.7	110	D	D	D	152	3 511	477.2	155.4
Bloomington	208	3 531	636.9	184.3	618	D	D	D	145	8 561	1 444.5	478.0
Brooklyn Center	30	D	D	D	67	412	51.1	22.0	33	2 076	346.3	98.7
Brooklyn Park	57	298	43.3	10.2	144	813	155.4	45.3	117	5 704	1 325.6	320.7
Burnsville	119	564	87.3	21.8	301	D	D	D	109	3 522	824.3	162.6
Coon Rapids	78	227	31.9	5.5	131	780	94.4	37.5	67	3 318	866.4	178.9
Cottage Grove	28	69	10.5	1.2	44	99	9.7	3.3	14	1 580	719.9	93.3
Duluth	125	692	102.7	15.2	249	D	D	D	91	3 111	1 081.1	139.8
Eagan	113	535	108.3	19.1	340	D	D	D	93	3 607	1 196.9	176.5
Eden Prairie	147	1 478	485.3	57.4	450	11 071	1 396.2	500.1	109	9 043	1 956.4	516.0
Edina	229	1 990	338.3	73.1	518	D	D	D	73	1 847	578.8	91.8
Fridley	34	274	83.6	5.5	82	446	58.3	27.2	130	7 953	2 612.6	447.6
Inver Grove Heights	30	77	14.5	2.5	108	678	46.3	50.6	29	856	284.9	44.9
Lakeville	87	228	33.3	6.5	162	396	54.2	21.6	74	3 057	714.3	132.5
Mankato	71	620	72.7	13.1	109	D	D	D	51	2 838	2 349.3	116.0
Maple Grove	93	269	41.3	9.9	291	1 120	141.5	74.2	105	7 124	2 443.1	436.8
Maplewood	60	235	43.6	4.3	90	580	123.3	28.5	26	562	165.0	23.7
Minneapolis	651	4 429	3 014.6	159.5	2 305	D	D	D	499	15 783	4 107.5	778.0
Minnetonka	157	1 087	344.2	73.9	485	4 586	698.7	323.6	86	4 543	1 393.9	263.1
Moorhead	31	167	16.0	3.0	44	D	D	D	29	D	D	D
Oakdale	24	90	16.5	2.8	87	596	82.4	28.7	40	997	275.7	46.8
Owatonna	24	241	12.4	4.2	45	142	14.2	4.7	43	5 287	1 309.6	244.8
Plymouth	168	758	827.3	38.2	468	5 079	1 119.4	310.9	194	11 757	3 583.4	662.4
Richfield	26	D	D	D	96	373	42.5	17.8	NA	NA	NA	NA
Rochester	136	735	108.7	19.6	231	D	D	D	62	8 002	2 798.6	535.3
Roseville	74	702	137.2	28.4	210	D	D	D	66	2 435	568.5	111.6
St. Cloud	106	802	91.9	20.3	172	D	D	D	71	7 544	1 926.4	302.6
St. Louis Park	135	1 867	191.1	54.0	359	D	D	D	78	3 302	720.0	158.0
St. Paul	362	3 273	474.6	126.4	968	D	D	D	263	9 382	3 509.0	527.8
Savage	45	105	22.2	3.2	109	254	39.0	11.2	39	1 270	486.9	60.9
Shakopee	44	124	17.6	3.1	90	D	D	D	41	3 413	1 194.9	227.1
Shoreview	36	120	19.2	3.0	124	429	52.6	22.0	30	1 157	295.2	62.1
Winona	39	108	14.4	2.0	60	D	D	D	68	3 313	D	133.5
Woodbury	99	288	63.3	7.8	248	901	141.8	44.0	20	918	202.6	44.5
MISSISSIPPI	2 517	10 169	1 734.6	283.7	4 751	30 855	3 971.9	1 350.3	2 598	159 235	59 869.5	5 756.6
Biloxi	82	326	58.5	9.3	147	D	D	D	NA	NA	NA	NA
Clinton	27	74	10.4	1.4	52	206	20.4	7.3	14	D	D	46.8
Greenville	49	245	27.8	7.5	72	D	D	D	32	1 435	652.9	55.6
Gulfport	118	448	85.5	15.5	189	D	D	D	56	1 809	346.6	65.4
Hattiesburg	111	442	65.4	12.5	201	D	D	D	60	3 846	788.4	117.6
Horn Lake	16	57	13.2	1.3	14	56	3.8	1.1	15	640	187.7	32.5
Jackson	241	1 605	402.4	58.9	613	D	D	D	122	3 732	893.3	157.6
Meridian	65	262	35.7	5.5	105	D	D	D	48	1 662	330.1	50.6
Olive Branch	35	164	26.2	4.9	34	127	10.8	3.4	71	2 903	1 139.9	129.4
Pearl	33	180	30.2	5.4	24	135	26.7	5.4	28	582	407.0	25.7
Southaven	37	144	42.1	4.2	75	509	37.3	14.0	NA	NA	NA	NA
Tupelo	80	365	69.8	10.3	163	D	D	D	89	5 055	1 348.5	188.8

1. Establishments subject to federal tax.

City	Accommodation and food services, 2007				Arts, entertainment, and recreation,[1] 2007				Health care and social assistance,[1] 2007			
	Number of establish-ments	Number of employees	Sales (mil dol)	Annual payroll (mil dol)	Number of establish-ments	Number of employees	Receipts (mil dol)	Annual payroll (mil dol)	Number of establish-ments	Number of employees	Receipts (mil dol)	Annual payroll (mil dol)
	92	93	94	95	96	97	98	99	100	101	102	103
MICHIGAN—Cont'd												
Oak Park	39	454	19.6	5.5	3	3	0.1	0.0	69	604	39.3	14.9
Pontiac	116	1 491	82.8	21.7	14	D	D	D	112	1 117	138.3	61.8
Portage	133	3 641	121.4	37.7	13	D	D	D	161	1 836	152.3	69.7
Port Huron	69	1 059	43.2	12.5	15	D	D	D	133	1 244	156.8	78.8
Rochester Hills	121	D	D	D	15	D	D	D	264	3 063	268.1	123.7
Roseville	107	2 900	116.2	36.1	9	106	5.0	1.2	101	1 071	81.4	37.8
Royal Oak	142	2 966	135.0	39.6	20	D	D	D	165	D	D	D
Saginaw	92	1 172	42.2	11.5	3	D	D	D	118	1 715	167.8	73.4
St. Clair Shores	116	1 995	80.8	23.1	26	D	D	D	193	1 934	200.9	94.2
Southfield	254	4 114	213.8	59.4	27	486	24.2	8.8	682	9 139	988.0	396.1
Southgate	86	2 234	98.5	28.7	2	D	D	D	98	718	90.9	31.6
Sterling Heights	232	5 096	207.6	66.9	30	345	28.5	7.9	292	3 412	282.9	122.9
Taylor	138	2 486	97.9	28.2	11	D	D	D	111	1 632	138.1	54.5
Troy	277	6 365	325.4	96.9	33	D	D	D	432	D	D	D
Warren	309	4 992	216.1	60.1	21	309	14.8	4.1	334	D	D	D
Westland	143	2 825	114.1	32.2	14	D	D	D	139	1 694	129.0	57.2
Wyandotte	58	668	27.7	7.4	5	D	D	D	45	D	D	D
Wyoming	124	2 182	87.9	23.8	16	D	D	D	86	1 035	88.2	38.1
MINNESOTA	11 340	221 081	10 423.7	2 978.4	1 990	28 038	2 185.6	796.1	10 263	157 035	13 229.6	6 021.1
Andover	23	424	15.7	4.5	6	D	D	D	27	D	D	D
Apple Valley	69	1 736	77.6	23.4	12	116	9.5	1.4	105	993	104.0	36.4
Blaine	97	2 430	93.3	29.3	12	D	D	D	69	D	D	D
Bloomington	258	7 752	459.7	137.3	35	684	31.0	9.2	181	3 061	249.3	111.4
Brooklyn Center	50	976	50.5	14.2	5	65	2.5	0.9	79	1 174	91.5	36.6
Brooklyn Park	79	1 745	75.5	23.0	12	D	D	D	103	1 411	81.8	34.2
Burnsville	128	3 128	126.2	39.4	25	760	16.8	4.7	188	D	D	D
Coon Rapids	106	2 918	110.1	33.8	19	D	D	D	130	D	D	D
Cottage Grove	38	693	25.9	7.2	6	84	3.3	1.0	37	453	44.9	15.0
Duluth	230	5 249	211.0	61.8	31	193	9.6	2.4	264	4 379	380.4	174.5
Eagan	128	3 250	155.2	45.4	13	D	D	D	138	2 553	211.5	85.6
Eden Prairie	139	3 182	154.2	51.5	34	D	D	D	119	1 914	229.2	94.8
Edina	100	2 950	161.0	48.2	23	98	7.1	2.2	340	D	D	D
Fridley	47	680	34.8	9.8	7	D	D	D	66	D	D	D
Inver Grove Heights	50	944	41.1	11.9	11	D	D	D	56	526	43.4	19.8
Lakeville	59	1 682	54.4	18.0	19	224	15.0	4.9	77	795	60.7	23.1
Mankato	144	3 813	132.8	39.4	14	110	10.2	1.8	112	D	D	D
Maple Grove	103	3 326	147.6	45.5	18	D	D	D	118	2 183	192.1	80.1
Maplewood	92	2 367	97.5	29.1	16	D	D	D	132	1 808	301.0	98.4
Minneapolis	1 095	24 428	1 333.5	421.5	167	2 758	502.7	235.6	746	13 034	1 258.1	627.4
Minnetonka	108	2 708	142.2	43.9	24	356	22.3	8.0	124	1 749	211.0	84.2
Moorhead	63	1 354	50.0	14.6	7	D	D	D	65	639	39.1	17.2
Oakdale	39	992	66.0	15.6	9	D	D	D	40	248	24.5	7.3
Owatonna	72	1 373	62.7	15.6	7	D	D	D	69	D	D	D
Plymouth	128	2 771	122.3	37.5	25	346	25.0	5.9	190	1 995	262.5	131.3
Richfield	64	1 254	68.6	18.2	6	D	D	D	72	1 414	101.2	42.8
Rochester	278	6 882	312.8	89.6	23	D	D	D	197	D	D	D
Roseville	124	3 672	151.0	51.6	18	D	D	D	129	3 307	285.6	119.5
St. Cloud	160	4 467	164.2	47.3	24	242	19.9	4.1	178	3 917	360.2	212.9
St. Louis Park	93	2 341	106.0	34.6	19	D	D	D	178	D	D	D
St. Paul	598	10 672	499.5	148.0	82	2 225	153.2	70.7	643	12 304	992.8	472.5
Savage	38	D	D	D	9	236	10.0	2.8	38	D	D	D
Shakopee	72	1 520	69.0	21.3	18	D	D	D	67	611	56.2	25.0
Shoreview	29	569	26.2	7.3	4	D	D	D	55	556	48.7	21.0
Winona	78	1 654	58.7	14.8	16	D	D	D	53	D	D	D
Woodbury	97	2 512	96.2	30.0	14	D	D	D	141	D	D	D
MISSISSIPPI	4 817	119 626	7 045.1	1 812.3	506	5 960	425.4	112.4	4 858	72 601	7 228.8	2 752.9
Biloxi	104	11 235	1 247.1	331.2	15	D	D	D	126	2 213	256.7	86.9
Clinton	54	1 168	45.1	11.2	5	D	D	D	46	782	47.3	17.5
Greenville	75	1 462	91.0	19.7	9	D	D	D	113	951	71.5	28.4
Gulfport	162	5 009	304.1	84.3	16	161	10.7	3.8	208	D	D	D
Hattiesburg	213	5 429	217.0	60.2	16	D	D	D	180	D	D	D
Horn Lake	46	1 176	50.9	13.1	5	42	1.4	0.4	11	D	D	D
Jackson	363	7 472	335.7	90.3	24	524	47.3	10.2	505	8 491	1 066.8	406.5
Meridian	140	3 511	131.8	36.9	10	D	D	D	155	D	D	D
Olive Branch	66	1 609	64.5	17.6	9	D	D	D	44	D	D	D
Pearl	62	1 455	61.2	16.6	6	D	D	D	26	250	29.4	9.9
Southaven	118	2 967	124.6	31.9	13	D	D	D	106	D	D	D
Tupelo	164	3 657	131.9	37.0	8	D	D	D	166	D	D	D

1. Establishments subject to federal tax.

Table D. Cities — **Other Services and Government Employment and Payroll**

City	Other services[1], 2007				Government employment and payroll, 2012								
						March payroll							
							Percent of total for:						
	Number of establish-ments	Number of employees	Receipts (mil dol)	Annual payroll (mil dol)	Full-time equivalent employees	Total (dollars)	Adminis-tration, judicial, and legal	Police and Corrections	Fire Protection	Highways and trans-portation	Health and welfare	Natural resources and utilities	Education and libraries
	104	105	106	107	108	109	110	111	112	113	114	115	116
MICHIGAN—Cont'd													
Oak Park	34	139	12.3	4.4	185	937 924	18.6	60.3	0.0	10.5	1.9	3.7	3.3
Pontiac	65	476	43.0	13.7	430	1 925 926	17.1	26.9	21.9	5.4	1.8	16.6	1.4
Portage	91	D	D	D	226	1 051 828	15.4	37.7	18.1	12.3	4.6	4.9	0.0
Port Huron	40	228	14.0	4.7	265	1 254 174	10.2	26.7	19.4	6.8	0.5	25.3	0.0
Rochester Hills	95	606	40.1	13.4	212	1 126 747	28.0	1.5	20.1	6.3	0.0	29.2	0.0
Roseville	86	464	34.9	10.8	272	1 442 763	17.1	38.9	18.8	5.1	2.8	6.5	2.7
Royal Oak	110	687	48.8	16.2	321	1 931 268	16.4	25.4	37.1	2.0	1.2	5.2	3.3
Saginaw	57	243	16.9	4.8	613	1 804 633	11.1	28.9	17.4	6.3	2.1	29.3	0.0
St. Clair Shores	97	497	28.1	8.9	289	1 541 860	15.0	42.8	21.6	1.7	0.7	11.6	5.1
Southfield	142	808	65.8	21.5	690	3 446 012	19.1	28.8	18.1	5.7	1.0	8.4	6.3
Southgate	54	506	79.9	19.3	177	773 845	14.0	43.0	18.7	6.4	1.2	9.7	2.6
Sterling Heights	158	809	62.6	20.5	579	3 290 094	12.5	40.0	22.0	5.0	1.9	8.5	3.7
Taylor	112	1 122	99.2	39.2	369	1 754 345	13.6	40.4	19.0	6.4	4.2	14.1	0.3
Troy	198	1 515	117.1	40.1	515	2 464 478	14.8	42.0	3.2	8.2	0.0	17.1	6.8
Warren	222	1 615	168.9	56.0	409	1 654 082	24.5	41.8	6.8	11.2	1.1	10.9	0.0
Westland	118	741	67.2	20.8	341	1 711 074	17.2	33.4	26.3	2.7	4.2	10.7	4.8
Wyandotte	55	237	20.5	5.3	264	1 258 764	6.9	21.7	11.9	10.2	0.2	39.9	0.0
Wyoming	124	790	67.5	23.6	303	1 910 038	15.8	32.7	7.9	12.1	3.7	22.2	0.0
MINNESOTA	8 519	52 215	4 106.5	1 281.6	X	X	X	X	X	X	X	X	X
Andover	36	D	D	D	57	306 532	24.8	0.0	6.4	37.0	5.8	20.9	0.0
Apple Valley	61	422	31.8	11.4	229	1 179 963	20.1	31.5	5.2	9.3	0.0	23.8	0.0
Blaine	113	D	D	D	193	1 113 430	14.4	41.7	4.5	11.3	3.0	15.1	0.0
Bloomington	166	1 575	101.7	41.3	580	3 330 394	17.4	31.1	1.2	8.0	13.9	19.4	0.0
Brooklyn Center	23	146	6.8	2.5	190	907 979	13.2	39.3	1.8	9.0	0.9	16.1	0.0
Brooklyn Park	86	613	46.2	16.4	439	1 758 756	8.0	36.5	10.9	10.9	10.0	15.7	0.0
Burnsville	106	819	58.8	20.6	283	1 681 229	9.1	34.0	19.2	3.9	1.0	16.7	0.0
Coon Rapids	77	D	D	D	274	1 545 147	17.1	30.9	13.2	6.2	5.6	15.0	0.0
Cottage Grove	28	D	D	D	144	711 248	12.8	41.8	9.7	7.9	5.8	15.7	0.0
Duluth	137	942	54.3	19.5	1 045	5 036 775	9.3	20.6	16.0	20.5	3.8	18.3	4.0
Eagan	112	1 216	117.9	37.0	268	1 561 646	13.0	28.8	3.4	11.0	7.1	30.5	0.0
Eden Prairie	114	947	70.7	24.8	328	1 743 608	14.5	34.2	4.6	8.2	2.3	23.7	0.0
Edina	81	997	75.1	26.5	352	1 123 601	13.6	25.8	14.8	13.3	1.1	27.2	0.0
Fridley	54	D	D	D	159	814 545	21.9	36.8	8.3	11.3	0.0	18.0	0.0
Inver Grove Heights	50	291	19.4	6.9	165	851 190	11.3	30.5	5.7	13.8	7.8	30.9	0.0
Lakeville	79	506	45.2	15.6	211	1 082 740	14.0	36.0	3.4	11.5	2.5	18.7	0.0
Mankato	87	D	D	D	247	1 231 381	15.7	27.7	8.8	14.5	6.7	19.1	0.0
Maple Grove	87	841	59.3	20.9	296	1 469 495	14.2	34.1	4.5	6.8	2.2	24.2	0.0
Maplewood	82	D	D	D	213	1 114 986	14.1	35.4	13.8	12.7	0.3	17.3	0.0
Minneapolis	685	5 055	426.7	130.5	5 068	26 103 507	17.5	27.4	10.3	12.5	9.5	21.9	0.0
Minnetonka	85	703	38.2	14.8	278	1 451 759	17.2	30.1	6.4	12.6	6.1	22.6	0.0
Moorhead	62	D	D	D	325	1 425 672	7.7	22.3	13.7	9.6	0.7	41.4	0.0
Oakdale	34	114	10.3	3.3	111	601 791	15.3	41.9	9.3	5.0	3.9	15.6	0.0
Owatonna	49	D	D	D	211	1 033 223	2.7	19.8	4.9	11.0	1.6	48.8	5.9
Plymouth	89	593	42.6	14.7	284	1 540 683	14.5	33.6	5.5	10.0	5.3	23.7	0.0
Richfield	56	337	24.7	9.2	152	758 629	14.7	33.6	0.0	13.7	5.8	23.9	0.0
Rochester	147	D	D	D	902	4 970 436	6.7	22.3	13.1	9.3	0.0	38.4	6.2
Roseville	83	940	73.5	25.1	191	1 032 673	11.9	37.1	9.1	3.6	4.1	15.9	0.0
St. Cloud	119	916	76.5	24.6	476	2 084 342	8.3	31.7	16.1	9.7	5.9	21.3	0.0
St. Louis Park	97	501	36.4	11.3	270	1 697 664	10.1	28.0	11.9	8.0	13.9	19.8	0.0
St. Paul	398	2 848	216.0	71.5	3 092	18 028 194	10.8	29.1	17.9	10.0	8.1	20.1	4.0
Savage	50	D	D	D	118	627 032	15.4	38.4	2.4	14.5	0.0	16.4	0.0
Shakopee	56	D	D	D	200	1 024 903	11.0	30.0	5.6	7.6	0.0	27.1	0.0
Shoreview	25	D	D	D	99	459 573	15.0	0.0	37.1	15.7	12.0	15.7	0.0
Winona	46	D	D	D	178	771 072	9.5	27.9	14.3	9.5	3.1	24.9	4.4
Woodbury	73	663	38.4	14.7	208	1 116 340	7.1	20.7	13.8	10.0	0.0	38.6	5.6
MISSISSIPPI	3 076	16 201	1 295.3	373.2	X	X	X	X	X	X	X	X	X
Biloxi	48	331	28.7	8.7	618	2 485 229	7.2	33.9	31.9	11.2	2.3	9.3	0.0
Clinton	24	142	10.8	3.9	200	583 437	12.6	31.2	23.8	11.1	0.0	20.4	0.0
Greenville	55	D	D	D	418	1 079 087	14.6	25.9	20.6	12.0	0.0	22.1	0.0
Gulfport	119	720	74.6	20.5	2 468	12 266 312	2.9	7.1	4.8	1.2	81.1	1.5	0.0
Hattiesburg	89	644	37.1	12.0	695	1 732 465	13.4	28.5	23.1	10.4	3.7	17.8	0.0
Horn Lake	24	D	D	D	207	963 937	6.8	40.4	27.4	12.4	0.0	9.9	0.0
Jackson	239	1 797	108.9	36.2	1 879	5 259 822	12.8	36.0	22.9	4.9	6.7	16.7	0.0
Meridian	95	D	D	D	506	1 342 577	12.8	26.9	25.1	9.4	2.6	19.3	0.0
Olive Branch	38	D	D	D	339	1 161 405	13.8	24.1	23.4	3.7	6.6	20.3	0.0
Pearl	50	233	20.9	6.1	218	812 891	8.6	31.3	29.5	10.4	2.5	17.7	0.0
Southaven	57	385	29.8	9.9	376	1 251 638	8.3	38.8	36.0	1.8	0.0	15.2	0.0
Tupelo	87	D	D	D	513	1 717 455	12.7	24.9	21.1	9.8	0.0	29.0	0.0

1. Establishments subject to federal tax.

City	City government finances, 2007									
	General revenue							General expenditure		
		Intergovernmental		Taxes					Per capita[1] (dollars)	
					Per capita[1] (dollars)					
	Total (mil dol)	Total (mil dol)	Percent from state government	Total (mil dol)	Total	Property	Sales and gross receipts	Total (mil dol)	Total	Capital outlays
	117	118	119	120	121	122	123	124	125	126
MICHIGAN—Cont'd										
Oak Park	34.3	6.1	77.1	15.3	515	501	14	32.4	1 094	25
Pontiac	80.8	29.4	48.1	29.2	491	278	50	91.7	1 541	157
Portage	42.4	7.6	94.6	24.0	508	481	26	39.8	842	89
Port Huron	56.4	17.9	36.7	21.0	712	492	23	60.3	2 048	427
Rochester Hills	71.4	14.4	64.9	31.6	437	403	34	59.2	819	60
Roseville	60.4	8.9	82.4	25.0	527	511	16	53.3	1 126	43
Royal Oak	80.5	15.1	59.4	31.4	537	481	56	82.6	1 412	97
Saginaw	92.8	33.0	36.6	21.3	420	150	24	92.8	1 827	78
St. Clair Shores	68.3	10.3	86.2	32.7	546	515	32	62.0	1 037	61
Southfield	103.2	22.5	49.8	64.7	892	863	29	95.5	1 316	49
Southgate	30.9	6.3	84.0	16.4	550	533	17	30.8	1 034	2
Sterling Heights	116.0	21.5	85.9	55.5	426	408	17	126.6	970	137
Taylor	98.5	28.2	37.2	43.0	688	652	36	96.7	1 549	17
Troy	91.2	12.7	89.5	49.2	600	579	21	79.5	969	131
Warren	142.5	27.4	77.3	78.9	588	570	18	136.7	1 019	40
Westland	82.4	25.5	58.5	27.2	327	312	14	78.6	943	2
Wyandotte	44.6	7.8	56.0	16.7	656	640	16	53.7	2 107	160
Wyoming	74.0	21.7	50.6	26.8	365	333	32	64.1	874	19
MINNESOTA	X	X	X	X	X	X	X	X	X	X
Andover	22.9	1.9	92.9	12.6	406	393	12	18.3	588	147
Apple Valley	46.2	2.4	99.7	25.9	518	476	43	38.3	766	170
Blaine	45.6	3.0	81.8	23.5	396	359	37	44.2	746	172
Bloomington	120.6	11.3	85.5	69.9	812	609	203	137.2	1 595	316
Brooklyn Center	39.3	5.0	72.8	18.2	595	514	59	39.3	1 280	319
Brooklyn Park	79.5	9.0	54.3	44.0	566	543	23	69.8	898	50
Burnsville	55.1	4.0	78.6	33.5	547	501	46	54.1	885	185
Coon Rapids	50.6	4.4	75.2	28.1	453	367	86	69.6	1 124	385
Cottage Grove	32.6	4.1	86.1	13.7	391	358	32	30.2	858	186
Duluth	206.7	90.6	73.8	42.1	488	216	272	223.1	2 586	972
Eagan	55.0	3.8	90.8	28.6	442	413	29	57.4	885	201
Eden Prairie	70.0	5.2	80.2	37.9	610	555	54	67.1	1 079	147
Edina	63.6	3.2	88.7	32.5	663	592	70	63.8	1 301	290
Fridley	25.2	2.5	85.3	13.4	485	445	39	22.0	798	53
Inver Grove Heights	31.7	4.0	89.5	15.9	466	442	24	53.2	1 557	670
Lakeville	38.7	2.8	74.0	25.0	436	404	32	42.0	732	180
Mankato	77.8	20.6	42.2	21.6	539	345	195	74.6	1 863	805
Maple Grove	94.0	6.8	98.0	34.4	534	494	40	87.7	1 362	607
Maplewood	49.5	5.8	59.6	18.9	481	447	34	51.2	1 300	407
Minneapolis	1 017.5	148.8	51.2	459.8	1 170	858	312	1 439.6	3 663	222
Minnetonka	66.8	15.6	62.1	35.1	686	601	85	65.7	1 286	502
Moorhead	71.8	30.0	77.2	8.2	210	171	39	91.5	2 342	1 042
Oakdale	20.9	1.3	73.5	10.5	379	346	33	27.2	981	403
Owatonna	26.3	7.8	88.0	10.8	426	355	71	25.3	995	237
Plymouth	77.8	8.1	86.5	32.3	443	399	45	66.3	909	162
Richfield	43.3	7.0	35.4	22.3	617	560	57	42.6	1 180	117
Rochester	216.6	36.4	96.7	62.4	572	415	158	238.9	2 190	743
Roseville	33.7	3.3	86.1	17.5	506	445	61	34.0	981	217
St. Cloud	89.0	22.7	89.2	36.3	550	348	201	105.0	1 592	659
St. Louis Park	76.4	3.2	86.2	35.3	760	659	101	77.7	1 676	320
St. Paul	510.2	119.9	59.1	175.4	602	412	190	504.8	1 733	219
Savage	32.0	3.4	94.3	16.3	584	537	46	22.4	802	183
Shakopee	36.9	5.1	99.9	15.9	410	373	37	36.0	928	217
Shoreview	25.3	1.3	99.9	11.3	441	424	17	23.1	899	137
Winona	24.8	11.9	97.0	7.9	284	213	71	23.2	837	90
Woodbury	61.1	3.7	75.8	30.7	475	432	44	55.7	863	229
MISSISSIPPI	X	X	X	X	X	X	X	X	X	X
Biloxi	102.9	58.6	70.6	23.1	518	393	125	110.6	2 484	715
Clinton	22.4	8.4	97.4	8.5	332	293	39	20.7	810	145
Greenville	30.6	10.5	67.0	12.3	368	293	75	32.5	970	190
Gulfport	510.2	92.4	40.6	32.6	466	348	117	508.4	7 267	1 373
Hattiesburg	68.9	33.4	74.6	25.2	537	368	168	64.6	1 378	307
Horn Lake	18.5	4.3	95.2	7.0	264	233	31	15.9	598	35
Jackson	222.7	65.9	65.5	79.3	452	389	63	212.1	1 210	208
Meridian	43.9	15.5	100.0	18.6	456	387	69	39.7	973	158
Olive Branch	42.4	15.2	100.0	15.0	434	379	55	33.8	978	185
Pearl	24.5	10.5	91.4	6.9	263	226	37	32.5	1 241	187
Southaven	49.4	12.7	100.0	25.8	512	457	55	48.7	966	118
Tupelo	65.5	32.8	96.4	15.7	442	418	24	62.2	1 751	529

1. Based on population estimated as of July 1 of the year shown.

City	Public welfare	Highways	Parking facilities	Education	Health and hospitals	Police protection	Sewerage and sanitation	Parks and recreation	Housing and community development	Interest on debt
	City government finances, 2012 (cont.)									
	General expenditure (cont.)									
	Percent of total for:									
	127	128	129	130	131	132	133	134	135	136
MICHIGAN—Cont'd										
Oak Park	0.0	4.6	0.0	0.0	0.0	26.1	25.4	3.4	1.7	4.4
Pontiac	0.0	7.1	0.9	0.0	0.0	12.5	18.4	0.4	15.4	3.8
Portage	0.3	15.3	0.0	0.0	0.0	16.1	25.8	5.4	0.7	6.0
Port Huron	0.0	9.9	0.2	0.0	0.0	12.5	24.6	6.6	19.9	4.4
Rochester Hills	0.0	16.6	0.0	0.0	0.0	14.1	16.0	17.9	0.0	1.7
Roseville	0.0	9.7	0.0	0.0	0.0	22.0	20.2	4.1	2.4	0.9
Royal Oak	0.0	8.3	2.6	0.0	0.9	15.6	28.0	4.9	2.8	4.3
Saginaw	0.0	6.8	0.3	0.0	0.0	19.4	19.6	0.4	17.3	1.0
St. Clair Shores	0.0	8.8	0.0	0.0	0.0	18.5	24.7	7.1	0.1	3.1
Southfield	0.0	8.3	0.0	0.0	0.0	25.8	3.3	9.2	0.8	2.2
Southgate	0.0	10.8	0.0	0.0	0.0	19.5	14.2	3.9	0.7	2.6
Sterling Heights	0.0	9.6	0.0	0.0	0.0	23.7	27.1	2.0	0.7	0.9
Taylor	0.0	6.6	0.0	0.0	0.0	13.8	11.6	3.9	20.5	5.2
Troy	0.0	17.7	0.0	0.0	0.0	27.5	18.5	11.2	0.2	3.2
Warren	0.0	10.2	0.0	0.0	0.0	25.5	15.8	5.4	3.9	3.3
Westland	0.0	7.6	0.0	0.0	0.0	18.9	22.4	3.3	2.0	0.4
Wyandotte	0.0	10.3	0.0	0.0	0.0	12.1	10.3	3.8	0.0	1.2
Wyoming	0.0	10.0	0.0	0.0	0.0	23.8	19.2	7.1	14.4	1.7
MINNESOTA	X	X	X	X	X	X	X	X	X	X
Andover	0.0	21.8	0.0	0.0	0.1	14.3	10.5	11.4	13.2	10.2
Apple Valley	0.0	23.5	0.0	0.0	0.1	20.0	12.9	18.3	1.6	4.4
Blaine	0.0	19.5	0.0	0.0	0.0	20.6	22.6	3.2	4.5	4.2
Bloomington	0.0	15.1	0.0	0.0	4.6	18.4	9.8	10.4	0.3	2.3
Brooklyn Center	0.0	19.6	0.0	0.0	0.0	18.2	16.1	7.6	5.8	2.3
Brooklyn Park	0.0	12.2	0.0	0.0	0.0	24.2	11.5	13.9	1.1	5.9
Burnsville	0.0	20.0	0.0	0.0	0.0	22.5	13.2	12.7	0.0	4.0
Coon Rapids	0.0	11.5	0.9	0.0	0.1	12.5	11.3	29.9	4.5	4.1
Cottage Grove	0.0	33.1	0.0	0.0	3.9	16.5	6.7	11.5	4.3	12.1
Duluth	0.0	10.1	0.4	0.0	0.0	13.3	14.3	13.0	4.6	4.5
Eagan	0.0	20.7	0.0	0.0	0.0	19.5	13.7	14.3	0.0	5.8
Eden Prairie	1.2	12.6	0.0	0.0	0.2	17.7	14.4	15.9	4.9	12.0
Edina	0.0	27.8	0.0	0.0	0.8	13.8	14.5	20.4	1.1	3.7
Fridley	0.0	16.8	0.0	0.0	0.0	23.9	27.0	6.0	5.6	0.1
Inver Grove Heights	0.0	24.4	0.0	0.0	0.0	10.4	20.8	20.6	1.3	4.3
Lakeville	0.0	25.3	0.0	0.0	0.0	21.3	9.7	9.7	1.2	8.8
Mankato	0.0	18.4	5.3	0.0	0.0	11.5	15.6	4.6	16.8	3.8
Maple Grove	0.0	38.8	0.0	0.0	0.0	10.9	8.6	15.2	1.5	5.0
Maplewood	0.0	30.5	0.0	0.0	0.3	15.2	9.0	8.7	0.7	17.9
Minneapolis	0.0	6.6	3.3	0.0	1.1	10.1	41.6	7.3	9.6	8.6
Minnetonka	0.0	31.5	0.0	0.0	0.5	16.6	9.2	10.9	8.2	3.8
Moorhead	0.0	11.8	0.0	0.0	0.4	8.0	8.7	5.0	1.2	11.2
Oakdale	0.0	28.1	0.0	0.0	0.0	15.5	10.8	5.0	0.0	3.0
Owatonna	0.0	25.9	0.0	0.0	0.0	16.3	14.0	13.5	3.4	3.0
Plymouth	0.0	16.9	0.0	0.0	0.0	14.7	11.2	18.8	2.0	8.3
Richfield	0.0	7.8	0.0	0.0	0.3	17.0	11.9	11.5	23.0	12.9
Rochester	0.0	14.1	1.4	0.0	0.1	8.6	5.1	7.5	0.2	27.8
Roseville	0.0	14.4	0.0	0.0	0.0	18.2	17.2	12.1	4.2	1.3
St. Cloud	0.0	11.6	1.2	0.0	0.9	15.3	22.1	22.3	1.4	4.9
St. Louis Park	0.0	9.2	0.0	0.0	0.0	9.0	10.3	10.9	1.1	25.9
St. Paul	0.0	12.4	1.3	0.0	0.7	17.5	8.3	15.6	9.7	6.3
Savage	0.0	30.8	0.0	0.0	0.0	19.3	12.0	7.6	0.9	11.4
Shakopee	0.0	22.2	0.0	0.0	0.0	18.6	16.8	12.4	0.0	13.3
Shoreview	0.0	15.7	0.0	0.0	0.0	7.9	23.0	26.0	3.7	6.4
Winona	0.0	12.5	0.0	0.0	0.5	18.9	18.0	13.8	3.7	0.8
Woodbury	0.0	22.0	2.9	0.0	3.0	20.7	11.9	11.7	3.2	3.7
MISSISSIPPI	X	X	X	X	X	X	X	X	X	X
Biloxi	1.0	7.1	0.0	0.0	0.2	13.5	15.9	12.3	0.7	2.1
Clinton	0.0	13.3	0.0	0.0	0.0	19.0	28.7	7.7	0.0	3.8
Greenville	0.4	16.8	0.0	0.0	0.9	22.4	13.5	2.6	0.0	1.1
Gulfport	0.0	5.6	0.0	0.0	72.1	4.7	4.9	3.1	2.1	1.8
Hattiesburg	0.0	16.5	0.3	0.0	1.6	16.2	16.4	6.6	2.8	2.3
Horn Lake	0.0	6.3	0.0	0.0	0.7	27.6	15.3	6.7	0.7	6.2
Jackson	0.5	9.5	0.0	0.0	0.5	15.4	16.2	6.3	0.9	4.0
Meridian	0.0	13.7	0.4	0.0	0.0	18.3	14.0	5.1	2.6	5.1
Olive Branch	0.0	10.9	0.0	0.0	2.5	22.3	22.4	4.0	0.0	5.9
Pearl	0.0	22.1	0.0	0.0	1.4	19.0	18.3	4.3	0.0	6.3
Southaven	0.0	2.9	0.0	0.0	0.6	21.9	9.2	9.5	0.0	8.5
Tupelo	0.0	24.5	0.0	0.0	0.0	16.4	11.5	9.2	0.1	4.2

City	City government finances, 2012 (cont.)			Climate[2]						
	Debt outstanding			Average daily temperature (degrees Fahrenheit)						
				Mean		Limits				
	Total (mil dol)	Per capita[1] (dollars)	Debt issued during year	January	July	January[3]	July[4]	Annual precipitation (inches)	Heating degree days	Cooling degree days
	137	138	139	140	141	142	143	144	145	146
MICHIGAN—Cont'd										
Oak Park	45.1	1 521	0.0	24.7	73.7	16.1	85.7	33.58	6 224	788
Pontiac	80.8	1 357	5.6	22.9	71.9	15.9	82.3	30.03	6 680	626
Portage	90.1	1 908	15.0	24.3	73.2	17.0	84.2	37.41	6 235	773
Port Huron	122.4	4 160	21.5	22.8	72.2	15.1	81.9	31.39	6 845	626
Rochester Hills	31.9	441	5.0	22.0	70.6	13.7	82.7	35.74	7 046	523
Roseville	13.3	282	0.3	25.3	73.6	18.8	83.3	33.97	6 160	757
Royal Oak	117.8	2 013	0.0	24.7	73.7	16.1	85.7	33.58	6 224	788
Saginaw	81.9	1 612	13.5	21.4	71.2	14.9	81.9	31.61	7 099	548
St. Clair Shores	53.2	890	9.1	25.3	73.6	18.8	83.3	33.97	6 160	757
Southfield	64.8	893	0.0	24.7	73.7	16.1	85.7	33.58	6 224	788
Southgate	22.5	757	0.3	24.5	73.5	17.8	83.4	32.89	6 422	736
Sterling Heights	63.9	490	13.6	24.4	71.9	18.0	81.8	32.24	6 620	597
Taylor	147.4	2 362	1.4	24.5	73.5	17.8	83.4	32.89	6 422	736
Troy	55.0	669	0.0	22.9	71.9	15.9	82.3	30.03	6 680	626
Warren	159.2	1 186	8.8	24.7	73.7	16.1	85.7	33.58	6 224	788
Westland	12.4	149	0.8	24.6	73.9	17.6	84.7	32.80	6 167	828
Wyandotte	63.3	2 483	0.8	24.5	73.5	17.8	83.4	32.89	6 422	736
Wyoming	117.0	1 595	7.3	22.4	71.4	15.6	82.3	37.13	6 896	613
MINNESOTA	X	X	X	X	X	X	X	X	X	X
Andover	55.4	1 776	0.3	10.9	70.4	1.8	80.5	31.36	8 367	500
Apple Valley	71.3	1 426	9.2	9.2	69.4	-1.1	80.5	29.19	8 805	416
Blaine	51.9	874	1.6	10.9	70.4	1.8	80.5	31.36	8 367	500
Bloomington	158.7	1 844	27.0	13.1	73.2	4.3	83.3	29.41	7 876	699
Brooklyn Center	47.5	1 549	0.0	13.0	71.4	2.8	82.8	30.50	7 983	587
Brooklyn Park	95.6	1 229	16.1	13.0	71.4	2.8	82.8	30.50	7 983	587
Burnsville	62.7	1 026	8.4	13.8	74.0	3.4	85.8	30.44	7 549	803
Coon Rapids	87.0	1 407	9.1	13.0	71.4	2.8	82.8	30.50	7 983	587
Cottage Grove	57.0	1 618	0.0	12.0	72.1	2.5	82.6	29.95	8 032	617
Duluth	251.3	2 914	21.9	8.4	65.5	-1.2	76.3	31.00	9 724	189
Eagan	61.1	943	0.0	13.1	73.2	4.3	83.3	29.41	7 876	699
Eden Prairie	202.7	3 258	11.3	10.2	71.4	-0.3	82.2	28.82	8 429	567
Edina	119.7	2 440	15.0	13.8	74.0	3.4	85.8	30.44	7 549	803
Fridley	14.9	541	0.0	10.9	70.4	1.8	80.5	31.36	8 367	500
Inver Grove Heights	55.6	1 626	4.6	10.1	71.0	0.0	81.3	34.60	8 345	533
Lakeville	90.0	1 570	4.3	13.1	72.2	3.8	83.6	31.43	7 773	658
Mankato	117.0	2 921	4.6	12.5	72.1	2.4	83.4	33.42	8 029	650
Maple Grove	207.8	3 225	5.4	13.0	71.4	2.8	82.8	30.50	7 983	587
Maplewood	157.8	4 004	10.0	14.5	73.0	6.2	83.2	32.59	7 606	715
Minneapolis	3 439.9	8 754	233.0	13.1	73.2	4.3	83.3	29.41	7 876	699
Minnetonka	91.2	1 784	0.0	13.1	73.2	4.3	83.3	29.41	7 876	699
Moorhead	252.1	6 451	10.0	3.8	69.8	-7.1	81.5	21.56	9 628	478
Oakdale	31.2	1 124	10.6	14.5	73.0	6.2	83.2	32.59	7 606	715
Owatonna	49.7	1 954	8.3	NA	NA	NA	NA	NA	NA	NA
Plymouth	108.6	1 490	0.0	13.0	71.4	2.8	82.8	30.50	7 983	587
Richfield	105.3	2 917	11.9	13.1	73.2	4.3	83.3	29.41	7 876	699
Rochester	2 086.4	19 128	285.0	9.8	70.0	0.0	80.9	29.10	8 703	474
Roseville	20.1	581	10.0	14.5	73.0	6.2	83.2	32.59	7 606	715
St. Cloud	413.3	6 266	35.1	8.8	69.8	-1.2	81.7	27.13	8 815	443
St. Louis Park	499.7	10 778	0.0	13.0	71.4	2.8	82.8	30.50	7 983	587
St. Paul	770.7	2 646	98.7	14.5	73.0	6.2	83.2	32.59	7 606	715
Savage	84.5	3 021	10.7	NA	NA	NA	NA	NA	NA	NA
Shakopee	92.8	2 394	0.0	NA	NA	NA	NA	NA	NA	NA
Shoreview	51.1	1 990	8.6	14.5	73.0	6.2	83.2	32.59	7 606	715
Winona	7.0	254	0.0	17.6	75.8	9.2	85.3	34.20	6 839	990
Woodbury	92.0	1 427	1.5	11.5	72.1	1.9	81.9	29.92	8 104	621
MISSISSIPPI	X	X	X	X	X	X	X	X	X	X
Biloxi	68.0	1 528	0.5	50.7	81.7	43.5	88.5	64.84	1 645	2 517
Clinton	36.4	1 422	1.7	NA	NA	NA	NA	NA	NA	NA
Greenville	22.8	681	10.5	42.3	82.6	33.0	92.6	54.20	2 715	2 216
Gulfport	212.6	3 038	5.0	51.6	82.6	42.6	91.3	65.20	1 514	2 679
Hattiesburg	89.3	1 904	5.4	47.9	81.7	36.0	92.1	62.47	2 024	2 327
Horn Lake	35.8	1 350	0.0	NA	NA	NA	NA	NA	NA	NA
Jackson	322.3	1 839	62.9	45.0	81.4	35.0	91.4	55.95	2 401	2 264
Meridian	61.0	1 493	9.3	46.1	81.7	34.7	92.9	58.65	2 352	2 173
Olive Branch	57.9	1 676	15.0	NA	NA	NA	NA	NA	NA	NA
Pearl	99.8	3 814	6.4	NA	NA	NA	NA	NA	NA	NA
Southaven	96.2	1 909	8.0	37.9	80.4	27.8	90.3	55.06	3 442	1 749
Tupelo	82.1	2 311	14.6	40.4	80.6	30.5	91.4	55.86	3 086	1 884

1. Based on the population estimated as of July 1 of the year shown. 2. Represents normal values based on the 30-year period, 1971–2000. 3. Average daily minimum. 4. Average daily maximum.

STATE Place code	City	Land area,[1] 2010 (sq km)	Population, 2014: Total persons	Population, 2014: Rank	Population, 2014: Per square kilometer	Race alone or in combination (percent), 2011-2013: White	Race: Black	Race: American Indian, Alaska Native	Race: Asian	Race: Hawaiian Pacific Islander	Percent Hispanic or Latino[2], 2011-2013	Percent foreign born 2011–2013
		1	2	3	4	5	6	7	8	9	10	11
29 00000	MISSOURI	178 039.7	6 063 589	X	34.1	85.0	12.5	1.3	2.2	0.2	3.7	4.0
29 03160	Ballwin	23.3	30 505	1 211	1 309.2	89.4	3.8	1.3	8.4	NA	1.7	7.2
29 06652	Blue Springs	57.7	53 573	693	928.5	88.4	8.8	1.0	3.0	NA	4.3	3.0
29 11242	Cape Girardeau	73.6	39 167	948	532.2	82.4	15.0	1.1	2.5	0.2	2.7	4.0
29 13600	Chesterfield	82.3	47 777	788	580.5	85.2	4.1	0.2	11.1	NA	3.1	11.8
29 15670	Columbia	163.4	116 906	232	715.5	83.1	12.1	1.9	6.5	0.1	3.6	8.1
29 24778	Florissant	32.5	52 303	712	1 609.3	67.4	32.4	1.6	2.2	NA	1.4	2.4
29 27190	Gladstone	20.9	26 800	1 369	1 282.3	91.0	7.4	2.2	1.7	NA	5.9	5.3
29 31276	Hazelwood	41.5	25 666	1 403	618.5	64.4	33.0	1.0	4.3	NA	3.8	6.6
29 35000	Independence	200.9	117 494	231	584.8	86.8	8.2	1.4	1.4	0.6	8.9	4.5
29 37000	Jefferson City	93.1	43 132	859	463.3	78.4	18.6	1.2	2.2	0.4	1.9	3.4
29 37592	Joplin	92.1	51 316	729	557.2	92.0	5.7	3.9	2.2	0.4	3.6	2.7
29 38000	Kansas City	815.7	470 800	37	577.2	62.6	30.5	1.4	3.3	0.5	10.0	7.7
29 39044	Kirkwood	23.7	27 660	1 325	1 167.1	91.6	7.5	0.8	1.8	NA	1.7	3.0
29 41348	Lee's Summit	164.1	93 864	323	572.0	86.1	11.4	0.5	2.2	0.6	4.4	3.2
29 42032	Liberty	75.2	30 376	1 220	403.9	94.3	4.8	1.1	1.5	NA	2.9	2.8
29 46586	Maryland Heights	56.5	27 405	1 343	485.0	72.4	14.9	2.5	12.0	NA	7.6	16.2
29 54074	O'Fallon	75.6	84 009	386	1 111.2	90.7	5.8	1.0	4.9	NA	2.3	4.7
29 60788	Raytown	25.7	29 481	1 250	1 147.1	66.7	29.7	1.5	2.0	NA	5.8	2.9
29 64082	St. Charles	61.3	68 090	509	1 110.8	89.5	7.6	1.3	2.9	NA	4.8	6.7
29 64550	St. Joseph	113.9	76 967	436	675.7	92.1	7.8	1.5	1.5	0.5	6.1	4.4
29 65000	St. Louis	160.3	317 419	60	1 980.2	47.6	49.6	1.2	3.6	0.1	3.7	7.0
29 65126	St. Peters	57.9	56 076	655	968.5	93.5	4.3	0.3	2.5	NA	3.1	3.6
29 70000	Springfield	211.7	165 378	149	781.2	91.7	5.4	1.8	2.5	0.5	4.1	4.2
29 75220	University City	15.3	35 115	1 063	2 295.1	58.3	39.2	1.8	3.8	NA	5.1	7.7
29 78442	Wentzville	51.7	33 912	1 097	655.9	93.8	6.9	1.0	0.4	NA	3.1	1.0
29 79820	Wildwood	172.0	35 820	1 044	208.3	94.0	1.4	0.6	4.1	NA	2.4	6.2
30 00000	MONTANA	376 961.9	1 023 579	X	2.7	91.6	0.9	8.1	1.2	0.2	3.2	2.0
30 06550	Billings	112.4	108 869	262	968.6	91.6	1.8	6.2	1.5	0.1	5.5	1.8
30 08950	Bozeman	49.5	41 660	885	841.6	94.0	1.3	3.1	3.7	NA	3.2	4.3
30 11390	Butte-Silver Bow	1 855.1	33 980	1 096	18.3	97.4	1.1	2.6	0.8	NA	3.7	1.7
30 32800	Great Falls	56.4	59 152	617	1 048.8	91.2	2.0	8.2	1.6	NA	4.3	1.9
30 35600	Helena	42.3	29 943	1 238	707.9	95.8	1.7	3.3	1.1	NA	2.4	1.6
30 50200	Missoula	71.3	69 821	492	979.3	95.2	1.2	4.1	2.4	0.3	3.4	3.0
31 00000	NEBRASKA	198 973.7	1 881 503	X	9.5	90.2	5.5	1.6	2.4	0.2	9.7	6.5
31 03950	Bellevue	41.1	53 936	689	1 312.3	88.9	6.5	2.3	3.6	0.7	12.9	8.7
31 17670	Fremont	22.8	26 500	1 381	1 162.3	97.5	0.6	0.8	2.0	NA	13.5	6.9
31 19595	Grand Island	73.6	51 236	730	696.1	93.2	2.9	0.9	1.9	NA	28.5	15.1
31 25055	Kearney	33.1	32 469	1 145	980.9	94.3	1.6	0.8	2.3	NA	8.5	4.6
31 28000	Lincoln	230.8	272 996	72	1 182.8	89.6	5.5	1.6	4.7	0.2	6.7	7.6
31 37000	Omaha	329.2	446 599	41	1 356.6	78.6	14.6	1.7	3.4	0.2	13.3	9.9
32 00000	NEVADA	284 331.9	2 839 099	X	10.0	73.1	9.6	1.9	9.4	1.3	27.2	19.2
32 09700	Carson City	374.7	54 522	681	145.5	86.5	2.6	3.3	2.7	0.8	22.4	11.8
32 31900	Henderson	279.0	277 440	71	994.4	81.7	7.2	1.2	10.1	1.2	14.1	12.0
32 40000	Las Vegas	351.8	613 599	29	1 744.2	68.8	13.2	1.4	8.6	1.3	31.7	21.3
32 51800	North Las Vegas	262.5	230 788	94	879.2	54.8	21.4	1.3	6.8	2.0	39.1	20.9
32 60600	Reno	266.8	236 995	89	888.3	81.6	3.7	1.9	7.7	1.2	25.4	17.0
32 68400	Sparks	92.6	94 708	319	1 022.8	81.0	3.2	2.6	7.9	1.9	26.4	16.6
33 00000	NEW HAMPSHIRE	23 187.3	1 326 813	X	57.2	95.6	1.8	0.8	2.8	0.1	3.0	5.6
33 14200	Concord	166.4	42 444	868	255.1	93.7	3.7	1.0	3.3	NA	2.2	5.9
33 18820	Dover	69.2	30 665	1 206	443.1	93.5	3.0	2.0	5.3	NA	1.8	7.3
33 45140	Manchester	85.7	110 448	254	1 288.8	88.1	6.0	0.9	5.0	NA	8.1	13.2
33 50260	Nashua	79.9	87 259	362	1 092.1	88.3	4.5	1.0	8.1	NA	10.6	13.5
33 65140	Rochester	117.6	29 991	1 236	255.0	97.6	1.7	0.5	1.6	NA	2.0	2.5
34 00000	NEW JERSEY	19 047.3	8 938 175	X	469.3	70.7	14.8	0.7	9.5	0.1	18.6	21.4
34 02080	Atlantic City	27.8	39 415	942	1 417.8	39.1	39.6	2.6	16.1	0.4	26.9	30.8
34 03580	Bayonne	15.0	65 975	531	4 398.3	74.8	11.9	1.0	10.0	0.3	19.7	28.2
34 05170	Bergenfield	7.5	27 406	1 342	3 654.1	46.0	7.0	0.7	27.5	NA	30.9	41.3
34 07600	Bridgeton	16.0	25 347	1 414	1 584.2	40.1	38.0	3.6	0.5	NA	48.0	23.2
34 10000	Camden	23.1	77 332	433	3 347.7	16.0	53.3	1.7	2.9	0.1	48.0	12.2
34 13690	Clifton	29.2	85 927	372	2 942.7	76.7	6.1	0.9	9.8	NA	33.1	34.9
34 19390	East Orange	10.2	65 078	543	6 380.2	4.6	91.2	0.6	1.3	NA	6.0	25.1
34 21000	Elizabeth	31.9	128 705	204	4 034.6	50.6	20.7	0.7	2.7	NA	63.2	46.9
34 21480	Englewood	12.7	27 670	1 323	2 178.7	38.9	36.9	0.7	14.1	NA	22.2	35.6
34 22470	Fair Lawn	13.3	33 549	1 109	2 522.5	80.9	2.3	0.8	13.5	NA	15.0	32.7
34 24420	Fort Lee	6.6	37 026	1 004	5 610.0	59.8	2.2	0.5	37.7	NA	11.4	50.0

1. Dry land or land partially or temporarily covered by water. 2. May be of any race.

City	Age of population (percent), 2011-2013									Median age 2011-2013	Percent female 2011-2013	Population			
												Census counts		Percent change	
	Under 5 years	5 to 17 years	18 to 24 years	25 to 34 years	35 to 44 years	45 to 54 years	55 to 64 years	65 to 74 years	75 years and over			2000	2010	2000–2010	2010–2014
	12	13	14	15	16	17	18	19	20	21	22	23	24	25	26
MISSOURI	6.3	17.0	9.9	13.2	12.2	14.2	12.7	8.0	6.6	38.1	51.0	5 595 211	5 988 927	7.0	1.2
Ballwin	5.5	19.2	8.8	10.1	13.2	14.6	13.6	8.9	6.1	39.4	53.3	31 283	30 404	-2.8	0.3
Blue Springs	6.8	21.1	7.4	13.9	13.8	13.7	12.9	6.1	4.3	35.6	51.3	48 080	52 575	9.3	1.8
Cape Girardeau	6.1	13.5	18.7	14.6	9.1	11.6	11.2	6.9	8.3	32.4	52.5	35 349	37 941	7.3	3.1
Chesterfield	4.9	18.1	6.2	8.6	10.9	16.5	14.1	10.9	9.7	45.8	51.8	46 802	47 484	1.5	0.6
Columbia	6.2	13.0	26.9	16.4	10.0	9.9	8.8	4.4	4.4	26.7	52.0	84 531	108 500	28.4	7.4
Florissant	6.9	17.9	8.5	12.6	12.7	13.6	11.1	7.1	9.5	38.0	53.6	50 497	52 158	3.3	0.0
Gladstone	8.2	12.6	8.2	14.4	10.8	14.1	13.7	9.0	8.9	40.9	52.7	26 365	25 410	-3.6	5.5
Hazelwood	5.9	16.9	12.1	13.0	12.2	14.9	12.8	5.5	6.7	35.9	50.5	26 206	25 703	-1.9	-0.1
Independence	6.6	15.1	8.1	14.0	11.3	14.2	13.2	9.2	8.3	40.8	52.8	113 288	116 830	3.1	0.6
Jefferson City	6.4	15.1	9.6	16.4	11.7	14.1	12.2	7.4	7.1	37.2	48.6	39 636	43 079	8.7	0.1
Joplin	6.6	15.4	12.4	14.2	12.6	12.2	11.7	7.5	7.4	35.7	50.6	45 504	50 150	10.2	1.0
Kansas City	7.2	16.4	9.7	16.6	13.2	13.6	11.8	6.4	5.2	35.0	51.4	441 545	459 787	4.1	2.4
Kirkwood	6.6	14.9	5.4	13.6	11.9	14.1	15.2	9.0	9.2	43.1	55.1	27 324	27 540	0.8	0.4
Lee's Summit	6.9	21.0	7.0	12.6	13.8	15.1	11.6	6.0	5.9	36.7	52.3	70 700	91 364	29.2	2.7
Liberty	4.7	21.1	11.3	10.5	15.3	13.7	11.4	6.8	5.3	36.3	49.7	26 232	29 149	11.1	4.2
Maryland Heights	7.6	12.8	9.7	18.9	13.6	12.6	12.2	7.7	4.8	35.8	49.8	25 756	27 472	6.7	-0.2
O'Fallon	7.1	21.9	7.4	13.7	16.2	14.8	9.3	5.1	4.5	34.9	50.3	46 169	79 329	71.8	5.6
Raytown	6.8	18.9	9.2	9.7	14.0	14.9	11.5	7.3	7.7	40.0	49.8	30 388	29 526	-2.8	-0.2
St. Charles	5.4	14.2	14.6	14.4	11.4	14.4	11.8	6.8	6.9	35.9	51.0	60 321	65 794	9.1	3.4
St. Joseph	7.3	16.1	11.4	14.2	12.0	13.5	11.8	7.0	6.7	35.7	50.4	73 990	76 780	3.8	0.2
St. Louis	6.7	13.9	11.4	19.0	12.6	13.4	12.0	5.8	5.2	34.4	51.7	348 189	319 294	-8.3	-0.6
St. Peters	7.1	15.5	8.3	15.0	12.5	15.2	14.0	6.9	5.6	38.5	53.2	51 381	52 575	2.3	6.6
Springfield	6.2	11.9	19.1	15.8	10.9	10.7	10.6	7.2	7.5	32.9	51.9	151 580	159 498	5.2	3.7
University City	6.1	11.9	11.4	16.4	12.7	12.3	12.6	8.2	8.4	38.9	53.6	37 428	35 371	-5.5	-0.7
Wentzville	8.7	22.7	5.2	15.5	17.8	10.3	10.1	6.4	3.4	34.2	51.4	6 896	29 070	321.5	15.6
Wildwood	5.9	23.9	6.2	6.4	11.7	20.7	15.1	6.6	3.6	42.2	50.0	32 884	35 517	8.0	0.8
MONTANA	6.0	16.2	9.9	12.5	11.3	13.8	14.7	8.8	6.8	39.8	49.8	902 195	989 415	9.7	3.5
Billings	6.6	16.0	9.8	14.5	12.0	13.3	12.9	7.8	7.2	37.4	52.0	89 847	104 170	15.9	4.5
Bozeman	5.3	9.1	29.3	20.3	11.8	8.2	8.1	3.9	3.9	27.7	47.6	27 509	37 280	35.5	11.7
Butte-Silver Bow	5.1	15.3	11.4	11.3	11.2	14.8	14.1	9.1	7.6	41.4	49.5	34 606	33 525	-1.1	1.4
Great Falls	7.3	15.3	9.7	14.4	10.7	13.6	12.6	8.1	8.3	37.9	51.0	56 690	58 505	3.2	0.9
Helena	6.3	12.4	11.1	13.1	12.0	13.6	15.0	8.6	7.8	40.0	50.5	25 780	28 190	9.3	6.1
Missoula	5.4	12.1	19.5	17.3	11.8	11.6	10.5	6.1	5.8	32.1	50.3	57 053	66 788	17.1	4.4
NEBRASKA	7.0	17.9	10.1	13.5	12.0	13.4	12.3	7.1	6.7	36.2	50.3	1 711 263	1 826 341	6.7	3.0
Bellevue	7.2	19.5	9.3	14.2	12.0	14.1	11.4	7.5	4.8	34.8	51.2	44 382	50 137	13.0	5.7
Fremont	7.1	17.5	9.3	14.1	12.6	12.0	11.3	7.3	8.8	36.0	51.7	25 174	26 397	4.9	0.3
Grand Island	8.0	19.0	9.0	14.0	12.9	12.8	11.4	6.2	6.7	35.0	50.1	42 940	48 520	13.0	5.3
Kearney	7.8	14.0	21.3	14.9	9.7	10.8	9.9	6.5	5.1	28.9	50.8	27 431	30 787	12.2	5.4
Lincoln	7.0	15.7	15.9	15.6	12.0	11.7	11.0	6.0	5.3	32.0	49.9	225 581	258 379	14.5	5.6
Omaha	7.4	17.5	10.4	16.2	12.3	13.1	11.5	6.2	5.5	34.0	51.1	390 007	408 958	4.9	5.5
NEVADA	6.6	17.4	9.2	14.2	13.8	13.7	12.0	8.1	5.0	36.9	49.6	1 998 257	2 700 551	35.1	5.1
Carson City	5.3	16.2	8.3	12.3	12.1	13.9	14.0	10.0	7.9	42.0	48.8	52 457	55 274	5.4	-1.4
Henderson	5.1	17.0	7.9	12.2	14.0	14.8	12.7	10.2	6.2	40.8	52.3	175 381	257 729	47.0	7.8
Las Vegas	6.8	17.8	9.0	14.2	14.2	13.6	11.3	7.7	5.5	36.6	49.5	478 434	583 756	22.0	5.0
North Las Vegas	8.2	23.1	9.9	15.4	15.3	11.9	8.6	5.2	2.5	30.6	49.8	115 488	216 961	87.9	6.5
Reno	6.7	16.4	11.7	15.9	12.4	13.1	11.5	7.2	5.1	34.5	49.1	180 480	225 221	24.8	4.9
Sparks	7.0	17.3	8.4	13.4	14.4	13.3	12.7	8.5	4.9	37.7	51.3	66 346	90 264	36.1	4.9
NEW HAMPSHIRE	5.0	15.8	9.5	11.2	12.7	16.7	14.4	8.3	6.4	41.9	50.7	1 235 786	1 316 470	6.5	0.8
Concord	5.6	14.5	8.8	14.8	13.9	15.1	13.0	7.1	7.2	40.2	51.5	40 687	42 695	4.9	-0.6
Dover	5.7	14.5	12.0	15.2	12.8	13.8	12.5	6.6	7.0	37.3	51.0	26 884	29 987	11.5	2.3
Manchester	5.6	14.8	10.6	16.4	14.0	13.8	11.8	7.0	6.0	36.7	50.0	107 006	109 565	2.4	0.8
Nashua	7.2	15.4	8.9	15.1	13.3	15.6	11.7	6.8	6.1	37.5	51.1	86 605	86 494	-0.1	0.9
Rochester	6.3	12.5	9.7	14.3	13.2	15.2	12.8	9.3	6.6	40.9	53.5	28 461	29 752	4.5	0.8
NEW JERSEY	6.0	16.9	8.9	12.8	13.5	15.4	12.5	7.5	6.5	39.3	51.2	8 414 350	8 791 894	4.5	1.7
Atlantic City	8.3	17.2	10.2	13.1	10.8	15.6	11.5	6.8	6.4	36.0	51.8	40 517	39 558	-2.4	-0.4
Bayonne	6.6	14.9	8.2	14.6	15.8	14.2	12.3	7.0	6.3	38.7	51.4	61 842	63 024	1.9	4.7
Bergenfield	5.3	17.0	8.7	11.8	16.0	14.3	12.0	7.2	7.1	39.9	50.7	26 247	26 764	2.0	2.4
Bridgeton	9.6	17.6	11.7	20.5	15.3	11.6	6.4	4.7	2.7	30.5	41.2	22 771	25 349	11.3	0.0
Camden	8.8	23.0	11.9	15.3	12.5	11.7	9.0	5.1	2.7	29.1	52.3	79 904	77 344	-3.2	0.0
Clifton	6.6	15.6	9.4	15.3	13.8	13.8	12.1	6.9	6.4	37.1	49.7	78 672	84 136	6.9	2.1
East Orange	6.7	16.4	10.4	13.3	13.9	13.9	12.2	7.7	5.4	37.4	56.6	69 824	64 270	-8.0	1.5
Elizabeth	9.3	18.4	10.5	16.4	14.1	12.5	9.1	5.6	4.0	31.9	51.9	120 568	124 969	3.7	3.0
Englewood	6.9	15.4	7.8	14.8	15.9	12.9	11.9	8.7	5.6	37.6	53.1	26 203	27 147	3.6	2.0
Fair Lawn	5.1	16.4	6.3	12.5	14.7	13.2	16.0	8.1	7.6	41.8	51.7	31 637	32 457	2.6	3.4
Fort Lee	4.7	10.6	4.8	12.6	15.8	12.1	15.5	11.3	12.5	46.5	54.4	35 461	35 345	-0.3	4.8

Table D. Cities — **Households, Group Quarters, Crime, and Education**

City	Households, 2011-2013				Persons in group quarters, 2010				Serious crimes known to police,[2] 2013				Educational attainment, 2011–2013		
			Percent			Institutional			Total		Rate[3]			Attainment[4] (percent)	
	Number	Persons per house-hold	Female family house-holder[1]	One-person	Total	Total	Persons in nursing facilities	Non-institu-tional	Number	Rate[3]	Violent	Property	Population age 25 and older	High school graduate or less	Bachelor's degree or more
	27	28	29	30	31	32	33	34	35	36	37	38	39	40	41
MISSOURI	2 353 778	2.49	12.3	29.0	174 142	93 274	44 866	80 868	215 803	3 570	433	3 137	4 027 255	43.5	26.5
Ballwin	11 033	2.76	11.7	17.8	2	0	0	2	272	893	72	821	20 271	16.7	54.4
Blue Springs	18 951	2.79	13.9	18.7	218	182	182	36	1 590	2 993	250	2 742	34 315	35.9	29.8
Cape Girardeau	15 146	2.34	12.9	32.8	3 466	789	712	2 677	2 248	5 806	666	5 140	23 829	38.3	32.9
Chesterfield	18 660	2.50	7.6	23.9	934	925	925	9	710	1 487	52	1 435	33 727	13.7	65.5
Columbia	44 069	2.37	9.4	33.1	8 804	1 146	624	7 658	4 775	4 167	363	3 804	60 963	20.9	55.2
Florissant	21 038	2.45	18.7	32.1	788	668	542	120	1 078	2 062	163	1 899	34 932	39.8	22.6
Gladstone	10 867	2.38	13.5	33.0	42	36	36	6	568	2 178	192	1 986	18 419	41.7	24.5
Hazelwood	10 872	2.34	15.2	33.4	140	0	0	140	1 002	3 903	370	3 533	16 725	41.1	22.1
Independence	48 778	2.37	14.2	34.0	1 225	1 048	982	177	7 651	6 518	463	6 055	82 229	51.1	17.5
Jefferson City	16 791	2.30	14.9	33.8	4 964	3 990	456	974	1 646	3 811	463	3 348	29 828	36.9	34.5
Joplin	21 390	2.31	11.7	33.8	1 988	743	653	1 245	4 174	8 471	489	7 982	33 541	45.5	23.2
Kansas City	191 728	2.38	15.8	36.3	8 812	4 192	2 499	4 620	30 531	6 559	1 262	5 296	309 807	38.0	31.9
Kirkwood	12 047	2.26	6.6	33.5	257	223	218	34	576	2 090	73	2 018	20 104	17.1	61.2
Lee's Summit	33 473	2.75	11.7	20.9	714	626	573	88	2 049	2 209	98	2 111	60 411	25.4	40.1
Liberty	10 506	2.71	11.3	24.3	1 358	585	277	773	595	1 983	193	1 790	18 748	34.0	36.1
Maryland Heights	11 823	2.27	11.6	36.1	559	522	473	37	610	2 223	171	2 052	19 151	31.0	38.4
O'Fallon	29 376	2.78	11.0	21.3	294	254	247	40	1 281	1 549	76	1 473	52 067	32.2	37.6
Raytown	11 422	2.53	17.7	30.9	559	401	395	158	1 415	4 796	383	4 413	19 217	43.1	22.7
St. Charles	26 536	2.31	13.2	32.2	4 623	917	508	3 706	1 892	2 840	170	2 670	43 865	34.9	35.3
St. Joseph	28 245	2.60	14.0	31.5	4 493	3 104	673	1 389	4 712	6 092	484	5 608	50 286	51.8	18.7
St. Louis	138 531	2.22	18.0	44.1	11 978	4 822	2 060	7 156	26 164	8 213	1 594	6 619	217 085	40.8	30.3
St. Peters	21 113	2.55	8.4	27.0	203	184	184	19	1 405	2 578	215	2 363	37 397	30.1	34.8
Springfield	71 025	2.14	11.9	37.1	10 739	3 302	1 443	7 437	16 585	10 171	1 162	9 009	101 855	40.0	26.2
University City	16 268	2.15	14.1	38.5	232	200	169	32	1 559	4 431	540	3 891	24 861	21.6	51.5
Wentzville	10 959	2.86	9.5	17.0	137	133	133	4	622	1 955	126	1 829	19 988	33.3	30.5
Wildwood	11 996	2.97	5.5	13.7	66	62	40	4	NA	NA	NA	NA	22 869	11.3	65.8
MONTANA	405 504	2.41	9.2	30.1	28 849	11 929	5 200	16 920	28 520	2 809	253	2 557	683 938	37.2	28.9
Billings	43 610	2.38	12.8	32.3	3 351	1 750	753	1 601	6 040	5 603	395	5 208	72 469	36.9	29.0
Bozeman	16 008	2.21	6.9	32.6	3 030	199	145	2 831	1 273	3 250	179	3 071	21 910	13.3	56.8
Butte-Silver Bow	14 574	2.23	12.2	34.9	998	610	276	388	1 419	4 097	251	3 846	22 808	45.7	23.0
Great Falls	24 629	2.34	12.1	34.0	1 263	798	482	465	2 865	4 861	283	4 578	40 030	41.6	23.1
Helena	12 851	2.15	9.3	39.5	1 682	432	191	1 250	1 409	4 791	445	4 345	20 476	23.5	46.9
Missoula	29 299	2.23	10.6	35.1	3 519	766	374	2 753	3 142	4 562	354	4 208	43 137	22.4	45.5
NEBRASKA	729 572	2.47	9.8	29.1	51 165	23 633	13 519	27 532	53 915	2 885	262	2 623	1 205 830	37.4	28.7
Bellevue	19 651	2.68	14.6	23.6	74	31	15	43	1 033	1 948	132	1 816	33 735	35.7	27.2
Fremont	10 537	2.43	10.0	23.2	832	468	386	364	708	2 713	172	2 540	17 484	48.8	20.5
Grand Island	18 638	2.64	12.2	28.7	1 058	781	546	277	2 525	5 006	270	4 736	32 023	53.7	15.6
Kearney	12 180	2.44	10.2	29.0	2 002	390	284	1 612	889	2 768	174	2 594	18 102	28.0	34.6
Lincoln	105 851	2.38	9.9	31.1	13 579	4 236	1 001	9 343	10 344	3 866	370	3 496	163 129	29.1	36.7
Omaha	169 114	2.47	13.7	33.9	11 183	4 676	2 002	6 507	21 557	5 071	576	4 495	277 341	35.6	33.3
NEVADA	995 980	2.73	13.2	27.9	36 154	25 835	5 005	10 319	96 001	3 441	603	2 838	1 840 605	44.1	22.5
Carson City	21 206	2.47	12.3	33.6	3 625	3 560	313	65	1 057	1 924	242	1 682	38 266	42.7	19.8
Henderson	100 943	2.61	11.8	26.6	1 104	787	585	317	5 725	2 134	137	1 997	185 916	34.4	30.4
Las Vegas	211 734	2.78	15.3	28.7	9 482	6 514	1 628	2 968	59 342	3 955	758	3 197	395 500	46.3	21.7
North Las Vegas	67 487	3.27	16.3	20.9	2 441	2 167	683	274	7 775	3 446	800	2 645	131 276	54.2	14.7
Reno	89 770	2.50	12.0	34.6	4 583	1 679	323	2 904	8 334	3 584	496	3 087	150 364	37.3	29.7
Sparks	34 474	2.66	13.9	27.4	321	256	256	65	2 793	3 011	292	2 719	62 036	42.0	21.9
NEW HAMPSHIRE	518 088	2.47	9.9	25.5	40 104	13 113	7 767	26 991	31 889	2 410	215	2 194	919 616	37.3	34.2
Concord	16 876	2.35	10.6	33.5	2 903	2 282	454	621	1 139	2 673	244	2 429	30 200	32.4	35.6
Dover	12 653	2.32	12.4	28.8	896	789	358	107	608	2 007	162	1 846	20 604	27.9	36.6
Manchester	45 549	2.36	13.8	32.7	2 578	1 547	662	1 031	4 940	4 474	676	3 799	76 053	45.6	26.3
Nashua	33 885	2.51	12.4	28.8	1 685	546	505	1 139	2 428	2 789	209	2 580	59 533	35.8	35.7
Rochester	12 870	2.30	13.7	29.8	240	192	181	48	1 395	4 674	355	4 318	21 301	50.3	19.5
NEW JERSEY	3 181 152	2.73	13.6	25.8	186 876	100 621	45 512	86 255	193 230	2 171	288	1 883	6 047 398	40.6	36.1
Atlantic City	15 862	2.44	26.1	40.3	802	186	186	616	3 160	8 004	1 735	6 269	25 420	64.6	14.8
Bayonne	25 649	2.50	18.9	30.3	276	0	0	276	966	1 487	212	1 275	45 286	48.6	29.5
Bergenfield	8 818	3.06	13.2	18.6	38	0	0	38	121	446	59	387	18 665	39.3	38.0
Bridgeton	5 833	3.62	27.2	25.3	4 276	4 257	0	19	1 526	6 036	1 345	4 691	15 449	75.5	6.6
Camden	25 354	2.94	36.6	30.5	3 321	2 229	290	1 092	5 210	6 739	2 522	4 217	43 517	69.5	7.7
Clifton	29 055	2.89	13.4	26.1	254	192	182	62	1 696	1 995	206	1 789	58 174	45.3	29.0
East Orange	25 921	2.44	27.3	40.5	1 235	780	716	455	1 610	2 499	629	1 870	42 812	51.8	16.1
Elizabeth	38 987	3.19	24.7	24.4	2 545	1 833	398	712	4 654	3 663	786	2 876	78 431	68.0	11.5
Englewood	10 590	2.57	14.1	32.5	164	136	136	28	551	1 983	392	1 591	19 177	32.4	48.0
Fair Lawn	11 776	2.77	10.9	20.0	187	152	152	35	335	1 015	51	963	23 705	26.7	51.5
Fort Lee	16 792	2.13	8.7	42.3	7	0	0	7	314	875	78	797	28 595	27.6	55.7

1. No spouse present. 2. Data for serious crimes have not been adjusted for underreporting. This may affect comparability between geographic areas and over time. 3. Per 100,000 population estimated by the FBI. 4. Persons 25 years old and over.

Table D. Cities — **Income, Poverty, and Housing**

City	Money income, 2011–2013					Housing units, 2010			Occupied housing units 2011–2013				
		Households								Owner-occupied		Median owner costs as a percent of income	
	Per capita income[1] (dollars)	Median income	Percent with income of $200,000 or more	Percent with income of less than $25,000	Families with income below poverty (percent)	Total	Percent change, 2000–2010	Vacant units for sale or rent[2]	Total	Percent	Median value[3] (dollars)	With a mortgage[4]	Without a mortgage[5]
	42	43	44	45	46	47	48	49	50	51	52	53	54
MISSOURI	25 332	46 640	2.9	26.3	11.6	2 712 729	11.1	337 118	2 353 778	67.6	135 100	21.6	11.8
Ballwin	37 662	85 192	8.9	11.6	2.4	12 435	3.2	561	11 033	79.7	236 500	21.4	10.2
Blue Springs	27 471	63 106	3.2	14.3	7.0	20 643	16.0	1 121	18 951	67.9	141 600	22.0	10.6
Cape Girardeau	21 643	38 128	1.6	34.8	17.6	16 760	6.0	1 555	15 146	53.4	126 200	19.7	11.3
Chesterfield	49 685	92 837	15.1	10.3	2.7	20 393	8.5	1 169	18 660	77.4	325 600	20.7	12.9
Columbia	26 555	42 945	4.1	31.6	11.0	46 758	30.0	3 693	44 069	47.6	170 800	20.1	10.0
Florissant	25 368	50 435	1.2	21.4	8.1	22 632	8.0	1 385	21 038	71.0	95 900	20.6	12.7
Gladstone	26 567	50 087	1.8	21.1	7.3	12 148	1.8	966	10 867	70.0	132 700	22.8	13.7
Hazelwood	23 384	41 327	0.9	24.4	13.1	11 730	2.9	797	10 872	63.8	103 700	25.9	12.6
Independence	23 089	42 696	1.0	28.2	13.3	53 834	7.3	5 092	48 778	64.7	97 100	22.4	13.5
Jefferson City	24 456	45 947	2.1	26.1	11.2	18 852	10.9	1 574	16 791	57.8	137 100	18.4	10.0
Joplin	22 473	35 781	1.7	35.3	12.4	23 322	9.2	2 462	21 390	56.1	103 000	20.0	12.9
Kansas City	26 546	44 613	2.9	28.4	15.6	221 860	9.7	29 454	191 728	55.0	130 800	22.1	13.5
Kirkwood	44 151	71 766	11.5	14.8	3.7	12 895	4.6	1 001	12 047	74.1	241 200	21.3	11.6
Lee's Summit	33 390	76 104	6.1	13.0	5.5	36 679	33.9	2 250	33 473	73.9	186 700	20.7	10.2
Liberty	30 112	62 515	4.0	15.6	7.9	11 284	14.5	702	10 506	74.3	167 300	21.1	12.5
Maryland Heights	29 204	54 230	2.5	16.8	7.2	13 092	10.7	912	11 823	56.5	144 500	21.4	12.6
O'Fallon	30 817	76 691	4.0	11.0	4.1	29 376	84.8	1 142	29 376	79.8	186 400	21.4	11.1
Raytown	22 207	47 899	0.9	22.3	11.4	13 276	-0.2	1 172	11 422	65.6	98 500	22.2	13.8
St. Charles	28 991	55 838	3.6	17.6	8.6	28 590	13.4	1 875	26 536	65.6	171 200	20.1	13.3
St. Joseph	20 036	41 077	1.4	32.1	16.2	33 189	4.7	3 462	28 245	59.6	98 600	19.8	11.9
St. Louis	22 735	33 770	1.9	38.7	22.6	176 002	-0.2	33 945	138 531	44.5	116 300	23.2	14.4
St. Peters	31 107	68 329	2.7	12.1	3.1	21 717	15.5	856	21 113	81.0	165 900	21.2	10.9
Springfield	20 751	32 322	1.6	37.7	18.7	77 620	11.1	7 866	71 025	45.7	106 200	21.4	10.4
University City	37 100	50 968	8.1	24.2	12.3	18 021	3.0	1 867	16 268	58.0	193 700	22.2	14.7
Wentzville	29 407	68 765	4.2	10.5	4.6	10 305	NA	538	10 959	84.4	183 200	22.5	11.2
Wildwood	49 599	120 600	21.4	7.4	4.1	12 604	11.5	492	11 996	91.4	350 300	21.1	10.0
MONTANA	25 383	45 951	2.6	26.9	10.5	482 825	17.0	73 218	405 504	67.3	186 600	23.3	11.5
Billings	27 024	47 196	3.0	26.8	11.5	46 317	18.3	2 372	43 610	62.1	183 100	21.7	11.0
Bozeman	26 962	47 354	2.9	27.0	7.1	17 464	50.0	1 689	16 008	44.6	242 300	26.0	11.5
Butte-Silver Bow	24 313	38 347	2.3	32.9	13.7	16 717	3.3	1 785	14 574	64.4	129 100	19.4	12.4
Great Falls	23 577	42 487	1.8	29.1	14.4	26 854	6.3	1 553	24 629	61.6	157 800	22.1	10.0
Helena	29 174	49 375	2.6	25.5	9.0	13 457	11.0	677	12 851	57.6	200 100	20.5	10.4
Missoula	24 809	41 319	2.4	32.4	10.7	30 682	22.3	1 601	29 299	45.3	237 300	23.6	12.1
NEBRASKA	26 930	51 370	3.2	22.6	9.0	796 793	10.3	75 663	729 572	66.4	129 400	20.7	12.1
Bellevue	25 199	55 653	2.1	17.8	9.6	20 591	18.0	1 449	19 651	66.0	133 500	21.0	11.7
Fremont	22 323	46 657	1.1	24.2	8.8	11 427	8.0	702	10 537	61.7	117 700	19.0	14.5
Grand Island	21 944	44 747	1.7	25.6	15.5	19 426	11.7	1 100	18 638	61.7	108 600	21.1	12.7
Kearney	24 539	47 729	2.2	24.7	8.9	12 738	15.7	537	12 180	57.7	149 700	20.7	10.0
Lincoln	26 047	48 329	3.0	24.1	10.4	110 546	16.1	7 000	105 851	57.0	144 800	20.6	11.2
Omaha	26 700	47 275	3.7	26.3	12.7	177 518	7.1	14 891	169 114	57.6	132 600	21.6	13.0
NEVADA	25 826	50 773	3.2	22.6	12.0	1 173 814	41.9	167 564	995 980	55.2	157 900	25.5	10.8
Carson City	25 491	50 233	2.7	25.7	10.2	23 534	10.6	2 107	21 206	55.3	174 800	25.3	11.0
Henderson	32 233	61 538	5.0	16.4	7.6	113 586	59.0	12 272	100 943	62.0	194 400	25.2	10.0
Las Vegas	24 945	48 676	3.5	24.2	13.8	243 701	27.7	32 012	211 734	51.8	152 300	25.4	11.2
North Las Vegas	20 047	51 186	1.4	21.0	14.3	76 073	107.9	9 574	67 487	55.5	127 300	26.8	10.0
Reno	25 716	46 348	3.1	28.7	13.5	102 582	28.9	11 658	89 770	46.4	184 800	24.3	11.4
Sparks	25 582	51 350	2.0	20.8	10.6	36 455	39.8	2 953	34 474	58.1	162 900	26.0	10.9
NEW HAMPSHIRE	33 101	64 689	5.4	17.2	5.7	614 754	12.4	95 781	518 088	70.9	236 000	25.3	16.9
Concord	30 824	54 790	4.8	19.9	7.1	18 852	11.7	1 260	16 876	56.6	213 600	24.0	17.9
Dover	30 932	59 673	2.5	18.9	5.0	13 685	14.8	858	12 653	50.4	239 300	26.6	16.6
Manchester	26 965	52 462	1.8	24.1	11.0	49 288	7.4	3 522	45 549	46.7	208 500	26.5	15.1
Nashua	31 596	64 154	4.9	19.4	7.7	37 168	5.0	2 124	33 885	56.1	233 500	24.3	15.2
Rochester	25 790	46 083	1.3	22.6	12.8	13 372	13.0	994	12 870	62.0	168 400	26.6	22.3
NEW JERSEY	35 506	70 324	9.2	17.9	8.2	3 553 562	7.3	339 202	3 181 152	64.9	315 100	27.7	18.5
Atlantic City	18 435	26 511	1.6	48.5	32.8	20 013	-1.0	4 509	15 862	27.4	207 000	48.6	22.9
Bayonne	28 135	53 484	3.2	23.3	13.8	27 799	3.6	2 562	25 649	37.2	321 100	33.6	25.3
Bergenfield	30 085	74 879	7.3	16.4	9.3	9 200	0.6	348	8 818	68.4	338 600	31.7	19.4
Bridgeton	14 041	38 967	1.2	33.9	31.5	6 782	-0.2	517	6 833	45.2	110 700	28.2	20.1
Camden	12 748	22 617	0.5	53.2	37.2	28 358	-4.7	3 883	25 354	38.6	84 900	30.2	19.5
Clifton	30 716	67 376	5.6	17.0	6.7	31 946	2.9	1 285	29 055	62.0	337 400	30.2	22.5
East Orange	20 549	35 568	0.6	37.2	20.0	28 803	1.1	3 858	25 921	26.4	213 500	39.1	21.1
Elizabeth	18 402	42 214	1.8	27.6	16.4	45 516	6.3	3 920	38 987	25.5	261 100	35.5	24.9
Englewood	45 384	73 050	10.8	16.6	9.9	10 695	11.2	638	10 590	50.8	374 000	29.5	21.3
Fair Lawn	40 863	96 340	11.4	13.0	4.3	12 266	2.2	336	11 776	77.6	387 200	27.6	17.6
Fort Lee	44 798	70 374	10.2	18.9	6.4	17 818	2.1	1 447	16 792	59.0	323 800	27.3	16.8

1. Based on population estimated by the American Community Survey. 2. Includes units rented or sold but not occupied. 3. Specified owner-occupied units; $1,000,000 represents $1,000,000 or more 4. 50.0 represents 50 percent or more. 5. 10.0 represents 10 percent or less.

City	Occupied housing units, 2011–2013 (cont.): Percent renter occupied	Occupied housing units, 2011–2013 (cont.): Median gross rent[1]	Occupied housing units, 2011–2013 (cont.): Median rent as a percent of income[2]	Occupied housing units, 2011–2013 (cont.): Percent with no vehicle available	Migration, 2011–2013: Percent who lived in the same house one year ago	Migration, 2011–2013: Percent who lived outside current city one year ago	Civilian labor force, 2014: Total	Civilian labor force, 2014: Percent change, 2013–2014	Civilian labor force, 2014: Unemployment: Total	Civilian labor force, 2014: Unemployment: Rate[3]	Civilian employment[4], 2011–2013: Population age 16 and older	Civilian employment[4], 2011–2013: Percent: In labor force	Civilian employment[4], 2011–2013: Percent: Civilian full-year full-time workers	Civilian employment[4], 2011–2013: Households with no workers (percent)
	55	56	57	58	59	60	61	62	63	64	65	66	67	68
MISSOURI	32.4	728	29.9	7.4	83.7	11.5	3 058 118	1.4	186 901	6.1	4 779 258	63.9	40.1	28.6
Ballwin	20.3	1 022	29.1	1.7	86.3	12.2	16 936	1.8	720	4.3	23 735	69.9	43.5	19.8
Blue Springs	32.1	870	24.9	2.0	86.6	9.2	29 893	2.0	1 595	5.3	39 921	70.1	46.3	20.2
Cape Girardeau	46.6	650	34.7	9.7	75.7	14.9	20 069	-0.1	1 128	5.6	31 478	62.1	34.6	29.7
Chesterfield	22.6	1 049	29.6	3.4	86.7	10.4	24 709	1.6	1 022	4.1	37 954	63.6	42.0	24.3
Columbia	52.4	785	35.6	7.1	66.9	16.9	66 315	1.0	2 625	4.0	93 508	68.4	38.7	21.1
Florissant	29.0	879	31.0	6.3	84.7	11.5	28 409	1.6	1 715	6.0	41 291	67.2	43.4	27.3
Gladstone	30.0	727	30.3	5.6	84.1	12.1	14 278	2.0	862	6.0	21 036	66.4	42.4	28.9
Hazelwood	36.2	785	33.7	9.3	83.0	15.8	13 957	1.3	909	6.5	20 468	70.3	46.1	25.6
Independence	35.3	760	32.3	6.7	89.2	6.7	58 318	1.9	3 940	6.8	94 115	61.5	40.4	31.9
Jefferson City	42.2	570	26.8	9.9	80.4	10.0	21 379	0.7	1 058	4.9	34 921	57.7	40.3	29.2
Joplin	43.9	648	30.9	10.3	78.5	9.8	25 972	0.2	1 313	5.1	41 118	65.3	40.0	31.4
Kansas City	45.0	789	30.7	11.2	79.4	9.5	251 057	2.0	16 845	6.7	365 978	68.3	43.3	26.0
Kirkwood	25.9	1 049	30.1	5.9	87.6	9.8	15 671	1.7	653	4.2	22 216	68.1	46.9	25.2
Lee's Summit	26.1	1 001	32.9	5.1	88.6	7.5	52 775	2.3	2 427	4.6	69 789	73.1	49.9	19.7
Liberty	25.7	795	31.4	4.2	82.4	13.8	15 835	1.7	826	5.2	23 032	66.3	42.3	25.3
Maryland Heights	43.5	841	23.7	4.5	79.7	16.9	16 226	1.7	784	4.8	22 378	73.7	48.4	17.7
O'Fallon	20.2	975	26.3	3.9	89.4	8.3	46 084	1.5	1 922	4.2	60 399	75.8	52.7	15.3
Raytown	34.4	873	31.3	7.0	90.0	7.5	15 619	2.5	1 195	7.7	22 770	64.5	40.5	30.3
St. Charles	34.4	806	27.9	5.7	81.7	12.6	37 307	1.5	1 881	5.0	55 053	67.8	43.1	24.1
St. Joseph	40.4	684	33.0	10.1	78.1	10.9	39 479	0.7	2 231	5.7	60 867	62.9	37.5	29.0
St. Louis	55.5	725	33.1	22.2	79.2	9.3	161 379	1.0	12 395	7.7	260 386	64.3	38.2	32.2
St. Peters	19.0	861	24.0	4.4	89.8	7.6	32 489	1.5	1 506	4.6	43 428	72.7	48.8	20.4
Springfield	54.3	656	32.2	9.4	73.6	13.5	85 598	2.6	4 270	5.0	136 125	63.0	34.8	30.4
University City	42.0	952	31.8	12.6	83.2	12.9	18 932	1.5	1 053	5.6	29 389	67.8	44.0	28.8
Wentzville	15.6	914	27.3	4.5	88.0	9.1	17 372	1.7	707	4.1	22 431	74.4	51.7	13.5
Wildwood	8.6	1 135	25.2	1.2	90.9	6.2	18 910	1.5	765	4.0	26 663	69.3	46.3	15.5
MONTANA	32.7	683	28.8	5.2	83.2	11.4	516 437	0.5	24 346	4.7	808 159	64.5	38.1	28.5
Billings	37.9	718	30.6	6.3	79.8	10.5	56 666	0.4	2 092	3.7	85 409	67.4	41.2	26.0
Bozeman	55.4	832	28.8	6.8	64.2	24.1	24 846	3.8	759	3.1	33 728	73.4	38.8	19.2
Butte-Silver Bow	35.6	620	29.8	9.1	80.3	9.9	17 134	-0.8	854	5.0	27 615	63.5	37.0	34.4
Great Falls	38.4	608	28.2	8.7	82.0	7.2	28 449	-0.1	1 197	4.2	47 057	64.3	36.9	29.6
Helena	42.4	694	28.2	8.7	76.8	10.4	16 732	0.7	591	3.5	24 258	67.0	44.5	26.8
Missoula	54.7	748	32.2	7.0	71.8	12.5	38 100	1.0	1 575	4.1	57 625	70.8	35.9	24.8
NEBRASKA	33.6	704	27.3	6.0	83.6	8.8	1 022 152	0.0	33 903	3.3	1 442 988	70.3	46.5	22.9
Bellevue	34.0	843	28.1	5.1	81.3	13.2	27 601	0.6	936	3.4	40 318	69.8	45.1	24.4
Fremont	38.3	696	24.2	7.3	82.0	7.1	13 846	0.2	489	3.5	20 465	66.5	42.3	25.6
Grand Island	38.3	637	26.0	7.2	81.7	7.6	27 039	0.0	1 004	3.7	37 952	72.1	44.6	23.6
Kearney	42.3	693	28.8	6.1	73.4	12.2	18 977	0.4	469	2.5	25 268	75.1	45.8	17.8
Lincoln	43.0	704	29.6	7.4	77.1	7.7	153 268	0.5	4 377	2.9	211 299	72.3	45.2	21.1
Omaha	42.4	771	29.9	9.0	81.8	6.8	230 047	0.5	8 199	3.6	333 478	70.2	44.2	23.6
NEVADA	44.8	959	30.5	7.9	77.8	13.7	1 394 599	0.7	108 125	7.8	2 168 375	64.9	38.7	26.5
Carson City	44.7	819	28.5	9.4	77.3	10.5	25 068	-1.5	2 128	8.5	44 234	59.4	33.4	37.8
Henderson	38.0	1 137	28.5	3.8	82.0	10.3	141 757	1.5	11 095	7.8	213 523	64.6	39.8	26.4
Las Vegas	48.2	959	31.5	10.1	75.0	11.5	292 750	1.1	23 400	8.0	464 998	64.4	37.3	27.5
North Las Vegas	44.5	1 093	32.3	6.9	74.7	15.4	105 686	1.0	8 996	8.5	161 338	66.5	40.4	21.4
Reno	53.6	837	31.4	10.4	76.9	10.7	119 904	0.4	8 984	7.5	183 314	66.7	39.2	26.1
Sparks	41.9	945	30.8	8.0	77.1	14.0	48 063	-0.1	3 626	7.5	72 516	68.3	41.1	27.6
NEW HAMPSHIRE	29.1	980	29.6	5.1	86.6	10.3	741 178	-0.1	31 959	4.3	1 080 471	68.5	43.2	24.1
Concord	43.4	924	29.4	9.1	82.5	10.0	22 526	0.2	846	3.8	35 019	64.7	42.2	26.6
Dover	49.6	992	30.2	5.3	79.0	13.1	17 638	0.6	631	3.6	24 844	71.5	44.2	21.9
Manchester	53.3	989	31.3	10.0	79.8	8.9	61 986	0.6	2 866	4.6	90 599	68.4	44.7	26.1
Nashua	43.9	1 080	28.9	8.6	82.9	9.5	48 851	-0.3	2 474	5.1	68 820	70.5	45.2	23.6
Rochester	38.0	910	32.4	6.8	84.7	9.7	16 790	0.1	708	4.2	25 048	68.1	43.8	31.6
NEW JERSEY	35.1	1 165	32.4	11.9	90.1	7.6	4 518 712	-0.3	300 277	6.6	7 072 194	66.2	41.7	24.9
Atlantic City	72.6	849	37.7	47.6	83.4	7.6	16 745	-2.7	2 479	14.8	30 333	62.0	30.4	38.4
Bayonne	62.8	1 111	27.2	23.1	94.1	4.0	33 161	-0.6	2 430	7.3	52 166	61.6	44.7	27.7
Bergenfield	31.6	1 181	35.8	10.7	90.3	6.7	14 688	-0.2	726	4.9	21 930	68.6	44.9	20.1
Bridgeton	54.8	1 021	35.0	20.2	82.1	11.0	8 357	-2.2	951	11.4	18 995	52.6	28.1	32.6
Camden	61.4	845	44.0	36.6	84.1	6.0	27 003	-2.4	3 431	12.7	55 149	55.7	28.4	45.7
Clifton	38.0	1 234	32.0	9.2	93.3	4.8	45 391	-0.4	3 120	6.9	68 120	66.9	47.0	21.8
East Orange	73.6	961	34.9	33.7	86.4	7.3	30 454	-0.7	3 030	9.9	51 044	65.6	37.0	34.2
Elizabeth	74.5	1 047	33.2	24.4	83.6	7.7	63 858	-0.5	5 352	8.4	94 340	70.7	43.5	23.6
Englewood	49.2	1 343	32.2	16.6	91.6	6.7	14 679	0.2	854	5.8	21 910	68.8	49.9	22.0
Fair Lawn	22.4	1 401	26.9	5.0	92.6	5.9	18 099	-0.2	903	5.0	26 526	70.3	47.4	20.0
Fort Lee	41.0	1 471	30.5	12.8	91.1	7.5	18 705	0.1	788	4.2	30 853	61.2	42.8	31.1

1. $2,000 represents $2,000 or more. 2. 50.0 represents 50 percent or more. 3. Percent of civilian labor force. 4. Persons 16 years old and over.

Table D. Cities — **Construction, Wholesale Trade, and Retail Trade**

City	Value of residential construction authorized by building permits, 2014: New construction ($1,000)	Number of housing units	Percent single family	Wholesale trade,[1] 2007: Number of establish-ments	Number of employees	Sales (mil dol)	Annual payroll (mil dol)	Retail trade,[2] 2007: Number of establish-ments	Number of employees	Sales (mil dol)	Annual payroll (mil dol)
	69	70	71	72	73	74	75	76	77	78	79
MISSOURI	2 682 665	16 003	56.7	6 903	96 451	81 032.9	4 533.6	23 360	317 318	76 575.2	7 155.3
Ballwin	11 568	37	100.0	17	55	44.9	2.7	101	1 905	523.1	45.9
Blue Springs	28 083	273	44.3	43	278	236.6	13.5	182	2 854	788.5	67.0
Cape Girardeau	17 031	115	79.1	84	1 611	1 625.5	63.3	313	4 809	1 018.2	93.6
Chesterfield	NA	NA	NA	144	1 712	1 194.1	122.5	340	5 576	1 047.6	112.3
Columbia	216 174	1 183	37.5	96	1 170	508.3	46.3	542	10 194	2 672.8	214.8
Florissant	140	1	100.0	24	126	29.7	3.6	190	3 586	737.2	83.9
Gladstone	726	6	100.0	17	59	19.5	2.2	84	1 873	436.2	43.4
Hazelwood	877	6	100.0	61	1 472	870.0	75.6	149	2 975	978.0	83.2
Independence	9 662	64	93.8	81	578	176.3	20.9	490	9 020	1 878.5	186.1
Jefferson City	13 208	79	70.9	53	2 277	620.8	67.1	306	5 229	1 134.4	110.0
Joplin	24 336	263	78.7	88	1 199	487.1	46.8	426	6 272	1 543.5	126.5
Kansas City	281 796	2 734	24.0	627	12 675	15 540.1	691.5	1 558	25 485	6 713.0	592.7
Kirkwood	20 438	61	100.0	38	237	94.2	13.3	134	2 394	649.0	63.3
Lee's Summit	117 028	571	56.2	94	1 304	589.6	60.6	253	4 732	1 092.0	105.7
Liberty	5 742	30	100.0	20	282	279.6	15.0	97	1 847	411.9	40.9
Maryland Heights	0	0	0.0	232	5 738	3 732.8	322.9	131	3 697	987.0	312.5
O'Fallon	49 889	442	77.8	73	724	705.6	37.5	202	3 285	776.7	75.2
Raytown	665	6	66.7	31	233	78.3	10.2	99	1 519	367.1	36.7
St. Charles	76 206	395	44.6	80	1 449	3 807.1	74.0	295	4 714	1 093.7	104.8
St. Joseph	11 680	60	90.0	92	1 358	1 001.8	54.0	358	5 847	1 419.1	126.9
St. Louis	123 458	758	12.7	522	9 422	5 042.1	462.3	1 028	11 368	2 496.7	263.5
St. Peters	87 449	405	64.4	76	D	D	D	334	5 810	1 545.1	138.2
Springfield	65 835	1 116	13.1	373	6 953	4 816.0	293.0	1 064	17 200	4 176.4	379.3
University City	839	3	100.0	29	284	147.9	20.5	94	987	183.4	22.8
Wentzville	148 798	626	90.1	33	D	D	D	89	1 678	468.7	46.7
Wildwood	NA	NA	NA	41	131	51.9	6.0	37	474	93.6	11.5
MONTANA	647 022	3 884	52.6	1 254	12 849	8 202.8	503.4	5 258	58 883	14 686.9	1 317.8
Billings	122 415	605	78.2	235	3 630	2 226.0	157.6	645	8 951	2 406.3	219.8
Bozeman	115 449	671	44.0	57	722	253.2	27.1	371	5 400	1 210.2	128.6
Butte-Silver Bow	4 887	58	55.2	31	D	D	D	189	2 183	504.7	44.3
Great Falls	43 724	356	13.5	94	942	597.0	37.8	346	5 153	1 226.0	114.3
Helena	37 605	338	15.4	32	335	167.3	12.9	251	3 597	775.5	79.5
Missoula	30 607	494	31.4	118	1 371	688.1	54.3	485	7 019	1 718.6	158.6
NEBRASKA	1 205 827	7 605	62.4	2 668	32 329	24 019.9	1 323.5	7 888	108 209	26 486.6	2 230.5
Bellevue	78 929	415	29.2	13	39	9.0	1.3	99	2 080	573.1	49.1
Fremont	6 365	31	100.0	33	396	363.0	15.2	142	2 060	580.6	47.3
Grand Island	32 482	198	71.7	81	899	553.4	39.0	306	4 795	962.9	94.1
Kearney	43 019	265	54.7	32	558	473.3	25.7	209	3 197	593.4	59.5
Lincoln	251 646	1 792	47.7	239	3 562	2 557.8	157.1	996	16 660	3 526.9	333.6
Omaha	280 516	2 453	53.2	675	9 809	5 606.0	460.7	1 707	34 372	7 495.1	759.5
NEVADA	1 754 597	13 016	68.3	2 614	36 052	19 255.9	1 698.5	8 492	139 829	37 434.0	3 691.7
Carson City	11 679	35	94.3	92	D	D	D	262	3 698	991.5	99.5
Henderson	251 384	2 256	56.0	183	1 292	566.3	57.1	704	15 060	4 803.0	404.1
Las Vegas	202 296	1 453	100.0	410	3 578	1 566.6	157.5	1 791	32 904	9 178.9	892.6
North Las Vegas	66 571	522	90.2	179	5 661	2 698.7	269.5	276	5 885	1 443.4	137.6
Reno	291 806	1 557	55.1	294	5 486	3 017.5	234.7	1 087	18 504	5 014.9	503.1
Sparks	85 609	377	97.9	247	4 534	2 998.8	208.4	323	5 092	1 166.4	128.6
NEW HAMPSHIRE	653 428	3 403	64.3	1 561	21 457	14 564.5	1 196.3	6 603	98 333	25 353.9	2 380.5
Concord	16 168	116	36.2	49	1 232	778.0	63.9	318	6 020	1 412.6	133.9
Dover	17 664	107	64.5	37	480	216.3	30.8	113	1 482	381.5	41.8
Manchester	19 720	114	91.2	171	2 531	1 350.6	126.6	489	8 057	2 132.5	196.9
Nashua	36 803	396	14.6	112	1 566	1 250.1	121.2	492	10 041	2 925.2	244.1
Rochester	4 992	44	100.0	13	D	D	D	144	2 419	651.6	65.8
NEW JERSEY	4 069 959	28 155	39.1	14 033	221 729	233 413.0	13 266.6	34 482	460 843	124 813.6	12 050.0
Atlantic City	15 643	114	17.5	13	355	70.9	8.7	316	2 692	554.0	59.5
Bayonne	23 792	193	28.5	46	1 380	622.0	76.0	216	1 605	369.8	36.5
Bergenfield	2 046	8	100.0	39	239	150.0	10.9	102	955	206.9	23.1
Bridgeton	1 150	14	100.0	14	D	D	D	112	908	241.8	22.4
Camden	13 285	687	0.9	64	1 222	849.4	58.5	192	1 256	270.5	28.0
Clifton	13 076	121	62.8	175	2 801	1 178.8	132.3	306	4 611	1 263.4	119.5
East Orange	1 776	24	29.2	15	148	143.5	6.8	137	896	237.2	21.9
Elizabeth	25 616	224	0.4	113	3 926	3 548.4	231.2	556	5 925	1 304.0	112.8
Englewood	43 335	542	0.6	113	1 476	933.8	84.4	165	2 048	1 004.5	92.0
Fair Lawn	5 575	66	15.2	57	739	801.1	32.1	112	1 374	440.5	55.4
Fort Lee	13 157	52	28.8	167	2 065	3 797.2	181.2	148	1 126	311.8	28.0

1. Merchant wholesalers except manufacturers' sales branches and offices. 2. Establishments with payroll.

City	Real estate and rental and leasing, 2007				Professional, scientific, and technical services,[1] 2007				Manufacturing, 2007			
	Number of establish-ments	Number of employees	Receipts (mil dol)	Annual payroll (mil dol)	Number of establish-ments	Number of employees	Receipts (mil dol)	Annual payroll (mil dol)	Number of establish-ments	Number of employees	Receipts (mil dol)	Annual payroll (mil dol)
	80	81	82	83	84	85	86	87	88	89	90	91
MISSOURI	7 003	39 625	7 186.3	1 248.8	13 524	130 786	19 749.8	7 454.7	6 886	295 313	110 907.6	12 996.5
Ballwin	29	94	11.5	1.8	85	187	23.6	8.5	NA	NA	NA	NA
Blue Springs	78	250	43.1	6.1	132	D	D	D	34	1 037	D	48.0
Cape Girardeau	88	312	51.9	6.9	106	D	D	D	39	2 650	2 605.4	134.8
Chesterfield	146	895	186.9	37.2	370	9 133	1 567.9	614.1	48	1 858	479.1	92.4
Columbia	202	903	136.4	23.4	325	D	D	D	63	3 354	1 259.9	129.9
Florissant	43	223	29.7	6.2	67	466	22.5	10.1	NA	NA	NA	NA
Gladstone	44	206	30.1	8.0	75	D	D	D	NA	NA	NA	NA
Hazelwood	38	384	60.1	15.5	40	1 940	526.5	152.4	39	3 413	1 112.2	202.9
Independence	121	569	137.7	13.8	237	D	D	D	97	4 394	1 039.4	201.1
Jefferson City	59	207	36.3	5.0	200	1 312	161.2	59.8	43	3 117	D	134.9
Joplin	92	489	53.9	13.2	148	D	D	D	91	5 843	1 902.5	218.0
Kansas City	622	5 816	1 381.0	213.3	1 543	D	D	D	434	19 070	7 789.3	897.7
Kirkwood	51	180	26.5	5.2	136	675	85.1	31.4	32	591	123.0	27.5
Lee's Summit	136	499	73.0	14.0	291	1 539	256.9	83.6	76	2 143	421.7	89.5
Liberty	41	185	28.1	4.9	102	D	D	D	20	1 311	D	62.4
Maryland Heights	67	345	97.0	16.4	179	2 947	620.4	234.6	111	3 673	1 082.3	173.5
O'Fallon	73	310	46.3	7.7	116	737	74.0	27.7	62	5 519	1 132.9	224.8
Raytown	22	124	13.5	2.8	76	499	37.9	17.2	NA	NA	NA	NA
St. Charles	120	666	256.7	24.7	265	4 800	287.1	121.1	77	2 392	D	121.9
St. Joseph	99	449	48.8	9.4	169	D	D	D	93	D	D	D
St. Louis	418	2 633	606.6	94.7	1 005	D	D	D	543	21 432	10 920.6	998.2
St. Peters	68	302	57.6	8.0	132	768	80.4	25.7	53	1 825	695.2	D
Springfield	375	2 593	322.7	63.7	675	D	D	D	273	13 588	3 554.2	520.0
University City	50	589	67.5	14.0	91	352	39.2	13.7	NA	NA	NA	NA
Wentzville	15	63	9.5	1.5	46	205	18.2	6.4	23	3 095	D	D
Wildwood	34	58	13.2	2.5	97	226	38.2	14.6	NA	NA	NA	NA
MONTANA	1 892	6 410	848.3	153.3	3 403	16 547	1 770.9	670.6	1 324	19 525	10 638.1	808.2
Billings	226	805	121.9	23.7	489	D	D	D	126	2 484	D	128.1
Bozeman	169	518	86.8	13.7	394	1 859	229.8	86.8	71	985	228.0	35.9
Butte-Silver Bow	45	144	14.9	3.0	107	D	D	D	NA	NA	NA	NA
Great Falls	119	349	53.9	7.8	177	D	D	D	53	938	640.2	39.5
Helena	80	603	75.0	13.0	206	1 625	198.6	81.4	NA	NA	NA	NA
Missoula	174	843	105.3	18.9	378	D	D	D	67	D	D	21.0
NEBRASKA	2 032	9 974	1 645.5	292.0	4 205	40 692	4 836.4	2 011.0	1 984	99 547	40 158.0	3 788.6
Bellevue	46	193	26.8	3.2	75	1 757	324.3	119.9	13	608	123.7	23.3
Fremont	43	D	D	D	43	189	15.4	5.5	33	929	395.7	36.8
Grand Island	64	256	44.4	7.2	91	D	D	D	63	6 524	D	240.2
Kearney	48	161	26.9	4.1	66	442	36.3	16.2	23	538	D	D
Lincoln	343	1 536	247.5	42.6	727	7 989	1 082.1	373.8	223	11 908	3 932.9	486.9
Omaha	599	5 226	775.7	168.3	1 385	D	D	D	448	20 354	8 853.9	817.4
NEVADA	4 613	31 603	6 187.3	1 106.5	7 895	57 357	8 881.4	3 241.1	2 035	51 958	15 735.8	2 290.8
Carson City	147	569	73.4	16.0	381	D	D	D	143	3 528	621.6	141.7
Henderson	431	1 532	361.9	58.5	678	D	D	D	128	5 086	1 634.7	197.1
Las Vegas	1 099	5 391	1 048.7	209.8	2 220	14 869	2 496.1	865.1	233	3 744	872.9	137.2
North Las Vegas	139	3 182	318.0	97.1	136	D	D	D	137	5 728	1 311.6	213.5
Reno	505	2 847	509.0	91.0	1 236	D	D	D	249	9 355	3 875.0	496.6
Sparks	126	795	134.7	25.8	157	D	D	D	196	4 760	1 522.3	210.7
NEW HAMPSHIRE	1 534	7 266	1 371.8	248.2	3 961	29 160	3 730.8	1 570.2	2 104	81 592	18 592.4	4 196.2
Concord	78	447	83.9	14.2	241	1 820	254.3	113.7	66	2 606	567.4	112.2
Dover	42	189	31.5	4.9	91	D	D	D	45	1 215	167.1	48.9
Manchester	141	1 161	234.3	38.9	398	D	D	D	153	6 970	1 493.4	309.1
Nashua	121	520	118.5	21.6	336	D	D	D	134	9 964	2 693.5	924.0
Rochester	30	113	15.3	2.4	45	302	25.5	10.7	42	1 531	281.0	60.3
NEW JERSEY	9 618	64 021	16 347.6	2 939.1	31 040	330 133	52 442.8	23 639.9	9 250	310 606	116 608.1	16 399.3
Atlantic City	63	739	139.4	20.7	69	D	D	D	NA	NA	NA	NA
Bayonne	52	243	48.6	9.0	79	290	27.7	10.0	39	1 208	470.9	58.1
Bergenfield	19	44	6.4	1.1	59	146	26.1	6.4	NA	NA	NA	NA
Bridgeton	10	90	10.5	2.0	40	D	D	D	15	659	254.8	29.0
Camden	35	196	32.8	5.4	54	D	D	D	56	2 851	641.1	192.0
Clifton	99	733	107.0	29.5	263	3 746	472.3	198.9	176	5 671	1 429.0	295.7
East Orange	70	385	66.9	10.4	56	D	D	D	NA	NA	NA	NA
Elizabeth	110	358	140.0	12.1	114	D	D	D	81	3 314	808.7	154.7
Englewood	74	250	59.0	11.4	125	791	154.8	50.3	61	1 582	468.2	67.2
Fair Lawn	34	100	36.4	2.9	218	1 037	257.2	71.3	40	2 031	634.7	97.5
Fort Lee	120	574	142.7	22.7	257	1 127	255.0	73.6	NA	NA	NA	NA

1. Establishments subject to federal tax.

Table D. Cities — Accommodation and Food Services, Arts, Entertainment, and Recreation, and Health Care and Social Assistance

City	Accommodation and food services, 2007				Arts, entertainment, and recreation,[1] 2007				Health care and social assistance,[1] 2007			
	Number of establish-ments	Number of employees	Sales (mil dol)	Annual payroll (mil dol)	Number of establish-ments	Number of employees	Receipts (mil dol)	Annual payroll (mil dol)	Number of establish-ments	Number of employees	Receipts (mil dol)	Annual payroll (mil dol)
	92	93	94	95	96	97	98	99	100	101	102	103
MISSOURI	12 261	241 438	11 070.6	3 109.1	1 696	25 744	2 735.9	1 026.2	12 881	159 529	14 101.7	5 911.6
Ballwin	37	787	27.1	8.4	10	D	D	D	38	D	D	D
Blue Springs	107	2 203	83.7	22.7	18	D	D	D	113	D	D	D
Cape Girardeau	126	3 284	119.7	35.1	14	136	7.9	2.6	194	D	D	D
Chesterfield	161	4 566	191.9	61.2	32	286	17.2	4.4	223	3 750	389.8	176.4
Columbia	362	7 659	286.3	83.7	33	546	17.9	6.8	387	4 126	423.1	177.8
Florissant	123	2 577	96.4	28.7	9	D	D	D	146	1 867	146.9	64.1
Gladstone	37	824	33.3	10.1	5	D	D	D	82	806	65.6	27.2
Hazelwood	66	1 148	59.2	17.4	6	D	D	D	47	378	41.0	14.2
Independence	217	5 267	216.8	67.9	17	D	D	D	224	3 795	432.7	165.1
Jefferson City	140	2 963	118.9	35.2	16	D	D	D	163	D	D	D
Joplin	190	4 200	168.3	48.5	9	D	D	D	263	2 508	233.5	113.7
Kansas City	1 110	26 835	1 668.7	426.6	104	2 464	503.4	281.6	886	13 090	1 483.9	645.2
Kirkwood	59	1 585	58.5	17.8	12	116	7.3	2.2	111	832	114.5	40.6
Lee's Summit	153	3 172	119.9	37.5	36	D	D	D	195	3 005	334.7	127.1
Liberty	55	1 020	42.7	13.0	5	74	2.6	0.8	85	D	D	D
Maryland Heights	93	4 251	438.0	98.4	9	D	D	D	64	2 747	329.8	103.7
O'Fallon	143	3 286	113.2	35.3	25	322	18.1	6.7	133	D	D	D
Raytown	43	693	28.7	8.4	8	D	D	D	50	D	D	D
St. Charles	196	4 467	178.1	52.2	23	D	D	D	158	1 753	181.9	69.3
St. Joseph	189	4 084	151.7	44.8	14	D	D	D	229	D	D	D
St. Louis	934	20 372	1 059.3	311.4	62	2 672	450.0	226.8	722	11 401	1 052.1	365.9
St. Peters	190	3 702	135.2	41.2	24	D	D	D	191	1 766	179.9	74.3
Springfield	598	13 951	540.5	160.7	54	470	28.7	7.4	506	D	D	D
University City	77	1 250	52.6	16.3	9	81	2.8	0.8	74	1 240	59.2	23.5
Wentzville	62	1 374	45.7	14.4	6	D	D	D	59	551	52.2	18.1
Wildwood	24	D	D	D	11	125	5.6	1.4	40	395	24.7	11.8
MONTANA	3 360	46 137	2 079.4	554.2	881	8 207	589.4	110.3	2 438	21 763	1 944.6	801.7
Billings	312	7 102	335.8	91.1	82	792	68.6	10.2	368	D	D	D
Bozeman	153	3 297	141.0	38.0	44	318	31.9	5.2	206	1 608	150.6	60.2
Butte-Silver Bow	133	1 946	78.3	22.7	34	276	33.0	3.9	113	1 458	85.9	36.9
Great Falls	209	3 588	157.7	44.4	54	D	D	D	197	D	D	D
Helena	145	2 729	106.9	30.3	25	337	14.4	3.0	172	1 531	134.3	56.3
Missoula	260	5 473	233.1	60.8	61	695	53.0	8.9	319	D	D	D
NEBRASKA	4 241	69 142	2 685.6	749.1	573	6 394	396.8	92.8	3 830	49 338	4 447.4	1 888.7
Bellevue	91	1 808	70.8	20.3	9	D	D	D	61	977	59.7	25.7
Fremont	77	1 233	47.5	12.4	4	D	D	D	79	D	D	D
Grand Island	122	2 330	86.2	25.1	13	230	9.3	2.6	129	D	D	D
Kearney	118	2 480	98.4	27.2	15	D	D	D	91	1 133	132.1	63.8
Lincoln	619	11 603	457.9	128.2	80	1 447	54.4	16.8	677	D	D	D
Omaha	1 123	23 858	1 041.5	298.0	129	1 976	119.2	29.4	1 156	17 234	1 853.5	787.1
NEVADA	5 570	325 544	28 815.5	8 594.6	1 153	28 815	3 275.5	752.7	5 269	72 716	9 225.8	3 345.0
Carson City	167	2 664	127.7	37.8	48	1 762	138.4	39.5	192	2 048	278.5	101.3
Henderson	463	15 786	1 145.5	333.9	128	D	D	D	612	D	D	D
Las Vegas	1 128	42 712	3 134.0	924.7	226	4 369	521.9	120.4	1 593	28 718	4 019.0	1 373.4
North Las Vegas	199	6 458	476.1	127.8	33	1 554	107.8	28.5	141	D	D	D
Reno	702	27 677	1 918.0	580.7	103	1 816	161.5	39.0	757	9 418	1 226.5	542.7
Sparks	202	5 809	340.3	105.4	24	D	D	D	167	2 083	168.3	68.1
NEW HAMPSHIRE	3 508	55 268	2 631.0	799.8	548	9 606	659.1	205.7	2 655	32 711	3 095.7	1 386.1
Concord	135	2 769	132.4	41.1	13	217	6.9	2.2	158	2 267	248.0	124.6
Dover	79	1 364	58.7	18.8	8	D	D	D	116	1 286	129.6	64.0
Manchester	294	5 777	265.3	82.3	30	858	73.4	34.4	236	3 281	322.1	157.8
Nashua	228	4 574	231.7	70.4	25	428	28.1	8.0	248	3 236	353.7	151.0
Rochester	66	1 048	43.1	12.0	3	D	D	D	66	662	68.3	31.6
NEW JERSEY	19 526	291 327	19 993.6	5 232.4	2 939	35 241	2 958.6	921.7	22 050	250 070	28 415.5	10 529.7
Atlantic City	238	47 392	5 602.5	1 369.0	16	131	15.8	4.0	48	490	39.5	16.7
Bayonne	112	983	49.5	12.4	8	D	D	D	152	1 042	119.0	44.3
Bergenfield	44	342	22.3	5.3	4	D	D	D	52	302	37.3	11.1
Bridgeton	35	441	21.2	5.2	1	D	D	D	31	D	D	D
Camden	93	600	42.2	9.7	7	84	27.9	3.8	76	1 342	126.6	66.0
Clifton	157	D	D	D	17	D	D	D	330	2 687	294.0	110.7
East Orange	47	703	33.6	8.3	2	D	D	D	130	2 371	139.0	61.0
Elizabeth	253	2 627	192.0	49.1	6	D	D	D	188	1 860	175.7	68.7
Englewood	54	744	43.8	10.2	14	D	D	D	216	D	D	D
Fair Lawn	69	751	44.2	11.2	12	D	D	D	198	1 872	216.1	88.4
Fort Lee	107	1 209	80.6	18.6	25	D	D	D	190	D	D	D

1. Establishments subject to federal tax.

City	Other services[1], 2007				Government employment and payroll, 2012								
						March payroll							
							Percent of total for:						
	Number of establish-ments	Number of employees	Receipts (mil dol)	Annual payroll (mil dol)	Full-time equivalent employees	Total (dollars)	Adminis-tration, judicial, and legal	Police and Corrections	Fire Protection	Highways and trans-portation	Health and welfare	Natural resources and utilities	Education and libraries
	104	105	106	107	108	109	110	111	112	113	114	115	116
MISSOURI	9 114	53 749	4 220.1	1 361.4	X	X	X	X	X	X	X	X	X
Ballwin	41	233	14.6	5.6	0	0	0.0	0.0	0.0	0.0	0.0	0.0	0.0
Blue Springs	86	418	30.4	9.7	262	1 043 733	19.7	47.3	0.0	9.7	0.9	18.0	0.0
Cape Girardeau	87	433	29.7	9.8	634	1 734 259	10.2	18.8	19.9	13.6	0.0	29.9	5.9
Chesterfield	85	876	48.8	16.0	272	943 362	17.5	48.7	0.0	16.3	0.0	12.9	0.0
Columbia	203	1 451	108.9	31.6	1 462	5 497 108	19.3	10.6	11.4	6.9	6.7	33.2	0.0
Florissant	94	597	46.2	14.8	357	1 267 576	12.1	34.2	0.4	11.1	12.2	29.7	0.0
Gladstone	46	275	20.1	6.3	214	773 534	15.6	32.5	18.4	8.2	3.9	21.3	0.0
Hazelwood	38	271	22.1	7.1	195	925 216	9.7	45.0	25.1	8.3	0.5	6.9	0.0
Independence	174	833	64.7	19.5	1 064	6 218 560	8.1	26.4	15.4	4.9	2.8	41.9	0.0
Jefferson City	98	D	D	D	415	1 606 150	17.3	28.1	18.7	13.4	4.3	18.2	0.0
Joplin	133	716	44.3	13.5	548	1 718 395	9.6	29.9	20.7	11.8	6.0	12.5	4.3
Kansas City	734	5 132	416.6	131.9	6 482	21 087 489	9.4	47.9	29.2	7.6	1.6	0.9	0.0
Kirkwood	52	403	26.7	9.8	247	1 279 082	4.4	28.6	22.0	4.0	0.0	32.0	0.0
Lee's Summit	112	668	46.0	14.7	662	3 026 236	14.1	26.0	24.8	12.2	1.2	15.7	0.0
Liberty	44	259	17.6	6.3	236	903 212	17.2	26.6	21.9	6.0	2.2	21.9	0.0
Maryland Heights	59	549	52.7	19.9	213	1 068 259	19.4	51.3	0.0	8.8	0.8	12.2	0.0
O'Fallon	122	862	54.5	18.8	411	1 761 725	11.2	39.0	0.0	8.3	0.2	28.0	0.0
Raytown	65	470	26.5	13.5	163	693 572	15.3	25.3	23.0	16.1	0.7	19.6	0.0
St. Charles	127	884	67.0	21.9	509	2 509 796	9.9	33.7	23.0	9.7	0.0	13.6	0.0
St. Joseph	150	D	D	D	663	2 327 632	8.6	25.3	21.9	12.5	6.9	20.6	0.0
St. Louis	517	3 996	306.0	106.8	6 234	25 364 525	13.6	42.1	13.8	12.2	1.8	10.5	0.0
St. Peters	144	1 123	74.1	26.2	494	2 194 343	14.2	29.0	0.0	11.7	1.0	34.9	0.0
Springfield	449	D	D	D	2 692	13 095 113	4.7	15.6	8.4	9.6	2.7	34.5	0.0
University City	56	408	34.1	11.7	298	1 365 064	15.3	34.6	18.6	11.0	0.0	13.0	5.7
Wentzville	46	D	D	D	193	721 735	12.9	42.6	0.0	13.1	0.0	18.1	0.0
Wildwood	17	97	5.1	1.5	22	125 285	42.6	1.4	0.0	18.0	0.0	3.7	0.0
MONTANA	1 619	7 260	647.7	164.8	X	X	X	X	X	X	X	X	X
Billings	241	1 418	117.5	34.1	872	4 012 052	9.7	22.7	20.9	15.3	1.0	18.6	2.7
Bozeman	80	396	28.2	9.1	338	1 647 964	17.1	21.0	15.4	5.9	2.9	25.5	4.6
Butte-Silver Bow	51	240	19.7	4.8	430	1 750 790	15.7	24.3	18.9	14.2	2.0	21.6	0.0
Great Falls	102	D	D	D	488	2 209 954	12.9	30.2	16.9	10.2	6.8	19.7	3.2
Helena	70	427	32.7	9.4	301	1 298 064	13.5	27.1	14.7	7.9	4.9	23.7	0.0
Missoula	161	955	71.4	21.2	447	1 919 831	13.5	30.6	24.9	10.1	1.2	12.0	0.0
NEBRASKA	3 226	17 286	1 299.7	406.5	X	X	X	X	X	X	X	X	X
Bellevue	60	403	31.3	10.5	265	938 368	6.4	36.6	4.0	16.6	2.5	17.7	7.0
Fremont	49	D	D	D	278	1 259 723	10.6	16.8	8.8	6.2	0.0	47.0	2.3
Grand Island	115	567	45.6	11.3	596	2 645 689	9.6	16.2	16.0	8.3	0.3	43.9	3.6
Kearney	59	281	20.2	5.6	270	1 071 385	12.0	30.1	5.2	9.0	0.0	29.1	4.9
Lincoln	425	2 627	154.9	57.2	2 609	13 359 820	7.8	16.2	13.7	9.9	9.9	36.2	2.7
Omaha	782	6 236	425.1	161.9	2 835	15 258 712	6.3	39.2	26.1	8.5	2.6	11.0	3.8
NEVADA	2 989	22 756	1 750.6	564.6	X	X	X	X	X	X	X	X	X
Carson City	117	820	57.8	20.1	599	3 175 867	20.0	28.1	15.2	8.9	6.6	14.1	2.2
Henderson	271	1 908	155.8	49.7	2 239	13 759 509	18.4	29.3	14.7	1.2	2.0	25.6	0.0
Las Vegas	665	4 876	370.4	119.6	2 582	17 371 881	20.0	12.6	31.6	6.1	2.8	17.6	0.0
North Las Vegas	131	2 797	198.0	70.6	1 363	9 456 660	14.1	46.1	18.2	3.1	4.2	11.5	1.3
Reno	365	2 887	183.0	67.5	1 190	7 727 021	13.9	33.3	27.4	3.9	0.0	11.5	0.0
Sparks	178	1 227	126.6	36.1	500	2 883 097	19.7	31.5	22.6	3.6	0.0	21.4	0.0
NEW HAMPSHIRE	2 281	12 269	1 117.9	346.5	X	X	X	X	X	X	X	X	X
Concord	105	549	48.0	16.0	511	2 745 870	14.5	22.9	23.9	13.9	5.1	10.5	4.7
Dover	50	300	22.4	6.9	877	3 404 621	4.9	9.4	7.4	1.9	0.4	5.5	67.4
Manchester	227	1 570	130.1	43.3	3 353	14 363 066	3.8	12.5	9.5	7.7	2.7	7.3	55.0
Nashua	151	1 172	109.7	36.7	2 841	11 458 659	3.6	11.3	8.2	3.9	1.1	3.4	67.9
Rochester	51	327	26.2	8.3	998	3 938 623	4.0	9.1	4.3	1.9	0.5	3.1	75.7
NEW JERSEY	16 350	85 202	7 212.2	2 257.6	X	X	X	X	X	X	X	X	X
Atlantic City	55	665	45.1	14.8	1 521	8 728 573	8.1	41.3	24.3	1.3	7.3	9.0	1.9
Bayonne	110	410	30.8	8.3	2 167	12 420 526	2.7	16.8	11.4	3.3	4.4	2.0	58.3
Bergenfield	62	178	15.9	3.9	255	1 134 735	8.1	48.9	3.6	7.5	2.5	16.0	6.5
Bridgeton	26	117	9.6	2.5	17	61 842	0.0	0.0	0.0	0.0	100.0	0.0	0.0
Camden	56	323	28.2	8.4	98	380 956	0.0	0.0	0.0	0.0	100.0	0.0	0.0
Clifton	184	747	64.8	20.7	557	3 601 939	8.2	40.5	27.4	6.6	4.9	6.5	4.0
East Orange	49	D	D	D	2 832	17 819 602	3.5	12.8	6.9	1.2	5.1	2.4	67.4
Elizabeth	191	917	90.6	23.5	1 367	7 810 360	7.8	38.8	26.4	7.8	8.7	0.5	1.8
Englewood	85	381	31.1	9.7	885	5 644 368	2.5	19.1	9.9	1.8	4.0	3.8	56.7
Fair Lawn	76	342	32.6	10.3	256	1 498 256	15.9	40.2	1.4	5.4	2.1	22.3	7.1
Fort Lee	103	381	33.3	10.2	326	1 959 502	8.0	51.4	17.5	5.4	6.0	4.7	4.2

1. Establishments subject to federal tax.

City	City government finances, 2007									
	General revenue							General expenditure		
		Intergovernmental		Taxes					Per capita[1] (dollars)	
					Per capita[1] (dollars)					
	Total (mil dol)	Total (mil dol)	Percent from state government	Total (mil dol)	Total	Property	Sales and gross receipts	Total (mil dol)	Total	Capital outlays
	117	118	119	120	121	122	123	124	125	126
MISSOURI	X	X	X	X	X	X	X	X	X	X
Ballwin	18.7	9.4	1.9	5.3	173	15	159	18.7	613	106
Blue Springs	53.1	13.3	54.5	24.5	462	193	260	57.4	1 082	459
Cape Girardeau	57.8	5.4	100.0	35.6	921	61	860	52.2	1 349	435
Chesterfield	34.7	22.0	9.0	9.6	202	20	182	34.5	723	209
Columbia	138.4	19.3	25.9	63.8	563	95	468	212.6	1 877	640
Florissant	33.1	18.3	15.6	8.4	161	11	147	32.8	626	96
Gladstone	29.7	4.2	55.7	15.5	597	132	465	27.7	1 069	194
Hazelwood	38.3	16.6	5.6	17.5	683	419	264	41.8	1 627	196
Independence	188.3	31.9	65.8	87.8	748	125	624	191.9	1 636	278
Jefferson City	59.3	4.3	100.0	36.2	838	120	718	57.9	1 340	163
Joplin	79.1	7.5	60.0	45.9	914	50	864	75.9	1 511	421
Kansas City	1 256.7	117.6	15.8	742.9	1 599	266	877	1 156.0	2 489	448
Kirkwood	31.5	7.3	39.6	15.7	568	296	272	30.7	1 115	279
Lee's Summit	126.6	6.4	34.2	72.9	788	290	499	116.7	1 263	277
Liberty	33.0	1.0	69.8	19.8	663	218	445	32.0	1 073	157
Maryland Heights	47.8	14.1	52.2	24.5	891	113	778	36.8	1 340	394
O'Fallon	65.0	5.7	97.0	39.2	478	97	381	58.2	710	117
Raytown	24.5	1.7	100.0	13.8	468	60	405	23.7	802	108
St. Charles	85.0	6.1	40.0	58.8	884	225	659	87.4	1 314	334
St. Joseph	112.7	24.2	75.0	53.0	685	173	513	85.5	1 107	153
St. Louis	986.4	175.2	99.4	544.6	1 706	233	878	1 082.7	3 391	490
St. Peters	69.7	8.7	23.6	38.5	712	244	469	72.3	1 337	393
Springfield	302.8	56.5	34.5	151.6	934	123	811	276.2	1 702	333
University City	39.5	14.2	32.7	14.1	401	174	227	40.5	1 149	172
Wentzville	32.7	2.6	11.6	20.8	663	174	488	39.1	1 245	374
Wildwood	13.3	6.4	6.0	5.9	164	64	100	11.4	318	100
MONTANA	X	X	X	X	X	X	X	X	X	X
Billings	139.3	26.8	53.7	38.1	356	286	52	121.4	1 134	258
Bozeman	47.2	7.7	100.0	17.3	446	415	31	47.1	1 218	295
Butte-Silver Bow	75.8	25.6	85.0	27.7	820	793	27	64.6	1 913	455
Great Falls	59.8	11.2	86.2	17.7	300	264	36	59.2	1 004	125
Helena	39.8	8.5	54.5	9.3	320	301	19	38.1	1 306	175
Missoula	74.2	24.8	96.6	28.9	422	381	42	74.8	1 093	151
NEBRASKA	X	X	X	X	X	X	X	X	X	X
Bellevue	47.3	5.6	93.3	31.0	589	275	302	46.0	874	117
Fremont	32.4	11.1	42.3	11.6	439	202	237	26.6	1 007	230
Grand Island	57.1	7.8	100.0	23.4	468	139	329	52.8	1 053	87
Kearney	41.2	6.7	95.0	15.3	478	83	395	40.5	1 270	296
Lincoln	295.4	84.6	29.9	137.0	516	178	338	277.5	1 045	307
Omaha	610.0	80.9	60.1	392.9	903	317	586	580.3	1 333	325
NEVADA	X	X	X	X	X	X	X	X	X	X
Carson City	111.3	36.0	61.3	38.3	701	418	283	103.8	1 902	301
Henderson	402.5	181.2	47.5	129.1	487	256	231	422.6	1 594	454
Las Vegas	801.6	407.6	63.4	200.6	336	186	150	876.8	1 470	462
North Las Vegas	281.9	110.2	80.4	84.1	377	246	131	281.1	1 260	340
Reno	315.2	72.0	57.4	121.3	526	255	271	287.2	1 245	153
Sparks	93.5	28.6	69.1	34.8	378	260	118	85.8	933	92
NEW HAMPSHIRE	X	X	X	X	X	X	X	X	X	X
Concord	62.7	3.7	75.0	39.6	931	895	36	59.6	1 402	31
Dover	105.4	21.2	95.8	64.9	2 139	2 120	18	90.6	2 982	200
Manchester	391.9	151.9	74.0	152.0	1 379	1 330	50	436.7	3 964	479
Nashua	282.0	81.9	99.2	176.1	2 033	2 010	23	264.6	3 055	177
Rochester	102.0	39.7	96.1	54.8	1 835	1 692	143	100.7	3 371	643
NEW JERSEY	X	X	X	X	X	X	X	X	X	X
Atlantic City	265.6	40.5	25.2	107.6	4 993	4 875	117	225.7	5 703	269
Bayonne	247.8	88.4	85.4	137.0	2 113	2 095	18	277.8	4 287	148
Bergenfield	32.3	2.9	94.6	28.1	1 033	1 005	28	28.7	1 057	46
Bridgeton	34.1	9.2	55.7	12.4	491	454	37	34.9	1 382	155
Camden	232.9	174.8	71.9	30.2	391	338	53	160.2	2 073	195
Clifton	115.4	15.5	73.5	84.3	990	936	54	103.5	1 216	37
East Orange	399.7	273.1	95.8	111.4	1 730	1 712	17	362.6	5 630	108
Elizabeth	263.2	59.9	65.7	151.2	1 191	1 058	134	254.8	2 007	251
Englewood	130.4	25.5	71.3	98.9	3 607	3 555	52	132.8	4 840	411
Fair Lawn	44.1	4.4	97.6	38.3	1 166	1 116	50	39.3	1 195	65
Fort Lee	75.6	8.8	24.0	61.9	1 726	1 666	61	78.8	2 198	328

1. Based on population estimated as of July 1 of the year shown.

City	City government finances, 2012 (cont.)									
	General expenditure (cont.)									
	Percent of total for:									
	Public welfare	Highways	Parking facilities	Education	Health and hospitals	Police protection	Sewerage and sanitation	Parks and recreation	Housing and community development	Interest on debt
	127	128	129	130	131	132	133	134	135	136
MISSOURI	X	X	X	X	X	X	X	X	X	X
Ballwin	0.0	26.8	0.0	0.0	0.0	25.3	1.6	20.8	0.0	6.3
Blue Springs	0.0	4.3	0.0	0.0	0.0	16.3	33.2	7.3	0.0	6.1
Cape Girardeau	0.0	23.1	0.0	0.0	0.6	13.1	19.5	15.6	0.7	2.2
Chesterfield	0.0	20.9	0.0	0.0	0.0	22.6	0.8	28.1	0.0	8.7
Columbia	0.3	9.2	2.5	0.0	2.7	7.7	25.4	7.7	0.9	2.5
Florissant	0.0	13.2	0.0	0.0	1.9	30.6	0.5	18.0	2.8	1.4
Gladstone	0.0	11.8	0.0	0.0	0.8	18.2	17.1	13.9	1.8	5.2
Hazelwood	0.0	0.9	0.0	0.0	0.0	19.1	0.3	8.1	0.0	2.2
Independence	1.9	13.2	0.0	0.0	1.6	15.3	15.0	3.9	0.4	8.1
Jefferson City	0.0	20.0	1.2	0.0	1.0	18.7	8.8	13.4	0.7	3.2
Joplin	0.3	11.6	0.1	0.0	3.2	12.8	22.9	7.3	2.2	0.8
Kansas City	0.5	13.1	0.4	0.0	4.6	17.1	7.8	4.6	3.5	8.1
Kirkwood	0.0	5.0	0.0	0.0	0.0	21.3	10.0	12.4	0.0	1.8
Lee's Summit	0.0	15.2	0.0	0.0	0.0	15.6	11.5	6.5	1.2	3.3
Liberty	0.0	13.8	0.0	0.0	0.0	14.6	20.9	11.7	4.7	6.1
Maryland Heights	0.9	36.0	0.0	0.0	0.0	26.9	8.2	10.0	3.4	3.1
O'Fallon	0.0	16.9	0.0	0.0	0.0	20.3	13.7	13.5	0.3	7.4
Raytown	0.0	5.9	0.0	0.0	0.0	28.8	18.1	6.2	2.8	11.3
St. Charles	0.0	22.9	0.1	0.0	0.0	21.1	5.4	10.0	0.6	8.9
St. Joseph	2.1	11.2	0.4	0.0	5.5	11.2	14.3	7.0	1.5	5.9
St. Louis	0.0	2.3	0.9	0.0	3.6	23.2	1.7	2.2	2.7	8.4
St. Peters	0.0	24.8	0.0	0.0	0.7	19.4	20.1	17.9	0.2	4.6
Springfield	0.4	10.7	0.1	0.0	2.9	23.9	12.1	10.6	0.9	5.3
University City	0.0	18.3	0.5	0.0	0.0	18.1	6.7	8.2	3.5	2.0
Wentzville	0.0	14.6	0.0	0.0	0.0	18.0	37.0	7.4	0.0	5.5
Wildwood	0.0	34.1	0.0	0.0	0.0	26.6	0.1	4.4	0.0	1.4
MONTANA	X	X	X	X	X	X	X	X	X	X
Billings	0.0	16.9	1.9	0.0	0.6	16.1	21.3	3.4	2.8	1.8
Bozeman	11.0	10.4	0.8	0.0	0.0	20.0	29.4	0.9	0.2	3.2
Butte-Silver Bow	0.2	7.2	0.2	0.0	7.7	10.3	23.9	4.7	0.4	2.6
Great Falls	0.0	12.3	1.1	0.0	0.0	20.7	22.3	10.6	4.0	2.1
Helena	0.0	10.7	5.1	0.0	0.4	18.4	19.1	15.1	0.1	3.1
Missoula	0.2	13.6	1.8	0.0	1.9	17.8	14.7	6.3	1.4	3.5
NEBRASKA	X	X	X	X	X	X	X	X	X	X
Bellevue	0.0	10.3	0.0	0.0	0.0	34.9	13.4	5.1	0.4	3.6
Fremont	0.0	16.1	0.0	0.0	0.0	16.9	17.3	8.7	9.2	1.3
Grand Island	0.0	12.5	0.1	0.0	0.0	16.4	18.8	8.4	1.9	2.1
Kearney	0.0	21.9	0.1	0.0	0.0	16.5	18.4	15.8	3.0	0.7
Lincoln	2.3	19.2	1.4	0.0	4.4	12.9	12.2	4.2	3.8	1.5
Omaha	0.3	10.5	0.8	0.0	0.0	16.3	19.0	13.1	0.3	7.2
NEVADA	X	X	X	X	X	X	X	X	X	X
Carson City	2.3	10.5	0.0	0.0	4.2	15.9	10.8	10.1	1.5	9.1
Henderson	0.0	1.7	0.0	0.0	0.0	17.2	10.2	28.6	2.7	2.3
Las Vegas	0.1	6.9	0.4	0.0	0.4	14.6	13.4	11.0	2.7	3.5
North Las Vegas	0.0	13.1	0.0	0.0	0.0	26.3	10.0	10.6	2.4	3.8
Reno	0.0	9.4	0.0	0.0	0.0	18.6	14.1	3.8	6.8	15.2
Sparks	0.0	7.6	0.0	0.0	0.0	23.2	17.6	6.4	0.6	13.5
NEW HAMPSHIRE	X	X	X	X	X	X	X	X	X	X
Concord	1.8	11.5	1.5	0.0	0.3	16.9	15.6	4.2	0.0	4.5
Dover	0.9	5.5	0.4	50.9	0.0	7.9	7.8	2.6	0.3	5.1
Manchester	0.3	5.2	0.6	39.2	1.3	7.0	4.3	1.3	0.9	5.3
Nashua	0.3	2.6	0.0	55.6	0.3	6.6	7.7	1.0	0.5	4.0
Rochester	0.6	7.4	0.0	57.0	0.0	6.1	4.6	0.7	0.3	2.9
NEW JERSEY	X	X	X	X	X	X	X	X	X	X
Atlantic City	0.6	1.1	0.0	0.0	1.7	16.6	1.7	3.0	11.8	1.9
Bayonne	0.0	0.6	0.5	41.0	0.5	9.0	4.6	1.2	21.6	4.2
Bergenfield	0.0	7.1	0.0	0.0	1.5	23.3	16.4	2.7	0.0	1.9
Bridgeton	0.0	3.9	0.0	0.0	0.4	15.8	23.3	1.5	13.4	0.5
Camden	0.0	2.8	0.0	0.0	1.1	17.8	5.7	1.0	24.6	2.6
Clifton	0.1	2.8	0.0	0.0	1.0	20.0	12.8	1.5	3.1	2.4
East Orange	0.0	0.5	0.1	63.0	1.4	7.5	2.7	0.7	4.4	0.7
Elizabeth	0.0	2.3	0.8	0.0	2.2	17.0	12.9	4.9	15.8	1.7
Englewood	0.0	2.1	0.0	52.5	0.6	9.2	4.3	0.7	5.2	1.0
Fair Lawn	0.2	2.9	0.0	0.0	1.8	20.0	13.4	4.5	0.0	3.4
Fort Lee	0.3	3.2	1.7	0.0	1.8	18.2	8.2	2.4	8.3	3.6

Table D. Cities — City Government Finances, City Government Employment, and Climate

City	City government finances, 2012 (cont.): Debt outstanding: Total (mil dol)	City government finances, 2012 (cont.): Debt outstanding: Per capita[1] (dollars)	City government finances, 2012 (cont.): Debt issued during year	Climate[2]: Average daily temperature (degrees Fahrenheit): Mean: January	Climate[2]: Average daily temperature (degrees Fahrenheit): Mean: July	Climate[2]: Average daily temperature (degrees Fahrenheit): Limits: January[3]	Climate[2]: Average daily temperature (degrees Fahrenheit): Limits: July[4]	Climate[2]: Annual precipitation (inches)	Climate[2]: Heating degree days	Climate[2]: Cooling degree days
	137	138	139	140	141	142	143	144	145	146
MISSOURI	X	X	X	X	X	X	X	X	X	X
Ballwin	17.1	563	0.0	27.5	78.1	17.3	89.2	38.00	5 199	1 293
Blue Springs	129.0	2 432	12.5	24.6	76.6	14.9	87.2	41.18	5 623	1 137
Cape Girardeau	56.2	1 453	14.5	32.4	79.5	24.0	90.1	46.54	4 344	1 515
Chesterfield	69.9	1 467	0.0	27.5	78.1	17.3	89.2	38.00	5 199	1 293
Columbia	354.5	3 130	121.7	27.8	77.4	18.2	88.6	40.28	5 177	1 246
Florissant	22.1	421	7.2	29.6	80.2	21.2	89.8	38.75	4 758	1 561
Gladstone	41.1	1 585	0.0	29.3	81.3	20.7	90.5	35.51	4 734	1 676
Hazelwood	43.7	1 703	7.9	29.6	80.2	21.2	89.8	38.75	4 758	1 561
Independence	427.5	3 645	74.2	26.6	77.1	17.1	87.5	43.14	5 373	1 176
Jefferson City	62.3	1 443	0.0	28.2	77.9	17.7	89.4	39.59	5 158	1 261
Joplin	15.0	299	1.4	33.1	79.9	23.7	90.4	46.07	4 253	1 555
Kansas City	2 948.0	6 347	651.3	29.3	81.3	20.7	90.5	35.51	4 734	1 676
Kirkwood	23.0	833	0.0	29.6	80.2	21.2	89.8	38.75	4 758	1 561
Lee's Summit	98.3	1 064	7.9	24.6	76.6	14.9	87.2	41.18	5 623	1 137
Liberty	47.2	1 585	5.9	26.6	77.1	17.1	87.5	43.14	5 373	1 176
Maryland Heights	17.8	647	0.0	29.5	80.7	21.2	90.5	38.84	4 650	1 633
O'Fallon	231.0	2 818	8.6	28.3	79.0	19.0	90.2	38.28	5 020	1 399
Raytown	54.1	1 832	0.0	24.6	76.6	14.9	87.2	41.18	5 623	1 137
St. Charles	217.8	3 273	9.9	27.5	78.1	17.3	89.2	38.00	5 199	1 293
St. Joseph	532.1	6 888	30.2	26.4	78.7	15.9	89.9	35.24	5 345	1 339
St. Louis	1 862.1	5 832	143.8	29.5	80.7	21.2	90.5	38.84	4 650	1 633
St. Peters	126.3	2 335	11.7	28.3	79.0	19.0	90.2	38.28	5 020	1 399
Springfield	1 021.0	6 292	42.8	31.7	78.5	21.8	89.9	44.97	4 602	1 366
University City	13.5	382	6.6	29.5	80.7	21.2	90.5	38.84	4 650	1 633
Wentzville	64.6	2 058	31.8	NA	NA	NA	NA	NA	NA	NA
Wildwood	5.1	142	0.0	27.5	78.1	17.3	89.2	38.00	5 199	1 293
MONTANA	X	X	X	X	X	X	X	X	X	X
Billings	108.2	1 011	7.4	24.0	72.0	15.1	85.8	14.77	7 006	583
Bozeman	35.1	906	4.1	22.6	65.3	12.0	81.8	16.45	7 984	216
Butte-Silver Bow	42.1	1 246	15.8	17.6	62.7	5.4	79.8	12.78	9 399	127
Great Falls	39.4	668	0.9	21.7	66.2	11.3	82.0	14.89	7 828	288
Helena	45.1	1 546	0.5	20.2	67.8	9.9	83.4	11.32	7 975	277
Missoula	84.9	1 240	6.4	23.5	66.9	16.2	83.6	13.82	7 622	256
NEBRASKA	X	X	X	X	X	X	X	X	X	X
Bellevue	65.0	1 234	8.2	21.7	76.7	11.6	87.4	30.22	6 311	1 095
Fremont	38.9	1 473	4.0	21.1	76.2	10.4	87.7	29.80	6 444	1 004
Grand Island	50.6	1 010	9.3	22.4	75.8	12.2	87.1	25.89	6 385	1 027
Kearney	40.8	1 277	10.8	22.4	74.7	11.0	85.7	25.20	6 652	852
Lincoln	1 294.9	4 876	354.0	22.4	77.8	11.5	89.6	28.37	6 242	1 154
Omaha	1 049.9	2 411	111.5	21.7	76.7	11.6	87.4	30.22	6 311	1 095
NEVADA	X	X	X	X	X	X	X	X	X	X
Carson City	282.0	5 168	35.1	33.7	70.0	21.7	89.2	10.36	5 661	419
Henderson	308.8	1 165	35.1	47.0	91.2	36.8	104.1	4.49	2 239	3 214
Las Vegas	637.5	1 069	51.5	47.0	91.2	36.8	104.1	4.49	2 239	3 214
North Las Vegas	473.2	2 122	27.1	47.0	91.2	36.8	104.1	4.49	2 239	3 214
Reno	1 243.0	5 389	55.4	33.6	71.3	21.8	91.2	7.48	5 600	493
Sparks	243.8	2 649	0.0	33.6	71.3	21.8	91.2	7.48	5 600	493
NEW HAMPSHIRE	X	X	X	X	X	X	X	X	X	X
Concord	67.0	1 577	8.1	20.1	70.0	9.7	82.9	37.60	7 478	442
Dover	72.6	2 392	9.7	23.3	70.7	13.1	83.2	42.80	6 748	427
Manchester	566.8	5 145	160.3	18.8	68.4	5.2	82.1	39.82	7 742	263
Nashua	156.2	1 803	14.8	22.8	70.8	12.1	82.5	45.43	6 834	445
Rochester	80.7	2 701	11.6	23.3	70.7	13.1	83.2	42.80	6 748	427
NEW JERSEY	X	X	X	X	X	X	X	X	X	X
Atlantic City	164.0	4 143	51.6	35.2	75.2	29.0	80.6	38.37	4 480	951
Bayonne	460.2	7 102	0.0	31.3	77.2	24.4	85.2	46.25	4 843	1 220
Bergenfield	14.8	544	0.0	28.6	75.0	19.5	85.5	51.50	5 522	824
Bridgeton	15.0	593	0.0	NA	NA	NA	NA	NA	NA	NA
Camden	77.8	1 007	0.0	32.3	76.3	23.2	87.8	48.25	4 801	1 054
Clifton	71.7	842	15.7	28.6	75.0	19.5	85.5	51.50	5 522	824
East Orange	100.2	1 556	0.0	31.3	77.2	24.4	85.2	46.25	4 843	1 220
Elizabeth	124.1	978	19.1	29.6	74.5	19.8	85.7	50.94	5 450	787
Englewood	44.8	1 633	0.0	29.6	75.3	22.7	82.5	46.33	5 367	882
Fair Lawn	38.7	1 176	0.0	28.6	75.0	19.5	85.5	51.50	5 522	824
Fort Lee	62.2	1 736	14.1	29.6	75.3	22.7	82.5	46.33	5 367	882

1. Based on the population estimated as of July 1 of the year shown. 2. Represents normal values based on the 30-year period, 1971–2000. 3. Average daily minimum. 4. Average daily maximum.

STATE Place code	City	Land area,[1] 2010 (sq km)	Population, 2014: Total persons	Population, 2014: Rank	Population, 2014: Per square kilometer	Race alone or in combination (percent), 2011-2013: White	Black	American Indian, Alaska Native	Asian	Hawaiian Pacific Islander	Percent Hispanic or Latino[2], 2011-2013	Percent foreign born 2011–2013
		1	2	3	4	5	6	7	8	9	10	11
	NEW JERSEY—Cont'd											
34 25770	Garfield	5.4	31 486	1 182	5 830.7	86.9	8.1	NA	1.4	NA	35.9	44.6
34 28680	Hackensack	10.8	44 519	831	4 122.1	41.8	24.3	0.8	11.9	NA	33.2	39.5
34 32250	Hoboken	3.3	53 312	695	16 155.2	86.8	4.8	0.3	8.9	NA	16.0	15.9
34 36000	Jersey City	38.3	262 146	74	6 844.5	37.3	26.5	1.0	26.2	0.1	27.3	39.9
34 36510	Kearny	22.7	41 837	881	1 843.0	62.2	3.9	0.6	5.6	NA	44.7	40.8
34 40350	Linden	27.7	41 651	886	1 503.6	60.1	30.5	0.9	3.0	NA	28.8	32.6
34 41310	Long Branch	13.7	30 522	1 209	2 227.9	73.7	17.1	2.4	3.0	NA	28.2	28.9
34 46680	Millville	108.8	28 497	1 290	261.9	74.1	21.4	1.7	0.8	NA	18.3	3.1
34 51000	Newark	62.6	280 579	69	4 482.1	27.5	53.7	0.8	1.8	0.2	34.7	28.5
34 51210	New Brunswick	13.5	57 080	641	4 228.1	69.1	15.6	0.5	8.5	NA	55.9	38.7
34 55950	Paramus	27.1	26 832	1 368	990.1	72.7	1.9	NA	24.7	NA	9.1	29.3
34 56550	Passaic	8.2	71 509	479	8 720.6	58.2	15.4	3.3	3.0	0.4	73.0	44.3
34 57000	Paterson	21.8	146 753	177	6 731.8	52.1	39.4	1.0	4.3	0.3	59.1	34.8
34 58200	Perth Amboy	12.2	52 328	711	4 289.2	81.8	8.3	0.3	2.2	NA	80.6	41.9
34 59190	Plainfield	15.6	50 955	735	3 266.3	13.7	45.4	0.3	2.5	0.4	37.8	39.5
34 61530	Rahway	10.1	28 528	1 287	2 824.6	51.5	32.2	NA	5.5	NA	25.9	23.0
34 65790	Sayreville	41.0	45 262	822	1 104.0	66.6	14.3	NA	18.3	NA	12.0	26.3
34 74000	Trenton	19.8	84 034	385	4 244.1	31.0	53.8	0.6	1.3	0.1	33.3	22.8
34 74630	Union City	3.3	68 668	500	20 808.5	66.8	5.9	NA	2.5	NA	87.0	57.8
34 76070	Vineland	177.2	61 171	584	345.2	65.1	17.5	1.3	2.3	NA	36.5	10.6
34 79040	Westfield	17.4	30 890	1 198	1 775.3	86.7	5.6	0.5	7.0	NA	6.2	11.1
34 79610	West New York	2.6	52 597	704	20 229.6	65.4	4.4	2.9	4.6	NA	80.4	58.6
35 00000	NEW MEXICO	314 160.8	2 085 572	X	6.6	75.6	2.8	10.4	2.0	0.2	47.0	9.8
35 01780	Alamogordo	55.5	31 060	1 191	559.6	80.3	8.4	2.5	3.4	NA	34.8	8.9
35 02000	Albuquerque	486.2	557 169	32	1 146.0	75.2	4.5	5.7	3.6	0.3	46.9	10.6
35 12150	Carlsbad	74.9	28 103	1 305	375.2	90.8	2.1	2.1	NA	NA	47.0	5.4
35 16420	Clovis	58.8	39 860	932	677.9	72.2	9.3	2.7	1.9	NA	42.1	8.4
35 25800	Farmington	81.6	44 445	832	544.7	68.4	2.7	24.1	1.2	0.3	24.3	4.9
35 32520	Hobbs	62.0	37 118	1 000	598.7	89.1	6.9	1.6	NA	NA	54.1	16.5
35 39380	Las Cruces	198.1	101 408	294	511.9	90.1	2.4	2.6	2.5	0.2	57.7	10.2
35 63460	Rio Rancho	267.7	93 820	324	350.5	86.7	5.3	3.7	2.9	0.2	40.2	5.3
35 64930	Roswell	77.3	48 608	776	628.8	78.6	3.0	2.6	1.7	NA	55.8	12.1
35 70500	Santa Fe	119.1	70 297	489	590.2	87.1	1.7	2.8	2.3	0.2	48.0	13.6
36 00000	NEW YORK	122 056.8	19 746 227	X	161.8	67.2	16.9	0.9	8.5	0.1	18.1	22.4
36 01000	Albany	55.4	98 566	305	1 779.2	60.6	33.9	1.0	6.9	NA	8.4	11.1
36 03078	Auburn	21.6	27 019	1 358	1 250.9	89.0	12.3	0.9	1.2	NA	3.9	3.2
36 06607	Binghamton	27.2	46 299	810	1 702.2	79.5	15.3	1.3	6.0	0.2	6.9	9.4
36 11000	Buffalo	104.6	258 703	76	2 473.3	52.2	39.6	1.5	4.6	0.1	10.7	8.5
36 24229	Elmira	18.8	28 647	1 281	1 523.8	84.0	19.2	0.5	0.5	NA	4.3	2.2
36 27485	Freeport	12.0	43 304	854	3 608.7	47.0	37.1	5.8	2.2	NA	42.2	32.9
36 29113	Glen Cove	17.2	27 314	1 347	1 588.0	66.3	7.6	NA	4.4	NA	29.8	33.2
36 32402	Harrison	43.4	28 151	1 301	648.6	82.9	4.1	0.8	8.2	NA	16.3	23.7
36 33139	Hempstead	9.5	55 527	663	5 844.9	21.9	49.4	1.0	1.8	NA	41.7	38.3
36 38077	Ithaca	14.0	30 720	1 205	2 194.3	74.0	9.0	0.4	19.4	NA	8.0	16.9
36 38264	Jamestown	23.1	30 429	1 215	1 317.3	90.5	6.1	1.3	0.8	NA	9.9	1.5
36 42554	Lindenhurst	9.7	27 321	1 346	2 816.6	95.1	1.8	0.8	1.5	NA	13.4	13.9
36 43335	Long Beach	5.7	33 664	1 103	5 906.0	85.9	5.8	1.1	3.2	NA	14.4	16.5
36 47042	Middletown	13.2	27 728	1 319	2 100.6	48.9	26.4	1.9	4.4	NA	37.3	21.0
36 49121	Mount Vernon	11.4	68 458	503	6 005.1	26.0	65.9	1.1	2.9	NA	14.6	33.4
36 50034	Newburgh	9.9	28 358	1 292	2 864.4	39.8	33.1	2.3	1.0	NA	52.5	25.0
36 50617	New Rochelle	26.8	79 637	413	2 971.5	70.2	19.9	0.5	4.4	NA	28.7	27.8
36 51000	New York	783.8	8 491 079	1	10 833.2	45.8	26.2	0.9	14.2	0.2	28.8	37.3
36 51055	Niagara Falls	36.5	49 219	761	1 348.5	73.4	25.2	2.1	1.5	0.4	2.3	5.7
36 53682	North Tonawanda	26.2	30 929	1 197	1 180.5	97.3	1.4	NA	0.9	NA	1.3	3.1
36 55530	Ossining	8.2	25 359	1 413	3 092.6	50.7	14.3	NA	5.0	NA	48.8	37.6
36 59223	Port Chester	6.0	29 522	1 247	4 920.3	41.8	8.3	NA	1.6	NA	60.6	45.6
36 59641	Poughkeepsie	13.3	30 513	1 210	2 294.2	50.6	39.0	1.5	3.0	0.2	22.7	19.1
36 63000	Rochester	92.7	209 983	103	2 265.2	48.1	44.0	1.4	3.7	0.3	17.5	8.8
36 63418	Rome	193.7	32 645	1 135	168.5	91.2	6.2	1.2	1.7	NA	5.9	3.5
36 65255	Saratoga Springs	72.7	27 436	1 340	377.4	94.7	3.6	1.1	2.7	NA	4.1	6.8
36 65508	Schenectady	27.9	65 936	533	2 363.3	66.0	24.4	1.4	6.7	NA	10.9	12.5
36 70420	Spring Valley	5.2	32 510	1 142	6 251.9	29.5	39.7	NA	3.2	NA	31.8	44.4
36 73000	Syracuse	64.9	144 263	182	2 222.9	59.7	32.9	2.8	7.1	0.1	7.9	11.4
36 75484	Troy	26.8	49 910	747	1 862.3	79.7	20.9	1.3	4.5	0.3	8.7	7.8
36 76540	Utica	43.4	61 332	582	1 413.2	70.9	20.6	1.2	9.2	NA	11.3	19.3
36 76705	Valley Stream	9.0	37 832	980	4 203.6	50.7	19.4	0.5	14.7	NA	30.6	35.5
36 78608	Watertown	23.4	27 590	1 330	1 179.1	87.7	9.8	1.9	2.9	NA	7.8	4.4
36 81677	White Plains	25.3	58 035	632	2 293.9	66.9	17.0	1.2	7.3	NA	33.1	32.5

1. Dry land or land partially or temporarily covered by water. 2. May be of any race.

City	Age of population (percent), 2011-2013: Under 5 years	5 to 17 years	18 to 24 years	25 to 34 years	35 to 44 years	45 to 54 years	55 to 64 years	65 to 74 years	75 years and over	Median age 2011-2013	Percent female 2011-2013	Population: Census counts: 2000	2010	Percent change: 2000–2010	2010–2014
	12	13	14	15	16	17	18	19	20	21	22	23	24	25	26
NEW JERSEY—Cont'd															
Garfield	8.1	14.7	10.2	16.2	13.4	15.9	9.7	5.7	6.0	35.4	51.3	29 786	30 487	2.4	3.3
Hackensack	6.8	11.0	9.8	16.0	16.3	14.4	12.3	7.5	5.9	38.6	48.6	42 677	43 010	0.8	3.5
Hoboken	6.6	6.7	11.1	37.8	17.2	8.8	5.2	3.1	3.4	31.1	50.2	38 577	50 005	29.6	6.6
Jersey City	7.0	13.5	9.3	22.8	15.0	12.6	10.0	5.8	4.0	33.6	50.7	240 055	247 597	3.1	5.9
Kearny	6.9	17.3	8.9	13.9	15.8	14.8	11.8	6.2	4.4	37.0	48.5	40 513	40 684	0.4	2.8
Linden	5.1	14.6	9.7	15.6	13.3	15.7	13.2	6.8	6.0	38.8	51.8	39 394	40 499	2.8	2.8
Long Branch	7.8	17.0	8.9	15.9	13.3	13.5	11.1	7.2	5.2	35.3	51.8	31 340	30 719	-2.0	-0.6
Millville	8.0	16.7	10.2	13.5	11.6	11.9	14.5	7.6	6.1	36.4	53.2	26 847	28 400	5.8	0.3
Newark	7.7	17.9	11.6	16.8	14.4	13.9	9.2	5.0	3.5	32.4	49.9	273 546	277 140	1.3	1.2
New Brunswick	8.3	14.7	30.8	17.4	12.0	6.6	5.5	2.5	2.1	23.2	50.0	48 573	55 181	13.6	4.6
Paramus	4.7	14.7	6.8	8.3	12.4	15.3	15.9	9.1	12.8	47.4	52.1	25 737	26 342	2.4	1.9
Passaic	9.8	23.3	10.4	16.0	13.8	11.1	8.2	3.9	3.7	29.7	49.9	67 861	69 781	2.8	2.5
Paterson	8.1	18.8	12.2	14.3	13.2	14.0	9.6	6.1	3.6	32.5	52.6	149 222	146 199	-2.0	0.4
Perth Amboy	8.0	18.1	10.9	15.4	13.5	13.9	9.9	5.5	4.8	33.4	50.8	47 303	50 814	7.4	3.0
Plainfield	6.9	16.5	12.2	17.0	14.4	13.4	10.2	4.9	4.5	33.4	48.8	47 829	49 808	4.1	2.3
Rahway	6.2	16.7	8.1	14.7	14.1	16.0	10.8	6.3	7.0	38.3	49.8	26 500	27 346	3.2	4.3
Sayreville	5.8	15.7	8.3	13.7	13.9	16.3	12.9	7.7	5.6	39.6	49.9	40 377	42 704	5.8	6.0
Trenton	7.6	17.7	11.0	16.8	15.0	13.9	9.9	4.7	3.5	33.6	49.2	85 403	84 913	-0.6	-1.0
Union City	6.6	16.2	10.8	17.3	14.4	14.6	10.1	6.1	3.9	34.4	48.4	67 088	66 455	-0.9	3.4
Vineland	6.5	19.1	8.7	12.6	12.4	14.1	12.1	7.8	6.6	37.7	53.1	56 271	60 724	7.9	0.7
Westfield	6.0	22.4	5.2	8.1	15.9	16.4	14.1	5.0	6.9	41.1	51.1	29 644	30 316	2.3	1.9
West New York	7.9	13.0	9.2	20.8	17.7	12.0	8.4	5.1	5.8	34.5	50.2	45 768	49 708	8.6	5.8
NEW MEXICO	6.7	17.8	10.2	13.1	11.9	13.3	12.8	8.2	6.0	36.8	50.4	1 819 046	2 059 179	13.2	1.3
Alamogordo	7.4	16.7	8.8	15.6	10.5	12.8	11.8	9.4	7.0	35.9	51.0	35 582	30 403	-14.6	2.1
Albuquerque	6.7	16.8	10.1	15.6	12.7	13.3	12.0	7.1	5.8	35.6	51.4	448 607	545 852	21.7	2.0
Carlsbad	6.1	19.8	8.2	11.7	13.4	13.1	12.6	7.7	7.3	37.6	49.6	25 625	26 138	2.0	7.3
Clovis	8.9	18.3	12.0	15.7	11.8	11.3	10.7	6.2	5.1	30.8	49.3	32 667	37 775	15.6	5.5
Farmington	7.3	19.7	9.2	15.5	11.7	12.8	11.8	6.7	5.3	33.6	50.4	37 844	45 877	21.2	-3.1
Hobbs	9.6	20.1	10.3	15.4	12.9	11.7	10.0	5.3	4.6	31.3	48.2	28 657	34 122	19.1	8.7
Las Cruces	8.0	17.3	15.4	14.8	10.8	11.2	9.5	7.0	6.1	31.1	50.5	74 267	97 618	31.4	3.9
Rio Rancho	6.7	20.8	8.2	12.8	13.5	14.4	11.5	7.2	4.9	36.4	51.1	51 765	87 521	69.1	7.4
Roswell	8.3	19.8	10.8	13.4	10.8	11.0	11.4	7.7	6.9	33.1	51.4	45 293	48 366	6.8	0.4
Santa Fe	5.1	14.0	7.3	12.3	12.1	13.5	16.3	11.4	8.1	44.5	53.5	62 203	67 947	9.2	3.4
NEW YORK	6.0	15.8	10.2	14.1	13.0	14.5	12.4	7.5	6.5	38.1	51.5	18 976 457	19 378 102	2.1	1.9
Albany	5.6	12.0	21.1	16.2	10.4	11.1	11.2	6.3	6.1	31.4	52.4	95 658	97 856	2.3	0.7
Auburn	5.8	13.4	11.3	13.7	12.9	14.6	11.7	7.1	9.5	40.5	49.4	28 574	27 687	-3.1	-2.4
Binghamton	5.2	12.6	17.2	13.7	10.2	12.9	11.5	7.7	9.1	36.6	50.7	47 380	47 376	0.0	-2.3
Buffalo	6.5	16.3	13.7	15.8	11.5	12.8	12.0	5.7	5.7	33.3	52.0	292 648	261 310	-10.7	-1.0
Elmira	7.3	16.6	14.0	14.6	13.1	13.3	10.8	5.6	4.9	33.8	48.3	30 940	29 200	-5.6	-1.9
Freeport	7.7	16.2	8.8	13.7	14.8	14.7	11.3	7.2	5.5	37.5	51.2	43 783	42 860	-2.1	1.0
Glen Cove	5.5	14.3	9.0	16.1	12.9	12.3	12.0	8.6	9.3	39.0	50.0	26 622	26 964	1.3	1.3
Harrison	2.8	18.0	19.6	8.6	11.3	15.8	10.5	6.9	6.4	36.0	51.0	24 154	27 472	13.7	2.5
Hempstead	8.2	16.3	10.6	16.5	14.9	13.4	10.0	5.3	4.7	33.8	49.7	56 554	53 891	-4.7	3.0
Ithaca	3.4	6.3	54.5	14.0	6.3	4.5	5.7	1.7	3.5	21.9	49.2	29 287	30 014	2.5	2.3
Jamestown	6.7	18.8	8.5	13.4	12.1	14.1	12.1	6.4	7.9	36.9	51.1	31 730	31 146	-1.8	-2.3
Lindenhurst	4.0	15.9	10.1	13.4	12.2	17.7	14.0	6.8	5.9	40.7	51.9	27 819	27 253	-2.0	0.2
Long Beach	3.6	11.8	6.9	16.8	13.6	18.6	12.2	9.2	7.4	43.7	54.8	35 462	33 275	-6.2	1.2
Middletown	7.0	18.2	12.6	16.6	13.2	12.7	10.0	4.6	5.1	31.8	50.1	25 388	28 086	10.6	-1.3
Mount Vernon	7.7	15.5	9.3	13.9	14.0	14.2	11.7	7.4	6.2	37.9	54.6	68 381	67 292	-1.6	1.7
Newburgh	9.6	22.8	14.9	14.5	11.4	10.5	8.9	4.1	3.4	27.8	51.2	28 259	28 866	2.1	-1.8
New Rochelle	5.8	16.1	10.2	12.5	11.8	14.8	13.8	7.1	7.9	39.4	50.6	72 182	77 062	6.8	3.3
New York	6.6	14.8	10.1	17.4	14.0	13.3	11.2	6.8	5.7	35.7	52.3	8 008 278	8 175 133	2.1	3.9
Niagara Falls	5.7	15.7	9.9	13.1	11.2	15.3	13.6	7.6	7.9	40.1	51.7	55 593	50 193	-9.7	-1.9
North Tonawanda	5.6	13.9	9.5	13.4	10.8	16.0	15.2	6.9	8.6	41.6	52.3	33 262	31 568	-5.1	-2.0
Ossining	6.0	16.8	7.1	16.8	16.5	15.9	11.8	4.0	5.1	37.2	46.3	24 010	25 060	4.4	1.1
Port Chester	6.1	15.7	8.9	18.7	16.1	13.8	10.6	4.8	5.4	35.4	47.8	27 867	28 967	3.9	1.9
Poughkeepsie	5.9	16.3	11.2	15.0	12.2	12.3	12.5	7.9	6.7	36.8	51.2	29 871	32 736	9.6	-1.3
Rochester	7.0	17.2	13.2	18.0	11.7	12.6	10.4	5.6	4.2	31.0	51.4	219 773	210 565	-4.2	-0.3
Rome	6.1	14.4	7.6	14.1	12.7	13.7	14.4	8.6	8.4	40.8	48.3	34 950	33 725	-3.5	-0.2
Saratoga Springs	4.5	12.9	15.5	14.1	11.2	12.3	12.3	8.8	8.4	37.8	50.0	26 186	26 586	1.5	3.3
Schenectady	6.6	16.0	13.5	14.9	12.4	13.3	11.2	6.5	5.6	34.2	51.2	61 821	66 135	7.0	-0.3
Spring Valley	11.2	22.2	11.3	18.0	12.0	10.0	8.5	4.5	2.4	27.7	49.4	25 464	31 347	23.1	3.9
Syracuse	7.1	15.7	18.9	15.4	9.9	11.6	10.3	5.6	5.6	29.7	52.8	147 306	145 170	-1.5	-0.6
Troy	6.0	13.2	21.7	16.0	11.4	11.2	9.3	5.5	5.7	30.3	50.6	49 170	50 129	2.0	-0.4
Utica	7.6	17.6	12.3	13.1	10.3	12.7	11.6	6.8	8.0	34.6	51.0	60 651	62 235	2.6	-1.5
Valley Stream	7.5	16.7	7.9	14.2	12.8	14.3	13.4	7.0	6.2	38.0	50.3	36 368	37 511	3.1	0.7
Watertown	10.3	13.8	13.8	18.1	10.8	10.3	9.8	6.4	6.6	30.6	51.3	26 705	27 023	1.2	2.1
White Plains	6.2	14.3	8.9	15.1	15.1	12.6	12.0	7.8	8.0	38.3	52.1	53 077	56 853	7.1	2.1

City	Households, 2011-2013				Persons in group quarters, 2010				Serious crimes known to police,[2] 2013				Educational attainment, 2011–2013		
	Number	Persons per household	Percent: Female family householder[1]	Percent: One-person	Total	Institutional: Total	Institutional: Persons in nursing facilities	Non-institutional	Total: Number	Total: Rate[3]	Rate[3]: Violent	Rate[3]: Property	Population age 25 and older	Attainment[4] (percent): High school graduate or less	Attainment[4] (percent): Bachelor's degree or more
	27	28	29	30	31	32	33	34	35	36	37	38	39	40	41
NEW JERSEY—Cont'd															
Garfield	10 747	2.88	21.4	23.0	32	0	0	32	762	2 455	200	2 256	20 736	59.8	18.7
Hackensack	18 421	2.30	15.3	37.4	1 301	985	172	316	963	2 180	251	1 928	31 683	43.6	34.7
Hoboken	24 670	2.04	7.9	38.9	1 574	0	0	1 574	1 122	2 126	288	1 838	39 236	14.5	75.6
Jersey City	97 364	2.59	17.4	30.1	2 843	984	914	1 859	6 491	2 527	644	1 883	178 975	38.2	42.3
Kearny	13 692	2.97	15.1	19.6	2 570	2 501	167	69	966	2 318	187	2 131	27 767	55.4	21.0
Linden	14 167	2.87	18.7	26.0	245	242	214	3	1 339	3 263	300	2 963	28 908	54.1	18.8
Long Branch	11 966	2.54	15.9	33.4	184	75	70	109	966	3 157	405	2 751	20 232	50.1	28.4
Millville	10 276	2.77	21.3	27.5	212	117	117	95	2 571	8 970	886	8 084	18 721	54.1	19.1
Newark	91 436	2.89	28.7	30.3	16 367	8 545	1 015	7 822	12 481	4 486	1 264	3 222	174 461	64.0	13.0
New Brunswick	13 920	3.46	24.9	26.4	7 745	182	147	7 563	1 968	3 481	536	2 945	25 705	65.3	18.7
Paramus	8 633	2.93	8.3	17.9	1 165	1 110	521	55	1 347	5 059	120	4 938	19 618	29.1	49.4
Passaic	20 395	3.44	28.5	23.5	458	232	224	226	1 652	2 345	727	1 618	39 919	71.7	12.7
Paterson	43 383	3.31	31.9	23.1	2 628	1 353	212	1 275	5 656	3 898	1 072	2 827	88 810	69.6	10.1
Perth Amboy	16 343	3.13	22.8	22.1	667	445	445	222	1 284	2 465	466	1 998	32 600	66.0	15.0
Plainfield	14 330	3.45	27.1	23.7	732	342	327	390	1 711	3 393	847	2 546	32 413	58.2	18.4
Rahway	10 187	2.73	13.9	31.5	124	109	109	15	502	1 797	179	1 618	19 259	45.5	26.6
Sayreville	15 672	2.78	13.0	21.9	200	193	193	7	573	1 297	86	1 211	30 757	35.0	34.0
Trenton	28 179	2.79	26.7	31.5	5 123	4 250	1 166	873	3 443	4 077	1 329	2 749	53 749	68.6	9.9
Union City	22 367	3.01	25.9	23.8	649	342	341	307	1 337	1 959	362	1 597	45 017	64.3	15.3
Vineland	20 728	2.86	18.6	23.9	1 491	897	593	594	2 544	4 180	342	3 838	40 037	59.4	18.0
Westfield	10 291	2.96	5.3	20.2	220	204	204	16	260	845	39	806	20 345	16.5	66.7
West New York	18 394	2.79	18.6	27.4	14	0	0	14	679	1 303	309	994	35 912	56.1	22.8
NEW MEXICO	760 251	2.68	14.3	28.9	42 629	25 266	5 567	17 363	90 038	4 318	613	3 705	1 358 996	42.6	26.0
Alamogordo	12 212	2.52	15.9	29.8	611	515	278	96	880	2 768	252	2 517	21 030	44.8	14.6
Albuquerque	222 510	2.46	14.5	32.4	7 659	2 897	1 712	4 762	34 856	6 245	775	5 470	368 304	34.1	33.6
Carlsbad	10 424	2.54	14.8	31.1	533	470	217	63	1 117	4 156	513	3 643	17 717	51.5	17.5
Clovis	14 370	2.70	15.7	26.8	597	503	188	94	2 296	5 810	681	5 129	23 888	43.2	20.8
Farmington	15 171	2.93	14.1	25.9	1 465	979	164	486	1 965	4 289	635	3 653	29 126	43.2	20.0
Hobbs	11 191	3.03	14.8	23.2	1 494	1 316	146	178	1 899	5 377	844	4 533	21 064	54.3	15.0
Las Cruces	38 254	2.58	16.8	30.2	1 610	1 186	251	424	4 681	4 589	325	4 263	59 887	34.4	32.5
Rio Rancho	32 347	2.80	12.2	24.3	197	141	141	56	1 883	2 052	182	1 870	58 438	33.1	27.2
Roswell	17 589	2.66	19.0	27.4	1 489	452	216	1 037	3 539	7 301	642	6 660	29 671	44.7	20.2
Santa Fe	31 604	2.15	10.9	41.3	1 119	270	247	849	886	1 274	83	1 190	51 106	30.2	44.6
NEW YORK	7 214 163	2.63	14.8	29.8	585 678	231 163	116 558	354 515	435 970	2 219	394	1 825	13 319 715	41.7	33.5
Albany	39 470	2.23	15.3	44.1	10 248	1 452	941	8 796	4 881	4 983	808	4 175	60 255	37.6	36.3
Auburn	10 942	2.31	16.7	40.0	2 328	2 139	370	189	955	3 502	352	3 150	19 087	52.2	16.6
Binghamton	20 120	2.24	14.4	40.7	1 262	846	458	416	2 633	5 686	613	5 073	30 393	49.1	23.5
Buffalo	110 374	2.27	22.1	39.4	9 371	2 530	1 201	6 841	15 740	6 082	1 255	4 827	165 033	45.4	24.8
Elmira	10 509	2.31	21.8	34.0	3 458	2 380	296	1 078	1 108	3 831	280	3 551	18 100	57.9	14.7
Freeport	13 488	3.16	20.1	24.2	574	354	346	220	1 085	2 511	352	2 159	28 983	50.4	24.8
Glen Cove	9 630	2.74	12.6	25.4	723	404	396	319	65	240	11	228	19 309	46.5	34.5
Harrison	8 227	2.90	9.1	19.6	4 285	0	0	4 285	231	829	22	807	16 567	30.0	50.8
Hempstead	16 430	3.28	24.5	24.6	1 306	686	678	620	1 391	2 520	784	1 736	35 518	62.0	15.5
Ithaca	9 432	2.37	7.9	42.2	7 701	179	172	7 522	1 303	4 282	158	4 124	10 826	20.1	61.9
Jamestown	13 117	2.29	17.2	33.9	1 134	399	353	735	1 308	4 266	548	3 718	20 357	48.9	17.6
Lindenhurst	8 911	3.06	13.6	18.6	29	0	0	29	NA	NA	NA	NA	19 101	48.0	24.6
Long Beach	14 611	2.21	11.8	39.9	1 094	920	822	174	372	1 109	104	1 005	26 025	28.6	45.0
Middletown	9 533	2.88	20.8	27.2	489	190	181	299	966	3 474	410	3 064	17 325	45.2	20.1
Mount Vernon	25 507	2.63	24.3	33.0	833	429	418	404	1 990	2 923	814	2 110	45 833	44.3	26.8
Newburgh	8 769	3.16	25.1	27.9	945	24	0	921	1 475	5 163	1 523	3 640	15 119	67.3	10.6
New Rochelle	28 658	2.63	12.9	29.7	3 277	1 256	999	2 021	1 566	1 987	222	1 765	53 236	38.8	40.4
New York	3 066 297	2.66	18.3	33.1	185 530	70 041	45 516	115 489	194 355	2 315	624	1 691	5 715 484	44.5	34.9
Niagara Falls	21 652	2.28	17.9	37.6	376	159	157	217	3 391	6 840	1 178	5 662	34 131	53.5	16.1
North Tonawanda	13 804	2.25	10.8	36.5	142	74	70	68	627	2 011	132	1 880	22 186	41.8	25.1
Ossining	7 565	3.07	13.4	23.3	1 858	1 830	102	28	279	1 102	142	960	17 735	51.6	31.0
Port Chester	9 215	3.15	20.8	23.1	465	154	154	311	620	2 114	164	1 950	20 311	59.7	18.8
Poughkeepsie	12 088	2.44	22.1	35.2	2 904	921	540	1 983	1 073	3 486	929	2 557	20 505	48.7	24.0
Rochester	86 413	2.32	24.1	40.3	10 200	3 657	1 960	6 543	12 158	5 774	1 001	4 773	131 685	47.1	24.5
Rome	13 456	2.27	15.4	38.8	2 882	2 581	462	301	709	2 178	144	2 033	23 798	49.2	19.1
Saratoga Springs	11 095	2.19	4.3	37.7	2 510	445	352	2 065	675	2 493	122	2 371	18 122	26.4	47.1
Schenectady	24 507	2.56	16.1	40.7	3 470	677	296	2 793	3 407	5 159	919	4 240	42 122	50.9	19.7
Spring Valley	8 398	3.74	22.8	18.7	216	0	0	216	536	1 660	409	1 251	17 397	59.4	17.1
Syracuse	54 520	2.38	21.0	40.4	12 782	2 332	1 523	10 450	7 665	5 329	829	4 500	84 184	48.3	25.0
Troy	19 921	2.27	21.2	37.4	4 508	493	202	4 015	2 356	4 722	744	3 978	29 569	45.1	25.7
Utica	23 325	2.53	20.1	37.2	3 076	1 171	983	1 905	2 889	4 683	585	4 098	38 706	53.4	17.0
Valley Stream	11 076	3.39	13.5	16.2	41	0	0	41	NA	NA	NA	NA	25 547	38.1	34.5
Watertown	11 732	2.30	13.7	37.5	905	667	473	238	1 274	4 521	387	4 134	17 248	45.5	19.7
White Plains	21 471	2.60	13.4	34.9	1 755	704	460	1 051	1 310	2 276	136	2 140	40 576	33.2	47.5

1. No spouse present. 2. Data for serious crimes have not been adjusted for underreporting. This may affect comparability between geographic areas and over time. 3. Per 100,000 population estimated by the FBI. 4. Persons 25 years old and over.

City	Money income, 2011–2013					Housing units, 2010			Occupied housing units 2011–2013				
	Per capita income[1] (dollars)	Households			Families with income below poverty (percent)					Owner-occupied		Median owner costs as a percent of income	
		Median income	Percent with income of $200,000 or more	Percent with income of less than $25,000		Total	Percent change, 2000–2010	Vacant units for sale or rent[2]	Total	Percent	Median value[3] (dollars)	With a mortgage[4]	Without a mortgage[5]
	42	43	44	45	46	47	48	49	50	51	52	53	54
NEW JERSEY—Cont'd													
Garfield	20 731	43 071	2.2	27.5	11.9	11 788	0.8	715	10 747	36.7	333 000	41.3	27.8
Hackensack	31 438	53 903	3.5	22.6	15.8	19 375	2.3	1 233	18 421	36.0	277 600	33.5	21.0
Hoboken	68 277	105 833	19.5	15.1	11.2	26 855	34.3	1 814	24 670	31.0	536 900	22.2	18.0
Jersey City	32 179	57 076	7.3	25.7	16.2	108 720	16.1	11 861	97 364	29.4	313 100	30.6	21.9
Kearny	25 904	58 987	3.7	17.7	9.1	14 180	2.2	718	13 692	46.1	321 600	33.4	22.5
Linden	27 085	61 826	2.5	18.9	7.0	15 872	2.0	963	14 167	59.2	268 100	33.0	25.1
Long Branch	26 726	47 442	5.3	26.9	14.3	14 170	1.3	2 417	11 966	38.6	322 400	32.1	15.6
Millville	22 995	47 850	1.2	27.1	14.9	11 435	7.4	787	10 276	63.3	163 600	27.0	17.8
Newark	16 174	32 338	0.9	39.8	27.1	109 520	9.4	14 978	91 436	22.1	222 600	41.0	23.4
New Brunswick	13 616	35 462	1.1	34.9	27.3	15 053	8.3	934	13 920	21.7	233 000	34.0	17.2
Paramus	44 972	100 801	18.6	10.7	2.4	8 915	8.6	285	8 633	88.6	545 500	26.7	17.6
Passaic	14 949	33 037	1.0	39.1	28.8	20 432	1.2	1 021	20 395	23.7	298 400	41.1	22.1
Paterson	15 966	32 056	1.5	39.7	27.3	47 946	1.6	3 617	43 383	25.5	257 700	46.3	24.1
Perth Amboy	18 302	41 531	1.2	32.0	22.5	16 556	8.7	1 137	16 343	33.6	238 700	29.2	23.4
Plainfield	20 974	51 628	3.3	27.7	21.6	16 621	2.7	1 441	14 330	46.2	248 300	31.7	21.1
Rahway	26 988	56 493	2.7	20.1	7.8	11 300	8.9	767	10 187	57.1	274 400	34.6	23.1
Sayreville	34 263	80 277	7.3	12.4	5.3	16 393	7.6	757	15 672	68.3	296 100	28.0	17.7
Trenton	16 854	34 309	1.5	39.1	22.5	33 035	-2.6	4 457	28 179	37.8	110 000	27.8	20.3
Union City	19 192	39 674	2.0	32.3	24.4	24 931	5.0	2 117	22 367	18.5	288 000	38.1	26.4
Vineland	23 986	47 750	2.9	26.1	14.9	22 661	8.1	1 211	20 728	65.5	165 500	26.1	18.1
Westfield	61 168	133 591	33.8	7.9	1.3	10 950	1.2	384	10 291	78.7	654 900	23.9	15.5
West New York	24 943	45 367	4.2	29.7	18.5	20 018	15.3	1 166	18 394	18.9	307 700	31.3	26.7
NEW MEXICO	23 411	43 747	2.8	29.8	16.6	901 388	15.5	109 993	760 251	68.1	159 000	23.1	10.0
Alamogordo	22 020	39 745	2.3	31.2	17.8	14 052	-11.2	1 289	12 212	57.9	107 100	22.4	10.0
Albuquerque	26 403	46 668	3.1	27.3	14.8	239 166	20.4	14 836	222 510	59.4	183 600	23.5	10.0
Carlsbad	25 159	45 287	2.4	30.6	11.2	11 243	-2.4	986	10 424	67.2	105 400	16.8	10.7
Clovis	20 441	40 539	0.9	33.9	18.4	15 573	8.9	1 285	14 370	62.2	126 200	20.1	10.0
Farmington	24 137	48 891	2.8	24.5	12.2	17 548	16.6	1 102	15 171	70.2	168 800	22.2	10.0
Hobbs	22 079	51 407	3.7	23.1	14.0	12 900	7.5	1 271	11 191	64.4	104 700	18.2	10.0
Las Cruces	21 055	39 155	1.7	35.8	19.1	42 370	33.9	2 937	38 254	56.4	147 600	22.4	10.0
Rio Rancho	26 122	58 281	2.3	20.4	10.3	33 964	68.3	2 072	32 347	78.8	171 500	24.7	10.0
Roswell	20 936	40 469	1.5	28.3	17.2	19 743	2.4	2 089	17 589	62.7	97 900	19.3	10.0
Santa Fe	33 120	49 305	5.1	26.2	14.1	37 200	22.0	5 305	31 604	59.8	274 200	27.0	10.0
NEW YORK	32 083	57 327	7.0	23.6	12.2	8 108 103	5.6	790 348	7 214 163	53.7	281 000	25.3	14.9
Albany	23 460	40 416	1.2	34.4	17.7	46 362	2.4	5 205	39 470	39.5	176 900	23.4	14.2
Auburn	19 829	36 690	0.8	37.2	16.4	12 639	0.0	948	10 942	46.1	95 600	19.9	14.3
Binghamton	20 289	30 075	1.4	44.9	22.8	23 842	-0.5	2 692	20 120	45.0	86 300	20.3	14.5
Buffalo	19 963	30 859	1.4	42.5	26.6	133 444	-8.3	20 908	110 374	41.2	66 900	21.0	13.4
Elmira	16 404	29 019	1.4	43.4	29.4	12 313	-4.5	1 322	10 509	45.6	68 700	18.8	14.0
Freeport	28 018	69 275	8.2	19.6	12.2	13 865	0.3	586	13 488	66.6	315 100	33.5	20.3
Glen Cove	34 164	62 331	10.5	17.6	9.7	10 352	6.3	588	9 630	51.2	455 100	31.0	24.8
Harrison	61 564	104 340	26.6	11.8	7.5	8 956	3.5	581	8 227	64.4	764 600	29.5	15.2
Hempstead	21 310	49 971	3.0	27.2	16.1	16 034	3.0	800	16 430	39.6	316 400	35.8	19.9
Ithaca	16 168	28 208	2.8	46.0	18.4	10 950	2.2	542	9 432	25.7	207 300	23.0	13.7
Jamestown	19 071	31 160	1.0	39.1	24.4	14 738	-1.9	1 616	13 117	51.6	63 100	19.2	13.2
Lindenhurst	33 040	84 966	7.8	10.4	3.0	9 665	4.1	349	8 911	79.3	345 200	32.0	19.8
Long Beach	45 001	85 813	8.7	15.1	6.4	16 450	2.0	1 641	14 611	56.2	466 900	31.0	19.5
Middletown	22 552	53 433	1.9	26.3	16.5	10 866	7.1	890	9 533	51.3	199 000	31.1	19.2
Mount Vernon	26 731	48 458	4.7	27.3	13.7	28 990	7.2	2 730	25 507	38.2	364 600	34.3	22.3
Newburgh	16 033	33 991	0.7	37.6	31.6	10 505	0.2	1 475	8 769	30.1	160 700	28.4	25.7
New Rochelle	39 477	64 619	12.7	19.7	8.1	29 586	9.6	1 633	28 658	50.1	535 700	29.3	19.4
New York	31 746	51 526	7.2	27.9	17.9	3 371 062	5.3	261 278	3 066 297	31.7	485 700	29.9	14.6
Niagara Falls	19 529	31 450	1.1	39.8	20.8	26 220	-5.8	3 617	21 652	56.3	66 700	21.0	15.5
North Tonawanda	28 438	46 677	1.2	23.2	9.4	14 757	2.3	753	13 804	67.0	102 800	19.9	15.5
Ossining	28 305	63 131	8.6	18.8	13.3	8 862	4.1	518	7 565	48.8	389 100	29.9	19.5
Port Chester	26 373	54 182	5.7	20.7	12.2	10 046	2.8	806	9 215	39.8	432 900	35.1	24.1
Poughkeepsie	23 496	37 435	2.9	34.6	19.9	13 984	6.3	1 584	12 088	38.5	205 700	26.9	20.6
Rochester	18 866	30 741	1.4	42.7	31.5	97 158	-2.7	10 131	86 413	37.8	75 500	22.8	13.9
Rome	23 896	41 180	1.7	29.2	12.9	14 893	-8.6	1 367	13 456	55.7	91 000	22.1	13.1
Saratoga Springs	38 076	68 233	7.9	19.9	2.5	12 930	11.7	1 024	11 006	64.8	294 300	22.5	12.8
Schenectady	20 070	36 947	1.0	35.7	20.8	30 095	-0.8	3 462	24 507	46.3	112 200	23.5	16.5
Spring Valley	16 435	46 180	2.1	22.7	22.4	9 374	20.2	619	8 398	29.3	245 000	36.0	16.0
Syracuse	18 471	30 391	1.4	43.0	29.3	64 356	-5.6	7 001	54 520	38.9	86 700	21.2	14.3
Troy	21 431	39 371	0.8	34.5	23.3	23 474	1.6	2 969	19 921	38.2	146 000	23.3	15.6
Utica	16 768	30 016	0.7	43.1	26.0	28 166	-3.4	3 261	23 325	47.0	89 600	22.3	15.2
Valley Stream	31 665	91 073	8.8	13.8	8.1	12 625	-0.6	436	11 076	81.5	367 400	30.6	21.1
Watertown	20 861	38 736	0.8	32.6	18.4	12 562	0.9	1 153	11 732	39.1	117 600	20.9	13.7
White Plains	44 762	82 422	13.4	17.0	9.3	24 382	13.0	1 472	21 471	52.5	496 800	24.3	17.4

1. Based on population estimated by the American Community Survey. 2. Includes units rented or sold but not occupied. 3. Specified owner-occupied units; $1,000,000 represents $1,000,000 or more 4. 50.0 represents 50 percent or more. 5. 10.0 represents 10 percent or less.

City	Occupied housing units, 2011–2013 (cont.)				Migration, 2011–2013		Civilian labor force, 2014				Civilian employment[4], 2011–2013			
									Unemployment			Percent		
	Percent renter occupied	Median gross rent[1]	Median rent as a percent of income[2]	Percent with no vehicle available	Percent who lived in the same house one year ago	Percent who lived outside current city one year ago	Total	Percent change, 2013–2014	Total	Rate[3]	Population age 16 and older	In labor force	Civilian full-year full-time workers	Households with no workers (percent)
	55	56	57	58	59	60	61	62	63	64	65	66	67	68
NEW JERSEY—Cont'd														
Garfield	63.3	1 172	36.6	11.1	95.8	3.1	16 017	-0.5	1 439	9.0	24 452	62.0	42.4	25.2
Hackensack	64.0	1 242	31.1	16.9	85.2	10.3	24 177	0.1	1 551	6.4	36 734	66.0	50.4	23.9
Hoboken	69.0	1 743	23.2	35.1	77.8	14.8	35 786	0.4	1 176	3.3	45 414	78.8	62.6	14.9
Jersey City	70.6	1 166	29.2	38.6	85.8	7.4	138 335	-0.5	9 140	6.6	207 932	68.1	46.6	20.9
Kearny	53.9	1 170	31.6	12.8	89.8	5.3	20 863	-0.5	1 566	7.5	32 592	69.0	46.1	21.3
Linden	40.8	1 153	29.2	9.0	88.5	7.3	21 824	-0.7	1 592	7.3	33 903	68.6	43.3	25.5
Long Branch	61.4	1 228	38.2	13.6	86.4	6.9	16 000	0.2	1 082	6.8	23 607	65.5	37.2	27.9
Millville	36.7	904	33.3	11.7	85.2	6.4	13 341	-2.9	1 264	9.5	22 192	64.7	34.7	33.9
Newark	77.9	951	34.4	40.4	84.9	6.1	118 917	-1.0	12 160	10.2	214 059	63.1	32.7	32.1
New Brunswick	78.3	1 336	45.7	34.8	72.1	13.9	26 382	0.2	1 628	6.2	43 773	60.3	34.4	23.1
Paramus	11.4	1 801	50.0	6.6	95.1	3.9	12 833	0.5	698	5.4	22 123	60.8	40.1	29.1
Passaic	76.3	1 031	38.4	38.2	94.9	2.6	30 221	-0.8	2 844	9.4	50 136	61.1	38.9	28.5
Paterson	74.5	1 102	41.5	30.9	89.9	2.7	62 767	-1.2	7 474	11.9	110 884	57.1	37.4	33.5
Perth Amboy	66.4	1 124	36.6	23.4	93.5	4.0	24 981	-1.3	2 657	10.6	39 727	58.0	41.6	23.9
Plainfield	53.8	1 138	41.4	17.9	83.7	6.6	27 441	-0.7	2 346	8.5	39 858	73.9	41.2	22.5
Rahway	42.9	1 190	35.7	14.3	91.9	6.2	14 612	-0.3	1 103	7.5	22 370	69.8	40.5	26.2
Sayreville	31.7	1 121	29.4	5.0	94.4	4.2	23 597	0.2	1 438	6.1	35 872	67.8	43.5	17.5
Trenton	62.2	954	37.0	30.3	83.0	8.6	38 548	-0.3	3 509	9.1	65 485	62.1	33.4	34.9
Union City	81.5	1 074	34.7	46.3	84.7	8.3	35 043	-0.3	2 796	8.0	54 563	68.5	38.8	22.1
Vineland	34.5	1 011	38.6	9.1	90.4	4.7	28 184	-2.9	2 722	9.7	47 108	61.1	37.6	31.1
Westfield	21.3	1 505	26.6	4.7	90.8	7.7	14 573	0.4	609	4.2	23 051	68.6	45.4	17.5
West New York	81.1	1 151	31.4	36.3	83.3	9.1	28 177	-0.2	1 880	6.7	41 831	71.9	43.9	23.5
NEW MEXICO	31.9	762	31.1	5.9	85.6	8.3	918 206	-0.5	60 057	6.5	1 627 194	60.2	36.7	30.2
Alamogordo	42.1	714	27.7	6.9	79.4	11.8	13 025	-2.7	706	5.4	24 434	58.8	29.2	36.3
Albuquerque	40.6	786	31.5	7.3	82.6	6.4	267 082	-0.5	15 667	5.9	438 368	65.1	40.8	27.3
Carlsbad	32.8	718	27.8	4.0	82.4	8.1	14 305	3.6	649	4.5	20 709	63.1	44.2	29.1
Clovis	37.8	741	33.5	6.8	77.4	9.7	16 952	0.4	835	4.9	29 769	64.6	40.4	27.2
Farmington	29.8	767	33.1	3.6	84.8	10.4	21 266	1.3	1 078	5.1	34 492	61.7	39.0	24.9
Hobbs	35.6	827	23.8	2.1	88.8	6.9	15 594	3.3	680	4.4	25 594	62.3	41.6	20.6
Las Cruces	43.6	689	33.6	6.5	76.7	9.8	45 047	-0.7	2 687	6.0	77 838	62.9	35.4	30.0
Rio Rancho	21.2	1 004	31.7	3.1	88.7	6.5	41 728	-0.5	2 753	6.6	68 667	62.8	41.4	27.2
Roswell	37.3	692	31.6	6.6	80.5	8.5	19 863	0.5	1 202	6.1	36 352	60.1	37.9	28.6
Santa Fe	40.2	928	31.4	6.1	81.1	9.1	34 730	-1.7	1 760	5.1	57 628	65.4	39.4	31.3
NEW YORK	46.3	1 096	32.2	29.4	88.8	6.3	9 569 062	-0.7	605 041	6.3	15 822 996	63.5	40.1	27.3
Albany	60.5	825	32.2	25.4	80.4	11.6	47 151	-2.0	2 742	5.8	82 975	60.3	35.7	33.1
Auburn	53.9	624	29.1	20.9	81.9	8.2	12 154	-2.8	806	6.6	22 897	56.9	29.0	39.0
Binghamton	55.0	642	36.9	24.2	77.0	13.8	18 981	-3.3	1 379	7.3	39 566	53.9	27.0	41.5
Buffalo	58.8	679	33.2	30.2	81.2	8.1	111 847	-2.7	8 842	7.9	207 345	59.0	31.6	37.9
Elmira	54.4	635	35.0	23.3	76.1	11.2	10 573	-3.4	843	8.0	22 828	48.2	26.2	37.6
Freeport	33.4	1 336	35.8	14.0	93.2	4.6	22 303	-1.7	1 316	5.9	33 688	68.7	44.3	23.6
Glen Cove	48.8	1 604	36.9	11.9	89.5	8.8	13 767	-1.4	677	4.9	22 171	64.1	44.2	24.9
Harrison	35.6	1 804	28.4	7.5	84.7	12.4	13 015	-1.0	682	5.2	23 101	60.6	37.2	18.0
Hempstead	60.4	1 253	38.8	31.3	89.9	7.0	27 151	-1.6	1 739	6.4	42 597	66.6	40.5	26.4
Ithaca	74.3	1 017	46.7	28.6	58.6	25.7	14 280	-2.1	687	4.8	27 774	47.6	16.5	42.3
Jamestown	48.4	601	34.0	19.5	80.5	9.7	12 466	-3.6	1 000	8.0	23 811	59.9	34.1	37.2
Lindenhurst	20.7	1 341	29.9	6.2	93.7	5.3	15 128	-1.7	815	5.4	22 903	67.7	41.4	19.5
Long Beach	43.8	1 590	27.2	14.1	87.3	8.6	19 320	-2.2	904	4.7	29 228	70.0	47.9	22.7
Middletown	48.7	1 115	38.3	19.4	86.1	6.7	13 442	-1.5	798	5.9	21 626	71.3	40.7	26.3
Mount Vernon	61.8	1 187	36.5	27.7	89.8	4.5	32 814	-1.2	2 368	7.2	53 945	68.3	41.4	27.1
Newburgh	69.9	1 046	45.4	36.0	87.0	6.4	12 153	-2.1	843	6.9	20 258	65.0	37.8	31.9
New Rochelle	49.9	1 290	34.4	18.5	87.8	6.7	38 359	-1.2	2 221	5.8	63 571	62.8	40.5	25.0
New York	68.3	1 210	32.3	55.7	88.9	3.2	4 125 596	1.2	298 923	7.2	6 756 892	63.4	41.0	26.8
Niagara Falls	43.7	618	34.6	22.5	89.0	4.1	21 796	-2.7	1 842	8.5	40 394	58.4	32.1	39.7
North Tonawanda	33.0	667	28.5	6.9	88.1	5.7	15 947	-2.2	980	6.1	25 888	67.8	41.2	29.1
Ossining	51.2	1 381	38.7	15.5	90.2	5.5	13 009	-0.9	601	4.6	20 212	69.5	41.4	17.1
Port Chester	60.2	1 409	35.9	19.5	83.7	8.7	16 257	-0.9	660	4.1	23 618	75.3	43.0	18.1
Poughkeepsie	61.5	982	37.2	26.7	85.2	7.2	13 288	-2.2	878	6.6	24 835	60.8	33.3	32.4
Rochester	62.2	754	37.9	25.9	75.5	8.6	91 732	-2.6	7 380	8.0	164 424	61.6	34.0	35.1
Rome	44.3	690	27.9	16.2	83.7	9.7	13 676	-3.4	851	6.2	27 159	53.9	35.6	36.2
Saratoga Springs	45.2	982	26.0	9.2	77.5	16.7	13 575	-1.7	620	4.6	22 791	62.5	35.5	28.8
Schenectady	53.7	805	35.7	21.1	85.2	7.7	30 353	-2.4	1 992	6.6	52 681	64.1	38.0	31.7
Spring Valley	70.7	1 174	36.9	22.4	83.6	7.1	14 487	-1.3	678	4.7	22 136	73.5	39.6	17.6
Syracuse	61.1	706	35.4	29.8	74.8	11.9	59 450	-2.9	4 298	7.2	114 885	55.8	29.5	37.2
Troy	61.8	809	30.9	22.7	74.8	14.7	23 326	-2.3	1 563	6.7	41 274	61.1	33.1	34.8
Utica	53.0	636	34.2	24.6	80.5	7.7	24 257	-3.1	1 823	7.5	48 153	55.7	28.5	40.0
Valley Stream	18.5	1 489	33.2	6.2	94.4	4.0	19 271	-1.4	1 021	5.3	29 793	69.3	43.5	20.8
Watertown	60.9	793	29.5	16.8	69.5	18.2	11 269	-3.3	731	6.5	21 474	64.1	32.8	32.1
White Plains	47.5	1 495	34.5	16.8	87.4	7.0	31 086	-1.1	1 339	4.3	46 732	69.0	44.5	22.8

1. $2,000 represents $2,000 or more. 2. 50.0 represents 50 percent or more. 3. Percent of civilian labor force. 4. Persons 16 years old and over.

City	Value of residential construction authorized by building permits, 2014			Wholesale trade,[1] 2007				Retail trade,[2] 2007			
	New construction ($1,000)	Number of housing units	Percent single family	Number of establish-ments	Number of employees	Sales (mil dol)	Annual payroll (mil dol)	Number of establish-ments	Number of employees	Sales (mil dol)	Annual payroll (mil dol)
	69	70	71	72	73	74	75	76	77	78	79
NEW JERSEY—Cont'd											
Garfield	3 390	129	11.6	51	755	236.7	23.4	76	531	152.0	15.6
Hackensack	5 257	119	7.6	223	2 147	1 699.4	131.2	278	4 052	1 144.3	108.5
Hoboken	133 571	475	0.8	36	245	575.9	16.6	153	1 351	312.4	31.4
Jersey City	487 563	2 180	9.0	210	4 366	3 264.5	227.9	818	8 754	2 210.1	201.6
Kearny	25 251	151	0.7	85	1 623	1 154.2	86.6	129	1 789	443.4	46.2
Linden	12 366	312	7.1	119	1 629	1 957.5	84.0	192	2 864	725.3	67.6
Long Branch	16 966	139	30.2	27	D	D	D	93	1 066	248.4	32.3
Millville	1 971	19	100.0	28	D	D	D	98	2 075	484.9	51.5
Newark	69 735	507	6.3	324	4 954	3 119.2	245.3	935	6 467	1 637.2	147.8
New Brunswick	139 436	728	1.2	65	843	623.7	45.7	135	958	201.5	20.3
Paramus	8 515	17	100.0	112	932	1 641.0	67.7	611	15 080	3 621.1	359.8
Passaic	2 181	37	18.9	93	814	422.7	32.9	274	1 874	415.4	42.2
Paterson	11 683	147	2.7	190	2 064	852.2	99.2	492	2 700	642.1	61.6
Perth Amboy	547	5	60.0	50	582	361.4	27.1	189	1 336	340.7	32.1
Plainfield	266	3	100.0	26	155	41.4	4.8	125	685	169.3	17.3
Rahway	3 079	123	6.5	61	767	961.2	45.1	87	798	265.7	26.1
Sayreville	2 716	17	100.0	53	420	547.5	23.3	98	1 221	328.7	30.1
Trenton	55	10	0.0	60	854	663.7	45.3	234	1 470	402.3	36.4
Union City	5 836	43	0.0	59	289	110.8	10.2	297	1 367	341.7	28.9
Vineland	7 451	71	100.0	86	1 357	980.4	55.3	281	3 885	1 052.0	94.5
Westfield	25 608	72	100.0	19	99	27.1	3.3	138	1 546	323.5	33.9
West New York	3 673	58	0.0	43	163	48.6	4.1	241	1 284	270.2	27.0
NEW MEXICO	881 907	4 799	84.5	1 763	19 891	10 589.3	805.8	7 208	97 385	24 470.0	2 250.8
Alamogordo	NA	NA	NA	15	62	27.2	2.0	146	2 128	491.4	42.4
Albuquerque	209 154	1 416	78.4	735	10 490	5 165.6	433.3	2 030	34 923	8 951.7	859.0
Carlsbad	34 318	290	40.7	26	182	66.2	6.6	125	1 512	361.4	34.7
Clovis	27 344	141	62.4	40	196	144.6	6.5	186	2 425	562.4	50.1
Farmington	21 596	109	100.0	107	1 111	606.3	54.9	346	5 296	1 368.3	123.4
Hobbs	39 784	276	68.5	67	631	285.1	29.6	142	2 189	628.5	53.4
Las Cruces	59 479	298	96.3	83	812	272.0	25.7	425	7 046	1 723.8	144.4
Rio Rancho	142 023	820	90.4	22	111	57.6	6.4	108	2 501	905.3	64.1
Roswell	7 614	44	100.0	38	350	237.6	10.8	233	3 102	788.3	66.3
Santa Fe	37 092	161	100.0	98	1 010	512.6	51.2	763	8 769	2 183.9	236.2
NEW YORK	5 581 783	36 286	28.6	30 863	357 459	313 461.9	19 609.0	76 637	892 863	230 718.1	22 336.7
Albany	11 321	79	43.0	130	1 777	1 352.9	95.4	381	5 687	1 362.3	134.1
Auburn	9 861	114	3.5	26	396	188.9	17.7	161	2 699	583.4	57.0
Binghamton	370	3	100.0	51	622	191.9	22.0	191	2 280	471.7	46.2
Buffalo	19 388	118	55.9	281	4 538	2 037.3	182.5	795	8 315	1 449.6	159.4
Elmira	0	0	0.0	33	404	151.7	16.5	101	1 367	308.3	30.2
Freeport	1 551	8	100.0	87	793	310.0	32.0	185	1 734	665.9	57.4
Glen Cove	4 367	36	11.1	49	192	130.8	8.8	131	1 337	581.8	45.0
Harrison	29 038	31	100.0	71	2 150	5 874.5	176.7	70	310	92.9	10.4
Hempstead	0	0	0.0	46	461	177.8	22.4	197	2 166	839.8	63.5
Ithaca	8 924	79	2.5	21	158	40.6	5.1	187	2 879	610.4	63.3
Jamestown	0	0	0.0	37	D	D	D	127	1 511	359.2	34.1
Lindenhurst	1 408	9	100.0	39	D	D	D	88	720	243.0	23.4
Long Beach	3 000	15	100.0	25	34	17.9	1.5	87	624	178.3	18.1
Middletown	16 658	69	100.0	33	361	128.5	12.4	131	1 394	457.1	37.5
Mount Vernon	529	6	33.3	100	1 185	541.4	51.8	222	2 491	583.8	64.6
Newburgh	1 255	10	100.0	57	768	1 365.4	34.9	117	1 397	359.9	31.6
New Rochelle	2 537	5	100.0	88	1 020	865.4	79.4	267	2 886	1 031.5	88.5
New York	185 203	1 885	0.0	16 230	164 336	147 228.0	9 512.3	31 459	287 574	78 206.5	8 041.7
Niagara Falls	964	6	0.0	35	362	160.6	14.7	182	2 429	513.0	46.5
North Tonawanda	1 789	12	100.0	36	1 071	220.0	51.6	74	741	137.2	15.7
Ossining	175	1	100.0	22	92	33.5	4.0	73	546	171.3	13.7
Port Chester	2 235	12	50.0	47	477	174.2	25.9	152	2 037	613.2	56.8
Poughkeepsie	250	2	100.0	34	340	160.1	16.3	153	1 599	405.5	39.3
Rochester	28 816	223	31.4	301	4 041	1 647.9	177.9	695	6 232	1 181.7	128.0
Rome	3 707	22	27.3	16	81	57.0	4.1	137	2 150	461.0	49.0
Saratoga Springs	38 834	198	36.4	22	121	113.6	6.3	169	2 419	614.0	53.8
Schenectady	367	2	100.0	47	588	340.6	21.9	183	1 712	441.7	42.4
Spring Valley	3 139	17	41.2	42	264	233.3	12.8	114	1 310	460.2	34.1
Syracuse	14 798	216	6.9	161	3 049	1 109.2	139.7	601	7 597	1 654.5	162.4
Troy	1 484	12	100.0	41	457	908.6	16.8	130	1 544	380.1	40.1
Utica	0	0	0.0	59	989	524.7	38.6	179	2 604	580.1	55.7
Valley Stream	7 608	40	2.5	72	418	317.2	22.3	209	2 558	697.9	58.7
Watertown	0	0	0.0	32	583	182.9	19.1	222	3 738	905.9	79.7
White Plains	14 338	111	7.2	111	1 426	3 327.6	109.3	471	8 610	2 004.6	221.0

1. Merchant wholesalers except manufacturers' sales branches and offices. 2. Establishments with payroll.

City	Real estate and rental and leasing, 2007: Number of establishments	Real estate: Number of employees	Real estate: Receipts (mil dol)	Real estate: Annual payroll (mil dol)	Professional, scientific, and technical services,[1] 2007: Number of establishments	Professional: Number of employees	Professional: Receipts (mil dol)	Professional: Annual payroll (mil dol)	Manufacturing, 2007: Number of establishments	Manufacturing: Number of employees	Manufacturing: Receipts (mil dol)	Manufacturing: Annual payroll (mil dol)
	80	81	82	83	84	85	86	87	88	89	90	91
NEW JERSEY—Cont'd												
Garfield	13	63	9.2	1.5	29	194	11.7	4.1	71	1 136	205.2	46.8
Hackensack	143	727	203.5	35.2	475	2 896	528.2	210.3	105	1 503	269.3	64.0
Hoboken	106	673	136.9	26.9	210	1 310	307.2	96.0	NA	NA	NA	NA
Jersey City	241	1 328	543.9	48.4	534	D	D	D	105	2 649	745.3	97.2
Kearny	43	368	103.6	19.2	58	213	27.7	8.1	62	1 850	552.9	82.0
Linden	41	295	46.0	8.7	57	914	88.3	58.2	112	3 886	D	236.8
Long Branch	30	79	21.1	2.2	49	D	D	D	NA	NA	NA	NA
Millville	18	78	10.9	2.0	49	264	29.4	8.7	48	3 201	829.8	122.5
Newark	222	2 181	533.1	76.1	413	8 444	1 706.2	660.1	309	9 590	3 209.2	413.2
New Brunswick	41	201	61.2	8.9	153	D	D	D	59	1 726	518.5	81.0
Paramus	65	609	355.3	36.9	227	D	D	D	NA	NA	NA	NA
Passaic	61	217	42.8	5.6	55	212	25.0	8.5	119	1 886	313.7	61.3
Paterson	73	353	63.4	11.0	101	517	53.2	18.0	278	5 473	1 153.7	226.4
Perth Amboy	29	109	34.2	4.4	45	D	D	D	49	2 139	938.5	87.4
Plainfield	30	95	24.9	2.4	44	220	22.0	10.7	23	600	82.0	20.7
Rahway	21	174	22.9	9.4	28	299	27.6	13.8	37	4 650	D	D
Sayreville	21	111	25.8	3.7	103	640	82.1	40.7	44	1 867	1 093.5	106.9
Trenton	50	352	51.9	10.9	117	D	D	D	67	1 609	333.8	68.7
Union City	67	178	27.3	4.1	87	270	28.8	8.9	55	505	77.2	14.1
Vineland	79	332	60.9	11.1	125	705	68.3	27.7	90	4 456	1 149.4	156.4
Westfield	33	117	50.8	4.7	170	1 160	215.4	82.2	NA	NA	NA	NA
West New York	69	690	171.2	25.4	67	174	26.1	8.2	NA	NA	NA	NA
NEW MEXICO	2 525	11 678	1 954.7	355.6	4 789	43 001	5 975.8	2 516.7	1 574	35 409	17 122.7	1 560.5
Alamogordo	50	224	23.5	3.7	55	264	16.4	6.6	NA	NA	NA	NA
Albuquerque	886	4 949	848.5	144.4	2 023	D	D	D	559	14 761	3 779.2	653.3
Carlsbad	24	149	15.6	4.2	44	D	D	D	NA	NA	NA	NA
Clovis	48	D	D	D	65	320	22.4	8.6	NA	NA	NA	NA
Farmington	88	686	168.5	37.2	173	D	D	D	50	660	74.6	22.1
Hobbs	44	397	100.5	23.3	50	418	46.8	21.2	NA	NA	NA	NA
Las Cruces	175	789	116.6	17.8	239	D	D	D	69	747	262.4	23.1
Rio Rancho	49	183	27.7	4.4	95	503	47.0	19.1	29	5 323	D	307.4
Roswell	78	240	35.7	6.2	97	745	102.6	33.4	30	520	D	15.3
Santa Fe	241	934	183.5	36.3	547	D	D	D	117	736	106.4	26.6
NEW YORK	32 588	171 601	49 867.2	7 941.7	58 087	539 635	112 045.6	41 604.5	18 629	533 835	162 720.2	24 268.0
Albany	164	1 181	249.5	32.7	434	D	D	D	71	1 791	544.3	76.7
Auburn	44	148	23.8	3.3	64	446	32.8	14.7	56	2 151	789.1	100.0
Binghamton	59	378	34.9	8.3	141	D	D	D	63	2 080	589.3	64.3
Buffalo	253	1 884	281.4	48.4	655	D	D	D	360	12 848	4 499.8	614.4
Elmira	38	212	39.1	5.6	55	D	D	D	27	2 156	403.0	86.0
Freeport	46	164	25.7	5.7	114	344	49.7	16.3	90	2 505	569.2	109.9
Glen Cove	29	101	19.9	3.7	88	367	56.3	17.4	NA	NA	NA	NA
Harrison	98	642	117.5	33.6	184	D	D	D	NA	NA	NA	NA
Hempstead	68	341	50.3	10.8	94	D	D	D	NA	NA	NA	NA
Ithaca	51	339	60.0	8.1	121	D	D	D	38	1 462	D	62.1
Jamestown	27	109	14.0	2.3	73	D	D	D	61	1 872	262.4	71.1
Lindenhurst	15	31	3.6	0.9	62	D	D	D	51	530	93.2	21.5
Long Beach	54	163	43.9	5.4	93	200	25.1	8.1	NA	NA	NA	NA
Middletown	31	100	22.4	2.4	64	342	31.8	13.4	36	1 005	198.2	38.2
Mount Vernon	172	511	102.3	17.3	99	319	53.7	12.2	112	2 784	548.7	115.6
Newburgh	47	176	17.3	4.6	62	D	D	D	43	753	122.4	25.3
New Rochelle	165	556	123.2	22.4	252	1 843	112.0	42.0	57	896	182.4	38.5
New York	18 972	106 396	36 279.1	5 588.3	24 909	300 564	76 850.6	27 940.7	6 626	101 310	20 411.6	3 818.4
Niagara Falls	37	248	27.3	6.9	93	D	D	D	51	1 877	1 073.3	114.9
North Tonawanda	11	30	2.6	0.6	41	283	15.5	6.9	58	1 468	416.2	60.5
Ossining	29	129	23.5	3.0	62	574	54.1	29.4	NA	NA	NA	NA
Port Chester	39	D	D	D	69	204	29.6	8.5	34	1 085	148.8	41.9
Poughkeepsie	83	412	71.9	11.3	143	D	D	D	39	6 649	D	D
Rochester	257	1 792	249.3	55.8	679	D	D	D	463	29 362	9 084.3	1 317.6
Rome	44	183	31.8	4.4	71	D	D	D	40	1 377	754.7	63.3
Saratoga Springs	42	244	50.1	7.0	156	D	D	D	24	1 696	540.3	75.4
Schenectady	57	281	35.1	8.3	142	1 173	140.5	65.5	60	2 171	1 096.5	112.7
Spring Valley	50	135	27.5	3.6	45	119	12.6	3.9	NA	NA	NA	NA
Syracuse	260	1 523	294.1	62.3	487	D	D	D	131	5 249	1 558.7	270.4
Troy	39	220	30.5	4.7	116	D	D	D	38	729	103.6	26.8
Utica	71	268	38.7	5.1	137	D	D	D	83	2 200	543.0	83.5
Valley Stream	59	202	45.2	7.6	151	962	99.5	39.4	NA	NA	NA	NA
Watertown	54	268	50.3	6.3	56	468	45.4	18.5	24	1 218	393.0	56.7
White Plains	198	1 206	425.2	71.3	676	D	D	D	NA	NA	NA	NA

1. Establishments subject to federal tax.

Table D. Cities — **Accommodation and Food Services, Arts, Entertainment, and Recreation, and Health Care and Social Assistance**

City	Accommodation and food services, 2007				Arts, entertainment, and recreation,[1] 2007				Health care and social assistance,[1] 2007			
	Number of establish-ments	Number of employees	Sales (mil dol)	Annual payroll (mil dol)	Number of establish-ments	Number of employees	Receipts (mil dol)	Annual payroll (mil dol)	Number of establish-ments	Number of employees	Receipts (mil dol)	Annual payroll (mil dol)
	92	93	94	95	96	97	98	99	100	101	102	103
NEW JERSEY—Cont'd												
Garfield	51	345	22.9	5.7	4	D	D	D	29	D	D	D
Hackensack	120	2 033	134.7	38.3	13	229	13.5	4.7	317	D	D	D
Hoboken	200	1 894	121.9	31.2	21	D	D	D	98	D	D	D
Jersey City	433	4 265	324.8	75.4	38	D	D	D	404	4 546	371.8	145.0
Kearny	67	538	34.8	9.1	3	D	D	D	71	523	52.7	17.7
Linden	98	793	45.6	11.5	6	62	3.6	1.0	65	956	66.8	28.2
Long Branch	96	D	D	D	6	D	D	D	93	D	D	D
Millville	59	691	32.0	8.7	2	D	D	D	55	761	53.5	24.0
Newark	542	6 939	552.6	135.8	25	344	118.4	85.5	289	3 577	376.9	138.4
New Brunswick	152	1 992	114.7	36.1	6	D	D	D	77	787	93.7	40.6
Paramus	122	2 686	151.5	41.4	16	D	D	D	199	2 216	253.3	89.2
Passaic	88	D	D	D	8	D	D	D	91	D	D	D
Paterson	198	D	D	D	5	D	D	D	147	1 298	137.4	58.6
Perth Amboy	97	512	32.5	7.3	4	14	1.0	0.3	68	D	D	D
Plainfield	70	595	29.6	8.0	4	D	D	D	68	790	70.3	29.5
Rahway	66	592	32.6	8.2	3	72	4.0	1.1	42	D	D	D
Sayreville	86	811	40.0	11.0	13	283	18.3	4.4	55	531	47.3	18.0
Trenton	157	1 107	66.2	16.7	3	D	D	D	104	1 367	150.2	69.1
Union City	130	910	47.7	11.1	4	27	2.9	0.6	152	1 766	102.4	45.1
Vineland	124	1 769	88.9	22.2	11	76	7.8	2.0	156	2 111	245.5	94.8
Westfield	64	719	42.1	11.5	12	205	7.4	2.8	154	1 599	174.2	74.3
West New York	84	D	D	D	7	22	1.8	0.7	96	D	D	D
NEW MEXICO	4 090	80 415	3 734.3	1 054.8	516	12 527	1 335.5	258.5	3 713	57 423	4 854.5	1 958.2
Alamogordo	79	1 293	48.5	13.6	6	D	D	D	75	D	D	D
Albuquerque	1 222	28 156	1 321.6	386.8	148	2 889	468.1	49.9	1 296	21 688	2 043.3	846.3
Carlsbad	73	1 081	51.3	13.1	4	D	D	D	60	1 145	137.7	47.7
Clovis	82	1 925	68.0	17.7	7	D	D	D	79	D	D	D
Farmington	126	3 003	127.8	33.9	9	D	D	D	192	D	D	D
Hobbs	80	1 493	69.1	16.8	9	D	D	D	72	D	D	D
Las Cruces	247	5 276	211.6	57.6	13	D	D	D	361	7 504	637.2	249.4
Rio Rancho	75	1 582	62.9	18.4	14	326	9.9	3.8	93	D	D	D
Roswell	108	2 235	88.9	24.3	2	D	D	D	138	D	D	D
Santa Fe	333	7 985	480.8	144.0	60	282	26.3	8.6	367	3 684	374.4	152.8
NEW YORK	43 791	591 653	39 813.5	10 956.3	9 289	101 381	15 566.1	4 656.2	41 201	459 964	46 577.9	18 427.7
Albany	413	5 321	309.7	76.8	26	811	14.3	5.3	241	3 540	468.7	175.5
Auburn	93	1 392	53.0	13.0	12	D	D	D	115	1 259	101.5	43.0
Binghamton	146	2 387	104.7	27.9	12	122	9.5	2.3	108	1 295	152.1	59.2
Buffalo	600	9 962	414.7	121.0	42	578	114.2	63.3	403	6 236	565.7	263.0
Elmira	66	955	33.3	9.5	4	104	2.2	0.8	82	849	103.7	41.3
Freeport	80	591	38.9	10.1	19	111	18.1	3.4	98	D	D	D
Glen Cove	72	660	36.5	12.1	16	D	D	D	110	D	D	D
Harrison	72	977	88.1	23.4	20	D	D	D	52	D	D	D
Hempstead	94	802	53.3	14.3	4	D	D	D	118	1 756	177.3	63.6
Ithaca	194	2 448	118.8	35.7	13	76	4.9	1.2	63	650	50.6	19.1
Jamestown	74	854	31.4	9.2	9	D	D	D	81	D	D	D
Lindenhurst	64	721	37.2	9.5	7	48	2.2	0.5	35	D	D	D
Long Beach	82	733	39.1	9.5	16	153	10.1	3.5	111	1 050	128.4	43.2
Middletown	88	1 654	77.3	22.0	5	D	D	D	83	974	116.1	63.5
Mount Vernon	97	649	40.8	10.4	14	D	D	D	115	1 524	85.8	36.7
Newburgh	90	1 042	54.0	15.3	9	D	D	D	86	738	77.4	30.4
New Rochelle	156	1 997	132.3	36.1	41	D	D	D	252	1 940	236.9	83.9
New York	17 494	249 519	22 095.1	6 009.6	4 574	49 339	10 570.7	3 162.4	16 239	185 098	18 567.4	7 309.4
Niagara Falls	154	5 174	520.9	110.8	12	D	D	D	82	980	62.7	27.5
North Tonawanda	56	624	24.6	6.6	9	22	2.9	0.5	52	398	27.2	11.4
Ossining	42	427	21.7	8.1	6	D	D	D	44	309	25.3	10.2
Port Chester	86	757	55.0	14.2	8	D	D	D	41	397	46.3	17.6
Poughkeepsie	104	1 518	81.7	22.6	9	174	8.3	2.3	118	1 886	233.4	105.3
Rochester	529	6 870	324.0	90.5	61	1 005	49.0	16.4	281	4 375	402.6	170.2
Rome	81	942	39.5	11.5	10	58	2.4	1.0	88	1 219	84.1	34.8
Saratoga Springs	163	2 358	131.5	40.5	28	D	D	D	102	1 081	113.0	41.7
Schenectady	156	1 452	72.5	18.9	11	D	D	D	155	1 652	163.2	72.0
Spring Valley	41	186	15.3	3.4	1	D	D	D	38	381	32.1	10.3
Syracuse	392	5 488	251.0	75.8	22	143	11.3	3.0	328	4 611	592.5	230.9
Troy	120	1 535	66.8	18.6	9	69	5.4	1.4	124	1 487	158.9	67.7
Utica	140	1 875	85.9	24.8	9	48	2.9	0.6	160	1 647	193.7	73.3
Valley Stream	76	923	48.7	12.7	20	D	D	D	121	D	D	D
Watertown	111	2 076	97.3	27.0	11	48	2.9	0.8	102	1 263	123.2	59.3
White Plains	194	2 668	177.9	50.8	23	465	26.9	9.1	362	5 152	566.8	266.4

1. Establishments subject to federal tax.

City	Other services[1], 2007				Government employment and payroll, 2012								
						March payroll							
							Percent of total for:						
	Number of establish-ments	Number of employees	Receipts (mil dol)	Annual payroll (mil dol)	Full-time equivalent employees	Total (dollars)	Adminis-tration, judicial, and legal	Police and Corrections	Fire Protection	Highways and trans-portation	Health and welfare	Natural resources and utilities	Education and libraries
	104	105	106	107	108	109	110	111	112	113	114	115	116
NEW JERSEY—Cont'd													
Garfield	63	D	D	D	172	1 065 564	10.9	55.4	1.4	9.0	14.1	5.5	3.1
Hackensack	129	749	63.5	20.2	540	2 983 931	6.1	38.2	33.3	3.4	8.9	5.9	3.9
Hoboken	105	D	D	D	712	4 180 854	7.4	42.5	22.9	2.8	7.1	10.6	3.1
Jersey City	341	1 286	119.1	30.3	2 936	18 762 329	8.1	43.6	27.3	3.2	7.6	6.7	2.0
Kearny	69	D	D	D	326	2 506 387	6.0	43.9	30.5	0.2	2.6	7.9	1.8
Linden	105	529	50.3	17.0	585	3 237 694	11.7	49.9	25.1	3.6	5.9	2.5	0.8
Long Branch	60	238	19.0	5.6	338	2 021 115	9.6	41.0	10.8	0.7	12.9	21.3	3.7
Millville	35	163	12.3	3.8	210	1 102 759	14.1	44.9	6.7	4.0	8.6	14.2	0.0
Newark	476	3 232	346.3	112.8	3 857	25 580 741	14.8	36.1	19.3	0.6	13.6	10.8	2.2
New Brunswick	72	305	25.7	8.5	1 983	11 480 514	2.4	14.2	6.5	0.7	1.8	3.7	67.3
Paramus	66	525	45.6	15.8	293	1 879 108	9.0	31.6	18.6	10.8	1.2	13.4	8.4
Passaic	94	346	26.4	8.5	563	3 095 395	9.0	45.4	25.9	6.9	9.0	1.7	2.3
Paterson	193	1 211	100.1	30.8	1 472	8 450 610	6.5	42.6	30.2	1.1	8.2	5.3	1.6
Perth Amboy	85	D	D	D	401	2 317 835	10.2	44.0	15.6	5.1	10.9	6.6	1.8
Plainfield	75	269	22.3	6.8	551	3 548 125	11.6	36.0	23.0	0.9	9.8	7.5	2.9
Rahway	45	232	22.0	7.0	277	1 741 702	7.4	40.4	21.7	9.0	8.1	6.9	4.4
Sayreville	82	D	D	D	240	1 549 628	10.5	59.2	0.8	2.5	2.2	9.8	4.9
Trenton	92	286	26.5	7.5	2 747	16 968 078	3.1	14.5	9.4	0.5	3.5	5.2	60.7
Union City	94	253	18.0	4.6	2 174	11 223 072	2.5	14.9	0.8	0.1	2.4	3.3	73.7
Vineland	137	636	47.0	14.3	718	3 828 158	13.3	30.7	5.0	1.6	10.8	34.6	2.3
Westfield	76	427	39.0	12.4	238	1 357 302	9.1	33.5	21.3	15.6	9.8	5.2	5.0
West New York	80	D	D	D	1 416	9 134 998	2.4	10.3	4.4	1.4	1.5	0.3	79.2
NEW MEXICO	2 202	13 461	1 108.3	324.9	X	X	X	X	X	X	X	X	X
Alamogordo	42	D	D	D	280	741 098	18.0	39.9	1.3	4.0	10.8	22.4	3.5
Albuquerque	739	5 676	410.1	138.9	6 438	33 331 138	10.6	29.5	14.1	15.4	8.8	17.0	1.5
Carlsbad	39	212	17.3	4.7	381	1 625 310	11.0	22.8	19.6	11.1	0.7	23.8	1.9
Clovis	58	D	D	D	383	1 169 467	11.4	25.1	25.2	9.8	5.3	18.8	2.8
Farmington	101	838	115.1	22.8	882	3 555 193	11.2	22.9	12.7	4.9	2.4	35.0	4.8
Hobbs	61	D	D	D	403	1 643 293	10.3	27.3	18.4	9.1	3.7	22.7	2.5
Las Cruces	127	767	45.9	14.6	1 337	4 708 150	16.1	21.4	12.0	10.4	4.2	18.4	1.9
Rio Rancho	56	350	30.6	8.3	606	2 382 289	13.5	29.4	20.0	10.8	8.8	12.6	4.3
Roswell	52	D	D	D	548	1 751 942	8.5	26.4	20.7	10.4	1.6	25.5	3.2
Santa Fe	175	891	67.8	21.5	1 540	6 258 370	13.8	15.1	12.9	7.7	6.4	28.1	2.3
NEW YORK	32 231	155 249	13 318.0	3 874.0	X	X	X	X	X	X	X	X	X
Albany	132	778	60.6	18.7	1 455	6 784 879	6.9	38.4	23.1	4.0	10.7	16.1	0.0
Auburn	56	255	19.8	5.2	306	1 503 241	6.8	27.5	30.2	4.3	6.2	19.5	0.0
Binghamton	78	469	33.8	11.3	581	2 791 570	8.2	32.5	25.6	1.7	4.0	21.6	0.0
Buffalo	307	1 649	144.2	43.6	8 627	45 770 501	2.5	13.0	9.3	1.2	2.8	5.8	63.6
Elmira	32	211	14.8	4.3	297	1 470 047	6.0	34.4	27.9	5.6	6.2	16.6	0.0
Freeport	107	349	34.3	8.7	414	2 410 577	14.5	41.4	0.5	2.6	0.9	35.0	0.0
Glen Cove	74	204	16.5	4.2	313	2 051 266	16.9	46.0	2.4	7.0	7.0	17.7	0.0
Harrison	43	D	D	D	272	1 502 544	14.2	43.3	8.0	7.9	2.8	13.9	7.7
Hempstead	92	751	59.3	18.9	437	2 884 577	9.4	54.8	2.8	5.5	2.5	17.0	3.8
Ithaca	42	279	19.7	6.0	454	2 158 827	9.3	24.0	19.7	8.1	0.9	28.6	0.0
Jamestown	38	192	15.5	4.6	658	3 048 026	3.6	13.9	18.8	8.5	1.7	2.6	51.0
Lindenhurst	76	276	26.1	6.6	72	206 485	20.7	0.0	5.1	24.6	6.2	32.4	0.0
Long Beach	54	169	8.9	2.5	484	2 657 473	9.3	32.7	12.4	11.0	4.5	25.8	0.0
Middletown	75	613	118.5	18.5	283	1 449 586	12.4	41.3	15.8	7.3	3.0	20.2	0.0
Mount Vernon	125	697	82.7	22.5	873	4 489 959	6.4	36.3	23.8	1.9	2.2	13.5	2.9
Newburgh	57	232	19.7	5.4	258	1 411 393	6.5	44.1	27.5	10.5	1.6	9.6	0.0
New Rochelle	146	651	56.6	15.0	652	4 204 505	7.5	35.0	29.4	4.5	9.0	14.1	0.0
New York	13 086	60 996	5 070.5	1 503.3	404 260	2 380 283 176	3.2	19.0	5.4	13.7	18.1	4.4	34.0
Niagara Falls	66	285	21.8	6.9	687	3 126 887	0.0	30.2	23.2	0.0	6.6	0.0	0.0
North Tonawanda	60	194	13.1	4.1	281	1 334 637	8.0	28.4	16.0	17.6	0.8	25.8	0.0
Ossining	37	110	9.4	2.8	186	1 201 283	12.6	41.7	0.4	13.3	0.9	24.9	0.0
Port Chester	72	260	33.4	8.6	227	2 070 548	10.9	52.5	7.8	6.0	2.3	13.1	0.0
Poughkeepsie	88	373	28.2	8.2	365	2 055 377	6.9	43.5	19.1	6.3	5.4	15.8	0.0
Rochester	307	1 973	180.9	55.1	9 049	47 150 145	2.7	13.0	6.6	0.8	3.9	4.3	67.0
Rome	48	189	19.1	4.9	373	1 669 365	8.0	27.2	30.1	12.6	4.5	16.3	0.0
Saratoga Springs	41	267	17.5	5.5	349	1 565 062	9.5	32.3	19.4	23.7	4.3	7.4	0.0
Schenectady	96	815	69.2	17.9	637	3 109 293	5.4	38.3	21.7	5.1	10.0	14.6	0.0
Spring Valley	35	89	10.7	2.1	298	901 316	12.0	64.5	0.6	10.1	7.0	0.4	0.0
Syracuse	206	1 374	110.7	34.9	5 644	31 187 441	1.4	12.0	7.9	4.1	2.4	3.2	68.9
Troy	58	284	27.1	7.8	598	3 268 327	9.0	41.8	17.7	4.1	9.7	13.5	0.0
Utica	87	513	33.4	9.7	614	2 894 903	5.7	39.6	26.6	3.3	11.4	9.1	0.0
Valley Stream	123	D	D	D	225	1 128 453	12.8	3.8	0.6	18.2	0.6	37.3	6.6
Watertown	56	330	27.4	7.7	370	1 573 042	9.1	22.3	27.5	9.6	5.8	20.8	2.5
White Plains	141	969	77.4	22.9	1 041	6 536 682	8.4	25.5	18.2	8.2	6.7	11.5	3.6

1. Establishments subject to federal tax.

City	City government finances, 2007									
	General revenue							General expenditure		
		Intergovernmental		Taxes					Per capita[1] (dollars)	
					Per capita[1] (dollars)					
	Total (mil dol)	Total (mil dol)	Percent from state government	Total (mil dol)	Total	Property	Sales and gross receipts	Total (mil dol)	Total	Capital outlays
	117	118	119	120	121	122	123	124	125	126
NEW JERSEY—Cont'd										
Garfield	35.0	4.4	66.3	24.7	798	774	23	30.5	985	29
Hackensack	89.8	9.7	58.1	74.7	1 693	1 640	53	81.7	1 851	0
Hoboken	112.1	26.1	53.1	59.5	1 137	1 071	66	110.1	2 106	65
Jersey City	597.9	170.1	64.9	235.7	918	842	76	580.2	2 260	102
Kearny	76.1	28.2	95.1	41.5	994	966	27	71.6	1 713	127
Linden	93.5	30.9	71.2	55.1	1 345	1 310	36	93.7	2 288	123
Long Branch	71.9	21.4	25.7	37.9	1 241	1 202	40	74.6	2 445	343
Millville	50.7	12.0	68.9	21.9	765	691	74	49.8	1 738	61
Newark	845.2	438.4	36.2	305.9	1 099	784	156	860.7	3 093	368
New Brunswick	273.2	161.6	90.4	60.6	1 087	1 034	52	308.3	5 532	930
Paramus	60.6	4.7	91.3	49.5	1 859	1 738	120	49.8	1 869	77
Passaic	116.8	43.8	42.5	59.3	840	818	22	115.2	1 634	39
Paterson	273.4	94.3	64.3	140.1	959	943	17	265.5	1 818	72
Perth Amboy	99.9	23.5	45.3	58.9	1 136	1 119	17	92.3	1 780	148
Plainfield	100.9	20.9	40.2	54.9	1 089	1 063	26	102.8	2 039	6
Rahway	52.2	8.2	52.9	35.2	1 263	1 210	53	40.3	1 445	119
Sayreville	48.5	12.4	79.2	29.1	663	632	31	48.1	1 097	44
Trenton	505.3	395.0	94.6	79.2	938	887	51	482.0	5 714	70
Union City	355.1	263.5	96.4	81.0	1 184	1 161	23	313.3	4 583	154
Vineland	73.4	16.1	56.5	36.7	602	549	53	67.7	1 110	67
Westfield	37.4	4.0	79.9	29.6	967	909	57	39.3	1 283	88
West New York	209.6	134.4	93.8	51.2	986	966	20	216.0	4 160	249
NEW MEXICO	X	X	X	X	X	X	X	X	X	X
Alamogordo	41.0	11.2	83.4	17.7	560	107	454	39.0	1 236	363
Albuquerque	951.2	282.5	80.4	367.8	663	244	419	827.4	1 491	292
Carlsbad	58.1	6.7	35.3	37.8	1 412	97	1 316	48.5	1 811	487
Clovis	56.3	14.0	34.5	27.9	706	44	662	57.5	1 457	483
Farmington	92.1	35.8	11.0	27.5	600	38	562	99.0	2 161	207
Hobbs	89.8	35.4	93.8	38.4	1 098	56	1 042	69.8	1 994	1 088
Las Cruces	182.5	39.2	26.8	96.3	953	139	815	144.3	1 429	190
Rio Rancho	95.2	13.7	34.9	54.3	599	175	424	87.0	959	166
Roswell	55.1	34.8	96.0	9.3	192	110	82	56.9	1 173	255
Santa Fe	162.5	78.1	73.2	35.9	518	123	395	178.9	2 584	479
NEW YORK	X	X	X	X	X	X	X	X	X	X
Albany	252.8	90.3	28.3	61.5	625	548	77	277.7	2 820	454
Auburn	42.1	14.9	40.5	12.2	447	408	39	47.1	1 722	251
Binghamton	80.6	30.7	45.7	35.7	765	729	37	75.4	1 615	190
Buffalo	1 438.1	1 151.5	83.0	149.0	573	504	69	1 532.1	5 896	790
Elmira	41.8	23.4	53.0	11.6	398	367	31	41.7	1 427	358
Freeport	62.3	3.3	46.3	42.5	985	940	44	67.6	1 566	34
Glen Cove	53.4	17.4	54.0	30.6	1 125	1 054	71	56.1	2 063	478
Harrison	13.5	1.5	60.8	10.7	385	338	47	12.1	434	112
Hempstead	71.2	3.7	54.3	55.6	1 013	971	42	80.4	1 463	51
Ithaca	58.8	12.2	65.1	33.1	1 088	633	455	57.2	1 881	235
Jamestown	70.2	29.9	76.1	15.0	487	459	28	77.7	2 528	164
Lindenhurst	11.6	1.7	75.6	7.0	257	207	50	11.3	413	55
Long Beach	66.7	9.4	52.8	33.6	1 002	859	144	74.0	2 210	91
Middletown	41.5	13.3	24.7	19.0	681	633	47	38.9	1 397	51
Mount Vernon	96.7	15.2	70.5	70.8	1 042	724	319	104.4	1 537	169
Newburgh	57.5	23.9	52.4	21.2	742	667	74	56.9	1 989	235
New Rochelle	134.5	29.2	42.3	80.1	1 022	628	394	133.3	1 700	146
New York	85 078.0	30 398.8	83.5	42 476.1	5 077	2 176	970	81 160.8	9 701	1 196
Niagara Falls	98.1	50.3	53.9	40.9	824	581	243	127.6	2 570	657
North Tonawanda	43.9	17.1	37.3	18.6	596	510	86	41.6	1 330	104
Ossining	33.4	8.9	10.1	20.3	805	760	45	37.3	1 479	39
Port Chester	36.3	5.3	14.4	23.6	808	753	54	37.3	1 275	86
Poughkeepsie	58.3	29.4	22.7	19.2	624	566	58	54.6	1 777	206
Rochester	1 215.0	931.5	73.2	180.9	859	798	61	1 222.9	5 805	517
Rome	49.4	15.0	77.6	25.0	760	462	298	50.7	1 538	140
Saratoga Springs	48.9	5.5	67.4	32.2	1 193	719	474	43.3	1 605	81
Schenectady	89.2	31.5	44.8	29.9	453	405	48	98.0	1 484	180
Spring Valley	34.8	11.4	13.6	21.9	684	651	33	34.7	1 083	29
Syracuse	822.4	598.0	72.4	96.4	668	613	55	858.4	5 950	640
Troy	90.3	48.5	30.6	21.6	433	387	47	91.3	1 830	238
Utica	93.1	41.6	48.0	37.0	597	363	234	94.1	1 521	162
Valley Stream	33.6	2.5	57.9	27.0	716	656	60	37.3	987	118
Watertown	42.6	26.8	23.3	8.9	316	265	50	49.0	1 746	140
White Plains	165.8	12.3	50.2	108.8	1 897	862	1 035	178.6	3 112	124

1. Based on population estimated as of July 1 of the year shown.

City	City government finances, 2012 (cont.)									
	General expenditure (cont.)									
	Percent of total for:									
	Public welfare	Highways	Parking facilities	Education	Health and hospitals	Police protection	Sewerage and sanitation	Parks and recreation	Housing and community development	Interest on debt
	127	128	129	130	131	132	133	134	135	136
NEW JERSEY—Cont'd										
Garfield	0.0	4.9	0.0	0.0	1.2	28.2	11.9	2.8	13.2	2.5
Hackensack	0.3	1.3	0.4	0.0	1.2	17.9	12.8	1.5	6.5	1.4
Hoboken	0.0	2.5	7.0	0.0	0.5	13.9	4.0	1.6	15.2	3.1
Jersey City	0.0	2.1	1.3	0.0	2.2	16.2	14.1	1.4	13.6	4.6
Kearny	0.0	7.5	0.1	0.0	1.0	20.6	13.2	0.8	0.0	3.6
Linden	0.8	2.4	0.6	0.0	0.9	15.3	6.7	2.6	6.2	1.7
Long Branch	0.0	2.4	0.0	0.0	1.1	15.9	20.9	1.9	20.8	3.0
Millville	0.0	2.0	0.0	0.0	0.0	13.2	16.0	1.1	16.4	2.3
Newark	0.3	0.7	0.4	0.2	4.3	15.3	9.7	2.5	24.4	3.2
New Brunswick	0.0	1.0	16.5	54.0	0.2	6.3	3.2	1.5	2.1	2.1
Paramus	0.1	3.7	0.0	0.0	3.0	23.8	11.3	5.3	0.0	2.7
Passaic	0.0	2.5	0.6	0.0	2.3	17.6	7.6	3.5	20.1	0.7
Paterson	0.0	3.0	1.9	0.0	4.0	17.4	9.1	2.0	10.5	1.2
Perth Amboy	0.1	2.3	0.6	0.0	0.6	15.2	8.7	1.9	19.0	3.0
Plainfield	0.0	6.3	0.0	0.0	0.6	15.9	18.4	1.4	13.0	1.7
Rahway	0.0	12.8	2.0	0.0	0.8	23.3	11.5	1.3	12.1	2.9
Sayreville	0.0	4.9	0.0	0.0	0.6	24.7	13.2	3.4	5.0	3.8
Trenton	0.0	0.8	0.8	58.2	0.5	6.3	3.8	0.3	4.5	2.6
Union City	0.0	2.3	0.7	64.8	0.6	6.4	1.9	0.7	4.1	0.9
Vineland	0.0	5.5	0.0	0.0	6.5	25.3	10.8	1.0	11.4	1.3
Westfield	0.0	5.2	0.5	0.0	2.2	16.1	8.8	2.6	0.0	1.6
West New York	0.0	1.4	0.6	65.2	0.6	5.6	1.5	0.6	5.1	1.0
NEW MEXICO	X	X	X	X	X	X	X	X	X	X
Alamogordo	3.1	26.7	0.0	0.0	0.0	16.5	10.5	11.1	3.1	3.2
Albuquerque	3.0	8.8	0.6	0.0	3.4	19.6	11.0	13.3	4.4	3.2
Carlsbad	0.0	11.5	0.0	0.0	1.6	17.0	21.2	11.8	0.0	0.8
Clovis	0.0	8.5	0.0	0.0	0.2	12.6	18.1	12.9	5.5	1.0
Farmington	0.0	12.8	0.0	0.0	1.2	15.7	9.6	13.8	1.3	0.6
Hobbs	0.0	29.3	0.0	0.0	1.5	6.2	12.9	10.4	0.0	0.0
Las Cruces	0.0	12.7	0.0	0.0	0.2	17.7	14.3	7.1	8.6	3.4
Rio Rancho	0.5	17.8	0.0	1.7	0.0	19.1	15.5	6.6	0.4	4.5
Roswell	0.0	8.7	0.0	0.0	0.0	19.1	9.7	11.3	0.0	1.5
Santa Fe	2.8	5.9	2.5	0.0	1.6	12.5	12.4	13.0	6.7	6.9
NEW YORK	X	X	X	X	X	X	X	X	X	X
Albany	0.0	5.6	0.0	0.0	0.2	17.8	5.3	1.6	23.5	17.5
Auburn	0.0	13.1	0.7	0.0	0.1	17.6	14.0	3.7	9.5	4.2
Binghamton	0.0	7.1	1.1	0.0	0.2	14.2	12.9	3.0	6.5	4.6
Buffalo	0.0	2.4	0.1	58.2	0.1	5.2	5.6	0.8	7.1	2.0
Elmira	0.0	21.6	0.6	0.0	0.5	16.9	2.2	3.1	4.9	2.6
Freeport	0.0	3.4	0.1	0.0	0.0	22.9	5.8	6.0	1.8	4.8
Glen Cove	0.0	9.1	0.0	0.0	0.6	22.5	4.1	13.1	9.0	6.4
Harrison	0.0	7.9	0.0	0.0	0.0	4.4	33.2	0.4	0.0	15.8
Hempstead	0.0	2.8	0.3	0.0	0.0	25.2	3.6	3.9	1.3	2.5
Ithaca	0.0	9.6	2.5	0.0	0.1	13.5	10.9	10.1	0.0	4.4
Jamestown	0.0	6.4	0.1	44.5	0.1	7.1	9.8	2.5	0.0	1.1
Lindenhurst	0.0	23.9	0.2	0.0	0.0	0.7	5.7	10.7	1.3	4.1
Long Beach	0.0	0.4	0.0	0.0	0.0	16.1	15.3	10.1	0.0	2.7
Middletown	0.0	5.3	0.0	0.0	0.0	19.0	11.9	6.4	5.3	3.9
Mount Vernon	0.0	2.6	0.1	0.0	0.4	19.2	7.2	5.0	2.7	3.0
Newburgh	0.0	3.7	0.2	0.0	0.1	24.8	13.6	2.8	1.7	4.8
New Rochelle	0.0	5.4	1.6	0.0	0.3	22.3	5.0	4.2	10.9	6.0
New York	15.7	1.8	0.1	27.7	10.4	6.2	5.6	1.3	5.8	5.3
Niagara Falls	0.0	16.1	0.0	0.0	0.1	14.7	2.8	4.1	5.6	2.1
North Tonawanda	0.0	12.9	0.0	0.0	0.1	13.1	15.2	4.4	0.0	1.2
Ossining	0.0	7.2	0.1	0.0	0.3	20.5	6.4	6.1	8.8	5.0
Port Chester	0.0	4.5	0.2	0.0	0.7	20.4	7.3	4.6	1.8	9.9
Poughkeepsie	0.0	9.9	0.9	0.0	0.2	23.5	8.9	1.2	1.5	3.8
Rochester	0.0	1.8	0.6	55.2	0.1	6.7	2.7	1.4	7.0	0.4
Rome	0.0	13.1	0.6	0.0	0.1	12.0	8.8	4.1	5.0	4.1
Saratoga Springs	0.0	10.1	0.2	0.0	0.1	23.1	9.2	8.2	0.6	3.2
Schenectady	0.0	7.4	0.7	0.0	0.1	16.3	15.5	2.0	4.8	6.5
Spring Valley	0.0	3.7	0.1	0.0	0.1	24.6	0.3	1.4	24.9	4.1
Syracuse	0.0	4.0	0.0	53.9	0.1	5.2	1.8	0.9	7.1	6.5
Troy	0.0	7.6	0.0	0.0	0.2	18.6	6.2	3.0	21.6	5.7
Utica	0.0	8.1	0.5	0.0	0.8	16.1	5.0	3.3	19.4	5.5
Valley Stream	0.0	15.7	0.7	0.0	0.4	0.6	12.9	12.6	0.0	5.6
Watertown	0.0	10.7	0.1	0.0	0.0	15.9	10.4	3.1	0.9	3.8
White Plains	0.0	8.2	7.1	0.0	0.0	18.6	5.2	4.4	3.7	1.8

City	City government finances, 2012 (cont.)			Climate[2]						
	Debt outstanding			Average daily temperature (degrees Fahrenheit)						
				Mean		Limits				
	Total (mil dol)	Per capita[1] (dollars)	Debt issued during year	January	July	January[3]	July[4]	Annual precipitation (inches)	Heating degree days	Cooling degree days
	137	138	139	140	141	142	143	144	145	146
NEW JERSEY—Cont'd										
Garfield	21.5	693	2.6	28.6	75.0	19.5	85.5	51.50	5 522	824
Hackensack	36.0	817	0.0	28.6	75.0	19.5	85.5	51.50	5 522	824
Hoboken	101.0	1 932	0.0	29.6	75.3	22.7	82.5	46.33	5 367	882
Jersey City	847.1	3 300	36.1	29.6	75.3	22.7	82.5	46.33	5 367	882
Kearny	83.3	1 995	9.1	31.3	77.2	24.4	85.2	46.25	4 843	1 220
Linden	46.6	1 137	15.0	28.5	74.0	18.2	85.8	51.61	5 595	757
Long Branch	70.9	2 322	0.0	31.7	74.1	22.8	82.6	48.63	5 168	750
Millville	39.9	1 390	9.2	32.7	76.3	24.1	85.9	43.20	4 835	1 009
Newark	658.6	2 366	2.2	31.3	77.2	24.4	85.2	46.25	4 843	1 220
New Brunswick	406.3	7 289	53.2	29.7	74.8	21.1	85.4	48.78	5 346	816
Paramus	39.3	1 477	0.0	28.6	75.0	19.5	85.5	51.50	5 522	824
Passaic	18.9	269	0.0	28.6	75.0	19.5	85.5	51.50	5 522	824
Paterson	119.6	819	5.1	28.6	75.0	19.5	85.5	51.50	5 522	824
Perth Amboy	91.3	1 761	13.7	29.7	74.8	21.1	85.4	48.78	5 346	816
Plainfield	48.0	952	0.1	30.0	74.9	21.5	86.6	49.63	5 266	854
Rahway	64.7	2 321	0.0	29.6	74.5	19.8	85.7	50.94	5 450	787
Sayreville	53.0	1 208	6.3	29.7	74.8	21.1	85.4	48.78	5 346	816
Trenton	390.2	4 626	34.2	30.4	75.2	21.3	86.9	48.83	5 262	903
Union City	82.9	1 213	0.0	29.6	75.3	22.7	82.5	46.33	5 367	882
Vineland	133.2	2 183	0.0	26.7	70.4	16.8	81.7	53.28	6 281	438
Westfield	20.7	675	0.0	30.0	74.9	21.5	86.6	49.63	5 266	854
West New York	52.4	1 010	0.0	29.6	75.3	22.7	82.5	46.33	5 367	882
NEW MEXICO	X	X	X	X	X	X	X	X	X	X
Alamogordo	58.7	1 859	25.6	42.2	79.7	28.9	93.0	13.20	31	1 715
Albuquerque	2 091.8	3 769	165.1	35.7	78.5	23.8	92.3	9.47	4 281	1 290
Carlsbad	40.7	1 520	8.7	42.7	81.7	27.5	95.8	14.15	2 823	2 029
Clovis	25.6	649	13.2	37.9	77.5	25.0	91.0	18.50	3 955	1 305
Farmington	1 802.6	39 348	11.1	29.8	74.9	17.9	90.7	8.39	5 508	805
Hobbs	58.7	1 677	0.0	42.9	80.1	29.1	93.5	18.15	2 849	1 842
Las Cruces	152.7	1 512	18.5	39.0	78.7	21.1	94.9	11.44	3 818	1 364
Rio Rancho	236.5	2 609	12.4	33.8	73.9	19.7	90.0	9.28	4 981	773
Roswell	18.0	371	0.0	40.0	80.8	24.4	94.8	13.34	3 332	1 814
Santa Fe	381.4	5 509	62.7	29.3	69.8	15.5	85.6	14.22	6 073	414
NEW YORK	X	X	X	X	X	X	X	X	X	X
Albany	773.1	7 851	27.8	22.2	71.1	13.3	82.2	38.60	6 860	544
Auburn	52.9	1 933	0.0	23.7	71.2	16.0	81.5	36.98	6 694	528
Binghamton	115.0	2 462	10.4	21.7	68.7	15.0	78.1	38.65	7 237	396
Buffalo	609.4	2 345	116.7	24.5	70.8	17.8	79.6	40.54	6 692	548
Elmira	36.3	1 243	8.5	23.9	70.3	15.0	82.3	34.95	6 806	446
Freeport	138.4	3 205	19.4	30.7	73.8	24.2	81.0	42.97	5 504	779
Glen Cove	81.8	3 010	11.6	31.9	74.2	25.4	82.8	46.36	5 231	839
Harrison	65.6	2 358	21.0	NA	NA	NA	NA	NA	NA	NA
Hempstead	47.9	872	0.0	31.9	74.2	25.4	82.8	46.36	5 231	839
Ithaca	76.9	2 530	0.0	22.6	68.7	13.9	80.1	36.71	7 182	312
Jamestown	36.2	1 179	4.0	22.3	69.2	14.1	80.1	45.68	7 048	389
Lindenhurst	5.9	218	0.0	30.7	73.8	24.2	81.0	42.97	5 504	779
Long Beach	54.6	1 631	2.5	31.8	74.8	24.7	82.9	42.46	4 947	949
Middletown	84.2	3 024	23.7	26.5	73.0	17.5	84.0	44.00	5 820	674
Mount Vernon	56.4	831	0.0	29.7	74.2	20.1	86.0	46.46	5 400	770
Newburgh	100.8	3 527	0.0	26.6	74.3	17.1	84.9	45.79	5 813	790
New Rochelle	141.5	1 805	20.0	29.7	74.2	20.1	86.0	46.46	5 400	770
New York	131 462.0	15 714	16 736.2	32.1	76.5	26.2	84.2	49.69	4 754	1 151
Niagara Falls	72.6	1 461	7.4	24.2	71.4	16.8	81.8	33.93	6 752	508
North Tonawanda	13.9	445	3.3	24.2	71.4	16.8	81.8	33.93	6 752	508
Ossining	25.9	1 027	2.3	NA	NA	NA	NA	NA	NA	NA
Port Chester	50.5	1 727	13.4	28.4	73.8	21.0	82.5	50.45	5 660	716
Poughkeepsie	86.8	2 825	12.4	24.5	71.9	14.7	83.6	44.12	6 438	550
Rochester	496.9	2 359	124.1	23.9	70.7	16.6	81.4	33.98	6 728	576
Rome	46.6	1 415	0.8	20.8	70.2	11.9	81.3	46.27	7 116	416
Saratoga Springs	36.7	1 362	3.4	20.9	71.2	11.6	83.0	43.31	6 904	477
Schenectady	159.7	2 417	13.3	22.2	71.1	13.3	82.2	38.60	6 860	544
Spring Valley	16.9	528	0.2	27.3	73.1	18.2	83.8	51.01	5 809	642
Syracuse	1 117.3	7 744	121.3	22.7	70.9	14.0	81.7	40.05	6 803	551
Troy	99.0	1 985	0.0	22.2	71.1	13.3	82.2	38.60	6 860	544
Utica	95.0	1 535	6.0	22.2	70.5	12.6	83.2	41.90	6 855	441
Valley Stream	28.5	756	3.5	22.2	70.5	12.6	83.2	41.90	6 855	441
Watertown	24.2	862	0.0	18.6	70.2	9.1	79.4	42.57	7 517	421
White Plains	106.6	1 858	45.7	29.7	74.2	20.1	86.0	46.46	5 400	770

1. Based on the population estimated as of July 1 of the year shown. 2. Represents normal values based on the 30-year period, 1971–2000. 3. Average daily minimum.
4. Average daily maximum.

STATE Place code	City	Land area,[1] 2010 (sq km)	Population, 2014			Race alone or in combination (percent), 2011-2013					Percent Hispanic or Latino[2], 2011-2013	Percent foreign born 2011–2013
			Total persons	Rank	Per square kilometer	White	Black	American Indian, Alaska Native	Asian	Hawaiian Pacific Islander		
		1	2	3	4	5	6	7	8	9	10	11
	NEW YORK—Cont'd											
36 84000	Yonkers	46.7	200 667	113	4 296.9	58.4	19.5	0.6	7.0	0.1	36.1	30.4
37 00000	NORTH CAROLINA	125 919.8	9 943 964	X	79.0	71.7	22.7	1.9	2.8	0.1	8.7	7.6
37 01520	Apex	39.8	43 907	844	1 103.2	84.1	10.0	0.4	5.7	NA	8.3	9.8
37 02080	Asheboro	48.0	25 886	1 400	539.3	84.2	12.1	NA	0.6	NA	24.8	14.1
37 02140	Asheville	116.4	87 882	355	755.0	84.0	13.6	0.7	2.7	NA	6.7	6.7
37 09060	Burlington	65.2	51 812	721	794.7	59.3	31.2	1.2	3.2	NA	12.9	8.8
37 10740	Cary	140.8	155 227	160	1 102.5	74.0	8.4	1.2	15.5	NA	8.8	21.1
37 11800	Chapel Hill	54.7	59 376	610	1 085.5	76.1	9.4	0.6	15.4	NA	5.2	16.4
37 12000	Charlotte	771.0	809 958	17	1 050.5	54.2	36.7	1.4	6.0	0.1	13.4	15.3
37 14100	Concord	156.1	85 560	377	548.1	75.8	19.0	0.8	3.2	NA	12.0	9.1
37 19000	Durham	278.1	251 893	81	905.8	50.9	42.1	1.3	5.8	0.2	13.8	14.6
37 22920	Fayetteville	377.7	203 948	109	540.0	51.3	44.1	2.5	4.1	1.0	11.1	5.9
37 25480	Garner	38.2	27 814	1 312	728.1	57.7	38.4	3.7	1.7	NA	5.1	4.1
37 25580	Gastonia	130.8	73 698	459	563.4	64.2	29.0	1.3	1.0	NA	10.9	7.7
37 26880	Goldsboro	72.9	35 947	1 041	493.1	39.1	57.6	0.7	1.6	NA	6.1	5.8
37 28000	Greensboro	327.7	282 586	67	862.3	50.8	43.3	1.0	4.4	0.1	7.4	10.4
37 28080	Greenville	89.6	89 852	346	1 002.8	58.3	38.0	0.6	3.6	NA	4.1	5.1
37 31060	Hickory	76.9	40 143	926	522.0	75.5	15.4	0.8	3.8	NA	13.5	11.5
37 31400	High Point	139.4	108 629	263	779.3	55.8	33.3	1.2	8.5	NA	9.1	11.9
37 33120	Huntersville	102.6	51 567	723	502.6	87.4	10.2	0.9	2.4	0.4	5.9	6.6
37 33560	Indian Trail	56.2	36 360	1 022	647.0	82.6	13.3	0.9	2.5	NA	9.4	7.9
37 34200	Jacksonville	120.5	69 047	497	573.0	68.9	24.7	1.3	4.3	0.5	15.0	4.8
37 35200	Kannapolis	82.7	45 245	823	547.1	71.6	23.5	1.3	2.3	NA	9.6	7.0
37 41960	Matthews	44.3	30 008	1 233	677.4	82.6	12.4	0.5	3.9	NA	5.1	9.5
37 43920	Monroe	77.1	34 331	1 081	445.3	66.4	24.7	0.8	NA	NA	30.5	22.6
37 44220	Mooresville	54.2	35 300	1 057	651.3	84.9	10.2	NA	3.7	NA	6.5	6.8
37 46340	New Bern	73.1	30 291	1 224	414.4	58.3	32.5	1.1	6.7	NA	7.4	9.0
37 55000	Raleigh	370.1	439 896	43	1 188.6	62.1	30.6	0.7	5.1	0.1	11.3	13.1
37 57500	Rocky Mount	113.4	56 325	652	496.7	33.0	64.0	1.3	1.7	NA	4.2	3.6
37 58860	Salisbury	57.4	33 710	1 101	587.3	57.5	38.6	1.8	1.4	NA	9.4	5.0
37 59280	Sanford	69.4	29 116	1 266	419.5	62.3	28.1	1.0	2.2	NA	22.4	14.0
37 67420	Thomasville	43.4	27 002	1 360	622.2	74.4	23.3	1.2	0.9	NA	14.8	8.2
37 70540	Wake Forest	39.1	36 693	1 012	938.4	82.3	15.3	NA	3.3	NA	4.7	6.0
37 74440	Wilmington	133.4	113 657	241	852.0	76.5	20.4	0.6	2.2	NA	5.2	6.5
37 74540	Wilson	74.5	49 395	757	663.0	45.0	48.4	1.4	1.5	0.5	9.3	7.8
37 75000	Winston-Salem	343.0	239 269	87	697.6	60.2	35.3	0.7	2.4	NA	15.5	10.7
38 00000	NORTH DAKOTA	178 711.2	739 482	X	4.1	91.3	1.9	6.5	1.4	0.2	2.5	2.8
38 07200	Bismarck	79.9	68 896	498	862.3	94.0	1.3	4.7	1.2	0.3	1.6	1.7
38 25700	Fargo	126.5	115 863	235	915.9	92.2	4.0	2.4	3.3	0.0	2.9	7.0
38 32060	Grand Forks	51.6	56 057	657	1 086.4	91.6	3.5	4.2	3.1	NA	3.3	4.2
38 53380	Minot	45.1	47 997	782	1 064.2	94.1	3.7	3.7	1.3	NA	3.6	3.2
38 84780	West Fargo	37.4	31 771	1 169	849.5	94.2	3.7	1.4	2.8	NA	0.5	4.4
39 00000	OHIO	105 828.7	11 594 163	X	109.6	84.8	13.6	0.8	2.2	0.1	3.3	4.0
39 01000	Akron	160.7	197 859	118	1 231.2	65.6	33.8	1.3	3.2	0.1	2.2	4.7
39 03828	Barberton	23.4	26 302	1 387	1 124.0	94.3	6.4	0.7	0.5	NA	1.5	3.0
39 04720	Beavercreek	68.4	45 934	813	671.5	90.8	4.1	0.7	6.2	NA	3.2	6.6
39 07972	Bowling Green	32.5	31 591	1 178	972.0	90.3	7.0	0.6	1.8	NA	6.2	5.6
39 09680	Brunswick	33.5	34 604	1 074	1 033.0	98.0	2.1	NA	0.8	NA	2.2	3.7
39 12000	Canton	66.0	72 297	471	1 095.4	76.1	28.5	1.7	0.9	NA	2.5	2.5
39 15000	Cincinnati	201.9	298 165	65	1 476.8	53.5	45.1	0.8	2.4	0.1	2.9	5.4
39 16000	Cleveland	201.2	389 521	48	1 936.0	43.4	53.7	1.1	2.2	0.1	10.5	4.8
39 16014	Cleveland Heights	21.0	45 181	824	2 151.5	51.5	45.4	0.7	5.2	0.1	1.6	7.7
39 18000	Columbus	562.5	835 957	15	1 486.1	64.7	30.3	1.3	5.1	0.2	5.8	11.1
39 19778	Cuyahoga Falls	66.4	49 210	763	741.1	95.6	3.3	0.6	1.9	NA	2.8	3.3
39 21000	Dayton	144.1	141 003	183	978.5	56.4	42.7	0.9	1.7	0.1	3.7	4.0
39 21434	Delaware	49.1	37 372	990	761.1	94.0	5.3	0.9	1.1	NA	1.7	2.7
39 22694	Dublin	63.3	44 214	835	698.5	80.7	1.8	NA	19.0	NA	4.5	16.5
39 25256	Elyria	53.3	53 972	688	1 012.6	82.0	19.0	1.3	1.0	0.7	5.5	1.5
39 25704	Euclid	27.5	47 893	784	1 741.6	41.6	59.0	0.6	1.2	NA	1.3	3.7
39 25914	Fairborn	34.1	33 329	1 118	977.4	86.6	12.0	0.9	4.8	NA	3.3	5.6
39 25970	Fairfield	54.2	42 770	864	789.1	84.8	15.1	1.0	1.5	NA	4.6	7.0
39 27048	Findlay	49.6	41 098	898	828.6	93.9	3.6	0.2	2.7	NA	6.5	3.6
39 29106	Gahanna	32.2	34 257	1 084	1 063.9	83.0	13.8	0.9	3.6	NA	1.5	5.9
39 29428	Garfield Heights	18.7	28 229	1 297	1 509.6	57.9	41.7	0.6	1.2	NA	2.0	3.7
39 31860	Green	83.0	25 917	1 396	312.3	96.3	3.1	1.0	2.0	NA	0.5	3.0
39 32592	Grove City	42.0	38 519	963	917.1	95.7	2.2	NA	2.4	NA	1.8	1.8

1. Dry land or land partially or temporarily covered by water. 2. May be of any race.

City	Age of population (percent), 2011-2013: Under 5 years	5 to 17 years	18 to 24 years	25 to 34 years	35 to 44 years	45 to 54 years	55 to 64 years	65 to 74 years	75 years and over	Median age 2011-2013	Percent female 2011-2013	Population: Census counts: 2000	2010	Percent change: 2000–2010	2010–2014
	12	13	14	15	16	17	18	19	20	21	22	23	24	25	26
NEW YORK—Cont'd															
Yonkers	6.8	15.7	9.2	14.4	13.0	13.9	11.8	8.0	7.2	37.6	52.9	196 086	195 976	-0.1	2.4
NORTH CAROLINA	6.3	17.1	10.0	12.9	13.5	14.0	12.3	8.0	5.8	37.8	51.3	8 049 313	9 535 483	18.5	4.3
Apex	6.6	24.3	6.8	9.9	20.6	16.9	8.7	4.0	2.3	37.3	52.1	20 212	37 476	85.4	17.1
Asheboro	8.4	19.6	9.8	12.2	14.4	11.4	10.9	6.9	6.3	34.9	52.6	21 672	25 012	15.4	2.7
Asheville	6.5	13.2	10.2	16.7	12.9	11.8	12.3	8.4	7.9	37.2	52.9	68 889	83 393	21.1	5.4
Burlington	6.5	16.5	9.5	13.6	11.2	12.4	14.0	8.2	8.1	38.9	53.7	44 917	49 963	11.2	1.7
Cary	7.1	19.9	6.6	13.7	16.6	16.2	10.6	5.6	3.8	36.9	50.6	94 536	135 234	43.1	14.7
Chapel Hill	3.4	12.9	33.6	11.5	10.0	10.5	8.7	4.9	4.4	25.1	53.5	48 715	57 233	17.5	3.7
Charlotte	7.4	17.6	9.9	17.4	15.5	13.3	10.0	5.1	3.8	33.6	52.0	540 828	731 424	35.2	10.1
Concord	7.0	20.3	8.4	12.8	16.8	14.3	9.3	6.6	4.5	35.7	51.3	55 977	79 066	41.2	8.0
Durham	7.5	14.9	12.1	19.6	14.3	12.0	10.3	5.4	4.0	32.7	52.7	187 035	228 330	22.1	10.3
Fayetteville	8.4	16.8	13.6	17.9	11.6	11.5	9.8	5.7	4.7	30.3	51.1	121 015	200 564	65.7	1.7
Garner	6.3	18.4	7.3	14.4	14.4	15.1	10.9	8.0	5.2	38.2	59.1	17 757	25 745	45.0	8.0
Gastonia	8.1	18.7	9.6	11.5	13.6	14.1	11.7	7.1	5.6	36.5	52.2	66 277	71 741	8.2	2.7
Goldsboro	9.1	14.9	10.7	17.4	9.0	12.4	12.5	7.0	7.0	33.6	51.7	39 043	36 437	-6.7	1.2
Greensboro	6.5	15.7	13.6	15.5	12.8	12.9	11.1	6.5	5.5	34.1	52.7	223 891	269 666	20.4	5.1
Greenville	5.6	13.2	28.6	16.2	11.4	8.4	8.7	4.3	3.7	25.9	55.1	60 476	84 554	39.8	6.2
Hickory	6.1	17.2	10.8	12.5	14.7	12.7	11.2	7.5	7.3	37.4	53.9	37 222	40 010	7.5	0.2
High Point	6.7	17.5	10.5	13.3	14.8	13.5	11.4	6.7	5.7	36.3	53.2	85 839	104 371	21.6	4.1
Huntersville	7.6	20.6	5.7	15.3	19.1	16.2	7.6	5.3	2.5	35.3	48.5	24 960	46 773	87.4	10.2
Indian Trail	7.1	25.0	9.1	10.3	17.8	13.8	7.9	6.1	3.0	34.0	52.8	11 905	33 518	181.5	8.2
Jacksonville	10.8	14.9	30.4	18.0	6.9	6.9	5.3	3.8	2.9	23.2	42.4	66 715	70 145	5.1	-1.6
Kannapolis	6.5	18.6	8.0	14.4	13.4	15.0	11.9	7.4	4.8	36.8	52.0	36 910	42 625	15.5	6.2
Matthews	4.2	19.3	8.6	10.3	12.4	16.4	14.0	8.7	6.2	41.3	52.8	22 127	27 198	22.9	10.3
Monroe	8.8	21.4	8.2	14.2	15.8	12.2	9.3	5.6	4.7	33.7	51.0	26 228	32 797	25.0	4.7
Mooresville	5.1	22.8	8.7	13.5	17.4	13.9	9.4	4.8	4.5	34.9	49.6	18 823	32 711	73.8	4.9
New Bern	7.7	17.0	10.2	14.3	10.7	11.3	11.5	8.3	9.0	35.7	53.3	23 128	29 524	27.7	2.5
Raleigh	6.9	16.0	13.6	18.1	15.2	12.3	9.1	4.9	3.9	32.6	51.9	276 093	403 892	46.3	8.9
Rocky Mount	6.3	18.3	9.6	11.6	12.4	13.1	12.6	8.8	7.3	38.8	53.3	55 893	57 477	2.8	-2.4
Salisbury	7.4	16.4	11.4	13.8	11.5	12.4	9.9	8.3	8.9	36.3	52.1	26 462	33 662	27.2	0.6
Sanford	7.8	20.3	9.7	12.1	13.1	13.9	10.1	7.1	5.9	35.2	51.5	23 220	28 094	21.0	3.5
Thomasville	9.8	18.0	9.7	12.5	12.5	13.2	9.0	7.3	8.0	34.9	52.6	19 788	26 757	35.2	0.9
Wake Forest	9.1	23.6	5.5	12.9	17.7	14.6	7.4	6.2	3.0	34.5	48.5	12 588	30 117	139.3	21.9
Wilmington	4.9	13.1	16.9	15.6	11.6	12.1	12.1	7.5	6.3	34.7	52.9	75 838	106 476	40.4	6.7
Wilson	7.2	17.7	10.3	11.9	11.7	13.5	12.4	8.3	7.0	37.3	54.5	44 405	49 167	10.7	0.5
Winston-Salem	7.3	17.2	12.0	14.1	12.7	12.9	11.0	6.8	6.0	34.6	53.0	185 776	229 617	23.6	4.2
NORTH DAKOTA	6.6	15.7	12.6	14.0	11.0	13.2	12.5	7.1	7.2	35.9	49.1	642 200	672 591	4.7	9.9
Bismarck	6.4	14.8	10.6	16.1	10.9	12.8	12.9	7.7	7.9	36.7	51.9	55 532	61 272	10.3	12.5
Fargo	6.4	13.3	19.9	17.6	11.1	10.9	10.2	4.8	5.7	30.4	50.2	90 599	105 549	16.5	9.8
Grand Forks	5.8	12.4	25.7	15.3	8.9	11.0	10.1	5.6	5.2	28.5	48.7	49 321	52 838	7.1	6.0
Minot	7.0	14.4	15.5	16.0	11.3	11.9	10.4	6.2	7.3	33.0	48.7	36 567	40 888	11.8	17.2
West Fargo	8.0	17.0	9.0	18.7	14.1	13.1	10.8	5.9	3.3	33.1	48.3	14 940	25 830	72.9	23.0
OHIO	6.0	17.1	9.6	12.4	12.4	14.5	13.3	8.0	6.8	39.2	51.1	11 353 140	11 536 504	1.6	0.5
Akron	7.0	15.4	12.8	13.6	11.8	13.2	13.1	7.1	6.1	36.1	52.0	217 074	199 110	-8.3	-0.6
Barberton	5.7	16.9	8.0	13.8	11.4	14.1	12.6	8.6	8.8	40.7	54.0	27 899	26 550	-4.8	-1.0
Beavercreek	4.7	17.2	8.2	12.9	12.3	14.3	14.6	9.4	6.4	40.9	50.5	37 984	45 193	19.0	1.6
Bowling Green	5.1	9.0	42.0	11.5	7.5	7.5	8.9	4.4	4.0	23.0	53.1	29 636	30 028	1.3	5.1
Brunswick	4.7	17.3	9.2	13.0	14.0	16.4	12.6	8.0	4.8	39.4	51.6	33 388	34 255	2.6	1.0
Canton	7.9	17.6	9.6	13.7	11.0	13.0	13.2	6.5	7.6	36.2	55.0	80 806	73 007	-9.7	-1.0
Cincinnati	7.4	14.7	14.2	17.3	11.4	12.6	11.3	6.0	5.2	32.4	52.2	331 285	296 943	-10.4	0.4
Cleveland	6.6	16.5	11.5	14.2	11.7	14.6	12.5	6.6	5.8	36.0	52.1	478 403	396 815	-17.1	-1.8
Cleveland Heights	6.6	16.8	10.7	16.8	11.2	10.9	13.2	7.8	5.9	34.3	55.2	49 958	46 121	-7.7	-2.3
Columbus	7.7	15.4	12.7	19.6	13.5	12.2	10.1	5.0	3.9	31.9	51.2	711 470	787 033	10.6	6.0
Cuyahoga Falls	5.7	14.6	7.5	15.5	13.2	13.6	14.8	7.3	7.7	39.9	51.0	49 374	49 652	0.6	-0.8
Dayton	6.4	14.8	16.9	13.9	11.7	12.0	12.2	6.4	5.6	33.5	51.1	166 179	141 527	-14.8	-0.5
Delaware	7.1	17.2	12.8	15.0	14.1	12.9	9.2	6.2	5.5	33.7	51.4	25 243	34 753	37.7	7.5
Dublin	6.8	24.0	4.8	9.3	15.7	17.2	12.9	6.4	2.9	38.6	52.1	31 392	41 751	33.0	6.9
Elyria	7.0	15.3	10.4	14.0	12.9	13.3	13.0	7.4	6.7	37.6	53.0	55 953	54 533	-2.5	-1.0
Euclid	5.5	16.7	7.8	11.7	12.3	16.5	14.1	6.8	8.4	41.4	54.2	52 717	48 920	-7.2	-2.1
Fairborn	6.5	12.9	17.2	14.6	10.5	13.0	11.3	6.9	7.2	34.0	50.9	32 052	32 352	0.9	1.7
Fairfield	5.5	15.9	8.0	14.9	12.9	14.3	14.7	7.7	6.0	39.3	50.3	42 097	42 510	1.0	0.6
Findlay	6.2	15.4	13.5	13.8	11.8	12.2	12.0	8.0	7.0	35.6	52.7	38 967	41 202	5.7	-0.2
Gahanna	5.1	18.6	10.2	11.9	12.1	17.0	13.5	5.7	5.9	38.4	51.3	32 636	33 248	1.9	3.1
Garfield Heights	6.0	16.8	9.3	12.0	12.2	14.9	12.5	7.4	8.8	39.7	54.9	30 734	28 849	-6.1	-2.1
Green	3.5	17.9	9.3	10.0	10.8	17.2	14.7	10.2	6.4	43.9	49.5	22 817	25 699	12.6	0.7
Grove City	6.5	17.0	6.9	14.0	13.0	15.8	12.9	8.3	5.7	39.2	52.0	27 075	35 575	31.4	8.3

City	Households, 2011-2013				Persons in group quarters, 2010				Serious crimes known to police,[2] 2013				Educational attainment, 2011–2013		
	Number	Persons per household	Percent: Female family householder[1]	Percent: One-person	Total	Institutional: Total	Institutional: Persons in nursing facilities	Non-institutional	Total: Number	Total: Rate[3]	Rate[3]: Violent	Rate[3]: Property	Population age 25 and older	Attainment[4] (percent): High school graduate or less	Attainment[4] (percent): Bachelor's degree or more
	27	28	29	30	31	32	33	34	35	36	37	38	39	40	41
NEW YORK—Cont'd															
Yonkers	73 092	2.68	19.7	31.2	3 286	1 099	864	2 187	3 404	1 709	520	1 189	135 670	45.5	30.0
NORTH CAROLINA	3 721 358	2.55	13.8	27.9	257 246	113 296	46 638	143 950	341 749	3 470	342	3 128	6 489 102	41.7	27.6
Apex	13 888	2.91	8.6	19.4	121	98	97	23	571	1 381	87	1 294	25 224	13.4	59.7
Asheboro	9 703	2.57	22.4	30.6	665	565	357	100	1 724	6 717	320	6 398	15 956	57.3	15.5
Asheville	36 653	2.24	12.2	39.9	4 249	2 292	1 047	1 957	5 514	6 379	516	5 863	60 257	27.0	46.1
Burlington	21 814	2.34	16.4	33.6	906	464	445	442	2 997	5 831	704	5 126	35 035	45.7	23.3
Cary	53 786	2.71	7.2	23.8	260	211	193	49	2 177	1 462	69	1 394	97 098	17.8	61.7
Chapel Hill	20 057	2.42	6.8	32.8	9 003	258	227	8 745	1 350	2 298	121	2 177	29 163	10.3	76.5
Charlotte	297 666	2.56	15.9	31.5	13 369	5 104	2 595	8 265	35 662	4 257	608	3 649	504 341	31.2	40.6
Concord	28 889	2.80	12.4	25.7	893	797	431	96	2 671	3 222	147	3 075	52 777	37.8	29.9
Durham	97 515	2.35	15.8	34.2	9 936	1 962	1 136	7 974	11 364	4 679	600	4 079	156 985	29.6	46.1
Fayetteville	78 104	2.48	19.0	29.6	8 841	1 253	689	7 588	13 431	6 632	578	6 054	123 859	34.1	24.2
Garner	10 591	2.48	15.5	31.3	284	243	232	41	1 230	4 552	192	4 360	18 117	31.9	34.0
Gastonia	26 642	2.67	19.3	25.3	1 745	1 149	691	596	4 376	5 990	698	5 292	46 203	44.5	22.2
Goldsboro	14 231	2.39	22.9	36.2	2 422	1 606	394	816	2 627	7 056	760	6 296	23 601	44.9	17.9
Greensboro	113 303	2.34	17.0	33.9	11 389	2 110	1 407	9 279	12 986	4 649	519	4 130	177 423	34.4	36.7
Greenville	34 944	2.35	17.8	33.8	5 858	760	734	5 098	4 417	5 018	631	4 388	46 183	30.8	37.6
Hickory	15 641	2.49	13.2	30.4	1 351	312	312	1 039	2 375	5 921	416	5 505	26 505	40.9	32.1
High Point	41 576	2.51	18.8	29.3	3 577	940	599	2 637	5 045	4 703	518	4 185	70 339	40.4	28.4
Huntersville	17 569	2.79	6.5	21.8	268	260	260	8	989	1 972	98	1 874	32 566	21.7	53.5
Indian Trail	10 937	3.19	12.0	15.2	0	0	0	0	NA	NA	NA	NA	20 510	32.5	33.4
Jacksonville	20 583	2.74	14.8	22.8	16 413	825	379	15 588	980	1 426	115	1 311	30 246	34.1	23.3
Kannapolis	16 886	2.57	15.7	32.2	330	303	278	27	1 004	2 274	197	2 077	29 273	50.0	16.9
Matthews	10 877	2.61	10.4	23.3	269	259	254	10	881	3 019	199	2 821	19 465	22.0	47.8
Monroe	10 972	3.02	21.1	18.2	379	273	248	106	1 975	5 827	602	5 225	20 753	58.2	16.9
Mooresville	12 093	2.82	12.1	24.4	372	252	252	120	1 476	4 383	229	4 154	21 848	31.2	32.3
New Bern	12 417	2.41	14.2	37.5	753	618	433	135	1 687	5 529	393	5 135	19 725	43.2	26.3
Raleigh	165 620	2.43	14.5	33.1	19 526	5 387	1 443	14 139	14 823	3 455	392	3 063	268 780	26.8	47.0
Rocky Mount	22 153	2.51	24.0	31.9	1 597	906	377	691	3 881	6 806	1 050	5 756	37 723	51.0	19.4
Salisbury	11 966	2.49	19.9	32.5	3 775	2 057	622	1 718	2 099	6 242	779	5 463	21 729	46.7	23.0
Sanford	10 084	2.78	17.5	28.9	858	684	289	174	213	725	92	633	18 075	51.1	21.7
Thomasville	10 445	2.55	18.5	33.0	390	315	275	75	1 213	4 515	435	4 080	16 866	53.8	14.8
Wake Forest	11 301	2.91	9.2	19.0	303	138	138	165	774	2 286	127	2 159	20 619	19.2	53.1
Wilmington	47 733	2.20	12.6	36.3	5 118	430	382	4 688	6 236	5 619	619	5 000	71 711	30.0	40.1
Wilson	19 054	2.52	19.9	33.4	1 534	1 003	756	531	2 239	4 502	474	4 027	32 045	48.8	22.5
Winston-Salem	92 302	2.43	16.5	34.8	9 431	2 480	1 268	6 951	14 279	6 055	605	5 451	148 857	40.0	32.9
NORTH DAKOTA	291 468	2.32	7.8	31.3	25 056	9 675	6 433	15 381	17 102	2 364	270	2 094	457 771	36.1	27.2
Bismarck	28 234	2.23	10.0	34.8	1 815	1 371	534	444	1 925	2 923	293	2 630	44 249	31.7	33.4
Fargo	48 440	2.18	7.9	36.3	4 924	1 011	678	3 913	3 669	3 302	394	2 908	66 724	25.3	38.7
Grand Forks	22 766	2.18	7.4	37.9	3 754	478	285	3 276	1 507	2 810	285	2 525	30 153	32.6	34.4
Minot	18 326	2.35	8.5	36.7	1 524	527	421	997	1 119	2 507	273	2 234	28 020	34.8	26.1
West Fargo	11 490	2.43	7.0	29.3	51	0	0	51	583	2 081	161	1 920	18 473	23.7	34.0
OHIO	4 551 497	2.47	12.9	30.0	306 266	166 042	83 019	140 224	371 852	3 214	286	2 927	7 776 454	45.8	25.4
Akron	82 592	2.34	19.7	37.6	6 133	1 981	878	4 152	11 277	5 684	794	4 889	128 766	49.6	20.0
Barberton	10 669	2.44	16.6	35.0	371	259	259	112	1 053	4 012	331	3 681	18 302	67.4	10.2
Beavercreek	18 317	2.51	8.4	25.3	278	257	257	21	1 162	2 528	26	2 502	32 398	23.3	48.1
Bowling Green	10 939	2.33	8.6	35.1	5 632	503	278	5 129	830	2 606	154	2 453	13 877	34.4	40.2
Brunswick	13 299	2.57	9.6	24.2	200	147	147	53	304	884	47	837	23 705	45.5	20.2
Canton	29 845	2.35	20.2	35.5	3 102	1 256	701	1 846	4 926	6 785	927	5 858	47 239	54.1	14.2
Cincinnati	130 360	2.18	19.5	44.0	14 443	4 531	2 199	9 912	20 160	6 800	964	5 836	189 199	42.4	31.4
Cleveland	166 093	2.28	23.4	42.2	13 742	6 258	3 062	7 484	29 049	7 464	1 486	5 978	255 725	55.6	15.5
Cleveland Heights	18 962	2.36	17.3	37.4	738	118	118	620	1 700	3 671	311	3 360	30 019	22.3	50.0
Columbus	327 023	2.41	15.8	36.7	21 099	6 086	3 236	15 013	45 022	5 515	545	4 970	520 385	38.2	33.0
Cuyahoga Falls	21 667	2.25	11.5	35.7	530	345	345	185	1 356	2 760	140	2 619	35 543	40.3	30.6
Dayton	57 250	2.27	21.4	42.3	9 365	2 099	773	7 266	8 954	6 343	878	5 464	88 783	48.9	17.0
Delaware	13 808	2.45	10.5	33.2	2 041	572	377	1 469	981	2 705	146	2 559	22 801	36.0	33.1
Dublin	15 202	2.82	7.0	18.5	127	127	127	0	570	1 314	23	1 291	27 718	9.0	74.0
Elyria	22 819	2.34	17.8	30.4	1 040	881	430	159	NA	NA	NA	NA	36 400	49.4	14.7
Euclid	22 509	2.12	20.5	45.2	675	489	391	186	565	1 175	193	981	33 787	44.8	19.3
Fairborn	14 694	2.20	13.4	36.4	275	229	229	46	1 001	3 050	192	2 858	20 959	44.5	24.0
Fairfield	17 303	2.43	13.2	29.1	506	404	384	102	1 220	2 859	281	2 578	30 085	42.7	27.1
Findlay	17 144	2.32	11.9	35.4	1 506	504	383	1 002	1 535	3 685	182	3 502	26 872	42.4	26.1
Gahanna	12 763	2.68	11.2	23.6	171	166	158	5	737	2 167	68	2 099	22 690	26.3	47.5
Garfield Heights	11 774	2.38	21.7	34.2	391	308	265	83	644	2 272	138	2 135	19 341	53.7	15.8
Green	10 478	2.45	7.4	27.8	141	133	130	8	NA	NA	NA	NA	17 879	37.2	33.2
Grove City	15 030	2.55	12.5	26.4	282	248	165	34	1 312	3 526	108	3 419	26 894	37.5	26.8

1. No spouse present. 2. Data for serious crimes have not been adjusted for underreporting. This may affect comparability between geographic areas and over time. 3. Per 100,000 population estimated by the FBI. 4. Persons 25 years old and over.

City	Money income, 2011–2013					Housing units, 2010			Occupied housing units 2011–2013				
		Households								Owner-occupied		Median owner costs as a percent of income	
	Per capita income[1] (dollars)	Median income	Percent with income of $200,000 or more	Percent with income of less than $25,000	Families with income below poverty (percent)	Total	Percent change, 2000–2010	Vacant units for sale or rent[2]	Total	Percent	Median value[3] (dollars)	With a mortgage[4]	Without a mortgage[5]
	42	43	44	45	46	47	48	49	50	51	52	53	54
NEW YORK—Cont'd													
Yonkers	29 110	57 301	5.8	25.0	14.1	80 389	3.6	5 839	73 092	46.4	397 100	27.8	18.5
NORTH CAROLINA	25 065	45 696	3.3	27.1	13.2	4 327 528	22.8	582 373	3 721 358	65.4	153 100	22.5	11.8
Apex	35 170	89 269	5.8	6.9	2.3	13 922	72.9	697	13 888	70.4	261 000	18.2	10.0
Asheboro	16 824	31 650	0.8	38.6	25.6	11 158	16.7	1 278	9 703	50.0	116 800	24.0	13.8
Asheville	26 965	42 218	3.3	29.3	13.5	41 626	23.9	4 246	36 653	50.4	197 500	24.4	12.5
Burlington	22 625	36 357	2.3	35.1	17.7	23 414	19.9	2 782	21 814	55.4	124 000	22.8	13.4
Cary	40 786	88 853	11.7	10.3	4.9	55 303	50.1	3 512	53 786	68.2	307 600	19.0	10.0
Chapel Hill	37 159	63 757	13.1	23.7	7.6	22 254	16.6	1 690	20 057	49.9	368 400	21.7	10.0
Charlotte	31 262	51 271	6.2	22.5	14.0	319 918	38.8	30 058	297 666	54.9	166 700	22.1	11.5
Concord	25 577	53 264	3.2	20.5	9.6	32 130	43.1	2 993	28 889	66.8	163 700	21.9	12.2
Durham	28 758	48 046	4.5	25.7	14.2	103 221	27.6	9 780	97 515	48.9	176 200	21.0	11.3
Fayetteville	22 842	44 770	1.9	25.5	15.5	87 005	62.7	8 731	78 104	48.6	129 300	23.4	10.6
Garner	27 241	58 760	0.9	16.4	8.7	10 993	51.9	786	10 591	66.2	163 500	22.2	11.1
Gastonia	20 825	40 581	2.0	33.6	18.2	31 238	12.2	3 468	26 642	53.1	140 400	23.4	11.5
Goldsboro	18 900	33 403	0.5	39.2	22.2	16 824	2.3	1 859	14 231	36.9	112 200	25.0	13.1
Greensboro	25 496	40 415	3.2	30.2	15.7	124 074	25.2	12 343	113 303	52.1	148 000	22.5	11.4
Greenville	22 106	34 295	2.5	39.4	17.5	40 564	43.5	4 493	34 944	35.4	152 000	21.3	11.4
Hickory	25 551	42 334	4.2	28.3	13.7	18 719	12.0	2 105	15 641	53.5	157 600	21.1	10.7
High Point	22 864	42 194	2.3	29.9	18.4	46 677	29.9	5 765	41 576	56.0	141 200	24.4	12.5
Huntersville	38 580	86 212	9.6	10.6	2.4	18 477	87.2	1 054	17 569	73.7	243 400	19.5	11.9
Indian Trail	24 391	63 097	3.4	10.0	7.0	11 700	166.4	579	10 937	81.6	172 300	23.0	11.0
Jacksonville	20 266	41 443	1.1	24.3	13.3	21 135	15.2	1 150	20 583	37.0	159 500	24.5	12.1
Kannapolis	21 133	37 192	1.3	33.9	15.7	18 645	17.4	2 270	16 886	56.1	120 100	24.3	14.0
Matthews	33 335	68 644	6.4	13.9	5.9	11 021	33.2	495	10 877	73.2	209 600	19.4	10.7
Monroe	18 840	43 041	1.2	28.6	19.8	12 375	27.4	1 255	10 972	58.9	145 100	24.3	13.5
Mooresville	27 080	66 042	3.2	21.1	7.1	13 655	74.1	1 281	12 093	69.2	184 100	22.5	12.6
New Bern	22 471	42 691	1.4	33.2	15.2	14 471	31.0	1 701	12 417	51.4	143 100	23.8	14.2
Raleigh	30 174	54 088	5.1	20.0	11.5	176 124	45.9	13 125	165 620	52.4	201 800	21.5	10.0
Rocky Mount	18 835	36 308	1.3	34.9	20.6	26 953	11.1	3 856	22 153	53.8	101 800	24.4	14.4
Salisbury	18 282	35 036	1.6	38.4	18.7	14 626	28.5	2 059	11 966	49.9	121 400	22.7	12.6
Sanford	18 974	38 950	1.3	34.1	20.4	11 411	23.1	953	10 084	52.5	136 000	22.4	13.0
Thomasville	16 827	33 436	0.5	36.3	21.2	11 870	39.2	1 333	10 445	59.4	103 100	25.1	12.0
Wake Forest	31 555	78 791	6.6	12.3	6.8	11 370	123.8	849	11 301	72.9	261 000	20.8	11.0
Wilmington	29 410	41 724	4.3	30.7	15.7	53 400	38.3	6 452	47 733	44.8	209 300	24.1	14.2
Wilson	20 940	37 312	1.6	34.8	20.3	21 870	17.1	2 285	19 054	52.2	127 300	26.1	15.6
Winston-Salem	24 319	38 566	4.1	32.9	19.1	103 974	25.8	11 637	92 302	55.6	141 000	22.5	11.2
NORTH DAKOTA	30 436	54 920	4.1	21.6	7.4	317 498	9.6	36 306	291 468	65.2	142 100	18.9	10.0
Bismarck	32 632	56 266	3.5	19.2	5.2	28 648	18.6	1 385	28 234	66.0	167 500	19.1	10.9
Fargo	29 475	45 227	4.0	25.2	9.5	49 956	21.0	3 165	48 440	44.4	161 600	21.2	10.0
Grand Forks	26 923	43 647	4.0	31.1	8.6	23 449	12.6	1 189	22 766	46.5	159 000	19.4	10.3
Minot	30 021	57 374	2.9	17.3	5.5	18 744	13.7	881	18 326	59.4	171 400	20.0	10.0
West Fargo	31 752	66 747	3.3	15.7	4.0	10 760	83.8	412	11 490	69.3	158 200	20.7	13.1
OHIO	25 967	47 782	3.1	26.2	11.8	5 127 508	7.2	524 073	4 551 497	66.5	128 100	21.8	12.5
Akron	19 845	33 209	1.4	38.8	21.5	96 288	-1.0	12 576	82 592	52.5	81 400	22.4	13.6
Barberton	20 224	35 958	0.7	34.2	16.0	12 191	0.2	1 137	10 669	64.7	83 000	21.3	13.2
Beavercreek	37 885	78 388	6.9	12.0	2.4	19 449	31.1	1 254	18 317	72.1	173 400	19.7	12.1
Bowling Green	18 495	35 595	0.9	36.0	13.5	12 301	15.9	1 013	10 939	41.5	148 200	21.8	10.0
Brunswick	28 377	62 918	2.3	14.2	5.6	13 600	10.9	633	13 299	74.4	156 500	21.3	10.0
Canton	16 471	29 574	0.6	44.2	26.8	34 571	-2.6	4 866	29 845	53.0	75 000	23.3	11.8
Cincinnati	24 325	32 316	2.9	41.5	26.0	161 095	-2.9	27 675	130 360	39.2	120 900	22.9	13.5
Cleveland	17 123	25 696	1.2	48.9	30.7	207 536	-3.8	40 046	166 093	43.0	71 600	25.4	14.5
Cleveland Heights	30 471	51 142	5.0	26.6	15.2	22 465	2.9	2 508	18 962	56.5	128 200	23.2	13.4
Columbus	23 998	43 441	1.8	28.7	17.1	370 965	13.3	39 363	327 023	45.4	126 000	22.6	12.8
Cuyahoga Falls	26 243	49 682	0.8	24.1	10.7	23 859	4.9	1 609	21 667	60.4	118 600	21.2	11.7
Dayton	16 442	27 304	0.8	46.3	29.5	74 065	-4.2	15 661	57 250	47.7	67 200	23.8	14.2
Delaware	26 986	52 779	2.2	20.6	7.2	14 192	37.9	939	13 808	62.2	155 100	22.8	12.4
Dublin	53 051	111 290	20.4	4.9	2.6	15 779	31.1	795	15 202	78.6	330 400	21.7	10.0
Elyria	21 387	41 292	0.6	29.8	17.1	25 085	5.2	2 685	22 819	59.2	95 200	22.2	13.9
Euclid	22 078	34 290	1.3	38.3	17.7	26 037	-0.3	3 352	22 509	50.0	83 900	23.1	14.6
Fairborn	23 299	39 580	1.8	33.7	18.3	15 893	10.3	1 587	14 694	46.8	105 100	22.1	11.6
Fairfield	27 673	54 230	2.5	18.1	6.3	18 803	5.7	1 388	17 303	64.2	146 000	22.1	12.4
Findlay	23 870	40 739	2.1	32.4	15.5	19 318	12.5	1 964	17 144	62.4	119 600	20.4	11.9
Gahanna	34 551	72 474	6.0	12.5	2.3	13 577	9.9	540	12 763	74.6	185 400	22.0	12.5
Garfield Heights	21 082	39 770	1.3	30.6	13.8	13 125	1.6	1 434	11 774	70.7	78 100	25.8	13.3
Green	31 602	58 968	5.3	15.0	6.5	10 858	18.3	788	10 478	74.5	172 700	21.9	10.6
Grove City	30 353	66 124	2.3	15.7	5.9	14 720	38.2	774	15 030	69.6	156 400	20.6	14.7

1. Based on population estimated by the American Community Survey. 2. Includes units rented or sold but not occupied. 3. Specified owner-occupied units; $1,000,000 represents $1,000,000 or more 4. 50.0 represents 50 percent or more. 5. 10.0 represents 10 percent or less.

City	Occupied housing units, 2011–2013 (cont.)				Migration, 2011–2013		Civilian labor force, 2014				Civilian employment[4], 2011–2013			
									Unemployment			Percent		
	Percent renter occupied	Median gross rent[1]	Median rent as a percent of income[2]	Percent with no vehicle available	Percent who lived in the same house one year ago	Percent who lived outside current city one year ago	Total	Percent change, 2013–2014	Total	Rate[3]	Population age 16 and older	In labor force	Civilian full-year full-time workers	Households with no workers (percent)
	55	56	57	58	59	60	61	62	63	64	65	66	67	68
NEW YORK—Cont'd														
Yonkers	53.6	1 180	33.7	25.8	89.8	4.7	93 439	-1.3	5 769	6.2	158 953	61.9	40.3	27.8
NORTH CAROLINA	34.6	772	30.4	6.7	84.6	10.9	4 656 194	-0.5	285 815	6.1	7 717 778	63.1	38.1	28.6
Apex	29.6	1 111	23.0	1.5	82.6	14.8	22 265	1.9	830	3.7	29 056	78.2	51.8	11.3
Asheboro	50.0	602	29.9	11.3	80.6	10.8	10 964	-2.3	648	5.9	18 937	59.2	35.3	35.6
Asheville	49.6	836	28.8	10.5	77.7	13.8	45 853	0.0	1 862	4.1	70 437	64.7	37.4	31.6
Burlington	44.6	696	33.1	8.5	83.3	7.4	24 940	-1.2	1 381	5.5	41 233	62.0	37.3	33.0
Cary	31.8	986	24.9	2.5	83.4	12.6	81 798	1.8	2 993	3.7	111 175	71.9	50.4	15.7
Chapel Hill	50.1	944	35.8	7.4	65.6	23.1	29 236	0.9	1 436	4.9	50 311	58.0	30.0	26.0
Charlotte	45.1	882	30.1	7.9	79.7	8.4	428 049	1.1	21 790	5.1	600 354	72.2	44.9	20.0
Concord	33.2	779	27.8	5.3	84.0	9.7	41 035	1.6	1 759	4.3	62 394	67.2	43.7	22.9
Durham	51.1	856	30.5	10.4	74.9	12.4	129 421	0.6	5 862	4.5	190 365	68.9	43.5	22.3
Fayetteville	51.4	866	29.1	6.9	75.5	14.5	74 028	-2.5	4 618	6.2	156 604	65.2	31.1	25.9
Garner	33.8	905	26.2	4.7	86.2	11.9	14 714	1.3	657	4.5	20 515	71.3	47.5	19.7
Gastonia	46.9	748	34.4	9.1	82.9	8.5	33 884	0.4	2 143	6.3	55 074	64.9	38.1	28.4
Goldsboro	63.1	714	33.0	16.9	72.7	17.3	12 562	-2.0	989	7.9	28 314	58.6	29.1	37.2
Greensboro	47.9	737	30.6	8.4	83.0	8.2	138 418	-1.5	8 226	5.9	221 569	65.5	39.6	25.6
Greenville	64.6	716	36.1	10.2	67.9	17.9	45 380	-0.6	2 582	5.7	72 998	66.5	35.0	24.1
Hickory	46.5	669	26.1	7.6	82.8	9.2	19 377	-1.4	1 115	5.8	31 768	63.2	40.7	27.7
High Point	44.0	755	30.7	10.0	82.4	8.4	51 826	-1.4	3 339	6.4	84 225	65.4	37.4	27.8
Huntersville	26.3	1 082	22.7	2.2	83.1	12.1	28 392	1.7	1 034	3.6	36 416	76.0	54.7	15.6
Indian Trail	18.4	1 038	29.1	0.7	85.4	12.9	18 040	1.7	724	4.0	24 701	72.6	47.7	15.1
Jacksonville	63.0	1 008	33.6	7.4	67.4	25.2	19 374	-0.1	1 227	6.3	52 607	73.7	21.6	20.2
Kannapolis	43.9	767	33.0	7.8	90.0	5.7	20 375	0.8	1 246	6.1	33 717	65.5	40.5	28.7
Matthews	26.8	917	37.2	4.5	84.9	12.8	15 578	1.7	676	4.3	22 683	71.0	42.1	20.2
Monroe	41.1	782	30.8	7.5	84.2	8.2	15 999	1.3	874	5.5	24 750	67.8	42.0	24.2
Mooresville	30.8	885	26.4	4.5	84.0	9.4	17 990	1.3	907	5.0	26 035	68.9	45.5	22.4
New Bern	48.6	855	30.8	16.0	78.4	13.9	12 147	-1.0	736	6.1	23 156	64.5	33.1	35.1
Raleigh	47.6	890	29.6	6.4	78.5	10.8	230 415	1.5	10 365	4.5	334 922	70.6	46.4	18.8
Rocky Mount	46.2	742	35.0	12.5	80.6	8.2	23 985	-3.4	2 184	9.1	45 303	60.0	33.2	32.9
Salisbury	50.1	715	33.1	11.4	78.0	14.5	13 250	0.4	950	7.2	26 339	51.5	28.1	38.1
Sanford	47.5	649	28.6	10.2	80.1	9.6	11 655	-4.6	906	7.8	21 648	61.0	37.6	32.1
Thomasville	40.6	592	31.7	8.9	79.6	10.2	12 038	-1.4	763	6.3	20 272	63.8	36.1	32.2
Wake Forest	27.1	938	27.9	4.3	84.8	11.1	17 418	1.9	594	3.4	23 176	71.0	46.0	18.0
Wilmington	55.2	849	32.4	9.4	73.5	13.8	56 774	0.5	3 025	5.3	92 500	65.1	34.6	29.7
Wilson	47.8	726	32.7	11.8	81.5	7.9	21 782	-1.7	2 001	9.2	38 330	61.8	37.2	32.5
Winston-Salem	44.4	703	33.0	10.3	81.1	7.7	110 952	-1.0	6 258	5.6	182 475	63.5	37.0	29.3
NORTH DAKOTA	34.8	664	25.2	5.6	82.6	11.4	416 367	2.4	11 503	2.8	562 803	70.5	46.8	22.0
Bismarck	34.0	701	23.2	5.4	83.1	9.3	36 149	0.7	893	2.5	52 240	72.2	50.4	21.9
Fargo	55.6	677	27.0	9.5	73.5	14.7	65 038	1.7	1 603	2.5	90 424	75.2	47.5	19.6
Grand Forks	53.5	690	31.4	8.1	77.2	12.5	30 704	-0.1	829	2.7	45 069	70.9	41.3	21.6
Minot	40.6	756	25.4	5.4	73.8	12.8	24 947	0.3	640	2.6	35 896	72.6	46.3	20.8
West Fargo	30.7	711	23.1	3.1	85.4	12.1	17 828	2.0	431	2.4	22 021	79.4	57.5	15.1
OHIO	33.5	711	29.8	8.4	85.3	9.8	5 719 472	-0.1	327 969	5.7	9 198 469	63.4	39.1	29.8
Akron	47.5	671	34.3	15.5	84.4	6.6	91 004	-0.3	6 019	6.6	158 894	62.3	35.4	34.7
Barberton	35.3	632	30.7	11.8	89.1	7.2	12 634	-0.4	778	6.2	21 334	62.2	36.8	34.7
Beavercreek	27.9	1 084	24.7	3.4	85.6	11.2	22 511	0.0	1 010	4.5	37 580	63.5	40.5	25.2
Bowling Green	58.5	629	40.2	10.3	56.6	27.1	16 707	-0.4	868	5.2	27 635	63.6	27.3	22.5
Brunswick	25.6	801	25.1	4.7	90.3	5.6	20 025	0.5	1 002	5.0	27 950	71.0	45.5	20.1
Canton	47.0	593	34.1	16.7	83.2	9.1	32 404	-0.8	2 211	6.8	55 810	61.1	31.7	37.3
Cincinnati	60.8	631	32.4	21.9	75.5	10.1	143 005	0.1	8 430	5.9	237 490	65.0	36.4	33.3
Cleveland	57.0	651	34.8	25.6	79.7	8.0	163 085	0.1	13 102	8.0	310 810	58.4	30.5	41.1
Cleveland Heights	43.5	829	29.8	13.4	80.8	15.2	23 377	0.5	1 275	5.5	36 520	64.9	40.6	28.8
Columbus	54.6	805	29.5	10.0	77.5	10.0	438 501	0.8	20 939	4.8	640 064	69.0	43.9	23.8
Cuyahoga Falls	39.6	759	26.4	7.0	91.2	6.8	26 424	0.1	1 393	5.3	40 290	67.9	46.2	25.8
Dayton	52.3	620	35.8	20.2	74.2	12.6	59 145	-1.0	4 212	7.1	115 803	56.8	27.0	41.4
Delaware	37.8	809	28.6	7.1	85.0	10.0	19 647	1.0	817	4.2	28 179	67.0	46.4	21.7
Dublin	21.4	1 180	19.0	2.7	85.5	10.6	23 622	1.3	838	3.5	31 472	72.3	50.6	12.4
Elyria	40.8	705	30.6	10.1	82.8	8.8	27 425	0.0	1 837	6.7	43 394	65.7	38.4	31.4
Euclid	50.0	711	35.1	17.0	84.5	9.1	23 296	0.4	1 719	7.4	38 756	63.4	38.3	36.2
Fairborn	53.2	745	29.4	7.0	81.6	11.4	16 516	-0.2	831	5.0	27 221	64.6	34.8	30.2
Fairfield	35.8	829	25.5	3.0	85.9	11.0	24 073	0.2	1 203	5.0	34 568	70.4	46.5	22.0
Findlay	37.6	620	31.2	9.4	80.3	11.4	21 414	0.7	976	4.6	33 485	65.4	36.6	32.5
Gahanna	25.4	937	28.1	4.7	84.8	8.7	19 565	1.3	811	4.1	27 343	73.5	47.8	17.8
Garfield Heights	29.3	747	41.4	10.5	87.6	9.4	14 069	0.3	1 020	7.2	22 823	64.0	36.9	32.0
Green	25.5	793	27.5	3.3	90.6	7.3	13 875	0.2	705	5.1	20 959	66.3	46.0	26.7
Grove City	30.4	851	27.2	4.0	91.1	6.4	20 314	1.2	883	4.3	30 674	67.9	48.9	22.2

1. $2,000 represents $2,000 or more. 2. 50.0 represents 50 percent or more. 3. Percent of civilian labor force. 4. Persons 16 years old and over.

Table D. Cities — **Construction, Wholesale Trade, and Retail Trade**

City	Value of residential construction authorized by building permits, 2014: New construction ($1,000)	Number of housing units	Percent single family	Wholesale trade,[1] 2007: Number of establish-ments	Number of employees	Sales (mil dol)	Annual payroll (mil dol)	Retail trade,[2] 2007: Number of establish-ments	Number of employees	Sales (mil dol)	Annual payroll (mil dol)
	69	70	71	72	73	74	75	76	77	78	79
NEW YORK—Cont'd											
Yonkers	20 098	81	28.4	182	1 594	1 058.6	79.4	638	8 802	2 591.1	230.5
NORTH CAROLINA	8 619 650	49 911	70.2	10 049	142 342	88 795.9	6 969.2	36 592	466 577	114 578.2	10 342.7
Apex	95 823	578	100.0	43	469	320.3	26.9	108	1 908	439.9	41.9
Asheboro	3 150	24	100.0	35	339	154.0	14.9	215	2 503	570.9	52.9
Asheville	67 125	312	80.8	134	1 508	785.3	67.0	804	11 457	2 616.9	254.2
Burlington	17 761	147	100.0	67	934	318.7	35.2	415	5 832	1 216.9	117.0
Cary	281 116	1 676	67.4	127	1 999	2 236.7	152.1	524	9 274	2 293.0	209.5
Chapel Hill	17 870	51	100.0	23	398	403.0	35.9	196	2 888	569.5	62.7
Charlotte	NA	NA	NA	1 552	24 881	15 551.6	1 369.3	2 544	38 969	10 101.4	970.9
Concord	NA	NA	NA	100	2 237	1 145.9	103.8	478	7 685	1 995.1	167.7
Durham	238 122	1 514	76.2	183	2 669	2 648.8	169.1	868	13 805	2 978.1	297.3
Fayetteville	59 897	423	81.8	111	1 243	552.7	54.6	843	13 255	3 298.5	291.0
Garner	16 235	94	100.0	58	1 009	801.5	50.7	124	2 120	541.1	48.3
Gastonia	59 401	243	96.7	81	692	559.5	28.2	397	6 645	1 391.5	132.2
Goldsboro	9 360	59	100.0	57	1 365	862.8	53.7	347	4 309	1 027.1	85.8
Greensboro	188 669	1 229	33.8	567	8 524	7 790.2	412.6	1 293	21 155	5 080.7	502.1
Greenville	83 309	755	24.5	67	905	463.2	40.1	457	6 652	1 503.2	140.0
Hickory	NA	NA	NA	140	4 304	2 975.0	181.3	511	7 297	1 807.2	162.9
High Point	86 462	594	41.4	320	4 722	2 663.4	222.5	467	5 734	1 343.0	131.2
Huntersville	NA	NA	NA	51	517	224.5	28.5	156	2 832	823.7	66.5
Indian Trail	NA	NA	NA	86	826	321.2	36.0	97	1 552	462.8	42.0
Jacksonville	6 566	48	58.3	16	103	36.3	5.4	332	5 647	1 473.9	121.2
Kannapolis	NA	NA	NA	19	158	71.2	6.3	191	2 419	596.5	52.5
Matthews	NA	NA	NA	54	605	264.1	39.6	188	3 373	853.6	77.0
Monroe	8 799	83	95.2	73	1 298	653.5	51.5	246	3 583	884.0	76.2
Mooresville	NA	NA	NA	67	694	313.6	33.8	242	3 659	1 054.3	87.3
New Bern	18 760	107	100.0	35	473	698.7	18.3	249	3 150	728.8	67.8
Raleigh	626 797	4 655	28.3	589	8 369	4 243.2	447.4	1 761	28 116	7 066.4	672.2
Rocky Mount	1 935	17	100.0	66	1 408	975.5	55.7	392	4 811	1 045.6	96.1
Salisbury	NA	NA	NA	48	887	442.7	35.0	223	3 161	782.6	68.1
Sanford	10 160	42	100.0	35	673	572.9	26.2	201	2 340	583.0	50.6
Thomasville	5 740	35	88.6	36	577	230.7	22.6	139	1 716	419.6	37.6
Wake Forest	83 946	548	84.7	16	101	42.3	5.1	80	1 593	454.6	38.7
Wilmington	NA	NA	NA	150	1 293	744.6	53.7	845	12 145	3 076.1	284.9
Wilson	22 886	134	46.3	74	842	654.7	42.1	309	3 695	953.7	81.3
Winston-Salem	89 747	783	65.6	268	5 166	2 841.7	217.1	1 081	16 204	3 886.0	357.7
NORTH DAKOTA	1 636 051	12 178	37.2	1 332	14 866	13 099.3	627.1	3 361	44 054	10 527.3	891.4
Bismarck	152 357	1 134	50.6	118	1 531	845.9	68.8	375	6 653	1 377.0	133.6
Fargo	218 628	2 170	17.4	249	4 419	3 067.3	208.5	545	10 379	2 552.5	224.8
Grand Forks	121 309	898	23.7	61	841	528.9	36.9	297	5 634	1 181.5	110.5
Minot	89 936	719	25.7	56	825	943.8	35.9	252	4 392	1 005.7	89.4
West Fargo	145 309	982	55.1	38	464	165.1	20.0	80	1 405	269.1	27.9
OHIO	3 753 786	19 872	63.1	12 591	192 403	135 575.3	8 914.0	40 075	591 237	138 816.0	12 729.5
Akron	NA	NA	NA	236	3 404	1 540.3	158.8	676	8 221	1 720.2	174.3
Barberton	675	5	100.0	30	1 501	177.8	37.0	68	781	170.5	16.3
Beavercreek	NA	NA	NA	23	D	D	D	232	5 106	887.4	84.4
Bowling Green	NA	NA	NA	15	130	34.0	3.5	111	1 839	394.7	33.9
Brunswick	14 638	128	39.1	56	654	268.9	30.2	115	1 553	594.4	41.6
Canton	1 670	12	100.0	100	1 407	612.4	62.0	232	3 215	725.7	71.0
Cincinnati	50 826	601	16.5	390	6 264	5 749.5	324.4	1 016	13 048	3 310.5	320.4
Cleveland	7 350	124	77.4	606	9 806	4 912.5	506.4	1 314	10 259	2 298.1	232.5
Cleveland Heights	1 383	9	100.0	6	D	D	D	123	1 748	378.8	40.2
Columbus	449 879	3 642	19.9	825	16 326	11 029.4	769.7	2 641	48 684	12 077.0	1 132.2
Cuyahoga Falls	NA	NA	NA	46	527	184.1	22.2	184	3 674	986.5	81.3
Dayton	630	7	100.0	187	3 202	1 370.4	145.3	422	4 514	961.3	107.4
Delaware	41 671	196	83.2	24	174	63.5	7.5	115	1 606	419.7	37.1
Dublin	66 256	202	100.0	83	3 800	2 040.4	200.1	130	4 095	1 435.3	133.8
Elyria	2 431	24	100.0	57	527	401.3	24.0	257	4 814	930.8	90.6
Euclid	0	0	0.0	36	511	336.0	27.3	104	1 178	337.1	31.7
Fairborn	9 052	35	100.0	9	308	316.1	18.3	82	1 114	269.0	25.4
Fairfield	1 467	9	100.0	77	1 495	825.4	67.5	172	4 303	1 518.4	127.1
Findlay	6 646	28	92.9	42	D	D	D	245	3 701	819.3	74.4
Gahanna	5 041	24	54.2	43	520	406.0	21.6	90	1 861	587.2	50.1
Garfield Heights	0	0	0.0	28	347	137.2	12.8	83	1 359	256.1	24.0
Green	NA	NA	NA	34	744	501.9	44.7	64	1 416	639.9	43.2
Grove City	46 847	234	73.5	33	980	1 745.0	35.8	115	2 554	557.0	58.7

1. Merchant wholesalers except manufacturers' sales branches and offices. 2. Establishments with payroll.

City	Real estate and rental and leasing, 2007: Number of establish-ments	Number of employees	Receipts (mil dol)	Annual payroll (mil dol)	Professional, scientific, and technical services,[1] 2007: Number of establish-ments	Number of employees	Receipts (mil dol)	Annual payroll (mil dol)	Manufacturing, 2007: Number of establish-ments	Number of employees	Receipts (mil dol)	Annual payroll (mil dol)
	80	81	82	83	84	85	86	87	88	89	90	91
NEW YORK—Cont'd												
Yonkers	433	1 372	408.8	52.7	272	D	D	D	114	3 698	960.3	185.6
NORTH CAROLINA	11 258	53 563	11 175.1	1 881.4	22 385	182 224	26 003.8	10 698.3	10 150	506 013	205 867.3	19 589.8
Apex	34	88	14.9	2.6	167	419	52.1	19.8	33	1 181	D	61.1
Asheboro	37	173	31.6	4.3	73	376	33.6	11.0	80	8 766	2 758.2	283.2
Asheville	245	900	186.6	33.3	556	D	D	D	115	3 100	D	112.6
Burlington	79	307	51.0	8.1	114	D	D	D	100	5 331	1 001.0	182.3
Cary	213	880	207.0	38.7	806	D	D	D	75	1 808	606.9	86.4
Chapel Hill	88	D	D	D	286	3 208	317.4	126.3	NA	NA	NA	NA
Charlotte	1 460	10 841	2 676.3	513.2	3 009	D	D	D	716	24 523	8 996.3	1 103.9
Concord	127	459	69.4	13.7	208	D	D	D	84	5 967	D	319.3
Durham	289	1 832	351.7	71.0	838	D	D	D	147	8 554	D	514.2
Fayetteville	261	1 238	191.1	33.5	375	D	D	D	62	D	D	D
Garner	34	94	21.3	2.9	76	413	40.3	14.8	22	1 263	606.5	60.5
Gastonia	99	877	143.1	24.6	166	D	D	D	129	6 225	1 805.4	226.1
Goldsboro	57	244	29.8	5.6	109	736	59.4	21.0	46	2 489	399.9	86.3
Greensboro	465	3 336	1 225.1	108.5	992	D	D	D	350	18 969	19 687.6	925.5
Greenville	147	644	90.5	17.0	221	1 223	139.8	53.6	39	2 412	D	118.5
Hickory	111	404	96.4	12.1	210	1 360	146.1	51.9	188	10 207	1 770.4	351.5
High Point	119	790	168.5	26.4	306	2 445	343.1	131.1	284	15 048	3 380.2	540.7
Huntersville	69	139	33.1	4.9	152	660	92.4	37.0	29	1 065	228.7	48.1
Indian Trail	29	104	21.8	4.1	45	207	20.2	8.2	61	1 354	D	49.0
Jacksonville	99	468	79.9	11.6	127	D	D	D	NA	NA	NA	NA
Kannapolis	44	173	21.7	4.6	54	392	40.9	11.4	31	596	D	16.9
Matthews	52	189	24.5	6.2	138	642	98.3	37.4	40	990	277.7	38.6
Monroe	57	241	55.0	8.2	100	538	51.2	19.6	91	7 591	2 721.0	319.0
Mooresville	88	273	60.6	10.8	149	1 900	188.9	75.3	62	1 999	655.5	80.9
New Bern	60	220	33.8	6.5	127	D	D	D	35	3 110	911.8	133.7
Raleigh	787	4 794	1 356.2	235.6	2 132	D	D	D	294	6 235	2 285.7	280.8
Rocky Mount	81	413	75.4	11.4	141	883	95.5	35.8	56	5 697	1 481.0	223.9
Salisbury	57	190	37.1	6.0	109	907	70.1	28.9	68	2 995	D	D
Sanford	49	175	29.1	5.4	68	D	D	D	49	4 633	1 089.8	150.6
Thomasville	26	78	9.7	1.5	51	191	20.3	5.2	82	3 166	D	114.9
Wake Forest	35	68	14.4	2.6	95	326	35.6	13.7	NA	NA	NA	NA
Wilmington	289	1 318	239.5	43.4	647	D	D	D	102	4 009	1 725.8	224.2
Wilson	63	173	28.2	4.1	105	D	D	D	65	6 950	8 024.2	281.4
Winston-Salem	341	D	D	D	711	D	D	D	232	11 806	9 391.1	529.9
NORTH DAKOTA	770	3 748	668.8	96.0	1 432	9 707	1 110.7	416.9	767	26 361	11 349.8	991.4
Bismarck	105	358	53.3	8.2	249	D	D	D	65	1 991	D	81.7
Fargo	223	1 526	215.9	43.8	349	D	D	D	136	6 055	1 805.1	226.1
Grand Forks	53	386	54.7	8.8	107	912	88.7	45.4	43	2 512	D	78.5
Minot	64	433	142.3	10.2	85	D	D	D	NA	NA	NA	NA
West Fargo	25	73	6.3	1.4	33	D	D	D	47	1 842	D	71.8
OHIO	10 973	67 048	15 011.3	2 339.2	24 963	224 265	32 285.4	12 304.2	16 237	760 267	295 890.9	35 485.5
Akron	168	1 083	154.9	33.3	536	D	D	D	306	8 736	2 379.8	404.7
Barberton	7	50	5.0	0.7	43	D	D	D	65	2 292	679.3	88.3
Beavercreek	44	203	49.6	4.8	173	D	D	D	NA	NA	NA	NA
Bowling Green	40	193	20.0	4.4	56	D	D	D	39	2 637	910.1	112.4
Brunswick	27	105	12.9	1.8	71	371	32.6	13.2	48	938	178.3	40.1
Canton	75	282	48.0	7.3	175	861	101.5	32.0	146	9 975	3 526.9	467.2
Cincinnati	450	2 423	505.9	102.3	1 157	20 569	3 124.8	1 408.7	428	18 795	6 446.6	877.5
Cleveland	361	5 548	1 866.6	287.2	1 260	D	D	D	922	26 961	7 497.0	1 271.1
Cleveland Heights	51	183	24.8	3.7	113	229	30.8	10.6	NA	NA	NA	NA
Columbus	993	8 129	1 767.2	325.0	2 122	D	D	D	600	24 027	11 317.9	1 102.5
Cuyahoga Falls	53	282	33.6	8.3	116	699	71.0	29.9	81	4 091	1 170.2	165.4
Dayton	138	918	129.3	26.4	358	D	D	D	303	12 820	3 197.1	571.1
Delaware	44	131	18.6	3.6	53	233	25.7	9.8	34	2 728	1 584.5	142.1
Dublin	82	540	134.9	24.7	341	3 427	499.9	200.8	29	1 978	437.2	86.6
Elyria	54	334	41.9	8.6	77	D	D	D	108	5 650	1 538.0	260.8
Euclid	51	319	37.0	8.7	49	D	D	D	80	5 429	1 671.5	290.5
Fairborn	30	141	14.0	3.3	77	D	D	D	12	572	D	23.5
Fairfield	49	319	132.9	10.9	84	512	50.0	21.2	90	4 636	1 155.8	173.9
Findlay	55	436	46.2	11.5	106	861	74.3	31.0	63	6 513	1 769.5	300.0
Gahanna	41	154	39.4	5.7	146	892	107.1	42.9	34	1 107	238.8	42.3
Garfield Heights	18	73	17.6	2.7	52	376	39.6	19.0	38	1 223	233.3	51.9
Green	26	224	39.0	4.8	63	968	75.5	50.9	44	1 529	403.3	57.6
Grove City	36	145	19.6	4.2	54	321	28.2	10.2	30	1 714	379.7	74.1

1. Establishments subject to federal tax.

Table D. Cities — Accommodation and Food Services, Arts, Entertainment, and Recreation, and Health Care and Social Assistance

City	Accommodation and food services, 2007				Arts, entertainment, and recreation,[1] 2007				Health care and social assistance,[1] 2007			
	Number of establishments	Number of employees	Sales (mil dol)	Annual payroll (mil dol)	Number of establishments	Number of employees	Receipts (mil dol)	Annual payroll (mil dol)	Number of establishments	Number of employees	Receipts (mil dol)	Annual payroll (mil dol)
	92	93	94	95	96	97	98	99	100	101	102	103
NEW YORK—Cont'd												
Yonkers	301	3 128	175.9	47.3	50	D	D	D	383	3 989	362.9	147.3
NORTH CAROLINA	18 268	343 235	16 126.9	4 395.1	2 676	37 489	3 588.0	1 148.8	17 964	286 998	22 794.8	10 132.8
Apex	75	1 237	57.1	15.8	10	D	D	D	87	762	51.7	23.1
Asheboro	88	1 649	67.5	18.5	6	D	D	D	122	1 552	125.2	58.2
Asheville	478	11 166	560.1	167.5	51	480	23.7	7.9	464	6 999	776.0	339.8
Burlington	183	3 616	151.8	44.4	17	D	D	D	174	2 696	214.0	103.9
Cary	322	6 654	317.5	88.6	46	821	48.1	15.5	395	4 388	438.8	180.7
Chapel Hill	222	4 683	219.7	64.8	21	229	7.1	3.2	191	D	D	D
Charlotte	1 803	37 995	2 107.7	578.3	211	5 136	559.0	265.3	1 542	24 083	2 463.3	1 129.8
Concord	206	4 796	239.3	67.8	36	1 593	497.4	129.2	196	3 580	288.6	142.9
Durham	550	11 809	652.1	179.5	56	D	D	D	560	D	D	D
Fayetteville	453	10 088	408.1	108.3	36	D	D	D	571	D	D	D
Garner	71	1 637	69.7	18.9	7	D	D	D	69	1 222	78.6	34.7
Gastonia	179	4 008	182.2	49.8	24	186	10.5	2.4	265	D	D	D
Goldsboro	150	2 791	110.0	29.7	15	D	D	D	190	3 116	244.8	102.6
Greensboro	759	16 581	769.6	218.6	80	D	D	D	700	11 476	1 044.9	496.8
Greenville	252	6 365	265.1	71.8	25	305	13.7	4.1	267	D	D	D
Hickory	232	4 776	196.6	56.6	15	173	15.6	3.6	226	5 072	585.7	231.6
High Point	249	4 994	206.3	59.1	24	D	D	D	229	4 335	486.7	194.2
Huntersville	86	2 164	103.9	27.7	30	706	129.9	44.3	113	1 380	141.3	55.3
Indian Trail	51	568	29.0	7.1	9	87	6.3	1.2	21	D	D	D
Jacksonville	174	4 352	183.7	47.4	17	456	16.0	5.3	170	D	D	D
Kannapolis	81	1 275	55.2	15.3	8	D	D	D	58	838	57.8	25.5
Matthews	90	1 940	89.1	23.5	18	D	D	D	109	D	D	D
Monroe	105	2 151	99.7	23.1	5	D	D	D	106	1 726	142.5	64.0
Mooresville	150	2 908	126.7	35.1	51	D	D	D	132	D	D	D
New Bern	103	2 352	91.2	23.8	11	D	D	D	163	D	D	D
Raleigh	980	20 611	999.7	280.6	131	3 172	275.0	90.1	1 111	16 932	1 652.4	771.8
Rocky Mount	155	3 695	150.3	41.0	19	D	D	D	201	3 504	268.0	117.1
Salisbury	128	2 500	103.7	29.1	18	D	D	D	131	2 223	177.0	82.5
Sanford	85	1 643	61.2	15.9	7	D	D	D	127	2 277	168.7	68.6
Thomasville	60	995	36.8	10.6	4	D	D	D	37	687	43.7	20.7
Wake Forest	52	771	34.5	10.0	18	D	D	D	68	D	D	D
Wilmington	418	8 924	373.2	107.0	55	701	33.7	9.7	506	D	D	D
Wilson	117	2 394	105.2	27.0	13	D	D	D	138	D	D	D
Winston-Salem	527	10 856	508.1	142.4	63	557	26.6	7.3	541	D	D	D
NORTH DAKOTA	1 840	30 307	1 214.2	337.8	267	2 539	131.1	35.4	1 176	14 135	1 426.8	570.7
Bismarck	162	4 332	166.9	49.6	20	D	D	D	178	D	D	D
Fargo	296	7 976	314.2	93.5	45	608	44.4	8.2	285	5 745	785.3	304.6
Grand Forks	162	3 980	135.4	39.7	20	170	7.9	2.2	93	D	D	D
Minot	124	2 687	100.2	28.3	17	D	D	D	101	D	D	D
West Fargo	32	528	19.8	5.7	1	D	D	D	36	D	D	D
OHIO	23 959	436 598	17 779.9	5 078.5	3 122	40 269	4 067.9	1 360.1	22 693	346 386	28 636.8	12 631.1
Akron	443	6 065	247.8	67.8	40	570	49.7	13.2	367	6 681	617.6	304.4
Barberton	46	703	23.2	6.3	4	D	D	D	80	1 893	204.9	82.4
Beavercreek	100	D	D	D	4	48	3.3	0.8	108	D	D	D
Bowling Green	96	2 026	62.4	18.8	13	D	D	D	72	870	72.4	32.4
Brunswick	73	1 093	41.0	10.8	8	D	D	D	53	666	40.9	17.9
Canton	160	2 224	79.9	21.8	11	208	5.9	2.1	159	3 037	316.4	150.4
Cincinnati	730	13 938	712.8	207.1	83	1 379	389.9	257.8	698	15 502	1 549.1	811.2
Cleveland	995	16 038	868.1	235.2	97	3 115	589.0	298.8	447	7 487	492.6	220.4
Cleveland Heights	86	1 162	50.8	14.6	12	61	3.4	0.9	96	1 245	80.4	35.3
Columbus	1 852	41 282	1 944.8	553.4	145	3 364	254.2	101.1	1 457	24 611	2 450.4	1 105.0
Cuyahoga Falls	117	2 514	106.8	31.5	6	D	D	D	134	D	D	D
Dayton	294	4 483	190.9	54.7	20	270	21.4	5.5	302	5 700	602.4	316.1
Delaware	85	1 401	55.0	14.2	9	48	4.7	1.2	75	930	68.0	28.9
Dublin	114	3 032	147.4	45.6	26	D	D	D	167	D	D	D
Elyria	139	2 501	89.3	25.9	10	D	D	D	116	1 509	137.7	57.4
Euclid	78	683	26.1	6.8	7	D	D	D	90	D	D	D
Fairborn	84	1 573	64.7	18.2	4	64	1.5	0.4	35	388	25.3	10.1
Fairfield	95	2 099	94.6	25.2	12	D	D	D	152	D	D	D
Findlay	135	2 981	108.5	31.8	8	D	D	D	127	D	D	D
Gahanna	95	1 907	78.2	21.0	10	D	D	D	114	1 989	137.6	67.9
Garfield Heights	55	712	27.5	7.3	3	9	0.5	0.2	66	1 086	153.8	45.0
Green	58	1 195	46.5	13.1	12	140	10.5	3.0	66	D	D	D
Grove City	113	2 551	104.6	32.2	14	D	D	D	85	D	D	D

1. Establishments subject to federal tax.

City	Other services[1], 2007				Government employment and payroll, 2012								
						March payroll							
							Percent of total for:						
	Number of establish-ments	Number of employees	Receipts (mil dol)	Annual payroll (mil dol)	Full-time equivalent employees	Total (dollars)	Adminis-tration, judicial, and legal	Police and Corrections	Fire Protection	Highways and trans-portation	Health and welfare	Natural resources and utilities	Education and libraries
	104	105	106	107	108	109	110	111	112	113	114	115	116
NEW YORK—Cont'd													
Yonkers	294	1 016	108.7	27.5	5 538	39 341 604	3.2	17.5	10.4	1.0	2.7	6.0	58.2
NORTH CAROLINA	11 846	67 498	5 307.6	1 628.9	X	X	X	X	X	X	X	X	X
Apex	51	D	D	D	344	1 509 120	15.4	23.1	14.9	7.4	4.6	28.3	0.0
Asheboro	45	D	D	D	349	1 396 592	5.9	23.8	15.1	5.8	2.2	22.5	0.0
Asheville	200	1 206	80.4	27.3	1 057	3 889 185	9.1	23.7	24.5	5.3	3.3	19.0	0.0
Burlington	90	528	31.1	10.5	628	2 130 883	10.7	32.6	15.8	5.7	0.1	29.4	0.0
Cary	194	1 823	134.4	48.3	1 135	5 112 012	14.8	23.3	19.4	15.6	0.0	21.6	0.0
Chapel Hill	61	558	34.0	12.6	840	3 017 788	12.7	26.8	15.1	19.0	2.7	8.1	3.9
Charlotte	1 090	8 624	685.8	231.6	7 449	34 348 745	9.7	36.0	16.2	12.9	2.2	17.0	0.0
Concord	116	700	46.1	14.0	923	3 576 064	7.2	20.8	21.3	7.1	4.4	23.7	0.0
Durham	309	2 641	282.8	77.1	1 086	4 030 398	25.2	0.0	0.0	16.5	6.6	47.8	0.0
Fayetteville	252	1 824	116.4	39.3	1 960	7 748 728	4.9	24.8	14.8	6.6	0.8	30.0	0.0
Garner	52	314	26.0	8.1	177	821 893	16.4	47.7	0.0	3.4	1.0	15.0	0.0
Gastonia	122	759	45.7	14.7	935	3 494 489	15.2	23.5	14.9	10.2	1.1	28.7	0.0
Goldsboro	83	D	D	D	449	1 502 437	12.1	25.9	19.1	3.7	0.8	27.4	0.0
Greensboro	425	2 632	213.4	68.6	3 098	11 503 988	8.8	28.2	17.9	6.9	2.9	20.8	2.5
Greenville	109	707	49.7	13.3	1 347	5 208 426	6.5	18.6	12.5	6.2	2.4	34.6	0.0
Hickory	114	D	D	D	636	2 107 555	11.1	23.4	23.3	9.5	0.2	23.5	3.6
High Point	171	1 165	91.8	28.1	1 446	5 797 223	10.4	32.4	13.1	5.0	2.2	31.9	3.2
Huntersville	65	387	23.4	7.7	161	688 375	25.1	57.8	0.0	7.5	0.0	9.6	0.0
Indian Trail	56	D	D	D	48	144 392	56.2	0.0	0.0	9.0	0.0	9.0	0.0
Jacksonville	117	758	42.2	14.2	542	2 172 480	13.1	25.3	14.1	6.1	0.2	19.4	0.0
Kannapolis	58	D	D	D	289	1 109 005	13.6	30.3	23.4	4.8	0.0	27.8	0.0
Matthews	56	292	22.1	6.8	163	577 637	14.5	49.3	6.0	9.7	1.3	6.1	0.0
Monroe	94	518	43.4	13.5	511	1 971 029	15.1	20.8	15.3	6.0	0.0	37.8	0.0
Mooresville	89	436	34.1	10.2	760	1 406 044	10.4	25.8	21.5	3.5	0.0	23.4	4.8
New Bern	64	309	19.4	5.4	449	1 701 922	12.5	25.9	16.3	4.6	1.3	33.6	0.0
Raleigh	693	5 015	345.4	118.8	3 936	15 850 858	10.6	25.2	16.4	6.4	0.7	28.5	0.0
Rocky Mount	102	D	D	D	1 002	3 610 762	13.3	21.6	15.9	8.8	1.5	39.0	0.0
Salisbury	49	286	20.0	6.7	458	1 569 483	17.2	19.6	16.0	10.0	0.7	25.8	0.0
Sanford	57	326	21.0	7.1	345	1 295 948	13.5	31.2	15.8	6.0	2.5	21.9	0.0
Thomasville	56	D	D	D	377	1 184 674	5.8	27.3	23.1	5.5	0.0	20.8	0.0
Wake Forest	43	246	24.3	7.6	200	792 417	16.8	36.0	0.0	10.9	6.1	19.0	0.0
Wilmington	272	1 638	120.7	36.7	949	3 706 301	13.1	34.8	22.0	7.7	2.3	17.8	0.0
Wilson	74	D	D	D	776	2 938 961	12.7	19.6	12.6	8.5	5.3	36.1	0.0
Winston-Salem	330	2 049	137.4	52.4	2 489	8 460 457	12.1	31.4	15.9	7.1	5.7	23.1	0.0
NORTH DAKOTA	1 241	6 059	487.1	140.7	X	X	X	X	X	X	X	X	X
Bismarck	140	D	D	D	605	2 280 206	9.2	23.4	16.3	8.9	10.4	15.3	4.2
Fargo	225	1 703	112.8	44.1	836	3 889 052	10.7	22.5	14.1	18.2	12.7	15.1	3.8
Grand Forks	103	672	46.2	13.9	549	2 249 631	11.5	21.4	13.7	14.6	8.9	22.9	0.0
Minot	86	505	36.8	10.7	348	1 359 688	12.5	26.4	15.9	13.9	0.0	20.0	3.8
West Fargo	38	239	23.1	7.2	120	521 710	16.1	47.5	0.0	0.0	0.0	30.4	6.0
OHIO	16 338	106 072	8 483.2	2 613.6	X	X	X	X	X	X	X	X	X
Akron	313	2 040	166.1	49.7	1 872	8 159 087	15.0	31.5	21.9	4.1	0.5	18.7	0.0
Barberton	46	250	19.2	6.3	256	1 078 359	17.1	23.7	20.5	6.9	9.7	22.1	0.0
Beavercreek	48	D	D	D	144	794 411	6.5	49.4	0.0	17.6	4.9	14.0	0.0
Bowling Green	47	222	14.5	4.4	302	1 389 538	15.6	20.6	19.6	2.1	0.6	31.6	0.0
Brunswick	55	368	29.0	8.1	156	716 777	14.6	38.7	22.6	9.5	2.3	6.8	0.0
Canton	132	670	43.7	13.4	914	3 932 055	14.5	23.0	20.1	7.9	7.6	22.3	0.0
Cincinnati	418	2 971	238.8	78.3	5 222	26 843 252	9.4	25.7	17.7	5.4	8.4	28.9	0.0
Cleveland	624	3 972	355.6	93.2	7 389	33 318 506	12.7	29.1	13.0	9.9	7.8	25.3	0.0
Cleveland Heights	53	321	27.3	8.5	461	2 098 391	11.2	30.1	23.8	3.9	3.6	16.1	0.0
Columbus	1 150	9 379	673.5	215.0	8 035	42 573 757	14.7	32.2	23.9	4.3	5.7	16.8	0.0
Cuyahoga Falls	95	550	39.6	13.2	489	2 562 538	13.6	24.8	17.8	10.3	2.3	25.4	0.0
Dayton	195	1 702	150.5	52.6	1 940	9 617 585	13.2	22.8	17.4	11.8	4.6	25.3	0.0
Delaware	34	169	13.9	4.7	269	1 371 645	23.1	26.5	19.6	10.0	0.0	17.2	0.0
Dublin	40	524	42.5	15.1	836	2 882 615	15.9	35.7	0.0	4.5	15.6	11.3	0.0
Elyria	76	583	67.9	17.2	532	2 415 086	14.1	27.3	15.3	5.3	6.2	26.7	0.0
Euclid	63	289	20.6	10.8	454	1 882 329	12.3	36.1	22.3	4.1	5.6	15.3	0.0
Fairborn	40	187	11.3	3.7	222	557 607	20.8	22.1	26.3	4.5	1.3	11.4	0.0
Fairfield	96	594	48.3	15.6	340	1 631 218	20.0	30.2	17.2	8.1	0.0	22.3	0.0
Findlay	85	542	45.8	14.8	325	1 499 497	13.1	24.6	25.6	9.6	3.8	22.6	0.0
Gahanna	56	663	46.2	15.6	274	1 378 735	13.1	50.2	0.0	7.2	1.6	18.8	0.0
Garfield Heights	42	230	11.6	3.7	204	993 260	15.9	40.2	25.6	1.0	4.0	2.4	0.0
Green	37	D	D	D	131	615 958	19.2	0.0	49.5	27.4	0.0	2.9	0.0
Grove City	63	522	38.7	18.1	169	893 462	12.9	61.0	0.0	6.2	0.0	15.6	0.0

1. Establishments subject to federal tax.

City	City government finances, 2007									
	General revenue							General expenditure		
		Intergovernmental		Taxes					Per capita[1] (dollars)	
					Per capita[1] (dollars)					
	Total (mil dol)	Total (mil dol)	Percent from state government	Total (mil dol)	Total	Property	Sales and gross receipts	Total (mil dol)	Total	Capital outlays
	117	118	119	120	121	122	123	124	125	126
NEW YORK—Cont'd										
Yonkers	973.8	463.3	98.2	426.2	2 146	1 487	460	967.5	4 872	267
NORTH CAROLINA	X	X	X	X	X	X	X	X	X	X
Apex	41.1	5.4	89.2	23.2	575	413	161	41.1	1 016	152
Asheboro	28.8	4.7	94.5	15.9	623	480	143	29.2	1 140	28
Asheville	115.3	28.1	51.3	66.5	775	542	233	121.5	1 415	244
Burlington	64.2	9.0	59.4	35.6	695	482	213	62.8	1 224	7
Cary	187.2	16.9	75.1	100.1	687	482	205	218.0	1 496	577
Chapel Hill	80.0	23.1	43.6	48.5	826	614	212	68.9	1 174	154
Charlotte	1 401.8	250.6	43.7	622.1	803	489	314	1 294.8	1 671	438
Concord	109.3	19.4	51.2	56.1	682	525	158	107.7	1 311	79
Durham	303.7	47.0	61.0	171.9	717	538	179	302.6	1 262	129
Fayetteville	208.3	50.9	51.4	95.2	472	298	174	235.1	1 166	340
Garner	26.6	2.9	28.3	20.3	760	553	207	24.8	926	110
Gastonia	81.0	9.5	71.1	46.3	636	418	218	85.6	1 176	76
Goldsboro	41.9	6.6	92.5	22.8	633	417	216	47.0	1 303	68
Greensboro	371.9	60.4	63.7	196.6	711	528	183	412.3	1 492	244
Greenville	116.0	31.1	70.0	46.0	525	360	165	107.6	1 228	125
Hickory	61.0	10.1	62.0	33.9	844	579	265	60.2	1 500	170
High Point	158.5	22.3	59.1	81.9	768	572	196	167.5	1 571	282
Huntersville	34.2	5.5	74.2	22.2	450	329	122	35.6	722	217
Indian Trail	10.0	2.4	32.5	6.4	182	142	41	7.7	220	16
Jacksonville	66.3	10.7	56.8	31.8	458	272	186	75.1	1 079	221
Kannapolis	41.5	5.6	64.3	25.1	572	425	147	48.1	1 099	338
Matthews	20.9	3.5	73.5	14.5	506	361	145	19.8	691	109
Monroe	55.3	6.6	75.2	24.8	738	578	160	69.9	2 080	827
Mooresville	65.3	6.7	75.3	35.6	1 034	845	189	71.2	2 068	563
New Bern	44.8	7.8	87.0	19.3	636	440	196	43.0	1 416	135
Raleigh	555.4	92.1	53.9	287.3	679	448	231	527.4	1 245	199
Rocky Mount	82.1	24.8	46.4	31.3	549	385	164	81.9	1 437	161
Salisbury	55.5	5.3	90.5	21.9	656	510	146	64.5	1 931	175
Sanford	35.2	4.6	61.9	18.2	628	419	210	34.4	1 189	24
Thomasville	26.0	4.5	82.6	14.1	525	395	129	26.2	973	39
Wake Forest	31.1	3.1	92.3	26.4	802	585	216	34.4	1 042	231
Wilmington	128.8	25.2	52.9	76.2	693	481	212	132.5	1 206	224
Wilson	71.8	10.0	67.7	27.6	557	410	147	70.7	1 427	69
Winston-Salem	293.3	50.8	63.3	139.2	594	431	163	303.3	1 294	272
NORTH DAKOTA	X	X	X	X	X	X	X	X	X	X
Bismarck	128.3	46.0	40.5	37.1	571	261	310	118.8	1 827	623
Fargo	237.9	83.4	99.5	72.5	658	188	465	229.3	2 080	749
Grand Forks	100.1	20.7	28.9	38.0	709	279	430	59.4	1 106	129
Minot	75.0	19.3	56.5	37.3	849	247	603	44.2	1 005	135
West Fargo	34.8	5.1	100.0	10.6	384	237	147	41.1	1 488	814
OHIO	X	X	X	X	X	X	X	X	X	X
Akron	350.3	65.6	64.3	174.5	879	131	9	337.8	1 701	101
Barberton	31.7	6.9	86.9	14.0	533	53	31	30.8	1 170	202
Beavercreek	25.7	8.8	100.0	12.8	279	249	24	26.8	583	125
Bowling Green	36.0	6.4	100.0	21.2	667	71	53	36.9	1 161	103
Brunswick	26.4	4.7	51.4	15.9	463	47	13	22.8	662	108
Canton	118.3	36.4	85.3	46.7	642	37	21	113.3	1 558	208
Cincinnati	947.1	392.8	17.6	415.4	1 400	180	74	783.9	2 641	864
Cleveland	897.0	231.8	58.8	419.1	1 071	143	124	897.7	2 294	222
Cleveland Heights	55.8	10.6	84.0	31.9	699	210	54	57.2	1 254	119
Columbus	1 434.3	260.4	47.1	776.6	958	53	57	1 353.3	1 670	431
Cuyahoga Falls	65.4	9.3	91.5	31.4	637	219	19	59.4	1 207	245
Dayton	304.4	74.9	66.0	118.0	832	117	10	297.8	2 099	314
Delaware	45.0	6.0	28.6	20.7	578	47	21	56.6	1 578	458
Dublin	103.4	6.6	100.0	74.6	1 709	85	81	90.8	2 117	497
Elyria	65.0	18.3	87.1	27.5	508	62	44	62.4	1 153	112
Euclid	62.8	10.1	90.8	28.1	581	104	4	73.1	1 514	131
Fairborn	38.1	6.6	99.9	16.6	498	73	74	37.4	1 124	168
Fairfield	52.2	6.6	100.0	29.3	686	121	80	61.3	1 438	11
Findlay	47.4	7.7	100.0	24.9	599	67	8	43.6	1 050	149
Gahanna	35.0	5.1	65.6	19.0	562	61	37	38.9	1 150	171
Garfield Heights	34.7	4.5	59.7	21.3	748	365	31	32.2	1 130	3
Green	27.4	4.6	79.0	20.6	800	59	29	25.0	969	123
Grove City	38.4	8.3	45.2	24.0	651	84	43	33.8	917	213

1. Based on population estimated as of July 1 of the year shown.

City	City government finances, 2012 (cont.)									
	General expenditure (cont.)									
	Percent of total for:									
	Public welfare	Highways	Parking facilities	Education	Health and hospitals	Police protection	Sewerage and sanitation	Parks and recreation	Housing and community development	Interest on debt
	127	128	129	130	131	132	133	134	135	136
NEW YORK—Cont'd										
Yonkers	0.0	0.9	0.5	52.5	0.1	8.5	2.4	1.0	0.9	3.4
NORTH CAROLINA	X	X	X	X	X	X	X	X	X	X
Apex	0.0	9.5	0.0	0.0	2.8	16.4	27.0	10.3	2.5	2.0
Asheboro	0.0	8.3	0.0	0.0	0.1	21.9	25.3	5.2	4.4	0.7
Asheville	0.0	11.4	6.4	0.0	0.1	18.3	8.4	17.4	4.6	1.0
Burlington	0.0	3.6	0.0	0.0	0.0	23.7	18.2	9.5	2.5	2.6
Cary	0.0	5.6	0.0	0.0	0.0	10.3	37.2	10.3	1.6	2.8
Chapel Hill	0.0	7.2	2.8	0.0	0.0	17.7	7.9	9.7	8.4	3.6
Charlotte	0.0	9.3	0.1	0.0	0.0	19.2	21.6	2.2	6.0	10.5
Concord	0.0	5.4	0.0	0.0	0.0	16.5	22.1	5.5	14.1	2.4
Durham	0.0	10.6	0.6	0.0	0.0	20.7	18.7	6.5	7.1	5.9
Fayetteville	0.0	4.9	1.7	0.0	0.0	18.9	35.9	6.3	3.1	2.1
Garner	0.0	19.6	0.0	0.0	0.0	27.7	7.0	11.0	3.5	2.1
Gastonia	0.0	10.5	1.2	0.0	0.0	19.9	26.7	5.9	5.3	3.9
Goldsboro	0.0	9.3	0.0	0.0	0.0	21.0	16.1	5.8	8.1	2.6
Greensboro	0.0	9.9	0.4	0.0	0.1	17.5	24.6	17.5	4.9	2.7
Greenville	0.0	8.9	0.1	0.0	0.0	22.4	22.7	8.4	5.4	2.9
Hickory	0.0	10.0	0.0	0.0	0.1	18.2	21.0	5.9	0.9	0.8
High Point	0.0	8.3	0.2	0.0	0.1	15.8	29.1	8.4	4.3	4.7
Huntersville	0.0	24.6	0.0	0.0	1.1	36.8	1.5	16.6	4.1	3.6
Indian Trail	0.0	12.0	0.0	0.0	0.2	17.8	38.0	0.6	12.1	1.2
Jacksonville	0.0	5.6	0.0	0.0	0.0	20.5	39.6	8.4	2.4	3.8
Kannapolis	0.0	7.6	0.0	0.0	0.0	14.6	9.5	9.7	2.7	4.1
Matthews	0.0	12.0	0.0	0.0	0.0	32.5	9.0	16.0	2.3	1.5
Monroe	0.0	3.6	0.0	0.0	0.1	13.8	9.2	5.7	1.3	0.9
Mooresville	0.0	5.1	0.0	0.0	0.0	9.5	29.1	9.2	9.4	12.4
New Bern	0.0	7.7	0.0	0.0	0.0	30.7	26.9	5.0	4.4	3.1
Raleigh	0.2	6.1	1.7	0.0	0.0	19.1	14.8	23.5	4.8	5.4
Rocky Mount	0.0	9.3	0.0	0.0	0.0	18.5	26.3	9.8	4.8	1.0
Salisbury	0.0	7.1	0.0	0.0	0.0	10.8	24.8	3.7	1.0	4.6
Sanford	0.0	6.4	0.0	0.0	0.2	24.4	26.0	2.5	7.0	4.5
Thomasville	0.0	7.7	0.0	0.0	0.1	20.4	26.1	8.1	3.0	3.4
Wake Forest	0.0	17.8	0.0	0.0	0.0	19.6	7.2	10.3	0.0	2.7
Wilmington	0.0	10.5	2.9	0.0	0.0	20.7	15.0	8.1	1.1	7.7
Wilson	0.6	5.3	0.2	0.0	0.0	18.4	20.5	7.6	5.6	3.2
Winston-Salem	0.0	6.9	0.9	0.0	0.0	21.2	27.1	7.5	5.2	7.0
NORTH DAKOTA	X	X	X	X	X	X	X	X	X	X
Bismarck	0.0	24.2	0.9	0.0	2.1	9.9	17.2	6.8	0.7	2.1
Fargo	4.1	24.0	0.3	0.0	0.0	12.3	6.2	5.9	0.9	7.6
Grand Forks	0.0	6.9	0.6	0.0	2.9	14.2	20.7	2.9	5.6	13.8
Minot	0.0	12.9	0.3	0.0	0.0	16.1	18.8	4.7	0.0	1.5
West Fargo	0.0	39.8	0.0	0.0	0.0	11.7	25.6	0.8	0.0	9.2
OHIO	X	X	X	X	X	X	X	X	X	X
Akron	0.0	2.5	1.8	0.0	1.6	10.0	12.3	1.6	3.3	7.7
Barberton	0.0	7.0	0.0	0.0	0.0	16.3	30.7	3.3	3.5	1.0
Beavercreek	0.0	39.4	0.0	0.0	0.6	27.4	0.0	12.8	2.3	3.6
Bowling Green	0.0	18.5	0.0	0.0	0.2	14.7	20.9	5.0	0.0	3.1
Brunswick	0.0	16.1	0.0	0.0	0.4	28.0	10.3	6.3	1.3	1.4
Canton	0.0	11.9	0.3	0.0	5.6	18.0	15.3	1.7	0.0	0.9
Cincinnati	0.0	7.1	1.4	0.0	3.5	14.5	34.1	4.3	5.1	2.9
Cleveland	1.2	3.1	0.7	0.0	4.6	19.2	6.3	4.4	9.1	9.8
Cleveland Heights	0.0	12.2	1.9	0.0	2.4	15.6	7.3	6.2	7.6	1.5
Columbus	0.0	9.9	0.2	0.0	2.8	18.9	20.2	10.2	2.3	6.4
Cuyahoga Falls	0.0	8.0	0.0	0.0	0.0	15.5	16.0	12.1	2.4	2.6
Dayton	0.8	8.7	0.0	0.0	0.0	14.5	12.3	2.9	7.3	0.8
Delaware	0.0	8.1	0.1	0.0	0.0	10.0	11.3	20.5	0.8	7.8
Dublin	0.0	5.5	0.0	0.0	0.3	11.4	6.9	18.8	0.0	2.5
Elyria	0.0	9.1	0.0	0.0	5.9	20.7	28.4	3.7	2.1	2.2
Euclid	0.0	2.8	0.0	0.0	0.5	15.6	17.9	2.5	1.4	1.9
Fairborn	0.0	14.7	0.0	0.0	0.0	15.7	20.6	0.7	1.8	2.3
Fairfield	0.0	27.4	0.0	0.0	0.0	16.3	11.4	7.3	0.0	2.2
Findlay	0.0	12.0	0.2	0.0	4.9	14.8	17.2	3.5	0.0	3.6
Gahanna	0.0	13.2	0.2	2.8	1.0	22.0	20.7	10.3	0.0	2.6
Garfield Heights	0.8	3.9	0.0	1.6	0.6	19.0	5.9	2.2	0.4	4.5
Green	0.0	27.0	0.0	0.0	3.3	7.4	0.7	5.3	0.0	7.8
Grove City	0.0	24.3	0.0	0.0	0.0	28.2	2.0	7.8	0.0	4.8

City	City government finances, 2012 (cont.)			Climate[2]						
	Debt outstanding			Average daily temperature (degrees Fahrenheit)						
				Mean		Limits				
	Total (mil dol)	Per capita[1] (dollars)	Debt issued during year	January	July	January[3]	July[4]	Annual precipitation (inches)	Heating degree days	Cooling degree days
	137	138	139	140	141	142	143	144	145	146
NEW YORK—Cont'd										
Yonkers	757.7	3 815	113.7	29.7	74.2	20.1	86.0	46.46	5 400	770
NORTH CAROLINA	X	X	X	X	X	X	X	X	X	X
Apex	63.3	1 566	35.0	NA	NA	NA	NA	NA	NA	NA
Asheboro	9.3	363	0.0	NA	NA	NA	NA	NA	NA	NA
Asheville	110.4	1 286	39.2	36.4	73.9	26.6	84.3	37.32	4 237	877
Burlington	62.0	1 208	18.4	38.7	79.3	27.6	90.6	45.08	3 588	1 489
Cary	243.8	1 672	11.3	39.5	78.7	30.1	87.9	46.49	3 431	1 456
Chapel Hill	60.5	1 030	33.5	38.5	79.4	27.8	88.6	48.04	3 650	1 491
Charlotte	3 227.6	4 165	470.5	41.7	80.3	32.1	90.1	43.51	3 162	1 681
Concord	100.3	1 221	19.4	39.4	79.2	27.9	90.3	47.30	3 463	1 540
Durham	398.4	1 661	15.6	39.7	78.8	29.6	89.1	43.05	3 465	1 521
Fayetteville	204.6	1 014	10.6	41.7	80.4	31.1	90.4	46.78	3 097	1 721
Garner	13.9	520	0.0	NA	NA	NA	NA	NA	NA	NA
Gastonia	94.3	1 295	6.0	42.0	79.9	31.7	89.9	49.19	3 009	1 701
Goldsboro	50.9	1 411	14.3	43.4	81.2	33.0	91.4	49.84	2 771	1 922
Greensboro	443.1	1 603	48.7	39.7	78.6	29.0	88.9	42.89	3 443	1 438
Greenville	143.1	1 633	4.3	42.0	78.8	31.9	88.4	49.30	3 113	1 516
Hickory	38.0	947	3.4	39.0	77.7	29.2	87.8	48.98	3 608	1 333
High Point	267.0	2 504	53.4	39.7	78.2	29.6	89.0	46.19	3 399	1 424
Huntersville	41.4	839	24.3	NA	NA	NA	NA	NA	NA	NA
Indian Trail	2.4	69	0.0	NA	NA	NA	NA	NA	NA	NA
Jacksonville	103.2	1 484	51.6	44.7	80.2	33.9	89.5	54.07	2 656	1 832
Kannapolis	67.9	1 550	17.0	39.4	79.2	27.9	90.3	47.30	3 463	1 540
Matthews	6.0	211	0.0	NA	NA	NA	NA	NA	NA	NA
Monroe	59.6	1 773	2.8	41.5	79.0	31.0	89.7	48.73	3 125	1 538
Mooresville	220.0	6 392	65.4	NA	NA	NA	NA	NA	NA	NA
New Bern	76.1	2 504	3.5	NA	NA	NA	NA	NA	NA	NA
Raleigh	1 004.7	2 373	218.5	39.1	79.4	28.1	89.9	45.70	3 514	1 550
Rocky Mount	10.0	175	2.4	41.1	79.2	30.8	89.7	46.51	3 215	1 518
Salisbury	81.1	2 426	8.3	40.2	78.7	29.5	89.5	42.86	3 356	1 466
Sanford	51.3	1 774	0.0	NA	NA	NA	NA	NA	NA	NA
Thomasville	42.9	1 594	11.3	NA	NA	NA	NA	NA	NA	NA
Wake Forest	32.8	993	6.3	NA	NA	NA	NA	NA	NA	NA
Wilmington	205.6	1 872	30.7	44.8	80.1	33.3	90.0	58.44	2 606	1 791
Wilson	113.0	2 279	12.2	40.4	79.2	29.5	90.2	47.18	3 328	1 575
Winston-Salem	727.7	3 105	38.5	39.7	78.2	29.6	89.0	46.19	3 399	1 424
NORTH DAKOTA	X	X	X	X	X	X	X	X	X	X
Bismarck	97.9	1 506	12.3	10.2	70.4	-0.6	84.5	16.84	8 802	471
Fargo	566.3	5 136	79.8	6.8	70.6	-2.3	82.2	21.19	9 092	533
Grand Forks	382.8	7 136	24.1	5.3	69.4	-4.3	81.9	19.60	9 489	420
Minot	41.8	952	7.0	7.5	68.4	-1.8	80.4	18.65	9 479	422
West Fargo	120.7	4 372	17.9	NA	NA	NA	NA	NA	NA	NA
OHIO	X	X	X	X	X	X	X	X	X	X
Akron	794.0	3 998	96.9	27.2	74.1	20.1	83.9	36.07	5 752	856
Barberton	16.6	631	0.0	29.1	73.6	20.3	85.0	39.16	5 348	813
Beavercreek	12.0	260	4.2	27.6	73.1	19.5	83.5	40.06	5 531	768
Bowling Green	24.2	761	3.4	23.1	72.9	15.2	84.2	33.18	6 492	690
Brunswick	11.1	322	0.4	25.7	71.9	18.8	81.4	38.71	6 121	702
Canton	20.1	276	0.0	25.2	71.8	17.4	82.3	38.47	6 154	678
Cincinnati	917.4	3 091	175.8	30.6	76.8	22.7	86.8	39.57	4 841	1 210
Cleveland	2 530.4	6 465	194.4	25.7	71.9	18.8	81.4	38.71	6 121	702
Cleveland Heights	18.6	407	0.0	25.7	71.9	18.8	81.4	38.71	6 121	702
Columbus	2 555.4	3 153	190.4	28.3	74.7	20.2	85.6	40.03	5 349	935
Cuyahoga Falls	55.8	1 133	3.3	29.1	73.6	20.3	85.0	39.16	5 348	813
Dayton	131.3	926	0.2	26.3	74.3	19.0	84.2	39.58	5 690	935
Delaware	89.4	2 492	2.2	25.1	73.0	16.6	84.6	37.58	6 178	739
Dublin	57.2	1 334	0.0	28.3	74.7	20.2	85.6	40.03	5 349	935
Elyria	50.5	934	13.2	27.1	73.0	19.3	85.0	38.02	5 731	818
Euclid	40.5	839	19.4	23.0	68.8	14.3	80.0	47.33	6 956	372
Fairborn	21.9	657	0.0	27.9	77.0	20.6	87.2	39.41	5 343	1 214
Fairfield	32.0	750	0.0	28.7	76.6	19.9	88.1	43.36	5 261	1 135
Findlay	18.2	439	2.7	24.5	73.6	17.4	83.5	36.91	6 194	809
Gahanna	26.3	777	5.8	28.3	75.1	20.3	85.3	38.52	5 492	951
Garfield Heights	27.3	959	0.0	25.7	71.9	18.8	81.4	38.71	6 121	702
Green	58.3	2 261	7.2	NA	NA	NA	NA	NA	NA	NA
Grove City	35.9	973	0.0	28.3	74.7	20.2	85.6	40.03	5 349	935

1. Based on the population estimated as of July 1 of the year shown. 2. Represents normal values based on the 30-year period, 1971–2000. 3. Average daily minimum.
4. Average daily maximum.

STATE Place code	City	Land area,[1] 2010 (sq km)	Population, 2014: Total persons	Population, 2014: Rank	Population, 2014: Per square kilometer	Race alone or in combination (percent), 2011-2013: White	Black	American Indian, Alaska Native	Asian	Hawaiian Pacific Islander	Percent Hispanic or Latino[2], 2011-2013	Percent foreign born 2011–2013
		1	2	3	4	5	6	7	8	9	10	11
	OHIO—Cont'd											
39 33012	Hamilton	55.9	62 486	566	1 117.8	88.5	10.9	0.8	0.6	NA	4.2	2.9
39 35476	Hilliard	34.1	32 465	1 147	952.1	91.0	3.4	NA	6.4	NA	1.7	6.1
39 36610	Huber Heights	57.7	38 162	971	661.4	83.3	16.8	1.8	2.1	NA	3.2	3.2
39 39872	Kent	23.8	29 639	1 244	1 245.3	85.9	12.1	0.2	5.9	NA	1.9	6.9
39 40040	Kettering	48.4	55 705	660	1 150.9	93.8	5.2	0.4	2.4	NA	2.2	4.0
39 41664	Lakewood	14.3	50 926	737	3 561.3	90.8	8.8	0.8	2.7	NA	3.8	8.7
39 41720	Lancaster	48.8	39 595	941	811.4	96.8	2.7	1.1	0.9	NA	0.7	1.0
39 43554	Lima	35.1	38 265	969	1 090.2	71.5	29.8	1.4	0.7	NA	2.8	1.1
39 44856	Lorain	61.3	63 776	553	1 040.4	78.7	19.0	2.1	1.5	0.2	26.0	2.5
39 47138	Mansfield	80.0	46 824	802	585.3	77.7	24.1	2.5	0.6	NA	2.3	1.7
39 47754	Marion	30.4	36 620	1 016	1 204.6	87.5	11.4	1.4	0.9	NA	3.0	1.9
39 48188	Mason	48.3	31 613	1 177	654.5	84.7	5.1	0.9	11.1	NA	4.2	11.6
39 48244	Massillon	48.1	32 274	1 155	671.0	91.9	9.1	0.2	NA	NA	2.7	1.2
39 48790	Medina	30.0	26 523	1 379	884.1	94.2	4.9	0.5	1.5	NA	2.7	3.2
39 49056	Mentor	69.0	46 870	800	679.3	97.5	1.1	0.4	1.5	NA	1.2	3.7
39 49840	Middletown	67.8	48 791	772	719.6	85.7	13.9	1.8	0.8	NA	5.8	3.4
39 54040	Newark	54.1	47 839	786	884.3	95.6	6.0	2.0	1.0	NA	1.2	0.9
39 56882	North Olmsted	30.2	32 130	1 161	1 063.9	93.7	2.9	0.5	3.3	NA	4.3	8.3
39 56966	North Ridgeville	60.7	31 871	1 168	525.1	95.6	1.9	NA	2.4	NA	3.7	5.3
39 57008	North Royalton	55.2	30 327	1 222	549.4	94.4	3.4	NA	3.7	NA	1.9	10.2
39 61000	Parma	51.9	80 015	410	1 541.7	94.2	3.6	0.8	2.7	NA	4.3	9.7
39 66390	Reynoldsburg	28.9	36 711	1 011	1 270.3	74.1	26.5	1.2	3.4	NA	5.2	6.5
39 67468	Riverside	25.2	25 040	1 420	993.7	90.2	8.1	0.3	2.8	NA	3.4	3.6
39 70380	Sandusky	25.2	25 346	1 416	1 005.8	75.4	25.6	1.7	0.7	NA	5.4	1.9
39 71682	Shaker Heights	16.3	27 790	1 314	1 704.9	58.6	36.9	0.7	5.8	NA	2.5	8.7
39 74118	Springfield	65.5	59 956	604	915.4	79.2	22.0	1.1	1.2	0.2	3.1	2.2
39 74944	Stow	44.3	34 773	1 070	784.9	95.2	2.6	0.4	3.1	0.2	1.3	4.5
39 75098	Strongsville	63.8	44 654	828	699.9	91.6	2.5	NA	5.0	NA	2.2	7.7
39 77000	Toledo	209.0	281 031	68	1 344.6	68.4	29.7	1.4	1.7	0.2	7.8	3.1
39 77588	Troy	30.4	25 564	1 406	840.9	93.2	5.5	1.1	3.5	NA	2.2	3.0
39 79002	Upper Arlington	25.5	34 609	1 073	1 357.2	93.7	1.5	0.7	5.7	NA	1.8	6.9
39 80892	Warren	41.8	40 633	912	972.1	71.2	31.3	0.9	NA	NA	2.9	2.1
39 83342	Westerville	32.3	37 667	982	1 166.2	90.5	7.6	0.3	2.9	NA	1.5	4.7
39 83622	Westlake	41.3	32 424	1 148	785.1	92.2	2.3	NA	7.7	NA	3.4	9.5
39 86548	Wooster	42.2	26 540	1 377	628.9	94.1	4.5	0.6	2.3	NA	2.4	3.5
39 86772	Xenia	34.4	25 911	1 397	753.2	84.8	16.0	1.6	1.7	NA	1.3	1.7
39 88000	Youngstown	87.9	65 062	544	740.2	52.4	46.9	1.5	0.8	NA	9.9	4.0
39 88084	Zanesville	30.5	25 372	1 412	831.9	90.5	13.1	1.8	NA	NA	1.4	2.0
40 00000	OKLAHOMA	177 660.0	3 878 051	X	21.8	80.5	8.9	13.3	2.4	0.2	9.4	5.6
40 04450	Bartlesville	58.9	36 498	1 019	619.7	85.7	4.7	12.6	2.0	NA	6.5	3.9
40 09050	Broken Arrow	159.5	104 726	280	656.6	86.4	5.8	10.3	4.5	0.3	6.6	5.6
40 23200	Edmond	219.4	88 605	351	403.9	86.7	6.4	4.2	4.5	0.4	4.7	6.3
40 23950	Enid	190.8	51 386	728	269.3	84.5	5.1	4.0	1.9	2.2	11.3	7.3
40 41850	Lawton	209.9	97 017	309	462.2	67.9	24.0	7.3	4.9	1.1	14.4	7.3
40 48350	Midwest City	63.2	57 039	643	902.5	71.3	24.3	7.6	2.7	NA	5.9	3.7
40 49200	Moore	56.5	59 196	615	1 047.7	87.9	6.0	10.0	3.2	0.4	10.3	4.5
40 50050	Muskogee	109.8	38 616	960	351.7	66.7	18.3	20.4	1.4	NA	6.7	3.6
40 52500	Norman	463.0	118 040	228	254.9	86.1	5.6	7.6	5.1	0.3	5.9	6.0
40 55000	Oklahoma City	1 570.6	620 602	27	395.1	73.5	16.7	7.6	4.8	0.1	18.3	12.5
40 56650	Owasso	42.2	33 773	1 099	800.3	85.2	3.5	12.0	2.8	NA	9.1	4.6
40 59850	Ponca City	47.6	24 766	1 427	520.3	84.9	4.8	13.6	1.1	NA	7.2	2.8
40 66800	Shawnee	114.3	31 254	1 186	273.4	79.2	5.2	21.4	1.6	0.2	5.6	2.7
40 70300	Stillwater	76.5	48 406	777	632.8	84.5	6.7	6.9	7.4	NA	4.6	8.5
40 75000	Tulsa	509.6	399 682	47	784.3	72.5	17.9	9.6	3.1	0.2	14.6	10.1
41 00000	OREGON	248 607.8	3 970 239	X	16.0	88.7	2.6	2.9	5.2	0.7	12.1	9.8
41 01000	Albany	45.4	51 980	714	1 144.9	93.5	1.0	3.0	3.0	NA	12.3	5.1
41 05350	Beaverton	48.5	95 109	315	1 961.0	74.5	3.9	2.2	14.5	0.9	15.4	21.9
41 05800	Bend	85.5	84 080	384	983.4	94.0	1.2	1.0	2.7	0.7	8.4	5.3
41 15800	Corvallis	36.6	54 953	672	1 501.4	88.0	1.4	1.5	9.9	0.7	7.9	11.3
41 23850	Eugene	113.2	160 561	155	1 418.4	90.0	2.4	2.9	5.9	0.8	8.3	7.9
41 30550	Grants Pass	28.2	35 272	1 059	1 250.8	96.1	0.7	3.7	1.6	NA	8.8	2.5
41 31250	Gresham	60.1	109 892	256	1 828.5	83.3	5.3	2.3	6.0	2.2	18.8	17.4
41 34100	Hillsboro	61.9	99 393	299	1 605.7	78.2	2.5	2.7	10.9	1.5	24.6	20.4
41 38500	Keizer	18.4	37 303	993	2 027.3	90.2	1.7	2.4	3.6	0.8	21.5	11.1
41 40550	Lake Oswego	27.7	37 999	975	1 371.8	91.4	0.8	0.6	8.6	NA	2.9	11.7
41 45000	McMinnville	27.4	33 393	1 113	1 218.7	87.3	2.1	2.3	1.3	NA	22.3	10.5
41 47000	Medford	66.7	78 557	421	1 177.8	93.4	1.7	2.2	2.7	0.9	14.2	8.3
41 55200	Oregon City	23.5	35 266	1 060	1 500.7	93.8	0.8	2.9	4.2	NA	7.9	5.4
41 59000	Portland	345.6	619 360	28	1 792.1	81.6	7.4	2.3	9.3	0.8	9.6	14.1

1. Dry land or land partially or temporarily covered by water. 2. May be of any race.

City	Age of population (percent), 2011-2013: Under 5 years	5 to 17 years	18 to 24 years	25 to 34 years	35 to 44 years	45 to 54 years	55 to 64 years	65 to 74 years	75 years and over	Median age 2011-2013	Percent female 2011-2013	Population: Census counts: 2000	2010	Percent change: 2000–2010	2010–2014
	12	13	14	15	16	17	18	19	20	21	22	23	24	25	26
OHIO—Cont'd															
Hamilton	8.0	16.5	9.2	14.4	12.3	14.6	12.2	6.1	6.7	37.0	54.1	60 690	62 477	2.9	0.3
Hilliard	6.3	23.5	6.3	11.6	14.5	17.8	10.0	5.5	4.6	37.3	52.0	24 230	28 435	17.4	15.0
Huber Heights	7.4	19.2	7.6	14.8	11.7	13.6	12.1	8.7	4.9	35.6	52.6	38 212	38 101	-0.3	0.2
Kent	4.0	10.1	42.6	13.2	6.8	6.8	8.2	4.5	3.7	23.0	52.6	27 906	28 904	3.6	2.5
Kettering	5.2	16.3	7.9	14.3	11.3	14.5	12.9	8.7	9.0	40.6	51.9	57 502	56 163	-2.3	-0.8
Lakewood	5.8	13.5	9.2	21.4	12.8	14.0	11.9	5.7	5.7	35.0	51.7	56 646	52 131	-8.0	-2.3
Lancaster	6.1	17.0	9.7	13.8	12.2	12.8	12.5	8.1	7.7	38.2	52.0	35 335	38 780	9.7	2.1
Lima	7.5	18.8	14.1	13.3	11.2	12.8	11.3	5.9	5.3	32.4	47.8	40 081	38 771	-3.3	-1.3
Lorain	5.9	19.9	8.7	11.4	12.6	14.6	11.9	7.8	7.1	37.9	53.5	68 652	64 097	-6.6	-0.5
Mansfield	6.1	14.4	9.5	14.8	12.5	13.3	12.3	8.2	8.9	39.0	47.0	49 346	47 821	-3.1	-2.1
Marion	6.4	14.5	10.3	14.9	14.2	15.1	12.0	6.9	5.8	38.4	41.6	35 318	36 837	4.3	-0.6
Mason	5.5	23.8	5.7	9.8	14.0	18.5	10.6	6.7	5.3	39.9	53.1	22 016	30 712	39.5	2.5
Massillon	6.6	16.1	8.5	13.7	10.1	13.1	15.3	8.1	8.5	40.8	50.5	31 325	32 149	2.6	0.2
Medina	7.2	21.3	8.0	10.0	14.9	15.8	10.8	5.2	6.8	37.6	53.3	25 139	26 678	6.1	-0.5
Mentor	5.6	14.9	6.4	10.5	11.8	17.9	15.8	9.7	7.4	45.9	51.6	50 278	47 159	-6.2	-0.6
Middletown	8.1	15.9	9.9	13.2	11.1	13.9	12.6	9.1	6.3	37.5	51.7	51 605	48 694	-5.6	0.2
Newark	7.4	17.9	8.9	13.5	12.7	13.2	11.9	8.1	6.6	36.8	52.0	46 279	47 573	2.8	0.6
North Olmsted	5.0	16.3	6.2	10.9	12.4	15.0	15.3	10.3	8.7	44.5	51.4	34 113	32 718	-4.1	-1.8
North Ridgeville	7.5	15.3	5.1	11.9	13.9	15.6	13.6	10.9	6.1	41.5	49.7	22 338	29 465	31.9	8.2
North Royalton	3.9	16.8	6.1	12.6	12.5	17.7	14.7	8.3	7.4	43.8	51.5	28 648	30 444	6.3	-0.4
Parma	5.7	14.2	9.8	12.5	11.4	15.4	13.0	8.4	9.5	42.2	51.8	85 655	81 601	-4.7	-1.9
Reynoldsburg	5.9	18.7	10.5	13.5	12.7	15.0	11.7	7.2	4.9	36.3	52.0	32 069	35 893	11.9	2.3
Riverside	6.6	17.8	10.8	13.6	12.4	13.4	11.9	6.7	6.8	36.1	48.9	23 545	25 201	7.0	-0.6
Sandusky	6.4	14.7	8.2	16.2	8.9	14.1	14.8	9.0	7.7	39.2	51.1	27 844	25 793	-7.4	-2.2
Shaker Heights	6.0	19.3	6.5	11.0	13.3	13.9	13.9	7.9	8.0	41.3	54.3	29 405	28 448	-3.3	-2.3
Springfield	7.5	17.3	11.4	12.3	10.7	12.6	12.9	7.7	7.5	36.6	52.6	65 358	60 608	-7.3	-1.1
Stow	5.6	16.4	7.7	13.9	11.7	14.5	14.2	8.1	7.8	40.8	53.7	32 139	34 837	8.4	-0.2
Strongsville	4.9	17.5	6.2	9.1	12.4	16.8	15.2	9.7	8.2	44.9	51.2	43 858	44 750	2.0	-0.2
Toledo	6.9	16.4	12.1	14.3	11.9	13.7	12.0	6.5	6.2	35.3	51.0	313 619	287 208	-8.4	-2.2
Troy	4.7	19.0	7.9	14.2	14.1	13.6	12.0	8.7	5.8	39.1	51.1	21 999	25 058	13.9	1.3
Upper Arlington	6.5	19.7	5.1	11.1	13.6	14.5	13.8	8.1	7.5	41.2	51.7	33 686	33 771	0.3	2.8
Warren	6.6	16.5	9.1	13.0	11.7	14.1	11.9	8.4	8.7	39.5	52.7	46 832	41 557	-11.3	-2.2
Westerville	4.4	16.6	11.7	8.8	13.5	14.9	14.6	8.6	6.9	41.3	52.7	35 318	36 120	2.3	4.3
Westlake	5.1	17.5	4.6	10.4	13.2	15.1	15.0	8.9	10.2	44.1	53.8	31 719	32 729	3.2	-0.9
Wooster	6.8	12.9	17.7	13.8	10.2	9.8	11.9	9.6	7.4	34.3	51.9	24 811	26 119	5.3	1.6
Xenia	7.9	18.9	6.3	16.7	11.8	11.4	11.4	8.3	7.3	35.2	52.7	24 164	25 719	6.4	1.0
Youngstown	6.6	15.9	11.6	11.5	11.4	13.7	13.8	6.6	8.9	39.4	51.4	82 026	66 982	-18.3	-2.9
Zanesville	8.7	17.4	9.5	15.9	9.1	13.7	10.7	7.6	7.3	33.5	50.9	25 586	25 487	-0.4	-0.4
OKLAHOMA	6.9	17.7	10.2	13.6	12.2	13.2	12.1	7.9	6.1	36.2	50.5	3 450 654	3 751 351	8.7	3.4
Bartlesville	7.2	16.6	9.4	12.5	11.8	11.8	13.0	9.3	8.4	38.5	52.3	34 748	35 750	2.9	2.1
Broken Arrow	7.1	19.3	8.1	13.2	13.8	14.8	12.5	6.8	4.5	36.9	50.8	74 859	98 850	32.0	6.0
Edmond	6.1	18.4	11.8	12.5	12.2	14.6	12.2	7.3	4.8	35.8	50.7	68 315	81 405	19.2	8.9
Enid	7.9	16.6	9.6	14.7	10.6	13.0	12.1	7.7	7.9	36.2	51.2	47 045	49 379	5.0	4.1
Lawton	8.2	16.6	15.2	17.9	11.7	11.5	9.3	5.3	4.4	30.1	47.8	92 757	96 867	4.4	0.2
Midwest City	6.4	17.8	9.5	14.7	13.0	13.6	11.5	6.6	6.9	36.1	52.5	54 088	54 371	0.5	4.9
Moore	7.4	19.3	10.2	18.8	12.4	13.7	9.8	5.3	3.1	32.2	51.8	41 138	55 081	33.9	7.5
Muskogee	7.8	18.5	10.1	12.8	10.9	12.6	12.3	8.1	6.8	35.7	53.1	38 310	39 223	2.4	-1.5
Norman	5.7	14.2	21.3	15.1	11.0	10.8	10.4	6.5	4.9	30.4	50.0	95 694	110 925	15.9	6.4
Oklahoma City	8.0	17.7	9.7	16.6	12.6	12.7	11.5	6.2	5.0	33.6	50.7	506 132	579 999	14.6	7.0
Owasso	5.8	23.3	8.3	13.3	17.4	13.1	8.9	5.7	4.1	34.6	50.8	18 502	28 915	56.3	13.6
Ponca City	7.6	18.3	8.9	12.2	10.9	12.2	12.5	8.4	8.9	37.2	50.8	25 919	25 387	-2.1	-2.5
Shawnee	8.8	16.3	14.1	12.4	11.1	11.6	11.4	7.3	7.1	33.6	52.0	28 692	29 857	4.1	4.7
Stillwater	5.3	10.6	38.4	13.7	8.0	8.1	7.1	4.7	4.1	23.7	50.1	39 065	45 688	17.0	5.9
Tulsa	7.6	16.9	10.6	15.2	12.0	13.0	12.0	6.8	6.0	34.9	51.5	393 049	391 906	-0.3	2.0
OREGON	6.0	16.1	9.4	13.6	13.0	13.4	13.7	8.5	6.4	38.9	50.5	3 421 399	3 831 074	12.0	3.6
Albany	6.8	18.5	8.8	15.1	13.2	12.5	12.0	7.7	5.5	35.6	49.6	40 852	50 158	22.8	3.6
Beaverton	6.3	17.1	8.7	18.0	15.0	12.9	11.2	6.2	4.6	35.0	51.6	76 129	89 803	18.0	5.9
Bend	6.6	16.7	7.8	14.5	14.2	13.1	12.7	8.0	6.4	38.4	50.9	52 029	76 639	47.3	9.7
Corvallis	4.4	10.2	32.2	12.9	9.9	9.6	9.9	5.4	5.6	27.0	49.2	49 322	54 462	10.4	0.9
Eugene	4.7	12.8	20.0	13.7	11.9	11.3	12.1	7.2	6.2	34.1	50.8	137 893	156 185	13.3	2.7
Grants Pass	6.9	16.6	8.6	11.7	10.3	13.8	11.8	9.3	11.2	40.0	53.0	23 003	34 533	50.1	1.8
Gresham	7.7	18.6	10.2	14.6	12.2	14.0	11.2	5.9	5.6	34.4	50.3	90 205	105 594	17.1	4.1
Hillsboro	8.5	18.0	8.6	18.8	15.9	12.6	9.2	5.1	3.2	32.7	51.7	70 186	91 611	30.5	7.9
Keizer	7.5	19.0	8.8	15.5	11.1	12.3	11.3	7.6	6.8	34.6	51.8	32 203	36 478	13.3	2.2
Lake Oswego	4.5	17.4	6.1	8.9	13.3	15.1	16.6	10.6	7.4	44.9	52.9	35 278	36 619	3.8	3.7
McMinnville	7.1	19.4	11.9	11.9	10.9	11.9	10.7	7.8	8.4	34.9	53.2	26 499	32 187	21.5	3.7
Medford	7.3	16.1	9.4	14.6	11.1	12.8	11.8	7.7	9.1	37.4	50.4	63 154	74 907	18.6	4.8
Oregon City	6.0	19.6	8.1	13.2	14.6	16.0	11.9	6.5	4.0	37.5	50.4	25 754	31 859	23.7	8.1
Portland	5.8	12.8	9.0	19.7	16.7	12.9	12.2	6.3	4.7	36.4	50.5	529 121	583 776	10.3	6.1

City	Households, 2011-2013: Number	Households, 2011-2013: Persons per household	Households, 2011-2013: Percent: Female family householder[1]	Households, 2011-2013: Percent: One-person	Persons in group quarters, 2010: Total	Persons in group quarters, 2010: Institutional: Total	Persons in group quarters, 2010: Institutional: Persons in nursing facilities	Persons in group quarters, 2010: Non-institutional	Serious crimes known to police,[2] 2013: Total: Number	Serious crimes known to police,[2] 2013: Total: Rate[3]	Serious crimes known to police,[2] 2013: Rate[3]: Violent	Serious crimes known to police,[2] 2013: Rate[3]: Property	Educational attainment, 2011–2013: Population age 25 and older	Educational attainment, 2011–2013: Attainment[4] (percent): High school graduate or less	Educational attainment, 2011–2013: Attainment[4] (percent): Bachelor's degree or more
	27	28	29	30	31	32	33	34	35	36	37	38	39	40	41
OHIO—Cont'd															
Hamilton	23 789	2.55	18.0	29.0	1 663	1 354	436	309	4 303	6 910	607	6 303	41 341	57.9	15.2
Hilliard	10 639	2.79	8.1	22.5	155	155	155	0	745	2 376	83	2 293	19 060	24.6	47.4
Huber Heights	14 945	2.58	18.1	26.1	184	64	64	120	1 457	3 822	157	3 665	25 544	37.9	22.4
Kent	10 685	2.53	13.3	27.9	6 067	81	81	5 986	717	2 380	186	2 194	13 860	27.8	45.4
Kettering	24 785	2.25	12.4	35.9	427	304	304	123	1 340	2 397	95	2 302	39 802	33.5	30.1
Lakewood	24 700	2.07	10.4	46.3	370	304	303	66	1 001	1 956	94	1 863	36 736	29.7	40.5
Lancaster	16 218	2.35	13.8	33.9	871	692	383	179	2 079	5 344	342	5 002	26 191	52.7	16.1
Lima	14 240	2.50	23.5	34.5	4 300	3 401	279	899	2 298	6 014	958	5 056	22 923	56.5	10.8
Lorain	25 571	2.47	21.7	32.4	662	444	423	218	3 107	4 887	477	4 410	41 811	54.7	11.1
Mansfield	18 244	2.23	17.1	40.6	6 594	5 881	519	713	3 372	7 200	384	6 816	32 840	58.1	12.7
Marion	12 853	2.43	14.9	30.5	5 267	5 112	363	155	2 111	5 715	365	5 350	26 074	61.8	9.5
Mason	10 989	2.81	6.6	22.3	186	76	76	110	433	1 388	35	1 352	20 216	23.5	54.9
Massillon	13 337	2.35	14.2	35.2	951	683	348	268	1 060	3 296	227	3 069	22 111	54.6	16.2
Medina	10 200	2.57	11.6	26.8	361	345	186	16	1	2	2	0	16 910	37.1	32.0
Mentor	19 121	2.44	7.8	28.3	403	381	381	22	1 102	2 346	92	2 254	34 405	35.1	31.2
Middletown	19 780	2.44	15.6	32.9	573	472	399	101	4 275	8 780	618	8 162	32 270	57.7	15.9
Newark	19 325	2.42	14.7	32.8	1 011	750	486	261	2 636	5 526	164	5 362	31 461	54.1	15.3
North Olmsted	13 160	2.43	9.5	30.3	323	264	264	59	NA	NA	NA	NA	23 493	36.0	29.7
North Ridgeville	12 170	2.50	9.0	26.0	225	213	213	12	280	906	45	861	22 075	36.9	30.2
North Royalton	12 396	2.43	9.1	29.9	247	226	226	21	NA	NA	NA	NA	22 212	37.6	32.7
Parma	32 850	2.42	13.3	31.6	1 063	897	792	166	943	1 174	108	1 066	56 713	47.8	18.9
Reynoldsburg	14 195	2.55	13.1	28.9	25	0	0	25	1 196	3 279	195	3 085	23 547	36.1	31.3
Riverside	9 990	2.52	14.7	30.6	0	0	0	0	670	2 668	179	2 489	16 292	47.8	15.7
Sandusky	11 460	2.17	17.6	40.5	579	305	240	274	1 221	4 807	307	4 500	18 007	55.1	16.3
Shaker Heights	11 170	2.50	14.4	29.3	156	119	44	37	690	2 471	147	2 324	19 100	13.6	65.4
Springfield	24 082	2.37	18.7	35.4	2 497	1 128	854	1 369	4 890	8 148	712	7 437	38 202	54.6	16.4
Stow	13 766	2.49	7.8	29.6	454	405	405	49	733	2 117	66	2 051	24 418	31.7	39.5
Strongsville	17 294	2.56	5.9	24.8	304	277	264	27	773	1 734	61	1 673	31 869	29.6	43.1
Toledo	117 008	2.36	19.2	36.7	8 475	2 987	1 239	5 488	10 069	3 558	1 025	2 532	183 481	49.6	16.9
Troy	10 037	2.43	15.1	26.1	420	263	163	157	817	3 213	79	3 135	16 888	47.8	20.6
Upper Arlington	13 156	2.59	6.2	24.3	254	254	254	0	466	1 356	29	1 327	23 454	10.0	73.6
Warren	17 618	2.18	19.3	42.4	2 517	2 302	525	215	2 186	5 401	655	4 746	27 708	63.8	10.9
Westerville	14 261	2.47	7.1	26.5	1 685	454	454	1 231	865	2 315	35	2 280	25 043	23.4	52.4
Westlake	13 553	2.33	5.8	35.5	871	830	830	41	58	179	9	170	23 684	18.8	55.0
Wooster	10 546	2.20	11.2	35.9	2 381	387	230	1 994	1 024	3 869	159	3 710	16 521	47.1	27.9
Xenia	10 038	2.46	14.4	37.9	925	700	312	225	1 110	4 263	211	4 052	17 347	50.0	18.7
Youngstown	26 296	2.28	26.0	39.5	5 831	3 929	644	1 902	4 109	6 328	813	5 514	43 299	60.6	11.2
Zanesville	10 505	2.37	20.9	35.2	582	514	290	68	1 723	6 789	430	6 360	16 385	63.1	11.0
OKLAHOMA	1 445 059	2.57	12.4	28.2	112 017	64 411	21 678	47 606	143 046	3 715	441	3 274	2 487 647	45.2	23.8
Bartlesville	14 925	2.39	13.1	31.2	658	256	145	402	955	2 624	239	2 385	24 231	37.5	29.7
Broken Arrow	36 770	2.76	11.8	20.3	468	466	466	2	2 181	2 118	143	1 976	66 830	32.9	31.3
Edmond	31 566	2.64	7.9	23.7	1 586	313	268	1 273	1 682	1 956	101	1 855	54 070	19.6	51.9
Enid	19 073	2.53	14.1	25.9	1 824	1 005	593	819	2 522	5 048	456	4 591	32 973	50.1	20.6
Lawton	34 025	2.63	15.9	30.8	10 143	3 772	523	6 371	5 946	6 034	933	5 101	58 805	44.6	19.4
Midwest City	23 062	2.42	17.3	31.4	285	260	235	25	3 285	5 805	634	5 171	37 153	40.3	20.4
Moore	20 954	2.73	15.4	21.4	309	179	179	130	1 959	3 341	123	3 219	36 374	42.2	21.3
Muskogee	15 100	2.49	17.9	29.2	1 353	834	430	519	2 132	5 483	815	4 668	24 760	49.7	19.0
Norman	44 942	2.41	9.6	32.2	6 757	1 124	566	5 633	3 119	2 666	152	2 514	68 057	27.3	43.5
Oklahoma City	228 435	2.57	13.2	31.1	12 144	6 609	2 521	5 535	37 477	6 194	826	5 368	388 150	40.8	28.3
Owasso	11 896	2.72	9.5	24.5	242	214	173	28	797	2 493	188	2 305	20 336	33.7	30.3
Ponca City	10 060	2.42	13.1	33.6	700	433	245	267	1 412	5 680	515	5 165	16 283	45.9	20.2
Shawnee	12 043	2.41	15.8	34.5	1 670	468	249	1 202	1 874	6 067	550	5 517	18 659	45.6	21.4
Stillwater	18 352	2.14	7.7	38.3	6 945	367	180	6 578	630	1 345	122	1 223	21 318	23.3	50.2
Tulsa	162 775	2.38	15.6	34.8	8 386	4 284	2 033	4 102	24 805	6 288	970	5 318	256 749	38.4	30.4
OREGON	1 516 591	2.51	10.5	28.1	86 642	36 612	11 491	50 030	134 721	3 428	254	3 174	2 673 399	35.1	30.0
Albany	19 370	2.62	15.6	25.4	824	560	256	264	2 059	3 987	77	3 909	33 921	36.4	22.6
Beaverton	36 433	2.52	10.6	30.7	945	460	393	485	1 595	1 705	133	1 572	62 896	28.2	42.1
Bend	32 018	2.46	8.3	29.9	578	183	157	395	2 471	3 092	229	2 863	54 592	22.6	39.7
Corvallis	21 148	2.35	8.6	32.8	4 899	116	74	4 783	1 653	2 994	116	2 878	29 260	15.0	58.9
Eugene	65 814	2.30	10.4	33.0	7 249	1 131	585	6 118	8 322	5 251	254	4 997	98 971	24.9	38.3
Grants Pass	14 409	2.35	13.6	36.7	1 051	627	355	424	2 701	7 747	321	7 426	23 690	43.3	14.4
Gresham	38 931	2.75	17.0	26.7	1 514	553	491	961	5 164	4 696	556	4 140	68 932	44.2	19.2
Hillsboro	33 250	2.83	12.4	25.4	1 528	989	220	539	2 301	2 389	146	2 243	61 958	35.4	32.1
Keizer	13 542	2.70	13.8	21.9	364	190	190	174	970	2 620	167	2 453	23 881	38.1	24.9
Lake Oswego	16 123	2.29	7.1	32.5	222	187	148	35	637	1 702	59	1 643	26 821	11.4	65.6
McMinnville	11 577	2.69	12.1	27.1	1 716	396	183	1 320	1 041	3 189	230	2 959	20 252	47.5	20.8
Medford	29 726	2.52	12.5	29.1	1 553	691	450	862	5 303	6 892	587	6 304	51 441	42.1	23.8
Oregon City	12 451	2.66	10.7	23.2	650	555	157	95	1 041	3 152	100	3 052	22 367	31.6	23.4
Portland	251 027	2.34	9.6	35.1	17 754	4 821	2 160	12 933	32 574	5 348	483	4 865	436 489	26.3	44.4

1. No spouse present. 2. Data for serious crimes have not been adjusted for underreporting. This may affect comparability between geographic areas and over time. 3. Per 100,000 population estimated by the FBI. 4. Persons 25 years old and over.

City	Money income, 2011–2013: Per capita income[1] (dollars)	Money income, 2011–2013: Households: Median income	Money income, 2011–2013: Households: Percent with income of $200,000 or more	Money income, 2011–2013: Households: Percent with income of less than $25,000	Money income, 2011–2013: Families with income below poverty (percent)	Housing units, 2010: Total	Housing units, 2010: Percent change, 2000–2010	Housing units, 2010: Vacant units for sale or rent[2]	Occupied housing units 2011–2013: Total	Occupied housing units 2011–2013: Owner-occupied: Percent	Occupied housing units 2011–2013: Owner-occupied: Median value[3] (dollars)	Occupied housing units 2011–2013: Median owner costs as a percent of income: With a mortgage[4]	Occupied housing units 2011–2013: Median owner costs as a percent of income: Without a mortgage[5]
	42	43	44	45	46	47	48	49	50	51	52	53	54
OHIO—Cont'd													
Hamilton	20 689	40 189	0.5	31.6	17.7	27 878	7.5	3 220	23 789	56.9	101 500	21.1	10.9
Hilliard	35 769	81 948	8.2	9.3	2.8	10 637	19.6	439	10 639	77.0	206 000	22.5	12.5
Huber Heights	24 125	47 899	2.0	22.2	11.2	15 875	6.2	1 155	14 945	69.7	105 300	23.0	12.8
Kent	19 722	33 280	2.2	41.0	21.3	11 174	6.8	886	10 685	38.6	142 000	17.4	10.7
Kettering	28 945	48 618	3.1	22.7	9.0	27 602	2.5	2 175	24 785	60.4	127 500	21.6	12.9
Lakewood	28 195	42 987	2.1	29.2	14.5	28 498	0.3	3 224	24 700	43.6	127 600	21.4	14.9
Lancaster	21 134	34 711	1.2	36.3	15.8	17 685	11.6	1 637	16 218	53.2	113 400	22.8	10.8
Lima	15 072	28 421	0.4	45.4	26.9	16 784	-5.0	2 563	14 240	45.6	68 600	20.9	12.8
Lorain	18 649	33 298	0.6	38.4	24.2	29 144	3.3	3 615	25 571	58.3	88 000	21.2	13.5
Mansfield	17 390	31 575	0.8	39.5	22.1	22 022	-1.4	3 326	18 244	55.8	80 600	21.7	12.2
Marion	15 221	31 889	0.9	38.8	19.2	15 066	2.3	2 198	12 853	57.8	76 000	22.7	12.4
Mason	38 112	87 677	12.0	8.8	2.3	11 471	41.1	455	10 989	81.2	222 800	20.2	10.0
Massillon	21 496	37 288	1.1	32.9	14.3	14 497	7.1	1 357	13 337	63.7	95 500	21.2	14.5
Medina	26 890	51 636	3.4	22.3	10.2	11 152	13.9	770	10 200	65.1	156 100	19.6	10.6
Mentor	32 776	68 104	3.7	15.8	5.5	20 218	4.8	1 052	19 121	85.0	167 600	20.5	11.6
Middletown	20 288	35 932	1.9	35.3	19.8	23 296	0.5	3 058	19 780	53.9	94 000	23.6	13.5
Newark	21 027	37 877	1.5	34.6	19.2	21 976	6.3	2 136	19 325	53.8	110 600	20.5	13.1
North Olmsted	29 684	61 296	1.6	15.0	5.8	14 500	3.1	855	13 160	76.0	146 800	21.8	14.2
North Ridgeville	29 958	65 255	3.2	12.1	4.9	12 109	41.0	609	12 170	86.3	161 700	21.7	12.7
North Royalton	33 696	65 735	5.2	14.3	1.9	13 710	16.6	766	12 396	70.6	188 600	22.2	13.7
Parma	24 000	49 167	1.0	23.7	9.8	36 608	0.5	2 119	32 850	74.5	110 100	21.6	14.0
Reynoldsburg	28 336	60 557	2.9	18.7	10.2	15 611	15.9	1 224	14 195	61.1	142 200	21.7	14.0
Riverside	20 720	39 914	0.3	28.3	11.8	11 304	8.8	1 020	9 990	53.5	90 200	21.8	12.9
Sandusky	22 469	36 353	1.6	36.6	16.2	13 386	0.4	2 304	11 460	53.2	85 000	21.7	13.0
Shaker Heights	48 192	76 034	16.4	18.0	5.0	13 318	2.5	1 478	11 170	62.5	217 000	20.6	13.2
Springfield	18 445	30 508	1.1	41.4	24.4	28 437	-2.9	3 978	24 082	50.7	79 700	21.0	12.2
Stow	31 197	63 442	2.8	13.9	3.4	15 141	17.8	915	13 766	72.4	165 900	21.1	10.9
Strongsville	38 191	77 234	7.1	11.7	2.3	18 476	9.6	817	17 294	80.0	190 700	19.8	11.9
Toledo	18 414	32 263	0.7	40.3	24.0	138 039	-1.3	18 309	117 008	53.8	78 400	22.7	13.6
Troy	23 471	45 705	0.3	24.2	13.6	11 166	17.1	813	10 037	57.1	124 000	20.3	10.0
Upper Arlington	51 648	95 056	18.6	9.8	2.9	14 544	0.8	790	13 156	81.5	309 500	21.6	13.3
Warren	16 624	27 612	0.5	45.0	28.9	20 384	-4.5	3 381	17 618	52.7	61 400	21.5	13.8
Westerville	37 072	79 971	8.1	12.9	4.0	14 467	10.1	608	14 261	73.3	202 000	20.7	10.0
Westlake	49 194	77 274	11.7	12.5	3.0	14 843	8.4	973	13 553	74.5	225 300	19.6	11.9
Wooster	22 212	39 022	1.9	31.0	14.0	11 822	10.0	1 089	10 546	55.0	120 500	22.4	12.2
Xenia	20 083	38 411	0.7	32.9	21.0	11 424	15.4	1 034	10 038	62.9	96 400	23.5	12.4
Youngstown	14 603	24 012	0.5	51.8	30.8	33 123	-10.9	6 284	26 296	56.5	44 100	22.0	13.3
Zanesville	15 521	24 751	0.3	50.6	30.9	12 385	5.4	1 521	10 505	45.4	73 800	23.2	13.9
OKLAHOMA	24 120	45 171	2.8	27.2	12.8	1 664 378	9.9	203 928	1 445 059	66.3	114 600	20.9	10.9
Bartlesville	27 221	47 928	3.5	24.9	12.8	16 768	4.1	1 791	14 925	67.9	112 200	19.3	10.0
Broken Arrow	28 646	64 789	3.6	14.2	6.1	38 013	40.2	1 872	36 770	77.6	153 100	20.8	11.0
Edmond	37 974	71 607	9.1	17.4	5.7	33 178	25.8	1 703	31 566	70.8	197 000	20.6	10.0
Enid	24 193	45 749	2.8	23.2	9.9	21 936	3.2	2 210	19 073	63.2	91 300	20.5	10.0
Lawton	20 755	42 326	1.4	27.6	16.1	39 409	8.2	4 508	34 025	48.9	105 300	21.0	10.9
Midwest City	22 696	43 555	0.9	24.6	12.4	24 723	3.9	1 997	23 062	57.8	102 000	21.4	11.6
Moore	24 468	56 671	2.3	15.6	8.0	21 444	34.8	998	20 954	71.0	121 900	20.8	11.4
Muskogee	17 624	31 870	0.4	39.5	21.9	18 055	2.8	2 351	15 100	57.3	83 400	19.5	11.0
Norman	28 796	49 772	4.3	26.0	10.3	47 965	15.5	3 304	44 942	56.8	155 300	19.8	10.0
Oklahoma City	25 085	45 073	3.1	26.3	14.6	256 930	12.6	26 697	228 435	58.4	134 300	22.1	11.8
Owasso	26 081	59 926	1.4	14.6	5.4	11 346	64.9	657	11 896	65.7	148 800	19.9	10.5
Ponca City	21 638	40 059	1.9	30.8	15.1	11 950	0.5	1 555	10 060	64.7	80 200	20.3	12.2
Shawnee	20 545	35 326	2.6	37.1	19.2	13 205	4.0	1 586	12 043	57.6	91 800	20.6	12.6
Stillwater	19 679	30 134	3.4	43.7	19.2	19 753	17.5	1 812	18 352	37.1	148 300	23.4	11.1
Tulsa	27 071	41 162	4.0	30.1	16.2	185 127	3.1	21 152	162 775	52.5	121 300	21.5	11.6
OREGON	26 553	49 519	3.3	25.0	11.8	1 675 562	15.3	156 624	1 516 591	61.1	228 700	25.5	12.7
Albany	21 718	47 390	1.1	28.1	16.3	20 979	20.6	1 274	19 370	60.4	176 000	24.0	12.1
Beaverton	29 616	54 685	3.3	20.7	13.0	39 500	21.5	2 287	36 433	47.1	269 000	24.6	12.8
Bend	29 133	51 041	4.0	24.0	7.9	36 110	60.5	4 320	32 018	57.0	239 900	25.8	13.8
Corvallis	24 171	39 483	2.8	36.3	11.9	23 423	12.1	1 140	21 148	45.2	270 800	22.5	10.1
Eugene	25 688	40 628	2.8	33.2	13.5	69 951	14.1	3 532	65 814	48.1	232 500	24.9	13.5
Grants Pass	19 906	31 384	1.7	39.6	19.1	15 561	57.8	1 248	14 409	49.3	170 700	26.2	14.0
Gresham	21 431	45 711	1.2	27.1	17.0	41 016	16.2	2 311	38 931	52.5	201 500	26.8	13.9
Hillsboro	27 444	64 826	4.0	17.2	11.1	35 487	30.5	2 198	33 250	53.8	228 200	24.7	11.6
Keizer	22 327	48 872	0.8	19.7	13.2	14 445	13.1	742	13 542	58.6	187 400	26.6	12.1
Lake Oswego	57 431	78 555	17.3	15.1	5.8	16 995	8.5	1 102	16 123	65.8	464 400	23.5	13.3
McMinnville	20 969	41 535	1.5	27.2	14.8	12 389	26.0	715	11 577	56.1	182 400	23.1	13.3
Medford	22 597	41 257	2.0	29.0	16.9	32 430	23.3	2 351	29 726	50.7	194 200	27.2	13.5
Oregon City	26 861	61 904	2.3	17.4	7.3	12 900	26.9	927	12 451	65.4	239 700	26.3	12.3
Portland	31 812	52 421	5.1	24.6	12.2	265 439	11.9	16 893	251 027	52.7	278 500	25.2	14.5

1. Based on population estimated by the American Community Survey. 2. Includes units rented or sold but not occupied. 3. Specified owner-occupied units; $1,000,000 represents $1,000,000 or more 4. 50.0 represents 50 percent or more. 5. 10.0 represents 10 percent or less.

City	Occupied housing units, 2011–2013 (cont.): Percent renter occupied	Occupied housing units, 2011–2013 (cont.): Median gross rent[1]	Occupied housing units, 2011–2013 (cont.): Median rent as a percent of income[2]	Occupied housing units, 2011–2013 (cont.): Percent with no vehicle available	Migration, 2011–2013: Percent who lived in the same house one year ago	Migration, 2011–2013: Percent who lived outside current city one year ago	Civilian labor force, 2014: Total	Civilian labor force, 2014: Percent change, 2013–2014	Civilian labor force, 2014: Unemployment: Total	Civilian labor force, 2014: Unemployment: Rate[3]	Civilian employment[4], 2011–2013: Population age 16 and older	Civilian employment[4], 2011–2013: Percent: In labor force	Civilian employment[4], 2011–2013: Percent: Civilian full-year full-time workers	Civilian employment[4], 2011–2013: Households with no workers (percent)
	55	56	57	58	59	60	61	62	63	64	65	66	67	68
OHIO—Cont'd														
Hamilton	43.1	717	31.0	9.9	81.8	9.6	27 891	-0.5	1 683	6.0	48 545	61.5	36.7	33.6
Hilliard	23.0	868	28.0	5.5	86.8	9.5	16 888	1.1	654	3.9	21 717	74.3	53.5	18.4
Huber Heights	30.3	851	33.2	5.3	82.1	9.6	17 990	-0.7	1 073	6.0	29 334	63.6	39.8	30.0
Kent	61.4	726	44.4	10.0	62.2	22.1	18 079	0.0	972	5.4	28 067	68.7	26.6	24.2
Kettering	39.6	715	27.4	6.5	82.8	11.0	28 934	-0.3	1 464	5.1	45 674	65.6	41.0	30.1
Lakewood	56.4	686	27.7	13.1	79.2	14.0	30 620	0.5	1 541	5.0	42 324	72.6	46.6	24.6
Lancaster	46.8	714	35.9	11.3	78.0	9.0	17 878	0.9	1 042	5.8	30 800	58.9	32.7	38.2
Lima	54.4	613	34.6	13.7	73.4	12.4	14 935	-2.9	1 045	7.0	29 500	60.6	27.2	35.9
Lorain	41.7	638	33.2	11.1	84.4	7.2	27 816	0.0	2 412	8.7	49 358	60.9	35.0	37.0
Mansfield	44.2	563	29.6	14.1	77.7	11.3	18 058	-0.6	1 295	7.2	38 393	48.3	26.0	40.8
Marion	42.2	660	34.7	11.9	72.4	13.0	13 737	-1.3	908	6.6	30 830	45.8	26.7	37.3
Mason	18.8	963	26.8	0.6	89.4	8.6	15 875	0.4	670	4.2	23 060	67.4	48.1	16.3
Massillon	36.3	642	29.9	9.8	88.0	7.8	15 404	-0.6	973	6.3	26 051	62.6	36.5	36.8
Medina	34.9	827	32.9	10.3	85.7	9.3	13 504	0.1	702	5.2	19 907	66.5	41.8	26.1
Mentor	15.0	843	30.9	4.5	93.6	5.1	26 637	0.4	1 347	5.1	38 893	67.3	45.8	24.9
Middletown	46.1	749	33.4	7.9	81.0	9.7	20 833	-0.4	1 414	6.8	38 007	62.5	34.1	35.8
Newark	46.2	675	32.0	9.9	77.9	10.3	23 380	0.5	1 306	5.6	37 231	64.2	37.7	31.5
North Olmsted	24.0	833	26.0	4.5	92.6	6.3	17 822	0.6	957	5.4	26 310	65.4	42.4	28.7
North Ridgeville	13.7	816	29.0	2.7	90.8	6.0	16 828	0.3	885	5.3	24 274	66.7	42.2	25.0
North Royalton	29.4	763	23.7	3.9	91.1	5.7	17 639	0.5	908	5.1	25 242	70.4	47.1	23.6
Parma	25.5	742	29.9	7.1	88.5	8.1	43 091	0.4	2 582	6.0	66 526	65.1	40.3	30.2
Reynoldsburg	38.9	842	27.3	5.2	86.0	9.7	20 268	1.0	963	4.8	28 231	72.0	46.1	23.0
Riverside	46.5	723	28.6	6.0	78.2	16.4	10 707	-0.6	692	6.5	19 709	63.0	36.2	33.4
Sandusky	46.8	614	27.3	12.7	79.8	9.3	11 942	-2.0	831	7.0	20 566	62.7	35.8	34.0
Shaker Heights	37.5	895	29.2	7.6	90.4	7.1	14 510	0.7	749	5.2	21 868	65.0	43.5	24.2
Springfield	49.3	633	34.3	13.8	79.0	8.0	25 915	-1.0	1 566	6.0	46 445	57.7	30.9	39.5
Stow	27.6	844	24.6	4.8	92.6	5.3	18 592	0.4	940	5.1	28 005	66.9	46.1	23.0
Strongsville	20.0	890	25.7	4.2	90.4	8.0	24 592	0.4	1 238	5.0	36 082	67.5	45.3	23.8
Toledo	46.2	623	33.7	14.6	80.8	6.2	128 945	-1.2	8 899	6.9	224 338	61.9	32.3	37.5
Troy	42.9	711	27.1	7.9	80.5	10.2	13 285	-0.1	666	5.0	19 563	68.6	46.3	25.9
Upper Arlington	18.5	1 038	23.8	3.2	88.5	8.9	17 995	1.4	683	3.8	26 193	67.8	46.2	22.9
Warren	47.3	571	35.4	13.5	84.7	8.2	14 872	-2.1	1 242	8.4	32 386	48.0	27.0	45.1
Westerville	26.7	896	26.7	6.1	85.6	12.1	21 005	1.1	838	4.0	30 670	68.5	43.7	21.2
Westlake	25.5	992	23.9	6.6	88.8	10.0	17 243	0.6	834	4.8	26 049	65.1	45.9	24.2
Wooster	45.0	656	29.8	9.6	71.9	14.9	13 464	-0.5	610	4.5	21 445	62.2	33.6	30.1
Xenia	37.1	652	32.6	10.7	85.1	9.6	11 050	-0.3	709	6.4	19 589	58.0	34.3	36.3
Youngstown	43.5	590	38.9	18.0	82.8	9.4	23 424	-2.1	1 999	8.5	52 896	49.8	23.1	44.9
Zanesville	54.6	599	32.8	15.4	76.0	11.1	9 886	-2.4	788	8.0	19 285	54.3	28.0	40.5
OKLAHOMA	33.7	702	28.7	5.8	82.6	10.6	1 784 035	-1.1	80 203	4.5	2 976 147	61.8	41.1	28.0
Bartlesville	32.1	634	26.5	6.5	80.1	10.9	17 183	-1.5	670	3.9	28 435	59.9	40.9	32.3
Broken Arrow	22.4	928	27.7	2.9	86.2	9.4	54 104	-0.6	1 818	3.4	78 203	70.4	49.8	18.6
Edmond	29.2	895	31.0	4.3	81.8	12.4	44 999	-0.5	1 386	3.1	66 140	68.7	45.5	20.3
Enid	36.8	683	22.4	4.6	76.3	12.1	23 194	-0.4	821	3.5	38 731	63.1	40.6	25.6
Lawton	51.1	775	28.5	8.7	67.1	19.7	36 548	-2.7	1 695	4.6	76 052	66.3	34.2	24.2
Midwest City	42.2	755	28.4	6.1	82.0	11.3	26 374	-0.8	1 232	4.7	43 788	63.7	42.1	29.1
Moore	29.0	883	28.1	3.2	83.8	11.5	29 576	-0.9	1 030	3.5	43 784	70.6	49.0	17.4
Muskogee	42.7	632	34.1	11.4	79.0	8.4	16 223	-2.4	848	5.2	29 736	56.4	35.8	37.4
Norman	43.2	757	32.0	5.1	74.1	13.0	60 021	-0.7	2 078	3.5	94 989	64.4	40.2	24.1
Oklahoma City	41.6	756	30.4	7.1	79.3	9.3	300 489	-0.8	11 647	3.9	461 193	66.7	44.2	24.3
Owasso	34.3	865	29.7	3.8	84.6	11.0	16 865	-0.7	547	3.2	24 021	70.7	48.3	17.3
Ponca City	35.3	639	27.7	7.7	79.9	9.2	10 498	-4.1	585	5.6	19 217	60.6	39.0	32.2
Shawnee	42.4	641	29.6	7.7	79.5	11.4	14 114	-0.8	618	4.4	23 652	60.6	38.0	30.9
Stillwater	62.9	699	43.4	7.2	63.0	19.5	23 461	1.6	789	3.4	39 934	58.9	27.5	28.3
Tulsa	47.5	720	29.5	8.3	79.5	7.8	193 582	-0.8	8 208	4.2	308 081	65.7	43.1	26.7
OREGON	38.9	877	32.4	8.1	81.6	12.3	1 942 025	1.6	134 956	6.9	3 137 983	62.4	34.8	30.7
Albany	39.6	776	37.3	8.1	80.3	10.3	23 878	1.2	1 818	7.6	39 893	62.2	33.2	32.6
Beaverton	52.9	979	29.6	8.6	79.1	14.5	51 391	2.0	2 811	5.5	72 970	70.4	42.1	20.2
Bend	43.0	928	31.0	6.2	77.0	10.9	42 836	3.8	2 816	6.6	62 673	67.7	33.9	29.3
Corvallis	54.8	825	42.8	9.1	72.1	17.6	28 442	0.9	1 486	5.2	47 946	57.7	24.5	32.5
Eugene	51.9	864	40.8	11.6	70.6	13.8	77 839	1.4	4 919	6.3	133 751	59.4	28.6	33.8
Grants Pass	50.7	829	39.2	11.8	78.8	10.9	14 184	2.6	1 232	8.7	27 562	49.2	26.9	47.5
Gresham	47.5	870	34.4	10.4	81.3	13.0	53 421	1.8	3 567	6.7	83 347	65.9	35.2	28.0
Hillsboro	46.2	1 073	28.2	7.1	79.1	14.2	51 392	2.3	2 881	5.6	73 009	70.6	44.9	18.1
Keizer	41.4	791	30.7	6.8	80.2	15.2	18 120	1.9	1 329	7.3	28 192	64.5	39.3	24.6
Lake Oswego	34.2	1 235	34.9	6.1	80.6	14.6	19 539	2.0	997	5.1	30 326	63.5	36.3	30.8
McMinnville	43.9	863	32.2	11.0	83.3	9.9	15 777	1.9	1 075	6.8	25 314	60.5	31.5	37.2
Medford	49.3	870	37.0	11.4	79.1	10.0	36 900	1.3	2 985	8.1	60 507	61.4	30.8	34.1
Oregon City	34.6	954	32.0	7.2	82.4	11.9	17 611	1.7	1 182	6.7	26 163	66.2	40.2	26.2
Portland	47.3	929	32.2	15.0	78.9	9.6	342 875	2.1	20 163	5.9	501 394	69.3	39.0	25.1

1. $2,000 represents $2,000 or more. 2. 50.0 represents 50 percent or more. 3. Percent of civilian labor force. 4. Persons 16 years old and over.

Table D. Cities — **Construction, Wholesale Trade, and Retail Trade**

City	Value of residential construction authorized by building permits, 2014			Wholesale trade,[1] 2007				Retail trade,[2] 2007			
	New construction ($1,000)	Number of housing units	Percent single family	Number of establish-ments	Number of employees	Sales (mil dol)	Annual payroll (mil dol)	Number of establish-ments	Number of employees	Sales (mil dol)	Annual payroll (mil dol)
	69	70	71	72	73	74	75	76	77	78	79
OHIO—Cont'd											
Hamilton	1 474	9	100.0	39	585	496.6	32.5	217	3 416	694.0	66.1
Hilliard	52 553	338	46.7	46	782	331.4	37.8	84	1 376	360.5	35.6
Huber Heights	NA	NA	NA	23	516	233.1	25.1	99	1 893	377.3	35.6
Kent	8 856	79	10.1	17	209	130.3	11.5	81	916	318.7	27.1
Kettering	937	7	100.0	32	255	116.5	11.7	170	3 629	1 550.1	81.4
Lakewood	1 200	1	100.0	32	D	D	D	124	1 273	238.5	25.4
Lancaster	9 761	70	40.0	32	231	81.9	7.5	238	3 172	576.4	59.3
Lima	175	2	100.0	48	725	401.2	29.5	129	1 423	289.0	29.6
Lorain	7 451	72	100.0	35	488	233.7	21.3	123	1 662	319.1	30.5
Mansfield	2 080	10	100.0	74	1 215	630.1	48.7	196	2 510	531.3	56.9
Marion	50	1	100.0	24	401	277.3	14.9	86	893	206.5	20.0
Mason	51 268	423	33.6	45	1 409	634.4	80.6	84	1 168	226.1	23.7
Massillon	7 295	75	56.0	33	474	318.4	20.7	124	2 536	574.1	54.8
Medina	0	0	0.0	46	550	349.8	23.3	115	1 894	334.8	32.4
Mentor	24 936	117	76.1	116	1 431	631.3	65.7	325	6 577	1 478.8	139.4
Middletown	2 801	20	100.0	40	838	482.0	40.0	173	3 252	852.3	70.6
Newark	NA	NA	NA	42	569	495.1	22.6	162	2 071	496.3	43.0
North Olmsted	125	1	100.0	22	129	144.8	8.6	283	5 132	1 130.5	102.4
North Ridgeville	34 692	310	74.5	33	182	79.2	7.8	64	885	195.1	20.3
North Royalton	12 211	44	100.0	58	408	247.5	18.2	69	715	147.9	14.9
Parma	4 500	125	0.0	61	735	199.2	34.6	301	4 662	963.1	86.1
Reynoldsburg	13 444	86	59.3	17	67	43.8	2.8	113	1 938	416.2	41.2
Riverside	NA	NA	NA	12	115	49.5	3.7	57	506	130.4	10.9
Sandusky	1 474	3	100.0	28	272	105.5	11.6	121	1 424	283.4	27.8
Shaker Heights	0	0	0.0	9	17	6.7	1.0	62	698	134.7	13.9
Springfield	1 349	8	100.0	51	1 482	1 706.1	55.5	242	4 072	914.8	84.6
Stow	8 956	41	100.0	40	801	625.0	47.5	106	2 302	481.4	43.7
Strongsville	24 869	73	100.0	72	1 741	950.5	88.4	246	4 691	831.5	87.7
Toledo	26 614	493	5.3	302	4 740	2 924.2	206.8	1 065	14 799	2 831.8	292.7
Troy	NA	NA	NA	17	D	D	D	104	1 786	413.7	38.1
Upper Arlington	20 560	23	100.0	16	47	13.6	1.9	90	1 040	159.9	19.0
Warren	0	0	0.0	41	551	1 168.1	21.1	168	2 240	589.2	50.1
Westerville	20 905	187	3.7	49	860	379.7	40.6	134	2 286	442.6	49.7
Westlake	23 691	57	100.0	105	1 567	915.2	87.2	159	2 544	481.6	48.9
Wooster	5 919	25	100.0	35	530	579.1	20.0	182	2 890	608.7	59.4
Xenia	NA	NA	NA	13	D	D	D	83	1 398	307.1	32.4
Youngstown	0	0	0.0	104	2 226	872.0	81.8	230	2 075	365.4	41.3
Zanesville	250	1	100.0	27	D	D	D	232	3 437	726.1	62.4
OKLAHOMA	2 457 497	14 179	72.2	3 917	52 262	48 074.7	2 312.2	13 554	170 984	43 095.4	3 610.4
Bartlesville	17 959	90	93.3	22	D	D	D	172	2 369	588.9	50.8
Broken Arrow	116 618	622	78.1	126	1 625	713.9	82.7	237	4 185	1 164.6	96.9
Edmond	173 217	585	95.9	88	D	D	D	341	4 480	999.1	91.8
Enid	14 693	63	100.0	62	637	763.9	28.7	242	3 211	716.7	66.5
Lawton	10 679	62	74.2	46	366	117.2	9.5	375	5 143	1 152.2	103.1
Midwest City	14 781	92	100.0	16	413	94.7	10.9	174	3 585	1 011.5	87.5
Moore	82 954	541	90.2	40	524	159.8	18.4	122	2 117	440.7	43.1
Muskogee	4 074	21	100.0	53	864	498.9	46.3	232	3 029	763.8	63.2
Norman	168 704	1 154	46.7	58	957	442.9	39.5	437	6 907	1 768.0	147.1
Oklahoma City	770 619	4 461	74.1	1 008	D	D	D	2 223	32 456	8 430.8	751.0
Owasso	56 709	270	98.5	15	111	28.8	3.7	102	2 258	490.6	43.7
Ponca City	7 023	69	30.4	26	127	45.7	4.7	141	1 812	391.5	35.6
Shawnee	9 781	51	100.0	23	205	70.8	6.8	199	2 598	631.8	52.3
Stillwater	35 184	299	29.4	22	291	387.0	14.0	213	3 137	632.9	59.8
Tulsa	183 107	1 365	29.5	806	13 655	8 307.1	712.7	1 800	28 095	7 081.7	626.9
OREGON	3 243 361	16 645	51.5	4 806	67 040	51 910.8	3 215.5	14 991	204 793	50 370.9	4 916.3
Albany	38 938	224	54.5	40	377	225.6	13.2	188	2 997	770.9	70.3
Beaverton	46 567	308	42.5	215	2 525	2 952.0	172.3	425	7 793	2 594.3	215.3
Bend	190 056	847	93.4	145	1 590	1 001.4	73.7	572	7 977	2 087.9	201.0
Corvallis	71 703	406	18.2	26	416	323.4	16.2	224	3 185	633.6	67.1
Eugene	172 793	1 032	21.7	278	3 362	1 569.6	154.5	780	12 435	2 582.5	279.3
Grants Pass	15 210	75	94.7	31	328	270.9	9.7	264	3 713	862.5	93.2
Gresham	14 984	63	96.8	60	1 182	1 428.5	55.3	290	4 468	1 256.9	111.0
Hillsboro	102 448	886	20.9	102	2 073	1 072.3	130.8	330	6 609	1 902.9	152.0
Keizer	20 828	125	44.8	15	63	34.3	1.5	75	1 053	198.4	21.7
Lake Oswego	41 879	105	73.3	84	1 115	764.0	66.5	161	1 540	322.4	35.5
McMinnville	26 098	170	54.7	24	305	160.7	14.0	125	1 928	518.7	46.9
Medford	89 822	407	65.6	122	1 478	711.7	58.3	547	7 889	2 045.7	189.1
Oregon City	21 027	83	95.2	17	296	109.5	12.3	117	1 799	395.8	39.3
Portland	773 329	5 016	15.8	1 176	21 291	20 566.4	1 053.0	2 562	33 811	8 174.1	888.5

1. Merchant wholesalers except manufacturers' sales branches and offices. 2. Establishments with payroll.

City	Real estate and rental and leasing, 2007				Professional, scientific, and technical services,[1] 2007				Manufacturing, 2007			
	Number of establish-ments	Number of employees	Receipts (mil dol)	Annual payroll (mil dol)	Number of establish-ments	Number of employees	Receipts (mil dol)	Annual payroll (mil dol)	Number of establish-ments	Number of employees	Receipts (mil dol)	Annual payroll (mil dol)
	80	81	82	83	84	85	86	87	88	89	90	91
OHIO—Cont'd												
Hamilton	47	248	36.8	6.6	112	D	D	D	79	2 827	1 034.2	125.6
Hilliard	49	154	20.0	4.2	76	404	48.6	23.0	31	1 514	355.4	65.5
Huber Heights	24	126	20.4	5.8	34	330	26.9	10.0	34	1 348	432.8	73.7
Kent	24	89	12.5	2.3	50	321	36.4	13.5	63	1 855	D	74.3
Kettering	57	339	62.2	9.9	132	D	D	D	47	2 164	530.9	100.9
Lakewood	56	189	32.5	4.6	116	424	45.8	18.8	35	535	106.1	24.5
Lancaster	58	206	23.4	4.2	77	D	D	D	58	2 919	669.0	131.1
Lima	41	244	23.0	6.6	83	D	D	D	38	2 845	7 330.7	D
Lorain	48	166	19.2	4.1	76	D	D	D	52	2 517	1 744.2	165.6
Mansfield	59	306	24.0	6.3	123	704	65.6	27.0	118	6 538	2 130.7	281.7
Marion	37	132	18.5	3.7	45	D	D	D	35	2 030	1 159.2	86.5
Mason	32	132	18.2	3.8	110	1 112	106.8	107.4	40	4 128	1 148.1	182.7
Massillon	28	126	15.1	2.7	52	301	20.7	10.7	65	3 810	1 199.6	155.3
Medina	34	107	18.7	2.7	110	504	55.5	20.6	60	3 216	1 031.3	138.9
Mentor	68	576	95.1	15.5	173	868	103.9	33.8	232	7 497	1 944.1	326.7
Middletown	60	233	36.5	6.6	74	538	54.6	23.8	58	3 834	4 793.1	239.5
Newark	42	239	22.2	5.4	86	D	D	D	45	3 198	927.0	128.5
North Olmsted	36	160	42.3	5.1	83	366	30.6	11.6	NA	NA	NA	NA
North Ridgeville	16	52	6.9	0.8	44	224	24.5	12.0	41	1 325	253.5	49.2
North Royalton	23	D	D	D	86	287	27.3	11.0	77	862	131.5	36.4
Parma	67	364	50.1	9.7	116	D	D	D	51	2 492	890.4	184.3
Reynoldsburg	39	131	14.7	2.4	80	444	42.0	14.3	NA	NA	NA	NA
Riverside	26	101	22.7	2.7	42	D	D	D	NA	NA	NA	NA
Sandusky	33	132	19.6	3.9	54	D	D	D	47	1 805	473.5	86.6
Shaker Heights	38	122	20.0	3.8	101	438	83.2	30.3	NA	NA	NA	NA
Springfield	62	313	38.1	7.2	103	D	D	D	94	3 997	967.5	164.5
Stow	35	165	23.0	3.7	95	593	60.0	25.1	52	1 695	320.0	87.2
Strongsville	50	231	51.8	5.1	127	495	62.6	19.7	75	2 988	659.1	132.5
Toledo	276	2 022	745.1	76.3	510	D	D	D	365	15 647	10 634.8	908.7
Troy	33	157	29.4	4.1	60	326	33.7	14.5	64	4 033	1 431.6	187.6
Upper Arlington	53	196	37.4	6.4	136	D	D	D	NA	NA	NA	NA
Warren	33	150	18.5	3.4	107	449	38.1	13.2	55	7 339	1 882.4	445.7
Westerville	66	362	39.1	10.7	216	D	D	D	38	1 384	297.4	48.7
Westlake	67	925	124.1	26.7	221	1 618	154.4	102.5	52	1 764	426.8	73.0
Wooster	43	131	15.6	3.4	75	461	49.1	16.0	35	3 887	1 245.0	177.8
Xenia	27	95	9.6	1.7	38	175	12.8	3.5	34	699	133.5	D
Youngstown	60	283	30.7	6.5	106	D	D	D	115	3 210	1 147.8	143.6
Zanesville	41	205	29.1	5.1	67	D	D	D	39	1 582	537.6	76.1
OKLAHOMA	4 003	24 887	3 852.3	806.2	9 128	D	D	D	3 964	142 351	60 681.4	5 971.2
Bartlesville	45	213	28.3	5.1	80	D	D	D	37	978	293.6	42.8
Broken Arrow	95	D	D	D	237	1 159	132.2	52.9	132	4 754	1 504.2	223.6
Edmond	158	2 132	237.5	58.2	378	D	D	D	NA	NA	NA	NA
Enid	68	324	39.0	8.1	119	544	56.0	19.6	56	2 120	D	64.3
Lawton	128	D	D	D	146	D	D	D	42	3 395	D	D
Midwest City	72	290	47.8	6.3	87	D	D	D	NA	NA	NA	NA
Moore	35	136	29.8	4.5	49	346	26.5	12.4	NA	NA	NA	NA
Muskogee	56	533	43.5	10.1	88	D	D	D	50	2 857	972.6	129.2
Norman	197	884	162.6	27.7	426	D	D	D	80	2 255	931.0	95.5
Oklahoma City	879	5 974	996.7	238.7	2 253	D	D	D	702	23 758	7 711.8	954.0
Owasso	39	109	22.8	2.9	61	214	21.1	7.6	23	786	191.9	29.0
Ponca City	31	D	D	D	68	381	35.8	13.9	37	2 093	D	66.8
Shawnee	36	168	19.1	3.6	83	D	D	D	41	2 624	864.3	113.1
Stillwater	56	193	27.5	4.0	114	D	D	D	36	1 900	984.6	71.3
Tulsa	744	5 083	871.9	170.6	1 958	14 698	2 170.9	811.8	725	24 382	8 815.2	1 108.2
OREGON	6 391	30 978	5 077.2	950.3	11 363	83 190	9 750.4	4 869.5	5 717	183 953	66 880.7	8 138.9
Albany	65	254	32.3	5.7	101	D	D	D	69	2 289	714.5	100.4
Beaverton	249	1 173	221.0	40.5	446	D	D	D	123	6 822	1 855.8	406.1
Bend	284	872	138.6	25.9	445	D	D	D	171	3 198	529.7	122.9
Corvallis	98	495	53.6	10.0	210	D	D	D	54	3 506	408.6	178.5
Eugene	323	1 547	257.1	39.1	714	D	D	D	305	9 542	2 276.1	400.3
Grants Pass	78	355	39.3	8.3	95	D	D	D	79	2 170	340.1	70.3
Gresham	136	476	62.7	11.2	128	425	33.7	13.8	71	6 000	1 939.5	319.4
Hillsboro	103	656	172.4	21.4	214	D	D	D	164	8 924	9 152.2	500.0
Keizer	46	147	19.1	2.9	55	188	20.2	5.9	NA	NA	NA	NA
Lake Oswego	151	612	210.2	40.1	314	D	D	D	43	993	D	52.4
McMinnville	39	122	17.4	3.1	85	D	D	D	54	2 304	868.8	93.6
Medford	183	947	135.6	24.9	255	D	D	D	101	1 756	375.9	63.7
Oregon City	46	129	27.0	3.4	104	D	D	D	44	923	243.5	41.2
Portland	1 307	9 115	1 676.4	350.8	3 116	D	D	D	1 035	30 694	8 434.6	1 315.5

1. Establishments subject to federal tax.

City	Accommodation and food services, 2007				Arts, entertainment, and recreation,[1] 2007				Health care and social assistance,[1] 2007			
	Number of establish-ments	Number of employees	Sales (mil dol)	Annual payroll (mil dol)	Number of establish-ments	Number of employees	Receipts (mil dol)	Annual payroll (mil dol)	Number of establish-ments	Number of employees	Receipts (mil dol)	Annual payroll (mil dol)
	92	93	94	95	96	97	98	99	100	101	102	103
OHIO—Cont'd												
Hamilton	119	2 341	88.6	26.2	7	D	D	D	113	1 409	143.4	55.7
Hilliard	57	1 514	58.1	17.7	18	257	26.4	9.2	77	783	62.6	23.0
Huber Heights	69	1 389	55.6	16.0	8	D	D	D	68	D	D	D
Kent	74	1 308	54.4	13.4	5	D	D	D	40	520	36.6	16.1
Kettering	109	2 389	88.9	26.9	12	D	D	D	181	D	D	D
Lakewood	114	1 420	61.1	16.6	13	85	5.0	1.3	117	1 145	87.1	38.2
Lancaster	110	2 550	90.9	26.2	8	D	D	D	148	D	D	D
Lima	78	1 161	47.1	12.4	5	D	D	D	170	D	D	D
Lorain	84	1 044	40.4	10.2	14	122	7.5	1.8	105	1 493	149.1	68.4
Mansfield	132	2 036	73.8	21.6	11	D	D	D	211	D	D	D
Marion	50	830	30.6	8.8	5	D	D	D	107	D	D	D
Mason	66	2 038	87.6	25.3	18	330	24.9	7.8	90	1 251	97.1	42.4
Massillon	84	1 330	51.7	13.7	3	9	0.2	0.1	55	1 636	81.3	34.5
Medina	66	1 245	43.8	12.4	6	D	D	D	103	1 396	106.7	48.5
Mentor	168	3 812	157.8	43.4	13	D	D	D	138	D	D	D
Middletown	107	2 584	97.0	29.0	8	103	2.8	1.0	116	D	D	D
Newark	107	2 198	84.2	23.1	12	D	D	D	115	2 879	189.7	102.0
North Olmsted	124	2 467	103.5	28.7	8	84	2.8	0.9	74	1 055	73.8	28.6
North Ridgeville	40	548	20.6	5.1	8	74	3.2	1.0	31	D	D	D
North Royalton	41	475	18.3	4.8	1	D	D	D	57	D	D	D
Parma	190	2 915	103.2	29.3	14	D	D	D	194	2 895	266.8	119.2
Reynoldsburg	71	1 175	51.2	14.8	7	44	1.8	0.5	85	1 158	58.0	27.2
Riverside	52	847	33.6	9.4	4	D	D	D	35	D	D	D
Sandusky	82	1 116	70.9	14.2	16	D	D	D	62	D	D	D
Shaker Heights	37	540	19.1	5.4	6	140	6.4	2.6	61	742	44.0	21.0
Springfield	162	3 379	129.4	36.8	10	94	4.2	1.4	202	2 889	237.9	104.5
Stow	76	1 795	62.3	18.3	10	D	D	D	69	D	D	D
Strongsville	114	2 769	104.4	28.1	12	151	4.1	1.2	93	971	102.9	39.0
Toledo	624	11 505	428.7	120.7	64	893	39.2	10.6	592	9 105	801.1	411.8
Troy	69	1 555	62.0	17.9	6	D	D	D	72	D	D	D
Upper Arlington	60	D	D	D	6	D	D	D	79	1 010	94.8	51.1
Warren	97	1 207	45.1	12.6	11	83	2.3	0.8	161	2 126	144.1	65.0
Westerville	96	2 085	86.8	22.5	13	D	D	D	203	D	D	D
Westlake	101	2 665	124.4	35.2	7	D	D	D	228	3 251	287.4	129.5
Wooster	71	1 798	61.1	19.0	5	D	D	D	77	1 327	118.1	53.4
Xenia	50	894	35.6	10.1	5	D	D	D	61	486	51.1	16.7
Youngstown	111	1 191	47.2	12.5	10	D	D	D	141	2 528	198.3	90.5
Zanesville	109	2 213	83.7	23.7	5	D	D	D	126	D	D	D
OKLAHOMA	6 900	129 159	5 106.6	1 401.3	862	22 167	2 330.9	412.6	8 577	121 175	10 860.0	4 171.7
Bartlesville	100	1 740	67.7	16.8	11	D	D	D	124	D	D	D
Broken Arrow	151	3 392	125.5	35.9	28	D	D	D	170	D	D	D
Edmond	189	4 635	155.0	46.0	28	424	23.1	8.2	346	3 152	320.9	117.6
Enid	108	D	D	D	10	49	3.7	0.7	180	D	D	D
Lawton	179	3 665	131.4	34.6	15	D	D	D	216	2 748	230.5	78.0
Midwest City	114	2 485	99.3	26.6	12	D	D	D	174	3 258	409.5	128.7
Moore	83	1 963	74.3	20.3	9	D	D	D	66	D	D	D
Muskogee	109	2 203	80.6	21.0	12	71	2.0	0.5	156	D	D	D
Norman	285	7 112	281.6	79.0	40	1 059	92.4	19.3	358	D	D	D
Oklahoma City	1 239	27 218	1 163.9	325.0	136	2 409	190.8	49.5	1 883	31 441	3 405.0	1 278.7
Owasso	79	1 748	67.0	17.9	6	44	1.7	0.5	68	D	D	D
Ponca City	67	1 217	43.6	10.9	4	D	D	D	92	D	D	D
Shawnee	105	2 393	90.7	24.1	5	D	D	D	89	1 283	95.5	39.1
Stillwater	120	2 746	98.2	26.3	9	D	D	D	104	D	D	D
Tulsa	1 051	21 344	929.0	264.5	110	2 142	232.5	42.9	1 415	21 613	2 657.9	1 049.8
OREGON	10 241	150 538	7 555.8	2 152.9	1 211	17 801	1 105.7	408.0	9 011	91 816	9 444.8	3 751.5
Albany	116	1 783	86.3	22.6	15	D	D	D	96	1 060	86.6	34.3
Beaverton	275	4 565	226.6	69.2	41	605	63.5	9.5	277	3 488	322.9	119.8
Bend	302	4 742	231.3	67.7	49	1 493	60.4	19.4	341	D	D	D
Corvallis	179	2 966	120.3	34.3	19	D	D	D	148	D	D	D
Eugene	508	8 243	369.8	107.5	43	656	22.9	7.5	503	6 188	737.8	256.7
Grants Pass	149	2 034	92.1	27.7	15	D	D	D	189	2 364	205.8	71.5
Gresham	223	3 640	166.2	50.3	22	D	D	D	266	2 517	229.1	89.8
Hillsboro	230	3 770	194.3	54.5	18	235	13.0	3.3	217	2 137	212.0	81.9
Keizer	47	1 014	42.0	11.3	12	159	7.2	3.1	52	583	45.4	16.5
Lake Oswego	102	1 742	85.7	26.7	16	79	5.2	1.4	161	D	D	D
McMinnville	82	1 212	52.5	15.3	6	D	D	D	107	1 735	167.1	66.6
Medford	263	4 248	202.0	58.7	28	437	21.8	6.6	294	D	D	D
Oregon City	71	1 085	57.3	16.0	8	100	5.1	1.6	102	D	D	D
Portland	2 205	34 188	1 842.4	539.5	227	2 730	311.5	166.5	1 725	16 888	2 022.3	822.3

1. Establishments subject to federal tax.

Table D. Cities — **Other Services and Government Employment and Payroll**

City	Other services[1], 2007				Government employment and payroll, 2012								
						March payroll							
							Percent of total for:						
	Number of establish-ments	Number of employees	Receipts (mil dol)	Annual payroll (mil dol)	Full-time equivalent employees	Total (dollars)	Adminis-tration, judicial, and legal	Police and Corrections	Fire Protection	Highways and trans-portation	Health and welfare	Natural resources and utilities	Education and libraries
	104	105	106	107	108	109	110	111	112	113	114	115	116
OHIO—Cont'd													
Hamilton	78	380	35.4	10.7	648	3 715 041	12.3	21.8	20.8	4.6	2.2	31.0	0.0
Hilliard	43	269	26.1	7.3	138	630 071	19.0	53.4	0.0	3.8	0.0	18.6	0.0
Huber Heights	52	226	15.1	6.1	178	969 065	15.5	36.2	31.4	11.5	0.0	0.2	0.0
Kent	45	237	11.7	4.6	203	1 021 262	8.2	30.7	21.0	16.4	6.0	15.0	0.0
Kettering	87	560	30.7	10.6	489	2 337 531	21.1	27.0	15.6	13.9	0.8	14.6	0.0
Lakewood	50	295	18.5	6.2	462	2 388 158	12.9	31.2	24.7	3.8	7.9	16.6	0.0
Lancaster	68	D	D	D	414	1 841 272	17.3	24.9	20.9	5.2	0.7	29.3	0.9
Lima	58	376	28.9	7.6	375	1 604 715	20.6	25.2	20.8	9.0	2.6	21.4	0.0
Lorain	70	515	30.7	9.9	466	2 344 000	9.9	33.0	23.6	4.0	5.6	19.7	4.2
Mansfield	91	829	52.0	15.6	423	1 865 914	20.0	26.6	23.0	4.6	1.3	17.6	0.0
Marion	39	228	15.1	4.9	241	1 067 754	11.2	34.1	23.1	9.9	0.0	17.7	0.0
Mason	39	287	13.2	5.5	266	1 194 447	18.2	24.2	20.0	7.6	0.0	21.7	0.0
Massillon	56	389	40.0	12.9	321	1 362 818	15.6	16.2	16.6	5.0	6.2	34.1	0.0
Medina	60	457	30.7	10.4	221	904 261	23.8	27.5	4.7	5.0	3.8	26.8	0.0
Mentor	135	1 109	90.6	29.1	500	2 127 362	11.3	29.5	28.5	14.3	5.5	10.9	0.0
Middletown	58	288	21.8	6.7	404	1 752 509	12.7	30.0	25.2	6.7	4.9	15.7	0.0
Newark	63	469	32.6	11.6	384	1 681 225	15.2	30.1	24.2	8.0	3.0	18.9	0.0
North Olmsted	93	557	33.8	12.1	255	1 250 704	8.6	28.1	19.4	3.8	2.7	29.3	0.0
North Ridgeville	44	168	11.3	3.4	199	885 287	13.3	28.1	21.5	10.7	2.1	18.6	0.0
North Royalton	59	279	26.5	8.3	185	949 689	9.7	32.8	24.0	9.0	2.8	17.2	0.0
Parma	136	1 003	90.2	30.1	468	1 957 354	15.6	32.5	28.4	11.6	3.1	4.2	0.0
Reynoldsburg	47	253	19.4	6.2	136	685 686	14.7	61.7	0.0	5.3	1.2	11.6	0.0
Riverside	17	78	6.2	2.2	85	380 891	12.2	46.1	28.8	12.4	0.0	0.0	0.0
Sandusky	35	190	11.9	3.4	231	1 023 311	17.4	23.9	23.6	4.8	2.8	23.4	0.0
Shaker Heights	23	131	6.8	2.2	356	1 867 638	14.5	30.2	20.9	14.6	4.9	6.2	0.0
Springfield	101	694	115.6	19.7	591	2 580 272	18.3	27.7	26.1	4.8	3.8	16.2	0.0
Stow	51	448	26.4	8.7	268	1 324 714	23.7	25.9	29.3	6.1	0.7	9.3	0.0
Strongsville	62	716	54.5	19.2	365	1 769 488	7.3	33.1	24.7	16.5	5.3	11.6	0.0
Toledo	415	2 866	240.0	67.9	2 146	10 282 276	15.9	23.9	36.8	7.3	1.5	13.8	0.0
Troy	44	358	17.0	5.9	184	972 285	13.3	25.7	22.4	11.8	1.3	24.4	0.0
Upper Arlington	31	266	13.9	4.8	239	1 342 741	13.2	27.2	31.7	10.1	4.0	11.5	0.0
Warren	65	329	22.5	6.2	445	1 785 083	16.7	23.0	19.1	3.3	3.9	30.7	0.0
Westerville	64	D	D	D	484	2 542 559	12.4	27.1	26.3	4.3	0.0	26.7	0.0
Westlake	65	592	29.5	11.6	288	1 367 977	13.6	30.0	24.5	2.8	3.2	21.7	0.0
Wooster	46	328	19.8	7.1	879	3 824 028	2.0	5.4	6.8	4.2	78.8	2.8	0.0
Xenia	35	182	12.6	4.2	219	1 060 316	20.5	35.1	21.7	3.3	0.9	13.1	0.0
Youngstown	83	D	D	D	757	3 252 504	14.0	28.1	18.4	6.3	4.9	27.3	0.0
Zanesville	78	702	44.4	14.2	297	1 096 683	10.0	29.7	21.1	6.3	2.8	25.1	0.0
OKLAHOMA	4 462	25 063	1 975.4	564.4	X	X	X	X	X	X	X	X	X
Bartlesville	51	D	D	D	344	1 284 794	8.5	23.4	23.5	6.4	0.4	26.0	5.4
Broken Arrow	125	922	70.7	25.1	618	2 786 415	13.1	30.6	27.6	5.5	0.0	17.1	0.0
Edmond	140	844	52.4	17.4	688	3 323 448	15.6	22.5	27.9	6.2	1.5	21.4	0.0
Enid	94	487	39.9	10.4	477	1 757 022	12.4	27.9	23.3	7.6	2.5	18.8	2.4
Lawton	122	628	37.5	11.2	892	3 414 778	14.9	29.7	19.3	9.4	2.0	20.6	1.8
Midwest City	60	439	26.7	8.3	494	2 315 063	15.2	28.4	24.6	3.8	4.3	18.9	0.0
Moore	52	D	D	D	275	1 722 367	12.5	35.2	32.5	2.3	5.4	6.1	0.0
Muskogee	58	422	26.4	8.0	497	1 548 570	8.5	26.0	24.8	12.1	0.0	24.8	0.0
Norman	117	D	D	D	3 161	15 136 504	3.2	7.5	5.5	2.7	74.3	5.6	0.0
Oklahoma City	838	6 390	516.6	151.1	4 418	24 268 820	9.9	32.6	28.7	9.3	4.5	15.0	0.0
Owasso	34	D	D	D	219	910 478	15.5	28.5	31.9	5.8	0.7	11.3	0.0
Ponca City	41	198	16.2	4.3	400	1 441 141	9.1	18.8	20.4	7.8	0.7	35.3	2.6
Shawnee	43	D	D	D	279	1 055 211	16.1	30.3	23.8	5.8	1.6	22.2	0.0
Stillwater	59	360	20.0	5.6	1 308	5 630 416	4.6	9.5	6.8	1.6	62.0	12.2	1.1
Tulsa	717	4 694	374.5	115.4	3 932	16 951 552	11.3	27.1	20.9	14.4	1.8	12.8	0.0
OREGON	5 333	29 509	2 595.4	799.5	X	X	X	X	X	X	X	X	X
Albany	66	D	D	D	389	2 123 666	12.9	24.2	24.6	13.2	0.1	18.7	3.7
Beaverton	160	1 240	105.3	33.0	488	2 217 436	38.8	23.9	0.0	5.4	0.0	10.8	12.0
Bend	157	895	73.5	23.1	432	2 556 081	14.4	29.2	23.0	5.2	3.3	12.8	0.0
Corvallis	63	384	21.2	8.2	430	2 437 922	9.9	21.5	18.9	5.8	8.1	18.9	8.1
Eugene	284	1 930	158.6	51.6	1 983	11 796 504	9.0	18.2	12.2	8.0	1.2	26.1	3.1
Grants Pass	76	328	24.6	7.0	214	1 160 951	18.8	44.3	16.7	2.1	0.0	13.1	0.0
Gresham	117	569	45.9	13.1	515	3 198 886	13.0	29.6	21.1	3.3	0.6	22.0	0.0
Hillsboro	135	926	110.5	42.3	759	4 281 252	14.6	24.9	17.5	3.5	0.0	24.7	6.8
Keizer	36	174	10.4	3.4	89	489 891	18.6	57.2	0.0	2.5	4.8	16.6	0.0
Lake Oswego	71	292	25.7	7.7	325	1 928 696	17.6	21.1	21.4	8.6	1.3	17.6	6.5
McMinnville	36	170	12.5	4.2	252	1 307 113	16.9	18.4	16.1	4.8	2.3	34.2	4.5
Medford	151	1 154	96.6	35.5	452	2 575 154	14.2	34.5	21.7	15.1	0.1	9.8	0.0
Oregon City	47	222	19.3	6.3	159	835 368	19.0	32.4	0.0	14.2	0.0	19.2	5.8
Portland	1 164	7 975	784.9	231.9	5 804	35 656 383	18.1	25.5	15.0	10.2	0.9	27.3	0.0

1. Establishments subject to federal tax.

City	City government finances, 2007									
	General revenue							General expenditure		
		Intergovernmental		Taxes					Per capita[1] (dollars)	
					Per capita[1] (dollars)					
	Total (mil dol)	Total (mil dol)	Percent from state government	Total (mil dol)	Total	Property	Sales and gross receipts	Total (mil dol)	Total	Capital outlays
	117	118	119	120	121	122	123	124	125	126
OHIO—Cont'd										
Hamilton	89.3	12.8	82.9	38.5	618	143	14	83.9	1 348	178
Hilliard	35.0	7.3	60.4	23.3	762	41	50	31.8	1 040	211
Huber Heights	30.3	5.3	52.2	16.8	442	90	32	34.7	911	258
Kent	26.7	4.8	93.2	14.4	488	94	24	31.0	1 046	271
Kettering	81.4	18.4	94.3	48.4	863	160	8	83.8	1 495	462
Lakewood	61.0	11.1	71.9	35.2	685	265	25	53.0	1 032	61
Lancaster	74.4	14.1	95.8	19.9	511	72	1	62.8	1 614	139
Lima	73.9	31.0	93.2	18.5	482	32	28	56.9	1 483	345
Lorain	67.9	22.6	96.7	25.7	402	58	34	56.8	890	61
Mansfield	55.9	12.3	51.1	27.7	588	43	15	51.8	1 101	78
Marion	39.4	10.3	100.0	13.8	375	33	10	36.5	989	43
Mason	54.1	7.0	87.3	29.3	937	192	66	56.2	1 798	343
Massillon	35.7	5.9	26.8	17.4	540	50	45	33.4	1 036	44
Medina	27.0	2.3	92.3	16.9	636	121	21	24.7	931	114
Mentor	61.5	10.0	90.4	40.5	862	94	40	59.9	1 274	0
Middletown	84.2	23.4	47.0	24.4	501	100	5	78.5	1 612	138
Newark	52.3	16.1	92.8	22.0	462	55	6	52.1	1 091	140
North Olmsted	41.3	6.2	95.2	23.4	724	285	44	35.0	1 082	136
North Ridgeville	32.6	5.0	88.6	15.8	516	189	54	29.7	972	100
North Royalton	28.1	4.2	100.0	16.8	554	150	19	25.8	852	47
Parma	80.5	21.4	100.0	48.3	599	109	29	75.6	937	31
Reynoldsburg	27.3	3.4	100.0	14.8	406	60	10	25.5	702	31
Riverside	11.8	3.1	96.7	6.6	263	93	1	11.2	447	11
Sandusky	39.2	10.7	84.2	17.6	686	79	317	32.3	1 262	169
Shaker Heights	52.5	8.5	41.5	33.5	1 195	272	23	57.7	2 057	258
Springfield	86.7	27.8	35.7	38.2	635	49	32	79.9	1 328	177
Stow	35.8	7.4	100.0	21.6	623	215	21	32.9	950	128
Strongsville	63.9	10.5	39.1	39.3	881	209	21	66.8	1 498	383
Toledo	451.3	105.2	62.6	175.0	618	42	23	399.2	1 408	377
Troy	33.3	3.4	70.1	17.1	674	74	29	30.1	1 187	140
Upper Arlington	43.7	6.5	59.0	27.9	815	255	41	52.7	1 538	476
Warren	62.9	13.4	36.4	19.8	486	36	24	56.8	1 394	127
Westerville	85.6	17.7	81.5	50.6	1 359	332	29	96.9	2 605	855
Westlake	58.8	5.1	53.1	39.7	1 222	403	54	49.3	1 518	310
Wooster	134.0	6.0	94.8	14.0	532	83	27	128.8	4 877	371
Xenia	28.5	5.5	95.4	13.4	514	62	40	28.4	1 089	214
Youngstown	104.6	20.7	41.1	54.6	826	37	116	89.8	1 358	37
Zanesville	44.9	17.1	96.5	17.8	701	46	54	34.3	1 347	67
OKLAHOMA	X	X	X	X	X	X	X	X	X	X
Bartlesville	40.2	4.0	79.0	22.5	619	96	523	44.1	1 213	354
Broken Arrow	90.6	4.1	24.8	53.9	528	119	409	91.4	896	239
Edmond	93.1	6.8	73.5	55.3	651	0	651	115.9	1 364	281
Enid	67.3	6.0	81.8	38.4	769	57	712	80.2	1 606	728
Lawton	96.6	12.3	38.3	56.7	575	41	534	92.9	943	108
Midwest City	69.8	4.9	68.6	36.3	646	46	600	62.1	1 107	89
Moore	45.7	1.5	65.9	32.5	561	58	503	41.5	717	95
Muskogee	130.4	3.3	45.2	28.4	729	5	724	134.9	3 462	322
Norman	443.4	6.4	56.7	79.6	687	68	619	422.1	3 646	294
Oklahoma City	1 107.5	90.6	50.5	601.9	1 003	139	865	835.1	1 392	272
Owasso	32.7	0.8	93.6	20.7	658	0	658	29.0	924	98
Ponca City	41.3	2.3	61.5	16.3	655	21	635	56.7	2 278	730
Shawnee	34.1	5.6	40.8	20.1	656	2	653	30.7	1 003	220
Stillwater	49.0	2.9	45.6	29.0	622	29	593	48.2	1 033	155
Tulsa	741.9	77.4	11.3	340.0	862	161	701	712.6	1 806	561
OREGON	X	X	X	X	X	X	X	X	X	X
Albany	59.2	9.0	56.9	32.7	638	505	133	56.1	1 094	127
Beaverton	79.4	16.3	57.8	44.0	475	344	131	78.1	842	126
Bend	88.7	15.0	61.7	44.0	558	331	227	81.1	1 029	162
Corvallis	71.4	12.8	43.7	35.6	647	446	202	62.4	1 135	94
Eugene	265.1	45.3	46.0	119.6	757	620	138	254.5	1 612	275
Grants Pass	36.2	6.8	64.2	20.5	589	453	136	35.8	1 028	164
Gresham	102.2	33.7	52.1	39.5	363	243	120	106.4	979	155
Hillsboro	134.5	12.8	83.8	79.4	832	541	291	124.8	1 309	91
Keizer	21.2	3.3	99.7	10.7	290	216	74	18.1	490	50
Lake Oswego	80.7	14.9	44.5	43.4	1 164	919	245	69.2	1 857	263
McMinnville	37.5	4.1	96.1	15.2	459	360	99	30.1	909	86
Medford	102.4	14.5	49.3	58.0	758	455	303	104.2	1 361	306
Oregon City	52.1	16.8	99.0	19.9	594	337	257	43.8	1 308	472
Portland	1 298.8	266.5	44.2	612.5	1 016	708	308	1 280.8	2 124	548

1. Based on population estimated as of July 1 of the year shown.

City	City government finances, 2012 (cont.)									
	General expenditure (cont.)									
	Percent of total for:									
	Public welfare	Highways	Parking facilities	Education	Health and hospitals	Police protection	Sewerage and sanitation	Parks and recreation	Housing and community development	Interest on debt
	127	128	129	130	131	132	133	134	135	136
OHIO—Cont'd										
Hamilton	0.0	6.1	0.5	0.0	1.5	24.9	20.3	0.9	3.4	4.7
Hilliard	0.0	24.2	0.0	0.0	0.5	19.2	1.2	7.4	0.0	8.3
Huber Heights	0.0	13.8	0.0	0.0	0.0	17.2	7.9	12.9	4.7	5.3
Kent	0.4	5.1	0.0	0.0	3.0	20.7	13.4	5.7	2.8	0.8
Kettering	0.0	11.2	0.0	0.0	0.0	17.2	0.0	14.9	1.4	0.8
Lakewood	3.1	12.4	0.5	0.0	0.8	19.5	15.5	4.3	5.6	4.7
Lancaster	0.0	5.4	0.0	0.0	0.4	12.7	21.9	2.9	0.9	23.9
Lima	0.0	16.0	0.0	0.0	0.0	15.9	21.7	1.8	6.7	2.8
Lorain	1.5	5.3	0.0	0.0	2.1	22.9	25.4	0.6	7.9	2.8
Mansfield	0.0	13.1	0.0	1.8	0.0	16.3	8.4	0.5	3.4	0.6
Marion	0.0	8.9	0.0	0.0	1.3	18.4	33.3	2.5	0.0	2.0
Mason	0.0	17.2	0.0	0.0	0.0	10.0	9.1	17.8	0.0	7.0
Massillon	0.0	11.0	0.1	0.0	1.8	14.9	25.5	10.7	0.9	5.3
Medina	0.0	17.5	8.9	0.0	0.0	17.4	12.9	13.7	0.0	1.6
Mentor	0.0	24.6	0.0	0.0	0.0	19.1	0.0	11.9	0.8	2.7
Middletown	0.0	12.5	0.0	0.0	1.0	10.4	16.2	3.7	18.8	2.3
Newark	0.0	9.2	0.0	0.0	0.0	16.1	17.8	0.0	0.0	2.0
North Olmsted	0.9	13.9	0.0	0.0	0.0	15.9	22.0	12.1	0.5	5.6
North Ridgeville	0.0	12.1	0.0	0.0	8.5	17.4	25.4	1.3	4.6	3.6
North Royalton	0.0	20.6	0.0	0.0	0.7	23.5	21.0	1.5	2.7	1.6
Parma	0.0	5.8	0.0	0.0	0.4	40.5	0.5	5.1	11.3	1.6
Reynoldsburg	0.0	5.9	0.0	0.0	0.8	30.8	31.8	3.9	0.0	1.4
Riverside	0.0	14.6	0.0	0.0	0.0	41.2	0.0	0.4	0.0	0.8
Sandusky	0.0	8.5	0.0	0.0	0.0	15.5	25.9	1.2	2.8	6.9
Shaker Heights	0.0	7.5	0.0	0.0	1.0	20.4	8.3	8.9	8.8	1.6
Springfield	0.0	3.0	0.0	0.0	0.0	15.5	8.1	0.0	5.0	1.9
Stow	0.0	10.2	0.0	0.0	0.9	18.9	2.2	7.6	0.0	3.2
Strongsville	0.0	30.1	0.0	0.0	0.5	17.2	11.8	7.8	0.0	4.3
Toledo	0.4	8.8	0.2	0.0	3.7	23.7	22.4	1.8	3.2	5.8
Troy	0.0	7.4	0.4	0.0	1.1	12.4	14.3	12.0	6.3	2.2
Upper Arlington	0.0	34.9	0.0	0.0	0.4	13.2	6.2	6.9	2.2	3.4
Warren	0.0	8.6	0.2	0.0	1.6	12.9	18.9	4.3	7.2	1.3
Westerville	0.0	2.3	0.0	0.0	0.0	14.8	10.3	17.5	0.0	1.5
Westlake	0.0	17.5	0.0	0.0	0.0	13.8	11.8	6.6	0.0	1.6
Wooster	0.0	1.4	0.0	0.0	76.3	4.9	6.2	1.1	0.2	0.4
Xenia	0.0	1.1	0.3	0.0	0.0	19.2	20.9	0.6	1.7	1.4
Youngstown	0.0	6.3	0.1	0.0	1.5	22.0	27.0	2.7	6.8	1.8
Zanesville	0.0	10.9	0.0	0.0	1.2	22.8	24.7	2.4	0.0	3.0
OKLAHOMA	X	X	X	X	X	X	X	X	X	X
Bartlesville	0.0	15.9	0.0	0.0	0.0	12.6	20.7	12.2	2.0	1.5
Broken Arrow	0.0	7.8	0.0	0.0	0.8	18.6	18.5	7.7	0.8	5.5
Edmond	1.6	24.4	0.0	0.0	1.5	11.6	15.1	8.3	0.6	0.3
Enid	0.3	12.1	0.0	0.0	5.1	10.6	19.3	6.6	17.6	0.7
Lawton	0.0	9.4	0.0	5.7	0.9	21.2	15.2	1.3	1.1	1.4
Midwest City	0.0	8.1	0.0	0.0	0.0	23.9	12.5	4.6	7.6	6.6
Moore	0.0	14.8	0.0	0.0	0.0	23.2	14.3	3.7	3.2	1.9
Muskogee	0.0	3.1	0.0	0.0	65.8	5.4	5.9	4.1	0.6	0.1
Norman	0.0	6.6	0.0	0.0	68.5	5.5	5.8	1.8	0.4	3.1
Oklahoma City	0.0	8.8	0.7	2.5	0.9	18.5	8.3	17.3	3.5	5.8
Owasso	0.0	4.3	0.0	0.0	4.7	22.5	13.0	6.5	1.6	5.2
Ponca City	0.0	7.2	0.0	0.0	1.8	11.7	12.2	6.8	1.4	3.7
Shawnee	0.0	12.2	0.0	0.0	0.0	22.5	9.6	3.8	2.4	0.3
Stillwater	0.4	18.2	0.0	0.0	0.2	21.6	13.9	8.0	0.0	2.1
Tulsa	2.1	19.7	1.1	0.0	8.8	12.2	19.9	4.8	0.0	6.0
OREGON	X	X	X	X	X	X	X	X	X	X
Albany	0.0	7.1	0.0	0.0	3.9	21.6	16.2	10.8	0.1	1.7
Beaverton	0.0	7.6	0.0	0.0	0.0	31.5	10.8	0.2	1.1	0.8
Bend	0.0	12.0	0.8	0.0	0.0	21.4	12.9	0.0	4.1	3.6
Corvallis	0.0	5.9	0.2	0.0	0.0	20.1	18.1	9.1	2.8	3.7
Eugene	0.0	2.5	1.5	0.0	0.0	18.2	14.0	9.7	2.9	0.9
Grants Pass	0.0	8.4	0.0	0.0	0.0	30.5	11.8	5.8	3.1	1.3
Gresham	0.0	10.0	0.0	0.0	0.0	20.1	23.2	3.0	1.4	3.3
Hillsboro	0.0	8.1	0.1	0.0	0.0	20.0	22.0	13.5	1.2	2.5
Keizer	0.0	10.4	0.0	0.0	0.0	28.9	33.1	2.7	4.7	7.4
Lake Oswego	0.0	4.0	0.0	0.0	0.0	13.3	14.8	11.9	0.0	6.6
McMinnville	0.0	5.9	0.0	0.0	10.6	19.5	16.7	11.4	0.0	3.2
Medford	0.0	12.8	0.4	0.0	0.0	19.0	14.3	5.7	5.9	15.0
Oregon City	0.0	35.9	0.8	0.0	0.0	15.8	13.8	8.7	1.1	3.8
Portland	0.0	13.9	0.6	0.0	0.0	13.5	20.3	7.8	7.5	7.6

City	City government finances, 2012 (cont.)			Climate[2]						
	Debt outstanding			Average daily temperature (degrees Fahrenheit)						
				Mean		Limits				
	Total (mil dol)	Per capita[1] (dollars)	Debt issued during year	January	July	January[3]	July[4]	Annual precipitation (inches)	Heating degree days	Cooling degree days
	137	138	139	140	141	142	143	144	145	146
OHIO—Cont'd										
Hamilton	315.7	5 070	50.5	28.7	76.6	19.9	88.1	43.36	5 261	1 135
Hilliard	62.6	2 046	8.0	NA	NA	NA	NA	NA	NA	NA
Huber Heights	57.3	1 501	0.6	27.9	77.0	20.6	87.2	39.41	5 343	1 214
Kent	19.1	645	0.0	27.2	74.1	20.1	83.9	36.07	5 752	856
Kettering	18.1	324	0.0	27.9	77.0	20.6	87.2	39.41	5 343	1 214
Lakewood	92.2	1 795	12.3	25.7	71.9	18.8	81.4	38.71	6 121	702
Lancaster	375.7	9 659	0.2	26.5	73.1	17.8	84.4	36.55	5 887	764
Lima	36.5	953	1.1	25.5	73.6	18.1	84.0	37.20	5 932	835
Lorain	48.2	755	6.9	27.1	73.8	19.3	85.0	38.02	5 731	818
Mansfield	9.9	210	0.4	24.3	71.0	16.2	81.8	43.24	6 364	653
Marion	44.8	1 215	0.0	24.5	72.7	16.0	83.7	38.35	6 300	703
Mason	120.3	3 846	16.6	NA	NA	NA	NA	NA	NA	NA
Massillon	22.4	697	0.1	25.2	71.8	17.4	82.3	38.47	6 154	678
Medina	45.6	1 720	0.0	23.7	71.3	16.2	82.0	38.34	6 525	558
Mentor	34.9	742	4.4	23.0	68.8	14.3	80.0	47.33	6 956	372
Middletown	241.5	4 959	0.3	27.5	74.2	18.3	86.3	39.54	5 609	879
Newark	24.5	514	2.9	25.8	72.7	17.3	83.8	41.62	6 084	687
North Olmsted	38.8	1 199	1.4	25.7	71.9	18.8	81.4	38.71	6 121	702
North Ridgeville	34.1	1 115	4.1	NA	NA	NA	NA	NA	NA	NA
North Royalton	40.3	1 328	15.0	25.7	71.9	18.8	81.4	38.71	6 121	702
Parma	37.5	465	0.0	25.7	71.9	18.8	81.4	38.71	6 121	702
Reynoldsburg	22.9	631	0.0	28.3	75.1	20.3	85.3	38.52	5 492	951
Riverside	2.0	79	0.0	NA	NA	NA	NA	NA	NA	NA
Sandusky	27.6	1 078	4.1	25.6	73.8	18.9	81.8	34.46	6 065	785
Shaker Heights	27.3	972	0.3	25.7	71.9	18.8	81.4	38.71	6 121	702
Springfield	42.8	711	0.0	26.1	73.5	18.2	83.8	37.70	5 921	796
Stow	28.9	832	0.0	27.2	74.1	20.1	83.9	36.07	5 752	856
Strongsville	60.3	1 353	10.7	25.7	71.9	18.8	81.4	38.71	6 121	702
Toledo	357.2	1 260	8.3	27.5	77.6	21.7	87.1	33.52	5 464	1 257
Troy	19.5	768	0.0	NA	NA	NA	NA	NA	NA	NA
Upper Arlington	51.9	1 515	6.0	28.3	75.1	20.3	85.3	38.52	5 492	951
Warren	33.9	832	0.0	24.0	70.2	15.3	82.4	37.80	6 678	458
Westerville	75.5	2 027	10.0	27.7	74.4	19.7	85.4	39.35	5 434	924
Westlake	43.8	1 350	7.4	27.1	73.8	19.3	85.0	38.02	5 731	818
Wooster	10.1	381	0.0	NA	NA	NA	NA	NA	NA	NA
Xenia	7.4	286	1.1	NA	NA	NA	NA	NA	NA	NA
Youngstown	32.0	483	0.0	24.9	69.9	17.4	81.0	38.02	6 451	552
Zanesville	6.6	261	0.0	24.3	68.4	16.3	78.7	36.91	6 639	373
OKLAHOMA	X	X	X	X	X	X	X	X	X	X
Bartlesville	60.7	1 673	0.0	35.4	82.2	23.7	94.5	38.99	3 743	1 894
Broken Arrow	183.9	1 802	48.4	34.8	81.3	23.5	92.9	40.46	3 917	1 746
Edmond	136.7	1 609	0.0	36.7	82.0	26.2	93.1	35.85	3 663	1 907
Enid	78.5	1 572	17.0	33.1	82.6	21.9	94.4	34.25	4 269	1 852
Lawton	141.0	1 431	38.0	38.2	84.2	26.4	95.7	31.64	3 326	2 199
Midwest City	106.7	1 901	73.2	36.7	82.0	26.2	93.1	35.85	3 663	1 907
Moore	71.4	1 232	25.2	36.7	82.0	26.2	93.1	35.85	3 663	1 907
Muskogee	44.3	1 136	5.0	36.1	82.1	25.2	93.1	43.77	3 667	1 858
Norman	372.5	3 217	23.4	35.8	82.1	23.2	93.9	41.65	3 713	1 906
Oklahoma City	1 318.9	2 199	185.3	36.7	82.0	26.2	93.1	35.85	3 663	1 907
Owasso	39.4	1 254	0.0	NA	NA	NA	NA	NA	NA	NA
Ponca City	59.4	2 385	24.9	33.8	82.9	23.8	94.1	36.41	4 053	1 964
Shawnee	23.5	767	3.5	37.3	83.0	25.5	94.5	40.87	3 460	2 024
Stillwater	38.1	817	4.6	34.5	82.3	21.9	93.6	36.71	3 899	1 881
Tulsa	1 254.1	3 179	126.1	37.4	81.9	27.1	92.2	45.10	3 413	1 905
OREGON	X	X	X	X	X	X	X	X	X	X
Albany	122.1	2 381	0.0	40.3	66.5	33.6	81.2	43.66	4 715	247
Beaverton	26.4	285	0.0	40.0	66.8	33.8	79.2	39.95	4 723	287
Bend	92.3	1 171	10.9	31.2	63.5	22.6	80.7	11.73	7 042	147
Corvallis	59.4	1 080	0.0	38.1	63.8	31.6	77.4	67.76	5 501	139
Eugene	418.2	2 649	112.5	39.8	66.2	33.0	81.5	50.90	4 780	242
Grants Pass	12.2	350	0.0	NA	NA	NA	NA	NA	NA	NA
Gresham	82.4	758	3.0	40.0	68.3	33.5	81.5	45.70	4 491	450
Hillsboro	62.2	652	0.0	40.5	67.6	35.1	80.4	38.19	4 532	323
Keizer	28.7	779	0.0	40.3	66.8	33.5	81.5	40.00	4 784	257
Lake Oswego	156.3	4 196	37.7	41.8	69.3	35.7	82.6	46.05	4 132	475
McMinnville	22.1	668	5.6	39.6	66.6	33.0	81.9	41.66	4 815	288
Medford	380.1	4 966	26.6	39.1	72.7	30.9	90.2	18.37	4 539	711
Oregon City	33.8	1 009	0.0	41.8	69.3	35.7	82.6	46.05	4 132	475
Portland	3 381.1	5 608	353.6	41.8	69.3	35.7	82.6	46.05	4 132	475

1. Based on the population estimated as of July 1 of the year shown. 2. Represents normal values based on the 30-year period, 1971–2000. 3. Average daily minimum.
4. Average daily maximum.

STATE Place code	City	Land area,[1] 2010 (sq km)	Population, 2014: Total persons	Population, 2014: Rank	Population, 2014: Per square kilometer	Race alone or in combination (percent), 2011-2013: White	Black	American Indian, Alaska Native	Asian	Hawaiian Pacific Islander	Percent Hispanic or Latino[2], 2011-2013	Percent foreign born 2011–2013
		1	2	3	4	5	6	7	8	9	10	11
	OREGON—Cont'd											
41 61200	Redmond	43.5	27 941	1 309	642.3	95.3	NA	2.5	1.5	1.2	11.0	6.0
41 64900	Salem	124.1	161 637	152	1 302.5	84.7	2.3	2.9	4.3	1.3	20.7	11.2
41 69600	Springfield	40.8	60 263	597	1 477.0	91.7	1.6	2.6	3.2	0.8	12.8	5.9
41 73650	Tigard	30.6	50 787	739	1 659.7	86.8	2.4	1.7	8.6	1.2	12.6	13.9
41 74950	Tualatin	21.3	26 907	1 366	1 263.2	91.8	3.8	2.4	3.0	0.5	17.5	11.5
41 80150	West Linn	19.1	26 289	1 389	1 376.4	92.5	1.5	0.4	6.7	NA	4.6	9.1
42 00000	PENNSYLVANIA	115 883.1	12 787 209	X	110.3	83.7	12.1	0.6	3.4	0.1	6.1	6.1
42 02000	Allentown	45.4	119 104	226	2 623.4	66.9	16.6	0.6	2.1	0.2	45.1	15.6
42 02184	Altoona	25.7	45 558	818	1 772.7	96.0	5.0	0.8	0.8	NA	1.1	1.0
42 06064	Bethel Park	30.2	32 257	1 157	1 068.1	96.0	2.6	0.5	1.6	NA	1.2	2.5
42 06088	Bethlehem	49.5	75 135	450	1 517.9	82.6	9.2	1.0	3.2	0.2	25.3	8.4
42 13208	Chester	12.5	34 133	1 090	2 730.6	21.3	74.0	1.1	0.9	0.1	10.8	5.2
42 21648	Easton	10.6	27 052	1 355	2 552.1	70.1	23.5	2.3	3.1	NA	24.1	13.7
42 24000	Erie	49.4	99 452	297	2 013.2	79.3	19.1	0.7	2.5	0.1	6.8	6.5
42 32800	Harrisburg	21.1	49 082	765	2 326.2	37.0	54.6	2.2	4.0	NA	19.4	9.3
42 33408	Hazleton	15.6	24 932	1 422	1 598.2	79.3	4.9	NA	1.2	NA	44.9	26.8
42 41216	Lancaster	18.7	59 302	612	3 171.2	62.3	19.3	1.5	3.9	0.4	39.6	7.8
42 42168	Lebanon	10.8	25 573	1 405	2 367.9	69.3	5.9	0.7	1.0	NA	37.1	7.0
42 50528	Monroeville	51.1	28 285	1 295	553.5	82.7	14.3	0.4	5.2	NA	1.5	7.6
42 54656	Norristown	9.1	34 484	1 077	3 789.5	59.8	36.1	1.0	3.1	1.0	24.0	19.3
42 60000	Philadelphia	347.3	1 560 297	5	4 492.6	43.4	44.6	0.9	7.2	0.3	13.0	12.4
42 61000	Pittsburgh	143.4	305 412	62	2 129.8	69.0	26.9	1.2	5.6	0.2	2.5	7.9
42 61536	Plum	74.0	27 532	1 335	372.1	93.9	4.6	NA	1.5	NA	1.4	2.3
42 63624	Reading	25.6	87 812	356	3 430.2	60.7	16.8	3.4	1.2	0.7	59.3	18.2
42 69000	Scranton	65.6	75 281	449	1 147.6	88.1	7.8	0.5	4.1	NA	10.4	8.4
42 73808	State College	11.8	42 100	875	3 567.8	83.6	5.4	0.5	12.0	NA	3.5	12.0
42 85152	Wilkes-Barre	18.1	40 814	908	2 254.9	78.2	15.3	0.6	1.4	NA	14.9	5.6
42 85312	Williamsport	22.6	29 197	1 260	1 291.9	82.3	18.9	0.5	0.6	NA	3.3	1.6
42 87048	York	13.7	43 865	846	3 201.8	59.6	33.3	1.0	0.6	NA	28.6	5.8
44 00000	RHODE ISLAND	2 677.6	1 055 173	X	394.1	83.3	7.9	1.2	3.7	0.2	13.2	13.2
44 19180	Cranston	73.4	81 037	404	1 104.0	83.7	6.5	1.5	6.3	NA	12.2	12.7
44 22960	East Providence	34.3	47 331	794	1 379.9	86.8	10.1	1.7	2.9	NA	4.5	15.2
44 54640	Pawtucket	22.5	71 499	480	3 177.7	67.5	19.7	1.4	1.9	0.5	20.5	24.3
44 59000	Providence	47.7	179 154	134	3 755.8	53.1	18.7	2.1	7.1	0.4	40.0	29.6
44 74300	Warwick	90.8	81 963	399	902.7	93.1	2.4	0.8	3.4	NA	4.6	6.6
44 80780	Woonsocket	20.0	41 228	895	2 061.4	84.6	8.0	0.3	7.1	NA	14.4	9.6
45 00000	SOUTH CAROLINA	77 856.8	4 832 482	X	62.1	68.8	28.7	0.9	1.7	0.1	5.3	4.8
45 00550	Aiken	53.6	30 258	1 228	564.5	65.6	32.2	NA	2.2	NA	3.0	3.6
45 01360	Anderson	37.8	27 181	1 348	719.1	61.2	37.1	0.8	2.0	NA	4.4	3.2
45 13330	Charleston	282.3	130 113	200	460.9	72.9	25.3	0.6	2.0	0.3	2.9	3.6
45 16000	Columbia	342.4	132 067	195	385.7	52.6	43.5	1.2	2.8	0.2	6.1	5.5
45 25810	Florence	54.1	37 961	977	701.7	54.7	44.5	0.6	1.7	NA	1.9	2.3
45 29815	Goose Creek	103.8	40 370	918	388.9	73.3	20.1	1.2	7.7	NA	5.7	5.9
45 30850	Greenville	74.3	62 252	569	837.8	65.8	31.5	0.7	2.4	0.1	5.5	7.2
45 30985	Greer	53.5	27 676	1 322	517.3	76.6	18.5	0.5	2.1	NA	17.7	10.9
45 34045	Hilton Head Island	107.1	40 039	928	373.8	82.7	6.7	0.6	2.3	NA	16.0	17.2
45 48535	Mount Pleasant	116.8	77 796	429	666.1	93.6	4.9	0.2	2.6	NA	2.7	5.0
45 49075	Myrtle Beach	60.4	29 992	1 235	496.6	83.7	12.7	0.8	1.4	0.8	11.0	15.6
45 50875	North Charleston	189.6	106 749	271	563.0	46.8	49.3	1.1	3.0	NA	9.6	8.6
45 61405	Rock Hill	92.5	69 967	491	756.4	57.7	40.0	0.5	2.6	NA	5.3	4.7
45 68290	Spartanburg	51.2	37 525	987	732.9	49.4	48.7	0.7	2.2	NA	3.1	4.0
45 70270	Summerville	46.7	46 974	799	1 005.9	78.2	20.5	NA	1.9	NA	4.5	4.1
45 70405	Sumter	83.1	40 929	905	492.5	48.8	49.0	1.5	2.4	NA	2.7	3.7
46 00000	SOUTH DAKOTA	196 349.6	853 175	X	4.3	87.6	2.1	10.3	1.3	0.1	3.1	2.8
46 00100	Aberdeen	40.2	27 800	1 313	691.5	93.1	1.2	5.5	1.1	NA	2.2	2.4
46 52980	Rapid City	143.5	72 638	470	506.2	85.2	2.7	15.8	2.0	NA	5.0	1.9
46 59020	Sioux Falls	189.0	168 586	147	892.0	88.0	5.5	3.5	2.5	0.1	4.9	6.7
47 00000	TENNESSEE	106 797.9	6 549 352	X	61.3	79.7	17.6	1.0	1.9	0.1	4.8	4.7
47 03440	Bartlett	69.0	58 264	630	844.4	78.6	19.0	0.4	2.5	NA	2.1	4.4
47 08280	Brentwood	106.7	40 982	901	384.1	91.6	3.2	0.4	6.6	NA	2.1	6.7
47 08540	Bristol	83.7	26 729	1 371	319.3	93.9	3.8	0.5	1.0	NA	2.6	1.7
47 14000	Chattanooga	355.2	173 778	141	489.2	61.2	35.6	0.8	2.4	0.1	5.3	5.2
47 15160	Clarksville	252.8	146 806	176	580.7	70.7	25.7	2.4	3.5	0.7	10.2	6.6
47 15400	Cleveland	69.7	43 182	856	619.5	89.0	9.4	0.6	1.3	NA	8.0	6.0
47 16420	Collierville	75.9	48 655	774	641.0	78.2	13.5	1.1	7.8	NA	2.1	6.6

1. Dry land or land partially or temporarily covered by water. 2. May be of any race.

City	Age of population (percent), 2011-2013									Median age 2011-2013	Percent female 2011-2013	Population			
												Census counts		Percent change	
	Under 5 years	5 to 17 years	18 to 24 years	25 to 34 years	35 to 44 years	45 to 54 years	55 to 64 years	65 to 74 years	75 years and over			2000	2010	2000–2010	2010–2014
	12	13	14	15	16	17	18	19	20	21	22	23	24	25	26
OREGON—Cont'd															
Redmond	7.0	19.2	9.9	13.1	11.8	10.2	13.7	8.1	6.9	36.3	52.9	13 481	26 215	94.5	6.6
Salem	7.4	18.0	10.5	14.1	12.9	12.5	11.7	7.1	5.9	35.0	50.9	136 924	154 637	12.9	4.5
Springfield	6.9	16.8	11.3	15.0	12.8	13.2	13.3	5.9	4.8	35.0	51.5	52 864	59 403	12.4	1.5
Tigard	5.9	16.7	9.0	13.8	14.4	14.4	13.2	7.0	5.5	38.2	50.4	41 223	48 035	16.5	5.6
Tualatin	7.3	18.9	8.1	13.2	17.0	13.4	14.1	4.8	3.2	36.2	51.3	22 791	26 054	14.3	3.3
West Linn	3.8	19.2	6.9	8.2	12.8	19.1	15.8	8.6	5.5	44.4	49.1	22 261	25 109	12.8	4.7
PENNSYLVANIA	5.6	15.8	9.9	12.4	12.2	14.7	13.5	8.3	7.7	40.4	51.2	12 281 054	12 702 379	3.4	0.7
Allentown	7.5	18.6	12.4	14.5	12.7	12.4	10.3	5.6	6.1	32.9	51.6	106 632	118 032	10.7	0.8
Altoona	6.6	16.3	9.8	12.4	12.2	12.6	13.6	8.8	7.8	39.0	50.1	49 523	46 320	-6.5	-1.6
Bethel Park	5.0	16.0	5.5	11.5	11.6	17.1	13.2	9.4	10.6	45.5	53.2	33 556	32 313	-3.7	-0.2
Bethlehem	4.8	14.8	15.3	14.3	11.3	12.4	11.7	7.6	7.9	35.7	51.1	71 329	74 982	5.1	0.2
Chester	6.7	16.0	17.2	13.9	11.2	11.0	11.8	7.5	4.7	30.9	52.7	36 854	33 972	-7.8	0.5
Easton	6.6	15.5	17.0	15.3	12.6	11.6	10.2	5.9	5.3	32.3	52.0	26 263	26 800	2.0	0.9
Erie	7.0	15.7	13.3	15.1	11.5	12.8	11.4	6.6	6.6	34.2	50.8	103 717	101 786	-1.9	-2.3
Harrisburg	8.6	18.4	11.0	15.4	13.8	11.5	11.7	5.5	4.1	32.5	52.4	48 950	49 528	1.2	-0.9
Hazleton	7.5	17.0	12.2	13.0	11.3	14.5	10.0	6.8	7.8	35.5	50.2	23 329	25 340	8.6	-1.6
Lancaster	7.7	17.9	14.0	18.2	11.9	12.3	9.4	4.9	3.6	30.5	52.1	56 348	59 322	5.3	0.0
Lebanon	7.3	19.7	10.2	12.4	12.1	13.4	11.4	6.6	6.8	35.4	51.3	24 461	25 477	4.2	0.4
Monroeville	4.5	13.0	6.0	14.6	11.1	13.0	15.7	9.5	12.6	46.1	52.6	29 349	28 386	-3.3	-0.2
Norristown	7.7	15.5	11.2	18.1	14.3	12.7	10.7	5.3	4.5	33.8	48.7	31 282	34 324	9.7	0.5
Philadelphia	6.9	15.4	12.4	17.2	12.2	12.6	11.1	6.5	5.8	33.6	52.8	1 517 550	1 526 006	0.6	2.2
Pittsburgh	5.0	11.1	17.4	18.8	10.4	11.4	11.9	6.7	7.2	33.5	51.6	334 563	305 704	-8.6	-0.1
Plum	5.2	17.2	6.6	10.0	12.2	18.0	12.2	9.4	9.2	44.1	51.8	26 940	27 126	0.7	1.5
Reading	8.9	21.5	12.4	14.2	12.3	12.1	8.8	5.0	4.7	29.6	50.8	81 207	88 082	8.5	-0.3
Scranton	6.0	14.4	14.7	12.9	9.8	13.3	12.2	7.7	9.1	37.4	52.3	76 415	76 089	-0.4	-1.1
State College	2.0	2.6	69.2	10.4	4.1	4.0	3.4	1.9	2.3	21.5	46.5	38 420	42 034	9.4	0.2
Wilkes-Barre	6.5	16.9	14.6	14.0	10.9	11.2	11.0	7.2	7.8	33.0	50.7	43 123	41 498	-3.8	-1.6
Williamsport	7.2	14.6	18.6	15.3	10.3	12.3	10.8	5.8	5.1	30.9	50.8	30 706	29 381	-4.3	-0.6
York	9.0	19.0	11.7	16.5	11.9	12.2	10.8	5.3	3.6	30.6	52.0	40 862	43 718	7.0	0.1
RHODE ISLAND	5.2	15.4	11.4	12.5	12.3	15.0	13.1	7.7	7.3	39.7	51.6	1 048 319	1 052 567	0.4	0.2
Cranston	6.0	14.2	10.0	12.4	13.0	16.7	12.8	7.2	7.8	40.9	49.9	79 269	80 387	1.4	0.8
East Providence	6.9	14.3	6.7	14.2	12.3	15.2	12.3	7.9	10.1	40.9	54.7	48 688	47 037	-3.4	0.6
Pawtucket	6.9	15.9	9.3	16.1	12.9	14.1	12.7	6.4	5.7	36.5	50.7	72 958	71 148	-2.5	0.5
Providence	5.9	17.0	19.6	16.7	12.1	11.1	8.9	4.5	4.1	28.9	51.3	173 618	178 042	2.5	0.6
Warwick	4.9	14.1	7.0	13.0	13.0	15.5	14.9	8.8	8.9	43.7	52.8	85 808	82 672	-3.7	-0.9
Woonsocket	7.2	15.2	8.7	15.1	11.9	14.9	12.3	7.3	7.4	37.8	50.0	43 224	41 186	-4.7	0.1
SOUTH CAROLINA	6.2	16.6	10.3	12.8	12.6	13.8	13.0	8.8	5.9	38.4	51.4	4 012 012	4 625 364	15.3	4.5
Aiken	5.0	13.7	13.0	9.1	8.6	11.8	15.7	12.4	10.6	45.5	55.7	25 337	29 524	16.5	2.4
Anderson	6.8	16.9	11.9	11.4	12.8	12.8	9.3	8.5	9.5	37.7	54.1	25 514	26 686	4.6	3.0
Charleston	6.2	11.5	15.4	18.7	12.1	11.6	11.7	7.5	5.3	33.9	52.8	96 650	120 083	24.2	8.2
Columbia	5.8	11.5	26.6	17.0	10.7	10.6	8.7	4.7	4.4	27.8	47.9	116 278	129 272	11.2	1.5
Florence	6.6	18.3	6.7	13.9	12.9	13.0	13.9	8.7	6.0	38.8	55.1	30 248	37 056	22.5	2.5
Goose Creek	7.5	16.9	15.9	15.6	11.9	14.4	9.8	5.7	2.3	30.4	46.7	29 208	35 938	23.0	11.7
Greenville	6.4	14.0	12.2	18.4	13.4	12.3	11.4	6.5	5.3	34.4	50.1	56 002	58 409	4.3	5.2
Greer	8.1	17.6	9.7	17.0	13.5	12.8	10.4	6.0	4.9	33.5	51.8	16 843	25 515	51.5	8.1
Hilton Head Island	3.0	11.9	5.0	9.5	10.1	13.1	15.5	18.4	13.3	53.1	49.3	33 862	37 099	9.6	7.9
Mount Pleasant	5.5	18.7	6.4	14.0	15.2	13.8	12.6	7.5	6.2	38.2	51.8	47 609	67 843	42.5	14.7
Myrtle Beach	6.0	10.3	7.0	16.0	13.5	13.1	15.9	10.6	7.6	42.0	51.3	22 759	27 109	19.1	10.7
North Charleston	8.6	15.8	12.0	19.6	11.9	12.9	10.6	5.3	3.2	31.2	50.5	79 641	97 471	22.4	9.4
Rock Hill	7.0	16.6	14.7	16.0	12.4	11.8	10.5	5.7	5.2	32.0	52.3	49 765	66 154	32.9	5.3
Spartanburg	8.1	13.7	15.6	11.2	11.4	13.0	11.5	7.6	7.8	36.5	56.7	39 673	37 013	-6.7	2.1
Summerville	7.6	19.4	9.6	12.6	14.9	14.2	10.3	5.8	5.6	35.4	53.1	27 752	43 392	56.4	10.3
Sumter	6.2	17.3	12.3	14.1	11.2	13.2	10.7	7.3	7.6	35.0	54.0	39 643	40 524	2.2	1.0
SOUTH DAKOTA	7.1	17.5	10.1	13.1	11.4	13.4	12.8	7.4	7.1	36.8	49.8	754 844	814 180	7.9	4.8
Aberdeen	7.4	15.5	12.0	15.3	10.5	11.5	11.9	6.7	9.2	34.8	51.8	24 658	26 091	5.8	6.6
Rapid City	7.9	15.9	10.0	14.8	11.3	12.3	12.7	7.5	7.5	35.9	50.2	59 607	67 956	14.0	6.9
Sioux Falls	8.2	16.1	10.0	17.4	12.6	12.9	11.8	5.9	5.3	33.9	50.2	123 975	153 888	24.1	9.5
TENNESSEE	6.2	16.9	9.7	13.0	13.1	14.1	12.8	8.3	5.9	38.3	51.2	5 689 283	6 346 105	11.5	3.2
Bartlett	6.5	19.6	7.4	10.2	13.9	14.9	14.0	7.8	5.7	39.6	51.2	40 543	54 613	34.7	2.4
Brentwood	5.7	24.7	5.2	5.9	14.4	18.5	14.1	7.5	4.1	41.6	50.6	23 445	37 060	58.1	10.6
Bristol	5.0	14.7	10.0	11.3	13.2	13.4	14.8	9.7	7.8	41.4	50.6	24 821	26 702	7.6	0.1
Chattanooga	6.3	15.0	11.2	14.7	12.3	12.9	12.9	7.7	7.1	37.0	51.9	155 554	167 674	7.8	2.9
Clarksville	9.2	18.5	13.6	19.6	13.3	10.9	7.7	4.2	2.8	28.7	50.5	103 455	132 929	28.5	10.4
Cleveland	6.4	17.1	14.7	13.5	12.0	12.2	9.9	6.9	7.2	33.3	50.6	37 192	41 285	11.0	4.6
Collierville	5.6	22.9	7.1	9.5	14.1	18.0	12.8	6.1	3.9	38.7	52.3	31 872	43 965	37.9	6.7

City	Households, 2011-2013				Persons in group quarters, 2010				Serious crimes known to police,[2] 2013				Educational attainment, 2011–2013		
			Percent			Institutional			Total		Rate[3]			Attainment[4] (percent)	
	Number	Persons per household	Female family householder[1]	One-person	Total	Total	Persons in nursing facilities	Noninstitutional	Number	Rate[3]	Violent	Property	Population age 25 and older	High school graduate or less	Bachelor's degree or more
	27	28	29	30	31	32	33	34	35	36	37	38	39	40	41
OREGON—Cont'd															
Redmond	10 503	2.53	18.0	25.4	300	181	181	119	1 165	4 291	320	3 970	17 200	39.3	22.1
Salem	57 939	2.59	13.6	29.7	8 635	5 610	639	3 025	7 352	4 646	329	4 318	101 833	38.6	26.6
Springfield	23 734	2.51	13.8	29.1	587	181	140	406	3 296	5 491	163	5 328	38 968	45.0	15.0
Tigard	19 225	2.57	9.7	26.2	347	111	78	236	1 683	3 345	113	3 232	34 024	22.9	39.9
Tualatin	10 613	2.54	8.0	27.4	87	45	45	42	807	2 997	89	2 908	17 760	26.9	40.7
West Linn	9 927	2.57	8.7	20.9	127	63	60	64	285	1 107	23	1 084	18 004	14.0	55.2
PENNSYLVANIA	4 945 140	2.49	12.0	29.7	426 113	197 112	87 775	229 001	306 089	2 396	335	2 061	8 764 132	48.0	27.9
Allentown	41 299	2.75	23.3	29.4	5 070	2 089	885	2 981	4 952	4 152	527	3 625	73 038	59.5	15.6
Altoona	18 770	2.40	15.4	34.0	1 189	452	443	737	1 166	2 529	284	2 245	31 013	61.3	15.8
Bethel Park	12 958	2.48	9.5	27.2	217	184	184	33	275	849	59	790	23 806	30.8	45.6
Bethlehem	29 670	2.33	15.5	35.6	6 265	955	882	5 310	2 193	2 919	244	2 675	48 894	47.6	26.4
Chester	11 647	2.61	33.9	34.2	3 151	1 328	143	1 823	1 912	5 617	2 148	3 470	20 392	65.5	10.8
Easton	9 249	2.57	21.0	30.0	3 087	1 093	311	1 994	820	3 037	356	2 681	16 456	59.2	15.9
Erie	41 187	2.33	18.2	36.6	5 244	1 578	715	3 666	3 665	3 635	453	3 182	64 746	55.3	21.6
Harrisburg	20 312	2.38	25.5	38.1	987	265	89	722	2 667	5 420	1 295	4 126	30 560	55.2	19.1
Hazleton	9 202	2.68	22.9	29.9	410	384	218	26	714	2 834	329	2 505	15 975	66.2	10.8
Lancaster	21 416	2.57	20.3	35.3	3 189	1 214	121	1 975	3 189	5 371	837	4 534	35 852	60.6	17.3
Lebanon	9 999	2.52	20.5	36.9	364	106	102	258	888	3 471	403	3 068	16 034	70.0	11.9
Monroeville	12 451	2.23	11.2	34.8	520	457	457	63	457	1 609	208	1 401	21 708	34.4	36.1
Norristown	12 726	2.64	20.3	33.7	947	224	224	723	1 392	4 040	940	3 100	22 576	57.0	19.0
Philadelphia	579 165	2.58	20.3	40.0	57 383	19 376	7 877	38 007	70 526	4 541	1 099	3 442	1 009 705	52.7	24.4
Pittsburgh	132 160	2.14	14.5	41.3	24 329	6 967	2 242	17 362	12 306	4 000	734	3 266	203 465	38.1	37.3
Plum	10 875	2.51	7.0	29.0	132	132	122	0	241	877	258	619	19 476	36.7	33.3
Reading	30 716	2.77	25.4	31.3	2 545	485	265	2 060	3 540	4 018	844	3 173	50 280	71.6	9.0
Scranton	28 886	2.44	14.5	35.8	5 472	2 380	1 444	3 092	2 443	3 226	219	3 007	49 312	53.8	21.6
State College	12 323	2.39	3.6	33.9	13 071	194	155	12 877	748	1 321	72	1 249	10 982	14.3	70.3
Wilkes-Barre	15 441	2.46	19.1	37.7	3 065	1 115	420	1 950	1 597	3 879	505	3 374	25 592	58.3	14.6
Williamsport	10 712	2.48	21.0	32.2	2 896	408	143	2 488	1 262	4 273	352	3 921	17 523	54.6	16.6
York	16 100	2.65	25.0	33.8	1 121	113	0	1 008	1 829	4 172	794	3 378	26 412	72.0	10.2
RHODE ISLAND	410 347	2.46	13.9	30.2	42 663	12 932	8 420	29 731	28 383	2 699	257	2 442	714 525	41.3	31.8
Cranston	29 757	2.55	12.8	30.0	4 523	4 004	224	519	1 901	2 355	181	2 174	56 283	44.2	29.7
East Providence	20 144	2.30	17.1	34.5	800	759	680	41	785	1 663	121	1 542	33 953	47.3	27.1
Pawtucket	27 855	2.54	19.6	33.0	524	357	335	167	2 604	3 652	393	3 259	48 271	54.0	17.4
Providence	61 368	2.67	21.8	30.8	15 086	1 200	1 152	13 886	9 144	5 112	628	4 483	102 372	49.2	28.8
Warwick	35 283	2.30	10.2	32.9	660	502	494	158	2 108	2 577	114	2 464	60 735	36.0	31.6
Woonsocket	17 220	2.33	16.7	35.6	802	568	568	234	1 466	3 571	585	2 986	28 249	58.3	14.1
SOUTH CAROLINA	1 781 957	2.57	15.3	27.6	139 154	63 765	19 020	75 389	197 327	4 133	508	3 624	3 156 752	45.1	25.0
Aiken	12 065	2.35	13.7	33.6	1 382	469	427	913	1 577	5 263	317	4 946	20 557	33.2	40.7
Anderson	10 522	2.38	21.1	37.8	1 751	716	577	1 035	2 700	10 070	1 041	9 030	17 259	50.9	20.5
Charleston	52 621	2.28	11.0	36.8	5 770	300	291	5 470	3 425	2 692	183	2 509	84 035	25.4	48.7
Columbia	43 571	2.35	17.4	38.5	29 919	7 777	920	22 142	8 956	6 773	723	6 050	74 068	32.9	39.4
Florence	15 059	2.45	21.5	32.1	654	389	384	265	3 238	8 609	779	7 830	25 693	38.2	30.3
Goose Creek	13 169	2.78	12.9	19.8	2 322	0	0	2 322	1 049	2 661	216	2 445	23 184	33.4	26.2
Greenville	25 667	2.19	14.1	41.7	5 129	1 393	208	3 736	3 708	6 060	740	5 320	40 894	34.5	39.6
Greer	9 748	2.66	17.0	29.1	272	130	130	142	898	3 331	464	2 868	16 789	43.0	28.3
Hilton Head Island	16 464	2.33	6.8	27.6	202	202	202	0	NA	NA	NA	NA	30 814	27.4	46.9
Mount Pleasant	28 423	2.52	8.4	27.1	568	544	544	24	1 559	2 130	167	1 963	50 001	15.7	57.4
Myrtle Beach	12 380	2.28	13.0	34.5	217	22	22	195	5 058	17 646	1 664	15 982	21 810	43.6	27.9
North Charleston	36 567	2.63	21.1	30.0	3 859	2 139	283	1 720	6 512	6 303	676	5 627	64 828	49.5	19.1
Rock Hill	26 825	2.43	20.2	31.7	3 005	612	442	2 393	2 960	4 314	544	3 770	42 093	40.8	27.1
Spartanburg	15 760	2.24	25.2	37.1	2 489	302	175	2 187	3 200	8 528	1 405	7 124	23 468	44.6	26.7
Summerville	17 092	2.67	15.4	26.2	318	251	160	67	1 744	3 858	232	3 625	29 168	34.2	30.3
Sumter	16 350	2.41	19.4	32.3	1 790	364	330	1 426	2 407	5 881	943	4 938	26 288	39.0	25.7
SOUTH DAKOTA	326 086	2.45	9.9	29.3	34 050	14 797	7 005	19 253	18 851	2 231	316	1 915	544 876	41.1	26.4
Aberdeen	11 716	2.18	10.5	35.9	1 191	433	351	758	720	2 667	293	2 374	17 469	43.1	28.5
Rapid City	27 858	2.40	12.4	33.1	2 471	1 331	491	1 140	3 039	4 316	581	3 735	46 205	36.9	27.8
Sioux Falls	64 020	2.43	11.9	29.6	6 085	3 336	982	2 749	5 602	3 463	401	3 063	105 576	36.6	32.5
TENNESSEE	2 480 467	2.54	13.4	28.4	153 472	84 371	33 041	69 101	244 993	3 771	591	3 181	4 333 913	48.1	24.2
Bartlett	19 526	2.93	12.3	16.5	703	688	244	15	1 220	2 165	186	1 978	38 531	31.4	35.4
Brentwood	12 814	3.04	5.0	10.3	349	312	275	37	464	1 171	43	1 128	25 164	10.2	69.5
Bristol	11 117	2.32	12.5	32.4	833	226	218	607	1 224	4 591	368	4 224	18 737	48.6	22.5
Chattanooga	69 391	2.37	17.5	35.8	7 562	3 067	1 212	4 495	13 215	7 670	986	6 684	116 251	42.5	25.7
Clarksville	50 581	2.72	16.2	22.0	2 921	904	419	2 017	4 937	3 391	534	2 856	82 446	37.6	24.1
Cleveland	15 951	2.48	13.9	32.1	2 703	786	430	1 917	2 787	6 522	791	5 731	26 158	46.1	22.6
Collierville	15 276	3.04	8.2	15.6	62	62	62	0	859	1 838	182	1 656	29 981	19.4	54.8

1. No spouse present. 2. Data for serious crimes have not been adjusted for underreporting. This may affect comparability between geographic areas and over time. 3. Per 100,000 population estimated by the FBI. 4. Persons 25 years old and over.

City	Money income, 2011–2013					Housing units, 2010			Occupied housing units 2011–2013				
		Households								Owner-occupied		Median owner costs as a percent of income	
	Per capita income[1] (dollars)	Median income	Percent with income of $200,000 or more	Percent with income of less than $25,000	Families with income below poverty (percent)	Total	Percent change, 2000–2010	Vacant units for sale or rent[2]	Total	Percent	Median value[3] (dollars)	With a mortgage[4]	Without a mortgage[5]
	42	43	44	45	46	47	48	49	50	51	52	53	54
OREGON—Cont'd													
Redmond	18 576	38 675	NA	32.2	19.7	10 965	92.8	1 018	10 503	55.3	147 700	26.7	12.5
Salem	22 242	44 773	2.0	27.4	16.2	61 276	14.0	3 986	57 939	52.4	178 600	25.0	13.0
Springfield	19 312	39 598	0.7	32.1	18.2	24 809	15.0	1 144	23 734	52.0	162 000	27.1	15.4
Tigard	34 316	62 240	5.1	18.6	9.7	20 068	15.4	911	19 225	58.9	290 900	24.2	10.7
Tualatin	33 331	66 834	6.6	20.6	8.0	10 528	14.2	528	10 613	54.4	296 900	22.3	10.1
West Linn	42 764	80 479	10.9	11.3	3.2	10 035	14.8	512	9 927	76.5	382 800	25.4	11.5
PENNSYLVANIA	28 257	51 953	4.2	23.8	9.4	5 567 315	6.0	548 411	4 945 140	69.2	164 300	22.7	13.6
Allentown	17 048	36 022	0.8	34.7	22.1	46 921	2.1	4 117	41 299	47.3	125 900	27.2	17.0
Altoona	18 985	35 290	0.9	37.3	15.5	21 179	-2.3	1 878	18 770	65.7	82 000	21.1	12.7
Bethel Park	33 602	71 229	3.2	13.6	2.9	14 311	3.2	652	12 958	79.3	159 000	19.3	13.1
Bethlehem	23 748	45 436	1.7	29.2	15.9	31 221	5.4	1 856	29 670	52.9	169 300	26.2	14.3
Chester	14 573	27 152	0.7	46.2	25.9	13 745	-8.2	2 083	11 647	39.9	67 800	28.4	14.4
Easton	18 059	37 078	1.0	35.2	17.2	10 356	-1.8	1 049	9 249	46.7	124 100	26.0	14.9
Erie	18 383	32 672	0.7	39.6	22.3	44 790	-0.4	3 877	41 187	51.3	84 600	22.2	14.3
Harrisburg	18 345	34 068	0.6	37.9	28.6	24 269	-0.3	3 664	20 312	39.8	89 700	23.8	12.9
Hazleton	16 854	29 623	1.1	38.2	22.6	11 409	-1.0	1 611	9 202	53.1	81 600	25.7	16.8
Lancaster	16 056	32 661	0.6	39.3	26.4	23 377	1.5	1 584	21 416	43.6	109 100	25.3	13.9
Lebanon	17 675	28 513	0.3	46.5	25.8	11 278	0.5	920	9 999	43.6	89 900	19.9	13.6
Monroeville	32 188	59 145	3.5	22.2	5.5	13 496	2.6	884	12 451	65.2	130 200	19.4	11.2
Norristown	20 950	41 444	0.8	32.1	18.9	13 420	-0.8	1 457	12 726	39.6	152 400	26.2	16.6
Philadelphia	21 902	36 222	2.4	36.9	21.6	670 171	1.2	70 435	579 165	52.4	140 200	25.1	15.3
Pittsburgh	27 159	39 527	3.8	34.0	16.1	156 165	-4.4	19 948	132 160	47.9	90 900	19.3	13.1
Plum	30 173	65 725	3.5	15.0	3.2	11 494	8.2	608	10 875	80.7	136 300	20.4	11.6
Reading	13 097	25 507	0.4	49.3	37.6	34 208	-0.3	4 229	30 716	42.2	66 300	28.0	16.2
Scranton	20 019	37 212	1.4	34.7	16.0	33 853	-4.2	3 784	28 886	50.9	108 000	22.1	15.6
State College	14 920	26 529	2.0	48.4	13.9	13 007	4.2	397	12 323	19.2	269 500	19.3	10.0
Wilkes-Barre	16 738	31 280	0.5	41.2	22.8	19 595	-3.4	2 721	15 441	46.1	78 600	22.2	14.0
Williamsport	17 292	35 096	1.0	35.5	24.0	12 864	-4.9	1 218	10 712	42.9	95 800	23.7	14.4
York	14 774	28 447	0.4	45.2	36.9	18 496	-0.2	2 243	16 100	42.2	82 900	27.7	15.6
RHODE ISLAND	30 356	55 675	4.7	23.8	10.2	463 388	5.4	49 788	410 347	60.2	238 800	25.6	15.9
Cranston	29 319	59 448	4.6	20.2	6.8	33 117	3.3	2 105	29 757	64.9	215 500	25.8	17.3
East Providence	27 272	48 145	2.8	27.6	10.3	21 440	0.6	1 239	20 144	57.1	214 300	26.5	17.4
Pawtucket	21 327	41 025	0.9	32.3	15.7	32 055	0.7	3 033	27 855	44.4	169 600	29.7	18.4
Providence	21 500	36 700	3.5	38.4	25.7	71 530	5.3	8 812	61 368	34.8	178 800	27.8	16.2
Warwick	34 591	63 706	3.8	19.5	4.4	37 730	1.7	2 496	35 283	71.5	195 300	24.6	15.4
Woonsocket	21 736	34 168	1.7	37.2	23.2	19 214	2.4	2 152	17 220	37.9	166 600	27.7	17.6
SOUTH CAROLINA	23 602	43 973	2.6	28.8	14.2	2 137 683	21.9	336 502	1 781 957	68.6	136 600	22.5	11.3
Aiken	30 255	51 627	4.6	26.4	11.6	14 162	25.3	1 389	12 065	68.8	181 400	21.2	10.1
Anderson	18 239	30 290	1.2	42.7	22.1	12 938	7.3	1 858	10 522	50.4	118 200	23.6	10.6
Charleston	32 832	52 066	6.7	26.5	12.0	59 522	34.8	7 181	52 621	54.0	242 200	24.3	14.0
Columbia	23 749	41 263	4.5	30.9	17.5	52 471	13.9	6 805	43 571	47.1	161 300	22.2	11.5
Florence	25 006	41 271	3.6	32.1	14.6	16 665	27.5	1 686	15 059	58.8	149 700	21.6	10.0
Goose Creek	25 314	61 254	1.2	15.4	9.9	13 484	42.4	1 128	13 169	63.7	166 800	21.1	10.0
Greenville	29 330	39 591	5.7	34.7	17.6	29 418	7.5	3 819	25 667	42.2	197 300	21.4	11.8
Greer	23 682	40 195	1.7	33.5	19.7	11 127	48.5	1 115	9 748	53.1	142 900	21.5	10.0
Hilton Head Island	44 628	67 643	9.7	15.0	5.2	33 306	35.0	16 771	16 464	73.6	421 000	30.7	12.3
Mount Pleasant	39 913	75 829	8.9	13.1	5.6	30 674	52.4	2 932	28 423	73.0	351 300	24.1	10.7
Myrtle Beach	28 065	34 621	4.7	37.4	19.7	23 262	59.2	11 149	12 380	52.1	167 800	28.4	10.6
North Charleston	19 763	38 842	1.2	32.8	19.7	42 219	25.5	5 304	36 567	48.1	135 100	26.3	13.3
Rock Hill	22 327	40 705	1.3	31.0	13.6	29 159	42.4	3 193	26 825	51.4	129 600	22.9	13.4
Spartanburg	19 772	33 381	2.2	41.3	27.6	17 516	-1.1	2 332	15 760	49.0	124 800	23.7	11.3
Summerville	24 338	51 804	2.1	20.7	12.0	18 557	64.9	1 691	17 092	60.8	180 600	23.1	13.8
Sumter	22 697	38 825	2.6	29.8	14.8	18 150	12.6	2 517	16 350	51.7	132 500	21.8	10.3
SOUTH DAKOTA	25 788	49 332	3.0	23.2	9.3	363 438	12.4	41 156	326 086	67.7	134 500	21.0	10.9
Aberdeen	26 603	47 283	3.0	24.9	5.1	12 158	8.1	740	11 716	60.6	136 600	19.5	12.7
Rapid City	25 151	46 244	2.7	25.4	11.2	30 254	20.4	1 668	27 858	58.1	155 200	22.8	11.9
Sioux Falls	27 527	51 099	3.2	20.1	8.8	66 283	28.1	4 576	64 020	61.1	152 600	21.5	10.0
TENNESSEE	24 331	43 697	2.9	28.5	13.6	2 812 133	15.3	318 581	2 480 467	66.7	139 000	22.6	11.0
Bartlett	31 998	79 116	4.2	6.9	2.2	20 143	43.9	687	19 526	82.8	169 800	21.7	10.6
Brentwood	59 885	134 702	32.0	3.6	1.7	12 577	58.5	407	12 814	91.7	486 500	20.3	10.0
Bristol	21 033	35 921	1.2	33.5	14.6	12 773	10.9	1 317	11 117	67.9	104 400	23.1	11.5
Chattanooga	23 743	37 652	2.8	34.5	18.9	79 607	10.4	8 858	69 391	53.4	141 800	23.2	11.8
Clarksville	21 017	46 100	1.4	24.3	14.8	54 815	36.9	5 376	50 581	52.8	137 500	22.5	10.6
Cleveland	20 712	32 489	1.6	39.4	24.7	17 841	8.4	1 734	15 951	47.9	154 100	24.4	10.9
Collierville	41 238	105 723	13.6	6.3	2.5	15 781	46.7	602	15 276	85.9	274 200	22.9	10.1

1. Based on population estimated by the American Community Survey. 2. Includes units rented or sold but not occupied. 3. Specified owner-occupied units; $1,000,000 represents $1,000,000 or more 4. 50.0 represents 50 percent or more. 5. 10.0 represents 10 percent or less.

City	Occupied housing units, 2011–2013 (cont.): Percent renter occupied	Occupied housing units, 2011–2013 (cont.): Median gross rent[1]	Occupied housing units, 2011–2013 (cont.): Median rent as a percent of income[2]	Occupied housing units, 2011–2013 (cont.): Percent with no vehicle available	Migration, 2011–2013: Percent who lived in the same house one year ago	Migration, 2011–2013: Percent who lived outside current city one year ago	Civilian labor force, 2014: Total	Civilian labor force, 2014: Percent change, 2013–2014	Civilian labor force, 2014: Unemployment: Total	Civilian labor force, 2014: Unemployment: Rate[3]	Civilian employment[4], 2011–2013: Population age 16 and older	Civilian employment[4], 2011–2013: Percent: In labor force	Civilian employment[4], 2011–2013: Percent: Civilian full-year full-time workers	Civilian employment[4], 2011–2013: Households with no workers (percent)
	55	56	57	58	59	60	61	62	63	64	65	66	67	68
OREGON—Cont'd														
Redmond	44.7	832	37.0	6.8	79.5	10.0	11 179	3.9	909	8.1	20 477	57.3	26.0	42.0
Salem	47.6	775	31.4	9.0	78.0	12.0	74 200	1.6	5 399	7.3	122 570	61.3	32.9	31.5
Springfield	48.0	798	31.3	8.8	74.5	15.1	29 568	1.4	2 222	7.5	47 417	64.6	34.6	30.6
Tigard	41.1	945	32.5	5.3	80.8	16.5	28 113	2.2	1 476	5.3	39 832	70.9	42.3	22.0
Tualatin	45.6	973	29.4	6.4	86.3	11.2	14 412	2.0	758	5.3	20 707	71.6	45.2	21.3
West Linn	23.5	1 316	32.8	2.7	85.5	11.5	13 904	2.1	740	5.3	20 667	65.1	38.3	22.0
PENNSYLVANIA	30.8	815	30.3	11.6	88.0	8.9	6 378 495	-1.0	369 962	5.8	10 354 784	62.8	39.2	29.7
Allentown	52.7	873	38.0	20.1	77.5	10.6	53 325	-1.6	4 489	8.4	91 190	62.5	33.6	32.0
Altoona	34.3	554	31.8	13.7	88.6	5.2	20 658	-1.4	1 289	6.2	36 697	58.1	33.6	36.0
Bethel Park	20.7	861	27.2	5.6	92.0	7.1	17 193	-0.7	743	4.3	26 294	64.6	42.7	26.4
Bethlehem	47.1	884	33.2	14.6	78.8	10.8	36 754	-0.9	2 487	6.8	62 598	58.4	35.3	34.4
Chester	60.1	787	37.3	32.9	85.1	8.8	13 305	-1.6	1 379	10.4	27 086	55.9	27.6	40.2
Easton	53.3	884	35.0	19.2	70.5	14.3	11 877	-1.2	919	7.7	21 750	57.3	33.5	27.9
Erie	48.7	631	33.3	19.5	81.5	8.7	45 774	-1.4	3 171	6.9	80 439	60.9	34.7	35.0
Harrisburg	60.2	747	32.0	27.8	79.1	10.2	21 517	-1.5	1 730	8.0	37 044	65.2	38.8	33.2
Hazleton	46.9	644	31.4	16.4	82.9	8.8	11 782	-1.6	1 339	11.4	19 919	61.6	34.0	35.3
Lancaster	56.4	770	36.5	22.2	80.6	11.4	26 623	-0.9	1 866	7.0	46 039	63.7	33.8	29.5
Lebanon	56.4	637	36.0	22.8	81.4	7.4	11 795	-0.9	918	7.8	19 350	62.9	35.8	37.7
Monroeville	34.8	867	28.3	6.4	87.5	9.4	14 720	-0.8	759	5.2	23 801	61.9	40.4	32.3
Norristown	60.4	961	40.1	22.4	86.5	7.7	17 826	-0.3	1 038	5.8	27 129	68.9	39.6	25.6
Philadelphia	47.6	894	34.6	33.1	85.6	4.6	689 205	-1.3	55 169	8.0	1 239 805	59.0	34.4	36.2
Pittsburgh	52.1	770	29.9	25.2	79.2	11.5	157 318	-1.0	8 800	5.6	262 663	62.0	37.1	32.3
Plum	19.3	884	26.4	5.5	94.8	3.5	14 920	-0.7	743	5.0	22 212	66.7	45.7	26.8
Reading	57.8	720	39.3	31.4	77.7	7.6	34 121	-1.4	2 967	8.7	64 141	59.6	28.7	38.2
Scranton	49.1	689	29.9	16.2	81.7	9.8	35 927	-1.0	2 585	7.2	62 033	57.8	34.0	35.7
State College	80.8	920	50.0	20.6	43.7	37.4	16 764	-0.7	853	5.1	40 229	45.4	15.0	31.3
Wilkes-Barre	53.9	630	29.2	22.2	77.2	13.9	18 600	-1.7	1 539	8.3	32 619	56.0	31.8	37.5
Williamsport	57.1	721	31.8	17.1	75.7	13.5	14 416	-1.3	1 017	7.1	23 462	61.7	30.6	29.7
York	57.8	694	36.7	26.6	73.9	11.3	17 844	-2.2	1 793	10.0	32 940	60.5	29.9	38.5
RHODE ISLAND	39.8	904	30.6	9.6	86.7	9.5	553 332	-0.6	42 430	7.7	861 216	66.2	38.8	28.4
Cranston	35.1	983	29.8	5.8	89.8	7.5	41 218	-0.8	3 162	7.7	66 481	63.5	38.5	28.4
East Providence	42.9	887	28.8	10.6	84.2	9.3	24 266	-0.9	2 010	8.3	38 192	64.8	38.3	34.3
Pawtucket	55.6	809	29.8	15.7	85.0	8.6	36 398	-1.0	3 271	9.0	56 518	67.9	39.2	30.3
Providence	65.2	882	32.7	19.6	78.4	10.7	86 333	-0.8	7 768	9.0	142 723	64.9	33.5	30.1
Warwick	28.5	1 032	30.6	6.3	90.9	5.1	46 138	-0.7	3 148	6.8	68 476	70.3	45.1	27.5
Woonsocket	62.1	797	31.1	18.1	91.4	4.4	19 005	-1.3	1 851	9.7	32 818	57.7	36.6	36.9
SOUTH CAROLINA	31.4	766	31.6	7.0	84.5	13.0	2 197 587	0.8	141 451	6.4	3 764 538	61.0	37.2	30.7
Aiken	31.2	845	33.7	7.8	84.6	10.6	13 060	1.2	867	6.6	25 107	52.7	33.2	39.6
Anderson	49.6	588	32.8	12.0	80.3	13.9	11 327	0.5	725	6.4	21 061	54.8	30.5	40.7
Charleston	46.0	975	33.8	10.6	77.5	13.9	68 437	1.7	3 210	4.7	105 343	66.0	42.3	26.2
Columbia	52.9	814	31.7	11.0	64.3	25.4	58 909	1.0	3 865	6.6	111 883	64.9	31.5	27.6
Florence	41.2	666	32.0	11.7	86.4	7.0	18 106	-1.0	1 095	6.0	28 954	63.7	40.8	31.7
Goose Creek	36.3	1 081	33.8	2.1	75.4	19.7	18 197	1.7	991	5.4	30 005	74.7	43.4	16.5
Greenville	57.8	745	29.9	12.8	77.2	16.9	31 564	1.1	1 546	4.9	49 535	65.8	38.4	29.3
Greer	46.9	755	29.3	6.6	77.7	15.6	13 925	0.9	630	4.5	20 126	67.6	43.2	25.1
Hilton Head Island	26.4	1 005	29.4	5.0	84.0	11.4	17 247	2.7	780	4.5	33 288	56.5	33.1	39.9
Mount Pleasant	27.0	1 251	34.1	2.9	80.9	9.1	40 165	2.0	1 593	4.0	55 890	70.6	48.6	21.5
Myrtle Beach	47.9	795	39.7	12.4	79.4	11.7	14 350	0.6	1 095	7.6	24 299	64.7	34.7	32.3
North Charleston	51.9	843	33.3	10.8	74.7	15.9	49 367	1.5	2 893	5.9	78 955	68.9	43.3	23.0
Rock Hill	48.6	750	32.4	8.4	79.2	10.5	35 791	1.1	2 486	6.9	53 979	68.3	41.1	26.1
Spartanburg	51.0	660	33.1	18.2	79.9	13.2	16 331	-0.4	1 157	7.1	30 430	58.0	30.1	38.0
Summerville	39.2	980	29.6	4.1	76.5	17.5	21 816	1.7	1 146	5.3	34 807	67.4	42.7	24.8
Sumter	48.3	706	28.7	13.2	78.7	13.2	15 984	0.5	1 080	6.8	31 992	61.0	34.9	32.1
SOUTH DAKOTA	32.3	644	26.1	5.0	83.3	10.1	448 201	0.7	15 228	3.4	651 321	69.0	46.0	23.6
Aberdeen	39.4	592	24.9	7.1	78.3	12.0	15 126	0.1	467	3.1	21 278	70.6	47.9	22.1
Rapid City	41.9	755	28.8	6.7	76.3	10.0	34 999	0.6	1 322	3.8	54 705	67.1	39.5	26.4
Sioux Falls	38.9	712	26.7	5.7	81.8	7.4	95 705	1.7	2 883	3.0	125 142	74.3	52.0	19.6
TENNESSEE	33.3	743	30.8	6.4	84.5	10.2	3 011 495	-2.3	200 633	6.7	5 125 885	61.4	38.7	29.8
Bartlett	17.2	1 270	26.2	2.7	90.4	6.9	29 359	-2.5	1 751	6.0	44 470	67.9	47.2	16.5
Brentwood	8.3	2 000	24.8	2.4	90.6	6.7	19 316	-0.4	902	4.7	29 171	65.1	43.5	14.8
Bristol	32.1	598	28.4	7.2	81.5	11.0	11 600	-3.1	813	7.0	22 073	57.4	32.7	36.9
Chattanooga	46.6	729	31.5	11.8	80.8	9.6	77 790	-3.5	5 440	7.0	138 904	60.6	37.0	33.1
Clarksville	47.2	857	28.4	5.2	72.0	16.3	56 772	-2.1	3 908	6.9	105 410	67.6	34.0	21.5
Cleveland	52.1	662	34.0	9.5	74.2	11.8	19 672	-3.1	1 293	6.6	33 301	58.6	32.2	32.0
Collierville	14.1	1 137	21.3	1.1	87.8	10.7	23 218	-2.6	1 238	5.3	35 165	69.9	47.7	14.3

1. $2,000 represents $2,000 or more. 2. 50.0 represents 50 percent or more. 3. Percent of civilian labor force. 4. Persons 16 years old and over.

City	Value of residential construction authorized by building permits, 2014: New construction ($1,000)	Number of housing units	Percent single family	Wholesale trade,[1] 2007: Number of establish-ments	Number of employees	Sales (mil dol)	Annual payroll (mil dol)	Retail trade,[2] 2007: Number of establish-ments	Number of employees	Sales (mil dol)	Annual payroll (mil dol)
	69	70	71	72	73	74	75	76	77	78	79
OREGON—Cont'd											
Redmond	34 935	148	100.0	43	268	131.7	10.4	143	1 587	438.0	45.0
Salem	74 121	291	92.8	165	1 753	2 260.8	75.0	642	10 742	2 617.1	262.9
Springfield	8 042	37	94.6	52	1 101	499.1	47.0	227	3 650	755.6	75.1
Tigard	19 949	63	100.0	177	2 928	2 572.7	187.6	345	7 479	1 807.4	188.2
Tualatin	5 664	16	100.0	110	2 197	971.4	109.5	124	2 241	483.3	55.0
West Linn	13 047	38	100.0	24	78	106.6	4.1	50	550	113.6	11.9
PENNSYLVANIA	4 714 443	25 059	65.3	13 161	200 151	142 859.2	10 100.7	46 532	672 042	166 842.8	14 862.3
Allentown	5 594	345	6.1	150	2 980	1 576.9	218.5	368	5 329	1 299.7	126.0
Altoona	401	4	100.0	46	682	272.0	22.6	217	4 426	917.1	84.1
Bethel Park	610	2	100.0	37	357	123.7	13.4	168	3 786	684.6	69.9
Bethlehem	2 016	21	100.0	64	D	D	D	215	3 236	696.9	71.6
Chester	0	0	0.0	22	232	114.3	10.5	55	345	94.5	9.4
Easton	0	0	0.0	22	478	238.9	24.5	94	1 098	268.4	26.6
Erie	185	3	100.0	108	1 541	646.0	65.3	336	4 931	945.9	100.3
Harrisburg	430	3	100.0	52	2 143	2 551.3	93.5	214	2 871	560.9	57.1
Hazleton	0	0	0.0	32	477	199.0	21.0	145	1 748	540.3	38.5
Lancaster	2 503	16	100.0	64	868	412.4	31.5	339	5 062	950.9	101.1
Lebanon	0	0	0.0	19	232	95.0	7.2	120	1 263	232.6	26.2
Monroeville	1 520	7	100.0	50	542	242.5	24.4	314	6 621	1 497.4	127.2
Norristown	57	1	100.0	50	755	399.5	42.5	80	601	168.5	18.8
Philadelphia	879 066	3 973	19.0	1 067	18 338	11 566.1	956.3	4 420	50 225	11 167.8	1 158.1
Pittsburgh	46 476	338	26.3	396	6 948	7 097.2	353.4	1 161	16 455	3 413.0	367.6
Plum	7 492	41	100.0	32	350	178.0	14.2	52	558	121.2	14.1
Reading	0	0	0.0	60	1 233	569.3	60.1	225	2 954	733.6	69.0
Scranton	365 949	1 733	100.0	100	1 973	844.5	73.2	341	4 370	957.6	94.5
State College	1 200	6	100.0	9	17	10.8	1.0	164	2 560	363.1	39.7
Wilkes-Barre	850	4	100.0	51	581	230.2	24.4	249	5 134	1 878.7	113.6
Williamsport	9 680	99	4.0	40	795	363.6	26.3	114	1 524	270.6	29.4
York	15 693	65	100.0	70	911	786.0	45.1	134	1 624	328.9	38.0
RHODE ISLAND	195 030	952	83.6	1 277	18 128	9 182.8	914.9	4 080	50 865	12 286.5	1 215.4
Cranston	3 439	24	100.0	142	2 191	1 223.1	110.7	314	4 726	1 050.9	109.2
East Providence	303	3	100.0	87	1 474	885.4	75.7	147	2 058	554.2	53.7
Pawtucket	1 237	7	71.4	70	753	291.6	31.2	194	1 765	468.1	45.2
Providence	3 318	27	51.9	195	1 785	1 001.7	89.1	660	7 461	1 474.0	156.0
Warwick	6 450	45	80.0	161	1 720	774.5	84.1	484	8 503	2 153.7	211.9
Woonsocket	764	8	100.0	42	480	192.8	23.4	148	1 885	441.9	43.0
SOUTH CAROLINA	5 424 387	27 537	77.9	4 323	58 524	40 498.0	2 599.4	18 886	231 685	54 298.4	4 878.1
Aiken	26 123	182	72.5	23	D	D	D	229	2 711	529.5	49.6
Anderson	3 695	32	56.3	44	478	178.0	14.9	315	4 231	761.9	78.4
Charleston	114 237	978	61.3	106	1 362	856.2	67.2	796	10 386	2 183.7	228.3
Columbia	63 341	546	37.4	173	2 737	1 449.0	124.0	723	12 683	2 720.2	265.8
Florence	NA	NA	NA	49	946	366.4	40.1	364	5 512	1 173.1	106.2
Goose Creek	20 045	124	100.0	12	447	201.4	22.4	84	1 439	336.5	30.3
Greenville	116 948	1 037	18.0	178	3 685	4 957.4	197.9	713	10 133	2 356.7	221.1
Greer	41 896	230	100.0	42	335	145.1	16.3	152	2 450	737.4	59.3
Hilton Head Island	73 028	146	100.0	57	227	95.9	12.3	326	3 375	736.0	82.4
Mount Pleasant	326 540	1 332	55.5	66	260	121.2	13.0	366	5 072	1 016.2	106.7
Myrtle Beach	137 719	452	98.0	81	591	234.9	22.3	606	7 762	1 773.1	171.9
North Charleston	45 780	450	85.8	215	4 229	2 186.1	198.8	599	9 752	2 321.2	222.8
Rock Hill	139 828	834	28.1	58	718	425.8	33.8	320	4 361	1 059.8	89.4
Spartanburg	3 547	15	100.0	67	749	640.5	28.2	372	5 963	1 251.1	117.5
Summerville	101 302	594	56.1	43	358	133.4	15.5	206	3 142	751.9	63.4
Sumter	NA	NA	NA	33	347	120.8	13.9	313	4 079	826.3	74.9
SOUTH DAKOTA	689 248	4 722	59.3	1 248	13 402	11 400.5	550.8	4 172	50 842	12 266.2	1 045.3
Aberdeen	7 623	119	52.1	42	600	1 121.6	25.4	176	2 761	622.7	59.9
Rapid City	47 733	323	62.2	137	1 725	889.4	67.1	406	7 009	1 055.7	167.8
Sioux Falls	233 076	1 878	44.8	282	4 460	2 681.5	207.3	775	14 756	3 875.9	334.2
TENNESSEE	4 550 319	27 632	64.7	6 282	99 238	80 116.5	4 593.4	24 234	320 739	77 547.3	7 244.6
Bartlett	39 831	202	100.0	60	1 035	472.6	57.6	151	3 196	986.7	88.2
Brentwood	98 465	251	100.0	61	848	505.7	49.3	172	2 949	931.0	84.3
Bristol	6 011	32	87.5	48	741	455.7	45.9	140	2 079	610.6	51.7
Chattanooga	133 327	1 127	31.0	416	5 506	2 799.8	251.2	1 188	17 322	4 054.0	395.5
Clarksville	104 767	987	86.1	62	562	320.1	24.2	478	7 524	1 753.2	170.7
Cleveland	25 554	330	21.2	35	D	D	D	320	3 756	977.7	90.1
Collierville	50 351	142	100.0	53	734	510.9	40.3	186	3 698	800.2	88.5

1. Merchant wholesalers except manufacturers' sales branches and offices. 2. Establishments with payroll.

City	Real estate and rental and leasing, 2007				Professional, scientific, and technical services,[1] 2007				Manufacturing, 2007			
	Number of establish-ments	Number of employees	Receipts (mil dol)	Annual payroll (mil dol)	Number of establish-ments	Number of employees	Receipts (mil dol)	Annual payroll (mil dol)	Number of establish-ments	Number of employees	Receipts (mil dol)	Annual payroll (mil dol)
	80	81	82	83	84	85	86	87	88	89	90	91
OREGON—Cont'd												
Redmond	59	267	34.2	7.0	39	201	18.5	6.2	63	1 228	217.6	44.3
Salem	303	1 658	240.3	48.2	520	D	D	D	188	5 541	1 294.1	191.4
Springfield	79	342	57.6	8.2	86	510	39.6	15.6	86	2 164	1 029.2	94.6
Tigard	144	799	287.7	34.9	365	4 087	445.4	216.6	108	2 596	D	129.7
Tualatin	41	773	123.1	26.7	92	D	D	D	128	7 068	2 007.1	331.1
West Linn	46	103	20.9	3.1	125	365	38.1	15.2	NA	NA	NA	NA
PENNSYLVANIA	9 904	68 954	13 602.6	2 611.8	29 534	292 791	45 888.3	18 184.2	15 406	650 804	234 840.4	29 433.0
Allentown	98	603	95.1	17.0	223	D	D	D	184	3 350	779.3	135.5
Altoona	37	213	40.8	5.3	101	924	78.2	32.7	51	1 060	227.6	35.1
Bethel Park	31	153	55.5	3.6	96	374	48.6	17.1	41	522	79.6	16.7
Bethlehem	55	286	50.0	7.5	187	1 196	185.2	71.1	65	5 383	1 509.9	286.6
Chester	11	54	8.4	1.2	19	D	D	D	29	1 625	D	108.5
Easton	19	71	14.1	1.6	79	329	34.4	12.1	26	1 076	299.7	50.5
Erie	64	406	45.2	12.1	194	D	D	D	158	6 486	1 595.3	284.4
Harrisburg	36	238	210.7	13.4	282	3 327	641.9	216.3	43	1 269	348.0	48.5
Hazleton	27	340	64.7	6.7	54	257	21.4	8.8	53	2 977	1 063.3	113.2
Lancaster	52	278	77.5	9.2	230	D	D	D	95	5 270	1 517.8	234.6
Lebanon	29	169	25.3	4.7	52	D	D	D	50	1 749	381.8	55.9
Monroeville	47	309	55.0	10.3	114	3 036	662.6	199.5	18	622	119.1	31.4
Norristown	26	125	23.2	4.0	94	D	D	D	31	827	185.5	28.2
Philadelphia	1 088	9 813	1 956.1	433.9	2 703	44 302	9 243.3	3 533.1	946	32 672	18 069.4	1 396.7
Pittsburgh	433	3 813	681.0	170.9	1 539	D	D	D	341	8 408	2 535.0	362.8
Plum	16	76	5.5	2.3	39	329	49.5	24.1	33	546	137.0	20.4
Reading	53	360	46.7	10.5	137	D	D	D	116	8 043	2 783.0	424.7
Scranton	49	347	32.4	9.1	210	D	D	D	89	3 023	662.4	110.9
State College	58	486	78.4	13.3	112	714	86.6	35.9	NA	NA	NA	NA
Wilkes-Barre	28	214	47.7	7.5	132	D	D	D	35	1 440	315.1	58.4
Williamsport	26	81	10.3	1.8	81	769	54.6	22.8	55	4 329	1 418.0	178.5
York	33	257	32.9	8.3	164	D	D	D	89	5 749	2 800.8	284.6
RHODE ISLAND	1 233	6 493	1 462.8	227.2	3 096	22 732	2 777.8	1 173.9	1 831	53 718	12 061.5	2 374.8
Cranston	96	616	90.1	17.8	238	1 598	181.8	68.1	192	4 815	1 606.7	214.0
East Providence	68	383	462.5	17.7	148	1 408	163.5	61.0	101	3 128	740.2	126.8
Pawtucket	55	263	33.7	8.8	114	D	D	D	163	4 805	912.4	204.9
Providence	218	1 458	244.9	53.6	799	7 799	1 057.1	512.3	303	5 828	1 050.5	214.2
Warwick	128	1 219	213.8	44.9	346	1 958	252.8	92.5	174	4 581	1 414.1	185.5
Woonsocket	39	161	20.4	4.0	48	260	40.3	11.9	59	1 306	192.6	45.2
SOUTH CAROLINA	5 473	30 417	5 194.1	989.8	9 459	74 372	9 343.3	3 622.6	4 335	242 153	93 977.5	10 061.5
Aiken	67	266	37.3	6.5	117	D	D	D	23	D	D	D
Anderson	60	240	44.5	7.3	143	D	D	D	59	3 230	860.3	126.8
Charleston	297	1 593	263.2	57.6	608	4 331	688.8	265.4	61	1 024	409.9	43.7
Columbia	262	2 385	616.0	92.9	865	D	D	D	93	3 888	D	203.4
Florence	76	439	61.8	10.2	127	D	D	D	21	D	D	D
Goose Creek	32	434	51.2	9.3	62	699	107.1	26.8	14	1 025	666.6	62.4
Greenville	245	1 822	429.6	73.8	728	6 866	1 376.5	450.7	107	4 053	978.4	162.0
Greer	37	191	27.9	4.4	70	273	24.2	9.6	37	5 333	D	D
Hilton Head Island	250	2 482	306.3	98.3	263	1 287	193.2	91.3	NA	NA	NA	NA
Mount Pleasant	187	507	136.1	18.7	354	D	D	D	NA	NA	NA	NA
Myrtle Beach	256	2 495	441.3	81.8	227	1 281	162.3	62.9	47	1 561	D	71.1
North Charleston	152	1 278	221.9	37.0	292	D	D	D	138	7 832	3 944.9	369.0
Rock Hill	87	459	66.8	12.4	168	D	D	D	57	3 000	1 145.1	139.1
Spartanburg	103	532	79.8	22.3	217	D	D	D	42	D	D	D
Summerville	78	214	40.2	5.8	106	503	41.3	15.7	27	D	D	D
Sumter	62	240	28.5	5.5	110	520	43.2	12.7	35	1 661	345.6	60.3
SOUTH DAKOTA	888	3 844	523.9	90.3	1 735	10 073	1 093.4	385.9	1 052	40 961	13 051.1	1 539.3
Aberdeen	53	D	D	D	70	364	34.4	13.5	32	D	D	D
Rapid City	134	637	106.0	15.5	258	D	D	D	100	2 575	623.6	90.9
Sioux Falls	202	1 288	214.6	38.7	460	D	D	D	160	10 329	3 113.0	428.1
TENNESSEE	6 087	37 737	6 950.4	1 243.0	11 278	D	D	D	6 752	369 165	140 447.8	15 165.6
Bartlett	44	242	96.6	5.5	110	741	104.5	37.4	33	937	299.3	39.4
Brentwood	115	739	121.1	25.6	344	3 706	627.9	274.2	NA	NA	NA	NA
Bristol	38	151	27.7	4.1	66	491	44.0	21.1	51	D	1 445.1	110.2
Chattanooga	314	2 049	326.2	93.6	620	D	D	D	370	18 580	6 159.7	798.8
Clarksville	139	559	109.1	14.9	150	D	D	D	53	3 604	1 827.2	145.7
Cleveland	68	378	82.1	10.7	131	D	D	D	92	D	4 222.7	D
Collierville	49	211	36.0	5.1	100	385	42.0	16.0	32	3 466	1 582.4	130.3

1. Establishments subject to federal tax.

Table D. Cities — Accommodation and Food Services, Arts, Entertainment, and Recreation, and Health Care and Social Assistance

City	Accommodation and food services, 2007				Arts, entertainment, and recreation,[1] 2007				Health care and social assistance,[1] 2007			
	Number of establish-ments	Number of employees	Sales (mil dol)	Annual payroll (mil dol)	Number of establish-ments	Number of employees	Receipts (mil dol)	Annual payroll (mil dol)	Number of establish-ments	Number of employees	Receipts (mil dol)	Annual payroll (mil dol)
	92	93	94	95	96	97	98	99	100	101	102	103
OREGON—Cont'd												
Redmond	89	1 355	57.3	15.8	6	D	D	D	73	D	D	D
Salem	393	6 630	309.5	86.5	34	605	37.8	13.4	509	6 251	587.2	248.5
Springfield	157	2 502	120.7	33.2	20	D	D	D	126	2 539	312.7	126.3
Tigard	165	2 940	147.0	43.0	13	D	D	D	175	1 904	183.6	72.0
Tualatin	82	1 487	75.4	23.4	11	D	D	D	126	D	D	D
West Linn	43	707	29.9	8.8	12	D	D	D	81	546	44.8	18.9
PENNSYLVANIA	26 910	420 209	19 625.4	5 454.0	3 420	53 939	4 743.5	1 682.1	27 138	368 531	35 089.4	15 093.0
Allentown	258	3 250	150.3	42.5	25	425	17.4	5.8	296	3 821	400.4	169.8
Altoona	113	1 750	64.1	17.1	10	D	D	D	151	D	D	D
Bethel Park	73	1 621	61.4	17.2	13	D	D	D	98	1 201	109.0	49.0
Bethlehem	213	2 815	141.4	39.5	10	157	5.0	1.3	195	2 197	223.0	105.6
Chester	39	295	16.2	4.0	NA	NA	NA	NA	45	1 401	197.0	90.8
Easton	87	1 117	50.1	12.3	1	D	D	D	44	1 657	226.4	67.7
Erie	220	3 227	122.7	32.5	26	D	D	D	351	5 218	481.3	257.4
Harrisburg	183	2 657	137.7	39.1	18	158	8.8	2.2	103	1 513	157.7	71.1
Hazleton	84	944	38.2	10.8	4	D	D	D	107	955	108.4	36.3
Lancaster	145	2 614	127.4	38.8	14	61	4.9	1.6	149	3 072	349.5	151.9
Lebanon	64	547	25.2	5.9	4	D	D	D	77	850	71.9	36.8
Monroeville	121	3 138	144.2	39.6	11	221	6.1	2.2	171	2 784	241.5	107.6
Norristown	55	410	21.7	4.8	3	D	D	D	72	1 391	148.1	74.6
Philadelphia	3 396	48 552	3 051.4	837.9	214	7 245	1 000.8	595.0	2 382	38 459	4 274.2	1 818.6
Pittsburgh	1 144	20 474	1 042.9	310.8	102	2 542	563.1	278.1	885	18 910	2 173.7	1 068.3
Plum	34	602	17.1	4.8	12	76	3.5	1.0	22	133	7.3	3.2
Reading	137	D	D	D	13	332	20.5	6.1	100	1 522	110.2	44.3
Scranton	195	3 044	128.2	34.7	15	D	D	D	212	2 712	286.2	138.6
State College	125	2 827	100.0	28.9	8	44	4.8	1.2	85	1 179	118.2	55.1
Wilkes-Barre	122	2 044	91.1	23.9	7	D	D	D	115	1 147	116.7	48.6
Williamsport	81	1 105	47.2	12.3	3	D	D	D	96	1 712	145.6	78.5
York	92	1 492	65.3	17.5	4	49	1.3	0.4	56	848	75.9	37.8
RHODE ISLAND	2 926	44 426	2 148.7	622.1	395	6 863	526.8	143.4	2 502	34 762	3 015.1	1 309.5
Cranston	188	3 227	144.4	40.7	20	D	D	D	231	3 318	230.5	109.8
East Providence	113	1 600	68.6	17.9	16	D	D	D	129	2 288	231.3	112.0
Pawtucket	144	1 668	65.2	18.1	10	74	14.8	6.3	139	2 060	153.7	72.5
Providence	517	9 156	472.0	138.1	37	1 596	44.6	14.0	447	5 447	639.0	294.3
Warwick	249	5 817	264.4	77.6	39	D	D	D	307	4 301	359.8	156.2
Woonsocket	95	1 249	53.9	14.5	6	D	D	D	82	1 394	105.0	49.9
SOUTH CAROLINA	9 291	182 899	8 383.5	2 311.0	1 271	19 444	1 105.6	316.1	7 883	115 669	11 213.4	4 523.3
Aiken	108	2 160	80.4	21.7	24	423	25.2	7.2	140	3 129	300.1	103.3
Anderson	155	3 447	126.8	35.1	12	140	5.8	2.3	195	D	D	D
Charleston	435	10 992	641.3	173.6	61	1 169	89.2	29.5	419	4 511	626.3	260.7
Columbia	491	10 913	496.0	140.7	41	D	D	D	472	7 864	863.7	373.3
Florence	140	3 211	135.7	37.1	12	D	D	D	217	D	D	D
Goose Creek	63	1 014	43.7	11.2	3	D	D	D	42	D	D	D
Greenville	367	8 250	385.6	112.2	41	851	36.1	12.6	298	4 660	537.5	241.2
Greer	82	1 307	53.0	13.7	8	D	D	D	71	D	D	D
Hilton Head Island	218	5 313	321.6	120.9	53	D	D	D	148	D	D	D
Mount Pleasant	196	3 810	181.1	54.1	43	D	D	D	269	D	D	D
Myrtle Beach	532	13 682	797.8	218.5	69	1 893	128.3	29.2	210	D	D	D
North Charleston	275	6 474	306.8	78.2	17	681	22.6	7.3	253	5 838	741.3	228.4
Rock Hill	170	3 829	157.9	43.5	15	D	D	D	183	4 639	563.8	202.6
Spartanburg	202	4 322	176.3	51.1	16	92	5.7	1.7	178	D	D	D
Summerville	114	3 049	116.1	32.4	8	D	D	D	125	D	D	D
Sumter	118	2 837	96.4	26.6	10	48	1.9	0.4	139	2 065	178.6	74.4
SOUTH DAKOTA	2 426	36 710	1 622.8	436.2	535	4 868	399.3	75.8	1 535	17 404	1 697.4	666.9
Aberdeen	97	1 858	70.5	18.9	21	D	D	D	116	D	D	D
Rapid City	229	5 384	231.9	67.8	60	467	36.1	6.7	259	D	D	D
Sioux Falls	391	9 548	387.3	118.4	96	1 475	118.7	19.6	343	4 728	612.1	266.5
TENNESSEE	11 592	239 379	10 626.8	3 009.2	2 006	21 937	2 873.8	885.3	11 720	185 582	19 249.5	7 599.6
Bartlett	87	1 956	75.8	21.0	8	153	4.8	1.6	98	D	D	D
Brentwood	83	2 193	107.9	30.2	64	D	D	D	273	D	D	D
Bristol	85	1 725	61.2	16.0	10	D	D	D	118	D	D	D
Chattanooga	586	12 921	554.8	164.9	65	1 169	49.9	14.6	699	11 422	1 395.6	547.2
Clarksville	279	5 871	235.5	61.4	19	D	D	D	222	D	D	D
Cleveland	143	D	D	D	14	D	D	D	159	D	D	D
Collierville	81	1 605	66.1	19.4	13	D	D	D	61	D	D	D

1. Establishments subject to federal tax.

City	Other services[1], 2007				Government employment and payroll, 2012								
						March payroll							
							Percent of total for:						
	Number of establish-ments	Number of employees	Receipts (mil dol)	Annual payroll (mil dol)	Full-time equivalent employees	Total (dollars)	Adminis-tration, judicial, and legal	Police and Corrections	Fire Protection	Highways and trans-portation	Health and welfare	Natural resources and utilities	Education and libraries
	104	105	106	107	108	109	110	111	112	113	114	115	116
OREGON—Cont'd													
Redmond	35	D	D	D	145	696 980	14.3	31.9	0.0	20.4	5.5	20.4	0.0
Salem	233	1 204	93.1	29.9	1 201	6 557 144	12.3	26.5	18.4	2.9	8.3	17.5	2.8
Springfield	83	437	34.9	11.0	535	3 245 769	12.3	22.4	20.4	10.8	4.0	18.1	2.0
Tigard	119	780	68.6	22.1	286	1 551 160	26.2	36.8	0.0	7.7	0.0	11.2	12.8
Tualatin	65	490	49.8	15.3	147	818 379	22.2	35.7	0.0	9.0	1.8	13.6	10.1
West Linn	31	139	7.8	2.9	104	541 464	20.2	40.2	0.0	4.2	0.0	22.8	12.6
PENNSYLVANIA	20 165	113 790	9 502.5	2 798.3	X	X	X	X	X	X	X	X	X
Allentown	200	1 202	95.1	28.6	870	4 561 766	8.4	33.3	19.8	5.0	8.9	19.7	0.0
Altoona	112	582	38.8	11.9	242	1 031 472	8.7	39.4	29.9	15.7	4.9	1.4	0.0
Bethel Park	80	552	31.8	11.4	127	577 790	11.9	56.2	0.0	16.0	0.0	15.3	0.0
Bethlehem	102	788	80.6	27.9	680	3 090 583	7.7	30.1	17.3	3.5	8.2	18.8	0.0
Chester	32	275	17.8	5.7	305	1 818 516	31.3	36.7	17.7	3.5	2.3	3.4	0.0
Easton	44	246	19.1	6.8	246	1 153 107	13.0	32.8	24.1	5.8	1.5	12.2	0.0
Erie	165	744	53.6	16.4	656	3 187 505	6.2	34.9	25.5	9.0	2.8	15.7	0.0
Harrisburg	71	355	33.8	10.5	534	2 458 452	13.1	41.4	17.4	3.7	6.0	16.7	0.0
Hazleton	55	209	14.1	4.3	93	424 630	10.3	46.4	20.8	13.6	6.5	0.6	0.0
Lancaster	99	566	37.6	12.8	519	2 372 327	5.8	43.9	17.4	3.9	3.7	21.3	0.0
Lebanon	51	215	14.7	4.6	153	662 861	5.0	39.2	17.2	5.8	2.6	30.3	0.0
Monroeville	89	594	31.3	10.9	148	872 947	9.5	53.2	0.0	15.7	2.8	6.5	6.5
Norristown	41	237	18.0	4.4	170	899 425	10.6	61.2	15.6	6.4	0.0	0.7	0.0
Philadelphia	1 903	10 803	836.4	252.6	29 409	148 399 324	18.0	39.0	9.6	3.4	11.1	15.4	1.7
Pittsburgh	574	3 536	265.6	81.6	4 176	16 527 485	9.4	38.3	25.1	11.2	8.9	5.4	0.0
Plum	34	178	16.7	3.6	67	358 089	66.3	0.0	0.0	0.0	0.0	0.0	0.0
Reading	97	823	63.8	24.0	730	12 558 088	5.8	44.6	24.9	0.6	5.6	13.5	1.3
Scranton	138	794	62.7	17.7	484	2 233 185	4.0	40.2	30.7	5.1	1.7	7.2	6.5
State College	41	257	15.3	5.0	165	866 140	14.2	48.6	0.0	13.8	4.0	4.8	0.0
Wilkes-Barre	74	329	22.2	5.7	284	1 342 714	13.0	34.7	27.3	0.0	8.1	12.4	0.0
Williamsport	51	364	37.1	9.5	201	913 971	5.1	32.7	21.3	35.2	1.9	3.5	0.0
York	46	338	34.5	9.9	379	1 772 634	9.4	43.1	18.8	1.0	6.2	13.8	0.0
RHODE ISLAND	1 929	10 073	820.0	264.1	X	X	X	X	X	X	X	X	X
Cranston	180	1 110	79.0	28.9	2 144	11 389 033	1.9	8.5	6.8	1.5	0.6	0.6	78.6
East Providence	97	482	50.8	15.2	1 234	5 386 925	3.6	8.7	7.8	3.2	0.6	4.6	71.2
Pawtucket	120	706	67.6	19.1	1 817	9 164 839	2.7	8.8	7.2	0.8	1.4	4.4	72.6
Providence	269	2 010	151.1	51.7	5 219	27 174 708	5.3	17.6	13.9	1.5	0.0	6.7	54.9
Warwick	184	983	83.6	25.8	2 400	12 798 555	2.8	10.0	12.2	1.9	0.5	3.3	67.2
Woonsocket	65	312	29.5	8.6	1 167	6 516 930	2.3	7.1	7.8	1.5	0.3	1.7	77.9
SOUTH CAROLINA	5 842	35 233	2 710.9	846.7	X	X	X	X	X	X	X	X	X
Aiken	61	526	24.0	8.0	346	1 255 386	18.9	27.9	10.5	14.5	0.0	24.7	0.0
Anderson	77	D	D	D	420	924 851	13.0	31.8	14.8	8.6	2.0	25.1	0.0
Charleston	182	1 296	73.1	25.9	2 045	7 787 974	9.2	27.1	16.5	1.2	1.0	37.8	0.0
Columbia	234	1 828	120.5	42.0	2 261	7 098 669	11.6	20.9	23.5	2.0	2.7	24.7	0.0
Florence	57	576	36.0	10.8	510	1 554 745	9.4	29.2	16.4	5.2	3.3	35.0	0.0
Goose Creek	40	165	10.5	3.0	271	928 636	14.9	34.9	20.4	3.8	0.0	23.9	0.0
Greenville	186	1 133	69.3	24.3	1 049	3 701 819	9.4	20.4	14.8	5.7	1.5	42.0	0.0
Greer	58	D	D	D	189	659 763	25.5	37.5	20.6	2.5	0.0	13.8	0.0
Hilton Head Island	95	399	32.7	10.3	242	1 283 504	30.6	0.0	57.1	4.6	0.0	0.5	0.0
Mount Pleasant	142	963	64.6	23.8	569	1 912 550	16.4	33.5	20.8	2.0	0.8	24.2	0.0
Myrtle Beach	125	653	47.7	12.9	889	3 176 078	16.3	31.5	18.5	3.8	0.5	25.7	1.3
North Charleston	192	1 863	193.6	62.9	1 049	3 596 992	11.5	39.1	21.3	5.5	0.4	16.7	0.0
Rock Hill	103	858	60.5	19.8	836	2 857 047	21.2	21.2	14.2	3.9	6.3	29.3	0.0
Spartanburg	101	784	57.5	14.8	616	2 210 757	10.5	25.6	11.1	4.0	2.5	41.1	0.0
Summerville	89	449	34.5	10.7	357	1 158 866	7.9	29.3	23.7	1.9	0.0	33.0	0.0
Sumter	84	564	38.1	11.6	550	1 497 205	11.8	29.7	18.8	1.8	1.1	29.5	0.0
SOUTH DAKOTA	1 359	6 196	465.7	129.1	X	X	X	X	X	X	X	X	X
Aberdeen	52	D	D	D	287	1 030 395	10.5	20.7	18.3	13.5	0.0	31.3	4.3
Rapid City	166	988	71.6	22.2	868	1 798 797	7.6	17.7	12.4	6.9	0.0	24.6	3.9
Sioux Falls	262	1 905	128.4	40.0	1 148	5 118 747	9.5	24.6	18.4	10.7	7.0	21.1	5.6
TENNESSEE	7 153	50 425	3 847.7	1 234.7	X	X	X	X	X	X	X	X	X
Bartlett	78	582	45.0	14.4	511	2 039 502	14.7	30.7	21.1	6.5	0.0	20.1	0.0
Brentwood	67	623	46.9	15.6	256	1 094 815	19.4	23.6	26.3	6.2	0.0	13.8	5.5
Bristol	57	761	71.3	20.9	919	3 282 369	4.6	12.4	6.6	3.8	0.6	7.7	61.5
Chattanooga	369	3 439	222.7	82.0	3 133	11 941 830	7.9	16.8	12.6	11.2	5.0	42.3	2.0
Clarksville	165	946	62.8	18.6	1 114	3 666 316	6.5	29.4	19.3	13.3	0.6	26.7	0.0
Cleveland	76	D	D	D	1 030	3 567 674	2.1	10.1	17.6	4.9	1.2	2.8	59.7
Collierville	50	D	D	D	435	1 694 955	11.6	31.7	20.1	7.3	1.0	19.2	0.0

1. Establishments subject to federal tax.

City	City government finances, 2007									
	General revenue							General expenditure		
		Intergovernmental		Taxes					Per capita[1] (dollars)	
					Per capita[1] (dollars)					
	Total (mil dol)	Total (mil dol)	Percent from state government	Total (mil dol)	Total	Property	Sales and gross receipts	Total (mil dol)	Total	Capital outlays
	117	118	119	120	121	122	123	124	125	126
OREGON—Cont'd										
Redmond	35.3	5.9	60.8	13.4	502	328	174	32.9	1 229	258
Salem	251.3	76.0	63.8	101.3	642	489	153	240.9	1 527	209
Springfield	103.6	9.1	99.1	32.9	549	452	97	90.7	1 514	262
Tigard	45.1	9.8	49.5	26.0	522	305	217	43.3	870	90
Tualatin	29.9	5.6	64.3	13.3	498	310	188	27.4	1 025	191
West Linn	24.0	5.0	70.0	11.3	439	271	168	22.2	865	100
PENNSYLVANIA	X	X	X	X	X	X	X	X	X	X
Allentown	129.2	30.4	47.0	56.8	477	247	115	175.0	1 471	88
Altoona	29.3	7.5	47.2	17.6	381	194	73	27.1	587	40
Bethel Park	24.5	2.7	71.8	13.8	427	131	46	25.6	790	60
Bethlehem	101.1	27.5	100.0	47.5	632	280	117	89.6	1 193	0
Chester	47.9	12.2	79.6	19.2	563	252	84	45.6	1 340	83
Easton	52.4	14.3	75.3	14.8	546	331	69	53.4	1 967	129
Erie	113.3	23.8	46.1	46.9	464	337	53	105.0	1 039	74
Harrisburg	93.9	6.2	90.0	30.4	616	345	171	78.7	1 595	121
Hazleton	18.6	7.2	55.0	8.3	329	113	39	13.3	528	65
Lancaster	69.1	11.7	71.8	31.0	522	384	54	87.4	1 472	261
Lebanon	21.7	10.2	34.6	8.3	325	116	37	26.5	1 036	259
Monroeville	23.1	1.7	95.3	19.7	695	159	284	30.1	1 058	116
Norristown	28.2	3.4	47.9	21.6	627	320	95	30.2	875	85
Philadelphia	6 411.8	2 254.7	74.3	3 239.1	2 089	323	474	5 483.2	3 537	209
Pittsburgh	607.0	163.6	87.2	357.2	1 166	443	419	548.9	1 791	25
Plum	13.3	1.8	85.5	9.6	352	192	32	13.6	498	25
Reading	139.8	30.8	89.3	42.9	488	220	111	135.9	1 543	96
Scranton	67.6	10.7	95.5	45.2	593	179	69	70.2	923	3
State College	36.3	5.5	55.6	11.4	272	114	42	35.4	843	78
Wilkes-Barre	52.9	20.4	46.2	24.1	583	208	78	57.3	1 386	201
Williamsport	41.3	20.3	45.8	15.5	526	329	123	30.5	1 035	151
York	68.7	9.7	51.4	24.7	566	395	110	63.2	1 448	39
RHODE ISLAND	X	X	X	X	X	X	X	X	X	X
Cranston	282.2	60.2	92.5	187.4	2 322	2 290	32	256.9	3 184	42
East Providence	148.4	43.6	95.5	91.6	1 942	1 918	24	155.3	3 292	150
Pawtucket	197.7	91.3	77.8	95.5	1 339	1 328	10	192.3	2 697	24
Providence	747.8	292.1	91.6	325.5	1 822	1 765	57	715.3	4 004	160
Warwick	318.8	59.3	98.4	219.5	2 682	2 607	74	303.4	3 707	110
Woonsocket	147.2	67.5	95.5	57.6	1 401	1 352	50	147.3	3 584	80
SOUTH CAROLINA	X	X	X	X	X	X	X	X	X	X
Aiken	42.7	5.6	22.9	23.7	790	330	460	40.3	1 341	206
Anderson	40.2	4.0	38.2	19.7	735	460	275	43.2	1 613	63
Charleston	207.6	27.8	72.1	132.3	1 053	446	607	178.8	1 424	222
Columbia	222.0	28.7	56.5	95.1	721	383	339	189.3	1 435	255
Florence	47.5	3.6	40.8	22.6	603	96	506	40.8	1 086	63
Goose Creek	19.6	0.7	100.0	11.6	298	47	251	20.5	528	67
Greenville	95.3	5.9	100.0	64.6	1 066	598	468	99.6	1 643	290
Greer	28.9	2.8	31.9	15.7	593	370	223	45.5	1 711	36
Hilton Head Island	89.1	35.5	16.2	48.4	1 261	625	586	94.8	2 471	1 299
Mount Pleasant	114.5	34.1	60.2	59.9	833	385	448	106.8	1 486	667
Myrtle Beach	161.3	12.2	83.8	82.5	2 918	878	2 040	123.3	4 360	375
North Charleston	122.2	14.2	23.7	93.4	915	471	408	119.1	1 168	208
Rock Hill	88.3	12.8	15.4	35.8	525	351	174	102.2	1 502	271
Spartanburg	53.3	13.1	6.6	33.4	895	449	446	42.1	1 130	160
Summerville	29.5	3.1	88.8	21.9	494	238	255	26.9	608	53
Sumter	43.8	6.9	24.7	24.0	587	218	369	40.1	980	178
SOUTH DAKOTA	X	X	X	X	X	X	X	X	X	X
Aberdeen	39.6	5.1	70.4	24.2	900	292	609	38.1	1 414	18
Rapid City	138.0	19.9	85.8	75.4	1 077	309	768	126.9	1 813	706
Sioux Falls	226.3	20.3	62.2	149.5	933	282	651	225.7	1 408	474
TENNESSEE	X	X	X	X	X	X	X	X	X	X
Bartlett	55.6	18.3	51.6	21.0	361	305	56	47.7	820	25
Brentwood	49.5	19.7	38.7	18.1	463	278	185	45.0	1 153	330
Bristol	75.0	35.6	60.9	26.6	999	899	101	74.6	2 797	336
Chattanooga	485.4	165.9	19.7	139.3	809	668	141	396.3	2 300	197
Clarksville	137.4	38.8	51.1	37.5	262	197	65	103.9	725	103
Cleveland	109.5	65.6	56.3	19.7	464	400	64	96.6	2 278	237
Collierville	56.6	15.9	37.4	25.4	547	460	87	51.4	1 107	164

1. Based on population estimated as of July 1 of the year shown.

City	Public welfare	Highways	Parking facilities	Education	Health and hospitals	Police protection	Sewerage and sanitation	Parks and recreation	Housing and community development	Interest on debt
	City government finances, 2012 (cont.)									
	General expenditure (cont.)									
	Percent of total for:									
	127	128	129	130	131	132	133	134	135	136
OREGON—Cont'd										
Redmond	0.0	21.1	0.0	0.0	0.0	15.5	10.0	8.1	3.5	10.2
Salem	0.0	14.5	0.7	0.0	0.5	13.9	12.1	3.7	13.0	8.7
Springfield	0.0	5.4	0.0	0.0	5.6	16.9	38.3	0.0	1.1	4.0
Tigard	0.3	7.7	0.0	0.0	0.0	32.1	6.0	8.9	0.0	3.8
Tualatin	0.0	6.8	0.1	0.0	0.0	16.5	24.6	7.3	13.2	1.4
West Linn	0.0	8.3	0.0	0.0	0.0	26.6	11.1	13.8	0.0	1.9
PENNSYLVANIA	X	X	X	X	X	X	X	X	X	X
Allentown	0.0	8.9	0.0	0.0	3.5	18.4	23.6	4.4	6.1	2.8
Altoona	0.0	14.2	0.0	0.0	0.0	19.2	3.2	1.2	0.4	4.1
Bethel Park	0.0	22.7	0.0	0.0	0.0	23.6	35.2	3.1	0.5	0.9
Bethlehem	0.0	9.0	0.0	0.0	4.0	14.3	14.7	6.1	3.7	7.6
Chester	0.0	7.2	0.0	0.0	1.1	32.8	3.0	11.5	2.2	2.3
Easton	0.0	6.5	0.4	0.0	0.1	15.5	18.0	5.8	18.7	5.4
Erie	0.0	11.3	0.0	0.0	0.0	14.0	14.2	2.1	11.8	7.3
Harrisburg	0.0	7.4	0.0	0.0	0.2	24.9	23.4	3.9	8.6	3.8
Hazleton	0.0	13.4	0.0	0.0	1.1	27.9	2.4	0.8	7.7	3.1
Lancaster	0.0	5.5	0.0	0.0	0.0	20.9	23.8	6.2	5.6	9.3
Lebanon	0.0	53.3	0.1	0.0	0.7	15.7	0.8	1.4	6.1	0.1
Monroeville	0.0	20.1	0.0	0.0	0.3	34.5	4.7	6.1	1.2	3.1
Norristown	0.0	15.4	0.0	0.0	1.6	24.2	5.2	2.1	0.0	4.5
Philadelphia	10.4	2.1	0.0	1.4	24.8	11.1	7.0	1.5	3.5	3.9
Pittsburgh	0.0	0.6	0.0	0.0	2.5	14.1	2.8	3.0	16.9	6.6
Plum	0.0	28.0	0.0	0.0	0.0	29.8	11.8	0.2	0.0	4.0
Reading	0.0	8.0	0.0	0.0	2.7	20.8	21.1	2.8	14.3	8.1
Scranton	0.0	4.2	3.7	0.0	2.3	23.1	4.8	1.1	0.2	11.1
State College	0.0	15.4	4.9	0.0	0.9	24.5	27.4	3.1	3.2	2.6
Wilkes-Barre	0.0	23.8	0.5	0.0	4.6	16.0	7.5	7.7	7.2	7.7
Williamsport	0.0	28.5	0.0	0.0	0.0	21.9	14.1	2.4	3.5	1.1
York	0.0	6.2	0.9	0.0	3.2	15.4	23.5	4.9	6.1	8.0
RHODE ISLAND	X	X	X	X	X	X	X	X	X	X
Cranston	0.0	6.7	0.0	55.8	1.1	9.1	6.7	0.9	0.6	2.1
East Providence	0.0	3.8	0.0	57.0	0.3	7.9	7.4	1.5	0.8	1.9
Pawtucket	0.0	1.0	0.0	62.2	0.0	8.3	1.9	0.8	1.8	1.1
Providence	0.0	1.4	0.0	53.6	0.0	11.5	1.4	1.2	2.1	5.7
Warwick	0.4	2.3	0.0	56.7	0.1	6.4	4.3	0.7	0.4	1.6
Woonsocket	0.2	1.6	0.0	53.4	0.1	6.0	10.2	0.1	1.1	8.0
SOUTH CAROLINA	X	X	X	X	X	X	X	X	X	X
Aiken	0.0	7.0	0.0	0.0	0.0	22.5	13.8	12.3	1.7	0.1
Anderson	0.0	8.9	1.2	0.0	0.0	14.1	22.7	7.2	3.6	9.8
Charleston	0.4	3.1	5.1	0.0	0.0	22.4	4.6	13.3	3.8	1.7
Columbia	0.0	4.0	1.7	0.0	0.7	13.1	43.5	7.0	3.2	2.4
Florence	0.0	6.9	0.0	0.0	0.1	23.0	19.5	15.0	6.8	1.0
Goose Creek	0.0	12.8	0.0	0.0	0.0	27.9	5.4	24.9	0.0	0.3
Greenville	0.0	7.1	3.2	0.0	0.5	18.3	13.4	14.0	4.6	2.4
Greer	0.0	2.8	0.0	0.0	0.0	10.2	60.8	3.3	1.8	7.7
Hilton Head Island	0.0	1.9	0.0	0.0	0.0	6.5	2.0	0.0	30.1	4.5
Mount Pleasant	0.0	41.5	0.0	0.0	0.0	10.2	14.4	4.9	1.7	4.1
Myrtle Beach	0.0	3.8	1.5	0.0	0.0	16.0	11.8	19.5	3.8	7.6
North Charleston	0.0	4.5	0.5	0.0	0.0	25.1	8.9	5.1	1.0	5.2
Rock Hill	0.0	2.7	0.0	0.0	0.0	13.2	22.9	12.5	2.9	3.6
Spartanburg	0.0	6.2	2.3	0.0	0.0	22.3	4.7	7.7	4.1	5.1
Summerville	0.0	11.9	0.0	0.0	0.0	23.8	8.6	7.7	0.1	1.8
Sumter	0.0	1.7	0.0	0.0	0.0	23.3	16.2	12.9	8.3	0.8
SOUTH DAKOTA	X	X	X	X	X	X	X	X	X	X
Aberdeen	0.0	29.4	0.0	0.0	3.2	9.7	7.1	15.7	0.0	2.8
Rapid City	0.6	19.1	0.5	0.0	2.8	10.2	14.4	12.7	1.8	3.0
Sioux Falls	0.0	19.1	0.9	0.0	4.2	12.3	22.3	14.2	2.2	3.2
TENNESSEE	X	X	X	X	X	X	X	X	X	X
Bartlett	0.7	8.5	0.0	0.0	5.6	26.6	15.0	11.0	0.0	2.2
Brentwood	0.0	19.3	0.0	0.5	0.2	13.3	16.6	5.6	0.0	3.8
Bristol	0.0	4.9	0.0	54.1	0.0	9.0	9.0	5.1	0.9	1.0
Chattanooga	3.7	5.6	0.4	0.0	0.6	13.8	18.8	6.1	2.6	4.4
Clarksville	0.0	10.6	0.3	0.0	0.0	22.6	26.1	6.1	1.6	6.6
Cleveland	0.0	6.0	0.0	47.1	0.6	9.4	11.6	2.5	1.3	2.9
Collierville	0.7	12.6	0.0	0.0	1.6	20.1	14.9	7.5	0.0	2.6

City	City government finances, 2012 (cont.)			Climate[2]						
	Debt outstanding			Average daily temperature (degrees Fahrenheit)						
				Mean		Limits				
	Total (mil dol)	Per capita[1] (dollars)	Debt issued during year	January	July	January[3]	July[4]	Annual precipitation (inches)	Heating degree days	Cooling degree days
	137	138	139	140	141	142	143	144	145	146
OREGON—Cont'd										
Redmond	73.6	2 750	12.3	NA	NA	NA	NA	NA	NA	NA
Salem	711.5	4 509	94.7	40.3	66.8	33.5	81.5	40.00	4 784	257
Springfield	151.8	2 534	3.8	39.8	66.2	33.0	81.5	50.90	4 786	242
Tigard	131.8	2 649	100.1	40.0	66.8	33.8	79.2	39.95	4 723	287
Tualatin	14.5	544	0.0	NA	NA	NA	NA	NA	NA	NA
West Linn	21.7	847	8.5	NA	NA	NA	NA	NA	NA	NA
PENNSYLVANIA	X	X	X	X	X	X	X	X	X	X
Allentown	119.4	1 003	11.6	27.1	73.3	19.1	83.9	45.17	5 830	787
Altoona	38.9	844	1.0	26.5	71.1	18.2	81.9	42.69	6 055	546
Bethel Park	4.8	147	0.0	28.6	73.1	19.8	84.5	37.78	5 727	709
Bethlehem	228.4	3 041	27.6	27.1	73.3	19.1	83.9	45.17	5 830	787
Chester	8.1	239	0.0	33.7	78.7	27.9	87.5	40.66	4 469	1 333
Easton	33.9	1 250	7.7	27.1	73.3	19.1	83.9	45.17	5 830	787
Erie	189.6	1 876	47.4	26.9	72.1	20.3	80.4	42.77	6 243	620
Harrisburg	110.0	2 230	0.0	30.3	75.9	23.1	85.7	41.45	5 201	955
Hazleton	11.6	460	5.6	NA	NA	NA	NA	NA	NA	NA
Lancaster	221.6	3 732	38.9	29.1	74.4	20.7	84.7	43.47	5 448	809
Lebanon	0.3	12	0.0	NA	NA	NA	NA	NA	NA	NA
Monroeville	30.2	1 064	7.5	28.6	73.1	19.8	84.5	37.78	5 727	709
Norristown	23.9	694	0.0	30.2	75.1	20.4	86.6	43.87	5 174	884
Philadelphia	7 729.2	4 985	667.1	32.3	77.6	25.5	85.5	42.05	4 759	1 235
Pittsburgh	704.7	2 300	0.0	27.5	72.6	19.9	82.7	37.85	5 829	726
Plum	50.0	1 825	11.3	28.6	73.1	19.8	84.5	37.78	5 727	709
Reading	256.9	2 918	24.4	27.1	73.6	19.1	83.8	45.28	5 876	723
Scranton	61.9	814	0.0	26.3	72.1	18.5	82.6	37.56	6 234	611
State College	28.2	673	0.0	25.4	71.2	18.3	80.7	39.76	6 345	538
Wilkes-Barre	73.4	1 775	9.2	21.5	67.7	13.2	77.4	47.89	7 466	234
Williamsport	5.4	183	2.3	25.5	72.4	17.9	83.2	41.59	6 063	709
York	128.7	2 949	22.1	30.0	74.6	20.9	86.5	43.00	5 233	862
RHODE ISLAND	X	X	X	X	X	X	X	X	X	X
Cranston	88.4	1 096	19.4	28.7	73.3	20.3	82.6	46.45	5 754	714
East Providence	75.2	1 595	23.3	28.7	73.3	20.3	82.6	46.45	5 754	714
Pawtucket	159.7	2 239	9.4	28.7	73.3	20.3	82.6	46.45	5 754	714
Providence	735.9	4 120	5.4	28.7	73.3	20.3	82.6	46.45	5 754	714
Warwick	170.1	2 078	2.4	28.7	73.3	20.3	82.6	46.45	5 754	714
Woonsocket	202.3	4 921	1.0	25.4	72.3	13.3	84.3	48.75	6 302	534
SOUTH CAROLINA	X	X	X	X	X	X	X	X	X	X
Aiken	2.8	92	0.0	45.6	81.7	33.4	93.7	52.43	2 413	2 081
Anderson	125.4	4 687	53.2	41.7	79.7	31.3	90.5	46.67	3 087	1 700
Charleston	74.3	592	0.0	49.8	82.8	42.4	88.5	46.39	1 755	2 473
Columbia	505.3	3 832	205.7	47.3	83.6	36.5	95.2	47.14	2 044	2 475
Florence	139.9	3 725	7.4	45.0	81.2	35.2	90.7	44.76	2 523	2 029
Goose Creek	1.4	36	0.0	47.9	81.7	36.9	90.9	51.53	2 005	2 306
Greenville	94.3	1 556	17.3	40.8	78.8	31.4	88.8	50.24	3 272	1 526
Greer	93.7	3 527	1.7	NA	NA	NA	NA	NA	NA	NA
Hilton Head Island	127.7	3 326	46.9	47.9	80.5	37.3	88.2	52.52	2 128	2 012
Mount Pleasant	99.4	1 383	0.0	47.1	81.1	37.5	88.5	49.38	2 260	2 124
Myrtle Beach	216.4	7 653	27.5	NA	NA	NA	NA	NA	NA	NA
North Charleston	186.0	1 823	52.5	47.9	81.7	36.9	90.9	51.53	2 005	2 306
Rock Hill	186.9	2 745	54.5	42.2	80.1	32.5	90.1	48.32	2 934	1 721
Spartanburg	205.6	5 518	0.0	42.1	79.3	30.1	91.1	49.95	3 080	1 591
Summerville	7.9	179	0.0	49.1	81.8	38.0	91.8	48.24	1 907	2 251
Sumter	45.0	1 100	4.2	44.9	80.7	33.6	91.8	48.65	2 577	1 913
SOUTH DAKOTA	X	X	X	X	X	X	X	X	X	X
Aberdeen	63.9	2 375	5.3	NA	NA	NA	NA	NA	NA	NA
Rapid City	113.7	1 624	24.2	22.3	70.2	10.3	82.7	18.45	7 623	480
Sioux Falls	307.2	1 916	24.4	14.0	73.0	2.9	85.6	24.69	7 812	747
TENNESSEE	X	X	X	X	X	X	X	X	X	X
Bartlett	40.8	701	9.5	37.3	79.6	27.3	89.9	55.09	3 665	1 635
Brentwood	29.8	765	16.6	NA	NA	NA	NA	NA	NA	NA
Bristol	50.2	1 884	3.1	NA	NA	NA	NA	NA	NA	NA
Chattanooga	733.3	4 256	51.6	39.4	79.6	29.9	89.8	54.52	3 427	1 608
Clarksville	870.1	6 075	29.2	35.2	79.0	25.0	90.4	51.78	4 058	1 512
Cleveland	130.0	3 067	3.1	38.0	77.5	27.7	88.5	55.42	3 782	1 333
Collierville	60.9	1 313	5.0	37.9	81.1	28.2	91.1	53.63	3 491	1 838

1. Based on the population estimated as of July 1 of the year shown. 2. Represents normal values based on the 30-year period, 1971–2000. 3. Average daily minimum.
4. Average daily maximum.

STATE Place code	City	Land area,[1] 2010 (sq km)	Population, 2014: Total persons	Population, 2014: Rank	Population, 2014: Per square kilometer	Race alone or in combination (percent), 2011-2013: White	Race alone or in combination (percent), 2011-2013: Black	Race alone or in combination (percent), 2011-2013: American Indian, Alaska Native	Race alone or in combination (percent), 2011-2013: Asian	Race alone or in combination (percent), 2011-2013: Hawaiian Pacific Islander	Percent Hispanic or Latino[2], 2011-2013	Percent foreign born 2011–2013
		1	2	3	4	5	6	7	8	9	10	11
	TENNESSEE—Cont'd											
47 16540	Columbia	81.7	36 071	1 036	441.5	76.8	21.8	0.8	1.0	NA	9.3	5.2
47 16920	Cookeville	84.6	31 335	1 184	370.4	93.2	3.8	1.2	2.9	NA	6.2	8.0
47 27740	Franklin	106.8	70 612	488	661.2	87.8	6.8	0.3	5.1	NA	7.1	9.9
47 28540	Gallatin	80.8	33 347	1 117	412.7	82.1	15.7	0.4	1.3	NA	7.8	5.7
47 28960	Germantown	51.7	39 267	946	759.5	88.1	5.9	0.2	6.2	NA	3.4	6.6
47 33280	Hendersonville	81.3	55 153	668	678.4	88.2	8.1	0.9	2.6	NA	4.3	4.8
47 37640	Jackson	139.2	67 319	514	483.6	53.6	45.2	0.4	1.7	NA	4.0	3.9
47 38320	Johnson City	111.2	65 813	536	591.8	89.7	8.6	0.6	2.6	NA	3.9	4.9
47 39560	Kingsport	129.0	53 028	700	411.1	94.1	5.3	1.4	1.2	0.2	2.6	2.1
47 40000	Knoxville	255.2	184 281	129	722.1	79.3	18.4	1.0	2.1	0.1	4.4	5.6
47 41200	La Vergne	64.6	34 274	1 082	530.6	71.8	24.1	1.3	3.4	NA	14.4	10.5
47 41520	Lebanon	100.1	29 427	1 252	294.0	80.3	14.0	0.5	1.9	NA	7.1	7.4
47 46380	Maryville	43.5	28 329	1 293	651.2	94.8	2.6	0.5	3.3	NA	2.0	4.6
47 48000	Memphis	816.0	656 861	23	805.0	31.3	64.1	0.8	2.1	0.1	6.7	6.2
47 50280	Morristown	72.3	29 304	1 255	405.3	86.3	9.0	1.8	0.8	NA	20.5	11.8
47 51560	Murfreesboro	143.4	120 954	222	843.5	79.5	17.6	1.2	4.1	0.3	5.4	6.5
47 52004	Nashville-Davidson	1 230.6	644 014	25	523.3	63.0	29.5	0.7	3.9	0.1	10.1	12.0
47 55120	Oak Ridge	220.8	29 303	1 256	132.7	87.0	11.7	1.3	2.8	NA	4.9	4.8
47 69420	Smyrna	76.7	45 274	821	590.3	82.5	12.9	1.7	3.6	NA	12.1	10.3
47 70580	Spring Hill	70.1	34 269	1 083	488.9	90.2	5.4	0.8	1.7	NA	6.8	2.7
48 00000	TEXAS	676 587.0	26 956 958	X	39.8	76.9	12.7	1.2	4.7	0.2	38.2	16.4
48 01000	Abilene	276.6	120 958	221	437.3	81.8	11.7	1.0	2.6	NA	25.3	5.7
48 01924	Allen	68.1	94 179	321	1 383.0	77.4	9.3	1.3	13.3	0.2	12.3	16.4
48 03000	Amarillo	257.6	197 254	120	765.7	85.8	7.9	1.6	4.1	0.4	30.2	10.2
48 04000	Arlington	248.3	383 204	51	1 543.3	69.3	20.1	1.0	7.8	0.2	28.3	19.6
48 05000	Austin	771.6	912 791	11	1 183.0	77.6	9.0	1.3	7.9	0.2	33.9	18.3
48 06128	Baytown	91.8	76 127	439	829.3	69.0	17.8	1.2	1.0	NA	44.9	19.0
48 07000	Beaumont	214.5	117 585	230	548.2	45.9	47.8	0.8	3.5	0.1	13.9	9.8
48 07132	Bedford	25.9	48 908	768	1 888.3	82.7	7.6	0.6	4.6	1.4	13.5	9.0
48 08236	Big Spring	49.5	28 472	1 291	575.2	82.5	8.3	2.7	0.7	NA	44.5	9.7
48 10768	Brownsville	342.7	183 046	130	534.1	92.4	0.5	0.3	1.3	0.2	93.4	30.3
48 10912	Bryan	115.0	80 913	405	703.6	65.6	18.5	1.5	3.2	NA	37.6	14.9
48 11428	Burleson	67.4	41 818	882	620.4	95.0	4.0	0.4	NA	NA	11.4	2.5
48 13024	Carrollton	94.0	128 353	207	1 365.5	70.2	10.0	1.4	14.7	NA	30.9	25.7
48 13492	Cedar Hill	92.8	48 084	780	518.1	40.3	55.2	0.7	4.6	NA	17.3	9.3
48 13552	Cedar Park	59.2	63 574	555	1 073.9	86.7	4.5	1.0	8.5	NA	18.4	11.5
48 15364	Cleburne	76.6	29 848	1 241	389.7	93.0	5.7	1.5	0.7	NA	27.5	10.2
48 15976	College Station	128.1	103 483	282	807.8	81.3	7.8	0.9	9.5	0.1	14.3	13.0
48 16432	Conroe	136.5	65 871	535	482.6	82.6	12.8	0.6	1.9	NA	35.8	19.7
48 16612	Coppell	37.3	40 678	911	1 090.6	72.3	4.6	0.6	21.8	NA	11.8	21.3
48 16624	Copperas Cove	46.7	32 943	1 126	705.4	75.2	18.4	1.2	3.9	1.7	16.6	7.2
48 17000	Corpus Christi	416.0	320 434	58	770.3	85.9	5.1	1.1	2.3	0.2	60.7	8.4
48 19000	Dallas	881.9	1 281 047	9	1 452.6	60.2	25.6	1.1	3.3	0.1	41.8	24.4
48 19624	Deer Park	27.1	33 719	1 100	1 244.2	93.0	1.1	1.4	2.1	NA	25.3	7.1
48 19792	Del Rio	52.2	36 079	1 035	691.2	93.1	1.1	NA	0.4	NA	84.7	24.0
48 19972	Denton	227.8	128 205	209	562.8	80.8	13.3	1.5	5.2	0.7	22.0	12.9
48 20092	DeSoto	56.0	51 934	715	927.4	26.8	70.2	0.5	0.6	NA	13.4	5.6
48 21628	Duncanville	29.1	39 707	936	1 364.5	60.9	32.3	0.2	2.4	NA	35.5	15.3
48 21892	Eagle Pass	24.8	28 329	1 293	1 142.3	94.3	0.5	NA	0.4	NA	95.3	32.6
48 22660	Edinburg	97.5	83 014	394	851.4	89.1	1.5	0.4	3.4	NA	87.3	19.8
48 24000	El Paso	661.1	679 036	19	1 027.1	85.1	4.2	0.9	1.8	0.3	79.7	24.9
48 24768	Euless	42.0	53 630	692	1 276.9	68.9	13.6	1.6	12.4	1.5	19.0	18.5
48 25452	Farmers Branch	30.6	32 560	1 140	1 064.1	83.2	3.6	0.6	4.9	NA	43.6	23.6
48 26232	Flower Mound	107.2	69 650	494	649.7	85.8	4.3	1.1	9.5	NA	8.5	10.5
48 27000	Fort Worth	880.1	812 238	16	922.9	68.7	19.9	1.7	4.4	0.4	34.5	17.8
48 27648	Friendswood	53.7	38 248	970	712.3	89.4	5.2	1.2	5.7	NA	15.6	9.2
48 27684	Frisco	160.1	145 035	179	905.9	77.9	9.0	0.9	13.4	0.5	12.3	14.2
48 28068	Galveston	106.8	49 608	752	464.5	73.8	21.4	0.9	4.3	NA	28.4	13.6
48 29000	Garland	147.9	235 501	91	1 592.3	47.2	15.3	3.9	10.8	0.1	41.5	27.0
48 29336	Georgetown	124.0	59 102	618	476.6	93.2	3.4	1.2	0.9	NA	21.5	9.6
48 30464	Grand Prairie	186.8	185 453	127	992.8	65.1	22.1	0.9	7.0	NA	43.3	21.7
48 30644	Grapevine	82.7	50 844	738	614.8	86.5	2.4	1.6	5.5	NA	19.8	13.3
48 30920	Greenville	84.5	26 180	1 392	309.8	64.6	15.8	1.6	1.8	NA	23.5	11.0
48 31928	Haltom City	32.0	43 913	842	1 372.3	79.1	5.9	0.6	8.0	NA	43.2	24.4
48 32312	Harker Heights	39.3	28 526	1 288	725.9	73.2	21.3	1.3	6.9	NA	22.2	9.2
48 32372	Harlingen	103.1	65 914	534	639.3	94.3	1.7	0.8	0.9	NA	78.5	15.4
48 35000	Houston	1 552.9	2 239 558	4	1 442.2	59.7	23.8	0.9	6.9	0.1	43.8	28.0
48 35528	Huntsville	92.9	40 435	916	435.3	68.3	28.1	0.6	1.8	NA	20.3	9.3
48 35576	Hurst	25.7	38 733	957	1 507.1	87.5	7.1	1.5	3.0	NA	21.8	10.8

1. Dry land or land partially or temporarily covered by water. 2. May be of any race.

City	Age of population (percent), 2011-2013: Under 5 years	5 to 17 years	18 to 24 years	25 to 34 years	35 to 44 years	45 to 54 years	55 to 64 years	65 to 74 years	75 years and over	Median age 2011-2013	Percent female 2011-2013	Population: Census counts: 2000	Census counts: 2010	Percent change: 2000–2010	Percent change: 2010–2014
	12	13	14	15	16	17	18	19	20	21	22	23	24	25	26
TENNESSEE—Cont'd															
Columbia	8.0	17.6	9.3	13.8	11.0	12.0	13.4	7.1	7.8	36.0	54.0	33 055	34 681	4.9	4.0
Cookeville	4.9	13.9	23.3	15.1	10.0	10.2	10.2	6.6	5.9	29.0	52.3	23 923	30 435	27.2	2.5
Franklin	5.7	20.6	6.9	11.5	16.5	15.1	12.9	5.2	5.5	38.4	51.9	41 842	62 487	49.3	12.8
Gallatin	7.2	15.9	8.6	17.0	11.1	13.9	12.2	7.9	6.0	36.1	52.2	23 230	30 278	30.3	9.7
Germantown	5.9	18.4	6.2	6.9	12.8	15.6	16.9	10.3	7.0	44.8	50.0	37 348	38 844	4.0	1.1
Hendersonville	5.4	19.5	7.9	11.2	15.5	15.3	11.6	7.8	5.9	39.4	51.6	40 620	51 372	26.5	7.5
Jackson	7.3	17.2	13.1	13.5	11.0	13.0	11.6	7.2	6.3	34.2	53.8	59 643	65 211	9.3	0.6
Johnson City	4.6	14.1	16.0	13.3	12.0	12.2	12.4	9.0	6.5	37.2	52.4	55 469	63 152	13.9	3.7
Kingsport	5.7	15.6	7.3	10.4	13.1	13.9	12.7	11.2	10.1	43.8	53.2	44 905	48 205	7.3	0.5
Knoxville	6.1	11.6	17.3	16.5	11.4	12.0	11.0	7.7	6.4	33.9	51.8	173 890	178 874	2.9	3.1
La Vergne	8.1	22.7	7.2	16.2	18.2	13.1	8.9	3.6	2.0	33.1	48.8	18 687	32 588	74.4	5.2
Lebanon	6.8	16.9	9.4	13.3	14.6	12.8	11.2	8.3	6.6	37.0	51.3	20 235	26 190	29.4	12.5
Maryville	5.1	18.4	11.0	9.5	14.5	13.4	11.7	8.1	8.4	40.0	52.8	23 120	27 465	18.8	3.1
Memphis	7.6	17.6	11.6	15.6	12.4	12.9	11.9	5.9	4.7	33.2	52.4	650 100	646 889	-0.5	0.8
Morristown	7.3	17.5	7.8	16.7	12.7	12.6	9.9	7.4	8.1	35.4	53.1	24 965	29 137	16.7	1.1
Murfreesboro	6.8	15.3	18.2	17.4	13.2	11.0	8.7	5.5	3.9	30.2	50.2	68 816	108 755	58.0	10.9
Nashville-Davidson	7.1	14.6	11.0	19.0	13.8	12.9	11.1	5.8	4.6	33.8	51.6	569 891	601 222	10.2	6.7
Oak Ridge	5.9	16.4	9.6	11.4	12.0	13.9	13.2	8.7	8.9	40.7	51.5	27 387	29 330	7.1	-0.1
Smyrna	8.0	20.7	9.0	15.2	15.7	12.8	10.0	5.4	3.2	33.0	52.7	25 569	39 974	56.3	13.3
Spring Hill	9.4	23.4	5.6	15.9	18.2	15.6	6.3	4.6	0.9	32.8	51.4	7 715	29 036	276.4	18.0
TEXAS	7.4	19.4	10.3	14.4	13.6	13.2	10.8	6.3	4.6	33.9	50.3	20 851 820	25 145 561	20.6	7.2
Abilene	7.4	15.5	16.3	15.8	11.1	11.8	9.7	6.5	5.9	31.1	48.3	115 930	117 063	1.0	3.0
Allen	7.9	23.4	6.8	11.1	17.9	17.3	8.8	4.1	2.6	35.4	52.9	43 554	84 246	93.4	11.7
Amarillo	7.9	19.5	9.5	15.5	12.3	12.0	10.9	6.5	5.8	33.3	51.2	173 627	190 695	9.8	3.5
Arlington	8.0	19.0	11.3	15.5	13.8	13.7	9.9	5.4	3.4	32.2	50.9	332 969	365 438	9.8	4.9
Austin	6.8	14.9	12.8	21.3	15.4	12.1	9.3	4.2	3.1	31.9	49.7	656 562	790 390	20.4	12.5
Baytown	8.8	21.3	9.4	14.7	12.2	12.8	11.0	4.4	5.3	31.7	51.0	66 430	71 802	8.1	5.7
Beaumont	7.4	17.2	11.5	14.6	11.3	12.9	11.8	6.9	6.3	34.5	52.3	113 866	118 296	3.9	0.3
Bedford	5.8	13.6	7.9	15.4	13.4	14.7	13.7	8.4	7.1	40.6	51.1	47 152	46 979	-0.4	4.1
Big Spring	6.5	15.2	11.4	15.8	15.1	13.6	10.8	5.9	5.6	35.5	41.9	25 233	27 282	8.1	4.4
Brownsville	8.8	24.1	10.7	12.9	12.8	11.7	8.8	5.7	4.6	30.3	52.3	139 722	175 023	25.3	4.6
Bryan	7.5	16.7	16.5	17.7	12.0	10.8	8.6	5.2	4.9	29.8	48.4	65 660	76 201	16.1	6.2
Burleson	7.8	23.2	7.4	14.9	14.1	12.5	9.7	6.7	3.6	33.2	52.9	20 976	36 690	74.9	14.0
Carrollton	6.2	18.4	8.7	15.3	14.1	16.5	11.9	5.8	3.2	36.1	50.6	109 576	119 097	8.7	7.8
Cedar Hill	7.5	22.6	7.6	12.5	16.2	14.2	12.3	4.9	2.4	34.9	54.1	32 093	45 028	40.3	6.8
Cedar Park	6.5	22.5	8.5	14.0	17.3	14.0	10.2	4.3	2.7	34.2	51.1	26 049	48 937	87.9	22.9
Cleburne	9.6	20.0	11.1	12.6	12.3	12.8	9.3	6.3	6.1	32.2	51.5	26 005	29 337	12.8	0.3
College Station	4.8	10.9	45.3	14.3	8.0	6.4	5.5	3.3	1.7	22.5	49.1	67 890	93 857	38.2	10.0
Conroe	8.8	18.9	10.2	16.3	15.3	11.1	9.1	5.5	4.9	32.5	52.7	36 811	56 207	52.7	15.6
Coppell	5.5	23.5	6.4	9.4	16.3	20.2	12.2	4.2	2.3	38.4	50.6	35 958	38 659	7.5	5.2
Copperas Cove	8.2	20.9	9.6	17.6	13.1	13.1	7.7	6.2	3.7	31.4	52.4	29 592	32 032	8.2	2.4
Corpus Christi	6.7	18.8	10.5	14.3	12.3	13.2	12.0	6.8	5.5	34.7	51.0	277 454	305 215	10.0	5.0
Dallas	8.1	17.7	10.4	18.5	14.0	12.4	9.8	5.1	4.0	32.2	49.9	1 188 580	1 197 816	0.8	7.0
Deer Park	7.9	18.1	9.7	14.7	15.1	13.2	12.0	5.6	3.8	34.6	51.5	28 520	32 010	12.2	5.3
Del Rio	9.2	20.5	9.9	13.5	11.7	12.0	9.6	6.7	6.9	32.6	50.0	33 867	35 591	5.1	0.4
Denton	5.5	14.9	23.7	16.6	11.3	10.8	8.4	5.9	3.0	27.7	51.9	80 537	113 383	40.8	10.3
DeSoto	4.7	19.1	9.1	10.3	13.2	15.2	15.3	7.9	5.4	40.4	53.3	37 646	49 047	30.3	5.9
Duncanville	8.1	18.5	9.1	12.2	13.7	13.2	12.1	8.1	5.0	36.4	52.7	36 081	38 524	6.8	3.0
Eagle Pass	9.3	22.5	10.1	11.5	12.5	11.6	9.6	6.9	5.9	31.8	50.4	22 413	26 248	17.1	7.9
Edinburg	9.6	20.7	14.0	16.5	13.1	11.4	6.7	4.1	3.8	28.0	50.3	48 465	77 100	59.1	11.3
El Paso	7.9	20.2	11.3	14.1	12.5	12.5	10.0	6.2	5.3	32.2	51.7	563 662	649 121	15.2	4.6
Euless	6.3	18.1	10.2	17.1	15.6	13.8	10.5	5.3	2.9	33.6	50.5	46 005	51 277	11.5	4.6
Farmers Branch	6.5	18.8	8.4	14.6	14.1	14.0	10.9	6.2	6.6	36.8	52.5	27 508	28 616	4.0	13.8
Flower Mound	5.9	24.8	6.6	7.2	17.9	21.0	10.7	4.1	1.9	38.7	50.5	50 702	64 669	27.5	7.7
Fort Worth	8.6	20.4	10.0	16.2	14.3	12.5	9.3	4.8	3.7	31.7	51.4	534 694	741 206	38.6	9.5
Friendswood	4.3	21.2	8.3	10.3	12.0	18.1	12.7	8.9	4.2	40.3	49.2	29 037	35 805	23.3	6.8
Frisco	8.0	25.1	6.1	11.6	22.1	13.2	7.2	4.5	2.1	34.5	49.6	33 714	116 989	247.0	23.9
Galveston	5.5	13.7	13.0	15.6	10.7	14.4	13.1	7.4	6.5	36.8	51.2	57 247	47 743	-16.6	3.9
Garland	8.0	21.5	9.6	13.4	14.0	13.8	10.2	5.6	3.9	33.2	51.1	215 768	226 876	5.1	3.8
Georgetown	5.4	15.1	6.2	11.2	11.1	8.6	13.6	16.4	12.3	46.4	51.6	28 339	47 400	67.3	24.5
Grand Prairie	7.9	21.9	9.9	15.4	14.9	14.1	9.2	4.5	2.3	32.0	50.2	127 427	175 396	37.6	5.7
Grapevine	6.2	19.6	7.0	13.2	15.6	17.6	12.3	5.2	3.3	37.4	52.4	42 059	46 334	10.2	9.7
Greenville	8.9	16.2	9.2	15.1	12.6	11.2	11.9	7.1	7.8	35.4	53.4	23 960	25 557	6.7	2.4
Haltom City	7.6	19.5	11.2	12.6	13.4	14.9	9.7	7.3	3.9	34.5	49.5	39 018	42 409	8.7	3.5
Harker Heights	8.1	22.5	10.9	14.2	16.0	12.7	8.2	4.4	3.0	31.8	49.9	17 308	26 700	54.3	6.8
Harlingen	9.5	22.3	9.2	12.2	13.8	10.5	10.2	6.5	5.9	31.8	50.7	57 564	64 849	12.7	1.5
Houston	7.8	17.6	10.6	17.8	14.0	12.6	10.2	5.5	4.0	32.6	49.9	1 953 631	2 099 451	7.5	6.8
Huntsville	4.8	9.0	27.3	18.3	14.1	11.5	7.7	3.9	3.3	29.2	38.7	35 078	38 548	9.9	4.9
Hurst	7.0	17.1	9.6	13.2	12.3	12.9	11.7	9.1	7.1	37.4	50.1	36 273	37 337	2.9	3.7

City	Households, 2011-2013: Number	Households: Persons per household	Households: Percent: Female family householder[1]	Households: Percent: One-person	Persons in group quarters, 2010: Total	Persons in group quarters: Institutional: Total	Persons in group quarters: Institutional: Persons in nursing facilities	Persons in group quarters: Non-institutional	Serious crimes known to police,[2] 2013: Total: Number	Serious crimes: Total: Rate[3]	Serious crimes: Rate[3]: Violent	Serious crimes: Rate[3]: Property	Educational attainment, 2011–2013: Population age 25 and older	Attainment[4] (percent): High school graduate or less	Attainment[4] (percent): Bachelor's degree or more
	27	28	29	30	31	32	33	34	35	36	37	38	39	40	41
TENNESSEE—Cont'd															
Columbia	14 003	2.43	19.0	34.1	863	795	462	68	1 713	4 901	781	4 120	22 844	52.5	16.1
Cookeville	12 483	2.26	14.3	34.4	2 410	431	201	1 979	1 743	5 591	459	5 132	17 972	47.1	28.6
Franklin	25 978	2.54	7.9	29.8	795	792	491	3	1 113	1 650	178	1 472	44 467	20.0	56.4
Gallatin	12 290	2.50	15.9	25.9	890	870	308	20	742	2 322	347	1 974	21 597	45.3	22.1
Germantown	14 059	2.79	5.2	18.9	43	43	43	0	559	1 411	73	1 337	27 309	12.8	65.1
Hendersonville	20 329	2.61	11.3	24.0	139	128	128	11	850	1 585	166	1 419	35 733	37.9	30.9
Jackson	24 546	2.58	18.0	34.5	4 297	1 456	557	2 841	4 335	6 435	1 278	5 157	42 017	44.4	27.8
Johnson City	27 610	2.19	11.4	36.7	3 936	750	626	3 186	2 852	4 393	419	3 974	42 151	36.6	36.6
Kingsport	23 413	2.22	12.6	33.9	887	744	660	143	2 920	5 670	493	5 177	37 824	46.7	25.7
Knoxville	82 824	2.08	11.3	43.3	10 048	1 723	1 287	8 325	13 005	7 097	843	6 254	118 297	39.1	30.3
La Vergne	10 916	3.08	13.1	18.2	5	0	0	5	901	2 639	630	2 009	20 884	49.3	20.3
Lebanon	10 406	2.55	17.4	32.8	1 101	609	375	492	1 190	4 219	656	3 563	18 611	55.2	21.8
Maryville	10 550	2.49	11.5	30.3	1 644	886	529	758	796	2 842	218	2 624	18 212	35.3	35.1
Memphis	247 638	2.58	23.9	35.8	16 536	10 165	2 710	6 371	50 766	7 719	1 656	6 063	413 153	46.2	24.5
Morristown	10 849	2.62	20.5	27.0	903	763	487	140	1 748	5 966	539	5 427	19 676	61.7	14.5
Murfreesboro	43 205	2.53	11.0	28.0	4 434	1 348	458	3 086	4 764	4 122	605	3 517	68 217	30.7	37.0
Nashville-Davidson	249 063	2.41	14.1	36.8	25 870	9 226	2 169	16 644	31 271	4 919	1 049	3 871	419 691	37.9	35.7
Oak Ridge	12 435	2.33	11.9	35.9	483	226	218	257	112	382	41	341	20 018	30.0	40.4
Smyrna	14 822	2.81	12.7	25.7	365	353	215	12	1 137	2 692	265	2 427	26 092	42.8	25.5
Spring Hill	10 015	3.08	7.3	17.9	47	30	0	17	350	1 100	151	949	NA	NA	NA
TEXAS	8 965 352	2.84	14.4	25.1	581 139	375 392	94 278	205 747	969 732	3 667	408	3 258	16 386 630	43.8	26.9
Abilene	42 169	2.57	12.9	30.9	9 592	5 306	816	4 286	5 246	4 394	399	3 994	73 819	46.5	22.6
Allen	29 396	3.05	11.3	16.1	171	171	164	0	1 262	1 382	68	1 315	55 522	16.8	51.6
Amarillo	74 851	2.58	14.5	28.9	1 881	1 419	1 019	462	9 535	4 851	661	4 189	123 242	41.5	22.4
Arlington	133 292	2.79	15.7	25.9	3 132	1 061	1 053	2 071	16 837	4 445	485	3 960	231 899	38.5	29.2
Austin	342 196	2.46	11.8	33.8	20 261	4 199	1 869	16 062	44 790	5 213	363	4 850	564 414	29.3	45.8
Baytown	24 560	2.98	18.8	25.5	601	507	507	94	3 938	5 343	387	4 956	44 563	53.8	13.0
Beaumont	45 268	2.50	19.7	35.1	5 133	2 634	513	2 499	7 417	6 276	1 037	5 240	75 037	47.2	22.0
Bedford	20 936	2.28	11.0	33.1	331	325	287	6	1 555	3 205	425	2 781	35 053	27.1	33.5
Big Spring	8 163	2.72	18.2	32.0	6 080	5 768	280	312	1 323	4 787	532	4 255	18 495	54.2	14.3
Brownsville	51 362	3.48	23.5	18.9	1 637	963	671	674	8 311	4 577	260	4 316	101 839	58.9	17.0
Bryan	27 563	2.69	15.9	32.3	3 097	2 822	361	275	2 669	3 397	456	2 941	46 169	49.0	27.3
Burleson	13 959	2.81	8.5	23.8	108	108	108	0	1 060	2 669	144	2 526	24 238	38.0	22.5
Carrollton	44 313	2.81	12.7	22.0	376	350	350	26	3 145	2 467	145	2 322	83 242	34.3	36.3
Cedar Hill	15 867	2.88	19.6	23.0	293	171	171	122	1 595	3 400	190	3 210	28 757	31.0	32.1
Cedar Park	19 007	3.02	11.0	20.0	137	107	107	30	920	1 535	115	1 420	35 988	21.3	41.9
Cleburne	10 061	2.84	14.3	23.9	876	794	316	82	1 113	3 795	310	3 485	17 648	52.4	14.8
College Station	34 015	2.56	8.1	28.1	10 347	201	201	10 146	2 609	2 638	383	2 254	38 178	19.7	53.0
Conroe	20 933	2.85	19.7	25.8	2 263	2 088	291	175	2 287	3 632	343	3 289	38 207	53.8	19.6
Coppell	14 336	2.80	9.2	18.2	3	0	0	3	597	1 476	42	1 434	25 988	16.8	61.7
Copperas Cove	11 448	2.85	16.4	21.3	284	174	174	110	1 221	3 615	278	3 336	20 187	31.4	19.2
Corpus Christi	112 390	2.71	17.5	25.2	5 640	3 199	1 344	2 441	16 540	5 259	616	4 642	199 693	46.5	20.6
Dallas	466 448	2.62	16.0	34.6	18 725	12 739	3 693	5 986	60 604	4 829	664	4 165	790 589	47.7	29.6
Deer Park	11 160	2.94	14.0	15.4	109	87	87	22	700	2 102	123	1 979	21 183	39.2	18.7
Del Rio	10 951	3.16	13.6	24.5	1 373	1 347	203	26	840	2 366	203	2 163	21 513	64.8	14.6
Denton	41 890	2.64	12.2	27.6	8 976	1 646	391	7 330	3 161	2 564	274	2 290	67 584	30.1	37.0
DeSoto	19 110	2.64	18.4	27.7	304	275	275	29	1 906	3 686	346	3 340	34 209	32.1	29.6
Duncanville	13 685	2.86	18.7	22.8	176	165	165	11	1 504	3 778	367	3 411	25 317	42.0	25.3
Eagle Pass	8 537	3.17	22.3	19.5	342	311	59	31	899	3 260	105	3 155	15 887	57.7	17.6
Edinburg	23 876	3.23	17.3	19.6	4 072	3 008	169	1 064	4 569	5 554	337	5 217	43 920	43.1	29.8
El Paso	219 972	3.01	19.8	23.2	9 414	5 777	1 482	3 637	18 080	2 660	371	2 289	406 419	46.1	23.0
Euless	20 852	2.52	13.3	31.5	109	99	99	10	1 657	3 113	167	2 945	34 433	31.5	32.5
Farmers Branch	10 793	2.77	13.9	27.9	103	0	0	103	1 120	3 783	220	3 563	19 941	42.8	30.7
Flower Mound	21 633	3.11	8.4	12.9	159	155	110	4	530	770	57	713	42 399	14.9	56.8
Fort Worth	266 098	2.87	16.2	27.1	13 977	8 117	2 410	5 860	38 806	4 918	563	4 355	473 922	44.7	26.6
Friendswood	12 994	2.83	7.8	20.8	207	201	201	6	429	1 152	30	1 123	24 424	20.8	50.7
Frisco	42 844	3.02	10.5	15.3	225	225	225	0	2 632	1 997	78	1 919	78 647	16.1	58.9
Galveston	20 000	2.26	16.1	38.8	2 477	1 261	86	1 216	2 571	5 349	491	4 858	32 681	43.5	28.0
Garland	73 915	3.14	17.7	20.3	567	478	463	89	8 885	3 770	218	3 552	141 872	48.9	20.9
Georgetown	21 328	2.38	6.6	30.6	2 499	1 436	389	1 063	843	1 566	132	1 434	38 480	29.6	45.7
Grand Prairie	58 172	3.11	16.3	21.7	257	188	188	69	5 669	3 084	278	2 806	109 222	46.6	23.4
Grapevine	18 934	2.55	10.1	26.0	242	226	226	16	1 642	3 346	179	3 167	32 670	25.9	46.2
Greenville	9 553	2.62	12.2	35.8	678	604	316	74	1 483	5 727	788	4 939	16 987	51.7	16.7
Haltom City	15 299	2.82	14.5	30.9	96	96	96	0	1 565	3 583	252	3 331	26 703	60.0	11.6
Harker Heights	8 439	3.27	14.8	18.2	166	166	166	0	1 040	3 698	320	3 378	16 239	32.2	25.6
Harlingen	20 158	3.21	18.8	20.8	1 070	457	415	613	2 848	4 323	401	3 922	38 769	52.4	19.5
Houston	788 096	2.70	16.3	32.2	37 071	18 243	4 778	18 828	131 912	6 049	963	5 087	1 384 622	46.4	30.0
Huntsville	10 083	2.31	19.4	29.7	11 239	8 489	190	2 750	1 291	3 228	533	2 696	23 349	56.8	15.8
Hurst	14 544	2.60	16.4	28.7	245	239	224	6	2 183	5 677	533	5 144	25 311	40.2	26.7

1. No spouse present. 2. Data for serious crimes have not been adjusted for underreporting. This may affect comparability between geographic areas and over time. 3. Per 100,000 population estimated by the FBI. 4. Persons 25 years old and over.

City	Money income, 2011–2013					Housing units, 2010			Occupied housing units 2011–2013				
		Households								Owner-occupied		Median owner costs as a percent of income	
	Per capita income[1] (dollars)	Median income	Percent with income of $200,000 or more	Percent with income of less than $25,000	Families with income below poverty (percent)	Total	Percent change, 2000–2010	Vacant units for sale or rent[2]	Total	Percent	Median value[3] (dollars)	With a mortgage[4]	Without a mortgage[5]
	42	43	44	45	46	47	48	49	50	51	52	53	54
TENNESSEE—Cont'd													
Columbia	18 527	31 584	1.4	38.5	21.4	15 906	10.7	1 894	14 003	56.3	116 100	25.1	13.7
Cookeville	22 203	27 090	2.4	46.8	27.4	13 706	26.9	1 235	12 483	42.4	166 700	22.7	11.1
Franklin	40 821	82 719	11.3	13.0	6.4	25 586	48.6	1 546	25 978	68.1	303 900	21.9	10.0
Gallatin	27 566	47 036	2.9	21.5	9.9	13 093	35.8	1 222	12 290	58.4	162 300	22.1	11.6
Germantown	50 940	111 200	20.0	7.6	2.5	15 536	13.4	626	14 059	87.1	280 000	20.4	10.0
Hendersonville	32 647	60 645	6.7	16.2	5.3	21 543	30.6	1 432	20 329	70.4	193 800	23.0	10.0
Jackson	22 842	36 332	3.7	35.8	18.2	28 052	9.8	2 861	24 546	56.9	119 900	23.7	12.7
Johnson City	27 006	38 337	3.9	35.4	15.6	30 583	19.5	3 566	27 610	54.9	147 900	20.8	10.0
Kingsport	25 924	38 140	2.5	34.8	15.0	23 784	9.0	2 495	23 413	63.9	138 800	19.6	10.0
Knoxville	23 051	33 761	2.2	35.9	16.7	88 009	3.7	9 961	82 824	47.9	116 700	23.5	12.7
La Vergne	21 778	53 498	1.2	11.5	6.2	11 612	66.3	696	10 916	78.2	130 200	22.8	10.0
Lebanon	21 459	38 756	3.1	31.0	13.4	11 030	26.1	900	10 406	53.6	163 800	23.2	11.9
Maryville	26 049	53 147	3.0	25.3	10.9	11 629	19.1	917	10 550	60.9	188 900	22.0	10.0
Memphis	21 391	35 455	2.4	36.2	23.2	291 883	7.4	41 539	247 638	49.2	92 700	25.6	13.3
Morristown	17 245	29 563	1.8	42.9	27.4	12 705	15.2	1 293	10 849	51.1	110 500	22.9	12.4
Murfreesboro	25 474	49 233	2.7	23.1	9.8	45 500	57.2	3 560	43 205	51.6	174 600	22.2	11.0
Nashville-Davidson	26 976	45 542	3.5	26.0	14.0	283 978	12.3	24 479	249 063	53.2	163 100	23.7	11.4
Oak Ridge	29 217	45 856	3.8	30.0	14.6	14 494	8.0	1 722	12 435	57.5	145 800	20.5	10.0
Smyrna	24 123	52 064	2.5	21.2	11.5	15 787	57.9	980	14 822	62.8	147 000	21.8	10.7
Spring Hill	27 838	75 390	1.8	7.8	4.1	10 569	NA	708	10 015	78.1	192 900	19.9	10.0
TEXAS	25 900	51 375	4.8	24.1	14.0	9 977 436	22.3	1 054 503	8 965 352	62.4	129 800	22.1	11.8
Abilene	20 016	41 470	1.8	30.0	13.7	47 783	4.8	4 171	42 169	56.0	90 500	20.2	12.0
Allen	38 862	99 563	13.6	7.8	5.0	28 877	89.4	1 007	29 396	76.0	198 600	20.6	10.4
Amarillo	23 974	45 744	2.2	27.4	13.7	80 298	11.0	6 380	74 851	61.3	116 500	20.9	11.9
Arlington	24 899	52 407	3.1	21.8	14.1	144 805	10.7	11 733	133 292	57.2	128 600	22.1	12.0
Austin	32 091	54 331	5.9	21.9	13.3	354 241	28.1	29 349	342 196	44.4	225 500	23.4	12.3
Baytown	20 494	44 650	1.7	27.5	18.4	28 998	10.2	4 043	24 560	59.7	93 100	22.2	11.3
Beaumont	23 705	38 049	3.5	34.4	18.1	50 689	3.8	5 041	45 268	59.0	98 400	23.7	12.3
Bedford	34 218	62 034	3.9	16.0	5.5	22 301	5.5	1 285	20 936	56.3	160 200	21.0	10.3
Big Spring	18 225	43 993	1.2	27.1	15.0	9 640	-2.4	1 373	8 163	59.1	64 900	16.4	11.3
Brownsville	14 307	31 770	1.8	40.5	30.7	53 936	28.8	4 065	51 362	61.7	83 000	26.4	13.7
Bryan	19 669	37 669	2.5	34.6	19.0	30 582	18.6	2 857	27 563	47.0	112 200	23.6	12.3
Burleson	27 500	67 572	3.3	13.3	6.2	13 591	74.5	703	13 959	68.9	125 100	19.1	14.5
Carrollton	31 771	68 789	5.1	11.0	6.5	45 508	12.3	2 209	44 313	61.4	165 900	21.6	11.9
Cedar Hill	29 184	68 164	4.8	13.5	9.2	16 338	47.0	832	15 867	73.5	133 800	23.4	12.1
Cedar Park	31 388	77 435	7.0	10.4	4.6	18 726	108.8	909	19 007	68.5	194 300	23.7	10.0
Cleburne	19 474	45 508	1.1	27.1	16.9	11 418	14.5	979	10 061	56.6	99 200	23.1	13.5
College Station	20 240	30 947	3.6	42.5	14.6	37 226	43.1	2 189	34 015	34.6	177 100	21.6	11.0
Conroe	21 707	43 701	2.1	30.0	18.1	22 215	54.5	2 198	20 933	48.0	129 900	24.3	12.3
Coppell	47 752	110 831	17.2	7.6	3.8	14 343	14.2	537	14 336	69.9	290 500	20.5	11.0
Copperas Cove	22 114	51 340	0.7	20.1	9.0	13 094	16.7	1 236	11 448	57.2	99 100	19.6	11.4
Corpus Christi	24 381	49 036	2.9	25.2	13.6	125 469	16.3	12 674	112 390	55.9	111 700	21.9	11.9
Dallas	27 380	42 026	5.8	29.5	21.1	516 639	6.7	58 582	466 448	42.8	127 700	24.6	13.5
Deer Park	30 906	78 660	4.2	11.2	3.3	11 742	18.6	609	11 160	75.4	136 300	18.9	10.0
Del Rio	16 732	39 981	1.2	33.9	16.2	12 958	9.5	1 359	10 951	63.6	92 000	20.8	13.0
Denton	23 835	47 136	3.2	26.6	9.9	46 211	41.1	3 576	41 890	48.0	146 800	22.9	13.1
DeSoto	28 484	57 223	2.6	19.3	7.5	19 488	38.1	1 278	19 110	64.3	143 100	26.0	12.3
Duncanville	23 763	55 619	2.0	15.9	7.5	14 011	5.6	731	13 685	67.5	113 500	24.1	12.4
Eagle Pass	17 283	36 971	1.6	36.9	20.4	9 019	17.6	747	8 537	64.6	111 200	25.9	13.5
Edinburg	17 401	44 066	1.2	32.7	23.0	25 167	57.8	2 068	23 876	54.2	101 400	21.5	13.1
El Paso	19 895	41 657	2.6	30.9	18.6	227 605	17.5	10 711	219 972	58.7	118 200	22.7	11.4
Euless	28 522	50 589	3.1	18.8	12.1	23 447	16.8	1 916	20 852	41.9	149 100	21.4	10.3
Farmers Branch	26 703	57 982	2.9	16.7	9.3	11 549	13.0	752	10 793	61.0	143 500	22.2	14.7
Flower Mound	45 236	121 605	18.2	4.0	1.6	21 570	27.1	559	21 633	88.3	270 900	19.5	10.2
Fort Worth	24 059	51 168	3.6	24.5	16.0	291 086	37.8	28 434	266 098	57.3	118 400	22.5	12.6
Friendswood	41 556	92 381	17.0	8.9	4.0	13 254	28.3	528	12 994	79.2	238 600	21.4	10.4
Frisco	41 926	110 461	13.6	6.8	3.5	42 306	209.0	2 405	42 844	73.4	252 700	20.4	10.5
Galveston	26 667	38 218	4.9	36.0	19.5	32 368	8.0	12 425	20 000	44.5	144 200	24.1	12.4
Garland	20 818	49 637	2.3	20.0	14.6	80 834	7.4	5 138	73 915	62.8	112 700	25.0	12.3
Georgetown	31 412	60 633	2.6	16.1	6.5	20 037	81.6	1 207	21 328	71.9	187 700	24.1	11.6
Grand Prairie	22 430	53 620	2.1	19.0	13.0	62 424	34.9	4 250	58 172	60.9	124 500	24.5	11.9
Grapevine	40 147	77 816	9.9	11.8	8.0	19 685	19.2	1 183	18 934	59.2	227 300	20.4	10.0
Greenville	19 094	37 108	0.5	31.9	20.5	10 838	9.3	1 122	9 553	54.5	74 200	22.8	12.0
Haltom City	20 410	41 639	0.9	27.1	15.0	16 626	5.0	1 357	15 299	54.4	87 400	20.8	12.3
Harker Heights	24 929	62 821	4.6	19.4	14.8	10 347	51.2	859	8 439	66.2	162 600	20.1	10.1
Harlingen	16 607	33 555	2.4	36.6	25.0	25 585	10.1	3 940	20 158	58.0	82 400	24.5	12.3
Houston	27 328	44 451	6.0	28.8	19.9	892 646	14.1	110 003	788 096	44.0	124 200	22.8	12.1
Huntsville	10 674	28 833	1.9	44.8	30.1	12 853	12.7	1 062	10 083	34.7	121 700	19.8	13.4
Hurst	26 762	50 136	3.3	22.7	13.0	15 761	6.8	1 109	14 544	65.8	136 500	21.1	12.6

1. Based on population estimated by the American Community Survey. 2. Includes units rented or sold but not occupied. 3. Specified owner-occupied units; $1,000,000 represents $1,000,000 or more 4. 50.0 represents 50 percent or more. 5. 10.0 represents 10 percent or less.

Table D. Cities — **Housing, Labor Force, and Employment**

City	Occupied housing units, 2011–2013 (cont.)				Migration, 2011–2013		Civilian labor force, 2014				Civilian employment[4], 2011–2013			
									Unemployment			Percent		
	Percent renter occupied	Median gross rent[1]	Median rent as a percent of income[2]	Percent with no vehicle available	Percent who lived in the same house one year ago	Percent who lived outside current city one year ago	Total	Percent change, 2013–2014	Total	Rate[3]	Population age 16 and older	In labor force	Civilian full-year full-time workers	Households with no workers (percent)
	55	56	57	58	59	60	61	62	63	64	65	66	67	68
TENNESSEE—Cont'd														
Columbia	43.7	636	32.5	7.9	80.4	9.7	15 967	-1.2	1 127	7.1	26 769	61.9	36.3	31.6
Cookeville	57.6	592	36.1	5.0	80.3	11.6	12 760	-2.4	929	7.3	25 771	53.1	29.3	37.0
Franklin	31.9	1 050	25.6	2.9	79.5	13.6	37 042	-0.3	1 608	4.3	51 054	71.4	48.4	18.3
Gallatin	41.6	811	25.7	8.0	76.7	14.8	15 839	-0.8	852	5.4	24 973	63.0	43.6	25.5
Germantown	12.9	1 550	31.3	2.4	91.5	7.3	19 061	-2.8	968	5.1	31 311	61.5	44.2	23.9
Hendersonville	29.6	894	29.7	3.7	84.0	10.9	28 598	-0.6	1 441	5.0	41 559	69.1	46.4	18.5
Jackson	43.1	736	38.1	9.4	83.0	9.0	30 502	-3.2	2 219	7.3	52 797	59.8	36.2	32.3
Johnson City	45.1	655	31.4	8.1	81.5	9.6	30 006	-3.1	1 926	6.4	53 801	59.7	37.0	31.4
Kingsport	36.1	570	31.1	9.4	83.1	10.6	22 455	-3.4	1 465	6.5	43 077	54.8	34.7	40.6
Knoxville	52.1	750	32.0	9.8	83.8	7.5	91 524	-2.0	5 606	6.1	153 097	62.2	38.2	31.5
La Vergne	21.8	991	28.5	2.4	88.9	6.4	17 365	-0.3	1 020	5.9	24 238	74.1	53.2	12.1
Lebanon	46.4	806	35.1	7.7	81.6	11.7	12 736	-1.2	769	6.0	21 864	60.1	37.8	31.9
Maryville	39.1	807	28.5	6.0	82.1	13.4	12 923	-1.8	781	6.0	22 182	58.4	35.6	32.4
Memphis	50.8	807	35.8	12.7	80.1	5.8	285 163	-3.3	24 805	8.7	506 956	64.2	38.0	28.6
Morristown	48.9	646	35.0	10.1	82.5	10.7	11 141	-2.9	929	8.3	22 838	54.2	31.7	36.2
Murfreesboro	48.4	834	29.9	4.8	73.1	14.4	62 253	-0.8	3 338	5.4	91 222	68.8	43.1	22.0
Nashville-Davidson	46.8	833	30.0	7.7	79.1	8.7	353 770	-0.6	17 882	5.1	5 010 060	69.3	44.4	22.5
Oak Ridge	42.5	732	32.1	7.2	84.5	9.9	13 830	-2.0	858	6.2	23 505	60.7	39.1	33.5
Smyrna	37.2	869	29.9	4.5	80.6	14.3	22 412	-0.6	1 205	5.4	30 740	72.1	47.4	18.1
Spring Hill	21.9	1 023	28.5	1.1	89.7	7.5	16 707	-0.7	757	4.5	21 167	73.7	NA	14.5
TEXAS	37.6	847	29.4	6.0	83.0	10.3	13 111 548	1.6	663 997	5.1	19 816 588	64.8	42.8	22.0
Abilene	44.0	751	30.1	6.8	72.9	11.1	55 637	0.4	2 394	4.3	96 268	58.2	35.3	26.5
Allen	24.0	1 198	24.9	1.1	87.1	9.1	50 447	2.7	2 116	4.2	64 979	74.7	52.4	10.4
Amarillo	38.7	733	29.2	6.0	81.3	6.3	101 448	0.1	3 642	3.6	147 253	67.1	46.4	22.9
Arlington	42.8	820	30.4	4.8	79.7	9.9	205 170	1.4	10 210	5.0	285 356	71.2	46.7	18.0
Austin	55.6	984	30.2	6.9	74.3	10.8	529 958	2.8	19 393	3.7	692 929	73.4	47.7	16.8
Baytown	40.3	816	32.2	8.7	79.7	8.3	34 400	1.1	2 513	7.3	54 134	63.2	38.4	25.6
Beaumont	41.0	734	33.8	11.1	84.0	6.0	53 837	0.7	3 971	7.4	91 578	59.3	37.2	32.0
Bedford	43.7	876	27.4	4.8	82.8	13.6	29 101	1.4	1 378	4.7	40 221	71.1	51.1	21.3
Big Spring	40.9	709	24.4	9.8	78.5	11.3	9 994	0.5	475	4.8	22 171	48.5	31.8	29.7
Brownsville	38.3	617	32.7	11.0	87.1	4.2	75 927	0.3	6 264	8.3	128 245	58.4	35.2	26.0
Bryan	53.0	771	31.9	10.2	74.7	16.9	39 652	1.2	1 560	3.9	60 647	66.3	36.4	26.9
Burleson	31.1	1 035	26.0	2.2	81.1	10.3	21 651	1.5	889	4.1	28 452	73.5	50.8	19.1
Carrollton	38.6	986	25.5	2.2	84.9	9.0	75 007	2.7	3 429	4.6	97 755	76.3	52.0	13.2
Cedar Hill	26.5	1 095	31.2	4.3	90.7	7.8	25 600	2.3	1 536	6.0	33 695	73.2	50.6	17.0
Cedar Park	31.5	1 064	28.1	1.4	81.4	14.8	33 436	2.8	1 275	3.8	42 640	73.4	48.6	14.0
Cleburne	43.4	788	27.2	4.9	72.9	15.3	13 419	1.4	688	5.1	21 837	59.8	36.2	28.4
College Station	65.4	890	50.0	5.3	59.8	24.1	51 890	1.4	2 033	3.9	84 271	59.8	27.7	23.5
Conroe	52.0	852	29.1	7.1	77.5	13.6	31 531	2.0	1 233	3.9	45 950	62.1	38.3	24.0
Coppell	30.1	1 158	22.9	1.5	85.3	11.7	22 928	2.7	1 042	4.5	30 293	73.0	51.9	10.1
Copperas Cove	42.8	831	26.0	4.5	79.6	13.2	13 159	0.0	733	5.6	24 405	63.1	34.7	21.5
Corpus Christi	44.1	851	29.0	8.5	79.7	7.7	154 540	1.2	7 542	4.9	241 359	65.4	43.4	22.6
Dallas	57.2	828	29.1	10.1	80.4	8.2	638 792	2.4	33 291	5.2	948 643	67.9	45.3	21.4
Deer Park	24.6	942	25.8	3.1	86.8	11.5	17 396	2.1	900	5.2	25 163	68.5	47.9	16.6
Del Rio	36.4	610	26.9	9.7	85.1	5.9	14 407	-0.4	821	5.7	26 196	60.1	35.1	29.5
Denton	52.0	871	36.1	5.6	68.8	17.8	66 312	2.6	2 744	4.1	100 069	67.6	35.8	22.5
DeSoto	35.7	893	33.6	5.9	89.9	8.2	27 417	2.5	1 787	6.5	40 640	67.9	46.2	23.9
Duncanville	32.5	934	26.2	3.8	90.5	8.0	20 302	2.1	1 212	6.0	30 044	69.2	47.3	19.6
Eagle Pass	35.4	500	26.0	9.5	88.8	6.0	12 372	-0.9	1 492	12.1	19 398	56.9	35.7	28.2
Edinburg	45.8	680	27.2	5.7	80.6	10.0	37 441	1.2	2 169	5.8	57 446	65.9	41.1	18.4
El Paso	41.3	742	30.2	8.4	84.7	6.1	290 333	-0.3	17 374	6.0	504 039	61.1	36.9	24.0
Euless	58.1	922	26.3	3.4	78.2	16.0	30 739	1.4	1 473	4.8	41 055	74.0	50.4	15.4
Farmers Branch	39.0	1 017	25.2	3.3	82.5	13.5	16 907	2.7	813	4.8	23 338	70.0	45.3	19.9
Flower Mound	11.7	1 595	23.8	1.2	90.3	7.1	37 894	2.5	1 507	4.0	49 645	73.8	53.5	11.2
Fort Worth	42.7	851	30.1	6.5	81.5	8.8	390 808	1.4	19 147	4.9	571 901	67.4	45.3	21.0
Friendswood	20.8	1 157	28.4	1.8	86.6	8.8	19 805	2.2	857	4.3	28 768	65.1	45.0	17.6
Frisco	26.6	1 277	24.7	1.1	85.3	11.1	74 702	2.9	2 806	3.8	90 318	76.8	56.5	10.4
Galveston	55.5	829	34.5	14.4	69.1	15.4	24 454	1.8	1 363	5.6	40 052	60.5	34.4	30.3
Garland	37.2	915	32.4	4.8	84.5	8.1	121 708	2.2	6 448	5.3	171 665	71.0	47.4	17.9
Georgetown	28.1	1 011	30.1	4.0	85.7	11.1	22 845	2.6	1 098	4.8	42 482	49.7	34.5	42.9
Grand Prairie	39.1	880	30.2	3.3	88.5	7.6	94 636	2.1	4 935	5.2	133 047	71.3	49.3	15.2
Grapevine	40.8	1 035	27.0	2.7	80.5	11.2	30 608	1.9	1 269	4.1	37 403	77.5	55.1	12.9
Greenville	45.5	736	34.1	9.8	76.7	13.6	10 797	1.7	639	5.9	19 811	59.5	37.3	33.2
Haltom City	45.6	779	27.8	2.2	83.4	14.6	22 336	1.4	1 120	5.0	32 662	67.8	48.3	18.6
Harker Heights	33.8	743	27.5	2.8	78.2	15.6	11 652	-0.2	657	5.6	20 203	63.7	38.3	25.8
Harlingen	42.0	704	29.2	8.3	89.9	4.8	25 009	-0.1	1 781	7.1	46 960	48.6	34.3	33.1
Houston	56.0	837	29.7	10.0	79.0	7.5	1 150 435	2.0	54 487	4.7	1 668 380	68.4	44.6	20.3
Huntsville	65.3	747	43.6	8.0	74.3	19.9	11 628	0.1	710	6.1	34 730	34.2	17.3	28.3
Hurst	34.2	804	32.0	2.1	85.1	12.0	20 363	1.6	1 012	5.0	29 666	66.5	44.0	25.1

1. $2,000 represents $2,000 or more. 2. 50.0 represents 50 percent or more. 3. Percent of civilian labor force. 4. Persons 16 years old and over.

City	Value of residential construction authorized by building permits, 2014			Wholesale trade,[1] 2007				Retail trade,[2] 2007			
	New construction ($1,000)	Number of housing units	Percent single family	Number of establish-ments	Number of employees	Sales (mil dol)	Annual payroll (mil dol)	Number of establish-ments	Number of employees	Sales (mil dol)	Annual payroll (mil dol)
	69	70	71	72	73	74	75	76	77	78	79
TENNESSEE—Cont'd											
Columbia	9 246	77	100.0	39	515	194.3	24.1	246	3 073	743.0	67.0
Cookeville	24 777	209	63.2	55	472	300.4	16.7	295	3 940	979.2	89.8
Franklin	203 262	801	59.6	115	1 321	2 156.7	94.0	483	8 846	2 024.0	198.1
Gallatin	78 927	368	100.0	46	669	470.3	25.4	146	1 904	477.8	45.9
Germantown	NA	NA	NA	42	467	265.5	20.0	176	2 293	365.0	44.0
Hendersonville	32 797	198	100.0	49	D	D	D	168	2 571	621.0	58.0
Jackson	31 835	149	100.0	125	1 774	988.5	72.9	459	6 786	1 553.8	146.2
Johnson City	53 862	462	46.3	106	1 737	1 025.2	60.6	442	7 266	1 674.9	150.2
Kingsport	20 288	105	84.8	80	966	379.4	35.6	373	5 355	1 260.8	117.2
Knoxville	83 013	861	21.0	452	6 580	3 106.5	318.3	1 452	27 067	6 470.5	648.3
La Vergne	9 922	56	100.0	71	3 466	5 145.4	166.3	50	550	159.8	14.2
Lebanon	56 610	428	63.6	39	1 056	862.5	52.8	231	2 778	767.8	63.6
Maryville	18 208	102	100.0	26	205	527.4	9.1	184	2 788	543.8	53.6
Memphis	NA	NA	NA	1 048	22 822	25 485.6	1 173.2	2 571	36 773	8 975.2	880.5
Morristown	5 367	28	100.0	49	D	D	D	277	4 011	1 018.2	87.9
Murfreesboro	195 878	1 734	47.3	102	898	526.1	42.9	538	8 282	2 008.1	184.7
Nashville-Davidson	953 546	6 367	39.9	1 009	20 028	11 942.6	983.6	2 795	42 241	10 581.8	1 046.2
Oak Ridge	2 573	19	100.0	18	118	94.0	6.1	129	2 055	477.1	44.3
Smyrna	30 814	314	77.4	34	996	526.0	43.0	107	1 949	467.8	41.9
Spring Hill	101 627	575	99.3	7	77	45.3	3.8	46	734	159.2	14.4
TEXAS	26 295 841	166 982	59.7	27 066	386 370	424 238.2	20 260.6	78 795	1 138 440	311 334.8	26 395.2
Abilene	57 115	278	100.0	125	1 372	988.0	50.3	547	8 023	1 897.2	176.4
Allen	231 799	1 333	37.7	43	543	213.7	37.7	217	3 179	647.1	61.0
Amarillo	164 302	853	55.0	227	3 368	2 351.2	142.7	859	12 913	3 720.1	288.8
Arlington	127 751	870	54.0	357	5 707	4 470.0	280.8	1 091	18 017	4 890.4	421.7
Austin	1 105 477	9 442	29.7	918	17 256	12 730.5	1 254.5	3 094	51 460	13 493.5	1 300.7
Baytown	25 391	190	100.0	42	385	186.5	14.8	270	4 221	1 242.1	94.0
Beaumont	45 300	354	100.0	180	3 112	2 269.7	148.2	660	9 983	2 474.6	228.6
Bedford	7 435	30	100.0	35	233	470.6	14.2	127	1 957	618.8	56.0
Big Spring	3 694	33	87.9	16	98	48.3	4.1	103	1 202	320.4	26.4
Brownsville	64 924	609	90.1	193	1 618	783.0	41.2	617	9 329	2 024.3	177.7
Bryan	52 867	251	92.8	74	1 102	520.1	39.3	294	3 600	991.3	87.5
Burleson	95 002	593	69.6	18	109	42.5	3.8	146	2 738	674.7	61.2
Carrollton	206 458	1 586	22.9	376	7 000	4 226.5	346.5	361	5 154	1 808.8	163.4
Cedar Hill	22 755	106	100.0	13	164	97.9	7.3	105	2 466	478.1	46.8
Cedar Park	130 686	639	93.3	34	283	95.6	11.6	135	1 927	484.0	44.0
Cleburne	3 975	31	80.6	35	411	242.8	17.6	155	2 364	639.5	58.4
College Station	201 458	1 535	47.0	20	212	173.7	8.5	323	5 380	1 092.6	99.4
Conroe	196 962	1 111	78.4	114	1 420	4 002.7	61.2	367	6 146	1 921.9	154.1
Coppell	39 386	118	100.0	67	2 208	1 881.7	125.1	57	1 079	413.1	35.7
Copperas Cove	14 817	114	86.0	5	5	1.3	0.1	74	1 012	249.2	21.4
Corpus Christi	285 268	2 342	50.5	358	4 002	2 682.6	184.2	1 081	16 200	4 133.8	350.2
Dallas	801 685	7 856	15.0	2 101	31 471	19 169.4	1 546.6	4 209	60 028	16 256.5	1 563.1
Deer Park	16 000	59	100.0	35	713	406.9	45.3	60	1 067	258.1	24.2
Del Rio	7 829	63	87.3	23	127	39.3	3.7	163	2 136	512.8	40.8
Denton	201 483	830	78.9	83	1 685	1 266.8	59.5	408	6 516	1 695.3	140.9
DeSoto	34 277	164	100.0	34	535	256.8	26.9	82	1 363	345.8	32.1
Duncanville	3 860	14	100.0	23	237	67.0	11.7	133	1 482	462.3	37.7
Eagle Pass	9 610	99	70.7	29	161	94.7	7.1	171	2 263	493.5	40.6
Edinburg	54 221	495	57.0	68	1 320	524.1	40.1	199	3 256	890.2	64.5
El Paso	416 264	2 798	72.2	846	8 016	4 793.1	290.2	2 131	32 240	7 892.9	653.3
Euless	24 795	104	100.0	45	401	279.7	25.2	96	1 167	366.1	27.8
Farmers Branch	8 898	28	100.0	227	6 362	3 631.9	385.4	167	2 217	619.9	66.2
Flower Mound	160 319	355	100.0	54	515	251.2	25.6	144	2 799	547.5	49.4
Fort Worth	749 094	5 923	52.7	689	14 729	11 371.3	782.4	1 956	30 304	9 586.1	816.1
Friendswood	70 813	189	100.0	22	82	34.4	3.0	86	1 084	330.9	23.9
Frisco	688 442	3 188	67.9	83	1 047	2 266.8	75.5	421	7 750	1 918.3	175.4
Galveston	71 859	279	100.0	31	502	1 084.7	17.4	238	2 786	558.4	57.3
Garland	50 237	329	54.7	183	2 941	1 470.5	140.6	626	9 531	2 320.0	225.2
Georgetown	378 129	1 724	70.1	41	336	188.6	17.7	195	3 307	1 084.1	89.3
Grand Prairie	100 024	593	66.4	258	5 486	3 794.6	249.8	299	4 954	1 470.6	129.9
Grapevine	40 004	122	96.7	87	1 813	3 263.3	93.2	365	5 623	1 611.4	133.0
Greenville	7 446	47	93.6	21	198	101.5	5.1	138	2 265	600.8	60.2
Haltom City	651	4	100.0	87	1 034	381.5	44.8	164	1 611	496.6	43.6
Harker Heights	43 524	203	100.0	2	D	D	D	55	1 064	279.4	25.0
Harlingen	13 916	123	100.0	75	866	374.3	25.3	329	5 074	1 149.5	102.4
Houston	2 399 526	20 304	26.6	4 409	78 172	189 998.4	4 899.1	8 646	130 578	36 570.2	3 266.0
Huntsville	22 744	222	36.0	27	233	152.6	8.7	130	2 171	589.1	45.2
Hurst	2 814	15	73.3	29	187	151.9	8.0	292	5 835	1 227.8	117.2

1. Merchant wholesalers except manufacturers' sales branches and offices. 2. Establishments with payroll.

Table D. Cities — **Real Estate, Professional Services, and Manufacturing**

City	Real estate and rental and leasing, 2007				Professional, scientific, and technical services,[1] 2007				Manufacturing, 2007			
	Number of establish-ments	Number of employees	Receipts (mil dol)	Annual payroll (mil dol)	Number of establish-ments	Number of employees	Receipts (mil dol)	Annual payroll (mil dol)	Number of establish-ments	Number of employees	Receipts (mil dol)	Annual payroll (mil dol)
	80	81	82	83	84	85	86	87	88	89	90	91
TENNESSEE—Cont'd												
Columbia	67	241	38.9	5.9	80	D	D	D	39	D	D	D
Cookeville	60	204	36.9	4.8	121	D	D	D	91	4 100	D	153.4
Franklin	125	1 838	273.5	56.7	324	D	D	D	81	2 501	848.9	93.6
Gallatin	45	400	121.9	19.3	54	D	D	D	74	3 000	860.8	111.7
Germantown	64	D	D	D	107	478	71.6	23.6	NA	NA	NA	NA
Hendersonville	73	297	49.5	8.8	117	601	72.1	36.3	62	852	139.3	32.6
Jackson	98	728	97.0	17.4	178	D	D	D	89	8 828	4 012.9	389.3
Johnson City	112	911	107.7	16.9	192	D	D	D	101	5 611	1 433.3	194.7
Kingsport	70	305	54.4	8.1	133	877	135.2	35.6	45	11 452	D	D
Knoxville	385	2 497	477.4	79.9	831	D	D	D	270	D	D	D
La Vergne	16	144	41.9	4.9	12	D	D	D	52	4 422	1 401.8	221.1
Lebanon	61	271	57.4	8.1	89	D	D	D	54	5 236	D	233.9
Maryville	33	138	25.1	3.6	99	D	D	D	35	3 628	D	176.8
Memphis	818	7 093	1 240.3	274.1	1 467	14 364	1 936.2	802.6	569	23 906	14 709.6	1 174.0
Morristown	54	265	41.0	6.3	70	D	D	D	88	12 463	3 142.6	438.5
Murfreesboro	150	800	297.6	20.2	234	D	D	D	93	5 328	2 273.3	223.4
Nashville-Davidson	934	6 617	1 588.0	252.2	1 912	23 798	2 943.3	1 285.4	633	23 715	7 347.2	999.0
Oak Ridge	47	246	36.0	6.0	159	D	D	D	52	5 916	1 006.6	395.2
Smyrna	39	145	35.5	3.9	51	353	38.9	16.8	33	7 897	D	428.2
Spring Hill	20	110	18.0	3.9	21	D	D	D	5	D	D	D
TEXAS	26 593	173 745	36 399.2	7 067.2	57 373	534 386	90 668.7	35 376.4	21 115	893 842	593 541.5	42 835.7
Abilene	156	628	132.2	19.1	260	D	D	D	88	2 282	D	D
Allen	61	285	54.2	9.4	218	1 252	174.5	69.1	20	1 545	440.6	D
Amarillo	256	1 199	203.0	35.0	429	D	D	D	164	6 376	D	235.2
Arlington	380	1 742	326.4	56.7	774	D	D	D	261	12 392	12 265.1	616.6
Austin	1 537	11 708	2 286.4	471.0	4 095	45 252	6 926.2	3 401.9	590	31 091	27 028.0	1 615.5
Baytown	84	483	102.5	13.7	117	1 482	85.4	114.3	48	4 833	D	464.1
Beaumont	194	988	175.9	34.5	386	D	D	D	116	6 480	D	396.9
Bedford	71	302	66.9	12.5	155	981	172.9	55.1	NA	NA	NA	NA
Big Spring	35	178	36.0	3.4	42	183	13.9	4.9	16	572	D	25.2
Brownsville	141	604	60.9	12.4	252	D	D	D	102	2 889	928.6	108.0
Bryan	95	487	80.8	14.6	164	D	D	D	73	3 948	788.6	129.6
Burleson	31	130	25.9	5.1	68	310	25.5	8.6	38	1 078	192.0	38.4
Carrollton	140	985	211.8	50.3	411	D	D	D	199	11 698	3 090.8	554.4
Cedar Hill	16	31	7.7	0.8	44	118	13.4	4.2	26	1 318	160.5	38.4
Cedar Park	58	318	35.3	14.0	110	460	60.5	22.5	25	981	419.8	50.0
Cleburne	39	119	26.7	3.6	72	356	42.1	13.3	37	1 725	698.9	83.7
College Station	115	566	83.2	14.3	177	D	D	D	21	613	D	24.5
Conroe	78	357	89.7	12.8	185	1 087	102.6	38.3	97	3 278	D	148.3
Coppell	56	504	52.8	14.3	155	921	145.7	53.2	22	1 203	297.2	38.3
Copperas Cove	43	136	15.9	2.6	29	247	34.5	17.6	NA	NA	NA	NA
Corpus Christi	394	2 413	384.7	73.2	757	D	D	D	191	5 961	D	310.6
Dallas	2 179	23 891	5 259.0	1 361.5	5 402	D	D	D	1 318	71 657	21 239.9	3 722.1
Deer Park	30	295	135.6	18.0	54	982	89.1	55.4	37	3 892	14 234.2	327.2
Del Rio	26	92	11.3	2.1	39	D	D	D	NA	NA	NA	NA
Denton	143	661	113.3	19.9	233	D	D	D	85	4 346	2 411.0	211.0
DeSoto	33	129	17.9	3.5	64	194	18.1	6.3	29	1 314	459.1	64.3
Duncanville	32	181	26.6	4.6	54	199	21.1	6.7	26	1 154	186.1	37.4
Eagle Pass	34	84	15.1	1.9	39	D	D	D	NA	NA	NA	NA
Edinburg	63	225	36.8	6.5	154	D	D	D	39	970	276.0	32.2
El Paso	635	3 439	612.6	104.3	1 109	D	D	D	513	14 792	14 103.1	577.0
Euless	47	308	68.0	8.8	84	316	41.4	14.4	39	983	148.6	40.5
Farmers Branch	98	1 008	222.4	45.6	283	3 421	518.7	208.5	110	5 769	1 417.5	267.6
Flower Mound	72	314	51.5	10.6	247	D	D	D	17	547	125.0	D
Fort Worth	656	3 915	1 555.2	175.9	1 534	15 959	2 246.6	1 113.6	731	65 224	24 367.5	3 606.7
Friendswood	33	126	16.0	3.1	115	336	41.7	15.9	NA	NA	NA	NA
Frisco	104	492	153.6	22.4	323	D	D	D	28	551	253.6	D
Galveston	75	388	57.6	10.1	113	480	83.4	30.7	NA	NA	NA	NA
Garland	183	1 137	197.3	31.7	301	3 291	757.9	278.3	297	10 604	4 338.5	445.1
Georgetown	65	246	77.1	10.7	144	513	59.2	22.3	45	943	227.6	42.5
Grand Prairie	116	2 146	333.5	90.0	183	1 128	124.6	44.4	210	14 061	3 733.7	736.5
Grapevine	72	580	184.1	25.5	190	1 141	135.7	43.5	47	1 533	427.7	56.9
Greenville	46	206	28.9	5.1	61	D	D	D	43	13 016	2 784.1	D
Haltom City	45	251	57.0	8.1	55	275	24.7	9.0	113	2 884	614.7	96.0
Harker Heights	37	149	17.9	3.8	26	D	D	D	NA	NA	NA	NA
Harlingen	107	559	71.7	10.2	144	D	D	D	62	1 246	229.8	35.1
Houston	3 576	31 940	7 873.4	1 462.7	8 915	D	D	D	2 582	97 035	49 122.0	4 774.3
Huntsville	44	D	D	D	68	354	23.8	6.9	22	585	D	25.1
Hurst	63	279	79.1	9.0	167	749	97.7	37.5	NA	NA	NA	NA

1. Establishments subject to federal tax.

Table D. Cities — Accommodation and Food Services, Arts, Entertainment, and Recreation, and Health Care and Social Assistance

City	Accommodation and food services, 2007				Arts, entertainment, and recreation,[1] 2007				Health care and social assistance,[1] 2007			
	Number of establishments	Number of employees	Sales (mil dol)	Annual payroll (mil dol)	Number of establishments	Number of employees	Receipts (mil dol)	Annual payroll (mil dol)	Number of establishments	Number of employees	Receipts (mil dol)	Annual payroll (mil dol)
	92	93	94	95	96	97	98	99	100	101	102	103
TENNESSEE—Cont'd												
Columbia	105	2 321	81.8	23.6	8	51	1.7	0.7	134	D	D	D
Cookeville	132	3 106	128.5	36.2	10	D	D	D	162	1 720	164.3	59.8
Franklin	220	4 926	229.4	65.9	80	567	70.9	15.2	220	3 880	434.2	221.3
Gallatin	75	1 073	45.6	11.5	7	D	D	D	76	D	D	D
Germantown	73	1 638	70.7	20.4	13	D	D	D	149	D	D	D
Hendersonville	97	2 018	78.0	23.8	26	D	D	D	131	D	D	D
Jackson	206	5 457	203.7	54.9	19	D	D	D	240	D	D	D
Johnson City	212	5 577	220.3	66.6	19	207	11.4	2.8	245	D	D	D
Kingsport	186	4 302	172.0	47.6	20	D	D	D	223	D	D	D
Knoxville	696	18 112	780.3	233.8	58	998	45.6	13.2	746	10 784	1 375.2	604.9
La Vergne	30	399	18.0	4.5	3	D	D	D	16	D	D	D
Lebanon	105	2 138	90.8	26.8	10	D	D	D	132	2 661	236.9	91.6
Maryville	90	1 877	73.1	22.3	8	D	D	D	134	D	D	D
Memphis	1 345	31 224	1 463.1	407.8	96	2 244	231.5	123.8	1 424	22 942	2 471.7	997.2
Morristown	100	D	D	D	11	38	2.0	0.7	134	D	D	D
Murfreesboro	266	6 483	257.7	73.3	18	159	9.5	2.0	277	D	D	D
Nashville-Davidson	1 605	38 979	2 203.0	626.4	622	5 305	1 557.7	484.8	1 504	29 785	3 704.3	1 365.8
Oak Ridge	72	1 756	79.4	22.4	4	D	D	D	101	1 385	152.5	72.4
Smyrna	92	1 884	76.0	22.0	5	D	D	D	88	D	D	D
Spring Hill	36	578	19.1	5.8	6	56	2.0	0.6	23	D	D	D
TEXAS	43 509	866 189	42 054.6	11 502.3	5 002	79 475	6 731.7	2 220.8	48 875	780 459	71 221.3	27 771.8
Abilene	268	D	D	D	39	272	16.9	3.4	301	D	D	D
Allen	109	2 152	99.5	26.7	13	D	D	D	194	D	D	D
Amarillo	462	9 616	428.3	113.5	43	521	28.6	6.5	569	8 906	1 017.5	349.2
Arlington	625	13 989	647.1	176.3	76	2 190	419.7	247.2	806	11 518	1 402.2	495.8
Austin	2 121	49 569	2 655.7	745.4	255	4 457	388.8	115.8	2 005	31 869	3 705.7	1 457.1
Baytown	139	2 846	133.0	34.4	12	D	D	D	190	D	D	D
Beaumont	261	6 190	258.4	75.4	37	D	D	D	503	6 944	570.7	228.2
Bedford	89	2 232	102.3	27.1	17	D	D	D	219	D	D	D
Big Spring	68	D	D	D	2	D	D	D	66	D	D	D
Brownsville	280	4 870	200.9	51.3	24	288	11.1	3.5	388	10 497	575.3	236.2
Bryan	130	2 153	89.6	23.3	16	385	17.6	7.9	217	2 468	279.7	104.9
Burleson	93	2 061	83.8	24.2	8	28	1.1	0.3	63	1 591	79.3	37.3
Carrollton	197	2 857	147.9	38.4	33	D	D	D	297	3 531	324.6	125.3
Cedar Hill	72	D	D	D	10	89	4.9	1.7	58	706	41.1	18.9
Cedar Park	82	1 424	65.6	16.8	15	D	D	D	103	D	D	D
Cleburne	70	1 338	54.1	14.2	8	61	2.5	0.6	87	D	D	D
College Station	230	6 283	248.7	67.8	16	D	D	D	114	2 192	268.9	87.7
Conroe	145	3 242	148.2	40.3	19	190	9.8	2.5	169	3 820	597.1	167.9
Coppell	66	D	D	D	10	D	D	D	80	D	D	D
Copperas Cove	48	921	32.1	8.4	5	37	1.2	0.3	28	311	14.9	5.9
Corpus Christi	717	14 005	607.1	170.7	59	1 304	68.2	19.4	890	D	D	D
Dallas	2 647	57 958	3 378.6	954.1	301	5 043	547.3	200.0	3 180	45 235	6 245.5	2 727.9
Deer Park	42	736	32.9	8.0	3	7	0.3	0.1	50	D	D	D
Del Rio	80	1 415	57.8	15.2	8	D	D	D	71	2 335	75.1	34.0
Denton	229	4 995	207.5	56.8	22	231	11.7	3.0	339	5 726	722.4	243.6
DeSoto	60	1 235	46.0	14.9	6	106	7.9	2.2	144	D	D	D
Duncanville	57	1 491	66.3	17.5	6	D	D	D	103	1 137	79.1	30.3
Eagle Pass	60	D	D	D	6	D	D	D	72	D	D	D
Edinburg	108	2 037	80.3	21.5	12	D	D	D	256	8 284	476.9	224.0
El Paso	1 194	23 499	990.6	258.0	82	1 288	134.0	22.5	1 137	D	D	D
Euless	83	2 182	131.5	39.2	8	140	7.6	2.1	69	747	75.4	26.8
Farmers Branch	93	1 321	76.8	21.8	13	370	19.2	7.6	136	D	D	D
Flower Mound	100	2 056	79.9	24.4	24	D	D	D	140	D	D	D
Fort Worth	1 103	23 998	1 246.1	339.1	128	2 245	243.5	50.1	1 325	19 388	2 197.9	856.8
Friendswood	74	D	D	D	11	159	9.7	3.2	94	D	D	D
Frisco	178	4 689	257.7	74.7	29	D	D	D	225	D	D	D
Galveston	203	5 316	275.9	76.6	19	D	D	D	84	D	D	D
Garland	299	5 150	227.9	62.9	31	681	41.9	10.4	378	D	D	D
Georgetown	96	1 727	77.5	21.3	12	D	D	D	126	2 146	170.6	75.7
Grand Prairie	190	3 784	191.2	49.2	26	D	D	D	185	2 236	138.7	58.4
Grapevine	221	9 432	697.9	195.5	19	449	19.1	5.8	184	D	D	D
Greenville	64	1 319	55.0	16.2	6	66	1.7	0.5	100	1 165	107.6	45.2
Haltom City	67	889	33.8	8.8	6	106	4.5	1.5	33	D	D	D
Harker Heights	48	583	24.5	5.6	10	60	5.0	0.6	28	D	D	D
Harlingen	155	3 136	129.6	33.6	15	268	9.1	2.7	311	D	D	D
Houston	5 177	111 291	6 263.9	1 660.1	464	8 787	1 445.8	509.2	5 956	85 100	8 718.9	3 273.8
Huntsville	84	1 740	63.8	16.7	4	D	D	D	83	D	D	D
Hurst	97	2 035	100.4	25.7	12	D	D	D	104	1 196	109.7	42.4

1. Establishments subject to federal tax.

City	Other services[1], 2007				Government employment and payroll, 2012								
						March payroll							
							Percent of total for:						
	Number of establishments	Number of employees	Receipts (mil dol)	Annual payroll (mil dol)	Full-time equivalent employees	Total (dollars)	Administration, judicial, and legal	Police and Corrections	Fire Protection	Highways and transportation	Health and welfare	Natural resources and utilities	Education and libraries
	104	105	106	107	108	109	110	111	112	113	114	115	116
TENNESSEE—Cont'd													
Columbia	57	D	D	D	492	1 828 149	7.0	18.8	18.5	8.4	0.0	42.6	0.0
Cookeville	81	D	D	D	2 260	9 757 664	1.2	3.6	1.9	1.3	85.3	5.8	0.0
Franklin	130	998	77.1	23.4	635	2 507 514	14.1	24.5	24.1	7.9	2.9	21.9	0.0
Gallatin	50	324	17.6	5.4	429	1 515 188	8.8	22.7	17.5	5.7	0.0	40.3	0.0
Germantown	51	512	23.3	10.1	286	1 166 262	0.4	46.4	32.0	8.9	0.0	6.3	0.0
Hendersonville	84	522	38.9	11.2	317	1 225 951	9.7	37.8	33.9	3.9	0.4	5.6	0.0
Jackson	106	772	57.4	20.9	732	2 706 306	10.3	39.0	26.4	6.9	0.2	15.5	0.0
Johnson City	128	756	51.2	16.2	2 069	7 207 080	4.3	9.1	5.7	7.6	0.0	24.2	46.3
Kingsport	94	730	47.4	14.6	2 088	7 112 728	4.6	8.2	5.7	3.4	0.1	9.0	66.2
Knoxville	429	3 172	228.3	77.7	2 544	10 707 196	7.3	20.0	11.8	5.2	1.3	49.6	0.0
La Vergne	27	674	88.8	26.4	165	495 446	15.9	42.8	0.0	4.2	0.0	26.3	4.3
Lebanon	52	305	26.1	7.0	337	1 064 568	9.9	34.9	13.8	8.3	1.8	27.1	0.0
Maryville	65	D	D	D	929	3 586 065	5.2	6.5	5.0	4.0	0.0	15.5	63.0
Memphis	857	7 640	632.5	192.5	24 196	79 305 378	2.0	15.7	10.1	4.9	0.8	25.5	40.2
Morristown	52	263	17.8	5.3	417	1 625 386	6.0	20.1	18.2	6.1	0.3	38.5	0.0
Murfreesboro	162	927	70.6	23.5	2 265	7 333 077	3.8	13.4	9.7	3.3	0.2	20.3	45.7
Nashville-Davidson	981	10 214	724.8	273.9	21 697	83 700 973	6.4	13.3	7.5	1.1	9.0	11.1	49.9
Oak Ridge	46	D	D	D	1 132	4 632 934	5.5	7.1	8.2	4.8	1.0	10.3	62.3
Smyrna	41	D	D	D	426	1 763 154	14.1	27.9	24.5	2.1	0.0	27.9	0.0
Spring Hill	21	D	D	D	153	514 319	5.2	29.3	24.9	4.9	0.0	23.4	4.4
TEXAS	28 404	209 702	17 917.8	5 592.5	X	X	X	X	X	X	X	X	X
Abilene	176	1 144	82.2	23.3	1 115	4 154 689	10.5	32.0	23.1	4.8	5.7	16.9	2.3
Allen	67	499	28.6	11.1	662	2 925 255	11.5	28.9	20.0	3.9	2.3	27.3	4.5
Amarillo	302	2 230	169.5	46.6	2 117	7 521 677	9.3	27.1	24.7	8.3	4.8	19.1	2.1
Arlington	406	3 093	225.6	71.3	2 551	12 130 944	13.1	38.1	20.5	5.1	4.7	13.8	2.7
Austin	1 246	11 182	899.4	315.4	12 580	64 599 610	10.4	24.1	13.4	7.1	8.1	30.6	1.9
Baytown	105	D	D	D	748	3 193 832	12.8	28.9	19.0	2.5	7.2	18.6	3.5
Beaumont	191	1 680	141.1	43.6	1 387	7 544 738	11.5	29.5	22.1	6.9	9.1	14.8	1.6
Bedford	51	329	21.0	7.6	396	1 910 062	12.2	44.6	25.8	2.3	0.9	11.0	3.3
Big Spring	38	D	D	D	255	860 648	10.2	23.3	19.7	6.6	10.8	21.6	0.0
Brownsville	126	570	33.7	8.6	1 660	6 576 268	6.3	28.3	16.9	10.1	3.1	22.4	2.2
Bryan	119	D	D	D	926	4 516 110	3.1	19.6	11.5	1.8	0.7	38.5	3.0
Burleson	50	D	D	D	314	1 837 857	11.3	27.1	16.3	3.9	5.4	20.8	2.6
Carrollton	166	1 685	192.9	64.0	750	3 791 660	11.3	30.8	28.1	4.7	3.6	12.4	3.2
Cedar Hill	39	D	D	D	345	1 415 937	9.4	29.5	24.7	6.8	4.1	17.5	2.3
Cedar Park	72	D	D	D	366	1 608 634	12.6	30.9	18.4	2.3	0.5	20.7	3.2
Cleburne	56	375	29.4	8.6	331	1 384 254	10.9	25.9	23.1	7.1	3.7	23.7	1.6
College Station	67	458	23.2	7.5	818	3 487 614	20.0	22.9	18.5	6.9	0.0	27.4	0.0
Conroe	111	758	73.6	19.7	506	2 148 894	13.0	28.8	20.3	9.4	1.3	18.9	0.0
Coppell	46	D	D	D	374	2 007 729	18.0	24.0	25.7	6.8	0.9	15.3	4.2
Copperas Cove	43	336	39.8	10.7	265	875 963	7.7	30.2	19.1	1.6	1.2	17.4	2.0
Corpus Christi	408	3 133	308.9	98.3	2 747	10 789 288	5.1	28.6	19.2	4.2	3.3	21.1	1.6
Dallas	1 567	12 760	1 252.6	351.6	14 235	67 511 933	7.3	31.8	17.3	19.3	4.4	14.9	1.2
Deer Park	67	D	D	D	328	1 382 968	18.7	32.7	5.3	2.7	0.0	31.9	2.9
Del Rio	30	D	D	D	479	1 348 047	13.5	25.7	21.8	5.8	8.4	17.9	0.0
Denton	139	766	57.5	17.6	1 265	6 238 827	15.5	19.1	17.6	2.9	1.6	38.3	2.8
DeSoto	37	156	16.2	4.1	317	1 509 174	9.4	33.2	25.8	4.2	5.1	12.0	3.0
Duncanville	70	376	31.2	9.4	262	1 180 545	13.5	32.0	24.0	4.8	0.9	15.2	3.2
Eagle Pass	26	D	D	D	351	916 457	7.8	31.5	17.9	15.9	3.9	20.4	1.6
Edinburg	77	253	18.6	4.9	687	2 190 991	12.2	35.3	5.2	5.7	1.0	33.1	3.3
El Paso	705	4 510	278.2	84.6	5 996	23 812 936	7.0	28.9	21.6	16.9	1.4	12.9	2.2
Euless	52	D	D	D	434	2 144 456	12.6	34.2	21.4	3.9	1.0	17.4	4.5
Farmers Branch	74	1 254	71.1	31.3	372	1 986 448	11.5	30.7	24.2	3.4	5.2	21.2	0.0
Flower Mound	79	696	29.9	14.5	440	1 883 026	25.4	26.1	22.5	3.5	4.1	11.7	3.5
Fort Worth	699	6 713	548.7	177.5	6 536	32 292 472	9.5	36.9	20.2	4.1	1.8	17.7	2.4
Friendswood	54	D	D	D	194	961 732	21.4	48.5	0.4	6.3	7.0	10.9	5.4
Frisco	115	935	58.5	20.2	594	2 715 180	9.9	30.4	23.9	5.3	1.2	19.8	3.8
Galveston	73	422	27.9	8.5	808	3 423 101	7.9	29.1	17.6	21.5	3.7	16.9	0.0
Garland	256	1 263	107.1	33.9	1 920	9 882 194	9.5	22.2	17.3	5.1	4.8	30.5	2.2
Georgetown	71	475	30.2	9.5	540	2 310 226	14.5	21.6	17.8	5.7	3.2	24.6	2.8
Grand Prairie	122	1 761	110.1	43.4	1 169	5 599 824	10.7	29.3	27.8	5.1	5.9	13.3	1.6
Grapevine	78	866	76.3	20.1	572	2 942 808	10.6	24.3	22.7	7.0	1.2	13.7	2.9
Greenville	45	202	15.7	4.6	403	1 671 286	7.6	21.2	16.8	3.9	1.7	41.0	1.8
Haltom City	67	728	72.3	16.5	281	1 111 357	13.5	36.6	17.0	6.0	1.5	13.9	4.9
Harker Heights	22	83	6.6	1.6	218	830 939	17.0	29.4	23.6	4.0	1.0	16.2	3.2
Harlingen	91	570	36.2	10.2	751	2 448 262	8.2	27.6	19.8	7.2	2.5	27.1	1.8
Houston	3 343	32 243	2 860.5	952.6	21 007	99 616 057	8.7	36.5	20.9	7.6	4.6	8.9	1.5
Huntsville	47	298	19.2	5.1	308	1 115 825	24.2	27.0	5.3	6.6	0.0	23.7	2.4
Hurst	73	D	D	D	371	1 783 347	13.7	36.1	21.5	5.6	0.0	15.6	6.0

1. Establishments subject to federal tax.

City	City government finances, 2007									
	General revenue							General expenditure		
		Intergovernmental		Taxes					Per capita[1] (dollars)	
					Per capita[1] (dollars)					
	Total (mil dol)	Total (mil dol)	Percent from state government	Total (mil dol)	Total	Property	Sales and gross receipts	Total (mil dol)	Total	Capital outlays
	117	118	119	120	121	122	123	124	125	126
TENNESSEE—Cont'd										
Columbia	41.4	15.4	53.0	12.6	360	269	88	40.7	1 166	252
Cookeville	277.1	19.0	22.5	9.4	303	201	101	277.4	8 954	919
Franklin	87.6	39.1	37.2	24.4	368	176	192	85.2	1 285	230
Gallatin	34.4	11.7	42.9	11.9	376	302	74	33.1	1 045	154
Germantown	61.8	21.1	73.1	24.7	627	570	58	65.4	1 661	429
Hendersonville	35.8	16.0	45.5	13.8	260	194	66	34.8	655	51
Jackson	87.7	28.3	31.7	40.9	609	491	118	83.5	1 243	137
Johnson City	163.0	78.4	55.6	47.4	732	608	124	167.9	2 594	204
Kingsport	166.0	83.1	48.9	57.0	1 080	915	166	164.5	3 118	644
Knoxville	351.6	81.3	38.7	163.6	898	585	313	318.2	1 747	425
La Vergne	25.4	7.8	50.3	10.3	306	225	80	18.7	553	55
Lebanon	28.1	13.4	31.2	6.1	218	112	106	31.0	1 113	106
Maryville	74.6	37.7	68.6	28.4	1 027	932	95	71.2	2 571	85
Memphis	2 270.7	1 329.3	61.2	520.3	789	551	237	2 276.9	3 451	425
Morristown	51.1	16.0	22.3	12.8	440	314	127	46.1	1 582	230
Murfreesboro	157.1	75.8	58.2	48.0	422	310	112	168.1	1 476	135
Nashville-Davidson	2 398.7	624.4	98.0	1 220.6	1 952	1 260	691	2 431.3	3 888	403
Oak Ridge	134.1	83.4	33.6	34.7	1 182	710	463	107.5	3 666	210
Smyrna	53.2	16.9	24.7	11.2	269	186	83	50.3	1 205	109
Spring Hill	19.8	7.0	49.1	5.7	182	127	55	26.7	857	343
TEXAS	X	X	X	X	X	X	X	X	X	X
Abilene	137.0	15.0	30.9	83.5	697	279	418	116.5	972	130
Allen	117.2	4.4	12.3	78.6	873	457	416	125.1	1 390	272
Amarillo	243.2	33.1	39.3	120.2	614	172	442	262.0	1 339	339
Arlington	460.5	35.2	25.8	242.5	644	301	343	480.0	1 275	145
Austin	1 410.8	92.8	27.1	613.6	709	410	298	1 511.5	1 746	382
Baytown	105.9	8.6	14.0	43.5	589	251	339	126.1	1 710	339
Beaumont	168.9	28.1	23.8	91.4	782	377	405	178.4	1 526	395
Bedford	41.1	0.8	100.0	27.1	562	290	272	42.9	889	121
Big Spring	26.6	1.5	86.7	14.4	521	200	321	29.9	1 081	134
Brownsville	224.1	50.4	11.0	74.7	415	197	218	175.9	976	181
Bryan	85.5	6.5	55.6	40.7	522	297	225	96.3	1 235	236
Burleson	54.3	0.2	84.0	35.0	897	409	488	43.5	1 115	101
Carrollton	128.2	6.2	86.1	88.8	708	435	273	119.3	951	184
Cedar Hill	54.5	2.8	12.5	34.8	748	403	345	54.1	1 163	158
Cedar Park	71.9	5.6	100.0	42.4	732	349	383	67.0	1 156	349
Cleburne	51.2	3.4	11.5	26.3	884	463	421	43.9	1 472	106
College Station	94.1	3.3	25.7	53.8	549	255	294	101.4	1 036	172
Conroe	70.6	1.0	16.8	50.6	824	235	589	74.4	1 211	375
Coppell	72.0	0.3	100.0	58.2	1 451	828	624	65.6	1 638	306
Copperas Cove	25.8	0.6	100.0	14.2	425	258	167	73.0	2 187	1 475
Corpus Christi	357.9	29.6	42.3	191.7	614	280	333	389.3	1 246	290
Dallas	2 544.8	172.7	56.8	1 084.4	872	545	327	2 543.0	2 045	435
Deer Park	42.3	0.3	34.3	19.4	585	370	215	36.3	1 097	77
Del Rio	34.7	4.3	47.7	15.1	418	189	229	37.0	1 026	201
Denton	169.7	11.5	79.7	94.5	765	357	408	149.1	1 207	175
DeSoto	50.0	1.3	100.0	32.7	640	413	227	48.8	954	113
Duncanville	37.1	1.0	60.3	22.7	573	320	253	42.9	1 085	220
Eagle Pass	32.1	2.3	62.3	10.6	387	159	228	32.6	1 184	237
Edinburg	72.5	6.4	81.8	40.8	518	269	249	71.1	903	197
El Paso	743.5	92.0	24.8	386.6	572	287	285	621.6	920	181
Euless	66.2	1.7	13.5	42.6	806	223	583	61.4	1 162	109
Farmers Branch	55.4	0.8	73.5	41.0	1 395	732	663	53.3	1 813	185
Flower Mound	74.2	2.2	6.5	54.3	800	457	343	76.4	1 125	247
Fort Worth	1 108.5	81.2	53.9	609.6	783	466	317	1 116.7	1 434	341
Friendswood	32.1	3.1	8.8	20.8	562	394	168	35.6	963	285
Frisco	214.9	32.8	2.5	125.6	977	507	469	202.2	1 572	466
Galveston	180.4	62.3	54.6	58.9	1 217	502	716	182.3	3 769	1 529
Garland	228.5	19.9	12.3	106.8	457	312	145	234.9	1 004	127
Georgetown	65.1	3.9	87.5	35.5	675	289	386	70.7	1 345	298
Grand Prairie	252.2	40.5	30.9	131.5	723	393	330	217.4	1 195	147
Grapevine	125.9	3.7	100.0	94.8	1 953	609	1 344	92.9	1 916	312
Greenville	39.6	2.4	41.3	19.8	762	371	392	43.8	1 690	468
Haltom City	42.3	2.2	23.7	24.5	565	230	336	38.1	878	131
Harker Heights	24.0	0.5	27.3	15.5	558	324	234	26.5	951	239
Harlingen	87.2	13.1	29.3	40.5	615	250	365	112.2	1 703	650
Houston	3 667.9	315.0	27.9	1 921.4	888	474	414	3 697.9	1 708	274
Huntsville	32.1	1.0	50.9	14.9	376	122	253	30.5	766	52
Hurst	51.1	2.4	26.0	34.8	911	328	583	49.1	1 285	225

1. Based on population estimated as of July 1 of the year shown.

City	City government finances, 2012 (cont.)									
	General expenditure (cont.)									
	Percent of total for:									
	Public welfare	Highways	Parking facilities	Education	Health and hospitals	Police protection	Sewerage and sanitation	Parks and recreation	Housing and community development	Interest on debt
	127	128	129	130	131	132	133	134	135	136
TENNESSEE—Cont'd										
Columbia	0.0	10.7	0.0	0.0	0.0	16.5	23.4	4.1	0.0	2.9
Cookeville	0.0	1.2	0.0	0.0	84.6	2.6	1.6	1.0	0.0	1.2
Franklin	0.0	10.0	0.0	0.0	0.0	16.6	17.5	4.0	0.2	6.0
Gallatin	0.0	5.6	0.0	0.0	0.4	19.4	17.8	11.9	0.0	1.4
Germantown	0.0	27.4	0.0	0.0	0.5	17.1	10.4	14.4	2.9	1.4
Hendersonville	0.0	12.3	0.0	0.0	0.0	27.4	13.2	7.3	0.0	1.2
Jackson	0.0	14.0	0.0	0.0	0.2	25.1	12.3	11.3	3.2	3.2
Johnson City	0.5	5.3	0.0	40.8	0.0	8.8	12.9	8.4	0.3	4.0
Kingsport	0.0	3.2	0.0	40.7	0.0	7.2	9.4	4.1	0.3	3.0
Knoxville	0.0	3.1	0.3	0.0	0.0	15.7	31.2	5.9	3.8	8.0
La Vergne	0.7	9.0	0.0	0.0	0.1	30.0	21.7	6.8	0.0	2.9
Lebanon	0.0	8.4	0.0	0.0	0.0	25.7	25.8	7.6	0.0	1.0
Maryville	0.0	3.8	0.0	66.8	0.3	6.3	5.5	2.0	0.0	3.6
Memphis	0.0	1.2	0.0	52.3	0.0	9.9	4.8	1.6	6.4	4.4
Morristown	0.6	10.0	0.0	0.0	0.0	15.5	27.8	3.8	1.6	1.5
Murfreesboro	0.1	11.1	0.1	38.8	0.0	13.6	8.2	6.7	0.8	2.6
Nashville-Davidson	1.3	1.6	0.0	34.8	9.5	8.0	6.5	3.3	0.0	7.0
Oak Ridge	0.0	2.3	0.0	52.8	0.0	6.5	10.1	3.7	0.6	3.4
Smyrna	0.5	5.1	0.0	0.0	0.0	18.7	11.2	12.4	0.3	2.6
Spring Hill	0.0	9.8	0.0	0.0	0.0	14.6	51.6	2.8	0.0	0.9
TEXAS	X	X	X	X	X	X	X	X	X	X
Abilene	0.0	7.3	0.0	0.0	3.8	18.8	16.3	6.3	1.0	2.9
Allen	0.0	4.2	0.0	0.0	0.2	15.6	11.7	22.6	1.0	5.9
Amarillo	0.0	6.1	0.0	0.0	6.0	13.9	17.9	6.7	4.4	2.1
Arlington	0.1	9.3	0.0	0.0	0.9	17.6	13.8	7.7	1.1	26.6
Austin	0.0	7.5	0.0	0.0	6.9	17.8	18.1	8.2	3.3	5.9
Baytown	0.0	9.2	0.0	0.0	3.4	15.7	9.1	9.2	2.3	5.4
Beaumont	0.0	21.9	0.0	0.0	5.1	21.4	8.4	9.5	1.2	4.0
Bedford	0.0	4.8	0.0	0.0	0.8	24.7	12.9	6.3	0.0	5.0
Big Spring	0.0	5.1	0.0	0.0	7.7	15.7	16.2	15.7	0.0	2.1
Brownsville	1.3	7.1	0.3	0.0	1.0	18.2	22.3	5.7	1.0	5.9
Bryan	0.0	9.9	0.0	0.0	0.0	16.0	19.2	3.8	1.3	6.5
Burleson	0.0	9.7	0.0	0.0	1.7	16.8	16.6	12.8	0.0	9.0
Carrollton	0.0	12.5	0.0	0.0	2.0	17.5	10.3	7.8	2.6	6.3
Cedar Hill	0.1	6.3	0.0	0.0	0.3	19.0	15.2	8.6	0.0	7.0
Cedar Park	0.0	19.4	0.0	0.0	0.4	11.4	13.6	7.0	0.0	10.8
Cleburne	0.0	5.5	0.0	0.0	1.7	16.6	19.7	9.4	3.6	4.0
College Station	0.0	15.6	1.2	0.0	0.0	13.7	18.3	9.5	1.4	5.1
Conroe	0.0	11.1	0.0	0.0	0.0	18.9	12.0	15.3	0.4	6.4
Coppell	0.0	7.8	0.0	0.0	0.5	14.6	6.7	17.0	0.0	5.6
Copperas Cove	0.0	63.3	0.0	0.0	0.5	6.3	7.5	2.6	0.0	4.4
Corpus Christi	0.0	10.6	0.1	0.0	1.8	18.9	23.2	9.8	3.9	3.6
Dallas	0.7	5.5	0.0	0.0	1.0	14.0	11.3	7.1	1.9	16.7
Deer Park	0.0	3.7	0.0	0.0	0.6	17.6	14.8	15.5	0.0	4.5
Del Rio	3.2	16.9	0.0	0.0	1.4	17.0	15.7	4.1	0.0	4.6
Denton	0.0	8.4	0.0	0.0	0.6	14.7	25.1	9.1	1.2	4.9
DeSoto	0.0	7.2	0.0	0.0	1.1	16.2	19.1	6.8	0.0	10.7
Duncanville	0.0	7.7	0.0	0.0	0.7	17.1	17.5	22.4	0.0	2.2
Eagle Pass	0.0	20.2	0.0	0.0	0.2	16.0	19.6	9.2	0.0	4.5
Edinburg	0.0	4.6	0.0	0.0	2.0	17.8	26.4	14.6	1.5	3.2
El Paso	0.4	3.1	0.0	0.0	3.3	18.8	16.2	4.6	2.2	8.5
Euless	0.0	6.2	0.0	0.0	0.5	16.4	4.4	12.4	0.1	3.2
Farmers Branch	0.0	11.0	0.0	0.0	1.5	20.8	10.8	13.5	0.0	2.3
Flower Mound	0.2	27.9	0.0	0.0	1.1	16.1	10.1	9.8	0.1	4.3
Fort Worth	0.0	9.2	0.3	0.0	1.3	21.0	19.0	7.6	3.1	5.7
Friendswood	0.0	4.5	0.0	0.0	3.2	21.8	12.3	5.4	1.7	2.4
Frisco	0.0	14.8	0.0	4.9	0.6	9.4	9.2	9.5	0.2	12.3
Galveston	0.0	12.7	0.0	0.0	0.3	9.8	11.8	9.1	14.0	5.5
Garland	0.0	6.6	0.0	0.0	1.3	19.5	18.2	8.0	6.9	6.4
Georgetown	0.0	19.8	0.0	0.0	0.9	12.7	17.5	8.6	0.0	5.3
Grand Prairie	0.0	8.1	0.0	0.0	0.7	16.1	13.9	10.7	14.8	6.4
Grapevine	0.0	8.5	0.0	0.0	0.0	14.9	6.7	16.5	0.0	4.9
Greenville	0.0	8.7	0.0	0.0	0.0	15.0	24.1	3.8	3.9	3.5
Haltom City	0.0	7.6	0.0	0.0	0.9	19.6	15.2	2.7	0.0	5.1
Harker Heights	0.0	3.6	0.0	0.0	0.0	18.2	17.1	6.8	0.0	4.4
Harlingen	0.0	5.5	0.0	0.0	0.6	11.9	13.7	4.7	0.7	3.1
Houston	0.0	10.0	0.2	0.0	3.0	16.1	6.5	2.7	2.5	13.3
Huntsville	0.0	8.0	0.0	0.0	1.5	17.2	34.7	4.6	0.0	4.1
Hurst	0.0	11.9	0.0	0.0	2.5	22.9	10.3	15.1	0.0	3.7

City	City government finances, 2012 (cont.)			Climate[2]						
	Debt outstanding			Average daily temperature (degrees Fahrenheit)						
				Mean		Limits				
	Total (mil dol)	Per capita[1] (dollars)	Debt issued during year	January	July	January[3]	July[4]	Annual precipitation (inches)	Heating degree days	Cooling degree days
	137	138	139	140	141	142	143	144	145	146
TENNESSEE—Cont'd										
Columbia	73.5	2 105	17.0	35.6	77.2	25.0	88.5	56.13	4 183	1 267
Cookeville	143.9	4 643	5.1	NA	NA	NA	NA	NA	NA	NA
Franklin	172.8	2 606	19.4	35.1	77.4	25.2	88.9	54.33	4 199	1 294
Gallatin	47.2	1 492	8.7	NA	NA	NA	NA	NA	NA	NA
Germantown	32.1	815	6.0	37.9	81.1	28.2	91.1	53.63	3 491	1 838
Hendersonville	11.8	222	0.3	36.8	79.1	27.9	88.7	48.11	3 677	1 652
Jackson	119.1	1 772	10.0	37.1	79.6	28.2	89.4	54.86	3 649	1 648
Johnson City	422.8	6 531	15.0	34.2	74.2	24.3	84.8	41.33	4 445	956
Kingsport	225.1	4 268	41.5	35.6	76.2	26.2	86.9	44.44	4 178	1 139
Knoxville	920.7	5 055	198.0	38.5	78.7	30.3	88.2	48.22	3 531	1 527
La Vergne	25.9	769	1.0	NA	NA	NA	NA	NA	NA	NA
Lebanon	61.0	2 191	5.9	NA	NA	NA	NA	NA	NA	NA
Maryville	130.5	4 709	0.0	NA	NA	NA	NA	NA	NA	NA
Memphis	2 500.9	3 791	107.2	39.9	82.5	31.3	92.1	54.65	3 041	2 187
Morristown	126.8	4 355	37.3	NA	NA	NA	NA	NA	NA	NA
Murfreesboro	318.3	2 795	1.6	35.4	78.1	25.3	89.1	54.98	4 107	1 388
Nashville-Davidson	4 895.0	7 828	800.3	36.8	79.1	27.9	88.7	48.11	3 677	1 652
Oak Ridge	170.4	5 812	11.1	36.6	77.3	27.2	88.1	55.05	3 993	1 301
Smyrna	71.6	1 717	2.4	36.8	79.1	27.9	88.7	48.11	3 677	1 652
Spring Hill	21.6	692	10.8	NA	NA	NA	NA	NA	NA	NA
TEXAS	X	X	X	X	X	X	X	X	X	X
Abilene	132.7	1 106	22.6	43.5	83.5	31.8	94.8	23.78	2 659	2 386
Allen	179.7	1 997	8.8	41.8	82.4	31.1	92.7	41.01	2 843	2 060
Amarillo	366.9	1 876	40.4	35.8	78.2	22.6	91.0	19.71	4 318	1 344
Arlington	2 154.5	5 724	564.5	44.1	85.0	34.0	95.4	34.73	2 370	2 568
Austin	5 572.8	6 438	681.1	50.2	84.2	40.0	95.0	33.65	1 648	2 974
Baytown	189.8	2 575	22.4	51.6	83.6	41.9	91.6	53.75	1 471	2 841
Beaumont	353.3	3 022	53.2	51.1	83.1	41.1	92.7	57.38	1 548	2 734
Bedford	61.2	1 268	14.8	44.1	85.0	34.0	95.4	34.73	2 370	2 568
Big Spring	23.3	843	0.0	42.7	82.7	29.6	94.3	20.12	2 724	2 243
Brownsville	528.4	2 931	23.6	59.6	83.9	50.5	92.4	27.55	644	3 874
Bryan	362.9	4 655	34.6	50.2	84.6	39.8	95.6	39.67	1 616	2 938
Burleson	130.3	3 340	17.8	NA	NA	NA	NA	NA	NA	NA
Carrollton	168.5	1 343	0.0	44.1	85.0	34.0	95.4	34.73	2 370	2 568
Cedar Hill	156.9	3 375	18.0	43.7	84.3	33.2	94.9	34.54	2 437	2 508
Cedar Park	214.5	3 700	8.4	47.2	83.8	35.1	95.7	36.42	1 998	2 584
Cleburne	132.4	4 443	26.5	45.9	84.5	34.0	97.0	36.25	2 158	2 604
College Station	242.2	2 475	47.0	50.2	84.6	39.8	95.6	39.67	1 616	2 938
Conroe	196.2	3 194	37.9	50.3	83.7	40.0	94.3	49.32	1 647	2 793
Coppell	93.5	2 332	21.3	44.1	85.0	34.0	95.4	34.73	2 370	2 568
Copperas Cove	98.1	2 937	52.5	46.0	83.5	34.0	95.3	32.88	2 190	2 477
Corpus Christi	1 152.6	3 689	80.5	56.1	83.8	46.2	93.2	32.26	950	3 497
Dallas	7 943.6	6 389	1 246.4	45.9	86.5	36.4	96.1	37.05	2 219	2 878
Deer Park	44.9	1 359	0.0	54.3	84.5	45.2	93.6	53.96	1 174	3 179
Del Rio	64.8	1 795	0.1	51.3	85.3	39.7	96.2	18.80	1 417	3 226
Denton	501.7	4 062	45.1	42.7	83.6	32.0	94.1	37.79	2 650	2 269
DeSoto	130.8	2 556	20.2	46.0	84.6	35.0	96.0	38.81	2 130	2 608
Duncanville	19.1	483	6.9	45.9	86.5	36.4	96.1	37.05	2 219	2 878
Eagle Pass	61.2	2 224	14.7	NA	NA	NA	NA	NA	NA	NA
Edinburg	98.1	1 246	24.2	58.7	85.1	48.2	95.5	22.61	719	3 898
El Paso	1 534.1	2 270	166.5	45.1	83.3	32.9	94.5	9.43	2 543	2 254
Euless	51.8	980	9.6	44.1	85.0	34.0	95.4	34.73	2 370	2 568
Farmers Branch	24.3	827	0.0	45.9	86.5	36.4	96.1	37.05	2 219	2 878
Flower Mound	129.5	1 908	3.6	44.1	85.0	34.0	95.4	34.73	2 370	2 568
Fort Worth	2 401.8	3 084	394.8	43.3	84.5	31.4	96.6	34.01	2 509	2 466
Friendswood	66.6	1 804	17.5	54.3	84.5	45.2	93.6	53.96	1 174	3 179
Frisco	640.8	4 982	148.2	41.8	82.4	31.1	92.7	41.01	2 843	2 060
Galveston	316.3	6 539	9.9	55.8	84.3	49.7	88.7	43.84	1 008	3 268
Garland	905.7	3 873	152.4	45.9	86.5	36.4	96.1	37.05	2 219	2 878
Georgetown	168.4	3 205	21.7	47.2	83.8	35.1	95.7	36.42	1 998	2 584
Grand Prairie	447.1	2 458	34.9	44.1	85.0	34.0	95.4	34.73	2 370	2 568
Grapevine	142.7	2 942	0.0	42.4	84.0	30.8	95.5	34.66	2 649	2 340
Greenville	148.3	5 723	11.5	NA	NA	NA	NA	NA	NA	NA
Haltom City	60.4	1 392	15.4	43.0	84.1	31.4	95.7	34.12	2 608	2 358
Harker Heights	50.6	1 819	8.0	NA	NA	NA	NA	NA	NA	NA
Harlingen	118.7	1 803	50.3	58.6	84.4	48.4	94.5	28.13	737	3 736
Houston	13 983.7	6 459	2 478.6	54.3	84.5	45.2	93.6	53.96	1 174	3 179
Huntsville	38.9	977	5.0	48.5	83.2	39.0	93.8	48.51	1 835	2 600
Hurst	57.6	1 508	9.1	44.1	85.0	34.0	95.4	34.73	2 370	2 568

1. Based on the population estimated as of July 1 of the year shown. 2. Represents normal values based on the 30-year period, 1971–2000. 3. Average daily minimum. 4. Average daily maximum.

STATE Place code	City	Land area,[1] 2010 (sq km)	Population, 2014: Total persons	Population, 2014: Rank	Population, 2014: Per square kilometer	Race alone or in combination (percent), 2011-2013: White	Black	American Indian, Alaska Native	Asian	Hawaiian Pacific Islander	Percent Hispanic or Latino[2], 2011-2013	Percent foreign born 2011–2013
		1	2	3	4	5	6	7	8	9	10	11
	TEXAS—Cont'd											
48 37000	Irving	173.6	232 406	93	1 338.7	56.4	13.8	1.0	16.5	0.1	39.7	34.3
48 38632	Keller	47.8	43 924	841	918.9	91.5	2.9	0.4	5.2	NA	7.3	6.6
48 39148	Killeen	138.8	138 154	188	995.3	53.1	37.3	2.2	6.1	1.9	25.1	8.3
48 39352	Kingsville	35.8	26 529	1 378	741.0	85.8	5.0	1.0	3.0	NA	75.6	8.9
48 39952	Kyle	49.4	32 881	1 128	665.6	74.9	7.3	NA	1.1	NA	49.4	8.1
48 40588	Lake Jackson	50.4	27 604	1 329	547.7	83.3	6.2	0.4	5.5	NA	23.2	6.9
48 41212	Lancaster	78.4	38 453	966	490.5	32.7	66.6	0.5	NA	NA	22.1	8.4
48 41440	La Porte	48.3	35 039	1 066	725.4	86.5	6.2	2.3	1.4	NA	31.1	10.2
48 41464	Laredo	230.3	252 309	80	1 095.6	94.6	0.5	0.5	0.7	0.0	95.2	26.4
48 41980	League City	132.8	94 403	320	710.9	84.0	8.9	1.2	6.5	NA	18.0	8.5
48 42016	Leander	59.2	34 172	1 086	577.2	91.8	5.4	NA	3.1	NA	29.2	6.9
48 42508	Lewisville	94.3	102 889	287	1 091.1	77.9	11.8	2.1	9.5	0.6	30.4	19.9
48 43012	Little Elm	37.7	35 414	1 053	939.4	76.3	14.9	0.6	5.6	NA	26.3	15.7
48 43888	Longview	144.2	81 593	402	565.8	73.4	22.8	1.3	1.7	NA	19.8	10.3
48 45000	Lubbock	317.0	243 839	85	769.2	80.4	9.3	1.4	3.0	0.3	33.6	5.9
48 45072	Lufkin	86.4	36 141	1 034	418.3	65.6	29.6	0.5	1.4	NA	24.5	10.5
48 45384	McAllen	125.2	138 596	187	1 107.0	89.2	1.3	0.9	2.8	NA	84.8	29.9
48 45744	McKinney	161.1	156 767	157	973.1	82.6	11.3	0.9	5.8	0.1	19.9	12.2
48 46452	Mansfield	94.2	62 246	570	660.8	75.9	17.8	1.1	5.4	NA	14.0	9.6
48 47892	Mesquite	119.2	144 416	180	1 211.5	69.1	24.1	0.9	3.7	NA	35.4	16.7
48 48072	Midland	186.7	128 037	210	685.8	80.7	8.7	1.1	1.9	NA	39.9	9.8
48 48768	Mission	88.0	82 431	397	936.7	93.6	0.8	NA	1.4	NA	85.9	28.2
48 48804	Missouri City	73.6	71 710	477	974.3	35.4	44.4	1.0	16.2	NA	15.1	20.4
48 50256	Nacogdoches	70.1	33 687	1 102	480.6	65.9	29.2	1.6	2.2	NA	18.1	10.3
48 50820	New Braunfels	113.6	66 394	527	584.5	93.3	3.0	NA	1.2	NA	38.8	7.5
48 52356	North Richland Hills	47.1	68 529	502	1 455.0	86.8	5.4	1.5	4.5	NA	17.8	9.8
48 53388	Odessa	108.7	114 597	239	1 054.3	86.6	7.1	1.7	1.8	NA	53.3	12.8
48 55080	Paris	94.5	24 895	1 423	263.4	71.9	25.9	3.0	1.5	NA	6.9	4.4
48 56000	Pasadena	110.8	153 887	163	1 388.9	81.3	3.0	2.5	2.5	NA	63.5	24.4
48 56348	Pearland	121.8	103 441	283	849.3	63.1	17.8	0.7	14.3	NA	21.7	17.3
48 57176	Pflugerville	57.8	54 644	678	945.4	76.0	14.8	1.4	8.0	NA	31.1	15.9
48 57200	Pharr	60.7	75 382	446	1 241.9	94.2	0.3	0.3	0.5	NA	94.0	32.7
48 58016	Plano	185.4	278 480	70	1 502.0	72.0	8.4	1.0	19.9	0.1	14.2	24.0
48 58820	Port Arthur	199.2	54 548	680	273.8	50.6	38.1	0.8	7.7	NA	32.6	22.0
48 61796	Richardson	74.0	108 617	264	1 467.8	69.0	9.7	1.3	17.0	0.6	17.7	24.3
48 62828	Rockwall	71.7	41 785	883	582.8	88.6	7.5	1.9	3.3	0.9	17.4	8.7
48 63284	Rosenberg	58.2	34 468	1 078	592.2	77.9	13.0	0.4	2.1	NA	61.1	16.9
48 63500	Round Rock	88.4	112 744	244	1 275.4	80.2	11.6	1.2	7.0	0.1	30.8	14.5
48 63572	Rowlett	51.5	58 407	628	1 134.1	74.7	18.6	1.0	7.0	NA	18.1	12.5
48 64472	San Angelo	147.3	98 975	301	671.9	86.8	5.7	1.2	1.9	NA	39.4	6.1
48 65000	San Antonio	1 193.8	1 436 697	7	1 203.5	78.5	7.9	1.4	3.1	0.3	63.0	14.1
48 65516	San Juan	29.7	36 174	1 032	1 218.0	97.2	NA	NA	NA	NA	98.5	31.1
48 65600	San Marcos	78.3	58 892	621	752.1	87.4	5.5	1.5	2.0	0.5	40.7	5.2
48 66128	Schertz	73.6	36 896	1 006	501.3	85.9	11.0	0.7	4.9	NA	27.2	6.5
48 66644	Seguin	89.3	27 041	1 357	302.8	81.2	10.9	1.7	2.1	NA	51.6	8.2
48 67496	Sherman	107.2	39 943	930	372.6	79.5	13.9	2.7	2.6	NA	21.1	10.5
48 68636	Socorro	57.1	32 909	1 127	576.3	81.4	0.7	2.9	NA	NA	96.1	34.3
48 69032	Southlake	56.7	29 086	1 268	513.0	90.3	2.9	0.2	8.1	NA	7.3	9.0
48 70808	Sugar Land	83.9	86 777	366	1 034.3	52.6	7.9	0.8	38.9	NA	10.7	34.5
48 72176	Temple	178.7	70 765	484	396.0	78.5	17.2	0.7	3.6	NA	22.7	8.0
48 72368	Texarkana	75.2	37 225	996	495.0	58.2	39.7	1.4	1.7	NA	6.3	4.0
48 72392	Texas City	165.3	46 639	805	282.1	70.8	26.2	0.8	NA	NA	30.2	7.3
48 72530	The Colony	36.3	41 352	893	1 139.2	83.4	7.6	1.4	8.0	NA	18.5	15.0
48 74144	Tyler	139.5	101 421	293	727.0	70.7	24.3	0.7	2.7	0.1	22.8	12.2
48 75428	Victoria	91.9	66 094	529	719.2	85.6	8.5	3.1	1.7	NA	48.9	5.7
48 76000	Waco	230.4	130 194	199	565.1	70.9	22.0	0.7	2.3	0.1	31.6	11.2
48 76816	Waxahachie	123.4	32 344	1 152	262.1	80.0	14.1	1.6	0.3	NA	25.8	7.4
48 76864	Weatherford	64.4	27 769	1 317	431.2	92.1	3.6	2.6	1.9	NA	14.9	4.8
48 77272	Weslaco	38.1	37 601	983	986.9	94.7	0.9	0.2	1.0	NA	85.8	19.7
48 79000	Wichita Falls	186.8	105 114	277	562.7	81.7	13.9	1.6	3.3	0.2	20.0	7.4
48 80356	Wylie	54.5	45 913	814	842.4	76.7	14.6	1.4	6.1	NA	19.4	11.0
49 00000	UTAH	212 818.3	2 942 902	X	13.8	90.1	1.6	1.7	3.0	1.4	13.2	8.4
49 01310	American Fork	23.8	28 152	1 300	1 182.9	95.7	0.9	1.4	2.8	0.9	5.0	5.1
49 07690	Bountiful	34.8	43 385	853	1 246.7	94.3	0.9	0.9	2.7	1.0	7.4	3.9
49 11320	Cedar City	95.4	29 483	1 249	309.0	94.5	1.3	2.7	1.9	1.2	7.6	3.8
49 13850	Clearfield	19.7	30 484	1 212	1 547.4	86.7	3.8	1.5	3.3	NA	16.6	5.2
49 16270	Cottonwood Heights	22.9	34 166	1 088	1 492.0	92.6	1.6	1.6	5.9	1.8	4.8	7.4
49 20120	Draper	77.9	46 202	811	593.1	92.7	1.2	1.4	3.2	0.7	6.0	5.6
49 36070	Holladay	20.5	27 129	1 352	1 323.4	95.9	0.7	NA	2.2	NA	4.6	6.8

1. Dry land or land partially or temporarily covered by water. 2. May be of any race.

City	Age of population (percent), 2011-2013									Median age 2011-2013	Percent female 2011-2013	Population			
												Census counts		Percent change	
	Under 5 years	5 to 17 years	18 to 24 years	25 to 34 years	35 to 44 years	45 to 54 years	55 to 64 years	65 to 74 years	75 years and over			2000	2010	2000–2010	2010–2014
	12	13	14	15	16	17	18	19	20	21	22	23	24	25	26
TEXAS—Cont'd															
Irving	8.9	17.5	9.1	20.0	16.2	12.6	8.2	4.2	3.1	31.9	50.4	191 615	216 290	12.9	7.5
Keller	4.9	25.1	6.0	7.9	16.0	18.0	12.1	6.5	3.4	40.0	50.2	27 345	39 627	44.9	10.8
Killeen	10.4	20.4	12.7	19.8	13.8	10.7	6.7	3.5	2.0	27.8	50.7	86 911	127 921	47.2	8.0
Kingsville	7.6	17.6	21.8	14.4	10.4	8.2	8.7	5.9	5.3	26.5	47.7	25 575	26 213	2.5	1.2
Kyle	9.4	26.1	7.2	17.3	19.1	10.5	6.0	2.7	1.7	30.1	51.3	5 314	28 016	427.2	17.4
Lake Jackson	5.6	20.7	9.3	13.1	12.8	15.6	11.4	5.9	5.5	36.1	51.1	26 386	26 849	1.8	2.9
Lancaster	8.2	23.3	8.9	11.9	16.7	13.6	9.1	4.4	3.8	32.8	54.1	25 894	36 361	40.4	4.9
La Porte	6.9	19.5	9.4	13.5	14.4	14.6	12.6	5.8	3.4	35.4	48.0	31 880	33 800	6.0	3.7
Laredo	9.8	24.5	11.1	13.7	13.8	10.9	7.9	4.7	3.6	28.6	51.3	176 576	236 091	33.7	6.9
League City	7.3	19.4	8.0	14.6	15.1	16.3	10.7	5.4	3.4	35.4	50.3	45 444	83 560	83.9	13.0
Leander	9.1	25.3	6.1	12.1	21.3	13.9	6.3	4.2	1.7	33.1	51.6	7 596	26 521	249.1	30.1
Lewisville	7.7	19.3	8.8	19.3	16.3	12.7	8.3	4.8	2.7	32.4	51.5	77 737	95 290	22.6	8.0
Little Elm	10.7	23.5	3.8	19.0	20.3	10.8	7.3	2.8	1.7	31.2	49.0	3 646	25 898	610.3	36.8
Longview	7.6	18.1	10.6	14.1	12.2	12.8	11.1	6.6	7.0	34.8	50.8	73 344	80 455	9.7	1.4
Lubbock	7.1	16.8	18.9	15.1	10.5	11.1	9.5	5.8	5.2	29.2	50.8	199 564	229 573	15.0	6.3
Lufkin	7.5	19.3	11.7	12.0	10.8	11.8	12.0	6.0	8.9	34.6	51.1	32 709	35 067	7.2	3.1
McAllen	7.5	21.3	10.7	13.8	13.9	11.8	10.1	6.4	4.6	32.7	51.0	106 414	129 877	22.0	6.4
McKinney	8.4	22.6	7.9	13.6	17.4	13.9	8.3	4.6	3.4	33.7	50.2	54 369	131 117	141.2	19.6
Mansfield	7.3	23.6	7.0	11.2	16.8	16.3	9.6	5.6	2.7	35.9	49.4	28 031	56 368	101.1	10.4
Mesquite	8.2	21.5	10.1	14.6	13.3	13.6	10.1	4.8	3.8	31.9	53.1	124 523	139 824	12.3	3.4
Midland	8.5	18.9	10.6	15.9	12.0	12.2	11.0	5.4	5.5	31.9	51.3	94 996	111 147	17.0	15.2
Mission	9.0	25.4	9.7	11.1	14.0	11.6	7.8	7.0	4.5	30.2	51.5	45 408	77 058	69.7	6.1
Missouri City	4.8	18.7	10.0	10.5	13.3	16.2	15.1	7.5	4.0	39.8	52.3	52 913	67 358	27.3	7.3
Nacogdoches	7.1	12.9	30.0	12.8	9.8	9.5	7.4	5.2	5.4	25.0	55.4	29 914	32 996	10.3	2.4
New Braunfels	7.3	20.7	8.2	15.4	13.1	11.6	9.9	7.3	6.6	33.9	51.3	36 494	57 740	58.2	15.0
North Richland Hills	6.8	16.9	9.5	14.9	11.8	15.2	12.6	6.1	6.3	36.8	51.5	55 635	63 343	13.9	8.2
Odessa	8.7	19.8	11.0	16.6	11.9	11.8	10.6	4.8	4.9	31.1	49.7	90 943	99 940	9.9	14.7
Paris	8.0	16.7	10.7	12.9	11.5	13.1	10.7	9.5	7.0	36.3	55.0	25 898	25 171	-2.8	-1.1
Pasadena	8.1	21.9	11.3	14.4	12.8	12.5	10.4	4.7	4.0	30.8	50.0	141 674	149 043	5.2	3.1
Pearland	8.2	20.7	8.0	13.5	17.1	13.8	9.7	4.7	4.2	34.8	50.8	37 640	91 252	142.4	15.1
Pflugerville	8.2	21.0	6.9	11.1	15.8	17.4	12.1	5.1	2.4	37.1	51.3	16 335	46 936	187.3	13.0
Pharr	9.6	25.9	10.6	14.2	13.5	8.6	7.5	4.7	5.3	28.0	52.1	46 660	70 400	50.9	7.0
Plano	6.2	19.1	7.5	13.3	15.3	16.3	12.0	6.6	3.7	37.8	50.5	222 030	259 841	17.0	7.2
Port Arthur	8.8	19.9	9.8	13.3	11.8	13.4	11.2	5.4	6.5	33.4	49.9	57 755	53 818	-6.8	0.3
Richardson	6.2	16.7	10.5	13.0	14.8	14.4	11.5	7.2	5.7	37.3	49.7	91 802	99 223	8.1	9.5
Rockwall	5.0	23.3	7.4	12.0	14.9	14.4	11.4	7.7	4.0	36.5	51.8	17 976	37 490	108.6	11.2
Rosenberg	9.6	21.3	12.2	15.3	13.6	10.2	7.9	5.6	4.3	28.8	52.2	24 043	30 618	27.3	9.8
Round Rock	9.9	21.4	9.3	15.9	16.2	13.6	7.4	4.2	2.0	31.4	51.8	61 136	99 887	63.4	12.8
Rowlett	4.8	20.6	9.8	9.5	15.5	18.5	11.5	6.2	3.6	37.9	50.3	44 503	56 199	26.3	3.8
San Angelo	7.3	16.1	14.9	15.1	9.8	11.8	10.8	7.5	6.7	32.3	51.0	88 439	93 200	5.4	6.2
San Antonio	7.4	18.8	11.3	15.5	13.0	12.9	10.2	6.1	4.9	32.8	51.2	1 144 646	1 327 407	16.0	8.2
San Juan	9.6	24.3	10.9	13.6	13.5	10.0	9.2	4.9	3.9	28.7	51.5	26 229	33 856	29.1	6.8
San Marcos	4.6	10.1	41.8	17.0	8.5	6.2	5.2	3.7	3.1	23.5	50.9	34 733	44 894	29.3	30.7
Schertz	7.0	18.9	9.2	13.8	13.0	15.5	11.1	6.7	4.7	35.8	51.3	18 694	31 465	68.3	16.1
Seguin	6.3	19.3	12.9	11.1	11.7	12.6	10.0	7.7	8.4	35.4	50.5	22 011	25 175	14.4	7.4
Sherman	6.7	17.7	13.8	14.0	11.3	12.2	11.5	6.5	6.4	33.1	51.6	35 082	38 521	9.8	4.2
Socorro	7.3	23.3	11.8	11.4	13.8	11.4	11.6	6.2	3.3	31.3	50.2	27 152	32 013	17.9	2.7
Southlake	4.4	28.6	3.8	4.3	13.7	22.3	14.4	4.4	4.1	42.5	49.7	21 519	26 575	23.5	9.4
Sugar Land	5.1	17.9	8.1	10.0	13.3	17.0	16.5	7.5	4.5	41.8	51.1	63 328	78 817	24.5	10.4
Temple	7.6	17.7	8.2	16.2	11.6	12.5	12.0	7.3	7.0	35.4	51.0	54 514	66 102	21.3	6.7
Texarkana	7.9	16.9	10.3	13.9	11.9	12.4	12.5	7.0	7.1	35.5	52.4	34 782	36 411	4.7	2.2
Texas City	8.4	18.4	8.2	14.6	12.4	11.7	13.2	7.3	5.8	35.3	51.0	41 521	45 099	8.6	3.4
The Colony	6.9	16.8	10.0	17.3	15.8	15.4	11.5	3.8	2.5	34.4	49.6	26 531	36 328	36.9	13.8
Tyler	6.2	16.9	14.1	14.4	11.5	11.0	10.8	7.1	8.0	33.7	53.6	83 650	96 900	15.8	4.6
Victoria	7.3	18.9	9.9	13.5	11.8	13.2	11.7	7.3	6.4	35.3	51.0	60 603	62 592	3.3	5.6
Waco	8.1	16.4	19.5	13.6	10.7	10.8	9.4	5.2	6.2	29.1	51.7	113 726	124 805	9.7	4.3
Waxahachie	7.7	21.4	9.9	15.0	13.0	11.7	11.0	5.7	4.7	31.6	52.3	21 426	29 621	38.2	9.3
Weatherford	7.5	19.9	9.8	13.8	13.2	12.0	9.2	7.9	6.9	34.6	53.7	19 000	25 250	32.9	10.0
Weslaco	9.1	22.7	7.0	12.1	12.1	10.3	9.6	9.2	8.0	33.8	53.2	26 935	35 670	32.4	6.1
Wichita Falls	6.3	16.3	15.3	14.8	11.3	12.5	10.6	6.6	6.2	32.7	47.6	104 197	104 553	0.3	0.4
Wylie	6.9	23.4	8.6	12.7	20.9	13.0	7.8	3.9	2.7	33.8	51.7	15 132	41 427	173.8	10.9
UTAH	9.0	22.1	11.4	15.5	12.6	10.7	9.2	5.4	4.1	29.9	49.7	2 233 169	2 763 885	23.8	6.5
American Fork	8.5	27.3	11.3	11.3	13.8	10.0	7.5	5.3	5.0	27.9	49.6	21 941	26 263	19.7	6.5
Bountiful	7.5	21.2	9.0	13.1	11.0	12.0	9.5	7.1	9.6	34.2	52.2	41 301	42 552	3.0	1.9
Cedar City	10.2	17.5	21.2	15.6	9.4	8.9	7.8	5.2	4.1	25.5	51.5	20 527	28 857	40.6	2.2
Clearfield	10.6	24.5	10.8	18.5	12.8	9.5	7.4	3.6	2.4	27.9	48.8	25 974	30 112	15.9	1.2
Cottonwood Heights	5.9	16.5	11.0	15.3	11.8	13.1	12.7	8.7	5.0	35.9	51.5	27 569	33 433	21.3	2.2
Draper	9.6	24.4	6.9	14.6	17.0	12.8	8.9	3.7	2.1	30.9	47.5	25 220	42 274	67.6	9.3
Holladay	5.5	17.8	6.4	14.6	11.7	12.1	13.3	9.5	9.3	40.1	51.6	14 561	26 472	81.8	2.5

City	Households, 2011-2013: Number	Households: Persons per household	Households: Percent: Female family householder[1]	Households: Percent: One-person	Persons in group quarters, 2010: Total	Institutional: Total	Institutional: Persons in nursing facilities	Non-institutional	Serious crimes known to police,[2] 2013: Total: Number	Total: Rate[3]	Rate[3]: Violent	Rate[3]: Property	Educational attainment, 2011-2013: Population age 25 and older	Attainment[4] (percent): High school graduate or less	Attainment[4] (percent): Bachelor's degree or more
	27	28	29	30	31	32	33	34	35	36	37	38	39	40	41
TEXAS—Cont'd															
Irving	83 099	2.69	12.7	30.9	873	393	393	480	6 705	2 936	232	2 704	144 634	40.3	35.2
Keller	14 042	2.97	5.4	15.6	251	251	251	0	417	978	63	915	26 807	14.3	57.0
Killeen	43 715	3.07	18.6	25.4	179	97	60	82	5 544	4 060	551	3 509	76 040	36.0	19.5
Kingsville	9 073	2.65	18.8	23.0	1 791	293	173	1 498	1 066	4 069	393	3 676	13 652	48.9	24.8
Kyle	9 142	3.30	9.3	14.4	391	388	0	3	581	1 831	284	1 547	17 568	36.4	26.7
Lake Jackson	10 343	2.62	12.7	26.8	57	56	56	1	629	2 306	147	2 160	17 511	28.0	30.7
Lancaster	12 743	2.93	21.7	26.7	360	359	359	1	1 712	4 481	468	4 012	22 498	42.4	16.8
La Porte	11 528	2.98	12.9	17.3	64	46	46	18	633	1 826	115	1 710	22 101	48.0	14.3
Laredo	64 782	3.72	22.3	15.1	3 479	2 014	367	1 465	11 509	4 653	415	4 238	133 525	58.0	16.8
League City	32 597	2.71	8.2	23.4	471	471	368	0	2 014	2 248	107	2 141	58 100	22.7	43.1
Leander	8 983	3.29	11.6	15.1	0	0	0	0	362	1 181	85	1 096	17 603	32.2	31.3
Lewisville	38 336	2.58	13.2	28.8	399	286	264	113	2 995	2 974	243	2 731	63 749	36.1	31.0
Little Elm	9 055	3.28	15.7	15.9	0	0	0	0	394	1 315	160	1 155	18 402	31.7	27.9
Longview	30 419	2.58	16.8	30.4	3 690	1 913	767	1 777	3 823	4 704	555	4 149	52 063	44.2	20.0
Lubbock	88 352	2.55	14.1	29.5	9 933	2 400	1 214	7 533	13 386	5 627	769	4 858	135 184	39.1	28.8
Lufkin	13 067	2.64	18.3	26.0	1 239	823	536	416	2 052	5 651	350	5 301	22 028	49.0	19.6
McAllen	41 915	3.20	16.2	21.9	1 110	899	890	211	5 595	4 109	126	3 983	81 763	47.0	26.5
McKinney	46 836	3.01	12.5	16.8	2 192	1 454	439	738	3 265	2 223	141	2 082	87 405	25.4	45.6
Mansfield	19 735	2.98	9.7	17.8	363	355	159	8	1 122	1 864	133	1 732	36 786	24.8	42.5
Mesquite	47 814	2.97	19.9	21.5	663	644	644	19	6 734	4 666	279	4 388	85 903	47.6	17.9
Midland	41 885	2.80	13.5	24.3	1 567	684	362	883	3 541	2 896	286	2 610	73 833	41.2	25.4
Mission	23 544	3.40	14.7	16.2	179	162	162	17	3 017	3 708	88	3 620	44 956	53.0	23.0
Missouri City	22 733	2.99	14.9	18.3	180	138	138	42	1 223	1 760	104	1 656	45 426	26.0	43.2
Nacogdoches	12 195	2.35	17.8	36.8	5 025	632	428	4 393	1 223	3 554	282	3 272	16 926	40.7	30.4
New Braunfels	21 656	2.78	15.3	24.1	940	666	411	274	2 300	3 731	238	3 492	39 033	38.2	27.7
North Richland Hills	24 946	2.62	11.2	25.5	294	267	267	27	1 794	2 722	238	2 484	43 885	31.6	29.9
Odessa	38 466	2.74	16.8	24.9	2 143	1 285	437	858	5 454	5 038	998	4 040	64 860	50.8	16.7
Paris	10 058	2.43	19.2	34.3	614	406	258	208	1 389	5 545	679	4 867	16 213	50.3	14.7
Pasadena	47 449	3.18	16.6	22.8	884	737	547	147	6 093	3 977	386	3 591	89 312	59.1	14.1
Pearland	33 563	2.91	12.4	17.6	318	312	299	6	2 088	2 127	156	1 971	61 883	27.4	45.1
Pflugerville	18 361	2.86	13.4	21.9	183	131	131	52	881	1 662	111	1 551	33 685	29.3	35.1
Pharr	20 380	3.58	22.6	16.3	19	15	0	4	2 739	3 705	311	3 394	39 330	64.0	13.4
Plano	102 489	2.64	10.1	23.7	859	791	733	68	6 400	2 321	148	2 173	182 333	19.6	53.7
Port Arthur	19 584	2.73	19.4	35.1	687	515	501	172	2 749	5 088	664	4 423	33 392	62.2	10.4
Richardson	38 930	2.63	11.5	24.6	931	517	501	414	2 886	2 760	122	2 637	68 832	24.4	49.5
Rockwall	13 781	2.87	11.9	17.2	325	325	158	0	758	1 866	62	1 804	25 753	27.3	38.6
Rosenberg	10 132	3.20	23.4	21.9	134	129	129	5	770	2 402	293	2 109	18 541	63.2	9.2
Round Rock	34 930	3.05	11.1	22.1	454	398	251	56	2 577	2 373	137	2 236	63 643	29.9	36.9
Rowlett	18 713	3.13	13.0	12.6	335	335	334	0	985	1 693	144	1 549	38 119	31.7	33.1
San Angelo	35 897	2.51	15.0	31.6	4 858	788	365	4 070	3 916	4 051	279	3 772	59 376	48.1	22.0
San Antonio	482 686	2.82	17.8	28.5	27 800	11 979	5 617	15 821	88 822	6 346	631	5 715	865 299	44.5	25.1
San Juan	8 877	3.95	18.3	9.8	121	112	112	9	1 262	3 546	537	3 009	19 413	68.8	9.5
San Marcos	18 357	2.44	12.4	33.0	6 202	729	300	5 473	2 105	4 065	425	3 640	22 012	36.4	31.0
Schertz	12 384	2.84	10.2	21.2	188	188	188	0	655	1 825	190	1 636	22 938	34.2	29.2
Seguin	8 878	2.79	17.1	33.1	1 644	881	396	763	1 179	4 427	229	4 197	16 170	58.7	14.0
Sherman	15 171	2.48	15.9	31.6	1 368	509	285	859	1 436	3 647	305	3 342	24 177	43.1	20.9
Socorro	8 855	3.67	26.0	13.0	25	0	0	25	517	1 572	176	1 396	18 745	70.4	6.7
Southlake	8 822	3.13	5.4	12.4	0	0	0	0	470	1 675	50	1 625	17 442	11.1	67.7
Sugar Land	27 030	3.00	8.1	16.3	1 413	1 245	313	168	1 721	2 062	129	1 933	56 598	19.5	53.9
Temple	24 176	2.79	12.4	29.3	1 613	989	908	624	2 264	3 237	242	2 996	45 969	45.3	24.5
Texarkana	13 955	2.57	21.1	32.0	1 641	1 469	554	172	2 629	7 017	878	6 139	24 108	42.2	28.1
Texas City	15 976	2.79	21.2	26.8	937	916	470	21	1 871	4 086	275	3 811	29 671	50.7	12.2
The Colony	14 403	2.68	8.7	30.0	0	0	0	0	604	1 514	120	1 393	25 573	29.0	32.5
Tyler	38 389	2.49	15.8	32.7	3 647	1 709	893	1 938	4 492	4 491	376	4 115	62 406	36.7	29.6
Victoria	23 960	2.63	17.3	27.8	1 324	1 053	478	271	2 902	4 466	611	3 855	41 083	49.5	16.6
Waco	46 225	2.59	16.2	32.6	8 019	3 026	1 488	4 993	5 937	4 654	404	4 250	71 560	48.6	21.3
Waxahachie	10 215	2.91	14.8	18.7	1 209	715	232	494	1 066	3 381	105	3 276	18 938	42.3	23.8
Weatherford	9 884	2.57	11.5	27.2	1 077	845	450	232	667	2 498	26	2 472	16 622	33.1	26.6
Weslaco	11 878	3.04	23.8	21.3	637	590	488	47	3 305	8 873	1 044	7 829	22 523	60.9	16.5
Wichita Falls	37 377	2.43	15.8	31.2	11 889	5 334	1 072	6 555	4 959	4 745	384	4 361	64 858	45.6	22.3
Wylie	13 495	3.22	12.8	14.7	155	155	155	0	563	1 247	73	1 174	26 631	28.8	34.4
UTAH	891 240	3.15	9.9	19.7	46 152	22 161	5 854	23 991	92 084	3 174	224	2 950	1 641 750	32.2	30.8
American Fork	7 748	3.49	10.8	18.2	283	72	62	211	843	2 245	69	2 176	14 499	25.7	32.6
Bountiful	14 131	3.01	9.2	19.7	330	318	318	12	1 232	2 867	151	2 715	26 741	23.0	38.2
Cedar City	9 471	2.98	10.5	24.3	986	259	83	727	755	2 587	267	2 320	14 905	29.7	30.0
Clearfield	9 632	3.14	12.0	20.9	1 263	144	96	1 119	671	2 205	131	2 073	16 467	41.1	19.4
Cottonwood Heights	12 155	2.79	8.7	18.6	14	0	0	14	919	2 687	108	2 578	22 619	21.4	45.8
Draper	12 090	3.42	11.3	11.1	3 960	3 960	71	0	1 139	2 549	90	2 460	26 232	21.5	38.9
Holladay	10 820	2.47	8.3	30.4	166	160	160	6	NA	NA	NA	NA	18 954	16.4	54.5

1. No spouse present. 2. Data for serious crimes have not been adjusted for underreporting. This may affect comparability between geographic areas and over time. 3. Per 100,000 population estimated by the FBI. 4. Persons 25 years old and over.

City	Money income, 2011–2013					Housing units, 2010			Occupied housing units 2011–2013				
		Households								Owner-occupied		Median owner costs as a percent of income	
	Per capita income[1] (dollars)	Median income	Percent with income of $200,000 or more	Percent with income of less than $25,000	Families with income below poverty (percent)	Total	Percent change, 2000–2010	Vacant units for sale or rent[2]	Total	Percent	Median value[3] (dollars)	With a mortgage[4]	Without a mortgage[5]
	42	43	44	45	46	47	48	49	50	51	52	53	54
TEXAS—Cont'd													
Irving	27 094	50 810	4.1	21.1	12.4	91 128	13.5	8 590	83 099	37.7	136 400	22.9	11.6
Keller	45 296	116 280	16.4	8.6	2.7	14 051	52.9	537	14 042	84.1	290 100	21.4	13.1
Killeen	19 325	45 575	0.9	24.5	13.2	53 913	52.8	5 861	43 715	48.0	119 200	23.7	10.0
Kingsville	16 334	35 692	0.8	38.4	24.1	10 354	-0.6	1 259	9 073	46.1	76 000	24.3	11.7
Kyle	24 754	76 141	1.0	9.6	3.1	9 226	NA	467	9 142	78.7	146 800	21.4	13.2
Lake Jackson	33 020	70 871	5.8	13.7	2.9	11 149	6.3	830	10 343	65.6	145 000	19.2	10.0
Lancaster	18 717	47 897	0.4	23.9	15.0	13 622	41.7	1 102	12 743	62.9	97 000	27.2	12.1
La Porte	26 982	68 037	1.9	16.3	9.0	12 875	10.2	985	11 528	72.1	120 300	18.9	10.7
Laredo	14 496	38 517	1.6	34.4	27.8	68 610	36.2	5 065	64 782	62.1	110 000	26.0	14.3
League City	37 689	84 271	6.9	8.6	3.2	32 119	86.3	1 927	32 597	71.5	173 000	20.8	11.4
Leander	29 072	77 766	4.3	9.3	5.5	8 949	NA	392	8 983	75.8	154 300	21.7	12.8
Lewisville	27 026	56 487	2.0	15.9	9.7	39 967	26.0	2 471	38 336	44.0	153 800	21.4	11.1
Little Elm	27 437	77 612	3.1	9.9	4.0	8 581	NA	421	9 055	81.4	159 800	25.0	10.0
Longview	23 604	41 365	2.5	29.2	14.0	32 751	6.8	2 189	30 419	54.7	125 500	21.2	11.7
Lubbock	23 537	43 413	3.1	29.6	13.4	95 926	14.2	7 420	88 352	53.9	110 800	20.8	11.9
Lufkin	21 508	36 512	2.8	32.7	17.1	14 183	5.9	1 255	13 067	51.4	95 100	19.9	12.4
McAllen	21 205	40 651	4.0	34.3	23.8	45 862	21.0	4 289	41 915	60.5	112 600	23.1	13.6
McKinney	32 808	81 076	8.5	12.3	7.3	47 915	146.7	3 562	46 836	67.0	190 400	21.4	13.0
Mansfield	36 235	89 200	8.8	12.9	5.7	19 106	103.0	801	19 735	77.6	179 600	21.8	12.1
Mesquite	20 815	47 298	1.3	21.9	14.1	51 952	11.9	3 562	47 814	58.0	106 800	23.6	11.6
Midland	34 306	63 819	8.2	17.1	8.1	44 708	12.3	2 821	41 885	63.4	159 000	20.2	10.0
Mission	17 454	41 579	2.0	30.6	22.2	27 291	54.0	4 174	23 544	72.9	94 100	24.0	12.6
Missouri City	33 903	84 963	7.8	10.0	3.9	23 374	34.0	998	22 733	84.0	159 600	21.4	12.1
Nacogdoches	19 600	31 593	2.5	41.1	23.7	13 635	10.3	1 493	12 195	39.8	121 900	21.6	11.2
New Braunfels	24 175	56 391	1.5	18.1	7.4	23 381	55.7	2 122	21 656	65.1	167 200	21.5	11.3
North Richland Hills	30 339	61 741	4.1	14.1	6.1	26 395	22.8	1 541	24 946	61.4	148 800	21.2	12.8
Odessa	25 868	54 009	3.0	21.4	11.1	39 806	4.8	3 198	38 466	61.1	105 600	18.3	10.3
Paris	18 641	30 556	1.3	40.0	24.6	11 883	1.0	1 577	10 058	49.5	69 800	21.5	13.4
Pasadena	20 159	46 948	2.7	27.5	18.0	53 899	6.9	5 428	47 449	55.0	101 800	22.9	11.5
Pearland	36 456	91 528	7.1	9.3	3.6	33 169	138.7	1 947	33 563	79.0	180 000	21.9	10.9
Pflugerville	29 946	71 729	5.5	13.9	7.2	16 418	209.9	629	18 361	78.2	163 600	22.6	10.0
Pharr	13 125	31 705	0.7	43.5	33.5	22 796	37.4	3 097	20 380	58.6	74 000	23.3	13.4
Plano	41 190	81 800	10.7	10.7	5.5	103 672	20.4	4 541	102 489	62.2	218 600	21.3	10.5
Port Arthur	17 698	31 473	1.2	41.9	28.3	23 577	-4.6	3 394	19 584	60.3	64 600	21.3	12.5
Richardson	34 300	70 031	7.4	15.8	6.2	40 630	11.7	1 916	38 930	60.1	190 300	20.4	12.1
Rockwall	37 584	93 070	7.2	10.4	2.5	13 957	96.1	745	13 781	76.4	184 200	19.3	12.5
Rosenberg	16 988	41 341	0.5	29.2	20.8	11 162	32.2	999	10 132	49.8	110 500	25.0	11.7
Round Rock	28 326	68 959	5.0	13.5	6.8	37 223	71.9	2 173	34 930	59.9	169 000	21.5	10.2
Rowlett	30 346	83 002	5.3	9.8	4.9	18 969	30.1	598	18 713	84.6	158 700	22.7	12.5
San Angelo	23 166	42 958	2.5	27.5	12.9	39 548	4.8	3 431	35 897	57.6	102 400	21.1	11.8
San Antonio	22 311	45 253	2.9	27.7	16.6	524 246	21.0	44 604	482 686	54.4	113 700	22.1	11.7
San Juan	13 650	36 732	1.8	30.7	29.2	9 740	25.8	858	8 877	74.8	81 600	26.7	12.7
San Marcos	16 697	28 381	1.5	41.8	15.7	18 179	36.8	1 148	18 357	28.8	122 600	24.7	13.7
Schertz	29 594	69 735	3.3	13.0	6.6	12 047	74.5	668	12 384	75.2	165 100	19.6	10.3
Seguin	17 697	33 583	1.7	38.9	18.7	9 714	18.7	920	8 878	62.9	96 100	24.3	15.4
Sherman	21 550	41 279	2.0	30.1	15.7	16 404	10.0	1 599	15 171	53.7	100 200	23.2	12.3
Socorro	11 585	30 741	0.2	39.2	31.5	9 313	28.0	521	8 855	74.6	80 600	28.6	12.3
Southlake	72 943	163 892	41.9	7.3	NA	8 494	28.7	301	8 822	92.6	508 600	24.0	12.9
Sugar Land	45 958	101 360	18.4	7.7	3.7	27 727	31.0	1 018	27 030	81.1	263 600	21.3	11.6
Temple	23 946	47 688	2.9	24.6	10.9	28 422	21.2	2 309	24 176	57.8	119 400	19.5	11.7
Texarkana	23 692	38 826	3.0	38.1	22.4	16 115	6.5	1 693	13 955	54.0	97 300	22.2	12.4
Texas City	19 937	42 780	0.9	29.6	17.5	18 773	12.6	2 145	15 976	58.6	98 200	21.8	11.2
The Colony	31 992	66 625	4.5	11.0	5.0	14 052	59.0	884	14 403	63.3	137 600	21.4	10.0
Tyler	26 733	43 239	4.8	28.9	14.0	41 742	17.4	3 846	38 389	53.0	129 300	22.3	11.7
Victoria	24 243	46 851	2.7	26.5	14.8	25 660	6.1	2 239	23 960	58.8	113 600	20.7	12.7
Waco	19 265	32 705	2.1	38.7	21.3	51 452	12.2	5 050	46 225	47.0	95 300	23.3	13.6
Waxahachie	21 721	53 719	1.6	22.3	11.7	11 554	47.0	1 097	10 215	58.3	128 400	21.4	12.8
Weatherford	25 026	51 983	2.0	22.3	9.3	10 853	31.3	1 083	9 884	59.8	136 700	21.7	12.1
Weslaco	15 149	34 647	1.0	38.9	26.2	14 394	41.0	3 182	11 878	63.3	71 600	23.7	14.7
Wichita Falls	22 574	43 903	2.4	28.6	14.4	43 632	4.3	5 178	37 377	57.3	90 900	21.2	12.7
Wylie	28 027	82 036	2.4	7.6	4.4	13 840	162.5	603	13 495	86.1	155 900	21.9	17.5
UTAH	23 760	58 561	3.8	18.5	9.7	979 709	27.5	102 017	891 240	69.5	206 600	23.5	10.0
American Fork	21 786	63 611	3.0	18.2	10.4	7 598	24.2	324	7 748	69.6	218 600	23.6	10.1
Bountiful	27 615	63 868	5.0	14.8	6.3	15 193	10.1	689	14 131	73.0	238 900	22.7	10.0
Cedar City	18 619	41 757	2.8	31.4	16.7	10 860	52.2	1 391	9 471	54.3	161 100	23.4	10.0
Clearfield	18 603	48 733	1.4	23.1	11.9	10 062	19.7	701	9 632	55.0	151 300	23.2	10.0
Cottonwood Heights	38 021	74 768	10.8	9.6	4.3	13 194	33.2	735	12 155	69.6	296 900	22.5	10.0
Draper	31 833	90 583	10.6	9.1	2.9	12 125	84.3	581	12 090	78.9	370 200	23.9	10.0
Holladay	42 042	69 779	10.8	18.1	4.6	10 537	99.0	610	10 820	72.5	347 800	24.1	10.0

1. Based on population estimated by the American Community Survey. 2. Includes units rented or sold but not occupied. 3. Specified owner-occupied units; $1,000,000 represents $1,000,000 or more 4. 50.0 represents 50 percent or more. 5. 10.0 represents 10 percent or less.

City	Occupied housing units, 2011–2013 (cont.): Percent renter occupied	Occupied housing units, 2011–2013 (cont.): Median gross rent[1]	Occupied housing units, 2011–2013 (cont.): Median rent as a percent of income[2]	Occupied housing units, 2011–2013 (cont.): Percent with no vehicle available	Migration, 2011–2013: Percent who lived in the same house one year ago	Migration, 2011–2013: Percent who lived outside current city one year ago	Civilian labor force, 2014: Total	Civilian labor force, 2014: Percent change, 2013–2014	Civilian labor force, 2014: Unemployment: Total	Civilian labor force, 2014: Unemployment: Rate[3]	Civilian employment[4], 2011–2013: Population age 16 and older	Civilian employment[4], 2011–2013: Percent: In labor force	Civilian employment[4], 2011–2013: Percent: Civilian full-year full-time workers	Civilian employment[4], 2011–2013: Households with no workers (percent)
	55	56	57	58	59	60	61	62	63	64	65	66	67	68
TEXAS—Cont'd														
Irving	62.3	880	26.1	5.5	76.9	11.7	124 307	2.4	5 953	4.8	170 604	73.0	51.0	14.1
Keller	15.9	1 170	30.4	1.7	85.2	11.4	22 372	1.3	919	4.1	31 079	67.0	46.9	17.4
Killeen	52.0	859	29.4	6.4	73.6	16.8	53 506	0.0	3 308	6.2	96 081	69.1	35.6	20.7
Kingsville	53.9	706	31.2	10.9	81.0	7.6	12 508	-0.3	658	5.3	20 005	61.4	32.0	27.0
Kyle	21.3	1 214	27.4	2.7	83.6	13.7	16 674	3.0	518	3.1	20 445	75.8	58.4	8.4
Lake Jackson	34.4	840	26.9	4.3	83.6	10.3	14 342	2.2	692	4.8	21 213	68.5	47.9	18.3
Lancaster	37.1	914	35.5	6.7	89.7	8.9	18 294	2.1	1 383	7.6	27 258	65.3	46.3	20.0
La Porte	27.9	1 016	28.2	3.1	84.7	11.0	19 019	1.7	1 000	5.3	26 567	70.2	47.6	18.8
Laredo	37.9	738	34.8	8.0	86.2	3.3	106 494	1.0	5 111	4.8	169 011	56.8	38.2	20.5
League City	28.5	1 135	23.9	2.5	85.3	11.7	52 156	2.0	2 106	4.0	67 230	73.2	53.2	15.4
Leander	24.2	1 306	31.7	2.4	77.0	18.8	16 460	2.8	573	3.5	20 374	76.1	51.7	11.1
Lewisville	56.0	932	26.9	4.5	75.9	16.3	61 268	2.7	2 564	4.2	75 036	77.2	54.6	13.9
Little Elm	18.6	1 376	27.3	1.3	89.8	8.3	16 672	2.9	583	3.5	20 479	74.5	54.5	11.3
Longview	45.3	772	30.0	7.0	77.2	10.7	40 659	0.5	1 962	4.8	63 120	61.9	40.4	27.4
Lubbock	46.1	799	33.8	5.7	72.6	12.3	124 444	0.5	4 802	3.9	185 496	67.4	41.3	23.4
Lufkin	48.6	768	34.0	6.1	76.0	11.5	16 014	0.0	813	5.1	26 907	61.5	36.1	33.2
McAllen	39.5	722	30.5	6.8	84.5	8.6	63 375	1.0	3 571	5.6	100 909	61.2	38.7	23.4
McKinney	33.0	1 102	29.1	3.3	84.6	9.0	78 040	2.6	3 476	4.5	103 564	69.9	52.6	13.4
Mansfield	22.4	1 134	32.5	2.2	87.1	10.0	32 790	1.5	1 392	4.2	42 926	73.5	51.4	14.3
Mesquite	42.0	944	30.9	4.9	83.6	10.4	75 487	2.3	4 065	5.4	105 327	70.8	48.1	17.4
Midland	36.6	991	27.5	4.4	81.5	9.2	74 825	6.0	2 115	2.8	89 271	69.1	50.1	16.4
Mission	27.1	683	31.8	7.0	92.4	5.3	33 186	1.1	2 318	7.0	55 818	57.3	35.3	26.1
Missouri City	16.0	1 309	26.4	2.2	91.7	6.0	38 960	2.2	1 933	5.0	54 374	70.9	49.8	15.9
Nacogdoches	60.2	714	33.8	11.7	68.3	15.9	14 879	-1.9	825	5.5	27 607	58.2	35.1	30.0
New Braunfels	34.9	941	30.8	4.1	82.1	10.1	32 389	1.5	1 222	3.8	45 582	67.0	46.1	23.1
North Richland Hills	38.6	926	28.9	4.2	84.3	11.5	38 300	1.5	1 728	4.5	52 255	70.4	50.9	18.0
Odessa	38.9	866	24.9	5.4	78.4	10.8	63 389	5.1	2 040	3.2	79 497	68.2	48.8	18.6
Paris	50.5	637	30.7	12.9	75.2	10.2	10 805	-0.9	701	6.5	19 510	59.4	34.3	36.8
Pasadena	45.0	772	29.7	6.6	79.2	11.1	70 591	1.7	4 247	6.0	111 913	64.2	40.4	22.9
Pearland	21.0	1 009	25.6	2.2	90.6	8.3	56 646	2.4	2 117	3.7	72 603	74.2	56.3	12.6
Pflugerville	21.8	1 078	34.6	3.3	92.2	6.7	30 225	2.8	1 115	3.7	39 030	74.3	54.5	15.2
Pharr	41.4	656	34.8	7.6	87.6	8.3	28 866	0.9	2 171	7.5	49 134	58.8	36.3	27.9
Plano	37.8	1 104	25.8	3.5	86.4	9.4	153 708	2.5	6 904	4.5	211 134	71.4	51.7	14.2
Port Arthur	39.7	648	31.4	12.1	83.7	7.9	22 896	-2.3	2 603	11.4	40 364	58.6	34.4	34.5
Richardson	39.9	1 057	27.2	3.7	83.4	12.5	56 910	2.4	2 629	4.6	82 244	69.4	47.0	18.3
Rockwall	23.6	1 256	26.8	2.8	88.3	9.4	20 933	2.3	910	4.3	29 911	69.0	49.9	19.2
Rosenberg	50.2	863	32.0	9.2	83.6	7.0	16 521	1.5	711	4.3	22 969	65.7	44.6	16.3
Round Rock	40.1	983	28.2	3.1	77.0	16.7	59 925	2.9	2 474	4.1	76 906	74.5	52.5	10.4
Rowlett	15.4	1 340	25.5	1.0	91.6	6.8	32 403	2.7	1 604	5.0	46 137	70.9	50.5	12.6
San Angelo	42.4	722	27.8	6.9	72.5	15.2	45 851	0.6	1 874	4.1	75 762	64.8	37.3	27.6
San Antonio	45.6	817	30.0	9.3	80.8	6.5	675 709	1.7	30 514	4.5	1 061 815	64.5	41.0	23.2
San Juan	25.2	578	27.0	5.6	91.6	6.2	14 627	0.7	1 162	7.9	24 082	60.9	37.9	22.9
San Marcos	71.2	903	45.2	5.4	60.5	23.0	27 936	2.6	1 199	4.3	44 240	64.6	28.2	23.1
Schertz	24.8	1 008	25.9	2.8	88.0	10.0	17 182	1.7	693	4.0	27 291	67.4	43.3	21.0
Seguin	37.1	725	30.1	9.9	82.8	9.1	12 298	1.7	551	4.5	20 509	60.4	38.0	30.6
Sherman	46.3	791	28.8	8.6	77.7	12.5	19 221	0.7	935	4.9	30 787	62.8	40.1	28.9
Socorro	25.4	690	37.4	6.1	92.8	6.4	13 353	-0.1	913	6.8	23 751	56.9	31.7	27.0
Southlake	7.4	781	28.5	1.5	91.1	6.7	13 441	1.6	594	4.4	20 047	62.7	43.8	13.9
Sugar Land	18.9	1 446	23.6	2.2	89.7	8.3	45 233	2.2	1 751	3.9	65 497	64.9	46.5	14.3
Temple	42.2	770	27.9	7.9	85.7	8.5	33 257	0.3	1 555	4.7	53 108	61.9	43.5	27.9
Texarkana	46.0	681	29.8	11.8	83.2	10.5	15 719	-1.6	949	6.0	29 073	55.6	34.1	34.2
Texas City	41.4	798	33.4	8.1	76.4	12.1	21 624	1.1	1 516	7.0	34 773	59.0	33.9	30.0
The Colony	36.7	1 103	28.4	1.3	85.6	12.5	25 051	2.8	1 119	4.5	30 544	80.1	58.8	11.6
Tyler	47.0	810	31.8	7.4	74.2	15.7	49 136	1.0	2 488	5.1	78 798	62.5	38.3	27.0
Victoria	41.2	769	29.2	7.6	78.7	9.6	33 369	1.2	1 384	4.1	49 535	65.3	42.8	25.7
Waco	53.0	719	34.0	10.4	73.1	13.1	56 892	-0.1	3 057	5.4	99 542	59.0	34.0	28.7
Waxahachie	41.7	892	32.4	6.5	74.7	12.3	15 960	2.4	715	4.5	22 734	65.8	45.0	20.9
Weatherford	40.2	896	29.1	6.5	81.7	10.2	12 382	1.4	579	4.7	19 881	64.0	42.2	26.0
Weslaco	36.7	648	32.9	7.6	82.2	10.5	14 545	-0.7	1 198	8.2	26 290	55.0	31.3	36.7
Wichita Falls	42.7	725	28.2	7.1	79.9	11.7	44 206	-0.8	2 177	4.9	83 315	61.8	36.7	26.7
Wylie	13.9	986	24.9	1.2	86.7	11.4	24 272	2.6	1 025	4.2	31 867	74.7	51.7	10.6
UTAH	30.5	863	29.5	4.7	82.8	12.4	1 431 104	1.5	54 158	3.8	2 057 343	68.0	40.6	19.4
American Fork	30.4	1 061	29.1	3.5	84.7	12.6	12 244	2.2	467	3.8	18 547	66.0	39.5	21.4
Bountiful	27.0	867	27.0	3.6	87.2	9.7	19 974	1.5	749	3.7	32 026	62.0	38.8	24.9
Cedar City	45.7	617	29.0	5.6	80.9	9.9	12 761	2.5	575	4.5	21 688	65.8	33.2	24.4
Clearfield	45.0	904	31.4	7.4	80.2	17.6	13 864	1.3	584	4.2	20 507	72.0	44.2	18.0
Cottonwood Heights	30.4	972	24.2	2.4	86.2	11.3	19 380	1.2	669	3.5	27 213	70.0	44.5	16.7
Draper	21.1	1 153	26.1	1.7	83.1	12.4	20 992	1.3	745	3.5	30 901	65.3	43.6	9.8
Holladay	27.5	945	27.8	2.6	88.0	10.5	13 638	1.0	464	3.4	21 112	65.0	40.0	26.5

1. $2,000 represents $2,000 or more. 2. 50.0 represents 50 percent or more. 3. Percent of civilian labor force. 4. Persons 16 years old and over.

City	Value of residential construction authorized by building permits, 2014			Wholesale trade,[1] 2007				Retail trade,[2] 2007			
	New construction ($1,000)	Number of housing units	Percent single family	Number of establish-ments	Number of employees	Sales (mil dol)	Annual payroll (mil dol)	Number of establish-ments	Number of employees	Sales (mil dol)	Annual payroll (mil dol)
	69	70	71	72	73	74	75	76	77	78	79
TEXAS—Cont'd											
Irving	284 366	1 553	31.6	380	9 717	13 529.5	643.1	645	14 897	4 784.6	376.6
Keller	114 560	526	64.4	26	185	43.9	4.8	91	1 417	355.5	30.1
Killeen	131 283	963	86.1	21	153	72.5	9.5	384	5 886	1 525.1	129.7
Kingsville	5 809	36	100.0	3	D	D	D	102	1 868	624.2	46.3
Kyle	84 325	751	67.2	7	111	51.8	3.7	27	273	112.7	12.0
Lake Jackson	1 509	8	100.0	11	48	16.1	2.1	120	2 683	582.4	52.6
Lancaster	18 977	89	100.0	14	264	97.6	11.2	60	1 004	227.1	23.6
La Porte	19 067	62	100.0	33	407	211.3	26.9	72	752	259.6	19.1
Laredo	186 839	1 719	55.5	348	2 501	1 468.1	78.8	811	12 789	2 900.5	234.5
League City	218 186	1 358	72.9	38	339	100.9	12.9	154	2 159	728.9	62.0
Leander	261 740	1 079	100.0	8	47	44.7	1.7	30	698	112.1	12.1
Lewisville	40 307	201	90.0	105	2 012	1 233.9	106.7	446	8 523	2 488.5	209.8
Little Elm	304 835	892	100.0	3	D	D	D	22	280	65.0	5.6
Longview	35 566	235	71.5	162	2 394	1 051.7	99.3	551	7 414	1 855.9	176.3
Lubbock	275 162	2 049	43.3	321	4 431	3 536.4	197.3	946	16 033	3 715.9	329.8
Lufkin	10 255	56	85.7	50	595	276.0	22.3	293	4 327	1 018.7	93.4
McAllen	99 003	608	67.8	255	2 504	1 828.8	86.8	893	15 462	3 599.1	303.1
McKinney	626 257	2 237	76.4	92	910	730.6	46.6	300	6 504	2 002.3	165.3
Mansfield	118 436	532	42.1	62	1 129	408.0	48.5	115	2 134	574.7	46.3
Mesquite	2 085	18	61.1	66	968	782.6	48.8	455	7 872	1 871.5	165.7
Midland	235 573	1 553	59.0	147	1 525	1 562.3	73.8	501	7 285	2 137.6	169.5
Mission	36 968	299	100.0	54	312	140.0	8.8	205	3 440	845.8	69.6
Missouri City	130 193	783	57.0	48	167	108.5	7.1	132	2 544	696.9	51.9
Nacogdoches	7 445	68	47.1	33	449	265.6	15.1	212	2 652	640.7	57.1
New Braunfels	257 981	1 506	70.1	46	451	712.2	20.3	285	4 089	1 284.6	105.3
North Richland Hills	25 541	95	100.0	35	325	91.6	15.1	190	4 220	1 376.9	116.7
Odessa	108 454	556	77.3	180	2 138	1 052.8	106.4	417	6 188	1 903.7	157.5
Paris	2 462	28	50.0	37	290	115.2	10.9	205	2 467	596.4	52.4
Pasadena	10 600	78	97.4	110	1 134	549.5	56.2	410	6 236	1 479.8	134.9
Pearland	304 884	2 076	51.4	47	646	334.8	32.1	181	3 135	779.6	71.3
Pflugerville	100 322	873	68.4	13	146	62.8	6.8	61	807	218.6	20.5
Pharr	24 169	364	68.7	105	1 221	622.4	44.1	183	2 416	613.2	51.4
Plano	287 925	2 017	26.0	372	5 651	4 512.4	422.8	1 086	22 006	7 210.4	585.7
Port Arthur	36 670	430	57.2	26	297	165.1	12.5	197	3 366	1 078.3	73.9
Richardson	90 964	627	15.2	270	9 924	12 498.2	900.6	353	5 001	1 910.8	165.3
Rockwall	64 327	266	100.0	41	173	63.9	7.8	168	2 790	787.0	64.6
Rosenberg	70 988	339	73.2	18	372	187.8	14.5	159	2 827	814.8	75.4
Round Rock	78 638	797	52.6	106	1 450	817.4	86.1	366	8 635	6 550.1	226.0
Rowlett	75 057	562	20.3	33	186	80.2	8.5	91	1 407	364.5	31.7
San Angelo	69 568	629	36.4	105	791	280.3	29.8	426	5 873	1 511.3	128.3
San Antonio	745 110	5 638	40.3	1 284	20 806	11 116.9	946.1	4 104	71 703	20 252.1	1 669.4
San Juan	7 443	110	100.0	10	93	53.9	3.3	57	666	156.6	12.6
San Marcos	39 493	243	100.0	31	353	208.8	14.2	379	6 463	1 331.8	112.8
Schertz	80 094	299	100.0	31	1 199	706.3	61.8	54	1 254	392.5	28.9
Seguin	14 634	87	100.0	32	414	143.8	11.4	144	1 744	433.7	39.5
Sherman	16 890	119	100.0	44	471	444.4	14.9	244	4 147	1 014.8	90.3
Socorro	14 187	161	96.3	15	67	24.5	1.4	61	334	69.0	5.6
Southlake	138 278	202	100.0	61	639	656.5	35.9	207	4 324	1 219.6	112.9
Sugar Land	89 475	429	40.8	152	2 248	3 573.1	110.8	410	7 114	1 719.9	154.9
Temple	109 120	622	99.5	62	2 387	3 972.4	103.4	302	4 084	1 133.8	98.0
Texarkana	6 660	82	100.0	75	874	1 459.9	31.9	368	5 330	1 241.0	118.0
Texas City	44 903	364	100.0	30	222	149.9	11.9	155	1 978	499.7	43.2
The Colony	36 902	77	100.0	11	146	121.5	10.3	53	808	204.6	18.2
Tyler	97 026	280	95.7	150	1 455	608.4	65.8	650	10 390	2 653.4	246.5
Victoria	85 491	835	19.5	79	1 046	461.9	45.0	371	5 694	1 346.2	123.6
Waco	156 358	1 245	30.9	137	2 251	4 248.8	90.8	601	8 393	1 970.7	176.8
Waxahachie	46 444	314	100.0	31	267	116.9	11.4	145	2 102	537.2	48.6
Weatherford	35 312	195	100.0	25	339	317.3	12.0	166	2 770	1 032.0	74.5
Weslaco	14 309	199	71.9	33	481	215.9	13.3	160	2 502	671.3	48.5
Wichita Falls	19 442	122	60.7	120	1 197	429.1	44.9	468	7 054	1 597.3	148.0
Wylie	59 932	251	100.0	21	434	80.9	7.3	43	000	221.5	24.5
UTAH	3 360 911	17 510	64.4	3 043	43 900	25 417.4	2 012.0	8 984	142 266	36 574.2	3 240.7
American Fork	19 693	93	86.0	29	322	160.0	15.2	132	2 605	724.2	57.9
Bountiful	17 976	65	63.1	25	137	19.7	2.8	138	2 165	594.5	52.5
Cedar City	23 285	142	71.8	28	338	250.6	12.7	163	2 016	558.5	43.0
Clearfield	5 433	40	100.0	26	492	349.9	22.4	57	629	123.9	9.7
Cottonwood Heights	7 401	21	100.0	32	349	357.4	25.4	69	1 641	1 048.5	65.4
Draper	58 084	219	78.5	49	481	165.4	26.6	157	2 957	820.7	78.6
Holladay	10 732	26	100.0	24	148	42.7	5.7	105	1 010	142.6	17.9

1. Merchant wholesalers except manufacturers' sales branches and offices. 2. Establishments with payroll.

City	Real estate and rental and leasing, 2007				Professional, scientific, and technical services,[1] 2007				Manufacturing, 2007			
	Number of establishments	Number of employees	Receipts (mil dol)	Annual payroll (mil dol)	Number of establishments	Number of employees	Receipts (mil dol)	Annual payroll (mil dol)	Number of establishments	Number of employees	Receipts (mil dol)	Annual payroll (mil dol)
	80	81	82	83	84	85	86	87	88	89	90	91
TEXAS—Cont'd												
Irving	351	4 341	1 571.2	242.7	844	D	D	D	187	9 661	3 441.1	465.2
Keller	34	189	44.8	6.4	148	476	69.8	20.1	NA	NA	NA	NA
Killeen	147	754	100.0	17.1	112	1 247	119.2	47.4	NA	NA	NA	NA
Kingsville	30	D	D	D	33	151	10.4	3.2	NA	NA	NA	NA
Kyle	5	17	1.2	0.4	17	46	12.6	2.2	NA	NA	NA	NA
Lake Jackson	35	326	59.6	11.0	46	D	D	D	NA	NA	NA	NA
Lancaster	20	87	12.4	2.2	18	107	7.6	3.3	30	1 351	259.8	48.3
La Porte	34	378	81.1	18.7	50	2 420	238.0	123.0	28	1 463	D	108.1
Laredo	201	D	D	D	309	D	D	D	89	914	242.4	30.7
League City	47	215	33.5	5.9	135	627	95.8	37.8	NA	NA	NA	NA
Leander	13	30	7.1	1.2	27	131	9.5	3.5	NA	NA	NA	NA
Lewisville	108	496	126.8	16.1	215	D	D	D	99	2 834	597.6	103.7
Little Elm	9	16	2.5	0.3	14	52	4.4	2.0	NA	NA	NA	NA
Longview	137	653	131.0	22.7	289	D	D	D	131	8 125	3 834.7	339.5
Lubbock	352	2 182	227.8	49.3	545	3 289	357.0	122.4	200	4 544	1 256.7	164.5
Lufkin	67	318	39.4	8.3	139	634	77.1	27.4	42	4 309	760.8	148.0
McAllen	234	959	202.2	26.8	427	D	D	D	95	2 197	605.0	70.0
McKinney	113	430	77.9	14.4	302	D	D	D	65	6 134	3 171.6	320.2
Mansfield	35	121	15.5	2.8	92	508	45.0	18.4	80	3 452	964.6	141.2
Mesquite	92	426	103.8	11.9	126	965	87.7	31.4	83	2 849	987.5	135.6
Midland	194	920	176.6	33.5	407	D	D	D	83	1 271	D	42.6
Mission	50	181	25.4	4.2	48	190	19.1	7.0	30	543	117.8	14.6
Missouri City	36	114	19.9	4.0	123	309	32.5	12.2	NA	NA	NA	NA
Nacogdoches	39	130	18.2	2.7	83	D	D	D	46	3 801	1 374.7	119.7
New Braunfels	95	380	63.0	10.1	131	458	44.8	15.6	64	2 516	655.8	89.8
North Richland Hills	61	403	43.6	10.1	111	D	D	D	22	832	385.5	35.9
Odessa	130	673	149.8	22.8	184	D	D	D	116	1 542	366.8	69.7
Paris	42	D	D	D	55	D	D	D	39	3 734	2 232.2	164.5
Pasadena	130	764	133.8	23.1	160	D	D	D	112	5 184	10 066.1	304.5
Pearland	66	430	123.7	15.2	137	512	53.7	22.4	65	2 462	450.0	101.3
Pflugerville	19	77	12.2	1.9	35	211	17.1	7.8	NA	NA	NA	NA
Pharr	40	321	36.0	6.3	54	584	30.6	10.4	NA	NA	NA	NA
Plano	394	3 094	533.4	133.4	1 281	D	D	D	164	4 870	1 072.4	282.7
Port Arthur	40	212	49.1	6.3	54	300	31.9	12.3	35	5 297	26 687.7	362.3
Richardson	166	799	134.4	31.8	667	D	D	D	146	6 824	1 883.9	429.3
Rockwall	36	D	D	D	138	D	D	D	50	D	247.8	D
Rosenberg	37	132	21.8	3.5	34	176	12.3	4.5	35	1 171	D	42.3
Round Rock	127	585	123.1	17.6	239	1 521	212.7	92.9	71	3 203	1 038.1	185.6
Rowlett	28	65	11.0	1.7	80	195	27.3	8.4	47	585	67.6	D
San Angelo	132	620	74.4	15.6	170	D	D	D	104	2 500	791.6	98.0
San Antonio	1 555	10 279	1 917.9	364.3	3 143	D	D	D	865	33 695	11 971.4	1 298.5
San Juan	6	40	2.3	0.4	11	D	D	D	NA	NA	NA	NA
San Marcos	78	306	56.3	7.6	76	1 226	58.4	24.6	38	2 060	532.4	84.8
Schertz	20	125	18.6	3.8	24	77	8.3	3.0	NA	NA	NA	NA
Seguin	35	215	24.7	5.5	48	184	13.3	5.4	49	4 371	1 145.3	176.0
Sherman	57	274	43.7	6.7	124	500	49.4	18.1	53	3 429	1 669.4	193.2
Socorro	7	29	2.3	0.4	4	30	1.2	0.4	NA	NA	NA	NA
Southlake	84	360	52.7	15.5	188	D	D	D	NA	NA	NA	NA
Sugar Land	154	652	175.5	27.8	408	2 930	486.4	182.1	63	4 819	1 577.9	227.7
Temple	82	400	64.5	11.1	100	D	D	D	62	5 283	1 604.2	191.9
Texarkana	79	376	49.5	9.8	133	D	D	D	37	D	D	D
Texas City	45	244	77.4	9.2	47	401	49.0	19.3	29	4 412	23 145.7	449.7
The Colony	17	109	29.6	3.7	35	135	7.5	2.7	NA	NA	NA	NA
Tyler	170	1 055	145.5	30.7	435	D	D	D	120	7 320	4 644.6	351.6
Victoria	107	697	112.6	26.9	138	D	D	D	56	D	D	D
Waco	146	1 150	246.9	47.4	268	D	D	D	153	11 568	5 303.2	463.8
Waxahachie	48	142	27.0	4.4	69	D	D	D	57	3 951	1 276.4	161.1
Weatherford	48	199	29.0	5.7	82	D	D	D	43	1 008	211.4	36.2
Weslaco	37	216	19.5	3.4	47	D	D	D	NA	NA	NA	NA
Wichita Falls	163	798	95.2	18.6	207	D	D	D	104	3 904	932.1	170.8
Wylie	20	84	10.9	1.7	39	D	D	D	38	1 963	608.9	85.1
UTAH	4 886	20 413	3 390.8	617.4	8 203	67 426	8 197.7	3 157.3	3 368	123 249	42 431.7	5 508.5
American Fork	65	193	16.8	6.7	106	2 245	133.1	64.1	24	687	202.2	38.3
Bountiful	78	200	22.7	5.1	180	D	D	D	NA	NA	NA	NA
Cedar City	75	160	26.9	3.5	95	D	D	D	63	D	729.3	57.8
Clearfield	33	117	38.1	3.6	49	1 225	285.8	97.7	45	5 091	1 388.6	209.8
Cottonwood Heights	176	785	146.4	33.9	208	1 630	289.3	121.4	27	834	120.1	36.0
Draper	105	277	55.7	9.1	200	1 172	170.2	58.1	45	1 259	299.9	50.3
Holladay	107	290	57.9	11.2	159	D	D	D	NA	NA	NA	NA

1. Establishments subject to federal tax.

City	Accommodation and food services, 2007				Arts, entertainment, and recreation,[1] 2007				Health care and social assistance,[1] 2007			
	Number of establish-ments	Number of employees	Sales (mil dol)	Annual payroll (mil dol)	Number of establish-ments	Number of employees	Receipts (mil dol)	Annual payroll (mil dol)	Number of establish-ments	Number of employees	Receipts (mil dol)	Annual payroll (mil dol)
	92	93	94	95	96	97	98	99	100	101	102	103
TEXAS—Cont'd												
Irving	489	12 088	722.7	199.5	49	D	D	D	450	D	D	D
Keller	69	1 042	48.9	13.5	9	188	8.4	2.0	105	939	86.9	32.9
Killeen	215	4 508	191.3	49.9	22	D	D	D	156	1 651	125.0	50.8
Kingsville	62	1 087	39.5	11.1	6	D	D	D	50	D	D	D
Kyle	19	227	11.4	2.3	3	D	D	D	12	D	D	D
Lake Jackson	53	1 227	56.3	14.7	6	146	4.8	1.8	126	D	D	D
Lancaster	34	497	22.3	5.6	6	26	1.7	0.5	40	D	D	D
La Porte	48	934	42.4	11.5	3	D	D	D	46	D	D	D
Laredo	358	D	D	D	29	D	D	D	399	11 210	654.6	258.7
League City	85	1 565	74.8	19.9	21	D	D	D	114	D	D	D
Leander	12	142	5.3	1.5	3	D	D	D	22	D	D	D
Lewisville	217	4 751	240.8	65.3	23	418	19.6	5.4	235	3 693	401.0	150.7
Little Elm	28	361	12.7	3.2	3	D	D	D	8	64	5.5	1.9
Longview	219	4 860	199.7	58.8	19	D	D	D	335	D	D	D
Lubbock	544	12 781	522.9	139.0	53	D	D	D	664	D	D	D
Lufkin	116	2 561	105.6	29.8	13	90	4.2	0.9	203	4 695	309.7	131.4
McAllen	335	7 776	357.5	91.1	22	348	20.7	4.4	627	13 300	1 031.1	402.2
McKinney	180	3 937	178.3	49.7	25	607	28.3	10.3	240	3 278	410.5	142.9
Mansfield	81	1 828	75.9	20.7	19	197	12.0	3.5	117	D	D	D
Mesquite	206	5 128	219.7	63.4	23	D	D	D	294	5 276	379.9	157.3
Midland	242	5 162	246.7	66.0	30	D	D	D	294	D	D	D
Mission	123	1 885	80.8	18.7	12	D	D	D	212	D	D	D
Missouri City	74	1 253	53.2	14.6	13	D	D	D	128	D	D	D
Nacogdoches	101	2 220	86.9	23.0	6	D	D	D	166	D	D	D
New Braunfels	173	3 494	151.3	41.0	24	520	34.4	12.6	196	1 913	185.9	69.9
North Richland Hills	110	2 639	106.3	31.2	14	D	D	D	126	D	D	D
Odessa	214	4 986	219.5	57.3	22	377	11.3	2.9	265	D	D	D
Paris	77	1 326	56.5	15.7	6	D	D	D	156	D	D	D
Pasadena	194	4 157	176.7	45.3	10	124	8.9	2.3	298	4 418	580.8	191.3
Pearland	115	2 679	99.3	29.0	16	D	D	D	144	1 206	96.7	39.5
Pflugerville	49	923	36.6	10.1	6	46	2.9	0.5	29	D	D	D
Pharr	83	1 588	76.1	16.1	9	114	4.2	1.3	116	4 821	106.5	53.6
Plano	596	13 066	655.3	188.1	64	1 364	80.9	21.8	1 099	D	D	D
Port Arthur	82	1 651	73.6	20.7	9	102	4.7	1.6	123	2 001	231.3	74.5
Richardson	263	4 515	254.4	68.3	30	D	D	D	438	D	D	D
Rockwall	89	1 918	81.4	24.3	17	231	9.8	3.2	117	D	D	D
Rosenberg	80	1 511	66.6	19.6	2	D	D	D	41	576	37.5	13.6
Round Rock	229	5 138	271.2	70.8	33	D	D	D	229	3 061	396.4	151.2
Rowlett	65	977	44.8	11.7	11	D	D	D	76	D	D	D
San Angelo	202	4 150	174.1	47.7	21	228	11.9	3.7	215	D	D	D
San Antonio	2 872	68 118	3 545.9	985.1	272	7 854	618.7	208.5	3 221	64 987	6 306.5	2 305.7
San Juan	23	D	D	D	3	D	D	D	36	D	D	D
San Marcos	178	3 896	158.7	43.7	12	D	D	D	125	D	D	D
Schertz	47	980	42.7	11.6	2	D	D	D	23	D	D	D
Seguin	77	1 306	56.1	15.6	10	D	D	D	94	D	D	D
Sherman	101	2 304	102.2	28.8	10	D	D	D	202	D	D	D
Socorro	14	183	8.5	1.9	3	D	D	D	5	D	D	D
Southlake	83	2 199	108.6	31.0	21	389	21.3	6.1	115	D	D	D
Sugar Land	239	5 017	244.4	67.7	23	D	D	D	398	D	D	D
Temple	150	2 943	133.0	34.8	15	241	8.7	2.5	155	D	D	D
Texarkana	118	2 975	139.3	42.4	16	176	7.0	2.3	228	D	D	D
Texas City	75	1 495	60.3	16.2	7	D	D	D	98	D	D	D
The Colony	40	733	33.3	8.7	9	144	8.3	2.2	28	222	15.4	6.5
Tyler	260	6 187	273.9	74.6	31	D	D	D	454	8 564	858.2	390.5
Victoria	160	3 119	128.4	34.8	22	255	12.0	3.2	283	4 405	425.6	167.1
Waco	320	7 206	287.0	80.4	34	D	D	D	337	6 716	458.5	211.6
Waxahachie	75	1 351	58.7	16.8	10	D	D	D	67	1 039	70.2	28.0
Weatherford	90	1 426	63.9	17.1	7	D	D	D	107	D	D	D
Weslaco	83	1 745	70.1	18.3	8	D	D	D	150	D	D	D
Wichita Falls	248	6 052	231.0	72.1	25	310	14.4	3.7	282	4 632	391.5	145.4
Wylie	34	573	27.1	7.5	5	46	2.7	0.6	36	D	D	D
UTAH	4 541	91 808	3 980.6	1 148.6	727	16 419	807.9	282.7	5 731	67 064	6 411.4	2 364.8
American Fork	53	1 253	48.1	13.4	5	D	D	D	117	D	D	D
Bountiful	69	D	D	D	11	D	D	D	173	2 362	208.4	77.9
Cedar City	92	1 517	56.6	15.9	7	D	D	D	91	D	D	D
Clearfield	34	711	23.6	6.1	6	78	1.5	0.4	40	D	D	D
Cottonwood Heights	41	605	31.7	9.4	12	D	D	D	108	D	D	D
Draper	69	1 049	49.9	13.2	8	D	D	D	91	D	D	D
Holladay	52	784	35.5	9.9	9	D	D	D	101	D	D	D

1. Establishments subject to federal tax.

City	Other services[1], 2007				Government employment and payroll, 2012								
						March payroll							
							Percent of total for:						
	Number of establish-ments	Number of employees	Receipts (mil dol)	Annual payroll (mil dol)	Full-time equivalent employees	Total (dollars)	Adminis-tration, judicial, and legal	Police and Corrections	Fire Protection	Highways and trans-portation	Health and welfare	Natural resources and utilities	Education and libraries
	104	105	106	107	108	109	110	111	112	113	114	115	116
TEXAS—Cont'd													
Irving	248	2 866	292.5	89.9	1 743	8 046 007	11.8	31.8	18.7	7.1	2.9	19.2	3.6
Keller	46	D	D	D	322	1 442 647	19.7	27.3	24.3	2.1	4.2	18.4	3.8
Killeen	140	949	64.7	20.7	1 394	4 447 306	9.5	31.5	19.2	10.2	0.6	25.4	2.0
Kingsville	36	D	D	D	241	740 345	13.5	34.2	17.7	5.2	3.4	18.4	2.6
Kyle	12	D	D	D	143	570 004	14.8	39.7	0.0	1.7	5.7	18.1	3.7
Lake Jackson	28	148	8.5	2.6	223	1 137 302	14.0	31.7	0.5	2.3	1.6	37.2	0.0
Lancaster	24	230	33.8	8.9	197	872 132	6.8	31.3	33.7	2.6	3.3	16.0	2.4
La Porte	45	1 632	251.4	84.2	386	1 606 505	14.9	33.6	6.2	5.1	7.8	22.0	0.0
Laredo	223	D	D	D	2 366	9 931 436	6.8	30.9	24.7	11.9	8.6	14.4	1.1
League City	80	686	50.7	17.7	495	2 096 779	14.9	38.2	2.0	7.5	5.2	20.9	5.0
Leander	14	53	5.2	1.4	176	773 154	15.8	34.3	18.9	9.2	0.8	16.9	0.0
Lewisville	145	948	82.0	25.4	702	3 410 758	13.2	32.7	24.8	4.3	1.7	15.0	2.1
Little Elm	10	30	2.3	0.6	174	691 106	17.2	23.6	29.0	9.8	0.8	13.6	2.1
Longview	168	1 301	133.7	37.6	813	3 225 874	7.0	26.2	26.9	3.4	3.3	21.3	2.7
Lubbock	347	2 670	204.5	61.5	2 120	8 958 861	10.0	27.2	23.3	4.5	2.1	29.5	1.5
Lufkin	80	D	D	D	429	1 543 350	10.3	27.6	23.6	6.7	2.2	23.4	1.9
McAllen	155	1 103	83.2	24.8	1 664	5 174 843	11.6	30.2	15.6	10.8	1.0	24.6	3.0
McKinney	103	665	48.0	15.7	813	4 047 327	14.6	26.8	24.0	4.8	0.1	11.7	2.8
Mansfield	54	338	22.7	7.3	451	2 111 359	10.1	41.1	18.9	1.8	1.4	11.7	1.5
Mesquite	141	1 005	92.0	26.2	1 105	5 253 222	10.9	34.0	25.7	3.7	4.0	15.6	2.0
Midland	161	D	D	D	894	4 038 726	12.2	27.1	26.9	7.2	3.1	13.6	0.0
Mission	63	338	21.3	5.7	597	1 943 490	10.4	37.6	17.4	3.6	1.5	22.5	3.1
Missouri City	66	D	D	D	283	1 318 714	9.4	42.4	22.9	9.3	0.0	4.5	0.0
Nacogdoches	58	323	22.6	6.3	302	1 195 157	10.1	30.1	23.9	1.7	1.3	26.6	1.9
New Braunfels	90	D	D	D	732	3 498 442	7.2	20.5	22.3	4.6	3.6	21.9	2.5
North Richland Hills	76	D	D	D	574	2 442 427	13.2	35.1	19.1	9.2	9.3	9.3	4.0
Odessa	153	D	D	D	873	3 249 214	13.9	28.3	26.0	7.1	3.0	16.3	0.0
Paris	58	D	D	D	203	911 303	16.1	38.4	1.6	2.6	5.8	17.2	7.9
Pasadena	144	1 312	148.3	53.1	960	4 082 891	10.8	48.1	2.1	4.7	5.5	18.7	2.8
Pearland	103	687	74.1	24.6	598	2 337 139	14.4	37.4	8.4	4.4	15.8	16.8	0.0
Pflugerville	41	201	16.9	4.3	253	1 010 931	16.1	44.8	0.0	8.0	1.3	21.6	3.5
Pharr	41	241	23.5	4.7	558	1 780 708	10.5	35.0	15.9	8.1	1.9	18.2	3.4
Plano	354	2 884	226.2	72.2	2 089	10 395 648	9.8	32.0	22.2	2.2	0.0	14.1	5.2
Port Arthur	40	177	12.0	3.6	668	2 985 904	7.8	28.2	20.4	6.1	9.3	23.9	1.7
Richardson	151	1 623	151.0	56.8	1 085	4 745 385	14.8	25.0	17.8	5.0	3.3	20.5	3.5
Rockwall	49	377	20.9	7.4	286	1 221 546	32.3	33.7	9.6	3.1	0.0	16.3	0.0
Rosenberg	55	D	D	D	213	967 179	15.7	34.7	16.7	5.1	5.0	18.2	0.0
Round Rock	135	1 676	113.9	45.7	471	2 565 694	21.2	46.9	28.7	0.0	0.0	0.7	2.5
Rowlett	73	D	D	D	332	1 590 040	18.8	30.9	25.7	4.7	2.6	10.7	1.9
San Angelo	166	D	D	D	915	3 145 374	16.7	27.8	25.3	3.8	3.2	19.2	0.0
San Antonio	1 765	13 495	918.4	304.5	15 382	70 371 976	6.9	20.9	12.5	5.3	3.5	46.3	2.1
San Juan	21	55	3.7	0.7	204	595 583	10.6	35.0	12.1	4.4	4.5	31.9	0.4
San Marcos	69	487	32.2	11.2	528	2 976 832	13.7	28.7	14.8	4.1	4.9	21.3	2.7
Schertz	34	332	24.4	8.4	292	1 152 930	17.4	24.7	12.8	2.8	16.4	9.2	3.8
Seguin	51	304	19.1	6.3	907	3 729 350	5.2	8.3	6.1	1.8	68.5	7.0	0.7
Sherman	54	380	26.1	7.7	387	1 528 362	13.7	25.7	23.1	4.3	3.0	22.7	2.2
Socorro	23	D	D	D	92	274 728	24.8	59.5	0.0	13.4	2.2	0.0	0.0
Southlake	55	498	27.8	10.0	274	1 309 065	24.1	24.8	21.4	7.0	0.0	20.0	2.7
Sugar Land	120	813	58.7	20.8	631	3 018 681	23.4	31.1	19.1	10.0	1.3	10.4	0.0
Temple	115	584	43.1	13.2	731	2 585 537	12.4	26.7	22.3	6.4	2.4	25.4	2.6
Texarkana	95	714	57.3	16.4	562	2 018 866	13.1	24.0	17.3	8.1	4.9	29.4	1.7
Texas City	40	364	36.4	12.6	481	1 954 986	8.1	29.3	20.9	5.9	1.6	25.9	2.0
The Colony	28	D	D	D	311	1 270 659	11.9	29.0	21.2	3.8	7.3	20.1	4.5
Tyler	165	1 330	81.3	29.6	778	3 106 473	9.1	34.9	25.5	3.1	3.1	18.2	1.7
Victoria	124	D	D	D	566	2 159 618	10.1	31.7	22.5	6.4	0.0	22.4	3.2
Waco	184	1 288	90.7	28.8	1 507	5 739 695	9.4	29.8	17.3	5.4	5.9	25.5	2.4
Waxahachie	40	212	16.1	4.4	264	1 145 356	12.3	28.0	25.5	3.4	3.0	21.1	0.0
Weatherford	56	380	24.1	7.2	345	1 550 071	17.4	23.4	20.0	5.7	2.6	21.9	3.2
Weslaco	36	175	14.3	3.2	368	1 252 682	6.2	31.0	27.7	5.1	2.2	17.8	3.2
Wichita Falls	164	1 024	79.3	24.1	1 213	4 712 736	7.8	25.5	27.3	8.3	5.3	16.8	1.2
Wylie	29	142	10.9	3.5	191	622 464	4.4	29.0	33.5	4.3	0.0	22.4	6.3
UTAH	3 537	21 934	1 751.2	520.6	X	X	X	X	X	X	X	X	X
American Fork	46	D	D	D	215	711 482	13.8	21.8	14.3	3.1	1.3	25.9	5.2
Bountiful	57	282	21.1	5.5	195	922 673	14.7	32.2	0.0	14.9	0.0	37.8	0.0
Cedar City	45	D	D	D	172	568 537	11.0	28.7	7.6	11.9	1.2	27.7	2.2
Clearfield	37	188	10.0	3.2	150	543 342	19.4	32.7	17.0	4.0	0.9	22.9	0.0
Cottonwood Heights	24	132	5.9	2.1	68	323 642	24.8	70.5	0.0	4.6	0.0	0.0	0.0
Draper	65	459	31.7	8.9	152	605 204	26.7	28.9	0.0	17.1	3.4	14.1	0.0
Holladay	38	D	D	D	18	69 533	64.5	0.0	0.0	0.0	22.6	12.9	0.0

1. Establishments subject to federal tax.

City	City government finances, 2007									
	General revenue							General expenditure		
		Intergovernmental		Taxes					Per capita[1] (dollars)	
					Per capita[1] (dollars)					
	Total (mil dol)	Total (mil dol)	Percent from state government	Total (mil dol)	Total	Property	Sales and gross receipts	Total (mil dol)	Total	Capital outlays
	117	118	119	120	121	122	123	124	125	126
TEXAS—Cont'd										
Irving	281.4	21.9	71.5	189.3	839	427	411	289.2	1 281	200
Keller	52.3	5.6	60.6	32.1	765	471	294	46.9	1 117	201
Killeen	120.2	5.4	5.6	62.9	466	248	219	125.1	928	204
Kingsville	22.9	0.6	12.6	12.2	464	228	236	21.7	825	89
Kyle	18.5	1.7	25.7	10.7	346	201	145	21.9	709	200
Lake Jackson	29.0	0.4	54.4	14.7	543	207	335	25.6	942	152
Lancaster	48.5	11.5	23.8	24.6	649	359	290	46.9	1 238	111
La Porte	56.7	0.9	100.0	26.5	769	497	272	48.6	1 407	246
Laredo	394.6	81.6	35.0	126.6	516	281	235	350.9	1 429	400
League City	86.5	3.8	100.0	58.1	658	411	247	73.3	829	130
Leander	26.5	2.2	9.7	17.9	606	377	229	29.0	981	234
Lewisville	95.9	2.2	49.8	62.5	628	286	342	100.9	1 013	207
Little Elm	30.5	4.2	98.1	18.2	629	354	275	39.3	1 357	641
Longview	103.8	12.8	28.3	64.9	798	306	492	94.8	1 166	149
Lubbock	270.7	38.4	30.0	127.0	538	245	293	310.3	1 313	386
Lufkin	50.9	0.7	59.9	25.8	716	272	443	52.9	1 468	203
McAllen	185.3	20.0	21.5	98.4	727	242	485	201.4	1 488	430
McKinney	171.7	14.0	23.8	109.6	764	437	327	184.3	1 284	234
Mansfield	76.9	0.3	100.0	53.1	894	514	381	67.5	1 136	167
Mesquite	149.0	15.9	19.4	81.9	571	255	316	164.5	1 147	212
Midland	147.3	7.4	38.3	94.6	790	273	516	126.0	1 052	145
Mission	73.0	7.2	12.2	38.7	478	266	212	68.7	850	112
Missouri City	57.5	9.1	36.1	36.0	524	363	161	66.1	963	354
Nacogdoches	37.5	1.3	98.2	17.4	514	223	291	34.0	1 005	86
New Braunfels	75.8	2.4	48.3	46.1	754	263	491	79.1	1 294	279
North Richland Hills	83.8	11.2	100.0	46.1	705	344	361	93.1	1 424	490
Odessa	103.9	3.9	38.2	61.7	580	196	384	93.2	877	116
Paris	30.9	2.2	100.0	18.1	722	303	419	29.3	1 166	79
Pasadena	146.5	20.4	12.6	75.9	497	217	280	138.9	910	167
Pearland	113.9	0.6	58.8	76.6	794	500	295	118.6	1 230	308
Pflugerville	42.9	1.9	93.4	26.5	509	326	184	44.6	858	248
Pharr	63.4	5.8	5.1	30.9	422	211	211	59.7	815	150
Plano	386.2	19.2	55.2	247.7	907	528	380	338.6	1 240	181
Port Arthur	104.3	23.2	53.0	35.6	652	306	346	92.8	1 701	263
Richardson	156.9	3.8	94.5	105.8	1 020	591	428	174.7	1 684	269
Rockwall	44.0	0.7	30.2	36.4	910	434	476	49.9	1 249	367
Rosenberg	36.1	5.0	24.6	21.6	665	231	434	29.5	906	207
Round Rock	146.3	3.6	66.0	112.0	1 050	315	735	119.5	1 120	243
Rowlett	58.1	2.1	65.8	33.9	587	420	167	55.7	965	142
San Angelo	93.6	7.0	10.4	55.3	575	299	276	98.6	1 026	216
San Antonio	1 748.6	300.5	51.3	740.3	534	275	253	1 743.3	1 258	188
San Juan	18.0	1.1	32.3	9.7	275	168	107	18.5	524	97
San Marcos	67.7	3.7	100.0	38.5	769	285	485	82.3	1 643	440
Schertz	37.4	1.3	65.0	21.3	611	306	305	31.5	902	81
Seguin	116.5	6.1	85.0	13.9	529	240	289	116.4	4 428	511
Sherman	47.8	2.7	3.7	27.5	704	182	522	48.9	1 254	120
Socorro	7.7	0.5	0.0	6.1	185	124	61	9.8	298	92
Southlake	68.2	0.6	38.4	54.7	1 972	1 139	834	66.5	2 398	864
Sugar Land	160.2	31.2	93.8	77.6	948	347	601	161.5	1 972	729
Temple	85.5	3.7	93.7	46.0	666	317	349	91.2	1 319	299
Texarkana	47.9	0.8	78.3	31.7	853	368	485	49.1	1 322	277
Texas City	68.4	8.3	43.2	43.1	944	451	493	58.5	1 280	147
The Colony	38.4	2.1	73.4	25.5	652	384	268	46.1	1 181	397
Tyler	128.9	15.0	13.7	61.9	623	142	481	120.1	1 209	168
Victoria	78.7	5.7	39.9	49.8	773	320	453	89.3	1 386	576
Waco	359.0	127.8	9.2	97.3	762	414	348	344.8	2 700	343
Waxahachie	40.4	0.2	100.0	28.8	928	477	451	33.9	1 090	82
Weatherford	34.6	3.2	80.9	20.7	782	306	475	43.0	1 627	441
Weslaco	37.6	0.7	25.3	22.1	599	267	332	35.9	972	114
Wichita Falls	120.3	13.6	34.0	66.3	633	276	357	114.0	1 088	129
Wylie	43.1	1.6	92.9	30.5	688	467	221	53.2	1 190	374
UTAH	X	X	X	X	X	X	X	X	X	X
American Fork	30.4	2.8	100.0	13.6	497	205	291	29.8	1 092	170
Bountiful	25.9	3.0	48.4	13.7	320	93	227	21.6	504	27
Cedar City	26.1	3.3	64.2	13.5	465	185	280	21.4	736	103
Clearfield	27.3	4.4	91.5	11.8	387	164	223	21.4	704	59
Cottonwood Heights	14.9	1.2	96.8	12.7	374	206	168	16.8	494	109
Draper	36.2	2.5	98.9	24.0	544	247	297	32.8	742	114
Holladay	17.7	2.0	70.1	11.7	434	197	236	15.0	555	0

1. Based on population estimated as of July 1 of the year shown.

City	Public welfare	Highways	Parking facilities	Education	Health and hospitals	Police protection	Sewerage and sanitation	Parks and recreation	Housing and community development	Interest on debt
	City government finances, 2012 (cont.)									
	General expenditure (cont.)									
	Percent of total for:									
	127	128	129	130	131	132	133	134	135	136
TEXAS—Cont'd										
Irving	0.0	6.3	0.0	0.0	0.3	18.5	10.7	16.0	1.7	6.2
Keller	0.0	17.7	0.0	0.0	0.0	17.1	7.0	11.8	0.0	10.1
Killeen	0.2	9.1	0.0	0.0	0.4	19.5	23.3	5.7	0.3	4.1
Kingsville	0.0	9.8	0.0	0.0	1.5	31.1	19.6	0.9	0.0	1.3
Kyle	0.0	2.5	0.0	0.0	0.7	17.1	24.0	10.5	0.0	11.7
Lake Jackson	0.0	11.4	0.0	0.0	3.4	18.2	19.4	20.7	0.0	5.0
Lancaster	0.0	1.7	0.0	0.0	0.3	12.2	16.8	4.5	18.4	8.3
La Porte	0.0	8.4	0.0	0.0	0.0	21.8	10.5	11.3	0.0	3.9
Laredo	0.2	2.1	0.4	0.0	4.1	15.0	11.2	3.3	3.8	5.2
League City	0.0	10.6	0.0	0.0	3.9	20.7	11.4	6.2	0.2	5.1
Leander	0.0	21.6	0.0	0.0	0.6	14.8	12.0	7.8	0.0	17.7
Lewisville	0.0	16.6	0.0	0.0	1.2	21.6	6.1	10.4	2.2	6.4
Little Elm	0.0	4.0	0.0	0.0	0.3	8.7	13.3	2.7	0.0	4.5
Longview	0.0	10.3	0.0	0.0	1.5	21.3	12.6	8.8	7.2	2.4
Lubbock	0.0	7.3	0.0	0.0	1.8	16.3	18.4	5.2	1.4	10.2
Lufkin	0.0	14.7	0.0	0.0	1.2	15.2	18.1	7.6	0.3	13.8
McAllen	0.6	11.5	0.4	0.0	0.8	16.5	22.1	10.4	1.7	2.6
McKinney	0.0	8.4	0.0	0.0	0.8	10.9	11.9	6.8	0.3	6.0
Mansfield	0.0	9.9	0.0	0.0	0.6	14.5	12.1	8.2	0.0	8.1
Mesquite	0.0	6.4	0.0	0.0	0.8	18.5	13.6	7.0	8.4	4.2
Midland	0.0	5.4	0.0	0.0	3.3	17.0	15.9	13.4	0.6	2.3
Mission	0.0	8.3	0.0	0.0	0.5	20.0	10.6	12.1	1.7	18.9
Missouri City	0.0	12.6	0.0	0.0	0.3	16.3	9.7	12.1	0.5	7.8
Nacogdoches	0.0	4.3	0.0	0.0	0.0	20.6	28.3	4.4	0.0	1.2
New Braunfels	0.0	16.3	0.0	0.0	0.9	17.7	16.5	7.8	0.3	6.0
North Richland Hills	0.0	7.5	0.0	0.0	0.9	17.6	8.3	14.6	0.0	2.6
Odessa	0.1	14.4	0.0	0.0	0.7	18.6	16.0	6.7	2.6	1.6
Paris	0.0	12.8	0.0	0.0	10.9	19.7	12.9	3.9	4.1	2.1
Pasadena	0.3	19.6	0.0	0.0	2.5	30.9	13.9	6.5	7.8	3.5
Pearland	0.0	21.9	0.0	0.0	3.6	13.1	14.4	6.1	0.0	12.2
Pflugerville	0.0	14.9	0.0	0.0	0.0	22.4	18.1	6.3	0.0	7.6
Pharr	0.0	17.9	0.0	0.0	3.4	23.5	9.1	9.1	2.3	3.4
Plano	0.0	5.1	0.0	0.0	1.0	16.3	18.5	12.9	0.8	4.2
Port Arthur	2.1	10.7	0.0	0.0	3.3	19.4	20.8	2.7	3.2	3.5
Richardson	0.0	11.9	0.0	0.0	1.1	13.7	17.6	8.7	0.0	6.6
Rockwall	0.0	20.4	0.0	0.0	1.1	16.8	11.8	16.8	0.0	11.1
Rosenberg	0.0	19.1	0.0	0.0	0.8	23.4	17.4	3.5	0.0	6.0
Round Rock	0.0	13.0	0.0	0.0	0.7	19.5	9.2	7.3	0.4	5.1
Rowlett	0.0	13.1	0.0	0.0	1.6	18.1	14.7	6.6	0.0	6.4
San Angelo	0.0	7.5	0.0	0.0	3.5	15.8	10.8	5.9	3.1	4.7
San Antonio	7.8	6.4	0.3	0.0	1.9	17.7	19.6	7.8	2.9	1.6
San Juan	0.0	7.7	0.0	0.0	0.0	18.3	23.7	7.5	0.0	4.2
San Marcos	0.0	3.2	0.0	0.0	2.0	17.4	16.7	3.5	0.8	8.8
Schertz	0.0	7.2	0.0	0.0	12.4	14.7	16.9	4.0	0.0	6.6
Seguin	0.0	2.2	0.0	0.0	64.9	4.6	5.0	2.7	0.0	6.7
Sherman	0.1	14.6	0.0	0.0	1.2	15.7	18.0	4.8	0.6	2.0
Socorro	0.0	16.3	0.0	0.0	4.1	19.1	0.0	1.1	2.7	3.8
Southlake	0.0	16.1	0.0	0.0	0.0	12.5	7.7	19.6	0.0	8.2
Sugar Land	0.0	21.1	0.0	0.0	0.4	10.2	11.7	4.0	0.2	5.9
Temple	0.0	5.4	0.0	0.0	0.9	17.8	21.2	9.8	0.0	5.0
Texarkana	0.0	16.5	0.0	0.0	1.7	19.3	24.5	4.0	0.9	4.9
Texas City	0.0	17.5	0.0	0.0	0.7	18.1	12.1	12.9	0.8	4.6
The Colony	0.0	20.7	0.0	0.0	0.0	26.6	8.9	7.9	0.0	5.3
Tyler	0.0	11.3	0.0	0.0	0.0	18.5	17.1	3.5	6.7	14.7
Victoria	0.0	29.4	0.0	0.0	0.0	15.1	11.6	3.8	1.2	5.0
Waco	0.0	2.2	0.0	0.0	2.2	10.3	12.3	7.5	1.0	48.3
Waxahachie	0.0	7.3	0.0	0.0	2.2	18.4	13.9	8.1	0.0	10.0
Weatherford	0.0	29.0	0.0	0.0	0.1	15.8	13.4	5.2	0.0	6.7
Weslaco	0.0	3.7	0.0	0.0	1.2	15.5	23.6	1.3	0.0	10.1
Wichita Falls	0.0	8.9	0.0	0.0	4.1	17.6	17.4	5.8	5.2	1.7
Wylie	0.0	21.8	0.0	0.0	0.5	9.5	11.2	16.0	0.0	9.1
UTAH	X	X	X	X	X	X	X	X	X	X
American Fork	0.0	15.1	0.0	0.0	4.9	14.4	17.4	12.8	0.9	3.0
Bountiful	0.0	19.3	0.0	0.0	0.0	26.9	15.0	11.0	3.2	0.7
Cedar City	0.0	17.1	0.0	0.0	0.0	18.7	14.8	18.3	3.1	4.1
Clearfield	0.0	8.5	0.0	0.0	0.0	19.0	14.3	16.1	2.4	4.6
Cottonwood Heights	0.0	31.0	0.0	0.0	0.0	0.9	1.2	1.1	0.0	0.0
Draper	0.0	22.1	0.0	0.0	0.6	12.1	7.5	9.8	9.4	3.2
Holladay	0.0	9.9	0.0	0.0	0.0	21.1	1.5	5.1	20.2	6.0

City	City government finances, 2012 (cont.): Debt outstanding: Total (mil dol)	City government finances, 2012 (cont.): Debt outstanding: Per capita[1] (dollars)	City government finances, 2012 (cont.): Debt issued during year	Climate[2]: Average daily temperature (degrees Fahrenheit): Mean: January	Climate[2]: Average daily temperature: Mean: July	Climate[2]: Average daily temperature: Limits: January[3]	Climate[2]: Average daily temperature: Limits: July[4]	Climate[2]: Annual precipitation (inches)	Climate[2]: Heating degree days	Climate[2]: Cooling degree days
	137	138	139	140	141	142	143	144	145	146
TEXAS—Cont'd										
Irving	567.8	2 515	137.2	45.9	86.5	36.4	96.1	37.05	2 219	2 878
Keller	128.2	3 054	0.0	43.0	84.1	31.4	95.7	34.12	2 608	2 358
Killeen	238.9	1 773	75.1	46.0	83.5	34.0	95.3	32.88	2 190	2 477
Kingsville	28.3	1 072	10.0	55.9	84.3	43.4	95.5	29.03	1 001	3 404
Kyle	69.4	2 246	7.7	NA	NA	NA	NA	NA	NA	NA
Lake Jackson	42.1	1 549	0.0	54.0	83.7	45.4	90.2	50.66	1 234	3 003
Lancaster	96.3	2 540	0.0	44.4	84.0	33.3	95.7	38.69	2 380	2 452
La Porte	45.1	1 307	0.0	51.6	83.6	41.9	91.6	53.75	1 471	2 841
Laredo	576.1	2 347	109.7	55.6	88.5	43.7	101.6	21.53	931	4 213
League City	210.1	2 379	39.8	52.7	82.7	43.1	91.2	51.73	1 365	2 815
Leander	176.0	5 952	0.0	NA	NA	NA	NA	NA	NA	NA
Lewisville	244.1	2 452	15.1	42.7	83.6	32.0	94.1	37.79	2 650	2 269
Little Elm	74.2	2 564	0.0	NA	NA	NA	NA	NA	NA	NA
Longview	160.6	1 975	39.2	45.4	83.4	33.7	94.5	49.06	2 319	2 355
Lubbock	1 342.1	5 681	257.0	38.1	79.8	24.4	91.9	18.69	3 508	1 769
Lufkin	179.5	4 983	21.3	48.6	82.6	37.9	93.5	46.62	1 900	2 480
McAllen	182.6	1 349	18.6	58.7	85.1	48.2	95.5	22.61	719	3 898
McKinney	313.4	2 184	16.9	41.8	82.4	31.1	92.7	41.01	2 843	2 060
Mansfield	183.2	3 084	26.8	43.7	84.3	33.2	94.9	34.54	2 437	2 508
Mesquite	242.0	1 687	42.9	45.9	86.5	36.4	96.1	37.05	2 219	2 878
Midland	125.3	1 046	6.0	44.5	81.8	29.5	95.6	14.84	2 479	2 241
Mission	387.2	4 787	51.7	58.8	86.3	47.5	97.7	22.13	740	4 128
Missouri City	174.1	2 535	5.1	51.8	84.1	41.6	93.7	49.34	1 475	2 950
Nacogdoches	62.8	1 856	1.7	46.5	83.9	36.4	93.5	48.36	2 150	2 555
New Braunfels	122.5	2 004	19.1	48.6	82.7	35.5	94.7	35.74	1 840	2 545
North Richland Hills	95.6	1 463	9.4	44.1	85.0	34.0	95.4	34.73	2 370	2 568
Odessa	124.0	1 168	0.0	43.2	81.7	29.6	94.3	14.80	2 716	2 139
Paris	25.2	1 004	0.0	40.6	83.1	29.9	94.3	47.82	2 972	2 197
Pasadena	223.9	1 467	34.6	54.3	84.5	45.2	93.6	53.96	1 174	3 179
Pearland	497.5	5 162	21.5	54.3	84.5	45.2	93.6	53.96	1 174	3 179
Pflugerville	167.6	3 224	21.9	NA	NA	NA	NA	NA	NA	NA
Pharr	103.3	1 410	2.2	60.1	85.9	50.3	96.1	22.96	624	4 181
Plano	352.8	1 293	21.4	44.1	85.0	34.0	95.4	34.73	2 370	2 568
Port Arthur	88.1	1 615	9.5	52.2	82.7	42.9	91.6	59.89	1 447	2 823
Richardson	311.9	3 007	21.2	45.9	86.5	36.4	96.1	37.05	2 219	2 878
Rockwall	163.4	4 091	17.3	NA	NA	NA	NA	NA	NA	NA
Rosenberg	52.3	1 608	15.4	NA	NA	NA	NA	NA	NA	NA
Round Rock	260.2	2 439	16.1	47.2	83.8	35.1	95.7	36.42	1 998	2 584
Rowlett	119.6	2 070	9.2	42.1	82.8	30.8	94.2	40.06	2 710	2 212
San Angelo	234.6	2 440	163.8	44.9	82.4	31.8	94.4	20.91	2 396	2 383
San Antonio	8 830.9	6 374	589.4	50.3	84.3	38.6	94.6	32.92	1 573	3 038
San Juan	24.6	697	5.9	60.1	85.9	50.3	96.1	22.96	624	4 181
San Marcos	264.7	5 283	17.2	49.9	84.4	38.6	95.1	37.19	1 629	2 913
Schertz	73.9	2 118	13.8	NA	NA	NA	NA	NA	NA	NA
Seguin	172.6	6 568	18.6	NA	NA	NA	NA	NA	NA	NA
Sherman	23.5	602	0.0	41.5	82.8	32.2	92.7	42.04	2 850	2 137
Socorro	12.3	374	8.1	44.9	83.6	29.2	98.7	9.71	2 557	2 372
Southlake	179.6	6 478	11.1	NA	NA	NA	NA	NA	NA	NA
Sugar Land	363.3	4 437	130.2	51.8	84.1	41.6	93.7	49.34	1 475	2 950
Temple	177.8	2 572	24.1	46.1	83.7	34.9	95.0	35.81	2 191	2 551
Texarkana	69.8	1 880	0.0	41.6	82.6	30.7	93.1	51.24	2 893	2 138
Texas City	91.3	1 997	31.9	55.8	84.3	49.7	88.7	43.84	1 008	3 268
The Colony	97.6	2 499	7.6	42.7	83.6	32.0	94.1	37.79	2 650	2 269
Tyler	428.2	4 307	9.4	47.5	83.4	37.7	93.6	45.27	1 958	2 521
Victoria	179.1	2 780	9.7	53.2	84.2	43.6	93.4	40.10	1 248	3 203
Waco	8 413.1	65 880	7.3	46.1	85.4	35.1	96.7	33.34	2 164	2 840
Waxahachie	170.0	5 475	0.0	NA	NA	NA	NA	NA	NA	NA
Weatherford	117.6	4 447	33.5	NA	NA	NA	NA	NA	NA	NA
Weslaco	115.6	3 134	11.5	58.6	84.5	47.7	95.4	25.37	755	3 791
Wichita Falls	168.4	1 607	0.0	40.5	84.8	28.9	97.2	28.83	3 024	2 396
Wylie	119.8	2 699	5.4	NA	NA	NA	NA	NA	NA	NA
UTAH	X	X	X	X	X	X	X	X	X	X
American Fork	62.3	2 284	1.7	NA	NA	NA	NA	NA	NA	NA
Bountiful	18.1	421	0.0	29.1	75.8	21.6	88.4	22.40	5 937	861
Cedar City	21.1	725	0.0	NA	NA	NA	NA	NA	NA	NA
Clearfield	24.6	809	0.0	27.6	74.2	18.6	89.9	20.75	6 142	746
Cottonwood Heights	0.0	0	0.0	NA	NA	NA	NA	NA	NA	NA
Draper	33.1	749	0.0	31.6	78.0	22.0	95.3	15.76	5 251	1 172
Holladay	20.8	770	9.2	NA	NA	NA	NA	NA	NA	NA

1. Based on the population estimated as of July 1 of the year shown. 2. Represents normal values based on the 30-year period, 1971–2000. 3. Average daily minimum. 4. Average daily maximum.

STATE Place code	City	Land area,[1] 2010 (sq km)	Population, 2014: Total persons	Population, 2014: Rank	Population, 2014: Per square kilometer	Race alone or in combination (percent), 2011-2013: White	Black	American Indian, Alaska Native	Asian	Hawaiian Pacific Islander	Percent Hispanic or Latino[2], 2011-2013	Percent foreign born 2011–2013
		1	2	3	4	5	6	7	8	9	10	11
	UTAH—Cont'd											
49 40360	Kaysville	27.1	29 494	1 248	1 088.3	97.1	0.8	NA	2.5	NA	4.2	2.0
49 43660	Layton	57.0	72 231	472	1 267.2	90.6	2.2	0.9	4.0	1.1	10.8	6.4
49 44320	Lehi	68.2	56 275	653	825.1	95.3	0.5	0.4	1.5	1.5	6.5	4.0
49 45860	Logan	46.5	48 997	767	1 053.7	90.0	1.7	1.3	4.0	NA	14.6	10.5
49 49710	Midvale	15.4	31 725	1 171	2 060.1	86.4	3.1	1.1	4.2	1.8	25.4	15.1
49 53230	Murray	31.8	48 822	769	1 535.3	93.1	1.8	1.2	2.2	0.2	9.4	6.9
49 55980	Ogden	70.2	84 316	383	1 201.1	82.0	2.7	2.0	1.9	0.7	30.8	12.8
49 57300	Orem	47.4	91 781	336	1 936.3	92.8	1.3	1.3	3.0	1.7	15.3	10.5
49 60930	Pleasant Grove	23.7	37 064	1 003	1 563.9	98.0	0.8	NA	1.0	0.2	10.0	4.2
49 62470	Provo	107.9	114 801	237	1 064.0	90.1	1.6	1.3	4.5	2.0	18.2	12.4
49 64340	Riverton	32.7	41 457	892	1 267.8	96.4	0.4	NA	2.5	1.4	3.5	2.8
49 65110	Roy	20.5	37 877	978	1 847.7	91.7	1.3	1.1	1.5	0.8	17.0	6.2
49 65330	St. George	182.3	78 505	422	430.6	93.6	1.4	1.9	1.4	1.6	13.2	8.4
49 67000	Salt Lake City	287.8	190 884	124	663.3	75.8	3.6	2.0	6.3	2.6	20.2	17.5
49 67440	Sandy	59.2	91 148	344	1 539.7	92.3	0.9	0.5	4.4	0.9	7.3	6.7
49 70850	South Jordan	57.1	62 781	564	1 099.5	95.2	0.7	0.4	3.4	0.9	6.5	5.1
49 71290	Spanish Fork	39.9	37 527	986	940.5	94.8	1.0	0.8	0.2	2.1	9.3	5.3
49 72280	Springville	37.3	31 464	1 183	843.5	94.2	0.3	2.9	1.9	1.0	8.5	6.1
49 75360	Taylorsville	28.1	60 433	591	2 150.6	83.7	3.1	1.7	4.0	1.7	21.8	14.2
49 76680	Tooele	55.6	32 573	1 137	585.8	92.9	1.3	3.2	1.5	NA	13.6	3.5
49 82950	West Jordan	84.1	110 920	252	1 318.9	90.0	2.3	1.6	2.9	1.8	18.7	9.9
49 83470	West Valley City	92.1	134 495	193	1 460.3	71.5	3.7	1.9	5.9	5.3	37.3	22.8
50 00000	VERMONT	23 871.0	626 562	X	26.2	97.0	1.5	1.3	1.8	0.1	1.6	4.2
50 10675	Burlington	26.7	42 211	873	1 580.9	90.3	4.6	1.5	5.5	0.1	3.1	9.3
51 00000	VIRGINIA	102 278.9	8 326 289	X	81.4	72.0	20.8	1.0	6.9	0.2	8.4	11.5
51 01000	Alexandria	38.9	150 575	166	3 870.8	67.8	23.2	1.1	8.1	0.1	16.7	27.6
51 07784	Blacksburg	51.5	43 985	839	854.1	81.8	6.1	0.8	13.0	0.2	3.5	15.3
51 14968	Charlottesville	26.5	45 593	817	1 720.5	72.6	20.5	0.3	8.0	0.3	5.0	12.7
51 16000	Chesapeake	882.7	233 371	92	264.4	65.2	31.3	1.1	4.5	0.2	4.8	5.0
51 21344	Danville	111.2	42 444	868	381.7	48.4	50.1	0.5	1.3	NA	3.0	3.2
51 35000	Hampton	133.2	136 879	189	1 027.6	45.4	52.4	1.3	3.3	0.1	5.0	4.6
51 35624	Harrisonburg	45.1	52 478	706	1 163.6	87.6	8.7	0.6	4.7	NA	17.4	17.4
51 44984	Leesburg	32.1	49 496	755	1 541.9	76.0	9.7	NA	10.1	0.3	20.6	23.1
51 47672	Lynchburg	127.2	79 047	415	621.4	67.1	30.3	1.1	3.3	NA	3.3	5.3
51 48952	Manassas	25.6	42 081	876	1 643.8	76.3	16.7	0.8	6.1	NA	32.4	27.7
51 56000	Newport News	178.0	182 965	132	1 027.9	53.9	42.8	1.6	4.1	0.4	8.0	7.3
51 57000	Norfolk	140.2	245 428	84	1 750.6	51.1	44.4	1.5	4.4	0.5	7.1	6.6
51 61832	Petersburg	59.4	32 701	1 133	550.5	19.2	79.8	0.5	0.4	NA	4.1	3.0
51 64000	Portsmouth	87.2	96 004	312	1 101.0	43.6	55.0	1.3	1.8	0.2	3.4	2.3
51 67000	Richmond	154.9	217 853	98	1 406.4	46.3	51.1	1.9	3.0	0.1	6.3	6.5
51 68000	Roanoke	110.2	99 428	298	902.3	68.8	30.7	1.8	2.5	NA	5.7	6.7
51 76432	Suffolk	1 036.4	86 806	365	83.8	55.9	44.4	1.8	2.6	NA	3.3	3.5
51 82000	Virginia Beach	645.0	450 980	40	699.2	71.8	21.7	1.2	8.0	0.4	7.2	8.6
51 86720	Winchester	23.9	27 543	1 334	1 152.4	84.7	12.0	1.6	2.9	NA	16.0	10.1
53 00000	WASHINGTON	172 119.0	7 061 530	X	41.0	82.5	5.0	3.0	9.4	1.1	11.7	13.4
53 03180	Auburn	76.7	76 347	438	995.4	76.6	7.5	4.7	12.0	2.7	12.8	17.8
53 05210	Bellevue	82.8	136 426	190	1 647.7	65.1	3.1	1.2	32.3	0.6	5.9	35.5
53 05280	Bellingham	70.1	83 365	388	1 189.2	89.8	2.3	2.7	7.0	0.4	9.0	11.2
53 07380	Bothell	31.4	36 567	1 018	1 164.6	81.4	1.8	1.5	15.9	NA	9.4	18.5
53 07695	Bremerton	73.6	38 572	962	524.1	79.8	9.5	6.1	6.5	1.1	11.7	7.9
53 08850	Burien	19.2	50 188	745	2 614.0	72.7	10.6	5.1	13.6	2.9	22.0	23.8
53 17635	Des Moines	16.8	31 011	1 193	1 845.9	72.4	9.4	2.3	15.4	3.3	16.1	23.7
53 20750	Edmonds	23.1	40 896	906	1 770.4	85.7	3.4	1.3	11.0	NA	4.4	13.3
53 22640	Everett	86.6	106 736	272	1 232.5	81.2	6.7	2.7	11.2	2.0	15.2	19.1
53 23515	Federal Way	57.7	93 425	325	1 619.2	66.7	12.5	3.1	16.2	2.4	18.3	22.8
53 33805	Issaquah	29.5	34 056	1 095	1 154.4	81.0	4.2	0.9	17.9	NA	6.8	16.0
53 35275	Kennewick	69.8	77 421	432	1 109.2	78.1	3.3	1.9	4.0	0.2	23.8	10.8
53 35415	Kent	74.1	125 560	217	1 694.5	61.9	12.0	1.7	20.7	4.9	16.7	28.2
53 35940	Kirkland	27.9	85 763	374	3 073.9	82.0	2.5	1.9	17.3	0.5	7.3	20.4
53 36745	Lacey	41.6	45 446	819	1 092.5	77.3	7.1	2.2	13.0	2.4	8.6	12.1
53 37900	Lake Stevens	23.0	30 284	1 226	1 316.7	92.8	0.8	1.7	6.7	NA	9.6	7.0
53 38038	Lakewood	44.5	59 610	608	1 339.6	69.3	12.4	3.9	12.3	3.3	18.1	17.3
53 40245	Longview	37.5	36 483	1 020	972.9	94.4	1.9	3.9	3.4	1.2	8.7	5.3
53 40840	Lynnwood	20.3	36 687	1 013	1 807.2	69.9	8.6	3.5	20.2	0.9	12.2	28.1
53 43955	Marysville	53.6	65 087	542	1 214.3	88.4	3.1	2.1	6.4	1.4	10.3	9.0
53 47560	Mount Vernon	31.9	33 132	1 122	1 038.6	84.8	1.5	2.5	3.9	NA	35.0	16.3
53 51300	Olympia	46.2	49 218	762	1 065.3	89.1	2.3	2.6	7.8	0.6	8.0	8.9

1. Dry land or land partially or temporarily covered by water. 2. May be of any race.

City	Age of population (percent), 2011-2013									Median age 2011-2013	Percent female 2011-2013	Population			
												Census counts		Percent change	
	Under 5 years	5 to 17 years	18 to 24 years	25 to 34 years	35 to 44 years	45 to 54 years	55 to 64 years	65 to 74 years	75 years and over			2000	2010	2000–2010	2010–2014
	12	13	14	15	16	17	18	19	20	21	22	23	24	25	26
UTAH—Cont'd															
Kaysville	9.2	27.0	8.9	12.1	14.7	12.0	9.4	3.8	2.9	29.4	50.4	20 351	27 300	34.1	7.6
Layton	9.8	21.7	10.8	16.4	12.7	10.6	10.2	4.3	3.5	29.6	49.4	58 474	67 311	15.1	7.3
Lehi	13.9	29.5	8.7	15.8	14.3	7.3	5.6	2.9	2.0	23.8	48.7	19 028	47 407	149.1	17.9
Logan	9.3	15.0	30.8	19.1	8.7	5.9	5.2	2.9	3.3	23.9	51.5	42 670	48 174	12.9	1.6
Midvale	6.5	17.9	10.7	23.4	12.8	10.0	8.8	5.3	4.5	30.9	51.3	27 029	27 964	3.5	13.4
Murray	5.8	15.7	11.5	16.2	12.8	11.4	12.6	7.0	7.1	35.5	50.6	34 024	46 746	37.4	4.6
Ogden	9.6	17.9	12.2	18.4	11.5	10.9	9.6	5.1	4.8	30.3	48.8	77 226	82 825	7.3	1.8
Orem	10.8	19.4	16.9	17.3	9.3	9.0	8.6	5.0	3.5	26.6	50.3	84 324	88 328	4.7	3.9
Pleasant Grove	11.8	26.8	12.1	14.0	13.5	9.3	6.0	3.8	2.6	24.6	50.4	23 468	33 509	42.8	10.5
Provo	8.7	14.7	34.7	18.0	7.5	5.4	5.2	2.7	3.0	23.6	50.4	105 166	112 488	7.0	2.1
Riverton	11.1	26.0	8.2	15.8	13.3	11.8	8.2	3.2	2.5	28.7	50.0	25 011	38 753	54.9	6.8
Roy	8.6	23.2	7.8	15.9	14.7	11.7	8.0	5.7	4.5	31.3	50.0	32 885	36 884	12.2	2.7
St. George	7.8	20.6	10.7	12.4	10.2	9.2	10.3	9.7	9.2	33.7	51.2	49 663	72 897	46.8	7.9
Salt Lake City	7.4	14.7	13.2	20.8	13.4	11.2	9.5	5.2	4.7	31.7	48.5	181 743	186 440	2.6	2.4
Sandy	7.1	21.2	8.6	13.3	13.7	13.0	12.5	6.9	3.6	34.8	49.9	88 418	87 461	-1.1	3.9
South Jordan	8.4	25.3	8.7	14.8	13.6	11.7	9.7	4.6	3.3	30.1	49.4	29 437	50 418	71.3	24.5
Spanish Fork	10.6	29.3	10.3	17.8	12.4	8.8	5.0	3.3	2.4	24.9	48.9	20 246	34 691	71.3	8.0
Springville	12.4	24.3	13.2	14.6	12.4	8.3	6.8	4.0	4.1	25.1	49.4	20 424	29 466	44.3	6.7
Taylorsville	9.3	18.7	9.5	17.6	12.4	11.2	11.2	6.1	3.8	31.6	51.3	57 439	58 652	2.1	3.1
Tooele	8.8	25.0	8.9	14.6	14.7	10.7	9.3	4.6	3.4	30.3	50.7	22 502	31 605	40.5	3.1
West Jordan	9.8	23.9	10.0	15.7	15.3	11.7	8.2	3.4	2.0	29.6	49.5	68 336	103 712	51.8	7.0
West Valley City	9.7	22.5	10.0	16.9	13.9	11.2	8.7	4.6	2.4	29.9	49.7	108 896	129 480	18.9	3.9
VERMONT	4.9	15.0	10.6	11.3	11.9	15.5	15.1	8.9	6.8	42.2	50.7	608 827	625 741	2.8	0.1
Burlington	3.2	8.9	34.0	16.6	9.2	9.3	8.4	5.1	5.3	26.9	50.1	38 889	42 417	9.1	-0.5
VIRGINIA	6.2	16.5	10.1	13.9	13.4	14.7	12.3	7.5	5.4	37.6	50.9	7 078 515	8 001 024	13.0	4.1
Alexandria	7.4	10.1	6.4	24.4	17.9	13.4	10.9	5.6	3.9	35.8	51.5	128 283	139 966	9.1	7.5
Blacksburg	3.2	6.4	57.6	11.9	5.9	5.4	4.6	2.7	2.3	21.9	44.9	39 573	42 620	7.7	3.2
Charlottesville	5.4	9.7	25.1	20.0	11.3	9.7	9.7	5.1	4.1	29.0	51.7	45 049	43 475	-3.5	5.0
Chesapeake	6.3	18.7	9.4	13.3	13.4	15.8	11.9	6.5	4.6	36.6	51.2	199 184	222 209	11.6	5.0
Danville	6.8	15.0	9.7	11.7	10.2	13.3	14.4	9.3	9.6	41.8	54.3	48 411	43 055	-11.1	-1.4
Hampton	6.2	15.9	12.5	14.5	11.1	14.4	12.4	7.3	5.6	35.6	51.9	146 437	137 436	-6.1	-0.5
Harrisonburg	4.8	10.9	38.2	14.6	9.3	7.6	7.0	3.7	4.0	22.8	53.0	40 468	48 914	20.9	7.3
Leesburg	7.4	21.7	7.9	15.0	15.6	16.8	9.3	3.7	2.7	33.8	50.5	28 311	42 616	50.5	16.1
Lynchburg	6.1	13.6	23.8	12.9	9.0	10.8	10.2	6.8	7.0	29.2	52.8	65 269	75 568	15.8	4.5
Manassas	8.4	19.1	10.2	16.5	13.3	15.0	9.4	5.1	3.1	32.7	50.9	35 135	37 821	7.6	11.2
Newport News	7.5	16.3	13.1	16.4	11.7	13.3	10.6	6.2	5.0	32.7	51.7	180 150	180 719	0.3	1.1
Norfolk	6.9	13.6	19.3	18.1	11.2	11.6	9.8	5.1	4.5	29.9	47.9	234 403	242 803	3.6	1.1
Petersburg	8.1	13.1	11.1	13.2	10.7	15.1	13.8	8.1	6.8	39.9	53.7	33 740	32 420	-3.9	0.9
Portsmouth	7.6	16.0	10.9	15.7	11.4	13.3	11.8	7.1	6.3	34.9	51.7	100 565	95 535	-5.0	0.5
Richmond	6.4	12.2	15.3	19.2	11.5	12.4	11.7	6.0	5.3	32.7	52.4	197 790	204 214	3.2	6.7
Roanoke	7.3	14.5	8.7	15.3	13.0	13.9	13.1	7.3	6.9	38.0	52.3	94 911	97 032	2.2	2.6
Suffolk	6.7	18.7	9.0	12.0	13.8	15.6	12.1	7.1	4.9	38.2	51.8	63 677	84 585	32.8	2.6
Virginia Beach	6.7	16.7	10.6	16.2	13.1	14.2	11.2	6.5	4.9	34.9	50.9	425 257	437 994	3.0	3.0
Winchester	6.7	16.2	11.8	14.8	11.8	13.1	11.6	7.1	6.9	35.4	50.6	23 585	26 203	11.1	5.1
WASHINGTON	6.4	16.6	9.7	14.1	13.2	13.9	12.8	7.6	5.6	37.4	50.1	5 894 121	6 724 540	14.1	5.0
Auburn	6.9	17.3	9.9	13.2	14.5	13.1	12.9	6.5	5.7	37.0	51.6	40 314	70 180	74.1	8.8
Bellevue	6.0	14.3	6.8	17.6	15.2	14.1	12.1	7.1	6.9	37.9	48.5	109 569	122 363	11.7	6.7
Bellingham	5.4	11.0	23.9	15.3	10.3	9.3	11.9	6.7	6.2	31.0	51.0	67 171	80 885	20.4	3.1
Bothell	5.5	16.6	7.3	12.0	17.6	15.5	12.4	7.2	6.1	40.2	50.9	30 150	33 505	11.1	9.1
Bremerton	7.2	11.9	17.9	19.6	11.2	10.8	10.3	6.6	4.5	30.8	46.0	37 259	37 729	1.3	2.0
Burien	7.3	16.3	9.0	13.8	12.7	16.0	11.6	8.1	5.3	38.4	49.0	31 881	33 313	4.5	4.4
Des Moines	5.9	14.1	11.0	17.6	11.5	13.6	12.5	5.9	7.8	36.2	48.2	29 267	29 673	1.4	4.5
Edmonds	5.1	12.1	6.9	10.3	11.9	14.7	19.1	10.6	9.3	48.1	53.2	39 515	39 709	0.5	3.0
Everett	7.5	14.4	11.1	17.2	13.2	14.7	11.2	5.9	4.8	34.9	48.9	91 488	103 019	12.6	3.6
Federal Way	6.8	17.5	11.2	13.5	12.6	14.9	11.8	6.3	5.4	35.8	51.2	83 259	89 306	7.3	4.6
Issaquah	7.5	17.4	5.5	15.4	16.0	17.0	9.7	4.9	6.4	37.5	52.2	11 212	30 434	171.4	11.9
Kennewick	8.2	19.3	10.2	14.6	13.1	12.5	10.5	6.1	5.5	33.2	50.1	54 693	73 917	35.1	4.8
Kent	7.6	18.3	9.7	16.0	14.1	14.3	10.4	5.7	3.8	33.9	49.4	79 524	92 411	16.2	5.9
Kirkland	6.9	15.2	6.8	17.6	15.3	15.1	12.0	6.8	4.2	37.2	51.0	45 054	48 787	8.3	6.1
Lacey	7.5	16.7	9.7	17.0	14.6	9.6	10.4	7.1	7.5	33.9	51.2	31 226	42 393	35.8	7.2
Lake Stevens	8.0	20.1	7.9	14.3	17.1	14.3	10.3	4.7	3.4	34.8	48.5	6 361	28 069	341.3	7.9
Lakewood	6.9	14.2	10.0	16.0	10.5	13.9	13.9	7.7	6.8	37.3	51.5	58 211	58 163	-0.1	2.5
Longview	5.7	16.1	7.3	13.0	11.8	13.7	14.1	9.5	8.9	41.6	52.1	34 660	36 648	5.7	-1.0
Lynnwood	4.3	16.7	9.2	16.4	13.5	13.0	12.7	6.8	7.4	37.4	48.4	33 847	35 836	5.9	2.3
Marysville	8.3	18.7	9.2	15.4	14.1	13.6	10.4	5.6	4.7	34.0	49.6	25 315	60 020	137.1	8.4
Mount Vernon	8.9	20.2	11.7	11.9	12.3	11.1	10.2	7.0	6.6	33.0	49.7	26 232	31 743	21.0	4.3
Olympia	5.7	13.6	11.7	15.2	13.7	13.8	12.7	7.1	6.5	37.3	52.2	42 514	46 478	9.3	5.9

City	Households, 2011-2013: Number	Households, 2011-2013: Persons per household	Households, 2011-2013: Percent: Female family householder[1]	Households, 2011-2013: Percent: One-person	Persons in group quarters, 2010: Total	Persons in group quarters, 2010: Institutional: Total	Persons in group quarters, 2010: Institutional: Persons in nursing facilities	Persons in group quarters, 2010: Non-institutional	Serious crimes known to police,[2] 2013: Total: Number	Serious crimes known to police,[2] 2013: Total: Rate[3]	Serious crimes known to police,[2] 2013: Rate[3]: Violent	Serious crimes known to police,[2] 2013: Rate[3]: Property	Educational attainment, 2011–2013: Population age 25 and older	Educational attainment, 2011–2013: Attainment[4] (percent): High school graduate or less	Educational attainment, 2011–2013: Attainment[4] (percent): Bachelor's degree or more
	27	28	29	30	31	32	33	34	35	36	37	38	39	40	41
UTAH—Cont'd															
Kaysville	8 026	3.54	7.2	14.3	24	0	0	24	272	952	42	910	15 607	19.0	46.2
Layton	21 954	3.15	10.9	16.4	44	26	0	18	1 861	2 695	154	2 542	39 947	27.1	30.9
Lehi	12 950	4.00	7.1	9.1	107	16	16	91	795	1 516	61	1 455	24 877	21.6	38.7
Logan	15 521	2.90	10.3	22.0	3 529	502	160	3 027	899	1 833	73	1 759	22 016	27.8	40.2
Midvale	11 272	2.64	15.4	28.6	85	10	0	75	NA	NA	NA	NA	19 394	41.5	21.9
Murray	18 712	2.56	10.9	27.3	175	124	97	51	2 675	5 485	424	5 061	32 168	30.1	29.8
Ogden	29 270	2.77	14.7	26.3	2 061	1 421	260	640	4 513	5 370	514	4 856	50 506	48.1	18.2
Orem	25 949	3.42	10.0	16.0	1 790	461	301	1 329	2 112	2 310	36	2 274	47 886	24.6	35.9
Pleasant Grove	9 316	3.70	9.8	12.1	51	42	42	9	437	1 256	46	1 210	17 038	24.3	37.7
Provo	32 215	3.30	8.3	14.0	10 353	1 037	223	9 316	2 994	2 560	142	2 418	48 307	23.3	38.8
Riverton	10 691	3.76	7.3	9.7	45	14	14	31	NA	NA	NA	NA	22 040	22.7	32.7
Roy	12 063	3.10	11.4	17.1	124	115	93	9	823	2 177	108	2 068	22 701	40.4	19.2
St. George	25 039	2.97	8.0	22.3	1 053	648	303	405	1 889	2 472	181	2 291	45 893	32.5	28.6
Salt Lake City	74 362	2.48	10.3	36.1	4 795	822	539	3 973	16 938	8 903	782	8 122	122 639	30.4	42.8
Sandy	28 748	3.10	8.0	17.7	365	287	287	78	3 099	3 446	150	3 295	56 411	23.7	39.6
South Jordan	15 490	3.63	4.9	9.7	7	7	7	0	1 279	2 221	49	2 172	32 361	20.4	39.7
Spanish Fork	9 251	3.78	8.3	13.5	832	813	27	19	495	1 349	27	1 322	18 090	32.0	26.7
Springville	8 772	3.48	7.8	13.3	119	119	55	0	715	2 311	107	2 204	15 410	26.3	36.5
Taylorsville	19 232	3.12	13.0	22.9	112	82	82	30	NA	NA	NA	NA	37 531	38.7	20.5
Tooele	10 065	3.16	11.1	20.9	243	237	103	6	1 421	4 407	223	4 184	18 420	43.0	18.7
West Jordan	31 471	3.42	10.4	17.8	502	394	162	108	2 932	2 670	180	2 489	60 988	37.5	23.1
West Valley City	36 434	3.62	15.9	15.5	193	158	77	35	7 290	5 466	531	4 935	76 470	54.2	12.7
VERMONT	256 563	2.34	9.1	28.3	25 329	5 571	3 588	19 758	14 634	2 335	121	2 214	435 144	38.7	35.7
Burlington	15 983	2.20	7.5	34.9	7 060	539	476	6 521	1 531	3 625	180	3 445	22 816	29.0	50.4
VIRGINIA	3 026 761	2.62	12.4	26.5	239 834	101 333	30 324	138 501	186 859	2 262	196	2 066	5 499 463	37.3	35.5
Alexandria	65 294	2.23	7.6	42.4	1 827	974	506	853	3 239	2 181	174	2 007	111 619	20.5	61.7
Blacksburg	13 274	2.59	5.1	25.9	8 718	150	134	8 568	560	1 314	75	1 239	14 118	14.2	69.6
Charlottesville	17 098	2.41	10.6	37.9	2 438	228	167	2 210	1 690	3 825	482	3 343	26 262	33.4	50.6
Chesapeake	79 431	2.79	14.9	21.2	3 721	3 258	650	463	6 979	3 027	321	2 705	149 627	35.9	28.6
Danville	18 239	2.26	19.4	36.8	1 483	987	558	496	2 192	5 082	352	4 730	29 355	50.5	17.4
Hampton	52 274	2.53	18.4	31.5	4 454	902	516	3 552	4 775	3 487	214	3 273	89 120	38.5	22.2
Harrisonburg	15 872	2.75	10.4	28.1	7 583	681	378	6 902	1 475	2 849	205	2 645	23 458	45.2	33.3
Leesburg	14 887	3.08	10.8	18.2	256	247	247	9	944	2 011	162	1 849	29 042	27.9	47.8
Lynchburg	28 904	2.31	15.1	36.4	10 198	1 534	863	8 664	2 311	2 972	426	2 546	43 632	37.7	33.1
Manassas	12 353	3.28	17.5	20.2	46	0	0	46	969	2 334	294	2 040	25 246	45.6	27.7
Newport News	68 120	2.53	18.7	30.9	7 499	1 555	633	5 944	6 397	3 533	440	3 093	114 160	40.3	23.6
Norfolk	86 075	2.56	18.5	31.6	32 780	2 746	924	30 034	12 293	4 971	579	4 392	147 781	40.4	25.7
Petersburg	12 368	2.54	25.9	36.8	1 058	587	273	471	1 271	3 991	518	3 473	21 843	57.7	14.9
Portsmouth	36 360	2.57	23.1	30.6	3 416	2 541	454	875	5 979	6 163	612	5 551	63 105	46.8	19.9
Richmond	85 303	2.34	18.9	40.6	12 725	2 884	1 312	9 841	10 059	4 726	623	4 104	139 224	41.4	34.7
Roanoke	41 993	2.27	17.4	36.7	2 126	1 083	517	1 043	4 907	5 011	469	4 542	67 896	47.9	23.0
Suffolk	30 573	2.76	16.9	22.7	1 128	1 029	267	99	2 860	3 346	318	3 028	55 911	40.7	26.0
Virginia Beach	164 444	2.64	14.7	24.2	9 253	2 961	1 520	6 292	12 007	2 664	164	2 500	294 372	28.9	33.7
Winchester	10 537	2.46	12.9	35.6	976	157	125	819	1 097	4 039	331	3 707	17 572	47.5	26.3
WASHINGTON	2 634 496	2.56	10.4	27.8	139 375	57 844	22 156	81 531	278 815	3 999	289	3 710	4 640 203	33.4	32.1
Auburn	28 051	2.57	13.9	28.1	668	289	228	379	4 261	5 714	396	5 319	47 915	43.3	21.9
Bellevue	53 460	2.45	7.0	26.5	1 110	154	154	956	4 074	3 191	98	3 093	96 356	16.0	62.1
Bellingham	33 715	2.29	11.5	33.8	5 172	1 065	570	4 107	4 405	5 330	270	5 060	49 049	26.4	38.7
Bothell	13 650	2.52	7.5	26.0	321	188	188	133	867	2 477	54	2 422	24 552	25.5	42.7
Bremerton	15 247	2.33	13.7	35.7	4 255	428	350	3 827	2 177	5 476	576	4 900	24 709	33.3	19.4
Burien	18 371	2.66	13.9	29.8	300	209	119	91	2 789	5 598	355	5 243	33 258	42.7	24.1
Des Moines	11 559	2.58	12.2	28.0	596	382	382	214	1 274	4 152	319	3 833	20 957	41.2	22.9
Edmonds	17 705	2.26	9.9	32.1	476	220	220	256	1 061	2 612	172	2 440	30 660	19.8	46.8
Everett	41 521	2.43	12.1	36.2	4 145	1 706	404	2 439	7 308	6 951	421	6 530	70 022	38.8	21.0
Federal Way	33 194	2.74	16.6	24.4	831	445	421	386	5 481	5 910	316	5 594	59 239	39.8	23.6
Issaquah	13 431	2.41	7.3	29.1	443	242	242	201	835	2 503	63	2 440	22 758	13.0	58.2
Kennewick	27 542	2.71	12.7	30.2	1 081	930	200	151	2 727	3 564	314	3 251	47 410	42.6	21.3
Kent	42 213	2.86	14.1	27.3	1 390	888	86	502	5 928	4 767	257	4 510	78 955	43.8	24.0
Kirkland	34 592	2.39	8.2	30.6	630	175	150	455	NA	NA	NA	NA	59 257	16.7	54.7
Lacey	16 742	2.58	11.6	28.0	998	207	204	791	1 573	3 551	178	3 373	29 104	30.5	32.7
Lake Stevens	10 104	2.89	12.0	18.9	29	5	5	24	781	2 658	153	2 504	18 732	37.0	21.0
Lakewood	24 204	2.39	12.4	36.7	1 268	992	152	276	3 074	5 205	696	4 509	40 579	38.9	21.0
Longview	15 107	2.37	13.0	33.9	962	769	389	193	2 598	7 142	470	6 672	25 974	42.4	15.2
Lynnwood	13 580	2.62	12.5	30.8	618	237	195	381	2 568	7 056	288	6 767	25 315	35.7	28.1
Marysville	21 755	2.84	12.6	21.5	600	225	191	375	2 526	4 000	219	3 781	39 778	39.8	17.2
Mount Vernon	11 102	2.84	17.3	21.0	639	399	173	240	1 753	5 402	274	5 128	19 110	46.5	21.0
Olympia	20 377	2.28	10.4	37.1	1 283	942	415	341	1 949	4 057	281	3 776	33 060	26.1	41.9

1. No spouse present. 2. Data for serious crimes have not been adjusted for underreporting. This may affect comparability between geographic areas and over time. 3. Per 100,000 population estimated by the FBI. 4. Persons 25 years old and over.

Table D. Cities — **Income, Poverty, and Housing**

City	Money income, 2011–2013					Housing units, 2010			Occupied housing units 2011–2013				
		Households								Owner-occupied		Median owner costs as a percent of income	
	Per capita income[1] (dollars)	Median income	Percent with income of $200,000 or more	Percent with income of less than $25,000	Families with income below poverty (percent)	Total	Percent change, 2000–2010	Vacant units for sale or rent[2]	Total	Percent	Median value[3] (dollars)	With a mortgage[4]	Without a mortgage[5]
	42	43	44	45	46	47	48	49	50	51	52	53	54
UTAH—Cont'd													
Kaysville	28 048	84 125	6.0	14.3	6.3	7 700	35.3	176	8 026	84.4	276 700	21.7	10.0
Layton	26 301	68 080	3.4	14.2	7.3	22 356	16.8	981	21 954	74.3	195 100	21.8	10.0
Lehi	22 424	74 566	4.4	7.9	4.4	13 064	146.5	662	12 950	80.0	239 200	22.5	10.0
Logan	16 929	35 770	2.1	33.3	18.8	16 790	14.0	962	15 521	42.8	162 500	25.8	10.0
Midvale	21 873	47 452	1.4	25.0	16.6	11 764	9.6	851	11 272	44.2	187 200	26.6	12.4
Murray	27 571	51 549	3.0	21.2	8.8	19 181	44.1	955	18 712	64.9	219 500	22.7	10.0
Ogden	18 706	40 110	1.7	27.7	16.6	32 482	9.1	2 851	29 270	55.4	126 400	23.6	11.5
Orem	20 602	53 229	2.7	20.5	13.8	26 970	11.6	1 154	25 949	61.5	199 500	23.3	10.0
Pleasant Grove	20 131	62 178	2.7	15.1	8.7	9 841	55.1	460	9 316	65.9	218 300	22.6	10.0
Provo	16 496	38 542	2.2	32.7	23.5	33 212	9.2	1 688	32 215	40.6	187 800	24.6	10.0
Riverton	26 042	82 373	5.6	5.8	2.2	10 810	63.9	350	10 691	89.0	260 300	24.6	10.0
Roy	21 485	59 468	0.8	13.5	9.0	12 599	14.3	425	12 063	85.0	156 800	23.4	10.0
St. George	21 782	46 493	3.2	23.6	10.4	32 089	52.2	6 569	25 039	64.7	198 900	26.5	10.0
Salt Lake City	28 892	45 774	5.2	28.5	14.3	80 724	4.8	6 211	74 362	48.4	231 900	23.2	10.0
Sandy	31 631	75 700	7.3	10.8	5.6	29 501	10.8	1 205	28 748	77.8	264 700	22.6	10.0
South Jordan	28 455	86 775	6.7	5.7	3.5	14 943	92.5	610	15 490	80.2	314 700	23.7	10.0
Spanish Fork	18 415	62 073	1.2	12.8	5.7	9 440	62.3	371	9 251	74.9	185 800	24.3	10.0
Springville	20 469	58 333	2.3	14.5	6.3	8 927	42.7	396	8 772	68.2	182 200	24.2	10.0
Taylorsville	22 462	56 601	1.9	17.4	9.3	20 671	7.8	910	19 232	69.6	182 400	22.7	10.0
Tooele	20 677	54 183	0.8	14.9	7.4	10 646	33.6	687	10 065	73.1	156 100	23.1	10.5
West Jordan	22 234	66 263	1.5	12.0	8.2	31 366	60.2	1 517	31 471	74.9	213 300	24.5	10.0
West Valley City	17 350	50 122	1.0	20.9	18.3	38 978	16.4	1 839	36 434	67.0	162 300	24.6	10.0
VERMONT	29 181	53 853	3.5	21.8	7.2	322 539	9.6	66 097	256 563	71.2	216 800	24.9	16.8
Burlington	24 820	43 620	3.4	30.4	11.1	16 897	3.1	778	15 983	40.2	262 200	24.5	17.2
VIRGINIA	33 103	63 056	7.6	18.8	8.4	3 364 939	15.9	308 881	3 026 761	66.3	240 200	23.2	10.7
Alexandria	53 079	85 762	13.8	10.6	5.8	72 376	12.6	4 294	65 294	43.0	477 900	22.2	11.3
Blacksburg	19 103	30 883	5.0	45.3	13.8	15 342	12.5	887	13 274	28.6	276 000	18.9	10.0
Charlottesville	27 632	44 215	5.2	30.6	10.1	19 189	9.1	1 411	17 098	42.0	288 200	23.5	12.8
Chesapeake	29 039	67 213	4.7	15.3	8.0	83 196	14.5	3 622	79 431	71.0	252 800	25.9	12.7
Danville	20 137	32 066	1.8	39.3	19.6	22 438	-2.9	3 607	18 239	54.5	87 700	20.8	11.7
Hampton	24 839	48 295	2.1	25.5	12.7	59 566	3.9	4 535	52 274	59.8	191 800	25.0	12.8
Harrisonburg	16 627	36 157	1.7	33.7	14.1	17 444	27.4	1 456	15 872	34.7	197 800	22.7	11.2
Leesburg	38 422	96 221	11.8	7.3	5.3	15 119	41.7	678	14 887	66.2	371 600	23.7	10.0
Lynchburg	20 941	38 568	2.1	34.3	18.5	31 992	15.7	3 516	28 904	51.2	146 800	22.8	12.2
Manassas	27 924	69 377	6.0	12.2	8.5	13 123	8.3	596	12 353	64.3	252 300	23.3	13.7
Newport News	24 710	49 096	2.3	23.5	12.9	76 198	2.8	5 534	68 120	50.8	195 200	24.6	12.9
Norfolk	23 938	43 864	2.5	28.8	16.5	95 018	0.6	8 533	86 075	43.2	193 300	27.9	13.8
Petersburg	18 039	31 526	0.7	40.5	22.9	16 326	2.3	2 692	12 368	42.9	117 700	24.2	13.4
Portsmouth	22 507	44 123	1.9	27.7	15.9	40 806	-1.9	3 482	36 360	54.9	171 000	27.6	16.2
Richmond	26 307	39 469	3.9	33.4	20.8	98 349	6.6	11 198	85 303	42.8	187 100	26.5	14.7
Roanoke	23 049	37 710	1.7	32.9	16.6	47 453	4.9	4 741	41 993	54.8	130 900	24.2	13.3
Suffolk	28 880	64 795	3.9	15.1	7.4	33 035	33.7	2 167	30 573	71.0	234 800	26.0	12.0
Virginia Beach	31 665	64 771	4.9	13.9	6.9	177 879	9.6	12 790	164 444	63.2	261 000	25.8	12.0
Winchester	25 073	42 858	4.0	29.7	11.2	11 872	12.1	1 265	10 537	44.7	207 500	22.9	12.0
WASHINGTON	30 432	58 592	5.0	20.0	9.4	2 885 677	17.7	265 601	2 634 496	62.4	249 200	25.0	12.1
Auburn	26 732	52 918	2.8	20.7	11.0	27 834	66.3	1 776	28 051	59.7	215 700	26.0	16.8
Bellevue	49 013	91 260	14.3	12.1	5.7	55 551	15.0	5 196	53 460	55.2	520 900	24.0	13.1
Bellingham	24 244	41 109	2.1	31.9	15.5	36 760	24.9	2 089	33 715	45.3	272 800	24.3	10.9
Bothell	37 854	75 266	7.6	15.2	7.7	14 255	15.3	758	13 650	66.0	335 700	22.9	15.3
Bremerton	23 830	43 240	1.1	28.5	17.4	17 273	3.9	2 341	15 247	42.1	181 900	25.9	11.4
Burien	24 900	50 161	2.6	24.0	15.5	14 322	2.1	1 069	18 371	52.8	255 500	28.9	12.4
Des Moines	26 325	54 090	4.0	19.5	11.7	12 588	6.2	924	11 559	58.2	244 800	28.7	15.8
Edmonds	40 892	67 228	7.9	15.3	5.4	18 378	4.9	997	17 705	68.7	371 700	26.6	13.3
Everett	25 453	46 914	1.6	26.9	14.2	44 609	15.6	3 297	41 521	43.0	221 600	27.3	13.4
Federal Way	26 176	53 131	3.2	21.8	13.7	35 444	8.8	2 256	33 194	55.1	236 300	25.5	13.1
Issaquah	48 225	86 178	14.7	11.5	2.5	13 914	173.6	1 073	13 431	58.6	438 700	24.4	17.8
Kennewick	24 716	51 170	3.2	24.5	12.4	28 507	29.3	1 241	27 542	60.8	166 600	19.9	10.0
Kent	25 060	54 302	2.9	21.4	14.6	36 424	12.0	2 380	42 213	51.1	236 400	25.7	13.1
Kirkland	48 123	85 684	12.7	11.1	4.9	24 345	11.0	1 900	34 592	63.7	399 200	26.7	12.7
Lacey	25 380	58 271	1.0	14.1	6.7	18 493	41.4	1 544	16 742	53.7	213 900	25.8	11.4
Lake Stevens	27 042	71 163	1.4	13.0	5.7	10 414	NA	604	10 104	70.4	232 500	27.6	14.8
Lakewood	25 061	44 859	3.1	29.7	16.4	26 548	4.7	2 479	24 204	46.2	199 700	26.5	13.5
Longview	21 415	36 229	1.5	36.6	17.0	16 380	7.7	1 099	15 107	55.2	165 700	25.5	13.4
Lynnwood	25 066	50 553	2.1	26.3	10.9	14 939	8.5	832	13 580	51.4	260 100	25.5	15.5
Marysville	26 448	62 312	1.7	17.3	7.4	22 363	130.6	1 144	21 755	67.5	214 600	25.7	14.0
Mount Vernon	21 787	46 390	1.9	26.3	17.3	12 058	24.0	716	11 102	55.3	205 800	23.8	13.4
Olympia	29 185	52 393	2.9	23.7	10.4	22 086	12.1	1 325	20 377	50.7	237 200	23.9	13.0

1. Based on population estimated by the American Community Survey. 2. Includes units rented or sold but not occupied. 3. Specified owner-occupied units; $1,000,000 represents $1,000,000 or more 4. 50.0 represents 50 percent or more. 5. 10.0 represents 10 percent or less.

City	Occupied housing units, 2011–2013 (cont.)				Migration, 2011–2013		Civilian labor force, 2014				Civilian employment[4], 2011–2013			
									Unemployment			Percent		
	Percent renter occupied	Median gross rent[1]	Median rent as a percent of income[2]	Percent with no vehicle available	Percent who lived in the same house one year ago	Percent who lived outside current city one year ago	Total	Percent change, 2013–2014	Total	Rate[3]	Population age 16 and older	In labor force	Civilian full-year full-time workers	Households with no workers (percent)
	55	56	57	58	59	60	61	62	63	64	65	66	67	68
UTAH—Cont'd														
Kaysville	15.6	639	28.2	2.1	91.5	7.2	13 095	1.6	419	3.2	19 158	68.4	41.6	14.0
Layton	25.7	855	26.6	5.4	84.1	12.3	35 273	1.5	1 303	3.7	49 588	70.1	45.2	15.4
Lehi	20.0	1 183	30.0	2.2	85.8	11.6	22 412	2.6	798	3.6	31 193	70.0	41.7	12.2
Logan	57.2	650	29.7	6.2	65.7	19.6	26 507	1.6	852	3.2	38 304	70.5	30.8	17.2
Midvale	55.8	941	28.6	8.5	78.5	17.4	18 303	1.0	691	3.8	23 455	72.3	45.9	17.8
Murray	35.1	900	33.0	7.0	81.3	16.3	28 234	1.2	1 071	3.8	38 704	70.9	44.2	22.7
Ogden	44.6	722	30.2	10.1	78.2	12.1	39 589	0.9	1 969	5.0	62 864	64.0	36.9	25.5
Orem	38.5	862	31.1	3.8	80.4	13.4	44 906	2.4	1 509	3.4	66 033	66.4	35.4	18.6
Pleasant Grove	34.1	1 055	29.5	3.3	77.6	18.2	16 265	2.5	561	3.4	22 428	68.6	37.6	14.1
Provo	59.4	723	33.1	4.6	61.2	21.8	62 401	2.5	2 064	3.3	90 866	68.8	24.0	17.3
Riverton	11.0	1 050	22.3	1.9	89.5	8.9	21 927	1.3	714	3.3	26 769	76.0	49.5	7.7
Roy	15.0	928	22.5	1.6	87.6	11.2	18 400	1.2	852	4.6	26 799	67.6	44.7	20.3
St. George	35.3	858	32.5	4.8	78.7	11.3	32 094	3.3	1 352	4.2	56 500	57.2	29.9	35.5
Salt Lake City	51.6	794	30.2	12.8	78.1	12.5	107 275	1.1	3 755	3.5	151 890	69.8	42.0	23.3
Sandy	22.2	1 138	27.6	3.6	88.1	9.5	49 304	1.1	1 752	3.6	67 010	71.6	45.3	15.5
South Jordan	19.8	1 455	29.0	2.8	83.4	13.9	29 543	1.2	996	3.4	39 142	70.1	45.4	12.7
Spanish Fork	25.1	988	29.1	2.6	81.6	13.4	15 807	2.3	577	3.7	22 928	65.5	38.6	13.8
Springville	31.8	895	26.8	3.2	81.1	13.8	14 631	2.5	518	3.5	20 500	69.0	42.1	14.5
Taylorsville	30.4	905	30.2	4.2	84.5	12.1	33 422	1.0	1 335	4.0	44 805	72.9	45.2	19.1
Tooele	26.9	866	28.2	3.3	84.7	9.5	15 434	0.9	775	5.0	22 387	66.3	43.5	17.6
West Jordan	25.1	1 021	29.8	2.0	86.4	10.0	59 109	1.2	2 145	3.6	75 691	76.1	49.8	11.2
West Valley City	33.0	915	36.3	4.8	81.3	12.8	68 073	0.9	2 821	4.1	93 553	71.8	44.7	16.2
VERMONT	28.8	871	31.1	6.7	86.6	11.2	348 868	-0.7	14 305	4.1	517 549	67.1	40.7	26.7
Burlington	59.8	987	35.1	14.8	66.5	19.3	24 200	-0.3	805	3.3	37 812	64.7	31.6	27.1
VIRGINIA	33.7	1 088	30.0	6.4	84.6	11.6	4 261 175	0.4	220 070	5.2	6 530 686	66.3	43.1	23.4
Alexandria	57.0	1 506	28.0	9.4	78.5	15.4	94 209	0.4	3 528	3.7	122 922	78.7	57.8	13.9
Blacksburg	71.4	898	49.8	7.7	57.3	24.1	20 686	0.9	1 280	6.2	39 382	48.6	22.1	29.1
Charlottesville	58.0	971	33.5	10.7	73.8	17.5	24 106	2.8	1 031	4.3	37 912	59.2	34.9	26.3
Chesapeake	29.0	1 159	31.1	4.2	85.9	9.2	116 496	-0.1	6 134	5.3	177 839	67.5	43.9	18.5
Danville	45.5	590	28.7	16.3	82.8	7.8	19 714	-0.7	1 710	8.7	34 469	56.2	32.1	40.6
Hampton	40.2	969	36.2	8.6	83.9	8.1	65 819	-0.2	4 406	6.7	109 642	64.9	38.6	27.1
Harrisonburg	65.3	850	36.0	9.7	65.7	24.2	24 121	0.2	1 466	6.1	43 503	56.2	28.7	24.4
Leesburg	33.8	1 333	28.9	2.8	85.3	11.7	26 276	0.5	1 090	4.1	34 286	77.2	53.5	8.3
Lynchburg	48.8	728	33.9	15.5	71.7	16.1	35 955	0.4	2 283	6.3	63 798	57.7	30.6	32.2
Manassas	35.7	1 305	31.4	6.5	83.4	9.4	22 330	0.2	1 103	4.9	30 714	74.6	49.7	15.4
Newport News	49.2	956	31.8	8.3	76.4	12.4	90 692	0.1	5 645	6.2	142 102	69.7	40.1	24.2
Norfolk	56.8	956	33.8	12.8	75.9	12.3	112 971	0.0	7 182	6.4	199 696	69.3	34.3	25.2
Petersburg	57.1	826	36.1	17.5	79.8	9.5	13 909	0.8	1 481	10.6	26 148	56.9	34.2	38.7
Portsmouth	45.1	939	34.1	11.2	80.0	10.0	45 364	-0.3	3 236	7.1	76 010	63.6	38.6	28.3
Richmond	57.2	869	33.0	17.2	77.2	11.2	111 992	1.2	6 858	6.1	174 584	64.6	36.8	30.4
Roanoke	45.2	700	28.9	13.8	81.7	7.8	50 175	0.6	2 945	5.9	78 292	63.8	40.9	30.6
Suffolk	29.0	977	31.3	5.3	84.8	8.2	42 076	0.0	2 428	5.8	65 942	67.6	42.8	22.4
Virginia Beach	36.8	1 221	31.8	4.0	82.4	8.9	231 784	0.1	11 442	4.9	352 886	70.6	43.8	19.5
Winchester	55.3	890	33.5	10.4	78.5	15.6	14 501	0.8	726	5.0	21 305	62.7	39.2	30.4
WASHINGTON	37.6	974	30.3	7.0	82.7	12.4	3 488 183	0.8	217 821	6.2	5 485 286	64.7	38.6	26.6
Auburn	40.3	969	34.4	7.9	81.9	12.1	37 975	1.5	1 967	5.2	57 130	64.6	40.1	26.8
Bellevue	44.8	1 425	24.4	6.4	79.2	14.4	73 858	1.9	3 031	4.1	108 734	67.0	44.8	20.8
Bellingham	54.7	893	35.9	11.0	75.9	12.6	42 512	0.1	2 690	6.3	70 290	65.4	31.6	29.1
Bothell	34.0	1 316	33.8	5.0	84.7	11.9	19 971	1.9	913	4.6	27 727	70.7	44.8	21.3
Bremerton	57.9	874	33.1	13.4	69.4	20.4	16 053	-0.2	1 236	7.7	32 455	64.2	30.7	33.1
Burien	47.2	972	32.3	9.4	79.8	14.4	26 123	1.7	1 191	4.6	38 926	66.0	40.6	25.6
Des Moines	41.8	1 039	29.7	6.2	83.4	11.7	16 094	1.7	884	5.5	25 125	65.8	39.1	25.9
Edmonds	31.3	1 057	30.4	2.7	87.4	10.0	22 166	1.9	1 057	4.8	34 125	62.1	39.8	28.3
Everett	57.0	937	31.7	12.0	77.6	15.1	53 856	1.4	3 094	5.7	83 873	68.1	37.7	26.0
Federal Way	44.9	990	34.2	10.2	79.7	13.5	47 761	1.6	2 586	5.4	72 443	65.7	40.4	23.4
Issaquah	41.4	1 431	25.1	6.1	76.0	18.8	18 627	1.8	723	3.9	25 398	72.0	47.5	21.8
Kennewick	39.2	789	29.1	7.0	81.3	10.8	37 429	0.1	2 817	7.5	57 324	63.9	40.9	26.1
Kent	48.9	986	33.1	7.0	81.6	12.6	63 141	1.6	3 423	5.4	94 599	66.1	40.6	22.0
Kirkland	36.3	1 325	26.6	4.2	82.4	12.2	49 683	2.2	1 958	3.9	66 720	72.4	47.9	17.7
Lacey	46.3	1 088	30.1	5.3	73.7	21.8	18 704	0.2	1 341	7.2	34 612	61.7	33.6	28.2
Lake Stevens	29.6	1 211	29.6	2.4	82.1	12.2	15 364	2.0	527	3.4	21 882	71.6	42.9	17.4
Lakewood	53.8	825	32.9	9.5	77.0	17.5	24 807	-0.1	1 887	7.6	47 950	59.9	31.3	33.1
Longview	44.8	700	37.3	12.4	77.2	10.2	15 011	1.8	1 269	8.5	29 504	52.3	28.0	42.9
Lynnwood	48.6	978	33.8	10.6	82.6	11.3	19 290	1.6	1 029	5.3	29 564	64.4	38.0	30.6
Marysville	32.5	1 146	32.1	4.4	83.6	11.0	31 855	1.7	1 366	4.3	47 084	69.7	43.3	23.6
Mount Vernon	44.7	880	36.7	6.0	81.3	10.3	14 445	-0.1	1 083	7.5	24 046	62.9	33.7	25.6
Olympia	49.3	937	32.6	11.8	77.6	14.8	24 543	0.6	1 467	6.0	39 759	65.2	38.3	28.7

1. $2,000 represents $2,000 or more. 2. 50.0 represents 50 percent or more. 3. Percent of civilian labor force. 4. Persons 16 years old and over.

City	Value of residential construction authorized by building permits, 2014			Wholesale trade,[1] 2007				Retail trade,[2] 2007			
	New construction ($1,000)	Number of housing units	Percent single family	Number of establish-ments	Number of employees	Sales (mil dol)	Annual payroll (mil dol)	Number of establish-ments	Number of employees	Sales (mil dol)	Annual payroll (mil dol)
	69	70	71	72	73	74	75	76	77	78	79
UTAH—Cont'd											
Kaysville	53 969	184	100.0	22	289	112.1	11.7	51	676	149.9	15.8
Layton	69 947	452	57.1	47	414	188.9	14.7	300	5 530	1 225.3	108.9
Lehi	140 201	719	63.0	19	148	57.3	6.3	72	2 005	596.4	61.9
Logan	35 706	260	38.8	69	591	315.1	24.1	247	3 611	709.3	63.1
Midvale	59 790	385	43.9	56	664	287.1	29.3	146	2 108	629.0	47.3
Murray	33 465	179	34.1	114	1 184	449.2	53.5	351	6 832	2 046.1	187.2
Ogden	29 763	321	17.8	126	1 276	696.7	51.0	356	4 207	1 018.2	96.1
Orem	149 896	1 028	22.9	134	1 447	569.2	59.8	464	8 311	1 734.3	165.6
Pleasant Grove	62 953	365	44.1	21	71	32.9	2.8	50	855	215.6	16.9
Provo	40 136	291	44.0	66	1 478	619.5	87.6	316	5 033	1 202.5	103.6
Riverton	28 619	116	64.7	19	70	31.8	2.8	53	725	167.7	15.8
Roy	1 452	11	100.0	6	D	D	D	67	963	217.1	19.3
St. George	120 943	792	95.1	98	848	342.3	31.5	446	6 242	1 672.5	151.1
Salt Lake City	47 290	340	27.9	567	9 776	7 486.3	475.7	972	15 888	4 213.6	398.1
Sandy	51 544	503	15.7	138	1 487	428.8	54.9	380	6 843	2 042.0	169.2
South Jordan	213 288	1 130	71.3	39	707	577.2	53.8	85	2 045	543.5	46.7
Spanish Fork	53 945	190	100.0	19	692	232.4	17.2	76	998	202.7	16.3
Springville	23 970	328	18.3	27	684	213.2	30.7	71	1 213	303.6	25.4
Taylorsville	7 629	34	100.0	18	D	D	D	107	1 934	457.1	41.0
Tooele	17 324	157	54.1	8	D	D	D	75	1 391	366.6	31.6
West Jordan	75 647	364	77.2	61	1 351	824.0	63.4	203	4 672	931.6	83.8
West Valley City	61 239	563	24.5	154	3 351	2 250.8	191.7	299	5 823	1 563.7	145.7
VERMONT	281 490	1 546	63.3	762	9 852	5 121.7	424.8	3 852	40 416	9 310.1	938.7
Burlington	612	4	100.0	47	561	418.2	29.0	252	3 435	575.2	71.5
VIRGINIA	4 655 664	28 682	65.7	6 502	98 304	60 513.4	4 787.4	29 633	431 634	105 663.3	9 991.9
Alexandria	170 552	1 324	13.1	91	1 262	525.7	65.2	528	8 052	2 353.8	232.5
Blacksburg	21 969	117	55.6	12	71	20.7	4.2	109	1 271	212.4	19.8
Charlottesville	30 030	173	35.8	55	473	203.4	20.4	349	3 880	699.4	78.1
Chesapeake	182 896	886	95.5	239	3 428	2 123.3	156.1	869	16 523	3 977.8	345.5
Danville	1 638	12	100.0	55	462	204.1	18.8	330	4 395	892.2	81.8
Hampton	7 087	160	100.0	60	800	288.9	33.5	436	7 295	1 805.7	162.3
Harrisonburg	14 080	152	47.4	55	1 033	378.5	42.7	376	6 265	1 465.3	158.1
Leesburg	NA	NA	NA	21	128	55.4	8.4	266	4 750	1 238.4	112.5
Lynchburg	17 863	92	100.0	82	1 125	541.5	43.2	419	7 266	1 665.1	151.2
Manassas	17 617	125	100.0	44	D	D	D	187	2 635	921.2	85.3
Newport News	19 582	330	33.0	116	1 470	902.0	68.5	727	10 894	2 431.3	233.8
Norfolk	62 419	650	60.5	250	8 577	3 280.4	247.2	975	13 764	2 724.1	293.5
Petersburg	1 145	8	100.0	29	647	356.1	19.0	155	1 569	324.2	37.5
Portsmouth	29 789	153	92.2	48	611	173.6	27.4	296	3 428	682.1	75.7
Richmond	58 844	551	33.0	289	4 408	2 843.3	231.1	883	9 029	1 922.8	211.6
Roanoke	5 918	49	71.4	198	3 098	2 233.6	130.4	588	9 765	2 039.8	215.4
Suffolk	56 647	348	85.3	50	1 105	715.8	55.7	228	3 174	820.3	70.4
Virginia Beach	158 800	1 208	57.0	374	5 069	2 835.1	207.4	1 625	25 639	5 579.9	568.5
Winchester	3 220	23	91.3	30	D	D	D	307	4 695	998.7	101.1
WASHINGTON	7 016 518	33 898	52.8	8 181	111 294	76 791.0	5 557.6	23 075	328 053	92 968.5	8 585.3
Auburn	85 126	362	100.0	175	4 037	3 732.6	196.9	294	5 123	1 417.2	141.6
Bellevue	266 975	1 292	18.2	345	3 999	3 754.5	279.3	729	13 684	4 141.0	407.3
Bellingham	73 475	541	25.0	145	1 746	776.8	79.3	552	8 450	1 944.6	200.3
Bothell	46 633	151	68.9	76	1 391	1 148.6	115.3	107	1 602	505.5	43.1
Bremerton	20 808	136	47.8	25	281	177.4	10.9	153	2 230	696.4	67.9
Burien	17 475	57	100.0	20	88	15.5	3.6	154	2 070	586.8	57.8
Des Moines	13 107	50	66.0	12	131	113.0	21.8	52	730	177.5	19.1
Edmonds	23 105	99	46.5	38	140	197.7	7.7	143	1 636	484.2	53.9
Everett	33 889	270	51.9	139	2 039	1 436.1	114.8	481	7 619	2 079.9	215.7
Federal Way	88 474	559	13.8	59	562	421.7	37.2	285	4 774	1 261.5	118.2
Issaquah	181 984	855	22.1	51	361	299.7	21.7	167	3 547	2 352.3	106.2
Kennewick	78 409	328	92.1	60	594	344.3	26.5	364	5 973	1 404.0	136.7
Kent	84 780	375	48.0	419	9 140	7 016.4	463.9	362	5 401	1 504.4	155.7
Kirkland	136 067	671	35.9	126	1 106	645.8	70.1	241	5 069	1 591.5	151.5
Lacey	77 888	314	100.0	26	242	107.2	11.7	150	3 528	853.7	89.5
Lake Stevens	41 041	148	98.6	8	52	20.2	1.6	39	929	198.9	21.7
Lakewood	11 589	49	57.1	61	871	1 130.6	39.0	274	3 213	743.7	80.6
Longview	3 063	13	100.0	38	560	339.8	26.7	188	3 334	827.7	81.2
Lynnwood	11 460	34	100.0	87	921	332.5	41.0	445	8 594	2 053.2	212.8
Marysville	62 755	477	20.1	37	339	146.3	12.9	171	2 719	706.0	72.1
Mount Vernon	18 729	114	100.0	35	506	151.3	21.5	155	2 186	596.9	60.0
Olympia	41 543	191	77.0	46	351	209.5	17.3	387	5 524	1 335.0	138.6

1. Merchant wholesalers except manufacturers' sales branches and offices. 2. Establishments with payroll.

City	Real estate and rental and leasing, 2007				Professional, scientific, and technical services,[1] 2007				Manufacturing, 2007			
	Number of establish-ments	Number of employees	Receipts (mil dol)	Annual payroll (mil dol)	Number of establish-ments	Number of employees	Receipts (mil dol)	Annual payroll (mil dol)	Number of establish-ments	Number of employees	Receipts (mil dol)	Annual payroll (mil dol)
	80	81	82	83	84	85	86	87	88	89	90	91
UTAH—Cont'd												
Kaysville	33	D	D	D	88	591	52.4	20.9	NA	NA	NA	NA
Layton	118	293	38.4	6.9	179	D	D	D	40	985	332.0	34.8
Lehi	50	53	10.7	2.0	110	1 606	99.6	56.9	35	1 720	D	102.1
Logan	107	415	48.3	10.9	171	D	D	D	109	6 969	2 130.6	284.5
Midvale	71	1 243	133.8	43.1	108	688	100.5	43.4	38	604	96.0	29.7
Murray	159	1 994	215.4	58.7	308	2 658	318.4	135.0	129	2 400	402.2	97.5
Ogden	133	499	59.2	9.6	258	D	D	D	146	9 325	2 752.7	374.6
Orem	210	555	103.3	14.2	385	D	D	D	113	3 629	780.6	153.3
Pleasant Grove	46	98	16.7	2.8	73	386	30.4	10.4	NA	NA	NA	NA
Provo	130	996	109.8	18.8	353	D	D	D	104	2 796	416.6	115.5
Riverton	62	148	10.2	2.7	77	243	13.9	5.3	NA	NA	NA	NA
Roy	17	65	5.8	1.0	38	390	57.7	20.8	NA	NA	NA	NA
St. George	271	675	99.0	15.3	315	D	D	D	93	2 305	465.9	83.5
Salt Lake City	536	3 371	920.2	123.1	1 336	14 855	2 364.4	1 010.1	480	24 868	9 175.7	1 203.5
Sandy	223	772	124.2	23.9	368	1 793	276.2	93.2	97	2 551	608.5	115.9
South Jordan	103	276	38.8	8.4	158	1 469	244.4	71.6	19	D	D	D
Spanish Fork	29	80	14.4	3.2	45	193	19.7	5.8	40	2 040	356.3	80.5
Springville	34	69	7.2	1.1	55	157	18.0	5.8	55	3 659	905.5	192.9
Taylorsville	50	190	20.9	4.5	80	D	D	D	19	699	114.5	31.7
Tooele	22	75	11.0	1.5	29	D	D	D	20	817	D	30.2
West Jordan	113	250	38.0	5.7	122	D	D	D	124	3 679	906.2	153.7
West Valley City	73	339	74.5	11.8	136	D	D	D	190	5 785	1 443.1	256.2
VERMONT	797	3 395	497.3	95.9	2 100	16 346	1 615.6	649.5	1 108	35 571	10 751.5	1 650.1
Burlington	72	464	75.5	13.4	249	D	D	D	33	1 264	224.3	65.4
VIRGINIA	9 475	60 502	12 636.8	2 408.7	27 078	376 172	66 543.7	26 936.8	5 777	277 456	92 417.8	12 169.6
Alexandria	229	2 484	811.8	127.1	1 166	D	D	D	88	1 483	284.5	56.3
Blacksburg	54	353	56.6	10.2	147	D	D	D	27	1 454	D	76.1
Charlottesville	98	557	86.5	19.7	290	D	D	D	51	1 589	677.1	79.1
Chesapeake	273	1 355	274.7	49.0	485	D	D	D	139	4 487	1 437.1	200.1
Danville	66	332	41.4	8.8	76	D	D	D	43	4 485	1 275.9	212.7
Hampton	115	873	113.9	24.2	280	D	D	D	77	2 790	522.4	122.0
Harrisonburg	80	346	68.3	8.8	150	D	D	D	47	2 824	746.3	103.1
Leesburg	54	240	66.9	9.5	262	D	D	D	NA	NA	NA	NA
Lynchburg	107	466	72.4	15.3	203	D	D	D	96	9 486	2 801.6	500.1
Manassas	59	230	41.7	8.3	218	D	D	D	41	4 038	1 408.7	340.5
Newport News	273	2 884	374.2	84.2	345	D	D	D	107	24 155	4 702.7	1 216.0
Norfolk	324	2 898	385.8	98.3	653	D	D	D	166	7 448	1 280.8	300.0
Petersburg	36	192	21.4	4.6	35	D	D	D	42	2 114	595.9	102.1
Portsmouth	93	383	48.6	8.5	144	D	D	D	63	2 360	652.9	105.2
Richmond	302	2 361	636.4	126.2	826	10 582	1 682.7	785.0	224	9 341	10 192.1	545.8
Roanoke	161	1 274	188.6	33.5	321	D	D	D	115	4 544	1 582.4	182.7
Suffolk	74	287	44.5	10.6	122	D	D	D	48	2 362	1 307.8	109.7
Virginia Beach	717	6 190	830.7	197.8	1 310	D	D	D	243	6 544	1 806.5	236.9
Winchester	76	329	63.3	12.0	147	D	D	D	30	D	D	D
WASHINGTON	10 480	51 196	10 467.3	1 818.7	19 242	150 367	23 394.7	9 778.0	7 650	269 851	112 053.3	13 274.5
Auburn	82	280	75.9	9.4	124	646	105.3	25.3	186	8 019	1 767.4	397.5
Bellevue	589	3 913	1 240.4	197.4	1 185	13 914	2 535.2	1 051.0	130	2 358	813.6	102.5
Bellingham	219	907	189.8	25.2	416	2 307	260.1	102.3	136	3 297	614.5	114.1
Bothell	89	326	91.0	10.7	187	D	D	D	37	2 063	D	127.7
Bremerton	70	250	34.0	6.5	74	D	D	D	NA	NA	NA	NA
Burien	72	329	119.3	10.7	90	553	41.6	15.9	NA	NA	NA	NA
Des Moines	29	86	17.0	2.6	29	91	7.7	2.6	NA	NA	NA	NA
Edmonds	98	311	65.3	12.2	176	721	103.5	39.9	NA	NA	NA	NA
Everett	191	926	134.1	30.1	291	3 107	403.0	164.3	136	29 991	18 143.4	1 933.6
Federal Way	125	636	238.7	22.8	185	1 829	147.1	87.5	NA	NA	NA	NA
Issaquah	77	361	92.7	16.4	169	3 278	1 038.9	251.3	24	1 277	510.4	D
Kennewick	119	734	158.3	22.9	176	D	D	D	42	612	D	26.6
Kent	149	890	180.4	28.8	203	D	D	D	264	19 431	6 922.6	1 279.1
Kirkland	191	1 074	337.0	42.6	403	D	D	D	63	877	D	40.3
Lacey	55	262	33.7	5.6	80	2 591	335.6	137.5	NA	NA	NA	NA
Lake Stevens	34	82	13.4	2.5	16	59	4.0	1.3	NA	NA	NA	NA
Lakewood	123	688	86.2	18.8	109	867	64.7	33.7	44	608	125.4	21.6
Longview	62	296	37.7	7.0	83	D	D	D	41	1 657	751.5	88.7
Lynnwood	106	448	138.6	17.8	142	D	D	D	62	686	91.1	23.5
Marysville	59	228	52.9	7.7	63	396	53.3	12.2	74	2 586	300.4	81.8
Mount Vernon	63	209	39.1	5.7	126	498	51.5	17.0	36	860	164.2	27.2
Olympia	117	477	127.3	12.4	297	D	D	D	35	672	237.5	29.0

1. Establishments subject to federal tax.

Table D. Cities — **Accommodation and Food Services, Arts, Entertainment, and Recreation, and Health Care and Social Assistance**

City	Accommodation and food services, 2007				Arts, entertainment, and recreation,[1] 2007				Health care and social assistance,[1] 2007			
	Number of establish-ments	Number of employees	Sales (mil dol)	Annual payroll (mil dol)	Number of establish-ments	Number of employees	Receipts (mil dol)	Annual payroll (mil dol)	Number of establish-ments	Number of employees	Receipts (mil dol)	Annual payroll (mil dol)
	92	93	94	95	96	97	98	99	100	101	102	103
UTAH—Cont'd												
Kaysville	23	D	D	D	10	38	1.0	0.3	40	D	D	D
Layton	126	2 945	112.9	33.2	15	D	D	D	139	2 196	241.7	83.3
Lehi	33	551	24.9	6.3	8	18	1.1	0.2	47	D	D	D
Logan	94	2 018	71.6	22.0	14	D	D	D	163	D	D	D
Midvale	72	1 459	60.4	17.2	8	115	3.9	1.0	47	D	D	D
Murray	97	2 203	92.4	27.6	12	D	D	D	259	D	D	D
Ogden	195	3 097	120.8	33.2	14	D	D	D	270	3 051	308.1	118.7
Orem	127	3 081	123.7	36.6	33	D	D	D	214	3 522	265.7	102.4
Pleasant Grove	25	381	12.2	3.1	8	25	3.6	0.6	51	D	D	D
Provo	182	3 840	150.9	43.6	33	D	D	D	265	D	D	D
Riverton	26	565	20.7	6.1	6	6	0.4	0.2	52	D	D	D
Roy	40	672	28.0	6.9	3	D	D	D	50	D	D	D
St. George	193	4 211	187.2	55.5	26	D	D	D	302	D	D	D
Salt Lake City	669	16 676	880.8	264.5	76	2 059	203.9	96.3	594	6 808	820.0	267.9
Sandy	168	3 812	148.3	45.2	37	525	21.2	5.6	237	D	D	D
South Jordan	44	785	34.2	10.5	8	D	D	D	77	627	67.1	21.0
Spanish Fork	35	D	D	D	4	D	D	D	46	D	D	D
Springville	30	534	22.3	5.7	3	D	D	D	53	D	D	D
Taylorsville	93	1 691	71.3	18.6	7	D	D	D	80	833	65.9	23.9
Tooele	41	760	27.5	6.9	4	D	D	D	62	D	D	D
West Jordan	95	D	D	D	9	D	D	D	144	2 053	259.0	74.7
West Valley City	160	2 746	125.5	33.0	18	D	D	D	104	D	D	D
VERMONT	1 942	31 176	1 367.6	427.9	323	6 554	280.4	79.3	1 469	15 381	1 147.3	531.8
Burlington	138	2 343	108.6	34.3	12	94	4.1	1.4	106	D	D	D
VIRGINIA	15 765	302 446	15 340.5	4 273.0	2 011	32 788	2 621.1	713.5	14 942	203 981	19 704.5	8 418.1
Alexandria	355	6 961	471.7	135.1	32	574	41.5	15.6	335	2 688	318.7	134.3
Blacksburg	93	1 679	57.5	17.8	4	D	D	D	77	D	D	D
Charlottesville	261	5 617	303.6	85.8	23	D	D	D	142	D	D	D
Chesapeake	431	8 991	369.8	105.5	43	D	D	D	431	D	D	D
Danville	140	2 741	110.3	30.0	11	D	D	D	182	D	D	D
Hampton	233	5 888	233.6	69.2	27	D	D	D	206	2 377	206.4	95.9
Harrisonburg	175	4 284	168.6	46.7	10	D	D	D	128	D	D	D
Leesburg	106	2 300	124.6	43.0	13	D	D	D	119	1 231	107.0	45.1
Lynchburg	234	5 226	190.0	58.3	21	161	6.8	1.9	202	D	D	D
Manassas	101	1 307	75.6	19.0	8	42	4.5	2.6	160	D	D	D
Newport News	384	7 660	329.1	89.9	36	351	17.5	4.3	328	5 716	497.9	269.1
Norfolk	551	11 667	505.0	140.2	58	600	45.0	13.0	427	7 517	792.0	367.7
Petersburg	70	864	36.6	9.7	4	56	1.8	0.4	99	D	D	D
Portsmouth	169	2 513	106.2	28.8	15	D	D	D	174	3 121	238.8	108.2
Richmond	547	10 136	476.8	143.5	51	490	41.0	7.6	462	11 317	1 110.4	453.7
Roanoke	294	6 162	267.2	83.3	19	144	6.1	2.0	232	3 993	443.2	173.6
Suffolk	121	1 981	72.8	20.2	14	106	5.5	1.9	124	D	D	D
Virginia Beach	1 134	21 694	1 074.2	294.9	146	1 585	111.9	27.4	855	10 228	985.2	424.2
Winchester	123	2 343	104.6	29.5	12	D	D	D	200	D	D	D
WASHINGTON	15 893	233 235	12 389.4	3 618.1	2 021	45 093	4 116.5	1 255.9	15 513	172 010	16 738.9	6 870.8
Auburn	153	2 150	103.8	29.9	24	D	D	D	146	2 235	241.9	89.2
Bellevue	387	7 861	505.9	147.2	61	1 714	128.5	33.5	753	7 473	793.2	322.3
Bellingham	336	5 623	226.6	71.1	37	638	22.2	6.9	408	D	D	D
Bothell	110	1 457	82.7	21.4	5	D	D	D	126	1 156	93.4	39.1
Bremerton	121	1 498	64.9	19.6	10	305	9.7	3.8	115	1 864	182.4	70.8
Burien	90	1 165	57.0	17.3	8	D	D	D	157	1 217	142.8	53.0
Des Moines	43	788	38.8	12.6	3	D	D	D	50	852	58.3	25.2
Edmonds	121	1 482	75.4	23.8	8	264	16.0	4.2	186	D	D	D
Everett	332	4 661	249.5	71.7	27	422	19.5	6.4	344	4 847	537.8	247.3
Federal Way	235	3 505	172.1	47.6	22	519	35.5	10.1	310	D	D	D
Issaquah	113	1 793	91.1	26.5	9	136	4.2	1.4	143	1 635	184.1	62.0
Kennewick	174	2 835	127.8	35.7	21	D	D	D	217	2 526	223.3	78.0
Kent	259	3 331	170.9	47.9	23	240	33.0	6.2	215	2 101	153.7	57.4
Kirkland	187	3 354	176.9	58.0	22	D	D	D	286	D	D	D
Lacey	106	1 796	83.8	23.6	8	175	7.3	2.6	98	1 189	101.3	35.7
Lake Stevens	37	489	28.2	6.3	2	D	D	D	31	D	D	D
Lakewood	189	2 632	125.5	37.5	12	D	D	D	167	1 790	150.0	57.5
Longview	104	1 489	66.5	18.5	8	D	D	D	136	2 377	225.3	90.9
Lynnwood	199	3 384	200.3	52.1	11	D	D	D	177	D	D	D
Marysville	90	1 256	62.4	18.1	6	D	D	D	93	1 060	89.6	36.8
Mount Vernon	92	1 246	53.8	16.2	7	D	D	D	124	1 944	224.5	87.0
Olympia	212	3 628	165.4	52.3	15	195	13.1	3.5	350	3 914	444.9	166.7

1. Establishments subject to federal tax.

Table D. Cities — **Other Services and Government Employment and Payroll**

City	Other services[1], 2007				Government employment and payroll, 2012								
						March payroll							
							Percent of total for:						
	Number of establishments	Number of employees	Receipts (mil dol)	Annual payroll (mil dol)	Full-time equivalent employees	Total (dollars)	Administration, judicial, and legal	Police and Corrections	Fire Protection	Highways and transportation	Health and welfare	Natural resources and utilities	Education and libraries
	104	105	106	107	108	109	110	111	112	113	114	115	116
UTAH—Cont'd													
Kaysville	27	D	D	D	134	462 338	10.8	22.9	9.0	7.6	0.0	39.1	0.0
Layton	84	579	39.7	10.8	349	1 449 599	18.3	33.6	21.9	4.9	0.0	21.4	0.0
Lehi	25	D	D	D	336	1 214 483	12.5	20.4	13.7	4.2	0.0	36.3	4.1
Logan	75	469	37.0	9.1	471	1 727 277	13.4	20.5	14.4	3.6	0.0	36.1	3.5
Midvale	65	456	41.5	11.3	75	305 262	65.6	0.0	0.0	6.5	2.9	20.3	0.0
Murray	134	933	66.6	19.7	431	1 925 114	16.4	23.1	16.8	2.6	0.0	30.9	3.1
Ogden	140	1 010	77.6	24.7	634	2 507 571	18.7	28.7	20.1	7.0	5.2	16.9	0.0
Orem	142	851	60.2	18.6	516	2 194 808	19.2	27.2	17.2	4.8	2.4	19.7	7.3
Pleasant Grove	32	119	11.5	2.6	245	686 046	17.4	27.3	9.0	3.6	2.6	26.1	8.0
Provo	114	598	42.9	11.7	702	2 815 201	17.2	23.0	14.4	5.6	1.8	29.5	4.4
Riverton	35	148	11.1	2.9	91	415 613	39.8	2.6	0.0	25.0	0.6	22.8	0.0
Roy	37	213	14.3	4.0	176	633 604	20.3	31.4	22.5	4.2	0.0	16.1	0.0
St. George	132	702	63.5	17.5	700	2 450 568	9.2	24.3	5.4	10.7	2.4	44.2	0.0
Salt Lake City	465	3 690	278.8	85.8	2 853	13 446 478	15.0	21.7	15.0	20.9	2.4	14.9	4.1
Sandy	141	1 460	89.7	45.6	496	2 122 916	21.0	24.1	15.6	9.8	7.5	20.1	0.0
South Jordan	36	193	14.3	4.3	333	1 224 842	20.3	19.7	17.6	6.1	2.9	18.3	0.0
Spanish Fork	35	D	D	D	215	776 827	12.0	18.4	0.0	6.4	4.3	34.7	2.8
Springville	24	D	D	D	213	858 647	17.7	20.4	1.6	8.5	0.6	42.5	4.7
Taylorsville	42	178	13.5	4.2	122	499 977	35.5	62.2	0.0	0.0	0.4	0.3	0.0
Tooele	37	D	D	D	184	603 981	20.7	27.5	3.3	5.6	6.8	29.9	3.6
West Jordan	96	720	57.2	19.0	409	1 901 684	7.2	32.4	23.5	4.1	0.0	8.0	0.0
West Valley City	134	750	76.1	20.8	699	2 859 122	17.7	37.1	17.3	7.1	8.8	9.1	0.0
VERMONT	1 107	4 439	389.2	104.8	X	X	X	X	X	X	X	X	X
Burlington	64	323	20.9	7.6	741	3 858 642	9.5	18.3	12.6	11.2	3.0	32.5	2.0
VIRGINIA	11 978	76 121	6 677.6	2 125.9	X	X	X	X	X	X	X	X	X
Alexandria	254	2 071	181.2	63.9	5 221	27 072 935	10.0	12.5	7.7	2.6	12.6	6.5	44.7
Blacksburg	48	D	D	D	360	1 254 541	15.3	27.9	0.6	24.0	1.6	12.0	0.0
Charlottesville	113	929	66.5	23.2	2 140	8 097 522	10.3	6.1	3.5	6.3	5.6	8.0	55.6
Chesapeake	375	2 791	314.0	86.9	9 069	32 784 817	5.1	11.5	6.3	2.1	5.7	4.5	62.1
Danville	108	D	D	D	2 451	7 816 325	9.2	11.3	5.7	3.0	5.2	9.6	51.6
Hampton	165	1 046	76.5	25.7	6 070	20 036 058	6.9	11.2	6.1	1.0	5.7	6.3	61.8
Harrisonburg	107	590	49.3	15.6	1 474	5 157 943	4.1	7.6	6.7	5.8	0.3	15.0	53.6
Leesburg	81	483	37.6	11.8	378	1 973 445	18.8	28.6	0.0	10.5	0.0	34.5	1.1
Lynchburg	135	852	55.1	19.2	3 057	9 313 489	8.7	9.6	8.0	2.9	8.1	7.5	52.5
Manassas	114	698	58.5	18.1	1 551	7 149 920	5.0	8.7	4.1	2.5	3.1	8.0	67.1
Newport News	276	1 885	133.5	46.0	8 390	34 469 339	6.2	10.2	4.6	1.3	4.5	9.2	63.2
Norfolk	351	2 706	258.2	86.8	11 723	42 393 144	6.3	13.5	5.5	3.7	10.1	7.2	51.8
Petersburg	69	520	35.2	12.3	1 422	4 584 024	6.0	20.2	8.9	4.5	6.2	4.0	47.4
Portsmouth	154	1 437	105.2	39.0	4 082	15 197 404	6.6	10.7	7.0	0.8	8.6	5.3	58.8
Richmond	408	2 897	233.4	79.8	8 746	33 243 527	9.0	18.5	6.0	1.8	8.7	7.9	42.5
Roanoke	218	1 429	110.6	37.1	3 839	13 972 707	8.1	12.9	8.3	1.7	8.0	2.4	56.6
Suffolk	84	D	D	D	3 545	11 901 204	10.3	7.7	9.6	2.9	3.6	6.8	58.2
Virginia Beach	783	4 883	310.0	104.4	18 286	64 539 702	3.7	9.5	3.6	0.3	6.6	7.3	60.5
Winchester	73	491	35.0	12.3	1 441	5 056 458	6.8	23.0	6.6	2.0	4.0	7.0	48.8
WASHINGTON	9 809	54 544	4 643.2	1 461.8	X	X	X	X	X	X	X	X	X
Auburn	141	852	98.4	29.8	428	2 532 346	24.2	34.3	0.0	15.0	4.6	18.9	0.0
Bellevue	300	2 031	193.1	65.6	1 278	8 997 838	17.4	19.2	22.6	7.6	8.6	23.3	0.0
Bellingham	189	1 065	81.2	25.1	813	4 462 504	14.2	23.4	26.3	8.6	0.9	16.4	3.3
Bothell	52	330	38.0	10.3	290	2 203 744	15.3	29.0	30.7	8.0	5.8	5.8	0.0
Bremerton	56	294	24.6	7.6	363	2 283 752	11.7	25.1	21.9	5.4	0.6	29.5	0.0
Burien	81	494	36.8	12.2	70	380 590	32.7	0.0	0.0	22.6	20.3	22.5	0.0
Des Moines	29	104	9.7	3.2	130	840 420	26.3	37.5	0.0	7.8	4.0	18.8	0.0
Edmonds	56	261	19.0	7.1	206	1 296 656	16.1	35.4	0.0	8.9	4.8	28.4	0.0
Everett	197	1 496	126.6	48.7	1 193	7 513 828	9.0	22.1	21.2	14.6	2.1	22.6	3.2
Federal Way	128	661	47.7	15.3	338	1 899 108	20.8	52.5	0.0	7.2	0.0	15.6	0.0
Issaquah	72	364	30.3	9.5	241	1 458 971	48.2	24.1	0.0	5.7	0.0	22.0	0.0
Kennewick	118	652	47.6	14.7	365	2 339 914	19.2	32.4	27.2	7.2	0.0	14.0	0.0
Kent	193	1 418	126.4	37.5	659	3 957 128	25.4	33.2	0.0	11.4	1.3	24.6	0.0
Kirkland	176	884	70.9	22.5	575	3 364 380	21.8	25.2	24.8	2.6	0.0	12.1	0.0
Lacey	64	410	26.5	9.0	244	1 204 776	6.5	40.8	0.0	5.7	7.4	37.2	0.0
Lake Stevens	25	D	D	D	60	371 914	10.4	53.2	0.0	21.3	10.4	0.0	0.0
Lakewood	128	701	62.9	20.3	252	1 631 866	29.1	53.0	0.0	11.9	1.0	3.8	0.0
Longview	71	508	39.3	14.6	291	1 531 626	13.5	28.3	20.6	13.2	0.0	18.9	5.5
Lynnwood	122	956	87.5	26.8	514	3 172 400	18.5	30.1	20.2	2.4	0.0	17.3	0.0
Marysville	86	D	D	D	244	1 573 886	23.0	37.9	0.0	9.3	0.0	24.8	0.0
Mount Vernon	60	318	21.5	6.8	209	1 138 810	14.6	30.5	21.7	3.5	0.0	18.1	5.0
Olympia	122	598	50.7	16.2	524	3 201 082	31.0	21.7	21.0	4.7	0.3	21.2	0.0

1. Establishments subject to federal tax.

City	City government finances, 2007									
	General revenue							General expenditure		
		Intergovernmental		Taxes					Per capita[1] (dollars)	
					Per capita[1] (dollars)					
	Total (mil dol)	Total (mil dol)	Percent from state government	Total (mil dol)	Total	Property	Sales and gross receipts	Total (mil dol)	Total	Capital outlays
	117	118	119	120	121	122	123	124	125	126
UTAH—Cont'd										
Kaysville	15.6	1.7	75.8	6.7	236	50	186	10.3	364	62
Layton	45.3	3.8	61.6	25.7	375	112	263	40.3	587	14
Lehi	47.8	1.8	100.0	28.4	552	308	244	36.9	718	82
Logan	58.6	7.2	21.6	20.1	408	111	297	49.7	1 011	194
Midvale	17.3	1.8	50.9	11.1	368	138	230	17.2	568	9
Murray	52.5	4.5	36.2	29.2	604	209	395	48.5	1 005	89
Ogden	102.4	13.2	30.0	48.5	578	280	298	114.7	1 367	205
Orem	78.3	6.3	49.6	38.7	427	131	296	65.7	725	49
Pleasant Grove	23.6	2.0	81.2	9.0	261	99	162	21.4	621	39
Provo	87.3	11.8	35.6	39.2	339	125	214	98.1	850	250
Riverton	19.6	1.5	82.4	10.7	264	47	217	34.9	864	199
Roy	21.0	1.5	77.3	10.5	279	86	193	16.4	436	23
St. George	76.3	3.8	65.5	38.0	504	165	340	76.8	1 020	221
Salt Lake City	529.4	30.7	31.4	201.1	1 062	642	419	382.9	2 021	145
Sandy	79.3	5.3	56.3	44.9	502	168	334	64.8	724	74
South Jordan	55.2	2.4	79.1	34.3	614	349	265	50.1	895	75
Spanish Fork	37.6	1.4	82.8	10.0	277	75	202	31.9	880	170
Springville	25.9	1.1	90.9	10.0	325	103	223	30.3	989	165
Taylorsville	24.7	2.8	76.1	17.3	287	79	208	28.5	473	69
Tooele	20.4	1.8	85.9	11.5	358	130	227	20.7	645	92
West Jordan	65.0	6.3	62.5	35.7	329	119	210	59.0	544	60
West Valley City	134.8	12.6	33.4	67.2	507	262	245	154.8	1 168	359
VERMONT	X	X	X	X	X	X	X	X	X	X
Burlington	110.0	17.7	38.0	38.4	908	674	234	92.8	2 192	417
VIRGINIA	X	X	X	X	X	X	X	X	X	X
Alexandria	694.5	112.0	62.0	498.6	3 394	2 493	843	697.3	4 746	514
Blacksburg	40.4	14.5	48.6	16.4	382	130	252	36.6	855	218
Charlottesville	233.9	98.5	67.6	93.0	2 089	1 298	743	229.9	5 163	617
Chesapeake	886.7	369.8	97.8	422.6	1 852	1 303	538	865.4	3 792	475
Danville	173.3	85.4	95.4	50.7	1 186	638	544	179.2	4 189	318
Hampton	525.3	220.7	90.2	218.7	1 599	1 068	519	516.8	3 777	217
Harrisonburg	165.0	51.6	74.2	63.4	1 238	628	603	166.3	3 246	275
Leesburg	59.3	13.1	95.3	31.9	693	279	414	58.7	1 273	249
Lynchburg	266.8	110.8	87.0	117.5	1 510	897	597	268.3	3 449	589
Manassas	181.8	62.5	84.3	83.5	2 049	1 559	467	169.8	4 168	200
Newport News	774.9	330.7	85.5	322.2	1 785	1 271	515	806.2	4 467	333
Norfolk	1 105.0	447.5	74.8	416.3	1 691	1 027	664	1 153.5	4 686	548
Petersburg	125.4	70.3	87.3	45.2	1 406	1 038	357	129.9	4 039	140
Portsmouth	430.0	216.4	85.2	161.2	1 669	1 218	439	514.7	5 331	1 170
Richmond	1 063.0	471.0	79.9	412.6	1 951	1 242	709	1 029.3	4 866	638
Roanoke	385.6	172.3	96.1	172.9	1 766	1 081	685	378.3	3 865	222
Suffolk	304.8	145.8	82.7	134.3	1 577	1 160	411	324.3	3 808	436
Virginia Beach	1 602.6	600.6	84.2	810.1	1 817	1 221	583	1 799.1	4 036	628
Winchester	116.1	39.1	89.9	61.6	2 267	1 283	983	112.7	4 147	231
WASHINGTON	X	X	X	X	X	X	X	X	X	X
Auburn	109.0	17.7	41.8	43.9	598	200	378	107.6	1 464	393
Bellevue	284.5	33.1	23.5	153.0	1 157	275	833	257.3	1 947	276
Bellingham	120.9	15.0	39.1	67.7	825	212	593	118.7	1 446	280
Bothell	54.5	14.0	63.8	29.4	848	273	531	61.1	1 763	521
Bremerton	57.7	6.4	49.1	25.4	646	218	419	58.3	1 484	236
Burien	28.1	4.7	75.2	18.7	378	142	222	34.9	705	215
Des Moines	29.2	4.6	73.5	12.6	412	142	257	26.8	881	214
Edmonds	45.6	4.4	75.7	28.0	693	332	334	42.6	1 054	137
Everett	182.2	16.6	67.5	108.1	1 033	367	650	170.4	1 629	324
Federal Way	65.3	12.0	93.7	40.0	435	107	311	59.1	643	167
Issaquah	59.7	10.5	71.1	31.0	949	250	650	53.3	1 633	344
Kennewick	68.6	6.5	60.3	41.7	550	142	391	69.4	914	179
Kent	137.7	20.6	82.9	62.9	511	157	335	140.6	1 143	354
Kirkland	106.7	9.7	53.2	61.0	731	262	428	105.7	1 267	159
Lacey	56.2	9.1	68.1	26.8	611	136	454	60.0	1 365	347
Lake Stevens	14.7	2.9	47.3	9.7	333	139	178	9.2	318	2
Lakewood	45.5	9.7	66.3	28.3	480	104	367	49.0	831	168
Longview	58.1	10.3	61.4	25.0	685	222	460	58.2	1 593	375
Lynnwood	66.8	5.6	76.9	38.6	1 065	319	731	58.4	1 610	230
Marysville	60.6	3.7	74.9	30.1	483	246	222	58.8	943	114
Mount Vernon	38.0	3.3	70.9	17.8	552	222	318	33.3	1 033	107
Olympia	99.6	9.9	54.8	50.0	1 045	267	761	116.3	2 434	673

1. Based on population estimated as of July 1 of the year shown.

City	City government finances, 2012 (cont.)									
	General expenditure (cont.)									
	Percent of total for:									
	Public welfare	Highways	Parking facilities	Education	Health and hospitals	Police protection	Sewerage and sanitation	Parks and recreation	Housing and community development	Interest on debt
	127	128	129	130	131	132	133	134	135	136
UTAH—Cont'd										
Kaysville	0.0	10.3	0.0	0.0	0.0	7.6	51.5	11.5	0.0	0.4
Layton	0.0	16.8	0.0	0.0	0.0	26.0	19.4	9.8	1.1	0.5
Lehi	0.0	39.4	0.0	0.0	0.0	13.0	21.2	1.1	0.0	4.8
Logan	0.0	14.4	0.0	0.0	0.0	16.5	26.1	11.6	5.4	0.7
Midvale	0.0	9.4	0.0	0.0	0.0	30.1	15.3	2.0	3.5	7.1
Murray	0.0	15.6	0.0	0.0	0.0	19.8	13.0	13.4	2.1	1.2
Ogden	0.0	4.7	0.0	0.0	0.0	14.8	16.3	5.7	17.8	2.5
Orem	0.0	11.1	0.0	0.0	0.0	20.7	17.2	10.0	3.7	2.9
Pleasant Grove	0.0	3.1	0.0	0.0	0.0	20.0	22.6	14.2	0.0	8.8
Provo	0.0	10.5	0.0	0.0	0.0	15.5	9.1	27.2	5.6	4.5
Riverton	0.0	25.5	0.0	0.0	0.0	7.2	8.5	5.8	2.0	36.7
Roy	0.0	7.7	0.0	0.0	0.0	26.4	11.6	13.2	2.1	0.2
St. George	0.0	18.8	0.0	0.0	0.0	16.5	19.8	18.3	1.4	6.6
Salt Lake City	0.0	10.9	0.0	0.0	0.0	14.9	5.8	5.6	9.0	3.8
Sandy	0.0	7.4	0.0	0.0	0.0	18.4	13.6	11.7	1.0	5.4
South Jordan	0.0	14.1	0.0	0.0	0.0	10.9	6.1	12.5	9.7	3.6
Spanish Fork	0.0	10.9	0.0	0.0	0.0	11.9	16.0	20.8	0.0	2.7
Springville	0.0	7.8	0.0	0.0	0.9	12.7	15.8	12.5	0.0	5.5
Taylorsville	0.0	10.3	0.0	0.0	0.0	27.4	1.8	1.8	4.8	1.3
Tooele	0.0	12.0	0.0	0.0	0.0	16.2	9.4	17.6	12.8	5.1
West Jordan	0.0	17.8	0.0	0.0	0.0	22.3	18.1	4.0	3.7	2.0
West Valley City	0.0	7.4	0.0	0.0	1.1	13.1	5.3	16.7	25.5	4.1
VERMONT	X	X	X	X	X	X	X	X	X	X
Burlington	0.0	9.2	5.2	0.0	0.0	11.3	8.3	8.8	5.6	3.9
VIRGINIA	X	X	X	X	X	X	X	X	X	X
Alexandria	6.3	3.7	0.0	34.5	6.0	9.6	6.1	3.7	2.0	2.8
Blacksburg	0.0	22.9	0.0	0.0	1.6	19.2	16.1	5.9	6.9	2.2
Charlottesville	11.0	6.3	0.1	31.0	8.0	7.1	5.8	5.3	2.3	1.6
Chesapeake	3.3	5.6	0.0	54.2	3.3	4.6	3.4	2.3	0.4	2.3
Danville	4.2	5.7	0.0	41.3	2.3	5.5	6.6	2.2	2.3	1.7
Hampton	5.7	1.3	0.1	45.5	0.8	5.2	4.9	6.8	8.5	3.2
Harrisonburg	1.8	11.3	0.1	38.9	0.7	4.7	9.4	3.1	0.3	18.0
Leesburg	0.0	9.2	0.0	0.0	0.0	19.2	10.4	11.6	0.0	4.3
Lynchburg	7.1	2.8	0.1	35.8	0.7	6.4	15.5	2.2	2.9	2.8
Manassas	0.7	6.2	0.1	54.0	2.2	7.8	7.8	0.2	2.3	3.2
Newport News	5.1	3.9	0.0	42.3	8.5	5.7	4.8	3.1	5.8	3.6
Norfolk	6.6	4.6	1.0	36.0	3.2	5.9	5.3	4.1	9.5	3.1
Petersburg	11.4	4.7	0.0	40.0	1.0	9.0	4.0	1.3	1.0	1.0
Portsmouth	5.0	1.3	0.2	33.2	2.1	6.8	5.2	2.1	6.8	2.7
Richmond	1.6	2.7	0.0	31.6	4.5	8.9	10.5	2.5	9.1	0.8
Roanoke	15.3	3.5	0.4	39.4	0.9	6.1	2.2	2.5	6.6	3.1
Suffolk	4.4	6.8	0.0	45.2	0.2	6.3	2.0	1.6	1.2	2.8
Virginia Beach	3.8	4.8	0.1	46.8	3.0	5.0	7.1	5.9	1.4	3.0
Winchester	6.4	5.0	0.8	43.4	1.0	6.4	10.1	2.6	1.9	4.9
WASHINGTON	X	X	X	X	X	X	X	X	X	X
Auburn	0.0	19.6	0.0	0.0	0.5	15.0	33.6	9.0	0.2	2.2
Bellevue	0.0	15.0	0.0	0.0	6.3	11.9	18.4	15.2	5.3	2.8
Bellingham	0.0	10.0	1.2	0.0	7.0	13.4	14.1	16.3	1.8	1.6
Bothell	0.0	30.3	0.0	0.0	0.2	16.3	12.8	2.0	1.6	0.9
Bremerton	0.0	5.7	0.8	0.0	4.2	18.7	14.8	21.3	1.8	3.3
Burien	0.0	31.7	0.0	0.0	3.0	27.1	2.7	8.9	2.0	2.6
Des Moines	0.1	19.9	0.0	0.0	0.8	24.9	4.7	24.1	0.0	1.4
Edmonds	0.0	7.5	0.0	0.0	0.1	18.8	16.6	11.8	0.0	2.5
Everett	0.2	7.5	0.1	0.0	4.4	15.4	24.4	7.7	1.3	4.0
Federal Way	0.2	28.9	0.0	0.0	1.1	27.6	4.7	10.0	2.0	1.0
Issaquah	0.0	14.9	0.0	0.0	0.0	8.3	20.1	9.3	2.9	3.0
Kennewick	0.0	11.4	0.0	0.0	5.3	18.7	4.5	20.4	0.8	2.9
Kent	0.2	5.1	0.0	0.0	1.2	15.6	40.1	11.7	2.0	3.1
Kirkland	0.0	10.8	0.1	0.0	0.7	17.1	22.2	8.0	0.0	2.1
Lacey	0.0	19.2	0.0	0.0	2.9	14.1	25.7	13.0	0.0	1.6
Lake Stevens	0.2	13.5	0.0	0.0	0.4	40.6	12.7	1.9	2.0	3.5
Lakewood	1.0	17.8	0.0	0.0	0.6	40.2	7.5	3.3	4.9	0.3
Longview	0.2	8.3	0.0	0.0	0.0	15.9	40.1	5.9	2.7	1.2
Lynnwood	0.0	8.5	0.0	0.0	7.2	19.4	9.5	17.2	1.2	1.4
Marysville	0.0	17.7	0.0	0.0	4.9	14.4	17.3	5.1	0.0	5.8
Mount Vernon	0.0	9.6	0.0	0.0	0.5	19.0	29.6	4.4	0.0	2.1
Olympia	0.0	6.3	0.0	0.0	1.9	9.4	24.8	12.3	0.4	3.4

City	City government finances, 2012 (cont.)			Climate[2]						
	Debt outstanding			Average daily temperature (degrees Fahrenheit)						
				Mean		Limits				
	Total (mil dol)	Per capita[1] (dollars)	Debt issued during year	January	July	January[3]	July[4]	Annual precipitation (inches)	Heating degree days	Cooling degree days
	137	138	139	140	141	142	143	144	145	146
UTAH—Cont'd										
Kaysville	2.6	91	0.0	NA	NA	NA	NA	NA	NA	NA
Layton	4.9	71	0.0	27.6	74.2	18.6	89.9	20.75	6 142	746
Lehi	97.2	1 889	0.7	NA	NA	NA	NA	NA	NA	NA
Logan	43.8	891	0.0	21.8	71.6	12.7	88.3	17.86	7 174	522
Midvale	50.8	1 678	1.5	30.4	78.5	22.1	90.9	26.19	5 441	1 197
Murray	36.9	765	6.1	29.2	77.0	21.3	90.6	16.50	5 631	1 066
Ogden	115.6	1 378	7.1	28.1	76.6	20.1	90.0	23.67	5 868	980
Orem	67.1	740	4.3	28.6	76.5	20.3	92.3	12.84	5 564	1 016
Pleasant Grove	62.2	1 801	22.8	NA	NA	NA	NA	NA	NA	NA
Provo	115.1	997	34.5	30.9	76.9	22.5	93.4	20.13	5 264	1 028
Riverton	482.2	11 921	4.6	31.6	78.0	22.0	95.3	15.76	5 251	1 172
Roy	7.2	193	0.6	27.6	74.2	18.6	89.9	20.75	6 142	746
St. George	157.4	2 090	6.1	41.8	86.3	28.9	102.8	8.77	3 103	2 471
Salt Lake City	393.2	2 075	81.7	32.0	78.1	25.4	89.0	17.75	5 095	1 190
Sandy	93.6	1 045	8.3	30.4	78.5	22.1	90.9	26.19	5 441	1 197
South Jordan	71.6	1 279	6.9	31.6	78.0	22.0	95.3	15.76	5 251	1 172
Spanish Fork	24.7	681	0.0	NA	NA	NA	NA	NA	NA	NA
Springville	37.6	1 229	0.0	NA	NA	NA	NA	NA	NA	NA
Taylorsville	10.9	182	0.7	29.2	77.0	21.3	90.6	16.50	5 631	1 066
Tooele	36.8	1 147	15.2	NA	NA	NA	NA	NA	NA	NA
West Jordan	23.2	214	3.3	30.4	78.5	22.1	90.9	26.19	5 441	1 197
West Valley City	149.0	1 125	33.1	29.2	77.0	21.3	90.6	16.50	5 631	1 066
VERMONT	X	X	X	X	X	X	X	X	X	X
Burlington	192.6	4 550	24.3	18.0	70.6	9.3	81.4	36.05	7 665	489
VIRGINIA	X	X	X	X	X	X	X	X	X	X
Alexandria	580.7	3 952	133.6	34.9	79.2	27.3	88.3	39.35	4 055	1 531
Blacksburg	23.1	541	9.5	30.9	71.1	20.6	82.5	42.63	5 559	533
Charlottesville	117.7	2 645	34.1	35.5	76.9	26.2	88.0	48.87	4 103	1 212
Chesapeake	635.5	2 785	137.5	40.1	79.1	32.3	86.8	45.74	3 368	1 612
Danville	152.0	3 554	3.9	36.6	78.8	25.8	90.0	44.98	3 970	1 418
Hampton	359.9	2 630	78.5	39.4	78.5	32.0	85.2	47.90	3 535	1 432
Harrisonburg	500.6	9 773	28.6	30.5	73.5	20.4	85.3	36.12	5 333	758
Leesburg	126.9	2 753	33.9	31.5	75.2	20.8	87.1	43.21	5 031	911
Lynchburg	330.4	4 247	7.0	34.5	75.1	24.5	86.4	43.31	4 354	1 075
Manassas	130.5	3 202	0.0	31.7	75.7	21.9	87.4	41.80	4 925	1 075
Newport News	797.6	4 419	228.9	41.2	80.3	33.8	87.9	43.53	3 179	1 682
Norfolk	1 752.2	7 119	414.1	40.1	79.1	32.3	86.8	45.74	3 368	1 612
Petersburg	34.6	1 076	1.5	39.7	79.6	29.2	91.0	45.26	3 334	1 619
Portsmouth	519.2	5 378	88.9	40.1	79.1	32.3	86.8	45.74	3 368	1 612
Richmond	1 340.2	6 336	260.0	36.4	77.9	27.6	87.5	43.91	3 919	1 435
Roanoke	544.5	5 563	52.3	35.8	76.2	26.6	87.5	42.49	4 284	1 134
Suffolk	538.4	6 320	114.6	39.6	78.5	30.3	88.1	48.71	3 467	1 427
Virginia Beach	1 698.8	3 811	173.0	40.7	78.8	32.2	86.9	44.50	3 336	1 482
Winchester	201.0	7 395	51.9	NA	NA	NA	NA	NA	NA	NA
WASHINGTON	X	X	X	X	X	X	X	X	X	X
Auburn	68.3	929	0.0	40.8	66.4	34.6	77.4	39.59	4 624	219
Bellevue	176.9	1 338	0.0	41.5	65.5	36.0	74.5	38.25	4 615	192
Bellingham	92.2	1 124	49.1	40.5	63.3	34.8	72.5	34.84	4 980	68
Bothell	43.3	1 251	30.0	40.8	65.2	35.2	75.0	35.96	4 756	174
Bremerton	75.6	1 923	12.7	40.1	64.6	34.7	75.2	53.96	4 994	158
Burien	33.0	667	8.6	40.9	65.3	35.9	75.3	37.07	4 797	173
Des Moines	14.4	471	2.0	40.9	65.3	35.9	75.3	37.07	4 797	173
Edmonds	37.6	929	13.8	40.8	65.2	35.2	75.0	35.96	4 756	174
Everett	252.3	2 410	52.2	39.7	63.6	33.6	73.0	37.54	5 199	121
Federal Way	13.7	149	0.0	41.0	65.6	35.1	76.1	38.95	4 650	167
Issaquah	38.5	1 180	5.4	NA	NA	NA	NA	NA	NA	NA
Kennewick	63.3	834	5.4	34.2	75.2	28.0	89.3	8.01	4 731	909
Kent	164.6	1 338	0.0	40.8	66.4	34.6	77.4	39.59	4 624	219
Kirkland	53.5	641	8.3	40.8	65.2	35.2	75.0	35.96	4 756	174
Lacey	24.6	561	1.6	38.1	62.8	31.8	76.1	50.79	5 531	97
Lake Stevens	22.3	768	0.0	NA	NA	NA	NA	NA	NA	NA
Lakewood	12.0	203	1.3	41.0	65.6	35.1	76.1	38.95	4 650	167
Longview	34.6	948	15.4	39.9	64.5	33.8	76.5	48.02	4 900	148
Lynnwood	46.2	1 274	6.4	40.8	65.2	35.2	75.0	35.96	4 756	174
Marysville	92.8	1 487	4.8	39.7	63.6	33.6	73.0	37.54	5 199	121
Mount Vernon	37.4	1 161	0.0	39.9	62.3	34.1	73.0	32.70	5 197	47
Olympia	95.1	1 989	3.4	38.1	62.8	31.8	76.1	50.79	5 531	97

1. Based on the population estimated as of July 1 of the year shown. 2. Represents normal values based on the 30-year period, 1971–2000. 3. Average daily minimum.
4. Average daily maximum.

STATE Place code	City	Land area,[1] 2010 (sq km)	Population, 2014			Race alone or in combination (percent), 2011-2013					Percent Hispanic or Latino[2], 2011-2013	Percent foreign born 2011–2013
			Total persons	Rank	Per square kilometer	White	Black	American Indian, Alaska Native	Asian	Hawaiian Pacific Islander		
		1	2	3	4	5	6	7	8	9	10	11
	WASHINGTON—Cont'd											
53 53545	Pasco	79.0	68 648	501	869.0	64.8	2.9	1.1	2.5	0.1	55.3	26.0
53 56625	Pullman	25.6	31 682	1 173	1 237.6	84.6	3.6	2.0	13.5	1.2	6.6	13.6
53 56695	Puyallup	36.1	39 105	950	1 083.2	89.2	6.5	2.3	5.4	0.5	6.1	6.7
53 57535	Redmond	42.2	59 285	613	1 404.9	65.3	2.4	0.8	31.5	0.6	10.0	37.3
53 57745	Renton	59.9	98 404	306	1 642.8	62.9	13.0	2.6	23.7	1.0	11.7	26.3
53 58235	Richland	92.5	53 019	701	573.2	89.0	1.3	2.4	5.8	0.6	9.5	8.0
53 61115	Sammamish	47.2	51 229	731	1 085.4	77.4	1.9	1.4	22.7	NA	3.4	23.7
53 62288	SeaTac	26.0	28 126	1 302	1 081.8	56.5	23.4	3.3	18.0	3.1	17.9	36.5
53 63000	Seattle	217.4	668 342	20	3 074.3	74.9	9.4	2.3	16.9	0.8	6.8	18.3
53 63960	Shoreline	30.2	55 174	667	1 827.0	73.9	8.1	3.2	14.0	1.0	9.5	19.6
53 67000	Spokane	153.5	212 052	102	1 381.4	91.5	3.8	3.6	3.9	0.6	5.5	7.0
53 67167	Spokane Valley	97.8	91 729	338	937.9	92.6	3.1	2.9	3.6	0.7	4.8	5.3
53 70000	Tacoma	128.8	205 159	107	1 592.8	73.1	14.7	3.3	11.8	1.9	11.2	13.0
53 73465	University Place	21.8	32 282	1 154	1 480.8	78.9	10.9	3.1	11.2	2.5	7.6	12.0
53 74060	Vancouver	120.3	169 294	145	1 407.3	83.7	4.9	2.5	6.7	2.1	11.1	12.6
53 75775	Walla Walla	33.2	31 910	1 166	961.1	88.3	3.7	4.3	3.9	0.4	24.7	12.0
53 77105	Wenatchee	20.1	33 261	1 120	1 654.8	87.5	1.0	2.7	1.5	0.4	31.7	14.7
53 80010	Yakima	70.4	93 357	328	1 326.1	73.3	2.2	2.2	1.6	0.4	45.1	18.7
54 00000	WEST VIRGINIA	62 258.7	1 850 326	X	29.7	95.5	4.0	1.2	0.9	0.1	1.3	1.5
54 14600	Charleston	81.6	50 404	742	617.7	87.1	11.3	5.7	3.4	0.3	1.6	3.0
54 39460	Huntington	42.0	48 807	770	1 162.1	91.0	10.6	1.1	1.4	NA	1.4	2.9
54 55756	Morgantown	26.3	31 073	1 190	1 181.5	89.9	7.6	0.9	3.9	NA	2.7	5.2
54 62140	Parkersburg	30.6	30 981	1 195	1 012.5	97.2	3.1	1.4	0.4	NA	0.7	0.6
54 86452	Wheeling	35.7	27 790	1 314	778.4	92.9	6.6	1.2	1.2	NA	1.1	1.9
55 00000	WISCONSIN	140 268.1	5 757 564	X	41.0	88.7	7.2	1.6	2.8	0.1	6.2	4.8
55 02375	Appleton	63.0	73 971	457	1 174.1	89.0	2.6	1.6	7.0	0.1	4.5	6.2
55 06500	Beloit	45.0	36 881	1 007	819.6	83.1	14.9	2.9	1.9	NA	16.7	8.7
55 10025	Brookfield	70.2	37 982	976	541.1	92.5	1.8	0.4	6.1	NA	3.1	7.5
55 22300	Eau Claire	83.0	67 684	511	815.5	94.5	2.2	0.8	4.7	NA	2.4	3.5
55 25950	Fitchburg	90.6	27 154	1 350	299.7	66.5	13.6	1.3	6.8	NA	24.6	19.1
55 26275	Fond du Lac	48.8	42 917	862	879.4	91.1	3.5	1.2	2.6	NA	7.1	5.8
55 27300	Franklin	89.6	36 278	1 028	404.9	86.1	4.8	0.8	9.2	NA	3.7	8.2
55 31000	Green Bay	117.8	104 891	279	890.4	86.1	5.3	4.6	4.8	NA	12.3	8.1
55 31175	Greenfield	29.8	37 157	998	1 246.9	90.6	2.5	1.0	5.8	NA	10.7	8.6
55 37825	Janesville	87.7	64 009	549	729.9	95.5	2.6	1.7	2.0	NA	5.7	3.8
55 39225	Kenosha	69.8	99 894	296	1 431.1	85.4	11.7	0.9	2.2	0.1	16.3	7.9
55 40775	La Crosse	53.1	52 440	707	987.6	89.9	3.4	1.3	5.3	NA	2.2	3.8
55 48000	Madison	198.9	245 691	83	1 235.2	82.6	8.9	1.1	8.7	0.1	6.9	10.8
55 48500	Manitowoc	45.7	33 102	1 123	724.3	92.6	1.4	0.8	5.8	NA	4.8	3.5
55 51000	Menomonee Falls	85.3	35 974	1 040	421.7	93.7	2.2	NA	4.7	NA	2.0	5.6
55 53000	Milwaukee	249.0	599 642	31	2 408.2	50.0	41.7	1.9	4.0	0.1	17.6	10.1
55 54875	Mount Pleasant	87.4	26 293	1 388	300.8	88.5	7.7	0.9	1.5	NA	10.0	4.0
55 55750	Neenah	23.9	25 855	1 401	1 081.8	93.2	1.8	1.9	2.5	NA	4.5	2.8
55 56375	New Berlin	94.4	39 842	934	422.1	94.5	1.5	0.6	4.6	NA	2.1	4.8
55 58800	Oak Creek	73.7	35 053	1 065	475.6	92.1	2.9	NA	4.0	NA	9.3	7.4
55 60500	Oshkosh	66.3	66 621	526	1 004.8	93.6	4.2	0.9	2.9	0.1	3.3	3.0
55 66000	Racine	40.1	78 065	427	1 946.8	69.5	24.2	1.4	1.3	NA	21.2	7.6
55 72975	Sheboygan	36.2	48 775	773	1 347.4	84.4	2.9	0.6	10.3	NA	10.7	10.4
55 77200	Stevens Point	41.3	26 658	1 375	645.5	93.5	1.6	1.4	5.2	NA	2.5	3.7
55 78600	Sun Prairie	31.7	31 752	1 170	1 001.6	88.7	8.8	NA	4.5	NA	2.4	4.3
55 78650	Superior	95.7	26 705	1 373	279.0	95.1	2.5	3.3	1.5	NA	0.9	2.5
55 84250	Waukesha	64.3	71 489	481	1 111.8	89.1	3.9	0.8	4.9	NA	12.5	8.6
55 84475	Wausau	48.6	39 302	944	808.7	85.3	3.3	1.8	13.3	NA	3.6	7.5
55 84675	Wauwatosa	34.3	47 102	795	1 373.2	91.8	6.0	0.8	3.7	NA	2.8	4.9
55 85300	West Allis	29.5	60 624	589	2 055.1	90.9	4.9	1.1	3.2	NA	9.8	5.5
55 85350	West Bend	37.7	31 692	1 172	840.6	97.1	1.2	0.7	1.0	NA	3.4	2.6
56 00000	WYOMING	251 470.1	584 153	X	2.3	93.4	1.7	3.9	1.3	0.2	9.4	3.5
56 13150	Casper	69.7	60 086	600	862.1	95.0	2.9	2.9	1.6	0.2	7.8	2.4
56 13900	Cheyenne	63.5	62 845	563	989.7	89.9	4.7	2.2	2.6	0.4	14.2	2.8
56 31855	Gillette	49.1	31 971	1 165	651.1	92.5	1.4	1.9	0.8	NA	10.1	4.6
56 45050	Laramie	45.9	32 081	1 163	698.9	91.5	2.0	1.3	4.0	NA	9.2	5.7

1. Dry land or land partially or temporarily covered by water. 2. May be of any race.

City	Age of population (percent), 2011-2013: Under 5 years	5 to 17 years	18 to 24 years	25 to 34 years	35 to 44 years	45 to 54 years	55 to 64 years	65 to 74 years	75 years and over	Median age 2011-2013	Percent female 2011-2013	Population: Census counts: 2000	2010	Percent change: 2000–2010	2010–2014
	12	13	14	15	16	17	18	19	20	21	22	23	24	25	26
WASHINGTON—Cont'd															
Pasco	10.7	24.3	10.1	16.9	12.9	10.4	7.6	4.0	3.2	28.1	49.4	32 066	59 781	86.4	12.4
Pullman	3.7	7.7	53.7	14.3	6.5	4.8	4.8	2.2	2.3	22.0	49.2	24 675	29 799	20.8	6.3
Puyallup	5.5	15.3	11.2	15.0	13.1	13.0	14.6	6.5	5.9	38.2	49.2	33 011	37 022	12.2	5.6
Redmond	7.7	13.9	7.1	23.3	17.3	12.4	9.4	4.3	4.6	34.1	48.9	45 256	54 144	19.6	9.2
Renton	7.6	15.4	7.5	17.7	17.1	13.8	11.1	5.1	4.7	36.0	50.6	50 052	90 927	81.7	7.2
Richland	7.2	18.3	8.5	13.4	11.2	14.5	12.1	8.8	6.0	37.3	49.5	38 708	48 058	24.2	10.2
Sammamish	7.2	25.1	5.4	7.5	19.2	18.6	10.8	4.2	2.0	38.2	50.2	34 104	45 780	34.2	9.6
SeaTac	7.6	14.6	11.2	17.8	13.9	13.5	10.8	6.7	3.9	34.2	45.8	25 496	26 909	5.5	4.5
Seattle	5.3	10.5	11.2	21.6	15.7	12.7	11.7	6.4	4.9	35.9	50.2	563 374	608 660	8.0	9.8
Shoreline	4.5	14.6	8.6	14.1	13.4	14.1	13.8	8.6	8.3	41.2	51.0	53 025	53 007	0.0	4.0
Spokane	7.1	15.0	11.8	15.7	11.9	12.4	12.1	7.2	6.9	35.3	51.0	195 629	208 916	6.8	1.2
Spokane Valley	5.5	17.4	8.4	14.0	12.2	14.9	12.8	8.1	6.8	38.9	49.3	NA	89 755	NA	2.2
Tacoma	6.8	15.8	10.7	15.5	13.4	13.6	11.9	6.7	5.5	35.8	50.8	193 556	198 397	2.5	3.4
University Place	6.1	19.0	10.8	11.3	12.8	12.9	13.3	6.8	6.9	36.8	52.9	29 933	31 144	4.0	3.6
Vancouver	6.8	16.8	9.0	15.2	14.1	12.9	11.9	7.5	5.9	36.7	51.1	143 560	161 791	12.7	4.6
Walla Walla	4.7	16.3	14.6	12.8	13.9	12.5	11.3	6.9	7.0	36.3	46.9	29 686	31 731	6.9	0.6
Wenatchee	9.4	18.8	8.6	16.7	8.6	12.4	11.2	5.8	8.4	31.9	52.0	27 856	31 925	14.6	3.6
Yakima	8.9	18.4	11.1	14.8	11.7	11.1	10.4	7.0	6.5	32.8	50.0	71 845	91 067	26.8	2.3
WEST VIRGINIA	5.5	15.1	9.3	11.8	12.6	14.2	14.7	9.4	7.3	41.6	50.7	1 808 344	1 852 994	2.5	-0.1
Charleston	5.6	14.7	9.2	13.3	11.4	14.5	14.4	8.8	8.1	41.2	51.4	53 421	51 400	-3.8	-1.8
Huntington	5.2	12.8	16.7	14.2	10.7	11.4	13.9	7.9	7.3	35.8	52.3	51 475	49 138	-4.5	-0.7
Morgantown	2.5	6.9	43.7	16.9	7.3	6.4	8.2	3.5	4.7	23.8	44.1	26 809	29 660	10.6	7.8
Parkersburg	6.0	14.9	8.9	11.0	11.9	16.1	13.1	9.2	8.9	42.8	54.1	33 099	31 492	-4.9	-1.3
Wheeling	6.2	12.7	8.4	10.6	10.5	13.6	16.5	10.2	11.3	46.7	51.4	31 419	28 486	-9.3	-2.4
WISCONSIN	6.1	16.9	9.7	12.7	12.3	14.8	13.1	7.7	6.7	38.9	50.4	5 363 675	5 686 986	6.0	1.2
Appleton	6.5	18.3	9.8	14.5	13.3	14.6	11.5	6.0	5.6	35.7	51.1	70 087	72 623	3.6	1.8
Beloit	6.3	19.5	13.1	11.8	12.6	13.0	11.0	6.2	6.5	34.4	52.7	35 775	36 966	3.3	-0.3
Brookfield	4.0	18.3	6.5	6.6	12.0	16.3	15.3	9.6	11.4	47.2	53.9	38 649	37 920	-1.9	0.1
Eau Claire	4.9	14.6	21.3	15.2	10.4	11.5	10.4	6.1	5.6	30.6	51.8	61 704	65 883	6.8	2.3
Fitchburg	7.2	18.2	7.6	19.8	15.3	11.1	11.4	6.7	2.7	33.5	46.7	20 501	25 260	23.2	7.9
Fond du Lac	6.5	15.0	9.8	13.7	13.8	13.4	12.4	7.3	8.1	38.2	51.1	42 203	43 021	1.9	-0.2
Franklin	5.2	16.7	7.5	12.6	14.7	14.9	14.6	6.9	6.8	40.7	48.0	29 494	35 451	20.2	2.3
Green Bay	7.7	16.0	11.1	16.3	11.8	13.3	11.7	5.8	6.3	34.0	51.0	102 313	104 057	1.7	0.9
Greenfield	5.6	11.1	6.6	15.7	11.6	13.1	16.3	8.6	11.3	44.3	53.1	35 476	36 720	3.5	1.1
Janesville	7.1	17.5	8.4	14.6	13.0	14.3	11.1	7.5	6.6	36.8	51.2	59 498	63 575	6.9	0.6
Kenosha	7.0	19.7	10.5	13.6	13.7	14.2	10.3	5.5	5.5	34.4	51.3	90 352	99 218	9.8	0.7
La Crosse	4.6	11.1	27.6	13.2	9.0	11.5	10.3	5.5	7.2	29.1	51.8	51 818	51 320	-1.0	2.2
Madison	5.7	11.6	20.5	19.5	11.5	11.2	10.1	5.3	4.7	30.9	50.7	208 054	233 209	12.1	5.4
Manitowoc	6.6	15.7	8.1	11.5	11.0	13.7	14.2	7.8	11.5	42.8	52.4	34 053	33 736	-0.9	-1.9
Menomonee Falls	5.3	16.5	6.9	10.1	11.4	16.7	14.1	9.2	9.9	44.9	51.6	32 647	35 626	9.1	1.0
Milwaukee	7.8	18.9	12.9	16.7	12.4	11.9	10.0	4.8	4.5	30.9	51.9	596 974	594 833	-0.4	0.8
Mount Pleasant	6.3	15.1	6.6	10.1	11.3	15.3	16.0	9.6	9.7	45.5	51.7	NA	26 197	NA	0.4
Neenah	5.7	18.9	8.8	12.9	13.0	16.1	11.6	6.0	7.1	37.8	52.8	24 507	25 501	4.1	1.4
New Berlin	4.1	16.7	6.8	9.6	11.7	17.8	15.6	8.8	8.9	46.1	51.0	38 220	39 584	3.6	0.7
Oak Creek	7.6	15.5	7.3	15.3	15.2	16.2	12.1	6.6	4.2	38.0	51.3	28 456	34 451	21.1	1.7
Oshkosh	5.1	13.9	19.8	13.8	11.8	12.5	10.3	6.3	6.7	33.2	48.0	62 916	66 083	5.0	0.8
Racine	7.3	20.4	9.9	13.3	14.2	12.9	10.8	6.1	5.2	34.0	52.3	81 855	78 860	-3.7	-1.0
Sheboygan	7.1	17.5	8.6	15.3	11.9	14.4	10.9	7.5	6.8	36.3	51.2	50 792	49 288	-3.0	-1.0
Stevens Point	3.6	11.6	31.0	14.4	7.6	11.0	9.2	6.1	5.5	26.4	52.3	24 551	26 717	8.8	-0.2
Sun Prairie	8.8	20.2	7.6	15.4	14.8	13.3	10.6	5.9	3.6	33.8	52.4	20 369	29 364	44.2	7.5
Superior	5.9	14.9	12.4	15.0	11.0	13.6	13.8	7.1	6.2	36.4	51.3	27 368	27 244	-0.5	-2.0
Waukesha	7.2	15.5	11.0	17.3	13.5	12.9	11.4	5.9	5.3	34.1	50.1	64 825	70 718	9.1	1.1
Wausau	7.6	15.5	8.4	14.4	10.0	14.5	12.5	7.4	9.6	39.4	51.5	38 426	39 106	1.8	0.5
Wauwatosa	7.1	15.2	5.9	16.1	12.7	13.5	13.8	6.8	9.0	39.3	52.4	47 271	46 396	-1.9	1.4
West Allis	6.6	13.9	8.4	18.3	11.5	14.9	12.1	6.2	8.1	37.3	50.5	61 254	60 411	-1.4	0.3
West Bend	6.1	18.8	7.2	14.8	13.9	13.8	11.5	6.7	7.3	36.6	50.1	28 152	31 078	10.4	1.6
WYOMING	6.7	17.2	9.9	14.0	12.0	13.5	13.7	7.5	5.4	36.8	49.0	493 782	563 626	14.1	3.6
Casper	6.8	16.9	9.9	16.2	11.7	12.5	13.2	6.6	6.2	35.2	49.7	49 644	55 316	11.4	0.0
Cheyenne	6.4	17.8	9.6	15.8	12.3	12.3	12.6	7.1	6.1	35.6	50.8	53 011	59 466	12.2	5.4
Gillette	9.7	20.1	10.2	17.9	13.9	11.1	11.2	3.7	2.3	30.4	47.6	19 646	29 087	48.1	7.2
Laramie	5.4	11.2	32.9	17.5	10.0	7.5	9.1	3.4	3.1	25.2	47.5	27 204	30 816	13.3	4.1

City	Households, 2011-2013				Persons in group quarters, 2010				Serious crimes known to police,[2] 2013				Educational attainment, 2011–2013		
			Percent			Institutional			Total		Rate[3]			Attainment[4] (percent)	
	Number	Persons per house-hold	Female family house-holder[1]	One-person	Total	Total	Persons in nursing facilities	Non-institu-tional	Number	Rate[3]	Violent	Property	Population age 25 and older	High school graduate or less	Bachelor's degree or more
	27	28	29	30	31	32	33	34	35	36	37	38	39	40	41
WASHINGTON—Cont'd															
Pasco	18 908	3.48	17.9	17.7	385	276	98	109	1 795	2 675	238	2 437	36 390	55.0	14.8
Pullman	10 560	2.34	7.3	27.9	5 788	18	18	5 770	484	1 517	107	1 411	10 760	12.5	67.5
Puyallup	14 837	2.52	15.0	28.5	710	443	403	267	3 138	8 144	280	7 864	25 959	36.9	25.3
Redmond	23 651	2.38	5.8	30.5	274	171	171	103	1 705	2 977	68	2 909	40 283	14.5	61.6
Renton	37 350	2.54	11.7	32.0	685	263	191	422	5 209	5 389	265	5 124	66 465	35.9	32.1
Richland	20 368	2.51	10.4	28.4	285	163	163	122	1 267	2 415	183	2 232	33 937	23.1	44.8
Sammamish	15 757	3.11	4.0	9.0	99	0	0	99	286	574	22	552	30 581	8.7	71.5
SeaTac	9 589	2.78	13.5	30.2	1 014	905	74	109	1 742	6 245	617	5 628	18 376	48.2	17.8
Seattle	289 153	2.12	7.2	41.3	24 925	4 904	2 588	20 021	39 724	6 180	585	5 595	464 557	18.4	57.8
Shoreline	21 056	2.49	11.4	29.9	1 415	581	578	834	1 777	3 245	146	3 099	39 278	25.9	40.1
Spokane	87 021	2.33	12.1	34.4	6 949	1 972	1 236	4 977	20 896	9 973	651	9 322	138 805	35.3	28.5
Spokane Valley	36 909	2.44	12.1	30.1	802	439	418	363	5 544	6 103	254	5 849	62 458	37.1	20.5
Tacoma	78 223	2.51	13.3	33.1	6 693	4 084	1 392	2 609	15 127	7 443	870	6 573	134 692	40.8	25.2
University Place	12 665	2.48	13.4	30.7	206	118	118	88	888	2 801	296	2 504	20 299	25.7	34.0
Vancouver	65 418	2.49	14.1	30.4	2 056	1 192	429	864	6 526	3 919	356	3 563	111 731	37.1	25.5
Walla Walla	10 916	2.51	11.9	35.5	3 651	2 600	190	1 051	1 487	4 663	304	4 359	20 546	38.3	21.2
Wenatchee	11 350	2.82	10.7	28.9	582	402	88	180	1 292	3 954	226	3 727	20 561	47.5	23.8
Yakima	32 791	2.76	13.6	30.6	2 448	1 841	650	607	5 165	5 519	505	5 013	57 267	54.4	16.4
WEST VIRGINIA	739 759	2.44	11.5	30.3	49 382	28 323	9 748	21 059	44 581	2 404	300	2 104	1 298 503	56.1	18.8
Charleston	22 854	2.14	13.7	40.4	1 940	675	220	1 265	2 978	5 849	858	4 990	35 977	35.1	40.0
Huntington	21 447	2.16	14.6	42.3	3 012	676	412	2 336	2 135	4 342	242	4 100	32 239	41.9	30.2
Morgantown	9 879	2.38	6.8	47.8	5 636	86	19	5 550	784	2 496	299	2 197	14 200	28.2	48.4
Parkersburg	13 413	2.29	14.5	39.8	547	341	326	206	1 521	4 874	413	4 461	21 940	56.5	14.6
Wheeling	12 857	2.09	11.6	43.4	1 436	523	413	913	786	2 794	661	2 133	20 477	43.4	28.2
WISCONSIN	2 281 781	2.44	10.1	29.1	150 214	74 295	33 808	75 919	141 649	2 467	278	2 189	3 853 730	41.7	27.2
Appleton	28 320	2.48	11.3	29.9	2 429	864	487	1 565	1 481	2 025	242	1 783	47 523	35.7	31.9
Beloit	14 147	2.48	19.6	31.1	1 553	242	242	1 311	1 324	3 596	350	3 246	22 542	56.9	14.9
Brookfield	14 665	2.56	5.3	24.8	513	460	460	53	1 116	2 937	79	2 858	27 029	19.7	54.0
Eau Claire	27 077	2.32	9.2	34.8	4 536	613	256	3 923	1 693	2 515	183	2 333	39 605	31.7	32.3
Fitchburg	10 088	2.46	10.5	30.3	822	815	0	7	505	1 933	234	1 700	17 372	31.4	43.1
Fond du Lac	18 277	2.24	11.2	35.7	2 087	1 481	480	606	1 334	3 099	358	2 742	29 541	45.5	23.1
Franklin	13 054	2.59	7.4	27.3	1 982	1 908	42	74	746	2 056	11	2 045	25 417	34.6	33.3
Green Bay	42 623	2.38	12.6	32.8	3 206	1 362	617	1 844	3 185	3 030	480	2 551	68 277	46.6	23.2
Greenfield	16 594	2.18	8.0	38.7	821	728	728	93	1 323	3 559	137	3 422	28 370	42.7	28.6
Janesville	26 089	2.42	13.5	29.1	930	756	309	174	2 109	3 316	261	3 055	42 588	47.2	19.7
Kenosha	37 414	2.58	18.4	28.5	3 488	1 620	736	1 868	2 736	2 725	273	2 452	62 743	45.1	22.0
La Crosse	20 434	2.29	10.3	35.0	4 681	827	540	3 854	1 659	3 206	207	3 000	29 159	34.5	31.0
Madison	104 028	2.20	8.9	37.1	10 740	2 171	1 173	8 569	8 617	3 553	365	3 188	149 513	21.0	53.7
Manitowoc	14 550	2.23	10.8	35.4	956	532	524	424	969	2 911	225	2 686	23 311	48.6	21.9
Menomonee Falls	14 556	2.45	6.3	27.7	217	202	202	15	409	1 141	39	1 102	25 575	31.7	38.2
Milwaukee	229 611	2.53	22.2	35.3	18 401	5 302	2 512	13 099	35 208	5 860	1 364	4 496	361 421	48.6	22.5
Mount Pleasant	10 971	2.36	8.8	31.2	290	268	265	22	779	2 976	53	2 922	18 867	34.4	33.4
Neenah	10 664	2.39	10.0	31.9	277	233	211	44	546	2 112	159	1 954	17 153	39.1	30.4
New Berlin	16 339	2.42	5.2	28.6	161	125	125	36	NA	NA	NA	NA	28 783	29.2	40.7
Oak Creek	14 131	2.46	6.1	30.6	125	0	0	125	1 063	3 033	131	2 902	24 266	38.2	30.2
Oshkosh	25 618	2.30	11.4	35.7	7 520	4 056	974	3 464	1 576	2 358	232	2 126	40 795	47.2	24.7
Racine	29 727	2.59	17.5	33.5	1 548	1 276	152	272	3 307	4 232	380	3 852	48 861	51.4	16.4
Sheboygan	20 141	2.38	11.8	32.2	953	766	472	187	1 373	2 814	271	2 544	32 667	51.1	17.6
Stevens Point	10 473	2.24	7.6	35.1	3 330	178	94	3 152	604	2 257	153	2 104	14 397	34.2	32.1
Sun Prairie	11 658	2.60	13.2	25.1	102	82	82	20	818	2 662	98	2 564	19 314	22.6	44.1
Superior	11 600	2.21	13.0	37.7	1 191	393	234	798	1 714	6 411	344	6 066	17 988	39.5	22.4
Waukesha	28 349	2.40	9.6	31.5	2 911	892	228	2 019	1 418	1 998	127	1 871	46 908	32.2	34.2
Wausau	16 524	2.30	11.3	34.7	1 100	820	526	280	1 055	2 693	217	2 476	26 831	46.4	24.6
Wauwatosa	20 351	2.27	9.2	35.0	871	732	615	139	1 691	3 577	125	3 452	33 629	19.0	54.9
West Allis	27 185	2.20	10.3	40.1	829	591	583	238	3 047	5 009	322	4 687	43 132	44.2	23.6
West Bend	12 629	2.45	8.6	29.2	530	429	215	101	894	2 823	57	2 766	21 394	36.6	27.1
WYOMING	222 679	2.52	9.0	27.5	13 712	6 701	2 450	7 011	14 004	2 403	205	2 198	380 967	37.8	25.3
Casper	23 646	2.40	10.5	29.1	1 125	548	483	577	2 124	3 619	150	3 469	38 462	33.6	23.7
Cheyenne	24 094	2.52	11.0	30.4	865	636	330	229	2 198	3 537	214	3 323	40 672	33.1	27.9
Gillette	11 324	2.72	11.3	24.4	422	260	123	162	1 061	3 328	166	3 161	18 719	48.1	15.3
Laramie	13 151	2.26	7.6	30.1	2 176	78	70	2 098	707	2 214	116	2 098	16 165	16.0	54.8

1. No spouse present. 2. Data for serious crimes have not been adjusted for underreporting. This may affect comparability between geographic areas and over time. 3. Per 100,000 population estimated by the FBI. 4. Persons 25 years old and over.

City	Money income, 2011–2013					Housing units, 2010			Occupied housing units 2011–2013				
		Households								Owner-occupied		Median owner costs as a percent of income	
	Per capita income[1] (dollars)	Median income	Percent with income of $200,000 or more	Percent with income of less than $25,000	Families with income below poverty (percent)	Total	Percent change, 2000–2010	Vacant units for sale or rent[2]	Total	Percent	Median value[3] (dollars)	With a mortgage[4]	Without a mortgage[5]
	42	43	44	45	46	47	48	49	50	51	52	53	54
WASHINGTON—Cont'd													
Pasco	18 539	53 473	2.0	24.1	19.0	18 782	81.7	799	18 908	65.2	160 300	22.1	10.0
Pullman	17 508	23 885	4.5	51.6	18.1	11 966	27.4	937	10 560	28.0	217 300	19.5	10.0
Puyallup	30 440	63 382	3.6	17.1	4.7	16 171	20.8	1 221	14 837	51.2	252 600	24.0	11.8
Redmond	50 634	97 378	14.6	11.0	5.2	24 177	19.1	1 627	23 651	50.2	464 800	20.2	10.0
Renton	31 020	62 154	4.7	17.4	9.3	38 930	71.5	2 921	37 350	52.2	272 900	26.4	13.0
Richland	35 848	68 825	7.0	15.9	8.2	20 876	26.9	1 169	20 368	67.1	203 300	18.0	10.0
Sammamish	54 824	143 239	28.2	5.1	2.2	15 736	34.7	582	15 757	87.6	569 000	22.1	10.0
SeaTac	19 927	44 558	1.0	24.2	19.5	10 360	3.3	827	9 589	50.9	222 200	32.2	16.2
Seattle	42 929	65 454	9.0	19.7	8.0	308 516	14.0	25 006	289 153	45.8	426 300	24.5	12.8
Shoreline	32 791	59 935	4.6	18.9	6.8	22 787	6.8	1 226	21 056	60.9	311 400	27.2	14.5
Spokane	23 781	41 200	2.2	30.6	13.6	94 291	7.0	7 020	87 021	56.3	157 600	24.1	12.1
Spokane Valley	23 916	47 530	1.2	25.6	10.3	38 851	NA	2 293	36 909	60.3	168 400	23.8	11.3
Tacoma	26 117	50 653	2.7	24.5	13.7	85 786	5.9	7 245	78 223	50.8	198 800	26.5	14.0
University Place	30 862	56 620	4.7	21.5	8.7	13 573	6.8	754	12 665	54.4	274 700	23.7	12.3
Vancouver	25 240	48 230	2.6	23.5	13.7	70 005	16.6	4 314	65 418	49.5	189 300	24.8	11.7
Walla Walla	19 394	40 697	1.9	32.8	17.1	12 514	9.3	977	10 916	58.5	171 900	25.0	13.5
Wenatchee	21 982	47 780	2.7	26.2	12.0	13 175	14.6	796	11 350	54.5	199 900	25.7	11.2
Yakima	19 052	39 268	1.5	32.2	18.6	34 829	21.2	1 755	32 791	52.3	156 700	23.0	12.4
WEST VIRGINIA	23 003	40 830	2.0	32.0	13.1	881 917	4.4	118 086	739 759	72.4	101 000	19.5	10.0
Charleston	36 190	48 427	7.3	28.7	15.7	26 205	-3.2	2 752	22 854	58.3	149 300	17.9	10.0
Huntington	21 684	29 753	3.1	45.2	20.2	25 146	-3.0	3 372	21 447	52.8	88 000	20.8	10.1
Morgantown	20 479	31 408	3.7	44.7	12.9	12 664	7.2	963	9 879	42.1	172 700	16.0	10.0
Parkersburg	18 512	29 985	0.7	41.8	20.4	15 562	-3.2	1 755	13 413	60.6	83 600	21.2	11.6
Wheeling	25 293	35 702	2.0	35.7	11.0	14 661	-6.2	1 845	12 857	62.3	94 500	18.2	10.0
WISCONSIN	27 347	51 768	3.0	22.8	8.9	2 624 358	13.1	344 590	2 281 781	67.4	165 200	23.2	13.7
Appleton	27 389	52 391	3.1	21.4	9.1	30 348	9.7	1 474	28 320	68.2	137 400	21.2	13.8
Beloit	18 514	35 810	1.2	32.4	19.4	15 177	6.5	1 396	14 147	58.8	84 300	23.9	15.4
Brookfield	44 570	86 703	13.5	10.0	1.8	15 317	7.5	741	14 665	86.0	274 500	21.9	13.8
Eau Claire	23 223	42 711	1.5	29.0	8.4	28 134	13.7	1 331	27 077	54.2	139 300	21.5	12.1
Fitchburg	32 809	60 625	6.1	17.5	13.5	10 668	23.2	713	10 088	50.2	258 800	22.9	12.8
Fond du Lac	24 352	46 389	1.1	25.7	10.4	19 181	9.2	1 239	18 277	57.0	122 100	21.6	14.3
Franklin	33 940	68 926	6.2	15.1	5.8	14 356	31.0	714	13 054	77.2	224 500	23.9	13.8
Green Bay	24 054	42 088	2.8	28.2	14.5	45 241	4.8	2 997	42 623	57.9	125 100	22.4	13.0
Greenfield	30 980	50 791	2.1	21.1	5.6	17 790	9.9	930	16 594	58.8	171 600	24.1	16.2
Janesville	23 343	45 877	1.1	26.2	13.1	27 996	11.7	2 168	26 089	65.1	126 400	23.5	12.8
Kenosha	22 923	48 313	1.9	27.8	14.2	40 643	12.4	3 267	37 414	57.1	143 200	25.1	13.8
La Crosse	21 377	41 090	1.7	29.8	10.6	22 628	1.9	1 200	20 434	50.0	128 000	22.6	14.8
Madison	31 208	51 833	3.8	24.4	10.1	108 843	17.9	6 327	104 028	48.0	209 200	23.9	12.5
Manitowoc	23 786	40 695	1.7	27.8	7.5	15 955	6.4	1 332	14 550	66.2	106 600	21.8	13.4
Menomonee Falls	35 300	71 444	6.4	16.0	3.3	15 142	15.1	575	14 556	73.0	223 300	21.5	14.5
Milwaukee	19 077	34 664	1.1	37.5	25.4	255 569	2.5	25 348	229 611	42.2	121 700	26.6	16.1
Mount Pleasant	34 312	60 792	4.4	15.0	4.2	11 827	NA	691	10 971	79.0	181 100	22.8	15.1
Neenah	30 041	51 737	4.1	22.5	10.3	11 313	11.2	619	10 664	64.7	133 300	22.0	12.1
New Berlin	38 623	74 478	6.8	11.5	3.6	16 829	12.7	537	16 339	76.6	232 400	21.5	13.6
Oak Creek	31 605	63 297	3.2	17.9	5.1	14 754	24.0	690	14 131	60.0	209 700	22.5	15.3
Oshkosh	21 441	41 493	1.3	30.8	11.1	28 179	11.1	2 041	25 618	53.7	114 000	21.8	14.1
Racine	20 102	40 174	0.8	32.1	20.1	33 887	1.3	3 357	29 727	54.3	116 500	23.5	15.7
Sheboygan	21 756	42 362	1.0	27.2	13.4	22 339	2.4	2 031	20 141	60.2	110 200	21.1	13.5
Stevens Point	20 856	38 449	1.5	34.8	10.1	11 220	15.0	622	10 473	50.1	111 500	21.8	12.6
Sun Prairie	30 303	66 402	2.3	11.6	4.1	12 413	53.0	777	11 658	59.2	199 300	24.0	12.1
Superior	22 908	39 261	1.0	33.4	18.8	12 328	1.0	658	11 600	55.2	111 500	21.6	12.6
Waukesha	28 059	56 709	2.4	20.6	8.2	29 843	11.1	1 548	28 349	58.5	192 800	22.7	15.2
Wausau	24 889	40 132	2.0	33.4	14.5	18 154	8.8	1 667	16 524	58.4	114 000	22.6	13.9
Wauwatosa	37 377	68 059	5.0	15.8	3.3	21 520	2.9	1 085	20 351	64.6	221 700	22.2	12.3
West Allis	24 134	43 138	0.5	29.8	11.0	29 353	2.2	1 899	27 185	54.3	143 400	24.9	17.4
West Bend	28 138	60 485	2.7	18.7	6.8	13 546	13.7	777	12 629	65.5	165 100	22.2	14.2
WYOMING	28 592	57 197	2.9	19.7	8.4	261 868	17.0	34 989	222 679	69.6	188 700	21.1	10.0
Casper	29 916	56 756	3.9	20.0	8.4	24 536	11.6	1 742	23 646	65.5	176 100	21.0	10.0
Cheyenne	28 415	57 173	2.0	17.7	6.5	27 283	14.6	1 726	24 094	63.2	179 600	21.1	10.0
Gillette	32 423	73 105	3.8	15.2	8.3	12 153	52.3	1 178	11 324	69.5	207 000	19.8	10.0
Laramie	22 457	37 446	1.8	36.2	19.6	14 307	19.2	913	13 151	44.3	199 800	21.6	10.0

1. Based on population estimated by the American Community Survey. 2. Includes units rented or sold but not occupied. 3. Specified owner-occupied units; $1,000,000 represents $1,000,000 or more 4. 50.0 represents 50 percent or more. 5. 10.0 represents 10 percent or less.

City	Occupied housing units, 2011–2013 (cont.): Percent renter occupied	Occupied housing units, 2011–2013 (cont.): Median gross rent[1]	Occupied housing units, 2011–2013 (cont.): Median rent as a percent of income[2]	Occupied housing units, 2011–2013 (cont.): Percent with no vehicle available	Migration, 2011–2013: Percent who lived in the same house one year ago	Migration, 2011–2013: Percent who lived outside current city one year ago	Civilian labor force, 2014: Total	Civilian labor force, 2014: Percent change, 2013–2014	Civilian labor force, 2014: Unemployment: Total	Civilian labor force, 2014: Unemployment: Rate[3]	Civilian employment[4], 2011–2013: Population age 16 and older	Civilian employment[4], 2011–2013: Percent: In labor force	Civilian employment[4], 2011–2013: Percent: Civilian full-year full-time workers	Civilian employment[4], 2011–2013: Households with no workers (percent)
	55	56	57	58	59	60	61	62	63	64	65	66	67	68
WASHINGTON—Cont'd														
Pasco	34.8	755	29.8	5.8	85.3	7.4	30 444	-0.1	2 671	8.8	45 019	68.4	43.9	18.7
Pullman	72.0	725	50.0	11.1	51.0	28.4	14 958	-0.6	846	5.7	27 647	56.5	18.8	29.1
Puyallup	48.8	1 025	29.7	8.8	76.7	18.4	19 935	0.2	1 364	6.8	31 254	68.3	41.5	23.7
Redmond	49.8	1 419	24.4	6.0	79.4	15.8	33 238	2.1	1 319	4.0	45 281	72.0	49.8	16.2
Renton	47.8	1 135	30.6	8.1	77.7	14.9	54 806	1.7	2 362	4.3	76 033	71.6	48.2	21.7
Richland	32.9	872	27.9	5.7	82.1	12.5	25 942	-0.2	1 757	6.8	40 022	63.4	42.9	25.9
Sammamish	12.4	1 920	22.7	1.4	89.8	8.0	25 507	2.2	1 063	4.2	34 966	69.5	49.4	10.1
SeaTac	49.1	912	31.6	8.1	79.0	14.8	14 145	1.5	788	5.6	21 914	65.9	35.9	20.0
Seattle	54.2	1 104	28.8	16.2	77.6	11.3	408 102	1.9	16 912	4.1	544 732	72.4	44.7	22.1
Shoreline	39.1	1 126	31.4	7.6	84.2	13.4	29 540	1.8	1 372	4.6	45 444	65.7	38.5	24.8
Spokane	43.7	732	33.4	10.8	81.9	8.9	99 174	-0.7	7 295	7.4	168 030	61.4	35.0	31.6
Spokane Valley	39.7	757	31.4	7.3	84.7	10.0	44 386	-0.9	3 254	7.3	72 589	62.7	37.1	31.5
Tacoma	49.2	925	32.0	9.6	80.7	11.2	96 586	0.2	7 277	7.5	162 112	64.7	37.3	28.5
University Place	45.6	911	33.3	4.9	83.6	13.7	15 709	0.3	951	6.1	24 570	68.0	37.7	26.1
Vancouver	50.5	903	31.1	7.6	79.9	11.3	79 676	-0.2	6 027	7.6	131 002	64.2	36.8	28.8
Walla Walla	41.5	729	33.5	12.9	81.2	11.0	14 124	-0.6	984	7.0	25 792	52.6	30.5	39.4
Wenatchee	45.5	794	29.5	10.5	87.4	6.9	17 652	1.5	1 174	6.7	24 394	61.4	39.7	29.8
Yakima	47.7	763	34.8	9.1	77.6	8.7	44 414	0.6	3 435	7.7	70 207	61.7	34.2	32.3
WEST VIRGINIA	27.6	618	29.1	8.7	87.9	10.1	790 035	-1.2	51 508	6.5	1 514 736	54.4	35.2	36.9
Charleston	41.7	676	28.2	14.4	81.3	9.8	24 267	-1.6	1 360	5.6	41 716	62.0	40.4	31.3
Huntington	47.2	588	33.8	18.3	77.2	11.5	20 595	-1.1	1 198	5.8	41 473	51.7	29.3	42.0
Morgantown	57.9	645	44.8	14.7	64.0	27.1	14 287	0.0	742	5.2	27 797	55.6	24.4	30.7
Parkersburg	39.4	585	35.1	14.2	88.0	7.7	12 935	-1.7	862	6.7	25 376	53.6	32.3	43.1
Wheeling	37.7	523	30.4	18.1	85.6	7.9	12 994	-0.9	758	5.8	23 390	58.0	34.2	39.0
WISCONSIN	32.6	758	29.3	7.2	85.8	8.9	3 093 918	0.3	170 385	5.5	4 562 266	67.3	41.4	26.6
Appleton	31.8	648	26.7	4.9	84.0	10.9	39 935	-1.3	1 970	4.9	57 055	70.1	43.7	21.8
Beloit	41.2	719	32.9	9.3	81.6	7.9	17 148	-0.9	1 298	7.6	28 314	63.0	33.2	32.9
Brookfield	14.0	1 307	27.1	1.9	91.5	7.2	19 264	0.4	838	4.4	30 537	62.9	40.4	29.2
Eau Claire	45.8	713	31.9	6.9	77.0	11.1	39 762	0.0	1 796	4.5	55 451	70.8	37.7	24.2
Fitchburg	49.8	842	29.6	8.1	79.1	16.2	15 079	0.7	556	3.7	19 870	73.1	45.1	19.2
Fond du Lac	43.0	674	27.0	8.5	80.5	8.0	23 155	-0.8	1 220	5.3	34 484	66.0	42.5	29.5
Franklin	22.8	923	29.3	3.2	85.9	12.5	18 475	0.5	928	5.0	29 033	59.6	41.5	26.7
Green Bay	42.1	646	28.5	8.2	84.0	7.7	54 971	-2.0	3 061	5.6	82 467	66.9	40.5	28.4
Greenfield	41.2	857	26.9	6.6	87.2	9.0	20 040	0.6	1 179	5.9	31 374	63.5	41.1	30.6
Janesville	34.9	727	31.7	6.4	83.4	6.8	33 038	0.3	2 069	6.3	49 515	66.2	39.4	30.8
Kenosha	42.9	800	33.3	7.6	83.4	7.5	49 915	-0.6	3 325	6.7	76 605	67.0	39.0	26.7
La Crosse	50.0	705	30.8	7.5	69.8	15.1	29 642	-0.9	1 396	4.7	44 558	67.0	32.7	24.2
Madison	52.0	897	32.7	13.1	71.8	13.9	149 599	1.4	5 470	3.7	202 768	72.4	40.2	20.3
Manitowoc	33.8	619	26.5	8.4	91.4	4.1	16 577	-1.8	1 100	6.6	27 023	63.5	37.9	31.8
Menomonee Falls	27.0	914	30.6	5.4	88.6	9.2	19 812	0.9	883	4.5	29 262	67.0	44.2	26.4
Milwaukee	57.8	766	34.9	19.2	78.6	6.1	285 195	-0.5	23 041	8.1	455 698	64.8	35.6	30.1
Mount Pleasant	21.0	786	25.8	5.1	89.1	8.7	14 161	-1.3	795	5.6	21 271	65.7	43.3	28.4
Neenah	35.3	672	27.5	6.7	82.4	10.7	14 060	-1.6	752	5.3	20 195	68.3	45.0	25.5
New Berlin	23.4	1 010	28.4	5.4	91.1	8.3	21 956	0.8	1 023	4.7	32 457	67.7	45.4	26.1
Oak Creek	40.0	951	25.0	2.8	87.5	10.4	20 310	0.2	988	4.9	27 693	73.0	49.8	21.0
Oshkosh	46.3	656	28.6	9.4	80.1	12.0	35 091	-0.5	1 966	5.6	55 396	61.2	35.2	27.9
Racine	45.7	718	32.5	14.4	87.3	4.5	36 607	-1.8	3 128	8.5	58 938	64.5	36.9	31.0
Sheboygan	39.8	611	27.6	9.4	82.7	6.4	25 406	0.3	1 328	5.2	38 004	69.6	40.4	28.6
Stevens Point	49.9	647	36.7	9.2	68.3	18.2	14 777	-2.0	776	5.3	23 081	67.6	29.4	28.8
Sun Prairie	40.8	995	26.2	4.5	84.9	9.4	18 480	0.7	728	3.9	22 466	78.2	51.6	17.1
Superior	44.8	673	31.2	12.9	82.8	9.6	14 921	-0.2	756	5.1	21 844	66.1	36.6	30.9
Waukesha	41.5	838	28.7	6.6	82.1	11.2	41 311	-0.3	2 001	4.8	56 302	72.0	45.8	25.1
Wausau	41.6	642	32.4	10.0	78.5	10.2	19 876	-0.7	1 106	5.6	31 281	65.5	37.0	29.3
Wauwatosa	35.4	905	27.9	8.4	88.5	8.5	26 888	0.8	1 142	4.2	37 620	70.7	48.1	24.5
West Allis	45.7	765	32.0	11.7	86.1	11.0	34 147	1.0	2 227	6.5	49 306	69.5	43.4	27.9
West Bend	34.5	767	26.3	6.0	86.2	6.3	17 034	-1.3	853	5.0	24 355	70.7	45.0	25.2
WYOMING	30.4	769	26.2	3.7	81.5	12.5	306 928	0.1	13 239	4.3	452 605	68.6	45.0	22.6
Casper	34.5	814	26.8	4.6	80.8	9.9	32 072	0.5	1 199	3.7	45 745	70.7	46.9	23.0
Cheyenne	36.8	759	26.2	5.7	79.1	12.9	31 842	0.6	1 368	4.3	48 355	68.2	45.0	23.5
Gillette	30.5	885	26.3	4.0	77.5	10.6	16 918	2.7	536	3.2	22 838	77.4	55.4	14.8
Laramie	55.7	714	40.8	5.5	63.5	19.5	17 291	-0.6	578	3.3	27 143	67.7	36.0	19.5

1. $2,000 represents $2,000 or more. 2. 50.0 represents 50 percent or more. 3. Percent of civilian labor force. 4. Persons 16 years old and over.

City	Value of residential construction authorized by building permits, 2014			Wholesale trade,[1] 2007				Retail trade,[2] 2007			
	New construction ($1,000)	Number of housing units	Percent single family	Number of establish-ments	Number of employees	Sales (mil dol)	Annual payroll (mil dol)	Number of establish-ments	Number of employees	Sales (mil dol)	Annual payroll (mil dol)
	69	70	71	72	73	74	75	76	77	78	79
WASHINGTON—Cont'd											
Pasco	58 315	261	83.9	66	876	550.1	36.7	155	2 388	706.2	66.1
Pullman	24 340	190	25.8	11	85	55.7	3.8	49	878	187.8	15.7
Puyallup	29 785	116	100.0	54	683	356.3	30.5	254	5 473	1 436.9	142.3
Redmond	111 736	480	45.0	192	3 567	6 602.3	236.5	260	4 178	916.8	108.1
Renton	114 261	605	35.5	108	4 360	2 572.5	235.1	216	4 945	1 584.9	157.7
Richland	85 061	343	67.3	22	307	365.3	11.0	154	2 145	550.7	54.8
Sammamish	107 616	278	100.0	33	52	28.2	2.3	43	512	122.8	12.9
SeaTac	1 271	11	9.1	23	204	146.8	8.9	40	351	125.1	9.2
Seattle	1 109 041	7 445	12.1	1 188	17 272	11 531.4	1 072.6	2 674	34 791	15 968.8	989.9
Shoreline	17 413	53	96.2	39	151	68.9	6.4	147	2 769	851.9	79.5
Spokane	112 488	519	43.0	296	3 929	1 944.3	169.6	914	14 446	3 115.8	362.5
Spokane Valley	62 156	491	30.3	230	2 936	1 774.4	129.1	475	7 990	2 121.9	210.1
Tacoma	170 709	1 059	24.6	204	3 168	2 055.2	159.3	779	12 385	3 064.9	331.0
University Place	28 186	207	24.2	22	219	96.6	10.1	58	860	185.0	20.1
Vancouver	70 593	818	23.1	197	2 247	2 952.5	130.4	563	10 489	2 630.6	250.1
Walla Walla	13 679	89	94.4	35	340	158.2	12.0	170	1 917	400.3	45.8
Wenatchee	7 414	55	67.3	62	976	536.6	36.5	193	2 737	655.6	67.9
Yakima	26 013	137	89.1	114	2 201	998.8	79.9	395	5 553	1 387.3	139.6
WEST VIRGINIA	395 354	2 677	71.3	1 372	16 790	11 036.5	656.0	7 047	92 227	20 538.8	1 776.5
Charleston	5 117	18	100.0	112	1 705	782.8	74.3	353	5 292	1 006.1	95.8
Huntington	383	10	0.0	83	1 327	477.6	55.0	236	2 896	548.1	57.2
Morgantown	4 063	57	19.3	22	201	53.3	6.1	212	3 569	743.3	63.5
Parkersburg	1 279	11	100.0	47	407	178.0	13.4	237	3 588	820.9	74.2
Wheeling	6 189	55	5.5	63	D	D	D	167	1 846	402.1	39.2
WISCONSIN	2 599 187	14 622	58.7	6 215	99 773	59 996.2	4 639.0	21 205	320 140	72 283.3	6 778.3
Appleton	31 639	198	29.3	94	1 428	486.0	60.8	290	4 596	1 008.6	97.4
Beloit	719	7	100.0	15	323	297.9	19.4	113	1 826	467.1	38.8
Brookfield	22 245	56	100.0	112	1 767	736.3	107.4	327	6 851	1 216.2	132.1
Eau Claire	10 958	65	100.0	80	1 557	818.4	59.2	363	7 046	1 334.9	130.3
Fitchburg	41 443	371	9.4	33	991	597.4	44.1	64	821	221.0	25.2
Fond du Lac	9 007	52	57.7	45	824	511.0	42.0	251	4 291	903.2	81.9
Franklin	14 893	51	96.1	40	331	212.9	19.3	75	1 831	460.1	43.1
Green Bay	19 446	180	38.9	119	2 134	1 327.7	98.1	395	6 406	1 474.6	132.6
Greenfield	9 815	96	10.4	20	75	22.4	2.9	159	3 492	858.3	83.2
Janesville	15 897	73	89.0	55	1 883	1 642.3	97.0	323	6 243	1 630.6	150.1
Kenosha	5 989	47	40.4	58	922	465.7	47.3	327	5 059	1 276.4	115.5
La Crosse	4 496	26	92.3	75	1 774	2 645.1	73.0	269	5 174	1 015.3	97.1
Madison	233 692	1 680	14.0	272	5 005	2 321.3	243.4	1 024	19 133	4 103.6	397.4
Manitowoc	5 457	65	13.8	23	242	170.8	10.3	169	2 578	529.4	51.2
Menomonee Falls	21 820	103	45.6	108	1 864	884.2	114.4	133	2 916	573.5	67.7
Milwaukee	17 811	206	16.5	490	9 788	5 599.5	486.5	1 447	18 937	4 001.7	410.5
Mount Pleasant	6 667	29	86.2	19	295	113.4	11.2	76	1 472	393.1	35.3
Neenah	10 698	54	96.3	26	430	199.4	21.5	93	1 603	408.8	34.1
New Berlin	9 825	31	100.0	131	2 743	1 404.6	147.4	104	2 274	515.3	56.0
Oak Creek	12 713	81	25.9	34	1 003	794.4	47.1	83	2 316	588.6	53.3
Oshkosh	15 564	157	9.6	62	1 467	600.7	54.3	277	4 853	1 021.0	96.2
Racine	415	3	100.0	62	637	278.0	30.1	314	4 240	710.5	70.0
Sheboygan	1 346	7	100.0	45	632	273.4	24.4	201	3 217	714.8	68.1
Stevens Point	5 585	40	55.0	31	717	380.6	18.6	147	2 708	530.4	51.1
Sun Prairie	38 354	266	42.9	29	652	271.2	28.4	68	1 376	293.3	37.8
Superior	395	3	100.0	40	D	D	D	123	1 959	468.0	45.4
Waukesha	31 448	319	24.5	127	2 032	1 261.0	110.1	222	4 498	1 248.1	111.8
Wausau	5 172	22	100.0	49	968	434.4	42.7	209	4 752	969.1	94.1
Wauwatosa	26 525	309	1.0	81	2 306	1 481.9	93.9	295	5 552	1 018.7	104.8
West Allis	1 519	23	17.4	107	2 026	1 003.8	104.5	276	4 827	1 386.5	116.9
West Bend	5 198	32	68.8	27	353	102.6	12.1	141	3 173	633.8	59.8
WYOMING	502 643	1 901	84.9	705	6 347	6 352.9	306.6	2 951	32 033	8 957.6	758.1
Casper	40 956	146	100.0	87	787	2 387.1	38.3	351	4 679	1 200.0	115.0
Cheyenne	40 981	283	65.4	77	691	354.6	31.0	313	5 108	1 382.7	122.5
Gillette	66 417	163	100.0	54	902	665.8	51.8	164	2 178	693.4	55.7
Laramie	8 407	51	100.0	16	118	107.5	4.3	157	1 871	444.6	36.8

1. Merchant wholesalers except manufacturers' sales branches and offices. 2. Establishments with payroll.

Table D. Cities — **Real Estate, Professional Services, and Manufacturing**

City	Real estate and rental and leasing, 2007				Professional, scientific, and technical services,[1] 2007				Manufacturing, 2007			
	Number of establish-ments	Number of employees	Receipts (mil dol)	Annual payroll (mil dol)	Number of establish-ments	Number of employees	Receipts (mil dol)	Annual payroll (mil dol)	Number of establish-ments	Number of employees	Receipts (mil dol)	Annual payroll (mil dol)
	80	81	82	83	84	85	86	87	88	89	90	91
WASHINGTON—Cont'd												
Pasco	49	240	44.3	6.3	68	D	D	D	39	D	D	D
Pullman	35	185	18.2	3.2	36	144	14.7	5.5	12	D	D	D
Puyallup	113	595	87.0	15.4	117	D	D	D	41	678	148.9	28.7
Redmond	127	1 324	283.2	60.3	352	D	D	D	147	9 662	4 379.9	603.2
Renton	102	1 284	239.2	47.4	180	1 848	177.4	75.6	62	11 491	D	719.1
Richland	69	231	32.3	6.4	163	4 779	796.8	361.3	35	1 361	511.7	83.9
Sammamish	61	113	34.6	3.4	158	322	53.0	16.5	NA	NA	NA	NA
SeaTac	35	374	132.9	13.1	19	186	25.0	9.5	NA	NA	NA	NA
Seattle	1 622	10 440	2 279.7	472.8	4 328	47 828	8 836.0	3 877.4	970	28 376	7 076.2	1 226.4
Shoreline	95	340	92.2	12.9	96	311	31.2	12.0	NA	NA	NA	NA
Spokane	321	1 767	333.4	54.6	733	5 625	728.8	297.1	230	4 866	965.5	192.7
Spokane Valley	135	774	170.9	24.6	205	1 197	169.6	54.8	209	7 472	1 886.9	313.1
Tacoma	343	2 193	334.9	58.3	499	D	D	D	240	8 785	2 257.3	407.5
University Place	51	D	D	D	71	220	23.3	10.7	NA	NA	NA	NA
Vancouver	282	1 895	281.9	70.5	540	D	D	D	197	7 993	2 689.2	357.5
Walla Walla	52	155	22.1	4.4	83	D	D	D	75	884	D	41.9
Wenatchee	61	276	41.8	7.2	118	D	D	D	31	586	D	D
Yakima	153	660	110.8	17.1	217	D	D	D	111	3 122	680.1	119.1
WEST VIRGINIA	1 586	7 055	1 171.0	175.3	2 906	20 766	2 341.1	857.5	1 413	59 981	25 080.6	2 645.8
Charleston	160	806	188.2	24.0	397	3 541	515.4	164.4	39	694	D	25.5
Huntington	89	325	58.8	8.7	141	D	D	D	57	3 839	1 725.1	174.5
Morgantown	82	323	44.7	7.7	127	D	D	D	NA	NA	NA	NA
Parkersburg	54	331	52.3	8.3	93	D	D	D	33	D	D	D
Wheeling	57	D	D	D	129	D	D	D	51	908	D	30.5
WISCONSIN	5 119	27 226	4 043.5	788.9	11 255	97 445	12 797.3	4 999.0	9 659	487 573	163 563.2	21 850.3
Appleton	69	326	37.3	8.6	193	3 091	276.4	120.9	108	7 032	2 651.0	318.5
Beloit	22	98	47.0	2.8	37	148	12.7	5.6	57	3 310	1 522.9	137.7
Brookfield	110	1 064	102.3	32.5	309	3 601	579.3	225.9	72	2 033	429.7	99.4
Eau Claire	98	677	80.7	14.9	148	1 008	104.1	47.5	89	4 706	1 141.0	196.0
Fitchburg	38	240	36.6	7.8	86	815	266.7	63.8	33	3 596	1 207.8	194.1
Fond du Lac	50	215	27.1	4.2	90	1 019	73.5	56.5	76	4 365	1 535.4	205.4
Franklin	18	83	13.2	1.8	56	429	85.1	18.1	55	3 081	1 014.7	160.6
Green Bay	111	724	98.5	24.1	221	D	D	D	144	11 058	5 193.4	484.8
Greenfield	47	231	50.7	6.3	76	518	43.6	19.1	NA	NA	NA	NA
Janesville	67	269	37.9	6.0	108	D	D	D	97	8 225	10 171.3	497.5
Kenosha	97	440	57.3	8.8	119	617	60.3	25.8	123	3 838	1 584.3	190.3
La Crosse	75	452	59.4	11.3	151	D	D	D	94	4 355	1 438.6	165.8
Madison	393	3 012	436.9	100.6	934	D	D	D	207	9 145	2 418.3	450.2
Manitowoc	22	138	13.1	2.3	52	411	45.2	14.1	86	7 191	1 995.2	289.8
Menomonee Falls	34	319	44.1	17.0	111	907	100.3	42.9	187	9 018	2 070.6	420.6
Milwaukee	437	3 183	572.7	136.3	1 131	17 521	2 458.6	1 110.0	652	28 510	9 058.9	1 406.3
Mount Pleasant	29	105	13.0	2.9	54	305	32.1	15.8	33	2 626	4 040.6	180.0
Neenah	17	193	41.5	7.2	58	420	37.6	29.6	62	6 070	2 197.2	271.6
New Berlin	32	237	44.1	6.4	111	D	D	D	139	5 303	1 312.8	262.9
Oak Creek	35	429	92.4	14.6	36	258	20.9	8.0	64	6 439	2 478.6	312.6
Oshkosh	66	432	35.4	8.0	100	D	D	D	125	8 592	3 869.1	425.8
Racine	58	214	28.0	4.8	140	D	D	D	170	7 717	2 174.1	399.0
Sheboygan	39	260	61.3	10.0	85	632	146.3	34.8	97	7 776	2 059.1	323.1
Stevens Point	21	104	10.7	1.7	54	400	39.6	15.1	36	1 939	539.8	80.0
Sun Prairie	21	66	22.2	2.9	45	318	31.2	14.0	35	1 393	281.7	56.9
Superior	30	D	D	D	54	285	24.7	10.6	41	D	D	D
Waukesha	70	348	79.3	12.1	184	1 658	222.3	90.1	152	10 719	7 548.7	707.2
Wausau	46	188	24.4	4.3	131	D	D	D	73	6 401	1 579.0	238.1
Wauwatosa	49	225	86.1	8.7	267	D	D	D	46	4 017	1 286.4	322.7
West Allis	55	405	89.5	14.9	115	1 324	110.9	52.3	101	3 692	753.1	169.0
West Bend	27	127	16.1	2.3	61	320	30.4	12.0	55	2 299	522.8	93.7
WYOMING	1 121	4 651	991.6	159.7	1 890	8 711	1 079.3	387.5	596	11 904	8 834.8	573.7
Casper	135	610	158.4	23.6	231	D	D	D	43	603	135.0	25.8
Cheyenne	108	438	86.4	12.2	274	1 251	165.1	58.0	47	1 576	2 390.9	76.4
Gillette	62	341	72.1	9.7	89	498	50.8	19.5	NA	NA	NA	NA
Laramie	51	D	D	D	107	D	D	D	NA	NA	NA	NA

1. Establishments subject to federal tax.

City	Accommodation and food services, 2007				Arts, entertainment, and recreation,[1] 2007				Health care and social assistance,[1] 2007			
	Number of establish-ments	Number of employees	Sales (mil dol)	Annual payroll (mil dol)	Number of establish-ments	Number of employees	Receipts (mil dol)	Annual payroll (mil dol)	Number of establish-ments	Number of employees	Receipts (mil dol)	Annual payroll (mil dol)
	92	93	94	95	96	97	98	99	100	101	102	103
WASHINGTON—Cont'd												
Pasco	83	934	46.3	12.9	8	D	D	D	86	632	54.3	18.8
Pullman	88	1 165	42.4	11.6	2	D	D	D	46	D	D	D
Puyallup	159	2 945	125.4	38.5	13	D	D	D	182	D	D	D
Redmond	257	4 434	306.7	88.5	22	D	D	D	169	1 580	161.4	60.4
Renton	219	3 446	229.0	60.7	17	D	D	D	211	2 103	270.6	97.3
Richland	111	1 806	83.1	25.0	10	D	D	D	199	D	D	D
Sammamish	31	532	23.9	7.8	10	177	10.6	3.1	63	413	36.5	15.3
SeaTac	80	2 817	236.4	60.4	6	D	D	D	26	915	19.0	10.7
Seattle	2 569	42 686	2 730.8	822.4	307	4 686	615.7	313.3	1 859	21 038	2 746.2	1 193.7
Shoreline	92	1 017	44.9	13.3	18	D	D	D	156	1 658	127.3	53.5
Spokane	552	10 324	477.3	145.5	56	875	50.4	13.9	703	11 330	1 154.8	510.2
Spokane Valley	215	3 525	164.7	48.1	26	506	22.7	7.4	291	4 759	313.9	139.4
Tacoma	534	7 979	380.7	114.7	44	1 890	248.9	52.0	613	8 885	938.0	427.7
University Place	34	399	17.8	5.4	4	D	D	D	73	D	D	D
Vancouver	404	7 159	326.2	97.3	40	605	29.0	8.6	444	6 682	651.1	283.8
Walla Walla	99	1 556	70.4	21.4	12	47	3.4	0.8	100	D	D	D
Wenatchee	108	1 588	77.4	22.8	9	83	2.4	0.9	121	D	D	D
Yakima	221	3 320	150.8	45.5	23	D	D	D	273	4 411	490.0	188.5
WEST VIRGINIA	3 650	61 711	2 553.3	712.8	563	8 488	1 257.9	149.7	3 741	51 790	4 338.6	1 708.4
Charleston	215	4 144	190.8	54.8	24	D	D	D	344	4 939	591.0	231.6
Huntington	171	3 145	122.0	33.6	13	215	5.2	1.7	205	D	D	D
Morgantown	160	3 183	118.2	30.1	28	205	9.6	2.8	79	D	D	D
Parkersburg	139	2 266	87.1	24.5	15	D	D	D	176	3 218	326.6	119.5
Wheeling	105	1 699	76.5	20.5	17	703	127.4	13.5	167	D	D	D
WISCONSIN	14 439	227 475	9 247.3	2 535.2	2 075	27 979	2 362.6	748.6	11 149	165 008	15 006.0	6 808.4
Appleton	203	3 949	139.1	39.9	23	298	7.2	2.9	198	3 521	423.6	197.4
Beloit	95	1 387	53.6	14.8	5	D	D	D	43	D	D	D
Brookfield	125	3 025	124.0	37.3	21	390	16.0	5.4	257	D	D	D
Eau Claire	208	4 579	157.0	46.2	24	401	21.4	4.1	186	4 608	494.7	274.0
Fitchburg	40	814	34.8	9.7	9	166	5.6	1.8	30	D	D	D
Fond du Lac	125	2 531	87.5	25.5	14	D	D	D	124	D	D	D
Franklin	51	853	33.9	9.3	4	D	D	D	70	1 009	83.6	33.3
Green Bay	274	5 245	203.7	56.7	33	D	D	D	219	6 217	839.7	317.3
Greenfield	85	D	D	D	15	D	D	D	143	D	D	D
Janesville	178	3 239	121.1	34.3	18	372	11.0	3.1	107	2 259	245.3	98.6
Kenosha	236	3 787	147.8	41.1	30	435	29.1	6.9	279	3 483	301.3	135.3
La Crosse	214	3 882	142.9	42.4	22	D	D	D	101	D	D	D
Madison	698	14 968	595.3	177.7	65	1 067	89.2	16.3	414	8 994	1 242.7	529.7
Manitowoc	94	1 783	57.4	16.5	11	89	5.2	1.5	104	D	D	D
Menomonee Falls	61	1 122	39.5	10.6	9	D	D	D	67	D	D	D
Milwaukee	1 134	20 453	949.1	265.9	75	3 629	661.7	251.0	1 313	16 744	1 439.5	768.1
Mount Pleasant	55	1 411	56.9	16.1	4	D	D	D	67	534	48.6	18.6
Neenah	79	1 219	47.3	12.3	8	48	2.9	1.0	83	1 029	136.3	69.8
New Berlin	61	1 363	48.6	13.3	17	D	D	D	76	1 031	111.5	56.2
Oak Creek	59	1 302	50.3	13.2	8	76	4.8	1.3	47	D	D	D
Oshkosh	186	3 694	125.2	35.7	18	D	D	D	146	2 253	206.8	102.0
Racine	167	D	D	D	26	221	16.8	3.7	144	2 238	214.4	119.6
Sheboygan	138	2 133	85.6	23.4	9	D	D	D	155	3 189	239.3	135.3
Stevens Point	102	1 858	61.0	16.9	10	D	D	D	71	D	D	D
Sun Prairie	52	863	27.8	8.2	5	D	D	D	48	784	75.5	27.9
Superior	112	1 840	64.9	18.3	14	D	D	D	48	940	51.5	23.0
Waukesha	149	2 686	100.2	28.1	21	260	11.5	3.1	183	2 386	236.5	116.6
Wausau	133	2 132	82.1	22.7	14	139	6.4	2.3	160	D	D	D
Wauwatosa	130	3 189	133.3	38.7	10	299	9.7	2.7	393	6 044	515.1	252.9
West Allis	168	D	D	D	20	299	21.3	4.4	189	4 352	308.9	148.8
West Bend	80	1 364	50.2	13.6	12	101	5.0	1.2	90	1 052	62.7	27.9
WYOMING	1 768	26 992	1 469.0	411.9	325	3 211	173.3	54.2	1 297	11 680	1 139.3	469.9
Casper	142	3 298	142.7	43.4	18	D	D	D	220	D	D	D
Cheyenne	154	3 278	144.0	44.2	12	D	D	D	209	2 494	213.7	94.1
Gillette	68	1 632	82.6	22.1	3	D	D	D	66	D	D	D
Laramie	94	1 500	58.7	16.8	9	62	2.2	0.6	84	D	D	D

1. Establishments subject to federal tax.

Table D. Cities — **Other Services and Government Employment and Payroll**

City	Other services[1], 2007				Government employment and payroll, 2012								
						March payroll							
							Percent of total for:						
	Number of establish-ments	Number of employees	Receipts (mil dol)	Annual payroll (mil dol)	Full-time equivalent employees	Total (dollars)	Adminis-tration, judicial, and legal	Police and Corrections	Fire Protection	Highways and trans-portation	Health and welfare	Natural resources and utilities	Education and libraries
	104	105	106	107	108	109	110	111	112	113	114	115	116
WASHINGTON—Cont'd													
Pasco	67	D	D	D	285	1 601 010	14.1	30.2	22.2	7.6	4.6	21.0	0.0
Pullman	26	D	D	D	232	989 864	6.3	23.6	22.8	32.0	0.0	11.6	3.7
Puyallup	74	715	67.5	22.6	469	3 001 181	14.9	30.0	21.9	6.7	0.0	16.4	3.2
Redmond	125	950	83.7	28.6	679	4 387 058	20.9	18.6	29.5	4.1	1.4	18.8	0.0
Renton	127	832	78.5	26.9	825	5 336 014	10.3	32.9	23.1	6.5	6.4	17.5	0.0
Richland	59	424	32.9	11.4	499	3 031 486	16.6	16.7	14.9	6.2	1.1	33.3	2.9
Sammamish	29	134	11.4	3.1	85	514 186	26.6	1.0	0.0	28.1	16.1	22.8	0.0
SeaTac	47	697	62.5	16.7	162	1 068 652	30.3	0.6	37.3	13.7	1.2	5.9	0.0
Seattle	1 382	8 585	751.4	239.8	10 193	71 586 796	7.4	21.3	13.4	5.8	3.3	38.0	3.4
Shoreline	70	386	31.4	10.0	222	1 123 950	28.0	39.9	0.0	5.5	0.6	22.6	0.0
Spokane	385	2 352	182.5	56.9	2 161	12 463 086	15.6	21.9	20.6	8.3	0.4	26.4	3.2
Spokane Valley	170	1 438	154.2	34.4	92	466 469	31.8	0.0	0.0	24.5	34.4	9.2	0.0
Tacoma	333	2 491	202.0	72.2	3 458	23 314 293	11.1	13.2	14.4	8.2	0.5	43.6	2.1
University Place	39	299	19.5	6.6	48	264 084	30.6	4.5	0.0	30.0	14.8	9.6	0.0
Vancouver	277	1 299	99.7	31.4	1 018	5 857 054	12.9	26.3	24.0	6.1	0.0	21.4	0.0
Walla Walla	37	D	D	D	251	1 313 753	15.6	33.8	26.5	0.9	0.3	16.4	3.3
Wenatchee	69	271	20.1	5.9	185	996 105	13.5	30.6	19.2	10.0	2.0	19.4	0.0
Yakima	140	900	61.7	18.6	615	3 330 932	12.9	39.5	16.4	10.4	0.9	18.9	0.0
WEST VIRGINIA	2 211	12 382	1 024.3	298.5	X	X	X	X	X	X	X	X	X
Charleston	124	1 051	53.1	17.2	826	2 940 542	13.0	28.6	24.9	0.8	1.4	16.3	0.0
Huntington	89	579	44.7	13.3	338	1 166 129	8.3	42.3	27.9	4.5	2.5	8.5	0.0
Morgantown	63	D	D	D	442	1 584 824	7.6	19.5	12.7	10.7	0.3	38.5	4.0
Parkersburg	76	426	28.3	8.5	347	1 079 226	8.0	24.0	18.5	10.1	1.5	34.7	0.0
Wheeling	74	673	52.9	15.3	828	2 250 153	5.6	14.0	15.9	7.2	0.0	55.8	0.0
WISCONSIN	8 822	51 066	3 865.8	1 235.7	X	X	X	X	X	X	X	X	X
Appleton	141	1 081	66.9	22.0	663	3 090 024	10.6	24.2	16.9	8.2	4.8	15.8	6.5
Beloit	45	193	11.1	3.7	368	1 795 646	10.7	25.3	19.5	14.3	3.6	17.7	4.9
Brookfield	103	1 042	104.2	28.3	333	1 844 609	12.7	28.6	21.1	12.3	0.0	14.9	6.1
Eau Claire	135	1 009	69.6	24.3	608	2 643 962	9.0	24.0	17.4	10.5	10.6	15.3	5.6
Fitchburg	29	309	15.6	5.6	168	745 550	17.6	38.6	15.3	7.5	2.7	10.2	0.8
Fond du Lac	94	695	48.8	14.8	344	1 652 329	8.9	25.7	21.9	14.0	1.9	15.0	6.8
Franklin	48	D	D	D	218	1 131 749	9.5	36.1	24.9	12.6	2.8	4.7	5.0
Green Bay	146	1 055	72.0	21.3	860	4 043 340	7.5	30.8	25.6	11.5	1.1	19.5	0.0
Greenfield	67	532	36.1	12.9	217	1 158 811	11.1	38.6	26.7	12.0	3.2	3.7	3.2
Janesville	105	584	39.1	12.6	482	2 513 217	10.6	24.7	21.6	15.6	3.3	16.1	7.3
Kenosha	152	1 024	60.3	20.3	811	3 859 872	5.8	28.1	22.1	10.6	2.7	18.1	7.7
La Crosse	99	672	44.9	17.9	567	2 357 551	9.7	24.1	19.2	17.7	2.0	14.4	9.6
Madison	337	2 878	242.6	78.8	3 036	14 945 308	10.6	21.2	12.9	22.9	2.3	18.7	5.5
Manitowoc	57	331	21.4	6.4	355	1 875 536	6.3	20.8	18.2	15.1	0.0	32.1	5.9
Menomonee Falls	69	482	41.0	10.9	252	1 124 295	9.0	39.6	11.5	12.7	2.5	9.8	5.9
Milwaukee	711	4 559	381.3	122.9	6 455	32 385 292	9.5	39.7	17.4	3.2	7.3	12.0	3.2
Mount Pleasant	35	243	17.4	5.4	206	856 388	12.7	34.6	41.4	6.6	0.0	4.6	0.0
Neenah	53	415	29.5	9.8	272	1 262 394	8.6	24.1	29.0	10.9	5.7	15.3	6.4
New Berlin	64	D	D	D	254	1 283 876	12.9	39.3	15.4	12.5	0.0	11.2	4.4
Oak Creek	40	D	D	D	266	1 412 700	9.6	31.2	21.6	13.5	2.3	15.7	2.7
Oshkosh	97	723	42.9	14.1	576	2 558 304	7.2	22.6	21.9	15.9	6.5	17.9	5.9
Racine	114	831	56.6	19.4	815	4 196 517	6.8	33.8	20.0	8.7	5.3	19.5	3.6
Sheboygan	85	526	32.5	9.6	431	1 929 836	9.1	27.3	17.8	18.6	2.9	13.8	7.8
Stevens Point	49	319	22.2	6.6	194	851 692	9.1	29.9	22.2	24.4	3.2	11.3	0.0
Sun Prairie	42	207	12.7	4.0	223	1 003 694	14.5	33.1	0.0	9.8	7.1	24.8	7.1
Superior	55	D	D	D	255	1 159 999	11.2	29.7	15.8	11.8	0.7	18.3	5.6
Waukesha	130	865	82.4	23.9	566	2 950 957	10.7	28.4	19.7	16.3	0.3	16.6	5.6
Wausau	64	304	22.5	5.9	306	1 383 873	11.0	27.3	21.3	24.5	3.8	8.0	0.0
Wauwatosa	78	713	48.2	18.9	414	2 166 975	10.9	28.6	27.5	10.0	3.1	9.0	5.3
West Allis	135	745	62.0	19.1	541	2 746 980	10.4	30.7	21.8	7.9	7.6	15.5	3.5
West Bend	72	500	33.7	10.2	261	1 244 682	11.9	33.2	19.5	9.0	0.0	16.8	5.0
WYOMING	996	4 850	520.2	141.5	X	X	X	X	X	X	X	X	X
Casper	108	D	D	D	563	2 490 135	12.1	24.0	15.7	5.9	2.6	30.8	0.0
Cheyenne	87	521	39.9	13.3	655	2 479 867	12.4	24.6	20.1	11.9	5.3	17.8	0.0
Gillette	71	D	D	D	278	1 359 171	21.1	29.1	0.0	9.2	3.7	24.3	0.0
Laramie	54	D	D	D	282	1 207 422	11.8	25.1	22.5	5.3	8.5	26.7	0.0

1. Establishments subject to federal tax.

City	City government finances, 2007									
	General revenue							General expenditure		
		Intergovernmental		Taxes					Per capita[1] (dollars)	
					Per capita[1] (dollars)					
	Total (mil dol)	Total (mil dol)	Percent from state government	Total (mil dol)	Total	Property	Sales and gross receipts	Total (mil dol)	Total	Capital outlays
	117	118	119	120	121	122	123	124	125	126
WASHINGTON—Cont'd										
Pasco	56.3	7.4	83.9	27.7	414	100	307	43.0	644	84
Pullman	28.8	6.2	79.9	14.1	450	166	280	23.2	740	102
Puyallup	56.2	6.0	83.5	28.9	756	220	514	45.2	1 184	149
Redmond	132.9	19.1	27.4	73.4	1 298	388	860	135.8	2 399	780
Renton	182.1	40.0	23.2	80.9	844	338	484	161.6	1 687	421
Richland	85.1	16.9	69.5	35.1	682	273	382	81.3	1 579	382
Sammamish	38.6	2.0	89.9	31.3	638	438	144	30.6	623	115
SeaTac	44.1	5.0	93.3	33.9	1 224	437	770	38.5	1 392	195
Seattle	1 849.1	193.2	68.5	913.5	1 438	626	809	1 658.2	2 611	430
Shoreline	64.6	27.8	75.5	28.7	527	212	300	61.5	1 129	532
Spokane	360.6	46.8	62.8	134.2	641	291	339	346.3	1 653	310
Spokane Valley	47.6	9.5	74.7	34.3	379	118	250	44.6	492	104
Tacoma	497.4	82.6	61.5	160.2	792	300	477	525.2	2 597	668
University Place	20.3	3.7	81.0	12.2	386	120	255	19.2	607	164
Vancouver	216.2	36.9	48.3	102.8	622	244	361	188.0	1 138	228
Walla Walla	47.0	7.8	77.4	16.3	512	186	320	48.0	1 505	391
Wenatchee	35.6	3.6	70.5	20.4	627	183	433	31.6	972	109
Yakima	108.8	28.2	59.7	50.2	539	163	367	101.0	1 085	250
WEST VIRGINIA	X	X	X	X	X	X	X	X	X	X
Charleston	119.9	8.4	43.3	74.5	1 461	237	1 224	118.2	2 318	327
Huntington	66.4	5.5	20.3	27.6	561	105	408	69.9	1 422	172
Morgantown	47.5	3.6	18.6	18.2	602	114	488	57.9	1 916	338
Parkersburg	38.3	2.2	14.9	16.0	512	159	345	37.9	1 214	142
Wheeling	68.9	4.3	9.3	21.9	776	214	556	77.9	2 759	267
WISCONSIN	X	X	X	X	X	X	X	X	X	X
Appleton	105.8	35.3	66.9	40.0	547	511	29	95.4	1 306	185
Beloit	62.8	26.8	88.2	19.9	542	506	31	62.9	1 709	281
Brookfield	58.1	9.5	75.4	37.1	977	878	98	58.2	1 531	164
Eau Claire	86.2	27.3	65.5	36.1	536	481	48	88.9	1 320	274
Fitchburg	30.2	5.5	88.9	18.6	718	696	22	39.3	1 517	661
Fond du Lac	60.5	20.6	71.8	21.1	490	445	41	63.0	1 465	223
Franklin	41.4	6.9	92.4	26.8	747	678	68	36.9	1 030	91
Green Bay	138.7	46.3	79.3	53.7	512	485	22	133.7	1 276	218
Greenfield	36.7	6.5	88.9	20.6	556	518	38	41.0	1 106	190
Janesville	81.1	21.4	60.8	31.0	488	455	30	86.4	1 359	476
Kenosha	136.7	40.5	74.7	66.5	666	635	29	121.2	1 213	141
La Crosse	96.0	32.3	81.3	41.7	801	727	63	83.2	1 597	241
Madison	476.1	163.1	64.2	192.4	802	725	69	469.3	1 956	262
Manitowoc	48.5	17.0	90.1	15.7	469	434	32	54.5	1 630	246
Menomonee Falls	46.2	6.0	94.8	25.0	698	656	42	54.6	1 523	188
Milwaukee	1 070.1	483.1	64.8	302.6	505	483	22	1 000.4	1 671	211
Mount Pleasant	34.1	6.0	62.3	15.7	601	545	49	36.3	1 387	0
Neenah	34.2	7.5	78.2	17.5	681	647	32	35.3	1 374	110
New Berlin	42.8	4.9	98.3	23.5	591	549	41	43.8	1 103	116
Oak Creek	39.6	9.3	95.7	20.6	591	532	53	40.8	1 169	139
Oshkosh	88.9	26.0	83.5	36.9	554	503	47	92.9	1 393	336
Racine	138.3	56.9	78.9	49.1	627	593	33	139.8	1 787	186
Sheboygan	64.8	24.2	81.4	26.8	549	494	49	58.7	1 204	114
Stevens Point	34.5	13.5	80.1	14.0	519	471	42	34.2	1 272	140
Sun Prairie	36.3	6.6	89.6	21.4	700	647	49	33.4	1 092	159
Superior	47.8	19.7	86.8	13.1	488	414	69	43.1	1 604	221
Waukesha	94.8	23.2	75.8	53.6	753	709	40	92.3	1 297	257
Wausau	59.2	21.8	72.8	26.1	667	628	35	52.5	1 340	306
Wauwatosa	76.5	14.7	62.5	41.9	891	830	51	68.2	1 451	107
West Allis	89.6	27.7	67.2	39.6	652	626	24	88.3	1 455	97
West Bend	37.8	8.6	79.5	22.6	714	667	45	36.4	1 152	223
WYOMING	X	X	X	X	X	X	X	X	X	X
Casper	90.9	48.4	57.4	10.7	185	79	91	91.8	1 586	372
Cheyenne	102.2	45.4	60.0	14.2	231	86	144	84.7	1 372	240
Gillette	102.0	79.8	46.5	4.1	129	81	48	73.4	2 334	563
Laramie	40.4	21.5	68.2	5.1	162	66	95	47.7	1 503	636

1. Based on population estimated as of July 1 of the year shown.

City	City government finances, 2012 (cont.)									
	General expenditure (cont.)									
	Percent of total for:									
	Public welfare	Highways	Parking facilities	Education	Health and hospitals	Police protection	Sewerage and sanitation	Parks and recreation	Housing and community development	Interest on debt
	127	128	129	130	131	132	133	134	135	136
WASHINGTON—Cont'd										
Pasco	0.0	12.0	0.0	0.0	5.4	17.4	11.1	11.5	2.3	5.8
Pullman	0.0	11.6	0.0	0.0	6.2	18.7	14.9	9.3	0.0	0.8
Puyallup	0.0	14.1	0.0	0.0	0.3	25.3	23.3	8.8	1.9	6.7
Redmond	0.1	20.2	0.0	0.0	3.2	9.2	16.1	13.1	0.8	2.8
Renton	0.0	13.1	0.0	0.0	0.2	11.9	18.6	6.2	1.5	5.1
Richland	0.0	12.0	0.0	0.0	3.2	11.2	16.4	9.6	5.1	3.3
Sammamish	0.0	22.0	0.0	0.0	0.5	13.9	5.2	17.5	3.3	0.4
SeaTac	0.0	17.5	0.0	0.0	0.0	22.5	3.5	7.6	3.2	0.3
Seattle	6.2	11.8	0.5	0.3	1.1	10.5	29.3	9.1	1.8	4.1
Shoreline	0.0	46.6	0.0	0.0	0.0	16.3	3.4	7.7	2.4	3.0
Spokane	1.1	10.6	0.1	0.0	0.1	12.3	34.0	5.6	2.9	2.6
Spokane Valley	0.0	29.1	0.0	0.0	0.7	37.4	3.1	8.3	3.7	0.9
Tacoma	1.2	12.1	1.0	0.0	2.6	11.0	24.3	5.6	2.6	4.8
University Place	0.0	26.2	0.0	0.0	0.9	17.4	7.1	4.1	4.1	14.1
Vancouver	0.0	18.7	0.7	0.0	0.1	13.2	12.4	8.6	1.9	4.8
Walla Walla	0.0	9.6	0.0	0.0	5.4	12.5	19.2	5.1	0.0	3.1
Wenatchee	0.0	8.3	0.0	0.0	0.6	18.3	19.6	9.2	4.5	4.1
Yakima	0.0	18.3	0.0	0.0	0.4	19.6	13.4	5.3	3.1	2.2
WEST VIRGINIA	X	X	X	X	X	X	X	X	X	X
Charleston	0.0	12.8	2.4	0.0	0.0	18.6	20.7	8.7	3.5	3.1
Huntington	1.1	3.4	1.2	0.0	0.5	17.3	19.7	5.0	6.2	1.0
Morgantown	0.0	7.3	3.3	0.0	0.1	10.7	27.2	11.8	9.3	1.9
Parkersburg	0.1	17.9	0.6	0.0	0.0	14.6	24.6	1.3	3.6	0.4
Wheeling	0.3	8.2	0.9	0.0	0.0	10.7	13.4	47.9	2.8	1.1
WISCONSIN	X	X	X	X	X	X	X	X	X	X
Appleton	0.5	20.7	1.8	0.0	1.3	17.2	14.6	5.8	1.5	8.6
Beloit	0.0	15.7	0.0	0.0	2.0	18.6	18.7	5.0	1.7	7.4
Brookfield	0.0	16.4	0.0	0.0	5.1	16.4	24.7	6.6	0.0	4.2
Eau Claire	0.0	26.3	0.5	0.0	7.7	17.5	7.2	8.4	1.3	5.0
Fitchburg	0.0	15.1	0.0	0.0	1.4	15.9	6.7	4.4	0.0	3.0
Fond du Lac	0.0	15.2	1.0	0.0	7.9	15.6	15.7	3.3	5.5	12.5
Franklin	0.0	12.4	0.0	0.0	6.0	25.2	13.8	0.9	1.9	3.9
Green Bay	0.0	15.6	1.6	0.0	0.1	19.6	17.1	7.5	0.1	7.7
Greenfield	0.0	24.5	0.0	0.0	6.1	25.0	12.3	4.7	0.0	3.4
Janesville	1.0	12.8	0.1	0.0	3.5	15.3	28.2	6.8	4.9	2.7
Kenosha	0.0	15.3	0.0	0.0	8.7	23.0	12.6	7.0	3.3	5.4
La Crosse	0.1	15.0	1.9	0.1	0.2	14.5	10.0	13.5	2.4	5.6
Madison	0.0	12.8	1.8	0.0	2.2	14.5	7.9	12.6	8.8	4.6
Manitowoc	0.0	15.2	0.1	0.0	0.4	14.2	10.4	6.0	0.2	12.4
Menomonee Falls	0.0	15.5	0.0	0.0	0.2	16.2	20.2	2.6	0.0	7.8
Milwaukee	0.0	12.7	2.5	0.0	2.4	25.6	14.5	0.3	4.2	5.0
Mount Pleasant	0.0	17.1	0.0	0.0	4.2	20.6	21.1	0.8	0.0	5.8
Neenah	0.0	16.2	0.6	0.0	1.9	17.0	13.8	6.1	0.8	10.8
New Berlin	0.0	19.7	0.0	0.0	2.8	23.9	21.2	4.8	0.0	3.7
Oak Creek	0.0	19.5	0.0	0.0	14.6	24.8	12.2	3.6	0.0	2.2
Oshkosh	0.0	23.8	0.5	0.0	2.4	13.2	11.8	12.9	0.2	8.2
Racine	0.0	14.3	1.2	0.0	5.6	23.4	15.4	8.0	2.0	7.2
Sheboygan	0.0	14.8	0.7	0.0	0.9	20.3	13.9	5.4	6.3	5.0
Stevens Point	0.0	23.7	0.0	0.0	4.9	16.2	9.8	7.6	0.0	4.2
Sun Prairie	0.0	21.7	0.0	0.0	4.2	20.7	12.6	6.0	0.0	10.6
Superior	0.0	18.0	0.0	0.0	0.4	17.5	22.0	4.7	2.4	3.9
Waukesha	0.0	16.2	0.8	0.0	2.6	18.4	16.2	9.4	0.3	5.9
Wausau	0.0	21.0	3.6	0.0	5.0	16.8	11.2	7.1	1.6	3.1
Wauwatosa	0.0	13.3	0.0	0.0	8.5	23.5	12.9	2.4	2.5	4.8
West Allis	0.0	15.5	0.1	0.0	4.5	22.8	11.5	0.5	5.7	4.1
West Bend	0.0	15.4	0.3	0.0	1.8	22.0	12.1	9.0	0.5	10.6
WYOMING	X	X	X	X	X	X	X	X	X	X
Casper	2.2	10.7	0.0	0.0	1.5	13.9	20.6	12.8	0.5	0.4
Cheyenne	1.4	15.7	0.8	0.0	2.2	15.2	14.6	13.7	0.4	1.9
Gillette	0.0	29.3	0.0	0.0	0.8	10.9	11.6	5.5	1.5	0.5
Laramie	0.0	22.8	0.0	0.0	3.0	15.4	15.8	9.0	1.0	1.4

Table D. Cities — City Government Finances, City Government Employment, and Climate

City	City government finances, 2012 (cont.)			Climate[2]						
	Debt outstanding			Average daily temperature (degrees Fahrenheit)						
				Mean		Limits				
	Total (mil dol)	Per capita[1] (dollars)	Debt issued during year	January	July	January[3]	July[4]	Annual precipitation (inches)	Heating degree days	Cooling degree days
	137	138	139	140	141	142	143	144	145	146
WASHINGTON—Cont'd										
Pasco	48.6	727	4.2	34.2	75.2	28.0	89.3	8.01	4 731	909
Pullman	7.0	224	0.3	NA	NA	NA	NA	NA	NA	NA
Puyallup	75.3	1 972	2.6	39.9	64.9	32.9	77.8	40.51	4 991	153
Redmond	82.8	1 463	8.0	25.1	55.0	20.0	65.0	82.86	9 630	12
Renton	184.1	1 921	26.1	40.9	65.3	35.9	75.3	37.07	4 797	173
Richland	147.2	2 861	0.3	33.0	73.2	26.0	87.9	7.55	5 133	739
Sammamish	7.7	157	0.0	40.8	65.2	35.2	75.0	35.96	4 756	174
SeaTac	5.8	208	0.0	40.9	65.3	35.9	75.3	37.07	4 797	173
Seattle	4 163.6	6 556	431.3	41.5	65.5	36.0	74.5	38.25	4 615	192
Shoreline	38.3	704	0.0	40.8	65.2	35.2	75.0	35.96	4 756	174
Spokane	189.9	906	0.0	27.3	68.6	21.7	82.5	16.67	6 820	394
Spokane Valley	7.9	88	0.0	NA	NA	NA	NA	NA	NA	NA
Tacoma	1 587.6	7 849	58.5	41.0	65.6	35.1	76.1	38.95	4 650	167
University Place	55.9	1 770	5.9	41.0	65.6	35.1	76.1	38.95	4 650	167
Vancouver	263.9	1 597	10.6	39.0	65.4	32.4	77.3	41.92	4 990	197
Walla Walla	62.5	1 959	0.0	34.7	75.3	28.8	89.9	20.88	4 882	957
Wenatchee	42.9	1 318	18.9	29.2	74.4	23.2	87.8	9.12	5 533	832
Yakima	60.7	653	2.8	29.1	69.1	20.5	87.2	8.26	6 104	431
WEST VIRGINIA	X	X	X	X	X	X	X	X	X	X
Charleston	118.0	2 315	9.2	33.4	73.9	24.2	84.9	44.05	4 644	978
Huntington	44.1	897	2.3	32.1	76.3	23.5	87.1	41.74	4 737	1 128
Morgantown	120.1	3 972	3.8	30.8	73.5	22.3	83.4	43.30	5 174	815
Parkersburg	67.9	2 176	4.9	30.7	75.4	22.3	85.8	40.69	5 091	1 038
Wheeling	49.6	1 759	8.3	29.6	74.8	21.4	85.2	40.34	5 313	926
WISCONSIN	X	X	X	X	X	X	X	X	X	X
Appleton	159.0	2 176	6.9	16.0	71.6	7.8	81.4	30.16	7 721	572
Beloit	93.8	2 547	28.1	19.1	72.4	11.6	82.5	35.25	6 969	664
Brookfield	66.3	1 745	9.1	20.0	74.3	11.5	85.1	32.09	6 886	791
Eau Claire	99.4	1 476	8.5	11.9	71.4	2.5	82.6	32.12	8 196	554
Fitchburg	29.6	1 143	6.6	NA	NA	NA	NA	NA	NA	NA
Fond du Lac	203.2	4 724	19.8	16.6	71.8	9.1	81.1	30.15	7 534	586
Franklin	32.5	906	0.0	20.7	72.0	13.4	81.1	34.81	7 087	616
Green Bay	209.5	1 998	5.7	15.6	69.9	7.1	81.2	29.19	7 963	463
Greenfield	32.8	886	7.3	19.9	73.8	12.7	81.9	33.86	6 847	764
Janesville	106.9	1 682	22.1	17.7	72.1	8.6	83.8	32.78	7 238	629
Kenosha	179.5	1 797	26.2	20.8	71.3	13.2	78.7	34.74	6 999	549
La Crosse	98.7	1 894	17.8	15.9	74.0	6.3	85.2	32.36	7 340	775
Madison	526.8	2 195	99.4	17.3	71.6	9.3	82.1	32.95	7 493	582
Manitowoc	154.4	4 618	11.6	18.7	69.9	10.8	79.6	30.49	7 563	425
Menomonee Falls	94.1	2 625	18.0	16.5	69.3	8.1	80.2	33.45	7 832	407
Milwaukee	1 306.0	2 181	454.0	20.0	74.3	11.5	85.1	32.09	6 886	791
Mount Pleasant	47.2	1 806	5.6	NA	NA	NA	NA	NA	NA	NA
Neenah	75.6	2 939	5.0	NA	NA	NA	NA	NA	NA	NA
New Berlin	45.0	1 133	6.4	19.9	73.8	12.7	81.9	33.86	6 847	764
Oak Creek	112.6	3 230	18.5	20.7	72.0	13.4	81.1	34.81	7 087	616
Oshkosh	221.7	3 326	42.5	16.1	72.0	7.8	81.8	31.57	7 639	591
Racine	233.6	2 986	30.0	20.7	71.3	13.3	78.6	35.35	7 032	567
Sheboygan	62.5	1 281	1.4	20.9	71.4	13.2	81.4	31.90	7 056	559
Stevens Point	44.4	1 651	18.4	NA	NA	NA	NA	NA	NA	NA
Sun Prairie	70.0	2 289	0.0	NA	NA	NA	NA	NA	NA	NA
Superior	54.2	2 019	18.4	12.1	66.6	3.4	76.2	30.78	9 006	241
Waukesha	127.7	1 793	19.3	19.5	73.8	11.4	84.2	34.64	6 893	784
Wausau	50.1	1 279	7.7	13.0	70.1	3.6	80.8	33.36	8 237	464
Wauwatosa	100.8	2 142	19.5	20.0	74.3	11.5	85.1	32.09	6 886	791
West Allis	78.5	1 294	5.9	19.9	73.8	12.7	81.9	33.86	6 847	764
West Bend	79.7	2 525	6.8	18.4	70.6	10.7	81.3	32.85	7 371	502
WYOMING	X	X	X	X	X	X	X	X	X	X
Casper	19.5	338	0.1	22.3	70.0	12.2	86.8	13.03	7 571	420
Cheyenne	86.1	1 395	14.1	25.9	67.7	14.8	81.9	15.45	7 388	273
Gillette	91.7	2 916	2.2	NA	NA	NA	NA	NA	NA	NA
Laramie	44.3	1 394	0.5	20.3	62.9	7.8	79.4	11.19	9 233	75

1. Based on the population estimated as of July 1 of the year shown. 2. Represents normal values based on the 30-year period, 1971–2000. 3. Average daily minimum.
4. Average daily maximum.

PART E.

Congressional Districts of the 113th Congress

(For explanation of symbols, see page viii)

Congressional District Highlights and Rankings

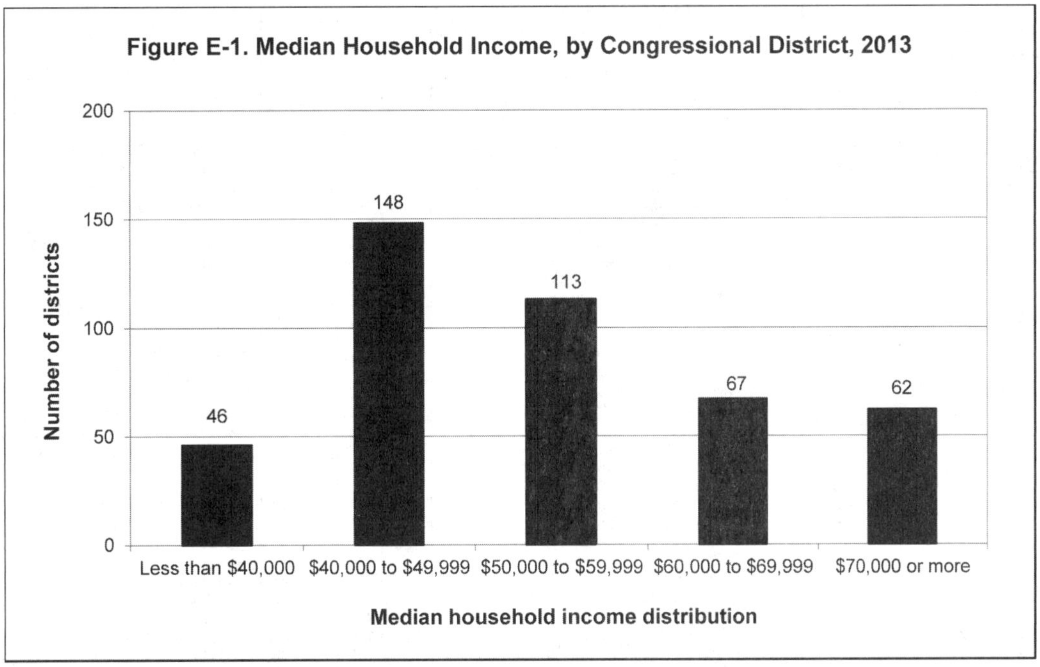

Every 10 years, the Census Bureau conducts a count to reapportion the seats in the U.S. House of Representatives. The House's 435 seats are divided among the 50 states. (The District of Columbia has no representative in Congress, although it has a nonvoting delegate.) The seats are reapportioned according to the population measured on April 1 of the census year in order to account for population changes among the states over the previous decade. The number of districts within a state may change after each decennial census, and the districts' boundaries may change more than once during a decade. The 113th Congress which convened in 2013 was the first to reflect the new boundaries based on the 2010 census. The data in Table E were gathered for the 113th Congress. The Representatives of the 114th Congress are listed. There were no boundary changes between the 113th and the 114th Congress.

As the state with the largest population, California had the most representatives with 53. Texas (36) and New York (27) were second and third largest, respectively. There were seven states with just one representative: Alaska, Delaware, Montana, North Dakota, South Dakota, Vermont, and Wyoming. These states' representatives were considered 'At Large,' as they represented an entire state instead of a specific congressional district within the state.

Because the number of representatives is limited to 435, states with larger population growth add seats, while states with little or no growth lose seats. When the 113th Congress convened in January 2013, eight states had more representatives in congress and 10 states had fewer. Based on the 2010 census, Texas gained four seats, Florida gained two, while Washington, Nevada, Utah, Arizona, Georgia, and South Carolina each gained one seat. New York and Ohio each lost two seats, while Massachusetts, New Jersey, Pennsylvania, Michigan, Illinois, Iowa, Missouri, and Louisiana each lost a seat.

As each decade progresses, population shifts alter the size of districts, leading up to the reapportionment of the next census. After the 2000 census, the population of each congressional district was about 645,000. Based on the 2013 population estimates, the new congressional districts average approximately 725,000 people. Montana's at-large congressional district had over a million people, while Delaware and South Dakota also had at-large seats with above average populations. Idaho's 1st district is the largest apportioned congressional district in the United States with a population over 812,000 in 2013. Rhode Island's two congressional districts have the smallest populations at 523,170 and 528,341. Congressional districts in Nebraska and West Virginia also have smaller populations. For years, Louisiana's 2nd district was the least populous congressional district in the nation due to outmigration after Hurricane Katrina.

While most of the congressional districts had about the same population size, they varied widely in other characteristics. In California's 33rd district, 95.5 percent of the residents were high school graduates, compared with just 51.7 percent in California's 40th district and 59.0 percent in California's 21st district. California's 21st and 40th districts had the lowest proportion of college graduates, with only 8.3 percent and 8.4 percent of their residents holding a bachelor's degrees respectively, followed by Texas' 29th district at 9.0 percent. In New York's 12th district, 69.2 percent of residents were college graduates.

The highest unemployment rates were found in Michigan's 13th district at 19.1 percent and Illinois' 2nd district at 17.5 percent. Two districts each from California, Illinois, and Michigan along with one district each from New York, New Jersey, Georgia, and Ohio ranked among the 10 highest. Ninety-one congressional districts had 20 percent or more of their populations living in poverty. New York's 15th district had the highest poverty rate in the nation at 39.8 percent and the lowest median household income at $25,801 in 2013. In Virginia's 10th district, the median household income was $110,444, the highest in the nation. Forty-four congressional districts had median household incomes exceeding $75,000 per year, while forty-six districts had median household incomes below $40,000. The U.S. median household income in 2013 was $52,250.

Congressional Districts of the 113th Congress of the United States

Selected Rankings

Population, 2013			Land area, 2010			Population density, 2013		
Population rank	State congressional district Representative	Population [col 2]	Land area rank	State congressional district Representative	Land area (square kilometers) [col 1]	Density rank	State congressional district Representative	Population density (per square kilometer) [col 3]
1	MT At-Large: Ryan K. Zinke (R)	1 015 165	1	AK At-Large: Don Young (R)	1 477 953	1	NY 13th: Charles B. Rangel (D)	28 348
2	DE At-Large: John C. Carney (D)	925 749	2	MT At-Large: Ryan K. Zinke (R)	376 962	2	NY 15th: José E. Serrano (D)	19 665
3	SD At-Large: Kristi Noem (R)	844 877	3	WY At-Large: Cynthia M. Lummis (R)	251 470	3	NY 10th: Jerrold Nadler (D)	19 370
4	ID 1st: Raul Labrador (R)	812 462	4	SD At-Large: Kristi Noem (R)	196 350	4	NY 12th: Carolyn B. Maloney (D)	18 962
5	ID 2nd: Michael K. Simpson (R)	799 674	5	NM 2nd: Steve Pearce (R)	185 804	5	NY 9th: Yvette D. Clarke (D)	18 385
6	OR 3rd: Earl Blumenauer (D)	797 199	6	OR 2nd: Greg Walden (R)	179 856	6	NY 7th: Nydia M. Velázquez (D)	18 103
7	OR 1st: Suzanne Bonamici (D)	796 901	7	ND-At Large: Kevin Cramer (R)	178 711	7	NY 14th: Joseph Crowley (D)	9 966
8	IA 3rd: David Young (R)	788 588	8	NE 3rd: Adrian Smith (R)	174 657	8	NY 8th: Hakeem S. Jeffries (D)	9 578
9	OR 5th: Kurt Schrader (D)	785 707	9	TX 23rd: Will Hurd (R)	150 373	9	NY 6th: Grace Meng (D)	9 365
10	OK 5th: Steve Russell (R)	785 441	10	NV 2nd: Mark E. Amodei (R)	144 598	10	CA 12th: Nancy Pelosi (D)	7 274
11	LA 2nd: Cedric Richmond (D)	784 928	11	AZ 1st: Ann Kirkpatrick (D)	142 552	11	CA 34th: Xavier Becerra (D)	5 792
12	TX 22nd: Pete Olson (R)	783 172	12	KS 1st: Tim Huelskamp (R)	136 084	12	NY 5th: Gregory W. Meeks (D)	5 736
13	NC 13th: George Holding (R)	782 722	13	NV 4th: Cresent Hardy (R)	132 084	13	NJ 8th: Albio Sires (D)	5 341
14	VA10th: Barbara Comstock (R)	781 947	14	CO 3rd: Scott R. Tipton (R)	128 805	14	IL 4th: Luis V. Gutierrez (D)	5 236
15	LA 1st: Steve Scalise (R)	781 134	15	NM 3rd: Ben Ray Luján (D)	116 442	15	CA 37th: Karen Bass (D)	5 123
16	NC 9th: Robert Pittenger (R)	780 211	16	ID 2nd: Michael K. Simpson (R)	111 952	16	CA 40th: Lucille Roybal-Allard (D)	4 822
17	OR 2nd: Greg Walden (R)	778 062	17	UT 2nd: Chris Stewart (R)	103 568	17	MA 7th: Michael E. Capuano (D)	4 636
18	NC 2nd: Renee Ellmers (R)	777 683	18	ID 1st: Raul Labrador (R)	102 092	18	IL 7th: Danny K. Davis (D)	4 447
19	OK 4th: Tom Cole (R)	776 394	19	TX 13th: Mac Thornberry (R)	99 324	19	NY 11th: Daniel M. Donovan Jr. (R)	4 259
20	VA 8th: Donald S. Beyer, Jr. (D)	774 396	20	CO 4th: Ken Buck (R)	98 685	20	DC At Large: Eleanor Holmes Norton (D)	4 091
21	IA 2nd: David Loebsack (D)	774 072	21	OK 3rd: Frank D. Lucas (R)	88 362	21	CA 46th: Loretta Sanchez (D)	3 907
22	NC 12th: Alma S. Adams (D)	773 617	22	MN 6th: Collin C. Peterson (D)	86 582	22	CA 43rd: Maxine Waters (D)	3 905
23	LA 6th: Garret Graves (R)	773 429	23	AZ 4th: Paul A. Gosar (R)	85 986	23	NJ 10th: Donald M. Payne, Jr. (D)	3 721
24	OK 1st: Jim Bridenstine (R)	773 208	24	CA 8th: Paul Cook (R)	85 126	24	PA 2nd: Chaka Fattah (D)	3 710
25	CO 1st: Diana DeGette (D)	772 255	25	CA 1st: Doug LaMalfa (R)	72 751	25	NY 16th: Eliot L. Engel (D)	3 600
26	OR 4th: Peter A. DeFazio (D)	772 196	26	MN 7th: Richard M. Nolan (D)	72 282	26	PA 1st: Robert A. Brady (D)	3 589
27	NC 4th: David E. Price (D)	769 734	27	TX 11th: K. Michael Conaway (R)	72 085	27	CA 44th: Janice Hahn (D)	3 431
28	LA 3rd: Charles W. Boustany Jr. (R)	769 331	28	ME 2nd: Bruce Poliquin (R)	71 373	28	NJ 9th: Bill Pascrell, Jr. (D)	3 077
29	NY 5th: Gregory W. Meeks (D)	768 603	29	TX 19th: Randy Neugebauer (R)	66 914	29	IL 5th: Michael Quigley (D)	2 962
30	FL 9th: Alan Grayson (D)	768 459	30	MI 1st: Dan Benishek (R)	64 822	30	CA 13th: Barbara Lee (D)	2 919
31	MO 2nd: Ann Wagner (R)	768 428	31	WI 7th: Sean P. Duffy (R)	59 666	31	CA 29th: Tony Cárdenas (D)	2 909
32	TX 26th: Michael C. Burgess (R)	768 246	32	IA 4th: Steve King (R)	58 940	32	CA 38th: Linda T. Sánchez (D)	2 759
33	TX 31st: John R. Carter (R)	767 721	33	AR 2nd: Bruce Westerman (R)	57 855	33	FL 24th: Frederica S. Wilson (D)	2 637
34	OK 3rd: Frank D. Lucas (R)	767 552	34	OK 2nd: Markwayne Mullin (R)	54 378	34	IL 9th: Janice D. Schakowsky (D)	2 599
35	IA 1st: Rod Blum (R)	766 821	35	UT 3rd: Jason Chaffetz (R)	51 982	35	NY 4th: Kathleen M. Rice (D)	2 492
36	VA11th: Gerald E. Connolly (D)	765 755	36	MO 8th: Jason T. Smith (R)	51 544	36	NV 1st: Dina Titus (D)	2 486
37	TX 3rd: Sam Johnson (R)	765 486	37	UT 1st: Rob Bishop (R)	50 662	37	CA 32nd: Grace F. Napolitano (D)	2 193
38	NY 13th: Charles B. Rangel (D)	765 391	38	AR 1st: Eric A. "Rick" Crawford (R)	50 034	38	WI 4th: Gwen Moore (D)	2 156
39	CO 6th: Mike Coffman (R)	765 338	39	WA 4th: Dan Newsome (R)	49 858	39	CA 30th: Brad Sherman (D)	2 115
40	VA 1st: Robert J. Wittman (R)	763 763	40	MO 6th: Sam Graves (R)	47 134	40	VA 8th: Donald S. Beyer, Jr. (D)	2 001
41	NC 7th: David Rouzer (R)	762 540	41	OR 4th: Peter A. DeFazio (D)	44 740	41	MN 5th: Keith Ellison (D)	1 988
42	LA 4th: John Fleming (R)	762 517	42	AZ 3rd: Raul M. Grijalva (D)	40 634	42	CA 48th: Dana Rohrabacher (R)	1 918
43	TX 8th: Kevin Brady (R)	761 764	43	MS 2nd: Bennie G. Thompson (D)	40 278	43	WA 7th: Jim McDermott (D)	1 894
44	IA 4th: Steve King (R)	760 935	44	WA 5th: Cathy McMorris Rodgers (R)	40 075	44	TX 7th: John Abney Culberson (R)	1 770
45	VA 7th: Dave Brat (R)	760 928	45	NY 21st: Elise M. Stefanik (R)	39 147	45	PA 13th: Brendan F. Boyle (D)	1 768
46	NC 6th: Howard Coble (R)	760 762	46	IL 15th: John Shimkus (R)	38 062	46	AZ 9th: Kyrsten Sinema (D)	1 736
47	MO 3rd: Blaine Luetkemeyer (R)	760 643	47	LA 5th: Ralph Lee Abraham (R)	37 433	47	TX 9th: Al Green (D)	1 718
48	NY 7th: Nydia M. Velázquez (D)	760 308	48	MO 4th: Vicky Hartzler (R)	37 299	48	CA 35th: Norma J. Torres (D)	1 667
49	NJ 9th: Bill Pascrell, Jr. (D)	760 064	49	KS 4th: Mike Pompeo (R)	37 077	49	FL 23rd: Debbie Wasserman Schultz (D)	1 643
50	MO 7th: Bill Long (R)	759 566	50	KS 2nd: Lynn Jenkins (R)	36 631	50	FL 22nd: Lois Frankel (D)	1 639
51	MA 8th: Stephen F. Lynch (D)	759 336	51	CA 2nd: Jared Huffman (D)	33 546	51	CA 6th: Doris O. Matsui (D)	1 610
52	AZ 5th: Matt Salmon (R)	759 102	52	CA 4th: Tom McClintock (R)	33 246	52	VA11th: Gerald E. Connolly (D)	1 599
53	MO 5th: Emanuel Cleaver (D)	758 911	53	MS 3rd: Gregg Harper (R)	33 034	53	CA 17th: Michael M. Honda (D)	1 528
54	TX 10th: Michael T. McCaul (R)	758 585	54	LA 4th: John Fleming (R)	32 207	54	NY 2nd: Peter T. King (R)	1 526
55	NJ 8th: Albio Sires (D)	758 406	55	IA 2nd: David Loebsack (D)	31 758	55	TX 29th: Gene Green (D)	1 505
56	MS 4th: Steven Palazzo (R)	758 257	56	KY 1st: Ed Whitfield (R)	31 286	56	MI 9th: Sander M. Levin (D)	1 502
57	AR 2nd: Steve Womack (R)	757 765	57	IA 1st: Rod Blum (R)	31 206	57	TX 32nd: Pete Sessions (R)	1 494
58	MS 1st: Trent Kelly (R)	756 459	58	MN 1st: Timothy J. Walz (D)	31 012	58	WA 9th: Adam Smith (D)	1 486
59	MO 4th: Vicky Hartzler (R)	756 407	59	KY 5th: Harold Rogers (R)	29 099	59	MI 14th: Brenda L. Lawrence (D)	1 469
60	MD 8th: Chris Van Hollen (D)	756 076	60	WI 3rd: Ron Kind (D)	28 779	60	TX 20th: Joaquin Castro (D)	1 457
61	CO 2nd: Jared Polis (D)	755 671	61	PA 5th: Glenn Thompson (R)	27 742	61	FL 13th: David W. Jolly (R)	1 451
62	CO 7th: Ed Perlmutter (D)	755 047	62	MS 1st: Trent Kelly (R)	27 383	62	AZ 7th: Ruben Gallego (D)	1 411
63	MO 6th: Sam Graves (R)	754 588	63	IL 18th: Vacancy	27 236	63	MI 13th: John Conyers Jr. (D)	1 406
64	LA 5th: Ralph Lee Abraham (R)	754 131	64	AL 7th: Terri A. Sewell (D)	26 304	64	CA 39th: Edward R. Royce (R)	1 363
65	MA 5th: Katherine Clark (D)	754 065	65	AL 2nd: Martha Roby (R)	26 267	65	IL 8th: Tammy Duckworth (D)	1 345
66	TX 20th: Joaquin Castro (D)	752 996	66	TX 4th: John Ratcliffe (R)	26 218	66	FL 27th: Ileana Ros-Lehtinen (R)	1 330
67	TX 35th: Lloyd Doggett (D)	752 749	67	VA 5th: Robert Hurt (R)	25 977	67	NJ 6th: Frank Pallone Jr. (D)	1 323
68	MD 5th: Steny H. Hoyer (D)	752 393	68	CA 23rd: Kevin McCarthy (R)	25 636	68	TX 33rd: Marc A. Veasey (D)	1 322
69	AR 2nd: J. French Hill (R)	751 463	69	OK 4th: Tom Cole (R)	25 323	69	PA 14th: Michael F. Doyle (D)	1 299
70	MA 7th: Michael E. Capuano (D)	751 062	70	WV 3rd: Evan H. Jenkins (R)	25 240	70	HI 1st: Mark Takai (D)	1 295
71	MA 6th: Seth Moulton (D)	750 623	71	GA 2nd: Sanford D. Bishop Jr. (D)	24 932	71	CA 47th: Alan S. Lowenthal (D)	1 289
72	NJ 12th: Bonnie Watson Coleman (D)	750 594	72	TX 28th: Henry Cuellar (D)	24 290	72	CA 31st: Pete Aguilar (D)	1 283
73	MS 3rd: Gregg Harper (R)	750 332	73	VT At-Large: Peter Welch (D)	23 871	73	MO 1st: William Lacy Clay (D)	1 262
74	CO 5th: Doug Lamborn (R)	749 815	74	TN 7th: Marsha Blackburn (R)	23 725	74	NY 26th: Brian Higgins (D)	1 260
75	NC 3rd: Walter B. Jones (R)	749 521	75	TX 27th: Blake Farenthold (R)	23 642	75	OH 3rd: Joyce Beatty (D)	1 252

Congressional Districts of the 113th Congress of the United States

Selected Rankings

Percent Non-Hispanic White alone, 2013			Percent Black alone, 2013			Percent American Indian, Alaska Native alone, 2013		
Non-Hispanic White alone rank	State congressional district Representative	Percent white [col 11]	Black rank	State congressional district Representative	Percent black [col 5]	American Indian Alaska Native rank	State congressional district Representative	Percent American Indian Alaska Native [col 6]
1	KY 5th: Harold Rogers (R)	96.0	1	MS 2nd: Bennie G. Thompson (D)	65.4	1	AZ 1st: Ann Kirkpatrick (D)	23.2
2	OH 6th: Bill Johnson (R)	94.9	2	TN 9th: Steve Cohen (D)	65.2	2	NM 3rd: Ben Ray Luján (D)	18.3
3	ME 2nd: Bruce Poliquin (R)	94.4	3	AL 7th: Terri A. Sewell (D)	62.9	3	OK 2nd: Markwayne Mullin (R)	16.6
4	VT At-Large: Peter Welch (D)	94.0	4	LA 2nd: Cedric Richmond (D)	62.4	4	AK: At-Large Don Young (R)	14.3
5	WV 1st: David McKinley (R)	93.9	5	GA 4th: Henry C. "Hank" Johnson Jr. (D)	58.7	5	SD At-Large: Kristi Noem (R)	8.5
6	ME 1st: Chellie Pingree (D)	93.4	6	PA 2nd: Chaka Fattah (D)	58.5	6	NC 8th: Richard Hudson (R)	7.2
7	PA 9th: Bill Shuster (R)	93.3	7	GA 5th: John Lewis (D)	58.0	7	MT At-Large: Ryan K. Zinke (R)	6.8
7	WV 3rd: Evan H. Jenkins (R)	93.3	8	MI 14th: Brenda L. Lawrence (D)	57.6	8	OK 3rd: Frank D. Lucas (R)	6.1
9	WI 3rd: Ron Kind (D)	92.7	8	SC 6th: James E. Clyburn (D)	57.6	9	ND-At Large Kevin Cramer (R)	5.6
10	PA 5th: Glenn Thompson (R)	92.5	10	NY 8th: Hakeem S. Jeffries (D)	57.5	10	OK 1st: Jim Bridenstine (R)	5.4
10	PA 12th: Keith J. Rothfus (R)	92.5	11	VA 3rd Robert C. "Bobby" Scott (D)	56.9	11	OK 4th: Tom Cole (R)	5.3
10	PA 18th: Tim Murphy (R)	92.5	12	GA 13th: David Scott (D)	56.4	12	NM 2nd: Steve Pearce (R)	5.2
13	WI 7th: Sean P. Duffy (R)	92.3	13	MI 13th: John Conyers Jr. (D)	56.2	13	OK 5th: Steve Russell (R)	4.6
14	IN 6th: Luke Messer (R)	92.2	14	IL 2nd: Robin L. Kelly (D)	55.7	14	AZ 3rd: Raul M. Grijalva (D)	4.0
14	MN 7th: Richard M. Nolan (D)	92.2	15	FL 24th: Frederica S. Wilson (D)	54.6	15	NM 1st: Michelle Lujan Grisham (D)	3.8
14	NY 27th: Chris Collins(R)	92.2	16	MD 7th: Elijah E. Cummings (D)	54.4	16	AZ 7th: Ruben Gallego (D)	3.0
17	OH 16th: James B. Renacci (R)	91.8	16	NC 1st: G. K. Butterfield (D)	54.4	17	MN 6th: Collin C. Peterson (D)	2.8
18	MO 3rd: Blaine Luetkemeyer (R)	91.7	18	OH 11th: Marcia L. Fudge (D)	53.8	17	MN 7th: Richard M. Nolan (D)	2.8
18	TN 1st: David P. Roe (R)	91.7	19	FL 20th: Alcee L. Hastings (D)	53.4	19	AZ 9th: Kyrsten Sinema (D)	2.7
20	IL 15th: John Shimkus (R)	91.6	20	NJ 10th: Donald M. Payne, Jr. (D)	53.2	19	MI 1st: Dan Benishek (R)	2.7
21	MI 4th: John L. Moolenar (R)	91.4	21	MD 4th: Donna F. Edwards (D)	52.8	21	WI 8th: Reid J. Ribble (R)	2.5
21	NH 1st: Frank C. Guinta (R)	91.4	22	FL 5th: Corrine Brown (D)	52.2	22	WA 4th: Dan Newsome (R)	2.4
23	NH 2nd: Ann M. Kuster (D)	91.3	23	NC 12th: Alma S. Adams (D)	51.6	23	WY At-Large Cynthia M. Lummis (R)	2.3
24	MO 8th: Jason T. Smith (R)	91.2	24	GA 2nd: Sanford D. Bishop Jr. (D)	51.3	23	NV 2nd: Mark E. Amodei (R)	2.3
25	PA 10th: Tom Marino (R)	91.1	25	IL 1st: Bobby L. Rush (D)	51.2	25	WI 7th: Sean P. Duffy (R)	2.1
26	MI 1st: Dan Benishek (R)	91.0	25	IL 7th: Danny K. Davis (D)	51.2	26	CA 2nd: Jared Huffman (D)	2.0
27	IN 8th: Larry Bucshon (R)	90.9	27	NY 9th: Yvette D. Clarke (D)	50.7	26	WA 6th: Derek Kilmer (D)	2.0
27	OH 7th: Bob Gibbs (R)	90.9	28	NY 5th: Gregory W. Meeks (D)	49.6	28	CO: 3rd Scott Tipton (R)	1.9
29	PA 3rd: Mike Kelly (R)	90.8	29	DC At Large: Eleanor Holmes Norton (D)	48.8	29	AZ 4th: Paul A. Gosar (R)	1.7
30	MI 10th: Candice S. Miller (R)	90.7	29	MO 1st: William Lacy Clay (D)	48.8	29	NC 7th: David Rouzer (R)	1.7
30	MN 5th: Tom Emmer (R)	90.7	31	TX 30th: Eddie Bernice Johnson (D)	43.4	29	OR 2nd: Greg Walden (R)	1.7
30	WV 2nd: David McKinley (R)	90.7	32	TX 9th: Al Green (D)	39.5	29	UT 3rd: Jason Chaffetz (R)	1.7
33	OH 15th: Steve Stivers (R)	90.5	33	MD 5th: Steny H. Hoyer (D)	38.3	33	CA 1st: Doug LaMalfa (R)	1.6
34	KY 4th: Thomas Massie (R)	90.4	34	TX 18th: Sheila Jackson-Lee (D)	37.6	33	CA 47th: Alan S. Lowenthal (D)	1.6
35	WI 6th: Glen Grothman(R)	90.3	35	PA 1st: Robert A. Brady (D)	36.0	35	WA 10th: Denny Heck (D)	1.5
36	NY 21st: Elise M. Stefanik (R)	90.2	36	LA 5th: Ralph Lee Abraham (R)	35.7	35	NC 11th: Mark Meadows (R)	1.5
37	IN 9th: Todd C. Young (R)	90.1	37	GA 12th: Rick W. Allen (R)	35.4	35	WA 5th: Cathy McMorris Rodgers (R)	1.5
37	MN 6th: Collin C. Peterson (D)	90.1	38	MS 3rd: Gregg Harper (R)	35.2	38	AZ 6th: David Schweikert (R)	1.4
39	OH 14th: David P. Joyce (R)	89.7	39	LA 4th: John Fleming (R)	33.7	38	CA 8th: Paul Cook (R)	1.4
39	VA 9th: Morgan Griffith (R)	89.7	39	WI 4th: Gwen Moore (D)	33.7	38	KS 2nd: Lynn Jenkins (R)	1.4
41	IA 1st: Rod Blum (R)	89.6	41	MD 2nd: C. A. Dutch Ruppersberger (D)	33.2	38	WA 2nd Rick Larsen (D)	1.4
42	IL 18th: Vacancy	89.2	42	NY 15th: José E. Serrano (D)	33.0	42	AZ 2nd: Martha McSally (R)	1.3
42	NY 23rd: Tom Reed (R)	89.2	43	OH 3rd: Joyce Beatty (D)	32.3	42	LA 1st: Steve Scalise (R)	1.3
42	TN 6th: Diane Black (R)	89.2	44	NY 16th: Eliot L. Engel (D)	31.8	42	ID 1st: Raul Labrador (R)	1.3
45	IA 4th: Steve King (R)	89.1	44	VA 4th: J. Randy Forbes (R)	31.8	45	AZ 8th: Trent Franks (R)	1.2
46	MO 7th: Bill Long (R)	89.0	46	NC 4th: David E. Price (D)	31.5	45	OR 4th: Peter A. DeFazio (D)	1.2
47	OH 4th: Jim Jordan (R)	88.9	47	AL 2nd: Martha Roby (R)	31.3	45	WA 1st Susan K. DelBene (D)	1.2
48	OH 5th: Robert E. Latta (R)	88.7	48	GA 8th: Austin Scott (R)	30.3	45	NE 1st: Jeff Fontenberry (R)	1.2
49	NY 22nd: Richard L. Hanna (R)	88.6	49	GA 1st: Earl L. "Buddy" Carter (R)	29.9	45	ID 2nd: Michael K. Simpson (R)	1.2
50	WI 5th: F. James Sensenbrenner Jr. (R)	88.5	50	IN 7th: André Carson (D)	29.7	45	UT 2ND: Chris Stewart (R)	1.2
51	MI 7th: Tim Walberg (R)	88.4	51	NY 13th: Charles B. Rangel (D)	29.3	51	AR 2nd: Steve Womack (R)	1.1
52	KY 1st: Ed Whitfield (R)	88.2	52	SC 7th: Tom Rice (R)	29.0	51	CA 3rd: John Garamendi (D)	1.1
53	MO 6th: Sam Graves (R)	88.0	53	AL 1st: Bradley Byrne (R)	27.9	51	CA 5th: Mike Thompson (D)	1.1
54	MA 9th: William R. Keating (D)	87.9	54	MS 1st: Trent Kelly (R)	27.5	51	CA 16th: Jim Costa (D)	1.1
54	WI 8th: Reid J. Ribble (R)	87.9	55	SC 5th: Mick Mulvaney (R)	26.4	51	CA 22nd: Devin Nunes (R)	1.1
56	KY 2nd: Brett Guthrie (R)	87.8	56	AL 3rd: Mike Rogers (R)	25.6	51	CA 23rd: Kevin McCarthy (R)	1.1
57	MN 1st: Timothy J. Walz (D)	87.5	57	FL 14th: Kathy Castor (D)	25.3	51	CA 44th: Janice Hahn (D)	1.1
58	ND-At Large: Kevin Cramer (R)	87.4	58	FL 2nd: Gwen Graham (D)	25.1	51	CA 50th: Duncan Hunter (R)	1.1
59	MO 4th: Vicky Hartzler (R)	87.3	59	GA 10th: Jody B. Hice (R)	24.9	51	TX 23rd: Will Hurd (R)	1.1
60	MO 2nd: Ann Wagner (R)	87.2	60	LA 3rd: Charles W. Boustany Jr. (R)	24.8	51	NV 4th: Cresent Hardy (R)	1.1
61	MT At-Large: Ryan K. Zinke (R)	87.0	60	MA 7th: Michael E. Capuano (D)	24.8	51	WA 3rd Jaime Herrera Beutler (R)	1.1
61	OH 8th: John A. Boehner (R)	87.0	60	TN 5th: Jim Cooper (D)	24.8	62	AZ 5th: Matt Salmon (R)	1.0
63	IA 2nd: David Loebsack (D)	86.9	63	LA 6th: Garret Graves (R)	24.3	62	CA 4th: Tom McClintock (R)	1.0
64	NC 11th: Mark Meadows (R)	86.8	64	GA 3rd: Lynn A. Westmoreland (R)	24.1	62	CA 34th: Xavier Becerra (D)	1.0
65	IN 4th: Todd Rokita (R)	86.6	65	MS 4th: Steven Palazzo (R)	23.9	62	CA 36th: Raul Ruiz (D)	1.0
65	TN 2nd: John J. Duncan Jr. (R)	86.6	66	SC 2nd: Joe Wilson (R)	23.4	62	MS 3rd: Gregg Harper (R)	1.0
67	OH 2nd: Brad R. Wenstrup (R)	86.2	67	CA 37th: Karen Bass (D)	23.0	62	UT 1st: Rob Bishop (R)	1.0
67	OH 12th: Patrick J. Tiberi (R)	86.2	68	CA 43rd: Maxine Waters (D)	22.4	68	AL 4th: Robert B. Aderholt (R)	0.9
69	PA 11th: Lou Barletta (R)	86.1	69	OH 1st: Steve Chabot (R)	21.9	68	CA 24th: Lois Capps (D)	0.9
70	NY 19th: Christopher P. Gibson (R)	85.8	70	AR 2nd: J. French Hill (R)	21.8	68	LA 4th: John Fleming (R)	0.9
71	PA 7th: Patrick Meehan (R)	85.7	70	MD 3rd: John P. Sarbanes (D)	21.8	68	MN 5th: Keth Ellison	0.9
72	NE 3rd: Adrian Smith (R)	85.4	72	DE At-Large: John C. Carney (D)	21.6	68	KS 4th: Mike Pompeo (R)	0.9
73	PA 8th: Michael G. Fitzpatrick (R)	85.2	73	MO 5th: Emanuel Cleaver (D)	21.5	68	MO 7th: Bill Long (R)	0.9
74	MA 4th:Joseph P. Kennedy III (D)	85.1	73	PA 14th: Michael F. Doyle (D)	21.5	68	OR 5th: Kurt Schrader (D)	0.9
75	OR 4th: Peter A. DeFazio (D)	85.0	75	VA 2nd: Scott Rigell (R)	21.4	68	WA 8th: David G. Reichert (R)	0.9

Congressional Districts of the 113th Congress of the United States

Selected Rankings

Percent Asian or Pacific Islander alone, 2013			Percent Hispanic or Latino,[1] 2013			Percent foreign born, 2013		
Asian or Pacific Islander rank	State congressional district Representative	Percent Asian or Pacific Islander [col 7]	Hispanic rank	State congressional district Representative	Percent Hispanic [col 10]	Foreign-born rank	State congressional district Representative	Percent foreign born [col 13]
1	HI 1st: Mark Takai (D)	58.2	1	CA 40th: Lucille Roybal-Allard (D)	87.7	1	FL 27th: Ileana Ros-Lehtinen (R)	52.9
2	CA 17th: Michael M. Honda (D)	52.2	2	TX 34th: Filemon Vela (D)	83.7	2	FL 25th: Mario Diaz-Balart (R)	52.7
3	NY 6th: Grace Meng (D)	38.9	3	TX 15th: Rubén Hinojosa (D)	80.7	3	NY 6th: Grace Meng (D)	51.7
4	CA 27th: Judy Chu (D)	38.6	4	TX 16th: Beto O'Rourke (D)	79.0	4	CA 34th: Xavier Becerra (D)	48.8
5	HI 2nd: Tulsi Gabbard (D)	37.1	5	TX 29th: Gene Green (D)	78.0	5	FL 26th: Carlos Curbelo (R)	47.8
6	CA 14th: Jackie Speier (D)	33.6	6	TX 28th: Henry Cuellar (D)	77.8	6	NY 14th: Joseph Crowley (D)	46.8
7	CA 12th: Nancy Pelosi (D)	32.1	7	FL 27th: Ileana Ros-Lehtinen (R)	75.4	7	CA 17th: Michael M. Honda (D)	46.1
8	CA 15th: Eric Swalwell (D)	31.0	8	CA 21st: David G. Valadao (R)	72.5	8	NJ 8th: Albio Sires (D)	44.7
9	CA 39th: Edward R. Royce (R)	29.8	9	FL 25th: Mario Diaz-Balart (R)	72.1	9	CA 29th: Tony Cárdenas (D)	44.6
10	CA 19th: Zoe Lofgren (D)	27.2	10	IL 4th: Luis V. Gutierrez (D)	70.5	10	NY 5th: Gregory W. Meeks (D)	42.5
11	WA 9th: Adam Smith (D)	22.8	11	CA 51st: Juan Vargas (D)	69.9	11	CA 40th: Lucille Roybal-Allard (D)	41.4
12	CA 45th: Mimi Walters (R)	22.4	11	TX 23rd: Will Hurd (R)	69.9	12	CA 28th: Adam B. Schiff (D)	40.7
13	CA 47th: Alan S. Lowenthal (D)	21.8	13	CA 44th: Janice Hahn (D)	69.4	13	FL 24th: Frederica S. Wilson (D)	40.3
14	CA 13th: Barbara Lee (D)	21.4	14	CA 29th: Tony Cárdenas (D)	68.7	14	CA 46th: Loretta Sanchez (D)	39.8
15	CA 52nd: Scott H. Peters (D)	20.7	15	TX 20th: Joaquin Castro (D)	68.3	15	NY 9th: Yvette D. Clarke (D)	39.7
16	CA 18th: Anna G. Eshoo (D)	20.5	16	CA 35th: Norma J. Torres (D)	67.5	16	CA 27th: Judy Chu (D)	38.4
17	CA 48th: Dana Rohrabacher (R)	19.2	17	FL 26th: Carlos Curbelo (R)	67.1	17	NJ 9th: Bill Pascrell, Jr. (D)	37.4
18	NY 7th: Nydia M. Velázquez (D)	19.1	18	CA 46th: Loretta Sanchez (D)	66.2	17	NY 7th: Nydia M. Velázquez (D)	37.4
19	CA 34th: Xavier Becerra (D)	18.8	19	CA 34th: Xavier Becerra (D)	65.9	19	CA 19th: Zoe Lofgren (D)	37.2
20	NY 10th: Jerrold Nadler (D)	18.2	20	NY 15th: José E. Serrano (D)	64.7	20	CA 14th: Jackie Speier (D)	36.7
21	VA11th: Gerald E. Connolly (D)	18.1	21	AZ 7th: Ruben Gallego (D)	64.6	21	FL 23rd: Debbie Wasserman Schultz (D)	36.5
22	NJ 6th: Frank Pallone Jr. (D)	17.6	21	TX 33rd: Marc A. Veasey (D)	64.6	22	NY 13th: Charles B. Rangel (D)	35.7
23	CA 6th: Doris O. Matsui (D)	17.1	23	TX 35th: Lloyd Doggett (D)	63.0	23	IL 4th: Luis V. Gutierrez (D)	35.3
23	CA 32nd: Grace F. Napolitano (D)	17.1	24	CA 32nd: Grace F. Napolitano (D)	61.7	24	NY 15th: José E. Serrano (D)	34.9
25	TX 22nd: Pete Olson (R)	16.8	25	AZ 3rd: Raul M. Grijalva (D)	61.3	25	CA 32nd: Grace F. Napolitano (D)	34.6
26	NJ 12th: Bonnie Watson Coleman (D)	16.5	26	CA 38th: Linda T. Sánchez (D)	60.6	26	CA 44th: Janice Hahn (D)	34.4
27	NY 14th: Joseph Crowley (D)	16.2	27	CA 16th: Jim Costa (D)	59.5	27	CA 51st: Juan Vargas (D)	34.2
28	CA 38th: Linda T. Sánchez (D)	15.7	28	CA 41st: Mark Takano (D)	59.3	28	CA 12th: Nancy Pelosi (D)	33.8
29	CA 7th: Ami Bera (D)	15.3	29	NJ 8th: Albio Sires (D)	55.1	29	NY 8th: Hakeem S. Jeffries (D)	33.1
30	CA 9th: Jerry McNerney (D)	14.9	30	NY 13th: Charles B. Rangel (D)	54.6	30	CA 30th: Brad Sherman (D)	33.0
31	NV 3rd: Joseph J. Heck (R)	14.5	31	NM 2nd: Steve Pearce (R)	53.1	31	CA 15th: Eric Swalwell (D)	32.8
32	NY 3rd: Steve Israel (D)	14.4	32	CA 20th: Sam Farr (D)	52.0	32	TX 29th: Gene Green (D)	32.7
33	CA 33rd: Ted Lieu (D)	14.2	33	CA 31st: Pete Aguilar (D)	51.6	33	TX 33rd: Marc A. Veasey (D)	32.4
34	NJ 9th: Bill Pascrell, Jr. (D)	13.8	34	TX 27th: Blake Farenthold (R)	50.6	34	FL 20th: Alcee L. Hastings (D)	31.9
35	CA 43rd: Maxine Waters (D)	13.4	35	NY 14th: Joseph Crowley (D)	49.8	35	CA 43rd: Maxine Waters (D)	31.8
35	NY 5th: Gregory W. Meeks (D)	13.4	36	NM 1st: Michelle Lujan Grisham (D)	48.9	36	CA 39th: Edward R. Royce (R)	31.7
37	NY 12th: Carolyn B. Maloney (D)	13.3	37	CA 36th: Raul Ruiz (D)	47.6	36	NY 10th: Jerrold Nadler (D)	31.7
38	CA 11th: Mark Desaulnier (D)	13.1	38	CA 43rd: Maxine Waters (D)	47.0	38	TX 9th: Al Green (D)	31.5
38	CA 28th: Adam B. Schiff (D)	13.1	39	FL 9th: Alan Grayson (D)	46.1	39	CA 37th: Karen Bass (D)	31.2
38	TX 3rd: Sam Johnson (R)	13.1	40	CA 22nd: Devin Nunes (R)	45.8	40	MA 7th: Michael E. Capuano (D)	31.0
41	IL 9th: Janice D. Schakowsky (D)	13.0	41	CA 26th: Julia Brownley (D)	44.7	41	VA11th: Gerald E. Connolly (D)	30.9
42	TX 24th: Kenny Marchant (R)	12.8	42	NV 1st: Dina Titus (D)	44.0	42	CA 35th: Norma J. Torres (D)	30.5
43	CA 46th: Loretta Sanchez (D)	12.6	43	NY 7th: Nydia M. Velázquez (D)	43.1	43	NV 1st: Dina Titus (D)	29.9
44	CA 30th: Brad Sherman (D)	12.5	44	CA 10th: Jeff Denham (R)	41.8	44	WA 9th: Adam Smith (D)	29.5
45	VA10th: Barbara Comstock (R)	12.4	45	CA 19th: Zoe Lofgren (D)	41.7	45	CA 38th: Linda T. Sánchez (D)	29.4
46	GA 7th: Robert Woodall (R)	12.3	46	TX 18th: Sheila Jackson-Lee (D)	40.4	45	CA 21st: David G. Valadao (R)	29.4
47	NY 11th: Daniel M. Donovan Jr. (R)	12.1	47	NM 3rd: Ben Ray Luján (D)	40.0	47	NY 16th: Eliot L. Engel (D)	29.1
48	IL 8th: Tammy Duckworth (D)	11.6	48	CA 8th: Paul Cook (R)	39.9	48	CA 47th: Alan S. Lowenthal (D)	29.0
49	MN 4th: Betty McCollum (D)	11.4	49	CA 37th: Karen Bass (D)	38.8	49	NY 11th: Daniel M. Donovan Jr. (R)	28.6
50	TX 7th: John Abney Culberson (R)	11.3	50	CA 23rd: Kevin McCarthy (R)	38.2	50	NJ 6th: Frank Pallone Jr. (D)	28.5
51	VA 8th: Donald S. Beyer, Jr. (D)	11.2	51	TX 30th: Eddie Bernice Johnson (D)	37.9	51	IL 8th: Tammy Duckworth (D)	27.9
51	WA 7th: Jim McDermott (D)	11.2	52	WA 4th: Dan Newsome (R)	37.7	52	IL 9th: Janice D. Schakowsky (D)	27.8
53	CA 5th: Mike Thompson (D)	11.1	53	CA 9th: Jerry McNerney (D)	37.4	52	NJ 12th: Bonnie Watson Coleman (D)	27.8
53	TX 9th: Al Green (D)	11.1	54	FL 23rd: Debbie Wasserman Schultz (D)	37.3	52	VA 8th: Donald S. Beyer, Jr. (D)	27.8
55	CA 3rd: John Garamendi (D)	10.9	55	TX 9th: Al Green (D)	36.8	55	CA 18th: Anna G. Eshoo (D)	27.6
56	MD 6th: John K. Delaney (D)	10.7	56	CA 25th: Stephen Knight (R)	36.6	56	NJ 10th: Donald M. Payne, Jr. (D)	27.5
57	WA 1st: Suzan K. DelBene (D)	10.2	56	CA 42nd: Ken Calvert (R)	36.6	57	TX 7th: John Abney Culberson (R)	27.3
58	CA 42nd: Ken Calvert (R)	10.0	58	TX 19th: Randy Neugebauer (R)	35.9	58	CA 13th: Barbara Lee (D)	26.8
58	NJ 5th: Scott Garrett (R)	10.0	59	TX 11th: K. Michael Conaway (R)	35.6	59	CA 45th: Mimi Walters (R)	26.7
60	GA 6th: Tom Price (R)	9.8	60	CA 47th: Alan S. Lowenthal (D)	35.4	60	AZ 7th: Ruben Gallego (D)	26.5
60	IL 10th: Robert J. Dold (R)	9.8	61	CA 24th: Lois Capps (D)	35.2	61	NY 12th: Carolyn B. Maloney (D)	26.0
60	MA 5th: Katherine Clark (D)	9.8	62	NJ 9th: Bill Pascrell, Jr. (D)	34.7	61	FL 22nd: Lois Frankel (D)	26.0
63	CA 16th: Jim Costa (D)	9.5	63	CA 39th: Edward R. Royce (R)	33.3	63	CA 20th: Sam Farr (D)	25.6
63	CA 37th: Karen Bass (D)	9.5	64	FL 24th: Frederica S. Wilson (D)	33.2	64	FL 21st: Theodore E. Deutch (D)	25.5
65	MD 8th: Chris Van Hollen (D)	9.4	65	CA 53rd: Susan A. Davis (D)	33.0	65	TX 16th: Beto O'Rourke (D)	25.3
65	MI 11th: David A.Trott (R)	9.4	66	TX 2nd: Ted Poe (R)	31.3	66	CA 48th: Dana Rohrabacher (R)	25.1
67	MA 7th: Michael E. Capuano (D)	9.3	67	IL 3rd: Daniel Lipinski (D)	31.2	67	IL 10th: Robert J. Dold (R)	24.8
67	NJ 11th: Rodney P. Frelinghuysen (R)	9.3	68	CA 30th: Brad Sherman (D)	30.6	68	CA 16th: Jim Costa (D)	24.4
69	NJ 7th: Leonard Lance (R)	9.0	68	CA 50th: Duncan Hunter (R)	30.6	68	CA 11th: Mark Desaulnier (D)	24.4
70	IL 6th: Peter J. Roskam (R)	8.9	70	NV 4th: Cresent Hardy (R)	30.2	70	CA 26th: Julia Brownley (D)	24.0
70	WA 8th: David G. Reichert (R)	8.9	71	CA 3rd: John Garamendi (D)	28.8	71	CA 41st: Mark Takano (D)	23.9
72	PA 13th: Brendan F. Boyle (D)	8.7	72	TX 10th: Michael T. McCaul (R)	28.6	72	MD 8th: Chris Van Hollen (D)	23.8
73	NV 1st: Dina Titus (D)	8.5	73	AZ 9th: Kyrsten Sinema (D)	28.4	73	CA 33rd: Ted Lieu (D)	23.7
74	CA 29th: Tony Cárdenas (D)	8.3	74	CO 1st: Diana DeGette (D)	28.3	74	NY 17th: Nita M. Lowey (D)	23.6
74	CA 51st: Juan Vargas (D)	8.3	74	TX 7th: John Abney Culberson (R)	28.3	74	CA 6th: Doris O. Matsui (D)	23.6

Congressional Districts of the 113th Congress of the United States

Selected Rankings

Percent under 18 years old, 2013			Percent 65 years old and over, 2013			Percent college graduates (bachelor's degree or more), 2013		
Under 18 years old rank	State congressional district Representative	Percent under 18 years old [col 15 and 16]	65 years old and over rank	State congressional district Representative	Percent 65 years old and over [col 22 and 23]	College graduates rank	State congressional district Representative	Percent college graduates [col 27]
1	TX 33rd: Marc A. Veasey (D)	32.8	1	FL 11th: Richard B. Nugent (R)	32.1	1	NY 12th: Carolyn B. Maloney (D)	69.2
2	TX 29th: Gene Green (D)	32.2	2	FL 16th: Vern Buchanan (R)	29.5	2	CA 33rd: Ted Lieu (D)	61.6
3	TX 15th: Rubén Hinojosa (D)	32.1	3	FL 19th: Curt Clawson (R)	28.7	3	VA 8th: Donald S. Beyer, Jr. (D)	61.4
4	CA 21st: David G. Valadao (R)	31.9	4	FL 17th: Thomas J. Rooney (R)	26.3	4	NY 10th: Jerrold Nadler (D)	60.6
4	UT 4th: Mia B. Love (R)	31.9	5	AZ 4th: Paul A. Gosar (R)	24.1	5	CA 18th: Anna G. Eshoo (D)	60.0
6	AZ 7th: Ruben Gallego (D)	31.7	6	FL 18th: Patrick Murphy (D)	24.0	6	WA 7th: Jim McDermott (D)	57.4
6	UT 1st: Rob Bishop (R)	31.7	7	FL 8th: Bill Posey (R)	23.5	7	GA 6th: Tom Price (R)	57.0
8	TX 28th: Henry Cuellar (D)	31.6	7	FL 13th: David W. Jolly (R)	23.5	8	DC At Large: Eleanor Holmes Norton (D)	55.1
9	UT 3rd: Jason Chaffetz (R)	31.5	9	FL 6th: Ron DeSantis (R)	23.0	9	CA 52nd: Scott H. Peters (D)	55.0
10	CA 16th: Jim Costa (D)	31.4	10	FL 21st: Theodore E. Deutch (D)	22.3	10	MA 5th: Katherine Clark (D)	54.5
11	CA 40th: Lucille Roybal-Allard (D)	30.3	11	FL 22nd: Lois Frankel (D)	21.4	11	CA 17th: Michael M. Honda (D)	54.3
12	TX 34th: Filemon Vela (D)	30.0	12	AZ 8th: Trent Franks (R)	21.2	12	CA 12th: Nancy Pelosi (D)	54.1
13	WA 4th: Dan Newsome (R)	29.5	13	FL 12th: Gus M. Bilirakis (R)	20.9	13	VA10th: Barbara Comstock (R)	53.8
14	TX 23rd: Will Hurd (R)	28.6	14	MI 1st: Dan Benishek (R)	20.6	14	VA11th: Gerald E. Connolly (D)	53.5
15	TX 16th: Beto O'Rourke (D)	28.5	14	NC 11th: Mark Meadows (R)	20.6	15	MD 8th: Chris Van Hollen (D)	52.2
15	UT 2nd: Chris Stewart (R)	28.5	16	MA 9th: William R. Keating (D)	20.2	15	NY 3rd: Steve Israel (D)	52.2
17	CA 44th: Janice Hahn (D)	28.4	17	PA 12th: Keith J. Rothfus (R)	19.3	17	IL 9th: Janice D. Schakowsky (D)	52.0
17	TX 22nd: Pete Olson (R)	28.4	18	CA 36th: Raul Ruiz (D)	19.2	18	NJ 11th: Rodney P. Frelinghuysen (R)	51.6
17	TX 30th: Eddie Bernice Johnson (D)	28.4	19	AZ 2nd: Martha McSally (R)	19.0	19	TX 3rd: Sam Johnson (R)	51.5
20	GA 7th: Robert Woodall (R)	28.3	20	CA 1st: Doug LaMalfa (R)	18.9	20	CO 2nd: Jared Polis (D)	51.4
21	CA 51st: Juan Vargas (D)	28.2	21	CA 4th:Tom McClintock (R)	18.8	21	CA 45th: Mimi Walters (R)	50.8
22	CA 22nd: Devin Nunes (R)	28.1	21	PA 18th: Tim Murphy (R)	18.8	21	IL 5th: Michael Quigley (D)	50.8
22	CA 35th: Norma J. Torres (D)	28.1	23	OR 2nd: Greg Walden (R)	18.6	23	NJ 7th: Leonard Lance (R)	50.3
22	NY 15th: José E. Serrano (D)	28.1	24	MN 6th: Collin C. Peterson (D)	18.3	24	IL 6th: Peter J. Roskam (R)	50.1
22	TX 26th: Michael C. Burgess (R)	28.1	24	PA 9th: Bill Shuster (R)	18.3	25	TX 7th: John Abney Culberson (R)	49.9
26	CA 10th: Jeff Denham (R)	28.0	26	MN 7th: Richard M. Nolan (D)	18.2	26	MO 2nd: Ann Wagner (R)	48.7
27	CA 9th: Jerry McNerney (D)	27.8	26	NY 3rd: Steve Israel (D)	18.2	27	MA 4th: Joseph P. Kennedy III (D)	48.4
27	CA 41st: Mark Takano (D)	27.8	26	OR 4th: Peter A. DeFazio (D)	18.2	28	CT 4th: James A. Himes (D)	48.3
27	TX 3rd: Sam Johnson (R)	27.8	26	PA 10th: Tom Marino (R)	18.2	28	NC 9th: Robert Pittenger (R)	48.3
30	VA10th: Barbara Comstock (R)	27.7	26	TN 1st: David P. Roe (R)	18.2	30	MN 3rd: Erik Paulsen (R)	46.7
31	AZ 3rd: Raul M. Grijalva (D)	27.6	26	VA 9th: Morgan Griffith (R)	18.2	31	MD 3rd: John P. Sarbanes (D)	45.9
31	CA 25th: Stephen Knight (R)	27.6	32	ME 2nd: Bruce Poliquin (R)	18.1	32	NJ 5th: Scott Garrett (R)	45.8
31	CA 31st: Pete Aguilar (D)	27.6	32	NE 3rd: Adrian Smith (R)	18.1	33	MI 11th: David A.Trott (R)	45.5
34	CA 42nd: Ken Calvert (R)	27.5	32	OH 16th: James B. Renacci (R)	18.1	34	NY 17th: Nita M. Lowey (D)	44.9
34	GA 13th: David Scott (D)	27.5	35	NJ 3rd: Thomas MacArthur (R)	18.0	35	TX 21st: Lamar Smith (R)	44.8
34	IL 4th: Luis V. Gutierrez (D)	27.5	35	NJ 4th: Christopher H. Smith (R)	18.0	36	CA 13th: Barbara Lee (D)	44.7
37	AZ 5th: Matt Salmon (R)	27.4	35	WI 7th: Sean P. Duffy (R)	18.0	36	KS 3rd: Kevin Yoder (R)	44.7
38	CA 23rd: Kevin McCarthy (R)	27.2	38	WV 3rd: Evan H. Jenkins (R)	17.9	38	CA 28th: Adam B. Schiff (D)	44.6
38	TX 31st: John R. Carter (R)	27.2	39	SC 7th: Tom Rice (R)	17.8	39	CO 1st: Diana DeGette (D)	43.9
40	CA 8th: Paul Cook (R)	27.1	40	OH 6th: Bill Johnson (R)	17.7	40	CA 14th: Jackie Speier (D)	43.7
40	IL 11th: Bill Foster (D)	27.1	40	VA 5th: Robert Hurt (R)	17.7	40	CA 48th: Dana Rohrabacher (R)	43.7
42	TX 6th: Joe Barton (R)	27.0	42	PA 11th: Lou Barletta (R)	17.6	42	TX 22nd: Pete Olson (R)	43.4
43	CA 46th: Loretta Sanchez (D)	26.9	43	FL 10th: Daniel Webster (R)	17.5	43	MA 8th: Stephen F. Lynch (D)	43.3
43	ID 2nd: Michael K. Simpson (R)	26.9	43	IL 15th: John Shimkus (R)	17.5	44	NJ 12th: Bonnie Watson Coleman (D)	43.1
43	TX 35th: Lloyd Doggett (D)	26.9	43	ME 1st: Chellie Pingree (D)	17.5	45	MN 5th: Keith Ellison (D)	43.0
46	IL 14th: Randy Hultgren (R)	26.8	43	NY 19th: Christopher P. Gibson (R)	17.5	45	TX 24th: Kenny Marchant (R)	43.0
47	TX 7th: John Abney Culberson (R)	26.7	43	WA 6th: Derek Kilmer (D)	17.5	47	IL 10th: Robert J. Dold (R)	42.9
47	TX 18th: Sheila Jackson-Lee (D)	26.7	48	CA 2nd: Jared Huffman (D)	17.4	48	TX 32nd: Pete Sessions (R)	42.7
49	NV 4th: Cresent Hardy (R)	26.6	48	IA 4th: Steve King (R)	17.4	49	IN 5th: Susan W. Brooks (R)	42.3
49	TX 20th: Joaquin Castro (D)	26.6	48	OH 14th: David P. Joyce (R)	17.4	49	MN 4th: Betty McCollum (D)	42.3
51	NE 2nd: Brad Ashford (D)	26.4	48	OK 2nd: Markwayne Mullin (R)	17.4	49	NC 4th: David E. Price (D)	42.3
51	TX 9th: Al Green (D)	26.4	48	PA 3rd: Mike Kelly (R)	17.4	49	PA 6th: Ryan A. Costello (R)	42.3
53	KS 3rd: Kevin Yoder (R)	26.2	48	PA 17th: Matt Cartwright (D)	17.4	53	MA 6th: Seth Moulton (D)	42.2
53	MN 5th: Tom Emmer (R)	26.2	54	AR 2nd: Bruce Westerman (R)	17.3	54	AZ 6th: David Schweikert (R)	41.6
53	TX 8th: Kevin Brady (R)	26.2	55	MO 8th: Jason T. Smith (R)	17.1	55	CA 27th: Judy Chu (D)	41.5
56	ID 1st: Raul Labrador (R)	26.1	55	WV 1st: David McKinley (R)	17.1	56	MD 6th: John K. Delaney (D)	41.1
57	KS 4th: Mike Pompeo (R)	26.0	57	MD 1st: Andrew Harris (R)	17.0	57	CA 11th: Mark Desaulnier (D)	41.0
57	NC 2nd: Renee Ellmers (R)	26.0	58	HI 1st: Mark Takai (D)	16.9	57	GA 5th: John Lewis (D)	41.0
57	TX 5th: Jeb Hensarling (R)	26.0	58	MO 2nd: Ann Wagner (R)	16.9	59	PA 7th: Patrick Meehan (R)	40.5
60	IN 3rd: Marlin Stutzman (R)	25.8	58	PA 5th: Glenn Thompson (R)	16.9	59	TX 26th: Michael C. Burgess (R)	40.5
60	MN 2nd: John Kline (R)	25.8	58	TN 3rd: Chuck Fleischmann (R)	16.9	61	CA 15th: Eric Swalwell (D)	40.4
62	IN 7th: André Carson (D)	25.7	62	AR 1st: Eric A. "Rick" Crawford (R)	16.8	61	CA 49th: Darrell E. Issa (R)	40.4
63	AK At-Large: Don Young (R)	25.6	62	KY 1st: Ed Whitfield (R)	16.8	63	CO 6th: Mike Coffman (R)	40.3
63	GA 14th: Tom Graves (R)	25.6	62	MI 4th: John L. Moolenar (R)	16.8	63	MA 7th: Michael E. Capuano (D)	40.3
63	IL 10th: Robert J. Dold (R)	25.6	62	SC 3rd: Jeff Duncan (R)	16.8	63	WA 1st: Suzan K. DelBene (D)	40.3
63	MS 2nd: Bennie G. Thompson (D)	25.6	62	VA 6th: Bob Goodlatte (R)	16.8	66	CA 30th: Brad Sherman (D)	39.9
63	NC 12th: Alma S. Adams (D)	25.6	62	WV 2nd: David McKinley (R)	16.8	66	WA 9th: Adam Smith (D)	39.9
63	TX 10th: Michael T. McCaul (R)	25.6	68	AL 4th: Robert B. Aderholt (R)	16.7	68	TX 2nd: Ted Poe (R)	39.5
69	OK 5th: Steve Russell (R)	25.5	68	NY 22nd: Richard L. Hanna (R)	16.7	69	NY 4th: Kathleen M. Rice (D)	39.4
70	AR 2nd: Steve Womack (R)	25.4	68	NY 27th: Chris Collins(R)	16.7	70	WI 2nd: Mark Pocan (D)	39.2
70	CA 20th: Sam Farr (D)	25.4	71	OH 13th: Tim Ryan (D)	16.6	71	CA 39th: Edward R. Royce (R)	39.1
70	GA 3rd: Lynn A. Westmoreland (R)	25.4	72	IL 17th: Cheri Bustos (D)	16.5	72	IL 7th: Danny K. Davis (D)	38.9
70	GA 4th: Henry C. "Hank" Johnson Jr. (D)	25.4	72	IL 18th: Vacancy	16.5	73	NY 16th: Eliot L. Engel (D)	38.8
70	IN 2nd: Jackie Walorski (R)	25.4	72	NJ 11th: Rodney P. Frelinghuysen (R)	16.5	74	CA 2nd: Jared Huffman (D)	38.7
70	TN 9th: Steve Cohen (D)	25.4	72	OH 7th: Bob Gibbs (R)	16.5	75	MI 8th: Mike Bishop (R)	38.6

Congressional Districts of the 113th Congress of the United States

Selected Rankings

Median value of owner-occupied housing units, 2013			Percent female-headed family households, 2013			Percent of households with one person, 2013		
Median value rank	State congressional district Representative	Median value (dollars) [col 43]	Female house-holder rank	State congressional district Representative	Percent with female house-holder [col 32]	One-person house-hold rank	State congressional district Representative	Percent one-person house-holds [col 33]
1	CA 33rd: Ted Lieu (D)	947 000	1	NY 15th: José E. Serrano (D)	48.7	1	NY 12th: Carolyn B. Maloney (D)	48.7
2	CA 18th: Anna G. Eshoo (D)	916 400	2	MS 2nd: Bennie G. Thompson (D)	45.3	2	PA 2nd: Chaka Fattah (D)	45.3
3	NY 12th: Carolyn B. Maloney (D)	845 900	3	NY 8th: Hakeem S. Jeffries (D)	43.8	3	NY 10th: Jerrold Nadler (D)	43.8
4	NY 10th: Jerrold Nadler (D)	799 100	4	NY 13th: Charles B. Rangel (D)	43.0	4	GA 5th: John Lewis (D)	43.0
5	CA 12th: Nancy Pelosi (D)	797 400	5	CA 40th: Lucille Roybal-Allard (D)	42.2	5	DC At Large: Eleanor Holmes Norton (D)	42.2
6	CA 14th: Jackie Speier (D)	705 200	6	MI 13th: John Conyers Jr. (D)	40.9	6	IL 7th: Danny K. Davis (D)	40.9
7	CA 17th: Michael M. Honda (D)	657 000	7	CA 44th: Janice Hahn (D)	40.4	7	OH 11th: Marcia L. Fudge (D)	40.4
8	CA 48th: Dana Rohrabacher (R)	639 400	8	TN 9th: Steve Cohen (D)	39.6	8	CA 12th: Nancy Pelosi (D)	39.6
9	CA 28th: Adam B. Schiff (D)	637 500	9	LA 2nd: Cedric Richmond (D)	39.4	9	CO 1st: Diana DeGette (D)	39.4
10	CA 45th: Mimi Walters (R)	590 200	10	NY 9th: Yvette D. Clarke (D)	39.3	10	FL 13th: David W. Jolly (R)	39.3
11	HI 1st: Mark Takai (D)	566 900	11	AL 7th: Terri A. Sewell (D)	39.0	11	MO 1st: William Lacy Clay (D)	39.0
12	CA 27th: Judy Chu (D)	557 800	11	FL 5th: Corrine Brown (D)	39.0	11	PA 14th: Michael F. Doyle (D)	39.0
13	CA 52nd: Scott H. Peters (D)	548 400	13	FL 20th: Alcee L. Hastings (D)	38.3	13	WA 7th: Jim McDermott (D)	38.3
14	CA 49th: Darrell E. Issa (R)	547 400	14	NY 5th: Gregory W. Meeks (D)	38.0	14	NY 13th: Charles B. Rangel (D)	38.0
15	CA 19th: Zoe Lofgren (D)	544 800	15	FL 24th: Frederica S. Wilson (D)	37.8	15	CA 28th: Adam B. Schiff (D)	37.8
16	NY 7th: Nydia M. Velázquez (D)	543 100	16	NJ 10th: Donald M. Payne, Jr. (D)	37.7	16	MN 5th: Keith Ellison (D)	37.7
17	CA 15th: Eric Swalwell (D)	536 600	17	VA 3rd: Robert C. "Bobby" Scott (D)	37.4	17	FL 22nd: Lois Frankel (D)	37.4
18	CA 37th: Karen Bass (D)	534 100	18	CA 21st: David G. Valadao (R)	37.1	18	MI 13th: John Conyers Jr. (D)	37.1
19	NY 3rd: Steve Israel (D)	525 000	19	CA 51st: Juan Vargas (D)	36.3	19	PA 1st: Robert A. Brady (D)	36.3
20	NY 9th: Yvette D. Clarke (D)	517 700	20	CA 16th: Jim Costa (D)	36.1	20	CA 33rd: Ted Lieu (D)	36.1
21	CA 39th: Edward R. Royce (R)	514 200	21	MI 14th: Brenda L. Lawrence (D)	35.8	21	IL 5th: Michael Quigley (D)	35.8
22	CT 4th: James A. Himes (D)	508 600	22	NC 12th: Alma S. Adams (D)	35.7	22	NY 26th: Brian Higgins (D)	35.7
23	CA 13th: Barbara Lee (D)	503 500	23	AZ 7th: Ruben Gallego (D)	35.4	23	OH 9th: Marcy Kaptur (D)	35.4
24	CA 30th: Brad Sherman (D)	503 200	24	GA 2nd: Sanford D. Bishop Jr. (D)	35.2	24	FL 14th: Kathy Castor (D)	35.2
25	NY 6th: Grace Meng (D)	495 700	24	IL 2nd: Robin L. Kelly (D)	35.2	24	LA 2nd: Cedric Richmond (D)	35.2
26	NY 8th: Hakeem S. Jeffries (D)	481 300	26	OH 11th: Marcia L. Fudge (D)	35.0	26	MO 5th: Emanuel Cleaver (D)	35.0
27	VA 8th: Donald S. Beyer, Jr. (D)	474 100	27	IL 1st: Bobby L. Rush (D)	34.9	27	OH 3rd: Joyce Beatty (D)	34.9
28	CA 2nd: Jared Huffman (D)	471 800	27	TX 30th: Eddie Bernice Johnson (D)	34.9	27	TN 5th: Jim Cooper (D)	34.9
29	CA 11th: Mark Desaulnier (D)	471 500	29	SC 6th: James E. Clyburn (D)	34.8	29	TN 9th: Steve Cohen (D)	34.8
30	DC At Large: Eleanor Holmes Norton (D)	470 500	30	TX 18th: Sheila Jackson-Lee (D)	34.7	30	AL 7th: Terri A. Sewell (D)	34.7
31	NY 11th: Daniel M. Donovan Jr. (R)	458 800	31	TX 29th: Gene Green (D)	34.4	31	IL 9th: Janice D. Schakowsky (D)	34.4
32	NY 13th: Charles B. Rangel (D)	454 100	32	NC 1st: G. K. Butterfield (D)	34.2	32	VA 3rd: Robert C. "Bobby" Scott (D)	34.2
33	HI 2nd: Tulsi Gabbard (D)	448 800	33	GA 13th: David Scott (D)	34.1	33	VA 8th: Donald S. Beyer, Jr. (D)	34.1
34	CA 47th: Alan S. Lowenthal (D)	448 300	33	TX 9th: Al Green (D)	34.1	33	WI 4th: Gwen Moore (D)	34.1
35	CA 26th: Julia Brownley (D)	442 000	35	TX 33rd: Marc A. Veasey (D)	34.0	35	IN 7th: André Carson (D)	34.0
36	NY 14th: Joseph Crowley (D)	440 800	36	MD 4th: Donna F. Edwards (D)	33.7	36	IL 2nd: Robin L. Kelly (D)	33.7
37	NY 17th: Nita M. Lowey (D)	438 900	37	GA 4th: Henry C. "Hank" Johnson Jr. (D)	33.6	37	MI 14th: Brenda L. Lawrence (D)	33.6
38	CA 24th: Lois Capps (D)	438 000	37	PA 1st: Robert A. Brady (D)	33.6	37	NC 1st: G. K. Butterfield (D)	33.6
39	NY 16th: Eliot L. Engel (D)	437 900	37	TX 15th: Rubén Hinojosa (D)	33.6	37	OH 13th: Tim Ryan (D)	33.6
40	MA 5th: Katherine Clark (D)	436 100	40	WI 4th: Gwen Moore (D)	33.4	40	MA 7th: Michael E. Capuano (D)	33.4
40	VA10th: Barbara Comstock (R)	436 100	41	MO 1st: William Lacy Clay (D)	33.3	41	KY 3rd: John A. Yarmuth (D)	33.3
42	VA11th: Gerald E. Connolly (D)	432 500	42	MD 7th: Elijah E. Cummings (D)	33.0	42	FL 23rd: Debbie Wasserman Schultz (D)	33.0
43	NY 4th: Kathleen M. Rice (D)	421 400	42	CA 43rd: Maxine Waters (D)	33.0	42	IL 1st: Bobby L. Rush (D)	33.0
44	WA 7th: Jim McDermott (D)	417 400	42	TX 16th: Beto O'Rourke (D)	33.0	42	MD 7th: Elijah E. Cummings (D)	33.0
45	NJ 7th: Leonard Lance (R)	416 500	45	IL 7th: Danny K. Davis (D)	32.9	45	NV 1st: Dina Titus (D)	32.9
46	NJ 11th: Rodney P. Frelinghuysen (R)	413 800	45	TX 35th: Lloyd Doggett (D)	32.9	45	NY 20th: Paul Tonko (D)	32.9
47	MD 8th: Chris Van Hollen (D)	410 900	47	IN 7th: André Carson (D)	32.8	47	AZ 2nd: Martha McSally (R)	32.8
48	CA 20th: Sam Farr (D)	407 700	47	CA 31st: Pete Aguilar (D)	32.8	47	NC 4th: David E. Price (D)	32.8
49	NJ 5th: Scott Garrett (R)	392 500	49	MA 7th: Michael E. Capuano (D)	32.7	49	AZ 9th: Kyrsten Sinema (D)	32.7
50	CA 34th: Xavier Becerra (D)	390 700	50	PA 2nd: Chaka Fattah (D)	32.6	50	CA 37th: Karen Bass (D)	32.6
51	NY 5th: Gregory W. Meeks (D)	384 400	50	NY 16th: Eliot L. Engel (D)	32.6	50	SC 6th: James E. Clyburn (D)	32.6
52	CA 43rd: Maxine Waters (D)	383 300	52	MD 2nd: C. A. Dutch Ruppersberger (D)	32.5	52	FL 16th: Vern Buchanan (R)	32.5
53	CA 53rd: Susan A. Davis (D)	379 900	52	NY 7th: Nydia M. Velázquez (D)	32.5	52	OH 10th: Michael R. Turner (R)	32.5
54	NY 15th: José E. Serrano (D)	376 600	54	TX 28th: Henry Cuellar (D)	32.4	54	CA 13th:Barbara Lee (D)	32.4
55	CA 38th: Linda T. Sánchez (D)	374 900	54	TX 34th: Filemon Vela (D)	32.4	54	PA 13th: Brendan F. Boyle (D)	32.4
56	CA 46th: Loretta Sanchez (D)	372 400	54	AZ 3rd: Raul M. Grijalva (D)	32.4	54	TX 21st: Lamar Smith (R)	32.4
57	MA 6th: Seth Moulton (D)	372 300	54	CA 29th: Tony Cárdenas (D)	32.4	54	WV 1st: David McKinley (R)	32.4
58	MA 4th: Joseph P. Kennedy III (D)	372 100	58	CA 41st: Mark Takano (D)	32.3	58	OK 5th: Steve Russell (R)	32.3
59	CA 50th: Duncan Hunter (R)	371 100	59	TX 20th: Joaquin Castro (D)	32.1	59	NY 25th: Louise McIntosh Slaughter (D)	32.1
60	MA 8th: Stephen F. Lynch (D)	362 700	60	CA 32nd: Grace F. Napolitano (D)	32.0	60	CT 3rd: Rosa L. DeLauro (D)	32.0
61	NY 1st: Lee M. Zeldin (R)	360 800	60	LA 5th: Ralph Lee Abraham (R)	32.0	60	NC 12th: Alma S. Adams (D)	32.0
62	NJ 9th: Bill Pascrell, Jr. (D)	360 300	62	CA 9th: Jerry McNerney (D)	31.7	62	NY 24th: John Katko (R)	31.7
63	CA 32nd: Grace F. Napolitano (D)	355 700	63	CA 46th: Loretta Sanchez (D)	31.5	63	MN 4th: Betty McCollum (D)	31.5
64	MA 7th: Michael E. Capuano (D)	355 400	64	FL 25th: Mario Diaz-Balart (R)	31.4	64	MI 9th: Sander M. Levin (D)	31.4
65	NY 2nd: Peter T. King (R)	354 800	64	NJ 8th: Albio Sires (D)	31.4	64	TX 24th: Kenny Marchant (R)	31.4
66	CA 5th: Mike Thompson (D)	345 200	66	CA 35th: Norma J. Torres (D)	31.3	66	LA 4th: John Fleming (R)	31.3
67	CA 29th: Tony Cárdenas (D)	342 800	67	CA 38th: Linda T. Sánchez (D)	31.2	67	FL 24th: Frederica S. Wilson (D)	31.2
68	WA 1st Suzan K. DelBene (D)	335 500	68	GA 5th: John Lewis (D)	31.1	68	IL 13th: Rodney Davis (R)	31.1
69	CA 25th: Stephen Knight (R)	334 800	68	CA 34th: Xavier Becerra (D)	31.1	68	NY 6th: Grace Meng (D)	31.1
70	NJ 4th: Christopher H. Smith (R)	327 200	68	NY 14th: Joseph Crowley (D)	31.1	68	OH 2nd: Brad R. Wenstrup (R)	31.1
71	CA 4th: Tom McClintock (R)	326 900	71	OH 3rd: Joyce Beatty (D)	31.0	71	IL 17th: Cheri Bustos (D)	31.0
71	MA 9th: William R. Keating (D)	326 900	71	GA 12th: Rick W. Allen (R)	31.0	71	RI 1st: David Cicilline (D)	31.0
73	WA 9th: Adam Smith (D)	324 000	73	IL 4th: Luis V. Gutierrez (D)	30.9	73	MD 3rd: John P. Sarbanes (D)	30.9
74	NJ 12th: Bonnie Watson Coleman (D)	321 400	73	NJ 9th: Bill Pascrell, Jr. (D)	30.9	73	OR 3rd: Earl Blumenauer (D)	30.9
75	CO: 2nd: Jared Polis (D)	318 800	75	LA 4th: John Fleming (R)	30.8	75	NY 8th: Hakeem S. Jeffries (D)	30.8

Congressional Districts of the 113th Congress of the United States

Selected Rankings

Median household income, 2013			Percent of persons below 65 years with no health insurance, 2013			Percent of persons below the poverty level, 2013		
Median income rank	State congressional district Representative	Median income (dollars) [col 47]	No health insurance rank	State congressional district Representative	Percent with no health insurance [col 59]	Poverty rate rank	State congressional district Representative	Poverty rate [col 49]
1	VA10th: Barbara Comstock (R)	110 444	1	TX 33rd: Marc A. Veasey (D)	41.1	1	NY 15th: José E. Serrano (D)	39.8
2	CA 18th: Anna G. Eshoo (D)	105 817	2	TX 29th: Gene Green (D)	38.9	2	AZ 7th: Ruben Gallego (D)	37.0
3	NY 3rd: Steve Israel (D)	101 695	3	CA 34th: Xavier Becerra (D)	36.1	3	MI 13th: John Conyers Jr. (D)	32.9
4	VA11th: Gerald E. Connolly (D)	101 226	4	TX 34th: Filemon Vela (D)	35.7	4	CA 16th: Jim Costa (D)	32.8
5	NJ 7th: Leonard Lance (R)	101 222	5	FL 24th: Frederica S. Wilson (D)	35.1	5	MS 2nd: Bennie G. Thompson (D)	32.5
6	CA 17th: Michael M. Honda (D)	100 282	6	TX 15th: Rubén Hinojosa (D)	34.6	6	NY 13th: Charles B. Rangel (D)	30.8
7	NJ 11th: Rodney P. Frelinghuysen (R)	100 143	7	TX 28th: Henry Cuellar (D)	34.2	7	TX 34th: Filemon Vela (D)	30.6
8	VA 8th: Donald S. Beyer, Jr. (D)	97 323	8	AZ 7th: Ruben Gallego (D)	33.8	8	CA 21st: David G. Valadao (R)	29.8
9	MD 8th: Chris Van Hollen (D)	97 192	9	CA 40th: Lucille Roybal-Allard (D)	33.5	9	CA 34th: Xavier Becerra (D)	29.4
10	NY 12th: Carolyn B. Maloney (D)	91 628	10	FL 25th: Mario Diaz-Balart (R)	33.3	9	TX 33rd: Marc A. Veasey (D)	29.4
11	CA 33rd: Ted Lieu (D)	90 541	11	NV 1st: Dina Titus (D)	32.9	11	CA 40th: Lucille Roybal-Allard (D)	29.3
12	CA 45th: Mimi Walters (R)	90 318	12	TX 9th: Al Green (D)	32.0	12	TX 15th: Rubén Hinojosa (D)	29.0
13	IL 6th: Peter J. Roskam (R)	89 683	13	FL 26th: Carlos Curbelo (R)	31.7	13	TX 29th: Gene Green (D)	28.3
14	NY 4th: Kathleen M. Rice (D)	89 600	14	FL 20th: Alcee L. Hastings (D)	31.3	14	FL 5th: Corrine Brown (D)	28.0
15	MD 5th: Steny H. Hoyer (D)	88 481	15	TX 18th: Sheila Jackson-Lee (D)	31.2	15	AL 7th: Terri A. Sewell (D)	27.6
16	NJ 5th: Scott Garrett (R)	88 280	16	FL 27th: Ileana Ros-Lehtinen (R)	30.6	15	OH 11th: Marcia L. Fudge (D)	27.6
17	NY 17th: Nita M. Lowey (D)	87 899	17	TX 16th: Beto O'Rourke (D)	29.8	17	PA 2nd: Chaka Fattah (D)	27.5
18	CA 15th: Eric Swalwell (D)	86 818	18	CA 29th: Tony Cárdenas (D)	29.6	18	NC 12th: Alma S. Adams (D)	27.3
19	TX 22nd: Pete Olson (R)	86 681	19	TX 30th: Eddie Bernice Johnson (D)	29.4	18	SC 6th: James E. Clyburn (D)	27.3
20	CT 4th: James A. Himes (D)	86 007	20	IL 4th: Luis V. Gutierrez (D)	28.8	20	GA 2nd: Sanford D. Bishop Jr. (D)	27.2
21	NY 2nd: Peter T. King (R)	85 976	21	CA 44th: Janice Hahn (D)	28.7	20	TN 9th: Steve Cohen (D)	27.2
22	CA 14th: Jackie Speier (D)	85 706	22	CA 46th: Loretta Sanchez (D)	28.6	22	NC 1st: G. K. Butterfield (D)	26.9
23	MA 4th: Joseph P. Kennedy III (D)	85 262	22	TX 5th: Jeb Hensarling (R)	28.6	23	KY 5th: Harold Rogers (R)	26.7
24	NY 1st: Lee M. Zeldin (R)	83 493	24	NJ 8th: Albio Sires (D)	28.2	23	NY 7th: Nydia M. Velázquez (D)	26.7
25	MA 5th: Katherine Clark (D)	83 430	25	TX 35th: Lloyd Doggett (D)	27.7	25	LA 2nd: Cedric Richmond (D)	26.5
26	CA 52nd: Scott H. Peters (D)	82 286	26	FL 9th: Alan Grayson (D)	27.6	26	MI 14th: Brenda L. Lawrence (D)	26.4
27	NY 10th: Jerrold Nadler (D)	81 810	27	FL 19th: Curt Clawson (R)	27.2	27	WI 4th: Gwen Moore (D)	26.1
28	PA 7th: Patrick Meehan (R)	81 186	28	CA 51st: Juan Vargas (D)	26.8	28	TX 28th: Henry Cuellar (D)	25.9
29	TX 3rd: Sam Johnson (R)	80 912	29	FL 22nd: Lois Frankel (D)	26.6	29	IL 7th: Danny K. Davis (D)	25.7
30	IL 14th: Randy Hultgren (R)	80 726	30	TX 23rd: Will Hurd (R)	26.5	30	PA 1st: Robert A. Brady (D)	25.4
31	CA 48th: Dana Rohrabacher (R)	80 502	31	CA 35th: Norma J. Torres (D)	26.4	31	GA 5th: John Lewis (D)	25.2
32	TX 26th: Michael C. Burgess (R)	80 124	32	TX 11th: K. Michael Conaway (R)	26.1	32	GA 12th: Rick W. Allen (R)	24.9
33	CA 39th: Edward R. Royce (R)	79 909	33	FL 5th: Corrine Brown (D)	25.5	33	FL 24th: Frederica S. Wilson (D)	24.8
34	WA 1st: Suzan K. DelBene (D)	79 145	33	FL 17th: Thomas J. Rooney (R)	25.5	33	LA 5th: Ralph Lee Abraham (R)	24.8
35	CA 19th: Zoe Lofgren (D)	78 169	35	CA 21st: David G. Valadao (R)	25.4	33	TX 30th: Eddie Bernice Johnson (D)	24.8
36	MN 3rd: Erik Paulsen (R)	77 647	36	TX 1st: Louie Gohmert (R)	25.3	36	CA 51st: Juan Vargas (D)	24.7
37	CA 12th: Nancy Pelosi (D)	77 577	37	CA 41st: Mark Takano (D)	25.1	36	NY 8th: Hakeem S. Jeffries (D)	24.7
38	CA 26th: Julia Brownley (D)	76 679	37	NC 12th: Alma S. Adams (D)	25.1	38	CA 44th: Janice Hahn (D)	24.3
39	GA 6th: Tom Price (R)	76 308	37	OK 2nd: Markwayne Mullin (R)	25.1	39	TX 18th: Sheila Jackson-Lee (D)	24.2
40	MA 6th: Seth Moulton (D)	76 182	40	CA 36th: Raul Ruiz (D)	25.0	40	CA 6th: Doris O. Matsui (D)	24.1
41	NJ 12th: Bonnie Watson Coleman (D)	75 927	41	FL 23rd: Debbie Wasserman Schultz (D)	24.9	40	IN 7th: André Carson (D)	24.1
42	VA 1st: Robert J. Wittman (R)	75 485	42	WA 4th: Dan Newsome (R)	24.8	42	TX 35th: Lloyd Doggett (D)	24.0
43	MD 3rd: John P. Sarbanes (D)	75 431	43	CA 43rd: Maxine Waters (D)	24.7	43	FL 20th: Alcee L. Hastings (D)	23.9
44	MA 8th: Stephen F. Lynch (D)	75 359	44	NY 14th: Joseph Crowley (D)	24.6	44	VA 3rd: Robert C. "Bobby" Scott (D)	23.8
45	NY 18th: Sean Patrick Maloney (D)	74 704	45	GA 4th: Henry C. "Hank" Johnson Jr. (D)	24.3	45	AZ 3rd: Raul M. Grijalva (D)	23.4
46	NJ 6th: Frank Pallone Jr. (D)	74 164	45	TX 19th: Randy Neugebauer (R)	24.3	45	NM 3rd: Ben Ray Luján (D)	23.4
47	CA 11th: Mark Desaulnier (D)	73 860	45	TX 36th: Brian Babin (R)	24.3	47	OH 3rd: Joyce Beatty (D)	23.3
48	MD 6th: John K. Delaney (D)	73 832	48	GA 13th: David Scott (D)	23.9	47	TX 9th: Al Green (D)	23.3
49	PA 6th: Ryan A. Costello (R)	73 826	49	AZ 3rd: Raul M. Grijalva (D)	23.8	49	WV 3rd: Evan H. Jenkins (R)	23.2
50	NJ 4th: Christopher H. Smith (R)	73 710	49	NV 4th: Cresent Hardy (R)	23.8	50	NM 2nd: Steve Pearce (R)	22.9
51	PA 8th: Michael G. Fitzpatrick (R)	73 522	49	TX 27th: Blake Farenthold (R)	23.8	51	IL 2nd: Robin L. Kelly (D)	22.7
52	MN 2nd: John Kline (R)	73 381	52	CA 37th: Karen Bass (D)	23.7	52	AR 2nd: Bruce Westerman (R)	22.6
53	MI 11th: David A.Trott (R)	73 294	52	GA 2nd: Sanford D. Bishop Jr. (D)	23.7	52	CA 29th: Tony Cárdenas (D)	22.6
54	MO 2nd: Ann Wagner (R)	72 888	54	FL 16th: Vern Buchanan (R)	23.5	52	IL 4th: Luis V. Gutierrez (D)	22.6
55	NJ 3rd: Thomas MacArthur (R)	72 798	55	TX 20th: Joaquin Castro (D)	23.4	52	NV 1st: Dina Titus (D)	22.6
56	HI 1st: Mark Takai (D)	72 302	56	TX 32nd: Pete Sessions (R)	23.3	56	CA 22nd: Devin Nunes (R)	22.5
57	MD 4th: Donna F. Edwards (D)	72 281	57	GA 8th: Austin Scott (R)	23.2	57	AZ 1st: Ann Kirkpatrick (D)	22.3
58	AK At-Large: Don Young (R)	72 237	58	LA 5th: Ralph Lee Abraham (R)	23.1	57	MS 3rd: Gregg Harper (R)	22.3
59	MN 5th: Tom Emmer (R)	71 340	59	CA 32nd: Grace F. Napolitano (D)	23.0	57	OH 9th: Marcy Kaptur (D)	22.3
60	WA 8th: David G. Reichert (R)	71 033	59	NJ 9th: Bill Pascrell, Jr. (D)	23.0	57	SC 7th: Tom Rice (R)	22.3
61	WA 7th: Jim McDermott (D)	70 596	59	NM 3rd: Ben Ray Luján (D)	23.0	61	CA 8th: Paul Cook (R)	21.8
62	CA 42nd: Ken Calvert (R)	70 261	62	CA 38th: Linda T. Sánchez (D)	22.9	61	FL 14th: Kathy Castor (D)	21.8
63	NC 9th: Robert Pittenger (R)	69 972	62	NM 2nd: Steve Pearce (R)	22.9	63	AR 1st: Eric A. "Rick" Crawford (R)	21.6
64	TX 2nd: Ted Poe (R)	69 833	64	CA 20th: Sam Farr (D)	22.8	63	GA 8th: Austin Scott (R)	21.6
65	IL 5th: Michael Quigley (D)	68 792	64	FL 21st: Theodore E. Deutch (D)	22.8	65	MO 1st: William Lacy Clay (D)	21.5
66	VA 7th: Dave Brat (R)	68 761	66	TX 4th: John Ratcliffe (R)	22.7	66	CA 43rd: Maxine Waters (D)	21.4
67	IL 10th: Robert J. Dold (R)	68 184	67	GA 9th: Doug Collins (R)	22.6	66	MI 5th: Daniel T. Kildee (D)	21.4
68	CA 27th: Judy Chu (D)	68 053	68	FL 11th: Richard B. Nugent (R)	22.5	68	LA 4th: John Fleming (R)	21.3
69	CA 30th: Brad Sherman (D)	67 819	68	GA 5th: John Lewis (D)	22.5	69	CA 31st: Pete Aguilar (D)	21.2
70	CT 2nd: Joe Courtney (D)	67 614	70	CA 28th: Adam B. Schiff (D)	22.4	69	CA 36th: Raul Ruiz (D)	21.2
71	DC At Large: Eleanor Holmes Norton (D)	67 572	70	FL 13th: David W. Jolly (R)	22.4	69	MS 4th: Steven Palazzo (R)	21.2
72	CA 25th: Stephen Knight (R)	67 293	72	TX 13th: Mac Thornberry (R)	22.2	72	MA 7th: Michael E. Capuano (D)	21.0
73	CA 49th: Darrell E. Issa (R)	67 018	73	CA 16th: Jim Costa (D)	22.1	72	TX 16th: Beto O'Rourke (D)	21.0
74	MA 3rd: Niki Tsongas (D)	67 009	73	FL 14th: Kathy Castor (D)	22.1	74	CA 46th: Loretta Sanchez (D)	20.9
75	IL 11th: Bill Foster (D)	66 747	73	OK 5th: Steve Russell (R)	22.1	74	FL 2nd: Gwen Graham (D)	20.9

Table E. Congressional Districts 113th Congress — **Land Area and Population Characteristics**

STATE District	Representative, 114th Congress	Land area,[1] 2010 (sq km)	Population and population characteristics, 2013											
					Percent									
					Race alone									
			Total persons	Per square kilometer	White	Black	American Indian, Alaska Native	Asian and Pacific Islander	Some other race (percent)	Two or more races (percent)	Hispanic or Latino[2] (percent)	Non-Hispanic White alone (percent)	Percent female	Percent foreign-born	Percent born in state of residence
		1	2	3	4	5	6	7	8	9	10	11	12	13	14

1. Dry land or land partially or temporarily covered by water. 2. May be of any race.

Table E. Congressional Districts 113th Congress — **Age and Education**

STATE District	Population and population characteristics, 2013 (cont.)										Education, 2013		
	Age (percent)											Attainment[2] (percent)	
	Under 5 years	5 to 17 years	18 to 24 years	25 to 34 years	35 to 44 years	45 to 54 years	55 to 64 years	65 to 74 years	75 years and over	Median age	Total Enrollment[1]	High school graduate or more	Bachelor's degree or more
	15	16	17	18	19	20	21	22	23	24	25	26	27

1. All persons 3 years old and over enrolled in nursery school through college and graduate or professional school. 2. Persons 25 years old and over.

Table E. Congressional Districts 113th Congress — **Households and Group Quarters**

STATE District	Households, 2013						Total in group quarters, 2013	Group quarters, 2010				
	Number	Average household size	Family households (percent)	Married-couple family (percent)	Female family householder[1]	One person households (percent)		Percent 65 years and over	Persons in correctional institutions	Persons in nursing facilities	Persons in college dormitories	Persons in military quarters
	28	29	30	31	32	33	34	35	36	37	38	39

1. No spouse present.

Table E. Congressional Districts 113th Congress — **Housing and Money Income**

STATE District	Housing units, 2013						Money income, 2013		
	Total	Occupied units					Per capita income (dollars)	Households	
			Owner-occupied			Renter-occupied			
		Occupied units as a percent of all units	Owner-occupied units as a percent of occupied units	Median value[1] (dollars)	Percent valued at $500,000 or more	Median rent[2]		Median income (dollars)	Percent with income of $100,000 or more
	40	41	42	43	44	45	46	47	48

1. Specified owner-occupied units. 2. Specified renter-occupied units.

Table E. Congressional Districts 113th Congress — **Poverty, Labor Force, Employment, and Social Security**

STATE District	Poverty, 2013			Civilian labor force, 2013			Civilian employment,[2] 2013				Persons under age 65 with no health insurance, 2013 (percent)	Social Security beneficiaries, December 2013		Supple-mental Security Income recipients, December 2013
					Unemployment			Percent						
	Persons below poverty level (percent)	Families below poverty level (percent)	Percent of households receiving food stamps in past 12 months	Total	Total	Rate[1]	Total	Manage-ment, business, science and arts occupa-tions	Service, sales, and office	Con-struction and production		Number	Rate[3]	
	49	50	51	52	53	54	55	56	57	58	59	60	61	62

1. Percent of civilian labor force. 2. Persons 16 years old and over. 3. Per 1,000 resident population estimated in the 2013 American Community Survey.

Table E. Congressional Districts 113th Congress — **Agriculture**

STATE District	Agriculture, 2012									
		Land in farms			Value of products sold				Government payments	
	Number of farms	Acres	Average size of farm (acres)	Irrigated land (acres)	Total ($1,000)	Average per farm (dollars)	Percent from crops	Percent from livestock and poultry products	Total ($1,000)	Average per farm receiving payments (dollars)
	63	64	65	66	67	68	69	70	71	72

STATE District	Representative, 114th Congress	Land area,[1] 2010 (sq km)	Population and population characteristics, 2013: Total persons	Per square kilometer	Percent: Race alone: White	Black	American Indian, Alaska Native	Asian and Pacific Islander	Some other race (percent)	Two or more races (percent)	Hispanic or Latino[2] (percent)	Non-Hispanic White alone (percent)	Percent female	Percent foreign-born	Percent born in state of residence
		1	2	3	4	5	6	7	8	9	10	11	12	13	14
UNITED STATES....		9 147 593	316 128 839	34.6	73.7	12.6	0.8	5.2	4.7	3.0	17.1	62.4	50.8	13.1	58.8
ALABAMA		131 171	4 833 722	36.9	68.9	26.6	0.5	1.2	1.1	1.7	3.9	66.3	51.6	3.4	70.0
District 1	Bradley Byrne (R)	15 713	695 176	44.2	67.7	27.9	0.8	1.4	0.4	1.7	3.0	65.4	51.7	2.6	68.0
District 2	Martha Roby (R)	26 267	690 074	26.3	64.5	31.3	0.3	1.0	1.1	1.8	3.2	62.6	51.4	2.7	68.9
District 3	Mike Rogers (R)	19 539	697 761	35.7	69.6	25.6	0.2	1.6	1.4	1.6	2.7	68.3	51.1	3.0	65.8
District 4	Robert B. Aderholt (R)	23 022	685 175	29.8	88.7	7.3	0.9	0.7	0.8	1.7	6.2	83.8	51.3	4.1	74.8
District 5	Mo Brooks (R)	9 524	701 220	73.6	77.0	17.3	0.6	1.8	1.0	2.3	4.9	73.4	51.0	4.3	61.7
District 6	Gary J. Palmer (R)	10 802	697 436	64.6	79.7	14.9	0.3	1.6	1.9	1.5	5.0	76.7	51.4	4.4	70.9
District 7	Terri A. Sewell (D)	26 304	666 880	25.4	33.8	62.9	0.2	0.6	1.3	1.2	2.4	32.6	53.0	2.4	80.2
ALASKA		1 477 953	735 132	0.5	66.4	3.4	14.3	6.9	1.3	7.7	6.6	62.5	47.8	6.9	42.9
At Large.....................	Don Young (R)	1 477 953	735 132	0.5	66.4	3.4	14.3	6.9	1.3	7.7	6.6	62.5	47.8	6.9	42.9
ARIZONA		294 207	6 626 624	22.5	79.0	4.2	4.4	3.1	6.2	3.2	30.3	56.6	50.3	13.5	38.7
District 1	Ann Kirkpatrick (D)	142 552	723 969	5.1	66.3	2.1	23.2	1.5	3.5	3.4	21.4	50.4	49.8	6.2	51.4
District 2	Martha McSally (R)	20 301	717 970	35.4	79.7	4.1	1.3	3.2	7.4	4.2	26.5	62.5	50.6	11.3	35.8
District 3	Raul M. Grijalva (D)	40 634	722 963	17.8	76.0	4.7	4.0	1.7	10.8	2.8	61.3	28.1	49.9	21.4	46.5
District 4	Paul A. Gosar (R)	85 986	732 689	8.5	88.6	2.0	1.7	1.3	3.9	2.5	19.1	74.4	49.3	8.9	27.3
District 5	Matt Salmon (R)	760	759 102	998.8	85.4	3.1	1.0	5.6	2.2	2.9	16.9	71.9	51.1	10.3	36.2
District 6	David Schweikert (R)	1 619	737 884	455.8	86.1	3.1	1.4	4.0	2.5	3.0	15.8	73.6	50.8	12.9	31.3
District 7	Ruben Gallego (D)	531	749 222	1 411.0	66.3	9.8	3.0	2.1	15.6	3.3	64.6	20.1	49.1	26.5	47.6
District 8	Trent Franks (R)	1 398	741 374	530.3	86.4	3.6	1.2	3.2	2.3	3.2	18.4	71.4	51.8	9.6	34.4
District 9	Kyrsten Sinema (D)	427	741 451	1 736.4	75.9	5.1	2.7	5.1	7.6	3.6	28.4	56.6	49.9	14.4	37.8
ARKANSAS............		134 771	2 959 373	22.0	77.9	15.7	0.6	1.3	2.3	2.2	6.9	73.6	50.9	4.5	62.2
District 1	Eric A. "Rick" Crawford (R)	50 034	729 971	14.6	78.6	18.0	0.4	0.4	0.9	1.6	3.2	76.5	50.5	2.0	66.6
District 2	J. French Hill (R)	12 893	751 463	58.3	72.8	21.8	0.3	1.4	1.1	2.7	5.0	69.3	51.4	3.9	68.0
District 3	Steve Womack (R)	13 988	757 765	54.2	85.1	3.4	1.1	2.9	4.4	3.0	13.6	76.2	50.5	9.1	49.5
District 4	Bruce Westerman (R)	57 855	720 174	12.4	75.0	19.8	0.6	0.6	2.5	1.5	5.4	72.4	51.0	2.9	64.9
CALIFORNIA..........		403 466	38 332 521	95.0	61.9	5.9	0.7	14.0	12.9	4.5	38.4	38.8	50.3	26.9	54.7
District 1	Doug LaMalfa (R)	72 751	707 992	9.7	86.5	1.4	1.6	2.9	3.1	4.4	12.9	78.1	49.7	6.7	68.9
District 2	Jared Huffman (D)	33 546	713 816	21.3	80.2	1.5	2.0	3.8	8.0	4.4	17.8	71.2	50.3	13.4	59.1
District 3	John Garamendi (D)	16 015	714 407	44.6	65.2	6.6	1.1	10.9	10.3	5.9	28.8	48.9	49.8	18.8	60.0
District 4	Tom McClintock (R)	33 246	703 377	21.2	85.2	1.3	1.0	4.7	3.0	4.8	12.3	77.4	50.1	8.9	64.8
District 5	Mike Thompson (D)	4 483	715 332	159.6	67.2	6.0	1.1	11.1	9.4	5.2	27.0	52.3	51.1	20.5	59.9
District 6	Doris O. Matsui (D)	453	729 428	1 610.2	53.6	12.3	0.7	17.1	9.0	7.2	27.1	38.4	51.2	23.6	59.6
District 7	Ami Bera (D)	1 421	721 042	507.4	66.1	7.5	0.8	15.3	3.9	6.5	17.2	55.1	50.9	18.3	60.5
District 8	Paul Cook (R)	85 126	709 384	8.3	75.5	8.2	1.4	2.8	7.3	4.8	39.9	46.8	50.0	12.2	65.3
District 9	Jerry McNerney (D)	3 225	724 907	224.8	54.5	8.5	0.6	14.9	13.2	8.2	37.4	35.9	50.7	23.0	63.0
District 10	Jeff Denham (R)	4 711	722 266	153.3	70.6	3.2	0.5	7.2	12.9	5.5	41.8	44.4	50.0	19.4	66.3
District 11	Mark Desaulnier (D)	1 278	733 916	574.3	62.7	8.9	0.5	13.1	9.3	5.6	26.4	47.0	51.3	24.4	54.1
District 12	Nancy Pelosi (D)	101	734 662	7 273.9	50.4	5.7	0.5	32.1	6.8	4.5	15.5	42.9	48.9	33.8	38.4
District 13	Barbara Lee (D)	251	732 753	2 919.3	44.9	18.5	0.7	21.4	7.9	6.6	21.4	33.8	51.1	26.8	49.7
District 14	Jackie Speier (D)	672	721 245	1 073.3	48.9	3.3	0.3	33.6	8.9	5.0	24.1	35.7	50.8	36.7	47.2
District 15	Eric Swalwell (D)	1 553	734 837	473.2	48.7	5.8	0.6	31.0	7.5	6.3	23.8	35.3	51.0	32.8	51.2
District 16	Jim Costa (D)	7 354	715 257	97.3	57.0	6.1	1.1	9.5	22.1	4.2	59.5	23.5	50.1	24.4	64.6
District 17	Michael M. Honda (D)	479	732 118	1 528.4	33.2	2.9	0.4	52.2	6.6	4.8	15.6	26.3	49.8	46.1	39.6
District 18	Anna G. Eshoo (D)	1 803	731 201	405.5	68.1	1.6	0.2	20.5	4.8	4.8	17.0	56.7	49.8	27.6	48.2
District 19	Zoe Lofgren (D)	2 371	746 071	314.7	43.9	3.6	0.7	27.2	19.8	4.9	41.7	25.3	49.9	37.2	49.8
District 20	Sam Farr (D)	12 624	725 199	57.4	78.2	2.0	0.8	5.8	9.2	3.9	52.0	37.7	49.4	25.6	57.8
District 21	David G. Valadao (R)	17 430	711 414	40.8	71.5	4.3	0.8	3.5	16.8	3.0	72.5	18.2	46.7	29.4	60.7
District 22	Devin Nunes (R)	3 018	730 271	242.0	75.6	3.3	1.1	8.1	8.1	3.8	45.8	40.9	50.7	18.5	67.5
District 23	Kevin McCarthy (R)	25 636	726 292	28.3	76.6	5.8	1.1	5.0	8.3	3.3	38.2	48.3	49.3	14.0	67.2
District 24	Lois Capps (D)	17 828	722 008	40.5	72.7	2.0	0.9	4.7	15.9	3.8	35.2	55.8	49.5	18.4	59.7
District 25	Stephen Knight (R)	4 378	716 815	163.7	65.4	7.9	0.7	7.8	13.4	4.8	36.6	44.4	49.8	20.8	60.8
District 26	Julia Brownley (D)	2 432	712 804	293.1	78.7	1.8	0.6	7.1	7.3	4.4	44.7	43.9	50.2	24.0	55.9
District 27	Judy Chu (D)	1 813	716 835	395.4	40.9	4.7	0.3	38.6	12.3	3.2	27.2	27.4	51.4	38.4	47.0
District 28	Adam B. Schiff (D)	566	708 212	1 251.3	67.9	2.9	0.3	13.1	12.0	3.8	25.2	55.8	50.1	40.7	36.9
District 29	Tony Cárdenas (D)	238	692 267	2 908.7	58.5	4.1	0.5	8.3	26.2	2.3	68.7	17.8	50.0	44.6	45.6
District 30	Brad Sherman (D)	352	744 617	2 115.4	65.6	4.1	0.3	12.5	12.5	5.1	30.6	49.6	50.5	33.0	46.4
District 31	Pete Aguilar (D)	565	725 024	1 283.2	63.7	11.2	0.7	7.6	13.0	3.8	51.6	28.5	50.3	21.2	63.4
District 32	Grace F. Napolitano (D)	322	706 167	2 193.1	49.9	3.3	0.7	17.1	25.3	3.8	61.7	16.5	50.9	34.6	56.4
District 33	Ted Lieu (D)	747	717 954	961.1	74.5	2.8	0.2	14.2	3.6	4.7	12.9	66.3	51.8	23.7	45.6
District 34	Xavier Becerra (D)	123	712 425	5 792.1	37.8	4.4	1.0	18.8	35.5	2.6	65.9	9.8	48.4	48.8	41.7
District 35	Norma J. Torres (D)	437	728 298	1 666.6	56.3	7.4	0.6	7.7	23.7	4.4	67.5	15.5	50.2	30.5	59.9
District 36	Raul Ruiz (D)	15 314	722 653	47.2	67.4	4.2	1.0	3.1	20.4	3.9	47.6	43.1	49.7	21.7	54.8
District 37	Karen Bass (D)	143	732 610	5 123.1	42.4	23.0	0.6	9.5	20.7	3.8	38.8	26.3	51.7	31.2	47.5

1. Dry land or land partially or temporarily covered by water. 2. May be of any race.

Table E. Congressional Districts 113th Congress — **Age and Education**

STATE District	Population and population characteristics, 2013 (cont.)										Education, 2013		
	Age (percent)											Attainment[2] (percent)	
	Under 5 years	5 to 17 years	18 to 24 years	25 to 34 years	35 to 44 years	45 to 54 years	55 to 64 years	65 to 74 years	75 years and over	Median age	Total Enrollment[1]	High school graduate or more	Bachelor's degree or more
	15	16	17	18	19	20	21	22	23	24	25	26	27
UNITED STATES	6.3	17.0	10.0	13.5	12.8	13.8	12.5	8.0	6.2	37.5	82 395 254	86.6	29.6
ALABAMA	6.0	16.9	10.3	12.7	12.6	13.7	12.8	8.7	6.2	38.3	1 209 237	84.5	23.5
District 1	6.2	17.4	9.4	12.6	12.2	13.5	13.1	9.1	6.4	38.5	167 025	86.7	22.8
District 2	6.0	17.5	9.9	13.1	12.5	13.5	12.5	8.7	6.3	37.9	178 199	83.8	20.4
District 3	6.0	16.2	12.2	12.5	12.7	13.1	13.0	8.7	5.7	37.4	180 610	83.2	21.0
District 4	6.0	16.8	8.8	11.8	12.8	13.8	13.3	9.9	6.8	40.3	152 854	80.2	15.9
District 5	5.9	16.7	10.1	12.5	12.5	14.9	12.7	8.5	6.2	38.7	173 707	85.8	29.6
District 6	5.9	18.0	8.2	13.2	14.0	13.8	12.6	8.5	5.9	38.7	179 495	89.3	34.8
District 7	6.4	15.8	13.7	13.1	11.4	13.0	12.9	7.4	6.3	35.7	177 347	82.5	19.0
ALASKA	7.4	18.2	11.4	15.6	12.3	13.8	12.6	5.9	3.1	33.1	200 784	91.6	28.0
At Large	7.4	18.2	11.4	15.6	12.3	13.8	12.6	5.9	3.1	33.1	200 784	91.6	28.0
ARIZONA	6.5	17.9	10.0	13.2	12.6	12.6	11.7	8.9	6.5	36.8	1 739 889	85.9	27.4
District 1	6.5	18.2	10.8	12.3	11.8	11.5	12.7	9.9	6.2	36.5	194 785	85.1	22.8
District 2	5.8	14.8	10.9	12.9	11.1	12.3	12.9	10.3	8.7	40.2	173 043	89.6	32.6
District 3	6.9	20.7	13.4	13.5	12.6	11.9	10.5	6.5	4.0	31.7	219 874	75.1	15.2
District 4	5.4	15.9	6.8	10.4	10.6	12.4	14.6	14.5	9.6	46.1	154 888	86.4	17.3
District 5	7.4	20.0	7.5	11.9	14.3	13.2	10.7	8.0	7.0	37.3	210 319	92.3	35.1
District 6	5.2	15.8	8.2	13.3	12.8	14.7	13.8	9.9	6.5	41.2	172 199	93.2	41.6
District 7	8.7	23.0	12.2	16.3	14.3	11.5	7.8	4.0	2.4	28.4	221 306	66.6	13.2
District 8	5.9	17.0	7.4	11.3	12.4	12.6	12.2	11.7	9.5	42.0	179 896	91.6	28.5
District 9	6.5	15.5	13.3	17.6	13.3	13.1	10.5	5.6	4.5	32.9	213 579	88.3	36.0
ARKANSAS	6.4	17.6	9.7	13.0	12.4	13.2	12.4	8.8	6.5	37.8	750 149	84.4	20.6
District 1	6.2	17.4	8.8	12.2	12.3	13.4	12.9	9.6	7.2	39.3	177 600	81.4	15.1
District 2	6.5	17.3	10.0	14.7	12.4	13.0	12.0	8.2	5.9	36.4	193 534	88.1	27.0
District 3	7.1	18.3	11.0	13.8	12.7	12.5	11.4	7.6	5.6	34.9	204 166	83.7	25.1
District 4	5.9	17.5	8.9	11.1	12.2	13.6	13.4	9.9	7.4	40.7	174 849	84.4	15.2
CALIFORNIA	6.5	17.4	10.5	14.6	13.4	13.6	11.5	7.0	5.5	35.7	10 548 455	81.7	31.0
District 1	5.0	15.3	10.7	11.1	10.5	13.3	15.0	10.7	8.2	42.4	171 913	88.1	22.6
District 2	5.4	15.1	8.1	11.1	12.8	14.3	15.9	10.2	7.2	43.1	168 461	90.4	38.7
District 3	6.5	18.0	13.2	13.1	12.2	13.0	11.5	7.2	5.3	34.4	214 935	83.5	23.8
District 4	5.0	16.3	7.8	10.5	11.7	14.6	15.4	11.2	7.6	43.8	164 609	92.8	31.8
District 5	5.6	15.4	9.6	13.4	12.2	14.4	14.1	8.9	6.4	40.2	179 916	86.5	29.5
District 6	7.4	17.6	10.7	16.8	12.8	12.5	11.0	6.2	5.1	33.5	203 234	83.4	25.4
District 7	6.2	18.2	8.8	13.3	13.5	14.3	12.2	7.7	6.0	37.8	204 184	90.0	31.6
District 8	7.4	19.7	10.3	14.3	11.5	13.0	11.7	7.2	5.0	33.7	195 028	83.1	14.4
District 9	7.1	20.7	10.3	12.6	12.8	13.0	11.3	7.1	5.0	34.5	215 485	79.4	19.0
District 10	7.4	20.6	10.4	13.8	13.0	13.3	10.4	6.3	4.6	33.4	209 513	79.1	16.5
District 11	6.0	16.7	8.7	13.2	13.1	14.5	13.0	8.3	6.6	39.3	184 173	87.5	41.0
District 12	4.7	8.6	7.2	23.5	16.7	13.5	11.6	7.3	6.7	38.4	140 395	86.9	54.1
District 13	5.6	13.8	11.0	17.1	14.7	13.2	12.1	7.1	5.5	36.7	198 767	85.1	44.7
District 14	5.7	14.4	8.6	14.2	14.5	14.4	13.5	7.8	7.0	39.7	182 554	89.0	43.7
District 15	6.7	17.7	8.1	13.4	14.9	14.9	12.4	7.0	5.0	37.9	190 613	88.4	40.4
District 16	9.2	22.2	11.5	15.3	11.8	11.5	9.1	5.5	4.0	29.6	222 975	66.4	12.4
District 17	6.3	15.9	8.2	16.7	16.1	15.0	10.8	6.3	4.7	36.5	188 737	91.1	54.3
District 18	5.5	17.3	7.5	12.6	14.8	16.3	12.1	7.6	6.2	40.3	193 716	93.2	60.0
District 19	7.1	17.6	9.7	15.0	15.0	13.3	11.1	6.1	5.0	35.3	209 178	78.8	31.0
District 20	7.3	18.1	12.6	14.0	12.6	12.3	11.5	6.5	5.1	33.6	214 377	76.6	25.8
District 21	8.8	23.1	12.1	15.6	13.1	11.5	7.9	4.5	3.3	28.5	223 469	59.0	8.3
District 22	7.8	20.3	11.0	13.8	12.5	12.2	10.6	6.5	5.2	32.8	215 677	78.7	23.6
District 23	7.5	19.7	10.2	13.9	12.4	13.4	11.3	6.8	4.7	33.9	209 084	81.5	18.2
District 24	5.8	14.9	15.8	12.5	11.2	12.3	12.4	8.1	6.8	35.9	212 735	82.9	32.0
District 25	7.0	20.6	9.7	11.9	13.0	15.5	11.6	6.7	4.0	35.7	215 788	84.5	27.2
District 26	6.6	18.4	10.5	13.2	12.6	14.0	12.1	7.1	5.6	36.2	198 901	81.8	31.6
District 27	4.4	15.3	9.1	13.7	13.3	14.6	13.3	8.5	7.7	41.0	186 804	85.1	41.5
District 28	4.8	11.1	8.0	19.1	15.9	14.0	12.8	7.4	6.8	39.2	146 901	85.9	11.6
District 29	6.7	18.1	11.4	16.6	15.1	13.3	9.8	5.2	3.7	33.0	192 779	65.7	18.3
District 30	5.9	15.0	9.1	14.7	14.6	14.1	12.7	7.5	6.3	38.9	186 866	87.7	39.9
District 31	7.9	19.7	12.0	14.9	13.6	12.4	10.2	5.5	3.9	31.8	223 946	79.7	23.9
District 32	6.1	17.6	11.3	14.8	12.5	13.9	11.1	6.9	5.7	35.1	204 148	74.7	19.8
District 33	5.3	13.7	9.4	13.9	13.9	15.6	12.2	8.3	7.8	40.8	181 816	95.5	61.6
District 34	6.4	15.6	11.5	18.6	15.6	12.5	9.5	5.8	4.4	33.7	185 508	61.7	22.4
District 35	7.2	20.9	12.7	14.7	13.7	13.1	9.4	5.0	3.4	31.1	230 853	69.0	14.9
District 36	6.9	18.1	8.4	12.4	11.6	12.1	11.3	10.4	8.8	38.6	176 340	78.8	20.5
District 37	6.4	14.6	11.6	18.0	14.5	13.2	10.3	6.3	5.1	34.6	197 080	79.5	36.9

1. All persons 3 years old and over enrolled in nursery school through college and graduate or professional school. 2. Persons 25 years old and over.

STATE District	Households, 2013							Group quarters, 2010				
	Number	Average household size	Family households (percent)	Married-couple family (percent)	Female family householder[1]	One person households (percent)	Total in group quarters, 2013	Percent 65 years and over	Persons in correctional institutions	Persons in nursing facilities	Persons in college dormitories	Persons in military quarters
	28	29	30	31	32	33	34	35	36	37	38	39
UNITED STATES	116 291 033	2.65	65.90	48.0	13.1	27.7	8 029 670	18.3	2 263 602	1 502 264	2 521 090	338 191
ALABAMA	1 822 439	2.59	67.10	47.1	15.6	29.0	115 032	18.7	41 177	22 995	36 341	2 152
District 1	248 388	2.74	67.80	47.7	15.7	28.5	15 693	19.1	5 651	2 671	2 579	0
District 2	262 483	2.55	66.00	45.8	16.1	30.1	19 884	15.4	13 081	3 727	3 107	1 274
District 3	265 548	2.56	67.30	46.5	16.1	27.5	19 087	15.9	7 014	3 016	6 949	0
District 4	258 120	2.63	71.50	53.0	13.5	25.7	7 566	39.0	2 922	3 652	791	0
District 5	274 535	2.50	67.10	49.3	13.2	29.4	15 986	17.5	5 087	2 879	5 347	823
District 6	260 766	2.63	69.60	54.5	11.9	27.0	12 056	23.8	4 884	2 733	2 830	0
District 7	252 599	2.54	60.20	32.3	23.0	34.7	24 760	15.1	2 538	4 317	14 738	55
ALASKA	246 015	2.88	67.20	51.4	10.1	25.5	26 599	5.9	4 206	1 626	1 872	5 055
At Large	246 015	2.88	67.20	51.4	10.1	25.5	26 599	5.9	4 206	1 626	1 872	5 055
ARIZONA	2 400 809	2.70	65.50	47.3	12.8	27.6	147 624	12.2	67 767	13 819	27 987	5 172
District 1	245 956	2.82	69.50	49.7	13.8	24.6	29 401	4.2	15 071	816	7 630	0
District 2	296 069	2.34	59.80	43.0	11.9	32.8	25 095	19.9	7 538	2 914	118	3 352
District 3	233 031	3.00	71.00	46.0	18.1	22.3	24 447	5.3	11 711	863	6 913	0
District 4	285 071	2.48	66.10	52.6	9.3	28.1	26 184	6.9	19 869	1 431	1 213	1 164
District 5	263 546	2.87	72.70	58.3	9.7	22.9	2 988	55.3	11	859	346	0
District 6	296 494	2.47	62.00	47.0	9.8	30.3	4 726	53.4	10	1 594	274	0
District 7	216 600	3.41	66.60	36.5	21.9	25.4	10 116	5.2	8 915	840	1 162	0
District 8	278 419	2.62	68.90	54.6	10.1	26.2	11 026	30.5	4 624	2 809	861	656
District 9	285 623	2.55	55.60	37.2	13.3	32.7	13 641	12.2	18	1 693	9 470	0
ARKANSAS	1 125 899	2.56	66.70	48.7	13.3	27.9	81 170	21.7	25 844	18 532	24 144	619
District 1	281 364	2.49	67.70	47.8	14.5	27.7	28 048	20.6	15 495	5 770	2 669	0
District 2	279 618	2.63	64.40	47.1	13.1	29.9	15 956	20.1	3 461	3 521	6 184	616
District 3	281 842	2.63	67.50	52.1	11.1	25.6	16 536	21.3	1 599	3 663	9 499	0
District 4	283 075	2.47	67.30	47.9	14.7	28.4	20 630	24.7	5 289	5 578	5 792	3
CALIFORNIA	12 650 592	2.97	68.30	48.7	13.7	24.3	806 174	15.4	256 807	111 884	172 843	57 628
District 1	271 790	2.52	62.50	47.2	11.2	29.4	23 555	14.1	11 908	2 834	2 728	5
District 2	277 735	2.50	61.00	46.7	9.9	30.1	20 091	13.5	9 975	2 246	2 645	393
District 3	239 633	2.89	68.70	50.4	12.5	23.7	22 364	9.1	12 154	1 728	4 981	1 321
District 4	266 965	2.58	68.40	56.6	8.3	25.6	13 673	15.3	8 633	1 677	458	0
District 5	261 333	2.69	64.40	46.0	12.8	26.9	12 388	22.6	1 940	3 657	3 581	0
District 6	260 198	2.76	61.10	38.9	15.8	29.7	10 104	19.4	2 254	1 789	1 493	0
District 7	257 540	2.75	69.60	49.1	14.3	23.7	12 514	23.1	6 682	1 704	22	0
District 8	225 136	3.09	72.80	50.4	15.6	22.4	14 665	10.8	6 717	1 325	117	4 748
District 9	224 464	3.17	75.30	51.9	17.7	20.2	13 189	21.5	1 358	2 403	2 194	0
District 10	226 317	3.15	75.00	51.9	15.7	19.3	9 413	24.1	4 848	2 580	584	0
District 11	265 358	2.73	68.90	50.5	12.5	24.5	8 923	35.3	865	3 004	1 568	0
District 12	321 110	2.24	42.50	31.4	7.8	39.6	16 500	18.3	1 573	2 810	5 993	0
District 13	280 846	2.54	55.70	37.2	13.2	32.4	20 709	13.2	1 044	2 600	11 927	661
District 14	249 155	2.85	68.00	52.3	10.5	24.2	10 971	29.2	1 090	1 939	2 487	0
District 15	240 034	3.01	74.10	57.1	11.7	20.8	11 815	23.6	5 669	2 136	1 076	0
District 16	205 264	3.38	74.90	44.6	22.0	19.8	21 658	11.0	12 113	2 113	1 443	0
District 17	246 583	2.93	72.50	59.6	9.1	20.6	9 583	20.8	2 564	1 666	2 592	0
District 18	269 197	2.66	68.40	56.5	7.6	24.3	15 065	24.9	4	2 889	6 712	5
District 19	222 742	3.29	75.00	53.8	14.1	18.1	12 550	11.7	1 448	916	3 356	0
District 20	221 689	3.14	68.40	50.2	12.9	23.3	30 175	8.9	11 516	2 072	8 411	2 504
District 21	179 503	3.72	81.60	50.0	22.2	15.0	44 281	4.1	44 549	1 252	239	2 038
District 22	235 463	3.07	73.60	50.9	15.6	21.3	7 960	28.5	1 349	1 709	1 566	0
District 23	239 071	2.96	70.80	50.5	14.0	23.0	18 896	9.1	17 160	2 293	560	329
District 24	249 899	2.75	64.00	49.1	9.9	25.9	36 034	7.2	11 387	1 805	15 714	475
District 25	223 651	3.15	77.00	56.9	14.3	18.3	11 818	5.7	7 129	251	1 775	0
District 26	222 462	3.15	73.20	55.4	12.3	20.4	11 831	18.2	1 535	1 644	2 316	1 349
District 27	244 187	2.88	70.30	51.2	13.3	23.8	13 688	25.4	331	3 659	5 809	0
District 28	294 206	2.37	51.50	36.7	10.1	37.8	10 062	32.8	183	3 356	647	0
District 29	197 344	3.47	71.80	44.7	18.0	20.5	6 527	35.7	307	2 842	151	0
District 30	269 268	2.73	63.40	45.6	12.0	27.4	9 959	41.0	20	2 996	2 746	0
District 31	212 481	3.31	73.00	46.3	18.6	22.0	22 026	15.4	5 464	2 391	2 739	0
District 32	192 446	3.61	79.20	52.6	17.8	16.0	11 635	29.1	74	2 895	3 298	0
District 33	301 385	2.31	54.10	43.6	7.0	36.1	20 319	11.2	98	1 851	14 107	0
District 34	232 312	2.96	60.60	34.8	17.4	29.9	24 396	11.7	8 722	3 270	2 438	0
District 35	184 712	3.85	77.60	51.6	17.5	18.0	16 933	11.5	6 996	2 041	1 948	0
District 36	254 442	2.79	66.10	47.9	13.3	27.7	12 756	16.9	9 107	1 504	70	0
District 37	265 643	2.70	56.80	33.8	16.5	32.6	14 611	14.0	155	2 263	7 976	0

1. No spouse present.

STATE District	Housing units, 2013						Money income, 2013		
		Occupied units						Households	
			Owner-occupied			Renter-occupied			
	Total	Occupied units as a percent of all units	Owner-occupied units as a percent of occupied units	Median value[1] (dollars)	Percent valued at $500,000 or more	Median rent[2]	Per capita income (dollars)	Median income (dollars)	Percent with income of $100,000 or more
	40	41	42	43	44	45	46	47	48
UNITED STATES	132 808 137	87.6	63.5	173 900	10.2	905	28 184	52 250	22.6
ALABAMA	2 190 027	83.2	68.0	122 700	2.9	694	23 384	42 849	15.7
District 1	326 125	76.2	67.7	130 700	3.1	761	21 946	42 309	14.9
District 2	310 496	84.5	65.5	112 400	1.6	694	21 997	41 862	13.5
District 3	318 694	83.3	68.7	111 700	2.3	656	22 338	40 990	13.9
District 4	310 413	83.2	73.4	102 600	2.0	581	20 508	39 993	11.7
District 5	307 189	89.4	68.9	141 500	3.2	671	27 396	49 974	21.1
District 6	295 253	88.3	74.3	169 900	6.5	876	30 642	57 367	24.5
District 7	321 857	78.5	57.5	87 200	1.3	676	18 559	31 953	10.1
ALASKA	307 417	80.0	63.5	254 000	7.0	1 117	32 474	72 237	33.1
At Large	307 417	80.0	63.5	254 000	7.0	1 117	32 474	72 237	33.1
ARIZONA	2 892 359	83.0	62.1	166 000	6.6	890	25 164	48 510	18.9
District 1	327 095	75.2	66.9	152 800	6.3	871	22 119	46 894	16.3
District 2	343 355	86.2	60.7	164 600	5.8	815	26 864	45 176	17.5
District 3	266 994	87.3	60.5	108 300	1.7	825	17 422	39 843	11.2
District 4	386 637	73.7	69.7	145 400	3.6	851	22 446	43 436	11.7
District 5	308 174	85.5	73.0	203 900	5.6	1 080	29 333	65 288	29.3
District 6	353 615	83.8	63.9	265 500	20.9	983	38 503	61 200	29.4
District 7	254 520	85.1	42.5	105 200	1.3	795	13 798	32 372	8.3
District 8	328 064	84.9	70.7	178 800	3.3	1 055	27 686	56 025	21.8
District 9	323 905	88.2	47.3	196 500	7.5	878	28 143	49 487	20.7
ARKANSAS	1 329 777	84.7	65.7	109 500	2.1	659	21 927	40 511	13.3
District 1	335 806	83.8	64.5	89 200	1.3	597	19 439	35 993	10.5
District 2	331 742	84.3	66.4	132 100	2.7	741	24 870	46 493	16.7
District 3	320 134	88.0	62.6	132 700	3.1	682	23 476	44 405	16.0
District 4	342 095	82.7	69.4	85 400	1.4	617	19 749	35 470	10.1
CALIFORNIA	13 791 262	91.7	53.8	373 100	34.1	1 224	29 513	60 190	28.7
District 1	320 474	84.8	64.8	227 600	9.2	882	24 596	44 689	16.8
District 2	319 742	86.9	62.5	471 800	47.2	1 214	39 830	62 176	31.8
District 3	261 538	91.6	56.8	237 600	11.4	1 109	24 852	54 398	23.4
District 4	350 509	76.2	70.6	326 900	20.1	1 170	32 985	63 712	30.3
District 5	284 588	91.8	59.0	345 200	24.4	1 254	31 786	62 432	28.6
District 6	283 368	91.8	45.5	204 500	7.5	963	22 743	45 584	17.6
District 7	273 331	94.2	61.6	265 200	10.5	1 093	29 687	60 735	27.4
District 8	305 316	73.7	61.1	159 800	4.0	973	19 687	45 976	16.5
District 9	244 230	91.9	59.3	226 500	9.9	1 004	22 980	52 739	24.3
District 10	242 477	93.3	57.6	200 000	5.3	1 014	23 179	52 992	22.2
District 11	280 933	94.5	61.7	471 500	47.1	1 332	39 655	73 860	37.1
District 12	345 956	92.8	32.7	797 400	84.5	1 480	53 403	77 577	41.1
District 13	301 497	93.2	43.1	503 500	50.3	1 210	36 060	60 417	30.0
District 14	261 571	95.3	59.9	705 200	79.2	1 680	42 155	85 706	43.1
District 15	249 805	96.1	61.9	536 600	54.7	1 470	36 626	86 818	43.1
District 16	223 069	92.0	46.6	141 300	4.1	830	15 112	36 190	10.7
District 17	256 842	96.0	54.9	657 000	70.8	1 778	42 409	100 282	50.3
District 18	282 284	95.4	61.2	916 400	84.7	1 670	58 296	105 817	52.7
District 19	228 926	97.3	57.4	544 800	56.1	1 467	32 168	78 169	39.6
District 20	245 427	90.3	51.0	407 700	39.2	1 246	25 237	59 131	26.7
District 21	194 290	92.4	47.4	141 400	3.6	770	13 870	36 777	11.1
District 22	250 934	93.8	56.8	204 800	6.6	931	22 607	50 389	20.1
District 23	269 729	88.6	57.7	178 100	3.5	949	23 169	52 207	21.4
District 24	277 128	90.2	53.5	438 000	42.6	1 271	30 876	60 796	28.1
District 25	240 051	93.2	67.6	334 800	22.5	1 346	28 920	67 293	33.1
District 26	237 714	93.6	62.1	442 000	40.5	1 529	32 858	76 679	37.8
District 27	261 652	93.3	55.7	557 800	57.9	1 276	32 994	68 053	32.8
District 28	314 042	93.7	33.2	637 500	66.6	1 243	38 293	52 887	26.5
District 29	207 749	95.0	40.9	342 800	12.3	1 122	18 348	45 233	16.4
District 30	282 541	95.3	51.1	503 200	50.4	1 401	36 169	67 819	33.0
District 31	229 671	92.5	53.8	260 400	12.0	1 105	21 977	52 503	22.8
District 32	204 727	94.0	58.7	355 700	16.0	1 206	20 750	55 839	23.5
District 33	328 790	91.7	47.8	947 000	85.5	1 785	61 317	90 541	46.3
District 34	249 169	93.2	20.4	390 700	29.0	978	18 604	34 752	12.6
District 35	196 906	93.8	59.2	254 400	4.3	1 165	18 062	54 425	18.4
District 36	343 756	74.0	63.3	184 200	10.9	983	23 762	42 939	17.6
District 37	283 474	93.7	35.3	534 100	53.3	1 255	29 617	50 127	24.1

1. Specified owner-occupied units. 2. Specified renter-occupied units.

STATE District	Poverty, 2013			Civilian labor force, 2013			Civilian employment,[2] 2013				Persons under age 65 with no health insurance, 2013 (percent)	Social Security beneficiaries, December 2013		Supplemental Security Income recipients, December 2013
	Persons below poverty level (percent)	Families below poverty level (percent)	Percent of households receiving food stamps in past 12 months	Total	Unemployment Total	Unemployment Rate[1]	Total	Percent Management, business, science and arts occupations	Percent Service, sales, and office	Percent Construction and production		Number	Rate[3]	
	49	50	51	52	53	54	55	56	57	58	59	60	61	62
UNITED STATES	15.8	11.6	13.5	158 498 347	13 369 671	8.4	145 128 676	36.3	42.6	21.1	16.7	56 480 451	178.7	8 362 414
ALABAMA	18.7	14.3	15.5	2 225 202	214 268	9.6	2 010 934	33.3	41.0	25.7	15.8	1 081 046	223.6	176 562
District 1	19.8	15.7	17.2	315 741	35 769	11.3	279 972	31.1	44.3	24.6	17.9	157 874	227.1	22 652
District 2	19.6	15.8	16.0	313 876	29 884	9.5	283 992	29.9	42.3	27.8	15.3	153 864	223.0	27 335
District 3	19.9	14.5	16.0	316 436	31 737	10.0	284 699	31.7	40.5	27.9	15.2	158 288	226.9	25 244
District 4	17.5	13.2	15.4	297 879	28 388	9.5	269 491	29.2	37.6	33.2	17.9	177 906	259.7	25 948
District 5	15.8	12.0	12.0	343 823	31 393	9.1	312 430	38.5	37.7	23.8	15.5	141 969	202.5	16 909
District 6	11.5	8.4	8.1	338 937	19 303	5.7	319 634	41.4	40.3	18.3	11.6	137 469	197.1	13 500
District 7	27.6	21.7	24.5	298 510	37 794	12.7	260 716	29.4	44.5	26.2	17.6	153 676	230.4	44 974
ALASKA	9.3	5.9	9.8	386 509	33 687	8.7	352 822	35.8	40.7	23.4	20.3	86 861	118.2	12 689
At Large	9.3	5.9	9.8	386 509	33 687	8.7	352 822	35.8	40.7	23.4	20.3	86 861	118.2	12 689
ARIZONA	18.6	13.6	13.5	3 065 156	273 610	8.9	2 791 546	35.1	46.2	18.7	20.1	1 174 944	177.3	118 216
District 1	22.3	16.4	16.0	302 344	36 250	12.0	266 094	33.3	43.6	23.1	20.0	137 407	189.8	19 436
District 2	17.1	11.8	12.7	335 092	30 873	9.2	304 219	37.8	46.7	15.5	15.9	155 904	217.1	13 128
District 3	23.4	18.4	22.5	330 341	40 716	12.3	289 625	26.0	47.0	26.9	23.8	100 906	139.6	18 458
District 4	17.4	12.0	12.0	287 401	30 629	10.7	256 772	28.8	48.9	22.2	21.0	192 089	262.2	11 786
District 5	9.1	6.5	6.9	360 428	20 916	5.8	339 512	43.4	41.7	14.9	13.0	119 909	158.0	5 645
District 6	11.2	8.4	7.1	389 569	26 972	6.9	362 597	43.6	45.5	11.0	15.6	132 306	179.3	8 010
District 7	37.0	32.4	30.3	319 800	37 671	11.8	282 129	20.3	50.0	29.6	33.8	77 526	103.5	23 670
District 8	11.1	7.5	7.1	324 635	19 715	6.1	304 920	36.3	47.2	16.4	15.4	160 943	217.1	7 784
District 9	19.4	14.2	12.4	415 546	29 868	7.2	385 678	39.9	45.7	14.4	20.4	97 954	132.1	10 299
ARKANSAS	19.7	14.5	15.3	1 351 145	109 317	8.1	1 241 828	31.9	41.0	27.1	18.8	666 172	225.1	112 741
District 1	21.6	16.2	19.9	315 393	31 412	10.0	283 981	29.2	40.0	30.8	20.8	182 719	250.3	36 328
District 2	15.8	11.0	11.8	367 199	25 781	7.0	341 418	35.6	43.9	20.5	17.1	152 384	202.8	27 043
District 3	19.0	13.3	11.6	356 896	22 469	6.3	334 427	33.2	40.3	26.4	18.0	146 466	193.3	17 826
District 4	22.6	17.3	17.9	311 657	29 655	9.5	282 002	28.6	39.3	32.2	19.4	184 603	256.3	31 544
CALIFORNIA	16.8	12.6	9.4	19 046 186	1 913 490	10.0	17 132 696	36.9	42.8	20.3	19.4	5 414 499	141.3	1 304 222
District 1	18.6	11.9	10.5	303 127	30 799	10.2	272 328	33.2	46.5	20.3	17.7	177 561	250.8	33 326
District 2	13.7	8.6	6.4	357 703	31 274	8.7	326 429	42.5	40.8	16.7	15.7	138 679	194.3	19 568
District 3	16.3	11.3	10.0	327 411	37 716	11.5	289 695	32.8	42.8	24.3	17.2	119 520	167.3	24 993
District 4	11.1	7.7	5.9	332 283	34 398	10.4	297 885	38.3	44.9	16.7	13.3	160 779	228.6	13 850
District 5	13.0	8.9	8.4	375 894	35 337	9.4	340 557	34.8	45.0	20.1	16.2	138 502	193.6	19 955
District 6	24.1	20.6	17.7	348 997	46 224	13.2	302 773	33.7	47.4	19.0	19.8	102 958	141.1	42 768
District 7	13.9	9.4	9.6	350 414	39 982	11.4	310 432	41.5	43.3	15.1	14.4	112 878	156.5	23 376
District 8	21.8	17.4	17.0	288 343	37 748	13.1	250 595	27.5	46.7	25.8	19.2	129 205	182.1	33 032
District 9	19.8	15.6	13.4	331 304	42 124	12.7	289 180	27.7	44.6	27.6	18.7	119 416	164.7	33 220
District 10	19.1	14.9	14.3	346 015	49 882	14.4	296 133	27.0	43.3	29.7	19.3	100 677	139.4	25 124
District 11	11.9	8.5	7.1	375 369	35 131	9.4	340 238	41.8	42.9	15.3	15.8	114 686	156.3	16 685
District 12	13.9	8.0	5.9	458 595	31 864	6.9	426 731	54.0	36.8	9.2	10.1	100 609	136.9	40 515
District 13	17.9	11.6	9.7	401 309	42 456	10.6	358 853	46.7	38.3	15.0	16.6	95 909	130.9	33 134
District 14	8.3	4.6	3.4	404 907	29 186	7.2	375 721	42.8	42.7	14.4	11.4	109 240	151.5	15 538
District 15	8.8	6.4	7.5	380 529	28 255	7.4	352 274	44.4	38.7	16.9	12.1	93 595	127.4	17 083
District 16	32.8	28.2	26.8	290 433	47 037	16.2	243 396	21.0	41.8	37.0	22.1	94 129	131.6	38 745
District 17	7.5	5.0	4.0	393 014	30 514	7.8	362 500	57.9	29.5	12.6	9.4	69 832	95.4	15 806
District 18	7.3	4.5	2.0	389 994	26 014	6.7	363 980	59.3	31.4	9.4	9.2	112 332	153.6	13 290
District 19	14.4	10.3	8.5	395 680	37 408	9.5	358 272	37.2	41.2	21.7	16.2	87 943	117.9	26 048
District 20	17.5	12.6	7.1	342 155	29 873	8.7	312 282	30.9	41.9	27.2	22.8	97 267	134.1	15 289
District 21	29.8	26.0	23.2	286 821	40 214	14.0	246 607	16.8	33.8	49.3	25.4	81 607	114.7	33 259
District 22	22.5	17.2	18.2	340 762	39 517	11.6	301 245	33.2	41.8	24.9	17.6	91 636	125.5	20 832
District 23	19.8	16.0	13.2	317 798	35 199	11.1	282 599	31.2	43.4	25.5	17.1	107 945	148.6	26 789
District 24	15.8	9.1	6.3	366 096	25 788	7.0	340 308	35.7	43.1	21.2	18.1	119 339	165.3	14 110
District 25	14.0	10.8	7.5	338 503	33 281	9.8	305 222	37.4	44.8	17.9	16.1	85 118	118.7	17 199
District 26	13.1	8.9	7.3	369 299	29 547	8.0	339 752	35.7	41.0	23.3	18.9	107 455	150.7	13 601
District 27	13.8	10.5	4.4	372 898	29 994	8.0	342 904	44.0	42.5	13.5	18.3	126 315	176.2	37 872
District 28	16.6	11.9	5.3	419 975	39 392	9.4	380 583	47.6	41.4	11.0	22.4	98 695	139.4	48 955
District 29	22.6	20.1	12.5	364 751	43 271	11.9	321 480	23.1	48.9	28.0	29.6	59 916	86.6	28 129
District 30	13.8	9.7	4.5	407 108	34 222	8.4	372 886	45.6	40.9	13.5	19.3	102 676	137.9	22 945
District 31	21.2	17.0	16.6	333 129	40 350	12.1	292 779	32.9	44.9	22.2	19.9	75 668	104.4	22 865
District 32	16.0	12.4	10.5	347 788	39 701	11.4	308 087	27.3	46.4	26.2	23.0	85 045	120.4	26 242
District 33	10.2	6.3	2.1	393 492	27 409	7.0	366 083	60.2	32.9	7.0	9.5	114 037	158.8	12 627
District 34	29.4	25.2	12.8	375 150	42 659	11.4	332 491	24.9	49.3	25.8	36.1	73 122	102.6	44 844
District 35	17.3	14.3	13.5	346 149	40 974	11.8	305 175	21.8	45.8	32.4	26.4	71 562	98.3	23 020
District 36	21.2	16.7	12.5	305 869	41 301	13.5	264 568	25.7	50.6	23.7	25.0	151 153	209.2	22 864
District 37	20.8	15.9	9.3	395 067	40 599	10.3	354 468	40.7	43.6	15.8	23.7	82 616	112.8	30 774

1. Percent of civilian labor force. 2. Persons 16 years old and over. 3. Per 1,000 resident population estimated in the 2013 American Community Survey.

STATE District	Agriculture, 2012									
		Land in farms			Value of products sold				Government payments	
	Number of farms	Acres	Average size of farm (acres)	Irrigated land (acres)	Total ($1,000)	Average per farm (dollars)	Percent from crops	Percent from livestock and poultry products	Total ($1,000)	Average per farm receiving payments (dollars)
	63	64	65	66	67	68	69	70	71	72
UNITED STATES	2 109 303	914 527 657	434	55 822 231	394 644 481	187 097	53.8	46.2	8 053 346	9 925
ALABAMA	43 223	8 902 654	206	113 008	5 571 173	128 894	23.6	76.4	88 145	6 802
District 1	3 041	621 188	204	11 518	337 273	110 909	78.6	21.4	9 284	10 125
District 2	8 890	2 339 433	263	40 808	1 477 342	166 180	24.7	75.3	29 691	6 929
District 3	5 244	1 101 850	210	15 725	685 901	130 797	22.0	78.0	7 690	7 180
District 4	12 450	1 691 155	136	11 693	1 879 383	150 954	9.7	90.3	15 683	5 528
District 5	6 283	1 043 516	166	19 334	507 359	80 751	46.8	53.2	12 988	6 559
District 6	2 759	414 441	150	2 353	211 764	76 754	16.5	83.5	2 073	5 498
District 7	4 556	1 691 071	371	11 577	472 151	103 633	16.9	83.1	10 736	7 201
ALASKA	762	833 861	1 094	2 451	58 925	77 329	42.2	57.8	2 432	12 472
At Large	762	833 861	1 094	2 451	58 925	77 329	42.2	57.8	2 432	12 473
ARIZONA	20 005	26 249 195	1 312	880 613	3 732 113	186 559	55.6	44.4	31 329	10 245
District 1	13 505	20 238 604	1 499	274 134	1 189 607	88 086	41.3	58.7	15 323	6 574
District 2	1 452	981 592	676	67 103	170 117	117 161	D	D	2 662	13 513
District 3	1 467	3 206 653	2 186	220 098	1 051 870	717 021	57.8	42.2	5 901	23 892
District 4	1 851	1 618 174	874	236 656	927 038	500 831	65.5	34.5	4 673	26 551
District 5	559	39 587	71	22 692	123 985	221 798	26.0	74.0	945	26 995
District 6	459	105 916	231	16 105	77 337	168 490	D	D	295	12 303
District 7	173	D	D	22 562	110 396	638 125	D	D	911	70 065
District 8	455	D	D	16 399	60 936	133 925	70.4	29.6	541	18 664
District 9	84	7 562	90	4 864	20 827	247 937	95.6	4.4	78	12 964
ARKANSAS	45 071	13 810 786	306	4 803 902	9 775 758	216 897	49.5	50.5	262 967	20 013
District 1	14 422	7 829 889	543	4 372 332	4 886 232	338 804	87.6	12.4	213 501	29 087
District 2	5 715	1 031 106	180	81 263	377 217	66 005	25.3	74.7	10 237	9 418
District 3	9 735	1 617 495	166	9 975	1 696 333	174 251	2.7	97.3	12 498	6 975
District 4	15 199	3 332 296	219	340 332	2 815 976	185 274	14.7	85.3	26 731	9 151
CALIFORNIA	77 857	25 569 001	328	7 861 964	42 627 472	547 510	71.2	28.8	146 919	19 349
District 1	8 970	3 605 203	402	823 662	1 598 258	178 178	80.2	19.8	20 753	19 414
District 2	5 047	2 066 839	410	103 785	1 213 224	240 385	57.7	42.3	5 084	16 453
District 3	6 350	2 502 923	394	1 126 206	2 636 257	415 159	91.0	9.0	44 654	27 770
District 4	5 257	1 451 586	276	204 969	866 959	164 915	81.3	18.7	3 025	15 672
District 5	3 592	544 785	152	92 050	851 570	237 074	89.4	10.6	1 043	10 032
District 6	171	23 658	138	9 578	16 301	95 328	89.6	10.4	240	21 799
District 7	814	154 475	190	34 153	158 078	194 199	55.6	44.4	846	14 582
District 8	1 016	451 523	444	63 093	298 555	293 853	16.4	83.6	379	17 209
District 9	3 238	689 573	213	404 975	1 895 907	585 518	74.5	25.5	4 447	15 548
District 10	4 768	895 191	188	411 475	2 605 175	546 387	51.5	48.5	8 320	16 030
District 11	327	112 764	345	18 602	54 849	167 734	78.3	21.7	219	10 418
District 12	X	X	X	X	X	X	X	X	X	X
District 13	32	D	D	25	1 386	43 320	34.8	65.2	4	1 300
District 14	180	24 402	136	1 370	59 526	330 702	97.6	2.4	116	12 909
District 15	395	122 196	309	8 413	47 578	120 450	83.5	16.5	44	2 921
District 16	4 025	1 389 192	345	718 961	4 429 651	1 100 534	52.4	47.6	11 620	17 396
District 17	74	13 886	188	993	10 881	147 042	93.7	6.3	4	1 466
District 18	523	80 723	154	10 387	186 955	357 466	96.2	3.8	66	13 263
District 19	736	204 524	278	10 694	176 147	239 330	95.6	4.4	6	802
District 20	2 323	1 938 924	835	309 691	3 603 918	1 551 407	97.3	2.7	822	6 273
District 21	5 300	2 806 804	530	1 670 398	9 238 009	1 743 021	61.6	38.4	22 328	21 449
District 22	3 817	673 040	176	413 405	2 735 381	716 631	50.6	49.4	8 027	19 158
District 23	3 373	2 214 121	656	465 834	2 351 633	697 193	84.5	15.5	4 352	13 068
District 24	4 487	2 092 601	466	195 967	2 176 789	485 132	95.4	4.6	4 079	15 162
District 25	505	58 321	115	29 580	80 815	160 030	D	D	186	5 806
District 26	1 885	231 273	123	69 082	1 105 491	586 467	99.5	0.5	134	3 612
District 27	154	4 357	28	1 448	24 375	158 280	99.0	1.0	7	1 167
District 28	133	3 668	28	46	1 007	14 009	33.0	67.0	47	15 759
District 29	59	1 703	29	245	8 994	152 438	99.1	0.9	0	0
District 30	51	2 077	41	592	3 853	75 553	95.5	4.5	8	2 733
District 31	181	3 547	20	2 222	5 777	31 918	96.2	3.8	10	3 386
District 32	58	767	13	128	13 127	226 320	99.9	0.1	0	0
District 33	133	8 247	62	1 982	6 266	47 110	93.0	7.0	D	D
District 34	X	X	X	X	X	X	X	X	X	X
District 35	195	7 032	36	1 442	311 590	1 597 900	7.8	92.2	569	21 901
District 36	1 148	201 280	175	111 349	734 534	639 838	78.6	21.4	1 447	16 439
District 37	23	448	19	439	2 725	118 471	D	D	0	0

1. Specified owner-occupied units. 2. Specified renter-occupied units.

STATE District	Representative, 114th Congress	Land area,[1] 2010 (sq km)	Population and population characteristics, 2013											
			Total persons	Per square kilometer	Percent									
					Race alone									
					White	Black	American Indian, Alaska Native	Asian and Pacific Islander	Some other race (percent)	Two or more races (percent)	Hispanic or Latino[2] (percent)	Non-Hispanic White alone (percent)	Percent female	Percent foreign-born	Percent born in state of residence
		1	2	3	4	5	6	7	8	9	10	11	12	13	14
CALIFORNIA—Cont'd															
District 38	Linda T. Sánchez (D)	263	725 481	2 758.5	58.6	4.2	0.8	15.7	17.1	3.6	60.6	17.6	51.3	29.4	61.1
District 39	Edward R. Royce (R)	529	721 014	1 363.0	55.3	2.3	0.3	29.8	8.1	4.1	33.3	32.6	50.7	31.7	53.0
District 40	Lucille Roybal-Allard (D)	149	718 451	4 821.8	53.8	4.7	0.4	2.3	37.1	1.8	87.7	4.9	50.6	41.4	54.1
District 41	Mark Takano (D)	820	734 942	896.3	57.9	9.1	0.7	5.3	22.8	4.3	59.3	24.6	50.7	23.9	63.3
District 42	Ken Calvert (R)	2 424	746 215	307.8	67.3	5.4	0.7	10.0	11.2	5.4	36.6	44.3	50.0	20.3	59.5
District 43	Maxine Waters (D)	187	730 217	3 904.9	35.7	22.4	0.4	13.4	22.6	5.5	47.0	14.4	52.1	31.8	53.3
District 44	Janice Hahn (D)	206	706 791	3 431.0	47.8	16.7	1.1	6.6	24.4	3.4	69.4	6.2	51.0	34.4	56.2
District 45	Mimi Walters (R)	856	733 706	857.1	64.4	1.9	0.4	22.4	6.8	4.1	18.8	53.4	51.1	26.7	50.4
District 46	Loretta Sanchez (D)	186	726 686	3 906.9	58.5	1.8	0.3	12.6	24.9	2.0	66.2	18.8	49.7	39.8	50.8
District 47	Alan S. Lowenthal (D)	560	721 957	1 289.2	55.1	7.8	1.6	21.8	9.2	4.5	35.4	32.3	50.8	29.0	54.8
District 48	Dana Rohrabacher (R)	377	723 140	1 918.1	67.1	1.0	0.2	19.2	8.5	4.0	21.0	55.8	50.5	25.1	51.4
District 49	Darrell E. Issa (R)	1 432	717 823	501.3	78.0	3.8	0.4	6.4	7.1	4.3	24.5	62.2	49.1	16.9	50.1
District 50	Duncan Hunter (R)	7 219	730 427	101.2	79.4	2.7	1.1	5.5	6.5	4.7	30.6	57.4	51.2	20.6	55.5
District 51	Juan Vargas (D)	12 410	743 982	60.0	64.8	7.0	0.7	8.3	15.0	4.2	69.9	13.1	49.4	34.2	52.5
District 52	Scott H. Peters (D)	692	713 904	1 031.7	69.3	3.0	0.5	20.7	2.0	4.5	13.4	59.3	49.6	22.7	42.1
District 53	Susan A. Davis (D)	351	741 909	2 113.7	66.3	7.3	0.6	14.1	5.6	6.1	33.0	41.8	49.7	23.5	49.3
COLORADO		268 431	5 268 367	19.6	83.8	4.0	0.8	3.0	4.8	3.6	21.0	69.1	49.8	9.5	43.4
District 1	Diana DeGette (D)	491	772 255	1 572.8	78.9	8.6	0.8	3.4	4.7	3.6	28.3	57.0	50.0	14.0	42.4
District 2	Jared Polis (D)	19 516	755 671	38.7	90.6	1.0	0.5	2.9	2.3	2.7	10.4	83.1	49.7	7.6	36.5
District 3	Scott R. Tipton (R)	128 805	721 617	5.6	87.6	1.2	1.9	0.8	5.4	2.9	24.1	71.2	49.8	5.9	51.0
District 4	Ken Buck (R)	98 685	748 624	7.6	86.0	1.2	0.8	1.9	7.0	3.1	21.9	72.8	49.4	7.4	49.2
District 5	Doug Lamborn (R)	18 818	749 815	39.8	81.4	5.5	0.6	2.9	4.3	5.3	15.0	72.6	49.2	6.2	32.6
District 6	Mike Coffman (R)	1 229	765 338	622.7	74.2	8.7	0.4	5.9	6.2	4.4	20.4	61.7	50.9	14.3	41.4
District 7	Ed Perlmutter (D)	886	755 047	852.2	88.3	1.3	0.8	3.1	3.4	3.0	27.1	66.1	49.8	10.6	50.7
CONNECTICUT		12 542	3 596 080	286.7	77.3	10.3	0.2	4.1	5.2	2.9	14.7	69.3	51.3	13.9	55.1
District 1	John B. Larson (D)	1 749	716 580	409.7	70.9	15.1	0.1	4.4	5.6	3.8	15.4	63.8	51.7	14.9	59.3
District 2	Joe Courtney (D)	5 148	714 637	138.8	87.1	3.8	0.5	3.1	1.9	3.6	7.7	82.7	49.9	7.2	57.0
District 3	Rosa L. DeLauro (D)	1 218	716 738	588.5	73.9	13.8	0.3	4.1	5.7	2.3	13.7	66.7	52.2	11.6	62.6
District 4	James A. Himes (D)	1 193	735 823	616.8	72.9	12.3	0.2	4.9	6.8	2.9	18.1	63.2	51.3	21.8	41.9
District 5	Elizabeth H. Esty (D)	3 233	712 302	220.3	81.6	6.5	0.0	4.1	5.8	2.0	18.2	70.4	51.2	13.7	54.9
DELAWARE		5 047	925 749	183.4	68.9	21.6	0.4	3.7	2.5	2.9	8.7	64.0	51.6	8.3	46.8
At Large	John C. Carney (D)	5 047	925 749	183.4	68.9	21.6	0.4	3.7	2.5	2.9	8.7	64.0	51.6	8.3	46.8
DISTRICT OF COLUMBIA		158	646 449	4 091.4	40.9	48.8	0.2	3.6	3.4	3.2	10.1	35.6	52.7	14.4	36.7
Delegate District (At Large)	Eleanor Holmes Norton (D)	158	646 449	4 091.4	40.9	48.8	0.2	3.6	3.4	3.2	10.1	35.6	52.7	14.4	36.7
FLORIDA		138 887	19 552 860	140.8	76.2	16.1	0.3	2.6	2.5	2.3	23.6	56.2	51.1	19.4	36.2
District 1	Jeff Miller (R)	10 402	729 553	70.1	77.4	13.5	0.5	2.7	1.9	4.1	6.1	73.8	49.8	5.0	39.4
District 2	Gwen Graham (D)	22 309	710 751	31.9	69.7	25.1	0.6	2.2	0.7	1.9	5.5	65.2	49.6	4.9	55.9
District 3	Ted S. Yoho (R)	18 923	707 112	37.4	79.5	13.4	0.2	3.3	1.0	2.6	8.1	72.9	49.6	6.9	50.5
District 4	Ander Crenshaw (R)	4 859	705 007	145.1	79.0	12.7	0.4	4.8	0.5	2.7	8.2	72.0	50.7	10.0	46.4
District 5	Corrine Brown (D)	3 510	729 368	207.8	38.5	52.2	0.3	2.8	3.0	3.3	12.5	30.0	51.8	11.7	55.7
District 6	Ron DeSantis (R)	6 493	722 788	111.3	85.5	8.3	0.2	2.3	1.7	2.0	7.2	80.0	51.6	6.6	35.9
District 7	John L. Mica (R)	1 330	716 811	539.0	80.8	9.3	0.1	3.7	3.1	3.0	21.2	64.1	50.8	11.1	37.1
District 8	Bill Posey (R)	4 538	704 053	155.1	83.9	10.2	0.3	2.1	1.0	2.4	9.6	76.3	51.3	8.6	33.8
District 9	Alan Grayson (D)	4 422	768 459	173.8	74.3	10.7	0.2	4.5	6.4	3.9	46.1	37.4	50.9	19.7	28.0
District 10	Daniel Webster (R)	2 925	732 296	250.4	75.1	12.0	0.5	3.6	6.2	2.6	17.3	64.5	51.0	13.8	36.4
District 11	Richard B. Nugent (R)	6 501	715 956	110.1	87.1	9.1	0.3	1.2	0.7	1.7	9.7	79.0	51.4	5.9	30.0
District 12	Gus M. Bilirakis (R)	2 289	719 044	314.1	88.8	4.5	0.3	2.5	1.4	2.4	13.0	78.4	51.7	9.5	32.5
District 13	David W. Jolly (R)	482	699 288	1 450.8	86.1	6.1	0.2	3.6	1.1	2.9	9.0	78.8	51.9	12.1	30.0
District 14	Kathy Castor (D)	687	733 381	1 067.5	63.7	25.3	0.3	3.0	4.8	2.8	28.2	41.6	51.1	16.7	40.7
District 15	Dennis A. Ross (R)	2 120	718 325	338.8	76.6	14.0	0.3	3.6	2.8	2.7	18.6	62.4	51.7	11.5	45.8
District 16	Vern Buchanan (R)	2 267	727 073	320.7	88.7	6.9	0.2	1.7	1.0	1.5	11.6	78.5	52.0	12.4	27.1
District 17	Thomas J. Rooney (R)	16 498	721 297	43.7	84.5	9.6	0.2	1.5	2.4	1.9	18.3	69.4	49.8	11.7	36.0
District 18	Patrick Murphy (D)	3 917	705 469	180.1	79.9	13.1	0.1	1.9	2.7	2.3	14.5	69.2	51.3	13.8	32.8
District 19	Curt Clawson (R)	1 943	738 554	380.1	86.4	7.8	0.3	1.3	2.8	1.5	17.7	72.2	51.3	16.0	23.0
District 20	Alcee L. Hastings (D)	6 287	728 883	115.9	40.6	53.4	0.2	1.7	2.2	1.9	20.3	24.2	51.4	31.9	41.0
District 21	Theodore E. Deutch (D)	676	738 875	1 093.0	77.5	13.0	0.2	3.9	2.9	2.5	22.8	58.5	52.3	25.5	27.5
District 22	Lois Frankel (D)	448	734 319	1 639.1	81.2	11.8	0.2	2.6	1.9	2.3	21.9	62.1	50.0	26.0	27.0
District 23	Debbie Wasserman Schultz (D)	438	719 732	1 643.2	77.3	10.7	0.2	3.4	5.5	2.9	37.3	46.9	51.3	36.5	30.4
District 24	Frederica S. Wilson (D)	275	725 282	2 637.4	39.0	54.6	0.1	2.1	3.0	1.1	33.2	11.5	52.2	40.3	42.6
District 25	Mario Diaz-Balart (R)	8 373	740 305	88.4	86.4	7.9	0.1	1.9	2.6	1.1	72.1	18.5	51.5	52.7	28.5
District 26	Carlos Curbelo (R)	5 435	741 247	136.4	83.8	10.4	0.1	2.2	1.8	1.6	67.1	20.0	51.0	47.8	34.1
District 27	Ileana Ros-Lehtinen (R)	541	719 632	1 330.2	87.5	7.5	0.2	1.5	1.5	1.8	75.4	16.5	50.5	52.9	30.4

1. Dry land or land partially or temporarily covered by water. 2. May be of any race.

STATE District	Population and population characteristics, 2013 (cont.)										Education, 2013		
	Age (percent)											Attainment[2] (percent)	
	Under 5 years	5 to 17 years	18 to 24 years	25 to 34 years	35 to 44 years	45 to 54 years	55 to 64 years	65 to 74 years	75 years and over	Median age	Total Enrollment[1]	High school graduate or more	Bachelor's degree or more
	15	16	17	18	19	20	21	22	23	24	25	26	27
CALIFORNIA—Cont'd													
District 38	6.6	17.5	10.8	13.5	13.1	13.5	11.9	6.9	6.1	36.0	206 272	78.0	21.5
District 39	5.4	16.9	10.4	13.8	13.1	15.0	12.7	7.1	5.7	37.7	203 807	88.1	39.1
District 40	8.7	21.6	13.4	14.8	15.1	11.2	7.8	4.4	3.2	29.3	224 296	51.7	8.4
District 41	7.0	20.8	13.9	14.3	12.8	12.9	9.8	4.7	3.8	30.4	231 512	74.1	17.0
District 42	6.8	20.7	9.2	13.7	14.0	13.9	10.5	6.6	4.6	34.6	223 124	86.0	24.3
District 43	7.0	17.6	11.0	15.5	13.0	14.5	10.6	6.4	4.6	34.2	206 366	75.7	23.9
District 44	8.2	20.2	11.9	14.6	13.1	13.2	9.6	5.3	4.0	31.5	216 358	61.7	11.9
District 45	5.0	16.5	10.2	12.6	13.3	16.0	12.6	7.4	6.4	39.9	208 421	93.5	50.8
District 46	7.9	19.0	11.8	16.7	14.3	12.6	8.5	5.1	3.9	31.4	207 602	64.7	16.7
District 47	6.1	17.8	10.6	14.6	14.2	13.5	11.4	6.7	5.3	35.8	206 775	81.5	28.7
District 48	5.2	15.7	8.7	13.6	14.5	14.8	12.6	8.5	6.3	40.3	185 334	89.3	43.7
District 49	6.5	15.6	10.4	13.5	13.7	14.6	12.5	7.4	5.8	37.9	170 160	89.4	40.4
District 50	6.2	17.6	10.4	13.1	13.3	13.8	12.6	7.5	5.5	36.9	195 414	82.9	24.3
District 51	8.1	20.1	12.9	15.3	12.5	11.3	9.6	5.7	4.7	30.4	224 547	68.1	13.4
District 52	6.0	14.0	11.5	17.7	13.1	13.6	11.0	7.4	6.0	35.6	190 545	94.6	55.0
District 53	6.2	15.4	11.0	17.4	13.7	13.6	10.9	6.4	5.5	35.0	206 464	89.1	34.6
COLORADO	6.3	17.3	9.7	14.7	13.7	13.6	12.5	7.2	5.0	36.4	1 400 453	90.5	37.8
District 1	6.8	14.3	8.9	20.6	15.2	12.2	11.1	6.2	4.8	34.8	180 147	87.6	43.9
District 2	4.9	15.6	13.4	13.5	12.9	13.8	13.7	7.3	4.9	36.9	216 982	95.3	51.4
District 3	5.7	16.8	9.2	12.6	12.2	13.4	14.4	9.3	6.3	40.0	178 116	89.4	29.8
District 4	6.6	19.2	8.7	12.5	13.9	14.4	12.5	7.3	4.8	37.3	203 801	89.4	33.3
District 5	6.6	17.5	10.7	14.7	12.4	13.8	12.1	7.3	4.9	35.4	209 331	92.7	33.8
District 6	6.9	20.0	8.2	14.0	15.3	13.8	11.3	6.5	3.9	35.6	217 013	91.3	40.3
District 7	6.8	17.3	9.1	15.2	13.6	13.4	12.2	7.2	5.2	35.9	195 063	88.4	31.4
CONNECTICUT	5.3	16.5	9.6	12.2	12.4	15.4	13.2	8.1	7.0	40.5	939 762	89.7	37.2
District 1	5.4	16.2	8.5	13.4	12.2	14.8	13.3	8.7	7.4	40.6	182 676	88.6	35.8
District 2	4.7	15.7	11.4	11.5	11.8	15.9	13.9	8.6	6.7	41.0	185 310	91.7	33.0
District 3	5.2	15.3	10.9	13.4	12.1	15.0	12.6	8.1	7.4	39.6	187 272	90.3	35.0
District 4	6.1	18.6	8.5	11.7	13.2	15.7	12.4	7.2	6.3	39.2	205 462	89.2	48.3
District 5	5.0	16.8	8.8	11.1	13.1	15.8	14.3	8.0	7.1	41.6	179 042	88.4	34.1
DELAWARE	6.1	15.9	10.0	12.9	12.0	14.1	13.1	9.3	6.6	39.1	229 133	88.3	29.8
At Large	6.1	15.9	10.0	12.9	12.0	14.1	13.1	9.3	6.6	39.1	229 133	88.3	29.8
DISTRICT OF COLUMBIA	6.4	11.0	12.7	22.4	13.9	11.8	10.6	6.3	5.1	33.8	162 510	90.1	55.1
Delegate District (At Large)	6.4	11.0	12.7	22.4	13.9	11.8	10.6	6.3	5.1	33.8	162 510	90.1	55.1
FLORIDA	5.5	15.1	9.2	12.4	12.3	14.0	12.9	10.1	8.5	41.5	4 643 948	86.8	27.2
District 1	6.0	15.6	10.7	13.9	11.5	14.3	12.8	8.8	6.4	38.3	173 319	88.5	25.3
District 2	5.5	14.3	14.7	13.8	12.3	13.1	12.5	8.1	5.7	36.6	201 829	85.3	26.2
District 3	5.5	15.9	13.3	12.1	11.0	13.2	12.6	9.4	6.9	37.9	200 313	87.2	23.8
District 4	6.0	15.0	9.0	15.6	13.2	14.0	13.2	8.2	5.6	38.3	165 231	91.6	30.4
District 5	7.4	17.8	11.3	14.6	12.5	13.1	11.4	6.8	4.9	34.1	195 127	81.6	16.9
District 6	4.6	14.1	8.5	9.7	11.3	13.8	14.8	13.0	10.0	46.4	161 092	90.4	27.1
District 7	4.9	16.1	12.1	13.9	11.5	14.4	13.0	7.9	6.3	37.8	206 284	92.2	35.1
District 8	4.6	14.1	7.8	9.8	10.7	14.8	14.7	12.4	11.1	47.7	148 992	90.1	26.3
District 9	6.4	17.7	10.6	15.2	14.9	13.4	10.4	7.1	4.1	35.0	212 484	84.1	23.7
District 10	5.7	15.7	8.2	12.7	14.0	14.3	11.8	9.7	7.8	40.7	169 139	88.9	30.3
District 11	4.0	12.6	6.6	8.8	9.5	11.6	14.8	18.3	13.8	52.3	130 004	87.4	19.8
District 12	5.0	15.6	7.2	10.5	12.6	14.6	13.8	11.5	9.4	44.5	159 536	90.3	28.3
District 13	4.6	12.2	7.0	11.4	11.2	15.1	15.0	12.1	11.4	48.0	129 295	89.5	27.8
District 14	6.5	15.9	9.8	16.7	13.4	13.6	11.7	6.9	5.6	35.6	182 952	85.4	27.7
District 15	5.9	17.7	10.2	12.9	12.4	14.3	12.6	8.5	5.6	37.9	192 793	86.9	27.0
District 16	4.4	13.1	7.0	8.8	9.8	12.7	14.6	15.2	14.3	50.5	134 928	90.2	30.8
District 17	5.5	14.6	7.7	9.5	11.0	11.7	13.7	13.6	12.7	46.7	146 216	82.8	18.2
District 18	4.8	14.4	6.8	10.7	11.2	14.1	13.9	12.4	11.6	46.5	153 937	89.9	29.0
District 19	4.5	13.2	7.0	10.2	10.2	12.5	13.7	16.0	12.7	49.1	137 279	87.7	30.7
District 20	6.8	17.3	10.0	13.5	13.2	14.0	11.4	7.3	6.6	36.8	193 127	80.6	18.8
District 21	5.8	15.9	8.0	10.2	12.8	13.1	11.8	10.4	11.9	43.1	181 913	90.9	33.4
District 22	4.3	12.1	7.8	13.0	12.5	15.1	13.9	10.7	10.7	45.2	149 894	88.3	35.7
District 23	5.7	15.0	7.6	13.6	13.4	16.1	12.7	8.1	7.7	41.4	176 568	90.3	37.5
District 24	6.5	16.7	10.6	15.4	14.0	13.5	11.4	6.8	5.1	35.6	193 900	79.4	21.2
District 25	5.5	15.8	9.9	13.0	14.1	15.4	10.8	8.5	7.0	39.5	189 750	80.8	23.7
District 26	5.5	14.7	10.3	12.9	13.4	15.8	12.7	8.3	6.5	40.3	185 751	83.0	28.0
District 27	6.0	14.8	8.5	13.7	14.7	14.5	11.4	8.2	8.1	39.9	172 295	79.2	29.0

1. All persons 3 years old and over enrolled in nursery school through college and graduate or professional school. 2. Persons 25 years old and over.

STATE District	Households, 2013							Group quarters, 2010				
	Number	Average household size	Family households (percent)	Married-couple family (percent)	Female family householder[1]	One person households (percent)	Total in group quarters, 2013	Percent 65 years and over	Persons in correctional institutions	Persons in nursing facilities	Persons in college dormitories	Persons in military quarters
	28	29	30	31	32	33	34	35	36	37	38	39
CALIFORNIA—Cont'd												
District 38	208 418	3.43	78.3	53.4	17.5	18.0	9 586	26.5	156	2 794	3 305	0
District 39	224 426	3.18	77.6	60.4	11.6	16.2	8 101	26.5	2	1 230	2 630	0
District 40	175 068	4.08	82.5	46.2	24.8	14.0	3 381	37.5	7	1 571	5	0
District 41	193 481	3.73	78.0	51.6	18.0	16.7	12 696	11.9	1 171	1 826	7 379	0
District 42	219 416	3.37	78.5	61.3	10.8	16.3	6 575	10.4	5 652	440	161	0
District 43	237 198	3.03	68.2	40.1	19.5	26.0	10 833	27.0	120	2 478	3 293	0
District 44	180 495	3.87	78.2	44.9	23.7	18.0	8 385	16.1	2 843	1 687	587	20
District 45	259 123	2.78	71.4	57.5	10.1	22.4	12 092	22.2	534	789	5 705	0
District 46	185 194	3.83	77.1	51.3	17.6	16.3	16 685	19.0	4 906	2 887	1 967	0
District 47	243 397	2.93	64.9	44.0	14.1	27.6	9 878	31.5	235	2 931	2 040	2
District 48	263 117	2.73	66.5	51.4	10.3	24.9	5 536	30.5	13	1 555	1 249	14
District 49	259 486	2.70	67.5	54.5	9.7	24.3	18 373	6.5	782	1 612	7 910	16 563
District 50	235 220	3.07	74.5	56.3	12.5	19.3	8 810	26.3	889	1 975	757	0
District 51	198 690	3.58	77.4	47.6	22.2	17.5	33 121	4.0	17 756	1 059	0	11 846
District 52	270 449	2.54	60.9	48.5	8.9	28.6	26 010	8.6	2 774	1 881	4 151	15 213
District 53	265 850	2.74	60.8	43.8	11.9	28.2	12 475	28.3	46	3 059	3 237	142
COLORADO	2 002 800	2.57	63.9	49.0	10.5	27.9	117 400	14.3	40 568	18 079	29 952	10 945
District 1	321 898	2.35	49.3	35.8	9.8	39.4	16 048	12.3	3 960	2 592	4 940	0
District 2	297 231	2.47	61.0	50.5	6.6	26.8	20 217	11.6	1 634	2 213	11 841	0
District 3	279 114	2.52	66.0	49.5	11.7	27.6	17 386	20.4	3 982	3 460	5 041	0
District 4	265 878	2.75	72.3	57.1	10.2	22.5	17 734	12.8	13 075	2 577	3 993	0
District 5	277 225	2.60	68.1	53.2	11.0	24.8	29 411	6.9	12 094	2 245	2 580	10 678
District 6	277 260	2.74	69.3	51.9	12.4	24.3	5 797	32.7	3 009	2 128	0	267
District 7	284 194	2.62	64.3	47.6	11.8	28.0	10 807	28.1	2 814	2 864	1 557	0
CONNECTICUT	1 339 860	2.60	66.4	49.1	13.1	27.7	118 129	20.9	20 059	26 371	48 537	3 977
District 1	280 887	2.49	65.1	45.6	15.0	29.5	17 385	33.0	1 335	6 778	5 649	0
District 2	268 569	2.50	67.1	51.0	11.4	26.2	42 132	10.7	12 975	4 306	16 779	3 977
District 3	270 267	2.56	62.0	44.7	13.8	32.0	25 957	17.9	902	5 257	16 566	0
District 4	254 241	2.84	70.7	54.5	12.5	23.2	13 926	31.6	1 159	4 719	5 030	0
District 5	265 896	2.61	67.6	50.2	12.5	27.2	18 729	28.1	3 688	5 311	4 513	0
DELAWARE	339 071	2.66	67.3	48.6	14.4	26.5	25 204	16.8	6 457	4 591	10 184	283
At Large	339 071	2.66	67.3	48.6	14.4	26.5	25 204	16.8	6 457	4 591	10 184	283
DISTRICT OF COLUMBIA	271 651	2.23	44.3	24.2	15.8	42.2	40 298	7.8	3 598	3 064	24 087	1 504
Delegate District (At Large)	271 651	2.23	44.3	24.2	15.8	42.2	40 298	7.8	3 598	3 064	24 087	1 504
FLORIDA	7 211 584	2.65	64.2	46.2	13.3	29.3	425 880	17.5	167 453	73 372	85 243	14 612
District 1	274 942	2.53	64.8	48.2	12.5	28.8	33 104	8.8	10 881	2 652	4 832	8 580
District 2	261 379	2.53	62.7	44.1	13.8	28.6	49 040	6.9	32 671	3 280	10 370	513
District 3	253 357	2.64	64.0	47.9	11.9	28.7	37 794	9.3	21 156	3 439	9 235	0
District 4	270 405	2.55	62.4	48.3	10.5	30.3	14 704	18.0	2 597	2 852	2 776	4 662
District 5	252 359	2.82	62.8	33.3	23.0	30.2	18 627	10.6	10 195	2 281	1 357	0
District 6	282 811	2.51	63.2	49.0	9.7	30.2	13 751	20.3	4 351	3 572	5 748	4
District 7	248 763	2.78	62.3	47.7	11.1	30.1	24 353	15.3	757	3 056	13 306	0
District 8	279 825	2.49	64.1	47.9	12.1	29.8	7 635	27.2	3 105	2 612	1 259	182
District 9	241 001	3.16	71.7	50.7	16.3	21.5	6 855	24.1	3 819	1 838	245	0
District 10	275 924	2.62	65.2	50.8	10.3	27.3	8 140	16.2	3 929	2 605	315	0
District 11	298 181	2.33	68.0	53.4	11.1	27.4	20 434	15.3	16 221	2 953	312	0
District 12	280 539	2.53	65.0	51.1	9.7	28.4	9 145	40.5	1 981	2 902	1 050	0
District 13	304 361	2.25	53.5	39.3	10.8	39.3	13 158	35.3	3 506	5 478	1 751	0
District 14	292 964	2.46	56.4	34.2	16.8	35.2	13 635	18.8	3 483	3 007	3 375	324
District 15	250 769	2.81	69.3	50.9	13.5	24.8	14 303	15.6	854	2 303	7 847	0
District 16	300 804	2.39	61.3	49.1	9.5	32.5	9 159	38.1	2 011	3 857	1 569	0
District 17	265 536	2.63	66.4	51.8	10.0	27.8	23 689	15.9	12 761	3 312	606	0
District 18	275 659	2.53	64.2	48.7	11.8	29.9	7 773	25.5	3 930	1 838	339	2
District 19	283 156	2.56	65.9	52.4	9.2	28.5	13 486	26.8	2 727	2 860	2 688	9
District 20	241 443	2.95	63.8	34.3	23.0	29.6	17 403	18.4	10 719	3 611	214	0
District 21	274 658	2.68	68.0	51.8	12.6	27.2	2 898	52.8	619	1 396	19	0
District 22	311 055	2.33	53.6	39.1	9.7	37.4	10 236	29.7	1 291	3 658	3 672	0
District 23	279 032	2.56	60.8	43.9	12.9	33.0	4 019	23.7	938	1 239	1 463	59
District 24	233 131	3.05	62.2	31.9	22.9	31.2	15 223	21.9	3 004	2 733	3 132	0
District 25	224 434	3.25	75.6	50.6	17.6	19.4	10 121	12.7	5 752	717	596	0
District 26	215 258	3.37	76.2	54.2	15.5	19.3	16 475	17.9	4 186	1 100	2 657	277
District 27	239 838	2.96	67.6	43.9	16.7	26.8	10 720	24.6	9	2 221	4 510	0

1. No spouse present.

STATE District	Housing units, 2013						Money income, 2013		
		Occupied units						Households	
			Owner-occupied			Renter-occupied			
	Total	Occupied units as a percent of all units	Owner-occupied units as a percent of occupied units	Median value[1] (dollars)	Percent valued at $500,000 or more	Median rent[2]	Per capita income (dollars)	Median income (dollars)	Percent with income of $100,000 or more
	40	41	42	43	44	45	46	47	48
CALIFORNIA—Cont'd									
District 38	220 354	94.6	61.2	374 900	21.6	1 249	23 017	61 015	26.5
District 39	236 526	94.9	66.4	514 200	52.0	1 442	31 874	79 909	38.3
District 40	183 667	95.3	33.2	317 900	11.6	1 032	13 540	38 981	10.9
District 41	205 948	93.9	57.5	218 600	5.3	1 171	18 894	52 546	18.9
District 42	232 908	94.2	70.0	293 600	9.6	1 423	26 027	70 261	32.0
District 43	251 877	94.2	42.0	383 300	28.2	1 114	22 025	47 145	18.9
District 44	190 356	94.8	49.1	289 600	7.7	1 047	16 356	44 909	16.7
District 45	272 012	95.3	65.6	590 200	63.7	1 757	41 561	90 318	45.5
District 46	192 425	96.2	41.8	372 400	16.4	1 315	18 687	52 409	19.9
District 47	256 889	94.7	46.5	448 300	37.9	1 181	26 658	56 829	25.5
District 48	282 630	93.1	56.9	639 400	68.7	1 655	43 773	80 502	40.6
District 49	280 470	92.5	59.6	547 400	54.2	1 490	38 197	67 018	34.1
District 50	252 592	93.1	61.9	371 100	23.9	1 215	26 975	61 533	28.1
District 51	218 441	91.0	42.9	235 300	4.1	982	16 114	41 477	13.4
District 52	295 068	91.7	53.8	548 400	55.8	1 614	44 061	82 286	42.2
District 53	284 893	93.3	48.7	379 900	25.7	1 224	29 241	61 021	26.3
COLORADO	2 247 291	89.1	64.5	240 500	11.9	971	31 421	58 823	25.7
District 1	345 330	93.2	54.1	264 800	16.1	913	34 754	53 271	25.1
District 2	361 196	82.3	67.1	318 800	22.9	1 100	37 692	68 653	32.2
District 3	356 843	78.2	67.1	199 100	11.1	854	27 017	47 419	17.4
District 4	289 253	91.9	72.4	231 000	10.2	915	30 839	64 525	28.8
District 5	310 481	89.3	64.3	209 500	6.7	946	28 541	55 295	22.7
District 6	288 292	96.2	64.4	253 000	10.4	1 078	31 746	65 987	30.4
District 7	295 896	96.0	64.1	224 500	5.3	984	29 053	58 609	23.2
CONNECTICUT	1 488 072	90.0	66.3	267 000	16.2	1 040	37 726	67 098	33.0
District 1	302 925	92.7	65.1	227 600	5.4	969	34 587	63 439	29.9
District 2	300 632	89.3	70.6	245 000	8.9	981	33 836	67 614	31.6
District 3	300 023	90.1	62.0	247 000	8.0	1 064	32 151	59 165	28.9
District 4	280 825	90.5	66.1	508 600	50.7	1 364	52 470	86 007	44.1
District 5	303 667	87.6	67.8	257 700	10.1	955	35 164	65 384	31.3
DELAWARE	412 015	82.3	71.7	226 200	6.6	999	29 484	57 846	24.5
At Large	412 015	82.3	71.7	226 200	6.6	999	29 484	57 846	24.5
DISTRICT OF COLUMBIA	302 975	89.7	40.7	470 500	46.2	1 307	45 477	67 572	35.8
Delegate District (At Large)	302 975	89.7	40.7	470 500	46.2	1 307	45 477	67 572	35.8
FLORIDA	9 047 973	79.7	64.8	153 300	6.9	972	25 834	46 036	17.7
District 1	349 746	78.6	65.3	149 200	5.0	923	24 912	49 416	16.4
District 2	338 820	77.1	60.1	136 900	3.0	826	22 219	42 184	15.3
District 3	300 392	84.3	68.3	123 500	2.4	838	22 553	43 169	14.8
District 4	314 878	85.9	65.1	157 600	5.4	1 000	30 364	55 461	22.5
District 5	312 189	80.8	50.8	88 600	1.3	847	16 981	33 024	8.7
District 6	366 967	77.1	72.2	159 600	7.7	924	27 724	44 505	17.6
District 7	295 696	84.1	66.9	154 200	4.6	1 025	25 889	52 197	20.3
District 8	353 286	79.2	71.9	138 400	4.7	872	26 089	45 570	16.3
District 9	317 005	76.0	57.8	138 800	1.5	1 028	19 715	44 995	13.6
District 10	335 647	82.2	66.0	152 200	5.9	975	26 604	49 060	18.1
District 11	362 904	82.2	76.6	121 200	2.8	808	23 144	41 275	11.3
District 12	339 767	82.6	72.4	143 100	4.5	938	27 911	50 115	20.8
District 13	386 949	78.7	65.5	133 300	6.4	916	29 004	44 118	15.8
District 14	335 940	87.2	48.2	121 400	6.4	921	24 999	40 362	15.3
District 15	291 017	86.2	65.0	139 300	2.9	887	24 949	50 941	19.5
District 16	402 062	74.8	72.8	167 300	8.8	956	29 900	48 202	18.7
District 17	357 048	74.4	75.2	112 300	2.8	801	22 202	41 798	13.0
District 18	359 631	76.7	72.4	174 500	10.6	1 072	32 588	51 068	22.1
District 19	447 911	63.2	69.6	190 800	15.6	962	31 468	49 135	21.6
District 20	292 673	82.5	54.5	109 800	0.8	1 024	17 775	37 105	9.7
District 21	328 145	83.7	74.9	201 000	7.0	1 227	30 493	54 696	24.1
District 22	405 408	76.7	63.6	222 900	18.1	1 177	38 441	53 679	24.2
District 23	381 682	73.1	59.6	232 800	17.2	1 202	32 146	52 013	24.5
District 24	279 159	83.5	47.1	147 300	5.7	995	19 662	36 748	12.9
District 25	261 732	85.7	61.2	190 800	6.1	1 134	21 434	45 697	17.1
District 26	257 527	83.6	66.8	215 900	6.3	1 231	21 845	50 582	20.9
District 27	273 792	87.6	51.2	233 400	20.4	1 023	27 074	42 262	20.6

1. Specified owner-occupied units. 2. Specified renter-occupied units.

STATE District	Poverty, 2013			Civilian labor force, 2013			Civilian employment,[2] 2013				Persons under age 65 with no health insurance, 2013 (percent)	Social Security beneficiaries, December 2013		Supple-mental Security Income recipients, December 2013
					Unemployment			Percent						
	Persons below poverty level (percent)	Families below poverty level (percent)	Percent of households receiving food stamps in past 12 months	Total	Total	Rate[1]	Total	Manage-ment, business, science and arts occupa-tions	Service, sales, and office	Con-struction and production		Number	Rate[3]	
	49	50	51	52	53	54	55	56	57	58	59	60	61	62
CALIFORNIA—Cont'd														
District 38	12.8	9.6	7.9	350 653	26 673	7.6	323 980	29.4	45.4	25.2	22.9	99 628	137.3	23 496
District 39	11.2	7.7	5.4	379 733	29 269	7.7	350 464	42.4	43.2	14.5	17.8	98 794	137.0	16 641
District 40	29.3	27.4	18.2	333 998	38 820	11.6	295 178	15.3	46.7	37.8	33.5	67 300	93.7	30 523
District 41	20.2	15.9	14.4	354 846	51 028	14.4	303 818	24.6	45.7	29.7	25.1	72 318	98.4	21 499
District 42	12.0	9.3	7.7	352 770	40 153	11.4	312 617	35.8	43.1	21.1	18.3	111 059	148.8	16 921
District 43	21.4	17.1	11.9	375 588	49 449	13.2	326 139	30.2	48.3	21.5	24.7	91 367	125.1	33 751
District 44	24.3	21.6	17.2	324 182	45 971	14.2	278 211	18.6	47.3	34.2	28.7	84 645	119.8	35 647
District 45	8.3	5.3	2.5	398 117	24 533	6.2	373 584	51.4	38.7	9.9	11.6	104 801	142.8	11 341
District 46	20.9	18.5	13.3	368 548	34 932	9.5	333 616	22.7	48.7	28.6	28.6	68 632	94.4	24 713
District 47	17.8	14.1	9.4	370 894	34 605	9.3	336 289	35.6	44.2	20.2	21.0	90 373	125.2	32 312
District 48	11.4	8.0	4.2	389 128	28 431	7.3	360 697	44.4	42.2	13.4	15.9	106 173	146.8	12 079
District 49	12.5	9.1	3.2	335 837	25 878	7.7	309 959	43.8	41.9	14.4	15.4	104 374	145.4	8 311
District 50	13.4	10.5	6.8	352 508	33 075	9.4	319 433	31.6	47.4	21.0	20.3	103 363	141.5	16 095
District 51	24.7	21.9	18.3	321 975	45 614	14.2	276 361	21.1	52.9	26.0	26.8	112 663	151.4	39 928
District 52	10.5	6.1	2.7	371 202	24 146	6.5	347 056	56.1	35.3	8.7	11.1	104 196	146.0	14 923
District 53	14.1	9.6	7.0	392 076	34 273	8.7	357 803	41.3	44.1	14.7	17.4	85 191	114.8	17 770
COLORADO	13.0	8.7	8.6	2 789 491	195 693	7.0	2 593 798	40.1	41.6	18.2	16.0	774 056	146.9	72 154
District 1	16.9	12.1	10.0	441 741	27 166	6.1	414 575	44.0	40.9	15.1	16.8	100 989	130.8	16 347
District 2	11.8	4.9	4.7	430 852	22 673	5.3	408 179	45.9	39.4	14.8	12.8	107 456	142.2	5 034
District 3	16.3	11.8	11.3	357 922	27 949	7.8	329 973	32.6	44.1	23.4	20.9	138 982	192.6	14 369
District 4	11.1	7.9	8.1	383 803	27 775	7.2	356 028	40.1	39.4	20.5	14.1	83 263	111.2	7 591
District 5	11.2	7.3	10.4	355 310	30 710	8.6	324 600	40.3	42.6	17.1	13.1	116 736	155.7	10 033
District 6	11.7	8.7	7.3	412 435	31 346	7.6	381 089	40.2	43.1	16.7	16.5	114 369	149.4	9 098
District 7	11.6	8.7	8.5	407 428	28 074	6.9	379 354	35.9	42.5	21.6	17.6	112 261	148.7	9 682
CONNECTICUT	10.7	7.6	12.3	1 951 694	180 553	9.3	1 771 141	40.4	42.4	17.1	10.9	648 466	180.3	62 537
District 1	12.4	9.6	15.3	387 943	39 839	10.3	348 104	42.1	41.4	16.6	10.0	137 435	191.8	16 804
District 2	8.5	5.9	10.7	392 961	35 405	9.0	357 556	38.7	42.3	19.0	8.4	134 322	188.0	8 038
District 3	11.9	8.1	12.8	386 819	34 212	8.8	352 607	40.4	43.2	16.4	9.9	131 573	183.6	13 860
District 4	10.0	7.0	9.8	396 878	38 003	9.6	358 875	43.7	41.9	14.4	14.8	113 544	154.3	10 242
District 5	10.8	7.4	12.9	387 093	33 094	8.5	353 999	37.3	43.7	19.0	10.9	131 592	184.7	13 593
DELAWARE	12.4	8.5	13.8	470 708	40 461	8.6	430 247	38.6	43.4	18.0	10.6	187 246	202.3	16 697
At Large	12.4	8.5	13.8	470 708	40 461	8.6	430 247	38.6	43.4	18.0	10.6	187 246	202.3	16 697
DISTRICT OF COLUMBIA	18.9	15.7	15.7	371 969	38 858	10.4	333 111	61.7	32.5	5.8	7.4	78 416	121.3	26 806
Delegate District (At Large)	18.9	15.7	15.7	371 969	38 858	10.4	333 111	61.7	32.5	5.8	7.4	78 416	121.3	26 806
FLORIDA	17.0	12.4	15.1	9 369 264	909 274	9.7	8 459 990	33.6	48.4	18.1	24.2	4 114 745	210.4	548 178
District 1	16.0	11.5	13.4	333 010	30 142	9.1	302 868	32.2	48.9	18.9	19.4	153 406	210.3	17 491
District 2	20.9	13.0	16.8	341 408	36 813	10.8	304 595	36.2	47.4	16.3	18.1	132 197	186.0	20 431
District 3	18.7	12.5	12.6	317 373	31 371	9.9	286 002	34.1	45.5	20.4	18.5	150 719	213.1	16 637
District 4	12.2	8.7	9.4	368 915	30 002	8.1	338 913	39.4	43.3	17.2	17.7	127 051	180.2	12 841
District 5	28.0	22.6	28.7	345 470	47 490	13.7	297 980	25.6	53.1	21.2	25.5	122 937	168.6	34 465
District 6	15.0	9.9	12.3	310 602	25 185	8.1	285 417	35.9	45.4	18.7	21.6	196 732	272.2	14 228
District 7	13.7	9.2	10.0	372 787	36 498	9.8	336 289	39.8	46.2	14.0	19.9	124 948	174.3	11 579
District 8	14.8	10.5	13.8	324 161	36 888	11.4	287 273	34.3	46.7	19.1	22.0	194 004	275.6	13 975
District 9	20.6	16.6	19.7	388 174	31 185	8.0	356 989	27.6	52.0	20.3	27.6	120 412	156.7	22 715
District 10	13.5	9.7	12.2	367 744	29 694	8.1	338 050	35.9	48.4	15.7	21.7	153 627	209.8	15 231
District 11	16.2	11.4	15.7	257 230	30 255	11.8	226 975	28.0	52.2	19.8	22.5	264 407	369.3	16 779
District 12	11.6	7.7	11.9	332 793	25 973	7.8	306 820	41.7	45.0	13.3	18.5	176 039	244.8	13 497
District 13	14.8	10.6	12.2	347 828	29 787	8.6	318 041	35.9	47.1	17.1	22.4	178 629	255.4	14 066
District 14	21.8	17.5	20.7	377 038	37 625	10.0	339 413	34.4	48.5	17.0	22.1	123 275	168.1	33 977
District 15	14.9	9.7	14.1	358 669	30 670	8.6	327 999	35.5	43.6	20.8	18.9	130 578	181.8	17 348
District 16	14.4	8.9	10.4	309 743	27 117	8.8	282 626	31.5	50.8	17.8	23.5	210 939	290.1	10 361
District 17	18.1	12.4	14.5	280 202	30 509	10.9	249 693	28.6	47.3	24.2	25.5	197 070	273.2	16 004
District 18	13.6	10.1	9.7	331 341	28 739	8.7	302 602	35.0	46.9	18.1	21.6	176 672	250.4	10 769
District 19	15.0	10.1	9.9	321 516	29 782	9.3	291 734	31.9	50.2	18.0	27.2	193 477	262.0	11 250
District 20	23.9	19.7	21.7	363 812	47 870	13.2	315 942	23.8	57.0	19.2	31.3	117 015	160.5	27 659
District 21	11.2	8.4	8.3	358 682	34 813	9.7	323 869	37.2	47.3	15.5	22.8	159 042	215.2	8 976
District 22	15.2	11.1	9.2	400 679	37 850	9.4	362 829	36.2	48.0	15.8	26.6	150 144	204.5	10 941
District 23	13.8	10.3	11.7	382 887	31 659	8.3	351 228	39.9	45.8	14.3	24.9	115 876	161.0	17 599
District 24	24.8	21.3	26.6	363 304	46 774	12.9	316 530	28.4	53.0	18.6	35.1	103 330	142.5	42 854
District 25	18.4	15.5	24.4	369 118	34 036	9.2	335 082	27.8	48.9	23.3	33.3	112 552	152.0	34 347
District 26	18.0	14.0	22.1	376 849	37 460	9.9	339 389	32.5	49.2	18.2	31.7	111 983	151.1	34 121
District 27	20.1	16.7	25.4	367 929	33 087	9.0	334 842	33.2	48.2	18.6	30.6	117 684	163.5	48 037

1. Percent of civilian labor force. 2. Persons 16 years old and over. 3. Per 1,000 resident population estimated in the 2013 American Community Survey.

Table E. Congressional Districts 113th Congress — **Agriculture**

STATE District	Agriculture, 2012									
		Land in farms			Value of products sold				Government payments	
	Number of farms	Acres	Average size of farm (acres)	Irrigated land (acres)	Total ($1,000)	Average per farm (dollars)	Percent from crops	Percent from livestock and poultry products	Total ($1,000)	Average per farm receiving payments (dollars)
	63	64	65	66	67	68	69	70	71	72
CALIFORNIA—Cont'd										
District 38	30	1 770	59	108	6 575	219 161	100.0	0.0	0	0
District 39	115	1 527	13	657	9 804	85 251	96.0	4.0	D	D
District 40	16	128	8	95	1 450	90 631	D	D	0	0
District 41	426	30 431	71	8 036	43 767	102 739	D	D	181	9 037
District 42	1 314	106 046	81	20 049	225 256	171 428	41.9	58.1	548	18 880
District 43	46	712	15	132	8 896	193 384	99.4	0.6	0	0
District 44	56	521	9	152	13 299	237 477	0.0	0.0	0	0
District 45	114	48 582	426	5 163	96 549	846 923	98.7	1.3	10	1 615
District 46	41	1 137	28	111	5 239	127 776	99.1	0.9	24	7 942
District 47	43	D	D	944	3 623	84 263	96.6	3.4	D	D
District 48	37	3 114	84	1 638	39 131	1 057 588	D	D	D	D
District 49	935	D	D	6 737	137 991	147 584	81.4	18.6	71	4 730
District 50	4 302	160 752	37	36 291	529 777	123 147	90.8	9.2	388	4 844
District 51	721	557 584	773	462 112	1 955 250	2 711 858	70.3	29.7	2 789	21 790
District 52	227	6 597	29	2 203	31 502	138 777	98.3	1.7	D	D
District 53	84	1 594	19	290	6 909	82 246	99.2	0.8	0	0
COLORADO	36 180	31 886 676	881	2 516 785	7 780 874	215 060	31.3	68.7	165 576	14 897
District 1	24	1 065	44	74	D	D	D	D	0	0
District 2	3 055	926 007	303	116 782	177 941	58 246	47.7	52.3	1 675	5 511
District 3	13 954	8 837 850	633	1 062 127	970 501	69 550	53.5	46.5	18 852	8 360
District 4	15 949	20 596 438	1 291	1 293 158	6 460 512	405 073	26.6	73.4	141 885	17 318
District 5	2 520	1 237 551	491	36 488	83 271	33 044	0.0	0.0	1 745	7 897
District 6	357	220 448	618	4 345	D	D	D	D	1 001	9 351
District 7	321	67 317	210	3 811	40 961	127 603	91.2	8.8	D	D
CONNECTICUT	5 977	436 539	73	9 272	550 620	92 123	70.7	29.3	4 841	9 328
District 1	826	46 562	56	4 128	106 344	128 745	96.7	3.3	325	5 908
District 2	2 762	200 857	73	3 001	272 398	98 624	57.4	42.6	2 729	10 579
District 3	579	35 645	62	1 080	34 176	59 026	78.6	21.4	238	5 409
District 4	348	53 930	155	319	30 068	86 401	55.1	44.9	78	6 487
District 5	1 462	99 545	68	744	107 634	73 621	80.5	19.5	1 471	9 808
DELAWARE	2 451	508 652	208	127 272	1 274 014	519 794	33.7	66.3	9 677	10 553
At Large	2 451	508 652	208	127 272	1 274 014	519 794	33.7	66.3	9 677	10 553
DISTRICT OF COLUMBIA	X	X	X	X	X	X	X	X	X	X
Delegate District (At Large)	X	X	X	X	X	X	X	X	X	X
FLORIDA	47 740	9 548 342	200	1 493 320	7 701 532	161 322	77.5	22.5	40 164	10 158
District 1	3 181	469 042	147	9 215	169 985	53 438	74.9	25.1	6 426	7 377
District 2	4 105	794 768	194	33 990	256 516	62 489	75.0	25.0	5 840	5 720
District 3	8 862	1 290 144	146	107 825	975 689	110 098	34.1	65.9	6 700	7 718
District 4	1 114	95 293	86	781	31 667	28 426	29.1	70.9	242	6 916
District 5	1 419	112 887	80	5 257	243 410	171 536	89.5	10.5	183	5 709
District 6	1 811	228 498	126	29 595	233 438	128 900	93.7	6.3	1 729	12 264
District 7	473	33 415	71	4 545	59 629	126 065	96.9	3.1	43	4 825
District 8	1 122	399 784	356	73 129	203 360	181 248	85.8	14.2	959	29 963
District 9	578	578 346	1 001	32 362	130 432	225 662	67.3	32.7	328	19 265
District 10	2 017	221 769	110	26 061	198 780	98 552	94.9	5.1	366	14 635
District 11	4 978	441 454	89	14 700	170 324	34 215	45.3	54.7	881	8 476
District 12	1 298	182 782	141	7 371	82 447	63 519	45.0	55.0	427	12 948
District 13	87	847	10	101	1 856	21 332	89.1	10.9	D	D
District 14	232	56 265	243	2 466	57 548	248 052	67.4	32.6	D	D
District 15	2 141	222 673	104	19 924	237 271	110 823	82.9	17.1	569	12 116
District 16	670	141 262	211	9 799	90 251	134 703	84.6	15.4	394	39 408
District 17	6 479	2 668 107	412	382 609	1 799 624	277 763	73.4	26.6	4 283	17 132
District 18	1 341	462 571	345	169 758	540 342	402 940	85.8	14.2	1 316	18 533
District 19	480	48 914	102	11 239	73 268	152 643	96.4	3.6	31	3 924
District 20	674	563 547	836	336 357	791 626	1 174 610	00.0	2.0	1 483	23 917
District 21	554	57 082	103	35 053	223 947	404 237	96.2	3.8	547	20 272
District 22	133	2 812	21	355	8 918	67 056	81.5	18.5	46	5 072
District 23	432	6 315	15	1 372	27 072	62 667	88.8	11.2	52	17 176
District 24	40	1 870	47	53	518	12 949	68.9	31.1	D	D
District 25	695	390 142	561	134 835	486 358	699 796	97.0	3.0	344	14 964
District 26	2 382	59 843	25	35 808	551 229	231 415	96.3	3.7	6 009	27 691
District 27	442	17 910	41	8 760	56 027	126 758	97.9	2.1	876	31 299

1. Specified owner-occupied units. 2. Specified renter-occupied units.

STATE District	Representative, 114th Congress	Land area,[1] 2010 (sq km)	Population and population characteristics, 2013: Total persons	Per square kilometer	Percent: Race alone: White	Black	American Indian, Alaska Native	Asian and Pacific Islander	Some other race (percent)	Two or more races (percent)	Hispanic or Latino[2] (percent)	Non-Hispanic White alone (percent)	Percent female	Percent foreign-born	Percent born in state of residence
		1	2	3	4	5	6	7	8	9	10	11	12	13	14
GEORGIA		148 959	9 992 167	67.1	60.4	31.0	0.2	3.6	2.7	2.1	9.1	54.6	51.1	9.7	55.1
District 1	Earl L. "Buddy" Carter (R)	20 675	721 388	34.9	63.6	29.9	0.3	1.6	1.7	2.9	6.3	59.8	50.8	5.0	56.8
District 2	Sanford D. Bishop Jr. (D)	24 932	696 006	27.9	43.3	51.3	0.1	1.2	2.2	1.8	5.1	40.8	50.9	4.2	71.0
District 3	Lynn A. Westmoreland (R)	9 941	713 143	71.7	69.7	24.1	0.2	1.9	1.6	2.6	5.4	66.4	51.7	4.8	62.6
District 4	Henry C. "Hank" Johnson Jr. (D)	1 286	721 682	561.2	30.0	58.7	0.2	5.4	3.7	2.0	8.7	25.3	52.9	15.8	44.6
District 5	John Lewis (D)	686	719 920	1 049.4	33.7	58.0	0.2	3.9	2.0	2.1	7.7	28.9	51.0	9.4	52.9
District 6	Tom Price (R)	774	726 129	938.2	70.6	15.0	0.3	9.8	1.7	2.6	12.4	60.7	50.2	22.0	32.3
District 7	Robert Woodall (R)	1 017	735 051	722.8	59.6	18.3	0.2	12.3	7.1	2.5	19.2	48.3	50.5	23.3	36.1
District 8	Austin Scott (R)	22 563	696 584	30.9	63.9	30.3	0.2	1.5	2.2	1.8	6.1	60.7	51.0	5.0	70.1
District 9	Doug Collins (R)	13 496	711 655	52.7	86.6	7.3	0.2	1.3	3.5	1.1	12.3	78.0	50.6	7.7	61.1
District 10	Jody B. Hice (R)	18 379	699 534	38.1	69.6	24.9	0.3	2.5	0.9	1.8	4.9	65.9	50.9	5.0	66.2
District 11	Barry Loudermilk (R)	2 775	730 150	263.1	74.5	15.6	0.1	3.1	4.6	2.2	12.2	67.5	51.1	11.6	43.9
District 12	Rick W. Allen (R)	21 200	706 182	33.3	58.9	35.4	0.2	1.8	1.8	2.0	5.7	55.5	50.6	4.1	67.2
District 13	David Scott (D)	1 852	718 624	388.0	36.4	56.4	0.1	2.7	2.2	2.1	9.9	29.7	53.0	10.5	50.9
District 14	Tom Graves (R)	9 384	696 119	74.2	86.1	8.9	0.2	0.8	2.1	1.9	10.7	77.9	50.9	6.5	59.1
HAWAII		16 635	1 404 054	84.4	25.6	2.2	0.2	47.6	1.0	23.5	9.8	23.0	49.7	17.6	54.2
District 1	Mark Takai (D)	542	702 026	1 295.3	18.2	2.7	0.1	58.2	1.0	19.9	8.4	16.4	49.7	22.3	53.3
District 2	Tulsi Gabbard (D)	16 093	702 028	43.6	32.9	1.6	0.2	37.1	1.0	27.1	11.3	29.6	49.6	12.8	55.1
IDAHO		214 045	1 612 136	7.5	91.5	0.6	1.2	1.7	2.6	2.4	11.8	83.2	49.9	5.9	47.1
District 1	Raul Labrador (R)	102 092	812 462	8.0	92.7	0.5	1.3	1.4	1.8	2.3	10.2	84.8	49.9	4.5	42.4
District 2	Michael K. Simpson (R)	111 952	799 674	7.1	90.3	0.6	1.2	1.9	3.5	2.5	13.4	81.5	49.9	7.4	51.7
ILLINOIS		143 793	12 882 135	89.6	72.7	14.2	0.2	5.0	5.7	2.2	16.4	62.7	50.9	14.0	67.2
District 1	Bobby L. Rush (D)	669	718 967	1 074.7	40.4	51.2	0.3	2.3	3.8	2.0	9.4	35.5	53.4	7.8	76.1
District 2	Robin L. Kelly (D)	2 799	699 363	249.9	39.3	55.7	0.2	0.7	2.3	1.9	12.3	30.4	52.9	6.8	75.7
District 3	Daniel Lipinski (D)	614	737 806	1 201.6	76.4	5.3	0.2	3.5	12.7	1.9	31.2	59.1	50.7	22.2	69.3
District 4	Luis V. Gutierrez (D)	136	712 077	5 235.9	61.7	4.5	0.5	3.4	27.9	2.0	70.5	20.8	49.3	35.3	52.9
District 5	Michael Quigley (D)	248	734 664	2 962.4	81.7	2.9	0.2	7.6	5.0	2.6	19.8	68.1	50.7	22.0	55.6
District 6	Peter J. Roskam (R)	981	727 718	741.8	84.8	2.3	0.1	8.9	2.0	1.8	10.0	77.5	51.1	14.4	65.8
District 7	Danny K. Davis (D)	162	720 325	4 446.5	34.4	51.2	0.0	6.2	5.8	2.3	12.6	28.4	52.6	11.8	64.0
District 8	Tammy Duckworth (D)	532	715 255	1 344.5	67.8	4.9	0.3	11.6	13.1	2.3	28.0	54.1	50.4	27.9	59.4
District 9	Janice D. Schakowsky (D)	273	709 590	2 599.2	72.5	8.7	0.3	13.0	2.8	2.7	11.8	63.9	51.1	27.8	53.1
District 10	Robert J. Dold (R)	776	716 308	923.1	74.8	6.8	0.3	9.8	5.7	2.6	22.7	58.8	50.4	24.8	55.8
District 11	Bill Foster (D)	728	709 493	974.6	66.0	10.8	0.2	7.3	12.6	3.1	26.9	52.7	50.7	19.4	64.4
District 12	Mike Bost (R)	12 971	702 625	54.2	79.2	16.7	0.2	1.1	0.4	2.3	3.0	77.0	50.6	2.3	69.3
District 13	Rodney Davis (R)	15 005	715 907	47.7	81.9	10.9	0.2	3.3	0.6	3.1	3.1	79.6	50.9	4.9	75.3
District 14	Randy Hultgren (R)	4 138	729 162	176.2	88.2	2.9	0.1	4.4	2.4	1.9	10.9	80.1	49.8	9.0	70.8
District 15	John Shimkus (R)	38 062	705 563	18.5	93.6	3.7	0.1	0.5	0.3	1.6	2.7	91.6	50.1	1.8	75.0
District 16	Adam Kinzinger (R)	20 506	697 856	34.0	91.5	3.9	0.1	1.2	1.5	1.8	9.0	84.6	50.4	4.8	77.4
District 17	Cheri Bustos (D)	17 957	710 667	39.6	82.1	11.1	0.1	1.5	2.5	2.7	8.7	76.7	50.8	4.9	72.1
District 18	Vacancy	27 236	718 789	26.4	91.3	3.8	0.1	2.6	0.6	1.7	2.9	89.2	50.7	4.0	77.5
INDIANA		92 789	6 570 902	70.8	84.2	9.2	0.2	1.8	2.5	2.2	6.4	80.6	50.8	4.8	68.5
District 1	Peter J. Visclosky (D)	2 997	719 164	240.0	70.1	19.6	0.4	1.4	6.2	2.3	14.6	63.3	51.0	5.4	58.8
District 2	Jackie Walorski (R)	10 253	719 730	70.2	86.9	6.5	0.4	1.1	2.2	2.9	9.0	80.8	50.6	5.5	70.2
District 3	Marlin Stutzman (R)	10 827	729 747	67.4	87.9	6.0	0.1	1.7	2.0	2.2	5.8	84.4	50.7	4.3	73.0
District 4	Todd Rokita (R)	16 453	738 647	44.9	90.9	3.4	0.2	2.5	1.0	1.9	5.8	86.6	49.8	4.9	70.1
District 5	Susan W. Brooks (R)	4 985	743 062	149.1	84.8	7.7	0.1	3.4	1.8	2.1	3.9	82.6	51.2	6.0	65.8
District 6	Luke Messer (R)	16 076	724 638	45.1	93.2	2.6	0.1	1.1	1.3	1.7	2.3	92.2	50.7	2.3	70.7
District 7	André Carson (D)	787	743 136	944.3	58.9	29.7	0.2	2.0	6.3	2.9	10.8	54.7	51.7	9.0	67.7
District 8	Larry Bucshon (R)	18 791	720 976	38.4	92.5	4.0	0.2	0.9	0.6	1.8	2.3	90.9	50.2	1.9	75.2
District 9	Todd C. Young (R)	11 621	731 802	63.0	92.5	2.8	0.2	2.1	0.6	1.8	3.3	90.1	50.7	3.8	65.6
IOWA		144 669	3 090 416	21.4	91.4	3.3	0.2	2.1	1.2	1.7	5.4	87.5	50.4	4.8	71.2
District 1	Rod Blum (R)	31 206	766 821	24.6	91.9	3.7	0.3	1.3	1.1	1.7	3.6	89.6	50.6	3.5	76.5
District 2	David Loebsack (D)	31 758	774 072	24.4	90.6	4.1	0.2	2.3	1.3	1.6	5.2	86.9	50.3	4.3	68.2
District 3	David Young (R)	22 765	788 588	34.6	89.5	4.1	0.2	2.8	1.3	2.1	6.5	84.5	50.8	6.6	67.5
District 4	Steve King (R)	58 940	760 935	12.9	93.5	1.4	0.3	2.0	1.3	1.4	6.2	89.1	50.1	4.8	72.9
KANSAS		211 754	2 893 957	13.7	85.6	5.8	0.8	2.6	1.9	3.3	11.1	77.1	50.3	6.8	58.8
District 1	Tim Huelskamp (R)	136 084	722 463	5.3	88.2	3.0	0.6	1.7	3.6	3.0	14.9	77.8	49.4	7.4	63.2
District 2	Lynn Jenkins (R)	36 631	715 785	19.5	87.8	4.4	1.4	1.3	1.0	4.1	6.2	83.3	50.3	3.4	63.7
District 3	Kevin Yoder (R)	1 961	738 508	376.6	81.6	8.8	0.4	4.2	2.1	2.9	11.6	72.8	50.9	9.6	43.6
District 4	Mike Pompeo (R)	37 077	717 201	19.3	84.8	7.0	0.9	3.1	1.0	3.3	11.8	74.5	50.5	6.9	65.3

1. Dry land or land partially or temporarily covered by water. 2. May be of any race.

STATE District	Population and population characteristics, 2013 (cont.)										Education, 2013		
	Age (percent)											Attainment[2] (percent)	
	Under 5 years	5 to 17 years	18 to 24 years	25 to 34 years	35 to 44 years	45 to 54 years	55 to 64 years	65 to 74 years	75 years and over	Median age	Total Enrollment[1]	High school graduate or more	Bachelor's degree or more
	15	16	17	18	19	20	21	22	23	24	25	26	27
GEORGIA	6.6	18.3	10.3	13.5	13.9	13.9	11.6	7.3	4.6	35.9	2 784 646	85.5	28.3
District 1	7.1	17.6	11.2	14.5	12.6	12.7	11.6	7.9	4.8	34.7	194 140	87.7	25.3
District 2	6.6	17.8	11.7	13.5	12.2	12.7	12.1	7.7	5.6	35.3	199 367	79.5	16.7
District 3	6.0	19.4	9.7	12.3	13.2	14.4	11.8	8.0	5.2	37.2	196 489	86.5	24.4
District 4	6.9	18.5	9.8	13.8	14.3	14.6	12.5	6.2	3.5	35.7	203 776	86.0	29.4
District 5	7.0	14.6	13.9	18.1	15.0	12.2	9.4	6.0	3.9	33.2	202 975	88.4	41.0
District 6	7.0	17.4	7.2	14.2	15.7	15.4	12.1	6.3	4.6	37.8	191 013	92.7	57.0
District 7	6.8	21.5	8.6	12.8	16.2	15.3	10.2	5.6	3.1	35.1	227 001	87.8	37.1
District 8	6.7	17.8	10.8	13.4	12.4	13.2	12.1	8.0	5.6	36.2	191 892	83.1	18.2
District 9	6.2	17.7	9.2	11.3	12.9	13.6	13.0	10.1	6.3	39.9	172 700	80.8	20.4
District 10	5.5	18.5	12.5	11.4	13.9	13.4	11.8	8.4	4.7	36.7	208 156	84.5	23.3
District 11	6.2	18.8	9.7	14.6	15.4	14.1	10.4	6.7	4.1	35.5	205 967	89.7	37.4
District 12	6.6	17.6	12.2	13.5	12.2	13.4	11.9	7.5	5.2	35.1	193 465	82.8	20.9
District 13	7.0	20.5	8.7	13.6	14.6	15.0	11.6	6.0	3.2	35.2	214 184	87.7	25.3
District 14	6.4	19.2	9.3	11.9	14.4	13.9	12.0	7.8	5.2	37.3	183 521	78.5	16.8
HAWAII	6.5	15.5	9.8	14.5	12.6	12.8	12.7	8.6	7.1	38.1	338 688	91.0	31.2
District 1	6.2	14.2	9.5	15.2	13.1	13.1	11.8	8.8	8.1	39.0	165 432	90.0	34.9
District 2	6.7	16.7	10.0	13.9	12.1	12.5	13.5	8.4	6.1	37.0	173 256	92.1	27.3
IDAHO	6.9	19.5	9.8	12.9	12.1	12.7	12.2	8.1	5.7	35.7	435 040	89.4	26.2
District 1	6.4	19.7	8.8	12.1	12.2	13.2	12.6	9.1	5.9	37.6	209 831	90.2	24.7
District 2	7.4	19.5	10.8	13.7	12.0	12.1	11.8	7.1	5.5	34.0	225 209	88.6	27.9
ILLINOIS	6.2	17.3	9.8	13.9	13.1	13.9	12.4	7.5	6.0	37.2	3 441 460	87.8	32.1
District 1	6.0	16.7	11.0	11.8	12.2	14.8	13.0	7.4	7.2	38.9	203 166	88.1	25.8
District 2	6.1	18.4	9.6	11.8	12.2	13.7	13.1	8.8	6.3	38.2	198 225	87.5	21.8
District 3	6.5	18.5	9.4	13.3	13.1	14.1	12.1	7.3	5.6	36.7	203 510	83.4	25.3
District 4	7.9	19.6	10.6	18.0	15.2	11.9	9.0	4.5	3.2	31.3	199 935	67.6	19.7
District 5	6.1	12.5	8.9	22.9	14.3	12.7	10.6	6.3	5.6	34.8	166 288	90.8	50.8
District 6	5.9	18.8	8.0	11.1	12.8	16.4	13.9	7.6	5.3	40.1	199 949	94.2	50.1
District 7	6.4	15.2	11.5	19.0	13.7	12.2	10.9	6.2	4.8	33.7	189 934	84.9	38.9
District 8	7.0	17.4	8.9	15.3	14.4	13.7	11.9	6.8	4.4	36.0	182 416	85.8	32.3
District 9	5.7	14.6	8.5	14.9	13.4	14.1	13.0	7.9	7.9	39.9	180 257	91.4	52.0
District 10	6.3	19.3	9.6	11.6	13.4	14.9	12.0	7.0	5.8	37.3	197 588	88.1	42.9
District 11	6.6	20.5	9.1	14.0	15.3	13.9	10.7	6.1	4.1	34.9	203 296	85.2	35.4
District 12	6.0	16.2	10.3	12.6	12.4	14.2	13.4	8.1	6.8	38.7	180 003	89.1	22.0
District 13	5.8	15.5	15.2	13.8	11.2	12.3	12.2	7.4	6.7	34.8	221 895	91.6	29.7
District 14	5.8	21.0	8.1	11.0	14.0	15.6	12.5	7.4	4.5	38.5	209 702	93.3	37.7
District 15	5.8	16.5	9.1	11.4	12.0	14.4	13.5	9.4	8.1	41.1	167 287	88.1	18.0
District 16	5.6	17.1	10.1	11.6	11.9	14.6	13.3	8.8	7.1	40.2	182 398	90.7	21.6
District 17	6.3	17.0	9.3	12.1	12.0	13.4	13.3	9.0	7.5	39.3	175 433	86.4	18.3
District 18	5.5	16.6	9.7	11.8	12.4	13.6	14.0	8.8	7.7	40.4	180 178	92.7	31.3
INDIANA	6.5	17.7	10.2	12.8	12.6	13.8	12.6	7.8	6.1	37.3	1 726 742	87.6	23.8
District 1	6.2	17.7	9.2	12.8	12.6	13.9	13.6	7.9	6.1	38.4	185 269	88.3	20.5
District 2	6.6	18.8	9.6	11.8	12.3	13.5	12.7	7.9	6.7	37.5	190 160	84.6	20.3
District 3	6.8	19.0	9.4	12.5	12.5	13.3	12.8	7.8	6.1	36.9	192 220	86.5	21.1
District 4	6.4	17.2	12.6	12.1	12.2	13.2	12.2	7.9	6.1	36.5	202 127	89.2	23.7
District 5	6.0	18.8	8.0	13.3	14.3	14.8	11.9	7.4	5.6	37.6	196 248	92.6	42.3
District 6	5.7	17.2	10.4	11.1	12.4	14.5	13.0	9.1	6.7	40.2	184 022	86.5	19.9
District 7	8.0	17.7	10.5	16.2	12.8	12.8	11.2	6.0	4.7	33.2	196 361	82.8	21.0
District 8	6.2	16.4	10.0	12.6	11.7	14.2	13.6	8.5	7.0	39.7	174 136	88.3	20.3
District 9	6.0	16.4	12.2	12.8	12.4	13.6	12.6	8.2	5.8	37.1	206 199	89.0	24.5
IOWA	6.2	17.1	10.3	12.6	11.8	13.4	13.0	8.0	7.5	38.0	815 675	91.6	26.4
District 1	6.1	17.0	10.6	12.1	11.4	13.5	13.1	8.3	7.8	38.6	199 236	91.6	23.8
District 2	6.1	16.7	10.8	12.9	11.3	13.5	13.3	8.3	7.2	37.9	208 183	91.5	27.9
District 3	6.9	18.1	8.5	14.3	13.3	13.4	12.1	7.3	6.0	36.7	202 147	92.6	31.3
District 4	5.8	16.9	11.4	11.1	10.9	13.2	13.5	8.4	9.0	39.4	206 109	90.7	22.5
KANSAS	6.9	18.1	10.4	13.4	12.0	12.9	12.3	7.5	6.5	36.0	797 058	90.1	31.1
District 1	7.0	17.2	12.8	13.0	10.8	11.8	12.1	7.7	7.5	35.0	197 396	88.1	23.9
District 2	6.0	17.2	11.3	12.7	11.7	12.9	12.9	8.2	6.9	37.1	195 150	90.8	27.0
District 3	7.2	19.0	8.0	14.4	13.6	13.9	12.0	6.8	5.2	36.0	203 082	91.5	44.7
District 4	7.3	18.7	9.6	13.5	11.7	13.0	12.6	7.3	6.5	35.8	201 430	89.7	27.9

1. All persons 3 years old and over enrolled in nursery school through college and graduate or professional school. 2. Persons 25 years old and over.

STATE District	Households, 2013							Group quarters, 2010				
	Number	Average household size	Family households (percent)	Married-couple family (percent)	Female family householder[1]	One person households (percent)	Total in group quarters, 2013	Percent 65 years and over	Persons in correctional institutions	Persons in nursing facilities	Persons in college dormitories	Persons in military quarters
	28	29	30	31	32	33	34	35	36	37	38	39
GEORGIA	3 546 965	2.74	67.40	47.2	15.3	27.0	260 701	12.5	104 012	34 738	72 288	16 072
District 1	258 808	2.69	68.70	47.3	15.9	26.2	24 449	10.4	10 733	3 028	5 798	5 069
District 2	245 676	2.65	65.90	39.0	21.8	29.8	45 247	8.4	17 145	3 559	7 343	5 167
District 3	255 014	2.75	72.10	53.3	14.0	24.0	12 402	20.6	4 777	2 837	4 020	64
District 4	245 266	2.91	67.80	41.8	20.1	26.2	6 963	17.9	4 367	1 472	653	0
District 5	281 992	2.41	48.00	27.0	17.5	43.0	41 646	5.3	6 731	2 500	22 635	78
District 6	276 007	2.62	65.80	52.8	9.2	27.4	2 872	49.0	89	1 109	620	0
District 7	235 938	3.09	76.00	58.2	12.7	19.3	5 147	18.9	4 093	1 167	0	0
District 8	250 053	2.69	67.80	47.2	15.5	26.5	24 985	13.4	13 355	4 044	5 390	401
District 9	256 649	2.72	71.00	54.4	11.8	23.9	12 741	17.7	4 824	2 514	4 115	44
District 10	244 205	2.77	69.20	51.3	13.0	24.8	22 652	12.0	10 678	2 840	9 699	74
District 11	266 188	2.7	65.60	48.8	11.5	28.1	10 130	14.1	3 520	1 539	4 296	36
District 12	241 413	2.79	66.00	43.7	17.3	28.6	33 073	10.7	15 029	3 980	5 294	5 139
District 13	247 210	2.88	69.20	43.2	20.4	26.0	5 635	21.4	3 437	1 322	0	0
District 14	242 546	2.82	73.40	54.4	13.8	22.3	12 759	21.5	5 234	2 827	2 425	0
HAWAII	450 120	3.02	69.10	52.3	11.8	24.1	43 282	12.2	5 673	5 198	7 540	12 551
District 1	231 882	2.93	66.90	51.1	11.3	26.2	23 017	13.3	3 581	2 672	4 641	5 332
District 2	218 238	3.12	71.50	53.5	12.3	21.9	20 265	10.9	2 092	2 526	2 899	7 219
IDAHO	588 489	2.69	69.70	55.2	9.8	24.1	29 416	16.9	11 275	4 820	7 223	466
District 1	294 247	2.7	71.20	56.7	9.8	23.4	17 297	15.4	7 951	2 375	4 359	0
District 2	294 242	2.68	68.20	53.7	9.7	24.7	12 119	19.2	3 324	2 445	2 864	466
ILLINOIS	4 783 421	2.63	65.40	48.1	12.7	28.9	299 479	22.6	70 828	81 516	92 960	12 483
District 1	265 363	2.66	63.10	36.6	21.5	33.0	12 282	21.7	0	4 063	5 957	0
District 2	261 661	2.63	62.80	35.8	21.7	33.7	11 765	31.1	685	5 037	2 054	0
District 3	240 005	3.03	73.30	54.5	13.0	22.6	10 940	30.2	3 160	3 740	1 890	0
District 4	219 830	3.22	69.10	43.3	17.2	23.6	3 294	34.4	1	1 268	285	0
District 5	303 624	2.38	52.20	41.0	7.9	35.8	10 656	32.7	0	3 882	4 823	0
District 6	259 772	2.77	73.90	62.8	7.7	22.1	8 981	36.8	786	4 034	3 517	0
District 7	287 935	2.41	51.10	27.7	18.8	40.9	27 056	6.3	11 612	3 240	7 992	16
District 8	253 568	2.8	68.40	52.2	11.1	26.1	5 069	45.7	0	2 564	744	0
District 9	278 596	2.47	58.60	47.3	8.0	34.4	22 242	27.4	31	8 543	8 803	0
District 10	250 517	2.78	72.40	57.5	10.9	23.9	20 076	19.5	704	5 665	2 088	12 155
District 11	237 136	2.96	72.30	54.4	12.6	23.0	6 691	33.9	1 085	2 891	1 495	0
District 12	278 694	2.44	65.00	45.7	14.3	29.8	21 394	22.6	10 700	5 209	3 332	307
District 13	279 000	2.41	60.60	43.7	12.7	31.1	43 049	12.5	5 125	5 481	27 454	0
District 14	252 437	2.87	75.20	62.6	9.0	20.8	4 495	33.0	1 364	1 562	158	0
District 15	275 846	2.46	67.60	52.3	10.5	28.7	26 027	23.2	12 642	6 376	3 900	0
District 16	268 223	2.53	67.50	52.6	10.5	26.9	19 355	26.0	6 821	5 619	6 178	0
District 17	284 747	2.41	64.00	45.5	13.7	31.0	23 263	21.2	8 864	5 921	5 835	0
District 18	286 467	2.43	67.00	54.6	8.4	27.9	22 844	27.7	7 248	6 421	6 455	5
INDIANA	2 498 395	2.55	66.00	49.1	12.3	28.2	188 594	20.5	48 694	41 158	75 434	228
District 1	271 596	2.58	67.80	46.9	15.7	27.4	18 078	19.0	7 380	3 116	3 194	0
District 2	270 169	2.58	67.00	48.8	12.9	27.7	21 448	20.0	5 936	4 482	8 659	0
District 3	278 250	2.57	67.00	51.6	11.3	28.0	13 362	33.2	2 229	4 852	3 948	0
District 4	277 481	2.56	67.80	53.5	9.5	25.6	29 184	15.3	7 233	4 934	15 651	0
District 5	289 240	2.51	65.40	51.6	10.4	29.1	16 258	25.1	4 416	4 444	5 257	0
District 6	278 245	2.53	67.10	51.1	11.2	26.9	21 410	23.8	5 096	5 532	8 541	178
District 7	282 975	2.57	59.20	35.0	18.7	34.0	15 564	18.3	3 216	3 152	5 162	0
District 8	275 819	2.5	65.70	51.8	9.7	29.0	30 342	19.4	10 561	5 980	10 509	50
District 9	274 620	2.58	66.90	51.7	11.4	26.3	22 948	17.9	2 627	4 666	14 513	0
IOWA	1 236 209	2.42	64.20	50.6	9.4	29.0	100 100	26.1	13 309	26 871	44 574	3
District 1	304 696	2.43	64.60	51.1	9.5	28.9	27 559	26.1	2 415	7 519	13 934	3
District 2	310 364	2.41	62.40	49.0	9.3	30.2	25 686	21.8	5 185	5 702	11 804	0
District 3	310 669	2.48	66.60	50.8	10.6	26.8	17 425	27.7	3 690	5 218	5 248	0
District 4	310 480	2.36	63.30	51.5	8.0	30.1	29 430	29.1	2 019	8 432	13 588	0
KANSAS	1 113 729	2.53	66.00	51.0	10.7	28.3	79 104	24.4	18 009	20 672	27 754	3 943
District 1	280 113	2.48	66.80	53.0	9.8	27.1	29 026	23.2	5 306	7 084	10 873	3 425
District 2	276 876	2.48	64.20	49.7	10.2	29.6	28 991	17.4	7 436	5 478	12 652	192
District 3	281 818	2.6	67.60	51.6	11.4	26.7	6 382	49.6	1 355	3 598	544	0
District 4	274 922	2.56	65.60	49.7	11.4	29.8	14 705	29.4	3 912	4 512	3 685	326

1. No spouse present.

STATE District	Housing units, 2013						Money income, 2013		
		Occupied units						Households	
			Owner-occupied			Renter-occupied			
	Total	Occupied units as a percent of all units	Owner-occupied units as a percent of occupied units	Median value[1] (dollars)	Percent valued at $500,000 or more	Median rent[2]	Per capita income (dollars)	Median income (dollars)	Percent with income of $100,000 or more
	40	41	42	43	44	45	46	47	48
GEORGIA	4 110 162	86.3	62.7	141 600	5.0	850	24 923	47 829	19.2
District 1	311 470	83.1	58.4	141 100	4.9	854	22 596	43 270	15.9
District 2	297 396	82.6	55.6	94 000	1.4	678	17 578	32 787	9.4
District 3	284 940	89.5	69.0	143 600	2.5	856	25 218	51 673	20.9
District 4	279 831	87.6	61.3	118 800	2.1	913	22 591	49 125	17.3
District 5	344 729	81.8	43.7	144 900	10.7	922	28 403	42 597	18.4
District 6	293 838	93.9	61.9	294 700	17.6	1 053	42 476	76 308	38.9
District 7	255 904	92.2	68.2	181 600	5.5	1 030	27 926	62 156	28.7
District 8	293 912	85.1	62.8	108 600	2.1	692	20 052	38 714	12.3
District 9	319 267	80.4	70.7	150 600	4.6	738	22 186	43 657	16.0
District 10	287 101	85.1	68.3	137 900	3.6	752	22 551	46 584	17.5
District 11	293 311	90.8	64.7	181 100	9.0	945	32 485	60 434	27.0
District 12	293 123	82.4	62.6	108 000	1.8	685	21 090	39 779	14.2
District 13	277 894	89.0	64.0	111 900	1.8	901	22 752	51 298	17.0
District 14	277 446	87.4	68.6	114 500	1.9	684	19 973	43 084	13.1
HAWAII	526 305	85.5	56.2	500 000	50.0	1 414	29 577	68 020	31.7
District 1	256 189	90.5	52.2	566 900	58.5	1 424	31 728	72 302	34.3
District 2	270 116	80.8	60.5	448 800	42.2	1 400	27 426	63 176	29.0
IDAHO	676 192	87.0	69.4	159 000	4.7	725	22 652	46 783	14.4
District 1	341 017	86.3	72.5	163 300	5.1	743	22 593	48 053	14.3
District 2	335 175	87.8	66.3	154 700	4.4	712	22 712	45 327	14.5
ILLINOIS	5 289 653	90.4	65.9	169 600	7.0	885	29 856	56 210	24.7
District 1	301 385	88.0	61.0	171 900	2.8	872	24 771	47 745	20.2
District 2	304 328	86.0	61.6	120 900	1.1	846	21 658	41 708	15.2
District 3	257 881	93.1	74.6	203 000	6.1	901	26 663	60 644	26.0
District 4	246 216	89.3	43.4	191 100	4.4	867	18 657	41 686	14.4
District 5	330 554	91.9	52.7	283 000	19.4	1 116	42 126	68 792	33.1
District 6	270 685	96.0	79.1	289 000	17.6	1 130	44 382	89 683	45.2
District 7	337 400	85.3	41.0	230 300	14.7	1 045	34 470	48 841	25.1
District 8	270 600	93.7	67.6	195 600	3.3	1 051	28 434	62 705	25.7
District 9	303 974	91.7	62.3	293 900	20.7	967	39 104	63 039	31.6
District 10	266 306	94.1	70.8	237 100	19.4	1 005	36 925	68 184	33.9
District 11	256 252	92.5	72.2	184 400	5.1	1 054	29 218	66 747	30.2
District 12	318 057	87.6	67.8	101 300	1.1	701	24 887	44 133	15.7
District 13	316 424	88.2	65.3	115 500	1.2	736	25 817	47 130	18.0
District 14	267 416	94.4	80.3	230 600	6.2	1 091	35 114	80 726	38.3
District 15	312 994	88.1	74.9	92 500	1.2	595	24 163	46 832	15.6
District 16	297 023	90.3	73.4	131 500	1.8	740	26 903	52 561	19.9
District 17	323 279	88.1	66.4	96 200	1.3	632	22 850	42 349	13.7
District 18	308 879	92.7	74.4	134 900	1.9	675	30 221	58 030	23.7
INDIANA	2 809 640	88.9	68.5	122 200	2.2	730	24 796	47 529	16.5
District 1	302 076	89.9	70.0	143 200	2.7	808	25 570	50 862	19.1
District 2	305 453	88.4	70.9	110 600	1.7	676	22 247	42 611	13.0
District 3	312 847	88.9	72.5	114 700	2.1	654	23 777	46 697	15.1
District 4	305 835	90.7	70.2	123 500	1.2	739	24 855	52 486	17.3
District 5	312 203	92.6	70.4	167 100	5.7	828	34 275	61 285	27.5
District 6	310 750	89.5	70.8	111 800	1.6	690	23 189	45 691	13.6
District 7	333 014	85.0	50.7	102 700	1.0	760	20 474	37 453	10.2
District 8	316 794	87.1	71.0	107 700	1.4	661	23 666	45 999	15.0
District 9	310 668	88.4	70.6	130 800	1.7	758	24 966	50 346	17.3
IOWA	1 349 607	91.6	70.8	126 900	2.1	679	27 740	52 229	19.1
District 1	334 674	91.0	73.3	133 100	2.0	653	26 856	52 237	18.2
District 2	336 722	92.2	68.8	125 000	1.9	666	27 116	50 855	18.8
District 3	333 462	93.2	69.5	147 800	2.7	766	30 328	57 593	22.8
District 4	344 749	90.1	71.7	106 200	1.8	627	26 583	49 497	16.6
KANSAS	1 239 755	89.8	66.1	129 700	2.6	745	27 175	50 972	19.6
District 1	315 746	88.7	66.0	100 700	1.4	666	23 973	45 273	13.4
District 2	314 355	88.1	66.9	110 900	1.5	711	24 644	48 926	16.8
District 3	300 939	93.6	65.7	192 700	5.8	888	34 658	64 266	30.0
District 4	308 715	89.1	65.6	115 000	1.6	696	25 220	48 560	18.1

1. Specified owner-occupied units. 2. Specified renter-occupied units.

STATE District	Poverty, 2013			Civilian labor force, 2013			Civilian employment,[2] 2013				Persons under age 65 with no health insurance, 2013 (percent)	Social Security beneficiaries, December 2013		Supplemental Security Income recipients, December 2013
					Unemployment			Percent						
	Persons below poverty level (percent)	Families below poverty level (percent)	Percent of households receiving food stamps in past 12 months	Total	Total	Rate[1]	Total	Management, business, science and arts occupations	Service, sales, and office	Construction and production		Number	Rate[3]	
	49	50	51	52	53	54	55	56	57	58	59	60	61	62
GEORGIA	19.0	14.5	16.2	4 846 590	498 751	10.3	4 347 839	35.6	42.3	22.1	21.2	1 632 953	163.4	253 498
District 1	19.4	15.4	14.9	329 910	35 696	10.8	294 214	32.4	42.8	25.0	21.2	121 461	168.4	17 648
District 2	27.2	23.2	26.6	292 275	43 294	14.8	248 981	27.7	47.2	25.2	23.7	131 467	188.9	31 036
District 3	16.3	11.8	15.9	335 550	32 557	9.7	302 993	32.5	39.7	27.8	16.0	136 310	191.1	17 297
District 4	18.2	14.5	19.0	376 150	46 412	12.3	329 738	33.8	45.3	20.9	24.3	106 277	147.3	19 469
District 5	25.2	20.3	19.7	378 477	48 372	12.8	330 105	42.6	43.4	13.9	22.5	90 042	125.1	26 600
District 6	10.7	7.4	6.0	400 409	23 228	5.8	377 181	51.6	38.1	10.2	15.9	87 166	120.0	6 269
District 7	12.2	9.3	11.0	382 446	33 143	8.7	349 303	40.5	42.5	17.0	21.7	78 856	107.3	8 505
District 8	21.6	17.5	18.5	299 398	30 653	10.2	268 745	32.0	43.7	24.3	23.2	135 765	194.9	25 183
District 9	20.1	14.9	15.4	331 132	31 076	9.4	300 056	29.3	41.2	29.4	22.6	153 249	215.3	16 180
District 10	19.5	13.2	14.9	332 223	29 921	9.0	302 302	32.6	42.9	24.4	18.6	131 238	187.6	18 095
District 11	14.0	9.9	10.3	389 036	31 005	8.0	358 031	41.8	40.9	17.3	20.7	99 065	135.7	8 692
District 12	24.9	19.1	18.3	301 292	34 267	11.4	267 025	32.5	42.9	24.6	20.7	130 239	184.4	24 677
District 13	18.4	14.2	19.7	369 068	46 952	12.7	322 116	32.1	43.7	24.1	23.9	101 141	140.7	16 714
District 14	19.3	15.3	18.2	329 224	32 175	9.8	297 049	28.1	40.7	31.3	21.9	130 677	187.7	17 133
HAWAII	10.8	7.1	11.3	685 185	41 614	6.1	643 571	34.2	47.5	18.2	7.8	246 477	175.5	25 342
District 1	8.9	5.7	9.3	344 861	15 556	4.5	329 305	36.0	46.7	17.4	6.3	123 923	176.5	12 188
District 2	12.8	8.5	13.5	340 324	26 058	7.7	314 266	32.4	48.3	19.2	9.4	122 554	174.6	13 154
IDAHO	15.6	10.4	13.0	765 759	55 466	7.2	710 293	33.0	42.2	24.7	18.6	298 269	185.0	30 317
District 1	15.6	10.4	13.6	370 122	28 585	7.7	341 537	32.5	43.2	24.4	18.7	167 899	206.7	16 279
District 2	15.6	10.4	12.3	395 637	26 881	6.8	368 756	33.6	41.4	25.0	18.5	130 370	163.0	14 038
ILLINOIS	14.7	10.8	13.5	6 712 311	638 222	9.5	6 074 089	36.6	42.2	21.2	14.5	2 133 829	165.6	278 543
District 1	20.2	15.2	21.5	358 868	55 158	15.4	303 710	32.7	48.5	18.8	15.6	124 094	172.6	29 054
District 2	22.7	18.1	23.6	340 905	59 773	17.5	281 132	29.4	46.8	23.8	18.4	132 374	189.3	28 289
District 3	13.1	10.2	12.1	376 476	39 159	10.4	337 317	30.5	43.6	25.9	16.7	114 823	155.6	11 780
District 4	22.6	19.8	21.2	362 242	37 710	10.4	324 532	23.1	44.9	32.1	28.8	82 833	116.3	22 573
District 5	10.7	7.3	6.5	446 986	28 273	6.3	418 713	48.3	39.1	12.7	14.8	104 200	141.8	14 454
District 6	5.2	3.5	4.1	399 669	25 827	6.5	373 842	47.4	39.0	13.7	7.7	102 779	141.2	5 193
District 7	25.7	21.6	23.9	367 819	53 148	14.4	314 671	45.4	40.6	14.0	18.7	89 806	124.7	32 756
District 8	11.1	8.2	10.8	406 312	32 281	7.9	374 031	32.4	43.1	24.6	16.3	95 079	132.9	8 093
District 9	12.8	7.8	10.0	383 636	28 079	7.3	355 557	48.9	38.5	12.6	14.7	120 218	169.4	17 974
District 10	9.9	7.6	9.9	369 106	28 362	7.7	340 744	41.3	40.5	18.2	14.1	99 088	138.3	8 961
District 11	10.3	7.6	10.9	379 545	32 626	8.6	346 919	36.6	42.2	21.1	14.8	84 989	119.8	7 996
District 12	18.4	13.2	16.6	335 532	31 765	9.5	303 767	30.4	46.1	23.5	13.1	137 047	195.0	19 784
District 13	18.9	11.7	15.0	364 917	33 201	9.1	331 716	37.0	43.5	19.5	11.1	129 432	180.8	15 234
District 14	6.4	5.2	5.9	394 846	30 816	7.8	364 030	39.8	41.7	18.5	8.8	114 653	157.2	4 857
District 15	15.1	11.0	13.8	344 299	30 080	8.7	314 219	29.1	40.9	30.0	13.0	161 467	228.8	15 672
District 16	13.0	9.3	11.4	360 321	34 872	9.7	325 449	30.9	41.2	27.9	11.1	149 367	214.0	10 722
District 17	18.3	13.4	17.7	349 615	34 307	9.8	315 308	28.2	43.2	28.7	13.3	141 617	199.3	15 212
District 18	10.8	7.2	8.4	371 217	22 785	6.1	348 432	38.8	40.3	21.0	8.2	149 963	208.6	9 939
INDIANA	15.9	11.9	13.1	3 282 793	257 007	7.8	3 025 786	32.1	40.4	27.5	16.1	1 267 542	192.9	127 355
District 1	16.6	13.5	13.8	350 445	31 044	8.9	319 401	30.3	42.3	27.5	15.1	140 045	194.7	16 456
District 2	18.3	14.2	14.2	354 263	30 259	8.5	324 004	28.0	39.6	32.4	18.8	141 670	196.8	13 312
District 3	15.3	11.3	12.0	364 174	27 174	7.5	337 000	29.0	37.3	33.8	18.7	140 241	192.2	12 454
District 4	12.6	7.8	10.0	373 054	24 728	6.6	348 326	31.3	39.6	29.1	13.5	139 206	188.5	9 794
District 5	11.1	8.7	9.5	391 773	23 073	5.9	368 700	45.0	38.5	16.5	12.2	129 023	173.6	9 675
District 6	15.3	10.8	13.8	354 708	31 016	8.7	323 692	30.5	40.4	29.2	15.9	161 099	222.3	14 674
District 7	24.1	20.2	21.8	376 813	44 155	11.7	332 658	29.6	44.4	25.9	20.9	117 312	157.9	23 484
District 8	15.1	10.8	12.3	346 922	22 208	6.4	324 714	30.7	40.8	28.5	15.8	154 035	213.6	15 194
District 9	15.0	10.7	10.3	370 641	23 350	6.3	347 291	32.8	41.4	25.8	13.5	144 911	198.0	12 312
IOWA	12.7	8.1	12.1	1 656 004	79 913	4.8	1 576 091	34.3	40.4	25.3	9.5	609 067	197.1	50 849
District 1	11.8	7.7	12.1	413 238	20 241	4.9	392 997	32.6	40.9	26.5	8.8	157 182	205.0	12 560
District 2	13.9	8.2	12.9	404 162	19 418	4.8	384 744	34.8	39.7	25.5	10.0	152 735	197.3	15 108
District 3	11.6	8.3	12.9	434 374	21 980	5.1	412 394	37.3	42.2	20.5	9.3	136 966	173.7	13 076
District 4	13.4	8.1	10.6	404 230	18 274	4.5	385 956	32.3	38.8	28.9	9.9	162 184	213.1	10 105
KANSAS	14.0	9.6	10.2	1 487 082	87 504	5.9	1 399 578	37.4	39.4	23.1	14.2	515 969	178.3	49 071
District 1	15.5	10.3	9.3	362 456	17 902	4.9	344 554	32.5	38.6	28.8	13.6	132 884	183.9	10 094
District 2	15.4	10.4	11.8	362 922	23 392	6.4	339 530	35.8	40.9	23.3	14.3	146 115	204.1	15 377
District 3	10.1	6.5	7.5	403 171	23 313	5.8	379 858	45.4	39.0	15.6	13.7	106 216	143.8	9 225
District 4	15.2	11.5	12.4	358 533	22 897	6.4	335 636	34.9	39.3	25.8	15.1	130 754	182.3	14 375

1. Percent of civilian labor force. 2. Persons 16 years old and over. 3. Per 1,000 resident population estimated in the 2013 American Community Survey.

Table E. Congressional Districts 113th Congress — **Agriculture**

STATE District	Agriculture, 2012									
		Land in farms			Value of products sold				Government payments	
	Number of farms	Acres	Average size of farm (acres)	Irrigated land (acres)	Total ($1,000)	Average per farm (dollars)	Percent from crops	Percent from livestock and poultry products	Total ($1,000)	Average per farm receiving payments (dollars)
	63	64	65	66	67	68	69	70	71	72
GEORGIA	42 257	9 620 836	228	1 125 355	9 255 125	219 020	39.7	60.3	142 322	9 793
District 1	2 069	417 353	202	37 955	290 617	140 462	58.1	41.9	4 870	7 356
District 2	5 559	2 470 948	444	D	1 887 305	339 504	70.0	30.0	49 436	14 669
District 3	3 475	447 816	129	6 652	357 673	102 928	12.5	87.5	1 939	4 683
District 4	248	18 707	75	45	2 149	8 664	52.8	47.2	20	997
District 5	30	2 801	93	D	211	7 025	90.0	10.0	12	2 007
District 6	105	7 064	67	245	1 378	13 119	60.5	39.5	28	3 540
District 7	209	13 328	64	81	10 188	48 748	72.3	27.7	37	2 651
District 8	6 419	2 068 738	322	343 268	1 501 791	233 960	71.7	28.3	40 267	11 375
District 9	7 080	666 984	94	4 291	2 135 687	301 651	2.4	97.6	4 110	4 160
District 10	5 566	1 082 225	194	39 355	784 526	140 950	22.5	77.5	9 360	6 138
District 11	936	88 216	94	2 474	140 080	149 658	15.8	84.2	1 056	9 183
District 12	6 035	1 793 019	297	163 770	1 211 704	200 779	61.3	38.7	26 685	8 290
District 13	342	24 390	71	279	5 701	16 671	70.3	29.7	128	3 464
District 14	4 184	519 247	124	4 551	926 116	221 347	5.7	94.3	4 374	7 112
HAWAII	7 000	1 129 317	161	81 813	661 347	94 478	81.5	18.5	5 228	8 325
District 1	291	21 133	73	3 760	28 230	97 009	82.6	17.4	101	5 617
District 2	6 709	1 108 184	165	78 053	633 117	94 368	81.4	18.6	5 127	8 405
IDAHO	24 816	11 760 109	474	3 365 292	7 801 446	314 372	44.1	55.9	99 789	10 673
District 1	11 404	4 227 137	371	612 775	1 790 850	157 037	48.6	51.4	33 991	9 847
District 2	13 412	7 532 972	562	2 752 517	6 010 597	448 151	42.8	57.2	65 798	11 156
ILLINOIS	75 087	26 937 721	359	522 479	17 187 052	228 895	82.3	17.7	553 300	9 829
District 1	191	66 255	347	387	47 865	250 604	91.7	8.3	923	10 487
District 2	1 204	451 866	375	14 622	367 131	304 926	90.6	9.4	7 554	8 898
District 3	97	13 188	136	326	8 734	90 045	0.0	0.0	212	8 140
District 4	X	X	X	X	X	X	X	X	X	X
District 5	21	349	17	D	D	D	D	D	D	D
District 6	187	17 561	94	462	30 306	162 064	95.9	4.1	420	9 765
District 7	X	X	X	X	X	X	X	X	X	X
District 8	21	4 457	212	D	3 655	174 060	99.7	0.3	D	D
District 9	X	X	X	X	X	X	X	X	X	X
District 10	141	8 223	58	407	13 357	94 727	95.6	4.4	126	8 421
District 11	131	31 383	240	D	23 965	182 943	95.8	4.2	559	9 172
District 12	6 959	1 905 115	274	15 491	688 176	98 890	85.7	14.3	29 651	6 488
District 13	7 760	2 974 971	383	13 854	1 842 362	237 418	88.1	11.9	53 882	9 103
District 14	2 132	625 197	293	18 015	560 569	262 931	83.2	16.8	13 128	13 274
District 15	22 203	7 559 605	340	102 777	3 613 564	162 751	78.7	21.3	155 644	8 968
District 16	10 468	4 292 328	410	48 782	3 466 237	331 127	84.7	15.3	92 879	11 381
District 17	9 730	3 458 529	355	118 763	2 861 291	294 069	75.5	24.5	85 811	11 696
District 18	13 826	5 528 495	400	187 608	3 658 219	264 590	84.0	16.0	112 453	10 343
INDIANA	58 695	14 720 396	251	437 445	11 210 818	191 001	67.2	32.8	267 287	8 331
District 1	1 212	348 046	287	38 398	300 726	248 123	D	D	6 174	9 572
District 2	7 547	1 747 268	232	183 555	1 685 428	223 324	61.1	38.9	32 668	8 128
District 3	11 801	1 957 311	166	53 255	1 877 293	159 079	54.8	45.2	38 957	6 794
District 4	8 570	3 273 095	382	47 054	2 697 593	314 772	72.4	27.6	59 486	10 747
District 5	2 682	803 313	300	5 904	690 258	257 367	89.1	10.9	13 671	8 507
District 6	10 531	2 532 278	240	20 206	1 686 224	160 120	69.8	30.2	50 568	8 006
District 7	185	17 001	92	163	26 173	141 475	D	D	201	6 708
District 8	9 529	2 812 457	295	79 188	1 677 310	176 022	65.2	34.8	45 753	8 707
District 9	6 638	1 229 627	185	9 722	569 814	85 841	61.2	38.8	19 809	6 733
IOWA	88 637	30 622 731	345	171 656	30 821 532	347 728	56.3	43.7	782 290	11 262
District 1	22 478	6 620 256	295	D	6 557 733	291 740	57.8	42.2	197 364	10 957
District 2	20 546	5 960 872	290	24 598	4 317 514	210 139	60.7	39.3	168 748	11 138
District 3	12 191	4 565 364	374	D	2 960 578	242 849	69.2	30.8	94 951	10 699
District 4	33 422	13 476 239	403	125 421	16 980 000	508 219	52.5	47.6	321 228	11 713
KANSAS	61 773	46 137 295	747	2 881 292	18 460 564	298 845	37.8	62.2	442 090	10 426
District 1	30 489	30 369 854	996	2 320 029	14 300 000	469 295	32.3	67.8	306 513	12 602
District 2	19 808	7 356 986	371	50 780	1 835 532	92 666	60.9	39.1	69 467	6 390
District 3	1 013	195 215	193	2 877	47 298	46 691	73.0	27.0	1 567	5 458
District 4	10 463	8 215 240	785	507 606	2 269 393	216 897	53.7	46.3	64 543	9 324

1. Specified owner-occupied units. 2. Specified renter-occupied units.

STATE District	Representative, 114th Congress	Land area,[1] 2010 (sq km)	Population and population characteristics, 2013: Total persons	Per square kilometer	Percent: Race alone: White	Black	American Indian, Alaska Native	Asian and Pacific Islander	Some other race (percent)	Two or more races (percent)	Hispanic or Latino[2] (percent)	Non-Hispanic White alone (percent)	Percent female	Percent foreign-born	Percent born in state of residence
		1	2	3	4	5	6	7	8	9	10	11	12	13	14
KENTUCKY		102 269	4 395 295	43.0	87.7	8.0	0.2	1.3	0.9	2.0	3.3	85.7	50.8	3.4	70.1
District 1	Ed Whitfield (R)	31 286	723 347	23.1	90.0	6.9	0.1	0.6	0.4	2.0	2.6	88.2	50.7	1.6	70.3
District 2	Brett Guthrie (R)	18 589	737 296	39.7	89.6	5.7	0.3	1.2	1.1	2.2	3.3	87.8	50.8	2.9	70.6
District 3	John A. Yarmuth (D)	827	739 047	893.6	73.0	21.2	0.1	2.3	0.5	3.0	4.7	69.3	51.8	6.8	69.3
District 4	Thomas Massie (R)	11 350	736 293	64.9	92.2	3.4	0.1	1.3	1.1	2.0	3.0	90.4	50.3	2.7	62.2
District 5	Harold Rogers (R)	29 099	714 729	24.6	96.9	1.3	0.2	0.4	0.2	1.0	1.2	96.0	50.4	0.9	79.8
District 6	Garland "Andy" Barr (R)	11 118	744 583	67.0	84.8	9.1	0.2	1.7	2.2	1.9	4.6	82.7	51.0	5.4	68.6
LOUISIANA		111 898	4 625 470	41.3	62.9	32.3	0.6	1.6	1.0	1.7	4.7	59.5	51.1	3.9	77.9
District 1	Steve Scalise (R)	10 438	781 134	74.8	81.1	12.7	1.3	2.1	1.4	1.5	8.8	74.1	51.3	6.4	74.3
District 2	Cedric Richmond (D)	3 285	784 928	238.9	31.4	62.4	0.2	2.9	1.7	1.5	5.8	27.8	52.2	6.2	78.4
District 3	Charles W. Boustany Jr. (R)	18 087	769 331	42.5	70.7	24.8	0.2	1.2	0.7	2.4	3.4	68.5	51.2	2.8	83.0
District 4	John Fleming (R)	32 207	762 517	23.7	61.7	33.7	0.9	0.9	1.0	1.8	3.9	59.3	50.8	2.4	74.1
District 5	Ralph Lee Abraham (R)	37 433	754 131	20.1	61.7	35.7	0.5	0.6	0.4	1.2	2.3	59.9	50.3	1.7	80.7
District 6	Garret Graves (R)	10 448	773 429	74.0	70.8	24.3	0.5	2.0	0.7	1.7	4.0	67.9	50.7	4.0	77.1
MAINE		79 883	1 328 302	16.6	94.9	1.0	0.6	1.1	0.3	2.1	1.4	93.9	51.0	3.4	63.7
District 1	Chellie Pingree (D)	8 509	670 714	78.8	94.5	1.5	0.4	1.4	0.3	1.9	1.5	93.4	51.4	4.0	57.4
District 2	Bruce Poliquin (R)	71 373	657 588	9.2	95.3	0.5	0.8	0.8	0.3	2.3	1.3	94.4	50.7	2.7	70.2
MARYLAND		25 142	5 928 814	235.8	57.6	29.6	0.3	6.0	3.6	2.9	9.0	53.2	51.6	14.2	47.6
District 1	Andrew Harris (R)	10 301	723 716	70.3	82.9	11.9	0.2	2.2	0.8	2.0	3.7	80.6	50.9	4.8	62.7
District 2	C. A. Dutch Ruppersberger (D)	904	745 135	824.3	55.7	33.2	0.3	5.6	2.0	3.1	6.4	52.5	52.8	10.6	62.4
District 3	John P. Sarbanes (D)	788	740 451	939.7	65.1	21.8	0.2	6.5	2.7	3.7	7.8	61.1	51.6	14.5	48.0
District 4	Donna F. Edwards (D)	771	739 293	958.9	32.6	52.8	0.3	3.1	9.1	2.1	15.7	26.9	51.9	18.2	30.2
District 5	Steny H. Hoyer (D)	3 836	752 393	196.1	51.9	38.3	0.5	4.3	2.3	2.7	7.4	47.8	51.1	10.5	39.1
District 6	John K. Delaney (D)	5 051	747 058	147.9	68.1	13.4	0.3	10.7	3.7	3.8	12.5	60.9	50.5	21.2	44.2
District 7	Elijah E. Cummings (D)	1 264	724 692	573.3	35.9	54.4	0.4	6.3	0.9	2.1	3.6	33.7	52.3	9.6	63.1
District 8	Chris Van Hollen (D)	2 227	756 076	339.5	68.6	11.6	0.2	9.4	7.0	3.3	14.4	61.9	51.4	23.8	32.4
MASSACHUSETTS		20 202	6 692 824	331.3	79.6	7.1	0.2	5.8	4.3	3.0	10.5	74.6	51.6	15.6	62.1
District 1	Richard E. Neal (D)	6 087	729 965	119.9	83.2	6.5	0.3	1.7	5.9	2.4	16.3	74.4	51.8	8.1	66.1
District 2	James P. McGovern (D)	4 216	738 642	175.2	84.9	5.1	0.2	5.3	1.8	2.7	9.0	79.4	51.4	12.2	64.9
District 3	Niki Tsongas (D)	1 963	742 932	378.5	76.2	4.1	0.1	7.3	9.2	3.0	17.9	69.6	50.3	16.9	62.3
District 4	Joseph P. Kennedy III (D)	1 731	746 358	431.2	87.4	2.6	0.1	5.9	1.1	2.8	3.6	85.1	52.0	12.3	61.1
District 5	Katherine Clark (D)	687	754 065	1 097.6	79.9	5.0	0.2	9.8	2.3	2.8	8.8	74.4	51.9	21.9	54.5
District 6	Seth Moulton (D)	1 364	750 623	550.3	85.7	3.4	0.0	4.6	3.9	2.3	7.8	82.9	51.6	12.2	70.2
District 7	Michael E. Capuano (D)	162	751 062	4 636.2	51.2	24.8	0.5	9.3	8.3	6.0	20.2	43.1	51.8	31.0	44.1
District 8	Stephen F. Lynch (D)	845	759 336	898.6	78.7	9.4	0.1	6.9	2.5	2.4	5.6	75.7	51.6	16.1	66.6
District 9	William R. Keating (D)	3 146	719 841	228.8	90.1	2.4	0.3	1.4	3.4	2.3	5.4	87.9	51.5	9.4	69.4
MICHIGAN		146 435	9 895 622	67.6	79.1	13.9	0.5	2.7	1.0	2.7	4.7	75.9	50.9	6.2	76.9
District 1	Dan Benishek (R)	64 822	704 991	10.9	92.0	1.6	2.7	0.7	0.2	2.8	1.6	91.0	49.2	1.7	80.2
District 2	Bill Huizenga (R)	8 498	717 114	84.4	87.1	5.6	0.5	2.0	1.8	3.0	9.4	80.4	50.5	5.0	79.9
District 3	Justin Amash (R)	6 808	720 731	105.9	84.0	9.1	0.6	1.8	1.2	3.3	6.7	79.7	50.7	4.9	78.2
District 4	John L. Moolenar (R)	21 906	709 423	32.4	93.7	2.2	0.6	1.0	0.5	2.0	3.0	91.4	50.1	2.0	85.7
District 5	Daniel T. Kildee (D)	6 083	682 848	112.3	77.8	17.5	0.3	0.8	0.8	2.7	4.8	74.3	51.6	2.0	84.3
District 6	Fred Upton (R)	9 186	709 976	77.3	85.1	8.4	0.4	1.6	1.3	3.3	5.6	81.4	50.8	4.2	70.2
District 7	Tim Walberg (R)	10 950	703 537	64.2	91.4	4.7	0.3	0.9	0.7	2.0	4.1	88.4	50.0	2.3	74.9
District 8	Mike Bishop (R)	3 893	713 867	183.4	86.4	5.0	0.3	3.8	0.8	3.6	5.2	83.0	50.7	7.3	75.9
District 9	Sander M. Levin (D)	475	713 212	1 501.5	80.6	11.8	0.3	4.2	0.3	2.7	2.1	79.1	51.6	11.5	76.6
District 10	Candice S. Miller (R)	10 724	711 342	66.3	93.1	2.8	0.3	1.5	0.3	1.9	3.0	90.7	50.4	6.2	83.4
District 11	David A.Trott (R)	1 086	717 393	660.6	82.9	5.0	0.2	9.4	0.5	2.0	3.2	80.4	50.9	13.4	71.2
District 12	Debbie Dingell (D)	1 044	711 313	681.3	79.7	10.2	0.4	5.1	1.4	3.2	5.4	76.0	51.3	11.1	68.1
District 13	John Conyers Jr. (D)	479	673 446	1 405.9	36.8	56.2	0.5	1.1	3.4	2.1	7.1	33.5	52.3	6.3	76.6
District 14	Brenda L. Lawrence (D)	481	706 429	1 468.7	34.7	57.6	0.2	3.7	1.1	2.8	4.7	31.4	52.9	9.2	72.3
MINNESOTA		206 232	5 420 380	26.3	84.8	5.4	1.1	4.3	1.6	2.7	4.9	81.9	50.3	7.4	68.1
District 1	Timothy J. Walz (D)	31 012	668 726	21.6	91.7	2.5	0.4	2.2	1.3	1.9	5.8	87.5	50.3	5.4	69.6
District 2	John Kline (R)	6 314	681 195	107.9	86.4	4.1	0.4	4.5	1.9	2.7	5.6	83.0	50.6	7.5	67.5
District 3	Erik Paulsen (R)	1 365	685 092	501.9	82.2	7.1	0.3	6.7	1.2	2.6	3.8	79.8	51.1	10.2	62.6
District 4	Betty McCollum (D)	861	686 098	796.9	73.0	9.6	0.8	11.4	1.6	3.7	6.5	69.2	51.2	12.8	60.6
District 5	Keith Ellison (D)	351	697 725	1 987.8	68.3	15.3	0.9	6.2	4.6	4.7	9.5	63.8	50.4	15.3	55.0
District 6	Tom Emmer (R)	7 465	675 687	90.5	92.2	2.4	0.5	2.1	0.8	1.9	2.6	90.7	49.6	3.6	78.5
District 7	Collin C. Peterson (D)	86 582	662 860	7.7	92.4	0.9	2.8	0.6	1.3	1.9	4.1	90.1	49.8	2.5	72.9
District 8	Richard M. Nolan (D)	72 282	662 997	9.2	93.2	1.1	2.8	0.7	0.1	2.1	1.3	92.2	49.4	1.5	78.8

1. Dry land or land partially or temporarily covered by water. 2. May be of any race.

Table E. Congressional Districts 113th Congress — **Age and Education**

STATE District	Population and population characteristics, 2013 (cont.)										Education, 2013		
	Age (percent)											Attainment[2] (percent)	
	Under 5 years	5 to 17 years	18 to 24 years	25 to 34 years	35 to 44 years	45 to 54 years	55 to 64 years	65 to 74 years	75 years and over	Median age	Total Enrollment[1]	High school graduate or more	Bachelor's degree or more
	15	16	17	18	19	20	21	22	23	24	25	26	27
KENTUCKY	6.2	16.9	9.7	12.9	12.9	14.1	13.0	8.4	6.0	38.5	1 105 248	84.1	22.6
District 1	6.1	16.8	9.8	11.9	12.0	13.5	13.0	9.8	7.0	39.9	174 734	81.2	15.5
District 2	6.2	17.4	10.0	12.5	12.4	14.2	13.0	8.3	6.1	38.5	190 199	85.7	19.8
District 3	6.4	16.3	9.0	14.5	12.8	13.6	13.2	7.6	6.5	38.1	183 997	88.3	30.3
District 4	6.6	18.2	8.2	12.8	13.4	14.7	13.0	7.9	5.3	38.4	184 658	88.7	26.3
District 5	5.9	16.1	8.9	11.9	13.1	14.6	14.0	9.4	6.1	40.5	164 242	74.5	13.4
District 6	5.9	16.6	12.4	13.5	13.4	13.4	12.0	7.6	5.2	36.1	207 418	86.1	30.1
LOUISIANA	6.6	17.5	10.3	14.3	12.3	13.4	12.6	7.6	5.5	36.0	1 168 161	83.1	22.5
District 1	6.1	16.8	9.2	14.1	12.1	14.2	13.0	8.5	5.9	37.9	195 828	85.4	27.5
District 2	6.8	16.3	10.7	15.8	12.8	13.3	12.7	7.0	4.7	35.3	195 685	81.0	21.9
District 3	6.9	18.1	10.3	13.8	12.0	14.1	12.4	7.1	5.4	35.8	191 276	80.7	20.0
District 4	7.0	17.7	10.2	13.7	12.1	12.7	12.5	7.9	6.3	36.0	184 292	83.6	20.4
District 5	6.6	17.9	10.2	13.7	12.0	12.7	12.7	8.0	6.0	36.1	186 034	80.0	16.5
District 6	6.3	17.9	11.3	14.3	12.4	13.5	12.2	7.1	4.9	35.1	215 046	87.5	28.5
MAINE	4.8	14.8	8.6	11.3	11.9	15.4	15.4	10.0	7.7	44.0	300 221	91.8	28.2
District 1	4.7	14.7	8.5	11.6	12.2	15.7	15.2	9.7	7.8	44.0	150 071	93.4	34.5
District 2	5.0	14.8	8.6	11.1	11.7	15.0	15.6	10.4	7.7	44.1	150 150	90.3	21.7
MARYLAND	6.2	16.5	9.5	13.8	13.0	15.0	12.6	7.7	5.7	38.2	1 562 663	89.1	37.4
District 1	5.4	16.3	9.6	10.6	11.6	15.6	14.1	9.9	7.1	42.4	176 225	89.6	30.3
District 2	6.4	16.0	10.1	15.2	13.2	14.7	12.1	7.0	5.4	36.8	199 545	88.0	29.4
District 3	6.1	15.6	9.1	16.4	13.3	13.2	12.5	7.5	6.3	37.3	196 092	91.3	45.9
District 4	6.9	16.6	9.4	15.2	13.5	15.3	11.6	7.1	4.5	36.5	188 975	85.2	30.4
District 5	6.0	17.3	11.2	12.1	13.2	16.4	12.7	6.9	4.3	37.8	216 261	91.0	32.9
District 6	6.3	17.3	8.8	13.1	14.1	14.9	12.4	7.5	5.6	38.1	197 319	90.5	41.1
District 7	6.4	16.0	10.6	14.3	11.6	14.9	12.8	7.6	5.8	37.1	194 251	86.2	36.1
District 8	6.0	16.8	7.6	13.3	13.2	15.2	13.1	8.1	6.7	40.3	193 995	91.1	52.2
MASSACHUSETTS	5.4	15.3	10.4	13.5	12.6	14.9	13.0	8.1	6.7	39.4	1 750 853	89.9	40.3
District 1	5.3	15.9	10.6	11.7	11.8	14.6	14.1	8.6	7.4	40.4	182 701	86.9	27.8
District 2	5.4	15.8	12.9	12.1	12.1	15.5	12.6	7.6	6.0	38.2	208 892	91.2	37.0
District 3	5.9	17.1	8.9	12.8	12.4	15.6	13.7	7.4	6.0	40.0	192 343	88.1	36.1
District 4	5.4	17.8	9.2	11.0	13.4	15.6	13.5	8.0	6.2	40.4	210 329	92.7	48.4
District 5	5.9	14.3	10.0	15.8	13.5	14.5	11.8	7.6	6.6	38.0	198 210	92.6	54.5
District 6	5.4	16.0	8.3	11.3	12.7	16.0	14.0	8.6	7.5	42.4	187 437	92.9	42.2
District 7	5.4	11.9	16.6	21.4	13.0	11.4	9.3	6.0	4.9	32.0	230 006	83.4	40.3
District 8	5.8	14.8	8.3	15.8	13.1	15.2	12.4	7.4	7.2	39.0	180 906	91.9	43.3
District 9	4.5	14.7	8.7	10.1	11.4	15.3	15.1	11.2	9.0	45.4	160 029	89.0	32.1
MICHIGAN	5.8	16.9	10.2	11.9	12.2	14.3	13.6	8.4	6.6	39.6	2 594 352	89.4	26.9
District 1	4.6	14.6	8.9	10.1	10.8	14.3	16.0	11.6	9.0	45.8	152 053	91.0	23.0
District 2	6.2	18.1	11.0	12.8	12.1	13.4	12.5	7.9	6.0	36.4	192 120	89.3	24.0
District 3	6.7	18.3	9.3	13.0	12.6	14.0	12.7	7.2	6.2	37.1	192 153	90.0	29.9
District 4	5.2	16.1	11.7	11.0	11.2	14.2	13.9	9.7	7.1	40.8	191 166	89.6	20.3
District 5	5.8	16.9	9.5	11.2	11.8	14.2	14.0	9.0	7.4	40.7	171 637	88.0	18.6
District 6	6.1	17.1	10.9	11.8	11.9	13.6	13.5	8.5	6.6	38.8	191 358	89.8	25.7
District 7	5.4	17.4	9.1	11.2	12.0	15.0	14.6	8.8	6.5	41.1	175 684	90.9	23.2
District 8	5.3	17.1	12.7	11.3	12.1	15.2	13.3	8.0	5.0	38.3	216 755	94.3	38.6
District 9	6.0	15.2	8.6	14.1	13.0	13.7	13.7	8.1	7.7	39.9	167 203	88.2	28.8
District 10	4.8	17.8	8.0	10.6	12.7	16.5	14.1	9.1	6.5	42.7	175 025	90.0	22.1
District 11	5.5	17.4	7.4	11.8	13.3	16.2	14.1	8.4	5.9	41.2	181 697	94.4	45.5
District 12	6.0	16.3	13.5	13.1	12.9	13.4	12.1	7.1	5.7	35.8	219 178	89.1	32.7
District 13	7.1	17.7	10.9	12.6	12.4	13.8	12.8	6.9	5.8	36.5	185 045	80.8	14.3
District 14	6.1	17.1	10.7	12.2	12.3	13.4	13.5	8.0	6.7	38.8	183 278	85.4	28.5
MINNESOTA	6.4	17.2	9.4	13.6	12.3	14.3	12.9	7.6	6.3	37.7	1 409 344	92.4	33.5
District 1	6.2	17.2	10.5	12.5	11.5	13.6	12.7	8.1	7.7	38.3	173 524	91.5	26.3
District 2	6.7	19.1	8.3	12.9	13.5	15.6	12.2	6.8	4.9	37.3	185 184	94.1	37.6
District 3	6.5	18.3	7.0	13.2	13.2	15.6	13.2	7.1	5.9	38.9	176 174	95.4	46.7
District 4	6.8	16.9	10.4	15.0	12.2	13.7	12.4	6.9	5.7	35.7	191 144	91.8	42.3
District 5	6.4	14.1	11.2	19.8	13.3	12.4	11.8	6.0	5.0	34.1	178 043	89.9	43.0
District 6	6.6	19.6	9.5	12.8	13.4	15.3	11.8	6.5	4.4	36.2	192 356	94.0	27.9
District 7	6.3	17.1	9.3	11.3	10.5	13.3	13.8	9.3	9.0	40.9	157 584	90.6	20.9
District 8	5.4	16.2	8.8	11.1	11.1	14.3	15.0	10.1	8.1	42.9	155 335	92.1	22.4

1. All persons 3 years old and over enrolled in nursery school through college and graduate or professional school. 2. Persons 25 years old and over.

STATE District	Households, 2013 Number	Average household size	Family households (percent)	Married-couple family (percent)	Female family householder[1]	One person households (percent)	Total in group quarters, 2013	Group quarters, 2010 Percent 65 years and over	Persons in correctional institutions	Persons in nursing facilities	Persons in college dormitories	Persons in military quarters
	28	29	30	31	32	33	34	35	36	37	38	39
KENTUCKY	1 705 623	2.5	66.80	48.9	12.9	27.7	126 139	19.2	41 122	26 044	36 340	5 856
District 1	279 371	2.5	67.20	50.7	11.8	28.7	26 076	20.4	7 869	5 548	4 101	3 843
District 2	280 248	2.56	69.70	53.4	11.4	25.4	20 386	21.3	4 501	4 378	7 527	2 013
District 3	303 418	2.39	59.80	39.9	15.0	33.3	14 613	30.7	2 662	4 723	3 307	0
District 4	272 731	2.64	71.50	53.4	12.4	23.7	16 840	21.9	9 255	3 657	1 768	0
District 5	277 070	2.49	68.80	49.6	13.3	27.7	24 012	15.1	12 451	4 570	5 039	0
District 6	292 785	2.46	64.70	47.2	13.1	27.0	24 212	12.1	4 384	3 168	14 598	0
LOUISIANA	1 728 149	2.6	65.40	43.1	17.0	29.3	128 357	16.7	60 804	24 524	24 891	2 861
District 1	295 271	2.6	66.60	47.9	13.2	27.4	13 379	24.4	1 182	2 957	5 469	57
District 2	302 127	2.53	58.50	29.9	23.4	35.2	19 434	12.0	11 687	3 058	4 007	138
District 3	291 285	2.6	67.00	44.7	16.2	27.4	13 007	26.9	4 329	4 273	2 935	0
District 4	282 896	2.62	64.80	43.3	16.9	31.3	22 632	18.4	13 410	5 425	2 390	2 524
District 5	271 501	2.6	66.90	44.4	17.8	29.0	48 916	11.6	28 559	5 925	6 333	142
District 6	285 069	2.67	68.60	49.3	14.1	25.3	10 989	23.4	1 637	2 886	3 757	0
MAINE	547 686	2.36	61.80	48.1	9.4	30.0	35 602	22.5	3 679	7 878	17 251	131
District 1	278 148	2.35	61.10	48.1	9.1	30.2	16 648	24.5	2 708	4 128	7 433	119
District 2	269 538	2.37	62.60	48.2	9.7	29.7	18 954	20.4	971	3 750	9 818	12
MARYLAND	2 161 680	2.68	66.80	47.3	14.8	27.2	140 959	19.4	35 832	28 001	48 141	7 534
District 1	265 390	2.66	71.10	55.9	11.8	23.7	17 216	20.6	5 648	3 465	5 803	7
District 2	280 069	2.59	64.30	40.9	18.4	29.5	18 865	17.1	7 411	3 533	3 971	2 113
District 3	284 780	2.54	60.80	44.5	12.0	30.9	18 317	19.9	583	3 399	6 910	4 515
District 4	260 778	2.81	67.30	40.2	20.2	27.4	5 529	42.2	1 149	2 597	410	115
District 5	253 925	2.88	71.10	52.0	14.0	23.4	20 758	11.8	1 111	2 598	14 602	387
District 6	269 193	2.69	71.00	54.2	11.7	24.2	22 121	17.6	12 569	3 716	2 766	93
District 7	271 652	2.57	60.20	36.6	19.6	33.0	27 270	14.8	6 305	4 677	10 895	0
District 8	275 893	2.7	69.20	54.5	10.5	24.9	10 883	37.8	1 056	4 016	2 784	304
MASSACHUSETTS	2 536 321	2.54	63.90	46.9	12.7	28.4	246 760	17.7	24 683	43 833	135 773	498
District 1	284 602	2.48	65.60	44.6	15.3	28.0	24 479	20.9	1 897	5 855	13 226	0
District 2	273 688	2.56	64.80	48.2	12.0	27.7	39 004	13.9	1 576	5 572	26 184	0
District 3	272 413	2.66	68.10	49.1	14.4	25.8	19 524	19.7	6 829	3 823	4 944	0
District 4	271 362	2.65	69.40	56.1	10.1	24.2	27 053	19.7	2 520	4 914	15 480	0
District 5	285 472	2.54	62.70	49.6	9.8	28.6	29 213	16.5	771	4 440	18 907	25
District 6	285 301	2.56	67.50	52.8	10.3	27.2	18 925	28.9	2 014	4 919	5 965	113
District 7	281 574	2.48	51.40	27.9	18.6	33.4	53 963	4.7	1 895	2 728	42 309	73
District 8	290 708	2.55	61.30	45.5	12.1	30.6	17 661	35.8	3 879	6 322	3 522	261
District 9	291 201	2.41	64.60	48.8	11.8	30.1	16 938	30.2	3 302	5 260	5 236	26
MICHIGAN	3 832 466	2.52	64.80	47.2	12.9	29.0	226 462	19.8	62 083	42 473	78 033	214
District 1	290 082	2.33	64.00	50.8	8.6	29.9	28 740	20.2	12 990	4 884	5 714	129
District 2	266 995	2.61	69.20	52.8	11.8	24.3	19 069	17.4	5 021	2 948	6 414	0
District 3	266 003	2.64	66.50	50.4	11.7	26.5	18 059	18.1	7 012	3 695	5 151	82
District 4	275 617	2.48	66.60	51.9	10.3	26.8	27 263	13.6	9 024	3 606	13 524	0
District 5	276 177	2.44	63.40	42.3	16.1	30.7	9 998	33.6	1 630	3 103	1 303	3
District 6	271 517	2.55	65.20	49.8	11.2	27.9	17 398	22.3	1 476	3 141	6 864	0
District 7	270 177	2.52	67.00	51.3	11.3	28.0	23 508	15.0	14 438	2 638	4 594	0
District 8	272 257	2.54	65.50	50.9	10.0	27.6	21 418	10.0	988	1 873	16 015	0
District 9	293 190	2.41	61.50	42.9	13.6	31.4	6 098	50.7	1 143	3 267	0	0
District 10	273 558	2.57	69.50	54.5	10.5	25.7	8 805	36.3	3 120	2 375	0	0
District 11	281 665	2.53	68.10	55.6	9.1	26.8	5 443	45.5	183	2 598	1 581	0
District 12	269 607	2.57	62.00	45.7	11.6	29.9	19 153	11.9	387	2 155	13 873	0
District 13	255 225	2.6	57.70	27.4	24.3	37.1	9 986	21.2	114	2 806	2 287	0
District 14	270 396	2.57	61.30	33.3	22.0	33.6	11 524	23.4	4 557	3 384	713	0
MINNESOTA	2 119 954	2.49	64.70	50.8	9.8	28.3	135 500	24.9	20 397	32 989	50 444	0
District 1	261 153	2.47	66.30	53.4	9.2	27.4	24 244	23.9	4 808	5 137	9 723	0
District 2	254 225	2.64	71.60	57.6	10.0	22.5	10 750	25.8	1 042	2 781	4 486	0
District 3	267 512	2.54	67.90	54.1	9.7	26.2	4 723	38.8	551	1 864	644	0
District 4	265 167	2.52	60.30	45.3	11.4	31.5	18 948	16.8	3 286	3 540	9 958	0
District 5	292 590	2.31	49.90	34.6	11.1	37.7	22 361	20.9	876	5 425	8 740	0
District 6	240 943	2.74	73.30	59.0	9.8	20.8	14 894	19.1	3 328	2 246	5 885	0
District 7	266 584	2.42	66.10	53.9	8.1	29.4	18 413	40.1	1 022	7 051	6 518	0
District 8	271 780	2.36	65.00	51.7	9.0	28.8	21 167	25.9	5 484	4 945	4 490	0

1. No spouse present.

Table E. Congressional Districts 113th Congress — **Housing and Money Income**

STATE District	Housing units, 2013						Money income, 2013		
		Occupied units						Households	
			Owner-occupied			Renter-occupied			
	Total	Occupied units as a percent of all units	Owner-occupied units as a percent of occupied units	Median value[1] (dollars)	Percent valued at $500,000 or more	Median rent[2]	Per capita income (dollars)	Median income (dollars)	Percent with income of $100,000 or more
	40	41	42	43	44	45	46	47	48
KENTUCKY	1 936 634	88.1	67.4	120 900	2.6	668	23 668	43 399	15.2
District 1	330 984	84.4	71.1	89 800	1.2	567	20 467	38 369	11.6
District 2	318 326	88.0	70.5	123 400	1.9	648	22 870	46 471	14.4
District 3	332 786	91.2	61.0	148 600	3.1	737	28 002	46 918	18.1
District 4	303 324	89.9	71.7	149 700	4.0	729	27 565	54 683	22.0
District 5	324 667	85.3	71.5	72 900	1.6	533	17 493	31 348	8.0
District 6	326 547	89.7	59.5	146 100	4.0	729	25 339	46 167	17.0
LOUISIANA	1 990 967	86.8	66.0	140 300	3.1	763	24 695	44 164	18.3
District 1	330 578	89.3	69.5	177 500	5.6	904	30 271	54 521	23.6
District 2	354 244	85.3	53.5	143 300	3.0	829	21 705	36 032	13.4
District 3	324 360	89.8	70.0	115 600	2.1	699	25 217	45 858	19.3
District 4	339 222	83.4	66.1	103 800	2.1	692	22 620	40 403	14.6
District 5	324 200	83.7	65.4	99 300	1.8	621	19 244	34 243	13.2
District 6	318 363	89.5	71.7	165 700	3.6	835	28 937	57 033	25.5
MAINE	723 140	75.7	70.2	172 800	5.5	760	26 630	46 974	16.4
District 1	349 553	79.6	69.8	219 100	8.5	856	29 846	52 680	21.0
District 2	373 587	72.1	70.5	134 100	2.4	683	23 350	41 499	11.6
MARYLAND	2 404 177	89.9	66.5	280 200	16.8	1 210	36 177	72 483	35.1
District 1	333 735	79.5	76.7	259 900	9.6	1 012	32 694	66 538	30.8
District 2	302 847	92.5	62.2	213 200	4.7	1 127	30 019	60 376	25.6
District 3	305 978	93.1	62.8	295 600	18.6	1 332	40 312	75 431	36.1
District 4	282 733	92.2	62.2	268 000	13.6	1 251	33 359	72 281	34.2
District 5	274 878	92.4	77.0	288 000	9.7	1 397	36 022	88 481	42.7
District 6	294 278	91.5	68.1	281 000	21.0	1 216	37 171	73 832	36.3
District 7	320 376	84.8	55.3	242 200	20.4	997	31 452	54 943	26.4
District 8	289 352	95.3	68.5	410 900	36.8	1 501	47 988	97 192	48.6
MASSACHUSETTS	2 813 641	90.1	61.5	327 200	21.3	1 077	35 879	66 768	32.5
District 1	317 802	89.6	64.6	204 200	4.9	816	27 857	52 300	22.5
District 2	296 442	92.3	62.9	250 900	7.9	943	30 389	61 313	27.8
District 3	289 596	94.1	62.9	289 300	15.8	1 014	33 012	67 009	31.6
District 4	288 657	94.0	70.9	372 100	32.6	1 144	44 957	85 262	43.3
District 5	301 653	94.6	60.3	436 100	37.9	1 364	45 632	83 430	42.3
District 6	304 075	93.8	67.8	372 300	23.9	1 128	38 016	76 182	37.1
District 7	305 507	92.2	33.3	355 400	26.2	1 261	30 232	52 036	24.8
District 8	309 869	93.8	60.6	362 700	23.2	1 247	39 862	75 359	37.3
District 9	400 040	72.8	70.7	326 900	20.7	883	32 439	59 245	25.8
MICHIGAN	4 525 266	84.7	70.6	117 500	2.6	768	25 918	48 273	18.3
District 1	441 743	65.7	77.5	116 600	4.2	640	23 451	41 971	11.2
District 2	311 213	85.8	73.0	120 300	1.9	716	23 382	48 717	15.9
District 3	294 941	90.2	72.6	128 100	2.5	759	25 614	51 202	18.4
District 4	344 432	80.0	75.8	108 200	1.1	677	22 388	42 813	13.1
District 5	326 006	84.7	71.1	82 800	0.7	674	22 052	39 662	12.0
District 6	324 399	83.7	71.3	123 300	2.9	685	24 032	46 738	15.5
District 7	302 832	89.2	75.2	127 100	1.8	743	25 408	50 462	18.3
District 8	293 616	92.7	71.4	168 200	2.7	830	31 068	61 456	27.4
District 9	316 995	92.5	69.9	104 800	2.8	833	29 041	51 154	19.9
District 10	307 729	88.9	78.5	142 200	1.8	784	27 285	55 027	21.1
District 11	299 104	94.2	74.2	180 300	5.8	937	37 682	73 294	34.5
District 12	292 753	92.1	64.3	114 400	3.7	878	28 327	52 193	22.5
District 13	336 035	76.0	54.7	52 800	0.3	742	16 870	30 706	7.1
District 14	333 468	81.1	56.5	81 900	3.2	838	25 473	41 588	18.7
MINNESOTA	2 368 754	89.5	71.6	180 100	5.6	832	31 358	60 702	25.5
District 1	283 195	92.2	75.2	149 700	3.2	689	28 640	55 397	20.6
District 2	264 410	96.1	77.0	215 700	5.5	939	34 187	73 381	33.4
District 3	281 430	95.1	73.5	241 100	12.6	1 067	41 104	77 647	37.6
District 4	279 200	95.0	63.9	200 800	7.1	872	31 942	61 574	28.2
District 5	308 945	94.7	53.6	187 000	7.1	865	32 334	52 468	23.1
District 6	257 930	93.4	79.9	188 300	3.7	866	30 403	71 040	29.9
District 7	325 917	81.8	75.2	136 300	2.9	611	26 243	50 655	16.2
District 8	367 727	73.9	76.9	152 200	3.0	664	25 483	49 860	16.1

1. Specified owner-occupied units. 2. Specified renter-occupied units.

STATE District	Poverty, 2013: Persons below poverty level (percent)	Poverty, 2013: Families below poverty level (percent)	Poverty, 2013: Percent of households receiving food stamps in past 12 months	Civilian labor force, 2013: Total	Civilian labor force, 2013: Unemployment: Total	Civilian labor force, 2013: Unemployment: Rate[1]	Civilian employment,[2] 2013: Total	Civilian employment,[2] 2013: Percent: Management, business, science and arts occupations	Civilian employment,[2] 2013: Percent: Service, sales, and office	Civilian employment,[2] 2013: Percent: Construction and production	Persons under age 65 with no health insurance, 2013 (percent)	Social Security beneficiaries, December 2013: Number	Social Security beneficiaries, December 2013: Rate[3]	Supplemental Security Income recipients, December 2013
	49	50	51	52	53	54	55	56	57	58	59	60	61	62
KENTUCKY	18.8	14.5	17.4	2 067 126	173 010	8.4	1 894 116	32.7	40.7	26.6	16.6	944 041	214.8	190 721
District 1	20.2	16.0	17.3	315 489	27 545	8.7	287 944	27.8	38.8	33.4	19.1	175 199	242.2	30 249
District 2	17.1	12.9	15.0	353 365	27 426	7.8	325 939	29.6	40.7	29.7	15.0	154 378	209.4	24 774
District 3	16.1	11.4	14.8	384 006	29 960	7.8	354 046	35.8	41.6	22.6	15.5	137 513	186.1	24 872
District 4	14.1	11.0	12.7	367 304	27 391	7.5	339 913	34.9	41.3	23.8	14.3	144 330	196.0	19 346
District 5	26.7	22.1	28.3	262 715	29 993	11.4	232 722	28.9	43.1	28.0	20.1	193 213	270.3	65 365
District 6	18.8	13.4	16.7	384 247	30 695	8.0	353 552	36.9	39.5	23.7	16.0	139 408	187.2	26 115
LOUISIANA	19.8	15.3	17.2	2 186 613	174 830	8.0	2 011 783	32.1	43.2	24.7	18.9	842 160	182.1	181 598
District 1	13.5	10.3	11.7	393 962	28 275	7.2	365 687	34.3	42.4	23.4	17.0	144 859	185.4	19 648
District 2	26.5	22.1	25.0	378 484	37 617	9.9	340 867	29.7	45.6	24.7	21.6	131 721	167.8	43 072
District 3	16.7	13.3	16.3	377 198	29 118	7.7	348 080	29.9	43.4	26.8	18.9	140 198	182.2	25 991
District 4	21.3	16.8	16.5	329 196	22 769	6.9	306 427	30.7	43.0	26.3	18.6	147 859	193.9	34 161
District 5	24.8	19.5	20.4	318 610	31 829	10.0	286 781	30.0	44.5	25.6	23.1	150 637	199.7	38 994
District 6	16.1	11.0	13.3	389 163	25 222	6.5	363 941	37.0	40.4	22.6	14.7	126 886	164.1	19 732
MAINE	14.0	9.6	18.0	691 352	47 974	6.9	643 378	34.6	42.5	22.9	13.5	320 482	241.3	37 428
District 1	12.0	8.3	14.4	365 996	23 034	6.3	342 962	38.1	41.7	20.2	12.7	152 467	227.3	14 560
District 2	16.0	10.9	21.6	325 356	24 940	7.7	300 416	30.7	43.4	26.0	14.3	168 015	255.5	22 868
MARYLAND	10.1	7.1	11.1	3 223 300	239 933	7.4	2 983 367	44.5	40.2	15.4	11.5	917 497	154.8	117 605
District 1	10.7	7.4	10.2	381 550	28 388	7.4	353 162	39.7	41.0	19.3	10.4	150 919	208.5	11 380
District 2	12.0	9.6	14.6	403 590	34 671	8.6	368 919	39.1	43.7	17.3	11.5	120 697	162.0	18 329
District 3	7.9	4.9	9.8	411 258	25 403	6.2	385 855	50.7	36.8	12.5	10.5	112 193	151.5	13 763
District 4	9.1	6.9	10.7	422 130	36 995	8.8	385 135	36.8	44.5	18.6	16.2	94 689	128.1	11 259
District 5	7.6	4.5	7.3	413 082	29 344	7.1	383 738	42.7	41.7	15.7	9.9	98 819	131.3	8 928
District 6	9.7	7.1	10.4	402 948	28 088	7.0	374 860	45.7	39.5	14.9	10.9	111 219	148.9	13 231
District 7	17.6	12.5	19.5	361 232	34 059	9.4	327 173	46.6	40.3	13.1	11.4	121 256	167.3	32 442
District 8	6.7	4.1	5.9	427 510	22 985	5.4	404 525	53.9	34.2	11.9	10.9	107 705	142.5	8 273
MASSACHUSETTS	11.9	8.6	12.9	3 684 771	286 768	7.8	3 398 003	44.0	40.4	15.6	4.3	1 206 184	180.2	188 015
District 1	15.7	12.3	19.2	379 134	35 574	9.4	343 560	36.3	43.6	20.1	4.2	160 268	219.6	36 701
District 2	14.0	8.9	12.4	399 335	29 828	7.5	369 507	42.3	40.7	17.0	4.2	130 251	176.3	20 135
District 3	12.2	9.2	14.4	401 119	35 398	8.8	365 721	41.2	39.0	19.9	4.6	123 617	166.4	23 679
District 4	7.4	5.2	8.4	411 001	26 457	6.4	384 544	49.6	36.1	14.3	3.0	125 935	168.7	11 282
District 5	8.2	5.4	7.3	434 020	26 357	6.1	407 663	53.2	35.9	10.9	3.9	118 798	157.5	11 564
District 6	8.8	5.9	10.0	414 692	27 995	6.8	386 697	44.6	40.3	15.1	3.9	141 781	188.9	14 248
District 7	21.0	17.0	21.6	436 104	39 245	9.0	396 859	43.1	44.8	12.1	5.6	92 614	123.3	35 288
District 8	9.2	6.6	10.8	433 387	31 318	7.2	402 069	47.1	40.0	13.0	3.9	131 905	173.7	16 600
District 9	11.4	8.3	12.4	375 979	34 596	9.2	341 383	35.7	44.2	20.1	5.4	181 015	251.5	18 518
MICHIGAN	17.0	12.3	16.9	4 846 296	476 509	9.8	4 369 787	34.4	42.4	23.2	12.8	2 098 078	212.0	277 210
District 1	15.6	10.3	14.8	323 302	31 009	9.6	292 293	29.0	46.3	24.8	15.6	198 134	281.0	15 851
District 2	15.6	11.0	16.3	362 275	28 429	7.8	333 846	29.9	41.2	28.9	11.3	146 608	204.4	16 580
District 3	14.9	10.0	15.1	361 049	30 266	8.4	330 783	35.1	41.1	23.7	11.2	136 730	189.7	18 614
District 4	18.4	12.7	16.7	330 993	35 624	10.8	295 369	29.8	42.8	27.4	13.7	169 987	239.6	17 177
District 5	21.4	16.5	22.4	306 849	35 281	11.5	271 568	29.5	46.5	24.0	12.3	170 962	250.4	29 247
District 6	16.8	11.4	15.8	350 674	31 323	8.9	319 351	33.2	41.0	25.8	14.1	151 542	213.4	17 775
District 7	14.6	11.2	14.6	341 202	30 244	8.9	310 958	30.7	42.2	27.0	11.7	156 889	223.0	14 021
District 8	12.1	7.4	10.5	377 185	30 318	8.0	346 867	42.2	41.0	16.8	9.1	125 751	176.2	11 427
District 9	14.8	11.6	15.7	369 749	31 924	8.6	337 825	36.4	43.8	19.8	12.4	153 361	215.0	19 671
District 10	11.6	8.8	12.9	357 343	29 950	8.4	327 393	32.9	40.5	26.5	11.2	152 415	214.3	11 894
District 11	6.7	4.4	6.7	385 517	22 439	5.8	363 078	47.8	37.2	15.0	8.7	131 708	183.6	8 045
District 12	17.9	12.6	14.3	353 209	30 836	8.7	322 373	39.3	39.7	20.9	10.5	130 068	182.9	16 651
District 13	32.9	26.7	35.4	294 908	56 354	19.1	238 554	23.7	49.3	26.8	20.0	135 211	200.8	43 927
District 14	26.4	21.7	26.4	332 041	52 512	15.8	279 529	35.1	45.8	19.1	17.6	138 712	196.4	36 330
MINNESOTA	11.2	7.2	9.2	2 991 160	162 880	5.4	2 828 280	38.8	40.5	20.7	9.4	948 229	174.9	93 748
District 1	11.5	7.3	8.8	368 999	18 676	5.1	350 323	34.1	40.1	25.8	9.2	130 344	194.9	9 206
District 2	8.4	5.6	6.5	388 634	18 973	4.9	369 661	41.5	39.9	18.6	8.0	99 413	145.9	6 647
District 3	6.4	4.8	5.9	383 523	19 488	5.1	364 035	46.3	38.9	14.7	7.3	109 935	160.5	7 589
District 4	13.6	9.1	11.0	375 910	24 627	6.6	351 283	43.6	40.1	16.3	10.5	107 587	156.8	18 127
District 5	16.8	11.2	13.9	406 880	29 413	7.2	377 467	45.0	40.3	14.6	13.4	94 393	135.3	21 621
District 6	8.2	5.1	6.8	387 411	17 100	4.4	370 311	34.8	41.4	23.8	6.3	99 597	147.4	6 607
District 7	11.9	7.7	9.7	344 250	15 308	4.4	328 942	32.1	38.7	29.2	10.0	148 143	223.5	10 567
District 8	12.9	8.1	10.5	335 553	19 295	5.8	316 258	30.9	44.7	24.4	10.7	158 817	239.5	13 384

1. Percent of civilian labor force. 2. Persons 16 years old and over. 3. Per 1,000 resident population estimated in the 2013 American Community Survey.

Table E. Congressional Districts 113th Congress — **Agriculture**

STATE District	Agriculture, 2012									
		Land in farms			Value of products sold				Government payments	
	Number of farms	Acres	Average size of farm (acres)	Irrigated land (acres)	Total ($1,000)	Average per farm (dollars)	Percent from crops	Percent from livestock and poultry products	Total ($1,000)	Average per farm receiving payments (dollars)
	63	64	65	66	67	68	69	70	71	72
KENTUCKY	77 064	13 049 347	169	73 573	5 067 334	65 755	45.0	55.0	169 821	5 087
District 1	22 897	4 970 288	217	46 542	2 738 196	119 588	47.8	52.2	88 556	6 975
District 2	19 734	3 055 139	155	14 508	1 059 346	53 681	48.6	51.4	44 239	5 052
District 3	223	13 572	61	101	5 973	26 784	82.2	17.8	184	4 611
District 4	11 411	1 595 512	140	6 248	311 349	27 285	62.8	37.2	13 820	3 421
District 5	11 144	1 522 271	137	1 494	277 300	24 883	32.6	67.4	8 668	2 468
District 6	11 655	1 892 565	162	4 680	675 171	57 930	24.4	75.6	14 353	3 310
LOUISIANA	28 093	7 900 864	281	1 092 881	3 809 401	135 600	73.1	26.9	138 164	14 625
District 1	1 386	376 150	271	1 242	101 752	73 414	48.0	52.0	291	4 037
District 2	404	234 199	580	1 175	103 689	256 656	95.7	4.3	277	6 915
District 3	5 363	1 709 327	319	246 622	646 950	120 632	83.8	16.2	23 708	11 824
District 4	7 545	1 535 386	203	104 062	737 447	97 740	29.8	70.2	19 192	11 980
District 5	11 106	3 503 066	315	730 933	1 891 903	170 350	84.7	15.3	90 840	16 970
District 6	2 289	542 736	237	8 847	327 660	143 146	83.0	17.0	3 857	10 285
MAINE	8 173	1 454 104	178	30 887	763 062	93 364	62.1	37.9	10 162	7 629
District 1	2 650	234 530	89	2 884	91 532	34 540	66.5	33.5	1 525	6 809
District 2	5 523	1 219 574	221	28 003	671 531	121 588	61.5	38.5	8 637	7 795
MARYLAND	12 256	2 030 745	166	104 910	2 271 397	185 329	46.3	53.7	36 024	7 784
District 1	5 451	1 180 832	217	97 880	1 731 665	317 678	41.3	58.7	25 698	8 696
District 2	115	7 376	64	182	5 909	51 381	89.3	10.7	304	17 878
District 3	204	20 466	100	112	27 937	136 945	86.8	13.2	118	7 345
District 4	114	7 095	62	628	11 343	99 500	98.2	1.8	38	2 916
District 5	1 850	198 919	108	1 755	70 566	38 144	87.3	12.7	2 074	5 171
District 6	2 360	341 624	145	1 644	199 544	84 552	49.6	50.4	3 123	5 385
District 7	604	69 173	115	305	53 048	87 827	D	D	673	5 342
District 8	1 558	205 260	132	2 404	171 386	110 004	D	D	3 997	7 686
MASSACHUSETTS	7 755	523 517	68	23 433	492 211	63 470	77.8	22.2	8 124	10 415
District 1	2 043	189 425	93	1 513	72 106	35 294	56.3	43.7	2 293	10 059
District 2	1 832	142 899	78	3 554	125 634	68 578	75.5	24.5	1 671	8 033
District 3	936	37 576	40	1 304	40 736	43 522	71.8	28.2	565	8 972
District 4	750	33 528	45	2 149	41 671	55 562	88.0	12.0	467	6 578
District 5	196	6 332	32	700	43 367	221 262	99.3	0.7	D	D
District 6	464	18 673	40	464	20 476	44 129	74.9	25.1	174	9 141
District 7	23	282	12	30	164	7 113	86.0	13.4	D	D
District 8	162	5 471	34	612	9 196	56 763	66.6	33.4	120	7 031
District 9	1 349	89 331	66	13 107	138 861	102 936	84.1	15.9	2 740	18 269
MICHIGAN	52 194	9 948 564	191	592 243	8 678 050	166 265	63.5	36.5	155 919	7 567
District 1	7 028	1 174 716	167	17 529	304 476	43 323	55.8	44.2	12 542	7 241
District 2	3 913	596 787	153	48 685	927 761	237 097	58.1	41.9	7 836	8 257
District 3	4 328	804 218	186	32 235	865 263	199 922	45.6	54.4	13 587	7 922
District 4	10 328	2 076 879	201	100 624	1 711 590	165 723	58.5	41.5	29 973	6 191
District 5	2 837	598 773	211	9 459	462 461	163 011	87.4	12.6	9 239	6 103
District 6	6 072	1 155 210	190	289 103	1 603 431	264 070	63.2	36.8	18 373	9 379
District 7	8 650	1 623 909	188	76 959	991 129	114 581	77.1	22.9	34 636	8 108
District 8	2 057	316 696	154	3 079	200 689	97 564	76.9	23.1	4 270	10 363
District 9	26	D	D	13	1 700	65 380	94.0	6.0	D	D
District 10	6 328	1 559 304	246	13 305	1 561 544	246 767	65.2	34.8	25 149	8 030
District 11	191	8 146	43	513	13 673	71 587	94.7	5.3	21	1 935
District 12	379	30 066	79	562	30 614	80 777	98.6	1.4	282	4 780
District 13	44	2 399	55	173	3 605	81 921	99.6	0.4	6	1 443
District 14	13	D	D	4	115	8 857	100.0	0.0	D	D
MINNESOTA	74 542	26 035 838	349	524 016	21 280 184	285 479	65.2	34.8	467 867	8 962
District 1	19 041	6 309 496	331	22 341	7 132 552	374 589	58.9	41.1	133 151	8 920
District 2	4 642	1 121 134	242	58 464	1 146 580	247 001	62.6	37.4	21 757	7 489
District 3	699	78 393	112	625	65 380	93 534	81.2	18.8	1 223	4 703
District 4	372	34 196	92	1 069	37 456	100 689	92.5	7.5	448	4 766
District 5	32	1 477	46	26	4 610	144 055	99.7	0.3	9	2 266
District 6	5 739	1 084 584	189	69 319	939 820	163 760	57.5	42.5	18 404	5 481
District 7	33 431	15 157 479	453	276 423	11 010 000	329 444	71.8	28.3	276 140	10 362
District 8	10 586	2 249 079	212	95 749	940 152	88 811	45.7	54.3	16 736	4 177

1. Specified owner-occupied units. 2. Specified renter-occupied units.

STATE District	Representative, 114th Congress	Land area,[1] 2010 (sq km)	Population and population characteristics, 2013: Total persons	Per square kilometer	Percent: Race alone: White	Black	American Indian, Alaska Native	Asian and Pacific Islander	Some other race (percent)	Two or more races (percent)	Hispanic or Latino[2] (percent)	Non-Hispanic White alone (percent)	Percent female	Percent foreign-born	Percent born in state of residence
		1	2	3	4	5	6	7	8	9	10	11	12	13	14
MISSISSIPPI		121 531	2 991 207	24.6	59.0	37.7	0.4	1.0	0.8	1.1	2.7	57.4	51.4	2.1	71.7
District 1	Trent Kelly (R)	27 383	756 459	27.6	69.8	27.5	0.1	0.9	0.6	1.1	2.8	67.7	51.5	2.1	63.5
District 2	Bennie G. Thompson (D)	40 278	726 159	18.0	31.9	65.4	0.4	0.5	1.0	0.9	1.9	31.5	51.9	1.4	83.0
District 3	Gregg Harper (R)	33 034	750 332	22.7	61.2	35.2	1.0	0.8	0.8	1.0	2.2	60.1	51.6	2.3	77.2
District 4	Steven Palazzo (R)	20 835	758 257	36.4	72.0	23.9	0.3	1.6	0.9	1.4	3.8	69.2	50.7	2.6	63.6
MISSOURI		178 040	6 044 171	33.9	82.8	11.5	0.4	1.8	1.1	2.5	3.8	80.4	51.0	3.9	66.2
District 1	William Lacy Clay (D)	584	737 033	1 262.0	44.3	48.8	0.2	2.7	0.7	3.3	3.0	42.1	52.8	5.6	69.5
District 2	Ann Wagner (R)	1 206	768 428	637.2	89.4	4.0	0.2	4.2	0.4	1.7	2.7	87.2	51.7	6.5	66.1
District 3	Blaine Luetkemeyer (R)	17 745	760 643	42.9	93.4	3.2	0.3	1.0	0.5	1.7	2.4	91.7	50.2	2.4	74.4
District 4	Vicky Hartzler (R)	37 299	756 407	20.3	89.7	4.1	0.4	1.8	0.7	3.3	3.5	87.3	49.9	3.1	62.1
District 5	Emanuel Cleaver (D)	6 280	758 911	120.8	69.3	21.5	0.4	1.8	3.9	3.0	8.4	65.5	51.5	5.9	61.1
District 6	Sam Graves (R)	47 134	754 588	16.0	90.6	4.5	0.3	1.2	0.9	2.5	4.1	88.0	50.4	2.9	65.6
District 7	Bill Long (R)	16 247	759 566	46.8	92.0	1.8	0.9	1.2	1.2	3.0	4.6	89.0	51.1	3.3	57.3
District 8	Jason T. Smith (R)	51 544	748 595	14.5	92.5	4.8	0.4	0.4	0.3	1.7	1.7	91.2	50.2	1.1	74.0
MONTANA		376 962	1 015 165	2.7	89.1	0.3	6.8	0.7	0.5	2.6	3.3	87.0	49.8	1.9	54.5
At Large	Robert K. Zinke (R)	376 962	1 015 165	2.7	89.1	0.3	6.8	0.7	0.5	2.6	3.3	87.0	49.8	1.9	54.5
NEBRASKA		198 974	1 868 516	9.4	88.3	4.6	0.8	2.1	1.9	2.3	9.8	81.0	50.3	6.6	65.0
District 1	Jeff Fortenberry (R)	22 997	628 082	27.3	89.0	2.9	1.2	2.3	1.9	2.6	8.1	83.8	50.1	6.1	67.4
District 2	Brad Ashford (D)	1 320	634 418	480.6	82.3	9.6	0.3	2.9	2.1	2.8	10.6	73.9	50.6	8.6	59.9
District 3	Adrian Smith (R)	174 657	606 016	3.5	93.9	1.1	0.8	1.0	1.7	1.4	10.8	85.4	50.3	5.0	67.9
NEVADA		284 332	2 790 136	9.8	68.3	8.4	1.1	8.4	9.6	4.2	27.5	52.1	49.6	19.0	25.7
District 1	Dina Titus (D)	271	673 794	2 486.3	58.4	11.1	0.4	8.5	17.7	3.9	44.0	34.0	48.5	29.9	23.6
District 2	Mark E. Amodei (R)	144 598	690 786	4.8	83.5	2.0	2.3	4.3	4.3	3.6	21.4	68.0	49.3	12.2	29.7
District 3	Joseph J. Heck (R)	7 379	720 438	97.6	70.3	6.8	0.5	14.5	3.3	4.6	15.3	59.6	51.2	18.2	21.8
District 4	Cresent Hardy (R)	132 084	705 118	5.3	61.0	13.7	1.1	6.0	13.5	4.7	30.2	46.1	49.4	15.9	27.8
NEW HAMPSHIRE		23 187	1 323 459	57.1	93.4	1.2	0.2	2.4	0.8	1.9	3.2	91.4	50.7	5.7	42.2
District 1	Frank C. Guinta (R)	6 381	662 473	103.8	93.6	1.3	0.2	2.3	0.8	1.8	3.2	91.4	50.7	5.7	42.4
District 2	Ann M. Kuster (D)	16 806	660 986	39.3	93.3	1.1	0.2	2.5	0.9	2.0	3.1	91.3	50.6	5.6	42.0
NEW JERSEY		19 047	8 899 339	467.2	68.2	13.7	0.2	9.0	6.5	2.4	18.9	57.3	51.2	21.6	52.6
District 1	Donald Norcross (D)	907	730 895	805.8	68.1	17.7	0.1	4.9	6.4	2.9	12.9	64.1	51.7	9.5	55.3
District 2	Frank A. LoBiondo (R)	5 419	732 764	135.2	74.9	13.2	0.2	3.9	4.9	2.9	15.1	66.4	50.9	10.1	59.7
District 3	Thomas MacArthur (R)	2 330	742 640	318.7	81.0	10.6	0.1	3.6	2.2	2.5	7.4	76.1	51.3	7.7	61.0
District 4	Christopher H. Smith (R)	1 792	735 064	410.2	85.4	6.4	0.1	4.2	2.5	1.4	10.1	78.3	51.6	12.3	59.4
District 5	Scott Garrett (R)	2 567	733 032	285.6	77.9	5.4	0.2	10.0	5.1	1.5	12.9	70.9	51.5	18.8	52.6
District 6	Frank Pallone Jr. (D)	558	738 398	1 323.3	64.9	10.1	0.2	17.6	4.9	2.3	21.7	49.6	50.6	28.5	49.4
District 7	Leonard Lance (R)	2 513	748 580	297.9	80.3	4.6	0.1	9.0	4.4	1.6	12.0	73.0	50.8	16.3	56.6
District 8	Albio Sires (D)	142	758 406	5 340.9	55.7	10.6	0.4	8.3	21.2	3.8	55.1	25.5	50.0	44.7	37.1
District 9	Bill Pascrell, Jr. (D)	247	760 064	3 077.2	60.5	11.3	0.4	13.8	10.2	3.8	34.7	40.6	51.2	37.4	43.6
District 10	Donald M. Payne, Jr. (D)	197	733 056	3 721.1	30.1	53.2	0.2	6.8	7.1	2.5	18.5	20.6	52.4	27.5	51.4
District 11	Rodney P. Frelinghuysen (R)	1 308	735 846	562.6	83.7	3.4	0.0	9.3	1.4	2.1	10.5	75.1	51.7	17.8	59.3
District 12	Bonnie Watson Coleman (D)	1 068	750 594	702.8	56.5	17.8	0.1	16.5	7.1	2.0	14.8	48.8	51.0	27.8	46.6
NEW MEXICO		314 161	2 085 287	6.6	75.3	2.0	9.1	1.4	8.9	3.3	47.3	39.3	50.4	10.1	52.0
District 1	Michelle Lujan Grisham (D)	11 914	694 442	58.3	77.7	3.0	3.8	2.6	9.6	3.4	48.9	40.9	50.9	11.1	51.7
District 2	Steve Pearce (R)	185 804	697 027	3.8	82.9	1.6	5.2	0.7	6.8	2.8	53.1	38.4	49.7	12.8	48.4
District 3	Ben Ray Luján (D)	116 442	693 818	6.0	65.2	1.3	18.3	1.1	10.3	3.8	40.0	38.5	50.6	6.5	55.9
NEW YORK		122 057	19 651 127	161.0	64.6	15.7	0.4	8.0	8.5	2.9	18.4	56.9	51.5	22.3	63.6
District 1	Lee M. Zeldin (R)	1 684	722 480	429.0	87.6	4.9	0.3	4.3	1.3	1.5	13.6	76.4	50.1	12.8	77.4
District 2	Peter T. King (R)	471	718 587	1 525.7	74.2	10.3	0.3	2.8	8.7	3.7	22.1	64.0	51.5	17.2	76.4
District 3	Steve Israel (D)	660	724 490	1 097.7	76.2	3.6	0.2	14.4	3.6	2.1	10.2	70.1	51.7	22.1	70.0
District 4	Kathleen M. Rice (D)	287	715 109	2 491.7	66.6	13.4	0.4	6.4	7.4	5.9	19.3	59.6	51.4	21.6	71.2
District 5	Gregory W. Meeks (D)	134	768 603	5 735.8	19.1	49.6	0.4	13.4	13.2	4.2	19.1	11.5	53.1	42.5	49.5
District 6	Grace Meng (D)	77	721 108	9 365.0	48.4	3.4	0.2	38.9	6.3	2.8	18.6	37.6	51.9	51.7	43.2
District 7	Nydia M. Velázquez (D)	42	760 308	18 102.6	49.0	11.6	0.5	19.1	16.5	3.3	43.1	28.2	50.1	37.4	45.3
District 8	Hakeem S. Jeffries (D)	77	737 529	9 578.3	27.5	57.5	0.3	5.1	7.4	2.3	16.8	21.8	54.6	33.1	53.1
District 9	Yvette D. Clarke (D)	40	735 408	18 385.2	34.3	50.7	0.2	7.4	5.4	2.0	10.5	31.3	54.4	39.7	47.9
District 10	Jerrold Nadler (D)	37	716 682	19 369.8	69.6	4.9	0.3	18.2	4.6	2.4	12.1	63.8	50.7	31.7	44.3
District 11	Daniel M. Donovan Jr. (R)	171	728 307	4 259.1	73.6	7.8	0.4	12.1	4.5	1.7	16.2	63.0	51.7	28.6	64.0
District 12	Carolyn B. Maloney (D)	38	720 538	18 961.5	73.6	5.3	0.2	13.3	4.5	3.1	13.6	65.5	53.6	26.0	42.9
District 13	Charles B. Rangel (D)	27	765 391	28 347.8	27.5	29.3	0.7	4.2	33.0	5.3	54.6	14.3	52.4	35.7	47.2
District 14	Joseph Crowley (D)	73	727 544	9 966.4	47.8	11.3	0.2	16.2	21.5	3.1	49.8	22.8	49.0	46.8	43.3

1. Dry land or land partially or temporarily covered by water. 2. May be of any race.

Table E. Congressional Districts 113th Congress — **Age and Education**

STATE District	Population and population characteristics, 2013 (cont.)										Education, 2013		
	Age (percent)											Attainment[2] (percent)	
	Under 5 years	5 to 17 years	18 to 24 years	25 to 34 years	35 to 44 years	45 to 54 years	55 to 64 years	65 to 74 years	75 years and over	Median age	Total Enrollment[1]	High school graduate or more	Bachelor's degree or more
	15	16	17	18	19	20	21	22	23	24	25	26	27
MISSISSIPPI	6.6	18.1	10.8	12.6	12.8	13.0	12.4	8.0	5.8	36.6	810 969	82.4	20.4
District 1	6.3	18.2	11.0	11.5	13.6	13.0	12.4	8.2	5.8	37.8	205 055	81.0	18.0
District 2	6.9	18.7	11.2	12.8	11.8	13.0	12.5	7.7	5.5	35.4	206 902	79.0	18.9
District 3	6.5	17.7	10.3	12.5	13.4	12.7	12.5	8.0	6.4	37.2	204 492	84.3	24.9
District 4	6.8	17.5	10.7	13.4	12.2	13.4	12.1	8.3	5.6	36.1	194 520	84.9	19.6
MISSOURI	6.2	17.0	9.9	13.2	11.9	13.9	12.9	8.4	6.6	38.1	1 549 456	88.7	27.0
District 1	6.4	15.7	10.8	16.5	12.5	13.3	12.6	6.5	5.7	35.5	195 462	87.1	29.8
District 2	5.9	16.9	7.5	11.5	12.1	15.0	14.2	9.0	7.9	42.0	197 060	94.8	48.7
District 3	6.1	18.1	8.8	13.1	12.1	15.1	12.6	8.4	5.7	38.3	197 058	89.7	23.5
District 4	6.1	16.5	12.9	12.8	11.2	12.9	12.5	8.5	6.6	36.6	207 873	87.9	23.3
District 5	7.0	16.4	9.1	15.2	12.3	13.8	12.4	7.7	6.3	36.8	180 564	88.9	25.3
District 6	6.0	18.2	9.5	12.5	12.3	13.8	12.8	8.2	6.7	38.2	194 884	90.7	25.7
District 7	6.2	16.9	11.2	12.6	11.8	13.1	12.3	9.2	6.8	37.6	196 967	88.7	22.8
District 8	6.0	17.0	9.5	11.3	11.5	14.0	13.6	9.7	7.4	40.4	179 588	81.4	15.0
MONTANA	6.0	16.1	10.0	12.4	11.3	13.2	14.6	9.3	6.9	39.6	238 510	92.7	29.0
At Large	6.0	16.1	10.0	12.4	11.3	13.2	14.6	9.3	6.9	39.6	238 510	92.7	29.0
NEBRASKA	6.9	18.0	10.1	13.4	12.0	13.2	12.3	7.4	6.7	36.3	517 420	90.2	29.4
District 1	6.7	17.7	12.1	13.3	11.6	13.1	11.9	7.3	6.4	35.2	178 251	92.0	30.1
District 2	7.6	18.8	9.1	15.9	13.5	13.2	11.2	6.1	4.8	34.1	188 179	89.7	36.9
District 3	6.3	17.2	9.2	11.0	11.0	13.2	13.9	8.9	9.2	40.9	150 990	89.1	21.1
NEVADA	6.4	17.4	9.2	14.3	13.6	13.6	12.1	8.5	5.2	37.1	682 666	85.2	22.5
District 1	6.4	16.6	10.5	15.5	13.8	13.3	11.9	6.8	5.2	35.7	156 420	75.4	14.5
District 2	6.1	16.7	9.5	13.2	12.2	13.6	13.7	9.4	5.6	38.7	169 692	87.1	24.9
District 3	6.0	16.4	7.1	14.5	14.9	14.2	11.9	10.0	5.1	39.2	166 269	92.2	30.7
District 4	6.9	19.7	9.7	13.9	13.5	13.0	10.7	7.7	4.8	34.8	190 285	84.9	18.9
NEW HAMPSHIRE	5.0	15.5	9.7	11.3	12.3	16.3	14.6	8.9	6.5	42.3	318 912	92.8	34.6
District 1	5.0	15.6	9.5	11.7	12.5	16.1	14.7	8.8	6.2	41.9	161 024	93.2	35.4
District 2	5.0	15.5	9.8	11.0	12.1	16.4	14.5	8.9	6.8	42.7	157 888	92.3	33.7
NEW JERSEY	6.0	16.8	8.9	12.8	13.3	15.2	12.7	7.9	6.5	39.4	2 265 632	88.5	36.6
District 1	6.2	16.9	9.1	13.4	12.9	14.6	12.7	7.9	6.2	38.6	186 026	89.3	28.5
District 2	6.0	16.1	8.8	12.1	11.9	15.0	13.8	9.2	7.2	41.2	169 410	85.8	24.1
District 3	5.5	16.2	7.8	11.0	12.7	15.4	13.5	9.6	8.4	42.9	176 938	91.9	31.2
District 4	5.9	18.3	8.0	10.6	11.1	15.4	12.7	9.2	8.8	42.3	196 396	90.5	37.4
District 5	4.8	18.0	8.2	9.3	12.8	16.9	14.0	8.9	7.0	42.8	188 291	93.5	45.8
District 6	6.3	16.2	10.3	14.1	13.7	14.6	12.5	7.0	5.2	37.2	195 407	87.5	38.0
District 7	5.0	18.5	7.9	9.4	13.6	17.8	13.8	7.9	6.4	42.2	197 464	93.5	50.3
District 8	7.3	14.1	9.6	20.3	15.6	13.3	10.0	5.5	4.4	34.3	178 584	77.3	28.7
District 9	6.6	16.4	8.9	14.7	14.0	14.4	11.6	7.1	6.3	37.2	192 100	84.7	32.1
District 10	6.7	17.3	10.6	15.0	14.2	13.8	11.1	6.6	4.6	35.2	208 179	85.8	27.5
District 11	5.4	16.8	7.7	10.6	13.3	16.0	13.8	8.8	7.7	42.6	185 217	94.1	51.6
District 12	5.8	16.3	9.7	13.0	13.9	15.3	12.3	7.3	6.3	39.2	191 620	88.5	43.1
NEW MEXICO	6.6	17.7	10.3	13.0	12.0	12.9	12.8	8.6	6.1	36.9	565 242	84.3	26.4
District 1	6.2	16.7	10.1	14.6	12.0	13.5	13.0	8.1	5.7	36.9	186 291	87.2	32.3
District 2	7.0	18.3	11.5	12.2	11.1	12.3	12.1	8.8	6.6	35.8	193 564	79.4	20.3
District 3	6.7	18.1	9.4	12.0	12.8	12.8	13.3	8.9	6.0	38.1	185 387	86.0	26.2
NEW YORK	6.0	15.6	10.1	14.2	12.8	14.3	12.5	7.9	6.6	38.2	4 957 486	85.6	34.1
District 1	5.5	16.4	9.3	11.2	12.9	15.7	13.2	9.0	6.8	41.0	184 288	91.1	34.9
District 2	5.5	16.7	9.5	12.0	13.2	16.3	13.1	7.4	6.3	40.3	178 720	87.9	27.3
District 3	4.9	17.7	7.9	9.7	12.0	16.5	13.2	9.2	9.0	43.4	187 725	92.6	52.2
District 4	5.7	16.7	9.3	11.8	12.5	15.0	13.5	8.3	7.3	40.5	182 869	88.4	39.4
District 5	6.8	16.5	10.6	14.1	12.7	15.0	11.8	7.1	5.3	36.6	208 298	81.6	23.7
District 6	5.4	13.2	7.6	14.7	14.8	14.4	14.0	8.2	7.7	41.1	161 092	83.0	37.0
District 7	7.4	15.4	10.1	19.8	15.3	11.9	9.8	5.8	4.4	33.4	185 788	68.8	29.9
District 8	6.7	15.9	10.1	15.6	13.2	13.7	11.6	7.0	6.2	36.0	190 027	80.3	29.0
District 9	7.1	15.5	10.0	16.8	13.4	12.7	11.9	7.4	5.2	35.4	193 147	84.4	35.1
District 10	6.9	12.6	9.0	21.3	14.4	12.0	11.1	7.1	5.6	35.0	170 370	88.5	60.6
District 11	6.2	15.9	8.6	14.0	13.5	14.5	12.6	8.1	6.6	39.3	181 578	86.1	32.9
District 12	4.4	7.1	9.1	27.1	15.7	11.4	10.8	7.9	6.6	36.2	126 023	92.7	69.2
District 13	7.0	14.2	11.4	18.7	13.6	13.0	10.8	6.4	5.0	34.4	196 700	73.0	29.7
District 14	6.3	14.0	9.9	18.6	14.7	13.8	10.5	6.6	5.8	35.7	167 608	74.9	25.4

1. All persons 3 years old and over enrolled in nursery school through college and graduate or professional school. 2. Persons 25 years old and over.

STATE District	Households, 2013							Group quarters, 2010				
	Number	Average household size	Family households (percent)	Married-couple family (percent)	Female family householder[1]	One person households (percent)	Total in group quarters, 2013	Percent 65 years and over	Persons in correctional institutions	Persons in nursing facilities	Persons in college dormitories	Persons in military quarters
	28	29	30	31	32	33	34	35	36	37	38	39
MISSISSIPPI	1 091 002	2.66	68.30	44.7	18.7	27.2	94 460	16.0	34 273	16 496	26 472	3 938
District 1	278 788	2.65	69.90	48.5	16.0	25.4	17 784	22.9	2 943	4 381	7 786	0
District 2	253 355	2.74	67.60	36.2	26.5	29.3	31 321	11.7	14 994	4 226	8 476	8
District 3	280 713	2.58	67.50	47.1	16.0	28.5	25 683	18.4	9 560	4 625	5 828	601
District 4	278 146	2.66	68.20	46.2	16.9	25.8	19 672	14.6	6 776	3 264	4 382	3 329
MISSOURI	2 362 853	2.48	64.50	48.0	12.2	29.3	174 538	22.7	41 956	44 866	52 869	10 217
District 1	309 673	2.32	53.90	29.0	19.7	39.0	19 874	17.6	1 344	4 741	9 050	0
District 2	301 232	2.51	69.50	57.1	9.5	26.3	11 809	55.7	2 300	7 231	1 046	0
District 3	283 891	2.62	70.00	54.7	10.8	25.1	18 191	19.1	6 107	3 662	5 666	0
District 4	287 375	2.51	65.90	52.0	9.8	26.0	36 000	13.4	6 015	5 555	11 262	10 217
District 5	309 920	2.41	57.70	37.8	15.4	35.0	13 293	31.8	1 420	5 172	2 626	0
District 6	284 105	2.55	67.70	52.9	10.9	26.3	29 214	20.5	11 433	6 573	8 326	0
District 7	301 393	2.45	65.00	50.7	9.9	28.0	20 193	22.7	2 358	4 919	9 841	0
District 8	285 264	2.53	67.00	51.5	11.0	27.8	25 964	23.9	10 979	7 013	5 052	0
MONTANA	406 288	2.43	63.00	49.0	9.3	30.3	28 797	19.2	5 338	5 200	8 332	678
At Large	406 288	2.43	63.00	49.0	9.3	30.3	28 797	19.2	5 338	5 200	8 332	678
NEBRASKA	730 579	2.49	65.00	51.0	9.8	28.8	51 436	24.4	8 084	13 519	22 073	443
District 1	243 060	2.5	65.10	50.9	9.5	27.8	19 295	19.1	3 362	4 124	10 719	443
District 2	243 694	2.55	63.40	47.5	11.6	30.1	12 749	17.6	2 325	2 632	4 750	0
District 3	243 825	2.41	66.50	54.8	8.2	28.7	19 392	35.5	2 397	6 763	6 604	0
NEVADA	1 002 571	2.75	63.80	45.5	12.7	28.6	36 315	15.2	19 891	5 005	3 336	1 022
District 1	237 234	2.8	58.80	36.6	15.2	32.9	9 094	11.3	4 771	954	1 211	0
District 2	261 723	2.59	62.20	46.7	10.5	29.4	12 361	12.8	6 685	1 334	2 125	166
District 3	272 429	2.64	64.10	49.0	10.5	28.4	2 331	58.1	352	1 044	0	0
District 4	231 185	3.0	70.40	49.2	15.1	23.5	12 529	14.2	8 083	1 673	0	856
NEW HAMPSHIRE	519 246	2.47	66.90	52.4	10.1	25.5	40 871	19.5	4 851	7 767	22 820	454
District 1	264 954	2.43	66.50	52.1	10.2	25.4	18 937	21.5	1 640	3 963	10 357	454
District 2	254 292	2.51	67.20	52.8	9.9	25.7	21 934	17.9	3 211	3 804	12 463	0
NEW JERSEY	3 176 139	2.74	69.50	50.7	13.8	25.5	186 622	23.7	44 468	45 512	55 483	1 452
District 1	266 632	2.7	67.50	45.7	16.3	27.2	11 356	33.0	2 221	3 995	2 424	0
District 2	265 245	2.67	69.70	49.0	14.8	25.1	23 754	17.9	11 704	4 360	2 376	768
District 3	274 012	2.66	69.40	53.9	11.1	26.3	14 768	26.5	6 383	4 169	0	360
District 4	267 573	2.72	69.60	54.8	10.8	25.9	8 174	50.3	1 319	4 614	1 306	254
District 5	266 456	2.69	73.10	58.2	10.7	23.0	15 208	39.2	1 041	5 005	4 364	0
District 6	250 817	2.84	71.40	53.3	13.0	24.1	26 549	12.3	2 976	3 169	15 266	70
District 7	262 582	2.8	74.30	62.4	8.5	22.2	12 523	37.9	2 789	3 543	129	0
District 8	274 813	2.73	61.40	36.3	17.6	28.9	7 906	22.0	3 043	2 492	1 409	0
District 9	261 665	2.88	70.60	47.3	17.0	24.6	5 487	26.3	1 068	1 145	468	0
District 10	259 002	2.75	64.10	34.5	22.6	30.5	21 342	11.0	7 245	2 896	6 771	0
District 11	264 247	2.72	73.30	60.8	9.4	22.7	16 574	30.3	411	5 741	9 278	0
District 12	263 095	2.77	69.70	52.3	13.7	24.9	22 981	16.9	4 268	4 383	11 692	0
NEW MEXICO	753 507	2.71	64.00	44.7	14.2	29.6	43 123	14.3	17 907	5 567	8 478	1 789
District 1	265 627	2.57	62.60	42.5	14.4	30.6	11 361	15.9	4 489	1 768	2 750	530
District 2	245 274	2.76	65.20	46.7	13.7	28.1	20 118	11.7	9 874	2 334	3 613	815
District 3	242 606	2.81	64.40	45.0	14.4	30.2	11 644	17.2	3 544	1 465	2 115	444
NEW YORK	7 219 356	2.64	63.50	43.7	14.7	29.9	583 811	19.7	95 306	116 558	218 960	8 100
District 1	248 292	2.82	72.90	57.3	11.5	22.5	23 111	20.6	1 648	4 504	9 203	6
District 2	226 339	3.14	76.30	57.3	13.9	20.2	6 925	46.7	6	2 952	720	4
District 3	247 476	2.87	73.60	61.9	8.7	23.3	13 191	41.2	10	5 607	3 982	4
District 4	232 488	3.02	73.60	55.5	13.6	22.5	12 451	28.5	1 657	4 200	4 748	0
District 5	228 051	3.31	75.80	45.0	23.0	20.8	13 467	30.2	234	5 713	2 367	0
District 6	268 775	2.66	63.80	47.7	11.0	31.1	6 089	62.0	17	4 179	812	0
District 7	251 133	2.97	64.50	38.8	18.3	25.4	14 375	12.2	3 636	1 600	1 803	0
District 8	272 812	2.64	63.00	30.9	25.4	30.8	16 817	26.0	256	4 120	2 056	0
District 9	270 250	2.69	62.80	34.0	23.3	29.7	9 102	27.0	0	2 585	611	0
District 10	300 575	2.31	45.70	36.7	6.1	43.8	21 893	10.2	165	2 076	16 711	0
District 11	264 033	2.73	69.60	50.7	13.4	26.5	8 635	36.4	924	3 540	1 457	60
District 12	358 889	1.93	37.60	28.8	7.0	48.7	26 962	10.4	414	3 896	16 755	0
District 13	271 292	2.77	54.50	23.0	25.4	38.0	15 046	29.6	334	5 101	1 924	0
District 14	245 436	2.89	63.80	38.6	17.4	28.1	17 617	21.9	11 095	5 195	2 355	0

1. No spouse present.

STATE District	Housing units, 2013						Money income, 2013		
		Occupied units						Households	
			Owner-occupied			Renter-occupied			
	Total	Occupied units as a percent of all units	Owner-occupied units as a percent of occupied units	Median value[1] (dollars)	Percent valued at $500,000 or more	Median rent[2]	Per capita income (dollars)	Median income (dollars)	Percent with income of $100,000 or more
	40	41	42	43	44	45	46	47	48
MISSISSIPPI	1 283 192	85.0	67.2	97 500	1.8	708	20 156	37 963	12.5
District 1	320 204	87.1	70.0	99 500	1.7	672	20 387	40 887	12.5
District 2	306 376	82.7	62.5	78 600	1.0	644	16 939	30 582	9.0
District 3	325 878	86.1	70.1	103 800	2.7	742	22 522	39 890	15.2
District 4	330 734	84.1	65.8	113 300	1.6	761	20 666	41 374	12.9
MISSOURI	2 719 109	86.9	67.0	133 200	3.1	734	25 384	46 931	17.0
District 1	368 142	84.1	53.2	99 700	2.1	780	23 848	40 372	12.6
District 2	318 047	94.7	78.3	207 900	8.7	921	39 316	72 888	35.2
District 3	331 528	85.6	76.2	152 600	2.5	743	25 402	53 371	19.7
District 4	341 216	84.2	67.0	125 600	3.3	712	22 477	43 857	13.7
District 5	355 035	87.3	57.9	112 400	2.1	772	24 704	44 496	14.6
District 6	323 027	88.0	69.5	133 200	2.2	713	25 326	51 219	19.0
District 7	345 022	87.4	64.6	119 500	1.9	675	22 274	40 364	12.0
District 8	337 092	84.6	70.5	99 100	1.1	579	19 421	37 617	9.3
MONTANA	485 767	83.6	66.9	190 100	7.1	690	26 054	46 972	16.7
At Large	485 767	83.6	66.9	190 100	7.1	690	26 054	46 972	16.7
NEBRASKA	806 888	90.5	66.0	132 700	2.3	714	27 093	51 440	19.1
District 1	264 656	91.8	65.7	142 000	2.4	704	26 732	52 195	19.5
District 2	259 627	93.9	62.6	148 700	2.9	788	28 912	54 879	23.1
District 3	282 605	86.3	69.8	98 700	1.8	624	25 564	48 263	14.7
NEVADA	1 186 936	84.5	54.3	165 300	4.8	952	25 918	51 230	19.3
District 1	300 644	78.9	40.6	110 200	1.7	836	19 803	39 265	10.8
District 2	296 324	88.3	59.4	185 100	7.7	871	28 322	53 093	22.1
District 3	317 356	85.8	58.9	209 300	6.3	1 153	32 608	61 217	25.5
District 4	272 612	84.8	57.2	151 700	1.9	1 019	22 571	51 708	17.6
NEW HAMPSHIRE	616 496	84.2	70.2	233 300	6.6	995	33 269	64 230	27.8
District 1	313 383	84.5	68.5	240 000	7.1	1 037	34 293	64 681	28.0
District 2	303 113	83.9	71.8	226 000	6.2	955	32 242	63 835	27.6
NEW JERSEY	3 578 260	88.8	64.0	307 700	19.5	1 171	35 728	70 165	34.6
District 1	293 077	91.0	68.2	191 800	3.0	978	30 043	61 369	27.7
District 2	384 317	69.0	71.0	219 100	9.5	1 009	27 871	56 532	24.5
District 3	317 919	86.2	81.6	252 700	8.3	1 254	34 819	72 798	33.6
District 4	294 366	90.9	75.2	327 200	22.1	1 235	36 712	73 710	36.7
District 5	282 735	94.2	74.3	392 500	30.9	1 308	44 470	88 280	44.7
District 6	272 381	92.1	62.1	314 300	14.7	1 241	32 517	74 164	35.6
District 7	280 740	93.5	77.6	416 500	36.3	1 355	49 920	101 222	51.0
District 8	302 789	90.8	27.1	297 500	16.2	1 142	28 686	52 524	23.6
District 9	283 740	92.2	48.9	360 300	20.3	1 242	30 562	60 439	29.4
District 10	298 391	86.8	39.6	261 100	11.0	1 039	25 479	45 421	20.4
District 11	280 961	94.1	77.4	413 800	33.3	1 350	49 892	100 143	50.1
District 12	286 844	91.7	65.5	321 400	20.5	1 195	37 805	75 927	38.2
NEW MEXICO	905 134	83.2	67.9	159 200	5.1	772	23 334	43 872	16.7
District 1	295 647	89.8	62.2	182 100	5.3	799	26 107	47 124	18.3
District 2	302 099	81.2	69.1	119 600	2.5	691	20 917	41 367	14.0
District 3	307 388	78.9	73.0	170 700	7.4	812	22 987	44 400	17.5
NEW YORK	8 126 399	88.8	53.7	277 600	22.5	1 109	32 514	57 369	27.6
District 1	305 545	81.3	81.4	360 800	23.8	1 564	36 759	83 493	41.2
District 2	241 405	93.8	79.7	354 800	12.6	1 452	32 989	85 976	41.8
District 3	261 104	94.8	80.2	525 000	52.7	1 676	50 166	101 695	51.4
District 4	247 833	93.8	76.3	421 400	29.8	1 438	38 227	89 600	45.3
District 5	246 762	92.4	54.4	384 400	20.1	1 243	23 050	58 470	25.5
District 6	286 900	93.7	47.2	495 700	49.4	1 339	29 380	57 001	25.3
District 7	270 714	92.8	22.2	543 100	54.6	1 188	26 620	48 813	24.0
District 8	302 168	90.3	33.3	481 300	46.2	1 106	26 830	45 117	20.1
District 9	293 079	92.2	30.2	517 700	52.1	1 170	27 170	47 355	21.5
District 10	357 284	84.1	29.9	799 100	78.2	1 699	60 098	81 810	42.1
District 11	281 769	93.7	56.4	458 800	41.5	1 204	31 451	63 750	30.8
District 12	419 465	85.6	26.9	845 900	78.3	1 817	79 560	91 628	47.0
District 13	294 550	92.1	10.2	454 100	45.2	1 045	21 539	33 607	13.1
District 14	262 554	93.5	30.1	440 800	37.9	1 307	24 012	50 804	20.1

1. Specified owner-occupied units. 2. Specified renter-occupied units.

STATE District	Poverty, 2013			Civilian labor force, 2013			Civilian employment,[2] 2013					Social Security beneficiaries, December 2013		
					Unemployment			Percent						
	Persons below poverty level (percent)	Families below poverty level (percent)	Percent of households receiving food stamps in past 12 months	Total	Total	Rate[1]	Total	Management, business, science and arts occupations	Service, sales, and office	Construction and production	Persons under age 65 with no health insurance, 2013 (percent)	Number	Rate[3]	Supplemental Security Income recipients, December 2013
	49	50	51	52	53	54	55	56	57	58	59	60	61	62
MISSISSIPPI	24.0	19.0	19.4	1 338 290	141 506	10.6	1 196 784	30.5	42.5	27.0	19.8	632 191	211.3	126 240
District 1	20.7	16.0	15.7	350 403	34 216	9.8	316 187	27.3	41.6	31.2	18.4	164 683	217.7	25 771
District 2	32.5	26.8	26.6	306 263	40 673	13.3	265 590	29.5	44.5	26.0	21.8	156 912	216.1	47 945
District 3	22.3	17.1	16.2	337 951	31 959	9.5	305 992	35.9	39.7	24.4	17.4	154 754	206.2	27 991
District 4	21.2	16.8	19.9	343 673	34 658	10.1	309 015	29.3	44.3	26.4	21.5	155 842	205.5	24 533
MISSOURI	15.9	11.5	13.7	3 035 251	226 716	7.5	2 808 535	34.8	43.2	22.0	15.2	1 232 526	203.9	142 219
District 1	21.5	17.2	20.4	389 401	43 868	11.3	345 533	35.4	48.0	16.6	17.8	134 811	182.9	30 555
District 2	5.9	4.2	5.2	417 414	20 102	4.8	397 312	48.8	38.5	12.7	7.4	146 487	190.6	5 497
District 3	11.2	8.7	10.2	392 095	27 955	7.1	364 140	33.4	42.5	24.2	12.4	150 053	197.3	10 521
District 4	19.6	13.5	15.1	356 514	26 171	7.3	330 343	34.3	41.7	23.9	15.6	156 017	206.3	16 144
District 5	18.0	13.5	14.2	394 829	26 891	6.8	367 938	32.6	46.0	21.4	19.0	144 020	189.8	19 409
District 6	13.3	9.3	11.0	380 926	23 333	6.1	357 593	33.7	41.7	24.6	13.4	145 666	193.0	12 310
District 7	17.9	12.7	14.4	373 261	29 530	7.9	343 731	31.2	45.2	23.7	19.4	166 200	218.8	17 601
District 8	20.2	14.9	19.2	330 811	28 866	8.7	301 945	26.5	42.6	30.9	16.5	189 272	252.8	30 182
MONTANA	16.5	11.3	10.7	516 204	33 601	6.5	482 603	34.8	43.7	21.5	19.5	208 546	205.4	18 673
At Large	16.5	11.3	10.7	516 204	33 601	6.5	482 603	34.8	43.7	21.5	19.5	208 546	205.4	18 673
NEBRASKA	13.2	8.8	9.1	1 012 431	46 652	4.6	965 779	35.7	40.7	23.7	13.0	321 882	172.3	27 457
District 1	12.9	7.9	8.5	345 083	16 581	4.8	328 502	34.6	41.6	23.8	12.3	104 354	166.1	8 405
District 2	13.6	9.5	10.5	347 368	15 554	4.5	331 814	40.6	41.4	18.0	12.7	89 613	141.3	10 317
District 3	13.1	8.9	8.1	319 980	14 517	4.5	305 463	31.4	39.0	29.5	14.2	127 915	211.1	8 735
NEVADA	15.8	11.6	11.8	1 418 167	155 437	11.0	1 262 730	28.0	53.0	18.9	23.6	459 536	164.7	48 817
District 1	22.6	17.7	19.0	350 712	45 199	12.9	305 513	18.4	61.8	19.8	32.9	90 653	134.5	16 969
District 2	14.3	9.8	9.7	352 735	34 230	9.7	318 505	31.7	45.5	22.7	20.8	129 141	186.9	10 062
District 3	9.7	7.1	5.6	379 503	30 911	8.1	348 592	34.5	51.5	14.0	17.1	120 038	166.6	8 143
District 4	16.9	12.9	14.1	335 217	45 097	13.5	290 120	26.2	53.8	19.9	23.8	119 704	169.8	13 643
NEW HAMPSHIRE	8.7	5.1	8.6	739 152	44 644	6.0	694 508	39.0	40.1	20.8	12.6	278 664	210.6	19 507
District 1	7.9	4.9	8.6	374 676	22 215	5.9	352 461	38.9	41.4	19.7	12.4	137 938	208.2	9 786
District 2	9.6	5.3	8.5	364 476	22 429	6.2	342 047	39.1	38.9	22.0	12.7	140 726	212.9	9 721
NEW JERSEY	11.4	8.7	9.6	4 677 032	424 406	9.1	4 252 626	40.4	42.0	17.6	15.1	1 548 525	174.0	180 354
District 1	13.5	10.9	12.6	384 713	38 969	10.1	345 744	37.3	44.5	18.2	13.1	137 304	187.9	20 039
District 2	15.6	12.9	13.3	362 342	43 434	12.0	318 908	31.8	48.3	19.9	15.5	158 359	216.1	17 648
District 3	5.4	3.9	5.5	385 902	32 218	8.3	353 684	39.2	43.6	17.2	8.8	166 034	223.6	9 272
District 4	9.6	6.1	6.5	360 723	27 709	7.7	333 014	40.4	43.4	16.1	12.5	155 468	211.5	8 923
District 5	7.1	5.4	4.5	391 607	27 406	7.0	364 201	46.9	39.3	13.7	10.5	131 969	180.0	8 010
District 6	11.8	8.1	7.9	387 855	34 809	9.0	353 046	40.8	40.1	19.0	14.5	111 629	151.2	13 263
District 7	4.8	3.4	3.6	406 006	24 782	6.1	381 224	49.6	37.4	13.1	8.5	119 834	160.1	5 855
District 8	19.2	16.2	17.7	428 635	43 729	10.2	384 906	31.5	42.8	25.7	28.2	90 542	119.4	27 287
District 9	15.1	12.8	15.0	380 482	30 492	8.0	349 990	36.1	41.0	22.8	23.0	115 320	151.7	19 236
District 10	20.8	17.3	17.8	378 596	55 461	14.6	323 135	33.3	47.5	19.2	21.5	104 369	142.4	30 026
District 11	4.7	3.0	2.8	401 308	29 170	7.3	372 138	51.2	38.0	10.7	8.5	134 235	182.4	6 717
District 12	9.6	6.5	7.9	408 863	36 227	8.9	372 636	43.8	40.2	16.1	14.6	123 462	164.5	14 078
NEW MEXICO	21.9	16.3	16.7	960 616	88 129	9.2	872 487	34.7	43.5	21.8	21.6	392 306	188.1	64 300
District 1	19.5	15.1	16.3	343 449	27 943	8.1	315 506	38.3	43.1	18.5	18.9	125 166	180.2	18 746
District 2	22.9	16.9	19.1	311 141	32 538	10.5	278 603	28.7	44.7	26.6	22.9	136 987	196.5	23 960
District 3	23.4	17.1	14.8	306 026	27 648	9.0	278 378	36.6	42.8	20.5	23.0	130 153	187.6	21 594
NEW YORK	16.0	12.1	15.8	10 086 197	872 645	8.7	9 213 552	39.2	44.2	16.7	12.3	3 444 200	175.3	698 928
District 1	7.0	5.1	6.3	372 869	23 962	6.4	348 907	38.8	41.9	19.4	9.6	145 343	201.2	11 094
District 2	6.6	5.5	6.8	388 001	26 023	6.7	361 978	32.2	46.9	21.0	11.1	130 376	181.4	11 443
District 3	5.5	3.8	3.7	371 407	22 245	6.0	349 162	50.1	39.4	10.4	8.2	144 798	199.9	8 643
District 4	7.2	5.1	6.6	373 545	26 883	7.2	346 662	41.2	43.8	15.0	12.8	132 808	185.7	11 210
District 5	14.6	11.5	20.6	397 189	48 182	12.1	349 007	28.0	51.6	20.4	15.8	100 427	130.7	28 663
District 6	13.5	10.5	10.1	370 954	27 459	7.4	343 495	37.8	45.8	16.3	17.7	111 049	154.0	24 106
District 7	26.7	23.4	28.4	393 822	39 890	10.1	353 932	36.1	46.1	17.8	18.6	83 345	109.6	42 081
District 8	24.7	20.2	26.9	362 937	45 482	12.5	317 455	37.5	48.0	14.5	11.9	104 813	142.1	51 980
District 9	20.1	17.4	22.3	370 441	37 962	10.2	332 479	37.3	49.5	13.1	14.8	93 593	127.3	36 378
District 10	17.0	13.4	11.8	405 149	26 733	6.6	378 416	60.7	31.7	7.6	9.3	101 250	141.3	26 952
District 11	13.7	11.0	15.3	349 797	27 166	7.8	322 631	39.8	43.8	16.5	10.9	123 093	169.0	27 724
District 12	12.5	7.6	6.4	467 846	23 883	5.1	443 963	64.6	30.6	4.8	10.5	104 844	145.5	16 852
District 13	30.8	27.1	34.3	378 870	50 698	13.4	328 172	33.7	52.4	13.9	16.4	101 999	133.3	61 394
District 14	18.7	16.0	18.7	378 473	33 322	8.8	345 151	27.7	50.9	21.4	24.6	92 066	126.5	25 766

1. Percent of civilian labor force. 2. Persons 16 years old and over. 3. Per 1,000 resident population estimated in the 2013 American Community Survey.

STATE District	Agriculture, 2012									
		Land in farms			Value of products sold				Government payments	
	Number of farms	Acres	Average size of farm (acres)	Irrigated land (acres)	Total ($1,000)	Average per farm (dollars)	Percent from crops	Percent from livestock and poultry products	Total ($1,000)	Average per farm receiving payments (dollars)
	63	64	65	66	67	68	69	70	71	72
MISSISSIPPI	38 076	10 931 080	287	1 651 978	6 441 025	169 162	46.2	53.8	181 205	10 983
District 1	10 989	2 650 855	241	41 049	785 235	71 456	59.0	41.0	32 055	5 487
District 2	10 256	5 182 018	505	1 580 386	2 848 319	277 722	79.4	20.6	124 539	19 898
District 3	10 656	2 250 486	211	25 717	2 096 730	196 765	7.7	92.3	17 972	5 567
District 4	6 175	847 721	137	4 826	710 741	115 100	12.0	88.0	6 640	5 680
MISSOURI	99 171	28 266 137	285	1 180 886	9 164 886	92 415	49.8	50.2	323 953	7 834
District 1	60	6 587	110	218	3 893	64 882	92.6	7.4	62	3 422
District 2	209	28 798	138	300	17 733	84 847	98.2	1.8	285	6 059
District 3	11 580	2 688 776	232	19 373	684 080	59 074	41.2	58.8	19 580	4 688
District 4	23 699	6 461 439	273	50 614	1 917 653	80 917	37.2	62.8	54 640	6 422
District 5	3 727	1 121 876	301	13 153	444 240	119 195	75.8	24.2	14 699	6 789
District 6	27 780	9 406 377	339	66 257	2 807 585	101 065	60.0	40.0	160 256	8 483
District 7	12 894	2 269 377	176	11 727	1 301 247	100 919	7.6	92.4	9 439	4 762
District 8	19 222	6 282 907	327	1 019 244	1 988 454	103 447	72.0	28.0	64 993	11 677
MONTANA	28 008	59 758 917	2 134	1 903 019	4 230 083	151 031	53.3	46.7	209 846	16 865
At Large	28 008	59 758 917	2 134	1 903 019	4 230 083	151 031	53.3	46.7	209 846	16 865
NEBRASKA	49 969	45 331 783	907	8 296 573	23 068 756	461 661	49.3	50.7	392 428	11 436
District 1	13 381	5 484 143	410	1 187 864	5 270 537	393 882	46.5	53.5	90 779	9 562
District 2	738	169 478	230	28 590	115 796	156 905	83.2	16.8	2 519	6 845
District 3	35 850	39 678 162	1 107	7 080 119	17 680 000	493 234	49.9	50.1	299 130	12 232
NEVADA	4 137	5 913 761	1 429	687 790	764 144	184 710	47.9	52.1	3 253	9 568
District 1	X	X	X	X	X	X	X	X	X	X
District 2	2 991	5 105 484	1 707	528 164	552 567	184 743	49.0	51.0	2 568	9 303
District 3	66	6 105	93	D	D	D	D	D	D	D
District 4	1 074	802 153	747	159 045	210 323	195 831	44.9	55.1	D	D
NEW HAMPSHIRE	4 391	474 065	108	2 630	190 907	43 477	52.8	47.2	3 472	7 435
District 1	1 576	118 543	75	1 011	42 022	26 664	58.4	41.6	1 110	7 761
District 2	2 815	355 522	126	1 619	148 885	52 890	51.2	48.8	2 362	7 290
NEW JERSEY	9 071	715 057	79	88 376	1 006 936	111 006	88.5	11.5	7 596	7 332
District 1	357	21 147	59	5 235	39 064	109 422	96.3	3.7	226	8 707
District 2	2 409	235 314	98	57 342	482 153	200 147	93.7	6.3	2 652	7 245
District 3	860	94 990	110	13 112	101 201	117 676	95.4	4.6	1 939	17 315
District 4	906	45 690	50	4 542	93 422	103 115	82.2	17.8	296	4 479
District 5	1 571	109 563	70	1 993	97 306	61 939	58.1	41.9	884	5 357
District 6	122	6 224	51	606	12 143	99 531	79.7	20.3	5	752
District 7	2 154	155 495	72	2 042	114 738	53 267	86.0	14.0	1 142	4 989
District 8	X	X	X	X	X	X	X	X	X	X
District 9	11	D	D	D	D	D	D	D	D	D
District 10	X	X	X	X	X	X	X	X	X	X
District 11	264	11 276	43	286	24 624	93 272	D	D	5	1 176
District 12	416	35 112	84	3 207	41 520	99 808	92.7	7.3	447	7 320
NEW MEXICO	24 721	43 201 023	1 748	680 318	2 550 147	103 157	24.2	75.8	70 588	12 830
District 1	1 868	2 249 327	1 204	33 967	73 029	39 095	44.7	55.3	3 559	14 829
District 2	10 130	21 702 074	2 142	369 030	1 599 576	157 905	27.4	72.6	37 277	16 257
District 3	12 723	19 249 622	1 513	277 321	877 541	68 973	16.6	83.4	29 752	10 021
NEW YORK	35 537	7 183 576	202	59 807	5 415 125	152 380	41.5	58.5	74 511	7 955
District 1	499	27 475	55	8 672	196 009	392 803	83.0	17.0	605	15 508
District 2	39	1 088	28	265	4 469	114 580	98.0	2.0	D	D
District 3	112	10 121	90	2 954	45 149	403 114	88.6	11.4	185	61 793
District 4	10	20	2	14	492	49 170	D	D	0	0
District 5	X	X	X	X	X	X	X	X	X	X
District 6	X	X	X	X	X	X	X	X	X	X
District 7	X	X	X	X	X	X	X	X	X	X
District 8	X	X	X	X	X	X	X	X	X	X
District 9	X	X	X	X	X	X	X	X	X	X
District 10	X	X	X	X	X	X	X	X	X	X
District 11	X	X	X	X	X	X	X	X	X	X
District 12	X	X	X	X	X	X	X	X	X	X
District 13	X	X	X	X	X	X	X	X	X	X
District 14	X	X	X	X	X	X	X	X	X	X

1. Specified owner-occupied units. 2. Specified renter-occupied units.

STATE District	Representative, 114th Congress	Land area,[1] 2010 (sq km)	Population and population characteristics, 2013: Total persons	Per square kilometer	Percent: Race alone: White	Black	American Indian, Alaska Native	Asian and Pacific Islander	Some other race (percent)	Two or more races (percent)	Hispanic or Latino[2] (percent)	Non-Hispanic White alone (percent)	Percent female	Percent foreign-born	Percent born in state of residence
		1	2	3	4	5	6	7	8	9	10	11	12	13	14
NEW YORK—Cont'd															
District 15	José E. Serrano (D)	38	747 271	19 665.0	14.6	33.0	0.5	2.4	45.9	3.6	64.7	2.9	53.2	34.9	51.1
District 16	Eliot L. Engel (D)	203	730 795	3 600.0	49.2	31.8	0.1	4.4	11.9	2.6	23.4	39.4	53.4	29.1	57.1
District 17	Nita M. Lowey (D)	991	742 344	749.1	68.1	11.1	0.4	6.2	11.7	2.5	21.9	59.6	50.8	23.6	62.6
District 18	Sean Patrick Maloney (D)	3 505	718 210	204.9	77.8	9.5	0.2	3.1	6.2	3.3	16.1	69.9	50.5	12.0	70.8
District 19	Christopher P. Gibson (R)	20 557	709 970	34.5	90.2	4.2	0.2	1.5	1.0	3.0	6.5	85.8	49.6	5.9	76.1
District 20	Paul Tonko (D)	3 189	724 345	227.1	81.6	9.2	0.2	4.4	1.6	3.0	5.9	78.1	51.5	8.2	76.9
District 21	Elise M. Stefanik (R)	39 147	716 340	18.3	91.8	3.1	0.9	0.9	0.9	2.5	3.2	90.2	48.8	3.4	77.3
District 22	Richard L. Hanna (R)	13 151	713 145	54.2	90.3	4.1	0.3	2.4	0.9	2.0	3.5	88.6	50.6	5.0	80.7
District 23	Tom Reed (R)	19 092	716 427	37.5	91.6	3.0	0.6	2.2	0.6	2.0	3.6	89.2	50.3	3.6	74.8
District 24	John Katko (R)	6 186	715 192	115.6	84.8	8.2	0.5	2.6	1.2	2.7	4.1	82.6	51.0	5.4	79.6
District 25	Louise McIntosh Slaughter (D)	1 321	724 587	548.5	74.6	16.1	0.4	3.7	2.6	2.5	8.1	70.8	51.8	8.0	74.1
District 26	Brian Higgins (D)	568	715 554	1 259.8	72.3	18.4	0.4	3.3	2.9	2.6	6.0	70.3	52.1	7.4	79.5
District 27	Chris Collins(R)	10 290	714 863	69.5	93.6	2.4	0.7	1.3	0.5	1.5	2.3	92.2	50.3	3.3	84.8
NORTH CAROLINA		125 920	9 848 060	78.2	69.2	21.5	1.1	2.5	3.3	2.4	8.8	#DIV/0!	51.3	7.6	57.4
District 1	G. K. Butterfield (D)	14 230	724 668	50.9	38.7	54.4	0.7	1.5	2.2	2.6	7.4	34.0	52.8	6.0	69.4
District 2	Renee Ellmers (R)	8 409	777 683	92.5	72.5	16.1	0.8	3.4	3.5	3.6	11.9	65.1	50.8	8.7	52.2
District 3	Walter B. Jones (R)	20 228	749 521	37.1	74.9	18.1	0.4	1.7	2.4	2.5	7.5	70.5	49.4	4.3	52.5
District 4	David E. Price (D)	2 707	769 734	284.3	55.1	31.5	0.5	5.6	3.9	3.3	11.7	48.5	51.9	12.7	46.6
District 5	Virginia Foxx (R)	9 251	745 928	80.6	81.2	12.8	0.3	1.4	2.7	1.6	8.2	76.0	51.6	5.9	63.7
District 6	Mark Walker (R)	9 517	760 762	79.9	77.1	16.0	0.7	2.0	2.4	1.7	6.7	73.5	51.5	6.0	63.7
District 7	David Rouzer (R)	15 959	762 540	47.8	73.4	17.6	1.7	0.9	4.4	1.9	9.6	68.7	51.1	6.6	60.9
District 8	Richard Hudson (R)	11 688	744 074	63.7	68.3	18.4	7.2	1.3	2.8	2.0	8.5	62.8	51.0	6.0	68.0
District 9	Robert Pittenger (R)	2 219	780 211	351.6	78.0	12.7	0.3	4.2	2.7	2.1	7.8	73.2	51.5	10.4	40.2
District 10	Patrick T. McHenry (R)	6 670	739 282	110.8	81.7	11.3	0.3	1.3	2.9	2.5	6.2	79.0	51.6	5.3	63.7
District 11	Mark Meadows (R)	17 711	737 318	41.6	89.8	2.9	1.5	1.1	2.4	2.3	5.4	86.8	50.9	4.3	61.1
District 12	Alma S. Adams (D)	1 424	773 617	543.3	34.6	51.6	0.4	4.8	6.4	2.3	14.8	27.7	51.8	14.3	53.8
District 13	George Holding (R)	5 907	782 722	132.5	73.9	17.0	0.3	2.6	3.5	2.7	8.2	69.5	51.1	7.9	52.7
NORTH DAKOTA		178 711	723 393	4.0	89.0	1.5	5.6	1.3	0.6	2.0	2.4	87.4	49.1	2.9	65.1
At Large	Kevin Cramer (R)	178 711	723 393	4.0	89.0	1.5	5.6	1.3	0.6	2.0	2.4	87.4	49.1	2.9	65.1
OHIO		105 829	11 570 808	109.3	82.5	12.1	0.2	1.9	0.8	2.6	3.3	80.3	51.1	4.1	75.4
District 1	Steve Chabot (R)	1 779	724 914	407.5	72.2	21.9	0.1	3.0	0.6	2.2	2.9	70.0	51.3	5.5	72.1
District 2	Brad R. Wenstrup (R)	8 344	727 391	87.2	87.6	8.4	0.2	1.6	0.2	2.0	1.7	86.2	51.1	3.1	75.1
District 3	Joyce Beatty (D)	591	739 980	1 252.1	57.2	32.3	0.1	3.7	2.4	4.3	5.9	54.2	51.5	10.4	68.4
District 4	Jim Jordan (R)	12 082	709 122	58.7	90.9	4.9	0.2	0.7	0.8	2.5	3.2	88.9	50.1	1.5	82.3
District 5	Robert E. Latta (R)	14 572	730 642	50.1	91.5	3.2	0.1	1.5	1.5	2.3	4.8	88.7	51.2	2.4	79.8
District 6	Bill Johnson (R)	18 687	713 464	38.2	95.5	2.1	0.1	0.5	0.3	1.6	1.0	94.9	50.3	1.0	69.7
District 7	Bob Gibbs (R)	10 010	719 276	71.9	92.3	4.2	0.1	0.7	0.3	2.4	1.8	90.9	51.0	1.9	82.6
District 8	John A. Boehner (R)	6 347	721 486	113.7	89.4	5.7	0.1	1.6	0.7	2.6	3.2	87.0	51.0	3.6	74.5
District 9	Marcy Kaptur (D)	1 203	715 447	594.7	76.4	15.4	0.4	1.1	2.6	4.1	10.2	70.8	51.2	4.3	76.3
District 10	Michael R. Turner (R)	2 926	723 987	247.4	77.3	16.9	0.1	2.0	0.7	2.9	2.5	75.6	51.7	3.9	69.9
District 11	Marcia L. Fudge (D)	633	692 794	1 094.5	39.7	53.8	0.2	2.1	1.2	2.9	3.8	37.6	53.4	5.0	73.2
District 12	Patrick J. Tiberi (R)	5 884	744 647	126.6	88.2	4.7	0.2	3.4	0.6	3.0	2.8	86.2	50.6	5.3	73.3
District 13	Tim Ryan (D)	2 316	719 201	310.5	83.0	12.2	0.2	1.3	0.7	2.6	3.4	80.9	51.4	3.7	77.4
District 14	David P. Joyce (R)	5 059	725 681	143.4	91.5	4.2	0.1	2.1	0.2	1.9	2.3	89.7	51.2	5.2	76.3
District 15	Steve Stivers (R)	12 274	742 133	60.5	91.9	3.8	0.1	1.9	0.2	2.2	1.6	90.5	49.7	3.6	77.6
District 16	James B. Renacci (R)	3 122	720 643	230.8	93.4	2.2	0.1	2.5	0.2	1.7	1.9	91.8	51.1	5.4	78.5
OKLAHOMA		177 660	3 850 568	21.7	73.1	7.2	7.5	2.0	2.7	7.5	9.6	67.4	50.5	5.7	61.1
District 1	Jim Bridenstine (R)	4 226	773 208	183.0	72.4	8.5	5.4	2.2	2.9	8.7	10.4	65.9	51.2	7.1	58.4
District 2	Markwayne Mullin (R)	54 378	747 973	13.8	67.3	3.5	16.6	0.6	1.7	10.2	4.7	65.3	50.3	1.9	62.1
District 3	Frank D. Lucas (R)	88 362	767 552	8.7	79.6	3.7	6.1	1.7	3.8	5.1	9.3	75.1	49.7	4.4	64.2
District 4	Tom Cole (R)	25 323	776 394	30.7	76.7	6.5	5.3	2.5	1.8	7.2	7.9	72.1	50.1	4.5	60.7
District 5	Steve Russell (R)	5 371	785 441	146.2	69.4	13.5	4.6	2.9	3.3	6.2	15.5	58.9	51.1	10.2	59.9
OREGON		248 608	3 930 065	15.8	85.8	1.8	1.1	4.2	2.8	4.2	12.3	77.3	50.5	10.0	46.2
District 1	Suzanne Bonamici (D)	7 788	796 901	102.3	82.8	1.7	0.8	7.2	3.2	4.4	14.2	72.9	50.6	13.9	45.3
District 2	Greg Walden (R)	179 856	778 062	4.3	90.4	0.5	1.7	1.2	2.4	3.7	13.1	80.7	50.3	6.1	44.5
District 3	Earl Blumenauer (D)	2 783	797 199	286.5	79.1	5.2	0.9	6.9	2.9	5.0	11.0	72.5	50.4	14.0	44.6
District 4	Peter A. DeFazio (D)	44 740	772 196	17.3	89.6	0.9	1.2	2.4	2.0	3.8	7.3	85.0	50.5	5.1	46.5
District 5	Kurt Schrader (D)	13 441	785 707	58.5	87.1	0.9	0.9	3.3	3.7	4.1	15.9	76.0	50.8	10.5	50.2
PENNSYLVANIA		115 883	12 773 801	110.2	81.6	11.0	0.2	3.0	2.1	2.1	6.3	78.2	51.2	6.2	73.5
District 1	Robert A. Brady (D)	202	725 059	3 589.4	45.2	36.0	0.2	7.3	8.4	2.8	17.1	38.7	52.2	13.7	65.8
District 2	Chaka Fattah (D)	192	712 372	3 710.3	32.9	58.5	0.2	4.7	1.6	2.2	5.8	29.8	54.0	8.1	67.2
District 3	Mike Kelly (R)	9 974	703 010	70.5	92.1	4.7	0.1	0.9	0.6	1.6	2.0	90.8	50.8	2.1	82.4

1. Dry land or land partially or temporarily covered by water. 2. May be of any race.

STATE District	Population and population characteristics, 2013 (cont.)										Education, 2013		
	Age (percent)											Attainment[2] (percent)	
	Under 5 years	5 to 17 years	18 to 24 years	25 to 34 years	35 to 44 years	45 to 54 years	55 to 64 years	65 to 74 years	75 years and over	Median age	Total Enrollment[1]	High school graduate or more	Bachelor's degree or more
	15	16	17	18	19	20	21	22	23	24	25	26	27
NEW YORK—Cont'd													
District 15	8.3	19.8	12.4	15.0	13.0	13.0	9.6	5.2	3.6	31.0	223 870	65.9	13.1
District 16	6.6	16.8	9.5	12.2	12.5	14.7	12.1	8.2	7.5	39.4	200 428	85.8	38.8
District 17	6.4	18.8	9.2	11.5	12.6	14.6	12.5	7.7	6.8	38.1	209 209	87.1	44.9
District 18	5.5	18.5	10.2	10.6	12.6	16.1	12.6	7.9	5.7	39.3	202 912	90.4	33.9
District 19	4.8	14.5	10.8	9.9	11.3	16.3	15.0	10.1	7.4	43.9	163 660	89.3	26.8
District 20	5.1	15.3	12.2	13.1	11.8	14.3	13.3	7.7	7.1	38.6	191 515	91.9	36.0
District 21	5.8	15.3	10.5	12.6	11.8	15.0	13.2	9.0	6.8	40.4	165 114	87.6	20.9
District 22	5.1	15.7	11.7	11.0	11.1	14.6	14.0	8.9	7.8	40.8	179 386	88.6	23.3
District 23	5.1	15.7	12.5	11.3	11.1	14.0	13.9	9.0	7.4	40.0	184 168	89.1	24.2
District 24	5.7	16.1	10.8	12.4	11.4	15.0	13.4	8.2	7.1	39.6	187 101	90.1	29.0
District 25	5.7	15.9	11.2	13.5	11.6	14.1	12.9	8.1	7.0	38.2	190 610	90.3	36.0
District 26	5.6	15.1	11.5	13.8	11.2	13.5	13.5	8.1	7.7	38.7	181 633	89.0	29.5
District 27	5.0	15.8	8.8	11.1	11.8	16.3	14.5	9.1	7.6	43.2	163 647	91.5	28.8
NORTH CAROLINA	6.2	17.0	10.1	12.9	13.4	13.7	12.4	8.4	5.9	37.9	2 560 742	85.7	28.4
District 1	7.1	15.9	11.4	13.9	12.0	12.1	12.8	8.1	6.7	36.2	187 159	79.8	20.0
District 2	7.2	18.8	8.9	13.2	13.8	13.6	11.4	7.6	5.4	36.0	205 752	86.8	29.2
District 3	6.1	15.1	15.5	13.6	11.5	12.2	11.6	8.8	5.6	34.9	196 598	87.5	21.3
District 4	6.5	16.1	13.9	17.4	14.4	11.6	9.9	5.9	4.3	32.7	240 488	88.2	42.3
District 5	5.6	15.8	10.9	11.2	12.7	14.0	13.5	9.4	6.9	40.6	187 158	85.8	26.8
District 6	5.4	16.5	8.8	11.2	12.9	15.0	14.1	9.0	7.1	41.7	180 936	86.8	29.8
District 7	6.2	17.0	8.3	11.4	13.5	13.4	13.6	10.2	6.2	40.3	183 230	83.9	23.6
District 8	6.2	18.3	9.5	11.7	13.5	14.3	12.5	8.3	5.7	38.5	192 637	81.5	17.8
District 9	6.2	19.1	7.2	13.1	16.2	15.5	11.2	6.9	4.6	38.2	205 552	93.6	48.3
District 10	5.6	16.3	8.8	11.6	13.1	14.5	13.7	9.7	6.6	41.2	173 530	84.2	24.2
District 11	4.7	15.2	8.7	10.4	12.0	13.8	14.6	11.8	8.8	44.3	166 147	84.0	22.5
District 12	7.5	18.1	12.3	16.9	13.8	12.4	9.6	5.7	3.9	32.0	231 987	81.2	23.3
District 13	6.0	18.8	7.4	11.6	14.5	16.3	12.7	7.8	4.8	39.4	209 568	90.1	37.9
NORTH DAKOTA	6.6	15.6	13.1	14.0	11.3	12.6	12.6	7.1	7.1	35.5	180 316	91.5	27.1
At Large	6.6	15.6	13.1	14.0	11.3	12.6	12.6	7.1	7.1	35.5	180 316	91.5	27.1
OHIO	6.0	16.9	9.7	12.5	12.2	14.1	13.5	8.3	6.8	39.3	2 952 357	89.0	26.1
District 1	6.6	18.2	9.9	13.0	12.0	14.6	12.5	7.6	5.8	37.3	198 369	88.4	31.8
District 2	5.9	17.2	8.1	13.1	13.0	14.2	13.8	8.1	6.7	40.0	171 083	88.2	30.1
District 3	7.7	17.0	11.8	17.5	13.0	12.7	10.4	5.5	4.4	32.5	207 833	86.1	26.6
District 4	6.0	16.8	9.2	11.2	12.2	14.5	14.2	8.8	7.1	40.7	169 412	89.6	17.2
District 5	6.1	17.3	10.6	11.8	12.1	13.3	13.6	8.3	6.9	38.6	197 717	92.2	24.6
District 6	5.4	16.2	8.3	11.1	12.2	14.2	15.0	10.1	7.6	42.6	160 647	87.3	15.2
District 7	6.1	17.5	8.6	11.2	11.8	14.0	14.2	9.4	7.1	40.6	174 406	87.4	20.0
District 8	6.0	17.9	10.4	11.3	12.1	14.0	13.2	8.5	6.6	38.7	189 241	88.8	22.9
District 9	5.9	16.4	10.1	13.5	12.2	14.4	13.0	7.8	6.8	38.4	182 035	85.7	21.4
District 10	5.9	16.2	10.7	12.6	11.6	13.7	13.2	8.7	7.4	38.9	199 060	89.5	27.4
District 11	6.1	16.2	11.1	13.3	11.2	13.2	13.8	8.0	7.3	38.1	184 130	85.4	27.3
District 12	6.3	18.2	9.0	12.5	13.8	14.6	12.6	7.7	5.3	37.8	198 405	92.0	38.4
District 13	5.0	14.6	11.6	12.2	11.6	13.7	14.7	8.8	7.8	40.9	175 357	88.9	21.6
District 14	5.2	17.3	7.5	10.6	11.7	15.7	14.6	9.3	8.1	43.3	175 495	91.9	33.4
District 15	5.7	16.4	10.2	14.1	13.4	13.9	12.7	8.2	5.5	38.1	191 236	90.4	28.9
District 16	5.4	17.2	7.3	10.9	12.2	15.1	14.1	9.8	8.3	42.9	177 931	92.2	31.0
OKLAHOMA	6.8	17.8	10.3	13.6	12.3	12.8	12.1	8.1	6.1	36.2	994 407	86.7	23.8
District 1	7.2	18.1	9.3	14.1	12.9	13.0	12.3	7.5	5.7	36.0	198 535	88.9	28.6
District 2	6.2	17.7	9.4	11.5	11.9	13.1	12.7	10.1	7.3	39.6	179 486	84.3	16.1
District 3	6.6	18.0	10.9	13.0	11.7	12.8	12.4	8.3	6.3	36.2	203 398	87.3	22.1
District 4	6.5	17.4	11.9	13.7	12.7	12.8	11.8	7.6	5.7	35.4	206 832	88.6	23.4
District 5	7.7	17.8	9.9	15.5	12.3	12.5	11.7	7.2	5.4	34.4	206 156	84.6	28.6
OREGON	5.8	16.1	9.3	13.7	13.1	13.0	13.7	9.0	6.4	39.1	961 860	89.7	30.7
District 1	6.2	17.4	8.3	14.6	14.6	13.8	12.4	7.5	5.3	37.4	197 751	90.6	36.6
District 2	5.9	16.3	8.3	11.8	11.7	12.9	14.7	10.8	7.8	42.1	179 442	88.2	24.2
District 3	6.1	14.5	8.7	17.8	15.4	13.1	12.7	7.0	4.8	36.8	194 580	90.0	37.8
District 4	5.0	14.5	11.9	11.7	11.0	12.5	15.1	10.4	7.8	41.4	193 662	91.3	26.2
District 5	5.8	17.6	9.5	12.1	12.6	13.0	13.5	9.2	6.6	39.2	196 425	88.6	28.4
PENNSYLVANIA	5.6	15.7	9.8	12.6	12.0	14.4	13.6	8.7	7.7	40.6	3 053 479	89.2	28.7
District 1	7.7	16.4	10.6	18.6	13.3	12.2	10.1	5.9	5.1	32.7	184 053	81.6	25.8
District 2	5.9	14.2	14.5	16.8	11.2	12.1	11.9	7.5	5.9	34.0	204 206	84.9	32.6
District 3	5.2	15.6	9.7	11.1	11.7	15.0	14.4	9.2	8.2	42.5	158 745	89.5	24.2

1. All persons 3 years old and over enrolled in nursery school through college and graduate or professional school. 2. Persons 25 years old and over.

STATE District	Households, 2013							Group quarters, 2010				
	Number	Average household size	Family households (percent)	Married-couple family (percent)	Female family householder[1]	One person households (percent)	Total in group quarters, 2013	Percent 65 years and over	Persons in correctional institutions	Persons in nursing facilities	Persons in college dormitories	Persons in military quarters
	28	29	30	31	32	33	34	35	36	37	38	39
NEW YORK—Cont'd												
District 15	244 865	2.98	67.80	22.5	36.7	28.0	18 530	8.9	981	2 145	2 352	0
District 16	266 219	2.68	66.80	42.9	18.5	29.7	16 772	41.8	0	7 221	5 113	0
District 17	240 044	2.99	72.40	56.7	11.5	23.0	23 658	23.3	3 245	4 756	8 571	0
District 18	242 882	2.84	72.50	55.7	12.8	23.2	27 294	14.3	8 143	3 627	7 046	4 409
District 19	270 168	2.48	63.90	49.5	9.8	29.2	39 385	13.1	9 986	4 771	12 644	3
District 20	287 147	2.41	58.80	44.5	10.9	32.9	31 527	16.3	1 298	4 651	18 920	0
District 21	272 734	2.47	65.30	49.2	11.0	28.3	41 777	10.4	18 001	3 692	11 032	3 614
District 22	274 813	2.47	62.30	45.0	11.6	30.0	35 547	18.0	6 104	6 243	17 830	0
District 23	283 672	2.37	62.30	46.4	11.5	30.0	43 291	13.9	6 988	5 257	23 896	0
District 24	278 347	2.47	61.70	44.3	12.8	31.7	27 527	17.7	4 484	4 882	14 806	0
District 25	288 509	2.42	60.50	42.0	14.2	32.1	26 140	20.7	1 499	4 931	14 361	0
District 26	304 142	2.29	57.00	36.8	14.5	35.7	20 550	20.0	926	3 778	11 661	0
District 27	279 973	2.46	67.10	52.6	9.8	27.3	26 132	20.3	13 255	5 336	5 224	0
NORTH CAROLINA	3 757 480	2.55	65.90	47.5	13.8	28.1	253 994	16.6	61 680	46 638	89 795	26 326
District 1	280 488	2.46	59.80	34.5	20.8	33.6	34 287	15.6	13 922	6 285	10 496	594
District 2	285 535	2.67	70.70	54.1	12.2	24.9	14 444	21.8	1 132	3 214	1 773	5 949
District 3	282 136	2.54	66.70	49.6	12.6	26.4	33 504	6.2	6 616	2 817	8 725	19 749
District 4	302 535	2.42	57.10	38.8	14.3	32.8	37 495	7.0	5 518	2 406	22 784	0
District 5	294 718	2.47	64.90	49.8	11.4	29.1	18 401	18.3	2 268	3 598	10 492	0
District 6	299 854	2.47	68.50	52.0	11.6	26.7	18 997	23.6	2 493	3 811	6 738	0
District 7	286 754	2.62	69.10	50.7	13.7	25.4	11 054	29.2	5 511	3 495	9	33
District 8	268 850	2.71	68.90	48.1	15.7	26.5	15 924	17.1	8 325	3 469	3 449	0
District 9	295 058	2.63	67.60	53.7	10.3	26.8	5 334	45.8	50	2 736	2 155	1
District 10	290 882	2.49	65.70	48.6	12.9	29.0	13 999	30.8	2 503	4 741	4 033	0
District 11	293 360	2.45	65.80	50.3	11.4	29.0	18 096	23.1	5 915	4 622	4 965	0
District 12	285 188	2.62	59.30	30.8	22.0	32.0	25 955	10.1	4 648	3 049	13 560	0
District 13	292 122	2.66	72.20	56.5	11.6	22.9	6 504	28.6	2 779	2 395	616	0
NORTH DAKOTA	298 298	2.33	60.40	48.6	7.4	30.5	26 953	25.3	2 489	6 433	10 570	1 380
At Large	298 298	2.33	60.40	48.6	7.4	30.5	26 953	25.3	2 489	6 433	10 570	1 380
OHIO	4 564 745	2.47	64.00	46.4	13.0	29.9	312 375	25.3	76 590	83 019	106 042	571
District 1	281 464	2.5	64.30	44.5	14.5	29.3	22 010	17.7	6 431	4 486	7 060	0
District 2	292 576	2.45	63.00	46.3	12.2	31.1	10 246	55.0	880	5 887	712	0
District 3	289 214	2.49	54.70	32.5	17.4	34.9	21 177	10.7	2 353	2 793	11 851	0
District 4	273 190	2.49	69.00	52.0	11.9	26.2	27 863	17.6	15 892	5 563	5 261	0
District 5	287 029	2.48	65.70	51.2	9.8	28.8	18 171	31.9	971	6 014	8 367	0
District 6	279 247	2.47	67.90	50.7	11.5	27.2	22 606	30.8	9 881	6 354	3 595	0
District 7	275 287	2.56	69.00	53.5	10.8	26.0	15 454	35.8	795	6 223	5 129	0
District 8	272 564	2.58	69.50	52.9	11.7	24.8	17 112	24.8	1 369	4 682	8 537	0
District 9	296 986	2.36	57.50	35.9	16.9	35.4	14 490	26.5	1 894	4 930	5 512	0
District 10	292 994	2.38	62.00	42.4	15.2	32.5	25 733	21.5	1 997	5 845	12 267	547
District 11	296 855	2.25	53.70	27.2	21.6	40.4	23 804	21.5	3 906	6 243	7 446	0
District 12	280 649	2.59	67.90	53.3	10.5	25.6	18 016	19.4	6 071	3 929	6 352	0
District 13	297 889	2.34	59.90	40.2	14.4	33.6	21 827	20.6	5 134	5 394	10 204	0
District 14	284 163	2.51	67.60	54.0	9.8	27.5	12 074	40.5	2 076	5 260	1 338	24
District 15	278 193	2.56	67.70	53.1	10.2	24.9	31 303	11.1	16 670	3 476	9 591	0
District 16	286 445	2.48	67.40	55.5	8.2	28.2	10 489	51.7	270	5 940	2 820	0
OKLAHOMA	1 447 277	2.58	66.10	48.6	12.5	28.6	109 803	24.0	40 562	21 678	30 148	7 203
District 1	301 476	2.53	65.40	47.4	13.1	29.1	9 523	28.8	2 371	3 656	2 981	0
District 2	280 361	2.58	67.80	49.7	12.8	28.2	24 701	19.9	9 915	5 506	4 623	0
District 3	279 994	2.64	68.60	53.5	10.4	26.6	29 437	13.8	15 091	4 818	10 089	463
District 4	286 269	2.62	67.10	50.1	12.0	26.6	26 912	12.1	7 991	3 797	7 490	6 740
District 5	299 177	2.56	61.80	42.5	14.0	32.3	19 230	18.8	5 194	3 901	4 965	0
OREGON	1 523 799	2.52	63.10	48.0	10.7	28.3	87 687	18.0	22 203	11 491	23 704	178
District 1	301 239	2.6	65.40	51.9	9.3	27.4	13 930	20.7	4 641	1 964	3 338	127
District 2	303 835	2.5	65.40	50.2	10.9	28.1	19 905	19.0	8 762	2 660	1 775	13
District 3	314 702	2.47	56.80	41.1	10.8	30.9	18 458	15.5	2 065	2 399	6 604	0
District 4	310 326	2.43	60.80	46.4	10.7	29.4	17 886	16.5	1 354	2 067	8 825	21
District 5	293 697	2.62	67.50	51.0	11.8	25.4	17 508	19.1	5 381	2 401	3 162	17
PENNSYLVANIA	4 938 894	2.5	63.80	47.7	11.9	30.1	430 361	21.0	97 820	87 775	177 332	259
District 1	258 651	2.73	55.70	29.4	19.9	36.3	20 033	9.2	10 896	2 024	7 108	14
District 2	283 007	2.39	45.70	23.4	18.6	45.3	36 121	13.8	680	4 909	23 446	0
District 3	280 905	2.41	65.10	49.2	11.3	29.4	27 069	19.5	6 328	5 188	11 315	11

1. No spouse present.

STATE District	Housing units, 2013						Money income, 2013		
		Occupied units						Households	
			Owner-occupied			Renter-occupied			
	Total	Occupied units as a percent of all units	Owner-occupied units as a percent of occupied units	Median value[1] (dollars)	Percent valued at $500,000 or more	Median rent[2]	Per capita income (dollars)	Median income (dollars)	Percent with income of $100,000 or more
	40	41	42	43	44	45	46	47	48
NEW YORK—Cont'd									
District 15	261 438	93.7	9.0	376 600	17.5	974	13 283	25 801	6.2
District 16	291 686	91.3	49.5	437 900	40.6	1 223	38 666	63 710	31.7
District 17	253 139	94.8	66.7	438 900	38.1	1 410	40 461	87 899	45.0
District 18	271 021	89.6	71.0	288 600	15.8	1 160	35 452	74 704	36.7
District 19	361 572	74.7	73.6	197 500	6.6	880	29 844	56 757	24.3
District 20	322 568	89.0	60.9	196 000	3.8	882	31 327	58 095	25.6
District 21	368 039	74.1	69.7	133 400	3.8	778	24 873	48 898	18.2
District 22	319 248	86.1	68.4	109 300	1.4	661	24 205	46 648	16.0
District 23	337 296	84.1	68.8	97 900	2.0	666	24 443	44 819	15.1
District 24	312 142	89.2	68.4	123 100	1.7	725	27 317	51 028	19.8
District 25	310 445	92.9	62.6	139 600	2.0	815	28 354	51 129	20.6
District 26	340 234	89.4	59.1	106 900	1.3	722	25 549	44 688	15.3
District 27	306 439	91.4	76.9	141 300	2.6	713	29 443	57 149	23.4
NORTH CAROLINA	4 394 515	85.5	64.3	154 300	5.1	778	25 377	45 906	17.2
District 1	332 481	84.4	52.4	101 900	2.0	731	18 772	32 916	9.2
District 2	321 472	88.8	66.0	168 300	5.3	818	26 055	50 713	20.6
District 3	370 338	76.2	62.7	158 200	4.0	827	23 749	44 147	14.3
District 4	332 994	90.9	51.2	172 000	6.6	873	28 292	49 637	19.6
District 5	350 580	84.1	68.5	149 500	4.5	698	24 881	42 904	15.8
District 6	333 005	90.0	71.2	156 600	4.0	715	27 502	49 980	18.4
District 7	362 823	79.0	69.3	148 400	5.2	766	23 621	45 545	15.2
District 8	310 894	86.5	67.6	123 500	1.9	671	20 181	40 669	11.6
District 9	318 455	92.7	71.1	225 000	13.6	987	38 902	69 972	34.4
District 10	332 227	87.6	66.7	138 000	4.5	699	23 629	42 148	14.4
District 11	391 946	74.8	72.2	145 200	4.3	656	21 866	39 355	11.0
District 12	322 559	88.4	43.2	115 900	0.8	773	18 956	35 679	9.9
District 13	314 741	92.8	72.8	195 700	6.8	883	32 394	63 686	27.7
NORTH DAKOTA	339 293	87.9	64.8	155 400	2.6	690	30 855	55 759	22.1
At Large	339 293	87.9	64.8	155 400	2.6	690	30 855	55 759	22.1
OHIO	5 124 126	89.1	66.1	127 000	2.4	709	26 354	48 081	18.4
District 1	315 872	89.1	60.7	148 700	4.1	696	28 880	50 461	22.8
District 2	326 172	89.7	67.6	136 800	4.6	685	28 955	50 802	20.9
District 3	332 466	87.0	47.5	112 800	1.8	765	22 897	41 020	12.9
District 4	306 428	89.2	71.2	117 100	1.4	667	24 234	47 605	15.3
District 5	309 124	92.9	71.5	122 900	1.4	668	26 006	50 823	18.1
District 6	322 923	86.5	74.5	97 100	1.3	595	22 306	41 719	12.6
District 7	301 496	91.3	72.1	124 000	1.3	665	24 206	48 382	16.2
District 8	301 315	90.5	68.5	135 600	1.5	722	25 420	50 750	19.2
District 9	348 614	85.2	60.0	94 300	1.1	650	22 811	40 150	12.1
District 10	333 902	87.7	62.5	118 500	1.4	730	26 179	45 903	18.0
District 11	363 465	81.7	50.1	90 200	3.3	686	24 275	33 935	13.8
District 12	302 430	92.8	71.4	176 200	4.6	823	32 003	61 180	28.8
District 13	335 606	88.8	63.2	94 900	0.6	666	22 938	40 835	11.6
District 14	309 721	91.7	76.6	167 000	4.2	830	31 445	59 111	25.2
District 15	308 785	90.1	67.4	150 900	2.5	804	26 820	53 720	21.9
District 16	305 807	93.7	74.4	156 300	2.5	759	31 922	60 353	25.2
OKLAHOMA	1 682 358	86.0	65.5	116 500	2.3	705	24 284	45 690	16.2
District 1	337 738	89.3	62.2	135 400	3.4	748	27 097	48 746	18.5
District 2	349 765	80.2	71.7	90 000	1.7	597	20 082	37 949	11.0
District 3	330 151	84.8	69.8	103 800	1.5	669	23 916	47 563	16.6
District 4	326 592	87.7	65.3	124 600	1.3	764	24 442	49 738	16.7
District 5	338 112	88.5	59.4	128 900	3.7	724	25 718	44 597	17.7
OREGON	1 684 107	90.5	60.8	229 700	9.2	887	27 048	50 251	19.4
District 1	324 356	92.9	60.5	272 000	12.2	992	31 133	61 908	27.5
District 2	355 061	85.6	63.3	184 300	7.7	800	23 439	42 583	13.7
District 3	333 332	94.4	56.4	269 800	11.5	941	29 785	54 300	22.2
District 4	342 723	90.5	61.8	195 400	5.1	826	23 917	42 103	13.4
District 5	328 635	89.4	62.3	227 000	9.9	874	26 776	53 431	20.2
PENNSYLVANIA	5 565 354	88.7	68.9	164 200	5.1	828	28 647	52 007	21.6
District 1	294 910	87.7	54.2	126 700	3.8	929	22 337	40 731	14.1
District 2	332 666	85.1	46.7	133 300	11.5	905	27 407	34 928	16.1
District 3	315 583	89.0	72.3	118 500	2.3	658	25 634	46 627	16.6

1. Specified owner-occupied units. 2. Specified renter-occupied units.

Table E. Congressional Districts 113th Congress — **Poverty, Labor Force, Employment, and Social Security**

STATE District	Poverty, 2013: Persons below poverty level (percent)	Poverty, 2013: Families below poverty level (percent)	Poverty, 2013: Percent of households receiving food stamps in past 12 months	Civilian labor force, 2013: Total	Civilian labor force, 2013: Unemployment: Total	Civilian labor force, 2013: Unemployment: Rate[1]	Civilian employment,[2] 2013: Total	Civilian employment,[2] 2013: Percent: Management, business, science and arts occupations	Civilian employment,[2] 2013: Percent: Service, sales, and office	Civilian employment,[2] 2013: Percent: Construction and production	Persons under age 65 with no health insurance, 2013 (percent)	Social Security beneficiaries, December 2013: Number	Social Security beneficiaries, December 2013: Rate[3]	Supplemental Security Income recipients, December 2013
	49	50	51	52	53	54	55	56	57	58	59	60	61	62
NEW YORK—Cont'd														
District 15	39.8	36.1	48.5	320 905	50 679	15.8	270 226	17.2	63.0	19.8	17.3	86 642	115.9	71 151
District 16	13.0	10.1	15.4	366 995	37 830	10.3	329 165	42.9	44.0	13.2	11.7	123 494	169.0	23 786
District 17	11.3	8.3	7.8	393 287	32 426	8.2	360 861	44.1	42.9	13.0	12.1	125 041	168.4	11 509
District 18	10.5	7.7	10.1	373 240	29 140	7.8	344 100	38.3	44.7	17.0	9.4	127 073	176.9	12 810
District 19	12.5	7.3	10.2	361 278	31 411	8.7	329 867	37.6	41.3	21.0	11.0	159 328	224.4	17 674
District 20	13.6	9.3	12.1	384 585	26 937	7.0	357 648	42.3	42.6	15.1	7.9	147 021	203.0	20 096
District 21	15.1	10.5	15.5	338 755	32 606	9.6	306 149	32.1	45.2	22.8	10.5	161 101	224.9	21 636
District 22	16.5	10.9	16.8	345 319	25 958	7.5	319 361	34.8	42.2	23.0	8.6	164 028	230.0	23 444
District 23	17.0	11.5	15.7	347 829	27 886	8.0	319 943	35.1	41.5	23.4	12.2	161 376	225.3	22 099
District 24	15.1	10.5	13.9	364 683	28 491	7.8	336 192	37.3	42.4	20.2	10.7	150 360	210.2	21 734
District 25	16.1	11.8	14.8	377 617	33 314	8.8	344 303	42.1	42.1	15.7	8.5	148 853	205.4	26 625
District 26	19.3	14.2	20.9	363 644	31 249	8.6	332 395	35.8	47.1	17.1	8.0	158 033	220.9	30 605
District 27	9.8	6.5	8.9	366 760	24 828	6.8	341 932	37.7	39.9	22.5	7.6	162 046	226.7	11 473
NORTH CAROLINA	17.9	13.1	14.7	4 820 861	465 380	9.7	4 355 481	35.9	41.9	22.2	18.1	1 907 394	193.7	234 362
District 1	26.9	20.6	25.0	327 098	41 644	12.7	285 454	30.5	44.7	24.8	20.1	157 548	217.4	36 735
District 2	16.2	12.0	12.2	347 193	33 380	9.6	313 813	38.7	40.4	20.9	16.7	136 310	175.3	15 180
District 3	17.3	11.7	13.4	348 654	36 596	10.5	312 058	31.3	45.5	23.3	19.1	143 404	191.3	16 739
District 4	18.2	13.6	12.0	401 392	34 151	8.5	367 241	44.8	39.5	15.7	16.8	106 125	137.9	16 432
District 5	19.0	13.2	12.7	370 923	35 400	9.5	335 523	35.6	40.4	24.0	16.5	162 882	218.4	14 562
District 6	15.1	11.1	11.2	375 652	30 007	8.0	345 645	37.2	40.6	22.1	14.6	164 083	215.7	13 715
District 7	19.3	14.6	16.4	363 584	37 355	10.3	326 229	32.5	40.4	27.1	20.7	168 303	220.7	20 344
District 8	20.5	14.9	18.9	350 416	39 043	11.1	311 373	28.0	42.7	29.3	19.0	153 297	206.0	21 543
District 9	7.9	5.4	6.2	423 630	26 212	6.2	397 418	47.2	39.5	13.4	13.2	110 874	142.1	6 884
District 10	17.7	13.4	17.8	371 131	36 882	9.9	334 249	32.3	41.9	25.8	19.5	169 824	229.7	18 227
District 11	19.0	13.6	14.5	327 203	29 725	9.1	297 478	30.5	44.2	25.3	22.0	199 765	270.9	17 557
District 12	27.3	22.6	23.1	401 302	55 506	13.8	345 796	27.5	47.8	24.7	25.1	109 924	142.1	25 391
District 13	9.7	6.4	8.9	412 683	29 479	7.1	383 204	44.7	38.1	17.2	13.2	125 055	159.8	11 053
NORTH DAKOTA	11.8	7.0	7.6	401 046	10 399	2.6	390 647	34.3	39.6	26.1	12.0	123 363	170.5	8 350
At Large	11.8	7.0	7.6	401 046	10 399	2.6	390 647	34.3	39.6	26.1	12.0	123 363	170.5	8 350
OHIO	16.0	11.6	15.4	5 820 829	473 028	8.1	5 347 801	34.9	41.6	23.5	12.9	2 239 797	193.6	311 195
District 1	17.9	13.0	15.3	362 198	35 752	9.9	326 446	38.8	43.1	18.1	12.5	123 443	170.3	20 491
District 2	15.5	11.3	14.3	362 027	22 577	6.2	339 450	38.7	40.1	21.2	12.2	141 796	194.9	20 933
District 3	23.3	17.8	21.6	383 619	32 758	8.5	350 861	33.3	45.7	21.0	17.0	101 808	137.6	28 531
District 4	13.4	9.8	14.5	356 776	28 465	8.0	328 311	28.5	38.7	32.8	11.2	148 564	209.5	15 327
District 5	12.6	9.2	10.2	381 097	26 261	6.9	354 836	31.8	38.9	29.3	10.0	143 771	196.8	10 563
District 6	17.9	12.6	17.4	322 155	23 432	7.3	298 723	27.6	42.3	30.1	15.0	168 449	236.1	25 766
District 7	13.0	10.2	13.9	357 888	26 611	7.4	331 277	28.8	41.0	30.2	15.5	151 985	211.3	14 746
District 8	13.8	9.7	13.2	360 828	26 701	7.4	334 127	32.7	41.5	25.9	11.7	139 468	193.3	14 512
District 9	22.3	17.6	21.4	362 101	39 236	10.8	322 865	29.9	46.1	24.0	15.8	138 576	193.7	31 089
District 10	17.6	13.7	15.7	358 533	34 268	9.6	324 265	38.6	41.8	19.7	13.0	141 830	195.9	19 335
District 11	27.6	21.6	28.2	335 446	50 571	15.1	284 875	36.9	44.9	18.2	14.4	138 057	199.3	43 247
District 12	11.1	7.3	11.5	393 784	21 568	5.5	372 216	44.8	38.6	16.6	10.4	124 554	167.3	11 984
District 13	19.8	14.6	17.7	362 668	35 986	9.9	326 682	29.0	45.5	25.4	13.9	156 696	217.9	22 721
District 14	9.0	6.9	9.0	373 943	22 934	6.1	351 009	39.3	40.1	20.7	11.5	148 078	204.1	9 448
District 15	13.5	9.0	14.2	374 729	25 711	6.9	349 018	38.3	40.1	21.5	12.1	126 375	170.3	14 900
District 16	8.2	5.4	7.3	373 037	20 197	5.4	352 840	39.1	39.2	21.8	9.4	146 347	203.1	7 602
OKLAHOMA	16.8	12.5	14.3	1 830 662	113 878	6.2	1 716 784	32.5	42.4	25.1	20.4	741 822	192.7	97 616
District 1	15.3	11.7	13.3	394 433	25 531	6.5	368 902	34.8	43.4	21.9	19.5	137 920	178.4	16 880
District 2	20.6	15.8	17.4	319 459	25 026	7.8	294 433	27.6	42.4	29.9	25.1	181 226	242.3	27 978
District 3	14.3	10.5	12.0	360 194	15 450	4.3	344 744	31.0	39.5	29.5	18.1	148 684	193.7	15 326
District 4	15.1	10.5	13.1	370 687	23 646	6.4	347 041	34.1	43.0	23.0	17.5	140 762	181.3	16 070
District 5	18.7	14.0	15.9	385 889	24 225	6.3	361 664	34.1	43.4	22.5	22.1	133 230	169.6	21 362
OREGON	16.7	11.3	19.8	1 966 661	181 042	9.2	1 785 619	36.7	42.3	21.0	17.2	777 832	197.9	83 264
District 1	11.3	8.2	14.7	421 232	33 339	7.9	387 893	42.7	38.9	18.4	15.0	124 840	156.7	10 922
District 2	18.0	13.4	22.7	356 458	34 242	9.6	322 216	31.0	45.8	23.2	20.6	186 829	240.1	17 079
District 3	18.0	11.8	20.4	439 672	40 727	9.3	398 945	41.0	40.9	18.2	17.4	122 170	153.2	20 485
District 4	20.9	12.6	21.5	361 396	37 847	10.5	323 549	34.3	42.9	22.8	17.1	187 247	242.5	19 730
District 5	15.3	10.6	19.7	387 903	34 887	9.0	353 016	32.8	44.0	23.2	16.4	156 746	199.5	15 048
PENNSYLVANIA	13.7	9.3	12.5	6 526 914	539 153	8.3	5 987 761	36.5	42.0	21.6	11.5	2 697 111	211.1	379 194
District 1	25.4	21.1	23.8	353 195	47 179	13.4	306 016	35.8	47.1	17.1	18.0	113 390	156.4	50 489
District 2	27.5	19.4	23.0	332 144	45 202	13.6	286 942	43.5	43.7	12.8	14.3	124 352	174.6	50 136
District 3	14.3	9.5	14.8	347 515	24 416	7.0	323 099	32.3	42.5	25.2	10.6	167 320	238.0	25 248

1. Percent of civilian labor force. 2. Persons 16 years old and over. 3. Per 1,000 resident population estimated in the 2013 American Community Survey.

STATE District	Agriculture, 2012									
		Land in farms			Value of products sold				Government payments	
	Number of farms	Acres	Average size of farm (acres)	Irrigated land (acres)	Total ($1,000)	Average per farm (dollars)	Percent from crops	Percent from livestock and poultry products	Total ($1,000)	Average per farm receiving payments (dollars)
	63	64	65	66	67	68	69	70	71	72
NEW YORK—Cont'd										
District 15	X	X	X	X	X	X	X	X	X	X
District 16	10	1 017	102	9	828	82 774	91.8	8.2	0	0
District 17	70	2 001	29	113	6 584	94 053	62.7	37.3	D	D
District 18	871	110 109	126	3 066	113 514	130 326	71.9	28.1	2 102	10 778
District 19	5 314	957 846	180	8 894	462 961	87 121	44.3	55.7	8 095	6 581
District 20	1 181	161 612	137	804	113 423	96 040	44.2	55.8	1 111	5 142
District 21	6 108	1 496 682	245	2 668	977 396	160 019	23.1	76.9	15 284	9 983
District 22	4 770	941 790	197	2 123	493 919	103 547	26.9	73.1	10 122	7 174
District 23	8 716	1 667 821	191	5 848	1 054 998	121 042	39.1	60.9	14 867	6 541
District 24	2 712	603 589	223	3 754	667 658	246 187	46.4	53.6	6 666	8 199
District 25	364	56 344	155	810	47 235	129 766	88.4	11.6	760	9 266
District 26	58	10 225	176	38	8 791	151 564	99.2	0.8	D	D
District 27	4 674	1 135 393	243	19 756	1 218 619	260 723	46.4	53.6	14 616	9 351
NORTH CAROLINA	50 218	8 414 756	168	174 526	12 588 142	250 670	34.2	65.8	120 129	8 332
District 1	3 457	1 267 552	367	37 421	1 411 910	408 421	48.5	51.5	29 500	13 176
District 2	4 319	540 316	125	9 955	794 538	183 963	20.7	79.3	6 417	7 902
District 3	3 115	1 258 856	404	23 466	1 667 112	535 188	52.2	47.8	25 085	13 663
District 4	1 051	113 099	108	2 044	117 955	112 231	33.8	66.2	1 419	5 609
District 5	7 523	782 829	104	3 009	863 937	114 839	22.6	77.4	4 295	3 873
District 6	6 051	744 474	123	12 316	442 156	73 072	44.1	55.9	6 752	4 271
District 7	5 330	1 205 092	226	46 178	3 720 633	698 055	21.0	79.0	19 390	8 106
District 8	5 065	901 322	178	11 176	1 694 602	334 571	21.9	78.1	9 344	7 205
District 9	1 068	128 936	121	1 065	282 689	264 690	68.8	31.2	819	7 805
District 10	4 082	385 987	95	1 696	307 645	75 366	22.2	77.8	2 462	3 558
District 11	6 428	461 764	72	8 510	305 338	47 501	65.3	34.7	6 241	6 125
District 12	483	49 775	103	918	36 733	76 052	71.7	28.3	289	3 849
District 13	2 246	574 754	256	16 772	942 895	419 811	54.3	45.7	8 114	8 058
NORTH DAKOTA	30 961	39 262 613	1 268	218 407	10 950 680	353 693	88.3	11.7	381 710	15 398
At Large	30 961	39 262 613	1 268	218 407	10 950 000	353 693	88.3	11.7	381 710	15 398
OHIO	75 462	13 960 604	185	46 569	10 064 085	133 366	65.6	34.4	228 858	6 603
District 1	1 200	124 692	104	970	80 571	67 142	89.9	10.1	1 194	4 593
District 2	6 107	983 627	161	1 478	373 277	61 123	82.8	17.2	17 161	5 529
District 3	92	16 593	180	144	19 539	212 376	94.4	5.6	120	4 435
District 4	9 348	2 307 012	247	6 343	1 844 009	197 262	76.8	23.2	45 190	6 949
District 5	10 792	2 847 931	264	6 809	2 386 632	221 148	70.5	29.5	61 441	7 107
District 6	11 766	1 584 934	135	4 365	426 139	36 218	46.0	54.0	10 048	4 426
District 7	9 520	1 354 995	142	6 634	1 072 386	112 646	50.5	49.5	15 873	5 529
District 8	6 055	1 174 229	194	5 577	1 371 101	226 441	43.7	56.3	23 599	6 752
District 9	506	76 485	151	1 354	82 288	162 624	97.9	2.1	1 493	4 993
District 10	1 898	378 015	199	1 868	254 837	134 266	86.2	13.8	6 374	6 612
District 11	81	2 497	31	197	3 575	44 131	94.0	6.0	37	7 391
District 12	4 307	712 235	165	1 331	536 943	124 668	67.4	32.6	9 618	6 438
District 13	1 038	107 448	104	184	57 947	55 825	69.0	31.0	962	4 413
District 14	3 053	342 898	112	2 734	265 078	86 825	77.1	22.9	2 865	4 783
District 15	6 879	1 598 791	232	5 392	850 104	123 580	83.2	16.8	27 660	8 745
District 16	2 820	348 222	123	1 189	439 660	155 908	32.6	67.4	5 223	7 048
OKLAHOMA	80 245	34 356 110	428	479 750	7 129 584	88 848	26.3	73.7	256 845	8 634
District 1	3 160	575 332	182	D	99 709	31 553	42.0	58.0	2 618	4 392
District 2	29 692	8 013 419	270	38 897	2 053 254	69 152	16.2	83.8	37 636	5 317
District 3	30 326	19 992 205	659	395 097	4 172 753	137 597	30.6	69.4	182 507	10 572
District 4	13 283	5 059 287	381	33 614	711 085	53 533	28.0	72.0	31 371	7 483
District 5	3 784	715 867	189	D	92 783	24 520	28.2	71.8	2 714	4 391
OREGON	35 439	16 301 578	460	1 629 735	4 883 674	137 805	66.5	33.5	85 840	16 054
District 1	4 759	400 597	84	46 715	584 568	122 834	84.9	15.1	4 343	6 861
District 2	13 284	13 924 323	1 048	1 349 942	2 419 047	182 102	58.7	41.3	72 580	21 038
District 3	2 500	86 297	35	12 384	210 983	84 393	85.5	14.5	448	6 395
District 4	8 820	1 301 199	148	95 961	646 366	73 284	67.3	32.7	3 986	7 157
District 5	6 076	589 162	97	124 733	1 022 711	168 320	70.1	29.9	4 483	7 038
PENNSYLVANIA	59 309	7 704 444	130	38 990	7 400 781	124 783	37.6	62.4	86 359	5 395
District 1	X	X	X	X	X	X	X	X	X	X
District 2	17	548	32	17	330	19 408	90.6	9.4	0	0
District 3	5 489	808 725	147	1 426	353 468	64 396	55.9	44.1	7 271	4 835

1. Specified owner-occupied units. 2. Specified renter-occupied units.

STATE District	Representative, 114th Congress	Land area,[1] 2010 (sq km)	Population and population characteristics, 2013: Total persons	Per square kilometer	Percent: Race alone: White	Black	American Indian, Alaska Native	Asian and Pacific Islander	Some other race (percent)	Two or more races (percent)	Hispanic or Latino[2] (percent)	Non-Hispanic White alone (percent)	Percent female	Percent foreign-born	Percent born in state of residence
		1	2	3	4	5	6	7	8	9	10	11	12	13	14
PENNSYLVANIA—Cont'd															
District 4	Scott Perry (R)	3 931	710 120	180.6	85.5	7.9	0.1	2.2	1.9	2.4	6.5	82.0	50.7	4.6	65.8
District 5	Glenn Thompson (R)	27 742	701 630	25.3	93.8	2.4	0.3	1.7	0.3	1.5	1.9	92.5	49.3	2.6	80.4
District 6	Ryan A. Costello (R)	2 229	721 522	323.7	87.8	4.1	0.2	3.7	2.0	2.2	6.3	84.0	51.3	6.7	72.0
District 7	Patrick Meehan (R)	2 234	722 495	323.4	87.8	5.3	0.0	4.7	0.6	1.6	3.0	85.7	50.9	7.0	74.4
District 8	Michael G. Fitzpatrick (R)	1 831	708 333	386.9	88.6	3.6	0.2	4.7	1.0	1.9	4.6	85.2	51.0	8.5	69.1
District 9	Bill Shuster (R)	14 841	701 622	47.3	94.8	2.9	0.1	0.5	0.3	1.5	1.9	93.3	50.8	1.3	80.7
District 10	Tom Marino (R)	21 699	707 291	32.6	93.4	3.4	0.2	0.9	0.8	1.4	3.3	91.1	49.9	3.3	69.5
District 11	Lou Barletta (R)	8 693	705 647	81.2	89.1	5.1	0.2	1.5	2.0	2.1	5.9	86.1	50.9	4.5	77.5
District 12	Keith J. Rothfus (R)	5 602	703 938	125.7	93.4	3.0	0.1	1.7	0.2	1.6	1.3	92.5	51.1	2.8	83.4
District 13	Brendan F. Boyle (D)	402	710 615	1 767.7	66.1	19.1	0.1	8.7	3.7	2.3	10.3	61.1	51.7	16.5	68.8
District 14	Michael F. Doyle (D)	542	704 276	1 299.4	72.1	21.5	0.2	2.8	0.3	3.1	1.9	70.9	52.3	5.4	78.4
District 15	Charles W. Dent (R)	3 328	713 008	214.2	84.3	4.8	0.2	2.8	5.8	2.0	14.4	77.4	50.9	7.7	67.9
District 16	Joseph R. Pitts (R)	2 584	712 447	275.7	82.0	6.7	0.5	1.9	5.6	3.3	17.3	73.4	51.2	7.4	69.8
District 17	Matt Cartwright (D)	4 489	699 632	155.9	88.1	6.1	0.3	1.5	1.7	2.3	8.1	83.0	51.0	5.6	69.0
District 18	Tim Murphy (R)	5 368	710 784	132.4	93.8	2.5	0.1	2.1	0.3	1.3	1.6	92.5	51.1	3.9	81.1
RHODE ISLAND		2 678	1 051 511	392.6	80.5	6.4	0.4	3.2	6.9	2.6	13.6	74.6	51.6	12.9	57.8
District 1	David Cicilline (D)	695	528 341	760.2	75.6	9.0	0.4	3.3	8.7	3.0	16.3	69.1	51.7	16.5	51.4
District 2	James R. Langevin (D)	1 982	523 170	264.0	85.4	3.8	0.3	3.2	5.2	2.1	10.8	80.2	51.5	9.3	64.2
SOUTH CAROLINA		77 857	4 774 839	61.3	67.2	27.6	0.3	1.4	1.5	1.9	5.3	63.8	51.4	4.8	57.8
District 1	Mark Sanford (R)	4 009	715 200	178.4	74.1	19.3	0.2	1.8	2.3	2.3	6.4	70.6	51.6	6.7	42.9
District 2	Joe Wilson (R)	7 827	671 907	85.8	71.1	23.4	0.2	1.9	1.3	2.1	5.3	67.6	51.2	4.7	52.7
District 3	Jeff Duncan (R)	13 645	663 437	48.6	77.0	18.9	0.2	0.8	1.7	1.4	4.2	74.8	50.8	3.4	67.4
District 4	Trey Gowdy (R)	3 365	690 796	205.3	74.9	19.3	0.3	2.4	1.5	1.5	8.2	68.4	51.6	7.4	56.2
District 5	Mick Mulvaney (R)	14 259	678 788	47.6	69.0	26.4	0.3	1.1	1.0	2.2	4.1	66.1	51.5	3.5	58.9
District 6	James E. Clyburn (D)	20 883	678 025	32.5	37.4	57.6	0.2	1.1	1.6	2.2	4.4	35.3	51.0	3.5	69.5
District 7	Tom Rice (R)	13 868	676 686	48.8	66.8	29.0	0.7	0.9	0.9	1.6	4.2	63.7	51.9	4.6	57.8
SOUTH DAKOTA		196 350	844 877	4.3	85.1	1.5	8.5	1.1	0.8	2.9	3.2	83.4	49.8	2.9	64.3
At Large	Kristi Noem (R)	196 350	844 877	4.3	85.1	1.5	8.5	1.1	0.8	2.9	3.2	83.4	49.8	2.9	64.3
TENNESSEE		106 798	6 495 978	60.8	77.9	17.0	0.2	1.6	1.4	1.9	4.8	74.8	51.2	4.7	61.1
District 1	David P. Roe (R)	10 728	709 547	66.1	93.7	2.4	0.3	0.6	1.2	1.8	3.4	91.7	51.2	2.5	62.6
District 2	John J. Duncan Jr. (R)	6 011	722 761	120.2	89.4	6.5	0.3	1.4	0.3	2.1	3.7	86.6	51.4	4.6	61.0
District 3	Chuck Fleischmann (R)	11 837	721 988	61.0	85.3	11.2	0.2	1.3	0.5	1.6	3.2	82.7	51.2	2.9	65.4
District 4	Scott DesJarlais (R)	15 501	726 649	46.9	86.3	8.7	0.2	1.5	0.9	2.4	5.5	81.8	50.8	4.8	60.3
District 5	Jim Cooper (D)	3 234	739 937	228.8	65.7	24.8	0.3	3.0	3.9	2.2	9.1	60.8	51.5	10.7	53.8
District 6	Diane Black (R)	16 768	724 274	43.2	92.1	4.6	0.2	0.9	0.7	1.5	3.8	89.2	51.0	3.5	63.3
District 7	Marsha Blackburn (R)	23 725	728 823	30.7	84.9	9.5	0.3	1.7	1.2	2.4	4.7	81.6	50.3	3.6	53.6
District 8	Stephen Lee Fincher (R)	17 743	710 335	40.0	75.3	20.3	0.2	2.0	0.7	1.4	2.6	73.5	51.3	3.4	65.9
District 9	Steve Cohen (D)	1 252	711 664	568.4	28.1	65.2	0.2	1.6	3.3	1.7	6.7	25.3	52.6	6.2	64.6
TEXAS		676 587	26 448 193	39.1	75.0	11.9	0.4	4.2	6.0	2.4	38.4	43.9	50.3	16.5	60.2
District 1	Louie Gohmert (R)	20 354	712 524	35.0	77.2	17.9	0.1	0.9	2.2	1.7	16.6	63.3	51.1	8.0	71.0
District 2	Ted Poe (R)	800	722 575	903.2	72.5	8.1	0.5	7.5	9.0	2.4	31.3	51.3	49.2	21.7	50.2
District 3	Sam Johnson (R)	1 245	765 486	614.8	73.2	8.9	0.4	13.1	1.6	2.9	15.1	60.3	50.6	18.4	45.2
District 4	John Ratcliffe (R)	26 218	710 641	27.1	81.8	11.0	0.6	1.0	3.0	2.6	12.5	73.0	50.8	5.9	66.8
District 5	Jeb Hensarling (R)	13 064	726 896	55.6	73.8	14.4	0.5	1.9	7.1	2.2	27.9	54.0	50.0	14.3	64.8
District 6	Joe Barton (R)	5 564	730 955	131.4	69.1	19.4	0.7	4.9	3.1	2.9	21.1	52.6	51.2	12.2	59.9
District 7	John Abney Culberson (R)	419	741 599	1 769.9	67.5	14.2	0.4	11.3	3.5	3.1	28.3	44.0	50.4	27.3	46.2
District 8	Kevin Brady (R)	15 679	761 764	48.6	82.0	8.6	0.3	2.3	5.1	1.7	22.4	65.5	48.9	12.6	59.1
District 9	Al Green (D)	429	736 852	1 717.6	36.7	39.5	0.2	11.1	10.6	1.9	36.8	11.7	51.3	31.5	50.1
District 10	Michael T. McCaul (R)	13 134	758 585	57.8	76.4	11.0	0.5	5.3	4.2	2.6	28.6	53.1	50.0	15.5	58.9
District 11	K. Michael Conaway (R)	72 085	729 613	10.1	85.5	3.7	0.6	1.1	6.8	2.2	35.6	58.2	49.9	9.2	69.7
District 12	Kay Granger (R)	3 733	732 246	196.2	80.9	7.1	0.6	3.2	5.2	3.0	22.4	65.0	51.0	10.7	61.4
District 13	Mac Thornberry (R)	99 324	700 874	7.1	86.0	5.6	0.7	2.0	2.8	3.0	25.6	65.0	49.2	8.6	67.3
District 14	Randy K. Weber, Sr. (R)	6 323	716 592	113.3	71.7	19.7	0.4	3.1	3.1	2.0	23.9	52.1	49.3	10.5	66.1
District 15	Rubén Hinojosa (D)	20 212	731 065	36.2	89.0	2.0	0.2	1.2	6.4	1.1	80.7	15.9	50.7	22.6	64.1
District 16	Beto O'Rourke (D)	1 840	728 654	396.0	83.5	3.9	0.7	1.4	8.4	2.1	79.0	14.9	51.1	25.3	54.8
District 17	Bill Flores (R)	19 816	726 128	36.6	74.1	12.9	0.4	4.1	5.7	2.8	24.7	56.3	50.4	12.2	66.0
District 18	Sheila Jackson-Lee (D)	609	741 385	1 217.4	46.3	37.6	0.4	3.8	9.8	2.2	40.4	17.2	50.5	21.7	59.7
District 19	Randy Neugebauer (R)	66 914	719 455	10.8	83.6	6.1	0.6	1.2	5.8	2.6	35.9	55.3	49.3	7.2	74.7
District 20	Joaquin Castro (D)	517	752 996	1 456.5	79.5	5.6	0.3	3.4	8.5	2.6	68.3	21.6	50.7	15.8	65.1
District 21	Lamar Smith (R)	15 335	743 443	48.5	88.8	3.5	0.2	3.2	1.8	2.5	26.9	64.8	51.1	9.2	57.1
District 22	Pete Olson (R)	2 675	783 172	292.8	62.2	14.1	0.3	16.8	4.4	2.2	24.3	43.2	50.5	23.4	52.2
District 23	Will Hurd (R)	150 373	723 867	4.8	84.4	2.8	1.1	1.4	7.9	2.3	69.9	24.5	49.6	17.5	65.4
District 24	Kenny Marchant (R)	681	741 164	1 088.3	66.2	10.5	0.2	12.8	7.2	3.0	23.7	50.6	50.7	22.6	45.6

1. Dry land or land partially or temporarily covered by water. 2. May be of any race.

STATE District	Population and population characteristics, 2013 (cont.)										Education, 2013		
	Age (percent)											Attainment[2] (percent)	
	Under 5 years	5 to 17 years	18 to 24 years	25 to 34 years	35 to 44 years	45 to 54 years	55 to 64 years	65 to 74 years	75 years and over	Median age	Total Enrollment[1]	High school graduate or more	Bachelor's degree or more
	15	16	17	18	19	20	21	22	23	24	25	26	27
PENNSYLVANIA—Cont'd													
District 4	5.7	16.4	9.0	11.4	13.1	15.1	13.6	8.8	6.9	40.9	166 129	89.0	24.6
District 5	4.8	14.4	13.7	11.5	11.3	13.4	13.9	9.1	7.8	40.4	177 946	89.6	22.3
District 6	5.9	17.5	8.8	11.5	12.6	15.3	13.0	8.5	6.9	40.6	183 167	92.4	42.3
District 7	5.6	17.0	8.7	11.3	12.1	15.0	14.2	8.3	7.9	41.4	185 245	92.1	40.5
District 8	5.2	16.5	7.8	11.0	12.2	16.4	14.7	8.7	7.4	42.7	165 897	93.7	37.1
District 9	5.3	15.4	9.8	10.9	11.8	14.3	14.4	9.7	8.6	42.7	154 272	88.1	17.4
District 10	5.3	15.3	9.5	10.8	11.5	14.8	14.5	10.1	8.1	42.9	152 068	88.3	20.3
District 11	5.3	15.1	9.7	12.1	11.6	14.5	14.1	9.5	8.1	42.1	157 932	89.2	23.1
District 12	5.1	15.4	6.8	11.6	11.6	15.0	15.2	9.8	9.5	44.7	152 112	92.8	31.8
District 13	6.7	16.0	8.3	14.3	12.3	14.5	12.8	7.6	7.7	39.0	170 398	88.2	32.0
District 14	4.9	12.4	12.3	16.2	10.7	12.6	14.4	8.2	8.3	38.4	171 451	92.1	32.1
District 15	5.3	15.5	10.1	11.8	12.3	14.8	13.7	8.8	7.7	41.3	170 810	88.1	27.9
District 16	6.6	18.3	9.9	12.1	12.2	14.0	12.1	7.7	7.1	37.7	179 302	83.2	25.9
District 17	5.2	15.7	9.1	11.5	12.4	14.6	14.1	9.0	8.4	42.0	163 097	88.3	20.7
District 18	5.0	14.8	7.7	10.8	12.3	15.7	14.9	10.1	8.7	44.5	156 649	93.3	34.7
RHODE ISLAND	5.2	15.1	11.3	12.9	12.1	14.8	13.4	8.2	7.3	39.9	263 971	85.9	32.4
District 1	5.2	15.0	11.2	13.9	11.8	14.3	13.1	8.2	7.5	39.4	132 237	83.5	31.5
District 2	5.1	15.3	11.3	11.8	12.4	15.2	13.7	8.2	7.1	40.5	131 734	88.3	33.3
SOUTH CAROLINA	6.1	16.4	10.4	12.7	12.5	13.6	12.9	9.2	6.0	38.6	1 210 706	85.6	26.1
District 1	6.0	16.0	9.3	14.6	12.8	13.5	12.3	9.5	6.0	37.7	174 876	92.3	38.3
District 2	6.0	17.1	9.9	12.9	12.9	14.0	13.2	8.5	5.5	38.5	175 966	88.5	32.3
District 3	5.6	16.0	10.8	11.6	12.4	13.6	13.1	10.1	6.7	40.3	166 989	82.7	20.2
District 4	6.4	17.5	9.9	12.9	13.0	14.0	12.3	8.2	5.8	37.8	176 728	85.7	29.9
District 5	6.7	17.2	9.2	11.8	12.9	14.3	13.2	8.9	6.0	39.6	166 712	83.9	22.1
District 6	6.6	15.8	14.5	13.5	10.9	12.8	12.5	8.0	5.4	34.6	190 255	82.0	18.0
District 7	5.7	15.6	9.2	11.6	12.4	13.3	14.4	11.2	6.6	41.5	159 180	83.5	20.4
SOUTH DAKOTA	6.9	17.7	10.1	13.1	11.4	12.9	13.0	7.7	7.1	36.6	219 960	91.6	26.6
At Large	6.9	17.7	10.1	13.1	11.4	12.9	13.0	7.7	7.1	36.6	219 960	91.6	26.6
TENNESSEE	6.1	16.9	9.8	13.0	13.0	13.8	12.8	8.6	6.0	38.5	1 597 851	85.6	24.8
District 1	5.1	15.7	8.7	10.8	12.8	14.3	14.3	10.8	7.4	42.9	157 825	84.0	18.6
District 2	5.7	15.6	10.7	12.5	12.8	13.6	12.9	9.4	6.6	39.5	172 314	88.2	28.6
District 3	5.6	15.7	8.9	12.0	12.8	14.0	14.2	9.8	7.1	41.1	161 330	83.7	20.7
District 4	5.9	18.0	10.4	13.0	13.1	13.8	12.1	8.6	5.2	37.0	181 940	85.5	21.1
District 5	7.0	15.0	10.3	18.2	13.9	13.0	11.7	6.3	4.7	34.7	185 447	87.2	35.0
District 6	5.7	17.2	8.9	11.3	12.8	14.5	13.1	9.8	6.6	40.8	167 533	84.4	19.5
District 7	6.6	18.7	9.4	12.3	13.6	13.8	12.1	8.0	5.5	37.1	191 630	87.4	27.8
District 8	5.8	18.0	8.8	10.8	13.2	14.4	13.5	9.0	6.4	40.4	185 979	87.1	28.4
District 9	7.6	17.8	11.6	15.7	12.6	12.9	11.5	6.1	4.2	32.9	193 853	82.6	23.1
TEXAS	7.3	19.3	10.3	14.4	13.5	13.0	10.8	6.6	4.6	34.0	7 416 105	81.9	27.5
District 1	7.0	18.1	10.7	12.3	12.1	12.4	12.3	8.6	6.5	36.3	186 370	82.7	19.7
District 2	7.0	17.1	9.1	16.6	14.2	14.0	11.6	6.7	3.6	35.1	179 541	87.7	39.5
District 3	6.6	21.2	7.9	13.0	16.7	15.1	10.3	5.9	3.3	35.9	223 179	94.0	51.5
District 4	6.4	18.0	8.7	11.7	12.6	13.9	12.7	9.5	6.5	39.0	172 242	85.1	19.3
District 5	6.8	19.2	9.6	13.3	13.8	13.2	11.2	7.7	5.2	35.8	189 336	79.4	19.4
District 6	7.4	19.6	9.4	13.8	14.0	14.4	11.0	6.4	4.0	34.9	212 499	87.9	29.4
District 7	7.4	19.3	7.4	17.0	15.3	12.7	11.3	5.4	3.9	34.3	205 808	89.8	49.9
District 8	6.8	19.4	9.2	12.7	13.9	13.8	12.0	7.5	4.7	36.1	206 474	85.2	27.1
District 9	7.4	19.0	11.8	16.2	14.0	12.7	10.7	5.0	3.3	32.1	212 866	76.9	26.7
District 10	7.5	18.1	9.6	14.3	14.6	13.8	11.0	6.5	4.5	35.4	208 148	87.0	36.6
District 11	7.0	17.9	10.4	14.0	11.0	12.3	12.1	8.5	6.7	35.6	175 900	80.0	20.1
District 12	6.2	18.5	9.4	15.5	12.9	14.0	11.7	6.9	4.9	35.2	191 950	88.8	31.2
District 13	6.9	18.2	10.2	13.6	12.1	12.6	12.0	7.8	6.4	35.7	179 297	83.1	20.0
District 14	6.5	18.1	9.9	13.1	13.1	14.4	12.7	7.1	5.1	36.6	189 525	85.2	22.2
District 15	8.7	23.4	10.9	13.2	13.3	11.2	9.1	5.8	4.5	30.4	227 432	68.0	17.7
District 16	8.1	20.4	11.9	14.3	12.5	11.9	9.8	6.0	5.0	31.6	227 841	76.6	22.8
District 17	6.7	16.4	16.3	15.1	12.1	11.7	10.3	6.5	5.0	31.7	226 240	85.0	27.9
District 18	8.5	18.2	10.8	17.6	13.7	12.2	10.4	5.3	3.3	32.0	208 111	76.2	20.3
District 19	6.9	17.8	14.2	13.6	12.0	11.5	11.0	6.9	6.0	33.1	208 650	80.4	21.2
District 20	7.2	19.4	12.1	14.9	14.2	12.6	9.6	5.8	4.3	32.6	228 873	80.9	24.0
District 21	5.4	14.9	10.7	15.9	12.2	13.6	12.6	8.3	6.2	37.9	191 628	92.7	44.8
District 22	7.1	21.3	8.0	12.8	15.0	14.4	11.3	6.2	3.7	35.4	240 263	89.4	43.4
District 23	7.6	21.0	10.0	13.8	12.5	12.1	10.6	7.2	5.0	33.0	208 372	75.3	20.0
District 24	6.7	17.0	8.7	17.0	15.4	14.4	10.8	5.8	4.1	35.4	188 933	89.8	43.0

1. All persons 3 years old and over enrolled in nursery school through college and graduate or professional school. 2. Persons 25 years old and over.

STATE District	Households, 2013						Total in group quarters, 2013	Group quarters, 2010				
	Number	Average household size	Family households (percent)	Married-couple family (percent)	Female family householder[1]	One person households (percent)		Percent 65 years and over	Persons in correctional institutions	Persons in nursing facilities	Persons in college dormitories	Persons in military quarters
	28	29	30	31	32	33	34	35	36	37	38	39
PENNSYLVANIA—Cont'd												
District 4	272 246	2.53	66.70	51.5	10.8	27.4	20 967	20.4	6 485	3 922	7 205	37
District 5	270 099	2.42	64.10	49.8	10.1	29.3	46 739	11.4	14 533	5 088	23 276	0
District 6	270 650	2.59	68.50	55.5	9.0	25.0	19 993	24.0	3 336	4 461	7 424	0
District 7	258 286	2.7	71.00	58.4	9.8	24.5	24 755	21.2	5 890	5 118	10 160	0
District 8	261 432	2.67	71.90	58.2	9.7	24.2	10 471	46.3	1 039	4 098	1 569	0
District 9	274 917	2.46	64.60	50.4	10.3	29.8	24 076	23.8	6 117	5 134	8 771	0
District 10	268 372	2.53	68.30	54.0	10.1	26.1	28 928	15.5	11 878	4 486	10 876	0
District 11	282 911	2.4	64.80	48.7	11.1	29.0	26 452	22.1	7 333	6 231	9 991	6
District 12	289 860	2.37	65.90	52.7	9.4	29.7	15 676	32.7	4 480	4 694	3 073	6
District 13	263 951	2.65	62.40	43.2	14.6	32.4	11 956	57.8	2	6 384	1 329	121
District 14	312 676	2.16	51.40	32.6	14.8	39.0	27 704	15.0	4 663	4 194	15 905	0
District 15	271 399	2.54	66.40	51.0	11.3	27.4	24 722	21.1	1 424	5 210	13 039	63
District 16	259 894	2.66	69.40	53.3	11.6	24.7	21 549	27.5	1 132	5 327	9 156	0
District 17	268 516	2.51	64.90	47.6	12.6	29.4	25 057	25.7	7 876	6 346	7 783	1
District 18	291 122	2.38	65.00	52.2	9.5	30.6	18 093	30.3	3 728	4 961	5 906	0
RHODE ISLAND	406 366	2.49	63.90	44.5	14.2	29.8	40 842	18.5	3 783	8 420	24 687	1 385
District 1	205 884	2.47	62.90	41.2	16.3	31.0	20 358	21.3	350	4 996	13 035	1 385
District 2	200 482	2.51	65.00	47.9	12.1	28.6	20 484	15.5	3 433	3 424	11 652	0
SOUTH CAROLINA	1 794 989	2.58	66.60	46.8	15.2	28.0	139 109	13.0	41 649	19 020	46 463	19 413
District 1	273 999	2.57	64.40	49.8	11.0	27.7	10 031	15.4	531	1 662	2 560	4 436
District 2	254 015	2.57	66.90	49.7	13.4	27.6	19 306	12.8	1 458	2 391	823	11 567
District 3	253 222	2.53	69.40	50.1	14.2	25.9	22 857	14.3	7 044	3 116	9 817	0
District 4	258 583	2.6	67.20	48.2	14.8	28.7	17 637	14.5	3 776	2 832	9 668	0
District 5	250 372	2.66	70.20	49.1	16.1	25.9	12 543	20.0	5 318	2 792	3 289	611
District 6	244 686	2.59	60.40	34.1	21.1	32.6	43 657	6.5	18 400	3 087	17 383	2 799
District 7	260 112	2.55	67.50	46.3	16.5	27.8	13 078	22.4	5 122	3 140	2 923	0
SOUTH DAKOTA	331 406	2.45	64.50	50.3	9.6	29.2	34 014	21.1	6 327	7 005	10 248	597
At Large	331 406	2.45	64.50	50.3	9.6	29.2	34 014	21.1	6 327	7 005	10 248	597
TENNESSEE	2 490 249	2.55	66.60	48.5	13.4	28.1	153 924	19.8	46 957	33 041	53 136	1 544
District 1	286 871	2.41	66.70	50.1	11.7	29.5	16 757	26.7	4 577	4 466	4 176	0
District 2	287 727	2.45	64.70	50.4	10.4	28.4	17 551	19.1	1 901	3 686	10 443	0
District 3	280 472	2.51	68.50	51.8	12.6	26.8	18 164	23.8	4 913	4 071	4 884	3
District 4	271 069	2.62	70.00	52.4	11.9	24.3	15 697	21.1	3 301	3 584	6 619	0
District 5	291 595	2.46	56.70	38.2	13.9	34.9	22 881	9.0	6 769	2 588	13 660	0
District 6	275 503	2.59	70.00	53.8	11.4	26.2	10 970	36.4	2 385	3 730	2 283	0
District 7	266 069	2.67	72.90	56.8	11.7	23.4	17 126	21.2	8 311	3 918	2 350	1 250
District 8	262 930	2.63	71.50	53.7	13.3	24.2	19 285	21.3	7 494	4 158	4 748	10
District 9	268 013	2.6	59.30	30.1	23.7	34.8	15 493	14.0	7 306	2 840	3 973	281
TEXAS	9 110 853	2.84	69.40	50.0	14.4	25.0	589 844	14.9	267 405	94 278	119 834	35 260
District 1	254 626	2.7	68.40	49.6	14.4	27.7	25 344	17.3	8 132	5 093	9 123	0
District 2	266 417	2.68	67.50	51.4	10.9	25.8	8 376	18.4	2 441	1 873	2 921	0
District 3	278 461	2.74	72.40	58.5	10.6	22.1	2 616	31.9	1 061	1 326	387	0
District 4	254 974	2.72	71.80	54.1	12.8	24.1	17 163	25.8	8 850	5 078	2 237	0
District 5	244 309	2.88	71.00	50.1	15.1	24.0	23 672	14.9	17 768	3 964	938	0
District 6	258 472	2.8	71.50	53.1	14.4	23.5	6 507	32.8	689	2 419	2 137	0
District 7	284 082	2.61	63.70	49.0	11.3	29.7	1 283	58.1	3	774	5	0
District 8	253 535	2.86	72.60	57.4	11.6	22.9	37 747	8.5	23 107	2 021	2 615	0
District 9	249 863	2.94	68.60	42.1	20.4	26.5	3 033	32.7	154	1 629	1 520	0
District 10	270 596	2.75	69.80	53.7	11.8	24.4	13 746	25.7	2 453	3 156	4 344	0
District 11	265 082	2.67	68.10	50.6	12.3	26.2	21 326	18.3	9 050	3 721	3 615	1 924
District 12	270 683	2.64	66.90	49.7	11.5	27.3	17 069	20.3	5 807	3 540	3 405	202
District 13	259 758	2.57	67.40	50.0	12.7	27.4	34 373	11.8	17 511	4 208	2 479	5 487
District 14	254 952	2.69	67.90	49.3	14.2	27.9	29 867	9.5	22 748	2 861	2 869	40
District 15	208 210	3.43	78.50	54.3	19.8	18.4	16 524	14.6	8 632	2 035	1 514	0
District 16	232 564	3.07	73.10	48.9	19.4	24.1	15 431	9.8	6 076	1 482	491	5 683
District 17	269 975	2.58	60.30	42.4	13.8	29.5	28 920	11.1	8 355	3 792	14 831	0
District 18	257 258	2.8	63.10	35.2	20.9	29.3	21 155	3.8	12 624	783	5 661	0
District 19	251 294	2.7	66.70	48.9	13.1	26.6	41 659	10.0	19 845	4 073	10 748	621
District 20	250 710	2.95	67.00	43.8	18.0	26.9	12 710	11.9	4	2 081	4 846	9 322
District 21	302 882	2.4	58.30	45.4	9.9	32.4	17 491	19.9	600	4 024	7 505	3 793
District 22	256 442	3.03	79.10	63.3	11.5	17.8	6 145	21.6	4 494	1 409	4	0
District 23	217 563	3.24	75.60	55.4	14.7	21.2	18 691	7.6	16 613	1 566	193	877
District 24	295 241	2.5	62.00	46.3	11.4	31.4	2 697	65.8	53	1 913	480	0

1. No spouse present.

STATE District	Housing units, 2013 Total	Occupied units: Occupied units as a percent of all units	Owner-occupied: Owner-occupied units as a percent of occupied units	Owner-occupied: Median value[1] (dollars)	Owner-occupied: Percent valued at $500,000 or more	Renter-occupied: Median rent[2]	Money income, 2013 Per capita income (dollars)	Households: Median income (dollars)	Households: Percent with income of $100,000 or more
	40	41	42	43	44	45	46	47	48
PENNSYLVANIA—Cont'd									
District 4	296 867	91.7	71.1	171 200	3.0	841	28 195	56 287	21.9
District 5	339 294	79.6	71.8	112 300	2.0	678	22 969	45 001	13.9
District 6	283 375	95.5	74.8	249 100	11.6	1 052	37 567	73 826	35.8
District 7	273 906	94.3	77.9	279 800	14.6	1 112	39 991	81 186	40.3
District 8	277 146	94.3	75.6	299 000	14.3	1 079	37 165	73 522	35.3
District 9	316 962	86.7	73.8	116 800	2.0	627	23 343	45 942	14.0
District 10	344 983	77.8	75.5	154 900	3.3	735	24 835	50 007	16.2
District 11	321 397	88.0	71.5	149 900	2.2	744	26 950	51 135	18.3
District 12	321 093	90.3	76.9	139 000	3.0	679	30 815	54 765	22.8
District 13	287 116	91.9	63.8	221 900	5.3	977	29 428	54 355	25.2
District 14	357 993	87.3	55.9	89 300	2.1	723	26 319	41 213	13.9
District 15	290 467	93.4	70.0	188 700	4.0	892	29 097	57 598	22.7
District 16	277 750	93.6	66.1	181 900	4.0	869	25 686	54 033	20.3
District 17	317 670	84.5	68.1	139 100	1.8	732	24 354	45 896	17.2
District 18	316 176	92.1	76.3	155 900	3.0	736	33 125	59 277	25.8
RHODE ISLAND	461 658	88.0	60.4	232 300	9.0	918	30 748	55 902	24.7
District 1	233 677	88.1	54.9	236 700	10.9	898	29 480	50 796	21.4
District 2	227 981	87.9	66.0	228 800	7.4	943	32 027	61 822	28.0
SOUTH CAROLINA	2 158 784	83.1	68.2	139 200	5.0	766	23 687	44 163	15.9
District 1	331 860	82.6	67.3	213 500	14.2	992	31 529	59 318	25.1
District 2	289 493	87.7	73.7	143 100	3.7	827	26 786	51 984	20.1
District 3	296 801	85.3	71.7	119 200	3.0	639	21 368	40 365	12.9
District 4	292 930	88.3	65.2	146 500	4.4	726	24 263	46 532	17.8
District 5	288 857	86.7	72.4	127 000	2.8	704	22 489	42 920	15.8
District 6	293 018	83.5	58.4	99 600	3.0	756	17 717	33 001	7.9
District 7	365 825	71.1	68.3	123 800	3.6	701	21 192	38 707	10.5
SOUTH DAKOTA	370 207	89.5	67.2	138 400	3.1	637	25 860	48 947	16.2
At Large	370 207	89.5	67.2	138 400	3.1	637	25 860	48 947	16.2
TENNESSEE	2 840 998	87.7	66.4	140 300	4.1	748	24 678	44 297	15.8
District 1	343 952	83.4	70.8	126 000	1.8	603	21 466	37 176	11.2
District 2	322 944	89.1	66.1	154 500	5.2	753	26 437	46 594	17.2
District 3	323 775	86.6	70.1	133 900	3.4	689	23 475	41 906	14.7
District 4	299 719	90.4	69.4	137 800	2.1	733	22 738	47 369	14.6
District 5	321 833	90.6	56.8	163 100	7.6	850	27 784	47 039	17.4
District 6	309 958	88.9	72.5	152 000	3.0	720	24 249	43 709	14.7
District 7	307 947	86.4	71.4	151 000	8.0	763	26 370	50 273	19.5
District 8	293 438	89.6	71.9	147 600	4.1	680	29 007	51 290	22.5
District 9	317 432	84.4	48.6	89 600	1.4	812	20 448	37 087	11.0
TEXAS	10 256 203	88.8	61.8	132 000	4.4	857	26 327	51 704	22.7
District 1	301 297	84.5	67.1	110 300	1.9	739	23 331	43 301	16.0
District 2	285 059	93.5	61.4	161 600	6.2	966	37 242	69 833	33.9
District 3	289 221	96.3	62.4	226 200	7.7	1 106	39 053	80 912	40.1
District 4	300 192	84.9	70.5	105 900	2.8	723	24 134	45 384	17.6
District 5	286 382	85.3	63.4	109 200	2.5	776	22 348	43 698	17.8
District 6	277 990	93.0	66.0	137 500	1.2	873	26 923	57 477	25.7
District 7	309 712	91.7	52.4	209 800	20.1	1 002	42 687	66 451	34.8
District 8	290 582	87.3	72.5	152 600	6.4	911	28 940	61 012	28.6
District 9	280 355	89.1	45.8	101 600	1.0	823	20 595	41 772	15.6
District 10	298 797	90.6	67.2	168 900	6.2	958	31 017	64 220	29.5
District 11	320 581	82.7	67.7	106 500	4.0	825	27 665	50 412	21.6
District 12	295 366	91.6	61.6	136 200	4.9	900	30 490	58 905	24.6
District 13	302 878	85.8	67.0	96 600	1.7	712	24 393	46 847	17.3
District 14	307 142	83.0	67.4	121 300	2.6	773	26 461	52 469	22.9
District 15	237 852	87.5	67.9	88 500	1.9	694	16 721	40 440	14.0
District 16	254 145	91.5	59.4	116 300	1.6	762	19 339	41 207	13.9
District 17	305 402	88.4	54.3	128 900	2.1	845	23 904	45 373	17.0
District 18	293 064	87.8	47.5	101 500	2.8	810	22 005	41 043	15.9
District 19	293 139	85.7	64.3	88 900	1.1	746	23 086	46 020	16.8
District 20	270 108	92.8	54.7	111 900	0.8	821	20 872	45 222	16.1
District 21	339 840	89.1	57.4	221 400	11.2	978	35 092	60 543	28.1
District 22	269 047	95.3	75.5	194 200	3.9	1 049	35 786	86 681	43.5
District 23	251 423	86.5	71.8	102 700	4.1	740	21 362	47 748	19.6
District 24	315 779	93.5	48.5	198 600	9.4	940	37 337	63 223	29.3

1. Specified owner-occupied units. 2. Specified renter-occupied units.

STATE District	Poverty, 2013: Persons below poverty level (percent)	Poverty, 2013: Families below poverty level (percent)	Poverty, 2013: Percent of households receiving food stamps in past 12 months	Civilian labor force, 2013: Total	Civilian labor force, 2013: Unemployment: Total	Civilian labor force, 2013: Unemployment: Rate[1]	Civilian employment,[2] 2013: Total	Civilian employment,[2] 2013: Percent: Management, business, science and arts occupations	Civilian employment,[2] 2013: Percent: Service, sales, and office	Civilian employment,[2] 2013: Percent: Construction and production	Persons under age 65 with no health insurance, 2013 (percent)	Social Security beneficiaries, December 2013: Number	Social Security beneficiaries, December 2013: Rate[3]	Supplemental Security Income recipients, December 2013
	49	50	51	52	53	54	55	56	57	58	59	60	61	62
PENNSYLVANIA—Cont'd														
District 4	11.0	7.9	10.9	378 332	30 426	8.0	347 906	33.5	41.3	25.3	11.3	145 849	205.4	14 447
District 5	16.4	10.1	13.0	332 190	22 356	6.7	309 834	31.5	40.7	27.7	11.3	159 990	228.0	17 913
District 6	7.8	4.7	6.5	391 618	24 359	6.2	367 259	44.4	39.1	16.4	7.5	132 573	183.7	7 250
District 7	5.6	3.8	4.5	385 887	26 601	6.9	359 286	46.3	37.7	16.0	9.1	138 963	192.3	6 857
District 8	6.1	4.1	5.2	393 816	30 463	7.7	363 353	41.2	40.4	18.4	8.0	140 315	198.1	7 808
District 9	15.6	10.6	15.0	334 630	25 417	7.6	309 213	28.8	42.5	28.7	13.0	172 942	246.5	26 027
District 10	11.6	8.2	9.9	341 712	27 993	8.2	313 719	29.9	41.4	28.7	12.8	164 774	233.0	15 508
District 11	12.9	8.9	11.4	362 268	23 855	6.6	338 413	32.6	43.1	24.2	11.0	165 181	234.1	16 823
District 12	9.6	6.2	9.4	359 350	22 289	6.2	337 061	39.0	40.8	20.3	7.5	174 472	247.9	16 006
District 13	13.6	10.2	12.8	378 257	38 893	10.3	339 364	37.9	44.9	17.3	13.5	123 223	173.4	24 476
District 14	19.2	13.3	17.5	379 181	34 827	9.2	344 354	38.9	46.4	14.6	11.4	152 005	215.8	32 278
District 15	12.1	8.1	10.3	375 771	30 148	8.0	345 623	35.7	41.2	23.2	11.7	151 334	212.2	16 374
District 16	14.5	10.8	13.7	367 271	32 132	8.7	335 139	32.5	40.1	27.4	14.7	139 055	195.2	19 478
District 17	14.7	10.9	14.3	341 548	29 790	8.7	311 758	29.2	45.3	25.6	12.0	165 228	236.2	19 318
District 18	9.1	6.3	8.4	372 229	22 807	6.1	349 422	40.1	38.8	21.1	7.9	166 145	233.7	12 758
RHODE ISLAND	14.3	10.7	16.0	567 622	52 282	9.2	515 340	36.8	44.2	19.0	13.6	214 095	203.6	33 133
District 1	16.5	13.3	17.7	283 155	28 381	10.0	254 774	36.0	44.2	19.9	16.1	106 621	201.8	19 214
District 2	12.1	8.0	14.2	284 467	23 901	8.4	260 566	37.7	44.2	18.1	11.1	107 474	205.4	13 919
SOUTH CAROLINA	18.6	14.1	15.5	2 297 871	217 153	9.5	2 080 718	32.8	43.7	23.4	18.5	1 014 683	212.5	118 384
District 1	13.3	9.3	8.4	373 470	27 470	7.4	346 000	38.6	44.1	17.3	18.0	138 641	193.8	9 508
District 2	13.6	9.9	13.3	341 735	29 593	8.7	312 142	37.3	42.1	20.6	14.5	127 785	190.2	12 858
District 3	19.2	14.2	16.3	303 248	28 626	9.4	274 622	29.5	40.8	29.6	17.9	160 965	242.6	15 605
District 4	17.5	13.5	12.7	342 691	27 015	7.9	315 676	35.0	42.0	23.1	19.0	138 783	200.9	14 793
District 5	17.5	14.1	15.9	317 158	29 711	9.4	287 447	32.1	41.1	26.7	16.4	147 373	217.1	16 812
District 6	27.3	21.3	22.8	303 522	40 031	13.2	263 491	27.5	46.3	26.2	21.8	133 429	196.8	27 628
District 7	22.3	17.4	20.1	316 047	34 707	11.0	281 340	27.3	50.4	22.4	22.0	167 707	247.8	21 180
SOUTH DAKOTA	14.2	9.2	12.5	449 367	18 111	4.0	431 256	33.6	43.0	23.4	13.1	162 695	192.6	14 833
At Large	14.2	9.2	12.5	449 367	18 111	4.0	431 256	33.6	43.0	23.4	13.1	162 695	192.6	14 833
TENNESSEE	17.8	13.3	17.2	3 157 372	275 941	8.7	2 881 431	33.7	42.1	24.3	16.1	1 348 004	207.5	183 784
District 1	19.5	14.9	19.3	326 041	26 737	8.2	299 304	29.2	44.4	26.5	18.3	192 636	271.5	23 478
District 2	16.3	10.9	14.9	357 401	29 053	8.1	328 348	35.4	42.7	22.0	14.0	155 543	215.2	18 202
District 3	18.5	13.7	18.5	332 662	29 280	8.8	303 382	32.9	43.2	24.0	14.5	170 359	236.0	23 203
District 4	15.5	11.8	15.3	356 207	30 322	8.5	325 885	31.6	40.7	27.7	17.3	147 221	202.6	17 282
District 5	17.4	12.8	14.9	408 146	29 206	7.2	378 940	38.2	41.8	20.1	17.7	112 969	152.7	17 336
District 6	16.5	12.4	15.3	341 640	26 800	7.8	314 840	30.4	42.4	27.2	15.0	167 272	231.0	17 767
District 7	14.8	11.4	14.3	333 679	27 800	8.3	305 879	37.5	38.6	23.9	13.6	142 783	195.9	16 447
District 8	14.4	10.4	15.8	343 211	29 077	8.5	314 134	36.5	40.8	22.7	13.1	149 075	209.9	18 123
District 9	27.2	22.8	26.4	358 385	47 666	13.3	310 719	30.9	44.0	25.1	21.1	110 146	154.8	31 946
TEXAS	17.5	13.6	14.1	12 992 119	917 139	7.1	12 074 980	34.9	42.2	22.9	24.6	3 756 420	142.0	666 258
District 1	19.1	13.2	12.9	326 165	23 899	7.3	302 266	27.8	41.4	30.7	25.3	142 509	200.0	21 585
District 2	10.9	8.1	7.3	404 492	21 576	5.3	382 916	44.9	36.3	18.8	19.9	84 467	116.9	9 824
District 3	8.0	5.9	4.0	418 176	21 275	5.1	396 901	51.6	38.2	10.2	15.8	79 612	104.0	6 743
District 4	16.9	12.5	14.9	326 675	27 059	8.3	299 616	31.1	41.3	27.6	22.7	147 470	207.5	20 192
District 5	17.3	14.2	15.7	345 098	27 050	7.8	318 048	29.3	44.9	25.9	28.6	122 203	168.1	18 638
District 6	13.6	10.8	11.5	385 331	28 098	7.3	357 233	37.2	40.8	22.1	21.5	99 392	136.0	13 556
District 7	13.0	10.5	8.0	396 287	19 634	5.0	376 653	51.0	35.8	13.2	20.5	78 493	105.8	9 847
District 8	14.8	11.2	8.5	338 892	19 329	5.7	319 563	34.5	43.3	22.2	20.4	121 636	159.7	13 189
District 9	23.3	20.3	20.6	396 984	39 755	10.0	357 229	29.4	46.9	23.7	32.0	77 777	105.6	27 581
District 10	12.6	8.8	9.3	399 692	22 726	5.7	376 966	42.3	38.4	19.3	19.9	99 932	131.7	11 726
District 11	14.2	10.1	11.9	341 931	16 467	4.8	325 464	28.5	40.2	31.3	26.1	134 969	185.0	16 820
District 12	12.6	8.7	9.6	377 790	21 338	5.6	356 452	37.3	41.1	21.6	20.0	108 115	147.6	12 042
District 13	17.1	13.0	13.4	333 431	18 020	5.4	315 411	29.5	42.8	27.7	22.2	124 619	177.8	14 307
District 14	17.5	13.6	14.3	336 074	24 208	7.2	311 866	34.7	41.3	24.0	22.0	120 041	167.5	19 043
District 15	29.0	23.9	27.2	307 922	24 138	7.8	283 784	27.4	48.1	24.5	34.6	96 197	131.6	33 143
District 16	21.0	18.3	23.3	315 856	26 467	8.4	289 389	32.1	47.2	20.8	29.8	105 206	144.4	25 590
District 17	20.7	14.1	12.2	374 994	25 130	6.7	349 864	35.9	43.6	20.5	20.7	104 130	143.4	16 974
District 18	24.2	20.8	19.4	369 751	34 680	9.4	335 071	27.8	44.6	27.7	31.2	88 143	118.9	30 295
District 19	17.5	12.3	13.9	345 526	22 372	6.5	323 154	30.8	44.0	25.2	24.3	118 710	165.0	17 621
District 20	20.2	16.3	17.4	366 852	27 949	7.6	338 903	30.8	50.6	18.7	23.4	105 740	140.4	23 942
District 21	12.4	7.4	7.7	403 926	23 036	5.7	380 890	47.0	40.2	12.7	17.7	126 126	169.7	9 220
District 22	8.0	6.3	7.2	400 767	18 540	4.6	382 227	50.0	33.4	16.6	15.2	79 253	101.2	10 304
District 23	18.8	15.8	18.8	316 693	25 586	8.1	291 107	29.3	43.1	27.7	26.5	114 589	158.3	26 140
District 24	11.1	8.6	6.4	437 805	24 236	5.5	413 569	43.4	40.9	15.8	20.6	81 092	109.4	7 300

1. Percent of civilian labor force. 2. Persons 16 years old and over. 3. Per 1,000 resident population estimated in the 2013 American Community Survey.

STATE District	Agriculture, 2012									
		Land in farms			Value of products sold				Government payments	
	Number of farms	Acres	Average size of farm (acres)	Irrigated land (acres)	Total ($1,000)	Average per farm (dollars)	Percent from crops	Percent from livestock and poultry products	Total ($1,000)	Average per farm receiving payments (dollars)
	63	64	65	66	67	68	69	70	71	72
PENNSYLVANIA—Cont'd										
District 4	3 470	442 692	128	3 131	445 123	128 277	60.2	39.8	4 659	5 508
District 5	7 119	1 025 582	144	3 772	448 440	62 992	39.2	60.8	10 295	5 589
District 6	1 821	161 792	89	1 708	433 872	238 260	45.4	54.6	2 446	7 109
District 7	2 521	214 656	85	2 080	682 479	270 718	64.7	35.3	2 325	5 033
District 8	1 048	75 181	72	922	74 095	70 701	74.0	26.0	D	D
District 9	7 608	1 178 741	155	5 850	886 733	116 553	27.1	72.9	12 005	5 333
District 10	10 157	1 530 318	151	3 931	1 036 895	102 087	22.8	77.2	21 819	6 165
District 11	5 191	681 540	131	3 494	535 209	103 103	42.4	57.6	8 608	4 435
District 12	2 312	289 072	125	639	128 146	55 427	44.2	55.8	2 453	4 576
District 13	60	1 550	26	74	2 026	33 774	97.6	2.4	D	D
District 14	52	3 737	72	14	679	13 064	86.6	13.4	D	D
District 15	2 654	327 761	123	2 862	600 645	226 317	27.8	72.2	4 326	5 769
District 16	5 054	416 310	82	6 010	1 498 795	296 556	25.2	74.8	5 716	6 226
District 17	1 388	170 812	123	1 943	198 442	142 969	51.0	49.0	2 205	4 641
District 18	3 340	375 166	112	1 112	74 892	22 423	53.2	46.8	1 538	3 395
RHODE ISLAND	1 243	69 589	56	3 954	59 652	47 990	82.1	17.9	2 345	12 342
District 1	344	15 923	46	647	19 582	56 923	80.6	19.4	875	13 059
District 2	899	53 666	60	3 307	40 070	44 572	82.9	17.1	1 470	11 955
SOUTH CAROLINA	25 266	4 971 244	197	159 239	3 040 069	120 323	42.6	57.4	46 616	6 867
District 1	544	82 106	151	4 774	39 179	72 021	95.4	4.6	310	4 996
District 2	3 158	453 236	144	24 868	388 653	123 069	30.6	69.4	3 820	5 343
District 3	6 630	878 661	133	14 298	540 476	81 520	19.8	80.2	5 673	6 107
District 4	1 912	135 628	71	2 756	42 760	22 364	61.8	38.2	898	7 240
District 5	4 848	858 012	177	17 565	683 746	141 037	26.1	73.9	6 325	6 164
District 6	4 690	1 601 949	342	74 041	713 033	152 033	67.5	32.5	16 616	7 434
District 7	3 484	961 652	276	20 937	632 221	181 464	54.3	45.7	12 974	7 645
SOUTH DAKOTA	31 989	43 257 079	1 352	378 678	10 170 227	317 929	59.7	40.3	283 797	12 451
At Large	31 989	43 257 079	1 352	378 678	10 170 000	317 929	59.7	40.3	283 797	12 451
TENNESSEE	68 050	10 867 812	160	146 442	3 611 037	53 064	57.8	42.2	67 665	4 184
District 1	9 853	905 084	92	D	255 474	25 929	24.2	75.8	3 479	1 706
District 2	5 214	522 807	100	1 856	168 328	32 284	54.7	45.3	1 492	1 565
District 3	5 665	627 645	111	826	240 743	42 497	9.6	90.4	1 616	2 726
District 4	10 696	1 649 872	154	14 838	625 877	58 515	35.3	64.7	5 744	3 258
District 5	1 918	237 050	124	881	35 345	18 428	64.2	35.8	335	1 573
District 6	13 698	1 963 227	143	7 539	601 843	43 937	53.2	46.8	9 216	3 391
District 7	13 249	2 330 708	176	10 200	433 743	32 738	58.1	41.9	11 722	3 232
District 8	7 529	2 581 642	343	103 713	1 227 122	162 986	87.4	12.6	33 653	7 990
District 9	228	49 777	218	D	22 562	98 957	95.9	4.1	408	7 425
TEXAS	248 809	130 153 438	523	4 489 163	25 375 581	101 988	29.0	71.0	643 993	12 293
District 1	12 033	1 894 203	157	7 229	1 248 621	103 766	9.3	90.7	2 219	5 604
District 2	277	26 687	96	696	24 812	89 575	93.6	6.4	135	8 991
District 3	1 239	181 470	146	1 483	49 687	40 103	63.7	36.3	1 063	10 738
District 4	23 397	4 272 976	183	35 066	1 185 301	50 660	25.1	74.9	18 210	6 358
District 5	12 498	1 955 349	156	9 102	447 708	35 822	44.0	56.0	3 504	8 505
District 6	5 164	1 029 961	199	1 486	161 229	31 222	63.1	36.9	5 425	6 082
District 7	145	22 255	153	613	1 872	12 911	64.6	35.5	237	9 112
District 8	9 297	2 007 965	216	12 705	286 726	30 841	39.9	60.1	4 791	7 557
District 9	138	14 387	104	19	1 778	12 886	62.3	37.7	98	6 540
District 10	14 453	2 579 215	178	39 297	388 941	26 911	48.1	51.9	12 664	6 758
District 11	21 093	15 735 425	746	231 436	1 140 013	54 047	30.5	69.5	71 961	11 722
District 12	5 466	663 119	121	2 653	92 035	16 838	24.2	75.8	459	2 871
District 13	20 372	22 410 589	1 100	1 321 922	8 593 468	421 827	16.1	83.9	142 997	14 697
District 14	3 818	1 023 671	268	43 308	144 002	37 717	57.4	42.6	9 058	19 231
District 15	8 704	4 303 286	494	154 612	506 516	58 193	67.4	32.6	17 789	9 165
District 16	370	120 411	325	10 427	23 588	63 753	94.9	5.1	409	14 114
District 17	16 124	4 032 650	250	59 093	1 003 696	62 249	27.5	72.5	21 247	9 123
District 18	119	4 478	38	28	3 789	31 843	10.5	89.5	20	4 904
District 19	15 781	14 714 801	932	1 783 134	5 205 921	329 885	27.7	72.3	191 903	17 292
District 20	221	18 965	86	770	1 394	6 306	62.3	37.6	35	2 345
District 21	7 738	2 997 190	387	7 650	103 517	13 378	30.3	69.7	4 697	5 820
District 22	1 965	414 170	211	12 771	128 234	65 259	86.2	13.8	4 359	10 209
District 23	9 377	28 460 973	3 035	314 787	966 721	103 095	51.4	48.6	35 825	16 647
District 24	158	10 534	67	93	3 807	24 094	92.4	7.6	61	8 648

1. Specified owner-occupied units. 2. Specified renter-occupied units.

STATE District	Representative, 114th Congress	Land area,[1] 2010 (sq km)	Population and population characteristics, 2013: Total persons	Per square kilometer	Percent: Race alone: White	Black	American Indian, Alaska Native	Asian and Pacific Islander	Some other race (percent)	Two or more races (percent)	Hispanic or Latino[2] (percent)	Non-Hispanic White alone (percent)	Percent female	Percent foreign-born	Percent born in state of residence
		1	2	3	4	5	6	7	8	9	10	11	12	13	14
TEXAS—Cont'd															
District 25	Roger Williams (R)	19 738	731 689	37.1	85.8	6.5	0.4	2.8	1.8	2.7	18.2	70.3	50.4	8.3	58.8
District 26	Michael C. Burgess (R)	2 350	768 246	326.9	80.4	7.1	0.4	5.2	2.7	4.2	17.5	66.5	50.7	11.9	49.9
District 27	Blake Farenthold (R)	23 642	714 527	30.2	84.1	5.4	0.3	1.6	6.5	2.0	50.6	41.6	50.8	7.6	75.3
District 28	Henry Cuellar (D)	24 290	724 080	29.8	88.6	3.7	0.4	0.7	4.8	1.8	77.8	16.8	50.9	22.0	63.5
District 29	Gene Green (D)	485	729 827	1 504.8	74.0	10.6	0.6	1.2	12.2	1.6	78.0	10.0	49.5	32.7	57.8
District 30	Eddie Bernice Johnson (D)	923	746 336	808.6	47.3	43.4	0.2	1.8	5.4	2.0	37.9	16.1	50.9	17.6	64.6
District 31	John R. Carter (R)	5 580	767 721	137.6	76.1	11.7	0.5	4.5	3.2	4.0	23.2	57.9	50.6	9.7	52.9
District 32	Pete Sessions (R)	481	718 713	1 494.2	62.6	13.4	0.3	7.6	11.9	4.1	25.6	50.5	50.6	20.2	51.5
District 33	Marc A. Veasey (D)	549	725 761	1 322.0	62.7	17.1	0.6	2.1	15.8	1.8	64.6	15.8	49.2	32.4	54.7
District 34	Filemon Vela (D)	21 213	720 005	33.9	92.0	1.1	0.3	0.7	5.1	0.8	83.7	14.3	50.5	20.8	68.5
District 35	Lloyd Doggett (D)	1 538	752 749	489.4	76.5	9.9	0.7	1.2	8.6	3.1	63.0	24.8	49.8	16.5	64.9
District 36	Brian Babin (R)	18 456	710 008	38.5	81.2	8.6	0.6	1.7	5.4	2.4	23.2	64.5	50.0	9.9	68.0
UTAH		212 818	2 900 872	13.6	87.4	1.1	1.1	3.1	4.8	2.4	13.4	79.5	49.7	8.2	62.7
District 1	Rob Bishop (R)	50 662	720 959	14.2	90.6	1.1	1.0	1.8	2.9	2.6	12.2	82.3	49.5	5.5	65.3
District 2	Chris Stewart (R)	103 568	715 552	6.9	84.9	1.2	1.2	3.9	6.4	2.5	14.3	77.7	49.6	9.0	60.0
District 3	Jason Chaffetz (R)	51 982	718 575	13.8	90.5	0.5	1.7	2.5	2.7	2.2	10.4	83.1	50.1	7.4	61.2
District 4	Mia B. Love (R)	6 605	745 786	112.9	83.7	1.7	0.8	4.3	7.2	2.4	16.5	75.2	49.7	10.7	64.4
VERMONT		23 871	626 630	26.3	95.0	1.1	0.3	1.3	0.3	2.1	1.5	94.0	50.7	4.3	50.5
At Large	Peter Welch (D)	23 871	626 630	26.3	95.0	1.1	0.3	1.3	0.3	2.1	1.5	94.0	50.7	4.3	50.5
VIRGINIA		102 279	8 260 405	80.8	69.3	19.3	0.2	5.9	2.0	3.3	8.6	63.5	50.9	11.5	49.8
District 1	Robert J. Wittman (R)	9 542	763 763	80.0	74.0	17.2	0.3	3.8	1.6	3.1	9.2	66.9	50.7	9.1	45.5
District 2	Scott Rigell (R)	2 568	738 759	287.7	67.7	21.4	0.2	5.5	1.1	4.1	7.7	62.3	50.2	8.2	42.3
District 3	Robert C. "Bobby" Scott (D)	2 453	742 782	302.8	35.6	56.9	0.5	1.9	1.6	3.5	5.8	32.4	51.9	5.4	62.1
District 4	J. Randy Forbes (R)	11 164	739 602	66.2	60.9	31.8	0.3	2.1	1.8	3.2	5.1	58.3	50.4	4.6	59.8
District 5	Robert Hurt (R)	25 977	735 799	28.3	75.3	20.0	0.1	1.5	0.7	2.4	3.3	72.9	51.4	3.7	65.5
District 6	Bob Goodlatte (R)	15 359	735 143	47.9	84.2	10.4	0.2	1.9	0.8	2.6	4.6	80.8	51.5	5.0	65.0
District 7	Dave Brat (R)	7 191	760 928	105.8	75.7	14.9	0.1	4.8	1.7	2.9	5.5	72.5	51.6	7.6	55.8
District 8	Donald S. Beyer, Jr. (D)	387	774 396	2 001.0	63.5	14.8	0.3	11.2	6.7	3.5	18.8	52.6	50.6	27.8	23.4
District 9	Morgan Griffith (R)	23 605	721 531	30.6	91.3	5.3	0.1	1.2	0.6	1.6	2.2	89.7	50.3	2.7	66.6
District 10	Barbara Comstock (R)	3 554	781 947	220.0	73.6	7.1	0.3	12.4	2.3	4.4	12.3	64.3	50.5	19.3	37.2
District 11	Gerald E. Connolly (D)	479	765 755	1 598.7	61.7	13.1	0.2	18.1	2.6	4.3	18.5	47.4	50.5	30.9	28.4
WASHINGTON		172 119	6 971 406	40.5	78.0	3.7	1.4	8.3	3.7	4.9	11.9	70.9	50.1	13.5	47.4
District 1	Suzan K. DelBene (D)	16 023	709 693	44.3	81.3	1.2	1.2	10.2	2.2	3.9	9.6	74.7	50.0	16.0	48.5
District 2	Rick Larsen (D)	2 629	692 085	263.3	80.5	3.1	1.4	8.0	2.1	5.0	9.5	74.4	50.3	13.0	48.2
District 3	Jaime Herrera Beutler (R)	23 605	691 968	29.3	86.9	1.6	1.1	3.6	2.6	4.2	8.4	82.0	50.5	8.0	40.9
District 4	Dan Newsome (R)	49 858	698 426	14.0	74.4	1.1	2.4	2.0	16.9	3.1	37.7	55.4	49.4	16.9	55.9
District 5	Cathy McMorris Rodgers (R)	40 075	681 812	17.0	89.0	1.8	1.5	2.8	1.0	3.9	6.2	84.7	50.1	5.9	53.8
District 6	Derek Kilmer (D)	17 878	682 280	38.2	82.3	3.2	2.0	5.5	1.9	5.2	7.2	77.9	49.8	6.7	48.5
District 7	Jim McDermott (D)	373	706 603	1 894.4	76.1	4.0	0.9	11.2	2.3	5.6	7.6	71.6	50.3	15.7	41.0
District 8	David G. Reichert (R)	19 062	701 614	36.8	79.3	3.5	0.9	8.9	2.6	4.7	10.1	72.7	50.3	12.6	52.1
District 9	Adam Smith (D)	475	705 731	1 485.7	56.8	10.7	0.8	22.8	2.1	6.9	12.0	48.5	49.7	29.5	39.0
District 10	Denny Heck (D)	2 141	701 194	327.5	74.4	6.8	1.5	7.5	2.9	6.7	11.0	67.8	50.6	10.5	46.4
WEST VIRGINIA		62 259	1 854 304	29.8	93.7	3.4	0.1	0.6	0.3	1.8	1.4	92.6	50.7	1.4	70.0
District 1	David McKinley (R)	16 254	617 842	38.0	94.8	2.6	0.1	0.8	0.2	1.4	1.4	93.9	50.3	1.6	68.2
District 2	Alexander X. Mooney (R)	20 765	626 979	30.2	92.3	3.7	0.1	0.7	0.4	2.8	1.9	90.7	50.8	1.8	65.1
District 3	Evan H. Jenkins (R)	25 240	609 483	24.1	94.1	3.9	0.1	0.4	0.3	1.2	1.0	93.3	51.0	0.8	76.8
WISCONSIN		140 268	5 742 713	40.9	86.6	6.2	0.9	2.5	1.7	2.1	6.3	82.5	50.4	4.8	71.8
District 1	Paul Ryan (R)	4 475	709 472	158.5	87.7	5.6	0.3	1.9	2.2	2.4	9.6	81.1	50.3	5.7	66.9
District 2	Mark Pocan (D)	11 750	733 541	62.4	87.2	4.3	0.3	4.0	1.7	2.6	6.1	83.2	50.4	6.8	65.4
District 3	Ron Kind (D)	28 779	711 620	24.7	94.2	1.0	0.6	2.0	0.6	1.6	2.3	92.7	49.7	2.0	72.3
District 4	Gwen Moore (D)	332	715 840	2 156.1	53.9	33.7	0.5	3.5	4.5	3.8	15.9	43.8	51.8	9.3	66.7
District 5	F. James Sensenbrenner Jr. (R)	4 897	723 153	147.7	92.6	1.8	0.3	2.4	1.4	1.6	5.6	88.5	51.0	4.8	76.2
District 6	Glen Grothman(R)	12 739	713 224	56.0	93.3	1.3	0.4	2.3	1.1	1.5	4.3	90.3	49.8	3.5	79.9
District 7	Sean P. Duffy (R)	59 666	715 263	12.0	93.7	0.9	2.1	1.6	0.3	1.4	2.0	92.3	49.6	2.3	67.7
District 8	Reid J. Ribble (R)	17 629	720 600	40.9	90.3	1.4	2.5	2.3	1.6	2.0	4.7	87.9	50.1	3.8	79.3
WYOMING		251 470	582 658	2.3	90.7	1.3	2.3	1.0	1.9	2.7	8.9	84.7	49.0	3.1	41.9
At Large	Cynthia M. Lummis (R)	251 470	582 658	2.3	90.7	1.3	2.3	1.0	1.9	2.7	8.9	84.7	49.0	3.1	41.9

1. Dry land or land partially or temporarily covered by water. 2. May be of any race.

STATE District	Population and population characteristics, 2013 (cont.)										Education, 2013		
	Age (percent)											Attainment[2] (percent)	
	Under 5 years	5 to 17 years	18 to 24 years	25 to 34 years	35 to 44 years	45 to 54 years	55 to 64 years	65 to 74 years	75 years and over	Median age	Total Enrollment[1]	High school graduate or more	Bachelor's degree or more
	15	16	17	18	19	20	21	22	23	24	25	26	27
TEXAS—Cont'd													
District 25	6.5	18.5	10.1	13.1	14.0	13.4	11.4	8.0	5.0	36.1	206 511	88.8	35.6
District 26	6.9	21.2	9.3	13.6	16.5	14.3	10.0	5.4	2.8	34.4	243 152	91.7	40.5
District 27	6.7	18.6	9.8	12.7	12.1	13.0	12.5	8.2	6.3	36.5	176 094	80.9	17.1
District 28	9.0	22.6	10.3	12.6	13.3	12.3	9.3	6.2	4.4	31.4	223 936	68.9	16.5
District 29	9.1	23.1	12.0	15.5	13.9	11.4	8.0	4.2	2.9	28.4	225 763	58.9	9.0
District 30	8.3	20.1	9.7	15.5	13.3	13.1	10.7	5.5	3.8	32.6	205 169	75.6	20.0
District 31	7.4	19.8	9.8	15.2	14.7	12.7	9.9	6.4	4.0	33.5	220 137	91.3	33.0
District 32	6.8	17.0	9.7	15.4	13.9	14.4	12.0	6.3	4.6	35.7	192 693	86.7	42.7
District 33	9.6	23.2	11.1	15.4	14.0	11.4	7.6	4.5	3.0	28.9	215 035	58.1	9.5
District 34	8.1	21.9	11.1	12.7	12.2	11.3	9.9	7.1	5.6	32.1	215 124	64.8	14.6
District 35	7.6	19.3	13.7	17.0	13.8	11.4	9.0	4.7	3.4	30.4	226 741	76.1	18.6
District 36	6.4	18.3	8.9	13.3	12.9	14.3	12.6	8.0	5.4	37.7	176 272	83.5	18.7
UTAH	8.7	22.1	11.5	15.2	12.9	10.5	9.3	5.6	4.1	30.2	945 104	91.5	31.3
District 1	8.9	22.8	10.9	14.9	12.7	11.0	9.6	5.4	3.9	30.1	227 449	92.2	28.8
District 2	8.0	20.5	11.3	15.1	12.6	10.2	10.2	6.8	5.4	31.9	224 080	91.2	31.9
District 3	8.7	22.8	14.7	13.7	12.1	9.8	8.9	5.4	3.8	27.7	260 655	93.7	38.5
District 4	9.4	22.5	9.1	16.9	14.1	11.0	8.6	5.0	3.4	30.5	232 920	89.4	26.9
VERMONT	4.8	14.9	10.6	11.2	11.6	15.2	15.2	9.6	6.8	42.5	146 569	91.5	35.7
At Large	4.8	14.9	10.6	11.2	11.6	15.2	15.2	9.6	6.8	42.5	146 569	91.5	35.7
VIRGINIA	6.2	16.4	10.1	13.9	13.3	14.4	12.4	7.9	5.5	37.6	2 157 510	88.4	36.1
District 1	6.3	18.0	10.0	11.4	13.9	14.9	12.1	8.1	5.3	38.5	209 425	91.5	35.7
District 2	6.2	15.5	12.3	16.0	12.2	13.4	11.6	7.3	5.3	35.0	190 712	92.4	32.4
District 3	6.9	15.0	13.3	17.6	11.5	12.5	11.7	6.6	4.8	32.9	204 012	83.5	22.0
District 4	5.8	18.0	8.8	12.8	13.6	15.2	12.6	7.9	5.3	38.9	198 401	87.6	24.8
District 5	5.2	15.9	10.0	11.3	11.6	14.4	13.9	10.5	7.2	41.7	185 152	84.5	26.9
District 6	5.3	15.1	12.7	11.4	12.0	13.5	13.1	9.3	7.5	39.9	191 276	85.0	25.4
District 7	5.9	17.5	8.3	12.5	13.4	15.1	13.2	8.3	5.9	39.6	194 169	90.8	38.4
District 8	7.4	13.6	7.1	20.9	16.3	13.6	10.9	5.9	4.2	35.6	175 634	91.0	61.4
District 9	5.0	13.9	12.2	11.1	11.8	13.7	14.2	10.5	7.7	41.9	170 802	81.3	19.0
District 10	7.0	20.7	7.7	11.8	15.1	16.3	11.5	6.3	3.6	36.8	226 126	92.4	53.8
District 11	6.6	17.1	9.1	16.4	14.5	14.6	11.5	6.4	3.8	35.6	211 801	91.5	53.5
WASHINGTON	6.3	16.6	9.6	14.2	13.1	13.5	12.9	8.0	5.7	37.4	1 722 089	90.1	32.7
District 1	6.6	17.5	7.9	13.2	14.8	15.4	12.5	7.5	4.6	38.4	177 087	92.2	40.3
District 2	6.2	15.3	11.0	14.4	12.3	13.7	13.2	8.2	5.9	37.4	168 388	92.0	29.8
District 3	6.1	18.2	8.1	12.2	12.9	13.7	13.5	9.4	5.9	39.1	170 074	90.8	22.5
District 4	8.2	21.3	9.5	13.1	12.3	11.7	11.3	7.2	5.3	33.5	184 136	77.5	19.1
District 5	5.8	16.1	12.1	13.1	11.7	12.8	13.3	8.6	6.5	37.5	186 529	91.6	26.9
District 6	5.3	14.6	9.6	12.5	11.7	13.3	15.2	10.3	7.2	42.0	148 677	91.4	28.4
District 7	4.8	11.2	10.4	20.4	15.3	12.6	12.9	7.2	5.1	36.9	156 477	94.7	57.4
District 8	6.5	18.8	8.4	11.6	14.1	15.7	12.8	7.6	4.4	38.6	184 080	91.0	32.1
District 9	6.7	15.4	8.8	16.8	14.0	13.8	11.7	6.7	6.2	36.7	170 028	88.4	39.9
District 10	7.2	17.2	10.3	15.0	12.6	13.0	12.1	7.2	5.4	35.3	176 613	90.4	26.2
WEST VIRGINIA	5.5	15.0	9.6	11.5	12.6	13.7	14.7	9.9	7.4	41.7	414 610	84.6	18.9
District 1	5.3	14.4	11.7	11.6	12.1	13.5	14.2	9.7	7.4	40.7	151 830	88.0	21.1
District 2	5.6	16.0	8.5	11.4	12.7	14.4	14.6	9.6	7.2	42.0	138 708	86.0	20.6
District 3	5.8	14.8	8.6	11.5	13.0	13.2	15.3	10.3	7.6	42.2	124 072	79.8	15.1
WISCONSIN	5.9	16.8	9.7	12.8	12.1	14.5	13.4	8.1	6.7	39.0	1 485 800	90.9	27.7
District 1	5.7	17.9	8.1	12.0	12.9	15.8	13.5	7.7	6.3	39.9	183 984	91.3	26.2
District 2	6.0	16.0	11.8	14.4	12.8	13.5	12.7	7.2	5.5	36.4	207 376	92.7	39.2
District 3	5.6	15.8	13.0	11.9	11.0	13.6	13.3	8.5	7.2	38.7	192 811	91.9	23.4
District 4	7.5	17.9	11.7	16.4	12.3	12.3	11.1	5.8	5.0	32.5	211 733	83.8	26.8
District 5	5.7	16.5	8.3	12.6	12.3	15.0	13.9	8.2	7.5	40.7	181 626	93.7	35.2
District 6	5.4	16.4	9.0	11.7	11.8	15.1	14.3	8.9	7.6	41.7	171 368	90.8	24.4
District 7	5.7	16.5	7.1	11.2	11.4	15.2	14.8	10.0	8.0	43.4	158 667	90.9	21.2
District 8	5.9	17.3	8.6	12.0	12.3	15.5	13.4	8.2	6.7	39.8	178 235	91.6	25.3
WYOMING	6.6	17.4	10.1	14.0	12.1	12.8	13.8	8.0	5.3	36.6	151 054	93.5	26.6
At Large	6.6	17.4	10.1	14.0	12.1	12.8	13.8	8.0	5.3	36.6	151 054	93.5	26.6

1. All persons 3 years old and over enrolled in nursery school through college and graduate or professional school. 2. Persons 25 years old and over.

STATE District	Households, 2013							Group quarters, 2010				
	Number	Average household size	Family households (percent)	Married-couple family (percent)	Female family householder[1]	One person households (percent)	Total in group quarters, 2013	Percent 65 years and over	Persons in correctional institutions	Persons in nursing facilities	Persons in college dormitories	Persons in military quarters
	28	29	30	31	32	33	34	35	36	37	38	39
TEXAS—Cont'd												
District 25	258 158	2.71	69.30	56.7	8.8	24.2	32 750	9.6	11 967	3 274	10 926	2 822
District 26	259 845	2.91	76.30	59.3	11.6	17.8	12 678	14.1	1 179	1 636	6 475	0
District 27	255 892	2.74	70.10	49.3	14.3	23.5	13 926	31.7	3 832	4 197	1 365	103
District 28	212 066	3.39	80.00	56.0	18.2	17.4	6 101	32.3	3 252	2 888	740	146
District 29	211 463	3.44	75.40	46.3	20.9	19.5	2 444	36.1	31	1 008	0	0
District 30	251 686	2.89	66.80	38.9	21.4	27.7	19 346	9.2	11 108	2 286	2 507	0
District 31	255 663	2.95	72.40	56.0	11.7	23.5	12 540	16.1	3 442	2 183	2 041	4 084
District 32	274 989	2.59	63.50	46.5	12.3	29.7	5 497	38.4	22	2 226	2 437	0
District 33	215 406	3.34	73.70	43.6	20.3	21.4	5 939	19.3	2 147	1 389	534	0
District 34	208 952	3.36	76.90	53.4	18.2	20.5	18 685	13.7	13 244	2 881	2 180	41
District 35	247 354	2.96	63.50	38.0	18.8	26.1	19 558	9.9	7 971	2 563	5 761	115
District 36	251 430	2.76	71.60	54.1	12.6	24.1	16 835	16.7	12 140	2 926	0	0
UTAH	899 475	3.17	75.30	61.4	9.6	19.1	47 231	10.4	12 666	5 854	15 666	523
District 1	227 360	3.13	77.30	63.6	9.6	18.3	9 888	10.6	1 892	1 190	3 227	488
District 2	236 237	2.97	70.40	56.0	9.7	22.6	13 314	12.1	3 459	1 763	3 443	35
District 3	211 662	3.32	78.20	66.2	8.6	16.2	15 762	7.5	441	1 279	8 960	0
District 4	224 216	3.29	75.70	60.2	10.5	19.2	8 267	12.4	6 874	1 622	36	0
VERMONT	253 234	2.37	61.60	48.6	9.1	29.9	25 333	15.0	1 592	3 588	16 895	5
At Large	253 234	2.37	61.60	48.6	9.1	29.9	25 333	15.0	1 592	3 588	16 895	5
VIRGINIA	3 055 863	2.62	67.10	50.1	12.6	26.7	241 941	12.0	1 592	30 324	84 048	37 568
District 1	266 532	2.8	73.60	57.7	11.8	21.6	18 659	13.8	4 215	2 568	6 380	3 351
District 2	273 700	2.58	65.90	47.2	14.0	27.2	33 382	11.2	1 685	2 534	7 086	7 370
District 3	284 079	2.51	56.70	29.1	22.6	34.2	30 430	5.4	6 045	3 045	11 014	24 287
District 4	259 558	2.72	72.10	53.0	15.1	23.9	32 742	10.2	19 352	2 662	2 942	316
District 5	287 146	2.46	66.30	50.6	11.8	28.5	29 512	13.8	10 972	4 052	12 206	0
District 6	287 350	2.43	65.50	48.7	12.2	28.6	35 607	12.6	4 623	4 349	19 615	1 398
District 7	282 435	2.65	69.70	54.6	11.4	24.8	11 154	19.8	4 500	2 649	3 721	0
District 8	305 654	2.51	56.30	43.8	7.9	34.1	6 373	28.6	944	2 026	1 084	846
District 9	290 159	2.38	65.60	49.2	11.4	28.4	30 893	13.1	10 091	4 288	14 085	0
District 10	256 373	3.03	78.70	66.0	9.4	16.8	5 660	18.7	1 606	907	1 068	0
District 11	262 877	2.88	70.40	54.2	11.3	22.8	7 529	13.6	1 207	1 244	4 847	0
WASHINGTON	2 644 557	2.58	64.50	49.5	10.3	27.5	141 263	18.6	31 960	22 156	35 534	12 385
District 1	258 659	2.71	71.10	58.4	8.4	21.6	7 477	23.7	2 676	1 313	620	0
District 2	267 873	2.53	62.70	47.1	11.4	28.8	13 062	20.5	1 754	2 323	3 862	2 504
District 3	255 126	2.68	68.80	52.8	11.2	25.3	6 969	35.8	1 539	1 617	0	14
District 4	233 400	2.95	72.40	52.3	13.7	22.2	10 078	25.7	4 028	2 246	382	4
District 5	264 635	2.46	61.30	46.8	10.5	30.0	29 536	11.8	5 656	2 927	13 048	513
District 6	268 651	2.47	63.10	48.5	10.1	29.4	19 633	16.0	8 063	3 211	1 022	5 694
District 7	317 520	2.16	48.10	38.5	6.4	38.3	22 019	13.6	1 851	2 700	10 456	362
District 8	253 268	2.74	72.90	58.4	8.9	21.0	7 142	24.8	839	1 305	2 155	0
District 9	267 730	2.6	62.60	45.5	12.1	28.5	10 835	26.9	3 031	2 422	1 348	0
District 10	257 695	2.66	66.60	49.9	11.3	26.8	14 512	17.9	2 523	2 092	2 641	3 294
WEST VIRGINIA	738 653	2.44	64.90	48.2	11.7	30.2	49 679	18.9	16 591	9 748	17 113	79
District 1	243 731	2.45	62.10	47.4	10.7	32.4	21 609	15.8	6 965	3 632	10 300	0
District 2	250 370	2.46	65.30	48.6	11.4	30.0	11 099	23.6	2 583	2 791	3 447	79
District 3	244 552	2.42	67.20	48.6	13.0	28.3	16 971	20.1	7 043	3 325	3 366	0
WISCONSIN	2 289 424	2.44	63.70	49.1	10.2	29.2	147 362	23.1	38 102	33 808	56 773	132
District 1	270 357	2.57	67.90	53.4	9.9	26.7	15 182	21.6	6 723	3 632	2 368	0
District 2	299 626	2.39	60.00	47.0	9.3	29.9	17 246	19.7	2 269	2 791	8 805	0
District 3	278 988	2.44	62.90	50.7	8.1	28.5	31 732	15.5	6 311	3 325	18 297	122
District 4	280 639	2.49	56.60	31.2	19.8	34.1	18 239	17.5	2 539	3 173	9 814	0
District 5	292 046	2.43	64.70	53.0	8.2	28.7	14 222	33.1	1 490	4 832	5 703	0
District 6	285 679	2.41	65.30	52.3	8.6	29.2	23 869	20.2	12 174	5 078	6 097	0
District 7	295 121	2.38	66.50	53.0	8.6	28.5	12 292	42.6	3 541	5 073	1 198	0
District 8	286 968	2.46	65.90	52.2	9.2	27.6	14 580	31.5	3 055	4 742	4 491	10
WYOMING	224 003	2.54	66.30	52.7	9.0	27.1	14 017	18.4	3 576	2 450	4 443	503
At Large	224 003	2.54	66.30	52.7	9.0	27.1	14 017	18.4	3 576	2 450	4 443	503

1. No spouse present.

STATE District	Housing units, 2013						Money income, 2013		
		Occupied units						Households	
			Owner-occupied			Renter-occupied			
	Total	Occupied units as a percent of all units	Owner-occupied units as a percent of occupied units	Median value[1] (dollars)	Percent valued at $500,000 or more	Median rent[2]	Per capita income (dollars)	Median income (dollars)	Percent with income of $100,000 or more
	40	41	42	43	44	45	46	47	48
TEXAS—Cont'd									
District 25	297 519	86.8	69.1	180 000	12.5	959	31 582	60 847	28.8
District 26	275 107	94.5	70.2	188 100	5.4	1 021	34 191	80 124	38.7
District 27	305 039	83.9	63.0	109 500	1.7	796	23 829	49 518	19.1
District 28	240 959	88.0	70.1	96 900	1.0	751	17 367	44 275	15.5
District 29	237 163	89.2	49.6	86 700	0.4	750	14 787	36 628	9.5
District 30	276 320	91.1	53.7	101 100	1.6	865	20 682	41 863	14.1
District 31	289 951	88.2	65.2	170 100	2.5	923	27 989	61 693	26.6
District 32	297 080	92.6	56.6	175 700	15.0	971	39 314	60 247	30.5
District 33	241 120	89.3	47.8	80 800	0.3	756	14 463	35 827	8.0
District 34	254 151	82.2	69.1	77 000	1.1	631	15 974	35 144	12.3
District 35	274 984	90.0	51.2	107 400	0.8	853	18 121	40 714	11.3
District 36	291 457	86.3	70.9	117 100	1.6	824	26 313	52 708	23.2
UTAH	1 006 164	89.4	69.2	211 400	6.8	881	24 250	59 770	22.9
District 1	262 563	86.6	72.4	193 400	6.0	815	23 834	59 760	21.7
District 2	274 306	86.1	66.8	193 400	6.7	832	24 516	55 107	20.2
District 3	230 578	91.8	68.1	243 100	10.6	912	24 994	61 875	26.3
District 4	238 717	93.9	69.6	216 700	4.3	982	23 681	61 788	23.5
VERMONT	323 936	78.2	71.0	218 300	6.9	865	29 136	52 578	20.2
At Large	323 936	78.2	71.0	218 300	6.9	865	29 136	52 578	20.2
VIRGINIA	3 412 577	89.5	65.6	239 300	15.9	1 086	33 145	62 666	29.8
District 1	302 923	88.0	72.4	286 500	12.1	1 221	33 725	75 485	36.3
District 2	306 639	89.3	60.3	236 100	9.5	1 111	30 277	59 435	23.7
District 3	324 041	87.7	46.9	161 400	2.7	882	21 415	38 885	11.9
District 4	284 822	91.1	71.0	208 800	4.7	1 015	27 130	60 216	25.6
District 5	346 891	82.8	72.0	172 200	9.0	751	26 050	47 972	18.8
District 6	326 983	87.9	65.6	177 700	4.3	762	25 788	46 862	16.6
District 7	303 821	93.0	72.2	241 900	10.0	1 052	34 298	68 761	31.8
District 8	332 960	91.8	52.1	474 100	45.9	1 715	51 489	97 323	48.7
District 9	340 643	85.2	71.1	110 300	2.2	628	22 157	39 427	11.6
District 10	269 359	95.2	76.6	436 100	41.0	1 485	45 989	110 444	55.7
District 11	273 495	96.1	64.1	432 500	37.1	1 703	43 943	101 226	50.8
WASHINGTON	2 928 300	90.3	61.9	250 800	13.5	989	30 672	58 405	25.7
District 1	282 720	91.5	71.2	335 500	22.7	1 270	39 011	79 145	39.2
District 2	304 135	88.1	60.1	269 800	10.3	1 055	28 986	56 236	22.3
District 3	287 426	88.8	66.2	203 400	4.3	881	25 630	52 172	20.2
District 4	257 759	90.5	65.1	164 800	3.4	769	21 391	48 691	16.1
District 5	296 537	89.2	62.2	176 500	4.3	754	24 078	46 009	15.8
District 6	315 952	85.0	65.5	232 600	10.2	914	29 351	54 049	21.6
District 7	338 106	93.9	50.2	417 400	34.7	1 178	44 711	70 596	34.4
District 8	279 687	90.6	70.6	277 300	15.6	1 073	32 796	71 033	33.6
District 9	283 913	94.3	53.9	324 000	24.9	1 099	33 887	61 060	30.0
District 10	282 065	91.4	57.9	218 100	4.2	993	26 301	54 735	21.1
WEST VIRGINIA	879 424	84.0	72.3	103 200	1.5	620	23 159	41 253	13.7
District 1	287 450	84.8	71.1	105 200	1.9	610	23 652	41 436	14.5
District 2	293 831	85.2	72.7	125 100	2.0	670	24 844	45 474	15.4
District 3	298 143	82.0	73.2	83 300	0.7	595	20 926	36 473	11.2
WISCONSIN	2 633 420	86.9	67.2	163 000	3.6	758	27 448	51 467	19.0
District 1	301 469	89.7	71.5	178 600	3.7	813	28 741	57 471	24.1
District 2	317 548	94.4	61.8	201 500	5.3	855	30 996	56 861	23.4
District 3	317 756	87.8	69.9	143 200	2.1	679	24 454	49 461	14.9
District 4	311 191	90.2	45.4	127 600	3.1	779	21 927	38 242	12.2
District 5	308 351	94.7	70.4	207 300	5.6	834	32 664	62 665	26.4
District 6	321 642	88.8	71.1	151 300	3.3	682	27 527	51 404	17.7
District 7	414 689	71.2	75.5	145 100	2.8	671	26 048	47 849	15.5
District 8	340 774	84.2	71.6	155 000	2.6	694	27 080	52 169	17.9
WYOMING	265 471	84.4	69.1	195 500	5.7	780	28 889	58 752	23.3
At Large	265 471	84.4	69.1	195 500	5.7	780	28 889	58 752	23.3

1. Specified owner-occupied units. 2. Specified renter-occupied units.

STATE District	Poverty, 2013			Civilian labor force, 2013			Civilian employment,[2] 2013				Persons under age 65 with no health insurance, 2013 (percent)	Social Security beneficiaries, December 2013		Supplemental Security Income recipients, December 2013
					Unemployment			Percent						
	Persons below poverty level (percent)	Families below poverty level (percent)	Percent of households receiving food stamps in past 12 months	Total	Total	Rate[1]	Total	Management, business, science and arts occupations	Service, sales, and office	Construction and production		Number	Rate[3]	
	49	50	51	52	53	54	55	56	57	58	59	60	61	62
TEXAS—Cont'd														
District 25	12.1	8.2	7.8	345 171	24 708	7.2	320 463	43.7	37.2	19.0	16.8	114 108	156.0	11 596
District 26	8.0	5.3	6.8	416 548	22 215	5.3	394 333	43.8	41.1	15.1	14.6	80 078	104.2	5 876
District 27	17.3	13.2	14.7	347 244	18 454	5.3	328 790	25.5	46.6	27.9	23.8	132 709	185.7	23 571
District 28	25.9	22.5	25.5	303 949	25 119	8.3	278 830	25.0	48.6	26.5	34.2	103 238	142.6	31 583
District 29	28.3	25.1	22.3	342 114	31 752	9.3	310 362	15.2	41.6	43.2	38.9	72 029	98.7	20 708
District 30	24.8	20.8	23.3	352 730	29 851	8.5	322 879	27.8	45.6	26.7	29.4	96 875	129.8	30 644
District 31	10.8	7.8	8.8	379 440	30 341	8.0	349 099	40.5	41.2	18.2	16.8	101 329	132.0	10 943
District 32	14.4	10.9	10.0	400 097	28 578	7.1	371 519	43.5	39.8	16.7	23.3	90 780	126.3	11 466
District 33	29.4	26.7	27.8	341 717	35 082	10.3	306 635	15.3	44.6	40.2	41.1	75 771	104.4	23 015
District 34	30.6	26.2	27.4	281 650	29 170	10.4	252 480	28.2	46.4	25.4	35.7	109 899	152.6	38 116
District 35	24.0	18.9	20.8	381 795	29 148	7.6	352 647	25.8	49.6	24.6	27.7	95 359	126.7	26 275
District 36	14.5	10.8	13.5	332 554	30 153	9.1	302 401	31.6	38.8	29.6	24.3	123 824	174.4	16 843
UTAH	12.7	9.3	9.0	1 405 334	77 882	5.5	1 327 452	37.0	42.0	21.0	15.4	356 984	123.1	31 093
District 1	11.2	8.6	8.7	345 673	18 563	5.4	327 110	35.7	39.5	24.8	12.5	85 872	119.1	7 491
District 2	14.2	10.2	9.7	345 846	18 983	5.5	326 863	36.2	43.5	20.4	18.4	105 767	147.8	9 203
District 3	13.4	9.6	8.5	338 409	18 931	5.6	319 478	40.8	42.8	16.3	14.1	84 666	117.8	6 595
District 4	11.9	8.9	8.9	375 406	21 405	5.7	354 001	35.7	42.1	22.2	16.7	80 679	108.2	7 804
VERMONT	12.3	7.8	14.8	342 695	19 796	5.8	322 899	39.5	39.8	20.7	8.6	138 418	220.9	15 741
At Large	12.3	7.8	14.8	342 695	19 796	5.8	322 899	39.5	39.8	20.7	8.6	138 418	220.9	15 741
VIRGINIA	11.7	8.4	10.0	4 269 122	282 457	6.6	3 986 665	42.2	40.0	17.7	14.0	1 384 419	167.6	153 632
District 1	8.9	6.3	6.8	384 400	23 958	6.2	360 442	42.0	40.6	17.4	12.5	121 066	158.5	8 127
District 2	10.8	7.6	8.9	372 834	25 066	6.7	347 768	37.8	42.7	19.5	14.5	110 865	150.1	10 347
District 3	23.8	19.3	19.3	368 683	37 408	10.1	331 275	30.6	48.0	21.4	19.3	130 252	175.4	30 049
District 4	12.5	9.4	11.9	362 215	32 557	9.0	329 658	36.6	41.4	22.1	13.1	130 506	176.5	14 993
District 5	15.1	9.8	12.3	349 676	20 880	6.0	328 796	37.4	39.5	23.0	13.4	172 435	234.4	18 936
District 6	15.2	10.0	11.6	366 988	26 594	7.2	340 394	34.1	43.7	22.2	15.6	160 945	218.9	16 013
District 7	7.4	5.2	7.2	409 321	25 772	6.3	383 549	44.0	40.7	15.3	12.3	130 885	172.0	8 177
District 8	7.7	5.4	4.9	465 374	21 672	4.7	443 702	56.7	33.4	9.9	14.5	72 024	93.0	7 732
District 9	18.1	12.9	15.5	321 604	22 513	7.0	299 091	30.2	42.5	27.3	14.8	195 511	271.0	25 623
District 10	4.6	3.3	4.6	424 360	23 010	5.4	401 350	53.1	34.7	12.2	10.2	86 016	110.0	5 814
District 11	6.5	4.9	6.0	443 667	23 027	5.2	420 640	51.1	37.6	11.4	14.5	73 914	96.5	7 821
WASHINGTON	14.1	9.5	14.8	3 507 113	277 682	7.9	3 229 431	38.5	40.5	20.9	16.1	1 197 824	171.8	150 239
District 1	9.2	5.7	10.0	375 541	25 063	6.7	350 478	46.1	36.0	17.9	12.5	105 952	149.3	8 639
District 2	14.4	9.9	15.1	357 481	29 299	8.2	328 182	34.5	42.7	22.8	15.3	121 740	175.9	13 493
District 3	13.9	9.7	16.6	321 178	30 083	9.4	291 095	32.5	42.2	25.3	15.8	143 830	207.9	16 863
District 4	17.9	14.2	21.9	322 395	28 733	8.9	293 662	27.4	38.9	33.7	24.8	116 217	166.4	17 323
District 5	17.8	10.6	17.9	316 023	26 050	8.2	289 973	35.2	44.6	20.1	16.7	137 829	202.2	18 858
District 6	14.7	9.0	15.3	316 528	27 613	8.7	288 915	35.6	43.3	21.0	17.8	152 341	223.3	18 474
District 7	12.2	6.7	8.6	436 948	25 472	5.8	411 476	54.9	35.0	10.2	12.1	101 696	143.9	12 850
District 8	11.4	7.7	12.0	358 358	24 869	6.9	333 489	37.4	39.5	23.1	13.4	100 828	143.7	8 892
District 9	15.4	11.2	16.3	373 101	26 711	7.2	346 390	40.2	41.6	18.2	18.1	98 089	139.0	19 029
District 10	14.8	10.8	16.2	329 560	33 789	10.3	295 771	33.4	44.3	22.3	14.4	119 302	170.1	15 818
WEST VIRGINIA	18.5	13.5	16.2	822 237	69 927	8.5	752 310	30.9	43.3	25.8	16.8	460 494	248.3	79 136
District 1	17.1	11.7	12.4	289 689	20 941	7.2	268 748	31.6	42.1	26.2	16.0	144 670	234.2	20 932
District 2	15.2	10.5	14.4	292 364	26 553	9.1	265 811	32.1	42.6	25.3	15.9	149 117	237.8	21 800
District 3	23.2	18.2	21.8	240 184	22 433	9.3	217 751	28.5	45.7	25.8	18.6	166 707	273.5	36 404
WISCONSIN	13.5	9.2	13.3	3 072 549	199 318	6.5	2 873 231	33.9	40.7	25.5	10.6	1 134 358	197.5	116 715
District 1	11.8	8.1	12.5	374 523	31 448	8.4	343 075	34.4	40.0	25.7	10.6	139 143	196.1	13 131
District 2	14.1	7.7	10.9	418 739	21 516	5.1	397 223	43.0	38.2	18.9	9.6	122 534	167.0	11 390
District 3	13.9	8.0	12.2	382 410	22 673	5.9	359 737	31.0	41.6	27.5	11.0	150 300	211.2	12 638
District 4	26.1	21.8	28.7	358 969	37 340	10.4	321 629	31.6	46.0	22.4	15.8	113 522	158.6	39 431
District 5	8.7	5.9	8.7	400 278	20 222	5.1	380 056	38.6	40.1	21.3	7.5	141 254	195.3	7 010
District 6	10.2	6.7	10.6	378 499	19 315	5.1	359 184	29.4	39.4	31.2	8.6	150 763	211.4	9 771
District 7	12.3	8.8	12.3	371 602	23 325	6.3	348 277	30.0	40.8	29.2	11.8	171 395	239.6	12 392
District 8	11.1	8.2	10.9	387 529	23 479	6.1	364 050	31.4	40.3	28.3	9.9	145 447	201.8	10 952
WYOMING	10.9	8.4	5.9	310 967	15 775	5.1	295 192	34.1	39.1	26.8	15.4	99 134	170.1	6 888
At Large	10.9	8.4	5.9	310 967	15 775	5.1	295 192	34.1	39.1	26.8	15.4	99 134	170.1	6 888

1. Percent of civilian labor force. 2. Persons 16 years old and over. 3. Per 1,000 resident population estimated in the 2013 American Community Survey.

Table E. Congressional Districts 113th Congress — **Agriculture**

STATE / District	Agriculture, 2012									
		Land in farms			Value of products sold				Government payments	
	Number of farms	Acres	Average size of farm (acres)	Irrigated land (acres)	Total ($1,000)	Average per farm (dollars)	Percent from crops	Percent from livestock and poultry products	Total ($1,000)	Average per farm receiving payments (dollars)
	63	64	65	66	67	68	69	70	71	72
TEXAS—Cont'd										
District 25	13 361	3 908 812	293	11 239	538 906	40 334	39.2	60.8	9 765	5 694
District 26	3 302	378 816	115	3 483	144 039	43 622	28.8	71.2	1 060	4 400
District 27	12 248	4 802 357	392	136 796	1 227 580	100 227	54.0	46.0	42 540	14 347
District 28	7 794	5 145 001	660	79 700	406 827	52 197	36.3	63.7	11 471	7 439
District 29	100	3 742	37	9	1 099	10 995	81.8	18.3	0	0
District 30	387	38 849	100	1 212	24 876	64 280	95.4	4.6	135	4 657
District 31	4 996	953 480	191	4 435	212 132	42 460	62.2	37.8	5 772	5 305
District 32	220	28 677	130	58	9 079	41 269	40.2	59.8	108	6 012
District 33	107	8 001	75	27	7 499	70 083	96.0	3.9	2	300
District 34	8 326	4 632 760	556	174 856	931 238	111 847	44.1	55.9	17 803	9 825
District 35	1 133	250 124	221	1 547	39 002	34 423	73.0	27.0	873	6 616
District 36	6 888	1 108 089	161	25 421	119 925	17 411	53.7	46.3	5 295	17 534
UTAH	18 027	10 974 396	609	1 104 257	1 816 147	100 746	31.6	68.4	23 898	8 584
District 1	7 334	5 425 669	740	500 075	568 013	77 449	37.1	62.9	12 472	9 805
District 2	4 911	2 536 753	517	404 236	897 850	182 824	24.8	75.2	6 598	7 558
District 3	3 651	2 577 805	706	127 071	205 267	56 222	42.2	57.8	2 877	6 851
District 4	2 131	434 169	204	72 875	145 017	68 051	37.3	62.7	1 950	8 906
VERMONT	7 338	1 251 713	171	3 565	776 105	105 765	22.9	77.1	13 930	8 929
At Large	7 338	1 251 713	171	3 565	776 105	105 765	22.9	77.1	13 930	8 929
VIRGINIA	46 030	8 302 444	180	68 651	3 753 287	81 540	36.2	63.8	82 318	7 719
District 1	2 338	522 532	223	10 540	215 529	92 185	87.3	12.7	8 842	14 495
District 2	567	157 025	277	11 243	280 070	493 951	48.3	51.7	4 246	19 478
District 3	369	104 848	284	3 470	64 905	175 894	81.9	18.1	2 661	19 423
District 4	3 003	766 641	255	7 971	473 780	157 769	61.3	38.7	19 465	14 735
District 5	12 069	2 441 870	202	15 716	613 975	50 872	40.7	59.3	18 392	5 929
District 6	8 195	1 297 577	158	11 153	1 271 186	155 117	9.9	90.1	7 944	6 576
District 7	3 265	523 003	160	4 983	242 528	74 281	68.7	31.3	5 367	10 713
District 8	33	1 227	37	15	1 611	48 818	D	D	D	D
District 9	13 389	2 166 935	162	2 506	487 735	36 428	17.9	82.1	14 226	4 245
District 10	2 775	318 962	115	1 050	100 953	36 379	61.2	38.8	1 150	5 478
District 11	27	1 824	68	4	1 014	37 546	D	D	D	D
WASHINGTON	37 249	14 748 107	396	1 633 571	9 120 749	244 859	71.2	28.8	159 269	22 014
District 1	3 651	215 635	59	44 402	568 090	155 598	45.9	54.1	4 361	10 794
District 2	1 660	124 240	75	19 235	251 457	151 480	61.8	38.2	1 391	10 303
District 3	5 698	888 616	156	53 077	379 033	66 520	44.4	55.6	5 823	11 418
District 4	10 221	7 236 719	708	1 287 721	6 100 198	596 830	73.0	27.0	64 825	25 302
District 5	7 733	5 665 632	733	112 588	1 151 558	148 915	92.9	7.1	79 599	24 364
District 6	2 533	197 926	78	15 406	86 682	34 221	D	D	390	4 432
District 7	196	2 185	11	195	D	D	D	D	38	5 463
District 8	3 967	349 188	88	95 859	413 543	104 246	70.5	29.5	2 648	11 220
District 9	115	1 916	17	282	D	D	D	D	29	4 767
District 10	1 475	66 050	45	4 806	130 983	88 802	43.3	56.7	166	8 316
WEST VIRGINIA	21 489	3 606 674	168	2 064	806 775	37 544	17.2	82.8	7 034	3 203
District 1	8 458	1 305 274	154	D	D	D	D	D	1 923	3 162
District 2	7 563	1 366 085	181	1 238	473 385	62 592	16.2	83.8	3 203	3 632
District 3	5 468	935 315	171	D	D	D	D	D	1 909	2 703
WISCONSIN	69 754	14 568 926	209	421 721	11 744 476	168 370	39.2	60.8	237 304	6 093
District 1	2 667	563 204	211	12 892	485 265	181 952	D	D	D	D
District 2	9 962	2 127 676	214	42 496	1 553 585	155 951	38.1	61.9	44 895	6 876
District 3	19 895	4 295 732	216	218 340	2 936 452	147 597	45.4	54.6	61 572	5 263
District 4	37	455	12	23	4 098	110 746	D	D	D	D
District 5	3 462	635 541	184	11 247	611 624	176 668	43.5	56.5	12 337	6 184
District 6	8 882	1 813 360	204	52 490	1 824 851	205 455	38.0	62.0	34 602	6 821
District 7	16 175	3 418 268	211	70 755	2 438 450	150 754	36.2	63.8	39 552	5 465
District 8	8 674	1 714 690	198	13 478	1 890 152	217 910	28.1	71.9	32 326	6 516
WYOMING	11 736	30 363 641	2 587	1 435 710	1 689 416	143 952	26.0	74.0	28 146	10 027
At Large	11 736	30 363 641	2 587	1 435 710	1 689 416	143 952	26.0	74.0	28 146	10 027

APPENDIX A
GEOGRAPHIC CONCEPTS AND CODES

GEOGRAPHIC AREAS COVERED

County and City Extra presents data for states (Table A), states and counties (Table B), metropolitan areas (Table C), cities with populations of 25,000 or more in 2010 (Table D), and congressional districts (Table E).

STATES AND COUNTIES

Data are presented for each of the 50 states, the District of Columbia, and the United States as a whole. The states are arranged alphabetically, and counties in Table B are arranged alphabetically within each state. Data are presented for 3,143 counties and county equivalents.

County equivalents

In Louisiana, the primary divisions of the state are known as parishes rather than counties. In Alaska, the county equivalents are the organized boroughs, together with the census areas that were developed for general statistical purposes by the state of Alaska and the U.S. Census Bureau. Four states—Maryland, Missouri, Nevada, and Virginia—have one or more incorporated places that are legally independent of any county and thus constitute primary divisions of their states. Within each state, independent cities are listed alphabetically following the list of counties. The District of Columbia is not divided into counties or county equivalents—data for the entire district are presented as a county equivalent. New York City contains five counties: Bronx, Kings, New York, Queens, and Richmond.

County changes since the 2010 census

- The independent city of Bedford, Virginia changed to town status and was added to Bedford County effective July 1, 2013. Both entities are retained in this book because most data sources have not made the change.

County changes since the 2000 census

- Broomfield County, CO, was created from parts of Adams, Boulder, Jefferson, and Weld Counties, effective November 15, 2001. The boundaries of Broomfield County reflect the boundaries of Broomfield city legally in effect on that date.
- Clifton Forge city, VA, formerly an independent city, became a town within Alleghany County, effective July 1, 2001.
- Effective June 20, 2007, the Skagway-Hoonah-Angoon Census Area in Alaska was divided into the Skagway Municipality and the Hoonah-Angoon Census Area.
- In May and June 2008, the Wrangell-Petersburg and Prince of Wales-Outer Ketchikan Census Areas were dissolved and replaced by Wrangell City and Borough, Petersburg Census Area, and Prince of Wales Census Area. Some territory from the Prince of Wales Outer Ketchikan Census Area became part of the existing Ketchikan Gateway Borough.

METROPOLITAN AREAS

Table C presents data for 381 metropolitan statistical areas and 31 metropolitan divisions, which are located within the 11 largest metropolitan statistical areas. The metropolitan statistical areas are listed alphabetically, and the metropolitan divisions are listed alphabetically under the metropolitan statistical area of which they are components.

The U.S. Office of Management and Budget (OMB) defines metropolitan and micropolitan statistical areas according to published standards. The major purpose of defining these areas is to enable all U.S. government agencies to use the same geographic definitions in tabulating and publishing data. The general concept of a metropolitan or micropolitan statistical area is that of a core area containing a substantial population nucleus, together with adjacent communities that have a high degree of economic and social integration with the core.

New delineations of these Core Based Statistical Areas (CBSAs) based on the 2010 census were released in February 2013, and many federal agencies have started to use these new definitions. Table C in this book uses these new delineations for metropolitan areas and metropolitan divisions. Micropolitan areas are not included in Table C. Many of the data items in Table C were released under the old scheme but have been aggregated from county data to the newly defined metropolitan areas. This results in a higher level of data suppression for those items. Appendix B lists the metropolitan areas and metropolitan divisions with their component counties and 2010 census populations. Appendix C lists the new metropolitan and micropolitan areas, together with their 2010 census populations and their 2014 estimated populations.

Standard definitions of metropolitan areas were first issued in 1949 by the Bureau of the Budget (the predecessor of OMB), under the designation ''standard metropolitan area'' (SMA). The term was changed to ''standard metropolitan statistical area'' (SMSA) in 1959, and to ''metropolitan statistical area'' (MSA) in 1983. The term ''metropolitan area'' (MA) was adopted in 1990 and referred collectively to metropolitan statistical areas (MSAs), consolidated metropolitan statistical areas (CMSAs), and primary metropolitan statistical areas (PMSAs). The term ''core based statistical area'' (CBSA) became effective in 2000 and refers collectively to metropolitan and micropolitan statistical areas.

The 2010 standards provide that each CBSA must contain at least one urban area of 10,000 or more population. Each metropolitan statistical area must have at least one urbanized area of 50,000 or more inhabitants. Each micropolitan statistical area must have at least one urban cluster of at least 10,000 but less than 50,000 people.

Under the standards, a metro area contains a core urban area of 50,000 or more population, and a micro area contains an urban core of at least 10,000 (but less than 50,000) population. Each metro or micro area consists of one or more counties and includes the counties containing the core urban area, as well as any adjacent counties that have a high degree of social and economic integration (as measured by commuting to work) with the urban core.

If specified criteria are met, a metropolitan statistical area containing a single core with a population of 2.5 million or more may be subdivided to form smaller groupings of counties referred to as ''metropolitan divisions.''

As of February 28, 2013, there were 381 metropolitan statistical areas and 541 micropolitan statistical areas in the United States. Table C includes the 381 metropolitan statistical areas and the 31 metropolitan divisions. The metropolitan areas and metropolitan divisions are listed in Appendix B with their 2010 census population counts. The metropolitan areas, metropolitan divisions, and micropolitan areas are listed in Appendix C with their 2010 census populations and their 2014 estimated populations.

The largest city in each metropolitan or micropolitan statistical area is designated a ''principal city.'' Additional cities qualify if specified requirements are met concerning population size and employment. The title of each metropolitan or micropolitan statistical area consists of the names of up to three of its principal cities and the name of each state into which the metropolitan or micropolitan statistical area extends. Titles of metropolitan divisions also typically are based on principal city names, but in certain cases consist of county names. The principal city need not be an incorporated place if it meets the requirements of population size and employment. Usually such a principal city is a census designated place in decennial census data, but it is not included in most other data sources and is not in Table D (cities) in this volume.

In view of the importance of cities and towns in New England, the 2010 standards also provide for a set of geographic areas that are defined using cities and towns in the six New England states. These New England city and town areas (NECTAs) are not included in this volume.

Appendix B lists the 381 metropolitan statistical areas, together with their component metropolitan divisions, where appropriate, the component counties of each area, and their 2010 census populations Appendix C provides the same information for the 381 metropolitan areas, and it also includes the 541micropolitan statistical areas. Maps showing the metropolitan and micropolitan areas within each state can be found in Appendix D.

CITIES

Table D presents data for 1,437 cities with 2010 census populations of 25,000 or more. Corresponding data for states are also provided. The states are arranged alphabetically, and the cities are ordered alphabetically within each state.

As used in this volume, the term *city* refers to places that have been incorporated as cities, boroughs, towns, or villages under the laws of their respective states. Towns in the New England states and New York are treated as minor civil divisions (MCDs) and are not included in the cities database. For Hawaii, data for the census designated places (CDPs) are included in the cities table, since the Census Bureau does not recognize any incorporated places in Hawaii. CDPs are delineated by the Census Bureau, in cooperation with states and localities, as statistical counterparts of incorporated places for purposes of the decennial census. CDPs comprise densely settled concentrations of population that are identifiable by name but are not legally incorporated as places.

Appendix E lists the 1,437 cities followed by the county where each city is located. If a city includes portions of more than one county, the population in each part is specified.

A consolidated city is an incorporated place that has combined its government functions with a county or subcounty entity but contains one or more other semi-independent incorporated places that continue to function as local governments within the consolidated government. Each consolidated city contains a core city, the area of a consolidated city not included in another separately incorporated place. The census geographic term for this core is the ''balance'' of the consolidated city. Thus the ''balance'' is essentially the core city of the consolidated government. This volume includes the consolidated city data where possible, but some data sources include numbers only for the ''balance,'' and others do not specify which entity is represented.

Consolidated cities included in this volume are Milford, CT; Athens-Clarke County, GA; Augusta-Richmond County, GA; Indianapolis, IN; Louisville-Jefferson County, KY; Butte-Silver Bow, MT; and Nashville-Davidson, TN.

Appendix E lists these seven consolidated cities, followed by the component places and their 2010 census populations.

On January 1, 2014, Macon, Georgia consolidated with Bibb county. A small portion of Macon that was in Jones county was de-annexed. The total population for 2014 is the only data yet available for the new entity. This book includes Macon city, but the 2014 population is for Macon-Bibb County.

CONGRESSIONAL DISTRICTS

The congressional districts shown in this volume are the districts used for the election of the 113th Congress, which convened in January 2013. These are the districts that were established following the 2010 Census and are based on population data from that census. Data are shown for the 435 regular districts plus the District of Columbia, which has a non-voting delegate, but no representative. Corresponding data for each state also are included. States are listed alphabetically and districts numerically within each state. A map showing congressional districts for the 113th Congress is included in Appendix D.

GEOGRAPHIC CODES

Tables A, B, C, and D provide, in one or more columns at the beginning of the table, a geographic code or codes for each area.

In Table B (states and counties), a five-digit state and county code is given for each state and county. The first two digits indicate the state; the remaining three represent the county. Within each state, the counties are listed in order, beginning with 001, with even numbers usually omitted. Independent cities follow the counties and begin with the number 510. In the second column of Table B, a five-digit core based statistical area (CBSA) code is given for those counties that are within metropolitan and micropolitan areas. In Table A, a two-digit state code is provided. The state code is a sequential numbering, with some gaps, of the states and the District of Columbia in alphabetical order from Alabama (01) to Wyoming (56).

These codes have been established by the U.S. government as Federal Information Processing Standards and are often referred to as *FIPS codes*. They are used by U.S. government agencies and many other organizations for data presentation. The codes are provided in this volume for use in matching the data given here with other data sources in which counties are identified by FIPS code. The metro area codes will also enable the user to identify the metro area of which a county is a component. Table C (metropolitan areas) provides the same metro area codes for each metropolitan area, as well as metropolitan division codes where appropriate.

Table D (cities) provides, in the first column, a seven-digit state and place code. The first two digits identify the state and are the same as the FIPS codes described above. The remaining five digits are the place FIPS codes established by the U.S. government.

INDEPENDENT CITIES

The following independent cities are not included in any county; their data are presented separately in this volume.

MARYLAND

Baltimore (separate from Baltimore County)

MISSOURI

St. Louis (separate from St. Louis County)

NEVADA

Carson City

VIRGINIA

Alexandria
Bedford[1]
Bristol
Buena Vista
Charlottesville
Chesapeake
Colonial Heights
Covington
Danville
Emporia
Fairfax
Falls Church
Franklin
Fredericksburg
Galax
Hampton
Harrisonburg
Hopewell
Lexington
Lynchburg
Manassas
Manassas Park
Martinsville
Newport News
Norfolk
Norton
Petersburg
Poquoson
Portsmouth
Radford
Richmond
Roanoke
Salem
Staunton
Suffolk
Virginia Beach
Waynesboro
Williamsburg
Winchester

[1] Bedford city became a town within Bedford county on July 1, 2013. Most of the data in this book, however, continues to reference the independent city.

COUNTY TYPE

Table B (states and counties) provides, in the third column, a *county type* code that identifies each county by its metropolitan/nonmetropolitan status and its size. These are the "rural-urban continuum codes" developed by the Economic Research Service of the U.S. Department of Agriculture.

The 2003 rural-urban continuum codes form a classification scheme that distinguishes metropolitan counties by size and nonmetropolitan counties by degree of urbanization and proximity to metro areas. The standard OMB metro and nonmetro categories have been subdivided into three metro and six nonmetro categories, resulting in a nine-part county codification. This scheme was originally developed in 1974. The codes were updated in 1983 and 1993, and slightly revised in 1988. The 1988 revision was first published in 1990. This scheme allows researchers to break county data into finer residential groups, beyond metro and nonmetro, particularly for the analysis of trends in nonmetro areas that are related to population density and metro influence. The 2003 rural-urban continuum codes are not directly comparable with the codes from previous years because of the new methodology used in developing the 2003 metropolitan areas.

Metropolitan counties

1. Counties in metro areas of 1 million population or more.
2. Counties in metro areas of 250,000 to 1 million population.
3. Counties in metro areas of fewer than 250,000 population.

Nonmetropolitan counties

4. Urban population of 20,000 or more, adjacent to a metro area.
5. Urban population of 20,000 or more, not adjacent to a metro area.
6. Urban population of 2,500 to 19,999, adjacent to a metro area.
7. Urban population of 2,500 to 19,999, not adjacent to a metro area.
8. Completely rural or less than 2,500 urban population, adjacent to a metro area.
9. Completely rural or less than 2,500 urban population, not adjacent to a metro area.

APPENDIX B
METROPOLITAN STATISTICAL AREAS, METROPOLITAN DIVISIONS, AND COMPONENTS (as defined February 2013)

Core based statistical area	State/ County FIPS code	Title and Geographic Components	2010 Census Population
10180		Abilene, TX	165 252
	48 059	Callahan County	13 544
	48 253	Jones County	20 202
	48 441	Taylor County	131 506
10420		Akron, OH	703 200
	39 133	Portage County	161 419
	39 153	Summit County	541 781
10500		Albany, GA	157 308
	13 007	Baker County	3 451
	13 095	Dougherty County	94 565
	13 177	Lee County	28 298
	13 273	Terrell County	9 315
	13 321	Worth County	21 679
10540		Albany, OR	116 672
	41 043	Linn County	116 672
10580		Albany-Schenectady-Troy, NY	870 716
	36 001	Albany County	304 204
	36 083	Rensselaer County	159 429
	36 091	Saratoga County	219 607
	36 093	Schenectady County	154 727
	36 095	Schoharie County	32 749
10740		Albuquerque, NM	887 077
	35 001	Bernalillo County	662 564
	35 043	Sandoval County	131 561
	35 057	Torrance County	16 383
	35 061	Valencia County	76 569
10780		Alexandria, LA	153 922
	22 043	Grant Parish	22 309
	22 079	Rapides Parish	131 613
10900		Allentown-Bethlehem-Easton, PA-NJ	821 173
	34 041	Warren County	108 692
	42 025	Carbon County	65 249
	42 077	Lehigh County	349 497
	42 095	Northampton County	297 735
11020		Altoona, PA	127 089
	42 013	Blair County	127 089
11100		Amarillo, TX	251 933
	48 011	Armstrong County	1 901
	48 065	Carson County	6 182
	48 359	Oldham County	2 052
	48 375	Potter County	121 073
	48 381	Randall County	120 725
11180		Ames, IA	89 542
	19 169	Story County	89 542
11260		Anchorage, AK	380 821
	02 020	Anchorage Municipality	291 826
	02 170	Matanuska-Susitna Borough	88 995
11460		Ann Arbor, MI	344 791
	26 161	Washtenaw County	344 791
11500		Anniston-Oxford-Jacksonville, AL	118 572
	01 015	Calhoun County	118 572
11540		Appleton, WI	225 666
	55 015	Calumet County	48 971
	55 087	Outagamie County	176 695
11700		Asheville, NC	424 858
	37 021	Buncombe County	238 318
	37 087	Haywood County	59 036
	37 089	Henderson County	106 740
	37 115	Madison County	20 764
12020		Athens-Clarke County, GA	192 541
	13 059	Clarke County	116 714
	13 195	Madison County	28 120
	13 219	Oconee County	32 808
	13 221	Oglethorpe County	14 899
12060		Atlanta-Sandy Springs-Roswell, GA	5 286 728
	13 013	Barrow County	69 367
	13 015	Bartow County	100 157
	13 035	Butts County	23 655
	13 045	Carroll County	110 527
	13 057	Cherokee County	214 346
	13 063	Clayton County	259 424
	13 067	Cobb County	688 078
	13 077	Coweta County	127 317
	13 085	Dawson County	22 330
	13 089	DeKalb County	691 893
	13 097	Douglas County	132 403
	13 113	Fayette County	106 567
	13 117	Forsyth County	175 511
	13 121	Fulton County	920 581
	13 135	Gwinnett County	805 321
	13 143	Haralson County	28 780
	13 149	Heard County	11 834
	13 151	Henry County	203 922
	13 159	Jasper County	13 900
	13 171	Lamar County	18 317
	13 199	Meriwether County	21 992
	13 211	Morgan County	17 868
	13 217	Newton County	99 958
	13 223	Paulding County	142 324
	13 227	Pickens County	29 431
	13 231	Pike County	17 869
	13 247	Rockdale County	85 215
	13 255	Spalding County	64 073
	13 297	Walton County	83 768
12100		Atlantic City-Hammonton, NJ	274 549
	34 001	Atlantic County	274 549
12220		Auburn-Opelika, AL	140 247
	01 081	Lee County	140 247
12260		Augusta-Richmond County, GA-SC	564 873
	13 033	Burke County	23 316
	13 073	Columbia County	124 053
	13 181	Lincoln County	7 996
	13 189	McDuffie County	21 875
	13 245	Richmond County	200 549
	45 003	Aiken County	160 099
	45 037	Edgefield County	26 985

Metropolitan Statistical Areas, Metropolitan Divisions, and Components (as defined February 2013)–*Continued*

Core based statistical area	State/ County FIPS code	Title and Geographic Components	2010 Census Population
12420		Austin-Round Rock, TX	1716 289
	48 021	Bastrop County	74 171
	48 055	Caldwell County	38 066
	48 209	Hays County	157 107
	48 453	Travis County	1024 266
	48 491	Williamson County	422 679
12540		Bakersfield, CA	839 631
	06 029	Kern County	839 631
12580		Baltimore-Columbia-Towson, MD	2710 489
	24 003	Anne Arundel County	537 656
	24 005	Baltimore County	805 029
	24 013	Carroll County	167 134
	24 025	Harford County	244 826
	24 027	Howard County	287 085
	24 035	Queen Anne's County	47 798
	24 510	Baltimore city	620 961
12620		Bangor, ME	153 923
	23 019	Penobscot County	153 923
12700		Barnstable Town, MA	215 888
	25 001	Barnstable County	215 888
12940		Baton Rouge, LA	802 484
	22 005	Ascension Parish	107 215
	22 033	East Baton Rouge Parish	440 171
	22 037	East Feliciana Parish	20 267
	22 047	Iberville Parish	33 387
	22 063	Livingston Parish	128 026
	22 077	Pointe Coupee Parish	22 802
	22 091	St. Helena Parish	11 203
	22 121	West Baton Rouge Parish	23 788
	22 125	West Feliciana Parish	15 625
12980		Battle Creek, MI	136 146
	26 025	Calhoun County	136 146
13020		Bay City, MI	107 771
	26 017	Bay County	107 771
13140		Beaumont-Port Arthur, TX	403 190
	48 199	Hardin County	54 635
	48 245	Jefferson County	252 273
	48 351	Newton County	14 445
	48 361	Orange County	81 837
13220		Beckley, WV	124 898
	54 019	Fayette County	46 039
	54 081	Raleigh County	78 859
13380		Bellingham, WA	201 140
	53 073	Whatcom County	201 140
13460		Bend-Redmond, OR	157 733
	41 017	Deschutes County	157 733
13740		Billings, MT	158 934
	30 009	Carbon County	10 078
	30 037	Golden Valley County	884
	30 111	Yellowstone County	147 972
13780		Binghamton, NY	251 725
	36 007	Broome County	200 600
	36 107	Tioga County	51 125
13820		Birmingham-Hoover, AL	1128 047
	01 007	Bibb County	22 915
	01 009	Blount County	57 322
	01 021	Chilton County	43 643
	01 073	Jefferson County	658 466
	01 115	St. Clair County	83 593
	01 117	Shelby County	195 085
	01 127	Walker County	67 023
13900		Bismarck, ND	114 778
	38 015	Burleigh County	81 308
	38 059	Morton County	27 471
	38 065	Oliver County	1 846
	38 085	Sioux County	4 153
13980		Blacksburg-Christiansburg-Radford, VA	178 237
	51 063	Floyd County	15 279
	51 071	Giles County	17 286
	51 121	Montgomery County	94 392
	51 155	Pulaski County	34 872
	51 750	Radford city	16 408
14010		Bloomington, IL	186 133
	17 039	De Witt County	16 561
	17 113	McLean County	169 572
14020		Bloomington, IN	159 549
	18 105	Monroe County	137 974
	18 119	Owen County	21 575
14100		Bloomsburg-Berwick, PA	85 562
	42 037	Columbia County	67 295
	42 093	Montour County	18 267
14260		Boise City, ID	616 561
	16 001	Ada County	392 365
	16 015	Boise County	7 028
	16 027	Canyon County	188 923
	16 045	Gem County	16 719
	16 073	Owyhee County	11 526
14460		Boston-Cambridge-Newton, MA-NH	4552 402
		Boston, MA Div 14454	1887 792
	25 021	Norfolk County	670 850
	25 023	Plymouth County	494 919
	25 025	Suffolk County	722 023
		Cambridge-Newton-Framingham, MA Div 15764	2246 244
	25 009	Essex County	743 159
	25 017	Middlesex County	1503 085
		Rockingham County-Strafford County, NH Div 40484	418 366
	33 015	Rockingham County	295 223
	33 017	Strafford County	123 143
14500		Boulder, CO	294 567
	08 013	Boulder County	294 567

Metropolitan Statistical Areas, Metropolitan Divisions, and Components (as defined February 2013)–*Continued*

Core based statistical area	State/ County FIPS code	Title and Geographic Components	2010 Census Population
14540		Bowling Green, KY	158 599
	21 003	Allen County	19 956
	21 031	Butler County	12 690
	21 061	Edmonson County	12 161
	21 227	Warren County	113 792
14740		Bremerton-Silverdale, WA	251 133
	53 035	Kitsap County	251 133
14860		Bridgeport-Stamford-Norwalk, CT	916 829
	09 001	Fairfield County	916 829
15180		Brownsville-Harlingen, TX	406 220
	48 061	Cameron County	406 220
15260		Brunswick, GA	112 370
	13 025	Brantley County	18 411
	13 127	Glynn County	79 626
	13 191	McIntosh County	14 333
15380		Buffalo-Cheektowaga-Niagara Falls, NY	1135 509
	36 029	Erie County	919 040
	36 063	Niagara County	216 469
15500		Burlington, NC	151 131
	37 001	Alamance County	151 131
15540		Burlington-South Burlington, VT	211 261
	50 007	Chittenden County	156 545
	50 011	Franklin County	47 746
	50 013	Grand Isle County	6 970
15680		California-Lexington Park, MD	105 151
	24 037	St. Mary's County	105 151
15940		Canton-Massillon, OH	404 422
	39 019	Carroll County	28 836
	39 151	Stark County	375 586
15980		Cape Coral-Fort Myers, FL	618 754
	12 071	Lee County	618 754
16020		Cape Girardeau, MO-IL	96 275
	17 003	Alexander County	8 238
	29 017	Bollinger County	12 363
	29 031	Cape Girardeau County	75 674
16060		Carbondale-Marion, IL	126 575
	17 077	Jackson County	60 218
	17 199	Williamson County	66 357
16180		Carson City, NV	55 274
	32 510	Carson City	55 274
16220		Casper, WY	75 450
	56 025	Natrona County	75 450
16300		Cedar Rapids, IA	257 940
	19 011	Benton County	26 076
	19 105	Jones County	20 638
	19 113	Linn County	211 226
16540		Chambersburg-Waynesboro, PA	149 618
	42 055	Franklin County	149 618
16580		Champaign-Urbana, IL	231 891
	17 019	Champaign County	201 081
	17 053	Ford County	14 081
	17 147	Piatt County	16 729
16620		Charleston, WV	227 078
	54 005	Boone County	24 629
	54 015	Clay County	9 386
	54 039	Kanawha County	193 063
16700		Charleston-North Charleston, SC	664 607
	45 015	Berkeley County	177 843
	45 019	Charleston County	350 209
	45 035	Dorchester County	136 555
16740		Charlotte-Concord-Gastonia, NC-SC	2217 012
	37 025	Cabarrus County	178 011
	37 071	Gaston County	206 086
	37 097	Iredell County	159 437
	37 109	Lincoln County	78 265
	37 119	Mecklenburg County	919 628
	37 159	Rowan County	138 428
	37 179	Union County	201 292
	45 023	Chester County	33 140
	45 057	Lancaster County	76 652
	45 091	York County	226 073
16820		Charlottesville, VA	218 705
	51 003	Albemarle County	98 970
	51 029	Buckingham County	17 146
	51 065	Fluvanna County	25 691
	51 079	Greene County	18 403
	51 125	Nelson County	15 020
	51 540	Charlottesville city	43 475
16860		Chattanooga, TN-GA	528 143
	13 047	Catoosa County	63 942
	13 083	Dade County	16 633
	13 295	Walker County	68 756
	47 065	Hamilton County	336 463
	47 115	Marion County	28 237
	47 153	Sequatchie County	14 112
16940		Cheyenne, WY	91 738
	56 021	Laramie County	91 738

Metropolitan Statistical Areas, Metropolitan Divisions, and Components (as defined February 2013)–*Continued*

Core based statistical area	State/ County FIPS code	Title and Geographic Components	2010 Census Population
16980		Chicago-Naperville-Elgin, IL-IN-WI	9461 105
		Chicago-Naperville-Arlington Heights, IL Div 16974	7262 718
	17 031	Cook County	5194 675
	17 043	DuPage County	916 924
	17 063	Grundy County	50 063
	17 093	Kendall County	114 736
	17 111	McHenry County	308 760
	17 197	Will County	677 560
		Elgin, IL Div 20994	620 429
	17 037	DeKalb County	105 160
	17 089	Kane County	515 269
		Gary, IN Div 23844	708 070
	18 073	Jasper County	33 478
	18 089	Lake County	496 005
	18 111	Newton County	14 244
	18 127	Porter County	164 343
		Lake County-Kenosha County, IL-WI Div 29404	869 888
	17 097	Lake County	703 462
	55 059	Kenosha County	166 426
17020		Chico, CA	220 000
	06 007	Butte County	220 000
17140		Cincinnati, OH-KY-IN	2114 580
	18 029	Dearborn County	50 047
	18 115	Ohio County	6 128
	18 161	Union County	7 516
	21 015	Boone County	118 811
	21 023	Bracken County	8 488
	21 037	Campbell County	90 336
	21 077	Gallatin County	8 589
	21 081	Grant County	24 662
	21 117	Kenton County	159 720
	21 191	Pendleton County	14 877
	39 015	Brown County	44 846
	39 017	Butler County	368 130
	39 025	Clermont County	197 363
	39 061	Hamilton County	802 374
	39 165	Warren County	212 693
17300		Clarksville, TN-KY	260 625
	21 047	Christian County	73 955
	21 221	Trigg County	14 339
	47 125	Montgomery County	172 331
17420		Cleveland, TN	115 788
	47 011	Bradley County	98 963
	47 139	Polk County	16 825
17460		Cleveland-Elyria, OH	2077 240
	39 035	Cuyahoga County	1280 122
	39 055	Geauga County	93 389
	39 085	Lake County	230 041
	39 093	Lorain County	301 356
	39 103	Medina County	172 332
17660		Coeur d'Alene, ID	138 494
	16 055	Kootenai County	138 494

Core based statistical area	State/ County FIPS code	Title and Geographic Components	2010 Census Population
17780		College Station-Bryan, TX	228 660
	48 041	Brazos County	194 851
	48 051	Burleson County	17 187
	48 395	Robertson County	16 622
17820		Colorado Springs, CO	645 613
	08 041	El Paso County	622 263
	08 119	Teller County	23 350
17860		Columbia, MO	162 642
	29 019	Boone County	162 642
17900		Columbia, SC	767 598
	45 017	Calhoun County	15 175
	45 039	Fairfield County	23 956
	45 055	Kershaw County	61 697
	45 063	Lexington County	262 391
	45 079	Richland County	384 504
	45 081	Saluda County	19 875
17980		Columbus, GA-AL	294 865
	01 113	Russell County	52 947
	13 053	Chattahoochee County	11 267
	13 145	Harris County	32 024
	13 197	Marion County	8 742
	13 215	Muscogee County	189 885
18020		Columbus, IN	76 794
	18 005	Bartholomew County	76 794
18140		Columbus, OH	1901 974
	39 041	Delaware County	174 214
	39 045	Fairfield County	146 156
	39 049	Franklin County	1163 414
	39 073	Hocking County	29 380
	39 089	Licking County	166 492
	39 097	Madison County	43 435
	39 117	Morrow County	34 827
	39 127	Perry County	36 058
	39 129	Pickaway County	55 698
	39 159	Union County	52 300
18580		Corpus Christi, TX	428 185
	48 007	Aransas County	23 158
	48 355	Nueces County	340 223
	48 409	San Patricio County	64 804
18700		Corvallis, OR	85 579
	41 003	Benton County	85 579
18880		Crestview-Fort Walton Beach-Destin, FL	235 865
	12 091	Okaloosa County	180 822
	12 131	Walton County	55 043
19060		Cumberland, MD-WV	103 299
	24 001	Allegany County	75 087
	54 057	Mineral County	28 212

Metropolitan Statistical Areas, Metropolitan Divisions, and Components (as defined February 2013)–*Continued*

Core based statistical area	State/ County FIPS code	Title and Geographic Components	2010 Census Population
19100		Dallas-Fort Worth-Arlington, TX	6426 214
		Dallas-Plano-Irving, TX Div 19124	4230 520
	48 085	Collin County	782 341
	48 113	Dallas County	2368 139
	48 121	Denton County	662 614
	48 139	Ellis County	149 610
	48 231	Hunt County	86 129
	48 257	Kaufman County	103 350
	48 397	Rockwall County	78 337
		Fort Worth-Arlington, TX Div 23104	2195 694
	48 221	Hood County	51 182
	48 251	Johnson County	150 934
	48 367	Parker County	116 927
	48 425	Somervell County	8 490
	48 439	Tarrant County	1809 034
	48 497	Wise County	59 127
19140		Dalton, GA	142 227
	13 213	Murray County	39 628
	13 313	Whitfield County	102 599
19180		Danville, IL	81 625
	17 183	Vermilion County	81 625
19300		Daphne-Fairhope-Foley, AL	182 265
	01 003	Baldwin County	182 265
19340		Davenport-Moline-Rock Island, IA-IL	379 690
	17 073	Henry County	50 486
	17 131	Mercer County	16 434
	17 161	Rock Island County	147 546
	19 163	Scott County	165 224
19380		Dayton, OH	799 232
	39 057	Greene County	161 573
	39 109	Miami County	102 506
	39 113	Montgomery County	535 153
19460		Decatur, AL	153 829
	01 079	Lawrence County	34 339
	01 103	Morgan County	119 490
19500		Decatur, IL	110 768
	17 115	Macon County	110 768
19660		Deltona-Daytona Beach-Ormond Beach, FL	590 289
	12 035	Flagler County	95 696
	12 127	Volusia County	494 593
19740		Denver-Aurora-Lakewood, CO	2543 482
	08 001	Adams County	441 603
	08 005	Arapahoe County	572 003
	08 014	Broomfield County	55 889
	08 019	Clear Creek County	9 088
	08 031	Denver County	600 158
	08 035	Douglas County	285 465
	08 039	Elbert County	23 086
	08 047	Gilpin County	5 441
	08 059	Jefferson County	534 543
	08 093	Park County	16 206
19780		Des Moines-West Des Moines, IA	569 633
	19 049	Dallas County	66 135
	19 077	Guthrie County	10 954
	19 121	Madison County	15 679
	19 153	Polk County	430 640
	19 181	Warren County	46 225
19820		Detroit-Warren-Dearborn, MI	4296 250
		Detroit-Dearborn-Livonia, MI Div 19804	1820 584
	26 163	Wayne County	1820 584
		Warren-Troy-Farmington Hills, MI 47664	2475 666
	26 087	Lapeer County	88 319
	26 093	Livingston County	180 967
	26 099	Macomb County	840 978
	26 125	Oakland County	1202 362
	26 147	St. Clair County	163 040
20020		Dothan, AL	145 639
	01 061	Geneva County	26 790
	01 067	Henry County	17 302
	01 069	Houston County	101 547
20100		Dover, DE	162 310
	10 001	Kent County	162 310
20220		Dubuque, IA	93 653
	19 061	Dubuque County	93 653
20260		Duluth, MN-WI	279 771
	27 017	Carlton County	35 386
	27 137	St. Louis County	200 226
	55 031	Douglas County	44 159
20500		Durham-Chapel Hill, NC	504 357
	37 037	Chatham County	63 505
	37 063	Durham County	267 587
	37 135	Orange County	133 801
	37 145	Person County	39 464
20700		East Stroudsburg, PA	169 842
	42 089	Monroe County	169 842
20740		Eau Claire, WI	161 151
	55 017	Chippewa County	62 415
	55 035	Eau Claire County	98 736
20940		El Centro, CA	174 528
	06 025	Imperial County	174 528
21060		Elizabethtown-Fort Knox, KY	148 338
	21 093	Hardin County	105 543
	21 123	Larue County	14 193
	21 163	Meade County	28 602
21140		Elkhart-Goshen, IN	197 559
	18 039	Elkhart County	197 559
21300		Elmira, NY	88 830
	36 015	Chemung County	88 830
21340		El Paso, TX	804 123
	48 141	El Paso County	800 647
	48 229	Hudspeth County	3 476

Metropolitan Statistical Areas, Metropolitan Divisions, and Components (as defined February 2013)–*Continued*

Core based statistical area	State/ County FIPS code	Title and Geographic Components	2010 Census Population
21500		Erie, PA	280 566
	42 049	Erie County	280 566
21660		Eugene, OR	351 715
	41 039	Lane County	351 715
21780		Evansville, IN-KY	311 552
	18 129	Posey County	25 910
	18 163	Vanderburgh County	179 703
	18 173	Warrick County	59 689
	21 101	Henderson County	46 250
21820		Fairbanks, AK	97 581
	02 090	Fairbanks North Star Borough	97 581
22020		Fargo, ND-MN	208 777
	27 027	Clay County	58 999
	38 017	Cass County	149 778
22140		Farmington, NM	130 044
	35 045	San Juan County	130 044
22180		Fayetteville, NC	366 383
	37 051	Cumberland County	319 431
	37 093	Hoke County	46 952
22220		Fayetteville-Springdale-Rogers, AR-MO	463 204
	05 007	Benton County	221 339
	05 087	Madison County	15 717
	05 143	Washington County	203 065
	29 119	McDonald County	23 083
22380		Flagstaff, AZ	134 421
	04 005	Coconino County	134 421
22420		Flint, MI	425 790
	26 049	Genesee County	425 790
22500		Florence, SC	205 566
	45 031	Darlington County	68 681
	45 041	Florence County	136 885
22520		Florence-Muscle Shoals, AL	147 137
	01 033	Colbert County	54 428
	01 077	Lauderdale County	92 709
22540		Fond du Lac, WI	101 633
	55 039	Fond du Lac County	101 633
22660		Fort Collins, CO	299 630
	08 069	Larimer County	299 630
22900		Fort Smith, AR-OK	280 467
	05 033	Crawford County	61 948
	05 131	Sebastian County	125 744
	40 079	Le Flore County	50 384
	40 135	Sequoyah County	42 391
23060		Fort Wayne, IN	416 257
	18 003	Allen County	355 329
	18 179	Wells County	27 636
	18 183	Whitley County	33 292
23420		Fresno, CA	930 450
	06 019	Fresno County	930 450
23460		Gadsden, AL	104 430
	01 055	Etowah County	104 430
23540		Gainesville, FL	264 275
	12 001	Alachua County	247 336
	12 041	Gilchrist County	16 939
23580		Gainesville, GA	179 684
	13 139	Hall County	179 684
23900		Gettysburg, PA	101 407
	42 001	Adams County	101 407
24020		Glens Falls, NY	128 923
	36 113	Warren County	65 707
	36 115	Washington County	63 216
24140		Goldsboro, NC	122 623
	37 191	Wayne County	122 623
24220		Grand Forks, ND-MN	98 461
	27 119	Polk County	31 600
	38 035	Grand Forks County	66 861
24260		Grand Island, NE	81 850
	31 079	Hall County	58 607
	31 081	Hamilton County	9 124
	31 093	Howard County	6 274
	31 121	Merrick County	7 845
24300		Grand Junction, CO	146 723
	08 077	Mesa County	146 723
24340		Grand Rapids-Wyoming, MI	988 938
	26 015	Barry County	59 173
	26 081	Kent County	602 622
	26 117	Montcalm County	63 342
	26 139	Ottawa County	263 801
24420		Grants Pass, OR	82 713
	41 033	Josephine County	82 713
24500		Great Falls, MT	81 327
	30 013	Cascade County	81 327
24540		Greeley, CO	252 825
	08 123	Weld County	252 825
24580		Green Bay, WI	306 241
	55 009	Brown County	248 007
	55 061	Kewaunee County	20 574
	55 083	Oconto County	37 660
24660		Greensboro-High Point, NC	723 801
	37 081	Guilford County	488 406
	37 151	Randolph County	141 752
	37 157	Rockingham County	93 643
24780		Greenville, NC	168 148
	37 147	Pitt County	168 148

Metropolitan Statistical Areas, Metropolitan Divisions, and Components (as defined February 2013)–*Continued*

Core based statistical area	State/ County FIPS code	Title and Geographic Components	2010 Census Population
24860		Greenville-Anderson-Mauldin, SC	824 112
	45 007	Anderson County	187 126
	45 045	Greenville County	451 225
	45 059	Laurens County	66 537
	45 077	Pickens County	119 224
25060		Gulfport-Biloxi-Pascagoula, MS	370 702
	28 045	Hancock County	43 929
	28 047	Harrison County	187 105
	28 059	Jackson County	139 668
25180		Hagerstown-Martinsburg, MD-WV	251 599
	24 043	Washington County	147 430
	54 003	Berkeley County	104 169
25220		Hammond, LA	121 097
	22 105	Tangipahoa Parish	121 097
25260		Hanford-Corcoran, CA	152 982
	06 031	Kings County	152 982
25420		Harrisburg-Carlisle, PA	549 475
	42 041	Cumberland County	235 406
	42 043	Dauphin County	268 100
	42 099	Perry County	45 969
25500		Harrisonburg, VA	125 228
	51 165	Rockingham County	76 314
	51 660	Harrisonburg city	48 914
25540		Hartford-West Hartford-East Hartford, CT	1212 381
	09 003	Hartford County	894 014
	09 007	Middlesex County	165 676
	09 013	Tolland County	152 691
25620		Hattiesburg, MS	142 842
	28 035	Forrest County	74 934
	28 073	Lamar County	55 658
	28 111	Perry County	12 250
25860		Hickory-Lenoir-Morganton, NC	365 497
	37 003	Alexander County	37 198
	37 023	Burke County	90 912
	37 027	Caldwell County	83 029
	37 035	Catawba County	154 358
25940		Hilton Head Island-Bluffton-Beaufort, NC	187 010
	45 013	Beaufort County	162 233
	45 053	Jasper County	24 777
25980		Hinesville, GA	77 917
	13 179	Liberty County	63 453
	13 183	Long County	14 464
26140		Homosassa Springs, FL	141 236
	12 017	Citrus County	141 236
26300		Hot Springs, AR	96 024
	05 051	Garland County	96 024
26380		Houma-Thibodaux, LA	208 178
	22 057	Lafourche Parish	96 318
	22 109	Terrebonne Parish	111 860
26420		Houston-The Woodlands-Sugar Land, TX	5920 416
	48 015	Austin County	28 417
	48 039	Brazoria County	313 166
	48 071	Chambers County	35 096
	48 157	Fort Bend County	585 375
	48 167	Galveston County	291 309
	48 201	Harris County	4092 459
	48 291	Liberty County	75 643
	48 339	Montgomery County	455 746
	48 473	Waller County	43 205
26580		Huntington-Ashland, WV-KY-OH	364 908
	21 019	Boyd County	49 542
	21 089	Greenup County	36 910
	39 087	Lawrence County	62 450
	54 011	Cabell County	96 319
	54 043	Lincoln County	21 720
	54 079	Putnam County	55 486
	54 099	Wayne County	42 481
26620		Huntsville, AL	417 593
	01 083	Limestone County	82 782
	01 089	Madison County	334 811
26820		Idaho Falls, ID	133 265
	16 019	Bonneville County	104 234
	16 023	Butte County	2 891
	16 051	Jefferson County	26 140
26900		Indianapolis-Carmel-Anderson, IN	1887 877
	18 011	Boone County	56 640
	18 013	Brown County	15 242
	18 057	Hamilton County	274 569
	18 059	Hancock County	70 002
	18 063	Hendricks County	145 448
	18 081	Johnson County	139 654
	18 095	Madison County	131 636
	18 097	Marion County	903 393
	18 109	Morgan County	68 894
	18 133	Putnam County	37 963
	18 145	Shelby County	44 436
26980		Iowa City, IA	152 586
	19 103	Johnson County	130 882
	19 183	Washington County	21 704
27060		Ithaca, NY	101 564
	36 109	Tompkins County	101 564
27100		Jackson, MI	160 248
	26 075	Jackson County	160 248
27140		Jackson, MS	567 122
	28 029	Copiah County	29 449
	28 049	Hinds County	245 285
	28 089	Madison County	95 203
	28 121	Rankin County	141 617
	28 127	Simpson County	27 503
	28 163	Yazoo County	28 065
27180		Jackson, TN	130 011
	47 023	Chester County	17 131
	47 033	Crockett County	14 586
	47 113	Madison County	98 294

Metropolitan Statistical Areas, Metropolitan Divisions, and Components (as defined February 2013)–*Continued*

Core based statistical area	State/ County FIPS code	Title and Geographic Components	2010 Census Population
27260		Jacksonville, FL	1345 596
	12 003	Baker County	27 115
	12 019	Clay County	190 865
	12 031	Duval County	864 263
	12 089	Nassau County	73 314
	12 109	St. Johns County	190 039
27340		Jacksonville, NC	177 772
	37 133	Onslow County	177 772
27500		Janesville-Beloit, WI	160 331
	55 105	Rock County	160 331
27620		Jefferson City, MO	149 807
	29 027	Callaway County	44 332
	29 051	Cole County	75 990
	29 135	Moniteau County	15 607
	29 151	Osage County	13 878
27740		Johnson City, TN	198 716
	47 019	Carter County	57 424
	47 171	Unicoi County	18 313
	47 179	Washington County	122 979
27780		Johnstown, PA	143 679
	42 021	Cambria County	143 679
27860		Jonesboro, AR	121 026
	05 031	Craighead County	96 443
	05 111	Poinsett County	24 583
27900		Joplin, MO	175 518
	29 097	Jasper County	117 404
	29 145	Newton County	58 114
27980		Kahului-Wailuku-Lahaina, HI	154 924
	15 005	Kalawao County	90
	15 009	Maui County	154 834
28020		Kalamazoo-Portage, MI	326 589
	26 077	Kalamazoo County	250 331
	26 159	Van Buren County	76 258
28100		Kankakee, IL	113 449
	17 091	Kankakee County	113 449
28140		Kansas City, MO-KS	2009 342
	20 091	Johnson County	544 179
	20 103	Leavenworth County	76 227
	20 107	Linn County	9 656
	20 121	Miami County	32 787
	20 209	Wyandotte County	157 505
	29 013	Bates County	17 049
	29 025	Caldwell County	9 424
	29 037	Cass County	99 478
	29 047	Clay County	221 939
	29 049	Clinton County	20 743
	29 095	Jackson County	674 158
	29 107	Lafayette County	33 381
	29 165	Platte County	89 322
	29 177	Ray County	23 494
28420		Kennewick-Richland, WA	253 340
	53 005	Benton County	175 177
	53 021	Franklin County	78 163
28660		Killeen-Temple, TX	405 300
	48 027	Bell County	310 235
	48 099	Coryell County	75 388
	48 281	Lampasas County	19 677
28700		Kingsport-Bristol-Bristol, TN-VA	309 544
	47 073	Hawkins County	56 833
	47 163	Sullivan County	156 823
	51 169	Scott County	23 177
	51 191	Washington County	54 876
	51 520	Bristol city	17 835
28740		Kingston, NY	182 493
	36 111	Ulster County	182 493
28940		Knoxville, TN	837 571
	47 001	Anderson County	75 129
	47 009	Blount County	123 010
	47 013	Campbell County	40 716
	47 057	Grainger County	22 657
	47 093	Knox County	432 226
	47 105	Loudon County	48 556
	47 129	Morgan County	21 987
	47 145	Roane County	54 181
	47 173	Union County	19 109
29020		Kokomo, IN	82 752
	18 067	Howard County	82 752
29100		La Crosse-Onalaska, WI-MN	133 665
	27 055	Houston County	19 027
	55 063	La Crosse County	114 638
29180		Lafayette, LA	466 750
	22 001	Acadia Parish	61 773
	22 045	Iberia Parish	73 240
	22 055	Lafayette Parish	221 578
	22 099	St. Martin Parish	52 160
	22 113	Vermilion Parish	57 999
29200		Lafayette-West Lafayette, IN	201 789
	18 007	Benton County	8 854
	18 015	Carroll County	20 155
	18 157	Tippecanoe County	172 780
29340		Lake Charles, LA	199 607
	22 019	Calcasieu Parish	192 768
	22 023	Cameron Parish	6 839
29420		Lake Havasu City-Kingman, AZ	200 186
	04 015	Mohave County	200 186
29460		Lakeland-Winter Haven, FL	602 095
	12 105	Polk County	602 095
29540		Lancaster, PA	519 445
	42 071	Lancaster County	519 445

Metropolitan Statistical Areas, Metropolitan Divisions, and Components (as defined February 2013)–*Continued*

Core based statistical area	State/ County FIPS code	Title and Geographic Components	2010 Census Population
29620		Lansing-East Lansing, MI	464 036
	26 037	Clinton County	75 382
	26 045	Eaton County	107 759
	26 065	Ingham County	280 895
29700		Laredo, TX	250 304
	48 479	Webb County	250 304
29740		Las Cruces, NM	209 233
	35 013	Dona Ana County	209 233
29820		Las Vegas-Henderson-Paradise, NV	1951 269
	32 003	Clark County	1951 269
29940		Lawrence, KS	110 826
	20 045	Douglas County	110 826
30020		Lawton, OK	130 291
	40 031	Comanche County	124 098
	40 033	Cotton County	6 193
30140		Lebanon, PA	133 568
	42 075	Lebanon County	133 568
30300		Lewiston, ID-WA	60 888
	16 069	Nez Perce County	39 265
	53 003	Asotin County	21 623
30340		Lewiston-Auburn, ME	107 702
	23 001	Androscoggin County	107 702
30460		Lexington-Fayette, KY	472 099
	21 017	Bourbon County	19 985
	21 049	Clark County	35 613
	21 067	Fayette County	295 803
	21 113	Jessamine County	48 586
	21 209	Scott County	47 173
	21 239	Woodford County	24 939
30620		Lima, OH	106 331
	39 003	Allen County	106 331
30700		Lincoln, NE	302 157
	31 109	Lancaster County	285 407
	31 159	Seward County	16 750
30780		Little Rock-North Little Rock-Conway, AR	699 757
	05 045	Faulkner County	113 237
	05 053	Grant County	17 853
	05 085	Lonoke County	68 356
	05 105	Perry County	10 445
	05 119	Pulaski County	382 748
	05 125	Saline County	107 118
30860		Logan, UT-ID	125 442
	16 041	Franklin County	12 786
	49 005	Cache County	112 656
30980		Longview, TX	214 369
	48 183	Gregg County	121 730
	48 401	Rusk County	53 330
	48 459	Upshur County	39 309

Core based statistical area	State/ County FIPS code	Title and Geographic Components	2010 Census Population
31020		Longview, WA	102 410
	53 015	Cowlitz County	102 410
31080		Los Angeles-Long Beach-Anaheim, CA	12828 837
		Anaheim-Santa Ana-Irvine, CA Div 11244	3010 232
	06 059	Orange County	3010 232
		Los Angeles-Long Beach-Glendale, CA Div 31084	9818 605
	06 037	Los Angeles County	9818 605
31140		Louisville/Jefferson County, KY-IN	1235 708
	18 019	Clark County	110 232
	18 043	Floyd County	74 578
	18 061	Harrison County	39 364
	18 143	Scott County	24 181
	18 175	Washington County	28 262
	21 029	Bullitt County	74 319
	21 103	Henry County	15 416
	21 111	Jefferson County	741 096
	21 185	Oldham County	60 316
	21 211	Shelby County	42 074
	21 215	Spencer County	17 061
	21 223	Trimble County	8 809
31180		Lubbock, TX	290 805
	48 107	Crosby County	6 059
	48 303	Lubbock County	278 831
	48 305	Lynn County	5 915
31340		Lynchburg, VA	252 634
	51 009	Amherst County	32 353
	51 011	Appomattox County	14 973
	51 019	Bedford County	68 676
	51 031	Campbell County	54 842
	51 515	Bedford city	6 222
	51 680	Lynchburg city	75 568
31420		Macon, GA	232 293
	13 021	Bibb County	155 547
	13 079	Crawford County	12 630
	13 169	Jones County	28 669
	13 207	Monroe County	26 424
	13 289	Twiggs County	9 023
31460		Madera, CA	150 865
	06 039	Madera County	150 865
31540		Madison, WI	605 435
	55 021	Columbia County	56 833
	55 025	Dane County	488 073
	55 045	Green County	36 842
	55 049	Iowa County	23 687
31700		Manchester-Nashua, NH	400 721
	33 011	Hillsborough County	400 721
31740		Manhattan, KS	92 719
	20 149	Pottawatomie County	21 604
	20 161	Riley County	71 115
31860		Mankato-North Mankato, MN	96 740
	27 013	Blue Earth County	64 013
	27 103	Nicollet County	32 727

Metropolitan Statistical Areas, Metropolitan Divisions, and Components (as defined February 2013)–*Continued*

Core based statistical area	State/ County FIPS code	Title and Geographic Components	2010 Census Population
31900		Mansfield, OH	124 475
	39 139	Richland County	124 475
32580		McAllen-Edinburg-Mission, TX	774 769
	48 215	Hidalgo County	774 769
32780		Medford, OR	203 206
	41 029	Jackson County	203 206
32820		Memphis, TN-MS-AR	1324 829
	05 035	Crittenden County	50 902
	28 009	Benton County	8 729
	28 033	DeSoto County	161 252
	28 093	Marshall County	37 144
	28 137	Tate County	28 886
	28 143	Tunica County	10 778
	47 047	Fayette County	38 413
	47 157	Shelby County	927 644
	47 167	Tipton County	61 081
32900		Merced, CA	255 793
	06 047	Merced County	255 793
33100		Miami-Fort Lauderdale-West Palm Beach, FL	5564 635
		Fort Lauderdale-Pompano Beach-Deerfield Beach, FL Div 22744	1748 066
	12 011	Broward County	1748 066
		Miami-Miami Beach-Kendall, FL Div 33124	2496 435
	12 086	Miami-Dade County	2496 435
		West Palm Beach-Boca Raton-Delray Beach, FL Div 48424	1320 134
	12 099	Palm Beach County	1320 134
33140		Michigan City-La Porte, IN	111 467
	18 091	LaPorte County	111 467
33220		Midland, MI	83 629
	26 111	Midland County	83 629
33260		Midland, TX	141 671
	48 317	Martin County	4 799
	48 329	Midland County	136 872
33340		Milwaukee-Waukesha-West Allis, WI	1555 908
	55 079	Milwaukee County	947 735
	55 089	Ozaukee County	86 395
	55 131	Washington County	131 887
	55 133	Waukesha County	389 891
33460		Minneapolis-St. Paul-Bloomington, MN	3348 859
	27 003	Anoka County	330 844
	27 019	Carver County	91 042
	27 025	Chisago County	53 887
	27 037	Dakota County	398 552
	27 053	Hennepin County	1152 425
	27 059	Isanti County	37 816
	27 079	Le Sueur County	27 703
	27 095	Mille Lacs County	26 097
	27 123	Ramsey County	508 640
	27 139	Scott County	129 928
	27 141	Sherburne County	88 499
	27 143	Sibley County	15 226
	27 163	Washington County	238 136
	27 171	Wright County	124 700
	55 093	Pierce County	41 019
	55 109	St. Croix County	84 345
33540		Missoula, MT	109 299
	30 063	Missoula County	109 299
33660		Mobile, AL	412 992
	01 097	Mobile County	412 992
33700		Modesto, CA	514 453
	06 099	Stanislaus County	514 453
33740		Monroe, LA	176 441
	22 073	Ouachita Parish	153 720
	22 111	Union Parish	22 721
33780		Monroe, MI	152 021
	26 115	Monroe County	152 021
33860		Montgomery, AL	374 536
	01 001	Autauga County	54 571
	01 051	Elmore County	79 303
	01 085	Lowndes County	11 299
	01 101	Montgomery County	229 363
34060		Morgantown, WV	129 709
	54 061	Monongalia County	96 189
	54 077	Preston County	33 520
34100		Morristown, TN	113 951
	47 063	Hamblen County	62 544
	47 089	Jefferson County	51 407
34580		Mount Vernon-Anacortes, WA	116 901
	53 057	Skagit County	116 901
34620		Muncie, IN	117 671
	18 035	Delaware County	117 671
34740		Muskegon, MI	172 188
	26 121	Muskegon County	172 188
34820		Myrtle Beach-Conway-North Myrtle Beach, NC-SC	376 722
	37 019	Brunswick County	107 431
	45 051	Horry County	269 291
34900		Napa, CA	136 484
	06 055	Napa County	136 484

Metropolitan Statistical Areas, Metropolitan Divisions, and Components (as defined February 2013)–*Continued*

Core based statistical area	State/ County FIPS code	Title and Geographic Components	2010 Census Population
34940		Naples-Immokalee-Marco Island, FL	321 520
	12 021	Collier County	321 520
34980		Nashville-Davidson—Murfreesboro—Franklin, TN	1670 890
	47 015	Cannon County	13 801
	47 021	Cheatham County	39 105
	47 037	Davidson County	626 681
	47 043	Dickson County	49 666
	47 081	Hickman County	24 690
	47 111	Macon County	22 248
	47 119	Maury County	80 956
	47 147	Robertson County	66 283
	47 149	Rutherford County	262 604
	47 159	Smith County	19 166
	47 165	Sumner County	160 645
	47 169	Trousdale County	7 870
	47 187	Williamson County	183 182
	47 189	Wilson County	113 993
35100		New Bern, NC	126 802
	37 049	Craven County	103 505
	37 103	Jones County	10 153
	37 137	Pamlico County	13 144
35300		New Haven-Milford, CT	862 477
	09 009	New Haven County	862 477
35380		New Orleans-Metairie, LA	1189 866
	22 051	Jefferson Parish	432 552
	22 071	Orleans Parish	343 829
	22 075	Plaquemines Parish	23 042
	22 087	St. Bernard Parish	35 897
	22 089	St. Charles Parish	52 780
	22 093	St. James Parish	22 102
	22 095	St. John the Baptist Parish	45 924
	22 103	St. Tammany Parish	233 740

Core based statistical area	State/ County FIPS code	Title and Geographic Components	2010 Census Population
35620		New York-Newark-Jersey City, NY-NJ-PA	19567 410
		Dutchess County-Putnam County, NY Div 20524	397 198
	36 027	Dutchess County	297 488
	36 079	Putnam County	99 710
		Nassau County-Suffolk County, NY Div 35004	2832 882
	36 059	Nassau County	1339 532
	36 103	Suffolk County	1493 350
		Newark, NJ-PA Div 35084	2471 171
	34 013	Essex County	783 969
	34 019	Hunterdon County	128 349
	34 027	Morris County	492 276
	34 035	Somerset County	323 444
	34 037	Sussex County	149 265
	34 039	Union County	536 499
	42 103	Pike County	57 369
		New York-Jersey City-White Plains, NY-NJ Div 35614	13866 159
	34 003	Bergen County	905 116
	34 017	Hudson County	634 266
	34 023	Middlesex County	809 858
	34 025	Monmouth County	630 380
	34 029	Ocean County	576 567
	34 031	Passaic County	501 226
	36 005	Bronx County	1385 108
	36 047	Kings County	2504 700
	36 061	New York County	1585 873
	36 071	Orange County	372 813
	36 081	Queens County	2230 722
	36 085	Richmond County	468 730
	36 087	Rockland County	311 687
	36 119	Westchester County	949 113
35660		Niles-Benton Harbor, MI	156 813
	26 021	Berrien County	156 813
35840		North Port-Sarasota-Bradenton, FL	702 281
	12 081	Manatee County	322 833
	12 115	Sarasota County	379 448
35980		Norwich-New London, CT	274 055
	09 011	New London County	274 055
36100		Ocala, FL	331 298
	12 083	Marion County	331 298
36140		Ocean City, NJ	97 265
	34 009	Cape May County	97 265
36220		Odessa, TX	137 130
	48 135	Ector County	137 130
36260		Ogden-Clearfield, UT	597 159
	49 003	Box Elder County	49 975
	49 011	Davis County	306 479
	49 029	Morgan County	9 469
	49 057	Weber County	231 236

Metropolitan Statistical Areas, Metropolitan Divisions, and Components (as defined February 2013)–*Continued*

Core based statistical area	State/ County FIPS code	Title and Geographic Components	2010 Census Population
36420		Oklahoma City, OK	1252 987
	40 017	Canadian County	115 541
	40 027	Cleveland County	255 755
	40 051	Grady County	52 431
	40 081	Lincoln County	34 273
	40 083	Logan County	41 848
	40 087	McClain County	34 506
	40 109	Oklahoma County	718 633
36500		Olympia-Tumwater, WA	252 264
	53 067	Thurston County	252 264
36540		Omaha-Council Bluffs, NE-IA	865 350
	19 085	Harrison County	14 928
	19 129	Mills County	15 059
	19 155	Pottawattamie County	93 158
	31 025	Cass County	25 241
	31 055	Douglas County	517 110
	31 153	Sarpy County	158 840
	31 155	Saunders County	20 780
	31 177	Washington County	20 234
36740		Orlando-Kissimmee-Sanford, FL	2134 411
	12 069	Lake County	297 052
	12 095	Orange County	1145 956
	12 097	Osceola County	268 685
	12 117	Seminole County	422 718
36780		Oshkosh-Neenah, WI	166 994
	55 139	Winnebago County	166 994
36980		Owensboro, KY	114 752
	21 059	Daviess County	96 656
	21 091	Hancock County	8 565
	21 149	McLean County	9 531
37100		Oxnard-Thousand Oaks-Ventura, CA	823 318
	06 111	Ventura County	823 318
37340		Palm Bay-Melbourne-Titusville, FL	543 376
	12 009	Brevard County	543 376
37460		Panama City, FL	184 715
	12 005	Bay County	168 852
	12 045	Gulf County	15 863
37620		Parkersburg-Vienna, WV	92 673
	54 105	Wirt County	5 717
	54 107	Wood County	86 956
37860		Pensacola-Ferry Pass-Brent, FL	448 991
	12 033	Escambia County	297 619
	12 113	Santa Rosa County	151 372
37900		Peoria, IL	379 186
	17 123	Marshall County	12 640
	17 143	Peoria County	186 494
	17 175	Stark County	5 994
	17 179	Tazewell County	135 394
	17 203	Woodford County	38 664
37980		Philadelphia-Camden-Wilmington, PA-NJ-DE-MD	5965 343
		Camden, NJ Div 15804	1250 679
	34 005	Burlington County	448 734
	34 007	Camden County	513 657
	34 015	Gloucester County	288 288
		Montgomery County-Bucks County-Chester County, PA Div 33874	1924 009
	42 017	Bucks County	625 249
	42 029	Chester County	498 886
	42 091	Montgomery County	799 874
		Philadelphia, PA Div 37964	2084 985
	42 045	Delaware County	558 979
	42 101	Philadelphia County	1526 006
		Wilmington, DE-MD-NJ Div 48864	705 670
	10 003	New Castle County	538 479
	24 015	Cecil County	101 108
	34 033	Salem County	66 083
38060		Phoenix-Mesa-Scottsdale, AZ	4192 887
	04 013	Maricopa County	3817 117
	04 021	Pinal County	375 770
38220		Pine Bluff, AR	100 258
	05 025	Cleveland County	8 689
	05 069	Jefferson County	77 435
	05 079	Lincoln County	14 134
38300		Pittsburgh, PA	2356 285
	42 003	Allegheny County	1223 348
	42 005	Armstrong County	68 941
	42 007	Beaver County	170 539
	42 019	Butler County	183 862
	42 051	Fayette County	136 606
	42 125	Washington County	207 820
	42 129	Westmoreland County	365 169
38340		Pittsfield, MA	131 219
	25 003	Berkshire County	131 219
38540		Pocatello, ID	82 839
	16 005	Bannock County	82 839
38860		Portland-South Portland, ME	514 098
	23 005	Cumberland County	281 674
	23 023	Sagadahoc County	35 293
	23 031	York County	197 131
38900		Portland-Vancouver-Hillsboro, OR-WA	2226 009
	41 005	Clackamas County	375 992
	41 009	Columbia County	49 351
	41 051	Multnomah County	735 334
	41 067	Washington County	529 710
	41 071	Yamhill County	99 193
	53 011	Clark County	425 363
	53 059	Skamania County	11 066
38940		Port St. Lucie, FL	424 107
	12 085	Martin County	146 318
	12 111	St. Lucie County	277 789
39140		Prescott, AZ	211 033
	04 025	Yavapai County	211 033

Metropolitan Statistical Areas, Metropolitan Divisions, and Components (as defined February 2013)–*Continued*

Core based statistical area	State/ County FIPS code	Title and Geographic Components	2010 Census Population
39300		Providence-Warwick, RI-MA	1600 852
	25 005	Bristol County	548 285
	44 001	Bristol County	49 875
	44 003	Kent County	166 158
	44 005	Newport County	82 888
	44 007	Providence County	626 667
	44 009	Washington County	126 979
39340		Provo-Orem, UT	526 810
	49 023	Juab County	10 246
	49 049	Utah County	516 564
39380		Pueblo, CO	159 063
	08 101	Pueblo County	159 063
39460		Punta Gorda, FL	159 978
	12 015	Charlotte County	159 978
39540		Racine, WI	195 408
	55 101	Racine County	195 408
39580		Raleigh, NC	1130 490
	37 069	Franklin County	60 619
	37 101	Johnston County	168 878
	37 183	Wake County	900 993
39660		Rapid City, SD	134 598
	46 033	Custer County	8 216
	46 093	Meade County	25 434
	46 103	Pennington County	100 948
39740		Reading, PA	411 442
	42 011	Berks County	411 442
39820		Redding, CA	177 223
	06 089	Shasta County	177 223
39900		Reno, NV	425 417
	32 029	Storey County	4 010
	32 031	Washoe County	421 407
40060		Richmond, VA	1208 101
	51 007	Amelia County	12 690
	51 033	Caroline County	28 545
	51 036	Charles City County	7 256
	51 041	Chesterfield County	316 236
	51 053	Dinwiddie County	28 001
	51 075	Goochland County	21 717
	51 085	Hanover County	99 863
	51 087	Henrico County	306 935
	51 101	King William County	15 935
	51 127	New Kent County	18 429
	51 145	Powhatan County	28 046
	51 149	Prince George County	35 725
	51 183	Sussex County	12 087
	51 570	Colonial Heights city	17 411
	51 670	Hopewell city	22 591
	51 730	Petersburg city	32 420
	51 760	Richmond city	204 214
40140		Riverside-San Bernardino-Ontario, CA	4224 851
	06 065	Riverside County	2189 641
	06 071	San Bernardino County	2035 210
40220		Roanoke, VA	308 707
	51 023	Botetourt County	33 148
	51 045	Craig County	5 190
	51 067	Franklin County	56 159
	51 161	Roanoke County	92 376
	51 770	Roanoke city	97 032
	51 775	Salem city	24 802
40340		Rochester, MN	206 877
	27 039	Dodge County	20 087
	27 045	Fillmore County	20 866
	27 109	Olmsted County	144 248
	27 157	Wabasha County	21 676
40380		Rochester, NY	1079 671
	36 051	Livingston County	65 393
	36 055	Monroe County	744 344
	36 069	Ontario County	107 931
	36 073	Orleans County	42 883
	36 117	Wayne County	93 772
	36 123	Yates County	25 348
40420		Rockford, IL	349 431
	17 007	Boone County	54 165
	17 201	Winnebago County	295 266
40580		Rocky Mount, NC	152 392
	37 065	Edgecombe County	56 552
	37 127	Nash County	95 840
40660		Rome, GA	96 317
	13 115	Floyd County	96 317
40900		Sacramento—Roseville—Arden-Arcade, CA	2149 127
	06 017	El Dorado County	181 058
	06 061	Placer County	348 432
	06 067	Sacramento County	1418 788
	06 113	Yolo County	200 849
40980		Saginaw, MI	200 169
	26 145	Saginaw County	200 169
41060		St. Cloud, MN	189 093
	27 009	Benton County	38 451
	27 145	Stearns County	150 642
41100		St. George, UT	138 115
	49 053	Washington County	138 115
41140		St. Joseph, MO-KS	127 329
	20 043	Doniphan County	7 945
	29 003	Andrew County	17 291
	29 021	Buchanan County	89 201
	29 063	DeKalb County	12 892

Metropolitan Statistical Areas, Metropolitan Divisions, and Components (as defined February 2013)–*Continued*

Core based statistical area	State/ County FIPS code	Title and Geographic Components	2010 Census Population
41180		St. Louis, MO-IL	2787 701
	17 005	Bond County	17 768
	17 013	Calhoun County	5 089
	17 027	Clinton County	37 762
	17 083	Jersey County	22 985
	17 117	Macoupin County	47 765
	17 119	Madison County	269 282
	17 133	Monroe County	32 957
	17 163	St. Clair County	270 056
	29 071	Franklin County	101 492
	29 099	Jefferson County	218 733
	29 113	Lincoln County	52 566
	29 183	St. Charles County	360 485
	29 189	St. Louis County	998 954
	29 219	Warren County	32 513
	29 510	St. Louis city	319 294
41420		Salem, OR	390 738
	41 047	Marion County	315 335
	41 053	Polk County	75 403
41500		Salinas, CA	415 057
	06 053	Monterey County	415 057
41540		Salisbury, MD-DE	373 802
	10 005	Sussex County	197 145
	24 039	Somerset County	26 470
	24 045	Wicomico County	98 733
	24 047	Worcester County	51 454
41620		Salt Lake City, UT	1087 873
	49 035	Salt Lake County	1029 655
	49 045	Tooele County	58 218
41660		San Angelo, TX	111 823
	48 235	Irion County	1 599
	48 451	Tom Green County	110 224
41700		San Antonio-New Braunfels, TX	2142 508
	48 013	Atascosa County	44 911
	48 019	Bandera County	20 485
	48 029	Bexar County	1714 773
	48 091	Comal County	108 472
	48 187	Guadalupe County	131 533
	48 259	Kendall County	33 410
	48 325	Medina County	46 006
	48 493	Wilson County	42 918
41740		San Diego-Carlsbad, CA	3095 313
	06 073	San Diego County	3095 313
41860		San Francisco-Oakland-Hayward, CA	4335 391
		Oakland-Hayward-Berkeley, CA Div 36084	2559 296
	06 001	Alameda County	1510 271
	06 013	Contra Costa County	1049 025
		San Francisco-Redwood City-South San Francisco, CA Div 41884	1523 686
	06 075	San Francisco County	805 235
	06 081	San Mateo County	718 451
		San Rafael, CA Div 42034	252 409
	06 041	Marin County	252 409
41940		San Jose-Sunnyvale-Santa Clara, CA	1836 911
	06 069	San Benito County	55 269
	06 085	Santa Clara County	1781 642
42020		San Luis Obispo-Paso Robles-Arroyo Grande, CA	269 637
	06 079	San Luis Obispo County	269 637
42100		Santa Cruz-Watsonville, CA	262 382
	06 087	Santa Cruz County	262 382
42140		Santa Fe, NM	144 170
	35 049	Santa Fe County	144 170
42200		Santa Maria-Santa Barbara, CA	423 895
	06 083	Santa Barbara County	423 895
42220		Santa Rosa, CA	483 878
	06 097	Sonoma County	483 878
42340		Savannah, GA	347 611
	13 029	Bryan County	30 233
	13 051	Chatham County	265 128
	13 103	Effingham County	52 250
42540		Scranton—Wilkes-Barre—Hazleton, PA	563 631
	42 069	Lackawanna County	214 437
	42 079	Luzerne County	320 918
	42 131	Wyoming County	28 276
42660		Seattle-Tacoma-Bellevue, WA	3439 809
		Seattle-Bellevue-Everett, WA Div 42644	2644 584
	53 033	King County	1931 249
	53 061	Snohomish County	713 335
		Tacoma-Lakewood, WA Div 45104	795 225
	53 053	Pierce County	795 225
42680		Sebastian-Vero Beach, FL	138 028
	12 061	Indian River County	138 028
42700		Sebring, FL	98 786
	12 055	Highlands County	98 786
43100		Sheboygan, WI	115 507
	55 117	Sheboygan County	115 507
43300		Sherman-Denison, TX	120 877
	48 181	Grayson County	120 877
43340		Shreveport-Bossier City, LA	439 811
	22 015	Bossier Parish	116 979
	22 017	Caddo Parish	254 969
	22 031	De Soto Parish	26 656
	22 119	Webster Parish	41 207
43420		Sierra Vista-Douglas, AZ	131 346
	04 003	Cochise County	131 346
43580		Sioux City, IA-NE-SD	168 563
	19 149	Plymouth County	24 986
	19 193	Woodbury County	102 172
	31 043	Dakota County	21 006
	31 051	Dixon County	6 000
	46 127	Union County	14 399

Metropolitan Statistical Areas, Metropolitan Divisions, and Components (as defined February 2013)–*Continued*

Core based statistical area	State/ County FIPS code	Title and Geographic Components	2010 Census Population
43620		Sioux Falls, SD	228 261
	46 083	Lincoln County	44 828
	46 087	McCook County	5 618
	46 099	Minnehaha County	169 468
	46 125	Turner County	8 347
43780		South Bend-Mishawaka, IN-MI	319 224
	18 141	St. Joseph County	266 931
	26 027	Cass County	52 293
43900		Spartanburg, SC	313 268
	45 083	Spartanburg County	284 307
	45 087	Union County	28 961
44060		Spokane-Spokane Valley, WA	527 753
	53 051	Pend Oreille County	13 001
	53 063	Spokane County	471 221
	53 065	Stevens County	43 531
44100		Springfield, IL	210 170
	17 129	Menard County	12 705
	17 167	Sangamon County	197 465
44140		Springfield, MA	621 570
	25 013	Hampden County	463 490
	25 015	Hampshire County	158 080
44180		Springfield, MO	436 712
	29 043	Christian County	77 422
	29 059	Dallas County	16 777
	29 077	Greene County	275 174
	29 167	Polk County	31 137
	29 225	Webster County	36 202
44220		Springfield, OH	138 333
	39 023	Clark County	138 333
44300		State College, PA	153 990
	42 027	Centre County	153 990
44420		Staunton-Waynesboro, VA	118 502
	51 015	Augusta County	73 750
	51 790	Staunton city	23 746
	51 820	Waynesboro city	21 006
44700		Stockton-Lodi, CA	685 306
	06 077	San Joaquin County	685 306
44940		Sumter, SC	107 456
	45 085	Sumter County	107 456
45060		Syracuse, NY	662 577
	36 053	Madison County	73 442
	36 067	Onondaga County	467 026
	36 075	Oswego County	122 109
45220		Tallahassee, FL	367 413
	12 039	Gadsden County	46 389
	12 065	Jefferson County	14 761
	12 073	Leon County	275 487
	12 129	Wakulla County	30 776
45300		Tampa-St. Petersburg-Clearwater, FL	2783 243
	12 053	Hernando County	172 778
	12 057	Hillsborough County	1229 226
	12 101	Pasco County	464 697
	12 103	Pinellas County	916 542
45460		Terre Haute, IN	172 425
	18 021	Clay County	26 890
	18 153	Sullivan County	21 475
	18 165	Vermillion County	16 212
	18 167	Vigo County	107 848
45500		Texarkana, TX-AR	149 198
	05 081	Little River County	13 171
	05 091	Miller County	43 462
	48 037	Bowie County	92 565
45540		The Villages, FL	93 420
	12 119	Sumter County	93 420
45780		Toledo, OH	610 001
	39 051	Fulton County	42 698
	39 095	Lucas County	441 815
	39 173	Wood County	125 488
45820		Topeka, KS	233 870
	20 085	Jackson County	13 462
	20 087	Jefferson County	19 126
	20 139	Osage County	16 295
	20 177	Shawnee County	177 934
	20 197	Wabaunsee County	7 053
45940		Trenton, NJ	366 513
	34 021	Mercer County	366 513
46060		Tucson, AZ	980 263
	04 019	Pima County	980 263
46140		Tulsa, OK	937 478
	40 037	Creek County	69 967
	40 111	Okmulgee County	40 069
	40 113	Osage County	47 472
	40 117	Pawnee County	16 577
	40 131	Rogers County	86 905
	40 143	Tulsa County	603 403
	40 145	Wagoner County	73 085
46220		Tuscaloosa, AL	230 162
	01 065	Hale County	15 760
	01 107	Pickens County	19 746
	01 125	Tuscaloosa County	194 656
46340		Tyler, TX	209 714
	48 423	Smith County	209 714
46520		Urban Honolulu, HI	953 207
	15 003	Honolulu County	953 207
46540		Utica-Rome, NY	299 397
	36 043	Herkimer County	64 519
	36 065	Oneida County	234 878

Metropolitan Statistical Areas, Metropolitan Divisions, and Components (as defined February 2013)–*Continued*

Core based statistical area	State/ County FIPS code	Title and Geographic Components	2010 Census Population
46660		Valdosta, GA	139 588
	13 027	Brooks County	16 243
	13 101	Echols County	4 034
	13 173	Lanier County	10 078
	13 185	Lowndes County	109 233
46700		Vallejo-Fairfield, CA	413 344
	06 095	Solano County	413 344
47020		Victoria, TX	94 003
	48 175	Goliad County	7 210
	48 469	Victoria County	86 793
47220		Vineland-Bridgeton, NJ	156 898
	34 011	Cumberland County	156 898
47260		Virginia Beach-Norfolk-Newport News, VA-NC	1676 822
	37 053	Currituck County	23 547
	37 073	Gates County	12 197
	51 073	Gloucester County	36 858
	51 093	Isle of Wight County	35 270
	51 095	James City County	67 009
	51 115	Mathews County	8 978
	51 199	York County	65 464
	51 550	Chesapeake city	222 209
	51 650	Hampton city	137 436
	51 700	Newport News city	180 719
	51 710	Norfolk city	242 803
	51 735	Poquoson city	12 150
	51 740	Portsmouth city	95 535
	51 800	Suffolk city	84 585
	51 810	Virginia Beach city	437 994
	51 830	Williamsburg city	14 068
47300		Visalia-Porterville, CA	442 179
	06 107	Tulare County	442 179
47380		Waco, TX	252 772
	48 145	Falls County	17 866
	48 309	McLennan County	234 906
47460		Walla Walla, WA	62 859
	53 013	Columbia County	4 078
	53 071	Walla Walla County	58 781
47580		Warner Robins, GA	179 605
	13 153	Houston County	139 900
	13 225	Peach County	27 695
	13 235	Pulaski County	12 010
47900		Washington-Arlington-Alexandria, DC-VA-MD-WV	5636 232
		Silver Spring-Frederick-Rockville, MD Div 43524	1205 162
	24 021	Frederick County	233 385
	24 031	Montgomery County	971 777
		Washington-Arlington-Alexandria, DC-VA-MD-WV Div 47894	4431 070
	11 001	District of Columbia	601 723
	24 009	Calvert County	88 737
	24 017	Charles County	146 551
	24 033	Prince George's County	863 420
	51 013	Arlington County	207 627
	51 043	Clarke County	14 034
	51 047	Culpeper County	46 689
	51 059	Fairfax County	1081 726
	51 061	Fauquier County	65 203
	51 107	Loudoun County	312 311
	51 153	Prince William County	402 002
	51 157	Rappahannock County	7 373
	51 177	Spotsylvania County	122 397
	51 179	Stafford County	128 961
	51 187	Warren County	37 575
	51 510	Alexandria city	139 966
	51 600	Fairfax city	22 565
	51 610	Falls Church city	12 332
	51 630	Fredericksburg city	24 286
	51 683	Manassas city	37 821
	51 685	Manassas Park city	14 273
	54 037	Jefferson County	53 498
47940		Waterloo-Cedar Falls, IA	167 819
	19 013	Black Hawk County	131 090
	19 017	Bremer County	24 276
	19 075	Grundy County	12 453
48060		Watertown-Fort Drum, NY	116 229
	36 045	Jefferson County	116 229
48140		Wausau, WI	134 063
	55 073	Marathon County	134 063
48260		Weirton-Steubenville, WV-OH	124 454
	39 081	Jefferson County	69 709
	54 009	Brooke County	24 069
	54 029	Hancock County	30 676
48300		Wenatchee, WA	110 884
	53 007	Chelan County	72 453
	53 017	Douglas County	38 431
48540		Wheeling, WV-OH	147 950
	39 013	Belmont County	70 400
	54 051	Marshall County	33 107
	54 069	Ohio County	44 443
48620		Wichita, KS	630 919
	20 015	Butler County	65 880
	20 079	Harvey County	34 684
	20 095	Kingman County	7 858
	20 173	Sedgwick County	498 365
	20 191	Sumner County	24 132

Metropolitan Statistical Areas, Metropolitan Divisions, and Components (as defined February 2013)–*Continued*

Core based statistical area	State/ County FIPS code	Title and Geographic Components	2010 Census Population
48660		Wichita Falls, TX	151 306
	48 009	Archer County	9 054
	48 077	Clay County	10 752
	48 485	Wichita County	131 500
48700		Williamsport, PA	116 111
	42 081	Lycoming County	116 111
48900		Wilmington, NC	254 884
	37 129	New Hanover County	202 667
	37 141	Pender County	52 217
49020		Winchester, VA-WV	128 472
	51 069	Frederick County	78 305
	51 840	Winchester city	26 203
	54 027	Hampshire County	23 964
49180		Winston-Salem, NC	640 595
	37 057	Davidson County	162 878
	37 059	Davie County	41 240
	37 067	Forsyth County	350 670
	37 169	Stokes County	47 401
	37 197	Yadkin County	38 406
49340		Worcester, MA-CT	916 980
	09 015	Windham County	118 428
	25 027	Worcester County	798 552
49420		Yakima, WA	243 231
	53 077	Yakima County	243 231
49620		York-Hanover, PA	434 972
	42 133	York County	434 972
49660		Youngstown-Warren-Boardman, OH-PA	565 773
	39 099	Mahoning County	238 823
	39 155	Trumbull County	210 312
	42 085	Mercer County	116 638
49700		Yuba City, CA	166 892
	06 101	Sutter County	94 737
	06 115	Yuba County	72 155
49740		Yuma, AZ	195 751
	04 027	Yuma County	195 751

APPENDIX C
CORE BASED STATISTICAL AREAS (Metropolitan and Micropolitan), METROPOLITAN DIVISIONS, AND COMPONENTS (as defined February 2013)

Core Based Statistical Area	State/ County FIPS Code	Title and Geographic Components	2010 Census Population	2014 Estimated Population
10100		Aberdeen, SD Micro area	40 602	42 391
	46013	Brown County, SD	36 531	38 408
	46045	Edmunds County, SD	4 071	3 983
10140		Aberdeen, WA Micro area	72 797	70 818
	53027	Grays Harbor County, WA	72 797	70 818
10180		Abilene, TX Metro area	165 252	168 592
	48059	Callahan County, TX	13 544	13 513
	48253	Jones County, TX	20 202	19 936
	48441	Taylor County, TX	131 506	135 143
10220		Ada, OK Micro area	37 492	38 005
	40123	Pontotoc County, OK	37 492	38 005
10300		Adrian, MI Micro area	99 892	99 047
	26091	Lenawee County, MI	99 892	99 047
10420		Akron, OH Metro area	703 200	703 825
	39133	Portage County, OH	161 419	161 882
	39153	Summit County, OH	541 781	541 943
10460		Alamogordo, NM Micro area	63 797	65 082
	35035	Otero County, NM	63 797	65 082
10500		Albany, GA Metro area	157 308	154 925
	13007	Baker County, GA	3 451	3 255
	13095	Dougherty County, GA	94 565	92 407
	13177	Lee County, GA	28 298	29 191
	13273	Terrell County, GA	9 315	9 132
	13321	Worth County, GA	21 679	20 940
10540		Albany, OR Metro area	116 672	119 356
	41043	Linn County, OR	116 672	119 356
10580		Albany-Schenectady-Troy, NY Metro area	870 716	880 167
	36001	Albany County, NY	304 204	308 171
	36083	Rensselaer County, NY	159 429	159 774
	36091	Saratoga County, NY	219 607	224 921
	36093	Schenectady County, NY	154 727	155 735
	36095	Schoharie County, NY	32 749	31 566
10620		Albemarle, NC Micro area	60 585	60 600
	37167	Stanly County, NC	60 585	60 600
10660		Albert Lea, MN Micro area	31 255	30 840
	27047	Freeborn County, MN	31 255	30 840
10700		Albertville, AL Micro area	93 019	94 636
	01095	Marshall County, AL	93 019	94 636
10740		Albuquerque, NM Metro area	887 077	904 587
	35001	Bernalillo County, NM	662 564	675 551
	35043	Sandoval County, NM	131 561	137 608
	35057	Torrance County, NM	16 383	15 611
	35061	Valencia County, NM	76 569	75 817
10780		Alexandria, LA Metro area	153 922	154 872
	22043	Grant Parish, LA	22 309	22 384
	22079	Rapides Parish, LA	131 613	132 488
10820		Alexandria, MN Micro area	36 009	36 790
	27041	Douglas County, MN	36 009	36 790
10860		Alice, TX Micro area	40 838	41 353
	48249	Jim Wells County, TX	40 838	41 353
10900		Allentown-Bethlehem-Easton, PA-NJ Metro area	821 173	829 835
	34041	Warren County, NJ	108 692	106 917
	42025	Carbon County, PA	65 249	64 441
	42077	Lehigh County, PA	349 497	357 823
	42095	Northampton County, PA	297 735	300 654
10940		Alma, MI Micro area	42 476	41 665
	26057	Gratiot County, MI	42 476	41 665
10980		Alpena, MI Micro area	29 598	28 988
	26007	Alpena County, MI	29 598	28 988
11020		Altoona, PA Metro area	127 089	125 955
	42013	Blair County, PA	127 089	125 955
11060		Altus, OK Micro area	26 446	25 998
	40065	Jackson County, OK	26 446	25 998
11100		Amarillo, TX Metro area	251 933	259 885
	48011	Armstrong County, TX	1 901	1 955
	48065	Carson County, TX	6 182	6 013
	48359	Oldham County, TX	2 052	2 070
	48375	Potter County, TX	121 073	121 627
	48381	Randall County, TX	120 725	128 220
11140		Americus, GA Micro area	37 829	36 395
	13249	Schley County, GA	5 010	5 163
	13261	Sumter County, GA	32 819	31 232
11180		Ames, IA Metro area	89 542	94 073
	19169	Story County, IA	89 542	94 073
11220		Amsterdam, NY Micro area	50 219	49 779
	36057	Montgomery County, NY	50 219	49 779
11260		Anchorage, AK Metro area	380 821	398 892
	02020	Anchorage Municipality, AK	291 826	301 010
	02170	Matanuska-Susitna Borough, AK	88 995	97 882
11380		Andrews, TX Micro area	14 786	17 477
	48003	Andrews County, TX	14 786	17 477
11420		Angola, IN Micro area	34 185	34 308
	18151	Steuben County, IN	34 185	34 308
11460		Ann Arbor, MI Metro area	344 791	356 874
	26161	Washtenaw County, MI	344 791	356 874
11500		Anniston-Oxford-Jacksonville, AL Metro area	118 572	115 916
	01015	Calhoun County, AL	118 572	115 916
11540		Appleton, WI Metro area	225 666	231 497
	55015	Calumet County, WI	48 971	49 491
	55087	Outagamie County, WI	176 695	182 006

Core Based Statistical Areas (Metropolitan and Micropolitan), Metropolitan Divisions, and Components (as defined February 2013)–*Continued*

Core Based Statistical Area	State/ County FIPS Code	Title and Geographic Components	2010 Census Population	2014 Estimated Population
11580		Arcadia, FL Micro area	34 862	35 012
	12027	DeSoto County, FL	34 862	35 012
11620		Ardmore, OK Micro area	47 557	48 821
	40019	Carter County, OK	47 557	48 821
11660		Arkadelphia, AR Micro area	22 995	22 576
	05019	Clark County, AR	22 995	22 576
11680		Arkansas City-Winfield, KS Micro area	36 311	35 963
	20035	Cowley County, KS	36 311	35 963
11700		Asheville, NC Metro area	424 858	442 316
	37021	Buncombe County, NC	238 318	250 539
	37087	Haywood County, NC	59 036	59 471
	37089	Henderson County, NC	106 740	111 149
	37115	Madison County, NC	20 764	21 157
11740		Ashland, OH Micro area	53 139	53 035
	39005	Ashland County, OH	53 139	53 035
11780		Ashtabula, OH Micro area	101 497	99 175
	39007	Ashtabula County, OH	101 497	99 175
11820		Astoria, OR Micro area	37 039	37 474
	41007	Clatsop County, OR	37 039	37 474
11860		Atchison, KS Micro area	16 924	16 513
	20005	Atchison County, KS	16 924	16 513
11900		Athens, OH Micro area	64 757	64 713
	39009	Athens County, OH	64 757	64 713
11940		Athens, TN Micro area	52 266	52 626
	47107	McMinn County, TN	52 266	52 626
11980		Athens, TX Micro area	78 532	79 290
	48213	Henderson County, TX	78 532	79 290
12020		Athens-Clarke County, GA Metro area	192 541	199 016
	13059	Clarke County, GA	116 714	120 938
	13195	Madison County, GA	28 120	28 312
	13219	Oconee County, GA	32 808	35 093
	13221	Oglethorpe County, GA	14 899	14 673
12060		Atlanta-Sandy Springs-Roswell, GA Metro area	5 286 728	5 614 323
	13013	Barrow County, GA	69 367	73 240
	13015	Bartow County, GA	100 157	101 736
	13035	Butts County, GA	23 655	23 368
	13045	Carroll County, GA	110 527	114 093
	13057	Cherokee County, GA	214 346	230 985
	13063	Clayton County, GA	259 424	267 542
	13067	Cobb County, GA	688 078	730 981
	13077	Coweta County, GA	127 317	135 571
	13085	Dawson County, GA	22 330	22 957
	13089	DeKalb County, GA	691 893	722 161
	13097	Douglas County, GA	132 403	138 776
	13113	Fayette County, GA	106 567	109 664
	13117	Forsyth County, GA	175 511	204 302
	13121	Fulton County, GA	920 581	996 319
	13135	Gwinnett County, GA	805 321	877 922
	13143	Haralson County, GA	28 780	28 641
	13149	Heard County, GA	11 834	11 603
	13151	Henry County, GA	203 922	213 869
	13159	Jasper County, GA	13 900	13 432
	13171	Lamar County, GA	18 317	18 207
	13199	Meriwether County, GA	21 992	21 198
	13211	Morgan County, GA	17 868	17 956
	13217	Newton County, GA	99 958	103 675
	13223	Paulding County, GA	142 324	148 987
	13227	Pickens County, GA	29 431	29 997
	13231	Pike County, GA	17 869	17 784
	13247	Rockdale County, GA	85 215	87 754
	13255	Spalding County, GA	64 073	63 988
	13297	Walton County, GA	83 768	87 615
12100		Atlantic City-Hammonton, NJ Metro area	274 549	275 209
	34001	Atlantic County, NJ	274 549	275 209
12140		Auburn, IN Micro area	42 223	42 383
	18033	DeKalb County, IN	42 223	42 383
12180		Auburn, NY Micro area	80 026	78 823
	36011	Cayuga County, NY	80 026	78 823
12220		Auburn-Opelika, AL Metro area	140 247	154 255
	01081	Lee County, AL	140 247	154 255
12260		Augusta-Richmond County, GA-SC Metro area	564 873	583 632
	13033	Burke County, GA	23 316	22 709
	13073	Columbia County, GA	124 053	139 257
	13181	Lincoln County, GA	7 996	7 622
	13189	McDuffie County, GA	21 875	21 370
	13245	Richmond County, GA	200 549	201 368
	45003	Aiken County, SC	160 099	164 753
	45037	Edgefield County, SC	26 985	26 553
12300		Augusta-Waterville, ME Micro area	122 151	121 112
	23011	Kennebec County, ME	122 151	121 112
12380		Austin, MN Micro area	39 163	39 323
	27099	Mower County, MN	39 163	39 323
12420		Austin-Round Rock, TX Metro area	1 716 289	1 943 299
	48021	Bastrop County, TX	74 171	78 069
	48055	Caldwell County, TX	38 066	39 810
	48209	Hays County, TX	157 107	185 025
	48453	Travis County, TX	1 024 266	1 151 145
	48491	Williamson County, TX	422 679	489 250
12460		Bainbridge, GA Micro area	27 842	27 220
	13087	Decatur County, GA	27 842	27 220
12540		Bakersfield, CA Metro area	839 631	874 589
	06029	Kern County, CA	839 631	874 589
12580		Baltimore-Columbia-Towson, MD Metro area	2 710 489	2 785 874
	24003	Anne Arundel County, MD	537 656	560 133
	24005	Baltimore County, MD	805 029	826 925
	24013	Carroll County, MD	167 134	167 830
	24025	Harford County, MD	244 826	250 105
	24027	Howard County, MD	287 085	309 284
	24035	Queen Anne's County, MD	47 798	48 804
	24510	Baltimore city, MD	620 961	622 793
12620		Bangor, ME Metro area	153 923	153 414
	23019	Penobscot County, ME	153 923	153 414
12660		Baraboo, WI Micro area	61 976	63 379
	55111	Sauk County, WI Micro area	61 976	63 379

Core Based Statistical Areas (Metropolitan and Micropolitan), Metropolitan Divisions, and Components (as defined February 2013)–*Continued*

Core Based Statistical Area	State/ County FIPS Code	Title and Geographic Components	2010 Census Population	2014 Estimated Population
12680		Bardstown, KY Micro area	43 437	44 812
	21179	Nelson County, KY	43 437	44 812
12700		Barnstable Town, MA Metro area	215 888	214 914
	25001	Barnstable County, MA	215 888	214 914
12740		Barre, VT Micro area	59 534	58 998
	50023	Washington County, VT	59 534	58 998
12780		Bartlesville, OK Micro area	50 976	51 937
	40147	Washington County, OK	50 976	51 937
12820		Bastrop, LA Micro area	27 979	26 760
	22067	Morehouse Parish, LA	27 979	26 760
12860		Batavia, NY Micro area	60 079	59 162
	36037	Genesee County, NY	60 079	59 162
12900		Batesville, AR Micro area	36 647	36 959
	05063	Independence County, AR	36 647	36 959
12940		Baton Rouge, LA Metro area	802 484	825 478
	22005	Ascension Parish, LA	107 215	117 029
	22033	East Baton Rouge Parish, LA	440 171	446 042
	22037	East Feliciana Parish, LA	20 267	19 813
	22047	Iberville Parish, LA	33 387	33 327
	22063	Livingston Parish, LA	128 026	135 751
	22077	Pointe Coupee Parish, LA	22 802	22 406
	22091	St. Helena Parish, LA	11 203	10 619
	22121	West Baton Rouge Parish, LA	23 788	25 085
	22125	West Feliciana Parish, LA	15 625	15 406
12980		Battle Creek, MI Metro area	136 146	134 878
	26025	Calhoun County, MI	136 146	134 878
13020		Bay City, MI Metro area	107 771	106 179
	26017	Bay County, MI	107 771	106 179
13060		Bay City, TX Micro area	36 702	36 519
	48321	Matagorda County, TX	36 702	36 519
13100		Beatrice, NE Micro area	22 311	21 663
	31067	Gage County, NE Micro area	22 311	21 663
13140		Beaumont-Port Arthur, TX Metro area	403 190	405 427
	48199	Hardin County, TX	54 635	55 621
	48245	Jefferson County, TX	252 273	252 235
	48351	Newton County, TX	14 445	14 138
	48361	Orange County, TX	81 837	83 433
13180		Beaver Dam, WI Micro area	88 759	88 574
	55027	Dodge County, WI	88 759	88 574
13220		Beckley, WV Metro area	124 898	123 373
	54019	Fayette County, WV	46 039	45 132
	54081	Raleigh County, WV	78 859	78 241
13260		Bedford, IN Micro area	46 134	45 704
	18093	Lawrence County, IN	46 134	45 704
13300		Beeville, TX Micro area	31 861	32 863
	48025	Bee County, TX	31 861	32 863
13340		Bellefontaine, OH Micro area	45 858	45 507
	39091	Logan County, OH	45 858	45 507
13380		Bellingham, WA Metro area	201 140	208 351
	53073	Whatcom County, WA	201 140	208 351
13420		Bemidji, MN Micro area	44 442	45 664
	27007	Beltrami County, MN	44 442	45 664
13460		Bend-Redmond, OR Metro area	157 733	170 388
	41017	Deschutes County, OR	157 733	170 388
13500		Bennettsville, SC Micro area	28 933	27 924
	45069	Marlboro County, SC	28 933	27 924
13540		Bennington, VT Micro area	37 125	36 445
	50003	Bennington County, VT	37 125	36 445
13620		Berlin, NH-VT Micro area	39 361	37 778
	33007	Coos County, NH	33 055	31 653
	50009	Essex County, VT	6 306	6 125
13660		Big Rapids, MI Micro area	42 798	43 186
	26107	Mecosta County, MI	42 798	43 186
13700		Big Spring, TX Micro area	36 238	37 942
	48173	Glasscock County, TX	1 226	1 291
	48227	Howard County, TX	35 012	36 651
13720		Big Stone Gap, VA Micro area	61 313	59 274
	51051	Dickenson County, VA	15 903	15 308
	51195	Wise County, VA	41 452	39 935
	51720	Norton city, VA	3 958	4 031
13740		Billings, MT Metro area	158 934	166 885
	30009	Carbon County, MT	10 078	10 399
	30037	Golden Valley County, MT	884	852
	30111	Yellowstone County, MT	147 972	155 634
13780		Binghamton, NY Metro area	251 725	247 219
	36007	Broome County, NY	200 600	197 349
	36107	Tioga County, NY	51 125	49 870
13820		Birmingham-Hoover, AL Metro area	1 128 047	1 143 772
	01007	Bibb County, AL	22 915	22 506
	01009	Blount County, AL	57 322	57 719
	01021	Chilton County, AL	43 643	43 931
	01073	Jefferson County, AL	658 466	660 793
	01115	St. Clair County, AL	83 593	86 697
	01117	Shelby County, AL	195 085	206 655
	01127	Walker County, AL	67 023	65 471
13900		Bismarck, ND Metro area	114 778	126 597
	38015	Burleigh County, ND	81 308	90 503
	38059	Morton County, ND	27 471	29 822
	38065	Oliver County, ND	1 846	1 850
	38085	Sioux County, ND	4 153	4 422
13940		Blackfoot, ID Micro area	45 607	45 269
	16011	Bingham County, ID	45 607	45 269
13980		Blacksburg-Christiansburg-Radford, VA Metro area	178 237	181 605
	51063	Floyd County, VA	15 279	15 578
	51071	Giles County, VA	17 286	16 815
	51121	Montgomery County, VA	94 392	97 244
	51155	Pulaski County, VA	34 872	34 322
	51750	Radford city, VA	16 408	17 646
14010		Bloomington, IL Metro area	186 133	190 345
	17039	De Witt County, IL	16 561	16 284
	17113	McLean County, IL	169 572	174 061

Core Based Statistical Areas (Metropolitan and Micropolitan), Metropolitan Divisions, and Components (as defined February 2013)–*Continued*

Core Based Statistical Area	State/ County FIPS Code	Title and Geographic Components	2010 Census Population	2014 Estimated Population
14020		Bloomington, IN Metro area	159 549	164 308
	18105	Monroe County, IN	137 974	143 339
	18119	Owen County, IN	21 575	20 969
14100		Bloomsburg-Berwick, PA Metro area	85 562	85 763
	42037	Columbia County, PA	67 295	67 122
	42093	Montour County, PA	18 267	18 641
14140		Bluefield, WV-VA Micro area	107 342	105 237
	51185	Tazewell County, VA	45 078	43 452
	54055	Mercer County, WV	62 264	61 785
14180		Blytheville, AR Micro area	46 480	44 235
	05093	Mississippi County, AR	46 480	44 235
14220		Bogalusa, LA Micro area	47 168	46 286
	22117	Washington Parish, LA	47 168	46 286
14260		Boise City, ID Metro area	616 561	664 422
	16001	Ada County, ID	392 365	426 236
	16015	Boise County, ID	7 028	6 824
	16027	Canyon County, ID	188 923	203 143
	16045	Gem County, ID	16 719	16 866
	16073	Owyhee County, ID	11 526	11 353
14340		Boone, IA Micro area	26 306	26 433
	19015	Boone County, IA	26 306	26 433
14380		Boone, NC Micro area	51 079	52 560
	37189	Watauga County, NC	51 079	52 560
14420		Borger, TX Micro area	22 150	21 773
	48233	Hutchinson County, TX	22 150	21 773
14460		Boston-Cambridge Newton, MA-NH Metro area	4 552 402	4 732 161
		Boston, MA Metro Div 14454	1 887 792	1 966 530
	25021	Norfolk County, MA	670 850	692 254
	25023	Plymouth County, MA	494 919	507 022
	25025	Suffolk County, MA	722 023	767 254
14460		Cambridge-Newton-Framingham, MA Metro Div 15764	2 246 244	2 339 406
	25009	Essex County, MA	743 159	769 091
	25017	Middlesex County, MA	1 503 085	1 570 315
14460		Rockingham County-Strafford County-NH Metro Div 40484	418 366	426 225
	33015	Rockingham County, NH	295 223	300 621
	33017	Strafford County, NH	123 143	125 604
14500		Boulder, CO Metro area	294 567	313 333
	08013	Boulder County, CO	294 567	313 333
14540		Bowling Green, KY Metro area	158 599	165 732
	21003	Allen County, KY	19 956	20 384
	21031	Butler County, KY	12 690	12 875
	21061	Edmonson County, KY	12 161	12 013
	21227	Warren County, KY	113 792	120 460
14580		Bozeman, MT Micro area	89 513	97 308
	30031	Gallatin County, MT	89 513	97 308
14620		Bradford, PA Micro area	43 450	42 554
	42083	McKean County, PA	43 450	42 554
14660		Brainerd, MN Micro area	91 067	91 824
	27021	Cass County, MN	28 567	28 559
	27035	Crow Wing County, MN	62 500	63 265
14700		Branson, MO Micro area	83 877	85 334
	29209	Stone County, MO Micro area	32 202	31 104
	29213	Taney County, MO Micro area	51 675	54 230
14720		Breckenridge, CO Micro area	27 994	29 404
	08117	Summit County, CO	27 994	29 404
14740		Bremerton-Silverdale, WA Metro area	251 133	254 183
	53035	Kitsap County, WA	251 133	254 183
14780		Brenham, TX Micro area	33 718	34 438
	48477	Washington County, TX	33 718	34 438
14820		Brevard, NC Micro area	33 090	33 045
	37175	Transylvania County, NC	33 090	33 045
14860		Bridgeport-Stamford-Norwalk, CT Metro area	916 829	945 438
	09001	Fairfield County, CT	916 829	945 438
15020		Brookhaven, MS Micro area	34 869	34 775
	28085	Lincoln County, MS	34 869	34 775
15060		Brookings, OR Micro area	22 364	22 335
	41015	Curry County, OR	22 364	22 335
15100		Brookings, SD Micro area	31 965	33 314
	46011	Brookings County, SD	31 965	33 314
15180		Brownsville-Harlingen, TX Metro area	406 220	420 392
	48061	Cameron County, TX	406 220	420 392
15220		Brownwood, TX Micro area	38 106	37 653
	48049	Brown County, TX	38 106	37 653
15260		Brunswick, GA Metro area	112 370	114 806
	13025	Brantley County, GA	18 411	18 417
	13127	Glynn County, GA	79 626	82 175
	13191	McIntosh County, GA	14 333	14 214
15340		Bucyrus, OH Micro area	43 784	42 480
	39033	Crawford County, OH	43 784	42 480
15380		Buffalo-Cheektowaga-Niagara Falls, NY Metro area	1 135 509	1 136 360
	36029	Erie County, NY	919 040	922 835
	36063	Niagara County, NY	216 469	213 525
15420		Burley, ID Micro area	43 021	43 863
	16031	Cassia County, ID	22 952	23 540
	16067	Minidoka County, ID	20 069	20 323
15460		Burlington, IA-IL Micro area	47 656	47 171
	17071	Henderson County, IL	7 331	6 916
	19057	Des Moines County, IA	40 325	40 255
15500		Burlington, NC Metro area	151 131	155 792
	37001	Alamance County, NC	151 131	155 792
15540		Burlington-South Burlington, VT Metro area	211 261	216 167

Core Based Statistical Areas (Metropolitan and Micropolitan), Metropolitan Divisions, and Components (as defined February 2013)–*Continued*

Core Based Statistical Area	State/ County FIPS Code	Title and Geographic Components	2010 Census Population	2014 Estimated Population
	50007	Chittenden County, VT	156 545	160 531
	50011	Franklin County, VT	47 746	48 642
	50013	Grand Isle County, VT	6 970	6 994
15580		Butte-Silver Bow, MT Micro area	34 200	34 680
	30093	Silver Bow County, MT	34 200	34 680
15620		Cadillac, MI Micro area	47 584	47 923
	26113	Missaukee County, MI	14 849	15 037
	26165	Wexford County, MI	32 735	32 886
15660		Calhoun, GA Micro area	55 186	56 047
	13129	Gordon County, GA	55 186	56 047
15680		California-Lexington Park, MD Metro area	105 151	110 382
	24037	St. Mary's County, MD	105 151	110 382
15700		Cambridge, MD Micro area	32 618	32 578
	24019	Dorchester County, MD	32 618	32 578
15740		Cambridge, OH Micro area	40 087	39 590
	39059	Guernsey County, OH	40 087	39 590
15780		Camden, AR Micro area	31 488	30 030
	05013	Calhoun County, AR	5 368	5 202
	05103	Ouachita County, AR	26 120	24 828
15820		Campbellsville, KY Micro area	24 512	25 257
	21217	Taylor County, KY	24 512	25 257
15860		Cañon City, CO Micro area	46 824	46 502
	08043	Fremont County, CO	46 824	46 502
15900		Canton, IL Micro area	37 069	36 007
	17057	Fulton County, IL	37 069	36 007
15940		Canton-Massillon, OH Metro area	404 422	403 923
	39019	Carroll County, OH	28 836	28 187
	39151	Stark County, OH	375 586	375 736
15980		Cape Coral-Fort Myers, FL Metro area	618 754	679 513
	12071	Lee County, FL	618 754	679 513
16020		Cape Girardeau, MO-IL Metro area	96 275	97 929
	17003	Alexander County, IL	8 238	7 492
	29017	Bollinger County, MO	12 363	12 394
	29031	Cape Girardeau County, MO	75 674	78 043
16060		Carbondale-Marion, IL Metro area	126 575	126 685
	17077	Jackson County, IL	60 218	59 677
	17199	Williamson County, IL	66 357	67 008
16100		Carlsbad-Artesia, NM Micro area	53 829	56 395
	35015	Eddy County, NM	53 829	56 395
16180		Carson City, NV Metro area	55 274	54 522
	32510	Carson City, NV Metro area	55 274	54 522
16220		Casper, WY Metro area	75 450	81 624
	56025	Natrona County, WY	75 450	81 624
16260		Cedar City, UT Micro area	46 163	47 269
	49021	Iron County, UT	46 163	47 269
16300		Cedar Rapids, IA Metro area	257 940	263 885
	19011	Benton County, IA	26 076	25 680
	19105	Jones County, IA	20 638	20 454

Core Based Statistical Area	State/ County FIPS Code	Title and Geographic Components	2010 Census Population	2014 Estimated Population
	19113	Linn County, IA	211 226	217 751
16340		Cedartown, GA Micro area	41 475	41 133
	13233	Polk County, GA	41 475	41 133
16380		Celina, OH Micro area	40 814	40 831
	39107	Mercer County, OH	40 814	40 831
16460		Centralia, IL Micro area	39 437	38 571
	17121	Marion County, IL	39 437	38 571
16500		Centralia, WA Micro area	75 455	75 128
	53041	Lewis County, WA	75 455	75 128
16540		Chambersburg-Waynesboro, PA Metro area	149 618	152 892
	42055	Franklin County, PA	149 618	152 892
16580		Champaign-Urbana, IL Metro area	231 891	237 252
	17019	Champaign County, IL	201 081	207 133
	17053	Ford County, IL	14 081	13 688
	17147	Piatt County, IL	16 729	16 431
16620		Charleston, WV Metro area	227 078	222 878
	54005	Boone County, WV	24 629	23 714
	54015	Clay County, WV	9 386	8 941
	54039	Kanawha County, WV	193 063	190 223
16660		Charleston-Mattoon, IL Micro area	64 921	64 153
	17029	Coles County, IL	53 873	53 320
	17035	Cumberland County, IL	11 048	10 833
16700		Charleston-North Charleston, SC Metro area	664 607	727 689
	45015	Berkeley County, SC	177 843	198 205
	45019	Charleston County, SC	350 209	381 015
	45035	Dorchester County, SC	136 555	148 469
16740		Charlotte-Concord-Gastonia, NC-SC Metro area	2 217 012	2 380 314
	37025	Cabarrus County, NC	178 011	192 103
	37071	Gaston County, NC	206 086	211 127
	37097	Iredell County, NC	159 437	166 675
	37109	Lincoln County, NC	78 265	79 829
	37119	Mecklenburg County, NC	919 628	1 012 539
	37159	Rowan County, NC	138 428	138 630
	37179	Union County, NC	201 292	218 568
	45023	Chester County, SC	33 140	32 337
	45057	Lancaster County, SC	76 652	83 160
	45091	York County, SC	226 073	245 346
16820		Charlottesville, VA Metro area	218 705	226 968
	51003	Albemarle County, VA	98 970	104 489
	51029	Buckingham County, VA	17 146	16 913
	51065	Fluvanna County, VA	25 691	26 092
	51079	Greene County, VA	18 403	19 031
	51125	Nelson County, VA	15 020	14 850
	51540	Charlottesville city, VA	43 475	45 593
16860		Chattanooga, TN-GA Metro area	528 143	544 559
	13047	Catoosa County, GA	63 942	65 621
	13083	Dade County, GA	16 633	16 389
	13295	Walker County, GA	68 756	68 218
	47065	Hamilton County, TN	336 463	351 220
	47115	Marion County, TN	28 237	28 407
	47153	Sequatchie County, TN	14 112	14 704
16940		Cheyenne, WY Metro area	91 738	96 389
	56021	Laramie County, WY	91 738	96 389

Core Based Statistical Areas (Metropolitan and Micropolitan), Metropolitan Divisions, and Components (as defined February 2013)–*Continued*

Core Based Statistical Area	State/ County FIPS Code	Title and Geographic Components	2010 Census Population	2014 Estimated Population
16980		Chicago-Naperville-Elgin, IL-IN-WI Metro area	9 461 105	9 554 598
16980		Chicago-Naperville-Arlington Heights, IL Metro Div 16974	7 262 718	7 343 641
	17031	Cook County, IL	5 194 675	5 246 456
	17043	DuPage County, IL	916 924	932 708
	17063	Grundy County, IL	50 063	50 425
	17093	Kendall County, IL	114 736	121 350
	17111	McHenry County, IL	308 760	307 283
	17197	Will County, IL	677 560	685 419
16980		Elgin, IL Metro Div 20994	620 429	632 768
	17037	DeKalb County, IL	105 160	105 462
	17089	Kane County, IL	515 269	527 306
16980		Gary, IN Metro Div 23844	708 070	704 935
	18073	Jasper County, IN	33 478	33 475
	18089	Lake County, IN	496 005	490 228
	18111	Newton County, IN	14 244	14 156
	18127	Porter County, IN	164 343	167 076
16980		Lake County-Kenosha County, IL-WI Metro Div 29404	869 888	873 254
	17097	Lake County, IL	703 462	705 186
	55059	Kenosha County, WI	166 426	168 068
17020		Chico, CA Metro area	220 000	224 241
	06007	Butte County, CA	220 000	224 241
17060		Chillicothe, OH Micro area	78 064	77 159
	39141	Ross County, OH	78 064	77 159
17140		Cincinnati, OH-KY-IN Metro area	2 114 580	2 149 449
	18029	Dearborn County, IN	50 047	49 506
	18115	Ohio County, IN	6 128	6 035
	18161	Union County, IN	7 516	7 246
	21015	Boone County, KY	118 811	126 413
	21023	Bracken County, KY	8 488	8 406
	21037	Campbell County, KY	90 336	91 833
	21077	Gallatin County, KY	8 589	8 589
	21081	Grant County, KY	24 662	24 875
	21117	Kenton County, KY	159 720	163 929
	21191	Pendleton County, KY	14 877	14 493
	39015	Brown County, OH	44 846	44 116
	39017	Butler County, OH	368 130	374 158
	39025	Clermont County, OH	197 363	201 560
	39061	Hamilton County, OH	802 374	806 631
	39165	Warren County, OH	212 693	221 659
17200		Claremont-Lebanon, NH-VT Micro area	218 466	217 634
	33009	Grafton County, NH	89 118	89 658
	33019	Sullivan County, NH	43 742	43 103
	50017	Orange County, VT	28 936	28 859
	50027	Windsor County, VT	56 670	56 014
17220		Clarksburg, WV Micro area	94 196	94 221
	54017	Doddridge County, WV	8 202	8 391
	54033	Harrison County, WV	69 099	68 761
	54091	Taylor County, WV	16 895	17 069
17260		Clarksdale, MS Micro area	26 151	24 807
	28027	Coahoma County, MS	26 151	24 807
17300		Clarksville, TN-KY Metro area	260 625	278 353
	21047	Christian County, KY	73 955	74 250
	21221	Trigg County, KY	14 339	14 142
	47125	Montgomery County, TN	172 331	189 961
17340		Clearlake, CA Micro area	64 665	64 184
	06033	Lake County, CA	64 665	64 184
17380		Cleveland, MS Micro area	34 145	33 768
	28011	Bolivar County, MS	34 145	33 768
17420		Cleveland, TN Metro area	115 788	119 705
	47011	Bradley County, TN	98 963	102 975
	47139	Polk County, TN	16 825	16 730
17460		Cleveland-Elyria, OH Metro area	2 077 240	2 063 598
	39035	Cuyahoga County, OH	1 280 122	1 259 828
	39055	Geauga County, OH	93 389	94 295
	39085	Lake County, OH	230 041	229 230
	39093	Lorain County, OH	301 356	304 216
	39103	Medina County, OH	172 332	176 029
17500		Clewiston, FL Micro area	39 140	38 505
	12051	Hendry County, FL	39 140	38 505
17540		Clinton, IA Micro area	49 116	48 051
	19045	Clinton County, IA	49 116	48 051
17580		Clovis, NM Micro area	48 376	50 969
	35009	Curry County, NM	48 376	50 969
17660		Coeur d'Alene, ID Metro area	138 494	147 326
	16055	Kootenai County, ID	138 494	147 326
17700		Coffeyville, KS Micro area	35 471	34 065
	20125	Montgomery County, KS	35 471	34 065
17740		Coldwater, MI Micro area	45 248	43 545
	26023	Branch County, MI	45 248	43 545
17780		College Station-Bryan, TX Metro area	228 660	242 905
	48041	Brazos County, TX	194 851	209 152
	48051	Burleson County, TX	17 187	17 253
	48395	Robertson County, TX	16 622	16 500
17820		Colorado Springs, CO Metro area	645 613	686 908
	08041	El Paso County, CO	622 263	663 519
	08119	Teller County, CO	23 350	23 389
17860		Columbia, MO Metro area	162 642	172 717
	29019	Boone County, MO	162 642	172 717
17900		Columbia, SC Metro area	767 598	800 495
	45017	Calhoun County, SC	15 175	14 878
	45039	Fairfield County, SC	23 956	22 976
	45055	Kershaw County, SC	61 697	63 161
	45063	Lexington County, SC	262 391	277 888
	45079	Richland County, SC	384 504	401 566
	45081	Saluda County, SC	19 875	20 026
17980		Columbus, GA-AL Metro area	294 865	314 005
	01113	Russell County, AL	52 947	59 608
	13053	Chattahoochee County, GA	11 267	11 837
	13145	Harris County, GA	32 024	32 876
	13197	Marion County, GA	8 742	8 797
	13215	Muscogee County, GA	189 885	200 887
18020		Columbus, IN Metro area	76 794	80 217
	18005	Bartholomew County, IN	76 794	80 217
18060		Columbus, MS Micro area	59 779	59 730
	28087	Lowndes County, MS	59 779	59 730

Core Based Statistical Areas (Metropolitan and Micropolitan), Metropolitan Divisions, and Components (as defined February 2013)–*Continued*

Core Based Statistical Area	State/ County FIPS Code	Title and Geographic Components	2010 Census Population	2014 Estimated Population
18100		Columbus, NE Micro area	32 237	32 666
	31141	Platte County, NE	32 237	32 666
18140		Columbus, OH Metro area	1 901 974	1 994 536
	39041	Delaware County, OH	174 214	189 113
	39045	Fairfield County, OH	146 156	150 381
	39049	Franklin County, OH	1 163 414	1 231 393
	39073	Hocking County, OH	29 380	28 725
	39089	Licking County, OH	166 492	169 390
	39097	Madison County, OH	43 435	43 918
	39117	Morrow County, OH	34 827	35 152
	39127	Perry County, OH	36 058	35 812
	39129	Pickaway County, OH	55 698	56 876
	39159	Union County, OH	52 300	53 776
18180		Concord, NH Micro area	146 445	147 171
	33013	Merrimack County, NH	146 445	147 171
18220		Connersville, IN Micro area	24 277	23 468
	18041	Fayette County, IN	24 277	23 468
18260		Cookeville, TN Micro area	106 042	107 761
	47087	Jackson County, TN	11 638	11 568
	47133	Overton County, TN	22 083	22 028
	47141	Putnam County, TN	72 321	74 165
18300		Coos Bay, OR Micro area	63 043	62 475
	41011	Coos County, OR	63 043	62 475
18380		Cordele, GA Micro area	23 439	22 934
	13081	Crisp County, GA	23 439	22 934
18420		Corinth, MS Micro area	37 057	37 380
	28003	Alcorn County, MS	37 057	37 380
18460		Cornelia, GA Micro area	43 041	43 752
	13137	Habersham County, GA	43 041	43 752
18500		Corning, NY Micro area	98 990	98 394
	36101	Steuben County, NY	98 990	98 394
18580		Corpus Christi, TX Metro area	428 185	448 108
	48007	Aransas County, TX	23 158	24 972
	48355	Nueces County, TX	340 223	356 221
	48409	San Patricio County, TX	64 804	66 915
18620		Corsicana, TX Micro area	47 735	48 195
	48349	Navarro County, TX	47 735	48 195
18660		Cortland, NY Micro area	49 336	49 024
	36023	Cortland County, NY	49 336	49 024
18700		Corvallis, OR Metro area	85 579	86 316
	41003	Benton County, OR	85 579	86 316
18740		Coshocton, OH Micro area	36 901	36 516
	39031	Coshocton County, OH	36 901	36 516
18780		Craig, CO Micro area	13 795	12 928
	08081	Moffat County, CO	13 795	12 928
18820		Crawfordsville, IN Micro area	38 124	38 146
	18107	Montgomery County, IN	38 124	38 146
18860		Crescent City, CA Micro area	28 610	27 212
	06015	Del Norte County, CA	28 610	27 212
18880		Crestview-Fort Walton Beach-Destin, FL Metro area	235 865	258 042
	12091	Okaloosa County, FL	180 822	196 512
	12131	Walton County, FL	55 043	61 530
18900		Crossville, TN Micro area	56 053	57 985
	47035	Cumberland County, TN	56 053	57 985
18980		Cullman, AL Micro area	80 406	81 289
	01043	Cullman County, AL	80 406	81 289
19000		Cullowhee, NC Micro area	40 271	40 981
	37099	Jackson County, NC	40 271	40 981
19060		Cumberland, MD-WV Metro area	103 299	100 530
	24001	Allegany County, MD	75 087	72 952
	54057	Mineral County, WV	28 212	27 578
19100		Dallas-Fort Worth-Arlington, TX Metro area	6 426 214	6 954 330
19100		Dallas-Plano-Irving, TX Metro Div 19124	4 230 520	4 604 097
	48085	Collin County, TX	782 341	885 241
	48113	Dallas County, TX	2 368 139	2 518 638
	48121	Denton County, TX	662 614	753 363
	48139	Ellis County, TX	149 610	159 317
	48231	Hunt County, TX	86 129	88 493
	48257	Kaufman County, TX	103 350	111 236
	48397	Rockwall County, TX	78 337	87 809
19100		Fort Worth-Arlington, TX Metro Div 23104	2 195 694	2 350 233
	48221	Hood County, TX	51 182	53 921
	48251	Johnson County, TX	150 934	157 456
	48367	Parker County, TX	116 927	123 164
	48425	Somervell County, TX	8 490	8 694
	48439	Tarrant County, TX	1 809 034	1 945 360
	48497	Wise County, TX	59 127	61 638
19140		Dalton, GA Metro area	142 227	142 952
	13213	Murray County, GA	39 628	39 410
	13313	Whitfield County, GA	102 599	103 542
19180		Danville, IL Metro area	81 625	79 728
	17183	Vermilion County, IL	81 625	79 728
19220		Danville, KY Micro area	53 174	54 151
	21021	Boyle County, KY	28 432	29 706
	21137	Lincoln County, KY	24 742	24 445
19260		Danville, VA Micro area	106 561	104 827
	51143	Pittsylvania County, VA	63 506	62 383
	51590	Danville city, VA	43 055	42 444
19300		Daphne-Fairhope-Foley, AL Metro area	182 265	200 111
	01003	Baldwin County, AL	182 265	200 111
19340		Davenport-Moline-Rock Island, IA-IL Metro area	379 690	383 030
	17073	Henry County, IL	50 486	49 635
	17131	Mercer County, IL	16 434	15 945
	17161	Rock Island County, IL	147 546	146 063
	19163	Scott County, IA	165 224	171 387

Core Based Statistical Areas (Metropolitan and Micropolitan), Metropolitan Divisions, and Components (as defined February 2013)–*Continued*

Core Based Statistical Area	State/ County FIPS Code	Title and Geographic Components	2010 Census Population	2014 Estimated Population
19380		Dayton, OH Metro area	799 232	800 836
	39057	Greene County, OH	161 573	163 820
	39109	Miami County, OH	102 506	103 900
	39113	Montgomery County, OH	535 153	533 116
19420		Dayton, TN Micro area	31 809	32 641
	47143	Rhea County, TN	31 809	32 641
19460		Decatur, AL Metro area	153 829	153 084
	01079	Lawrence County, AL	34 339	33 477
	01103	Morgan County, AL	119 490	119 607
19500		Decatur, IL Metro area	110 768	108 350
	17115	Macon County, IL	110 768	108 350
19540		Decatur, IN Micro area	34 387	34 791
	18001	Adams County, IN	34 387	34 791
19580		Defiance, OH Micro area	39 037	38 510
	39039	Defiance County, OH	39 037	38 510
19620		Del Rio, TX Micro area	48 879	48 974
	48465	Val Verde County, TX	48 879	48 974
19660		Deltona-Daytona Beach-Ormond Beach, FL Metro area	590 289	609 939
	12035	Flagler County, FL	95 696	102 408
	12127	Volusia County, FL	494 593	507 531
19700		Deming, NM Micro area	25 095	24 673
	35029	Luna County, NM	25 095	24 673
19740		Denver-Aurora-Lakewood, CO Metro area	2 543 482	2 754 258
	08001	Adams County, CO	441 603	480 718
	08005	Arapahoe County, CO	572 003	618 821
	08014	Broomfield County, CO	55 889	62 138
	08019	Clear Creek County, CO	9 088	9 187
	08031	Denver County, CO	600 158	663 862
	08035	Douglas County, CO	285 465	314 638
	08039	Elbert County, CO	23 086	24 195
	08047	Gilpin County, CO	5 441	5 851
	08059	Jefferson County, CO	534 543	558 503
	08093	Park County, CO	16 206	16 345
19760		DeRidder, LA Micro area	35 654	36 198
	22011	Beauregard Parish, LA	35 654	36 198
19780		Des Moines-West Des Moines, IA Metro area	569 633	611 549
	19049	Dallas County, IA	66 135	77 400
	19077	Guthrie County, IA	10 954	10 722
	19121	Madison County, IA	15 679	15 609
	19153	Polk County, IA	430 640	459 862
	19181	Warren County, IA	46 225	47 956
19820		Detroit-Warren-Dearborn, MI Metro area	4 296 250	4 296 611
19820		Detroit-Dearborn-Livonia, MI Metro Div 19804	1 820 584	1 764 804
	26163	Wayne County, MI	1 820 584	1 764 804
19820		Warren-Troy-Farmington Hills, MI Metro Div 47664	2 475 666	2 531 807
	26087	Lapeer County, MI	88 319	88 153
	26093	Livingston County, MI	180 967	185 596
	26099	Macomb County, MI	840 978	860 112
	26125	Oakland County, MI	1 202 362	1 237 868
	26147	St. Clair County, MI	163 040	160 078
19860		Dickinson, ND Micro area	24 199	30 372
	38089	Stark County, ND	24 199	30 372
19940		Dixon, IL Micro area	36 031	34 735
	17103	Lee County, IL	36 031	34 735
19980		Dodge City, KS Micro area	33 848	34 795
	20057	Ford County, KS	33 848	34 795
20020		Dothan, AL Metro area	145 639	148 095
	01061	Geneva County, AL	26 790	26 712
	01067	Henry County, AL	17 302	17 190
	01069	Houston County, AL	101 547	104 193
20060		Douglas, GA Micro area	42 356	42 811
	13069	Coffee County, GA	42 356	42 811
20100		Dover, DE Metro area	162 310	171 987
	10001	Kent County, Delaware	162 310	171 987
20140		Dublin, GA Micro area	58 414	57 552
	13167	Johnson County, GA	9 980	9 701
	13175	Laurens County, GA	48 434	47 851
20180		DuBois, PA Micro area	81 642	81 191
	42033	Clearfield County, PA	81 642	81 191
20220		Dubuque, IA Metro area	93 653	96 370
	19061	Dubuque County, IA	93 653	96 370
20260		Duluth, MN-WI Metro area	279 771	280 218
	27017	Carlton County, MN	35 386	35 571
	27137	St. Louis County, MN	200 226	200 949
	55031	Douglas County, WI	44 159	43 698
20300		Dumas, TX Micro area	21 904	22 148
	48341	Moore County, TX	21 904	22 148
20340		Duncan, OK Micro area	45 048	44 493
	40137	Stephens County, OK	45 048	44 493
20380		Dunn, NC Micro area	114 678	126 666
	37085	Harnett County, NC	114 678	126 666
20420		Durango, CO Micro area	51 334	53 989
	08067	La Plata County, CO	51 334	53 989
20460		Durant, OK Micro area	42 416	44 486
	40013	Bryan County, OK	42 416	44 486
20500		Durham-Chapel Hill, NC Metro area	504 357	542 710
	37037	Chatham County, NC	63 505	68 698
	37063	Durham County, NC	267 587	294 460
	37135	Orange County, NC	133 801	140 420
	37145	Person County, NC	39 464	39 132
20540		Dyersburg, TN Micro area	38 335	37 935
	47045	Dyer County, TN	38 335	37 935
20580		Eagle Pass, TX Micro area	54 258	57 023
	48323	Maverick County, TX	54 258	57 023

Core Based Statistical Areas (Metropolitan and Micropolitan), Metropolitan Divisions, and Components (as defined February 2013)–*Continued*

Core Based Statistical Area	State/ County FIPS Code	Title and Geographic Components	2010 Census Population	2014 Estimated Population
20660		Easton, MD Micro area	37 782	37 643
	24041	Talbot County, MD	37 782	37 643
20700		East Stroudsburg, PA Metro area	169 842	166 314
	42089	Monroe County, PA	169 842	166 314
20740		Eau Claire, WI Metro area	161 151	165 024
	55017	Chippewa County, WI	62 415	63 460
	55035	Eau Claire County, WI	98 736	101 564
20780		Edwards, CO Micro area	52 197	52 921
	08037	Eagle County, CO	52 197	52 921
20820		Effingham, IL Micro area	34 242	34 320
	17049	Effingham County, IL	34 242	34 320
20900		El Campo, TX Micro area	41 280	41 168
	48481	Wharton County, TX	41 280	41 168
20940		El Centro, CA Metro area	174 528	179 091
	06025	Imperial County, CA	174 528	179 091
20980		El Dorado, AR Micro area	41 639	40 227
	05139	Union County, AR	41 639	40 227
21020		Elizabeth City, NC Micro area	64 094	63 584
	37029	Camden County, NC	9 980	10 331
	37139	Pasquotank County, NC	40 661	39 787
	37143	Perquimans County, NC	13 453	13 466
21060		Elizabethtown-Fort Knox, KY Metro area	148 338	151 585
	21093	Hardin County, KY	105 543	108 266
	21123	Larue County, KY	14 193	14 180
	21163	Meade County, KY	28 602	29 139
21120		Elk City, OK Micro area	22 119	23 691
	40009	Beckham County, OK	22 119	23 691
21140		Elkhart-Goshen, IN Metro area	197 559	201 971
	18039	Elkhart County, IN	197 559	201 971
21180		Elkins, WV Micro area	29 405	29 429
	54083	Randolph County, WV	29 405	29 429
21220		Elko, NV Micro area	50 805	54 784
	32007	Elko County, NV	48 818	52 766
	32011	Eureka County, NV	1 987	2 018
21260		Ellensburg, WA Micro area	40 915	42 522
	53037	Kittitas County, WA	40 915	42 522
21300		Elmira, NY Metro area	88 830	87 770
	36015	Chemung County, NY	88 830	87 770
21340		El Paso, TX Metro area	804 123	836 698
	48141	El Paso County, TX	800 647	833 487
	48229	Hudspeth County, TX	3 476	3 211
21380		Emporia, KS Micro area	33 690	33 212
	20111	Lyon County, KS	33 690	33 212
21420		Enid, OK Micro area	60 580	63 091
	40047	Garfield County, OK	60 580	63 091
21460		Enterprise, AL Micro area	49 948	50 909
	01031	Coffee County, AL	49 948	50 909
21500		Erie, PA Metro area	280 566	278 443
	42049	Erie County, PA	280 566	278 443
21540		Escanaba, MI Micro area	37 069	36 559
	26041	Delta County, MI	37 069	36 559
21580		Española, NM Micro area	40 246	39 777
	35039	Rio Arriba County, NM	40 246	39 777
21660		Eugene, OR Metro area	351 715	358 337
	41039	Lane County, OR	351 715	358 337
21700		Eureka-Arcata-Fortuna, CA Micro area	134 623	134 809
	06023	Humboldt County, CA	134 623	134 809
21740		Evanston, WY Micro area	21 118	20 904
	56041	Uinta County, WY	21 118	20 904
21780		Evansville, IN-KY Metro area	311 552	315 162
	18129	Posey County, IN	25 910	25 540
	18163	Vanderburgh County, IN	179 703	182 006
	18173	Warrick County, IN	59 689	61 149
	21101	Henderson County, KY	46 250	46 467
21820		Fairbanks, AK Metro area	97 581	99 357
	02090	Fairbanks North Star Borough, AK	97 581	99 357
21840		Fairfield, IA Micro area	16 843	17 325
	19101	Jefferson County, IA	16 843	17 325
21900		Fairmont, WV Micro area	56 418	56 803
	54049	Marion County, WV	56 418	56 803
21980		Fallon, NV Micro area	24 877	23 989
	32001	Churchill County, NV	24 877	23 989
22020		Fargo, ND-MN Metro area	208 777	228 291
	27027	Clay County, MN	58 999	61 286
	38017	Cass County, ND	149 778	167 005
22060		Faribault-Northfield, MN Micro area	64 142	65 151
	27131	Rice County, MN	64 142	65 151
22100		Farmington, MO Micro area	65 359	65 960
	29187	St. Francois County, MO	65 359	65 960
22140		Farmington, NM Metro area	130 044	123 785
	35045	San Juan County, NM	130 044	123 785
22180		Fayetteville, NC Metro area	366 383	377 939
	37051	Cumberland County, NC	319 431	326 328
	37093	Hoke County, NC	46 952	51 611
22220		Fayetteville-Springdale-Rogers, AR-MO Metro area	463 204	501 653
	05007	Benton County, AR	221 339	242 321
	05087	Madison County, AR	15 717	15 740
	05143	Washington County, AR	203 065	220 792
	29119	McDonald County, MO	23 083	22 800
22260		Fergus Falls, MN Micro area	57 303	57 635
	27111	Otter Tail County, MN	57 303	57 635
22280		Fernley, NV Micro area	51 980	51 789
	32019	Lyon County, NV	51 980	51 789

Core Based Statistical Areas (Metropolitan and Micropolitan), Metropolitan Divisions, and Components (as defined February 2013)–*Continued*

Core Based Statistical Area	State/ County FIPS Code	Title and Geographic Components	2010 Census Population	2014 Estimated Population
22300		Findlay, OH Micro area	74 782	75 337
	39063	Hancock County, OH	74 782	75 337
22340		Fitzgerald, GA Micro area	17 634	17 464
	13017	Ben Hill County, GA	17 634	17 464
22380		Flagstaff, AZ Metro area	134 421	137 682
	04005	Coconino County, AZ	134 421	137 682
22420		Flint, MI Metro area	425 790	412 895
	26049	Genesee County, MI	425 790	412 895
22500		Florence, SC Metro area	205 566	207 030
	45031	Darlington County, SC	68 681	67 799
	45041	Florence County, SC	136 885	139 231
22520		Florence-Muscle Shoals, AL Metro area	147 137	147 639
	01033	Colbert County, AL	54 428	54 543
	01077	Lauderdale County, AL	92 709	93 096
22540		Fond du Lac, WI Metro area	101 633	101 759
	55039	Fond du Lac County, WI	101 633	101 759
22580		Forest City, NC Micro area	67 810	66 600
	37161	Rutherford County, NC	67 810	66 600
22620		Forrest City, AR Micro area	28 258	26 899
	05123	St. Francis County, AR	28 258	26 899
22660		Fort Collins, CO Metro area	299 630	324 122
	08069	Larimer County, CO	299 630	324 122
22700		Fort Dodge, IA Micro area	38 013	36 955
	19187	Webster County, IA	38 013	36 955
22780		Fort Leonard Wood, MO Micro area	52 274	53 436
	29169	Pulaski County, MO	52 274	53 436
22800		Fort Madison-Keokuk, IA-IL-MO Micro area	62 105	60 767
	17067	Hancock County, IL	19 104	18 564
	19111	Lee County, IA	35 862	35 286
	29045	Clark County, MO	7 139	6 917
22820		Fort Morgan, CO Micro area	28 159	28 328
	08087	Morgan County, CO	28 159	28 328
22860		Fort Polk South, LA Micro area	52 334	52 132
	22115	Vernon Parish, LA	52 334	52 132
22900		Fort Smith, AR-OK Metro area	280 467	279 592
	05033	Crawford County, AR	61 948	61 697
	05131	Sebastian County, AR	125 744	126 776
	40079	Le Flore County, OK	50 384	49 761
	40135	Sequoyah County, OK	42 391	41 358
23060		Fort Wayne, IN Metro area	416 257	427 183
	18003	Allen County, IN	355 329	365 918
	18179	Wells County, IN	27 636	27 862
	18183	Whitley County, IN	33 292	33 403
23140		Frankfort, IN Micro area	33 224	32 776
	18023	Clinton County, IN	33 224	32 776
23180		Frankfort, KY Micro area	70 706	71 768
	21005	Anderson County, KY	21 421	21 888
	21073	Franklin County, KY	49 285	49 880
23240		Fredericksburg, TX Micro area	24 837	25 520
	48171	Gillespie County, TX	24 837	25 520
23300		Freeport, IL Micro area	47 711	46 435
	17177	Stephenson County, IL	47 711	46 435
23340		Fremont, NE Micro area	36 691	36 744
	31053	Dodge County, NE	36 691	36 744
23380		Fremont, OH Micro area	60 944	60 179
	39143	Sandusky County, OH	60 944	60 179
23420		Fresno, CA Metro area	930 450	965 974
	06019	Fresno County, CA	930 450	965 974
23460		Gadsden, AL Metro area	104 430	103 531
	01055	Etowah County, AL	104 430	103 531
23500		Gaffney, SC Micro area	55 342	56 024
	45021	Cherokee County, SC	55 342	56 024
23540		Gainesville, FL Metro area	264 275	273 377
	12001	Alachua County, FL	247 336	256 380
	12041	Gilchrist County, FL	16 939	16 997
23580		Gainesville, GA Metro area	179 684	190 761
	13139	Hall County, GA	179 684	190 761
23620		Gainesville, TX Micro area	38 437	38 761
	48097	Cooke County, TX	38 437	38 761
23660		Galesburg, IL Micro area	52 919	52 069
	17095	Knox County, IL	52 919	52 069
23700		Gallup, NM Micro area	71 492	74 098
	35031	McKinley County, NM	71 492	74 098
23780		Garden City, KS Micro area	40 753	41 099
	20055	Finney County, KS	36 776	37 184
	20093	Kearny County, KS	3 977	3 915
23820		Gardnerville Ranchos, NV Micro area	46 997	47 536
	32005	Douglas County, NV	46 997	47 536
23860		Georgetown, SC Micro area	60 158	60 773
	45043	Georgetown County, SC	60 158	60 773
23900		Gettysburg, PA Metro area	101 407	101 714
	42001	Adams County, PA	101 407	101 714
23940		Gillette, WY Micro area	46 133	48 320
	56005	Campbell County, WY	46 133	48 320
23980		Glasgow, KY Micro area	52 272	53 138
	21009	Barren County, KY	42 173	43 148
	21169	Metcalfe County, KY	10 099	9 990
24020		Glens Falls, NY Metro area	128 923	127 345
	36113	Warren County, NY	65 707	64 973
	36115	Washington County, NY	63 216	62 372
24060		Glenwood Springs, CO Micro area	73 537	75 087
	08045	Garfield County, CO	56 389	57 461
	08097	Pitkin County, CO	17 148	17 626
24100		Gloversville, NY Micro area	55 531	54 105
	36035	Fulton County, NY	55 531	54 105

Core Based Statistical Areas (Metropolitan and Micropolitan), Metropolitan Divisions, and Components (as defined February 2013)–*Continued*

Core Based Statistical Area	State/ County FIPS Code	Title and Geographic Components	2010 Census Population	2014 Estimated Population
24140		Goldsboro, NC Metro area	122 623	124 456
	37191	Wayne County, NC	122 623	124 456
24220		Grand Forks, ND-MN Metro area	98 461	101 842
	27119	Polk County, MN	31 600	31 704
	38035	Grand Forks County, ND	66 861	70 138
24260		Grand Island, NE Metro area	81 850	84 755
	31079	Hall County, NE	58 607	61 492
	31081	Hamilton County, NE	9 124	9 135
	31093	Howard County, NE	6 274	6 362
	31121	Merrick County, NE	7 845	7 766
24300		Grand Junction, CO Metro area	146 723	148 255
	08077	Mesa County, CO	146 723	148 255
24340		Grand Rapids-Wyoming, MI Metro area	988 938	1 027 703
	26015	Barry County, MI	59 173	59 281
	26081	Kent County, MI	602 622	629 237
	26117	Montcalm County, MI	63 342	62 893
	26139	Ottawa County, MI	263 801	276 292
24380		Grants, NM Micro area	27 213	27 349
	35006	Cibola County, NM	27 213	27 349
24420		Grants Pass, OR Metro area	82 713	83 599
	41033	Josephine County, OR	82 713	83 599
24460		Great Bend, KS Micro area	27 674	27 385
	20009	Barton County, KS	27 674	27 385
24500		Great Falls, MT Metro area	81 327	82 344
	30013	Cascade County, MT	81 327	82 344
24540		Greeley, CO Metro area	252 825	277 670
	08123	Weld County, CO	252 825	277 670
24580		Green Bay, WI Metro area	306 241	314 531
	55009	Brown County, WI	248 007	256 670
	55061	Kewaunee County, WI	20 574	20 444
	55083	Oconto County, WI	37 660	37 417
24620		Greeneville, TN Micro area	68 831	68 335
	47059	Greene County, TN	68 831	68 335
24640		Greenfield Town, MA Micro area	71 372	70 862
	25011	Franklin County, MA	71 372	70 862
24660		Greensboro-High Point, NC Metro area	723 801	746 593
	37081	Guilford County, NC	488 406	512 119
	37151	Randolph County, NC	141 752	142 778
	37157	Rockingham County, NC	93 643	91 696
24700		Greensburg, IN Micro area	25 740	26 524
	18031	Decatur County, IN	25 740	26 524
24740		Greenville, MS Micro area	51 137	48 958
	28151	Washington County, MS	51 137	48 958
24780		Greenville, NC Metro area	168 148	175 354
	37147	Pitt County, NC	168 148	175 354
24820		Greenville, OH Micro area	52 959	52 196
	39037	Darke County, OH	52 959	52 196
24860		Greenville-Anderson-Mauldin, SC Metro area	824 112	862 463
	45007	Anderson County, SC	187 126	192 810
	45045	Greenville County, SC	451 225	482 752
	45059	Laurens County, SC	66 537	66 533
	45077	Pickens County, SC	119 224	120 368
24900		Greenwood, MS Micro area	42 914	41 676
	28015	Carroll County, MS	10 597	10 254
	28083	Leflore County, MS	32 317	31 422
24940		Greenwood, SC Micro area	95 078	94 485
	45001	Abbeville County, SC	25 417	24 965
	45047	Greenwood County, SC	69 661	69 520
24980		Grenada, MS Micro area	21 906	21 666
	28043	Grenada County, MS	21 906	21 666
25060		Gulfport-Biloxi-Pascagoula, MS Metro area	370 702	386 144
	28045	Hancock County, MS	43 929	45 949
	28047	Harrison County, MS	187 105	199 058
	28059	Jackson County, MS	139 668	141 137
25100		Guymon, OK Micro area	20 640	21 853
	40139	Texas County, OK	20 640	21 853
25180		Hagerstown-Martinsburg, MD-WV Metro area	251 599	260 070
	24043	Washington County, MD	147 430	149 573
	54003	Berkeley County, WV	104 169	110 497
25200		Hailey, ID Micro area	27 701	27 837
	16013	Blaine County, ID	21 376	21 482
	16025	Camas County, ID	1 117	1 039
	16063	Lincoln County, ID	5 208	5 316
25220		Hammond, LA Metro area	121 097	127 049
	22105	Tangipahoa Parish, LA	121 097	127 049
25260		Hanford-Corcoran, CA Metro area	152 982	150 269
	06031	Kings County, CA	152 982	150 269
25300		Hannibal, MO Micro area	38 948	39 175
	29127	Marion County, MO	28 781	28 920
	29173	Ralls County, MO	10 167	10 255
25420		Harrisburg-Carlisle, PA Metro area	549 475	560 849
	42041	Cumberland County, PA	235 406	243 762
	42043	Dauphin County, PA	268 100	271 453
	42099	Perry County, PA	45 969	45 634
25460		Harrison, AR Micro area	45 233	45 100
	05009	Boone County, AR	36 903	37 196
	05101	Newton County, AR	8 330	7 904
25500		Harrisonburg, VA Metro area	125 228	130 649
	51165	Rockingham County, VA	76 314	78 171
	51660	Harrisonburg city, VA	48 914	52 478
25540		Hartford-West Hartford-East Hartford, CT Metro area	1 212 381	1 214 295
	09003	Hartford County, CT	894 014	897 985
	09007	Middlesex County, CT	165 676	164 943
	09013	Tolland County, CT	152 691	151 367
25580		Hastings, NE Micro area	31 364	31 457
	31001	Adams County, NE	31 364	31 457

Core Based Statistical Areas (Metropolitan and Micropolitan), Metropolitan Divisions, and Components (as defined February 2013)–*Continued*

Core Based Statistical Area	State/ County FIPS Code	Title and Geographic Components	2010 Census Population	2014 Estimated Population
25620		Hattiesburg, MS Metro area	142 842	148 656
	28035	Forrest County, MS	74 934	76 330
	28073	Lamar County, MS	55 658	60 099
	28111	Perry County, MS	12 250	12 227
25700		Hays, KS Micro area	28 452	29 013
	20051	Ellis County, KS	28 452	29 013
25720		Heber, UT Micro area	23 530	27 714
	49051	Wasatch County, UT	23 530	27 714
25740		Helena, MT Micro area	74 801	77 414
	30043	Jefferson County, MT	11 406	11 558
	30049	Lewis and Clark County, MT	63 395	65 856
25760		Helena-West Helena, AR Micro area	21 757	19 930
	05107	Phillips County, AR	21 757	19 930
25780		Henderson, NC Micro area	45 422	44 614
	37181	Vance County, NC	45 422	44 614
25820		Hereford, TX Micro area	19 372	19 195
	48117	Deaf Smith County, TX	19 372	19 195
25840		Hermiston-Pendleton, OR Micro area	87 062	87 892
	41049	Morrow County, OR	11 173	11 187
	41059	Umatilla County, OR	75 889	76 705
25860		Hickory-Lenoir-Morganton, NC Metro area	365 497	362 896
	37003	Alexander County, NC	37 198	37 392
	37023	Burke County, NC	90 912	89 486
	37027	Caldwell County, NC	83 029	81 484
	37035	Catawba County, NC	154 358	154 534
25880		Hillsdale, MI Micro area	46 688	45 830
	26059	Hillsdale County, MI	46 688	45 830
25900		Hilo, HI Micro area	185 079	194 190
	15001	Hawaii County, HI	185 079	194 190
25940		Hilton Head Island-Bluffton-Beaufort, SC Metro area	187 010	203 022
	45013	Beaufort County, SC	162 233	175 852
	45053	Jasper County, SC	24 777	27 170
25980		Hinesville, GA Metro area	77 917	82 311
	13179	Liberty County, GA	63 453	65 198
	13183	Long County, GA	14 464	17 113
26020		Hobbs, NM Micro area	64 727	69 999
	35025	Lea County, NM	64 727	69 999
26090		Holland, MI Micro area	111 408	113 847
	26005	Allegan County, MI	111 408	113 847
26140		Homosassa Springs, FL Metro area	141 236	139 377
	12017	Citrus County, FL	141 236	139 377
26220		Hood River, OR Micro area	22 346	22 885
	41027	Hood River County, OR	22 346	22 885
26300		Hot Springs, AR Metro area	96 024	97 322
	05051	Garland County, AR	96 024	97 322
26340		Houghton, MI Micro area	38 784	38 712
	26061	Houghton County, MI	36 628	36 495
	26083	Keweenaw County, MI	2 156	2 217
26380		Houma-Thibodaux, LA Metro area	208 178	211 348
	22057	Lafourche Parish, LA	96 318	98 020
	22109	Terrebonne Parish, LA	111 860	113 328
26420		Houston-The Woodlands-Sugar Land, TX Metro area	5 920 416	6 490 180
	48015	Austin County, TX	28 417	29 114
	48039	Brazoria County, TX	313 166	338 124
	48071	Chambers County, TX	35 096	38 145
	48157	Fort Bend County, TX	585 375	685 345
	48167	Galveston County, TX	291 309	314 198
	48201	Harris County, TX	4 092 459	4 441 370
	48291	Liberty County, TX	75 643	78 117
	48339	Montgomery County, TX	455 746	518 947
	48473	Waller County, TX	43 205	46 820
26460		Hudson, NY Micro area	63 096	62 122
	36021	Columbia County, NY	63 096	62 122
26500		Huntingdon, PA Micro area	45 913	45 750
	42061	Huntingdon County, PA	45 913	45 750
26540		Huntington, IN Micro area	37 124	36 706
	18069	Huntington County, IN	37 124	36 706
26580		Huntington-Ashland, WV-KY-OH Metro area	364 908	363 325
	21019	Boyd County, KY	49 542	48 832
	21089	Greenup County, KY	36 910	36 308
	39087	Lawrence County, OH	62 450	61 623
	54011	Cabell County, WV	96 319	97 109
	54043	Lincoln County, WV	21 720	21 561
	54079	Putnam County, WV	55 486	56 770
	54099	Wayne County, WV	42 481	41 122
26620		Huntsville, AL Metro area	417 593	441 086
	01083	Limestone County, AL	82 782	90 787
	01089	Madison County, AL	334 811	350 299
26660		Huntsville, TX Micro area	82 446	84 013
	48455	Trinity County, TX	14 585	14 224
	48471	Walker County, TX	67 861	69 789
26700		Huron, SD Micro area	17 398	18 169
	46005	Beadle County, SD	17 398	18 169
26740		Hutchinson, KS Micro area	64 511	63 794
	20155	Reno County, KS	64 511	63 794
26780		Hutchinson, MN Micro area	36 651	35 882
	27085	McLeod County, MN	36 651	35 882
26820		Idaho Falls, ID Metro area	133 265	138 266
	16019	Bonneville County, ID	104 234	108 623
	16023	Butte County, ID	2 891	2 622
	16051	Jefferson County, ID	26 140	27 021
26860		Indiana, PA Micro area	88 880	87 706
	42063	Indiana County, PA	88 880	87 706

Core Based Statistical Areas (Metropolitan and Micropolitan), Metropolitan Divisions, and Components (as defined February 2013)–*Continued*

Core Based Statistical Area	State/ County FIPS Code	Title and Geographic Components	2010 Census Population	2014 Estimated Population
26900		Indianapolis-Carmel-Anderson, IN Metro area	1 887 877	1 971 274
	18011	Boone County, IN	56 640	61 915
	18013	Brown County, IN	15 242	14 962
	18057	Hamilton County, IN	274 569	302 623
	18059	Hancock County, IN	70 002	71 978
	18063	Hendricks County, IN	145 448	156 056
	18081	Johnson County, IN	139 654	147 538
	18095	Madison County, IN	131 636	130 069
	18097	Marion County, IN	903 393	934 243
	18109	Morgan County, IN	68 894	69 693
	18133	Putnam County, IN	37 963	37 618
	18145	Shelby County, IN	44 436	44 579
26940		Indianola, MS Micro area	29 450	27 496
	28133	Sunflower County, MS	29 450	27 496
26960		Ionia, MI Micro area	63 905	64 294
	26067	Ionia County, MI	63 905	64 294
26980		Iowa City, IA Metro area	152 586	164 357
	19103	Johnson County, IA	130 882	142 287
	19183	Washington County, IA	21 704	22 070
27020		Iron Mountain, MI-WI Micro area	30 591	30 438
	26043	Dickinson County, MI	26 168	25 957
	55037	Florence County, WI	4 423	4 481
27060		Ithaca, NY Metro area	101 564	104 691
	36109	Tompkins County, NY	101 564	104 691
27100		Jackson, MI Metro area	160 248	159 741
	26075	Jackson County, MI	160 248	159 741
27140		Jackson, MS Metro area	567 122	577 564
	28029	Copiah County, MS	29 449	28 797
	28049	Hinds County, MS	245 285	243 729
	28089	Madison County, MS	95 203	101 688
	28121	Rankin County, MS	141 617	148 070
	28127	Simpson County, MS	27 503	27 463
	28163	Yazoo County, MS	28 065	27 817
27160		Jackson, OH Micro area	33 225	32 748
	39079	Jackson County, OH	33 225	32 748
27180		Jackson, TN Metro area	130 011	130 225
	47023	Chester County, TN	17 131	17 379
	47033	Crockett County, TN	14 586	14 668
	47113	Madison County, TN	98 294	98 178
27220		Jackson, WY-ID Micro area	31 464	33 271
	16081	Teton County, ID	10 170	10 341
	56039	Teton County, WY	21 294	22 930
27260		Jacksonville, FL Metro area	1 345 596	1 419 127
	12003	Baker County, FL	27 115	27 093
	12019	Clay County, FL	190 865	199 798
	12031	Duval County, FL	864 263	897 698
	12089	Nassau County, FL	73 314	76 619
	12109	St. Johns County, FL	190 039	217 919
27300		Jacksonville, IL Micro area	40 902	40 133
	17137	Morgan County, IL	35 547	34 929
	17171	Scott County, IL	5 355	5 204
27340		Jacksonville, NC Metro area	177 772	187 589
	37133	Onslow County, NC	177 772	187 589
27380		Jacksonville, TX Micro area	50 845	50 902
	48073	Cherokee County, TX	50 845	50 902
27420		Jamestown, ND Micro area	21 100	21 129
	38093	Stutsman County, ND	21 100	21 129
27460		Jamestown-Dunkirk-Fredonia, NY Micro area	134 905	132 053
	36013	Chautauqua County, NY	134 905	132 053
27500		Janesville-Beloit, WI Metro area	160 331	161 188
	55105	Rock County, WI	160 331	161 188
27540		Jasper, IN Micro area	54 734	54 969
	18037	Dubois County, IN	41 889	42 345
	18125	Pike County, IN	12 845	12 624
27600		Jefferson, GA Micro area	60 485	61 870
	13157	Jackson County, GA	60 485	61 870
27620		Jefferson City, MO Metro area	149 807	150 866
	29027	Callaway County, MO	44 332	44 750
	29051	Cole County, MO	75 990	76 557
	29135	Moniteau County, MO	15 607	15 856
	29151	Osage County, MO	13 878	13 703
27700		Jesup, GA Micro area	30 099	29 949
	13305	Wayne County, GA	30 099	29 949
27740		Johnson City, TN Metro area	198 716	201 091
	47019	Carter County, TN	57 424	56 886
	47171	Unicoi County, TN	18 313	17 963
	47179	Washington County, TN	122 979	126 242
27780		Johnstown, PA Metro area	143 679	137 732
	42021	Cambria County, PA	143 679	137 732
27860		Jonesboro, AR Metro area	121 026	126 764
	05031	Craighead County, AR	96 443	102 518
	05111	Poinsett County, AR	24 583	24 246
27900		Joplin, MO Metro area	175 518	176 141
	29097	Jasper County, MO	117 404	117 543
	29145	Newton County, MO	58 114	58 598
27920		Junction City, KS Micro area	34 362	36 713
	20061	Geary County, KS	34 362	36 713
27940		Juneau, AK Micro area	31 275	32 406
	02110	Juneau City and Borough, AK	31 275	32 406
27980		Kahului-Wailuku-Lahaina, HI Metro area	154 924	163 108
	15005	Kalawao County, HI	90	89
	15009	Maui County, HI	154 834	163 019
28020		Kalamazoo-Portage, MI Metro area	326 589	334 017
	26077	Kalamazoo County, MI	250 331	258 818
	26159	Van Buren County, MI	76 258	75 199
28060		Kalispell, MT Micro area	90 928	94 924
	30029	Flathead County, MT	90 928	94 924
28100		Kankakee, IL Metro area	113 449	111 375
	17091	Kankakee County, IL	113 449	111 375

Core Based Statistical Areas (Metropolitan and Micropolitan), Metropolitan Divisions, and Components (as defined February 2013)–*Continued*

Core Based Statistical Area	State/ County FIPS Code	Title and Geographic Components	2010 Census Population	2014 Estimated Population
28140		Kansas City, MO-KS Metro area	2 009 342	2 071 133
	20091	Johnson County, KS	544 179	574 272
	20103	Leavenworth County, KS	76 227	78 797
	20107	Linn County, KS	9 656	9 502
	20121	Miami County, KS	32 787	32 822
	20209	Wyandotte County, KS	157 505	161 636
	29013	Bates County, MO	17 049	16 584
	29025	Caldwell County, MO	9 424	9 034
	29037	Cass County, MO	99 478	100 889
	29047	Clay County, MO	221 939	233 682
	29049	Clinton County, MO	20 743	20 299
	29095	Jackson County, MO	674 158	683 191
	29107	Lafayette County, MO	33 381	32 688
	29165	Platte County, MO	89 322	94 788
	29177	Ray County, MO	23 494	22 949
28180		Kapaa, HI Micro area	67 091	70 475
	15007	Kauai County, HI	67 091	70 475
28260		Kearney, NE Micro area	52 591	54 868
	31019	Buffalo County, NE	46 102	48 224
	31099	Kearney County, NE	6 489	6 644
28300		Keene, NH Micro area	77 117	76 115
	33005	Cheshire County, NH	77 117	76 115
28340		Kendallville, IN Micro area	47 536	47 618
	18113	Noble County, IN	47 536	47 618
28380		Kennett, MO Micro area	31 953	31 344
	29069	Dunklin County, MO	31 953	31 344
28420		Kennewick-Richland, WA Metro area	253 340	274 295
	53005	Benton County, WA	175 177	186 486
	53021	Franklin County, WA	78 163	87 809
28500		Kerrville, TX Micro area	49 625	50 562
	48265	Kerr County, TX	49 625	50 562
28540		Ketchikan, AK Micro area	13 477	13 787
	02130	Ketchikan Gateway Borough, AK	13 477	13 787
28580		Key West, FL Micro area	73 090	77 136
	12087	Monroe County, FL	73 090	77 136
28620		Kill Devil Hills, NC Micro area	38 327	39 219
	37055	Dare County, NC	33 920	35 104
	37177	Tyrrell County, NC	4 407	4 115
28660		Killeen-Temple, TX Metro area	405 300	424 858
	48027	Bell County, TX	310 235	329 140
	48099	Coryell County, TX	75 388	75 562
	48281	Lampasas County, TX	19 677	20 156
28700		Kingsport-Bristol-Bristol, TN-VA Metro area	309 544	308 079
	47073	Hawkins County, TN	56 833	56 735
	47163	Sullivan County, TN	156 823	157 047
	51169	Scott County, VA	23 177	22 384
	51191	Washington County, VA	54 876	54 729
	51520	Bristol city, VA	17 835	17 184
28740		Kingston, NY Metro area	182 493	180 445
	36111	Ulster County, NY	182 493	180 445
28780		Kingsville, TX Micro area	32 477	32 590
	48261	Kenedy County, TX	416	400
	48273	Kleberg County, TX	32 061	32 190
28820		Kinston, NC Micro area	59 495	58 485
	37107	Lenoir County, NC	59 495	58 485
28860		Kirksville, MO Micro area	30 038	29 972
	29001	Adair County, MO	25 607	25 602
	29197	Schuyler County, MO	4 431	4 370
28900		Klamath Falls, OR Micro area	66 380	65 455
	41035	Klamath County, OR	66 380	65 455
28940		Knoxville, TN Metro area	837 571	857 585
	47001	Anderson County, TN	75 129	75 528
	47009	Blount County, TN	123 010	126 339
	47013	Campbell County, TN	40 716	39 918
	47057	Grainger County, TN	22 657	22 864
	47093	Knox County, TN	432 226	448 644
	47105	Loudon County, TN	48 556	50 771
	47129	Morgan County, TN	21 987	21 660
	47145	Roane County, TN	54 181	52 748
	47173	Union County, TN	19 109	19 113
29020		Kokomo, IN Metro area	82 752	82 982
	18067	Howard County, IN	82 752	82 982
29060		Laconia, NH Micro area	60 088	60 305
	33001	Belknap County, NH	60 088	60 305
29100		La Crosse-Onalaska, WI-MN Metro area	133 665	136 749
	27055	Houston County, MN	19 027	18 738
	55063	La Crosse County, WI	114 638	118 011
29180		Lafayette, LA Metro area	466 750	484 974
	22001	Acadia Parish, LA	61 773	62 486
	22045	Iberia Parish, LA	73 240	73 913
	22055	Lafayette Parish, LA	221 578	235 644
	22099	St. Martin Parish, LA	52 160	53 315
	22113	Vermilion Parish, LA	57 999	59 616
29200		Lafayette-West Lafayette, IN Metro area	201 789	211 697
	18007	Benton County, IN	8 854	8 700
	18015	Carroll County, IN	20 155	19 923
	18157	Tippecanoe County, IN	172 780	183 074
29260		La Grande, OR Micro area	25 748	25 691
	41061	Union County, OR	25 748	25 691
29300		LaGrange, GA Micro area	67 044	69 469
	13285	Troup County, GA	67 044	69 469
29340		Lake Charles, LA Metro area	199 607	203 883
	22019	Calcasieu Parish, LA	192 768	197 204
	22023	Cameron Parish, LA	6 839	6 679
29380		Lake City, FL Micro area	67 531	67 857
	12023	Columbia County, FL	67 531	67 857
29420		Lake Havasu City-Kingman, AZ Metro area	200 186	203 361
	04015	Mohave County, AZ	200 186	203 361
29460		Lakeland-Winter Haven, FL Metro area	602 095	634 638
	12105	Polk County, FL	602 095	634 638
29500		Lamesa, TX Micro area	13 833	13 372
	48115	Dawson County, TX	13 833	13 372

Core Based Statistical Areas (Metropolitan and Micropolitan), Metropolitan Divisions, and Components (as defined February 2013)–*Continued*

Core Based Statistical Area	State/ County FIPS Code	Title and Geographic Components	2010 Census Population	2014 Estimated Population
29540		Lancaster, PA Metro area	519 445	533 320
	42071	Lancaster County, PA	519 445	533 320
29620		Lansing-East Lansing, MI Metro area	464 036	470 458
	26037	Clinton County, MI	75 382	77 297
	26045	Eaton County, MI	107 759	108 579
	26065	Ingham County, MI	280 895	284 582
29660		Laramie, WY Micro area	36 299	37 811
	56001	Albany County, WY	36 299	37 811
29700		Laredo, TX Metro area	250 304	266 673
	48479	Webb County, TX	250 304	266 673
29740		Las Cruces, NM Metro area	209 233	213 676
	35013	Doña Ana County, NM	209 233	213 676
29780		Las Vegas, NM Micro area	29 393	28 239
	35047	San Miguel County, NM	29 393	28 239
29820		Las Vegas-Henderson-Paradise, NV Metro area	1 951 269	2 069 681
	32003	Clark County, NV	1 951 269	2 069 681
29860		Laurel, MS Micro area	84 823	84 891
	28061	Jasper County, MS	17 062	16 601
	28067	Jones County, MS	67 761	68 290
29900		Laurinburg, NC Micro area	36 157	35 576
	37165	Scotland County, NC	36 157	35 576
29940		Lawrence, KS Metro area	110 826	116 585
	20045	Douglas County, KS	110 826	116 585
29980		Lawrenceburg, TN Micro area	41 869	42 274
	47099	Lawrence County, TN	41 869	42 274
30020		Lawton, OK Metro area	130 291	131 183
	40031	Comanche County, OK	124 098	125 033
	40033	Cotton County, OK	6 193	6 150
30060		Lebanon, MO Micro area	35 571	35 439
	29105	Laclede County, MO	35 571	35 439
30140		Lebanon, PA Metro area	133 568	136 359
	42075	Lebanon County, PA	133 568	136 359
30220		Levelland, TX Micro area	22 935	23 577
	48219	Hockley County, TX	22 935	23 577
30200		Lewisburg, PA Micro area	44 947	44 874
	42119	Union County, PA	44 947	44 874
30280		Lewisburg, TN Micro area	30 617	31 269
	47117	Marshall County, TN	30 617	31 269
30300		Lewiston, ID-WA Metro area	60 888	62 196
	16069	Nez Perce County, ID	39 265	40 007
	53003	Asotin County, WA	21 623	22 189
30340		Lewiston-Auburn, ME Metro area	107 702	107 440
	23001	Androscoggin County, ME	107 702	107 440
30380		Lewistown, PA Micro area	46 682	46 552
	42087	Mifflin County, PA	46 682	46 552
30420		Lexington, NE Micro area	26 370	26 066
	31047	Dawson County, NE	24 326	24 096
	31073	Gosper County, NE	2 044	1 970
30460		Lexington-Fayette, KY Metro area	472 099	494 189
	21017	Bourbon County, KY	19 985	19 972
	21049	Clark County, KY	35 613	35 758
	21067	Fayette County, KY	295 803	310 797
	21113	Jessamine County, KY	48 586	50 815
	21209	Scott County, KY	47 173	51 284
	21239	Woodford County, KY	24 939	25 563
30580		Liberal, KS Micro area	22 952	23 465
	20175	Seward County, KS	22 952	23 465
30620		Lima, OH Metro area	106 331	105 040
	39003	Allen County, OH	106 331	105 040
30660		Lincoln, IL Micro area	30 305	29 746
	17107	Logan County, IL	30 305	29 746
30700		Lincoln, NE Metro area	302 157	318 945
	31109	Lancaster County, NE	285 407	301 795
	31159	Seward County, NE	16 750	17 150
30780		Little Rock-North Little Rock-Conway, AR Metro area	699 757	729 135
	05045	Faulkner County, AR	113 237	120 768
	05053	Grant County, AR	17 853	18 144
	05085	Lonoke County, AR	68 356	71 557
	05105	Perry County, AR	10 445	10 245
	05119	Pulaski County, AR	382 748	392 702
	05125	Saline County, AR	107 118	115 719
30820		Lock Haven, PA Micro area	39 238	39 745
	42035	Clinton County, PA	39 238	39 745
30860		Logan, UT-ID Metro area	125 442	131 364
	16041	Franklin County, ID	12 786	13 021
	49005	Cache County, UT	112 656	118 343
30880		Logan, WV Micro area	36 743	35 348
	54045	Logan County, WV	36 743	35 348
30900		Logansport, IN Micro area	38 966	38 438
	18017	Cass County, IN	38 966	38 438
30940		London, KY Micro area	126 369	127 316
	21121	Knox County, KY	31 883	31 798
	21125	Laurel County, KY	58 849	60 015
	21235	Whitley County, KY	35 637	35 503
30980		Longview, TX Metro area	214 369	217 481
	48183	Gregg County, TX	121 730	123 204
	48401	Rusk County, TX	53 330	53 923
	48459	Upshur County, TX	39 309	40 354
31020		Longview, WA Metro area	102 410	102 133
	53015	Cowlitz County, WA	102 410	102 133
31060		Los Alamos, NM Micro area	17 950	17 682
	35028	Los Alamos County, NM	17 950	17 682
31080		Los Angeles-Long Beach-Anaheim, CA Metro area	12 828 837	13 262 220
31080		Anaheim-Santa Ana-Irvine, CA Metro Div 11244	3 010 232	3 145 515
	06059	Orange County, CA	3 010 232	3 145 515

Core Based Statistical Areas (Metropolitan and Micropolitan), Metropolitan Divisions, and Components (as defined February 2013)–*Continued*

Core Based Statis-tical Area	State/ County FIPS Code	Title and Geographic Components	2010 Census Population	2014 Estimated Population
31080		Los Angeles-Long Beach-Glendale, CA Metro Div 31084	9 818 605	10 116 705
	06037	Los Angeles County, CA	9 818 605	10 116 705
31140		Louisville/Jefferson County, KY-IN Metro area	1 235 708	1 269 702
	18019	Clark County, IN	110 232	114 262
	18043	Floyd County, IN	74 578	76 179
	18061	Harrison County, IN	39 364	39 299
	18143	Scott County, IN	24 181	23 712
	18175	Washington County, IN	28 262	27 878
	21029	Bullitt County, KY	74 319	77 955
	21103	Henry County, KY	15 416	15 572
	21111	Jefferson County, KY	741 096	760 026
	21185	Oldham County, KY	60 316	63 490
	21211	Shelby County, KY	42 074	44 875
	21215	Spencer County, KY	17 061	17 668
	21223	Trimble County, KY	8 809	8 786
31180		Lubbock, TX Metro area	290 805	305 644
	48107	Crosby County, TX	6 059	5 899
	48303	Lubbock County, TX	278 831	293 974
	48305	Lynn County, TX	5 915	5 771
31220		Ludington, MI Micro area	28 705	28 824
	26105	Mason County, MI	28 705	28 824
31260		Lufkin, TX Micro area	86 771	87 750
	48005	Angelina County, TX	86 771	87 750
31300		Lumberton, NC Micro area	134 168	134 760
	37155	Robeson County, NC	134 168	134 760
31340		Lynchburg, VA Metro area	252 634	257 835
	51009	Amherst County, VA	32 353	32 041
	51011	Appomattox County, VA	14 973	15 279
	51019	Bedford County, VA	74 866	76 583
	51031	Campbell County, VA	54 842	54 885
	51680	Lynchburg city, VA	75 568	79 047
31380		Macomb, IL Micro area	32 612	31 880
	17109	McDonough County, IL	32 612	31 880
31420		Macon, GA Metro area	232 293	230 450
	13021	Bibb County, GA	155 547	153 905
	13079	Crawford County, GA	12 630	12 387
	13169	Jones County, GA	28 669	28 787
	13207	Monroe County, GA	26 424	27 051
	13289	Twiggs County, GA	9 023	8 320
31460		Madera, CA Metro area	150 865	154 548
	06039	Madera County, CA	150 865	154 548
31500		Madison, IN Micro area	32 428	32 494
	18077	Jefferson County, IN	32 428	32 494
31540		Madison, WI Metro area	605 435	633 787
	55021	Columbia County, WI	56 833	56 615
	55025	Dane County, WI	488 073	516 284
	55045	Green County, WI	36 842	37 063
	55049	Iowa County, WI	23 687	23 825
31580		Madisonville, KY Micro area	46 920	46 376
	21107	Hopkins County, KY	46 920	46 376
31620		Magnolia, AR Micro area	24 552	23 933
	05027	Columbia County, AR	24 552	23 933
31660		Malone, NY Micro area	51 599	51 262
	36033	Franklin County, NY	51 599	51 262
31680		Malvern, AR Micro area	32 923	33 368
	05059	Hot Spring County, AR	32 923	33 368
31700		Manchester-Nashua, NH Metro area	400 721	405 184
	33011	Hillsborough County, NH	400 721	405 184
31740		Manhattan, KS Metro area	92 719	98 091
	20149	Pottawatomie County, KS	21 604	22 897
	20161	Riley County, KS	71 115	75 194
31820		Manitowoc, WI Micro area	81 442	80 160
	55071	Manitowoc County, WI	81 442	80 160
31860		Mankato-North Mankato, MN Metro area	96 740	98 478
	27013	Blue Earth County, MN	64 013	65 385
	27103	Nicollet County, MN	32 727	33 093
31900		Mansfield, OH Metro area	124 475	121 942
	39139	Richland County, OH	124 475	121 942
31930		Marietta, OH Micro area	61 778	61 213
	39167	Washington County, OH	61 778	61 213
31940		Marinette, WI-MI Micro area	65 778	65 012
	26109	Menominee County, MI	24 029	23 714
	55075	Marinette County, WI	41 749	41 298
31980		Marion, IN Micro area	70 061	68 569
	18053	Grant County, IN	70 061	68 569
32000		Marion, NC Micro area	44 996	44 965
	37111	McDowell County, NC	44 996	44 965
32020		Marion, OH Micro area	66 501	65 720
	39101	Marion County, OH	66 501	65 720
32100		Marquette, MI Micro area	67 077	67 676
	26103	Marquette County, MI	67 077	67 676
32140		Marshall, MN Micro area	25 857	25 665
	27083	Lyon County, MN	25 857	25 665
32180		Marshall, MO Micro area	23 370	23 347
	29195	Saline County, MO	23 370	23 347
32220		Marshall, TX Micro area	65 631	67 336
	48203	Harrison County, TX	65 631	67 336
32260		Marshalltown, IA Micro area	40 648	40 866
	19127	Marshall County, IA	40 648	40 866
32280		Martin, TN Micro area	35 021	34 373
	47183	Weakley County, TN	35 021	34 373
32300		Martinsville, VA Micro area	67 972	65 792
	51089	Henry County, VA	54 151	52 081
	51690	Martinsville city, VA	13 821	13 711
32340		Maryville, MO Micro area	23 370	23 081
	29147	Nodaway County, MO	23 370	23 081
32380		Mason City, IA Micro area	51 749	50 878
	19033	Cerro Gordo County, IA	44 151	43 254
	19195	Worth County, IA	7 598	7 624

Core Based Statistical Areas (Metropolitan and Micropolitan), Metropolitan Divisions, and Components (as defined February 2013)–*Continued*

Core Based Statistical Area	State/ County FIPS Code	Title and Geographic Components	2010 Census Population	2014 Estimated Population
32460		Mayfield, KY Micro area	37 121	37 618
	21083	Graves County, KY	37 121	37 618
32500		Maysville, KY Micro area	17 490	17 166
	21161	Mason County, KY	17 490	17 166
32540		McAlester, OK Micro area	45 837	44 626
	40121	Pittsburg County, OK	45 837	44 626
32580		McAllen-Edinburg-Mission, TX Metro area	774 769	831 073
	48215	Hidalgo County, TX	774 769	831 073
32620		McComb, MS Micro area	53 535	52 687
	28005	Amite County, MS	13 131	12 629
	28113	Pike County, MS	40 404	40 058
32660		McMinnville, TN Micro area	39 839	39 969
	47177	Warren County, TN	39 839	39 969
32700		McPherson, KS Micro area	29 180	29 241
	20113	McPherson County, KS	29 180	29 241
32740		Meadville, PA Micro area	88 765	87 175
	42039	Crawford County, PA	88 765	87 175
32780		Medford, OR Metro area	203 206	210 287
	41029	Jackson County, OR	203 206	210 287
32820		Memphis, TN-MS-AR Metro area	1 324 829	1 343 230
	05035	Crittenden County, AR	50 902	49 548
	28009	Benton County, MS	8 729	8 296
	28033	DeSoto County, MS	161 252	170 913
	28093	Marshall County, MS	37 144	36 234
	28137	Tate County, MS	28 886	28 204
	28143	Tunica County, MS	10 778	10 598
	47047	Fayette County, TN	38 413	39 011
	47157	Shelby County, TN	927 644	938 803
	47167	Tipton County, TN	61 081	61 623
32860		Menomonie, WI Micro area	43 857	44 305
	55033	Dunn County, WI	43 857	44 305
32900		Merced, CA Metro area	255 793	266 353
	06047	Merced County, CA	255 793	266 353
32940		Meridian, MS Micro area	107 449	106 201
	28023	Clarke County, MS	16 732	16 299
	28069	Kemper County, MS	10 456	10 163
	28075	Lauderdale County, MS	80 261	79 739
32980		Merrill, WI Micro area	28 743	28 493
	55069	Lincoln County, WI	28 743	28 493
33020		Mexico, MO Micro area	25 529	25 887
	29007	Audrain County, MO	25 529	25 887
33060		Miami, OK Micro area	31 848	32 105
	40115	Ottawa County, OK	31 848	32 105
33100		Miami-Fort Lauderdale-West Palm Beach, FL Metro area	5 564 635	5 929 819
33100		Fort Lauderdale-Pompano Beach-Deerfield Beach, FL Metro Div 22744	1 748 066	1 869 235
	12011	Broward County, FL	1 748 066	1 869 235
33100		Miami-Miami Beach-Kendall, FL Metro Div 33124	2 496 435	2 662 874
	12086	Miami-Dade County, FL	2 496 435	2 662 874
33100		West Palm Beach-Boca Raton-Delray Beach, FL Metro Div 48424	1 320 134	1 397 710
	12099	Palm Beach County, FL	1 320 134	1 397 710
33140		Michigan City-La Porte, IN Metro area	111 467	111 444
	18091	LaPorte County, IN	111 467	111 444
33180		Middlesborough, KY Micro area	28 691	27 778
	21013	Bell County, KY	28 691	27 778
33220		Midland, MI Metro area	83 629	83 427
	26111	Midland County, MI	83 629	83 427
33260		Midland, TX Metro area	141 671	161 290
	48317	Martin County, TX	4 799	5 460
	48329	Midland County, TX	136 872	155 830
33300		Milledgeville, GA Micro area	55 149	54 418
	13009	Baldwin County, GA	45 720	45 909
	13141	Hancock County, GA	9 429	8 509
33340		Milwaukee-Waukesha-West Allis, WI Metro area	1 555 908	1 572 245
	55079	Milwaukee County, WI	947 735	956 406
	55089	Ozaukee County, WI	86 395	87 470
	55131	Washington County, WI	131 887	133 251
	55133	Waukesha County, WI	389 891	395 118
33420		Mineral Wells, TX Micro area	28 111	28 096
	48363	Palo Pinto County, TX	28 111	28 096
33460		Minneapolis-St. Paul-Bloomington, MN Metro area	3 348 859	3 495 176
	27003	Anoka County, MN	330 844	341 864
	27019	Carver County, MN	91 042	97 338
	27025	Chisago County, MN	53 887	54 025
	27037	Dakota County, MN	398 552	412 529
	27053	Hennepin County, MN	1 152 425	1 212 064
	27059	Isanti County, MN	37 816	38 413
	27079	Le Sueur County, MN	27 703	27 770
	27095	Mille Lacs County, MN	26 097	25 884
	27123	Ramsey County, MN	508 640	532 655
	27139	Scott County, MN	129 928	139 672
	27141	Sherburne County, MN	88 499	91 126
	27143	Sibley County, MN	15 226	14 918
	27163	Washington County, MN	238 136	249 283
	27171	Wright County, MN	124 700	129 918
	55093	Pierce County, WI	41 019	40 958
	55109	St. Croix County, WI	84 345	86 759
33500		Minot, ND Micro area	69 540	77 959
	38049	McHenry County, ND	5 395	5 988
	38075	Renville County, ND	2 470	2 587
	38101	Ward County, ND	61 675	69 384
33540		Missoula, MT Metro area	109 299	112 684
	30063	Missoula County, MT	109 299	112 684
33580		Mitchell, SD Micro area	22 835	23 304
	46035	Davison County, SD	19 504	19 885
	46061	Hanson County, SD	3 331	3 419
33620		Moberly, MO Micro area	25 414	25 072
	29175	Randolph County, MO	25 414	25 072

Core Based Statistical Areas (Metropolitan and Micropolitan), Metropolitan Divisions, and Components (as defined February 2013)–*Continued*

Core Based Statis-tical Area	State/ County FIPS Code	Title and Geographic Components	2010 Census Population	2014 Estimated Population
33660		Mobile, AL Metro area	412 992	415 123
	01097	Mobile County, AL	412 992	415 123
33700		Modesto, CA Metro area	514 453	531 997
	06099	Stanislaus County, CA	514 453	531 997
33740		Monroe, LA Metro area	176 441	178 864
	22073	Ouachita Parish, LA	153 720	156 325
	22111	Union Parish, LA	22 721	22 539
33780		Monroe, MI Metro area	152 021	149 824
	26115	Monroe County, MI	152 021	149 824
33860		Montgomery, AL Metro area	374 536	373 141
	01001	Autauga County, AL	54 571	55 395
	01051	Elmore County, AL	79 303	80 977
	01085	Lowndes County, AL	11 299	10 580
	01101	Montgomery County, AL	229 363	226 189
33940		Montrose, CO Micro area	41 276	40 873
	08085	Montrose County, CO	41 276	40 873
33980		Morehead City, NC Micro area	66 469	68 811
	37031	Carteret County, NC	66 469	68 811
34020		Morgan City, LA Micro area	54 650	53 162
	22101	St. Mary Parish, LA	54 650	53 162
34060		Morgantown, WV Metro area	129 709	137 251
	54061	Monongalia County, WV	96 189	103 463
	54077	Preston County, WV	33 520	33 788
34100		Morristown, TN Metro area	113 951	115 713
	47063	Hamblen County, TN	62 544	63 036
	47089	Jefferson County, TN	51 407	52 677
34140		Moscow, ID Micro area	37 244	38 411
	16057	Latah County, ID	37 244	38 411
34180		Moses Lake, WA Micro area	89 120	93 147
	53025	Grant County, WA	89 120	93 147
34220		Moultrie, GA Micro area	45 498	46 102
	13071	Colquitt County, GA	45 498	46 102
34260		Mountain Home, AR Micro area	41 513	40 857
	05005	Baxter County, AR	41 513	40 857
34300		Mountain Home, ID Micro area	27 038	26 094
	16039	Elmore County, ID	27 038	26 094
34340		Mount Airy, NC Micro area	73 673	72 968
	37171	Surry County, NC	73 673	72 968
34380		Mount Pleasant, MI Micro area	70 311	70 616
	26073	Isabella County, MI	70 311	70 616
34420		Mount Pleasant, TX Micro area	32 334	32 506
	48449	Titus County, TX	32 334	32 506
34460		Mount Sterling, KY Micro area	44 396	45 967
	21011	Bath County, KY	11 591	12 206
	21165	Menifee County, KY	6 306	6 287
	21173	Montgomery County, KY	26 499	27 474
34500		Mount Vernon, IL Micro area	38 827	38 534
	17081	Jefferson County, IL	38 827	38 534

Core Based Statis-tical Area	State/ County FIPS Code	Title and Geographic Components	2010 Census Population	2014 Estimated Population
34540		Mount Vernon, OH Micro area	60 921	61 167
	39083	Knox County, OH	60 921	61 167
34580		Mount Vernon-Anacortes, WA Metro area	116 901	120 365
	53057	Skagit County, WA	116 901	120 365
34620		Muncie, IN Metro area	117 671	117 074
	18035	Delaware County, IN	117 671	117 074
34660		Murray, KY Micro area	37 191	38 282
	21035	Calloway County, KY	37 191	38 282
34700		Muscatine, IA Micro area	42 745	42 903
	19139	Muscatine County, IA	42 745	42 903
34740		Muskegon, MI Metro area	172 188	172 344
	26121	Muskegon County, MI	172 188	172 344
34780		Muskogee, OK Micro area	70 990	69 966
	40101	Muskogee County, OK	70 990	69 966
34820		Myrtle Beach-Conway-North Myrtle Beach, NC-SC Metro area	376 722	417 668
	37019	Brunswick County, NC	107 431	118 836
	45051	Horry County, SC	269 291	298 832
34860		Nacogdoches, TX Micro area	64 524	65 301
	48347	Nacogdoches County, TX	64 524	65 301
34900		Napa, CA Metro area	136 484	141 667
	06055	Napa County, CA	136 484	141 667
34940		Naples-Immokalee-Marco Island, FL Metro area	321 520	348 777
	12021	Collier County, FL	321 520	348 777
34980		Nashville-Davidson-Murfreesboro-Franklin, TN Metro area	1 670 890	1 792 649
	47015	Cannon County, TN	13 801	13 757
	47021	Cheatham County, TN	39 105	39 764
	47037	Davidson County, TN	626 681	668 347
	47043	Dickson County, TN	49 666	50 575
	47081	Hickman County, TN	24 690	24 384
	47111	Macon County, TN	22 248	23 003
	47119	Maury County, TN	80 956	85 515
	47147	Robertson County, TN	66 283	68 079
	47149	Rutherford County, TN	262 604	288 906
	47159	Smith County, TN	19 166	19 009
	47165	Sumner County, TN	160 645	172 706
	47169	Trousdale County, TN	7 870	8 002
	47187	Williamson County, TN	183 182	205 226
	47189	Wilson County, TN	113 993	125 376
35020		Natchez, MS-LA Micro area	53 119	52 203
	22029	Concordia Parish, LA	20 822	20 466
	28001	Adams County, MS	32 297	31 737
35060		Natchitoches, LA Micro area	39 566	39 166
	22069	Natchitoches Parish, LA	39 566	39 166
35100		New Bern, NC Metro area	126 802	127 534
	37049	Craven County, NC	103 505	104 510
	37103	Jones County, NC	10 153	10 076
	37137	Pamlico County, NC	13 144	12 948
35140		Newberry, SC Micro area	37 508	37 783
	45071	Newberry County, SC	37 508	37 783

Core Based Statistical Areas (Metropolitan and Micropolitan), Metropolitan Divisions, and Components (as defined February 2013)–*Continued*

Core Based Statistical Area	State/ County FIPS Code	Title and Geographic Components	2010 Census Population	2014 Estimated Population
35220		New Castle, IN Micro area	49 462	48 995
	18065	Henry County, IN	49 462	48 995
35260		New Castle, PA Micro area	91 108	88 771
	42073	Lawrence County, PA	91 108	88 771
35300		New Haven-Milford, CT Metro area	862 477	861 277
	09009	New Haven County, CT	862 477	861 277
35380		New Orleans-Metairie, LA Metro area	1 189 866	1 251 849
	22051	Jefferson Parish, LA	432 552	435 716
	22071	Orleans Parish, LA	343 829	384 320
	22075	Plaquemines Parish, LA	23 042	23 447
	22087	St. Bernard Parish, LA	35 897	44 409
	22089	St. Charles Parish, LA	52 780	52 745
	22093	St. James Parish, LA	22 102	21 638
	22095	St. John the Baptist Parish, LA	45 924	43 745
	22103	St. Tammany Parish, LA	233 740	245 829
35420		New Philadelphia-Dover, OH Micro area	92 582	92 788
	39157	Tuscarawas County, OH	92 582	92 788
35440		Newport, OR Micro area	46 034	46 406
	41041	Lincoln County, OR	46 034	46 406
35460		Newport, TN Micro area	35 662	35 374
	47029	Cocke County, TN	35 662	35 374
35500		Newton, IA Micro area	36 842	36 872
	19099	Jasper County, IA	36 842	36 872
35580		New Ulm, MN Micro area	25 893	25 292
	27015	Brown County, MN	25 893	25 292
35620		New York-Newark-Jersey City, NY-NJ-PA Metro area	19 567 410	20 092 883
35620		Dutchess County-Putnam County, NY Metro Div 20524	397 198	396 066
	36027	Dutchess County, NY	297 488	296 579
	36079	Putnam County, NY	99 710	99 487
35620		Nassau County-Suffolk County, NY Metro Div 35004	2 832 882	2 861 595
	36059	Nassau County, NY	1 339 532	1 358 627
	36103	Suffolk County, NY	1 493 350	1 502 968
35620		Newark, NJ-PA Metro Div 35084	2 471 171	2 508 124
	34013	Essex County, NJ	783 969	795 723
	34019	Hunterdon County, NJ	128 349	126 067
	34027	Morris County, NJ	492 276	499 727
	34035	Somerset County, NJ	323 444	332 568
	34037	Sussex County, NJ	149 265	144 909
	34039	Union County, NJ	536 499	552 939
	42103	Pike County, PA	57 369	56 191
35620		New York-Jersey City-White Plains, NY-NJ Metro Div 35614	13 866 159	14 327 098
	34003	Bergen County, NJ	905 116	933 572
	34017	Hudson County, NJ	634 266	669 115
	34023	Middlesex County, NJ	809 858	836 297
	34025	Monmouth County, NJ	630 380	629 279
	34029	Ocean County, NJ	576 567	586 301
	34031	Passaic County, NJ	501 226	508 856
	36005	Bronx County, NY	1 385 108	1 438 159
	36047	Kings County, NY	2 504 700	2 621 793
	36061	New York County, NY	1 585 873	1 636 268
	36071	Orange County, NY	372 813	376 099
	36081	Queens County, NY	2 230 722	2 321 580
	36085	Richmond County, NY	468 730	473 279
	36087	Rockland County, NY	311 687	323 866
	36119	Westchester County, NY	949 113	972 634
35660		Niles-Benton Harbor, MI Metro area	156 813	155 233
	26021	Berrien County, MI	156 813	155 233
35700		Nogales, AZ Micro area	47 420	46 695
	04023	Santa Cruz County, AZ	47 420	46 695
35740		Norfolk, NE Micro area	48 271	48 445
	31119	Madison County, NE	34 876	35 174
	31139	Pierce County, NE	7 266	7 202
	31167	Stanton County, NE	6 129	6 069
35820		North Platte, NE Micro area	37 590	37 063
	31111	Lincoln County, NE	36 288	35 815
	31113	Logan County, NE	763	750
	31117	McPherson County, NE	539	498
35840		North Port-Sarasota-Bradenton, FL Metro area	702 281	748 708
	12081	Manatee County, FL	322 833	351 746
	12115	Sarasota County, FL	379 448	396 962
35860		North Vernon, IN Micro area	28 525	28 000
	18079	Jennings County, IN	28 525	28 000
35900		North Wilkesboro, NC Micro area	69 340	68 838
	37193	Wilkes County, NC	69 340	68 838
35940		Norwalk, OH Micro area	59 626	58 714
	39077	Huron County, OH	59 626	58 714
35980		Norwich-New London, CT Metro area	274 055	273 676
	09011	New London County, CT	274 055	273 676
36020		Oak Harbor, WA Micro area	78 506	79 275
	53029	Island County, WA	78 506	79 275
36100		Ocala, FL Metro area	331 298	339 167
	12083	Marion County, FL	331 298	339 167
36140		Ocean City, NJ Metro area	97 265	95 344
	34009	Cape May County, NJ	97 265	95 344
36220		Odessa, TX Metro area	137 130	153 904
	48135	Ector County, TX	137 130	153 904
36260		Ogden-Clearfield, UT Metro area	597 159	632 293
	49003	Box Elder County, UT	49 975	51 518
	49011	Davis County, UT	306 479	329 692
	49029	Morgan County, UT	9 469	10 608
	49057	Weber County, UT	231 236	240 475

Core Based Statistical Areas (Metropolitan and Micropolitan), Metropolitan Divisions, and Components (as defined February 2013)–*Continued*

Core Based Statistical Area	State/ County FIPS Code	Title and Geographic Components	2010 Census Population	2014 Estimated Population
36300		Ogdensburg-Massena, NY Micro area	111 944	111 400
	36089	St. Lawrence County, NY	111 944	111 400
36340		Oil City, PA Micro area	54 984	53 529
	42121	Venango County, PA	54 984	53 529
36380		Okeechobee, FL Micro area	39 996	39 149
	12093	Okeechobee County, FL	39 996	39 149
36420		Oklahoma City, OK Metro area	1 252 987	1 336 767
	40017	Canadian County, OK	115 541	129 582
	40027	Cleveland County, OK	255 755	269 908
	40051	Grady County, OK	52 431	53 854
	40081	Lincoln County, OK	34 273	34 619
	40083	Logan County, OK	41 848	45 276
	40087	McClain County, OK	34 506	37 313
	40109	Oklahoma County, OK	718 633	766 215
36460		Olean, NY Micro area	80 317	78 600
	36009	Cattaraugus County, NY	80 317	78 600
36500		Olympia-Tumwater, WA Metro area	252 264	265 851
	53067	Thurston County, WA	252 264	265 851
36540		Omaha-Council Bluffs, NE-IA Metro area	865 350	904 421
	19085	Harrison County, IA	14 928	14 324
	19129	Mills County, IA	15 059	14 831
	19155	Pottawattamie County, IA	93 158	93 128
	31025	Cass County, NE	25 241	25 524
	31055	Douglas County, NE	517 110	543 244
	31153	Sarpy County, NE	158 840	172 193
	31155	Saunders County, NE	20 780	20 919
	31177	Washington County, NE	20 234	20 258
36580		Oneonta, NY Micro area	62 259	61 128
	36077	Otsego County, NY	62 259	61 128
36620		Ontario, OR-ID Micro area	53 936	53 195
	16075	Payette County, ID	22 623	22 836
	41045	Malheur County, OR	31 313	30 359
36660		Opelousas, LA Micro area	83 384	83 709
	22097	St. Landry Parish, LA	83 384	83 709
36700		Orangeburg, SC Micro area	92 501	90 090
	45075	Orangeburg County, SC	92 501	90 090
36740		Orlando-Kissimmee-Sanford, FL Metro	2 134 411	2 321 418
	12069	Lake County, FL	297 052	315 690
	12095	Orange County, FL	1 145 956	1 253 001
	12097	Osceola County, FL	268 685	310 211
	12117	Seminole County, FL	422 718	442 516
36780		Oshkosh-Neenah, WI Metro area	166 994	169 511
	55139	Winnebago County, WI	166 994	169 511
36820		Oskaloosa, IA Micro area	22 381	22 370
	19123	Mahaska County, IA	22 381	22 370
36830		Othello, WA Micro area	18 728	19 179
	53001	Adams County, WA	18 728	19 179
36840		Ottawa, KS Micro area	25 992	25 611
	20059	Franklin County, KS	25 992	25 611
36860		Ottawa-Peru, IL Micro area	154 908	150 895
	17011	Bureau County, IL	34 978	33 840
	17099	LaSalle County, IL	113 924	111 241
	17155	Putnam County, IL	6 006	5 814
36900		Ottumwa, IA Micro area	44 378	43 993
	19051	Davis County, IA	8 753	8 781
	19179	Wapello County, IA	35 625	35 212
36940		Owatonna, MN Micro area	36 576	36 573
	27147	Steele County, MN	36 576	36 573
36980		Owensboro, KY Metro area	114 752	116 506
	21059	Daviess County, KY	96 656	98 275
	21091	Hancock County, KY	8 565	8 753
	21149	McLean County, KY	9 531	9 478
37020		Owosso, MI Micro area	70 648	68 933
	26155	Shiawassee County, MI	70 648	68 933
37060		Oxford, MS Micro area	47 351	52 930
	28071	Lafayette County, MS	47 351	52 930
37080		Oxford, NC Micro area	59 916	58 500
	37077	Granville County, NC	59 916	58 500
37100		Oxnard-Thousand Oaks-Ventura, CA Metro area	823 318	846 178
	06111	Ventura County, CA	823 318	846 178
37120		Ozark, AL Micro area	50 251	49 484
	01045	Dale County, AL	50 251	49 484
37140		Paducah, KY-IL Micro area	98 762	97 820
	17127	Massac County, IL	15 429	14 905
	21007	Ballard County, KY	8 249	8 240
	21139	Livingston County, KY	9 519	9 359
	21145	McCracken County, KY	65 565	65 316
37220		Pahrump, NV Micro area	43 946	42 282
	32023	Nye County, NV	43 946	42 282
37260		Palatka, FL Micro area	74 364	72 143
	12107	Putnam County, FL	74 364	72 143
37300		Palestine, TX Micro area	58 458	57 627
	48001	Anderson County, TX	58 458	57 627
37340		Palm Bay-Melbourne-Titusville, FL Metro area	543 376	556 885
	12009	Brevard County, FL	543 376	556 885
37420		Pampa, TX Micro area	22 535	23 044
	48179	Gray County, TX	22 535	23 044
37460		Panama City, FL Metro area	184 715	194 929
	12005	Bay County, FL	168 852	178 985
	12045	Gulf County, FL	15 863	15 944
37500		Paragould, AR Micro area	42 090	43 694
	05055	Greene County, AR	42 090	43 694
37540		Paris, TN Micro area	32 330	32 204
	47079	Henry County, TN	32 330	32 204
37580		Paris, TX Micro area	49 793	49 523
	48277	Lamar County, TX	49 793	49 523

Core Based Statistical Areas (Metropolitan and Micropolitan), Metropolitan Divisions, and Components (as defined February 2013)–*Continued*

Core Based Statis-tical Area	State/ County FIPS Code	Title and Geographic Components	2010 Census Population	2014 Estimated Population
37620		Parkersburg-Vienna, WV Metro area	92 673	92 082
	54105	Wirt County, WV	5 717	5 845
	54107	Wood County, WV	86 956	86 237
37660		Parsons, KS Micro area	21 607	20 960
	20099	Labette County, KS	21 607	20 960
37740		Payson, AZ Micro area	53 597	53 119
	04007	Gila County, AZ	53 597	53 119
37780		Pecos, TX Micro area	13 783	14 349
	48389	Reeves County, TX	13 783	14 349
37860		Pensacola-Ferry Pass-Brent, FL Metro area	448 991	474 081
	12033	Escambia County, FL	297 619	310 659
	12113	Santa Rosa County, FL	151 372	163 422
37900		Peoria, IL Metro area	379 186	380 040
	17123	Marshall County, IL	12 640	12 014
	17143	Peoria County, IL	186 494	187 319
	17175	Stark County, IL	5 994	5 813
	17179	Tazewell County, IL	135 394	135 707
	17203	Woodford County, IL	38 664	39 187
37940		Peru, IN Micro area	36 903	35 954
	18103	Miami County, IN	36 903	35 954
37980		Philadelphia-Camden-Wilmington, PA-NJ-DE-MD Metro area	5 965 343	6 051 170
		Camden, NJ Metro Div 15804	1 250 679	1 251 711
	34005	Burlington County, NJ	448 734	449 722
	34007	Camden County, NJ	513 657	511 038
	34015	Gloucester County, NJ	288 288	290 951
37980		Montgomery County-Bucks County-Chester County, PA Metro Div 33874	1 924 009	1 956 326
	42017	Bucks County, PA	625 249	626 685
	42029	Chester County, PA	498 886	512 784
	42091	Montgomery County, PA	799 874	816 857
37980		Philadelphia, PA Metro Div 37964	2 084 985	2 123 257
	42045	Delaware County, PA	558 979	562 960
	42101	Philadelphia County, PA	1 526 006	1 560 297
37980		Wilmington, DE-MD-NJ Metro Div 48864	705 670	719 876
	10003	New Castle County, Delaware	538 479	552 778
	24015	Cecil County, MD	101 108	102 383
	34033	Salom County, NJ	66 083	64 715
38060		Phoenix-Mesa-Scottsdale, AZ Metro area	4 192 887	4 489 109
	04013	Maricopa County, AZ	3 817 117	4 087 191
	04021	Pinal County, AZ	375 770	401 918
38100		Picayune, MS Micro area	55 834	55 224
	28109	Pearl River County, MS	55 834	55 224
38180		Pierre, SD Micro area	21 361	22 063
	46065	Hughes County, SD	17 022	17 642
	46117	Stanley County, SD	2 966	2 983
	46119	Sully County, SD	1 373	1 438
38220		Pine Bluff, AR Metro area	100 258	94 716
	05025	Cleveland County, AR	8 689	8 449
	05069	Jefferson County, AR	77 435	72 297
	05079	Lincoln County, AR	14 134	13 970
38240		Pinehurst-Southern Pines, NC Micro area	88 247	93 077
	37125	Moore County, NC	88 247	93 077
38260		Pittsburg, KS Micro area	39 134	39 290
	20037	Crawford County, KS	39 134	39 290
38300		Pittsburgh, PA Metro area	2 356 285	2 355 968
	42003	Allegheny County, PA	1 223 348	1 231 255
	42005	Armstrong County, PA	68 941	67 785
	42007	Beaver County, PA	170 539	169 392
	42019	Butler County, PA	183 862	185 943
	42051	Fayette County, PA	136 606	134 086
	42125	Washington County, PA	207 820	208 187
	42129	Westmoreland County, PA	365 169	359 320
38340		Pittsfield, MA Metro area	131 219	128 715
	25003	Berkshire County, MA	131 219	128 715
38380		Plainview, TX Micro area	36 273	34 720
	48189	Hale County, TX	36 273	34 720
38420		Platteville, WI Micro area	51 208	51 829
	55043	Grant County, WI	51 208	51 829
38460		Plattsburgh, NY Micro area	82 128	81 632
	36019	Clinton County, NY	82 128	81 632
38500		Plymouth, IN Micro area	47 051	47 107
	18099	Marshall County, IN	47 051	47 107
38540		Pocatello, ID Metro area	82 839	83 347
	16005	Bannock County, ID	82 839	83 347
38580		Point Pleasant, WV-OH Micro area	58 258	57 413
	39053	Gallia County, OH	30 934	30 397
	54053	Mason County, WV	27 324	27 016
38620		Ponca City, OK Micro area	46 562	45 478
	40071	Kay County, OK	46 562	45 478
38700		Pontiac, IL Micro area	38 950	37 903
	17105	Livingston County, IL	38 950	37 903
38740		Poplar Bluff, MO Micro area	42 794	42 972
	29023	Butler County, MO	42 794	42 972
38780		Portales, NM Micro area	19 846	19 536
	35041	Roosevelt County, NM	19 846	19 536
38820		Port Angeles, WA Micro area	71 404	72 715
	53009	Clallam County, WA	71 404	72 715
38840		Port Clinton, OH Micro area	41 428	41 154
	39123	Ottawa County, OH	41 428	41 154
38860		Portland-South Portland, ME Metro area	514 098	523 552
	23005	Cumberland County, ME	281 674	287 797
	23023	Sagadahoc County, ME	35 293	35 045
	23031	York County, ME	197 131	200 710

Core Based Statistical Areas (Metropolitan and Micropolitan), Metropolitan Divisions, and Components (as defined February 2013)–*Continued*

Core Based Statistical Area	State/ County FIPS Code	Title and Geographic Components	2010 Census Population	2014 Estimated Population
38900		Portland-Vancouver-Hillsboro, OR-WA Metro area	2 226 009	2 348 247
	41005	Clackamas County, OR	375 992	394 972
	41009	Columbia County, OR	49 351	49 459
	41051	Multnomah County, OR	735 334	776 712
	41067	Washington County, OR	529 710	562 998
	41071	Yamhill County, OR	99 193	101 758
	53011	Clark County, WA	425 363	451 008
	53059	Skamania County, WA	11 066	11 340
38920		Port Lavaca, TX Micro area	21 381	21 797
	48057	Calhoun County, TX	21 381	21 797
38940		Port St. Lucie, FL Metro area	424 107	444 420
	12085	Martin County, FL	146 318	153 392
	12111	St. Lucie County, FL	277 789	291 028
39020		Portsmouth, OH Micro area	79 499	77 258
	39145	Scioto County, OH	79 499	77 258
39060		Pottsville, PA Micro area	148 289	145 797
	42107	Schuylkill County, PA	148 289	145 797
39140		Prescott, AZ Metro area	211 033	218 844
	04025	Yavapai County, AZ	211 033	218 844
39220		Price, UT Micro area	21 403	20 660
	49007	Carbon County, UT	21 403	20 660
39260		Prineville, OR Micro area	20 978	20 998
	41013	Crook County, OR	20 978	20 998
39300		Providence-Warwick, RI-MA Metro area	1 600 852	1 609 367
	25005	Bristol County, MA	548 285	554 194
	44001	Bristol County, RI	49 875	49 060
	44003	Kent County, RI	166 158	165 128
	44005	Newport County, RI	82 888	82 358
	44007	Providence County, RI	626 667	631 974
	44009	Washington County, RI	126 979	126 653
39340		Provo-Orem, UT Metro area	526 810	571 460
	49023	Juab County, UT	10 246	10 486
	49049	Utah County, UT	516 564	560 974
39380		Pueblo, CO Metro area	159 063	161 875
	08101	Pueblo County, CO	159 063	161 875
39420		Pullman, WA Micro area	44 776	46 827
	53075	Whitman County, WA	44 776	46 827
39460		Punta Gorda, FL Metro area	159 978	168 474
	12015	Charlotte County, FL	159 978	168 474
39500		Quincy, IL-MO Micro area	77 314	77 126
	17001	Adams County, IL	67 103	66 988
	29111	Lewis County, MO	10 211	10 138
39540		Racine, WI Metro area	195 408	195 163
	55101	Racine County, WI	195 408	195 163
39580		Raleigh, NC Metro area	1 130 490	1 242 974
	37069	Franklin County, NC	60 619	62 860
	37101	Johnston County, NC	168 878	181 423
	37183	Wake County, NC	900 993	998 691
39660		Rapid City, SD Metro area	134 598	143 638
	46033	Custer County, SD	8 216	8 445
	46093	Meade County, SD	25 434	26 951
	46103	Pennington County, SD	100 948	108 242
39700		Raymondville, TX Micro area	22 134	21 903
	48489	Willacy County, TX	22 134	21 903
39740		Reading, PA Metro area	411 442	413 691
	42011	Berks County, PA	411 442	413 691
39780		Red Bluff, CA Micro area	63 463	63 067
	06103	Tehama County, CA	63 463	63 067
39820		Redding, CA Metro area	177 223	179 804
	06089	Shasta County, CA	177 223	179 804
39860		Red Wing, MN Micro area	46 183	46 423
	27049	Goodhue County, MN	46 183	46 423
39900		Reno, NV Metro area	425 417	443 990
	32029	Storey County, NV	4 010	3 912
	32031	Washoe County, NV	421 407	440 078
39940		Rexburg, ID Micro area	50 778	50 905
	16043	Fremont County, ID	13 242	12 867
	16065	Madison County, ID	37 536	38 038
39980		Richmond, IN Micro area	68 917	67 671
	18177	Wayne County, IN	68 917	67 671
40060		Richmond, VA Metro area	1 208 101	1 260 029
	51007	Amelia County, VA	12 690	12 855
	51033	Caroline County, VA	28 545	29 778
	51036	Charles City County, VA	7 256	7 023
	51041	Chesterfield County, VA	316 236	332 499
	51053	Dinwiddie County, VA	28 001	27 859
	51075	Goochland County, VA	21 717	21 936
	51085	Hanover County, VA	99 863	101 918
	51087	Henrico County, VA	306 935	321 924
	51101	King William County, VA	15 935	16 186
	51127	New Kent County, VA	18 429	20 021
	51145	Powhatan County, VA	28 046	28 449
	51149	Prince George County, VA	35 725	37 333
	51183	Sussex County, VA	12 087	11 767
	51570	Colonial Heights city, VA	17 411	17 731
	51670	Hopewell city, VA	22 591	22 196
	51730	Petersburg city, VA	32 420	32 701
	51760	Richmond city, VA	204 214	217 853
40080		Richmond-Berea, KY Micro area	99 972	104 166
	21151	Madison County, KY	82 916	87 340
	21203	Rockcastle County, KY	17 056	16 826
40100		Rio Grande City, TX Micro area	60 968	62 955
	48427	Starr County, TX	60 968	62 955
40140		Riverside-San Bernardino-Ontario, CA	4 224 851	4 441 890
	06065	Riverside County, CA	2 189 641	2 329 271
	06071	San Bernardino County, CA	2 035 210	2 112 619
40180		Riverton, WY Micro area	40 123	40 703
	56013	Fremont County, WY	40 123	40 703

Core Based Statistical Areas (Metropolitan and Micropolitan), Metropolitan Divisions, and Components (as defined February 2013)–*Continued*

Core Based Statistical Area	State/ County FIPS Code	Title and Geographic Components	2010 Census Population	2014 Estimated Population
40220		Roanoke, VA Metro area	308 707	313 388
	51023	Botetourt County, VA	33 148	33 100
	51045	Craig County, VA	5 190	5 234
	51067	Franklin County, VA	56 159	56 358
	51161	Roanoke County, VA	92 376	93 785
	51770	Roanoke city, VA	97 032	99 428
	51775	Salem city, VA	24 802	25 483
40260		Roanoke Rapids, NC Micro area	76 790	73 433
	37083	Halifax County, NC	54 691	52 970
	37131	Northampton County, NC	22 099	20 463
40300		Rochelle, IL Micro area	53 497	52 085
	17141	Ogle County, IL	53 497	52 085
40340		Rochester, MN Metro area	206 877	212 778
	27039	Dodge County, MN	20 087	20 353
	27045	Fillmore County, MN	20 866	20 776
	27109	Olmsted County, MN	144 248	150 287
	27157	Wabasha County, MN	21 676	21 362
40380		Rochester, NY Metro area	1 079 671	1 083 393
	36051	Livingston County, NY	65 393	64 586
	36055	Monroe County, NY	744 344	749 857
	36069	Ontario County, NY	107 931	109 707
	36073	Orleans County, NY	42 883	41 984
	36117	Wayne County, NY	93 772	92 051
	36123	Yates County, NY	25 348	25 208
40420		Rockford, IL Metro area	349 431	342 411
	17007	Boone County, IL	54 165	53 869
	17201	Winnebago County, IL	295 266	288 542
40460		Rockingham, NC Micro area	46 639	45 733
	37153	Richmond County, NC	46 639	45 733
40540		Rock Springs, WY Micro area	43 806	45 010
	56037	Sweetwater County, WY	43 806	45 010
40580		Rocky Mount, NC Metro area	152 392	149 290
	37065	Edgecombe County, NC	56 552	54 933
	37127	Nash County, NC	95 840	94 357
40620		Rolla, MO Micro area	45 156	44 847
	29161	Phelps County, MO	45 156	44 847
40660		Rome, GA Metro area	96 317	96 063
	13115	Floyd County, GA	96 317	96 063
40700		Roseburg, OR Micro area	107 667	106 972
	41019	Douglas County, OR	107 667	106 972
40740		Roswell, NM Micro area	65 645	65 878
	35005	Chaves County, NM	65 645	65 878
40780		Russellville, AR Micro area	83 939	85 152
	05115	Pope County, AR	61 754	63 201
	05149	Yell County, AR	22 185	21 951
40820		Ruston, LA Micro area	46 735	47 617
	22061	Lincoln Parish, LA	46 735	47 617
40860		Rutland, VT Micro area	61 642	60 086
	50021	Rutland County, VT	61 642	60 086
40900		Sacramento—Roseville—Arden-Arcade, CA Metro area	2 149 127	2 244 397
	06017	El Dorado County, CA	181 058	183 087
	06061	Placer County, CA	348 432	371 694
	06067	Sacramento County, CA	1 418 788	1 482 026
	06113	Yolo County, CA	200 849	207 590
40940		Safford, AZ Micro area	37 220	37 957
	04009	Graham County, AZ	37 220	37 957
40980		Saginaw, MI Metro area	200 169	195 012
	26145	Saginaw County, MI	200 169	195 012
41060		St. Cloud, MN Metro area	189 093	192 418
	27009	Benton County, MN	38 451	39 506
	27145	Stearns County, MN	150 642	152 912
41100		St. George, UT Metro area	138 115	151 948
	49053	Washington County, UT	138 115	151 948
41140		St. Joseph, MO-KS Metro area	127 329	127 431
	20043	Doniphan County, KS	7 945	7 874
	29003	Andrew County, MO	17 291	17 379
	29021	Buchanan County, MO	89 201	89 486
	29063	DeKalb County, MO	12 892	12 692
41180		St. Louis, MO-IL Metro area	2 787 701	2 806 207
	17005	Bond County, IL	17 768	17 269
	17013	Calhoun County, IL	5 089	4 956
	17027	Clinton County, IL	37 762	37 857
	17083	Jersey County, IL	22 985	22 571
	17117	Macoupin County, IL	47 765	46 453
	17119	Madison County, IL	269 282	266 560
	17133	Monroe County, IL	32 957	33 722
	17163	St. Clair County, IL	270 056	265 729
	29071	Franklin County, MO	101 492	102 084
	29099	Jefferson County, MO	218 733	222 716
	29113	Lincoln County, MO	52 566	54 249
	29183	St. Charles County, MO	360 485	379 493
	29189	St. Louis County, MO	998 954	1 001 876
	29219	Warren County, MO	32 513	33 253
	29510	St. Louis city, MO	319 294	317 419
41220		St. Marys, GA Micro area	50 513	52 027
	13039	Camden County, GA	50 513	52 027
41400		Salem, OH Micro area	107 841	105 686
	39029	Columbiana County, OH	107 841	105 686
41420		Salem, OR Metro area	390 738	404 026
	41047	Marion County, OR	315 335	326 110
	41053	Polk County, OR	75 403	77 916
41460		Salina, KS Micro area	61 697	61 820
	20143	Ottawa County, KS	6 091	6 065
	20169	Saline County, KS	55 606	55 755
41500		Salinas, CA Metro area	415 057	431 344
	06053	Monterey County, CA	415 057	431 344
41540		Salisbury, MD-DE Metro area	373 802	389 922
	10005	Sussex County, DE	197 145	210 849
	24039	Somerset County, MD	26 470	25 859
	24045	Wicomico County, MD	98 733	101 539
	24047	Worcester County, MD	51 454	51 675
41620		Salt Lake City, UT Metro area	1 087 873	1 153 340
	49035	Salt Lake County, UT	1 029 655	1 091 742
	49045	Tooele County, UT	58 218	61 598

Core Based Statistical Areas (Metropolitan and Micropolitan), Metropolitan Divisions, and Components (as defined February 2013)–*Continued*

Core Based Statistical Area	State/ County FIPS Code	Title and Geographic Components	2010 Census Population	2014 Estimated Population
41660		San Angelo, TX Metro area	111 823	118 182
	48235	Irion County, TX	1 599	1 574
	48451	Tom Green County, TX	110 224	116 608
41700		San Antonio-New Braunfels, TX Metro	2 142 508	2 328 652
	48013	Atascosa County, TX	44 911	47 774
	48019	Bandera County, TX	20 485	20 892
	48029	Bexar County, TX	1 714 773	1 855 866
	48091	Comal County, TX	108 472	123 694
	48187	Guadalupe County, TX	131 533	147 250
	48259	Kendall County, TX	33 410	38 880
	48325	Medina County, TX	46 006	47 894
	48493	Wilson County, TX	42 918	46 402
41740		San Diego-Carlsbad, CA Metro area	3 095 313	3 263 431
	06073	San Diego County, CA	3 095 313	3 263 431
41760		Sandpoint, ID Micro area	40 877	41 585
	16017	Bonner County, ID	40 877	41 585
41780		Sandusky, OH Micro area	77 079	75 828
	39043	Erie County, OH	77 079	75 828
41820		Sanford, NC Micro area	57 866	59 662
	37105	Lee County, NC	57 866	59 662
41860		San Francisco-Oakland-Hayward, CA Metro area	4 335 391	4 594 060
41860		Oakland-Hayward-Berkeley, CA Metro Div 36084	2 559 296	2 722 260
	06001	Alameda County, CA	1 510 271	1 610 921
	06013	Contra Costa County, CA	1 049 025	1 111 339
41860		San Francisco-Redwood City-South San Francisco, CA Metro Div 41884	1 523 686	1 611 050
	06075	San Francisco County, CA	805 235	852 469
	06081	San Mateo County, CA	718 451	758 581
41860		San Rafael, CA Metropolitan Div 42034	252 409	260 750
	06041	Marin County, CA	252 409	260 750
41940		San Jose-Sunnyvale-Santa Clara, CA Metro area	1 836 911	1 952 872
	06069	San Benito County, CA	55 269	58 267
	06085	Santa Clara County, CA	1 781 642	1 894 605
42020		San Luis Obispo-Paso Robles-Arroyo Grande, CA Metro area	269 637	279 083
	06079	San Luis Obispo County, CA	269 637	279 083
42100		Santa Cruz-Watsonville, CA Metro area	262 382	271 804
	06087	Santa Cruz County, CA	262 382	271 804
42140		Santa Fe, NM Metro area	144 170	148 164
	35049	Santa Fe County, NM	144 170	148 164
42200		Santa Maria-Santa Barbara, CA Metro	423 895	440 668
	06083	Santa Barbara County, CA	423 895	440 668
42220		Santa Rosa, CA Metro area	483 878	500 292
	06097	Sonoma County, CA	483 878	500 292
42300		Sault Ste. Marie, MI Micro area	38 520	38 321
	26033	Chippewa County, MI	38 520	38 321
42340		Savannah, GA Metro area	347 611	372 708
	13029	Bryan County, GA	30 233	33 906
	13051	Chatham County, GA	265 128	283 379
	13103	Effingham County, GA	52 250	55 423
42380		Sayre, PA Micro area	62 622	61 784
	42015	Bradford County, PA	62 622	61 784
42420		Scottsbluff, NE Micro area	38 971	38 532
	31007	Banner County, NE	690	764
	31157	Scotts Bluff County, NE	36 970	36 465
	31165	Sioux County, NE	1 311	1 303
42460		Scottsboro, AL Micro area	53 227	52 665
	01071	Jackson County, AL	53 227	52 665
42540		Scranton-Wilkes-Barre-Hazleton, PA Metro area	563 631	559 679
	42069	Lackawanna County, PA	214 437	212 719
	42079	Luzerne County, PA	320 918	318 829
	42131	Wyoming County, PA	28 276	28 131
42620		Searcy, AR Micro area	77 076	78 592
	05145	White County, AR	77 076	78 592
42660		Seattle-Tacoma-Bellevue, WA Metro area	3 439 809	3 671 478
42660		Seattle-Bellevue-Everett, WA Metro Div 42644	2 644 584	2 839 550
	53033	King County, WA	1 931 249	2 079 967
	53061	Snohomish County, WA	713 335	759 583
42660		Tacoma-Lakewood, WA Metro Div 45104	795 225	831 928
	53053	Pierce County, WA	795 225	831 928
42680		Sebastian-Vero Beach, FL Metro area	138 028	144 755
	12061	Indian River County, FL	138 028	144 755
42700		Sebring, FL Metro area	98 786	98 236
	12055	Highlands County, FL	98 786	98 236
42740		Sedalia, MO Micro area	42 201	42 225
	29159	Pettis County, MO	42 201	42 225
42780		Selinsgrove, PA Micro area	39 702	40 323
	42109	Snyder County, PA	39 702	40 323
42820		Selma, AL Micro area	43 820	41 711
	01047	Dallas County, AL	43 820	41 711
42860		Seneca, SC Micro area	74 273	75 192
	45073	Oconee County, SC	74 273	75 192
42900		Seneca Falls, NY Micro area	35 251	34 884
	36099	Seneca County, NY	35 251	34 884
42940		Sevierville, TN Micro area	89 889	95 110
	47155	Sevier County, TN	89 889	95 110
42980		Seymour, IN Micro area	42 376	43 705
	18071	Jackson County, IN	42 376	43 705
43020		Shawano, WI Micro area	46 181	46 101
	55078	Menominee County, WI	4 232	4 522
	55115	Shawano County, WI	41 949	41 579

Core Based Statistical Areas (Metropolitan and Micropolitan), Metropolitan Divisions, and Components (as defined February 2013)–*Continued*

Core Based Statistical Area	State/ County FIPS Code	Title and Geographic Components	2010 Census Population	2014 Estimated Population
43060		Shawnee, OK Micro area	69 442	71 811
	40125	Pottawatomie County, OK	69 442	71 811
43100		Sheboygan, WI Metro area	115 507	115 290
	55117	Sheboygan County, WI	115 507	115 290
43140		Shelby, NC Micro area	98 078	97 076
	37045	Cleveland County, NC	98 078	97 076
43180		Shelbyville, TN Micro area	45 058	46 627
	47003	Bedford County, TN	45 058	46 627
43220		Shelton, WA Micro area	60 699	60 711
	53045	Mason County, WA	60 699	60 711
43260		Sheridan, WY Micro area	29 116	30 032
	56033	Sheridan County, WY	29 116	30 032
43300		Sherman-Denison, TX Metro area	120 877	123 534
	48181	Grayson County, TX	120 877	123 534
43320		Show Low, AZ Micro area	107 449	108 101
	04017	Navajo County, AZ	107 449	108 101
43340		Shreveport-Bossier City, LA Metro area	439 811	445 142
	22015	Bossier Parish, LA	116 979	125 064
	22017	Caddo Parish, LA	254 969	252 603
	22031	De Soto Parish, LA	26 656	27 142
	22119	Webster Parish, LA	41 207	40 333
43380		Sidney, OH Micro area	49 423	48 951
	39149	Shelby County, OH	49 423	48 951
43420		Sierra Vista-Douglas, AZ Metro area	131 346	127 448
	04003	Cochise County, AZ	131 346	127 448
43460		Sikeston, MO Micro area	39 191	38 903
	29201	Scott County, MO	39 191	38 903
43500		Silver City, NM Micro area	29 514	29 096
	35017	Grant County, NM	29 514	29 096
43580		Sioux City, IA-NE-SD Metro area	168 563	168 806
	19149	Plymouth County, IA	24 986	24 874
	19193	Woodbury County, IA	102 172	102 271
	31043	Dakota County, NE	21 006	20 850
	31051	Dixon County, NE	6 000	5 782
	46127	Union County, SD	14 399	15 029
43620		Sioux Falls, SD Metro area	228 261	248 351
	46083	Lincoln County, SD	44 828	51 548
	46087	McCook County, SD	5 618	5 649
	46099	Minnehaha County, SD	169 468	182 882
	46125	Turner County, SD	8 347	8 272
43660		Snyder, TX Micro area	16 921	17 328
	48415	Scurry County, TX	16 921	17 328
43700		Somerset, KY Micro area	63 063	63 825
	21199	Pulaski County, KY	63 063	63 825
43740		Somerset, PA Micro area	77 742	76 218
	42111	Somerset County, PA	77 742	76 218
43760		Sonora, CA Micro area	55 365	53 831
	06109	Tuolumne County, CA	55 365	53 831

Core Based Statistical Area	State/ County FIPS Code	Title and Geographic Components	2010 Census Population	2014 Estimated Population
43780		South Bend-Mishawaka, IN-MI Metro area	319 224	319 226
	18141	St. Joseph County, IN	266 931	267 618
	26027	Cass County, MI	52 293	51 608
43900		Spartanburg, SC Metro area	313 268	321 418
	45083	Spartanburg County, SC	284 307	293 542
	45087	Union County, SC	28 961	27 876
43940		Spearfish, SD Micro area	24 097	24 657
	46081	Lawrence County, SD	24 097	24 657
43980		Spencer, IA Micro area	16 667	16 515
	19041	Clay County, IA	16 667	16 515
44020		Spirit Lake, IA Micro area	16 667	16 935
	19059	Dickinson County, IA	16 667	16 935
44060		Spokane-Spokane Valley, WA Metro area	527 753	540 953
	53051	Pend Oreille County, WA	13 001	12 985
	53063	Spokane County, WA	471 221	484 318
	53065	Stevens County, WA	43 531	43 650
44100		Springfield, IL Metro area	210 170	211 567
	17129	Menard County, IL	12 705	12 570
	17167	Sangamon County, IL	197 465	198 997
44140		Springfield, MA Metro area	621 570	629 100
	25013	Hampden County, MA	463 490	468 161
	25015	Hampshire County, MA	158 080	160 939
44180		Springfield, MO Metro area	436 712	452 297
	29043	Christian County, MO	77 422	82 101
	29059	Dallas County, MO	16 777	16 389
	29077	Greene County, MO	275 174	285 865
	29167	Polk County, MO	31 137	31 054
	29225	Webster County, MO	36 202	36 888
44220		Springfield, OH Metro area	138 333	136 554
	39023	Clark County, OH	138 333	136 554
44260		Starkville, MS Micro area	47 671	49 414
	28105	Oktibbeha County, MS	47 671	49 414
44300		State College, PA Metro area	153 990	158 742
	42027	Centre County, PA	153 990	158 742
44340		Statesboro, GA Micro area	70 217	72 087
	13031	Bulloch County, GA	70 217	72 087
44420		Staunton-Waynesboro, VA Metro area	118 502	119 766
	51015	Augusta County, VA	73 750	73 862
	51790	Staunton city, VA	23 746	24 538
	51820	Waynesboro city, VA	21 006	21 366
44460		Steamboat Springs, CO Micro area	23 509	23 865
	08107	Routt County, CO	23 509	23 865
44500		Stephenville, TX Micro area	37 890	40 147
	48143	Erath County, TX	37 890	40 147
44540		Sterling, CO Micro area	22 709	22 524
	08075	Logan County, CO	22 709	22 524
44580		Sterling, IL Micro area	58 498	56 876
	17195	Whiteside County, IL	58 498	56 876

Core Based Statistical Areas (Metropolitan and Micropolitan), Metropolitan Divisions, and Components (as defined February 2013)–*Continued*

Core Based Statistical Area	State/ County FIPS Code	Title and Geographic Components	2010 Census Population	2014 Estimated Population
44620		Stevens Point, WI Micro area	70 019	70 482
	55097	Portage County, WI	70 019	70 482
44660		Stillwater, OK Micro area	77 350	80 264
	40119	Payne County, OK	77 350	80 264
44700		Stockton-Lodi, CA Metro area	685 306	715 597
	06077	San Joaquin County, CA	685 306	715 597
44740		Storm Lake, IA Micro area	20 260	20 578
	19021	Buena Vista County, IA	20 260	20 578
44780		Sturgis, MI Micro area	61 295	60 946
	26149	St. Joseph County, MI	61 295	60 946
44860		Sulphur Springs, TX Micro area	35 161	35 921
	48223	Hopkins County, TX	35 161	35 921
44900		Summerville, GA Micro area	26 015	24 939
	13055	Chattooga County, GA	26 015	24 939
44920		Summit Park, UT Micro area	36 324	39 105
	49043	Summit County, UT	36 324	39 105
44940		Sumter, SC Metro area	107 456	107 919
	45085	Sumter County, SC	107 456	107 919
44980		Sunbury, PA Micro area	94 528	93 944
	42097	Northumberland County, PA	94 528	93 944
45000		Susanville, CA Micro area	34 895	31 749
	06035	Lassen County, CA	34 895	31 749
45020		Sweetwater, TX Micro area	15 216	15 093
	48353	Nolan County, TX	15 216	15 093
45060		Syracuse, NY Metro area	662 577	661 478
	36053	Madison County, NY	73 442	72 369
	36067	Onondaga County, NY	467 026	468 196
	36075	Oswego County, NY	122 109	120 913
45140		Tahlequah, OK Micro area	46 987	48 341
	40021	Cherokee County, OK	46 987	48 341
45180		Talladega-Sylacauga, AL Micro area	93 830	92 208
	01037	Coosa County, AL	11 539	10 886
	01121	Talladega County, AL	82 291	81 322
45220		Tallahassee, FL Metro area	367 413	375 751
	12039	Gadsden County, FL	46 389	46 281
	12065	Jefferson County, FL	14 761	14 050
	12073	Leon County, FL	275 487	283 988
	12129	Wakulla County, FL	30 776	31 432
45300		Tampa-St. Petersburg-Clearwater, FL Metro area	2 783 243	2 915 582
	12053	Hernando County, FL	172 778	175 855
	12057	Hillsborough County, FL	1 229 226	1 316 298
	12101	Pasco County, FL	464 697	485 331
	12103	Pinellas County, FL	916 542	938 098
45340		Taos, NM Micro area	32 937	33 084
	35055	Taos County, NM	32 937	33 084
45380		Taylorville, IL Micro area	34 800	33 892
	17021	Christian County, IL	34 800	33 892
45460		Terre Haute, IN Metro area	172 425	171 480
	18021	Clay County, IN	26 890	26 562
	18153	Sullivan County, IN	21 475	21 050
	18165	Vermillion County, IN	16 212	15 693
	18167	Vigo County, IN	107 848	108 175
45500		Texarkana, TX-AR Metro area	149 198	149 235
	05081	Little River County, AR	13 171	12 532
	05091	Miller County, AR	43 462	43 428
	48037	Bowie County, TX	92 565	93 275
45520		The Dalles, OR Micro area	25 213	25 515
	41065	Wasco County, OR	25 213	25 515
45540		The Villages, FL Metro area	93 420	114 350
	12119	Sumter County, FL	93 420	114 350
45580		Thomaston, GA Micro area	27 153	26 256
	13293	Upson County, GA	27 153	26 256
45620		Thomasville, GA Micro area	44 720	44 959
	13275	Thomas County, GA	44 720	44 959
45660		Tiffin, OH Micro area	56 745	55 669
	39147	Seneca County, OH	56 745	55 669
45700		Tifton, GA Micro area	40 118	40 704
	13277	Tift County, GA	40 118	40 704
45740		Toccoa, GA Micro area	26 175	25 480
	13257	Stephens County, GA	26 175	25 480
45780		Toledo, OH Metro area	610 001	607 456
	39051	Fulton County, OH	42 698	42 580
	39095	Lucas County, OH	441 815	435 286
	39173	Wood County, OH	125 488	129 590
45820		Topeka, KS Metro area	233 870	233 758
	20085	Jackson County, KS	13 462	13 539
	20087	Jefferson County, KS	19 126	18 855
	20139	Osage County, KS	16 295	15 936
	20177	Shawnee County, KS	177 934	178 406
	20197	Wabaunsee County, KS	7 053	7 022
45860		Torrington, CT Micro area	189 927	184 993
	09005	Litchfield County, CT	189 927	184 993
45900		Traverse City, MI Micro area	143 372	147 610
	26019	Benzie County, MI	17 525	17 519
	26055	Grand Traverse County, MI	86 986	90 782
	26079	Kalkaska County, MI	17 153	17 394
	26089	Leelanau County, MI	21 708	21 915
45940		Trenton, NJ Metro area	366 513	371 537
	34021	Mercer County, NJ	366 513	371 537
45980		Troy, AL Micro area	32 899	33 389
	01109	Pike County, AL	32 899	33 389
46020		Truckee-Grass Valley, CA Micro area	98 764	98 893
	06057	Nevada County, CA	98 764	98 893
46060		Tucson, AZ Metro area	980 263	1 004 516
	04019	Pima County, AZ	980 263	1 004 516

Core Based Statistical Areas (Metropolitan and Micropolitan), Metropolitan Divisions, and Components (as defined February 2013)–*Continued*

Core Based Statistical Area	State/ County FIPS Code	Title and Geographic Components	2010 Census Population	2014 Estimated Population
46100		Tullahoma-Manchester, TN Micro area	100 210	101 344
	47031	Coffee County, TN	52 796	53 623
	47051	Franklin County, TN	41 052	41 402
	47127	Moore County, TN	6 362	6 319
46140		Tulsa, OK Metro area	937 478	969 224
	40037	Creek County, OK	69 967	70 632
	40111	Okmulgee County, OK	40 069	39 095
	40113	Osage County, OK	47 472	47 981
	40117	Pawnee County, OK	16 577	16 401
	40131	Rogers County, OK	86 905	89 815
	40143	Tulsa County, OK	603 403	629 598
	40145	Wagoner County, OK	73 085	75 702
46180		Tupelo, MS Micro area	136 268	139 723
	28057	Itawamba County, MS	23 401	23 527
	28081	Lee County, MS	82 910	85 246
	28115	Pontotoc County, MS	29 957	30 950
46220		Tuscaloosa, AL Metro area	230 162	237 761
	01065	Hale County, AL	15 760	15 184
	01107	Pickens County, AL	19 746	20 365
	01125	Tuscaloosa County, AL	194 656	202 212
46300		Twin Falls, ID Micro area	99 604	103 732
	16053	Jerome County, ID	22 374	22 818
	16083	Twin Falls County, ID	77 230	80 914
46340		Tyler, TX Metro area	209 714	218 842
	48423	Smith County, TX	209 714	218 842
46380		Ukiah, CA Micro area	87 841	87 869
	06045	Mendocino County, CA	87 841	87 869
46460		Union City, TN-KY Micro area	38 620	37 206
	21075	Fulton County, KY	6 813	6 265
	47131	Obion County, TN	31 807	30 941
46500		Urbana, OH Micro area	40 097	39 128
	39021	Champaign County, OH	40 097	39 128
46520		Urban Honolulu, HI Metro area	953 207	991 788
	15003	Honolulu County, HI	953 207	991 788
46540		Utica-Rome, NY Metro area	299 397	296 615
	36043	Herkimer County, NY	64 519	63 744
	36065	Oneida County, NY	234 878	232 871
46620		Uvalde, TX Micro area	26 405	27 117
	48463	Uvalde County, TX	26 405	27 117
46660		Valdosta, GA Metro area	139 588	143 317
	13027	Brooks County, GA	16 243	15 418
	13101	Echols County, GA	4 034	4 003
	13173	Lanier County, GA	10 078	10 373
	13185	Lowndes County, GA	109 233	113 523
46700		Vallejo-Fairfield, CA Metro area	413 344	431 131
	06095	Solano County, CA	413 344	431 131
46740		Valley, AL Micro area	34 215	34 076
	01017	Chambers County, AL	34 215	34 076
46780		Van Wert, OH Micro area	28 744	28 462
	39161	Van Wert County, OH	28 744	28 462
46820		Vermillion, SD Micro area	13 864	13 932
	46027	Clay County, SD	13 864	13 932
46860		Vernal, UT Micro area	32 588	36 867
	49047	Uintah County, UT	32 588	36 867
46900		Vernon, TX Micro area	13 535	12 973
	48487	Wilbarger County, TX	13 535	12 973
46980		Vicksburg, MS Micro area	58 377	57 063
	28021	Claiborne County, MS	9 604	9 080
	28149	Warren County, MS	48 773	47 983
47020		Victoria, TX Metro area	94 003	98 630
	48175	Goliad County, TX	7 210	7 549
	48469	Victoria County, TX	86 793	91 081
47080		Vidalia, GA Micro area	36 346	36 273
	13209	Montgomery County, GA	9 123	8 991
	13279	Toombs County, GA	27 223	27 282
47180		Vincennes, IN Micro area	38 440	37 938
	18083	Knox County, IN	38 440	37 938
47220		Vineland-Bridgeton, NJ Metro area	156 898	157 389
	34011	Cumberland County, NJ	156 898	157 389
47240		Vineyard Haven, MA Micro area	16 535	17 356
	25007	Dukes County, MA	16 535	17 356
47260		Virginia Beach-Norfolk-Newport News, VA-NC Metro area	1 676 822	1 716 624
	37053	Currituck County, NC	23 547	24 976
	37073	Gates County, NC	12 197	11 567
	51073	Gloucester County, VA	36 858	37 141
	51093	Isle of Wight County, VA	35 270	36 007
	51095	James City County, VA	67 009	72 583
	51115	Mathews County, VA	8 978	8 836
	51199	York County, VA	65 464	66 342
	51550	Chesapeake city, VA	222 209	233 371
	51650	Hampton city, VA	137 436	136 879
	51700	Newport News city, VA	180 719	182 965
	51710	Norfolk city, VA	242 803	245 428
	51735	Poquoson city, VA	12 150	12 048
	51740	Portsmouth city, VA	95 535	96 004
	51800	Suffolk city, VA	84 585	86 806
	51810	Virginia Beach city, VA	437 994	450 980
	51830	Williamsburg city, VA	14 068	14 691
47300		Visalia-Porterville, CA Metro area	442 179	458 198
	06107	Tulare County, CA	442 179	458 198
47340		Wabash, IN Micro area	32 888	32 252
	18169	Wabash County, IN	32 888	32 252
47380		Waco, TX Metro area	252 772	260 430
	48145	Falls County, TX	17 866	16 989
	48309	McLennan County, TX	234 906	243 441
47420		Wahpeton, ND-MN Micro area	22 897	22 927
	27167	Wilkin County, MN	6 576	6 495
	38077	Richland County, ND	16 321	16 432
47460		Walla Walla, WA Metro area	62 859	63 829
	53013	Columbia County, WA	4 078	3 985
	53071	Walla Walla County, WA	58 781	59 844
47540		Wapakoneta, OH Micro area	45 949	45 841
	39011	Auglaize County, OH	45 949	45 841

Core Based Statistical Areas (Metropolitan and Micropolitan), Metropolitan Divisions, and Components (as defined February 2013)–*Continued*

Core Based Statistical Area	State/County FIPS Code	Title and Geographic Components	2010 Census Population	2014 Estimated Population
47580		Warner Robins, GA Metro area	179 605	187 516
	13153	Houston County, GA	139 900	149 111
	13225	Peach County, GA	27 695	26 922
	13235	Pulaski County, GA	12 010	11 483
47620		Warren, PA Micro area	41 815	40 703
	42123	Warren County, PA	41 815	40 703
47660		Warrensburg, MO Micro area	52 595	54 362
	29101	Johnson County, MO	52 595	54 362
47700		Warsaw, IN Micro area	77 358	78 564
	18085	Kosciusko County, IN	77 358	78 564
47780		Washington, IN Micro area	31 648	32 729
	18027	Daviess County, IN	31 648	32 729
47820		Washington, NC Micro area	47 759	47 585
	37013	Beaufort County, NC	47 759	47 585
47900		Washington-Arlington-Alexandria, DC-VA-MD-WV Metro area	5 636 232	6 033 737
47900		Silver Spring-Frederick-Rockville, MD Metro Div 43524	1 205 162	1 274 122
	24021	Frederick County, MD	233 385	243 675
	24031	Montgomery County, MD	971 777	1 030 447
47900		Washington-Arlington-Alexandria, DC-VA-MD-WV Metro Div 47894	4 431 070	4 759 615
	11001	District of Columbia, DC	601 723	658 893
	24009	Calvert County, MD	88 737	90 613
	24017	Charles County, MD	146 551	154 747
	24033	Prince George's County, MD	863 420	904 430
	51013	Arlington County, VA	207 627	226 908
	51043	Clarke County, VA	14 034	14 423
	51047	Culpeper County, VA	46 689	49 166
	51059	Fairfax County, VA	1 081 726	1 137 538
	51061	Fauquier County, VA	65 203	68 248
	51107	Loudoun County, VA	312 311	363 050
	51153	Prince William County, VA	402 002	446 094
	51157	Rappahannock County, VA	7 373	7 361
	51177	Spotsylvania County, VA	122 397	129 188
	51179	Stafford County, VA	128 961	139 992
	51187	Warren County, VA	37 575	38 987
	51510	Alexandria city, VA	139 966	150 575
	51600	Fairfax city, VA	22 565	24 483
	51610	Falls Church city, VA	12 332	13 601
	51630	Fredericksburg city, VA	24 286	28 350
	51683	Manassas city, VA	37 821	42 081
	51685	Manassas Park city, VA	14 273	15 174
	54037	Jefferson County, WV	53 498	55 713
47920		Washington Court House, OH Micro area	29 030	28 800
	39047	Fayette County, OH	29 030	28 800
47940		Waterloo-Cedar Falls, IA Metro area	167 819	169 993
	19013	Black Hawk County, IA	131 090	132 897
	19017	Bremer County, IA	24 276	24 721
	19075	Grundy County, IA	12 453	12 375
47980		Watertown, SD Micro area	27 227	27 938
	46029	Codington County, SD	27 227	27 938
48020		Watertown-Fort Atkinson, WI Micro area	83 686	84 395
	55055	Jefferson County, WI	83 686	84 395

Core Based Statistical Area	State/County FIPS Code	Title and Geographic Components	2010 Census Population	2014 Estimated Population
48060		Watertown-Fort Drum, NY Metro area	116 229	119 103
	36045	Jefferson County, NY	116 229	119 103
48100		Wauchula, FL Micro area	27 731	27 469
	12049	Hardee County, FL	27 731	27 469
48140		Wausau, WI Metro area	134 063	135 780
	55073	Marathon County, WI	134 063	135 780
48180		Waycross, GA Micro area	55 070	54 506
	13229	Pierce County, GA	18 758	18 991
	13299	Ware County, GA	36 312	35 515
48220		Weatherford, OK Micro area	27 469	29 500
	40039	Custer County, OK	27 469	29 500
48260		Weirton-Steubenville, WV-OH Metro area	124 454	121 336
	39081	Jefferson County, OH	69 709	67 694
	54009	Brooke County, WV	24 069	23 530
	54029	Hancock County, WV	30 676	30 112
48300		Wenatchee, WA Metro area	110 884	114 392
	53007	Chelan County, WA	72 453	74 588
	53017	Douglas County, WA	38 431	39 804
48460		West Plains, MO Micro area	40 400	40 173
	29091	Howell County, MO	40 400	40 173
48540		Wheeling, WV-OH Metro area	147 950	145 205
	39013	Belmont County, OH	70 400	69 461
	54051	Marshall County, WV	33 107	32 416
	54069	Ohio County, WV	44 443	43 328
48580		Whitewater-Elkhorn, WI Micro area	102 228	103 527
	55127	Walworth County, WI	102 228	103 527
48620		Wichita, KS Metro area	630 919	641 076
	20015	Butler County, KS	65 880	66 227
	20079	Harvey County, KS	34 684	34 820
	20095	Kingman County, KS	7 858	7 698
	20173	Sedgwick County, KS	498 365	508 803
	20191	Sumner County, KS	24 132	23 528
48660		Wichita Falls, TX Metro area	151 306	151 536
	48009	Archer County, TX	9 054	8 811
	48077	Clay County, TX	10 752	10 370
	48485	Wichita County, TX	131 500	132 355
48700		Williamsport, PA Metro area	116 111	116 508
	42081	Lycoming County, PA	116 111	116 508
48780		Williston, ND Micro area	22 398	32 130
	38105	Williams County, ND	22 398	32 130
48820		Willmar, MN Micro area	42 239	42 285
	27067	Kandiyohi County, MN	42 239	42 285
48900		Wilmington, NC Metro area	254 884	272 548
	37129	New Hanover County, NC	202 667	216 298
	37141	Pender County, NC	52 217	56 250
48940		Wilmington, OH Micro area	42 040	41 835
	39027	Clinton County, OH	42 040	41 835
48980		Wilson, NC Micro area	81 234	81 401
	37195	Wilson County, NC	81 234	81 401

Core Based Statistical Areas (Metropolitan and Micropolitan), Metropolitan Divisions, and Components (as defined February 2013)–*Continued*

Core Based Statistical Area	State/ County FIPS Code	Title and Geographic Components	2010 Census Population	2014 Estimated Population
49020		Winchester, VA-WV Metro area	128 472	133 403
	51069	Frederick County, VA	78 305	82 377
	51840	Winchester city, VA	26 203	27 543
	54027	Hampshire County, WV	23 964	23 483
49080		Winnemucca, NV Micro area	16 528	17 279
	32013	Humboldt County, NV	16 528	17 279
49100		Winona, MN Micro area	51 461	51 097
	27169	Winona County, MN	51 461	51 097
49180		Winston-Salem, NC Metro area	640 595	655 015
	37057	Davidson County, NC	162 878	164 072
	37059	Davie County, NC	41 240	41 434
	37067	Forsyth County, NC	350 670	365 298
	37169	Stokes County, NC	47 401	46 419
	37197	Yadkin County, NC	38 406	37 792
49220		Wisconsin Rapids-Marshfield, WI Micro area	74 749	73 608
	55141	Wood County, WI	74 749	73 608
49260		Woodward, OK Micro area	20 081	21 529
	40153	Woodward County, OK	20 081	21 529
49300		Wooster, OH Micro area	114 520	115 537
	39169	Wayne County, OH	114 520	115 537
49340		Worcester, MA-CT Metro area	916 980	930 473
	09015	Windham County, CT	118 428	116 998
	25027	Worcester County, MA	798 552	813 475
49380		Worthington, MN Micro area	21 378	21 590
	27105	Nobles County, MN	21 378	21 590
49420		Yakima, WA Metro area	243 231	247 687
	53077	Yakima County, WA	243 231	247 687
49460		Yankton, SD Micro area	22 438	22 684
	46135	Yankton County, SD	22 438	22 684
49620		York-Hanover, PA Metro area	434 972	440 755
	42133	York County, PA	434 972	440 755
49660		Youngstown-Warren-Boardman, OH-PA Metro area	565 773	553 263
	39099	Mahoning County, OH	238 823	233 204
	39155	Trumbull County, OH	210 312	205 175
	42085	Mercer County, PA	116 638	114 884
49700		Yuba City, CA Metro area	166 892	169 813
	06101	Sutter County, CA	94 737	95 847
	06115	Yuba County, CA	72 155	73 966
49740		Yuma, AZ Metro area	195 751	203 247
	04027	Yuma County, AZ	195 751	203 247
49780		Zanesville, OH Micro area	86 074	85 818
	39119	Muskingum County, OH	86 074	85 818
49820		Zapata, TX Micro area	14 018	14 319
	48505	Zapata County, TX	14 018	14 319

APPENDIX D
MAPS OF CONGRESSIONAL DISTRICTS AND STATES

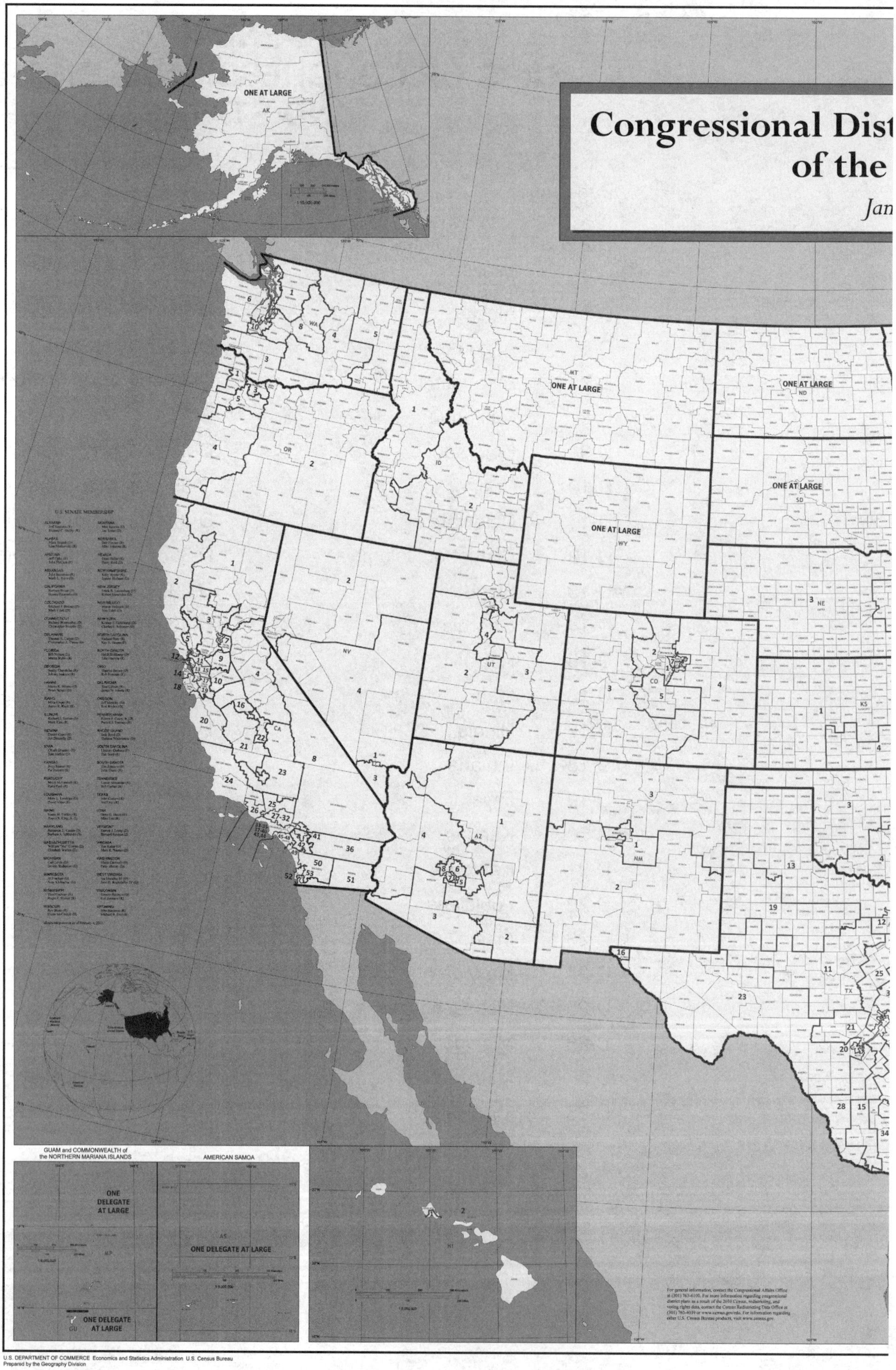

U.S. DEPARTMENT OF COMMERCE Economics and Statistics Administration U.S. Census Bureau
Prepared by the Geography Division

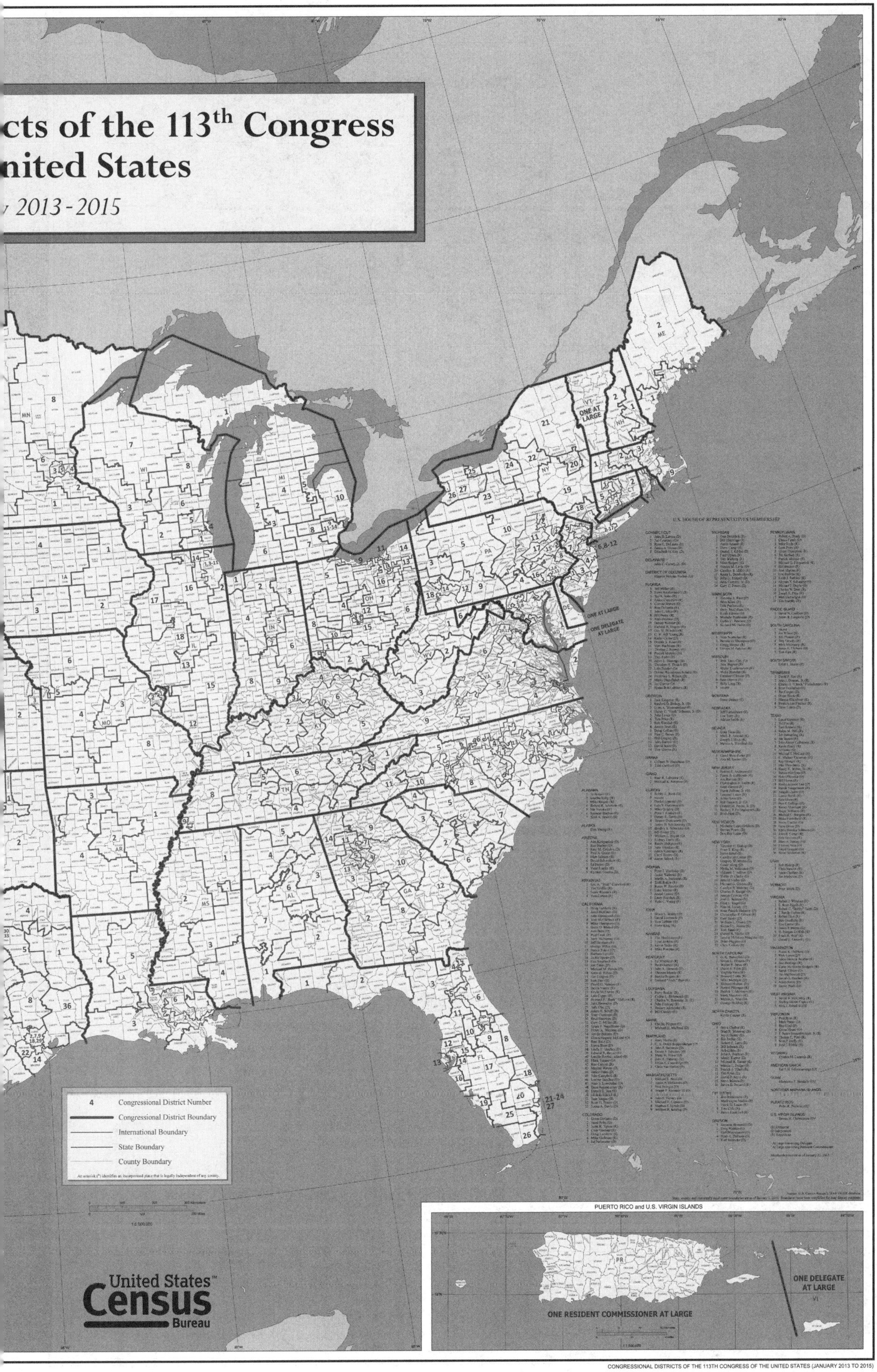

CONGRESSIONAL DISTRICTS OF THE 113TH CONGRESS OF THE UNITED STATES (JANUARY 2013 TO 2015)

ALABAMA - Core Based Statistical Areas (CBSAs) and Counties

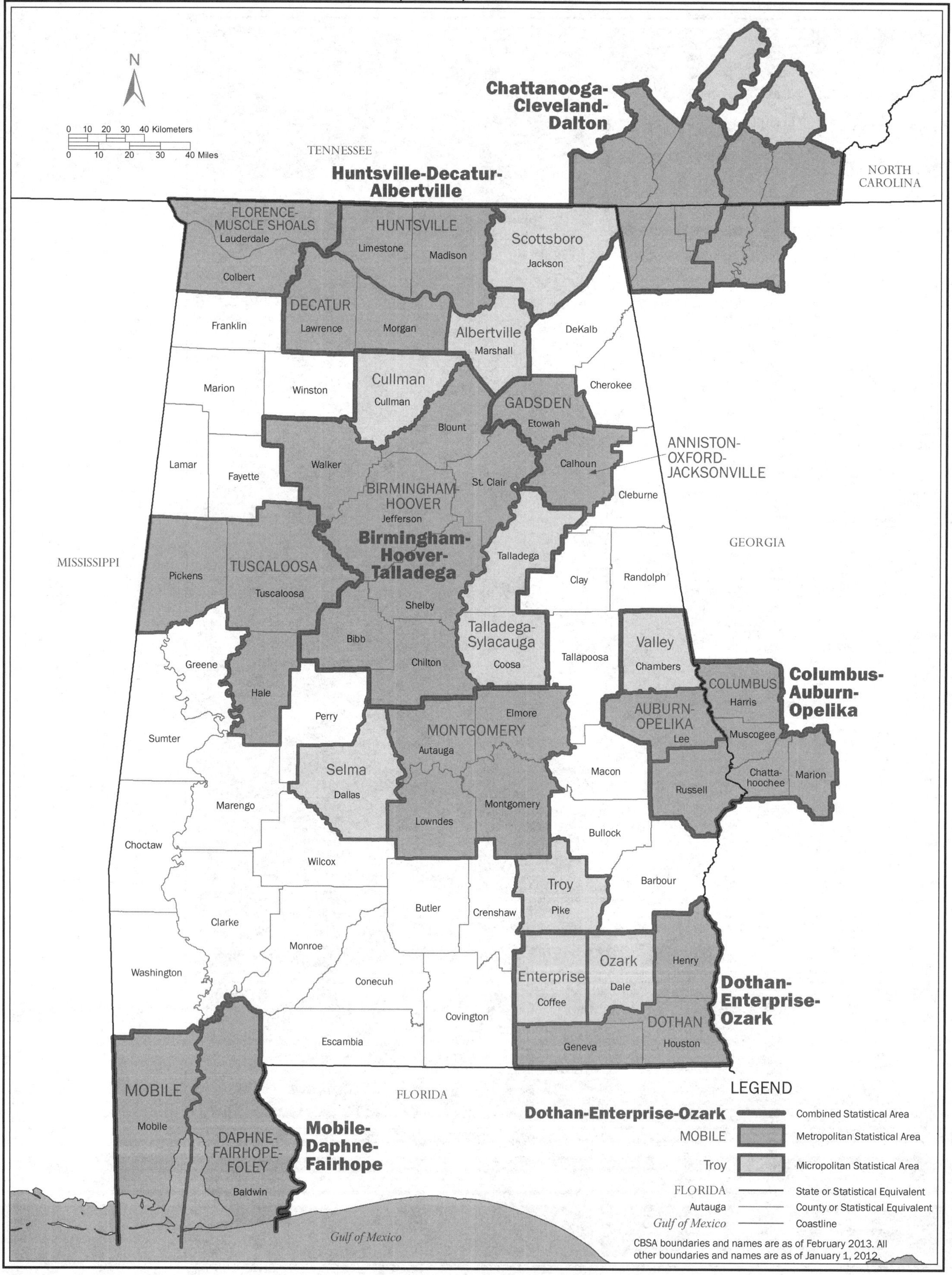

ALASKA - Core Based Statistical Areas (CBSAs) and Counties

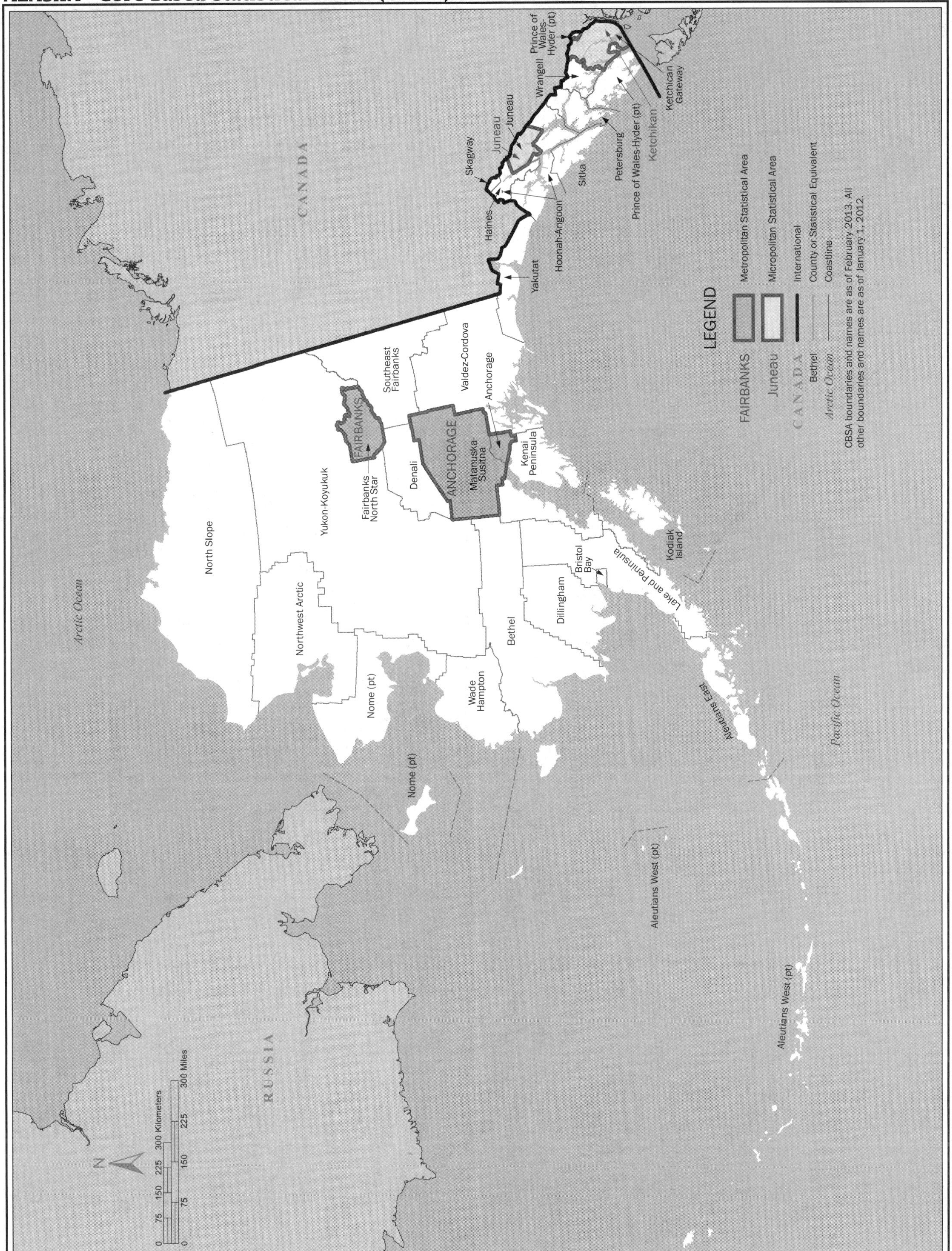

ARIZONA - Core Based Statistical Areas (CBSAs) and Counties

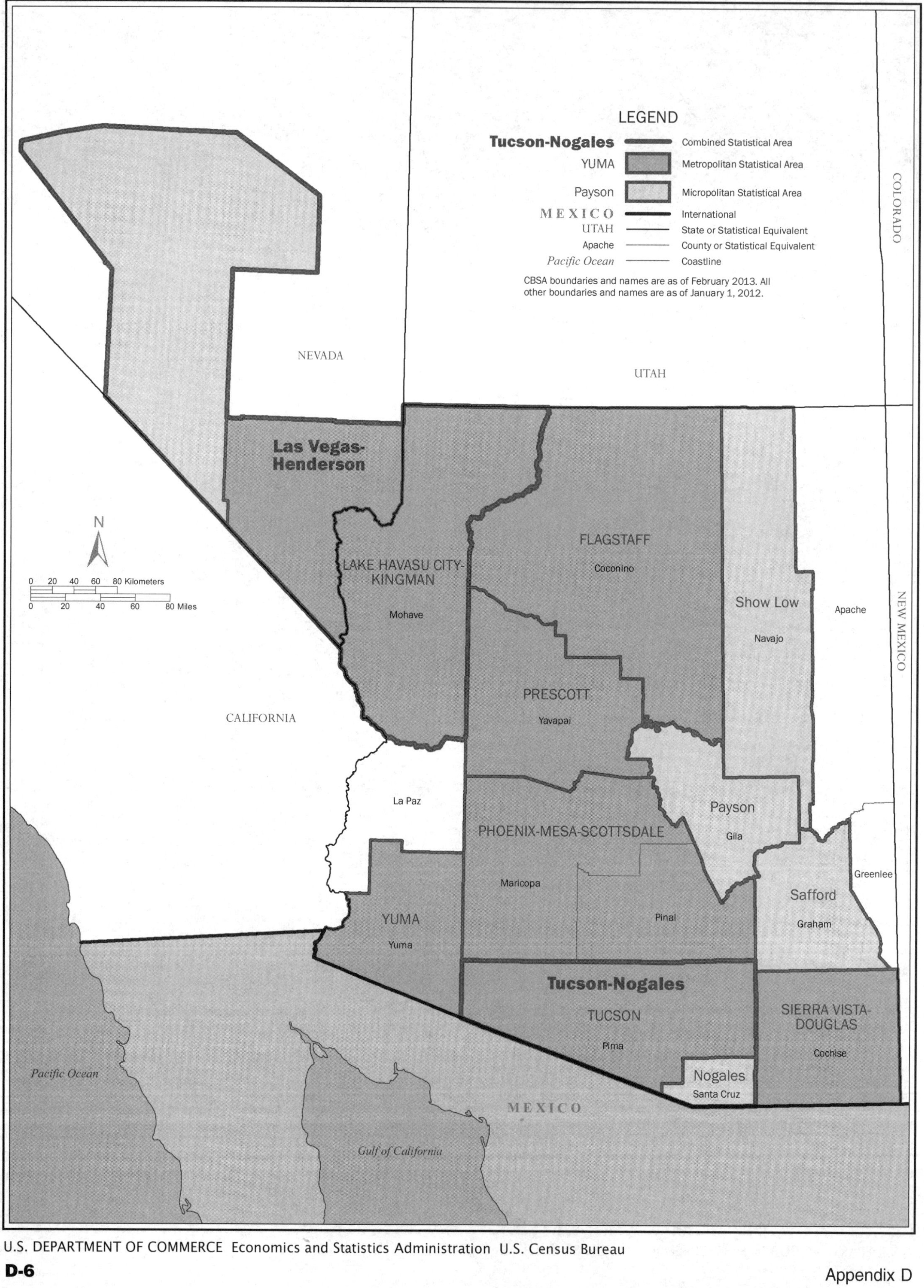

ARKANSAS - Core Based Statistical Areas (CBSAs) and Counties

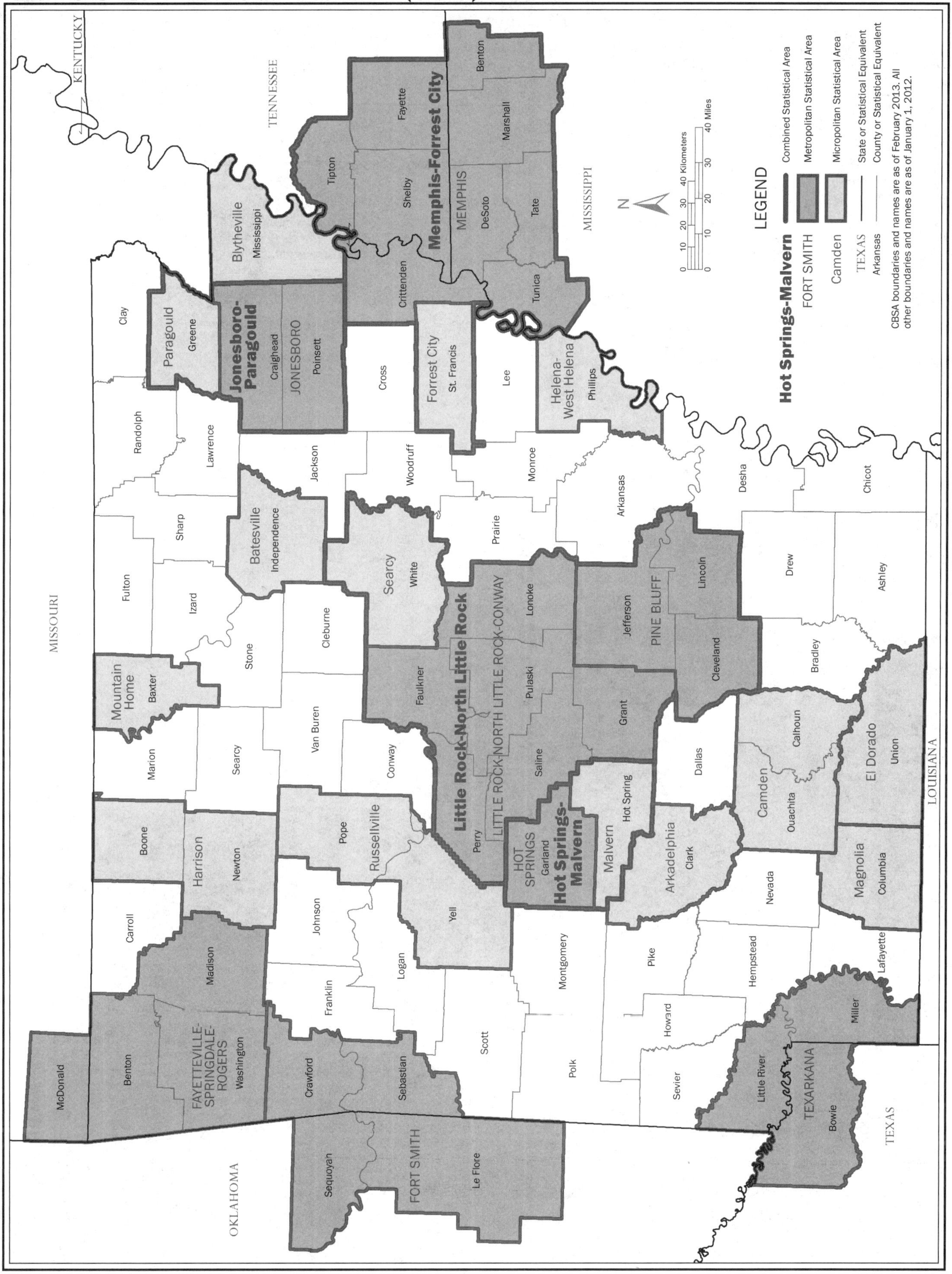

CALIFORNIA - Core Based Statistical Areas (CBSAs) and Counties

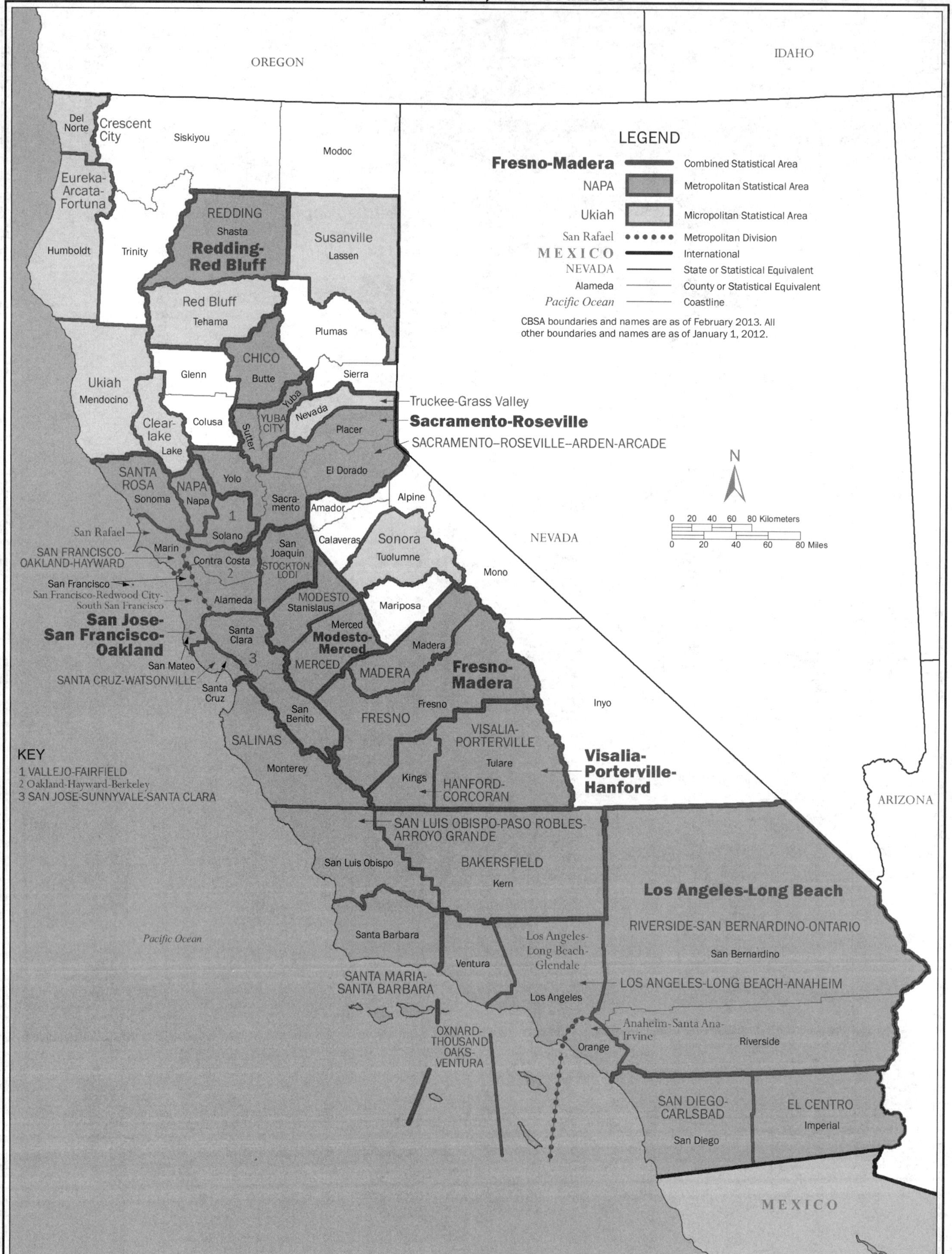

COLORADO - Core Based Statistical Areas (CBSAs) and Counties

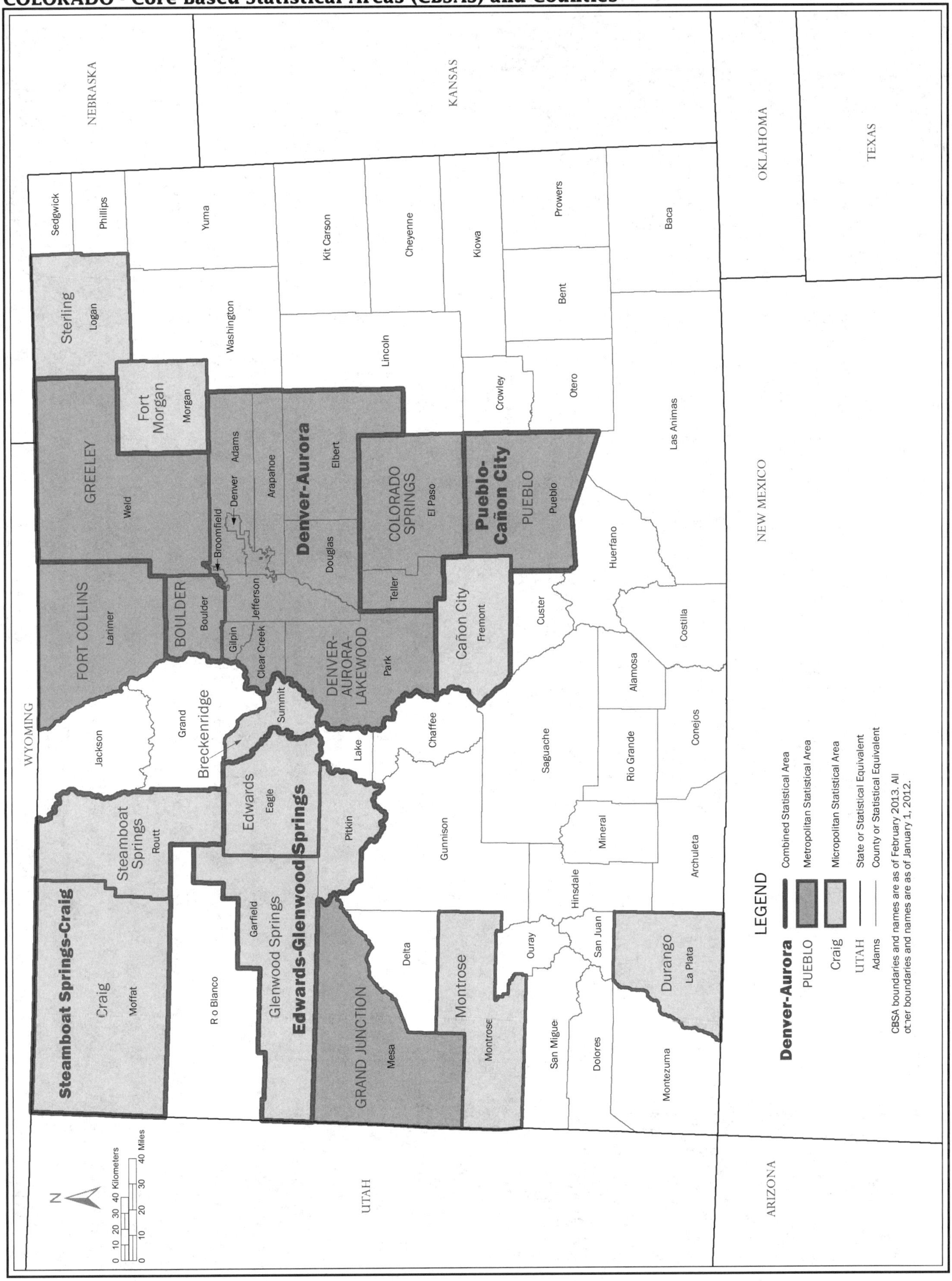

CONNECTICUT - Core Based Statistical Areas (CBSAs) and Counties

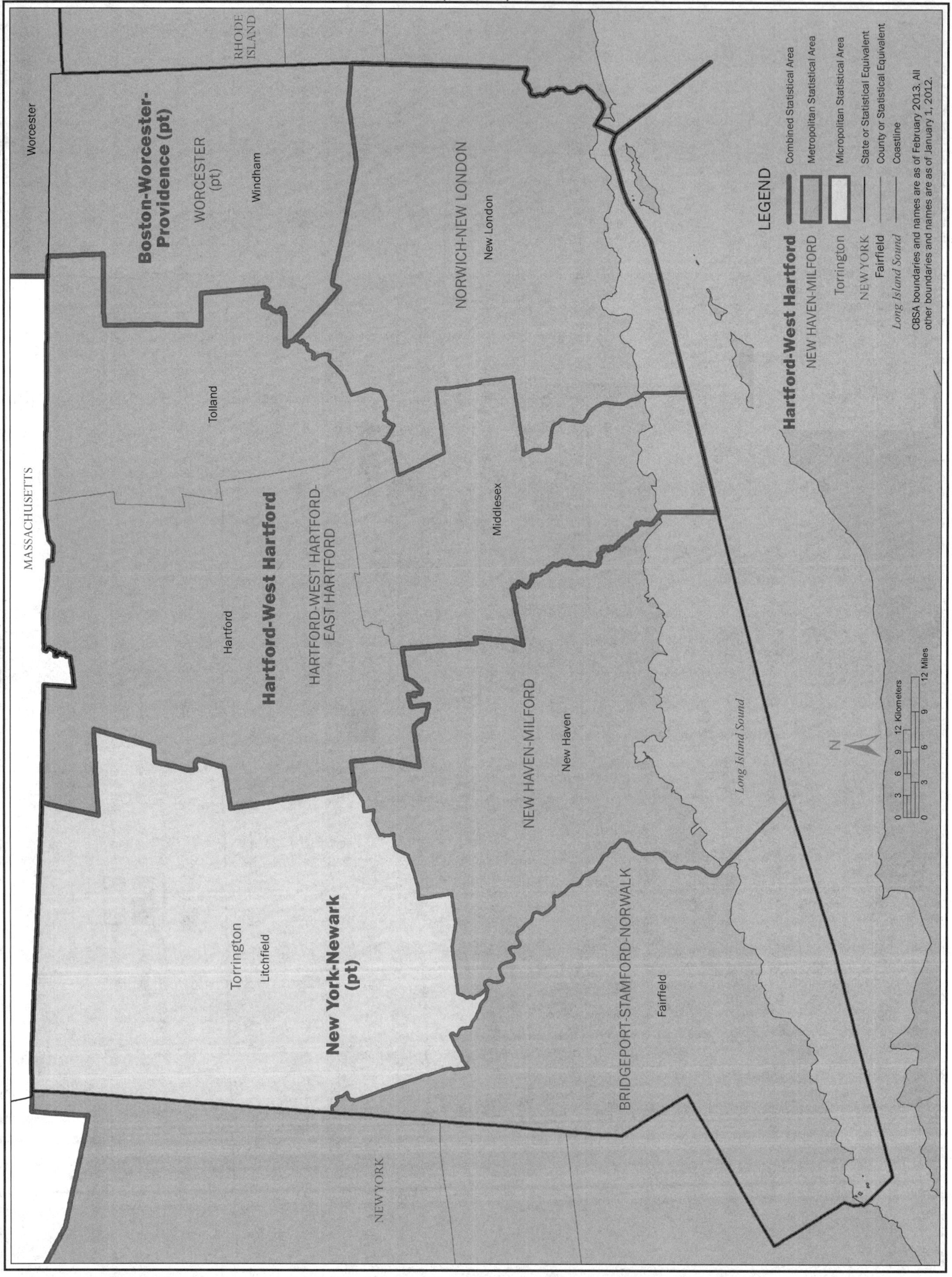

DELAWARE - Core Based Statistical Areas (CBSAs) and Counties

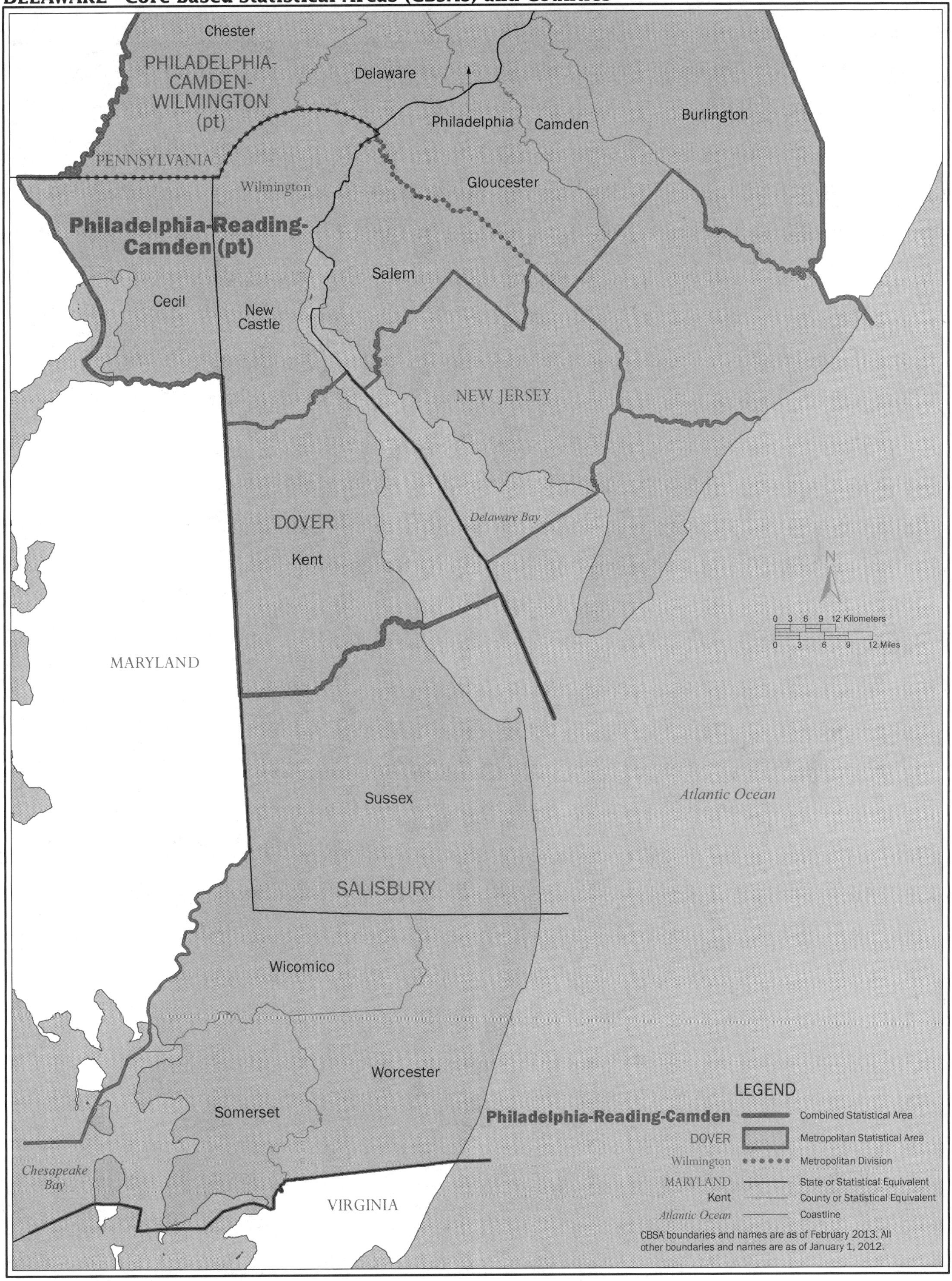

DISTRICT OF COLUMBIA - Core Based Statistical Areas (CBSAs) and Counties

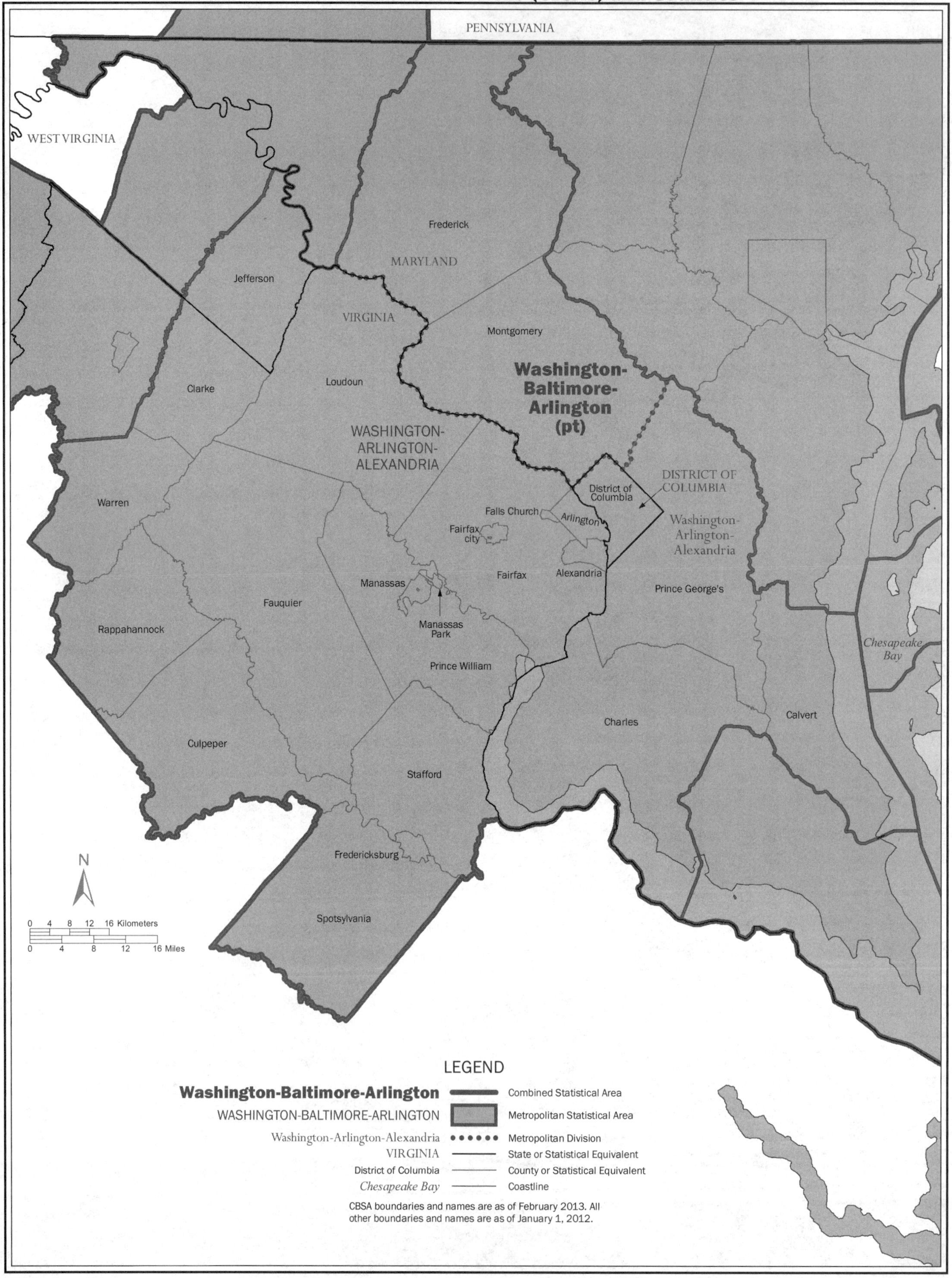

FLORIDA - Core Based Statistical Areas (CBSAs) and Counties

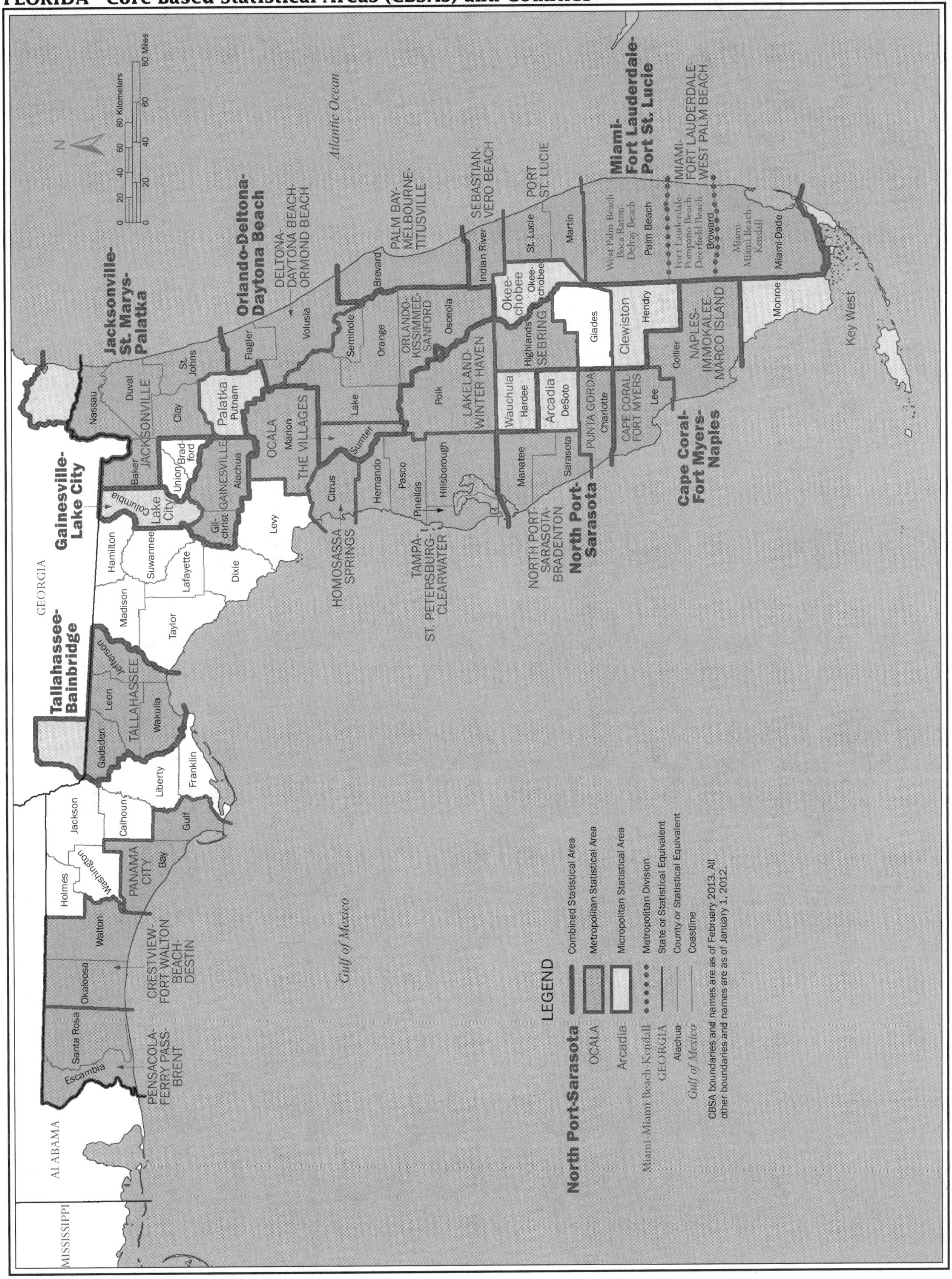

GEORGIA - Core Based Statistical Areas (CBSAs) and Counties

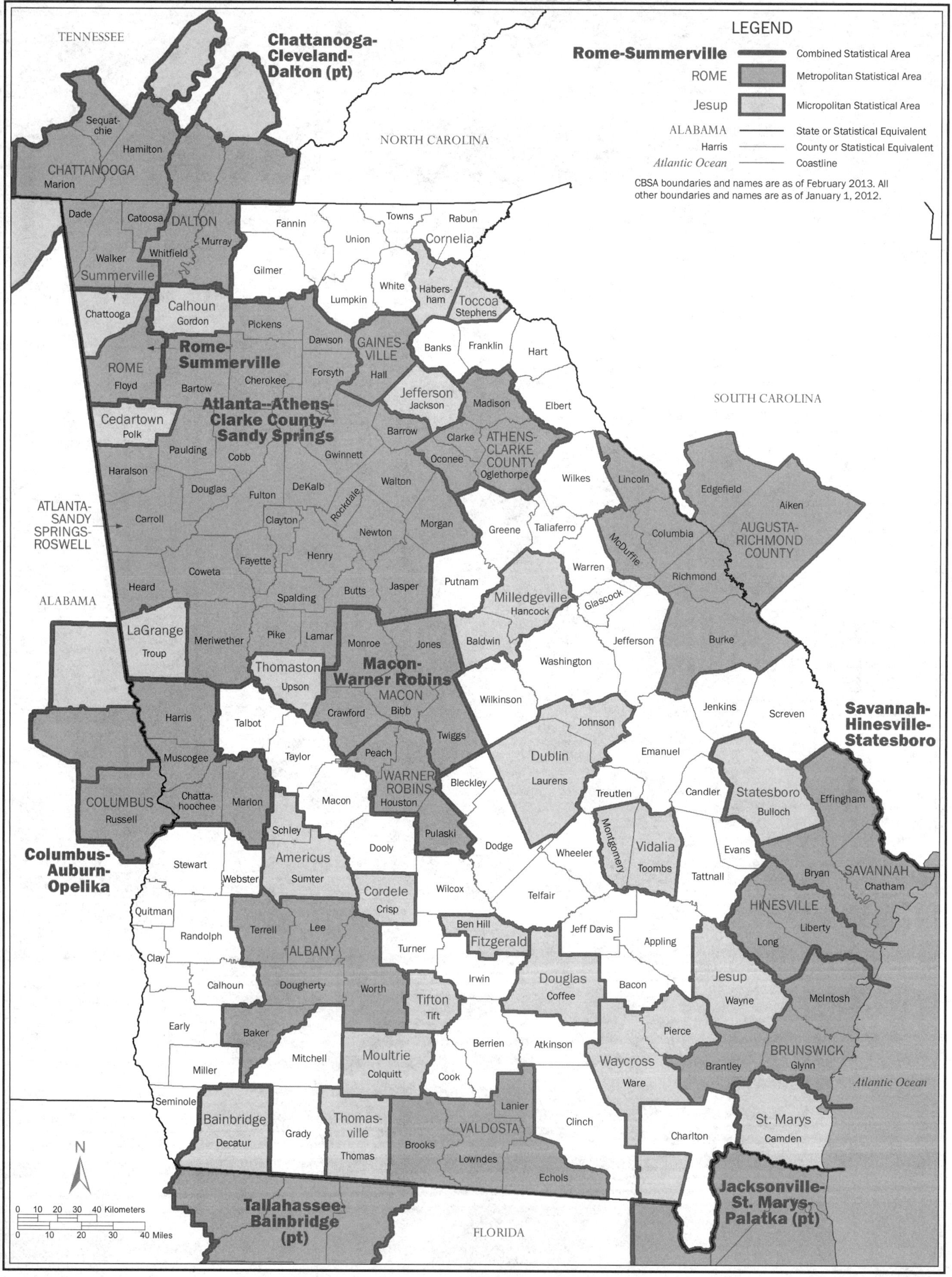

HAWAII - Core Based Statistical Areas (CBSAs) and Counties

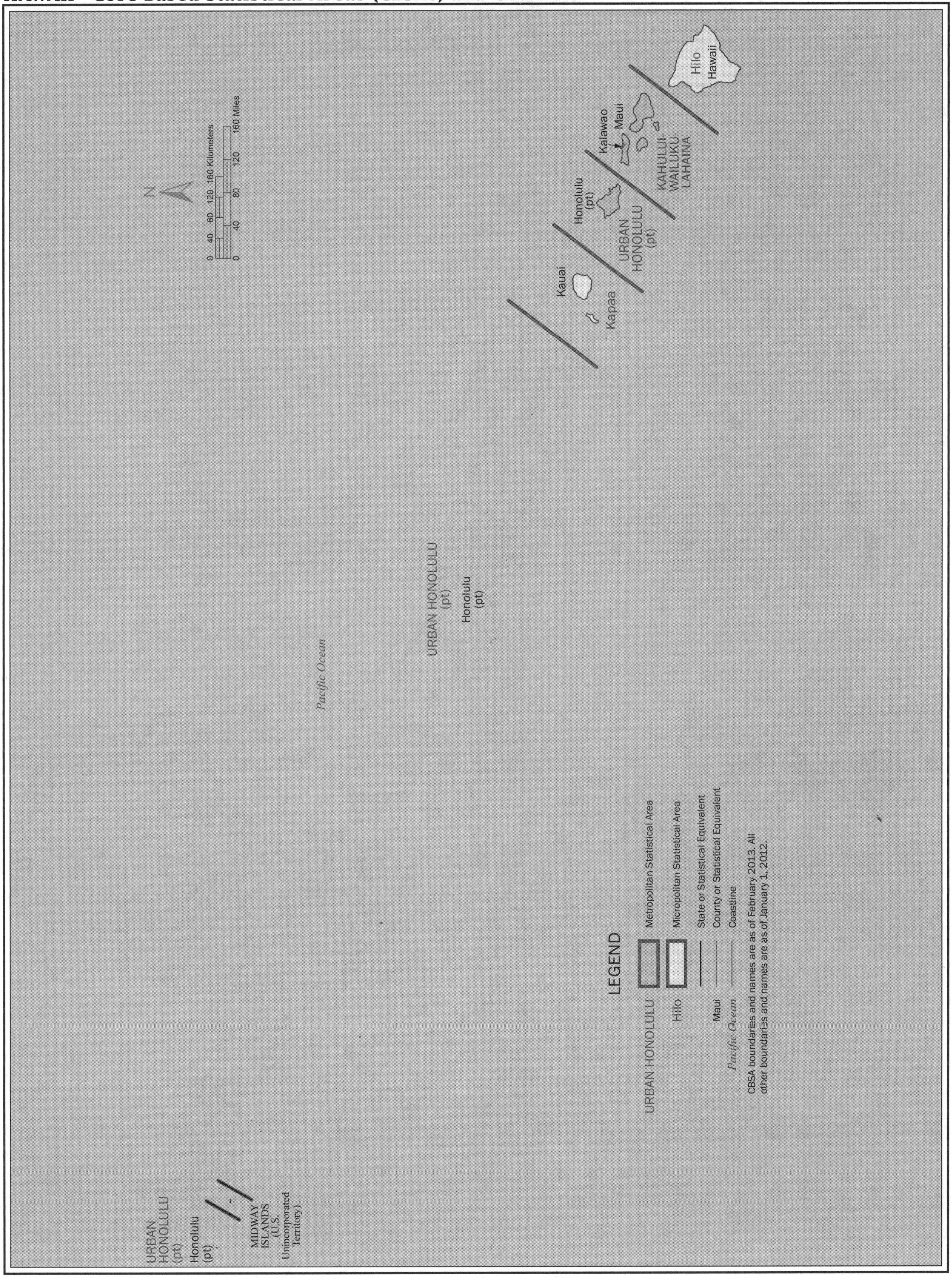

IDAHO - Core Based Statistical Areas (CBSAs) and Counties

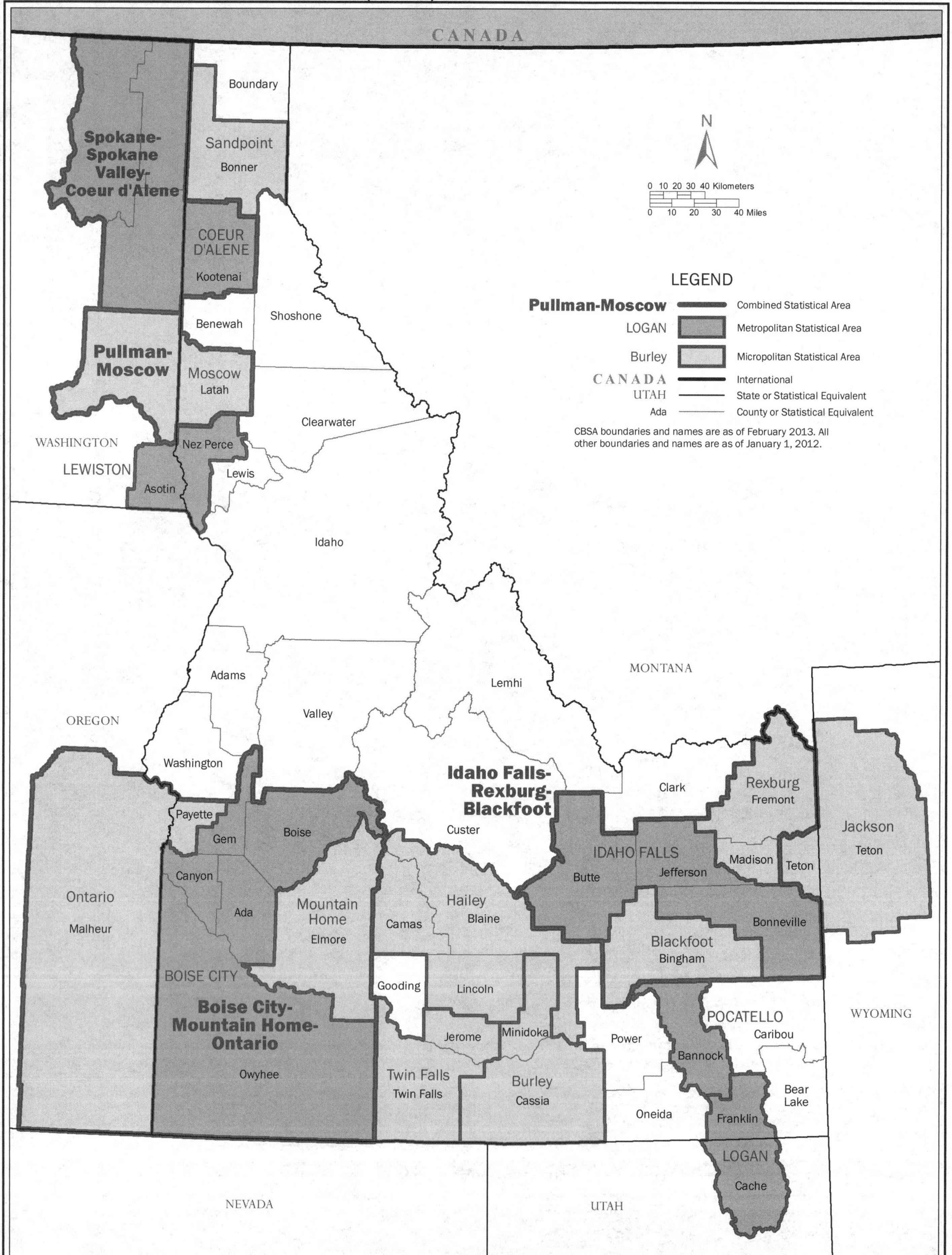

ILLINOIS - Core Based Statistical Areas (CBSAs) and Counties

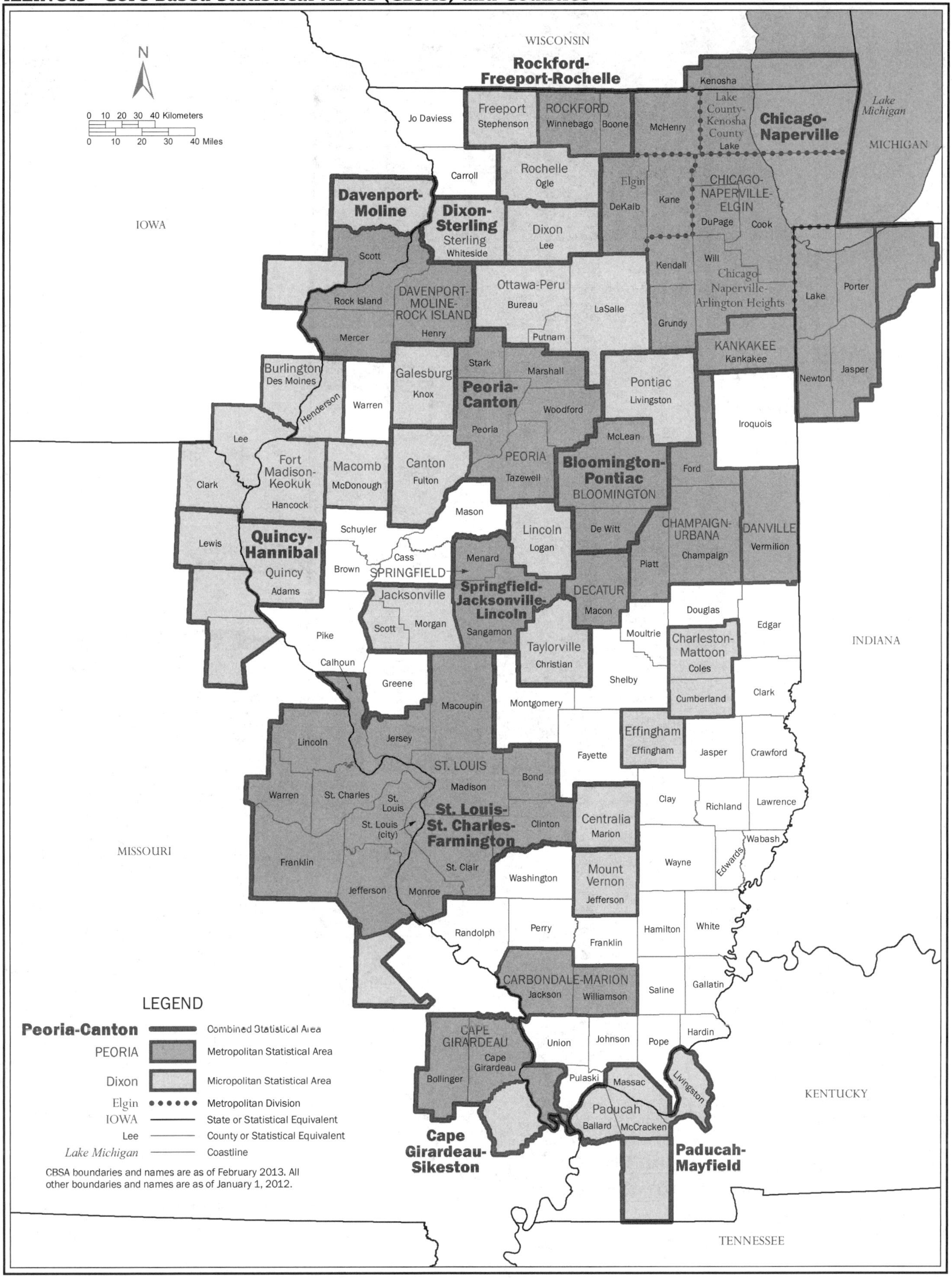

INDIANA - Core Based Statistical Areas (CBSAs) and Counties

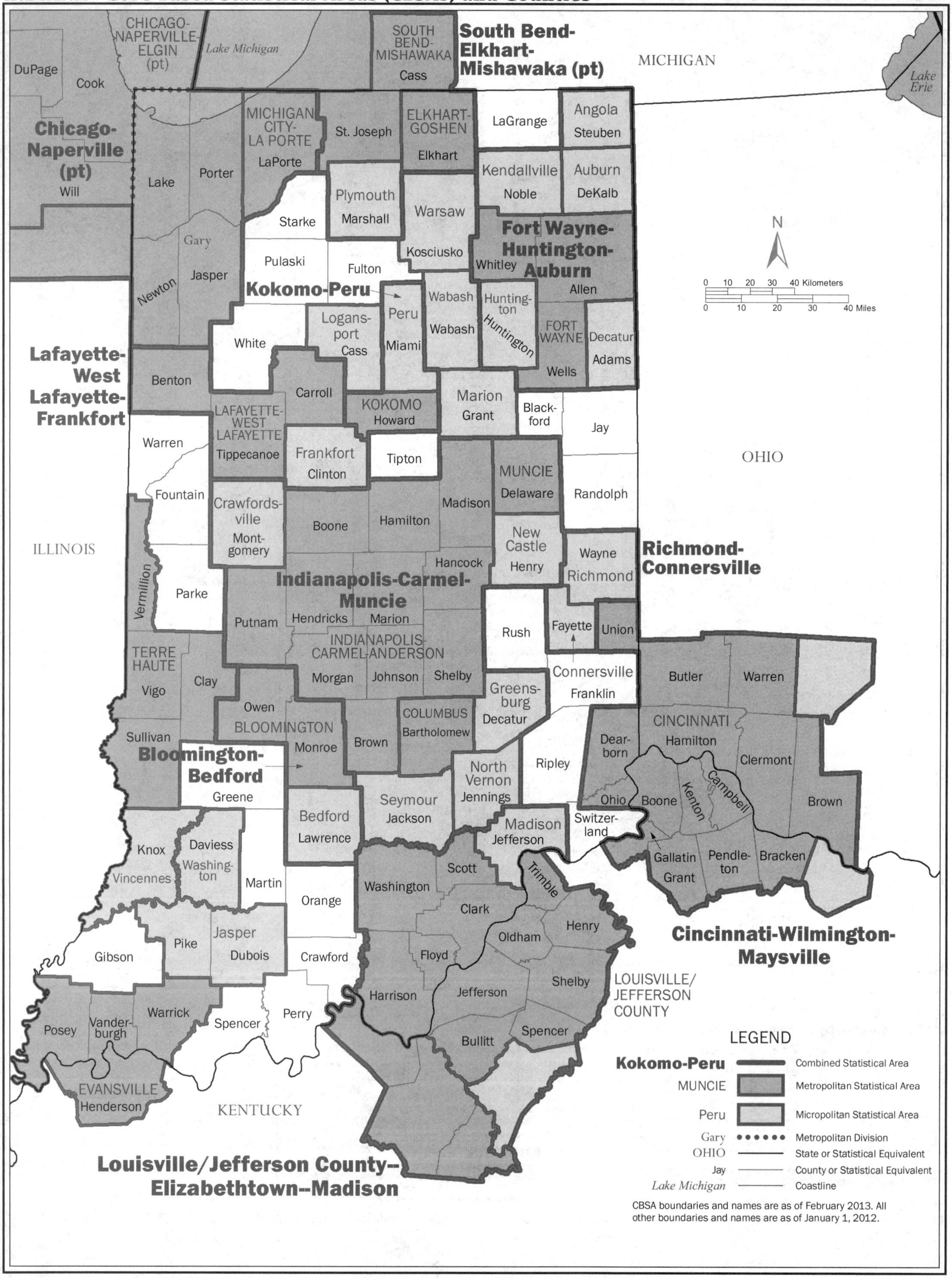

IOWA - Core Based Statistical Areas (CBSAs) and Counties

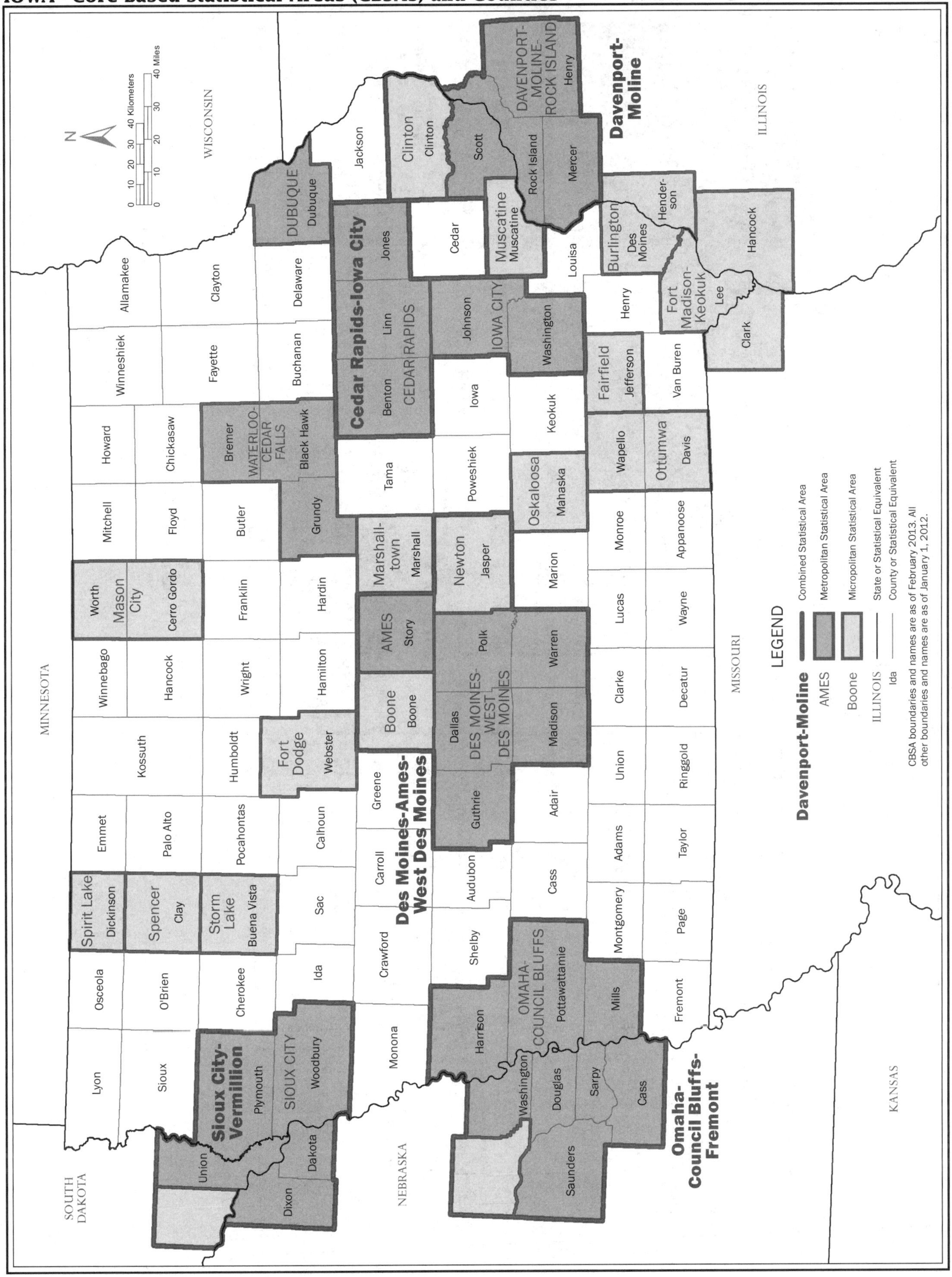

KANSAS - Core Based Statistical Areas (CBSAs) and Counties

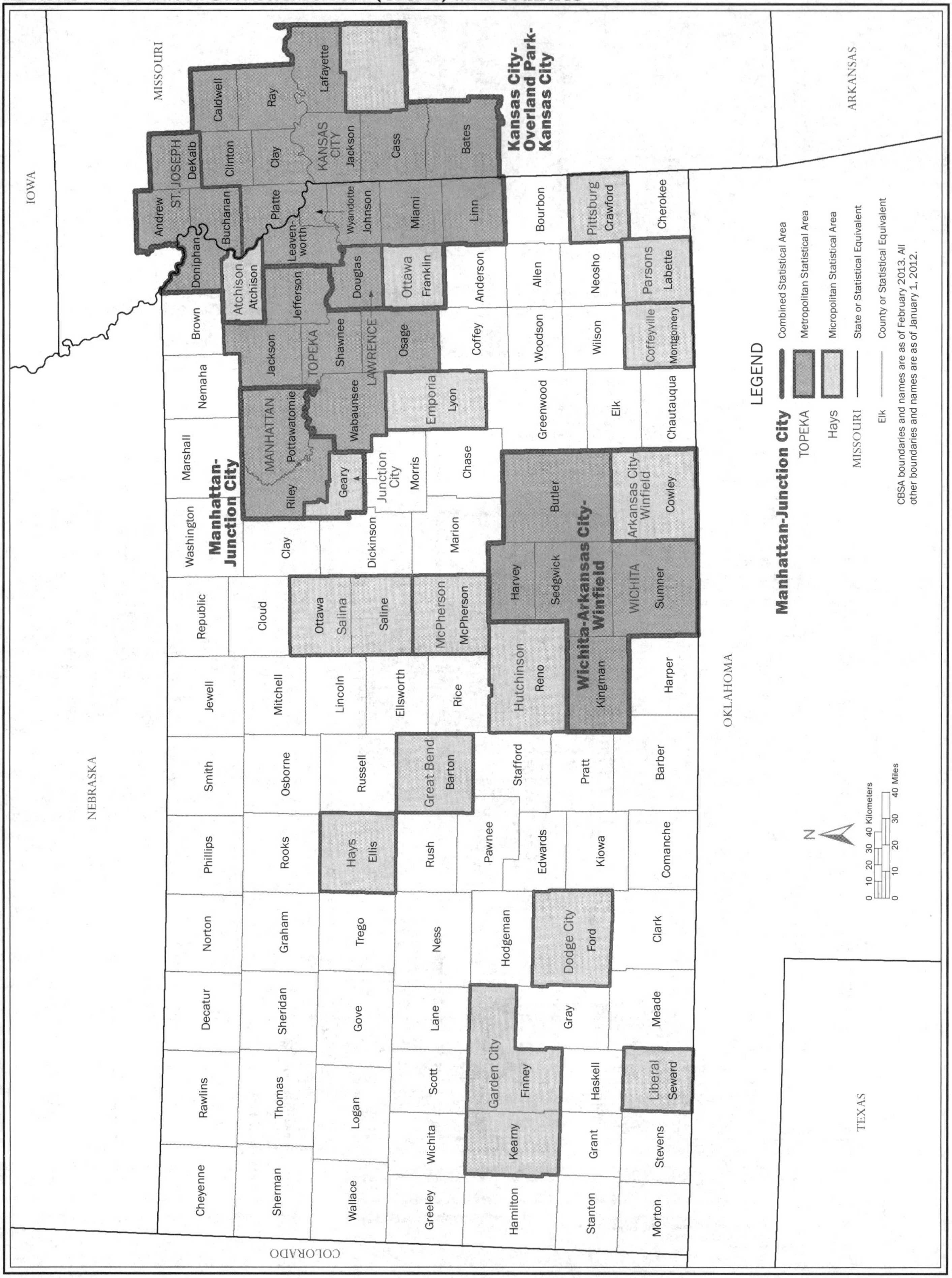

KENTUCKY - Core Based Statistical Areas (CBSAs) and Counties

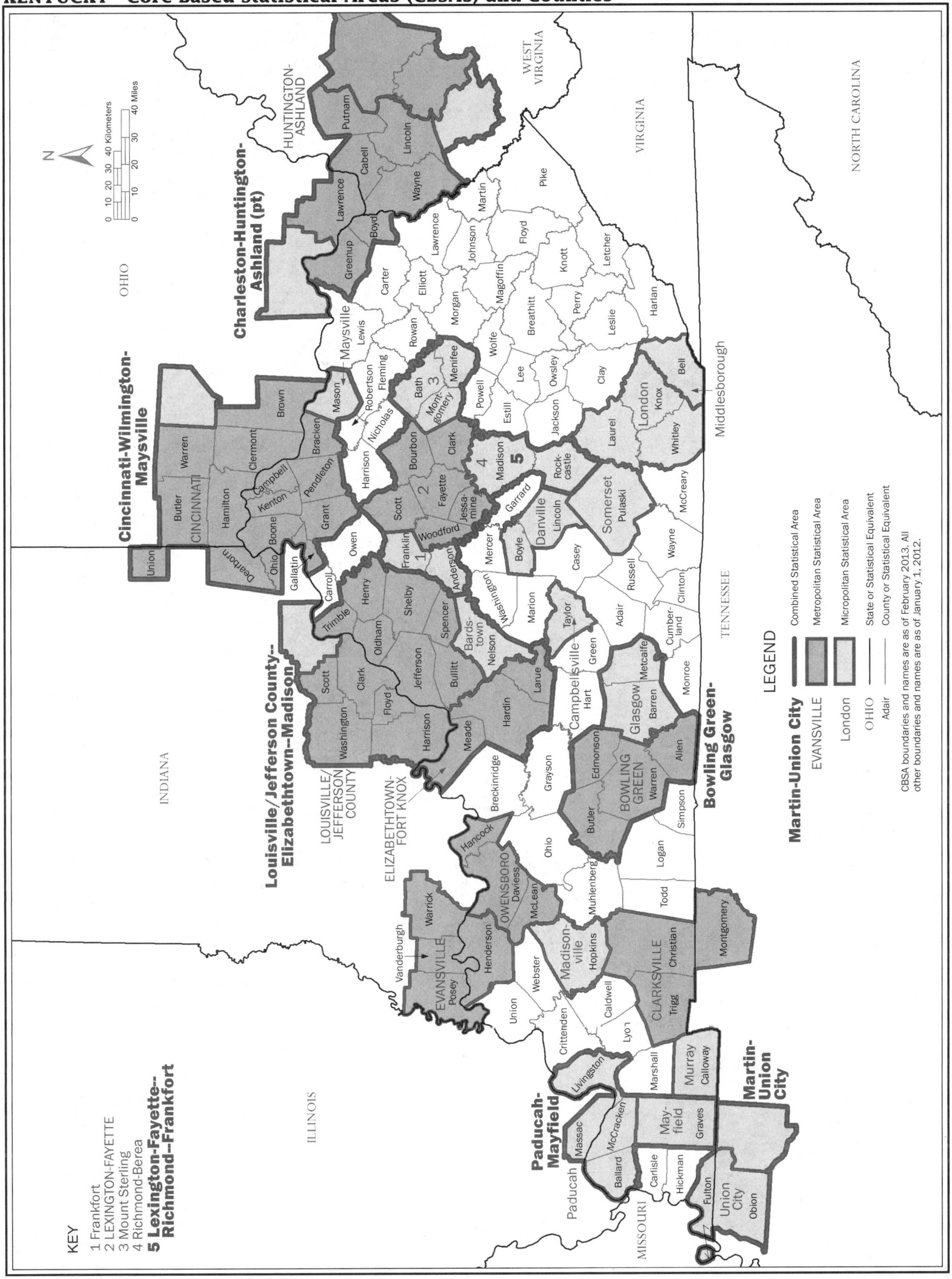

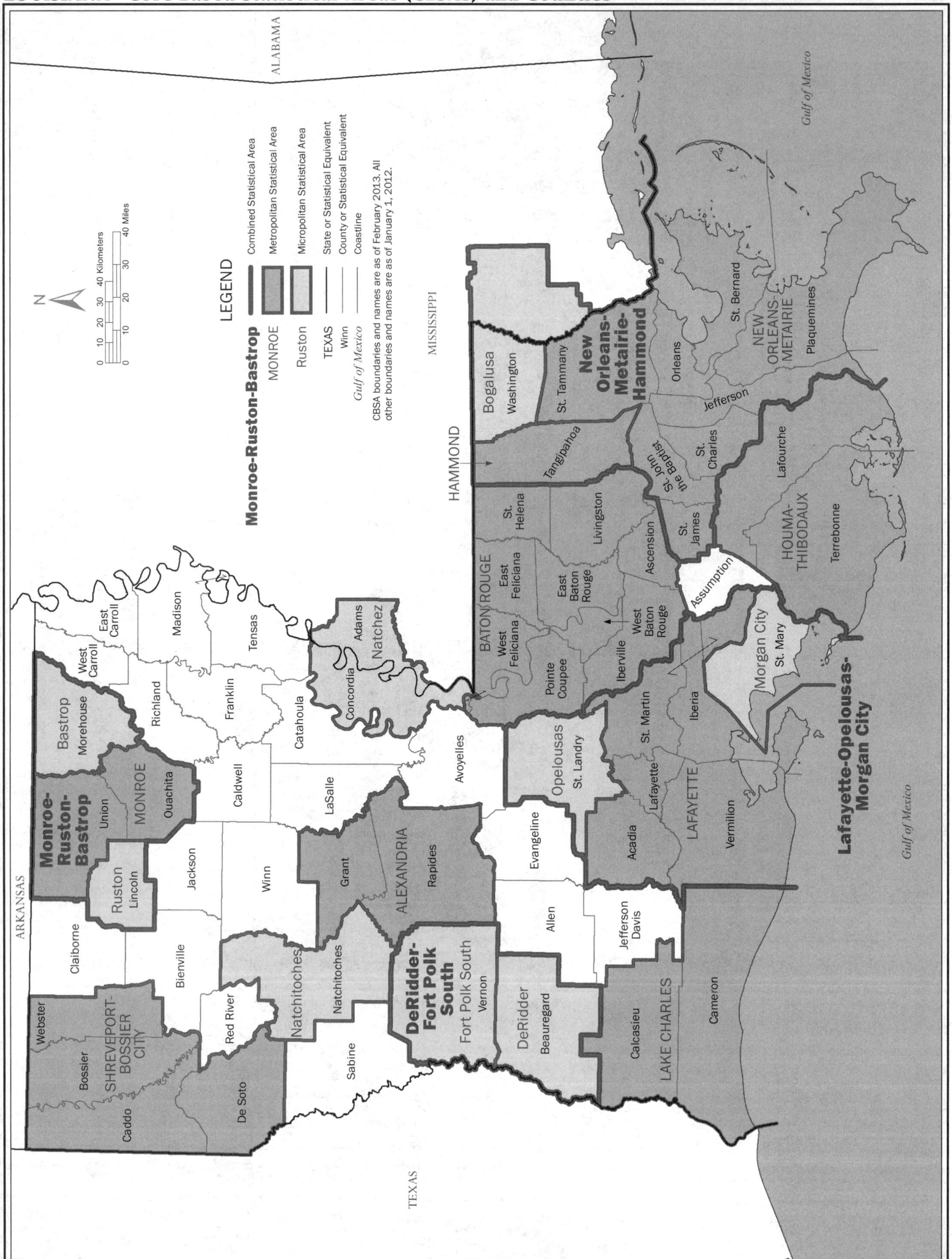
LEGEND
Monroe-Ruston-Bastrop Combined Statistical Area
MONROE Metropolitan Statistical Area
Ruston Micropolitan Statistical Area
TEXAS State or Statistical Equivalent
Winn County or Statistical Equivalent
Gulf of Mexico Coastline
CBSA boundaries and names are as of February 2013. All other boundaries and names are as of January 1, 2012.
0 10 20 30 40 Kilometers
0 10 20 30 40 Miles
N
ARKANSAS
MISSISSIPPI
ALABAMA
TEXAS
Gulf of Mexico
Monroe-Ruston-Bastrop
MONROE
Bastrop
Ruston
SHREVEPORT-BOSSIER CITY
Natchitoches
ALEXANDRIA
DeRidder-Fort Polk South
Fort Polk South
DeRidder
LAKE CHARLES
LAFAYETTE
Lafayette-Opelousas-Morgan City
Opelousas
Morgan City
BATON ROUGE
HAMMOND
New Orleans-Metairie-Hammond
NEW ORLEANS-METAIRIE
Bogalusa
HOUMA-THIBODAUX
Natchez
Caddo
Bossier
Webster
Claiborne
De Soto
Red River
Bienville
Lincoln
Union
Morehouse
West Carroll
East Carroll
Ouachita
Jackson
Winn
Caldwell
Richland
Madison
Franklin
Tensas
Catahoula
Concordia
Adams
LaSalle
Grant
Rapides
Avoyelles
Sabine
Vernon
Beauregard
Allen
Evangeline
St. Landry
Jefferson Davis
Calcasieu
Cameron
Acadia
Lafayette
Vermilion
St. Martin
Iberia
St. Mary
Pointe Coupee
West Feliciana
East Feliciana
West Baton Rouge
East Baton Rouge
Iberville
Ascension
Assumption
St. Helena
Livingston
Tangipahoa
Washington
St. Tammany
St. James
St. John the Baptist
St. Charles
Lafourche
Terrebonne
Jefferson
Orleans
St. Bernard
Plaquemines

MAINE - Core Based Statistical Areas (CBSAs) and Counties

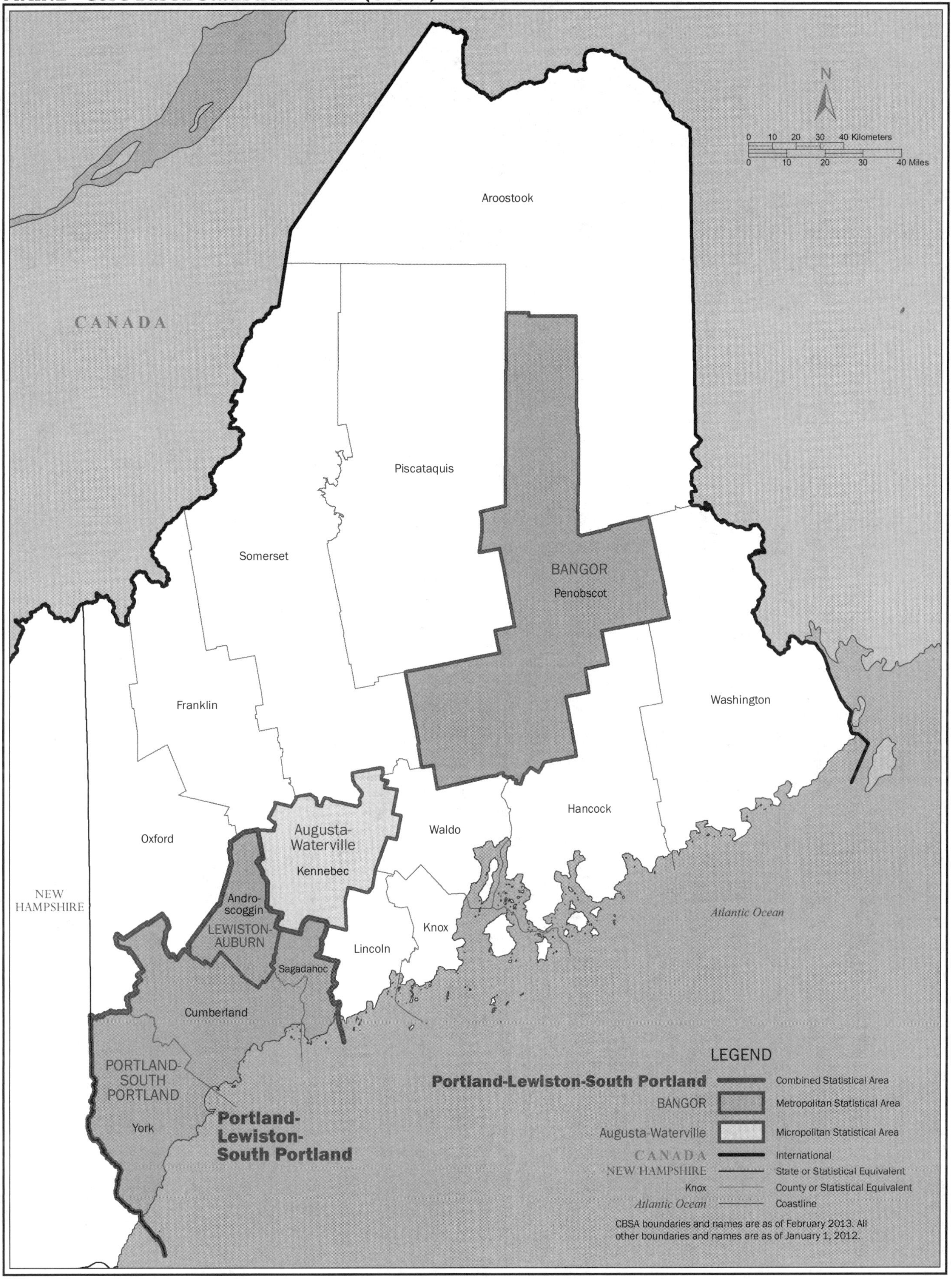

MARYLAND - Core Based Statistical Areas (CBSAs) and Counties

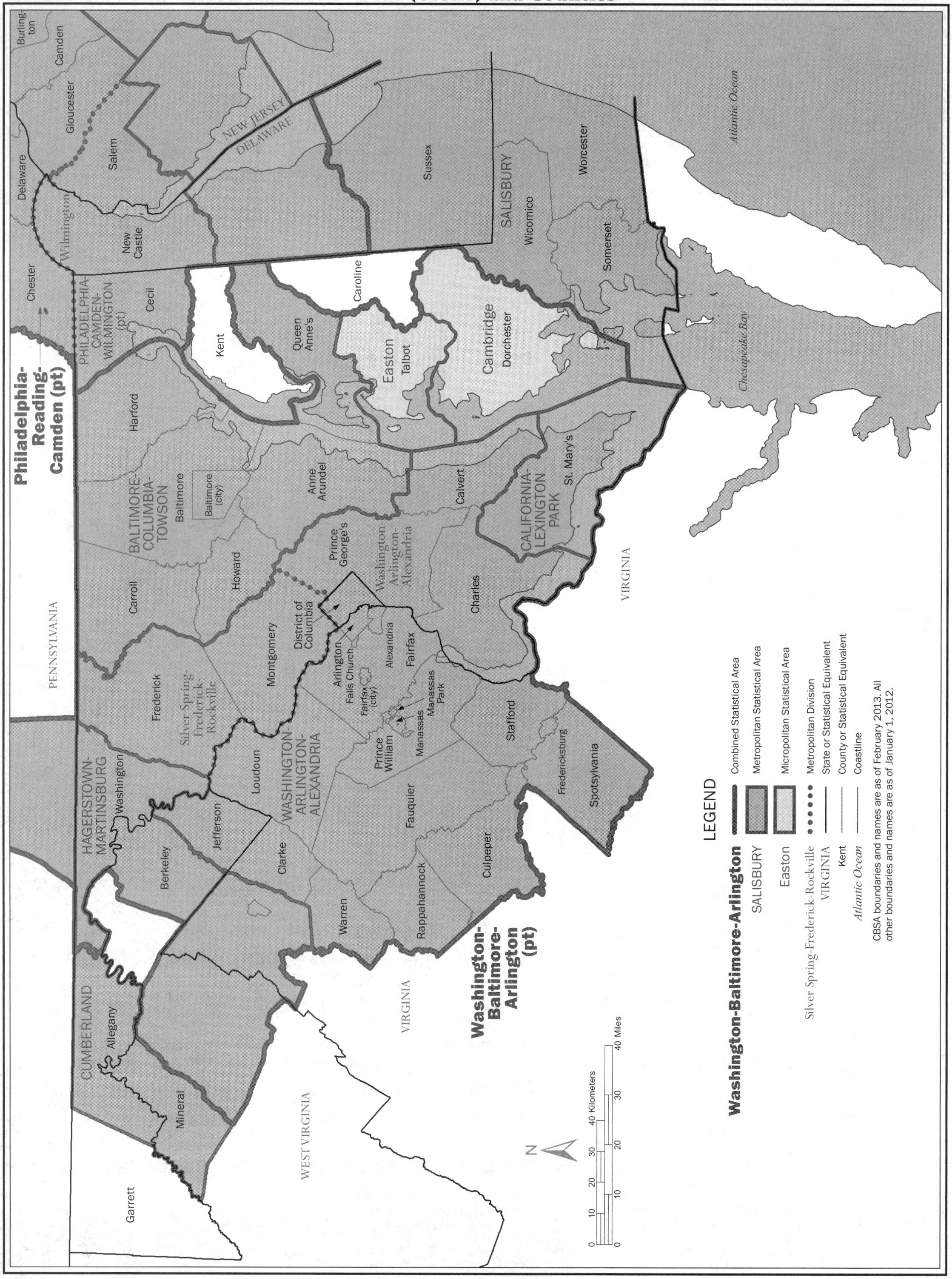

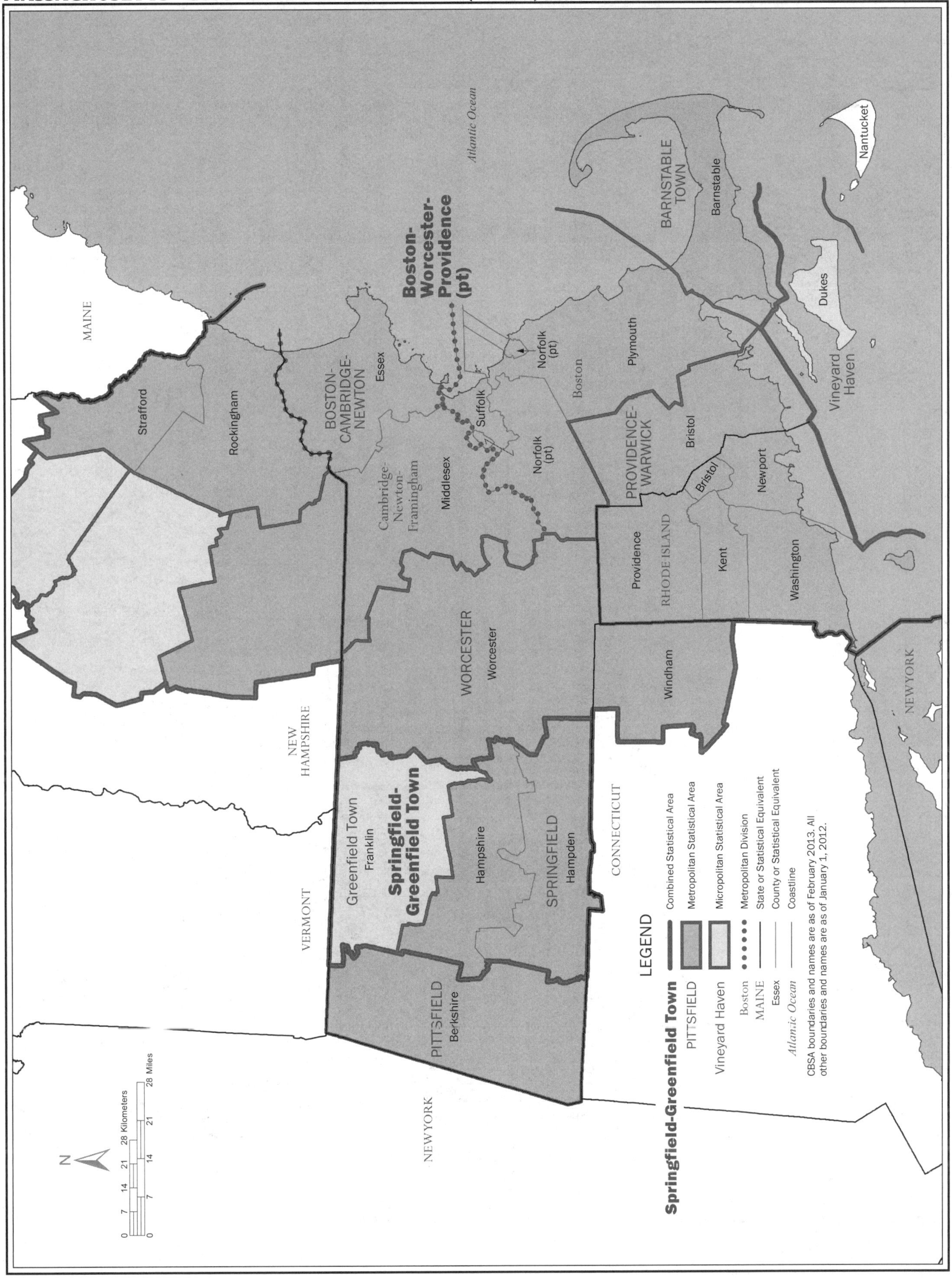
MAINE
Atlantic Ocean
Boston-Worcester-Providence (pt)
BARNSTABLE TOWN
Barnstable
Nantucket
Dukes
Vineyard Haven
Strafford
Rockingham
BOSTON-CAMBRIDGE-NEWTON
Essex
Suffolk
Norfolk (pt)
Boston
Plymouth
Cambridge-Newton-Framingham
Middlesex
PROVIDENCE-WARWICK
Bristol
Newport
RHODE ISLAND
Providence
Kent
Washington
WORCESTER
Worcester
Windham
NEW YORK
NEW HAMPSHIRE
Greenfield Town
Franklin
Springfield-Greenfield Town
Hampshire
SPRINGFIELD
Hampden
CONNECTICUT
VERMONT
PITTSFIELD
Berkshire
LEGEND
Springfield-Greenfield Town Combined Statistical Area
PITTSFIELD Metropolitan Statistical Area
Vineyard Haven Micropolitan Statistical Area
Boston Metropolitan Division
MAINE State or Statistical Equivalent
Essex County or Statistical Equivalent
Atlantic Ocean Coastline
CBSA boundaries and names are as of February 2013. All other boundaries and names are as of January 1, 2012.
0 7 14 21 28 Kilometers
0 7 14 21 28 Miles
N

MICHIGAN - Core Based Statistical Areas (CBSAs) and Counties

MINNESOTA - Core Based Statistical Areas (CBSAs) and Counties

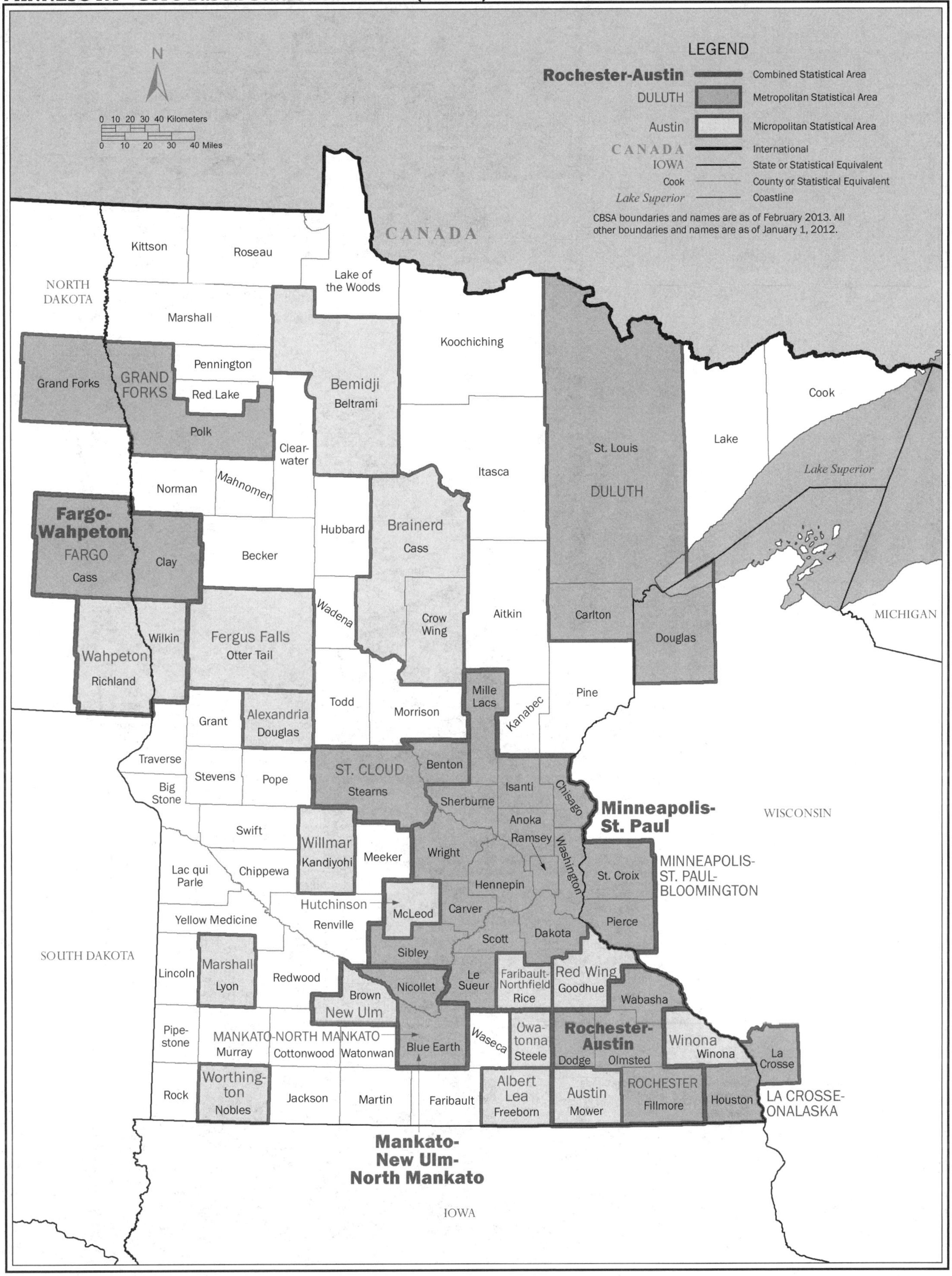

MISSISSIPPI - Core Based Statistical Areas (CBSAs) and Counties

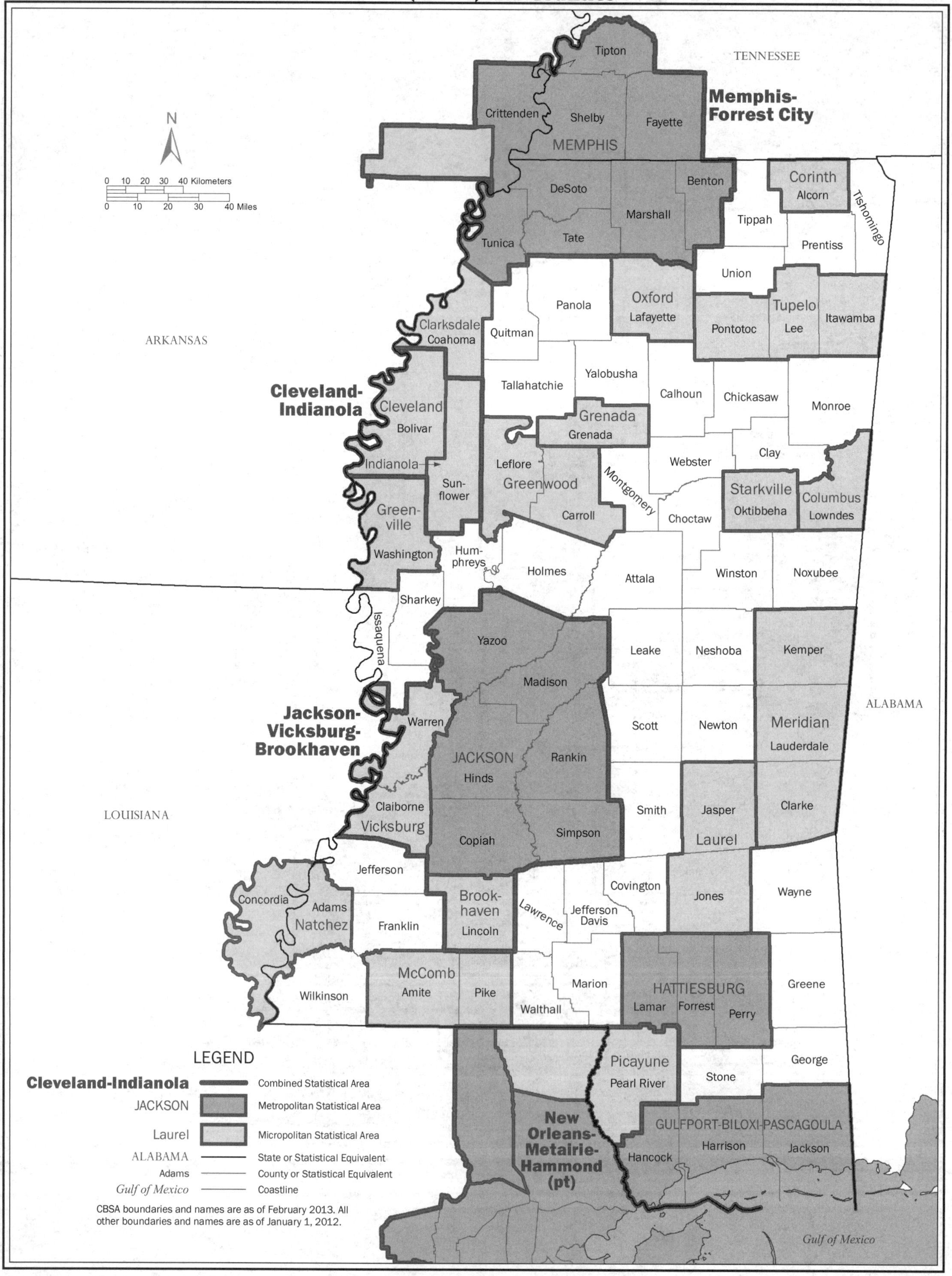

MISSOURI - Core Based Statistical Areas (CBSAs) and Counties

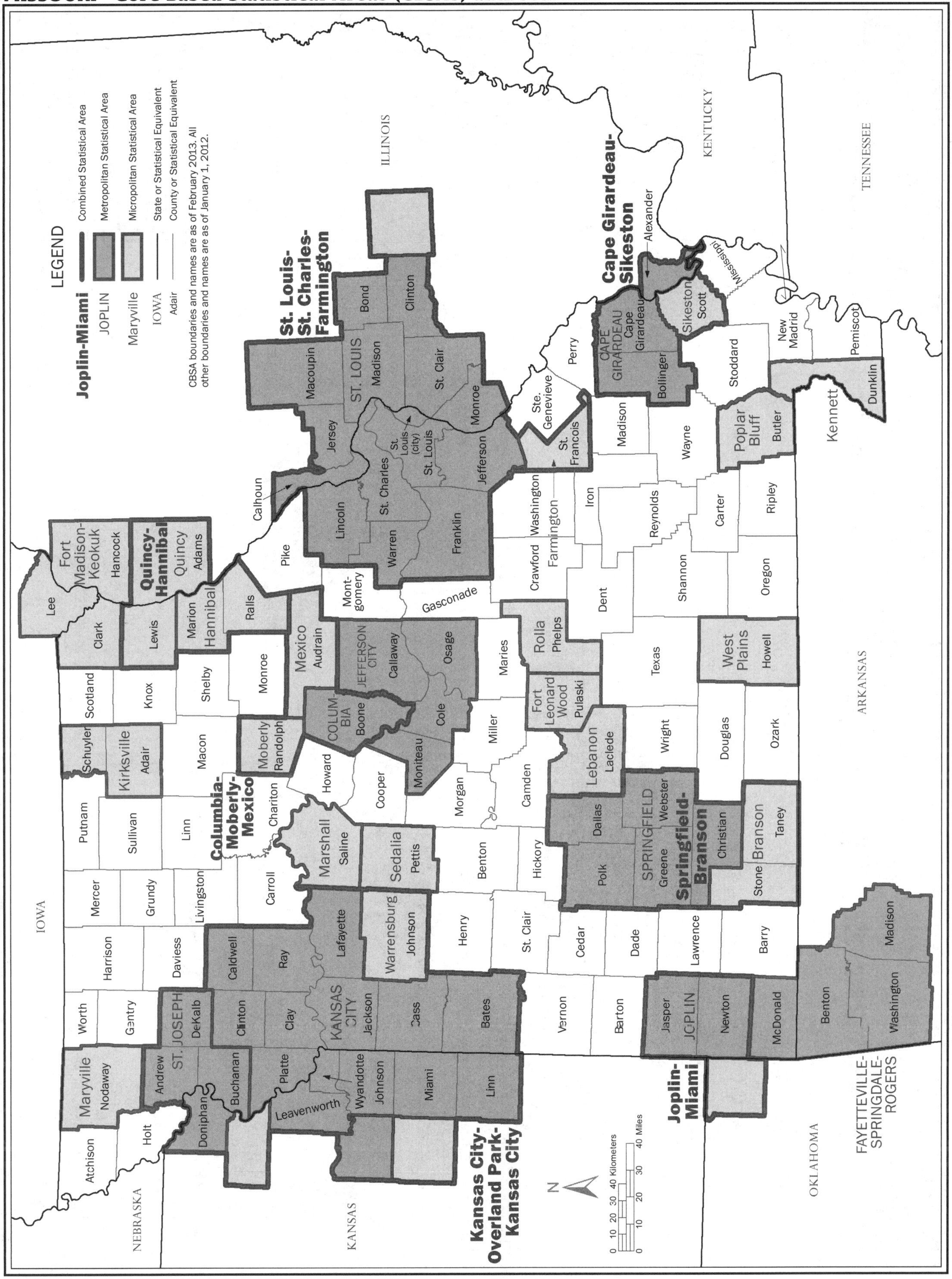

MONTANA - Core Based Statistical Areas (CBSAs) and Counties

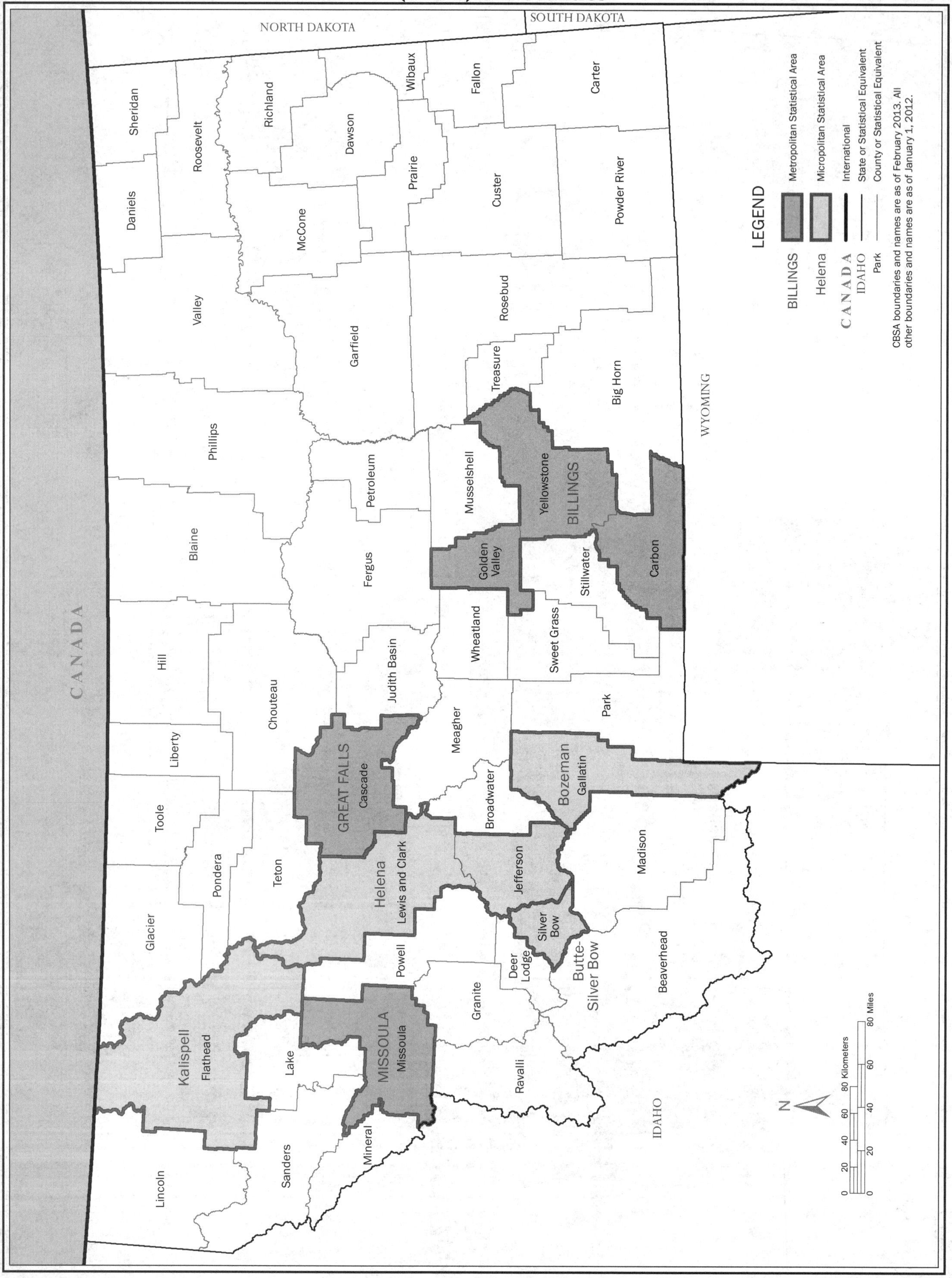

NEBRASKA - Core Based Statistical Areas (CBSAs) and Counties

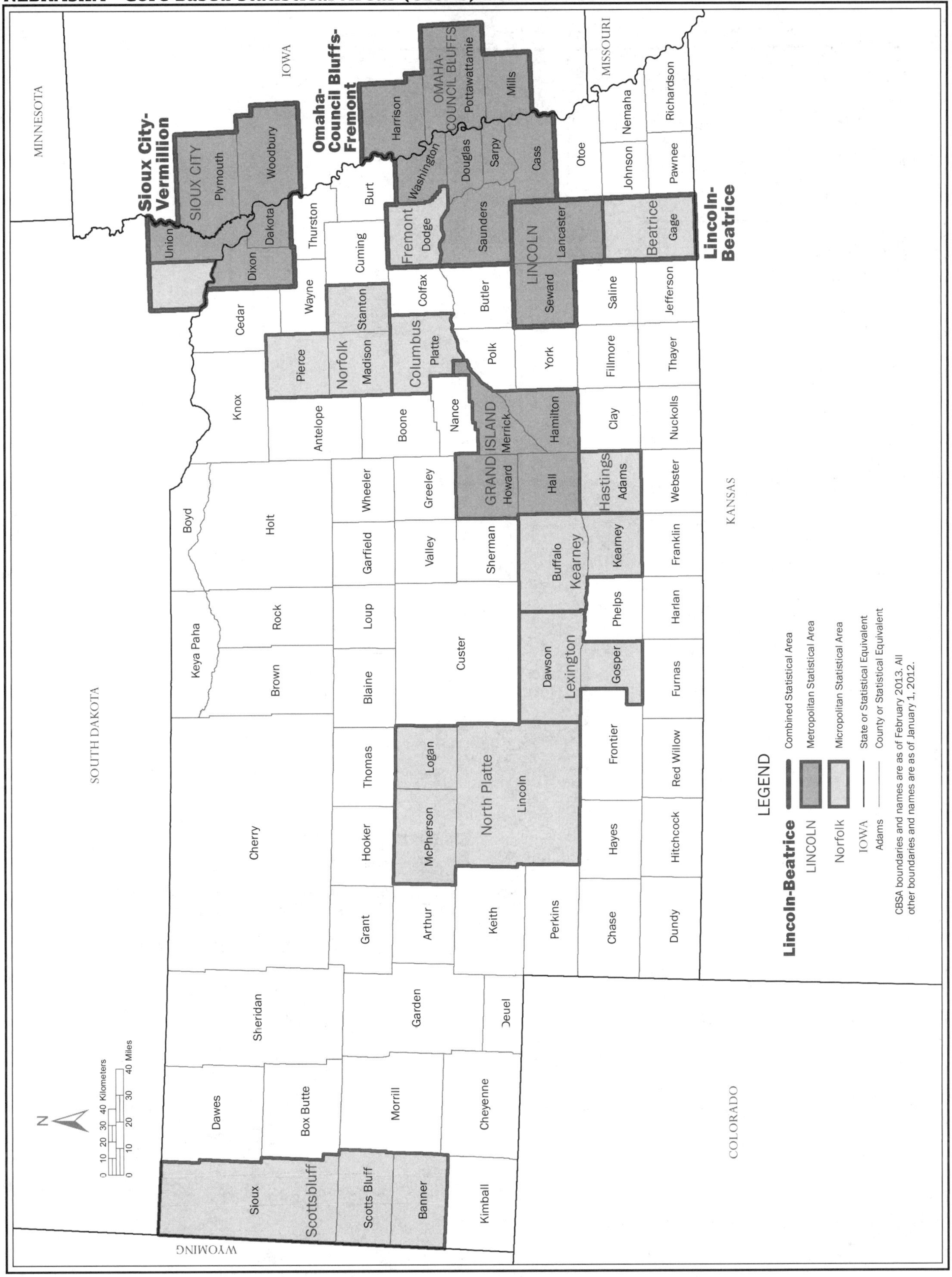

NEVADA - Core Based Statistical Areas (CBSAs) and Counties

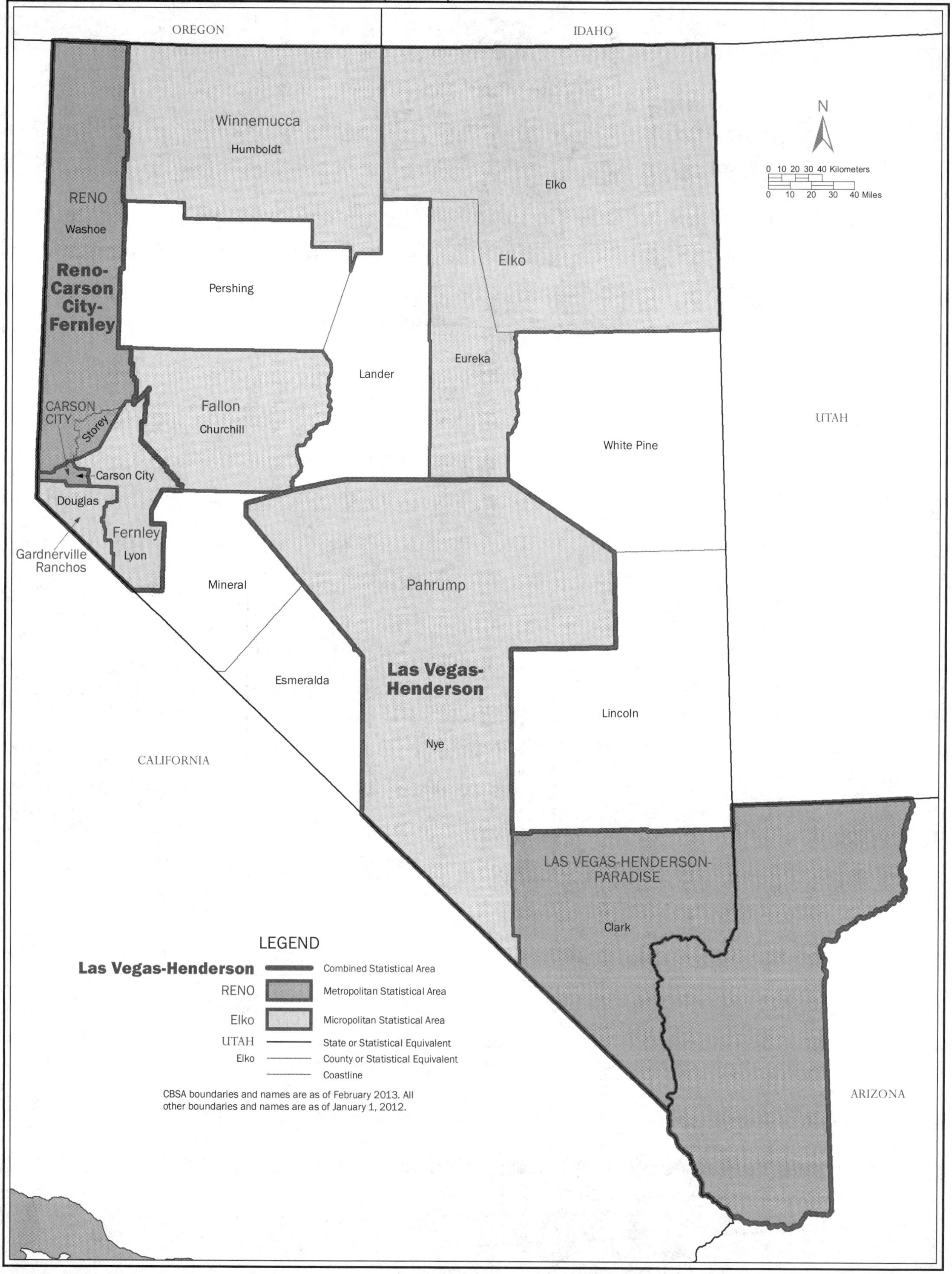

NEW HAMPSHIRE - Core Based Statistical Areas (CBSAs) and Counties

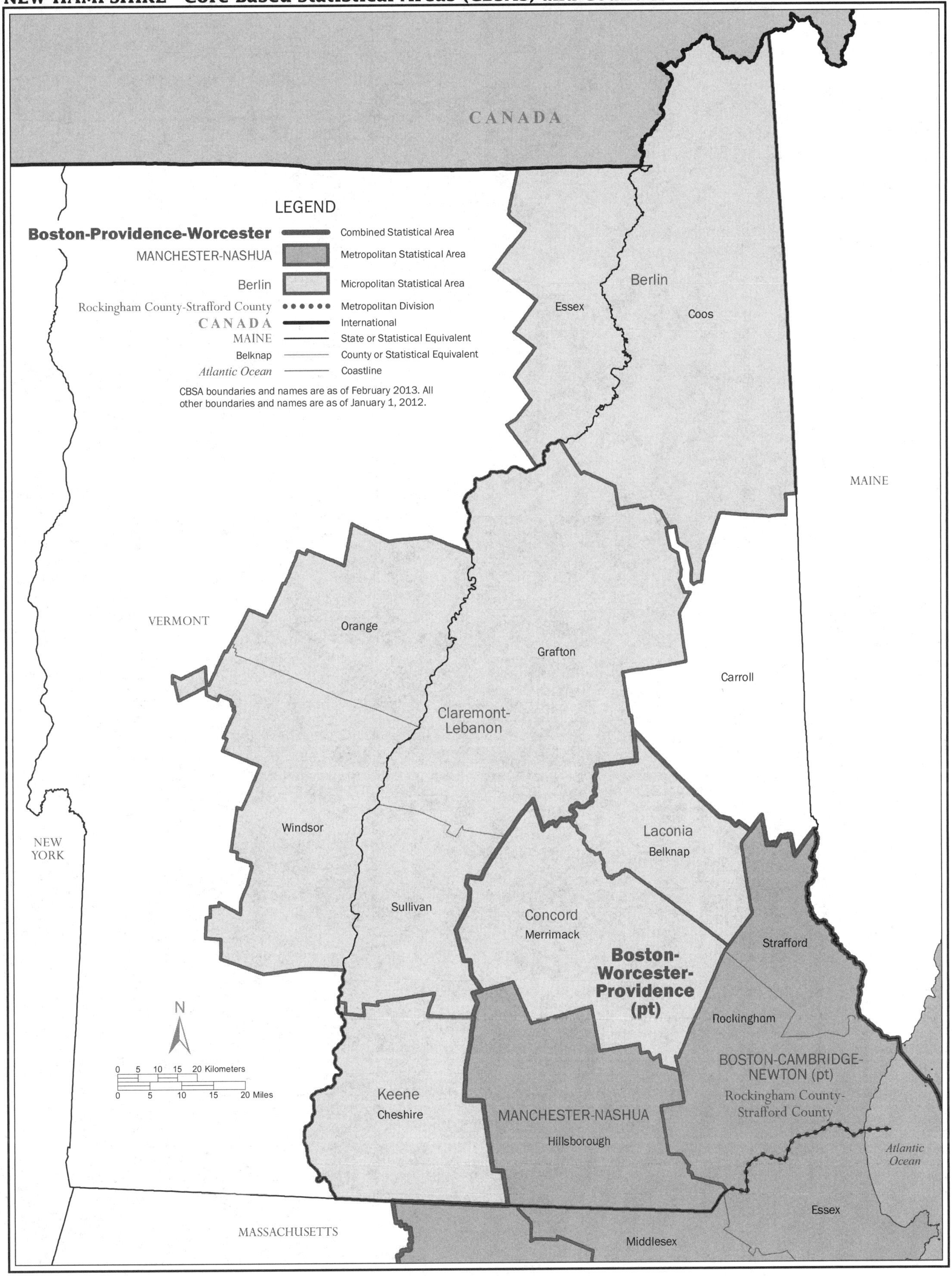

NEW JERSEY - Core Based Statistical Areas (CBSAs) and Counties

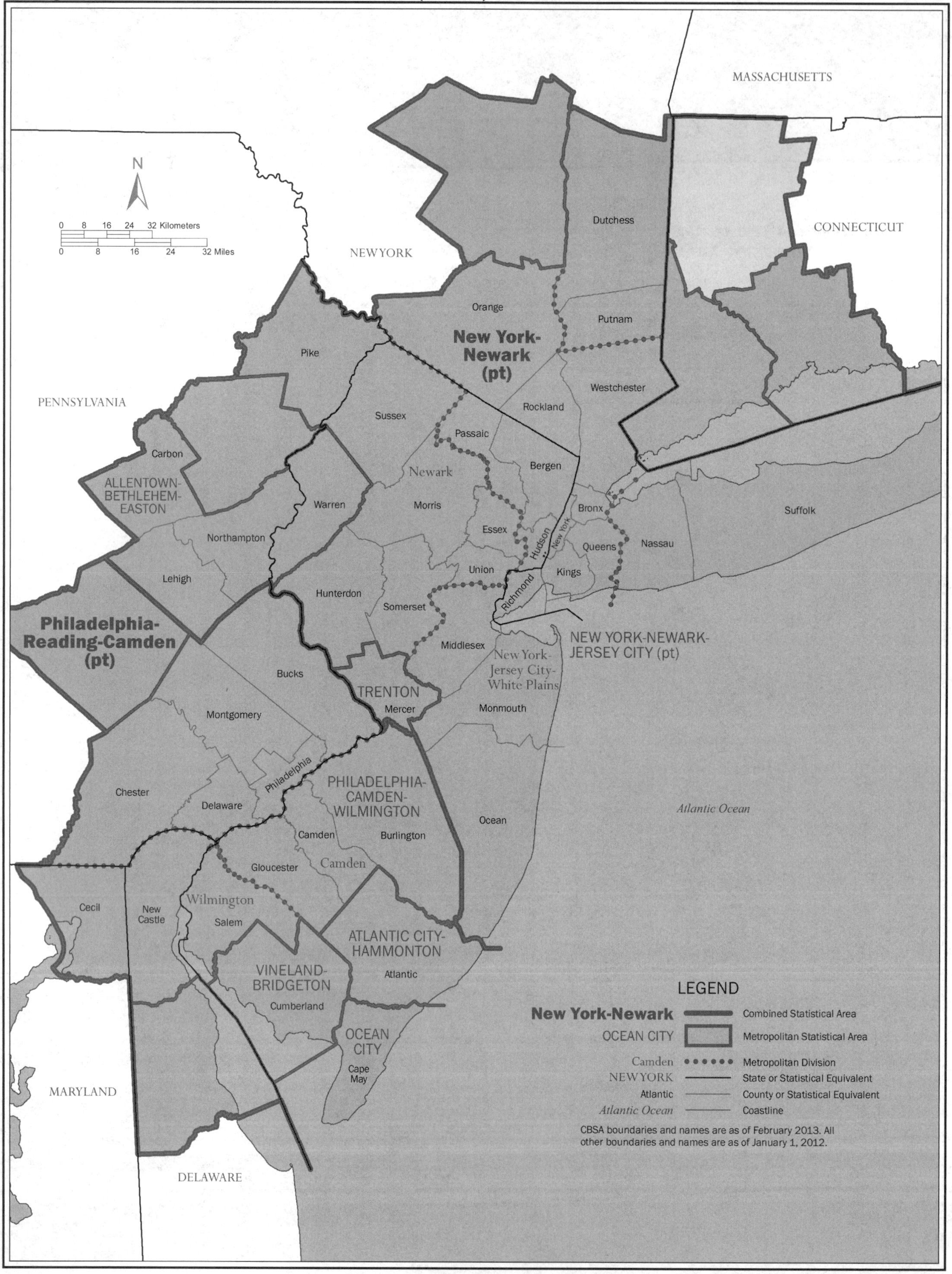

NEW MEXICO - Core Based Statistical Areas (CBSAs) and Counties

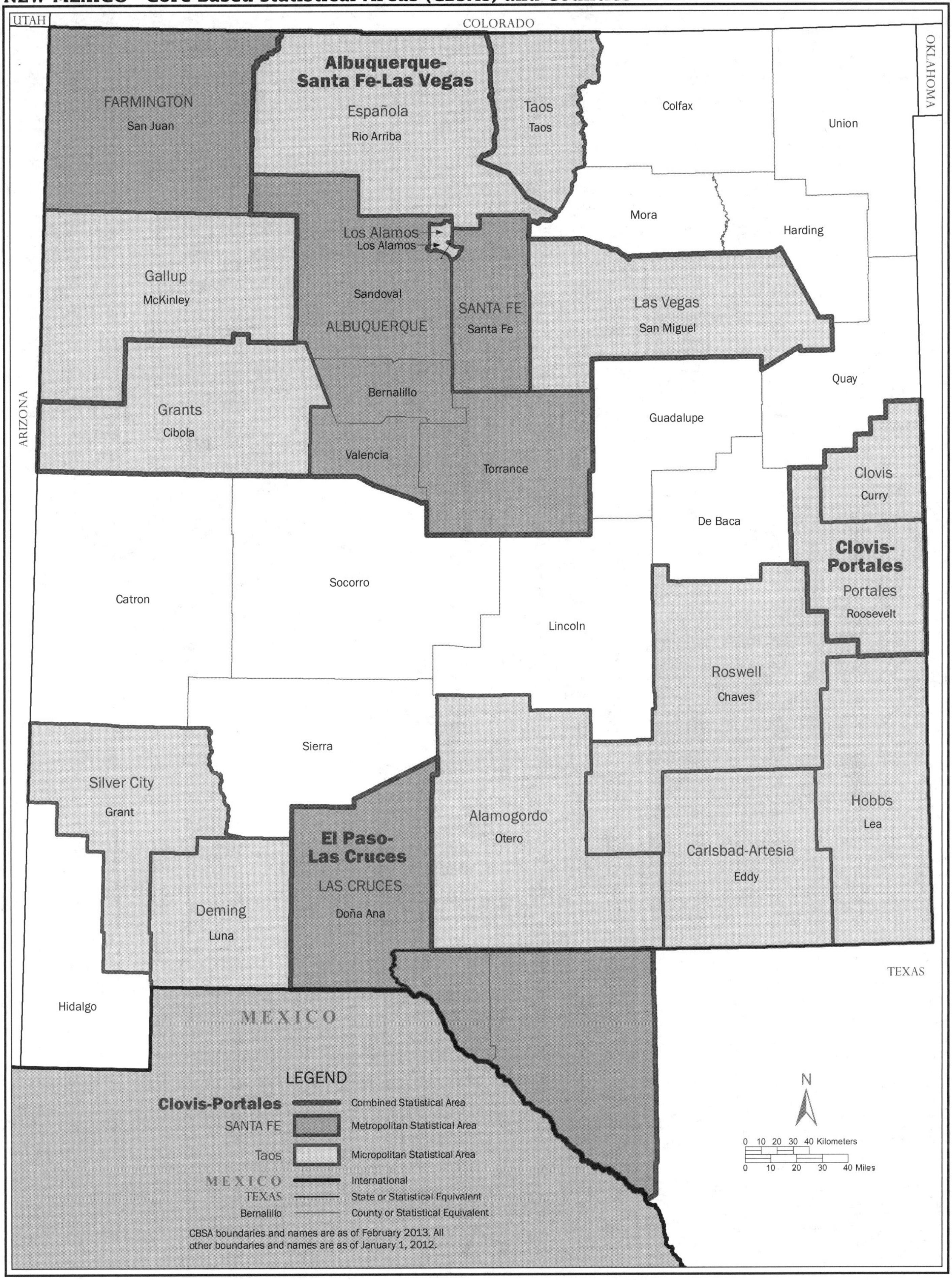

NEW YORK - Core Based Statistical Areas (CBSAs) and Counties

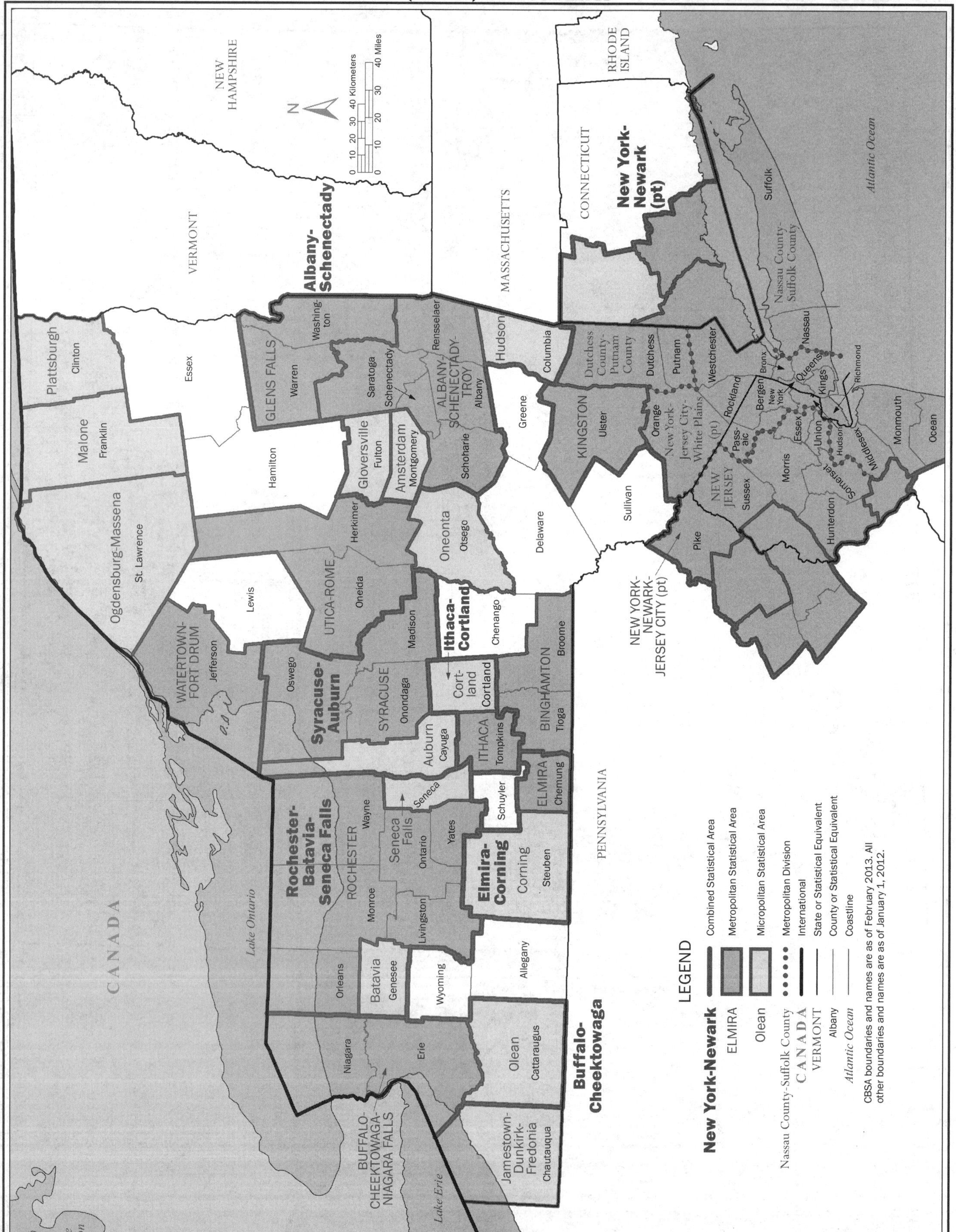

NORTH CAROLINA - Core Based Statistical Areas (CBSAs) and Counties

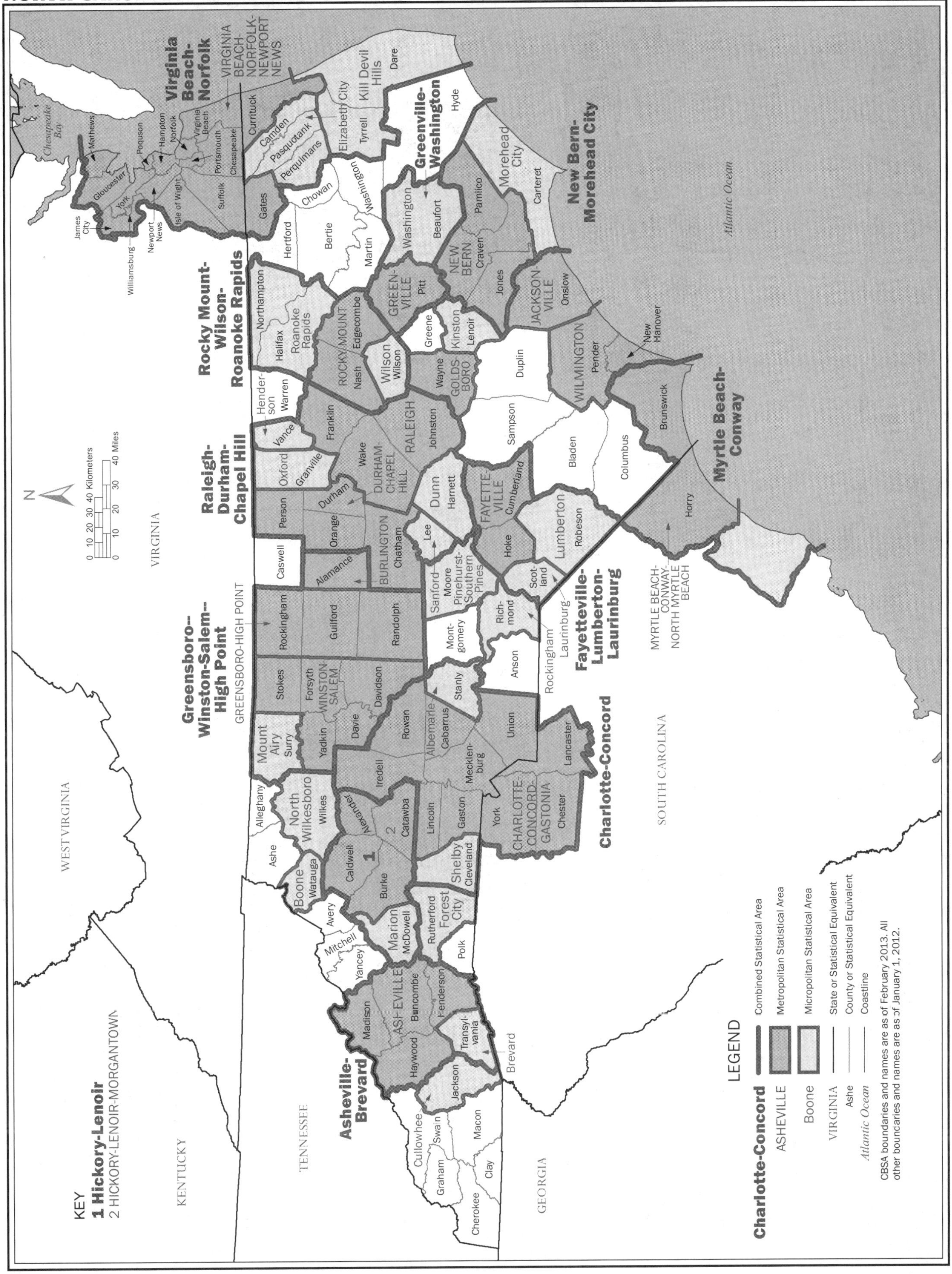

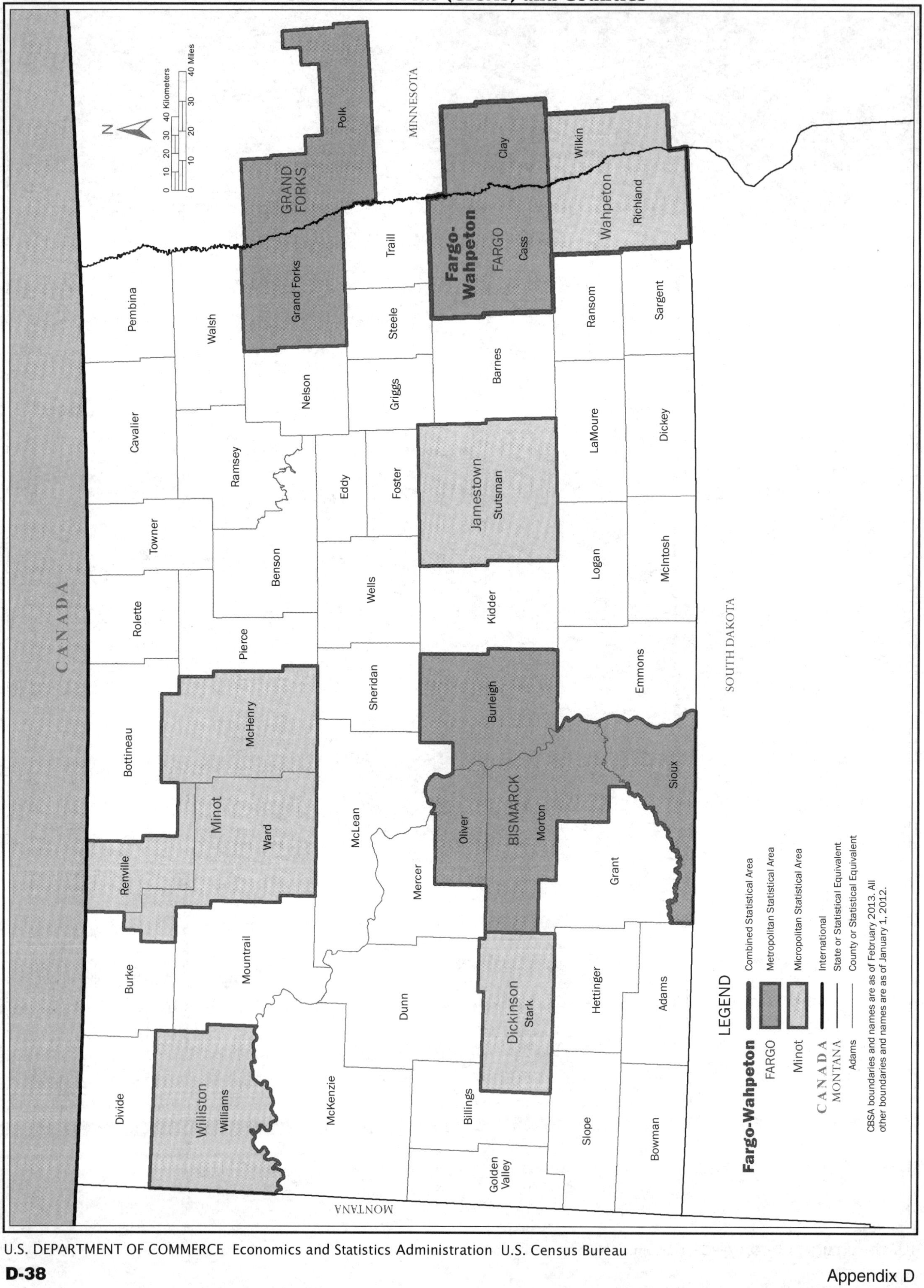
CANADA
MINNESOTA
SOUTH DAKOTA
MONTANA
0 10 20 30 40 Kilometers
0 10 20 30 40 Miles
N
GRAND FORKS
Polk
Grand Forks
Fargo-Wahpeton
FARGO
Cass
Clay
Wilkin
Wahpeton
Richland
Pembina
Walsh
Traill
Steele
Ransom
Sargent
Cavalier
Nelson
Griggs
Barnes
LaMoure
Dickey
Ramsey
Eddy
Foster
Jamestown
Stutsman
Towner
Benson
Wells
Kidder
Logan
McIntosh
Rolette
Pierce
Sheridan
Burleigh
Emmons
Bottineau
McHenry
Minot
Ward
Renville
McLean
Oliver
BISMARCK
Morton
Sioux
Grant
Mercer
Burke
Mountrail
Dunn
Dickinson
Stark
Hettinger
Adams
Divide
Williston
Williams
McKenzie
Billings
Golden Valley
Slope
Bowman
LEGEND
Fargo-Wahpeton Combined Statistical Area
FARGO Metropolitan Statistical Area
Minot Micropolitan Statistical Area
CANADA International
MONTANA State or Statistical Equivalent
Adams County or Statistical Equivalent
CBSA boundaries and names are as of February 2013. All other boundaries and names are as of January 1, 2012.

OHIO - Core Based Statistical Areas (CBSAs) and Counties

OKLAHOMA - Core Based Statistical Areas (CBSAs) and Counties

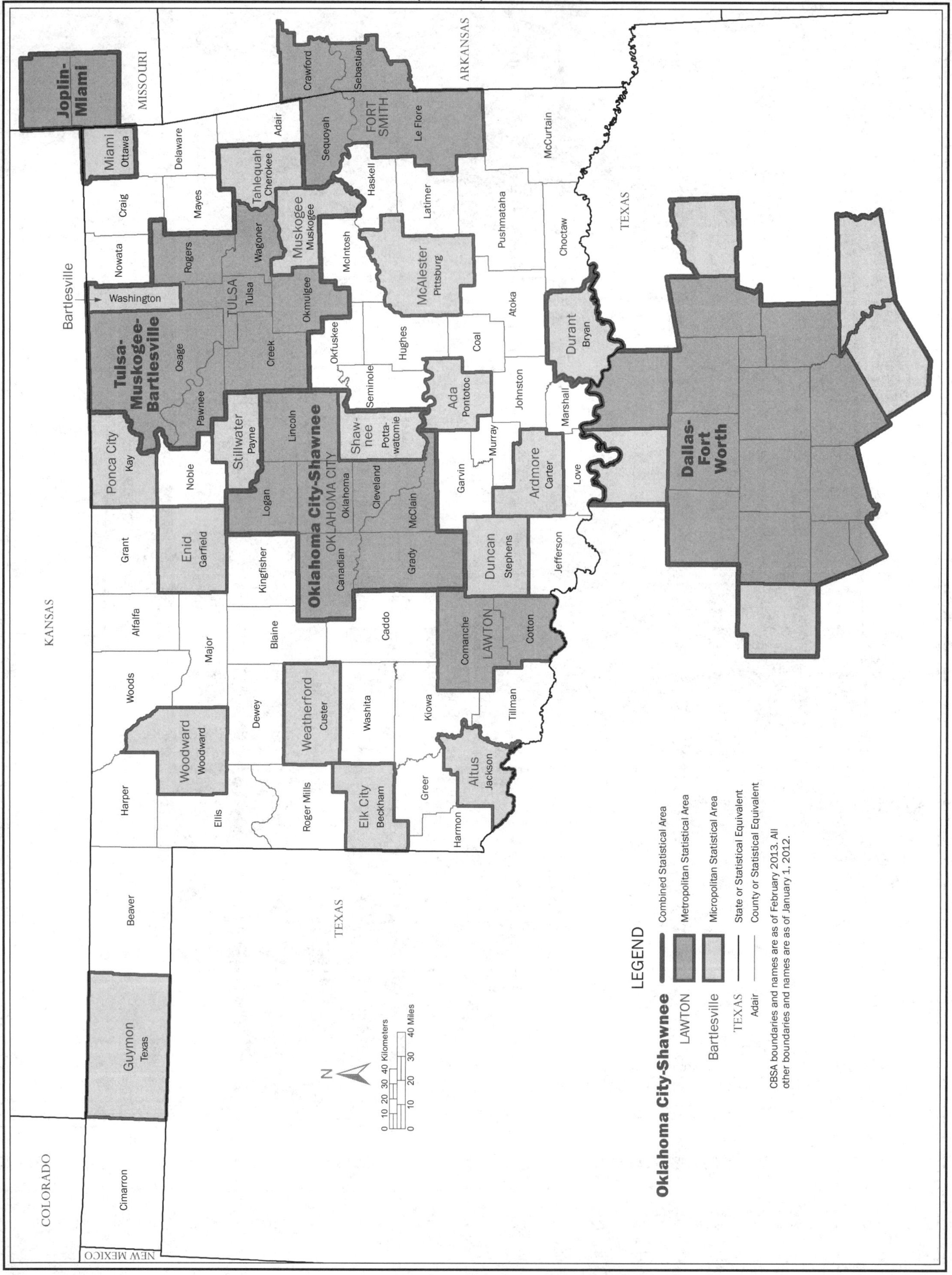

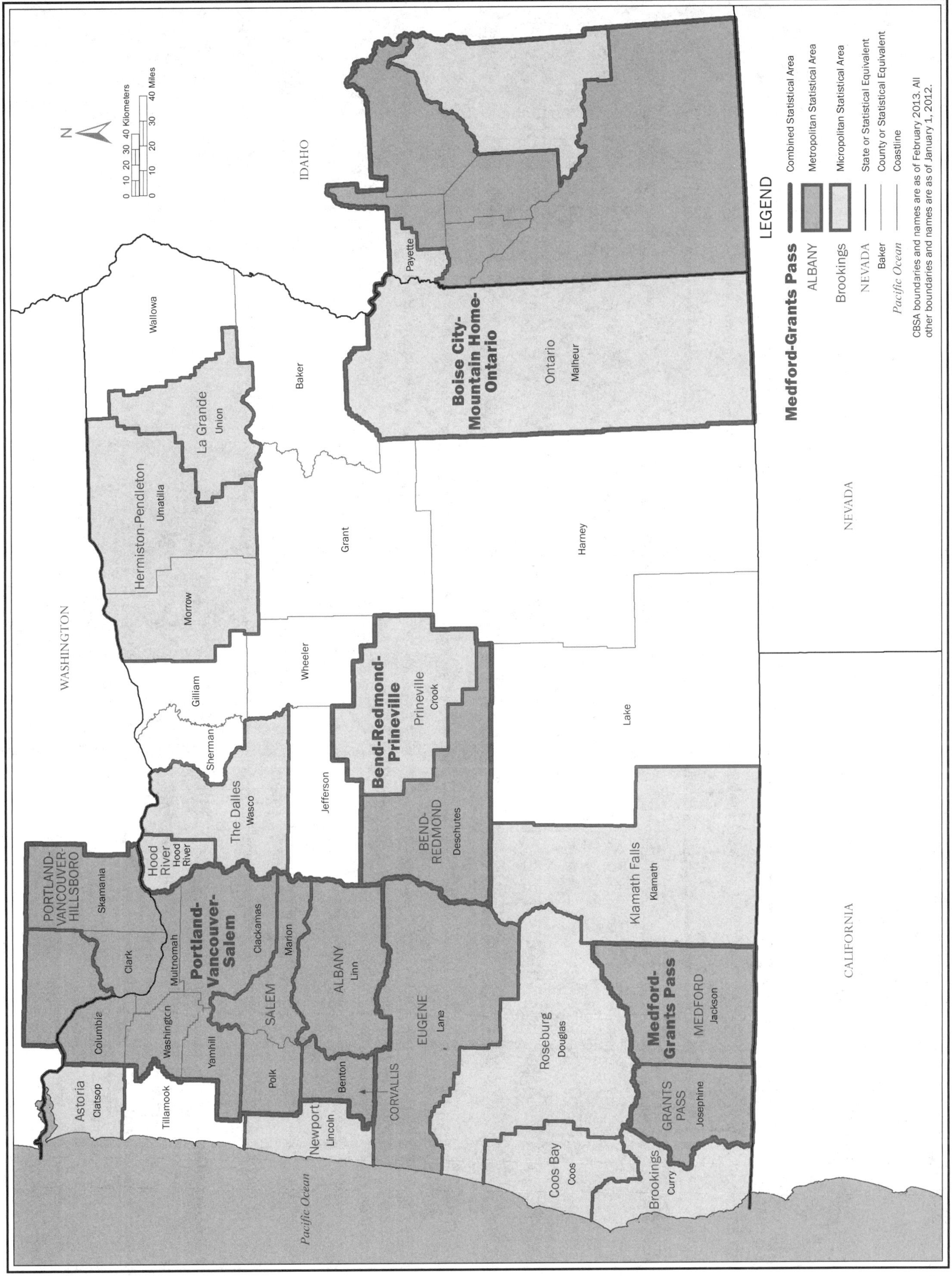
WASHINGTON
IDAHO
NEVADA
CALIFORNIA
Pacific Ocean
0 10 20 30 40 Kilometers
0 10 20 30 40 Miles
N
Portland-Vancouver-Salem
PORTLAND-VANCOUVER-HILLSBORO
Skamania
Clark
Multnomah
Columbia
Washington
Yamhill
Clackamas
Marion
SALEM
Polk
ALBANY
Linn
CORVALLIS
Benton
EUGENE
Lane
Astoria
Clatsop
Tillamook
Newport
Lincoln
Hood River
Hood River
The Dalles
Wasco
Sherman
Gilliam
Wheeler
Jefferson
Bend-Redmond-Prineville
Prineville
Crook
BEND-REDMOND
Deschutes
Hermiston-Pendleton
Umatilla
Morrow
La Grande
Union
Wallowa
Baker
Grant
Boise City-Mountain Home-Ontario
Ontario
Malheur
Payette
Harney
Lake
Klamath Falls
Klamath
Medford-Grants Pass
MEDFORD
Jackson
GRANTS PASS
Josephine
Roseburg
Douglas
Coos Bay
Coos
Brookings
Curry
LEGEND
Medford-Grants Pass Combined Statistical Area
ALBANY Metropolitan Statistical Area
Brookings Micropolitan Statistical Area
NEVADA State or Statistical Equivalent
Baker County or Statistical Equivalent
Pacific Ocean Coastline
CBSA boundaries and names are as of February 2013. All other boundaries and names are as of January 1, 2012.

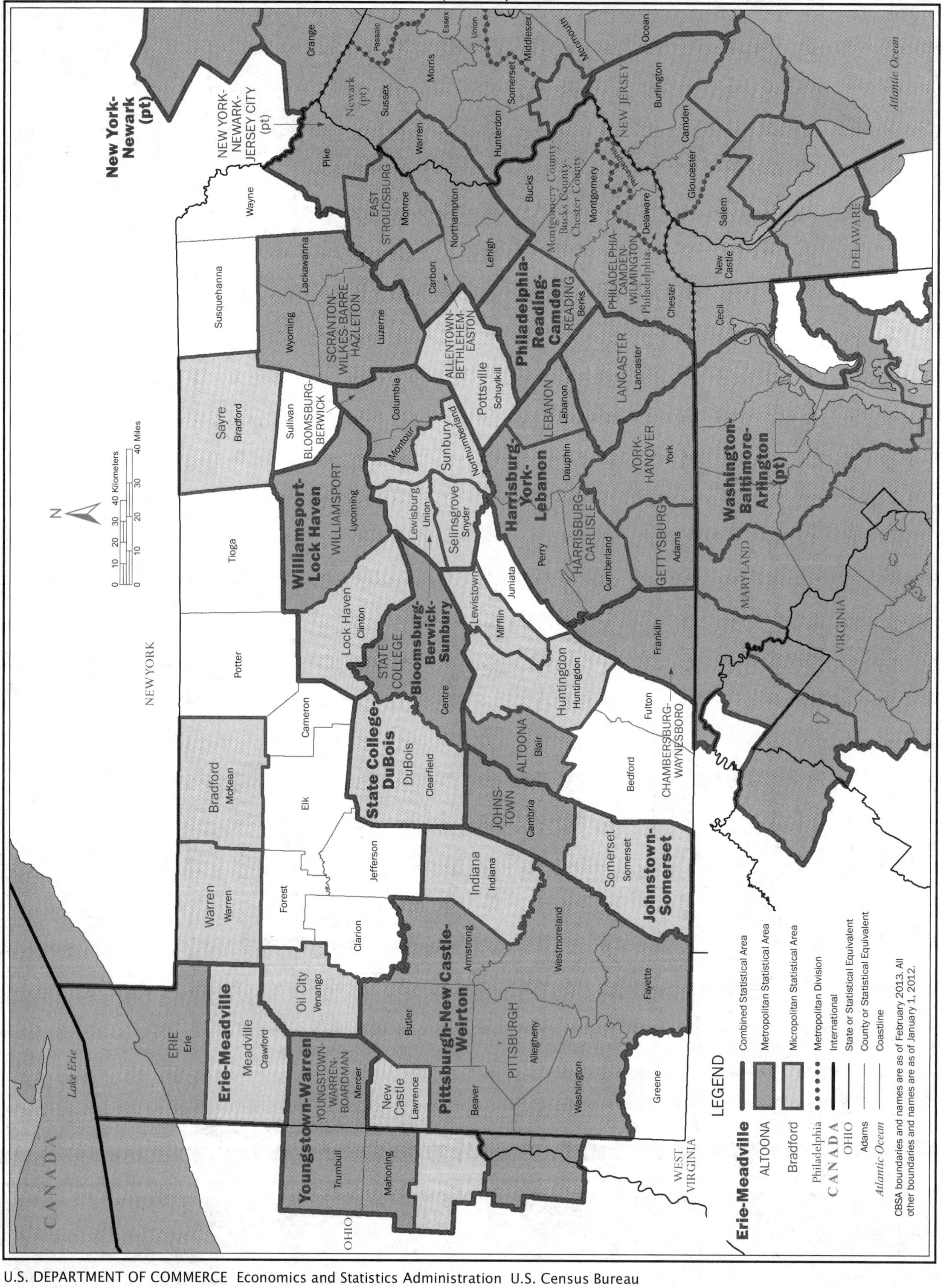
LEGEND
Erie-Meadville Combined Statistical Area
ALTOONA Metropolitan Statistical Area
Bradford Micropolitan Statistical Area
Philadelphia Metropolitan Division
CANADA International
OHIO State or Statistical Equivalent
Adams County or Statistical Equivalent
Atlantic Ocean Coastline
CBSA boundaries and names are as of February 2013. All other boundaries and names are as of January 1, 2012.
New York-Newark (pt)
Philadelphia-Reading-Camden
Harrisburg-York-Lebanon
Washington-Baltimore-Arlington (pt)
Williamsport-Lock Haven
Bloomsburg-Berwick-Sunbury
State College-DuBois
Johnstown-Somerset
Pittsburgh-New Castle-Weirton
Erie-Meadville
Youngstown-Warren
NEW YORK
NEW JERSEY
DELAWARE
MARYLAND
VIRGINIA
WEST VIRGINIA
OHIO
CANADA
Lake Erie
Atlantic Ocean

RHODE ISLAND - Core Based Statistical Areas (CBSAs) and Counties

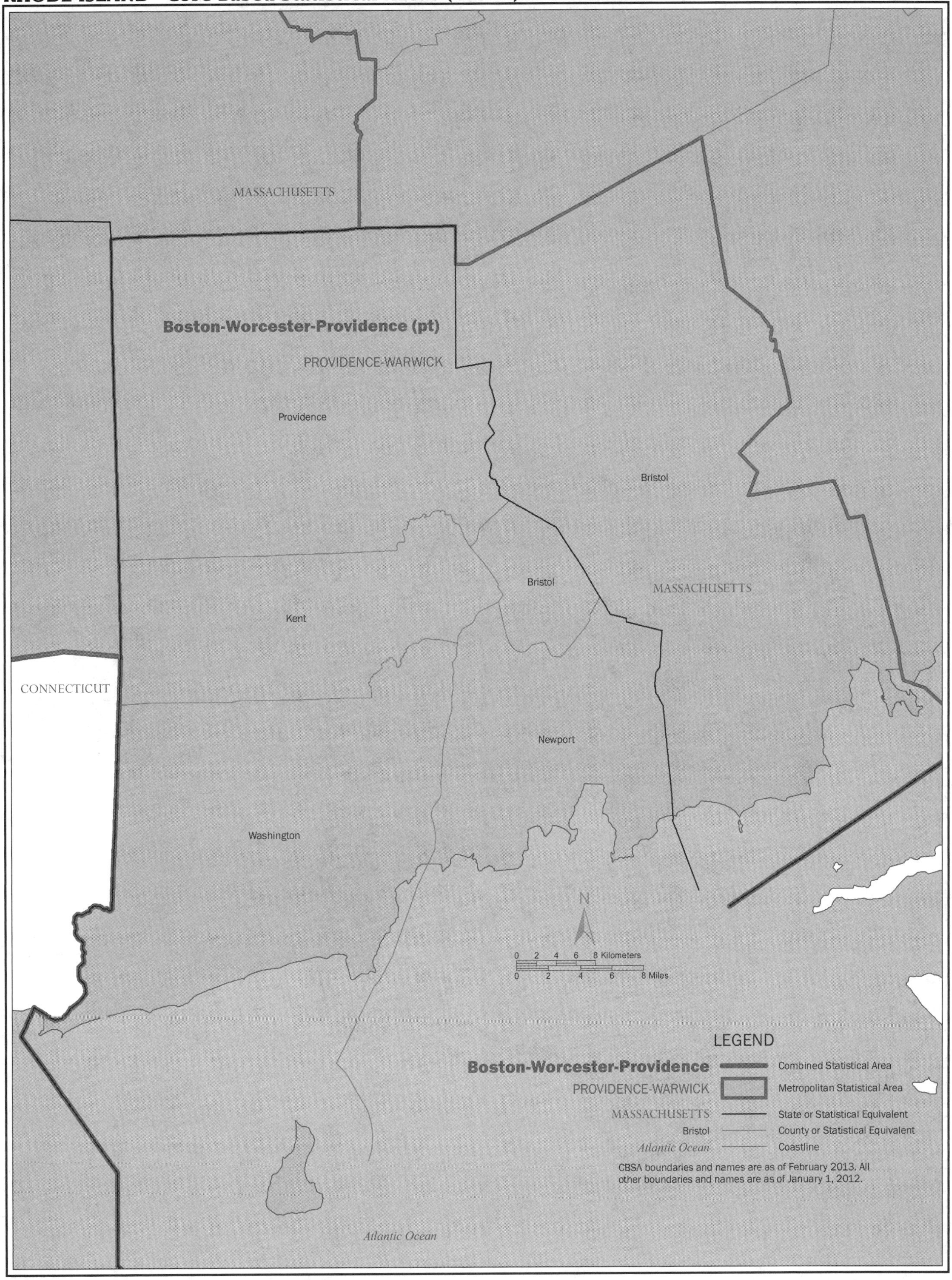

SOUTH CAROLINA - Core Based Statistical Areas (CBSAs) and Counties

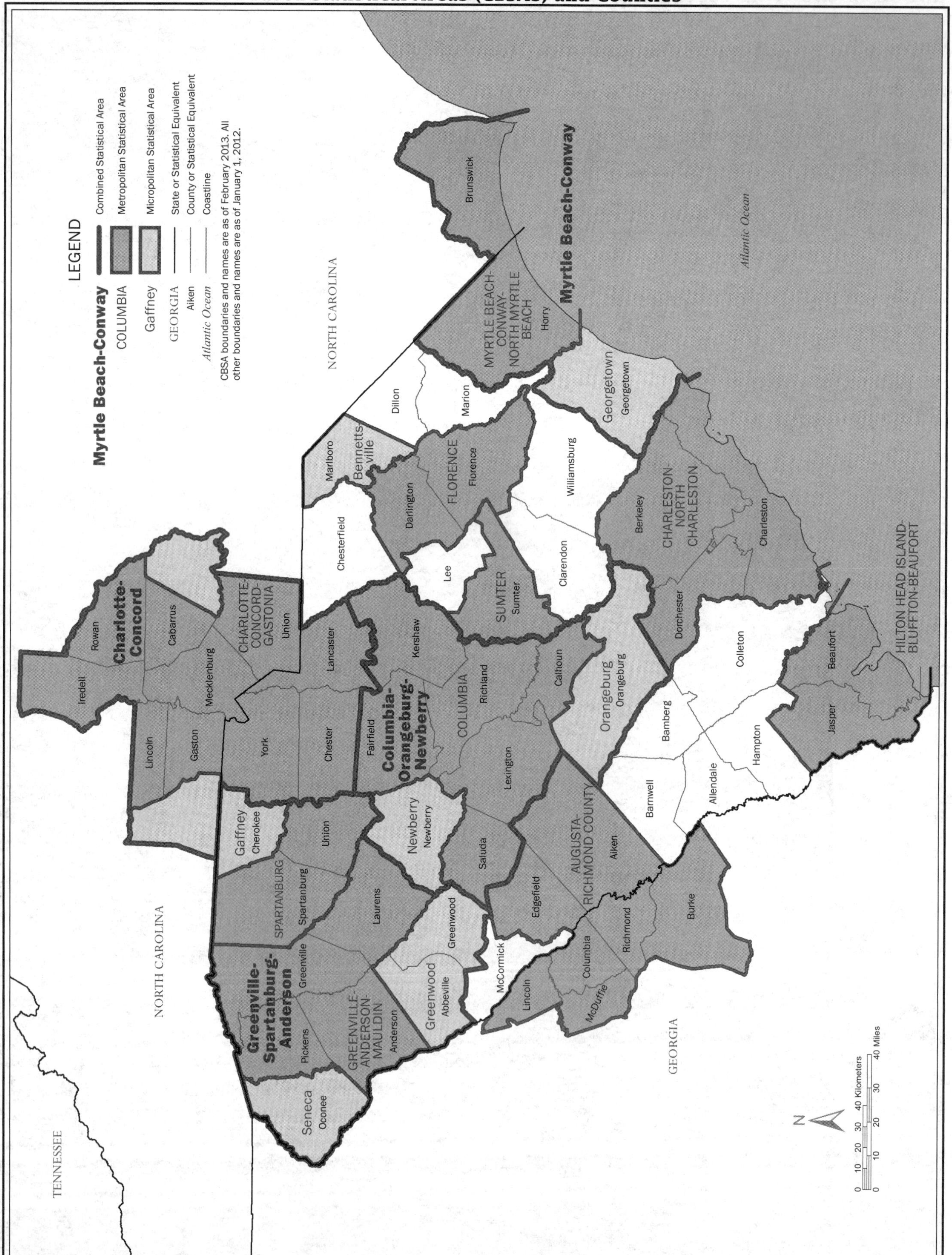

SOUTH DAKOTA - Core Based Statistical Areas (CBSAs) and Counties

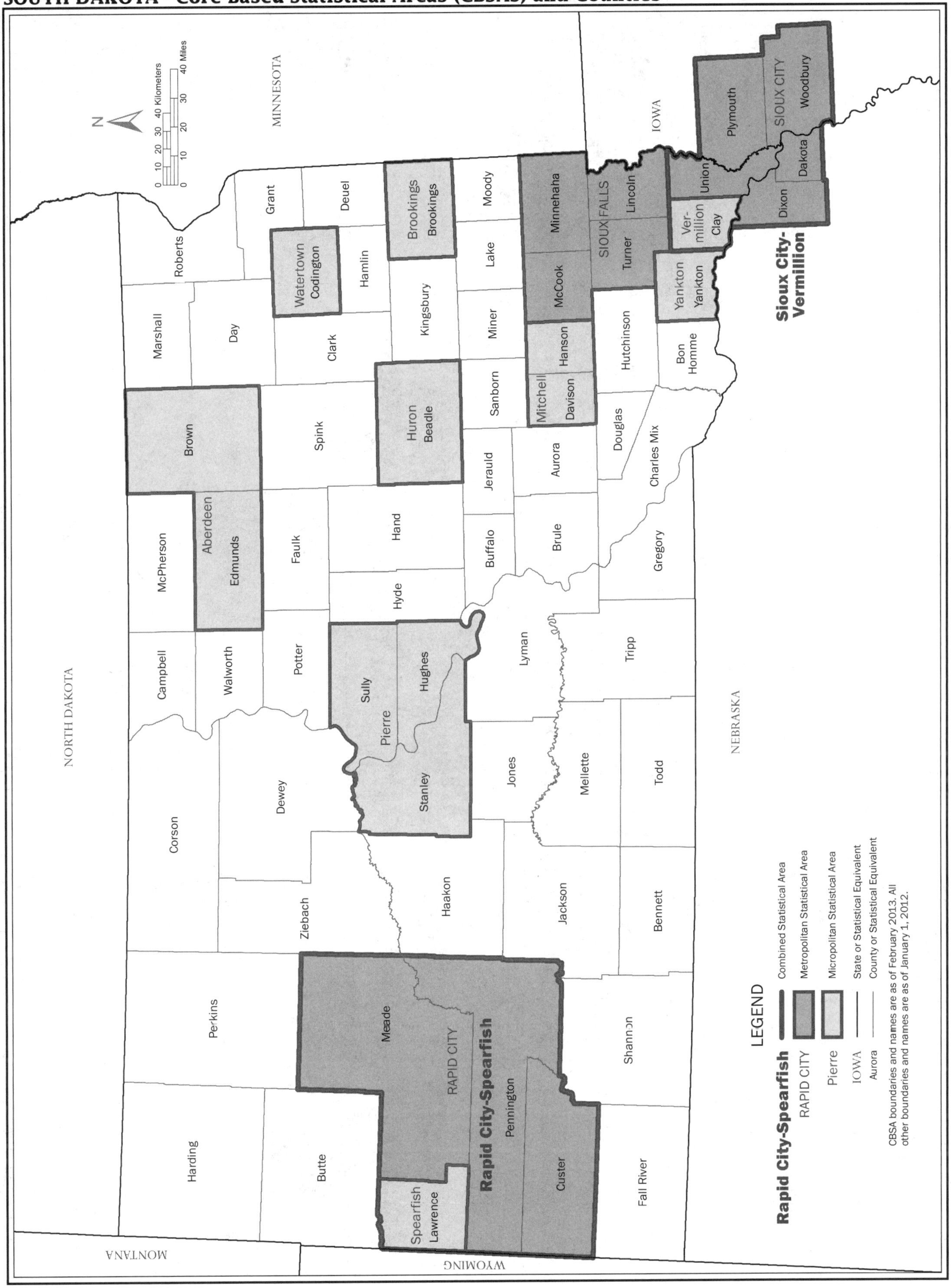

TENNESSEE - Core Based Statistical Areas (CBSAs) and Counties

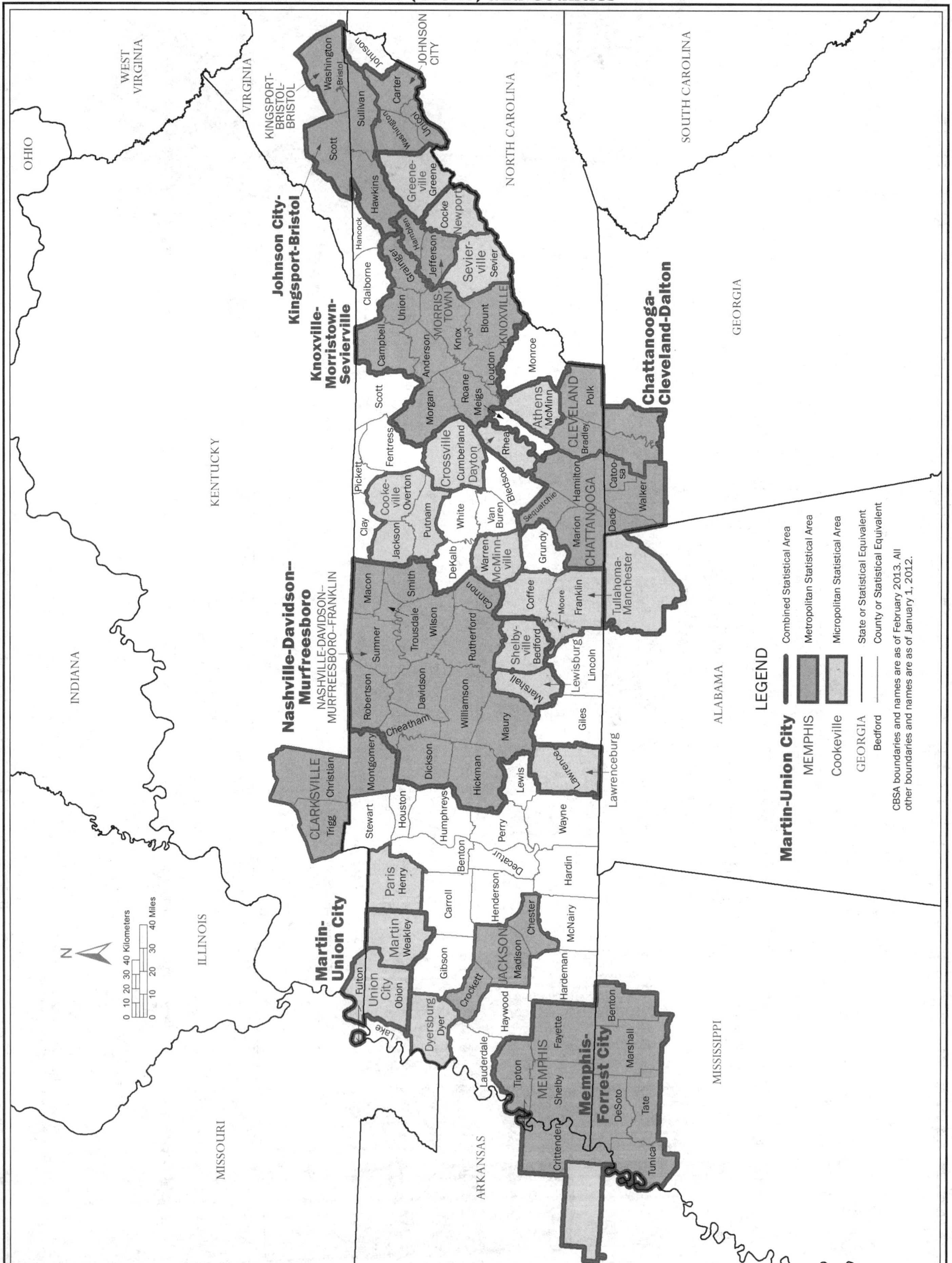

TEXAS - Core Based Statistical Areas (CBSAs) and Counties

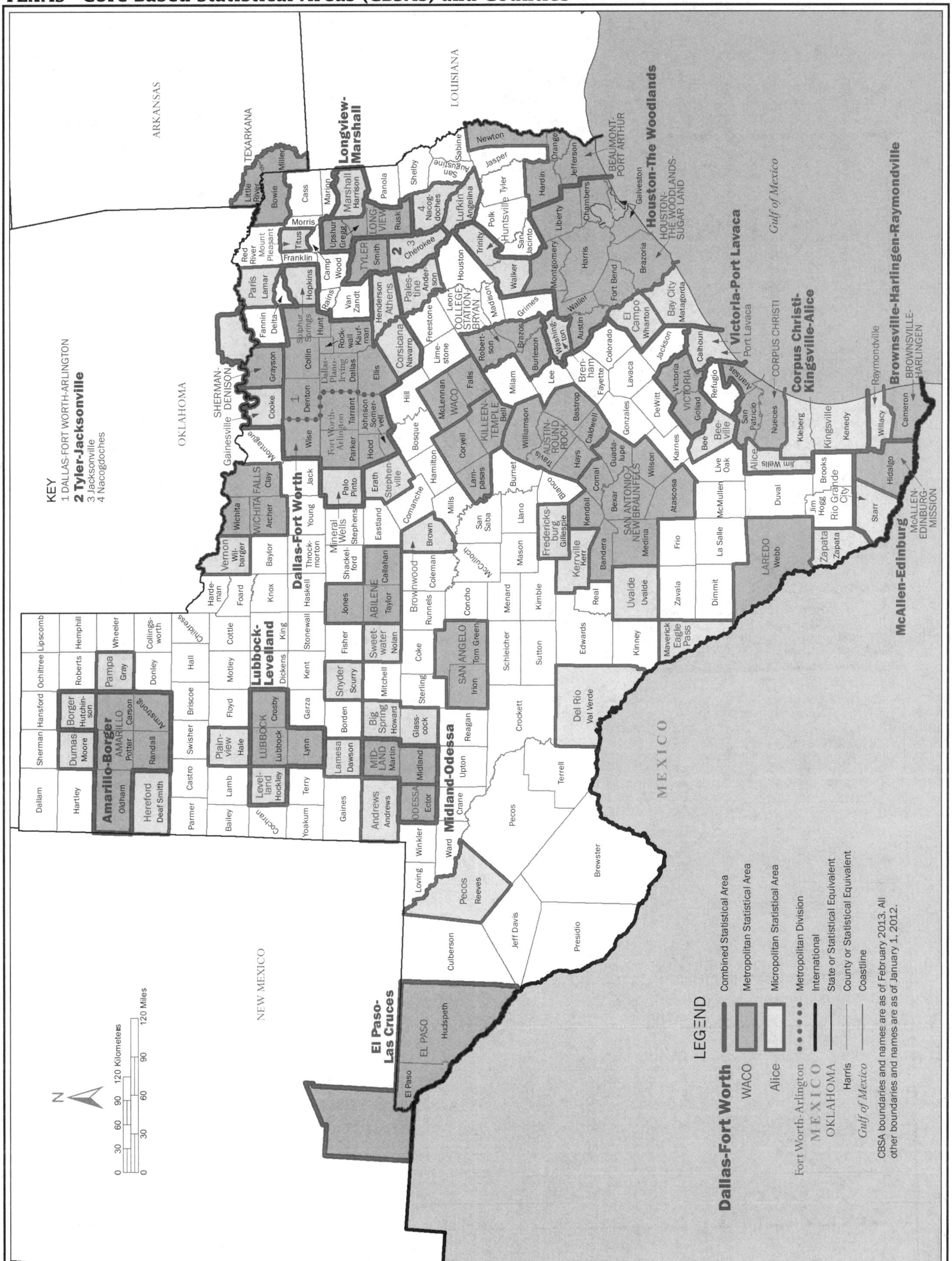

UTAH - Core Based Statistical Areas (CBSAs) and Counties

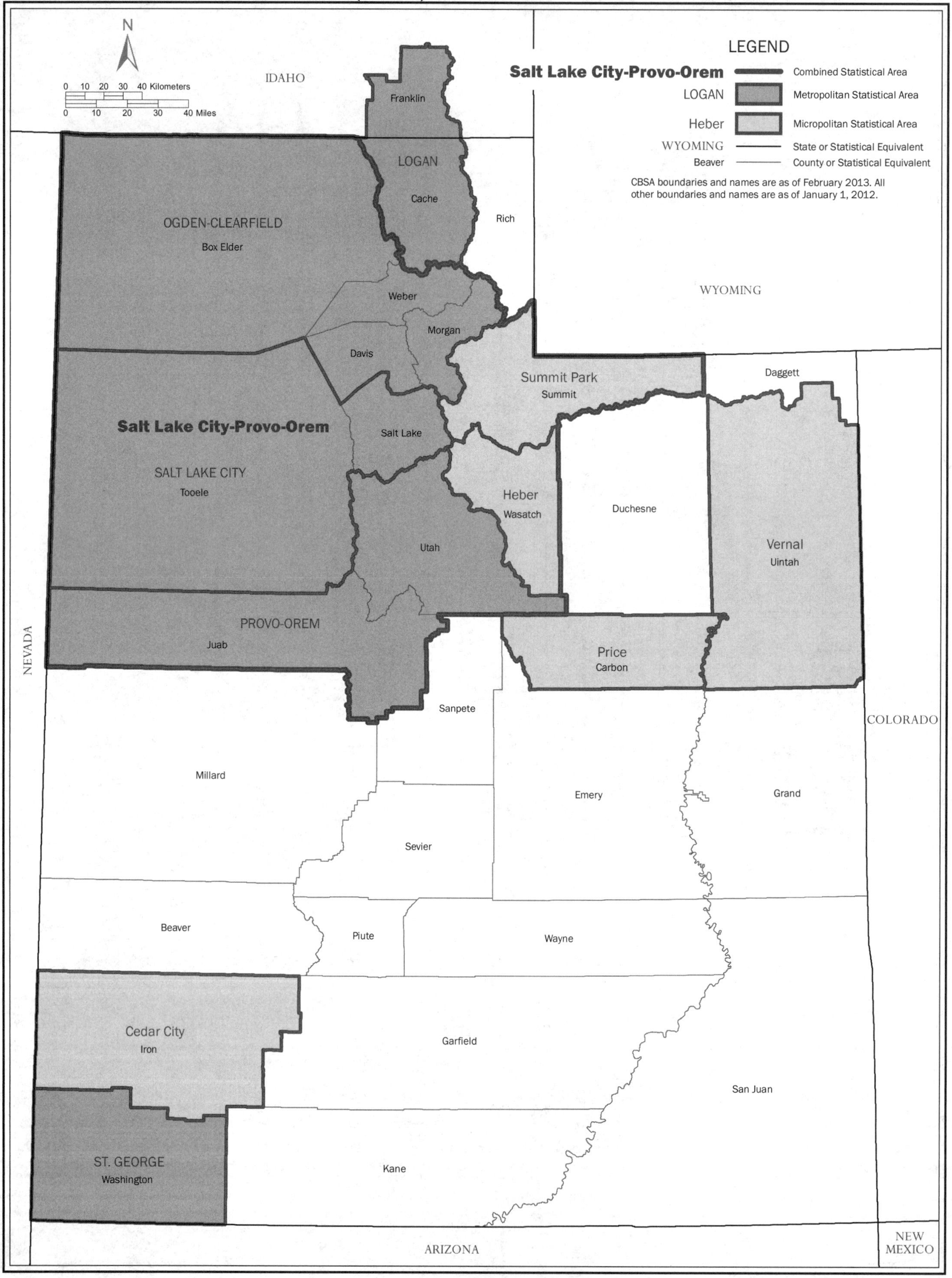

VERMONT - Core Based Statistical Areas (CBSAs) and Counties

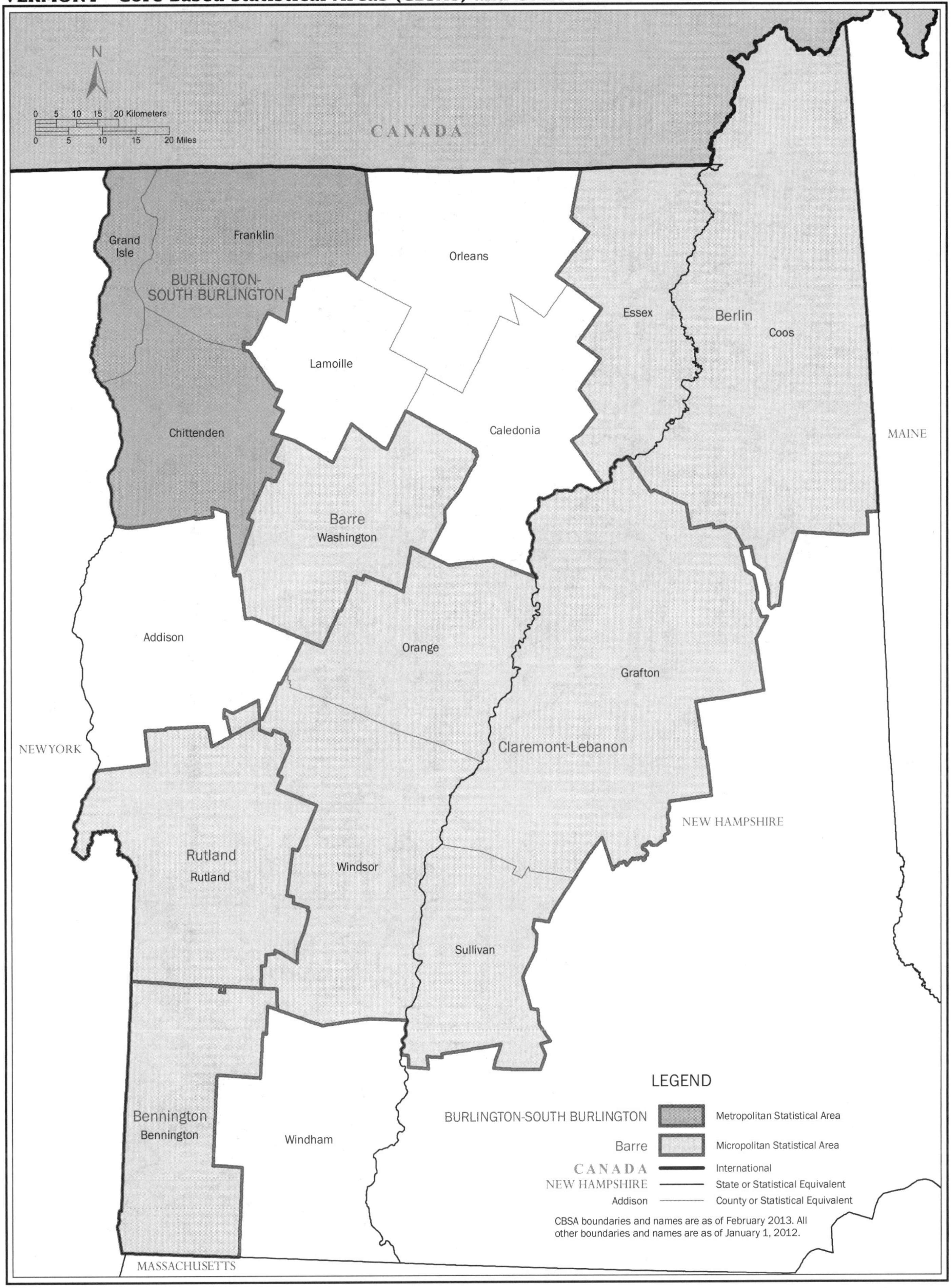

VIRGINIA - Core Based Statistical Areas (CBSAs) and Counties

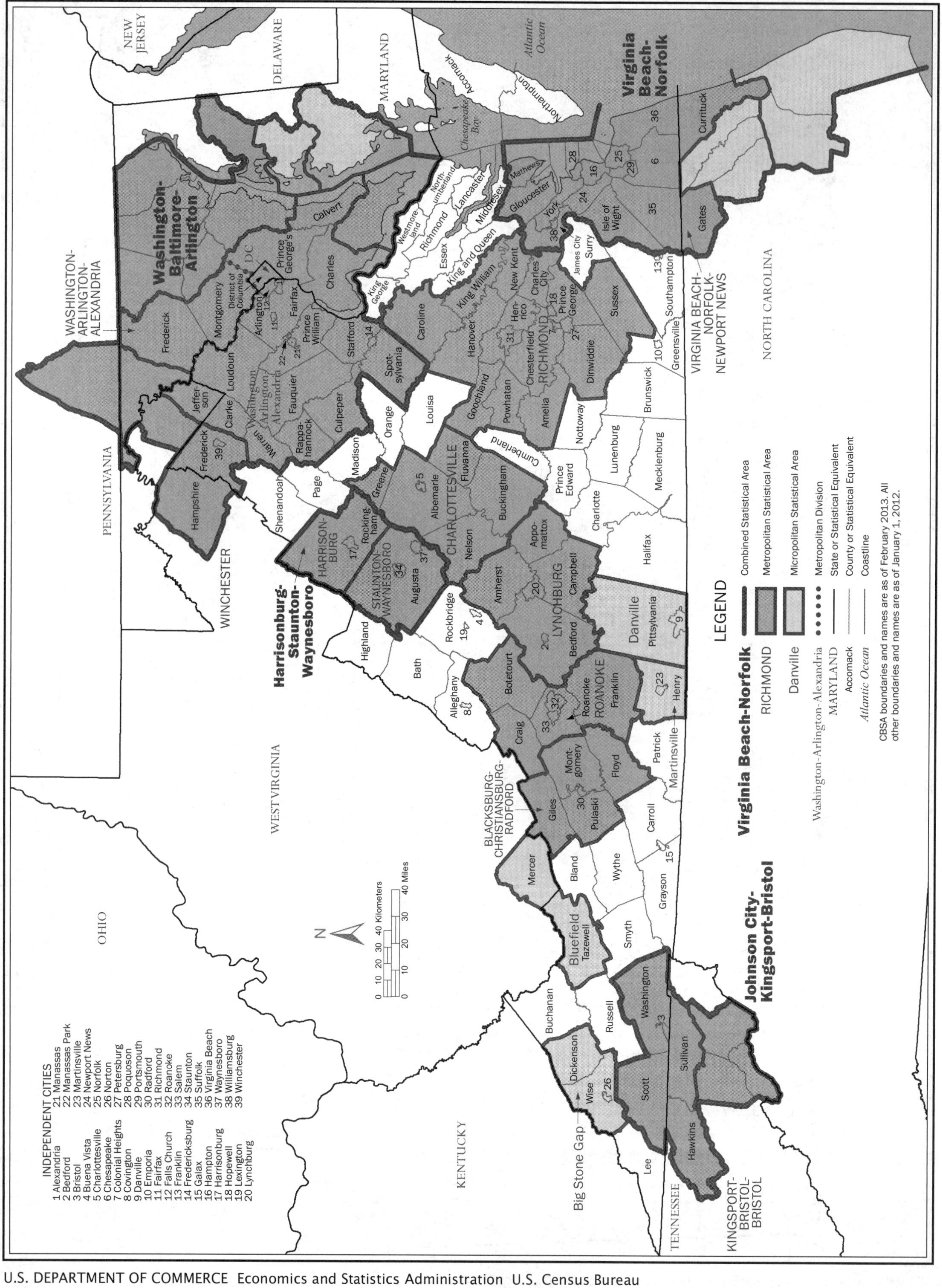

WASHINGTON - Core Based Statistical Areas (CBSAs) and Counties

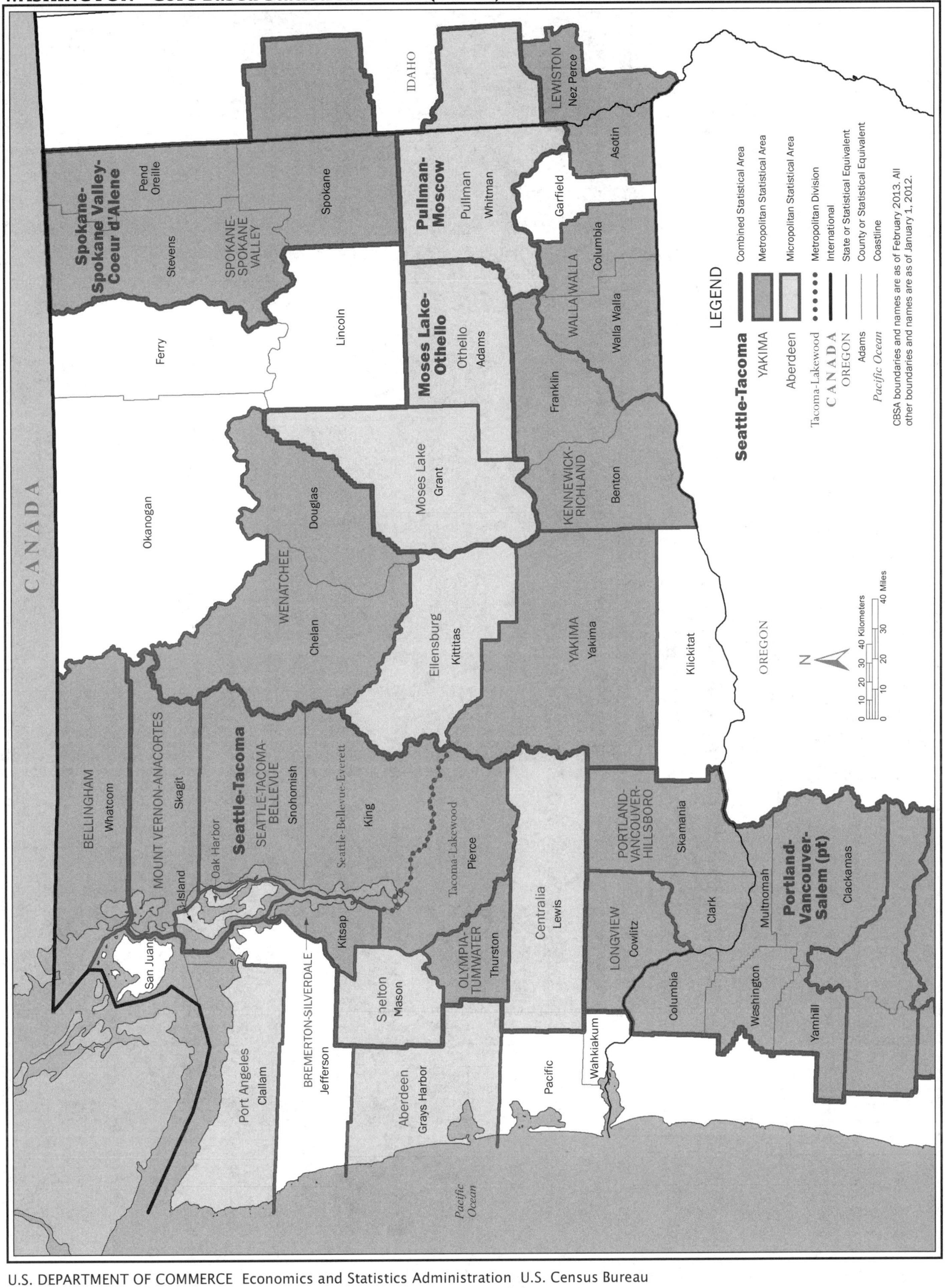

WEST VIRGINIA - Core Based Statistical Areas (CBSAs) and Counties

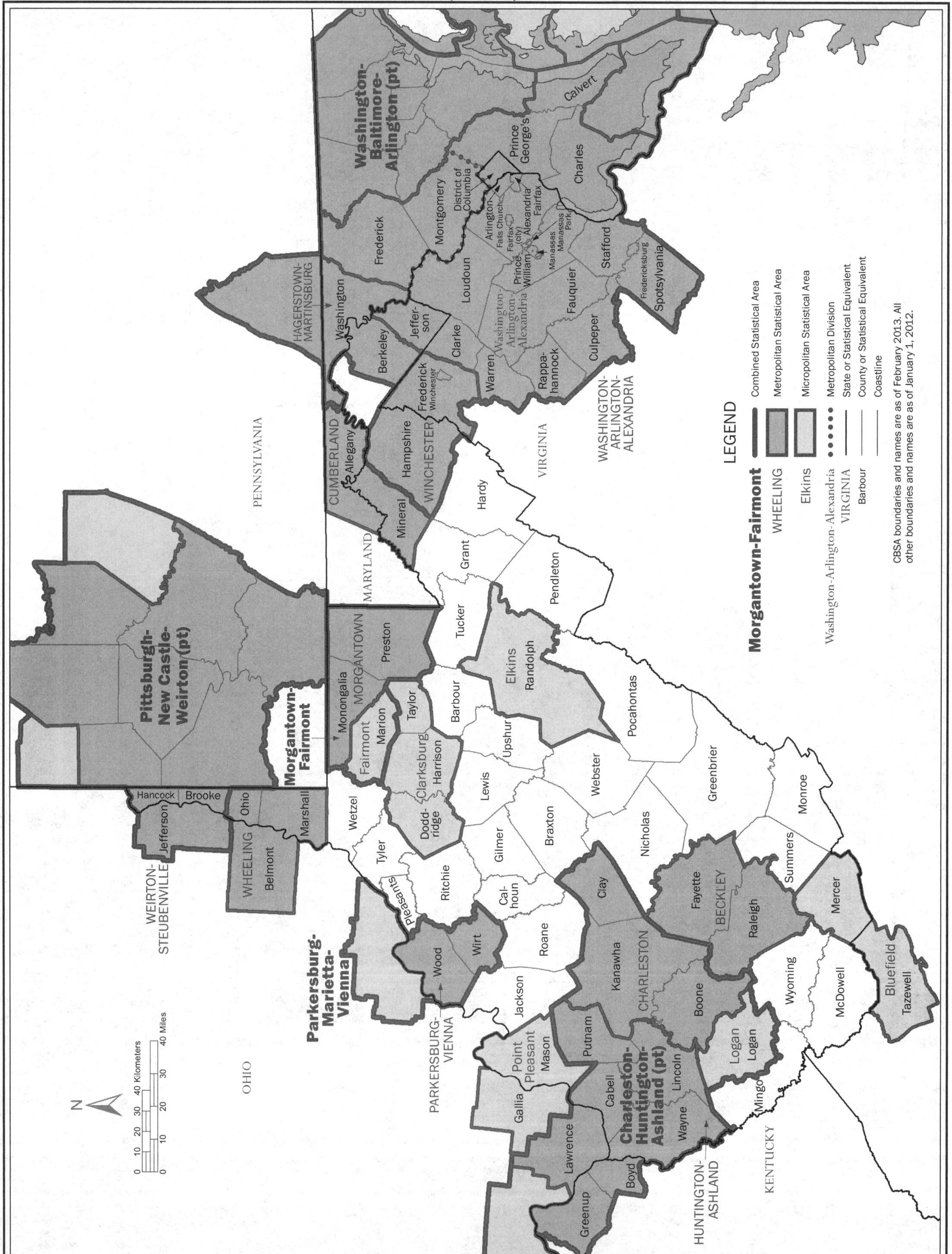

WISCONSIN - Core Based Statistical Areas (CBSAs) and Counties

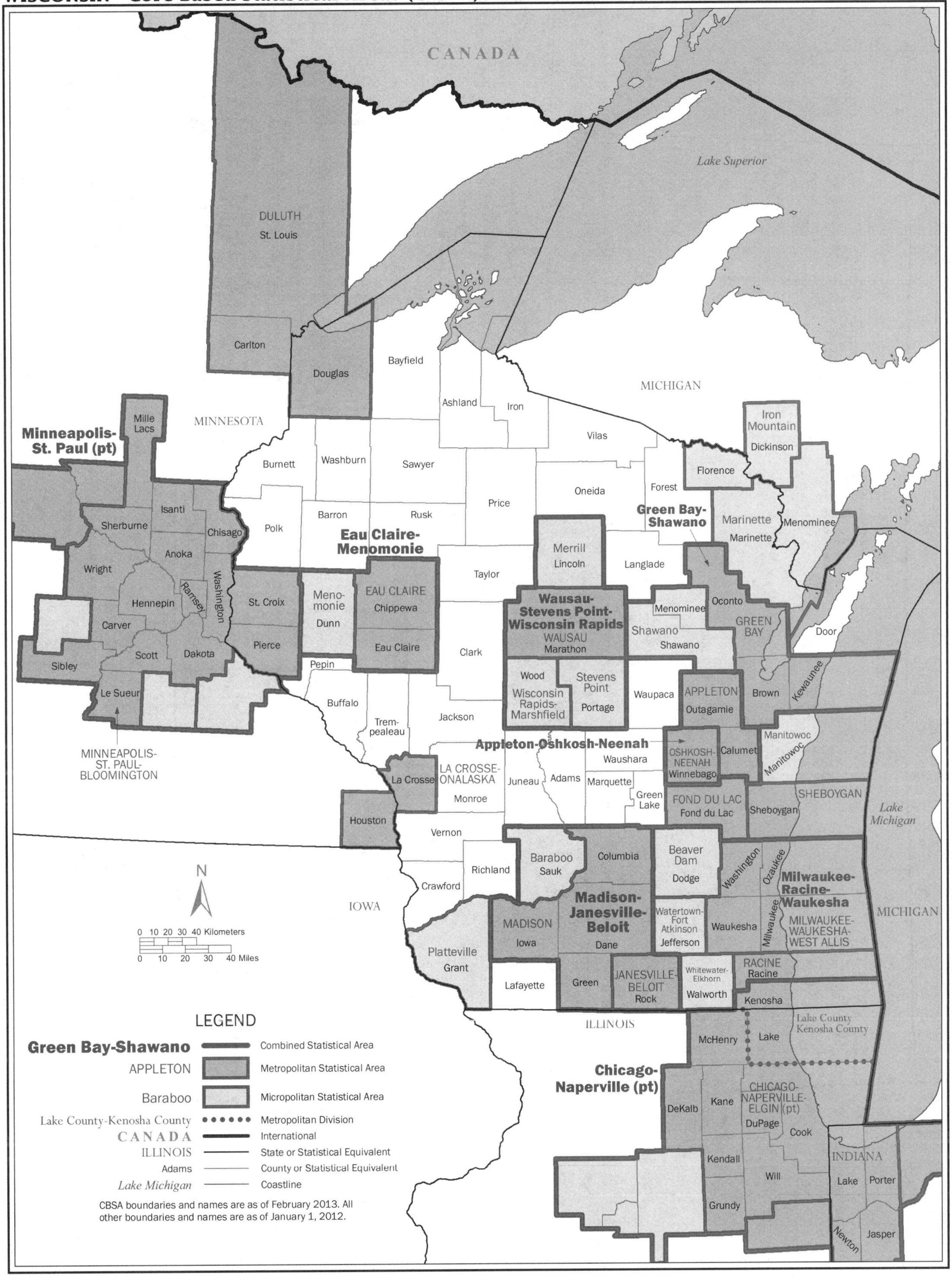

WYOMING - Core Based Statistical Areas (CBSAs) and Counties

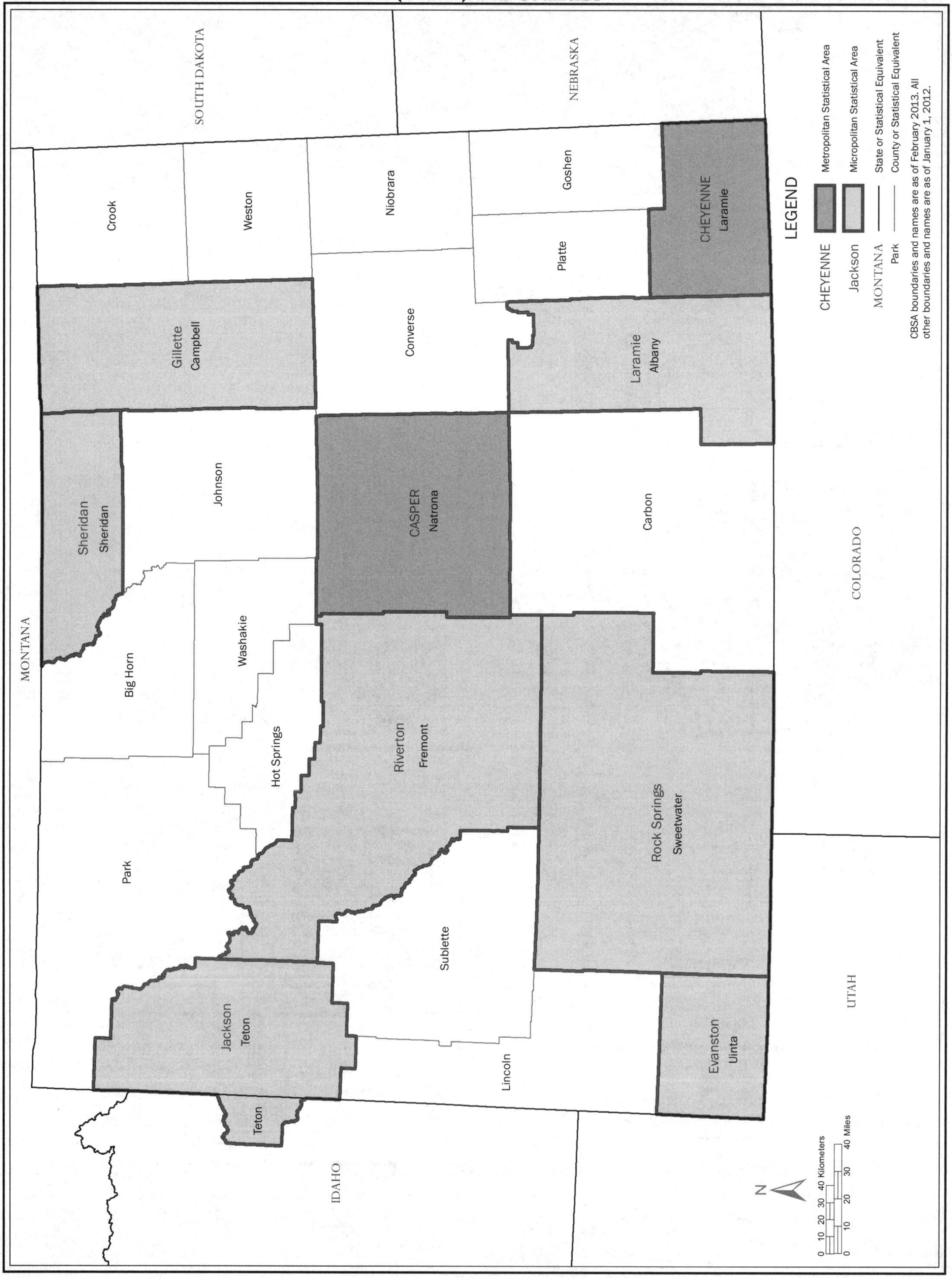

APPENDIX E
CITIES BY COUNTY

The following table is arranged alphabetically by state. Under each state heading are listed all cities with a 2010 census population over 25,000 along with their component counties and the population in each component.

State Code	Place Code	County Code	Geographic Area Name	2010 Census Population
01			**ALABAMA**	4 779 736
01	00820		Alabaster city	30 352
01	00820	117	Shelby County	30 352
01	03076		Auburn city	53 380
01	03076	081	Lee County	53 380
01	05980		Bessemer city	27 456
01	05980	073	Jefferson County	27 456
01	07000		Birmingham city	212 237
01	07000	073	Jefferson County	210 609
01	07000	117	Shelby County	1 628
01	20104		Decatur city	55 683
01	20104	083	Limestone County	84
01	20104	103	Morgan County	55 599
01	21184		Dothan city	65 496
01	21184	045	Dale County	887
01	21184	067	Henry County	5
01	21184	069	Houston County	64 604
01	24184		Enterprise city	26 562
01	24184	031	Coffee County	26 139
01	24184	045	Dale County	423
01	26896		Florence city	39 319
01	26896	077	Lauderdale County	39 319
01	28696		Gadsden city	36 856
01	28696	055	Etowah County	36 856
01	35800		Homewood city	25 167
01	35800	073	Jefferson County	25 167
01	35896		Hoover city	81 619
01	35896	073	Jefferson County	58 582
01	35896	117	Shelby County	23 037
01	37000		Huntsville city	180 105
01	37000	083	Limestone County	1 521
01	37000	089	Madison County	178 584
01	45784		Madison city	42 938
01	45784	083	Limestone County	3 453
01	45784	089	Madison County	39 485
01	50000		Mobile city	195 111
01	50000	097	Mobile County	195 111
01	51000		Montgomery city	205 764
01	51000	101	Montgomery County	205 764
01	57048		Opelika city	26 477
01	57048	081	Lee County	26 477
01	59472		Phenix City city	32 822
01	59472	081	Lee County	4 153
01	59472	113	Russell County	28 669
01	62328		Prattville city	33 960
01	62328	001	Autauga County	32 168
01	62328	051	Elmore County	1 792
01	77256		Tuscaloosa city	90 468
01	77256	125	Tuscaloosa County	90 468
01	78552		Vestavia Hills city	34 033
01	78552	073	Jefferson County	34 019
01	78552	117	Shelby County	14
02			**ALASKA**	710 231
02	03000		Anchorage municipality	291 826
02	03000	020	Anchorage Municipality	291 826
02	24230		Fairbanks city	31 535
02	24230	090	Fairbanks North Star Borough	31 535
02	36400		Juneau city and borough	31 275
02	36400	110	Juneau City and Borough	31 275
04			**ARIZONA**	6 392 017
04	02830		Apache Junction city	35 840
04	02830	013	Maricopa County	294
04	02830	021	Pinal County	35 546
04	04720		Avondale city	76 238
04	04720	013	Maricopa County	76 238
04	07940		Buckeye town	50 876
04	07940	013	Maricopa County	50 876
04	08220		Bullhead City city	39 540
04	08220	015	Mohave County	39 540
04	10530		Casa Grande city	48 571
04	10530	021	Pinal County	48 571
04	12000		Chandler city	236 123
04	12000	013	Maricopa County	236 123
04	22220		El Mirage city	31 797
04	22220	013	Maricopa County	31 797
04	23620		Flagstaff city	65 870
04	23620	005	Coconino County	65 870
04	23760		Florence town	25 536
04	23760	021	Pinal County	25 536
04	27400		Gilbert town	208 453
04	27400	013	Maricopa County	208 453
04	27820		Glendale city	226 721
04	27820	013	Maricopa County	226 721
04	28380		Goodyear city	65 275
04	28380	013	Maricopa County	65 275
04	37620		Kingman city	28 068
04	37620	015	Mohave County	28 068
04	39370		Lake Havasu City city	52 527
04	39370	015	Mohave County	52 527
04	44270		Marana town	34 961
04	44270	019	Pima County	34 961
04	44270	021	Pinal County	0
04	44410		Maricopa city	43 482
04	44410	021	Pinal County	43 482
04	46000		Mesa city	439 041
04	46000	013	Maricopa County	439 041

Cities by County–*Continued*

State Code	Place Code	County Code	Geographic Area Name	2010 Census Population
04	51600		Oro Valley town	41 011
04	51600	019	Pima County	41 011
04	54050		Peoria city	154 065
04	54050	013	Maricopa County	154 058
04	54050	025	Yavapai County	7
04	55000		Phoenix city	1 445 632
04	55000	013	Maricopa County	1 445 632
04	57380		Prescott city	39 843
04	57380	025	Yavapai County	39 843
04	57450		Prescott Valley town	38 822
04	57450	025	Yavapai County	38 822
04	58150		Queen Creek town	26 361
04	58150	013	Maricopa County	25 912
04	58150	021	Pinal County	449
04	62140		Sahuarita town	25 259
04	62140	019	Pima County	25 259
04	63470		San Luis city	25 505
04	63470	027	Yuma County	25 505
04	65000		Scottsdale city	217 385
04	65000	013	Maricopa County	217 385
04	66820		Sierra Vista city	43 888
04	66820	003	Cochise County	43 888
04	71510		Surprise city	117 517
04	71510	013	Maricopa County	117 517
04	73000		Tempe city	161 719
04	73000	013	Maricopa County	161 719
04	77000		Tucson city	520 116
04	77000	019	Pima County	520 116
04	85540		Yuma city	93 064
04	85540	027	Yuma County	93 064
05			**ARKANSAS**	2 915 918
05	04840		Bella Vista town	26 461
05	04840	007	Benton County	26 461
05	05290		Benton city	30 681
05	05290	125	Saline County	30 681
05	05320		Bentonville city	35 301
05	05320	007	Benton County	35 301
05	15190		Conway city	58 908
05	15190	045	Faulkner County	58 908
05	23290		Fayetteville city	73 580
05	23290	143	Washington County	73 580
05	24550		Fort Smith city	86 209
05	24550	131	Sebastian County	86 209
05	33400		Hot Springs city	35 193
05	33400	051	Garland County	35 193
05	34750		Jacksonville city	28 364
05	34750	119	Pulaski County	28 364
05	35710		Jonesboro city	67 263
05	35710	031	Craighead County	67 263
05	41000		Little Rock city	193 524
05	41000	119	Pulaski County	193 524
05	50450		North Little Rock city	62 304
05	50450	119	Pulaski County	62 304
05	53390		Paragould city	26 113
05	53390	055	Greene County	26 113
05	55310		Pine Bluff city	49 083
05	55310	069	Jefferson County	49 083
05	60410		Rogers city	55 964
05	60410	007	Benton County	55 964
05	61670		Russellville city	27 920
05	61670	115	Pope County	27 920
05	63800		Sherwood city	29 523
05	63800	119	Pulaski County	29 523
05	66080		Springdale city	69 797
05	66080	007	Benton County	6 054
05	66080	143	Washington County	63 743
05	68810		Texarkana city	29 919
05	68810	091	Miller County	29 919
05	74540		West Memphis city	26 245
05	74540	035	Crittenden County	26 245
06			**CALIFORNIA**	37 253 956
06	00296		Adelanto city	31 765
06	00296	071	San Bernardino County	31 765
06	00562		Alameda city	73 812
06	00562	001	Alameda County	73 812
06	00884		Alhambra city	83 089
06	00884	037	Los Angeles County	83 089
06	00947		Aliso Viejo city	47 823
06	00947	059	Orange County	47 823
06	02000		Anaheim city	336 265
06	02000	059	Orange County	336 265
06	02252		Antioch city	102 372
06	02252	013	Contra Costa County	102 372
06	02364		Apple Valley town	69 135
06	02364	071	San Bernardino County	69 135
06	02462		Arcadia city	56 364
06	02462	037	Los Angeles County	56 364
06	03064		Atascadero city	28 310
06	03064	079	San Luis Obispo County	28 310
06	03162		Atwater city	28 168
06	03162	047	Merced County	28 168
06	03386		Azusa city	46 361
06	03386	037	Los Angeles County	46 361
06	03526		Bakersfield city	347 483
06	03526	029	Kern County	347 483
06	03666		Baldwin Park city	75 390
06	03666	037	Los Angeles County	75 390

Cities by County–*Continued*

State Code	Place Code	County Code	Geographic Area Name	2010 Census Population
06	03820		Banning city	29 603
06	03820	065	Riverside County	29 603
06	04758		Beaumont city	36 877
06	04758	065	Riverside County	36 877
06	04870		Bell city	35 477
06	04870	037	Los Angeles County	35 477
06	04982		Bellflower city	76 616
06	04982	037	Los Angeles County	76 616
06	04996		Bell Gardens city	42 072
06	04996	037	Los Angeles County	42 072
06	05108		Belmont city	25 835
06	05108	081	San Mateo County	25 835
06	05290		Benicia city	26 997
06	05290	095	Solano County	26 997
06	06000		Berkeley city	112 580
06	06000	001	Alameda County	112 580
06	06308		Beverly Hills city	34 109
06	06308	037	Los Angeles County	34 109
06	08100		Brea city	39 282
06	08100	059	Orange County	39 282
06	08142		Brentwood city	51 481
06	08142	013	Contra Costa County	51 481
06	08786		Buena Park city	80 530
06	08786	059	Orange County	80 530
06	08954		Burbank city	103 340
06	08954	037	Los Angeles County	103 340
06	09066		Burlingame city	28 806
06	09066	081	San Mateo County	28 806
06	09710		Calexico city	38 572
06	09710	025	Imperial County	38 572
06	10046		Camarillo city	65 201
06	10046	111	Ventura County	65 201
06	10345		Campbell city	39 349
06	10345	085	Santa Clara County	39 349
06	11194		Carlsbad city	105 328
06	11194	073	San Diego County	105 328
06	11530		Carson city	91 714
06	11530	037	Los Angeles County	91 714
06	12048		Cathedral City city	51 200
06	12048	065	Riverside County	51 200
06	12524		Ceres city	45 417
06	12524	099	Stanislaus County	45 417
06	12552		Cerritos city	49 041
06	12552	037	Los Angeles County	49 041
06	13014		Chico city	86 187
06	13014	007	Butte County	86 187
06	13210		Chino city	77 983
06	13210	071	San Bernardino County	77 983
06	13214		Chino Hills city	74 799
06	13214	071	San Bernardino County	74 799
06	13392		Chula Vista city	243 916
06	13392	073	San Diego County	243 916
06	13588		Citrus Heights city	83 301
06	13588	067	Sacramento County	83 301
06	13756		Claremont city	34 926
06	13756	037	Los Angeles County	34 926
06	14218		Clovis city	95 631
06	14218	019	Fresno County	95 631
06	14260		Coachella city	40 704
06	14260	065	Riverside County	40 704
06	14890		Colton city	52 154
06	14890	071	San Bernardino County	52 154
06	15044		Compton city	96 455
06	15044	037	Los Angeles County	96 455
06	16000		Concord city	122 067
06	16000	013	Contra Costa County	122 067
06	16350		Corona city	152 374
06	16350	065	Riverside County	152 374
06	16532		Costa Mesa city	109 960
06	16532	059	Orange County	109 960
06	16742		Covina city	47 796
06	16742	037	Los Angeles County	47 796
06	17568		Culver City city	38 883
06	17568	037	Los Angeles County	38 883
06	17610		Cupertino city	58 302
06	17610	085	Santa Clara County	58 302
06	17750		Cypress city	47 802
06	17750	059	Orange County	47 802
06	17918		Daly City city	101 123
06	17918	081	San Mateo County	101 123
06	17946		Dana Point city	33 351
06	17946	059	Orange County	33 351
06	17988		Danville town	42 039
06	17988	013	Contra Costa County	42 039
06	18100		Davis city	65 622
06	18100	113	Yolo County	65 622
06	18394		Delano city	53 041
06	18394	029	Kern County	53 041
06	18996		Desert Hot Springs city	25 938
06	18996	065	Riverside County	25 938
06	19192		Diamond Bar city	55 544
06	19192	037	Los Angeles County	55 544
06	19766		Downey city	111 772
06	19766	037	Los Angeles County	111 772
06	20018		Dublin city	46 036
06	20018	001	Alameda County	46 036

Cities by County–*Continued*

State Code	Place Code	County Code	Geographic Area Name	2010 Census Population	State Code	Place Code	County Code	Geographic Area Name	2010 Census Population
06	20956		East Palo Alto city	28 155	06	32548		Hawthorne city	84 293
06	20956	081	San Mateo County	28 155	06	32548	037	Los Angeles County	84 293
06	21712		El Cajon city	99 478	06	33000		Hayward city	144 186
06	21712	073	San Diego County	99 478	06	33000	001	Alameda County	144 186
06	21782		El Centro city	42 598	06	33182		Hemet city	78 657
06	21782	025	Imperial County	42 598	06	33182	065	Riverside County	78 657
06	22020		Elk Grove city	153 015	06	33434		Hesperia city	90 173
06	22020	067	Sacramento County	153 015	06	33434	071	San Bernardino County	90 173
06	22230		El Monte city	113 475	06	33588		Highland city	53 104
06	22230	037	Los Angeles County	113 475	06	33588	071	San Bernardino County	53 104
06	22300		El Paso de Robles (Paso Robles)	29 793	06	34120		Hollister city	34 928
06	22300	079	San Luis Obispo County	29 793	06	34120	069	San Benito County	34 928
06	22678		Encinitas city	59 518	06	36000		Huntington Beach city	189 992
06	22678	073	San Diego County	59 518	06	36000	059	Orange County	189 992
06	22804		Escondido city	143 911	06	36056		Huntington Park city	58 114
06	22804	073	San Diego County	143 911	06	36056	037	Los Angeles County	58 114
06	23042		Eureka city	27 191	06	36294		Imperial Beach city	26 324
06	23042	023	Humboldt County	27 191	06	36294	073	San Diego County	26 324
06	23182		Fairfield city	105 321	06	36448		Indio city	76 036
06	23182	095	Solano County	105 321	06	36448	065	Riverside County	76 036
06	24638		Folsom city	72 203	06	36546		Inglewood city	109 673
06	24638	067	Sacramento County	72 203	06	36546	037	Los Angeles County	109 673
06	24680		Fontana city	196 069	06	36770		Irvine city	212 375
06	24680	071	San Bernardino County	196 069	06	36770	059	Orange County	212 375
06	25338		Foster City city	30 567	06	39220		Laguna Hills city	30 344
06	25338	081	San Mateo County	30 567	06	39220	059	Orange County	30 344
06	25380		Fountain Valley city	55 313	06	39248		Laguna Niguel city	62 979
06	25380	059	Orange County	55 313	06	39248	059	Orange County	62 979
06	26000		Fremont city	214 089	06	39290		La Habra city	60 239
06	26000	001	Alameda County	214 089	06	39290	059	Orange County	60 239
06	27000		Fresno city	494 665	06	39486		Lake Elsinore city	51 821
06	27000	019	Fresno County	494 665	06	39486	065	Riverside County	51 821
06	28000		Fullerton city	135 161	06	39496		Lake Forest city	77 264
06	28000	059	Orange County	135 161	06	39496	059	Orange County	77 264
06	28168		Gardena city	58 829	06	39892		Lakewood city	80 048
06	28168	037	Los Angeles County	58 829	06	39892	037	Los Angeles County	80 048
06	29000		Garden Grove city	170 883	06	40004		La Mesa city	57 065
06	29000	059	Orange County	170 883	06	40004	073	San Diego County	57 065
06	29504		Gilroy city	48 821	06	40032		La Mirada city	48 527
06	29504	085	Santa Clara County	48 821	06	40032	037	Los Angeles County	48 527
06	30000		Glendale city	191 719	06	40130		Lancaster city	156 633
06	30000	037	Los Angeles County	191 719	06	40130	037	Los Angeles County	156 633
06	30014		Glendora city	50 073	06	40340		La Puente city	39 816
06	30014	037	Los Angeles County	50 073	06	40340	037	Los Angeles County	39 816
06	30378		Goleta city	29 888	06	40354		La Quinta city	37 467
06	30378	083	Santa Barbara County	29 888	06	40354	065	Riverside County	37 467
06	31960		Hanford city	53 967	06	40830		La Verne city	31 063
06	31960	031	Kings County	53 967	06	40830	037	Los Angeles County	31 063

Cities by County–*Continued*

State Code	Place Code	County Code	Geographic Area Name	2010 Census Population
06	40886		Lawndale city	32 769
06	40886	037	Los Angeles County	32 769
06	41124		Lemon Grove city	25 320
06	41124	073	San Diego County	25 320
06	41474		Lincoln city	42 819
06	41474	061	Placer County	42 819
06	41992		Livermore city	80 968
06	41992	001	Alameda County	80 968
06	42202		Lodi city	62 134
06	42202	077	San Joaquin County	62 134
06	42524		Lompoc city	42 434
06	42524	083	Santa Barbara County	42 434
06	43000		Long Beach city	462 257
06	43000	037	Los Angeles County	462 257
06	43280		Los Altos city	28 976
06	43280	085	Santa Clara County	28 976
06	44000		Los Angeles city	3 792 621
06	44000	037	Los Angeles County	3 792 621
06	44028		Los Banos city	35 972
06	44028	047	Merced County	35 972
06	44112		Los Gatos town	29 413
06	44112	085	Santa Clara County	29 413
06	44574		Lynwood city	69 772
06	44574	037	Los Angeles County	69 772
06	45022		Madera city	61 416
06	45022	039	Madera County	61 416
06	45400		Manhattan Beach city	35 135
06	45400	037	Los Angeles County	35 135
06	45484		Manteca city	67 096
06	45484	077	San Joaquin County	67 096
06	46114		Martinez city	35 824
06	46114	013	Contra Costa County	35 824
06	46492		Maywood city	27 395
06	46492	037	Los Angeles County	27 395
06	46842		Menifee city	77 519
06	46842	065	Riverside County	77 519
06	46870		Menlo Park city	32 026
06	46870	081	San Mateo County	32 026
06	46898		Merced city	78 958
06	46898	047	Merced County	78 958
06	47766		Milpitas city	66 790
06	47766	085	Santa Clara County	66 790
06	48256		Mission Viejo city	93 305
06	48256	059	Orange County	93 305
06	48354		Modesto city	201 165
06	48354	099	Stanislaus County	201 165
06	48648		Monrovia city	36 590
06	48648	037	Los Angeles County	36 590
06	48788		Montclair city	36 664
06	48788	071	San Bernardino County	36 664
06	48816		Montebello city	62 500
06	48816	037	Los Angeles County	62 500
06	48872		Monterey city	27 810
06	48872	053	Monterey County	27 810
06	48914		Monterey Park city	60 269
06	48914	037	Los Angeles County	60 269
06	49138		Moorpark city	34 421
06	49138	111	Ventura County	34 421
06	49270		Moreno Valley city	193 365
06	49270	065	Riverside County	193 365
06	49278		Morgan Hill city	37 882
06	49278	085	Santa Clara County	37 882
06	49670		Mountain View city	74 066
06	49670	085	Santa Clara County	74 066
06	50076		Murrieta city	103 466
06	50076	065	Riverside County	103 466
06	50258		Napa city	76 915
06	50258	055	Napa County	76 915
06	50398		National City city	58 582
06	50398	073	San Diego County	58 582
06	50916		Newark city	42 573
06	50916	001	Alameda County	42 573
06	51182		Newport Beach city	85 186
06	51182	059	Orange County	85 186
06	51560		Norco city	27 063
06	51560	065	Riverside County	27 063
06	52526		Norwalk city	105 549
06	52526	037	Los Angeles County	105 549
06	52582		Novato city	51 904
06	52582	041	Marin County	51 904
06	53000		Oakland city	390 724
06	53000	001	Alameda County	390 724
06	53070		Oakley city	35 432
06	53070	013	Contra Costa County	35 432
06	53322		Oceanside city	167 086
06	53322	073	San Diego County	167 086
06	53896		Ontario city	163 924
06	53896	071	San Bernardino County	163 924
06	53980		Orange city	136 416
06	53980	059	Orange County	136 416
06	54652		Oxnard city	197 899
06	54652	111	Ventura County	197 899
06	54806		Pacifica city	37 234
06	54806	081	San Mateo County	37 234
06	55156		Palmdale city	152 750
06	55156	037	Los Angeles County	152 750

Cities by County–*Continued*

State Code	Place Code	County Code	Geographic Area Name	2010 Census Population
06	55184		Palm Desert city	48 445
06	55184	065	Riverside County	48 445
06	55254		Palm Springs city	44 552
06	55254	065	Riverside County	44 552
06	55282		Palo Alto city	64 403
06	55282	085	Santa Clara County	64 403
06	55520		Paradise town	26 218
06	55520	007	Butte County	26 218
06	55618		Paramount city	54 098
06	55618	037	Los Angeles County	54 098
06	56000		Pasadena city	137 122
06	56000	037	Los Angeles County	137 122
06	56700		Perris city	68 386
06	56700	065	Riverside County	68 386
06	56784		Petaluma city	57 941
06	56784	097	Sonoma County	57 941
06	56924		Pico Rivera city	62 942
06	56924	037	Los Angeles County	62 942
06	57456		Pittsburg city	63 264
06	57456	013	Contra Costa County	63 264
06	57526		Placentia city	50 533
06	57526	059	Orange County	50 533
06	57764		Pleasant Hill city	33 152
06	57764	013	Contra Costa County	33 152
06	57792		Pleasanton city	70 285
06	57792	001	Alameda County	70 285
06	58072		Pomona city	149 058
06	58072	037	Los Angeles County	149 058
06	58240		Porterville city	54 165
06	58240	107	Tulare County	54 165
06	58520		Poway city	47 811
06	58520	073	San Diego County	47 811
06	59444		Rancho Cordova city	64 776
06	59444	067	Sacramento County	64 776
06	59451		Rancho Cucamonga city	165 269
06	59451	071	San Bernardino County	165 269
06	59514		Rancho Palos Verdes city	41 643
06	59514	037	Los Angeles County	41 643
06	59587		Rancho Santa Margarita city	47 853
06	59587	059	Orange County	47 853
06	59920		Redding city	89 861
06	59920	089	Shasta County	89 861
06	59962		Redlands city	68 747
06	59962	071	San Bernardino County	68 747
06	60018		Redondo Beach city	66 748
06	60018	037	Los Angeles County	66 748
06	60102		Redwood City city	76 815
06	60102	081	San Mateo County	76 815
06	60466		Rialto city	99 171
06	60466	071	San Bernardino County	99 171
06	60620		Richmond city	103 701
06	60620	013	Contra Costa County	103 701
06	60704		Ridgecrest city	27 616
06	60704	029	Kern County	27 616
06	62000		Riverside city	303 871
06	62000	065	Riverside County	303 871
06	62364		Rocklin city	56 974
06	62364	061	Placer County	56 974
06	62546		Rohnert Park city	40 971
06	62546	097	Sonoma County	40 971
06	62896		Rosemead city	53 764
06	62896	037	Los Angeles County	53 764
06	62938		Roseville city	118 788
06	62938	061	Placer County	118 788
06	64000		Sacramento city	466 488
06	64000	067	Sacramento County	466 488
06	64224		Salinas city	150 441
06	64224	053	Monterey County	150 441
06	65000		San Bernardino city	209 924
06	65000	071	San Bernardino County	209 924
06	65028		San Bruno city	41 114
06	65028	081	San Mateo County	41 114
06	65042		San Buenaventura (Ventura)	106 433
06	65042	111	Ventura County	106 433
06	65070		San Carlos city	28 406
06	65070	081	San Mateo County	28 406
06	65084		San Clemente city	63 522
06	65084	059	Orange County	63 522
06	66000		San Diego city	1 307 402
06	66000	073	San Diego County	1 307 402
06	66070		San Dimas city	33 371
06	66070	037	Los Angeles County	33 371
06	67000		San Francisco city	805 235
06	67000	075	San Francisco County	805 235
06	67042		San Gabriel city	39 718
06	67042	037	Los Angeles County	39 718
06	67112		San Jacinto city	44 199
06	67112	065	Riverside County	44 199
06	68000		San Jose city	945 942
06	68000	085	Santa Clara County	945 942
06	68028		San Juan Capistrano city	34 593
06	68028	059	Orange County	34 593
06	68084		San Leandro city	84 950
06	68084	001	Alameda County	84 950
06	68154		San Luis Obispo city	45 119
06	68154	079	San Luis Obispo County	45 119

Cities by County–*Continued*

State Code	Place Code	County Code	Geographic Area Name	2010 Census Population	State Code	Place Code	County Code	Geographic Area Name	2010 Census Population
06	68196		San Marcos city	83 781	06	75630		Suisun City city	28 111
06	68196	073	San Diego County	83 781	06	75630	095	Solano County	28 111
06	68252		San Mateo city	97 207	06	77000		Sunnyvale city	140 081
06	68252	081	San Mateo County	97 207	06	77000	085	Santa Clara County	140 081
06	68294		San Pablo city	29 139	06	78120		Temecula city	100 097
06	68294	013	Contra Costa County	29 139	06	78120	065	Riverside County	100 097
06	68364		San Rafael city	57 713	06	78148		Temple City city	35 558
06	68364	041	Marin County	57 713	06	78148	037	Los Angeles County	35 558
06	68378		San Ramon city	72 148	06	78582		Thousand Oaks city	126 683
06	68378	013	Contra Costa County	72 148	06	78582	111	Ventura County	126 683
06	69000		Santa Ana city	324 528	06	80000		Torrance city	145 438
06	69000	059	Orange County	324 528	06	80000	037	Los Angeles County	145 438
06	69070		Santa Barbara city	88 410	06	80238		Tracy city	82 922
06	69070	083	Santa Barbara County	88 410	06	80238	077	San Joaquin County	82 922
06	69084		Santa Clara city	116 468	06	80644		Tulare city	59 278
06	69084	085	Santa Clara County	116 468	06	80644	107	Tulare County	59 278
06	69088		Santa Clarita city	176 320	06	80812		Turlock city	68 549
06	69088	037	Los Angeles County	176 320	06	80812	099	Stanislaus County	68 549
06	69112		Santa Cruz city	59 946	06	80854		Tustin city	75 540
06	69112	087	Santa Cruz County	59 946	06	80854	059	Orange County	75 540
06	69196		Santa Maria city	99 553	06	80994		Twentynine Palms city	25 048
06	69196	083	Santa Barbara County	99 553	06	80994	071	San Bernardino County	25 048
06	70000		Santa Monica city	89 736	06	81204		Union City city	69 516
06	70000	037	Los Angeles County	89 736	06	81204	001	Alameda County	69 516
06	70042		Santa Paula city	29 321	06	81344		Upland city	73 732
06	70042	111	Ventura County	29 321	06	81344	071	San Bernardino County	73 732
06	70098		Santa Rosa city	167 815	06	81554		Vacaville city	92 428
06	70098	097	Sonoma County	167 815	06	81554	095	Solano County	92 428
06	70224		Santee city	53 413	06	81666		Vallejo city	115 942
06	70224	073	San Diego County	53 413	06	81666	095	Solano County	115 942
06	70280		Saratoga city	29 926	06	82590		Victorville city	115 903
06	70280	085	Santa Clara County	29 926	06	82590	071	San Bernardino County	115 903
06	70742		Seaside city	33 025	06	82954		Visalia city	124 442
06	70742	053	Monterey County	33 025	06	82954	107	Tulare County	124 442
06	72016		Simi Valley city	124 237	06	82996		Vista city	93 834
06	72016	111	Ventura County	124 237	06	82996	073	San Diego County	93 834
06	72520		Soledad city	25 738	06	83332		Walnut city	29 172
06	72520	053	Monterey County	25 738	06	83332	037	Los Angeles County	29 172
06	73080		South Gate city	94 396	06	83346		Walnut Creek city	64 173
06	73080	037	Los Angeles County	94 396	06	83346	013	Contra Costa County	64 173
06	73220		South Pasadena city	25 619	06	83542		Wasco city	25 545
06	73220	037	Los Angeles County	25 619	06	83542	029	Kern County	25 545
06	73262		South San Francisco city	63 632	06	83668		Watsonville city	51 199
06	73262	081	San Mateo County	63 632	06	83668	087	Santa Cruz County	51 199
06	73962		Stanton city	38 186	06	84200		West Covina city	106 098
06	73962	059	Orange County	38 186	06	84200	037	Los Angeles County	106 098
06	75000		Stockton city	291 707	06	84410		West Hollywood city	34 399
06	75000	077	San Joaquin County	291 707	06	84410	037	Los Angeles County	34 399

Cities by County–*Continued*

State Code	Place Code	County Code	Geographic Area Name	2010 Census Population
06	84550		Westminster city	89 701
06	84550	059	Orange County	89 701
06	84816		West Sacramento city	48 744
06	84816	113	Yolo County	48 744
06	85292		Whittier city	85 331
06	85292	037	Los Angeles County	85 331
06	85446		Wildomar city	32 176
06	85446	065	Riverside County	32 176
06	85922		Windsor town	26 801
06	85922	097	Sonoma County	26 801
06	86328		Woodland city	55 468
06	86328	113	Yolo County	55 468
06	86832		Yorba Linda city	64 234
06	86832	059	Orange County	64 234
06	86972		Yuba City city	64 925
06	86972	101	Sutter County	64 925
06	87042		Yucaipa city	51 367
06	87042	071	San Bernardino County	51 367
08			**COLORADO**	5 029 196
08	03455		Arvada city	106 433
08	03455	001	Adams County	2 849
08	03455	059	Jefferson County	103 584
08	04000		Aurora city	325 078
08	04000	001	Adams County	39 871
08	04000	005	Arapahoe County	285 090
08	04000	035	Douglas County	117
08	07850		Boulder city	97 385
08	07850	013	Boulder County	97 385
08	08675		Brighton city	33 352
08	08675	001	Adams County	33 009
08	08675	123	Weld County	343
08	09280		Broomfield city	55 889
08	09280	014	Broomfield County	55 889
08	12415		Castle Rock town	48 231
08	12415	035	Douglas County	48 231
08	12815		Centennial city	100 377
08	12815	005	Arapahoe County	100 377
08	16000		Colorado Springs city	416 427
08	16000	041	El Paso County	416 427
08	16495		Commerce City city	45 913
08	16495	001	Adams County	45 913
08	20000		Denver city	600 158
08	20000	031	Denver County	600 158
08	24785		Englewood city	30 255
08	24785	005	Arapahoe County	30 255
08	27425		Fort Collins city	143 986
08	27425	069	Larimer County	143 986
08	27865		Fountain city	25 846
08	27865	041	El Paso County	25 846
08	31660		Grand Junction city	58 566
08	31660	077	Mesa County	58 566
08	32155		Greeley city	92 889
08	32155	123	Weld County	92 889
08	43000		Lakewood city	142 980
08	43000	059	Jefferson County	142 980
08	45255		Littleton city	41 737
08	45255	005	Arapahoe County	39 328
08	45255	035	Douglas County	28
08	45255	059	Jefferson County	2 381
08	45970		Longmont city	86 270
08	45970	013	Boulder County	86 240
08	45970	123	Weld County	30
08	46465		Loveland city	66 859
08	46465	069	Larimer County	66 859
08	54330		Northglenn city	35 789
08	54330	001	Adams County	35 777
08	54330	123	Weld County	12
08	57630		Parker town	45 297
08	57630	035	Douglas County	45 297
08	62000		Pueblo city	106 595
08	62000	101	Pueblo County	106 595
08	77290		Thornton city	118 772
08	77290	001	Adams County	118 772
08	77290	123	Weld County	0
08	83835		Westminster city	106 114
08	83835	001	Adams County	63 696
08	83835	059	Jefferson County	42 418
08	84440		Wheat Ridge city	30 166
08	84440	059	Jefferson County	30 166
09			**CONNECTICUT**	3 574 097
09	08000		Bridgeport city	144 229
09	08000	001	Fairfield County	144 229
09	08420		Bristol city	60 477
09	08420	003	Hartford County	60 477
09	18430		Danbury city	80 893
09	18430	001	Fairfield County	80 893
09	37000		Hartford city	124 775
09	37000	003	Hartford County	124 775
09	46450		Meriden city	60 868
09	46450	009	New Haven County	60 868
09	47290		Middletown city	47 648
09	47290	007	Middlesex County	47 648
09	49880		Naugatuck borough	31 862
09	49880	009	New Haven County	31 862
09	50370		New Britain city	73 206
09	50370	003	Hartford County	73 206
09	52000		New Haven city	129 779
09	52000	009	New Haven County	129 779
09	52280		New London city	27 620
09	52280	011	New London County	27 620

Cities by County–*Continued*

State Code	Place Code	County Code	Geographic Area Name	2010 Census Population
09	55990		Norwalk city	85 603
09	55990	001	Fairfield County	85 603
09	56200		Norwich city	40 493
09	56200	011	New London County	40 493
09	68100		Shelton city	39 559
09	68100	001	Fairfield County	39 559
09	73000		Stamford city	122 643
09	73000	001	Fairfield County	122 643
09	76500		Torrington city	36 383
09	76500	005	Litchfield County	36 383
09	80000		Waterbury city	110 366
09	80000	009	New Haven County	110 366
09	82800		West Haven city	55 564
09	82800	009	New Haven County	55 564
10			**DELAWARE**	897 934
10	21200		Dover city	36 047
10	21200	001	Kent County	36 047
10	50670		Newark city	31 454
10	50670	003	New Castle County	31 454
10	77580		Wilmington city	70 851
10	77580	003	New Castle County	70 851
11			**DISTRICT OF COLUMBIA**	601 723
11	50000		Washington city	601 723
11	50000	001	District of Columbia	601 723
12			**FLORIDA**	18 801 310
12	00950		Altamonte Springs city	41 496
12	00950	117	Seminole County	41 496
12	01700		Apopka city	41 542
12	01700	095	Orange County	41 542
12	02681		Aventura city	35 762
12	02681	086	Miami-Dade County	35 762
12	07300		Boca Raton city	84 392
12	07300	099	Palm Beach County	84 392
12	07525		Bonita Springs city	43 914
12	07525	071	Lee County	43 914
12	07875		Boynton Beach city	68 217
12	07875	099	Palm Beach County	68 217
12	07950		Bradenton city	49 546
12	07950	081	Manatee County	49 546
12	10275		Cape Coral city	154 305
12	10275	071	Lee County	154 305
12	11050		Casselberry city	26 241
12	11050	117	Seminole County	26 241
12	12875		Clearwater city	107 685
12	12875	103	Pinellas County	107 685
12	12925		Clermont city	28 742
12	12925	069	Lake County	28 742
12	13275		Coconut Creek city	52 909
12	13275	011	Broward County	52 909
12	14125		Cooper City city	28 547
12	14125	011	Broward County	28 547
12	14250		Coral Gables city	46 780
12	14250	086	Miami-Dade County	46 780
12	14400		Coral Springs city	121 096
12	14400	011	Broward County	121 096
12	15968		Cutler Bay town	40 286
12	15968	086	Miami-Dade County	40 286
12	16335		Dania Beach city	29 639
12	16335	011	Broward County	29 639
12	16475		Davie town	91 992
12	16475	011	Broward County	91 992
12	16525		Daytona Beach city	61 005
12	16525	127	Volusia County	61 005
12	16725		Deerfield Beach city	75 018
12	16725	011	Broward County	75 018
12	16875		DeLand city	27 031
12	16875	127	Volusia County	27 031
12	17100		Delray Beach city	60 522
12	17100	099	Palm Beach County	60 522
12	17200		Deltona city	85 182
12	17200	127	Volusia County	85 182
12	17935		Doral city	45 704
12	17935	086	Miami-Dade County	45 704
12	18575		Dunedin city	35 321
12	18575	103	Pinellas County	35 321
12	24000		Fort Lauderdale city	165 521
12	24000	011	Broward County	165 521
12	24125		Fort Myers city	62 298
12	24125	071	Lee County	62 298
12	24300		Fort Pierce city	41 590
12	24300	111	St. Lucie County	41 590
12	25175		Gainesville city	124 354
12	25175	001	Alachua County	124 354
12	27322		Greenacres city	37 573
12	27322	099	Palm Beach County	37 573
12	28452		Hallandale Beach city	37 113
12	28452	011	Broward County	37 113
12	30000		Hialeah city	224 669
12	30000	086	Miami-Dade County	224 669
12	32000		Hollywood city	140 768
12	32000	011	Broward County	140 768
12	32275		Homestead city	60 512
12	32275	086	Miami-Dade County	60 512
12	35000		Jacksonville city	821 784
12	35000	031	Duval County	821 784
12	35875		Jupiter town	55 156
12	35875	099	Palm Beach County	55 156

Cities by County–*Continued*

State Code	Place Code	County Code	Geographic Area Name	2010 Census Population
12	36950		Kissimmee city	59 682
12	36950	097	Osceola County	59 682
12	38250		Lakeland city	97 422
12	38250	105	Polk County	97 422
12	39075		Lake Worth city	34 910
12	39075	099	Palm Beach County	34 910
12	39425		Largo city	77 648
12	39425	103	Pinellas County	77 648
12	39525		Lauderdale Lakes city	32 593
12	39525	011	Broward County	32 593
12	39550		Lauderhill city	66 887
12	39550	011	Broward County	66 887
12	43125		Margate city	53 284
12	43125	011	Broward County	53 284
12	43975		Melbourne city	76 068
12	43975	009	Brevard County	76 068
12	45000		Miami city	399 457
12	45000	086	Miami-Dade County	399 457
12	45025		Miami Beach city	87 779
12	45025	086	Miami-Dade County	87 779
12	45060		Miami Gardens city	107 167
12	45060	086	Miami-Dade County	107 167
12	45100		Miami Lakes town	29 361
12	45100	086	Miami-Dade County	29 361
12	45975		Miramar city	122 041
12	45975	011	Broward County	122 041
12	49425		North Lauderdale city	41 023
12	49425	011	Broward County	41 023
12	49450		North Miami city	58 786
12	49450	086	Miami-Dade County	58 786
12	49475		North Miami Beach city	41 523
12	49475	086	Miami-Dade County	41 523
12	49675		North Port city	57 357
12	49675	115	Sarasota County	57 357
12	50575		Oakland Park city	41 363
12	50575	011	Broward County	41 363
12	50750		Ocala city	56 315
12	50750	083	Marion County	56 315
12	51075		Ocoee city	35 579
12	51075	095	Orange County	35 579
12	53000		Orlando city	238 300
12	53000	095	Orange County	238 300
12	53150		Ormond Beach city	38 137
12	53150	127	Volusia County	38 137
12	53575		Oviedo city	33 342
12	53575	117	Seminole County	33 342
12	54000		Palm Bay city	103 190
12	54000	009	Brevard County	103 190
12	54075		Palm Beach Gardens city	48 452
12	54075	099	Palm Beach County	48 452
12	54200		Palm Coast city	75 180
12	54200	035	Flagler County	75 180
12	54700		Panama City city	36 484
12	54700	005	Bay County	36 484
12	55775		Pembroke Pines city	154 750
12	55775	011	Broward County	154 750
12	55925		Pensacola city	51 923
12	55925	033	Escambia County	51 923
12	56975		Pinellas Park city	49 079
12	56975	103	Pinellas County	49 079
12	57425		Plantation city	84 955
12	57425	011	Broward County	84 955
12	57550		Plant City city	34 721
12	57550	057	Hillsborough County	34 721
12	58050		Pompano Beach city	99 845
12	58050	011	Broward County	99 845
12	58575		Port Orange city	56 048
12	58575	127	Volusia County	56 048
12	58715		Port St. Lucie city	164 603
12	58715	111	St. Lucie County	164 603
12	60975		Riviera Beach city	32 488
12	60975	099	Palm Beach County	32 488
12	62100		Royal Palm Beach village	34 140
12	62100	099	Palm Beach County	34 140
12	62625		St. Cloud city	35 183
12	62625	097	Osceola County	35 183
12	63000		St. Petersburg city	244 769
12	63000	103	Pinellas County	244 769
12	63650		Sanford city	53 570
12	63650	117	Seminole County	53 570
12	64175		Sarasota city	51 917
12	64175	115	Sarasota County	51 917
12	69700		Sunrise city	84 439
12	69700	011	Broward County	84 439
12	70600		Tallahassee city	181 376
12	70600	073	Leon County	181 376
12	70675		Tamarac city	60 427
12	70675	011	Broward County	60 427
12	71000		Tampa city	335 709
12	71000	057	Hillsborough County	335 709
12	71900		Titusville city	43 761
12	71900	009	Brevard County	43 761
12	75812		Wellington village	56 508
12	75812	099	Palm Beach County	56 508
12	76582		Weston city	65 333
12	76582	011	Broward County	65 333

Cities by County–*Continued*

State Code	Place Code	County Code	Geographic Area Name	2010 Census Population
12	76600		West Palm Beach city	99 919
12	76600	099	Palm Beach County	99 919
12	78250		Winter Garden city	34 568
12	78250	095	Orange County	34 568
12	78275		Winter Haven city	33 874
12	78275	105	Polk County	33 874
12	78300		Winter Park city	27 852
12	78300	095	Orange County	27 852
12	78325		Winter Springs city	33 282
12	78325	117	Seminole County	33 282
13			**GEORGIA**	9 687 653
13	01052		Albany city	77 434
13	01052	095	Dougherty County	77 434
13	01696		Alpharetta city	57 551
13	01696	121	Fulton County	57 551
13	04000		Atlanta city	420 003
13	04000	089	DeKalb County	28 292
13	04000	121	Fulton County	391 711
13	19000		Columbus city	189 885
13	19000	215	Muscogee County	189 885
13	21380		Dalton city	33 128
13	21380	313	Whitfield County	33 128
13	23900		Douglasville city	30 961
13	23900	097	Douglas County	30 961
13	24600		Duluth city	26 600
13	24600	135	Gwinnett County	26 600
13	24768		Dunwoody city	46 267
13	24768	089	DeKalb County	46 267
13	25720		East Point city	33 712
13	25720	121	Fulton County	33 712
13	31908		Gainesville city	33 804
13	31908	139	Hall County	33 804
13	38964		Hinesville city	33 437
13	38964	179	Liberty County	33 437
13	42425		Johns Creek city	76 728
13	42425	121	Fulton County	76 728
13	43192		Kennesaw city	29 783
13	43192	067	Cobb County	29 783
13	44340		LaGrange city	29 588
13	44340	285	Troup County	29 588
13	45488		Lawrenceville city	28 546
13	45488	135	Gwinnett County	28 546
13	49000		Macon city	91 351
13	49000	021	Bibb County	90 885
13	49000	169	Jones County	466
13	49756		Marietta city	56 579
13	49756	067	Cobb County	56 579
13	51670		Milton city	32 661
13	51670	121	Fulton County	32 661
13	55020		Newnan city	33 039
13	55020	077	Coweta County	33 039
13	59724		Peachtree City city	34 364
13	59724	113	Fayette County	34 364
13	66668		Rome city	36 303
13	66668	115	Floyd County	36 303
13	67284		Roswell city	88 346
13	67284	121	Fulton County	88 346
13	68516		Sandy Springs city	93 853
13	68516	121	Fulton County	93 853
13	69000		Savannah city	136 286
13	69000	051	Chatham County	136 286
13	71492		Smyrna city	51 271
13	71492	067	Cobb County	51 271
13	73256		Statesboro city	28 422
13	73256	031	Bulloch County	28 422
13	73704		Stockbridge city	25 636
13	73704	151	Henry County	25 636
13	78800		Valdosta city	54 518
13	78800	185	Lowndes County	54 518
13	80508		Warner Robins city	66 588
13	80508	153	Houston County	66 224
13	80508	225	Peach County	364
15			**HAWAII**	1 360 301
15	06290		East Honolulu CDP	49 914
15	06290	003	Honolulu County	49 914
15	14650		Hilo CDP	43 263
15	14650	001	Hawaii County	43 263
15	22700		Kahului CDP	26 337
15	22700	009	Maui County	26 337
15	23150		Kailua CDP	38 635
15	23150	003	Honolulu County	38 635
15	28250		Kaneohe CDP	34 597
15	28250	003	Honolulu County	34 597
15	51050		Mililani Town CDP	27 629
15	51050	003	Honolulu County	27 629
15	62600		Pearl City CDP	47 698
15	62600	003	Honolulu County	47 698
15	71550		Urban Honolulu CDP	337 256
15	71550	003	Honolulu County	337 256
15	79700		Waipahu CDP	38 216
15	79700	003	Honolulu County	38 216
16			**IDAHO**	1 567 582
16	08830		Boise City city	205 671
16	08830	001	Ada County	205 671
16	12250		Caldwell city	46 237
16	12250	027	Canyon County	46 237
16	16750		Coeur d'Alene city	44 137
16	16750	055	Kootenai County	44 137

Cities by County–*Continued*

State Code	Place Code	County Code	Geographic Area Name	2010 Census Population
16	39700		Idaho Falls city	56 813
16	39700	019	Bonneville County	56 813
16	46540		Lewiston city	31 894
16	46540	069	Nez Perce County	31 894
16	52120		Meridian city	75 092
16	52120	001	Ada County	75 092
16	56260		Nampa city	81 557
16	56260	027	Canyon County	81 557
16	64090		Pocatello city	54 255
16	64090	005	Bannock County	54 239
16	64090	077	Power County	16
16	64810		Post Falls city	27 574
16	64810	055	Kootenai County	27 574
16	67420		Rexburg city	25 484
16	67420	065	Madison County	25 484
16	82810		Twin Falls city	44 125
16	82810	083	Twin Falls County	44 125
17			**ILLINOIS**	12 830 632
17	00243		Addison village	36 942
17	00243	043	DuPage County	36 942
17	00685		Algonquin village	30 046
17	00685	089	Kane County	8 433
17	00685	111	McHenry County	21 613
17	01114		Alton city	27 865
17	01114	119	Madison County	27 865
17	02154		Arlington Heights village	75 101
17	02154	031	Cook County	75 101
17	02154	097	Lake County	0
17	03012		Aurora city	197 899
17	03012	043	DuPage County	49 433
17	03012	089	Kane County	130 976
17	03012	093	Kendall County	6 019
17	03012	197	Will County	11 471
17	04013		Bartlett village	41 208
17	04013	031	Cook County	16 797
17	04013	043	DuPage County	24 411
17	04013	089	Kane County	0
17	04078		Batavia city	26 045
17	04078	043	DuPage County	0
17	04078	089	Kane County	26 045
17	04845		Belleville city	44 478
17	04845	163	St. Clair County	44 478
17	05092		Belvidere city	25 585
17	05092	007	Boone County	25 585
17	05573		Berwyn city	56 657
17	05573	031	Cook County	56 657
17	06613		Bloomington city	76 610
17	06613	113	McLean County	76 610
17	07133		Bolingbrook village	73 366
17	07133	043	DuPage County	1 571
17	07133	197	Will County	71 795
17	09447		Buffalo Grove village	41 496
17	09447	031	Cook County	13 644
17	09447	097	Lake County	27 852
17	09642		Burbank city	28 925
17	09642	031	Cook County	28 925
17	10487		Calumet City city	37 042
17	10487	031	Cook County	37 042
17	11163		Carbondale city	25 902
17	11163	077	Jackson County	25 902
17	11163	199	Williamson County	0
17	11332		Carol Stream village	39 711
17	11332	043	DuPage County	39 711
17	11358		Carpentersville village	37 691
17	11358	089	Kane County	37 691
17	12385		Champaign city	81 055
17	12385	019	Champaign County	81 055
17	14000		Chicago city	2 695 598
17	14000	031	Cook County	2 695 598
17	14000	043	DuPage County	0
17	14026		Chicago Heights city	30 276
17	14026	031	Cook County	30 276
17	14351		Cicero town	83 891
17	14351	031	Cook County	83 891
17	15599		Collinsville city	25 579
17	15599	119	Madison County	22 573
17	15599	163	St. Clair County	3 006
17	17887		Crystal Lake city	40 743
17	17887	111	McHenry County	40 743
17	18563		Danville city	33 027
17	18563	183	Vermilion County	33 027
17	18823		Decatur city	76 122
17	18823	115	Macon County	76 122
17	19161		DeKalb city	43 862
17	19161	037	DeKalb County	43 862
17	19642		Des Plaines city	58 364
17	19642	031	Cook County	58 364
17	20591		Downers Grove village	47 833
17	20591	043	DuPage County	47 833
17	22255		East St. Louis city	27 006
17	22255	163	St. Clair County	27 006
17	23074		Elgin city	108 188
17	23074	031	Cook County	24 032
17	23074	089	Kane County	84 156
17	23256		Elk Grove Village village	33 127
17	23256	031	Cook County	33 127
17	23256	043	DuPage County	0
17	23620		Elmhurst city	44 121
17	23620	031	Cook County	0
17	23620	043	DuPage County	44 121
17	24582		Evanston city	74 486
17	24582	031	Cook County	74 486

Cities by County–*Continued*

State Code	Place Code	County Code	Geographic Area Name	2010 Census Population
17	27884		Freeport city	25 638
17	27884	177	Stephenson County	25 638
17	28326		Galesburg city	32 195
17	28326	095	Knox County	32 195
17	29730		Glendale Heights village	34 208
17	29730	043	DuPage County	34 208
17	29756		Glen Ellyn village	27 450
17	29756	043	DuPage County	27 450
17	29938		Glenview village	44 692
17	29938	031	Cook County	44 692
17	30926		Granite City city	29 849
17	30926	119	Madison County	29 849
17	32018		Gurnee village	31 295
17	32018	097	Lake County	31 295
17	32746		Hanover Park village	37 973
17	32746	031	Cook County	20 636
17	32746	043	DuPage County	17 337
17	33383		Harvey city	25 282
17	33383	031	Cook County	25 282
17	34722		Highland Park city	29 763
17	34722	097	Lake County	29 763
17	35411		Hoffman Estates village	51 895
17	35411	031	Cook County	51 895
17	35411	089	Kane County	0
17	38570		Joliet city	147 433
17	38570	093	Kendall County	9 749
17	38570	197	Will County	137 684
17	38934		Kankakee city	27 537
17	38934	091	Kankakee County	27 537
17	41183		Lake in the Hills village	28 965
17	41183	111	McHenry County	28 965
17	42028		Lansing village	28 331
17	42028	031	Cook County	28 331
17	44407		Lombard village	43 165
17	44407	043	DuPage County	43 165
17	45694		McHenry city	26 992
17	45694	111	McHenry County	26 992
17	48242		Melrose Park village	25 411
17	48242	031	Cook County	25 411
17	49867		Moline city	43 483
17	49867	161	Rock Island County	43 483
17	51089		Mount Prospect village	54 167
17	51089	031	Cook County	54 167
17	51349		Mundelein village	31 064
17	51349	097	Lake County	31 064
17	51622		Naperville city	141 853
17	51622	043	DuPage County	94 533
17	51622	197	Will County	47 320
17	53000		Niles village	29 803
17	53000	031	Cook County	29 803
17	53234		Normal town	52 497
17	53234	113	McLean County	52 497
17	53481		Northbrook village	33 170
17	53481	031	Cook County	33 170
17	53559		North Chicago city	32 574
17	53559	097	Lake County	32 574
17	54638		Oak Forest city	27 962
17	54638	031	Cook County	27 962
17	54820		Oak Lawn village	56 690
17	54820	031	Cook County	56 690
17	54885		Oak Park village	51 878
17	54885	031	Cook County	51 878
17	55249		O'Fallon city	28 281
17	55249	163	St. Clair County	28 281
17	56640		Orland Park village	56 767
17	56640	031	Cook County	56 583
17	56640	197	Will County	184
17	56887		Oswego village	30 355
17	56887	093	Kendall County	30 355
17	57225		Palatine village	68 557
17	57225	031	Cook County	68 557
17	57225	097	Lake County	0
17	57875		Park Ridge city	37 480
17	57875	031	Cook County	37 480
17	58447		Pekin city	34 094
17	58447	143	Peoria County	0
17	58447	179	Tazewell County	34 094
17	59000		Peoria city	115 007
17	59000	143	Peoria County	115 007
17	60287		Plainfield village	39 581
17	60287	093	Kendall County	2 079
17	60287	197	Will County	37 502
17	62367		Quincy city	40 633
17	62367	001	Adams County	40 633
17	65000		Rockford city	152 871
17	65000	201	Winnebago County	152 871
17	65078		Rock Island city	39 018
17	65078	161	Rock Island County	39 018
17	65442		Romeoville village	39 680
17	65442	197	Will County	39 680
17	66040		Round Lake Beach village	28 175
17	66040	097	Lake County	28 175
17	66703		St. Charles city	32 974
17	66703	043	DuPage County	543
17	66703	089	Kane County	32 431
17	68003		Schaumburg village	74 227
17	68003	031	Cook County	74 227
17	68003	043	DuPage County	0
17	70122		Skokie village	64 784
17	70122	031	Cook County	64 784

Cities by County–*Continued*

State Code	Place Code	County Code	Geographic Area Name	2010 Census Population
17	72000		Springfield city	116 250
17	72000	167	Sangamon County	116 250
17	73157		Streamwood village	39 858
17	73157	031	Cook County	39 858
17	75484		Tinley Park village	56 703
17	75484	031	Cook County	49 236
17	75484	197	Will County	7 467
17	77005		Urbana city	41 250
17	77005	019	Champaign County	41 250
17	77694		Vernon Hills village	25 113
17	77694	097	Lake County	25 113
17	79293		Waukegan city	89 078
17	79293	097	Lake County	89 078
17	80060		West Chicago city	27 086
17	80060	043	DuPage County	27 086
17	81048		Wheaton city	52 894
17	81048	043	DuPage County	52 894
17	81087		Wheeling village	37 648
17	81087	031	Cook County	37 642
17	81087	097	Lake County	6
17	82075		Wilmette village	27 087
17	82075	031	Cook County	27 087
17	83245		Woodridge village	32 971
17	83245	031	Cook County	0
17	83245	043	DuPage County	32 949
17	83245	197	Will County	22
18			**INDIANA**	6 483 802
18	01468		Anderson city	56 129
18	01468	095	Madison County	56 129
18	05860		Bloomington city	80 405
18	05860	105	Monroe County	80 405
18	10342		Carmel city	79 191
18	10342	057	Hamilton County	79 191
18	14734		Columbus city	44 061
18	14734	005	Bartholomew County	44 061
18	16138		Crown Point city	27 317
18	16138	089	Lake County	27 317
18	19486		East Chicago city	29 698
18	19486	089	Lake County	29 698
18	20728		Elkhart city	50 949
18	20728	039	Elkhart County	50 949
18	22000		Evansville city	117 429
18	22000	163	Vanderburgh County	117 429
18	23278		Fishers town	76 794
18	23278	057	Hamilton County	76 794
18	25000		Fort Wayne city	253 691
18	25000	003	Allen County	253 691
18	27000		Gary city	80 294
18	27000	089	Lake County	80 294
18	28386		Goshen city	31 719
18	28386	039	Elkhart County	31 719
18	29898		Greenwood city	49 791
18	29898	081	Johnson County	49 791
18	31000		Hammond city	80 830
18	31000	089	Lake County	80 830
18	34114		Hobart city	29 059
18	34114	089	Lake County	29 059
18	38358		Jeffersonville city	44 953
18	38358	019	Clark County	44 953
18	40392		Kokomo city	45 468
18	40392	067	Howard County	45 468
18	40788		Lafayette city	67 140
18	40788	157	Tippecanoe County	67 140
18	42426		Lawrence city	46 001
18	42426	097	Marion County	46 001
18	46908		Marion city	29 948
18	46908	053	Grant County	29 948
18	48528		Merrillville town	35 246
18	48528	089	Lake County	35 246
18	48798		Michigan City city	31 479
18	48798	091	LaPorte County	31 479
18	49932		Mishawaka city	48 252
18	49932	141	St. Joseph County	48 252
18	51876		Muncie city	70 085
18	51876	035	Delaware County	70 085
18	52326		New Albany city	36 372
18	52326	043	Floyd County	36 372
18	54180		Noblesville city	51 969
18	54180	057	Hamilton County	51 969
18	60246		Plainfield town	27 631
18	60246	063	Hendricks County	27 631
18	61092		Portage city	36 828
18	61092	127	Porter County	36 828
18	64260		Richmond city	36 812
18	64260	177	Wayne County	36 812
18	68220		Schererville town	29 243
18	68220	089	Lake County	29 243
18	71000		South Bend city	101 168
18	71000	141	St. Joseph County	101 168
18	75428		Terre Haute city	60 785
18	75428	167	Vigo County	60 785
18	78326		Valparaiso city	31 730
18	78326	127	Porter County	31 730
18	82700		Westfield town	30 068
18	82700	057	Hamilton County	30 068
18	82862		West Lafayette city	29 596
18	82862	157	Tippecanoe County	29 596

Cities by County–*Continued*

State Code	Place Code	County Code	Geographic Area Name	2010 Census Population
19			**IOWA**	3 046 355
19	01855		Ames city	58 965
19	01855	169	Story County	58 965
19	02305		Ankeny city	45 582
19	02305	153	Polk County	45 582
19	06355		Bettendorf city	33 217
19	06355	163	Scott County	33 217
19	09550		Burlington city	25 663
19	09550	057	Des Moines County	25 663
19	11755		Cedar Falls city	39 260
19	11755	013	Black Hawk County	39 260
19	12000		Cedar Rapids city	126 326
19	12000	113	Linn County	126 326
19	14430		Clinton city	26 885
19	14430	045	Clinton County	26 885
19	16860		Council Bluffs city	62 230
19	16860	155	Pottawattamie County	62 230
19	19000		Davenport city	99 685
19	19000	163	Scott County	99 685
19	21000		Des Moines city	203 433
19	21000	153	Polk County	203 419
19	21000	181	Warren County	14
19	22395		Dubuque city	57 637
19	22395	061	Dubuque County	57 637
19	28515		Fort Dodge city	25 206
19	28515	187	Webster County	25 206
19	38595		Iowa City city	67 862
19	38595	103	Johnson County	67 862
19	49485		Marion city	34 768
19	49485	113	Linn County	34 768
19	49755		Marshalltown city	27 552
19	49755	127	Marshall County	27 552
19	50160		Mason City city	28 079
19	50160	033	Cerro Gordo County	28 079
19	60465		Ottumwa city	25 023
19	60465	179	Wapello County	25 023
19	73335		Sioux City city	82 684
19	73335	149	Plymouth County	6
19	73335	193	Woodbury County	82 678
19	79950		Urbandale city	39 463
19	79950	049	Dallas County	6 337
19	79950	153	Polk County	33 126
19	82425		Waterloo city	68 406
19	82425	013	Black Hawk County	68 406
19	83910		West Des Moines city	56 609
19	83910	049	Dallas County	11 569
19	83910	153	Polk County	44 999
19	83910	181	Warren County	41
20			**KANSAS**	2 853 118
20	18250		Dodge City city	27 340
20	18250	057	Ford County	27 340
20	25325		Garden City city	26 658
20	25325	055	Finney County	26 658
20	33625		Hutchinson city	42 080
20	33625	155	Reno County	42 080
20	36000		Kansas City city	145 786
20	36000	209	Wyandotte County	145 786
20	38900		Lawrence city	87 643
20	38900	045	Douglas County	87 643
20	39000		Leavenworth city	35 251
20	39000	103	Leavenworth County	35 251
20	39075		Leawood city	31 867
20	39075	091	Johnson County	31 867
20	39350		Lenexa city	48 190
20	39350	091	Johnson County	48 190
20	44250		Manhattan city	52 281
20	44250	149	Pottawatomie County	146
20	44250	161	Riley County	52 135
20	52575		Olathe city	125 872
20	52575	091	Johnson County	125 872
20	53775		Overland Park city	173 372
20	53775	091	Johnson County	173 372
20	62700		Salina city	47 707
20	62700	169	Saline County	47 707
20	64500		Shawnee city	62 209
20	64500	091	Johnson County	62 209
20	71000		Topeka city	127 473
20	71000	177	Shawnee County	127 473
20	79000		Wichita city	382 368
20	79000	173	Sedgwick County	382 368
21			**KENTUCKY**	4 339 367
21	08902		Bowling Green city	58 067
21	08902	227	Warren County	58 067
21	17848		Covington city	40 640
21	17848	117	Kenton County	40 640
21	24274		Elizabethtown city	28 531
21	24274	093	Hardin County	28 531
21	27982		Florence city	29 951
21	27982	015	Boone County	29 951
21	28900		Frankfort city	25 527
21	28900	073	Franklin County	25 527
21	30700		Georgetown city	29 098
21	30700	209	Scott County	29 098
21	35866		Henderson city	28 757
21	35866	101	Henderson County	28 757
21	37918		Hopkinsville city	31 577
21	37918	047	Christian County	31 577
21	40222		Jeffersontown city	26 595
21	40222	111	Jefferson County	26 595

Cities by County–*Continued*

State Code	Place Code	County Code	Geographic Area Name	2010 Census Population
21	46027		Lexington-Fayette urban county	295 803
21	46027	067	Fayette County	295 803
21	56136		Nicholasville city	28 015
21	56136	113	Jessamine County	28 015
21	58620		Owensboro city	57 265
21	58620	059	Daviess County	57 265
21	58836		Paducah city	25 024
21	58836	145	McCracken County	25 024
21	65226		Richmond city	31 364
21	65226	151	Madison County	31 364
22			**LOUISIANA**	4 533 372
22	00975		Alexandria city	47 723
22	00975	079	Rapides Parish	47 723
22	05000		Baton Rouge city	229 493
22	05000	033	East Baton Rouge Parish	229 493
22	08920		Bossier City city	61 315
22	08920	015	Bossier Parish	61 315
22	13960		Central city	26 864
22	13960	033	East Baton Rouge Parish	26 864
22	36255		Houma city	33 727
22	36255	109	Terrebonne Parish	33 727
22	39475		Kenner city	66 702
22	39475	051	Jefferson Parish	66 702
22	40735		Lafayette city	120 623
22	40735	055	Lafayette Parish	120 623
22	41155		Lake Charles city	71 993
22	41155	019	Calcasieu Parish	71 993
22	51410		Monroe city	48 815
22	51410	073	Ouachita Parish	48 815
22	54035		New Iberia city	30 617
22	54035	045	Iberia Parish	30 617
22	55000		New Orleans city	343 829
22	55000	071	Orleans Parish	343 829
22	70000		Shreveport city	199 311
22	70000	015	Bossier Parish	2 702
22	70000	017	Caddo Parish	196 609
22	70805		Slidell city	27 068
22	70805	103	St. Tammany Parish	27 068
23			**MAINE**	1 328 361
23	02795		Bangor city	33 039
23	02795	019	Penobscot County	33 039
23	38740		Lewiston city	36 592
23	38740	001	Androscoggin County	36 592
23	60545		Portland city	66 194
23	60545	005	Cumberland County	66 194
23	71990		South Portland city	25 002
23	71990	005	Cumberland County	25 002
24			**MARYLAND**	5 773 552
24	01600		Annapolis city	38 394
24	01600	003	Anne Arundel County	38 394
24	04000		Baltimore city	620 961
24	04000	510	Baltimore city	620 961
24	08775		Bowie city	54 727
24	08775	033	Prince George's County	54 727
24	18750		College Park city	30 413
24	18750	033	Prince George's County	30 413
24	30325		Frederick city	65 239
24	30325	021	Frederick County	65 239
24	31175		Gaithersburg city	59 933
24	31175	031	Montgomery County	59 933
24	36075		Hagerstown city	39 662
24	36075	043	Washington County	39 662
24	45900		Laurel city	25 115
24	45900	033	Prince George's County	25 115
24	67675		Rockville city	61 209
24	67675	031	Montgomery County	61 209
24	69925		Salisbury city	30 343
24	69925	045	Wicomico County	30 343
25			**MASSACHUSETTS**	6 547 629
25	00840		Agawam Town city	28 438
25	00840	013	Hampden County	28 438
25	02690		Attleboro city	43 593
25	02690	005	Bristol County	43 593
25	03690		Barnstable Town city	45 193
25	03690	001	Barnstable County	45 193
25	05595		Beverly city	39 502
25	05595	009	Essex County	39 502
25	07000		Boston city	617 594
25	07000	025	Suffolk County	617 594
25	07740		Braintree Town city	35 744
25	07740	021	Norfolk County	35 744
25	09000		Brockton city	93 810
25	09000	023	Plymouth County	93 810
25	11000		Cambridge city	105 162
25	11000	017	Middlesex County	105 162
25	13205		Chelsea city	35 177
25	13205	025	Suffolk County	35 177
25	13660		Chicopee city	55 298
25	13660	013	Hampden County	55 298
25	21990		Everett city	41 667
25	21990	017	Middlesex County	41 667
25	23000		Fall River city	88 857
25	23000	005	Bristol County	88 857
25	23875		Fitchburg city	40 318
25	23875	027	Worcester County	40 318
25	25172		Franklin Town city	31 635
25	25172	021	Norfolk County	31 635
25	26150		Gloucester city	28 789
25	26150	009	Essex County	28 789

Cities by County–*Continued*

State Code	Place Code	County Code	Geographic Area Name	2010 Census Population
25	29405		Haverhill city	60 879
25	29405	009	Essex County	60 879
25	30840		Holyoke city	39 880
25	30840	013	Hampden County	39 880
25	34550		Lawrence city	76 377
25	34550	009	Essex County	76 377
25	35075		Leominster city	40 759
25	35075	027	Worcester County	40 759
25	37000		Lowell city	106 519
25	37000	017	Middlesex County	106 519
25	37490		Lynn city	90 329
25	37490	009	Essex County	90 329
25	37875		Malden city	59 450
25	37875	017	Middlesex County	59 450
25	38715		Marlborough city	38 499
25	38715	017	Middlesex County	38 499
25	39835		Medford city	56 173
25	39835	017	Middlesex County	56 173
25	40115		Melrose city	26 983
25	40115	017	Middlesex County	26 983
25	40710		Methuen Town city	47 255
25	40710	009	Essex County	47 255
25	45000		New Bedford city	95 072
25	45000	005	Bristol County	95 072
25	45560		Newton city	85 146
25	45560	017	Middlesex County	85 146
25	46330		Northampton city	28 549
25	46330	015	Hampshire County	28 549
25	52490		Peabody city	51 251
25	52490	009	Essex County	51 251
25	53960		Pittsfield city	44 737
25	53960	003	Berkshire County	44 737
25	55745		Quincy city	92 271
25	55745	021	Norfolk County	92 271
25	56585		Revere city	51 755
25	56585	025	Suffolk County	51 755
25	59105		Salem city	41 340
25	59105	009	Essex County	41 340
25	62535		Somerville city	75 754
25	62535	017	Middlesex County	75 754
25	67000		Springfield city	153 060
25	67000	013	Hampden County	153 060
25	69170		Taunton city	55 874
25	69170	005	Bristol County	55 874
25	72600		Waltham city	60 632
25	72600	017	Middlesex County	60 632
25	73440		Watertown Town city	31 915
25	73440	017	Middlesex County	31 915
25	76030		Westfield city	41 094
25	76030	013	Hampden County	41 094
25	77890		West Springfield Town city	28 391
25	77890	013	Hampden County	28 391
25	78972		Weymouth Town city	53 743
25	78972	021	Norfolk County	53 743
25	81035		Woburn city	38 120
25	81035	017	Middlesex County	38 120
25	82000		Worcester city	181 045
25	82000	027	Worcester County	181 045
26			**MICHIGAN**	9 883 640
26	01380		Allen Park city	28 210
26	01380	163	Wayne County	28 210
26	03000		Ann Arbor city	113 934
26	03000	161	Washtenaw County	113 934
26	05920		Battle Creek city	52 347
26	05920	025	Calhoun County	52 347
26	06020		Bay City city	34 932
26	06020	017	Bay County	34 932
26	12060		Burton city	29 999
26	12060	049	Genesee County	29 999
26	21000		Dearborn city	98 153
26	21000	163	Wayne County	98 153
26	21020		Dearborn Heights city	57 774
26	21020	163	Wayne County	57 774
26	22000		Detroit city	713 777
26	22000	163	Wayne County	713 777
26	24120		East Lansing city	48 579
26	24120	037	Clinton County	1 969
26	24120	065	Ingham County	46 610
26	24290		Eastpointe city	32 442
26	24290	099	Macomb County	32 442
26	27440		Farmington Hills city	79 740
26	27440	125	Oakland County	79 740
26	29000		Flint city	102 434
26	29000	049	Genesee County	102 434
26	31420		Garden City city	27 692
26	31420	163	Wayne County	27 692
26	34000		Grand Rapids city	188 040
26	34000	081	Kent County	188 040
26	38640		Holland city	33 051
26	38640	005	Allegan County	7 016
26	38640	139	Ottawa County	26 035
26	40680		Inkster city	25 369
26	40680	163	Wayne County	25 369
26	41420		Jackson city	33 534
26	41420	075	Jackson County	33 534
26	42160		Kalamazoo city	74 262
26	42160	077	Kalamazoo County	74 262

Cities by County–*Continued*

State Code	Place Code	County Code	Geographic Area Name	2010 Census Population
26	42820		Kentwood city	48 707
26	42820	081	Kent County	48 707
26	46000		Lansing city	114 297
26	46000	045	Eaton County	4 734
26	46000	065	Ingham County	109 563
26	47800		Lincoln Park city	38 144
26	47800	163	Wayne County	38 144
26	49000		Livonia city	96 942
26	49000	163	Wayne County	96 942
26	50560		Madison Heights city	29 694
26	50560	125	Oakland County	29 694
26	53780		Midland city	41 863
26	53780	017	Bay County	157
26	53780	111	Midland County	41 706
26	56020		Mount Pleasant city	26 016
26	56020	073	Isabella County	26 016
26	56320		Muskegon city	38 401
26	56320	121	Muskegon County	38 401
26	59440		Novi city	55 224
26	59440	125	Oakland County	55 224
26	59920		Oak Park city	29 319
26	59920	125	Oakland County	29 319
26	65440		Pontiac city	59 515
26	65440	125	Oakland County	59 515
26	65560		Portage city	46 292
26	65560	077	Kalamazoo County	46 292
26	65820		Port Huron city	30 184
26	65820	147	St. Clair County	30 184
26	69035		Rochester Hills city	70 995
26	69035	125	Oakland County	70 995
26	69800		Roseville city	47 299
26	69800	099	Macomb County	47 299
26	70040		Royal Oak city	57 236
26	70040	125	Oakland County	57 236
26	70520		Saginaw city	51 508
26	70520	145	Saginaw County	51 508
26	70760		St. Clair Shores city	59 715
26	70760	099	Macomb County	59 715
26	74900		Southfield city	71 739
26	74900	125	Oakland County	71 739
26	74960		Southgate city	30 047
26	74960	163	Wayne County	30 047
26	76460		Sterling Heights city	129 699
26	76460	099	Macomb County	129 699
26	79000		Taylor city	63 131
26	79000	163	Wayne County	63 131
26	80700		Troy city	80 980
26	80700	125	Oakland County	80 980
26	84000		Warren city	134 056
26	84000	099	Macomb County	134 056
26	86000		Westland city	84 094
26	86000	163	Wayne County	84 094
26	88900		Wyandotte city	25 883
26	88900	163	Wayne County	25 883
26	88940		Wyoming city	72 125
26	88940	081	Kent County	72 125
27			**MINNESOTA**	5 303 925
27	01486		Andover city	30 598
27	01486	003	Anoka County	30 598
27	01900		Apple Valley city	49 084
27	01900	037	Dakota County	49 084
27	06382		Blaine city	57 186
27	06382	003	Anoka County	57 186
27	06382	123	Ramsey County	0
27	06616		Bloomington city	82 893
27	06616	053	Hennepin County	82 893
27	07948		Brooklyn Center city	30 104
27	07948	053	Hennepin County	30 104
27	07966		Brooklyn Park city	75 781
27	07966	053	Hennepin County	75 781
27	08794		Burnsville city	60 306
27	08794	037	Dakota County	60 306
27	13114		Coon Rapids city	61 476
27	13114	003	Anoka County	61 476
27	13456		Cottage Grove city	34 589
27	13456	163	Washington County	34 589
27	17000		Duluth city	86 265
27	17000	137	St. Louis County	86 265
27	17288		Eagan city	64 206
27	17288	037	Dakota County	64 206
27	18116		Eden Prairie city	60 797
27	18116	053	Hennepin County	60 797
27	18188		Edina city	47 941
27	18188	053	Hennepin County	47 941
27	22814		Fridley city	27 208
27	22814	003	Anoka County	27 208
27	31076		Inver Grove Heights city	33 880
27	31076	037	Dakota County	33 880
27	35180		Lakeville city	55 954
27	35180	037	Dakota County	55 954
27	39878		Mankato city	39 309
27	39878	013	Blue Earth County	39 305
27	39878	079	Le Sueur County	4
27	39878	103	Nicollet County	0
27	40166		Maple Grove city	61 567
27	40166	053	Hennepin County	61 567
27	40382		Maplewood city	38 018
27	40382	123	Ramsey County	38 018

Cities by County–*Continued*

State Code	Place Code	County Code	Geographic Area Name	2010 Census Population
27	43000		Minneapolis city	382 578
27	43000	053	Hennepin County	382 578
27	43252		Minnetonka city	49 734
27	43252	053	Hennepin County	49 734
27	43864		Moorhead city	38 065
27	43864	027	Clay County	38 065
27	47680		Oakdale city	27 378
27	47680	163	Washington County	27 378
27	49300		Owatonna city	25 599
27	49300	147	Steele County	25 599
27	51730		Plymouth city	70 576
27	51730	053	Hennepin County	70 576
27	54214		Richfield city	35 228
27	54214	053	Hennepin County	35 228
27	54880		Rochester city	106 769
27	54880	109	Olmsted County	106 769
27	55852		Roseville city	33 660
27	55852	123	Ramsey County	33 660
27	56896		St. Cloud city	65 842
27	56896	009	Benton County	6 396
27	56896	141	Sherburne County	6 785
27	56896	145	Stearns County	52 661
27	57220		St. Louis Park city	45 250
27	57220	053	Hennepin County	45 250
27	58000		St. Paul city	285 068
27	58000	123	Ramsey County	285 068
27	58738		Savage city	26 911
27	58738	139	Scott County	26 911
27	59350		Shakopee city	37 076
27	59350	139	Scott County	37 076
27	59998		Shoreview city	25 043
27	59998	123	Ramsey County	25 043
27	71032		Winona city	27 592
27	71032	169	Winona County	27 592
27	71428		Woodbury city	61 961
27	71428	163	Washington County	61 961
28			**MISSISSIPPI**	2 967 297
28	06220		Biloxi city	44 054
28	06220	047	Harrison County	44 054
28	14420		Clinton city	25 216
28	14420	049	Hinds County	25 216
28	29180		Greenville city	34 400
28	29180	151	Washington County	34 400
28	29700		Gulfport city	67 793
28	29700	047	Harrison County	67 793
28	31020		Hattiesburg city	45 989
28	31020	035	Forrest County	41 000
28	31020	073	Lamar County	4 989
28	33700		Horn Lake city	26 066
28	33700	033	DeSoto County	26 066
28	36000		Jackson city	173 514
28	36000	049	Hinds County	172 891
28	36000	089	Madison County	622
28	36000	121	Rankin County	1
28	46640		Meridian city	41 148
28	46640	075	Lauderdale County	41 148
28	54040		Olive Branch city	33 484
28	54040	033	DeSoto County	33 484
28	55760		Pearl city	25 092
28	55760	121	Rankin County	25 092
28	69280		Southaven city	48 982
28	69280	033	DeSoto County	48 982
28	74840		Tupelo city	34 546
28	74840	081	Lee County	34 546
29			**MISSOURI**	5 988 927
29	03160		Ballwin city	30 404
29	03160	189	St. Louis County	30 404
29	06652		Blue Springs city	52 575
29	06652	095	Jackson County	52 575
29	11242		Cape Girardeau city	37 941
29	11242	031	Cape Girardeau County	37 941
29	11242	201	Scott County	0
29	13600		Chesterfield city	47 484
29	13600	189	St. Louis County	47 484
29	15670		Columbia city	108 500
29	15670	019	Boone County	108 500
29	24778		Florissant city	52 158
29	24778	189	St. Louis County	52 158
29	27190		Gladstone city	25 410
29	27190	047	Clay County	25 410
29	31276		Hazelwood city	25 703
29	31276	189	St. Louis County	25 703
29	35000		Independence city	116 830
29	35000	047	Clay County	0
29	35000	095	Jackson County	116 830
29	37000		Jefferson City city	43 079
29	37000	027	Callaway County	22
29	37000	051	Cole County	43 057
29	37592		Joplin city	50 150
29	37592	097	Jasper County	43 955
29	37592	145	Newton County	6 195
29	38000		Kansas City city	459 787
29	38000	037	Cass County	197
29	38000	047	Clay County	113 415
29	38000	095	Jackson County	302 499
29	38000	165	Platte County	43 676
29	39044		Kirkwood city	27 540
29	39044	189	St. Louis County	27 540
29	41348		Lee's Summit city	91 364
29	41348	037	Cass County	1 917
29	41348	095	Jackson County	89 447

Cities by County–*Continued*

State Code	Place Code	County Code	Geographic Area Name	2010 Census Population
29	42032		Liberty city	29 149
29	42032	047	Clay County	29 149
29	46586		Maryland Heights city	27 472
29	46586	189	St. Louis County	27 472
29	54074		O'Fallon city	79 329
29	54074	183	St. Charles County	79 329
29	60788		Raytown city	29 526
29	60788	095	Jackson County	29 526
29	64082		St. Charles city	65 794
29	64082	183	St. Charles County	65 794
29	64550		St. Joseph city	76 780
29	64550	021	Buchanan County	76 780
29	65000		St. Louis city	319 294
29	65000	510	St. Louis city	319 294
29	65126		St. Peters city	52 575
29	65126	183	St. Charles County	52 575
29	70000		Springfield city	159 498
29	70000	043	Christian County	2
29	70000	077	Greene County	159 496
29	75220		University City city	35 371
29	75220	189	St. Louis County	35 371
29	78442		Wentzville city	29 070
29	78442	183	St. Charles County	29 070
29	79820		Wildwood city	35 517
29	79820	189	St. Louis County	35 517
30			**MONTANA**	989 415
30	06550		Billings city	104 170
30	06550	111	Yellowstone County	104 170
30	08950		Bozeman city	37 280
30	08950	031	Gallatin County	37 280
30	32800		Great Falls city	58 505
30	32800	013	Cascade County	58 505
30	35600		Helena city	28 190
30	35600	049	Lewis and Clark County	28 190
30	50200		Missoula city	66 788
30	50200	063	Missoula County	66 788
31			**NEBRASKA**	1 826 341
31	03950		Bellevue city	50 137
31	03950	153	Sarpy County	50 137
31	17670		Fremont city	26 397
31	17670	053	Dodge County	26 397
31	19595		Grand Island city	48 520
31	19595	079	Hall County	48 520
31	25055		Kearney city	30 787
31	25055	019	Buffalo County	30 787
31	28000		Lincoln city	258 379
31	28000	109	Lancaster County	258 379
31	37000		Omaha city	408 958
31	37000	055	Douglas County	408 958
32			**NEVADA**	2 700 551
32	09700		Carson City	55 274
32	09700	510	Carson City	55 274
32	31900		Henderson city	257 729
32	31900	003	Clark County	257 729
32	40000		Las Vegas city	583 756
32	40000	003	Clark County	583 756
32	51800		North Las Vegas city	216 961
32	51800	003	Clark County	216 961
32	60600		Reno city	225 221
32	60600	031	Washoe County	225 221
32	68400		Sparks city	90 264
32	68400	031	Washoe County	90 264
33			**NEW HAMPSHIRE**	1 316 470
33	14200		Concord city	42 695
33	14200	013	Merrimack County	42 695
33	18820		Dover city	29 987
33	18820	017	Strafford County	29 987
33	45140		Manchester city	109 565
33	45140	011	Hillsborough County	109 565
33	50260		Nashua city	86 494
33	50260	011	Hillsborough County	86 494
33	65140		Rochester city	29 752
33	65140	017	Strafford County	29 752
34			**NEW JERSEY**	8 791 894
34	02080		Atlantic City city	39 558
34	02080	001	Atlantic County	39 558
34	03580		Bayonne city	63 024
34	03580	017	Hudson County	63 024
34	05170		Bergenfield borough	26 764
34	05170	003	Bergen County	26 764
34	07600		Bridgeton city	25 349
34	07600	011	Cumberland County	25 349
34	10000		Camden city	77 344
34	10000	007	Camden County	77 344
34	13690		Clifton city	84 136
34	13690	031	Passaic County	84 136
34	19390		East Orange city	64 270
34	19390	013	Essex County	64 270
34	21000		Elizabeth city	124 969
34	21000	039	Union County	124 969
34	21480		Englewood city	27 147
34	21480	003	Bergen County	27 147
34	22470		Fair Lawn borough	32 457
34	22470	003	Bergen County	32 457
34	24420		Fort Lee borough	35 345
34	24420	003	Bergen County	35 345
34	25770		Garfield city	30 487
34	25770	003	Bergen County	30 487

Cities by County–*Continued*

State Code	Place Code	County Code	Geographic Area Name	2010 Census Population
34	28680		Hackensack city	43 010
34	28680	003	Bergen County	43 010
34	32250		Hoboken city	50 005
34	32250	017	Hudson County	50 005
34	36000		Jersey City city	247 597
34	36000	017	Hudson County	247 597
34	36510		Kearny town	40 684
34	36510	017	Hudson County	40 684
34	40350		Linden city	40 499
34	40350	039	Union County	40 499
34	41310		Long Branch city	30 719
34	41310	025	Monmouth County	30 719
34	46680		Millville city	28 400
34	46680	011	Cumberland County	28 400
34	51000		Newark city	277 140
34	51000	013	Essex County	277 140
34	51210		New Brunswick city	55 181
34	51210	023	Middlesex County	55 181
34	55950		Paramus borough	26 342
34	55950	003	Bergen County	26 342
34	56550		Passaic city	69 781
34	56550	031	Passaic County	69 781
34	57000		Paterson city	146 199
34	57000	031	Passaic County	146 199
34	58200		Perth Amboy city	50 814
34	58200	023	Middlesex County	50 814
34	59190		Plainfield city	49 808
34	59190	039	Union County	49 808
34	61530		Rahway city	27 346
34	61530	039	Union County	27 346
34	65790		Sayreville borough	42 704
34	65790	023	Middlesex County	42 704
34	74000		Trenton city	84 913
34	74000	021	Mercer County	84 913
34	74630		Union City city	66 455
34	74630	017	Hudson County	66 455
34	76070		Vineland city	60 724
34	76070	011	Cumberland County	60 724
34	79040		Westfield town	30 316
34	79040	039	Union County	30 316
34	79610		West New York town	49 708
34	79610	017	Hudson County	49 708
35			**NEW MEXICO**	2 059 179
35	01780		Alamogordo city	30 403
35	01780	035	Otero County	30 403
35	02000		Albuquerque city	545 852
35	02000	001	Bernalillo County	545 852
35	12150		Carlsbad city	26 138
35	12150	015	Eddy County	26 138
35	16420		Clovis city	37 775
35	16420	009	Curry County	37 775
35	25800		Farmington city	45 877
35	25800	045	San Juan County	45 877
35	32520		Hobbs city	34 122
35	32520	025	Lea County	34 122
35	39380		Las Cruces city	97 618
35	39380	013	Doña Ana County	97 618
35	63460		Rio Rancho city	87 521
35	63460	001	Bernalillo County	130
35	63460	043	Sandoval County	87 391
35	64930		Roswell city	48 366
35	64930	005	Chaves County	48 366
35	70500		Santa Fe city	67 947
35	70500	049	Santa Fe County	67 947
36			**NEW YORK**	19 378 102
36	01000		Albany city	97 856
36	01000	001	Albany County	97 856
36	03078		Auburn city	27 687
36	03078	011	Cayuga County	27 687
36	06607		Binghamton city	47 376
36	06607	007	Broome County	47 376
36	11000		Buffalo city	261 310
36	11000	029	Erie County	261 310
36	24229		Elmira city	29 200
36	24229	015	Chemung County	29 200
36	27485		Freeport village	42 860
36	27485	059	Nassau County	42 860
36	29113		Glen Cove city	26 964
36	29113	059	Nassau County	26 964
36	32402		Harrison village	27 472
36	32402	119	Westchester County	27 472
36	33139		Hempstead village	53 891
36	33139	059	Nassau County	53 891
36	38077		Ithaca city	30 014
36	38077	109	Tompkins County	30 014
36	38264		Jamestown city	31 146
36	38264	013	Chautauqua County	31 146
36	42554		Lindenhurst village	27 253
36	42554	103	Suffolk County	27 253
36	43335		Long Beach city	33 275
36	43335	059	Nassau County	33 275
36	47042		Middletown city	28 086
36	47042	071	Orange County	28 086
36	49121		Mount Vernon city	67 292
36	49121	119	Westchester County	67 292
36	50034		Newburgh city	28 866
36	50034	071	Orange County	28 866

Cities by County–*Continued*

State Code	Place Code	County Code	Geographic Area Name	2010 Census Population
36	50617		New Rochelle city	77 062
36	50617	119	Westchester County	77 062
36	51000		New York city	8 175 133
36	51000	005	Bronx County	1 385 108
36	51000	047	Kings County	2 504 700
36	51000	061	New York County	1 585 873
36	51000	081	Queens County	2 230 722
36	51000	085	Richmond County	468 730
36	51055		Niagara Falls city	50 193
36	51055	063	Niagara County	50 193
36	53682		North Tonawanda city	31 568
36	53682	063	Niagara County	31 568
36	55530		Ossining village	25 060
36	55530	119	Westchester County	25 060
36	59223		Port Chester village	28 967
36	59223	119	Westchester County	28 967
36	59641		Poughkeepsie city	32 736
36	59641	027	Dutchess County	32 736
36	63000		Rochester city	210 565
36	63000	055	Monroe County	210 565
36	63418		Rome city	33 725
36	63418	065	Oneida County	33 725
36	65255		Saratoga Springs city	26 586
36	65255	091	Saratoga County	26 586
36	65508		Schenectady city	66 135
36	65508	093	Schenectady County	66 135
36	70420		Spring Valley village	31 347
36	70420	087	Rockland County	31 347
36	73000		Syracuse city	145 170
36	73000	067	Onondaga County	145 170
36	75484		Troy city	50 129
36	75484	083	Rensselaer County	50 129
36	76540		Utica city	62 235
36	76540	065	Oneida County	62 235
36	76705		Valley Stream village	37 511
36	76705	059	Nassau County	37 511
36	78608		Watertown city	27 023
36	78608	045	Jefferson County	27 023
36	81677		White Plains city	56 853
36	81677	119	Westchester County	56 853
37			**NORTH CAROLINA**	9 535 483
37	01520		Apex town	37 476
37	01520	183	Wake County	37 476
37	02080		Asheboro city	25 012
37	02080	151	Randolph County	25 012
37	02140		Asheville city	83 393
37	02140	021	Buncombe County	83 393
37	09060		Burlington city	49 963
37	09060	001	Alamance County	49 308
37	09060	081	Guilford County	655

State Code	Place Code	County Code	Geographic Area Name	2010 Census Population
37	10740		Cary town	135 234
37	10740	037	Chatham County	1 422
37	10740	183	Wake County	133 812
37	11800		Chapel Hill town	57 233
37	11800	063	Durham County	2 836
37	11800	135	Orange County	54 397
37	12000		Charlotte city	731 424
37	12000	119	Mecklenburg County	731 424
37	14100		Concord city	79 066
37	14100	025	Cabarrus County	79 066
37	19000		Durham city	228 330
37	19000	063	Durham County	228 300
37	19000	135	Orange County	30
37	19000	183	Wake County	0
37	22920		Fayetteville city	200 564
37	22920	051	Cumberland County	200 564
37	25480		Garner town	25 745
37	25480	183	Wake County	25 745
37	25580		Gastonia city	71 741
37	25580	071	Gaston County	71 741
37	26880		Goldsboro city	36 437
37	26880	191	Wayne County	36 437
37	28000		Greensboro city	269 666
37	28000	081	Guilford County	269 666
37	28080		Greenville city	84 554
37	28080	147	Pitt County	84 554
37	31060		Hickory city	40 010
37	31060	023	Burke County	66
37	31060	027	Caldwell County	18
37	31060	035	Catawba County	39 926
37	31400		High Point city	104 371
37	31400	057	Davidson County	5 310
37	31400	067	Forsyth County	8
37	31400	081	Guilford County	99 042
37	31400	151	Randolph County	11
37	33120		Huntersville town	46 773
37	33120	119	Mecklenburg County	46 773
37	33560		Indian Trail town	33 518
37	33560	179	Union County	33 518
37	34200		Jacksonville city	70 145
37	34200	133	Onslow County	70 145
37	35200		Kannapolis city	42 625
37	35200	025	Cabarrus County	33 194
37	35200	159	Rowan County	9 431
37	41960		Matthews town	27 198
37	41960	119	Mecklenburg County	27 198
37	43920		Monroe city	32 797
37	43920	179	Union County	32 797
37	44220		Mooresville town	32 711
37	44220	097	Iredell County	32 711
37	46340		New Bern city	29 524
37	46340	049	Craven County	29 524

Cities by County–*Continued*

State Code	Place Code	County Code	Geographic Area Name	2010 Census Population
37	55000		Raleigh city	403 892
37	55000	063	Durham County	1 067
37	55000	183	Wake County	402 825
37	57500		Rocky Mount city	57 477
37	57500	065	Edgecombe County	17 524
37	57500	127	Nash County	39 953
37	58860		Salisbury city	33 662
37	58860	159	Rowan County	33 662
37	59280		Sanford city	28 094
37	59280	105	Lee County	28 094
37	67420		Thomasville city	26 757
37	67420	057	Davidson County	26 493
37	67420	151	Randolph County	264
37	70540		Wake Forest town	30 117
37	70540	069	Franklin County	899
37	70540	183	Wake County	29 218
37	74440		Wilmington city	106 476
37	74440	129	New Hanover County	106 476
37	74540		Wilson city	49 167
37	74540	195	Wilson County	49 167
37	75000		Winston-Salem city	229 617
37	75000	067	Forsyth County	229 617
38			**NORTH DAKOTA**	672 591
38	07200		Bismarck city	61 272
38	07200	015	Burleigh County	61 272
38	25700		Fargo city	105 549
38	25700	017	Cass County	105 549
38	32060		Grand Forks city	52 838
38	32060	035	Grand Forks County	52 838
38	53380		Minot city	40 888
38	53380	101	Ward County	40 888
38	84780		West Fargo city	25 830
38	84780	017	Cass County	25 830
39			**OHIO**	11 536 504
39	01000		Akron city	199 110
39	01000	153	Summit County	199 110
39	03828		Barberton city	26 550
39	03828	153	Summit County	26 550
39	04720		Beavercreek city	45 193
39	04720	057	Greene County	45 193
39	07972		Bowling Green city	30 028
39	07972	173	Wood County	30 028
39	09680		Brunswick city	34 255
39	09680	103	Medina County	34 255
39	12000		Canton city	73 007
39	12000	151	Stark County	73 007
39	15000		Cincinnati city	296 943
39	15000	061	Hamilton County	296 943
39	16000		Cleveland city	396 815
39	16000	035	Cuyahoga County	396 815
39	16014		Cleveland Heights city	46 121
39	16014	035	Cuyahoga County	46 121
39	18000		Columbus city	787 033
39	18000	041	Delaware County	7 245
39	18000	045	Fairfield County	9 666
39	18000	049	Franklin County	770 122
39	19778		Cuyahoga Falls city	49 652
39	19778	153	Summit County	49 652
39	21000		Dayton city	141 527
39	21000	113	Montgomery County	141 527
39	21434		Delaware city	34 753
39	21434	041	Delaware County	34 753
39	22694		Dublin city	41 751
39	22694	041	Delaware County	4 018
39	22694	049	Franklin County	35 367
39	22694	159	Union County	2 366
39	25256		Elyria city	54 533
39	25256	093	Lorain County	54 533
39	25704		Euclid city	48 920
39	25704	035	Cuyahoga County	48 920
39	25914		Fairborn city	32 352
39	25914	057	Greene County	32 352
39	25970		Fairfield city	42 510
39	25970	017	Butler County	42 510
39	25970	061	Hamilton County	0
39	27048		Findlay city	41 202
39	27048	063	Hancock County	41 202
39	29106		Gahanna city	33 248
39	29106	049	Franklin County	33 248
39	29428		Garfield Heights city	28 849
39	29428	035	Cuyahoga County	28 849
39	31860		Green city	25 699
39	31860	153	Summit County	25 699
39	32592		Grove City city	35 575
39	32592	049	Franklin County	35 575
39	33012		Hamilton city	62 477
39	33012	017	Butler County	62 477
39	35476		Hilliard city	28 435
39	35476	049	Franklin County	28 435
39	36610		Huber Heights city	38 101
39	36610	057	Greene County	0
39	36610	109	Miami County	959
39	36610	113	Montgomery County	37 142
39	39872		Kent city	28 904
39	39872	133	Portage County	28 904
39	40040		Kettering city	56 163
39	40040	057	Greene County	467
39	40040	113	Montgomery County	55 696
39	41664		Lakewood city	52 131
39	41664	035	Cuyahoga County	52 131

Cities by County–*Continued*

State Code	Place Code	County Code	Geographic Area Name	2010 Census Population
39	41720		Lancaster city	38 780
39	41720	045	Fairfield County	38 780
39	43554		Lima city	38 771
39	43554	003	Allen County	38 771
39	44856		Lorain city	64 097
39	44856	093	Lorain County	64 097
39	47138		Mansfield city	47 821
39	47138	139	Richland County	47 821
39	47754		Marion city	36 837
39	47754	101	Marion County	36 837
39	48188		Mason city	30 712
39	48188	165	Warren County	30 712
39	48244		Massillon city	32 149
39	48244	151	Stark County	32 149
39	48790		Medina city	26 678
39	48790	103	Medina County	26 678
39	49056		Mentor city	47 159
39	49056	085	Lake County	47 159
39	49840		Middletown city	48 694
39	49840	017	Butler County	45 994
39	49840	165	Warren County	2 700
39	54040		Newark city	47 573
39	54040	089	Licking County	47 573
39	56882		North Olmsted city	32 718
39	56882	035	Cuyahoga County	32 718
39	56966		North Ridgeville city	29 465
39	56966	093	Lorain County	29 465
39	57008		North Royalton city	30 444
39	57008	035	Cuyahoga County	30 444
39	61000		Parma city	81 601
39	61000	035	Cuyahoga County	81 601
39	66390		Reynoldsburg city	35 893
39	66390	045	Fairfield County	910
39	66390	049	Franklin County	26 157
39	66390	089	Licking County	8 826
39	67468		Riverside city	25 201
39	67468	113	Montgomery County	25 201
39	70380		Sandusky city	25 793
39	70380	043	Erie County	25 793
39	71682		Shaker Heights city	28 448
39	71682	035	Cuyahoga County	28 448
39	74118		Springfield city	60 608
39	74118	023	Clark County	60 608
39	74944		Stow city	34 837
39	74944	153	Summit County	34 837
39	75098		Strongsville city	44 750
39	75098	035	Cuyahoga County	44 750
39	77000		Toledo city	287 208
39	77000	095	Lucas County	287 208

State Code	Place Code	County Code	Geographic Area Name	2010 Census Population
39	77588		Troy city	25 058
39	77588	109	Miami County	25 058
39	79002		Upper Arlington city	33 771
39	79002	049	Franklin County	33 771
39	80892		Warren city	41 557
39	80892	155	Trumbull County	41 557
39	83342		Westerville city	36 120
39	83342	041	Delaware County	7 792
39	83342	049	Franklin County	28 328
39	83622		Westlake city	32 729
39	83622	035	Cuyahoga County	32 729
39	86548		Wooster city	26 119
39	86548	169	Wayne County	26 119
39	86772		Xenia city	25 719
39	86772	057	Greene County	25 719
39	88000		Youngstown city	66 982
39	88000	099	Mahoning County	66 971
39	88000	155	Trumbull County	11
39	88084		Zanesville city	25 487
39	88084	119	Muskingum County	25 487
40			**OKLAHOMA**	3 751 351
40	04450		Bartlesville city	35 750
40	04450	113	Osage County	3
40	04450	147	Washington County	35 747
40	09050		Broken Arrow city	98 850
40	09050	143	Tulsa County	80 634
40	09050	145	Wagoner County	18 216
40	23200		Edmond city	81 405
40	23200	109	Oklahoma County	81 405
40	23950		Enid city	49 379
40	23950	047	Garfield County	49 379
40	41850		Lawton city	96 867
40	41850	031	Comanche County	96 867
40	48350		Midwest City city	54 371
40	48350	109	Oklahoma County	54 371
40	49200		Moore city	55 081
40	49200	027	Cleveland County	55 081
40	50050		Muskogee city	39 223
40	50050	101	Muskogee County	39 223
40	52500		Norman city	110 925
40	52500	027	Cleveland County	110 925
40	55000		Oklahoma City city	579 999
40	55000	017	Canadian County	44 541
40	55000	027	Cleveland County	63 723
40	55000	109	Oklahoma County	471 671
40	55000	125	Pottawatomie County	64
40	56650		Owasso city	28 915
40	56650	131	Rogers County	2 614
40	56650	143	Tulsa County	26 301
40	59850		Ponca City city	25 387
40	59850	071	Kay County	25 387

Cities by County–*Continued*

State Code	Place Code	County Code	Geographic Area Name	2010 Census Population
40	66800		Shawnee city	29 857
40	66800	125	Pottawatomie County	29 857
40	70300		Stillwater city	45 688
40	70300	119	Payne County	45 688
40	75000		Tulsa city	391 906
40	75000	113	Osage County	6 136
40	75000	131	Rogers County	0
40	75000	143	Tulsa County	385 613
40	75000	145	Wagoner County	157
41			**OREGON**	3 831 074
41	01000		Albany city	50 158
41	01000	003	Benton County	6 463
41	01000	043	Linn County	43 695
41	05350		Beaverton city	89 803
41	05350	067	Washington County	89 803
41	05800		Bend city	76 639
41	05800	017	Deschutes County	76 639
41	15800		Corvallis city	54 462
41	15800	003	Benton County	54 462
41	23850		Eugene city	156 185
41	23850	039	Lane County	156 185
41	30550		Grants Pass city	34 533
41	30550	033	Josephine County	34 533
41	31250		Gresham city	105 594
41	31250	051	Multnomah County	105 594
41	34100		Hillsboro city	91 611
41	34100	067	Washington County	91 611
41	38500		Keizer city	36 478
41	38500	047	Marion County	36 478
41	40550		Lake Oswego city	36 619
41	40550	005	Clackamas County	34 066
41	40550	051	Multnomah County	2 544
41	40550	067	Washington County	9
41	45000		McMinnville city	32 187
41	45000	071	Yamhill County	32 187
41	47000		Medford city	74 907
41	47000	029	Jackson County	74 907
41	55200		Oregon City city	31 859
41	55200	005	Clackamas County	31 859
41	59000		Portland city	583 776
41	59000	005	Clackamas County	744
41	59000	051	Multnomah County	581 485
41	59000	067	Washington County	1 547
41	61200		Redmond city	26 215
41	61200	017	Deschutes County	26 215
41	64900		Salem city	154 637
41	64900	047	Marion County	130 398
41	64900	053	Polk County	24 239
41	69600		Springfield city	59 403
41	69600	039	Lane County	59 403
41	73650		Tigard city	48 035
41	73650	067	Washington County	48 035
41	74950		Tualatin city	26 054
41	74950	005	Clackamas County	2 862
41	74950	067	Washington County	23 192
41	80150		West Linn city	25 109
41	80150	005	Clackamas County	25 109
42			**PENNSYLVANIA**	12 702 379
42	02000		Allentown city	118 032
42	02000	077	Lehigh County	118 032
42	02184		Altoona city	46 320
42	02184	013	Blair County	46 320
42	06064		Bethel Park municipality	32 313
42	06064	003	Allegheny County	32 313
42	06088		Bethlehem city	74 982
42	06088	077	Lehigh County	19 343
42	06088	095	Northampton County	55 639
42	13208		Chester city	33 972
42	13208	045	Delaware County	33 972
42	21648		Easton city	26 800
42	21648	095	Northampton County	26 800
42	24000		Erie city	101 786
42	24000	049	Erie County	101 786
42	32800		Harrisburg city	49 528
42	32800	043	Dauphin County	49 528
42	33408		Hazleton city	25 340
42	33408	079	Luzerne County	25 340
42	41216		Lancaster city	59 322
42	41216	071	Lancaster County	59 322
42	42168		Lebanon city	25 477
42	42168	075	Lebanon County	25 477
42	50528		Monroeville municipality	28 386
42	50528	003	Allegheny County	28 386
42	54656		Norristown borough	34 324
42	54656	091	Montgomery County	34 324
42	60000		Philadelphia city	1 526 006
42	60000	101	Philadelphia County	1 526 006
42	61000		Pittsburgh city	305 704
42	61000	003	Allegheny County	305 704
42	61536		Plum borough	27 126
42	61536	003	Allegheny County	27 126
42	63624		Reading city	88 082
42	63624	011	Berks County	88 082
42	69000		Scranton city	76 089
42	69000	069	Lackawanna County	76 089
42	73808		State College borough	42 034
42	73808	027	Centre County	42 034
42	85152		Wilkes-Barre city	41 498
42	85152	079	Luzerne County	41 498
42	85312		Williamsport city	29 381
42	85312	081	Lycoming County	29 381

Cities by County–*Continued*

State Code	Place Code	County Code	Geographic Area Name	2010 Census Population
42	87048		York city	43 718
42	87048	133	York County	43 718
44			**RHODE ISLAND**	1 052 567
44	19180		Cranston city	80 387
44	19180	007	Providence County	80 387
44	22960		East Providence city	47 037
44	22960	007	Providence County	47 037
44	54640		Pawtucket city	71 148
44	54640	007	Providence County	71 148
44	59000		Providence city	178 042
44	59000	007	Providence County	178 042
44	74300		Warwick city	82 672
44	74300	003	Kent County	82 672
44	80780		Woonsocket city	41 186
44	80780	007	Providence County	41 186
45			**SOUTH CAROLINA**	4 625 364
45	00550		Aiken city	29 524
45	00550	003	Aiken County	29 524
45	01360		Anderson city	26 686
45	01360	007	Anderson County	26 686
45	13330		Charleston city	120 083
45	13330	015	Berkeley County	8 095
45	13330	019	Charleston County	111 988
45	16000		Columbia city	129 272
45	16000	063	Lexington County	559
45	16000	079	Richland County	128 713
45	25810		Florence city	37 056
45	25810	041	Florence County	37 056
45	29815		Goose Creek city	35 938
45	29815	015	Berkeley County	35 933
45	29815	019	Charleston County	5
45	30850		Greenville city	58 409
45	30850	045	Greenville County	58 409
45	30985		Greer city	25 515
45	30985	045	Greenville County	18 635
45	30985	083	Spartanburg County	6 880
45	34045		Hilton Head Island town	37 099
45	34045	013	Beaufort County	37 099
45	48535		Mount Pleasant town	67 843
45	48535	019	Charleston County	67 843
45	49075		Myrtle Beach city	27 109
45	49075	051	Horry County	27 109
45	50875		North Charleston city	97 471
45	50875	015	Berkeley County	0
45	50875	019	Charleston County	78 393
45	50875	035	Dorchester County	19 078
45	61405		Rock Hill city	66 154
45	61405	091	York County	66 154
45	68290		Spartanburg city	37 013
45	68290	083	Spartanburg County	37 013
45	70270		Summerville town	43 392
45	70270	015	Berkeley County	3 643
45	70270	019	Charleston County	1 010
45	70270	035	Dorchester County	38 739
45	70405		Sumter city	40 524
45	70405	085	Sumter County	40 524
46			**SOUTH DAKOTA**	814 180
46	00100		Aberdeen city	26 091
46	00100	013	Brown County	26 091
46	52980		Rapid City city	67 956
46	52980	103	Pennington County	67 956
46	59020		Sioux Falls city	153 888
46	59020	083	Lincoln County	21 095
46	59020	099	Minnehaha County	132 793
47			**TENNESSEE**	6 346 105
47	03440		Bartlett city	54 613
47	03440	157	Shelby County	54 613
47	08280		Brentwood city	37 060
47	08280	187	Williamson County	37 060
47	08540		Bristol city	26 702
47	08540	163	Sullivan County	26 702
47	14000		Chattanooga city	167 674
47	14000	065	Hamilton County	167 674
47	15160		Clarksville city	132 929
47	15160	125	Montgomery County	132 929
47	15400		Cleveland city	41 285
47	15400	011	Bradley County	41 285
47	16420		Collierville town	43 965
47	16420	047	Fayette County	0
47	16420	157	Shelby County	43 965
47	16540		Columbia city	34 681
47	16540	119	Maury County	34 681
47	16920		Cookeville city	30 435
47	16920	141	Putnam County	30 435
47	27740		Franklin city	62 487
47	27740	187	Williamson County	62 487
47	28540		Gallatin city	30 278
47	28540	165	Sumner County	30 278
47	28960		Germantown city	38 844
47	28960	157	Shelby County	38 844
47	33280		Hendersonville city	51 372
47	33280	165	Sumner County	51 372
47	37640		Jackson city	65 211
47	37640	113	Madison County	65 211
47	38320		Johnson City city	63 152
47	38320	019	Carter County	1 252
47	38320	163	Sullivan County	367
47	38320	179	Washington County	61 533
47	39560		Kingsport city	48 205
47	39560	073	Hawkins County	2 854
47	39560	163	Sullivan County	45 351

Cities by County–*Continued*

State Code	Place Code	County Code	Geographic Area Name	2010 Census Population
47	40000		Knoxville city	178 874
47	40000	093	Knox County	178 874
47	41200		La Vergne city	32 588
47	41200	149	Rutherford County	32 588
47	41520		Lebanon city	26 190
47	41520	189	Wilson County	26 190
47	46380		Maryville city	27 465
47	46380	009	Blount County	27 465
47	48000		Memphis city	646 889
47	48000	157	Shelby County	646 889
47	50280		Morristown city	29 137
47	50280	063	Hamblen County	29 131
47	50280	089	Jefferson County	6
47	51560		Murfreesboro city	108 755
47	51560	149	Rutherford County	108 755
47	55120		Oak Ridge city	29 330
47	55120	001	Anderson County	26 271
47	55120	145	Roane County	3 059
47	69420		Smyrna town	39 974
47	69420	149	Rutherford County	39 974
47	70580		Spring Hill city	29 036
47	70580	119	Maury County	7 023
47	70580	187	Williamson County	22 013
48			**TEXAS**	25 145 561
48	01000		Abilene city	117 063
48	01000	253	Jones County	5 145
48	01000	441	Taylor County	111 918
48	01924		Allen city	84 246
48	01924	085	Collin County	84 246
48	03000		Amarillo city	190 695
48	03000	375	Potter County	105 486
48	03000	381	Randall County	85 209
48	04000		Arlington city	365 438
48	04000	439	Tarrant County	365 438
48	05000		Austin city	790 390
48	05000	209	Hays County	2
48	05000	453	Travis County	754 691
48	05000	491	Williamson County	35 697
48	06128		Baytown city	71 802
48	06128	071	Chambers County	4 116
48	06128	201	Harris County	67 686
48	07000		Beaumont city	118 296
48	07000	245	Jefferson County	118 296
48	07132		Bedford city	46 979
48	07132	439	Tarrant County	46 979
48	08236		Big Spring city	27 282
48	08236	227	Howard County	27 282
48	10768		Brownsville city	175 023
48	10768	061	Cameron County	175 023
48	10912		Bryan city	76 201
48	10912	041	Brazos County	76 201
48	11428		Burleson city	36 690
48	11428	251	Johnson County	29 111
48	11428	439	Tarrant County	7 579
48	13024		Carrollton city	119 097
48	13024	085	Collin County	2
48	13024	113	Dallas County	49 352
48	13024	121	Denton County	69 743
48	13492		Cedar Hill city	45 028
48	13492	113	Dallas County	44 477
48	13492	139	Ellis County	551
48	13552		Cedar Park city	48 937
48	13552	453	Travis County	489
48	13552	491	Williamson County	48 448
48	15364		Cleburne city	29 337
48	15364	251	Johnson County	29 337
48	15976		College Station city	93 857
48	15976	041	Brazos County	93 857
48	16432		Conroe city	56 207
48	16432	339	Montgomery County	56 207
48	16612		Coppell city	38 659
48	16612	113	Dallas County	37 905
48	16612	121	Denton County	754
48	16624		Copperas Cove city	32 032
48	16624	027	Bell County	0
48	16624	099	Coryell County	31 457
48	16624	281	Lampasas County	575
48	17000		Corpus Christi city	305 215
48	17000	007	Aransas County	0
48	17000	273	Kleberg County	0
48	17000	355	Nueces County	305 215
48	17000	409	San Patricio County	0
48	19000		Dallas city	1 197 816
48	19000	085	Collin County	46 885
48	19000	113	Dallas County	1 124 296
48	19000	121	Denton County	26 579
48	19000	257	Kaufman County	0
48	19000	397	Rockwall County	56
48	19624		Deer Park city	32 010
48	19624	201	Harris County	32 010
48	19792		Del Rio city	35 591
48	19792	465	Val Verde County	35 591
48	19972		Denton city	113 383
48	19972	121	Denton County	113 383
48	20092		DeSoto city	49 047
48	20092	113	Dallas County	49 047
48	21628		Duncanville city	38 524
48	21628	113	Dallas County	38 524
48	21892		Eagle Pass city	26 248
48	21892	323	Maverick County	26 248
48	22660		Edinburg city	77 100
48	22660	215	Hidalgo County	77 100
48	24000		El Paso city	649 121
48	24000	141	El Paso County	649 121

Cities by County–*Continued*

State Code	Place Code	County Code	Geographic Area Name	2010 Census Population
48	24768		Euless city	51 277
48	24768	439	Tarrant County	51 277
48	25452		Farmers Branch city	28 616
48	25452	113	Dallas County	28 616
48	26232		Flower Mound town	64 669
48	26232	121	Denton County	64 457
48	26232	439	Tarrant County	212
48	27000		Fort Worth city	741 206
48	27000	121	Denton County	7 813
48	27000	367	Parker County	7
48	27000	439	Tarrant County	733 386
48	27000	497	Wise County	0
48	27648		Friendswood city	35 805
48	27648	167	Galveston County	25 510
48	27648	201	Harris County	10 295
48	27684		Frisco city	116 989
48	27684	085	Collin County	72 489
48	27684	121	Denton County	44 500
48	28068		Galveston city	47 743
48	28068	167	Galveston County	47 743
48	29000		Garland city	226 876
48	29000	085	Collin County	266
48	29000	113	Dallas County	226 608
48	29000	397	Rockwall County	2
48	29336		Georgetown city	47 400
48	29336	491	Williamson County	47 400
48	30464		Grand Prairie city	175 396
48	30464	113	Dallas County	123 487
48	30464	139	Ellis County	45
48	30464	439	Tarrant County	51 864
48	30644		Grapevine city	46 334
48	30644	113	Dallas County	0
48	30644	121	Denton County	0
48	30644	439	Tarrant County	46 334
48	30920		Greenville city	25 557
48	30920	231	Hunt County	25 557
48	31928		Haltom City city	42 409
48	31928	439	Tarrant County	42 409
48	32312		Harker Heights city	26 700
48	32312	027	Bell County	26 700
48	32372		Harlingen city	64 849
48	32372	061	Cameron County	64 849
48	35000		Houston city	2 099 451
48	35000	157	Fort Bend County	38 124
48	35000	201	Harris County	2 057 280
48	35000	339	Montgomery County	4 047
48	35528		Huntsville city	38 548
48	35528	471	Walker County	38 548
48	35576		Hurst city	37 337
48	35576	439	Tarrant County	37 337
48	37000		Irving city	216 290
48	37000	113	Dallas County	216 290
48	38632		Keller city	39 627
48	38632	439	Tarrant County	39 627
48	39148		Killeen city	127 921
48	39148	027	Bell County	127 921
48	39352		Kingsville city	26 213
48	39352	273	Kleberg County	26 213
48	39952		Kyle city	28 016
48	39952	209	Hays County	28 016
48	40588		Lake Jackson city	26 849
48	40588	039	Brazoria County	26 849
48	41212		Lancaster city	36 361
48	41212	113	Dallas County	36 361
48	41440		La Porte city	33 800
48	41440	201	Harris County	33 800
48	41464		Laredo city	236 091
48	41464	479	Webb County	236 091
48	41980		League City city	83 560
48	41980	167	Galveston County	81 998
48	41980	201	Harris County	1 562
48	42016		Leander city	26 521
48	42016	453	Travis County	1 077
48	42016	491	Williamson County	25 444
48	42508		Lewisville city	95 290
48	42508	113	Dallas County	841
48	42508	121	Denton County	94 449
48	43012		Little Elm city	25 898
48	43012	121	Denton County	25 898
48	43888		Longview city	80 455
48	43888	183	Gregg County	78 585
48	43888	203	Harrison County	1 870
48	45000		Lubbock city	229 573
48	45000	303	Lubbock County	229 573
48	45072		Lufkin city	35 067
48	45072	005	Angelina County	35 067
48	45384		McAllen city	129 877
48	45384	215	Hidalgo County	129 877
48	45744		McKinney city	131 117
48	45744	085	Collin County	131 117
48	46452		Mansfield city	56 368
48	46452	139	Ellis County	95
48	46452	251	Johnson County	1 652
48	46452	439	Tarrant County	54 621
48	47892		Mesquite city	139 824
48	47892	113	Dallas County	139 731
48	47892	257	Kaufman County	93
48	48072		Midland city	111 147
48	48072	317	Martin County	0
48	48072	329	Midland County	111 147
48	48768		Mission city	77 058
48	48768	215	Hidalgo County	77 058

Cities by County–*Continued*

State Code	Place Code	County Code	Geographic Area Name	2010 Census Population
48	48804		Missouri City city	67 358
48	48804	157	Fort Bend County	61 755
48	48804	201	Harris County	5 603
48	50256		Nacogdoches city	32 996
48	50256	347	Nacogdoches County	32 996
48	50820		New Braunfels city	57 740
48	50820	091	Comal County	47 586
48	50820	187	Guadalupe County	10 154
48	52356		North Richland Hills city	63 343
48	52356	439	Tarrant County	63 343
48	53388		Odessa city	99 940
48	53388	135	Ector County	98 270
48	53388	329	Midland County	1 670
48	55080		Paris city	25 171
48	55080	277	Lamar County	25 171
48	56000		Pasadena city	149 043
48	56000	201	Harris County	149 043
48	56348		Pearland city	91 252
48	56348	039	Brazoria County	86 706
48	56348	157	Fort Bend County	721
48	56348	201	Harris County	3 825
48	57176		Pflugerville city	46 936
48	57176	453	Travis County	46 636
48	57176	491	Williamson County	300
48	57200		Pharr city	70 400
48	57200	215	Hidalgo County	70 400
48	58016		Plano city	259 841
48	58016	085	Collin County	254 525
48	58016	121	Denton County	5 316
48	58820		Port Arthur city	53 818
48	58820	245	Jefferson County	53 814
48	58820	361	Orange County	4
48	61796		Richardson city	99 223
48	61796	085	Collin County	28 569
48	61796	113	Dallas County	70 654
48	62828		Rockwall city	37 490
48	62828	397	Rockwall County	37 490
48	63284		Rosenberg city	30 618
48	63284	157	Fort Bend County	30 618
48	63500		Round Rock city	99 887
48	63500	453	Travis County	1 362
48	63500	491	Williamson County	98 525
48	63572		Rowlett city	56 199
48	63572	113	Dallas County	49 188
48	63572	397	Rockwall County	7 011
48	64472		San Angelo city	93 200
48	64472	451	Tom Green County	93 200
48	65000		San Antonio city	1 327 407
48	65000	029	Bexar County	1 327 381
48	65000	091	Comal County	0
48	65000	325	Medina County	26
48	65516		San Juan city	33 856
48	65516	215	Hidalgo County	33 856
48	65600		San Marcos city	44 894
48	65600	055	Caldwell County	3
48	65600	187	Guadalupe County	0
48	65600	209	Hays County	44 891
48	66128		Schertz city	31 465
48	66128	029	Bexar County	1 157
48	66128	091	Comal County	845
48	66128	187	Guadalupe County	29 463
48	66644		Seguin city	25 175
48	66644	187	Guadalupe County	25 175
48	67496		Sherman city	38 521
48	67496	181	Grayson County	38 521
48	68636		Socorro city	32 013
48	68636	141	El Paso County	32 013
48	69032		Southlake city	26 575
48	69032	121	Denton County	773
48	69032	439	Tarrant County	25 802
48	70808		Sugar Land city	78 817
48	70808	157	Fort Bend County	78 817
48	72176		Temple city	66 102
48	72176	027	Bell County	66 102
48	72368		Texarkana city	36 411
48	72368	037	Bowie County	36 411
48	72392		Texas City city	45 099
48	72392	071	Chambers County	0
48	72392	167	Galveston County	45 099
48	72530		The Colony city	36 328
48	72530	121	Denton County	36 328
48	74144		Tyler city	96 900
48	74144	423	Smith County	96 900
48	75428		Victoria city	62 592
48	75428	469	Victoria County	62 592
48	76000		Waco city	124 805
48	76000	309	McLennan County	124 805
48	76816		Waxahachie city	29 621
48	76816	139	Ellis County	29 621
48	76864		Weatherford city	25 250
48	76864	367	Parker County	25 250
48	77272		Weslaco city	35 670
48	77272	215	Hidalgo County	35 670
48	79000		Wichita Falls city	104 553
48	79000	485	Wichita County	104 553
48	80356		Wylie city	41 427
48	80356	085	Collin County	39 957
48	80356	113	Dallas County	415
48	80356	397	Rockwall County	1 055
49			**UTAH**	2 763 885
49	01310		American Fork city	26 263
49	01310	049	Utah County	26 263
49	07690		Bountiful city	42 552
49	07690	011	Davis County	42 552

Cities by County–*Continued*

State Code	Place Code	County Code	Geographic Area Name	2010 Census Population
49	11320		Cedar City city	28 857
49	11320	021	Iron County	28 857
49	13850		Clearfield city	30 112
49	13850	011	Davis County	30 112
49	16270		Cottonwood Heights city	33 433
49	16270	035	Salt Lake County	33 433
49	20120		Draper city	42 274
49	20120	035	Salt Lake County	40 532
49	20120	049	Utah County	1 742
49	36070		Holladay city	26 472
49	36070	035	Salt Lake County	26 472
49	40360		Kaysville city	27 300
49	40360	011	Davis County	27 300
49	43660		Layton city	67 311
49	43660	011	Davis County	67 311
49	44320		Lehi city	47 407
49	44320	049	Utah County	47 407
49	45860		Logan city	48 174
49	45860	005	Cache County	48 174
49	49710		Midvale city	27 964
49	49710	035	Salt Lake County	27 964
49	53230		Murray city	46 746
49	53230	035	Salt Lake County	46 746
49	55980		Ogden city	82 825
49	55980	057	Weber County	82 825
49	57300		Orem city	88 328
49	57300	049	Utah County	88 328
49	60930		Pleasant Grove city	33 509
49	60930	049	Utah County	33 509
49	62470		Provo city	112 488
49	62470	049	Utah County	112 488
49	64340		Riverton city	38 753
49	64340	035	Salt Lake County	38 753
49	65110		Roy city	36 884
49	65110	057	Weber County	36 884
49	65330		St. George city	72 897
49	65330	053	Washington County	72 897
49	67000		Salt Lake City city	186 440
49	67000	035	Salt Lake County	186 440
49	67440		Sandy city	87 461
49	67440	035	Salt Lake County	87 461
49	70850		South Jordan city	50 418
49	70850	035	Salt Lake County	50 418
49	71290		Spanish Fork city	34 691
49	71290	049	Utah County	34 691
49	72280		Springville city	29 466
49	72280	049	Utah County	29 466
49	75360		Taylorsville city	58 652
49	75360	035	Salt Lake County	58 652
49	76680		Tooele city	31 605
49	76680	045	Tooele County	31 605
49	82950		West Jordan city	103 712
49	82950	035	Salt Lake County	103 712
49	83470		West Valley City city	129 480
49	83470	035	Salt Lake County	129 480
50			**VERMONT**	625 741
50	10675		Burlington city	42 417
50	10675	007	Chittenden County	42 417
51			**VIRGINIA**	8 001 024
51	01000		Alexandria city	139 966
51	01000	510	Alexandria city	139 966
51	07784		Blacksburg town	42 620
51	07784	121	Montgomery County	42 620
51	14968		Charlottesville city	43 475
51	14968	540	Charlottesville city	43 475
51	16000		Chesapeake city	222 209
51	16000	550	Chesapeake city	222 209
51	21344		Danville city	43 055
51	21344	590	Danville city	43 055
51	35000		Hampton city	137 436
51	35000	650	Hampton city	137 436
51	35624		Harrisonburg city	48 914
51	35624	660	Harrisonburg city	48 914
51	44984		Leesburg town	42 616
51	44984	107	Loudoun County	42 616
51	47672		Lynchburg city	75 568
51	47672	680	Lynchburg city	75 568
51	48952		Manassas city	37 821
51	48952	683	Manassas city	37 821
51	56000		Newport News city	180 719
51	56000	700	Newport News city	180 719
51	57000		Norfolk city	242 803
51	57000	710	Norfolk city	242 803
51	61832		Petersburg city	32 420
51	61832	730	Petersburg city	32 420
51	64000		Portsmouth city	95 535
51	64000	740	Portsmouth city	95 535
51	67000		Richmond city	204 214
51	67000	760	Richmond city	204 214
51	68000		Roanoke city	97 032
51	68000	770	Roanoke city	97 032
51	76432		Suffolk city	84 585
51	76432	800	Suffolk city	84 585
51	82000		Virginia Beach city	437 994
51	82000	810	Virginia Beach city	437 994
51	86720		Winchester city	26 203
51	86720	840	Winchester city	26 203

Cities by County–*Continued*

State Code	Place Code	County Code	Geographic Area Name	2010 Census Population
53			**WASHINGTON**	6 724 540
53	03180		Auburn city	70 180
53	03180	033	King County	62 761
53	03180	053	Pierce County	7 419
53	05210		Bellevue city	122 363
53	05210	033	King County	122 363
53	05280		Bellingham city	80 885
53	05280	073	Whatcom County	80 885
53	07380		Bothell city	33 505
53	07380	033	King County	17 090
53	07380	061	Snohomish County	16 415
53	07695		Bremerton city	37 729
53	07695	035	Kitsap County	37 729
53	08850		Burien city	33 313
53	08850	033	King County	33 313
53	17635		Des Moines city	29 673
53	17635	033	King County	29 673
53	20750		Edmonds city	39 709
53	20750	061	Snohomish County	39 709
53	22640		Everett city	103 019
53	22640	061	Snohomish County	103 019
53	23515		Federal Way city	89 306
53	23515	033	King County	89 306
53	33805		Issaquah city	30 434
53	33805	033	King County	30 434
53	35275		Kennewick city	73 917
53	35275	005	Benton County	73 917
53	35415		Kent city	92 411
53	35415	033	King County	92 411
53	35940		Kirkland city	48 787
53	35940	033	King County	48 787
53	36745		Lacey city	42 393
53	36745	067	Thurston County	42 393
53	37900		Lake Stevens city	28 069
53	37900	061	Snohomish County	28 069
53	38038		Lakewood city	58 163
53	38038	053	Pierce County	58 163
53	40245		Longview city	36 648
53	40245	015	Cowlitz County	36 648
53	40840		Lynnwood city	35 836
53	40840	061	Snohomish County	35 836
53	43955		Marysville city	60 020
53	43955	061	Snohomish County	60 020
53	47560		Mount Vernon city	31 743
53	47560	057	Skagit County	31 743
53	51300		Olympia city	46 478
53	51300	067	Thurston County	46 478
53	53545		Pasco city	59 781
53	53545	021	Franklin County	59 781
53	56625		Pullman city	29 799
53	56625	075	Whitman County	29 799
53	56695		Puyallup city	37 022
53	56695	053	Pierce County	37 022
53	57535		Redmond city	54 144
53	57535	033	King County	54 144
53	57745		Renton city	90 927
53	57745	033	King County	90 927
53	58235		Richland city	48 058
53	58235	005	Benton County	48 058
53	61115		Sammamish city	45 780
53	61115	033	King County	45 780
53	62288		SeaTac city	26 909
53	62288	033	King County	26 909
53	63000		Seattle city	608 660
53	63000	033	King County	608 660
53	63960		Shoreline city	53 007
53	63960	033	King County	53 007
53	67000		Spokane city	208 916
53	67000	063	Spokane County	208 916
53	67167		Spokane Valley city	89 755
53	67167	063	Spokane County	89 755
53	70000		Tacoma city	198 397
53	70000	053	Pierce County	198 397
53	73465		University Place city	31 144
53	73465	053	Pierce County	31 144
53	74060		Vancouver city	161 791
53	74060	011	Clark County	161 791
53	75775		Walla Walla city	31 731
53	75775	071	Walla Walla County	31 731
53	77105		Wenatchee city	31 925
53	77105	007	Chelan County	31 925
53	80010		Yakima city	91 067
53	80010	077	Yakima County	91 067
54			**WEST VIRGINIA**	1 852 994
54	14600		Charleston city	51 400
54	14600	039	Kanawha County	51 400
54	39460		Huntington city	49 138
54	39460	011	Cabell County	45 214
54	39460	099	Wayne County	3 924
54	55756		Morgantown city	29 660
54	55756	061	Monongalia County	29 660
54	62140		Parkersburg city	31 492
54	62140	107	Wood County	31 492
54	86452		Wheeling city	28 486
54	86452	051	Marshall County	276
54	86452	069	Ohio County	28 210

Cities by County–*Continued*

State Code	Place Code	County Code	Geographic Area Name	2010 Census Population
55			**WISCONSIN**	5 686 986
55	02375		Appleton city	72 623
55	02375	015	Calumet County	11 088
55	02375	087	Outagamie County	60 045
55	02375	139	Winnebago County	1 490
55	06500		Beloit city	36 966
55	06500	105	Rock County	36 966
55	10025		Brookfield city	37 920
55	10025	133	Waukesha County	37 920
55	22300		Eau Claire city	65 883
55	22300	017	Chippewa County	1 981
55	22300	035	Eau Claire County	63 902
55	25950		Fitchburg city	25 260
55	25950	025	Dane County	25 260
55	26275		Fond du Lac city	43 021
55	26275	039	Fond du Lac County	43 021
55	27300		Franklin city	35 451
55	27300	079	Milwaukee County	35 451
55	31000		Green Bay city	104 057
55	31000	009	Brown County	104 057
55	31175		Greenfield city	36 720
55	31175	079	Milwaukee County	36 720
55	37825		Janesville city	63 575
55	37825	105	Rock County	63 575
55	39225		Kenosha city	99 218
55	39225	059	Kenosha County	99 218
55	40775		La Crosse city	51 320
55	40775	063	La Crosse County	51 320
55	48000		Madison city	233 209
55	48000	025	Dane County	233 209
55	48500		Manitowoc city	33 736
55	48500	071	Manitowoc County	33 736
55	51000		Menomonee Falls village	35 626
55	51000	133	Waukesha County	35 626
55	53000		Milwaukee city	594 833
55	53000	079	Milwaukee County	594 833
55	53000	131	Washington County	0
55	53000	133	Waukesha County	0
55	54875		Mount Pleasant village	26 197
55	54875	101	Racine County	26 197
55	55750		Neenah city	25 501
55	55750	139	Winnebago County	25 501
55	56375		New Berlin city	39 584
55	56375	133	Waukesha County	39 584
55	58800		Oak Creek city	34 451
55	58800	079	Milwaukee County	34 451
55	60500		Oshkosh city	66 083
55	60500	139	Winnebago County	66 083
55	66000		Racine city	78 860
55	66000	101	Racine County	78 860
55	72975		Sheboygan city	49 288
55	72975	117	Sheboygan County	49 288
55	77200		Stevens Point city	26 717
55	77200	097	Portage County	26 717
55	78600		Sun Prairie city	29 364
55	78600	025	Dane County	29 364
55	78650		Superior city	27 244
55	78650	031	Douglas County	27 244
55	84250		Waukesha city	70 718
55	84250	133	Waukesha County	70 718
55	84475		Wausau city	39 106
55	84475	073	Marathon County	39 106
55	84675		Wauwatosa city	46 396
55	84675	079	Milwaukee County	46 396
55	85300		West Allis city	60 411
55	85300	079	Milwaukee County	60 411
55	85350		West Bend city	31 078
55	85350	131	Washington County	31 078
56			**WYOMING**	563 626
56	13150		Casper city	55 316
56	13150	025	Natrona County	55 316
56	13900		Cheyenne city	59 466
56	13900	021	Laramie County	59 466
56	31855		Gillette city	29 087
56	31855	005	Campbell County	29 087
56	45050		Laramie city	30 816
56	45050	001	Albany County	30 816

Cities by County–*Continued*

The following consolidated cities are included in Table D. They are listed here with their 2010 census populations followed by the separate entities that make up the consolidated city. Data from the American Community Survey include only the "balance," the major city of each consolidated city.

State Code	Place Code	County Code	Geographic Area Name	2010 Census Population
09			**CONNECTICUT**	3 574 097
09	47500		Milford city	52 759
			Milford city (balance)	51 271
	88050		Woodmont borough	1 488
13			**GEORGIA**	9 687 653
13	03436		Athens-Clark county	116 714
13	03440		Athens-Clark county (balance)	115 452
13	09068		Bogart town	140
13	83728		Winterville city	1 122
13	04200		Augusta-Richmond county	200 549
13	04204		Augusta-Richmond county (balance)	195 844
13	09040		Blythe city	694
13	38040		Hephzibah city	4 011
18			**INDIANA**	6 483 802
18	36000		Indianapolis city	829 718
18	04204		Beech Grove city	0
18	13492		Clermont town	1 356
18	16156		Crows Nest town	73
18	16336		Cumberland town	2 597
18	34420		Homecroft town	722
18	36003		Indianapolis city (balance)	820 445
18	42426		Lawrence city	42
18	48456		Meridian Hills town	1 616
18	54612		North Crows Nest town	45
18	65556		Rocky Ripple town	606
18	72232		Spring Hill town	98
18	80234		Warren Park town	1 480
18	84374		Williams Creek town	407
18	85742		Wynnedale town	231
21			**KENTUCKY**	4 339 367
21	46003		Louisville/Jefferson County	741 096
21	01504		Anchorage city	2 348
21	02656		Audubon Park city	1 473
21	03376		Bancroft city	494
21	03556		Barbourmeade city	1 218
21	05068		Beechwood Village city	1 324
21	05392		Bellemeade city	865
21	05464		Bellewood city	321
21	07858		Blue Ridge Manor city	767
21	09532		Briarwood city	435
21	09847		Broeck Pointe city	272
21	10162		Brownsboro Farm city	648
21	10198		Brownsboro Village city	319
21	12066		Cambridge city	175
21	16395		Coldstream city	1 100
21	18270		Creekside city	305
21	18766		Crossgate city	225
21	22204		Douglass Hills city	5 484
21	22474		Druid Hills city	308
21	27262		Fincastle city	817
21	28342		Forest Hills city	444
21	31348		Glenview city	531
21	31402		Glenview Hills city	319
21	31420		Glenview Manor city	191
21	31870		Goose Creek city	294
21	32523		Graymoor-Devondale city	2 870
21	32986		Green Spring city	715
21	36102		Heritage Creek city	1 076
21	36374		Hickory Hill city	114
21	36865		Hills and Dales city	142
21	37576		Hollow Creek city	783
21	37630		Hollyvilla city	537
21	38170		Houston Acres city	507
21	38814		Hurstbourne city	4 216
21	38818		Hurstbourne Acres city	1 811
21	39304		Indian Hills city	2 868
21	40222		Jeffersontown city	26 595
21	42598		Kingsley city	381
21	43900		Langdon Place city	936
21	46540		Lincolnshire city	148
21	48006		Louisville/Jefferson County (balance)	597 337
21	48558		Lyndon city	11 002
21	48648		Lynnview city	914
21	49800		Manor Creek city	140
21	50412		Maryhill Estates city	179
21	51193		Meadowbrook Farm city	136
21	51258		Meadow Vale city	736
21	51294		Meadowview Estates city	363
21	51978		Middletown city	7 218
21	52842		Mockingbird Valley city	167
21	53328		Moorland city	431
21	54660		Murray Hill city	582
21	56550		Norbourne Estates city	441
21	56730		Northfield city	1 020
21	56928		Norwood city	370
21	57658		Old Brownsboro Place city	353
21	59322		Parkway Village city	650
21	61554		Plantation city	832
21	62370		Poplar Hills city	362
21	63264		Prospect city	4 636
21	65208		Richlawn city	405
21	65766		Riverwood city	446
21	66486		Rolling Fields city	646
21	66504		Rolling Hills city	959
21	67944		St. Matthews city	17 472
21	67998		St. Regis Park city	1 454
21	69384		Seneca Gardens city	696
21	70284		Shively city	15 264
21	72138		South Park View city	7
21	72770		Spring Mill city	287
21	72790		Spring Valley city	654
21	74064		Strathmoor Manor city	337
21	74082		Strathmoor Village city	648
21	75190		Sycamore city	160
21	75963		Ten Broeck city	103
21	76380		Thornhill city	178
21	80913		Watterson Park city	976
21	81372		Wellington city	565
21	81624		West Buechel city	1 230
21	82164		Westwood city	634
21	83208		Wildwood city	261
21	83784		Windy Hills city	2 385
21	84486		Woodland Hills city	696
21	84576		Woodlawn Park city	942
21	84891		Worthington Hills city	1 446
30			**MONTANA**	989 415
30	11390		Butte-Silver Bow	34 200
30	11397		Butte-Silver Bow (balance)	33 525
30	77650		Walkerville town	675
47			**TENNESSEE**	6 346 105
47	52004		Nashville-Davidson	626 681
47	04620		Belle Meade city	2 912
47	05140		Berry Hill city	537
47	27020		Forest Hills city	4 812
47	29920		Goodlettsville city	10 319
47	40720		Lakewood city	2 302
47	52006		Nashville-Davidson (balance)	601 222
47	54780		Oak Hill city	4 529
47	63140		Ridgetop city	48

APPENDIX F
SOURCE NOTES AND EXPLANATIONS

The following documentation is provided in the order in which items appear in the tables. Internet addresses are provided for the sources of the data. Some of the links refer to the specific data tables. Others provide information about the general data source.

TABLE A—STATES

Table A presents 355 items for the United States as a whole, for each individual state, and for the District of Columbia. The states are presented in alphabetical order.

LAND AREA, Items 1 and 4

Source: U.S. Census Bureau—Decennial Censuses and Population Estimates
http://www.census.gov/2010census/

Land area measurements are shown to the nearest square kilometer. Land area includes dry land and land temporarily or partially covered by water, such as marshlands, swamps, and river floodplains.

POPULATION AND COMPONENTS OF CHANGE, Items 2–4, 31–41

Source: U.S. Census Bureau—Decennial Censuses and Population Estimates
http://www.census.gov/popest/estimates.html
http://www.census.gov/2010census/data/

The population data for 2014 are Census Bureau estimates of the resident population as of July 1, 2014.

The population data for 1990, 2000, and 2010 are from the decennial censuses and represent the resident population as of April 1 of those years.

The change in population between 2010 and 2014 is made up of (a) natural increase—births minus deaths, and (b) net migration—the difference between the number of persons moving into a particular state and the number of persons moving out of the state. Net migration is composed of internal and international migration.

POPULATION PROJECTIONS, Items 42–44

Source: U.S. Census Bureau—Population Projections Branch
http://www.census.gov/population/projections/l

Projections are estimates of the population for future dates. They illustrate plausible courses of future population change based on assumptions about future births, deaths, international migration, and domestic migration. Projected numbers are based on an estimated population consistent with the most recent decennial census as enumerated. The Census Bureau does not have a current set of state population projections and currently has no plans to produce them. This volume includes projections released in 2005, based on the 2000 census. The Census Bureau notes that these projections should be used with caution because population trends may have changed substantially since their release.

POPULATION AND POPULATION CHARACTERISTICS, Items 5–23 and 45–63

Source: U.S. Census Bureau—Population Estimates and 2013 American Community Survey
http://www.census.gov/popest/estimates.html
http://www.census.gov/acs/www/

Data on age, sex, race, and Hispanic origin are from the Population Estimates program. Data on place of birth are from the 2013 American Community Survey, a nationwide continuous survey designed to replace the long form questionnaire used in previous censuses.

Data on race were derived from answers to the question on race that was asked of all persons. The concept of race, as used by the Census Bureau, reflects self-identification by respondents according to the race or races with which they most closely identify. These categories are sociopolitical constructs and should not be interpreted as being scientific or anthropological in nature. Furthermore, the race categories include both racial and national origin groups.

The **White** population is defined as persons who indicated their race as White, as well as persons who did not classify themselves in one of the specific race categories listed on the questionnaire but entered a nationality such as Irish, German, Italian, Lebanese, Near Easterner, Arab, or Polish.

The **Black** population includes persons who indicated their race as ''Black, African Am., or Negro,'' as well as persons who did not classify themselves in one of the specific race categories but reported entries such as African American, Afro American, Kenyan, Nigerian, or Haitian.

The **American Indian or Alaska Native** population includes persons who indicated their race as American Indian or Alaska Native, as well as persons who did not classify themselves in one of the specific race categories but reported entries such as Canadian Indian, French-American Indian, Spanish-American Indian, Eskimo, Aleut, Alaska Indian, or any of the American Indian or Alaska Native tribes.

The **Asian and Pacific Islander** population combines two census groupings: **Asian** and **Native Hawaiian or Other Pacific Islander**. The **Asian** population includes persons who indicated their race as Asian Indian, Chinese, Filipino, Japanese, Korean, Vietnamese, or ''Other Asian,'' as well as persons who provided write-in entries of such groups as Cambodian, Laotian, Hmong, Pakistani, or Taiwanese. The **Native Hawaiian or Other Pacific Islander** population includes persons who indicated their race as ''Native Hawaiian,'' ''Guamanian or Chamorro,'' ''Samoan,'' or ''Other Pacific Islander,'' as well as persons who reported entries such as Part Hawaiian, American Samoan, Fijian, Melanesian, or Tahitian.

The **Hispanic** population is based on a question that asked respondents ''Is this person Spanish/Hispanic/Latino?'' Persons marking any one of the four Hispanic categories (i.e., Mexican, Puerto Rican, Cuban, or other Spanish) are collectively referred to as Hispanic.

Age is defined as age at last birthday (number of completed years since birth), as of April 1 of the census year.

The **median age** is the age that divides the population into two equal-size groups. Half of the population is older than the median age and half is younger. Median age is based on a standard distribution of the population by single years of age and is shown to the nearest tenth of a year.

The **female** population is shown as a percentage of total population.

The **foreign-born** population includes all persons who were not U.S. citizens at birth. Foreign-born persons are those who indicated they were either a U.S. citizen by naturalization or were not a citizen of the United States. Neither the census nor the American Community Survey asked about immigration status. The population surveyed included all persons who indicated that the United States was their usual place of residence. The foreign-born population consists of immigrants (legal permanent residents), temporary migrants (students), humanitarian migrants (refugees), and unauthorized migrants (persons illegally residing in the United States).

Percent born in state of residence is shown as a percentage of total population.

IMMIGRANTS, Item 24

Source: Department of Homeland Security, U.S. Citizenship and Immigration Services http://www.dhs.gov/yearbook-immigration-statistics

The number of immigrants by state of intended residence is summarized from the administrative records of the Citizenship and Immigration Services. This information is compiled from immigrant visas and forms granting legal permanent resident status.

An **immigrant** is an alien admitted to the United States as a lawful permanent resident. Immigrants are those persons lawfully accorded the privilege of residing permanently in the United States. They may be newly arrived individuals who were issued immigrant visas by the Department of State overseas, or they may be U.S. residents who were admitted to permanent resident status in 2012 by the U.S. Citizenship and Immigration Services.

HOUSEHOLDS, Items 25–30 and 64–68

Source: U.S. Census Bureau—2013 American Community Survey http://www.census.gov/acs/www/

A **household** includes all of the persons who occupy a housing unit. Persons not living in households are classified as living in group quarters. A housing unit is a house, an apartment, a mobile home, a group of rooms, or a single room occupied (or, if vacant, intended for occupancy) as separate living quarters. Separate living quarters are those in which the occupants live separately from any other persons in the building and have direct access from the outside of the building or through a common hall. The occupants may be a single family, one person living alone, two or more families living together, or any other group of related or unrelated persons who share living quarters. The number of households is the same as the number of year-round occupied housing units.

The measure of **persons per household** is obtained by dividing the number of persons in households by the number of households or householders. One person in each household is designated as the householder. In most cases, this is the person, (or one of the persons) in whose name the house is owned, being bought, or rented. If there is no such person in the household, any adult household member 15 years old and over can be designated as the householder.

A **family** includes a householder and one or more other persons living in the same household who are related to the householder by birth, marriage, or adoption. All persons in a household who are related to the householder are regarded as members of his or her family. A **family household** may contain persons not related to the householder; thus, family households may include more members than families do. A household can contain only one family for the purposes of census tabulations. Not all households contain families, as a household may comprise a group of unrelated persons or one person living alone. Families are classified by type as either a ''husband-wife family'' or ''other family'' according to the presence of a spouse.

The category **female family householder** includes only female-headed family households with no spouse present.

HOUSING, Items 69–92

Source: U.S. Census Bureau—2010 and 2013 American Community Survey http://www.census.gov/acs/www/

Housing data for 2010 and 2013 are from the American Community Survey, a nationwide continuous survey designed to replace the long form questionnaire used in previous censuses. A sample of households is surveyed to provide estimates.

A **housing unit** is a house, apartment, mobile home or trailer, group of rooms, or single room occupied or, if vacant, intended for occupancy as separate living quarters. Separate living quarters are those in which the occupants do not live and eat with any other person in the structure and which have direct access from the outside of the building or through a common hall. For vacant units, the criteria of separateness and direct access are applied to the intended occupants whenever possible. If that information cannot be obtained, the criteria are applied to the previous occupants.

The occupants of a housing unit may be a single family, one person living alone, two or more families living together, or any other group of related or unrelated persons who share living arrangements. Both occupied and vacant housing units are included in the housing inventory, although recreational vehicles, tents, caves, boats, railroad cars, and the like are included only if they are occupied as a person's usual place of residence.

A housing unit is classified as **occupied** if it is the usual place of residence of the person or group of persons living in it at the time of enumeration, or if the occupants are only temporarily absent (away on vacation). A household consists of all persons who occupy a housing unit as their usual place of residence.

Housing cost, as a percentage of income, is shown separately for owners with mortgages, owners without mortgages, and renters. Also shown is the percentage of mortgaged owners and renters who pay 30 percent or more of household income on selected monthly costs. Rent as a percent of income is a computed ratio of gross rent and monthly household income (total household income divided by 12). Selected owner costs include utilities and fuels, mortgage payments, insurance, taxes, etc. In each case, the ratio of housing cost to income is computed separately for each housing unit. The housing cost ratios for half of all units are above the median shown in this book, and half are below the median. Median monthly housing costs divides the monthly housing costs distribution into two equal parts, one-half of the cases falling below the median monthly housing costs and one-half above the median.

Median value is the dollar amount that divides the distribution of specified owner-occupied housing units into two equal parts, with half of all units below the median value and half above the median value. Value is defined as the respondent's estimate of what the house would sell for if it were for sale. Data are presented for single-family units on fewer than 10 acres of land that have no business or medical office on the property.

Median rent divides the distribution of renter-occupied housing units into two equal parts. The rent concept used in this volume is gross rent, which includes the amount of cash rent a renter pays (contract rent) plus the estimated average cost of utilities and fuels, if these are paid by the renter. The rent is the amount of rent only for living quarters and excludes any business or other space occupied. Single-family houses on lots of 10 or more acres of land are excluded.

Substandard units are occupied units that are overcrowded or lack complete plumbing facilities. For the purposes of this item, ''overcrowded'' is defined as having 1.01 persons or more per room. Complete plumbing facilities include hot and cold piped water, a flush toilet, and a bathtub or shower. These facilities must be located inside the housing unit, but do not have to be in the same room.

Different house includes all people 1 year old and over who, a year earlier, lived in a different house or apartment from the one they occupied at the time of interview.

BUILDING PERMITS, Items 93–95

Source: U.S. Census Bureau—Building Permits Survey http://www.census.gov/construction/bps/

These figures represent private residential construction authorized by building permits in approximately 20,000 places in the United States. Valuation represents the expected cost of construction as recorded on the building permit. This figure usually excludes the cost of on-site and off-site development and improvements, as well as the cost of heating, plumbing, electrical, and elevator installations.

National, state, and county totals were obtained by adding the data for permit-issuing places within each jurisdiction. These totals thus are limited to permits issued in the 20,000 place universe covered by the Census Bureau and may not include all permits issued within a state. Current surveys indicate that construction is undertaken for all but a very small percentage of housing units authorized by building permits.

Residential building permits include buildings with any number of housing units. Housing units exclude group quarters (such as dormitories and rooming houses), transient accommodations (such as transient hotels, motels, and tourist courts), ''HUD-code'' manufactured (mobile) homes, moved or relocated units, and housing units created in an existing residential or nonresidential structure.

MANUFACTURED HOUSING UNITS, Item 96

Source: U.S. Census Bureau—Manufactured Housing Survey http://www.census.gov/construction/mhs/placbystate.html

The Manufactured Housing Survey involves a monthly sample of new mobile homes shipped by manufacturers. The dealer to whom the sampled unit was shipped is contacted by telephone and asked about the status of the unit. This is done each month until that unit is reported as placed.

A mobile home, often referred to as a manufactured housing unit, is defined as a movable dwelling, 8 feet or more wide and 40 feet or more long, that is designed to be towed on its own chassis (with transportation gear integral to the unit when it leaves the factory) and without need of a permanent foundation. These mobile homes include multiwides, which are counted as single units, and expandable mobile homes. Excluded are travel trailers, motor homes, and modular housing.

There was not an increase in placements due to Hurricane Katrina, as federally owned FEMA units are not included in the private placement data collected by the Manufactured Housing Survey.

BIRTHS AND DEATHS, Items 97–103

Source: U.S. Centers for Disease Control and Prevention, National Center for Health Statistics http://www.cdc.gov/nchs/data/nvsr/nvsr62/nvsr62_01.pdf http://www.cdc.gov/nchs/data/nvsr/nvsr61/nvsr61_04.pdf http://www.cdc.gov/nchs/data/nvsr/nvsr59/nvsr59_10.pdf

The registration of births, deaths, and other vital events in the United States is primarily a state and local function. The civil laws of every state provide for continuous and permanent birth and death registration systems. Through the National Vital Statistics System, the National Center for Health Statistics (NCHS) obtains data on births and deaths from the registration offices of each state, New York City, and the District of Columbia.

Birth and death statistics are limited to events occurring during the year. The data are by place of residence and exclude events for nonresidents of the United States. Births or deaths occurring outside the United States are excluded.

Birth and death rates represent the number of births and deaths per 1,000 resident population enumerated as of April 1 for decennial census years and estimated as of July 1 for other years.

Figures for infant deaths include deaths of children under 1 year of age but exclude fetal deaths. The infant death rate is per 1,000 live births.

The rates of almost all causes of disease, injury, and death vary by age. Age adjustment is a technique for ''removing'' the effects of age from crude rates, in order to allow meaningful comparisons across populations with different underlying age structures. For example, comparing the crude death rate in Florida to that of California is misleading, since the relatively older population in Florida will lead to a higher crude death rate. For such a comparison, age-adjusted death rates are preferable.

The population estimates were developed by the Census Bureau's Population Division using a traditional cohort component method. Starting with a basic population from the 2000 census, each component of population change—births, deaths, domestic migration, and international migration—is estimated separately for each birth cohort by sex, race, and Hispanic or Latino origin.

Age-adjusted rates are calculated by applying the age-specific rates of various populations to a single standard population. In this volume, the standard population is 2000. The Centers for Disease Control and Prevention recently switched to the year 2000, after many years of using the year 1940 as the standard population for age-adjusted death rates. For this reason, the 2006 age-adjusted rates are close to the actual death rates.

PERSONS LACKING HEALTH INSURANCE, Items 104–105

Source: U.S. Census Bureau—American Community Survey http://www.census.gov/hhes/www/hlthins/data/incpovhlth/2013/acs-tables.html

These estimates are from the American Community Survey, an ongoing nationwide survey that is conducted throughout the year. About 250,000 addresses per month receive the ACS. Respondents are asked whether each household member is currently covered (by specific types of health coverage) at the time of interview. The 2013 estimates were the first to use the ACS. Prior year estimates were based on the Annual Social and Economic Supplement (ASEC) of the Current Population Survey (CPS).

Those lacking coverage are the percentage of the population of each state who were not covered by private health plans purchased directly or provided by an employer, Medicaid, Medicare, or military health care.

MEDICARE ENROLLEES, Item 106

Source: U.S. Department of Health and Human Services, Centers for Medicare and Medicaid Services http://www.cms.gov/Research-Statistics-Data-and-Systems/Statistics-Trends-and-Reports/MedicareEnrpts/index.html/

The Centers for Medicare and Medicaid Services (CMS) administers Medicare, which provides health insurance to persons 65 years old and over, persons with permanent kidney failure, and certain persons with disabilities. Medicare has two parts: Hospital Insurance and Supplemental Medical Insurance. The numbers in this volume include persons enrolled in either or both parts of the program as of July 1 of the year shown for their state of residence.

CRIME, Items 107–110

Source: U.S. Federal Bureau of Investigation—Uniform Crime Reports http://www.fbi.gov/ucr/ucr.htm

Crime data are as reported to the Federal Bureau of Investigation (FBI) by law enforcement agencies and have not been adjusted for underreporting. This may affect comparability between geographic areas or over time.

Through the voluntary contribution of crime statistics by law enforcement agencies across the United States, the Uniform Crime Reporting (UCR) Program provides periodic assessments of crime in the nation as measured by offenses that have come to the attention of the law enforcement community. The Committee on Uniform Crime Records of the International Association of Chiefs of Police initiated this voluntary national data-collection effort in 1930. The UCR Program contributors compile and submit their crime data either directly to the FBI or through state-level UCR Programs.

Seven offenses, because of their severity, frequency of occurrence, and likelihood of being reported to police, were initially selected to serve as an index for evaluating fluctuations in the volume of crime. These serious crimes were murder and nonnegligent manslaughter, forcible rape, robbery, aggravated assault, burglary, larceny-theft, and motor vehicle theft. By congressional mandate, arson was added as the eighth index offense in 1979. The totals shown in this volume do not include arson.

In 2004, the FBI discontinued the use of the Crime Index in the UCR Program and its publications, stating that the Crime Index was driven upward by the offense with the highest number of cases (in this case, larceny-theft) creating a bias against jurisdictions with a high number of larceny-thefts but a low number of other serious crimes, such as murder and forcible rape. The FBI is currently publishing a violent crime total and a property crime total until a more viable index is developed.

In 2013, the FBI adopted a new definition of rape. Rape is now defined as, ''Penetration, no matter how slight, of the vagina or anus with any body part or object, or oral penetration by a sex organ of another person, without the consent of the victim.'' The new definition updated the 80-year-old historical definition of rape which was ''carnal knowledge of a female forcibly and against her will.'' Effectively, the revised definition expands rape to include both male and female victims and offenders, and reflects the various forms of sexual penetration understood to be rape, especially nonconsenting acts of sodomy, and sexual assaults with objects.

Violent crimes include four categories of offenses: (1) Murder and nonnegligent manslaughter, as defined in the UCR Program, is the willful (nonnegligent) killing of one human being by another. This offense excludes deaths caused by negligence, suicide, or accident; justifiable homicides; and attempts to murder or assaults to murder. (2) Rape is the penetration, no matter how slight, of the vagina or anus with any body part or object, or oral penetration by a sex organ of another person, without the consent of the victim. Assaults or attempts to commit rape by force or threat of force are also included; however, statutory rape (without force) and other sex offenses are excluded. (3) Robbery is the taking or attempting to take anything of value from the care, custody, or control of a person or persons by force or threat of force or violence and/or by putting the victim in fear. (4) Aggravated assault is an unlawful attack by one person upon another for the purpose of inflicting severe or aggravated bodily injury. This type of assault is usually accompanied by the use of a weapon or by other means likely to produce death or great bodily harm. Attempts are included, since injury does not necessarily have to result when a gun, knife, or other weapon is used, as these incidents could and probably would result in a serious personal injury if the crime were successfully completed.

Property crimes include three categories: (1) Burglary, or breaking and entering, is the unlawful entry of a structure to commit a felony or theft, even though no force was used to gain entrance. (2) Larceny-theft is the unauthorized taking of the personal property of another, without the use of force. (3) Motor vehicle theft is the unauthorized taking of any motor vehicle.

Rates are based on population estimates provided by the FBI. For some states, reporting is not sufficiently complete to be representative of the state as a whole. The FBI has estimated state totals for those states.

ELEMENTARY AND SECONDARY SCHOOL ENROLLMENT, Items 111 and 112

Source: U.S. Department of Education, National Center for Education Statistics—Common Core of Data
http://nces.ed.gov/ccd/elsi/

Data on public school enrollment is from the Common Core of Data 2012–2013 survey. Public school enrollment includes pre-kindergarten through grade 12 and ungraded students. The student/teacher ratio is calculated by dividing the number of students in all schools by the number of full-time equivalent teachers employed by all schools and agencies.

EDUCATIONAL ATTAINMENT, Items 113–116

Source: U.S. Census Bureau—2010 and 2013 American Community Survey
http://www.census.gov/acs/www/

Data on **educational attainment** are tabulated for the population 25 years old and over. The data were derived from a question that asked respondents for the highest level of school completed or the highest degree received. Persons who had passed a high school equivalency examination were considered high school graduates. Schooling received in foreign schools was to be reported as the equivalent grade or years in the regular American school system. Vocational and technical training, such as barber school training; business, trade, technical, and vocational schools; or other training for a specific trade are specifically excluded.

High school graduate or more. This category includes persons whose highest degree was a high school diploma or its equivalent, and those who reported any level higher than a high school diploma.

Bachelor's degree or more. This category includes persons who have received bachelor's degrees, master's degrees, professional school degrees (such as law school or medical school degrees), and doctoral degrees.

LOCAL GOVERNMENT EDUCATION EXPENDITURES, Items 117 and 118

Source: U.S. Department of Education, National Center for Education Statistics—Common Core of Data
http://nces.ed.gov/ccd/

Total expenditure for education includes provision or support of schools and facilities for elementary and secondary education. It encompasses instructional, support, and auxiliary services (school lunch, student activities, and community service) offered by public school systems. Retirement benefits paid to former education employees and interest payments are not included. Current expenditure includes all components of total expenditure except capital outlay. Expenditure data are obtained by the Census Bureau through its annual survey of government finances and are supplied to the National Center for Education Statistics (NCES). Current expenditure per student is current expenditure divided by the number of students enrolled. The number of students enrolled is based on an annual ''membership'' count of students on or about October 1.

NCES uses the Common Core of Data (CCD) Survey system to acquire and maintain statistical data from each of the 50 states, the District of Columbia, and the outlying areas. State education agencies compile and submit data for approximately 94,000 schools and 17,000 local school districts. Typically, this results in varying interpretation of NCES definitions and different record keeping systems, leading to large amounts of missing data for several states; this absence is reflected in the data in this publication. The numbers in Table A reflect imputations and adjustments as published in *Revenues and Expenditures for Public Elementary and Secondary Education: School Year 2011–12 (Fiscal Year 2012).*

EXPORTS, Items 119–121

Source: U.S. Department of Commerce, International Trade Administration
http://www.census.gov/foreign-trade/statistics/state/origin_movement/index.html

The data on exports of goods by state of origin are based on the location of the exporter (the principal party responsible for exportation from the United States). Exporters are often intermediaries, so the data do not necessarily represent the states in which the goods were actually produced. The total includes re-exports of foreign goods.

INCOME AND POVERTY, Items 122–133

Source: U.S. Census Bureau—2013 American Community Survey
http://www.census.gov/acs/www/

The data on income were derived from answers to questions which were asked of the population 15 years old and over. **Total income** is the sum of the amounts reported separately for wage or salary income; net self-employment income; interest, dividends, or net rental or royalty income or income from estates and trusts; Social Security or railroad retirement income; Supplemental Security Income (SSI); public assistance or welfare payments;

retirement, survivor, or disability pensions; and all other income. Receipts from the following sources are not included as income: capital gains; money received from the sale of property (unless the recipient was engaged in the business of selling such property); the value of income ''in kind'' from food stamps, public housing subsidies, medical care, employer contributions for individuals, etc.; withdrawal of bank deposits; money borrowed; tax refunds; exchange of money between relatives living in the same household; and gifts and lump-sum inheritances, insurance payments, and other types of lump-sum receipts.

Per capita income is the mean income computed for every man, woman, and child in a particular group. It is derived by dividing the aggregate income of a particular group by the total population in that group. Per capita income is rounded to the nearest whole dollar.

Household income includes the income of the householder and all other individuals 15 years old and over in the household, whether or not they are related to the householder. Since many households consist of only one person, average household income is usually less than average family income. Although the household income statistics cover the past 12 months, the characteristics of individuals and the composition of households refer to the time of enumeration. Thus, the income of the household does not include amounts received by individuals who were members of the household during all or part of the past 12 months if these individuals no longer resided in the household at the time of interview. Similarly, income amounts reported by individuals who did not reside in the household during the past 12 months but who were members of the household at the time of interview are included. However, the composition of most households was the same during the past 12 months as at the time of interview.

Median income divides the income distribution into two equal parts, with half of all cases below the median income level and half of all cases above the median income level. For households and families, the median income is based on the distribution of the total number of households and families, including those with no income. Median income for households is computed on the basis of a standard distribution with a minimum value of less than $2,500 and a maximum value of $200,000 or more and is rounded to the nearest whole dollar.

For **family income**, the incomes of all household members 15 years old and over related to the householder are summed and treated as a single amount. Although the family income statistics cover the past 12 months, the characteristics of individuals and the composition of families refer to the time of interview. Thus, the income of the family does not include amounts received by individuals who were members of the family during all of part of the past 12 months if these individuals no longer resided with the family at the time of interview. Similarly, income amounts reported by individuals who did not reside with the family during the past 12 months but who were members of the family at the time of interview are included. However, the composition of most families was the same during the past 12 months as at the time of interview.

The **poverty status** data were derived from data collected on the number of persons in the household, each person's relationship to the householder, and the income data. The Social Security Administration (SSA) developed the original poverty definition in 1964, which federal interagency committees subsequently revised in 1969 and 1980. The Office of Management and Budget's (OMB) *Directive 14* prescribes the SSA's definition as the official poverty measure for federal agencies to use in their statistical work. Poverty statistics presented in American Community Survey products adhere to the standards defined by OMB in *Directive 14*.

The poverty thresholds vary depending on three criteria: size of family, number of children, and, for one- and two-person families, age of householder. In determining the poverty status of families and unrelated individuals, the Census Bureau uses thresholds (income cutoffs) arranged in a two-dimensional matrix. The matrix consists of family size (from one person to nine or more persons), cross-classified by presence and number of family members under 18 years old (from no children present to eight or more children present). Unrelated individuals and two-person families are further differentiated by age of reference person (under 65 years old and 65 years old and over). To determine a person's poverty status, the person's total family income in the last 12 months is compared to the poverty threshold appropriate for that person's family size and composition. If the total income of that person's family is less than the threshold appropriate for that family, then the person is considered poor or ''below the poverty level,'' together with every member of his or her family. If a person is not living with anyone related by birth, marriage, or adoption, then the person's own income is compared with his or her poverty threshold. The total number of persons below the poverty level is the sum of persons in families and the number of unrelated individuals with incomes below the poverty level in the last 12 months. The average poverty threshold for a four-person family was $23,834 in 2013.

The data on **poverty status of households** were derived from answers to the income questions. Since poverty is defined at the family level and not the household level, the poverty status of the household is determined by the poverty status of the householder. Households are classified as poor when the total income of the householder's family in the previous 12 months is below the appropriate poverty threshold. (For nonfamily householders, the person's income is compared with the appropriate threshold.) The income of persons living in the household who are unrelated to the householder is not considered when determining the poverty status of a household, nor does their presence affect the family size in determining the appropriate threshold. The poverty thresholds vary depending upon three criteria: size of family, number of children, and, for one- and two-person families, age of the householder.

Poverty status of children by **family type** is the percentage of children living in that particular type of family that has a family income below the poverty threshold based on family size and composition.

PERSONAL INCOME AND EARNINGS, Items 134–158

Source: U.S. Bureau of Economic Analysis, Regional Economic Accounts
http://www.bea.gov/regional/index.htm#state

Total personal income is the current income received by residents of an area from all sources. It is measured before deductions of income and other personal taxes but after deductions of personal contributions for Social Security, government retirement, and other social insurance programs. It consists of **wage and salary disbursements** (covering all employee earnings, including executive salaries, bonuses, commissions, payments-in-kind, incentive payments, and tips); various types of supplementary earnings, such as employers' contributions to pension funds (termed ''other labor income'' or ''supplements to wages and salaries''); proprietors' income; rental income of persons; dividends; personal interest income; and government and business transfer payments.

Proprietors' income is the monetary income and income-in-kind of proprietorships and partnerships (including the independent professions), and the income of tax-exempt cooperatives. **Dividends** are cash payments by corporations to stockholders who are U.S. residents. **Interest** is the monetary and imputed interest income of persons from all sources. **Rent** is the monetary income of persons from the rental of real property, except the income of persons primarily engaged in the real estate business; the imputed net rental income of owner-occupants of nonfarm dwellings; and the royalties received by persons.

Transfer payments are income for which services are not currently rendered. They consist of both government and business transfer payments. Government transfer payments include payments under the following programs: Federal Old-Age, Survivors, and Disability Insurance (''Social Security''); Medicare and medical vendor payments; unemployment insurance; railroad and government retirement; federal- and state-government-insured workers' compensation; veterans' benefits, including veterans' life insurance; food stamps; black lung payments; Supplemental Security Income; and Temporary Assistance for Needy Families. Government payments to nonprofit institutions, other than for work under research and development contracts, are also included. Business transfer payments consist primarily of liability payments for personal injury and of corporate gifts to nonprofit institutions.

Per capita personal income is based on resident population estimated as of July 1 of the year shown.

Personal tax payments include taxes paid by individuals to federal, state, and local governments. Personal taxes include individual income taxes, estate and gift taxes, motor vehicle license taxes, and personal property taxes. Personal contributions to social insurance (''Social Security taxes'') are not included, nor are sales taxes.

Disposable personal income equals personal income less personal tax payments. It is a measure of the income available to persons for spending or saving.

Earnings cover wage and salary disbursements, other labor income, and proprietors' income.

The data for earnings obtained from the Bureau of Economic Analysis (BEA) are based on place of work. In computing personal income, BEA makes an ''adjustment for residence'' to earnings based on commuting patterns; thus, personal income is presented on a place-of-residence basis.

Farm earnings include the income of farm workers (wages and salaries and other labor income) and farm proprietors. Farm proprietors' income includes only the income of sole proprietorships and partnerships.

Farm earnings estimates are benchmarked to data collected in the Census of Agriculture and the revised Department of Agriculture state totals of income and expense items.

Goods-related industries include mining, construction, and manufacturing. **Service-related** and other industries includes private-sector earnings in forestry, related activities, and other; utilities; transportation and warehousing; information; wholesale trade; retail trade; finance and insurance; real estate and rental and leasing; services, which includes professional, scientific, and technical services; management of companies and enterprises; administrative and waste services; educational services; health care and social assistance; arts, entertainment, and recreation; accommodation and food services; and other services, except public administration. Government earnings include all levels of government. Industries are categorized under the North American Industry Classification System (NAICS) and are not directly comparable to years prior to 2002.

GROSS STATE PRODUCT, Item 159

Source: U.S. Bureau of Economic Analysis, Regional Economic Accounts
http://www.bea.gov/regional/index.htm#state

Gross state product (GSP) for a state is derived as the sum of gross state product originating in all industries in the state. In concept, an industry's GSP, referred to as its ''value added,'' is equivalent to its gross output (sales or receipts and other operating income, commodity taxes, and inventory changes) minus its intermediate inputs (consumption of goods and services purchased from other industries or imported from other countries). As such, it is often referred to as the state counterpart to the nation's gross domestic product (GDP). In practice, GSP estimates are measured as the sum of distributions by industry of the components of gross domestic income—that is, the sum of the costs incurred (such as compensation of employees, net interest, and indirect business taxes) and the profits earned in production.

SOCIAL SECURITY AND SUPPLEMENTAL SECURITY INCOME, Items 160–162

Source: U.S. Social Security Administration
http://www.ssa.gov/policy/docs/statcomps/oasdi_sc/
http://www.ssa.gov/policy/docs/statcomps/ssi_sc/

Social Security beneficiaries are persons receiving benefits under the Old-Age, Survivors, and Disability Insurance Program. These include retired or disabled workers covered by the program, their spouses and dependent children, and the surviving spouses and dependent children of deceased workers.

Supplemental Security Income (SSI) recipients are persons receiving SSI payments. The SSI program is a cash assistance program that provides monthly benefits to low-income aged, blind, or disabled persons.

Data are as of December of the year shown.

CIVILIAN EMPLOYMENT, Items 163–166

Source: U.S. Census Bureau—2013 American Community Survey
http://www.census.gov/acs/www/

The data on occupation were derived from answers to questions that were asked of all persons 15 years old and over who had worked in the past five years. **Occupation** describes the kind of work the person does on the job. For employed persons, the data refer to the person's job during the previous week. For those who worked two or more jobs, the data refer to the job at which the person worked the greatest number of hours. For unemployed persons, the data refer to their last job. The American Community Survey uses the occupational classification system that was developed for the 2000 census and modified in 2002 and again in 2010. This system consists of 539 specific occupational categories for employed persons arranged into 23 major occupational groups. This classification was developed based on the *Standard Occupational Classification (SOC) Manual: 2010*, published by the Executive Office of the President, Office of Management and Budget.

CIVILIAN LABOR FORCE AND UNEMPLOYMENT, Items 167–171

Source: U.S. Bureau of Labor Statistics—Local Areas Unemployment Statistics http://www.bls.gov/lau/#tables

Data for the civilian labor force are the product of a federal-state cooperative program in which state employment security agencies prepare labor force and unemployment estimates under concepts, definitions, and technical procedures established by the Bureau of Labor Statistics (BLS). The **civilian labor force** consists of all civilians 16 years old and over who are either employed or unemployed.

Unemployment includes all persons who did not work during the survey week, made specific efforts to find a job during the prior four weeks, and were available for work during the survey week (except for temporary illness). Persons waiting to be called back to a job from which they had been laid off and those waiting to report to a new job within the next 30 days are included in unemployment figures.

PRIVATE NONFARM EMPLOYMENT AND EARNINGS, Items 172–183

Source: U.S. Bureau of Labor Statistics—Current Employment Survey http://www.bls.gov/ces/#tables

Data for private nonfarm employment and earnings are compiled from payroll information reported monthly on a voluntary basis to the BLS and its cooperating state agencies. More than 350,000 establishments represent all industries except agriculture.

Employment is the annual average of monthly totals of persons who received pay for any part of the pay period including the 12th day of the month. Included are all full-time and part-time workers in nonfarm establishments. Not covered are government employees, proprietors, the self-employed, unpaid volunteers or family workers, farm workers, and domestic workers in households. The data by industry conform to the definitions established in the North American Industry Classification System (NAICS).

Earnings of **production workers** in **manufacturing** industries are derived from reports of gross payrolls and corresponding paid hours. Payroll is reported before deductions of any kinds. Total hours during the pay period include all hours worked (including overtime hours) and hours paid for holidays, vacations, and sick leave.

AGRICULTURE, ITEMS 184–202

Source: U.S. Department of Agriculture, National Agricultural Statistics Service—2012 Census of Agriculture http://agcensus.usda.gov/index.php

The Census Bureau took a census of agriculture every 10 years from 1840 to 1920; since 1925, this census has been taken roughly once every five years. The 1997 Census of Agriculture was the first one conducted by the National Agricultural Statistics Service of the U.S. Department of Agriculture. Over time, the definition of a farm has varied. For recent censuses (including the 2012 census), a farm has been defined as any place from which $1,000 or more of agricultural products were produced and sold or normally would have been sold during the census year. Dollar figures are expressed in current dollars and have not been adjusted for inflation or deflation.

The term **operator** refers to a person who operates a farm by either doing the work or making day-to-day decisions about such activities as planting, harvesting, feeding, marketing, etc. The operator may be the owner, a member of the owner's household, a salaried manager, a tenant, a renter, or a sharecropper. If a person rents land to others or has land worked on shares by others, he/she is considered the operator only of the land that is retained for his/her own operation. The census collected information on the total number of operators, the total number of women operators, and demographic information for up to three operators per farm.

Government payments consists of direct payments as defined by the 2002 Farm Bill; payments from Conservation Reserve Program (CRP), Wetlands reserve Program (WRP), Farmable Wetlands Program (FWP), and Conservation Reserve Enhancement Program (CREP); loan deficiency payments; disaster payments; other conservation programs; and all other federal farm programs under which payments were made directly to farm operators. Commodity Credit Corporation (CCC) proceeds, amount from state and local federal crop insurance payments were not included in this category.

The acreage designated as **land in farms** consists primarily of agricultural land used for crops, pasture, or grazing. It also includes woodland and wasteland not actually under cultivation or used for pasture or grazing, provided that this land was part of the farm operator's total operation.

Land in farms is an operating-unit concept and includes all land owned and operated, as well as all land rented from others. Land used rent-free is classified as land rented from others. All land in Indian reservations used for growing crops or grazing livestock is classified as land in farms.

Irrigated land includes all land watered by any artificial or controlled means, such as sprinklers, flooding, furrows or ditches, sub-irrigation, and spreader dikes. Included are supplemental, partial, and preplant irrigation. Each acre was counted only once regardless of the number of times it was irrigated or harvested. Livestock lagoon waste water distributed by sprinkler or flood systems was also included.

Total cropland includes cropland harvested, cropland used only for pasture or grazing, cropland on which all crops failed or were abandoned, cropland in cultivated summer fallow, and cropland idle or used for cover crops or soil improvement but not harvested and not pastured or grazed.

Respondents were asked to report their estimate of the current market **value of land and buildings** owned, rented, or leased from others and rented and leased to others. Market value refers to the respondent's estimate of what the land and buildings would sell for under current market conditions.

The **value of machinery and equipment** was estimated by the respondent as the current market value of all cars, trucks, tractors, combines, balers, irrigation equipment, etc., used on the farm. This value is an estimate of what the machinery and equipment would sell for in its present condition and not the replacement of depreciated value. Share interests are reported at full value at the farm where the equipment and machinery are usually kept. Only equipment that was physically located at the farm on December 31, 2012, is included.

Market **value of agricultural products sold** by farms represents the gross market value before taxes and the production expenses of all agricultural products sold or removed from the place in 2012, regardless of who received the payment. It is equivalent to total sales and it includes sales by the operator as well as the value of any share received by partners, landlords, contractors, and others associated with the operation. It includes value of direct sales and the value of commodities placed in the Commodity Credit Corporation (CCC) loan program. Market value of agricultural products sold does not include payments received for participation in other federal farm programs. Also, it does not include income from farm-related sources such as customwork and other agricultural services, or income from nonfarm sources.

LAND USE, ITEMS 203 to 205

Source: U.S. Department of Agriculture, Natural Resources Conservation Service—2010 National Resources Inventory http://www.nrcs.usda.gov/technical/NRI/

The National Resources Inventory (NRI) has been conducted every five years since 1982. The 2010 NRI is based on a sample of about 800,000 locations throughout the United States (excluding Alaska and the District of Columbia). Acreages for federal land and total surface area are established through geospatial processes and administrative records. Total surface area of the contiguous United States is 1,937.7 million acres.

Cropland includes cultivated and non-cultivated cropland. **Federally-owned lands** include military bases, national forests, wildlife refuges, parks, grassland game preserves, scenic waterways, wilderness areas, monuments, lakeshore, parkways, battlefields, Bureau of Land Management lands, and other federal lands. **Developed land** includes any built-up area greater than one fourth of an acre. Built-up areas include residential, industrial, commercial, and institutional land; construction sites; public administrative sites; railroad yards; cemeteries; airports; golf courses; sanitary landfills; sewage treatment plants; water control structures and spillways; other land used for such purpose; small parks (fewer than 10 acres of land) within urban and built-up areas; and highways, railroads, and other transportation facilities that are surrounded by urban areas. Also included are tracts of fewer than 10 acres that do not meet the above definition but are completely surrounded by urban and built-up land, as well as all highways, roads, railroads, and associated rights-of-way outside of urban and built-up areas (including private roads to farmsteads or ranch headquarters, logging roads, and other private roads).

WATER CONSUMPTION, Item 206

Source: U.S. Geological Survey, National Water Use Information Program—2010 Water Use Data http://pubs.usgs.gov/circ/1344/

Every five years, the U.S. Geological Survey compiles national water-use estimates. This volume includes the total fresh and saline water withdrawals expressed as million gallons per day. Estimate of withdrawals of ground and surface water are given for the following categories of use: public water supplies, domestic, commercial, irrigation, livestock, industrial, mining, and thermoelectric power.

MANUFACTURES, Items 207–216

Source: U.S. Census Bureau—2013 Annual Survey of Manufactures http://www.census.gov/manufacturing/asm/

The Annual Survey of Manufactures (ASM) has been conducted annually every year since 1949, except for years ending in "2" and "7," at which time ASM data are included in the manufacturing sector of the Economic Census. The ASM provides statistics on employment, payroll, worker hours, payroll supplements, cost of materials, value added by manufacturing, capital expenditures, inventories, and energy consumption. It also provides estimates of value of shipments for over 1,400 classes of manufactured products. The Annual Survey of Manufactures includes approximately 50,000 establishments selected from the census universe of 350,000 manufacturing establishments.

The **all employees** number is the average number of production workers for the payroll periods including the 12th of March, May, August, and November plus the number of other employees in mid-March. Included are all persons on paid sick leave, paid holidays, and paid vacations during the pay period. Officers of corporations are included as employees, while proprietors and partners of unincorporated firms are excluded.

Payroll figures include the gross annual earnings of all employees on the payroll of operating manufacturing establishments. The definition, which is the same as the one used for calculating the federal withholding tax, includes all forms of compensation, such as salaries, wages, commissions, dismissal pay, bonuses, vacation and sick leave pay, and compensation-in-kind, prior to such deductions as employees' Social Security contributions, withholding taxes, group insurance, union dues, and savings bonds. The total includes salaries of officers of corporations; it excludes payments to proprietors or partners of unincorporated concerns. Also excluded are payments to members of armed forces and to pensioners carried on the active payrolls of manufacturing establishments.

Production workers include workers (up through the line-supervisor level) engaged in fabricating, processing, assembling, inspecting, receiving, storing, handling, packing, warehousing, shipping (but not delivering), maintenance, repair, janitorial and guard services, product development, auxiliary production for the plant's own use (for example, power plant), record keeping, and other services closely associated with these production operations at the establishment covered by the report. Employees above the working-supervisor level are excluded.

The number of production workers is the average for the payroll periods including the 12th of March, May, August, and November. Not included in this classification are all other employees, defined as non-production employees, including those engaged in factory supervision above the line-supervisor level.

Production worker hours cover hours worked or paid for at the manufacturing plant, including actual overtime hours (not straight-time equivalent hours). The data exclude hours paid for vacations, holidays, or sick leave when the employee is not at the establishment. Production wages represent all compensation paid to production workers.

Value added by manufacture is derived by subtracting the cost of materials, supplies, containers, fuel, purchased electricity, and contract work from the value of shipments (products manufactured plus receipts for services rendered). The result of this calculation is adjusted by the addition of value added by merchandising operations (the difference between the sales value and the cost of merchandise sold without further manufacture, processing, or assembly) plus the net change in finished goods and work-in-process between the beginning- and end-of-year inventories.

Value of shipments covers the received or receivable net selling values; free on board plant (excluding of freight and taxes), of all products shipped, both primary and secondary; and all miscellaneous receipts, such as receipts for contract work performed for others, installation and repair, sales of scrap, and sales of products bought and sold without further processing. Included are all items made by or for the establishments from material owned by it, whether sold, transferred to other plants of the same company, or shipped on consignment. The net selling value of products made in one plant on a contract basis from materials owned by another was reported by the plant providing the materials.

In the case of multi-unit companies, the manufacturer was asked to report the value of products transferred to other establishments of the same company at full economic or commercial value, including both the direct cost of production and a reasonable proportion of "all other costs" (including company overhead) and profit (interplant transfers).

The aggregate of the value of shipments figure for industry groups and for all manufacturing industries includes large amounts of duplications, as the products of some industries are used as materials by others. Estimates as to the overall extent of this duplication indicate that the value of manufactured products exclusive of such duplication (the value of finished manufactures) tends to approximate two-thirds of the total value of products reported in the census of manufactures.

Total cost of materials refers to direct charges actually paid or payable for items consumed or put into production during the year, including freight charges and other direct charges incurred by the establishment in acquiring these materials. It includes the cost of materials or fuel consumed, whether purchased by the individual establishment from other companies, transferred to it from other establishments of the same company, or withdrawn from inventory during the year. Included in this item are cost of parts, components, containers, etc.; cost of products bought and sold in the same condition; cost of fuels consumed for heat and power; cost of purchased electricity; and cost of contract work. Aggregate of total cost of materials and total value of shipments includes extensive duplication, since products of some industries are used as materials of others.

2007 ECONOMIC CENSUS: OVERVIEW, Items 217–308

Source: U.S. Census Bureau
http://www.census.gov/econ/census07/

The Economic Census provides a detailed portrait of the nation's economy, from the national to the local level, once every five years. The 2007 Economic Census covers nearly all of the U.S. economy in its basic collection of establishment statistics. The 1997 Economic Census was the first major data source to use the new North American Industry Classification System (NAICS); therefore, data are not comparable to economic data from prior years, which were based on the Standard Industrial Classification (SIC) system.

NAICS, developed in cooperation with Canada and Mexico, classifies North America's economic activities at two-, three-, four-, and five-digit levels of detail; the U.S. version of NAICS further defines industries to a sixth digit. The Economic Census takes advantage of this hierarchy to publish data at these successive levels of detail: sector (two-digit); subsector (three-digit); industry group (four-digit); industry (five-digit); and U.S. industry (six-digit). Information in Table A is at the two-digit level, with a few three- and four-digit items.

Several key statistics are tabulated for all industries included in this volume: number of establishments (or companies); number of employees; payroll; and a measure of output (sales, receipts, revenue, value of shipments, or value of construction work done).

Number of establishments. An establishment is a single physical location at which business is conducted. It is not necessarily identical with a company or enterprise, which may consist of one establishment or more. Economic Census figures represent a summary of reports for individual establishments rather than companies. For cases in which a census report was received, separate information was obtained for each location where business was conducted. When administrative records of other federal agencies were used instead of a census report, no information was available on the number of locations operated. Each Economic Census establishment was tabulated according to the physical location at which the business was conducted. The count of establishments represents those in business at any time during 2007.

When two activities or more were carried on at a single location under a single ownership, all activities were generally grouped together as a single establishment. The entire establishment was classified on the basis of its major activity and all of its data were included in that classification. However, when distinct and separate economic activities (for which different industry classification codes were appropriate) were conducted at a single location under a single ownership, separate establishment reports for each of the different activities were obtained in the census.

Number of employees. Paid employees consist of the full-time and part-time employees, including salaried officers and executives of corporations. Included are employees on paid sick leave, paid holidays, and paid vacations; not included are proprietors and partners of unincorporated businesses. The definition of paid employees is the same as that used by the Internal Revenue Service (IRS) on form 941.

For some industries, the Economic Census gives codes representing the number of employees as a range of numbers (for example, ''100 to 249 employees'' or ''1,000 to 2,499'' employees). In this volume, those codes have been replaced by the standard suppression code ''D''.

Payroll. Payroll includes all forms of compensation, such as salaries, wages, commissions, dismissal pay, bonuses, vacation allowances, sick-leave pay, and employee contributions to qualified pension plans paid during the year to all employees. For corporations, payroll includes amounts paid to officers and executives; for unincorporated businesses, it does not include profit or other compensation of proprietors or partners. Payroll is reported before deductions for Social Security, income tax, insurance, union dues, etc. This definition of payroll is the same as that used on IRS form 941.

Sales, shipments, receipts, revenue, or business done. This measure includes the total sales, shipments, receipts, revenue, or business done by establishments within the scope of the Economic Census. The definition of each of these items is specific to the economic sector measured.

CONSTRUCTION, Items 217–221

Source: U.S. Census Bureau—2007 Economic Census (See Overview of 2007 Economic Census prior to Item 217)

The Construction sector (sector 23) comprises establishments primarily engaged in the construction of buildings and other structures, heavy construction (except buildings), additions, alterations, reconstruction, installation, and maintenance and repairs. Establishments engaged in the demolition or wrecking of buildings and other structures, the clearing of building sites, and the sale of materials from demolished structures are also included. This sector also contains those establishments engaged in blasting, test drilling, landfill, leveling, earthmoving, excavating, land drainage, and other land preparation. The industries within this sector have been defined on the basis of their unique production processes. As with all industries, the production processes are distinguished by their use of specialized human resources and specialized physical capital. Construction activities are generally administered or managed at a relatively fixed place of business, but the actual construction work can be performed at one or more different project sites. This sector is divided into three subsectors of construction activities: (1) building construction and land subdivision and land development; (2) heavy construction (except buildings), such as highways, power plants, and pipelines; and (3) construction activity by special trade contractors.

WHOLESALE TRADE, Items 222–226

Source: U.S. Census Bureau—2007 Economic Census (See Overview of 2007 Economic Census prior to Item 217)

The Wholesale Trade sector (sector 42) comprises establishments engaged in wholesaling merchandise, generally without transformation, and rendering services incidental to the sale of merchandise. The wholesaling process is an intermediate step in the distribution of merchandise. Wholesalers are organized to sell or arrange the purchase or sale of (1) goods for resale (i.e., goods sold to other wholesalers or retailers), (2) capital or durable nonconsumer goods, and (3) raw and intermediate materials and supplies used in production.

Wholesalers sell merchandise to other businesses and normally operate from a warehouse or office. These warehouses and offices are characterized by having little or no display of merchandise. In addition, neither the design nor the location of the premises is intended to solicit walk-in traffic. Wholesalers do not normally use advertising directed to the general public. Customers are generally first reached via telephone, in-person marketing, or by specialized advertising that may include internet and other electronic means. Follow-up orders are either vendor-initiated or client-initiated, are usually based on previous sales, and typically exhibit strong ties between sellers and buyers. In fact, transactions are often conducted between wholesalers and clients that have long-standing business relationships.

This sector is made up of two main types of wholesalers: those that sell goods on their own account and those that arrange sales and purchases for others for a commission or fee.

(1) Establishments that sell goods on their own account are known as wholesale merchants, distributors, jobbers, drop shippers, import/export merchants, and sales branches. These establishments typically maintain their own warehouse, where they receive and handle goods for their customers. Goods are generally sold without transformation, but may include integral functions, such as sorting, packaging, labeling, and other marketing services.

(2) Establishments arranging for the purchase or sale of goods owned by others or purchasing goods on a commission basis are known as agents and brokers, commission merchants, import/export agents and brokers, auction companies, and manufacturers' representatives. These establishments operate from offices and generally do not own or handle the goods they sell.

Some wholesale establishments may be connected with a single manufacturer and/or promote and sell that particular manufacturer's products to a wide range of other wholesalers or retailers. Other wholesalers may be connected to a retail chain or a limited number of retail chains and only provide a variety of products needed by the particular retail operation(s). These wholesalers may obtain the products from a wide range of manufacturers. Still other wholesalers may not take title to the goods but act as agents and brokers for a commission.

Although, in general, wholesaling normally denotes sales in large volumes, durable nonconsumer goods may be sold in single units. Sales of capital or durable nonconsumer goods used in the production of goods and services, such as farm machinery, medium- and heavy-duty trucks, and industrial machinery, are always included in Wholesale Trade.

RETAIL TRADE, Items 227–235

Source: U.S. Census Bureau—2007 Economic Census (See Overview of 2007 Economic Census prior to Item 217)

The Retail Trade sector (44–45) is made up of establishments engaged in retailing merchandise, generally without transformation, and rendering services incidental to the sale of merchandise.

The retailing process is the final step in the distribution of merchandise; retailers are, therefore, organized to sell merchandise in small quantities to the general public. This sector comprises two main types of retailers: store and nonstore retailers.

Store retailers operate fixed point-of-sale locations, located and designed to attract a high volume of walk-in customers. In general, retail stores have extensive displays of merchandise and use mass-media advertising to attract customers. They typically sell merchandise to the general public for personal or household consumption; some also serve business and institutional clients. These include establishments, such as office supply stores, computer and software stores, building materials dealers, plumbing supply stores, and electrical supply stores. Catalog showrooms, gasoline service stations, automotive dealers, and mobile home dealers are treated as store retailers.

In addition to retailing merchandise, some types of store retailers are also engaged in the provision of after-sales services, such as repair and installation. For example, new automobile dealers, electronic and appliance stores, and musical instrument and supply stores often provide repair services. As a general rule, establishments engaged in retailing merchandise and providing after-sales services are classified in this sector.

Nonstore retailers, like store retailers, are organized to serve the general public, although their retailing methods differ. The establishments of this subsector reach customers and market merchandise with methods, such as the broadcasting of ''infomercials,'' the broadcasting and publishing of direct-response advertising, the publishing of paper and electronic catalogs, door-to-door solicitation, in-home demonstration, selling from portable stalls (street vendors, except food), and distribution through vending machines. Establishments engaged in the direct sale (nonstore) of products, such as home heating oil dealers and home-delivery newspaper routes are included in this sector.

The buying of goods for resale is a characteristic of retail trade establishments that distinguishes them from establishments in the Agriculture, Manufacturing, and Construction sectors. For example, farms that sell their products at or from the point of production are classified in Agriculture instead of in Retail Trade. Similarly, establishments that both manufacture and sell their products to the general public are classified in Manufacturing instead of Retail Trade. However, establishments that engage in processing activities incidental to retailing are classified in retail.

Industries in the **Motor Vehicle and Parts Dealers** subsector (441) retail motor vehicle and parts merchandise from fixed point-of-sale locations. Establishments in this subsector typically operate from a showroom and/or an open lot where the vehicles are on display. The display of vehicles and the related parts require little by way of display equipment. Personnel generally include both sales and sales support staff familiar with the requirements for registering and financing a vehicle as well as a staff of parts experts and mechanics trained to provide vehicle repair and maintenance services. Specific industries have been included in this subsector to identify the type of vehicle being retailed. Sales of capital or durable nonconsumer goods, such as medium and heavy-duty trucks, are always included in the Wholesale Trade sector. These goods are virtually never sold through retail methods.

Industries in the **Food and Beverage Stores** subsector (445) usually retail food and beverage merchandise from fixed point-of-sale locations. Establishments in this subsector have special equipment (e.g., freezers, refrigerated display cases, and refrigerators) for displaying food and beverage goods. They have staff trained in the processing of food products to guarantee the proper storage and sanitary conditions, as mandated by regulatory authority.

Industries in the **Clothing and Clothing Accessories Stores** subsector (448) retail new clothing and clothing accessories merchandise from fixed point-of-sale locations. Establishments in this subsector have similar types of display equipment, as well as employees who are knowledgeable regarding fashion trends and who can match styles, colors, and combinations of clothing and accessories to the characteristics and tastes of the customer.

Industries in the **General Merchandise Stores** subsector (452) retail new general merchandise from fixed point-of-sale locations. Establishments in this subsector are unique in that they have the equipment and staff capable of retailing a large variety of goods from a single location. This includes a variety of display equipment and staff trained to provide information on many lines of products.

INFORMATION, Items 236–246

Source: U.S. Census Bureau—2007 Economic Census (See Overview of 2007 Economic Census prior to Item 217)

The Information sector (51) comprises establishments engaged in the following processes: (1) producing and distributing information and cultural products, (2) providing the means to transmit or distribute these products as well as data or communications, and (3) processing data.

The main components of this sector are the publishing industries, including software publishing; the motion picture and sound recording industries; the broadcasting and telecommunications industries; and the information services and data processing industries.

For the purpose of NAICS, the transformation of information into a commodity that is produced and distributed by a number of growing industries is at issue. The Information sector groups three types of establishments: (1) those engaged in producing and distributing information and cultural products; (2) those that provide the means to transmit or distribute these products as well as data or communications; and (3) those that process data. Cultural products are those that directly express attitudes, opinions, ideas, values, and artistic creativity; provide entertainment; or offer information and analysis concerning the past and present. Included in this definition are popular, mass-produced products, as well as cultural products that normally have a more limited audience, such as poetry books, literary magazines, or classical records. These activities were formerly classified throughout the existing national classifications. Traditional publishing was in manufacturing; broadcasting in communications; software production in business services; film production in amusement services; and so forth.

Industries in the **Publishing Industries, Except Internet** subsector (511) include establishments engaged in the publishing of newspapers, magazines, other periodicals, and books, as well as database and software publishing. In general, these establishments, which are known as publishers, issue copies of works for which they usually possess copyright. Works may be in one or more formats, including traditional print format, CD-ROM format, or online format. Publishers may publish works originally created by others for which they have obtained the rights and/or works that they have created in-house. Software publishing is included here because the activity (creation of a copyrighted product and bringing it to market) is equivalent to the creation process for other types of intellectual products.

In NAICS, publishing—the reporting, writing, editing, and other processes that are required to create an edition of a book or a newspaper—is treated as a major economic activity in its own right, rather than as a subsidiary activity to printing, which is a manufacturing activity. Thus, publishing is classified in the Information sector, while printing remains in the NAICS Manufacturing sector. In part, the NAICS classification reflects the fact that publishing increasingly takes place in establishments that are physically separate from the associated printing establishments. More crucially, the NAICS classification of book and newspaper publishing is intended to portray their roles in a modern economy—roles that do not resemble manufacturing activities.

Music publishers are not included in the Publishing Industries subsector, but can be found in the Motion Picture and Sound Recording Industries subsector. Reproduction of prepackaged software is treated in NAICS as a manufacturing activity; online distribution of software products is in the Information sector, and custom design of software to client specifications is included in the Professional, Scientific, and Technical Services sector. These distinctions arise because of the different ways that software is created, reproduced, and distributed.

The Information sector does not include products, such as manifold business forms. Information is not the essential component of these items. Establishments producing these items are included in subsector 323, Printing and Related Support Activities.

Industries in the **Motion Picture and Sound Recording Industries** subsector (512) group establishments involved in the production and distribution of motion pictures and sound recordings. While producers and distributors of motion pictures and sound recordings issue works for sale as traditional publishers do, the processes are different enough to warrant placing the establishments engaged in these activities in separate subsectors. Production is typically a complex process that involves several distinct types of establishments engaged in activities, such as contracting with performers, creating the film or sound content, and providing technical postproduction services. Film distribution is often to exhibitors, such as theaters and broadcasters, rather than to a wholesale or retail distribution chain. When the product is in a mass-produced form, NAICS treats production and distribution as the major economic activity, rather than as a subsidiary activity to the manufacture of such products.

This subsector does not include establishments primarily engaged in the wholesale distribution of video cassettes and sound recordings, such as compact discs and audio tapes; these establishments are included in the Wholesale Trade sector. Reproduction of video cassettes and sound recordings that is carried out separately from establishments engaged in production and distribution is treated in NAICS as a manufacturing activity.

Industries in the **Broadcasting, except Internet** subsector (515) include establishments that create content or acquire the right to distribute and subsequently broadcast content. The industry groups (Radio and Television Broadcasting and Cable and Other Subscription Programming) are based on differences in the methods of communication and the nature of services provided. The Radio and Television Broadcasting industry group includes establishments that operate broadcasting studios and facilities for over-the-air or satellite delivery of radio and television programs, including entertainment, news, and talk programs. These establishments are often engaged in production and purchase of programs and generating revenues from the sale of air time to advertisers, as well as from donations, subsidies, and/or the sale of programs. The Cable and Other Subscription Programming industry group includes establishments that operate studios and facilities for the broadcasting of limited-format programs (such as news, sports, educational, and youth-oriented programs) that are typically narrowly-focused in nature; these programs are usually available on a subscription or fee basis. The distribution of cable and other subscription programming is included in subsector 517, Telecommunications.

Industries in the **Internet Publishing and Broadcasting and Web search portals** subsector (51913) consist of establishments that publish and/or broadcast content exclusively for the internet. The unique combination of text, audio, video, and interactive features present in informational and/or cultural products on the internet justifies the separation of internet publishers and broadcasters from the more traditional publishers included in subsector 511, Publishing Industries, Except Internet, and subsector 515, Broadcasting, Except Internet.

Industries in the **Telecommunications** subsector (517) include establishments that provide telecommunications and services related to that activity. The Telecommunications subsector is primarily engaged in operating, maintaining, and/or providing access to facilities for the transmission of voice, data, text, sound, and video. A transmission facility may be based on a single technology or a combination of technologies. Establishments primarily engaged as independent contractors in the maintenance and installation of broadcasting and telecommunications systems are classified in sector 23, Construction.

Industries in the **Internet Service Providers, Web Search Portals, and Data Processing Services** subsector (518) group establishments that provide: (1) access to the internet; (2) search facilities for the internet; and (3) data processing, hosting, and related services. The industry groups (Internet Service Providers and Web Search Portals, Data Processing Hosting, and Related Services) are based on differences in the processes used to access information and process information. The Internet Service Providers and Web Search Portals industry group includes establishments that provide access to the internet or assist users in their navigations on the Web. The Data Processing, Hosting, and

Related Services industry group includes establishments that process data. These establishments can transform data, prepare data for dissemination, or place data or content on the internet for others. In addition, the shared use of computer resources is included in the Data Processing, Hosting, and Related Services industry group.

Establishments that are publishing exclusively on the internet are included in subsector 516, Internet Publishing and Broadcasting; establishments that sell goods over the internet are included in sector 44–45, Retail Trade.

UTILITIES, Items 247–252

Source: U.S. Census Bureau—2007 Economic Census (See Overview of 2007 Economic Census prior to Item 217)

The Utilities sector (22) comprises establishments engaged in the provision of the following utility services: electric power, natural gas, steam supply, water supply, and sewage removal. Within this sector, the specific activities associated with the utility services provided vary by utility: electric power includes generation, transmission, and distribution; natural gas includes distribution; steam supply includes provision and/or distribution; water supply includes treatment and distribution; and sewage removal includes collection, treatment, and disposal of waste through sewer systems and sewage treatment facilities.

Excluded from this sector are establishments primarily engaged in waste management. These services are classified in subsector 562, Waste Management and Remediation Services, which also collect, treat, and dispose of waste materials; however, establishments in this subsector do not use sewer systems or sewage treatment facilities.

TRANSPORTATION AND WAREHOUSING, Items 252–256

Source: U.S. Census Bureau—2007 Economic Census (See Overview of 2007 Economic Census prior to Item 217)

The Transportation and Warehousing sector (48–49) includes industries that provide transportation of passengers and cargo, warehousing and storage for goods, scenic and sightseeing transportation, and support activities related to modes of transportation. Establishments in these industries use transportation equipment or transportation related facilities as a productive asset. The type of equipment depends on the mode of transportation, which includes air, rail, water, road, and pipeline.

The transportation and warehousing sector distinguishes three basic types of activities: subsectors for each mode of transportation, a subsector for warehousing and storage, and a subsector for establishments providing support activities for transportation. In addition, there are subsectors for establishments that provide passenger transportation for scenic and sightseeing purposes, postal services, and courier services.

FINANCE AND INSURANCE, Items 257–261

Source: U.S. Census Bureau—2007 Economic Census (See Overview of 2007 Economic Census prior to Item 217)

The Finance and Insurance sector (52) comprises establishments primarily engaged in financial transactions (transactions involving the creation, liquidation, or change in ownership of financial assets) and/or in facilitating financial transactions. Three principal types of activities are identified:

(1) Raising funds by taking deposits and/or issuing securities and, in the process, incurring liabilities. Establishments engaged in this activity use raised funds to acquire financial assets by making loans and/or purchasing securities. Putting themselves at risk, they channel funds from lenders to borrowers and transform or repackage the funds with respect to maturity, scale, and risk. This activity is known as financial intermediation.

(2) Pooling of risk by underwriting insurance and annuities. Establishments engaged in this activity collect fees, insurance premiums, or annuity considerations; build up reserves; invest those reserves; and make contractual payments. Fees are based on the expected incidence of the insured risk and the expected return on investment.

(3) Providing specialized services facilitating or supporting financial intermediation, insurance, and employee benefit programs.

In addition, monetary authorities charged with monetary control are included in this sector.

REAL ESTATE AND RENTAL AND LEASING, Items 262–266

Source: U.S. Census Bureau—2007 Economic Census (See Overview of 2007 Economic Census prior to Item 217)

The Real Estate and Rental and Leasing sector (53) comprises establishments primarily engaged in renting, leasing, or otherwise allowing the use of tangible or intangible assets, and establishments providing related services. The major portion of this sector comprises establishments that rent, lease, or otherwise allow the use of their own assets by others. The assets may be tangible, such as real estate and equipment, or intangible, such as patents and trademarks.

This sector also includes establishments primarily engaged in managing real estate for others, selling, renting, and/or buying real estate for others, and appraising real estate. These activities are closely related to this sector's main activity. In addition, a substantial proportion of property management is self-performed by lessors.

The main components of this sector are the real estate lessors industries; equipment lessors industries (including motor vehicles, computers, and consumer goods); and lessors of nonfinancial intangible assets (except copyrighted works).

PROFESSIONAL, SCIENTIFIC, AND TECHNICAL SERVICES, Items 267–275

Source: U.S. Census Bureau—2007 Economic Census (See Overview of 2007 Economic Census prior to Item 217)

The Professional, Scientific, and Technical Services sector (54) is made up of establishments that specialize in performing professional, scientific, and technical activities for others. These activities require a high degree of expertise and training. The establishments in this sector specialize according to expertise and provide services to clients in a variety of industries (and, in some cases, to households). Activities performed include legal advice and representation; accounting, bookkeeping, and payroll services; architectural, engineering, and specialized design services; computer services; consulting services; research services; advertising services; photographic services; translation and interpretation services; veterinary services; and other professional, scientific, and technical services.

This sector excludes establishments primarily engaged in providing a range of day-to-day office administrative services, such as financial planning, billing and record keeping, personnel services, and physical distribution and logistics services. These establishments are classified in sector 56, Administrative and Support and Waste Management and Remediation Services.

Legal Services is a NAICS industry group (5411) that includes establishments classified in the following NAICS industries: 54111, Offices of Lawyers, and 54119, Other Legal Services.

Accounting, Tax Preparation, Bookkeeping, and Payroll Services is a NAICS industry group (5412) that comprises establishments primarily engaged in providing services such as auditing of accounting records, designing accounting systems, preparing financial statements, developing budgets, preparing tax returns, processing payrolls, bookkeeping, and billing.

Architectural, Engineering, and Related Services is a NAICS industry group (5413) that includes establishments classified in the following NAICS industries: 54131, Architectural Services; 54133, Engineering Services; 54134, Drafting Services; 54135, Building Inspection Services; 54136, Geophysical Surveying and Mapping Services; 54137, Surveying and Mapping (Except Geophysical) Services; and 54138, Testing Laboratories.

Computer Systems Design and Related Services is a NAICS industry group (5415) that consists of establishments primarily engaged in providing expertise in the field of information technologies through one or more of the following activities: (1) writing, modifying, testing, and supporting software to meet the needs of a particular customer; (2) planning and designing computer systems that integrate computer hardware, software, and communication technologies; (3) on-site management and operation of clients' computer systems and/or data processing facilities; and (4) other professional and technical computer-related advice and services.

HEALTH CARE AND SOCIAL ASSISTANCE, Items 276–289

Source: U.S. Census Bureau—2007 Economic Census (See Overview of 2007 Economic Census prior to Item 217)

The Health Care and Social Assistance sector (62) consists of establishments that provide health care and social assistance services to individuals. The sector includes both health care and social assistance, because it is sometimes difficult to distinguish between the boundaries of these two activities. The industries in this sector are arranged on a continuum starting with those that provide medical care exclusively, continuing with those that provide health care and social assistance, and finishing with those that provide only social assistance. The services provided by establishments in this sector are delivered by trained professionals. All industries in the sector share this commonality of process-namely, labor inputs of health practitioners or social workers with the requisite expertise. Many of the industries in the sector are defined based on the educational degree held by the practitioners included in the industry.

In this volume, taxable and tax-exempt establishments are presented separately.

Excluded from this sector are aerobic classes, which can be found in subsector 713, Amusement, Gambling and Recreation Industries; and nonmedical diet and weight-reducing centers, which can be found in subsector 812, Personal and Laundry Services. Although these can be viewed as health services, they are not typically delivered by health practitioners.

Industries in the **Ambulatory Health Care Services** subsector (621) provide health care services directly or indirectly to ambulatory patients and do not typically provide inpatient services. Health practitioners in this subsector provide outpatient services, and facilities and equipment do not usually play the most significant part in this sector's production process.

Industries in the **Hospitals** subsector (622) provide medical, diagnostic, and treatment services, including physician, nursing, specialized accommodation, and other health services, to inpatients. Hospitals may provide outpatient services as a secondary activity. Many of the services provided by establishments in the Hospitals subsector require the use of specialized facilities and equipment, both of which form a significant and integral part of the production process.

ARTS, ENTERTAINMENT, AND RECREATION, Items 290–294

Source: U.S. Census Bureau—2007 Economic Census (See Overview of 2007 Economic Census prior to Item 217)

The Arts, Entertainment, and Recreation sector (71) includes a wide range of establishments that operate facilities or provide services that meet the diverse cultural, entertainment, and recreational interests of their patrons. This sector is made up of: (1) establishments that are involved in producing, promoting, or participating in live performances, events, or exhibits intended for public viewing; (2) establishments that preserve and exhibit objects and sites of historical, cultural, or educational interest; and (3) establishments that operate facilities or provide services that enable patrons to participate in recreational activities or pursue amusement, hobby, and leisure time interests.

Some establishments that provide cultural, entertainment, or recreational facilities and services are classified in other sectors. Excluded from this sector are: (1) establishments that provide both accommodations and recreational facilities—such as hunting and fishing camps and resort and casino hotels—are classified in subsector 721, Accommodation; (2) restaurants and night clubs that provide live entertainment in addition to the sale of food and beverages are classified in subsector 722, Food Services and Drinking Places; (3) motion picture theaters, libraries and archives, and publishers of newspapers, magazines, books, periodicals, and computer software are classified in sector 51, Information; and (4) establishments that use transportation equipment to provide recreational and entertainment services, such as those operating sightseeing buses, dinner cruises, or helicopter rides, are classified in subsector 487, Scenic and Sightseeing Transportation.

ACCOMMODATION AND FOOD SERVICES, Items 295–300

Source: U.S. Census Bureau—2007 Economic Census (See Overview of 2007 Economic Census prior to Item 217)

The Accommodation and Food Services sector (72) consists of establishments that provide customers with lodging and/or meals, snacks, and beverages for immediate consumption. The sector includes both accommodation and food services establishments because the two activities are often combined at the same establishment. Excluded from this sector are civic and social organizations, amusement and recreation parks, theaters, and other recreation or entertainment facilities providing food and beverage services.

Industries in the **Food Services and Drinking Places** subsector (722) prepare meals, snacks, and beverages to customer order for immediate on-premises and off-premises consumption. There is a wide range of establishments in these industries. Some provide food and drink only; while others provide various combinations of seating space, waiter/waitress services and incidental amenities, such as limited entertainment. The industries in the subsector are grouped based on the type and level of services provided. The industry groups are full-service restaurants; limited-service eating places; special food services, such as food service contractors, caterers, and mobile food services; and drinking places. Food services and drink activities at hotels and motels; amusement parks, theaters, casinos, country clubs, and similar recreational facilities; and civic and social organizations are included in this subsector only if these services are provided by a separate establishment primarily engaged in providing food and beverage services. Excluded from this subsector are establishments operating dinner cruises. These establishments are classified in subsector 487, Scenic and Sightseeing Transportation, because they utilize transportation equipment to provide scenic recreational entertainment.

OTHER SERVICES, EXCEPT PUBLIC ADMINISTRATION Items 301–308

Source: U.S. Census Bureau—2007 Economic Census (See Overview of 2007 Economic Census prior to Item 217)

The Other Services, Except Public Administration sector (81) comprises establishments engaged in providing services not specifically categorized elsewhere in the classification system. Establishments in this sector are primarily engaged in activities such as equipment and machinery repairing, promoting or administering religious activities, grant making, and advocacy; this sector also includes establishments that provide dry-cleaning and laundry services, personal care services, death care services, pet care services, photofinishing services, temporary parking services, and dating services.

Private households that employ workers on or about the premises in activities primarily concerned with the operation of the household are included in this sector.

Excluded from this sector are establishments primarily engaged in retailing new equipment and performing repairs and general maintenance on equipment. These establishments are classified in sector 44–45, Retail Trade.

Industries in the **Repair and Maintenance** subsector (811) restore machinery, equipment, and other products to working order. These establishments also typically provide general or routine maintenance (i.e., servicing) on such products to ensure they work efficiently; this maintenance also helps prevent breakdowns and make certain repairs unnecessary.

The NAICS structure for this subsector brings together most types of repair and maintenance establishments and categorizes them based on production processes (i.e., on the type of repair and maintenance activity performed, and the necessary skills, expertise, and processes required for different repair and maintenance establishments). This NAICS classification does not delineate between repair services provided to businesses versus those provided to households. Although some industries primarily serve either businesses or households, separation by class of customer is limited by the fact that many establishments serve both types. Establishments that repair computers and consumer electronics products are examples of such overlap.

The Repair and Maintenance subsector does not include all establishments engaged in repair and maintenance. For example, a substantial amount of repair is done by establishments that also manufacture machinery, equipment, and other goods. These establishments are included in the Manufacturing sector in NAICS. In addition, the repairing of transportation equipment is often provided by or based at transportation facilities, such as airports and seaports; these activities are included in the Transportation and Warehousing sector.

A particularly unique situation exists with repair of buildings. Plumbing, electrical installation and repair, painting and decorating, and other construction-related establishments are often involved in performing installation or other work on new construction, while also providing repair services on existing structures. Although some establishments do specialize in repair, it is difficult to distinguish between these two types. Thus, all such establishments are included in the Construction sector.

Excluded from this subsector are establishments primarily engaged in rebuilding or remanufacturing machinery and equipment. These are classified in sector 31–33, Manufacturing. Also excluded are retail establishments that provide after-sale services and repair. These are classified in sector 44–45, Retail Trade.

Industries in the **Personal and Laundry Services** subsector (812) include establishments that provide personal and laundry services to individuals, households, and businesses. Services performed include personal care services, death care services, laundry and dry-cleaning services, and a wide range of other personal services, such as pet care (except veterinary) services, photofinishing services, temporary parking services, and dating services.

The Personal and Laundry Services subsector is by no means all-inclusive of the activities that could be termed personal services (i.e., those provided to individuals rather than businesses). There are many other sectors and subsectors that provide services to persons. Establishments providing legal, accounting, tax preparation, architectural, portrait photography, and similar professional services are classified in sector 54, Professional, Scientific, and Technical Services; those providing job placement, travel arrangement, home security, interior and exterior house cleaning, exterminating, lawn and garden care, and similar support services are classified in sector 56, Administrative and Support and Waste Management and Remediation Services; those providing health and social services are classified in sector 62, Health Care and Social Assistance; those providing amusement and recreation services are classified in sector 71, Arts, Entertainment and Recreation; those providing educational instruction are classified in sector 61, Educational Services; those providing repair services are classified in subsector 811, Repair and Maintenance; and those providing spiritual, civic, and advocacy services are classified in subsector 813, Religious, Grantmaking, Civic, Professional, and Similar Organizations.

Industries in the **Religious, Grantmaking, Civic, Professional, and Similar Organizations** subsector (813) include establishments that organize and promote religious activities, support various causes through grant making, advocate various social and political causes, and promote and defend the interests of their members. This category includes only tax-exempt establishments.

The industry groups within the subsector are defined in terms of their activities, separately grouping establishments that provide funding for specific causes or for a variety of charitable causes, establishments that advocate and actively promote causes and beliefs for the public good, and establishments that have an active membership structure to promote causes and represent the interests of their members. Establishments in this subsector may publish newsletters, books, and periodicals for distribution to their membership.

GOVERNMENT EMPLOYMENT, Items 309–311

Source: U.S. Bureau of Economic Analysis—Regional Economic Accounts
http://www.bea.gov/regional/index.htm#state

Employment is measured as the average annual sum of full-time and part-time jobs. The estimates are on a place-of-work basis. Data for federal civilian employment include civilian employees of the Department of Defense. Military employment includes all persons on active duty status.

STATE GOVERNMENT EMPLOYMENT AND PAYROLL, Items 312–330

Source: U.S. Census Bureau—2012 Census of Governments
http://www.census.gov/govs/cog2012/

The Census of Governments identifies the scope and nature of the nation's state and local government sector; provides authoritative benchmark figures of public finance and public employment; classifies local government organizations, powers, and activities; and measures federal, state, and local fiscal relationships. The Employment component was mailed **March 2012** to collect information on the number of state and local government civilian employees and their payrolls.

State government employees include all persons paid for personal services performed, including persons paid from federally funded programs, paid elected or appointed officials, persons in a paid leave status, and persons paid on a per meeting, annual, semiannual, or quarterly basis. Unpaid officials, pensioners, persons whose work is performed on a fee basis, and contractors and their employees are excluded from the count of employees. **Full-time employees** are persons employed during the pay period to work the number of hours per week that represents regular full-time employment. Included are full-time temporary or seasonal employees who are working the number of hours that represent full-time employment. **Part-time employees** are persons paid on a part-time basis during the designated pay period. Included are those daily or hourly employees usually engaged for less than the regular full-time workweek, as well as any part-time paid officials. **Full-Time Equivalent employees** is a computed statistic representing the number of full-time employees that could have been employed if the reported number of hours worked by part-time employees had been worked by full-time employees. This statistic is calculated separately for each function of a government by dividing the ''part-time hours paid'' by the standard number of hours for full-time employees in the particular government and then adding the resulting quotient to the number of full-time employees.

Full-time payroll represents gross payroll amounts for the one-month period of March for full-time employees. **Part-time pay** represents gross payroll amounts for the one-month period of March for part-time employees. Gross payroll includes all salaries, wages, fees, commissions, and overtime paid to employees **before** withholdings for taxes, insurance, etc. It also includes incentive payments that are paid at regular pay intervals. It excludes employer share of fringe benefits like retirement, Social Security, health and life insurance, lump sum payments, and so forth.

Administration combines **Financial administration** and **Other government administration**. **Financial administration** includes activities concerned with tax assessment and collection, custody and disbursement of funds, debt management, administration of trust funds, budgeting, and other government-wide financial management activities. This function is not applied to school district or special district governments. **Other government administration** applies to the legislative and government-wide administrative agencies of governments. Included here are overall planning and zoning activities, and central personnel and administrative activities. This function is not applied to school district or special district governments.

Judicial and legal includes all court and court related activities (except probation and parole activities that are included at the ''Correction'' function), court activities of sheriff's offices, prosecuting attorneys' and public defenders' offices, legal departments, and attorneys providing government-wide legal service.

Police includes all activities concerned with the enforcement of law and order, including coroner's offices, police training academies, investigation bureaus, and local jails, ''lockups,'' or other detention facilities not intended to serve as correctional facilities.

Corrections includes activities pertaining to the confinement and correction of adults and minors convicted of criminal offenses. Pardon, probation, and parole activities are also included here.

Highways and transportation includes activities associated with the maintenance and operation of streets, roads, sidewalks, bridges, tunnels, toll roads, and ferries. Snow and ice removal, street lighting, and highway and traffic engineering activities are also included here. Also included are the operation, maintenance, and construction of public mass transit systems, including subways, surface rails, and buses; and the provision, construction, operation, maintenance, and support of public waterways, harbors, docks, wharves, and related marine terminal facilities; and activities associated with the operation and support of publicly operated airport facilities.

Public welfare includes the administration of various public assistance programs for the needy, veteran services, operation of nursing homes, indigent care institutions, and programs that provide payments for medical care, handicap transportation, and other services for the needy.

Health includes administration of public health programs, community and visiting nurse services, immunization programs, drug abuse rehabilitation programs, health and food inspection activities, operation of outpatient clinics, and environmental pollution control activities.

Hospitals includes only government operated medical care facilities that provide inpatient care. Employees and payrolls of private corporations that lease and operate government-owned hospital facilities are excluded.

Social insurance administration includes the administration of unemployment compensation systems, public employment services, and the Federal Social Security, Medicare, and Railroad Retirement trusts.

Natural resources and parks includes activities primarily concerned with the conservation and development of natural resources (soil, water, energy, minerals, etc.) and the regulation of industries that develop, utilize, or affect natural resources, as well as the operation and maintenance of parks, playgrounds, swimming pools, public beaches, auditoriums, public golf courses, museums, marinas, botanical gardens, and zoological parks.

Utilities, sewerage, and waste management includes operation, maintenance, and construction of public water supply systems, including production, acquisition, and distribution of water to general public or to other public or private utilities, for residential, commercial, and industrial use; activities associated with the production or acquisition and distribution of electric power; provision, maintenance, and operation of sanitary and storm sewer systems and sewage disposal and treatment facilities; and refuse collection and disposal, operation of sanitary landfills, and street cleaning activities.

Elementary and secondary education and libraries includes activities associated with the operation of public elementary and secondary schools and locally operated vocational-technical schools. Special education programs operated by elementary and secondary school systems are also included as are all ancillary services associated with the operation of schools, such as pupil transportation and food service. Also included are the establishment and provision of libraries for use by the general public and the technical support of privately operated libraries. This category includes classroom teachers, principals, supervisors of instruction, librarians, teacher aides, library aides, and guidance and psychological personnel as well as school superintendents and other administrative personnel, clerical and secretarial staffs, plant operation and maintenance personnel, health and recreation employees, transportation and food service personnel, and any student employees.

Higher education includes state government degree-granting institutions that provide academic training above grade 12. This includes persons engaged in teaching and related academic research as well as administrative, clerical, custodial, cafeteria, health personnel, noninstructional employees engaged in organized research, law enforcement personnel, and paid student employees.

STATE GOVERNMENT FINANCES, Items 331–350

Source: U.S. Census Bureau—State Government Finances
http://www.census.gov/govs/state/

Data are from an annual survey conducted by the Census Bureau and pertain to state government fiscal years ending on June 30, except for four states with other ending dates: Alabama and Michigan (September 30), New York (March 31), and Texas (August 31).

The state government finance data presented in this publication may differ from data published by state governments because the Census Bureau may be using a different definition of which organizations are covered under the term, ''state government.''

For the purpose of Census Bureau statistics, the term ''state government'' refers not only to the executive, legislative, and judicial branches of a given state, but it also includes agencies, institutions, commissions, and public authorities that operate separately or somewhat autonomously from the central state government but where the state government maintains administrative or fiscal control over their activities as defined by the Census Bureau.

Total **general revenue** includes all revenue except utility, liquor stores, and insurance trust revenue. All tax revenue and intergovernmental revenue, even if designated for employee-retirement or local utility purpose, are classified as general revenue.

Intergovernmental revenue covers amounts received from the federal government as fiscal aid, reimbursements for performance of general government functions and specific services for the paying government, or in lieu of taxes. It excludes any amounts received from other governments from the sale of property, commodities, and utility services.

Taxes consist of compulsory contributions exacted by governments for public purposes. However, this category excludes employer and employee payments for retirement and social insurance purposes, which are classified as insurance trust revenue; it also excludes special assessments, which are classified as nontax general revenue. Sales and gross receipts taxes do not include dealer discounts, or ''commissions'' allowed to merchants for collection of taxes from consumers. General sales taxes and selected taxes on sales of motor fuels, tobacco products, and other particular commodities and services are included.

General government expenditure includes capital outlay, a major portion of which is commonly financed by borrowing. Government revenue does not include receipts from borrowing. Among other things, this distorts the relationship between totals of revenue and expenditure figures that are presented and renders it useless as a direct measure of the degree of budgetary ''balance'' (as that term is generally applied).

Direct general expenditure comprises all expenditures of the state governments, excluding utility, liquor stores, insurance trust expenditures, and any intergovernmental payments.

State government expenditure for **education** is mainly for the provision and general support of schools and other educational facilities and services, including those for educational institutions beyond high school. They cover such related services as student transportation; school lunch and other cafeteria operations; school health, recreation, and library services; and dormitories, dining halls, and bookstores operated by public institutions of higher education.

Health and hospitals expenditure includes health research; clinics; nursing; immunization; other categorical, environmental, and general health services provided by health agencies; establishment and operation of hospital facilities; provision of hospital care; and support of other public and private hospitals.

Highways expenditure is for the provision and maintenance of highway facilities, including toll turnpikes, bridges, tunnels, and ferries, as well as regular roads, highways, and streets. Also included are expenditures for street lighting and for snow and ice removal. Not included are highway policing and traffic control, which are considered part of police protection

Public safety expenditure includes police and correctional institution expenditures.

Public welfare expenditure covers support of and assistance to needy persons; this aid is contingent upon the person's needs. Included are cash assistance paid directly to needy persons under categorical (Old Age Assistance, Temporary Assistance for Needy Families, Aid to the Blind, and Aid to the Disabled) and other welfare programs; vendor payments made directly to private purveyors for medical care, burials, and other commodities and services provided under welfare programs; welfare institutions; and any intergovernmental or other direct expenditure for welfare purposes. Pensions to former employees and other benefits not contingent on need are excluded.

Natural resources, parks, and recreation includes expenditures for conservation, promotion, and development of natural resources (soil, water, energy, minerals, etc.) and the regulation of industries which develop, utilize, or affect natural resources. It also includes the provision and support of recreational and cultural-scientific facilities, such as golf courses, playgrounds, tennis courts, public beaches, swimming pools, play fields, parks, camping areas, recreational piers and marinas, galleries, museums, zoos, botanical gardens, auditoriums, stadiums, recreational centers, convention centers, exhibition halls, community music, drama, and celebrations.

Debt outstanding includes all long-term debt obligations of the government and its agencies (exclusive of utility debt) and all interest-bearing, short-term (repayable within one year) debt obligations remaining unpaid at the close of the fiscal year. It includes judgments, mortgages, and revenue bonds, as well as general obligation bonds, notes, and interest-bearing warrants. This category consists of non-interest-bearing, short-term obligations; inter-fund obligations; amounts owed in a trust or agency capacity; advances and contingent loans from other governments; and rights of individuals to benefit from government-administered employee-retirement funds.

VOTING AND REGISTRATION, Items 351 and 352

Source: U.S. Census Bureau—Current Population Survey
http://www.census.gov/hhes/www/socdemo/voting/index.html

These estimates are based on the November 2014 Voting and Registration Supplement to the Current Population Survey (CPS).

Voting rates are calculated using the voting-age population, which includes both citizens and noncitizens. Statistics from surveys are subject to sampling and nonsampling error. The CPS estimate of overall turnout differs from the ''official'' turnout reported by the Clerk of the House of Representatives.

ELECTION STATISTICS, Items 353–355

Source: Election Data Services, Inc. Washington, DC (copyright)
http://www.electiondataservices.com/

Election results show the percentage of the total vote cast for the Democratic and Republican candidates, as well as the combined percentage for all other candidates in the 2012 presidential election.

TABLE B—STATES AND COUNTIES

Table B presents 199 items for the United States as a whole, each individual state, and the District of Columbia and every county, county equivalent, and independent city. The counties are presented in alphabetical order within each state, and the states are also presented in alphabetical order. Independent cities, which are found in Maryland, Missouri, Nevada, and Virginia, are placed in alphabetical order at the end of the list of counties for those states. The District of Columbia is included in Table B as both a county and a state. It is also included as a city in Table D.

LAND AREA, Items 1 and 4

Source: U.S. Census Bureau—2010 Census of Population and Housing
http://www.census.gov/2010census/data/

Land area measurements are shown to the nearest square kilometer. Land area includes dry land and land temporarily or partially covered by water, such as marshlands, swamps, and river floodplains.

POPULATION, Items 2–4

Source: U.S. Census Bureau—Population Estimates
http://www.census.gov/popest/estimates.html

The population data are Census Bureau estimates of the resident population as of July 1 of the year shown. The ranks are shown for counties (including independent cities and the District of Columbia).

POPULATION AND POPULATION CHARACTERISTICS, Items 5–19

Source: U.S. Census Bureau—Population Estimates
http://www.census.gov/popest/estimates.html

The concept of race, as used by the Census Bureau, reflects self-identification by persons according to the race or races with which they most closely identify. These categories are sociopolitical constructs and should not be interpreted as being scientific or anthropological in nature. Furthermore, race categories include both racial and national origin groups.

Beginning with the 2000 census, respondents were offered the option of selecting one or more races. This option was not available in prior censuses; thus, comparisons between censuses should be made with caution. In Table B, Columns 5 through 8 refer to individuals who identified with each racial category, either alone or in combination with other races. The estimates exclude persons of Hispanic or Latino origin from all race groups. Because respondents could include as many categories as they wished, and because the columns refer to the percentage of the population, the total will often exceed 100 percent.

The **White** population is defined as persons who indicated their race as White, as well as persons who did not classify themselves in one of the specific race categories listed on the questionnaire but entered a nationality such as Irish, German, Italian, Lebanese, Near Easterner, Arab, or Polish.

The **Black** population includes persons who indicated their race as ''Black, African Am., or Negro,'' as well as persons who did not classify themselves in one of the specific race categories but reported entries such as African American, Afro American, Kenyan, Nigerian, or Haitian.

The **American Indian or Alaska Native** population includes persons who indicated their race as American Indian or Alaska Native, as well as persons who did not classify themselves in one of the specific race categories but reported entries such as Canadian Indian, French-American Indian, Spanish-American Indian, Eskimo, Aleut, Alaska Indian, or any of the American Indian or Alaska Native tribes.

The **Asian and Pacific Islander** population combines two census groupings: **Asian** and **Native Hawaiian or Other Pacific Islander**. The **Asian** population includes persons who indicated their race as Asian Indian, Chinese, Filipino, Japanese, Korean, Vietnamese, or ''Other Asian,'' as well as persons who provided write-in entries of such groups as Cambodian, Laotian, Hmong, Pakistani, or Taiwanese. The **Native Hawaiian or Other Pacific Islander** population includes persons who indicated their race as ''Native Hawaiian,'' ''Guamanian or Chamorro,'' ''Samoan,'' or ''Other Pacific Islander,'' as well as persons who reported entries such as Part Hawaiian, American Samoan, Fijian, Melanesian, or Tahitian.

The **Hispanic population** is based on a question that asked respondents ''Is this person Spanish/Hispanic/Latino?'' Persons marking any one of the four Hispanic categories (i.e., Mexican, Puerto Rican, Cuban, or other Spanish) are collectively referred to as Hispanic.

In the census, the Hispanic origin question was placed before the race question and specific instructions indicated that both questions should be answered. These changes were designed to improve accuracy and may affect comparability with data prior to the 2000 census.

Age is defined as age at last birthday (number of completed years since birth), as of April 1 of the census year. The census also asked for the specific date of birth of the respondent, and census procedures used the birth date for deriving age data. For this reason, it is likely that the data have fewer problems than data from censuses prior to 2000, such as the tendency of respondents to round ages or to report their ages on the date the questionnaire was filled out rather than on April 1.

The **female** population is shown as a percentage of total population.

POPULATION AND COMPONENTS OF CHANGE, Items 20–26

Source: U.S. Census Bureau—Decennial Censuses and Population Estimates
http://www.census.gov/main/www/cen2000.html
http://www.census.gov/popest/estimates.html
http://www.census.gov/2010census/data/

The population data for 1990, 2000, and 2010 are from the decennial censuses and represent the resident population as of April 1 of those years. The components of change are based on Census Bureau estimates of the resident population as of July 1, 2014. The change in population between 2010 and 2014 is made up of (a) natural increase—births minus deaths, and (b) net migration—the difference between the number of persons moving into a particular area and the number of persons moving out of the area. Net migration is composed of internal and international migration.

Because the 2014 population estimates are based on a model that begins with a national population estimate, the county components of change do not always exactly add up to the difference between the 2010 census population and the 2014 estimates.

HOUSEHOLDS, Items 27–31

Source: U.S. Census Bureau—American Community Survey
http://www.census.gov/acs/www/

A **household** includes all of the persons who occupy a housing unit. (Persons not living in households are classified as living in group quarters.) A housing unit is a house, an apartment, a mobile home, a group of rooms, or a single room occupied (or, if vacant, intended for occupancy) as separate living quarters. Separate living quarters are those in which the occupants live separately from any other persons in the building and have direct access from the outside of the building or through a common hall. The occupants may be a single family, one person living alone, two or more families living together, or any other group of related or unrelated persons who share living quarters. The number of households is the same as the number of year-round occupied housing units.

A **family** includes a householder and one or more other persons living in the same household who are related to the householder by birth, marriage, or adoption. All persons in a household who are related to the householder are regarded as members of his or her family. A **family household** may contain persons not related to the householder; thus, family households may include more members than families do. A household can contain only one family for the purposes of census tabulations. Not all households contain families, as a household may comprise a group of unrelated persons or of one person living alone. Families are classified by type as either a ''husband-wife family'' or ''other family,'' according to the presence or absence of a spouse.

The measure of **persons per household** is obtained by dividing the number of persons in households by the number of households or householders. One person in each household is designated as the householder. In most cases, this is the person (or one of the persons) in whose name the house is owned, being bought, or rented. If there is no such person in the household, any adult household member 15 years old and over can be designated as the householder.

The category **female family householder** includes only female-headed family households with no spouse present.

GROUP QUARTERS, Item 32

Source:
Source: U.S. Census Bureau—Population Estimates
http://www.census.gov/popest/estimates.html

The Census Bureau classifies all persons not living in households as living in group quarters; this category includes both the institutional and noninstitutional populations. The institutionalized population includes persons under formally authorized, supervised care or custody in institutions, such as correctional institutions, nursing homes, mental (psychiatric) hospitals, and juvenile institutions. The noninstitutionalized population includes persons who live in group quarters other than institutions, such as college dormitories, military quarters, and group homes. This volume includes the total number of persons in group quarters.

DAYTIME POPULATION, Items 33 and 34

Source: U.S. Census Bureau—American Community Survey
http://www.census.gov/acs/www/

Daytime population refers to the number of persons who are present in an area or place during normal business hours, including workers. This can be contrasted with the ''resident'' population, which is present during the evening and nighttime hours. The daytime population estimate is calculated by adding the total resident population and the total workers working in the area/place, and then subtracting the total workers living in the area/place from that result. Information on the expansion or contraction experienced by different communities between their nighttime and daytime populations is important for many planning purposes, especially those concerning transportation, disaster, and relief operations.

The employment/residence ratio is a measure of the total number of workers working in an area or place, relative to the total number of workers living in the area or place. It is often used as a rough indication of the jobs-workers balance in an area/place, although it does not take into account whether the resident workers possess the skills needed for the jobs available in their particular area/place. The employment/residence ratio is calculated by dividing the number of total workers working in an area/place by the number of total workers residing in the area/place.

BIRTHS AND DEATHS, Items 35–38

Source: U.S. Census Bureau—Population Estimates
http://www.census.gov/popest/estimates.html

The numbers of births and deaths are from the Census Bureau's Population Estimates Program. They represent the total number of live births and deaths occurring to residents of an area as estimated using reports from the National Center for Health Statistics (NCHS) and the Federal-State Cooperative for Population Estimates (FSCPE). The rates measure births and deaths during the specified time period as a proportion of an area's population. Rates are expressed per 1,000 population estimated as of July 1. These numbers and rates do not represent the calendar year, but rather the year-long period ending on July 1.

PERSONS UNDER 65 WITH NO HEALTH INSURANCE, Items 39 and 40

Source: U.S. Census Bureau—Small Area Health Insurance Estimates
http://www.census.gov/did/www/sahie/index.html

The Small Area Health Insurance Estimates (SAHIE) program develops model-based estimates of health insurance coverage for counties and states. This developmental program builds on the work of the Small Area Income and Poverty Estimates (SAIPE) program. The SAHIE program models health insurance coverage by combining survey data with population estimates and administrative records. These estimates combine data from administrative records, postcensal population estimates, and the decennial census with direct estimates from the American Community Survey to provide consistent and reliable single-year estimates. These model-based single-year estimates are more reflective of current conditions than multi-year survey estimates.

MEDICARE ENROLLMENT, Items 41–43

Source: U.S. Department of Health and Human Services, Centers for Medicare and Medicaid Services http://www.cms.hhs.gov/MCRAdvPartDEnrolData/

The Centers for Medicare and Medicaid Services (CMS) administers Medicare, which provides health insurance to persons 65 years old and over, persons with permanent kidney failure, and certain persons with disabilities. Original Medicare has two parts: Hospital Insurance and Supplemental Medical Insurance. In recent years, Medicare has been expanded to include two new programs: Medicare Advantage plans and prescription drug coverage. Medicare Advantage Plans are health plan options that are approved by Medicare but run by private companies. Medicare prescription drug plans can be part of Medicare Advantage plans or stand-alone drug plans.

Persons who are **eligible** for Medicare can enroll in Part A (Hospital Insurance) at no charge, and can choose to pay a monthly premium to enroll in Part B. Most eligible persons are enrolled in Part A, and more than 90 percent of enrollees in Part A are also enrolled in Part B (Supplemental Medical Insurance.) This table includes persons who were eligible as of December 2014.

Medicare Advantage enrollees were enrolled in a Medicare Advantage plan of some type at the end of 2014. These include Private Fee for Service plans, Preferred Provider Organizations, Health Maintenance Organizations, Medical Savings Account Plans, Demonstration plans, and Programs for All-Inclusive Care for the Elderly.

Persons enrolled in a **Medicare Prescription drug plan** were enrolled in stand-alone plans for prescription drug benefits. This number does not include Medicare enrollees who had prescription drug coverage through private or federal retiree health plans, through Medicare Advantage plans, or through Medicaid.

CRIME, Items 44–47

Source: U.S. Federal Bureau of Investigation—Uniform Crime Reports http://www.fbi.gov/ucr/ucr.htm

Crime data are as reported to the Federal Bureau of Investigation (FBI) by law enforcement agencies and have not been adjusted for underreporting. This may affect comparability between geographic areas or over time.

Through the voluntary contribution of crime statistics by law enforcement agencies across the United States, the Uniform Crime Reporting (UCR) Program provides periodic assessments of crime in the nation as measured by offenses that have come to the attention of the law enforcement community. The Committee on Uniform Crime Records of the International Association of Chiefs of Police initiated this voluntary national data collection effort in 1930. The UCR Program contributors compile and submit their crime data either directly to the FBI or through state-level UCR Programs.

Seven offenses, because of their severity, frequency of occurrence, and likelihood of being reported to police, were initially selected to serve as an index for evaluating fluctuations in the volume of crime. These serious crimes were murder and nonnegligent manslaughter, forcible rape, robbery, aggravated assault, burglary, larceny-theft, and motor vehicle theft. By congressional mandate, arson was added as the eighth index offense in 1979. The totals shown in this volume do not include arson.

In 2004, the FBI discontinued the use of the Crime Index in the UCR Program and its publications, stating that the Crime Index was driven upward by the offense with the highest number of cases (in this case, larceny-theft), creating a bias against jurisdictions with a high number of larceny-thefts but a low number of other serious crimes, such as murder and forcible rape. The FBI is currently publishing a violent crime total and property crime total until a more viable index is developed. This book includes the crime total, as well as violent crime and property crime rates.

In 2013, the FBI adopted a new definition of rape. Rape is now defined as, ''Penetration, no matter how slight, of the vagina or anus with any body part or object, or oral penetration by a sex organ of another person, without the consent of the victim.'' The new definition updated the 80-year-old historical definition of rape which was ''carnal knowledge of a female forcibly and against her will.'' Effectively, the revised definition expands rape to include both male and female victims and offenders, and reflects the various forms of sexual penetration understood to be rape, especially nonconsenting acts of sodomy, and sexual assaults with objects.

At the county level, the change had not been consistently adopted for the 2013 data, so many counties reflect the old definition while many others used the new one.

Violent crimes include four categories of offenses: (1) Murder and nonnegligent manslaughter, as defined in the UCR Program, is the willful (nonnegligent) killing of one human being by another. This offense excludes deaths caused by negligence, suicide, or accident; justifiable homicides; and attempts to murder or assaults to murder. (2) Rape is the penetration, no matter how slight, of the vagina or anus with any body part or object, or oral penetration by a sex organ of another person, without the consent of the victim. Assaults or attempts to commit rape by force or threat of force are also included; however, statutory rape (without force) and other sex offenses are excluded. (3) Robbery is the taking or attempting to take anything of value from the care, custody, or control of a person or persons by force or threat of force or violence and/or by putting the victim in fear. (4) Aggravated assault is an unlawful attack by one person upon another for the purpose of inflicting severe or aggravated bodily injury. This type of assault is usually accompanied by the use of a weapon or by other means likely to produce death or great bodily harm. Attempts are included, since injury does not necessarily have to result when a gun, knife, or other weapon is used, as these incidents could and probably would result in a serious personal injury if the crime were successfully completed.

Property crimes include three categories: (1) Burglary, or breaking and entering, is the unlawful entry of a structure to commit a felony or theft, even though no force was used to gain entrance. (2) Larceny-theft is the unauthorized taking of the personal property of another, without the use of force. (3) Motor vehicle theft is the unauthorized taking of any motor vehicle.

Rates are based on population estimates provided by the FBI. The county totals published in this volume were obtained by aggregating individual reporting units within each county and MSA. If the population total for the units aggregated was less than 75 percent of the county's population (as estimated by the Census Bureau), the total was not considered representative of the county as a whole and was not published. State and U.S. totals include FBI estimates for those areas. State and U.S. totals in this table are the adjusted totals as published in the FBI's *Crime in the United States.*

EDUCATION—SCHOOL ENROLLMENT AND EDUCATIONAL ATTAINMENT, Items 48–51

Source: U.S. Census Bureau—American Community Survey
http://www.census.gov/acs/www/

Persons were classified as enrolled in school if they reported attending a ''regular'' public or private school (or college) during the three months preceding the interview. The instructions were to include only nursery school, kindergarten, elementary school, and schooling which would lead to a high school diploma or a college degree as regular school. The Census Bureau defines a public school as ''any school or college controlled and supported by a local, county, state, or federal government.'' Schools primarily supported and controlled by religious organizations or other private groups are defined as private schools.

Data on **educational attainment** are tabulated for the population 25 years old and over. The data were derived from a question that asked respondents for the highest level of school completed or the highest degree received. Persons who had passed a high school equivalency examination were considered high school graduates. Schooling received in foreign schools was to be reported as the equivalent grade or years in the regular American school system.

Vocational and technical training, such as barber school training; business, trade, technical, and vocational schools; or other training for a specific trade are specifically excluded.

High school graduate or less. This category includes persons whose highest degree was a high school diploma or its equivalent, and those who reported any level lower than a high school diploma.

Bachelor's degree or more. This category includes persons who have received bachelor's degrees, master's degrees, professional school degrees (such as law school or medical school degrees), and doctoral degrees.

LOCAL GOVERNMENT EDUCATION EXPENDITURES, Items 52 and 53

Source: U.S. Census Bureau—Annual Survey of School System Finances
http://www.census.gov/govs/school/

Expenditures are for elementary and secondary education, which includes prekindergarten through twelfth grade regular, special, and vocational education, as well as cocurricular, community service, and adult education programs provided by a public school system. The financial activities of these systems for all instruction, support service, and noninstructional activities are included

Current Spending comprises current operation expenditure, payments made by the state government on behalf of school systems, and transfers made by school systems into their own retirement funds. Current operation expenditures include direct expenditure for salaries, employee benefits, purchased professional and technical services, purchased property and other services, and supplies. It includes gross school system expenditure for instruction, support services, and noninstructional functions. It excludes expenditure for debt service, capital outlay, and reimbursement to other governments (including other school systems).

Current expenditure per student is current expenditure divided by the number of students enrolled. The number of students enrolled is based on an annual ''membership'' count of students on or about October 1, collected by the National Center for Education Statistics on the Common Core of Data (CCD) agency universe file—''Local Education Agency (School District) Universe Survey.''

MONEY INCOME, Items 54–57

Source: U.S. Census Bureau—American Community Survey
http://www.census.gov/acs/www/

Total money income is the sum of the amounts reported separately for wage or salary income; net self-employment income; interest, dividends, or net rental or royalty income or income from estates and trusts; Social Security or railroad retirement income; Supplemental Security Income (SSI); public assistance or welfare payments; retirement, survivor, or disability pensions; and all other income. Receipts from the following sources are not included as income: capital gains; money received from the sale of property (unless the recipient was engaged in the business of selling such property); the value of income ''in kind'' from food stamps, public housing subsidies, medical care, employer contributions for individuals, etc.; withdrawal of bank deposits; money borrowed; tax refunds; exchange of money between relatives living in the same household; and gifts, lump-sum inheritances, insurance payments, and other types of lump-sum receipts.

Money income differs in definition from personal income (item 62). For example, money income does not include the pension rights, employer provided health insurance, food stamps, or Medicare payments that are included in personal income.

Per capita income is the mean income computed for every man, woman, and child in a particular group. It is derived by dividing the aggregate income of a particular group by the resident population in that group as estimated in the American Community Survey. Per capita income is rounded to the nearest whole dollar.

Household income includes the income of the householder and all other individuals 15 years old and over in the household, whether or not they are related to the householder. Since many households consist of only one person, median household income is usually less than median family income. Although the household income statistics cover the 12 months preceding the interview, the characteristics of individuals and the composition of households refer to the date of interview. Thus, the income of the household does not include amounts received by individuals who were no longer residing in the household at the time of interview. Similarly, income amounts reported by individuals who did not reside in the household during all of the past 12 months but who were members of the household at the time of interview are included. However, the composition of most households was the same during those 12 months as it was at the time of interview.

Median income divides the income distribution into two equal parts, with half of all cases below the median income level and half of all cases above the median income level. For households, the median income is based on the distribution of the total number of households, including those with no income. Median income for households is computed on the basis of a standard distribution with a minimum value of less than $2,500 and a maximum value of $200,000 or more and is rounded to the nearest whole dollar. Median income figures are calculated using linear interpolation if the width of the interval containing the estimate is $2,500 or less. If the width of the interval containing the estimate is greater than $2,500, Pareto interpolation is used.

Income amounts have been adjusted for inflation to represent the final year of multi-year estimates, in this case 2008–2012 estimates. The constant-dollar figures are based on an annual average Consumer Price Index from the Bureau of Labor Statistics. Constant-dollar figures are estimates representing an effort to remove the effects of price changes from statistical series reported in dollar terms. However, the estimates do not reflect the price and cost-of-living differences that may exist between areas.

INCOME AND POVERTY, Items 58–61

Source: U.S. Census Bureau—Small Area Income and Poverty Estimates Program
http://www.census.gov/did/www/saipe/index.html

The annual income and poverty estimates by county are constructed from statistical models that relate income and poverty to indicators based on summary data from federal income tax returns, data about participation in the Food Stamp program, and the previous census. A regression model predicts the number of people in poverty using county-level observations from the current year's American Community Survey (ACS) and administrative records and census data as the predictors. The 2005 estimates were the first to use the ACS. Prior year models were based on the Annual Social and Economic Supplement (ASEC) of the Current Population Survey (CPS). The ACS is a much larger survey than the ASEC, permitting income and poverty estimates based on a single year for many counties. Because of the differences between the two surveys, caution should be used when comparing these estimates with those from earlier years.

The **poverty status** data were derived from data collected on the number of persons in a household, each person's relationship to the householder, and income data. The Social Security Administration (SSA) developed the original poverty definition in 1964, which federal interagency committees subsequently revised in 1969 and 1980. The Office of Management and Budget's (OMB) *Directive 14* prescribes the SSA's definition as the official poverty measure for federal agencies to use in their statistical work. Poverty statistics presented in American Community Survey products adhere to the standards defined by OMB in *Directive 14.*

Poverty thresholds vary depending on three criteria: size of family, number of children, and, for one- and two-person families, age of householder. In determining the poverty status of families and unrelated individuals, the Census Bureau uses thresholds (income cutoffs) arranged in a two-dimensional matrix. The matrix consists of family size (from one person to nine or more persons), cross-classified by presence and number of family members under 18 years old (from no children present to eight or more children present). Unrelated individuals and two-person families are further differentiated by age of reference person (under 65 years old and 65 years old and over). To determine a person's poverty status, the person's total family income over the previous 12 months is compared with the poverty threshold appropriate for that person's family size and composition. If the total income of that person's family is less than the threshold appropriate for that family, then the person is considered poor or ''below the poverty level,'' together with every member of his or her family. If a person is not living with anyone related by birth, marriage, or adoption, then the person's own income is compared with his or her poverty threshold. The total number of persons below the poverty level is the sum of persons in families and the number of unrelated individuals with incomes below the poverty level over the previous 12 months.

Poverty Thresholds for 2013 by Size of Family and Number of Related Children Under 18 Years

Size of family unit	Weighted average thresholds
One person (unrelated individual)	11,888
Under 65 years	12,119
65 years and over	11,173
Two people	15,142
Householder under 65 years	15,679
Householder 65 years and over	14,095
Three people	18,552
Four people	23,834
Five people	28,265
Six people	31,925
Seven people	36,384
Eight people	40,484
Nine people or more	48,065

Source: U.S. Census Bureau.

PERSONAL INCOME AND EARNINGS, Items 62–83

Source: U.S. Bureau of Economic Analysis, Regional Economic Accounts
http://www.bea.gov/regional/index.htm#state

Total personal income is the current income received by residents of an area from all sources. It is measured before deductions of income and other personal taxes, but after deductions of personal contributions for Social Security, government retirement, and other social insurance programs. It consists of **wage and salary disbursements** (covering all employee earnings, including executive salaries, bonuses, commissions, payments-in-kind, incentive payments, and tips); various types of supplementary earnings, such as employers' contributions to pension funds (termed ''other labor income'' or ''supplements to wages and salaries''); proprietors' income; rental income of persons; dividends; personal interest income; and government and business transfer payments.

Per capita personal income is based on the resident population estimated as of July 1 of the year shown.

Proprietors' income is the monetary income and income-in-kind of proprietorships and partnerships (including the independent professions) and the income of tax-exempt cooperatives.

Dividends are cash payments by corporations to stockholders who are U.S. residents. **Interest** is the monetary and imputed interest income of persons from all sources. **Rent** is the monetary income of persons from the rental of real property, except the income of persons primarily engaged in the real estate business; the imputed net rental income of owner-occupants of nonfarm dwellings; and the royalties received by persons.

Transfer payments are income for which services are not currently rendered. They consist of both government and business transfer payments. Government transfer payments include payments under the following programs: Federal Old-Age, Survivors, and Disability Insurance (''Social Security''); Medicare and medical vendor payments; unemployment insurance; railroad and government retirement; federal- and state-government-insured workers' compensation; veterans' benefits, including veterans' life insurance; food stamps; black lung payments; Supplemental Security Income; and Temporary Assistance for Needy Families. Government payments to nonprofit institutions, other than for work under research and development contracts, are also included. Business transfer payments consist primarily of liability payments for personal injury and of corporate gifts to nonprofit institutions.

Personal income differs in definition from money income (items 54–57). For example, personal income includes pension rights, employer-provided health insurance, food stamps, and Medicare. These are not included in the definition of money income.

Earnings cover wage and salary disbursements, other labor income, and proprietors' income.

The data for earnings obtained from the Bureau of Economic Analysis (BEA) are based on place of work. In computing personal income, BEA makes an ''adjustment for residence'' to earnings, based on commuting patterns; personal income is thus presented on a place-of-residence basis.

Farm earnings include the income of farm workers (wages and salaries and other labor income) and farm proprietors. Farm proprietors' income includes only the income of sole proprietorships and partnerships. Farm earnings estimates are benchmarked to data collected in the Census of Agriculture and the revised Department of Agriculture statistical totals of income and expense items.

Goods-related industries include mining, construction, and manufacturing. **Service-related** and other industries include private-sector earnings in agricultural services, forestry, and fisheries; transportation and public utilities; wholesale trade; retail trade; finance, insurance, and real estate; and services. Government earnings include all levels of government. Industries are categorized under the North American Industry Classification System (NAICS) and are not comparable to years prior to 2002.

SOCIAL SECURITY AND SUPPLEMENTAL SECURITY INCOME, Items 84–86

Source: U.S. Social Security Administration
http://www.ssa.gov/policy/docs/statcomps/oasdi_sc/
http://www.ssa.gov/policy/docs/statcomps/ssi_sc/

Social Security beneficiaries are persons receiving benefits under the Old-Age, Survivors, and Disability Insurance Program. These include retired or disabled workers covered by the program, their spouses and dependent children, and the surviving spouses and dependent children of deceased workers.

Supplemental Security Income (SSI) recipients are persons receiving SSI payments. The SSI program is a cash assistance program that provides monthly benefits to low-income aged, blind, or disabled persons.

Data are as of December of the year shown.

HOUSING, Items 87–96

Source: U.S. Census Bureau—Population Estimates Program
http://www.census.gov/popest/
Source: U.S. Census Bureau—American Community Survey
http://www.census.gov/acs/www/

Housing data for 2014 are from the Population Estimates Program. Housing unit characteristics for 2009–2013 are from the American Community Survey.

A **housing unit** is a house, apartment, mobile home or trailer, group of rooms, or single room occupied or, if vacant, intended for occupancy as separate living quarters. Separate living quarters are those in which the occupants do not live and eat with any other person in the structure and which have direct access from the outside of the building or through a common hall.

The occupants of a housing unit may be a single family, one person living alone, two or more families living together, or any other group of related or unrelated persons who share living quarters. Both occupied and vacant housing units are included in the housing inventory, although recreational vehicles, tents, caves, boats, railroad cars, and the like are included only if they are occupied as a person's usual place of residence.

A housing unit is classified as occupied if it is the usual place of residence of the person or group of persons living in it at the time of enumeration, or if the occupants are only temporarily absent (away on vacation). A household consists of all persons who occupy a housing unit as their usual place of residence. Vacant units for sale or rent include units rented or sold but not occupied and any other units held off the market.

Median value is the dollar amount that divides the distribution of specified owner-occupied housing units into two equal parts, with half of all units below the median value and half of all units above the median value. Value is defined as the respondent's estimate of what the house would sell for if it were for sale. Data are presented for single-family units on fewer than 10 acres of land that have no business or medical offices on the property.

Median rent divides the distribution of renter-occupied housing units into two equal parts. The rent concept used in this volume is gross rent, which includes the amount of cash rent a renter pays (contract rent) plus the estimated average cost of utilities and fuels, if these are paid by the renter. The rent is the amount of rent only for living quarters and excludes amounts paid for any business or other space occupied. Single-family houses on lots of 10 or more acres of land are also excluded.

Housing cost as a percentage of income is shown separately for owners with mortgages, owners without mortgages, and renters. Rent as a percentage of income is a computed ratio of gross rent and monthly household income (total household income in 2014 divided by 12). Selected owner costs include utilities and fuels, mortgage payments, insurance, taxes, etc. In each case, the ratio of housing cost to income is computed separately for each housing unit. The housing cost ratios for half of all units are above the median shown in this book, and half are below the median shown in the book.

Substandard units are occupied units that are overcrowded or lack complete plumbing facilities. For the purposes of this item, ''overcrowded'' is defined as having 1.01 persons or more per room. Complete plumbing facilities include hot and cold piped water, a flush toilet, and a bathtub or shower. These facilities must be located inside the housing unit, but do not have to be in the same room.

CIVILIAN LABOR FORCE AND UNEMPLOYMENT, Items 97–100

Source: U.S. Bureau of Labor Statistics—Local Area Unemployment Statistics
http://www.bls.gov/lau/#tables

Data for the civilian labor force are the product of a federal-state cooperative program in which state employment security agencies prepare labor force and unemployment estimates under concepts, definitions, and technical procedures established by the Bureau of Labor Statistics (BLS). The civilian labor force consists of all civilians 16 years old and over who are either employed or unemployed.

Unemployment includes all persons who did not work during the survey week, made specific efforts to find a job during the previous four weeks, and were available for work during the survey week (except for temporary illness). Persons waiting to be called back to a job from which they had been laid off and those waiting to report to a new job within the next 30 days are included in unemployment figures.

Table B includes annual average data for the year shown. The Local Area Unemployment Statistics data are periodically updated to reflect revised inputs, reestimation, and controlling to new statewide totals.

CIVILIAN EMPLOYMENT, Items 101–103

Source: U.S. Census Bureau—American Community Survey
http://www.census.gov/acs/www/

Total employment includes all civilians 16 years old and over who were either (1) ''at work''—those who did any work at all during the reference week as paid employees, worked in either their own business or profession, worked on their own farm, or worked 15 hours or more as unpaid workers in a family farm or business; or were (2) ''with a job, but not at work''—those who had a job but were not at work that week due to illness, weather, industrial dispute, vacation, or other personal reasons.

The **occupational categories** are based on the occupational classification system that was developed for the 2000 census and revised in 2002 and 2010. This system consists of 539 specific occupational categories for employed persons arranged into 23 major occupational groups. This classification was developed based on the *Standard Occupational Classification (SOC) Manual: 2000*, published by the Executive Office of the President, Office of Management and Budget.

PRIVATE NONFARM EMPLOYMENT AND EARNINGS, Items 104–112

Source: U.S. Bureau of Labor Statistics—County Business Patterns
http://www.census.gov/econ/cbp/index.html

Data for private nonfarm employment and earnings are compiled from the payroll information reported monthly in the Census Bureau publication *County Business Patterns*. The estimates are based on surveys conducted by the Census Bureau and administrative records from the Internal Revenue Service (IRS).

The following types of employment are excluded from the tables: government employment, self-employed persons, farm workers, and domestic service workers. Railroad employment jointly covered by Social Security and railroad retirement programs, employment on oceanborne vessels, and employment in foreign countries are also excluded.

Annual payroll is the combined amount of wages paid, tips reported, and other compensation (including salaries, vacation allowances, bonuses, commissions, sick-leave pay, and the value of payments-in-kind such as free meals and lodging) paid to employees before deductions for Social Security, income tax, insurance, union dues, etc. All forms of compensation are included, regardless of whether they are subject to income tax or the Federal Insurance Contributions Act tax, with the exception of annuities, third-party sick pay, and supplemental unemployment compensation benefits (even if income tax was withheld). For corporations, total annual payroll includes compensation paid to officers and executives; for unincorporated businesses, it excludes profit or other compensation of proprietors or partners.

AGRICULTURE, ITEMS 113–132

Source: U.S. Department of Agriculture, National Agricultural Statistics Service—2012 Census of Agriculture
http://agcensus.usda.gov/index.php

Data for the 2012 Census of Agriculture were collected in 2013 but pertain to the year 2012.

The Census Bureau took a census of agriculture every 10 years from 1840 to 1920; since 1925, this census has been taken roughly once every five years. The 1997 Census of Agriculture was the first one conducted by the National Agricultural Statistics Service of the U.S. Department of Agriculture. Over time, the definition of a farm has varied. For recent censuses (including the 2012 census), a farm has been defined as any place from which $1,000 or more of agricultural products were produced and sold or normally would have been sold during the census year. Dollar figures are expressed in current dollars and have not been adjusted for inflation or deflation.

The term **operator** refers to a person who operates a farm by either doing the work or making day-to-day decisions about such activities as planting, harvesting, feeding, marketing, etc. The operator may be the owner, a member of the owner's household, a salaried manager, a tenant, a renter, or a sharecropper. If a person rents land to others or has land worked on shares by others, he/she is considered the operator only of the land that is retained for his/her own operation. The census collected information on the total number of operators, the total number of women operators, and demographic information for up to three operators per farm.

The acreage designated as **land in farms** consists primarily of agricultural land used for crops, pasture, or grazing. It also includes woodland and wasteland not actually under cultivation or used for pasture or grazing, provided that this land was part of the farm operator's total operation. Land in farms is an operating-unit concept and includes all land owned and operated, as well as all land rented from others. Land used rent-free is classified as land rented from others. All land in Indian reservations used for growing crops or grazing livestock is classified as land in farms.

Irrigated land includes all land watered by any artificial or controlled means, such as sprinklers, flooding, furrows or ditches, sub-irrigation, and spreader dikes. Included are supplemental, partial, and preplant irrigation. Each acre was counted only once regardless of the number of times it was irrigated or harvested. Livestock lagoon waste water distributed by sprinkler or flood systems was also included.

Total cropland includes cropland harvested, cropland used only for pasture or grazing, cropland on which all crops failed or were abandoned, cropland in cultivated summer fallow, and cropland idle or used for cover crops or soil improvement but not harvested and not pastured or grazed.

Respondents were asked to report their estimate of the current market **value of land and buildings** owned, rented, or leased from others, and rented and leased to others. Market value refers to the respondent's estimate of what the land and buildings would sell for under current market conditions. If the value of land and buildings was not reported, it was estimated during processing by using the average value of land and buildings from similar farms in the same geographic area.

The **value of machinery and equipment** was estimated by the respondent as the current market value of all cars, trucks, tractors, combines, balers, irrigation equipment, etc., used on the farm. This value is an estimate of what the machinery and equipment would sell for in its present condition and not the replacement or depreciated value. Share interests are reported at full value at the farm where the equipment and machinery are usually kept. Only equipment that was physically located at the farm on December 31, 2012, is included.

Market value of agricultural products sold by farms represents the gross market value before taxes and the production expenses of all agricultural products sold or removed from the place in 2007, regardless of who received the payment. It is equivalent to total sales, and it includes sales by the operator as well as the value of any share received by partners, landlords, contractors, and others associated with the operation. It includes value of direct sales and the value of commodities placed in the Commodity Credit Corporation (CCC) loan program. Market value of agricultural products sold does not include payments received for participation in other federal farm programs. Also, it does not include income from farm-related sources such as customwork and other agricultural services, or income from nonfarm sources.

Government payments consist of direct payments as defined by the 2002 Farm Bill; payments from Conservation Reserve Program (CRP), Wetlands Reserve Program (WRP), Farmable Wetlands Program (FWP), and Conservation Reserve Enhancement Program (CREP); loan deficiency payments; disaster payments; other conservation programs; and all other federal farm programs under which payments were made directly to farm operators. Commodity Credit Corporation (CCC) proceeds, amount from State and local federal crop insurance payments were not included in this category.

WATER CONSUMPTION, Items 133–134

Source: U.S. Geological Survey, National Water—Use Information Program
http://water.usgs.gov/watuse/

Every five years, the U.S. Geological Survey compiles county-level water-use estimates. This volume includes the total fresh and saline withdrawals expressed as million gallons per day. Estimate of withdrawals of ground and surface water are given for the following categories of use: public water supplies, domestic, commercial, irrigation, livestock, industrial, mining, and thermoelectric power. The number of gallons withdrawn per person is based on the county population, but the water is not necessarily used locally, providing an indicator of counties that serve as major water sources.

2007 ECONOMIC CENSUS: OVERVIEW, Items 135–166

Source: U.S. Census Bureau
http://www.census.gov/econ/census07/

The Economic Census provides a detailed portrait of the nation's economy, from the national to the local level, once every five years. The 2007 Economic Census covers nearly all of the

U.S. economy in its basic collection of establishment statistics. The 1997 Economic Census was the first major data source to use the new North American Industry Classification System (NAICS); therefore, data from this census are not comparable to economic data from prior years, which were based on the Standard Industrial Classification (SIC) system.

NAICS, developed in cooperation with Canada and Mexico, classifies North America's economic activities at two-, three-, four-, and five-digit levels of detail; the U.S. version of NAICS further defines industries to a sixth digit. The Economic Census takes advantage of this hierarchy to publish data at these successive levels of detail: sector (two-digit), subsector (three-digit), industry group (four-digit), industry (five-digit), and U.S. industry (six-digit). Information in Table A is at the two-digit level, with a few three- and four-digit items. The data in Table B are at the two-digit level.

Several key statistics are tabulated for all industries in this volume, including number of establishments (or companies), number of employees, payroll, and certain measures of output (sales, receipts, revenue, value of shipments, or value of construction work done).

Number of establishments. An establishment is a single physical location at which business is conducted. It is not necessarily identical with a company or enterprise, which may consist of one establishment or more. Economic Census figures represent a summary of reports for individual establishments rather than companies. For cases in which a census report was received, separate information was obtained for each location where business was conducted. When administrative records of other federal agencies were used instead of a census report, no information was available on the number of locations operated. Each Economic Census establishment was tabulated according to the physical location at which the business was conducted. The count of establishments represents those in business at any time during 2007.

When two activities or more were carried on at a single location under a single ownership, all activities were generally grouped together as a single establishment. The entire establishment was classified on the basis of its major activity, and all of its data were included in that classification. However, when distinct and separate economic activities (for which different industry classification codes were appropriate) were conducted at a single location under a single ownership, separate establishment reports for each of the different activities were obtained in the census.

Number of employees. Paid employees consist of the full-time and part-time employees, including salaried officers and executives of corporations. Included are employees on paid sick leave, paid holidays, and paid vacations; not included are proprietors and partners of unincorporated businesses. The definition of paid employees is the same as that used by the Internal Revenue Service (IRS) on form 941.

For some industries, the Economic Census gives codes representing the number of employees as a range of numbers (for example, ''100 to 249 employees'' or ''1,000 to 2,499'' employees). In this volume, those codes have been replaced by the standard suppression code ''D.''

Payroll. Payroll includes all forms of compensation, such as salaries, wages, commissions, dismissal pay, bonuses, vacation allowances, sick-leave pay, and employee contributions to qualified pension plans paid during the year to all employees. For corporations, payroll includes amounts paid to officers and executives; for unincorporated businesses, it does not include profit or other compensation of proprietors or partners. Payroll is reported before deductions for Social Security, income tax, insurance, union dues, etc. This definition of payroll is the same as that used by on IRS form 941.

Sales, shipments, receipts, revenue, or business done. This measure includes the total sales, shipments, receipts, revenue, or business done by establishments within the scope of the Economic Census. The definition of each of these items is specific to the economic sector measured.

WHOLESALE TRADE, Items 135–138

Source: U.S. Census Bureau—2007 Economic Census (See Overview of 2007 Economic Census prior to Item 135)

The Wholesale Trade sector (sector 42) comprises establishments engaged in wholesaling merchandise, generally without transformation, and rendering services incidental to the sale of merchandise. The wholesaling process is an intermediate step in the distribution of merchandise.

Wholesalers are organized to sell or arrange the purchase or sale of (1) goods for resale (i.e., goods sold to other wholesalers or retailers), (2) capital or durable nonconsumer goods, and (3) raw and intermediate materials and supplies used in production.

Wholesalers sell merchandise to other businesses and normally operate from a warehouse or office. These warehouses and offices are characterized by having little or no display of merchandise. In addition, neither the design nor the location of the premises is intended to solicit walk-in traffic. Wholesalers do not normally use advertising directed to the general public. In general, customers are initially reached via telephone, in-person marketing, or specialized advertising, which may include the internet and other electronic means. Follow-up orders are either vendor-initiated or client-initiated, are usually based on previous sales, and typically exhibit strong ties between sellers and buyers. In fact, transactions are often conducted between wholesalers and clients that have long-standing business relationships.

This sector is made up of two main types of wholesalers: those that sell goods on their own account and those that arrange sales and purchases for others for a commission or fee.

(1) Establishments that sell goods on their own account are known as wholesale merchants, distributors, jobbers, drop shippers, import/export merchants, and sales branches. These establishments typically maintain their own warehouse, where they receive and handle goods for their customers. Goods are generally sold without transformation but may include integral functions, such as sorting, packaging, labeling, and other marketing services.

(2) Establishments arranging for the purchase or sale of goods owned by others or purchasing goods on a commission basis are known as agents and brokers, commission merchants, import/export agents and brokers, auction companies, and manufacturers' representatives. These establishments operate from offices and generally do not own or handle the goods they sell.

Some wholesale establishments may be connected with a single manufacturer and promote and sell that particular manufacturer's products to a wide range of other wholesalers or retailers. Other wholesalers may be connected to a retail chain or a limited number of retail chains and only provide the products needed by the particular retail operation(s). These wholesalers may obtain the products from a wide range of manufacturers. Still other wholesalers may not take title to the goods, but act instead as agents and brokers for a commission.

Although wholesaling normally denotes sales in large volumes, durable nonconsumer goods may be sold in single units. Sales of capital or durable nonconsumer goods used in the production of goods and services, such as farm machinery, medium- and heavy-duty trucks, and industrial machinery, are always included in Wholesale Trade.

The county table includes only **Merchant wholesalers, except manufacturers' sales branches and offices,** establishments primarily engaged in buying and selling merchandise on their own account. Included here are such types of establishments as wholesale distributors and jobbers, importers, exporters, own-brand importers/marketers, terminal and country grain elevators, and farm products assemblers.

RETAIL TRADE, Items 139–142

Source: U.S. Census Bureau—2007 Economic Census (See Overview of 2007 Economic Census prior to Item 135)

The Retail Trade sector (44–45) is made up of establishments engaged in retailing merchandise, generally without transformation, and rendering services incidental to the sale of merchandise.

The retailing process is the final step in the distribution of merchandise; retailers are therefore organized to sell merchandise in small quantities to the general public. This sector comprises two main types of retailers: store and nonstore retailers.

Store retailers operate fixed point-of-sale locations, located and designed to attract a high volume of walk-in customers. In general, retail stores have extensive displays of merchandise and use mass-media advertising to attract customers. They typically sell merchandise to the general public for personal or household consumption; some also serve business and institutional clients. These include establishments such as office supply stores, computer and software stores, building materials dealers, plumbing supply stores, and electrical supply stores. Catalog showrooms, gasoline service stations, automotive dealers, and mobile home dealers are treated as store retailers.

In addition to retailing merchandise, some types of store retailers are also engaged in the provision of after-sales services, such as repair and installation. For example, new automobile dealers, electronic and appliance stores, and musical instrument and supply stores often provide repair services. As a general rule, establishments engaged in retailing merchandise and providing after-sales services are classified in this sector.

Nonstore retailers, like store retailers, are organized to serve the general public, although their retailing methods differ. The establishments of this subsector reach customers and market merchandise with methods including the broadcasting of ''infomercials,'' the broadcasting and publishing of direct-response advertising, the publishing of paper and electronic catalogs, door-to-door solicitation, in-home demonstration, selling from portable stalls (street vendors, except food), and distribution through vending machines. Establishments engaged in the direct sale (nonstore) of products, such as home heating oil dealers and home-delivery newspaper routes are included in this sector.

The buying of goods for resale is a characteristic of retail trade establishments that distinguishes them from establishments in the Agriculture, Manufacturing, and Construction sectors. For example, farms that sell their products at or from the point of production are classified in Agriculture instead of in Retail Trade. Similarly, establishments that both manufacture and sell their products to the general public are classified in Manufacturing instead of Retail Trade. However, establishments that engage in processing activities incidental to retailing are classified in Retail Trade.

REAL ESTATE AND RENTAL AND LEASING, Items 143–146

Source: U.S. Census Bureau—2007 Economic Census (See Overview of 2007 Economic Census prior to Item 135)

The Real Estate and Rental and Leasing sector (53) comprises establishments primarily engaged in renting, leasing, or otherwise allowing the use of tangible or intangible assets, and establishments providing related services. The major portion of this sector is made up of establishments that rent, lease, or otherwise allow the use of their own assets by others. The assets may be tangible, such as real estate and equipment, or intangible, such as patents and trademarks.

This sector also includes establishments primarily engaged in managing real estate for others, selling, renting, and/or buying real estate for others, and appraising real estate. These activities are closely related to this sector's main activity. In addition, a substantial proportion of property management is self-performed by lessors.

The main components of this sector are the real estate lessors industries; equipment lessors industries (including motor vehicles, computers, and consumer goods); and lessors of nonfinancial intangible assets (except copyrighted works).

PROFESSIONAL, SCIENTIFIC, AND TECHNICAL SERVICES, Items 147–150

Source: U.S. Census Bureau—2007 Economic Census (See Overview of 2007 Economic Census prior to Item 135)

The Professional, Scientific, and Technical Services sector (54) is made up of establishments that specialize in performing professional, scientific, and technical activities for others. These activities require a high degree of expertise and training. The establishments in this sector specialize in one or more areas and provide services to clients in a variety of industries (and, in some cases, to households). Activities performed include legal advice and representation; accounting, bookkeeping, and payroll services; architectural, engineering, and specialized design services;

computer services; consulting services; research services; advertising services; photographic services; translation and interpretation services; veterinary services; and other professional, scientific, and technical services.

Table B includes only those establishments subject to federal income tax.

This sector excludes establishments primarily engaged in providing a range of day-to-day office administrative services, such as financial planning, billing and record keeping, personnel services, and physical distribution and logistics services. These establishments are classified in sector 56, Administrative and Support and Waste Management and Remediation Services.

MANUFACTURING, Items 151–154

Source: U.S. Census Bureau—2007 Economic Census (See Overview of 2007 Economic Census prior to Item 135)

The Manufacturing sector (31–33) is made up of establishments engaged in the mechanical, physical, or chemical transformation of materials, substances, or components into new products. The assembling of component parts of manufactured products is considered manufacturing, except in cases in which the activity is appropriately classified in the Construction sector. Establishments in the Manufacturing sector are often described as plants, factories, or mills, and characteristically use power-driven machines and materials-handling equipment. However, establishments that transform materials or substances into new products by hand or in the worker's home, and establishments engaged in selling to the general public products made on the same premises from which they are sold (such as bakeries, candy stores, and custom tailors) may also be included in this sector. Manufacturing establishments may process materials or contract with other establishments to process their materials for them. Both types of establishments are included in the Manufacturing sector.

The materials, substances, or components transformed by manufacturing establishments are raw materials that are products of agriculture, forestry, fishing, mining, or quarrying, or are products of other manufacturing establishments. The materials used may be purchased directly from producers, obtained through customary trade channels, or secured without recourse to the market by transferring the product from one establishment to another, under the same ownership. The new product of a manufacturing establishment may be finished (in the sense that it is ready for utilization or consumption), or it may be semifinished to become an input for an establishment engaged in further manufacturing. For example, the product of the alumina refinery is the input used in the primary production of aluminum; primary aluminum is the input used in an aluminum wire drawing plant; and aluminum wire is the input used in a fabricated wire product manufacturing establishment.

Data are included for counties with 500 or more employees in the Manufacturing sector.

ACCOMMODATION AND FOOD SERVICES, Items 155–158

Source: U.S. Census Bureau—2007 Economic Census (See Overview of 2007 Economic Census prior to Item 135)

The Accommodation and Food Services sector (72) consists of establishments that provide customers with lodging and/or meals, snacks, and beverages for immediate consumption. This sector includes both accommodation and food services establishments because the two activities are often combined at the same establishment.

Excluded from this sector are civic and social organizations, amusement and recreation parks, theaters, and other recreation or entertainment facilities providing food and beverage services.

HEALTH CARE AND SOCIAL ASSISTANCE, Items 159–162

Source: U.S. Census Bureau—2007 Economic Census (See Overview of 2007 Economic Census prior to Item 135)

The Health Care and Social Assistance sector (62) consists of establishments that provide health care and social assistance services to individuals. The sector includes both health care and social assistance because it is sometimes difficult to distinguish between the boundaries of these two activities. The industries in this sector are arranged on a continuum, starting with establishments that provide medical care exclusively, continuing with those that provide health care and social assistance, and finishing with those that provide only social assistance. The services provided by establishments in this sector are delivered by trained professionals. All industries in the sector share this commonality of process—namely, labor inputs of health practitioners or social workers with the requisite expertise. Many of the industries in the sector are defined based on the educational degree held by the practitioners included in the industry.

Excluded from this sector are aerobic classes, which can be found in subsector 713, Amusement, Gambling, and Recreation Industries; and nonmedical diet and weight-reducing centers, which can be found in subsector 812, Personal and Laundry Services. Although these can be viewed as health services, they are not typically delivered by health practitioners.

OTHER SERVICES, EXCEPT PUBLIC ADMINISTRATION Items 163–166

Source: U.S. Census Bureau—2007 Economic Census (See Overview of 2007 Economic Census prior to Item 135)

The Other Services, Except Public Administration sector (81) comprises establishments engaged in providing services not specifically categorized elsewhere in the classification system. Establishments in this sector are primarily engaged in activities such as equipment and machinery repairing, promoting or administering religious activities, grant making, and advocacy; this sector also includes establishments that provide dry-cleaning and laundry services, personal care services, death care services, pet care services, photofinishing services, temporary parking services, and dating services.

Private households that employ workers on or about the premises in activities primarily concerned with the operation of the household are included in this sector.

Excluded from this sector are establishments primarily engaged in retailing new equipment and performing repairs and general maintenance on equipment. These establishments are classified in sector 44–45, Retail Trade.

NONEMPLOYER BUSINESSES, Items 167 and 168

Source: U.S. Census Bureau—Nonemployer Statistics http://www.census.gov/econ/nonemployer/

Nonemployer Statistics is an annual series that provides subnational economic data for businesses that have no paid employees and are subject to federal income tax. The data consist of the number of businesses and total receipts by industry. Most nonemployers are self-employed individuals operating unincorporated businesses (known as sole proprietorships), which may or may not be the owner's principal source of income.

The majority of all business establishments in the United States are nonemployers, yet these firms average less than 4 percent of all sales and receipts nationally. Due to their small economic impact, these firms are excluded from most other Census Bureau business statistics (the primary exception being the Survey of Business Owners). The Nonemployers Statistics series is the primary resource available to study the scope and activities of nonemployers at a detailed geographic level.

BUILDING PERMITS, Items 169 and 170

Source: U.S. Census Bureau—Building Permits Survey http://www.census.gov/construction/bps/

These figures represent private residential construction authorized by building permits in approximately 20,000 places in the United States. Valuation represents the expected cost of construction as recorded on the building permit. This figure usually excludes the cost of on-site and off-site development and improvements, as well as the cost of heating, plumbing, electrical, and elevator installations.

National, state, and county totals were obtained by adding the data for permit-issuing places within each jurisdiction. Not all areas of the country require a building or zoning permit. The statistics only represent those areas that do require a permit. These totals thus are limited to permits issued in the 20,000 place universe covered by the Census Bureau and may not include all permits issued within a state. Current surveys indicate that construction is undertaken for all but a very small percentage of housing units authorized by building permits.

Residential building permits include buildings with any number of housing units. Housing units exclude group quarters (such as dormitories and rooming houses), transient accommodations (such as transient hotels, motels, and tourist courts), ''HUD-code'' manufactured (mobile) homes, moved or relocated units, and housing units created in an existing residential or nonresidential structure.

COUNTY AREA LOCAL GOVERNMENT EMPLOYMENT AND PAYROLL, Items 171–179

Source: U.S. Census Bureau—2012 Census of Governments http://www.census.gov/govs/cog2012/

These items include data for all local governments (i.e., counties, municipalities, townships, special districts, and school districts) located within the county. The Census of Governments identifies the scope and nature of the nation's state and local government sector; provides authoritative benchmark figures of public finance and public employment; classifies local government organizations, powers, and activities; and measures federal, state, and local fiscal relationships. The Employment component was mailed March 2012 to collect information on the number of state and local government civilian employees and their payrolls.

Government employees include all persons paid for personal services performed, including persons paid from federally funded programs, paid elected or appointed officials, persons in a paid leave status, and persons paid on a per meeting, annual, semiannual, or quarterly basis. Unpaid officials, pensioners, persons whose work is performed on a fee basis, and contractors and their employees are excluded from the count of employees. **Full-Time Equivalent employees** is a computed statistic representing the number of full-time employees that could have been employed if the reported number of hours worked by part-time employees had been worked by full-time employees. This statistic is calculated separately for each function of a government by dividing the ''part-time hours paid'' by the standard number of hours for full-time employees in the particular government and then adding the resulting quotient to the number of full-time employees.

March payroll represents gross payroll amounts for the one-month period of March for full-time and part-time employees. Gross payroll includes all salaries, wages, fees, commissions, and overtime paid to employees **before** withholdings for taxes, insurance, etc. It also includes incentive payments that are paid at regular pay intervals. It excludes employer share of fringe benefits like retirement, Social Security, health and life insurance, lump sum payments, and so forth.

Administration and Judicial and Legal combines **Financial administration**, **Other government administration,** and **Judicial and legal** activities. **Financial administration** includes activities concerned with tax assessment and collection, custody and disbursement of funds, debt management, administration of trust funds, budgeting, and other government-wide financial management activities. This function is not applied to school district or special district governments. **Other government administration** applies to the legislative and government-wide administrative agencies of governments. Included here are overall planning and zoning activities, and central personnel and administrative activities. This function is not applied to school district or special district governments. **Judicial and legal** includes all court and court related activities (except probation and parole activities that are included at the ''Correction'' function), court activities of sheriff's offices, prosecuting attorneys' and public defenders' offices, legal departments, and attorneys providing government-wide legal service.

Police and Corrections includes all activities concerned, with the enforcement of law and order, including coroner's offices, police training academies, investigation bureaus, and local jails, "lockups," or other detention facilities not intended to serve as correctional facilities. **Corrections** includes activities pertaining to the confinement and correction of adults and minors convicted of criminal offenses. Pardon, probation, and parole activities are also included here.

Fire protection includes local government fire protection and prevention activities plus any ambulance, rescue, or other auxiliary services provided by a fire protection agency. Volunteer firefighters, if remunerated for their services on a "per fire" or some other basis, are included as part-time employees.

Highways and transportation includes activities associated with the maintenance and operation of streets, roads, sidewalks, bridges, tunnels, toll roads, and ferries. Snow and ice removal, street lighting, and highway and traffic engineering activities are also included here. Also included are the operation, maintenance, and construction of public mass transit systems, including subways, surface rails, and buses; the provision, construction, operation, maintenance and support of public waterways, harbors, docks, wharves, and related marine terminal facilities; and activities associated with the operation and support of publicly operated airport facilities.

Health and Welfare includes **Health, Hospitals,** and **Public welfare. Health** includes administration of public health programs, community and visiting nurse services, immunization programs, drug abuse rehabilitation programs, health and food inspection activities, operation of outpatient clinics, and environmental pollution control activities. **Hospitals** includes only government-operated medical care facilities that provide inpatient care. Employees and payrolls of private corporations that lease and operate government-owned hospital facilities are excluded. **Public welfare** includes the administration of various public assistance programs for the needy, veteran services, operation of nursing homes, indigent care institutions, and programs that provide payments for medical care, handicap transportation, and other services for the needy.

Natural resources and utilities includes activities primarily concerned with the conservation and development of natural resources (soil, water, energy, minerals, etc.) and the regulation of industries that develop, utilize, or affect natural resources, as well as the operation and maintenance of parks, playgrounds, swimming pools, public beaches, auditoriums, public golf courses, museums, marinas, botanical gardens, and zoological parks. **Utilities, sewerage, and waste management** includes operation, maintenance, and construction of public water supply systems, including production, acquisition, and distribution of water to general public or to other public or private utilities, for residential, commercial, and industrial use; activities associated with the production or acquisition and distribution of electric power; provision, maintenance, and operation of sanitary and storm sewer systems and sewage disposal and treatment facilities; and refuse collection and disposal, operation of sanitary landfills, and street cleaning activities.

Education and libraries includes activities associated with the operation of public elementary and secondary schools and locally operated vocational-technical schools. Special education programs operated by elementary and secondary school systems are also included, as are all ancillary services associated with the operation of schools, such as pupil transportation and food service. Also included are the establishment and provision of libraries for use by the general public and the technical support of privately operated libraries. This category includes classroom teachers, principals, supervisors of instruction, librarians, teacher aides, library aides, and guidance and psychological personnel as well as school superintendents and other administrative personnel, clerical and secretarial staff, plant operation and maintenance personnel, health and recreation employees, transportation and food service personnel, and any student employees. Also included are any degree-granting institutions that provide academic training above grade 12.

LOCAL GOVERNMENT FINANCES, Items 180–193

Source: U.S. Census Bureau—2012 Census of Governments

http://www.census.gov/govs/cog/

Data on local government finances are based on results of the 2012 Census of Governments. For each county area, the financial data comprise amounts for all local governments—not only the county government, but also any municipalities, townships, school districts, and special districts within the county. Statistics from governmental units located in two or more county areas are assigned to the county area containing the administrative office.

Revenue and expenditure items include all amounts of money received and paid out, respectively, by a government and its agencies (net of correcting transactions such as recoveries of refunds), with the exception of amounts for debt issuance and retirement and for loan and investment, agency, and private transactions.

Payments among the various funds and agencies of a particular government are excluded from revenue and expenditure items as representing internal transfers. Therefore, a government's contribution to a retirement fund that it administers is not counted as expenditure, nor is the receipt of this contribution by the retirement fund counted as revenue.

Total **general revenue** includes all revenue except utility, liquor stores, and insurance trust revenue. All tax revenue and intergovernmental revenue, even if designated for employee-retirement or local utility purpose, are classified as general revenue.

Intergovernmental revenue covers amounts received from the federal government as fiscal aid, reimbursements for performance of general government functions and specific services for the paying government, or in lieu of taxes. It excludes any amounts received from other governments from the sale of property, commodities, and utility services.

Taxes consist of compulsory contributions exacted by governments for public purposes. However, this category excludes employer and employee payments for retirement and social insurance purposes, which are classified as insurance trust revenue; it also excludes special assessments, which are classified as non-tax general revenue. Property taxes are taxes conditioned on ownership of property and assessed by its value. Sales and gross receipts taxes do not include dealer discounts, or ''commissions'' allowed to merchants for collection of taxes from consumers. General sales taxes and selected taxes on sales of motor fuels, tobacco products, and other particular commodities and services are included.

General government expenditure includes capital outlay, a major portion of which is commonly financed by borrowing. Government revenue does not include receipts from borrowing. Among other things, this distorts the relationship between totals of revenue and expenditure figures that are presented and renders it useless as a direct measure of the degree of budgetary ''balance'' (as that term is generally applied).

Direct general expenditure comprises all expenditures of the local governments, excluding utility, liquor stores, insurance trust expenditures, and any intergovernmental payments.

Local government expenditure for **education** is mainly for the provision and general support of schools and other educational facilities and services, including those for educational institutions beyond high school. They cover such related services as student transportation; school lunch and other cafeteria operations; school health, recreation, and library services; and dormitories, dining halls, and bookstores operated by public institutions of higher education.

Health and hospital expenditure includes health research; clinics; nursing; immunization; other categorical, environmental, and general health services provided by health agencies; establishment and operation of hospital facilities; provision of hospital care; and support of other public and private hospitals.

Police protection expenditure includes police activities such as patrols, communications, custody of persons awaiting trial, and vehicular inspection.

Public welfare expenditure covers support of and assistance to needy persons; this aid is contingent upon the person's needs. Included are cash assistance paid directly to needy persons under categorical (Old Age Assistance, Temporary Assistance for Needy Families, Aid to the Blind, and Aid to the Disabled) and other welfare programs; vendor payments made directly to private purveyors for medical care, burials, and other commodities and services provided under welfare programs; welfare institutions; and any intergovernmental or other direct expenditure for welfare purposes. Pensions to former employees and other benefits not contingent on need are excluded.

Highway expenditure is for the provision and maintenance of highway facilities, including toll turnpikes, bridges, tunnels, and ferries, as well as regular roads, highways, and streets. Also included are expenditures for street lighting and for snow and ice removal. Not included are highway policing and traffic control, which are considered part of police protection

Debt outstanding includes all long-term debt obligations of the government and its agencies (exclusive of utility debt) and all interest-bearing, short-term (repayable within one year) debt obligations remaining unpaid at the close of the fiscal year. It includes judgments, mortgages, and revenue bonds, as well as general obligation bonds, notes, and interest-bearing warrants. This category consists of non-interest-bearing, short-term obligations; inter-fund obligations; amounts owed in a trust or agency capacity; advances and contingent loans from other governments; and rights of individuals to benefit from government-administered employee-retirement funds.

GOVERNMENT EMPLOYMENT, Items 194–196

Source: U.S. Bureau of Economic Analysis—Regional Economic Accounts
http://www.bea.gov/regional/index.htm#state

Employment is measured as the average annual sum of full-time and part-time jobs. The estimates are on a place-of-work basis. State and local government employment includes persons employed in all state and local government agencies and enterprises. Data for federal civilian employment include civilian employees of the federal government, including civilian employees of the Department of Defense. Military employment includes all persons on active duty status.

ELECTION STATISTICS, Items 197–199

Source: Election Data Services, Inc. Washington, DC (copyright)
http://www.electiondataservices.com/index.php?content=elecdata

Election results show the percentage of the total vote cast for the Democratic and Republican candidates, as well as the combined percentage for all other candidates in the 2012 presidential election.

TABLE C—METROPOLITAN AREAS

Table C presents 199 items for the 381 metropolitan statistical areas (MSAs) and 31 metropolitan divisions in the United States. The metropolitan areas are presented in alphabetical order, and the metropolitan divisions are presented in alphabetical order within the appropriate metropolitan area. For some data items, the metropolitan area data have been aggregated from county data sources.

LAND AREA, Items 1 and 4

Source: U.S. Census Bureau—2010 Census of Population and Housing http://www.census.gov/2010census/data

Land area measurements are shown to the nearest square kilometer. Land area includes dry land and land temporarily or partially covered by water, such as marshlands, swamps, and river floodplains.

POPULATION, Items 2–4

Source: U.S. Census Bureau—Population Estimates http://www.census.gov/popest/estimates.html

The population data are Census Bureau estimates of the resident population as of July 1 of the year shown. The ranks are shown for metropolitan statistical areas, but exclude metropolitan divisions.

POPULATION AND POPULATION CHARACTERISTICS, Items 5–19

Source: U.S. Census Bureau—Population Estimates http://www.census.gov/popest/estimates.html

The concept of race, as used by the Census Bureau, reflects self-identification by persons according to the race or races with which they most closely identify. These categories are sociopolitical constructs and should not be interpreted as being scientific or anthropological in nature. Furthermore, race categories include both racial and national origin groups.

Beginning with the 2000 census, respondents were offered the option of selecting one or more races. This option was not available in prior censuses; thus, comparisons between censuses should be made with caution. In Table C, Columns 5 through 8 refer to individuals who identified with each racial category, either alone or in combination with other races. The estimates exclude persons of Hispanic or Latino origin from all race groups. Because respondents could include as many categories as they wished, and because the columns refer to the percentage of the population, the total will often exceed 100 percent.

The **White** population is defined as persons who indicated their race as White, as well as persons who did not classify themselves in one of the specific race categories listed on the questionnaire but entered a nationality such as Irish, German, Italian, Lebanese, Near Easterner, Arab, or Polish.

The **Black** population includes persons who indicated their race as ''Black, African Am., or Negro,'' as well as persons who did not classify themselves in one of the specific race categories but reported entries such as African American, Afro American, Kenyan, Nigerian, or Haitian.

The **American Indian or Alaska Native** population includes persons who indicated their race as American Indian or Alaska Native, as well as persons who did not classify themselves in one of the specific race categories but reported entries such as Canadian Indian, French-American Indian, Spanish-American Indian, Eskimo, Aleut, Alaska Indian, or any of the American Indian or Alaska Native tribes.

The **Asian and Pacific Islander** population combines two census groupings: **Asian** and **Native Hawaiian or Other Pacific Islander**. The **Asian** population includes persons who indicated their race as Asian Indian, Chinese, Filipino, Japanese, Korean, Vietnamese, or ''Other Asian,'' as well as persons who provided write-in entries of such groups as Cambodian, Laotian, Hmong, Pakistani, or Taiwanese. The **Native Hawaiian or Other Pacific Islander** population includes persons who indicated their race as ''Native Hawaiian,'' ''Guamanian or Chamorro,'' ''Samoan,'' or ''Other Pacific Islander,'' as well as persons who reported entries such as Part Hawaiian, American Samoan, Fijian, Melanesian, or Tahitian.

The **Hispanic population** is based on a complete-count question that asked respondents ''Is this person Spanish/Hispanic/Latino?'' Persons marking any one of the four Hispanic categories (i.e., Mexican, Puerto Rican, Cuban, or other Spanish) are collectively referred to as Hispanic.

Beginning with the 2000 census, the Hispanic origin question was placed before the race question and specific instructions indicated that both questions should be answered. These changes were designed to improve accuracy and may affect comparability with earlier data.

Age is defined as age at last birthday (number of completed years since birth), as of April 1 of the census year. The 2000 census also asked for the specific date of birth of the respondent, and 2000 census procedures used the birth date for deriving age data. For this reason, it is likely that the 2000 data have fewer problems than data from prior censuses, such as the tendency of respondents to round ages or to report their ages on the date the questionnaire was filled out rather than on April 1.

The **female** population is shown as a percentage of total population.

POPULATION AND COMPONENTS OF CHANGE, Items 20–26

Source: U.S. Census Bureau—Decennial Censuses and Population Estimates http://www.census.gov/main/www/cen2000.html http://www.census.gov/popest/estimates.html http://www.census.gov/2010census/data/

The population data for 2000 and 2010 are from the decennial censuses and represent the resident population as of April 1 of those years. The components of change are based on Census Bureau estimates of the resident population as of July 1 of 2014. The change in population between 2010 and 2014 is made up of (a) natural increase—births minus deaths, and (b) net migration—the difference between the number of persons moving into a particular area and the number of persons moving out of the area. Net migration is composed of internal and international migration.

Because the 2014 population estimates are based on a model that begins with a national population estimate, the county and msa components of change do not always exactly add up to the difference between the 2010 census population and the 2014 estimates.

HOUSEHOLDS, Items 27–31

Source: U.S. Census Bureau—American Community Survey
http://www.census.gov/acs/www/

A **household** includes all of the persons who occupy a housing unit. (Persons not living in households are classified as living in group quarters.) A housing unit is a house, an apartment, a mobile home, a group of rooms, or a single room occupied (or, if vacant, intended for occupancy) as separate living quarters. Separate living quarters are those in which the occupants live separately from any other persons in the building and have direct access from the outside of the building or through a common hall. The occupants may be a single family, one person living alone, two or more families living together, or any other group of related or unrelated persons who share living quarters. The number of households is the same as the number of year-round occupied housing units.

A **family** includes a householder and one or more other persons living in the same household who are related to the householder by birth, marriage, or adoption. All persons in a household who are related to the householder are regarded as members of his or her family. A **family household** may contain persons not related to the householder; thus, family households may include more members than families do. A household can contain only one family for the purposes of census tabulations. Not all households contain families, as a household may comprise a group of unrelated persons or of one person living alone. Families are classified by type as either a ''married couple family'' or ''other family,'' according to the presence or absence of a spouse.

The measure of **persons per household** is obtained by dividing the number of persons in households by the number of households or householders. One person in each household is designated as the householder. In most cases, this is the person (or one of the persons) in whose name the house is owned, being bought, or rented. If there is no such person in the household, any adult household member 15 years old and over can be designated as the householder.

The category **female family householder** includes only female-headed family households with no spouse present.

GROUP QUARTERS, Item 32

Source: U.S. Census Bureau—Population Estimates
http://www.census.gov/popest/estimates.html

The Census Bureau classifies all persons not living in households as living in group quarters; this category includes both the institutional and noninstitutional populations. The institutionalized population includes persons under formally authorized, supervised care or custody in institutions, such as correctional institutions, nursing homes, mental (psychiatric) hospitals, and juvenile institutions. The noninstitutionalized population includes persons who live in group quarters other than institutions, such as college dormitories, military quarters, and group homes. This volume includes the total number of persons in group quarters.

DAYTIME POPULATION, Items 33 and 34

Source: U.S. Census Bureau—American Community Survey
http://www.census.gov/acs/www/

Daytime population refers to the number of persons who are present in an area or place during normal business hours, including workers. This can be contrasted with the ''resident'' population, which is present during the evening and nighttime hours. The daytime population estimate is calculated by adding the total resident population and the total workers working in the area/place, and then subtracting the total workers living in the area/place from that result. Information on the expansion or contraction experienced by different communities between their nighttime and daytime populations is important for many planning purposes, especially those concerning transportation, disaster, and relief operations.

The employment/residence ratio is a measure of the total number of workers working in an area or place, relative to the total number of workers living in the area or place. It is often used as a rough indication of the jobs-workers balance in an area/place, although it does not take into account whether the resident workers possess the skills needed for the jobs available in their particular area/place. The employment/residence ratio is calculated by dividing the number of total workers working in an area/place by the number of total workers residing in the area/place.

BIRTHS AND DEATHS, Items 35–38

Source: U.S. Census Bureau—Population Estimates
http://www.census.gov/popest/estimates.html

The numbers of births and deaths are from the Census Bureau's Population Estimates Program. They represent the total number of live births and deaths occurring to residents of an area as estimated using reports from the National Center for Health Statistics (NCHS) and the Federal-State Cooperative for Population Estimates (FSCPE). The rates measure births and deaths during the specified time period as a proportion of an area's population. Rates are expressed per 1,000 population estimated as of July 1. These numbers and rates do not represent the calendar year, but rather the year-long period ending on July 1.

PERSONS UNDER 65 WITH NO HEALTH INSURANCE, Items 39 and 40

Source: U.S. Census Bureau—Small Area Health Insurance Estimates
http://www.census.gov/did/www/sahie/index.html

The Small Area Health Insurance Estimates (SAHIE) program develops model-based estimates of health insurance coverage for counties and states. This developmental program builds on the work of the Small Area Income and Poverty Estimates (SAIPE) program. The SAHIE program models health insurance coverage by combining survey data with population estimates and administrative records. These estimates combine data from administrative records, postcensal population estimates, and the decennial census with direct estimates from the American Community Survey to provide consistent and reliable single-year estimates. These model-based single-year estimates are more reflective of current conditions than multi-year survey estimates.

MEDICARE ENROLLMENT, Items 41–43

Source: U.S. Department of Health and Human Services, Centers for Medicare and Medicaid Services http://www.cms.hhs.gov/MCRAdvPartDEnrolData/

The Centers for Medicare and Medicaid Services (CMS) administers Medicare, which provides health insurance to persons 65 years old and over, persons with permanent kidney failure, and certain persons with disabilities. Original Medicare has two parts: Hospital Insurance and Supplemental Medical Insurance. In recent years, Medicare has been expanded to include two new programs: Medicare Advantage plans and prescription drug coverage. Medicare Advantage Plans are health plan options that are approved by Medicare but run by private companies. Medicare prescription drug plans can be part of Medicare Advantage plans or stand-alone drug plans.

Persons who are eligible for Medicare can enroll in Part A (Hospital Insurance) at no charge and can choose to pay a monthly premium to enroll in Part B. Most eligible persons are enrolled in Part A, and more than 90 percent of enrollees in Part A are also enrolled in Part B (Supplemental Medical Insurance). This table includes persons who were eligible as of December 2014.

Medicare Advantage enrollees were enrolled in a Medicare Advantage plan of some type at the end of 2014. These include Private Fee For Service plans, Preferred Provider Organizations, Health Maintenance Organizations, Medical Savings Account Plans, Demonstration plans, and Programs for All-Inclusive Care for the Elderly.

Persons enrolled in a Medicare Prescription drug plan were enrolled in stand-alone plans for prescription drug benefits. This number does not include Medicare enrollees who had prescription drug coverage through private or federal retiree health plans, through Medicare Advantage plans, or through Medicaid.

CRIME, Items 44–47

Source: U.S. Federal Bureau of Investigation—Uniform Crime Reports http://www.fbi.gov/ucr/ucr.htm

Crime data are as reported to the Federal Bureau of Investigation (FBI) by law enforcement agencies and have not been adjusted for underreporting. This may affect comparability between geographic areas or over time.

Through the voluntary contribution of crime statistics by law enforcement agencies across the United States, the Uniform Crime Reporting (UCR) Program provides periodic assessments of crime in the nation as measured by offenses that have come to the attention of the law enforcement community. The Committee on Uniform Crime Records of the International Association of Chiefs of Police initiated this voluntary national data collection effort in 1930. The UCR Program contributors compile and submit their crime data either directly to the FBI or through state-level UCR Programs.

Seven offenses, because of their severity, frequency of occurrence, and likelihood of being reported to police, were initially selected to serve as an index for evaluating fluctuations in the volume of crime. These serious crimes were murder and nonnegligent manslaughter, forcible rape, robbery, aggravated assault, burglary, larceny-theft, and motor vehicle theft. By congressional mandate, arson was added as the eighth index offense in 1979. The totals shown in this volume do not include arson.

In 2004, the FBI discontinued the use of the Crime Index in the UCR Program and its publications, stating that the Crime Index was driven upward by the offense with the highest number of cases (in this case, larceny-theft), creating a bias against jurisdictions with a high number of larceny-thefts but a low number of other serious crimes, such as murder and forcible rape. The FBI is currently publishing a violent crime total and property crime total until a more viable index is developed. This book includes the crime total, as well as violent crime and property crime rates.

In 2013, the FBI adopted a new definition of rape. Rape is now defined as, ''Penetration, no matter how slight, of the vagina or anus with any body part or object, or oral penetration by a sex organ of another person, without the consent of the victim.'' The new definition updated the 80-year-old historical definition of rape which was ''carnal knowledge of a female forcibly and against her will.'' Effectively, the revised definition expands rape to include both male and female victims and offenders, and reflects the various forms of sexual penetration understood to be rape, especially nonconsenting acts of sodomy, and sexual assaults with objects.

At the county level, the change had not been consistently adopted for the 2013 data, so many counties reflect the old definition while many others used the new one. The metropolitan area data reflect this inconsistency because they are aggregated from the county data.

Violent crimes include four categories of offenses: (1) Murder and nonnegligent manslaughter, as defined in the UCR Program, is the willful (nonnegligent) killing of one human being by another. This offense excludes deaths caused by negligence, suicide, or accident; justifiable homicides; and attempts to murder or assaults to murder. (2) Rape is the penetration, no matter how slight, of the vagina or anus with any body part or object, or oral penetration by a sex organ of another person, without the consent of the victim. Assaults or attempts to commit rape by force or threat of force are also included; however, statutory rape (without force) and other sex offenses are excluded. (3) Robbery is the taking or attempting to take anything of value from the care, custody, or control of a person or persons by force or threat of force or violence and/or by putting the victim in fear. (4) Aggravated assault is an unlawful attack by one person upon another for the purpose of inflicting severe or aggravated bodily injury. This type of assault is usually accompanied by the use of a weapon or by other means likely to produce death or great bodily harm. Attempts are included, since injury does not necessarily have to result when a gun, knife, or other weapon is used, as these incidents could and probably would result in a serious personal injury if the crime were successfully completed.

Property crimes include three categories: (1) Burglary, or breaking and entering, is the unlawful entry of a structure to commit a felony or theft, even though no force was used to gain entrance. (2) Larceny-theft is the unauthorized taking of the personal property of another, without the use of force. (3) Motor vehicle theft is the unauthorized taking of any motor vehicle.

Rates are based on population estimates provided by the FBI. The county totals published in this volume were obtained by aggregating individual reporting units within each county and MSA. If the population total for the units aggregated was less than 75 percent of the county's population (as estimated by the Census Bureau), the total was not considered representative of the county as a whole and was not published. State and U.S. totals include FBI estimates for those areas. State and U.S. totals in this table are the adjusted totals as published in the FBI's *Crime in the United States*.

EDUCATION—SCHOOL ENROLLMENT AND EDUCATIONAL ATTAINMENT, Items 48–51

Source: U.S. Census Bureau—American Community Survey
http://www.census.gov/acs/www/

Data on school enrollment and educational attainment were derived from a sample of the population. Persons were classified as enrolled in school if they reported attending a ''regular'' public or private school (or college) during the three months prior to the survey. The instructions were to ''include only nursery school, kindergarten, elementary school, and schooling which would lead to a high school diploma or a college degree'' as regular school. The Census Bureau defines a public school as ''any school or college controlled and supported by a local, county, state, or federal government.'' Schools primarily supported and controlled by religious organizations or other private groups are defined as private schools.

Data on **educational attainment** are tabulated for the population 25 years old and over. The data were derived from a question that asked respondents for the highest level of school completed or the highest degree received. Persons who had passed a high school equivalency examination were considered high school graduates. Schooling received in foreign schools was to be reported as the equivalent grade or years in the regular American school system.

Vocational and technical training, such as barber school training; business, trade, technical, and vocational schools; or other training for a specific trade are specifically excluded.

High school graduate or less. This category includes persons whose highest degree was a high school diploma or its equivalent, and those who reported any level lower than a high school diploma.

Bachelor's degree or more. This category includes persons who have received bachelor's degrees, master's degrees, professional school degrees (such as law school or medical school degrees), and doctoral degrees.

LOCAL GOVERNMENT EDUCATION EXPENDITURES, Items 52 and 53

Source: U.S. Census Bureau—Annual Survey of School System Finances
http://www.census.gov/govs/school/

Expenditures are for elementary and secondary education, which includes prekindergarten through twelfth grade regular, special, and vocational education, as well as cocurricular, community service, and adult education programs provided by a public school system. The financial activities of these systems for all instruction, support service, and noninstructional activities are included

Current spending comprises current operation expenditure, payments made by the state government on behalf of school systems, and transfers made by school systems into their own retirement funds. Current operation expenditures include direct expenditure for salaries, employee benefits, purchased professional and technical services, purchased property and other services, and supplies. It includes gross school system expenditure for instruction, support services, and noninstructional functions. It excludes expenditure for debt service, capital outlay, and reimbursement to other governments (including other school systems).

Current expenditure per student is current expenditure divided by the number of students enrolled. The number of students enrolled is based on an annual ''membership'' count of students on or about October 1.

INCOME AND POVERTY Items 54–61

Source: U.S. Census Bureau—American Community Survey
http://www.census.gov/acs/www/

The data on income were derived from responses of a sample of persons 15 years old and over. **Total money income** is the sum of the amounts reported separately for wage or salary income; net self-employment income; interest, dividends, or net rental or royalty income or income from estates and trusts; Social Security or railroad retirement income; Supplemental Security Income (SSI); public assistance or welfare payments; retirement, survivor, or disability pensions; and all other income. Receipts from the following sources are not included as income: capital gains; money received from the sale of property (unless the recipient was engaged in the business of selling such property); the value of income ''in kind'' from food stamps, public housing subsidies, medical care, employer contributions for individuals, etc.; withdrawal of bank deposits; money borrowed; tax refunds; exchange of money between relatives living in the same household; and gifts, lump-sum inheritances, insurance payments, and other types of lump-sum receipts.

Money income differs in definition from personal income (item 62). For example, money income does not include the pension rights, employer-provided health insurance, food stamps, or Medicare payments that are included in personal income.

Per capita income is the mean income computed for every man, woman, and child in a particular group. It is derived by dividing the aggregate income of a particular group by the resident population in that group in the survey year. Per capita income is rounded to the nearest whole dollar.

Household income includes the income of the householder and all other individuals 15 years old and over in the household, whether or not they are related to the householder. Since many households consist of only one person, median household income is usually less than median family income. Although the household income statistics cover the year preceding the survey, the characteristics of individuals and the composition of households refer to the date of the survey. Thus, the income of the household does not include amounts received by individuals who were members of the household during the year if these individuals were no longer residing in the household at the time of the survey. Similarly, income amounts reported by individuals who did not reside in the household during the year but who were members of the household at the time of the survey are included. However, the composition of most households was the same during the year as it was at the time of the survey.

Mean household income is the amount obtained by dividing the aggregate income of all households by the total number of households. The mean is based on the distribution of the total number of households including those with no income. Mean income is rounded to the nearest whole dollar. Care should be exercised in using and interpreting mean income values for small subgroups of the population. Because the mean is influenced strongly by extreme values in the distribution, it is especially susceptible to the effects of sampling variability, misreporting, and processing errors. The median, which is not affected by extreme values, is, therefore, a better measure than the mean when the population base is small.

Median income divides the income distribution into two equal parts, with half of all cases below the median income level and half of all cases above the median income level. For households, the median income is based on the distribution of the total number of households, including those with no income. Median income for households is computed on the basis of a standard distribution with a minimum value of less than $2,500 and a maximum value of $200,000 or more and is rounded to the nearest whole dollar. Median income figures are calculated using linear interpolation if the width of the interval containing the estimate is $2,500 or less. If the width of the interval containing the estimate is greater than $2,500, Pareto interpolation is used.

Income components were reported for the 12 months preceding the interview month. Monthly Consumer Price Indices (CPI) factors were used to inflation-adjust these components to a reference calendar year (January through December). For example, a household interviewed in March 2012 reports their income for March 2011 through February 2012. Their income is adjusted to the 2012 reference calendar year by multiplying their reported income by 2012 average annual CPI (January-December) and then dividing by the average CPI for March 2011–February 2012. However, the estimates do not reflect the price and cost-of-living differences that may exist between areas.

The **poverty status** data were derived from data collected on the number of persons in a household, each person's relationship to the householder, and income data. The Social Security Administration (SSA) developed the original poverty definition in 1964, which federal interagency committees subsequently revised in 1969 and 1980. The Office of Management and Budget's (OMB) *Directive 14* prescribes the SSA's definition as the official poverty measure for federal agencies to use in their statistical work. Poverty statistics presented in American Community Survey products adhere to the standards defined by OMB in *Directive 14*.

Poverty thresholds vary depending on three criteria: size of family, number of children, and, for one- and two-person families, age of householder. In determining the poverty status of families and unrelated individuals, the Census Bureau uses thresholds (income cutoffs) arranged in a two-dimensional matrix. The matrix consists of family size (from one person to nine or more persons), cross-classified by presence and number of family members under 18 years old (from no children present to eight or more children present). Unrelated individuals and two-person families are further differentiated by age of reference person (under 65 years old and 65 years old and over). To determine a person's poverty status, the person's total family income over the previous 12 months is compared with the poverty threshold appropriate for that person's family size and composition. If the total income of that person's family is less than the threshold appropriate for that family, then the person is considered poor or "below the poverty level," together with every member of his or her family. If a person is not living with anyone related by birth, marriage, or adoption, then the person's own income is compared with his or her poverty threshold. The total number of persons below the poverty level is the sum of persons in families and the number of unrelated individuals with incomes below the poverty level over the previous 12 months.

Poverty Thresholds for 2013 by Size of Family and Number of Related Children Under 18 Years

Size of family unit	Weighted average thresholds
One person (unrelated individual)	11,888
Under 65 years	12,119
65 years and over	11,173
Two people	15,142
Householder under 65 years	15,679
Householder 65 years and over	14,095
Three people	18,552
Four people	23,834
Five people	28,265
Six people	31,925
Seven people	36,384
Eight people	40,484
Nine people or more	48,065

Source: U.S. Census Bureau.

PERSONAL INCOME AND EARNINGS, Items 62–83

Source: U.S. Bureau of Economic Analysis, Regional Economic Accounts http://www.bea.gov/regional/index.htm#state

Total personal income is the current income received by residents of an area from all sources. It is measured before deductions of income and other personal taxes, but after deductions of personal contributions for Social Security, government retirement, and other social insurance programs. It consists of **wage and salary disbursements** (covering all employee earnings, including executive salaries, bonuses, commissions, payments-in-kind, incentive payments, and tips); various types of supplementary earnings, such as employers' contributions to pension funds (termed ''other labor income'' or ''supplements to wages and salaries''); proprietors' income; rental income of persons; dividends; personal interest income; and government and business transfer payments.

Per capita personal income is based on the resident population estimated as of July 1 of the year shown.

Proprietors' income is the monetary income and income-in-kind of proprietorships and partnerships (including the independent professions) and the income of tax-exempt cooperatives. **Dividends** are cash payments by corporations to stockholders who are U.S. residents. **Interest** is the monetary and imputed interest income of persons from all sources. **Rent** is the monetary income of persons from the rental of real property, except the income of persons primarily engaged in the real estate business; the imputed net rental income of owner-occupants of nonfarm dwellings; and the royalties received by persons.

Transfer payments are income for which services are not currently rendered. They consist of both government and business transfer payments. Government transfer payments include payments under the following programs: Federal Old-Age, Survivors, and Disability Insurance (''Social Security''); Medicare and medical vendor payments; unemployment insurance; railroad and government retirement; federal- and state-government-insured workers' compensation; veterans' benefits, including veterans' life insurance; food stamps; black lung payments; Supplemental Security Income; and Temporary Assistance for Needy Families. Government payments to nonprofit institutions, other than for work under research and development contracts, are also included. Business transfer payments consist primarily of liability payments for personal injury and of corporate gifts to nonprofit institutions.

Personal income differs in definition from money income (items 54–57). For example, personal income includes pension rights, employer-provided health insurance, food stamps, and Medicare. These are not included in the definition of money income.

Earnings cover wage and salary disbursements, other labor income, and proprietors' income.

The data for earnings obtained from the Bureau of Economic Analysis (BEA) are based on place of work. In computing personal income, BEA makes an ''adjustment for residence'' to earnings, based on commuting patterns; personal income is thus presented on a place-of-residence basis.

Farm earnings include the income of farm workers (wages and salaries and other labor income) and farm proprietors. Farm proprietors' income includes only the income of sole proprietorships and partnerships. Farm earnings estimates are benchmarked to data collected in the Census of Agriculture and the revised Department of Agriculture statistical totals of income and expense items.

Goods-related industries include mining, construction, and manufacturing. **Service-related** and other industries include private-sector earnings in agricultural services, forestry, and fisheries; transportation and public utilities; wholesale trade; retail trade; finance, insurance, and real estate; and services. Government earnings include all levels of government. Industries are categorized under the North American Industry Classification System (NAICS), and are not comparable to years prior to 2002.

SOCIAL SECURITY AND SUPPLEMENTAL SECURITY INCOME, Items 84–86

Source: U.S. Social Security Administration
http://www.ssa.gov/policy/docs/statcomps/oasdi_sc/
http://www.ssa.gov/policy/docs/statcomps/ssi_sc/

Social Security beneficiaries are persons receiving benefits under the Old-Age, Survivors, and Disability Insurance Program. These include retired or disabled workers covered by the program, their spouses and dependent children, and the surviving spouses and dependent children of deceased workers.

Supplemental Security Income (SSI) recipients are persons receiving SSI payments. The SSI program is a cash assistance program that provides monthly benefits to low-income aged, blind, or disabled persons.

Data are as of December of the year shown.

HOUSING, Items 87–96

Source: U.S. Census Bureau—Population Estimates Program
http://www.census.gov/popest/
Source: U.S. Census Bureau—American Community Surveyhttp://www.census.gov/acs/www/

Housing data for 2014 are from the Population Estimates Program. Housing unit characteristics for 2013 are from the American Community Survey.

A **housing unit** is a house, apartment, mobile home or trailer, group of rooms, or single room occupied or, if vacant, intended for occupancy as separate living quarters. Separate living quarters are those in which the occupants do not live and eat with any other person in the structure and which have direct access from the outside of the building through a common hall.

The occupants of a housing unit may be a single family, one person living alone, two or more families living together, or any other group of related or unrelated persons who share living quarters. Both occupied and vacant housing units are included in the housing inventory, although recreational vehicles, tents, caves, boats, railroad cars, and the like are included only if they are occupied as a person's usual place of residence.

A housing unit is classified as occupied if it is the usual place of residence of the person or group of persons living in it at the time of enumeration, or if the occupants are only temporarily absent (away on vacation). A household consists of all persons who occupy a housing unit as their usual place of residence. Vacant units for sale or rent include units rented or sold but not occupied and any other units held off the market.

Median value is the dollar amount that divides the distribution of specified owner-occupied housing units into two equal parts, with half of all units below the median value and half of all units above the median value. Value is defined as the respondent's estimate of what the house would sell for if it were for sale. Data are presented for single-family units on fewer than 10 acres of land that have no business or medical offices on the property.

Median rent divides the distribution of renter-occupied housing units into two equal parts. The rent concept used in this volume is gross rent, which includes the amount of cash rent a renter pays (contract rent) plus the estimated average cost of utilities and fuels, if these are paid by the renter. The rent is the amount of rent only for living quarters and excludes amounts paid for any business or other space occupied. Single-family houses on lots of 10 or more acres of land are also excluded.

Housing cost as a percentage of income is shown separately for owners with mortgages, owners without mortgages, and renters. Rent as a percentage of income is a computed ratio of gross rent and monthly household income (total household income in the past 12 months divided by 12). Selected owner costs include utilities and fuels, mortgage payments, insurance, taxes, etc. In each case, the ratio of housing cost to income is computed separately for each housing unit. The housing cost ratios for half of all units are above the median shown in this book, and half are below the median shown in the book.

Substandard units are occupied units that are overcrowded or lack complete plumbing facilities. For the purposes of this item, ''overcrowded'' is defined as having 1.01 persons or more per room. Complete plumbing facilities include hot and cold piped water, a flush toilet, and a bathtub or shower. These facilities must be located inside the housing unit, but do not have to be in the same room.

CIVILIAN LABOR FORCE AND UNEMPLOYMENT, Items 97–100

Source: U.S. Bureau of Labor Statistics—Local Area Unemployment Statistics
http://www.bls.gov/lau/#tables

Data for the civilian labor force are the product of a federal-state cooperative program in which state employment security agencies prepare labor force and unemployment estimates under concepts, definitions, and technical procedures established by the Bureau of Labor Statistics (BLS). The civilian labor force consists of all civilians 16 years old and over who are either employed or unemployed.

Unemployment includes all persons who did not work during the survey week, made specific efforts to find a job during the previous four weeks, and were available for work during the survey week (except for temporary illness). Persons waiting to be called back to a job from which they had been laid off and those waiting to report to a new job within the next 30 days are included in unemployment figures.

Table C includes annual average data for the year shown. The Local Area Unemployment Statistics data are periodically updated to reflect revised inputs, reestimation, and controlling to new statewide totals.

CIVILIAN EMPLOYMENT, Items 101–103

Source: U.S. Census Bureau—American Community Survey
http://www.census.gov/acs/www/

Total employment includes all civilians 16 years old and over who were either (1) ''at work''—those who did any work at all during the reference week as paid employees, worked in either their own business or profession, worked on their own farm, or worked 15 hours or more as unpaid workers in a family farm or business; or were (2) ''with a job, but not at work''—those who had a job but were not at work that week due to illness, weather, industrial dispute, vacation, or other personal reasons.

The **occupational categories** are based on the occupational classification system that was developed for the 2000 census. This system consists of 509 specific occupational categories for employed persons arranged into 23 major occupational groups. This classification was developed based on the *Standard Occupational Classification (SOC) Manual: 2000*, published by the Executive Office of the President, Office of Management and Budget.

PRIVATE NONFARM EMPLOYMENT AND EARNINGS, Items 104–112

Source: U.S. Bureau of Labor Statistics—County Business Patterns
http://www.census.gov/econ/cbp/index.html

Data for private nonfarm employment and earnings are compiled from the payroll information reported monthly in the Census Bureau publication *County Business Patterns*. The estimates are based on surveys conducted by the Census Bureau and administrative records from the Internal Revenue Service (IRS).

The following types of employment are excluded from the tables: government employment, self-employed persons, farm workers, and domestic service workers. Railroad employment jointly covered by Social Security and railroad retirement programs, employment on oceanborne vessels, and employment in foreign countries are also excluded.

Annual payroll is the combined amount of wages paid, tips reported, and other compensation (including salaries, vacation allowances, bonuses, commissions, sick-leave pay, and the value of payments-in-kind such as free meals and lodging) paid to employees before deductions for Social Security, income tax, insurance, union dues, etc. All forms of compensation are included, regardless of whether they are subject to income tax or the Federal Insurance Contributions Act tax, with the exception of annuities, third-party sick pay, and supplemental unemployment compensation benefits (even if income tax was withheld). For corporations, total annual payroll includes compensation paid to officers and executives; for unincorporated businesses, it excludes profit or other compensation of proprietors or partners.

AGRICULTURE, ITEMS 113–132

Source: U.S. Department of Agriculture, National Agricultural Statistics Service—2012 Census of Agriculture
http://agcensus.usda.gov/index.php

Data for the 2012 Census of Agriculture were collected in 2013, but pertain to the year 2012.

The Census Bureau took a census of agriculture every 10 years from 1840 to 1920; since 1925, this census has been taken roughly once every 5 years. The 1997 Census of Agriculture was the first one conducted by the National Agricultural Statistics Service of the U.S. Department of Agriculture. Over time, the definition of a farm has varied. For recent censuses (including the 2007 census), a farm has been defined as any place from which $1,000 or more of agricultural products were produced and sold or normally would have been sold during the census year. Dollar figures are expressed in current dollars and have not been adjusted for inflation or deflation.

The term **operator** refers to a person who operates a farm by either doing the work or making day-to-day decisions about such activities as planting, harvesting, feeding, marketing, etc. The operator may be the owner, a member of the owner's household, a salaried manager, a tenant, a renter, or a sharecropper. If a person rents land to others or has land worked on shares by others, he/she is considered the operator only of the land that is retained for his/her own operation. The census collected information on the total number of operators, the total number of women operators, and demographic information for up to three operators per farm.

The acreage designated as **land in farms** consists primarily of agricultural land used for crops, pasture, or grazing. It also includes woodland and wasteland not actually under cultivation or used for pasture or grazing, provided that this land was part of the farm operator's total operation. Land in farms is an operating-unit concept and includes all land owned and operated, as well as all land rented from others. Land used rent-free is classified as land rented from others. All land in Indian reservations used for growing crops or grazing livestock is classified as land in farms.

Irrigated land includes all land watered by any artificial or controlled means, such as sprinklers, flooding, furrows or ditches, sub-irrigation, and spreader dikes. Included are supplemental, partial, and preplant irrigation. Each acre was counted only once regardless of the number of times it was irrigated or harvested. Livestock lagoon waste water distributed by sprinkler or flood systems was also included.

Total cropland includes cropland harvested, cropland used only for pasture or grazing, cropland on which all crops failed or were abandoned, cropland in cultivated summer fallow, and cropland idle or used for cover crops or soil improvement but not harvested and not pastured or grazed.

Respondents were asked to report their estimate of the current market **value of land and buildings** owned, rented, or leased from others, and rented and leased to others. Market value refers to the respondent's estimate of what the land and buildings would sell for under current market conditions. If the value of land and buildings was not reported, it was estimated during processing by using the average value of land and buildings from similar farms in the same geographic area.

The **value of machinery and equipment** was estimated by the respondent as the current market value of all cars, trucks, tractors, combines, balers, irrigation equipment, etc., used on the farm. This value is an estimate of what the machinery and equipment would sell for in its present condition and not the replacement or depreciated value. Share interests are reported at full value at the farm where the equipment and machinery are usually kept. Only equipment that was physically located at the farm on December 31, 2012, is included.

Market value of agricultural products sold by farms represents the gross market value before taxes and the production expenses of all agricultural products sold or removed from the place in 2007, regardless of who received the payment. It is equivalent to total sales and it includes sales by the operator as well as the value of any share received by partners, landlords, contractors, and others associated with the operation. It includes value of direct sales and the value of commodities placed in the Commodity Credit Corporation (CCC) loan program. Market value of agricultural products sold does not include payments received for participation in other federal farm programs. Also, it does not include income from farm-related sources such as custom work and other agricultural services, or income from nonfarm sources.

Government payments consists of direct payments as defined by the 2002 Farm Bill; payments from Conservation Reserve Program (CRP), Wetlands Reserve Program (WRP), Farmable Wetlands Program (FWP), and Conservation Reserve Enhancement Program (CREP); loan deficiency payments; disaster payments; other conservation programs; and all other federal farm programs under which payments were made directly to farm operators. Commodity Credit Corporation (CCC) proceeds, amount from state and local federal crop insurance payments were not included in this category.

WATER CONSUMPTION, Items 133–134

Source: U.S. Geological Survey, National Water—Use Information Program
http://water.usgs.gov/watuse/

Every five years, the U.S. Geological Survey compiles county-level water-use estimates. This volume includes the total fresh and saline withdrawals expressed as million gallons per day. Estimate of withdrawals of ground and surface water are given for the following categories of use: public water supplies, domestic, commercial, irrigation, livestock, industrial, mining, and thermoelectric power. The number of gallons withdrawn per person is based on the metropolitan area population but the water is not necessarily used locally, providing an indicator of metropolitan areas that serve as major water sources.

2007 Economic CENSUS: OVERVIEW, Items 135–166

Source: U.S. Census Bureau
http://www.census.gov/econ/census07/

The Economic Census provides a detailed portrait of the nation's economy, from the national to the local level, once every five years. The 2007 Economic Census covers nearly all of the U.S. economy in its basic collection of establishment statistics. The 1997 Economic Census was the first major data source to use the new North American Industry Classification System (NAICS); therefore, data from this census are not comparable to economic data from prior years, which were based on the Standard Industrial Classification (SIC) system.

NAICS, developed in cooperation with Canada and Mexico, classifies North America's economic activities at two-, three-, four-, and five-digit levels of detail; the U.S. version of NAICS further defines industries to a sixth digit. The Economic Census takes advantage of this hierarchy to publish data at these successive levels of detail: sector (two-digit), subsector (three-digit), industry group (four-digit), industry (five-digit), and U.S. industry (six-digit). Information in Table A is at the two-digit level, with a few three- and four-digit items. The data in Tables B and C are at the two-digit level.

Several key statistics are tabulated for all industries in this volume, including number of establishments (or companies), number of employees, payroll, and certain measures of output (sales, receipts, revenue, value of shipments, or value of construction work done).

Number of establishments. An establishment is a single physical location at which business is conducted. It is not necessarily identical with a company or enterprise, which may consist of one establishment or more. Economic Census figures represent a summary of reports for individual establishments rather than companies. For cases in which a census report was received, separate information was obtained for each location where business was conducted. When administrative records of other federal agencies were used instead of a census report, no information was available on the number of locations operated. Each Economic Census establishment was tabulated according to the physical location at which the business was conducted. The count of establishments represents those in business at any time during 2002.

When two activities or more were carried on at a single location under a single ownership, all activities were generally grouped together as a single establishment. The entire establishment was classified on the basis of its major activity, and all of its data were included in that classification. However, when distinct and separate economic activities (for which different industry classification codes were appropriate) were conducted at a single location under a single ownership, separate establishment reports for each of the different activities were obtained in the census.

Number of employees. Paid employees consist of the full-time and part-time employees, including salaried officers and executives of corporations. Included are employees on paid sick leave, paid holidays, and paid vacations; not included are proprietors and partners of unincorporated businesses. The definition of paid employees is the same as that used by the Internal Revenue Service (IRS) on form 941.

For some industries, the Economic Census gives codes representing the number of employees as a range of numbers (for example, ''100 to 249 employees'' or ''1,000 to 2,499'' employees). In this volume, those codes have been replaced by the standard suppression code ''D.''

Payroll. Payroll includes all forms of compensation, such as salaries, wages, commissions, dismissal pay, bonuses, vacation allowances, sick-leave pay, and employee contributions to qualified pension plans paid during the year to all employees. For corporations, payroll includes amounts paid to officers and executives; for unincorporated businesses, it does not include profit or other compensation of proprietors or partners. Payroll is reported before deductions for Social Security, income tax, insurance, union dues, etc. This definition of payroll is the same as that used on IRS form 941.

Sales, shipments, receipts, revenue, or business done. This measure includes the total sales, shipments, receipts, revenue, or business done by establishments within the scope of the Economic Census. The definition of each of these items is specific to the economic sector measured.

WHOLESALE TRADE, Items 135–138

Source: U.S. Census Bureau—2007 Economic Census (See Overview of 2007 Economic Census prior to Item 135)

The Wholesale Trade sector (sector 42) comprises establishments engaged in wholesaling merchandise, generally without transformation, and rendering services incidental to the sale of merchandise. The wholesaling process is an intermediate step in the distribution of merchandise.

Wholesalers are organized to sell or arrange the purchase or sale of (1) goods for resale (i.e., goods sold to other wholesalers or retailers), (2) capital or durable nonconsumer goods, and (3) raw and intermediate materials and supplies used in production.

Wholesalers sell merchandise to other businesses and normally operate from a warehouse or office. These warehouses and offices are characterized by having little or no display of merchandise. In addition, neither the design nor the location of the premises is intended to solicit walk-in traffic. Wholesalers do not normally use advertising directed to the general public. In general, customers are initially reached via telephone, in-person marketing, or specialized advertising, which may include the internet and other electronic means. Follow-up orders are either vendor-initiated or client-initiated, are usually based on previous sales, and typically exhibit strong ties between sellers and buyers. In fact, transactions are often conducted between wholesalers and clients that have long-standing business relationships.

This sector is made up of two main types of wholesalers: those that sell goods on their own account and those that arrange sales and purchases for others for a commission or fee.

(1) Establishments that sell goods on their own account are known as wholesale merchants, distributors, jobbers, drop shippers, import/export merchants, and sales branches. These establishments typically maintain their own warehouse, where they receive and handle goods for their customers. Goods are generally sold without transformation, but may include integral functions, such as sorting, packaging, labeling, and other marketing services.

(2) Establishments arranging for the purchase or sale of goods owned by others or purchasing goods on a commission basis are known as agents and brokers, commission merchants, import/export agents and brokers, auction companies, and manufacturers' representatives. These establishments operate from offices and generally do not own or handle the goods they sell.

Some wholesale establishments may be connected with a single manufacturer and promote and sell that particular manufacturer's products to a wide range of other wholesalers or retailers. Other wholesalers may be connected to a retail chain or a limited number of retail chains and only provide the products needed by the particular retail operation(s). These wholesalers may obtain the products from a wide range of manufacturers. Still other wholesalers may not take title to the goods, but act instead as agents and brokers for a commission.

Although wholesaling normally denotes sales in large volumes, durable nonconsumer goods may be sold in single units. Sales of capital or durable nonconsumer goods used in the production of goods and services, such as farm machinery, medium- and heavy-duty trucks, and industrial machinery, are always included in Wholesale Trade.

The metropolitan area table includes only **Merchant wholesalers, except manufacturers' sales branches and offices,** establishments primarily engaged in buying and selling merchandise on their own account. Included here are such types of establishments as wholesale distributors and jobbers, importers, exporters, own-brand importers/marketers, terminal and country grain elevators, and farm products assemblers.

RETAIL TRADE, Items 139–142

Source: U.S. Census Bureau—2007 Economic Census (See Overview of 2007 Economic Census prior to Item 135)

The Retail Trade sector (44–45) is made up of establishments engaged in retailing merchandise, generally without transformation, and rendering services incidental to the sale of merchandise.

The retailing process is the final step in the distribution of merchandise; retailers are therefore organized to sell merchandise in small quantities to the general public. This sector comprises two main types of retailers: store and nonstore retailers.

Store retailers operate fixed point-of-sale locations, located and designed to attract a high volume of walk-in customers. In general, retail stores have extensive displays of merchandise and use mass-media advertising to attract customers. They typically sell merchandise to the general public for personal or household consumption; some also serve business and institutional clients. These include establishments such as office supply stores, computer and software stores, building materials dealers, plumbing supply stores, and electrical supply stores. Catalog showrooms, gasoline service stations, automotive dealers, and mobile home dealers are treated as store retailers.

In addition to retailing merchandise, some types of store retailers are also engaged in the provision of after-sales services, such as repair and installation. For example, new automobile dealers, electronic and appliance stores, and musical instrument and supply stores often provide repair services. As a general rule, establishments engaged in retailing merchandise and providing after-sales services are classified in this sector.

Nonstore retailers, like store retailers, are organized to serve the general public, although their retailing methods differ. The establishments of this subsector reach customers and market merchandise with methods including the broadcasting of ''infomercials,'' the broadcasting and publishing of direct-response advertising, the publishing of paper and electronic catalogs, door-to-door solicitation, in-home demonstration, selling from portable stalls (street vendors, except food), and distribution through vending machines. Establishments engaged in the direct sale (nonstore) of products, such as home heating oil dealers and home-delivery newspaper routes are included in this sector.

The buying of goods for resale is a characteristic of retail trade establishments that distinguishes them from establishments in the Agriculture, Manufacturing, and Construction sectors. For example, farms that sell their products at or from the point of production are classified in Agriculture instead of in Retail Trade. Similarly, establishments that both manufacture and sell their products to the general public are classified in Manufacturing instead of Retail Trade. However, establishments that engage in processing activities incidental to retailing are classified in Retail Trade.

REAL ESTATE AND RENTAL AND LEASING, Items 143–146

Source: U.S. Census Bureau—2007 Economic Census (See Overview of 2007 Economic Census prior to Item 135)

The Real Estate and Rental and Leasing sector (53) comprises establishments primarily engaged in renting, leasing, or otherwise allowing the use of tangible or intangible assets, and establishments providing related services. The major portion of this sector is made up of establishments that rent, lease, or otherwise allow the use of their own assets by others. The assets may be tangible, such as real estate and equipment, or intangible, such as patents and trademarks.

This sector also includes establishments primarily engaged in managing real estate for others, selling, renting, and/or buying real estate for others, and appraising real estate. These activities are closely related to this sector's main activity. In addition, a substantial proportion of property management is self-performed by lessors.

The main components of this sector are the real estate lessors industries; equipment lessors industries (including motor vehicles, computers, and consumer goods); and lessors of nonfinancial intangible assets (except copyrighted works).

PROFESSIONAL, SCIENTIFIC, AND TECHNICAL SERVICES, Items 147–150

Source: U.S. Census Bureau—2007 Economic Census (See Overview of 2007 Economic Census prior to Item 135)

The Professional, Scientific, and Technical Services sector (54) is made up of establishments that specialize in performing professional, scientific, and technical activities for others. These activities require a high degree of expertise and training. The establishments in this sector specialize in one or more areas and provide services to clients in a variety of industries (and, in some cases, to households). Activities performed include legal advice and representation; accounting, bookkeeping, and payroll services; architectural, engineering, and specialized design services; computer services; consulting services; research services; advertising services; photographic services; translation and interpretation services; veterinary services; and other professional, scientific, and technical services.

Table C includes only those establishments subject to federal income tax.

This sector excludes establishments primarily engaged in providing a range of day-to-day office administrative services, such as financial planning, billing and record keeping, personnel services, and physical distribution and logistics services. These establishments are classified in sector 56, Administrative and Support and Waste Management and Remediation Services.

MANUFACTURING, Items 151–154

Source: U.S. Census Bureau—2007 Economic Census (See Overview of 2007 Economic Census prior to Item 135)

The Manufacturing sector (31–33) is made up of establishments engaged in the mechanical, physical, or chemical transformation of materials, substances, or components into new products. The assembling of component parts of manufactured products is considered manufacturing, except in cases in which the activity is appropriately classified in the Construction sector. Establishments in the Manufacturing sector are often described as plants, factories, or mills, and characteristically use power-driven machines and materials-handling equipment. However, establishments that transform materials or substances into new products by hand or in the worker's home, and establishments engaged in selling to the general public products made on the same premises from which they are sold (such as bakeries, candy stores, and custom tailors) may also be included in this sector. Manufacturing establishments may process materials or contract with other establishments to process their materials for them. Both types of establishments are included in the Manufacturing sector.

The materials, substances, or components transformed by manufacturing establishments are raw materials that are products of agriculture, forestry, fishing, mining, or quarrying, or are products of other manufacturing establishments. The materials used may be purchased directly from producers, obtained through customary trade channels, or secured without recourse to the market by transferring the product from one establishment to another, under the same ownership. The new product of a manufacturing establishment may be finished (in the sense that it is ready for utilization or consumption), or it may be semifinished to become an input for an establishment engaged in further manufacturing. For example, the product of the alumina refinery is the input used in the primary production of aluminum; primary aluminum is the input used in an aluminum wire drawing plant; and aluminum wire is the input used in a fabricated wire product manufacturing establishment.

Data are included for counties with 500 or more employees in the Manufacturing sector.

ACCOMMODATION AND FOOD SERVICES, Items 155–158

Source: U.S. Census Bureau—2007 Economic Census (See Overview of 2007 Economic Census prior to Item 135)

The Accommodation and Food Services sector (72) consists of establishments that provide customers with lodging and/or meals, snacks, and beverages for immediate consumption. This sector includes both accommodation and food services establishments because the two activities are often combined at the same establishment.

Excluded from this sector are civic and social organizations, amusement and recreation parks, theaters, and other recreation or entertainment facilities providing food and beverage services.

HEALTH CARE AND SOCIAL ASSISTANCE, Items 159–162

Source: U.S. Census Bureau—2007 Economic Census (See Overview of 2007 Economic Census prior to Item 135)

The Health Care and Social Assistance sector (62) consists of establishments that provide health care and social assistance services to individuals. The sector includes both health care and social assistance because it is sometimes difficult to distinguish between the boundaries of these two activities. The industries in this sector are arranged on a continuum, starting with establishments that provide medical care exclusively, continuing with those that provide health care and social assistance, and finishing with those that provide only social assistance. The services provided by establishments in this sector are delivered by trained professionals. All industries in the sector share this commonality of process—namely, labor inputs of health practitioners or social workers with the requisite expertise. Many of the industries in the sector are defined based on the educational degree held by the practitioners included in the industry.

Excluded from this sector are aerobic classes, which can be found in subsector 713, Amusement, Gambling, and Recreation Industries; and nonmedical diet and weight-reducing centers, which can be found in subsector 812, Personal and Laundry Services. Although these can be viewed as health services, they are not typically delivered by health practitioners.

OTHER SERVICES, EXCEPT PUBLIC ADMINISTRATION Items 163–166

Source: U.S. Census Bureau—2007 Economic Census (See Overview of 2007 Economic Census prior to Item 135)

The Other Services, Except Public Administration sector (81) comprises establishments engaged in providing services not specifically categorized elsewhere in the classification system. Establishments in this sector are primarily engaged in activities such as equipment and machinery repairing, promoting or administering religious activities, grant making, and advocacy; this sector also includes establishments that provide dry-cleaning and laundry services, personal care services, death care services, pet care services, photofinishing services, temporary parking services, and dating services.

Private households that employ workers on or about the premises in activities primarily concerned with the operation of the household are included in this sector.

Excluded from this sector are establishments primarily engaged in retailing new equipment and performing repairs and general maintenance on equipment. These establishments are classified in sector 44–45, Retail Trade.

NONEMPLOYER BUSINESSES, Items 167 and 168

Source: U.S. Census Bureau—Nonemployer Statistics http://www.census.gov/econ/nonemployer/

Nonemployer Statistics is an annual series that provides subnational economic data for businesses that have no paid employees and are subject to federal income tax. The data consist of the number of businesses and total receipts by industry. Most nonemployers are self-employed individuals operating unincorporated businesses (known as sole proprietorships), which may or may not be the owner's principal source of income.

The majority of all business establishments in the United States are nonemployers, yet these firms average less than 4 percent of all sales and receipts nationally. Due to their small economic impact, these firms are excluded from most other Census Bureau business statistics (the primary exception being the Survey of Business Owners). The Nonemployers Statistics series is the primary resource available to study the scope and activities of nonemployers at a detailed geographic level.

BUILDING PERMITS, Items 169 and 170

Source: U.S. Census Bureau—Building Permits Survey http://www.census.gov/construction/bps/

These figures represent private residential construction authorized by building permits in approximately 20,000 places in the United States. Valuation represents the expected cost of construction as recorded on the building permit. This figure usually excludes the cost of on-site and off-site development and improvements, as well as the cost of heating, plumbing, electrical, and elevator installations.

National, state, and county totals were obtained by adding the data for permit-issuing places within each jurisdiction. Not all areas of the country require a building or zoning permit. The statistics only represent those areas that do require a permit. These totals thus are limited to permits issued in the 20,000 place universe covered by the Census Bureau and may not include all permits issued within a state. Current surveys indicate that construction is undertaken for all but a very small percentage of housing units authorized by building permits.

Residential building permits include buildings with any number of housing units. Housing units exclude group quarters (such as dormitories and rooming houses), transient accommodations (such as transient hotels, motels, and tourist courts), ''HUD-code'' manufactured (mobile) homes, moved or relocated units, and housing units created in an existing residential or nonresidential structure.

METROPOLITAN AREA LOCAL GOVERNMENT EMPLOYMENT AND PAYROLL, Items 171–179

Source: U.S. Census Bureau—2012 Census of Governments http://www.census.gov/govs/cog2012/

These items include data for all local governments (i.e., counties, municipalities, townships, special districts, and school districts) located within the metropolitan area. The Census of Governments identifies the scope and nature of the nation's state and local government sector; provides authoritative benchmark figures of public finance and public employment; classifies local government organizations, powers, and activities; and measures federal, state, and local fiscal relationships. The Employment component was mailed March 2012 to collect information on the number of state and local government civilian employees and their payrolls.

Government employees include all persons paid for personal services performed, including persons paid from federally funded programs, paid elected or appointed officials, persons in a paid leave status, and persons paid on a per meeting, annual, semiannual, or quarterly basis. Unpaid officials, pensioners, persons whose work is performed on a fee basis, and contractors and their employees are excluded from the count of employees. **Full-time equivalent employees** is a computed statistic representing the number of full-time employees that could have been employed if the reported number of hours worked by part-time employees had been worked by full-time employees. This statistic is calculated separately for each function of a government by dividing the ''part-time hours paid'' by the standard number of hours for full-time employees in the particular government and then adding the resulting quotient to the number of full-time employees.

March payroll represents gross payroll amounts for the one-month period of March for full-time and part-time employees. Gross payroll includes all salaries, wages, fees, commissions, and overtime paid to employees **before** withholdings for taxes, insurance, etc. It also includes incentive payments that are paid at regular pay intervals. It excludes employer share of fringe benefits like retirement, Social Security, health and life insurance, lump sum payments, and so forth.

Administration and Judicial and Legal combines **Financial administration**, **Other government administration, and Judicial and legal** activities. **Financial administration** includes activities concerned with tax assessment and collection, custody and disbursement of funds, debt management, administration of trust funds, budgeting, and other government-wide financial management activities. This function is not applied to school district or special district governments. **Other government administration** applies to the legislative and government-wide administrative agencies of governments. Included here are overall planning and zoning activities, and central personnel and administrative activities. This function is not applied to school district or special district governments. **Judicial and legal** includes all court and court related activities (except probation and parole activities that are included at the ''Correction'' function), court activities of sheriff's offices, prosecuting attorneys' and public defenders' offices, legal departments, and attorneys providing government-wide legal service.

Police and Corrections includes all activities concerned, with the enforcement of law and order, including coroner's offices, police training academies, investigation bureaus, and local jails, ''lockups,'' or other detention facilities not intended to serve as correctional facilities. **Corrections** includes activities pertaining to the confinement and correction of adults and minors convicted of criminal offenses. Pardon, probation, and parole activities are also included here.

Fire protection includes local government fire protection and prevention activities plus any ambulance, rescue, or other auxiliary services provided by a fire protection agency. Volunteer firefighters, if remunerated for their services on a ''per fire'' or some other basis, are included as part-time employees.

Highways and transportation includes activities associated with the maintenance and operation of streets, roads, sidewalks, bridges, tunnels, toll roads, and ferries. Snow and ice removal, street lighting, and highway and traffic engineering activities are also included here. Also included are the operation, maintenance, and construction of public mass transit systems, including subways, surface rails, and buses; the provision, construction, operation, maintenance, and support of public waterways, harbors, docks, wharves, and related marine terminal facilities; and activities associated with the operation and support of publicly operated airport facilities.

Health and Welfare includes **Health, Hospitals, and Public welfare. Health** includes administration of public health programs, community and visiting nurse services, immunization programs, drug abuse rehabilitation programs, health and food inspection activities, operation of outpatient clinics, and environmental pollution control activities. **Hospitals** includes only government-operated medical care facilities that provide inpatient care. Employees and payrolls of private corporations that lease and operate government-owned hospital facilities are excluded. **Public welfare** includes the administration of various public assistance programs for the needy, veteran services, operation of nursing homes, indigent care institutions, and programs that provide payments for medical care, handicap transportation, and other services for the needy.

Natural Resources and Utilities includes activities primarily concerned with the conservation and development of natural resources (soil, water, energy, minerals, etc.) and the regulation of industries that develop, utilize, or affect natural resources, as well as the operation and maintenance of parks, playgrounds, swimming pools, public beaches, auditoriums, public golf courses, museums, marinas, botanical gardens, and zoological parks. **Utilities, sewerage, and waste management** includes operation, maintenance, and construction of public water supply systems, including production, acquisition, and distribution of water to general public or to other public or private utilities, for residential, commercial, and industrial use; activities associated with the production or acquisition and distribution of electric power; provision, maintenance, and operation of sanitary and storm sewer systems and sewage disposal and treatment facilities; and refuse collection and disposal, operation of sanitary landfills, and street cleaning activities.

Education and libraries includes activities associated with the operation of public elementary and secondary schools and locally operated vocational-technical schools. Special education programs operated by elementary and secondary school systems are also included as are all ancillary services associated with the operation of schools, such as pupil transportation and food service. Also included are the establishment and provision of libraries for use by the general public and the technical support of privately operated libraries. This category includes classroom teachers, principals, supervisors of instruction, librarians, teacher aides, library aides, and guidance and psychological personnel as well as school superintendents and other administrative personnel, clerical and secretarial staffs, plant operation and maintenance personnel, health and recreation employees, transportation and food service personnel, and any student employees. Also included are any degree-granting institutions that provide academic training above grade 12.

LOCAL GOVERNMENT FINANCES, Items 180–193

Source: U.S. Census Bureau—2012 Census of Governments
http://www.census.gov/govs/cog/

Data on local government finances are based on result of the 2012 Census of Governments. For each metropolitan area, the data are aggregated from its component counties, and the financial data comprise amounts for all local governments—not only the county governments, but also any municipalities, townships, school districts, and special districts within the county. Statistics from governmental units located in two or more county areas are assigned to the county area containing the administrative office.

Revenue and expenditure items include all amounts of money received and paid out, respectively, by a government and its agencies (net of correcting transactions such as recoveries of refunds), with the exception of amounts for debt issuance and retirement and for loan and investment, agency, and private transactions.

Payments among the various funds and agencies of a particular government are excluded from revenue and expenditure items as representing internal transfers. Therefore, a government's contribution to a retirement fund that it administers is not counted as expenditure, nor is the receipt of this contribution by the retirement fund counted as revenue.

Total **general revenue** includes all revenue except utility, liquor stores, and insurance trust revenue. All tax revenue and intergovernmental revenue, even if designated for employee-retirement or local utility purpose, are classified as general revenue.

Intergovernmental revenue covers amounts received from the federal government as fiscal aid, reimbursements for performance of general government functions and specific services for the paying government, or in lieu of taxes. It excludes any amounts received from other governments from the sale of property, commodities, and utility services.

Taxes consist of compulsory contributions exacted by governments for public purposes. However, this category excludes employer and employee payments for retirement and social insurance purposes, which are classified as insurance trust revenue; it also excludes special assessments, which are classified as non-tax general revenue. Property taxes are taxes conditioned on ownership of property and assessed by its value. Sales and gross receipts taxes do not include dealer discounts, or ''commissions'' allowed to merchants for collection of taxes from consumers. General sales taxes and selected taxes on sales of motor fuels, tobacco products, and other particular commodities and services are included.

General government expenditure includes capital outlay, a major portion of which is commonly financed by borrowing. Government revenue does not include receipts from borrowing. Among other things, this distorts the relationship between totals of revenue and expenditure figures that are presented and renders it useless as a direct measure of the degree of budgetary ''balance'' (as that term is generally applied).

Direct general expenditure comprises all expenditures of the local governments, excluding utility, liquor stores, insurance trust expenditures, and any intergovernmental payments.

Local government expenditure for **education** is mainly for the provision and general support of schools and other educational facilities and services, including those for educational institutions beyond high school. They cover such related services as student transportation; school lunch and other cafeteria operations; school health, recreation, and library services; and dormitories, dining halls, and bookstores operated by public institutions of higher education.

Health and hospital expenditure includes health research; clinics; nursing; immunization; other categorical, environmental, and general health services provided by health agencies; establishment and operation of hospital facilities; provision of hospital care; and support of other public and private hospitals.

Police protection expenditure includes police activities such as patrols, communications, custody of persons awaiting trial, and vehicular inspection.

Public welfare expenditure covers support of and assistance to needy persons; this aid is contingent upon the person's needs. Included are cash assistance paid directly to needy persons under categorical (Old Age Assistance, Temporary Assistance for Needy Families, Aid to the Blind, and Aid to the Disabled) and other welfare programs; vendor payments made directly to private purveyors for medical care, burials, and other commodities and services provided under welfare programs; welfare institutions; and any intergovernmental or other direct expenditure for welfare purposes. Pensions to former employees and other benefits not contingent on need are excluded.

Highway expenditure is for the provision and maintenance of highway facilities, including toll turnpikes, bridges, tunnels, and ferries, as well as regular roads, highways, and streets. Also included are expenditures for street lighting and for snow and ice removal. Not included are highway policing and traffic control, which are considered part of police protection.

Debt outstanding includes all long-term debt obligations of the government and its agencies (exclusive of utility debt) and all interest-bearing, short-term (repayable within one year) debt obligations remaining unpaid at the close of the fiscal year. It includes judgments, mortgages, and revenue bonds, as well as general obligation bonds, notes, and interest-bearing warrants. This category consists of non-interest-bearing, short-term obligations; inter-fund obligations; amounts owed in a trust or agency capacity; advances and contingent loans from other governments; and rights of individuals to benefit from government-administered employee-retirement funds.

GOVERNMENT EMPLOYMENT, Items 194–196

Source: U.S. Bureau of Economic Analysis—Regional Economic Accounts
http://www.bea.gov/regional/index.htm#state

Employment is measured as the average annual sum of full-time and part-time jobs. The estimates are on a place-of-work basis. The estimates are on a place-of-work basis. State and local government employment includes person employed in all state and local government agencies and enterprises. Data for federal civilian employment include civilian employees of the federal government, including civilian employees of the Department of Defense. Military employment includes all persons on active duty status.

ELECTION STATISTICS, Items 197–199

Source: Election Data Services, Inc. Washington, DC (copyright)
http://www.electiondataservices.com/index.php?content=elecdata

Election results show the percentage of the total vote cast for the Democratic and Republican candidates, as well as the combined percentage for all other candidates in the 2012 presidential election.

TABLE D—CITIES

Table D present 146 items of data for cities with populations of 25,000 or more at the time of the 2010 census.

LAND AREA, Items 1 and 4

Source: U.S. Census Bureau—2010 Census of Population and Housing http://www.census.gov/2010census/data/

Land area measurements are shown to the nearest square kilometer. Land area includes dry land and land temporarily or partially covered by water, such as marshlands, swamps, and river floodplains.

POPULATION AND POPULATION CHARACTERISTICS, Items 5–22

Source: U.S. Census Bureau—American Community Survey http://www.census.gov/acs/www/

Source: US. Census Bureau—Population Estimates http://www.census.gov/popest/estimates.html

The population data are Census Bureau estimates of the resident population as of July 1 of the year shown.

Data on age, sex, race, and Hispanic origin, and place of birth are from the 2011–2013 American Community Survey, a nationwide continuous survey designed to replace the long form questionnaire used in previous censuses.

Data on race were derived from answers to the question on race that was asked of all persons. The concept of race, as used by the Census Bureau, reflects self-identification by respondents according to the race or races with which they most closely identify. These categories are sociopolitical constructs and should not be interpreted as being scientific or anthropological in nature. Furthermore, the race categories include both racial and national origin groups.

On the American Community Survey, respondents were offered the option of selecting one or more races. This option was not available prior to the 2000 census; thus, comparisons between censuses should be made with caution. In this table, Columns 5 through 9 refer to individuals who identified with each racial category, either alone or in combination with other races. Because respondents could include as many categories as they wished, and because the columns refer to the percentage of the population, the total will often exceed 100 percent.

The **White** population is defined as persons who indicated their race as White, as well as persons who did not classify themselves in one of the specific race categories listed on the questionnaire but entered a nationality such as Irish, German, Italian, Lebanese, Near Easterner, Arab, or Polish.

The **Black** population includes persons who indicated their race as ''Black, African Am., or Negro,'' as well as persons who did not classify themselves in one of the specific race categories but reported entries such as African American, Afro American, Kenyan, Nigerian, or Haitian.

The **American Indian or Alaska Native** population includes persons who indicated their race as American Indian or Alaska Native, as well as persons who did not classify themselves in one of the specific race categories but reported entries such as Canadian Indian, French-American Indian, Spanish-American Indian, Eskimo, Aleut, Alaska Indian, or any of the American Indian or Alaska Native tribes.

The **Asian and Pacific Islander** population combines two census groupings: **Asian** and **Native Hawaiian or Other Pacific Islander**. Because two separate groups are combined, this category occasionally represents more than 100 percent of a city's population. The **Asian** population includes persons who indicated their race as Asian Indian, Chinese, Filipino, Japanese, Korean, Vietnamese, or ''Other Asian,'' as well as persons who provided write-in entries of such groups as Cambodian, Laotian, Hmong, Pakistani, or Taiwanese. The **Native Hawaiian or Other Pacific Islander** population includes persons who indicated their race as ''Native Hawaiian,'' ''Guamanian or Chamorro,'' ''Samoan,'' or ''Other Pacific Islander,'' as well as persons who reported entries such as Part Hawaiian, American Samoan, Fijian, Melanesian, or Tahitian.

The **Hispanic population** is based on a separate question that asked respondents ''Is this person Spanish/Hispanic/Latino?'' Persons marking any one of the four Hispanic categories (i.e., Mexican, Puerto Rican, Cuban, or other Spanish) are collectively referred to as Hispanic.

The Hispanic origin question was placed before the race question and specific instructions indicated that both questions should be answered.

The **foreign-born** population includes all persons who were not U.S. citizens at birth. Foreign-born persons are those who indicated they were either a U.S. citizen by naturalization or were not a citizen of the United States. The foreign-born population consists of immigrants (legal permanent residents), temporary migrants (students), humanitarian migrants (refugees), and unauthorized migrants (persons illegally residing in the United States).

Age is defined as age at last birthday (number of completed years since birth), at the time of the interview. The American Community Survey also asked for the specific date of birth of the respondent. Both age and date of birth are used in combination to calculate the most accurate age at the time of the interview.

The **female** population is shown as a percentage of total population.

POPULATION CHANGE, Items 23–26

Source: U.S. Census Bureau—Decennial Censuses U.S. Census Bureau—Population Estimates http://www.census.gov/main/www/cen2000.html http://www.census.gov/2010census/data/ http://www.census.gov/popest/estimates.html

The population data for 2000 and 2010 are from the decennial censuses and represent the resident population as of April 1 of those years. The data for 2014 are from the Census Bureau's Population Estimates Program and represent the estimated resident population as of July 1.

The change in population from 2010 to 2014 is calculated from census data based on city boundaries as they existed in 2000 and 2010, respectively. No attempt was made to adjust the data to reflect boundary changes.

HOUSEHOLDS, Items 27–30

Source: U.S. Census Bureau—American Community Survey
http://www.census.gov/acs/www/

A **household** includes all of the persons who occupy a housing unit. (Persons not living in households are classified as living in group quarters.) A housing unit is a house, an apartment, a mobile home, a group of rooms, or a single room occupied (or, if vacant, intended for occupancy) as separate living quarters. Separate living quarters are those in which the occupants live separately from any other persons in the building and have direct access from the outside of the building or through a common hall. The occupants may be a single family, one person living alone, two or more families living together, or any other group of related or unrelated persons who share living quarters. The number of households is the same as the number of year-round occupied housing units.

A **family** includes a householder and one or more other persons living in the same household who are related to the householder by birth, marriage, or adoption. All persons in a household who are related to the householder are regarded as members of his or her family. A **family household** may contain persons not related to the householder; thus, family households may include more members than families do. A household can contain only one family for the purposes of census tabulations. Not all households contain families, as a household may comprise a group of unrelated persons or of one person living alone. Families are classified by type as either a ''husband-wife family'' or ''other family,'' according to the presence or absence of a spouse.

The measure of **persons per household** is obtained by dividing the number of persons in households by the number of households or householders. One person in each household is designated as the householder. In most cases, this is the person (or one of the persons) in whose name the house is owned, being bought, or rented. If there is no such person in the household, any adult household member 15 years old and over can be designated as the householder.

The category **female family householder** includes only female-headed family households with no spouse present.

GROUP QUARTERS, Item 31–34

Source: U.S. Census Bureau—2010 Census of Population and Housing
http://www.census.gov/2010census/data/

The Census Bureau classifies all persons not living in households as living in group quarters; this category includes both the institutional and noninstitutional populations. This volume includes the total number of persons in group quarters and in selected types of group quarters.

The **institutionalized population** includes persons who are primarily ineligible, unable, or unlikely to participate in the labor force while residents, including those in correctional institutions, skilled-nursing facilities, mental (psychiatric) hospitals, and juvenile institutions.

Nursing facilities include facilities licensed to provide medical care with 7-day, 24-hour coverage for people requiring long-term non-acute care. People in these facilities require nursing care, regardless of age. Included in this category are skilled-nursing facilities, intermediate-care facilities, long-term care rooms in wards or buildings on the grounds of hospitals, or long-term care rooms/nursing wings in congregate housing facilities. Also included are nursing, convalescent, and rest homes, such as soldiers', veterans', and fraternal or religious homes for the aged, with or without nursing care.

The **noninstitutionalized population** includes persons who live in group quarters other than institutions, such as college dormitories, military quarters, and group homes.

CRIME, Items 35–38

Source: U.S. Federal Bureau of Investigation—Uniform Crime Reports
http://www.fbi.gov/ucr/ucr.htm

Crime data are as reported to the Federal Bureau of Investigation (FBI) by law enforcement agencies and have not been adjusted for underreporting. This may affect comparability between geographic areas or over time.

Through the voluntary contribution of crime statistics by law enforcement agencies across the United States, the Uniform Crime Reporting (UCR) Program provides periodic assessments of crime in the nation as measured by offenses that have come to the attention of the law enforcement community. The Committee on Uniform Crime Records of the International Association of Chiefs of Police initiated this voluntary national data collection effort in 1930. The UCR Program contributors compile and submit their crime data either directly to the FBI or through state-level UCR Programs.

Seven offenses, because of their severity, frequency of occurrence, and likelihood of being reported to police, were initially selected to serve as an index for evaluating fluctuations in the volume of crime. These serious crimes were murder and nonnegligent manslaughter, forcible rape, robbery, aggravated assault, burglary, larceny-theft, and motor vehicle theft. By congressional mandate, arson was added as the eighth index offense in 1979. The totals shown in this volume do not include arson.

In 2004, the FBI discontinued the use of the Crime Index in the UCR Program and its publications, stating that the Crime Index was driven upward by the offense with the highest number of cases (in this case, larceny-theft), creating a bias against jurisdictions with a high number of larceny-thefts but a low number of other serious crimes, such as murder and forcible rape. The FBI is currently publishing a violent crime total and property crime total until a more viable index is developed. This book includes the total Crime Index, as well as violent crime and property crime rates.

In 2013, the FBI adopted a new definition of rape. Rape is now defined as, ''Penetration, no matter how slight, of the vagina or anus with any body part or object, or oral penetration by a sex organ of another person, without the consent of the victim.'' The new definition updated the 80-year-old historical definition of rape which was ''carnal knowledge of a female forcibly and against her will.'' Effectively, the revised definition expands rape to include both male and female victims and offenders, and reflects the various forms of sexual penetration understood to be rape, especially nonconsenting acts of sodomy, and sexual assaults with objects.

Violent crimes include four categories of offenses: (1) Murder and nonnegligent manslaughter, as defined in the UCR Program, is the willful (nonnegligent) killing of one human being by another. This offense excludes deaths caused by negligence, suicide, or accident; justifiable homicides; and attempts to murder or assaults to murder. (2) Rape is the penetration, no matter how slight, of the vagina or anus with any body part or object, or oral penetration by a sex organ of another person, without the consent of the victim Assaults or attempts to commit rape by force or threat of force are also included; however, statutory rape (without force) and other sex offenses are excluded. (3) Robbery is the taking or attempting to take anything of value from the care, custody, or control of a person or persons by force or threat of force or violence and/or by putting the victim in fear. (4) Aggravated assault is an unlawful attack by one person upon another for the purpose of inflicting severe or aggravated bodily injury. This type of assault is usually accompanied by the use of a weapon or by other means likely to produce death or great bodily harm. Attempts are included, since injury does not necessarily have to result when a gun, knife, or other weapon is used, as these incidents could and probably would result in a serious personal injury if the crime were successfully completed.

Property crimes include three categories: (1) Burglary, or breaking and entering, is the unlawful entry of a structure to commit a felony or theft, even though no force was used to gain entrance. (2) Larceny-theft is the unauthorized taking of the personal property of another, without the use of force. (3) Motor vehicle theft is the unauthorized taking of any motor vehicle.

Rates are based on population estimates provided by the FBI. If a city is not in the UCR database, or if the population total for the units aggregated was less than 75 percent of the city's population (as estimated by the Census Bureau), the total was not considered representative of the city as a whole and was not published. State and U.S. totals include FBI estimates for those areas.

EDUCATIONAL ATTAINMENT, Items 39–41

Source: U.S. Census Bureau—American Community Survey
http://www.census.gov/acs/www/

Data on **educational attainment** are tabulated for the population 25 years old and over. The data were derived from a question that asked respondents for the highest level of school completed or the highest degree received. Persons who had passed a high school equivalency examination were considered high school graduates. Schooling received in foreign schools was to be reported as the equivalent grade or years in the regular American school system.

Vocational and technical training, such as barber school training; business, trade, technical, and vocational schools; or other training for a specific trade are specifically excluded.

High school graduate or less. This category includes persons whose highest degree was a high school diploma or its equivalent, and those who reported any level lower than a high school diploma.

Bachelor's degree or more. This category includes persons who have received bachelor's degrees, master's degrees, professional school degrees (such as law school or medical school degrees), and doctoral degrees.

INCOME AND POVERTY, Items 42–46

Source: U.S. Census Bureau—American Community Survey
http://www.census.gov/acs/www/

Total money income is the sum of the amounts reported separately for wage or salary income; net self-employment income; interest, dividends, or net rental or royalty income or income from estates and trusts; Social Security or railroad retirement income; Supplemental Security Income (SSI); public assistance or welfare payments; retirement, survivor, or disability pensions; and all other income. Receipts from the following sources are not included as income: capital gains; money received from the sale of property (unless the recipient was engaged in the business of selling such property); the value of income ''in kind'' from food stamps, public housing subsidies, medical care, employer contributions for individuals, etc.; withdrawal of bank deposits; money borrowed; tax refunds; exchange of money between relatives living in the same household; and gifts, lump-sum inheritances, insurance payments, and other types of lump-sum receipts.

Per capita income is the mean income computed for every man, woman, and child in a particular group. It is derived by dividing the aggregate income of a particular group by the resident population in that group in the survey year. Per capita income is rounded to the nearest whole dollar.

Household income includes the income of the householder and all other individuals 15 years old and over in the household, whether or not they are related to the householder. Since many households consist of only one person, median household income is usually less than median family income. Although the household income statistics cover the twelve months prior to the survey, the characteristics of individuals and the composition of households refer to the date of the interview. Thus, the income of the household does not include amounts received by individuals who were members of the household during all or part of the year if these individuals were no longer residing in the household at the time of the interview. Similarly, income amounts reported by individuals who did not reside in the household during full year but who were members of the household at the time of the interview are included. However, the composition of most households was the same during the year as it was at the time of the interview.

Median income divides the income distribution into two equal parts, with half of all cases below the median income level and half of all cases above the median income level. For households, the median income is based on the distribution of the total number of households, including those with no income. Median income for households is computed on the basis of a standard distribution with a minimum value of less than $2,500 and a maximum value of $200,000 or more and is rounded to the nearest whole dollar. Median income figures are calculated using linear interpolation if the width of the interval containing the estimate is $2,500 or less. If the width of the interval containing the estimate is greater than $2,500, Pareto interpolation is used.

Income components were reported for the 12 months preceding the interview month. Monthly Consumer Price Index (CPI) factors were used to inflation-adjust these components to a reference calendar year (January through December). For example, a household interviewed in March 2013 reports their income for March 2012 through February 2013. Their income is adjusted to the 2013 reference calendar year by multiplying their reported income by 2013 average annual CPI (January-December 2013) and then dividing by the average CPI for March 2012-February 2013. In addition, the 3-year estimates are inflation-adjusted to the final year. However, the estimates do not reflect the price and cost-of-living differences that may exist between areas.

The **poverty status** data were derived from data collected on the number of persons in a household, each person's relationship to the householder, and each person's income during the past twelve months. The Social Security Administration (SSA) developed the original poverty definition in 1964, which federal interagency committees subsequently revised in 1969 and 1980. The Office of Management and Budget's (OMB) *Directive 14* prescribes the SSA's definition as the official poverty measure for federal agencies to use in their statistical work.

Poverty thresholds vary depending on three criteria: size of family, number of children, and, for one- and two-person families, age of householder. In determining the poverty status of families and unrelated individuals, the Census Bureau uses thresholds (income cutoffs) arranged in a two-dimensional matrix. The matrix consists of family size (from one person to nine or more persons), cross-classified by presence and number of family members under 18 years old (from no children present to eight or more children present). Unrelated individuals and two-person families are further differentiated by age of reference person (under 65 years old and 65 years old and over). To determine a person's poverty status, the person's total family income over the previous 12 months is compared with the poverty threshold appropriate for that person's family size and composition. If the total income of that person's family is less than the threshold appropriate for that family, then the person is considered poor or ''below the poverty level,'' together with every member of his or her family. If a person is not living with anyone related by birth, marriage, or adoption, then the person's own income is compared with his or her poverty threshold. The total number of persons below the poverty level is the sum of persons in families and the number of unrelated individuals with incomes below the poverty level.

Poverty Thresholds for 2013 by Size of Family and Number of Related Children Under 18 Years

Size of family unit	Weighted average thresholds
One person (unrelated individual)	11,888
Under 65 years	12,119
65 years and over	11,173
Two people	15,142
Householder under 65 years	15,679
Householder 65 years and over	14,095
Three people	18,552
Four people	23,834
Five people	28,265
Six people	31,925
Seven people	36,384
Eight people	40,484
Nine people or more	48,065

Source: U.S. Census Bureau.

HOUSING, Items 47–57

Source: U.S. Census Bureau—2010 Census of Population and Housing
http://www.census.gov/2010census/data/
Source: American Community Survey
http://www.census.gov/acs/www/

The housing unit counts in columns 47 through 49 are from the 2010 census. The characteristics of occupied housing units are from the 2011–2013 American Community Survey.

A **housing unit** is a house, apartment, mobile home or trailer, group of rooms, or single room occupied or, if vacant, intended for occupancy as separate living quarters. Separate living quarters are those in which the occupants do not live and eat with any other person in the structure and which have direct access from the outside of the building through a common hall. For vacant units, the criteria of separateness and direct access are applied to the intended occupants whenever possible. If that information cannot be obtained, the criteria are applied to the previous occupants.

The occupants of a housing unit may be a single family, one person living alone, two or more families living together, or any other group of related or unrelated persons who share living quarters. Both occupied and vacant housing units are included in the housing inventory, although recreational vehicles, tents, caves, boats, railroad cars, and the like are included only if they are occupied as a person's usual place of residence.

A housing unit is classified as occupied if it is the usual place of residence of the person or group of persons living in it at the time of enumeration, or if the occupants are only temporarily absent (away on vacation). A household consists of all persons who occupy a housing unit as their usual place of residence. Vacant units for sale or rent include units rented or sold but not occupied and any other units held off the market.

The percent change represents the difference in the number of total housing units in a specified area from 2000 to 2010.

A housing unit is **owner occupied** if the owner or co-owner lives in the unit, even if it is mortgaged or not fully paid for. The owner or co-owner must live in the unit and is usually the first person listed on the census or ACS questionnaire.

All occupied housing units that are not owner occupied, whether they are rented for cash rent or occupied without payment of cash rent, are classified as **renter occupied**.

Median value is the dollar amount that divides the distribution of specified owner-occupied housing units into two equal parts, with half of all units below the median value and half of all units above the median value. Value is defined as the respondent's estimate of what the house would sell for if it were for sale. Data are presented for single-family units on fewer than 10 acres of land that have no business or medical offices on the property.

Median rent divides the distribution of renter-occupied housing units into two equal parts. The rent concept used in this volume is gross rent, which includes the amount of cash rent a renter pays (contract rent) plus the estimated average cost of utilities and fuels, if these are paid by the renter. The rent is the amount of rent only for living quarters and excludes amounts paid for any business or other space occupied. Single-family houses on lots of 10 or more acres of land are also excluded.

Housing cost as a percentage of income is shown separately for owners with mortgages, owners without mortgages, and renters. Rent as a percentage of income is a computed ratio of gross rent and monthly household income (total household income during the year divided by 12). Selected owner costs include utilities and fuels, mortgage payments, insurance, taxes, etc. In each case, the ratio of housing cost to income is computed separately for each housing unit. The housing cost ratios for half of all units are above the median shown in this book, and half are below the median shown in the book.

Substandard units are occupied units that are overcrowded or lack complete plumbing facilities. For the purposes of this item, ''overcrowded'' is defined as having 1.01 persons or more per room. Complete plumbing facilities include hot and cold piped water, a flush toilet, and a bathtub or shower. These facilities must be located inside the housing unit, but do not have to be in the same room.

PERCENT WITH NO VEHICLES AVAILABLE, Item 58

Source: U.S. Census Bureau—American Community Survey
http://www.census.gov/acs/www/

The data on vehicles available show the number of passenger cars, vans, and pickup or panel trucks of one-ton capacity or less kept at home and available for the use of household members. Vehicles rented or leased for one month or more, company vehicles, and police and government vehicles are included if kept at home and used for non-business purposes. Dismantled or immobile vehicles are excluded. Vehicles kept at home but used only for business purposes also are excluded.

MIGRATION, Items 59 and 60

Source: U.S. Census Bureau—American Community Survey
http://www.census.gov/acs/www/

Residence one year ago is used in conjunction with location of current residence to determine the extent of residential mobility of the population and the resulting redistribution of the population across the various states, metropolitan areas, and regions of the country. **Same house** includes all people 1 year old and over who, a year before the survey date, lived in the same house or apartment that they occupied at the time of interview.

The **percent who lived outside this city** includes all persons who did not live in the listed city one year before the interview, whether their previous residence was in the same state, a different state, Puerto Rico, or abroad.

CIVILIAN LABOR FORCE AND UNEMPLOYMENT, Items 61–64

Source: U.S. Bureau of Labor Statistics—Local Areas Unemployment Statistics
http://www.bls.gov/lau/#tables

Data for the civilian labor force are the product of a federal-state cooperative program in which state employment security agencies prepare labor force and unemployment estimates under concepts, definitions, and technical procedures established by the Bureau of Labor Statistics (BLS). The civilian labor force consists of all civilians 16 years old and over who are either employed or unemployed.

Unemployment includes all persons who did not work during the survey week, made specific efforts to find a job during the previous four weeks, and were available for work during the survey week (except for temporary illness). Persons waiting to be called back to a job from which they had been laid off and those waiting to report to a new job within the next 30 days are included in unemployment figures.

Table D includes annual average data for the year shown. The Local Area Unemployment Statistics data are periodically updated to reflect revised inputs, reestimation, and controlling to new statewide totals.

CIVILIAN EMPLOYMENT, Items 65–68

Source: U.S. Census Bureau—American Community Survey
http://www.census.gov/acs/www/

The **labor force** includes all persons 16 years old and over who were either (1) ''at work''—those who did any work at all during the reference week as paid employees, worked in either their own business or profession, worked on their own farm, or worked 15 hours or more as unpaid workers in a family farm or business; or were (2) ''with a job, but not at work''—those who had a job but were not at work that week due to illness, weather, industrial dispute, vacation, or other personal reasons.

Full-year, Full-Time Workers includes all people 16 years old and over who usually worked 35 hours or more per week for 50 to 52 weeks in the past 12 months.

Households with no workers includes households where all members ''Did not work in the past 12 months.'' Workers include all people 16 years old and over who, for one or more weeks, did any work for pay or profit (including paid vacation and paid sick leave) or worked without pay on a family farm or in a family business. Weeks of active service in the Armed Forces are also included.

BUILDING PERMITS, Items 69–71

Source: U.S. Census Bureau—Building Permits Survey
http://www.census.gov/const/www/permitsindex.html

These figures represent private residential construction authorized by building permits in approximately 20,000 places in the United States. Valuation represents the expected cost of construction as recorded on the building permit. This figure usually excludes the cost of on-site and off-site development and improvements, as well as the cost of heating, plumbing, electrical, and elevator installations.

National, state, and county totals were obtained by adding the data for permit-issuing places within each jurisdiction. These totals thus are limited to permits issued in the 20,000 place universe covered by the Census Bureau and may not include all permits issued within a state. Current surveys indicate that construction is undertaken for all but a very small percentage of housing units authorized by building permits.

Residential building permits include buildings with any number of housing units. Housing units exclude group quarters (such as dormitories and rooming houses), transient accommodations (such as transient hotels, motels, and tourist courts), ''HUD-code'' manufactured (mobile) homes, moved or relocated units, and housing units created in an existing residential or nonresidential structure.

2007 ECONOMIC CENSUS: OVERVIEW, Items 72–107

Source: U.S. Census Bureau
http://www.census.gov/econ/census07/

The Economic Census provides a detailed portrait of the nation's economy, from the national to the local level, once every five years. The 2007 Economic Census covers nearly all of the U.S. economy in its basic collection of establishment statistics. The 1997 Economic Census was the first major data source to use the new North American Industry Classification System (NAICS); therefore, data from this census are not comparable to economic data from prior years, which were based on the Standard Industrial Classification (SIC) system.

NAICS, developed in cooperation with Canada and Mexico, classifies North America's economic activities at two-, three-, four-, and five-digit levels of detail; the U.S. version of NAICS further defines industries to a sixth digit. The Economic Census takes advantage of this hierarchy to publish data at these successive levels of detail: sector (two-digit), subsector (three-digit), industry group (four-digit), industry (five-digit), and U.S. industry (six-digit). Information in Table A is at the two-digit level, with a few three- and four-digit items. The data in Table D are at the two-digit level.

Several key statistics are tabulated for all industries in this volume, including number of establishments (or companies), number of employees, payroll, and certain measures of output (sales, receipts, revenue, value of shipments, or value of construction work done).

Number of establishments. An establishment is a single physical location at which business is conducted. It is not necessarily identical with a company or enterprise, which may consist of one establishment or more. Economic Census figures represent a summary of reports for individual establishments rather than companies. For cases in which a census report was received, separate information was obtained for each location where business was conducted. When administrative records of other federal agencies were used instead of a census report, no information was available on the number of locations operated. Each Economic Census establishment was tabulated according to the physical location at which the business was conducted. The count of establishments represents those in business at any time during 2002.

When two activities or more were carried on at a single location under a single ownership, all activities were generally grouped together as a single establishment. The entire establishment was classified on the basis of its major activity and all of its data were included in that classification. However, when distinct and separate economic activities (for which different industry classification codes were appropriate) were conducted at a single location under a single ownership, separate establishment reports for each of the different activities were obtained in the census.

Number of employees. Paid employees consist of the full-time and part-time employees, including salaried officers and executives of corporations. Included are employees on paid sick leave, paid holidays, and paid vacations; not included are proprietors and partners of unincorporated businesses. The definition of paid employees is the same as that used by the Internal Revenue Service (IRS) on form 941. For some industries, the Economic Census gives codes representing the number of employees as a range of numbers (for example, ''100 to 249 employees'' or ''1,000 to 2,499'' employees). In this volume, those codes have been replaced by the standard suppression code ''D.''

Payroll. Payroll includes all forms of compensation, such as salaries, wages, commissions, dismissal pay, bonuses, vacation allowances, sick-leave pay, and employee contributions to qualified pension plans paid during the year to all employees. For corporations, payroll includes amounts paid to officers and executives; for unincorporated businesses, it does not include profit or other compensation of proprietors or partners. Payroll is reported before deductions for Social Security, income tax, insurance, union dues, etc. This definition of payroll is the same as that used on IRS form 941.

Sales, shipments, receipts, revenue, or business done. This measure includes the total sales, shipments, receipts, revenue, or business done by establishments within the scope of the Economic Census. The definition of each of these items is specific to the economic sector measured.

WHOLESALE TRADE, Items 72–75

Source: U.S. Census Bureau—2007 Economic Census (See Overview of 2007 Economic Census prior to Item 72)

The Wholesale Trade sector (sector 42) comprises establishments engaged in wholesaling merchandise, generally without transformation, and rendering services incidental to the sale of merchandise. The wholesaling process is an intermediate step in the distribution of merchandise.

Wholesalers are organized to sell or arrange the purchase or sale of (1) goods for resale (i.e., goods sold to other wholesalers or retailers), (2) capital or durable nonconsumer goods, and (3) raw and intermediate materials and supplies used in production.

Wholesalers sell merchandise to other businesses and normally operate from a warehouse or office. These warehouses and offices are characterized by having little or no display of merchandise. In addition, neither the design nor the location of the premises is intended to solicit walk-in traffic. Wholesalers do not normally use advertising directed to the general public. In general, customers are initially reached via telephone, in-person marketing, or specialized advertising, which may include the internet and other electronic means. Follow-up orders are either vendor-initiated or client-initiated, are usually based on previous sales, and typically exhibit strong ties between sellers and buyers. In fact, transactions are often conducted between wholesalers and clients that have long-standing business relationships.

This sector is made up of two main types of wholesalers: those that sell goods on their own account and those that arrange sales and purchases for others for a commission or fee.

(1) Establishments that sell goods on their own account are known as wholesale merchants, distributors, jobbers, drop shippers, import/export merchants, and sales branches. These establishments typically maintain their own warehouse, where they receive and handle goods for their customers. Goods are generally sold without transformation, but may include integral functions, such as sorting, packaging, labeling, and other marketing services.

(2) Establishments arranging for the purchase or sale of goods owned by others or purchasing goods on a commission basis are known as agents and brokers, commission merchants, import/export agents and brokers, auction companies, and manufacturers' representatives. These establishments operate from offices and generally do not own or handle the goods they sell.

Some wholesale establishments may be connected with a single manufacturer and promote and sell that particular manufacturer's products to a wide range of other wholesalers or retailers. Other wholesalers may be connected to a retail chain or a limited number of retail chains and only provide the products needed by the particular retail operation(s). These wholesalers may obtain the products from a wide range of manufacturers. Still other wholesalers may not take title to the goods, but act instead as agents and brokers for a commission.

Although wholesaling normally denotes sales in large volumes, durable nonconsumer goods may be sold in single units. Sales of capital or durable nonconsumer goods used in the production of goods and services, such as farm machinery, medium- and heavy-duty trucks, and industrial machinery, are always included in Wholesale Trade.

The city table includes only **Merchant wholesalers,** except manufacturers' sales branches and offices, establishments primarily engaged in buying and selling merchandise on their own account. Included here are such types of establishments as wholesale distributors and jobbers, importers, exporters, own-brand importers/marketers, terminal and country grain elevators, and farm products assemblers.

RETAIL TRADE, Items 76–79

Source: U.S. Census Bureau—2007 Economic Census (See Overview of 2007 Economic Census prior to Item 72)

The Retail Trade sector (44–45) is made up of establishments engaged in retailing merchandise, generally without transformation, and rendering services incidental to the sale of merchandise.

The retailing process is the final step in the distribution of merchandise; retailers are therefore organized to sell merchandise in small quantities to the general public. This sector comprises two main types of retailers: store and nonstore retailers.

Store retailers operate fixed point-of-sale locations, located and designed to attract a high volume of walk-in customers. In general, retail stores have extensive displays of merchandise and use mass-media advertising to attract customers. They typically sell merchandise to the general public for personal or household consumption; some also serve business and institutional clients. These include establishments such as office supply stores, computer and software stores, building materials dealers, plumbing supply stores, and electrical supply stores. Catalog showrooms, gasoline service stations, automotive dealers, and mobile home dealers are treated as store retailers.

In addition to retailing merchandise, some types of store retailers are also engaged in the provision of after-sales services, such as repair and installation. For example, new automobile dealers, electronic and appliance stores, and musical instrument and supply stores often provide repair services. As a general rule, establishments engaged in retailing merchandise and providing after-sales services are classified in this sector.

Nonstore retailers, like store retailers, are organized to serve the general public, although their retailing methods differ. The establishments of this subsector reach customers and market merchandise with methods including the broadcasting of ''infomercials,'' the broadcasting and publishing of direct-response advertising, the publishing of paper and electronic catalogs, door-to-door solicitation, in-home demonstration, selling from portable stalls (street vendors, except food), and distribution through vending machines. Establishments engaged in the direct sale (nonstore) of products, such as home heating oil dealers and home-delivery newspaper routes are included in this sector.

The buying of goods for resale is a characteristic of retail trade establishments that distinguishes them from establishments in the Agriculture, Manufacturing, and Construction sectors. For example, farms that sell their products at or from the point of production are classified in Agriculture instead of in Retail Trade. Similarly, establishments that both manufacture and sell their products to the general public are classified in Manufacturing instead of Retail Trade. However, establishments that engage in processing activities incidental to retailing are classified in Retail Trade.

REAL ESTATE AND RENTAL AND LEASING, Items 80–83

Source: U.S. Census Bureau—2007 Economic Census (See Overview of 2007 Economic Census prior to Item 72)

The Real Estate and Rental and Leasing sector (53) comprises establishments primarily engaged in renting, leasing, or otherwise allowing the use of tangible or intangible assets, and establishments providing related services. The major portion of this sector is made up of establishments that rent, lease, or otherwise allow the use of their own assets by others. The assets may be tangible, such as real estate and equipment, or intangible, such as patents and trademarks.

This sector also includes establishments primarily engaged in managing real estate for others, selling, renting, and/or buying real estate for others, and appraising real estate. These activities are closely related to this sector's main activity. In addition, a substantial proportion of property management is self-performed by lessors.

The main components of this sector are the real estate lessors industries; equipment lessors industries (including motor vehicles, computers, and consumer goods); and lessors of nonfinancial intangible assets (except copyrighted works).

PROFESSIONAL, SCIENTIFIC, AND TECHNICAL SERVICES, Items 84–87

Source: U.S. Census Bureau—2007 Economic Census (See Overview of 2007 Economic Census prior to Item 72)

The Professional, Scientific, and Technical Services sector (54) is made up of establishments that specialize in performing professional, scientific, and technical activities for others. These activities require a high degree of expertise and training. The establishments in this sector specialize in one or more areas and provide services to clients in a variety of industries (and, in some cases, to households). Activities performed include legal advice and representation; accounting, bookkeeping, and payroll services; architectural, engineering, and specialized design services; computer services; consulting services; research services; advertising services; photographic services; translation and interpretation services; veterinary services; and other professional, scientific, and technical services.

Table D includes only those establishments subject to federal income tax.

This sector excludes establishments primarily engaged in providing a range of day-to-day office administrative services, such as financial planning, billing and record keeping, personnel services, and physical distribution and logistics services. These establishments are classified in sector 56, Administrative and Support and Waste Management and Remediation Services.

MANUFACTURING, Items 88–91

Source: U.S. Census Bureau—2007 Economic Census (See Overview of 2007 Economic Census prior to Item 72)

The Manufacturing sector (31–33) is made up of establishments engaged in the mechanical, physical, or chemical transformation of materials, substances, or components into new products. The assembling of component parts of manufactured products is considered manufacturing, except in cases in which the activity is appropriately classified in the Construction sector. Establishments in the Manufacturing sector are often described as plants, factories, or mills, and characteristically use power-driven machines and materials-handling equipment. However, establishments that transform materials or substances into new products by hand or in the worker's home, and establishments engaged in selling to the general public products made on the same premises from which they are sold (such as bakeries, candy stores, and custom tailors) may also be included in this sector. Manufacturing establishments may process materials or contract with other establishments to process their materials for them. Both types of establishments are included in the Manufacturing sector.

The materials, substances, or components transformed by manufacturing establishments are raw materials that are products of agriculture, forestry, fishing, mining, or quarrying, or are products of other manufacturing establishments. The materials used may be purchased directly from producers, obtained through customary trade channels, or secured without recourse to the market by transferring the product from one establishment to another, under the same ownership. The new product of a manufacturing establishment may be finished (in the sense that it is ready for utilization or consumption), or it may be semifinished to become an input for an establishment engaged in further manufacturing. For example, the product of the alumina refinery is the input used in the primary production of aluminum; primary aluminum is the input used in an aluminum wire drawing plant; and aluminum wire is the input used in a fabricated wire product manufacturing establishment.

Data are included for cities with 500 or more employees in the Manufacturing sector.

ACCOMMODATION AND FOOD SERVICES, Items 92–95

Source: U.S. Census Bureau—2007 Economic Census (See Overview of 2007 Economic Census prior to Item 72)

The Accommodation and Food Services sector (72) consists of establishments that provide customers with lodging and/or meals, snacks, and beverages for immediate consumption. This sector includes both accommodation and food services establishments because the two activities are often combined at the same establishment.

Excluded from this sector are civic and social organizations, amusement and recreation parks, theaters, and other recreation or entertainment facilities providing food and beverage services.

ARTS, ENTERTAINMENT, AND RECREATION, Items 96–99

Source: U.S. Census Bureau—2007 Economic Census (See Overview of 2007 Economic Census prior to Item 72)

The Arts, Entertainment, and Recreation sector (71) includes a wide range of establishments that operate facilities or provide services that meet the diverse cultural, entertainment, and recreational interests of their patrons. This sector is made up of: (1) establishments that are involved in producing, promoting, or participating in live performances, events, or exhibits intended for public viewing; (2) establishments that preserve and exhibit objects and sites of historical, cultural, or educational interest; and (3) establishments that operate facilities or provide services that enable patrons to participate in recreational activities or pursue amusement, hobby, and leisure time interests.

Some establishments that provide cultural, entertainment, or recreational facilities and services are classified in other sectors. Excluded from this sector are: (1) establishments that provide both accommodations and recreational facilities—such as hunting and fishing camps and resort and casino hotels—are classified in subsector 721, Accommodation; (2) restaurants and night clubs that provide live entertainment in addition to the sale of food and beverages are classified in subsector 722, Food Services and Drinking Places; (3) motion picture theaters, libraries and archives, and publishers of newspapers, magazines, books, periodicals, and computer software are classified in sector 51, Information; and (4) establishments that use transportation equipment to provide recreational and entertainment services, such as those operating sightseeing buses, dinner cruises, or helicopter rides, are classified in subsector 487, Scenic and Sightseeing Transportation.

Table D includes only those establishments subject to federal tax.

HEALTH CARE AND SOCIAL ASSISTANCE, Items 100–103

Source: U.S. Census Bureau—2007 Economic Census (See Overview of 2007 Economic Census prior to Item 72)

The Health Care and Social Assistance sector (62) consists of establishments that provide health care and social assistance services to individuals. The sector includes both health care and social assistance because it is sometimes difficult to distinguish between the boundaries of these two activities. The industries in this sector are arranged on a continuum, starting with establishments that provide medical care exclusively, continuing with those that provide health care and social assistance, and finishing with those that provide only social assistance. The services provided by establishments in this sector are delivered by trained professionals. All industries in the sector share this commonality of process—namely, labor inputs of health practitioners or social workers with the requisite expertise. Many of the industries in the sector are defined based on the educational degree held by the practitioners included in the industry.

Excluded from this sector are aerobic classes, which can be found in subsector 713, Amusement, Gambling, and Recreation Industries; and nonmedical diet and weight-reducing centers, which can be found in subsector 812, Personal and Laundry Services. Although these can be viewed as health services, they are not typically delivered by health practitioners.

Table D includes only those establishments subject to federal tax.

OTHER SERVICES, EXCEPT PUBLIC ADMINISTRATION Items 104–107

Source: U.S. Census Bureau—2007 Economic Census (See Overview of 2007 Economic Census prior to Item 72)

The Other Services, Except Public Administration sector (81) comprises establishments engaged in providing services not specifically categorized elsewhere in the classification system. Establishments in this sector are primarily engaged in activities such as equipment and machinery repairing, promoting or administering religious activities, grant making, and advocacy; this sector also includes establishments that provide dry-cleaning and laundry services, personal care services, death care services, pet care services, photofinishing services, temporary parking services, and dating services.

Private households that employ workers on or about the premises in activities primarily concerned with the operation of the household are included in this sector.

In Table D, only firms subject to federal tax are included.

Excluded from this sector are establishments primarily engaged in retailing new equipment and performing repairs and general maintenance on equipment. These establishments are classified in sector 44–45, Retail Trade.

CITY GOVERNMENT EMPLOYMENT AND PAYROLL, Items 171–179

Source: U.S. Census Bureau—2012 Census of Governments http://www.census.gov/govs/cog2012/

These items include data for municipal governments only. They do not include any special district government entities within the city. The Census of Governments identifies the scope and nature of the nation's state and local government sector; provides authoritative benchmark figures of public finance and public employment; classifies local government organizations, powers, and activities; and measures federal, state, and local fiscal relationships. The Employment component was mailed March 2012 to collect information on the number of state and local government civilian employees and their payrolls.

Government employees include all persons paid for personal services performed, including persons paid from federally funded programs, paid elected or appointed officials, persons in a paid leave status, and persons paid on a per meeting, annual, semiannual, or quarterly basis. Unpaid officials, pensioners, persons whose work is performed on a fee basis, and contractors and their employees are excluded from the count of employees. **Full-time equivalent employees** is a computed statistic representing the number of full-time employees that could have been employed if the reported number of hours worked by part-time employees had been worked by full-time employees. This statistic is calculated separately for each function of a government by dividing the ''part-time hours paid'' by the standard number of hours for full-time employees in the particular government and then adding the resulting quotient to the number of full-time employees.

March payroll represents gross payroll amounts for the one-month period of March for full-time and part-time employees. Gross payroll includes all salaries, wages, fees, commissions, and overtime paid to employees **before** withholdings for taxes, insurance, etc. It also includes incentive payments that are paid at regular pay intervals. It excludes employer share of fringe benefits like retirement, Social Security, health and life insurance, lump sum payments, and so forth.

Administration and Judicial and Legal combines **Financial administration**, **Other government administration, and Judicial and legal** activities. **Financial administration** includes activities concerned with tax assessment and collection, custody and disbursement of funds, debt management, administration of trust funds, budgeting, and other government-wide financial management activities. This function is not applied to school district or special district governments. **Other government administration** applies to the legislative and government-wide administrative agencies of governments. Included here are overall planning and zoning activities, and central personnel and administrative activities. This function is not applied to school district or special district governments. **Judicial and legal** includes all court and court related activities (except probation and parole activities that are included at the ''Correction'' function), court activities of sheriffs' offices, prosecuting attorneys' and public defenders' offices, legal departments, and attorneys providing government-wide legal service.

Police and Corrections includes all activities concerned, with the enforcement of law and order, including coroners' offices, police training academies, investigation bureaus, and local jails, ''lockups,'' or other detention facilities not intended to serve as correctional facilities. **Corrections** includes activities pertaining to the confinement and correction of adults and minors convicted of criminal offenses. Pardon, probation, and parole activities are also included here.

Fire protection includes local government fire protection and prevention activities plus any ambulance, rescue, or other auxiliary services provided by a fire protection agency. Volunteer firefighters, if remunerated for their services on a ''per fire'' or some other basis, are included as part-time employees.

Highways and transportation includes activities associated with the maintenance and operation of streets, roads, sidewalks, bridges, tunnels, toll roads, and ferries. Snow and ice removal, street lighting, and highway and traffic engineering activities are also included here. Also included are the operation, maintenance, and construction of public mass transit systems, including subways, surface rails, and buses; the provision, construction, operation, maintenance, and support of public waterways, harbors, docks, wharves, and related marine terminal facilities; and activities associated with the operation and support of publicly operated airport facilities.

Health and Welfare includes **Health, Hospitals,** and **Public welfare. Health** includes administration of public health programs, community and visiting nurse services, immunization programs, drug abuse rehabilitation programs, health and food inspection activities, operation of outpatient clinics, and environmental pollution control activities. **Hospitals** includes only government operated medical care facilities that provide inpatient care. Employees and payrolls of private corporations that lease and operate government-owned hospital facilities are excluded. **Public welfare** includes the administration of various public assistance programs for the needy, veteran services, operation of nursing homes, indigent care institutions, and programs that provide payments for medical care, handicap transportation, and other services for the needy.

Natural resources and utilities includes activities primarily concerned with the conservation and development of natural resources (soil, water, energy, minerals, etc.) and the regulation of industries that develop, utilize, or affect natural resources, as well as the operation and maintenance of parks, playgrounds, swimming pools, public beaches, auditoriums, public golf courses, museums, marinas, botanical gardens, and zoological parks. **Utilities, sewerage, and waste management** includes operation, maintenance, and construction of public water supply systems, including production, acquisition, and distribution of water to general public or to other public or private utilities, for residential, commercial, and industrial use; activities associated with the production or acquisition and distribution of electric power; provision, maintenance, and operation of sanitary and storm sewer systems and sewage disposal and treatment facilities; and refuse collection and disposal, operation of sanitary landfills, and street cleaning activities.

Education and libraries includes activities associated with the operation of public elementary and secondary schools and locally operated vocational-technical schools. Special education programs operated by elementary and secondary school systems are also included as are all ancillary services associated with the operation of schools, such as pupil transportation and food service. Also included are the establishment and provision of libraries for use by the general public and the technical support of privately operated libraries. This category includes classroom teachers, principals, supervisors of instruction, librarians, teacher aides, library aides, and guidance and psychological personnel as well as school superintendents and other administrative personnel, clerical and secretarial staffs, plant operation and maintenance personnel, health and recreation employees, transportation and food service personnel, and any student employees. Also included are any degree-granting institutions that provide academic training above grade 12.

CITY GOVERNMENT FINANCES, Items 117–139

Source: U.S. Census Bureau—2012 Census of Governments http://www.census.gov/govs/cog

Revenue and expenditure data are included in Table D for municipal governments only. The data do not include funds of any special district governments located in the city. For example, if a city's school district is a separate governmental unit, it is not included.

Total **general revenue** includes all revenue except utility, liquor stores, and insurance trust revenue. All tax revenue and intergovernmental revenue, even if designated for employee-retirement or local utility purpose, are classified as general revenue.

Intergovernmental revenue covers amounts received from other governments as fiscal aid in the form of shared revenues and grants-in-aid, as reimbursements for the performance of general government functions and specific services for the paying government (for example, care of prisoners or contractual research), or in lieu of taxes. It excludes any amounts received from other governments from the sale of property, commodities, and utility services. All intergovernmental revenue is classified as general revenue. Intergovernmental revenue from the state governments includes amounts originally from the federal government but channeled through the state.

Taxes consist of compulsory contributions exacted by governments for public purposes. However, this category excludes employer and employee payments for retirement and social insurance purposes, which are classified as insurance trust revenue. All tax revenue is classified as general revenue and comprises amounts received (including interest and penalties, but excluding protested amounts and refunds) from all taxes imposed by a government. Note that local government tax revenue excludes any amounts from shares of state-imposed and collected taxes, which are classified as intergovernmental revenue.

Property taxes are based on ownership of property and measured by its value. They include general property taxes related to property as a whole—real and personal, tangible or intangible—whether taxed at a single rate or at classified rates. Also included are taxes on selected types of property, such as motor vehicles or certain or all intangibles.

Sales and gross receipts taxes include "licenses" at more than nominal rates, based on volume or value of transfers of goods or services; taxes upon gross receipts or upon gross income; and related taxes based upon the use, storage, production (other than the severance of natural resources), importation, or consumption of goods. Dealer discounts "commissions," which are allowed to merchants for the collection of taxes from consumers, are excluded.

Total **general expenditure** includes all city expenditure other than specifically enumerated kinds of expenditure, including utility, liquor store, and employee-retirement and other insurance trust expenditures.

Capital outlays are direct expenditures for contract of force account construction or buildings, roads, and other improvements, and for purchases of equipment, land, and existing structures. They include amounts for additions, replacements, and major alterations to fixed work and structures. Expenditures for repair to such works and structures, however, is classified as current operation expenditure.

A major portion of capital outlay is commonly financed by borrowing, while governmental revenue does not include receipts from borrowing. Among other things, this distorts the relationship between the totals presented for revenue and expenditure and renders this relationship useless as a direct measure of the degree of budgetary "balance" (as that term is generally applied).

Public welfare expenditure covers support of and assistance to needy persons; this aid is contingent upon the person's needs. Included are cash assistance paid directly to needy persons; vendor payments made directly to private purveyors for medical care, burials, and other commodities and services provided under welfare programs; welfare institutions; and any intergovernmental or other direct expenditure for welfare purposes. Pensions to former employees and other benefits not contingent on need are excluded.

Highway expenditure is for the provision and maintenance of highway facilities, including toll turnpikes, bridges, tunnels, and ferries, as well as regular roads, highways, and streets. Also included are expenditures for street lighting and for snow and ice removal. Not included are highway policing and traffic control, which are considered part of police protection

Parking facilities include the construction, purchase, maintenance, and operation of public-use parking lots, garages, parking meters, and other distinctive parking facilities on a commercial basis.

Education is mainly for the provision and general support of schools and other educational facilities and services, including those for educational institutions beyond high school. Elementary and secondary education includes the provision of public kindergarten through high school education by local governments. It encompasses instructional, support, and auxiliary services (school lunch, student activities, and community services) offered by public school systems. Higher education consists of all local institutions of higher education.

Health expenditures include outpatient health services other than hospital care, such as public health administration; research and education; categorical health programs; treatment and immunization clinics; nursing; environmental health activities, such as air and water pollution control; ambulance service if provided separately from fire protection services; and other general public health activities, such as mosquito abatement. School health services provided by health agencies (rather than school agencies) are included here. Not included are sewage treatment operations, which are classified as part of sewerage and sanitation. **Hospital expenditures** include financing, construction, acquisition, maintenance and operation of hospital facilities, provision of hospital care, and support of public or private hospitals.

Police protection encompasses expenditures for the preservation of law and order, as well as for traffic safety. It includes police patrols and communications, crime prevention activities, detention and custody of persons awaiting trial, traffic safety, and vehicular inspection.

Sewerage and recreation include sanitary and storm sewers, sewage disposal facilities and services, and other government activities for such purposes. Street cleaning and the collection and disposal of garbage and other waste are also included.

Parks and recreation includes cultural and scientific activities, such as museums and art galleries; organized recreation, including playgrounds and playing fields, swimming pools, and bathing beaches; and municipal parks and special recreation facilities, such as auditoriums, stadiums, auto camps, recreation piers, and boat harbors.

Housing and community development includes city housing and redevelopment projects and the regulation, promotion, and support of private housing and redevelopment activities. Data from Arizona, Kentucky, Michigan, New Mexico, New York, and Virginia generally include municipal housing authorities. Housing authorities for other cities are usually classified as independent governments, and data from them are not included.

Interest on debt is the amount paid for the use of borrowed money.

Total **debt outstanding** is the total of debt obligations remaining unpaid on the date specified. **Debt issued during the year** is the amount of the outstanding debt that was recently borrowed.

CLIMATE, Items 140–146

Source: National Oceanic and Atmospheric Administration
http://cdo.ncdc.noaa.gov/cgi-bin/climatenormals/climatenormals.pl

All climate data are average values for the 30-year period from 1961 to 1990.

Mean temperatures for January and July were determined by adding the average daily maximum temperatures and the average daily minimum temperatures and dividing by two.

Temperature limits represent average daily minimum for January and average daily maximum for July.

Annual precipitation values are the average annual water equivalent of all precipitation for the 30-year period.

Heating and cooling degree days are used as relative measures of the energy required for heating and cooling buildings. One heating degree day is accumulated for each whole degree that the mean daily temperature is below 65 degrees Fahrenheit (a mean daily temperature of 62 degrees Fahrenheit will produce three heating degree days). Cooling degree days are accumulated in similar fashion for deviations of the mean daily temperature above 65 degrees Fahrenheit.

TABLE E—CONGRESSIONAL DISTRICTS OF THE 113TH CONGRESS

Members of the House of Representatives are for the 114th Congress.

LAND AREA, Items 1 and 3

Source: U.S. Census Bureau—2010 Census of Population and Housing
http://www.census.gov/2010census/data/

Land area measurements are shown to the nearest square kilometer. Land area includes dry land and land temporarily or partially covered by water, such as marshlands, swamps, and river floodplains.

POPULATION, Items 2–3

Source: U.S. Census Bureau—American Community Survey
http://www.census.gov/acs/www/

The population data are estimates from the American Community Survey.

POPULATION AND POPULATION CHARACTERISTICS, Items 4–24

Source: U.S. Census Bureau—American Community Survey, 2013
http://www.census.gov/acs/www/

Data on age, sex, race, Hispanic origin foreign-born residents, and percent born in state of residence are from the 2013 American Community Survey.

Data on race were derived from answers to the question on race that was asked of all respondents. The concept of race, as used by the Census Bureau, reflects self-identification by people according to the race or races with which they most closely identify. These categories are sociopolitical constructs and should not be interpreted as being scientific or anthropological in nature. Furthermore, the race categories include both racial and national origin groups.

In Table E, Columns 4 through 8 refer to individuals who identified with each racial category alone, while column 9 includes persons who identified with two or more races.

The **White** population is defined as persons who indicated their race as White, as well as persons who did not classify themselves in one of the specific race categories listed on the questionnaire but entered a nationality such as Irish, German, Italian, Lebanese, Near Easterner, Arab, or Polish.

The **Black** population includes persons who indicated their race as ''Black, African Am., or Negro,'' as well as persons who did not classify themselves in one of the specific race categories but reported entries such as African American, Afro American, Kenyan, Nigerian, or Haitian.

The **American Indian or Alaska Native** population includes persons who indicated their race as American Indian or Alaska Native, as well as persons who did not classify themselves in one of the specific race categories but reported entries such as Canadian Indian, French-American Indian, Spanish-American Indian, Eskimo, Aleut, Alaska Indian, or any of the American Indian or Alaska Native tribes.

The **Asian and Pacific Islander** population combines two census groupings: **Asian** and **Native Hawaiian or Other Pacific Islander**. The **Asian** population includes persons who indicated their race as Asian Indian, Chinese, Filipino, Japanese, Korean, Vietnamese, or ''Other Asian,'' as well as persons who provided write-in entries of such groups as Cambodian, Laotian, Hmong, Pakistani, or Taiwanese. The **Native Hawaiian or Other Pacific Islander** population includes persons who indicated their race as ''Native Hawaiian,'' ''Guamanian or Chamorro,'' ''Samoan,'' or ''Other Pacific Islander,'' as well as persons who reported entries such as Part Hawaiian, American Samoan, Fijian, Melanesian, or Tahitian.

The **Hispanic population** is based on a question that asked respondents ''Is this person Spanish/Hispanic/Latino?'' Persons marking any one of the four Hispanic categories (i.e., Mexican, Puerto Rican, Cuban, or other Spanish) are collectively referred to as Hispanic.

The **Non-Hispanic White alone** number in Column 11 includes only those persons who were not Hispanic and whose race was ''White only.''

The **female** population is shown as a percentage of total population.

The **foreign-born** population includes all persons who were not U.S. citizens at birth. Foreign-born persons are those who indicated they were either a U.S. citizen by naturalization or were not a citizen of the United States. The foreign-born population consists of immigrants (legal permanent residents), temporary migrants (students), humanitarian migrants (refugees), and unauthorized migrants (persons illegally residing in the United States).

Percent born in state of residence is shown as a percentage of total population.

Age is defined as age at last birthday (number of completed years since birth).

EDUCATION—SCHOOL ENROLLMENT AND EDUCATIONAL ATTAINMENT, Items 25–27

Source: U.S. Census Bureau—American Community Survey, 2013
http://www.census.gov/acs/www/

Data on school enrollment and educational attainment were derived from a sample of the population. Persons were classified as enrolled in school if they reported attending a ''regular'' public or private school (or college) during the year. The instructions were to ''include only nursery school, kindergarten, elementary school, and schooling which would lead to a high school diploma or a college degree'' as regular school. The Census Bureau defines a public school as ''any school or college controlled and supported by a local, county, state, or federal government.'' Schools primarily supported and controlled by religious organizations or other private groups are defined as private schools.

Data on **educational attainment** are tabulated for the population 25 years old and over. The data were derived from a question that asked respondents for the highest level of school completed or the highest degree received. Persons who had passed a high school equivalency examination were considered high school graduates. Schooling received in foreign schools was to be reported as the equivalent grade or years in the regular American school system.

Vocational and technical training, such as barber school training; business, trade, technical, and vocational schools; or other training for a specific trade are specifically excluded.

High school graduate or more. This category includes persons who have received a high school diploma or its equivalent, and those who reported any level higher than a high school diploma.

Bachelor's degree or more. This category includes persons who have received bachelor's degrees, master's degrees, professional school degrees (such as law school or medical school degrees), and doctoral degrees.

HOUSEHOLDS, Items 28–33

Source: U.S. Census Bureau—American Community Survey, 2013
http://www.census.gov/acs/www/

A **household** includes all persons who occupy a housing unit. (Persons not living in households are classified as living in group quarters.) A housing unit is a house, an apartment, a mobile home, a group of rooms, or a single room occupied (or, if vacant, intended for occupancy) as separate living quarters. Separate living quarters are those in which the occupants live separately from any other persons in the building and have direct access from the outside of the building or through a common hall. The occupants may be a single family, one person living alone, two or more families living together, or any other group of related or unrelated persons who share living quarters. The number of households is the same as the number of year-round occupied housing units.

A **family** includes a householder and one or more other persons living in the same household who are related to the householder by birth, marriage, or adoption. All persons in a household who are related to the householder are regarded as members of his or her family. A **family household** may contain persons not related to the householder; thus, family households may include more members than families do. A household can contain only one family for the purposes of census tabulations. Not all households contain families, as a household may comprise a group of unrelated persons or of one person living alone. Families are classified by type as either a ''husband-wife family'' or ''other family,'' according to the presence or absence of a spouse.

The measure of **persons per household** is obtained by dividing the number of persons in households by the number of households or householders. One person in each household is designated as the householder. In most cases, this is the person (or one of the persons) in whose name the house is owned, being bought, or rented. If there is no such person in the household, any adult household member 15 years old and over can be designated as the householder.

The category **female family householder** includes only female-headed family households with no spouse present.

GROUP QUARTERS, Items 34–39

Source: U.S. Census Bureau—American Community Survey, 2013
http://www.census.gov/acs/www/

The Census Bureau classifies all people not living in households as living in **group quarters**. There are two types of group quarters: institutional, including **correctional facilities**, **nursing homes**, and mental hospitals; and non-institutional, including **college dormitories**, **military quarters**, group homes, missions, and shelters.

HOUSING, Items 40–45

Source: U.S. Census Bureau—American Community Survey, 2013
http://www.census.gov/acs/www/

A **housing unit** is a house, apartment, mobile home or trailer, group of rooms, or single room occupied or, if vacant, intended for occupancy as separate living quarters. Separate living quarters are those in which the occupants do not live and eat with any other person in the structure and which have direct access from the outside of the building or through a common hall. For vacant units, the criteria of separateness and direct access are applied to the intended occupants whenever possible. If that information cannot be obtained, the criteria are applied to the previous occupants.

The occupants of a housing unit may be a single family, one person living alone, two or more families living together, or any other group of related or unrelated persons who share living quarters. Both occupied and vacant housing units are included in the housing inventory, although recreational vehicles, tents, caves, boats, railroad cars, and the like are included only if they are occupied as a person's usual place of residence.

A housing unit is classified as **occupied** if it is the usual place of residence of the person or group of persons living in it at the time of interview, or if the occupants are only temporarily absent (away on vacation). A household consists of all persons who occupy a housing unit as their usual place of residence. Vacant units for sale or rent include units rented or sold but not occupied and any other units held off the market.

A housing unit is **owner occupied** if the owner or co-owner lives in the unit, even if it is mortgaged or not fully paid for. The owner or co-owner must live in the unit and is usually the first person listed on the census questionnaire

All occupied housing units that are not owner occupied, whether they are rented for cash rent or occupied without payment of cash rent, are classified as **renter occupied**.

Median value is the dollar amount that divides the distribution of specified owner-occupied housing units into two equal parts, with half of all units below the median value and half of all units above the median value. Value is defined as the respondent's estimate of what the house would sell for if it was for sale. Data are presented for single-family units on fewer than 10 acres of land that have no business or medical offices on the property.

Median rent divides the distribution of renter-occupied housing units into two equal parts. The rent concept used in this volume is gross rent, which includes the amount of cash rent a renter pays (contract rent) plus the estimated average cost of utilities and fuels, if these are paid by the renter. The rent is the amount of rent only for living quarters and excludes amounts paid for any business or other space occupied. Single-family houses on lots of 10 or more acres of land are also excluded.

Housing cost as a percentage of income is shown separately for owners with mortgages, owners without mortgages, and renters. Rent as a percentage of income is a computed ratio of gross rent and monthly household income (total household income the past 12 months divided by 12). Selected owner costs include utilities and fuels, mortgage payments, insurance, taxes, etc. In each case, the ratio of housing cost to income is computed separately for each housing unit. The housing cost ratios for half of all units are above the median shown in this book, and half are below the median shown in the book.

Substandard units are occupied units that are overcrowded or lack complete plumbing facilities. For the purposes of this item, ''overcrowded'' is defined as having 1.01 persons or more per room. Complete plumbing facilities include hot and cold piped water, a flush toilet, and a bathtub or shower. These facilities must be located inside the housing unit, but do not have to be in the same room.

INCOME AND POVERTY, Items 46–51

Source: U.S. Census Bureau—American Community Survey, 2013
http://www.census.gov/acs/www/

The data on income were derived from responses of a sample of persons 15 years old and over. **Total money income** is the sum of the amounts reported separately for wage or salary income; net self-employment income; interest, dividends, or net rental or royalty income or income from estates and trusts; Social Security or railroad retirement income; Supplemental Security Income (SSI); public assistance or welfare payments; retirement, survivor, or disability pensions; and all other income. Receipts from the following sources are not included as income: capital gains; money received from the sale of property (unless the recipient was engaged in the business of selling such property); the value of income ''in kind'' from food stamps, public housing subsidies, medical care, employer contributions for individuals, etc.; withdrawal of bank deposits; money borrowed; tax refunds; exchange of money between relatives living in the same household; and gifts, lump-sum inheritances, insurance payments, and other types of lump-sum receipts.

Per capita income is the mean income computed for every man, woman, and child in a particular group. It is derived by dividing the aggregate income of a particular group by the resident population in that group. Per capita income is rounded to the nearest whole dollar.

Household income includes the income of the householder and all other individuals 15 years old and over in the household, whether or not they are related to the householder. Since many households consist of only one person, median household income is usually less than median family income.

The **poverty status** data were derived from data collected on the number of persons in a household, from questionnaire item 3, which provided data on each person's relationship to the householder, and questionnaire items 41 and 42, which were also used to derive the income data. The Social Security Administration (SSA) developed the original poverty definition in 1964, which federal interagency committees subsequently revised in 1969 and 1980. The Office of Management and Budget's (OMB) *Directive 14* prescribes the SSA's definition as the official poverty measure for federal agencies to use in their statistical work. Poverty statistics presented in American Community Survey products adhere to the standards defined by OMB in *Directive 14*.

Poverty thresholds vary depending on three criteria: size of family, number of children, and, for one- and two-person families, age of householder. In determining the poverty status of families and unrelated individuals, the Census Bureau uses thresholds (income cutoffs) arranged in a two-dimensional matrix. The matrix consists of family size (from one person to nine or more persons), cross-classified by presence and number of family members under 18 years old (from no children present to eight or more children present). Unrelated individuals and two-person families are further differentiated by age of reference person (under 65 years old and 65 years old and over). To determine a person's poverty status, the person's total family income over the previous 12 months is compared with the poverty threshold appropriate for that person's family size and composition. If the total income of that person's family is less than the threshold appropriate for that family, then the person is considered poor or ''below the poverty level,'' together with every member of his or her family. If a person is not living with anyone related by birth, marriage, or adoption, then the person's own income is compared with his or her poverty threshold. The total number of persons below the poverty level is the sum of persons in families and the number of unrelated individuals with incomes below the poverty level over the previous 12 months. The average poverty threshold for a four-person family was $23,834 in 2013.

The data on participation in the Food Stamp Program are designed to identify households in which one or more of the current members received food stamps during the past 12 months. Once a food stamp household was identified, a question was asked about the total value of all food stamps received by the household during that 12-month period. The Food Stamp Act of 1977 defines this federally funded program as one intended to ''permit low-income households to obtain a more nutritious diet.'' (From title XIII of P.L. 95–113, The Food Stamp Act of 1977, declaration of policy.) Providing eligible households with coupons that can be used to purchase food increases food purchasing power. The Food and Nutrition Service (FNS) of the U.S. Department of Agriculture (USDA) administers the Food Stamp program through state and local welfare offices. The Food Stamp program is the major national income support program to which all low-income and low-resource households, regardless of household characteristics, are eligible.

Poverty Thresholds for 2013 by Size of Family and Number of Related Children Under 18 Years

Size of family unit	Weighted average thresholds
One person (unrelated individual)	11,888
Under 65 years	12,119
65 years and over	11,173
Two people	15,142
Householder under 65 years	15,679
Householder 65 years and over	14,095
Three people	18,552
Four people	23,834
Five people	28,265
Six people	31,925
Seven people	36,384
Eight people	40,484
Nine people or more	48,065

Source: U.S. Census Bureau.

CIVILIAN LABOR FORCE, UNEMPLOYMENT, AND EMPLOYMENT, Items 52–58

Source: U.S. Census Bureau—American Community Survey, 2013
http://www.census.gov/acs/www/

The **civilian labor force** consists of all civilians 16 years old and over who are either employed or unemployed.

Unemployment includes all persons who did not work during the survey week, made specific efforts to find a job during the previous four weeks, and were available for work during the survey week (except for temporary illness). Persons waiting to be called back to a job from which they had been laid off and those waiting to report to a new job within the next 30 days are included in unemployment figures.

Total employment includes all civilians 16 years old and over who were either (1) ''at work''—those who did any work at all during the reference week as paid employees, worked in either their own business or profession, worked on their own farm, or worked 15 hours or more as unpaid workers in a family farm or business; or were (2) ''with a job, but not at work''—those who had a job but were not at work that week due to illness, weather, industrial dispute, vacation, or other personal reasons.

The **occupational categories** are based on the occupational classification system that was developed for the 2000 census. This system consists of 539 specific occupational categories for employed persons arranged into 23 major occupational groups. This classification was developed based on the *Standard Occupational Classification (SOC) Manual: 2010*, published by the Executive Office of the President, Office of Management and Budget.

PERSONS WITH NO HEALTH INSURANCE, Item 59

Source: U.S. Census Bureau—American Community Survey, 2013
http://www.census.gov/acs/www/

The percentage of persons under age 65 with no **health insurance** shows the percentage of the population of each congressional district who were not covered by private health plans purchased directly or provided by an employer, Medicaid, Medicare, or military health care.

SOCIAL SECURITY AND SUPPLEMENTAL SECURITY INCOME, Items 60–62

Source: U.S. Social Security Administration
Source: U.S. Social Security Administration
http://www.ssa.gov/policy/docs/factsheets/cong_stats/

Social Security beneficiaries are persons receiving benefits under the Old-Age, Survivors, and Disability Insurance Program. These include retired or disabled workers covered by the program, their spouses and dependent children, and the surviving spouses and dependent children of deceased workers.

Supplemental Security Income (SSI) recipients are persons receiving SSI payments. The SSI program is a cash assistance program that provides monthly benefits to low-income aged, blind, or disabled persons.

Data are as of December of the year shown.

AGRICULTURE, ITEMS 63–72

Source: U.S. Department of Agriculture, National Agricultural Statistics Service—2012 Census of Agriculture
http://agcensus.usda.gov/index.php

The Census Bureau took a census of agriculture every 10 years from 1840 to 1920; since 1925, this census has been taken roughly once every 5 years. The 1997 Census of Agriculture was the first one conducted by the National Agricultural Statistics Service of the U.S. Department of Agriculture. Over time, the definition of a farm has varied. For recent censuses (including the 2012 census), a farm has been defined as any place from which $1,000 or more of agricultural products were produced and sold or normally would have been sold during the census year. Dollar figures are expressed in current dollars and have not been adjusted for inflation or deflation.

The acreage designated as **land in farms** consists primarily of agricultural land used for crops, pasture, or grazing. It also includes woodland and wasteland not actually under cultivation or used for pasture or grazing, provided that this land was part of the farm operator's total operation.

Land in farms is an operating-unit concept and includes all land owned and operated, as well as all land rented from others. Land used rent-free is classified as land rented from others. All land in Indian reservations used for growing crops or grazing livestock is classified as land in farms.

The **value of farm products sold** by farms represents the gross market value before taxes and the production expenses of all agricultural products sold or removed from the place in 2007, regardless of who received the payment. It includes sales by the operator as well as the value of any share received by partners, landlords, contractors, and others associated with the operation. It represents the sum of all crops, including nursery products sold and livestock and poultry and their products sold.

The value of crops sold in 2012 does not necessarily represent the sales from crops harvested that year. The data include sales from crops produced in earlier years and exclude some crops that were produced in 2012 but held in storage and not sold during the census year. For crops sold through a co-op that made payments in several installments, only the total value received in the census year was reported.

Government payments consists of government payments received from the Conservation Reserve Program (CRP) and Wetlands Reserve Program (WRP), plus government payments received from federal programs other than the CRP, WRP, and Commodity Credit Corporation (CCC).